THE NBA
FAMILY TREE

76 75 73 72 71 70 69 68 67 66 65 63 62 60 59 58 57 56 55 54 52 51 49 48

THE OFFICIAL NBA ENCYCLOPEDIA

Basketball was invented because young male students found indoor sports such as gymnastics far less entertaining than misbehavior. So in 1891, instructor Dr. James A. Naismith had the gymnastics equipment (OPPOSITE) cleared off the floor of a YMCA training school in Springfield, Massachusetts, and a peach basket was nailed below the railing. The class had 18 male students, most of whom were in their 20s, and they were divided into teams of nine. A 30-minute game was held and the final score was 1-0. When the basket was scored, a custodian got a ladder and retrieved the ball.

The early game was brutal while athletes made the transition from traditional physical contact games like football and rugby to a game that would ultimately reward finesse. Steel mesh cages had to be constructed around courts to keep excited spectators from interfering with play, leading to the term "cagers" that is sometimes still used. "Players would be thrown against the wire and most of us would be cut," said one early player. "The court was covered with blood." Everyone was thankful in the early 1900s when a rope mesh cage (ABOVE) was substituted around a court in Paterson, New Jersey.

Basketball has undergone many changes, but there is also a sameness about the game. Whether it is the NBA Finals 2000 (TOP) or the late 1890s (BOTTOM), the jump ball always starts the game.

Modern-day players are taller and jump higher, but whether it is Bill MacDonald playing for the Oshkosh All-Stars of the National Basketball League in the 1940s (LEFT) or the Miami Heat's Alonzo Mourning (RIGHT), shotblocking has been a fundamental part of basketball for decades.

NAT HOLMAN

MARQUES HAYNES

Eight decades ago, a pioneering guard named Nat Holman played for the Original Celtics, who were a barnstorming team that also won championships in the American Basketball League, which existed from 1925-31. Holman was responsible for inventing passes and plays that are still used in today's game. As basketball advanced and techniques developed, there were many creative guards who added flair, starting with the Harlem Globetrotters' sensational Marques Haynes. The line of great playmakers and showmen continues to this day.

PETE MARAVICH

ISIAH THOMAS

BOB COUSY

MAGIC JOHNSON

JASON KIDD

JASON WILLIAMS

Naismith would have been stunned to see more than 40,000 fans watching the 1999 NBA Finals in a facility such as San Antonio's Alamodome (TOP), but he was gratified to live long enough to see basketball established as an Olympic sport in 1936 (BOTTOM), even though it was played outdoors. When the U.S. won the first gold medal game, however, it had to overcome significant weather obstacles. It was raining.

The conditions were considerably better in Barcelona in 1992, when NBA players Charles Barkley (LEFT) and Scottie Pippen (RIGHT) participated in the Olympics for the first time and helped make Naismith's game popular beyond his wildest dreams.

The NBA traces its beginning to 1946, but players were paid to play basketball, making them professionals, as early as 18
There were great touring teams and significant national leagues that played important roles in providing the roots that eventua
led to the creation and permanence of the NBA.

The Buffalo Germans once won 111 consecutive games. They are in the Hall of Fame.

The fabulous Rens toured the country from 1923-49 and they are also in the Hall of Fame.

The SPHAs had a 31-year run as a touring team, and they also won championships in three leagues.

George Mikan's career began with the Chicago American Gears of the National Basketball League.

During its nine-year existence, the colorful American Basketball Association was unable to attract great centers, but its collection of forwards and guards possessed sensational offensive talent. David Thompson (LEFT) may have been the greatest 6-4 leaper in history, and when four ABA teams joined the NBA in 1976, San Antonio's George Gervin, (RIGHT) "The Iceman," went on to win four scoring championships.

JOE FULKS

It wasn't until a half-century after basketball was invented that players regularly began elevating from the floor on field goal attempts. The jump shot was first used in the late 1920s but did not become a staple of the game until the '40s. While there are many players who were effective shooters with unique styles, over the years, the purists have always revered the classic jump shooter. Joe Fulks was one of the great practitioners in the early years of the NBA and the line of artists who followed him stretches through each decade, all the way to the present.

JERRY WEST

SAM JONES

RICK BARRY

ROLANDO BLACKMAN

REGGIE MILLER

ALLAN HOUSTON

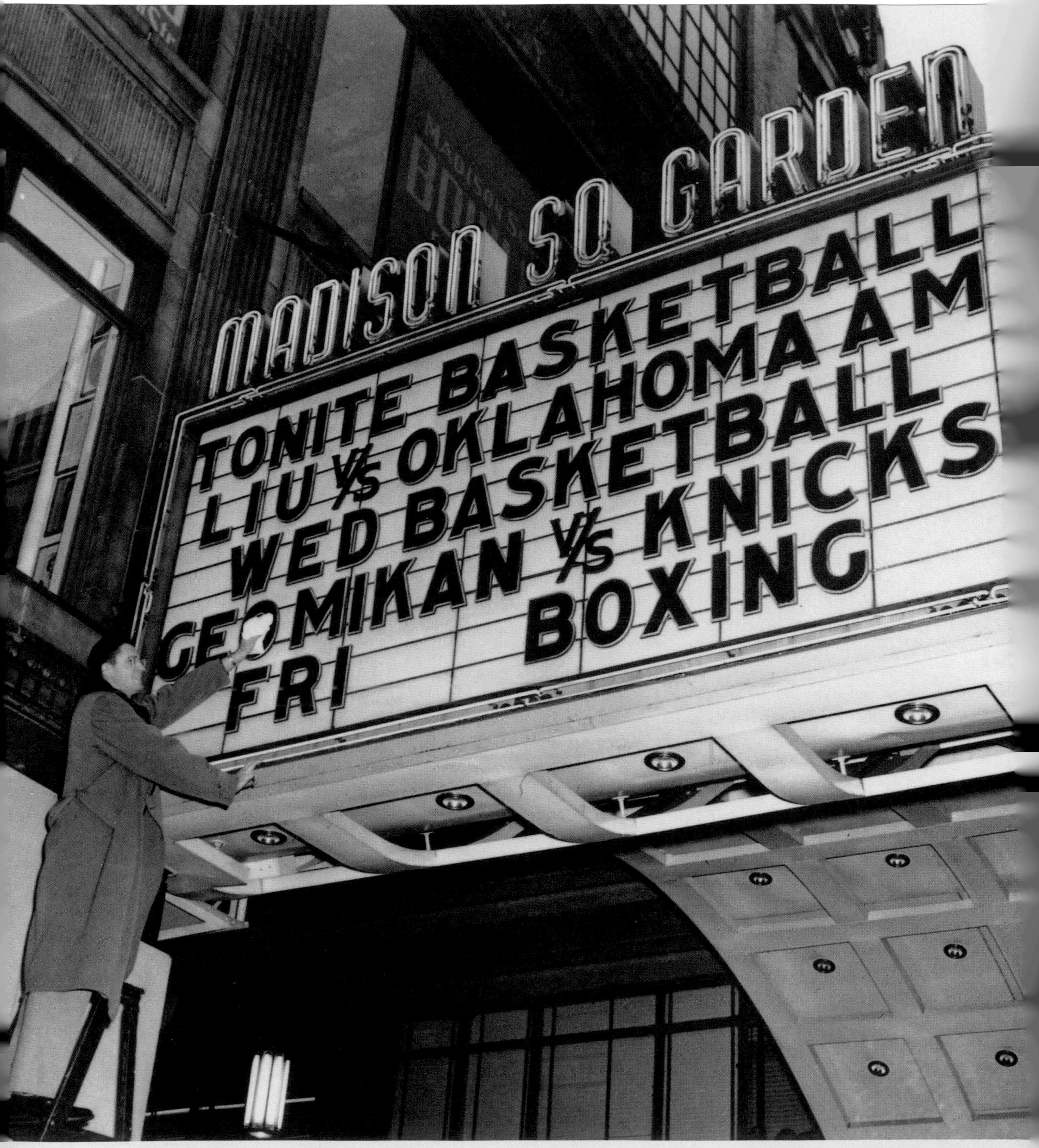

Although the NBA's global popularity is at an all-time high, the notion of a marquee player is almost as old as the league itself. George Mikan was the first dominant NBA player in the '50s and was so popular that when he came to Broadway, it was only proper to put his name in lights.

Michael Jordan advanced the legacy that began with Mikan into an art form. Jordan's impact on the court was so profound that off the court, he became a global icon. When he first announced that he was leaving the Chicago Bulls, it was necessary to honor his career in some sort of monumental way.

Individually, each was nothing less than Paul Bunyanesque, bigger than life, giants by any standard. Together, they became basketball's synonym for "rivalry." Wilt Chamberlain and Bill Russell matched up individually 142 times, more than any two players of superstar stature in NBA history. Their battles were epic and entertaining. The memories are everlasting.

Lighting the victory cigar, (ABOVE) a gesture designed to irritate opponents and remind them of their inferiority, became part of the lore of the Celtics, who won eight consecutive titles and 11 in 13 seasons. Red Auerbach built the dynasty and reveled in its success.

When it came to championships, Russell (LEFT) had the whole basketball world in his hands.

ELGIN BAYLOR

CONNIE HAWKINS

DOMINIQUE WILKINS

Elgin Baylor, the godfather of high flyers, took the game from the ground to the air in the '50s. And above the rim is where it has remained with a line of spectacular athletes who always have and always will explore the stratosphere with breathtaking grace and power.

JULIUS ERVING

MICHAEL JORDAN

KOBE BRYANT

VINCE CARTER

In the 1980s, the NBA was synonymous with Bird-Magic, whose teams won eight of the 10 titles in the decade. Magic had the edge as the Lakers defeated the Celtics two out of three times and won five titles while Boston won three.

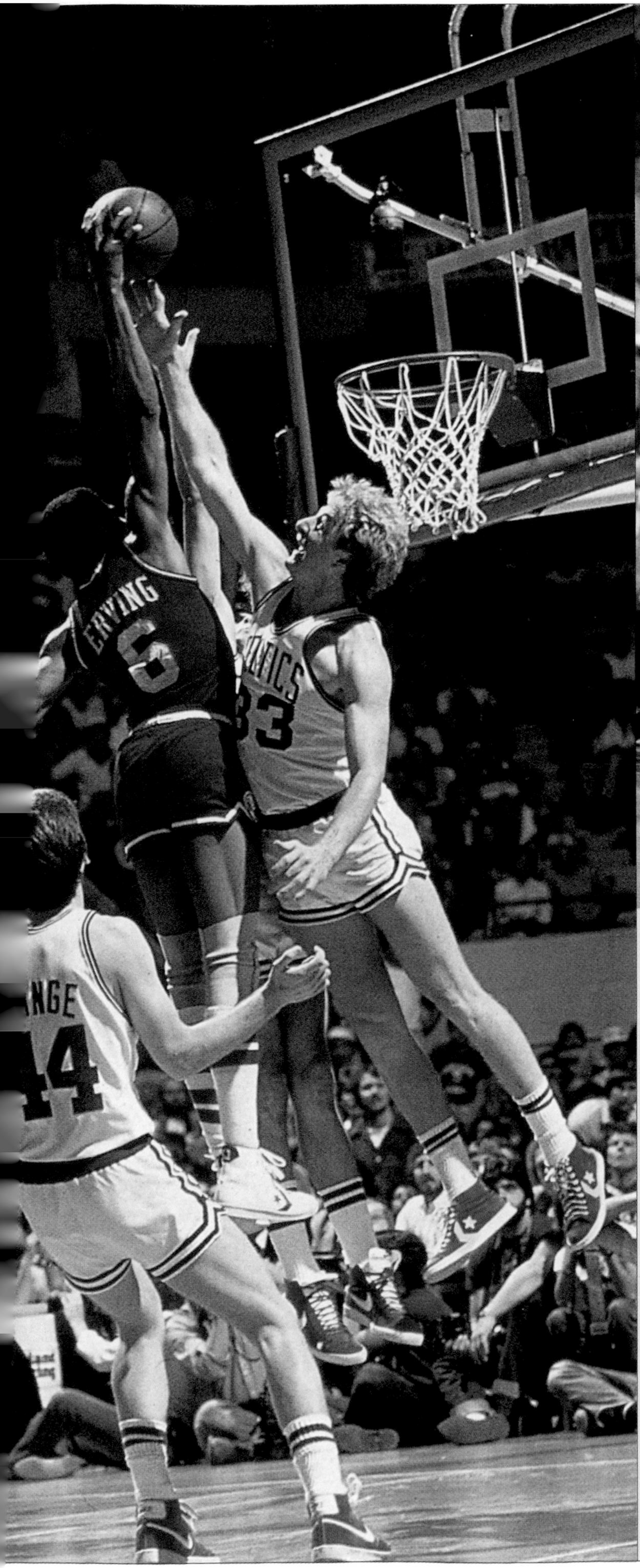

After a brilliant ABA career that was played before audiences often too small, but always in awe of his wondrous talents, Julius Erving (left) soared into the NBA and elevated the league to new levels of popularity and altitude. When Bird joined the NBA in 1979, the Celtics-Sixers rivalry that once featured Russell and Wilt was revived. The two teams met three consecutive years in the conference finals with the Sixers winning twice. From 1980-83, championships were won by the Lakers, Celtics, Lakers and Sixers, respectively, but then Philadelphia began fading slightly and the Magic-Bird rivalry dominated the rest of the decade. When the '90s began, Michael (ABOVE) muscled into the picture, defeating Magic's Lakers in the 1991 Finals, the first of six Bulls titles in the decade.

LENNY WILKENS

DON NELSON

LARRY BROWN

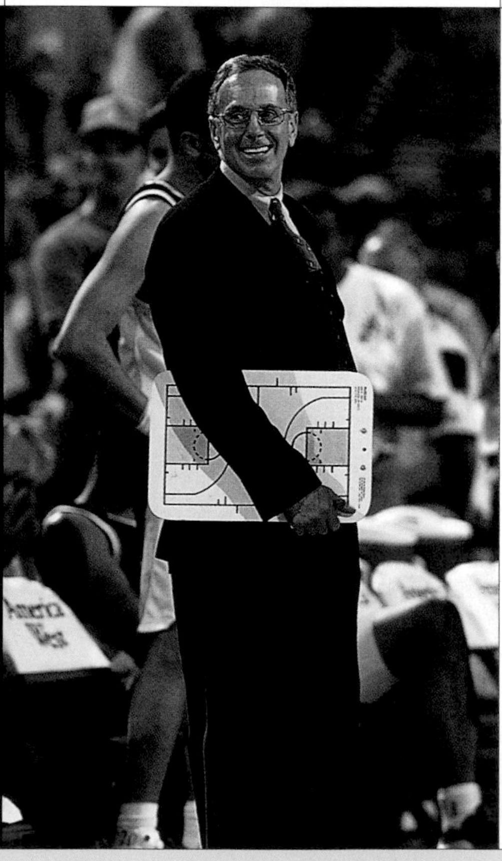

The NBA has a rich tradition of the best and the brightest players moving into leadership positions, teaching a new generation of players and extending their own legacies. The coaches had varying degrees of success as players. Lenny Wilkens was a nine-time All-Star who is one of only two men in the Hall of Fame as a player and coach (John Wooden is the other). Larry Brown led the ABA in assists three times and holds the single-game ABA record with 23 assists.

JERRY SLOAN | **PAT RILEY** | **PHIL JACKSON**

Jerry Sloan made the NBA All-Defensive first team four times and second team twice. Don Nelson, Pat Riley and Phil Jackson were valuable role players who were known for their competitiveness and toughness. But, besides being students of the game, all of the coaches were consummate team players who not only understood what it took to be an NBA player, but who ultimately were able to convey that to generations of new players.

The game provides the opportunity for greatness, and a special few have embraced it in dramatic ways. Sometimes brief moment. Sometimes it's an entire game. Each of these has become a permanent part of NBA lore.

APRIL 15, 1965:

Havlicek . . .

. . .

. . . stole the ball!

MAY 8, 1970: Despite a leg injury that should have prevented him from playing, Knicks center Willis Reed's inspirational appearance and two quick baskets helped New York defeat the Lakers and win the 1970 NBA championship.

MARCH 2, 1962: Going where no man ever has — and perhaps ever will — Wilt Chamberlain shattered the scoring mark with 100 points in a Warriors' victory over New York in Hershey, Pennsylvania.

JUNE 11, 1997: With a temperature of more than 100 degrees, Michael Jordan still scored 38 points in Chicago's 1997 Game 5 Finals victory over Utah, but needed help to get to the locker room.

There is no substitute for size, whether it comes in the form of height, bulk or strength. It has been that way from the beginning and the big man continues to dominate in the NBA.

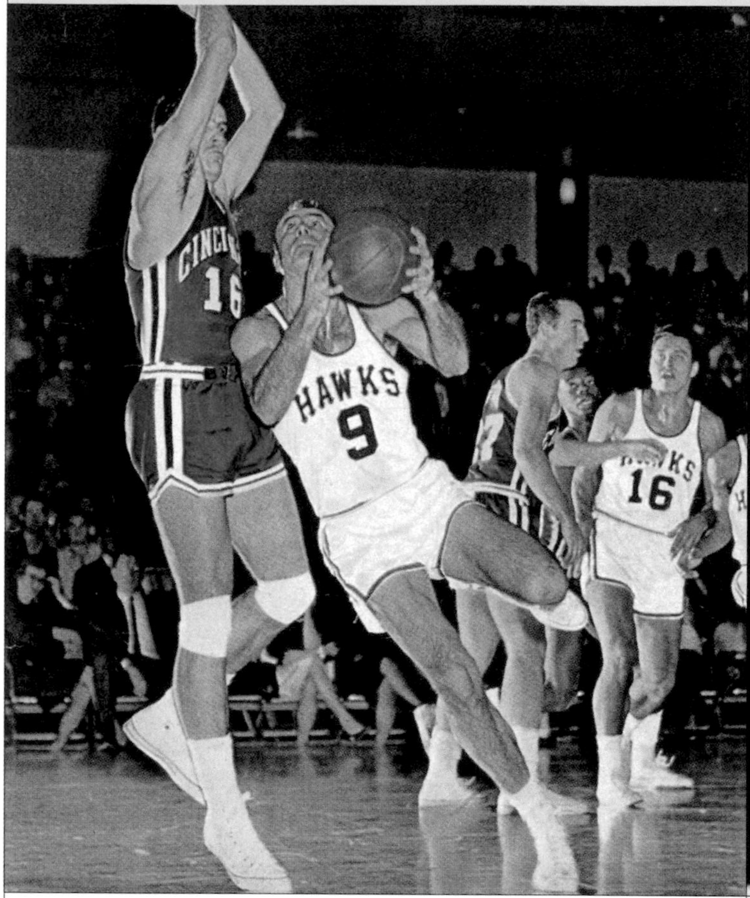

BOB PETTIT

WES UNSELD

BILL WALTON AND DAVE COWENS

MOSES MALONE

PATRICK EWING

HAKEEM OLAJUWON

DAVID ROBINSON

SHAQUILLE O'NEAL

One of the traits of the truly great ones is a mastery of the fundamentals. Whether it is classic '70s with Kareem Abdul-Jabbar and Oscar Robertson (OPPOSITE PAGE) or classic '90s with John Stockton and Karl Malone (ABOVE), a pick-and-roll run to perfection might not be labeled as spectacular, yet it is a thing of beauty to watch.

ANTONIO MCDYESS

GARY PAYTON

KEVIN GARNETT

Since its inception, the NBA has consistently had to replenish talent. Stars of the past move on and become legends, forever venerated by fans and the next generation of players. The game itself is measured by the skills of present players, and the promise of young superstars, who one day will pass on their legacy to the next generation. As great as any era has been in the NBA, there are always many reasons to be excited about the future.

MICHAEL FINLEY

STEVE SMITH

ALLEN IVERSON

TIM DUNCAN

RAY ALLEN

STEPHON MARBURY

CHRIS WEBBER

SHAREEF ABDUR-RAHIM

History, in fact, does sometimes repeat itself. Whether it is Wilt on *American Bandstand* or Shaq rapping a single from a platinum-selling CD, the giants of the NBA have always been entertainers. On and off the court.

FOREWORD BY MICHAEL JORDAN

THE OFFICIAL NBA ENCYCLOPEDIA

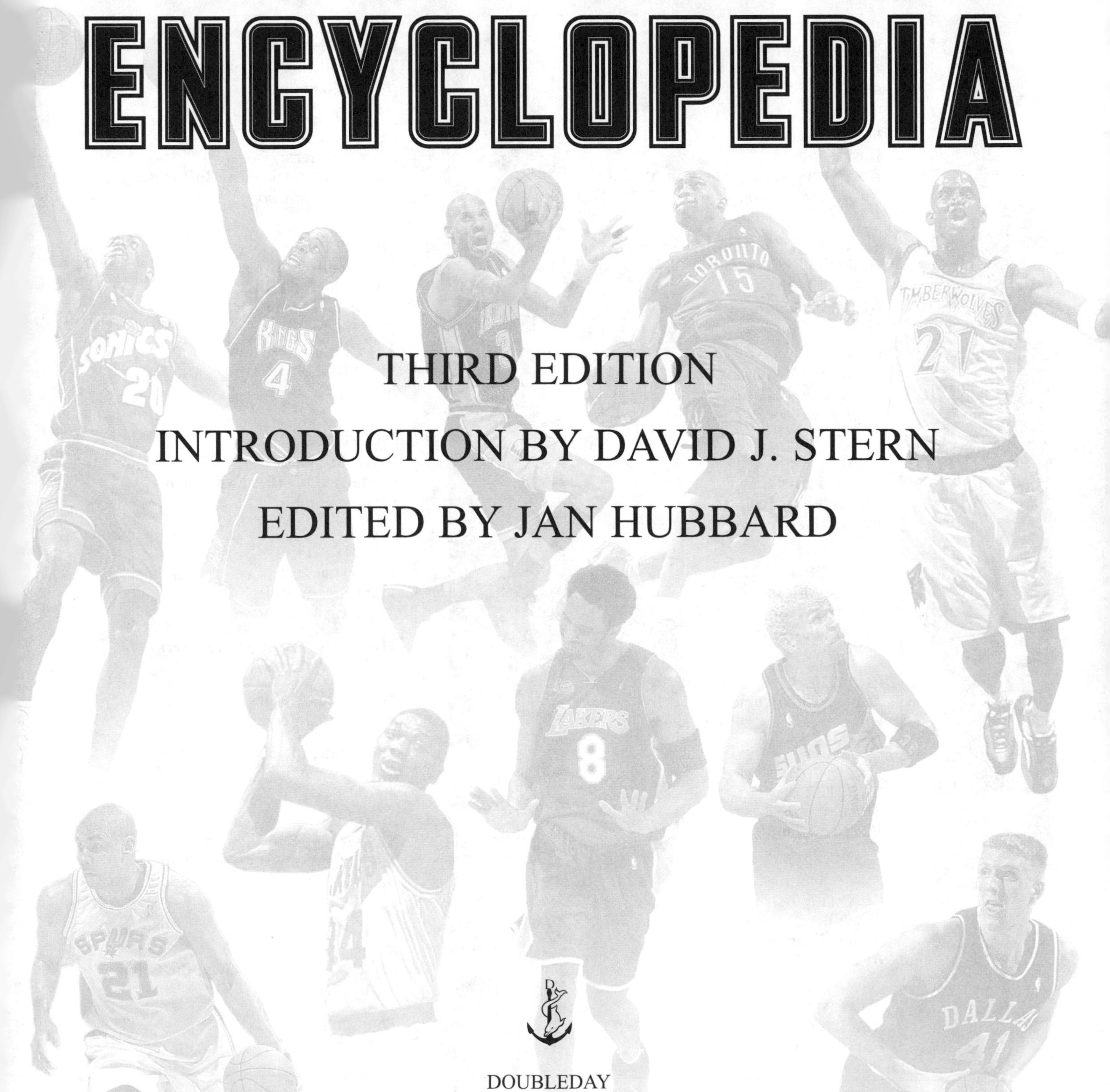

THIRD EDITION

INTRODUCTION BY DAVID J. STERN

EDITED BY JAN HUBBARD

DOUBLEDAY
NEW YORK — LONDON — TORONTO — SYDNEY — AUCKLAND

TABLE OF

4 INTRODUCTION
The Encyclopedia:
A Special, Exciting Endeavor
By David J. Stern

6 FOREWORD
Basketball:
An Overpowering Force in My Life
By Michael Jordan

10 CHAPTER 1
Basketball Forever:
It's Just One Game
By Jan Hubbard

16 CHAPTER 2
Tomorrow's Game:
It's in Good Hands
By Bryan Burwell

20 CHAPTER 3
Michael Jordan:
Modern-Day Icon
By Art Thiel

26 CHAPTER 4
George Mikan:
The First Icon
By Dan Barreiro

30 CHAPTER 5
The Great Rivalries:
Russell vs. Wilt * Bird vs. Magic
By Bob Ryan

36 CHAPTER 6
The Commissioners
By Mike Monroe

CAN YOU TOP
THIS?
Anyone Taller
6 Ft. 8 Inches
Free to

38 CHAPTER 7
The NBA:
A New League
By Leonard Koppett

42 CHAPTER 8
The Roots:
Early Professional Leagues
By Robin Deutsch and Douglas Stark

52 CHAPTER 9
Innovators:
The Rens and Globetrotters
By John Smallwood

58 CHAPTER 10
NBA Pioneers:
The African-American Influence
By John Smallwood

62 CHAPTER 11
Red, White & Blue:
The Colorful ABA
By John Gardella

The Forgotten League:
The ABL (1961-63)
By Paul Ladewski

72 CHAPTER 12
Coast to Coast:
Modern-Day NBA Expansion
By John Hareas

76 CHAPTER 13
The Dynasties:
The Chicago Bulls
By Jackie MacMullan

The 1980s Los Angeles Lakers
By Jack McCallum

The Boston Celtics
By Dan Shaughnessy

The Minneapolis Lakers
By Alex Sachare

94 CHAPTER 14
Nicknames:
The Origin of NBA Team Names
By Tracey Reavis

98 CHAPTER 15
Rules:
24-Second Clock Revived the Game
By Alex Sachare

The Long Ball
By Barry Rubinstein

CONTENTS

102 CHAPTER 16
The Coaches
By Paul Ladewski

112 CHAPTER 17
The Referees
By Alex Sachare

115 CHAPTER 18
NBA Seasons in Review
By Roland Lazenby

201 CHAPTER 19
ABA Seasons in Review
By Tracey Reavis

211 CHAPTER 20
The Naismith Memorial Basketball Hall of Fame
By Curtis Bunn and Mark Hale

228 CHAPTER 21
The NBA at 50: The Greatest Players in History
By Chris Ekstrand, Scott Ostler, Sam Goldaper, Fran Blinebury, Bruce Newman, Art Thiel, Fred Kerber and David DuPree

256 CHAPTER 22
The All-Star Experience
By Barry Rubinstein

288 CHAPTER 23
USA Basketball
By Rita Sullivan

290 CHAPTER 24
The Dream Team: A Global Explosion
By Jan Hubbard

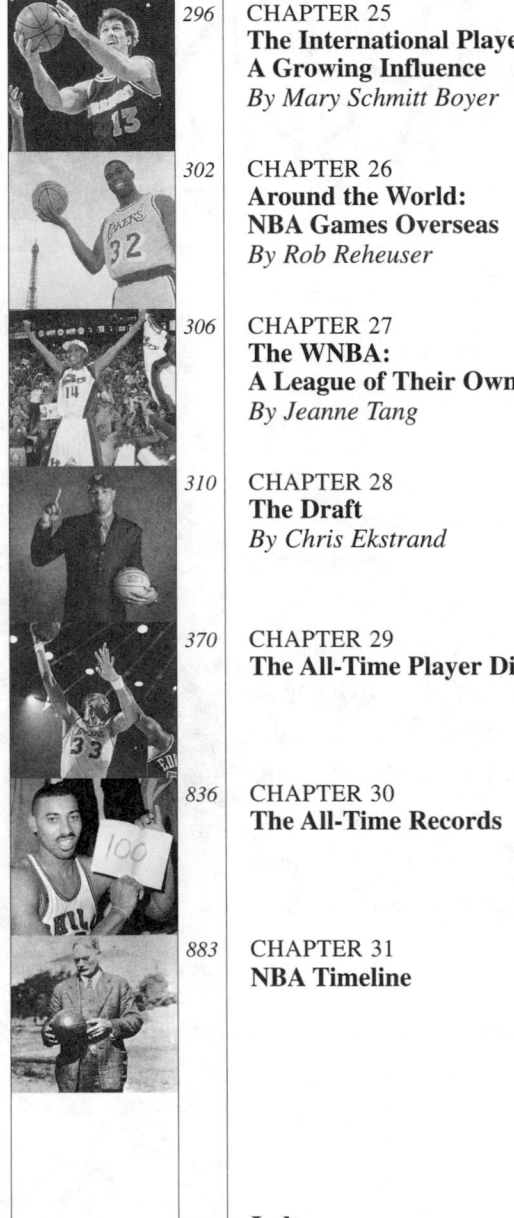

296 CHAPTER 25
The International Player: A Growing Influence
By Mary Schmitt Boyer

302 CHAPTER 26
Around the World: NBA Games Overseas
By Rob Reheuser

306 CHAPTER 27
The WNBA: A League of Their Own
By Jeanne Tang

310 CHAPTER 28
The Draft
By Chris Ekstrand

370 CHAPTER 29
The All-Time Player Directory

836 CHAPTER 30
The All-Time Records

883 CHAPTER 31
NBA Timeline

887 **Index**

906 **Copyright Information**

907 **Photo Credits**

908 **Acknowledgements**
By Jan Hubbard

909 **Special Thanks, Writers Bios**

INTRODUCTION

THE ENCYCLOPEDIA A SPECIAL, EXCITING ENDEAVOR

By David J. Stern

We have taken a new approach to presenting our history in this third edition of the NBA Encyclopedia, and we hope you find it entertaining as well as informative. We have included all the staples you expect in a sports encyclopedia, including complete statistics on every player who ever made it into an NBA box score, but we have formatted our text in a unique way. Rather than presenting information in a traditional chronological order, our overall approach is to begin in the present and then explore our past by focusing on key figures and stories in the league's history. At times, we juxtapose different eras, and we also attempt to capture our greatest moments and influences in vignettes written by some of basketball's best known and most accomplished writers.

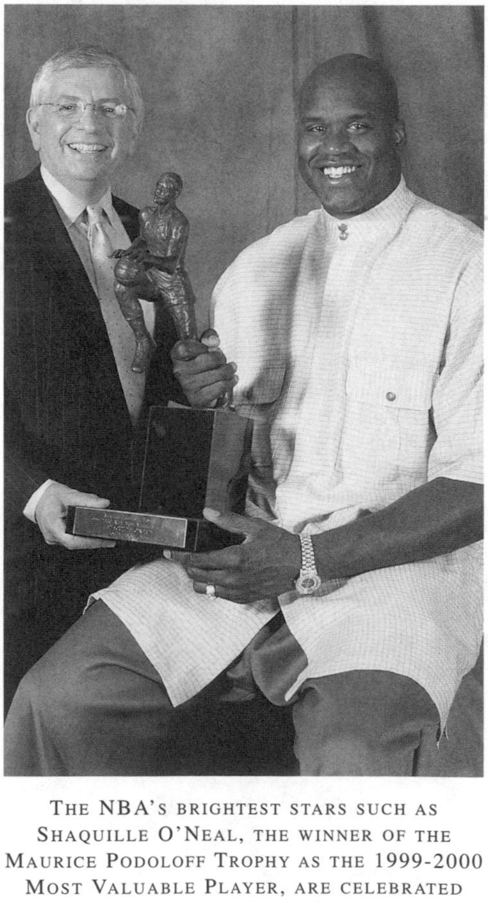

THE NBA'S BRIGHTEST STARS SUCH AS SHAQUILLE O'NEAL, THE WINNER OF THE MAURICE PODOLOFF TROPHY AS THE 1999-2000 MOST VALUABLE PLAYER, ARE CELEBRATED IN THIS THIRD EDITION...

By now, you have already seen our opening photo essay that illustrates many of our celebrated players and moments. We begin our text with a very personal foreword by Michael Jordan, followed by a section covering today's brightest stars, like Shaquille O'Neal, Kobe Bryant, Tim Duncan, Kevin Garnett, Jason Kidd, Vince Carter, Alonzo Mourning, Gary Payton, Chris Webber, Allen Iverson, Eddie Jones, Jalen Rose, Ray Allen and Grant Hill.

We examine the past with features on Jordan and George Mikan — icons of their respective generations a half-century apart; two legendary matchups — Magic vs. Bird and Russell vs. Wilt; the four greatest NBA dynasties; the leagues and players who formed our roots; and other features on the growth of the league, the international explosion, the NBA Draft, the Hall of Fame, the All-Star Game and much more.

Throughout its history, the NBA has been blessed with great players who have consistently taken our sport to new heights. Besides the players mentioned earlier, we have features on Kareem Abdul-Jabbar, the leading scorer in NBA history, and early superstars

...ALONG WITH LEGENDS — GEORGE MIKAN, WILT CHAMBERLAIN, BILL RUSSELL, JULIUS ERVING AND OSCAR ROBERTSON — WHO HAVE PROVIDED THE FOUNDATION FOR THE NBA'S GLOBAL SUCCESS.

Elgin Baylor, Bob Cousy, Bob Pettit, Oscar Robertson and Jerry West. We pay tribute to "Dr. J," Julius Erving, and we highlight the extraordinary play of two remarkable tandems, Walt Frazier and Earl Monroe, and Karl Malone and John Stockton. All of those players are part of our special section about the 50 Greatest Players in NBA History.

For us, the process of creating a new Encyclopedia is a special endeavor, for as we explore the NBA's past, it allows us to better understand and appreciate the game today. I have had the privilege of working on behalf of the NBA now for more than 30 years, the last 16 as Commissioner, and yet I still enjoy reflecting from time to time on the contributions of those players, coaches and others who have meant so much to the game. And for some of our younger NBA fans, who were not able to see Oscar and Cooz and Wilt in their prime, this book can at least give you some insight into their accomplishments on the court. The same is true for our growing legion of fans around the world who, through these pages, can learn about the people who were the foundation for the current global success of the NBA.

Fortunately, thanks to the wonders of modern technology, we no longer have to stop there. Besides this encyclopedia, we continue to have a large body of historical information on NBA.com. So whether it is in this book or on the Internet, it is always possible to look at the feats of our current and future players in the context of the achievements of those who came before them.

Speaking of the relationship between the players of the past and those of the future, it occurs to me that the previous two editions of the NBA Encyclopedia contained forewords by Julius Erving and this edition has a foreword written by Michael Jordan. And right now there is a player on some NBA team who will, some years down the road, be asked to pen the foreword for the next edition, having achieved his level of greatness in the league. I wonder who that might be?

FOREWORD

BASKETBALL
AN OVERPOWERING FORCE IN MY LIFE

By Michael Jordan

Basketball became my passion at a very painful time. When I was a sophomore in high school, my attitude towards success was the same as it is today. When I set a goal, it was at the very highest level, and at the time, I was intent on making the varsity basketball team. People who are familiar with my past know I didn't make the team and, instead, played on the jayvee squad that year.

My disappointment became my determination.

I also got an assist. The varsity coach was a man named Clifton Herring, and after he cut me, he set up a program where he picked me up at my house every morning at 6:30. He took me to the gym and worked with me on my ballhandling, my shooting and my game. I had been discouraged because I had not made the varsity and I felt like no one believed in me. But when the man who had cut me went out of his way to help me, it became obvious that he did believe in me, and that made me even more determined to succeed.

"TO SUCCEED IN THIS GAME, YOU HAVE TO LOVE IT, RESPECT ITS HISTORY AND UNDERSTAND THAT YOU HAVE A RESPONSIBILITY TO MAKE IT BETTER."

My determination became my dedication.

And basketball became more than a sport. It became a love and a passion, an overpowering force in my life that, to this day, drives me, moves me and motivates me.

The love of the game is why I was so happy to become president of basketball operations for the Washington Wizards. I see it as an opportunity to have an impact on the players of today and the future. I see it as an opportunity to teach them about the responsibility that all of us have to the game. I see it as a chance to teach them how to approach

"When I was in high school, David Thompson was the first player I admired. He had great moves, played the game way above the rim, and was an inspiration to me."

"I was a big Walter Davis fan because of his work ethic and his one-dribble, pullup shot. I implemented some of the things he did into my game."

the game because if you are approaching it the way you should, it doesn't matter if you get paid. True love of the game is knowing that you would play it even if you didn't get paid one dollar. That sometimes gets distorted in today's game because the dollars paid to players are so high. We also place a lot of emphasis on marketing players, and before anyone says anything, I admit that I helped create that situation. If it is a problem, I guess you can say that I'm a part of it.

But I never let money affect the way I approached the game. I always understood the difference between playing and what I did away from the game. It was far more important for me to know that I was going to be remembered for the way I played the game, not the commercials I made. That's the point I want to continue to get across to young players. Money provides security, and that's good. But the only way this game is going to continue to be as successful as the former players have made it is for each player to fulfill his responsibility.

That responsibility is very simple. It is to respect what came before you, build on it, and to leave the game in better shape. That's what I tried to do.

Throughout my career, I learned the game from other people – Dr. J, David Thompson, Walter Davis, Magic Johnson, Larry Bird, Phil Jackson and Dean Smith. I learned the love that you have to have for the game and the dedication that you have to have to perfect it. I always approached the game in the same way that someone with a black belt would approach the martial arts. I didn't want to be good; I wanted to be the master.

So I worked hard to make myself the best player I could be, and I also tried to learn as much about the game as I could. After I got to the NBA, I started meeting some of the great players like Jerry West, Mr. Clutch, and he became my favorite player because we played the same position and a lot of people compared me to him. When I started passing people in the record book, I had a goal of catching him because if I could somehow surpass Jerry West, then I was going to be very successful.

I also wanted to be an integral part of the evolution of the game. Each generation should make the game better. I know my generation did, although I sometimes get into a few friendly arguments with the older players who are proud of what they did for the game. I understand that, but for a number of reasons – advances in training, nutrition, etc. – we were better. It's like I tell them: I can no longer play in Chuck Taylors because they were canvas shoes and I'm used to leather shoes. In essence, the older players are the Chuck Taylors and we are the leather shoes. That is not disrespecting anyone. That's just progress and modernization.

One of the reasons we were better is that we took everything that we learned from players of a previous era and improved on it. I believe that will continue, although when I get older, I sometimes wonder if my pride will make me change my mind and I will end up like some of the former players – arguing that my era was the best.

I will say that right now, I do believe the current players as a group, are better athletes than players were a few short years ago. The danger, however, is that athleticism becomes

"WITH THE WIZARDS, I HAVE AN OPPORTUNITY TO HAVE AN IMPACT ON THE PLAYERS OF TODAY AND THE FUTURE. I SEE IT AS AN OPPORTUNITY TO TEACH THEM ABOUT THE RESPONSIBILITY THAT ALL OF US HAVE TO THE GAME."

"BILL RUSSELL HAS HAD A TREMENDOUS IMPACT ON ME. IT HAS BEEN REMARKABLE TO LISTEN TO HIM. WHEN I LISTEN TO HIM TALK, IT IS LIKE I AM LISTENING TO MY INNER VOICE BECAUSE IT IS EXACTLY HOW I FEEL."

such a focus that you forget about the other aspects of the game, like shooting and defense. I enjoyed dunking, but I worked much harder on shooting and defense. Again, I know I helped increase the popularity of the dunk and playing above the rim, but I try to practice what I preach. One day I came home and my kids had lowered the basket to nine feet so they could dunk. I raised it back to 10 and told them to learn how to shoot.

I'm confident that young players will continue advancing the game, and I hope they will be looking at me the same way I look at players from previous eras. Over the years, I've had enlightening conversations with guys who played in the '50s and '60s like Red Kerr and Bill Russell. I currently work with Wes Unseld, who was a great center in the '60s and '70s. They all have taught me a lot about players I had never heard of, but who were important parts in shaping the NBA.

I didn't really get to know Bill until after the NBA at 50 celebration, but I have talked to him a lot, spent time with him and he has had a tremendous impact on me. The knowledge that he gave me enhanced my attitude towards the history of the game because Bill is truly a historian. It has been remarkable to listen to him because his feelings are so similar to mine. When I listen to him talk, it is like I am listening to my inner voice because it is exactly how I feel.

So I have found a very strong connection between the present and the past, and I think everyone will be able to see it when reading the chapters in this new NBA Encyclopedia. I also believe very strongly that the love of the game is what links the past and the future and I am determined to make sure that the players of today do not forget that. That will be my assist.

MJ – May 2000

CHAPTER 1

BASKETBALL FOREVER

"It's Just One Game."

By Jan Hubbard

The beauty of the play stems from its simplicity and a reliance on nonverbal communication. When teammates understand body language, proper positioning on the court and the precision needed to execute the play successfully, they speak with their eyes.

The play begins with the center or power forward on the opposite side of the lane from the guard with the ball. He suddenly bolts toward the guard and seals off the defender with his back. He is in the *pivot* and prepared to accept the *entry pass*, which he gets without asking. The big man then has a variety of options, including spinning to the basket, shooting a fallaway jump shot, or perhaps moving through the lane for a hook. The players involved could be Karl Malone and John Stockton, Tim Duncan and Avery Johnson, Kevin Garnett and Terrell Brandon or any other tandem in the NBA.

FEW PLAYERS IN HISTORY SEAL OFF THE DEFENDER BETTER THAN UTAH'S KARL MALONE, WHO WILL RECEIVE THE ENTRY PASS FROM JOHN STOCKTON. THIS PLAY WAS FIRST UTILIZED IN THE EARLY 1920S.

The play is approximately eight decades old.

It began during the Roaring '20s at a time when basketball was so simple that after each basket, there was a jump ball. Yet the creativity that would become a staple of the game was already in bloom. The Original Celtics, a barnstorming professional team that operated throughout the East, South and Midwest, were constantly experimenting, dazzling fans with brilliant passing exhibitions and inventing new approaches to the game, such as switching on defense rather than trying to fight through screens. An innovative guard named Nat Holman instructed a strong forward named Dutch Dehnert to step toward Holman when receiving a pass. That enabled Dehnert to seal off

Lamar Odom of the Los Angeles Clippers utilizes the Mikan drill, developed more than half a century ago, to improve his dexterity around the basket.

George Mikan had sensational skills and work habits. It is a tribute to his impact and legend that "the Mikan drill" continues to be a teaching staple.

the player behind him and made the pass easier to catch. The players of today are bigger and stronger and years of practice may have enabled them to execute the play more precisely, but the play has not changed.

* * *

During a mid-morning practice in April 2000, rookie Lamar Odom of the Los Angeles Clippers began a figure-eight put-back drill that involved shooting the ball off the backboard with his left hand, then with his right hand, then left, then right, and doing it continuously until he felt comfortable scoring with either hand.

The drill was invented nearly 60 years ago.

Former DePaul coach Ray Meyer designed it to develop the stamina and coordination of center George Mikan, a player Odom has never even seen on tape or film.

"It's called the Mikan drill," Odom said. "It was named after George Mikan. I know that. I practice it every day to become a better low-post player."

* * *

Before NBA All-Star 2000 in Oakland, it would not have been surprising to read that Vince Carter "was capable of taking off at the foul line and flying to the hoop, where he would jam it through. It was a feat performed publicly by a select few through the years, notably Julius Erving and Michael Jordan, but [he] would do it only in practice for the enjoyment and amazement of his teammates."

The player was not Vince Carter, who obviously has no problem with public dunking displays, and the year was not 2000. The player described by sportswriter Leonard Lewin was Jim Pollard, a 6-5 forward who had such extraordinary jumping ability that he was called "The Kangaroo Kid." Pollard's eight-year career ended in 1955, long before the dunk became a staple of the game.

* * *

"The beautiful thing about basketball is that it never changes," said Orlando Magic Coach Doc Rivers, who played in the NBA for 13 years. "There might be new dunks or fancier plays, but for the most part, everything I did as a player, I did because I had seen it done before. Everything my sons will do will be because they have seen it done

ORLANDO COACH DOC RIVERS, WHO PLAYED IN THE NBA FOR 13 SEASONS, SAYS THE BEAUTY OF BASKETBALL IS THAT AS THE PLAYERS GET BETTER, THE GAME RETAINS ITS CONSISTENCY AND SIMPLICITY.

before. Each generation might take it to a new level, but there are only a certain number of ways that you can play the game. You can be a leaper, you can be a plodder, but you still have to play the game and it's just one game. You can play it fast or slow or at a medium speed, but when you get down to it, the game is about shooting, driving to the basket, setting picks and passing the ball on offense. On defense, it comes down to moving your feet, keeping the guy in front of you, contesting shots and helping or trapping. That has been the way it has been since Naismith invented the game, and none of that will ever change."

It is the consistency and continuity of the game that bond those who have played it. Odom, who was born in 1979, grew up idolizing Magic Johnson, who was born in 1959 and grew up admiring the 11 championships won by Bill Russell. Russell was born in 1934 and experienced a thrill in high school when he met George Mikan, who was born in 1924. Mikan played on one Minneapolis Lakers championship team with Clyde Lovellette, who played at the University of Kansas for Forrest "Phog" Allen, who was born in 1885 and was coached at Kansas by Dr. James A. Naismith, who was born in 1861. Allen also succeeded Naismith as the Kansas head coach in 1907 and coached for the next 49 years, with 39 of those at Kansas.

There is a very real link that connects basketball today with basketball in the beginning, even though the modern version bears little resemblance to the game Naismith conceived in 1891. Fifteen years earlier, Alexander Graham Bell had invented the telephone, and that instrument has about as much in common with a cell phone as today's NBA has with the first game played in Springfield, Mass. Yet there are connections that are as basic as talking on Bell's phone, or the cell phone.

"The main thing about today is that you have more outstanding players," said former Celtics coach Red Auerbach, who coached nine Boston teams to titles and was a club executive during seven other championship years. "But the bottom line is still putting the ball in the hole. That never changes."

It's been that way from the beginning, although the game Naismith created had a peach basket with no hole on the bottom. The basket height was 10 feet, but only because that was the height of the overhead running track where the peach basket was nailed. The first game lasted 30 minutes and was played in a recreation area that was approximately 55 feet long and 35 feet wide. The ball had to be retrieved from the basket exactly one time. William R. Chase made the shot from about midcourt, which is perfect. Even with the shorter floor, the first basket in history was from three-point range.

Once established, the game immediately began changing, but initially there were baby steps. At first, a janitor would sit on a ladder next to the peach basket to retrieve the ball. Later, a small hole was cut in the bottom of the basket so the ball could be popped out with a pole. Then an iron rim with braided cord netting that was stitched at the bottom was manufactured, and that made it easier to poke the ball out of the net. All of that happened within two years. There also was no backboard, but because the basket was nailed below a railing that was surrounded by a walkway, kids could sit above the basket and slap the ball before it went into the basket, which means goaltending is as old as the game. Naismith invented the

In two seasons, Vince Carter has proven to be a worthy successor to the pantheon of high-flying NBA stars like Elgin Baylor, Connie Hawkins, Julius Erving and Michael Jordan.

backboard in 1893 to eliminate that strategy, but for several decades, backboards were used in some places but not in others.

Since the beginning, when basketball was created by a scholar and inventor (Naismith also invented the football helmet), it has attracted great minds and great athletes. The combination of intellect and athletic skills led to a natural progression of the game that continues to this day. Basketball has never feared change. If something does not work, it must be altered. Almost every season, rules are modified in the NBA.

Naismith's original goal was to create a new indoor game that could be played during the cold winter months. There were 18 students in his 1891 gym class, so the first game had nine players to a side. There was no 10-second line, no three-second violation, no frontcourt, no backcourt and no out of bounds. There was not even a basketball — a soccer ball was used. And the game was not even spelled the same — it was two words, Basket Ball.

As early as 1896, players began earning money for games, thus becoming professionals. But it was a tough game — so tough that cages of steel mesh were placed around the court to separate players and fans. The game was more like football than the modern basketball game. Players would get pushed into the wire and would be bleeding, but play would continue. Before the 1999-2000 NBA season, new rules were implemented to reduce physical play. The early game, however, needed something stronger than new rules — perhaps a suit of armor, if an inscription on a plaque in the Naismith Memorial Basketball Hall of Fame is any indication.

Early basketball was a violent and sometimes brutal game. Players slammed into each other with abandon and injuries were common.

Padded pants, knee guards and elbow pads were standard issue. "The center tap was murderous," said one early star. "I've seen guys get crippled."

Gradually rules were changed. A rope net replaced the steel cage after only a few years, and by 1929, the cage had been eliminated (although the term "cagers" remained popular for many years and is still sometimes used). A few years later, the center jump that had occurred after each basket was also history. And basketball had become one word.

But there was still a long way to go. In 1936, 45 years after the game was invented, basketball was played in the Olympics for the first time, but on an outdoor court. The U.S. won the gold medal game over Canada 19-8, and it is accurate to say it was a sloppy game.

It was raining.

In 1986, an NBA game between Phoenix and Seattle was postponed because of a leak in the roof, which might have amused one of the Olympians because in '36, even a partial roof would have been a luxury.

Basketball taken as a whole offers many cases of history at least attempting to repeat itself. In some cases, ancient history was even more impressive on paper than modern times.

Consider that the NBA record of 33 consecutive victories was set in the 1971-72 season by the Los Angeles Lakers. The Buffalo Germans, a barnstorming team that has been enshrined in the Hall of Fame, won 111 consecutive games from 1908 to 1910.

In 1993, Micheal Williams of the Minnesota Timberwolves made 97 consecutive free throws, which is the NBA record. In the early 1930s, a player for the Indianapolis Kautskys, a barnstorming team, made 138 consecutive free throws in game competition. That is, perhaps, one of the more incredible, little-known facts about Hall of Fame coach John Wooden, who is also enshrined as a player.

The most points scored during a game in the 1999-2000 season were 61 by Shaquille O'Neal. In 1949, Joe Fulks of Philadelphia scored 63 points, and that was five years before the institution of the 24-second clock, which is credited with speeding up the game and increasing scoring.

Those examples are not to suggest that the old days necessarily were better — they simply demonstrate that no matter the era, certain players and teams reached an elite level. While athletic skills have continually improved, there still is that thread that is common to all champions.

"I've asked some of the older coaches, like Coach Wooden and Tex Winter, what made the players of earlier eras great, what separated them from all the others," said Bill Walton, who played on championship teams at UCLA as well as in Portland and Boston. "And it is the same simple answer that makes players excel today — heart, brains, soul and competitive greatness. Being a champion has always been more about human qualities than basketball strategy."

There is little doubt, however, that in each era, someone comes along and takes basketball to a higher level. Some of the advances are so fascinating because of the historical extremes they connect. One occurred in the early 1970s when Julius Erving was playing in the ABA. After a typically brilliant high-flying performance, Erving, who was born in 1950, encountered legendary Kentucky coach Adolph Rupp in a hallway near the locker room. Rupp, who was born in 1901, was the essence of basketball conservatism and the flamboyant Erving was the polar opposite of what Rupp wanted, and what he taught.

That, however, was before Rupp watched Erving play a game in Louisville. After the game, Rupp told Erving: "You made me realize that there's something I've been teaching all these years that I need to re-think. And that's that a player cannot leave his feet and not have his mind made up. I have always coached that any time you leave your feet, know exactly what you're going to do. But I have to re-think that."

Erving still smiles at the memory. "That left him open to thinking about leaving your feet and letting things happen," Erving said, and then added proudly: "That's changing a purist."

RECOGNIZE THIS LEGEND IN THE MAKING? JOHN WOODEN IS IN THE HALL OF FAME AS A COACH AND PLAYER AND ONCE MADE 138 CONSECUTIVE FREE THROWS AS A PRO.

to do because you've got to get your rhythm together. People never even noticed that. That was my way of improving on what Dr. J did. That was taking it to the next level — the evolution of the dunk. And then in the All-Star Game in 2000, Vince Carter took off with two hands from the free throw line. That's the evolution of how change happens. Dr. J ran, I dribbled and Vince Carter is adding the two hands, which is increasing the norm."

As the norm increases, however, the beauty of the game is that those who love it can stay connected with the roots and recognize the commonality that stretches across generations and eras.

"If Naismith saw the game now, he would be very proud," said Rivers. "He would say, 'Wow! The end product is the same thing that I started with. The difference is that guys can do more. They can jump higher, they're faster and stronger. But this is still basketball.' "

Michael Jordan has another example that involves the comparisons between Erving, his inspiration, and himself. Erving first dunked from the foul line in the slam dunk contest at the 1976 ABA All-Star Game in Denver. Jordan duplicated the feat at the 1985 NBA All-Star Weekend in Indianapolis.

"I'll give you a great example of the evolution of the game," Jordan said. "In the slam dunk contest, the major feat was to take off from the free throw line. Dr. J was the first to do it, then I did it. What was different about the way the two of us did it?"

When a pause produced no answer, Jordan said:

"When Dr. J took off, he ran. I dribbled, which is harder

It is that continuing evolution that enables basketball purists to connect the past with the future and the possibilities it offers.

"I respect the history of the game and that is what is most important," said Kevin Garnett. "Without the history of the game, there would be no KG, no Vince Carter, no Kobe Bryant. We have a lot more young people in the game right now, but our vision is no different from the players that came before us. You always have a goal to transcend the game itself. That is the vision, and it hasn't changed. That's the vision I have and I share it with all of the players who have had the same vision."

CHAPTER 2

TOMORROW'S GAME

It's in Good Hands

By Bryan Burwell

Pro basketball at the dawn of the 21st century is in a fascinating place, caught between the magnificent achievements of a brilliant past and the tantalizing potential of an uncertain future. In these early years of the post-Jordan/Dream Team era, there is a nervous vagueness about what lies ahead for the NBA.

We are looking for solutions to this uncertainty, so there seem to be more questions than answers. Who will lead pro basketball in the new millennium? Who will replace Michael Jordan as the next great American athletic icon? Will there ever be another Magic vs. Bird, or Lakers vs. Celtics — that compelling rivalry that captures not only our hearts and souls, but also drives the Nielsen ratings through the roof? And Lordy-be, can't we please find someone, anyone, who can be as outspoken and irreverent as Sir Charles?

KOBE BRYANT, WHO HELPED THE LOS ANGELES LAKERS TO THE NBA TITLE IN 2000, IS ONE OF A LARGE COMPLEMENT OF EXCITING STARS.

Well, I come loaded with answers. That's my job. Part of the reality of the NBA of the new millennium is its rich history. The NBA of the last quarter of the 20th century was so brilliant that it tends to blind us to the promising glow of what the future holds.

So, if for a moment, can we simply imagine the undeniable promise of an NBA with Shaquille O'Neal and Kobe Bryant fueling a new Laker dynasty? How about the anticipation of more monumental meetings between Shaq and Tim Duncan with the prospect of a latter-day Chamberlain vs. Russell rivalry? Beyond these dreams are more New Jack b-ballers, equally worthy of our passions. How much anxiety can you have about a sport that has Jason Kidd, Vince Carter, Kevin

THE SHEER POWER AND JAW-DROPPING ATHLETICISM OF THE LAKERS' SHAQUILLE O'NEAL ENSURE THE LEGACY OF GEORGE MIKAN AND WILT CHAMBERLAIN WILL ENDURE.

KEVIN GARNETT COMBINES THE SPEED AND AGILITY OF A GUARD WITH THE REBOUNDING AND SHOTBLOCKING OF A CENTER IN A NEAT PACKAGE AS A 7-FOOT FORWARD.

Garnett, Chris Webber, Allen Iverson, Eddie Jones, Jalen Rose, Allan Houston, Latrell Sprewell, Elton Brand and Grant Hill entertaining us?

If you look at Alonzo Mourning and Gary Payton, Steve Francis and Tracy McGrady, Ray Allen and Glenn Robinson, just to name a few, the reality is, there is that new prosperity right around the corner. The league has more than enough well-schooled veterans and up-and-coming young bucks to rebound from the post-Jordan years.

What, exactly, are we nervous about? Hasn't this all happened before? Aren't these anxious moments simply a part of pro basketball's timeless evolution? Before there was Magic, Bird or Isiah Thomas, there was Marques Haynes, Bob Cousy and Earl Monroe — below-the-rim masters of improvisation who dazzled fans with their sleight of hand and foot.

Aren't Kidd, Payton and Jason Williams the next of that generation?

Before there was a Hakeem Olajuwon, weren't there George Mikan, Bill Russell, Wilt Chamberlain and Kareem

CHRIS WEBBER'S SOFT HANDS, NIMBLE FOOTWORK AND DEEP SHOOTING RANGE MAY REWRITE THE DESCRIPTION OF THE POWER FORWARD POSITION ENTERING A NEW AGE.

A HUGE PIECE OF CHICAGO'S REBUILDING EFFORT, THE MULTI-TALENTED ELTON BRAND AVERAGED BETTER THAN 20 POINTS AND 10 REBOUNDS AS A ROOKIE.

Abdul-Jabbar — brilliant centers who altered our notions of the big man?

Tell me Shaq hasn't already climbed into that rarefied air with his first championship and MVP season.

And of course, the most breathless evolution of all came from that line of gravity-defying visionaries who allowed us to imagine the possibility of endless flight above the rim: from Elgin Baylor to Connie Hawkins, from Julius Erving to Dominique Wilkins and the highest flyer of them all, Michael Jordan.

And now we not only have a soaring Bryant on the West Coast, but we also have "Air Canada," Vince Carter, hang-gliding into our consciousness with even more spectacular 360-degree flights of fancy. We are going from air to space.

So as the old guard of Dream Teamers step aside now, loaded with their championship hardware and Hall of Fame

THE NEXT SKYWALKER IN THE NBA MAY EMULATE YOUNG HEROES LIKE STEVE FRANCIS OF THE HOUSTON ROCKETS, HERE EXHIBITING HIS POWERS OF LEVITATION.

PLAYERS WITH TRUE SCORING GENIUS COME IN ALL SHAPES AND SIZES. PHILADELPHIA'S ALLEN IVERSON STANDS SIX FEET TALL, BUT HE INVENTS NEW WAYS TO SCORE EVERY TIME HE PLAYS.

careers, let's take a deep breath and realize that the family business is in good hands after all.

A few years ago, upon being named one of the 50 Greatest Players in NBA History, Julius Erving took the time to write these words of thanks that today seem right for the times:

"For 16 years, the action within the black lines allowed my alter ego, 'Dr. J,' to soar, score and redefine my sport as an art form. My predecessors, Elgin Baylor and Connie Hawkins, paved the way for George Gervin and Michael Jordan. God bless you, and may the next in line live up to advance billing."

These were not the words of a nervous man. They were the words of a prophet. Erving was not wondering; he was predicting, envisioning. And his words have come true. The next ones in line are already here. All we need to do is enjoy the show . . . and imagine the possibilities.

CHAPTER 3

MICHAEL JORDAN

Modern-Day Icon

By Art Thiel

In a culture with an inexhaustible passion to rank, to quantify, to compare and contrast everything, Michael Jordan became the universal measuring device for appraising greatness. Jordan the athlete, as well as cultural icon, had such an effect on global society that descriptions of standout athletes in other sports, as well as top artists, business executives and elite achievers in any field, began with: "He/she is the Michael Jordan of … "

MICHAEL JORDAN DOMINATED THE NBA IN THE 1990S, BUT HIS TALENT AND CHARISMA ALLOWED HIM TO MAKE THE LEAP TO CULTURAL ICON.

The person being described was never quite "the Jordan of …" but it was a point of reference almost universally understood. The standard response?

"Oh, really? Wow."

Jordan so dominated the basketball world that, for the second half of a pro career that spanned 1984-98, there was no debate about the game's supreme player — an astonishing distinction in a time when superb athletes proliferate. Previous eras argued Wilt versus Russell, Robertson versus West, Magic versus Bird. But Jordan stood alone, so far ahead of his peers that individual rivalry ceased.

He was so far apart that he even broke a basic rule of literature: All protagonists must have antagonists. Jordan remained a great drama despite the lack of a persistent adversary. With attention unsplintered, the focus went to the ultimate player instead of the ultimate battle.

He even undid team rivalries. His Chicago Bulls won six of the eight championships from 1991-98 against five different teams from the Western Conference. The Bulls' misses were in 1994 and 1995 when Jordan missed most of two seasons while playing baseball. It was the only period in Jordan's pro athletic career when the phrase "minor league" could be attached with accuracy.

Even his Bulls teammates had a hard time keeping up. In spanning the decade of the '90s with championships, he had only a single teammate for the entire time — Scottie Pippen. The Bulls' roster was remade several times, but the Jordan-Pippen axis was invulnerable to any basketball force from outside or inside.

Most remarkably, neither Jordan nor Pippen was the 7-foot monolith previously believed to be the mandatory requirement for sustained NBA success. Basketball's presumed minimum physical virtue, height, was not a part of their games and almost no part of the Bulls' championships. Jordan was of mortal appearance, but not of mortal deed. Or as Larry Bird put it after he watched Jordan score 63 points in a playoff game against his Celtics in 1986, "I think he's God disguised as Michael Jordan."

A little hyperbolic, but it also seemed as if earth rules never applied. Even he seemed to sense something a little cosmic.

"I don't know about flying," Jordan said in 1995, "but sometimes it feels like I have these little wings on my feet."

The last image of Jordan's on-court career — a game-winning 20-foot jumper in Salt Lake City's Delta Center in June, 1998, to beat the Jazz for the Bulls' final Jordan-era championship — was a repeat of so many devastating knockout punches that it seemed he had been doing these feats forever. In fact, it took a long time to reach the pro pinnacle, a steady appreciation over nine years — from the skinny North Carolina freshman's jump shot to win the 1982 NCAA Championship to the Bulls' defeat of the Los Angeles Lakers for the 1991 NBA title — before his nonpareil status was certified.

Until then, the conventional wisdom was that Jordan was like many an individual scoring champion and/or highlight-video player — a part greater than the whole. But Jordan demonstrated that extraordinary physical gifts were not sufficient by themselves to create the game's greatest player.

"The thing about Michael is he takes nothing about his game for granted," said Phil Jackson, who shared Jordan's six title rings while coaching the Bulls. "When he first came into the league

NBA.COM FACT

Jordan led the league in scoring seven straight seasons from 1986-87 to 1992-93, a feat accomplished by only one other player — Wilt Chamberlain.

Jordan, who won five MVP awards, left the NBA as one of the most decorated players of all time.

Jordan's numerous game-winning shots and plays burnished his legend. Teammates and opponents alike agreed that Jordan was a step above the rest.

in 1984, he was primarily a penetrator. His outside shooting wasn't up to pro standards. So he put in his gym time in the offseason, shooting hundreds of shots each day. Eventually, he became a deadly three-point shooter."

He led the NBA in scoring a record 10 times with a 31.5 points per game average, another all-time mark. What made the achievement even more remarkable was that he did so while playing the other end of the floor as well. Nine times he was named to the NBA's All-Defensive First Team, and in 1988, he was named NBA Defensive Player of the Year.

"Playing outstanding defense didn't come automatically to him, either," Jackson said. "He had to study his opponents, learn their favorite moves and then dedicate himself to learning the techniques necessary to stop them. He has worked extremely hard to perfect his footwork and balance."

As Jordan embarked upon his teardown of the perception that a supreme scorer could never be a champion, he was also distinguishing himself personally from all other athletes. In a 1980s world newly impressed by ESPN, MTV and the worldwide media explosion, Jordan shaved his skull, wore audacious red sneakers and let the hem of his shorts flirt with his knees. He didn't invent the fashions, just as he didn't invent the smile and the wink, but he combined all of them in such an engaging manner that the once-unsightly affectations became trendy, and his image became nearly as admirable as his unsurpassed skills.

As his playing career was closing, Jordan created his own line of cologne and clothing, presuming shrewdly that while no one can be like Mike exactly, the chance to smell and dress like him will be, in a world given over to computer-generated simulations, virtually enough.

While some suggest that Jordan was already unreachable even for the most active imagination, his relative humanity is at the center of his appeal. A grandson of a sharecropper, Jordan was cut from his high school varsity basketball team as a sophomore, and could not afford his own bicycle until he was 16. Though his basketball skills are transcendent, they are not so freakish as to be unfathomable. He was a shorter, slender man dominating giants, and for that there is no shortage of projection from millions of people convinced they were built too closely to the planet surface.

Throw in eye contact, articulation, a handsome sexiness and acceptance from Bugs Bunny, and he became a ubiquitous pitchman who sold tight underwear and baggy outerwear to a mainstream America that would have considered such fashion delivered another way as a threat from the streets.

The distance that separated him from the second-best also created a suction that brought to basketball millions upon millions of casual fans, many of whom seldom paid attention to the playoff race but set their VCRs to his national TV schedule.

Following the electric rivalry between Magic Johnson and Larry Bird that dominated the 1980s, Jordan's wonders helped continue the NBA's huge leap in national and international popularity. The parallel ascensions of Jordan and the league were not coincidence. During the press conference announcing Jordan's retirement on January 13, 1999, Bulls owner Jerry Reinsdorf hit the trenchant point.

"The truth is that for what Michael has meant to the NBA," he said, "his number 23 could very well be retired in

Early in his career, Jordan vacationed in Paris, enjoying the anonymity. A few years later, he visited and found that he had become a landmark.

DESPITE HIS SCORING PROWESS, JORDAN DELIGHTED BASKETBALL PURISTS BY EXCELLING AT OTHER PARTS OF THE GAME.

every arena in the league."

His aura extended worldwide, often to countries where basketball had been only a minor diversion. Upon the Bulls' arrival in Paris for the McDonald's Championship in October 1997, the front-page story in France's *Le Soir* national newspaper began:

"Michael Jordan is in Paris. That's better than the Pope. It's God in person."

Jordan was among the handful of sports figures of the 20th century whose virtuosity and personality was so transcendent that he drew millions who otherwise would have no particular knowledge or affinity for the exercise. Jordan's predecessor in that regard was Muhammad Ali, and before him Joe DiMaggio. Before DiMaggio, there was Babe

NBA.COM FACT

Jordan topped the 50-point mark in the playoffs eight times. He has five of the top-10 highest scoring playoff games in history.

Ruth. Following Jordan is golfer Tiger Woods.

But no athlete reached Jordan's breadth of emotional impact. He hit notes normally reserved for pop music stars — Elvis, the Beatles, Frank Sinatra. Upon the death of Princess Diana, reporters rushed to Jordan to seek comparisons about skirmishes with the paparazzi.

Who better to speak about the perils of royalty?

That Jordan stimulated so many so deeply is a result of a unique confluence of events. His magnetism as well as his astonishing force of basketball will intertwined fortuitously with the invention of athletic-shoe marketing, a combination no veteran hoopster or wizened Wall Streeter could have foreseen 20 years ago. The timing coincided with an explosion of sports media, not only print and broadcast, but also advertising. The burgeoning sports-marketing wave sent his and the NBA's image around the world to millions who would not otherwise have noticed.

Cultural anthropologists will divine many explanations, and a few lamentations, for the spread of this seed, but there is no argument that the distribution was breathtaking. Jordan in December 1997, was the first athlete named No.1 in *The Sporting News'* annual list of the most powerful people in sports. In choosing Jordan, the magazine identified him as the lone one-sport athlete who touched multiple

WHEREVER JORDAN GOES, CROWDS FOLLOW.

industries and nations, a distinction normally reserved for media moguls whose influence is felt in multiple sports.

What has launched Jordan to this frontier was a competitive nature that apparently was unprecedented in the world of pro athletics. By now, anyone who followed the Bulls has a story of Jordan's relentless desire.

"He came into camp like a man possessed," said Steve Kerr, a teammate on three title teams. "Every practice, every shooting drill was just a huge competition. It set the tone for our season. There was definitely a purpose to it. He was trying to show us what we had to do to be champions."

Chuck Daly, the coach of the 1992 U.S. Olympic team, tells the story of his time at the Olympics when he edged Jordan in a round of golf. Jordan was beside himself in defeat, demanding another round. Daly, a man who knows when to quit while ahead, declined and ambled off to his hotel.

The knock on his door came at 4 a.m.

"Chuck, it's Michael," Daly recalled hearing. "Let's go play."

Nor can Jordan stand to be second in the game of one-upmanship. At the same Olympics, he was lounging at the hotel with two of sport's ultimate gamesmen, Magic Johnson

NBA.COM FACT

Michael Jordan's 63-point stat line against Boston in Game 2 of the '86 playoffs: 22-of-41 from the field, 19-of-21 at the free throw line, five rebounds, six assists, three steals and two blocked shots in 53 minutes.

When Jordan joined Magic Johnson and Larry Bird on the 1992 U.S. Olympic team, it was a dream come true . . . for all three and the rest of the basketball world.

and Larry Bird, when Johnson allowed as to how he was thinking of unretiring and returning to the Lakers.

"It's so easy [playing against] L.A. now," said a mockingly wistful Jordan, referring to the passage of the Showtime atmosphere when the Lakers under Johnson were formidable. "I think I'm going to start taking my two kids on road trips to L.A. But if you come back, out of respect to you, I'll only bring one."

As the championships piled up, Jordan had to search for ways to create a competitive edge. During the 1996 Finals against the Seattle SuperSonics, after the Bulls had won an NBA-record 72 regular-season games, Jordan was looking for something fresh, no matter how contrived. George Karl, a fellow North Carolina alum, provided it.

The Sonics coach was quoted in the papers saying Jordan no longer drove to the basket as much, preferring his fadeaway jumper. The observation was hardly a scoop, having been noted for years by many NBA observers. But Jordan made himself a mountain from Karl's molehill. He put up 38 points, saying afterwards, with a strong hint of sarcasm, that his skills probably had diminished, that Karl probably was right. Karl was left in the familiar position of Jordan victims: sputtering.

"I said it," he said, "but I didn't mean it that way."

Too late. With Jordan, there are no do-overs.

Four years later, as the NBA entered a new millennium, Jordan moved to the management side of the league. Almost two years after his retirement as a player, Jordan became president of basketball operations and part-owner of the Washington Wizards.

Jordan was back, albeit in a suit. Still, there was the same fierceness wrapped in grace that the world had witnessed. For Jordan, the job will be different because it can never be what he had before: "The easiest job in America," as he once described playing basketball. "You could go out and play for two hours and gain the notoriety and respect of millions, yet be the best at what you do."

No, the easiest job was watching Michael Jordan. It is foolish to say that there will never be another like him. Who imagined the first one? But he will be what all those who follow him are measured against — the standard bearer for the sports world, and worlds beyond.

NBA.COM FACT

Jordan holds the NBA Finals record for most consecutive games scoring 40 or more points, with four in the 1993 Finals against the Phoenix Suns. The Bulls defeated Phoenix four games to two.

JORDAN'S WORLDWIDE APPEAL HELPED TRANSFORM THE NBA FROM A SUCCESSFUL AMERICAN SPORT TO A GLOBAL PHENOMENON THAT TRANSCENDED NATIONAL BOUNDARIES.

CHAPTER 4

GEORGE MIKAN

The First Icon

By Dan Barreiro

On a cool Los Angeles morning in October 1998, Kareem Abdul-Jabbar climbed into his Ford Expedition to take a drive.

A long drive.

His objective was to clear his head a bit of the L.A. bustle and smog, and to try something new. So he headed for a little town called Whiteriver, Ariz. There, on the White Mountain Apache Reservation, he would become a volunteer coach for the Alchesay Falcons High School basketball team for one season. There, he would instruct the team's teenaged big men on the fundamentals. There, he would show them something called the Mikan drill, a drill conceived by DePaul coach Ray Meyer, but perfected by Mikan.

"The kids, of course, had never heard of George Mikan," Abdul-Jabbar wrote in his book, *A Season on the Reservation*.

Mikan, who started his nine-year pro career in 1946 with the Chicago American Gears of the National Basketball

NBA.COM FACT

In a nationwide poll of writers and broadcasters conducted by *The Associated Press* in January 1950, Mikan was chosen the greatest basketball player of the first half century.

AT 6-10 AND 245 POUNDS, MIKAN WAS SUCH A TOWERING PRESENCE IN THE EARLY GAME THAT THE RULES WERE CHANGED TO WIDEN THE LANE FROM SIX TO 12 FEET IN ORDER TO LESSEN MIKAN'S IMPACT.

LIKE MICHAEL JORDAN YEARS LATER, MIKAN EXCELLED AT BOTH ENDS OF THE COURT, INTIMIDATING OPPONENTS WITH HIS SIZE, ATHLETICISM AND SHOTBLOCKING SKILLS.

League, had done "something that up until then coaches and critics believed could not be done. He'd shown everyone that a truly big man – he was pushing seven feet – could develop the agility and skills needed to play basketball … Mikan quickly opened their minds," wrote Abdul-Jabbar.

"Along the way, George developed his own drill, in which he would stand close to the goal and shoot the ball off the backboard with his left hand, then with his right hand, then switching between his left hand and right hand again, back and forth, over and over again, until he was scoring with either hand in one fluid motion.

"His drill is still the best way to learn how to score under the basket. Since Mikan's day, his routine has been passed along to all the significant centers who have played pro basketball. That list includes Bill Russell and Wilt Chamberlain, Willis Reed and Dave Cowens and Nate Thurmond, Bill Walton and Wes Unseld and Moses Malone, myself and Hakeem Olajuwon."

There can be no greater testimonial to Mikan's influence on the pro game than from the center who would become arguably the most dominant college player of all time, then the most prolific scorer in the history of the NBA.

The kids may forget about Mikan, but Abdul-Jabbar has not, and others should not. Abdul-Jabbar is black, grew up in New York City and was molded by the turbulent '60s. Mikan is white, grew up in Joliet, Ill., and was molded by World War II.

Yet Abdul-Jabbar sees Mikan in himself, and sees Mikan's historic place in the continuum.

At the center position, Mikan was the start of the royal succession that, until Michael Jordan came along, virtually defined the game. Mikan was the first dominant big man. As a college center discovered and developed by Meyer, Mikan led the Blue Demons to the 1945 National Invitation Tournament title, the only college title that mattered at the time.

As a member of the Minneapolis Lakers, he was the anchor of a basketball dynasty. He led the Lakers to six championships in seven years from 1947-48 through 1953-54 – one in the old National Basketball League and five in the NBA. He also won another title with the American Gears in 1946-47, meaning he led his team to the league championship in seven of eight seasons.

He was named the game's best player for the first half of the 20th century, and was also named one of the 50 Greatest Players in NBA History.

He won scoring titles in six straight seasons, once averaging as many as 28.4 points. He developed a devastating hook shot that, some 20 years later, Abdul-Jabbar would further define as the sky-hook.

At 6-10, with broad shoulders and sharp elbows, the bespectacled Mikan was so dominant that the foul lane was

NBA.COM FACT

In an attempt to neutralize Mikan's immense presence in the middle and the Lakers' equally dominant home-court advantage, Fort Wayne played keep-away whenever it had possession of the ball on Nov. 22, 1950. The result was the lowest-scoring game in NBA history, one where Mikan still scored 15 points — including all of his team's four field goals — in a 19-18 loss. The defeat snapped the Lakers' streak of 29 consecutive home victories.

And, like Kareem Abdul-Jabbar years later, Mikan was equally proficient with the sky-hook with either hand. Mikan won six scoring titles and was so dominant that he once averaged 28.4 points while the second leading scorer in the league averaged 21.7—24 percent fewer points.

widened from six to 12 feet to move him away from the basket and the 24-second shot clock implemented so teams would not try to win 19-18.

"George changed the game," said Bud Grant, a Lakers teammate who went on to coach the NFL's Minnesota Vikings. "I have played with and coached many great players. But I'd have to say that George Mikan is the greatest competitor I've ever seen or been around in any sport."

Yet none of this captures Mikan's intangible quality the way a marquee at the old Madison Square Garden did the night of a Lakers-Knickerbockers game in the early 1950s: "Geo Mikan vs. Knicks."

It's not just Abdul-Jabbar's basketball roots that can be found in Mikan. It's also Jordan's.

Mikan was the game's first bigger-than-life star, a precursor of how far a team or league could go in marketing one player to stoke the business. He was on the back of national magazines endorsing beer and chewing gum. He was the subject of an Edward R. Murrow *Person-to-Person* national TV documentary. He was the one player everybody wanted to touch.

"In our time, George was Michael Jordan, Magic Johnson and Larry Bird all rolled into one," said teammate and fellow Hall of Famer Vern Mikkelsen.

"In those days," Mikan remembered, "I'd come in by train or plane a day ahead of the team to promote the game. They'd take me to a hotel and I'd do interview after interview with reporters trying to promote the game."

It is difficult to believe that this was the same gangly fellow

NBA.COM FACT

Mikan established a then-NBA record for rebounds on March 4, 1952, when he grabbed 36 in a game at Philadelphia. He also accounted for 41 of his team's 81 points in the two-point loss.

NBA.COM FACT

After Minneapolis defeated Syracuse in Game 7 of the 1954 NBA Finals to become the first team to capture three consecutive league titles, Mikan announced his retirement. The second-place Lakers were eliminated in the Western Division semifinals one year later and then Mikan came out of retirement to play 37 regular-season games in the 1955-56 campaign, his last.

who was cut from his freshman basketball team at Joliet Catholic High School. Yes, Mikan was even the first superstar, long before Jordan, who suffered this indignity. Those were the days when there were certain stereotypes about big, tall fellows trying to play basketball, especially with eyeglasses.

"You just can't play basketball with glasses on," his high school coach told him. "You better turn in your uniform."

Mikan did, but he would wear one again. He would work day after day to improve his agility. Not just on a court, but on a dance floor at DePaul.

"Coach Meyer had all kinds of ideas on improving my coordination," Mikan said. "When we had dances at school, he would tell me to dance with the shortest and smallest girls. He figured that it would force me to improve my footwork. Otherwise, I'd step on them and hurt them. He figured that would be a pretty good incentive."

Before long, Mikan being big and tall wasn't viewed as a hindrance to playing basketball. Before long, nobody was complaining about the footwork or the glasses.

MIKAN'S CELEBRITY WAS NATIONWIDE, AS EVIDENCED BY THIS PHOTO WITH PRESIDENT DWIGHT D. EISENHOWER.

This is what Abdul-Jabbar admires about the game's first significant big man. This is what he tried to tell the kids at the White Mountain Apache Reservation. Mikan broke down the stereotypes of what a big man can't be, and ultimately, Russell, Chamberlain, Abdul-Jabbar, Walton, Olajuwon and so many more big men followed in his legendary footsteps.

CHAPTER 5

THE GREAT RIVALRIES

Russell vs. Wilt ✦ Bird vs. Magic

By Bob Ryan

Bill Russell terrorized the NBA for three seasons. No one had ever seen anything quite like him.

Then came Wilt Chamberlain.

Bigger by at least three inches, stronger, arguably just as quick, and in possession of the greatest offensive skills from the center position the basketball world had yet seen, Chamberlain loomed as a major threat to Russell's supremacy. On the eve of the 1959-60 NBA season, many people automatically assumed the *Russell Era* was over, that the next dozen years or so would belong exclusively to Wilt Chamberlain.

THE WILT VS. RUSSELL RIVALRY TOWERS OVER ALL OTHERS.

Carl Braun was not one of those people. The veteran Knicks guard had played against each of the pivot greats during the exhibition season, and he figured he knew what made Bill Russell tick after watching him play from the moment he entered the NBA, fresh from winning an Olympic gold medal in December 1956.

"This challenge by Chamberlain is going to make [Russell] better than ever," Braun forecasted. "He's got a lot of pride, and nobody is going to knock him off that All-Star team without a fight."

Red Auerbach couldn't have said it better. Nor could Bill Russell, of course. You want to talk about an A-1 prophecy, start with this one: The Bill Russell reign of terror was only beginning.

But so was the greatest individual subplot in American team sports history. For Wilt Chamberlain was every bit as gifted as his advocates believed. He would rewrite the NBA record book many times over. He would become the greatest individual force in the sport's history. And he would prod Bill Russell into playing some of his very best basketball.

Absent Wilt Chamberlain, Bill Russell would have been

ALTHOUGH CHAMBERLAIN WAS THE MORE PROLIFIC OFFENSIVE PLAYER, RUSSELL WAS HIS EQUAL IN ATHLETICISM AND HAD A VARIETY OF CREATIVE MOVES AROUND THE PAINT.

great. But because of Wilt Chamberlain's Herculean presence, Bill Russell became, as the old Army ad said, all that he could be.

"People say it was the greatest individual rivalry they've ever seen," Russell said. "I agree with that. I have to laugh today. I'll turn on the TV and see the Knicks play the Lakers, and half the time Patrick [Ewing] isn't even guarding Shaq [O'Neal], and vice-versa. Let me assure you that if either Wilt's or Russ' coach had ever told one of them he couldn't guard the other guy, he would have lost that player forever!"

It was the great man-to-man confrontation of the '60s, and, unquestionably the greatest individual rivalry in NBA history. But there was one other that certainly qualifies as an easy No. 2. More than a decade later, fans would be treated to the other great meeting of basketball deities — Larry Bird and Earvin Johnson.

Bird and Magic. Unlike Russell and Chamberlain, their competition began in college. Michigan State's triumph over Bird's 33-0 Indiana State team in 1979 remains the highest-rated NCAA Championship Game of all time.

They were rivals caught up in a larger focus: namely, Boston versus L.A., both as teams and as cities. They also played at a time when the NBA was gaining popularity, particularly on national television. They had similar skills, with a great love for passing, but Bird was a forward and Magic was a guard, and as such, they seldom guarded each other. Their matchup was more of a one-upsmanship thing, but it was no less passionate than the legendary Russell

NBA.COM FACT

Chamberlain holds the NBA record for points in one game, but his most dominant performance may have come at the expense of Russell and the Celtics on Nov. 24, 1960. In a 132-129 loss at Philadelphia, Chamberlain bettered Russell's league mark with 55 rebounds, a record that may be even more unbreakable than the 100 points he would score against the last-place Knicks one season later.

WITH MORE THAN 45,000 REBOUNDS BETWEEN THEM, CHAMBERLAIN (23,924) AND RUSSELL (21,620) ARE THE TWO LEADING REBOUNDERS IN THE HISTORY OF THE NBA.

"Always," Magic confirmed. "He'd say, 'Bring it here. I've got this little one on me.'"

But by the time Bird and Magic came along, the NBA was a far different place from the days of Russell and Wilt. As much as people want to rhapsodize about the rivalry, because the league had grown in size, the two only played against each other 37 times, with Magic and the Lakers holding a 22-15 edge over Bird and the Celtics.

Bill Russell and Wilt Chamberlain went at each other — are you ready? — 142 times during the 10 years of their rivalry. Russell's Celtics won 85 while Wilt, who was with the Warriors, 76ers and Lakers during that period, was on the winning side 57 times. And that average of more than 14 meetings a year was only during the regular season and playoffs. They also played in many exhibitions against each other.

Now that, friends, is a *rivalry*.

Bird and Magic had their exhibition battles, too, since it was in the best business interests of both teams as well as the league to showcase these players and to promote this rivalry as much as possible. There was never any doubt where the great players themselves stood.

None of this "just another game" stuff for either of them. They were acutely aware of each other's movements.

"When the new schedule would come out each year," Magic said, "I'd grab it and circle the Boston games. To me

NBA.COM FACT

In their careers, Bird and Johnson captured three Most Valuable Player Awards apiece. Each was selected to the All-NBA First Team nine times and the Second Team once. In 1981-82, Johnson was bypassed for George Gervin and Gus Williams, and in 1989-90, Bird was beaten out by Charles Barkley and Karl Malone.

and Chamberlain meetings that had enthralled basketball fans in earlier times.

"About the only time we ever guarded each other was on a switch," Bird explained. "He'd be on me, and I'd say, 'Hey, I got a little one.'"

it was *The Two* and the other 80."

"The first thing I would do every morning was look at the box scores to see what Magic did," countered Bird. "I didn't care about anything else."

Now *that's* a rivalry.

What made each of these great rivalries take, of course, was that these epic confrontations were generally fought at the highest level. Russell and Chamberlain (that is to say, Boston and Philadelphia/San Francisco/Los Angeles, due to Wilt's perambulations) played for the Eastern Conference title in 1960, 1962, 1965, 1966, 1967 and 1968, and for the NBA championship in 1964 (San Francisco) and 1969 (Los Angeles). Bird and Magic, each of whom spent his entire career with one team, played for the NBA championship in 1984, 1985 and 1987.

If you were to look at the Russell-Chamberlain rivalry strictly in terms of the individual numbers, you'd say, "What's the fuss?"

Chamberlain averaged exactly 28.7 points and 28.7 rebounds during those 142 games, the point totals brought down a bit by his late-in-career transformation from relentless scoring machine to more well-rounded player. In the early years, Wilt scored 50 or more points seven times against Russell, including a high of 62 on January 14, 1962. By the time we could start referring to these men as "aging warriors," the numbers were a bit more back to earth. Wilt's high game in their final year was 35, and three times he scored in single figures.

Russell's totals against Wilt were 14.5 points and 23.7 rebounds per game. His highest-scoring game against his arch rival was 37.

But Russell had the ultimate trump card. He wound up on the winning side more often than not. In the 10 years in question, Russell won nine championships to Wilt's one. The argument will rage on forever: Did Wilt just not know how to win, or did he lack the supporting cast that Russell enjoyed?

Take the night Chamberlain scored the 62. The Celtics won the game, 145-136. The Celtics led by 31 in the fourth quarter. Wilt scored 42 in the second half, but his team was never in the game. Russell fans say that was an all-too-familiar scenario when these two played, especially in the first five or six years of their duels.

NBA.COM FACT

The All-Star Game was fairly indicative of the Russell-Wilt matchup: The individual statistics favored Chamberlain, while the final score favored Russell. In four such head-to-head meetings, Chamberlain averaged 15.0 points and 16.8 rebounds, compared to 13.0 points and 16.0 rebounds for Russell. But Russell's East team got the best of Chamberlain's West squad each time.

IN CHAMBERLAIN'S FIRST YEAR IN LOS ANGELES, HE TOOK THE LAKERS TO THE 1969 FINALS AGAINST BOSTON, BUT RUSSELL AND THE CELTICS WON GAME 7 IN L.A.

Russell would never go there. He had, and has, nothing but the utmost respect for Wilt Chamberlain, who impressed him from the get-go.

"After I played him for the first time," Russell said, "I said, 'Let's see. He's four or five inches taller. He's 40 or 50 pounds heavier. His vertical leap is at least as good as mine. He can get up and down the floor as well as I can. And he's smart. The real problem with all this is that I have to show up!'"

His appreciation grew with each passing year. By 1962, the third year of their rivalry, their teams would meet for the

The Bird-Magic rivalry, which began in the 1979 NCAA Championship Game, captivated the nation and expanded the NBA's popularity.

Eastern Division championship. Wilt was pluperfectly monstrous that season, averaging a record 50.4 points. The series went seven games, with Russell and friends able to keep the Big Dipper under some kind of control. (In 12 playoff games that year, Wilt averaged 35 points and 26.6 rebounds.) A Sam Jones jumper with two seconds remaining won the seventh game by a 109-107 score, and Russell (19 points and 26 rebounds a game) immediately requested to be left alone for a while.

"I haven't had any sleep all week," he said. "Every time I went out on the court, that guy seemed to grow a little taller."

The Celtics' championship tally grew as well, with Chamberlain being on the losing side in '64, '65 and '66. There was no doubt his frustration was mounting, but he was always civil in public when the issue was raised. After a 30-point, 39-rebound performance brought down the Celtics in Game 2 of the 1965 Eastern Division Finals, for example, Russell heaped praise on his rival.

"The Big Fella was great, real great," he observed. "That was the best game he ever played against me."

Wilt's response: "I don't want to talk about this being a victory over Russell, but a victory over Boston."

There always was a larger context in both the Russell-Wilt and Bird-Magic rivalries. None of the four played in a vacuum. Russell once played on a team with seven future Hall of Famers, not including himself.

Wilt, at various times, played with Nate Thurmond, Paul Arizin, Billy Cunningham, Tom Gola, Hal Greer, Jerry West and Elgin Baylor, who are all in the Hall of Fame, not to mention Chet Walker and Guy Rodgers, who could be. Bird played with Kevin McHale, Robert Parish, Dennis Johnson and Bill Walton. Magic played with Kareem Abdul-Jabbar, James Worthy, Jamaal Wilkes, Norm Nixon, Byron Scott and Michael Cooper.

So very seldom was it all about them as individuals. It usually was about how they fit into the team. That was surely the crux of the Bird-Magic thing — championships.

For a while there was a nice symmetry. Magic won in '80. Bird won in '81. Magic won in '82. Bird won in '84. Magic won in '85. Bird won in '86.

NBA.COM FACT

In three NBA Finals matchups between Bird and Johnson, the Lakers boasted an 11-8 edge in victories and a 2-1 advantage in league championships.

The Magic vs. Bird rivalry had the perfect elements: great teams with charismatic leaders playing on opposite coasts with contrasting playing styles.

ALTHOUGH THEY PLAYED DIFFERENT POSITIONS AND SELDOM MATCHED-UP ON THE COURT, JOHNSON AND BIRD WERE NEVER FAR FROM EACH OTHER'S THOUGHTS.

But Magic and the Lakers took over, even as Bird's body was starting to break down. The favored Lakers won in 1987, but it took a phenomenal effort to win the pivotal Game 4. Did someone say "one-upsmanship?" How about Bird drilling a nerveless corner three-pointer to put the Celtics ahead by two with seconds remaining, only to see Magic seize the moment. After Abdul-Jabbar split a pair of free throws, Magic hit a running hook over Bird, McHale and Parish — yes, all three — a shot Magic called his "junior, junior sky-hook."

Bird even had the last shot, another corner jumper that was a hair long.

"The thing between us was that neither team could ever relax," said Magic. "You never felt the game was over. That night was a great example.

"Even after Larry misses, we were afraid to move. It was like . . . *we won*? . . .With individuals like us, and with two cities going crazy — not just two cities, but *the world* — there will never be another rivalry like it again."

We'll see. It's *possible*, but not probable. No one will ever again play each other 142 times, at least not officially, as did Wilt and Russ. Nor are we likely to get another white guy-black guy, country bumpkin-city slicker matchup with such parallel skills and basketball sensibilities, as Bird-Magic.

Let's just say, with great conviction, that these are the two greatest rivalries in NBA history, and all future ones will be measured against them.

CHAPTER 6

THE COMMISSIONERS

By Mike Monroe

Like most pro sports leagues, the operation of the NBA requires that teams that are highly competitive on the court must operate together to function as a league. No such organization can exist, let alone thrive as the league has for more than 50 years, without outstanding leadership at the top.

Only four men have held the league's top position: David J. Stern, Larry O'Brien, J. Walter Kennedy and Maurice Podoloff. Each man, in his own way, made a significant impact on the league's success and put a particular imprint on its history.

An attorney, Stern began his association with the league in 1966 as an outside counsel and was named NBA General Counsel in 1978. After a promotion to Executive Vice President in 1980, he moved into the Commissioner's office when O'Brien retired in 1984.

DAVID J. STERN

During those years, Stern has participated in virtually every matter that has shaped the NBA, including the landmark 1976 settlement between the NBA and its players that created a free agency system; the collective bargaining agreement that introduced the salary cap and revenue sharing; professional sports' first anti-drug agreement; the development of NBA Properties as the league's marketing arm; and the creation of NBA Entertainment, an award-winning television and multi-media production company. More recently, Stern moved the NBA into the digital age with the development of NBA.com and NBA.com TV.

As Commissioner, he has presided over the expansion of the league to 29 teams and the globalization of the sport. NBA players compete in competitions worldwide, including the Olympic Games, under the aegis of the International Basketball Federation (FIBA), and the NBA has offices in Europe, Australia and Asia.

Under Stern's guidance the NBA has enjoyed its period of greatest growth and taken basketball to the forefront of the global sports scene.

O'Brien played an important role during a tumultuous time for the NBA. He had an unusual background for a sports commissioner. Before he was named Commissioner in 1975, he had served as National Chairman of the Democratic Party, Postmaster General and as a longtime adviser to President John F. Kennedy.

His experience proved to be very valuable. O'Brien applied all his considerable political savvy to both the NBA's absorption of four ABA teams, each of whom was required to pay an entry fee. In his first year on the job, O'Brien also solved one of the league's biggest problems, the so-called "Oscar Robertson Suit," which had both blocked a merger and cost the league dearly in legal fees. O'Brien then helped the league reach a collective bargaining agreement with its players' union.

With Stern serving as the point man, O'Brien presided over negotiations with the union to avert a strike in 1983. The result was a landmark collective bargaining agreement that became a blueprint for the stabilization and growth of the league and led to a unique anti-drug program hailed as the most far-reaching and innovative in professional sports.

The league's first publicity director, Kennedy had gone into business and then politics, serving as mayor of Stamford, Conn., before he rejoined the league in 1963 and was named to the position of NBA President. Kennedy's strengths were in marketing and advertising as well as publicity, but he also was a skillful administrator and negotiator. His legacy, however, was overseeing the expansion of the NBA from nine teams to 18, from coast to coast.

Kennedy served during the formation of the National Basketball Players Association, the players' union. Literally minutes before the scheduled start of the 1964 All-Star Game at Boston Garden, it was Kennedy's personal promise to use his best efforts to force the owners to create a pension plan that saved the event from what would have been a disastrous wildcat strike by the league's star players.

In 1967, Kennedy's title was changed to Commissioner, and in 1971 the owners gave him far-reaching authority to run the league, making him perhaps the most powerful administrative figure in American pro sports at that time.

Podoloff was a Yale-educated lawyer who was born in Russia in 1890 and had come to

LARRY O'BRIEN

J. WALTER KENNEDY

MAURICE PODOLOFF

the United States while still a child. He was selected as the first league president in 1946. Podoloff was a shrewd businessman and a keen negotiator whose brilliance lay in his ability to forge coalitions and recognize the common good, and those were the qualities that enabled him to guide the NBA, originally known as the Basketball Association of America (BAA), through its early years.

The BAA incurred significant losses in its first two years, in part because salaries were escalating, the result of a battle with the National Basketball League (NBL) for the top college players. Podoloff and some of the BAA's owners recognized the solution, thus leading to Podoloff's greatest triumph as league president — a merger in the summer of 1948. Podoloff used the lure of the BAA's big arenas, such as Madison Square Garden and Boston Garden, to convince the leaders of the Fort Wayne Zollner Pistons and the Indianapolis Kautskys that their future could be better served in the BAA.

The NBL team Podoloff really coveted, though, was the Minneapolis Lakers, with their 6-10 star, George Mikan. Podoloff convinced Minneapolis owners Max Winter and Ben Berger that since the NBL was weakened, they should also join the BAA, which they did. So, too, did the Rochester Royals, who had the NBL's best backcourt player, Bob Davies. The NBL survived one season without Mikan and Davies, but before the start of the 1949-50 season the BAA absorbed what remained of the NBL and adopted a new name: the National Basketball Association.

Podoloff presided over the league in 1954, when it adopted the 24-second shot clock, perhaps the most important rules change in pro basketball history. He would remain as the league's top executive until 1963, when he retired at age 73 and was replaced by Kennedy.

CHAPTER 7

THE NBA
1946: A New League

By Leonard Koppett

When Germany surrendered in May 1945, it became clear that World War II would soon end and the civilian world could start thinking about a future. In America, the sports world was no exception.

Baseball, the unquestioned top spectator sport for more than half a century, could look forward to a return to its established normality. Pro football, struggling for a foothold just before the war, was on the road to further development because an expanded college population would keep turning out stars. Hockey, reduced to two Canadian and four American cities during the war, nonetheless retained a firm grip on the northern half of the continent. Boxing and horse racing, the other two major commercial sports, could resume contexts that were as well defined as baseball's.

CAN YOU TOP
THIS?
Anyone Taller Than NOSTRAND 6 Ft. 8 Inches Will Be Admitted Free to OPENING GAME
Apply at Toronto Basketball Club Office Before Thursday Noon
Big-Time Basketball
TORONTO vs.
HUSKIES
NEW YORK
KNICKERBOCKERS
Friday, Nov. 1
SEATS ON SALE NOW
75¢, $1.25, $2.00, $2.50
NOSTRAND
Tallest Husky, 6 ft. 8 in.

WHEN THE BASKETBALL ASSOCIATION OF AMERICA PLAYED ITS FIRST GAME IN 1946, UNIQUE PROMOTIONAL METHODS WERE USED TO ATTRACT FANS.

A group very interested in looking ahead consisted of the operators of big arenas in New York, Boston, Philadelphia, Detroit, Chicago, Pittsburgh, Toronto and elsewhere. These had been built in the boom time of the 1920s to house boxing, the circus, track meets, horse shows, rodeos and other special events, and had brought hockey south of the border to fill their many other open dates. After the 1936 Winter Olympics, ice shows featuring Sonja Henie also became main moneymaking productions.

Dates had to be coordinated for such activities, so the operators formed close working relationships, and in the late 1930s found a new highly successful date-filler with college basketball doubleheaders.

At the time, professional basketball was in ill repute and a commercial failure. Attempts at establishing league play flourished in the 1920s but died in the Great Depression of the 1930s. Games were staged in dance halls and theaters, armories and

NBA.COM FACT

During the BAA's first season, the league set a salary cap of $55,000, and instructed teams to pay players between $3,000 and $10,000 (few made more than $6,000).

NBA.COM FACT

During the 1946-47 season, the New York Knickerbockers played only six games in Madison Square Garden, their "home" arena. The "Mecca of Basketball" scheduled so many college doubleheaders and other events that the Knicks had to play their 24 other home games at the 69th Regiment Armory.

MADISON SQUARE GARDEN IN NEW YORK WAS ONE OF THE ARENAS THAT MADE THE NBA POSSIBLE.

small gyms. A college star's reputation seldom extended beyond the school's immediate locality or region. Most did not continue their careers, and those who did had only two outlets, the small-income professional minor leagues or "amateur" teams subsidized by business firms, which also hired those players.

But from 1936 on, when basketball magnified its spectator appeal by abandoning the center jump after every score and creating a "racehorse" style of play, the college doubleheaders had become a big moneymaker. The college game flourished during the war because outstanding players could stay in school. Some of the best players were too tall for military service; and others who were in service were assigned to on-campus training; still others were too young to be drafted.

When the war ended, there would still be open dates to fill. Hockey, boxing and college basketball (with its short December-March season) took up only five nights a week. Why not a professional basketball league to continue cashing in on the reputations the college stars had built up?

The rudiments of an organization were in place. New York (Madison Square Garden), Boston (the Boston Garden), Detroit (Olympia), Chicago (the Stadium) and Toronto (Maple Leaf Gardens) were partners in the National Hockey League. Hockey's top minor league, the American Hockey League, had Cleveland, Philadelphia, Pittsburgh, Providence, New Haven and St. Louis.

Walter Brown, who owned the Boston Bruins, and Al Sutphin, who owned the AHL Cleveland team, took the lead within the arena operators' group in pushing for a basketball league. John Harris of Pittsburgh, the chief ice show impresario, was in favor. Ned Irish of Madison Square Garden, dedicated to the college basketball phenomenon he had created, was reluctant but unwilling to let an outsider in, so he went along.

On June 6, 1946 — two years to the day after the invasion of Normandy, exactly 10 months after the first atom bomb fell on Japan — they formed the Basketball Association of America during a meeting at New York's Commodore Hotel, next to Grand Central Station. There would be 11 teams playing a schedule of 60 games, each 48 minutes long, to make a full enough evening for ticket buyers accustomed to two 40-minute games.

They chose as league president Maurice Podoloff, who was also president of the American Hockey League, in whose office the BAA could be given some desk space. He knew as little about basketball as he did about hockey, and didn't pretend otherwise, but his knowledge of law and real estate and his familiarity with the club owners suited their needs. To handle publicity, they hired a truly knowledgeable J. Walter Kennedy, well known within the sports media establishment.

The concept was clear-cut: "clean" college boys, fresh from glamorous and well-publicized achievements, would be presented in a college-type (that is, lots of running) game, to continue developing their popularity.

It didn't work, for several reasons:

1. The teams had no identity, and many didn't last long enough to gain one.

2. The college doubleheaders were going stronger than ever.

3. Most of the best existing pros were in the 10-year-old

NBA.COM FACT

The Washington Capitols, coached by 29-year-old Red Auerbach, posted the best record (49-11) in the BAA's inaugural season. The Capitols' .817 winning percentage would not be surpassed for 20 years, when Philadelphia went 68-13 (.840) in 1966-67.

National Basketball League or with industrial teams playing within the structure of the Amateur Athletic Union. You couldn't claim to be "major league" when it was obvious that more proficient players and teams were not included.

4. The biggest arenas, such as Madison Square Garden, couldn't give their teams 30 home dates, and consigned them to smaller courts. So their moneymaking potential was back to square one.

With only seven teams left for the second season, they cut the schedule to 48 games and brought in the Baltimore Bullets from the American League, an eastern weekend league. The Bullets, an old-style pro team with old-pro tug-and-pull techniques, won the BAA championship.

NBA.COM FACT

Each of the Philadelphia Warriors received approximately $2,000 for winning the 1947 Finals.

NBA.COM FACT

The Boston Celtics, New York Knickerbockers, and Golden State Warriors (then the Philadelphia Warriors) are the only franchises remaining from the BAA's first season in 1946-47.

The problem was clear. The pro players to whom basketball fans could respond were in the NBL — operating in Minneapolis, Indianapolis, Fort Wayne (Ind.), Rochester (N.Y.), Syracuse (N.Y.), Sheboygan (Wis.), Oshkosh (Wis.), Moline (Ill.), Anderson (Ind.), Toledo (Ohio) and Youngstown (Ohio). The NBL had the players; the BAA had the arenas and population. They had to merge to thrive.

The key man was George Mikan, who had come out of DePaul in 1946. At 6-10, he was college basketball's dominant player, but instead of coming into the BAA he had joined the Chicago American Gears and led them to the 1947 NBL title. The Gears later folded after their owner tried to

The Philadelphia Warriors won the first NBA championship in 1947 despite having only the fourth best regular season record. The Warriors were led by high-scoring Joe Fulks, whose 23.2 average was 6.4 points more than the second leading scorer. The players are (front row from left): Jerry Rullo, Angelo Musi, general manager Peter A. Tyrell, Petey Rosenberg, Jerry Fleishman and (back row from left): assistant coach Cy Kaselman, George Senesky, Ralph Kaplowitz, Howie Dallmar, Art Hillhouse, Fulks, Matt Guokas and head coach Ed Gottlieb.

form a new league, and Mikan ended up with the NBL's Minneapolis Lakers, where he teamed with Jim Pollard, a superstar out of Stanford. If they came to New York or Philadelphia, they surely would sell out the building — but they weren't in the right league.

Podoloff succeeded in persuading Fort Wayne and Indianapolis to switch leagues on the eve of the 1948-49 season — so Minneapolis decided to come along also. The best team of all was Rochester, and it moved too. Now the BAA had 12 teams, most of the experienced pros and more room for emerging collegians, and it was playing a 60-game season again.

The 1948-49 season proved the BAA was viable; shaky, still unsound economically, but viable. The remains of the NBL were absorbed after the season. The name was changed to National Basketball Association, but in essence and power structure it was the BAA.

But the 1949-50 season, with 17 teams divided into three divisions, playing unequal schedules, and stretching as far west as Denver, nearly broke everyone. The original concept was destroyed. The Lakers and other stars would show up in the big cities too seldom, the old-pro style (rough, slow down) was winning games, and income could not cover expenses.

So the great shakeout took place in the summer of 1950, and when the 1950-51 season started, there were 11 teams. At this point, the NBA was living off two main attractions: Mikan's Lakers (on their way to five championships in six years) and the Harlem Globetrotters, who could (and did) sell out any building as a "preliminary" game. But it had made little headway against college basketball's popularity, and few were ready to predict long-range success.

Then it got its big break.

Point-fixing scandals tore through the college basketball world. Revelations began in January 1951, and continued past October. The New York District Attorney's office finally reported dozens of games in 22 cities in 17 states had been rigged, including tournament games. And no one doubted that this was just the tip of a huge iceberg. The colleges retreated to on-campus sites, away from the "evil" big-city arenas. Doubleheader dates dried up.

NBA.COM FACT

The Rochester Royals squad that won the 1946 NBL title included Otto Graham, the star quarterback of the Cleveland Browns; Chuck Connors, who would go on to gain stardom as *The Rifleman* on television; and Red Holzman, who would later become a Hall of Fame coach for the Knicks.

NBA.COM FACT

The Toronto Huskies, one of the BAA's original franchises, hired Ed Sadowski as their player-coach in 1946 — then traded him to Cleveland 12 games into the season.

That enabled the NBA teams to move in. Their arenas now had dates to fill. And the league, despite cynicism and suspicion, had produced no evidence of manipulated games. The very fact that the players had reasonably well paid careers at stake, and that hard-core gamblers had been concentrating on colleges, helped make pro honesty seem plausible. The situation gave the public's attention a chance to shift to the pros.

Competitive results helped. In the 1951 Finals, the Knickerbockers took Rochester to the seventh game before losing, and the Knicks lost the next two Finals to the Lakers and Mikan. Since New York was then so clearly the center of the world in communications, media and advertising, that period of Knickerbocker success helped the league gain increased prestige and attention. The NBA was becoming a permanent part of the major-league landscape.

One step remained to complete the originally sound idea, so often lost sight of. Post-graduate basketball had to be based in big markets with big arenas. Once the franchises themselves were stabilized, by 1952, the migration out of smaller cities could begin.

By 1960, Rochester was in Cincinnati, Fort Wayne was in Detroit, and Milwaukee was in St. Louis. Before the 1960-61 season, Minneapolis became Los Angeles, and when the Philadelphia Warriors moved to San Francisco in 1962, Syracuse became the Philadelphia 76ers the year after that. Chicago came back and so did Baltimore. That began a process of expansion that has never stopped and reached 29 teams by the end of the century.

It has proven three things.

1. The original vision was correct.
2. It's never easy to turn a vision into a reality.
3. The vision takes time to develop.

CHAPTER 8

THE ROOTS

Early Professional Leagues

By Robin Deutsch and Douglas Stark

While the NBA became a staple in the sports world during the last half of the 20th century, the vision and effort to create a professional basketball league is almost as old as the game. The first professional league began in 1898, only seven years after the sport was created, and many pro leagues came and went during the first half of the 20th century.

THE BUFFALO GERMANS WERE ORGANIZED IN 1895 AS A GROUP OF SIX TEENAGERS WHO PLAYED YMCA BASKETBALL. THEY LASTED UNTIL 1925 AS A TOURING TEAM, COMPILING A 792-86 RECORD.

Most of the leagues were regional, but two leagues — the American Basketball League and the National Basketball League — were somewhat national in scope, and they produced some great players and memorable stories. The barnstorming tradition made popular by the Harlem Globetrotters also has its roots in early basketball. There were a number of teams that went from town to town, earning a paycheck by playing a local team, and eventually three of those teams — the Original Celtics, Buffalo Germans and New York Renaissance — were enshrined into the Hall of Fame.

The first professional basketball game that can be documented took place on November 7, 1896, when the Trenton (N.J.) Basketball Team (formerly the Trenton YMCA team) rented the local Masonic Temple, charged admission and agreed to split the profits should there be any. Trenton defeated the Brooklyn YMCA team 16-1 and the Trenton players received $15 each, with the $1 that was left over going to team leader Fred Cooper — who thus became pro basketball's first "highest paid player." That game also marked the first appearance of the cage, a steel mesh that surrounded the court and separated the players from the fans.

The first pro league on record is the National Basketball League, founded in 1898 with six teams in Philadelphia and nearby parts of New Jersey — hardly "national" in scope. The National League lasted five seasons, but new leagues quickly were formed throughout New England and the Mid-Atlantic states, prominent among them were the Philadelphia Basketball League, Eastern League, Hudson River League, New York State League and the Interstate League.

History was made in 1902 in the New England League when Harry "Bucky" Lew entered a game for Lowell against Marlboro, becoming the first African-American to play in a

NBL TEAMS HAD A LOYAL FOLLOWING, BUT NOT MANY PLACES TO SIT AS EVIDENCED BY THE TWO ROWS (RIGHT BASELINE) OF FOLDING CHAIRS AT A 1941 GAME WHEN THE DETROIT EAGLES PLAYED THE SHEYBOYGAN REDSKINS.

professional basketball game. "At first this manager refused to put me in," he said years later. "He let them play us five on four but the fans got real mad and almost started a riot screaming to let me play. I took the bumps, the elbows in the gut, knees here and there and everything else that went with it. It was rough but worth it."

THE NBL

The most successful league — at least in terms of longevity — was the National Basketball League (NBL), which began as the Midwest Basketball Conference in 1935 but changed its name in 1937 in an attempt to attract a larger audience.

The league began rather informally with scheduling left to the discretion of each of the nine teams as long as the team played at least 10 games and four of them were on the road. Games consisted either of four 10-minute quarters or three 15-minute periods. The choice was made by the home team. Some of the teams were independent while others were owned by companies that also found jobs for their players. And for those who may think that professional sports are too commercialized, consider some of the team names in the NBL — the Akron Firestone Non-Skids, the Akron Goodyear Wingfoots, the Toledo Jim White Chevrolets, the Cleveland Allmen Transfers and the Chicago Duffy Florals.

"Our team was sponsored by the General Electric Company, so they gave me a job working in the factory," said Scott Armstrong, who played for the Fort Wayne General Electrics in 1936-37. "GE paid us $5 a game."

The history of the NBL falls into three eras, each contributing significantly to the growth of professional basketball and the emergence of the NBA. The first dynasty centered on

NBA.COM FACT

Hall of Famer Barney Sedran, who stood only 5-4 and weighed only 115 pounds, once scored 17 baskets in a game for Utica — without a backboard.

the Oshkosh All-Stars, who appeared in the championship series five consecutive years (1938-42) and won two titles. The middle years saw the emergence of the Fort Wayne Zollner Pistons, who were later instrumental in the survival of the NBA during its infancy. The final period of note during the NBL's existence centered around George Mikan and the emergence of the big man in basketball.

The Oshkosh All-Stars were led by rugged 6-4 center Leroy "Cowboy" Edwards. He used a deadly hook shot with either hand and an array of moves around the basket to lead the NBL in scoring three consecutive years (1937-40).

The Zollner Pistons — so nicknamed because they were owned by Fred Zollner, whose company made pistons for engines — were led by tough veteran Bobby McDermott. The Pistons finished second in 1942 and 1943 and won the league title in 1944 and 1945. Like many teams of that era, it wasn't uncommon for Fort Wayne to play its games in taverns, armories, high school gyms or ballrooms.

"In those days, you would drive into town and look for the biggest building," recalled the Pistons' Buddy Jeannette, like McDermott, a Basketball Hall of Famer. "We drove up to this bar and I got out of the car and ran inside and I said to the bartender, 'Hey, we are supposed to play a basketball game in this town today, can you tell me where it is?' He said, 'This is the place.' I looked around and there were tables all over the place. After we got dressed they had shoved all the tables back and put a basket on one wall, and on the other side they had a basket drawn up into the ceiling. The referee drew a big circle on the middle of the floor, and a net dropped down around the floor. And the damnedest fight you ever saw started. That was a real education."

Under Zollner, the Pistons would eventually play an important role in the survival and growth of the NBA. Zollner's financial support of the NBA helped the league stay afloat during its tumultuous formative years.

The NBL's third era was dominated by Mikan, the 6-10,

THE ORIGINAL CELTICS, WHO TOURED INDEPENDENTLY AND ALSO PLAYED IN SEVERAL LEAGUES, WERE A CREATIVE TEAM WELL AHEAD OF THEIR TIME. SOME OF THEIR DEFENSIVE AND OFFENSIVE INNOVATIONS ARE STILL USED IN TODAY'S GAME.

GEORGE MIKAN'S ILLUSTRIOUS CAREER BEGAN WITH THE CHICAGO AMERICAN GEARS. MIKAN LED THE GEARS TO THE NBL TITLE, AND THAT BEGAN A PERSONAL STREAK OF SEVEN CHAMPIONSHIPS OVER AN EIGHT-YEAR PERIOD.

three-time All-American center from DePaul who would emerge as the dominant player in the game. As a rookie, Mikan led the Chicago American Gears to the 1947 NBL title, but before the next season, owner Maurice White pulled his team out of the league and formed his own 24-team circuit called the National Professional Basketball League. That venture quickly failed, and Mikan was signed by the NBL's Minneapolis Lakers, where he teamed with the versatile Jim Pollard to win the 1948 championship.

But after the 1947-48 season, Mikan's Lakers and three other NBL clubs left to join the Basketball Association of America. The NBL, stripped of its best teams and prime gate attraction, lasted only one more season, the Anderson Duffey Packers winning the league's last championship before six of its members were absorbed by the BAA, which changed its name to the National Basketball Association.

The NBL obviously contributed significantly to the foundation of the NBA, but it also had major accomplishments in other areas, most notably in offering opportunities for African-American players. In the 1942-43 season, with many players in the armed forces, two NBL clubs, the Toledo Jim White Chevrolets and the Chicago Studebakers, filled their rosters by signing African-Americans — five years before Jackie Robinson would break baseball's color barrier with the Brooklyn Dodgers. Neither team fared well. Toledo signed several black players to start the season, including Bill Jones, who had starred at the University of Toledo, but the team lost its first four games and folded due to financial difficulties. Chicago stocked its roster with several members of the Harlem Globetrotters, who worked during the week at the Studebaker plant, but it also folded after compiling an 8-15 record.

NBA.COM FACT

In the early 1920s, the Original Celtics went on a 205-game road trip—and posted a remarkable 193-11-1 record.

During the final NBL season, the Detroit Vagabond Kings folded in midseason, their franchise was awarded to one of the most famous of the barnstorming teams, the New York Renaissance Five, comprised of all African-Americans. The team finished the year as the Dayton Rens, marking the first time that an all-black team competed in an all-white league.

THE ABL

The first league of any significance — and the one that paved the way for the NBL, was the American Basketball League, which was founded in 1925. It was the first "national" league with franchises that stretched from New York and Boston in the East to Chicago and Indiana in the Midwest. The ABL advanced the profession of basketball in several ways. It was the first league to sign players to exclusive contracts that prevented them from constantly changing teams, a problem that had plagued earlier regional leagues. It made backboards mandatory in each arena and eliminated the wire cage around the court that had separated fans from players in the sport's early years. The ABL also adopted amateur rules and made the double dribble a violation, creating a style of play that was predicated on speed and agility as opposed to brute strength.

At the time, however, basketball was not very popular, so the league would piggyback its games onto other events such as concerts or dances, a common practice during that era.

"At halftime of a game, fans would go down to the bar and have a drink," said Moe Spahn, an ABL player with

NBA.COM FACT

Chicago Bears owner George Halas, one of the founders of the National Football League, also owned the Chicago Bruins of the ABL and the NBL. Several Bears players served as reserves.

THE DETROIT PISTONS WERE ORIGINALLY BASED IN FORT WAYNE, IND., AND CALLED THE ZOLLNER PISTONS. OWNER FRED ZOLLNER WAS A MAN AHEAD OF HIS TIME, AND EVEN HAD A TEAM PLANE, A DC-3, IN THE EARLY '40S.

Kingston. "After the game the crowd would have a dance to canned music or a band. I think the dance was the real reason they came to the game."

The Cleveland Rosenblums, led by John "Honey" Russell, won the championship of the nine-team ABL in its inaugural season. The following season, the league strengthened itself by adding the Original Celtics, a barnstorming troupe that was arguably the world's best team with stars like Joe Lapchick, Dutch Dehnert, Nat Holman and Pete Barry. It also added the Philadelphia Warriors, an offshoot of another prominent barnstorming club, the SPHAs. That team was run by Eddie Gottlieb, a master promoter and lifelong basketball man who would go on to play a prominent role in the NBA for many years.

The Original Celtics overpowered the rest of the ABL, winning championships in their first two seasons in the league. They were so dominant that the league sought ways to break up the Celtics, finally getting the opportunity after the team's manager, Jim Furey, was convicted of embezzling. The team's players were dispersed, and the 1929 title went to the Cleveland Rosenblums — a team that had been strengthened by the additions of Lapchick, Dehnert and Barry. Those three joined ex-Celtics Johnny Beckman and Carl Husta, leading many to refer to the club as the Rosenblum Celtics.

Despite the crash of the stock market and the onset of the Great Depression, the ABL attempted to plow on. Cleveland won the title again in 1930 but folded early the following year, and after Brooklyn won the crown in 1931, the league suspended operations. Attempts would be made to revive it, but it would never again achieve the status of a national league.

EARLY LEAGUES

The ABL was a model of stability compared with pro basketball's earlier leagues, which folded almost as quickly as they sprang up. Each league operated under different rules and there were no contracts to bind one player to a team and a league. It was not uncommon to see players play for a team in one league one night and then travel to another city and play for another team in another league the next night. For example, in the 1914-15 season, Hall of Famer Barney Sedran led Carbondale, Pa., to 35 consecutive victories and the championship of the Tri County League while at the same time helping Utica to a 15-11 record in the New York State League.

The best players sold their services to the highest bidder on almost a nightly basis. In 1919, Lapchick, who is in the Hall of Fame, split his services among several teams including those in Holyoke, Mass., Schenectady, N.Y., and Brooklyn, N.Y.

"Sometimes there were important games in Schenectady or Brooklyn," Lapchick said. "I'd make a phone call and tell the Holyoke manager I had a chance to play for $45 in Schenectady. 'Don't let a few dollars stand in your way. I'll pay you $50,' he'd say. That would lead to several more phone calls and the first thing I knew I was selling myself to the highest bidder for $75 a game. Like the rest of the fellows, I'd play where the money was."

BARNSTORMING TEAMS

Some of the best teams of the era disdained affiliation with leagues, or moved in and out of leagues as it suited them. They found they could make more money by barnstorming — traveling around the country, playing one-night stands against local teams and then moving on. Among the best-

NBA.COM FACT

The Original Celtics became so popular that President Calvin Coolidge entertained them at the White House in 1925.

known of these teams were the Original Celtics, the SPHAs and the Buffalo Germans, who once won 111 consecutive games and compiled a 792-86 record from 1895 to 1929. One of the Germans' victories came against the Carlisle Indians, a team that featured the legendary Jim Thorpe. Other noteworthy barnstorming teams included the Trojans of New York, and two teams comprised of African-Americans, the New York Renaissance Five and the the Harlem Globetrotters.

The SPHAs, an outgrowth of a team created by Eddie Gottlieb, Harry Passon and Hughie Black in 1918 in Philadelphia, had a successful 31-year run before disbanding at the end of the 1948-49 season. One of professional basketball's pioneering teams, the SPHAs, an acronym that stood for South Philadelphia Hebrew Association, a social club from which the team derived its name, won championships in the Philadelphia League, the Eastern League and the ABL.

When the Philadelphia League disbanded, the SPHAs took their show on the road. In one stretch, they won nine of 11 games against the Cleveland Rosenblums — the ABL's premier team — the Original Celtics and the Rens.

The Original Celtics' impact on the game before they entered the ABL was profound — from the first individual contracts to the zone defense to working the ball into the pivot. Descendants of the New York Celtics, a team organized in 1914 to represent a settlement house on Manhattan's tough west side, the Original Celtics were formed after World War I by Jim Furey, a New York promoter, and his brother Tom.

The Original Celtics became one of the dominant teams by adding the best players, such as Dehnert, Holman, Lapchick, Barry, Swede Grimstead, Johnny Beckman and Horse Haggerty. Jim Furey created stability by renting the 71st Regiment Armory in Manhattan for Sunday night games and by signing the players to the first individual contracts in the history of basketball, which meant no more switching teams or leagues at the highest bidder.

The team experimented constantly with great success,

The Cleveland Rosenblums won two ABL championships and were led by Hall of Famers Dutch Dehnert (fourth from left) and Joe Lapchick (fifth from left).

averaging more than five victories for every six games. They were superb showmen, and none was better than Holman. He had Dehnert step toward the pivot pass, sealing the defender off with his back, a tactic that is still a basic of fundamental basketball. But Holman's biggest attribute on the court was the feint, which invariably drew fouls, often the results of imaginary contact. That move has survived, although it is now called the "flop."

Primarily a barnstorming team, the Original Celtics did play in a couple of professional leagues before their ABL days. They joined the Eastern League for the second half of the 1921-22 season, when they beat Trenton in a best-of-three championship.

The following season they joined the Metropolitan League, but dominated so thoroughly — 13-0 — they withdrew for lack of competition. They rejoined the Eastern League, replacing the Atlantic City team, but again won so easily they couldn't attract enough people to cover their $900 weekly guarantee. They dropped out when the owner sought to cut the salaries to $400.

So the Original Celtics went back to barnstorming, touring the country for appreciative fans.

THE CAGERS

By Barry Rubinstein

In its early stages, professional basketball was violent and chaotic. And that was on the court. Players armed themselves with knee, elbow and shin pads. At worst, it could resemble something closer to a riot with players vulnerable to physical attack from vitriolic, mean-spirited crowds cramped inside the tiny halls and gymnasiums where the games were played.

Frank Basloe, an early promoter and manager, remembered a Trenton player being knocked out cold during a game in Millville, Pa., as the fans "proceeded to kick him in the face. He ended up with a broken jaw." Indeed, home-court advantage certainly carried a much different connotation

The cage was an early staple of professional basketball, protecting unruly fans and tough, no-nonsense players from one another. At first, the cages were made of chicken wire or steel mesh. When the rope mesh cage (above) was invented, players had fewer concerns, and fewer cuts.

Barney Sedran, a Hall of Famer, played in the early 1900s during the "cage" era. "Players would be thrown against the wire," said Sedran. "And most of us would get cut. The court was covered with blood."

than it does today.

Such incidents resulted in drastic measures. The Trenton team took to playing its games inside a wire cage, designed to separate the players from the bellicose fans, and vice versa.

That was the intent, anyway. To Fred Paderatz, who managed the Trenton team part-time when he wasn't toiling at his regular job as a carpenter, fashioning the first cage from chicken wire seemed to provide adequate protection for all involved. Fred Cooper, the team captain, advanced the process by building a stronger cage of steel mesh.

The reality led to unexpected results; players learned to change direction and elude opponents by bouncing off the siding of the cage, ripping their skin apart in the process, despite the padding they wore. "Players would be thrown against the wire," recalled Barney Sedran, one of the great small players of the time, "and most of us would get cut. The court was covered in blood."

Not surprisingly, the players quickly developed an affinity to a net made of rope rather than steel, first introduced by a team from Bristol, Pa., and used extensively throughout Pennsylvania and neighboring states into the 1920s.

Whether using a cage fashioned of rope or metal, the players — particularly those on visiting teams, as well as officials — remained at the mercy of the often unruly spectators. Some took to jabbing players' legs with hatpins and lit cigarettes. Nails, heated with mining lamps, were the weapon of choice in hardscrabble Pennsylvania coal towns, as miners would throw them in the general direction of the referee or the opposing free-throw shooter. Heavily-waxed floors — in preparation for the social dances often held after games — added to the already treacherous playing conditions.

While trying to avoid being shoved into the cage, felled by a slippery floor or hit by sharp flying objects, teams generally employed two methods of scoring baskets. There was the layup — made more difficult by the practice of the opposition placing a "standing guard" in the free-throw lane — and the two-handed set shot, at times propelled by an underhand delivery.

The era did contribute what was at the time a literal description; players came to be known as "cagers," a phrase that would be a part of the game for generations.

DR. JAMES A. NAISMITH

By Robin Deutsch and Douglas Stark

The father of basketball was a high school dropout who eventually earned four college degrees. Dr. James A. Naismith was a modest man who neither sought publicity nor engaged in self-promotion. He was a remarkably versatile and humble man who in 1891 invented a game that is now played by more people than any game in the world.

It's doubtful that even Naismith's creative mind could have envisioned his game's vast global popularity little more than a century later, or a National Basketball Association consisting of 29 teams spanning North America. All he was seeking was an indoor activity that would provide an outlet for sometimes-unruly students during the long, cold New England winters.

In late 1891, Dr. Luther Halsey Gulick Jr., the superintendent of physical education at the International YMCA Training School (now Springfield College) in Springfield, Mass., challenged Naismith to create a new indoor game "that would be interesting, easy to learn, and easy to play in the winter and by artificial light." Naismith reflected on popular games of the day (baseball, football, lacrosse, rugby and soccer) and the games from his childhood (duck on a rock), and assembled the pieces that would become Basket Ball. It would be 30 years before it would be shortened to one word.

Naismith had the school janitor, Pop Stebbins, nail two peach baskets to the lower rail of the gymnasium balcony, one at each end, while the secretary, Mrs. Lyons, typed the original 13 rules. Then he nervously awaited his students' arrival.

"There were 18 in the class," Naismith said years later. "I selected two captains and had them choose sides. I placed the men on the floor. There were three forwards, three centers and three backs on each team. I chose two of the center men to jump, then threw the ball between them. It was the start of the first basketball game and the finish of trouble with that class."

The game was an immediate success. The students played the entire class period and finished the game with a 1-0 score. Within a few weeks, basketball quickly spread on campus by word of mouth and across the United States through the YMCA network.

A MAN OF MANY TALENTS AND INTERESTS, DR. JAMES A. NAISMITH NEVER ENVISIONED THE GAME HE CREATED BECOMING A GLOBAL SUCCESS. HE WAS ABLE TO SEE IT PLAYED IN THE 1936 OLYMPICS, THREE YEARS BEFORE HIS DEATH.

Naismith was a humanitarian who cared deeply about the well-being of others. He was a minister who regularly spoke to civic organizations later in life. He was a doctor by degree, although he never actually practiced medicine. He was a physical education instructor who lived by the credo "a sound mind is a sound body."

As a teen, Naismith worked as a lumberjack, but eventually he became a Presbyterian minister. At a time when he should have been contemplating retirement, the 55-year-old Naismith volunteered for the Kansas National Guard and served a short term of duty as a chaplain during the 1916 Mexican border war against Pancho Villa. And that was after

DR. JAMES NAISMITH'S ORIGINAL 13 RULES

The object of the game is to put the ball into your opponent's goal. This may be done by throwing the ball from any part of the grounds, with one or both hands, under the following conditions and rules.

1. The ball may be thrown in any direction with one or both hands.

2. The ball may be batted in any direction with one or both hands (never with a fist).

3. A player cannot run with the ball. The player must throw it from the spot on which he catches it, allowance to be made for a man who catches the ball when running if he tries to stop.

4. The ball must be held by the hands. The arms or body must not be used for holding it.

5. No shouldering, holding, pushing, tripping, or striking in any way the person of an opponent shall be allowed; the first infringement of this rule by any player shall count as a foul, the second shall disqualify him until the next goal is made, or, if there was evident intent to injure the person, for the whole of the game, no substitute allowed.

6. A foul is striking at the ball with the fist, violation of Rules 3, 4, and such as described in Rule 5.

7. If either side makes three consecutive fouls it shall count as a goal for the opponents (consecutive means without the opponents in the meantime making a foul).

8. A goal shall be made when the ball is thrown or batted from the grounds into the basket and stays there, providing those defending the goal do not touch or disturb the goal. If the ball rests on the edges, and the opponent moves the basket, it shall count as a goal.

9. When the ball goes out of bounds, it shall be thrown into the field of play by the person first touching it. He has a right to hold it unmolested for five seconds. In case of a dispute the umpire shall throw it straight into the field. The thrower-in is allowed five seconds; if he holds it longer it shall go to the opponent. If any side persists in delaying the game the umpire shall call a foul on that side.

10. The umpire shall be the judge of the men and shall note the fouls and notify the referee when three consecutive fouls have been made. He shall have power to disqualify men according to Rule 5.

11. The referee shall be judge of the ball and shall decide when the ball is in play, in bounds, to which side it belongs, and shall keep the time. He shall decide when a goal has been made and keep account of the goals, with any other duties that are usually performed by a referee.

12. The time shall be two fifteen-minute halves, with five minutes rest between.

13. The side making the most goals in that time shall be declared the winner. In the case of a draw the game may, by agreement of the captains, be continued until another goal is made.

PLAYERS IN NAISMITH'S (CENTER) FIRST GAME ARE IN THE HALL OF FAME AS A TEAM. WILLIAM CHASE (THIRD FROM LEFT, BOTTOM ROW) MADE THE ONLY BASKET.

he invented the football helmet. Basketball was only one piece of Naismith's colorful life.

Naismith always felt his mission was to improve the way people lived their lives, both athletically and socially. He earned a degree in religion from Presbyterian Theological Seminary in Montreal in 1890, but was never affiliated with a church because he wanted to combine his love of sports with his religious interests. In 1939, he was honored with a Doctor of Divinity degree from Presbyterian.

Although Naismith was particularly productive while in Massachusetts — inventing basketball in 1891 and the football helmet during the same period — he didn't rest on his laurels. He left Springfield in 1895 and traveled to Colorado, where he studied medicine at Gross Medical School and served as physical education director at the Denver YMCA. In 1898, Naismith moved to Kansas and embarked on a 39-year career as professor of physical education and chaplain at the University of Kansas. Ironically, the inventor of basketball is the only coach in Kansas men's history with a losing record (55-60).

While Naismith did not benefit financially from his invention, he was afforded a glimpse of the game's potential appeal in 1936 when he attended the Berlin Olympics, where basketball was played as a medal sport for the first time.

One popular historical textbook in 1995 listed Naismith as the fourth (of 100) most influential sports figures in America in the 20th century. If Naismith were alive to hear what he would consider nonsensical banter, he would laugh and wonder what all the fuss was about.

That was James Naismith.

CHAPTER 9

INNOVATORS

The Rens and Globetrotters

By John Smallwood

Although the NBA was not integrated until 1950, there is a rich African-American basketball history that dates back to the Roaring '20s. The two greatest African-American teams in the early days were the New York Renaissance Five and the Harlem Globetrotters, whose innovation, creativity and extraordinary skills have had a lasting impact on basketball.

THE RENS

Many claimed that they were the best basketball team of their day. But they were hardly America's darlings.

The New York Rens began as the Spartan Braves of Brooklyn, then became the Spartan Five and finally in 1923 emerged as the Renaissance, named after the famed Renaissance Ballroom on 138th Street and Seventh Avenue in Harlem. The Rens, as they were commonly called, were one of the most-watched traveling teams of the barnstorming era. Fans would fill auditoriums to root against them, often insult them and sometimes spit on them.

WILLIAM 'POP' GATES, WHO PLAYED FOR THE RENS AND LATER SERVED AS PLAYER-COACH FOR THE GLOBETROTTERS, WAS A COMPLETE PLAYER.

When the games were finished, their postgame meal often was eaten on the team's bus because many dining establishments refused to serve them. All because they were African-Americans.

Founded by Robert J. Douglas, who is now referred to as the father of black basketball, the Rens were the first full-salaried black professional basketball team, and games against them became sure money-makers. Contests with the Rens were so lucrative that their archrivals — the all-white Original Celtics — refused to join the American Basketball League in 1925, in part because the league did not invite the black club to join.

By the time the Rens had reached their prime in the early 1930s, the Celtics were on the decline, but their games were still drawing close to 15,000 fans in the Midwest and allowed promoters to put a premium on tickets for games in New

FROM 1923 TO 1949, THE NEW YORK RENAISSANCE FIVE WERE SYNONYMOUS WITH BASKETBALL EXCELLENCE. NAMED FOR HARLEM'S RENAISSANCE BALLROOM IN NEW YORK CITY, THE RENS, AS THEY WERE USUALLY CALLED, WERE A BARNSTORMING JUGGERNAUT, ONCE WINNING 88 STRAIGHT GAMES AND COMPILING A 2,588-529 RECORD.

York. The Celtics and Rens also staged the first game between whites and blacks in the South, and it was the Celtics who ended the Rens' 88-game winning streak in 1933. It was the Celtics' only victory in eight meetings with the Rens that year.

The Rens were led during their peak years by 6-4 Charles "Tarzan" Cooper, whom many called the best center of his day. Cooper and 6-5 "Wee" Willie Smith dominated the inside, while the 5-7 Clarence "Fat" Jenkins, called the "fastest man in basketball," orchestrated a devastating fast break. The outside shooting threats were Bill Yancey and Eyre "Bruiser" Saitch, with John Holt and James "Pappy" Ricks coming off the bench.

NBA.COM FACT

In a four-year period between 1932 and 1936, the Rens compiled a remarkable 473-49 record.

During their barnstorming days, the Rens often would play two or three games a day. Douglas took care of his players, paying them $800 to $1,000 a month. Considering that bread was a nickel a loaf and an apartment was $60 a month, those were remarkable salaries.

The Rens had a road secretary, Eric Illidge, who carried a tabulator and personally counted fans because the team was usually paid a percentage of the gate. Illidge also carried a gun, although he never had occasion to use it.

"Eric would tell guys not to come out on the court until he had the money," Smith said. "It was the only way we could survive."

Not surprisingly, in a still segregated America, fans often presented a threat for the Rens. During a game in Akron, Ohio, Smith got into a skirmish with a player and the crowd became so incensed that fans attacked the Rens. The Rens gathered in a circle and fought off the mob until someone turned out the lights in the building and ended the brawl. The Rens were given a police escort out of town.

On-court incidents were rare, however. John "Honey" Russell, a respected pro who played frequently against the Rens, once said they were "one of the cleanest teams I ever played against. They just played basketball."

The Rens posted a 112-7 record in 1939 and became the first all-black professional team to win a world title in any sport when they defeated the Oshkosh All-Stars of the National Basketball League in the World Pro Tournament in Chicago.

In 1948 the Rens became the Dayton Rens and joined the NBL as a replacement for the Detroit Vagabond Kings, an all-white team. Still owned by Douglas, the Rens played their last game against the Denver Nuggets on March 21, 1949 in Rockford, Ill. Their lifetime record was 2,588-529.

To those who marveled at the Rens' success amidst so much adversity, Illidge simply said, "We would not let anyone deny us our right to make a living."

THE GLOBETROTTERS

Long before they became internationally beloved as the clown princes of basketball and embarked on an endless string of victories over the hapless Washington Generals, the Harlem Globetrotters were a great team.

Organized five years after the Rens, the early Trotters hardly traveled the globe, and they weren't even based in Harlem. They were the vision of Jewish businessman Abe Saperstein, who was convinced that despite the prejudice of the day, another all-black team could be marketed. So he assumed control of the Savoy Big Five of Chicago and renamed them the Harlem Globetrotters.

Saperstein was a man of vision, and the path he took with the Globetrotters was based on smart business practices. No black teams belonged to the ABL and none were about to be added because that would give them access to Madison Square Garden. Black-versus-black basketball had little fan appeal at the time, so the Trotters became a barnstorming troupe of players who played well but also put on a good show.

As the team's first manager and coach, Saperstein outfitted his team in striped uniforms of red, white and blue that were made in his father's tailor shop. He drove the team through the rural Midwest, booking games wherever he could.

NBA.COM FACT

Due to discrimination, the Rens were forced to set up command posts in such cities as Chicago and Indianapolis and return from as far as 200 miles away because they were denied hotel space.

After the Trotters became a showtime team, Saperstein (in suit) still attracted top talent, including (left to right) Grady McCollum, Tex Harrison and Connie Hawkins.

In the winter of 1927, the Globetrotters won 101 of 117 games before crowds whose exposure to basketball had been minimal. Rarely did they leave with more than $75.

But while the first starting five of Walter "Toots" Wright, Byron "Fats" Long, Willis "Kid" Oliver, Andy Washington and Al "Runt" Pullins did not hit it big monetarily right away, they developed an entertaining style involving quick cuts and passes, perfected while they toyed with mostly inexperienced pick-up teams. In 1929, the Trotters added Inman Jackson, a tall, strong man with a good sense of humor who could perform tricks with a basketball. To entertain the crowds, and themselves, the Trotters would spin the ball on their fingers, drop-kick it toward the goal and even bounce it off their heads into the basket. Saperstein recognized that injecting

IN 1951, THE GLOBETROTTERS MADE A HISTORIC TRIP TO BERLIN, PLAYING BEFORE 75,000 FANS AT OLYMPIC STADIUM. AT HALFTIME, JESSE OWENS - WHO HAD BEEN SNUBBED AT THE 1936 OLYMPICS BY ADOLF HITLER - FLEW INTO THE STADIUM IN A HELICOPTER.

such antics into the game would make the defeats his team inflicted on its hosts easier to swallow, thus making for more return engagements.

Despite the showmanship, they still had ambition to become known as the best professional basketball team in the world. Their big break came in 1935 when Saperstein finally was able to arrange a game with the Original Celtics. With two minutes left and the score tied at 32, the Celtics called timeout and walked off the court rather than chance losing the game.

In 1939, the Trotters finished third in the *Chicago Herald American's* World Professional Tournament, losing to the Rens in the semifinal round. That was also the year they made their first trip out of the United States, going to Mexico.

The next year, the Trotters had finally surpassed the Rens, beating them 37-36 in the semifinal round of the professional

NBA.COM FACT

Although the team eventually lived up to its name by circumnavigating the world, the Trotters' first journey, on January 7, 1927, took them from Chicago to Hinckley, Ill. — all of 48 miles away.

BEFORE THEY BECAME ENTERTAINERS, THE TROTTERS WERE A SERIOUS BASKETBALL TEAM THAT COMPETED AGAINST THE TOP TOURING TEAMS IN THE COUNTRY, INCLUDING THE SPHAS FROM PHILADELPHIA.

REECE "GOOSE" TATUM, COMBINED AN 84-INCH WINGSPAN, A GREAT SENSE OF HUMOR AND EXCEPTIONAL BASKETBALL SKILLS TO BECOME THE ULTIMATE SHOWMAN.

NBA.COM FACT

In time, the Trotters fame led to them being the subject of two motion pictures, getting invited to appear behind the Iron Curtain and forming the basis of a children's television series.

tournament. The team of Jackson, Sonny Boswell, Babe Pressley, Hillary Brown, Ted Strong and Bernie Price rallied from a late five-point deficit to defeat the Chicago Bruins 31-29 in overtime to win the title.

The 1940s set the Trotters on the path to their destiny with the signings of Reece "Goose" Tatum and Marques Haynes. Tatum was a great athlete from Eldorado, Ark., with gigantic hands and an 84-inch wingspan, whom Saperstein lured away from a professional baseball career. Haynes was noticed by Saperstein when Haynes led Langston (Okla.) University to a 74-70 victory over the Trotters. These two players would be the backbone of Saperstein's team.

In 1950, the inevitable integration of the NBA began and the premier African-American players began play in the league. Subsequently, the Globetrotters shifted strictly to entertainment.

And they became frequent flyers. In 1949, the Trotters played 14 games in five days during a tour of Alaska. In 1950, they went on a tour of Western Europe and North Africa. In 1951, it was on to Central and South America, where they drew 50,000 fans to a game in Rio de Janeiro. Still, the highlight of those first world forays was a game in Berlin in the summer of 1951.

At the request of U.S. Commissioner for Germany John J. McCloy, who had sought to ease anti-American feelings in the defeated country, the Trotters agreed to play a game at the Olympic Stadium, where 15 years earlier Adolf Hitler had snubbed African-American Olympians. A huge crowd of 75,000 gave the Trotters a rousing round of applause.

Then at halftime, a helicopter flew over the open-air court and let off a lone figure in a track suit. As the unannounced figure began to circle the track, the crowd realized it was Jesse Owens, whose four gold medals had made him the star of the 1936 Berlin Olympic Games. The crowd erupted with a standing ovation. Both the Trotters and Owens were recognized as "ambassadors of goodwill" by the U.S. State Department.

WILT CHAMBERLAIN PLAYED FOR ONE YEAR WITH THE TROTTERS BECAUSE HE LEFT COLLEGE AFTER HIS JUNIOR YEAR AND THERE WAS NO EARLY ENTRY RULE AT THE TIME.

CHAMBERLAIN WAS A HUGE ATTRACTION, BUT WHEN IT CAME TO BASKETBALL, HE DID WHAT CAME NATURALLY, DOMINATING RATHER THAN SIMPLY ENTERTAINING.

The following year, the Trotters celebrated their 25th year with a 50,000-mile tour around the world. Five Trotters — Babe Pressley, Leon Hilliard, Bill Brown, Clarence Wilson and Josh Crider — performed their famous warm-up routine to the tune of "Sweet Georgia Brown" for Pope Pius XII during an audience at Castel Gandolfo.

While they never joined the NBA, the Trotters were nonetheless an important part of the league's early days. Because they were a draw, they were often used as part of doubleheaders with NBA teams.

And they were good. On Feb. 24, 1948, the Trotters defeated the Minneapolis Lakers and George Mikan in an exhibition game at Chicago Stadium, when Ermer Robinson took a pass from Haynes and sank a 20-foot set shot at the buzzer.

While the integration of the NBA turned the Trotters into a show team, they remain enormously popular throughout the world. Their fame also made them the subject of two motion pictures, including *The Globetrotter Story* in 1951 that starred African-American movie legend Dorothy Dandridge. The Trotters were invited to appear behind the Iron Curtain during the Cold War and have even been the basis of a children's television program.

They also served as the springboard for the Hall-of-Fame NBA career of Wilt Chamberlain, who suited up for the Globetrotters in 1958; and they broke down the gender barrier in 1985 when Lynette Woodard became the first woman to play for the Globetrotters.

Meadowlark Lemon and Curly Neal joined Tatum and Hayes as American entertainment icons, and to this day, a new generation of Globetrotters continues to entertain fans all over the world.

CHAPTER 10

NBA PIONEERS
The African-American Influence

By John Smallwood

The flame was first lit a half century ago. It happened on the night of October 31, 1950, when Earl Lloyd stepped onto the court for the Washington Capitols. The complexion of the NBA would not only change, but the very fabric of how the league would evolve was impacted in a very permanent and profound way.

EARL LLOYD MADE NBA HISTORY OCTOBER 31, 1950, WHEN HE PLAYED FOR WASHINGTON. HE ALSO PLAYED FOR SYRACUSE AND DETROIT DURING HIS NINE-YEAR NBA CAREER.

Lloyd was the first African-American to participate in an NBA game. Fifty years later, the league is predominantly comprised of African-Americans, and it seems almost naïve to think there was a time when the owners operating the NBA openly questioned whether its audience would accept players who were not white.

But back in 1946, when the Basketball Association of America — the league that would become the NBA — was founded, America was a different place. The general societal belief of interaction between the races was still separate and professional sports was no different.

Jackie Robinson was playing in the Brookyn Dodgers' farm system, so the shattering of Major League Baseball's color barrier was inevitable. But the founders of the BAA were starting a new professional league for a sport that did not register very highly in the public consciousness and was considered a shaky proposition at best. Thus the BAA owners had little passion to take up social concerns at the risk of failing economically.

During its early years, when many college teams were integrated, all-black teams competed regularly against all-white teams, and UCLA All-American Don Barksdale became the first African-American to play on a United States Olympic basketball team in 1948.

Fort Wayne Whips Celtics in Opener

FORT WAYNE, Ind., Nov. 2 (AP)—The Fort Wayne Pistons cut loose with their fast break in the second half and won a 107-84 victory over the Boston Celtics tonight.

Fort Wayne held only a 47-45 lead at the half. It was the opening game of the National Basket Ball Association for each team.

FORT WAYNE (107)	G	F	TP
Schaus f	3	8	14
Riffey f	4	0	8
Harris f	2	2	6
Burris f	3	0	6
Foust c	8	5	21
Kerris,c-f	3	6	12
Johnson g	5	2	12
Carpenter g	0	2	2
Oldham g	5	1	11
Klueh g	5	5	15
Totals	38	31	107

BOSTON (84)	G	F	TP
Walker f	0	0	0
Cooper f	3	1	7
Leede f	2	4	8
Stanczak f	1	7	9
Duncan f	2	3	7
Macauley c	3	3	9
Mahnken c	3	0	6
Herzberg g	1	4	6
Cousy g	4	8	16
Donham g	4	1	9
Sailors g	2	3	7
Totals	25	34	84

RED AUERBACH BROKE DOWN ONE BARRIER WHEN HE DRAFTED CHUCK COOPER FROM DUQUESNE IN 1950, MAKING COOPER THE FIRST AFRICAN-AMERICAN PLAYER TO BE DRAFTED INTO THE NBA. IN MAKING HIS NBA DEBUT, COOPER (BELOW) SCORED SEVEN POINTS IN BOSTON'S LOSS AGAINST FORT WAYNE.

By the end of the 1949-50 season, it had become clear that black players — albeit in extremely limited numbers — would be allowed into the league.

Chuck Cooper, from Duquesne University, was the first to be drafted, taken by the Boston Celtics in the second round of the 1950 draft. Nat "Sweetwater" Clifton, who attended Xavier University in Louisiana, was the first to sign an NBA contract with the New York Knickerbockers. Clifton had been playing with the Harlem Globetrotters. But through a scheduling quirk, Lloyd, who was drafted in the ninth round out of West Virginia State University, became the first to actually play in a game.

"I don't think my situation was anything like Jackie Robinson's — a guy who played in a hostile environment, where some of his teammates didn't want him around," Lloyd said. "In basketball, folks were used to seeing integrated college teams. There was a different mentality."

NBA.COM FACT

Both Earl Lloyd and Chuck Cooper wore No. 11 in the NBA and both attended West Virginia State. Cooper left West Virginia State after three semesters to join the U.S. Navy, then attended Duquesne after his discharge.

During that first year, Cooper had an impressive season, playing in 66 games with 615 points, 562 rebounds and 174 assists. Clifton played in 65 games and collected 562 points, 491 rebounds and 162 assists. Lloyd, however, played in only seven games because another team (the U.S. Army) drafted him; besides, the Capitols disbanded on Jan. 9, 1951, after only 35 games. Lloyd returned for the 1952-53 season and he and Jim Tucker became the first African-American players to be on an NBA championship team — the 1954-55 Syracuse Nationals.

The presence of the African-American player changed the way the NBA game was played. Because African-American athletes had been so long excluded from the structured white organizations of the game, they were not bound by the traditional approaches to basketball. The segregation of the era meant that basketball developed independently in the African-American community, separate from the more conservative style that dominated early professional leagues, such as the BAA. Since African-Americans could not play in the pro leagues, black semipro players continued with the styles they had utilized in college, which were more conducive to wide open play.

Cultural influences also played a large part in this development. For example, flamboyant or showy moves by an offensive player were considered bad sportsmanship in the white-dominated leagues. By contrast, African-American players and fans reveled in showmanship and flamboyance as a mode of self-expression.

Inspired by the play of the legendary all-black New York

Renaissance Five and Harlem Globetrotters, a distinctive "black" style of play developed, one that emphasized speed, agility, and took advantage of creative ballhandling.

While this style often conflicted with white coaching philosophies of the day, it was clearly a style of play that fans found more appealing. And at the start of the 1954-55 season, when the NBA adopted the 24-second clock because its slow methodical style was losing interest with fans, the "open style" of play exploded throughout the game.

Two seasons after the shot clock came into being, the first African-American superstar entered the league — Boston Celtics center Bill Russell who was unlike any other big man who had ever played the game.

"Nobody had ever blocked shots in the pros before Russell came along," legendary Celtics coach Arnold "Red" Auerbach said. "He upset everybody. And the thing about it is that he blocked shots with a purpose. You see today a lot of players will block a shot as hard as they can, and it goes out of bounds. Russell always tried to control the ball when he blocked it. He would block a shot and aim it towards a teammate. It was almost like a pass. Nobody else has ever done that."

NBA.COM FACT

Nat "Sweetwater" Clifton, who earned $7,500 for the 1950-51 season, received his nickname because of his love for soft drinks.

NAT "SWEETWATER" CLIFTON (WITH KNICKS COACH JOE LAPCHICK) AVERAGED 10 POINTS AND 8.2 REBOUNDS IN AN EIGHT-YEAR CAREER.

NBA.COM FACT

When Earl Lloyd of the Washington Capitols became the first African-American to play in the NBA on October 31, 1950, he pulled down 10 rebounds in a game against the Rochester Royals. Lloyd led all rebounders that night.

Auerbach was the first NBA coach to take advantage of this style of play by installing a full-court press and allowing black stars such as Russell, K.C. Jones and Sam Jones to freelance more on the court. In 1958, Russell became the first African-American to be named Most Valuable Player.

After St. Louis Hawks forward Bob Pettit in 1958-59, it would be 13 seasons before another white player — Boston Celtics center Dave Cowens in 1972-73 — would be named league MVP. Since Russell won his first MVP, only four white players — Pettit, Cowens, Portland Trail Blazers center Bill Walton (1977-78) and Boston Celtics forward Larry Bird (1983-84, 1984-85 and 1985-86) have been named MVP.

Within three years after Russell made his NBA debut, two more African-American players who would change the style and perception of the NBA entered the league — Wilt Chamberlain of the Philadelphia Warriors and Elgin Baylor of the Minneapolis Lakers.

Chamberlain, 7-1 and 275 pounds, was the original immovable object. The "Power-in-the-Paint" game that is the staple offense of today's big men had its genesis in Chamberlain. The "Big Dipper" became the NBA's first African-American scoring champion in 1959-60, beginning a 40-year era when only three non-African-American players — San Francisco Warriors forward Rick Barry in 1966-67, Los Angeles Lakers guard Jerry West in 1969-70 and New Orleans Jazz guard Pete Maravich in 1976-77 — won scoring titles.

Before Julius Erving, Michael Jordan and Vince Carter started walking on air, Baylor was the first player to show

NBA.COM FACT

In 1966, Bill Russell became player-coach of the Boston Celtics, the first African-American coach in a major professional sports league. He guided Boston to NBA titles in 1968 and 1969, becoming the first African-American coach to lead a pro sports team to a championship.

Bill Russell coached Seattle and Sacramento after starting his coaching career as a player-coach with Boston.

crowds that NBA players could seemingly defy gravity. Baylor and other black players transformed the NBA from a game played below the rim to one played above. Hal Greer and Guy Rodgers became prototypes for the faster, ball-controlling NBA guard whose job is to direct the offense, play pressure defense and dictate the pace of the game. At 6-5 and 220 pounds, Oscar Robertson was the first of the "big lead guards." His all-around play foreshadowed the comtemporary statistical "triple-double."

Erving, as "Dr. J," popularized the job of celebrity endorser for NBA players. Michael Jordan, as "Air Jordan," raised the connection between NBA players and Madison Avenue into the stratosphere. Long before the other major sports leagues would hire their first African-American head coaches, Russell had already guided the Celtics to championships. Later Al Attles, Lenny Wilkens and K. C. Jones also led teams to titles.

And Wayne Embry, who played 11 seasons in the NBA, became the first African-American general manager of a major sports team when he took the reins of the Milwaukee Bucks in 1972.

Today the overwhelming majority of NBA players are African-American. But rather than being shunned by an audience that is predominantly not African-American, as the league's original owners feared, the NBA has flourished and grown into a globally recognized and celebrated league in large part because of its African-American players.

Wayne Embry became the first African-American general manager in professional sports in 1972 with the Milwaukee Bucks.

CHAPTER 11

RED, WHITE & BLUE

The Colorful ABA

By John Gardella

When the American Basketball Association began play with a painted basketball in 1967, the NBA took one look at the tri-colored ball and the three-point shot and couldn't decide whether to laugh or yawn. Yes, the ABA did play basketball — or at least a form of it — in several cities that were worthy of NBA teams, but for the most part, NBA officials didn't take the new league seriously.

That changed, however. By the time the ABA folded in 1976 with four of its teams joining the NBA and the rest of its star players taken in a dispersal draft, the NBA knew the league with the red, white and blue ball was dead serious. The first NBA All-Star Game held after the four-team absorption made that evident. Of the 24 All-Stars, 10 were ABA graduates. Julius Erving, whose incredibly exciting talents probably were the most important reason that the NBA added the ABA teams, was named the Most Valuable Player in the game. And when the championship was decided at the end of the season, the Portland Trail Blazers had their first title, in no small part because their starting power forward was Maurice Lucas, an ABA alum who was the Blazers' leading scorer.

More than two decades later, Erving says the ABA continues to live — only now, it is in the form of every dunk, every buzzer-beating three-pointer, all that wide-open, above-the-rim play that occurs in NBA games.

"Every night I watch an NBA game I see the ABA," said Erving. "When you watch the up-tempo game and the three-point shot and much of what the strategy employed is, it is definitely an ABA game. There is no ques-

NBA.COM FACT

NBC's Bob Costas got his start as a radio announcer for the ABA's Spirits of St. Louis. In 1974, at the age of 22, the Spirits hired Costas for the princely sum of $11,000 per year.

Julius Erving (going against Indiana Pacer great Roger Brown) was the ABA's top attraction. His talent played a huge part in four teams eventually joining the NBA.

tion about it. You see the flair. You see the innovation. You see the accent on the entertainment."

And Julius Erving is the nexus that links the two leagues. "Dr. J was the single most important figure for making the league something that people wanted to see," said Jim O'Brien, a reporter who covered the ABA for the *New York Post* and *The Sporting News*. The 6-7 Erving signed with the Virginia Squires in 1971 after his junior year at the University of Massachusetts. He averaged 27.3 points and 15.7 rebounds as a rookie, and the league finally had its cleanup hitter. In his five-year ABA career, Dr. J averaged 28.7 points, utilizing into-the-stratosphere moves that shouldn't be attempted without a parachute. He won three scoring titles, three Most Valuable Player awards and two league championships.

Erving had played college basketball in an era when the dunk was not allowed, so when he entered the ABA, it was like freeing a caged bird.

"I went from doing it by the book in college to having the chains taken off and having the freedom to explore, experiment, dare to be great," said Erving.

Erving played two seasons with the Squires, where he teamed with George Gervin for half a season. But the Squires, like most ABA teams, struggled financially, and the ABA did not benefit from having its biggest star play in a small market. Before the 1973-74 season, Virginia traded Erving to the New York Nets, and midway through the season, the Squires sold Gervin's contract to the San Antonio Spurs. Coached by Kevin Loughery and led by Erving, the Nets won titles in 1974 and 1976.

The ABA was formed Feb. 1, 1967, by sports promoter Dennis Murphy and a group of investors. Franchises included the Houston Mavericks, Pittsburgh Pipers, Minnesota Muskies, Indiana Pacers, New Jersey Americans, New Orleans Buccaneers, Dallas Chaparrals, Anaheim Amigos and Oakland Oaks. Kansas City was awarded a franchise, but a month later it was moved to Denver to become the Denver Rockets, and later the Nuggets. Also within that month, the league awarded Kentucky Colonels a franchise. With credibility an issue, the league hired 43-year-old George Mikan as its first commissioner. Mikan came up with the idea for the red, white and blue ball because the traditional brownish-orange ball was hard to pick up on TV.

The NBA stopped laughing when it realized the ABA considered players fair game. Besides welcoming players such as Connie Hawkins, Doug Moe and Roger Brown, who

THE INDIANA PACERS WON THREE OF THE NINE ABA CHAMPIONSHIPS AND FEATURED ABA ALL-STARS MEL DANIELS, ROGER BROWN AND GEORGE MCGINNIS.

had been banned from the NBA when their names were linked to college basketball scandals in the early 1960s, the new league also went after players the NBA deemed its own.

When the Oakland Oaks hired Bruce Hale as coach, his then son-in-law, Rick Barry, who was playing for the San Francisco Warriors, was lured across the Bay. The Warriors filed suit — the first of many filed by both sides — and won, forcing Barry to either play for them or sit out the 1967-68 season (he chose the latter). But Barry was cleared to play in the 1968-69 season and with him, Larry Brown at the point and Moe at forward, Oakland won the 1969 title.

"When they started signing people like Charlie Scott, Artis Gilmore, Jim McDaniels, Rick Mount, Dan Issel, then they [the NBA] started paying attention," said O'Brien. "That's when the NBA started getting a little nervous about it."

The NBA became enraged in 1969, when agent Steve Arnold, who the ABA had hired to approach underclassmen about turning pro early, convinced college superstar Spencer Haywood to forego his junior and senior years of college. The Denver Rockets signed Haywood to a three-year deal worth $450,000 (actually the contract called for $50,000 a year, with $300,000 deferred until after Haywood's 40th

NBA.COM FACT

Only two players — Byron Beck of the Denver Rockets/Nuggets and Louie Dampier of the Kentucky Colonels — lasted all nine seasons of the ABA's existence. Beck, a 6-9 center, averaged 12.0 points during his ABA career. Dampier, a 6-0 guard, finished as the ABA's all-time leader in total points (13,726 for an average of 18.9 per game), assists (4,044), and minutes (27,770). Dampier also was the ABA's top three-point shooter, making 794 treys in 2,217 attempts for a .358 percentage.

birthday). The Indiana Pacers followed, signing George McGinnis after his sophomore year at Indiana. The New York Nets tapped Jim Chones out of Marquette after his junior year. And the Virginia Squires signed sophomore Gervin out of Eastern Michigan and junior Erving from UMass. In 1974, Utah selected Moses Malone right out of Petersburg (Va.) High School.

With a merger between the ABA and NBA seemingly imminent, the leagues agreed to interleague exhibition games in 1971. Although merger talks eventually collapsed, the NBA and ABA teams continued to play each other. The younger league didn't do that well against the NBA early, winning only eight of 22 contests in 1971 and eight of 35 the following year. But as better players entered the league, the tide turned. In 1973, ABA teams won 15 of 24 games, and a year later they posted a 16-7 record. In 1975, ABA teams posted a 30-18 mark against NBA opponents.

"I think the best players in the ABA were every bit as talented as the best players in the NBA," said Erving. "Down the line you probably had more depth on NBA teams, but I'm not so sure. When I got to Philadelphia it happened to be a

OFTEN DESPERATE FOR FANS, ABA TEAMS POSITIONED THEMSELVES AS REGIONAL ATTRACTIONS AND PLAYED IN SEVERAL CITIES, LIKE THE TEXAS CHAPARRALS.

DAN ISSEL AVERAGED 25.6 POINTS IN SIX ABA SEASONS, LED IN TOTAL POINTS THREE TIMES AND SET THE SINGLE-SEASON RECORD OF 2,538 POINTS IN 1971-72.

pretty deep team, and, I think, one through 12, that team was stronger than most ABA teams. But Philadelphia was a team destined to go to the Finals of the NBA. Of all those NBA teams that didn't make the playoffs, I'm sure my Nets team, the Denver Nuggets or the Kentucky Colonels would have wiped them out."

It was during the 1976 ABA All-Star Weekend in Denver that the high-flying Erving did something on a basketball court that had never been seen before and may have hastened the four teams' entrance into the NBA. The ABA was desperate. There were seven teams left by the All-Star break. It needed a big-time attraction to spark interest. The idea was a dunk contest. The contestants were 7-2 Artis Gilmore of the Kentucky Colonels, 6-7 George Gervin of the San Antonio Spurs, 6-9 Larry Kenon of the Spurs, 6-4 David Thompson of the host Nuggets and Erving.

Everyone knew the real contest was between Thompson and Erving. Thompson's performance included the first recorded 360-degree dunk. But Erving's best dunk of the evening was the kind of athletic feat that is seared into the public consciousness, like Babe Ruth's called home run. For his first dunk, Erving simply stood under the basket and dunked two balls during the same jump. For his second dunk,

NBA.COM FACT

The ABA posted a 79-76 record in exhibition games against NBA teams. The ABA's ball, three-point shot, and 30-second shot clock were used for one half, and the NBA's ball and rules were used during the other half.

THE NINTH AND FINAL ABA ALL-STAR GAME, PLAYED JANUARY 27, 1976, PITTED THE DENVER NUGGETS AGAINST A TEAM COMPRISED OF ABA ALL-STARS FROM THE SIX SURVIVING TEAMS. THE GAME IS BEST REMEMBERED NOT FOR THE GLEN CAMPBELL/CHARLIE RICH CONCERT, BUT FOR JULIUS ERVING'S DUNK FROM THE FOUL LINE IN THE SLAM DUNK CONTEST.

Erving walked up to the foul line and started measuring his steps back to the other end of the court. People guessed what was coming and they were frenzied. He started running and picked up speed at half-court. He hit the free throw line and took off . . . into basketball legend. The grainy tape of that dunk is still a favorite of basketball connoisseurs.

By the end of that season, the ABA's ninth, Virginia shut down its operations, leaving six teams — the Indiana Pacers, Denver Nuggets, New York Nets, San Antonio Spurs, Kentucky Colonels and the Spirits of St. Louis. The NBA agreed to admit Indiana, Denver, San Antonio and New York, raising the total teams to 22. It adopted the ABA's three-point shot in 1979. It incorporated the Slam Dunk contest into its All-Star festivities in 1984.

The Nets, faced with a $3.2 million fee to enter the NBA plus $480,000 a year in indemnity payments to the New York Knicks, had a cash crisis, so they sold Erving's contract to the Philadelphia 76ers for $3 million. The Sixers advanced to the Finals that season led by Erving and George McGinnis, another former ABA player.

"I think some of the NBA brain trust said, 'We don't want all of it, but we want the best of what the ABA has to offer,'" Erving said. "'We'll take the players and we'll take a few franchises, but we'll leave the maverick aspect of the league.' Little did they know those things were coming along, too. The spirit of the ABA actually made the transition, too. And it's still there."

NBA.COM FACT

Only three ABA franchises — Denver, Indiana, and Kentucky — finished in the cities where they started.

ABA CHAMPIONS (FOR MORE INFORMATION ON THE ABA, SEE PAGES 201-210.)

SEASON	CHAMPION	EASTERN DIVISION	W	L	WESTERN DIVISION	W	L
1967-68	Pittsburgh	Pittsburgh	54	24	New Orleans	48	30
1968-69	Oakland	Indiana	44	34	Oakland	60	18
1969-70	Indiana	Indiana	59	25	Denver	51	33
1970-71	Utah	Virginia	55	29	Indiana	58	26
1971-72	Indiana	Kentucky	68	16	Utah	60	24
1972-73	Indiana	Carolina	57	27	Utah	55	29
1973-74	New York	New York	55	29	Utah	51	33
1974-75	Kentucky	Kentucky	58	26	Denver	65	19
1975-76	New York	One division: Denver was first with				60	24

ABA POSTSEASON AWARDS

SEASON	MVP	ROOKIE OF THE YEAR	COACH OF THE YEAR
1967-68	Connie Hawkins, Pittsburgh	Mel Daniels, Minnesota	Vince Cazetta, Pittsburgh
1968-69	Mel Daniels, Indiana	Warren Armstrong, Oakland	Alex Hannum, Oakland
1969-70	Spencer Haywood, Denver	Spencer Haywood, Denver	Bill Sharman, Los Angeles, and Joe Belmont, Denver
1970-71	Mel Daniels, Indiana	Charlie Scott, Virginia, and Dan Issel, Kentucky	Al Bianchi, Virginia
1971-72	Artis Gilmore, Kentucky	Artis Gilmore, Kentucky	Tom Nissalke, Dallas
1972-73	Billy Cunningham, Carolina	Brian Taylor, New York	Larry Brown, Carolina
1973-74	Julius Erving, New York	Swen Nater, San Antonio	Babe McCarthy, Kentucky, and Joe Mullaney, Utah
1974-75	Julius Erving, New York, and George McGinnis, Indiana	Marvin Barnes, St. Louis	Larry Brown, Denver
1975-76	Julius Erving, New York	David Thompson, Denver	Larry Brown, Denver

ABA ALL-ROOKIE TEAMS

1968
Tom Washington, Pittsburgh
Bob Netolicky, Indiana
Mel Daniels, Minnesota
Louie Dampier, Kentucky
James Jones, New Orleans

1969
Larry Miller, Los Angeles
Walt Piatkowski, Denver
Gene Moore, Kentucky
Warren Armstrong, Oakland
Ron Boone, Dallas

1970
Willie Wise, Los Angeles
John Brisker, Pittsburgh
Spencer Haywood, Denver
Mike Barrett, Washington
Mack Calvin, Los Angeles

1971
Wendell Ladner, Memphis
Sam Robinson, Floridians
Dan Issel, Kentucky
Charlie Scott, Virginia
Joe Hamilton, Texas

1972
Julius Erving, Virginia
George McGinnis, Indiana
Artis Gilmore, Kentucky
John Roche, New York
Johnny Neumann, Memphis

1973
George Gervin, Virginia
Dennis Wuycik, Carolina
Jim Chones, New York
Brian Taylor, New York
James Silas, Dallas

1974
Larry Kenon, New York
Mike Green, Denver
Swen Nater, San Antonio
Dwight Lamar, San Antonio
John Williamson, New York

1975
Bobby Jones, Denver
Marvin Barnes, St. Louis
Moses Malone, Utah
Billy Knight, Indiana
Gus Gerard, St. Louis

1976
David Thompson, Denver
Mark Olberding, San Antonio
Kim Hughes, New York
M. L. Carr, St. Louis
Luther Burden, Virginia

ALL-ABA TEAMS

FIRST	SECOND
1967-68	
Connie Hawkins, Pittsburgh	Roger Brown, Indiana
Doug Moe, New Orleans	Cincy Powell, Dallas
Mel Daniels, Minnesota	John Beasley, Dallas
Larry Jones, Denver	Larry Brown, New Orleans
Charlie Williams, Pittsburgh	Louie Dampier, Kentucky
1968-69	
Connie Hawkins, Minnesota	John Beasley, Dallas
Rick Barry, Oakland	Doug Moe, Oakland
Mel Daniels, Indiana	Red Robbins, New Orleans
Larry Jones, Denver	Don Freeman, Miami
James Jones, New Orleans	Louie Dampier, Kentucky
1969-70	
Rick Barry, Washington	Roger Brown, Indiana
Spencer Haywood, Denver	Bob Netolicky, Indiana
Mel Daniels, Indiana	Red Robbins, New Orleans
Bob Verga, Carolina	Louie Dampier, Kentucky
Larry Jones, Denver	Don Freeman, Miami
1970-71	
Roger Brown, Indiana	John Brisker, Pittsburgh
Rick Barry, New York	Joe Caldwell, Carolina
Mel Daniels, Indiana	Zelmo Beaty, Utah
Mack Calvin, Floridians	Dan Issel, Kentucky
Charlie Scott, Virginia	Don Freeman, Texas
	Larry Cannon, Denver
1971-72	
Rick Barry, New York	Willie Wise, Utah
Dan Issel, Kentucky	Julius Erving, Virginia
Artis Gilmore, Kentucky	Zelmo Beaty, Utah
Don Freeman, Dallas	Ralph Simpson, Denver
Bill Melchionni, New York	Charlie Scott, Virginia
1972-73	
Billy Cunningham, Carolina	George McGinnis, Indiana
Julius Erving, Virginia	Dan Issel, Kentucky
Artis Gilmore, Kentucky	Mel Daniels, Indiana
James Jones, Utah	Ralph Simpson, Denver
Warren Jabali, Denver	Mack Calvin, Carolina
1973-74	
Julius Erving, New York	Dan Issel, Kentucky
George McGinnis, Indiana	Willie Wise, Utah
Artis Gilmore, Kentucky	Swen Nater, San Antonio
James Jones, Utah	Ron Boone, Utah
Mack Calvin, Carolina	Louie Dampier, Kentucky
1974-75	
Julius Erving, New York	Marvin Barnes, St. Louis
George McGinnis, Indiana	George Gervin, San Antonio
Artis Gilmore, Kentucky	Swen Nater, San Antonio
Mack Calvin, Denver	Brian Taylor, New York
Ron Boone, Utah	James Silas, San Antonio
1975-76	
Julius Erving, New York	David Thompson, Denver
Billy Knight, Indiana	Bobby Jones, Denver
Artis Gilmore, Kentucky	Dan Issel, Denver
James Silas, San Antonio	Don Buse, Indiana
Ralph Simpson, Denver	George Gervin, San Antonio

ABA ALL-STAR GAMES

YEAR	RESULT	LOCATION	MVP	ATTENDANCE
1968	East 126, West 120	Indianapolis	Larry Brown, New Orleans	10,872
1969	West 133, East 127	Louisville	John Beasley, Dallas	5,407
1970	West 128, East 98	Indianapolis	Spencer Haywood, Denver	11,932
1971	East 126, West 122	Greensboro	Mel Daniels, Indiana	14,407
1972	East 142, West 115	Louisville	Dan Issel, Kentucky	15,738
1973	West 123, East 111	Salt Lake City	Warren Jabali, Denver	12,556
1974	East 128, West 112	Norfolk	Artis Gilmore, Kentucky	10,624
1975	East 151, West 124	San Antonio	Freddie Lewis, St. Louis	10,449
1976	Denver 144, All-Stars 138	Denver	David Thompson, Denver	17,798

COMBINED NBA/ABA STATISTICAL LEADERS

CAREER SCORING
(Active 1999-2000 players in capital letters)

Player	Yrs	G	Pts	Avg
Kareem Abdul-Jabbar	20	1560	38,387	24.6
Wilt Chamberlain	14	1045	31,419	30.1
KARL MALONE	15	1192	31,041	26.0
Julius Erving	16	1243	30,026	24.2
Moses Malone	21	1455	29,580	20.3
Michael Jordan	13	930	29,277	31.5
Dan Issel	15	1218	27,482	22.6
Elvin Hayes	16	1303	27,313	21.0
Oscar Robertson	14	1040	26,710	25.7
Dominique Wilkins	15	1074	26,668	24.8
George Gervin	14	1060	26,595	25.1
John Havlicek	16	1270	26,395	20.8
HAKEEM OLAJUWON	16	1119	25,822	23.1
Alex English	15	1193	25,613	21.5
Rick Barry	14	1020	25,279	24.8
Jerry West	14	932	25,192	27.0
Artis Gilmore	17	1329	24,941	18.8
CHARLES BARKLEY	16	1073	23,757	22.1
PATRICK EWING	15	1039	23,665	22.8
Robert Parish	21	1611	23,334	14.5
Adrian Dantley	15	955	23,177	24.3
Elgin Baylor	14	846	23,149	27.4
Clyde Drexler	15	1086	22,195	20.4
Larry Bird	13	897	21,791	24.3
Hal Greer	15	1122	21,586	19.2
Walt Bellamy	14	1043	20,941	20.1
Bob Pettit	11	792	20,880	26.4
Tom Chambers	16	1107	20,049	18.1
REGGIE MILLER	13	1013	19,792	19.5
Bernard King	14	874	19,655	22.5
MITCH RICHMOND	12	875	19,639	22.4
Walter Davis	15	1033	19,521	18.9
TERRY CUMMINGS	18	1183	19,460	16.4
Dolph Schayes	16	1059	19,249	18.2
Bob Lanier	14	959	19,248	20.1
Eddie A. Johnson	17	1199	19,202	16.0
Gail Goodrich	14	1031	19,181	18.6
Reggie Theus	13	1026	19,015	18.5
DALE ELLIS	17	1209	19,004	15.7
Chet Walker	13	1032	18,831	18.2
Isiah Thomas	13	979	18,822	19.2
Bob McAdoo	14	852	18,787	22.1
Mark Aguirre	13	923	18,458	20.0
Dave Bing	12	901	18,327	20.3
DAVID ROBINSON	11	765	18,142	23.7
World B. Free	13	886	17,955	20.3
Calvin Murphy	13	1002	17,949	17.9
Lou Hudson	13	890	17,940	20.2
CHRIS MULLIN	15	966	17,796	18.4
Len Wilkens	15	1077	17,772	16.5
Bailey Howell	12	950	17,770	18.7
Magic Johnson	13	906	17,707	19.5
Rolando Blackman	13	980	17,623	18.0
OTIS THORPE	16	1208	17,462	14.5
Earl Monroe	13	926	17,454	18.8
Ron Boone	13	1041	17,437	16.8
Kevin McHale	13	971	17,335	17.9
Jack Sikma	14	1107	17,287	15.6
Jeff Malone	13	905	17,231	19.0
Spencer Haywood	13	844	17,111	20.3
George McGinnis	11	842	17,009	20.2
Bob Cousy	14	924	16,960	18.4
Buck Williams	17	1307	16,784	12.8
JOHN STOCKTON	16	1258	16,781	13.3
SCOTTIE PIPPEN	13	965	16,735	17.3
GLEN RICE	11	825	16,643	20.2
Nate Archibald	13	876	16,481	18.8
Joe Dumars	14	1018	16,401	16.1
James Worthy	12	926	16,320	17.6
Billy Cunningham	11	770	16,310	21.2
Paul Arizin	10	713	16,266	22.8
Randy Smith	12	976	16,262	16.7
Derek Harper	16	1199	16,006	13.3
Kiki Vandeweghe	13	810	15,980	19.7
Pete Maravich	10	658	15,948	24.2
Jack Twyman	11	823	15,840	19.2
Larry Nance	13	920	15,687	17.1
JEFF HORNACEK	14	1077	15,659	14.5
DETLEF SCHREMPF	15	1110	15,657	14.1
KEVIN WILLIS	15	1141	15,656	13.7
Walt Frazier	13	825	15,581	18.9
Dennis Johnson	14	1100	15,535	14.1
Bob Dandridge	13	839	15,530	18.5
Sam Jones	12	871	15,411	17.7
Dick Barnett	14	971	15,358	15.8
John Drew	11	739	15,291	20.7
Louie Dampier	12	960	15,279	15.9

HIGHEST SCORING AVERAGE (400 Games or 10,000 Points minimum)

Player	G	FGM	FTM	Pts	Avg
Michael Jordan	930	10,962	6,798	29,277	31.5
Wilt Chamberlain	1045	12,681	6,057	31,419	30.1
SHAQUILLE O'NEAL	534	5,896	2,894	14,687	27.5
Elgin Baylor	846	8,693	5,763	23,149	27.4
Jerry West	932	9,016	7,160	25,192	27.0
Bob Pettit	792	7,349	6,182	20,880	26.4
KARL MALONE	1192	11,435	8,100	31,041	26.0
Oscar Robertson	1040	9,508	7,694	26,710	25.7
George Gervin	1060	10,368	5,737	26,595	25.1
Dominique Wilkins	1074	9,963	6,031	26,668	24.8

HIGHEST FREE THROW PERCENTAGE (1,200 FTM Minimum)

Player	FTM	FTA	Pct
Mark Price	2,135	2,362	.904
Rick Barry	5,713	6,397	.893
Calvin Murphy	3,445	3,864	.892
Scott Skiles	1,548	1,741	.889
Larry Bird	3,960	4,471	.886
Bill Sharman	3,143	3,559	.883
REGGIE MILLER	5,015	5,690	.881
JEFF HORNACEK	2,973	3,390	.877
Ricky Pierce	3,389	3,871	.875
Billy Keller	1,202	1,378	.872

HIGHEST FIELD GOAL PERCENTAGE (2,000 FGM minimum)

Player	FGM	FGA	Pct
Artis Gilmore	9,403	16,158	.582
MARK WEST	2,528	4,356	.580
SHAQUILLE O'NEAL	5,896	10,210	.577
Steve Johnson	2,841	4,965	.572
Darryl Dawkins	3,477	6,079	.572
James Donaldson	3,105	5,442	.571
Jeff Ruland	2,105	3,734	.564
Bobby Jones	4,451	7,953	.560
Kareem Abdul-Jabbar	15,837	28,307	.559
Kevin McHale	6,830	12,334	.554

HIGHEST 3-POINT FIELD GOAL PERCENTAGE (250 3FGM Minimum)

Player	3FGM	3FGA	Pct
STEVE KERR	618	1,332	.464
HUBERT DAVIS	581	1,317	.441
Drazen Petrovic	255	583	.437
TIM LEGLER	260	603	.431
B.J. ARMSTRONG	436	1,026	.425
DANA BARROS	1,022	2,476	.413
WESLEY PERSON	777	1,890	.411
Trent Tucker	575	1,410	.408
ALLAN HOUSTON	777	1,917	.405
GLEN RICE	1,353	3,339	.405

COMBINED NBA/ABA STATISTICAL LEADERS (Continued)

POINTS

Kareem Abdul-Jabbar	38,387
Wilt Chamberlain	31,419
KARL MALONE	31,041
Julius Erving	30,026
Moses Malone	29,580
Michael Jordan	29,277
Dan Issel	27,482
Elvin Hayes	27,313
Oscar Robertson	26,710
Dominique Wilkins	26,668

GAMES

Robert Parish	1,611
Kareem Abdul-Jabbar	1,560
Moses Malone	1,455
Artis Gilmore	1,329
Buck Williams	1,307
Elvin Hayes	1,303
Caldwell Jones	1,299
John Havlicek	1,270
JOHN STOCKTON	1,258
Paul Silas	1,254

MINUTES

Kareem Abdul-Jabbar	57,446
Elvin Hayes	50,000
Moses Malone	49,444
Wilt Chamberlain	47,859
Artis Gilmore	47,134
John Havlicek	46,471
Robert Parish	45,704
Julius Erving	45,227
KARL MALONE	44,608
Oscar Robertson	43,886

FIELD GOALS MADE

Kareem Abdul-Jabbar	15,837
Wilt Chamberlain	12,681
Julius Erving	11,818
KARL MALONE	11,435
Elvin Hayes	10,976
Michael Jordan	10,962
Alex English	10,659
John Havlicek	10,513
Dan Issel	10,431
George Gervin	10,368

FIELD GOALS ATTEMPTED

Kareem Abdul-Jabbar	28,307
Elvin Hayes	24,272
John Havlicek	23,930
Wilt Chamberlain	23,497
Julius Erving	23,370
KARL MALONE	21,777
Michael Jordan	21,686
Dominique Wilkins	21,589
Rick Barry	21,283
Alex English	21,036

FREE THROWS MADE

Moses Malone	9,018
KARL MALONE	8,100
Oscar Robertson	7,694
Jerry West	7,160
Dolph Schayes	6,979
Adrian Dantley	6,832
Michael Jordan	6,798
Kareem Abdul-Jabbar	6,712
Dan Issel	6,591
CHARLES BARKLEY	6,349

FREE THROWS ATTEMPTED

Moses Malone	11,864
Wilt Chamberlain	11,862
KARL MALONE	11,027
Kareem Abdul-Jabbar	9,304
Oscar Robertson	9,185
Jerry West	8,801
Artis Gilmore	8,790
CHARLES BARKLEY	8,643
Adrian Dantley	8,351
Dan Issel	8,315

THREE POINT FIELD GOALS MADE

REGGIE MILLER	1,867
DALE ELLIS	1,719
GLEN RICE	1,353
MITCH RICHMOND	1,263
DAN MAJERLE	1,224
VERNON MAXWELL	1,222
CHUCK PERSON	1,220
TIM HARDAWAY	1,219
DENNIS SCOTT	1,214
HERSEY HAWKINS	1,209

THREE POINT FIELD GOALS ATTEMPTED

REGGIE MILLER	4,629
DALE ELLIS	4,266
VERNON MAXWELL	3,820
MOOKIE BLAYLOCK	3,549
TIM HARDAWAY	3,443
DAN MAJERLE	3,382
CHUCK PERSON	3,370
GLEN RICE	3,339
JOHN STARKS	3,314
MITCH RICHMOND	3,222

REBOUNDS

Wilt Chamberlain	23,924
Bill Russell	21,620
Moses Malone	17,834
Kareem Abdul-Jabbar	17,440
Artis Gilmore	16,330
Elvin Hayes	16,279
Robert Parish	14,715
Nate Thurmond	14,464
Walt Bellamy	14,241
Wes Unseld	13,769

ASSISTS

JOHN STOCKTON	13,790
Magic Johnson	10,141
Oscar Robertson	9,887
Isiah Thomas	9,061
MARK JACKSON	8,574
Maurice Cheeks	7,392
Lenny Wilkens	7,211
Bob Cousy	6,955
Guy Rodgers	6,917
ROD STRICKLAND	6,723

PERSONAL FOULS

Kareem Abdul-Jabbar	4,657
Artis Gilmore	4,529
Robert Parish	4,443
Caldwell Jones	4,436
Buck Williams	4,267
Elvin Hayes	4,193
HAKEEM OLAJUWON	4,095
James Edwards	4,042
OTIS THORPE	4,038
CHARLES OAKLEY	3,890

DISQUALIFICATIONS

Vern Mikkelsen	127
Walter Dukes	121
SHAWN KEMP	109
Charlie Share	105
Paul Arizin	101
Darryl Dawkins	100
James Edwards	96
Tom Gola	94
Tom Sanders	94
Steve Johnson	93

STEALS

JOHN STOCKTON	2,844
Maurice Cheeks	2,310
Michael Jordan	2,306
Julius Erving	2,272
Clyde Drexler	2,207
Alvin Robertson	2,112
HAKEEM OLAJUWON	2,018
SCOTTIE PIPPEN	1,986
Derek Harper	1,957
MOOKIE BLAYLOCK	1,888

BLOCKED SHOTS

HAKEEM OLAJUWON	3,652
Kareem Abdul-Jabbar	3,189
Artis Gilmore	3,178
Mark Eaton	3,064
PATRICK EWING	2,758
Tree Rollins	2,542
DAVID ROBINSON	2,506
DIKEMBE MUTOMBO	2,443
Robert Parish	2,361
Caldwell Jones	2,297

COACHES

By Victories

Coach	W	L	Pct
LENNY WILKENS	1,179	981	.546
PAT RILEY	999	434	.697
LARRY BROWN	961	693	.581
Bill Fitch	944	1,106	.460
Red Auerbach	938	479	.662
Dick Motta	935	1,017	.479
DON NELSON	926	752	.552
Jack Ramsay	864	783	.525
Cotton Fitzsimmons	832	775	.518
Gene Shue	784	861	.477
JERRY SLOAN	731	419	.636
John MacLeod	707	657	.518
Red Holzman	696	604	.535
Alex Hannum	649	564	.535
Kevin Loughery	642	746	.463
Chuck Daly	638	437	.593
Doug Moe	628	529	.543
PHIL JACKSON	612	208	.746
Bob Leonard	573	534	.518
GEORGE KARL	573	388	.596

By Games

Coach	G
LENNY WILKENS	2,160
Bill Fitch	2,050
Dick Motta	1,952
DON NELSON	1,678
LARRY BROWN	1,654
Jack Ramsay	1,647
Gene Shue	1,645
Cotton Fitzsimmons	1,607
PAT RILEY	1,433
Red Auerbach	1,417
Kevin Loughery	1,388
John MacLeod	1,364
Red Holzman	1,300
Alex Hannum	1,213
Doug Moe	1,157
JERRY SLOAN	1,150
Bob Leonard	1,107
Alvin Attles	1,075
Chuck Daly	1,075
Mike Fratello	1,037

By Winning Percentage NBA/ABA (Minimum: 400 games)

Coach	W	L	Pct
PHIL JACKSON	612	208	.746
Billy Cunningham	454	196	.698
PAT RILEY	999	434	.697
Red Auerbach	938	479	.662
K.C. Jones	552	306	.643
JERRY SLOAN	731	419	.636
PAUL WESTPHAL	261	150	.635
Les Harrison	295	181	.620
Tom Heinsohn	427	263	.619
GEORGE KARL	573	388	.596
Chuck Daly	638	437	.593
RUDY TOMJANOVICH	387	267	.592
Larry Costello	430	300	.589
Johnny Kundla	423	302	.583
LARRY BROWN	961	693	.581
RICK ADELMAN	428	313	.578
Al Cervi	326	241	.575
Bill Sharman	466	353	.569
Joe Lapchick	326	247	.569
Joe Mullaney	322	244	.569

THE FORGOTTEN LEAGUE: THE ABL (1961-63)

By Paul Ladewski

ABE SAPERSTEIN FOUNDED THE HARLEM GLOBETROTTERS, BUT HIS ATTEMPT TO LAUNCH THE ABL IN 1961 WAS NOT AS SUCCESSFUL, AND THE LEAGUE LASTED ONLY 19 MONTHS.

While the ABA had a significant impact on professional basketball, one league that sought major status but fell considerably short of that goal was second edition of the American Basketball League. The brainchild of Abe Saperstein, founder of the Harlem Globetrotters, the ABL was founded in 1961 in Chicago because Saperstein was convinced that professional basketball was ready for something new.

Ultimately, the ABL left its mark in one significant area. It was the first league to institute a three-point shot. What it had in creativity, however, it lacked in star power. While the league had some NBA-caliber talent, players like George Yardley and Los Angeles Jets player-coach Bill Sharman were at the end of their careers. Dick Barnett, Bill Bridges and a teenaged Connie Hawkins were excellent players who also played in the league, but they were not regarded as marquee talent.

Only two major markets were part of the original eight franchise cities, and those faced rough prospects: Chicago had been a graveyard for professional basketball, and Los Angeles already was mesmerized by Elgin Baylor, Jerry West and the Lakers, the new kids on the Hollywood block.

If the basketball public didn't know what to expect of the ABL from week to week, it was because the league wasn't quite sure itself. Three months into the debut season, Washington relocated to New York, where the Tapers became little more than a rumor at Long Island Arena. Los Angeles dropped out after the first half of the season to leave only seven teams. On the court, one of the few eventful moments took place at Cleveland on March 14, when Chicago guard Tony Jackson established a league mark for three-point field goals (12) in one game. Four decades later, his three-point barrage still stands as the most in an ABL, ABA or NBA game.

At the root of the instability was a growing divide among club owners, especially one in particular. After his team evened the best-of-five, championship series versus Kansas City at two games apiece, the brash, young president of the Cleveland team, a fellow named George Steinbrenner, argued that the decisive game be played at a neutral site such as St. Louis and not in Kansas City as scheduled. After the appeal was rejected, Steinbrenner's Pipers finally prevailed in Game 5 two nights later — but only after they failed to appear for the game the previous evening when it was originally scheduled. The Pipers were coached by Sharman, who retired as a player after the Jets folded, and then took over as the Cleveland coach. The title was the first for Sharman, who later won titles in the ABA and NBA – the only coach to win titles in three pro leagues.

The ABL's second season was marked by more franchise shifts — Hawaii to Long Beach, Calif., San Francisco to Oakland, New York to Philadelphia and Cleveland to oblivion — and more three-figure crowds. With the league a reported $1.25 million in the red, Saperstein pulled the plug on January 1, 1963. With a league-best 22-9 record, Kansas City was declared champion.

The decision to cease operations turned nearly 100 players into free agents, but only a handful of them immediately found jobs in the NBA – Bridges, Larry Staverman, Gene Tormohlen and Ben Warley. That was yet another indication of the ABL's lack of talent.

Unlike a predecessor with the same name (the 1925-1931 ABL) the latter-day ABL existed for only 19 months, but its legacy endures. It gave us the three-point goal and also started the sports career of Steinbrenner, who years later would buy the New York Yankees and become one of the most powerful owners in sports.

NBA.COM FACT

Bill Russell was the first African-American coach in the NBA. However, John McLendon preceded Russell as the first black coach in a professional league, although the ABL was so short-lived that it was not considered a "major" league. McLendon coached the ABL Cleveland Pipers for the first half of the 1961-62 season.

CHAPTER 12

COAST TO COAST

The NBA Expands

By John Hareas

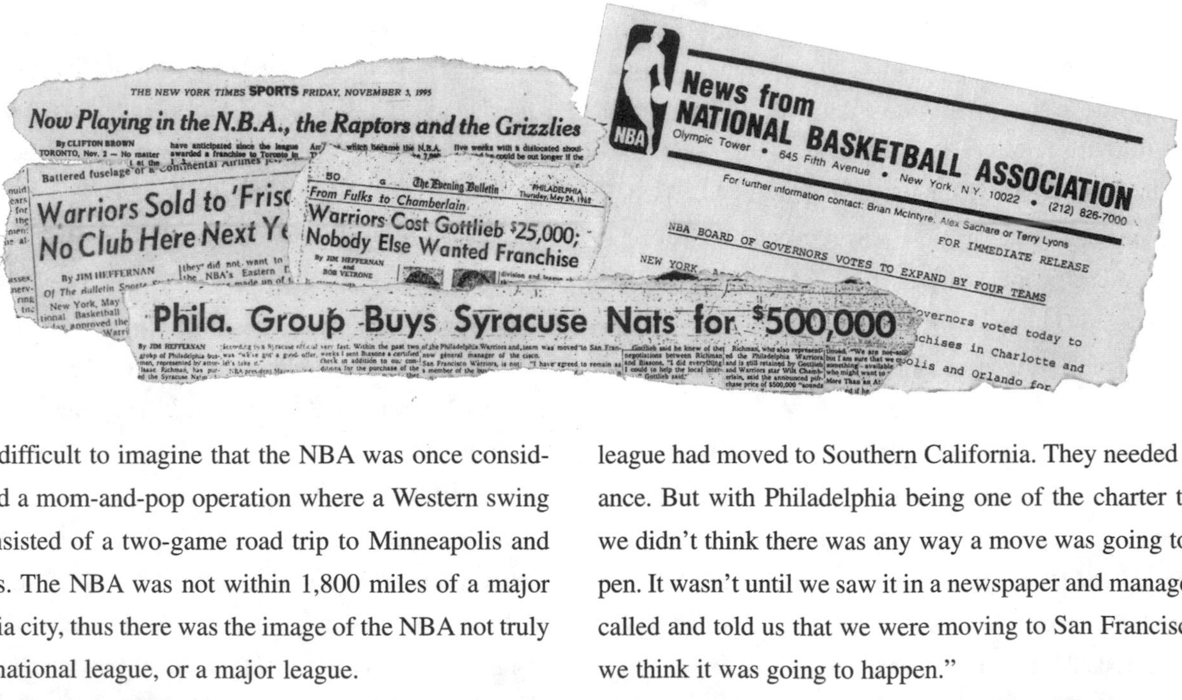

It's difficult to imagine that the NBA was once considered a mom-and-pop operation where a Western swing consisted of a two-game road trip to Minneapolis and St. Louis. The NBA was not within 1,800 miles of a major California city, thus there was the image of the NBA not truly being a national league, or a major league.

That changed in 1960 when the Lakers left Minneapolis after 13 years and five championships and moved to Los Angeles. Two years later, the Philadelphia Warriors stunned many people — including their own employees — by leaving one of the hotbeds of East Coast basketball for San Francisco.

"It was a revolutionary move," said Warriors Vice President Al Attles, who played for the Warriors in Philadelphia and in California. "From the league standpoint, they had to have a presence in Northern California since the league had moved to Southern California. They needed a balance. But with Philadelphia being one of the charter teams, we didn't think there was any way a move was going to happen. It wasn't until we saw it in a newspaper and management called and told us that we were moving to San Francisco did we think it was going to happen."

Other than the relocation of the Lakers, Warriors and then the Syracuse Nationals in 1963 to Philadelphia to become the 76ers, the only growth in the first six years of the '60s was to expand twice to Chicago. The Packers began play in Chicago in 1961 but were not well received. They decided to move to Baltimore, but had to wait a year until a new arena was built, so they changed their name to the Chicago Zephyrs for their second year in Chicago, then became the Baltimore Bullets in 1963. The NBA returned to Chicago for good in 1966

JERRY COLANGELO (LEFT), OWNER DICK KLEIN (CENTER) AND JOHNNY KERR (RIGHT) WITH LARGE FRIEND IN BACKGROUND USHER IN THE CHICAGO BULLS IN 1966.

when the Bulls were formed.

Still, at that point, the NBA was only a 10-team league. Four years later, there was a dramatic change with expansion into seven new cities: Seattle and San Diego (1967), Phoenix and Milwaukee (1968) and Buffalo, Cleveland and Portland (1970).

"We went from a mom and pop to a growth industry right then and there," said Jerry Colangelo, Chief Executive Officer of the Phoenix Suns, who began his NBA career as a scout with the Bulls in 1966 and was a part of the expansion movement when he became the Suns' first general manager.

There was little doubt that part of the NBA's expansion was a defensive tactic aimed at the American Basketball Association, which formed in 1967 and placed teams in cities such as Denver, Indianapolis, Minneapolis, Dallas and Houston. Eventually, each of those cities would have an NBA team.

After the 1970 NBA expansion, however, no team was added until 1974 when the New Orleans Jazz, a team that would play home games in the Superdome, joined the league.

"I think part of the reason New Orleans was awarded an expansion franchise was because of the Superdome," said Dave Fredman, Utah's assistant coach and director of scouting, who began his career as an intern in the Jazz public relations and ticket offices in 1974. "Since the Superdome wasn't ready, we ended up splitting our games between Loyola Fieldhouse and Municipal Auditorium. The Loyola Fieldhouse was an old gym that sat around 6,500 and had a raised floor. The players association made the team put a net all the way around the floor so players who dived for loose balls didn't fall into the stands."

The ABA had already abandoned New Orleans by that time, and it was evident that without a major television contract, the league could not survive. But it had accumulated tremendous talent and had teams in several areas where there was a strong fan base. So in 1976, the ABA folded, with four teams joining the NBA — Denver, Indiana, San Antonio and the New York Nets. The NBA was suddenly a 22-team league only 11 years after it consisted of nine teams.

"I think the competing league brought more interest in professional basketball because more markets were involved," said Colangelo. "Ultimately, the merger brought some strong franchises into the league, and of course all of the ABA stars — Julius Erving, George Gervin, David Thompson — brought a little bit of flair when the game needed it."

Pat Riley of Kentucky was the first college draft pick in the history of the expansion San Diego Rockets franchise.

Perhaps it was only natural that after such rapid expansion, the growth of the league slowed down considerably. In the 11 years after the ABA teams were admitted to the league, only one more team was added — the Dallas Mavericks in 1980. As the league entered the '80s, the overall economic health of the game was not very good, so the talk was of contraction not expansion. Generally referred to as the "Dark Days," many teams were losing money and rumors of mergers were running rampant.

"Franchises weren't making any money and we certainly were one of them," said Fredman who moved along with the Jazz from New Orleans to Salt Lake City. "There was talk about merging Utah and Denver. Those were the dark ages." So dark that the Jazz played 11 "home" games in Las Vegas during the 1983-1984 season.

A snapshot of the league's popularity at that time is perhaps best represented with the NBA Finals being shown on a tape-delay basis on network television in the late '70s and early '80s.

But the league addressed a number of issues — becoming partners with the players in a revenue sharing/salary cap economic system and also implementing a strong anti-drug program — and by the mid-'80s, the league began to grow in popularity. It obviously helped that superstars Magic Johnson and Larry Bird were in their prime and a rookie named Michael Jordan entered the league in 1984.

Suddenly, the NBA had reached new heights, and cities began clamoring to enter the league. The next wave of expansion was the main topic of conversation at the league meetings in Phoenix in October 1986 when representatives from six cities made their pitches to NBA owners with hopes of being awarded one of two new franchises. One writer who covered the expansion meetings called them "the most significant occurrence off the court in basketball history."

The competition to get into the NBA fraternity was fierce. "For 12 years it's been shut down other than the freak of Dallas," said Pat Williams, Orlando Magic's Senior Executive Vice President, referring to the NBA's expansion drought. "All of a sudden these owners whose franchises really don't have a lot of value are being bombarded by six communities, demanding to get in."

Overwhelmed by the presentations and the long-term growth possibilities that each city offered, the league decided to add not two but four teams. The Miami Heat and Charlotte Hornets entered in the 1988-89 season while the Minnesota Timberwolves and Orlando Magic entered the following season.

The expansion of the late '80s helped pave the way for the most recent additions of Toronto and Vancouver in 1995, even though the league wasn't necessarily planning on adding any teams at the time.

"Because of the great interest from Toronto, Commissioner Stern decided we had to take a look at that although we didn't have a game plan to continue with expansion," said Colangelo, who was appointed the chairman of the expansion committee.

So, on November 3, 1995, NBA basketball returned to Toronto, where on November 1, 1946 the Toronto Huskies tipped off against the New York Knickerbockers in the first game of the Basketball Association of America, which eventually became the NBA. This time the Raptors tipped off against the New Jersey Nets in front of 33,306 euphoric fans in the SkyDome. It was the largest crowd ever to watch a basketball game in Canada. On that same night, the Vancouver Grizzlies tipped off some 2,113 miles west against the Trail Blazers in Portland. Somewhere that night, the game's inventor, Canadian native Dr. James Naismith, was smiling. Even the veteran NBA executives were in awe. The league that grew from nine to 10 teams when Colangelo and the Bulls joined in 1966 now consisted of 29 teams.

"It would have been very hard to visualize this back in the '60s when I first got involved in the NBA because we were just trying to survive as a league — as our own franchise," Colangelo said. "We were a small player in the big scheme of things."

NBA EXPANSION FACTS

TEAM	FIRST SEASON	FIRST SEASON .500 OR BETTER	FIRST SEASON IN PLAYOFFS
Chicago Packers	1961-62 (18-62)	—	1964-65
Chicago Bulls	1966-67 (33-48)	1970-71 (51-31)	1966-67
San Diego Rockets	1967-68 (15-67)	1974-75 (41-41)	1968-69
Seattle SuperSonics	1967-68 (23-59)	1971-72 (47-35)	1974-75
Milwaukee Bucks	1968-69 (27-55)	1969-70 (56-26)	1969-70
Phoenix Suns	1968-69 (16-66)	1970-71 (48-34)	1969-70
Buffalo Braves	1970-71 (22-60)	1973-74 (42-20)	1973-74
Cleveland Cavaliers	1970-71 (15-67)	1975-76 (49-33)	1975-76
Portland Trail Blazers	1970-71 (29-53)	1976-77 (49-33)	1976-77
New Orleans Jazz	1974-75 (23-59)	1983-84 (45-37)	1983-84
Dallas Mavericks	1980-81 (15-67)	1983-84 (43-39)	1983-84
Charlotte Hornets	1988-89 (20-62)	1992-93 (44-38)	1992-93
Miami Heat	1988-89 (15-67)	1993-94 (42-40)	1991-92
Orlando Magic	1989-90 (18-64)	1992-93 (41-41)	1993-94
Minnesota Timberwolves	1989-90 (22-60)	1997-98 (45-37)	1996-97
Toronto Raptors	1995-96 (21-61)	1999-00 (45-37)	1999-2000
Vancouver Grizzlies	1995-96 (15-67)	—	—

Note: Packers became the Zephyrs for 1962-63 before becoming the Baltimore Bullets for 1963-64, the Capital Bullets (1973-74), the Washington Bullets (1974-1997) then the Washington Wizards. Rockets moved to Houston for 1971-72 season. Buffalo moved to San Diego and became the Clippers in 1978-79, then moved to Los Angeles in 1984-85. Jazz moved to Utah in 1979-80.

NBA EXPANSION TEAM PRICES

FIRST SEASON	TEAM	PRICE
1966-67	Chicago Bulls	$ 1,250,000
1967-68	San Diego Rockets	$ 1,750,000
	Seattle SuperSonics	$ 1,750,000
1968-69	Milwaukee Bucks	$ 2,000,000
	Phoenix Suns	$ 2,000,000
1970-71	Buffalo Braves	$ 3,700,000
	Cleveland Cavaliers	$ 3,700,000
	Portland Trail Blazers	$ 3,700,000
1974-75	New Orleans Jazz	$ 6,150,000
1980-81	Dallas Mavericks	$ 12,000,000
1988-89	Charlotte Hornets	$ 32,500,000
	Miami Heat	$ 32,500,000
1989-90	Minnesota Timberwolves	$ 32,500,000
	Orlando Magic	$ 32,500,000
1995-96	Toronto Raptors	$ 125,000,000
	Vancouver Grizzlies	$ 125,000,000

Note: The San Diego franchise is now in Houston, the New Orleans franchise is now in Salt Lake City, and the Buffalo franchise is now the L.A. Clippers. The NBA expanded in Chicago in 1961 (now the Washington Wizards), but the cost is not available. The NBA and ABA merged in 1976 with four ABA franchises admitted (Denver, Indiana, New Jersey and San Antonio). They each paid a $3.2 million entrance fee.

CHAPTER 13

THE DYNASTIES

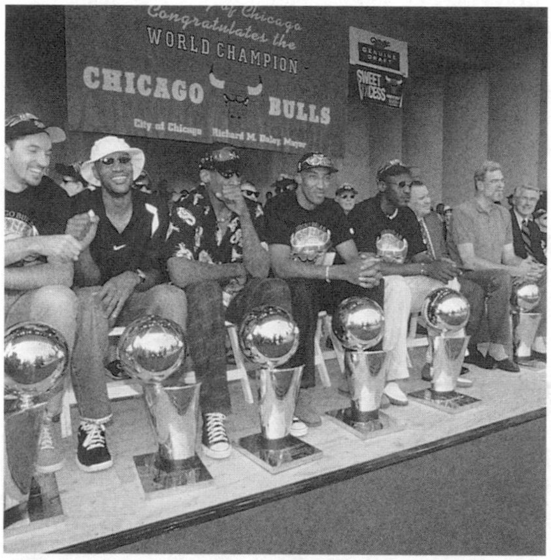

CHICAGO BULLS: 1990-91 TO 1997-98

LOS ANGELES LAKERS: 1979-80 TO 1987-88

BOSTON CELTICS: 1956-57 TO 1968-69

MINNEAPOLIS LAKERS: 1948-49 TO 1953-54

Chicago Bulls

By Jackie MacMullan

The very definition of a dynasty requires a franchise to be rooted in endurance, consistency and, above all, excellence. It is one thing to win a championship by capturing the fleeting combination of chemistry, talent and luck; it is quite another to be able to sustain that exquisite, delicate balance. Only a few teams in basketball history have been able to do that.

Perhaps that is why the dominance of the Chicago Bulls, who won six championships from 1991 to 1998, was so exceptional. At a time when parity ruled the sporting world, the Bulls emerged as the invincible force of the '90s, the team of the decade and, arguably, a team for the ages.

Michael Jordan, the most compelling athlete of his era, was at the epicenter of this collection of competitors, who varied in ages, backgrounds and temperament. Like any champions, they needed time together to nurture and grow, to allow their roots to take hold.

How do you measure when a dynasty is born?

Was it a balmy afternoon in Richfield, Ohio, in 1989, two years before the first championship was actually won, when Jordan, only 26 years old, soared above the outstretched arm of Cleveland guard Craig Ehlo, and willed in an 18-foot jump shot through the strings so neatly, it left the favored Cavaliers frozen in stunned disbelief? The basket secured a 101-100 Chicago victory, and eliminated Cleveland from the playoffs. For Jordan, it was validation that his gaudy individual skills could lead his team to greatness.

Although the Bulls would later fall to their nemesis, the Detroit Pistons, in the Eastern Conference Finals, Air Jordan's shot on May 7, 1989, elevated himself and the Bulls to a new level.

And yet, wasn't the evolution of another key figure, Coach Phil Jackson, equally important to the cause? Jackson, a free-spirited basketball junkie, was once considered too liberal for the palates of the button-down NBA owners. He was a man who practiced Zen Buddhism, shunned neckties and drove the team van of his Continental Basketball Association team, the Albany Patroons, who won the 1984 CBA title under him. Jackson's CBA training taught him how to handle the unexpected, to juggle personnel, to practice infinite patience, to understand sacrifice.

He was hired as a Chicago assistant to Doug Collins in 1987; two seasons later, he moved a few inches to the left on the bench, and became the league's resident Zen master. Jackson burned incense, chanted ancient Indian rites, passed out paperback books, massaged egos and laid down the law.

NBA.COM FACT

Michael Jordan, Scottie Pippen, head coach Phil Jackson and assistant coach Tex Winter were the constants for Chicago in its six championship seasons.

MICHAEL JORDAN'S MIRACULOUS SHOT OVER CLEVELAND'S CRAIG EHLO WAS A PORTENT OF DRAMAS TO COME.

CHICAGO'S CORE GROUP WAS A WONDERFUL MIX OF TALENTS AND PERSONALITIES THAT SLOWLY BECAME A UNIT.

The Bulls won 55 games in his first season as head coach, more than any other rookie coach had before him. But more importantly, Jordan grew to trust Jackson completely.

The coach and the player each had their trusted companions. Jordan's ally in this dance through history was Scottie Pippen, a wiry forward with long arms whose exceptional ballhandling skills and defensive instincts complemented Jordan's athletic gifts. Jackson's sidekick was an old-time basketball legend, Tex Winter, the proponent of the Triangle Offense, a man who demanded cooperation, selflessness and above all, the commitment of his players.

NBA.COM FACT

The most unlikely postseason hero in the Chicago dynasty was Bobby Hansen, a journeyman guard who averaged 6.9 points in his nine-season career. In the 1992 NBA Finals, Portland took a 15-point lead into the fourth quarter of Game 6, so Bulls head coach Phil Jackson called on a lineup that included four reserves and starter Scottie Pippen. The result was a 14-2 run with Hansen contributing a steal, an assist and a key three-pointer. The 97-93 victory completed the greatest fourth quarter comeback in NBA Finals history.

The assembly of this central cast cemented one firm fact from 1991 forward: As long as Jordan and the Bulls were prowling the NBA, everyone else was playing for second.

The NBA saw how special he was when he dropped 63 points on the Celtics on April 20, 1986, in a playoff game at storied Boston Garden. Yet he was dismissed as a preposterous individual talent that simply had not been able to grasp the team concept, or make others around him better.

Jordan dedicated himself to proving that theory incorrect, understanding the only way to eradicate that criticism was to win a title. By the 1990-91 season, Chicago had become more comfortable with Winter's Triangle, which centered on players cutting, passing, waiting for the most opportune place on the floor where they could score. Winter promised his players if they completed the cycle of cuts, the team would benefit, yet too often Jordan would identify a clear path to the basket and break the rules. More often than not he'd score successfully, but as Winter admonished him, throwing up his hands in disgust, he'd explain the offense was designed not only to get Jordan optimal shots — but also provide his less talented teammates with their highest percentage chances.

When Jordan finally bought into the concept, the others

NBA.COM FACT

So total and complete was its domination in six championship seasons that, in 24 playoff series, Chicago trailed only once after the third game. The lone comeback took place against New York in the 1993 Eastern Conference Finals. The Knicks captured the first two games at home before the Bulls responded with four consecutive victories.

Chicago's triumph in the 1991 NBA Finals came in the 25th year of the franchise's existence.

quickly followed suit. Horace Grant, the prototype power forward who was a solid defender and excellent rebounder, was a key piece of the 1991 title team. Veteran John Paxson, Jordan's close friend, epitomized what Winter was striving for — a player who made the right pass, the right cut, the right decision. Center Bill Cartwright, whose awkward gait and soft demeanor made him a favorite Jordan target of abuse, was happy to assume whatever role was asked of him.

That nucleus was a model of efficiency in 1990-91, winning 61 regular-season games and shooting 51 percent from the floor. The Bulls dismissed the Pistons in four games in the Eastern Conference Finals and won the championship against the Los Angeles Lakers, in a matchup billed as Michael versus Magic, in five games. When it ended, Jordan was weeping tears of joy, cradling the championship trophy as though it were his first-born child. In between gulps of champagne, his Airness vowed, "This is only the beginning."

How right he was. The following season, in 1991-92, Chicago won 67 regular-season games and stormed through Miami, New York (in the only tough, seven-game series), Cleveland and Portland. By the 1992-93 season, when the

When Magic Johnson hugged the victorious Jordan in 1991, the torch of supremacy had been passed.

THE BULLS THREE-PEAT IN 1993 WAS THE FIRST TIME SINCE 1966 AN NBA TEAM HAD WON THREE IN A ROW.

Bulls ousted Phoenix in a six-game Finals, it was clear the opponent was of little consequence — this was all about Chicago and its assault on history. Mindful both the Lakers and Pistons were able to win back-to-back titles. Jordan sought to separate himself from their superstars, Magic Johnson and Isiah Thomas, by winning three in a row.

After the third title, Jordan suffered an enormous personal loss when his father James, a fixture in the Bulls' locker room, was murdered. Jordan said later that he already had planned to retire, but certainly the loss of his dad sealed his departure at age 30.

Jordan, forever looking for a challenge, chased his childhood dream of playing baseball and spent one season in Double-A ball in Birmingham, Ala. Jordan had been an excellent baseball player in high school, but he found that pro ball was an entirely different world. After a season of humility, Jordan took off his spikes and rejoined the world where he was second to none. In returning to the Bulls, MJ merely announced, "I'm back."

What he discovered was a lineup of new faces, yet eerily similar personnel. It was a credit to Jackson and Chicago General Manager Jerry Krause that the Bulls so smoothly re-invented themselves with interchangeable parts that suited the Triangle Offense the way their predecessors had.

When Paxson retired in 1994, the Bulls signed veteran shooter Steve Kerr, who was on the verge of being cut from the league. Yet when he assumed his place in the Triangle Offense vacated by Paxson, he became a vital part of Chicago's offense.

When Grant bolted for Orlando in 1994, Chicago began searching for a clone who would provide the same tenacious rebounding and defense. Equally important, the player had to be willing to accept a subservient offensive role. One year later, the Bulls found their man: Dennis Rodman, the former

1990-1991

1991-1992

1992-1993

COLORFUL AND TENACIOUS, DENNIS RODMAN (RIGHT) WAS A KEY ELEMENT OF THE SECOND THREE-PEAT.

Pistons villain.

There were other key additions to the "second" championship roster. Toni Kukoc, a versatile, offensive-minded European, drove Jordan crazy because he was not tough-minded defensively, yet even his Airness could not dismiss Kukoc's considerable contributions. Conversely, Jordan's good friend, Ron Harper, never proved to be a consistent offensive threat, yet he endeared himself to Jackson and his teammates by willingly doing the "little things," such as taking charges, jumping into the passing lanes and slashing to the hoop in traffic.

With the new cast, the Bulls won a league-record 72 games in 1995-96. Their fourth trip to the Finals, this time against Gary Payton and Seattle, was as lethal and proficient as the first three had been. In 1997, the Bulls defended their championship against Utah, but not before Jordan shook off a case of the stomach flu with the series tied 2-2 and knocked down 38 points, including a game clinching three-pointer in the final 25 seconds in Game 5.

1995-1996

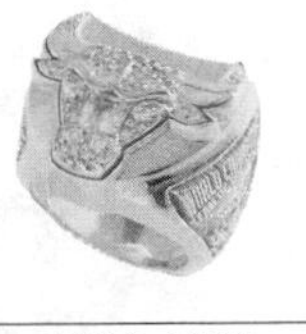

1996-1997

1997-1998

Would the Bulls' Reign of Terror ever end? Chicago showed signs of vulnerability in the 1998 Eastern Conference Finals when a rejuvenated Indiana team — led by rookie coach Larry Bird — pushed it to the brink in a thrilling seven-game series. Again, the experience of the Bulls prevailed.

That set the stage for a rematch with the Jazz in the Finals, the first time in the Jordan era that Chicago played the same opponent twice for the title. On June 14, 1998, in Game 6 of the Finals, with six and half seconds left on the clock, Jordan pulled up at the foul line and stroked in a game-winning jumper.

As the ball dropped through, he exaggerated his follow through, punctuating a career and a dynasty so extraordinary that only the greatest player and team of any future era would even dare dream of matching it.

Los Angeles Lakers

By Jack McCallum

The reign began on an evening beyond compare — May 16, 1980, a night that a sporting nation was touched by brilliance on delayed tape. NBA Commissioner David Stern, then the Executive Vice President in the league office, has said it was his darkest moment as a NBA executive: The deciding game of the NBA Finals was taped and shown in most markets after the late local news because of a lack of viewer interest.

But in that relative darkness, a dazzling explosion took place. A 20-year-old rookie named Earvin "Magic" Johnson took a team without the injured Kareem Abdul-Jabbar, who would become the leading scorer in the history of the league, to its first of five titles in the decade. Johnson electrified the

NBA.COM FACT

Magic Johnson owns the three highest single-game assist totals recorded in the NBA Finals: 21 against Boston in 1984, 20 against Boston in 1987 and Chicago in 1991. He also is the NBA Finals leader in career assists (584) and career steals (102).

MAGIC JOHNSON'S PERFORMANCE IN GAME 6 OF THE 1980 NBA FINALS MADE HIM AN NBA LEGEND AT 20.

NBA.COM FACT

Pat Riley posted a 533-194 record (.733 winning percentage) in his nine seasons as Lakers coach, plus a 102-47 mark (.685) in the postseason. Despite those numbers, he did not win Coach of the Year honors until the 1989-90 season, his last as the club's coach and the year of his earliest exit from the playoffs.

somnolent but faithful viewers with a 42-point, 15-rebound performance that staggered the Philadelphia 76ers, 123-107, in the deciding game of the 1980 NBA Finals. More importantly, Johnson's performance not only ignited interest in the NBA, it also established the Lakers as the team to beat in the decade.

"The Lakers that year, even with Kareem, Norm Nixon, Jamaal Wilkes and all those guys, were not thought of as a contender," said Pat Riley, who was on the Lakers bench as an assistant to Paul Westhead during the game. "He came in and he was just a smiley kid from Michigan State, but he changed the face of our team forever. We didn't realize how good this guy was. But he brought this unique, special attitude about winning, and how to win at that young an age. In that Game 6, he proved his greatness as a player. To do it on the road against Dr. J without Kareem and just demand and command your team to win, was absolutely remarkable. It was one of the greatest performances that I've ever seen.

"Greatness is never achieved until you get to those moments where greatness is respected and given out," continued Riley. "You can be called a great player but you are not of greatness until you play those kinds of games in those kinds of arenas for those kind of stakes. Magic found his greatness in Philadelphia in May of 1980."

There was little doubt that it added to the aura of Magic, who had, at the tender ages of 19 and 20, won consecutive titles in college at Michigan State and with the Lakers. The Lakers obviously benefited the most from Magic's presence, but he was also a breath of fresh air to the NBA. His team-oriented style of play, all-out hustle and boundless enthusiasm went a long way toward erasing the selfish, me-first attitude fans attributed to NBA players in the late '70s. He was the essence of Showtime, bringing excitement to the Forum and turning it into the place for the glamorous people to see and be seen in Tinseltown. On the court, his arrival as the consummate playmaker infused new life into Abdul-Jabbar, the stoic center who had been less productive each year since coming to Los Angeles from Milwaukee in 1975. With Johnson feeding him the ball and deflecting the glare of the spotlight Abdul-Jabbar so often found uncomfortable, the Big Fella went on to play effectively for 10 more years.

PAT RILEY WAS NOT ACKNOWLEDGED AS A COACHING GENIUS UNTIL THE LAKERS REIGN OF CHAMPIONSHIPS WAS CLOSING.

Together, Johnson and Abdul-Jabbar formed the nucleus of the team of the '80s. Aided by a strong supporting cast and coached for most of the decade by Riley, who took over in the 1981-82 season, they led the Lakers to championships in 1980, 1982, 1985, 1987 and 1988, with second-place finishes in 1983, 1984 and 1989.

It wasn't all Magic and Kareem, to be sure. With owner Jerry Buss letting savvy Hall of Famers Bill Sharman and Jerry West run the front office, the Lakers were constantly replenishing talent and picking up players who helped in clearly defined roles. Before Norm Nixon could get old, the Lakers dealt him for Byron Scott; similarly, James Worthy took over the small forward position from Wilkes. Need a scorer? Pick up an aging Bob McAdoo, who still had enough in the tank to contribute to two Lakers championships. Want a defensive stopper and wingman for the break? Find a raw talent no one ever heard of and watch Michael Cooper blos-

LARRY BIRD AND THE BOSTON CELTICS WON THREE TITLES IN THE 1980S, INCLUDING A WIN OVER THE LAKERS IN 1984.

som. Need a backup for Kareem? Trade for Mychal Thompson, who was instrumental in two title runs.

And then there was Riley. A college star who had modest success as a pro player, he held closed practices and communicated in pithy sayings (Riley would ask his players to "stay within themselves," at the same time urging them to "take it to the next level"), thus eliciting an intriguing fusion of West Coast style (did anyone look more Hollywood than the slickly coiffured Riley?) and East Coast toughness (the guy, after all, was from blue-collar Schenectady, N.Y.). As the decade wore

NBA.COM FACT

Only the Boston Celtics (16 titles) have more NBA championships than the Lakers (12, including five in Minneapolis). The Lakers have appeared in 25 NBA Finals, the most of any franchise.

NBA.COM FACT

Jamaal Wilkes also had a big night in Game 6 of the 1980 NBA Finals. The Lakers forward tallied 37 points and 10 rebounds in Los Angeles' series-clinching victory.

THE MATCHUP OF KAREEM ABDUL-JABBAR (33) VS. ROBERT PARISH WAS ONE OF MANY MONUMENTAL PAIRINGS.

on, rumors abounded that the players were perennially ready to revolt against Riley's strong hand on the throttle. But they never did, and Riley's Lakers became the consummate winners of the '80s.

NBA fans weaned on the Chicago Bulls' six titles in the '90s don't realize how extraordinary the Lakers' back-to-backs in '87 and '88 really were. Until L.A. beat the Detroit Pistons to win its second straight championship, no NBA team had repeated as champion since the 1968-69 Celtics. One of the enduring images of the '80s, in fact, came after the Lakers won their second straight title when an atypically exuberant Abdul-Jabbar shoved a towel in Riley's mouth before the coach could predict a third consecutive title. The message from Abdul-Jabbar was clear: The coach had coaxed and cajoled so much out of them to win two in a row (the Lakers had survived three consecutive seven-game series to win the title), it was going to be all but impossible to get three.

That turned out to be the case, though the Lakers reached the 1989 NBA Finals on an unprecedented roll. That squad swept three playoff series (11 consecutive games) to reach the NBA Finals, but injuries to Scott and Johnson left Los Angeles depleted and unable to prevent a sweep by the Detroit Pistons. Still, even at the end of their reign, they were nothing less than remarkable.

And they had to be very, very good, because lapping at their heels throughout most of the decade were the Boston Celtics, led by their own magical, do-everything talent, Larry Bird.

Bird's Celtics were more than perfect foils for Magic's Lakers, bordering on a dynasty in their own right with three championships and two more Finals appearances in seven years from 1981 through 1987. The media delighted in the rivalry between the Lakers and Celtics, the glamour boys from Hollywood and the lunch-pail guys from back East. L.A. played before a multitude of stars epitomized by Jack Nicholson and Dyan Cannon in the glitzy Forum, while Boston's home was the run-down Boston Garden. L.A.'s attack was up tempo Showtime, Boston's was measured blue-collar. Magic was ebullient and relished the spotlight. Bird preferred living away from prying eyes, only growing comfortable with his celebrity status in the latter half of his career.

Both the Lakers and Celtics were brilliant teams, and as a result, the message sent to fans in the '80s was that the NBA was not a selfish league. Its two best players, Magic and Larry, delighted in making the extra pass and bringing out the best in their teammates. Magic and Larry kept NBA basketball free-flowing enough to please those in search of up-tempo entertainment, yet old-fashioned enough to satisfy the purists. Both played better defense, as individuals and within the team concept, than casual observers might expect.

Most of all, however, each gave it his all every night, setting an example for teammates and an entire league. When they left the game, however, Magic had the edge in championships and the Lakers overshadowed the Celtics enough to earn the right to be called a dynasty.

NBA.COM FACT

Kareem Abdul-Jabbar, Michael Cooper and Magic Johnson were the only Lakers to play on all five of the club's championship teams during the 1980s.

JAMES WORTHY (GUARDED BY ADRIAN DANTLEY) WAS A KEY TO THE LAKERS' VAUNTED "SHOWTIME" STYLE.

Boston Celtics

By Dan Shaughnessy

If you grew up in a Massachusetts basketball culture in the 1950s and 1960s, a Boston Celtics championship was something of a birthright. Spring arrived, the forsythia bloomed, skinny guys ran 26 miles from Hopkington to Boston and the Celtics won the NBA title. Imagine making it all the way to the eighth grade before realizing that your team doesn't automatically win the crown. I don't expect any American professional sports fans will ever share this experience.

I was born in Central Massachusetts in 1953 and didn't know there was such a thing as pro basketball until a local pol named John F. Kennedy was running for the White House. Coming of age as a fan at that particular time, I was forever spoiled by the team that wore black sneakers and played on a parquet court. The Celtics won the championship every year of my youth.

It was a different NBA and the Celtics were always one step ahead of the other teams. They had the best coach in Red Auerbach and they had the best player in Bill Russell. Fans elsewhere in NBA America feared Wilt Chamberlain, and why not? The guy averaged 50 points a game for a season and seemed to be the strongest man in the world. In Boston, we didn't fear Wilt because Russell was Kryptonite to Chamberlain's Superman. Wilt might light up Big Bill for 50, but the Celtics would win in the end.

RED AUERBACH'S ACQUISITION OF BILL RUSSELL IN 1956 MADE THE CELTICS' DYNASTY POSSIBLE.

BOB COUSY WAS THE BALLHANDLING AND SCORING WIZARD WHO FUELED THE CELTIC MACHINE.

The Celtics were everything right about team sports. They never had a scoring champion, but it wasn't unusual to see eight guys in double figures. Russell, Satch Sanders and K. C. Jones were paid to play defense, not to score. It didn't matter who started — but who finished. Frank Ramsey and John Havlicek made it to the Hall of Fame while coming off the bench for much of their careers.

The Celtics were in better shape than other teams. At a time when America was grappling with civil rights, the Celtics were color-blind. Auerbach was the first NBA coach to draft an African-American player (Chuck Cooper), and the first to start five blacks. Russell became the first black head coach in major American professional sports. Auerbach sold Celtic Pride and Celtic Mystique and nobody snickered. The stuff really worked.

From 1957 through 1969 the Celtics won 11 championships in 13 NBA seasons, including a never-to-be-broken eight consecutive titles from 1959-66. The Celtics' reign spanned four presidential administrations. It started before Sputnik and ended the same year we landed on the moon. Eight straight championships elevates the Celtics above the New York Yankees, Montreal Canadiens, Green Bay Packers and every other pro sports juggernaut. Today it's fashionable to talk dynasty after two or three championships. Try eight in a row or 11 of 13. It's unfathomable in the 21st century sports world.

The first championship came in 1957 thanks to the potent additions of rookies Russell and Tommy Heinsohn. The pre-Russell Celtics were carried by Hall of Fame guards Bob Cousy and Bill Sharman, but the team needed more rebounding and defense. Russell delivered both. He arrived

NBA.COM FACT

The Celtics have retired an NBA-high 21 jerseys, including one (No. 18) twice (for Jim Loscutoff and Dave Cowens). They also have retired a microphone in honor of legendary announcer Johnny Most.

NBA.COM FACT

The Celtics made their home debut on November 5, 1946, at Boston Arena, which featured a glass backboard. Future television actor Chuck "The Rifleman" Connors, then a 6-7 forward for the Celtics, dunked during warm-ups and shattered the backboard. The Celtics found a spare (wooden) backboard at Boston Garden, which was hosting a rodeo, and installed it at the arena. After an hour delay, the teams tipped off.

24 games into the regular season after winning Olympic gold in Melbourne. The NBA had never seen anything like the 6-10 floor runner/shotblocker, and Boston beat the St. Louis Hawks in a thrilling seven-game Finals in '57. Game 7 was a 125-123 double-overtime victory at Boston Garden. Russell scored 19 with 32 rebounds and five blocks. Fellow rookie Heinsohn chipped in with 37 points and 23 rebounds.

Cousy said, "Once we won the first time, we were so certain that nobody would beat us."

Russell turned his ankle in the third game of the Finals the next year and St. Louis won the rematch, but it would be nine long years before the Celtics would lose again.

They won the 1959 title in four games against the Minneapolis Lakers, then beat the Hawks in seven again in 1960. But it was the conference finals series that got more attention. Chamberlain had made his dramatic entry into the league in 1959-60 (averaging 37.6 points and 27 rebounds) and there was speculation that he might dominate for the entire decade. But the Celtics beat Chamberlain's Philadelphia Warriors in six games, paving the way to a second straight title and establishing a pattern.

The 1960-61 Celtics were so deep they had three Hall of Famers on the bench (Ramsey, K.C. and Sam Jones). Counting Auerbach and owner Walter Brown, there are nine Hall of Famers in the '61 Celtic team photo. Six players averaged 15 or more points, but none of them ranked in the top 10 in league scoring. They routed the Hawks in five games and Auerbach declared, "This is the greatest team ever assembled." Sharman was the first Celtic Hall of Famer to retire after winning a championship. There would be many more.

A year later the Celtic leprechaun wove some magic when Frank Selvy missed an eight-footer that would have won the championship for the Lakers. This was the year Chamberlain averaged 50.4 points and Russell needed the full seven games to defeat Goliath in the conference finals.

The 1962-63 season was Cousy's last and Havlicek's first. They're pro basketball's answer to the 1951 Yankees, who had an outgoing Joe DiMaggio in center and rookie Mickey Mantle in right. The Celts beat the Lakers in six for the title, and the final seconds of the final game featured Cousy drib-

THE 1960-61 BOSTON CELTICS' CHAMPIONSHIP TEAM FEATURED NINE HALL OF FAMERS [IN BOLD]. FRONT ROW [FROM LEFT]: **K.C. JONES, BOB COUSY**, HEAD COACH **RED AUERBACH**, PRESIDENT **WALTER BROWN, BILL SHARMAN, FRANK RAMSEY**. BACK [FROM LEFT] TRAINER BUDDY LEROUX, TOM "SATCH" SANDERS, **TOM HEINSOHN**, GENE CONLEY, **BILL RUSSELL**, GENE GUARILLIA, JIM LOSCUTOFF, **SAM JONES**. INSET: TREASURER LOU PIERI.

John Havlicek won six NBA championships in his first seven seasons from 1963 to 1969.

bling out the clock, then chucking the ball toward the Los Angeles Sports Arena ceiling as the buzzer sounded.

Boston's sixth straight title in 1964 — the one that broke the record set by the Yankees and Canadiens — was one of the more unremarkable Celtic campaigns. They beat Wilt's San Francisco Warriors in five games for the championship. It was Ramsey's turn to retire.

The 1964-65 Celtics won a record 62 games, but almost lost the conference finals when Russell hit a basket support wire with an inbounds pass in the closing seconds of Game 7

NBA.COM FACT

Although no Boston player has won a scoring title while playing for the Celtics, the franchise boasts an NBA record 10 MVP Award winners (Russell, five; Bird, three; Cousy and Cowens, one).

NBA.COM FACT

From 1956 to 1969, Boston posted a regular-season record of 716-299 (.705) and a postseason mark of 108-59 (.647).

against the Philadelphia 76ers. The Sixers were led by Chamberlain, who'd been traded from the Warriors at mid-season. Boston led by one with five seconds left when Russell turned it over, but the blunder was forgotten because when Hal Greer inbounded . . . *Havlicek stole the ball!* Celtic radio legend Johnny Most made the most famous call of his career. To this day, "Havlicek Stole the Ball" is as much a part of Boston folklore as "The British Are Coming!" The Celts went on to beat the Lakers in five — a going-away championship gift for Heinsohn.

Auerbach announced that 1965-66 would be his last season on the bench and issued a challenge to the league. The Sixers thought they were up to the task, but Boston beat Philly in five and then took the Lakers in seven to send Red out in style. Auerbach named Russell his successor before the conclusion of the playoffs.

The 1967 Philadelphia 76ers snapped Boston's streak in Russell's first year as player-coach. It was bound to happen sooner or later, and the '67 Sixers are still regarded as one of the NBA's best teams. But it didn't take Russell and Co. long to dismantle the one-year Sixer dynasty. Growing long in the tooth, the Celtics bounced back to win two more championships in 1968 and '69 — beating Chamberlain-led teams both times. Russell and Auerbach still wear the 1969 ring. It's their favorite.

The Celtics never had a slick marketing machine that would churn out slogans designed to spur their continued greatness. Instead, they motivated from within. After winning the first title, they wanted to prove they could repeat. Then they wanted to win one for the Cooz, or for Walter Brown, or for Auerbach. According to Russell, "For a few years in there we couldn't think of anything special, so we won those on general principle."

A Celtics championship was so routine that it ultimately created its own slogan. Even today, more than three decades after the 11-in-13 run ended, "Celtics Tradition" remains a permanent part of American sports lore.

Minneapolis Lakers

By Alex Sachare

The Minneapolis Lakers are the forgotten dynasty, an afterthought when the discussion turns to the NBA's greatest teams. Part of that is because it has been 40 years since the franchise picked up stakes and moved to sunny Los Angeles, replaced a decade ago by an expansion team seeking to forge its own identity. What's more, a half-century has passed since the glory days, and the players who have not passed on are in their 70s and 80s now, several generations removed from the NBA of the new millennium.

But history cannot be changed and should not be forgotten.

NBA.COM FACT

Jim Pollard and George Mikan were the only Minneapolis players to be a part of each of its six league championship teams.

The Minneapolis Lakers were the NBA's first dynasty, winning five titles in six seasons from 1948-49 through 1953-54.

Add the championship the Lakers won in the National Basketball League before they entered the NBA and the count is six crowns in seven seasons — a dynasty by any standard.

George Mikan (with ball) was not only the Lakers' center, but the centerpiece attraction of the young NBA.

They won championships in their first two years in the NBA. Then, after a year when they were beaten in the division finals, they reeled off three consecutive titles.

They were built around 6-10 center George Mikan, who won five straight scoring championships and averaged 22.6 points in a career that came almost entirely before the 24-second shot clock.

"Mikan ran the whole show," said Larry Foust, a 6-9 center who played for the Fort Wayne Pistons in those days. "Nobody ever had better offensive moves under the basket. When George played, he owned that lane."

But the Lakers were far from a one-man team. They also featured Jim Pollard, perhaps the finest all-around player of his day. Slater Martin was a point guard who could distribute the ball and run an offense as well as anyone. Vern Mikkelsen and Clyde Lovellette provided more muscle up front, and there were always a couple of shooters on the roster to round things out.

Orchestrating it all was John Kundla, a man who never got his share of credit because of the array of talent at his disposal. Kundla was far from a push-button coach. He not only knew his Xs and Os, but how to deal with divergent personalities and the heightened expectations that come with winning year after year. He was a vital part of the Lakers' equation.

The Lakers rose from the ashes of the Detroit Gems, a team that compiled a 4-40 record in the NBL in 1946-47, its only season. The franchise was purchased by a group of Minneapolis businessmen fronted by a 24-year-old sports writer, Sid Hartman, and revamped for the 1947-48 NBL season.

Hartman signed Pollard, a Coast Guard veteran who had led the Oakland Bittners to the 1946 Amateur Athletic Union championship, when he agreed to take on three of Pollard's AAU teammates as well. He paid the Chicago Stags $25,000 for the rights to Tony Jaros and Don "Swede" Carlson, two veteran pros who were Minnesota natives and figured to be helpful in drawing fans.

For a coach he found Kundla at St. Thomas College in St. Paul, and a three-year contract convinced the 31-year-old Kundla to sign on with the fledgling team — after all, he didn't have to relocate.

The Lakers won their first game, against the Oshkosh

NBA.COM FACT

Minneapolis was extended to a seventh game twice in its run of five championships. The first took place on April 25, 1952, when the Lakers posted an 82-65 triumph against New York at Minneapolis. The second occurred on April 12, 1954 as the Lakers defeated Syracuse 87-80.

NBA.COM FACT

Sid Hartman was the creative force behind the Lakers' dynasty, but he was a general manager without portfolio. Since starting up a franchise, especially in those days, was a shaky proposition, he never gave up his "day job" as a Minneapolis sports writer. To avoid a conflict of interest, he did not write about the team and he kept his name out of stories about the team's operations, working behind the scenes while veteran promoter Max Winter served as the team's official general manager.

JIM POLLARD, GEORGE MIKAN, VERN MIKKELSEN (STANDING L TO R) AND SLATER MARTIN (KNEELING R) ARE ALL HALL OF FAMERS.

NBA.COM FACT

The Lakers enjoyed a home-court advantage in that their playing floor at the Minneapolis Auditorium actually was several feet narrower than the standard 50-foot court width. "When Mikan, Mikkelsen and Pollard stretched their arms across that narrow court, nobody could get through," said Syracuse player and coach Al Cervi.

All-Stars, and shortly thereafter added playmaking guard Herm Schaeffer from the Indianapolis Kautskys. Then, four games into the season, Mikan became available when the 24-team Professional Basketball League of America folded. The NBL parceled out the PBLA's players, and the Lakers got Mikan. The pieces of the dynasty were in place.

Kundla used the contrasting styles of Mikan and Pollard to the team's advantage. Most of the time the Lakers played at a leisurely pace, waiting for Mikan to lumber up the floor and set up house down low. But if an opponent was slow getting back on defense, Pollard or Martin or one of the other quicker Lakers would race right past, running what today is called an opportunity fast break.

The Lakers lost their first five games after Mikan joined the team, but they rebounded to finish the 1947-48 season at 43-17, tops in the Western Division. They beat the famous Rens in the championship game of the final Chicago World Tournament, then defeated the Rochester Royals 3-1 to win the NBL crown and complete their impressive debut season.

The Lakers and Royals (now the Sacramento Kings) were among four NBL clubs to jump to the better-financed BAA for the 1948-49 season, and they continued what would become one of basketball's best early rivalries. Over the next six seasons, the Lakers won 273 regular-season games, the Royals 266. The only championship the Lakers lost in that stretch was won by the Royals.

Mikan and the Lakers immediately became the BAA's biggest attraction and third champion when they defeated the Washington Capitols, coached by Red Auerbach, in six games to win the 1949 championship. Minneapolis now had a BAA title to go with its NBL crown.

The NBL fell apart the following summer and the BAA swallowed up its survivors, bloating to a 17-team league that

The Minneapolis Lakers won an NBL championship in 1948 before their run of five titles in six years in the NBA.

was renamed the National Basketball Association. The Lakers defeated Syracuse in six games to repeat as champions.

In 1950-51, Mikan led the league with a career-high 28.4 points per game but suffered a late-season hairline fracture of his ankle. The injury was enough to swing the balance of power to the Royals, who beat the Lakers in four games in the Western Division Finals and went on to capture the crown in a seven-game series with the New York Knickerbockers.

During the offseason the rules committee voted to double the width of the foul lane to 12 feet, but that actually made Mikan a better all-around player. He added a jump shot to his array of moves around the basket and began taking advantage of teammates who were able to use the wider lane to cut to the hoop. The result was better balance on the Lakers, and

EVEN A CHANGE IN THE WIDTH OF THE LANE COULD NOT STOP THE DOMINANCE OF GEORGE MIKAN.

another championship. After finishing one game behind Rochester during the regular season, Minneapolis turned the tables on the Royals by winning the division finals in four, then won the championship by beating New York 82-65 in Game 7 of the NBA Finals.

The same teams met in a rematch in 1953, and this time the Lakers needed only five games to repeat. And in 1954, some 35 years before Pat Riley would trademark the term "three-peat," these Lakers of another generation made it a reality. Minneapolis beat the Royals in three games in the division finals, then topped the Syracuse Nationals in a seven-game championship series.

The Lakers had their third consecutive title and their fifth in six years, but when Mikan was unable to come to terms on a new contract and went into retirement, the run came to an end. The Lakers were ousted from the 1955 playoffs by Fort Wayne, and Pollard subsequently hung up his sneakers. Mikan made a comeback the following year but could average only 10.5 points in 37 games before going back into retirement, taking with him the legacy of the NBA's first dynasty.

NBA.COM FACT

The Minneapolis Lakers are well represented in the Naismith Memorial Basketball Hall of Fame. George Mikan was a member of the first class of inductees in 1959. He was joined by Jim Pollard in 1977, Slater Martin in 1981, Clyde Lovellette in 1988, and Vern Mikkelsen and Coach John Kundla in 1995.

CHAPTER 14

THE NICKNAMES

By Tracey Reavis

NBA teams resorted to a variety of methods to get their team nicknames — fan vote, history of the area, inherited after team relocation, etc. Here are the stories of how the 29 NBA teams became who they are.

Atlanta

THE HAWKS

In 1946, the National Basketball League granted a franchise to three cities along the Mississippi River — Moline and Rock Island, Ill., and Davenport, Iowa. Because Sauk Indian Chief Black Hawk's tribe was located in Rock Island and a major part of the 1831 Black Hawk War was fought in the surrounding area, the team was named the Tri-Cities Blackhawks. The club joined the NBA in 1949, and in 1951, the franchise relocated to Milwaukee, where the nickname was shortened to Hawks. The team moved to St. Louis in 1955, and finally to Atlanta in 1968.

Boston

THE CELTICS

The birth of the Boston Celtics in 1946 coincided with the beginning of the Basketball Association of America, the forerunner of the NBA. Walter Brown headed the Boston Garden Arena Corporation and named the new basketball team. Various nicknames were batted around, including Whirlwinds, Olympians and Unicorns. But Brown wanted Celtics, explaining, "The name has a great basketball tradition from the old Original Celtics in New York (1914-1939). And Boston is full of Irishmen."

Charlotte

THE HORNETS

Before the city was awarded an NBA franchise, the club was to be called the Charlotte Spirit. But Carolinians objected and so a fan contest was held. Hornets was the winning nickname for the team, which took the court in 1988. The name goes back to the Revolutionary War, when British General Charles Cornwallis wrote to the King of England in his battle report from the Carolinas that "this place is like fighting in a hornet's nest."

Chicago

THE BULLS

Dick Klein, the Chicago basketball club's first owner, chose Bulls as the nickname for his team when it joined the NBA in 1966. Why Bulls? The mighty bull has a persistent fighting attitude along with the instinct to never say die. What more could you want from a basketball team?

Cleveland

THE CAVALIERS

In 1970, Cleveland's newspaper, *The Plain Dealer*, held a contest to name the city's new basketball club. Contest winner Jerry Tomko wrote that the Cavaliers "represent a group of daring, fearless men, whose life's pact was never surrender, no matter what the odds." The nickname is frequently shortened to Cavs.

Dallas

THE MAVERICKS

Dallas radio station WBAP held a contest to name the city's new basketball franchise. After making a selection from the pool of choices, the club's executive committee announced the name Dallas Mavericks on May 1, 1980. The name Mavericks was chosen because it ties in with the cowboy image of Texas.

Denver

THE NUGGETS

The franchise was known as the Denver Rockets when it entered the ABA in 1967. The same year, an NBA expansion franchise named the San Diego (now Houston) Rockets began play. After seven seasons, and with entry into the NBA looming, Denver team officials renamed their club. Nuggets refers to the 19th century mining boom in Colorado, when people rushed to the area, hoping to make their fortunes by panning for gold and silver nuggets. It also draws a connection to the defunct Denver Nuggets that played one season (1949-50) in the NBA.

Detroit

THE PISTONS

Originally a franchise in the National Basketball League (NBL), the Fort Wayne, Ind., team got its nickname from owner Fred Zollner. He chose the unique name after his business—a piston-making plant located in Fort Wayne. When the Fort Wayne Zollner Pistons, as the team originally called, relocated to Detroit in 1957, the name Pistons was still appropriate in the nation's automobile capital, although the "Zollner" had been dropped years earlier.

Golden State

THE WARRIORS

When Philadelphia was awarded a charter NBA franchise in 1946, the owners decided to name the team after an old Philadelphia basketball team, the Warriors, who played as a member of the American Basketball League in 1925. The team became the San Francisco Warriors after it relocated to the West Coast in 1962, and changed its name to the Golden State Warriors—symbolizing a team belonging to all of California, the Golden State—upon settling into a new home in Oakland in 1971.

Houston

THE ROCKETS

In 1967, San Diego became the 12th member of the NBA. Basketball fans there were asked to choose a nickname for the team. Rockets was picked because it reflected the outstanding growth of space-age industries in San Diego. Even though the team relocated to Houston in 1971, the nickname still fits because of the NASA space program's operation center there.

Indiana

THE PACERS

An original member of the ABA, the nickname was chosen by the group of investors. Indianapolis attorney Richard D. Tinkham said the nickname Pacers was chosen because it was reflective both of the state's rich history with harness racing pacers and the pace car used for the running of the Indianapolis 500. The team kept the name when it joined the NBA in 1976.

Los Angeles

THE CLIPPERS

In 1978, San Diego welcomed the relocation of the Buffalo Braves' franchise because the city had lost its Rockets to Houston seven years earlier. But San Diego team officials didn't think Braves was a representative nickname for the club. A contest decided on Clippers because the city was known for the great sailing ships that passed through San Diego Bay. When the Clippers moved to Los Angeles in 1984, they kept their nickname.

Los Angeles

THE LAKERS

The Minneapolis Lakers began play in the National Basketball League in 1947-48, moving to the Basketball Association of America (the NBA's forerunner) a year later. The nickname chosen for the team was based on the state motto, "The Land of 10,000 Lakes." Even though there are few lakes in Los Angeles, the nickname was retained when the team relocated there in 1960.

Miami

THE HEAT

When Miami was awarded an NBA franchise to begin play in 1988, team officials wanted to have the fans in South Florida involved in the naming, so a contest was held. Among more than 5,000 entries submitted were Sharks, Barracudas, Flamingos, Palm Trees, Beaches, Heat, Suntan, Shade, Tornadoes and Floridians. "The Heat was it," said the team's general partner, Zev Bufman. "When you think of Miami, that's what you think of."

Milwaukee

THE BUCKS

This team's nickname was selected in 1968 from more than 14,000 contest entries, and the winner was R.D. Treblicox of Whitefish Bay, Wis. who won a new car for his choice of Bucks. The name reflected the fish and game area "because it is indigenous to Wisconsin," said then-General Manager John Erickson. "The predominance of bucks led us to the name."

Minnesota

THE TIMBERWOLVES

A fan contest was held before the franchise began play in 1989. The decision was narrowed down to two names—Timberwolves and Polars. Team officials liked the name Timberwolves for two reasons. First, besides Alaska, Minnesota is the only state with a significant number of this breed of wolf. Secondly, no other professional sports team had used the nickname. The team is sometimes informally called the T'Wolves, or simply the Wolves.

New Jersey

THE NETS

The New Jersey Americans were charter members of the ABA in 1967. The team moved to Commack, N.Y., the following year and changed its name to the New York Nets, after one of the most important parts of the basketball game—the net. Also, Nets rhymed with other New York sports franchises, baseball's Mets and football's Jets. A season after joining the NBA in 1976, the team returned to the Garden State, kept its nickname and became the New Jersey Nets.

New York

THE KNICKS

The term Knickerbockers refers to the early Dutch settlers who came to what is now New York, and their rolled-up-just-below-the-knee trousers, called knickerbockers, or knickers. The name had become synonymous with the city. According to Fred Podesta, an aide to club founder Ned Irish, naming the team Knickerbockers in 1946 was simple. "We all put a name in a hat, and when we pulled them out, most of them said Knickerbockers." The nickname is generally shortened to Knicks.

Orlando

THE MAGIC

Orlando's basketball franchise was almost called the Juice. *The Orlando Sentinel* and team officials held a fan contest, and Juice and Magic were the two nicknames they liked best. Juice was representative of the area's orange and grapefruit groves, but a panel of local community leaders picked Magic for Orlando's new team, which took the floor in 1989, because of the city's tourism slogan, "Come to the Magic."

Philadelphia

THE 76ERS

Founded as a National Basketball League team (the Syracuse Nationals) in 1946, the club joined the NBA in 1949 and was purchased in 1963 by Irv Kosloff and Ike Richman and relocated to Philadelphia. The team was renamed the 76ers in honor of the signing of the Declaration of Independence on July 4, 1776, at Independence Hall, located in Philadelphia. The team also is frequently referred to as the Sixers.

Phoenix

THE SUNS

Out of the 28,000 suggestions submitted by contestants to name this expansion franchise in 1968, team officials hoped to find a nickname that best represented Arizona's year-round sunshine and desert terrain. Tumbleweeds, Scorpions and Rattlers were just a few of the names submitted that fit the Phoenix image. A drawing was held and Selinda King was the winner and the person credited with naming the Suns.

Portland

THE TRAIL BLAZERS

In 1970, Portland club founder Harry Glickman held a contest to select an original nickname for his new franchise. Of the 10,000-plus entries submitted, 172 were Trail Blazers. Said Glickman, "We feel Trail Blazers reflects both the ruggedness of the Pacific Northwest and the start of a major league era in our state." The name is frequently shortened to Blazers.

Sacramento

THE KINGS

The first majestic moniker for this club, which began as a member of the National Basketball League in 1945, was the Rochester Royals. The team relocated to Cincinnati in 1957, and became the Kansas City/Omaha Kings in 1972, choosing a new nickname to avoid confusion with Kansas City's baseball team. Three years later, the Kings stopped playing games in Omaha and became the Kansas City Kings. They kept their nickname when they relocated to Sacramento in 1985.

San Antonio

THE SPURS

An original member of the ABA, this franchise — which joined the NBA in 1976 — was born in Dallas as the Chaparrals. When the original investors agreed to start a team, they were dining in a posh club called the Chaparral Club. One of the owners noticed an image of the chaparral, which is a roadrunner, on the napkin, and everyone agreed the bird would make a nice, lively mascot. In 1970, they became a regional franchise called the Texas Chaparrals. When they relocated to San Antonio in 1973, team officials wanted a name that reflected the Western heritage of Texas, so a contest was held and the name Spurs was chosen.

Seattle

THE SUPERSONICS

The nickname for this franchise, which entered the NBA in 1967, was inspired by the Boeing plant in Seattle. One year earlier, the company had begun work on a Concorde-like airplane, which was to be called the Supersonic Transport. The plane never got off the ground, but Boeing's involvement left quite an impression on the citizens of Seattle. When asked to name the new club, SuperSonics won by a landslide. The nickname frequently is shortened to Sonics.

Toronto

THE RAPTORS

The team had a contest that generated more than 2,000 entries for the expansion franchise. Raptors, no doubt because of the popularity of dinosaurs amongst youngsters—not to mention the success of the movie Jurassic Park—was selected. The nickname Raptors was announced on May 15, 1994.

Utah

THE JAZZ

When the city of New Orleans was granted an NBA franchise in 1974, team officials chose the nickname Jazz to represent the city because of its reputation as the jazz capital of the world. After the team moved to Salt Lake City in 1979, it kept its musical moniker.

Vancouver

THE GRIZZLIES

When Vancouver entered the league before the 1995-96 season, the name Grizzlies was the owner's choice. Vancouver is Grizzly country. The British Columbia province is home to more than 20,000 of the indigenous Grizzly bears, and they are also prominent in northwestern native culture and mythology. Dragons, Ravens, Orcas and Mounties were also considered.

Washington

THE WIZARDS

In 1946, a franchise was nicknamed Bullets after a nearby ammunition foundry in Baltimore. Though the team disbanded, the Chicago Packers — who later became the Chicago Zephyrs — relocated to Baltimore, and in 1963, the Bullets nickname returned. In 1996, Washington team owner Abe Pollin decided to adopt a nickname that portrayed a non-violent image and selected Wizards. The name depicts energy and an omnipresent power, and brings to light what is hoped to be the wise and magical nature of the team.

CHAPTER 15

THE RULES

24-Second Clock Revived the Game

By Alex Sachare

Professional basketball was struggling in the early 1950s, and one look at what was taking place on the court explained why. The game was dull, all too often played at a snail's pace with one team opening up a lead and freezing the ball until time ran out. The only thing the trailing team could do was foul, thus games became rough, ragged, free throw-shooting contests.

"That was the way the game was played — get a lead and put the ball in the icebox," said Bob Cousy of the Boston Celtics, one of the game's best ballhandling guards. "Teams literally started sitting on the ball in the third quarter. Coaches are conservative by nature, and it didn't make much sense to play a wide-open game. We'd get a lead, and you'd see good ol' No. 14 doing his tricks out there."

If not Cousy, who was "good ol' No. 14," then it would be one of the other premier guards of that era like Dick McGuire, Slater Martin, Bob Davies or Andy Phillip, who would dribble until they were fouled, and the parade from one free throw line to the other would begin.

"The game had become a stalling game," Danny Biasone, owner of the Syracuse Nationals, said before his death in 1992. "A team would get ahead, even in the first half, and it would go into a stall. The other team would keep fouling, and it got to be a constant parade to the foul line. Boy, was it dull!"

Dull was the last thing NBA moguls wanted when the league was still in its infancy, struggling for a place on the American sports scene. But that's what it was:

• On November 22, 1950, the Fort Wayne Pistons edged the Minneapolis Lakers 19-18 in a game where the teams scored a total of eight baskets.

• Three years later, 106 fouls were called and 128 free throws shot in a playoff game between Boston and Syracuse. Cousy scored 30 points from the foul line alone.

• In 1954, Syracuse beat New York 75-69 in another playoff horror show where free throws outnumbered baskets 75-34.

"If you're a promoter, that won't do," Biasone said. "You've got to have offense, because offense excites people."

Something drastic was called for, and Biasone knew what it was. "We needed a time element in our game," he said. "Other sports had limits — in baseball you get three outs to score, in football you must make 10 yards in four downs or you lose the ball. But in basketball, if you had the lead and a good ballhandler, you could play around all night."

Biasone's idea was a shot clock, giving a team 24 seconds to attempt a shot or else lose possession of the ball. To deal with the matter of excessive fouling, the Board of Governors also adopted a rule limiting the number of fouls per team per quarter, with each foul became a shooting foul after the limit

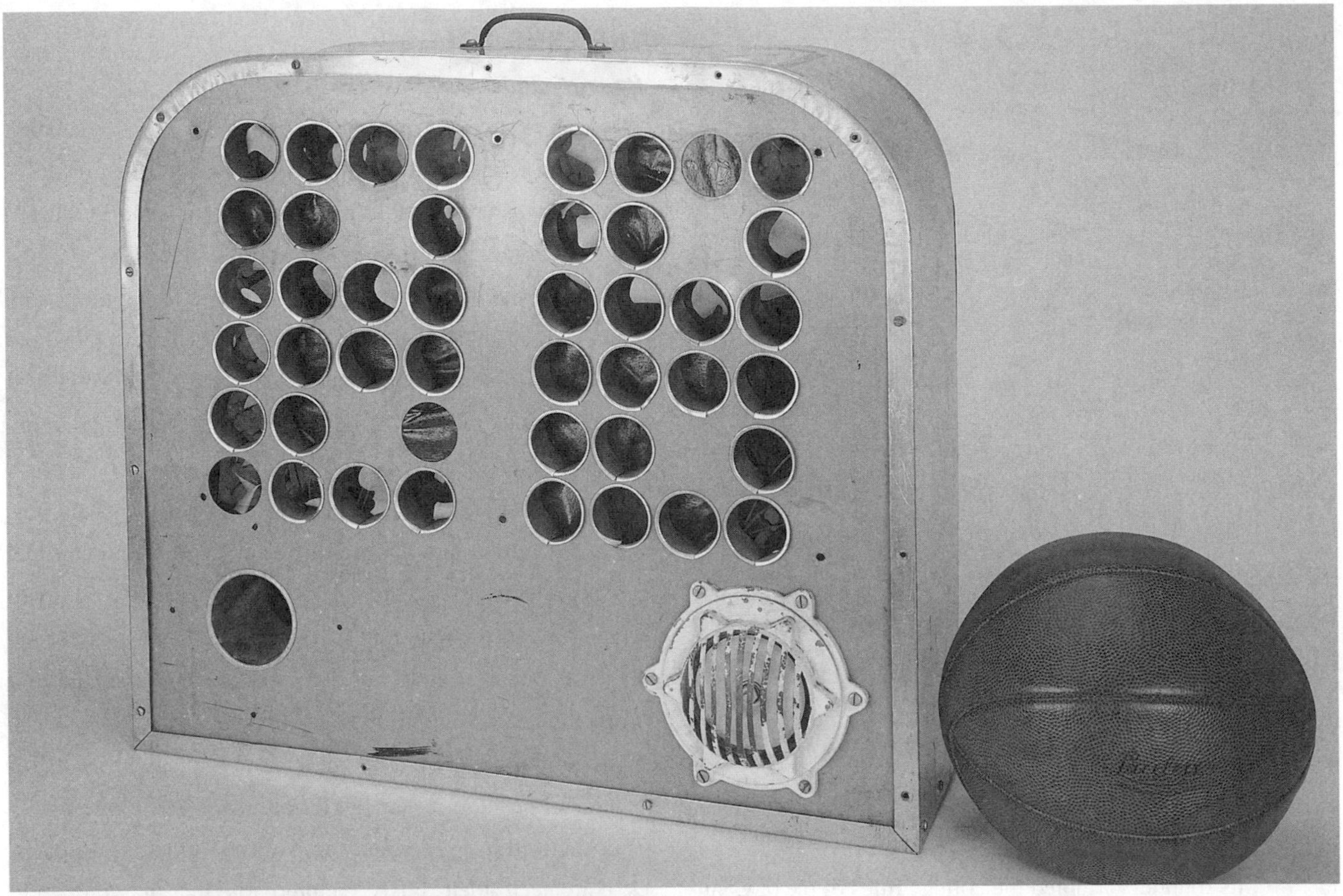

The introduction of the 24-second shot clock in 1954 ended slowdown tactics and made the game exciting.

Current players always know how much time is left in the quarter and on the shot clock with the clock mounted at the top of the backboard.

was reached. The two rules complemented each other perfectly.

The 24-second shot clock made an immediate impact. In 1954-55, its first season, NBA teams averaged 93.1 points, an increase of 13.6 points over the previous season. The Boston Celtics became the first team in NBA history to average more than 100 points per game for a season, and three years later, every team did it.

"Pro basketball would not have survived without a clock," said Biasone.

Others agreed. "The adoption of the clock was the most important event in the NBA," said Maurice Podoloff, the NBA's president, while longtime Celtics coach and executive Red Auerbach called it "the single most important rule change in the last 50 years."

The 24-second clock was the most dramatic change in a league where the rules are constantly undergoing fine-tuning, but only rarely seeing major changes. When the NBA's predecessor, the Basketball Association of America, was formed

IN 1992, SHORTLY BEFORE HIS DEATH, DANNY BIASONE POSED IN FRONT OF THE MODERN VERSION OF HIS SHOT CLOCK. THE 24-SECOND RULE WAS INSTITUTED IN 1954 AND IS REGARDED AS THE MOST SIGNIFICANT RULE CHANGE IN NBA HISTORY.

in 1946, its founders adopted the college rules of the day, but changed the length of games from two 20-minute halves to four 12-minute quarters in order to give the fans more for their money. Two months into the inaugural season, the league made another change, banning zone defenses. Prohibitions against what are now termed "illegal defenses" have been on the books ever since.

Most of the game's dimensions have remained the same — the height of the basket is 10 feet, the foul line is 15 feet away from the backboard, the rim is 18 inches in diameter, the ball exactly half that. Courts differed slightly in size in the league's early years as teams played in whatever buildings were available; in today's modern arenas, every court measures 50 x 94 feet.

The supreme skills of two of the NBA's greatest big men did force changes in the dimensions of the foul lane. The width of the lane was doubled from six to 12 feet in 1951 in an effort to limit the dominance of George Mikan; more than a decade later it was further widened to 16 feet in an attempt to contain Wilt Chamberlain. Both players proved skillful enough to adapt their games to the changes, and they continued to be dominant forces in their eras.

THE LONG BALL

By Barry Rubinstein

It is alive and well today in the familiar form of a dazzling missile from downtown. It is the polar opposite of a spectacular slam dunk, yet it is equally capable of igniting a crowd at home, and crushing one on the road.

Perhaps the three-point field goal began as a gimmick — first by the ill-fated American Basketball League in 1961 and then by the American Basketball Association in 1967. But it is now an integral part of the game at all levels, and simply one of the most electrifying and anticipated plays in basketball.

"I always liked the three-point shot because it could turn the game around in a hurry," said Dick Motta, who coached five NBA teams to 935 victories. "But it was also good if you weren't a good rebounding team because if you missed, the shot was taken from so far away that it sometimes led to a long rebound. I thought it was a great equalizer."

But at first, the NBA did not want to implement the three-point shot because it was not a traditional part of the game. That changed in 1979 when some of the former ABA coaches convinced their NBA counterparts that it would add excitement and unpredictability to the game.

They proved to be right. The fabric of the game quickly changed after the three-pointer was adopted as teams with confident outside shooters now had an immediate and tangible advantage, particularly with the clock winding down in a tight game. NBA basketball became more of a wide-open affair as defenses were forced to spread out to respect the threat of the three-pointer, thus opening up lanes for slashing and driving to the hoop.

"I think it's done a lot for the game," said Los Angeles Lakers Hall of Fame forward Elgin Baylor. "No play can change a game as quickly as a three-pointer. It gets the crowd going, and it can turn the momentum just like that. When I played, you knew it would take a while to get back in a game if you were down. Now, you hit a couple of threes, and next thing you know, you're right back in it.

"Sometimes I wonder what it would have been like if we'd have had it when I played. I had three-point range, like a lot of guys did. But the whole focus in those days was on getting closer to the bucket. If you had a 15-footer, you tried to get a 10-footer. The three-pointer has added a lot to the game."

LARRY BIRD NOT ONLY WON THREE CONSECUTIVE THREE-POINT SHOOTING CONTESTS, HE LOVED TO HIT A BACK-BREAKING THREE-POINTER THAT THWARTED AN OPPONENT'S COMEBACK.

Former Laker Magic Johnson's NBA career began the same year that the three-point shot was adopted.

"Michael Cooper, Byron Scott and I would work on three-point shots together every day before practice," Johnson said. "Sometimes we'd take crazy shots from behind the visitors' bench — and make 'em, too. That sort of thing really helps your confidence. When you make a shot like that, the regular three-pointer starts to look easy. I took a lot of pride in improving parts of my game from year to year. The three-pointer was part of that. I don't think fans realize how hard the great players work on their game. I always knew that Larry [Bird] was shooting hundreds of three-pointers at practice, and I didn't want him to get any advantage on me, so I started to do it, too."

Three-point shooters ultimately became specialists, plying their trade when their teams needed them most. Among the best were Bird and Craig Hodges, who played for San Diego, Milwaukee, Phoenix and Chicago. Both players were three-time winners of what has become one of the most popular events at NBA All-Star Weekend, the annual three-point shooting contest.

That contest is simply a reflection of the effect the three-point shot can have. The adoption of the rule has added immeasurably to the game. There are many times each year when a team wins a game because of a last-second shot. But when that shot is a three-pointer, it just seems to be that much more thrilling.

CHAPTER 16

THE COACHES

By Paul Ladewski

When Arnold "Red" Auerbach retired from coaching in 1966, his record for victories, winning championships and irritating opponents was unmatched. Auerbach directed the Boston Celtics to nine championships, recorded 938 victories and never worried about reminding adversaries of his team's superiority. Auerbach's habit of lighting a victory cigar when he felt the Celtics were comfortably in control was aggravating and annoying — unless you were a Celtics fan, and then it was celebrated.

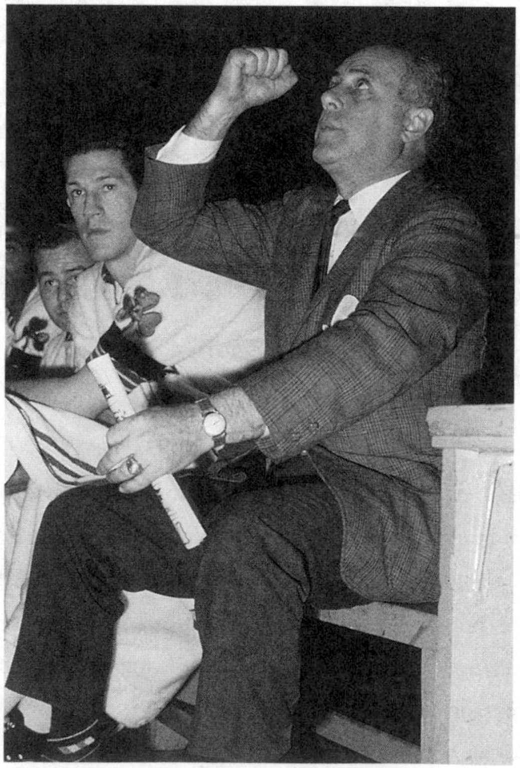

RED AUERBACH WON 938 GAMES AS A HEAD COACH, BUT HIS LOFTIEST ACHIEVEMENT WAS NINE CHAMPIONSHIPS.

Regardless, opponents knew that a meeting with Auerbach would be a meeting with a well-conditioned, disciplined, determined team. Auerbach was a master motivator and a "players" coach, who effectively employed the skills of his players, whether stars or substitutes. The Celtics lived off a Bill Russell-inspired defense, a nonstop fast break and an offensive scheme, that consisted of seven basic plays. "We don't really do anything different," Auerbach once said. "We just spend more time on it."

Indeed, the Celtics won more than any other team before or since because Red Auerbach the scout and general manager made sure that Red Auerbach the head coach had the best talent around. The greatest dynasty in NBA history took root in April 1956, when in one fell swoop Auerbach acquired the services of three future Hall of Famers — Russell, Tom Heinsohn and K.C. Jones — via draft or trade, although a military commitment would delay Jones' entry into the league for two years.

Four decades later, this is all one needs to know about Red Auerbach: "We came to play," said Auerbach, " and we came to win."

If Auerbach is the fire portion of the greatest coaches in league history, then **Lenny Wilkens** is the ice. For three decades, Wilkens has stood as a monument to quiet dignity

LENNY WILKENS RANKS NO. 1 IN COACHING VICTORIES AND IS ALSO IN THE HALL OF FAME AS A COACH AND A PLAYER.

while achieving unprecedented success. Wilkens moved from Atlanta to Toronto in 2000, and took 1,179 victories, the most in NBA history, with him.

After an All-America career as Providence's floor leader, Wilkens went on to become a nine-time All-Star with St. Louis, Seattle and Cleveland. In 1969, when he was named player-coach at Seattle, he was the second African-American head coach in league history.

Known for his ability to teach and his precise offensive schemes, Wilkens engineered one of the most sudden turnarounds ever in his second go-round in Seattle. After the SuperSonics got off to a 5-17 start in the 1977-78 season, Wilkens assumed the reins and guided the Sonics to within one victory of the NBA title. One year later, Seattle closed the deal in a rematch against Washington for its only league crown.

His other great victories as a head coach occurred two decades later. On January 6, 1995, Wilkens passed Auerbach as the winningest coach in NBA history when he won his 939th game. Then in 1996, the United States struck gold in the Olympics — eight years after Wilkens had been elected to the Naismith Memorial Hall of Fame as a player, and two years before he was elected as a coach.

Has there ever been a more unlikely head coach than **Phil Jackson**, the long-haired, tie-dyed flower child of the psychedelic '60s? Like, probably not, man.

But in Bill Fitch and Red Holzman, under whom he played at North Dakota and with the Knicks, respectively, Jackson could not have had better teachers. The fact that he boasts the best winning percentage (.745 through 1999-2000) in league history is evidence that Jackson has learned his lessons well.

In nine seasons with the Chicago Bulls, the Jackson five averaged nearly 61 regular-season victories and captured a half-dozen league titles. Still, because of the immense presence of Michael Jordan and Scottie Pippen, Jackson's share of the credit for team success was open to debate.

But not long after Jackson joined forces with Shaquille O'Neal, Kobe Bryant, and the Lakers in 1999, similar success followed in his first season: a 67-15 regular-season record and the franchise's first championship in 12 years.

In seven seasons, from 1981-82 to 1987-88, the Lakers of **Pat Riley** captured four league championships, the best run

WITH SEVEN CHAMPIONSHIPS IN 10 YEARS AS A HEAD COACH, PHIL JACKSON HAS HAD PHENOMENAL SUCCESS.

PAT RILEY HAS WON FOUR CHAMPIONSHIPS AND ENDED THE 1999-2000 SEASON WITH 999 CAREER VICTORIES.

since the Celtics' dynasty. Then again, with a star-studded Hollywood cast that included Kareem Abdul-Jabbar, Magic Johnson and James Worthy, among others, any head coach could have done as well, right? Or so went the theory in some circles.

It wasn't until Riley departed for New York and then Miami that his standing on the short list of all-time greats finally was confirmed. The only head coach to be afforded Coach of the Year honors with three franchises, Riley was among the select few who was willing and able to modify his style to fit the talent around him. Whether it was Showtime with the Lakers or slow time with the Knicks and Heat, his were teams of substance, as evidenced by his 999 career victories through the 1999-2000 season, second most in league history.

In the minds of many, what separates Riley from the rest is an innate ability to coax the most out of his players, regardless of their backgrounds and skill levels.

One more thing: From impeccable hair to Armani suits to Gucci shoes, no head coach ever did more to raise the fashion level of his profession.

Auerbach, Wilkens, Jackson, Riley and the following six coaches were among the Top 10 Coaches in NBA History as selected by a panel of basketball experts and honored in conjunction with the league's 50th anniversary celebration.

It wasn't until the 1988-89 campaign, at the ripe age of 58, that **Chuck Daly** received his gold card in the championship coaches club, as his Pistons muscled their way to the first of back-to-back championships. In the process, the Pistons changed the game with physical, in-your-face defense.

The fact remains, Daly had been big in the business long before heading to Detroit. In six seasons, his Penn teams gained four Ivy League titles. Head Coach Billy

CHUCK DALY COACHED THE DETROIT PISTONS TO TWO TITLES AND ALSO COACHED THE 1992 DREAM TEAM TO A GOLD MEDAL.

Cunningham said the expertise of Daly, his assistant, was vital in the Philadelphia 76ers' run to the 1983 NBA title. After Daly became the head coach in Detroit, the Pistons averaged 49 victories in five seasons before they reached the mountain top.

In the 1992 Summer Olympics, when the Dream Team struck gold with Daly at the controls, his ticket to the Hall of Fame was punched.

After four unproductive campaigns at the helm for Milwaukee and St. Louis, **William "Red" Holzman** was hired as the New York Knicks' chief scout in 1959, a position he held until being handed the coaching reins in December 1967. Under Holzman, the Knicks enjoyed immediate success.

RED HOLZMAN WAS THE CALMING FORCE BEHIND TWO KNICKS CHAMPIONSHIPS IN THE EARLY '70S.

Elevated by the team concept that Holzman preached, the Knicks advanced to the NBA Finals three times in a span of four seasons from 1970 to 1973 and twice bagged the big prize. In 1986, Holzman was elected to the Naismith Memorial Hall of Fame with his 696 career victories and the unofficial title of Comeback Coach of the Century.

Before there was Michael, Scottie, Phil and the Bulls, there was Magic, Kareem, Riley and the Lakers. Before that, there was Russ, Cooz, Red and the Celtics. And before that, there was George Mikan, Jim Pollard, **John Kundla** and the Lakers, the original NBA dynasty.

Kundla, who had coached in high school and at the University of St. Thomas (Minn.), guided Mikan and the Lakers to the National Basketball League title in 1948. The Lakers then jumped to the Basketball Association of America, the NBA's forerunner, and Kundla proceeded to guide them to five championships in the next six years. In 12 pro coaching seasons, he had a record of 466-319, a .594 winning percentage. He was enshrined in the Hall of Fame in 1995.

JOHN KUNDLA, FIVE TITLES IN MINNEAPOLIS.

Say this much for **Jack Ramsay**: For 20-plus seasons, his teams were some of the most precise and fundamentally sound teams in the NBA. Indeed, on any list of the premier teachers in the game, Dr. Jack's name is at or near the top.

Under his leadership, the Trail Blazers took the basics to new levels in the 1976-77 season, which culminated in his only league championship. Some believe the Trail Blazers were even better the following season, but a foot injury to center Bill Walton cut short a budding dynasty before it could take root.

DR. JACK RAMSAY HAD A HALL OF FAME CAREER THAT INCLUDED THE 1977 TITLE WITH THE PORTLAND TRAIL BLAZERS.

No matter. Ramsay still finished with 864 career victories — good enough for seventh in NBA history — and a spot in the Hall of Fame.

If there's a patron saint of perseverance in the religion of coaches, then **Bill Fitch** should be first in line to be canonized. After a 12-year college career, much of which was spent at tiny Coe College (Iowa) and North Dakota, he finally got his big chance in 1970 with the expansion Cavaliers. Four teams and 25 seasons later, Fitch had 944 career victories, third most in NBA history.

Fitch is best remembered as the bench leader who guided

Bill Fitch had a rugged start in Cleveland, but he won a championship while coaching the Celtics.

the Celtics to the first of their three league titles in the Larry Bird era. But perhaps his most notable effort took place in the 1975-76 season, when the overachieving Cavaliers advanced to the Eastern Conference Finals. The feat became known as the Miracle of Richfield. That season, Fitch earned the first of his two Coach of the Year Awards.

Some head coaches have won more games than **Don Nelson** in their careers. Five to be exact. He has 907 victories — sixth most in league history — to show for his 22 seasons (through 1999-2000). Though Nelson has never won an NBA championship as a coach, he did lead Team USA to a gold medal in the 1994 World Championship.

No one has been more creative than the three-time Coach of the Year in terms of matchups and strategies. Opponents swore they couldn't fall prey to Nellie's crazy-quilt pairings, but more times than not, they played into his hands before the night was over. And if ever there was a bench leader who could take advantage of a rule to benefit his team, then Nelson was the guy.

Don Nelson has led teams to 50 or more victories nine times during his 22-year career.

Other top coaches who have won 400-plus games (in alphabetical order):

Rick Adelman led the Portland Trail Blazers to the NBA Finals in 1990 and 1992, but was unable to win a title, losing to the Detroit Pistons and Chicago Bulls, respectively. He has taken Sacramento to the playoffs twice and has won 428 games in his career.

Rick Adelman, coached Blazers to Finals.

The mastermind of the greatest upset in NBA Finals history was **Al Attles**, one of 20 head coaches to total 550 or more regular-season victories in their careers. His Golden State team won 12 fewer games than Washington (60-22) in the 1974-75 campaign, but the Warriors relied on Rick Barry and depth to pull off the unthinkable in the NBA Finals — only the third sweep ever in the league's championship series.

Al Attles, led Warriors to '75 title.

Before he made his mark in the broadcast booth, **Hubie Brown** totaled 445 victories in the NBA and ABA. He also won one Coach of the Year Award in 10 seasons as an NBA head coach. His career highlight took place in the ABA,

Hubie Brown, premier X's and O's coach.

Larry Brown, one of the game's great teachers has finished .500 or better in 19 of 22 years.

where in his first season as a head coach, Brown led the Kentucky Colonels to their only league title.

Let the record show that nobody frets the details, with as much success, as **Larry Brown**. In 17 NBA seasons split between Denver, New Jersey, San Antonio, the Los Angeles Clippers, Indiana and Philadelphia, he has five division titles and finished below .500 only three times.

The fact is, wherever Brown goes, success is almost certain to follow. In four seasons in the ABA, he amassed 229 victories and his teams made two trips to the conference finals and one to the championship series.

Larry Costello, coach of '71 Bucks champion.

A solid guard who played 12 seasons in the NBA, **Larry Costello** was named the first head coach of the expansion Milwaukee Bucks in 1968. In his third season at the helm, he led a team built around Kareem Abdul-Jabbar and Oscar Robertson to 66 wins and the franchise's only NBA championship. For five seasons, from 1969-70 through 1973-74, the Bucks averaged more than 60 wins under Costello, who compiled an overall record of 430-300 (.589) in 10 seasons as an NBA head coach, all but one in Milwaukee.

Billy Cunningham, directed 76ers to 1983 title.

Through the 1999-2000 season, only Phil Jackson boasted a better regular-season winning percentage than **Billy Cunningham** (.698), whose Philadelphia teams never finished lower than second place and only once failed to reach the 50-win plateau in eight seasons. En route to the league title in 1983, Julius Erving, Moses Malone and the Sixers had a 12-1 playoff record that remains the standard for postseason dominance.

Cotton Fitzsimmons, always competitive.

In 21 seasons, he claimed only one division title, but championships don't begin to tell the **Cotton Fitzsimmons** story. As his 832 victories indicate, the Cotton clubs were almost always competitive. Phoenix enjoyed some of its greatest success under Fitzsimmons, who posted at least 48 victories in all six of his full seasons there.

Mike Fratello, 572 career victories.

In 1986, only his third full season at Atlanta, **Mike Fratello** was selected Coach of the Year. It was the first of four consecutive seasons of 50 or more victories, and Fratello went on to record 572 career triumphs with the Hawks and Cleveland Cavaliers. He embarked on a career as a television network analyst and was dubbed by broadcast partner Marv Albert the "Czar of the Telestrator" for his skill at diagramming and explaining plays.

From 1957 to 1969, only **Alex Hannum** dared to challenge the Celtics' dynasty. Boston won 11 championships in those 13 seasons, and the two that got away went to Hannum's St. Louis Hawks in 1958 and Hannum's Philadelphia 76ers in 1967.

While Hannum is renowned as a Celtics-killer, often overlooked is the fact that he coached two of the greatest pro bas-

No one could dismantle the Celtics dynasty, but Alex Hannum cracked it twice.

ketball teams ever in a span of three seasons. He guided the 1966-67 76ers (68-13) of Wilt Chamberlain, Chet Walker, Billy Cunningham and Hal Greer to the NBA title, then led the 1968-69 Oakland Oaks (60-18) of Rick Barry, Larry Brown and Doug Moe to the ABA title. The twin wins make him one of only two head coaches (with Bill Sharman) to boast championship rings in both leagues.

Del Harris, one of game's great teachers.

In 1979, after nine seasons as head coach at Earlham (Ind.) College and five more as an assistant at Utah (ABA) and Houston, **Del Harris** finally got his chance to call the shots for an NBA team. One season later, his Rockets became the third — and last — team to advance to the NBA Finals with a sub-.500 record in the regular season. His career résumé includes 556 victories, one Coach of the Year selection, and a striking resemblance to actor Leslie Nielsen.

Tom Heinsohn, two Boston Celtics titles.

After Bill Russell retired as player-coach in 1969, it was left for **Tom Heinsohn** to pick up the pieces of what could have been a crumbling Boston dynasty. With the same fire-and-brimstone approach that marked his career as a player, the Celtics soon recaptured their magic in the form of five division titles and a pair of league titles.

Which head coach owns the best winning percentage in the regular season and the postseason in Boston history? It's not Red Auerbach, but **K.C. Jones**, and Jones' overall regular-season mark of .674 (including stints in Washington and Seattle) ranked fourth in league history as of 2000. In his nine-plus seasons with Washington, Boston and Seattle, Jones' teams captured seven division titles and two league championships.

K.C. Jones, two titles with the Boston Celtics.

After four mostly forgettable campaigns with the Cavaliers and the Warriors, **George Karl** went back to his CBA roots, earning Coach of the Year honors with Albany in 1991 (he'd previously won the award twice with Montana). Then he went to Spain to coach Real Madrid. Upon his return to the NBA in 1992, Karl and the SuperSonics were all the better for the experience, as both enjoyed their greatest

George Karl, took Sonics to Finals in '96.

KEVIN LOUGHERY, TWO ABA TITLES WITH THE NETS.

success in the form of four division titles and an NBA Finals berth. Karl led the Milwaukee Bucks to two straight playoff appearances after the team had not made the playoffs for seven years.

A guard for 11 NBA seasons, **Kevin Loughery** coached for 17 seasons in the NBA with six different teams: Philadelphia (as a player-coach), the Nets (in both New York and New Jersey), Atlanta, Chicago, Washington and Miami. He also coached the Nets for their final three seasons in the ABA, leading them to league titles in 1974 and 1976. In 20 seasons as a professional coach, Loughery won 642 games.

JOHN MACLEOD, MORE THAN 700 VICTORIES.

In only his third season as an NBA head coach, **John MacLeod** was at the controls of one of the most unlikely conference champions.

After a regular season that saw Phoenix finish no better than third place with a 42-40 record, the Suns advanced to the NBA Finals and extended Boston to six games, including the memorable triple-overtime classic in Game 5. Four other MacLeod-coached teams would reach the conference finals in a career that totaled 707 victories, but none of his squads confounded the experts more than the Sunderella Suns of 1975-76.

DOUG MOE, MASTER OF THE RUN-AND-GUN.

As a certified genius, **Doug Moe** considered himself to be somewhere between Curly and Larry. Indeed, his critics claimed that he did little more than roll out the ball. The fact is, few teams scored and entertained more often than his. Under Moe's direction in 1981-82, Denver averaged a league-record 126.5 points per game. When the smoke finally cleared after 15 seasons, Moe's teams had posted .500 or better marks 12 times.

In 1968, when Chicago rolled the dice on a relative unknown out of Utah, the rest of the basketball world could only ask, "What's a Motta?" After all, the only previous experience for **Dick Motta** had come at Grace High School and Weber State. It wasn't long before he put his brand on the Bulls, however, whose wrecking-ball defense annually ranked among the league's best during his eight seasons on Chicago's bench.

DICK MOTTA LED FOUR TEAMS TO 935 VICTORIES AND WON THE 1978 TITLE IN WASHINGTON.

When Motta left for Washington in 1976, he adjusted his style to fit the Hall of Fame talents of Elvin Hayes and Wes Unseld. Under Motta, the Bullets captured their first and only NBA title in 1978. One season later, they were in the NBA Finals again.

After stops at Dallas, Sacramento and Denver, Motta

BILL SHARMAN, INNOVATOR AND LAKERS CHAMPION.

retired with 935 victories — fifth most in league history.

The only person to coach championship teams in the ABL, ABA and NBA was **Bill Sharman** who directed teams to 509 victories. As a player with the Boston Celtics, Sharman was a long-range shooter who was ahead of his time, an outstanding marksman whose totals would have been greatly enhanced had the three point arc been in place. As a coach, he was one of the first to place a premium on fundamentals and physical conditioning. After guiding Utah to the ABA crown in 1971, the Southern Cal product returned to Los Angeles for the 1971-72 season, when the Lakers posted a record 33-game winning streak and captured their first league title since moving to the West Coast. "He was our MVP that season," said center Wilt Chamberlain.

GENE SHUE, COACHED 76ERS TO FINALS.

JERRY SLOAN, ROCK-LIKE STABILITY IN UTAH, WHERE HE LED THE JAZZ TO THE FINALS TWICE.

After 10 seasons as an All-Star guard, **Gene Shue** returned to his Baltimore roots to lead the Bullets to four division titles as head coach. In a career that spanned 784 victories and 22 seasons, his personal highlight occurred in 1976-77, when Philadelphia secured division and conference titles en route to the NBA Finals.

In an era of short shelf lives for head coaches in all sports, the face of **Jerry Sloan** belongs on Mount Rushmore in terms of stability. In the last 12 seasons, Sloan has been the one and only band leader that the Jazz has known. In the same intense, blood-and-guts style that marked Sloan as a player, the Jazz has five division titles and a pair of trips to the NBA Finals to show for its efforts.

RUDY TOMJANOVICH, GREAT SHOOTER AS A PLAYER, STRAIGHT SHOOTER AS A COACH, AND WINNER OF TWO TITLES.

No sooner was former player and longtime assistant **Rudy Tomjanovich** promoted midway through the 1991-92 campaign than Houston gelled into a championship unit. On the heels of a club-record 55 victories in his first full season on the job, Rudy T fueled the Rockets to back-to-back league championships, the second as a No. 6 playoff seed. Tomjanovich also coached the 2000 U.S. Olympic team in the Sydney Olympics.

* * *

Winning 400 games is a sign of success and longevity, but there also have been some excellent coaches who simply did not coach long enough to reach that milestone. Among those who coached with distinction are (in alphabetical order):

Stan Albeck: Achieved his greatest success with a run-and-gun attack in San Antonio, where the Spurs were led by George Gervin. Also coached Chicago and New Jersey and once was Wilt Chamberlain's assistant with the San Diego Conquistadors of the ABA. Won 307 games.

Bernie Bickerstaff: A key assistant coach on the Bullets' team that played in the Finals in 1975 and then went on to coach in Seattle and Denver before returning to Washington as the head coach. Bickerstaff's teams won 338 games.

Al Cervi: A member of the Hall of Fame as a player, Cervi coached the Syracuse Nationals and the Philadelphia Warriors to a record of 326-241 for an outstanding winning percentage of .575.

Don Chaney: He is the answer to a trivia question as the only player to be a Boston teammate of both Bill Russell and Larry Bird. Chaney has spent much of his coaching career as an assistant, but in stints with Houston, the Clippers and Detroit, he won 265 games.

Doug Collins: The No. 1 pick by Philadelphia in the 1973 draft, Collins averaged 17.9 points in his eight-year career. He coached the Bulls and Pistons and won 258 games, and is now with NBC and is regarded as one of the top basketball analysts in the world.

Mike Dunleavy: He was a sixth-round draft pick who survived 11 years as a pro because of his toughness and basketball knowledge. He has carried that on into coaching, directing the Lakers to the Finals in his first year. In 10 years, Dunleavy's teams in Los Angeles, Milwaukee and Portland have won 348 games.

Chris Ford: A teammate of Larry Bird on the 1981 Celtics championship team, Ford was later a Boston assistant on two title teams. Ford was head coach for the Celtics, Milwaukee and L.A. Clippers and won 311 games.

Eddie Gottlieb: By the time he coached the Philadelphia Warriors to the first title in NBA (then BAA) history, Eddie Gottlieb had already been coaching for 30 years. His first coaching job was with the famed Philadelphia SPHAs in 1918. Gottlieb won 263 NBA games, but that was only a small part of his career.

Richie Guerin: An outstanding player who averaged 17.3 points per game during a 13-year playing career, Guerin also was a successful coach, leading the Hawks in St. Louis and Atlanta to 327 victories.

Les Harrison: A member of the Hall of Fame as a contributor, Harrison directed Rochester to the 1951 NBA title, breaking up a span of six years when the Minneapolis Lakers won five titles. Harrison won 295 games, but his winning percentage of .620 is seventh best in history.

Joe Lapchick: A great player in the early years of basketball (1917-36) and a member of the Original Celtics, Lapchick coached the Knicks to the playoffs eight times in nine seasons and won 326 NBA games. He also won 334 as a college coach at St. John's.

Frank Layden: A master of the one-liner, Layden deflected a lot of criticism from his struggling Utah Jazz team with his sense of humor. But his coaching and personnel moves gave the Jazz credibility and he led the team to its first division title. He won 277 games.

Bob Leonard: "Slick" had a successful 12-year coaching career, but only four of those were after Indiana joined the NBA. Only 142 of his 573 career victories came in the NBA, but he led the Pacers to three ABA titles.

Jim Lynam: A demonstrative leader, Jim Lynam coached the Los Angeles Clippers, Philadelphia 76ers and Washington Bullets. In nine seasons, Lynam's teams won 328 games.

Jack McMahon: Coached the Cincinnati Royals and guard Oscar Robertson to 55 victories in 1963-64. All together, McMahon won 300 games for the San Diego Rockets, Royals and Chicago Zephyrs.

Bill Russell: One of his greatest assets when he began coaching in 1966 was his ability to start himself at center. Russell was the first African-American coach in the NBA, won two titles in three seasons at Boston, and later coached Seattle and Sacramento. He won 341 games as a coach.

Fred Schaus: A victim of the Celtic dynasty, Schaus directed Laker teams led by Elgin Baylor and Jerry West to four NBA Finals, but each time, his team fell to the Celtics. He had a 315-245 career record.

Paul Seymour: He had a 15-year playing career and coached four NBA teams. Coached the St. Louis Hawks, Syracuse Nationals, Detroit Pistons and Baltimore Bullets to 271 victories and he had a winning percentage of .529.

Butch van Breda Kolff: Coached the Lakers to two NBA Finals, but Boston and Bill Russell were waiting both times and the Lakers could only get second place. Also coached the New Orleans Jazz. His teams won 287 games.

Paul Westphal: An outstanding scorer who once averaged 25.2 points for the Phoenix Suns, Westphal returned later to direct the Suns to the 1993 NBA Finals, where they lost to the Bulls. With Phoenix and Seattle, he has won 261 games.

CHAPTER 17

THE REFEREES

By Alex Sachare

An NBA game is a sprint, with players working above the rim, often making moves at Mach 2.

Realizing the game had progressed to the point where it was too swift and too potentially volatile to be handled by a pair of officials, the Board of Governors in 1988-89 voted to add a third official to each crew.

"Two officials have very little chance of consistently legislating contact off the ball," said Ed T. Rush, an NBA and ABA referee from 1966 to 1998 and currently the league's Director of Officiating. "With the type of athlete you have today, the strength, size, speed, you just have to have that extra pair of eyes."

Refereeing continues to evolve, with improvements in the training and technique of officials. Another step in this evolution took place in 1997 when the NBA dramatically broadened its pool of potential officials by adding the first female officials to its staff.

REFEREES SUCH AS THE COLORFUL PAT KENNEDY, WHO IS IN THE HALL OF FAME, ADDED HISTRIONICS TO THE GAME IN THE EARLY YEARS. TODAY'S REFEREES APPROACH THE GAME IN A MORE BUSINESSLIKE WAY.

Today the NBA pays greater attention than ever before to referee development, training and evaluation. Officials watch hundreds of hours of videotape to discover their strengths and work on their weaknesses, in terms of positioning as well as play-calling, and they are constantly being observed and graded. They have conditioning programs and their own preseason training camp to get ready to call the action.

Unlike years ago, when the referees were considered part of the entertainment, the notion of the referee as a marquee character is something the NBA today feels it can do without. The players are the unquestioned attractions in today's game, the most recognizable and popular of all pro athletes. "When I first came into the game, it

After more than 30 seasons as a pro basketball official in the NBA and ABA, Ed T. Rush was named NBA Director of Officiating on July 1, 1998.

Referees need comprehensive people skills to not only control the game but to allow players to express their viewpoints, at least within reason.

had some very strong officiating personalities," said Rush. "The game was played and officiated according to the personality of that individual. They almost put their stamp as to how the game would go. That was all part of the game. They were part of the whole picture as far as what you saw."

The NBA has come a long way since then, and so have its officials.

When 10 players are at their most frenetic, the three NBA referees on the NBA court are, like the players, the best at what they do. They have to keep up with the athletes, control emotions and make split-second decisions that have a huge impact on the way the game is played.

"The real good official knows what's important to call," observed retired NBA superstar Julius Erving. "Professional basketball is part of the entertainment business, but the first order of business is allowing the play to be at its highest level. An official can encourage that, or he can destroy it."

Being an NBA official is a demanding job, but a rewarding one. Veteran officials are paid well, travel the country, have an exciting and stimulating job and, like the players, have time off when there are no games.

"It is, in my opinion, the best job in sports," said Rush. "You're on the court, you're part of the game, you're connected to the game. It's competitive. Every night there is something different. There are tremendous challenges no matter how established you are. The compensation is very good and there is a long vacation."

It might be the best job, but no means is it an easy one. Officiating may be the only profession performed before crowds who pay tribute with their silence rather than their cheers. The official does his work in front of thousands of critical eyes, knowing that the best referee is the one who manages to appear the least conspicuous.

"There are few places in life where you're in charge, yet you're supposed to be anonymous," wrote longtime NBA official Earl Strom in his autobiography, *Calling the Shots*. "The whole show rests on your judgment, yet the better the job you do, the less anyone notices."

"I call it leadership through a quiet yet assertive efficiency," said Rush. "We are paid to be reactors, not initiators."

NBA referees have come a long way since the days when they were paid $30 and $40 a game to work in small, dimly lit arenas before often hostile and unruly crowds. One night in Syracuse many years ago, Sid Borgia and John Nucatola had to be escorted off the court and out of town to avoid the wrath of unruly fans. "We had to stay in the Knicks' locker room until everyone cleared out," recalled Borgia. "Then a detective pulled a car up to the back door and took us to the train station. We couldn't even go back to the hotel for our things."

John Nucatola was enshrined in the Hall of Fame in 1978. He retired in 1959 after officiating in more than 2,000 games. He also was the NBA's supervisor of officials from 1970-77.

The late Earl Strom was one of the NBA's outstanding officials, using talent and personality to command respect.

When the NBA was in its infancy, referees such as Borgia and colorful cohorts Pat Kennedy and Mendy Rudolph became showmen. Kennedy, for example, gained renown for his shrill whistle, his finger-wagging and his loud, resonant voice. Fans delighted in his style, watching gleefully as his neck would bulge, his face would turn purple and he'd blow his whistle several times before turning to the offending player and say, "I caught you this time!"

Kennedy's theatrics didn't always sit well with players, coaches or fellow referees, but the saving grace was that everyone conceded he was an outstanding official. Whatever his style, a good referee above all has to be even-handed and poised, knowledgeable about the rules and consistent in their application. Kennedy met these standards, as did other outstanding officials over the years, such as Rudolph, Borgia, Strom, Rush, Norm Drucker, Jake O'Donnell, Richie Powers, Darell Garretson and many more. The same goes for today's top officials, such as Hugh Evans, Steve Javie, Joe Crawford, Dick Bavetta, Hue Hollins, Ronnie Nunn, Danny Crawford, Bennett Salvatore and Ron Garretson.

Like the athletes they officiate, NBA referees are the best in the world.

CHAPTER 18

NBA SEASONS IN REVIEW

NBA CHAMPIONS 2000-1946

1999-2000 Los Angeles Lakers
1998-1999 San Antonio Spurs
1997-1998 Chicago Bulls
1996-1997 Chicago Bulls
1995-1996 Chicago Bulls
1994-1995 Houston Rockets
1993-1994 Houston Rockets
1992-1993 Chicago Bulls
1991-1992 Chicago Bulls
1990-1991 Chicago Bulls
1989-1990 Detroit Pistons
1988-1989 Detroit Pistons
1987-1988 Los Angeles Lakers
1986-1987 Los Angeles Lakers
1985-1986 Boston Celtics
1984-1985 Los Angeles Lakers
1983-1984 Boston Celtics
1982-1983 Philadelphia 76ers
1981-1982 Los Angeles Lakers
1980-1981 Boston Celtics
1979-1980 Los Angeles Lakers
1978-1979 Seattle SuperSonics
1977-1978 Washington Bullets
1976-1977 Portland Trail Blazers
1975-1976 Boston Celtics
1974-1975 Golden State Warriors
1973-1974 Boston Celtics
1972-1973 New York Knicks
1971-1972 Los Angeles Lakers
1970-1971 Milwaukee Bucks
1969-1970 New York Knicks
1968-1969 Boston Celtics
1967-1968 Boston Celtics
1966-1967 Philadelphia 76ers
1965-1966 Boston Celtics
1964-1965 Boston Celtics
1963-1964 Boston Celtics
1962-1963 Boston Celtics
1961-1962 Boston Celtics
1960-1961 Boston Celtics
1959-1960 Boston Celtics
1958-1959 Boston Celtics
1957-1958 St. Louis Hawks
1956-1957 Boston Celtics
1955-1956 Philadelphia Warriors
1954-1955 Syracuse Nationals
1953-1954 Minneapolis Lakers
1952-1953 Minneapolis Lakers
1951-1952 Minneapolis Lakers
1950-1951 Rochester Royals
1949-1950 Minneapolis Lakers
1948-1949 Minneapolis Lakers
1947-1948 Baltimore Bullets
1946-1947 Philadelphia Warriors

LOS ANGELES LAKERS—1999-2000 NATIONAL BASKETBALL ASSOCIATION CHAMPIONS
FRONT ROW, LEFT TO RIGHT—GLEN RICE, ROBERT HORRY, SHAQUILLE O'NEAL, DR. JERRY BUSS (OWNER), TRAVIS KNIGHT, JOHN SALLEY, A.C. GREEN. SECOND ROW, LEFT TO RIGHT—TYRONN LUE, DEVEAN GEORGE, RON HARPER, RICK FOX, KOBE BRYANT, BRIAN SHAW, JOHN CELESTAND, DEREK FISHER. BACK ROW LEFT TO RIGHT—GARY VITTI (ATHLETIC TRAINER), CHIP SCHAEFER (ATHLETIC PERFORMANCE COORDINATOR), BILL BERTKA (ASST. COACH), FRANK HAMBLEN (ASST. COACH), PHIL JACKSON (HEAD COACH), TEX WINTER (ASST. COACH), JIM CLEAMONS (ASST. COACH), JIM COTTA (STRENGTH AND CONDITIONING COACH), RUDY GARCIDUENAS (EQUIPMENT MANAGER).

1999-00 SEASON

Shaquille O'Neal

NBA.COM FACT

San Antonio failed to defend its NBA title, becoming the first league champion since the 1986 Celtics to not win consecutive crowns.

When he was coach of the Chicago Bulls, Phil Jackson observed that each NBA season is a mysterious journey, filled with twists, turns and surprises. The surprises began with Jackson's abrupt hiring as coach of the Lakers during the 1999 offseason. The twists and turns came mostly for opponents as they tried to contend with a breakout campaign from 7-1, 315-pound center Shaquille O'Neal.

"The ball is going into Shaq," Jackson said as training camp opened. "And he's going to have a responsibility to distribute the ball. It's going to be good for the team, and good for him."

Good indeed. O'Neal would go on to average 29.7 points per game while operating out of Jackson's triangle offense, good enough to lead the league in scoring and earn O'Neal his first MVP Award. The team's share of the spoils included 67 wins and the Lakers' first title in a dozen seasons.

For all the offensive excitement, Jackson reminded O'Neal and his teammates early and often that defense would distinguish them. To play it, Jackson wanted O'Neal in shape and filled with desire to block shots and defend the basket.

A preseason injury forced Kobe Bryant to miss the first 15 games on the schedule. Yet even that setback allowed the coaches to mold the team identity before Bryant returned in December. O'Neal was still dogged by his old free throw problems, a weakness that opponents continued to exploit, especially in the playoffs when team after team forced O'Neal to beat them from the line.

The parade of fouls, dubbed "Hack-A-Shaq," slowed the action, but the league still found a measure of success in its first full season after the retirement of Michael Jordan. New rules to bolster the offense did just that, with playoff scoring up significantly.

Besides the Lakers, the Western Conference featured an array of competitive teams, beginning with the Portland Trail Blazers, who were aided by the addition of Scottie Pippen in a trade with Houston. With Pippen's leadership and the rapid development of volatile forward Rasheed Wallace, the Blazers posted a 59-23 record, second best in the league. Their showdown with L.A. in the Western Conference Finals proved to be a great series, with the Lakers jumping out to a 3-1 lead only to have the Blazers battle back to tie it at three games apiece. In Game 7, Portland held a 15-point lead early in the fourth quarter, but the Lakers staged a miraculous comeback to advance to the championship round.

The defending champion San Antonio Spurs finished second in the Midwest Division with 53 wins, behind Utah's 55-27 record. The Spurs showed during the regular season that they could pose problems for the Lakers. But injury forced Tim Duncan out of the playoffs, which allowed Penny Hardaway's new team, the Phoenix Suns, to defeat the Spurs in the first round.

The Lakers also had first-round trouble, getting pushed to a full five games by Chris Webber and the Sacramento Kings.

In the Eastern Conference, the New York Knicks again broke hearts in Miami by overcoming a 3-2 deficit to defeat Pat Riley's Heat in the semifinals. But the Indiana Pacers ultimately prevailed in the East to make their first trip to the league championship series.

In the last season of his three-year run on the Pacers' bench, Coach Larry Bird watched his hot-shooting team battle the Lakers before finally falling 4-2. It was a dream ending for Hollywood's team, and O'Neal was openly emotional afterward.

"It's just a great moment," the Lakers' center said once his tears had subsided.

FINAL STANDINGS

EASTERN CONFERENCE

ATLANTIC DIVISION

	W	L	Pct.
Miami	52	30	.634
New York	50	32	.610
Philadelphia	49	33	.598
Orlando	41	41	.500
Boston	35	47	.427
New Jersey	31	51	.378
Washington	29	53	.354

CENTRAL DIVISION

	W	L	Pct.
Indiana	56	26	.683
Charlotte	49	33	.598
Toronto	45	37	.549
Detroit	42	40	.512
Milwaukee	42	40	.512
Cleveland	32	50	.390
Atlanta	28	54	.341
Chicago	17	65	.207

WESTERN CONFERENCE

MIDWEST DIVISION

	W	L	Pct.
Utah	55	27	.671
San Antonio	53	29	.646
Minnesota	50	32	.610
Dallas	40	42	.488
Denver	35	47	.427
Houston	34	48	.415
Vancouver	22	60	.268

PACIFIC DIVISION

	W	L	Pct.
L.A. Lakers	67	15	.817
Portland	59	23	.720
Phoenix	53	29	.646
Seattle	45	37	.549
Sacramento	44	38	.537
Golden State	19	63	.232
L.A. Clippers	15	67	.183

PLAYOFFS

EASTERN CONFERENCE

FIRST ROUND

Indiana 3, Milwaukee 2

Apr. 23 ....@Indiana 88, Milwaukee 85
Apr. 27 ....Milwaukee 104, @Indiana 91
Apr. 29 ....Indiana 109, @Milwaukee 96
May 1 ......@Milwaukee 100, Indiana 87
May 4 ......@Indiana 96, Milwaukee 95

Miami 3, Detroit 0

Apr. 22 ....@Miami 95, Detroit 85
Apr. 25 ....@Miami 84, Detroit 82
Apr. 29 ....Miami 91, @Detroit 72

New York 3, Toronto 0

Apr. 23 ....@New York 92, Toronto 88
Apr. 26 ....@New York 84, Toronto 83
Apr. 30 ....New York 87, @Toronto 80

Philadelphia 3, Charlotte 1

Apr. 22 ....Philadelphia 92, @Charlotte 82
Apr. 24 ....@Charlotte 108, Philadelphia 98*
Apr. 28 ....@Philadelphia 81, Charlotte 76
May 1 ......@Philadelphia 105, Charlotte 99

SEMIFINALS

Indiana 4, Philadelphia 2

May 6 .....@Indiana 108, Philadelphia 91
May 8 .....@Indiana 103, Philadelphia 97
May 10 ....Indiana 97, @Philadelphia 89
May 13 ....@Philadelphia 92, Indiana 90
May 15 ....Philadelphia 107, @Indiana 86
May 19 ....Indiana 106, @Philadelphia 90

New York 4, Miami 3

May 7 .....@Miami 87, New York 83
May 9 .....New York 82, @Miami 76
May 12 ....Miami 77, @New York 76*
May 14 ....@New York 91, Miami 83
May 17 ....@Miami 87, New York 81
May 19 ....@New York 72, Miami 70
May 21 ....New York 83, @Miami 82

FINALS

Indiana 4, New York 2

May 23 ....@Indiana 102, New York 88
May 25 ....@Indiana 88, New York 84
May 27 ....Indiana 95, @New York 98
May 29 ....@New York 91, Indiana 89
May 31 ....@Indiana 88, New York 79
June 2 I ...Indiana 93, @New York 80

WESTERN CONFERENCE

FIRST ROUND

Los Angeles 3, Sacramento 2

Apr. 23 ....@Los Angeles 117, Sacramento 107
Apr. 27 ....@Los Angeles 113, Sacramento 89
Apr. 30 ....@Sacramento 99, Los Angeles 91
May 2 ......@Sacramento 101, Los Angeles 88
May 5 ......@Los Angeles 113, Sacramento 86

Utah 3, Seattle 2

Apr. 22 ....@Utah 104, Seattle 93
Apr. 24 ....@Utah 101, Seattle 87
Apr. 29 ....@Seattle 89, Utah 78
May 3 ......@Seattle 104, Utah 93
May 5 ......@Utah 96, Seattle 93

Portland 3, Minnesota 1

Apr. 23 ....@Portland 91, Minnesota 88
Apr. 26 ....@Portland 86, Minnesota 82
Apr. 30 ....@Minnesota 94, Portland 87
May 2 ......Portland 85 @Minnesota 77

Phoenix 3, San Antonio 1

Apr. 22 ....Phoenix 72, @San Antonio 70
Apr. 25 ....@San Antonio 85, Phoenix 70
Apr. 29 ....@Phoenix 101, San Antonio 94
May 2 ......@Phoenix 89, San Antonio 78

SEMIFINALS

Los Angeles 4, Phoenix 1

May 7 ......@Los Angeles 105, Phoenix 77
May 10 ....@Los Angeles 97, Phoenix 96
May 12 ....Los Angeles 105, @Phoenix 99
May 14 ....@Phoenix 117, Los Angeles 98
May 16 ....@Los Angeles 87, Phoenix 65

Portland 4, Utah 1

May 7 ......@Portland 94, Utah 75
May 9 ......@Portland 103, Utah 85
May 11 ....Portland 103, @Utah 84
May 14 ....@Utah 88, Portland 85
May 16 ....@Portland 81, Utah 79

FINALS

Los Angeles 4, Portland 3

May 20 ....@Los Angeles 109, Portland 94
May 22 ....Portland 106, @Los Angeles 77
May 26 ....Los Angeles 93, @Portland 91
May 28 ....Los Angeles 103, @Portland 91
May 30 ....Portland 96, @Los Angeles 88
June 2 ....@Portland 103, Los Angeles 93
June 4 ....@Los Angeles 89, Portland 84

NBA FINALS

Los Angeles 4, Indiana 2

June 7 .....@Los Angeles 104, Indiana 87
June 9 .....@Los Angeles 111, Indiana 104
June 11 ...@Indiana 100, Los Angeles 91
June 14 ...Los Angeles 120, @Indiana 118*
June 16 ...@Indiana 120, Los Angeles 87
June 19 ...@Los Angeles 116, Indiana 111

*Denotes number of overtime periods.

INDIVIDUAL LEADERS

SCORING (minimum 70 games or 1,400 points)

	G	FGM	FTM	Pts.	Avg.
O'Neal, LA-L	79	956	432	2344	29.7
Iverson, Philadelphia	70	729	442	1989	28.4
Hill, Detroit	74	696	480	1906	25.8
Carter, Toronto	82	788	436	2107	25.7
Malone, Utah	82	75	589	2095	25.5
Webber, Sacramento	75	748	311	1834	24.5
Payton, Seattle	82	747	311	1982	24.2
Stackhouse, Detroit	82	619	618	1939	23.6
Duncan, San Antonio	74	628	459	1716	23.2
Garnett, Minnesota	81	759	309	1857	22.9

FIELD GOAL PCT. (minimum 300 made)

	FGM	FGA	Pct.
O'Neal, LA-L	956	1665	.574
Mutombo, Atlanta	322	573	.562
Mourning, Miami	652	1184	.551
Patterson, Seattle	354	661	.536
Wallace, Portland	542	1045	.519

THREE-POINT FIELD GOAL PCT. (minimum 55 made)

	FGM	FGA	Pct.
Davis, Dallas	82	167	.491
Hornacek, Utah	66	138	.478
Bullard, Houston	79	177	.446
Rogers, Phoenix	115	262	.439
Houston, New York	106	243	.436

FREE THROW PCT. (minimum 125 made)

	FTM	FTA	Pct.
Hornacek, Utah	171	180	.950
Miller, Indiana	373	406	.919
Armstrong, Orlando.	225	247	.911
Brandon, Minnesota.	187	208	.899
Allen, Milwaukee	353	398	.887

ASSISTS (minimum 70 games or 400 assists)

	G	No.	Avg.
Kidd, Phoenix.	67	678	10.1
Van Exel, Denver	79	714	9.0
Cassell, Milwaukee	81	729	9.0
Payton, Seattle	82	732	8.9
Brandon, Minnesota	71	629	8.9

REBOUNDS (minimum 70 games or 800 rebounds)

	G	Off.	Def.	Tot.	Avg.
Mutombo, Atlanta	82	304	853	1157	14.1
O'Neal, LA-L	79	336	742	1078	13.6
Duncan, San Antonio	74	262	656	918	12.4
Garnett, Minnesota	81	223	733	956	11.8
Webber, Sacramento	75	189	598	787	10.5

STEALS (minimum 70 games or 125 steals)

	G	No.	Avg.
Jones, Cha	72	192	2.67
Pierce, Bos	73	152	2.08
Armstrong, Orl	82	169	2.06
Iverson, Phi	70	144	2.06
Blaylock, G.S.	73	146	2.00

BLOCKED SHOTS (minimum 43 games or 61 blocked shots)

	G	No.	Avg.
Mourning, Mia	79	294	3.72
Mutombo, Atl.	82	269	3.28
O'Neal, LA-L	79	239	3.03
Ratliff, Phi	57	171	3.00
Bradley, Dal.	77	190	2.47

1998-99 SEASON

Tim Duncan

Recovering from the labor lockout that cut more than three months out of the 1998-99 schedule, the NBA played 50 games in 89 days. The season began in February, and teams had only two weeks to prepare. Another change was the retirement of Michael Jordan the league's longtime star attraction.

Still, the league's new look emerged in short time with Philadelphia's Allen Iverson (26.8 points per game) edging the Lakers' Shaquille O'Neal (26.3) for the scoring title and Toronto's Vince Carter earning Rookie of the Year distinction.

Team success was achieved by the Spurs and their overwhelming frontcourt — the gentlemanly David Robinson, in his 10th season, and Tim Duncan, the second-year star out of Wake Forest with a fundamentally pure game.

Making it all the sweeter for longtime fans, the Spurs became the first of the former American Basketball Association teams to reach the NBA championship round, ending a dry spell that stretched over a quarter-century.

San Antonio stumbled out of the gate to a 6-8 start. But March and April brought displays of dominance that extended the Spurs' record to 37-13 by season's end and gave them home-court advantage through the playoffs.

Throughout the whirl of days Alamodome fans serenaded Duncan with chants of "MVP!" The award would go to Utah's Karl Malone, but the postseason belonged to Duncan.

After their flourish to close the regular season, Spurs Coach Gregg Popovich refired the engines for an 11-1 dash through the Western Conference Playoffs. The Minnesota Timberwolves managed a Game 2 victory in the Alamodome during the first round, but after that the T-wolves went quickly, followed by the Lakers and Trail Blazers in sweeps. The Blazers did seem set to take Game 2 until Sean Elliott's late three-pointer, the so-called "Memorial Day Miracle," pushed the Spurs over the brink. With his team down 85-83 and all timeouts exhausted, Elliott rose up 24 feet from the basket with 12 seconds to go. "If he had put his heels down, he would have been out of bounds," Popovich said later.

In the East, the surprise of the playoffs, the New York Knicks, won a showdown with the Indiana Pacers to become the first No. 8 seed to reach the championship series.

When the Finals began there was little suspense for the crowd of 39,514 at the Alamodome once Duncan settled in to work on the Knicks' undermanned frontcourt. With Patrick Ewing out with an injured Achilles tendon the Knicks relied heavily on Latrell Sprewell and Allan Houston, but the Spurs took a 1-0 lead with an 89-77 victory. Game 2 had a similar feel and outcome, 80-67, with Duncan running his two-game totals to 58 points and 31 rebounds.

New York found an edge in Game 3, 89-81, but a strong defensive effort netted San Antonio a 96-89 triumph in Game 4 and then the Spurs settled the matter in Game 5, 78-77. Duncan, the Finals MVP, led the Spurs in the series-ending game with 31 points, while Sprewell scored 35. But the game-winner for San Antonio came on Avery Johnson's deep two-pointer from the left corner with 47 seconds to go.

The Knicks, trailing by one point, got the ball back with 2.1 seconds left. The Knicks inbounded but the Spurs promptly pinned Sprewell against the baseline. He executed a spin move and even managed to get off a shot through the foliage of outstretched arms, but it was off target. This was to be the Spurs' night and the Spurs' season.

NBA.COM FACT

For the first time since 1954-55 (the first year of the shot clock), only one team — Sacramento (100.2) — scored 100 points per game.

FINAL STANDINGS

EASTERN CONFERENCE

ATLANTIC DIVISION

	W	L	Pct.
Miami	33	17	.660
Orlando	33	17	.660
Philadelphia	28	22	.560
New York	27	23	.540
Boston	19	31	.380
Washington	18	32	.360
New Jersey	16	34	.320

CENTRAL DIVISION

	W	L	Pct.
Indiana	33	17	.660
Atlanta	31	19	.620
Detroit	29	21	.580
Milwaukee	28	22	.560
Charlotte	26	24	.520
Toronto	23	27	.460
Cleveland	22	28	.440
Chicago	13	37	.260

WESTERN CONFERENCE

MIDWEST DIVISION

	W	L	Pct.
San Antonio	37	13	.740
Utah	37	13	.740
Houston	31	19	.620
Minnesota	25	25	.500
Dallas	19	31	.380
Denver	14	36	.280
Vancouver	8	42	.160

PACIFIC DIVISION

	W	L	Pct.
Portland	35	15	.700
L.A. Lakers	31	19	.620
Phoenix	27	23	.540
Sacramento	27	23	.540
Seattle	25	25	.500
Golden State	21	29	.420
L.A. Clippers	9	41	.180

PLAYOFFS

EASTERN CONFERENCE

FIRST ROUND

New York 3, Miami 2
May 8......New York 95, @Miami 75
May 10....@Miami 83, New York 73
May 12....@New York 97, Miami 73
May 14....Miami 87, @New York 72
May 16....New York 78, @Miami 77

Atlanta 3, Detroit 2
May 8......@Atlanta 90, Detroit 70
May 10....@Atlanta 89, Detroit 69
May 12....@Detroit 79, Atlanta 63
May 14....@Detroit 103, Atlanta 82
May 16....@Atlanta 87, Detroit 75

Indiana 3, Milwaukee 0
May 9.....@Indiana 110, Milwaukee 88
May 11....@Indiana 108, Milwaukee 107*
May 13....Indiana 99, @Milwaukee 91

Philadelphia 3, Orlando 1
May 9......Philadelphia 104, @Orlando 90
May 11....@Orlando 79, Philadelphia 68
May 13....@Philadelphia 97, Orlando 85
May 15....@Philadelphia 101, Orlando 91

SEMIFINALS

Indiana 4, Philadelphia 0
May 17....@Indiana 94, Philadelphia 90
May 19....@Indiana 85, Philadelphia 82
May 21....Indiana 97, @Philadelphia 86
May 23....Indiana 89, @Philadelphia 86

New York 4, Atlanta 0
May 18....New York 100, @Atlanta 92
May 20....New York 77, @Atlanta 70
May 23....@New York 90, Atlanta 78
May 24....@New York 79, Atlanta 66

FINALS

New York 4, Indiana 2
May 30....New York 93, @Indiana 90
June 1.....@Indiana 88, New York 86
June 5.....@New York 92, Indiana 91
June 7.....Indiana 90, @New York 78
June 9.....New York 101, @Indiana 94
June 11...@New York 90, Indiana 82

WESTERN CONFERENCE

FIRST ROUND

San Antonio 3, Minnesota 1
May 9......@San Antonio 99, Minnesota 86
May 11....Minnesota 80, @San Antonio 71
May 13....San Antonio 85, @Minnesota 71
May 15....San Antonio 92, @Minnesota 85

L.A. Lakers 3, Houston 1
May 9......@L.A. Lakers 101, Houston 100
May 11....@L.A. Lakers 110, Houston 98
May 13....@Houston 102, L.A. Lakers 88
May 15....L.A. Lakers 98, @Houston 88

Portland 3, Phoenix 0
May 8......@Portland 95, Phoenix 85
May 10....@Portland 110, Phoenix 99
May 12....Portland 103, @Phoenix 93

Utah 3, Sacramento 2
May 8......@Utah 117, Sacramento 87
May 10....Sacramento 101, @Utah 90
May 12....@Sacramento 84, Utah 81*
May 14....Utah 90, @Sacramento 89
May 16....@Utah 99*, Sacramento 92

SEMIFINALS

San Antonio 4, L.A. Lakers 0
May 17....@San Antonio 87, L.A. Lakers 81
May 19....@San Antonio 79, L.A. Lakers 76
May 22....San Antonio 103, @L.A. Lakers 91
May 23....San Antonio 118, @L.A. Lakers 107

Portland 4, Utah 2
May 18....@Utah 93, Portland 83
May 20....Portland 84, @Utah 81
May 22....@Portland 97, Utah 87
May 23....@Portland 81, Utah 75
May 25....@Utah 88, Portland 71
May 27....@Portland 92, Utah 80

FINALS

San Antonio 4, Portland 0
May 29....@San Antonio 80, Portland 76
May 31....@San Antonio 86, Portland 85
June 4.....San Antonio 85, @Portland 63
June 6.....San Antonio 94, @Portland 80

NBA FINALS

San Antonio 4, New York 1
June 16...@San Antonio 89, New York 77
June 18...@San Antonio 80, New York 67
June 21...@New York 89, San Antonio 81
June 23...San Antonio 96, @New York 89
June 25...San Antonio 78, @New York 77

*Denotes number of overtime periods.

INDIVIDUAL LEADERS

SCORING (minimum 43 games or 854 points)

	G	FGM	FTM	Pts.	Avg.
Iverson, Philadelphia	48	435	356	1284	26.8
O'Neal, L.A. Lakers	49	510	269	1289	26.3
Malone, Utah	49	393	378	1164	23.8
Abdur-Rahim, Vancouver	50	386	369	1152	23.0
Van Horn, New Jersey	42	322	256	916	21.8
Duncan, San Antonio	50	418	247	1084	21.7
Payton, Seattle	50	401	199	1084	21.7
Marbury, Min.-N.J.	49	378	222	1044	21.3
McDyess, Denver	50	415	230	1061	21.2
Hill, Detroit	50	384	285	1053	21.1

FIELD GOAL PCT. (minimum 183 made)

	FGM	FGA	Pct.
O'Neal, L.A. Lakers	510	885	.576
Thorpe, Washington	240	440	.545
Olajuwon, Houston	373	725	.514
Mourning, Miami	324	634	.511
Robinson, San Antonio	268	527	.509

THREE-POINT FIELD GOAL PCT. (minimum 34 made)

	FGM	FGA	Pct.
Curry, Milwaukee	69	145	.476
Mullin, Indiana	73	157	.465
Davis, Dallas	65	144	.451
Williams, Portland	63	144	.438
Ellis, Seattle	94	217	.433

FREE THROW PCT. (minimum 76 made)

	FTM	FTA	Pct.
Miller, Indiana	226	247	.915
Billups, Denver	157	172	.913
Armstrong, Orlando	161	178	.904
Allen, Milwaukee	176	195	.903
Hawkins, Seattle	119	132	.902

ASSISTS (minimum 43 games or 244 assists)

	G	No.	Avg.
Kidd, Phoenix	50	539	10.8
Strickland, Washington	44	434	9.9
Marbury, Minnesota-New Jersey	49	437	8.9
Payton, Seattle	50	436	8.7
Brandon, Milwaukee-Minnesota	36	309	8.6

REBOUNDS (minimum 43 games or 488 rebounds)

	G	Off.	Def.	Tot.	Avg.
Webber, Sacramento	42	149	396	545	13.0
Barkley, Houston	42	167	349	516	12.3
Mutombo, Atlanta	50	192	418	610	12.2
Fortson, Denver	50	210	371	581	11.6
Duncan, San Antonio	50	159	412	571	11.4

STEALS (minimum 43 games or 76 steals)

	G	No.	Avg.
Gill, New Jersey	50	134	2.68
Jones, L.A. Lakers-Charlotte	50	125	2.50
Iverson, Philadelphia	48	110	2.29
Kidd, Phoenix	50	114	2.28
Christie, Toronto	50	113	2.26

BLOCKED SHOTS (minimum 43 games or 61 blocked shots)

	G	No.	Avg.
Mourning, Miami	46	180	3.91
Bradley, Dallas	49	159	3.24
Ratliff, Philadelphia	50	149	2.98
Mutombo, Atlanta	50	147	2.94
Ostertag, Utah	48	131	2.73

1997-98 SEASON

Scottie Pippen

Michael Jordan's long, brilliant career came down to an appropriate final sequence. In the last seconds of Game 6 of the NBA Finals, he stole the ball from Utah's Karl Malone, then executed a one-on-one move on Bryon Russell at the other end.

The jumper Jordan launched from just left of the top of the key hangs there still in the photographs that captured the scene — 6.6 seconds on the clock, the rows of fans in Utah's Delta Center waiting with faces transfixed, Jordan's arms outstretched in a fundamentally exact follow-through.

The ensuing swish gave the Chicago Bulls their sixth championship and capped a career that included five league MVP Awards. The fifth of those had come that spring, with the legendary Bill Russell presenting the award to Jordan.

Russell said he had often been asked his opinion on the greatest player of all time. "I never thought about it," he told Jordan. "But I'll just say this about you. To play the game you were introduced to, I cannot imagine anyone playing it any better."

This final season had brought Jordan his 10th scoring title, at 28.7 points per game, as well as his All-Star MVP recognition for the third time and his ninth appearance on the league's All-Defensive First Team.

His ability was so great that it often seemed to obscure the rest of the league. But there was much afoot during the season. Larry Bird returned to the game as the coach of the Indiana Pacers and guided his veteran club into the Eastern Conference Finals against the Bulls. Driven by Reggie Miller's fire, the Pacers pushed the Bulls through seven games before succumbing to Chicago's home-court advantage.

Additional excitement in the Eastern Conference came from the rivalry between the Miami Heat and New York Knicks, which boiled over yet again during the playoffs. Game 4 of the Eastern Conference First Round featured Knicks coach Jeff Van Gundy clutching Alonzo Mourning around the leg during a bench-clearing exchange. The subsequent suspension of Mourning cost the Heat dearly as the Knicks easily won Game 5 of the series 98-81 on Miami's home floor.

In the Western Conference, San Antonio experienced a resurgence, made possible by the addition of Rookie of the Year Tim Duncan, who formed a Twin Towers alignment alongside David Robinson. Duncan averaged 21.1 points and 11.9 rebounds.

Los Angeles center Shaquille O'Neal finished second in the scoring race with a 28.3 points-per-game average and his team topped the league with 105.5 points per game, but the Lakers fell in the playoffs for a second straight year to the graybeard Jazz. Malone and John Stockton worked their pick-and-roll magic yet again to deliver 62 regular-season victories for Utah and a second straight run to the Finals.

In the end, though, all eyes were turned to Jordan and the Bulls in a season that Coach Phil Jackson appropriately dubbed "The Last Dance."

With Scottie Pippen injured over the first two months of the season, the burden had fallen on Jordan, who responded by following Jackson's Zen philosophy of living and performing "in the moment." Sometimes those moments were hard to handle, especially in light of the behavior of Jordan's zany teammate, Dennis Rodman. Yet under the stern leadership of Jackson and Jordan, the forward with the dyed hair won his seventh consecutive league rebounding title.

When the Finals began, the burden fell squarely on Jordan.

He scored 45 points in the last game of his career, including the final brilliant sequence. "Things start to move very slowly and you start to see the court very well," Jordan said. "You start reading what the defense is trying to do. And I saw that. I saw the moment."

NBA.COM FACT

Dallas Mavericks forward A.C. Green played his 907th consecutive game November 26, 1997, to break Randy Smith's NBA mark. Green's streak stood at 1,110 games by the end of the 1999-2000 season.

FINAL STANDINGS

EASTERN CONFERENCE

ATLANTIC DIVISION

	W	L	Pct.
Miami	55	27	.671
New Jersey	43	39	.524
New York	43	39	.524
Washington	42	40	.512
Orlando	41	41	.500
Boston	36	46	.439
Philadelphia	31	51	.378

CENTRAL DIVISION

	W	L	Pct.
Chicago	62	20	.756
Indiana	58	24	.707
Charlotte	51	31	.622
Atlanta	50	32	.610
Cleveland	47	35	.573
Detroit	37	45	.451
Milwaukee	36	46	.439
Toronto	16	66	.195

WESTERN CONFERENCE

MIDWEST DIVISION

	W	L	Pct.
Utah	62	20	.756
San Antonio	56	26	.683
Minnesota	45	37	.549
Houston	41	41	.500
Dallas	20	62	.244
Vancouver	19	63	.232
Denver	11	71	.134

PACIFIC DIVISION

	W	L	Pct.
L.A. Lakers	61	21	.744
Seattle	61	21	.744
Phoenix	56	26	.683
Portland	46	36	.561
Sacramento	27	55	.329
Golden State	19	63	.232
L.A. Clippers	17	65	.207

PLAYOFFS

EASTERN CONFERENCE

FIRST ROUND

Chicago 3, New Jersey 0
Apr. 24 ....@Chicago 96, New Jersey 93*
Apr. 26 ....@Chicago 96, New Jersey 91
Apr. 29 ....Chicago 116, @New Jersey 101

New York 3, Miami 2
Apr. 24 ....@Miami 94, New York 79
Apr. 26 ....New York 96, @Miami 86
Apr. 28 ....Miami 91, @New York 85
Apr. 30 ....@New York 90, Miami 85
May 3 ......New York 98, @Miami 81

Indiana 3, Cleveland 1
Apr. 23 ....@Indiana 106, Cleveland 77
Apr. 25 ....@Indiana 92, Cleveland 86
Apr. 27 ....@Cleveland 86, Indiana 77
Apr. 30 ....Indiana 80, @Cleveland 74

Charlotte 3, Atlanta 1
Apr. 23 ....@Charlotte 97, Atlanta 87
Apr. 25 ....@Charlotte 92, Atlanta 85
Apr. 28 ....@Atlanta 96, Charlotte 64
May 1 ......Charlotte 91,@Atlanta 82

SEMIFINALS

Chicago 4, Charlotte 1
May 3 ......@Chicago 83, Charlotte 70
May 6 ......Charlotte 78, @Chicago 76
May 8 ......Chicago 103, @Charlotte 89
May 10 ....Chicago 94, @Charlotte 80
May 13 ....@Chicago 93, Charlotte 84

Indiana 4, New York 1
May 5 ......@Indiana 93, New York 83
May 7 ......@Indiana 85, New York 77
May 9 ......@New York 83, Indiana 76
May 10 ....Indiana 118, @New York 107*
May 13 ....@Indiana 99, New York 88

FINALS

Chicago 4, Indiana 3
May 17 ....@Chicago 85, Indiana 79
May 19 ....@Chicago 104, Indiana 98
May 23 ....@Indiana 107, Chicago 105
May 25 ....@Indiana 96, Chicago 94
May 27 ....@Chicago 106, Indiana 87
May 29 ....@Indiana 92, Chicago 89
May 31 ....@Chicago 88, Indiana 83

WESTERN CONFERENCE

FIRST ROUND

Utah 3, Houston 2
Apr. 23 ....Houston 103, @Utah 90
Apr. 25 ....@Utah 105, Houston 90
Apr. 29 ....@Houston 89, Utah 85
May 1 ......Utah 93, @Houston 71
May 3 ......@Utah 84, Houston 70

Seattle 3, Minnesota 2
Apr. 24 ....@Seattle 108, Minnesota 83
Apr. 26 ....Minnesota 98, @Seattle 93
Apr. 28 ....@Minnesota 98, Seattle 90
Apr. 30 ....Seattle 92, @Minnesota 88
May 2 ......@Seattle 97, Minnesota 84

L.A. Lakers 3, Portland 1
Apr. 24 ....@L.A. Lakers 104, Portland 102
Apr. 26 ....@L.A. Lakers 108, Portland 99
Apr. 28 ....@Portland 99, L.A. Lakers 94
Apr. 30 ....L.A. Lakers 110, @Portland 99

San Antonio 3, Phoenix 1
Apr. 23 ....San Antonio 102, @Phoenix 96
Apr. 25 ....@Phoenix 108, San Antonio 101
Apr. 27 ....@San Antonio 100, Phoenix 88
Apr. 29 ....@San Antonio 99, Phoenix 80

SEMIFINALS

Utah 4, San Antonio 1
May 5 ......@Utah 83, San Antonio 82
May 7 ......@Utah 109, San Antonio 106*
May 9 ......@San Antonio 86, Utah 64
May 10 ....Utah 82, @San Antonio 73
May 12 ....@Utah 87, San Antonio 77

L.A. Lakers 4, Seattle 1
May 4 ......@Seattle 106, L.A. Lakers 92
May 6 ......L.A. Lakers 92, @Seattle 68
May 8 ......@L.A. Lakers 119, Seattle 103
May 10 ....@L.A. Lakers 112, Seattle 100
May 12 ....L.A. Lakers 110, @Seattle 95

FINALS

Utah 4, L.A. Lakers 0
May 16 ....@Utah 112, L.A. Lakers 77
May 18 ....@Utah 99, L.A. Lakers 95
May 22 ....Utah 109, @L.A. Lakers 98
May 24 ....Utah 96, @L.A. Lakers 92

NBA FINALS

Chicago 4, Utah 2
June 3 .....@Utah 88, Chicago 85*
June 5 .....Chicago 93, @Utah 88
June 7 .....@Chicago 96, Utah 54
June 10 ...@Chicago 86, Utah 82
June 12. ..Utah 83, @Chicago 81
June 14 ...Chicago 87, @Utah 86

*Denotes number of overtime periods.

INDIVIDUAL LEADERS

SCORING (minimum 70 games or 1,400 points)

	G	FGM	FTM	Pts.	Avg.
Jordan, Chicago	82	881	565	2357	28.7
O'Neal, L.A. Lakers	60	670	359	1699	28.3
Malone, Utah	81	780	628	2190	27.0
Richmond, Sacramento	70	543	407	1623	23.2
Walker, Boston	82	722	305	1840	22.4
Abdur-Rahim, Vancouver	82	653	502	1829	22.3
Rice, Charlotte	82	634	428	1826	22.3
Iverson, Philadelphia	80	649	390	1758	22.0
Webber, Washington	71	647	196	1555	21.9
Robinson, San Antonio	73	544	485	1574	21.6

FIELD GOAL PCT. (minimum 300 made)

	FGM	FGA	Pct.
O'Neal, L.A. Lakers	670	1147	.584
Outlaw, Orlando	301	543	.554
Mourning, Miami	403	732	.551
Duncan, San Antonio	706	1287	.549
Baker, Seattle	631	1164	.542

THREE-POINT FIELD GOAL PCT. (minimum 55 made)

	FGM	FGA	Pct.
Ellis, Seattle	127	274	.464
Hornacek, Utah	56	127	.441
Mullin, Indiana	107	243	.440
Davis, Dallas	101	230	.439
Kerr, Chicago	57	130	.438

FREE THROW PCT. (minimum 125 made)

	FTM	FTA	Pct.
Mullin, Indiana	154	164	.939
Hornacek, Utah	285	322	.885
Allen, Milwaukee	342	391	.875
Anderson, Cleveland	275	315	.873
Johnson, Phoenix	162	186	.871

ASSISTS (minimum 70 games or 400 assists)

	G	No.	Avg.
Strickland, Washington	76	801	10.5
Kidd, Phoenix	82	745	9.1
Jackson, Indiana	82	713	8.7
Marbury, Minnesota	82	704	8.6
Stockton, Utah	64	543	8.5

REBOUNDS (minimum 70 games or 800 rebounds)

	G	Off.	Def.	Tot.	Avg.
Rodman, Chicago	80	421	780	1201	15.0
Williams, New Jersey	65	443	440	883	13.6
Duncan, San Antonio	82	274	703	977	11.9
Mutombo, Atlanta	82	276	656	932	11.4
Robinson, San Antonio	73	239	536	775	10.6

STEALS (minimum 70 games or 125 steals)

	G	No.	Avg.
Blaylock, Atlanta	70	183	2.61
Knight, Cleveland	80	196	2.45
Christie, Toronto	78	190	2.44
Payton, Seattle	82	185	2.26
Iverson, Philadelphia	80	176	2.20

BLOCKED SHOTS (minimum 70 games or 100 blocked shots)

	G	No.	Avg.
Camby, Toronto	63	230	3.65
Mutombo, Atlanta	82	277	3.38
Bradley, Dallas	64	214	3.34
Ratliff, Detroit-Philadelphia	82	258	3.15
Robinson, San Antonio	73	192	2.63

1996-97 SEASON

Karl Malone

This was the year of the upset stomachs, which occurred in the NBA Finals. Phil Jackson's Chicago Bulls met Jerry Sloan's Utah Jazz. In Game 4 at Utah's Delta Center a Bulls assistant mistakenly substituted a high-calorie supplement for the regular sports drink.

The result was like the Bulls having 10 baked potatoes in their bellies, explained Chicago trainer Chip Schaefer. Suddenly, Michael Jordan, Scottie Pippen and Dennis Rodman, who never asked out of games, were signaling Jackson to take them out because of upset stomachs. Late in the game the Bulls were dragging so badly they uncharacteristically blew a five-point lead and lost.

Then, with the series tied at 2-2, Jordan became afflicted with the stomach flu on the eve of Game 5 and spent all night and the next day fighting off waves of nausea. Yet he managed to score 38 points, and the Bulls were able to secure the key victory, which allowed them to claim their fifth title when the series returned to Chicago for Game 6.

Beyond that, 1996-97 marked a start of the changing of the guard in the NBA with the arrival of rookies Allen Iverson in Philadelphia, Kobe Bryant in Los Angeles (Lakers), Shareef Abdur-Rahim in Vancouver, Ray Allen in Milwaukee, Antoine Walker in Boston and Stephon Marbury in Minnesota. There also was a huge free agent move as Shaquille O'Neal left Orlando and signed with the Los Angeles Lakers.

Utah's Karl Malone tallied 27.4 ppg to finish second to Jordan in the scoring race (29.6 ppg), but Malone was voted the league's MVP. His effort was rewarded by Utah's first trip to the Finals. The Jazz emerged from a Western Conference bracket that found rebuilding Phoenix pushing defending finalist Seattle to the brink in the first round. Houston finished off the Sonics in the second round while Utah's experience helped deflate playoff hopes in Los Angeles.

In the East, the Knicks went for a new look, signing free agents Chris Childs and Allan Houston and trading for Larry Johnson, and Atlanta moved into the league's elite with the free agent signing of center Dikembe Mutombo. Miami, in particular, turned in a stellar regular season, with 61 victories. "It's all because of Pat Riley," guard Tim Hardaway said of his coach. "He's got everybody thinking big thoughts." But in the playoffs, Miami and Atlanta struggled in the first round. The Heat, though, managed to reach the conference finals for the first time in its history, but couldn't generate enough offense to overcome Chicago.

Jordan's team ran into some low moments, but the Bulls found a way to answer all challenges, beginning in October with a triumph at the McDonald's Championship in Paris and carrying right through to those stomach-churning moments against the Jazz in the Finals.

With Jackson, Rodman and Jordan working under contracts about to expire, Jordan used his media interview after winning the title to lobby Bulls Chairman Jerry Reinsdorf to bring the team and its coach back for another title run in 1998.

"I think this team is entitled to an opportunity to continue to be successful," Jordan said. "We're entitled to defend what we have until we lose it."

Ultimately, Reinsdorf decided to keep the team intact, which allowed Chicago's fairy tale to live for yet another season, upset stomachs or not.

NBA.COM FACT

Bulls center Robert Parish played his 21st and final campaign to break Kareem Abdul-Jabbar's record for most NBA seasons. Parish also holds the mark for most games (1,611).

FINAL STANDINGS

EASTERN CONFERENCE

ATLANTIC DIVISION

	W	L	Pct.
Miami	61	21	.744
New York	57	25	.695
Orlando	45	37	.549
Washington	44	38	.537
New Jersey	26	56	.317
Philadelphia	22	60	.268
Boston	15	67	.183

CENTRAL DIVISION

	W	L	Pct.
Chicago	69	13	.841
Atlanta	56	26	.683
Charlotte	54	28	.659
Detroit	54	28	.659
Cleveland	42	40	.512
Indiana	39	43	.476
Milwaukee	33	49	.402
Toronto	30	52	.366

WESTERN CONFERENCE

MIDWEST DIVISION

	W	L	Pct.
Utah	64	18	.780
Houston	57	25	.695
Minnesota	40	42	.488
Dallas	24	58	.293
Denver	21	61	.256
San Antonio	20	62	.244
Vancouver	14	68	.171

PACIFIC DIVISION

	W	L	Pct.
Seattle	57	25	.695
L.A. Lakers	56	26	.683
Portland	49	33	.598
Phoenix	40	42	.488
L.A. Clippers	36	46	.439
Sacramento	34	48	.415
Golden State	30	52	.366

PLAYOFFS

EASTERN CONFERENCE

FIRST ROUND

Chicago 3, Washington 0

Apr. 25 ....@Chicago 98, Washington 86
Apr. 27 ....@Chicago 109, Washington 104
Apr. 30 ....Chicago 96, @Washington 95

Miami 3, Orlando 2

Apr. 24 ....@Miami 99, Orlando 64
Apr. 27 ....@Miami 104, Orlando 87
Apr. 29 ....@Orlando 88, Miami 75
May 1 ......@Orlando 99, Miami 91
May 4 ......@Miami 91, Orlando 83

New York 3, Charlotte 0

Apr. 24 ....@New York 109, Charlotte 99
Apr. 26 ....@New York 100, Charlotte 93
Apr. 28 ....New York 104, @Charlotte 95

Atlanta 3, Detroit 2

Apr. 25 ....@Atlanta 89, Detroit 75
Apr. 27 ....Detroit 93, @Atlanta 80
Apr. 29 ....@Detroit 99, Atlanta 91
May 2 ......Atlanta 94, @Detroit 82
May 4 ......@Atlanta 84, Detroit 79

SEMIFINALS

Chicago 4, Atlanta 1

May 6 ......@Chicago 100, Atlanta 97
May 8 ......Atlanta 103, @Chicago 95
May 10 ....Chicago 100, @Atlanta 80
May 11 ....Chicago 89, @Atlanta 80
May 13 ....@Chicago 107, Atlanta 92

Miami 4, New York 3

May 7 ......New York 88, @Miami 79
May 9 ......@Miami 88, New York 84
May 11 ....@New York 77, Miami 73
May 12 ....@New York 89, Miami 76
May 14 ....@Miami 96, New York 81
May 16 ....Miami 95, @New York 90
May 18 ....@Miami 101, New York 90

FINALS

Chicago 4, Miami 1

May 20 ....@Chicago 84, Miami 77
May 22 ....@Chicago 75, Miami 68
May 24 ....Chicago 98, @Miami 74
May 26 ....@Miami 87, Chicago 80
May 28 ....@Chicago 100, Miami 87

WESTERN CONFERENCE

FIRST ROUND

Utah 3, L.A. Clippers 0

Apr. 24 ....@Utah 106, L.A. Clippers 86
Apr. 26 ....@Utah 105, L.A. Clippers 99
Apr. 28 ....Utah 104, @L.A. Clippers 92

Seattle 3, Phoenix 2

Apr. 25 ....Phoenix 106, @Seattle 101
Apr. 27 ....@Seattle 122, Phoenix 78
Apr. 29 ....@Phoenix 110, Seattle 103
May 1 ......Seattle 122, @Phoenix 115*
May 3 ......@Seattle 116, Phoenix 92

Houston 3, Minnesota 0

Apr. 24 ....@Houston 112, Minnesota 95
Apr. 26 ....@Houston 96, Minnesota 84
Apr. 29 ....Houston 125, @Minnesota 120

L.A. Lakers 3, Portland 1

Apr. 25 ....@L.A. Lakers 95, Portland 77
Apr. 27 ....@L.A. Lakers 107, Portland 93
Apr. 30 ....@Portland 98, L.A. Lakers 90
May 2 ......L.A. Lakers 95, @Portland 91

SEMIFINALS

Utah 4, L.A. Lakers 1

May 4 ......@Utah 93, L.A. Lakers 77
May 6 ......@Utah 103, L.A. Lakers 101
May 8 ......@L.A. Lakers 104, Utah 84
May 10 ....Utah 110, @L.A. Lakers 95
May 12 ....@Utah 98, L.A. Lakers 93*

Houston 4, Seattle 3

May 5 ......@Houston 112, Seattle 102
May 7 ......Seattle 106, @Houston 101
May 9 ......Houston 97, @Seattle 93
May 11 ....Houston 110, @Seattle 106*
May 13 ....Seattle 100, @Houston 94
May 15 ....@Seattle 99, Houston 96
May 17 ....@Houston 96, Seattle 91

FINALS

Utah 4, Houston 2

May 19 ....@Utah 101, Houston 86
May 21 ....@Utah 104, Houston 92
May 23 ....@Houston 118, Utah 100
May 25 ....@Houston 95, Utah 92
May 27 ....@Utah 96, Houston 91
May 29 ....Utah 103, @Houston 100

NBA FINALS

Chicago 4, Utah 2

June 1 .....@Chicago 84, Utah 82
June 4 .....@Chicago 97, Utah 85
June 6 .....@Utah 104, Chicago 93
June 8 .....@Utah 78, Chicago 73
June 11 ...Chicago 90, @Utah 88
June 13 ...@Chicago 90, Utah 86

*Denotes number of overtime periods.

INDIVIDUAL LEADERS

SCORING (minimum 70 games or 1,400 points)

	G	FGM	FTM	Pts.	Avg.
Jordan, Chicago	82	920	480	2431	29.6
Malone, Utah	82	864	521	2249	27.4
Rice, Charlotte	79	722	464	2115	26.8
Richmond, Sacramento	81	717	457	2095	25.9
Sprewell, Golden State	80	649	493	1938	24.2
Iverson, Philadelphia	76	625	382	1787	23.5
Olajuwon, Houston	78	727	351	1810	23.2
Ewing, New York	78	655	439	1751	22.4
Gill, New Jersey	82	644	427	1789	21.8
Payton, Seattle	82	706	254	1785	21.8

FIELD GOAL PCT. (minimum 300 made)

	FGM	FGA	Pct.
Muresan, Washington	327	541	.604
Hill, Cleveland	357	595	.600
Wallace, Portland	380	681	.558
O'Neal, L.A. Lakers	552	991	.557
Mullin, Golden State	438	792	.553

THREE-POINT FIELD GOAL PCT. (minimum 82 made)

	FGM	FGA	Pct.
Rice, Charlotte	207	440	.470
Kerr, Chicago	110	237	.464
Johnson, Phoenix	89	202	.441
Dumars, Detroit	166	384	.432
Richmond, Sacramento	204	477	.428

FREE THROW PCT. (minimum 125 made)

	FTM	FTA	Pct.
Price, Golden State	155	171	.906
Brandon, Cleveland	268	297	.902
Hornacek, Utah	293	326	.899
Pierce, Denver-Charlotte	139	155	.897
Elie, Houston	207	231	.896

ASSISTS (minimum 70 games or 400 assists)

	G	No.	Avg.
Jackson, Denver-Indiana	82	935	11.4
Stockton, Utah	82	860	10.5
Johnson, Phoenix	70	653	9.3
Kidd, Dallas-Phoenix	55	496	9.0
Strickland, Washington	82	727	8.9

REBOUNDS (minimum 70 games or 800 rebounds)

	G	Off.	Def.	Tot.	Avg.
Rodman, Chicago	55	320	563	883	16.1
Mutombo, Atlanta	80	268	661	929	11.6
Mason, Charlotte	73	186	643	829	11.4
Johnson, Denver	82	231	682	913	11.1
Ewing, New York	78	175	659	834	10.7

STEALS (minimum 70 games or 125 steals)

	G	No.	Avg.
Blaylock, Atlanta	78	212	2.72
Christie, Toronto	81	201	2.48
Payton, Seattle	82	197	2.40
Jones, L.A. Lakers	80	189	2.36
Fox, Boston	76	167	2.20

BLOCKED SHOTS (minimum 70 games or 100 blocked shots)

	G	No.	Avg.
Bradley, New Jersey-Dallas	73	248	3.40
Mutombo, Atlanta	80	264	3.30
O'Neal, L.A. Lakers	51	147	2.88
Mourning, Miami	66	189	2.86
Johnson, Denver	82	227	2.77

1995-96 SEASON

Dennis Rodman

Quite simply, this was The Year of the Bull, when Chicago's team rolled across the landscape gathering crowds and converts in every city on their way to a record 72-win finish and a fourth championship.

The campaign was largely the fruit of Michael Jordan's offseason conditioning work, his drive to prove that he wasn't washed up after returning to basketball from an 18-month layoff playing minor league baseball.

The season offered many other highs, lows and in-betweens, dating from its first days, when agent David Falk forced the trade of Alonzo Mourning from Charlotte to Miami. Pat Riley had left the Knicks to take over as the coach/part owner of the Heat and made the Mourning trade his first big move on the way to 42 wins.

In another turn, Magic Johnson attempted a comeback with the Lakers, but their season ended badly amid player unrest and confusion.

Certainly one of the strangest couplings was the Bulls trading for their sworn enemy, Dennis Rodman, who prospered surprisingly under the guidance of Coach Phil Jackson. Rodman won his sixth rebounding title (14.9 rebounds per game) while giving the team what Bulls executive Jerry Krause called "the nasty factor" in the frontcourt.

During Chicago's wildly successful season, Rodman's cross-dressing, tattooed persona scored a huge hit with Chicago fans, to the point that he stopped traffic with a late-season appearance at a downtown book store in a feather boa.

The real issues, though, were settled on the court where 13 teams averaged better than 100 points per game. Jordan reclaimed his status as league scoring champ with a 30.4 average. Houston's Hakeem Olajuwon, in his last truly fine season, finished second at 26.9 points per game.

Whatever gains Eastern Conference teams made were quickly lost in a playoff haze. Chicago's pressure defense, which featured three first All-Defensive performers in Pippen, Jordan and Rodman, simply discombobulated opponents.

The Bulls swept the Heat in the first round, dit the Knicks 4-1 in the second, then rolled past Orla 4-0 in the conference finals, a loss that prompted M center Shaquille O'Neal to depart for Los Angele the offseason.

In the West, San Antonio posted 59 regular-sea wins only to stumble in the playoffs, while Hous was felled hard by injuries, and the Lakers imploc Magic Johnson criticized teammate Nick Van Exel shoving a ref. But then Magic, too, bumped a man w a whistle, and was forced to apologize. Before L.A. w ousted by Houston, Johnson publicly questioned Coa Del Harris' strategy.

The survivors were the Sonics, who rode Ga Payton through the playoffs only to run aground agai the Bulls in the league championship series.

Chicago took a 3-0 lead, then watched the Soni lash back for a pair of wins at home. The Bulls clos out their fourth championship when the series return to Chicago for Game 6.

"All we do is go out and play hard and play smart Rodman told reporters, "and everyone thinks there something special going on."

Some observers, such as Tom Heinsohn, forme Boston player and coach, offered that Chicago's bi success was due to the league's recent expansion i Canada, which left the talent pool thinned. "I think yo have to see how expansion has played a part in all th big records – even with the team I coached in '72-73,' he said. "The Lakers went 69-13 in '72, and we wen 68-14 the year after. But a couple of years before that there was expansion. (Cleveland, Buffalo and Portland came into the NBA in 1970-71.)

"Whenever you add people to the league, there's a problem. You have older guys and injured guys leaving, and there aren't enough people prepared to fill that gap."

In this case, it was a matter of standing in the way of a stampede.

NBA.COM FACT

Utah's John Stockton led the NBA in assists for the ninth consecutive season to surpass Bob Cousy's NBA-record streak.

FINAL STANDINGS

EASTERN CONFERENCE

ATLANTIC DIVISION

	W	L	Pct.
Orlando	60	22	.732
New York	47	35	.573
Miami	42	40	.512
Washington	39	43	.476
Boston	33	49	.402
New Jersey	30	52	.366
Philadelphia	18	64	.220

CENTRAL DIVISION

	W	L	Pct.
Chicago	72	10	.878
Indiana	52	30	.634
Cleveland	47	35	.573
Atlanta	46	36	.561
Detroit	46	36	.561
Charlotte	41	41	.500
Milwaukee	25	57	.305
Toronto	21	61	.256

WESTERN CONFERENCE

MIDWEST DIVISION

	W	L	Pct.
San Antonio	59	23	.720
Utah	55	27	.671
Houston	48	34	.585
Denver	35	47	.427
Dallas	26	56	.317
Minnesota	26	56	.317
Vancouver	15	67	.183

PACIFIC DIVISION

	W	L	Pct.
Seattle	64	18	.780
L.A. Lakers	53	29	.646
Portland	44	38	.537
Phoenix	41	41	.500
Sacramento	39	43	.476
Golden State	36	46	.439
L.A. Clippers	29	53	.354

PLAYOFFS

EASTERN CONFERENCE

FIRST ROUND

Chicago 3, Miami 0
Apr. 26 ....@Chicago 102, Miami 85
Apr. 28 ....@Chicago 106, Miami 75
May 1 ......Chicago 112, @Miami 91

Orlando 3, Detroit 0
Apr. 26 ....@Orlando 112, Detroit 92
Apr. 28 ....@Orlando 92, Detroit 77
Apr. 30 ....Orlando 101, @Detroit 98

Atlanta 3, Indiana 2
Apr. 25 ....Atlanta 92, @Indiana 80
Apr. 27 ....@Indiana 102, Atlanta 94*
Apr. 29 ....@Atlanta 90, Indiana 83
May 2 ......Indiana 83, @Atlanta 75
May 5 ......Atlanta 89, @Indiana 87

New York 3, Cleveland 0
Apr. 25 ....New York 106, @Cleveland 83
Apr. 27 ....New York 84, @Cleveland 80
May 1 ......@New York 81, Cleveland 76

SEMIFINALS

Chicago 4, New York 1
May 5 ......@Chicago 91, New York 84
May 7 ......@Chicago 91, New York 80
May 11 ....@New York 102, Chicago 99*
May 12 ....Chicago 94, @New York 91
May 14 ....@Chicago 94, New York 81

Orlando 4, Atlanta 1
May 8 ......@Orlando 117, Atlanta 105
May 10 ....@Orlando 120, Atlanta 94
May 12 ....Orlando 102, @Atlanta 96
May 13 ....@Atlanta 104, Orlando 99
May 15 ....@Orlando 96, Atlanta 88

FINALS

Chicago 4, Orlando 0
May 19 ....@Chicago 121, Orlando 83
May 21 ....@Chicago 93, Orlando 88
May 25 ....Chicago 86, @Orlando 67
May 27 ....Chicago 106, @Orlando 101

WESTERN CONFERENCE

FIRST ROUND

Seattle 3, Sacramento 1
Apr. 26 ....@Seattle 97, Sacramento 85
Apr. 28 ....Sacramento 90, @Seattle 81
Apr. 30 ....Seattle 96, @Sacramento 89
May 2 ......Seattle 101, @Sacramento 87

San Antonio 3, Phoenix 1
Apr. 26 ....@San Antonio 120, Phoenix 98
Apr. 28 ....@San Antonio 110, Phoenix 105
May 1 ......@Phoenix 94, San Antonio 93
May 3 ......San Antonio 116, @Phoenix 98

Utah 3, Portland 2
Apr. 25 ....@Utah 110, Portland 102
Apr. 27 ....@Utah 105, Portland 90
Apr. 29 ....@Portland 94, Utah 91*
May 1 ......@Portland 98, Utah 90
May 5 ......@Utah 102, Portland 64

Houston 3, L.A. Lakers 1
Apr. 25 ....Houston 87, @L.A. Lakers 83
Apr. 27 ....@L.A. Lakers 104, Houston 94
Apr. 30 ....@Houston 104, L.A. Lakers 98
May 2 ......@Houston 102, L.A. Lakers 94

SEMIFINALS

Seattle 4, Houston 0
May 4 ......@Seattle 108, Houston 75
May 6 ......@Seattle 105, Houston 101
May 10 ....Seattle 115, @Houston 112
May 12 ....Seattle 114, @Houston 107*

Utah 4, San Antonio 2
May 7 ......Utah 95, @San Antonio 75
May 9 ......@San Antonio 88, Utah 77
May 11 ....@Utah 105, San Antonio 75
May 12 ....@Utah 101, San Antonio 86
May 14 ....@San Antonio 98, Utah 87
May 16 ....@Utah 108, San Antonio 81

FINALS

Seattle 4, Utah 3
May 18 ....@Seattle 102, Utah 72
May 20 ....@Seattle 91, Utah 87
May 24 ....@Utah 96, Seattle 76
May 26 ....Seattle 88, @Utah 86
May 28 ....Utah 98, @Seattle 95*
May 30 ....@Utah 118, Seattle 83
June 2 .....@Seattle 90, Utah 86

NBA FINALS

Chicago 4, Seattle 2
June 5 .....@Chicago 107, Seattle 90
June 7 .....@Chicago 92, Seattle 88
June 9 .....Chicago 108, @Seattle 86
June 12 ...@Seattle 107, Chicago 86
June 14 ...@Seattle 89, Chicago 78
June 16 ...@Chicago 87, Seattle 75

*Denotes number of overtime periods.

INDIVIDUAL LEADERS

SCORING (minimum 70 games or 1,400 points)

	G	FGM	FTM	Pts.	Avg.
Jordan, Chicago	82	916	548	2491	30.4
Olajuwon, Houston	72	768	397	1936	26.9
O'Neal, Orlando	54	592	249	1434	26.6
Malone, Utah	82	789	512	2106	25.7
Robinson, San Antonio	82	711	626	2051	25.0
Barkley, Phoenix	71	580	440	1649	23.2
Mourning, Miami	70	563	488	1623	23.2
Richmond, Sacramento	81	611	425	1872	23.1
Ewing, New York	76	678	351	1711	22.5
Howard, Washington	81	733	319	1789	22.1

FIELD GOAL PCT. (minimum 300 made)

	FGM	FGA	Pct.
Muresan, Washington	466	798	.584
Gatling, Golden State-Washington	326	567	.575
O'Neal, Orlando	592	1033	.573
Mason, New York	449	798	.563
Kemp, Seattle	526	937	.561

THREE-POINT FIELD GOAL PCT. (minimum 82 made)

	FGM	FGA	Pct.
Legler, Washington	128	245	.522
Kerr, Chicago	122	237	.515
Davis, New York	127	267	.476
Armstrong, Golden State	98	207	.473
Hornacek, Utah	104	223	.466

FREE THROW PCT. (minimum 125 made)

	FTM	FTA	Pct.
Abdul-Rauf, Denver	146	157	.930
Hornacek, Utah	259	290	.893
Brandon, Cleveland	338	381	.887
Barros, Boston	130	147	.884
Price, Washington	167	191	.874

ASSISTS (minimum 70 games or 400 assists)

	G	No.	Avg.
Stockton, Utah	82	916	11.2
Kidd, Dallas	81	783	9.7
Johnson, San Antonio	82	789	9.6
Strickland, Portland	67	640	9.6
Stoudamire, Toronto	70	653	9.3

REBOUNDS (minimum 70 games or 800 rebounds)

	G	Off.	Def.	Tot.	Avg.
Rodman, Chicago	64	356	596	952	14.9
Robinson, San Antonio	82	319	681	1000	12.2
Mutombo, Denver	74	249	622	871	11.8
Barkley, Phoenix	71	243	578	821	11.6
Kemp, Seattle	79	276	628	904	11.4

STEALS (minimum 70 games or 125 steals)

	G	No.	Avg.
Payton, Seattle	81	231	2.85
Blaylock, Atlanta	81	212	2.62
Jordan, Chicago	82	180	2.60
Kidd, Dallas	81	175	2.16
Robertson, Toronto	77	166	2.16

BLOCKED SHOTS (minimum 70 games or 100 blocked shots)

	G	No.	Avg.
Mutombo, Denver	74	332	4.49
Bradley, Philadelphia-New Jersey	79	288	3.65
Robinson, San Antonio	82	271	3.30
Olajuwon, Houston	72	207	2.88
Mourning, Miami	70	189	2.70

1994-95 SEASON

Kenny Smith

The Houston Rockets entered the season as NBA champions, yet something didn't feel quite right.

Michael Jordan had retired abruptly in the fall of 1993 and the Rockets, led by Hakeem Olajuwon, went on to the NBA title in June 1994. The victory was sweet, but the Houston center and his teammates felt they didn't get the respect due a champion since they won without Jordan around. So the Rockets figured the 1994-95 season would be an opportunity to establish their dominance.

By February, though, they had slipped into a funk and seemed to have little hope of repeating as champions. That's when the franchise made the daring move of trading forward Otis Thorpe, a key starter on their 1994 team, to get Clyde Drexler from Portland.

The Rockets needed a revived running game and the 6-7 Drexler was a strong finisher who had played at the University of Houston with Olajuwon.

In mid-March, Jordan announced his sudden return to the game after nearly two seasons away, part of which he spent playing minor league baseball. "I'm back," he said.

The story created intense media interest in his reappearance in a Bulls uniform, with No. 45 on his new jersey (his old No. 23 had been retired), for the final 17 games of the regular season. The Bulls had struggled to stay above .500 through most of the season, and his presence provided an obvious lift for Chicago. Still, the Bulls earned only a fifth seed in the Eastern Conference.

In the first round, Chicago eliminated the Charlotte Hornets but Jordan struggled in the next series against Orlando with Shaquille O'Neal, Anfernee Hardaway and Horace Grant. In Game 1 in Orlando Jordan committed two late turnovers that cost the Bulls the game. From there he missed shots, made miscues and watched Grant's play shift the balance in the series. At one point Jordan donned his old No. 23 to inspire a second victory, but the Magic took over from there to claim the series in six games.

Orlando then eliminated the Indiana Pacers in seven games in the Eastern Conference Finals.

Who should be there waiting but Olajuwon and his Rockets, who had made a magical playoff run of their own.

In the first round of the playoffs, the Utah Jazz took a 2-1 lead over Houston, but the Rockets managed to tie it with a key home triumph as Drexler scored 41 and Olajuwon 40. Houston then rallied in the fourth quarter to win Game 5 in Salt Lake City.

The Rockets moved on to the Western Conference Semifinals and dispatched Charles Barkley and the Phoenix Suns in similar wrenching fashion. Phoenix took a 3-1 series lead, but Houston again fought back and went on to take the final three games of the series including a 115-114 victory in Game 7 that had Olajuwon claiming, "This is a team of destiny."

Next up were David Robinson's Spurs who reached the conference finals for the first time in club history. Robinson had turned in an outstanding season and was voted the league MVP, yet the Spurs lost to the Rockets in a six-game series in which only one home team (Houston in Game 6) won a game.

The Magic had home-court advantage in the championship round, the benefit of their 57 regular-season triumphs. Orlando bullied its way to a 57-37 second quarter lead in Game 1 before Houston's Kenny Smith found his range and set a Finals record with seven three-pointers. After Nick Anderson missed four free throws late in regulation that would have won the game for Orlando, the Magic lost in overtime 120-118. Houston went on to a 4-0 sweep and became the first team to win four series without the home court advantage and defeat four 50-win teams.

NBA.COM FACT

Chicago's Steve Kerr made 89 of 170 three-point attempts for a record-setting .524 percentage. He shot only slightly better (.529) inside the arc.

FINAL STANDINGS

EASTERN CONFERENCE

ATLANTIC DIVISION

	W	L	Pct.
Orlando	57	25	.695
New York	55	27	.671
Boston	35	47	.427
Miami	32	50	.390
New Jersey	30	52	.366
Philadelphia	24	58	.293
Washington	21	61	.256

CENTRAL DIVISION

	W	L	Pct.
Indiana	52	30	.634
Charlotte	50	32	.610
Chicago	47	35	.573
Cleveland	43	39	.524
Atlanta	42	40	.512
Milwaukee	34	48	.415
Detroit	28	54	.341

WESTERN CONFERENCE

MIDWEST DIVISION

	W	L	Pct.
San Antonio	62	20	.756
Utah	60	22	.732
Houston	47	35	.573
Denver	41	41	.500
Dallas	36	46	.439
Minnesota	21	61	.256

PACIFIC DIVISION

	W	L	Pct.
Phoenix	59	23	.720
Seattle	57	25	.695
L.A. Lakers	48	34	.585
Portland	44	38	.537
Sacramento	39	43	.476
Golden State	26	56	.317
L.A. Clippers	17	65	.207

PLAYOFFS

EASTERN CONFERENCE

FIRST ROUND

Orlando 3, Boston 1
Apr. 28 ....@Orlando 124, Boston 77
Apr. 30 ....Boston 99, @Orlando 92
May 3 ......Orlando 82, @Boston 77
May 5 ......Orlando 95, @Boston 92

Indiana 3, Atlanta 0
Apr. 27 ....@Indiana 90, Atlanta 82
Apr. 29 ....@Indiana 105, Atlanta 97
May 2 ......Indiana 105, @Atlanta 89

New York 3, Cleveland 1
Apr. 27 ....@New York 103, Cleveland 79
Apr. 29 ....Cleveland 90, @New York 84
May 1 ......New York 83, @Cleveland 81
May 4 ......New York 93, @Cleveland 80

Chicago 3, Charlotte 1
Apr. 28 ....Chicago 108, @Charlotte 100*
Apr. 30 ....@Charlotte 106, Chicago 89
May 2 ......@Chicago 103, Charlotte 80
May 4 ......@Chicago 85, Charlotte 84

SEMIFINALS

Indiana 4, New York 3
May 7 ......Indiana 107, @New York 105
May 9 ......@New York 96, Indiana 77
May 11 ....@Indiana 97*, New York 95
May 13 ....@Indiana 98, New York 84
May 17 ....@New York 96, Indiana 95
May 19 ....New York 92, @Indiana 82
May 21 ....Indiana 97, @New York 95

Orlando 4, Chicago 2
May 7 ......@Orlando 94, Chicago 91
May 10 ....Chicago 104, @Orlando 94
May 12 ....Orlando 110, @Chicago 101
May 14 ....@Chicago 106, Orlando 95
May 16 ....@Orlando 103, Chicago 95
May 18 ....Orlando 108, @Chicago 102

FINALS

Orlando 4, Indiana 3
May 23 ....@Orlando 105, Indiana 101
May 25 ....@Orlando 119, Indiana 114
May 27 ....@Indiana 105, Orlando 100
May 29 ....@Indiana 94, Orlando 93
May 31 ....@Orlando 108, Indiana 106
June 2 .....@Indiana 123, Orlando 96
June 4 .....@Orlando 105, Indiana 81

WESTERN CONFERENCE

FIRST ROUND

San Antonio 3, Denver 0
Apr. 28 ....@San Antonio 104, Denver 88
Apr. 30 ....@San Antonio 122, Denver 96
May 2 ......San Antonio 99, @Denver 95

Phoenix 3, Portland 0
Apr. 28 ....@Phoenix 129, Portland 102
Apr. 30 ....@Phoenix 103, Portland 94
May 2 ......Phoenix 117, @Portland 109

Houston 3, Utah 2
Apr. 27 ....@Utah 102, Houston 100
Apr. 29 ....Houston 140, @Utah 126
May 3 ......Utah 95, @Houston 82
May 5 ......@Houston 123, Utah 106
May 7 ......Houston 95, @Utah 91

L.A. Lakers 3, Seattle 1
Apr. 27 ....@Seattle 96, L.A. Lakers 71
Apr. 29 ....L.A. Lakers 84, @Seattle 82
May 1 ......@L.A. Lakers 105, Seattle 101
May 4 ......@L.A. Lakers 114, Seattle 110

SEMIFINALS

San Antonio 4, L.A. Lakers 2
May 6 ......@San Antonio 110, L.A. Lakers 94
May 8 ......@San Antonio 97, L.A. Lakers 90*
May 12 ....@L.A. Lakers 92, San Antonio 85
May 14 ....San Antonio 80, @L.A. Lakers 71
May 16 ....L.A. Lakers 98, @San Antonio 96*
May 18 ....San Antonio 100, @L.A. Lakers 88

Houston 4, Phoenix 3
May 9 ......@Phoenix 130, Houston 108
May 11 ....@Phoenix 118, Houston 94
May 13 ....@Houston 118, Phoenix 85
May 14 ....Phoenix 114, @Houston 110
May 16 ....Houston 103, @Phoenix 97*
May 18 ....@Houston 116, Phoenix 103
May 20 ....Houston 115, @Phoenix 114

FINALS

Houston 4, San Antonio 2
May 22 ....Houston 94, @San Antonio 93
May 24 ....Houston 106, @San Antonio 96
May 26 ....San Antonio 107, @Houston 102
May 28 ....San Antonio 103, @Houston 81
May 30 ....Houston 111, @San Antonio 90
June 1 .....@Houston 100, San Antonio 95

NBA FINALS

Houston 4, Orlando 0
June 7 .....Houston 120, @Orlando 118*
June 9 .....Houston 117, @Orlando 106
June 11 ...@Houston 106, Orlando 103
June 14 ...@Houston 113, Orlando 101

*Denotes number of overtime periods.

INDIVIDUAL LEADERS

SCORING (minimum 70 games or 1,400 points)

	G	FGM	FTM	Pts.	Avg.
O'Neal, Orlando	79	930	455	2315	29.3
Olajuwon, Houston	72	798	406	2005	27.8
Robinson, San Antonio	81	788	656	2238	27.6
Malone, Utah	82	830	516	2187	26.7
Mashburn, Dallas	80	683	447	1926	24.1
Ewing, New York	79	730	420	1886	23.9
Barkley, Phoenix	68	554	379	1561	23.0
Richmond, Sacramento	82	668	375	1867	22.8
Rice, Miami	82	667	312	1831	22.3
Robinson, Milwaukee	80	636	397	1755	21.9

FIELD GOAL PCT. (minimum 300 made)

	FGM	FGA	Pct.
Gatling, Golden State	324	512	.633
O'Neal, Orlando	930	1594	.583
Grant, Orlando	401	707	.567
Thorpe, Houston-Portland	385	681	.565
Davis, Indiana	324	576	.563

THREE-POINT FIELD GOAL PCT. (minimum 82 made)

	FGM	FGA	Pct.
Kerr, Chicago	89	170	.524
Schrempf, Seattle	93	181	.514
Barros, Philadelphia	197	425	.464
Davis, New York	131	288	.455
Stockton, Utah	102	227	.449

FREE THROW PCT. (minimum 125 made)

	FTM	FTA	Pct.
Webb, Sacramento	226	242	.934
Price, Cleveland	148	162	.914
Barros, Philadelphia	347	386	.899
Miller, Indiana	383	427	.897
Bogues, Charlotte	160	180	.889

ASSISTS (minimum 70 games or 400 assists)

	G	No.	Avg.
Stockton, Utah	82	1011	12.3
Anderson, New Jersey	72	680	9.4
Hardaway, Golden State	62	578	9.3
Strickland, Portland	64	562	8.8
Bogues, Charlotte	78	675	8.7

REBOUNDS (minimum 70 games or 800 rebounds)

	G	Off.	Def.	Tot.	Avg.
Rodman, San Antonio	49	274	549	823	16.8
Mutombo, Denver	82	319	710	1029	12.5
O'Neal, Orlando	79	328	573	901	11.4
Ewing, New York	79	157	710	867	11.0
Kemp, Seattle	82	318	575	893	10.9

STEALS (minimum 70 games or 125 steals)

	G	No.	Avg.
Pippen, Chicago	79	232	2.94
Blaylock, Atlanta	80	200	2.50
Payton, Seattle	82	204	2.49
Stockton, Utah	82	194	2.37
McMillan, Seattle	80	165	2.06

BLOCKED SHOTS (minimum 70 games or 100 blocked shots)

	G	No.	Avg.
Mutombo, Denver	82	321	3.91
Olajuwon, Houston	72	242	3.36
Bradley, Philadelphia	82	274	3.34
Robinson, San Antonio	81	262	3.23
Mourning, Charlotte	77	225	2.92

1993-94 SEASON

Hakeem Olajuwon

NBA.COM FACT

Minnesota guard Micheal Williams missed a free throw on November 9, 1993, but only after he had made 97 consecutive shots from the foul line, an NBA record.

His team had just won three straight championships and he had just claimed his seventh consecutive scoring title. At age 30, that seemed like enough for Michael Jordan.

Staggered by his father's murder during the 1993 offseason, the Chicago Bulls' star shockingly announced his retirement on October 6, on the eve of training camp.

His mother, traveling in Africa on a goodwill mission was stunned by the news, as was the entire NBA. Jordan soon found his way into baseball, and pro basketball was suddenly struck with a sense of opportunity. He had lorded over the playoffs, winning three straight Finals MVP awards, but now it would be someone else's turn. In their eagerness to show they were worthy, seven teams went on to win at least 55 games during the regular season, led by Seattle which had come within one victory of reaching the 1993 NBA Finals. The SuperSonics won 63 games to lead the West, while Houston, led by NBA Most Valuable Player Hakeem Olajuwon, won 58.

In the East, a pair of defensive stalwarts, New York and Atlanta, won 57 games apiece, while the Jordan-less Chicago Bulls did surprisingly well, winning 55. Phoenix, which battled through injuries to Charles Barkley and Kevin Johnson, won 56 games, and San Antonio, with David Robinson enjoying his best season, won 55.

With Jordan's absence the playoffs presented a strange feel, it was emphasized when a young Denver squad achieved the improbable, becoming the first No. 8 seed to defeat a No. 1 seed when it came back from a 2-0 deficit and ousted Seattle in the first round.

Houston disposed of Portland easily, came back from a 2-0 deficit to beat Phoenix in seven games, and beat Utah in five games to advance to the NBA Finals for the first time since 1986.

Pat Riley's New York club, which took the hard road all season with its grinding defense, dismissed New Jersey in four games, then survived a pair of seven-game series against Chicago and Indiana to reach the Finals for the first time since 1973.

Olajuwon responded to the Knicks' gritty challenge, winning his private duel with Patrick Ewing and scoring 26.9 ppg in a series when Houston's other players managed only 59.3 ppg. He also averaged 9.1 rebounds, 3.6 assists and 3.86 blocked shots.

The Knicks found themselves in what would become their third straight seven-game series of the playoffs, and they responded by taking a 3-2 Finals lead with a Game 5 victory in Madison Square Garden. The momentum swung, however, with Houston's 86-84 victory in Game 6, preserved when Olajuwon blocked a last-second three-point attempt by John Starks.

The Rockets then won Game 7 at home 90-84 to close out the Finals.

"Now that Michael has left, Hakeem is the most complete player in the game — there's no doubt in my mind," Cleveland center Brad Daugherty said. "He's 31 years old, an age when you're considered to be on the downside of your career, but he's just exploded into the greatest player in the league."

Olajuwon had long been the NBA's most underrated superstar, quietly flourishing in the background while charismatic stars such as Jordan, Larry Bird, Magic Johnson, Isiah Thomas and Charles Barkley captured the spotlight. Olajuwon made it to the NBA Finals in his second NBA season in 1986, but didn't make it back to the NBA's premier stage until 1994 when he capped his MVP season by bringing the city of Houston its first major-league championship in any sport.

For the effort Olajuwon added a championship ring and the NBA Finals MVP Award to his regular-season MVP trophy.

FINAL STANDINGS

EASTERN CONFERENCE

ATLANTIC DIVISION

	W	L	Pct.
New York	57	25	.695
Orlando	50	32	.610
New Jersey	45	37	.549
Miami	42	40	.512
Boston	32	50	.390
Philadelphia	25	57	.305
Washington	24	58	.293

CENTRAL DIVISION

	W	L	Pct.
Atlanta	57	25	.695
Chicago	55	27	.671
Cleveland	47	35	.573
Indiana	47	35	.573
Charlotte	41	41	.500
Detroit	20	62	.244
Milwaukee	20	62	.244

WESTERN CONFERENCE

MIDWEST DIVISION

	W	L	Pct.
Houston	58	24	.707
San Antonio	55	27	.671
Utah	53	29	.646
Denver	42	40	.512
Minnesota	20	62	.244
Dallas	13	69	.159

PACIFIC DIVISION

	W	L	Pct.
Seattle	63	19	.768
Phoenix	56	26	.683
Golden State	50	32	.610
Portland	47	35	.573
L.A. Lakers	33	49	.402
Sacramento	28	54	.341
L.A. Clippers	27	55	.329

PLAYOFFS

EASTERN CONFERENCE

FIRST ROUND

Atlanta 3, Miami 2
- Apr. 28 ....Miami 93, @Atlanta 88
- Apr. 30 ....@Atlanta 104, Miami 86
- May 3 ......@Miami 90, Atlanta 86
- May 5 ......Atlanta 103, @Miami 89
- May 8 ......@Atlanta 102, Miami 91

New York 3, New Jersey 1
- Apr. 29 ....@New York 91, New Jersey 80
- May 1 ......@New York 90, New Jersey 81
- May 4 ......@New Jersey 93, New York 92*
- May 6 ......New York 102, @New Jersey 92

Chicago 3, Cleveland 0
- Apr. 29 ....@Chicago 104, Cleveland 96
- May 1 ......@Chicago 105, Cleveland 96
- May 3 ......Chicago 95, @Cleveland 92*

Indiana 3, Orlando 0
- Apr. 28 ....Indiana 89, @Orlando 88
- Apr. 30 ....Indiana 103, @Orlando 101
- May 2 ......@Indiana 99, Orlando 86

SEMIFINALS

New York 4, Chicago 3
- May 8 ......@New York 90, Chicago 86
- May 11 ....@New York 96, Chicago 91
- May 13 ....@Chicago 104, New York 102
- May 15 ....@Chicago 95, New York 83
- May 18 ....@New York 87, Chicago 86
- May 20 ....@Chicago 93, New York 79
- May 22 ....@New York 87, Chicago 77

Indiana 4, Atlanta 2
- May 10 ....Indiana 96, @Atlanta 85
- May 12 ....@Atlanta 92, Indiana 69
- May 14 ....@Indiana 101, Atlanta 81
- May 15 ....@Indiana 102, Atlanta 86
- May 17 ....@Atlanta 88, Indiana 76
- May 19 ....@Indiana 98, Atlanta 79

FINALS

New York 4, Indiana 3
- May 24 ....@New York 100, Indiana 89
- May 26 ....@New York 89, Indiana 78
- May 28 ....@Indiana 88, New York 68
- May 30 ....@Indiana 83, New York 77
- June 1 .....Indiana 93, @New York 86
- June 3 .....New York 98, @Indiana 91
- June 5 .....@New York 94, Indiana 90

*Denotes number of overtime periods.

WESTERN CONFERENCE

FIRST ROUND

Denver 3, Seattle 2
- Apr. 28 ....@Seattle 106, Denver 82
- Apr. 30 ....@Seattle 97, Denver 87
- May 2 ......@Denver 110, Seattle 93
- May 5 ......@Denver 94, Seattle 85*
- May 7 ......Denver 98, @Seattle 94*

Houston 3, Portland 1
- Apr. 29 ....@Houston 114, Portland 104
- May 1 ......@Houston 115, Portland 104
- May 3 ......@Portland 118, Houston 115
- May 6 ......Houston 92, @Portland 89

Phoenix 3, Golden State 0
- Apr. 29 ....@Phoenix 111, Golden State 104
- May 1 ......@Phoenix 117, Golden State 111
- May 4 ......Phoenix 140, @Golden State 133

Utah 3, San Antonio 1
- Apr. 28 ....@San Antonio 106, Utah 89
- Apr. 30 ....Utah 96, @San Antonio 84
- May 3 ......@Utah 105, San Antonio 72
- May 5 ......@Utah 95, San Antonio 90

SEMIFINALS

Houston 4, Phoenix 3
- May 8 ......Phoenix 91, @Houston 87
- May 11 ....Phoenix 124, @Houston 117*
- May 13 ....Houston 118, @Phoenix 102
- May 15 ....Houston 107, @Phoenix 96
- May 17 ....@Houston 109, Phoenix 86
- May 19 ....@Phoenix 103, Houston 89
- May 21 ....@Houston 104, Phoenix 94

Utah 4, Denver 3
- May 10 ....@Utah 100, Denver 91
- May 12 ....@Utah 104, Denver 94
- May 14 ....Utah 111, @Denver 109*
- May 15 ....@Denver 83, Utah 82
- May 17 ....Denver 109, @Utah 101**
- May 19 ....@Denver 94, Utah 91
- May 21 ....@Utah 91, Denver 81

FINALS

Houston 4, Utah 1
- May 23 ....@Houston 100, Utah 88
- May 25 ....@Houston 104, Utah 99
- May 27 ....@Utah 95, Houston 86
- May 29 ....Houston 80, @Utah 78
- May 31 ....@Houston 94, Utah 83

NBA FINALS

Houston 4, New York 3
- June 8 .....@Houston 85, New York 78
- June 10 ...New York 91, @Houston 83
- June 12 ...Houston 93, @New York 89
- June 15 ...@New York 91, Houston 82
- June 17 ...@New York 91, Houston 84
- June 19 ...@Houston 86, New York 84
- June 22 ...@Houston 90, New York 84

INDIVIDUAL LEADERS

SCORING (minimum 70 games or 1,400 points)

	G	FGM	FTM	Pts.	Avg.
Robinson, San Antonio	80	840	693	2383	29.8
O'Neal, Orlando	81	953	471	2377	29.3
Olajuwon, Houston	80	894	388	2184	27.3
Wilkins, Atl.-L.A. Clip.	74	698	442	1923	26.0
Malone, Utah	82	772	511	2063	25.2
Ewing, New York	79	745	445	1939	24.5
Richmond, Sacramento	78	635	426	1823	23.4
Pippen, Chicago	72	627	270	1587	22.0
Barkley, Phoenix	65	518	318	1402	21.6
Rice, Miami	81	663	250	1708	21.1

FIELD GOAL PCT. (minimum 300 made)

	FGM	FGA	Pct.
O'Neal, Orlando	953	1591	.599
Mutombo, Denver	365	642	.569
Thorpe, Houston	449	801	.561
Webber, Golden State	572	1037	.552
Kemp, Seattle	533	990	.538

THREE-POINT FIELD GOAL PCT. (minimum 50 made)

	FGA	FGM	Pct.
Murray, Portland	109	50	.459
Armstrong, Chicago	135	60	.444
Miller, Indiana	292	123	.421
Kerr, Chicago	124	52	.419
Skiles, Orlando	165	68	.412

FREE THROW PCT. (minimum 125 made)

	FTM	FTA	Pct.
Abdul-Rauf, Denver	219	229	.956
Miller, Indiana	403	444	.908
Pierce, Seattle	189	211	.896
Threatt, L.A. Lakers	138	155	.890
Price, Cleveland	238	268	.888

ASSISTS (minimum 70 games or 400 assists)

	G	No.	Avg.
Stockton, Utah	82	1031	12.6
Bogues, Charlotte	77	780	10.1
Blaylock, Atlanta	81	789	9.7
Anderson, New Jersey	82	784	9.6
Johnson, Phoenix	67	637	9.5

REBOUNDS (minimum 70 games or 800 rebounds)

	G	Off.	Def.	Tot.	Avg.
Rodman, San Antonio	79	453	914	1367	17.3
O'Neal, Orlando	81	384	688	1072	13.2
Willis, Atlanta	80	335	628	963	12.0
Olajuwon, Houston	80	229	726	955	11.9
Polynice, Detroit-Sac.	68	299	510	809	11.9

STEALS (minimum 70 games or 125 steals)

	G	No.	Avg.
McMillan, Seattle	73	216	2.96
Pippen, Chicago	72	211	2.93
Blaylock, Atlanta	81	212	2.62
Stockton, Utah	82	199	2.43
Murdock, Milwaukee	82	197	2.40

BLOCKED SHOTS (minimum 70 games or 100 blocked shots)

	G	No.	Avg.
Mutombo, Denver	82	336	4.10
Olajuwon, Houston	80	297	3.71
Robinson, San Antonio	80	265	3.31
Mourning, Charlotte	60	188	3.13
Bradley, Philadelphia	49	147	3.00

1992-93 SEASON

Dominique Wilkins

NBA.COM FACT

The Bulls became only the third franchise (after the Minneapolis Lakers and Boston Celtics) to win as many as three consecutive NBA titles.

Michael Jordan and Scottie Pippen played for the the Dream Team in the 1992 Olympic Games at Barcelona and despite the United States' easy road to the gold medal that August, they came home thoroughly exhausted.

With his stars having run through two championship seasons and the Olympics, Phil Jackson backed off from the Bulls' trademark pressure defense. But Jordan called an on-court conference and told his teammates to resume the pressure. "Maybe we gamble and we lose our legs," Jordan later explained. "I still don't think we get conservative now. When we try to slow down things get too deliberate."

The season, Jordan said, was "monotony." For the Bulls that meant another division championship, 57 victories (their fourth straight 50-win season) and a seventh straight scoring crown for Jordan (32.6 points per game), tying him with Wilt Chamberlain.

On January 8, Jordan surpassed 20,000 career points after just 620 games. Only Chamberlain got to that milestone faster, taking 499 games. "It looks like I fell short of Wilt again, which is a privilege," Jordan said.

Behind him in the scoring race was Atlanta's Dominique Wilkins at 29.9 points per game, while Utah's John Stockton again led the league in assists (12.0 per game) and Detroit's Dennis Rodman secured yet another rebounding title (18.3 per game).

For two years, the Knicks and Patrick Ewing had their championship hopes end in playoff battles with the Bulls. So Coach Pat Riley used the full force of his considerable intensity to drive New York to 60 victories and the home-court advantage in the East.

Once in the playoffs, the Bulls and Knicks easily advanced to the Eastern Conference Finals, where they split the first four games. "My favorite Michael move came from that series, where he went baseline, and [Charles] Oakley cut the baseline off," Pippen recalled. "Michael kind of turned his back to him, then he did a spin back and was able to get by him and dunk on Patrick. That was probably the most dominating move I've ever seen, to be able just to break that whole defense down like that."

Jordan scored 54 points to drive Chicago to a 105-95 triumph in Game 4, and it was Jordan's triple-double (29 points, 10 rebounds and 14 assists) that dominated the statistics column in Game 5, when Chicago took the series lead 3-2. But it was Pippen's successive blocks of putback attempts by New York's Charles Smith in the final minute that closed off the Knicks' hopes. Then, when the Bulls closed out the series in Chicago, it was Pippen again doing the final damage, a corner jumper and a trey in a 96-88 victory.

The Bulls had persevered to return to their third straight NBA Finals, this time to meet the Phoenix Suns who had traded for Charles Barkley and won a league-best 62 games, many of them in brand new America West Arena.

Under rookie coach Paul Westphal, Phoenix had survived a first-round scare against the Lakers, then defeated San Antonio and followed that by taking Seattle in seven games in the Western Conference Finals.

The Bulls claimed the first two games in Phoenix, but the Suns outlasted Jordan and Co. in triple overtime in Game 3 in Chicago Stadium. Chicago won Game 4 (the only time a home team won a game in the series), then lost Game 5, which left Jordan furious that his team had to board a plane for Game 6 in Phoenix. There a tight game came down to John Paxson's three-pointer with 3.9 seconds on the clock as the Bulls pulled out a 99-98 victory.

"I knew it was in as soon as Pax shot it," Jordan said.

"It was like a dream come true," Paxson said.

FINAL STANDINGS

EASTERN CONFERENCE

ATLANTIC DIVISION

	W	L	Pct.
New York	60	22	.732
Boston	48	34	.585
New Jersey	43	39	.524
Orlando	41	41	.500
Miami	36	46	.439
Philadelphia	26	56	.317
Washington	22	60	.268

CENTRAL DIVISION

	W	L	Pct.
Chicago	57	25	.695
Cleveland	54	28	.659
Charlotte	44	38	.537
Atlanta	43	39	.524
Indiana	41	41	.500
Detroit	40	42	.488
Milwaukee	28	54	.341

WESTERN CONFERENCE

MIDWEST DIVISION

	W	L	Pct.
Houston	55	27	.671
San Antonio	49	33	.598
Utah	47	35	.573
Denver	36	46	.439
Minnesota	19	63	.232
Dallas	11	71	.134

PACIFIC DIVISION

	W	L	Pct.
Phoenix	62	20	.756
Seattle	55	27	.671
Portland	51	31	.622
L.A. Clippers	41	41	.500
L.A. Lakers	39	43	.476
Golden State	34	48	.415
Sacramento	25	57	.305

PLAYOFFS

EASTERN CONFERENCE

FIRST ROUND

New York 3, Indiana 1

Apr. 30 ....@New York 107, Indiana 104
May 2 ......@New York 101, Indiana 91
May 4 ......@Indiana 116, New York 93
May 6 ......New York 109, @Indiana 100*

Chicago 3, Atlanta 0

Apr. 30 ....@Chicago 114, Atlanta 90
May 2 ......@Chicago 117, Atlanta 102
May 4 ......Chicago 98, @Atlanta 88

Cleveland 3, New Jersey 2

Apr. 29 ....@Cleveland 114, New Jersey 98
May 1 ......New Jersey 101, @Cleveland 99
May 5 ......Cleveland 93, @New Jersey 84
May 7 ......@New Jersey 96, Cleveland 79
May 9 ......@Cleveland 99, New Jersey 89

Charlotte 3, Boston 1

Apr. 29 ....@Boston 112, Charlotte 101
May 1 ......Charlotte 99, @Boston 98**
May 3 ......@Charlotte 119, Boston 89
May 5 ......@Charlotte 104, Boston 103

SEMIFINALS

New York 4, Charlotte 1

May 9 ......@New York 111, Charlotte 95
May 12 ....@New York 105, Charlotte 101*
May 14 ....@Charlotte 110, New York 106**
May 16 ....New York 94, @Charlotte 92
May 18 ....@New York 105, Charlotte 101

Chicago 4, Cleveland 0

May 11 ....@Chicago 91, Cleveland 84
May 13 ....@Chicago 104, Cleveland 85
May 15 ....Chicago 96, @Cleveland 90
May 17 ....Chicago 103, @Cleveland 101

FINALS

Chicago 4, New York 2

May 23 ....@New York 98, Chicago 90
May 25 ....@New York 96, Chicago 91
May 29 ....@Chicago 103, New York 83
May 31 ....@Chicago 105, New York 95
June 2 .....Chicago 97, @New York 94
June 4 .....@Chicago 96, New York 88

*Denotes number of overtime periods

WESTERN CONFERENCE

FIRST ROUND

Phoenix 3, L.A. Lakers 2

Apr. 30 ....L.A. Lakers 107, @Phoenix 103
May 2 ......L.A. Lakers 86, @Phoenix 81
May 4 ......Phoenix 107, @L.A. Lakers 102
May 6 ......Phoenix 101, @L.A. Lakers 86
May 9 ......@Phoenix 112, L.A. Lakers 104*

Houston 3, L.A. Clippers 2

Apr. 29 ....@Houston 117, L.A. Clippers 94
May 1 ......L.A. Clippers 95, @Houston 83
May 3 ......Houston 111, @L.A. Clippers 99
May 5 ......@L.A. Clippers 93, Houston 90
May 8 ......@Houston 84, L.A. Clippers 80

Seattle 3, Utah 2

Apr. 30 ....@Seattle 99, Utah 85
May 2 ......Utah 89, @Seattle 85
May 4 ......@Utah 90, Seattle 80
May 6 ......Seattle 93, @Utah 80
May 8 ......@Seattle 100, Utah 92

San Antonio 3, Portland 1

Apr. 29 ....San Antonio 87, @Portland 86
May 1 ......@Portland 105, San Antonio 96
May 5 ......@San Antonio 107, Portland 101
May 7 ......@San Antonio 100, Portland 97*

SEMIFINALS

Phoenix 4, San Antonio 2

May 11 ....@Phoenix 98, San Antonio 89
May 13 ....@Phoenix 109, San Antonio 103
May 15 ....@San Antonio 111, Phoenix 96
May 16 ....@San Antonio 117, Phoenix 103
May 18 ....@Phoenix 109, San Antonio 97
May 20 ....Phoenix 102, @San Antonio 100

Seattle 4, Houston 3

May 10 ....@Seattle 99, Houston 90
May 12 ....@Seattle 111, Houston 100
May 15 ....@Houston 97, Seattle 79
May 16 ....@Houston 103, Seattle 92
May 18 ....@Seattle 120, Houston 95
May 20 ....@Houston 103, Seattle 90
May 22 ....@Seattle 103, Houston 100*

FINALS

Phoenix 4, Seattle 3

May 24 ....@Phoenix 105, Seattle 91
May 26 ....Seattle 103, @Phoenix 99
May 28 ....Phoenix 104, @Seattle 97
May 30 ....@Seattle 120, Phoenix 101
June 1 .....@Phoenix 120, Seattle 114
June 3 .....@Seattle 118, Phoenix 102
June 5 .....@Phoenix 123, Seattle 110

NBA FINALS

Chicago 4, Phoenix 2

June 9 .....Chicago 100, @Phoenix 92
June 11 ...Chicago 111, @Phoenix 108
June 13 ...Phoenix 129, @Chicago 121***
June 16 ...@Chicago 111, Phoenix 105
June 18 ...Phoenix 108, @Chicago 98
June 20 ...Chicago 99, @Phoenix 98

INDIVIDUAL LEADERS

SCORING (minimum 70 games or 1,400 points)

	G	FGM	FTM	Pts.	Avg.
Jordan, Chicago	78	992	476	2541	32.6
Wilkins, Atlanta	71	741	519	2121	29.9
Malone, Utah	82	797	619	2217	27.0
Olajuwon, Houston	82	848	444	2140	26.1
Barkley, Phoenix	76	716	445	1944	25.6
Ewing, New York	81	779	400	1959	24.2
Dumars, Detroit	77	677	343	1809	23.5
O'Neal, Orlando	81	733	427	1893	23.4
Robinson, San Antonio	82	676	561	1916	23.4
Manning, L.A. Clippers	79	702	388	1800	22.8

FIELD GOAL PCT. (minimum 300 made)

	FGM	FGA	Pct.
Ceballos, Phoenix	381	662	.576
Daugherty, Cleveland	520	911	.571
Davis, Indiana	304	535	.568
O'Neal, Orlando	733	1304	.562
Thorpe, Houston	385	690	.558

THREE-POINT FIELD GOAL PCT. (minimum 50 made)

	FGA	FGM	Pct.
Armstrong, Chicago	139	63	.453
Mullin, Golden State	133	60	.451
Petrovic, New Jersey	167	75	.449
Smith, Houston	219	96	.438
Les, Sacramento	154	66	.429

FREE THROW PCT. (minimum 125 made)

	FTM	FTA	Pct.
Price, Cleveland	289	305	.948
Abdul-Rauf, Denver	217	232	.935
Johnson, Seattle	234	257	.911
Williams, Minnesota	419	462	.907
Skiles, Orlando	289	324	.892

ASSISTS (minimum 70 games or 400 assists)

	G	No.	Avg.
Stockton, Utah	82	987	12.0
Hardaway, Golden State	66	699	10.6
Skiles, Orlando	78	735	9.4
Jackson, L.A. Clippers	82	724	8.8
Bogues, Charlotte	81	711	8.8

REBOUNDS (minimum 70 games or 800 rebounds)

	G	Off.	Def.	Tot.	Avg.
Rodman, Detroit	62	367	765	1132	18.3
O'Neal, Orlando	81	342	780	1122	13.9
Mutombo, Denver	82	344	726	1070	13.0
Olajuwon, Houston	82	283	785	1068	13.0
Willis, Atlanta	80	335	693	1028	12.9

STEALS (minimum 70 games or 125 steals)

	G	No.	Avg.
Jordan, Chicago	78	221	2.83
Blaylock, Atlanta	80	203	2.54
Stockton, Utah	82	199	2.43
McMillan, Seattle	73	173	2.37
Robertson, Milwaukee-Detroit	69	155	2.25

BLOCKED SHOTS (minimum 70 games or 100 blocked shots)

	G	No.	Avg.
Olajuwon, Houston	82	342	4.17
O'Neal, Orlando	81	286	3.53
Mutombo, Denver	82	287	3.50
Mourning, Charlotte	78	271	3.47
Robinson, San Antonio	82	264	3.22

1991-92 SEASON

Mark Price

NBA.COM FACT

In the highest-scoring contest in playoff history, Portland defeated Phoenix 153-151 in double overtime to win Game 4 of the Western Conference Semifinals on May 11, 1992.

Kobe Bryant was a 13-year-old living in Europe when he heard the news. Magic Johnson was retiring from basketball. Bryant didn't understand why, but he cried anyway and hardly ate for a week. Johnson was his hero.

Fans everywhere had similar reactions to Johnson's revelation in October 1991 that he had contracted the human immunodeficiency virus (HIV), which causes AIDS. Johnson announced that he would retire immediately from the NBA and devote his time to educating the public about HIV and AIDS.

He would later attempt two comebacks, but in essence his 12-year NBA career, which included five titles and three MVP seasons, was over. The season would also prove to be the last for Larry Bird, who played through back pain to appear in 45 games, averaging 20.2 points.

The Bulls, meanwhile, showed their determination to win a second straight championship by rolling to a club-record 67 victories. Jordan won his third MVP award and sixth straight scoring title (though his average of 30.1 points was his lowest in six seasons). More than ever, Jordan worked to include teammates Scottie Pippen (21 ppg) and Horace Grant (14.2 ppg, 10 rpg).

Cleveland, with All-Stars Mark Price and Brad Daugherty, won 57 games to tie Portland for the league's second-best record. The Cavaliers played well all season but had no answer for Jordan and succumbed in six games in the Eastern Conference Finals.

Portland, hungry to get back to the Finals after a disappointing playoffs in 1991, defeated the Lakers, Phoenix and tough Utah, which had All-Stars John Stockton and Karl Malone, to gain a Finals berth for the second time in three seasons.

The Trail Blazers managed a split on the road in the first two games but Chicago took two of three in Portland and returned home with a huge advantage. Many observers expected an easy triumph for the Bulls in Game 6, but after three quarters the Trail Blazers led 79-64 and seemed ready to push the series to a seventh game. Then, an improbable lineup of Pippen and reserves Scott Williams, B.J. Armstrong, Bobby Hansen and Stacey King turned the tide, outscoring the Trail Blazers 14-2 to open the fourth quarter and cut the seemingly insurmountable lead to 81-78.

Jordan and Pippen took over from there, scoring the Bulls' last 19 points to grab the series from the stunned Trail Blazers.

"We needed a different matchup," Bulls coach Phil Jackson said afterward. "That's what we got from those guys. They had fresh legs. It's either daring or stupid, depending on which way it comes out."

The Bulls had long retreated to their locker room when they learned that their fans were still celebrating upstairs because it was the team's first title won in the Chicago Stadium. Jackson said, "Grab that trophy. We're going back up to celebrate with our fans!" And so they did.

"With that, Michael grabbed the trophy, and we went back upstairs," recalled Bulls VP Steve Schanwald. "When we started emerging through the tunnel, we started to play the opening to our introduction music. It's very dramatic, "Eye in the Sky" by the Alan Parsons Project. So the crowd knew when the music started playing that something was happening. The team came up through the tunnel, and all of a sudden the crowd just exploded. It was a 10,000-goose bump experience.

"All of a sudden some of the players — Scottie and Horace and Hansen— got up on the table so that everybody could see them in the crowd. Then Michael came up and joined them with the trophy and they started dancing. It was just an electrifying experience, and I think for anybody that was there, it was a moment that they will never forget as long as they live."

FINAL STANDINGS

EASTERN CONFERENCE

ATLANTIC DIVISION

	W	L	Pct.
Boston	51	31	.622
New York	51	31	.622
New Jersey	40	42	.488
Miami	38	44	.463
Philadelphia	35	47	.427
Washington	25	57	.305
Orlando	21	61	.256

CENTRAL DIVISION

	W	L	Pct.
Chicago	67	15	.817
Cleveland	57	25	.695
Detroit	48	34	.585
Indiana	40	42	.488
Atlanta	38	44	.463
Charlotte	31	51	.378
Milwaukee	31	51	.378

WESTERN CONFERENCE

MIDWEST DIVISION

	W	L	Pct.
Utah	55	27	.671
San Antonio	47	35	.573
Houston	42	40	.512
Denver	24	58	.293
Dallas	22	60	.268
Minnesota	15	67	.183

PACIFIC DIVISION

	W	L	Pct.
Portland	57	25	.695
Golden State	55	27	.671
Phoenix	53	29	.646
Seattle	47	35	.573
L.A. Clippers	45	37	.549
L.A. Lakers	43	39	.524
Sacramento	29	53	.354

PLAYOFFS

EASTERN CONFERENCE

FIRST ROUND

Chicago 3, Miami 0
Apr. 24 ....@Chicago 113, Miami 94
Apr. 26 ....@Chicago 120, Miami 90
Apr. 29 ....Chicago 119, @Miami 114

Boston 3, Indiana 0
Apr. 23 ....@Boston 124, Indiana 113
Apr. 25 ....@Boston 119, Indiana 112*
Apr. 27 ....Boston 102, @Indiana 98

Cleveland 3, New Jersey 1
Apr. 23 ....@Cleveland 120, New Jersey 113
Apr. 25 ....@Cleveland 118, New Jersey 96
Apr. 28 ....@New Jersey 109, Cleveland 104
Apr. 30 ....Cleveland 98, @New Jersey 89

New York 3, Detroit 2
Apr. 24 ....@New York 109, Detroit 75
Apr. 26 ....Detroit 89, @New York 88
Apr. 28 ....New York 90, @Detroit 87*
May 1 ......@Detroit 86, New York 82
May 3 ......@New York 94, Detroit 87

SEMIFINALS

Cleveland 4, Boston 3
May 2 ......@Cleveland 101, Boston 76
May 4 ......Boston 104, @Cleveland 98
May 8 ......@Boston 110, Cleveland 107
May 10 ....Cleveland 114, @Boston 112*
May 13 ....@Cleveland 114, Boston 98
May 15 ....@Boston 122, Cleveland 91
May 17 ....@Cleveland 122, Boston 104

Chicago 4, New York 3
May 5 ......New York 94, @Chicago 89
May 7 ......@Chicago 86, New York 78
May 9 ......Chicago 94, @New York 86
May 10 ....@New York 93, Chicago 86
May 12 ....@Chicago 96, New York 88
May 14 ....@New York 100, Chicago 86
May 17 ....@Chicago 110, New York 81

FINALS

Chicago 4, Cleveland 2
May 19 ....@Chicago 103, Cleveland 89
May 21 ....Cleveland 107, @Chicago 81
May 23 ....Chicago 105, @Cleveland 96
May 25 ....@Cleveland 99, Chicago 85
May 27 ....@Chicago 112, Cleveland 89
May 29 ....Chicago 99, @Cleveland 94

WESTERN CONFERENCE

FIRST ROUND

Portland 3, L.A. Lakers 1
Apr. 23 ....@Portland 115, L.A. Lakers 102
Apr. 25 ....@Portland 101, L.A. Lakers 79
Apr. 29 ....@L.A. Lakers 121, Portland 119*
May 3 ......Portland 102, @L.A. Lakers 76

Utah 3, L.A. Clippers 2
Apr. 24 ....@Utah 115, L.A. Clippers 97
Apr. 26 ....@Utah 103, L.A. Clippers 92
Apr. 28 ....@L.A. Clippers 98, Utah 88
May 3 ......@L.A. Clippers 115, Utah 107
May 4 ......@Utah 98, L.A. Clippers 89

Seattle 3, Golden State 1
Apr. 23 ....Seattle 117, @Golden State 109
Apr. 25 ....@Golden State 115, Seattle 101
Apr. 28 ....@Seattle 129, Golden State 128
Apr. 30 ....@Seattle 119, Golden State 116

Phoenix 3, San Antonio 0
Apr. 24 ....@Phoenix 117, San Antonio 111
Apr. 26 ....@Phoenix 119, San Antonio 107
Apr. 29 ....Phoenix 101, @San Antonio 92

SEMIFINALS

Portland 4, Phoenix 1
May 5 ......@Portland 113, Phoenix 111
May 7 ......@Portland 126, Phoenix 119
May 9 ......@Phoenix 124, Portland 117
May 11 ....Portland 153, @Phoenix 151**
May 14 ....@Portland 118, Phoenix 106

Utah 4, Seattle 1
May 6 ......@Utah 108, Seattle 100
May 8 ......@Utah 103, Seattle 97
May 10 ....@Seattle 104, Utah 98
May 12 ....Utah 89, @Seattle 83
May 14 ....@Utah 111, Seattle 100

FINALS

Portland 4, Utah 2
May 16 ....@Portland 113, Utah 88
May 19 ....@Portland 119, Utah 102
May 22 ....@Utah 97, Portland 89
May 24 ....@Utah 121, Portland 112
May 26 ....@Portland 127, Utah 121*
May 28 ....Portland 105, @Utah 97

NBA FINALS

Chicago 4, Portland 2
June 3 .....@Chicago 122, Portland 89
June 5 .....Portland 115, @Chicago 104*
June 7 .....Chicago 94, @Portland 84
June 10 ...@Portland 93, Chicago 88
June 12 ...Chicago 119, @Portland 106
June 14 ...@Chicago 97, Portland 93

*Denotes number of overtime periods.

INDIVIDUAL LEADERS

SCORING (minimum 70 games or 1,400 points)

	G	FGM	FTM	Pts.	Avg.
Jordan, Chicago	80	943	491	2404	30.1
K. Malone, Utah	81	798	673	2272	28.0
Mullin, Golden State	81	830	350	2074	25.6
Drexler, Portland	76	694	401	1903	25.0
Ewing, New York	82	796	377	1970	24.0
Hardaway, Golden State	81	734	298	1893	23.4
Robinson, San Antonio	68	592	393	1578	23.2
Barkley, Philadelphia	75	622	454	1730	23.1
Richmond, Sacramento	80	685	330	1803	22.5
Rice, Miami	79	672	266	1765	22.3

FIELD GOAL PCT. (minimum 300 made)

	FGM	FGA	Pct.
Williams, Portland	340	563	.604
Thorpe, Houston	558	943	.592
Grant, Chicago	457	790	.578
Daugherty, Cleveland	576	1010	.570
Cage, Seattle	307	542	.566

THREE-POINT FIELD GOAL PCT. (minimum 50 made)

	FGA	FGM	Pct.
Barros, Seattle	186	83	.446
Petrovic, New Jersey	277	123	.444
Hornacek, Phoenix	189	83	.439
Iuzzolino, Dallas	136	59	.434
Ellis, Milwaukee	329	138	.419

FREE THROW PCT. (minimum 125 made)

	FTM	FTA	Pct.
Price, Cleveland	270	285	.947
Bird, Boston	150	162	.926
Pierce, Seattle	417	455	.916
Blackman, Dallas	239	266	.898
J. Malone, Utah	256	285	.898

ASSISTS (minimum 70 games or 400 assists)

	G	No.	Avg.
Stockton, Utah	82	1126	13.7
Johnson, Phoenix	78	836	10.7
Hardaway, Golden State	81	807	10.0
Bogues, Charlotte	82	743	9.1
Strickland, San Antonio	57	491	8.6

REBOUNDS (minimum 70 games or 800 rebounds)

	G	Off.	Def.	Tot.	Avg.
Rodman, Detroit	82	523	1007	1530	18.7
Willis, Atlanta	81	418	840	1258	15.5
Mutombo, Denver	71	316	554	870	12.3
Robinson, San Antonio	68	261	568	829	12.2
Olajuwon, Houston	70	246	599	845	12.1

STEALS (minimum 70 games or 125 steals)

	G	No.	Avg.
Stockton, Utah	82	244	2.98
Williams, Indiana	79	233	2.95
Robertson, Milwaukee	82	210	2.56
Blaylock, New Jersey	72	170	2.36
Robinson, San Antonio	68	158	2.32

BLOCKED SHOTS (minimum 70 games or 100 blocked shots)

	G	No.	Avg.
Robinson, San Antonio	68	305	4.49
Olajuwon, Houston	70	304	4.34
Nance, Cleveland	81	243	3.00
Ewing, New York	82	245	2.99
Mutombo, Denver	71	210	2.96

1990-91 SEASON

Michael Jordan

NBA.COM FACT

On November 10, 1990, Phoenix scored a record 107 points in the first half against Denver, which had set the old mark of 90 first-half points three days earlier.

With each passing season, Michael Jordan's "greatness" had become an issue. He had won four straight NBA scoring titles, but was he the kind of player who could lead a team to a championship? Or was he the kind of superstar whose gifts were good only for show? Those questions haunted Jordan more than ever as training camp opened in 1990.

Never had his basketball skills been a question. But his leadership skills and his character, were. There was only one way to answer.

"I think there came a point where he understood his greatness was going to be defined by winning," Bulls guard John Paxson would later explain. "That's why I saw a change in his real commitment to winning championships."

Jordan's main frustrations grew out of the Bulls' failures against the physical Detroit Pistons in 1989 and 1990.

The Bulls matured into a determined unit over the 1990-91 season. The key development came with 6-7 Scottie Pippen. He had been stung by criticism, most of it stemming from his migraine headache against Detroit in Game 7 of the 1990 Eastern Conference Finals. Pippen answered with determination, averaging nearly 18 points, seven rebounds and six assists.

"I thought about it all summer," he said of the migraine. "I failed to produce last season."

"For Pippen," Bulls coach Phil Jackson observed, "it was ultimately taking him from being a wing into a point guard role. He became a guy who now had the ball as much as Michael. He became a dominant force."

The Bulls opened the playoffs against the Knicks, winning the first game by 41 points en route to a sweep. Next, Philadelphia fell in five games, setting up the only rematch the Bulls wanted: Detroit in the Eastern Conference Finals. Chicago hammered the Pistons, who were reeling from injuries, in four straight games, an outcome Jordan boldly forecasted.

The Portland Trail Blazers had ruled the regular season in the Western Conference with a 63-19 record, but Magic Johnson and the Lakers again survived in the playoffs, ousting Portland in six games in the Conference Finals.

For many observers, the NBA Finals seemed a dream matchup: Jordan and the Bulls against Magic and the Lakers. Many, including former Lakers coach Pat Riley, figured the Lakers' experience made them a sure bet. Los Angeles was making its ninth Finals appearance since 1980, and had five titles to show for it.

Los Angeles won Game 1, 93-91, on a late three-pointer by Sam Perkins. Although the Bulls blew out the Lakers, 107-86, in Game 2, the Lakers had gotten a split in Chicago Stadium and were headed home for three straight games in the Forum.

But the Bulls met the challenge in Game 3. Jordan hit a jumper with 3.4 seconds left to send the game into overtime. There, the Bulls ran off eight straight points for a 104-96 win and a 2-1 lead in the series. Chicago's Game 4 weapon was defense. The Bulls won 97-82, harassing the Lakers into shooting 37 percent from the floor.

"I didn't even dream this would happen," Johnson said.

The Bulls turned to their offense to claim the title in Game 5, 108-101. Pippen led the scoring parade with 32 points, and Paxson hit five buckets in the final four minutes to finish with 20 points and seal the victory.

Jordan's numbers for the series? 31.2 points, 11.4 assists and 6.6 rebounds per game. Afterward, Johnson tracked him down. "I saw tears in his eyes," Johnson said. "I told him, 'You proved everyone wrong. You're a winner as well as a great individual basketball player.'"

FINAL STANDINGS

EASTERN CONFERENCE

ATLANTIC DIVISION

	W	L	Pct.
Boston	56	26	.683
Philadelphia	44	38	.537
New York	39	43	.476
Washington	30	52	.366
New Jersey	26	56	.317
Miami	24	58	.293

CENTRAL DIVISION

	W	L	Pct.
Chicago	61	21	.744
Detroit	50	32	.610
Milwaukee	48	34	.585
Atlanta	43	39	.524
Indiana	41	41	.500
Cleveland	33	49	.402
Charlotte	26	56	.317

WESTERN CONFERENCE

MIDWEST DIVISION

	W	L	Pct.
San Antonio	55	27	.671
Utah	54	28	.659
Houston	52	30	.634
Orlando	31	51	.378
Minnesota	29	53	.354
Dallas	28	54	.341
Denver	20	62	.244

PACIFIC DIVISION

	W	L	Pct.
Portland	63	19	.768
L.A. Lakers	58	24	.707
Phoenix	55	27	.671
Golden State	44	38	.537
Seattle	41	41	.500
L.A. Clippers	31	51	.378
Sacramento	25	57	.305

PLAYOFFS

EASTERN CONFERENCE

FIRST ROUND

Chicago 3, New York 0
- Apr. 25 ....@Chicago 126, New York 85
- Apr. 28 ....@Chicago 89, New York 79
- Apr. 30 ....Chicago 103, @New York 94

Boston 3, Indiana 2
- Apr. 26 ....@Boston 127, Indiana 120
- Apr. 28 ....Indiana 130, @Boston 118
- May 1 ......Boston 112, @Indiana 105
- May 3 ......@Indiana 116, Boston 113
- May 5 ......@Boston 124, Indiana 121

Detroit 3, Atlanta 2
- Apr. 26 ....Atlanta 103, @Detroit 98
- Apr. 28 ....@Detroit 101, Atlanta 88
- Apr. 30 ....Detroit 103, @Atlanta 91
- May 2 ......@Atlanta 123, Detroit 111
- May 5 ......@Detroit 113, Atlanta 81

Philadelphia 3, Milwaukee 0
- Apr. 25 ....Philadelphia 99, @Milwaukee 90
- Apr. 27 ....Philadelphia 116, @Milwaukee 112*
- Apr. 30 ....@Philadelphia 121, Milwaukee 100

SEMIFINALS

Chicago 4, Philadelphia 1
- May 4 ......@Chicago 105, Philadelphia 92
- May 6 ......@Chicago 112, Philadelphia 100
- May 10 ....@Philadelphia 99, Chicago 97
- May 12 ....Chicago 101, @Philadelphia 85
- May 14 ....@Chicago 100, Philadelphia 95

Detroit 4, Boston 2
- May 7 ......Detroit 86, @Boston 75
- May 9 ......@Boston 109, Detroit 103
- May 11 ....Boston 115, @Detroit 83
- May 13 ....@Detroit 104, Boston 97
- May 15 ....Detroit 116, @Boston 111
- May 17 ....@Detroit 117, Boston 113*

FINALS

Chicago 4, Detroit 0
- May 19 ....@Chicago 94, Detroit 83
- May 21 ....@Chicago 105, Detroit 97
- May 25 ....Chicago 113, @Detroit 107
- May 27 ....Chicago 115, @Detroit 94

WESTERN CONFERENCE

FIRST ROUND

Portland 3, Seattle 2
- Apr. 26 ....@Portland 110, Seattle 102
- Apr. 28 ....@Portland 115, Seattle 106
- Apr. 30 ....@Seattle 102, Portland 99
- May 2 ......@Seattle 101, Portland 89
- May 4 ......@Portland 119, Seattle 107

Golden State 3, San Antonio 1
- Apr. 25 ....@San Antonio 130, Golden State 121
- Apr. 27 ....Golden State 111, @San Antonio 98
- May 1 ......@Golden State 109, San Antonio 106
- May 3 ......@Golden State 110, San Antonio 97

L.A. Lakers 3, Houston 0
- Apr. 25 ....@L.A. Lakers 94, Houston 92
- Apr. 27 ....@L.A. Lakers 109, Houston 98
- Apr. 30 ....L.A. Lakers 94, @Houston 90

Utah 3, Phoenix 1
- Apr. 25 ....Utah 129, @Phoenix 90
- Apr. 27 ....@Phoenix 102, Utah 92
- Apr. 30 ....@Utah 107, Phoenix 98
- May 2 ......@Utah 101, Phoenix 93

SEMIFINALS

L.A. Lakers 4, Golden State 1
- May 5 ......@L.A. Lakers 126, Golden State 116
- May 8 ......Golden State 125, @L.A. Lakers 124
- May 10 ....L.A. Lakers 115, @Golden State 112
- May 12 ....L.A. Lakers 123, @Golden State 107
- May 14 ....@L.A. Lakers 124, Golden State 119*

Portland 4, Utah 1
- May 7 ......@Portland 117, Utah 97
- May 9 ......@Portland 118, Utah 116
- May 11 ....@Utah 107, Portland 101
- May 12 ....Portland 104, @Utah 101
- May 14 ....@Portland 103, Utah 96

FINALS

L.A. Lakers 4, Portland 2
- May 18 ....L.A. Lakers 111, @Portland 106
- May 21 ....@Portland 109, L.A. Lakers 98
- May 24 ....@L.A. Lakers 106, Portland 92
- May 26 ....@L.A. Lakers 116, Portland 95
- May 28 ....@Portland 95, L.A. Lakers 84
- May 30 ....@L.A. Lakers 91, Portland 90

NBA FINALS

Chicago 4, L.A. Lakers 1
- June 2 .....L.A. Lakers 93, @Chicago 91
- June 5 .....@Chicago 107, L.A. Lakers 86
- June 7 .....Chicago 104, @L.A. Lakers 96*
- June 9 .....Chicago 97, @L.A. Lakers 82
- June 12 ...Chicago 108, @L.A. Lakers 101

*Denotes number of overtime periods.

INDIVIDUAL LEADERS

SCORING (minimum 70 games or 1,400 points)

	G	FGM	FTM	Pts.	Avg.
Jordan, Chicago	82	990	571	2580	31.5
K. Malone, Utah	82	847	684	2382	29.0
King, Washington	64	713	383	1817	28.4
Barkley, Philadelphia	67	665	475	1849	27.6
Ewing, New York	81	845	464	2154	26.6
Adams, Denver	66	560	465	1752	26.5
Wilkins, Atlanta	81	770	476	2101	25.9
Mullin, Golden State	82	777	513	2107	25.7
Robinson, San Antonio	82	754	592	2101	25.6
Richmond, Golden State	77	703	394	1840	23.9

FIELD GOAL PCT. (minimum 300 made)

	FGM	FGA	Pct.
Williams, Portland	358	595	.602
Parish, Boston	485	811	.598
Gamble, Boston	548	933	.587
Barkley, Philadelphia	665	1167	.570
Divac, L.A. Lakers	360	637	.565

THREE-POINT FIELD GOAL PCT. (minimum 50 made)

	FGA	FGM	Pct.
Les, Sacramento	154	71	.461
Tucker, New York	153	64	.418
Hornacek, Phoenix	146	61	.418
Porter, Portland	313	130	.415
Skiles, Orlando	228	93	.408

FREE THROW PCT. (minimum 125 made)

	FTM	FTA	Pct.
Miller, Indiana	551	600	.918
J. Malone, Utah	231	252	.917
Pierce, Milwaukee-Seattle	430	471	.913
Tripucka, Charlotte	152	167	.910
Johnson, L.A. Lakers	519	573	.906

ASSISTS (minimum 70 games or 400 assists)

	G	No.	Avg.
Stockton, Utah	82	1164	14.2
Johnson, L.A. Lakers	79	989	12.5
Adams, Denver	66	693	10.5
Johnson, Phoenix	77	781	10.1
Hardaway, Golden State	82	793	9.7

REBOUNDS (minimum 70 games or 800 rebounds)

	G	Off.	Def.	Tot.	Avg.
Robinson, San Antonio	82	335	728	1063	13.0
Rodman, Detroit	82	361	665	1026	12.5
Oakley, New York	76	305	615	920	12.1
K. Malone, Utah	82	236	731	967	11.8
Ewing, New York	81	194	711	905	11.2

STEALS (minimum 70 games or 125 steals)

	G	No.	Avg.
Robertson, Milwaukee	81	246	3.04
Stockton, Utah	82	234	2.85
Jordan, Chicago	82	223	2.72
Hardaway, Golden State	82	214	2.61
Pippen, Chicago	82	193	2.35

BLOCKED SHOTS (minimum 70 games or 100 blocked shots)

	G	No.	Avg.
Olajuwon, Houston	56	221	3.95
Robinson, San Antonio	82	320	3.90
Ewing, New York	81	258	3.19
Bol, Philadelphia	82	247	3.01
Dudley, New Jersey	61	153	2.51

1989-90 SEASON

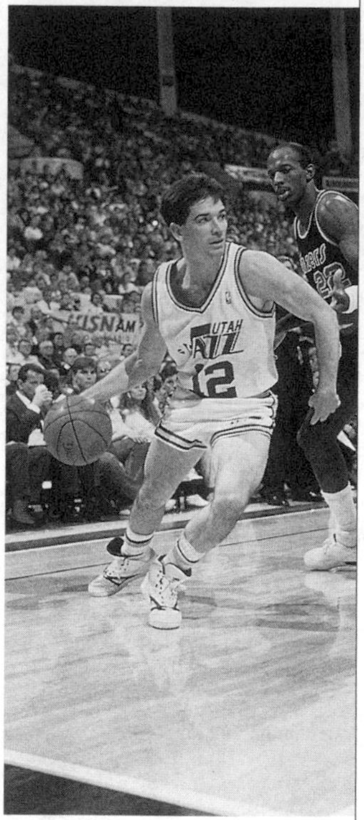

John Stockton

For two straight seasons, the Motor City Bad Boys ruled the NBA. For opponents of the physical Detroit Pistons, it wasn't a fun time.

Having claimed the 1989 championship in a sweep over the injury-ravaged Lakers, the Pistons came back to do it all again the next season, armed this time with what Detroit leader Isiah Thomas described as the knowledge of how to win.

Thomas had gained those secrets in late-night, long-distance phone calls with the Lakers' Magic Johnson. "I could kick myself," Johnson said after realizing he had revealed too much.

Besides the usual grind, the handicap for the Pistons in trying to repeat as champions was the loss of frontcourt enforcer Rick Mahorn in the NBA Expansion Draft. The NBA added new teams in Minnesota and Orlando, and each existing team had to dip into its talent pool to contribute. Mahorn was notified that he would not be protected shortly after the Pistons wrapped up their first championship. His departure meant more minutes for veteran James Edwards, nowhere near Mahorn's physical presence but a needed low-post scorer to complement small forward Mark Aguirre.

The Pistons won 59 games and their third straight Central Division title, but they also had to contend with the maturing Chicago Bulls, who had slowly built a team around Michael Jordan. The Bulls won 55 games under new coach Phil Jackson, the former Knicks forward from the 1970s.

The league's top scorers behind Jordan (33.6) were Karl Malone with 31.0 points per game and Patrick Ewing with 28.6. John Stockton averaged 14.5 assists and Hakeem Olajuwon 14 boards to take honors in each category.

For the first time in 20 seasons, the NBA drama unfolded without Kareem Abdul-Jabbar. The Lakers relied on Magic Johnson's all-around talents more than ever before, and he responded by scoring more than 22 points per game for the second straight year and also averaging 11.5 assists. Without Kareem, the Lakers used 35-year-old Mychal Thompson and rookie Vlade Divac at center. The new formula, with most of the old ingredients still intact, worked well enough for the Lakers to post a league-best 63-19 record, including a stellar 37-4 home record.

In the playoffs Detroit blitzed Indiana and New York, but needed seven games to dismiss the increasingly troublesome Bulls. The Lakers defeated Houston, but were stunned in the Western Conference Semifinals by Phoenix in five games. The Suns were in turn beaten by the Portland Trail Blazers, a team that had lost in the first round of the playoffs in each of the previous four years.

The Trail Blazers, led by high-scoring Clyde Drexler, won 59 games, but didn't get much respect until outlasting San Antonio in seven games to reach the Western Conference Finals, where they beat Phoenix in six games. When Portland won Game 2 in Detroit by one point in overtime to tie the Finals at 1-1, the young Blazers seemed poised to score a major upset. But the veteran Pistons, behind Thomas' 27.6 points per game, took three straight games in Portland to capture a second consecutive title. After going 19 years without back-to-back champions, the NBA now had back-to-back repeaters.

The Pistons felt they hadn't received their due for winning the NBA title in 1989 with the Lakers hobbled by injuries to Byron Scott and Magic Johnson. While the 1989 title may have been for the loyal Detroit fans, the 1990 crown was one the Pistons won more for themselves.

"You rank this one as more of a satisfaction for a job well done," said Pistons center Bill Laimbeer after it was over. "We wanted to repeat as champions, but not so much to prove it to anybody else. We wanted to do it for ourselves."

NBA.COM FACT

For the first time since 1979, neither the Lakers nor the Celtics reached the NBA Finals.

FINAL STANDINGS

EASTERN CONFERENCE

ATLANTIC DIVISION

	W	L	Pct.
Philadelphia	53	29	.646
Boston	52	30	.634
New York	45	37	.549
Washington	31	51	.378
Miami	18	64	.220
New Jersey	17	65	.207

CENTRAL DIVISION

	W	L	Pct.
Detroit	59	23	.720
Chicago	55	27	.671
Milwaukee	44	38	.537
Cleveland	42	40	.512
Indiana	42	40	.512
Atlanta	41	41	.500
Orlando	18	64	.220

WESTERN CONFERENCE

MIDWEST DIVISION

	W	L	Pct.
San Antonio	56	26	.683
Utah	55	27	.671
Dallas	47	35	.573
Denver	43	39	.524
Houston	41	41	.500
Minnesota	22	60	.268
Charlotte	19	63	.232

PACIFIC DIVISION

	W	L	Pct.
L.A. Lakers	63	19	.768
Portland	59	23	.720
Phoenix	54	28	.659
Seattle	41	41	.500
Golden State	37	45	.451
L.A. Clippers	30	52	.366
Sacramento	23	59	.280

PLAYOFFS

EASTERN CONFERENCE

FIRST ROUND

New York 3, Boston 2
Apr. 26 ....@Boston 116, New York 105
Apr. 28 ....@Boston 157, New York 128
May 2 ......@New York 102, Boston 99
May 4 ......@New York 135, Boston 108
May 6 ......New York 121, @Boston 114

Detroit 3, Indiana 0
Apr. 26 ....@Detroit 104, Indiana 92
Apr. 28 ....@Detroit 100, Indiana 87
May 1 ......Detroit 108, @Indiana 96

Philadelphia 3, Cleveland 2
Apr. 26 ....@Philadelphia 111, Cleveland 106
Apr. 29 ....@Philadelphia 107, Cleveland 101
May 1 ......@Cleveland 122, Philadelphia 95
May 3 ......@Cleveland 108, Philadelphia 96
May 5 ......@Philadelphia 113, Cleveland 97

Chicago 3, Milwaukee 1
Apr. 27 ....@Chicago 111, Milwaukee 97
Apr. 29 ....@Chicago 109, Milwaukee 102
May 1 ......@Milwaukee 119, Chicago 112
May 3 ......Chicago 110, @Milwaukee 86

SEMIFINALS

Chicago 4, Philadelphia 1
May 7 ......@Chicago 96, Philadelphia 85
May 9 ......@Chicago 101, Philadelphia 96
May 11 ....@Philadelphia 118, Chicago 112
May 13 ....Chicago 111, @Philadelphia 101
May 16 ....@Chicago 117, Philadelphia 99

Detroit 4, New York 1
May 8 ......@Detroit 112, New York 77
May 10 ....@Detroit 104, New York 97
May 12 ....@New York 111, Detroit 103
May 13 ....Detroit 102, @New York 90
May 15 ....@Detroit 95, New York 84

FINALS

Detroit 4, Chicago 3
May 20 ....@Detroit 86, Chicago 77
May 22 ....@Detroit 102, Chicago 93
May 26 ....@Chicago 107, Detroit 102
May 28 ....@Chicago 108, Detroit 101
May 30 ....@Detroit 97, Chicago 83
June 1 .....@Chicago 109, Detroit 91
June 3 .....@Detroit 93, Chicago 74

WESTERN CONFERENCE

FIRST ROUND

L.A. Lakers 3, Houston 1
Apr. 27 ....@L.A. Lakers 101, Houston 89
Apr. 29 ....@L.A. Lakers 104, Houston 100
May 1 ......@Houston 114, L.A. Lakers 108
May 3 ......L.A. Lakers 109, @Houston 88

Phoenix 3, Utah 2
Apr. 27 ....@Utah 113, Phoenix 96
Apr. 29 ....Phoenix 105, @Utah 87
May 2 ......@Phoenix 120, Utah 105
May 4 ......Utah 105, @Phoenix 94
May 6 ......Phoenix 104, @Utah 102

San Antonio 3, Denver 0
Apr. 26 ....@San Antonio 119, Denver 103
Apr. 28 ....@San Antonio 129, Denver 120
May 1 ......San Antonio 131, @Denver 120

Portland 3, Dallas 0
Apr. 26 ....@Portland 109, Dallas 102
Apr. 28 ....@Portland 114, Dallas 107
May 1 ......Portland 106, @Dallas 92

SEMIFINALS

Portland 4, San Antonio 3
May 5 ......@Portland 107, San Antonio 94
May 8 ......@Portland 122, San Antonio 112
May 10 ....@San Antonio 121, Portland 98
May 12 ....@San Antonio 115, Portland 105
May 15 ....@Portland 138, San Antonio 132**
May 17 ....@San Antonio 112, Portland 97
May 19 ....@Portland 108, San Antonio 105*

Phoenix 4, L.A. Lakers 1
May 8 ......Phoenix 104, @L.A. Lakers 102
May 10 ....@L.A. Lakers 124, Phoenix 100
May 12 ....@Phoenix 117, L.A. Lakers 103
May 13 ....@Phoenix 114, L.A. Lakers 101
May 15 ....Phoenix 106, @L.A. Lakers 103

FINALS

Portland 4, Phoenix 2
May 21 ....@Portland 100, Phoenix 98
May 23 ....@Portland 108, Phoenix 107
May 25 ....@Phoenix 123, Portland 89
May 27 ....@Phoenix 119, Portland 107
May 29 ....@Portland 120, Phoenix 114
May 31 ....Portland 112, @Phoenix 109

NBA FINALS

Detroit 4, Portland 1
June 5 .....@Detroit 105, Portland 99
June 7 .....Portland 106, @Detroit 105*
June 10 ...Detroit 121, @Portland 106
June 12 ...Detroit 112, @Portland 109
June 14 ...Detroit 92, @Portland 90

*Denotes number of overtime periods.

INDIVIDUAL LEADERS

SCORING (minimum 70 games or 1,400 points)

	G	FGM	FTM	Pts.	Avg.
Jordan, Chicago	82	1034	593	2753	33.6
Malone, Utah	82	914	696	2540	31.0
Ewing, New York	82	922	502	2347	28.6
Chambers, Phoenix	81	810	557	2201	27.2
Wilkins, Atlanta	80	810	459	2138	26.7
Barkley, Philadelphia	79	706	557	1989	25.2
Mullin, Golden State	78	682	505	1956	25.1
Miller, Indiana	82	661	544	2016	24.6
Olajuwon, Houston	82	806	382	1995	24.3
Robinson, San Antonio	82	690	613	1993	24.3
Bird, Boston	75	718	319	1820	24.3
Malone, Washington	75	781	257	1820	24.3

FIELD GOAL PCT. (minimum 300 made)

	FGM	FGA	Pct.
West, Phoenix	331	530	.625
Barkley, Philadelphia	706	1177	.600
Parish, Boston	505	871	.580
Malone, Utah	914	1627	.562
Woolridge, L.A. Lakers	306	550	.556

THREE-POINT FIELD GOAL PCT. (minimum 25 made)

	FGA	FGM	Pct.
Kerr, Cleveland	144	73	.507
Hodges, Chicago	181	87	.481
Petrovic, Portland	74	34	.459
Sundvold, Miami	100	44	.440
Scott, L.A. Lakers	220	93	.423

FREE THROW PCT. (minimum 125 made)

	FTM	FTA	Pct.
Bird, Boston	319	343	.930
Johnson, Phoenix	188	205	.917
Davis, Denver	207	227	.912
Dumars, Detroit	297	330	.900
McHale, Boston	393	440	.893

ASSISTS (minimum 70 games or 400 assists)

	G	No.	Avg.
Stockton, Utah	78	1134	14.5
Johnson, L.A. Lakers	79	907	11.5
Johnson, Phoenix	74	846	11.4
Bogues, Charlotte	81	867	10.7
Grant, L.A. Clippers	44	442	10.0

REBOUNDS (minimum 70 games or 800 rebounds)

	G	Off.	Def.	Tot.	Avg.
Olajuwon, Houston	82	299	850	1149	14.0
Robinson, San Antonio	82	303	680	983	12.0
Barkley, Philadelphia	79	361	548	909	11.5
Malone, Utah	82	232	679	911	11.1
Ewing, New York	82	235	658	893	10.9

STEALS (minimum 70 games or 125 steals)

	G	No.	Avg.
Jordan, Chicago	82	227	2.77
Stockton, Utah	78	207	2.65
Pippen, Chicago	82	211	2.57
Robertson, Milwaukee	81	207	2.56
Harper, Dallas	82	187	2.28

BLOCKED SHOTS (minimum 70 games or 100 blocked shots)

	G	No.	Avg.
Olajuwon, Houston	82	376	4.59
Ewing, New York	82	327	3.99
Robinson, San Antonio	82	319	3.89
Bol, Golden State	75	238	3.17
Benjamin, L.A. Clippers	71	187	2.63

1988-89 SEASON

Joe Dumars

Joe Dumars' father was a trucker, a man who labored long hours delivering groceries to stores across southern Louisiana. As a youth, Dumars rode along with his father so that the elder could teach the son what real work meant.

It was a lesson that never left him, even after he became an NBA star. So while Dumars contributed solid defense and pinpoint shooting for the Detroit Pistons, the work ethic and character instilled by his father are what made him a favorite of coaches, teammates, opponents and Pistons fans. And those attributes were a key factor in Detroit's 1989 NBA title run.

When it was pointed out that fans expect flashy play from big-time pro guards, Dumars replied, "I can understand that people want to see the fancy stuff. But believe me, we've got enough fancy stuff on the Detroit Pistons. I don't have to be fancy."

His work ethic would be rewarded with the MVP Award from the 1989 Finals, something that gave the season something of a theme because the 1988-89 campaign marked a transition for another work-ethic giant: Kareem Abdul-Jabbar played the last of his 20 NBA seasons.

The 42-year-old center, the Los Angeles Lakers' team captain, retired after winning league MVP honors six times, becoming the NBA's all-time scoring leader and playing on six NBA title teams.

There was also a strong element of the new in the NBA in 1988-89. Franchises began play in Charlotte and Miami, part of a four-team expansion that would next include Orlando and Minnesota in 1989-90.

In the business as usual category, Michael Jordan won his third straight NBA scoring crown and Magic Johnson won his second Most Valuable Player Award.

With Dumars in the lineup, the Pistons played the second-best defense in the NBA. But management sensed that the elusive team chemistry wasn't quite what it should be, so three days after the All-Star Game, the Pistons traded high-scoring Adrian Dantley and a draft pick for forward Mark Aguirre of the Dallas Mavericks, a close friend of Detroit guard Isiah Thomas. The trade seemed a gamble, but the Pistons responded and finished the regular season with a league-best 63-19 record.

Meanwhile, the Lakers swept through the first three rounds of the playoffs without a loss in 11 games, and it seemed Abdul-Jabbar's career might close with a fairy-tale ending. But Byron Scott tore his hamstring prior to Game 1 of the Finals and Magic Johnson also suffered a hamstring injury during Game 2.

"It's like you have a real nice sports car and a great driver," Abdul-Jabbar said of the circumstances, "and then all of a sudden you have to find somebody who has been driving a bus to be a driver. That's a learning experience."

The Pistons, who had nearly captured a championship the previous year, outplayed what was left of the Lakers and swept four straight games, including the clincher at the Forum.

Dumars got the hot hand in the series and his backcourt mate, Isiah Thomas, stayed busy feeding him the ball. "I just happened to get into one of those zones where a couple of shots went down and I wanted to touch the ball every time it came down the floor," Dumars explained.

"Was it a case where you would talk to Isiah and say, 'I'm hot?'" a writer asked. "Or does he just know that?"

"He knows it," Dumars said. "At one point he asked me, 'What do you want?' meaning what play do I want. I said, 'Just the ball.' That's about how it was. 'Just give me the ball.'"

NBA.COM FACT

No Pistons player finished in the top 20 in scoring, or top 10 in free throw percentage, steals, blocked shots or three-point field goals. The NBA champions had Isiah Thomas (ninth in assists) and Bill Laimbeer (ninth in rebounds) among the league leaders. Detroit's only league leader was Dennis Rodman, whose .595 field goal percentage was tops in the NBA.

FINAL STANDINGS

EASTERN CONFERENCE

ATLANTIC DIVISION

	W	L	Pct.
New York	52	30	.634
Philadelphia	46	36	.561
Boston	42	40	.512
Washington	40	42	.488
New Jersey	26	56	.317
Charlotte	20	62	.244

CENTRAL DIVISION

	W	L	Pct.
Detroit	63	19	.768
Cleveland	57	25	.695
Atlanta	52	30	.634
Milwaukee	49	33	.598
Chicago	47	35	.573
Indiana	28	54	.341

WESTERN CONFERENCE

MIDWEST DIVISION

	W	L	Pct.
Utah	51	31	.622
Houston	45	37	.549
Denver	44	38	.537
Dallas	38	44	.463
San Antonio	21	61	.256
Miami	15	67	.183

PACIFIC DIVISION

	W	L	Pct.
L.A. Lakers	57	25	.695
Phoenix	55	27	.671
Seattle	47	35	.573
Golden State	43	39	.524
Portland	39	43	.476
Sacramento	27	55	.329
L.A. Clippers	21	61	.256

PLAYOFFS

EASTERN CONFERENCE

FIRST ROUND

New York 3, Philadelphia 0

Apr. 27 ....@New York 102, Philadelphia 96
Apr. 29 ....@New York 107, Philadelphia 106
May 2......New York 116, @Philadelphia 115*

Detroit 3, Boston 0

Apr. 28 ....@Detroit 101, Boston 91
Apr. 30 ....@Detroit 102, Boston 95
May 2......Detroit 100, @Boston 85

Chicago 3, Cleveland 2

Apr. 28 ....Chicago 95, @Cleveland 88
Apr. 30 ....@Cleveland 96, Chicago 88
May 3......@Chicago 101, Cleveland 94
May 5......Cleveland 108, @Chicago 105*
May 7......Chicago 101, @Cleveland 100

Milwaukee 3, Atlanta 2

Apr. 27 ....@Atlanta 100, Milwaukee 92
Apr. 29 ....Milwaukee 108, @Atlanta 98
May 2......@Milwaukee 117, Atlanta 113*
May 5......Atlanta 113, @Milwaukee 106*
May 7......Milwaukee 96, @Atlanta 92

SEMIFINALS

Chicago 4, New York 2

May 9......Chicago 120, @New York 109*
May 11 ....@New York 114, Chicago 97
May 13 ....@Chicago 111, New York 88
May 14 ....@Chicago 106, New York 93
May 16 ....@New York 121, Chicago 114
May 19 ....@Chicago 113, New York 111

Detroit 4, Milwaukee 0

May 10 ....@Detroit 85, Milwaukee 80
May 12 ....@Detroit 112, Milwaukee 92
May 14 ....Detroit 110, @Milwaukee 90
May 15 ....Detroit 96, @Milwaukee 94

FINALS

Detroit 4, Chicago 2

May 21 ....Chicago 94, @Detroit 88
May 23 ....@Detroit 100, Chicago 91
May 27 ....@Chicago 99, Detroit 97
May 29 ....Detroit 86, @Chicago 80
May 31 ....@Detroit 94, Chicago 85
June 2 .....Detroit 103, @Chicago 94

WESTERN CONFERENCE

FIRST ROUND

L.A. Lakers 3, Portland 0

Apr. 27 ....@L.A. Lakers 128, Portland 108
Apr. 30 ....@L.A. Lakers 113, Portland 105
May 3......L.A. Lakers 116, @Portland 108

Golden State 3, Utah 0

Apr. 27 ....Golden State 123, @Utah 119
Apr. 29 ....Golden State 99, @Utah 91
May 2......@Golden State 120, Utah 106

Phoenix 3, Denver 0

Apr. 28 ....@Phoenix 104, Denver 103
Apr. 30 ....@Phoenix 132, Denver 114
May 2......Phoenix 130, @Denver 121

Seattle 3, Houston 1

Apr. 28 ....@Seattle 111, Houston 107
Apr. 30 ....@Seattle 109, Houston 97
May 3......@Houston 126, Seattle 107
May 5......Seattle 98, @Houston 96

SEMIFINALS

Phoenix 4, Golden State 1

May 6......@Phoenix 130, Golden State 103
May 9......Golden State 127, @Phoenix 122
May 11 ....Phoenix 113, @Golden State 104
May 13 ....Phoenix 135, @Golden State 99
May 16 ....@Phoenix 116, Golden State 104

L.A. Lakers 4, Seattle 0

May 7......@L.A. Lakers 113, Seattle 102
May 10 ....@L.A. Lakers 130, Seattle 108
May 12 ....L.A. Lakers 91, @Seattle 86
May 14 ....L.A. Lakers 97, @Seattle 95

FINALS

L.A. Lakers 4, Phoenix 0

May 20 ....@L.A. Lakers 127, Phoenix 119
May 23 ....@L.A. Lakers 101, Phoenix 95
May 26 ....L.A. Lakers 110, @Phoenix 107
May 28 ....L.A. Lakers 122, @Phoenix 117

NBA FINALS

Detroit 4, L.A. Lakers 0

June 6 .....@Detroit 109, L.A. Lakers 97
June 8 .....@Detroit 108, L.A. Lakers 105
June 11 ...Detroit 114, @L.A. Lakers 110
June 13 ...Detroit 105, @L.A. Lakers 97

*Denotes number of overtime periods.

INDIVIDUAL LEADERS

SCORING (minimum 70 games or 1,400 points)

	G	FGM	FTM	Pts.	Avg.
Jordan, Chicago	81	966	674	2633	32.5
Malone, Utah	80	809	703	2326	29.1
Ellis, Seattle	82	857	377	2253	27.5
Drexler, Portland	78	829	438	2123	27.2
Mullin, Golden State	82	830	493	2176	26.5
English, Denver	82	924	325	2175	26.5
Wilkins, Atlanta	80	814	442	2099	26.2
Barkley, Philadelphia	79	700	602	2037	25.8
Chambers, Phoenix	81	774	509	2085	25.7
Olajuwon, Houston	82	790	454	2034	24.8

FIELD GOAL PCT. (minimum 300 made)

	FGM	FGA	Pct.
Rodman, Detroit	316	531	.595
Barkley, Philadelphia	700	1208	.579
Parish, Boston	596	1045	.570
Ewing, New York	727	1282	.567
Worthy, L.A. Lakers	702	1282	.548

THREE-POINT FIELD GOAL PCT. (minimum 25 made)

	FGA	FGM	Pct.
Sundvold, Miami	92	48	.522
Ellis, Seattle	339	162	.478
Price, Cleveland	211	93	.441
Hawkins, Philadelphia	166	71	.428
Hodges, Phoenix-Chicago	180	75	.417

FREE THROW PCT. (minimum 125 made)

	FTM	FTA	Pct.
Johnson, L.A. Lakers	513	563	.911
Sikma, Milwaukee	266	294	.905
Skiles, Indiana	130	144	.903
Price, Cleveland	263	292	.901
Mullin, Golden State	493	553	.892

ASSISTS (minimum 70 games or 400 assists)

	G	No.	Avg.
Stockton, Utah	82	1118	13.6
Johnson, L.A. Lakers	77	988	12.8
Johnson, Phoenix	81	991	12.2
Porter, Portland	81	770	9.5
McMillan, Seattle	75	696	9.3

REBOUNDS (minimum 70 games or 800 rebounds)

	G	Off.	Def.	Tot.	Avg.
Olajuwon, Houston	82	338	767	1105	13.5
Barkley, Philadelphia	79	403	583	986	12.5
Parish, Boston	80	342	654	996	12.5
Malone, Atlanta	81	386	570	956	11.8
Malone, Utah	80	259	594	853	10.7

STEALS (minimum 70 games or 125 steals)

	G	No.	Avg.
Stockton, Utah	82	263	3.21
Robertson, San Antonio	65	197	3.03
Jordan, Chicago	81	234	2.89
Lever, Denver	71	195	2.75
Drexler, Portland	78	213	2.73

BLOCKED SHOTS (minimum 70 games or 100 blocked shots)

	G	No.	Avg.
Bol, Golden State	80	345	4.31
Eaton, Utah	82	315	3.84
Ewing, New York	80	281	3.51
Olajuwon, Houston	82	282	3.44
Nance, Cleveland	73	206	2.82

1987-88 SEASON

Rolando Blackman (22) and Derek Harper

NBA.COM FACT

The only triple-double of James Worthy's career came in Game 7 of the 1988 NBA Finals, when he had 36 points, 16 rebounds and 10 assists.

The Lakers had won four NBA titles in the 1980s, but after Los Angeles claimed the 1987 crown, Lakers coach Pat Riley immediately set his sights on another goal. No NBA team had won back-to-back championships since the Boston Celtics turned the trick in 1968 and 1969. Many believed that the league's expansion had spread the talent pool so widely that repeating had become nearly impossible.

Riley, though, wasn't satisfied with the Lakers' position as the "Team of the 1980s." He decided that back-to-back championships would stamp his team as one of the all-time greats. So he did a peculiar thing: While the players sprayed champagne in the locker room to celebrate their victory in the 1987 Finals, Riley guaranteed the Lakers would repeat.

That guarantee left his players unsettled. It put immense pressure on them as well as their coach.

The Lakers fashioned the NBA's best record at 62-20, as Byron Scott (21.7 points per game) and James Worthy (19.7 ppg) assumed a greater share of the scoring load from Kareem Abdul-Jabbar and Magic Johnson.

The Lakers were blessed with a deep bench. Mychal Thompson, a key reserve on the 1987 title team, was now sharing the center spot with Abdul-Jabbar. Third-year forward A.C. Green also came of age, and veterans Michael Cooper and Kurt Rambis made important contributions.

As the Lakers looked to repeat, a new challenger rose in the East. Detroit had pushed the Celtics to the limit before losing in the Eastern Finals in 1987. Boston responded in 1988 by winning a conference-high 57 games, but the Pistons came right after them, winning 54 games and the Central Division.

General Manager Jack McCloskey and Coach Chuck Daly had surrounded 6-1 superstar guard Isiah Thomas with rugged rebounders Bill Laimbeer and Rick Mahorn; scorers Adrian Dantley, Joe Dumars and Vinnie Johnson; and young, aggressive defensive forwards Dennis Rodman and John Salley.

Thomas yearned for a title to match the one he won in college at Indiana.

By Thomas' third season, the Pistons had a head coach, Daly, who had figured out how to maximize his superstar's strengths so that a team built around a point guard could contend.

The 1988 playoffs became their time to mature. The Pistons went 11-5 in the Eastern Conference Playoffs, and they finally vanquished the Celtics by winning two of three games in Boston Garden.

Driven by Riley, the Lakers outlasted Dallas in seven hard-fought games in the Western Conference Finals, with the home team winning each time. In the Finals, Los Angeles again needed every bit of its home-court advantage, coming back from a 3-2 deficit to win two close games in the Forum to become the first repeat champion since the 1968-69 Boston Celtics.

Although Detroit lost the 1988 NBA Finals in seven games, Thomas' effort in Game 6, when he sustained a seriously sprained ankle but still scored 43 points, stamped him as an NBA legend in the making. Motoring around on a bum ankle, Thomas scored 25 points in the third quarter, which remains an NBA Finals record.

"What Isiah Thomas did in the second half was just incredible," marveled Riley in his postgame interviews.

Also significant was James Worthy's offensive effort in the face of Detroit's physical defense, a strong enough performance to earn "Big Game James" Finals MVP honors. The only triple-double of his career came in Game 7, when he had 36 points, 16 rebounds, and 10 assists.

The victory gave Riley the repeat he had pushed for, but after Game 7 his players stood close by — to make sure he made no more guarantees about championships.

FINAL STANDINGS

EASTERN CONFERENCE

ATLANTIC DIVISION

	W	L	Pct.
Boston	57	25	.695
Washington	38	44	.463
New York	38	44	.463
Philadelphia	36	46	.439
New Jersey	19	63	.232

CENTRAL DIVISION

	W	L	Pct.
Detroit	54	28	.659
Atlanta	50	32	.610
Chicago	50	32	.610
Milwaukee	42	40	.512
Cleveland	42	40	.512
Indiana	38	44	.463

WESTERN CONFERENCE

MIDWEST DIVISION

	W	L	Pct.
Denver	54	28	.659
Dallas	53	29	.646
Utah	47	35	.573
Houston	46	36	.561
San Antonio	31	51	.378
Sacramento	24	58	.293

PACIFIC DIVISION

	W	L	Pct.
L.A. Lakers	62	20	.756
Portland	53	29	.646
Seattle	44	38	.537
Phoenix	28	54	.341
Golden State	20	62	.244
L.A. Clippers	17	65	.207

PLAYOFFS

EASTERN CONFERENCE

FIRST ROUND

Boston 3, New York 1

Apr. 29 ....@Boston 112, New York 92
May 1 ......@Boston 128, New York 102
May 4 ......@New York 109, Boston 100
May 6 ......Boston 102, @New York 94

Detroit 3, Washington 2

Apr. 28 ....@Detroit 96, Washington 87
Apr. 30 ....@Detroit 102, Washington 101
May 2 ......@Washington 114, Detroit 106*
May 4 ......@Washington 106, Detroit 103
May 8 ......@Detroit 99, Washington 78

Chicago 3, Cleveland 2

Apr. 28 ....@Chicago 104, Cleveland 93
May 1 ......@Chicago 106, Cleveland 101
May 3 ......@Cleveland 110, Chicago 102
May 5 ......@Cleveland 97, Chicago 91
May 8 ......@Chicago 107, Cleveland 101

Atlanta 3, Milwaukee 2

Apr. 29 ....@Atlanta 110, Milwaukee 107
May 1 ......@Atlanta 104, Milwaukee 97
May 4 ......@Milwaukee 123, Atlanta 115
May 6 ......@Milwaukee 105, Atlanta 99
May 8 ......@Atlanta 121, Milwaukee 111

SEMIFINALS

Boston 4, Atlanta 3

May 11 ....@Boston 110, Atlanta 101
May 13 ....@Boston 108, Atlanta 97
May 15 ....@Atlanta 110, Boston 92
May 16 ....@Atlanta 118, Boston 109
May 18 ....Atlanta 112, @Boston 104
May 20 ....Boston 102, @Atlanta 100
May 22 ....@Boston 118, Atlanta 116

Detroit 4, Chicago 1

May 10 ....@Detroit 93, Chicago 82
May 12 ....Chicago 105, @Detroit 95
May 14 ....Detroit 101, @Chicago 79
May 15 ....Detroit 96, @Chicago 77
May 18 ....@Detroit 102, Chicago 95

FINALS

Detroit 4, Boston 2

May 25 ....Detroit 104, @Boston 96
May 26 ....@Boston 119, Detroit 115**
May 28 ....@Detroit 98, Boston 94
May 30 ....Boston 79, @Detroit 78
June 1 .....Detroit 102, @Boston 96*
June 3 .....@Detroit 95, Boston 90

*Denotes number of overtime periods.

WESTERN CONFERENCE

FIRST ROUND

L.A. Lakers 3, San Antonio 0

Apr. 29 ....@L.A. Lakers 122, San Antonio 110
May 1 ......@L.A. Lakers 130, San Antonio 112
May 3 ......L.A. Lakers 109, @San Antonio 107

Denver 3, Seattle 2

Apr. 29 ....@Denver 126, Seattle 123
May 1 ......Seattle 111, @Denver 91
May 3 ......Denver 125, @Seattle 114
May 5 ......@Seattle 127, Denver 117
May 7 ......@Denver 115, Seattle 96

Dallas 3, Houston 1

Apr. 28 ....@Dallas 120, Houston 110
Apr. 30 ....Houston 119, @Dallas 108
May 3 ......Dallas 93, @Houston 92
May 5 ......Dallas 107, @Houston 97

Utah 3, Portland 1

Apr. 28 ....@Portland 108, Utah 96
Apr. 30 ....Utah 114, @Portland 105
May 4 ......@Utah 113, Portland 108
May 6 ......@Utah 111, Portland 96

SEMIFINALS

L.A. Lakers 4, Utah 3

May 8 ......@L.A. Lakers 110, Utah 91
May 10 ....Utah 101, @L.A. Lakers 97
May 13 ....@Utah 96, L.A. Lakers 89
May 15 ....L.A. Lakers 113, @Utah 100
May 17 ....@L.A. Lakers 111, Utah 109
May 19 ....@Utah 108, L.A. Lakers 80
May 21 ....@L.A. Lakers 109, Utah 98

Dallas 4, Denver 2

May 10 ....@Denver 126, Dallas 115
May 12 ....Dallas 112, @Denver 108
May 14 ....Denver 107, @Dallas 105
May 15 ....@Dallas 124, Denver 103
May 17 ....Dallas 110, @Denver 106
May 19 ....@Dallas 108, Denver 95

FINALS

L.A. Lakers 4, Dallas 3

May 23 ....@L.A. Lakers 113, Dallas 98
May 25 ....@L.A. Lakers 123, Dallas 101
May 27 ....@Dallas 106, L.A. Lakers 94
May 29 ....@Dallas 118, L.A. Lakers 104
May 31 ....@L.A. Lakers 119, Dallas 102
June 2 .....@Dallas 105, L.A. Lakers 103
June 4 .....@L.A. Lakers 117, Dallas 102

NBA FINALS

L.A. Lakers 4, Detroit 3

June 7 .....Detroit 105, @L.A. Lakers 93
June 9 .....@L.A. Lakers 108, Detroit 96
June 12 ...L.A. Lakers 99, @Detroit 86
June 14 ...@Detroit 111, L.A. Lakers 86
June 16 ...@Detroit 104, L.A. Lakers 94
June 19 ...@L.A. Lakers 103, Detroit 102
June 21 ...@L.A. Lakers 108, Detroit 105

INDIVIDUAL LEADERS

SCORING (minimum 70 games or 1,400 points)

	G	FGM	FTM	Pts.	Avg.
Jordan, Chicago	82	1069	723	2868	35.0
Wilkins, Atlanta	78	909	541	2397	30.7
Bird, Boston	76	881	415	2275	29.9
Barkley, Philadelphia	80	753	714	2264	28.3
Malone, Utah	82	858	552	2268	27.7
Drexler, Portland	81	849	476	2185	27.0
Ellis, Seattle	75	764	303	1938	25.8
Aguirre, Dallas	77	746	388	1932	25.1
English, Denver	80	843	314	2000	25.0
Olajuwon, Houston	79	712	381	1805	22.8

FIELD GOAL PCT. (minimum 300 made)

	FGM	FGA	Pct.
McHale, Boston	550	911	.604
Parish, Boston	442	750	.589
Barkley, Philadelphia	753	1283	.587
Stockton, Utah	454	791	.574
Berry, San Antonio	540	960	.563

THREE-POINT FIELD GOAL PCT. (minimum 25 made)

	FGA	FGM	Pct.
Hodges, Milwaukee-Phoenix	175	86	.491
Price, Cleveland	148	72	.486
Long, Indiana	77	34	.442
Henderson, New York-Philadelphia	163	69	.423
Tripucka, Utah	74	31	.419

FREE THROW PCT. (minimum 125 made)

	FTM	FTA	Pct.
Sikma, Milwaukee	321	348	.922
Bird, Boston	415	453	.916
Long, Indiana	166	183	.907
Gminski, New Jersey-Philadelphia	355	392	.906
Dawkins, San Antonio	198	221	.896

ASSISTS (minimum 70 games or 400 assists)

	G	No.	Avg.
Stockton, Utah	82	1128	13.8
Johnson, L.A. Lakers	72	858	11.9
Jackson, New York	82	868	10.6
Porter, Portland	82	831	10.1
Rivers, Atlanta	80	747	9.3

REBOUNDS (minimum 70 games or 800 rebounds)

	G	Off.	Def.	Tot.	Avg.
Cage, L.A. Clippers	72	371	567	938	13.03
Oakley, Chicago	82	326	740	1066	13.00
Olajuwon, Houston	79	302	657	959	12.1
Malone, Utah	82	277	709	986	12.0
Barkley, Philadelphia	80	385	566	951	11.9
Williams, N.J.	70	298	536	834	11.9

STEALS (minimum 70 games or 125 steals)

	G	No.	Avg.
Jordan, Chicago	82	259	3.16
Robertson, San Antonio	82	243	2.96
Stockton, Utah	82	242	2.95
Lever, Denver	82	223	2.72
Drexler, Portland	81	203	2.51

BLOCKED SHOTS (minimum 70 games or 100 blocked shots)

	G	No.	Avg.
Eaton, Utah	82	304	3.71
Benjamin, L.A. Clippers	66	225	3.41
Ewing, New York	82	245	2.99
Olajuwon, Houston	79	214	2.71
Bol, Washington	77	208	2.70

1986-87 SEASON

Magic Johnson

It was the season of the rubber match and the blazing star.

The Celtics and Lakers had each won three NBA championships in the 1980s, delivering for fans everywhere a cross-country showdown featuring two immensely popular players, Larry Bird and Magic Johnson.

Even better for the league, there was a growing subplot — the starburst of Michael Jordan.

Not since Wilt Chamberlain's exploits in the early 1960s had the NBA seen such individual scoring brilliance. Jordan tore through the league with a vengeance, scoring 3,041 points for a 37.1 average, marking the first time a player had eclipsed the 3,000-point mark since Chamberlain in 1962-63.

"I had to be the igniter, to get the fire going," Jordan said. "So a lot of my individual skills had to come out."

Thirty-seven times that season Jordan scored 40 or more points. Eight times he ran up 50 or more. During late November and early December he scored 40 or more points in nine straight games, six of them coming on a Western road trip.

After winning the All-Star Slam Dunk Championship, Jordan scored 58 points against the Nets, breaking Chet Walker's franchise regular-season record of 57. A few days later, despite a painful corn on his left foot, he blasted the Pistons for 61 in an overtime victory before 30,281 at the Pontiac Silverdome. "I don't know how he did it," teammate John Paxson said. "Every night someone else was standing in his face, and he never took a step back."

Aside from Jordan, the player who had been asked to do the biggest job for his team was Magic Johnson. As Kareem Abdul-Jabbar approached 40, Lakers coach Pat Riley asked Magic to take on more of the scoring load. Johnson responded by averaging a career-best 23.9 points per game while still leading the league in assists (12.2).

The Lakers won 65 games and devastated the competition in the West, going 11-1 in the Western Conference Playoffs on the way to a showdown with Boston.

The defending champion Celtics won 59 games, but injuries to Bill Walton and Scott Wedman decimated their bench. As a result, Bird, Robert Parish, Kevin McHale and Dennis Johnson each played more than 37 minutes per game and Danny Ainge played 35.

Boston showed fatigue while being extended to seven games by both Milwaukee and Detroit, though the Celtics still advanced to the Finals for the fourth straight year. But the rested Lakers jumped out to a 2-0 lead, living up to their "Showtime" aura.

Boston won Game 3 behind a 30-point effort from Bird. Game 4 came down to one memorable sequence. With the Lakers trailing 106-104 Abdul-Jabbar was fouled, and made the first free throw but missed the second. However the rebound was batted out of bounds and ruled Lakers' ball. Johnson took the inbounds pass on the left side and considered a 20-footer, but McHale came out to prevent that. So Johnson drove into the key and was met by Bird and Parish, with McHale still hounding him. Magic managed to loft a hook shot over Boston's tall trio, and when the shot found the net, the Lakers led by one. With two seconds left after a timeout, Bird somehow got open for a long jumper, but the shot rimmed out. The Lakers had stolen a game in Boston and would eventually win the series in six games after returning to Los Angeles.

"You expect to lose on a sky-hook," said Bird later. "You don't expect it to be from Magic."

NBA.COM FACT

The West defeated the East 154-149 in the NBA All-Star Game at Seattle's Kingdome on February 8, 1987. The combined 303 points set a record for the midwinter game.

FINAL STANDINGS

EASTERN CONFERENCE

ATLANTIC DIVISION

	W	L	Pct.
Boston	59	23	.720
Philadelphia	45	37	.549
Washington	42	40	.512
New Jersey	24	58	.293
New York	24	58	.293

CENTRAL DIVISION

	W	L	Pct.
Atlanta	57	25	.695
Detroit	52	30	.634
Milwaukee	50	32	.610
Indiana	41	41	.500
Chicago	40	42	.488
Cleveland	31	51	.378

WESTERN CONFERENCE

MIDWEST DIVISION

	W	L	Pct.
Dallas	55	27	.671
Utah	44	38	.537
Houston	42	40	.512
Denver	37	45	.451
Sacramento	29	53	.354
San Antonio	28	54	.341

PACIFIC DIVISION

	W	L	Pct.
L.A. Lakers	65	17	.793
Portland	49	33	.598
Golden State	42	40	.512
Seattle	39	43	.476
Phoenix	36	46	.439
L.A. Clippers	12	70	.146

PLAYOFFS

EASTERN CONFERENCE

FIRST ROUND

Boston 3, Chicago 0

Apr. 23 ....@Boston 108, Chicago 104
Apr. 26 ....@Boston 105, Chicago 96
Apr. 28 ....Boston 105, @Chicago 94

Milwaukee 3, Philadelphia 2

Apr. 24 ....@Milwaukee 107, Philadelphia 104
Apr. 26 ....Philadelphia 125, @Milwaukee 122*
Apr. 29 ....Milwaukee 121, @Philadelphia 120
May 1 ......@Philadelphia 124, Milwaukee 118
May 3 ......@Milwaukee 102, Philadelphia 89

Detroit 3, Washington 0

Apr. 24 ....@Detroit 106, Washington 92
Apr. 26 ....@Detroit 128, Washington 85
Apr. 29 ....Detroit 97, @Washington 96

Atlanta 3, Indiana 1

Apr. 24 ....@Atlanta 110, Indiana 94
Apr. 26 ....@Atlanta 94, Indiana 93
Apr. 29 ....@Indiana 96, Atlanta 87
May 1 ......Atlanta 101, @Indiana 97

SEMIFINALS

Detroit 4, Atlanta 1

May 3 ......Detroit 112, @Atlanta 111
May 5 ......@Atlanta 115, Detroit 102
May 8 ......@Detroit 108, Atlanta 99
May 10 ....@Detroit 89, Atlanta 88
May 13 ....Detroit 104, @Atlanta 96

Boston 4, Milwaukee 3

May 5 ......@Boston 111, Milwaukee 98
May 6 ......@Boston 126, Milwaukee 124
May 8 ......@Milwaukee 126, Boston 121*
May 10 ....Boston 138, @Milwaukee 137**
May 13 ....Milwaukee 129, @Boston 124
May 15 ....@Milwaukee 121, Boston 111
May 17 ....@Boston 119, Milwaukee 113

FINALS

Boston 4, Detroit 3

May 19 ....@Boston 104, Detroit 91
May 21 ....@Boston 110, Detroit 101
May 23 ....@Detroit 122, Boston 104
May 24 ....@Detroit 145, Boston 119
May 26 ....@Boston 108, Detroit 107
May 28 ....@Detroit 113, Boston 105
May 30 ....@Boston 117, Detroit 114

WESTERN CONFERENCE

FIRST ROUND

L.A. Lakers 3, Denver 0

Apr. 23 ....@L.A. Lakers 128, Denver 95
Apr. 25 ....@L.A. Lakers 139, Denver 127
Apr. 29 ....L.A. Lakers 140, @Denver 103

Golden State 3, Utah 2

Apr. 23 ....@Utah 99, Golden State 85
Apr. 25 ....@Utah 103, Golden State 100
Apr. 29 ....@Golden State 110, Utah 95
May 1 ......@Golden State 98, Utah 94
May 3 ......Golden State 118, @Utah 113

Houston 3, Portland 1

Apr. 24 ....Houston 125, @Portland 115
Apr. 26 ....@Portland 111, Houston 98
Apr. 28 ....@Houston 117, Portland 108
Apr. 30 ....@Houston 113, Portland 101

Seattle 3, Dallas 1

Apr. 23 ....@Dallas 151, Seattle 129
Apr. 25 ....Seattle 112, @Dallas 110
Apr. 28 ....@Seattle 117, Dallas 107
Apr. 30 ....@Seattle 124, Dallas 98

SEMIFINALS

Seattle 4, Houston 2

May 2 ......Seattle 111, @Houston 106*
May 5 ......Seattle 99, @Houston 97
May 7 ......Houston 102, @Seattle 84
May 9 ......@Seattle 117, Houston 102
May 12 ....@Houston 112, Seattle 107
May 14 ....@Seattle 128, Houston 125**

L.A. Lakers 4, Golden State 1

May 5 ......@L.A. Lakers 125, Golden State 116
May 7 ......@L.A. Lakers 116, Golden State 101
May 9 ......L.A. Lakers 133, @Golden State 108
May 10 ....@Golden State 129, L.A. Lakers 121
May 12 ....@L.A. Lakers 118, Golden State 106

FINALS

L.A. Lakers 4, Seattle 0

May 16 ....@L.A. Lakers 92, Seattle 87
May 19 ....@L.A. Lakers 112, Seattle 104
May 23 ....L.A. Lakers 122, @Seattle 121
May 25 ....L.A. Lakers 133, @Seattle 102

NBA FINALS

L.A. Lakers 4, Boston 2

June 2 .....@L.A. Lakers 126, Boston 113
June 4 .....@L.A. Lakers 141, Boston 122
June 7 .....@Boston 109, L.A. Lakers 103
June 9 .....L.A. Lakers 107, @Boston 106
June 11 ...@Boston 123, L.A. Lakers 108
June 14 ...@L.A. Lakers 106, Boston 93

*Denotes number of overtime periods.

INDIVIDUAL LEADERS

SCORING (minimum 70 games or 1,400 points)

	G	FGM	FTM	Pts.	Avg.
Jordan, Chicago	82	1098	833	3041	37.1
Wilkins, Atlanta	79	828	607	2294	29.0
English, Denver	82	965	411	2345	28.6
Bird, Boston	74	786	414	2076	28.1
Vandeweghe, Portland	79	808	467	2122	26.9
McHale, Boston	77	790	428	2008	26.1
Aguirre, Dallas	80	787	429	2056	25.7
Ellis, Seattle	82	785	385	2041	24.9
Malone, Washington	73	595	570	1760	24.1
Johnson, L.A. Lakers	80	683	535	1909	23.9

FIELD GOAL PCT. (minimum 300 made)

	FGM	FGA	Pct.
McHale, Boston	790	1307	.604
Gilmore, San Antonio	346	580	.597
Barkley, Philadelphia	557	937	.594
Donaldson, Dallas	311	531	.586
Abdul-Jabbar, L.A. Lakers	560	993	.564

THREE-POINT FIELD GOAL PCT. (minimum 25 made)

	FGA	FGM	Pct.
Vandeweghe, Portland	81	39	.481
Schrempf, Dallas	69	33	.478
Ainge, Boston	192	85	.443
Scott, L.A. Lakers	149	65	.436
Tucker, New York	161	68	.422

FREE THROW PCT. (minimum 125 made)

	FTM	FTA	Pct.
Bird, Boston	414	455	.910
Ainge, Boston	148	165	.897
Laimbeer, Detroit	245	274	.894
Scott, L.A. Lakers	224	251	.892
Hodges, Milwaukee	131	147	.891

ASSISTS (minimum 70 games or 400 assists)

	G	No.	Avg.
Johnson, L.A. Lakers	80	977	12.2
Floyd, Golden State	82	848	10.3
Thomas, Detroit	81	813	10.0
Rivers, Atlanta	82	823	10.0
Porter, Portland	80	715	8.9

REBOUNDS (minimum 70 games or 800 rebounds)

	G	Off.	Def.	Tot.	Avg.
Barkley, Philadelphia	68	390	604	994	14.6
Oakley, Chicago	82	299	775	1074	13.1
Williams, New Jersey	82	322	701	1023	12.5
Donaldson, Dallas	82	295	678	973	11.9
Laimbeer, Detroit	82	243	712	955	11.6

STEALS (minimum 70 games or 125 steals)

	G	No.	Avg.
Robertson, San Antonio	81	260	3.21
Jordan, Chicago	82	236	2.88
Cheeks, Philadelphia	68	180	2.65
Harper, Cleveland	82	209	2.55
Drexler, Portland	82	204	2.49

BLOCKED SHOTS (minimum 70 games or 100 blocked shots)

	G	No.	Avg.
Eaton, Utah	79	321	4.06
Bol, Washington	82	302	3.68
Olajuwon, Houston	75	254	3.39
Benjamin, L.A. Clippers	72	187	2.60
Lister, Seattle	75	180	2.40

1985-86 SEASON

Bill Walton

The NBA fostered the air of a podiatry convention as two key players found glory in the aftermath of foot injuries.

Both stories were huge. Bill Walton, long plagued with failing feet, joined the Boston Celtics and found a celebrated role as sixth man on a team headed to greatness.

And Michael Jordan, sidelined by a career-threatening injury just days into the season, came back despite the wishes of Bulls management to register a performance basketball fans will never forget.

Walton went to Boston from the Los Angeles Clippers in a trade for Cedric Maxwell, MVP of the Celtics' 1981 title run.

The acquisition of Walton gave Larry Bird hope, which he promptly cashed in, winning his third consecutive MVP while erasing the heavy memory of the loss to the Lakers in the 1985 Finals. The presence of Big Bill added yet another brilliant passer for the Celtics' ball-movement attack. And Bird headed the parade back to the top, finishing in the NBA's Top 10 in five categories: scoring (25.8 points per game, fourth), rebounding (9.8 per game, seventh), steals (2.02, ninth), free throw percentage (.896, first) and three-point field goal percentage (.423, fourth).

Walton shocked NBA observers by playing a career-high 80 games as a valuable backup to Robert Parish and Kevin McHale. The contributions of fellow reserves Scott Wedman and Jerry Sichting helped propel Boston to a franchise-best 67-15 record, including an astounding 40-1 record at home.

It was in the first round of the playoffs that the foot convention convened. Boston swept Chicago, but not before Jordan set the NBA abuzz with a playoff-record 63-point performance in a double-overtime loss on April 20 in Boston Garden. "I think he's God disguised as Michael Jordan," Bird said afterward.

"That was something I'll never forget," recalled Sidney Green, Jordan's teammate. "It was total silence in the locker room before the game. Michael was extremely focused, and we knew he was intent on doing something big."

"That game was when we began to realize just how great Michael could be," said Bulls Chairman Jerry Reinsdorf.

Having survived Jordan's aerials, the Celtics defeated Atlanta in five games and swept Milwaukee to reach the Finals for the third straight season.

The Lakers won 62 games, but were shocked in the Western Conference Finals in five games by the Houston Rockets. Coached by former Boston pilot Bill Fitch, the Rockets employed a Twin Towers look with the 7-4 Ralph Sampson and 7-0 Hakeem Olajuwon playing together. Houston had won the Midwest Division and two playoff series, but when the Lakers took Game 1 of the Western Finals, NBA fans anticipated another Boston-L.A. meeting. The Rockets surprised everyone by winning the next four games to advance to the championship series.

The Rockets brought a new wrinkle to the NBA by starting two uncommonly agile big players. But the Celtics, unlike most teams, had the answer up front with Parish, Bird and McHale, with Walton off the bench. Although the Celtics received much praise for their unselfish, crisp-passing offense, their defense was key in bringing down Houston in six games.

"I don't remember the last time I was hounded by a team more than I was today," Sampson said after Game 6. "Every time I touched the ball, there were two and three guys around me. And that went for Hakeem, too."

Playing at the top of his game, Bird averaged 24.0 points, 9.7 rebounds and 9.5 assists as Boston captured its 16th title.

NBA.COM FACT

The Portland Trail Blazers were the only team to defeat the Celtics in Boston Garden during the 1985-86 season. The Celtics finished 50-1 at home, including the playoffs.

FINAL STANDINGS

EASTERN CONFERENCE

ATLANTIC DIVISION

	W	L	Pct.
Boston	67	15	.817
Philadelphia	54	28	.659
New Jersey	39	43	.476
Washington	39	43	.476
New York	23	59	.280

CENTRAL DIVISION

	W	L	Pct.
Milwaukee	57	25	.695
Atlanta	50	32	.610
Detroit	46	36	.561
Chicago	30	52	.366
Cleveland	29	53	.354
Indiana	26	56	.317

WESTERN CONFERENCE

MIDWEST DIVISION

	W	L	Pct.
Houston	51	31	.622
Denver	47	35	.573
Dallas	44	38	.537
Utah	42	40	.512
Sacramento	37	45	.451
San Antonio	35	47	.427

PACIFIC DIVISION

	W	L	Pct.
L.A. Lakers	62	20	.756
Portland	40	42	.488
L.A. Clippers	32	50	.390
Phoenix	32	50	.390
Seattle	31	51	.378
Golden State	30	52	.366

PLAYOFFS

EASTERN CONFERENCE

FIRST ROUND

Boston 3, Chicago 0
Apr. 17 ....@Boston 123, Chicago 104
Apr. 20 ....@Boston 135, Chicago 131**
Apr. 22 ....Boston 122, @Chicago 104

Milwaukee 3, New Jersey 0
Apr. 18 ....@Milwaukee 119, New Jersey 107
Apr. 20 ....@Milwaukee 111, New Jersey 97
Apr. 22 ....Milwaukee 118, @New Jersey 113

Philadelphia 3, Washington 2
Apr. 18 ....Washington 95, @Philadelphia 94
Apr. 20 ....@Philadelphia 102, Washington 97
Apr. 22 ....Philadelphia 91, @Washington 86
Apr. 24 ....@Washington 116, Philadelphia 111
Apr. 27 ....@Philadelphia 134, Washington 109

Atlanta 3, Detroit 1
Apr. 17 ....@Atlanta 140, Detroit 122
Apr. 19 ....@Atlanta 137, Detroit 125
Apr. 22 ....@Detroit 106, Atlanta 97
Apr. 25 ....Atlanta 114, @Detroit 113**

SEMIFINALS

Boston 4, Atlanta 1
Apr. 27 ....@Boston 103, Atlanta 91
Apr. 29 ....@Boston 119, Atlanta 108
May 2 ......Boston 111, @Atlanta 107
May 4 ......@Atlanta 106, Boston 94
May 6 ......@Boston 132, Atlanta 99

Milwaukee 4, Philadelphia 3
Apr. 29 ....Philadelphia 118, @Milwaukee 112
May 1 ......@Milwaukee 119, Philadelphia 107
May 3 ......@Philadelphia 107, Milwaukee 103
May 5 ......Milwaukee 109, @Philadelphia 104
May 7 ......@Milwaukee 113, Philadelphia 108
May 9 ......@Philadelphia 126, Milwaukee 108
May 11 ....@Milwaukee 113, Philadelphia 112

FINALS

Boston 4, Milwaukee 0
May 13 ....@Boston 128, Milwaukee 96
May 15 ....@Boston 122, Milwaukee 111
May 17 ....Boston 111, @Milwaukee 107
May 18 ....Boston 111, @Milwaukee 98

WESTERN CONFERENCE

FIRST ROUND

L.A. Lakers 3, San Antonio 0
Apr. 17 ....@L.A. Lakers 135, San Antonio 88
Apr. 19 ....@L.A. Lakers 122, San Antonio 94
Apr. 23 ....L.A. Lakers 114, @San Antonio 94

Houston 3, Sacramento 0
Apr. 17 ....@Houston 107, Sacramento 87
Apr. 19 ....@Houston 111, Sacramento 103
Apr. 22 ....Houston 113, @Sacramento 98

Denver 3, Portland 1
Apr. 18 ....@Denver 133, Portland 126
Apr. 20 ....Portland 108, @Denver 106
Apr. 22 ....Denver 115, @Portland 104
Apr. 24 ....Denver 116, @Portland 112

Dallas 3, Utah 1
Apr. 18 ....@Dallas 101, Utah 93
Apr. 20 ....@Dallas 113, Utah 106
Apr. 23 ....@Utah 100, Dallas 98
Apr. 25 ....Dallas 117, @Utah 113

SEMIFINALS

L.A. Lakers 4, Dallas 2
Apr. 27 ....@L.A. Lakers 130, Dallas 116
Apr. 30 ....@L.A. Lakers 117, Dallas 113
May 2 ......@Dallas 110, L.A. Lakers 108
May 4 ......@Dallas 120, L.A. Lakers 118
May 6 ......@L.A. Lakers 116, Dallas 113
May 8 ......L.A. Lakers 120, @Dallas 107

Houston 4, Denver 2
Apr. 26 ....@Houston 126, Denver 119
Apr. 29 ....@Houston 119, Denver 101
May 2 ......@Denver 116, Houston 115
May 4 ......@Denver 114, Houston 111*
May 6 ......@Houston 131, Denver 103
May 8 ......Houston 126, @Denver 122**

FINALS

Houston 4, L.A. Lakers 1
May 10 ....@L.A. Lakers 119, Houston 107
May 13 ....Houston 112, @L.A. Lakers 102
May 16 ....@Houston 117, L.A. Lakers 109
May 18 ....@Houston 105, L.A. Lakers 95
May 21 ....Houston 114, @L.A. Lakers 112

NBA FINALS

Boston 4, Houston 2
May 26 ....@Boston 112, Houston 100
May 29 ....@Boston 117, Houston 95
June 1 .....@Houston 106, Boston 104
June 3 .....Boston 106, @Houston 103
June 5 .....@Houston 111, Boston 96
June 8 .....@Boston 114, Houston 97

*Denotes number of overtime periods.

INDIVIDUAL LEADERS

SCORING (minimum 70 games or 1,400 points)

	G	FGM	FTM	Pts.	Avg.
Wilkins, Atlanta	78	888	577	2366	30.3
Dantley, Utah	76	818	630	2267	29.8
English, Denver	81	951	511	2414	29.8
Bird, Boston	82	796	441	2115	25.8
Short, Golden State	64	633	351	1632	25.5
Vandeweghe, Portland	79	719	523	1962	24.8
Malone, Philadelphia	74	571	617	1759	23.8
Olajuwon, Houston	68	625	347	1597	23.5
Abdul-Jabbar, L.A. Lakers	79	755	336	1846	23.4
Free, Cleveland	75	652	379	1754	23.4
Mitchell, San Antonio	82	802	317	1921	23.4

FIELD GOAL PCT. (minimum 300 made)

	FGM	FGA	Pct.
Johnson, San Antonio	362	573	.632
Gilmore, San Antonio	423	684	.618
Nance, Phoenix	582	1001	.581
Worthy, L.A. Lakers	629	1086	.579
McHale, Boston	561	978	.574

THREE-POINT FIELD GOAL PCT. (minimum 25 made)

	FGA	FGM	Pct.
Hodges, Milwaukee	162	73	.451
Tucker, New York	91	41	.451
Grunfeld, New York	61	26	.426
Bird, Boston	194	82	.423
Free, Cleveland	169	71	.420

FREE THROW PCT. (minimum 125 made)

	FTM	FTA	Pct.
Bird, Boston	441	492	.896
Mullin, Golden State	189	211	.896
Gminski, New Jersey	351	393	.893
Paxson, Portland	217	244	.889
Gervin, Chicago	283	322	.879

ASSISTS (minimum 70 games or 400 assists)

	G	No.	Avg.
Johnson, L.A. Lakers	72	907	12.6
Thomas, Detroit	77	830	10.8
Theus, Sacramento	82	788	9.6
Bagley, Cleveland	78	735	9.4
Cheeks, Philadelphia	82	753	9.2

REBOUNDS (minimum 70 games or 800 rebounds)

	G	Off.	Def.	Tot.	Avg.
Laimbeer, Detroit	82	305	770	1075	13.1
Barkley, Philadelphia	80	354	672	1026	12.8
Williams, New Jersey	82	329	657	986	12.0
Malone, Philadelphia	74	339	533	872	11.8
Sampson, Houston	79	258	621	879	11.1

STEALS (minimum 70 games or 125 steals)

	G	No.	Avg.
Robertson, San Antonio	82	301	3.67
Richardson, New Jersey	47	125	2.66
Drexler, Portland	75	197	2.63
Cheeks, Philadelphia	82	207	2.52
Lever, Denver	78	178	2.28

BLOCKED SHOTS (minimum 70 games or 100 blocked shots)

	G	No.	Avg.
Bol, Washington	80	397	4.96
Eaton, Utah	80	369	4.61
Olajuwon, Houston	68	231	3.40
Cooper, Denver	78	227	2.91
Benjamin, L.A. Clippers	79	206	2.61

1984-85 SEASON

Pat Riley

It was the big hurt, Boston Celtics style. Favored to win the 1984 title, Los Angeles lost to Boston yet again, bowing to the same Celtics franchise that had defeated the Lakers seven previous times in the league championship series, an ache that stretched over parts of four decades and two cities.

Thus began the NBA's grandest tale of redemption. Lakers coach Pat Riley and his players spent the 1985 season aching for a rematch.

The main diversion from this intensity came with the bevy of young talent that had entered the league in the 1984 draft, including Michael Jordan, Hakeem Olajuwon, Charles Barkley and John Stockton. Olajuwon was chosen first by Houston, Jordan third by Chicago, Barkley fifth by Philadelphia and Stockton 16th by Utah.

That summer Jordan thrilled television audiences in leading the United States to the gold medal in the 1984 Olympic Games in Los Angeles. "When Michael gets the ball on the break only one thing's going to happen," said Olympic teammate Steve Alford. "Some kind of dunk. Sometimes the players get into the habit of just watching Michael, because he's usually going to do something you don't want to miss."

NBA observers said the same thing once he joined the Bulls that fall. Jordan scored 27 in an early loss to the Celtics at Chicago Stadium. "I've never seen one player turn a team around like that," Larry Bird said afterward. "All the Bulls have become better because of him … Pretty soon this place will be packed every night … They'll pay just to watch Jordan. Heck, there was one drive tonight. He had the ball up in his right hand, then he took it down. Then he brought it back up. I got a hand on it, fouled him, and he still scored. All the while, he's in the air.

"You have to play this game to know how difficult that is. You see that and say, 'Well, what the heck can you do?'"

In New York, Bernard King won the scoring title (32.9 points per game) despite suffering a serious knee injury with 27 games left in the season.

For the most part though, the NBA was focused intently on the Celtics-Lakers matchup. During the regular season, Boston was the class of the East with 63 victories, and Bird enjoyed his best season to date, averaging 28.7 points, 10.5 rebounds and 6.6 assists. Each member of Boston's starting five — Bird, Robert Parish, Kevin McHale, Dennis Johnson and Danny Ainge — played more than 2,500 minutes.

The Lakers, meanwhile, won 62 games and easily dispatched Phoenix, Portland and Denver to reach the Finals and a rematch with Boston, which had beaten Cleveland, Detroit and Philadelphia. Led by 38-year-old center Kareem Abdul-Jabbar and a revitalized James Worthy, the Lakers went to Boston Garden for Game 1 filled with hope, only to suffer a 148-114 defeat that became known as the Memorial Day Massacre.

"That game was a blessing in disguise," Riley said later. "It strengthened the fiber of this team."

Burning with humiliation, the Lakers won the next game in Boston, took two of the three games in Los Angeles and then closed out the series with a 111-100 decision in Game 6 on the parquet. The sound of silence in Boston Garden was sweet music indeed, for generations of frustrated Laker faithful.

"All of our skeletons are out of the closet," Riley said afterward. "I don't want to hear about history anymore. The history is this: This was our year. And we did it on the parquet floor. Maybe that's the ultimate test."

NBA.COM FACT

The Lakers set an NBA record for field goal percentage (.545), breaking the mark (.532) they had set the season before.

FINAL STANDINGS

EASTERN CONFERENCE

ATLANTIC DIVISION

	W	L	Pct.
Boston	63	19	.768
Philadelphia	58	24	.707
New Jersey	42	40	.512
Washington	40	42	.488
New York	24	58	.293

CENTRAL DIVISION

	W	L	Pct.
Milwaukee	59	23	.720
Detroit	46	36	.561
Chicago	38	44	.463
Cleveland	36	46	.439
Atlanta	34	48	.415
Indiana	22	60	.268

WESTERN CONFERENCE

MIDWEST DIVISION

	W	L	Pct.
Denver	52	30	.634
Houston	48	34	.585
Dallas	44	38	.537
San Antonio	41	41	.500
Utah	41	41	.500
Kansas City	31	51	.378

PACIFIC DIVISION

	W	L	Pct.
L.A. Lakers	62	20	.756
Portland	42	40	.512
Phoenix	36	46	.439
L.A. Clippers	31	51	.378
Seattle	31	51	.378
Golden State	22	60	.268

PLAYOFFS

EASTERN CONFERENCE

FIRST ROUND

Boston 3, Cleveland 1
Apr. 18 ....@Boston 126, Cleveland 123
Apr. 20 ....@Boston 108, Cleveland 106
Apr. 23 ....@Cleveland 105, Boston 98
Apr. 25 ....Boston 117, @Cleveland 115

Milwaukee 3, Chicago 1
Apr. 19 ....@Milwaukee 109, Chicago 100
Apr. 21 ....@Milwaukee 122, Chicago 115
Apr. 24 ....@Chicago 109, Milwaukee 107
Apr. 26 ....Milwaukee 105, @Chicago 97

Philadelphia 3, Washington 1
Apr. 17 ....@Philadelphia 104, Washington 97
Apr. 21 ....@Philadelphia 113, Washington 94
Apr. 24 ....@Washington 118, Philadelphia 100
Apr. 26 ....Philadelphia 106, @Washington 98

Detroit 3, New Jersey 0
Apr. 18 ....@Detroit 125, New Jersey 105
Apr. 21 ....@Detroit 121, New Jersey 111
Apr. 24 ....Detroit 116, @New Jersey 115

SEMIFINALS

Boston 4, Detroit 2
Apr. 28 ....@Boston 133, Detroit 99
Apr. 30 ....@Boston 121, Detroit 114
May 2......@Detroit 125, Boston 117
May 5......@Detroit 102, Boston 99
May 8......@Boston 130, Detroit 123
May 10 ....Boston 123, @Detroit 113

Philadelphia 4, Milwaukee 0
Apr. 28 ....Philadelphia 127, @Milwaukee 105
Apr. 30 ....Philadelphia 112, @Milwaukee 108
May 3......@Philadelphia 109, Milwaukee 104
May 5......@Philadelphia 121, Milwaukee 112

FINALS

Boston 4, Philadelphia 1
May 12....@Boston 108, Philadelphia 93
May 14....@Boston 106, Philadelphia 98
May 18....Boston 105, @Philadelphia 94
May 19....@Philadelphia 115, Boston 104
May 22....@Boston 102, Philadelphia 100

WESTERN CONFERENCE

FIRST ROUND

L.A. Lakers 3, Phoenix 0
Apr. 18 ....@L.A. Lakers 142, Phoenix 114
Apr. 20 ....@L.A. Lakers 147, Phoenix 130
Apr. 23 ....L.A. Lakers 119, @Phoenix 103

Denver 3, San Antonio 2
Apr. 18 ....@Denver 141, San Antonio 111
Apr. 20 ....San Antonio 113, @Denver 111
Apr. 23 ....Denver 115, @San Antonio 112
Apr. 26 ....@San Antonio 116, Denver 111
Apr. 28 ....@Denver 126, San Antonio 99

Utah 3, Houston 2
Apr. 19 ....Utah 115, @Houston 101
Apr. 21 ....@Houston 122, Utah 96
Apr. 24 ....@Utah 112, Houston 104
Apr. 26 ....Houston 96, @Utah 94
Apr. 28 ....Utah 104, @Houston 97

Portland 3, Dallas 1
Apr. 18 ....@Dallas 139, Portland 131**
Apr. 20 ....Portland 124, @Dallas 121*
Apr. 23 ....@Portland 122, Dallas 109
Apr. 25 ....@Portland 115, Dallas 113

SEMIFINALS

L.A. Lakers 4, Portland 1
Apr. 27 ....@L.A. Lakers 125, Portland 101
Apr. 30 ....@L.A. Lakers 134, Portland 118
May 3......L.A. Lakers 130, @Portland 126
May 5......@Portland 115, L.A. Lakers 107
May 7......@L.A. Lakers 139, Portland 120

Denver 4, Utah 1
Apr. 30 ....@Denver 130, Utah 113
May 2......@Denver 131, Utah 123*
May 4......@Utah 131, Denver 123
May 5......Denver 125, @Utah 118
May 7......@Denver 116, Utah 104

FINALS

L.A. Lakers 4, Denver 1
May 11 ....@L.A. Lakers 139, Denver 122
May 14....Denver 136, @L.A. Lakers 114
May 17....L.A. Lakers 136, @Denver 118
May 19....L.A. Lakers 120, @Denver 116
May 22 ....@L.A. Lakers 153, Denver 109

NBA FINALS

L.A. Lakers 4, Boston 2
May 27 ....@Boston 148, L.A. Lakers 114
May 30 ....L.A. Lakers 109, @Boston 102
June 2.....@L.A. Lakers 136, Boston 111
June 5.....Boston 107, @L.A. Lakers 105
June 7.....@L.A. Lakers 120, Boston 111
June 9.....L.A. Lakers 111, @Boston 100

*Denotes number of overtime periods.

INDIVIDUAL LEADERS

SCORING (minimum 70 games or 1,400 points)

	G	FGM	FTM	Pts.	Avg.
King, New York	55	691	426	1809	32.9
Bird, Boston	80	918	403	2295	28.7
Jordan, Chicago	82	837	630	2313	28.2
Short, Golden State	78	819	501	2186	28.0
English, Denver	81	939	383	2262	27.9
Wilkins, Atlanta	81	853	486	2217	27.4
Dantley, Utah	55	512	438	1462	26.6
Aguirre, Dallas	80	794	440	2055	25.7
Malone, Philadelphia	79	602	737	1941	24.6
Cummings, Milwaukee	79	759	343	1861	23.6

FIELD GOAL PCT. (minimum 300 made)

	FGM	FGA	Pct.
Donaldson, L.A. Clippers	351	551	.637
Gilmore, San Antonio	532	854	.623
Thorpe, Kansas City	411	685	.600
Abdul-Jabbar, L.A. Lakers	723	1207	.599
Nance, Phoenix	515	877	.587

THREE-POINT FIELD GOAL PCT. (minimum 25 made)

	FGA	FGM	Pct.
Scott, L.A. Lakers	60	26	.433
Bird, Boston	131	56	.427
Davis, Dallas	115	47	.409
Tucker, New York	72	29	.403
Ellis, Dallas	109	42	.385

FREE THROW PCT. (minimum 125 made)

	FTM	FTA	Pct.
Macy, Phoenix	127	140	.907
Vandeweghe, Portland	369	412	.896
Davis, Dallas	158	178	.888
Tripucka, Detroit	255	288	.885
Adams, Phoenix	250	283	.883

ASSISTS (minimum 70 games or 400 assists)

	G	No.	Avg.
Thomas, Detroit	81	1123	13.9
Johnson, L.A. Lakers	77	968	12.6
Moore, San Antonio	82	816	10.0
Nixon, L.A. Clippers	81	711	8.8
Bagley, Cleveland	81	697	8.6

REBOUNDS (minimum 70 games or 800 rebounds)

	G	Off.	Def.	Tot.	Avg.
Malone, Philadelphia	79	385	646	1031	13.1
Laimbeer, Detroit	82	295	718	1013	12.4
Williams, New Jersey	82	323	682	1005	12.3
Olajuwon, Houston	82	440	534	974	11.9
Eaton, Utah	82	207	720	927	11.3

STEALS (minimum 70 games or 125 steals)

	G	No.	Avg.
Richardson, New Jersey	82	243	2.96
Moore, San Antonio	82	229	2.79
Lever, Denver	82	202	2.46
Jordan, Chicago	82	196	2.39
Rivers, Atlanta	69	163	2.36

BLOCKED SHOTS (minimum 70 games or 100 blocked shots)

	G	No.	Avg.
Eaton, Utah	82	456	5.56
Olajuwon, Houston	82	220	2.68
Bowie, Portland	76	203	2.67
Cooper, Denver	80	197	2.46
Rollins, Atlanta	70	167	2.39

1983-84 SEASON

Bernard King

HIGHEST-SCORING GAME IN NBA HISTORY

December 13, 1983, At Denver

DETROIT PISTONS (186)

	FGM	FGA	FTM	FTA	Pts.
Kelly Tripucka	14	25	7	9	35
Cliff Levingston	1	2	0	0	2
Bill Laimbeer	6	10	5	9	17
Isiah Thomas	18	34	10	19	47
John Long	18	25	5	6	41
Terry Tyler	8	15	2	3	18
Vinnie Johnson	4	12	4	5	12
Earl Cureton	3	6	3	5	9
Ray Tolbert	1	4	1	4	3
Walker Russell	1	2	0	0	2
Kent Benson	0	1	0	0	0
David Thirdkill	0	0	0	0	0
Totals	**74**	**136**	**37**	**60**	**186**

DENVER NUGGETS (184)

	FGM	FGA	FTM	FTA	Pts.
Alex English	18	30	11	13	47
Kiki Vandeweghe	21	29	9	11	51
Dan Issel	11	19	6	8	28
Rob Williams	3	8	3	4	9
T.R. Dunn	3	3	1	2	7
Mike Evans	7	13	2	2	16
Richard Anderson	5	6	2	3	13
Danny Schayes	0	1	11	12	11
Bill Hanzlik	0	4	2	2	2
Howard Carter	0	1	0	0	0
Ken Dennard	0	1	0	0	0
Totals	**68**	**115**	**47**	**57**	**184**

SCORE BY PERIODS

	1st	2nd	3rd	4th	OT	OT	OT	Tot.
Detroit	38	36	34	37	14	12	15	186
Denver	34	40	39	32	14	12	13	184

3-pt. Field goals: Thomas 1-2, Anderson 1-1, Issel 0-1.

Officials: Joe Borgia, Jesse Hall.

Attendance: 9,655.

Time of game: 3:11.

Whoever wrote "When Irish Eyes Are Smiling" must have somehow foreseen the 1984 NBA Playoffs.

After four seasons in the league, Magic Johnson and Larry Bird would finally renew their college rivalry in a championship showdown. Johnson's Lakers had won two titles and Bird's Celtics had captured one, but not against each other. Their teams met only twice a year during the regular season, and they would both later admit to wanting more as they followed each other's progress in the morning papers.

The playoff system underwent a radical expansion. The field was expanded to include 16 teams instead of 12, which eliminated the first-round byes and the best-of-three miniseries. Instead, each first round series would be a best-of-five, and even the division winners would have to play in the first round. To be crowned NBA champion, a team would have to win four series for the first time in NBA history.

That hardly deterred Boston or L.A.

During the regular season, the Celtics rolled to 62 wins and took the Atlantic Division by 10 games over the defending champion 76ers. Philadelphia won 52 games but was ousted in the first round of the playoffs by New Jersey, the high point in that franchise's history. The Celtics eased past Washington, defeated the Bernard King-led New York Knicks in seven games and easily moved past Milwaukee to reach the Finals.

The Lakers had won 54 games during the regular season and had played especially well in the spring, finding the kind of chemistry that awed opponents, even the Celtics. By playoff time, Los Angeles appeared to be the best team in the league.

The Lakers' spring was further highlighted with Kareem Abdul-Jabbar's ascension to the NBA's career scoring leader. On April 5, in the unlikely locale of Las Vegas, where the Utah Jazz played some of their home games, he surpassed Wilt Chamberlain's mark of 31,419 points.

Once in the playoffs, the Lakers defeated Kansas City, Dallas and Phoenix, losing only three games along the way and building up a substantial head of steam for their meeting with Boston. The Lakers won the first game in Boston and led Game 2, 115-113 with possession of the ball and 18 seconds left. The thought of a series sweep was on the minds of players on both sides. But Boston's Gerald Henderson intercepted James Worthy's crosscourt pass and went in for an uncontested layup to tie the score. Boston won the game in overtime on a shot by Scott Wedman.

The Lakers easily won Game 3 in L.A. with Johnson setting a Finals record with 21 assists and Bird fussing afterward, "We played like a bunch of sissies." Spurred by that criticism, his teammates rebounded with a physical victory in Game 4. The Celtics forced overtime by overcoming a five-point deficit with a minute to play, in part because Johnson missed two key free throws. Boston then outmuscled the Lakers in the extra period after another crucial miss from the free throw line by Worthy.

"We had to go out and make things happen," Henderson said. "If being physical was gonna do it, then we had to do it."

Bird scored 34 in the pivotal Game 5 in a sweltering Boston Garden, where the temperature at courtside was 97 degrees at game time. L.A. took Game 6 at home, setting the table for Cedric Maxwell to come alive for the Celtics in Game 7 with 24 points, eight assists and eight rebounds.

The Lakers couldn't overcome the feeling that they had given away the championship in Games 2 and 4. Even the Celtics felt that way. "To be honest, they should have swept," Bird said.

The season also saw a significant change off the court. Larry O'Brien, who had presided over the merger of the NBA and the ABA, retired as commissioner. In his place came David Stern, the league's executive vice president, with a knack for marketing. He would oversee the development of a cohesive and profitable broadcasting strategy and lead the sport into a period of unprecedented global popularity.

FINAL STANDINGS

EASTERN CONFERENCE

ATLANTIC DIVISION

	W	L	Pct.
Boston	62	20	.756
Philadelphia	52	30	.634
New York	47	35	.573
New Jersey	45	37	.549
Washington	35	47	.427

CENTRAL DIVISION

	W	L	Pct.
Milwaukee	50	32	.610
Detroit	49	33	.598
Atlanta	40	42	.488
Cleveland	28	54	.341
Chicago	27	55	.329
Indiana	26	56	.317

WESTERN CONFERENCE

MIDWEST DIVISION

	W	L	Pct.
Utah	45	37	.549
Dallas	43	39	.524
Denver	38	44	.463
Kansas City	38	44	.463
San Antonio	37	45	.451
Houston	29	53	.354

PACIFIC DIVISION

	W	L	Pct.
Los Angeles	54	28	.659
Portland	48	34	.585
Seattle	42	40	.512
Phoenix	41	41	.500
Golden State	37	45	.451
San Diego	30	52	.366

PLAYOFFS

EASTERN CONFERENCE

FIRST ROUND

Boston 3, Washington 1

Apr. 17 ....@Boston 91, Washington 83
Apr. 19 ....@Boston 88, Washington 85
Apr. 21 ....@Washington 111, Boston 108*
Apr. 24 ....Boston 99, @Washington 96

Milwaukee 3, Atlanta 2

Apr. 17 ....@Milwaukee 105, Atlanta 89
Apr. 19 ....@Milwaukee 101, Atlanta 87
Apr. 21 ....@Atlanta 103, Milwaukee 94
Apr. 24 ....@Atlanta 100, Milwaukee 97
Apr. 26 ....@Milwaukee 118, Atlanta 89

New York 3, Detroit 2

Apr. 17 ....New York 94, @Detroit 93
Apr. 19 ....@Detroit 113, New York 105
Apr. 22 ....@New York 120, Detroit 113
Apr. 25 ....Detroit 119, @New York 112
Apr. 27 ....New York 127, @Detroit 123*

New Jersey 3, Philadelphia 2

Apr. 18 ....New Jersey 116, @Philadelphia 101
Apr. 20 ....New Jersey 116, @Philadelphia 102
Apr. 22 ....Philadelphia 108, @New Jersey 100
Apr. 24 ....Philadelphia 110, @New Jersey 102
Apr. 26 ....New Jersey 101, @Philadelphia 98

SEMIFINALS

Boston 4, New York 3

Apr. 29 ....@Boston 110, New York 92
May 2 ......@Boston 116, New York 102
May 4 ......@New York 100, Boston 92
May 6 ......@New York 118, Boston 113
May 9 ......@Boston 121, New York 99
May 11 ....@New York 106, Boston 104
May 13 ....@Boston 121, New York 104

Milwaukee 4, New Jersey 2

Apr. 29 ....New Jersey 106, @Milwaukee 100
May 1 ......@Milwaukee 98, New Jersey 94
May 3 ......Milwaukee 100, @New Jersey 93
May 5 ......@New Jersey 106, Milwaukee 99
May 8 ......@Milwaukee 94, New Jersey 82
May 10 ....Milwaukee 98, @New Jersey 97

FINALS

Boston 4, Milwaukee 1

May 15 ....@Boston 119, Milwaukee 96
May 17 ....@Boston 125, Milwaukee 110
May 19 ....Boston 109, @Milwaukee 100
May 21 ....@Milwaukee 122, Boston 113
May 23 ....@Boston 115, Milwaukee 108

*Denotes number of overtime periods.

WESTERN CONFERENCE

FIRST ROUND

Utah 3, Denver 2

Apr. 17 ....@Utah 123, Denver 121
Apr. 19 ....Denver 132, @Utah 116
Apr. 22 ....@Denver 121, Utah 117
Apr. 24 ....Utah 129, @Denver 124
Apr. 26 ....@Utah 127, Denver 111

Dallas 3, Seattle 2

Apr. 17 ....@Dallas 88, Seattle 86
Apr. 19 ....Seattle 95, @Dallas 92
Apr. 21 ....@Seattle 104, Dallas 94
Apr. 24 ....Dallas 107, @Seattle 96
Apr. 26 ....@Dallas 105, Seattle 104*

Phoenix 3, Portland 2

Apr. 18 ....Phoenix 113, @Portland 106
Apr. 20 ....@Portland 122, Phoenix 116
Apr. 22 ....@Phoenix 106, Portland 103
Apr. 24 ....Portland 113, @Phoenix 110
Apr. 26 ....Phoenix 117, @Portland 105

Los Angeles 3, Kansas City 0

Apr. 18 ....@Los Angeles 116, Kansas City 105
Apr. 20 ....@Los Angeles 109, Kansas City 102
Apr. 22 ....Los Angeles 108, @Kansas City 102

SEMIFINALS

Los Angeles 4, Dallas 1

Apr. 28 ....@Los Angeles 134, Dallas 91
May 1 ......@Los Angeles 117, Dallas 101
May 4 ......@Dallas 125, Los Angeles 115
May 6 ......Los Angeles 122, @Dallas 115*
May 8 ......@Los Angeles 115, Dallas 99

Phoenix 4, Utah 2

Apr. 29 ....@Utah 105, Phoenix 95
May 2......Phoenix 102, @Utah 97
May 4 ......@Phoenix 106, Utah 94
May 6 ......@Phoenix 111, Utah 110*
May 8 ......@Utah 118, Phoenix 106
May 10 ....@Phoenix 102, Utah 82

FINALS

Los Angeles 4, Phoenix 2

May 12 ....@Los Angeles 110, Phoenix 94
May 15 ....@Los Angeles 118, Phoenix 102
May 18 ....@Phoenix 135, Los Angeles 127*
May 20 ....Los Angeles 126, @Phoenix 115
May 23 ....Phoenix 126, @Los Angeles 121
May 25 ....Los Angeles 99, @Phoenix 97

NBA FINALS

Boston 4, Los Angeles 3

May 27 ....Los Angeles 115, @Boston 109
May 31 ....@Boston 124, Los Angeles 121*
June 3 .....@Los Angeles 137, Boston 104
June 6 .....Boston 129, @Los Angeles 125*
June 8 .....@Boston 121, Los Angeles 103
June 10 ...@Los Angeles 119, Boston 108
June 12 ...@Boston 111, Los Angeles 102

INDIVIDUAL LEADERS

SCORING (minimum 70 games or 1,400 points)

	G	FGM	FTM	Pts.	Avg.
Dantley, Utah	79	802	813	2418	30.6
Aguirre, Dallas	79	925	465	2330	29.5
Vandeweghe, Denver	78	895	494	2295	29.4
English, Denver	82	907	352	2167	26.4
King, New York	77	795	437	2027	26.3
Gervin, San Antonio	76	765	427	1967	25.9
Bird, Boston	79	758	374	1908	24.2
Mitchell, San Antonio	79	779	275	1839	23.3
Cummings, San Diego	81	737	380	1854	22.9
Short, Golden State	79	714	353	1803	22.8

FIELD GOAL PCT. (minimum 300 made)

	FGM	FGA	Pct.
Gilmore, San Antonio	351	556	.631
Donaldson, San Diego	360	604	.596
McGee, Los Angeles	347	584	.594
Dawkins, New Jersey	507	855	.593
Natt, Portland	500	857	.583

THREE-POINT FIELD GOAL PCT. (minimum 25 made)

	FGA	FGM	Pct.
Griffith, Utah	252	91	.361
Evans, Denver	89	32	.360
Moore, San Antonio	87	28	.322
Cooper, Los Angeles	121	38	.314
Williams, New York	81	25	.309

FREE THROW PCT. (minimum 125 made)

	FTM	FTA	Pct.
Bird, Boston	374	421	.888
Long, Detroit	243	275	.884
Laimbeer, Detroit	316	365	.866
Davis, Phoenix	233	270	.863
Pierce, San Diego	149	173	.861

ASSISTS (minimum 70 games or 400 assists)

	G	No.	Avg.
Johnson, Los Angeles	67	875	13.1
Nixon, San Diego	82	914	11.1
Thomas, Detroit	82	914	11.1
Lucas, San Antonio	63	673	10.7
Moore, San Antonio	59	566	9.6

REBOUNDS (minimum 70 games or 800 rebounds)

	G	Off.	Def.	Tot.	Avg.
Malone, Philadelphia	71	352	598	950	13.4
Williams, New Jersey	81	355	645	1000	12.3
Ruland, Washington	75	265	657	922	12.3
Laimbeer, Detroit	82	329	674	1003	12.2
Sampson, Houston	82	293	620	913	11.1

STEALS (minimum 70 games or 125 steals)

	G	No.	Avg.
Green, Utah	81	215	2.65
Thomas, Detroit	82	204	2.49
Williams, Seattle	80	189	2.36
Cheeks, Philadelphia	75	171	2.28
Johnson, Los Angeles	67	150	2.24

BLOCKED SHOTS (minimum 70 games or 100 blocked shots)

	G	No.	Avg.
Eaton, Utah	82	351	4.28
Rollins, Atlanta	77	277	3.60
Sampson, Houston	82	197	2.40
Nance, Phoenix	82	173	2.11
Gilmore, San Antonio	64	132	2.06

1982-83 SEASON

Moses Malone

They had waited a long time for it, but when their moment finally arrived, the Philadelphia 76ers seized it.

From the start of the 1982-83 schedule, the season had a championship feel to it in Philadelphia. That certainly had something to do with the acquisition of Moses Malone from the Houston Rockets in the offseason.

Sixers fans had expected a title since the arrival of Julius Erving prior to the 1976-77 season. Erving had won two ABA championships with the New York Nets in 1974 and 1976. His transition from one league to the other was marked by leading Philly to the 1977 Finals, although the 76ers lost in six games to Portland. In all, the 76ers made three trips to the NBA Finals in Dr. J's first six years with the team, but the big prize continued to elude them. Then Malone, a rebounding machine as well as a potent scorer who was the league's MVP, became available as a free agent. The Sixers swooped in and signed him, gladly giving up Caldwell Jones and a first-round draft pick to the Rockets as compensation.

The acquisition solidified the 76ers up front and sent the entire city surging on a rush of anticipation.

"Everybody had a sense that this was our opportunity," recalled forward Bobby Jones, who won the league's first Sixth Man Award in 1983. "The motivation was there, and we were healthy, too. We got off to a good start, got some confidence and didn't get cocky but kept that good work ethic. I think Moses really established a lot of that. Julius had always had it. But then a big guy comes in and does that, and it helps."

The measure of that help was 65 victories and the Atlantic Division title, capped with the three greatest words in the history of prognostications.

When asked how Philadelphia would perform in the playoffs, Malone issued what would become a famous prediction: "Fo', Fo', Fo'," meaning that the 76ers would win each round in a four-game sweep on their way to the championship.

It was just the kind of talk to get the Lakers cooked up. Bolstered by the addition of smooth forward James Worthy, the top pick in the 1982 NBA Draft, L.A. won 58 games and another Pacific Division title, its third in four years. But in the last week of the season, Worthy fractured his leg coming down from a tip-in. Just as his ability to finish in the open court and to score in the post had opened the Lakers' attack, his absence would now limit it.

Still, the Lakers easily moved past Portland and San Antonio in the playoffs to advance to the Finals, as did the Sixers. Philadelphia swept the Knicks, but a single loss against Milwaukee blemished Malone's brash prediction. The Lakers, already without Worthy, also lost Norm Nixon and Bob McAdoo for much of the Finals, opening the door for Philadelphia to sweep to its first title since the days of Wilt Chamberlain.

The 76ers had gone 12-1 in the playoffs, leaving the usually taciturn Malone with a smile that would last a long time.

"Let's not make believe," said 76ers coach Billy Cunningham, a member of the 76ers' last title team in 1967. "The difference from last year was Moses. He gave us the consistency inside that the Lakers had always gotten from Abdul-Jabbar. We got that and more from Moses."

For Erving, the victory erased years of disappointment. "I've always tried to tell myself that the work itself is the thing, that win, lose, or draw, the work is really what counts," he said. "As hard as it was to make myself believe that sometimes, it was the only thing I had to cling to each year, that every game, every night, I did the best I could."

NBA.COM FACT

The Lakers reached the NBA Finals despite making only 10 three-point field goals in 82 regular-season games, equaling the fewest in league history.

FINAL STANDINGS

EASTERN CONFERENCE

ATLANTIC DIVISION

	W	L	Pct.
Philadelphia	65	17	.793
Boston	56	26	.683
New Jersey	49	33	.598
New York	44	38	.537
Washington	42	40	.512

CENTRAL DIVISION

	W	L	Pct.
Milwaukee	51	31	.622
Atlanta	43	39	.524
Detroit	37	45	.451
Chicago	28	54	.341
Cleveland	23	59	.280
Indiana	20	62	.244

WESTERN CONFERENCE

MIDWEST DIVISION

	W	L	Pct.
San Antonio	53	29	.646
Denver	45	37	.549
Kansas City	45	37	.549
Dallas	38	44	.463
Utah	30	52	.366
Houston	14	68	.171

PACIFIC DIVISION

	W	L	Pct.
Los Angeles	58	24	.707
Phoenix	53	29	.646
Seattle	48	34	.585
Portland	46	36	.561
Golden State	30	52	.366
San Diego	25	57	.305

PLAYOFFS

EASTERN CONFERENCE

FIRST ROUND

New York 2, New Jersey 0

Apr. 20 ....New York 118, @New Jersey 107
Apr. 21 ....@New York 105, New Jersey 99

Boston 2, Atlanta 1

Apr. 19 ....@Boston 103, Atlanta 95
Apr. 22 ....@Atlanta 95, Boston 93
Apr. 24 ....@Boston 98, Atlanta 79

SEMIFINALS

Philadelphia 4, New York 0

Apr. 24 ....@Philadelphia 112, New York 102
Apr. 27 ....@Philadelphia 98, New York 91
Apr. 30 ....Philadelphia 107, @New York 105
May 1 ......Philadelphia 105, @New York 102

Milwaukee 4, Boston 0

Apr. 27 ....Milwaukee 116, @Boston 95
Apr. 29 ....Milwaukee 95, @Boston 91
May 1 ......@Milwaukee 107, Boston 99
May 2 ......@Milwaukee 107, Boston 93

FINALS

Philadelphia 4, Milwaukee 1

May 8 ......@Philadelphia 111, Milwaukee 109*
May 11 ....@Philadelphia 87, Milwaukee 81
May 14 ....Philadelphia 104, @Milwaukee 96
May 15 ....@Milwaukee 100, Philadelphia 94
May 18 ....@Philadelphia 115, Milwaukee 103

WESTERN CONFERENCE

FIRST ROUND

Portland 2, Seattle 0

Apr. 20 ....Portland 108, @Seattle 97
Apr. 22 ....@Portland 105, Seattle 96

Denver 2, Phoenix 1

Apr. 19 ....@Phoenix 121, Denver 108
Apr. 21 ....@Denver 113, Phoenix 99
Apr. 24 ....Denver 117, @Phoenix 112*

SEMIFINALS

Los Angeles 4, Portland 1

Apr. 24 ....@Los Angeles 118, Portland 97
Apr. 26 ....@Los Angeles 112, Portland 106
Apr. 29 ....Los Angeles 115, @Portland 109*
May 1 ......@Portland 108, Los Angeles 95
May 3 ......@Los Angeles 116, Portland 108

San Antonio 4, Denver 1

Apr. 26 ....@San Antonio 152, Denver 133
Apr. 27 ....@San Antonio 126, Denver 109
Apr. 29 ....San Antonio 127, @Denver 126*
May 2 ......@Denver 124, San Antonio 114
May 4 ......@San Antonio 145, Denver 105

FINALS

Los Angeles 4, San Antonio 2

May 8 ......@Los Angeles 119, San Antonio 107
May 10 ....San Antonio 122, @Los Angeles 113
May 13 ....Los Angeles 113, @San Antonio 100
May 15 ....Los Angeles 129, @San Antonio 121
May 18 ....San Antonio 117, @Los Angeles 112
May 20 ....Los Angeles 101, @San Antonio 100

NBA FINALS

Philadelphia 4, Los Angeles 0

May 22 ....@Philadelphia 113, Los Angeles 107
May 26 ....@Philadelphia 103, Los Angeles 93
May 29 ....Philadelphia 111, @Los Angeles 94
May 31 ....Philadelphia 115, @Los Angeles 108

*Denotes number of overtime periods.

INDIVIDUAL LEADERS

SCORING (minimum 70 games or 1,400 points)

	G	FGM	FTM	Pts.	Avg.
English, Denver	82	959	406	2326	28.4
Vandeweghe, Denver	82	841	489	2186	26.7
Tripucka, Detroit	58	565	392	1536	26.5
Gervin, San Antonio	78	757	517	2043	26.2
Malone, Philadelphia	78	654	600	1908	24.5
Aguirre, Dallas	81	767	429	1979	24.4
Carroll, Golden State	79	785	337	1907	24.1
Free, Golden State-Cle.	73	649	430	1743	23.9
Theus, Chicago	82	749	434	1953	23.8
Cummings, San Diego	70	684	292	1660	23.7

FIELD GOAL PCT. (minimum 300 made)

	FGM	FGA	Pct.
Gilmore, San Antonio	556	888	.626
Johnson, Kansas City	371	595	.624
Dawkins, New Jersey	401	669	.599
Abdul-Jabbar, Los Angeles	722	1228	.588
Williams, New Jersey	536	912	.588

THREE-POINT FIELD GOAL PCT. (minimum 25 made)

	FGA	FGM	Pct.
Dunleavy, San Antonio	194	67	.345
Griffith, Utah	132	38	.288
Thomas, Detroit	125	36	.288
Leavell, Houston	175	42	.240

FREE THROW PCT. (minimum 125 made)

	FTM	FTA	Pct.
Murphy, Houston	138	150	.920
Vandeweghe, Denver	489	559	.875
Macy, Phoenix	129	148	.872
Gervin, San Antonio	517	606	.853
Dantley, Utah	210	248	.847

ASSISTS (minimum 70 games or 400 assists)

	G	No.	Avg.
Johnson, Los Angeles	79	829	10.5
Moore, San Antonio	77	753	9.8
Green, Utah	78	697	8.9
Drew, Kansas City	75	610	8.1
Johnson, Washington	68	549	8.1

REBOUNDS (minimum 70 games or 800 rebounds)

	G	Off.	Def.	Tot.	Avg.
Malone, Philadelphia	78	445	749	1194	15.3
Williams, New Jersey	82	365	662	1027	12.5
Laimbeer, Detroit	82	282	711	993	12.1
Gilmore, San Antonio	82	299	685	984	12.0
Roundfield, Atlanta	77	259	621	880	11.4
Sikma, Seattle	75	213	645	858	11.4

STEALS (minimum 70 games or 125 steals)

	G	No.	Avg.
Richardson, Golden St.-New Jersey	64	182	2.84
Green, Utah	78	220	2.82
Moore, San Antonio	77	194	2.52
Thomas, Detroit	81	199	2.46
Cook, New Jersey	82	194	2.37

BLOCKED SHOTS (minimum 70 games or 100 blocked shots)

	G	No.	Avg.
Rollins, Atlanta	80	343	4.29
Walton, San Diego	33	119	3.61
Eaton, Utah	81	275	3.40
Nance, Phoenix	82	217	2.65
Gilmore, San Antonio	82	192	2.34

1981-82 SEASON

Jamaal Wilkes

It was the kind of soap opera that could be scripted only in L.A. How deep were the early season woes and conflicts for the Lakers in the fall of 1981?

Within weeks, the coach, a big-time winner, had been ousted, and the franchise had turned to a former broadcast analyst to get the running game back on track. Frustrated by their playoff failure in 1981, the Lakers started the season determined to make a better showing by emphasizing power instead of fast breaks. But a mediocre start and the plodding pace of the new offense led to the dismissal of Paul Westhead as coach 11 games into the season, despite the team having won at least 50 games in each of Westhead's two seasons at the Lakers' helm.

Magic Johnson, cast as the villain because the firing came the day after he had a heated on-court exchange with Westhead, was actually booed in his beloved Forum, which had previously been unthinkable. But out of the chaos emerged Pat Riley, the former Laker who had been part of the 1972 championship team. Two years earlier, Westhead had brought Riley over from the broadcast table to serve as an assistant. Now Riley was thrust into the top job when Jerry West, then a personnel consultant to the team, refused to take the head coaching duties but agreed to sit next to Riley on the bench to ease the transition.

Riley installed a freewheeling offense and aggressive, trapping defense, and the Lakers responded by winning 57 games.

Boston won a league-high 63 games and the Atlantic Division, and Philadelphia and Boston advanced to meet in the Eastern Conference Finals for the third straight year. Philadelphia went up 3-1 for the second straight year, but Boston again won two games to send it to a seventh game in Boston. This time, Philadelphia triumphed 120-106 and moved on to meet the Lakers in the Finals.

Los Angeles had swept Phoenix and San Antonio to reach the championship series and had been enduring two-a-day practice sessions in order not to be rusty for the Finals.

Key to the Lakers' success had been the addition of Bob McAdoo, who had won three consecutive scoring titles as a member of the Buffalo Braves. His Braves teams had never gotten past the Eastern Conference Semifinals. After several injuries and trades, the former All-Star had fallen into the category of many high-scoring players: admired for his point-producing ability but disdained for his team's lack of playoff success. The night before Christmas 1981, the 30-year-old McAdoo was traded to the Lakers, and he became a key player for Los Angeles, averaging 16.7 points in the playoffs. With McAdoo providing offense off the bench, the Lakers won Game 1 by seven points, the closest game of the Finals, and captured the series in six games.

"This is the happiest moment of my life," he said after the Lakers' victory. "People have said bad things about me during my career, but this makes up for it."

Johnson, with 13 points, 13 rebounds and 13 assists in Game 6, was named the series MVP, an award some in the media found controversial.

The Lakers, though, had had about all the controversy they could stand for one season. "There were times earlier in the year when I didn't think this would be possible," Lakers forward Jamaal Wilkes said as champagne cascaded over his face. "We had so many unhappy people around here you wouldn't believe it."

The Lakers had won another title with a rookie coach. Riley and team owner Jerry Buss smiled broadly as the Lakers owner accepted the trophy afterward. "It seems like a millennium since I took over," Riley said of his seven months as a head coach. "Yeah, a millennium. I've got brain drain right now, mush brain. I dug down for everything I could find. I need four months to rest up."

NBA.COM FACT

Denver averaged 126.5 points for the season to set an NBA record. The Nuggets scored 100 or more points in all 82 games, another record.

FINAL STANDINGS

EASTERN CONFERENCE

ATLANTIC DIVISION

	W	L	Pct.
Boston	63	19	.768
Philadelphia	58	24	.707
New Jersey	44	38	.537
Washington	43	39	.524
New York	33	49	.402

CENTRAL DIVISION

	W	L	Pct.
Milwaukee	55	27	.671
Atlanta	42	40	.512
Detroit	39	43	.476
Indiana	35	47	.427
Chicago	34	48	.415
Cleveland	15	67	.183

WESTERN CONFERENCE

MIDWEST DIVISION

	W	L	Pct.
San Antonio	48	34	.585
Denver	46	36	.561
Houston	46	36	.561
Kansas City	30	52	.366
Dallas	28	54	.341
Utah	25	57	.305

PACIFIC DIVISION

	W	L	Pct.
Los Angeles	57	25	.695
Seattle	52	30	.634
Phoenix	46	36	.561
Golden State	45	37	.549
Portland	42	40	.512
San Diego	17	65	.207

PLAYOFFS

EASTERN CONFERENCE

FIRST ROUND

Philadelphia 2, Atlanta 0

Apr. 21 ....@Philadelphia 111, Atlanta 76
Apr. 23 ....Philadelphia 98, @Atlanta 95*

Washington 2, New Jersey 0

Apr. 20 ....Washington 96, @New Jersey 83
Apr. 23 ....@Washington 103, New Jersey 92

SEMIFINALS

Boston 4, Washington 1

Apr. 25 ....@Boston 109, Washington 91
Apr. 28 ....Washington 103, @Boston 102
May 1 ......Boston 92, @Washington 83
May 2 ......Boston 103, @Washington 99*
May 5 ......@Boston 131, Washington 126**

Philadelphia 4, Milwaukee 2

Apr. 25 ....@Philadelphia 125, Milwaukee 122
Apr. 28 ....@Philadelphia 120, Milwaukee 108
May 1 ......@Milwaukee 92, Philadelphia 91
May 2 ......Philadelphia 100, @Milwaukee 93
May 5 ......Milwaukee 110, @Philadelphia 98
May 7 ......Philadelphia 102, @Milwaukee 90

FINALS

Philadelphia 4, Boston 3

May 9 ......@Boston 121, Philadelphia 81
May 12 ....Philadelphia 121, @Boston 113
May 15 ....@Philadelphia 99, Boston 97
May 16 ....@Philadelphia 119, Boston 94
May 19 ....@Boston 114, Philadelphia 85
May 21 ....Boston 88, @Philadelphia 75
May 23 ....Philadelphia 120, @Boston 106

WESTERN CONFERENCE

FIRST ROUND

Seattle 2, Houston 1

Apr. 21 ....@Seattle 102, Houston 87
Apr. 23 ....@Houston 91, Seattle 70
Apr. 25 ....@Seattle 104, Houston 83

Phoenix 2, Denver 1

Apr. 20 ....@Denver 129, Phoenix 113
Apr. 23 ....@Phoenix 126, Denver 110
Apr. 24 ....Phoenix 124, @Denver 119

SEMIFINALS

Los Angeles 4, Phoenix 0

Apr. 27 ....@Los Angeles 115, Phoenix 96
Apr. 28 ....@Los Angeles 117, Phoenix 98
Apr. 30 ....Los Angeles 114, @Phoenix 106
May 2 ......Los Angeles 112, @Phoenix 107

San Antonio 4, Seattle 1

Apr. 27 ....San Antonio 95, @Seattle 93
Apr. 28 ....@Seattle 114, San Antonio 99
Apr. 30 ....@San Antonio 99, Seattle 97
May 2 ......@San Antonio 115, Seattle 113
May 5 ......San Antonio 109, @Seattle 103

FINALS

Los Angeles 4, San Antonio 0

May 9 ......@Los Angeles 128, San Antonio 117
May 11 ....@Los Angeles 110, San Antonio 101
May 14 ....Los Angeles 118, @San Antonio 108
May 15 ....Los Angeles 128, @San Antonio 123

NBA FINALS

Los Angeles 4, Philadelphia 2

May 27 ....Los Angeles 124, @Philadelphia 117
May 30 ....@Philadelphia 110, Los Angeles 94
June 1 .....@Los Angeles 129, Philadelphia 108
June 3 .....@Los Angeles 111, Philadelphia 101
June 6 .....@Philadelphia 135, Los Angeles 102
June 8 .....@Los Angeles 114, Philadelphia 104

*Denotes number of overtime periods.

INDIVIDUAL LEADERS

SCORING (minimum 70 games or 1,400 points)

	G	FGM	FTM	Pts.	Avg.
Gervin, San Antonio	79	993	555	2551	32.3
Malone, Houston	81	945	630	2520	31.1
Dantley, Utah	81	904	648	2457	30.3
English, Denver	82	855	372	2082	25.4
Erving, Philadelphia	81	780	411	1974	24.4
Abdul-Jabbar, L.A.	76	753	312	1818	23.9
Williams, Seattle	80	773	320	1875	23.4
King, Golden State	79	740	352	1833	23.2
Free, Golden State	78	650	479	1789	22.9
Issel, Denver	81	651	546	1852	22.9
Bird, Boston	77	711	328	1761	22.9

FIELD GOAL PCT. (minimum 300 made)

	FGM	FGA	Pct.
Gilmore, Chicago	546	837	.652
Johnson, Kansas City	395	644	.613
Williams, New Jersey	513	881	.582
Abdul-Jabbar, Los Angeles	753	1301	.579
Natt, Portland	515	894	.576

THREE-POINT FIELD GOAL PCT. (minimum 25 made)

	FGA	FGM	Pct.
Russell, New York	57	25	.439
Toney, Philadelphia	59	25	.424
Macy, Phoenix	100	39	.390
Winters, Milwaukee	93	36	.387
Buse, Indiana	189	73	.386

FREE THROW PCT. (minimum 125 made)

	FTM	FTA	Pct.
Macy, Phoenix	152	169	.899
Criss, Atlanta-San Diego	141	159	.887
Long, Detroit	238	275	.865
Gervin, San Antonio	555	642	.864
Bird, Boston	328	380	.863

ASSISTS (minimum 70 games or 400 assists)

	G	No.	Avg.
Moore, San Antonio	79	762	9.6
Johnson, Los Angeles	78	743	9.5
Cheeks, Philadelphia	79	667	8.4
Archibald, Boston	68	541	8.0
Nixon, Los Angeles	82	652	8.0

REBOUNDS (minimum 70 games or 800 rebounds)

	G	Off.	Def.	Tot.	Avg.
Malone, Houston	81	558	630	1188	14.7
Sikma, Seattle	82	223	815	1038	12.7
Williams, New Jersey	82	347	658	1005	12.3
Thompson, Portland	79	258	663	921	11.7
Lucas, New York	80	274	629	903	11.3

STEALS (minimum 70 games or 125 steals)

	G	No.	Avg.
Johnson, Los Angeles	78	208	2.67
Cheeks, Philadelphia	79	209	2.65
Richardson, New York	82	213	2.60
Buckner, Milwaukee	70	174	2.49
Williams, New Jersey	82	199	2.43

BLOCKED SHOTS (minimum 70 games or 100 blocked shots)

	G	No.	Avg.
Johnson, San Antonio	75	234	3.12
Rollins, Atlanta	79	224	2.84
Abdul-Jabbar, Los Angeles	76	207	2.72
Gilmore, Chicago	82	221	2.70
Parish, Boston	80	192	2.40

1980-81 SEASON

Larry Bird

During their years together in Boston, Larry Bird, Kevin McHale and Robert Parish were known as The Big Three, the frontcourt that powered the Celtics to glory.

The 1980-81 season was their first together, made possible by a big heist. On June 9, 1980, Celtics General Manager Red Auerbach pulled off the type of trade that had earned him a reputation for thievery in his more than three decades in the league. Auerbach dealt the first and 13th picks in the 1980 NBA Draft to Golden State for the third pick in the draft and Parish, a four-year veteran center. The Warriors selected Purdue center Joe Barry Carroll with the first pick and Mississippi State forward Rickey Brown 13th. The Celtics took forward McHale, adding him and Parish to a frontcourt that already featured Bird and Cedric Maxwell.

In one trade, Auerbach had stocked a frontcourt that would lead the franchise to five NBA Finals appearances in seven seasons. The other two Celtics teams would reach the conference finals.

As if these gains weren't enough, Auerbach's strong year continued with his selection as the coach on the NBA's All-Time Team. In conjunction with the NBA's 35th anniversary, pro basketball writers also selected Bill Russell, Kareem Abdul-Jabbar, Elgin Baylor, Wilt Chamberlain, Bob Cousy, Julius Erving, John Havlicek, George Mikan, Bob Pettit, Oscar Robertson and Jerry West as the game's greatest players, with Auerbach at the helm.

The Lakers, meanwhile, were dealt a big blow when Magic Johnson suffered torn cartilage in his left knee one month into the season, forcing him to miss 45 games. As a result, the Lakers failed to win the Pacific Division and were knocked out of the playoffs in the first round by Houston, which made it all the way to the Finals despite a 40-42 record in the regular season.

Moses Malone of Houston, the 26-year-old center already in his seventh professional season, averaged 27.8 points and led the NBA in rebounding with 14.8 rebounds per game.

The Celtics swept Chicago (coached by Jerry Sloan), defeated Philadelphia in seven games after trailing 3-1 and overmatched Houston in six games to win their first title of the Bird-Parish-McHale era.

A shot by Bird late in the fourth quarter of Game 1 of the NBA Finals set the tone for the series. Bird launched an 18-footer from the right side, knew instantly that the shot was off, hustled to rebound his miss, caught the ball as his momentum was carrying him to the baseline, switched the ball to his left hand in midair and swished a 12-footer. The Boston Garden faithful fell about the place.

"It was the one best shot I've ever seen a player make," Auerbach claimed. Bird, though, spent much of the series mired in a slump until a huge performance in Game 6. Carrying the load offensively and in terms of leadership was Maxwell, whose efforts would be rewarded with series MVP honors.

It was Maxwell who led the charge after Houston's Malone told reporters he could get four guys off the streets of Petersburg, Va., his hometown, and beat the Celtics. "I don't think they're all that good," he said. "I don't think they can stop us from doing what we want to do."

Malone's comment provided the emotional spark the Celtics needed. "The man threw down a challenge," Maxwell explained, "and this is a team that responds well to challenges."

NBA.COM FACT

Diminutive Houston guard Calvin Murphy (5-9) notched the highest free throw percentage (.958) in NBA history, sinking all but nine of his 215 attempts.

FINAL STANDINGS

EASTERN CONFERENCE

ATLANTIC DIVISION

	W	L	Pct.
Boston	62	20	.756
Philadelphia	62	20	.756
New York	50	32	.610
Washington	39	43	.476
New Jersey	24	58	.293

CENTRAL DIVISION

	W	L	Pct.
Milwaukee	60	22	.732
Chicago	45	37	.549
Indiana	44	38	.537
Atlanta	31	51	.378
Cleveland	28	54	.341
Detroit	21	61	.256

WESTERN CONFERENCE

MIDWEST DIVISION

	W	L	Pct.
San Antonio	52	30	.634
Kansas City	40	42	.488
Houston	40	42	.488
Denver	37	45	.451
Utah	28	54	.341
Dallas	15	67	.183

PACIFIC DIVISION

	W	L	Pct.
Phoenix	57	25	.695
Los Angeles	54	28	.659
Portland	45	37	.549
Golden State	39	43	.476
San Diego	36	46	.439
Seattle	34	48	.415

PLAYOFFS

EASTERN CONFERENCE

FIRST ROUND

Chicago 2, New York 0

Mar. 31 ....Chicago 90, @New York 80
Apr. 3 ......@Chicago 115, New York 114*

Philadelphia 2, Indiana 0

Mar. 31 ....@Philadelphia 124, Indiana 108
Apr. 2 ......Philadelphia 96, @Indiana 85

SEMIFINALS

Philadelphia 4, Milwaukee 3

Apr. 5 ......@Philadelphia 125, Milwaukee 122
Apr. 7 ......Milwaukee 109, @Philadelphia 99
Apr. 10 ....Philadelphia 108, @Milwaukee 103
Apr. 12 ....@Milwaukee 109, Philadelphia 98
Apr. 15 ....@Philadelphia 116, Milwaukee 99
Apr. 17 ....@Milwaukee 109, Philadelphia 86
Apr. 19 ....@Philadelphia 99, Milwaukee 98

Boston 4, Chicago 0

Apr. 5 ......@Boston 121, Chicago 109
Apr. 7 ......@Boston 106, Chicago 97
Apr. 10 ....Boston 113, @Chicago 107
Apr. 12 ....Boston 109, @Chicago 103

FINALS

Boston 4, Philadelphia 3

Apr. 21 ....Philadelphia 105, @Boston 104
Apr. 22 ....@Boston 118, Philadelphia 99
Apr. 24 ....@Philadelphia 110, Boston 100
Apr. 26 ....@Philadelphia 107, Boston 105
Apr. 29 ....@Boston 111, Philadelphia 109
May 1 ......Boston 100, @Philadelphia 98
May 3 ......@Boston 91, Philadelphia 90

WESTERN CONFERENCE

FIRST ROUND

Houston 2, Los Angeles 1

Apr. 1 ......Houston 111, @Los Angeles 107
Apr. 3 ......Los Angeles 111, @Houston 106
Apr. 5 ......Houston 89, @Los Angeles 86

Kansas City 2, Portland 1

Apr. 1 ......Kansas City 98, @Portland 97*
Apr. 3 ......Portland 124, @Kansas City 119*
Apr. 5 ......Kansas City 104, @Portland 95

SEMIFINALS

Kansas City 4, Phoenix 3

Apr. 7 ......@Phoenix 102, Kansas City 80
Apr. 8 ......Kansas City 88, @Phoenix 83
Apr. 10 ....@Kansas City 93, Phoenix 92
Apr. 12 ....@Kansas City 102, Phoenix 95
Apr. 15 ....@Phoenix 101, Kansas City 89
Apr. 17 ....Phoenix 81, @Kansas City 76
Apr. 19 ....Kansas City 95, @Phoenix 88

Houston 4, San Antonio 3

Apr. 7 ......Houston 107, @San Antonio 98
Apr. 8 ......@San Antonio 125, Houston 113
Apr. 10 ....@Houston 112, San Antonio 99
Apr. 12 ....San Antonio 114, @Houston 112
Apr. 14 ....Houston 123, @San Antonio 117
Apr. 15 ....San Antonio 101, @Houston 96
Apr. 17 ....Houston 105, @San Antonio 100

FINALS

Houston 4, Kansas City 1

Apr. 21 ....Houston 97, @Kansas City 78
Apr. 22 ....@Kansas City 88, Houston 79
Apr. 24 ....@Houston 92, Kansas City 88
Apr. 26 ....@Houston 100, Kansas City 89
Apr. 29 ....Houston 97, @Kansas City 88

NBA FINALS

Boston 4, Houston 2

May 5 ......@Boston 98, Houston 95
May 7 ......Houston 92, @Boston 90
May 9 ......Boston 94, @Houston 71
May 10 ....@Houston 91, Boston 86
May 12 ....@Boston 109, Houston 80
May 14 ....Boston 102, @Houston 91

*Denotes number of overtime periods.

INDIVIDUAL LEADERS

SCORING (minimum 70 games or 1,400 points)

	G	FGM	FTM	Pts.	Avg.
Dantley, Utah	80	909	632	2452	30.7
Malone, Houston	80	806	609	2222	27.8
Gervin, San Antonio	82	850	512	2221	27.1
Abdul-Jabbar, L.A.	80	836	423	2095	26.2
Thompson, Denver	77	734	489	1967	25.5
Birdsong, Kansas City	71	710	317	1747	24.6
Erving, Philadelphia	82	794	422	2014	24.6
Mitchell, Cleveland	82	853	302	2012	24.5
Free, Golden State	65	516	528	1565	24.1
English, Denver	81	768	390	1929	23.8

FIELD GOAL PCT. (minimum 300 made)

	FGM	FGA	Pct.
Gilmore, Chicago	547	816	.670
Dawkins, Philadelphia	423	697	.607
King, Golden State	731	1244	.588
Maxwell, Boston	441	750	.588
Abdul-Jabbar, Los Angeles	836	1457	.574

THREE-POINT FIELD GOAL PCT. (minimum 25 made)

	FGA	FGM	Pct.
Taylor, San Diego	115	44	.383
Hassett, Dallas-Golden State	156	53	.340
Williams, San Diego	141	48	.340
Bratz, Cleveland	169	57	.337
Bibby, San Diego	95	32	.337

FREE THROW PCT. (minimum 125 made)

	FTM	FTA	Pct.
Murphy, Houston	206	215	.958
Sobers, Chicago	231	247	.935
Newlin, New Jersey	414	466	.888
Spanarkel, Dallas	375	423	.887
Bridgeman, Milwaukee	213	241	.884

ASSISTS (minimum 70 games or 400 assists)

	G	No.	Avg.
Porter, Washington	81	734	9.1
Nixon, Los Angeles	79	696	8.8
Ford, Kansas City	66	580	8.8
Richardson, New York	79	627	7.9
Archibald, Boston	80	618	7.7

REBOUNDS (minimum 70 games or 800 rebounds)

	G	Off.	Def.	Tot.	Avg.
Malone, Houston	80	474	706	1180	14.8
Nater, San Diego	82	295	722	1017	12.4
Smith, Golden State	82	433	561	994	12.1
Bird, Boston	82	191	704	895	10.9
Sikma, Seattle	82	184	668	852	10.4

STEALS (minimum 70 games or 125 steals)

	G	No.	Avg.
Johnson, Los Angeles	37	127	3.43
Richardson, New York	79	232	2.94
Buckner, Milwaukee	82	197	2.40
Cheeks, Philadelphia	81	193	2.38
Williams, New York	79	185	2.34

BLOCKED SHOTS (minimum 70 games or 100 blocked shots)

	G	No.	Avg.
Johnson, San Antonio	82	278	3.39
Rollins, Atlanta	40	117	2.93
Abdul-Jabbar, Los Angeles	80	228	2.85
Parish, Boston	82	214	2.61
Gilmore, Chicago	82	198	2.41

1979-80 SEASON

Magic Johnson

They came into the league together, linked by their competitive nature and the meeting of their teams in the 1979 NCAA championship game. It was Larry Bird who got the Rookie of the Year Award, but it was Magic Johnson who took home the ultimate prize.

"I'm asked a lot about what the greatest thing Earvin did," his college coach, Michigan State's Jud Heathcote, said. "Many say passing the ball, his great court sense, the fact that he could rebound. I say the greatest things Earvin did were intangible. He always made the guys he played with better. In summer pick-up games, Earvin would take three or four non-players, and he'd make those guys look so much better and they would win, not because he was making the baskets all by himself, but because he just made other players play better."

He certainly did that for Kareem Abdul-Jabbar and his other Lakers teammates.

Johnson and Bird happened upon the league as it was going through critical changes. The NBA adopted the three-point field goal, a popular facet of the ABA game; the New Orleans Jazz moved to Salt Lake City but kept their Bourbon St. nickname and became the Utah Jazz; and the league altered the schedule so teams faced rivals in their division more often than clubs from other divisions.

But the big story of the season was the arrival of the charismatic and talented rookies, each taking up residence on opposite coasts on the rosters of two of the NBA's most successful and tradition-steeped franchises. The turnaround in Boston was dramatic. John Havlicek had retired after the 1977-78 season, and Boston tumbled to a 29-53 record in 1978-79. Along with Bird, the Celtics had an aging Dave Cowens and third-year forward Cedric Maxwell up front, with Tiny Archibald and Chris Ford in the backcourt. The team posted a remarkable 61-21 record, a 32-game improvement but Philadelphia won 59 games, and behind Julius Erving's stellar play defeated the Celtics in five games to advance to the Finals.

In Los Angeles, Johnson's enthusiasm seemed to rejuvenate Abdul-Jabbar, propelling the Lakers to 60 victories and a berth in the NBA Finals for the first time since 1973.

Abdul-Jabbar, who hadn't won an NBA title since 1971 with Milwaukee, dominated the Finals as Johnson fed him the ball in the right spots in the first five games. But Abdul-Jabbar badly twisted an ankle in Game 5 and didn't make the trip to Philadelphia for Game 6, staying home to rest the injury for the expected Game 7 in Los Angeles.

The Lakers, figuring they had nothing to lose with a 3-2 series lead, came out and played loose in the Spectrum. Jamaal Wilkes enjoyed one of the finest games of his career and finished with 37 points. But the newspapers the next day heralded the only headline possible: "It's Magic!"

Johnson filled in for Abdul-Jabbar as the starting center and eventually played every position on the court. He scored 42 points, grabbed 15 rebounds and dished seven assists as the Lakers wrapped up the title with a 123-107 victory.

"It was amazing, just amazing," said Erving, who led Philly with 27 points.

"Magic was outstanding, unreal," agreed the Sixers' Doug Collins, who was injured and watched from the sidelines. "I knew he was good, but I never realized he was great."

Johnson, the hands-down choice as series MVP, was asked how the Lakers had won without their center. "Without Kareem, we couldn't play the halfcourt and think defensively. We had to play the full court and take our chances."

In other words, play Johnson's kind of game. "What position did I play?" he asked afterward. "Well, I played center, a little forward, some guard. I tried to think up a name for it, but the best I could come up with was CFG-Rover."

Center-forward-guard-rover. In other words, all over the court.

NBA.COM FACT

Fortuitous circumstances brought Magic Johnson to the Lakers, who received the Jazz's first-round pick in 1979 as compensation for Gail Goodrich, then won a coin toss with Chicago for the first overall selection.

FINAL STANDINGS

EASTERN CONFERENCE

ATLANTIC DIVISION

	W	L	Pct.
Boston	61	21	.744
Philadelphia	59	23	.720
Washington	39	43	.476
New York	39	43	.476
New Jersey	34	48	.415

CENTRAL DIVISION

	W	L	Pct.
Atlanta	50	32	.610
Houston	41	41	.500
San Antonio	41	41	.500
Cleveland	37	45	.451
Indiana	37	45	.451
Detroit	16	66	.195

WESTERN CONFERENCE

MIDWEST DIVISION

	W	L	Pct.
Milwaukee	49	33	.598
Kansas City	47	35	.573
Denver	30	52	.366
Chicago	30	52	.366
Utah	24	58	.293

PACIFIC DIVISION

	W	L	Pct.
Los Angeles	60	22	.732
Seattle	56	26	.683
Phoenix	55	27	.671
Portland	38	44	.463
San Diego	35	47	.427
Golden State	24	58	.293

PLAYOFFS

EASTERN CONFERENCE

FIRST ROUND

Philadelphia 2, Washington 0

Apr. 2 ......@Philadelphia 111, Washington 96
Apr. 4 ......Philadelphia 112, @Washington 104

Houston 2, San Antonio 1

Apr. 2 ......@Houston 95, San Antonio 85
Apr. 4 ......@San Antonio 106, Houston 101
Apr. 6 ......@Houston 141, San Antonio 120

SEMIFINALS

Boston 4, Houston 0

Apr. 9 ......@Boston 119, Houston 101
Apr. 11 ....@Boston 95, Houston 75
Apr. 13 ....Boston 100, @Houston 81
Apr. 14 ....Boston 138, @Houston 121

Philadelphia 4, Atlanta 1

Apr. 6 ......@Philadelphia 107, Atlanta 104
Apr. 9 ......@Philadelphia 99, Atlanta 92
Apr. 10 ....@Atlanta 105, Philadelphia 93
Apr. 13 ....Philadelphia 107, @Atlanta 83
Apr. 15 ....@Philadelphia 105, Atlanta 100

FINALS

Philadelphia 4, Boston 1

Apr. 18 ....Philadelphia 96, @Boston 93
Apr. 20 ....@Boston 96, Philadelphia 90
Apr. 23 ....@Philadelphia 99, Boston 97
Apr. 25 ....@Philadelphia 102, Boston 90
Apr. 27 ....Philadelphia 105, @Boston 94

WESTERN CONFERENCE

FIRST ROUND

Phoenix 2, Kansas City 1

Apr. 2 ......@Phoenix 96, Kansas City 93
Apr. 4 ......@Kansas City 106, Phoenix 96
Apr. 6 ......@Phoenix 114, Kansas City 99

Seattle 2, Portland 1

Apr. 2 ......@Seattle 120, Portland 110
Apr. 4 ......@Portland 105, Seattle 95*
Apr. 6 ......@Seattle 103, Portland 86

SEMIFINALS

Los Angeles 4, Phoenix 1

Apr. 8 ......@Los Angeles 119, Phoenix 110
Apr. 9 ......@Los Angeles 131, Phoenix 128*
Apr. 11 ....Los Angeles 108, @Phoenix 105
Apr. 13 ....@Phoenix 127, Los Angeles 101
Apr. 15 ....@Los Angeles 126, Phoenix 101

Seattle 4, Milwaukee 3

Apr. 8 ......@Seattle 114, Milwaukee 113*
Apr. 9 ......Milwaukee 114, @Seattle 112*
Apr. 11 ....@Milwaukee 95, Seattle 91
Apr. 13 ....Seattle 112, @Milwaukee 107
Apr. 15 ....Milwaukee 108, @Seattle 97
Apr. 18 ....Seattle 86, @Milwaukee 85
Apr. 20 ....@Seattle 98, Milwaukee 94

FINALS

Los Angeles 4, Seattle 1

Apr. 22 ....Seattle 108, @Los Angeles 107
Apr. 23 ....@Los Angeles 108, Seattle 99
Apr. 25 ....Los Angeles 104, @Seattle 100
Apr. 27 ....Los Angeles 98, @Seattle 93
Apr. 30 ....@Los Angeles 111, Seattle 105

NBA FINALS

Los Angeles 4, Philadelphia 2

May 4 ......@Los Angeles 109, Philadelphia 102
May 7 ......Philadelphia 107, @Los Angeles 104
May 10 ....Los Angeles 111, @Philadelphia 101
May 11 ....@Philadelphia 105, Los Angeles 102
May 14 ....@Los Angeles 108, Philadelphia 103
May 16 ....Los Angeles 123, @Philadelphia 107

*Denotes number of overtime periods.

INDIVIDUAL LEADERS

SCORING (minimum 70 games or 1,400 points)

	G	FGM	FTM	Pts.	Avg.
Gervin, San Antonio	78	1024	505	2585	33.1
Free, San Diego	68	737	572	2055	30.2
Dantley, Utah	68	730	443	1903	28.0
Erving, Philadelphia	78	838	420	2100	26.9
Malone, Houston	82	778	563	2119	25.8
Abdul-Jabbar, L.A.	82	835	364	2034	24.8
Issel, Denver	82	715	517	1951	23.8
Hayes, Washington	81	761	334	1859	23.0
Birdsong, Kansas City	82	781	286	1858	22.7
Mitchell, Cleveland	82	775	270	1820	22.2

FIELD GOAL PCT. (minimum 300 made)

	FGM	FGA	Pct.
Maxwell, Boston	457	750	.609
Abdul-Jabbar, Los Angeles	835	1383	.604
Gilmore, Chicago	305	513	.595
Dantley, Utah	730	1267	.576
Boswell, Denver-Utah	346	613	.564

THREE-POINT FIELD GOAL PCT. (minimum 25 made)

	FGA	FGM	Pct.
Brown, Seattle	88	39	.443
Ford, Boston	164	70	.427
Bird, Boston	143	58	.406
Roche, Denver	129	49	.380
Taylor, San Diego	239	90	.377

FREE THROW PCT. (minimum 125 made)

	FTM	FTA	Pct.
Barry, Houston	143	153	.935
Murphy, Houston	271	302	.897
Boone, Los Angeles-Utah	175	196	.893
Silas, San Antonio	339	382	.887
Newlin, New Jersey	367	415	.884

ASSISTS (minimum 70 games or 400 assists)

	G	No.	Avg.
Richardson, New York	82	832	10.2
Archibald, Boston	80	671	8.4
Walker, Cleveland	76	607	8.0
Nixon, Los Angeles	82	642	7.8
Lucas, Golden State	80	602	7.5

REBOUNDS (minimum 70 games or 800 rebounds)

	G	Off.	Def.	Tot.	Avg.
Nater, San Diego	81	352	864	1216	15.0
Malone, Houston	82	573	617	1190	14.5
Unseld, Washington	82	334	760	1094	13.3
Jones, Philadelphia	80	219	731	950	11.9
Sikma, Seattle	82	198	710	908	11.1

STEALS (minimum 70 games or 125 steals)

	G	No.	Avg.
Richardson, New York	82	265	3.23
Jordan, New Jersey	82	223	2.72
Bradley, Indiana	82	211	2.57
Williams, Seattle	82	200	2.44
Johnson, Los Angeles	77	187	2.43

BLOCKED SHOTS (minimum 70 games or 100 blocked shots)

	G	No.	Avg.
Abdul-Jabbar, Los Angeles	82	280	3.41
Johnson, New Jersey	81	258	3.19
Rollins, Atlanta	82	244	2.98
Tyler, Detroit	82	220	2.68
Hayes, Washington	81	189	2.33

1978-79 SEASON

George Gervin

Dennis Johnson had shot 0-for-14 from the field in Game 7 of the 1978 NBA Finals, and his Seattle SuperSonics had lost to the Washington Bullets, on their home floor, no less. But the redemption took one season, when Johnson again found himself in the championship series. He excelled at both ends of the court and led his Sonics to the title over those same Bullets, a performance that earned him the Finals MVP Award. "I really believe defense is an art," said Johnson, who would go on to help Boston to two titles later in his career.

Led by Elvin Hayes, Washington won a league-high 54 games and took the Atlantic Division title, but it wasn't easy. "It's all so different from last season when we were relaxed," Hayes said. "The pressure. The mental part. Everyone's after us. Defending [the championship] is the hardest thing I've ever done in my life."

San Antonio, behind repeat NBA scoring champion George Gervin (29.6 points per game), won the Central, and the two met in the Western Conference Finals. The Bullets fell behind the Spurs 3-1, but won three straight games to keep their hopes of two straight titles alive.

Coached by Lenny Wilkens, the Sonics took the Pacific with 52 victories and ditched Los Angeles in the Western Conference Semifinals. Seattle won the first two against Phoenix in the Western Finals, then lost three straight but managed to win the last two by a total of five points to set up a rematch with the Bullets.

"It all boils down to us against Washington one more time," Seattle guard Fred Brown observed. "They're deeper, but we make up for that with our backcourt. I think it will be wild and picturesque all over again."

In adjusting to the rigors of the season, Wilkens moved Jack Sikma from forward to center, then shifted Lonnie Shelton into the starting slot at power forward to go with guards Dennis Johnson and Gus Williams and versatile small forward John Johnson. "Downtown" Fred Brown came off the bench and provided instant offense with his long-range shooting. Another key was the veteran leadership provided by Paul Silas, the 35-year-old ex-Celtic who came off the bench and gave the Sonics the benefit of his toughness and savvy. "Look anywhere on our team and you'll see Paul's influence," Wilkens said.

In the NBA Finals, Washington claimed Game 1 when Larry Wright made two free throws with no time remaining. But the SuperSonics then found their stride, led by Johnson's search for redemption.

"The difference from last year is maturity," Wilkens said. "Last year we were so young we played on emotion. Last year we were questioning. Now we're playing with confidence."

Beginning with Game 2, that confidence soared to an all-time high. Secured with their ability to shut down Hayes and Bob Dandridge, the Sonics took home-court advantage with a 92-82 triumph in the second game.

Williams scored 31 to lead the charge in Game 3, a 10-point win that gave Seattle a 2-1 series edge. Game 4 was a foul-fest (59 were called) that went to overtime. Again Williams provided the key offense with 36 points while D.J. added 32 — the two backcourtmen would score more than half their team's points in the series. Johnson recorded his fourth block of the night on Kevin Grevey's last-ditch shot in overtime to preserve Seattle's 114-112 victory.

Johnson and Williams came through again in Game 5 when the Finals returned to Washington. Seattle won 97-93 for its fourth consecutive triumph and its first NBA title.

NBA.COM FACT

No period in league history was more competitive than the 1970s, which produced eight different league champions and saw each conference capture five All-Star Games. So how fitting that, as the curtain came down on the decade, no fewer than six of the 11 playoff series went the distance, and of those, only one was decided by more than six points.

FINAL STANDINGS

EASTERN CONFERENCE

ATLANTIC DIVISION

	W	L	Pct.
Washington	54	28	.659
Philadelphia	47	35	.573
New Jersey	37	45	.451
New York	31	51	.378
Boston	29	53	.354

CENTRAL DIVISION

	W	L	Pct.
San Antonio	48	34	.585
Houston	47	35	.573
Atlanta	46	36	.561
Cleveland	30	52	.366
Detroit	30	52	.366
New Orleans	26	56	.317

WESTERN CONFERENCE

MIDWEST DIVISION

	W	L	Pct.
Kansas City	48	34	.585
Denver	47	35	.573
Indiana	38	44	.463
Milwaukee	38	44	.463
Chicago	31	51	.378

PACIFIC DIVISION

	W	L	Pct.
Seattle	52	30	.634
Phoenix	50	32	.610
Los Angeles	47	35	.573
Portland	45	37	.549
San Diego	43	39	.524
Golden State	38	44	.463

PLAYOFFS

EASTERN CONFERENCE

FIRST ROUND

Philadelphia 2, New Jersey 0

Apr. 11 ....@Philadelphia 122, New Jersey 114
Apr. 13 ....Philadelphia 111, @New Jersey 101

Atlanta 2, Houston 0

Apr. 11 ....Atlanta 109, @Houston 106
Apr. 13 ....@Atlanta 100, Houston 91

SEMIFINALS

Washington 4, Atlanta 3

Apr. 15 ....@Washington 103, Atlanta 89
Apr. 17 ....Atlanta 107, @Washington 99
Apr. 20 ....Washington 89, @Atlanta 77
Apr. 22 ....Washington 120, @Atlanta 118*
Apr. 24 ....Atlanta 107, @Washington 103
Apr. 26 ....@Atlanta 104, Washington 86
Apr. 29 ....@Washington 100, Atlanta 94

San Antonio 4, Philadelphia 3

Apr. 15 ....@San Antonio 119, Philadelphia 106
Apr. 17 ....@San Antonio 121, Philadelphia 120
Apr. 20 ....@Philadelphia 123, San Antonio 115
Apr. 22 ....San Antonio 115, @Philadelphia 112
Apr. 26 ....Philadelphia 120, @San Antonio 97
Apr. 29 ....@Philadelphia 92, San Antonio 90
May 2 ......@San Antonio 111, Philadelphia 108

FINALS

Washington 4, San Antonio 3

May 4 ......San Antonio 118, @Washington 97
May 6 ......@Washington 115, San Antonio 95
May 9 ......@San Antonio 116, Washington 114
May 11 ....@San Antonio 118, Washington 102
May 13 ....@Washington 107, San Antonio 103
May 16 ....Washington 108, @San Antonio 100
May 18 ....@Washington 107, San Antonio 105

WESTERN CONFERENCE

FIRST ROUND

Phoenix 2, Portland 1

Apr. 10 ....@Phoenix 107, Portland 103
Apr. 13 ....@Portland 96, Phoenix 92
Apr. 15 ....@Phoenix 101, Portland 91

Los Angeles 2, Denver 1

Apr. 10 ....@Denver 110, Los Angeles 105
Apr. 13 ....@Los Angeles 121, Denver 109
Apr. 15 ....Los Angeles 112, @Denver 111

SEMIFINALS

Seattle 4, Los Angeles 1

Apr. 17 ....@Seattle 112, Los Angeles 101
Apr. 18 ....@Seattle 108, Los Angeles 103*
Apr. 20 ....@Los Angeles 118, Seattle 112*
Apr. 22 ....Seattle 117, @Los Angeles 115
Apr. 25 ....@Seattle 106, Los Angeles 100

Phoenix 4, Kansas City 1

Apr. 17 ....@Phoenix 102, Kansas City 99
Apr. 20 ....@Kansas City 111, Phoenix 91
Apr. 22 ....@Phoenix 108, Kansas City 93
Apr. 25 ....Phoenix 108, @Kansas City 94
Apr. 27 ....@Phoenix 120, Kansas City 99

FINALS

Seattle 4, Phoenix 3

May 1 ......@Seattle 108, Phoenix 93
May 4 ......@Seattle 103, Phoenix 97
May 6 ......@Phoenix 113, Seattle 103
May 8 ......@Phoenix 100, Seattle 91
May 11 ....Phoenix 99, @Seattle 93
May 13 ....Seattle 106, @Phoenix 105
May 17 ....@Seattle 114, Phoenix 110

NBA FINALS

Seattle 4, Washington 1

May 20 ....@Washington 99, Seattle 97
May 24 ....Seattle 92, @Washington 82
May 27 ....@Seattle 105, Washington 95
May 29 ....@Seattle 114, Washington 112*
June 1 .....Seattle 97, @Washington 93

*Denotes number of overtime periods.

INDIVIDUAL LEADERS

SCORING (minimum 70 games or 1,400 points)

	G	FGM	FTM	Pts.	Avg.
Gervin, San Antonio	80	947	471	2365	29.6
Free, San Diego	78	795	654	2244	28.8
Johnson, Milwaukee	77	820	332	1972	25.6
Malone, Houston	82	716	599	2031	24.8
McAdoo, New York-Boston	60	596	295	1487	24.8
Thompson, Denver	76	693	439	1825	24.0
Westphal, Phoenix	81	801	339	1941	24.0
Abdul-Jabbar, L.A.	80	777	349	1903	23.8
Gilmore, Chicago	82	753	434	1940	23.7
Davis, Phoenix	79	764	340	1868	23.6

FIELD GOAL PCT. (minimum 300 made)

	FGM	FGA	Pct.
Maxwell, Boston	472	808	.584
Abdul-Jabbar, Los Angeles	777	1347	.577
Unseld, Washington	346	600	.577
Gilmore, Chicago	753	1310	.575
Nater, San Diego	357	627	.569

FREE THROW PCT. (minimum 125 made)

	FTM	FTA	Pct.
Barry, Houston	160	169	.947
Murphy, Houston	246	265	.928
Brown, Seattle	183	206	.888
Smith, Denver	159	180	.883
Sobers, Indiana	298	338	.882

ASSISTS (minimum 70 games or 400 assists)

	G	No.	Avg.
Porter, Detroit	82	1099	13.4
Lucas, Golden State	82	762	9.3
Nixon, Los Angeles	82	737	9.0
Ford, Kansas City	79	681	8.6
Westphal, Phoenix	81	529	6.5

REBOUNDS (minimum 70 games or 800 rebounds)

	G	Off.	Def.	Tot.	Avg.
Malone, Houston	82	587	857	1444	17.6
Kelley, New Orleans	80	303	723	1026	12.8
Abdul-Jabbar, L.A.	80	207	818	1025	12.8
Gilmore, Chicago	82	293	750	1043	12.7
Sikma, Seattle	82	232	781	1013	12.4

STEALS (minimum 70 games or 125 steals)

	G	No.	Avg.
Carr, Detroit	80	197	2.46
Jordan, New Jersey	82	201	2.45
Nixon, Los Angeles	82	201	2.45
Walker, Cleveland	55	130	2.36
Ford, Kansas City	79	174	2.20

BLOCKED SHOTS (minimum 70 games or 100 blocked shots)

	G	No.	Avg.
Abdul-Jabbar, Los Angeles	80	316	3.95
Johnson, New Jersey	78	253	3.24
Rollins, Atlanta	81	254	3.14
Parish, Golden State	76	217	2.86
Tyler, Detroit	82	201	2.45

1977-78 SEASON

Elvin Hayes

Injuries to center Bill Walton derailed the hopes of the Portland Trail Blazers, the league's defending champions, and opened the door for two upstarts, the Washington Bullets and Seattle SuperSonics.

Somehow the Bullets found a chemistry in the strong-willed personalities of two of their key figures, hard-driving coach Dick Motta and veteran star Elvin Hayes, and won the first championship in the 17-year history of the franchise that began as the Chicago Packers in 1961-62.

"Dick demanded a lot of his players," Hayes recalled. "He demanded a lot of himself. He gave us direction, and we followed it."

"What we needed was an iron hand," Bullets center Wes Unseld would say later when asked about Motta.

"We had such diverse talent on that team," Hayes said. "We had Mitch Kupchak, Larry Wright, Charles Johnson and Greg Ballard all coming off the bench. Any one of those guys would have been a great starter on another team. For starters, we had Unseld, Kevin Grevey, Tommy Henderson, Bobby Dandridge and myself. From the bench to the starters, we had great balance."

The Bullets' franchise, which had been to the NBA Finals twice before without winning a single game, rebounded from a 3-2 deficit to defeat Seattle in seven games, winning the title on the Sonics' home floor. After tying the series at three games apiece at home, the Bullets had made a pensive flight back to Seattle for Game 7.

"I remember flying out to Seattle," Hayes said, "thinking about all of the things that I had gone through all of the years I had played in the NBA.

"All of that was coming down to one game, a championship game, and after that game I remember feeling a joy over the next 48 hours, just a spring of joy, a feeling of great accomplishment. Out of my 16 years of playing, I had waited for that moment, and that moment came and it was just tremendous."

It proved to be the only NBA championship for Hayes, who played in 1,303 regular-season games.

Two violent incidents during the regular season cast a shadow over the league. On opening night, the Lakers' Kareem Abdul-Jabbar punched Milwaukee rookie center Kent Benson, breaking his hand and drawing a $5,000 fine from Commissioner Larry O'Brien. Abdul-Jabbar missed 20 games.

In December, Kermit Washington, a powerfully built forward for the Lakers, got into a fight with Houston center Kevin Kunnert. As Houston's star forward Rudy Tomjanovich ran toward the combatants, Washington turned and swung his fist, inflicting massive injuries to Tomjanovich's jaw, eye and cheek. The league fined Washington and suspended him for two months, costing him more than $50,000 in salary.

"It was the most physical blow I've ever seen anybody throw or receive," said former Lakers General Manager Pete Newell. "He saw this uniform coming at him and from then on it was a blur. He responded almost instinctively."

"Kermit was into karate and happened to throw the right punch at the right time," said former Laker Lou Hudson.

"All Kermit did was turn and throw, just as Rudy was coming in," former Laker Stu Lantz said. "With those forces colliding, that's what made the damage as severe as it was."

His face shattered, Tomjanovich missed the rest of the season while undergoing a series of reconstructive surgeries. A former All-Star, he resumed his career the next season.

Shortly after the incident, the Lakers traded Washington and Don Chaney to the Boston Celtics for Charlie Scott.

NBA.COM FACT

When Denver's David Thompson dropped 73 points — 53 in the first half — on host Detroit in his season finale, it appeared that the scoring crown was his to wear. But seven hours later, San Antonio's George Gervin countered with 63 points — 53 in the first half — at New Orleans to claim the title by a 27.22-27.15 margin in the closest race in league history.

FINAL STANDINGS

EASTERN CONFERENCE

ATLANTIC DIVISION

	W	L	Pct.
Philadelphia	55	27	.671
New York	43	39	.524
Boston	32	50	.390
Buffalo	27	55	.329
New Jersey	24	58	.293

CENTRAL DIVISION

	W	L	Pct.
San Antonio	52	30	.634
Washington	44	38	.537
Cleveland	43	39	.524
Atlanta	41	41	.500
New Orleans	39	43	.476
Houston	28	54	.341

WESTERN CONFERENCE

MIDWEST DIVISION

	W	L	Pct.
Denver	48	34	.585
Milwaukee	44	38	.537
Chicago	40	42	.488
Detroit	38	44	.463
Indiana	31	51	.378
Kansas City	31	51	.378

PACIFIC DIVISION

	W	L	Pct.
Portland	58	24	.707
Phoenix	49	33	.598
Seattle	47	35	.573
Los Angeles	45	37	.549
Golden State	43	39	.524

PLAYOFFS

EASTERN CONFERENCE

FIRST ROUND

New York 2, Cleveland 0
Apr. 12 ....New York 132, @Cleveland 114
Apr. 14 ....@New York 109, Cleveland 107

Washington 2, Atlanta 0
Apr. 12 ....@Washington 103, Atlanta 94
Apr. 14 ....Washington 107, @Atlanta 103*

SEMIFINALS

Philadelphia 4, New York 0
Apr. 16 ....@Philadelphia 130, New York 90
Apr. 18 ....@Philadelphia 119, New York 100
Apr. 20 ....Philadelphia 137, @New York 126
Apr. 23 ....Philadelphia 112, @New York 107

Washington 4, San Antonio 2
Apr. 16 ....@San Antonio 114, Washington 103
Apr. 18 ....Washington 121, @San Antonio 117
Apr. 21 ....@Washington 118, San Antonio 105
Apr. 23 ....@Washington 98, San Antonio 95
Apr. 25 ....@San Antonio 116, Washington 105
Apr. 28 ....@Washington 103, San Antonio 100

FINALS

Washington 4, Philadelphia 2
Apr. 30 ....Washington 122, @Philadelphia 117*
May 3 ......@Philadelphia 110, Washington 104
May 5 ......@Washington 123, Philadelphia 108
May 7 ......@Washington 121, Philadelphia 105
May 10 ....@Philadelphia 107, Washington 94
May 12 ....@Washington 101, Philadelphia 99

WESTERN CONFERENCE

FIRST ROUND

Milwaukee 2, Phoenix 0
Apr. 11 ....Milwaukee 111, @Phoenix 103
Apr. 14 ....@Milwaukee 94, Phoenix 90

Seattle 2, Los Angeles 1
Apr. 12 ....@Seattle 102, Los Angeles 90
Apr. 14 ....@Los Angeles 105, Seattle 99
Apr. 16 ....@Seattle 111, Los Angeles 102

SEMIFINALS

Seattle 4, Portland 2
Apr. 18 ....Seattle 104, @Portland 95
Apr. 21 ....@Portland 96, Seattle 93
Apr. 23 ....@Seattle 99, Portland 84
Apr. 26 ....@Seattle 100, Portland 98
Apr. 30 ....@Portland 113, Seattle 89
May 1 ......@Seattle 105, Portland 94

Denver 4, Milwaukee 3
Apr. 18 ....@Denver 119, Milwaukee 103
Apr. 21 ....@Denver 127, Milwaukee 111
Apr. 23 ....@Milwaukee 143, Denver 112
Apr. 25 ....Denver 118, @Milwaukee 104
Apr. 28 ....Milwaukee 117, @Denver 112
Apr. 30 ....@Milwaukee 119, Denver 91
May 3 ......@Denver 116, Milwaukee 110

FINALS

Seattle 4, Denver 2
May 5 ......@Denver 116, Seattle 107
May 7 ......Seattle 121, @Denver 111
May 10 ....@Seattle 105, Denver 91
May 12 ....@Seattle 100, Denver 94
May 14 ....@Denver 123, Seattle 114
May 17 ....@Seattle 123, Denver 108

NBA FINALS

Washington 4, Seattle 3
May 21 ....@Seattle 106, Washington 102
May 25 ....@Washington 106, Seattle 98
May 28 ....Seattle 93, @Washington 92
May 30 ....Washington 120, @Seattle 116*
June 2 .....@Seattle 98, Washington 94
June 4 .....@Washington 117, Seattle 82
June 7 .....Washington 105, @Seattle 99

*Denotes number of overtime periods.

INDIVIDUAL LEADERS

SCORING (minimum 70 games or 1,400 points)

	G	FGM	FTM	Pts.	Avg.
Gervin, San Antonio	82	864	504	2232	27.2
Thompson, Denver	80	826	520	2172	27.2
McAdoo, New York	79	814	469	2097	26.5
Abdul-Jabbar, L.A.	62	663	274	1600	25.8
Murphy, Houston	76	852	245	1949	25.6
Westphal, Phoenix	80	809	396	2014	25.2
Smith, Buffalo	82	789	443	2021	24.6
Lanier, Detroit	63	622	298	1542	24.5
Davis, Phoenix	81	786	387	1959	24.2
King, New Jersey	79	798	313	1909	24.2

FIELD GOAL PCT. (minimum 300 made)

	FGM	FGA	Pct.
Jones, Denver	440	761	.578
Dawkins, Philadelphia	332	577	.575
Gilmore, Chicago	704	1260	.559
Abdul-Jabbar, Los Angeles	663	1205	.550
English, Milwaukee	343	633	.542

FREE THROW PCT. (minimum 125 made)

	FTM	FTA	Pct.
Barry, Golden State	378	409	.924
Murphy, Houston	245	267	.918
Brown, Seattle	176	196	.898
Newlin, Houston	152	174	.874
Maravich, New Orleans	240	276	.870
Wedman, Kansas-City	221	254	.870

ASSISTS (minimum 70 games or 400 assists)

	G	No.	Avg.
Porter, Detroit-New Jersey	82	837	10.2
Lucas, Houston	82	768	9.4
Sobers, Indiana	79	584	7.4
Nixon, Los Angeles	81	553	6.8
Van Lier, Chicago	78	531	6.8

REBOUNDS (minimum 70 games or 800 rebounds)

	G	Off.	Def.	Tot.	Avg.
Robinson, New Orleans	82	298	990	1288	15.7
Malone, Houston	59	380	506	886	15.0
Cowens, Boston	77	248	830	1078	14.0
Hayes, Washington	81	335	740	1075	13.3
Nater, Buffalo	78	278	751	1029	13.2

STEALS (minimum 70 games or 125 steals)

	G	No.	Avg.
Lee, Phoenix	82	225	2.74
Williams, Seattle	79	185	2.34
Buckner, Milwaukee	82	188	2.29
Gale, San Antonio	70	159	2.27
Buse, Phoenix	82	185	2.26

BLOCKED SHOTS (minimum 70 games or 100 blocked shots)

	G	No.	Avg.
Johnson, New Jersey	81	274	3.38
Abdul-Jabbar, Los Angeles	62	185	2.98
Rollins, Atlanta	80	218	2.73
Walton, Portland	58	146	2.52
Paultz, San Antonio	80	194	2.43

1976-77 SEASON

Bill Walton

The Portland Trail Blazers had lived six NBA seasons without a winning record. Then, for one special campaign, center Bill Walton got healthy and Blazer fans discovered they lived in Rip City.

Portland's success came at a time of change in pro basketball. Four teams from the disbanded ABA — the New York Nets, Indiana Pacers, Denver Nuggets and San Antonio Spurs — became NBA franchises for a fee of $3.2 million per team. The NBA used a dispersal draft to allocate the rest of the ABA players, including imposing 7-2 center Artis Gilmore of the Kentucky Colonels.

Portland, greatly improved under Coach Jack Ramsay, snared a scorer and rebounder from the ashes of the ABA in 6-9 Maurice Lucas, and he provided the toughness to complement the all-around skills of Walton. The rest of the team consisted of consummate role players: small forward Bobby Gross, point guard Dave Twardzik and shooting guard Lionel Hollins.

The central figure, of course, was Walton, the son of a San Diego social worker. Off the court, he was a counterculture kind of guy with long red hair. On the court, he was the picture of precision, the ultimate passing center, schooled and polished in every phase of the game.

"He's another one who made all the players around him better," said John Wooden, his coach at UCLA. "He was probably the greatest at getting the ball off the boards and initiating a fast break."

Those skills would enable Walton to become UCLA's career assists leader, a remarkable feat for a center, and a sign of his great pro potential, a potential that had gone largely unrealized during his first two seasons because of injuries.

The addition of four ABA franchises brought the NBA to 22 teams, and the playoffs were restructured so that 12 teams qualified, with the four division winners receiving first-round byes.

With that format, the Trail Blazers prospered despite not winning their division in the regular season. Ramsay's team beat Chicago, Denver and the Lakers on their way to the Finals, with the Blazers' big challenge coming in the first round against the revived Bulls.

In the ABA dispersal draft, Chicago had paid $1 million to acquire Gilmore, who had led the Kentucky Colonels to the 1975 ABA title. The presence of the 7-2, 265-pound Gilmore created a rush of hope in Chicago, but then the Bulls got off to a 4-15 start. By February, Chicago found a chemistry and charged from 21-31 and the bottom of the standings to a 44-38 finish and a tense playoff series against the eventual-champion Trail Blazers. The run, dubbed the "Miracle On Madison" by the media, excited all of Chicago and brought a string of sellout crowds to Chicago Stadium.

"The Bulls were our toughest series that year," Ramsay recalled. "They had a very good team. Artis Gilmore had probably his best season ever. We split the first two games, and the third and final game was in Portland. By the time we reached the closing minutes, several guys on each side had fouled out. We had a lead, but Chicago closed the gap. We got down to the nub of the game, and we were ahead by two." The Bulls had the ball with 15 seconds left, trailing by two, but in attempting to inbound the ball, Chicago's John Mengelt tossed it into the basket, a violation that allowed the Blazers to escape.

In the Finals, Portland met the 76ers, led by former ABA superstar Julius Erving. Philadelphia won the first two at home, but then Walton cut his long red hair and the Blazers got down to business, sweeping four straight.

Blazermania overwhelmed Portland, which became known as Rip City after one of radio announcer Bill Schonley's favorite calls, describing the sound a ball makes going through the net.

NBA.COM FACT

After nearly 19 hours of nonstop negotiations, Philadelphia General Manager Pat Williams finally emerged from an office to announce, "Dr. J is a 76er." The acquisition of Julius Erving from the financially strapped New York Nets helped the Sixers both on and off the court as the team won the Eastern Conference championship and became one of the league's top attractions.

FINAL STANDINGS

EASTERN CONFERENCE

ATLANTIC DIVISION

	W	L	Pct.
Philadelphia	50	32	.610
Boston	44	38	.537
N.Y. Knicks	40	42	.488
Buffalo	30	52	.366
N.Y. Nets	22	60	.268

CENTRAL DIVISION

	W	L	Pct.
Houston	49	33	.598
Washington	48	34	.585
San Antonio	44	38	.537
Cleveland	43	39	.524
New Orleans	35	47	.427
Atlanta	31	51	.378

WESTERN CONFERENCE

MIDWEST DIVISION

	W	L	Pct.
Denver	50	32	.610
Chicago	44	38	.537
Detroit	44	38	.537
Kansas City	40	42	.488
Indiana	36	46	.439
Milwaukee	30	52	.366

PACIFIC DIVISION

	W	L	Pct.
Los Angeles	53	29	.646
Portland	49	33	.598
Golden State	46	36	.561
Seattle	40	42	.488
Phoenix	34	48	.415

PLAYOFFS

EASTERN CONFERENCE

FIRST ROUND

Boston 2, San Antonio 0

Apr. 12 ....@Boston 104, San Antonio 94
Apr. 15 ....Boston 113, @San Antonio 109

Washington 2, Cleveland 1

Apr. 13 ....@Washington 109, Cleveland 100
Apr. 15 ....@Cleveland 91, Washington 83
Apr. 17 ....@Washington 104, Cleveland 98

SEMIFINALS

Philadelphia 4, Boston 3

Apr. 17 ....Boston 113, @Philadelphia 111
Apr. 20 ....@Philadelphia 113, Boston 101
Apr. 22 ....Philadelphia 109, @Boston 100
Apr. 24 ....@Boston 124, Philadelphia 119
Apr. 27 ....@Philadelphia 110, Boston 91
Apr. 29 ....@Boston 113, Philadelphia 108
May 1 ......@Philadelphia 83, Boston 77

Houston 4, Washington 2

Apr. 19 ....Washington 111, @Houston 101
Apr. 21 ....@Houston 124, Washington 118*
Apr. 24 ....@Washington 93, Houston 90
Apr. 26 ....Houston 107, @Washington 103
Apr. 29 ....@Houston 123, Washington 115
May 1 ......Houston 108, @Washington 103

FINALS

Philadelphia 4, Houston 2

May 5 ......@Philadelphia 128, Houston 117
May 8 ......@Philadelphia 106, Houston 97
May 11 ....@Houston 118, Philadelphia 94
May 13 ....Philadelphia 107, @Houston 95
May 15 ....Houston 118, @Philadelphia 115
May 17 ....Philadelphia 112, @Houston 109

WESTERN CONFERENCE

FIRST ROUND

Golden State 2, Detroit 1

Apr. 12 ....Detroit 95, @Golden State 90
Apr. 14 ....Golden State 138, @Detroit 108
Apr. 17 ....@Golden State 109, Detroit 101

Portland 2, Chicago 1

Apr. 12 ....@Portland 96, Chicago 83
Apr. 15 ....@Chicago 107, Portland 104
Apr. 17 ....@Portland 106, Chicago 98

SEMIFINALS

Los Angeles 4, Golden State 3

Apr. 20 ....@Los Angeles 115, Golden State 106
Apr. 22 ....@Los Angeles 95, Golden State 86
Apr. 24 ....@Golden State 109, Los Angeles 105
Apr. 26 ....@Golden State 114, Los Angeles 103
Apr. 29 ....@Los Angeles 112, Golden State 105
May 1 ......@Golden State 115, Los Angeles 106
May 4 ......@Los Angeles 97, Golden State 84

Portland 4, Denver 2

Apr. 20 ....Portland 101, @Denver 100
Apr. 22 ....@Denver 121, Portland 110
Apr. 24 ....@Portland 110, Denver 106
Apr. 26 ....@Portland 105, Denver 96
May 1 ......@Denver 114, Portland 105*
May 2 ......@Portland 108, Denver 92

FINALS

Portland 4, Los Angeles 0

May 6 ......Portland 121, @Los Angeles 109
May 8 ......Portland 99, @Los Angeles 97
May 10 ....@Portland 102, Los Angeles 97
May 13 ....@Portland 105, Los Angeles 101

NBA FINALS

Portland 4, Philadelphia 2

May 22 ....@Philadelphia 107, Portland 101
May 26 ....@Philadelphia 107, Portland 89
May 29 ....@Portland 129, Philadelphia 107
May 31 ....@Portland 130, Philadelphia 98
June 3 .....Portland 110, @Philadelphia 104
June 5 .....@Portland 109, Philadelphia 107

*Denotes number of overtime periods.

INDIVIDUAL LEADERS

SCORING (minimum 70 games or 1,400 points)

	G	FGM	FTM	Pts.	Avg.
Maravich, New Orleans	73	886	501	2273	31.1
Knight, Indiana	78	831	413	2075	26.6
Abdul-Jabbar, L.A.	82	888	376	2152	26.2
Thompson, Denver	82	824	477	2125	25.9
McAdoo, Buf.-N.Y. Knicks	72	740	381	1861	25.8
Lanier, Detroit	64	678	260	1616	25.3
Drew, Atlanta	74	689	412	1790	24.2
Hayes, Washington	82	760	422	1942	23.7
Gervin, San Antonio	82	726	443	1895	23.1
Issel, Denver	79	660	445	1765	22.3

FIELD GOAL PCT. (minimum 300 made)

	FGM	FGA	Pct.
Abdul-Jabbar, Los Angeles	888	1533	.579
Kupchak, Washington	341	596	.572
Jones, Denver	501	879	.570
Gervin, San Antonio	726	1335	.544
Lanier, Detroit	678	1269	.534

FREE THROW PCT. (minimum 125 made)

	FTM	FTA	Pct.
DiGregorio, Buffalo	138	146	.945
Barry, Golden State	359	392	.916
Murphy, Houston	272	307	.886
Newlin, Houston	269	304	.885
Brown, Seattle	168	190	.884

ASSISTS (minimum 70 games or 400 assists)

	G	No.	Avg.
Buse, Indiana	81	685	8.5
Watts, Seattle	79	630	8.0
Van Lier, Chicago	82	636	7.8
Porter, Detroit	81	592	7.3
Henderson, Atlanta-Washington	87	598	6.9

REBOUNDS (minimum 70 games or 800 rebounds)

	G	Off.	Def.	Tot.	Avg.
Walton, Portland	65	211	723	934	14.4
Abdul-Jabbar, L.A.	82	266	824	1090	13.3
Malone, Buffalo-Houston	82	437	635	1072	13.1
Gilmore, Chicago	82	313	757	1070	13.0
McAdoo, Buf.-N.Y. Knicks	72	199	727	926	12.9

STEALS (minimum 70 games or 125 steals)

	G	No.	Avg.
Buse, Indiana	81	281	3.47
Taylor, Kansas City	72	199	2.76
Watts, Seattle	79	214	2.71
Buckner, Milwaukee	79	192	2.43
Gale, San Antonio	82	191	2.33

BLOCKED SHOTS (minimum 70 games or 100 blocked shots)

	G	No.	Avg.
Walton, Portland	65	211	3.25
Abdul-Jabbar, Los Angeles	82	261	3.18
Hayes, Washington	82	220	2.68
Gilmore, Chicago	82	203	2.48
Jones, Philadelphia	82	200	2.44

1975-76 SEASON

Alvan Adams (33)

NBA.COM FACT

In Phoenix, which posted the eighth-best record (42–40) during the regular season, the league had its most unlikely conference champion. In 101 regular- and postseason games, the Suns were only three games over the break-even mark (52-49) and had outscored their opponents by just 30 points (10,625-10,595).

Boston fans never tired of swarming the parquet during Garden victory parties. At least that's the way it seemed to NBA opponents who saw the Celtics claim their 13th championship.

The Celtics — featuring Dave Cowens, Jo Jo White, John Havlicek, Charlie Scott, Don Nelson and Don Chaney and coached by Tommy Heinsohn — won their second title in three years.

As the season approached, two ABA teams, the New York Nets and Denver Nuggets, applied for NBA admission. The move signaled the end for the ABA, although it would last one more season.

The NBA, meanwhile, named its third commissioner. Larry O'Brien, former chairman of the Democratic National Committee, replaced retiring Walter Kennedy. The owners hoped O'Brien's skills as a mediator and lobbyist would hasten the merger.

In a stunning move, Milwaukee traded Kareem Abdul-Jabbar to the Lakers for four players. While Abdul-Jabbar went on to win MVP honors for the fourth time by averaging 27.7 points and a league-leading 16.9 rebounds, the Lakers went 40-42 and missed the playoffs.

The defending-champion Warriors won a league-high 59 games, but upstart Phoenix, with Rookie of the Year Alvan Adams, beat Seattle and defending champion Golden State in seven games to meet Boston in the Finals. Boston, having acquired Scott from Phoenix for Paul Westphal, won 54 games to top the East.

The six-game championship series featured a triple-overtime Game 5. "That was the most exciting basketball game I've ever seen," said Rick Barry, who worked the event as part of the CBS broadcast crew. "They just had one great play after another. I'll never forget the end. Jo Jo White was so exhausted, he just sat down on the court. It was such an emotional and physical game for everybody involved."

It didn't exactly begin as a classic, though. After nine minutes, Boston was up 32-12. The Celtics went on to score 38 points in the first quarter and seemed on the verge of breaking the Suns. Phoenix stayed in it somehow, cutting a 22-point deficit to 15 by the half. Then the Suns went to their defense, held Boston to a mere 34 points over the last two quarters and closed regulation at 95-95.

The first overtime brought six more points for each team. In the second overtime, Havlicek hit a 15-foot-jump shot for an apparent 111-110 victory. Celtics fans swarmed the court, but the officials ruled one second remained.

After the court was cleared, Westphal called a timeout the Suns didn't have so Phoenix could move the ball to half-court and have a chance for a shot. Boston made the technical free throw, but Phoenix inbounded to forward Gar Heard, who hit a 20-footer for yet another overtime.

With several regulars having fouled out, the unlikely hero for the Celtics was little-used Glenn McDonald, a 6-6 forward who had been the team's No. 1 draft pick out of Long Beach State in 1974. His NBA career would last only nine more games after the 1976 Finals, as he would be released in the 1976-77 season by Milwaukee. But he scored six points in that third overtime, the last two on a short jumper to give Boston a 128-126 triumph.

In Game 6 in Phoenix, White, Cowens, Havlicek and Scott took control. The Celtics rode a late surge to an 87-80 victory and their 13th championship. "We had to gut it out all the way," Heinsohn said. "Phoenix has a fine team with a great shooter. When the game was up for grabs, it was a question of pure guts."

White scored 15 in Game 6 and led Boston throughout the series, averaging 21.7 points in six games. For that performance, he was named the series MVP. "Our offense really wasn't that great," White said. "But defense will do it for you every time, and our defense did it."

FINAL STANDINGS

EASTERN CONFERENCE

ATLANTIC DIVISION

	W	L	Pct.
Boston	54	28	.659
Buffalo	46	36	.561
Philadelphia	46	36	.561
New York	38	44	.463

CENTRAL DIVISION

	W	L	Pct.
Cleveland	49	33	.598
Washington	48	34	.585
Houston	40	42	.488
New Orleans	38	44	.463
Atlanta	29	53	.354

WESTERN CONFERENCE

MIDWEST DIVISION

	W	L	Pct.
Milwaukee	38	44	.463
Detroit	36	46	.439
Kansas City	31	51	.378
Chicago	24	58	.293

PACIFIC DIVISION

	W	L	Pct.
Golden State	59	23	.720
Seattle	43	39	.524
Phoenix	42	40	.512
Los Angeles	40	42	.488
Portland	37	45	.451

PLAYOFFS

EASTERN CONFERENCE

FIRST ROUND

Buffalo 2, Philadelphia 1

Apr. 15 ....Buffalo 95, @Philadelphia 89
Apr. 16 ....Philadelphia 131, @Buffalo 106
Apr. 18 ....Buffalo 124, @Philadelphia 123*

SEMIFINALS

Boston 4, Buffalo 2

Apr. 21 ....@Boston 107, Buffalo 98
Apr. 23 ....@Boston 101, Buffalo 96
Apr. 25 ....@Buffalo 98, Boston 93
Apr. 28 ....@Buffalo 124, Boston 122
Apr. 30 ....@Boston 99, Buffalo 88
May 2......Boston 104, @Buffalo 100

Cleveland 4, Washington 3

Apr. 13 ....Washington 100, @Cleveland 95
Apr. 15 ....Cleveland 80, @Washington 79
Apr. 17 ....@Cleveland 88, Washington 76
Apr. 21 ....@Washington 109, Cleveland 98
Apr. 22 ....@Cleveland 92, Washington 91
Apr. 26 ....@Washington 102, Cleveland 98*
Apr. 29 ....@Cleveland 87, Washington 85

FINALS

Boston 4, Cleveland 2

May 6......@Boston 111, Cleveland 99
May 9......@Boston 94, Cleveland 89
May 11 ....@Cleveland 83, Boston 78
May 14 ....@Cleveland 106, Boston 87
May 16 ....@Boston 99, Cleveland 94
May 18 ....Boston 94, @Cleveland 87

WESTERN CONFERENCE

FIRST ROUND

Detroit 2, Milwaukee 1

Apr. 13 ....@Milwaukee 110, Detroit 107
Apr. 15 ....@Detroit 126, Milwaukee 123
Apr. 18 ....Detroit 107, @Milwaukee 104

SEMIFINALS

Golden State 4, Detroit 2

Apr. 20 ....@Golden State 127, Detroit 103
Apr. 22 ....Detroit 123, @Golden State 111
Apr. 24 ....Golden State 113, @Detroit 96
Apr. 26 ....@Detroit 106, Golden State 102
Apr. 28 ....@Golden State 128, Detroit 109
Apr. 30 ....Golden State 118, @Detroit 116*

Phoenix 4, Seattle 2

Apr. 13 ....@Seattle 102, Phoenix 99
Apr. 15 ....Phoenix 116, @Seattle 111
Apr. 18 ....@Phoenix 103, Seattle 91
Apr. 20 ....@Phoenix 130, Seattle 114
Apr. 25 ....@Seattle 114, Phoenix 108
Apr. 27 ....@Phoenix 123, Seattle 112

FINALS

Phoenix 4, Golden State 3

May 2......@Golden State 128, Phoenix 103
May 5......Phoenix 108, @Golden State 101
May 7......Golden State 99, @Phoenix 91
May 9......@Phoenix 133, Golden State 129**
May 12 ....@Golden State 111, Phoenix 95
May 14 ....@Phoenix 105, Golden State 104
May 16 ....Phoenix 94, @Golden State 86

NBA FINALS

Boston 4, Phoenix 2

May 23 ....@Boston 98, Phoenix 87
May 27 ....@Boston 105, Phoenix 90
May 30 ....@Phoenix 105, Boston 98
June 2 ....@Phoenix 109, Boston 107
June 4 .....@Boston 128, Phoenix 126***
June 6 .....Boston 87, @Phoenix 80

*Denotes number of overtime periods.

INDIVIDUAL LEADERS

SCORING (minimum 70 games or 1,400 points)

	G	FGM	FTM	Pts.	Avg.
McAdoo, Buffalo	78	934	559	2427	31.1
Abdul-Jabbar, L.A.	82	914	447	2275	27.7
Maravich, New Orleans	62	604	396	1604	25.9
Archibald, Kansas City	78	717	501	1935	24.8
Brown, Seattle	76	742	273	1757	23.1
McGinnis, Philadelphia	77	647	475	1769	23.0
Smith, Buffalo	82	702	383	1787	21.8
Drew, Atlanta	77	586	488	1660	21.6
Dandridge, Milwaukee	73	650	271	1571	21.5
Barry, Golden State	81	707	287	1701	21.0
Murphy, Houston	82	675	372	1722	21.0

FIELD GOAL PCT. (minimum 300 made)

	FGM	FGA	Pct.
Unseld, Washington	318	567	.56085
Shumate, Phoenix-Buffalo	332	592	.56081
McMillian, Buffalo	492	918	.536
Lanier, Detroit	541	1017	.532
Abdul-Jabbar, Los Angeles	914	1728	.529

FREE THROW PCT. (minimum 125 made)

	FTM	FTA	Pct.
Barry, Golden State	287	311	.923
Murphy, Houston	372	410	.907
Russell, Los Angeles	132	148	.892
Bradley, New York	130	148	.878
Brown, Seattle	273	314	.869

ASSISTS (minimum 70 games or 400 assists)

	G	No.	Avg.
Watts, Seattle	82	661	8.1
Archibald, Kansas City	78	615	7.9
Murphy, Houston	82	596	7.3
Van Lier, Chicago	76	500	6.6
Barry, Golden State	81	496	6.1

REBOUNDS (minimum 70 games or 800 rebounds)

	G	Off.	Def.	Tot.	Avg.
Abdul-Jabbar, L.A.	82	272	1111	1383	16.9
Cowens, Boston	78	335	911	1246	16.0
Unseld, Washington	78	271	765	1036	13.3
Silas, Boston	81	365	660	1025	12.7
Lacey, Kansas City	81	218	806	1024	12.6

STEALS (minimum 70 games or 125 steals)

	G	No.	Avg.
Watts, Seattle	82	261	3.18
McGinnis, Philadelphia	77	198	2.57
Westphal, Phoenix	82	210	2.56
Barry, Golden State	81	202	2.49
Ford, Detroit	82	178	2.17

BLOCKED SHOTS (minimum 70 games or 100 blocked shots)

	G	No.	Avg.
Abdul-Jabbar, Los Angeles	82	338	4.12
Smith, Milwaukee	78	238	3.05
Hayes, Washington	80	202	2.53
Catchings, Philadelphia	75	164	2.19
Johnson, Golden State	82	174	2.12

1974-75 SEASON

Bob McAdoo (11)

In their first eight years in the league, the Chicago Bulls believed they had to have a dominant center. Heading into the 1974-75 season, they got one. Along with him came a huge lesson in irony.

The Bulls traded pivot workhorse Clifford Ray and a first-round pick to Golden State for the brilliant but aging future Hall of Famer, Nate Thurmond. The two teams met that next spring in the Western Conference Finals, and Ray played a key role in overcoming his old team. The Warriors went on to sweep the favored Washington Bullets for the NBA championship.

"Our key change was getting Clifford Ray for Nate Thurmond," the Warriors' Rick Barry said later. "Ray was one of the best defensive centers in the game."

It was a season of individual brilliance, with three players — Bob McAdoo, Barry and Kareem Abdul-Jabbar — averaging 30 or more points, and five players — Wes Unseld, Dave Cowens, Sam Lacey, McAdoo and Abdul-Jabbar averaging better than 14 rebounds a game.

The retirements of Jerry West and Oscar Robertson left their teams weakened, and the Lakers and Milwaukee each fell to the bottom of their division. This spelled opportunity for hungry young teams in the Western Conference, and nobody was hungrier than the Warriors.

Al Attles, a fixture with the Warriors since 1960 as a player and a coach, had developed an 11-deep roster of role players. They complemented Barry, the high-scoring forward still in his prime (he turned 31 during the season) and he was nearly able to average his age at 30.6 points per game, second best in the league. In addition to acquiring Ray for the aging Thurmond, Attles also brought in scrappy guard Butch Beard and drafted forward Jamaal Wilkes from UCLA, who would emerge as Rookie of the Year.

This unlikely group won 48 games to top the Western Conference, defeated Coach Bill Russell's Seattle team in six games in the conference semifinals and used its endless hustle and desire to beat a talented Chicago Bulls team in seven games to reach the Finals. The Bulls, coached by Dick Motta and led by Jerry Sloan and Chet Walker, led 3-2 in the Western Finals, but the Warriors somehow persevered.

With former Celtic K.C. Jones coaching, the Washington Bullets won 60 games, matching defending champion Boston for the best record in the East. Point guard Kevin Porter posted the best assist numbers in the league at 8.0 per game while the muscular Unseld claimed the rebounding title with 14.8 a game. But it took the Bullets seven games to dispatch the Buffalo Braves, led by NBA scoring champ McAdoo (34.5 ppg), in the Eastern Conference Semifinals. Washington then used the inside-outside scoring combination of Elvin Hayes and Phil Chenier to turn back the Celtics in six games.

The Bullets were heavily favored to beat the Warriors in the Finals. Washington had an experienced team with Hayes, Unseld and feisty Mike Riordan up front and Porter and Chenier in the backcourt. On paper, the Bullets were far superior to the Warriors. But the pressure mounted on Jones' players with each succeeding close loss. Golden State stunned the Bullets and the basketball world by winning four straight tight games — the average margin of victory was just four points — to post only the third sweep in the 29-year history of the NBA Finals.

"It has to be the greatest upset in the history of the NBA Finals," Barry said. "It was like a fairytale season. Everything just fell into place. It's something I'll treasure for the rest of my life."

NBA.COM FACT

Team owners ended their 22-month search for a successor to the retiring Walter Kennedy with the unanimous selection Larry O'Brien, who was born in Springfield, Mass., the birthplace of basketball. A former national chairman of the Democratic party, O'Brien became the third commissioner in the 29-year history of the league.

FINAL STANDINGS

EASTERN CONFERENCE

ATLANTIC DIVISION

	W	L	Pct.
Boston	60	22	.732
Buffalo	49	33	.598
New York	40	42	.488
Philadelphia	34	48	.415

CENTRAL DIVISION

	W	L	Pct.
Washington	60	22	.732
Houston	41	41	.500
Cleveland	40	42	.488
Atlanta	31	51	.378
New Orleans	23	59	.280

WESTERN CONFERENCE

MIDWEST DIVISION

	W	L	Pct.
Chicago	47	35	.573
K.C./Omaha	44	38	.537
Detroit	40	42	.488
Milwaukee	38	44	.463

PACIFIC DIVISION

	W	L	Pct.
Golden State	48	34	.585
Seattle	43	39	.524
Portland	38	44	.463
Phoenix	32	50	.390
Los Angeles	30	52	.366

PLAYOFFS

EASTERN CONFERENCE

FIRST ROUND

Houston 2, New York 1

Apr. 8 ......@Houston 99, New York 84
Apr. 10 ....@New York 106, Houston 96
Apr. 12 ....@Houston 118, New York 86

SEMIFINALS

Boston 4, Houston 1

Apr. 14 ....@Boston 123, Houston 106
Apr. 16 ....@Boston 112, Houston 100
Apr. 19 ....@Houston 117, Boston 102
Apr. 22 ....Boston 122, @Houston 117
Apr. 24 ....@Boston 128, Houston 115

Washington 4, Buffalo 3

Apr. 10 ....Buffalo 113, @Washington 102
Apr. 12 ....Washington 120, @Buffalo 106
Apr. 16 ....@Washington 111, Buffalo 96
Apr. 18 ....@Buffalo 108, Washington 102
Apr. 20 ....@Washington 97, Buffalo 93
Apr. 23 ....@Buffalo 102, Washington 96
Apr. 25 ....@Washington 115, Buffalo 96

FINALS

Washington 4, Boston 2

Apr. 27 ....Washington 100, @Boston 95
Apr. 30 ....@Washington 117, Boston 92
May 3......@Boston 101, Washington 90
May 7......@Washington 119, Boston 108
May 9......@Boston 103, Washington 99
May 11 ....@Washington 98, Boston 92

WESTERN CONFERENCE

FIRST ROUND

Seattle 2, Detroit 1

Apr. 8 ......@Seattle 90, Detroit 77
Apr. 10 ....@Detroit 122, Seattle 106
Apr. 12 ....@Seattle 100, Detroit 93

SEMIFINALS

Golden State 4, Seattle 2

Apr. 14 ....@Golden State 123, Seattle 96
Apr. 16 ....Seattle 100, @Golden State 99
Apr. 17 ....Golden State 105, @Seattle 96
Apr. 19 ....@Seattle 111, Golden State 94
Apr. 22 ....@Golden State 124, Seattle 100
Apr. 24 ....Golden State 105, @Seattle 96

Chicago 4, Kansas City/Omaha 2

Apr. 9 ......@Chicago 95, Kansas City/Omaha 89
Apr. 13 ....@Kansas City/Omaha 102, Chicago 95
Apr. 16 ....@Chicago 93, Kansas City/Omaha 90
Apr. 18 ....@Kansas City/Omaha 104, Chicago 100*
Apr. 20 ....@Chicago 104, Kansas City/Omaha 77
Apr. 23 ....Chicago 101, @Kansas City/Omaha 89

FINALS

Golden State 4, Chicago 3

Apr. 27 ....@Golden State 107, Chicago 89
Apr. 30 ....@Chicago 90, Golden State 89
May 4......@Chicago 108, Golden State 101
May 6......@Golden State 111, Chicago 106
May 8......Chicago 89, @Golden State 79
May 11 ....Golden State 86, @Chicago 72
May 14 ....@Golden State 83, Chicago 79

NBA FINALS

Golden State 4, Washington 0

May 18 ....Golden State 101, @Washington 95
May 20 ....@Golden State 92, Washington 91
May 23 ....@Golden State 109, Washington 101
May 25 ....Golden State 96, @Washington 95

*Denotes number of overtime periods.

INDIVIDUAL LEADERS

SCORING (minimum 70 games or 1,400 points)

	G	FGM	FTM	Pts.	Avg.
McAdoo, Buffalo	82	1095	641	2831	34.5
Barry, Golden State	80	1028	394	2450	30.6
Abdul-Jabbar, Milwaukee	65	812	325	1949	30.0
Archibald, K.C./Omaha	82	759	652	2170	26.5
Scott, Phoenix	69	703	274	1680	24.3
Lanier, Detroit	76	731	361	1823	24.0
Hayes, Washington	82	739	409	1887	23.0
Goodrich, Los Angeles	72	656	318	1630	22.6
Haywood, Seattle	68	608	309	1525	22.4
Carter, Philadelphia	77	715	256	1686	21.9

FIELD GOAL PCT. (minimum 300 made)

	FGM	FGA	Pct.
Nelson, Boston	423	785	.539
Beard, Golden State	408	773	.528
Tomjanovich, Houston	694	1323	.525
Abdul-Jabbar, Milwaukee	812	1584	.513
McAdoo, Buffalo	1095	2138	.512

FREE THROW PCT. (minimum 125 made)

	FTM	FTA	Pct.
Barry, Golden State	394	436	.904
Murphy, Houston	341	386	.883
Bradley, New York	144	165	.873
Archibald, Kansas City/Omaha	652	748	.872
Price, Los Angeles-Milwaukee	169	194	.871

ASSISTS (minimum 70 games or 400 assists)

	G	No.	Avg.
Porter, Washington	81	650	8.0
Bing, Detroit	79	610	7.7
Archibald, Kansas City/Omaha	82	557	6.8
Smith, Buffalo	82	534	6.5
Pete Maravich, New Orleans	79	488	6.2

REBOUNDS (minimum 70 games or 800 rebounds)

	G	Off.	Def.	Tot.	Avg.
Unseld, Washington	73	318	759	1077	14.8
Cowens, Boston	65	229	729	958	14.7
Lacey, Kansas City/Omaha	81	228	921	1149	14.2
McAdoo, Buffalo	82	307	848	1155	14.1
Abdul-Jabbar, Milw.	65	194	718	912	14.0

STEALS (minimum 70 games or 125 steals)

	G	No.	Avg.
Barry, Golden State	80	228	2.85
Frazier, New York	78	190	2.44
Steele, Portland	76	183	2.41
Watts, Seattle	82	190	2.32
Brown, Seattle	81	187	2.31

BLOCKED SHOTS (minimum 70 games or 100 blocked shots)

	G	No.	Avg.
Abdul-Jabbar, Milwaukee	65	212	3.26
Smith, Los Angeles	74	216	2.92
Thurmond, Chicago	80	195	2.44
Hayes, Washington	82	187	2.28
Lanier, Detroit	76	172	2.26

1973-74 SEASON

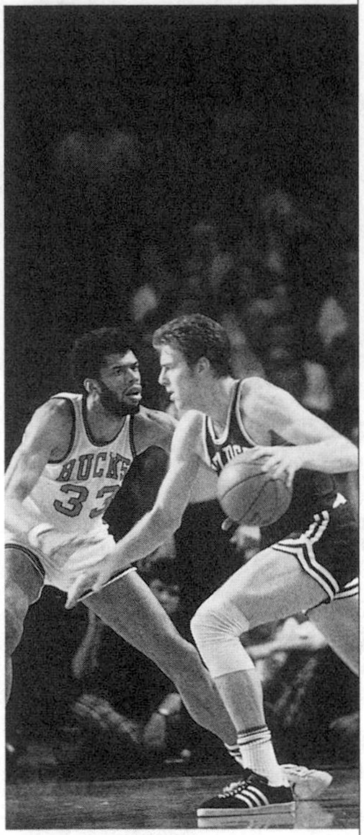

Dave Cowens driving on Kareem Abdul-Jabbar

The Boston Celtics wrote a new chapter in their championship saga in 1974.

To do so, the Celtics had to shake off profound disappointment. The franchise had won 11 championships between 1957 and 1969. Then Bill Russell retired, and the team fell on hard times — but only until Red Auerbach's new wave of players found time to mature.

Leading the charge was undersized 6-9 center Dave Cowens, whom Auerbach had drafted out of Florida State in 1970. Combined with John Havlicek, the main holdover from the Russell days, and the acquisitions of Jo Jo White, Don Chaney and a round of new faces, Boston soon moved back into contention. By 1972-73, Cowens had pushed Boston to a franchise-best 68 victories, but the campaign ended in supreme disappointment when the Celtics lost a seventh game playoff showdown with the New York Knicks in their beloved Boston Garden.

That embarrassment drove Cowens and his teammates as they opened play in the fall of 1973. It wouldn't be an easy run through the regular season, but come playoff time the Celtics would be ready.

The NBA was changing following the retirement of Wilt Chamberlain and his over 31,419 points and 23,924 rebounds. The old guard was gone or on its way out. Willis Reed, Dave DeBusschere and Jerry Lucas were playing their last seasons for New York, while Jerry West in L.A. and Oscar Robertson in Milwaukee were also moving through their final campaigns.

The beneficiary proved to be Boston, which had come of age with a mix of veterans and young stars. Havlicek was still good for a team-high 22.6 points a game, and Cowens hauled in 15.7 rebounds a game and baffled opposing centers with his quickness and fiery determination. Tom Heinsohn had nurtured the group as head coach for five years, and Auerbach was still making the key acquisitions to build another contender.

The Celtics won 56 games, 12 fewer than the previous year but still the most in the East. Boston romped past Buffalo and the aging Knicks to reach the Finals for the first time since 1969. In the West, Abdul-Jabbar won his third MVP Award after averaging 27 points and 14.5 rebounds in leading Milwaukee to a league-high 59 victories. The Bucks toppled the aging Lakers in five games and swept overmatched Chicago to reach the Finals.

The matchup of Cowens and Abdul-Jabbar headlined the series, and each man helped his team to wins as the teams split six games, including a pair of overtime Milwaukee victories.

But playing a huge role for Boston was the 34-year-old Havlicek, still a player in constant motion, able to outrun the opposition every game just as he had when he helped Russell's Celtics win NBA titles during the 1960s. A link to the Cousy/Russell Celtics, "Hondo" was still the critical player for the Celtics a decade later. He proved that by hitting key shots throughout the series, especially in the critical fifth game.

"When things are swinging easy, we all get in the flow of it," explained teammate Paul Silas, another valuable piece to the Boston machine. "And sometimes then it almost looks like we ignore John. But when things don't go well, we look to him all the time to make the tough play. We do this instinctively because he has usually been the guy who's turned bad moments into good ones for us."

In Game 7 the Celtics altered their strategy of having Cowens try to play Abdul-Jabbar by himself, and instead double- and triple-teamed the Milwaukee center. Cowens, freed for the first time in the series from having to focus on defense, scored 28 points and helped Boston to a 102-87 triumph.

Once again, the league faced a dreaded scene: Red Auerbach toasting another championship with a cigar.

NBA.COM FACT

For the first time in NBA history, steals and blocked shots were recorded as official statistics. The first league leaders: aptly named Portland guard Larry Steele (2.68 steals per game) and Los Angeles center Elmore Smith (4.85 blocks per game).

FINAL STANDINGS

EASTERN CONFERENCE

ATLANTIC DIVISION

	W	L	Pct.
Boston	56	26	.683
New York	49	33	.598
Buffalo	42	40	.512
Philadelphia	25	57	.305

CENTRAL DIVISION

	W	L	Pct.
Capital	47	35	.573
Atlanta	35	47	.427
Houston	32	50	.390
Cleveland	29	53	.354

WESTERN CONFERENCE

MIDWEST DIVISION

	W	L	Pct.
Milwaukee	59	23	.720
Chicago	54	28	.659
Detroit	52	30	.634
K.C./Omaha	33	49	.402

PACIFIC DIVISION

	W	L	Pct.
Los Angeles	47	35	.573
Golden State	44	38	.537
Seattle	36	46	.439
Phoenix	30	52	.366
Portland	27	55	.329

PLAYOFFS

EASTERN CONFERENCE
SEMIFINALS
Boston 4, Buffalo 2
Mar. 30....@Boston 107, Buffalo 97
Apr. 2......@Buffalo 115, Boston 105
Apr. 3......@Boston 120, Buffalo 107
Apr. 6......@Buffalo 104, Boston 102
Apr. 9......@Boston 100, Buffalo 97
Apr. 12....Boston 106, @Buffalo 104

New York 4, Capital 3
Mar. 29....@New York 102, Capital 91
Mar. 31....@Capital 99, New York 87
Apr. 2......Capital 88, @New York 79
Apr. 5......New York 101, @Capital 93*
Apr. 7......@New York 106, Capital 105
Apr. 10....@Capital 109, New York 92
Apr. 12....@New York 91, Capital 81

FINALS
Boston 4, New York 1
Apr. 14....@Boston 113, New York 88
Apr. 16....Boston 111, @New York 99
Apr. 19....New York 103, @Boston 100
Apr. 21....Boston 98, @New York 91
Apr. 24....@Boston 105, New York 94

WESTERN CONFERENCE
SEMIFINALS
Milwaukee 4, Los Angeles 1
Mar. 29....@Milwaukee 99, Los Angeles 95
Mar. 31....@Milwaukee 109, Los Angeles 90
Apr. 2......@Los Angeles 98, Milwaukee 96
Apr. 4......Milwaukee 112, @Los Angeles 90
Apr. 7......@Milwaukee 114, Los Angeles 92

Chicago 4, Detroit 3
Mar. 30....Detroit 97, @Chicago 88
Apr. 1......Chicago 108, @Detroit 103
Apr. 5......@Chicago 84, Detroit 83
Apr. 7......@Detroit 102, Chicago 87
Apr. 9......@Chicago 98, Detroit 94
Apr. 11....@Detroit 92, Chicago 88
Apr. 13....@Chicago 96, Detroit 94

FINALS
Milwaukee 4, Chicago 0
Apr. 16....@Milwaukee 101, Chicago 85
Apr. 18....Milwaukee 113, @Chicago 111
Apr. 20....@Milwaukee 113, Chicago 90
Apr. 22....Milwaukee 115, @Chicago 99

NBA FINALS
Boston 4, Milwaukee 3
Apr. 28....Boston 98, @Milwaukee 83
Apr. 30....@Milwaukee 105, Boston 96*
May 3......@Boston 95, Milwaukee 83
May 5......Milwaukee 97, @Boston 89
May 7......Boston 96, @Milwaukee 87
May 10....Milwaukee 102, @Boston 101**
May 12....Boston 102, @Milwaukee 87

*Denotes number of overtime periods.

INDIVIDUAL LEADERS

SCORING (minimum 70 games)

	G	FGM	FTM	Pts.	Avg.
McAdoo, Buffalo	74	901	459	2261	30.6
Maravich, Atlanta	76	819	469	2107	27.7
Abdul-Jabbar, Milwaukee	81	948	295	2191	27.0
Goodrich, Los Angeles	82	784	508	2076	25.3
Barry, Golden State	80	796	417	2009	25.1
Tomjanovich, Houston	80	788	385	1961	24.5
Petrie, Portland	73	740	291	1771	24.3
Haywood, Seattle	75	694	373	1761	23.5
Havlicek, Boston	76	685	346	1716	22.6
Lanier, Detroit	81	748	326	1822	22.5

FIELD GOAL PCT. (minimum 560 attempted)

	FGM	FGA	Pct.
McAdoo, Buffalo	901	1647	.547
Abdul-Jabbar, Milwaukee	948	1759	.539
Tomjanovich, Houston	788	1470	.536
Murphy, Houston	671	1285	.522
Beard, Golden State	316	617	.512

FREE THROW PCT. (minimum 160 attempted)

	FTM	FTA	Pct.
DiGregorio, Buffalo	174	193	.902
Barry, Golden State	417	464	.899
Mullins, Golden State	168	192	.875
Walker, Chicago	439	502	.875
Bradley, New York	146	167	.874

ASSISTS (minimum 70 games)

	G	No.	Avg.
DiGregorio, Buffalo	81	663	8.2
Murphy, Houston	81	603	7.4
Wilkens, Cleveland	74	522	7.1
Frazier, New York	80	551	6.9
Van Lier, Chicago	80	548	6.9
Bing, Detroit	81	555	6.9

REBOUNDS (minimum 70 games)

	G	Off.	Def.	Tot.	Avg.
Hayes, Capital	81	354	1109	1463	18.1
Cowens, Boston	80	264	993	1257	15.7
McAdoo, Buffalo	74	281	836	1117	15.1
Abdul-Jabbar, Milw.	81	287	891	1178	14.5
Hairston, Los Angeles	77	335	705	1040	13.5

STEALS (minimum 70 games)

	G	No.	Avg.
Steele, Portland	81	217	2.68
Mix, Philadelphia	82	212	2.59
Smith, Buffalo	82	203	2.48
Sloan, Chicago	77	183	2.38
Barry, Golden State	80	169	2.11

BLOCKED SHOTS (minimum 70 games)

	G	No.	Avg.
Smith, Los Angeles	81	393	4.85
Abdul-Jabbar, Milwaukee	81	283	3.49
McAdoo, Buffalo	74	246	3.32
Lanier, Detroit	81	247	3.05
Hayes, Capital	81	240	2.96

1972-73 SEASON

Nate "Tiny" Archibald

Tiny dominated.

It's not often in NBA history that you can say that.

But Nate "Tiny" Archibald, a showman with all the New York playground moves, pulled off an amazing feat in 1972-73, leading the league in scoring and assists. That, combined with his longtime excellence, earned him a place in the Hall of Fame.

It's hard to say what was more impressive, the fact that as a 6-1 guard he averaged 34 points, or that he also whipped an average of 11.4 assists each night to his teammates. Consider the remarkable degree of difficulty. He performed these feats for the Kings, a losing team that divided its home games between Kansas City, Mo., and Omaha, Neb., after moving from Cincinnati (where they had been the Royals) for the 1972-73 season. Although the Kings went 36-46 and didn't qualify for the playoffs, Archibald wowed the league in only his third pro season. Nearly three decades later, no one has come close to matching Archibald's dual achievement. And despite his slender frame, he played a league-leading 46 minutes per game.

Outside of Archibald's big numbers, the season belonged to the Boston Celtics and New York Knickerbockers. Willis Reed returned to the Knicks after injuries had limited him to 11 games the previous season. New York, which won the title in 1970 but lost the championship series to the Lakers in '72, was primed to make a run at a second trophy.

Jerry Lucas shared the center spot with Reed, giving New York a tag team of Hall of Famers. Bill Bradley and Dave DeBusschere were the sweet-shooting forwards, with rangy Phil Jackson in reserve. The backcourt provided an interesting chemistry lesson. In his years with the Baltimore Bullets, Earl Monroe had engaged the Knicks' Walt Frazier in some emotional battles. With Monroe coming to the Knicks (New York had traded Mike Riordan and Dave Stallworth to get him), the longtime adversaries not only learned to coexist, but brought out the best in each other by sharing the load.

The top team during the regular season was Boston, which had rebuilt around John Havlicek with young stars Jo Jo White and Dave Cowens; veteran Paul Silas; and 1969 title team holdovers Don Chaney, Don Nelson and Satch Sanders.

Boston won 68 games, only one shy of the league record the Lakers had established a season earlier. At the other end of the standings, the Philadelphia 76ers, who lost Billy Cunningham to the ABA, suffered through an NBA record-worst 9-73 season.

New York breezed past Baltimore in the Eastern Conference Semifinals, then battled tooth and nail with Boston before the Celtics succumbed 94-78 in a surprisingly easy Game 7 in the conference finals.

With Wilt Chamberlain, Jerry West, Gail Goodrich and Happy Hairston still pushing it, the Lakers made a run at defending their first title since moving to Los Angeles. They defeated Chicago (led by Jerry Sloan, Chet Walker and Bob Love) in seven games, then moved past a well-balanced Golden State team in five games to reach the Finals.

It was the Knicks against the Lakers for the third time in four years, so there were few secrets between the two teams. After the Lakers edged New York in Game 1, the Knicks won four straight closely contested games to bring a second NBA title to New York.

"The Knicks are so well-balanced," Chamberlain said afterward, "and have tremendous passing and so many good shooters, you can't concentrate on one man. The key to the series was that their defense stopped our running game."

The outcome marked the swan song for the big center in the league championship series. Chamberlain had taken three different teams to seven appearances in the Finals, winning twice.

NBA.COM FACT

The Players Association and club owners signed a bargaining agreement, the first in league history. Under the terms of the three-year contract, the minimum salary was set at $20,000. Beginning at age 50, former players were to receive a $720 pension for each year of service. Larry Fleisher represented the players in negotiations with a committee of club owners

FINAL STANDINGS

EASTERN CONFERENCE

ATLANTIC DIVISION

	W	L	Pct.
Boston	68	14	.829
New York	57	25	.695
Buffalo	21	61	.256
Philadelphia	9	73	.110

CENTRAL DIVISION

	W	L	Pct.
Baltimore	52	30	.634
Atlanta	46	36	.561
Houston	33	49	.402
Cleveland	32	50	.390

WESTERN CONFERENCE

MIDWEST DIVISION

	W	L	Pct.
Milwaukee	60	22	.732
Chicago	51	31	.622
Detroit	40	42	.488
K.C./Omaha	36	46	.439

PACIFIC DIVISION

	W	L	Pct.
Los Angeles	60	22	.732
Golden State	47	35	.573
Phoenix	38	44	.463
Seattle	26	56	.317
Portland	21	61	.256

PLAYOFFS

EASTERN CONFERENCE

SEMIFINALS

Boston 4, Atlanta 2

Apr. 1 ......@Boston 134, Atlanta 109
Apr. 4 ......Boston 126, @Atlanta 113
Apr. 6 ......Atlanta 118, @Boston 105
Apr. 8 ......@Atlanta 97, Boston 94
Apr. 11 ....@Boston 108, Atlanta 101
Apr. 13 ....Boston 121, @Atlanta 103

New York 4, Baltimore 1

Mar. 30....@New York 95, Baltimore 83
Apr. 1 ......@New York 123, Baltimore 103
Apr. 4 ......New York 103, @Baltimore 96
Apr. 6 ......@Baltimore 97, New York 89
Apr. 8 ......@New York 109, Baltimore 99

FINALS

New York 4, Boston 3

Apr. 15 ....@Boston 134, New York 108
Apr. 18 ....@New York 129, Boston 96
Apr. 20 ....New York 98, @Boston 91
Apr. 22 ....@New York 117, Boston 110**
Apr. 25 ....@Boston 98, New York 97
Apr. 27 ....Boston 110, @New York 100
Apr. 29 ....New York 94, @Boston 78

WESTERN CONFERENCE

SEMIFINALS

Golden State 4, Milwaukee 2

Mar. 30....@Milwaukee 110, Golden State 90
Apr. 1 ......Golden State 95, @Milwaukee 92
Apr. 5 ......Milwaukee 113, @Golden State 93
Apr. 7 ......@Golden State 102, Milwaukee 97
Apr. 10 ....Golden State 100, @Milwaukee 97
Apr. 13 ....@Golden State 100, Milwaukee 86

Los Angeles 4, Chicago 3

Mar. 30....@Los Angeles 107, Chicago 104*
Apr. 1 ......@Los Angeles 108, Chicago 93
Apr. 6 ......@Chicago 96, Los Angeles 86
Apr. 8 ......@Chicago 98, Los Angeles 94
Apr. 10 ....@Los Angeles 123, Chicago 102
Apr. 13 ....@Chicago 101, Los Angeles 93
Apr. 15 ....@Los Angeles 95, Chicago 92

FINALS

Los Angeles 4, Golden State 1

Apr. 17 ....@Los Angeles 101, Golden State 99
Apr. 19 ....@Los Angeles 104, Golden State 93
Apr. 21 ....Los Angeles 126, @Golden State 70
Apr. 23 ....@Golden State 117, Los Angeles 109
Apr. 25 ....@Los Angeles 128, Golden State 118

NBA FINALS

New York 4, Los Angeles 1

May 1 ......@Los Angeles 115, New York 112
May 3 ......New York 99, @Los Angeles 95
May 6 ......@New York 87, Los Angeles 83
May 8 ......@New York 103, Los Angeles 98
May 10 ....New York 102, @Los Angeles 93

*Denotes number of overtime periods.

INDIVIDUAL LEADERS

SCORING (minimum 70 games)

	G	FGM	FTM	Pts.	Avg.
Archibald, K.C./Omaha	80	1028	663	2719	34.0
Abdul-Jabbar, Milwaukee	76	982	328	2292	30.2
Haywood, Seattle	77	889	473	2251	29.2
Hudson, Atlanta	75	816	397	2029	27.1
Maravich, Atlanta	79	789	485	2063	26.1
Scott, Phoenix	81	806	436	2048	25.3
Petrie, Portland	79	836	298	1970	24.9
Goodrich, Los Angeles	76	750	314	1814	23.9
Lanier, Detroit	81	810	307	1927	23.8
Wicks, Portland	80	761	384	1906	23.8

FIELD GOAL PCT. (minimum 560 attempted)

	FGM	FGA	Pct.
Chamberlain, Los Angeles	426	586	.727
Guokas, Kansas City/Omaha	322	565	.570
Abdul-Jabbar, Milwaukee	982	1772	.554
Rowe, Detroit	547	1053	.519
Fox, Seattle	316	613	.515

FREE THROW PCT. (minimum 160 attempted)

	FTM	FTA	Pct.
Barry, Golden State	358	397	.902
Murphy, Houston	239	269	.888
Newlin, Houston	327	369	.886
Walker, Houston	244	276	.884
Bradley, New York	169	194	.871

ASSISTS (minimum 70 games)

	G	No.	Avg.
Archibald, Kansas City/Omaha	80	910	11.4
Wilkens, Cleveland	75	628	8.4
Bing, Detroit	82	637	7.8
Robertson, Milwaukee	73	551	7.6
Van Lier, Chicago	80	567	7.1

REBOUNDS (minimum 70 games)

	G	No.	Avg.
Chamberlain, Los Angeles	82	1526	18.6
Thurmond, Golden State	79	1349	17.1
Cowens, Boston	82	1329	16.2
Abdul-Jabbar, Milwaukee	76	1224	16.1
Unseld, Baltimore	79	1260	15.9

1971-72 SEASON

Jerry West

Somehow the Los Angeles Lakers made the right changes in 1971, which led to the right results. Finally.

Through the heyday of Elgin Baylor, the Lakers never beat the rival Boston Celtics in the NBA Finals. Baylor had been named to the All-NBA First Team 10 times in his career, but nine games into the 1971-72 season, he decided injuries and age (37) had caught up to him and announced his retirement.

The Lakers' other big change involved coaches. Out went Joe Mullaney, in came 45-year-old Bill Sharman, the former Boston Celtic who had just coached the Utah Stars to the 1971 American Basketball Association championship. He was a strange mix of fight and quiet innovation, a Southern California boy who was also a Celtic. The Lakers weren't quite sure what to make of him.

"It was difficult for us to relate to him in the beginning because he was covered with Boston green," recalled Pat Riley, a Laker reserve at the time. "But in time we came around. He was a low-key guy, but very competitive, very feisty."

With Chamberlain (35 years old) and West (33) approaching the end of their careers, Sharman needed to fit the other players around his aging stars to win now. Forwards Jim McMillian and Happy Hairston and guard Gail Goodrich were the perfect pieces.

Sharman asked the veteran Hairston to concentrate on rebounding, and the 6-7, 225-pound forward complied. While his scoring average dipped from 18.6 points per game in 1971 to 13.1 in '72, he averaged 15 boards over the last half of the season and became the first forward to pull down 1,000 rebounds while playing alongside Chamberlain.

That was one of a pack of firsts generated by the Lakers in 1971-72. They won more games than any team in NBA history, 69, a record that would stand for almost a quarter-century. They had the most games in which they scored more than 100 points, 81; the most wins on the road, 31; and the most at home, 38. Best of all, they had a record 33-game winning streak, which ran from November 5, when they defeated Baltimore, through January 9, when they lost a road game to Milwaukee 120-114.

Chamberlain led the league in field goal percentage (.649) and rebounding (19.2 per game), while Goodrich (25.9 ppg) and West (25.8 ppg) finished in the top 10 in scoring.

As the playoffs neared, the team sensed that old Laker luck hovered somewhere nearby. "We were waiting for something to happen, something bad to happen again," Riley said. "But it didn't."

Chicago, their first-round opponent, had won 57 games, but the Bulls lacked a dominating center and were forced to play a control game. They fell in four.

The Lakers' big challenge came in the Western Finals against the Bucks and Kareem Abdul-Jabbar. But Chamberlain outdueled Kareem, and the Lakers dismissed Milwaukee in six games.

The Knicks somehow prospered despite the loss of Willis Reed to injury. New York defeated Baltimore and Boston in the Eastern Conference Playoffs. But without Reed in the Finals, New York proved no match for the Lakers, who finally got their championship in five games. After seven losses in the NBA Finals since 1962, the eighth worked out just right. West had been brilliant in defeat for many years in the championship series. It almost didn't seem right that he was no longer a dominant player when the Lakers finally won the championship.

"I played terrible basketball in the Finals, and we won," West said. "That didn't seem to be justice for me personally because I had contributed so much in other years when we lost. Now, when we won, I was just another piece of the machinery. It was particularly frustrating because I was playing so poorly that the team overcame me.

"But maybe that's what a team is all about."

NBA.COM FACT

In a 134-90 march through Atlanta on Jan. 7, Los Angeles did the unthinkable: It won for a record 33rd consecutive time. Six players scored in double figures for Coach Bill Sharman's team, which shot 63 percent from the field in the first half. Incredibly, the Lakers had not lost a game since Oct. 31, a span of 68 days.

FINAL STANDINGS

EASTERN CONFERENCE

ATLANTIC DIVISION

	W	L	Pct.
Boston	56	26	.683
New York	48	34	.585
Philadelphia	30	52	.366
Buffalo	22	60	.268

CENTRAL DIVISION

	W	L	Pct.
Baltimore	38	44	.463
Atlanta	36	46	.439
Cincinnati	30	52	.366
Cleveland	23	59	.280

WESTERN CONFERENCE

MIDWEST DIVISION

	W	L	Pct.
Milwaukee	63	19	.768
Chicago	57	25	.695
Phoenix	49	33	.598
Detroit	26	56	.317

PACIFIC DIVISION

	W	L	Pct.
Los Angeles	69	13	.841
Golden State	51	31	.622
Seattle	47	35	.573
Houston	34	48	.415
Portland	18	64	.220

PLAYOFFS

EASTERN CONFERENCE

SEMIFINALS

Boston 4, Atlanta 2

Mar. 29....@Boston 126, Atlanta 108
Mar. 31....@Atlanta 113, Boston 104
Apr. 2......@Boston 136, Atlanta 113
Apr. 4......@Atlanta 112, Boston 110
Apr. 7......@Boston 124, Atlanta 114
Apr. 9......Boston 127, @Atlanta 118

New York 4, Baltimore 2

Mar. 31....@Baltimore 108, New York 105*
Apr. 2......@New York 110, Baltimore 88
Apr. 4......@Baltimore 104, New York 103
Apr. 6......@New York 104, Baltimore 98
Apr. 9......New York 106, @Baltimore 82
Apr. 11....@New York 107, Baltimore 101

FINALS

New York 4, Boston 1

Apr. 13....New York 116, @Boston 94
Apr. 16....@New York 106, Boston 105
Apr. 19....@Boston 115, New York 109
Apr. 21....@New York 116, Boston 98
Apr. 23....New York 111, @Boston 103

WESTERN CONFERENCE

SEMIFINALS

Milwaukee 4, Golden State 1

Mar. 28....Golden State 117, @Milwaukee 106
Mar. 30....@Milwaukee 118, Golden State 93
Apr. 1......Milwaukee 122, @Golden State 94
Apr. 4......Milwaukee 106, @Golden State 99
Apr. 6......@Milwaukee 108, Golden State 100

Los Angeles 4, Chicago 0

Mar. 28....@Los Angeles 95, Chicago 80
Mar. 30....@Los Angeles 131, Chicago 124
Apr. 2......Los Angeles 108, @Chicago 101
Apr. 4......Los Angeles 108, @Chicago 97

FINALS

Los Angeles 4, Milwaukee 2

Apr. 9......Milwaukee 93, @Los Angeles 72
Apr. 12....@Los Angeles 135, Milwaukee 134
Apr. 14....Los Angeles 108, @Milwaukee 105
Apr. 16....@Milwaukee 114, Los Angeles 88
Apr. 18....@Los Angeles 115, Milwaukee 90
Apr. 22....Los Angeles 104, @Milwaukee 100

NBA FINALS

Los Angeles 4, New York 1

Apr. 26....New York 114, @Los Angeles 92
Apr. 30....@Los Angeles 106, New York 92
May 3......Los Angeles 107, @New York 96
May 5......Los Angeles 116, @New York 111*
May 7......@Los Angeles 114, New York 100

*Denotes number of overtime periods.

INDIVIDUAL LEADERS

SCORING (minimum 70 games)

	G	FGM	FTM	Pts.	Avg.
Abdul-Jabbar, Milwaukee	81	1159	504	2822	34.8
Archibald, Cincinnati	76	734	677	2145	28.2
Havlicek, Boston	82	897	458	2252	27.5
Haywood, Seattle	73	717	480	1914	26.2
Goodrich, Los Angeles	82	826	475	2127	25.9
Love, Chicago	79	819	399	2037	25.8
West, Los Angeles	77	735	515	1985	25.8
Lanier, Detroit	80	834	388	2056	25.7
Hayes, Houston	82	832	399	2063	25.2
Clark, Philadelphia-Balt.	77	712	514	1938	25.2

FIELD GOAL PCT. (minimum 700 attempted)

	FGM	FGA	Pct.
Chamberlain, Los Angeles	496	764	.649
Abdul-Jabbar, Milwaukee	1159	2019	.574
Bellamy, Atlanta	593	1089	.545
Snyder, Seattle	496	937	.529
Frazier, New York	669	1307	.512
Lucas, New York	543	1060	.512

FREE THROW PCT. (minimum 350 attempted)

	FTM	FTA	Pct.
Marin, Baltimore	356	398	.894
Murphy, Houston	349	392	.890
Goodrich, Los Angeles	475	559	.850
Walker, Chicago	481	568	.847
Van Arsdale, Phoenix	529	626	.845

ASSISTS (minimum 70 games)

	G	No.	Avg.
West, Los Angeles	77	747	9.7
Wilkens, Seattle	80	766	9.6
Archibald, Cincinnati	76	701	9.2
Clark, Philadelphia-Baltimore	77	613	8.0
Havlicek, Boston	82	614	7.5

REBOUNDS

	G	No.	Avg.
Chamberlain, Los Angeles	82	1572	19.2
Unseld, Baltimore	76	1336	17.6
Abdul-Jabbar, Milwaukee	81	1346	16.6
Thurmond, Golden State	78	1252	16.1
Cowens, Boston	79	1203	15.2

1970-71 SEASON

Kareem Abdul-Jabbar

For years, Oscar Robertson had taught the entire league about greatness. He had won the Rookie of the Year and MVP Awards. He even averaged a triple-double for an entire season, a feat no other player has matched.

The only thing missing from his résumé was an NBA title, until, at 32, he joined the Milwaukee Bucks and added that last item.

"In his time, he was the greatest," said Ed Jucker, who coached "the Big O" at the University of Cincinnati. "No one was the equal to him. I always called him a complete ballplayer, and there are not many truly complete players. But he could play any position."

Not only was Robertson complete, but he was almost nonchalant about it, former Kansas coach Dick Harp said. "He had unbelievable control of a basketball game, and many times he looked like he was taking a walk in the country when he did it. He was so much in control of things. He had the size, the quickness, everything. He had all those great blessings, but among them he had great judgment about what to do with the ball."

"He was such a great passer," recalled Pete Newell, the hoops guru and former California coach and Lakers general manager. "He was so tough when he got the ball . . . There was no way you could stop Oscar one-on-one from penetrating and getting his shot."

As great as he was, it was Robertson's pairing with Kareem Abdul-Jabbar in Milwaukee that allowed him to realize the championship. Bucks coach Larry Costello had retired as a player after the 1968 season and was hired to bring along a young Milwaukee expansion team. But the schedule was accelerated after the Bucks drafted Abdul-Jabbar. Sensing that Abdul-Jabbar could be the focus of a championship contender, Bucks management went out and traded for veterans Robertson, Lucius Allen and Bob Boozer.

The group clicked almost immediately, due in part to the single-mindedness shared by Costello, Robertson and Abdul-Jabbar.

"Larry, Oscar and I have the same way about us," Abdul-Jabbar said. "We agree that being as efficient as possible cuts down on our chances for errors."

Abdul-Jabbar ruled the NBA with grace uncommon in a seven-footer. His sky-hook had become the most devastating weapon in the game, and he used it to lead the league in scoring (31.7 points per game) and also win the Most Valuable Player Award for the first time.

Abdul-Jabbar and Robertson were surrounded by a group of quality teammates, with Boozer, Greg Smith and Bob Dandridge at forward and Allen and Jon McGlocklin assisting Robertson at guard.

The new season brought with it expansion teams in Buffalo, Cleveland and Portland and a new wrinkle: the advent of four divisions, two in each newly formed conference. In 1964-65, nine teams played 360 games in a league with 108 players. Only five years later, the NBA season opened with 17 teams playing 697 games in a 204-player league.

Milwaukee won a league-high 66 games and brushed aside San Francisco and Los Angeles in five games, each in the Western Conference Playoffs. Baltimore surprised many by defeating defending champ New York in a rugged seven-game series in the Eastern Conference Finals. But Earl Monroe and Gus Johnson sustained injuries during the series, joining an already hobbled Wes Unseld. The Bucks swept to the championship in four straight, only the second Finals sweep in NBA history.

"It was almost like pure basketball," Robertson would say later about his championship season.

Pure basketball for pure players.

NBA.COM FACT

In an out-of-court settlement that prompted the league to revise its draft eligibility guidelines three months later, Seattle agreed to pay a $200,000 fine for a rules violation but was allowed to retain the rights to Spencer Haywood. The star forward had jumped to the SuperSonics from the ABA at mid-season even though he had not been subject to the NBA Draft.

FINAL STANDINGS

EASTERN CONFERENCE

ATLANTIC DIVISION

	W	L	Pct.
New York	52	30	.634
Philadelphia	47	35	.573
Boston	44	38	.537
Buffalo	22	60	.268

CENTRAL DIVISION

	W	L	Pct.
Baltimore	42	40	.512
Atlanta	36	46	.439
Cincinnati	33	49	.402
Cleveland	15	67	.183

WESTERN CONFERENCE

MIDWEST DIVISION

	W	L	Pct.
Milwaukee	66	16	.805
Chicago	51	31	.622
Phoenix	48	34	.585
Detroit	45	37	.549

PACIFIC DIVISION

	W	L	Pct.
Los Angeles	48	34	.585
San Francisco	41	41	.500
San Diego	40	42	.488
Seattle	38	44	.463
Portland	29	53	.354

PLAYOFFS

EASTERN CONFERENCE

SEMIFINALS

New York 4, Atlanta 1

Mar. 25....@New York 112, Atlanta 101
Mar. 27....Atlanta 113, @New York 104
Mar. 28....New York 110, @Atlanta 95
Mar. 30....New York 113, @Atlanta 107
Apr. 1 ......@New York 111, Atlanta 107

Baltimore 4, Philadelphia 3

Mar. 24....Philadelphia 126, @Baltimore 112
Mar. 26....Baltimore 119, @Philadelphia 107
Mar. 28....@Baltimore 111, Philadelphia 103
Mar. 30....Baltimore 120, @Philadelphia 105
Apr. 1 ......Philadelphia 104, @Baltimore 103
Apr. 3 ......@Philadelphia 98, Baltimore 94
Apr. 4 ......@Baltimore 128, Philadelphia 120

FINALS

Baltimore 4, New York 3

Apr. 6 ......@New York 112, Baltimore 111
Apr. 9 ......@New York 107, Baltimore 88
Apr. 11 ....@Baltimore 114, New York 88
Apr. 14 ....@Baltimore 101, New York 80
Apr. 16 ....@New York 89, Baltimore 84
Apr. 18 ....@Baltimore 113, New York 96
Apr. 19 ....Baltimore 93, @New York 91

WESTERN CONFERENCE

SEMIFINALS

Milwaukee 4, San Francisco 1

Mar. 27....Milwaukee 107, @San Francisco 96
Mar. 29....Milwaukee 104, San Francisco 90 (@ Madison, Wis.)
Mar. 30....Milwaukee 114, San Francisco 102 (@ Madison, Wis.)
Apr. 1 ......@San Francisco 106, Milwaukee 104
Apr. 4 ......Milwaukee 136, San Francisco 86 (@ Madison, Wis.)

Los Angeles 4, Chicago 3

Mar. 24....@Los Angeles 100, Chicago 99
Mar. 26....@Los Angeles 105, Chicago 95
Mar. 28....@Chicago 106, Los Angeles 98
Mar. 30....@Chicago 112, Los Angeles 102
Apr. 1 ......@Los Angeles 115, Chicago 89
Apr. 4 ......@Chicago 113, Los Angeles 99
Apr. 6 ......@Los Angeles 109, Chicago 98

FINALS

Milwaukee 4, Los Angeles 1

Apr. 9 ......@Milwaukee 106, Los Angeles 85
Apr. 11 ....@Milwaukee 91, Los Angeles 73
Apr. 14 ....@Los Angeles 118, Milwaukee 107
Apr. 16 ....Milwaukee 117, @Los Angeles 94
Apr. 18 ....@Milwaukee 116, Los Angeles 98

NBA FINALS

Milwaukee 4, Baltimore 0

Apr. 21 ....@Milwaukee 98, Baltimore 88
Apr. 25 ....Milwaukee 102, @Baltimore 83
Apr. 28 ....@Milwaukee 107, Baltimore 99
Apr. 30 ....Milwaukee 118, @Baltimore 106

INDIVIDUAL LEADERS

SCORING (minimum 70 games)

	G	FGM	FTM	Pts.	Avg.
Alcindor, Milwaukee	82	1063	470	2596	31.7
Havlicek, Boston	81	892	554	2338	28.9
Hayes, San Diego	82	948	454	2350	28.7
Bing, Detroit	82	799	615	2213	27.0
Hudson, Atlanta	76	829	381	2039	26.8
Love, Chicago	81	765	513	2043	25.2
Petrie, Portland	82	784	463	2031	24.8
Maravich, Atlanta	81	738	404	1880	23.2
Cunningham, Philadelphia	81	702	455	1859	23.0
Van Arsdale, Cincinnati	82	749	377	1875	22.9

FIELD GOAL PCT. (minimum 700 attempted)

	FGM	FGA	Pct.
Green, Cincinnati	502	855	.587
Alcindor, Milwaukee	1063	1843	.577
Chamberlain, Los Angeles	668	1226	.545
McGlocklin, Milwaukee	574	1073	.535
Snyder, Seattle	645	1215	.531

FREE THROW PCT. (minimum 350 attempted)

	FTM	FTA	Pct.
Walker, Chicago	480	559	.859
Robertson, Milwaukee	385	453	.850
Williams, San Francisco	331	392	.844
Mullins, San Francisco	302	358	.844
Snyder, Seattle	302	361	.837

ASSISTS (minimum 70 games)

	G	No.	Avg.
Van Lier, Cincinnati	82	832	10.2
Wilkens, Seattle	71	654	9.2
Robertson, Milwaukee	81	668	8.3
Havlicek, Boston	81	607	7.5
Frazier, New York	80	536	6.7

REBOUNDS (minimum 70 games)

	G	No.	Avg.
Chamberlain, Los Angeles	82	1493	18.2
Unseld, Baltimore	74	1253	16.9
Hayes, San Diego	82	1362	16.6
Alcindor, Milwaukee	82	1311	16.0
Lucas, San Francisco	80	1265	15.8

1969-70 SEASON

Willis Reed

After Bill Russell's retirement, the new team to beat in the East was the New York Knicks, who served notice by winning a league-record 18 straight games early in the season. They played as a team on both ends of the floor, no one player dominating the spotlight. The selfless play of starters Willis Reed, Dave DeBusschere, Bill Bradley, Walt Frazier and Dick Barnett made them immensely popular with fans at Madison Square Garden and throughout the city. The Knicks advanced to the Finals, where they met the Lakers.

The first six games were classic battles, with the Knicks winning one, then the Lakers tying the series. Reed, until he tore a leg muscle in Game 5, was marvelous, dominating the injury-slowed Wilt Chamberlain. The Knicks scrambled with undersized players against Chamberlain and hung on to win that game, but with Reed out of Game 6, Chamberlain poured in 45 points to tie the series.

The Knicks left the locker room before Game 7 in New York not knowing if Reed would be able to play. Before tipoff, Reed hobbled onto the floor of Madison Square Garden. The fans erupted and Reed scored New York's first two baskets and the inspired Knicks went on to a 113-99 victory.

Frazier finished with 36 points and 19 assists, Barnett scored 21 and DeBusschere had 17 rebounds, but their efforts were overshadowed by the drama of Reed's last-minute appearance.

It's a moment forever etched in basketball history.

"There isn't a day in my life that people don't remind me of that game," Reed said more than two decades later.

FINAL STANDINGS

EASTERN DIVISION

	W	L	Pct.
New York	60	22	.732
Milwaukee	56	26	.683
Baltimore	50	32	.610
Philadelphia	42	40	.512
Cincinnati	36	46	.439
Boston	34	48	.415
Detroit	31	51	.378

WESTERN DIVISION

	W	L	Pct.
Atlanta	48	34	.585
Los Angeles	46	36	.561
Chicago	39	43	.476
Phoenix	39	43	.476
Seattle	36	46	.439
San Francisco	30	52	.366
San Diego	27	55	.329

NBA.COM FACT

Playing in his 10th NBA season, Los Angeles guard Jerry West led the league in scoring (31.2 ppg) for the lone time in his career despite a career average of 27 points per game.

PLAYOFFS

EASTERN DIVISION

SEMIFINALS

Milwaukee 4, Philadelphia 1

Mar. 25....@Milwaukee 125, Philadelphia 118
Mar. 27....Philadelphia 112, @Milwaukee 105
Mar. 30....Milwaukee 156, @Philadelphia 120
Apr. 1 ......Milwaukee 118, @Philadelphia 111
Apr. 3 ......@Milwaukee 115, Philadelphia 106

New York 4, Baltimore 3

Mar. 26....@New York 120, Baltimore 117**
Mar. 27....New York 106, @Baltimore 99
Mar. 29....Baltimore 127, @New York 113
Mar. 31....@Baltimore 102, New York 92
Apr. 2 ......@New York 101, Baltimore 80
Apr. 5 ......@Baltimore 96, New York 87
Apr. 6 ......@New York 127, Baltimore 114

FINALS

New York 4, Milwaukee 1

Apr. 11 ....@New York 110, Milwaukee 102
Apr. 13 ....@New York 112, Milwaukee 111
Apr. 17 ....@Milwaukee 101, New York 96
Apr. 19 ....New York 117, @Milwaukee 105
Apr. 20 ....@New York 132, Milwaukee 96

WESTERN DIVISION

SEMIFINALS

Atlanta 4, Chicago 1

Mar. 25....@Atlanta 129, Chicago 111
Mar. 28....@Atlanta 124, Chicago 104
Mar. 31....Atlanta 106, @Chicago 101
Apr. 3 ......@Chicago 131, Atlanta 120
Apr. 5 ......@Atlanta 113, Chicago 107

Los Angeles 4, Phoenix 3

Mar. 25....@Los Angeles 128, Phoenix 112
Mar. 29....Phoenix 114, @Los Angeles 101
Apr. 2 ......@Phoenix 112, Los Angeles 98
Apr. 4 ......@Phoenix 112, Los Angeles 102
Apr. 5 ......@Los Angeles 138, Phoenix 121
Apr. 7 ......Los Angeles 104, @Phoenix 93
Apr. 9 ......@Los Angeles 129, Phoenix 94

FINALS

Los Angeles 4, Atlanta 0

Apr. 12 ....Los Angeles 119, @Atlanta 115
Apr. 14 ....Los Angeles 105, @Atlanta 94
Apr. 16 ....@Los Angeles 115, Atlanta 114*
Apr. 19 ....@Los Angeles 133, Atlanta 114

NBA FINALS

New York 4, Los Angeles 3

Apr. 24 ....@New York 124, Los Angeles 112
Apr. 27 ....Los Angeles 105, @New York 103
Apr. 29 ....New York 111, @Los Angeles 108*
May 1 ......@Los Angeles 121, New York 115*
May 4 ......@New York 107, Los Angeles 100
May 6 ......@Los Angeles 135, New York 113
May 8 ......@New York 113, Los Angeles 99

*Denotes number of overtime periods.

INDIVIDUAL LEADERS

SCORING (minimum 70 games)

	G	FGM	FTM	Pts.	Avg.
West, Los Angeles	74	831	647	2309	31.2
Alcindor, Milwaukee	82	938	485	2361	28.8
Hayes, San Diego	82	914	428	2256	27.5
Cunningham, Philadelphia	81	802	510	2114	26.1
Hudson, Atlanta	80	830	371	2031	25.4
Hawkins, Phoenix	81	709	577	1995	24.6
Rule, Seattle	80	789	387	1965	24.6
Havlicek, Boston	81	736	488	1960	24.2
Monroe, Baltimore	82	695	532	1922	23.4
Bing, Detroit	70	575	454	1604	22.9

FIELD GOAL PCT. (minimum 700 attempted in 70 games)

	FGM	FGA	Pct.
Green, Cincinnati	481	860	.559
Imhoff, Philadelphia	430	796	.540
Hudson, Atlanta	830	1564	.531
McGlocklin, Milwaukee	639	1206	.530
Snyder, Phoenix-Seattle	456	863	.528

FREE THROW PCT. (minimum 350 attempted in 70 games)

	FTM	FTA	Pct.
Robinson, Milwaukee	439	489	.898
Walker, Chicago	483	568	.850
Mullins, San Francisco	320	378	.847
Havlicek, Boston	488	578	.844
Love, Chicago	442	525	.842

ASSISTS (minimum 70 games)

	G	No.	Avg.
Wilkens, Seattle	75	683	9.1
Frazier, New York	77	629	8.2
Haskins, Chicago	82	624	7.6
West, Los Angeles	74	554	7.5
Goodrich, Phoenix	81	605	7.5

REBOUNDS (minimum 70 games)

	G	No.	Avg.
Hayes, San Diego	82	1386	16.9
Unseld, Baltimore	82	1370	16.7
Alcindor, Milwaukee	82	1190	14.5
Bridges, Atlanta	82	1181	14.4
Reed, New York	81	1126	13.9
Johnson, Baltimore	78	1086	13.9

1968-69 SEASON

Wes Unseld

It was supposed to be the Lakers' year. They had acquired center Wilt Chamberlain from Philadelphia and Lakers owner Jack Kent Cooke hoped the addition of Chamberlain would bring him a title.

It was also a year when two rookies had a huge immediate impact on the league. Elvin Hayes, a powerfully built forward for the San Diego Rockets, won the league scoring title with 28.4 points per game. Wes Unseld joined Chamberlain as the only players to win both the Most Valuable Player and Rookie of the Year awards in the same season.

In the Finals, Los Angeles had home-court advantage against Boston. When the series went to a seventh game, Cooke had hundreds of balloons placed in netting in the Forum ceiling to be released in a victory celebration. The sight of those balloons spurred Bill Russell and his teammates to make the Lakers pay.

With a little more than a minute left and Boston up 103-102, West knocked the ball loose on defense. Boston's Don Nelson picked it up at the free throw line and threw it up. It hit the back rim, rose up several feet in the air and dropped back through the net. The balloons were all but burst. The Celtics hung on to win 108-106.

Jerry West finished with 42 points, 13 rebounds and 12 assists, earning NBA Finals MVP honors, the first and only time the award has gone to a member of the losing team. "He is the master," said Boston's Larry Siegfried. "They can talk about the others, build them up, but he is the one. He is the only guard."

Three months after the season, Russell announced his retirement. The Boston dynasty was over. They had won 11 titles in 13 years, a string unmatched by any team in any major sport.

FINAL STANDINGS

EASTERN DIVISION

	W	L	Pct.
Baltimore	57	25	.695
Philadelphia	55	27	.671
New York	54	28	.659
Boston	48	34	.585
Cincinnati	41	41	.500
Detroit	32	50	.390
Milwaukee	27	55	.329

WESTERN DIVISION

	W	L	Pct.
Los Angeles	55	27	.671
Atlanta	48	34	.585
San Francisco	41	41	.500
San Diego	37	45	.451
Chicago	33	49	.402
Seattle	30	52	.366
Phoenix	16	66	.195

NBA.COM FACT

Walt Bellamy should have put in for overtime when he was traded from New York to Detroit in the middle of the 82-game season. Because the Knicks had a busier early season schedule, he played in a record 88 games.

PLAYOFFS

EASTERN DIVISION

SEMIFINALS

New York 4, Baltimore 0

- Mar. 27 ....New York 113, @Baltimore 101
- Mar. 29 ....@New York 107, Baltimore 91
- Mar. 30 ....New York 119, @Baltimore 116
- Apr. 2 ......@New York 115, Baltimore 108

Boston 4, Philadelphia 1

- Mar. 26 ....Boston 114, @Philadelphia 100
- Mar. 28 ....@Boston 134, Philadelphia 103
- Mar. 30 ....Boston 125, @Philadelphia 118
- Apr. 1 ......Philadelphia 119, @Boston 116
- Apr. 4 ......Boston 93, @Philadelphia 90

FINALS

Boston 4, New York 2

- Apr. 6 ......Boston 108, @New York 100
- Apr. 9 ......@Boston 112, New York 97
- Apr. 10 ....@New York 101, Boston 91
- Apr. 13 ....@Boston 97, New York 96
- Apr. 14 ....@New York 112, Boston 104
- Apr. 18 ....@Boston 106, New York 105

WESTERN DIVISION

SEMIFINALS

Los Angeles 4, San Francisco 2

- Mar. 26 ....San Francisco 99, @Los Angeles 94
- Mar. 28 ....San Francisco 107, @Los Angeles 101
- Mar. 31 ....Los Angeles 115, @San Francisco 98
- Apr. 2 ......Los Angeles 103, @San Francisco 88
- Apr. 4 ......@Los Angeles 103, San Francisco 98
- Apr. 5 ......Los Angeles 118, @San Francisco 78

Atlanta 4, San Diego 2

- Mar. 27 ....@Atlanta 107, San Diego 98
- Mar. 29 ....@Atlanta 116, San Diego 114
- Apr. 1 ......@San Diego 104, Atlanta 97
- Apr. 4 ......@San Diego 114, Atlanta 112
- Apr. 6 ......@Atlanta 112, San Diego 101
- Apr. 7 ......Atlanta 108, @San Diego 106

FINALS

Los Angeles 4, Atlanta 1

- Apr. 11 ....@Los Angeles 95, Atlanta 93
- Apr. 13 ....@Los Angeles 104, Atlanta 102
- Apr. 15 ....@Atlanta 99, Los Angeles 80
- Apr. 17 ....Los Angeles 100, @Atlanta 85
- Apr. 20 ....@Los Angeles 104, Atlanta 96

NBA FINALS

Boston 4, Los Angeles 3

- Apr. 23 ....@Los Angeles 120, Boston 118
- Apr. 25 ....@Los Angeles 118, Boston 112
- Apr. 27 ....@Boston 111, Los Angeles 105
- Apr. 29 ....@Boston 89, Los Angeles 88
- May 1 ......@Los Angeles 117, Boston 104
- May 3 ......@Boston 99, Los Angeles 90
- May 5 ......Boston 108, @Los Angeles 106

INDIVIDUAL LEADERS

SCORING

	G	FGM	FTM	Pts.	Avg.
Hayes, San Diego	82	930	467	2327	28.4
Monroe, Baltimore	80	809	447	2065	25.8
Cunningham, Philadelphia	82	739	556	2034	24.8
Rule, Seattle	82	776	413	1965	24.0
Robertson, Cincinnati	79	656	643	1955	24.7
Goodrich, Phoenix	81	718	495	1931	23.8
Greer, Philadelphia	82	732	432	1896	23.1
Baylor, Los Angeles	76	730	421	1881	24.8
Wilkens, Seattle	82	644	547	1835	22.4
Kojis, San Diego	81	687	446	1820	22.5

FIELD GOAL PCT. (minimum 230 made)

	FGM	FGA	Pct.
Chamberlain, Los Angeles	641	1099	.583
Lucas, Cincinnati	555	1007	.551
Reed, New York	704	1351	.521
Dischinger, Detroit	264	513	.515
Bellamy, New York-Detroit	563	1103	.510

FREE THROW PCT. (minimum 230 made)

	FTM	FTA	Pct.
Siegfried, Boston	336	389	.864
Mullins, San Francisco	381	452	.843
McGlocklin, Milwaukee	246	292	.842
Robinson, Chicago-Milwaukee	412	491	.839
Robertson, Cincinnati	643	767	.838

ASSISTS

	G	No.	Avg.
Robertson, Cincinnati	79	772	9.8
Wilkens, Seattle	82	674	8.2
Frazier, New York	80	635	7.9
Rodgers, Milwaukee	81	561	6.9
Bing, Detroit	77	546	7.1

REBOUNDS

	G	No.	Avg.
Chamberlain, Los Angeles	81	1712	21.1
Unseld, Baltimore	82	1491	18.2
Russell, Boston	77	1484	19.3
Hayes, San Diego	82	1406	17.1
Thurmond, San Francisco	71	1402	19.7

1967-68 SEASON

Dave Bing

Having lost to the 76ers in the 1967 playoffs, ending their string of eight straight championships, the Boston Celtics had to listen to a new tune the following season. "Everywhere we went, especially in Philadelphia, they had a chant: 'Boston's dead. Boston's dead,'" Bailey Howell said. "Everywhere we went, the fans were real vocal. But it just made you more determined, really. It helped you to play." Helped so well, in fact, that the Celtics claimed their 10th title.

The NBA greeted two more expansion franchises, Seattle and San Diego, which were installed in the Western Division while Detroit moved to the East. The NBA was now a 12-team league and played an 82-game schedule for the first time. The season also brought the birth of the rival ABA, with 11 teams playing a 78-game schedule in places such as Dallas, Denver, Houston and Oakland. The league gained credibility with the naming of NBA legend George Mikan as its first commissioner and with Rick Barry's decision to sign with the Oakland franchise. In the NBA, Detroit's Dave Bing became the first guard to lead the NBA in scoring (27.1 points per game) since 1948.

But the real story was the return of the Celtics, who came back from a 3-1 deficit to win the Eastern Finals over Philadelphia, then defeated the Lakers in six games to take the title. With the victory, Bill Russell proved he could play and coach at the same time, which meant the same old tune for opponents.

FINAL STANDINGS

EASTERN DIVISION

	W	L	Pct.
Philadelphia	62	20	.756
Boston	54	28	.659
New York	43	39	.524
Detroit	40	42	.488
Cincinnati	39	43	.476
Baltimore	36	46	.439

WESTERN DIVISION

	W	L	Pct.
St. Louis	56	26	.683
Los Angeles	52	30	.634
San Francisco	43	39	.524
Chicago	29	53	.354
Seattle	23	59	.280
San Diego	15	67	.183

NBA.COM FACT

Many said coach Bill Russell's best weapon was player Bill Russell, so the player-coach played himself a total of 292 minutes in the Celtics' NBA Finals triumph over the Lakers, a record for a six-game Finals.

PLAYOFFS

EASTERN DIVISION

SEMIFINALS

Philadelphia 4, New York 2

Mar. 22....@Philadelphia 118, New York 110
Mar. 23....@New York 128, Philadelphia 117
Mar. 27....@Philadelphia 138, New York 132**
Mar. 30....@New York 107, Philadelphia 98
Mar. 31....@Philadelphia 123, New York 105
Apr. 1......Philadelphia 113, @New York 97

Boston 4, Detroit 2

Mar. 24....@Boston 123, Detroit 116
Mar. 25....@Detroit 126, Boston 116
Mar. 27....Detroit 109, @Boston 98
Mar. 28....Boston 135, @Detroit 110
Mar. 31....@Boston 110, Detroit 96
Apr. 1......Boston 111, @Detroit 103

FINALS

Boston 4, Philadelphia 3

Apr. 5......Boston 127, @Philadelphia 118
Apr. 10....Philadelphia 115, @Boston 106
Apr. 11....@Philadelphia 122, Boston 114
Apr. 14....Philadelphia 110, @Boston 105
Apr. 15....Boston 122, @Philadelphia 104
Apr. 17....@Boston 114, Philadelphia 106
Apr. 19....Boston 100, @Philadelphia 96

WESTERN DIVISION

SEMIFINALS

San Francisco 4, St. Louis 2

Mar. 22....San Francisco 111, @St. Louis 106
Mar. 23....@St. Louis 111, San Francisco 103
Mar. 26....@San Francisco 124, St. Louis 109
Mar. 29....@San Francisco 108, St. Louis 107
Mar. 31....@St. Louis 129, San Francisco 103
Apr. 2......@San Francisco 111, St. Louis 106

Los Angeles 4, Chicago 1

Mar. 24....@Los Angeles 109, Chicago 101
Mar. 25....@Los Angeles 111, Chicago 106
Mar. 27....@Chicago 104, Los Angeles 98
Mar. 29....Los Angeles 93, @Chicago 87
Mar. 31....@Los Angeles 122, Chicago 99

FINALS

Los Angeles 4, San Francisco 0

Apr. 5......@Los Angeles 133, San Francisco 105
Apr. 10....@Los Angeles 115, San Francisco 112
Apr. 11....Los Angeles 128, @San Francisco 124
Apr. 13....Los Angeles 106, @San Francisco 100

NBA FINALS

Boston 4, Los Angeles 2

Apr. 21....@Boston 107, Los Angeles 101
Apr. 24....Los Angeles 123, @Boston 113
Apr. 26....Boston 127, @Los Angeles 119
Apr. 28....@Los Angeles 119, Boston 105
Apr. 30....@Boston 120, Los Angeles 117*
May 2......Boston 124, @Los Angeles 109

*Denotes number of overtime periods.

INDIVIDUAL LEADERS

SCORING

	G	FGM	FTM	Pts.	Avg.
Bing, Detroit	79	835	472	2142	27.1
Baylor, Los Angeles	77	757	488	2002	26.0
Chamberlain, Philadelphia	82	819	354	1992	24.3
Monroe, Baltimore	82	742	507	1991	24.3
Greer, Philadelphia	82	777	422	1976	24.1
Robertson, Cincinnati	65	660	576	1896	29.2
Hazzard, Seattle	79	733	428	1894	24.0
Lucas, Cincinnati	82	707	346	1760	21.5
Beaty, St. Louis	82	639	455	1733	21.1
LaRusso, San Francisco	79	602	522	1726	21.8

FIELD GOAL PCT. (minimum 220 made)

	FGM	FGA	Pct.
Chamberlain, Philadelphia	819	1377	.595
Bellamy, New York	511	944	.541
Lucas, Cincinnati	707	1361	.519
West, Los Angeles	476	926	.514
Chappell, Cincinnati-Detroit	235	458	.513

FREE THROW PCT. (minimum 220 made)

	FTM	FTA	Pct.
Robertson, Cincinnati	576	660	.873
Siegfried, Boston	236	272	.868
Gambee, San Diego	321	379	.847
Hetzel, San Francisco	395	474	.833
Smith, Cincinnati	320	386	.829

ASSISTS

	G	No.	Avg.
Chamberlain, Philadelphia	82	702	8.6
Wilkens, St. Louis	82	679	8.3
Robertson, Cincinnati	65	633	9.7
Bing, Detroit	79	509	6.4
Hazzard, Seattle	79	493	6.2

REBOUNDS

	G	No.	Avg.
Chamberlain, Philadelphia	82	1952	23.8
Lucas, Cincinnati	82	1560	19.0
Russell, Boston	78	1451	18.6
Lee, San Francisco	82	1141	13.9
Thurmond, San Francisco	51	1121	22.0

1966-67 SEASON

Chet Walker

Wilt Chamberlain sent the message early and often: This was the season he would finally silence his critics. Philadelphia, which had hired veteran Alex Hannum as coach, got off to a 46-4 start and never looked back, posting an NBA-best 68-13 record. Chet Walker and Billy Cunningham scored more points as Chamberlain concentrated on rebounding and defense. Chamberlain still finished third in scoring (24.1 points per game), but he led the league in rebounding (24.2 per game) and field goal percentage (.683) and was also third in assists (7.8 per game).

The Chicago Bulls were added as an expansion franchise, and the Baltimore Bullets moved to the Eastern Division. With two five-team divisions, the playoffs were changed so that the division winners no longer received first-round byes and instead played against the third-place team. Philadelphia polished off Cincinnati in the Eastern Division Semifinals, then crushed the Russell-coached Celtics in five games in the Eastern Division Finals, ending Boston's run of eight straight championships. The 76ers captured the title in six games over San Francisco, which featured the NBA's new scoring leader, Rick Barry (35.6 points per game). After so many years of failing to beat the Celtics, the 76ers needed a nearly flawless season to finally topple the champions. "The whole season was just magical, something where a team played almost perfect basketball," said Philadelphia's Wali Jones. "We played with a team/family concept." Even the Celtics had to admit the 76ers were better. "They're playing the same game we've played for the last nine years," said Boston's K.C. Jones. "In other words, team ball."

FINAL STANDINGS

EASTERN DIVISION

	W	L	Pct.
Philadelphia	68	13	.840
Boston	60	21	.741
Cincinnati	39	42	.481
New York	36	45	.444
Baltimore	20	61	.247

WESTERN DIVISION

	W	L	Pct.
San Francisco	44	37	.543
St. Louis	39	42	.481
Los Angeles	36	45	.444
Chicago	33	48	.407
Detroit	30	51	.370

NBA.COM FACT

On February 24, 1967, Wilt Chamberlain shot 18-for-18 from the field for the Philadelphia 76ers in a 149-118 rout of the Baltimore Bullets, an NBA record for most baskets in a game without a miss.

PLAYOFFS

EASTERN DIVISION

SEMIFINALS

Boston 3, New York 1

Mar. 21....@Boston 140, New York 110
Mar. 25....Boston 115, @New York 108
Mar. 26....New York 123, @Boston 112
Mar. 28....Boston 118, @New York 109

Philadelphia 3, Cincinnati 1

Mar. 21....Cincinnati 120, @Philadelphia 116
Mar. 22....Philadelphia 123, @Cincinnati 102
Mar. 24....@Philadelphia 121, Cincinnati 106
Mar. 25....Philadelphia 112, @Cincinnati 94

FINALS

Philadelphia 4, Boston 1

Mar. 31....@Philadelphia 127, Boston 113
Apr. 2 ......Philadelphia 107, @Boston 102
Apr. 5 ......@Philadelphia 115, Boston 104
Apr. 9 ......@Boston 121, Philadelphia 117
Apr. 11 ....@Philadelphia 140, Boston 116

WESTERN DIVISION

SEMIFINALS

St. Louis 3, Chicago 0

Mar. 21....@St. Louis 114, Chicago 100
Mar. 23....St. Louis 113, @Chicago 107
Mar. 25....@St. Louis 119, Chicago 106

San Francisco 3, Los Angeles 0

Mar. 21....@San Francisco 124, Los Angeles 108
Mar. 23....San Francisco 113, @Los Angeles 102
Mar. 26....@San Francisco 122, Los Angeles 115

FINALS

San Francisco 4, St. Louis 2

Mar. 30....@San Francisco 117, St. Louis 115
Apr. 1 ......@San Francisco 143, St. Louis 136
Apr. 5 ......@St. Louis 115, San Francisco 109
Apr. 8 ......@St. Louis 109, San Francisco 104
Apr. 10 ....@San Francisco 123, St. Louis 102
Apr. 12 ....San Francisco 112, @St. Louis 107

NBA FINALS

Philadelphia 4, San Francisco 2

Apr. 14 ....@Philadelphia 141, San Francisco 135*
Apr. 16 ....@Philadelphia 126, San Francisco 95
Apr. 18 ....@San Francisco 130, Philadelphia 124
Apr. 20 ....Philadelphia 122, @San Francisco 108
Apr. 23 ....San Francisco 117, @Philadelphia 109
Apr. 24 ....Philadelphia 125, @San Francisco 122

*Denotes number of overtime periods.

INDIVIDUAL LEADERS

SCORING

	G	FGM	FTM	Pts.	Avg.
Barry, San Francisco	78	1011	753	2775	35.6
Robertson, Cincinnati	79	838	736	2412	30.5
Chamberlain, Philadelphia	81	785	386	1956	24.1
West, Los Angeles	66	645	602	1892	28.7
Baylor, Los Angeles	70	711	440	1862	26.6
Greer, Philadelphia	80	699	367	1765	22.1
Havlicek, Boston	81	684	365	1733	21.4
Reed, New York	78	635	358	1628	20.9
Howell, Boston	81	636	349	1621	20.0
Bing, Detroit	80	664	273	1601	20.0

FIELD GOAL PCT. (minimum 220 made)

	FGM	FGA	Pct.
Chamberlain, Philadelphia	785	1150	.683
Bellamy, New York	565	1084	.521
Howell, Boston	636	1242	.512
Robertson, Cincinnati	838	1699	.493
Reed, New York	635	1298	.489

FREE THROW PCT. (minimum 220 made)

	FTM	FTA	Pct.
Smith, Cincinnati	343	380	.903
Barry, San Francisco	753	852	.884
West, Los Angeles	602	686	.878
Robertson, Cincinnati	736	843	.873
Jones, Boston	318	371	.857

ASSISTS

	G	No.	Avg.
Rodgers, Chicago	81	908	11.2
Robertson, Cincinnati	79	845	10.7
Chamberlain, Philadelphia	81	630	7.8
Russell, Boston	81	472	5.8
West, Los Angeles	66	447	6.8

REBOUNDS

	G	No.	Avg.
Chamberlain, Philadelphia	81	1957	24.2
Russell, Boston	81	1700	21.0
Lucas, Cincinnati	81	1547	19.1
Thurmond, San Francisco	65	1382	21.3
Bridges, St. Louis	79	1190	15.1

1965-66 SEASON

Red Auerbach

This campaign brought yet another shell game from Red Auerbach, the set-up being that the 76ers were allowed to hope. Philadelphia beat the Celtics six times in 10 meetings and won 55 games, taking the Eastern Division title away from Boston for the first time in 10 years. Wilt Chamberlain led the league in scoring for the seventh and final time, averaging 33.5 points and supplanting Bob Pettit as the NBA's all-time leading scorer. Rookie forward Billy Cunningham boosted the Philly cause, averaging 14.3 points.

For the playoffs, though, the Celtics had added incentive: Auerbach announced his coaching retirement and a move to the front office effective at season's end. Boston recovered from a 2-1 deficit to defeat Cincinnati in five games. The Sixers were rusty after resting for two weeks, and the Celtics disposed of them in five games.

Meanwhile, the Lakers sweated out a seven-game Western Finals series over the Hawks to advance to meet Boston. L.A. took the opener in overtime in Boston, but that's when Auerbach pulled out a trump card, announcing that Bill Russell would succeed him as head coach and become the first black head coach in a major American sports league. The bombshell announcement inspired the Celtics, who went on to win three in a row and eventually take the title in seven games. It was Boston's eighth straight championship and ninth in 10 seasons.

FINAL STANDINGS

EASTERN DIVISION

	W	L	Pct.
Philadelphia	55	25	.688
Boston	54	26	.675
Cincinnati	45	35	.563
New York	30	50	.375

WESTERN DIVISION

	W	L	Pct.
Los Angeles	45	35	.563
Baltimore	38	42	.475
St. Louis	36	44	.450
San Francisco	35	45	.438
Detroit	22	58	.275

NBA.COM FACT

Guard Adrian Smith of the host Cincinnati Royals, the last man selected to the East team and the least-heralded player in the All-Star Game, scored a game-high 24 points and captured MVP honors.

PLAYOFFS

EASTERN DIVISION

SEMIFINALS

Boston 3, Cincinnati 2

Mar. 23....Cincinnati 107, @Boston 103
Mar. 26....Boston 132, @Cincinnati 125
Mar. 27....Cincinnati 113, @Boston 107
Mar. 30....Boston 120, @Cincinnati 103
Apr. 1 ......@Boston 112, Cincinnati 103

FINALS

Boston 4, Philadelphia 1

Apr. 3 ......Boston 115, @Philadelphia 96
Apr. 6 ......@Boston 114, Philadelphia 93
Apr. 7 ......@Philadelphia 111, Boston 105
Apr. 10 ....@Boston 114, Philadelphia 108*
Apr. 12 ....Boston 120, @Philadelphia 112

WESTERN DIVISION

SEMIFINALS

St. Louis 3, Baltimore 0

Mar. 24....St. Louis 113, @Baltimore 111
Mar. 27....St. Louis 105, @Baltimore 100
Mar. 30....@St. Louis 121, Baltimore 112

FINALS

Los Angeles 4, St. Louis 3

Apr. 1 ......@Los Angeles 129, St. Louis 106
Apr. 3 ......@Los Angeles 125, St. Louis 116
Apr. 6 ......@St. Louis 120, Los Angeles 113
Apr. 9 ......Los Angeles 107, @St. Louis 95
Apr. 10 ....St. Louis 112, @Los Angeles 100
Apr. 13 ....@St. Louis 131, Los Angeles 127
Apr. 15 ....@Los Angeles 130, St. Louis 121

NBA FINALS

Boston 4, Los Angeles 3

Apr. 17 ....Los Angeles 133, @Boston 129*
Apr. 19 ....@Boston 129, Los Angeles 109
Apr. 20 ....Boston 120, @Los Angeles 106
Apr. 22 ....Boston 122, @Los Angeles 117
Apr. 24 ....Los Angeles 121, @Boston 117
Apr. 26 ....@Los Angeles 123, Boston 115
Apr. 28 ....@Boston 95, Los Angeles 93

*Denotes number of overtime periods.

INDIVIDUAL LEADERS

SCORING

	G	FGM	FTM	Pts.	Avg.
Chamberlain, Philadelphia	79	1074	501	2649	33.5
West, Los Angeles	79	818	840	2476	31.3
Robertson, Cincinnati	76	818	742	2378	31.3
Barry, San Francisco	80	745	569	2059	25.7
Bellamy, Baltimore-N.Y.	80	695	430	1820	22.8
Greer, Philadelphia	80	703	413	1819	22.7
Barnett, New York	75	631	467	1729	23.1
Lucas, Cincinnati	79	690	317	1697	21.5
Beaty, St. Louis	80	616	424	1656	20.7
S. Jones, Boston	67	626	325	1577	23.5

FIELD GOAL PCT. (minimum 210 made)

	FGM	FGA	Pct.
Chamberlain, Philadelphia	1074	1990	.540
Green, New York-Baltimore	358	668	.536
Bellamy, Baltimore-New York	695	1373	.506
Attles, San Francisco	364	724	.503
Hairston, Cincinnati	398	814	.489

FREE THROW PCT. (minimum 210 made)

	FTM	FTA	Pct.
Siegfried, Boston	274	311	.881
Barry, San Francisco	569	660	.862
Komives, New York	241	280	.861
West, Los Angeles	840	977	.860
Smith, Cincinnati	408	480	.850

ASSISTS

	G	No.	Avg.
Robertson, Cincinnati	76	847	11.1
Rodgers, San Francisco	79	846	10.7
K.C. Jones, Boston	80	503	6.3
West, Los Angeles	79	480	6.1
Wilkens, St. Louis	69	429	6.2

REBOUNDS

	G	No.	Avg.
Chamberlain, Philadelphia	79	1943	24.6
Russell, Boston	78	1779	22.8
Lucas, Cincinnati	79	1668	21.1
Thurmond, San Francisco	73	1312	18.0
Bellamy, Baltimore-New York	80	1254	15.7

1964-65 SEASON

John Havlicek

Something had to change. Bill Russell's Celtics kept on winning titles and Wilt Chamberlain continued to lead the league in scoring, so the NBA tried a move to lessen the dominance of big men and keep the action moving. The foul lane was widened from 12 to 16 feet. That helped some, but it didn't stop Chamberlain—or the celebrations in Boston.

A major trade took place at the All-Star break that would have far-reaching implications. The financially strapped San Francisco Warriors dealt Chamberlain, in the midst of his greatness at 28 years old, to the Philadelphia 76ers for Paul Neumann, Connie Dierking, Lee Shaffer and cash. The immediate results: San Francisco went from 48-32 the season before to 17-63, while Philadelphia, with Chamberlain leading the league at 34.7 points per game, improved from 34-46 to 40-40. More important, Chamberlain was back in the Celtics' division and would have to be dealt with before the Finals.

Celtics founder Walter Brown had died in August, putting more of the team's administrative load on Auerbach. Boston, however, broke its own league record with 62 victories despite the retirements of Frank Ramsey and Jim Loscutoff. The Lakers led the West with 49 wins as Jerry West (31.0) and Elgin Baylor (27.1) finished in the top five in scoring. While the Lakers defeated Baltimore in six games in the West Finals, Boston and Philadelphia used the full seven in the East. The Celtics won Game 7 by a point, with John Havlicek's deflection producing the famous "Havlicek stole the ball!" radio call from Celtics broadcaster Johnny Most. The Finals were almost anti-climactic as Boston closed out the Lakers, who were without the injured Baylor, in five games.

FINAL STANDINGS

EASTERN DIVISION

	W	L	Pct.
Boston	62	18	.775
Cincinnati	48	32	.600
Philadelphia	40	40	.500
New York	31	49	.388

WESTERN DIVISION

	W	L	Pct.
Los Angeles	49	31	.613
St. Louis	45	35	.563
Baltimore	37	43	.463
Detroit	31	49	.388
San Francisco	17	63	.213

NBA.COM FACT

Although it came in a losing effort, Jerry West's average of 46.3 points per game in the Lakers' five-game NBA Finals against the Boston Celtics is the highest for any player in an NBA Playoff series.

PLAYOFFS

EASTERN DIVISION

SEMIFINALS

Philadelphia 3, Cincinnati 1

Mar. 24....Philadelphia 119, @Cincinnati 117
Mar. 26....Cincinnati 121, @Philadelphia 120
Mar. 28....Philadelphia 108, @Cincinnati 94
Mar. 31....@Philadelphia 119, Cincinnati 112

FINALS

Boston 4, Philadelphia 3

Apr. 4 ......@Boston 108, Philadelphia 98
Apr. 6 ......@Philadelphia 109, Boston 103
Apr. 8 ......@Boston 112, Philadelphia 94
Apr. 9 ......@Philadelphia 134, Boston 131*
Apr. 11 ....@Boston 114, Philadelphia 108
Apr. 13 ....@Philadelphia 112, Boston 106
Apr. 15 ....@Boston 110, Philadelphia 109

WESTERN DIVISION

SEMIFINALS

Baltimore 3, St. Louis 1

Mar. 24....Baltimore 108, @St. Louis 105
Mar. 26....@St. Louis 129, Baltimore 105
Mar. 27....@Baltimore 131, St. Louis 99
Mar. 30....@Baltimore 109, St. Louis 103

FINALS

Los Angeles 4, Baltimore 2

Apr. 3 ......@Los Angeles 121, Baltimore 115
Apr. 5 ......@Los Angeles 118, Baltimore 115
Apr. 7 ......@Baltimore 122, Los Angeles 115
Apr. 9 ......@Baltimore 114, Los Angeles 112
Apr. 11 ....@Los Angeles 120, Baltimore 112
Apr. 13 ....Los Angeles 117, @Baltimore 115

NBA FINALS

Boston 4, Los Angeles 1

Apr. 18 ....@Boston 142, Los Angeles 110
Apr. 19 ....@Boston 129, Los Angeles 123
Apr. 21 ....@Los Angeles 126, Boston 105
Apr. 23 ....Boston 112, @Los Angeles 99
Apr. 25 ....@Boston 129, Los Angeles 96

*Denotes number of overtime periods.

INDIVIDUAL LEADERS

SCORING

	G	FGM	FTM	Pts.	Avg.
Chamberlain, S.F.-Phil.	73	1063	408	2534	34.7
West, Los Angeles	74	822	648	2292	31.0
Robertson, Cincinnati	75	807	665	2279	30.4
S. Jones, Boston	80	821	428	2070	25.9
Baylor, Los Angeles	74	763	483	2009	27.1
Bellamy, Baltimore	80	733	515	1981	24.8
Reed, New York	80	629	302	1560	19.5
Howell, Baltimore	80	515	504	1534	19.2
Dischinger, Detroit	80	568	320	1456	18.2
Ohl, Baltimore	77	568	284	1420	18.4

FIELD GOAL PCT. (minimum 220 made)

	FGM	FGA	Pct.
Chamberlain, S.F.-Phil.	1063	2083	.510
Bellamy, Baltimore	733	1441	.509
Lucas, Cincinnati	558	1121	.498
West, Los Angeles	822	1655	.497
Howell, Baltimore	515	1040	.495

FREE THROW PCT. (minimum 210 made)

	FTM	FTA	Pct.
Costello, Philadelphia	243	277	.877
Robertson, Cincinnati	665	793	.839
Komives, New York	212	254	.835
Smith, Cincinnati	284	342	.830
West, Los Angeles	648	789	.821

ASSISTS

	G	No.	Avg.
Robertson, Cincinnati	75	861	11.5
Rodgers, San Francisco	79	565	7.2
K.C. Jones, Boston	78	437	5.6
Wilkens, St. Louis	78	431	5.5
Russell, Boston	78	410	5.3

REBOUNDS

	G	No.	Avg.
Russell, Boston	78	1878	24.1
Chamberlain, S.F.-Phil.	73	1673	22.9
Thurmond, San Francisco	77	1395	18.1
Lucas, Cincinnati	66	1321	20.0
Reed, New York	80	1175	14.7

1963-64 SEASON

Jerry Lucas

Opponents didn't like Red Auerbach. They didn't like his cigar smoke and they didn't like his teams winning year after year. But there was little they could do about it. "The thrill never goes from winning," Boston's coach said. "But maybe the reasons change. First it was just trying to win a title. Now it is a question of going down as the greatest team of all time. That stimulates you." Bob Cousy retired, but the Celtics didn't skip a beat. K.C. Jones stepped in as a starter and the band played on.

Maurice Podoloff, the only president the league had ever known, retired before the season and was replaced by J. Walter Kennedy, who had earlier served as publicity director. In franchise shifts, the Chicago Zephyrs moved to Baltimore and became the new Baltimore Bullets, while the Syracuse Nationals moved to Philadelphia, vacated by the Warriors a season earlier, and became the 76ers.

A pair of impressive rookie big men came into the league, Jerry Lucas (Cincinnati) and Nate Thurmond (San Francisco). Alex Hannum became coach at San Francisco, where he instilled a defensive philosophy. Led by Chamberlain and Thurmond, the Warriors allowed a league-low 102.6 points per game and won the West by two games over St. Louis. The Warriors fought off a spirited challenge from Bob Pettit's Hawks to win the Western Division Finals in seven games, but were no match for Boston's depth as the Celtics polished them off in five games for a sixth straight title.

FINAL STANDINGS

EASTERN DIVISION

	W	L	Pct.
Boston	59	21	.738
Cincinnati	55	25	.688
Philadelphia	34	46	.425
New York	22	58	.275

WESTERN DIVISION

	W	L	Pct.
San Francisco	48	32	.600
St. Louis	46	34	.575
Los Angeles	42	38	.525
Baltimore	31	49	.388
Detroit	23	57	.288

NBA.COM FACT

The Boston Celtics' sixth successive NBA title broke the major professional sports record of five straight, which the Celtics had shared with baseball's New York Yankees (1949-53) and hockey's Montreal Canadiens (1956-60).

PLAYOFFS

EASTERN DIVISION

SEMIFINALS

Cincinnati 3, Philadelphia 2

Mar. 22 ....@Cincinnati 127, Philadelphia 102
Mar. 24 ....@Philadelphia 122, Cincinnati 114
Mar. 25 ....@Cincinnati 101, Philadelphia 89
Mar. 28 ....@Philadelphia 129, Cincinnati 120
Mar. 29 ....@Cincinnati 130, Philadelphia 124

FINALS

Boston 4, Cincinnati 1

Mar. 31 ....@Boston 103, Cincinnati 87
Apr. 2 ......@Boston 101, Cincinnati 90
Apr. 5 ......Boston 102, @Cincinnati 92
Apr. 7 ......@Cincinnati 102, Boston 93
Apr. 9 ......@Boston 109, Cincinnati 95

WESTERN DIVISION

SEMIFINALS

St. Louis 3, Los Angeles 2

Mar. 21 ....@St. Louis 115, Los Angeles 104
Mar. 22 ....@St. Louis 106, Los Angeles 90
Mar. 25 ....@Los Angeles 107, St. Louis 105
Mar. 28 ....@Los Angeles 97, St. Louis 88
Mar. 30 ....@St. Louis 121, Los Angeles 108

FINALS

San Francisco 4, St. Louis 3

Apr. 1 ......St. Louis 116, @San Francisco 111
Apr. 3 ......@San Francisco 120, St. Louis 85
Apr. 5 ......@St. Louis 113, San Francisco 109
Apr. 8 ......San Francisco 111, @St. Louis 109
Apr. 10 ....@San Francisco 121, St. Louis 97
Apr. 12 ....@St. Louis 123, San Francisco 95
Apr. 16 ....@San Francisco 105, St. Louis 95

NBA FINALS

Boston 4, San Francisco 1

Apr. 18 ....@Boston 108, San Francisco 96
Apr. 20 ....@Boston 124, San Francisco 101
Apr. 22 ....@San Francisco 115, Boston 91
Apr. 24 ....Boston 98, @San Francisco 95
Apr. 26 ....@Boston 105, San Francisco 99

INDIVIDUAL LEADERS

SCORING

	G	FGM	FTM	Pts.	Avg.
Chamberlain, San Francisco	80	1204	540	2948	36.9
Robertson, Cincinnati	79	840	800	2480	31.4
Pettit, St. Louis	80	791	608	2190	27.4
Bellamy, Baltimore	80	811	537	2159	27.0
West, Los Angeles	72	740	584	2064	28.7
Baylor, Los Angeles	78	756	471	1983	25.4
Greer, Philadelphia	80	715	435	1865	23.3
Howell, Detroit	77	598	470	1666	21.6
Dischinger, Baltimore	80	604	454	1662	20.8
Havlicek, Boston	80	640	315	1595	19.9

FIELD GOAL PCT. (minimum 210 made)

	FGM	FGA	Pct.
Lucas, Cincinnati	545	1035	.527
Chamberlain, San Francisco	1204	2298	.524
Bellamy, Baltimore	811	1582	.513
Dischinger, Baltimore	604	1217	.496
McGill, Baltimore-New York	456	937	.487

FREE THROW PCT. (minimum 210 made)

	FTM	FTA	Pct.
Robertson, Cincinnati	800	938	.853
West, Los Angeles	584	702	.832
Greer, Philadelphia	435	525	.829
Heinsohn, Boston	283	342	.827
Guerin, New York-St. Louis	347	424	.818

ASSISTS

	G	No.	Avg.
Robertson, Cincinnati	79	868	11.0
Rodgers, San Francisco	79	556	7.0
K.C. Jones, Boston	80	407	5.1
West, Los Angeles	72	403	5.6
Chamberlain, San Francisco	80	403	5.0

REBOUNDS

	G	No.	Avg.
Russell, Boston	78	1930	24.7
Chamberlain, San Francisco	80	1787	22.3
Lucas, Cincinnati	79	1375	17.4
Bellamy, Baltimore	80	1361	17.0
Pettit, St. Louis	80	1224	15.3

1962-63 SEASON

Dave DeBusschere

For the second straight year, Jerry West and Elgin Baylor drove the Lakers to the top. And once again they flamed out against that immutable force, the Boston Celtics. Significant changes took place prior to the season. The Warriors, who had the league's top gate attraction in Wilt Chamberlain, moved to San Francisco and the Western Division. To compensate, Cincinnati, with Oscar Robertson, was moved to the East. The Chicago franchise changed its name from Packers to Zephyrs. Bob Cousy, 34, announced before the season that it would be his final one. Exciting rookies Zelmo Beaty, John Havlicek and Dave DeBusschere came into the league. The Celtics didn't have a 20 points-per-game scorer, yet won 58 games and another Eastern title. The Lakers won 53 games and a second straight Western title.

Chamberlain posted astounding individual numbers with 44.8 points per game and 24.3 rebounds per game. Each divisional finals went to seven games. Boston belted Cincinnati 142-131 in the East's Game 7, while the Lakers held off a revived St. Louis team 115-100 to advance to the Finals. The Celtics helped Cousy go out on a high note by taking leads of 2-0 and 3-1 in the series before closing out the Lakers in six games, with the clincher coming in Los Angeles. Another Auerbach victory cigar gave his critics more to fume about.

"Anytime you're winning, you get criticism," he said. "Nothing instigates jealousy like winning." Jerry West recalled: "Red was outspoken. His sideline antics were funny. I happened to like him very much. When you talk to his ex-players, they all have great respect for him. I don't know many players who would tell you that about their former coaches."

FINAL STANDINGS

EASTERN DIVISION

	W	L	Pct.
Boston	58	22	.725
Syracuse	48	32	.600
Cincinnati	42	38	.525
New York	21	59	.263

WESTERN DIVISION

	W	L	Pct.
Los Angeles	53	27	.663
St. Louis	48	32	.600
Detroit	34	46	.425
San Francisco	31	49	.388
Chicago	25	55	.313

NBA.COM FACT

Walter Dukes, a seven-foot center, closed out an eight-year NBA career that he fouled out of 21.9 percent of the games he played in (121 of 553), a record.

PLAYOFFS

EASTERN DIVISION

SEMIFINALS

Cincinnati 3, Syracuse 2

Mar. 19....@Syracuse 123, Cincinnati 120
Mar. 21....@Cincinnati 133, Syracuse 115
Mar. 23....@Syracuse 121, Cincinnati 117
Mar. 24....@Cincinnati 125, Syracuse 118
Mar. 26....Cincinnati 131, @Syracuse 127*

FINALS

Boston 4, Cincinnati 3

Mar. 28....Cincinnati 135, @Boston 132
Mar. 29....Boston 125, @Cincinnati 102
Mar. 31....Cincinnati 121, @Boston 116
Apr. 3......Boston 128, @Cincinnati 110
Apr. 6......@Boston 125, Cincinnati 120
Apr. 7......@Cincinnati 109, Boston 99
Apr. 10....@Boston 142, Cincinnati 131

WESTERN DIVISION

SEMIFINALS

St. Louis 3, Detroit 1

Mar. 20....@St. Louis 118, Detroit 99
Mar. 22....@St. Louis 122, Detroit 108
Mar. 24....@Detroit 107, St. Louis 103
Mar. 26....St. Louis 104, @Detroit 100

FINALS

Los Angeles 4, St. Louis 3

Mar. 31....@Los Angeles 112, St. Louis 104
Apr. 2......@Los Angeles 101, St. Louis 99
Apr. 4......@St. Louis 125, Los Angeles 112
Apr. 6......@St. Louis 124, Los Angeles 114
Apr. 7......@Los Angeles 123, St. Louis 100
Apr. 9......@St. Louis 121, Los Angeles 113
Apr. 11....@Los Angeles 115, St. Louis 100

NBA FINALS

Boston 4, Los Angeles 2

Apr. 14....@Boston 117, Los Angeles 114
Apr. 16....@Boston 113, Los Angeles 106
Apr. 17....@Los Angeles 119, Boston 99
Apr. 19....Boston 108, @Los Angeles 105
Apr. 21....Los Angeles 126, @Boston 119
Apr. 24....Boston 112, @Los Angeles 109

*Denotes number of overtime periods.

INDIVIDUAL LEADERS

SCORING

	G	FGM	FTM	Pts.	Avg.
Chamberlain, San Francisco	80	1463	660	3586	44.8
Baylor, Los Angeles	80	1029	661	2719	34.0
Robertson, Cincinnati	80	825	614	2264	28.3
Pettit, St. Louis	79	778	685	2241	28.4
Bellamy, Chicago	80	840	553	2233	27.9
Howell, Detroit	79	637	519	1793	22.7
Guerin, New York	79	596	509	1701	21.5
Twyman, Cincinnati	80	641	304	1586	19.8
Greer, Syracuse	80	600	362	1562	19.5
Ohl, Detroit	80	636	275	1547	19.3

FIELD GOAL PCT. (minimum 210 made)

	FGM	FGA	Pct.
Chamberlain, San Francisco	1463	2770	.528
Bellamy, Chicago	840	1595	.527
Robertson, Cincinnati	825	1593	.518
Howell, Detroit	637	1235	.516
Dischinger, Chicago	525	1026	.512

FREE THROW PCT. (minimum 210 made)

	FTM	FTA	Pct.
Costello, Syracuse	288	327	.881
Guerin, New York	509	600	.848
Baylor, Los Angeles	661	790	.837
Heinsohn, Boston	340	407	.835
Greer, Syracuse	362	434	.834

ASSISTS

	G	No.	Avg.
Rodgers, San Francisco	79	825	10.4
Robertson, Cincinnati	80	758	9.5
Cousy, Boston	76	515	6.8
Green, Chicago	73	422	5.8
Baylor, Los Angeles	80	386	4.8

REBOUNDS

	G	No.	Avg.
Chamberlain, San Francisco	80	1946	24.3
Russell, Boston	78	1843	23.6
Bellamy, Chicago	80	1309	16.4
Pettit, St. Louis	79	1191	15.1
Baylor, Los Angeles	80	1146	14.3

1961-62 SEASON

Oscar Robertson

It was a season of amazing feats. Wilt Chamberlain, playing in all but eight possible minutes of the entire season for the Philadelphia Warriors, posted the staggering averages of 50.4 points and 48.5 minutes. On March 2, 1962, Chamberlain scored 100 points against the Knicks in Hershey, Pa., in a 169-147 triumph, a single-game NBA scoring mark that has never been approached.

Meanwhile, in Cincinnati, guard Oscar Robertson of the Royals averaged a triple-double of 30.8 points, 12.5 rebounds and 11.4 assists — another feat that has never been duplicated, though Robertson himself came close on a number of other occasions.

The Chicago Packers, an expansion franchise, watched their center, Walt Bellamy, win Rookie of the Year honors by averaging 31.6 points and 19.0 rebounds. Bellamy also led the league with a .519 shooting percentage. The Boston Celtics, meanwhile, went about the business of maintaining a dynasty, winning a record 60 games in an 80-game season even though no Boston player appeared among the NBA's Top 10 in scoring.

In the Eastern finals, Sam Jones hit a jump shot with two seconds left in Game 7 to give the Celtics a 109-107 win over Philadelphia. St. Louis' two-year run of Finals appearances ended when the Lakers won 54 games and advanced to a showdown with Boston. The series went to a seventh game, and Frank Selvy of the Lakers had a chance to put Boston away on the parquet. But with seconds remaining and the score tied in Game 7, Selvy, a 29-year-old guard who had played in two All-Star Games, had his eight-foot shot bounce off the rim. The game went into overtime and Boston prevailed 110-107 to win a fourth straight NBA title.

FINAL STANDINGS

EASTERN DIVISION

	W	L	Pct.
Boston	60	20	.750
Philadelphia	49	31	.613
Syracuse	41	39	.513
New York	29	51	.363

WESTERN DIVISION

	W	L	Pct.
Los Angeles	54	26	.675
Cincinnati	43	37	.538
Detroit	37	43	.463
St. Louis	29	51	.363
Chicago	18	62	.225

NBA.COM FACT

Elgin Baylor of the Lakers poured in 61 points in a 126-121 victory over the Celtics in Game 5 at Boston Garden, setting the individual scoring record for an NBA Finals contest.

PLAYOFFS

EASTERN DIVISION

SEMIFINALS

Philadelphia 3, Syracuse 2

Mar. 16....@Philadelphia 110, Syracuse 103
Mar. 18....Philadelphia 97, @Syracuse 82
Mar. 19....Syracuse 101, @Philadelphia 100
Mar. 20....@Syracuse 106, Philadelphia 99
Mar. 22....@Philadelphia 121, Syracuse 104

FINALS

Boston 4, Philadelphia 3

Mar. 24....@Boston 117, Philadelphia 89
Mar. 27....@Philadelphia 113, Boston 106
Mar. 28....@Boston 129, Philadelphia 114
Mar. 31....@Philadelphia 110, Boston 106
Apr. 1 ......@Boston 119, Philadelphia 104
Apr. 3 .....@Philadelphia 109, Boston 99
Apr. 5 .....@Boston 109, Philadelphia 107

WESTERN DIVISION

SEMIFINALS

Detroit 3, Cincinnati 1

Mar. 16 ...@Detroit 123, Cincinnati 122
Mar. 17....@Cincinnati 129, Detroit 107
Mar. 18....@Detroit 118, Cincinnati 107
Mar. 20....Detroit 112, @Cincinnati 111

FINALS

Los Angeles 4, Detroit 2

Mar. 24....@Los Angeles 132, Detroit 108
Mar. 25....@Los Angeles 127, Detroit 112
Mar. 27....Los Angeles 111, @Detroit 106
Mar. 29....@Detroit 118, Los Angeles 117
Mar. 31....Detroit 132, @Los Angeles 125
Apr. 3 ......Los Angeles 123, @Detroit 117

NBA FINALS

Boston 4, Los Angeles 3

Apr. 7 ......@Boston 122, Los Angeles 108
Apr. 8 ......Los Angeles 129, @Boston 122
Apr. 10 ....@Los Angeles 117, Boston 115
Apr. 11 ....Boston 115, @Los Angeles 103
Apr. 14 ....Los Angeles 126, @Boston 121
Apr. 16 ....Boston 119, @Los Angeles 105
Apr. 18 ....@Boston 110, Los Angeles 107*

*Denotes number of overtime periods.

INDIVIDUAL LEADERS

SCORING

	G	FGM	FTM	Pts.	Avg.
Chamberlain, Philadelphia	80	1597	835	4029	50.4
Bellamy, Chicago	79	973	549	2495	31.6
Robertson, Cincinnati	79	866	700	2432	30.8
Pettit, St. Louis	78	867	695	2429	31.1
West, Los Angeles	75	799	712	2310	30.8
Guerin, New York	78	839	625	2303	29.5
Naulls, New York	75	747	383	1877	25.0
Baylor, Los Angeles	48	680	476	1836	38.3
Twyman, Cincinnati	80	739	353	1831	22.9
Hagan, St. Louis	77	701	362	1764	22.9

FIELD GOAL PCT. (minimum 200 made)

	FGM	FGA	Pct.
Bellamy, Chicago	973	1875	.519
Chamberlain, Philadelphia	1597	3159	.506
Twyman, Cincinnati	739	1542	.479
Robertson, Cincinnati	866	1810	.478
Attles, Philadelphia	343	724	.474

FREE THROW PCT. (minimum 200 made)

	FTM	FTA	Pct.
Schayes, Syracuse	286	319	.897
Naulls, New York	383	455	.842
Costello, Syracuse	247	295	.837
Hagan, St. Louis	362	439	.825
Ramsey, Boston	334	405	.825

ASSISTS

	G	No.	Avg.
Robertson, Cincinnati	79	899	11.4
Rodgers, Philadelphia	80	643	8.0
Cousy, Boston	75	584	7.8
Guerin, New York	78	539	6.9
Shue, Detroit	80	465	5.8

REBOUNDS

	G	No.	Avg.
Chamberlain, Philadelphia	80	2052	25.7
Russell, Boston	76	1790	23.6
Bellamy, Chicago	79	1500	19.0
Pettit, St. Louis	78	1459	18.7
Kerr, Syracuse	80	1176	14.7

CHAMBERLAIN'S 100-POINT GAME

March 2, 1962, at Hersey, Pa.

PHILADELPHIA WARRIORS (169)

	FGM	FGA	FTM	FTA	Pts.
Paul Arizin	7	18	2	2	16
Tom Meschery	7	12	2	2	16
Wilt Chamberlain	36	63	28	32	100
Guy Rodgers	1	4	9	12	11
Al Attles	8	8	1	1	17
York Larese	4	5	1	1	9
Ed Conlin	0	4	0	0	0
Joe Ruklick	0	1	0	2	0
Ted Luckenbill	0	0	0	0	0
Totals	**63**	**115**	**43**	**52**	**169**

NEW YORK KNICKERBOCKERS (147)

	FGM	FGA	FTM	FTA	Pts.
Willie Naulls	9	22	13	15	31
Johnny Green	3	7	0	0	6
Darrall Imhoff	3	7	1	1	7
Richie Guerin	13	29	13	17	39
Al Butler	4	13	0	0	8
Cleveland Buckner	16	26	1	1	33
Dave Budd	6	8	1	1	13
Donnie Butcher	3	6	4	6	10
Totals	**57**	**118**	**33**	**41**	**147**

SCORE BY PERIODS

	1st	2nd	3rd	4th	Tot.
Philadelphia	42	37	46	44	169
New York	26	42	38	41	147

Officials: Willie Smith, Pete D'Ambrosio.

Attendance: 4,124.

WILT SCORES 100

by Alex Sachare

It was one of the greatest performances in NBA history, one that has grown in legend in the nearly four decades since it took place. On March 2, 1962, Wilt Chamberlain of the Philadelphia Warriors scored 100 points in leading his team to a 169-147 victory over the New York Knicks before 4,124 in Hershey, Pa.

The game was not televised, and thus is shrouded in mystery. The 7-1, 275-pound Chamberlain scored his final basket, on a dunk off a pass from Joe Ruklick, with 46 seconds to play. Fans poured onto the court, stopping the game, and Chamberlain went to the locker room where Warriors PR man Harvey Pollack wrote "100" on a sheet of paper and had Chamberlain hold it up for photographers. Years later, a tape of the radio broadcast was uncovered revealing that the game actually had been resumed and the final 46 seconds played, but since Pollack, who was also the official scorer and was writing the story for the local Philadelphia newspaper, called in the story and was not around when the game resumed. So the remaining 46 seconds were never officially logged.

"It is a mythic game because Wilt scored exactly 100, no more, no less," noted Pollack.

But it was no aberration. Chamberlain already had broken the NBA's single-game scoring record, notching 78 points against the Lakers on December 8, 1961, to surpass Elgin Baylor's mark of 71. He scored 60 or more points 18 times during the season and finished with an average of 50.4 points per game, another record.

The 100-pointer was his pièce de résistance, a performance for the ages, a game where he shot 36-for-63 from the field and 28-for-32 from the foul line.

"As time goes by," he said not long before his death in 1999, "I feel more and more a part of that 100-point game. It has become my handle, and I've come to realize just what I did. People will say to a little kid, 'See that guy right there? He scored 100 points in a game.' I'm definitely proud of it."

CHAMBERLAIN'S SCORING BY PERIODS

	MIN	FGM	FGA	FTM	FTA	REB	AST	PTS.
1st	12	7	14	9	9	10	0	23
2nd	12	7	12	4	5	4	1	18
3rd	12	10	16	8	8	6	1	28
4th	12	12	21	7	10	5	0	31
Totals	48	36	63	28	32	25	2	100

1960-61 SEASON

Jerry West

It didn't take long for observers to realize that Jerry West and Oscar Robertson were on their way to greatness. Robertson came out of Cincinnati and moved right in with the Royals. West graduated from West Virginia and learned he was headed to the Lakers, but not to Minneapolis. The two rising stars helped make the U.S. Olympic team dominant at the summer games in Rome that year, then returned home to find a rapidly changing pro league, one that was bicoastal for the first time.

In a sudden move, the Lakers had departed Minneapolis to take up a new home in Los Angeles. Robertson immediately used his strength and skills to average 30.5 points and lead the league with 9.7 assists per game. Robertson's presence gave the league three scorers averaging better than 30 a game for the first time.

Wilt Chamberlain led the NBA at 38.4 points per game followed by Elgin Baylor with 34.8. West finished with an impressive 17.6 points per game. The eight-team league expanded its schedule to 79 games, but little changed. Boston won 57 games, six better than second-best St. Louis. For the second straight season, St. Louis had to fight off the Lakers in seven games in the Western Division Finals to earn the right to meet the Celtics, who had defeated Syracuse in five games. The Hawks, with their own impressive rookie in Lenny Wilkens, had no better luck against Bill Russell and Co. in the NBA Finals. The Celtics needed just five games to claim their fourth title.

FINAL STANDINGS

EASTERN DIVISION

	W	L	Pct.
Boston	57	22	.722
Philadelphia	46	33	.582
Syracuse	38	41	.481
New York	21	58	.266

WESTERN DIVISION

	W	L	Pct.
St. Louis	51	28	.646
Los Angeles	36	43	.456
Detroit	34	45	.430
Cincinnati	33	46	.418

NBA.COM FACT

Philadelphia's Wilt Chamberlain set an NBA record by grabbing 2,149 rebounds in 79 games, an average of 27.2 rebounds per game, surpassing the mark of 27.0 rebounds per game he set the previous year as a rookie.

PLAYOFFS

EASTERN DIVISION

SEMIFINALS

Syracuse 3, Philadelphia 0

Mar. 14....Syracuse 115, @Philadelphia 107
Mar. 16....@Syracuse 115 , Philadelphia 114
Mar. 18....Syracuse 106, @Philadelphia 103

FINALS

Boston 4, Syracuse 1

Mar. 19....@Boston 128, Syracuse 115
Mar. 21....@Syracuse 115, Boston 98
Mar. 23....@Boston 133, Syracuse 110
Mar. 25....Boston 120, @Syracuse 107
Mar. 26....@Boston 123, Syracuse 101

WESTERN DIVISION

SEMIFINALS

Los Angeles 3, Detroit 2

Mar. 14....@Los Angeles 120, Detroit 102
Mar. 15....@Los Angeles 120, Detroit 118
Mar. 17....@Detroit 124, Los Angeles 113
Mar. 18....@Detroit 123, Los Angeles 114
Mar. 19....@Los Angeles 137, Detroit 120

FINALS

St. Louis 4, Los Angeles 3

Mar. 21....Los Angeles 122, @St. Louis 118
Mar. 22....@St. Louis 121, Los Angeles 106
Mar. 24....@Los Angeles 118, St. Louis 112
Mar. 25....St. Louis 118, @Los Angeles 117
Mar. 27....Los Angeles 121, @St. Louis 112
Mar. 29....St. Louis 114, @Los Angeles 113*
Apr. 1 ......@St. Louis 105, Los Angeles 103

NBA FINALS

Boston 4, St. Louis 1

Apr. 2 ......@Boston 129, St. Louis 95
Apr. 5 ......@Boston 116, St. Louis 108
Apr. 8 ......@St. Louis 124, Boston 120
Apr. 9 ......Boston 119, @St. Louis 104
Apr. 11 ....@Boston 121, St. Louis 112

*Denotes number of overtime periods.

INDIVIDUAL LEADERS

SCORING

	G	FGM	FTM	Pts.	Avg.
Chamberlain, Philadelphia	79	1251	531	3033	38.4
Baylor, Los Angeles	73	931	676	2538	34.8
Robertson, Cincinnati	71	756	653	2165	30.5
Pettit, St. Louis	76	769	582	2120	27.9
Twyman, Cincinnati	79	796	405	1997	25.3
Schayes, Syracuse	79	594	680	1868	23.6
Naulls, New York	79	737	372	1846	23.4
Arizin, Philadelphia	79	650	532	1832	23.2
Howell, Detroit	77	607	601	1815	23.6
Shue, Detroit	78	650	465	1765	22.6

FIELD GOAL PCT. (minimum 200 made)

	FGM	FGA	Pct.
Chamberlain, Philadelphia	1251	2457	.509
Twyman, Cincinnati	796	1632	.488
Costello, Syracuse	407	844	.482
Robertson, Cincinnati	756	1600	.473
Howell, Detroit	607	1293	.469

FREE THROW PCT. (minimum 200 made)

	FTM	FTA	Pct.
Sharman, Boston	210	228	.921
Schayes, Syracuse	680	783	.868
Shue, Detroit	465	543	.856
Arizin, Philadelphia	532	639	.833
Ramsey, Boston	295	354	.833

ASSISTS

	G	No.	Avg.
Robertson, Cincinnati	71	690	9.7
Rodgers, Philadelphia	78	677	8.7
Cousy, Boston	76	587	7.7
Shue, Detroit	78	530	6.8
Guerin, New York	79	503	6.4

REBOUNDS

	G	No.	Avg.
Chamberlain, Philadelphia	79	2149	27.2
Russell, Boston	78	1868	23.9
Pettit, St. Louis	76	1540	20.3
Baylor, Los Angeles	73	1447	19.8
Howell, Detroit	77	1111	14.4

1959-60 SEASON

Bill Sharman (21)

Never before, and never again, would a rookie have such an impact on the NBA. In the statistical categories. In ticket sales. In team standings. At 7-1 and nearly 275 pounds, Wilt Chamberlain towered over the centers of his time. In his rookie season with the Philadelphia Warriors, Chamberlain won both Rookie of the Year and Most Valuable Player honors, leading the league in scoring (37.6 points per game) and rebounding (27.0 rebounds per game). Chamberlain scored 50 or more points seven times. The Warriors had gone 32-40 the previous season, but with Chamberlain they improved to 49-26.

Not surprisingly, Wilt's Warriors attracted capacity crowds just about everywhere they went. Even so, the Celtics shook off this challenge and kept winning, this time an NBA-record 59 games and the Eastern Division. St. Louis won the West by 16 games in what was now a 75-game season. Boston defeated the Warriors and Chamberlain in six games to advance to the Finals. St. Louis was pushed to seven games by the Lakers before moving on to meet the Celtics.

With Red Auerbach at the controls, Boston had built a dynasty piece by piece, beginning with Cousy in 1950 and adding Bill Sharman in 1951, Frank Ramsey in 1954, Jim Loscutoff in 1955, and Tom Heinsohn and Bill Russell in 1956. But after the first championship in 1957, the Celtics didn't stop adding winners. Sam Jones came aboard in 1957, K.C. Jones and Gene Conley in 1958. They all had a hand in title number three. The Celtics and Hawks split the first six games of the championship series, but Boston easily won Game 7 at home, 122-103, as Russell starred with 22 points and 35 rebounds.

FINAL STANDINGS

EASTERN DIVISION

	W	L	Pct.
Boston	59	16	.787
Philadelphia	49	26	.653
Syracuse	45	30	.600
New York	27	48	.360

WESTERN DIVISION

	W	L	Pct.
St. Louis	46	29	.613
Detroit	30	45	.400
Minneapolis	25	50	.333
Cincinnati	19	56	.253

NBA.COM FACT

Bill Russell of the champion Celtics set an NBA Finals record by hauling down 40 rebounds in Game 2 of the Finals against the St. Louis Hawks, even though his team lost 113-103.

PLAYOFFS

EASTERN DIVISION

SEMIFINALS

Philadelphia 2, Syracuse 1

Mar. 11 ....@Philadelphia 115, Syracuse 92
Mar. 13 ...@Syracuse 125, Philadelphia 119
Mar. 14 ....@Philadelphia 132, Syracuse 112

FINALS

Boston 4, Philadelphia 2

Mar. 16 ....@Boston 111, Philadelphia 105
Mar. 18 ....@Philadelphia 115, Boston 110
Mar. 19 ....@Boston 120, Philadelphia 90
Mar. 20 ....Boston 112, @Philadelphia 104
Mar. 22 ....Philadelphia 128, @Boston 107
Mar. 24 ....Boston 119, @Philadelphia 117

WESTERN DIVISION

SEMIFINALS

Minneapolis 2, Detroit 0

Mar. 12 ....Minneapolis 113, @Detroit 112
Mar. 13 ....@Minneapolis 114, Detroit 99

FINALS

St. Louis 4, Minneapolis 3

Mar. 16 ....@St. Louis 112, Minneapolis 99
Mar. 17 ....Minneapolis 120, @St. Louis 113
Mar. 19 ....St. Louis 93, @Minneapolis 89
Mar. 20 ....@Minneapolis 103, St. Louis 101
Mar. 22 ....Minneapolis 117, @St. Louis 110*
Mar. 24 ....St. Louis 117, @Minneapolis 96
Mar. 26 ....@St. Louis 97, Minneapolis 86

NBA FINALS

Boston 4, St. Louis 3

Mar. 27 ....@Boston 140, St. Louis 122
Mar. 29 ....St. Louis 113, @Boston 103
Apr. 2 ......Boston 102, @St. Louis 86
Apr. 3 ......@St. Louis 106, Boston 96
Apr. 5 ......@Boston 127, St. Louis 102
Apr. 7 ......@St. Louis 105, Boston 102
Apr. 9 ......@Boston 122, St. Louis 103

*Denotes number of overtime periods.

INDIVIDUAL LEADERS

SCORING

	G	FGM	FTM	Pts.	Avg.
Chamberlain, Philadelphia	72	1065	577	2707	37.6
Twyman, Cincinnati	75	870	598	2338	31.2
Baylor, Minneapolis	70	755	564	2074	29.6
Pettit, St. Louis	72	669	544	1882	26.1
Hagan, St. Louis	75	719	421	1859	24.8
Shue, Detroit	75	620	472	1712	22.8
Schayes, Syracuse	75	578	533	1689	22.5
Heinsohn, Boston	75	673	283	1629	21.7
Guerin, New York	74	579	457	1615	21.8
Arizin, Philadelphia	72	593	420	1606	22.3

FIELD GOAL PCT. (minimum 190 made)

	FGM	FGA	Pct.
Sears, New York	412	863	.477
Greer, Syracuse	388	815	.476
Lovellette, St. Louis	550	1174	.468
Russell, Boston	555	1189	.467
Hagan, St. Louis	719	1549	.464

FREE THROW PCT. (minimum 185 made)

	FTM	FTA	Pct.
Schayes, Syracuse	533	597	.893
Shue, Detroit	472	541	.872
Sears, New York	363	418	.868
Sharman, Boston	252	291	.866
Costello, Syracuse	249	289	.862

ASSISTS

	G	No.	Avg.
Cousy, Boston	75	715	9.5
Rodgers, Philadelphia	68	482	7.1
Guerin, New York	74	468	6.3
Costello, Syracuse	71	449	6.3
Gola, Philadelphia	75	409	5.5

REBOUNDS

	G	No.	Avg.
Chamberlain, Philadelphia	72	1941	27.0
Russell, Boston	74	1778	24.0
Pettit, St. Louis	72	1221	17.0
Baylor, Minneapolis	70	1150	16.4
Schayes, Syracuse	75	959	12.8

1958-59 SEASON

Elgin Baylor

Elgin Baylor had a nervous tic that he turned into the NBA's most dreaded head fake. Add in his remarkable hang time and vast array of spectacular moves, and it's no wonder opponents were left spinning in confusion as they tried to adjust to the Minneapolis Lakers' exciting rookie. A 6-5 forward from the University of Seattle, Baylor helped a Lakers team that had been 19-53 a year before to a 33-39 record and a playoff berth. He averaged 24.9 points and 15.0 rebounds, making the All-NBA First Team. His early magic included a 55-point game that first season, the third highest in NBA history. It foreshadowed a surprising playoffs.

Boston won the East by 12 games, while St. Louis won the West by 16. The Celtics had a tough time with Syracuse, which added George Yardley to a front line that already boasted Dolph Schayes and Red Kerr. Pushed to the limit, Boston won the seventh game of the Eastern Finals, 130-125.

In the West, Baylor and the Lakers upset the Hawks, overcoming a 2-1 St. Louis lead by winning three straight games. Nobody gave the Lakers much chance against the Celtics, and although the Lakers kept three of the four games close, Boston recorded the first 4-0 sweep in NBA Finals history. It would be the first of eight NBA Finals appearances for Baylor — and the first of eight defeats. Without ever having won a title, the great forward would retire in early in the 1971-72 season, on the eve of the Lakers' first championship in Los Angeles.

FINAL STANDINGS

EASTERN DIVISION

	W	L	Pct.
Boston	52	20	.722
New York	40	32	.556
Syracuse	35	37	.486
Philadelphia	32	40	.444

WESTERN DIVISION

	W	L	Pct.
St. Louis	49	23	.681
Minneapolis	33	39	.458
Detroit	28	44	.389
Cincinnati	19	53	.264

NBA.COM FACT

By decade's end, the league had come full circle. On Feb. 27, Boston turned back visiting Minneapolis 173-139 in a game that saw seven league records fall. A shocked NBA President Maurice Podoloff immediately ordered an investigation to determine whether an attempt had been made to carry out defensive assignments or the participants merely "were goofing around."

PLAYOFFS

EASTERN DIVISION

SEMIFINALS

Syracuse 2, New York 0

Mar. 13....Syracuse 129, @New York 123
Mar. 15....@Syracuse 131, New York 115

FINALS

Boston 4, Syracuse 3

Mar. 18....@Boston 131, Syracuse 109
Mar. 21....@Syracuse 120, Boston 118
Mar. 22....@Boston 133, Syracuse 111
Mar. 25....@Syracuse 119, Boston 107
Mar. 28....@Boston 129, Syracuse 108
Mar. 29....@Syracuse 133, Boston 121
Apr. 1 ......@Boston 130, Syracuse 125

WESTERN DIVISION

SEMIFINALS

Minneapolis 2, Detroit 1

Mar. 14....@Minneapolis 92, Detroit 89
Mar. 15....@Detroit 117, Minneapolis 103
Mar. 18....@Minneapolis 129, Detroit 102

FINALS

Minneapolis 4, St. Louis 2

Mar. 21....@St. Louis 124, Minneapolis 90
Mar. 22....@Minneapolis 106, St. Louis 98
Mar. 24....@St. Louis 127, Minneapolis 97
Mar. 26....@Minneapolis 108, St. Louis 98
Mar. 28....Minneapolis 98, @St. Louis 97*
Mar. 29....@Minneapolis 106, St. Louis 104

NBA FINALS

Boston 4, Minneapolis 0

Apr. 4 ......@Boston 118, Minneapolis 115
Apr. 5 ......@Boston 128, Minneapolis 108
Apr. 7 ......Boston 123, Minneapolis 110 (@St. Paul)
Apr. 9 ......Boston 118, @Minneapolis 113

*Denotes number of overtime periods.

INDIVIDUAL LEADERS

SCORING

	G	FGM	FTM	Pts.	Avg.
Pettit, St. Louis	72	719	667	2105	29.2
Twyman, Cincinnati	72	710	437	1857	25.8
Arizin, Philadelphia	70	632	587	1851	26.4
Baylor, Minneapolis	70	605	532	1742	24.9
Hagan, St. Louis	72	646	415	1707	23.7
Schayes, Syracuse	72	504	526	1534	21.3
Sears, New York	71	491	506	1488	21.0
Sharman, Boston	72	562	342	1466	20.4
Cousy, Boston	65	484	329	1297	20.0
Guerin, New York	71	443	405	1291	18.2

FIELD GOAL PCT. (minimum 230 made)

	FGM	FGA	Pct.
Sears, New York	491	1002	.490
Russell, Boston	456	997	.457
Hagan, St. Louis	646	1417	.456
Lovellette, St. Louis	402	885	.454
Greer, Syracuse	308	679	.454

FREE THROW PCT. (minimum 190 made)

	FTM	FTA	Pct.
Sharman, Boston	342	367	.932
Schayes, Syracuse	526	609	.864
Sears, New York	506	588	.861
Cousy, Boston	329	385	.855
Naulls, New York	258	311	.830

ASSISTS

	G	No.	Avg.
Cousy, Boston	65	557	8.6
McGuire, Detroit	71	443	6.2
Costello, Syracuse	70	379	5.4
Guerin, New York	71	364	5.1
Braun, New York	72	349	4.9

REBOUNDS

	G	No.	Avg.
Russell, Boston	70	1612	23.0
Pettit, St. Louis	72	1182	16.4
Baylor, Minneapolis	70	1050	15.0
Kerr, Syracuse	72	1008	14.0
Schayes, Syracuse	72	962	13.4

1957-58 SEASON

George Yardley

He had the fire in his stomach. That sums up the drive of St. Louis Hawks star Bob Pettit. The 6-9, 215-pound forward from LSU never seemed satisfied with his play. "When I fall below what I know I can do, my belly growls and growls," Pettit once said. He led the Hawks to the NBA Finals four times but found his only reward in 1958, a victory over Boston after Bill Russell was injured. That avenged a seven-game loss to the Celtics in the Finals the year before and gave the Hawks the only championship in franchise history.

Before the season, the Fort Wayne Pistons moved to Detroit and the Rochester Royals moved to Cincinnati. Just three years earlier, half the NBA's teams had been based in metropolitan areas with less than a million people; now only Syracuse was in that category. Fans in Detroit were treated to the league's leading scorer. The Pistons' George Yardley became the first player to score 2,000 points in a season, leading the NBA in scoring at 27.8 points per game.

Boston in the East and St. Louis in the West were clearly the class of the league. Each won its division by eight games over a 72-game schedule. Boston took Philadelphia in five games to win what was now a best-of-seven Division Finals, while St. Louis bested Detroit in five games. St. Louis and Boston split the first two games in Boston, and it seemed another classic championship series was in the Hawks' favor. Boston showed gritty determination with a win in Game 4 without Russell (who had injured his ankle in the Celtics' Game 3 defeat), but St. Louis won Game 5 in Boston by two points. Then Pettit exploded for 50 points in Game 6 to give St. Louis a 110-109 victory and the club's only title.

FINAL STANDINGS

EASTERN DIVISION

	W	L	Pct.
Boston	49	23	.681
Syracuse	41	31	.569
Philadelphia	37	35	.514
New York	35	37	.486

WESTERN DIVISION

	W	L	Pct.
St. Louis	41	31	.569
Detroit	33	39	.458
Cincinnati	33	39	.458
Minneapolis	19	53	.264

NBA.COM FACT

In a 135-109 rout of visiting Detroit on Jan. 12, Syracuse's Dolph Schayes scored 23 points to surpass George Mikan as the all-time NBA scorer. Mikan scored 11,764 points in 439 regular-season games, compared to Schayes' totals of 11,770 points and 655 games at the time.

PLAYOFFS

EASTERN DIVISION

SEMIFINALS

Philadelphia 2, Syracuse 1

Mar. 15....@Syracuse 86, Philadelphia 82
Mar. 16....@Philadelphia 95, Syracuse 93
Mar. 18....Philadelphia 101, @Syracuse 88

FINALS

Boston 4, Philadelphia 1

Mar. 19....@Boston 107, Philadelphia 98
Mar. 22....Boston 109, @Philadelphia 87
Mar. 23....@Boston 106, Philadelphia 92
Mar. 26....@Philadelphia 111, Boston 97
Mar. 27....@Boston 93, Philadelphia 88

WESTERN DIVISION

SEMIFINALS

Detroit 2, Cincinnati 0

Mar. 15....@Detroit 100, Cincinnati 93
Mar. 16....Detroit 124, @Cincinnati 104

FINALS

St. Louis 4, Detroit 1

Mar. 19....@St. Louis 114, Detroit 111
Mar. 22....St. Louis 99, @Detroit 96
Mar. 23....Detroit 109, @St. Louis 89
Mar. 25....St. Louis 145, @Detroit 101
Mar. 27....@St. Louis 120, Detroit 96

NBA FINALS

St. Louis 4, Boston 2

Mar. 29....St. Louis 104, @Boston 102
Mar. 30....@Boston 136, St. Louis 112
Apr. 2......@St. Louis 111, Boston 108
Apr. 5......Boston 109, @St. Louis 98
Apr. 9......St. Louis 102, @Boston 100
Apr. 12....@St. Louis 110, Boston 109

INDIVIDUAL LEADERS

SCORING

	G	FGM	FTM	Pts.	Avg.
Yardley, Detroit	72	673	655	2001	27.8
Schayes, Syracuse	72	581	629	1791	24.9
Pettit, St. Louis	70	581	557	1719	24.6
Lovellette, Cincinnati	71	679	301	1659	23.4
Arizin, Philadelphia	68	483	440	1406	20.7
Sharman, Boston	63	550	302	1402	22.3
Hagan, St. Louis	70	503	385	1391	19.9
Johnston, Philadelphia	71	473	442	1388	19.5
Sears, New York	72	445	452	1342	18.6
Mikkelsen, Minneapolis	72	439	370	1248	17.3

FIELD GOAL PCT. (minimum 230 made)

	FGM	FGA	Pct.
Twyman, Cincinnati	465	1028	.452
Hagan, St. Louis	503	1135	.443
Russell, Boston	456	1032	.442
Felix, New York	304	688	.442
Lovellette, Cincinnati	679	1540	.441

FREE THROW PCT. (minimum 190 made)

	FTM	FTA	Pct.
Schayes, Syracuse	629	696	.904
Sharman, Boston	302	338	.893
Cousy, Boston	277	326	.850
Braun, New York	321	378	.849
Schnittker, Minneapolis	201	237	.848

ASSISTS

	G	No.	Avg.
Cousy, Boston	65	463	7.1
McGuire, Detroit	69	454	6.6
Stokes, Cincinnati	63	403	6.4
Braun, New York	71	393	5.5
King, Cincinnati	63	337	5.4

REBOUNDS

	G	No.	Avg.
Russell, Boston	69	1564	22.7
Pettit, St. Louis	70	1216	17.4
Stokes, Cincinnati	63	1142	18.1
Schayes, Syracuse	72	1022	14.2
Kerr, Syracuse	72	963	13.4

1956-57 SEASON

Bill Russell

The scoring title went to Philadelphia's Paul Arizin in 1957, but nobody paid much attention. The league had been overwhelmed by a shotblocking, rebounding revolution in the form of Bill Russell. Boston's exciting rookie would lead his team to 11 championships in 13 seasons, a drive he started immediately. For years the Celtics had been a fast-breaking bunch, but without rebounding and defense, so they hadn't gone very far in the playoffs. Then Red Auerbach traded veteran Ed Macauley and a young Cliff Hagan to St. Louis for the draft rights to Russell, a college standout at the University of San Francisco and a member of the 1956 U.S. Olympic team. Boston also drafted high-scoring, 6-7 forward Tom Heinsohn of Holy Cross.

With Russell and Heinsohn joining guards Bob Cousy and Bill Sharman, muscleman Jim Loscutoff and sixth man Frank Ramsey, the Celtics assembled a team that would be the scourge of the league for years to come. Sharman and Cousy still piled up the points, but with Russell (who arrived in midseason, after the Olympics were over) anchoring a tough Celtics defense, Boston won the Eastern Division by a comfortable six games. St. Louis, led by Bob Pettit (24.7 points per game) and buoyed by the addition of Macauley (16.5 points per game) and Hagan, advanced to the NBA Finals, a classic series won by the Celtics in a thrilling, 125-123 double-overtime Game 7 in Boston. That Game 7 would be talked about for years. Rookies Russell (19 points, 32 rebounds) and Heinsohn (37 points, 23 rebounds) stepped up and provided the win that would set the Celtic dynasty in motion. "The first one [championship] is always the hardest, and it's also the most satisfying," said Auerbach.

FINAL STANDINGS

EASTERN DIVISION

	W	L	Pct.
Boston	44	28	.611
Syracuse	38	34	.528
Philadelphia	37	35	.514
New York	36	36	.500

WESTERN DIVISION

	W	L	Pct.
St. Louis*	34	38	.472
Minneapolis	34	38	.472
Fort Wayne	34	38	.472
Rochester	31	41	.431

*Won playoff to break tie

NBA.COM FACT

In search of some needed local flavor for their new fans in St. Louis, the Hawks set their sights on Kentucky product Cliff Hagan and St. Louis University graduate Ed Macauley, both of whom were Boston property. With a first-round draft pick named Bill Russell as the bait for the defense-challenged Celtics, the trade was completed on April 29, 1956, and the rest of the league was history.

PLAYOFFS

EASTERN DIVISION

SEMIFINALS

Syracuse 2, Philadelphia 0

Mar. 16....Syracuse 103, @Philadelphia 96
Mar. 18....@Syracuse 91, Philadelphia 80

FINALS

Boston 3, Syracuse 0

Mar. 21....@Boston 108, Syracuse 90
Mar. 23....Boston 120, @Syracuse 105
Mar. 24....@Boston 83, Syracuse 80

WESTERN DIVISION

TIEBREAKERS

Mar. 14....@St. Louis 115, Fort Wayne 103
Mar. 16....@St. Louis 114, Minneapolis 111

SEMIFINALS

Minneapolis 2, Fort Wayne 0

Mar. 17....@Minneapolis 131, Fort Wayne 127
Mar. 19....Minneapolis 110, @Fort Wayne 108

FINALS

St. Louis 3, Minneapolis 0

Mar. 21....@St. Louis 118, Minneapolis 109
Mar. 24....@St. Louis 106, Minneapolis 104
Mar. 25....St. Louis 143, @Minneapolis 135**

NBA FINALS

Boston 4, St. Louis 3

Mar. 30....St. Louis 125, @Boston 123**
Mar. 31....@Boston 119, St. Louis 99
Apr. 6......@St. Louis 100, Boston 98
Apr. 7......Boston 123, @St. Louis 118
Apr. 9......@Boston 124, St. Louis 109
Apr. 11....@St. Louis 96, Boston 94
Apr. 13....@Boston 125, St. Louis 123**

*Denotes number of overtime periods.

INDIVIDUAL LEADERS

SCORING

	G	FGM	FTM	Pts.	Avg.
Arizin, Philadelphia	71	613	591	1817	25.6
Pettit, St. Louis	71	613	529	1755	24.7
Schayes, Syracuse	72	496	625	1617	22.5
Johnston, Philadelphia	69	520	535	1575	22.8
Yardley, Fort Wayne	72	522	503	1547	21.5
Lovellette, Minneapolis	69	574	286	1434	20.8
Sharman, Boston	67	516	381	1413	21.1
Cousy, Boston	64	478	363	1319	20.6
Macauley, St. Louis	72	414	359	1187	16.5
Garmaker, Minneapolis	72	406	365	1177	16.3

FIELD GOAL PCT. (minimum 230 made)

	FGM	FGA	Pct.
Johnston, Philadelphia	520	1163	.447
Twyman, Rochester	449	1023	.439
Share, St. Louis	235	535	.439
Houbregs, Fort Wayne	253	585	.432
Russell, Boston	277	649	.427

FREE THROW PCT. (minimum 190 made)

	FTM	FTA	Pct.
Sharman, Boston	381	421	.905
Schayes, Syracuse	625	691	.904
Garmaker, Minneapolis	365	435	.839
Arizin, Philadelphia	591	713	.829
Johnston, Philadelphia	535	648	.826

ASSISTS

	G	No.	Avg.
Cousy, Boston	64	478	7.5
McMahon, St. Louis	72	367	5.1
Stokes, Rochester	72	331	4.6
George, Philadelphia	67	307	4.6
Martin, New York-St. Louis	66	269	4.1

REBOUNDS

	G	No.	Avg.
Stokes, Rochester	72	1256	17.4
Pettit, St. Louis	71	1037	14.6
Schayes, Syracuse	72	1008	14.0
Russell, Boston	48	943	19.6
Lovellette, Minneapolis	69	932	13.5

1955-56 SEASON

Bob Pettit

The numbers do the talking — 25.7 points and 16.2 rebounds. That's the kind of year Bob Pettit had, leading the league in both categories. Pettit's big performance in his second NBA season also helped his Hawks make their move from Milwaukee to St. Louis. The NBA, too, was in its second season — of adjustment to the shot clock. The league was just beginning to comprehend the potential of the up-tempo game. Scoring surged to 99 points per team per game, and quickness and athleticism became very important. Gone were the Baltimore Bullets. Their demise, just 14 games into the previous season, left the NBA an eight-team league, six of which made the playoffs.

Philadelphia and Fort Wayne, the first-place teams in each division, received first-round byes, then dismissed Syracuse and St. Louis, respectively, to advance to the NBA Finals. The Warriors had won just 33 games the previous season, but with Paul Arizin loving the new rules and rookie Tom Gola displaying a nice floor game, they improved to 45-27. Owned by Eddie Gottlieb and coached by George Senesky, the Warriors got 22.1 points per game from Neil Johnston in the post to go along with Arizin's 24.2 points from the wing.

The Pistons were coached by former referee Charley Eckman, who liked to feature George Yardley in a loosely run offense. However, the 6-4 Arizin hit a hot streak at playoff time, scoring 289 points in 10 games, too much for the Pistons in the Finals. They fell in five games.

FINAL STANDINGS

EASTERN DIVISION

	W	L	Pct.
Philadelphia	45	27	.625
Boston	39	33	.542
Syracuse*	35	37	.486
New York	35	37	.486

WESTERN DIVISION

	W	L	Pct.
Fort Wayne	37	35	.514
Minneapolis*	33	39	.458
St. Louis	33	39	.458
Rochester	31	41	.431

*Won playoff to break tie

NBA.COM FACT

The up-tempo pace never was more apparent than on Dec. 15, when Minneapolis and Syracuse combined for 268 points to shatter the league record for one game. Led by Dolph Schayes with 34 points — one of seven players who scored 20 or more — the host Nationals prevailed in the triple-overtime thriller, 135-133.

PLAYOFFS

EASTERN DIVISION

THIRD-PLACE TIEBREAKER

Mar. 15....@Syracuse 82, New York 77

SEMIFINALS

Syracuse 2, Boston 1

Mar. 17....@Boston 110, Syracuse 93
Mar. 19....@Syracuse 101, Boston 98
Mar. 21....Syracuse 102, @Boston 97

FINALS

Philadelphia 3, Syracuse 2

Mar. 23....@Philadelphia 109, Syracuse 87
Mar. 25....@Syracuse 122, Philadelphia 118
Mar. 27....@Philadelphia 119, Syracuse 96
Mar. 28....@Syracuse 108, Philadelphia 104
Mar. 29....@Philadelphia 109, Syracuse 104

WESTERN DIVISION

SECOND-PLACE TIEBREAKER

Mar. 16....Minneapolis 103, @St. Louis 97

SEMIFINALS

St. Louis 2, Minneapolis 1

Mar. 17....@St. Louis 116, Minneapolis 115
Mar. 19....@Minneapolis 133, St. Louis 75
Mar. 21....St. Louis 116, @Minneapolis 115

FINALS

Fort Wayne 3, St. Louis 2

Mar. 22....St. Louis 86, @Fort Wayne 85
Mar. 24....@St. Louis 84, Fort Wayne 74
Mar. 25....@Fort Wayne 107, St. Louis 84
Mar. 27....Fort Wayne 93, @St. Louis 84
Mar. 29....@Fort Wayne 102, St. Louis 97

NBA FINALS

Philadelphia 4, Fort Wayne 1

Mar. 31....@Philadelphia 98, Fort Wayne 94
Apr. 1 ......@Fort Wayne 84, Philadelphia 83
Apr. 3 ......@Philadelphia 100, Fort Wayne 96
Apr. 5 ......Philadelphia 107, @Fort Wayne 105
Apr. 7 ......@Philadelphia 99, Fort Wayne 88

INDIVIDUAL LEADERS

SCORING

	G	FGM	FTM	Pts.	Avg.
Pettit, St. Louis	72	646	557	1849	25.7
Arizin, Philadelphia	72	617	507	1741	24.2
Johnston, Philadelphia	70	499	549	1547	22.1
Lovellette, Minneapolis	71	594	338	1526	21.5
Schayes, Syracuse	72	465	542	1472	20.4
Sharman, Boston	72	538	358	1434	19.9
Cousy, Boston	72	440	476	1356	18.8
Macauley, Boston	71	420	400	1240	17.5
Yardley, Fort Wayne	71	434	365	1233	17.4
Stokes, Rochester	67	403	319	1125	16.8
Foust, Fort Wayne	72	367	432	1166	16.2

FIELD GOAL PCT. (minimum 230 made)

	FGM	FGA	Pct.
Johnston, Philadelphia	499	1092	.457
Arizin, Philadelphia	617	1378	.448
Foust, Fort Wayne	367	821	.447
Sears, New York	319	728	.438
Sharman, Boston	538	1229	.438

FREE THROW PCT. (minimum 190 made)

	FTM	FTA	Pct.
Sharman, Boston	358	413	.867
Schayes, Syracuse	542	632	.858
Schnittker, Minneapolis	304	355	.856
Cousy, Boston	476	564	.844
Braun, New York	320	382	.838

ASSISTS

	G	No.	Avg.
Cousy, Boston	72	642	8.9
George, Philadelphia	72	457	6.4
Martin, Minneapolis	72	445	6.2
Phillip, Fort Wayne	70	410	5.9
King, Syracuse	72	410	5.7

REBOUNDS

	G	No.	Avg.
Pettit, St. Louis	72	1164	16.2
Stokes, Rochester	67	1094	16.3
Lovellette, Minneapolis	71	992	14.0
Schayes, Syracuse	72	891	12.4
Johnston, Philadelphia	70	872	12.5

1954-55 SEASON

Danny Biasone

You say you want a revolution? The league's adoption of Danny Biasone's 24-second shot clock during the 1954 offseason certainly brought one. The league also placed a limit on the number of fouls a team could commit in a quarter before free throws were awarded. Leonard Koppett of *The New York Times* later wrote, "This combination, the time limit on shooting and the team limit on fouls, saved the NBA. Literally."

George Mikan, pro basketball's original aircraft carrier, retired before the season, having led the Lakers to five NBA titles and the 1947 championship of the National Basketball League. Neil Johnston won another scoring title with a 22.7 points-per-game average (he also led the league with 15.1 rebounds per game), while Boston's Bob Cousy celebrated the new rules with 21.2 points per game. Paul Arizin, another player who would benefit from the changes, rejoined the Warriors after two years of military service and averaged 21.0 points.

The team story, though, was Biasone's Syracuse Nationals, led by Paul Seymour and Dolph Schayes and coached by Al Cervi. They won the East, beat Boston in the Division Finals, and then met the Fort Wayne Pistons in the NBA Finals. Charley Eckman, a former referee, had taken over the Pistons and coaxed them along to a 43-29 finish in the regular season, all the time insisting that his team ran no offensive plays. The Finals ran a wild course through seven hotly contested games. In the deciding game, Syracuse's George King made one of two foul shots with 12 seconds left and then stole the ball to secure a 92-91 victory.

FINAL STANDINGS

EASTERN DIVISION

	W	L	Pct.
Syracuse	43	29	.597
New York	38	34	.528
Boston	36	36	.500
Philadelphia	33	39	.458
Baltimore*	3	11	.214

* Team disbanded and did not finish season.

WESTERN DIVISION

	W	L	Pct.
Fort Wayne	43	29	.597
Minneapolis	40	32	.556
Rochester	29	43	.403
Milwaukee	26	46	.361

NBA.COM FACT

The impact of the 24-second clock couldn't have been more dramatic — or overdue. Each team attempted an average of 11 more field goals per game than in the previous campaign, which translated into an increase of nearly 14 points. At 101.4 per game, Boston became the first team in league history to score in triple figures in a season.

PLAYOFFS

EASTERN DIVISION

SEMIFINALS

Boston 2, New York 1

Mar. 15....@Boston 122, New York 101
Mar. 16....@New York 102, Boston 95
Mar. 19....Boston 116, @New York 109

FINALS

Syracuse 3, Boston 1

Mar. 22....@Syracuse 110, Boston 100
Mar. 24....@Syracuse 116, Boston 110
Mar. 26....@Boston 100, Syracuse 97*
Mar. 27....Syracuse 110, @Boston 94

WESTERN DIVISION

SEMIFINALS

Minneapolis 2, Rochester 1

Mar. 16....Minneapolis 82, Rochester 78 (@St. Paul)
Mar. 18....@Rochester 94, Minneapolis 92
Mar. 19....Minneapolis 119, Rochester 110 (@St. Paul)

FINALS

Fort Wayne 3, Minneapolis 1

Mar. 20....Fort Wayne 96, Minneapolis 79 (@Elkhart, Ind.)
Mar. 22....Fort Wayne 98, Minneapolis 97* (@Indianapolis)
Mar. 23....@Minneapolis 99, Fort Wayne 91*
Mar. 27....Fort Wayne 105, @Minneapolis 96

NBA FINALS

Syracuse 4, Fort Wayne 3

Mar. 31....@Syracuse 86, Fort Wayne 82
Apr. 2......@Syracuse 87, Fort Wayne 84
Apr. 3......Fort Wayne 96, Syracuse 89 (@Indianapolis)
Apr. 5......Fort Wayne 109, Syracuse 102 (@Indianapolis)
Apr. 7......Fort Wayne 74, Syracuse 71 (@Indianapolis)
Apr. 9......@Syracuse 109, Fort Wayne 104
Apr. 10....@Syracuse 92, Fort Wayne 91

*Denotes number of overtime periods.

INDIVIDUAL LEADERS

SCORING

	G	FGM	FTM	Pts.	Avg.
Johnston, Philadelphia	72	521	589	1631	22.7
Arizin, Philadelphia	72	529	454	1512	21.0
Cousy, Boston	71	522	460	1504	21.2
Pettit, Milwaukee	72	520	426	1466	20.4
Selvy, Balt.-Milwaukee	71	452	444	1348	19.0
Schayes, Syracuse	72	422	489	1333	18.5
Mikkelsen, Minneapolis	71	440	447	1327	18.7
Lovellette, Minneapolis	70	519	273	1311	18.7
Sharman, Boston	68	453	347	1253	18.4
Macauley, Boston	71	403	442	1248	17.6

FIELD GOAL PCT. (minimum 210 made)

	FGM	FGA	Pct.
Foust, Fort Wayne	398	818	.487
Coleman, Rochester	400	866	.462
Marshall, Rochester	223	505	.442
Johnston, Philadelphia	521	1184	.440
Felix, New York	364	832	.438

FREE THROW PCT. (minimum 180 made)

	FTM	FTA	Pct.
Sharman, Boston	347	387	.897
Brian, Fort Wayne	217	255	.851
Schayes, Syracuse	489	587	.833
Schnittker, Minneapolis	298	362	.823
Baechtold, New York	279	339	.823

ASSISTS

	G	No.	Avg.
Cousy, Boston	71	557	7.9
McGuire, New York	71	542	7.6
Phillip, Fort Wayne	64	491	7.7
Seymour, Syracuse	72	483	6.7
Martin, Minneapolis	72	427	5.9

REBOUNDS

	G	No.	Avg.
Johnston, Philadelphia	72	1085	15.1
Gallatin, New York	72	995	13.8
Pettit, Milwaukee	72	994	13.8
Schayes, Syracuse	72	887	12.3
Felix, New York	72	818	11.4

1953-54 SEASON

Bob Cousy

The Minneapolis Lakers liked to walk the ball up the floor, then wait for big George Mikan to set up in the post and go to work. At that lumbering pace, he controlled the game.

That was the crux of both the Lakers' success and the NBA's problem: The pace was too slow.

In yet another effort to tinker with the rules and hold back the excessive fouling used to counter Mikan's style, the league decided to limit each player to two fouls per quarter. The change brought the average number of fouls down to 51 a game, but did little to abate the flurry of fouls in late-game situations, when teams with a lead used their dribble kings to run out the clock, forcing the other team to foul.

Another sign that the league was failing to capture fans' hearts came when the Indianapolis franchise folded despite playing in a hoops-crazy state, leaving only four teams in the Western Division.

The big performers were Philly center Neil Johnston, who won the scoring title with a 24.4 average, and Cousy, who finished behind him with 19.2 points and a league-high 7.2 assists per game.

Mikan, meanwhile, was approaching 30 and was playing fewer minutes, although he still posted a healthy double-double (18.1 points and 14.3 rebounds per game). His presence was again the difference in the playoffs, which had been shifted to a round-robin in which the top three teams in each division played each other. Syracuse survived the East and challenged the Lakers through seven games for the title. In the end, though, it was Mikan and Co. again, completing the NBA's first three-peat by winning Game 7, 87-80.

FINAL STANDINGS

EASTERN DIVISION

	W	L	Pct.
New York	44	28	.611
Boston	42	30	.583
Syracuse	42	30	.583
Philadelphia	29	43	.403
Baltimore	16	56	.222

WESTERN DIVISION

	W	L	Pct.
Minneapolis	46	26	.639
Rochester	44	28	.611
Fort Wayne	40	32	.556
Milwaukee	21	51	.292

NBA.COM FACT

Well aware of the gambling problems that had rocked college basketball only years earlier, the board of directors denied entry to Kentucky All-America Bill Spivey, who had been tried but not convicted on perjury charges. Nine months later, budding star Jack Molinas was suspended indefinitely after he admitted that he had placed bets on his Fort Wayne team.

PLAYOFFS

EASTERN DIVISION

ROUND ROBIN

Mar. 16....Boston 93, @New York 71
Mar. 17....Syracuse 96, @Boston 95*
Mar. 18....@Syracuse 75, New York 68
Mar. 20....@Boston 79, New York 78
Mar. 21....Syracuse 103, @New York 99
Mar. 22....@Syracuse 98, Boston 85

FINALS

Syracuse 2, Boston 0

Mar. 25....@Syracuse 109, Boston 94
Mar. 27....Syracuse 83, @Boston 76

WESTERN DIVISION

ROUND ROBIN

Mar. 16....@Rochester 82, Fort Wayne 75
Mar. 17....@Minneapolis 109, Rochester 88
Mar. 18....Minneapolis 90, @Fort Wayne 85
Mar. 20....@Minneapolis 78, Fort Wayne 73
Mar. 21....Rochester 89, @Fort Wayne 71
Mar. 23....Minneapolis, @Rochester (canceled)

FINALS

Minneapolis 2, Rochester 1

Mar. 24....@Minneapolis 89, Rochester 76
Mar. 27....@Rochester 74, Minneapolis 73
Mar. 28....@Minneapolis 82, Rochester 72

NBA FINALS

Minneapolis 4, Syracuse 3

Mar. 31....@Minneapolis 79, Syracuse 68
Apr. 3......Syracuse 62, @Minneapolis 60
Apr. 4......Minneapolis 81, @Syracuse 67
Apr. 8......@Syracuse 80, Minneapolis 69
Apr. 10....Minneapolis 84, @Syracuse 73
Apr. 11....Syracuse 65, @Minneapolis 63
Apr. 12....@Minneapolis 87, Syracuse 80

*Denotes number of overtime periods.

INDIVIDUAL LEADERS

SCORING

	G	FGM	FTM	Pts.	Avg.
Johnston, Philadelphia	72	591	577	1759	24.4
Cousy, Boston	72	486	411	1383	19.2
Macauley, Boston	71	462	420	1344	18.9
Mikan, Minneapolis	72	441	424	1306	18.1
Felix, Baltimore	72	410	449	1269	17.6
Schayes, Syracuse	72	370	488	1228	17.1
Sharman, Boston	72	412	331	1155	16.0
Foust, Fort Wayne	72	376	338	1090	15.1
Braun, New York	72	354	354	1062	14.8
Wanzer, Rochester	72	322	314	958	13.3

FIELD GOAL PCT. (minimum 210 made)

	FGM	FGA	Pct.
Macauley, Boston	462	950	.486
Sharman, Boston	412	915	.450
Johnston, Philadelphia	591	1317	.449
Lovellette, Minneapolis	237	560	.423
Felix, Baltimore	410	983	.417

FREE THROW PCT. (minimum 180 made)

	FTM	FTA	Pct.
Sharman, Boston	331	392	.844
Schayes, Syracuse	488	590	.827
Braun, New York	354	429	.825
Seymour, Syracuse	299	368	.813
Zawoluk, Philadelphia	186	230	.809

ASSISTS

	G	No.	Avg.
Cousy, Boston	72	518	7.2
Phillip, Fort Wayne	71	449	6.3
Seymour, Syracuse	71	364	5.1
McGuire, New York	68	354	5.2
Davies, Rochester	72	323	4.5

REBOUNDS

	G	No.	Avg.
Gallatin, New York	72	1098	15.3
Mikan, Minneapolis	72	1028	14.3
Foust, Fort Wayne	72	967	13.4
Felix, Baltimore	72	958	13.3
Schayes, Syracuse	72	870	12.1

1952-53 SEASON

Carl Braun

John Kundla's coaching career presents a study in delayed gratification. He directed the Lakers to six pro championships in the 1940s and '50s and yet had to wait four decades to gain entry into the Hall of Fame.

Kundla's Lakers roster featured Mikan, Jim Pollard and Vern Mikkelsen, which left observers assuming that he had little coaching to do.

"I've seen a lot of great teams, at least on paper, that won nothing," Red Auerbach noted. "Sure, Kundla had a great team, but he did great things with them."

By the 1953 playoffs, Kundla was in the midst of driving his team to its fourth NBA crown and its fifth overall league title.

Opponents tried to counter Mikan's power game with furious foulfests, prompting officials to whistle an average of 58 per game. If teams weren't trying to stop Mikan, they were zeroing in on Philly center Neil Johnston, the great hook shooter who won the first of his three consecutive scoring titles with a 22.3 average. The season also featured the rise of Celtics guards Bob Cousy and Bill Sharman.

Again the playoffs brought more highlights in New York, where the Knickerbockers won the Eastern Division, then held off Baltimore and Boston to reach the NBA Finals for the third straight year.

The Knickerbockers, with a lineup that featured Carl Braun, Dick McGuire, Harry Gallatin and Nat "Sweetwater" Clifton, even took a 1-0 series lead on the Lakers with an upset in Minneapolis. Their hopes, however, didn't last long. Kundla's team won the next four.

FINAL STANDINGS

EASTERN DIVISION

	W	L	Pct.
New York	47	23	.671
Syracuse	47	24	.662
Boston	46	25	.648
Baltimore	16	54	.229
Philadelphia	12	57	.174

WESTERN DIVISION

	W	L	Pct.
Minneapolis	48	22	.686
Rochester	44	26	.629
Fort Wayne	36	33	.522
Indianapolis	28	43	.394
Milwaukee	27	44	.380

NBA.COM FACT

In one of the most remarkable performances in postseason history, Boston's Bob Cousy scored a then playoff-record 50 points in a four-overtime, 111-105 series clincher against Syracuse on March 21. His 30 free throws made remains a league record, five decades later.

PLAYOFFS

EASTERN DIVISION

SEMIFINALS

New York 2, Baltimore 0

Mar. 17....@New York 80, Baltimore 62
Mar. 20....New York 90, @Baltimore 81

Boston 2, Syracuse 0

Mar. 19....Boston 87, @Syracuse 81
Mar. 21....@Boston 111, Syracuse 105****

FINALS

New York 3, Boston 1

Mar. 25....@New York 95, Boston 91
Mar. 26....@Boston 86, New York 70
Mar. 28....@New York 101, Boston 82
Mar. 29....New York 82, @Boston 75

WESTERN DIVISION

SEMIFINALS

Fort Wayne 2, Rochester 1

Mar. 20....Fort Wayne 84, @Rochester 77
Mar. 22....Rochester 83, @Fort Wayne 71
Mar. 24....Fort Wayne 67, @Rochester 65

Minneapolis 2, Indianapolis 0

Mar. 22....@Minneapolis 85, Indianapolis 69
Mar. 23....Minneapolis 81, @Indianapolis 79

FINALS

Minneapolis 3, Fort Wayne 2

Mar. 26....@Minneapolis 83, Fort Wayne 73
Mar. 28....@Minneapolis 82, Fort Wayne 75
Mar. 30....@Fort Wayne 98, Minneapolis 95
Apr. 1 ......@Fort Wayne 85, Minneapolis 82
Apr. 2 ......@Minneapolis 74, Fort Wayne 58

NBA FINALS

Minneapolis 4, New York 1

Apr. 4 ......New York 96, @Minneapolis 88
Apr. 5 ......@Minneapolis 73, New York 71
Apr. 7 ......Minneapolis 90, @New York 75
Apr. 8 ......Minneapolis 71, @New York 69
Apr. 10 ....Minneapolis 91, @New York 84

*Denotes number of overtime periods.

INDIVIDUAL LEADERS

SCORING

	G	FGM	FTM	Pts.	Avg.
Johnston, Philadelphia	70	504	556	1564	22.3
Mikan, Minneapolis	70	500	442	1442	20.6
Cousy, Boston	71	464	479	1407	19.8
Macauley, Boston	69	451	500	1402	20.3
Schayes, Syracuse	71	375	512	1262	17.8
Sharman, Boston	71	403	341	1147	16.2
Nichols, Milwaukee	69	425	240	1090	15.8
Mikkelsen, Minneapolis	70	378	291	1047	15.0
Davies, Rochester	66	339	351	1029	15.6
Wanzer, Rochester	70	318	384	1020	14.6

FIELD GOAL PCT. (minimum 210 made)

	FGM	FGA	Pct.
Johnston, Philadelphia	504	1114	.452
Macauley, Boston	451	997	.452
Gallatin, New York	282	635	.444
Sharman, Boston	403	925	.436
Mikkelsen, Minneapolis	378	868	.435

FREE THROW PCT. (minimum 180 made)

	FTM	FTA	Pct.
Sharman, Boston	341	401	.850
Scolari, Fort Wayne	276	327	.844
Schayes, Syracuse	512	619	.827
Braun, New York	331	401	.825
Schaus, Fort Wayne	243	296	.821

ASSISTS

	G	No.	Avg.
Cousy, Boston	71	547	7.7
Phillip, Philadelphia-Fort Wayne	70	397	5.7
King, Syracuse	71	364	5.1
McGuire, New York	61	296	4.9
Seymour, Syracuse	67	294	4.4

REBOUNDS

	G	No.	Avg.
Mikan, Minneapolis	70	1007	14.4
Johnston, Philadelphia	70	976	13.9
Schayes, Syracuse	71	920	13.0
Gallatin, New York	70	916	13.1
Hutchins, Milwaukee	71	793	11.2

1951-52 SEASON

Paul Arizin

Slowed during the 1951 playoffs by an ankle injury, George Mikan returned to the game in the fall and found it had changed. The lane had been widened, from six to 12 feet, on account of rule makers who thought it would diminish his dominance. Mikan's scoring average dipped, from 28.4 to 23.8 points per game, which allowed the Warriors' Paul Arizin to move ahead of him in the scoring race at 25.4. What was even more eye-opening to basketball aficionados was that Arizin, one of the game's early jump shooters, also posted the top field goal percentage (.448).

Point-shaving scandals rocked college basketball in 1951, and the issue cost two young NBA stars their pro careers. Alex Groza and Ralph Beard, both of the Indianapolis Olympians, were implicated for misdeeds at the University of Kentucky and subsequently banned from the NBA.

For the fist time since 1948-49, all NBA teams played the same number of games (66), and also for the first time, all 10 teams that had finished the previous season started and completed the next season. Mikan, Arizin and Boston's Ed Macauley and Bob Cousy made the All-NBA First Team, with Rochester's Bob Davies and Syracuse's Dolph Schayes sharing the fifth spot.

The Knickerbockers managed only a third-place finish in the East during the regular season but navigated their way through the playoffs to reach the Finals. The Western Division had its annual battle between the Royals and Lakers. Mikan's team reasserted itself this time around after having watched the Royals take the title in '51. The Knickerbockers fought to extend the NBA Finals to seven games, but the Lakers held home-court advantage and claimed Game 7 easily, 82-65.

FINAL STANDINGS

EASTERN DIVISION

	W	L	Pct.
Syracuse	40	26	.606
Boston	39	27	.591
New York	37	29	.561
Philadelphia	33	33	.500
Baltimore	20	46	.303

WESTERN DIVISION

	W	L	Pct.
Rochester	41	25	.621
Minneapolis	40	26	.606
Indianapolis	34	32	.515
Fort Wayne	29	37	.439
Milwaukee	17	49	.258

NBA.COM FACT

No sooner was the free throw lane widened than the backcourt stepped to the forefront. A half-dozen guards — Leo Barnhorst (Indianapolis), Bob Cousy (Boston), Bob Davies (Rochester), Andy Phillip (Philadelphia), Fred Schaus (Fort Wayne) and Bobby Wanzer (Rochester) — ranked among the top 20 in points.

PLAYOFFS

EASTERN DIVISION

SEMIFINALS

Syracuse 2, Philadelphia 1

Mar. 20....@Syracuse 102, Philadelphia 83
Mar. 22....@Philadelphia 100, Syracuse 95
Mar. 23....@Syracuse 84, Philadelphia 73

New York 2, Boston 1

Mar. 19....@Boston 105, New York 94
Mar. 23....@New York 101, Boston 97
Mar. 26....New York 88, @Boston 87**

FINALS

New York 3, Syracuse 1

Apr. 2 ......New York 87, @Syracuse 85
Apr. 3 ......@Syracuse 102, New York 92
Apr. 4 ......@New York 99, Syracuse 92
Apr. 8 ......@New York 100, Syracuse 93

WESTERN DIVISION

SEMIFINALS

Minneapolis 2, Indianapolis 0

Mar. 23....@Minneapolis 78, Indianapolis 70
Mar. 25....Minneapolis 94, @Indianapolis 87

Rochester 2, Fort Wayne 0

Mar. 18....@Rochester 95, Fort Wayne 78
Mar. 20....Rochester 92, @Fort Wayne 86

FINALS

Minneapolis 3, Rochester 1

Mar. 29....@Rochester 88, Minneapolis 78
Mar. 30....Minneapolis 83, @Rochester 78
Apr. 5 ......@Minneapolis 77, Rochester 67
Apr. 6 ......@Minneapolis 82, Rochester 80

NBA FINALS

Minneapolis 4, New York 3

Apr. 12 ....Minneapolis 83, New York 79* (@St. Paul)
Apr. 13 ....New York 80, Minneapolis 72 (@St. Paul)
Apr. 16 ....Minneapolis 82, @New York 77
Apr. 18 ....@New York 90, Minneapolis 89*
Apr. 20 ....Minneapolis 102, New York 89 (@St. Paul)
Apr. 23 ....@New York 76, Minneapolis 68
Apr. 25 ....@Minneapolis 82, New York 65

*Denotes number of overtime periods.

INDIVIDUAL LEADERS

SCORING

	G	FGM	FTM	Pts.	Avg.
Arizin, Philadelphia	66	548	578	1674	25.4
Mikan, Minneapolis	64	545	433	1523	23.8
Cousy, Boston	66	512	409	1433	21.7
Macauley, Boston	66	384	496	1264	19.2
Davies, Rochester	65	379	294	1052	16.2
Brian, Fort Wayne	66	342	367	1051	15.9
Foust, Fort Wayne	66	390	267	1047	15.9
Wanzer, Rochester	66	328	377	1033	15.7
Risen, Rochester	66	365	302	1032	15.6
Mikkelsen, Minneapolis	66	363	283	1009	15.3

FIELD GOAL PCT. (minimum 210 made)

	FGM	FGA	Pct.
Arizin, Philadelphia	548	1222	.448
Gallatin, New York	233	527	.442
Macauley, Boston	384	888	.432
Wanzer, Rochester	328	772	.425
Mikkelsen, Minneapolis	363	866	.419

FREE THROW PCT. (minimum 180 made)

	FTM	FTA	Pct.
Wanzer, Rochester	377	417	.904
Cervi, Syracuse	219	248	.883
Sharman, Boston	183	213	.859
Brian, Fort Wayne	367	433	.848
Scolari, Baltimore	353	423	.835

ASSISTS

	G	No.	Avg.
Phillip, Philadelphia	66	539	8.2
Cousy, Boston	66	441	6.7
Davies, Rochester	65	390	6.0
McGuire, New York	64	388	6.1
Scolari, Baltimore	64	303	4.7

REBOUNDS

	G	No.	Avg.
Foust, Fort Wayne	66	880	13.3
Hutchins, Milwaukee	66	880	13.3
Mikan, Minneapolis	64	866	13.5
Risen, Rochester	66	841	12.7
Schayes, Syracuse	63	773	12.3

1950-51 SEASON

Chuck Cooper

It was a rough year for NBA franchises. Six — Chicago, St. Louis, Anderson, Sheboygan, Waterloo and Denver — expired in the offseason, shrinking the league from 17 teams to 11. Then the Washington Capitols, who had lost Coach Red Auerbach to Tri-Cities a year earlier, folded in January with a 10-25 record.

Chuck Cooper became the first African-American player to be drafted when he was chosen by Boston, New York's Nat "Sweetwater" Clifton became the first to sign an NBA contract, and Earl Lloyd became the first to play in an NBA regular-season game when Washington opened play first. Another first occurred March 2, 1951, when the East defeated the West 111-94 at Boston Garden in the first NBA All-Star Game.

The turmoil of losing franchises left the standings a mess, with teams playing different numbers of games. Philadelphia won the East while Minneapolis beat Rochester by three games in the West. In the playoffs, though, New York rolled past Boston and edged Syracuse to reach the Finals. Rochester, behind 6-9 Arnie Risen and backcourt star Bob Davies, defeated Fort Wayne and finally overcame Minneapolis (with Mikan slowed by an injury) to meet the Knickerbockers.

Coached by owner Les Harrison, Rochester took the first three games of the Finals, but New York fought back, winning the next three by margins of six, three and seven points to send the NBA Finals to its first seventh game. Playing at home, the Royals led by 16 early, but the Knickerbockers took a late two-point lead. With 40 seconds left, Davies sank two free throws that were key in Rochester's 79-75 victory.

FINAL STANDINGS

EASTERN DIVISION

	W	L	Pct.
Philadelphia	40	26	.606
Boston	39	30	.565
New York	36	30	.545
Syracuse	32	34	.485
Baltimore	24	42	.364
Washington*	10	25	.286

WESTERN DIVISION

	W	L	Pct.
Minneapolis	44	24	.647
Rochester	41	27	.603
Fort Wayne	32	36	.471
Indianapolis	31	37	.456
Tri-Cities	25	43	.368

*Washington team was disbanded January 9; players assigned to other teams.

NBA.COM FACT

In what remains the lowest-scoring game in NBA history, Larry Foust scored with six seconds left in regulation play to give Fort Wayne a 19-18 victory against host Minneapolis on Nov. 22. The game produced a total of eight field goals, four by each team.

PLAYOFFS

EASTERN DIVISION

SEMIFINALS

New York 2, Boston 0

Mar. 20....New York 83, @Boston 69
Mar. 22....@New York 92, Boston 78

Syracuse 2, Philadelphia 0

Mar. 20....Syracuse 91, @Philadelphia 89*
Mar. 22....@Syracuse 90, Philadelphia 78

FINALS

New York 3, Syracuse 2

Mar. 28....@New York 103, Syracuse 92
Mar. 29....@Syracuse 102, New York 80
Mar. 31....@New York 77, Syracuse 75
Apr. 1......@Syracuse 90, New York 83
Apr. 4......@New York 83, Syracuse 81

WESTERN DIVISION

SEMIFINALS

Rochester 2, Fort Wayne 1

Mar. 20....@Rochester 110, Fort Wayne 81
Mar. 22....@Fort Wayne 83, Rochester 78
Mar. 24....@Rochester 97, Fort Wayne 78

Minneapolis 2, Indianapolis 1

Mar. 21....@Minneapolis 95, Indianapolis 81
Mar. 23....@Indianapolis 108, Minneapolis 88
Mar. 25....@Minneapolis 85, Indianapolis 80

FINALS

Rochester 3, Minneapolis 1

Mar. 29....@Minneapolis 76, Rochester 73
Mar. 31....Rochester 70, @Minneapolis 66
Apr. 1......@Rochester 83, Minneapolis 70
Apr. 3......@Rochester 80, Minneapolis 75

NBA FINALS

Rochester 4, New York 3

Apr. 7......@Rochester 92, New York 65
Apr. 8......@Rochester 99, New York 84
Apr. 11....Rochester 78, @New York 71
Apr. 13....@New York 79, Rochester 73
Apr. 15....New York 92, @Rochester 89
Apr. 18....@New York 80, Rochester 73
Apr. 21....@Rochester 79, New York 75

*Denotes number of overtime periods.

INDIVIDUAL LEADERS

SCORING

	G	FGM	FTM	Pts.	Avg.
Mikan, Minneapolis	68	678	576	1932	28.4
Groza, Indianapolis	66	492	445	1429	21.7
Macauley, Boston	68	459	466	1384	20.4
Fulks, Philadelphia	66	429	378	1236	18.7
Brian, Tri-Cities	68	363	418	1144	16.8
Arizin, Philadelphia	65	352	417	1121	17.2
Schayes, Syracuse	66	332	457	1121	17.0
Beard, Indianapolis	66	409	293	1111	16.8
Cousy, Boston	69	401	276	1078	15.6
Risen, Rochester	66	377	323	1077	16.3

FIELD GOAL PCT. (minimum 200 made)

	FGM	FGA	Pct.
Groza, Indianapolis	492	1046	.470
Macauley, Boston	459	985	.466
Mikan, Minneapolis	678	1584	.428
Coleman, Rochester	315	749	.421
Gallatin, New York	293	705	.416

FREE THROW PCT. (minimum 170 made)

	FTM	FTA	Pct.
Fulks, Philadelphia	378	442	.855
Smawley, Syracuse-Baltimore	227	267	.850
Wanzer, Rochester	232	273	.850
Scolari, Washington-Syracuse	279	331	.843
Boryla, New York	278	332	.837

ASSISTS

	G	No.	Avg.
Phillip, Philadelphia	66	414	6.3
McGuire, New York	64	400	6.3
Senesky, Philadelphia	65	342	5.3
Cousy, Boston	69	341	4.9
Beard, Indianapolis	66	318	4.8

REBOUNDS

	G	No.	Avg.
Schayes, Syracuse	66	1080	16.4
Mikan, Minneapolis	68	958	14.1
Gallatin, New York	66	800	12.1
Risen, Rochester	66	795	12.0
Groza, Indianapolis	66	709	10.7

1949-50 SEASON

Dolph Schayes (4)

The Lakers, already loaded with talent, hauled in two Hall of Famers in the 1949 draft: point guard Slater Martin and power forward Vern Mikkelsen. So what if the Syracuse Nationals rang up a 51-13 record during the regular season? The Mikan Machine still rolled in the springtime. The season marked a major convergence in pro hoops: The six surviving teams of the National Basketball League joined the Basketball Association of America to form the newly named NBA. The league was split into Eastern, Central and Western divisions. Syracuse, the only original NBL team in the East, won that division behind the play of 6-8 Dolph Schayes, who averaged 16.8 points per game. Alex Groza averaged 23.4 points for a new Indianapolis team that won the West, while Mikan led the league again with 27.4 points and helped the Lakers win the Central Division. With three divisions, the playoffs were a jumble. Minneapolis had to beat Chicago, Fort Wayne and Anderson to reach the Finals, while Syracuse had to defeat only Philadelphia and New York to qualify. The Nationals, though, offered speed and finesse, something that was no match for the Lakers' power. Syracuse fell in six. Helping out the Lakers was Minneapolis Auditorium, a court several feet narrower than the standard. "They used to say that when Mikan, Mikkelsen and Pollard stretched their arms across that narrow court, nobody could get through," said Syracuse player-coach Al Cervi. "Those three made every court look narrow," Nationals guard Paul Seymour added.

FINAL STANDINGS

EASTERN DIVISION

	W	L	Pct.
Syracuse	51	13	.797
New York	40	28	.588
Washington	32	36	.471
Philadelphia	26	42	.382
Baltimore	25	43	.368
Boston	22	46	.324

CENTRAL DIVISION

	W	L	Pct.
Minneapolis*	51	17	.750
Rochester	51	17	.750
Fort Wayne*	40	28	.588
Chicago	40	28	.588
St. Louis	26	42	.382

*Won playoff to break tie

WESTERN DIVISION

	W	L	Pct.
Indianapolis	39	25	.609
Anderson	37	27	.578
Tri-Cities	29	35	.453
Sheboygan	22	40	.355
Waterloo	19	43	.306
Denver	11	51	.177

NBA.COM FACT

Indianapolis (23-5), Minneapolis (30-1), Ft. Wayne (28-6) and Syracuse (31-1) were virtually unbeatable at home. The trend continued in the postseason, when the home team prevailed in 23 of 32 games, including the last five in the NBA Finals.

PLAYOFFS

EASTERN DIVISION

SEMIFINALS

Syracuse 2, Philadelphia 0

Mar. 22....@Syracuse 93, Philadelphia 76
Mar. 23....Syracuse 59, @Philadelphia 53

New York 2, Washington 0

Mar. 21....New York 90, @Washington 87
Mar. 22....@New York 103, Washington 83

FINALS

Syracuse 2, New York 1

Mar. 26....@Syracuse 91, New York 83*
Mar. 30....@New York 80, Syracuse 76
Apr. 2......@Syracuse 91, New York 80

CENTRAL DIVISION

FIRST-PLACE TIEBREAKER

Mar. 21....Minneapolis 78, @Rochester 76

THIRD-PLACE TIEBREAKER

Mar. 20....@Fort Wayne 86, Chicago 69

SEMIFINALS

Minneapolis 2, Chicago 0

Mar. 22....@Minneapolis 85, Chicago 75
Mar. 25....Minneapolis 75, @Chicago 67

Fort Wayne 2, Rochester 0

Mar. 23....Fort Wayne 90, @Rochester 84
Mar. 25....@Fort Wayne 79, Rochester 78*

FINALS

Minneapolis 2, Fort Wayne 0

Mar. 27....@Minneapolis 93, Fort Wayne 79
Mar. 28....Minneapolis 89, @Fort Wayne 82

WESTERN DIVISION

SEMIFINALS

Indianapolis 2, Sheboygan 1

Mar. 21....@Indianapolis 86, Sheboygan 85
Mar. 23....@Sheboygan 95, Indianapolis 85
Mar. 25....@Indianapolis 91, Sheboygan 84

Anderson 2, Tri-Cities 1

Mar. 21....@Anderson 89, Tri-Cities 77
Mar. 23....@Tri-Cities 76, Anderson 75
Mar. 24....@Anderson 94, Tri-Cities 71

FINALS

Anderson 2, Indianapolis 1

Mar. 28....@Indianapolis 77, Anderson 74
Mar. 30....@Anderson 84, Indianapolis 67
Apr. 1......Anderson 67, @Indianapolis 65

NBA SEMIFINALS

Minneapolis 2, Anderson 0

Apr. 5......@Minneapolis 75, Anderson 50
Apr. 6......Minneapolis 90, @Anderson 71

NBA FINALS

Minneapolis 4, Syracuse 2

Apr. 8......Minneapolis 68, @Syracuse 66
Apr. 9......@Syracuse 91, Minneapolis 85
Apr. 14....Minneapolis 91, Syracuse 77 (@St. Paul)
Apr. 16....Minneapolis 77, Syracuse 69 (@St. Paul)
Apr. 20....@Syracuse 83, Minneapolis 76
Apr. 23....@Minneapolis 110, Syracuse 95

*Denotes number of overtime periods.

INDIVIDUAL LEADERS

SCORING

	G	FGM	FTM	Pts.	Avg.
Mikan, Minneapolis	68	649	567	1865	27.4
Groza, Indianapolis	64	521	454	1496	23.4
Brian, Anderson	64	368	402	1138	17.8
Zaslofsky, Chicago	68	397	321	1115	16.4
Macauley, St. Louis	67	351	379	1081	16.1
Schayes, Syracuse	64	348	376	1072	16.8
Braun, New York	67	373	285	1031	15.4
Sailors, Denver	57	329	329	987	17.3
Pollard, Minneapolis	66	394	185	973	14.7
Schaus, Fort Wayne	68	351	270	972	14.3

FIELD GOAL PCT. (minimum 200 made)

	FGM	FGA	Pct.
Groza, Indianapolis	521	1090	.478
Mehen, Waterloo	347	826	.420
Wanzer, Rochester	254	614	.414
Boykoff, Waterloo	288	698	.413
Mikan, Minneapolis	649	1595	.407

FREE THROW PCT. (minimum 170 made)

	FTM	FTA	Pct.
Zaslofsky, Chicago	321	381	.843
Reiser, Washington	212	254	.835
Cervi, Syracuse	287	346	.829
Smawley, St. Louis	260	314	.828
Curran, Rochester	199	241	.826

ASSISTS

	G	No.	Avg.
McGuire, New York	68	386	5.7
Phillip, Chicago	65	377	5.8
Davies, Rochester	64	294	4.6
Cervi, Syracuse	56	264	4.7
Senesky, Philadelphia	68	264	3.9

1948-49 SEASON

George Mikan

The Minneapolis Lakers won the 1948 National League title, then jumped to the Basketball Association of America the next year and won that one, too. The BAA clearly had the best arenas in the bigger cities, but the National Basketball League, featuring teams in smaller Midwestern cities, claimed the best players. This changed, however, prior to the 1948 season, when three other NBL teams — Fort Wayne, Rochester, and Indianapolis — joined the Lakers in moving to the BAA. George Mikan led the Lakers. At 6-10 and 245 pounds, he dominated the game with his inside scoring, hook shooting right and left. He shot .416 from the floor while averaging a league-leading 28.3 points, earning him the first of three consecutive league scoring titles. Just behind Mikan in the scoring race was jump-shooting Joe Fulks, the Kentucky hillbilly who rifled in 26.0 points per game for the Philadelphia Warriors. With 12 teams, the NBA played a 60-game schedule, with Washington (coached by Red Auerbach) finishing first in the Eastern Division and Rochester besting Minneapolis by one game in the West. The two teams went on to meet in the Finals. Mikan scored 42 points in Game 1 and, despite breaking his wrist in Game 4, led the Lakers over Auerbach's Capitols in six games. "He wore a cast that was as hard as a brick," recalled Washington's Horace "Bones" McKinney, who guarded Mikan in the series. "It fit right in with his elbows. It would kill you. And it didn't bother his shooting a bit."

FINAL STANDINGS

EASTERN DIVISION

	W	L	Pct.
Washington	38	22	.633
New York	32	28	.533
Baltimore	29	31	.483
Philadelphia	28	32	.467
Boston	25	35	.417
Providence	12	48	.200

WESTERN DIVISION

	W	L	Pct.
Rochester	45	15	.750
Minneapolis	44	16	.733
Chicago	38	22	.633
St. Louis	29	31	.483
Fort Wayne	22	38	.367
Indianapolis	18	42	.300

NBA.COM FACT

Although triple teamed for much of the game, Minneapolis center George Mikan erupted for 48 points in a 101-74 rout of New York on Feb. 22. At the time, the output was the third-highest total for one player in BAA history and the most ever at Madison Square Garden.

PLAYOFFS

EASTERN DIVISION

SEMIFINALS

Washington 2, Philadelphia 0

Mar. 23....Washington 92, @Philadelphia 70
Mar. 24....@Washington 80, Philadelphia 78

New York 2, Baltimore 1

Mar. 23....@Baltimore 82, New York 81
Mar. 24....@New York 84, Baltimore 82
Mar. 26....@New York 103, Baltimore 99*

FINALS

Washington 2, New York 1

Mar. 29....@Washington 77, New York 71
Mar. 31....@New York 86, Washington 84*
Apr. 2 ......@Washington 84, New York 76

WESTERN DIVISION

SEMIFINALS

Rochester 2, St. Louis 0

Mar. 22....@Rochester 93, St. Louis 64
Mar. 23....Rochester 66, @St. Louis 64

Minneapolis 2, Chicago 0

Mar. 23....@Minneapolis 84, Chicago 77
Mar. 24....Minneapolis 101, @Chicago 85

FINALS

Minneapolis 2, Rochester 0

Mar. 27..........Minneapolis 80, @Rochester 79
Mar. 29..........Minneapolis 67, Rochester 55 (@St. Paul)

NBA FINALS

Minneapolis 4, Washington 2

Apr. 4............@Minneapolis 88, Washington 84
Apr. 6............@Minneapolis 76, Washington 62
Apr. 8............Minneapolis 94, @Washington 74
Apr. 9............@Washington 83, Minneapolis 71
Apr. 11..........@Washington 74, Minneapolis 65
Apr. 13..........Minneapolis 77, Washington 56 (@St. Paul)

*Denotes number of overtime periods.

INDIVIDUAL LEADERS

SCORING

	G	FGM	FTM	Pts.	Avg.
Mikan, Minneapolis	60	583	532	1698	28.3
Fulks, Philadelphia	60	529	502	1560	26.0
Zaslofsky, Chicago	58	425	347	1197	20.6
Risen, Rochester	60	345	305	995	16.6
Sadowski, Philadelphia	60	340	240	920	15.3
Smawley, St. Louis	59	352	210	914	15.5
Davies, Rochester	60	317	270	904	15.1
Sailors, Providence	57	309	281	899	15.8
Braun, New York	57	299	212	810	14.2
Logan, St. Louis	57	282	239	803	14.1

FIELD GOAL PCT. (minimum 200 made)

	FGM	FGA	Pct.
Risen, Rochester	345	816	.423
Mikan, Minneapolis	583	1403	.416
Sadowski, Philadelphia	340	839	.405
Pollard, Minneapolis	314	792	.396
Rocha, St. Louis	223	574	.389

FREE THROW PCT. (minimum 150 made)

	FTM	FTA	Pct.
Feerick, Washington	256	298	.859
Zaslofsky, Chicago	347	413	.840
Wanzer, Rochester	209	254	.823
Schaefer, Minneapolis	174	213	.817
Shannon, Providence	152	189	.804

ASSISTS

	G	No.	Avg.
Davies, Rochester	60	321	5.4
Phillip, Chicago	60	319	5.3
Logan, St. Louis	57	276	4.8
Calverley, Providence	59	251	4.3
Senesky, Philadelphia	60	233	3.9

1947-48 SEASON

Joe Lapchick

Life was fragile for pro basketball teams in the 1940s. Heading into its second year of operation, the Basketball Association of America lost four of its original 11 franchises. Detroit, Cleveland, Toronto and Pittsburgh all slipped into past tense. To cut costs, the BAA reduced the schedule to 48 games. The league still needed an eighth team to fill out two divisions, so it added the Baltimore Bullets. The newcomer went all the way to the championship. The Bullets had a talented roster that included 5-11 player-coach Buddy Jeannette, 6-8 center Clarence "Kleggie" Hermsen, guard Chick Reiser, and forwards Paul Hoffman and Connie Simmons. Philadelphia's Jumpin' Joe Fulks averaged 22.1 points in leading the Warriors, but the scoring title in those days was awarded on total points. Fulks missed five games, which allowed Chicago's Max Zaslofsky to take it with a 21.0 average because he was the only player who broke the 1,000-point barrier. Perhaps the most telling stat was the field goal percentage, led by Washington's Bob Feerick at an icy .340. Only Baltimore shot at least .300. Interest jumped in New York when Joe Lapchick, who had played for the Original Celtics and coached at St. John's, signed on to coach the Knicks. The Bullets bested the Warriors in six games in the championship series, highlighted by Baltimore's comeback from a 21-point halftime deficit in Game 2, which stands as the best in NBA playoff history. The Bullets played in a dingy old coliseum in one of Baltimore's poorer neighborhoods. "I'll tell you how bad it was," said player-coach Jeannette. "When they quit using it as an arena, they made a garage out of it."

FINAL STANDINGS

EASTERN DIVISION

	W	L	Pct.
Philadelphia	27	21	.563
New York	26	22	.542
Boston	20	28	.417
Providence	6	42	.125

WESTERN DIVISION

	W	L	Pct.
St. Louis	29	19	.604
Baltimore*	28	20	.583
Chicago	28	20	.583
Washington	28	20	.583

*Won playoff to break tie

NBA.COM FACT

Prior to the start of the season, two significant rules changes were approved. Players were allowed six fouls before disqualification, an increase from five the previous season. And teams were limited to 10 members — two fewer than the previous season — of which a minimum of nine had to be in uniform for each game.

PLAYOFFS

WESTERN DIVISION TIEBREAKERS

Mar. 23....@Chicago 74, Washington 70
Mar. 25....Baltimore 75, @Chicago 72

QUARTERFINALS

Baltimore 2, New York 1

Mar. 27....@Baltimore 85, New York 81
Mar. 28....@New York 79, Baltimore 69
Apr. 1......@Baltimore 84, New York 77

Chicago 2, Boston 1

Mar. 28....Chicago 79, @Boston 72
Mar. 31....@Boston 81, Chicago 77
Apr. 2......Chicago 81, @Boston 74

SEMIFINALS

Philadelphia 4, St. Louis 3

Mar. 23....@St. Louis 60, Philadelphia 58
Mar. 25....Philadelphia 65, @St. Louis 64
Mar. 27....@Philadelphia 84, St. Louis 56
Mar. 30....St. Louis 56, @Philadelphia 51
Apr. 1......@St. Louis 69, Philadelphia 62
Apr. 3......@Philadelphia 84, St. Louis 61
Apr. 6......Philadelphia 85, @St. Louis 46

Baltimore 2, Chicago 0

Apr. 7......Baltimore 73, @Chicago 67
Apr. 8......@Baltimore 89, Chicago 72

NBA FINALS

Baltimore 4, Philadelphia 2

Apr. 10....@Philadelphia 71, Baltimore 60
Apr. 13....Baltimore 66, @Philadelphia 63
Apr. 15....@Baltimore 72, Philadelphia 70
Apr. 17....@Baltimore 78, Philadelphia 75
Apr. 20....@Philadelphia 91, Baltimore 82
Apr. 21....@Baltimore 88, Philadelphia 73

INDIVIDUAL LEADERS

SCORING

	G	FGM	FTM	Pts.	Avg.
Zaslofsky, Chicago	48	373	261	1007	21.0
Fulks, Philadelphia	43	326	297	949	22.1
Sadowski, Boston	47	308	294	910	19.4
Feerick, Washington	48	293	189	775	16.1
Miasek, Chicago	48	263	190	716	14.9
Braun, New York	47	276	119	671	14.3
Logan, St. Louis	48	221	202	644	13.4
Palmer, New York	48	224	174	622	13.0
Rocha, St. Louis	48	232	147	611	12.7
Scolari, Washington	47	229	131	589	12.5

FIELD GOAL PCT. (minimum 200 made)

	FGM	FGA	Pct.
Feerick, Washington	293	861	.340
Braun, New York	276	854	.323
Sadowski, Boston	308	953	.323
Zaslofsky, Chicago	373	1156	.323
Reiser, Baltimore	202	628	.322
Palmer, New York	224	710	.315
Rocha, St. Louis	232	740	.314
Riebe, Boston	202	653	.309
Smawley, St. Louis	212	688	.308
Miasek, Chicago	263	867	.303

FREE THROW PCT. (minimum 125 made)

	FTM	FTA	Pct.
Feerick, Washington	189	240	.788
Zaslofsky, Chicago	261	333	.784
Fulks, Philadelphia	297	390	.762
Jeannette, Baltimore	191	252	.758
Palmer, New York	174	234	.744

ASSISTS

	G	No.	Avg.
Dallmar, Philadelphia	48	120	2.5
Calverley, Providence	47	119	2.5
Seminoff, Chicago	48	89	1.9
Gilmur, Chicago	48	77	1.6
Phillip, Chicago	32	74	2.3

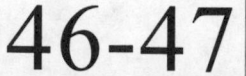

1946-47 SEASON

Joe Fulks (10)

When the Basketball Association of American was formed, Eddie Gottlieb knew the new league needed star power. So Gottlieb, the coach and general manager of the Philadelphia Warriors, made sure that Joe Fulks played as much as possible. The more Fulks played, the more he would score and the more fans would be interested, Gottlieb figured. He was right. The jump-shooting Fulks became a star, averaging 23.2 points (6.4 more than the next highest player) in the days of lopsided balls, dimly lit gyms, no 24-second shot clock, sparse crowds. Led by the 6-5 Fulks, they won the BAA's first title. Communication, though, was a bit of a problem. Fulks' city-bred teammates weren't sure what to make of his Kentucky twang. "It took me about a month and a half before I could understand him," Howie Dallmar recalled. Ernie Calverley of the Providence Steamrollers led the league with 3.4 assists per game. Other stars in the fledgling league were Washington's Bob Feerick and Bones McKinney, Detroit's Stan Miasek and Chicago's Max Zaslofsky. The 60-game regular season belonged to the Washington Capitols. Coached by Red Auerbach to a 49-11 record, they had a 29-1 mark at home. But the playoffs featured an old hockey format where the best teams played in the first round. Chicago shocked the Capitols behind the play of Zaslofsky and center Chuck Halbert to advance to the Finals. The Warriors defeated St. Louis and New York to reach the championship series, where Fulks, Dallmar and Angelo Musi led Philadelphia past Chicago 4-1. The Warriors' players pocketed about $2,000 per man in bonus money.

FINAL STANDINGS

EASTERN DIVISION

	W	L	Pct.
Washington	49	11	.817
Philadelphia	35	25	.583
New York	33	27	.550
Providence	28	32	.467
Boston	22	38	.367
Toronto	22	38	.367

WESTERN DIVISION

	W	L	Pct.
Chicago	39	22	.639
St. Louis	38	23	.623
Cleveland	30	30	.500
Detroit	20	40	.333
Pittsburgh	15	45	.250

NBA.COM FACT

The debut of professional basketball definitely wasn't your father's NBA. More like your grandfather's BAA, as in the Basketball Association of America. None of the original 11 teams shot as much as 30 percent from the field or averaged as many as 80 points for the season. Evidently, eliminating zone defenses in the middle of the season didn't help.

PLAYOFFS

QUARTERFINALS

New York 2, Cleveland 1

Apr. 2 ......@Cleveland 77, New York 51
Apr. 5 ......@New York 86, Cleveland 74
Apr. 9 ......@New York 93, Cleveland 71

Philadelphia 2, St. Louis 1

Apr. 2 ......@Philadelphia 73, St. Louis 68
Apr. 5 ......@St. Louis 73, Philadelphia 51
Apr. 6 ......Philadelphia 75, @St. Louis 59

SEMIFINALS

Chicago 4, Washington 2

Apr. 2 ......Chicago 81, @Washington 65
Apr. 3 ......Chicago 69, @Washington 53
Apr. 8 ......@Chicago 67, Washington 55
Apr. 10 ....@Washington 76, Chicago 69
Apr. 12 ....Washington 67, @Chicago 55
Apr. 13 ....@Chicago 66, Washington 61

Philadelphia 2, New York 0

Apr. 12 ....@Philadelphia 82, New York 70
Apr. 14 ....Philadelphia 72, @New York 53

NBA FINALS

Philadelphia 4, Chicago 1

Apr. 16 ....@Philadelphia 84, Chicago 71
Apr. 17 ....@Philadelphia 85, Chicago 74
Apr. 19 ....Philadelphia 75, @Chicago 72
Apr. 20 ....@Chicago 74, Philadelphia 73
Apr. 22 ....@Philadelphia 83, Chicago 80

INDIVIDUAL LEADERS

SCORING

	G	FGM	FTM	Pts.	Avg.
Fulks, Philadelphia	60	475	439	1389	23.2
Feerick, Washington	55	364	198	926	16.8
Miasek, Detroit	60	331	233	895	14.9
Sadowski, Toronto-Cleveland	53	329	219	877	16.5
Zaslofsky, Chicago	61	336	205	877	14.4
Calverley, Providence	59	323	199	845	14.3
Halbert, Chicago	61	280	213	773	12.7
Logan, St. Louis	61	290	190	770	12.6
Mogus, Cleveland-Toronto	58	259	235	753	13.0
Gunther, Pittsburgh	52	254	226	734	14.1

FIELD GOAL PCT. (minimum 200 made)

	FGM	FGA	Pct.
Feerick, Washington	364	908	.401
Sadowski, Toronto-Cleveland	329	891	.369
Shannon, Providence	245	722	.339
Gunther, Pittsburgh	254	756	.336
Zaslofsky, Chicago	336	1020	.329
Carlson, Chicago	272	845	.322
Simmons, Boston	246	768	.320
Norlander, Washington	223	698	.319
Sailors, Cleveland	229	741	.309
Riebe, Cleveland	276	898	.307

FREE THROW PCT. (minimum 125 made)

	FTM	FTA	Pct.
Scolari, Washington	146	180	.811
Kappen, Pittsburgh-Boston	128	161	.795
Stutz, New York	133	170	.782
Feerick, Washington	198	260	.762
Logan, St. Louis	190	254	.748

ASSISTS

	G	No.	Avg.
Calverley, Providence	59	202	3.4
Sailors, Cleveland	58	134	2.3
Schectman, New York	54	109	2.0
Dallmar, Philadelphia	60	104	1.7
Miasek, Detroit	60	93	1.6
Rottner, Chicago	56	93	1.7

CHAPTER 19

ABA SEASONS IN REVIEW

ABA Champions 1976-1967

1975-76	New York Nets
1974-75	Kentucky Colonels
1973-74	New York Nets
1972-73	Indiana Pacers
1971-72	Indiana Pacers
1970-71	Utah Stars
1969-70	Indiana Pacers
1968-69	Oakland Oaks
1967-68	Pittsburgh Pipers

The Oakland Oaks won the second ABA Championship in 1969 and several members of the team either already had or eventually would have an impact in the NBA. Alex Hannum, the coach, had won titles with two teams in the NBA: the 1958 St. Louis Hawks and the 1967 Philadelphia 76ers. Future coaches Larry Brown and Doug Moe were key members of the team, and the league's leading scorer was Rick Barry, who later would return to the NBA and go on to a Hall of Fame career.

OAKLAND OAKS—1968-69 AMERICAN BASKETBALL ASSOCIATION CHAMPIONS
FRONT ROW, LEFT TO RIGHT—JOHN CLAWSON, HENRY LOGAN,
LARRY BROWN, RUSS CRITCHFIELD, WARREN ARMSTRONG.
STANDING, LEFT TO RIGHT—COACH ALEX HANNUM, MEL PETERSON,
DOUG MOE, IRA HARGE, JIM EAKINS, GARY BRADDS, RICK BARRY.

1975-76 SEASON

Julius Erving

Dissension marred the start of the ninth and final season of the ABA. Before it began, both the New York Nets and Denver Nuggets — two of the more stable teams in the league — sought to join the NBA, and the season got underway with their applications in limbo. Meanwhile, Memphis had relocated and intended to start the season as the Baltimore Claws. But the franchise never got to play a game, folding before the season tipped off. San Diego began the season but folded after 11 games and Utah folded after 16, leaving seven teams to finish the season.

Julius Erving won his third ABA scoring title, leading the Nets to 55 victories. In two classic semifinal matchups, which both stretched to seven games, New York defeated San Antonio and Denver beat Kentucky.

In the Finals, the Nets beat the Nuggets in six games to win their second, and the league's last, ABA championship. Erving, again, captured both the regular season and playoffs MVP Awards.

On June 17, 1976, one month after the final ABA game was played, four ABA teams — Denver, Indiana, New York and San Antonio — were absorbed into the NBA.

FINAL STANDINGS

	W	L	PCT.
Denver	60	24	.714
New York	55	29	.655
San Antonio	50	34	.595
Kentucky	46	38	.548
Indiana	39	45	.464
St. Louis	35	49	.417
San Diego*	3	8	.273
Utah*	4	12	.250
Virginia	15	68	.181

*San Diego and Utah disbanded and did not finish the season

NBA.COM FACT

Going out in style: The playoffs consisted of two great semifinal rounds, with Kentucky extending Denver to seven games and San Antonio matching the feat against New York. Julius Erving dominated in his and the league's final postseason, averaging 34.7 points in 13 games.

PLAYOFFS

FIRST ROUND

Kentucky 2, Indiana 1

Apr. 8 ......Kentucky 120, Indiana 109
Apr. 10 ....Indiana 109, Kentucky 95
Apr. 12 ....Kentucky 100, Indiana 99

SEMIFINALS

Denver 4, Kentucky 3

Apr. 15 ....Denver 110, Kentucky 107
Apr. 17 ....Kentucky 138, Denver 119
Apr. 19 ....Kentucky 126, Denver 114
Apr. 21 ....Denver 108, Kentucky 106
Apr. 22 ....Denver 127, Kentucky 117
Apr. 25 ....Kentucky 119, Denver 115
Apr. 28 ....Denver 133, Kentucky 110

New York 4, San Antonio 3

Apr. 9 ......New York 116, San Antonio 101
Apr. 11 ....San Antonio 105, New York 79
Apr. 14 ....San Antonio 111, New York 103
Apr. 18 ....New York 110, San Antonio 108
Apr. 19 ....New York 110, San Antonio 108
Apr. 21 ....San Antonio 106, San Antonio 105
Apr. 24 ....New York 121, San Antonio 114

ABA FINALS

New York 4, Denver 2

May 1 ......New York 120, Denver 118
May 4 ......Denver 127, New York 121
May 6 ......New York 117, Denver 111
May 8 ......New York 121, Denver 112
May 11 ....Denver 118, New York 110
May 13 ....New York 112, Denver 106

INDIVIDUAL LEADERS

SCORING (Minimum 900 points)

	G.	FG	FT	PTS.	AVG
Erving, New York	84	949	530	2462	29.3
Knight, Indiana	70	774	415	1969	28.1
Thompson, Denver	83	807	541	2158	26.0
Gilmore, Kentucky	84	773	521	2067	24.6
Barnes, St. Louis	67	681	251	1616	24.1
Silas, San Antonio	84	718	564	2000	23.8
Issel, Denver	84	752	425	1930	23.0
Boone, Utah-St.L.	78	713	277	1719	22.0
Gervin, San Antonio	81	706	342	1768	21.8
Burden, Virginia	71	561	283	1413	19.9

3-PT. FIELD GOAL PCT. (Minimum 13 made)

	FGM	FGA	PCT.
Taylor, New York	32	76	.421
Boone, Utah-St.L.	16	43	.372
Dampier, Kentucky	32	87	.368
Keller, Indiana	123	349	.352
Buse, Indiana	72	208	.346

FIELD GOAL PCT. (Minimum 220 FG made)

	FGM	FGA	PCT.
Jones, Denver	510	878	.581
Gilmore, Kentucky	773	1401	.552
Hughes, New York	300	566	.530
Silas, San Antonio	718	1384	.519
Beck, Denver	334	646	.517

FREE THROW PCT. (Minimum 150 FT made)

	FTM	FTA	PCT.
Keller, Indiana	164	183	.896
Eakins, Utah-Vir.-NY	198	223	.888
Calvin, Virginia	253	285	.888
Silas, San Antonio	564	647	.872
Boone, Utah-St.L.	277	318	.871

ASSISTS (Minimum 225)

	G.	No.	AVG.
Buse, Indiana	84	689	8.2
Simpson, Denver	84	597	7.1
Calvin, Virginia	45	271	6.0
Dampier, Kentucky	82	467	5.7
Silas, San Antonio	84	452	5.4

REBOUNDS (Minimum 550)

	G.	OFF.	DEF.	TOT.	AVG.
Gilmore, Kentucky	84	402	901	1303	15.5
Lucas, St.L.-Ken.	86	297	673	970	11.3
Jones, S.D.-Ken.-St.L.	76	246	607	853	11.2
Kenon, San Antonio	81	287	610	897	11.1
Erving, New York	84	337	588	925	11.0

BLOCKED SHOTS (Minimum 110)

	G.	NO.	AVG.
Paultz, San Antonio	83	253	3.05
Jones, S.D.-Ken.-St.L.	76	218	2.87
Gilmore, Kentucky	84	205	2.44
Elmore, Indiana	76	178	2.34
Jones, Denver	83	184	2.22

STEALS (Minimum 110)

	G.	NO.	AVG.
Buse, Indiana	84	346	4.12
Taylor, Virginia	76	206	2.71
Erving, New York	84	207	2.46
Taylor, New York	54	125	2.31
Jones, Denver	83	170	2.05

1974-75 SEASON

Moses Malone

He was 6-10, 215 pounds, and the Utah Stars wanted him. The fact that Moses Malone had just graduated from high school did not prevent him from being drafted. The ABA had started the practice of allowing college players early entry; dipping into the list of high school grads was just a new wrinkle, albeit one that caused concern among many.

Malone's performance — 18.8 points and 14.6 rebounds per game — quieted even the most vocal of critics. And although Darryl Dawkins was drafted into the NBA out of high school the next season, it would be more than 20 years before other high school players would make an impact in the NBA.

The Denver Nuggets, who had Mack Calvin, Ralph Simpson and rookie Bobby Jones, won a league-best 65 games. But it was the Indiana Pacers, led by ABA scoring champion George McGinnis (29.8 points per game), who prevailed in the Western Division Finals.

Indiana, however, was no match for Kentucky, powered by Artis Gilmore and Dan Issel, in the Finals. In 15 playoff games — Kentucky defeated each playoff opponent 4-1 — Gilmore and Issel combined for more than 44 points and 25 rebounds per game as the Colonels went on to win their only ABA title.

FINAL STANDINGS

EASTERN DIVISION

	W	L	PCT.
Kentucky*	58	26	.690
New York	58	26	.690
St. Louis	32	52	.381
Memphis	27	57	.321
Virginia	15	69	.179

*Won special playoff for 1st place

WESTERN DIVISION

	W	L	PCT.
Denver	65	19	.774
San Antonio	51	33	.607
Indiana	45	39	.536
Utah	38	46	.452
San Diego	31	53	.369

NBA.COM FACT

One night when the ABA didn't have to worry about gate receipts was April 30, when Denver beat host Indiana 104-99 in the sixth game of their playoff series. A record 17,421 turned out for the game.

PLAYOFFS

EASTERN DIVISION SEMIFINALS

Kentucky 4, Memphis 1

Apr. 6 ......Kentucky 98, Memphis 91
Apr. 8 ......Kentucky 119, Memphis 105
Apr. 10 ....Kentucky 101, Memphis 80
Apr. 11 ....Memphis 107, Kentucky 93
Apr. 13 ....Kentucky 111, Memphis 99

St. Louis 4, New York 1

Apr. 6 ......New York 111, St. Louis 105
Apr. 9 ......St. Louis 115, New York 97
Apr. 11 ....St. Louis 113, New York108
Apr. 13 ....St. Louis 100, New York 89
Apr. 15 ....St. Louis 108, New York 107

WESTERN DIVISION SEMIFINALS

Denver 4, Utah 2

Apr. 6 ......Denver 122, Utah 107
Apr. 7 ......Denver 126, Utah 120
Apr. 9 ......Utah 122, Denver 108
Apr. 11 ....Utah 132, Denver 110
Apr. 12 ....Denver 130, Utah 119
Apr. 14 ....Denver 115, Utah 113

Indiana 4, San Antonio

Apr. 5 ......Indiana 122, San Antonio 119 (OT)
Apr. 7 ......Indiana 98, San Antonio 93
Apr. 10 ....Indiana 113, San Antonio 103
Apr. 12 ....San Antonio 110, Indiana 109
Apr. 14 ....San Antonio 123, Indiana 117
Apr. 16 ....Indiana 115, San Antonio 100

EASTERN DIVISION FINALS

Kentucky 4, St. Louis 1

Apr. 21 ....Kentucky 112, St. Louis 109
Apr. 23 ....Kentucky 108, St. Louis 103
Apr. 25 ....St. Louis 103, Kentucky 97
Apr. 27 ....Kentucky 117, St. Louis 98
Apr. 28 ....Kentucky 123, St. Louis 103

WESTERN DIVISION FINALS

Indiana 4, Denver 3

Apr. 20 ....Denver 131, Indiana 128
Apr. 22 ....Indiana 131, Denver 124
Apr. 24 ....Indiana 118, Denver 112
Apr. 25 ....Denver 126, Indiana 109
Apr. 27 ....Indiana 109, Denver 90
Apr. 30 ....Denver 104, Indiana 99
May 3......Indiana 104, Denver 96

ABA FINALS

Kentucky 4, Indiana 1

May 13 ....Kentucky 120, Indiana 94
May 15 ....Kentucky 95, Indiana 93
May 17 ....Kentucky 109, Indiana 101
May 19 ....Indiana 94, Kentucky 86
May 22 ....Kentucky 110, Indiana 105

INDIVIDUAL LEADERS

SCORING (Minimum 1000 points)

	G.	FG.	FT.	PTS.	AVG.
McGinnis, Indiana	79	873	545	2353	29.8
Erving, New York	84	914	486	2343	27.9
Boone, Utah	84	872	363	2117	25.2
Grant, San Diego	53	576	182	1335	25.2
Barnes, St. Louis	77	777	295	1849	24.0
Gilmore, Kentucky	84	784	412	1981	23.6
Gervin, San Antoni	84	784	380	1965	23.4
Lewis, Mem.-St.L.	69	579	355	1531	22.2
Lamar, San Diego	77	667	247	1606	20.9
Simpson, Denver	82	694	303	1692	20.6

FIELD GOAL PCT. (Minimum 250 FG made)

	FGM	FGA	PCT.
Jones, Denver	529	876	.604
Gilmore, Kentucky	784	1351	.580
Malone, Utah	591	1035	.571
Twardzik, Virginia	359	657	.546
Grant, San Diego	576	1058	.544

INDIVIDUAL LEADERS (con't)

3-PT. FIELD GOAL PCT. (Minimum 27 made)

	FGM	FGA	PCT.
Shepherd, Memphis	60	143	.420
Dampier, Kentucky	38	96	.396
Smith, Utah	34	94	.362
McGinnis, Indiana	62	175	.354
Brown, Mem.-Utah-Ind	35	100	.350

FREE THROW PCT. (Minimum 200 FT made)

	FTM	FTA	PCT.
Calvin, Denver	475	530	.896
Silas, San Antonio	430	486	.885
Robisch, Denver	304	346	.879
Boone, Utah	363	422	.860
Lewis, Mem.-St.L.	355	421	.843

ASSISTS (Minimum 250)

	G.	NO.	AVG.
Calvin, Denver	74	570	7.7
Williams, Memphis	81	576	7.1
McGinnis, Indiana	79	495	6.3
Jabali, San Diego	62	358	5.8
O'Brien, San Diego	79	443	5.6

REBOUNDS (Minimum 600)

	G.	OFF.	DEF.	TOT.	AVG.
Nater, San Antonio	78	369	910	1279	16.4
Gilmore, Kentucky	84	427	934	1361	16.2
Barnes, St. Louis	77	419	783	1202	15.6
Malone, Utah	83	455	754	1209	14.6
McGinnis, Indiana	79	396	730	1126	14.3

STEALS (Minimum 100)

	G.	NO.	AVG
Taylor, New York	79	221	2.80
McGinnis, Indiana	79	206	2.61
Taylor, Denver	76	172	2.26
Erving, New York	84	186	2.21
Lewis, Mem.-St.L.	69	147	2.13

BLOCKED SHOTS

	G.	NO.	AVG.
Jones, San Diego	76	246	3.24
Gilmore, Kentucky	84	258	3.07
Green, Denver	81	174	2.15
Erving, New York	84	157	1.87
Jones, Denver	84	153	1.82

1973-74 SEASON

Julius Erving

The battle lines between the ABA and the NBA had been drawn. In the summer of 1973, those lines again came close to being crossed.

Virginia Squires forward Julius Erving had signed a contract with the NBA's Atlanta Hawks before the 1972 NBA Draft (Erving, a junior, was eligible because his class graduated that year). The Hawks, however, did not have a first-round pick, and the Milwaukee Bucks snatched up Erving's NBA rights.

In 1973, Erving tried to jump to the Hawks when the Squires would not give him a new contract (he actually played two exhibition games with Atlanta). The matter ended up in court (where Erving tried to get out of his ABA contract) and in arbitration (where the Hawks and Bucks fought over Erving's NBA rights). The ABA managed to hang on to its brightest star when Roy Boe, owner of the New York Nets, acquired Erving in a complicated deal that involved two ABA teams and two NBA teams.

In New York, Erving captured his second scoring title and joined veterans Billy Paultz and Brian Taylor and rookies Larry Kenon and John Williamson to win a league-high 55 games. The Nets polished off Virginia and Kentucky to reach the Finals, then took out Utah in five games to win the ABA crown.

FINAL STANDINGS

EASTERN DIVISION

	W	L	PCT.
New York	55	29	.655
Kentucky	53	31	.631
Carolina	47	37	.560
Virginia	28	56	.333
Memphis	21	63	.250

WESTERN DIVISION

	W	L	PCT.
Utah	51	33	.607
Indiana	46	38	.548
San Antonio	45	39	.536
San Diego*	37	47	.440
Denver	37	47	.440

*Won playoff for 4th place

NBA.COM FACT

In Denver's 139-112 rout of San Diego during the regular season, Alan Smith paced the way with 26 points. He did have some help as four other Rockets teammates netted 20-plus points.

PLAYOFFS

EASTERN DIVISION SEMIFINALS

Kentucky 4, Carolina 0

Apr. 1 ......Kentucky 118, Carolina 102
Apr. 5 ......Kentucky 99, Carolina 96
Apr. 6 ......Kentucky 120, Carolina 110
Apr. 8 ......Kentucky 128, Carolina 119

New York 4, Virginia 1

Mar. 29....New York 108, Virginia 96
Apr. 1 ......New York 129, Virginia 110
Apr. 4 ......Virginia 116, New York 115
Apr. 7 ......New York 116, Virginia 88
Apr. 8 ......New York 108, Virginia 96

WESTERN DIVISION SEMIFINALS

Indiana 4, San Antonio 3

Mar. 30....San Antonio 113, Indiana 109
Apr. 1 ......Indiana 128, San Antonio 101
Apr. 3 ......San Antonio 115, Indiana 96
Apr. 4 ......Indiana 91, San Antonio 89
Apr. 6 ......Indiana 105, San Antonio 100
Apr. 10 ....San Antonio 102, Indiana 86
Apr. 12 ....Indiana 97, San Antonio 86

Utah 4, San Diego 2

Mar. 30....Utah 114, San Diego 99
Apr. 1 ......Utah 119, San Diego 105
Apr. 3 ......San Diego 97, Utah 96
Apr. 4 ......San Diego 100, Utah 98
Apr. 6 ......Utah 100, San Diego 93
Apr. 8 ......Utah 110, San Diego 99

EASTERN DIVISION FINALS

New York 4, Kentucky 0

Apr. 13 ....New York 119, Kentucky 106
Apr. 15 ....New York 99, Kentucky 80
Apr. 17 ....New York 89, Kentucky 87
Apr. 20 ....New York 103, Kentucky 90

WESTERN DIVISION FINALS

Utah 4, Indiana 3

Apr. 13 ....Utah 105, Indiana 96
Apr. 15 ....Utah 106, Indiana 102
Apr. 17 ....Utah 99, Indiana 90
Apr. 18 ....Indiana 118, Utah 107
Apr. 22 ....Indiana 110, Utah 101
Apr. 25 ....Indiana 91, Utah 89
Apr. 27 ....Utah 109, Indiana 87

ABA FINALS

New York 4, Utah 1

Apr. 30 ....New York 89, Utah 85
May 4......New York 118, Utah 94
May 6......New York 103, Utah 100 (OT)
May 8......Utah 97, New York 89
May 10 ....New York 111, Utah 100

INDIVIDUAL LEADERS

SCORING (Minimum 1000 points)

	G.	FG	FT	PTS.	AVG.
Erving, New York	84	914	454	2299	27.4
McGinnis, Indiana	80	789	488	2071	25.9
Issel, Kentucky	83	829	457	2118	25.5
Gervin, Vir.-S.A.	74	672	378	1730	23.4
Wise, Utah	82	714	396	1826	22.3
Lamar, San Diego	84	686	272	1713	20.4
Johnson, San Diego	84	716	199	1690	20.1
Carter, Virginia	80	561	392	1546	19.3
Thompson, Memphis	78	539	410	1498	19.2
Simpson, Denver	75	597	208	1404	18.7

FIELD GOAL PCT. (Minimum 200 FG made)

	FGM	FGA	PCT.
Nater, Vir.-S.A.	467	846	.552
Jones, Utah	583	1060	.550
Owens, Carolina	444	843	.527
Chones, Carolina	535	1017	.526
Grant, San Diego	357	681	.524

INDIVIDUAL LEADERS (con't)

3-PT. FIELD GOAL PCT. (Minimum 20 made)

	FGM	FGA	PCT.
Dampier, Kentucky	48	124	.387
Keller, Indiana	50	131	.382
Jabali, Denver	45	123	.366
Brown, Indiana	56	155	.361
Combs, Utah-Mem.	52	147	.354

FREE THROW PCT. (Minimum 135 FT made)

	FTM	FTA	PCT.
Jones, Utah	229	259	.884
Calvin, Carolina	490	560	.875
Boone, Utah	300	343	.875
Johnson, San Diego	199	235	.847
Carter, Virginia	392	466	.841

ASSISTS (Minimum 200)

	G.	NO.	AVG.
Smith, Denver	76	619	8.1
Jabali, Denver	49	358	7.3
Williams, S.D.-Ken.	90	557	6.2
Dampier, Kentucky	84	473	5.6
Taylor, Virginia	80	416	5.2

REBOUNDS (Minimum 500)

	G.	OFF.	DEF.	TOT.	AVG.
Gilmore, Kentucky	84	478	1060	1538	18.3
McGinnis, Indiana	80	422	775	1197	15.0
Jones, San Diego	79	322	773	1095	13.9
Nater, Vir.-S.A.	79	286	712	998	12.6
Daniels, Indiana	78	251	655	906	11.6

STEALS

	G.	NO.	AVG.
McClain, Carolina	84	250	2.98
Taylor, Virginia	80	215	2.69
Erving, New York	84	190	2.26
Caldwell, Carolina	79	170	2.15
Gale, Ken.-NY	80	167	2.09

BLOCKED SHOTS

	G.	NO.	AVG.
Jones, San Diego	79	316	4.00
Gilmore, Kentucky	84	287	3.42
Erving, New York	84	204	2.43
Hillman, Indiana	83	177	2.13
Paultz, New York	77	147	1.91

1972-73 SEASON

Billy Cunningham

Despite the many franchise relocations, the ABA's original 11 teams had survived — in some form or another — the first five years of the league's existence. But the 1972-73 season began with the Pittsburgh Condors and the Floridians folding because of financial problems. The San Diego Conquistadors became the league's first true expansion team.

Merger talk again surfaced as the U.S. Senate considered an antitrust exemption for a proposed ABA-NBA union. The players, fearing the effect a merger would have on salaries, lobbied the Senate to attach conditions that ultimately proved unacceptable to club owners.

The Carolina Cougars, led by forward Billy Cunningham, posted the league's best record at 57-27. Cunningham, a four-time NBA All-Star, grabbed the ABA MVP award and Carolina's head coach, Larry Brown, the ABA's all-time assist leader, was named Coach of the Year.

The Finals pitted Kentucky against Indiana, two teams that finished second in the regular season in their divisions. The series went to seven games, the third ABA Finals in six seasons to go the distance, with the Pacers winning their third championship in four years by taking Game 7 88-81.

FINAL STANDINGS

EASTERN DIVISION

	W	L	PCT.
Carolina	57	27	.679
Kentucky	56	28	.667
Virginia	42	42	.500
New York	30	54	.357
Memphis	24	60	.286

WESTERN DIVISION

	W	L	PCT.
Utah	55	29	.655
Indiana	51	33	.607
Denver	47	37	.560
San Diego	30	54	.357
Dallas	28	56	.333

NBA.COM FACT

Denver's Julius Keye had an ABA record 12 of his team's 17 blocked shots when Denver beat Virginia 103-99 on December 14.

PLAYOFFS

EASTERN DIVISION SEMIFINALS

Kentucky 4, Virginia 1

Mar. 30....Kentucky 129, Virginia 101
Apr. 1 ......Virginia 109, Kentucky 94
Apr. 3 ......Kentucky 115, Virginia 113
Apr. 6 ......Kentucky 108, Virginia 90
Apr. 7 ......Kentucky 114, Virginia 93

Carolina 4, New York 1

Mar. 30....Carolina 104, New York 96
Mar. 31....New York 114, Carolina 111
Apr. 3 ......Carolina 101, New York 91
Apr. 5 ......Carolina 112, New York 108
Apr. 6 ......Carolina 136, New York 113

WESTERN DIVISION SEMIFINALS

Indiana 4, Denver 1

Mar. 31....Indiana 114, Denver 91
Apr. 1 ......Indiana 106, Denver 93
Apr. 3 ......Denver 105, Indiana 94
Apr. 5 ......Indiana 97, Denver 95
Apr. 7 ......Indiana 121, Denver 107

Utah 4, San Diego 0

Apr. 2 ......Utah 107, San Diego 93
Apr. 4 ......Utah 103, San Diego 92
Apr. 7 ......Utah 97, San Diego 96
Apr. 8 ......Utah 120, San Diego 98

EASTERN DIVISION FINALS

Kentucky 4, Carolina 3

Apr. 11 ....Kentucky 113, Carolina 103
Apr. 14 ....Carolina 125, Kentucky 105
Apr. 16 ....Kentucky 108, Carolina 94
Apr. 18 ....Carolina 102, Kentucky 91
Apr. 20 ....Carolina 112, Kentucky 107
Apr. 21 ....Kentucky 119, Carolina 100
Apr. 24 ....Kentucky 107, Carolina 96

WESTERN DIVISION FINALS

Indiana 4, Utah 2

Apr. 12 ....Utah 124, Indiana 107
Apr. 14 ....Indiana 116, Utah 110
Apr. 16 ....Indiana 118, Utah 108
Apr. 18 ....Utah 104, Indiana 103
Apr. 19 ....Indiana 104, Utah 102
Apr. 21 ....Indiana 107, Utah 98

ABA FINALS

Indiana 4, Kentucky 3

Apr. 28 ....Indiana 111, Kentucky 107
Apr. 30 ....Kentucky 114, Indiana 102
May 3 ......Kentucky 92, Indiana 88
May 5 ......Indiana 90, Kentucky 86
May 8 ......Indiana 89, Kentucky 86
May 10 ....Kentucky 109, Indiana 93
May 12 ....Indiana 88, Kentucky 81

INDIVIDUAL LEADERS

SCORING (Minimum 1000 points)

	G.	FG	FT	PTS.	AVG.
Erving, Virginia	71	894	475	2268	31.9
McGinnis, Indiana	82	868	517	2261	27.6
Issel, Kentucky	84	902	485	2292	27.3
Cunningham, Carolina	84	771	472	2028	24.1
Simpson, Denver	81	732	421	1890	23.3
R. Jones, Dallas	67	564	324	1495	22.3
Johnson, San Diego	80	769	195	1770	22.1
Wise, Utah	83	672	476	1823	22.0
Thompson, Memphis	80	579	549	1727	21.6
Gilmore, Kentucky	84	687	368	1743	20.8

FIELD GOAL PCT. (Minimum 250 FG made)

	FGM	FGA	PCT.
Gilmore, Kentucky	687	1228	.559
Kennedy, Dallas	365	664	.550
Owens, Carolina	393	727	.541
Beck, Denver	466	879	.530
Irvine, Virginia	424	805	.527

3-PT. FIELD GOAL PCT. (Minimum 28 made)

	FGM	FGA	PCT.
Combs, Utah	51	134	.381
Brown, Indiana	42	118	.356
Dampier, Kentucky	54	155	.348
Hamilton, Dallas	66	191	.346
Lewis, Indiana	38	110	.345

FREE THROW PCT. (Minimum 200 FT made)

	FTM	FTA	PCT.
Keller, Indiana	234	269	.870
Boone, Utah	415	479	.866
Warren, Car.-Dal.-Utah	236	274	.861
Calvin, Carolina	500	582	.859
Silas, Dallas	389	467	.833

ASSISTS (Minimum 250)

	G.	NO.	AVG.
Melchionni, New York	61	453	7.4
Williams, San Diego	83	582	7.0
Jabali, Denver	82	539	6.6
Dampier, Kentucky	80	521	6.5
Cunningham, Carolina	84	530	6.3

REBOUNDS (Minimum 600)

	G	OFF.	DEF	TOT.	AVG.
Gilmore, Kentucky	84	449	1027	1476	17.6
Daniels, Indiana	81	348	899	1247	15.4
Paultz, New York	81	279	736	1015	12.5
McGinnis, Indiana	82	434	588	1022	12.5
Denton, Memphis	66	276	544	820	12.4

1971-72 SEASON

George McGinnis

Julius Erving, an unheralded forward from the University of Massachusetts, was drafted by the Virginia Squires. Nobody knew it then, but this young star would give the league credibility and, at the same time, the attention that would cause the ABA's eventual alliance with the NBA.

Dr. J, a nickname Erving had acquired from a high school friend, didn't just play basketball, he played with a particular style and grace. He played above the rim, soaring over opponents to score. People who hadn't watched the ABA before suddenly started paying attention.

In Kentucky, another rookie was leaving impressions. The 7-2 Artis Gilmore teamed with Dan Issel to lead the Colonels to a league-record 68 victories and captured the ABA Rookie of the Year award after averaging 23.8 points and 17.8 rebounds. But Kentucky was surprised by the 44-40 New York Nets in the first round of the playoffs, and New York made it all the way to the Finals.

There the Nets were overmatched against the Indiana Pacers, who won the championship in six games with a starting lineup of Roger Brown, George McGinnis, Mel Daniels, Freddie Lewis and Rick Mount.

FINAL STANDINGS

EASTERN DIVISION

	W	L	PCT.
Kentucky	68	16	.810
Virginia	45	39	.536
New York	44	40	.524
Floridians	36	48	.429
Carolina	35	49	.417
Pittsburgh	25	59	.298

WESTERN DIVISION

	W	L	PCT.
Utah	60	24	.714
Indiana	47	37	.560
Dallas	42	42	.500
Denver	34	50	.405
Memphis	26	58	.310

NBA.COM FACT

In Kentucky's 105-102 loss against Indiana during the regular season, 7-2 rookie Artis Gilmore, who would lead the league in rebounding (17.8 rebounds per game) and average 5.0 blocks per game, was called for goaltending seven times.

PLAYOFFS

EASTERN DIVISION SEMIFINALS

Virginia 4, Floridians 0

Mar. 31 ....Virginia 114, Floridians 107 (OT)
Apr. 1 ......Virginia 125, Floridians 100
Apr. 4 ......Virginia 118, Floridians 113
Apr. 6 ......Virginia 115, Floridians 106

New York 4, Kentucky 2

Apr. 1 ......New York 122, Kentucky 108
Apr. 4 ......New York 105, Kentucky 90
Apr. 5 ......Kentucky 105, New York 99
Apr. 7 ......New York 100, Kentucky 92
Apr. 8 ......Kentucky 109, New York 103
Apr. 10 ....New York 101, Kentucky 96

WESTERN DIVISION SEMIFINALS

Indiana 4, Denver 3

Mar. 31 ....Indiana 102, Denver 95
Apr. 1 ......Denver 106, Indiana 105
Apr. 4 ......Indiana 122, Denver 120 (OT)
Apr. 6 ......Denver 112, Indiana 96
Apr. 8 ......Indiana 91, Denver 79
Apr. 9 ......Denver 106, Indiana 99
Apr. 13 ....Indiana 91, Denver 89

Utah 4, Dallas 0

Apr. 1 ......Utah 106, Dallas 96
Apr. 3 ......Utah 113, Dallas 107
Apr. 5 ......Utah 96, Dallas 89
Apr. 7 ......Utah 103, Dallas 99

EASTERN DIVISION FINALS

New York 4, Virginia 3

Apr. 13 ....Virginia 138, New York 91
Apr. 15 ....Virginia 115, New York 106
Apr. 24 ....New York 119, Virginia 117
Apr. 26 ....New York 118, Virginia 107
Apr. 29 ....Virginia 116, New York 107
May 1 ......New York 146, Virginia 136
May 4 ......New York 94, Virginia 88

WESTERN DIVISION FINALS

Indiana 4, Utah 3

Apr. 15 ....Utah 108, Indiana 100
Apr. 17 ....Utah 117, Indiana 109
Apr. 19 ....Indiana 116, Utah 111
Apr. 22 ....Indiana 118, Utah 108
Apr. 24 ....Utah 139, Indiana 130
Apr. 26 ....Indiana 105, Utah 99
May 1 ......Indiana 117, Utah 113

ABA FINALS

Indiana 4, New York 2

May 6 ......Indiana 124, New York 103
May 9 ......New York 117, Indiana 115
May 12 ....Indiana 114, New York 108
May 15 ....New York 110, Indiana 105
May 18 ....Indiana 100, New York 99
May 20 ....Indiana 108, New York 105

INDIVIDUAL LEADERS

SCORING (Minimum 1000 points)

	G.	FG	FT	PTS.	AVG.
C. Scott, Virginia	73	985	525	2524	34.6
Barry, New York	80	902	641	2518	31.5
Issel, Kentucky	83	972	591	2538	30.6
Brisker, Pittsburgh	49	563	248	1417	28.9
Simpson, Denver	84	920	457	2300	27.4
Erving, Virginia	84	910	467	2290	27.3
Thompson, Pittsburgh	70	696	455	1888	27.0
McDaniels, Carolina	58	659	234	1552	26.8
Freeman, Dallas	72	628	475	1733	24.1
Gilmore, Kentucky	84	806	391	2003	23.8

FIELD GOAL PCT. (Minimum 375 FG made)

	FGM	FGA	PCT.
Gilmore, Kentucky	806	1348	.598
Washington, New York	387	678	.571
Lewis, Pittsburgh	385	713	.540
Beaty, Utah	729	1353	.539
Jones, Floridians	423	797	.531

3-PT. FIELD GOAL PCT. (Minimum 40 made)

	FGM	FGA	PCT.
Combs, Utah	103	254	.406
Dampier, Kentucky	84	233	.361
Jabali, Floridians	102	285	.358
Lehmann, Car.-Mem.	71	199	.357
Hamilton, Dallas	46	132	.348

FREE THROW PCT. (Minimum 300 FT made)

	FTM	FTA	PCT.
Barry, New York	641	730	.878
Calvin, Floridians	611	701	.872
S. Jones, Dallas	367	422	.870
Lewis, Indiana	341	396	.861
Combs, Utah	319	380	.839

ASSISTS (Minimum 335)

	G.	NO.	AVG.
Melchionni, New York	80	669	8.4
Lehmann, Car.-Mem.	53	411	7.8
Brown, Denver	76	549	7.2
Jones, Utah	78	485	6.2
Dampier, Kentucky	83	515	6.2

REBOUNDS (Minimum 700)

	G.	OFF.	DEF.	TOT.	AVG.
Gilmore, Kentucky	84	421	1070	1491	17.8
Daniels, Indiana	79	383	914	1297	16.4
Erving, Virginia	84	476	843	1319	15.7
Govan, Memphis	83	310	872	1182	14.2
McDaniels, Carolina	58	249	565	814	14.0

1970-71 SEASON

Dan Issel

"Change is good" must have been the mantra repeated around the league as the ABA embarked on its fourth season with more franchise relocations. The New Orleans Buccaneers became the Memphis Pros, the Los Angeles Stars became the Utah Stars, the Washington Capitols became the Virginia Squires and the Pittsburgh Pipers stayed put but were renamed the Condors. The Floridians and Chaparrals played at different locations throughout their respective states, effectively (or ineffectively, based on attendance) becoming regional franchises.

The hot topic was the possibility of the ABA joining the NBA, fueled by the NBA owners voting 13-4 to pursue merger talks, but the players soon squashed the idea with an antitrust lawsuit (known as the Oscar Robertson suit). Having two leagues had driven up player salaries, and the players were in no rush to end this surge.

Utah, behind powerful center Zelmo Beaty (22.9 points and 15.7 rebounds per game), defeated Kentucky in a seven-game Finals series that saw each team win its home games. In Game 7, Dan Issel scored 41 points, but Beaty's 36 points and 16 rebounds were enough for Utah to win 131-121.

FINAL STANDINGS

EASTERN DIVISION

	W	L	PCT.
Virginia	55	29	.655
Kentucky	44	40	.524
New York	40	44	.476
Floridians	37	47	.440
Pittsburgh	36	48	.429
Carolina	34	50	.405

WESTERN DIVISION

	W	L	PCT.
Indiana	58	26	.690
Utah	57	27	.679
Memphis	41	43	.488
Texas*	30	54	.357
Denver	30	54	.357

*Won special playoff for 4th place

NBA.COM FACT

Pittsburgh's John Brisker, who ranked third in the league in scoring with a 29.3-point-per-game average, had back-to-back 50-point games, hitting for 53 against Indiana on November 12 and netting 50 against Texas a night later.

PLAYOFFS

EASTERN DIVISION SEMIFINALS

Kentucky 4, Floridians 2

Apr. 2 ......Kentucky 116, Floridians 112
Apr. 4 ......Kentucky 120, Floridians 110
Apr. 6 ......Floridians 120, Kentucky 102
Apr. 8 ......Floridians 129, Kentucky 117
Apr. 10 ....Kentucky 118, Floridians 101
Apr. 12 ....Kentucky 112, Floridians 103

Virginia 4, New York 2

Apr. 2 ......Virginia 113, New York 105
Apr. 4 ......Virginia 114, New York 108
Apr. 6 ......New York 135, Virginia 131
Apr. 7 ......New York 130, Virginia 127
Apr. 9 ......Virginia 127, New York 124
Apr. 10 ....Virginia 118, New York 114

WESTERN DIVISION SEMIFINALS

Indiana 4, Memphis 0

Apr. 2 ......Indiana 114, Memphis 98
Apr. 3 ......Indiana 106, Memphis 104
Apr. 5 ......Indiana 91, Memphis 90
Apr. 7 ......Indiana 102, Memphis 101

Utah 4, Texas 0

Apr. 2 ......Utah 125, Texas 115
Apr. 3 ......Utah 137, Texas 107
Apr. 4 ......Utah 113, Texas 101
Apr. 6 ......Utah 128, Texas 107

EASTERN DIVISION FINALS

Kentucky 4, Virginia 2

Apr. 15 ....Kentucky 136, Virginia 132
Apr. 17 ....Virginia 142, Kentucky 122
Apr. 19 ....Virginia 150, Kentucky 137
Apr. 21 ....Kentucky 128, Virginia 110
Apr. 23 ....Kentucky 115, Virginia 107
Apr. 24 ....Kentucky 129, Virginia 117

WESTERN DIVISION FINALS

Utah 4, Indiana 3

Apr. 12 ....Utah 120, Indiana 118
Apr. 14 ....Indiana 120, Utah 107
Apr. 17 ....Utah 121, Indiana 107
Apr. 20 ....Utah 126, Indiana 99
Apr. 22 ....Indiana 127, Utah 109
Apr. 24 ....Indiana 105, Utah 102
Apr. 28 ....Utah 108, Indiana 101

ABA FINALS

Utah 4, Kentucky 3

May 3 ......Utah 136, Kentucky 117
May 5 ......Utah 138, Kentucky 125
May 7 ......Kentucky 116, Utah 110
May 8 ......Kentucky 129, Utah 125 (OT)
May 12 ....Utah 137, Kentucky 127
May 15 ....Kentucky 105, Utah 101
May 18 ....Utah 131, Kentucky 121

INDIVIDUAL LEADERS

SCORING (Minimum 1000 points)

	G.	FG	FT	PTS.	AVG.
Issel, Kentucky	83	938	604	2480	29.9
Barry, New York	59	632	451	1734	29.4
Brisker, Pittsburgh	79	898	430	2315	29.3
Calvin, Floridians	81	744	696	2201	27.2
C. Scott, Virginia	84	902	456	2276	27.1
Cannon, Denver	80	751	606	2126	26.6
Jones, Floridians	84	764	471	2044	24.3
Freeman, Utah-Texas	66	596	367	1559	23.6
Caldwell, Carolina	72	685	302	1678	23.3
Beaty, Utah	76	661	420	1744	22.9

FIELD GOAL PCT. (Minimum 450 FG made)

	FGM	FGA	PCT.
Beaty, Utah	661	1192	.555
Paultz, New York	510	973	.524
Daniels, Indiana	698	1357	.514
Netolicky, Indiana	651	1305	.499
J. Beasley, Texas	532	1070	.497

3-PT. FIELD GOAL PCT. (Minimum 35 made)

	FGM	FGA	PCT.
Lehmann, Carolina	154	382	.403
Carrier, Kentucky	63	161	.391
S. Jones, Memphis	40	108	.370
Dampier, Kentucky	103	280	.368
Combs, Texas - Utah	77	210	.367

FREE THROW PCT. (Minimum 225 FT made)

	FTM	FTA	PCT.
Barry, New York	451	507	.890
Carrier, Kentucky	327	377	.867
Keller, Indiana	267	308	.867
Calvin, Floridians	696	805	.865
Dampier, Kentucky	320	376	.851

ASSISTS (Minimum 275)

	G.	NO.	AVG.
Melchionni, New York	81	672	8.3
Calvin, Floridians	81	619	7.6
J. Jones, Memphis	80	468	5.9
C. Scott, Virginia	84	472	5.6
Lehmann, Carolina	83	464	5.6

REBOUNDS (Minimum 650)

	G.	OFF.	DEF.	TOT.	AVG.
Daniels, Indiana	82	394	1081	1475	18.0
Keye, Denver	83	370	1084	1454	17.5
Beaty, Utah	76	407	783	1190	15.7
Lewis, Pittsburgh	83	435	778	1213	14.6
Govan, Memphis	84	277	861	1138	13.5

1969-70 SEASON

Spencer Haywood

In its third season, the ABA expanded — its schedule. Teams played 84 games, up from 78. What the league gained in length it lost in sizzle, though, as two big events earmarked the 1969-70 season. First, Connie Hawkins jumped to the NBA. Then the league lost out in a bidding war for center Kareem Abdul-Jabbar, who was drafted and signed by the Milwaukee Bucks.

In franchise moves, the Houston Mavericks became the Carolina Cougars, the Oakland Oaks became the Washington Capitols and the Minnesota Pipers moved back to Pittsburgh, where they had won the league's first championship two years earlier.

The championship banner would again wave from an Eastern Division perch as Indiana proved the dominant power in the ABA. With the league's most productive frontcourt — forwards Roger Brown averaged 23.0 points, Bob Netolicky 20.6 points and center Mel Daniels 18.8 points and 17.6 rebounds — and the speedy backcourt of John Barnhill and Freddie Lewis, the Pacers compiled a 59-25 record. In the playoffs, they beat Carolina and Kentucky, then powered past the Los Angeles Stars in a six-game Finals matchup.

FINAL STANDINGS

EASTERN DIVISION

	W	L	PCT.
Indiana	59	25	.702
Kentucky	45	39	.536
Carolina	42	42	.500
New York	39	45	.464
Pittsburgh	29	55	.345
Miami	23	61	.274

WESTERN DIVISION

	W	L	PCT.
Denver	51	33	.607
Dallas	45	39	.536
Washington	44	40	.524
Los Angeles	43	41	.512
New Orleans	42	42	.500

NBA.COM FACT

The Indiana Pacers set ABA records for points and assists (43) in a 177-135 win against the Pittsburgh Pipers on April 12.

PLAYOFFS

EASTERN DIVISION SEMIFINALS

Indiana 4, Carolina 0

Apr. 18 ....Indiana 123, Carolina 105
Apr. 19 ....Indiana 103, Carolina 98
Apr. 22 ....Indiana 115, Carolina 106
Apr. 24 ....Indiana 110, Carolina 106

Kentucky 4, New York 3

Apr. 17 ....New York 122, Kentucky 118 (OT)
Apr. 18 ....Kentucky 113, New York 111
Apr. 19 ....New York 107, Kentucky 99
Apr. 22 ....Kentucky 128, New York 101
Apr. 26 ....New York 127, Kentucky 112
Apr. 28 ....Kentucky 116, New York 113
Apr. 29 ....Kentucky 112, New York 101

WESTERN DIVISION SEMIFINALS

Denver 4, Washington 3

Apr. 17 ....Denver 130, Washington 111
Apr. 18 ....Denver 143, Washington 133
Apr. 19 ....Washington 125, Denver 120
Apr. 22 ....Washington 131, Denver 114
Apr. 23 ....Denver 132, Washington 110
Apr. 25 ....Washington 116, Denver 111
Apr. 28 ....Denver 143, Washington 119

Los Angeles 4, Dallas 2

Apr. 17 ....Los Angeles 115, Dallas 103
Apr. 18 ....Dallas 129, Los Angeles 121
Apr. 20 ....Dallas 116, Los Angeles 104
Apr. 22 ....Los Angeles 144, Dallas 138
Apr. 24 ....Los Angeles 146, Dallas 139
Apr. 26 ....Los Angeles 124, Dallas 123

EASTERN DIVISION FINALS

Indiana 4, Kentucky 1

May 1 ......Kentucky 114, Indiana 110
May 2 ......Indiana 121, Kentucky 110
May 3 ......Indiana 114, Kentucky 110
May 5 ......Indiana 111, Kentucky 103
May 6 ......Indiana 117, Kentucky 103

WESTERN DIVISION FINALS

Los Angeles 4, Denver 1

Apr. 30 ....Denver 123, Los Angeles 113 (OT)
May 1 ......Los Angeles 114, Denver 105
May 4 ......Los Angeles 119, Denver 113
May 5 ......Los Angeles 114, Denver 110
May 9 ......Los Angeles 109, Denver 107

ABA FINALS

Indiana 4, Los Angeles 2

May 15 ....Indiana 109, Los Angeles 93
May 17 ....Indiana 114, Los Angeles 111
May 18 ....Los Angeles 109, Indiana 106
May 19 ....Indiana 142, Los Angeles 120
May 23 ....Los Angeles 117, Indiana 113
May 25 ....Indiana 111, Los Angeles 107

INDIVIDUAL LEADERS

SCORING (Minimum 1200 points)

	G.	FG	FT	PTS.	AVG.
Haywood, Denver	84	986	547	2519	30.0
Barry, Washington	52	517	400	1442	27.7
Verga, Carolina	82	867	458	2258	27.5
Freeman, Miami	79	766	626	2163	27.4
Dampier, Kentucky	82	743	447	2131	26.0
Jones, Denver	75	625	579	1870	24.9
Tart, New York	80	756	412	1935	24.2
Carrier, Kentucky	77	608	454	1775	23.1
Brown, Indiana	84	719	457	1935	23.0
Combs, Dallas	84	640	458	1868	22.2

FIELD GOAL PCT. (Minimum 300 FG made)

	FGM	FGA	PCT.
Washington, Pit.-LA	320	582	.550
Card, Washington	351	666	.527
Beck, Denver	440	841	.523
Becker, Indiana	309	593	.521
Ligon, Kentucky	507	1000	.507

3-PT. FIELD GOAL PCT. (Minimum 50 made)

	FGM	FGA	PCT.
Carrier, Kentucky	105	280	.375
Dampier, Kentucky	198	548	.361
Congdon, Denver	63	178	.354
Combs, Dallas	130	370	.351
Barrett, Washington	62	180	.344

FREE THROW PCT. (Minimum 250 FT made)

	FTM	FTA	PCT.
Carrier, Kentucky	454	509	.892
Barry, Washington	400	463	.864
Combs, Dallas	458	548	.836
S. Jones, New Orleans	412	495	.832
Dampier, Kentucky	447	538	.831

ASSISTS (Minimum 325)

	G.	NO.	AVG.
Brown, Washington	82	580	7.1
Melchionni, New York	80	457	5.7
Calvin, Los Angeles	84	478	5.7
Jones, Denver	75	426	5.7
Dampier, Kentucky	82	447	5.5

REBOUNDS (Minimum 750)

	G.	OFF.	DEF.	TOT.	AVG.
Haywood, Denver	84	533	1104	1637	19.5
Daniels, Indiana	83	423	1039	1462	17.6
Robbins, New Orleans	82	427	905	1332	16.2
Govan, New Orleans	84	285	932	1217	14.5
Harge, Washington	84	334	843	1177	14.0

1968-69 SEASON

Oakland Oaks

After two seasons in the NBA — and one when he led the league in scoring — forward Rick Barry signed with the Oakland Oaks of the ABA. In his first season, he led the league in scoring with 34.0 points per game, shot .511 from the field and a league-best .888 from the free throw line. Barry's offense helped the team improve from 22-56 in their first season to 60-18, the best record in the ABA.

Emerging stars without an NBA pedigree included Connie Hawkins of Minnesota (30.2 ppg), ABA MVP Mel Daniels of Indiana (24.0 ppg, league-best 16.5 rpg), Denver's Larry Jones (28.4 ppg) and James Jones of New Orleans (26.6 ppg, 5.7 apg).

In the Finals against Indiana, Oakland averaged 131.6 points and dropped only one game to earn the ABA title.

The relocation of several franchises prior to the start of the season began a trend that would mark the life of the ABA. Four teams changed cities during the offseason: the Anaheim Amigos became the Los Angeles Stars, the New Jersey Americans became the New York Nets, the Minnesota Muskies became the Miami Floridians and the defending champion Pittsburgh Pipers became the Minnesota Pipers.

FINAL STANDINGS

EASTERN DIVISION

	W	L	PCT.
Indiana	44	34	.564
Miami	43	35	.551
Kentucky	42	36	.538
Minnesota	36	42	.462
New York	17	61	.218

WESTERN DIVISION

	W	L	PCT.
Oakland	60	18	.769
New Orleans	46	32	.590
Denver	44	34	.564
Dallas	41	37	.526
Los Angeles	33	45	.423
Houston	23	55	.295

NBA.COM FACT

Alex Hannum had ridiculed the ABA's colorful ball as something that "belongs on the nose of a seal" when he was an NBA coach. But he changed his mind at least about the league. Hannum directed the Oakland Oaks to the ABA championship.

PLAYOFFS

EASTERN DIVISION SEMIFINALS

Miami 4, Minnesota 3

Apr. 7 ......Miami 119, Minnesota 110
Apr. 9 ......Minnesota 106, Miami 99
Apr. 10 ....Minnesota 109, Miami 93
Apr. 12 ....Miami 116, Minnesota 109
Apr. 13 ....Miami 122, Minnesota 107
Apr. 15 ....Minnesota 105, Miami 100
Apr. 19 ....Miami 137, Minnesota 128

Indiana 4, Kentucky 3

Apr. 8 ......Kentucky 128, Indiana 118
Apr. 9 ......Indiana 120, Kentucky 115
Apr. 10 ....Kentucky 130, Indiana 111
Apr. 13 ....Kentucky 105, Indiana 104 (OT)
Apr. 14 ....Indiana 116, Kentucky 97
Apr. 15 ....Indiana 107, Kentucky 89
Apr. 17 ....Indiana 120, Kentucky 111

WESTERN DIVISION SEMIFINALS

Oakland 4, Denver 3

Apr. 5 ......Oakland 129, Denver 99
Apr. 6 ......Denver 122, Oakland 119
Apr. 8 ......Oakland 121, Denver 99
Apr. 10 ....Denver 109, Oakland 108
Apr. 12 ....Oakland 128, Denver 118
Apr. 13 ....Denver 126, Oakland 115
Apr. 16 ....Oakland 115, Denver 102

New Orleans 4, Dallas 3

Apr. 5 ......New Orleans 129, Dallas 106
Apr. 7 ......New Orleans 122, Dallas 108
Apr. 10 ....Dallas 130, New Orleans 106
Apr. 12 ....New Orleans 114, Dallas 107
Apr. 14 ....Dallas 123, New Orleans 112
Apr. 15 ....Dallas 136, New Orleans 118
Apr. 17 ....New Orleans 101, Dallas 95

EASTERN DIVISION FINALS

Indiana 4, Miami 1

Apr. 20 ....Indiana 126, Miami 110
Apr. 22 ....Indiana 131, Miami 116
Apr. 23 ....Indiana 119, Miami 105
Apr. 25 ....Miami 114, Indiana 110
Apr. 26 ....Indiana 127, Miami 105

WESTERN DIVISION FINALS

Oakland 4, New Orleans 0

Apr. 19 ....Oakland 128, New Orleans 118
Apr. 21 ....Oakland 135, New Orleans 124
Apr. 23 ....Oakland 113, New Orleans 107
Apr. 25 ....Oakland 128, New Orleans 114

ABA FINALS

Oakland 4, Indiana 1

Apr. 30 ....Oakland 123, Indiana 114
May 2 ......Indiana 150, Oakland 122
May 3 ......Oakland 134, Indiana 126 (OT)
May 5 ......Oakland 144, Indiana 117
May 7 ......Oakland 135, Indiana 131 (OT)

INDIVIDUAL LEADERS

SCORING

	G	FGM	FTM	Pts.	Avg.
Barry, Oakland	35	392	403	1190	34.0
Hawkins, Minnesota	47	496	425	1420	30.2
Jones, Denver	75	759	591	2133	28.4
J. Jones, New Orleans	77	764	521	2050	26.6
Dampier, Kentucky	78	713	308	1933	24.8
Daniels, Indiana	76	712	400	1824	24.0
Somerset, Hou.-NY	74	619	484	1758	23.8
Carrier, Kentucky	73	559	447	1690	23.2
Freeman, Miami	78	651	420	1724	22.1
Armstrong, Oakland	71	573	373	1530	21.5

FIELD GOAL PCT.

	FGM	FGA	PCT.
McGill, Denver	411	745	.552
Hammond, Denver	329	601	.547
Eakins, Oakland	351	646	.543
J. Jones, New Orleans	764	1429	.535
Barry, Oakland	392	767	.511

3-PT. FIELD GOAL PCT.

	FGM	FGA	PCT.
Carrier, Kentucky	125	330	.379
Combs, Dallas	84	233	.361
Dampier, Kentucky	199	552	.361
Lehmann, Los Angeles	48	137	.350
Johnson, NY-Hou.	64	183	.350

FREE THROW PCT.

	FTM	FTA	PCT.
Barry, Oakland	403	454	.888
Jackson, NY-Min.-Hou.	299	337	.887
Lloyd, New York	218	246	.886
Becker, Houston	200	240	.833
Soemerset, Hou.-NY	484	583	.830

ASSISTS

	G.	NO.	AVG.
Brown, Oakland	77	544	7.1
Freeman, Miami	78	501	6.4
Dampier, Kentucky	78	456	5.8
J. Jones, New Orleans	77	437	5.7
Brown, Indiana	75	345	4.6

REBOUNDS

	G.	OFF.	DEF.	TOT.	AVG.
Daniels, Indiana	76	383	873	1256	16.5
Robbins, New Orleans	76	368	656	1024	13.5
Thoren, Miami	78	391	655	1046	13.4
Washington, Minnesota	69	367	501	868	12.6
Hawkins, Minnesota	47	367	367	534	11.4

1967-68 SEASON

Connie Hawkins

Perhaps it was doomed from the beginning, starting as it did on the unluckiest of days, Friday the 13th. On that day, in October 1967, the American Basketball Association began competing against the NBA. Could it combine the right mix of basketball talent and business savvy to survive where other leagues had failed before?

The ABA's first season tipped off with 11 teams playing a 78-game schedule, the Oakland Oaks defeating the Anaheim Amigos 134-129 in the opening game. The marquee player was the Pittsburgh Pipers' Connie Hawkins, a 25-year-old New York playground legend. Hawkins had been denied entry into the NBA after his name was associated with a college basketball betting scandal, even though he was never convicted of any wrongdoing. The 6-8, 215-pound Hawkins averaged 26.8 points and 13.5 rebounds and led the Pipers to the Eastern Division title.

Pittsburgh advanced to the Finals against New Orleans, winner of the Western Division. The Pipers fell behind 3-2, then won Game 6 on the road 118-112 and Game 7 at home 122-113 to capture the first ABA championship. Hawkins earned the league's MVP crown.

FINAL STANDINGS

EASTERN DIVISION

	W	L	PCT.
Pittsburgh	54	24	.692
Minnesota	50	28	.641
Indiana	38	40	.487
Kentucky*	36	42	.462
New Jersey	36	42	.462

* Qualified for playoffs via forfeit win over New Jersey

WESTERN DIVISION

	W	L	PCT.
New Orleans	48	30	.615
Dallas	46	32	.590
Denver	45	33	.577
Houston	29	49	.372
Anaheim	25	53	.321
Oakland	22	56	.282

NBA.COM FACT

The new league was looking for credibility, and what better place to start than at the top. So the ABA hired George Mikan as its commissioner. It was Mikan who is credited for coming up with the idea for the red, white and blue ball that was to become the league's most recognized symbol.

PLAYOFFS

EASTERN DIVISION SEMIFINALS

Minnesota 3, Kentucky 2

Mar. 24....Minnesota 115, Kentucky 102
Mar. 26....Kentucky 100, Minnesota 95
Mar. 27....Minnesota 116, Kentucky 107
Mar. 29....Kentucky 94, Minnesota 86
Mar. 30....Minnesota 114, Kentucky 108

Pittsburgh 3, Indiana 0

Mar. 25....Pittsburgh 146, Indiana 127
Mar. 26....Pittsburgh 121, Indiana 108
Mar. 27....Pittsburgh 133, Indiana 114

WESTERN DIVISION SEMIFINALS

New Orleans 3, Denver 2

Mar. 26....New Orleans 130, Denver 104
Mar. 27....New Orleans 105, Denver 93
Mar. 30....Denver 105, New Orleans 98
Mar. 31....Denver 108, New Orleans 100
Apr. 3......New Orleans 102, Denver 97

Dallas 3, Houston 0

Mar. 23....Dallas 111, Houston 110
Mar. 25....Dallas 115, Houston 97
Mar. 26....Dallas 116, Houston 103

EASTERN DIVISION FINALS

Pittsburgh 4, Minnesota 1

Apr. 4......Pittsburgh 125, Minnesota 117
Apr. 6......Minnesota 137, Pittsburgh 123
Apr. 10....Pittsburgh 107, Minnesota 99
Apr. 13....Pittsburgh 117, Minnesota 108
Apr. 14....Pittsburgh 114, Minnesota 105

WESTERN DIVISION FINALS

New Orleans 4, Dallas 1

Apr. 5......New Orleans 104, Dallas 99
Apr. 9......Dallas 112, New Orleans 109
Apr. 10....New Orleans 110, Dallas 107
Apr. 11....New Orleans 119, Dallas 103
Apr. 13....New Orleans 108, Dallas 107

ABA FINALS

Pittsburgh 4, New Orleans 3

Apr. 18....Pittsburgh 120, New Orleans 112
Apr. 20....New Orleans 109, Pittsburgh 100
Apr. 24....New Orleans 109, Pittsburgh 101
Apr. 25....Pittsburgh 106, New Orleans 105 (OT)
Apr. 27....New Orleans 111, Pittsburgh 108
May 1......Pittsburgh 118, New Orleans 112
May 4......Pittsburgh 122, New Orleans 113

INDIVIDUAL LEADERS

SCORING

	G.	FG	FT	PTS.	AVG.
Hawkins, Pittsburgh	70	635	603	1875	26.8
Moe, New Orleans	78	665	551	1884	24.2
Tart, Oak.-NJ	73	633	451	1718	23.5
Carrier, Kentucky	77	643	395	1765	22.9
Jones, Denver	76	602	530	1742	22.9
Daniels, Minnesota	78	669	390	1729	22.2
Somerset, Houston	61	467	359	1326	21.7
Williams, Pittsburgh	78	642	290	1625	20.8
Dampier, Kentucky	72	620	209	1487	20.7
Lewis, Indiana	76	542	465	1565	20.6

FIELD GOAL PCT.

	FGM	FGA	PCT.
Washington, Pittsburgh	312	596	.523
Hawkins, Pittsburgh	635	1223	.519
Netolicky, Indiana	468	928	.504
Anderson, New Jersey	463	938	.494
C. Beasley, Dallas	374	758	.493

3-PT. FIELD GOAL PCT.

	FGM	FGA	PCT.
Carrier, Kentucky	84	235	.357
Perry, Minnesota	62	178	.348
Vaughn, Pittsburgh	137	410	.334
Rayl, Indiana	57	175	.326
Selvage, Anaheim	147	461	.319

FREE THROW PCT.

	FTM	FTA	PCT.
C. Beasley, Dallas	285	327	.872
Lloyd, New Jersey	170	199	.854
J. Beasley, Dallas	271	322	.842
Jackson, New Jersey	450	543	.829
Nowell, New Jersey	176	213	.826

ASSISTS

	G.	NO.	AVG.
Brown, New Orleans	78	506	6.5
Hagan, Dallas	56	276	4.9
Chubin, Anaheim	77	364	4.7
Hawkins, Pittsburgh	70	320	4.6
Brown, Indiana	76	327	4.3

REBOUNDS

	G.	OFF.	DEF.	TOT.	AVG.
Daniels, Minnesota	78	502	711	1213	15.6
Hawkins, Pittsburgh	70	368	577	945	13.5
J. Beasley, Dallas	77	278	704	982	12.8
Harge, Pit.-Oak.	82	357	681	1038	12.7
Robbins, New Orleans	73	366	528	894	12.2

CHAPTER 20

THE HALL OF FAME

By Curtis Bunn

The thing about the Naismith Memorial Basketball Hall of Fame is this: It has something for everyone who has an interest in the game. And if you are not a hoops fan when you enter, you likely will be when you exit.

That is the magnitude of the shrine in basketball's birthplace in Springfield, Mass. For every age and gender, every level of interest, the Hall provides a cornucopia of knowledge, exhibits, games and more. And most significantly, it is the special place where most every player hopes to be enshrined after his playing career.

THE NAISMITH MEMORIAL BASKETBALL HALL OF FAME HAS A WEALTH OF PHOTOS, EXHIBITS AND MEMORABILIA THAT CAPTURE THE HISTORY OF THE SPORT.

"Just an unbelievable place with a wealth of knowledge," said Bill Walton, a 1993 enshrinee who starred at UCLA and in the NBA with the Portland Trail Blazers and the Boston Celtics.

Indeed, the Basketball Hall of Fame, which opened on February 17, 1968, is a celebration of the people — players, coaches, referees, and members of the media — and the teams that advanced the game into a worldwide phenomenon. It is dedicated to all levels of the sport internationally, with a unifying theme of "many faces, one game."

"What makes the Basketball Hall of Fame unique is that it represents all levels of basketball — amateur, professional, male, female, international," said Don Gibson, Chief Operating Officer of the Hall. "It's an education about basketball."

The core of the building is the Honors Court, which depicts the Hall's enshrined members. The Hall is the desired destination of most every player who laced up sneakers and hit the blacktop. The players in the Hall have exhibited outstanding prowess on the court, helping advance the game to unprecedented heights.

"It's one of the great days of my life," said former Denver Nuggets forward Alex English, who was enshrined into the

THE HALL OF FAME HAS A HUGE INTERACTIVE AREA THAT ALLOWS VISITORS TO PLAY THE SPORT.

Hall in 1997. "There's no greater validation of your career. You look at all the great players there and what the Basketball Hall of Fame represents, and you can't help but get caught up in the history of it all."

The coaches in the Hall have helped the players hone their skills while leading teams to great success and developing new strategies. "It's the ultimate honor," Toronto Raptors coach Lenny Wilkens said. The NBA's all-time winningest coach is one of two people (UCLA's John Wooden is the other) to be enshrined as a coach (1998) and a player ('89). "I didn't play the game or get into coaching thinking I wanted to be in the Hall of Fame," Wilkens said, "You strive to do your best. And when something like that happens, you're just so grateful because it represents the best in a great sport."

The contributors impacted basketball in various ways. The referees regulated the game and enforced the rules that changed and enshrined the game. The administrators safeguarded the integrity of the game. And the four teams represent the essence of basketball: the harmonious functioning of a group.

NBA.COM FACT

The Hall of Fame inducted its first class in 1959, nine years before it had a facility to call home. The Hall of Fame's charter class featured 17 inductees, including the game's founder (Dr. James Naismith), the NBA's first superstar (Lakers center George Mikan), and basketball's first great team (the Original Celtics from the 1920s). By the time the Hall of Fame opened in 1968, it already had inducted 66 individuals and four teams.

"I've been to the Hall of Fame," Los Angeles Lakers center Shaquille O'Neal said, "and there's a lot of knowledge there. All the old-timers, the growth of the game. The interactive stuff, the memorabilia. It's all about the history of the game."

The history of basketball began in December 1891, when Dr. James A. Naismith created the game with 13 rules, played by 18 young men in a YMCA gymnasium. The object of the game was simple: toss a ball into a peach basket. Literally, from the moment the first "basket" was scored, basketball was a success. Naismith's game rapidly grew, and by the start of World War I, the game had blossomed into a major sport.

In 1936, basketball made its mark around the world when it was introduced as a sport in the Olympic Games in Berlin. The National Association of Basketball Coaches sponsored Naismith's trip to the Olympics three years before his death. Naismith was thrilled to see that his game had become so successful.

Now, basketball is played in more than 170 countries. Of course, all of this progress is captured in the Basketball Hall of Fame — with photos, exhibits, interactive elements and video.

"The Hall is dedicated to the most popular sport in the world, the fastest-growing with the youngest demographic," Gibson said. "The mission of the Hall is to educate, from Dr. James Naismith's invention to today."

The Hall had a difficult beginning. Its existence speaks to the determination of the men who worked to get the structure up nearly 20 years after it was founded in 1949. On July 1, 1966, after countless delays for various reasons, a group called the Hall of Fame, Inc., hired Lee Williams, the longtime Colby College basketball coach and past president of the National Association of Basketball Coaches (NABC), as Basketball Hall of Fame executive director.

"When I came here, [the Hall of Fame] was still a hole in the ground," Williams recalled. "My motivation was given to me by a reporter. When I first took the job, there was a sign at the future building site that . . . a reporter took the liberty of referring to our site as the 'Hole of Fame.' That was all the inspiration I needed."

Williams went on a fund-raising campaign all over the country. On February 17, 1968, Williams' commitment was rewarded: The Naismith Memorial Basketball Hall of Fame opened its doors to the public on the campus of Springfield College, not far from where the first game was played.

It was a celebrated event, but the popularity of the Hall was slow in developing. It took five years to get its 100,000th visitor. In the next three years, another 200,000 patrons visited, and the Hall had to build a larger facility, which opened in 1985. Now, it receives 150,000 visitors a year.

Among Gibson's goals is to have as many NBA players as possible counted among the yearly visitors. "I've talked to a lot of NBA players," he said. "Many of them have visited in the past. And in all instances, they came away with a strong sense of the history of the game."

One of Gibson's ambitions is to have all NBA players visit the Hall during the season. "We can't make them come, but we'd like to set it up that they come in when they're visiting to play the Celtics in Boston," he said. "The wealth of information is so vast that we know all the players would be engulfed in it."

And the Hall is due to get even better with a new facility scheduled to open in 2002, a contemporary centerpiece of a $103-million, 18.5-acre complex on the bank of the Connecticut River. It will be resplendent with basketball-themed retail and restaurant promenades.

The need for another facility was simple: Ample space was necessary to adequately display all the growth and advancement of the game over the years. No major sport has been more advanced in technology and cultural development, and the Hall expresses it all.

NBA.COM FACT

Any person affiliated with basketball is eligible for election into the Hall of Fame. Players must be retired for five years before they become eligible. Coaches and referees must have coached or officiated for 25 years, or been retired for at least five years. Contributors are eligible.

A visitor's experience is multi-faceted. There are countless memorabilia items and exhibits chronicling the game's early days. There is footage from every era, showing the changes the game has made and the extraordinary talent.

The collection of memorabilia is astounding, from the display of early uniforms to former Pistons center Bob Lanier's size 22 shoes. From the peach basket to the 10-foot goal. And anything in between.

"You can't help but get caught up in all the stuff that they have there," Miami Heat guard Tim Hardaway said. "It's a great place. It's a place to take your kids to learn about the game. And the great thing is that you're learning just as much as they are."

Over the years, the Hall has transformed itself into one of the foremost sports museums in the world through the use of modern technology, the expansion of the museum's administrative capabilities through staff recruitment, computerization and more effective involvement of the Board of Trustees.

The enhancement of Enshrinement Weekend and the upgrading of the NBA Hall of Fame Game, the Tip-Off Classic and College Awards Day help bolster the Hall's appeal.

THE CURRENT HALL OF FAME OPENED IN 1985.

THE 21ST CENTURY HALL OF FAME WILL OPEN IN 2002.

BASKETBALL HALL OF FAME ENSHRINEES

PLAYERS

NAME	YEAR ELECTED
Abdul-Jabbar, Kareem	1995
Archibald, Nathaniel (Nate, "Tiny")	1991
Arizin, Paul J.	1977
*Barlow, Thomas B. (Tarzan)	1980
Barry, Richard F. (Rick)	1987
Baylor, Elgin	1976
*Beckman, John	1972
Bellamy, Walt	1993
Belov, Sergei	1992
Bing, Dave	1990
Bird, Larry J.	1998
Blazejowksi, Carol	1994
*Borgmann, Bernard (Bennie)	1961
Bradley, William W. (Bill)	1982
*Brennan, Joseph R.	1974
Cervi, Alfred N. (Al)	1984
*Chamberlain, Wilton N. (Wilt)	1978
*Cooper, Charles T. (Tarzan)	1976
*Cosic, Kresimir	1996
Cousy, Robert J. (Bob)	1970
Cowens, David W. (Dave)	1991
Crawford, Joan	1997
Cunningham, William J.	1986
Curry, Denise M.	1997
*Davies, Robert E. (Bob)	1969
*DeBernardi, Forrest S.	1961
DeBusschere, David A. (Dave)	1982
*Dehnert, Henry G. (Dutch)	1968
Donovan, Anne	1995
*Endacott, Paul	1971
English, Alexander (Alex)	1997
Erving, Julius W.	1993
*Foster, Harold E. (Bud)	1964
Frazier, Walter (Clyde)	1987
*Friedman, Max (Marty)	1971
*Fulks, Joseph F. (Joe)	1977
*Gale, Lauren (Laddie)	1976
Gallatin, Harry J.	1991
*Gates, William (Pop)	1989
Gervin, George	1996
Gola, Thomas J. (Tom)	1975
Goodrich, Gail	1996
Greer, Harold E. (Hal)	1981
*Gruenig, Robert F. (Ace)	1963
Hagan, Clifford O.	1977
*Hanson, Victor A.	1960
Harris-Stewart, Lusia	1992
Havlicek, John	1983
Hawkins, Connie	1992
Hayes, Elvin E.	1990
Haynes, Marques O.	1998
Heinsohn, Thomas W.	1986
*Holman, Nat	1964
Houbregs, Robert J.	1987
Howell, Bailey E.	1997
*Hyatt, Charles D. (Chuck)	1959
Issel, Dan P.	1993
*Jeannette, Harry (Buddy)	1994
*Johnson, William C.	1976
*Johnston, Donald Neil	1990
Jones, K.C.	1989
Jones, Samuel (Sam)	1983
*Krause, Edward W. (Moose)	1975
Kurland, Robert A. (Bob)	1961
Lanier, Robert J. (Bob)	1992
*Lapchick, Joe	1966
Lieberman-Cline, Nancy	1996
Lovellette, Clyde E.	1988
Lucas, Jerry R.	1979
Luisetti, Angelo (Hank)	1959
Macauley, Edward C. (Ed)	1960
*Maravich, Peter P. (Pete)	1987
Martin, Slater N.	1981
McAdoo, Robert (Bob)	2000
*McCracken, Branch	1960
*McCracken, Jack	1962
*McDermott, Robert (Bobby)	1988
McGuire, Richard S. (Dick)	1993
McHale, Kevin	1999
Meyers, Ann E.	1993
Mikan, George L.	1959
Mikkelsen, Vern	1995
Miller, Cheryl	1995
Monroe, Earl (The Pearl)	1990
Murphy, Calvin J.	1993
*Murphy, Charles C. (Stretch)	1960
*Page, Harlan O. (Pat)	1962
Pettit, Robert L. (Bob)	1970
Phillip, Andy	1961
*Pollard, James C. (Jim)	1977
Ramsey, Frank V.	1981
Reed, Willis	1981
Risen, Arnold D. (Arnie)	1998
Robertson, Oscar P.	1979
*Roosma, John S.	1961
*Russell, John D. (Honey)	1964
Russell, William F. (Bill)	1974
Schayes, Adolph (Dolph)	1972
*Schmidt, Ernest J.	1973
*Schommer, John J.	1959
*Sedran, Barney	1962
Semjonova, Uljana	1993
Sharman, William W. (Bill)	1975
*Steinmetz, Christian	1961
Thomas, Isiah	2000
Thompson, David	1996
*Thompson, John A. (Cat)	1962
Thurmond, Nate	1984
Twyman, John K. (Jack)	1982
Unseld, Westley S. (Wes)	1988
*Vandivier, Robert P. (Fuzzy)	1974
*Wachter, Edward A.	1961
Walton, William T. (Bill)	1993
Wanzer, Robert F.	1987
West, Jerry A.	1979
White, Nera	1992
**Wilkens, Leonard R. (Lenny)	1989
**Wooden, John R.	1960
Yardley, George	1996

COACHES

NAME	YEAR ELECTED
*Allen, Dr. Forrest C. (Phog)	1959
*Anderson, W. Harold	1984

Auerbach, Arnold J. (Red)	1968
*Barry, Justin M. (Sam)	1978
*Blood, Ernest A.	1960
*Cann, Howard G.	1967
*Carlson, Dr. H. Clifford	1959
Carnesecca, Louis P. (Lou)	1992
Carnevale, Bernard L. (Ben)	1969
Carril, Peter J. (Pete)	1997
*Case, Everett N.	1981
Conradt, Jody	1998
Crum, Denny E.	1994
Daly, Charles J. (Chuck)	1994
*Dean, Everett S.	1966
*Diaz-Miguel, Antonio	1997
*Diddle, Edgar A.	1971
*Drake, Bruce	1972
Gaines, Clarence E.	1981
*Gardner, James H. (Jack)	1983
*Gill, Amory T. (Slats)	1967
Gomelsky, Aleksandr	1995
Hannum, Alexander M. (Alex)	1998
Harshman, Marv K.	1984
Haskins, Donald L. (Don)	1997
*Hickey, Edgar S.	1978
*Hobson, Howard A.	1965
*Holzman, William (Red)	1986
*Iba, Henry P. (Hank)	1968
*Julian, Alvin F. (Doggie)	1967
*Keaney, Frank W.	1960
*Keogan, George E.	1961
Knight, Robert M. (Bob)	1991
Kundla, John	1995
*Lambert, Ward L.	1960
*Litwack, Harry	1975
*Loeffler, Kenneth D.	1964
*Lonborg, Arthur C. (Dutch)	1972
*McCutchan, Arad A.	1980
McGuire, Al	1992
*McGuire, Frank J.	1976
*McLendon, John B.	1978
*Meanwell, Dr. Walter E.	1959
Meyer, Raymond J.	1978
Miller, Ralph H.	1988
Moore, Billie	1999
Newell, Peter F.	1978
*Nikolic, Aleksandar G. (Aza)	1998
Ramsay, Jack T.	1992
Rubini, Cesare	1994
*Rupp, Adolph F.	1968
*Sachs, Leonard D.	1961
*Shelton, Everett G.	1979
Smith, Dean E.	1982
Summitt, Pat	2000
Taylor, Fred R.	1986
Thompson, John	1999
*Wade, Margaret	1984
*Watts, Stanley H.	1986
**Wilkens, Leonard R. (Lenny)	1998
**Wooden, John R.	1972
*Woolpert, Phillip D. (Phil)	1992
Wootten, Morgan	2000

CONTRIBUTORS

NAME	YEAR ELECTED
*Abbott, Senda Berenson	1984
*Bee, Clair F.	1967
*Biasone, Daniel (Danny)	2000
*Brown, Walter A.	1965
*Bunn, John W.	1964
*Douglas, Robert L. (Bob)	1971
*Duer, Alva O. (Al)	1981
Embry, Wayne	1999
*Fagan, Clifford B.	1983
*Fisher, Harry A.	1973
*Fleisher, Lawrence (Larry)	1991
*Gottlieb, Edward	1971
*Gulick, Dr. Luther H.	1959
*Harrison, Lester	1979
*Hepp, Ferenc	1980
*Hickox, Edward J.	1959
*Hinkle, Paul D. (Tony)	1965
*Irish, Edward S. (Ned)	1964
*Jones, R. William	1964
*Kennedy, J. Walter	1980
*Liston, Emil S.	1974
*Mokray, William G. (Bill)	1965
*Morgan, Ralph	1959
*Morgenweck, Frank	1962
*Naismith, Dr. James	1959
Newton, C.M.	2000
*O'Brien, John J.	1961
*O'Brien, Lawrence F. (Larry)	1991
*Olsen, Harold G.	1959
*Podoloff, Maurice	1973
*Porter, Henry V.	1960
*Reid, William A.	1963
*Ripley, Elmer H.	1972
*St. John, Lynn W.	1962
*Saperstein, Abraham (Abe)	1970
*Schabinger, Arthur A.	1961
*Stagg, Amos Alonzo	1959
Stankovic, Borislav	1991
*Steitz, Edward S.	1983
*Taylor, Charles H. (Chuck)	1968
*Teague, Bertha F.	1984
*Tower, Oswald	1959
*Trester, Arthur L.	1961
*Wells, W.R. Clifford	1971
*Wilke, Louis G. (Lou)	1982
*Zollner, Fred	1999

REFEREES

NAME	YEAR ELECTED
*Enright, James E.	1978
*Hepbron, George T.	1960
*Hoyt, George H.	1961
*Kennedy, Matthew P.	1959
*Leith, Lloyd R.	1982
*Mihalik, Zigmund J. (Red)	1986
*Nucatola, John P.	1977
*Quigley, Ernest C.	1961
*Shirley, J. Dallas	1979
*Strom, Earl	1995
*Tobey, David	1961
*Walsh, David H.	1961

TEAMS

NAME	YEAR ELECTED
Buffalo Germans	1961
First Team	1959
Original Celtics	1959
Renaissance	1963

**Deceased*

***John Wooden and Lenny Wilkens are enshrined as both a player and coach.*

DIRECTORY OF MEMBERS ASSOCIATED WITH THE NBA *(updates since 1994 written by Mark Hale)*

MEMBERS ARE LISTED ALPHABETICALLY IN THEIR RESPECTIVE CATEGORIES. DATE OF ELECTION IS NEXT TO THEIR NAMES.

PLAYERS

Kareem Abdul-Jabbar (1995) — One of the NBA's greatest players with both Milwaukee Bucks and Los Angeles Lakers ... At time of retirement in 1989, was NBA's all-time leader in points (38,387), seasons played (20), points in the playoffs (5,762), MVP awards (six), minutes (57,446), games (1,560), field goals (15,837), field goal attempts (28,307) and blocked shots (3,189) ... Was Rookie of the Year in 1969. ... Notched one championship with Milwaukee and five with L.A. ... Had career average of 24.6 points per game ... Won three NCAA titles at UCLA as Bruins went 88-2 over three seasons ... Selected as one of the 50 Greatest Players in NBA History in 1996 .

Nate Archibald (1991) — Only player ever to lead NBA in scoring and assists in the same season, 1973, when he averaged 34.0 points per game and 11.4 assists per game ... Played 14 seasons, averaging 18.8 points per game and 7.4 assists per game ... Six-time All-Star and MVP of 1981 contest ... All-NBA First Team three times ... Helped Boston Celtics to 1981 NBA Championship ... Selected as one of the 50 Greatest Players in NBA History in 1996.

Paul Arizin (1997) — All-American and College Player of the Year at Villanova in 1950 ... Averaged 17.2 points per game as Philadelphia Warrior rookie, more than 20 points per game for last nine pro seasons ... Retired as third-highest NBA scorer with 16,266 points ... A 10-time All-Star and Game's MVP in 1952 ... Led league in scoring twice ... Averaged 24.2 points per game while pacing Warriors to title in 1956 ... Selected as one of the 50 Greatest Players in NBA History in 1996.

Rick Barry (1986) — Led NCAA in scoring (37.4 points per game) in 1965 at Miami ... NBA Rookie of the Year with San Francisco the next season ... Had brilliant 14-year pro career — four in ABA (Oakland, Washington, New York Nets) and 10 in NBA (San Francisco, Golden State and Houston) ... Only player to lead both leagues in scoring (NBA 1967, ABA 1969) ... Led Golden State to 1975 NBA crown and was NBA Finals MVP ... Shot 90 percent from foul line using unorthodox underhand style ... Scored 25,279 points in his career for a 24.8 average ... Selected as one of the 50 Greatest Players in NBA History in 1996.

Elgin Baylor (1976) — All-American in 1958 at Seattle, averaging 32.5 points per game ... NBA Rookie of the Year in 1959 ... Selected to NBA All-Star team 11 times ... All-Star co-MVP with Bob Pettit in 1959 ... Scored L.A. Lakers' record 71 points in one game in 1960 ... Compiled 23,149 points and 27.4 average during 14-year career ... Retired as third-leading all-time NBA scorer ... Selected as one of the 50 Greatest Players in NBA History in 1996.

Walt Bellamy (1993) — Outstanding scorer and rebounder ... Two-time All-American at Indiana and gold medal winner at 1960 Olympics ... NBA Rookie of the Year in 1962 with Chicago, averaging 31.6 points per game and 19.0 rebounds per game ... Scored 20, 941 points (20.1 points per game) and grabbed 14,241 rebounds (13.6 rebounds per game.) in 14 NBA seasons ... Four-time NBA All-Star.

Dave Bing (1989) — All-American at Syracuse (1966) ... Played 12 seasons in NBA, nine with Detroit Pistons ... NBA Rookie of the Year in 1967 ... Twice named to the All-NBA First Team ... Seven-time All-Star and MVP of 1976 contest ... Averaged 20.3 points per game for career and led the NBA with 27.1 points per game in 1968 ... Founded Bing Steel in Detroit and has been honored for his business efforts ... Selected as one of the 50 Greatest Players in NBA History in 1996.

Larry Bird (1998) — After 13-year career with Boston Celtics, held or shared 27 team records ... Won three championships (1981, 1984, 1986) and reached Finals two other times ... All-Star 12 times and MVP in 1982 contest ... Rookie of the Year in 1980 ... Three-time MVP (1984, 1985, 1986) ... All-NBA First-Team pick from 1980-88 ... Had brilliant career at Indiana State, setting 30 school records and leading team to NCAA title game in 1979 ... Coached Indiana Pacers to NBA Finals in 2000 ... Selected as one of the 50 Greatest Players in NBA History in 1996.

Bill Bradley (1982) — Averaged 30 points per game and was a two-time All-American at Princeton ... Established an NCAA tourney record of 58 points as a senior in 1965 when he was College Player of the Year ... Member of the U.S. Olympic gold medal team at Tokyo in 1964 ... Spent two years as a Rhodes Scholar at Oxford before signing with New York Knicks ... Noted for team play during 10-year career in which he helped Knicks to NBA championships in 1970 and 1973 ... Elected to United States Senate from New Jersey in 1978.

Al Cervi (1984) — One of the game's greatest backcourt players in late 1940s and early 1950s ... Superb scorer and defensive player with Rochester Royals, he was MVP of the NBL in 1946-47 ... Became player-coach of the Syracuse Nationals in NBL in 1948 and brought them into NBA the following year ... One of his era's leading coaches, he retired as a player in 1953 and coached the Nats until the 1956-57 season.

Wilt Chamberlain (1978) — Considered by many as game's greatest offensive force ... Starred at Kansas and played one year with Globetrotters before joining NBA ... Holds NBA records for points in a season (4,029), points in a game (100 versus Knicks March 2, 1962), scoring average for season (50.4 in 1962), career rebounds (23,924), rebounds in a season (2,149) and rebounds in a game (55) ... Led NBA in assists in 1967-68 ... Played 47,859 minutes (including 48.5 mpg in 1962) and never fouled out in 1,045 games ... Led 1967 Philadelphia 76ers and 1972 Los Angeles Lakers to NBA titles ... NBA MVP four times ... Played in 13 All-Star Games ... Selected as one of the 50 Greatest Players in NBA History in 1996.

Bob Cousy (1970) — One of basketball's greatest playmakers ... Two-time All-American at Holy Cross (1949-1950) ... Superb playmaker and court general, "The Cooz" led Boston Celtics to six NBA championships in seven years, including five in a row (1959-63) ... All NBA First Team 10 consecutive years ... NBA MVP in 1957 ... A 13-time All-Star, winning MVP honors in 1954 and 1957 ... Once scored 50 points in an NBA playoff game ... Had 6,955 career assists and 16,960 points ... Selected as one of the 50 Greatest Players in NBA History in 1996.

Dave Cowens (1990) — Hardworking, competitive center who made up for lack of size (6-9) with tenacity ... Led Boston Celtics to NBA championships in 1974 and 1976 ... NBA co-Rookie of the Year (with Geoff Petrie) in 1971 ... NBA MVP in 1973 ...Played 10 seasons with Boston Celtics, including one as player-coach ... Also played one-half season with Milwaukee ... Averaged 17.6 points per game and 13.6 rebounds per game for career ... Selected as one of the 50 Greatest Players in NBA History in 1996.

Billy Cunningham (1985) — Two-time All-American at North Carolina, nicknamed "The Kangaroo Kid" for his jumping ability ... Played nine years with Philadelphia 76ers, two with Carolina Cougars of ABA ... Starred on Sixers' 1967 championship team and was MVP of ABA in 1973 ... Averaged 21.2 points per game in 770 pro games ... Coached Sixers from 1977 to 1985, compiling 454-196 record (.698) and winning NBA Championship in 1983 ... Former part-owner of Miami Heat ... Selected as one of the 50 Greatest Players in NBA History in 1996.

Bob Davies (1969) — Two-time All-American at Seton Hall, leading team to 43 straight wins ... Joined Rochester Royals in 1945 for a 10-year pro career in NBL and NBA ... Outstanding playmaker ... All-league seven times ... MVP of the NBL in 1947 ... Led Royals to titles in 1946, 1947 (NBL) and 1951 (NBA) ... Scored 7,771 points and annually ranked among league leaders in assists.

Dave DeBusschere (1982) — Three-time All-American at University of Detroit ... At 24, became the youngest coach in NBA history when, early in 1964-65 season, he became player-coach of Detroit Pistons ... Coached them until late in the 1966-67 season ... Also pitched for parts of two seasons for the Chicago White Sox (1962, 1963) ... Helped New York Knicks to NBA titles in 1970 and 1973 ... Outstanding shooter, also one of game's greatest defensive forwards ... Later served as New York Net's General Manager, ABA Commissioner and New York Knicks' Executive Vice President ... Selected as one of the 50 Greatest Players in NBA History in 1996

Alex English (1997) — NBA's leading scorer in 1980s (19,682 points) ... Spent 15 years in league, 10 with Denver Nuggets ... Owns Denver records for scoring (points and average), games and assists, among others ... First NBA player to score more than 2,000 points in eight consecutive seasons ... Appeared in eight straight All-Star Games ... Three-time All-NBA Second-Team pick ... League's top scorer in 1982-83 ... Ranks fourth in NBA history in field goals, seventh in games and ninth in scoring.

Julius Erving (1992) — At UMass, one of seven players in NCAA history to average over 20 points per game and 20 rebounds per game for career ... Played five seasons in ABA and 11 in NBA, making All-Star team every year ... ABA MVP in 1974, 1975 and 1976, NBA MVP in 1981 ... Led Nets to ABA titles in 1974 and 1976, Sixers to NBA title in 1983 ... One of the game's most exciting players, known for spectacular drives to the basket ending in dunks ... With 30,026 points, ranks fourth behind only Kareem Abdul-Jabbar, Wilt Chamberlain and Karl Malone on all-time NBA/ABA scoring list ... Selected as one of the 50 Greatest Players in NBA History in 1996.

Walt "Clyde" Frazier (1986) — Led Southern Illinois to NIT title in 1967 and was named tourney MVP ... One of the smoothest guards in the game, "Clyde" played for the New York Knicks for 10 seasons (1968-77) ... Outstanding at playing the passing lanes to come up with steals ... Known for style and flair on and off the court ... Starred on 1970 and 1973 Knick championship teams ... Had 36 points and 19 assists in Game 7 of 1970 NBA Finals against Lakers ... Selected as one of the 50 Greatest Players in NBA History in 1996.

Joe Fulks (1977) — "Jumpin' Joe" was one of the first great jump shooters, scoring 1,560 NBA points for 26-point average in his third pro season after starring for Murray State ... Scored 63 points for Philadelphia Warriors in 1949, and NBA record that stood for 10 years ... Won scoring title with 23.2 average and led Philadelphia Warriors to championship in NBA's inaugural season, 1946-47 ... Unanimous All-NBA First Team selection three times in eight-year career.

Harry Gallatin (1990) — One of the game's top players in the 1950s ... Played 10 pro seasons, nine with New York and one with Detroit ... Though only 6-6, played center for much of his career and led the NBA in rebounding at 15.3 rebounds per game in 1954 ... "The Horse" averaged 11.9 rebounds per game for eight seasons — rebounds were not kept as an official statistic during his first two years in the league ... Coached St. Louis and New York, earning Coach of the Year honors in 1963.

George Gervin (1996) — Nicknamed "The Iceman" ... One of three NBA players to win four or more scoring titles (1978-80, 1982) ... Played 14 seasons with the Virginia Squires, San Antonio Spurs and Chicago Bulls ... A 12-time All-Star (three ABA, nine NBA) ... Ranks 23rd on NBA's scoring list (20,708 points), 11th on combined ABA and NBA scoring list (26,595 points) and sixth in scoring average (26.2 points per game) ... San Antonio's all-time leader in points, games, field goals, free throws and steals ... Selected as one of the 50 Greatest Players in NBA History in 1996.

Tom Gola (1975) — Four-time All-American at LaSalle ... MVP in 1952 NIT and 1954 NCAA Tournament, leading LaSalle to both titles ... Spent outstanding 10-year NBA career with Philadelphia and San Francisco Warriors and New York Knicks ... All-NBA in 1958 ... Versatile player who was always among league leaders in scoring, rebounds and assists.

Gail Goodrich (1996) — Southpaw with sweet shooting touch posted career scoring average of 18.6 points per game over 14 NBA seasons with Los Angeles Lakers, Phoenix Suns and New Orleans Jazz ... Appeared in five All-Star Games ... Spearheaded Lakers' NBA title run in 1971-72 by averaging team-high 25.9 points per game ... Led UCLA to championships in 1964 and 1965 ... Finished college career as UCLA's all-time leading scorer ... Led conference in scoring in 1964, the first Bruin to ever do so.

Hal Greer (1981) — All-American at Marshall in 1958 ... Spent 15-year pro career with the same franchise, joining Syracuse Nationals in 1958 and moving with them to Philadelphia in 1963 ... Outstanding jump shooter ... Averaged 22.1 points per game for 1966-67 Sixers, who are regarded as one of the NBA's greatest teams ... Selected as one of the 50 Greatest Players in NBA History in 1996.

Cliff Hagan (1977) — Helped Kentucky win NCAA title in 1951 and go undefeated (25-0) in 1954 ... After 10 seasons with St. Louis Hawks in which he averaged 18.0 points per game, he completed 13-year pro career as player-coach of ABA Dallas Chaparrals ... Finished with 14,870 points ... One of the great all-time hook shooters ... Played in five NBA All-Star Games ... Key contributor as Hawks won five Western Division titles and NBA crown in 1958.

John Havlicek (1983) — Standout at Ohio State, leading Buckeyes to NCAA title and 78-6 record in three seasons ... Boston Celtics' No. 1 pick in 1962 ... At first known for his defense, later became outstanding scorer as well ... "Hondo" began illustrious 16-year career as sixth man ... Tireless, clutch, all-around performer ... Played in 13 All-Star Games ... Played in 1,270 games, scored 26,395 points for 20.8 points per game ... Selected as one of the 50 Greatest Players in NBA History in 1996.

Connie Hawkins (1991) — One of the great leapers in basketball history, a forerunner to Julius Erving and Michael Jordan at swooping to the basket ... A playground legend in New York ... Played seven NBA seasons with Phoenix, the L.A. Lakers and Atlanta ... Four-time NBA All-Star ... MVP of short-lived ABL with Pittsburgh Rens in 1961 ... Led Pittsburgh Pipers to 1968 ABA championship and won league MVP honors ... Also toured with Harlem Globetrotters.

Elvin Hayes (1989) — Among game's greatest scorers ... Tallied 27,313 points (21.0 points per game), third-highest total in NBA history ... All-American at Houston who played in famous Astrodome duel against Kareem Abdul-Jabbar's UCLA squad ... Led NBA in scoring as a rookie with 28.4 points per game for San Diego Rockets in 1969 ... Twelve-time All-Star and three-time All-NBA First Team ... Twice led league in rebounding (1970, 1974) ... Led Washington Bullets to 1978 NBA Championship ... Selected as one of the 50 Greatest Players in NBA History in 1996.

Tom Heinsohn (1985) — All-American at Holy Cross in 1955 and 1956 ... NBA Rookie of the Year in 1957, leading Boston Celtics to their first NBA title ... Starting forward on eight NBA Championship teams ... Averaged 18.6 points per game in nine-year career ... Compiled 427-263 record as Celtics coach 1969-78, winning NBA crowns in 1974 and 1976 ... An accomplished artist who has had many gallery exhibitions.

Robert Houbregs (1986) — NCAA Player of the Year in 1953, leading Washington to best-ever 30-3 record ... Ranks second in NCAA tournament history with 34.8 scoring average ... Drafted by Milwaukee, "Houby" played five years in the NBA (1953-58) with Milwaukee, Baltimore, Boston, Fort Wayne and Detroit ... Was Seattle SuperSonics general manager, 1970-73.

Bailey Howell (1997) — Played 12 seasons in NBA for Detroit Pistons, Baltimore Bullets, Boston Celtics and Philadelphia 76ers ... Upon retirement in 1971, ranked eighth in career points (17,770), fourth in games (950) and ninth in rebounds (9,383). . . Six-time All-Star ... Named to All-NBA Second Team in 1963 ... Won two titles with Boston (1968, 1969) ... Three-time All-SEC pick at Mississippi State and school's all-time leader in rebounding and free throws.

Dan Issel (1992) — Set 23 school records at Kentucky before starring in both ABA and NBA, averaging over 20 points per game in each league ... Ranks seventh on combined ABA/NBA career scoring list with 27,482 points, 22.6 average ... ABA Rookie of the Year in 1971 and All-Star MVP in 1972 ... Led Kentucky Colonels to ABA title in 1975 ... NBA All-Star in 1977 ... After serving as broadcaster for Denver Nuggets, became team's coach in 1992.

Harry (Buddy) Jeanette (1994) — Regarded as basketball's top backcourt player from 1938-48 ... Earned four MVP awards ... Won five championships in three different cities (Sheboygan, Fort Wayne and Baltimore) and captured five straight titles from 1941-48 ... Shared NBL Rookie of the Year honors with Lou Boudreau in 1938 ... In 1947-48 became the first player/coach to win a professional championship (with the Baltimore Bullets).

Neil Johnston (1989) — High-scoring frontcourtman played eight seasons for Philadelphia Warriors in 1950s ... Led NBA in scoring three consecutive years (1953-55) ... Topped NBA in rebounding in 1955 ... Averaged over 20 points per game in five of eight NBA seasons, two of them before the 24-second shot clock ... Six-time All-Star ... All-NBA First Team four times.

K. C. Jones (1988) — Teamed with Bill Russell for successive NCAA titles at the University of San Francisco in 1955 and 1956 and Olympic gold medal in 1956 ... As a backcourtman with the Boston Celtics starting in 1958-59, he was known for tenacious defense during a nine-year career in which Celtics won eight consecutive NBA championships ... Coached Brandeis University, San Diego (ABA), Washington, Boston and Seattle (NBA) ... Guided Celtics to NBA titles in 1984 and 1986.

Sam Jones (1983) — One of NBA's all-time great shooters ... Master of the bank shot, he scored 15,380 points for 17.7 points per game in fabulous 12-year career with Celtics ... Played on 10 Celtic championship teams ... A popular and supremely graceful player, teamed with K.C. Jones in great Celtics backcourt ... Selected as one of the 50 Greatest Players in NBA History in 1996.

Bob Lanier (1991) — Two-time All-American and all-time scoring and rebounding leader at St. Bonaventure ... Eight-time All-Star during 14-year NBA career with Detroit and Milwaukee ... Led Bucks to five consecutive division titles ... Retired with 19,248 points and 9,698 career rebounds, ranking among NBA's career Top 20 in both categories.

Joe Lapchick (1966) — Gained fame as first legitimate "star" center in game when he played for Original Celtics ... Played pro ball from 1917 to 1936 ... Later coached at St. John's University, where his teams won four NIT titles ... Twice college Coach of the Year ... Coached NBA's New York Knickerbockers (1947-56).

Clyde Lovellette (1987) — Three-time All-American at Kansas (1950-52) ... Captained the 1952 Jayhawks squad that won NCAA title and was named MVP of the Final Four ... Member of the U.S. Olympic gold medal team in Helsinki in 1952 ... Played on three NBA championship teams (Minneapolis Lakers in 1954 and Boston Celtics in 1963 and 1964) in 11-year pro career.

Jerry Lucas (1979) — Collegiate Player of the Year at Ohio State in 1961 and 1962 ... His Buckeyes were 78-6, won three Big Ten titles and NCAA crown in 1960 ... NBA Rookie of the Year with Cincinnati in 1964 ... Great rebounder who also had soft outside shooting touch ... NBA All-Star seven times, including MVP in 1965 game ... Helped New York to NBA Championship in 1973 ... Selected as one of the 50 Greatest Players in NBA History in 1996.

Ed Macauley (1960) — Two-time All-American at St. Louis University ... "Easy Ed" led nation in field-goal percentage with .524 in 1948-49 ... Played in seven NBA All-Star Games ... Traded by Boston Celtics along with rights to Cliff Hagan for rights to Bill Russell in 1956 ... Career high of 46 versus George Mikan and the Minneapolis Lakers, March 6, 1953 ... Coached St. Louis Hawks to Western Division titles 1959-1960.

Pete Maravich (1986) — "Pistol Pete" set NCAA scoring records with 3,667 career points and 44.2 points per game at LSU ... Known for his floppy socks and razzle-dazzle style of play, including no-look passes and fancy dribbling ... Played 10 years in NBA with Atlanta, New Orleans, Utah and Boston ... Led league in scoring in 1977 (31.1 points per game) ... Five-time NBA All-Star ... One of basketball's greatest showmen ... Selected as one of the 50 Greatest Players in NBA History in 1996.

Slater Martin (1981) — All-American at Texas in 1949 … Playmaker on Minneapolis Laker teams that won NBA titles in 1950, 1952, 1953 and 1954 … Helped St. Louis Hawks to crown in 1958 … "Dugie" was voted All-Star seven times in 11-year career … At 5-10, he's considered one of the great small men ever to play the game.

Bob McAdoo (2000) — Played for seven teams in 14 seasons, most notably the Buffalo Braves and Los Angeles Lakers … Rookie of the Year in 1973 … NBA scoring leader in 1974 (30.6 points per game), 1975 (34.5) and 1976 (31.1) … MVP and All-NBA First-Team pick in 1975 … League's 35th all-time leading scorer (18,787 points) … Won two NBA Championships with Lakers (1982, 1985) … Played in five straight All-Star Games … All-American at North Carolina in 1971-72.

Dick McGuire (1992) — One of the game's great early point guards …"Tricky Dick" starred at St. John's before 11-year NBA career, eight with New York Knicks … Ranked among league assist leaders every year … Later coached Detroit and New York … Currently is Knicks' director of scouting services.

Kevin McHale (1999) — Seven-time All-Star in 12-year career as power forward with Boston Celtics … All-NBA First Team in 1987 … Earned Sixth Man Award in 1984 and 1985 … NBA's ninth-best career shooting percentage (.554) … First player to shoot 60 percent from field and 80 percent from foul line in same season … All-Defensive First Team pick twice and Second Team selection three times … Among Boston's career leaders in field goal percentage (second), games (third), points (fourth) and rebounds (sixth) … Helped Boston win three championships (1981, 1984, 1986) … Selected as one of the 50 Greatest Players in NBA History in 1996.

George Mikan (1959) — Sport's first dominant big man … Three-time All-American center at DePaul … Voted AP Player of the Half Century in 1950 … One of all-time pro greats with Minneapolis Lakers … Led NBA in scoring three times, rebounding once … NBA All-Star Game MVP, 1953 … Led Lakers to five titles in six years as NBA's first dynasty … First commissioner of the American Basketball Association … Selected as one of the 50 Greatest Players in NBA History in 1996.

Vern Mikkelsen (1995) — One of the game's first true power forwards … An intense rebounder and defender … Part of dominating frontcourt of Minneapolis Lakers, who captured four NBA titles (1950, 1952-54) … A six-time NBA All-Star … Named to the All-NBA Second Team four times and served as Lakers captain for five seasons … Sixth player to score 10,000 career points … Averaged 14.4 points per game and 8.4 rebounds per game.

Earl Monroe (1989) — Crowd-pleasing showman with dazzling moves … Played 13 seasons for Baltimore and New York … "The Pearl" first gained national attention by averaging 41.5 points per game as a senior at Winston-Salem State (1967) … Rookie of the Year in 1968 and All-NBA First Team the following year … Blended his one-on-one moves into Knicks' team concept and helped them win 1973 NBA Championship … Averaged 18.8 points per game for pro career … Selected as one of the 50 Greatest Players in NBA History in 1996.

Calvin Murphy (1993) — One of the game's great little men … Three-time All-American at Niagara, where he averaged 33.1 points per game … Spent entire 13-year pro career with Rockets, first in San Diego and later in Houston … Team's all-time scoring leader with 17,949 points … Career free throw mark of .892 is among best in NBA history … Once held record with 78 consecutive free throws made … At 5-9, was one of sport's most popular players.

Bob Pettit (1970) — One of game's first great big forwards … Though 6-9, was mobile enough and shot well enough to play facing the basket … Three-time All-American at LSU … NBA Rookie of the Year in 1955 … All-NBA First Team 10 straight years for Milwaukee and St. Louis Hawks … NBA MVP 1956, 1959 … All-Star Game MVP three times and co-MVP once … Retired in 1965 as highest scorer in NBA history with 20,880 points … Selected as one of the 50 Greatest Players in NBA History in 1996.

Andy Phillip (1961) — One of the outstanding backcourtmen of his era, a solid scorer and playmaker ... Leader of famed "Whiz Kids" team at Illinois, where he was a two-time All-American ... Played 11 years in NBA with Chicago Stags, Philadelphia Warriors, Fort Wayne Pistons and Boston Celtics ... Member of 1957 Boston Celtics NBA Championship team.

Jim Pollard (1977) — All-American as sophomore at Stanford, which won NCAA championship in 1942 ... Smooth forward with great finesse moves ... Played eight seasons with Minneapolis Lakers, one in NBL and seven in NBA ... Four-time NBA All-Star ... Helped Minneapolis to five NBA titles in six-year span from 1949 through 1954, as well as NBL title in 1948.

Frank Ramsey (1981) — All-American at Kentucky in 1952 and 1954 ... Captained Adolph Rupp's NCAA champs in 1952 ... Helped pioneer "sixth man" concept for the Boston Celtics ... Played on seven NBA Championship teams in nine years, including six in a row (1959-64) ... Versatile guard who could score or set up teammates.

Willis Reed (1981) — Led Grambling to NAIA championship in 1961 ... Selected to all-time NAIA team in 1970 ... NBA Rookie of the Year in 1965 with New York Knicks ... Dominating and inspirational presence in 10-year Knick career ... "The Captain" led Knicks to NBA titles in 1970 and 1973 ... First player ever selected as MVP for regular season, All-Star Game and NBA Finals in same season (1970) ... Retired as Knicks' career rebound leader with 8,414 ... Coached Knicks, Creighton University and New Jersey Nets ... Selected as one of the 50 Greatest Players in NBA History in 1996.

Oscar Robertson (1979) — One of games' greatest all-around players ... Two-time NCAA Player of the Year and three-time All-American at Cincinnati ... Set 14 NCAA records ... Won Olympic gold medal in 1960 ... Played 14 NBA seasons, 10 with Cincinnati and four with Milwaukee ... NBA Rookie of the Year in 1961, MVP in 1964, All-Star MVP in 1961, 1964 and 1969 ... "The Big O" averaged a triple-double in 1962 ... Scored 26,710 points for a 25.7 average in 1,040 games, with then-record 9,887 assists ... Selected as one of the 50 Greatest Players in NBA History in 1996.

Arnold (Arnie) Risen (1998) — One of basketball's top rebounders, he played 13 seasons with Indianapolis of the NBL, Rochester of the NBL/NBA and Boston of the NBA... Led Rochester to 1951 NBA crown by averaging 16.3 points per game and 12.0 rebounds per game ... Also part of Boston's 1957 title-winning team ... Holds Rochester records for points and rebounds in a season, scoring average and career rebounds ... Three-time NBA All-Star ... Nicknamed "Stilts."

Bill Russell (1974) — Brilliant shotblocker who revolutionized NBA defensive concepts and brought Boston Celtics eight straight titles, 11 in 13 seasons ... Amassed 21,721 career rebounds and 15.1 scoring average ... Appeared in 12 All-Star Games, winning MVP in 1963 ... Five-time NBA MVP ... Led San Francisco to NCAA titles in 1955 and 1956 and U.S. to gold medal at 1956 Olympics ... Player-coach with Celtics for three seasons, winning NBA championships in 1968 and 1969 ... Later coached Seattle and Sacramento and served as general manager of both clubs ... Selected as one of the 50 Greatest Players in NBA History in 1996.

Dolph Schayes (1972) — All-American at NYU ... High-scoring forward helped Syracuse Nats become one of NBA's top teams in 1950s ... Owned outstanding shooting touch ... A 12-time All-Star ... Scored 19,249 points and played in a onetime record 1,059 games ... Later coached Philadelphia and Buffalo ... Also served as NBA supervisor of officials ... Son Danny also enjoyed a long NBA career ... Selected as one of the 50 Greatest Players in NBA History in 1996.

Bill Sharman (1975) — Two-time All-American at Southern Cal ... Broke into NBA with Washington in 1951, then on to 10 seasons with Boston Celtics ... Teamed with Bob Cousy in great early Celtic backcourt ... All-NBA seven times ... 1955 NBA All-Star Game MVP ... Scored 12,665 career points and ranks as one of the top all-time foul shooters with 88 percent lifetime mark … Selected to NBA Silver Anniversary Team in 1971 … Selected as one of the 50 Greatest Players in NBA History in 1996 … Only coach to win championships in three professional leagues — ABL (Cleveland, 1962), ABA (Utah, 1971) and NBA (LA Lakers, 1972) … Later served as Lakers' general manager and president.

Isiah Thomas (2000) — One of NBA's best point guards … Led Detroit Pistons to 1989 and 1990 titles, earning Finals MVP in latter … Played 13 seasons with Detroit, gaining All-Star recognition 12 times … Fourth in NBA career assists with 9,061 … Also Detroit's all-time leading scorer (18,822 points) … Rookie of the Year in 1982 … All-NBA First-Team in 1984, 1985 and 1986 … Led Indiana to 1981 NCAA championship … Selected as one of the 50 Greatest Players in NBA History in 1996.

David Thompson (1996) — A tremendous leaper, "The Skywalker" was a three-time All-American at North Carolina State … Three-time All-ACC pick and two-time AP Player of the Year … MVP of N.C. State's 1974 National Championship team … Named to NCAA All-Decade Team of the 1970s … ABA Rookie of the Year in 1975 … Four-time NBA All-Star … Two-time All-NBA First-Team pick … Averaged 22.1 points per game over nine seasons with Denver Nuggets and Seattle SuperSonics.

Nate Thurmond (1984) — Outstanding all-around center who made presence felt with scoring, rebounding and defensive skills … All-American in 1963 at Bowling Green, where he set NCAA Tournament record for most rebounds (31) in one game … Averaged 15 points and 15 rebounds per game in 14-year NBA career with San Francisco-Golden State, Chicago and Cleveland … In 1974, posted first quadruple double in NBA history with 22 points, 14 rebounds, 13 assists and 12 blocked shots in one game … Selected as one of the 50 Greatest Players in NBA History in 1996.

Jack Twyman (1982) — All-American at Cincinnati in 1955 … One of NBA's greatest shooting forwards … Scored 15,840 points (19.2 points per game) in 11 seasons with Royals in Rochester and Cincinnati … Played in 609 consecutive games … Recognized for his humanitarianism, he was legal guardian for Maurice Stokes, Royals teammate who was paralyzed in 1958.

Wes Unseld (1987) — Although he was only 6-7, his strength and skills made him one of game's best centers … Outstanding rebounder who was known for his solid picks and outlet passing … All-American at Louisville … Played 13 NBA season with Bullets … Was Rookie of the Year and MVP in 1969, a feat achieved by only one other player, Wilt Chamberlain … Led team to NBA Playoffs 12 consecutive seasons and was MVP of the 1978 NBA Finals in which Washington won its only championship … Scored 10,624 points (10.8 points per game) and grabbed 13,769 rebounds (14.0 rebounds per game) … Coached Bullets from 1987 to 1994 … Selected as one of the 50 Greatest Players in NBA History in 1996.

Bill Walton (1992) — One of the game's finest all-around centers, a brilliant passer, scorer and rebounder … Three-time All-American who led UCLA to 86-4 record, NCAA titles in 1972 and 1973 … Guided Portland to its only NBA Championship in 1977 … Was NBA's MVP in 1978 … Averaged 13.3 points per game and 10.5 rebounds per game in injury-plagued NBA career … Came back to win NBA Sixth Man Award in 1986 when he helped Boston Celtics to championship … Selected as one of the 50 Greatest Players in NBA History in 1996.

Bobby Wanzer (1986) — Played 10 seasons with Rochester Royals after earning All-American honors at Seton Hall … Five-time NBA All-Star … An uncanny shooter, he ranked among league leaders in field-goal percentage four times … Sparked Rochester to NBA crown in 1951 … Led league in free-throw shooting (90.4 percent) in 1952 … Coached Royals for three years in Rochester and Cincinnati.

Jerry West (1979) — Among the greatest shooting guards in NBA history … Two-time All-American at West Virginia State and co-captain of Olympic gold medalists in 1960 … Scored 25,192 points in 14 seasons with Los Angeles Lakers for an average of 27.0 points per game ... "Mr. Clutch" scored then-record 4,457 NBA playoff points (29.1 in 153 games), including 40.6 points per game in 1965 ... NBA Finals MVP in 1969 ... Made All-NBA First Team 10 times and All-Defensive First Team four times ... A 14-time All-Star ... Later coached Lakers for three seasons and currently serves as team's general manager ...Selected as one of the 50 Greatest Players in NBA History in 1996.

Leonard (Lenny) Wilkens (1988) — Brilliant playmaker ... Handed out 7,211 career assists, an NBA record, when he retired in 1975 ... After starring at Providence, played 15 NBA seasons with St. Louis, Seattle, Cleveland and Portland ... Averaged 16.5 points per game and 6.7 assists per game ... Nine-time All-Star, winning MVP honors in 1971 ... Player-coach for three years at Seattle and one year at Portland ... Selected as one of the 50 Greatest Players in NBA History in 1996 ... Also inducted as a head coach (1998), joining John Wooden as the only other person enshrined as both player and coach ... See Coaches Section for Wilkens bio.

George Yardley (1996) — Six-time All-Star averaged 19.2 points per game over seven seasons with Fort Wayne, Detroit and Syracuse ... First player in NBA history to score 2,000 points in one season, averaging 27.8 points per game and 10.7 rebounds per game in 1957-58 and earning All-NBA First-Team honors ... Averaged 20.3 points per game in 46 playoff contests and led Fort Wayne to two NBA Finals ... Nicknamed "Bird."

COACHES

Arnold "Red" Auerbach (1968) — Retired as winningest coach in NBA history with 938 regular-season victories, 1,037 overall ... Coached Washington and Tri-Cities before forging basketball's greatest dynasty with Boston Celtics ... Guided Celtics to nine NBA championships in 10 years, including eight in a row (1959-66) ... Later served as general manager and president of the Celtics ... Coached East NBA All-Star team 11 years in a row ... NBA's Coach of the Year trophy is named after him ... Selected as one of the Top Ten Coaches in NBA History in 1996.

Pete Carril (1997) — The only Division I coach to record 500 wins (525-273) without providing athletic scholarships ... Coached one season at Lehigh and 29 at Princeton before becoming assistant with the Sacramento Kings ... His fundamental team defense helped Princeton lead the nation in scoring defense in 14 of his final 21 seasons ... Won 13 Ivy League championships ... Led Princeton to 1975 NIT title and to first-round upset over defending champion UCLA in 1996 NCAA Tournament.

Charles J. (Chuck) Daly (1994)—One of NBA's top coaches with Cleveland Cavaliers, Detroit Pistons, New Jersey Nets and Orlando Magic ... At the time of induction, his 564 combined ABA/NBA wins ranked 17th all-time and 74 playoff wins ranked fourth ... Won back-to-back championships with Detroit (1989, 1990), the fifth coach in NBA history to do so ... One of two Hall of Fame coaches to win an NBA championship and an Olympic gold medal, achieving the latter with the Dream Team in 1992 ... Selected as one of the Top Ten Coaches in NBA History in 1996.

Alexander (Alex) Hannum (1998) — First coach to win both an ABA and NBA championship ... Coached 16 seasons (12 in NBA, four in ABA), posting a 471-412 NBA record and a 178-152 ABA mark ... Led St. Louis to 1958 NBA title and Philadelphia to 1967 championship, the latter with a then-record .840 winning percentage (68-14) ... Guided Oakland to 1969 ABA title ... NBA Coach of the Year in 1964 and ABA Coach of the Year in 1969.

William "Red" Holzman (1985) — Coached New York Knicks to 1970 and 1973 NBA championships, when "Dee-fense" was the popular chant ... Compiled 696 regular-season victories (second-highest when he retired in 1982) and 58 playoff wins in 18 years as an NBA coach, 14 with New York and four with Milwaukee-St. Louis ... Played nine pro seasons, eight with Rochester Royals in NBL and NBA ... Typified the smarts and savvy of New York guards ... Helped Rochester to NBL title in 1946 and NBA crown in 1951 ... Selected as one of the Top Ten Coaches in NBA History in 1996.

Alvin "Doggie" Julian (1967) — Coached Boston Celtics for two seasons prior to arrival of Red Auerbach in 1950 … Best known for college coaching success at Holy Cross, where he compiled 65-10 record and won 1947 NCAA title … Coached Bob Cousy, Joe Mullaney, George Kaftan, Frank Oftring and Bob Curran at Holy Cross … Also coached at Albright, Muhlenberg and Dartmouth.

John Kundla (1995) — A pro head coach at age 31, he quickly became the first of only three men in NBA history to guide teams to three consecutive NBA titles … Stressed defense and disciplined basketball … Led Lakers to six league titles (NBL 1948; BAA 1949; NBA 1950, 1952-54) … Compiled a 466-319 record, including a 70-38 postseason mark … Ranks third all-time in number of Hall of Famers coached (six) … Selected as one of the Top Ten Coaches in NBA History in 1996.

Ken Loeffler (1964) — Coached St. Louis Bombers for two seasons and Providence Steamrollers for one in NBA's early years … Also coached at Geneva, Yale, LaSalle and Texas A&M, winning 310 games … Compiled 145-27 record at LaSalle, winning NIT in 1952 and NCAA Tournament in 1954 … Tom Gola was among his LaSalle players.

Frank McGuire (1976) — Coached Philadelphia Warriors to 49-31 record in 1962, the year Wilt Chamberlain averaged 50.4 points per game and scored 100 points in one game … First coach to compile 100 victories at three colleges — St. John's (103), North Carolina (164) and South Carolina (283) … Three-time NCAA Coach of the Year, led North Carolina to 32-0 mark and NCAA crown in 1957.

Jack Ramsay (1991) — Compiled 864 victories in 21-year NBA coaching career, the second-highest total in league history at the time he retired in 1988 … After compiling 234-72 record in 11 years at St. Joseph's, became GM of Philadelphia 76ers in 1966 and coach of the team in 1968 … Guided Portland Trail Blazers to 1977 NBA Championship … Coached 10 years in Portland, four apiece at Philly and Buffalo and three in Indiana … Selected as one of the Top Ten Coaches in NBA History in 1996.

Leonard (Lenny) Wilkens (1998) — NBA's all-time winningest coach (1,179 victories entering 2000-2001) … Guided Seattle to 1979 NBA championship … Also coached Portland, Cleveland and Atlanta … Coach of the Year in 1994 … Ranks sixth in playoff wins (69) … Ranks third in regular-season games coached with 2,160 (entering 2000-2001) … Coached the 1996 U.S. Olympic Team to a gold medal … Selected as one of the Top Ten Coaches in NBA History in 1996.

CONTRIBUTORS

Daniel (Danny) Biasone (2000) — Introduced the 24-second clock in 1954-55 season, resulting in one-season team scoring increase from 79.5 points per game to 93.1 points per game … Also supported 1953 rule that awarded two foul shots for backcourt fouls … Founded Syracuse Nationals in 1946 and oversaw winning records in 11 of 14 seasons, including NBA title in 1955 … Earned Hall of Fame's John Bunn Award in 1982.

Clair Bee (1967) — Helped Danny Biasone in formulation of NBA's 24-second shot clock in 1954 … Instrumental in development of three-second rule … Coached for 29 years, including three with NBA Baltimore Bullets, 1952-54 … Highly successful college coach at Rider and LIU … Prolific author who wrote 21 instructional and nonfiction books and the 23-volume "Chip Hilton" fiction series for youth.

Walter Brown (1965) — One of the NBA's founding fathers … President of Boston Garden, organized the Boston Celtics as charter member of league … NBA's early championship trophy was named after him … Served as chairman of the Hall of Fame board of directors, 1961-64.

Wayne Embry (1999) — In 1972, became first African-American General Manager (of Milwaukee Bucks) … In 1994, became first African-American Team President (of Cleveland Cavaliers) … Served as Cleveland's Vice President and General Manager from 1985-92 … Guided team to nine playoff berths in last 13 years … The Sporting News' Executive of the Year in 1992 and 1998 … Played 11 seasons with Cincinnati Royals, Boston Celtics and Milwaukee Bucks ... Five-time All-Star.

Larry Fleisher (1990) — Served as general counsel of NBA Players Association for more than 25 years, from its inception in the early 1950s until his death in 1989 ... Innovative leader who worked with NBA to raise level of popularity of basketball ... Worked to improve player salaries, pensions and other benefits, including system of free agency.

Eddie Gottlieb (1971) — One of the NBA's founders ... Coached the famed Philadelphia SPHAs beginning in 1918 ... Teams enjoyed success barnstorming as well as in Eastern and American Basketball leagues ... Coached Philadelphia Warriors to championship in 1947, first year of NBA (when it was known as BAA) ... Coached team through 1954-55, then became owner ... Subsequently served as NBA consultant and schedule maker.

Lester Harrison (1979) — Organized teams and games throughout 1930s and 1940s ... Bought Rochester Pros in 1945, changed name to Royals and built them into one of the dominant teams of the late 1940s and early 1950s ... As owner-coach, led Royals to NBL title in 1946 and NBA title in 1951 ... Won 394 games before selling team in 1958.

Edward S. "Ned" Irish (1964) — One of the NBA's founders ... Became basketball director of Madison Square Garden in 1934 and introduced popular college doubleheaders, which were milestone in basketball's growth ... New York and the Garden became mecca of basketball as the game, because of Irish, went intersectional ... Founded New York Knickerbockers in 1946.

J. Walter Kennedy (1980) — Led NBA from 1963 to 1975, presiding over expansion from nine to 18 teams, a fourfold increase in attendance and acquisition of a national TV contract ... Served as league's first publicity director under Maurice Podoloff ... Was in second term as mayor of Stamford, Conn., when he was chosen as the NBA's second commissioner, although his title from 1963 to 1967 was president.

Bill Mokray (1965) — Edited Official NBA Guide, 1958-67 ... Worked with Boston Celtics and Walter Brown for 21 years as a scout and promotion director for Celtics and basketball director for Boston Garden ... First chairman, Hall of Fame Honors Committee, 1959-64.

Pete Newell (1978) — Legendary coach won NIT title in 1949 with San Francisco, NCAA crown in 1959 with California and Olympic gold medal in 1960 ... Runs highly regarded Big Man's Camp attended by many NBA centers and forwards each summer ... Regarded as one of the game's outstanding teachers, has organized countless clinics around the world ... Has served as personnel director and consultant to Golden State Warriors.

Larry O'Brien (1990) — NBA commissioner from 1975 to 1984 ... An aide to presidents Kennedy and Johnson and former Democratic national committee chairman, was brought to NBA to negotiate an end to costly war with ABA, which he quickly accomplished ... In his tenure NBA grew from 18 to 23 teams, attendance and TV revenues rose and the league formulated innovative and far-reaching collective bargaining and antidrug agreements with its players.

Harold Olsen (1959) — Coached Chicago Stags from 1946 to 1949, when league was known as BAA ... Team won division with 39-22 record and lost in championship series in first season ... Was president of the National Association of Basketball Coaches and chairman NCAA rules committee, NCAA tournament committee and 1948 Olympic basketball committee ... Helped introduce the 10-second rule.

Maurice Podoloff (1973) — Served as president of NBA from its founding in 1946 (as BAA) until 1963 ... Oversaw absorption of surviving NBL teams to larger markets in 1950s, including Lakers' move to Los Angeles in 1960 that made league truly national ... Prior to heading basketball league, was president of the American Hockey League.

Fred Zollner (1999) — Owner of NBL's Fort Wayne Zollner Pistons (who later became NBA's Fort Wayne Pistons and then Detroit Pistons) and won 1944 and 1945 NBL titles ... Helped oversee merger of Basketball Association of America (BAA) and National Basketball League (NBL) into National Basketball Association ... Advocate for several major rule changes, including 24-second clock and six-foul rule ... Named "Mr. Pro Basketball" at 1975 Silver Anniversary NBA All-Star Game for status as founder and longtime supporter of NBA.

REFEREES

Jim Enright (1978) — Refereed in NBA, BAA and NBL ... Also officiated for 24 years in Big Ten, Big Eight and Missouri Valley conferences ... Conducted officiating clinics in Europe ... Also a highly regarded sportswriter who was president of U.S. Basketball Writers in 1967.

Matthew "Pat" Kennedy (1959) — Perhaps the most famous referee in basketball history ... Renowned for his colorful, crowd-pleasing style of calling a game that made him a gate attraction in his own right ... Served as high school, college and professional official from 1928 through 1952 ... Was NBA supervisor officials, 1946-50 ... Toured with Harlem Globetrotters, 1950-57.

John Nucatola (1977) — Officiated more than 2,000 games, many of them while still coaching at his alma mater, Newtown (N.Y.) High School ... Worked collegiate games in ECAC, ACC, Southern and Big Eight conferences, as well as NCAA Tournament and NIT ... Refereed in pros in ABL, BAA and NBA until he hung up whistle in 1959 to concentrate on administrative career ... Served as NBA's supervisor of officials, 1970-77.

J. Dallas Shirley (1979) — Worked games in Southern, ACC ECAC, CBOA, Mason-Dixon conferences as well as NIT, NCAA tourneys, Sugar Bowl, Pan Am Games, Olympics and BAA during 32-year refereeing career ... Also officiated in Colombia, Iceland, Puerto Rico and Libya ... Received FIBA Award in 1979 for devoting lifetime to officiating development.

Earl Strom (1995) — One of basketball's top referees ... Nicknamed the "Pied Piper" for his ability to control the game with his whistle ... Had a 32-year career (29 NBA seasons and three ABA seasons) ... Officiated in 29 NBA and ABA Finals and some 50 NBA and ABA Final games ... Selected to referee seven NBA All-Star Games ... Officiated 2,400 regular season games and 295 playoff games.

THE FIRST NAISMITH MEMORIAL BASKETBALL HALL OF FAME OPENED IN 1968.

CHAPTER 21

NBA AT 50

The Greatest in History

By Chris Ekstrand

When the NBA turned 50 years old in 1996, the league asked an elite group of 50 basketball experts to select the 50 best players in NBA history. The criterion was very simple: Greatness.

The project produced lasting images. It officially began on June 6, 1996, at the Grand Hyatt in New York. Exactly 50 years earlier on June 6, 1946, the hotel was known as the Commodore and it is where a group of businessmen met to form a new basketball league.

In late October when the 50 Greatest Players in NBA History were officially announced, five of them were at the unveiling: George Mikan, Wilt Chamberlain, Bill Russell, Oscar Robertson and Julius Erving.

At the NBA All-Star Game in February 1997, the lineup of players introduced at halftime was the greatest collection of talent in basketball history under one roof at the same time. Players were almost giddy being around one another. They had each other autograph *NBA at 50* books almost as if they were kids waiting for their favorite players at the arena exit.

The NBA at 50 celebration was a premier event in NBA history. Here are the players who made it possible:

50 GREATEST PLAYERS IN NBA HISTORY

Kareem Abdul-Jabbar	Dave DeBusschere	Karl Malone	David Robinson
Nate Archibald	Clyde Drexler	Moses Malone	Bill Russell
Paul Arizin	Julius Erving	Pete Maravich	Dolph Schayes
Charles Barkley	Patrick Ewing	Kevin McHale	Bill Sharman
Rick Barry	Walt Frazier	George Mikan	John Stockton
Elgin Baylor	George Gervin	Earl Monroe	Isiah Thomas
Dave Bing	Hal Greer	Hakeem Olajuwon	Nate Thurmond
Larry Bird	John Havlicek	Shaquille O'Neal	Wes Unseld
Wilt Chamberlain	Elvin Hayes	Robert Parish	Bill Walton
Bob Cousy	Earvin Johnson	Bob Pettit	Jerry West
Dave Cowens	Sam Jones	Scottie Pippen	Lenny Wilkens
Billy Cunningham	Michael Jordan	Willis Reed	James Worthy
	Jerry Lucas	Oscar Robertson	

At the NBA at 50 celebration in Cleveland during the 1997 All-Star Weekend, Elgin Baylor, the "godfather of high flyers," gets a precious autograph from the heir, or air, apparent, Michael Jordan.

Charles Barkley and Bill Russell, the greatest 6-6 and 6-10 rebounders in NBA history, enjoy the moment.

Three decades separated George Mikan and Larry Bird, but both know about being marquee players.

Wilt Chamberlain was unstoppable, but Julius Erving demonstrates a technique that might have worked.

Clyde Drexler and John Havlicek glide through the book almost as easily as they slashed through defenses.

KAREEM ABDUL-JABBAR

By Scott Ostler

Like any artist, basketball performer Kareem Abdul-Jabbar had his critics. And he addressed them in the 1980 comedy *Airplane*, when he played airline pilot Roger Murdock.

A young passenger comes into the cockpit and recognizes the pilot as Kareem, and says, "My father says you don't [hustle] . . ." Abdul-Jabbar grabs the lad by the shirt and snarls, "Listen, kid . . . I'm out there busting my buns every night. Tell your old man to drag Walton and Lanier up and down the court for 48 minutes."

Kareem not only dragged the Bob Laniers and Bill Waltons up and down the court for 20 NBA seasons, he sky-hooked over them often enough to become the game's all-time leading scorer and hustled enough to win six MVP Awards and lead his teams to six NBA championships.

And he did it his way. In the violent, caveman-like world of the NBA paint, Kareem dominated with finesse and intelligence, his main weapon a graceful sky-hook he developed in the fourth grade.

"He's the most beautiful athlete in sports," Lakers teammate Earvin "Magic" Johnson said.

But he was much more — in basketball vernacular, "money." Former teammate Norm Nixon once was talking about the Lakers' turbo-charged offense — Showtime. And when he described a key reason the overall offense was so effective he dramatically slowed his speech for effect, saying, "Whenever the fast break isn't going, there is nothing more effective than the . . . 10 . . . foot . . . sky . . . hook."

Abdul-Jabbar was born Ferdinand Lewis Alcindor Jr., and grew to his 7-2 height while a prep superstar at Power Memorial in New York City. Coach John Wooden lured Lew to UCLA (LewCLA, some called it), and Alcindor made an immediate impact.

College rule makers, fearing Alcindor would dismantle backboards and dishearten foes, outlawed the dunk shot. Dunk, schmunk — Alcindor led the Bruins to an 88-2 record and three NCAA championships in his three varsity seasons, and twice was named collegiate player of the year.

He showed the strength of his convictions by boycotting the 1968 Olympics to protest U.S. treatment of African-Americans. At UCLA, Alcindor converted from Catholicism to Islam and changed his name to Kareem (noble and generous) Abdul (serves Allah) Jabbar (powerful), though he did not make the change public until his second NBA season.

That '70-71 season, Kareem and 11-year veteran Oscar Robertson took the Bucks to an NBA title and Abdul-Jabbar won his first MVP trophy. After six seasons in Milwaukee, he requested a trade to either New York or Los Angeles. The Bucks sent him to the Lakers, and Kareem was league MVP his first two seasons in L.A.

By the '78-79 season, Abdul-Jabbar, past 30, seemed to be slowing down, losing his fire. But when the Lakers drafted Magic Johnson, the young point guard and the veteran center inspired one another, and the result was an NBA title, the first of five in the 1980s for Kareem, Magic and the Lakers.

Kareem's lowest moment might have been Game 1 of the '85 Finals. In a 34-point loss to the Boston Celtics, the 38-year-old warhorse was held to 12 points and three rebounds.

But in Game 2, one of the great personal comebacks in NBA lore, Kareem had 30 points, 17 rebounds and eight assists. He finished the series strong and the Lakers won in six games. "What you saw," Lakers coach Pat Riley said of Kareem in Game 2, "was passion."

Abdul-Jabbar was one of the first NBA players to seriously practice yoga and tai chi. As Lakers General Manager Jerry West said, "Kareem is a master of fitness and grace."

Abdul-Jabbar is an avid collector of oriental rugs and jazz recordings, and has authored four books, including a biography of African-American cultural heroes, and the diary of a season he spent coaching a prep team on an Indian reservation. He has three sons and two daughters.

In 2000, 11 years after retiring, Abdul-Jabbar returned to the NBA as an assistant coach with the L.A. Clippers. The man Lakers teammates called Big Fella continues to make an impact on the game.

CAREER HIGHLIGHTS: NBA championships with Milwaukee Bucks (1971) and Los Angeles Lakers (1980, '82, '85, '87, '88); NBA Finals MVP (1971, '85); NBA MVP (1971, '72, '74, '76, '77, '80); NBA Rookie of the Year (1970); NBA All-Rookie Team (1970); All-NBA First Team (1971, '72, '73, '74, '76, '77, '80, '81, '84, '86); All-NBA Second Team (1970, '78, '79, '83, '85); NBA All-Defensive First Team (1974, '75, '79, '80, '81); NBA All-Defensive Second Team (1970, '71, '76, '77, '78, '84); Led NBA in scoring (1971, '72); Led NBA in rebounding (1976, '77); Led NBA in blocked shots (1975, '76, '79, '80); NBA All-Star (1970, '71, '72, '73, '74, '75, '76, '77, '79, '80, '81, '82, '83, '84, '85, '86, '87, '88, '89); Holds NBA career records for most minutes (57,446), most points (38,387), most field goals made (15,837) and most field goals attempted (28,307); NBA 35th Anniversary All-Time Team (1980); No. 33 retired by Los Angeles Lakers and Milwaukee Bucks; Naismith Memorial Basketball Hall of Fame (1995).

NATE "TINY" ARCHIBALD

Retired in 1984.

Began play in 1970.

Played 13 seasons.

Nate Archibald's career emphatically answered the question of whether a small player could dominate in the modern basketball era. When he used his breathtaking quickness to become the first NBA player to lead the NBA in scoring and assists in 1973, few realized the magnitude of his accomplishment. Nearly three decades later, no player has come close to duplicating his feat. Like all smaller players, the 6-1 "Tiny" — a native of New York who went to college at Texas-El Paso — had to prove himself time and again. He was only the 19th player picked in the 1970 NBA Draft, and even after he excelled for six seasons with the Royals/Kings, some felt he dominated the ball so much he was incapable of being part of a winner. That question, too, was put to rest when he quarterbacked the Boston Celtics to the 1981 NBA championship.

CAREER HIGHLIGHTS: NBA championship with Boston Celtics (1981); All-NBA First Team (1973, '75, '76); All-NBA Second Team (1972, '81); NBA All-Star (1973, '75, '76, '80, '81, '82); NBA All-Star Game MVP (1981); No. 1 retired by Sacamento Kings; Naismith Memorial Basketball Hall of Fame (1990).

PAUL ARIZIN

Retired in 1962.

Began play in 1950.

Played 10 seasons (missed two seasons because of military service).

Just as the jump shot started to replace the set shot, a uniquely coordinated athlete materialized out of Philadelphia to exhibit the possibilities of the modern style and become one of the game's top scorers. Paul Arizin didn't even play high school basketball, but he was the College Player of the Year for Villanova in 1950. With a jump shot so picture-perfect opposing coaches likened it to a painting by Rembrandt, Arizin exploded on the professional basketball scene, immediately becoming a star of the Philadelphia Warriors. The man they called "Pitchin' Paul" averaged more than 20 points for nine straight seasons and, with Neil Johnston, led the Warriors to the 1956 NBA title. When he retired, the 10-time NBA All-Star was the third-leading scorer in NBA history (16,266 points).

CAREER HIGHLIGHTS: NBA championship with Philadelphia Warriors (1956); All-NBA First Team (1952, '56, '57); All-NBA Second Team (1959); NBA All-Star (1951, '52, '55, '56, '57, '58, '59, '60, '61, '62); NBA All-Star Game MVP (1952); Led the NBA in scoring in 1952 (25.4 points per game) and 1957 (25.6 points per game); Retired as NBA's third all-time leading scorer (16,266); NBA 25th All-Time Anniversary Team (1970); Naismith Memorial Basketball Hall of Fame (1977).

CHARLES BARKLEY

Retired in 2000.
Began play in 1984.
Played 16 seasons.

There are four players in NBA history that have compiled 20,000 points, 10,000 rebounds and 4,000 assists: Kareem Abdul-Jabbar, Wilt Chamberlain, Karl Malone and Charles Barkley. But when the conversation turns to the exploits of Sir Charles, most people think first of the always entertaining, sometimes outrageous running commentary on basketball and life he provided throughout his celebrated 16-year NBA career. Everyone in basketball marveled at how Barkley would say things that others barely dared think. His pointed observations sometimes obscured this truth about Sir Charles: As a player, he was the greatest anomaly in basketball history. At about 6-6, he played power forward as well as anyone, often dominating players half a foot taller. That's the legacy this irrepressible man from Alabama and Auburn University leaves behind.

CAREER HIGHLIGHTS: NBA MVP (1993); All-NBA First Team (1988, '89, '90, '91, '93); All-NBA Second Team (1986, '87, '92, '94, '95); All-NBA Third Team (1996); NBA All-Star (1987, '88, '89, '90, '91, '92, '93, '94, '95, '96, '97); NBA All-Star Game MVP (1991); All-Rookie Team (1985); Member of gold medal-winning U.S. Olympic teams ('92, '96).

RICK BARRY

Retired in 1980.
Began play in 1965.
Played 14 seasons.

Most legendary scorers are known for either a deadly jump shot or the ability to create a shot while driving to the basket. Rick Barry did both equally well. During his 14 seasons in the NBA and ABA, Barry earned the reputation as a player who could score from anywhere on the floor, averaging 24.8 points in 1,020 games. But Barry, who went to the University of Miami, was much more than a scorer. In addition to being one of the greatest free throw shooters in pro basketball (90 percent success rate in the NBA) with his old-fashioned, underhand style, he was a skilled passer, averaging more than five assists from the forward position, and a capable rebounder as well. Barry played the game relentlessly, aggressively and was the driving force behind the 1975 Golden State Warriors team that shocked the basketball world by winning the NBA championship.

CAREER HIGHLIGHTS: NBA championship with Golden State Warriors (1975); NBA Finals MVP (1975); ABA championship with Oakland Oaks (1969); All-NBA First Team (1966, '67, '74, '75, '76); All-NBA Second Team (1973); All-ABA First Team (1969, '70, '71, '72); NBA leading scorer in 1966-67 season (35.6 points per game); Eight time NBA All-Star (1966, '67, '73, '74, '75, '76, '77, '78); NBA All-Star Game MVP (1967); Only player in history to lead the NCAA, ABA and NBA in scoring; NBA Rookie of the Year (1966); No. 24 retired by Golden State Warriors; Naismith Basketball Hall of Fame (1986).

ELGIN BAYLOR

By Lyle Spencer

Elgin Baylor is the source, the originator. From his incomparable style, grace, creativity and athleticism came the NBA that fans cheer today in all its spectacular forms.

The first true master of air, space and time, Baylor was the model for Connie Hawkins, Julius Erving, Michael Jordan and all the contemporary stars. Hanging suspended, creating shots in traffic, making it all up as he went along, elegant Elgin left teammates, rivals and fans in awe.

Baylor's genius came entirely from within. He copied and emulated no one. Growing up in Washington, D.C., he had no one to copy or emulate.

"I never tried to be like anybody," Baylor said. "I just played the game my way. I didn't know much about the NBA, and I didn't even play organized basketball until I was 15. We couldn't afford a television. I remember once, on a Saturday, we went to someone's house and I saw a playoff game on television. But I don't recall who was playing."

He was an All-American at Seattle University, having transferred there in 1955 after one season at the College of Idaho, when he finally saw NBA players in the flesh, courtesy of Bill Russell.

"I'd met Bill in college at Corvallis, Oregon, in the Far West Regional," Baylor said. "He was playing with a team of touring NBA all-stars and got me tickets for the game. R.C. Owens, who went on to be a great football player, was a friend of mine and he was in Seattle playing for an AAU team at the time. They needed an extra player and asked R.C. to play. He did OK, didn't embarrass himself. That was the first time I started thinking about the NBA. I got a little inspired watching R.C., because I knew I might be a little better than R.C., and he held his own with those great players."

Averaging 29.7 and 32.5 points in two seasons at Seattle, Baylor carried his team all the way to the 1958 NCAA championship game as a senior. Even though Seattle lost to Kentucky, Baylor was the tournament MVP. He became the first overall pick in the 1958 NBA Draft by the Minneapolis Lakers, a franchise in dire straits financially and artistically.

An instant hit with his soaring game and unassuming manner, the 6-5, 225-pound Baylor was the 1958-59 NBA Rookie of the Year. He also was an All-NBA First Team choice, a distinction he would earn nine more times.

After two brilliant seasons in Minneapolis, Baylor moved with the franchise to Los Angeles in 1960. He welcomed Jerry West as a teammate that season, and the two began a long odyssey as one of the greatest tandems in league history.

Baylor's first season in L.A. was the greatest of his career, statistically. He produced a then-record 71 points against New York and averaged 34.8 points, 19.8 rebounds and 5.1 assists, driving the Lakers to the conference finals while averaging 38.1 points in the postseason.

Baylor remained a force throughout the decade, but he never was quite as dominant after knee troubles began to surface in 1963. By the time the '70s rolled around, he didn't have much mileage left in that magnificent machine. Ironically, the Lakers finally won their elusive first championship in Los Angeles in 1972, the season when Baylor, who played in six Finals without winning a title, retired after nine games.

Still, Baylor's impact is transcendent. Along with Russell, Wilt Chamberlain, Oscar Robertson, Jerry West and a few others, he elevated the NBA in the 1960s to new levels of popularity. And in spite of his physical troubles, Baylor had career averages of 27.4 points (fourth all-time) and 13.5 rebounds (second among all forwards after Bob Pettit). He was elected to the Hall of Fame in 1976, and in 1996 he was named one of the 50 Greatest Players in NBA History.

CAREER HIGHLIGHTS: NBA Rookie of the Year (1959); All-NBA First Team (1959, '60, '61, '62, '63, '64, '65, '67, '68, '69); NBA All-Star (1959, '60, '61, '62, '63, '64, '65, '67, '68, '69, '70); NBA All-Star Game Co-MVP (1959); Holds NBA Finals single-game record for most points ('61) on April 24, 1962 against Boston; Retired as NBA's third all-time leading scorer; No. 22 retired by Los Angeles Lakers; NBA 35th Anniversary Team (1980); Naismith Memorial Basketball Hall of Fame (1976).

DAVE BING

Retired in 1978.

Began play in 1966.

Played 12 seasons.

If the average observer failed to appreciate the substance of Dave Bing's game, it was only because Bing made the difficult look easy. A fluid, graceful guard who scored and passed with seemingly effortless efficiency, Bing was the engine that made the Detroit Pistons go for nine seasons from 1966 to 1975. Bing, from Syracuse University, was the second player picked in the 1966 NBA Draft, and was named NBA

Rookie of the Year after averaging 20 points per game. In 1973-74, Bing led the Pistons to 52 victories, the most in the 26-year history of the franchise to that time. A seven-time All-Star who won MVP honors at the All-Star Game in 1976, Bing was able to rise over opponents and shoot his feathery jump shots with ease, or use his speed to whip by defenders on his way to an easy layup.

CAREER HIGHLIGHTS: All-NBA First Team (1968, '71); All-NBA Second Team (1974); Seven-time NBA All-Star (1968, '69, '71, '73, '74, '75, '76); NBA All-Star Game MVP (1976); NBA Rookie of the Year (1967); NBA All-Rookie Team (1967); No. 21 retired by Detroit Pistons; Naismith Memorial Basketball Hall of Fame (1989).

LARRY BIRD

Retired in 1992.

Began play in 1979.

Played 13 seasons.

If one player could embody the phrase "practice makes perfect," it would be Larry Bird. The Indiana native spent countless hours working on his game at every level of basketball, vowing that nobody would outwork him. Gifted with size, great hands and an inherent feel for the game, Bird was limited in foot speed and jumping ability, but the degree to which he overcame those deficiencies was startling. Bird played the game like he invented the rules. He seemed to know not only where players on the court were at any given time, but also where they were likely to go next. Bird's work ethic and skills made him a peerless perimeter shooter and passer, and his unshakable belief in himself made him a remarkable performer under pressure. After a spectacular college career at Indiana State, which he led to the 1979 NCAA Championship Game, Bird led the Boston Celtics to titles in 1981, 1984 and 1986. (For more on Larry Bird, see page 30).

CAREER HIGHLIGHTS: NBA championships with Boston Celtics (1981, '84, '86); NBA Finals MVP (1984, '86); NBA Most Valuable Player (1984, '85, '86); All-NBA First Team (1980, '81, '82, '83, '84, '85, '86, '87, '88); All-NBA Second Team (1990); NBA All-Defensive Second Team (1982, '83, '84); NBA All-Star (1980, '81, '82, '83, '84, '85, '86, '87, '88, '90, '91, '92); NBA All-Star Game MVP (1982); Long Distance Shootout Winner (1986, '87, '88); Led the NBA in free throw shooting (1984, '86, '87, '90); NBA Rookie of the Year (1980); NBA All-Rookie team (1980); Member of gold-medal-winning U.S. Olympic Team (1992); No. 33 retired by Boston Celtics; Naismith Memorial Basketball Hall of Fame (1998).

WILT CHAMBERLAIN

Retired in 1973.

Began play in 1959.

Played 14 seasons.

Dominant is a word that is thrown around a lot in sports, often unwisely. Few athletes actually measure up to the weighty word. Wilt Chamberlain exuded dominance. "The Big Dipper" was virtually impossible to stop with only one defender. An imposing presence who was the world's first fully coordinated seven-foot athlete — he set a school record in the high jump at the University of Kansas — the 7-1 Chamberlain's impact on the NBA was enormous. A bevy of rule changes enacted to keep him from lording over the game had little impact. Without the intrigue of Chamberlain's matchup against Bill Russell of the Boston Celtics, the NBA might never have captured the imagination of the sporting public. Chamberlain rewrote the NBA record book, scoring 100 points in one game and averaging 50.4 points for an entire season; many contemporary NBA scoring and rebounding achievements are dwarfed by his output. For 14 seasons, Chamberlain bestrode the NBA like a colossus. His impact resonates even today. (For more on Wilt Chamberlain, see page 30).

CAREER HIGHLIGHTS: NBA championships with the Philadelphia 76ers (1967) and Los Angeles Lakers (1972); NBA Finals MVP (1972); NBA Most Valuable Player (1960, '66, '67, '68); All-NBA First Team (1960, '61, '62, '64, '66, '67, '68); All-NBA Second Team (1963, '65, '72); NBA All-Defensive First Team (1972, '73); NBA All-Star (1960, '61, '62, '63, '64, '65, '66, '67, '68, '69, '71, '72, '73); NBA All-Star Game MVP (1960); NBA Rookie of the Year (1960); Scored 31,419 points (30.1 points per game) in 1,045 pro games, best in the league when he retired; currently second all-time behind Kareem Abdul-Jabbar; Led the NBA in scoring seven straight years (1960-66), including a career-high 50.4 points per game in 1962; Holds single game record for points in one game (100, March 2, 1962) against the New York Knicks in Hershey, Pa.; Scored 50 or more points 118 times; Scored 40 points or more 271 times; Holds single-game record for most points by a rookie (58, Jan. 25, 1960 vs. the Detroit Pistons); All-time rebounding leader (23,924 rebounds); Led the league in rebounding 11 times (1960-63, 1966-69, 1971-73); Led the league in minutes seven times (1961-64, 1966-68); One of only three players in NBA history to top 20,000 points, 6,000 rebounds, and 3,000 assists; No. 13 retired by Los Angeles Lakers and Philadelphia 76ers; NBA 35th Anniversary All-Time Team (1980); Naismith Memorial Basketball Hall of Fame (1978).

BOB COUSY

By Sam Goldaper

On March 17, 1963, a voice from the Boston Garden balcony cried out, "We love you Cooz!" It triggered a tumultuous ovation from the capacity St. Patrick's Day crowd for the man known as "The Houdini of the Hardwood." The regular season finale was the fans' tribute to the retiring Bob Cousy, a player who joined the Boston Celtics by the luck of the draw and stayed around for 13 seasons. His slick ballhandling and blind behind-the-back and look-away passes brought excitement to the NBA and six championships to the Celtics. He played in each of the first 13 All-Star Games, was an All-NBA First Team selection 10 times and led the league in assists for eight straight years.

As Cousy stood at center court and received the fans' adoration, he left behind a legacy for every youngster who ever dribbled a basketball.

In Cousy's day, a player's popularity was not measured by how much licensed apparel he sold or how many commercials he appeared in. Instead of identifying with Cousy's jersey No. 14, youngsters did it by trying to mimic his style. For decades, when a youngster on a playground would try to dribble behind his back and would lose the ball, some wisecracking bystander would call out,

"Who do you think you are — Cousy?"

By build, temperament and vision, Cousy was magnificently equipped to dazzle. Though only a shade over 6-1 and 175 pounds, Cousy was blessed with large hands, long arms, powerful thighs and uncommon peripheral vision. His lack of physical size became an advantage, for it spurred him to see things from a perspective no one else had. No one before him had even conceived ways to exploit those alleys and openings, much less tried those daring new passes and dribbles.

"Because of his shoulders, wrists and hands," explained Cousy's legendary coach, Arnold "Red" Auerbach, "Cooz could dribble from his front, either side or his back without breaking stride, twisting his body or changing the cadence of his dribble. I had never seen a player able to do that."

Despite the accolades and the success he brought to the Celtics, Cousy, an All-American at Holy Cross and a player renowned throughout New England, had to overcome Auerbach's skepticism when he became eligible for the 1950 draft. Named the coach of the Celtics only days before the draft, Auerbach spurned local pressure to select Cousy first. Instead, in need of a big man, he took 6-11 Charlie Share, the rugged All-American center from Bowling Green.

Cousy, picked ninth overall by the Tri-Cities Hawks, was promptly traded to Chicago. But the Stags folded before the season, and Cousy was parceled out in a dispersal draft. Boston, picking third and last in the dispersal, ended up with the unwanted Cousy, prompting the stubborn Auerbach to say, "He will have to make the team."

He not only made the team, he made it into a champion. Auerbach firmly believed in a running game and Cousy was just the player to take it to a new level, becoming the spark plug that powered the famed Celtics fast break. In 13 seasons, Cousy's teams never posted a losing record, and they won championships in six of his last seven seasons.

"Cooz was the absolute offensive master, the best playmaking guard that ever played the game," said long-time teammate Tom Heinsohn. "Once that ball reached his hands, the rest of us just took off, never bothering to look back. We didn't have to. He'd find us. When you got into a position to score, the ball would be there."

CAREER HIGHLIGHTS: NBA championships with the Boston Celtics (1957, '59, '60, '61, '62, '63); NBA MVP (1957); All-NBA First Team (1952, '53, '54, '55, '56, '57, '58, '59, '60, '61); All-NBA Second Team (1962, '63); NBA All-Star (1951, '52, '53, '54, '55, '56, '57, '58, '59, '60, '61, '62, '63); NBA All-Star Game MVP (1954, '57); Led the NBA in assists (1953, '54, '55, '56, '57, '58, '59, '60); NBA 25th Anniversary All-Time Team (1970); NBA 35th Anniversary All-Time Team (1980); No. 14 retired by Boston Celtics; Naismith Memorial Basketball Hall of Fame (1970).

DAVE COWENS

Retired in 1983.

Began play in 1970.

Played 11 seasons.

Everyone thought Dave Cowens was too short to play center, everyone except Cowens himself. At 6-9 on a good day, Cowens excelled at center in an era when giants such as Kareem Abdul-Jabbar, Wilt Chamberlain and Nate Thurmond provided the competition. Cowens was a few inches shorter and a few pounds lighter than his opposition most nights, but he was never outworked and never outhustled. Cowens, who went to college at Florida State, was a terrific outside shooter and excellent passer out of the high post. His jump shooting and ballhandling ability on the perimeter forced opposing centers out of the paint, increasing opportunities for his teammates to drive to the basket. Cowens led the Boston Celtics to NBA titles in 1974 and 1976, teaming with John Havlicek to start a new era in Celtics championship basketball after the retirements of Hall-of-Famers Bill Russell and Sam Jones.

CAREER HIGHLIGHTS: NBA championships with Boston Celtics (1974, '76); NBA MVP (1973); All-NBA Second Team (1973, '75, '76); NBA All-Defensive First Team (1976); NBA All-Defensive Second Team (1975, '80); NBA All-Star Game MVP (1973); NBA All-Star (1972, '73, '74, '75, '76, '77, '78); NBA Co-Rookie of the Year (1971); NBA All-Rookie Team (1971); No.18 retired by Boston Celtics; Naismith Memorial Basketball Hall of Fame (1990).

BILLY CUNNINGHAM

Retired in 1976.

Began play in 1965.

Played 11 seasons.

Some players don't need to be motivated by coaches, teammates or big-game situations. They play with a remarkable intensity at all times. Put that desire together with tremendous natural ability, and you have Billy Cunningham. Known as "The Kangaroo Kid" for his extraordinary leaping ability, Cunningham made a reputation as the best bench player in the NBA, helping his Philadelphia 76ers to the NBA title in 1967. Two years later, he had developed into one of the unstoppable scoring forces in the NBA. Able to score from the perimeter or in close, Cunningham played with a relentless fervor. When his playing career was cut short at age 32 by a devastating knee injury, he averaged 20.8 points and 10.1 rebounds during his career. Bringing the same intensity to the bench, Cunningham, who went to college at North Carolina, coached the 76ers to the NBA title in 1983.

CAREER HIGHLIGHTS: NBA championship with Philadelphia 76ers (1967); All-NBA First Team (1969, '70, '71); All-NBA Second Team (1972); NBA All-Star (1969, '70, '71, '72); All-NBA Rookie Team (1966); ABA MVP (1973); ABA All-Star First Team (1973); No. 32 retired by Philadelphia 76ers; Naismith Memorial Basketball Hall of Fame (1985).

DAVE DEBUSSCHERE

Retired in 1974.

Began play in 1962.

Played 12 seasons.

The New York Knicks were a playoff team in 1968, but there was something missing. On December 19, 1968, the Knicks acquired three-time All-Star forward Dave DeBusschere from Detroit for center Walt Bellamy and guard Howard Komives. Bellamy's departure meant Willis Reed would move to center, and DeBusschere would be inserted into Reed's power forward slot. Overnight, the Knicks dramatically improved. DeBusschere, out of the University of Detroit, provided rebounding, perimeter shooting and toughness New York hadn't had before. DeBusschere, who pitched in the major leagues for the Chicago White Sox, became the youngest coach in NBA history when he served as player-coach of the Detroit Pistons in 1964 at the age of 24. As a player, he helped the Knicks win NBA titles in 1970 and 1973, the only championships in the history of one of the NBA's original members. The tangible and intangible contributions of DeBusschere to New York's success were immense.

CAREER HIGHLIGHTS: NBA championships with New York Knicks (1970, '73); All-NBA Second Team (1969); NBA All-Defensive First Team (1969, '70, '71, '72, '73, '74); NBA All-Star (1966, '67, '68, '70, '71, '72, '73); NBA All-Rookie Team (1963); No. 22 retired by New York Knicks; Naismith Memorial Basketball Hall of Fame (1982).

CLYDE DREXLER

Retired in 1998.

Began play in 1983.

Played 15 seasons.

When Clyde Drexler came into the NBA from the University of Houston in 1983, he was billed as an incredible leaper. By the time he departed in 1998, Drexler had shown his excellence in every facet of the game. It was rare to see a sentence describing Drexler's game without seeing the word versatility. One of the best passers in NBA history from the big guard position, Drexler went from being a suspect outside shooter to a feared three-point bomber. He blew by defenders with quickness, then often topped off his drives with spectacular slam dunks. Drexler was the driving force behind Portland teams that advanced to the NBA Finals in 1990 and 1992, before staging a dramatic homecoming to Houston. On February 14, 1995, Drexler was traded to the defending NBA champion Houston Rockets, and teamed with former college teammate Hakeem Olajuwon to bring the Rockets a second straight NBA title.

CAREER HIGHLIGHTS: NBA championship with Houston Rockets (1995); All-NBA First Team (1992); All-NBA Second Team (1988, '91); All-NBA Third Team (1990, '95); NBA All-Star (1986, '88, '89, '90, '91, '92, '93, '94, '96, '97); Member of gold medal-winning U.S. Olympic team (1992); Portland Trail Blazers all time leader in scoring, rebounds, field goals, free throws, steals, games and minutes; One of only three players in NBA history to top 20,000 points, 6,000 rebounds, and 3,000 assists; Teamed with Cynthia Cooper to win inaugural All-Star 2ball championship (1998).

JULIUS ERVING

By Fran Blinebury

Julius Erving did for basketball what the Wright Brothers did for passenger travel — he took it airborne. He could wrap his long fingers around a basketball and brandish it like a tomahawk as he floated along the baseline for a rim-jarring, mind-rattling dunk.

He could make the backboard shake on its moorings from the explosive power of an all-out assault on the hoop, or barely move the net with a delicate finger roll at the end of a tip-toe drive on cat's feet.

He could launch himself into the air like one of NASA's rockets and remain suspended in orbit for what seemed like minutes, just beyond the long arm of the law of gravity.

It wasn't what he did, but the way he did it. He didn't

invent the dunk, but he brought it to the masses.

He was Dr. J and he could fly.

"Julius Erving did more to popularize basketball than anybody else who's ever played the game," said Magic Johnson. "I remember going to the schoolyard as a kid, the day after one of his games would be on TV.

"Everybody there would be saying, 'Did you see The Doctor?' And we'd all start trying to do those moves. There were other big players, talented players and great players before him. But it was Dr. J who put the 'Wow!' into the game."

He came quietly out of the University of Massachusetts in 1971, yet quickly became the feature attraction with the Virginia Squires and New York Nets of the American Basketball Association, where he was named MVP three times and twice won league championships. Yet in the upstart league, Erving remained mostly a cult figure without a spotlight.

When four ABA teams joined the NBA in 1976, Erving was traded for financial reasons from the New York Nets to the Philadelphia 76ers. That's when The Doctor began to operate as a national phenomenon, and for the next decade was the sport's greatest ambassador. He was Luke Skywalker in high-tops, driven by The Force within. He was a 6-7 E.T. who could levitate without special effects and make magical things happen with the touch of a finger. He was Astaire and Nureyev, Travolta and Baryshnikov, a pied piper with a flamboyant streak and hypnotizing tune who took basketball on an enchanted journey and forever changed the perception of how the game was to be played.

"I had my own style," Erving said. "Call it playground, call it street ball or whatever. It was about pushing at the limits, testing my own imagination."

He was an All-Star in each of his 16 pro seasons and the only player to win MVP awards and team championships in both the ABA and NBA. He led the Sixers to the NBA Finals four times, winning the title in 1983.

Combining his totals from both leagues, he scored the fourth-most points in pro basketball history, behind only Kareem Abdul-Jabbar, Wilt Chamberlain and Karl Malone.

Yet the record book barely hints at the brilliance of Dr. J. Elgin Baylor had the agility, Connie Hawkins the flash and David Thompson the leaping ability. But Erving was the embodiment of the best of all those attributes and, in addition to an artist's palette of colors, gave the game a touch of class. At a time when Chamberlain and Bill Russell had just retired and when the likes of Magic and Larry Bird and Michael Jordan were still in gym class, Erving was a galvanizing force in the NBA's dramatic rise in popularity. Dr. J blazed the path for Air Jordan to follow.

"I've seen a lot of great players, people who can do some amazing things on the court," said Magic. "But I've never seen anyone coming up who looks like another Julius. He was better. He was different. He was special."

He was Dr. J. And he could fly.

CAREER HIGHLIGHTS: NBA championship with Philadelphia 76ers (1983); NBA MVP (1981); All-NBA First Team (1978, '80, '81, '82, '83); All-NBA Second Team (1977, '84); NBA All-Star (1977, '78, '79, '80, '81, '82, '83, '84, '85, '86, '87); All-Star Game MVP (1977, '83); ABA championship with New York Nets (1974, '76); ABA MVP (1974, '76); ABA co-MVP (1975); All-ABA First Team (1973, '74, '75 '76); Led ABA in scoring (1973, '74); ABA All-Star (1972, '73, '74, '75, '76); No. 32 retired by New Jersey Nets; No. 6 retired by Philadelphia 76ers; NBA 35th Anniversary All-Time Team (1980); Walter J. Kennedy Citizenship Award (1983); Naismith Memorial Basketball Hall of Fame (1993).

PATRICK EWING

Began play in 1985.

The proud New York Knicks franchise had fallen on hard times in 1985. A string of injuries to key players and a lucky lottery outcome combined to give the Knicks the No. 1 pick in the 1985 NBA Draft. Patrick Ewing had been a defensive force at Georgetown, but as a professional, Ewing blossomed into one of the greatest shooters ever to play the center position. He elevated the Knicks into the playoffs by his third season, and helped them reach the NBA Finals in 1994 and 1999. On March 26, 1999, he became only the 12th player in NBA history to record 20,000 career points and 10,000 career rebounds. With Ewing in the middle, the Knicks have made the playoffs for 13 straight seasons. The big man resurrected the Knicks' franchise and filled Madison Square Garden with championship dreams again.

CAREER HIGHLIGHTS: All-NBA First Team (1990); All-NBA Second Team (1988, '89, '91, '92, '93, '97); All-NBA Defensive Team (1988, '89, '92); NBA All-Star (1986, '88, '89, '90, '91, '92, '93, '94, '95, '96, '97); NBA Rookie of the Year (1986); NBA All-Rookie Team (1986); Member of gold medal-winning U.S. Olympic teams (1984, '92); Knicks franchise leader in points (23,665), field goals made (9,260) and attempted (18,224), free throws made (5,126) and attempted (6,904), rebounds (10,759), blocked shots (2,758) and steals (1,061).

WALT FRAZIER/EARL MONROE

By Bruce Newman

Even at the apex of their careers, their distinctly rural names — Walt and Earl — were a contradiction to their personas on and off the court. Earl and Walt. It was as if at any moment they might burst into a Willie Nelson song, or a discussion of crop-rotation techniques.

In 1973, when Walt Frazier and Earl Monroe propelled the New York Knickerbockers to the franchise's second NBA title, they were rarely called by their given names. Instead, they were Clyde and Pearl. (The Pearl, to be exact, because in those days not only did the great players have nicknames, they had articles.) They were that rarest of all backcourt combinations, both instant offense and instant defense.

Fire and ice.

The 1971 trade that brought Monroe to New York forged one of the great backcourts of all time and gave Monroe his best opportunity to win a title. Frazier already had one championship ring from the '70 Knicks, had made the All-NBA First Team once and the All-Defensive Team three times. But Earl the Pearl, who averaged 23.7 points during his four years with the Baltimore Bullets and established himself as one of the game's great individual talents, had experienced lesser team success. He reached the NBA Finals the previous spring only to be swept by Kareem Abdul-Jabbar, Oscar Robertson and the Milwaukee Bucks.

The acquisition of Monroe gave the Knicks a chance to regain the title they had won in 1970, in no small part because Monroe left much of his Pearl character in Baltimore.

"Not many guys get the chance to have their own team, one that revolves around you, and that's what I left in Baltimore," Monroe said. "I felt it was like protocol. I was coming to New York; I had to acquiesce to whatever was going on in New York. And it was Clyde's ball. I wasn't going to try to impede on that. If it was the opposite way, I'm quite sure Clyde would have felt the same way."

Despite being drafted by different franchises, they were almost connected at the hip from the beginning. Monroe was the second pick in the 1967 draft out of Winston-Salem State, while Frazier was the fifth pick out of Southern Illinois. They played together for almost six seasons, retired in the same year, and ended up with almost identical career scoring averages — Frazier averaged 18.9 points while Monroe averaged 18.8.

When they began their successful partnership with the Knicks, it clearly was a deferential relationship. In their first season together, Monroe, suffering from bone spurs in his foot and struggling to find his way in the Knicks' ball-movement offense, had the worst scoring year of his career, averaging only 11.9 points. Frazier's average climbed to 23.2, his career-best.

"When they made that trade and they got Earl, I think it

took a burden off of Clyde," said Hall of Fame guard Nate "Tiny" Archibald. "He was smart and he wouldn't handle the ball as much on you outside. He would go in there and post you up and use his height and his ability to score. He was a great player and I'm kind of glad that I didn't have to play against him consistently. He was a great competitor."

As a historic figure in the development of basketball's current aesthetic, Monroe has been vastly overlooked and underappreciated. Certainly he did not invent "moves," but Monroe was the first player to mythologize them. His schoolmates in Philadelphia called him "Thomas Edison" because of his inventiveness, but his later playground nickname (Earl the Pearl was a newspaper coinage Monroe acquired at Winston-Salem State) seemed a better fit: Black Jesus.

"When we used to play him with the Bullets, the crowd would be in a frenzy," said Frazier, who had to try to guard him. "He didn't know what he was going to do, so how could I? He had the spin move, which was new at the time. He was the first guy who would post and toast — just back you inside, man, all the herky-jerky moves. Swirling dervish! When Earl scored on you it was humiliating. He's throwing up stuff from behind his back, and the people are screaming, 'Earl! Earl! Best in the world!' It takes a lot of fortitude to come back from that."

With Monroe, the Knicks' starting lineup had no weak spots, and New York devastated the Lakers in five games in the 1973 Finals. In two more seasons his scoring average climbed back over 20 points, but by then Earl the Pearl was only a memory. "I could still turn it on," he said, "but I wasn't as physical as I was before. That was all part of the process of understanding the game, the science of it. I started analyzing the game and that allowed me to do a lot of things I was doing before, but with less effort."

Frazier was always the ultimate in efficiency, so his coolness, combined with Earl's Pearlness, created something special, and memorable.

"As far as I was concerned," Monroe said, "we were the best backcourt to play."

CAREER HIGHLIGHTS (FRAZIER): NBA championships with New York Knicks (1970, '73); All-NBA First Team (1970, '72, '74, '75); All-NBA Second Team (1971, '73); NBA All-Rookie Team (1968); NBA All-Star (1970, '71, '72, '73, '74, '75, '76); NBA All-Star Game MVP (1975); NBA All-Defensive First Team (1969, '70, '71, '72, '73, '74 '75); New York Knicks all-time assist leader (4,791); No. 10 retired by New York Knicks; Naismith Memorial Basketball Hall of Fame (1987).

CAREER HIGHLIGHTS (MONROE): NBA championship with New York Knicks (1973); All-NBA First Team (1969); NBA Rookie of the Year (1968); NBA All-Rookie Team (1968); NBA All-Star (1969, '71, '75, '77); No. 15 retired by New York Knicks; Naismith Memorial Basketball Hall of Fame (1989).

GEORGE GERVIN

Retired in 1986.

Began play in 1972.

Played 14 seasons.

Coaches watch hours of videotape of top players, trying to find out that player's favorite shooting spots. For the "Iceman," also known as George Gervin, such an effort was futile. An unlikely looking superstar, the reed-thin Gervin not only was comfortable shooting from anywhere on the floor, he seemed to invent new ways to release his shots in every game. A one-handed, 15-foot flip off the backboard while on the move is a horrible shot for anyone else, but for Ice, it was just another reliable shot in his arsenal. Gervin, who turned pro with the ABA's Virginia Squires out of Eastern Michigan University, won four NBA scoring titles, and owns the seventh-highest scoring average in NBA history (26.2). Players such as Gervin and Julius Erving entered the NBA after the ABA folded and brought an exciting, wide-open brand of basketball that created a new generation of NBA fans.

CAREER HIGHLIGHTS: All-NBA First Team (1978, '79, '80, '81, '82); All-NBA Second Team (1977, '83); San Antonio Spurs All-Time leading scorer (19,383); NBA All-Star (1977, '78, '79, '80, '81, '82, '83, '84, '85); NBA All-Star Game MVP (1980); All-ABA Second Team (1975, '76); ABA All-Star (1974, '75, '76); All-ABA Rookie team (1973); Joined by Michael Jordan and Wilt Chamberlain as the only players to win four or more NBA scoring titles (1978-80, 1982); Career scoring average of 26.2 points per game; Scored 26,595 career points; Scored 50 or more points four times and 40 or more points 64 times in the NBA; Scored 1,000 points or more for 13 consecutive years; No. 44 retired by San Antonio Spurs; Naismith Memorial Basketball Hall of Fame (1996).

HAL GREER

Retired in 1973.

Began play in 1958.

Played 15 seasons.

Before modern training techniques enabled players to extend their careers well into their 30s, there was a durable marvel named Hal Greer. The West Virginia native, who played at Marshall University, was a quick and athletic guard who had no weaknesses in his game. He played in an era when players normally retired after about 10 seasons, but in 1968-69, his 11th NBA season, Greer averaged 23.1 points. He went on to average 22 points the next season. Greer played his entire 1,122-game NBA career for one franchise, the Syracuse Nationals/ Philadelphia 76ers. He was a starter and star for the 76ers' team that won the 1967 NBA championship, breaking the string of eight straight titles won by the Boston Celtics. Greer was a top defender, unselfish passer and effective rebounder from the backcourt. He remains the franchise's all-time leader in scoring with 21,586 points.

CAREER HIGHLIGHTS: NBA championship with Philadelphia 76ers (1967); All-NBA Second Team (1963, '64, '65, '66, '67, '68, '69); NBA All-Star (1961, '62, '63, '64, '65, '66, '67, '68, '69, '70); All-Star Game MVP (1968); No. 15 retired by Philadelphia 76ers; Naismith Memorial Basketball Hall of Fame (1981).

JOHN HAVLICEK

Retired in 1978.

Began play in 1962.

Played 16 seasons.

Only three players in NBA history — Kareem Abdul-Jabbar, Elvin Hayes and Wilt Chamberlain — played more minutes in their NBA careers than John Havlicek. The man from Ohio State whom they called "Hondo" bridged the years between Boston Celtics dynasties, playing for the Celtics for 16 seasons and winning eight championships from 1962 to 1978. Havlicek won six championships with Bill Russell in the 1960s, then teamed with Dave Cowens to bring the franchise titles in 1974 and 1976. Havlicek is undoubtedly the best sixth man of all time, maximizing the role legendary Celtics coach Red Auerbach first popularized with Frank Ramsey. A rugged 6-5 and 205 pounds, Havlicek could play either guard or forward and could shoot, pass, rebound and defend. At 37 years old, Havlicek averaged 34.1 minutes and 16.1 points in 1977-78, his final season.

CAREER HIGHLIGHTS: NBA championships with Boston Celtics (1963, '64, '65, '66, '68, '69, '74, '76); NBA Finals MVP (1974); All-NBA First Team (1971, '72, '73, '74); All-NBA Second Team (1964, '66, '68, '69, '70, '75, '76); All-NBA Defensive First Team (1972, '73, '74, '75, '76); All-NBA Defensive Second Team (1969, '70, '71); NBA All-Star (1966, '67, '68, '69, '70, '71, '72, '73, '74, '75, '76, '77, '78); Became first player to score 1,000 points in 16 consecutive seasons; Regarded as the best sixth man in NBA history; NBA 35th Anniversary Team (1980); No. 17 retired by Boston Celtics; Naismith Memorial Basketball Hall of Fame (1983).

ELVIN HAYES

Retired in 1984.

Began play in 1968.

Played 16 seasons.

Few players define a position in sport the way Elvin Hayes did the power forward position. His unique combination of strength and agility embodied the modern power forward, becoming the measuring stick for all who played against him and all who would follow. In the years since his retirement in 1984, only Karl Malone has come close to his achievements. Hayes played center at the University of Houston, and will forever be remembered for his Astrodome matchup against UCLA's Kareem Abdul-Jabbar (then known as Lew Alcindor) in one of the sport's seminal games. Hayes was a spectacular scorer and rebounder in his first four NBA seasons as a center for the Rockets, but came into his own after a trade to Baltimore in 1972. That resulted in a move to power forward alongside Wes Unseld. Hayes scored many of his points with an unstoppable turnaround jump shot, but he is also the fourth-leading rebounder in NBA history (16,279) and is fifth in career games played (1,303). Hayes led the Bullets to the NBA Finals three times, winning the NBA championship in 1978.

CAREER HIGHLIGHTS: NBA championship with Washington Bullets (1978); All-NBA First Team (1975, '77, '79); All-NBA Second Team (1973, '74, '76); All-NBA Defensive Second Team (1974, '75); NBA All-Star (1969, '70, '71, '72, '73, '74, '75, '76, '77, '78, '79, '80); Scored 27,313 points (21.0 points per game) in 1,303 professional games, third best in history upon retirement; NBA All-Rookie Team (1969); Grabbed 16,279 rebounds (12.5) in 1,303 professional games, third best in history upon retirement; Upon retirement, played more minutes (49,006, 37.6 mpg) than any player in history; Upon retirement, ranked third all-time in games played (1,303) and blocked shots (1,743); Washington Wizards franchise all-time leader in scoring (15,551) and blocked shots (1,558); No. 11 retired by Washington Wizards; Naismith Memorial Basketball Hall of Fame (1989).

EARVIN "MAGIC" JOHNSON

Retired in 1996.

Began play in 1979.

Played 13 seasons.

Rare is the player who can dominate a basketball game without scoring a point. That player is as hard to find as, say, a 6-9 point guard. Magic Johnson entered the NBA after winning an NCAA championship with Michigan State, beating Larry Bird's Indiana State team in the title game. He would continue to be a champion as he ruled the NBA during the 1980s, leading his Los Angeles Lakers to five NBA titles in a nine-year period, and his rivalry with Bird and the Boston Celtics took the sport to new heights of popularity. Magic held the baton as the conductor of what many believe was the most entertaining basketball symphony of all-time. The Lakers were dubbed "Showtime," and there was no doubt who ran the show. Magic was never the fastest NBA player, but he always seemed to be leading another Lakers' fast break. When Magic had the ball in the middle of a break, there was no telling how he would choose to pass the ball, or if he would fake the pass left, then right, then go right to the rim for a layup. Magic made passing the basketball exciting and cool, and that will be his enduring legacy to the game he loved so much. (For more on Magic Johnson, see page 30).

CAREER HIGHLIGHTS: NBA championships with Los Angeles Lakers (1980, '82, '85, '87, '88); NBA MVP (1987, '89, '90); NBA Finals MVP (1980, '82, '87); Became First Rookie ever to win NBA Finals MVP; All-NBA First Team (1983, '84, '85, '86, '87, '88, '89, '90, '91); All-NBA Second Team (1982); NBA All-Star (1980, '82, '83, '84, '85, '86, '87, '88, '89, '90, '91, '92); All-Star Game MVP (1990, '92); NBA All-Rookie Team (1980); Member of gold medal-winning U.S. Olympic team (1992); L.A. Lakers franchise leader in assists (10,141) and steals (1,724); Led league in steals (1981, 82); Four league assist titles (1983, '84, '86, '87); Ninth place on the all-time career steals list (1,724); No. 32 retired by Los Angeles Lakers.

SAM JONES

Retired in 1969.

Began play in 1957.

Played 12 seasons.

While it's not true that Sam Jones invented the bank shot, you might say he perfected it. The sweet-shooting guard from North Carolina Central was a scoring machine for the Boston Celtics' dynasty of the 1960s. From 1963 to 1966, Jones was either first or second on the Celtics in scoring as the team completed an NBA-record eight straight NBA championships. Jones could score on anyone, at any time, from anywhere. When the Celtics were in a tight spot late in a game, they called for Sam Jones to take the big shot. Almost every time, he delivered. Jones averaged more than 19 points for six straight seasons, with a high mark of 25.9 points (fourth in the NBA) during the 1964-65 season. An excellent all-around player, he teamed with K.C. Jones to give the Celtics one of the best backcourts in the league. One more thing about Sam Jones: he has 10 NBA championship rings, second only to Bill Russell's 11.

CAREER HIGHLIGHTS: NBA championships with Boston Celtics (1959, '60, '61, '62, '63, '64, '65, '66, '68, '69); All-NBA Second Team (1965, '66, '67); No. 24 retired by Boston Celtics; NBA 25th Anniversary Team (1970); Naismith Memorial Basketball Hall of Fame (1983).

MICHAEL JORDAN (see page 20).

JERRY LUCAS

Retired in 1974.
Began play in 1963.
Played 11 seasons.

One of the top rebounders in NBA history, Jerry Lucas is also remembered for his distinctive and accurate perimeter shot. Few men of his size (6-8, 235 pounds) have ever shot the ball from long range as well as Lucas, who energized the Cincinnati Royals for six seasons during the 1960s as a teammate of all-time great Oscar Robertson. If the three-point shot were around in his day, Lucas easily would have added several points per game to his scoring average. Lucas, a graduate of Ohio State who played center and power forward equally well, was not the highest jumping player in the league, but his tenacious desire for rebounds enabled him to average more than 17 rebounds for six straight seasons from 1963-64 to 1968-69. Late in his career, Lucas was traded to the New York Knicks, where he played his final three seasons and was a key performer on the 1973 NBA championship team.

CAREER HIGHLIGHTS: NBA championship team with New York Knicks (1973); All-NBA First Team (1965, '66, '68); All-NBA Second Team (1964, '67); All Star (1964, '65, '66, '67, '68, '69, '71); NBA All-Star MVP (1965); NBA Rookie of the Year (1964); NBA All-Rookie Team (1964); Member of gold medal-winning U.S. Olympic team (1960); Naismith Memorial Basketball Hall of Fame (1979).

KARL MALONE/JOHN STOCKTON

By Art Thiel

Championships. Statistics. Trademark moves. A momentous event. All can make an athletic legacy. But in the NBA, there is only one legacy defined by a simple basketball play. Pick and roll. Stockton and Malone.

Although the accomplishments of John Stockton and Karl Malone are far greater than the mastery of the game's most elemental two-man maneuver, it is also representative of their essence — turning the mundane into sports art.

Often a pair of brown shoes in the tuxedoed world of the NBA, Stockton and Malone nevertheless are, for basketball aficionados, the personification of the game as it appears in the hoops textbook. From execution to consistency to grace to power, they are greatness perfected and maintained.

And they have maintained it in one place — Salt Lake City, Utah, one of the NBA's smallest markets. Since the 1985-86 season, when Malone joined one-year veteran Stockton, the pair set up shop at the foot of the Wasatch Mountains and, ignoring the temptations of vagabond free agency, never left. They made the NBA world come to them.

The Jazz has yet to win a championship with the tandem. But the pair and the team achieved a level of consistent excellence nearly unmatched in NBA history. The 1999-2000 season marked the 15th consecutive season the Jazz had a winning record, a mark second only to the 16 of the Los Angeles Lakers (1976-77 through 1991-92). During that time, Stockton and Malone played together in 1,170 games. No two players in NBA history have played as many games as teammates. It was fitting that when the NBA All-Star Game was played in Salt Lake City in 1993, Stockton and Malone would share MVP honors, and fitting that in 1996, they would both be named among the 50 Greatest Players in NBA History.

Stockton and Malone were teammates in two Olympics — with the original Dream Team in 1992 in Barcelona, and in the 1996 Atlanta Olympics. Each has two gold medals. But their greatest feat was transforming a moribund franchise into a perennial power. Their first season as teammates resulted in only the second winning record in club history, but eventually Malone and Stockton took the Jazz to five Western Conference Finals during a seven-year period with trips to the NBA Finals in 1997 and 1998, where it took the greatness of Michael Jordan and the Chicago Bulls to beat them.

The fortuitous blend of their talents — each became the definition of their positions of point guard and power forward — made each greater. Stockton is the all-time leader in assists (as well as steals) and Malone in 2000 passed Michael Jordan to become the NBA's third-leading career scorer, trailing only Kareem Abdul-Jabbar and Wilt Chamberlain.

The tandem developed an unparalleled seamlessness, each having a sense for the other's presence, while making the Jazz a splendid example of a whole greater than the sum of its parts.

Identifying them with the pick and roll minimizes the impact of their mastery. They developed so many options from the play that the original is seldom seen. It made the Jazz one of the most efficient teams ever, minimizing mistakes and wasted energy, which allowed the team to flourish throughout the 1990s despite a roster usually loaded with veterans in their mid-to-late 30s.

Malone and Stockton also personify "work ethic." Each maintains a rigorous offseason regimen that helps each defy age and injury. Through 1999-2000, Stockton had played in 98 percent of all possible games, and had 13 seasons of a full 82 games, tying the NBA record. Malone had played in an incredible 99.5 percent of his games, missing three due to injury and three by suspension.

Longtime Jazz coach Jerry Sloan tells the story of a time during Malone's first year when the two were having a long talk. Sloan asked him, "When are you going to change?" referring to the young Malone's relentless sessions of weight lifting and running that sculpted his massive body.

"He told me, 'Coach, I'll never change,'" Sloan said. "He never did."

Malone was the ninth player to win two or more Most Valuable Player awards. His second, for the 1998-99 season, made him, at 35 years, 10 months, the oldest such achiever. He was also the fourth player to reach 20,000 points, 10,000 rebounds and 4,000 assists.

Entering the 2000-01 season, only six players had appeared in more NBA games than Stockton, a remarkable plateau for a 6-1, 175-pounder who not only was fearless about taking the ball inside among the behemoths, but played the other end, too. Five times Stockton was named to the All-Defensive Second Team. He set the career assists mark in 1995, and the steals mark in 1996, so his continued play into a fresh decade may set Cal Ripken-like standards that never will be broached.

In a sports world increasingly given over to glamour, hype and instant gratification, Karl Malone and John Stockton are the epitome of substance, excellence and consistency.

CAREER HIGHLIGHTS (MALONE): NBA Most Valuable Player (1997, '99); All-NBA First Team (1989, '90, '91, '92, '93, '94, '95, '96, '97, '98, '99); All-NBA Second Team (1988, 2000); NBA All-Defensive First Team (1997, '98, '99); NBA All-Defensive Second Team (1988); NBA All-Rookie Team (1986); NBA All-Star (1988, '89, '90, '91, '92, '93, '94, '95, '96, '97, '98, 2000); All-Star MVP (1989); All-Star co-MVP (1993); Holds career records for most consecutive seasons with 2,000 or more points (11) and most seasons leading league in free throws made (8).

CAREER HIGHLIGHTS (STOCKTON): All-NBA First Team (1994, '95); All-NBA Second Team (1988, '89, '90, '92, '93, '96); All-NBA Third Team (1991, '97, '99), NBA All-Defensive Second Team (1989, '91, '92, '95, '97); NBA All-Star (1989, '90, '91, '92, '93, '94, '95, '96, '97, 2000); All-Star co-MVP (1993); Led league in assists (1988, '89, '90, '91, '92, '93, '94, '95, '96); Led league in steals (1989, '92); Career leader assists and steals.

MOSES MALONE

Retired in 1995.

Began play in 1974.

Played 21 seasons.

The greatest offensive rebounder in NBA history, Moses Malone was the epitome of relentless hard work in the NBA's trenches for two decades. Only Robert Parish and Kareem Abdul-Jabbar played more NBA games than Malone, who was the league's Most Valuable Player in 1979, 1982 and 1983. When you were playing against Malone, the defensive play started only after his team missed a shot. Malone, who went straight from Petersburg (Va.) High School to the ABA, went over, around and through the opposition for 6,731 offensive rebounds in his NBA career, more than 2,000 ahead of second-place Parish. Moses commanded a full arsenal of offensive moves: post-ups, mid-range jump shots and bank shots. Malone was a career 77-percent free throw shooter, important since no one in NBA history made more than his 8,531 free throws. In 1983, Malone and Julius Erving led Philadelphia to 12 victories in 13 playoff games as the 76ers won the NBA title.

CAREER HIGHLIGHTS: NBA championship with Philadelphia 76ers (1983); NBA Finals MVP (1983); NBA MVP (1979, '82, '83); All-NBA First Team (1979, '82, '83, '85); All-NBA Second Team (1980, '81, '84, '87); NBA All-Defensive First Team (1983); NBA All-Defensive Second Team (1979); NBA All-Star (1978, '79, '80, '81, '82, '83, '84, '85, '86, '87, '88, '89); NBA's third leading rebounder in history (16,212); NBA's fifth leading scorer (27,409); Made more free throws than any other player in NBA history (8,531); Third most NBA games played in NBA history (1,329); Sixth most NBA minutes played (45,071); Has most NBA offensive rebounds ever in NBA history (6,731); Second most defensive rebounds (9,481); NBA's leading rebounder six times in a seven year span; ABA All-Rookie Team (1975); No. 24 retired by Houston Rockets.

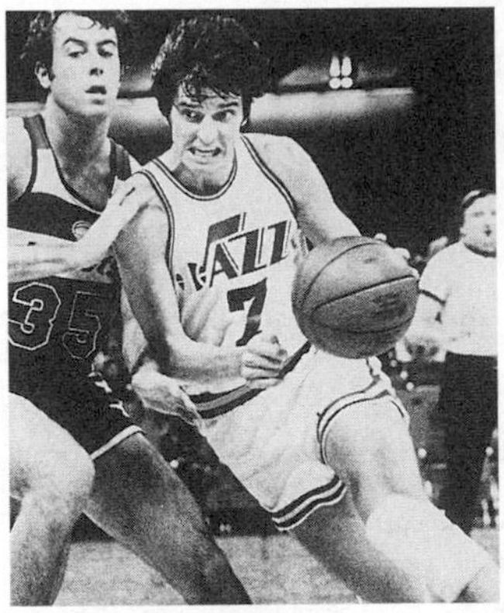

PETE MARAVICH

Retired in 1980.

Began play in 1970.

Played 10 seasons.

It speaks well for the late Pete Maravich that when his legacy is examined today, the spectacular passes to teammates are what people remember best. One of the most gifted scorers in NCAA history at LSU, Maravich's exploits continued in the pros, where he did everything with a flourish, whether he was draining a 30-foot shot or whipping a pass through a phalanx of defenders to a wide-open teammate. In an era when the safe, sure pass was highly prized, Maravich pushed the envelope with a derring-do that confounded the establishment. Maravich was a scorer who handled the ball better than any point guard. "Pistol Pete" led the NBA in scoring with 31.1 points per game in 1976-77, and averaged 24.2 points during his career. He once scored 68 points against the New York Knicks, the third-highest total by a guard in NBA history. Maravich won new fans for the game with his flamboyant style, and set the stage for the exploits of showmen such as Magic Johnson and Isiah Thomas.

CAREER HIGHLIGHTS: All-NBA First Team (1976, '77); All-NBA Second Team (1973, '78); Led NBA in scoring in 1976-77 season (31.1 points per game); NBA All-Rookie Team (1971); No. 7 retired by Utah Jazz; Elected to Naismith Memorial Basketball Hall of Fame (1986).

KEVIN MCHALE

Retired in 1993.

Began play in 1980.

Played 13 seasons.

Not every great athlete has a prototypical athletic physique. Kevin McHale was one of the most unstoppable post-up players in the history of the NBA, and was the X-factor that propelled the Boston Celtics to three championships in the 1980s. Joining with Larry Bird and Robert Parish to form the greatest NBA frontcourt in the modern era, McHale's long arms, great hands and superior intellect were an unbeatable combination. When he got the ball close to the basket, McHale, from the University of Minnesota, gave hapless defenders a clinic on post play, using a variety of head and shoulder fakes, up-and-under moves and different release points on his shots. Since McHale lacked the strength of many post players, he invented countless other ways to beat his man down low. In 13 NBA seasons, no team ever found a defender able to consistently stop McHale. And as good as McHale was during the season, he always seemed to perform even better when the postseason began.

CAREER HIGHLIGHTS: NBA championships with Boston Celtics (1981, '84, '86); All-NBA First Team (1987); All-NBA Defensive First Team (1986, '87, '88); NBA All-Defensive Second Team (1983, '89, '90); NBA Sixth Man Award (1984, '85); NBA All-Star (1984, '86, '87, '88, '89, '90, '91); NBA All-Rookie Team (1981); No. 32 retired by Boston Celtics; Naismith Memorial Basketball Hall of Fame (1999).

GEORGE MIKAN (See page 26).

HAKEEM OLAJUWON

Began play in 1984.

No big man ever embodied the grace and balance of basketball better than Hakeem "The Dream" Olajuwon. The native of Nigeria came to the game of basketball late in his youth after a childhood spent playing soccer and handball. His peerless footwork, a remnant from those days, enabled him to weave in and out of the post with balletic ease. Olajuwon, who played at the University of Houston, has spent his entire career playing against centers who had a height advantage against him (he was listed at seven feet but stood closer to 6-10). But he used his superior athletic ability, and his shrewd use of fakes and positioning often put him in the driver's seat. Olajuwon runs the court like a small forward, often chasing down much smaller opponents from behind to make a steal or block a shot. At the close of the 1999-2000 season, Olajuwon was in the NBA's all-time top 10 in points and steals and was first in blocked shots. He led the Houston Rockets to back-to-back championships in 1994 and 1995, securing a prominent place in NBA history.

CAREER HIGHLIGHTS: NBA championships with Houston Rockets (1994, '95); NBA Finals MVP (1994, '95); NBA MVP (1994); NBA All-Star (1985, '86, '87, '88, '89, '90, '92, '93, '94, '95, '96, '97); All-NBA First Team (1987, '88, '89, '93, '94, '97); All-NBA Second Team (1986, '90, '96); All-NBA Third Team (1991, '95, '99); NBA All-Defensive First Team (1987, '88, '90, '93, '94); NBA All-Defensive Second Team (1985, '91, '96, '97); NBA All-Rookie Team (1985); Member of gold medal-winning U.S. Olympic team (1996).

SHAQUILLE O'NEAL

Began play in 1992.

The most prolific scoring big man since Wilt Chamberlain terrorized NBA centers in the 1960s and 1970s, Shaquille O'Neal has evolved into an unstoppable force. At 7-1 and more than 300 pounds, O'Neal, who went to LSU, possesses a mix of power and athleticism not seen since Wilt. When O'Neal posts up close to the basket, no player is strong enough to deny him position; once the ball arrives, the defender has two choices: get out of the way, or quickly foul before O'Neal attacks the rim for one of his ferocious slam dunks. In his eighth season in the league at a mere 28 years old, O'Neal earned regular-season and NBA Finals MVP honors in the 1999-2000 regular season and the NBA Finals as he led the Los Angeles Lakers to the NBA title. Still only entering his prime years, O'Neal, who led the NBA in scoring in 1999-00, is poised to keep his team at the championship level for years to come.

CAREER HIGHLIGHTS: NBA championship with Los Angeles Lakers (2000); NBA Finals MVP (2000); NBA MVP (2000); NBA All-Star (1993, '94, '95, '96, '97, '98, '00); NBA All-Star Co-MVP 2000; All-NBA First Team (1998, '00); All-NBA Second Team (1995, '99); All-NBA Third Team (1994, '96, '97); NBA Rookie of the Year (1993); Led NBA in scoring twice (1995, '00); Member of gold medal-winning U.S. World Championship team (1994); Member of gold medal-winning U.S. Olympic team (1996).

ROBERT PARISH

Retired in 1997.

Began play in 1976.

Played 21 seasons.

The center for what many call the finest NBA frontcourt of the modern era always took a back seat to Larry Bird and Kevin McHale. But true basketball insiders knew that the talents of Robert Parish enabled Bird and McHale to excel to the degree they did. Without Parish, the stone-faced 7-1 pivot man teammates called "Chief," the Celtics would not have won NBA titles in 1981, 1984 and 1986. Parish, from Centenary College in Louisiana, was the perfect defensive complement to the offensive-minded Bird and McHale. He rebounded and blocked shots with the top centers of his era, while mastering the pick and roll and running the floor like few big men ever have. Parish also possessed a reliable and nearly unblockable jump shot that he released from somewhere far behind his head. Parish played more games (1,611) than any player in NBA history and retired in the top 10 in rebounds and blocks.

CAREER HIGHLIGHTS: NBA championships with Boston Celtics (1981, '84, '86) and Chicago Bulls (1997); All-NBA Second Team (1982); All-NBA Third Team (1989); NBA All-Star (1981, '82, '83, '84, '85, '86, '87, '90, '91); Boston Celtics franchise all-time leader in games played (1,611), minutes (45,704) and blocks (1,703); No. 00 retired by Boston Celtics.

BOB PETTIT

By Fred Kerber

In his first two years at Baton Rouge High School in Louisiana, Bob Pettit's seat at basketball games was in the stands, not on the team bench. Lacking in pure athleticism, he was cut the first two times he tried out for the team.

It was the best thing that could have happened to him because Pettit possessed attributes far more important than size and coordination: He had drive. Desire. Determination. If coaches felt he was not good enough, then he simply would get good enough. No, he'd get even better.

"Basically, getting cut made me more determined. Probably it was a good thing that I was not good to start with," recalled Pettit, the son of a county sheriff. "If you walk out and you're naturally good at something, you don't work to develop it like you do if you're struggling. I had to work very hard. I'd go home and practice two, three hours an afternoon just shooting around at a goal in the backyard trying to get better. When I did start getting coordinated, started getting size, I was a lot further advanced than a lot of these guys who picked it up and found it easy to start."

Pettit made his high school team as a 6-4 junior, then starred at Louisiana State where he grew to 6-9 and averaged 27.4 points and 14.6 rebounds in his varsity career. Selected by the then-Milwaukee Hawks in the first round of the 1954 NBA Draft, he spent 11 seasons in the league, making the All-Star team and averaging more than 20 points and 12 rebounds every year.

Before Elvin Hayes and Karl Malone, both Louisiana products, came along, the big forward position was defined and dominated by Pettit, a 6-9 all-purpose performer for the Milwaukee and St. Louis Hawks. He was unquestionably the premier forward of his time and one of the greatest players ever to grace the game.

Drafted in the same summer the NBA adopted the 24-second shot clock, Pettit, with a rare blend of outside and inside skills, was an instant hit in the new, up-tempo style. The 1954-55 Rookie of the Year, he moved with the Hawks to St. Louis in his second season and went on to become the first player in NBA history to top 20,000 points. Ten straight years he was voted to the All-NBA First Team, and he was a second team pick in his final season. On his way to the Hall of Fame, Pettit picked up two MVP awards, won two scoring titles and gathered an NBA championship ring with the Hawks, who upended Bill Russell's Celtics in 1958. Pettit scored 50 points in the Hawks' title-clinching game.

"Bob made 'second effort' a part of the sport's vocabulary," said Russell. "He kept coming at you more than any man in the game."

"He was a power forward and a power forward who could really score. You didn't find guys like that in those days," said fellow Hall of Famer Lenny Wilkens, Pettit's teammate for five seasons.

Pettit never finished below seventh among the league scoring leaders in any of his 10 full seasons, but he was more than just a scorer. He ranks as the greatest rebounder in Hawks history, having grabbed 12,851 boards. During his career, he averaged 16.2 rebounds and 26.4 points.

And it was his drive that made it happen. "I was never satisfied, never totally happy with the way I played," said Pettit, who went into banking and the financial services field after his basketball career ended in 1965. "I always felt there was room for improvement.

"One thing I had was a drive to succeed, and as I kept reaching plateaus, I was not satisfied," continued Pettit, the All-Star Game MVP three times and a co-MVP a fourth time. "Overall, if you asked for one highlight it would be the year we won it and I scored 50 points in the final game. When you combine the other honors I was fortunate enough to win or be awarded, then looking back, I'm pretty proud. It was a good career, one I'm very proud of and one that not a lot of guys have done a lot better than."

Not even those who made their high school teams all four years.

CAREER HIGHLIGHTS: NBA championship with St. Louis Hawks (1958); NBA Rookie of the Year (1955); NBA MVP (1956, '59); All-NBA First Team (1955, '56, '57, '58, '59, '60, '61, '62, '63, '64); All-NBA Second Team (1965); NBA All-Star (1955, '56, '57, '58, '59, '60, '61, '62, '63, '64, '65); NBA All-Star Game MVP (1956, '58, '62); Led the league in scoring (1956, '59); Led the league in rebounding (1956); Atlanta Hawks franchise all-time leading rebounder (12,849); No. 9 retired by Atlanta Hawks; NBA 25th Anniversary All-Time Team (1970); NBA 35th Anniversary All-Time Team (1980); Naismith Memorial Basketball Hall of Fame (1989).

SCOTTIE PIPPEN

Began play in 1987.

If one player best captured the excellence of the versatile, athletic mid-sized player who helped change the face of the NBA in the last decade of the 20th century, that player would be Scottie Pippen. The alter-ego of Michael Jordan when the Chicago Bulls were winning six NBA championships in the 1990s, Pippen, out of Central Arkansas, was the best defensive player and top passer during those years. While Jordan poured in the points, Pippen was his team's defensive mastermind, able to thwart smaller, quicker players and frustrate bigger, beefier types alike. Pippen's enormous wingspan, quick feet and knowledge of an opponent's tendencies made him an eight-time NBA All-Defensive First Team member. Pippen also was a creative scorer, mixing post-ups and slashing moves to the basket. It's often said Jordan's presence made people pay attention to Pippen's excellence. While it is obvious the Bulls would not have won six titles without Michael Jordan, it's also apparent that Jordan benefited from Pippen's all-around excellence.

CAREER HIGHLIGHTS: NBA championships with Chicago Bulls (1991, '92, '93, '96, '97, '98); All-NBA First Team (1994, '95, '96); All-NBA Second Team (1992, '97); All-NBA Third Team (1993, '98); NBA All-Defensive first team (1992, '93, '94, '95, '96, '97, '98, '99); NBA All-Defensive second team (1991); NBA All-Star (1990, '92, '93, '94, '95, '96, '97); All-Star Game MVP (1994); Member of gold medal-winning U.S. Olympic teams (1992, '96).

WILLIS REED

Retired in 1974.

Began play in 1964.

Played 10 seasons.

More than a quarter century after his playing career concluded, Willis Reed remains nothing less than the personification of courage in athletic competition. His determination in fighting through the searing pain of a torn thigh muscle to play in Game 7 of the 1970 NBA Finals not only lifted the Knicks to the championship, it made America pay attention to the drama that was pro basketball. New York's triumph in 1970 is credited by basketball historians as the moment that vaulted professional basketball from cult-only status to equal footing with other major professional sports, and Reed made that happen. One of the top team players ever to suit up in the NBA, Reed, out of Grambling State University, used his mind as much as his brawn to compete against taller opponents. While his career was shortened by injuries, Reed's place in history was assured by the events of May 8, 1970.

CAREER HIGHLIGHTS: NBA championships with New York Knicks (1970, '73); NBA Finals MVP (1970, '73); NBA MVP (1970); All-NBA First Team (1970); All-NBA Second Team (1967, '68, '69, '71); NBA All-Defensive First Team (1970); NBA All Star (1965, '66, '67, '68, '69, '70, '71) ; NBA All-Star Game MVP (1970); NBA Rookie of the Year (1965); NBA All-Rookie Team (1965); Upon retirement in 1974, was New York Knicks franchise leader in points (12,183, 18.7 points per game) and rebounds (8,414, 12.9 rebounds per game); Was the first player in NBA history to win regular season MVP, All-Star and Finals MVP in same year (1970); No. 19 retired by New York Knicks; Naismith Memorial Basketball Hall of Fame (1981).

OSCAR ROBERTSON

By David DuPree

Oscar Robertson was so good, it often looked as if the game was being played in slow motion just so you could appreciate everything he did.

He controlled the game not with fancy moves or sleight of hand, but with fundamentally sound play. He did things the right way, and throughout the history of the game, no one has done it better.

Others have won more championships, scored more points, dished more assists and collected more rebounds, but none mastered all phases of the game as well as the man known as "The Big O."

If the triple-double is the standard we now use to measure a player's versatility, then Robertson is the most versatile player the sport has ever produced.

In 1961-62, his second season in the NBA, he averaged a triple-double for the entire season — 30.8 points, 12.5 rebounds and 11.4 assists. He missed averaging a triple-double in four other seasons by no more than one rebound or one assist per game. For the first five seasons of his career (384 games), he averaged 30.3 points, 10.4 rebounds and 10.6 assists.

"My game was just to go out and start playing," he said. "If you play hard enough, you're going to get your shots, you're going to get your rebounds and you're going to get your assists. I never put an emphasis on one area of the game, but to play successfully and win, you have to do two things — rebound and play defense. That hasn't changed throughout the history of the game."

For all the legendary feats he performed on the basketball court, his most meaningful contribution has nothing to do with putting a ball in a basket. In 1997, he donated a kidney to his daughter, Tia. "I'm no hero," he said. "I'm just a father."

Calling Robertson "just" anything is under-appreciating the man. His style, grace, intelligence and leadership, to say nothing of his sheer talent, helped lay the foundation for what the NBA is today.

He grew up in a segregated housing project in Indianapolis and learned how to shoot a basketball by tossing tennis balls and rags with rubber bands wrapped around them into a rickety peach basket. He battled racial discrimination throughout his career and never wavered from his drive to make things better for those who came after him.

His trademark became an unblockable one-handed shot where he held the ball almost directly over his head.

He went on to win the national scoring title three times at the University of Cincinnati, was a three-time College Player of the Year honoree and co-captain of the gold medal-winning 1960 U.S. Olympic team.

He was just as dominant in the NBA, finishing third in the league in scoring his rookie season with a 30.5 average. He was Rookie of the Year and went on to play in 12 consecutive All-Star Games.

Robertson has always been a leader, on and off the court. He served as president of the NBA Players Association from 1963-1974 and has been president of the Retired NBA Players Association as well. The famed Oscar Robertson lawsuit, so-named because he was the president of the players' union at the time (1970), led to free agency in the NBA.

He won one NBA title, directing the Milwaukee Bucks to the crown in 1971, only their third season of existence.

The Bucks had drafted Lew Alcindor (Kareem Abdul-Jabbar) in 1969 and made it to the Eastern Conference Finals in his rookie season. The next season they acquired Robertson, who had played his entire career with the Cincinnati Royals, and they cruised through the regular season with 14 more victories than any other team and swept the Baltimore Bullets in four straight in the NBA Finals. Winning the title seemed almost effortless once they acquired Robertson.

"Oscar made everything simple," said K.C. Jones, who for years as a Boston Celtic went up against Robertson. "Nobody ever wants to admit they're afraid of another player, but it was scary the things that Oscar could do to you. He had a certain presence. They call it a lot of things today, but back then it was just something that he emitted. He was a basketball player, plain and simple, and he could do it all."

CAREER HIGHLIGHTS: NBA championship with Milwaukee Bucks (1971); NBA Rookie of the Year (1961); NBA MVP (1964); All-NBA First Team (1961, '62, '63, '64, '65, '66, '67, '68, '69); All-NBA Second Team (1970, '71); NBA All-Star (1961, '62, '63, '64, '65, '66, '67, '68, '69, '70, '71, '72); All-Star Game MVP (1961, '64, '69); Member of gold medal-winning U.S. Olympic Team (1960); Retired as the NBA's second all-time leading scorer; Led the NBA in scoring (1968); Averaged the only triple-double (30.8 ppg, 12.5 rpg, 11.4 apg) in league history in 1962; Led the league in assists in 1961, '62, '64, '65, '66, '67, '68, '69; Sacramento Kings franchise all-time leader in points (22,009) and assists (7,731); No. 1 retired by Milwaukee Bucks; No. 14 retired by Sacramento Kings; NBA 35th Anniversary All-Time Team (1980); Naismith Memorial Basketball Hall of Fame (1979).

DAVID ROBINSON

Began play in 1989.

The intellect of David Robinson could have taken him in any number of directions after a fine academic and athletic career at the U.S. Naval Academy. Fortunately for the San Antonio Spurs and the NBA, Robinson chose to put his exceptional talents to good use on the court. At 7-1 and 250 sculpted pounds, Robinson possessed the total package of skills necessary to become one of the best centers in NBA history. After a two-year service commitment was satisfied, Robinson burst on the NBA scene in 1989-90 as the league's Rookie of the Year. Over the next decade, Robinson scored, rebounded and defended his way to an MVP Award and a Defensive Player of the Year Award, as well as scoring, rebounding and blocked shots titles. In 1999, Robinson teamed with young superstar

Tim Duncan to complete his trophy case by bringing the Spurs the franchise's first NBA championship.

CAREER HIGHLIGHTS: NBA championship with San Antonio Spurs (1999); NBA MVP (1995); All-NBA First Team (1991, '92, '95, '96); All-NBA Second Team (1994, '98); All NBA-Third Team (1990, '93, 2000); NBA All-Star (1990, '91, '92, '93, '94, '95, '96, '98); NBA Defensive Player of the Year (1992); All-Defensive first team (1991, '92, '95, '96); All-Defensive second team (1990, '93, '94, '98); NBA Rookie of the Year (1990); NBA All-Rookie First Team (1990); Member of bronze medal-winning U.S. Olympic team (1988); Member of gold medal-winning U.S. Olympic teams (1992, '96).

BILL RUSSELL

Retired in 1969.

Began play in 1956.

Played 13 seasons.

After their careers are over, some players are remembered as scorers, or rebounders, or defenders. Bill Russell left the game in 1969 with the only title that ever mattered to him: winner. When it came to winning, nobody did it like Russell. The centerpiece of the Boston Celtics dynasty, Russell led the Celtics, often by the force of his will, to 11 championships in 13 seasons, the greatest run in the history of professional sports. Add two NCAA titles at the University of San Francisco and one Olympic gold medal, and it's obvious that winning and Russell are basketball synonyms. Russell redefined the sport, showing how basketball could be won on the defensive end of the court. Russell used his mind as well as his body to outthink and outsmart opponents. When his man made a move, Russell was already there, waiting for him. Shotblocking records were not kept when Russell played, but if they had been, the numbers would have been staggering. When it came to discovering and then implementing what it took to win, Russell had no peer. (For more on Bill Russell, see page 30).

CAREER HIGHLIGHTS: NBA championships with Boston Celtics (1957, '59, '60, '61, '62, '63, '64, '65, '66, '68, '69); NBA MVP (1958, '61, '62, '63, '65); NBA All-First Team (1959, '63, '65); NBA All-Second Team (1958, '60, '61, '62, '64, '66, '67, '68); NBA All-Defensive First Team (1969); NBA All-Star (1958, '59, '60, '61, '62, '63, '64, '65, '66, '67, '68, '69); All-Star Game MVP (1963); Boston Celtics franchise all time leading rebounder (21,620); Member of gold medal-winning U.S. Olympic team (1956); Declared Greatest Player in the History of the NBA by the Professional Basketball Writers Association of America (1980); No. 6 retired by Boston Celtics; NBA 25th Anniversary All-Time Team (1970); NBA 35th Anniversary All-Time Team (1980); Naismith Memorial Basketball Hall of Fame (1974).

DOLPH SCHAYES

Retired in 1964.

Began play in 1948.

Played 16 seasons.

One of the most consistent scorers and rebounders in NBA history, Dolph Schayes entered the NBA when it was only three years old and helped spur the growth of the league with his excellence. For nine straight seasons, from 1952-53 through 1960-61, Schayes averaged more than 17 points and 12 rebounds for the Syracuse Nationals, leading his team in scoring and rebounding for eight of those seasons. Schayes, a graduate of NYU, was a capable set shooter, but he scored many of his points with creative drives and shots around the basket. He was also one of the greatest free throw shooting big men in NBA history, three times leading the league in that category and shooting better than 84 percent for his career. Schayes was the driving force that led Syracuse to its only NBA title in 1955, and he guided the Nationals to the NBA Finals on two other occasions. Schayes was able to maintain a high level of play much longer than anyone playing in his era, and was named to the All-NBA First or Second Team for 12 consecutive years.

CAREER HIGHLIGHTS: NBA championship with Syracuse Nationals (1955); All-NBA First Team (1952, '53, '54, '55, '57, '58); All-NBA Second Team (1950, '51, '56, '59, '60, '61); NBL Rookie of the Year (1949) NBA All-Star (1951, '52, '53, '54, '55, '56, '57, '58, '59, '60, '61, '62); Retired playing more games than anyone else in NBA history (1,059); Played in a record 764 straight games (including playoffs) until fracturing a cheek bone; In 1957 and 1958, led the NBA in minutes (39.5 mpg, 40.5 mpg); Led the NBA in free throw shooting (1958-.904; 1960- .893; 1962-.897) and shot .843 for a career (6,979 of 8,274); Retired as the NBA leader in free throws attempted and made; Averaged 19.2 points a game in 103 playoff contests; Led the NBA in rebounding (1951, 16.4 per game) and had three seasons with 1,000 or more rebounds (1951, '57, '58); NBA 25th Anniversary All-Team (1970); Naismith Basketball Memorial Hall of Fame (1972).

BILL SHARMAN

Retired 1961.

Began play in 1950.

Played 11 seasons.

Make a list of great pure shooters in NBA history, and Bill Sharman's name would have to be near the top. When the Boston Celtics were beginning to establish themselves as a good team in the early 1950s, Sharman teamed with Bob Cousy to form one of the NBA's best backcourts. Sharman, who played college ball at Southern Cal, also played five seasons of minor league baseball while he was starting his NBA career. He was a man of perpetual motion, constantly coming off a screen or running to an open spot and then displaying one of the quickest releases in the game. His pure mechanics were also in evidence at the free throw line, where he led the NBA in accuracy seven times in his career and ranks sixth all-time in that department at better than 88 percent. But Sharman was more than a shooter — he was an excellent defensive player as well. Sharman was named All-NBA First or Second Team seven times in his career, and he was a starter on four NBA championship teams with the Celtics. Sharman also became an accomplished pro coach and executive, and was responsible for a number of innovations including the game-day shootaround.

CAREER HIGHLIGHTS: NBA championships with Boston Celtics (1957, '59, '60, '61); All-NBA First Team (1956, '57, '58, '59); All-NBA Second Team (1953, '55, '60); NBA All-Star (1953, '54, '55, '56, '57, '58, '59, '60); All-Star Game MVP (1955); Led Celtics in free throw shooting 10 straight years; NBA 25th Anniversary All-Time Team (1970); No. 21 retired by Boston Celtics; Naismith Memorial Basketball Hall of Fame (1975).

ISIAH THOMAS

Retired in 1994.

Began play in 1981.

Played 13 seasons.

After teams led by multitalented big men Magic Johnson and Larry Bird dominated for most of the 1980s, some basketball fans wondered if a team led by a small player would ever rise to the top of the NBA again. Isiah Thomas already had done it in college, winning a championship at Indiana, and then in 1989, he proved he could do it at the pro level when he led the Pistons to the first of two consecutive titles. Thomas had long been a vibrant scorer who was also among the league leaders in assists. But when Thomas and the Pistons realized their best chance to win a title rested on how well they could play defense, they became one of the most tenacious defensive teams the league had ever seen. Thomas, one of the quickest players in the history of the NBA, became one of the most mentally tough players ever, challenging his teammates to play every play as if a championship depended on it. Thomas retired as one of only four players in NBA history to record 9,000 assists, but he is better remembered as one of the toughest 6-1 players of all time.

CAREER HIGHLIGHTS: NBA championships with Detroit Pistons (1989, '90); NBA Finals MVP (1990); All-NBA First Team (1984, '85, '86); All-NBA Second Team (1983, '87); NBA All-Rookie Team (1982); NBA All-Star (1982, '83, '84, '85, '86, '87, '88, '89, '90, '91, '92, '93); NBA All-Star Game MVP (1984, '86); Detroit Pistons franchise leader in points (18,822), assists (9,061), steals (1,861) and games played (979); No. 11 retired by Detroit Pistons; Naismith Memorial Basketball Hall of Fame (2000).

NATE THURMOND

Retired in 1977.

Began play in 1963.

Played 14 seasons.

One of the great shot-blocking and defensive centers to ever play in the NBA, Nate Thurmond was often overlooked during his career, coming as it did during the era when Bill Russell and Wilt Chamberlain received almost all of the attention. But those great centers and all-time scoring leader Kareem Abdul-Jabbar often remarked how tough it was to score against the long arms and iron will of Big Nate. Thurmond was a defensive superstar, reducing the success of opponent's forays into the lane dramatically. Thurmond — the pride of Bowling Green University — used his physical talents along with accrued knowledge of opposing players to make the paint his own. Although Thurmond was a good offensive player, averaging 15.0 points for his career and averaging 20 or more points five times, he made a lasting reputation with his defense and rebounding. Thurmond ranks fifth in NBA history in rebounds (15.0 per game) and is seventh in total rebounds.

CAREER HIGHLIGHTS: NBA All-Defensive First Team (1969, '71); NBA All-Defensive Second Team (1972, '73, '74); NBA All-Rookie Team (1964); Golden State Warriors franchise all-time leading rebounder with 12,771; NBA All-Star (1965, '66, '67, '68, '70, '73, '74); First player to record a quadruple-double (1974) with 22 points, 14 rebounds, 13 assists and 12 blocked shots in an overtime victory against the Atlanta Hawks; No. 42 retired by Cleveland Cavaliers and Golden State Warriors; Naismith Memorial Basketball Hall of Fame (1984).

WES UNSELD

Retired in 1981.

Began play in 1968.

Played 13 seasons.

It's a short conversation when talk turns to who were the strongest men in NBA history. Wilt Chamberlain. Wes Unseld. Artis Gilmore. Shaquille O'Neal. The only man not taller than seven feet in the group is Unseld, who stands 6-7. Playing center and giving away inches to every opponent, Unseld was merely named NBA Rookie of the Year and NBA Most Valuable Player in the same year (1969), joining Chamberlain as the only two to achieve that feat. He went on to average more than 10 rebounds in 12 of the 13 seasons he played, play in five NBA All-Star Games and lead the Washington Bullets to the 1978 NBA championship. Unseld was never the tallest player in any game he played, nor was he ever the highest jumper. But Unseld made a science of using body positioning and strength to keep taller opponents off the backboards. Unseld is also widely regarded as the best outlet passer in NBA history, able to throw a two-handed pass from one end of the court to the other with accuracy.

CAREER HIGHLIGHTS: NBA championship with Washington Bullets (1978); NBA MVP (1969); NBA Finals MVP (1978); All-NBA First Team (1969); NBA Rookie of the Year (1969); NBA All-Rookie Team (1969); NBA All-Star (1969, '71, '72, '73, '75); Washington Bullets' franchise all-time leading rebounder (13,769); Retired as seventh best rebounder in history; currently ranks ninth; Recipient of the inaugural J. Walter Kennedy Award (1975); Upon retirement, was Washington's all-time leader in games played (984), minutes played (35,832; 36.4 minutes per game and assists (3,822); No. 41 retired by Washington Wizards; Naismith Basketball Memorial Hall of Fame (1987).

BILL WALTON

Retired in 1988.

Began play in 1974.

Played 10 seasons.

It's a testament to Bill Walton's greatness that he was selected among the 50 Greatest Players in NBA History despite playing in only 468 NBA games, equivalent to less than six full seasons. Injuries curtailed Walton's career after he had been a key part of two NBA championship teams. Walton was a different kind of center, one whose presence left an indelible stamp on every aspect of games in which he played. A winner of two national championships at UCLA, Walton was a complete player who applied his skills in whatever area his team required on a given night. Adept at playing in the low post or out at the free throw line, Walton was masterful at hitting teammates cutting to the basket for easy layups. He had a soft touch on his shots, whether operating close to the basket or venturing out to 15 feet. And he managed to grab nearly every important rebound. He led the Portland Trail Blazers to the 1977 NBA title, then was a major player off the bench for the Boston Celtics' title team in 1986.

CAREER HIGHLIGHTS: NBA championships with the Portland Trail Blazers (1977) and Boston Celtics (1986); NBA Finals MVP (1977); NBA MVP (1978); All-NBA First Team (1978); All-NBA Second Team (1977); NBA All-Defensive First Team (1977, '78); NBA Sixth Man Award (1986); NBA All-Star (1977, '78); No. 32 retired by Portland Trail Blazers; Naismith Basketball Memorial Hall of Fame (1993).

JERRY WEST

By Scott Ostler

When the Lakers were about to move from Minneapolis to Los Angeles in 1960, their top draft choice (and the second pick overall) was a skinny 6-2 guard from West Virginia, Jerry West. The Lakers waited two days to phone West and inform him he'd been drafted. If they had known what they were getting, they would have called much earlier.

Elgin Baylor nicknamed his new teammate "Zeke from Cabin Creek," but he soon earned another nickname — Mr. Clutch. West led the Lakers to the NBA Finals in nine of his 13 seasons, was a 10-time All-NBA First Team selection, coached the Lakers for three seasons, and served 21 years in the front office.

In the 40 seasons since West joined the Lakers, they have missed the playoffs three times, two of them during West's two-year "retirement."

As a player he was not flashy, but dazzlingly efficient. West had speed to lead the Lakers' sizzling fast break, excellent leaping ability, a classic jump shot, a slashing drive, uncanny court sense and consummate defensive skills.

But what set West apart was his knack for performing under pressure. He played Game 7 of the 1969 Finals with an injured hamstring and had 42 points, 13 rebounds and 12 assists. The Lakers lost by two to the Celtics but West was series MVP.

Jerome Allen West grew up not in Cabin Creek, but in nearby Chelyan (pop. 500), the fifth of six children of a coal-mine electrician. Jerry was short, scrawny and bashful, and was cut from his freshman football, baseball and track squads.

"I think I became a basketball player because it's a game you can play by yourself," he said. He spent countless hours practicing alone on a neighbor's dirt court.

West led his high school team to the state championship in 1956 and led West Virginia to the 1959 NCAA Championship Game (losing to the University of California). He then starred with Oscar Robertson on the 1960 U.S. Olympic team that won the gold medal in Rome.

The Lakers gave West a $1,500 bonus, a $15,000 salary, and the ball. His stats were always impressive — he once had a quadruple-double (44 points, 10 rebounds, 12 assists, 10 steals while making 16-of-17 field goals and 12-of-12 from the line). But his major contribution to the Lakers was attitude.

"If you didn't come into the game breathing fire every night, Jerry couldn't understand," said Tommy Hawkins, a Lakers teammate. "And I never saw him have back-to-back bad nights. Until he could replace a bad performance with a good one, his soul was not at rest."

West's career was marked by frustration. His first seven trips to the Finals were losses, six of them to the Boston Celtics, four of those losses in Game 7. West finally got his ring in 1972 when the Lakers beat the Knicks in five, after winning a record 33 consecutive regular-season games.

West retired in 1974 and quickly became a scratch golfer, but was lured back to coach the Lakers. Despite success, he felt temperamentally unsuited to the job. He took losing so hard, one writer called him Zeke the Bleak. West fired himself and moved into the front office.

As a player, coach and executive, West has never been remotely laid back. Call it creative anxiety. "You'd think the more successful a team is, the more relaxed you'd be," he once said. "I'd say it's the opposite."

West is known for his bold moves and genius-level judgment. He uncovered draft gems such as Vlade Divac and A.C. Green, landed key free agents to keep alive the dynasty of the 1980s, and assembled the Shaquille O'Neal/Kobe Bryant team that won the 1999-2000 NBA title.

As TV commentator and former coach Hubie Brown said of West, "He was born to basketball."

CAREER HIGHLIGHTS: NBA championship with Los Angeles Lakers (1972); All-NBA First Team (1962, '63, '64, '65, '66, '67, '70, '71, '72, '73); All-NBA Second Team (1968, '69); NBA All-Defensive First Team (1970, '71, '72, '73); NBA All-Defensive Second Team (1969); NBA All-Star (1961, '62, '63, '64, '65, '66, '67, '68, '69, '70, '71, '72, '73, '74); NBA All-Star MVP (1972); NBA Finals MVP (1969); Member of 1972 Lakers that compiled a 69-13 record and 33-game winning streak; Led NBA in scoring (1970); Led the NBA in assists (1972); Led NBA in most free throws made (1966, '70); Holds single-season record for most free throws made (840, 1966); Holds single-series playoff record for highest points-per-game average (46.3) against Baltimore (1965); Holds record for highest point average in playoffs for one season (40.6 in 11 games 1966); NBA 35th Anniversary Team (1980); No. 44 retired by Los Angeles Lakers; Naismith Memorial Basketball Hall of Fame (1979).

LENNY WILKENS

Retired in 1975.

Began play in 1960.

Played 15 seasons.

Sometimes a player is so good, even when you know he's going to do something, you can't stop him from doing it. That was the case with Lenny Wilkens beginning at Providence College and then for 15 superb NBA seasons. Wilkens went to his left when everybody knew he wanted to do that. Once he did, Wilkens either used his exceptional quickness to go to the basket or penetrated and set up a teammate for a shot. One of the game's top playmakers, Wilkens was a thinking man's player who used his head as well as his legs to beat you. That intelligent approach to the game foreshadowed Wilkens' long, successful coaching career. A consistent player who was named an NBA All-Star nine times, Wilkens averaged more than eight assists for six straight seasons from 1967-68 to 1972-73. Wilkens coached the Seattle SuperSonics to the 1979 NBA championship and the 1996 U.S. Olympic team to a gold medal in Atlanta. He is the winningest coach in NBA history. In 1998, Wilkens joined John Wooden as the only two people enshrined in the Basketball Hall of Fame as both a player and a coach. (For more on Wilkens see page 102).

CAREER HIGHLIGHTS: NBA All-Star (1963, '64, '65, '67, '68, '69, '70, '71, '73); NBA All-Star MVP (1971); Retired second on all-time assists list (7,211); Played in 1,077 career games; Served as a player/coach for three seasons with Seattle (1969-70 through 1971-72) and one with Portland (1974-75); No. 19 retired by Seattle SuperSonics; One of only two individuals enshrined in the Naismith Memorial Basketball Hall of Fame as a player (1988) and as a coach (1998). The other is John Wooden; Head coach, gold medal-winning U.S. Olympic team (1996).

JAMES WORTHY

Retired in 1994.

Began play in 1982.

Played 12 seasons.

There was something majestic about James Worthy's drives to the basket for dunks, an indefinable quality that served notice this was more than a mere two points being scored. Worthy not only played the game exceptionally well, contributing his dynamic scoring ability to the Los Angeles Lakers' NBA championship teams in 1985, 1987 and 1988, he competed with a grace rarely seen in a rugged sport. And Worthy always seemed to rise the highest when championships were on the line, his catalogue of outstanding playoff performances earning him the nickname "Big Game James." Whether he was shooting his unstoppable turnaround jumper from the perimeter, posting up his man or soaring above an opponent for a picturesque one-handed slam, Worthy embodied the Lakers' "Showtime" attack. He will always be remembered as a major force that helped drive one of the best and most exciting teams in NBA history.

CAREER HIGHLIGHTS: NBA championships with Los Angeles Lakers (1985, '87, '88); NBA Finals MVP (1988); All-NBA Third Team (1990, '91); NBA All-Rookie Team (1983); NBA All-Star (1986, '87, '88, '89, '90, '91, '92); No. 42 retired by Los Angeles Lakers.

CHAPTER 22

THE ALL-STAR EXPERIENCE

By Barry Rubinstein

The 18,325 pairs of eyes couldn't believe what they had seen, but they knew it was something special. The response was explosive vocal approval that was equal parts awe and appreciation. In one move so glorious that it demanded superlatives not yet invented, the language of All-Star Weekend was rewritten.

It began with a burst from midcourt, continued with a leap into the heavens, became surreal with an airborne between-the-legs pass from the left to the right hand, and defied reality with a thundering dunk that was almost too quick for the naked eye to see. No matter. There would be plenty of replays of Vince Carter's moment of magnificence and if the NBA's founding fathers could have been there, well . . .

VINCE CARTER'S ACROBATIC DUNK AT NBA ALL-STAR 2000 IS ONE OF THE MOST SPECTACULAR DUNKS IN SLAM DUNK CONTEST HISTORY.

The first NBA All-Star Game was played in 1951, and it was the brainchild of a trio of men whose goal was to spike interest in professional basketball. The actual idea for the game came from NBA Public Relations Director Haskell Cohen, who got his inspiration from baseball's midsummer All-Star Game. Cohen's proposal was quickly supported by NBA President Maurice Podoloff and Boston Celtics President Walter Brown, who supplied the use of Boston Garden to the NBA for no charge.

The first game on March 2, 1951, drew 10,094 fans, but those three visionaries could not have possibly conceived how big the NBA All-Star Game would eventually become.

And that was when it was only a game. In 1984, it became something much bigger, thanks in part to Julius Erving and

WHILE ALL-STAR WEEKEND HAS BECOME AN EXTRAVAGANZA, IT HAS NOT CHANGED FROM THE BEGINNING IN ONE RESPECT. THE GREATEST PLAYERS IN THE WORLD HAVE ALWAYS BEEN FEATURED, INCLUDING IN THE EARLY '50S WHEN (FROM LEFT) BILL SHARMAN, "EASY" ED MACAULEY AND BOB COUSY REPRESENTED THE EAST.

the heritage of the American Basketball Association. At the last ABA All-Star Game in 1976, Erving mesmerized a sell-out crowd in Denver with a soaring dunk from the free throw line in the first slam dunk contest. After that season, the ABA folded with four of its teams — Denver, Indiana, the Nets and San Antonio — entering the NBA.

In 1984, the NBA brought its All-Star Game to Denver and decided to revive the slam dunk event. Erving agreed to enter, although he placed second to Larry Nance of the Phoenix Suns. The event was held on Saturday, the day before the All-Star Game, and it was so well-received that the NBA decided that the All-Star Game had now become All-Star Weekend.

It would only get bigger. By All-Star 2000 in Oakland, there was a full week's worth of activities, none providing a setting for a feat more spectacular than Carter's, whose creativity and power fit perfectly into the slam dunk tradition established by Erving, Michael Jordan, Dominique Wilkins and others.

One thing, however, never changes and that is that the weekend is all centered around the game. Over the years, there have been many classics. To name a few:

• In 1960 when a rookie named Wilt Chamberlain put on a show for his hometown fans at Philadelphia's Convention Hall by scoring 23 points and grabbing 25 rebounds in a 125-115 East decision.

• In 1972 when Jerry West's 20-foot jumper at the buzzer gave the West a 112-110 triumph in Los Angeles.

• In 1980 when Larry Bird made the first three-point shot in All-Star competition during the East's 144-136 victory in 1980 in Landover, Md.

NBA.COM FACT

St. Louis' Bob Pettit made the All-Star Game his own little showcase, winning a record four MVP awards. His last came in the 1959 All-Star Game when he and rookie Elgin Baylor shared the honors as the West All-Stars won 124-108. It was the first time co-MVP awards were given out.

Utah's Jeff Hornacek was always a premier All-Star Saturday competitor. Hornacek won the three-point contest twice.

Larry Nance of the Phoenix Suns won the first NBA slam dunk contest in Denver in 1984, defeating the sentimental favorite Julius Erving.

Bird's shot was a preview of another All-Star Saturday staple. In 1986 in Dallas, the three-point shooting contest debuted as contestants shot five three-point shots from five different locations. Bird was unstoppable during the first three contests, winning all three and leaving nothing to the imagination. In Dallas, Bird's last three-point attempt was halfway to the basket when he began running down the court waving his index finger, signifying that he was No. 1. The shot hit nothing but net.

The three-point contest produced many memorable performances, particularly from Craig Hodges, who also won three times and once made 19 consecutive three-point shots.

But perhaps the most memorable All-Star moment occurred in 1992 when Magic Johnson, who had retired three months earlier after announcing that he was HIV positive, made an All-Star appearance. Johnson did not retire until after the season began and was already on the All-Star ballot. So when fans voted him to the starting lineup, the league allowed him to play in the game. Johnson responded with an

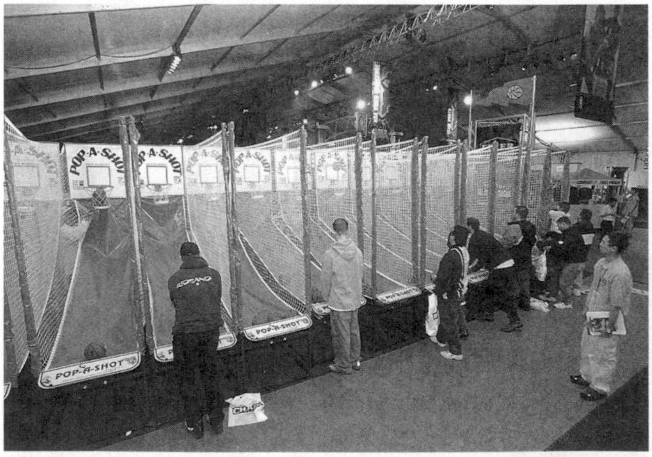

All-Star Weekend has something for everyone. In 1993 in Salt Lake City, NBA fans got their first taste of Jam Session with a wide range of interactive events.

NBA.COM FACT

The nets at the Seattle Kingdome were screaming for mercy in 1987 when the two teams combined for an All-Star record 303 points, with the West All-Stars earning a 154-149 overtime victory.

NBA.COM FACT

In the All-Star Game's 49-year history, hometown players have won the MVP Award 11 times. They include: Boston's Ed Macauley, 1951; Boston's Bob Cousy, 1957; St. Louis' Bob Pettit, 1958, '62; Philadelphia's Wilt Chamberlain, 1960; Cincinnati's Adrian Smith, 1966; San Francisco's Rick Barry, 1967; Los Angeles' Jerry West, 1972; Seattle's Tom Chambers, 1987; Chicago's Michael Jordan, 1998; and Utah's Karl Malone and John Stockton, 1993.

incredible performance for someone who had not played a game all season — 25 points and nine assists in a 153-113 West victory.

Johnson even hit his final All-Star shot — a fallaway three-pointer — with 14.5 seconds to play. After the ball popped the net, he was the center of a mass embrace by his All-Star brethren.

"It was the first game ever called on account of hugs," Johnson said after his 12th and final All-Star Game. "That final moment, oh boy, I don't know. It's like I've been writing this script all weekend, and I couldn't come up with an ending. But that was it. That was my dot."

John Stockton, who has played in 10 All-Star Games, cites his first appearance in 1989 as his most memorable.

"I remember Magic was supposed to start and was sick," Stockton said, "and I ended up playing almost the whole game. It was a lot of fun. I remember trying to pass the ball to Kareem [Abdul-Jabbar] and Alex English, and just a number of great games and great players. It's fun to look back on it."

Stockton and longtime Utah Jazz teammate Karl Malone share a significant All-Star distinction, as they became the first players from the same NBA team to share the All-Star Game MVP Award. And they did it on their home court, as Malone had 28 points and 10 rebounds and Stockton nine points and 15 assists in the West's 135-132 overtime victory in Salt Lake City in 1993.

As time went on, NBA All-Star Weekend continued to blossom and grow. In 1994, the Legends Classic, a game featuring former greats of the game, was replaced by the Rookie Game, a forum for showcasing the stars of tomorrow. And 1998 brought the introduction of All-Star 2ball, which teams NBA and WNBA players from the same cities facing other duos in a timed shooting contest.

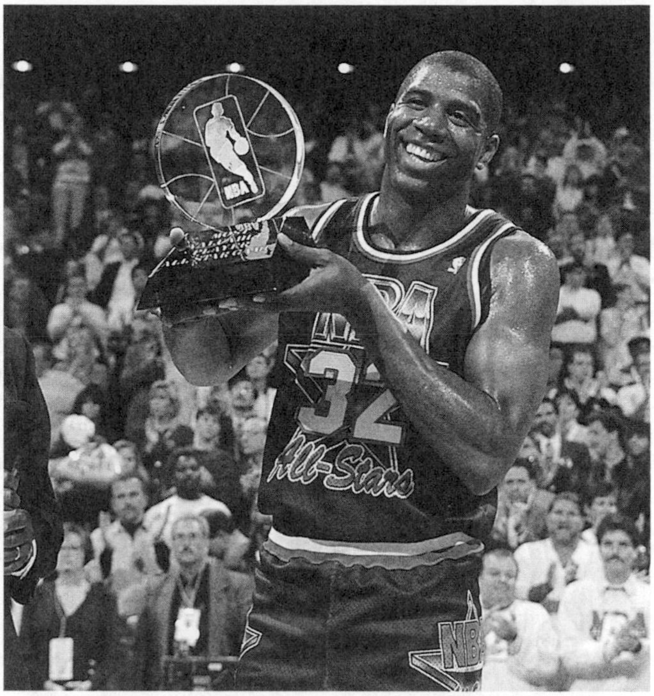

One of the most dramatic performances was by Magic Johnson in the 1992 All-Star Game in Orlando, where he was the MVP.

NBA All-Star 2000 signaled another first, as Jeff Hornacek of the Jazz won both the three-point shootout and the 2ball competition, teamed with Natalie Williams of the Utah Starzz.

Not all the thrills of NBA All-Star Weekend are left on the court. There is NBA Jam Session, an interactive theme park for basketball fans of all ages, along with the All-Star TeamUp Celebration, which honors youth around the country for their community service involvement. Such events help make the NBA All-Star experience an unforgettable one.

And for players such as Carter, born 26 years after that first NBA All-Star Game, the scope of the extravaganza continues to astound.

"You can't prepare for it," he said before a bevy of microphones and cameras during a media interview session before NBA All-Star 2000. "It's amazing. I just pinch myself and say, 'Wow, it is really happening.'"

"Look where it is today," said 11-time All-Star Bob Pettit. "I think the things off the court are what have changed so much. In the years that I played, you wouldn't have anywhere near the publicity or the interest or anything. Today it's a real happening, it's a real event. It's a celebration of where it started and where it's gotten."

ALL-STAR GAME RESULTS

YEAR	RESULT & LOCATION	WINNING COACH	LOSING COACH	MOST VALUABLE PLAYER
2000	West 137, East 126 at Oakland	Phil Jackson	Jeff Van Gundy	Tim Duncan, San Antonio Shaquille O'Neal, L.A. Lakers
1999	No game played.			
1998	East 135, West 114 at New York	Larry Bird	George Karl	Michael Jordan, Chicago
1997	East 132, West 120 at Cleveland	Doug Collins	Rudy Tomjanovich	Glen Rice, Charlotte
1996	East 129, West 118 at San Antonio	Phil Jackson	George Karl	Michael Jordan, Chicago
1995	West 139, East 112 at Phoenix	Paul Westphal	Brian Hill	Mitch Richmond, Sacramento
1994	East 127, West 118 at Minneapolis	Lenny Wilkens	George Karl	Scottie Pippen, Chicago
1993	West 135, East 132 (OT) at Salt Lake City	Paul Westphal	Pat Riley	Karl Malone, Utah John Stockton, Utah
1992	West 153, East 113 at Orlando	Don Nelson	Phil Jackson	Magic Johnson, L.A. Lakers
1991	East 116, West 114 at Charlotte	Chris Ford	Rick Adelman	Charles Barkley, Philadelphia
1990	East 130, West 113 at Miami	Chuck Daly	Pat Riley	Magic Johnson, L.A. Lakers
1989	West 143, East 134 at Houston	Pat Riley	Lenny Wilkens	Karl Malone, Utah
1988	East 138, West 133 at Chicago	Mike Fratello	Pat Riley	Michael Jordan, Chicago
1987	West 154, East 149 (OT) at Seattle	Pat Riley	K.C. Jones	Tom Chambers, Seattle
1986	East 139, West 132 at Dallas	K.C. Jones	Pat Riley	Isiah Thomas, Detroit
1985	West 140, East 129 at Indianapolis	Pat Riley	K.C. Jones	Ralph Sampson, Houston
1984	East 154, West 145 (OT) at Denver	K.C. Jones	Frank Layden	Isiah Thomas, Detroit
1983	East 132, West 123 at Los Angeles	Billy Cunningham	Pat Riley	Julius Erving, Philadelphia
1982	East 120, West 118 at E. Rutherford	Bill Fitch	Pat Riley	Larry Bird, Boston
1981	East 123, West 120 at Cleveland	Billy Cunningham	John MacLeod	Nate Archibald, Boston
1980	East 144, West 136 (OT) at Landover	Billy Cunningham	Lenny Wilkens	George Gervin, San Antonio
1979	West 134, East 129 at Detroit	Lenny Wilkens	Dick Motta	David Thompson, Denver
1978	East 133, West 125 at Atlanta	Billy Cunningham	Jack Ramsay	Randy Smith, Buffalo
1977	West 125, East 124 at Milwaukee	Larry Brown	Gene Shue	Julius Erving, Philadelphia
1976	East 123, West 109 at Philadelphia	Tom Heinsohn	Al Attles	Dave Bing, Washington
1975	East 108, West 102 at Phoenix	K.C. Jones	Al Attles	Walt Frazier, New York
1974	West 134, East 123 at Seattle	Larry Costello	Tom Heinsohn	Bob Lanier, Detroit
1973	East 104, West 84 at Chicago	Tom Heinsohn	Bill Sharman	Dave Cowens, Boston
1972	West 112, East 110 at Los Angeles	Bill Sharman	Tom Heinsohn	Jerry West, Los Angeles
1971	West 108, East 107 at San Diego	Larry Costello	Red Holzman	Lenny Wilkens, Seattle
1970	East 142, West 135 at Philadelphia	Red Holzman	Richie Guerin	Willis Reed, New York
1969	East 123, West 112 at Baltimore	Gene Shue	Richie Guerin	Oscar Robertson, Cincinnati
1968	East 144, West 124 at New York	Alex Hannum	Bill Sharman	Hal Greer, Philadelphia
1967	West 135, East 120 at San Francisco	Fred Schaus	Red Auerbach	Rick Barry, San Francisco
1966	East 137, West 94 at Cincinnati	Red Auerbach	Fred Schaus	Adrian Smith, Cincinnati
1965	East 124, West 123 at St. Louis	Red Auerbach	Alex Hannum	Jerry Lucas, Cincinnati
1964	East 111, West 107 at Boston	Red Auerbach	Fred Schaus	Oscar Robertson, Cincinnati
1963	East 115, West 108 at Los Angeles	Red Auerbach	Fred Schaus	Bill Russell, Boston

YEAR	RESULT & LOCATION	WINNING COACH	LOSING COACH	MOST VALUABLE PLAYER
1962	West 150, East 130 at St. Louis	Fred Schaus	Red Auerbach	Bob Pettit, St. Louis
1961	West 153, East 131 at Syracuse	Paul Seymour	Red Auerbach	Oscar Robertson, Cincinnati
1960	East 125, West 115 at Philadelphia	Red Auerbach	Ed Macauley	Wilt Chamberlain, Phil.
1959	West 124, East 108 at Detroit	Ed Macauley	Red Auerbach	Elgin Baylor, Minneapolis Bob Pettit, St. Louis
1958	East 130, West 118 at St. Louis	Red Auerbach	Alex Hannum	Bob Pettit, St. Louis
1957	East 109, West 97 at Boston	Red Auerbach	Bobby Wanzer	Bob Cousy, Boston
1956	West 108, East 94 at Rochester	Charley Eckman	George Senesky	Bob Pettit, St. Louis
1955	East 100, West 91 at New York	Al Cervi	Charley Eckman	Bill Sharman, Boston
1954	East 98, West 93 (OT) at New York	Joe Lapchick	John Kundla	Bob Cousy, Boston
1953	West 79, East 75 at Fort Wayne	John Kundla	Joe Lapchick	George Mikan, Minneapolis
1952	East 108, West 91 at Boston	Al Cervi	John Kundla	Paul Arizin, Philadelphia
1951	East 111, West 94 at Boston	Joe Lapchick	John Kundla	Ed Macauley, Boston

ALL-STAR SATURDAY RESULTS

AT&T SHOOTOUT

2000 Jeff Hornacek, Utah
1999 No competition held.
1998 Jeff Hornacek, Utah
1997 Steve Kerr, Chicago
1996 Tim Legler, Washington
1995 Glen Rice, Miami
1994 Mark Price, Cleveland
1993 Mark Price, Cleveland
1992 Craig Hodges, Chicago
1991 Craig Hodges, Chicago
1990 Craig Hodges, Chicago
1989 Dale Ellis, Seattle
1988 Larry Bird, Boston
1987 Larry Bird, Boston
1986 Larry Bird, Boston

NBA.COM SLAM DUNK

2000 Vince Carter, Toronto Raptors
1999 No competition held.
1998 No competition held.
1997 Kobe Bryant, L.A. Lakers
1996 Brent Barry, L.A. Clippers
1995 Harold Miner, Miami
1994 Isaiah Rider, Minnesota
1993 Harold Miner, Miami
1992 Cedric Ceballos, Phoenix
1991 Dee Brown, Boston
1990 Dominique Wilkins, Atlanta
1989 Kenny Walker, New York
1988 Michael Jordan, Chicago
1987 Michael Jordan, Chicago
1986 Spud Webb, Atlanta
1985 Dominique Wilkins, Atlanta
1984 Larry Nance, Phoenix

SONY ALL-STAR 2BALL

2000 Jeff Hornacek, Utah Jazz
Natalie Williams, Utah Starzz (WNBA)
1999 No competition held.
1998 Clyde Drexler, Houston Rockets
Cynthia Cooper, Houston Comets (WNBA)

SCHICK LEGENDS CLASSIC

1993 East 58, West 45
1992 West 46, East 38
1991 East 41, West 34
1990 East 37, West 36
1989 West 54, East 53
1988 East 47, West 45 (OT)
1987 West 54, East 43
1986 West 53, East 44
1985 East 63, West 53
1984 West 64, East 63

SCHICK ROOKIE CHALLENGE

2000 Freshmen 92, Sophomores 83 (OT)
1999 No competition held.
1998 East 85, West 80
1997 East 96, West 91
1996 East 94, West 92
1995 White 83, Green 79 (OT)
1994 Phenoms 74, Sensations 68

ALL-STAR GAME RECORDS—INDIVIDUAL

GAMES
Most games
18 Kareem Abdul-Jabbar
13 Wilt Chamberlain
Bob Cousy
John Havlicek
12 Elvin Hayes
Hakeem Olajuwon
Oscar Robertson
Bill Russell
Jerry West

MINUTES
Most minutes, career
449 Kareem Abdul-Jabbar
388 Wilt Chamberlain
380 Oscar Robertson
Most minutes, game
42 Oscar Robertson, 1964
Bill Russell, 1964
Jerry West, 1964
Nate Thurmond, 1967

SCORING
Highest average, points per game, career (minimum 60 points)
21.3 Michael Jordan
20.5 Oscar Robertson
20.4 Bob Pettit
Most points, game
42 Wilt Chamberlain, 1962
Most points, one half
24 Glen Rice, 1997
Most points, one quarter
20 Glen Rice, 1997

FIELD GOAL PERCENTAGE
Highest field goal percentage, career (minimum 15 made)
.714 Larry Nance
Randy Smith
.673 David Thompson

FIELD GOALS
Most field goals, career
105 Kareem Abdul-Jabbar
97 Michael Jordan
88 Oscar Robertson
Most field goals, game
17 Wilt Chamberlain, 1962
Michael Jordan, 1988
Most field goals, one half
10 Wilt Chamberlain, 1962
Most field goals, one quarter
8 Dave DeBusschere, 1967
Glen Rice, 1997

FIELD GOAL ATTEMPTS
Most field goal attempts, career
213 Kareem Abdul-Jabbar
193 Bob Pettit
Michael Jordan
178 Julius Erving
Most field goal attempts, game
27 Rick Barry, 1967
Most field goal attempts, one half
17 Glen Rice, 1997
Most field goal attempts, one quarter
12 Bill Sharman, 1960

FREE THROW PERCENTAGE
Highest free throw percentage, career (minimum 10 made)
1.00 Archie Clark
Clyde Drexler
Gary Payton
.938 Larry Foust

FREE THROWS
Most free throws, career
78 Elgin Baylor
70 Oscar Robertson
62 Bob Pettit
Most free throws, game
12 Elgin Baylor, 1962
Oscar Robertson, 1965
Most free throws, one half
10 Zelmo Beaty, 1966
Most free throws, one quarter
9 Zelmo Beaty, 1966
Julius Erving, 1978

FREE THROW ATTEMPTS
Most free throw attempts, career
98 Elgin Baylor
Oscar Robertson
94 Wilt Chamberlain
Most free throw attempts, game
16 Wilt Chamberlain, 1962
Most free throw attempts, one half
12 Zelmo Beaty, 1966
Most free throw attempts, one quarter
11 Julius Erving, 1978

THREE-POINT FIELD GOALS
Most three-point field goals, career
10 Magic Johnson
9 Mark Price
Glen Rice
8 Tim Hardaway
Most three-point field goals, game
6 Mark Price, 1993 (OT)
5 Scottie Pippen, 1994
Most three-point field goals, one half
6 Mark Price, 1993
Most three-point field goals, one quarter
4 Glen Rice, 1997

THREE-POINT FIELD GOAL ATTEMPTS
Most three-point field goal attempts, career
22 Scottie Pippen
21 Magic Johnson
Tim Hardaway
John Stockton
19 Reggie Miller
Mark Price
Most three-point field goal attempts, game
9 Mark Price, 1993 (OT)
Scottie Pippen, 1994
Most three-point field goal attempts, one half
7 Scottie Pippen, 1994

REBOUNDS
Most rebounds, career
197 Wilt Chamberlain
178 Bob Pettit
149 Kareem Abdul-Jabbar
Most rebounds, game
27 Bob Pettit, 1962
Most offensive rebounds, game
9 Dan Roundfield, 1980 (OT)
Hakeem Olajuwon, 1990
Most defensive rebounds, game
14 Charles Barkley, 1991
Most rebounds, one half
16 Wilt Chamberlain, 1960
Bob Pettit, 1962
Most rebounds, one quarter
10 Bob Pettit, 1962

ASSISTS
Most assists, career
127 Magic Johnson
97 Isiah Thomas
86 Bob Cousy
Most assists, game
22 Magic Johnson, 1984 (OT)
19 Magic Johnson, 1988
Most assists, one half
13 Magic Johnson, 1984
Most assists, one quarter
9 John Stockton, 1989

PERSONAL FOULS
Most personal fouls, career
57 Kareem Abdul-Jabbar
41 Oscar Robertson
37 Elvin Hayes
Bill Russell
Most personal fouls, game
6 Bob Wanzer, 1954
Paul Arizin, 1956
Bob Cousy, 1956, 1961
Dolph Schayes, 1959
Walt Bellamy, 1962
Richie Guerin, 1962
Bill Russell, 1965
John Green, 1965
Rick Barry, 1966, 1978
Kareem Abdul-Jabbar, 1970
Willis Reed, 1970
Hakeem Olajuwon, 1987
Most personal fouls, one half
5 Randy Smith, 1978
Most personal fouls, one quarter
4 Vern Mikkelsen, 1955
Cliff Hagan, 1959
Bob McAdoo, 1976
Randy Smith, 1978
David Robinson, 1991

STEALS
Most steals, career
33 Michael Jordan
31 Isiah Thomas
23 Larry Bird
Most steals, game
8 Rick Barry, 1975
Most steals, one half
5 Larry Bird, 1986
Most steals, one quarter
4 Fred Brown, 1976
Larry Bird, 1986
Isiah Thomas, 1989

BLOCKED SHOTS
Most blocked shots, career
31 Kareem Abdul-Jabbar
23 Hakeem Olajuwon
16 Patrick Ewing
Most blocked shots, game
6 Kareem Abdul-Jabbar, 1980 (OT)
5 Patrick Ewing, 1990
Hakeem Olajuwon, 1994
Most blocked shots, one half
4 Kareem Abdul-Jabbar, 1980
Kareem Abdul-Jabbar, 1981
Michael Jordan, 1988
Hakeem Olajuwon, 1994
Most blocked shots, one quarter
4 Kareem Abdul-Jabbar, 1981

ALL-STAR GAME RECORDS—TEAM

SCORING

Most points, game
154 East, 1984 (OT)
West, 1987 (OT)
153 West, 1961
West, 1992

Most points, both teams, game
303 West (154) vs. East (149), 1987 (OT)
299 East (154) vs. West (145), 1984 (OT)
284 West (153) vs. East (131), 1961

Most points, one half
87 West, 1989

Most points, both teams, one half
157 West (79) vs. East (78), 1988

Most points, one quarter
50 West, 1970

Most points, both teams, one quarter
86 West (50) vs. East (36), 1970

FIELD GOALS

Most field goals, game
64 West, 1992

Most field goals, both teams, game
126 East (63) vs. West (63), 1984 (OT)
115 West (61) vs. East (54), 1989
West (64) vs. East (51), 1992

Most field goals, one half
36 West, 1989

Most field goals, both teams, one half
65 West (35) vs. East (30), 1962

Most field goals, one quarter
19 West, 1962
West, 1979
East, 1983
West, 1989

Most field goals, both teams, one quarter
36 West (19) vs. East (17), 1962

FIELD GOAL ATTEMPTS

Most field goal attempts, game
135 East, 1960

Most field goal attempts, both teams, game
256 East (135) vs. West (121), 1960

Most field goal attempts, one half
73 East, 1960

Most field goal attempts, both teams, one half
135 East (73) vs. West (62), 1960

Most field goal attempts, one quarter
38 East, 1960

Most field goal attempts, both teams, one quarter
71 East (37) vs. West (34), 1962

THREE-POINT FIELD GOALS

Most three-point field goals, game
12 East, 1997

Most three-point field goals, both teams, game
21 East (12) vs. West (9), 1997

THREE-POINT FIELD GOAL ATTEMPTS

Most three-point field goal attempts, game
29 East, 1997

Most three-point field goal attempts, both teams, game
50 East (29) vs. West (21), 1997

FREE THROWS

Most free throws, game
40 East, 1959

Most free throws, both teams, game
71 West (39) vs. East (32), 1987 (OT)
70 West (37) vs. East (33), 1961

Most free throws, one half
26 East, 1959

Most free throws, both teams, one half
36 West (20) vs. East (16), 1961

Most free throws, one quarter
19 East, 1986

Most free throws, both teams, one quarter
27 East (19) vs. West (8), 1986

FREE THROW ATTEMPTS

Most free throw attempts, game
57 West, 1970

Most free throw attempts, both teams, game
95 East (53) vs. West (42), 1956

Most free throw attempts, one half
31 East, 1959

Most free throw attempts, both teams, one half
57 West (29) vs. East (28), 1962

Most free throw attempts, one quarter
25 West, 1970

Most free throw attempts, both teams, one quarter
33 East (20) vs. West (13), 1962
West (21) vs. East (12), 1993

REBOUNDS

Most rebounds, game
83 East, 1966

Most rebounds, both teams, game
151 East (79) vs. West (72), 1960

Most offensive rebounds, game
33 East, 1985

Most offensive rebounds, both teams, game
55 East (31) vs. West (24), 1980 (OT)
51 West (28) vs. East (23), 1987 (OT)
45 West (24) vs. East (21), 1994

Most defensive rebounds, game
44 East, 1982
West, 1993 (OT)

Most defensive rebounds, both teams, game
81 East (44) vs. West (37), 1982

Most rebounds, one half
51 East, 1966

Most rebounds, both teams, one half
98 East (50) vs. West (48), 1962
East (51) vs. West (47), 1966

Most rebounds, one quarter
30 West, 1966

Most rebounds, both teams, one quarter
58 West (30) vs. East (28), 1966

ASSISTS

Most assists, game
46 West, 1984 (OT)
45 West, 1986

Most assists, both teams, game
85 West (46) vs. East (39), 1984 (OT)
77 West (45) vs. East (32), 1986
West (44) vs. East (33), 1995

Most assists, one half
28 West, 1984

Most assists, both teams, one half
45 West (28) vs. East (17), 1984

Most assists, one quarter
15 West, 1977
West, 1984

Most assists, both teams, one quarter
25 West (15) vs. East (10), 1984

PERSONAL FOULS

Most personal fouls, game
36 East, 1965

Most personal fouls, both teams, game
64 East (36) vs. West (28), 1965

Most personal fouls, one half
22 West, 1980

Most personal fouls, both teams, one half
37 West (22) vs. East (15), 1980

Most personal fouls, one quarter
13 East, 1970

Most personal fouls, both teams, one quarter
20 East (11) vs. West (9), 1985
East (12) vs. West (8), 1987

STEALS

Most steals, game
24 East, 1989

Most steals, both teams, game
40 East (24) vs. West (16), 1989

BLOCKED SHOTS

Most blocked shots, game
16 West, 1980 (OT)
12 West, 1994

Most blocked shots, both teams, game
25 West (16) vs. East (9), 1980 (OT)
21 West (12) vs. East (9), 1994

DISQUALIFICATIONS

Most disqualifications, game
2 East, 1956
East, 1965
East, 1970

Most disqualifications, both teams, game
2 East (2) vs. West (0), 1956
East (1) vs. West (1), 1962
East (2) vs. West (0), 1965
East (2) vs. West (0), 1970

Most disqualifications, one half
2 East, 1956
East, 1970

Most disqualifications, both teams, one half
2 East (2) vs. West (0), 1956
East (1) vs. West (1), 1962
East (2) vs. West (0), 1970

Most disqualifications, one quarter
2 East, 1956
East, 1970

Most disqualifications, both teams, one quarter
2 East (2) vs. West (0), 1956
East (1) vs. West (1), 1962
East (2) vs. West (0), 1970

GAME 49: February 13, 2000 — West 137, East 126 at Golden State — The Spurs' Tim Duncan (24 points, 14 rebounds and four assists) and the Lakers' Shaquille O'Neal (22 points, nine rebounds, three blocked shots) were co-MVPs in the West's triumph.

GAME 48: February 8, 1998 – East 135, West 114 at New York — Michael Jordan won his third All-Star Game MVP by leading all scorers with 23 points, grabbing six rebounds and also dishing a team-high eight assists in the East's win.

GAME 47: February 9, 1997 — East 132, West 120 at Cleveland — Charlotte's Glen Rice set a pair of All-Star Game scoring records — most points in a quarter (20) and half (24) — and Michael Jordan recorded the first-ever All-Star Game triple-double in the Eastern Conference's win.

GAME 46: February 11, 1996 — East 129, West 118 at San Antonio — The Bulls' Michael Jordan (20 points) and the Magic's Shaquille O'Neal (25 points) fueled the East's victory, with Jordan winning his second All-Star Game MVP award.

GAME 45: February 12, 1995 — West 139, East 112 at Phoenix — Sacramento's Mitch Richmond, a third-time All-Star, garnered MVP honors by scoring a game-high 23 points — including all three of his three-point attempts — in 22 minutes in the West's victory.

GAME 44: February 13, 1994 — East 127, West 118 at Minneapolis — Chicago's Scottie Pippen gained MVP honors by scoring 29 points, including five three-point field goals, and grabbing 11 rebounds in the East's victory.

GAME 43: February 21, 1993 — West 135, East 132, OT, at Salt Lake City — Utah teammates Karl Malone and John Stockton shared MVP honors, Malone tallying 28 points and Stockton handing out 15 assists.

GAME 42: February 9, 1992 — West 153, East 113 at Orlando — Magic Johnson came out of retirement with 25 points, nine assists, and a dazzling all-around performance as the West routed the East.

GAME 41: February 10, 1991 — East 116, West 114 at Charlotte, N.C. — Chicago's Michael Jordan scored 26 points and Philadelphia's Charles Barkley scored 17 points and hauled down 22 rebounds as the East edged the West.

GAME 40: February 11, 1990 — East 130, West 113 at Miami — With seven players scoring in double figures, the East jumped ahead 40-23 in the first quarter and never trailed, shooting .543 for the game.

GAME 39: February 12, 1989 — West 143, East 134 at Houston — Before a record crowd of 44,735 at the Astrodome, Utah's Karl Malone had 28 points and nine rebounds and teammate John Stockton contributed 17 assists.

GAME 38: February 7, 1988 — East 138, West 133 at Chicago — Michael Jordan scored 16 of his 40 points in the final 5:51 to clinch the East victory in a game in which Kareem Abdul-Jabbar of Los Angeles became the leading career All-Star scorer.

GAME 37: February 8, 1987 — West 154, East 149, OT, at Seattle — Late replacement Tom Chambers of Seattle tallied 34 points and Dallas' Rolando Blackman sent the game into overtime with two free throws after time had expired before 34,275 at the Kingdome.

GAME 36: February 9, 1986 — East 139, West 132 at Dallas — Detroit's Isiah Thomas, used in a one-guard offense late in the game, finished with 30 points and 10 assists and won his second MVP Award in three years.

GAME 35: February 10, 1985 — West 140, East 129 at Indianapolis — Before 43,146 at the Hoosier Dome, the West broke a five-game losing streak as 7-4 Ralph Sampson of Houston scored 24 points and grabbed 10 rebounds.

GAME 34: January 29, 1984 — East 154, West 145, OT, at Denver — Detroit's Isiah Thomas scored all 21 of his points after halftime and Philadelphia's Julius Erving poured in a game-high 34 to offset Magic Johnson's record 22 assists.

GAME 33: February 13, 1983 — East 132, West 123 at Inglewood, Cal. — Julius Erving's dazzling dunks and drives led to a game-high 25 points for the Philadelphia forward in the East's victory.

GAME 32: January 31, 1982 — East 120, West 118 at East Rutherford, N.J. — Boston's Larry Bird scored 12 of his team's last 15 points in the final 6 minutes as the East edged the West.

GAME 31: February 1, 1981 — East 123, West 120 at Richfield, Ohio — Boston's 6-1 Nate "Tiny" Archibald had nine points, nine assists and controlled play with his ballhandling down the stretch to gain MVP honors.

GAME 30: February 4, 1980 — East 144, West 136, OT, at Landover, Md. — George Gervin of San Antonio scored 34 points and Boston rookie Larry Bird scored the first All-Star three-pointer to put the East ahead to stay in overtime.

GAME 29: February 4, 1979 — West 134, East 129 at Pontiac, Mich. — Denver's David Thompson scored 25 points as the West jumped to an 80-58 halftime lead and held on to win before 31,745 at the Silverdome.

GAME 28: February 5, 1978 — East 133, West 125 at Atlanta — Buffalo's Randy Smith scored 27 points and shot 11-for-14 from the field, connecting on 30- and 40-foot jumpers at the buzzers ending the first and second quarters.

GAME 27: February 13, 1977 — West 125, East 124 at Milwaukee — Paul Westphal of Phoenix had two baskets and a steal in the closing minutes to clinch the West's victory, although Julius Erving of the East was voted MVP.

GAME 26: February 3, 1976 — East 123, West 109 at Philadelphia — Former Piston Dave Bing, now playing for the Washington Bullets near the end of his career, had 16 points and four assists and was voted MVP.

GAME 25: January 14, 1975 — East 108, West 102 at Phoenix — New York's Walt Frazier led all scorers with 30 points and dribbled off with the MVP award for the East.

GAME 24: January 15, 1974 — West 134, East 123 at Seattle — Detroit's Bob Lanier and Seattle's Spencer Haywood combined for 47 points, Lanier getting half of his 24 in the fourth quarter for the West.

GAME 23: January 23, 1973 — East 104, West 84 at Chicago — Boston's Dave Cowens had 15 points and 13 rebounds as the East held the West to the fewest points since the advent of the shot clock.

GAME 22: January 18, 1972 — West 112, East 110 at Inglewood, Cal. — Laker Jerry West thrilled the hometown Forum fans by scoring the winning basket on a 20-foot jumper at the buzzer.

GAME 21: January 12, 1971 — West 108, East 107 at San Diego — Milwaukee's Kareem Abdul-Jabbar (then known as Lew Alcindor) scored on a five-foot jumper and converted a free throw with 48 seconds left for the West.

GAME 20: January 20, 1970 — East 142, West 135 at Philadelphia — New York's Willis Reed and Cincinnati's Oscar Robertson scored 21 points apiece as the East won the 20th NBA All-Star Game.

GAME 19: January 14, 1969 — East 123, West 112 at Baltimore — Cincinnati's Oscar Robertson walked off with his third MVP trophy by scoring 24 points for the East.

GAME 18: January 23, 1968 — East 144, West 124 at New York — Philadelphia's Hal Greer shot 8-for-8 from the field and scored 21 points in only 17 minutes for the East.

GAME 17: January 10, 1967 — West 135, East 120 at San Francisco — The West ended four years of frustration as San Francisco's Rick Barry scored 38 points in 34 minutes.

GAME 16: January 11, 1966 — East 137, West 94 at Cincinnati — A late addition to the East team, Adrian Smith of the host Royals scored 24 points and was selected MVP.

GAME 15: January 13, 1965 — East 124, West 123 at St. Louis — Jerry Lucas of Cincinnati gained MVP honors in a game overshadowed by the trade of superstar Wilt Chamberlain from San Francisco to Philadelphia.

GAME 14: January 14, 1964 — East 111, West 107 at Boston — Cincinnati's Oscar Robertson gained MVP honors for the second time in four years in a game that was threatened by a possible players' strike until close to game time.

GAME 13: January 16, 1963 — East 115, West 108 at Los Angeles — Boston's Bill Russell outscored San Francisco's Wilt Chamberlain 19-17 and outrebounded him 24-19 in their first All-Star confrontation.

GAME 12: January 16, 1962 — West 150, East 130 at St. Louis — Four West players scored 23 points or more to offset an All-Star record 42-point ourburst by Philadelphia's Wilt Chamberlain.

GAME 11: January 17, 1961 — West 153, East 131 at Syracuse, N.Y. — Rookie Oscar Robertson of Cincinnati upstaged the veterans with 23 points and 14 assists in the West's high-scoring victory.

GAME 10: January 22, 1960 — East 125, West 115 at Philadelphia — Philadelphia's Wilt Chamberlain celebrated his rookie season by taking MVP honors with 23 points and 25 rebounds for the East.

GAME 9: January 23, 1959 — West 124, East 108 at Detroit — St. Louis veteran Bob Pettit and Minneapolis rookie Elgin Baylor became the first co-MVPs in the West's third All-Star triumph.

GAME 8: January 21, 1958 — East 130, West 118 at St. Louis — Philadelphia's Paul Arizin had 24 points for the East, but Bob Pettit of St. Louis became the first losing team member to gain MVP honors with 28 points and 26 rebounds.

GAME 7: January 15, 1957 — East 109, West 97 at Boston — Boston's Bob Cousy controlled the game with his playmaking, and Celtics teammate Bill Sharman ended the first half with a 70-foot basket in the East's victory.

GAME 6: January 24, 1956 — West 108, East 94 at Rochester, N.Y. — Bob Pettit of the St. Louis Hawks, in only his second pro season, chalked up a game-high 20 points and 24 rebounds to pace the West.

GAME 5: January 18, 1955 — East 100, West 91 at New York — Boston's Bill Sharman scored 10 of his 15 points in the fourth quarter, and Celtics teammate Bob Cousy had 20 points for the East.

GAME 4: January 21, 1954 — East 98, West 93, OT, at New York — Before a sellout crowd at Madison Square Garden, Boston's Bob Cousy scored 10 of the East's 14 overtime points.

GAME 3: January 13, 1953 — West 79, East 75 at Fort Wayne, Ind. — Rochester guard Bob Davies helped the West to its first All-Star victory with eight fourth quarter points.

GAME 2: February 11, 1952 — East 108, West 91 at Boston — Paul Arizin of Philadelphia shot 9-for-13 for 26 points, and the East pulled away with a 16-3 spurt in the fourth quarter.

GAME 1: March 2, 1951 — East 111, West 94 at Boston — Boston's "Easy" Ed Macauley scored a game-high 20 points and held George Mikan of Minneapolis to just four field goals in the first NBA All-Star Game.

RESULTS OF ABA ALL-STAR GAMES

YEAR	RESULT & LOCATION	MOST VALUABLE PLAYER	ATTENDANCE
1968	East 126, West 120 at Indianapolis	Larry Brown, New Orleans	10,872
1969	West 133, East 127 at Louisville	John Beasley, Dallas	5,407
1970	West 128, East 98 at Indianapolis	Spencer Haywood, Denver	11,932
1971	East 126, West 122 at Greensboro	Mel Daniels, Indiana	14,407
1972	East 142, West 115 at Louisville	Dan Issel, Kentucky	15,738
1973	West 123, East 111 at Salt Lake City	Warren Jabali, Denver	12,556
1974	East 128, West 112 at Norfolk	Artis Gilmore, Kentucky	10,624
1975	East 151, West 124 at San Antonio	Freddie Lewis, St. Louis	10,449
1976	Denver 144, All-Stars 138 at Denver	David Thompson, Denver	17,798

GAME 1: January 9, 1968 — East 126, West 120 at Indianapolis — Minnesota's Mel Daniels, with 22 points and 15 rebounds, powered the East to victory in the first ABA All-Star Game.

GAME 2: January 28, 1969 — West 133, East 127 at Louisville — John Beasley of Dallas had 19 points and 14 rebounds and Alex Hannum, who had coached the NBA East All-Stars to victory a year earlier, led the West to the win.

GAME 3: January 24, 1970 — West 128, East 98 at Indianapolis — Denver rookie Spencer Haywood had 23 points, 19 rebounds and seven blocked shots and teammate Larry Jones scored 30 points in the West rout.

GAME 4: January 23, 1971 — East 126, West 122 at Greensboro, N.C. — Rick Barry of New York scored four points in the final 49 seconds as the East overcame an 18-point third-quarter deficit.

GAME 5: January 29, 1972 — East 142, West 115 at Louisville — Carolina's Jim McDaniels scored 18 of his 24 points in a 45-point fourth quarter as the East pulled away at the end.

GAME 6: February 6, 1973 — West 123, East 111 at Salt Lake City — Warren Jabali of Denver led the West to a 39-19 edge over the East in the final period for the victory.

GAME 7: January 30, 1974 — East 128, West 112 at Norfolk, Va. — Despite 29 points and 22 rebounds by San Antonio rookie Swen Nater for the West, the East shot .552 from the field to win.

GAME 8: January 28, 1975 — East 151, West 124 at San Antonio — Freddie Lewis of St. Louis scored 12 of his game-high 26 points in the first period as the East won easily.

GAME 9: January 27, 1976 — Denver 144, All-Stars 138 at Denver — The first-place Denver Nuggets, led by rookie David Thompson's 29 points, outscored a team of stars from the league's other six clubs.

NBA ALL STAR GAMES

GAME 49: February 13, 2000

LOCATION	EAST COACH	WEST COACH	MOST VALUABLE PLAYER	OFFICIALS	ATTENDANCE
The Arena in Oakland	Jeff Van Gundy, New York	Phil Jackson, Los Angeles	Tim Duncan, San Antonio Shaquille O'Neal, L.A. Lakers	Joe Crawford, Terry Durham, Joe Forte	18,325

East (126)

PLAYER	MIN	FGM-FGA	3PM-3PT	FT	REBOUNDS OFF	DEF	TOT	AST	PF	ST	TO	BS	PTS
Vince Carter, Toronto	28	6-11	0-2	0-0	2	2	4	2	0	2	2	0	12
Grant Hill, Detroit	19	3-7	0-1	1-1	0	3	3	5	0	1	3	0	7
Alonzo Mourning, Miami	27	7-11	0-0	1-2	2	5	7	1	4	3	1	4	15
Eddie Jones, Charlotte	21	4-7	2-3	0-0	1	3	4	3	1	1	1	0	10
Allen Iverson, Philadelphia	28	10-18	2-2	4-5	2	0	2	9	0	2	5	0	26
Allan Houston, New York	18	3-10	1-3	4-4	0	0	0	2	1	1	1	0	11
Glenn Robinson, Milwaukee	17	5-10	0-0	0-0	2	4	6	0	0	0	0	0	10
Ray Allen, Milwaukee	17	4-13	1-6	5-6	1	0	1	2	2	3	3	1	14
Dikembe Mutombo, Atlanta	16	2-4	0-0	0-0	2	6	8	0	0	0	2	0	4
Antonio Davis, Indiana	14	2-3	0-0	0-0	3	5	8	1	0	0	0	0	4
Jerry Stackhouse, Detroit	14	4-7	0-0	0-0	0	1	1	2	2	0	1	0	8
Reggie Miller, Indiana	21	1-7	1-6	2-2	0	2	2	3	1	1	1	0	5
TOTAL	240	51-108	7-23	17-20	15	31	46	30	11	14	20	5	126

Team Rebs: 8 — Total TO: 20 (24 Pts)

West (137)

PLAYER	MIN	FGM-FGA	3PM-3PT	FT	REBOUNDS OFF	DEF	TOT	AST	PF	ST	TO	BS	PTS
Kevin Garnett, Minnesota	35	10-19	0-1	4-4	3	7	10	5	1	1	0	1	24
Tim Duncan, San Antonio	33	12-14	0-0	0-0	7	7	14	4	3	1	2	1	24
Shaquille O'Neal, L.A. Lakers	25	11-20	0-0	0-2	4	5	9	3	2	0	4	3	22
Kobe Bryant, L.A. Lakers	28	7-16	1-4	0-0	1	0	1	3	3	2	1	0	15
Jason Kidd, Phoenix	34	4-9	3-6	0-0	0	5	5	14	0	4	6	0	11
Gary Payton, Seattle	20	1-8	0-4	3-3	0	4	4	8	1	2	2	0	5
Chris Webber, Sacramento	13	3-10	0-0	0-0	3	5	8	3	2	1	2	0	6
Rasheed Wallace, Portland	21	3-6	0-0	3-4	2	2	4	0	0	1	0	1	9
Michael Finley, Dallas	10	5-6	1-2	0-0	0	1	1	0	0	0	1	0	11
David Robinson, San Antonio	7	0-1	0-0	0-0	1	1	2	0	1	0	1	0	0
John Stockton, Utah	11	5-5	0-0	0-0	0	0	0	2	2	1	0	0	10
Karl Malone, Utah	3	0-1	0-0	0-0	0	0	0	0	0	0	0	0	0
TOTAL	240	61-115	5-17	10-13	21	37	58	42	15	13	19	6	137

Team Rebs: 5 — Total TO: 19 (19 Pts)

SCORE BY PERIODS:	1	2	3	4	FINAL
EAST	26	33	38	29	126
WEST	33	31	35	38	137

1999: No Game Played

GAME 48: February 8, 1998

LOCATION	EAST COACH	WEST COACH	MOST VALUABLE PLAYER	OFFICIALS	ATTENDANCE
New York	Larry Bird, Indiana	George Karl, Seattle	Michael Jordan, Chicago	Hue Hollins, Bernie Fryer, Bob Delaney	18,323

East (135)

		FGM-	3PM-		REBOUNDS								
PLAYER	MIN	FGA	3PT	FT	OFF	DEF	TOT	AST	PF	ST	TO	BS	PTS
Grant Hill, Detroit	28	7-11	1-1	0-0	0	3	3	5	1	1	0	0	15
Shawn Kemp, Cleveland	25	5-10	0-1	2-2	2	9	11	2	2	4	4	0	12
Dikembe Mutombo, Atlanta	19	4-5	0-0	1-2	1	6	7	0	3	0	0	1	9
Michael Jordan, Chicago	32	10-18	1-1	2-3	1	5	6	8	0	3	2	0	23
Anfernee Hardaway, Orlando	12	3-5	0-1	0-0	0	0	0	3	0	0	1	0	6
Tim Hardaway, Miami	17	3-8	2-5	0-0	0	1	1	6	0	0	6	0	8
Jayson Williams, New Jersey	19	2-3	0-0	0-0	3	7	10	1	2	0	0	0	4
Rik Smits, Indiana	21	3-7	0-0	4-4	2	5	7	4	3	0	0	2	10
Reggie Miller, Indiana	20	6-8	1-2	1-2	0	0	0	0	2	1	0	0	14
Glen Rice, Charlotte	16	6-14	4-6	0-0	1	0	1	0	0	0	1	0	16
Steve Smith, Atlanta	16	6-12	2-5	0-0	2	1	3	0	0	0	0	0	14
Antoine Walker, Boston	15	2-8	0-3	0-0	1	2	3	3	0	1	1	0	4
Totals	240	57-109	11-25	10-13	13	39	52	32	13	10	15	3	135

West (114)

		FGM-	3PM-		REBOUNDS								
PLAYER	MIN	FGA	3PT	FT	OFF	DEF	TOT	AST	PF	ST	TO	BS	PTS
Karl Malone, Utah	17	2-4	0-0	0-0	0	3	3	2	1	2	0	0	4
Kevin Garnett, Minnesota	21	6-11	0-1	0-0	1	3	4	2	0	2	3	1	12
Shaquille O'Neal, L.A. Lakers	18	5-10	0-0	2-4	2	2	4	1	2	0	2	0	12
Kobe Bryant, L.A. Lakers	22	7-16	2-3	2-2	2	4	6	1	1	2	1	0	18
Gary Payton, Seattle	24	3-7	1-3	0-0	2	1	3	13	0	2	4	0	7
Vin Baker, Seattle	21	3-12	0-0	2-2	6	2	8	0	1	1	0	0	8
Eddie Jones, L.A. Lakers	25	7-19	0-7	1-2	7	4	11	1	1	2	0	0	15
David Robinson, San Antonio	22	3-4	0-0	9-10	2	4	6	0	1	2	2	2	15
Mitch Richmond, Sacramento	17	4-11	0-2	0-0	0	1	1	2	0	0	0	0	8
Jason Kidd, Phoenix	19	0-1	0-0	0-0	0	1	1	9	2	0	2	0	0
Tim Duncan, San Antonio	14	1-4	0-1	0-0	1	10	11	1	0	0	2	0	2
Nick Van Exel, L.A. Lakers	20	5-14	1-6	2-2	1	2	3	2	0	0	2	0	13
Totals	240	46-113	4-23	18-22	24	37	61	34	9	13	18	3	114

SCORE BY PERIODS:	1	2	3	4	FINAL
WEST	25	33	33	23	114
EAST	33	34	34	34	135

GAME 47: February 9, 1997

LOCATION	EAST COACH	WEST COACH	MOST VALUABLE PLAYER	OFFICIALS	ATTENDANCE
Cleveland	Doug Collins, Detroit	Rudy Tomjanovich, Houston	Glen Rice, Charlotte	Hugh Evans, Ron Garretson, Bill Oakes	20,592

East (132)

		FGM-	3PM-		REBOUNDS								
PLAYER	MIN	FGA	3PT	FT	OFF	DEF	TOT	AST	PF	ST	TO	BS	PTS
Scottie Pippen, Chicago	25	4-9	0-3	0-0	0	3	3	2	0	0	2	0	8
Grant Hill, Detroit	22	4-7	0-0	3-4	2	1	3	2	2	1	3	1	11
Dikembe Mutombo, Atlanta	15	1-5	0-0	1-2	2	6	8	0	0	0	1	1	3
Michael Jordan, Chicago	26	5-14	0-0	4-7	3	8	11	11	4	2	3	0	14
Anfernee Hardaway, Orlando	24	7-10	3-5	2-2	4	3	7	3	2	2	1	0	19
Vin Baker, Milwaukee	24	8-12	0-0	3-4	7	5	12	1	2	0	0	0	19
Terrell Brandon, Cleveland	17	4-11	2-4	0-0	1	2	3	8	2	2	0	0	10
Chris Webber, Washington	14	1-4	0-0	0-0	1	3	4	3	3	1	3	0	2
Tim Hardaway, Miami	14	4-10	2-6	0-0	0	3	3	2	1	1	2	0	10
Glen Rice, Charlotte	25	10-24	4-7	2-2	1	0	1	1	2	2	1	0	26
Joe Dumars, Detroit	10	1-4	1-4	0-0	0	1	1	1	0	0	0	0	3
Christian Laettner, Atlanta	24	3-5	0-0	1-1	4	7	11	2	4	1	2	1	7
Patrick Ewing, New York *(Selected but did not play due to injury.)*													
Alonzo Mourning, Miami *(Selected but did not play due to injury.)*													
TOTALS	240	52-115	12-29	16-22	25	42	67	36	22	12	18	3	132

West (120)

	FGM-		3PM-REBOUNDS										
PLAYER	MIN	FGA	3PT	FT	OFF	DEF	TOT	AST	PF	ST	TO	BS	PTS
Shawn Kemp, Seattle	19	4-7	1-2	1-2	1	3	4	1	1	1	1	0	10
Karl Malone, Utah	20	2-8	0-0	0-0	1	3	4	0	0	1	0	1	4
Hakeem Olajuwon, Houston	20	5-8	0-0	1-2	0	3	3	1	1	0	1	1	11
Gary Payton, Seattle	28	7-15	1-5	2-2	0	1	1	10	2	2	4	0	17
John Stockton, Utah	20	5-6	2-2	0-0	0	0	0	5	2	1	1	0	12
Mitch Richmond, Sacramento	22	3-7	3-4	0-0	1	2	3	4	1	0	1	0	9
Tom Gugliotta, Minnesota	19	3-7	0-1	3-4	1	7	8	3	3	2	3	0	9
Latrell Sprewell, Golden State	25	7-12	1-3	4-6	1	2	3	1	2	2	1	0	19
Eddie Jones, L.A. Lakers	17	3-4	0-1	4-7	1	0	1	1	1	1	3	2	10
Kevin Garnett, Minnesota	18	1-7	0-0	4-4	1	8	9	1	2	0	0	1	6
Detlef Schrempf, Seattle	20	5-8	1-3	0-1	1	3	4	2	3	0	1	1	11
Chris Gatling, Dallas	12	1-8	0-0	0-0	0	2	2	0	1	1	0	0	2
Charles Barkley, Houston *(Selected but did not play due to injury.)*													
Clyde Drexler, Houston *(Selected but did not play due to injury.)*													
Shaquille O'Neal, L.A. Lakers *(Selected but did not play due to injury.)*													
TOTALS	240	46-97	9-21	19-28	8	34	42	29	19	11	16	6	120

SCORE BY PERIODS:	1	2	3	4	FINAL
WEST	34	26	27	33	120
EAST	21	36	40	35	132

GAME 46: February 11, 1996

LOCATION	EAST COACH	WEST COACH	MOST VALUABLE PLAYER	OFFICIALS	ATTENDANCE
San Antonio	Phil Jackson, Chicago	George Karl, Seattle	Michael Jordan, Chicago	Ed T. Rush, Ed Middleton, Ronnie Nunn	36,037

East (129)

PLAYER	MIN	FGM-FGA	3PM-3PT	FT	REBOUNDS OFF	DEF	TOT	AST	PF	ST	TO	BS	PTS
Scottie Pippen, Chicago	25	4-7	0-1	0-0	2	6	8	5	0	3	6	0	8
Grant Hill, Detroit	26	6-10	0-0	2-2	1	2	3	2	1	1	2	0	14
Shaquille O'Neal, Orlando	28	10-16	0-0	5-11	3	7	10	1	3	1	1	2	25
Michael Jordan, Chicago	22	8-11	0-0	4-4	1	3	4	1	1	1	0	0	20
Anfernee Hardaway, Orlando	31	6-8	2-4	4-4	0	3	3	7	0	2	3	0	18
Patrick Ewing, New York	12	3-7	0-0	2-2	1	2	3	1	2	3	0	1	8
Reggie Miller, Indiana	18	4-8	0-4	0-0	0	2	2	2	2	1	1	0	8
Vin Baker, Milwaukee	14	2-5	0-0	2-2	1	1	2	2	4	1	0	0	6
Terrell Brandon, Cleveland	20	4-10	1-4	2-2	1	0	1	3	1	1	3	1	11
Glen Rice, Charlotte	15	1-5	1-2	4-4	0	1	1	2	2	0	2	0	7
Juwan Howard, Washington	16	1-5	0-0	0-0	4	2	6	2	3	1	0	0	2
Alonzo Mourning, Miami	13	1-6	0-0	0-0	0	1	1	0	2	0	2	1	2
TOTALS	240	50-98	4-15	25-31	14	30	44	28	21	15	20	5	129

West (118)

PLAYER	MIN	FGM-FGA	3PM-3PT	FT	REBOUNDS OFF	DEF	TOT	AST	PF	ST	TO	BS	PTS
Charles Barkley, Phoenix	16	4-6	0-0	0-0	0	0	0	1	1	0	2	0	8
Shawn Kemp, Seattle	22	6-12	0-2	1-2	2	2	4	1	4	0	3	1	13
Hakeem Olajuwon, Houston	14	2-8	0-0	0-0	1	2	3	0	2	0	0	0	4
Clyde Drexler, Houston	19	5-8	1-4	0-0	0	2	2	3	0	3	3	0	11
Jason Kidd, Dallas	22	3-4	1-2	0-0	2	4	6	10	1	2	2	0	7
David Robinson, San Antonio	23	8-13	0-0	2-2	6	5	11	2	4	2	1	2	18
Gary Payton, Seattle	28	6-10	0-1	6-6	3	2	5	5	1	5	6	0	18
Sean Elliott, San Antonio	22	5-12	2-6	1-1	2	3	5	2	4	0	2	0	13
Karl Malone, Utah	20	2-6	0-0	7-8	0	9	9	2	1	1	1	0	11
Mitch Richmond, Sacramento	25	3-10	0-3	1-2	0	2	2	2	0	1	2	0	7
Dikembe Mutombo, Denver	11	2-4	0-0	0-0	6	3	9	0	3	0	3	0	4
John Stockton, Utah	18	2-9	0-7	0-0	0	1	1	3	2	0	1	0	4
TOTALS	240	48-102	4-25	18-21	22	35	57	31	23	14	26	3	118

SCORE BY PERIODS:	1	2	3	4	FINAL
EAST	33	28	41	27	129
WEST	32	26	22	38	118

GAME 45: February 12, 1995

LOCATION	EAST COACH	WEST COACH	MOST VALUABLE PLAYER	OFFICIALS	ATTENDANCE
Phoenix	Brian Hill, Orlando	Paul Westphal, Phoenix	Mitch Richmond, Sacramento	Dick Bavetta, Steve Javie, Jack Nies	18,755

East (112)

PLAYER	MIN	FGM-FGA	3PM-3PT	FT	REBOUNDS OFF	DEF	TOT	AST	PF	ST	TO	BS	PTS
Grant Hill, Detroit	20	5-8	0-0	0-4	0	0	0	3	2	2	1	0	10
Scottie Pippen, Chicago	30	5-15	2-6	0-0	0	7	7	3	1	2	4	1	12
Shaquille O'Neal, Orlando	26	9-16	0-1	4-7	4	3	7	1	2	3	2	2	22
Anfernee Hardaway, Orlando	31	4-9	0-2	4-6	4	1	5	11	1	0	3	0	12
Reggie Miller, Indiana	23	3-9	3-6	0-0	0	0	0	2	0	1	1	1	9
Joe Dumars, Detroit	21	5-8	1-2	0-0	0	0	0	6	1	1	1	0	11
Patrick Ewing, New York	22	4-7	0-0	2-2	0	3	3	1	3	1	5	0	10
Dana Barros, Philadelphia	11	2-5	1-3	0-0	0	1	1	3	0	0	0	0	5
Larry Johnson, Charlotte	20	2-3	1-1	2-2	1	3	4	2	0	0	1	0	7
Alonzo Mourning, Charlotte	19	4-9	0-1	2-3	0	8	8	1	5	0	1	1	10
Vin Baker, Milwaukee	11	0-2	0-0	2-4	2	0	2	0	1	0	1	1	2
Tyrone Hill, Cleveland	6	1-1	0-0	0-0	2	2	4	0	1	0	0	0	2
Totals	240	44-92	8-22	16-28	13	28	41	33	17	10	20	6	112

West (139)

PLAYER	MIN	FGM-FGA	3PM-3PT	FT	REBOUNDS OFF	DEF	TOT	AST	PF	ST	TO	BS	PTS
Charles Barkley, Phoenix	23	7-12	1-4	0-0	5	4	9	2	1	2	2	0	15
Shawn Kemp, Seattle	23	4-6	0-0	5-6	0	2	2	2	5	1	4	0	13
Hakeem Olajuwon, Houston	25	6-13	1-1	0-2	4	7	11	1	2	2	3	2	13
Dan Majerle, Phoenix	20	4-12	2-7	0-0	1	4	5	3	1	0	0	0	10
Latrell Sprewell, Golden State	22	4-9	0-2	1-1	2	2	4	4	0	3	1	0	9
Gary Payton, Seattle	23	3-10	0-3	0-0	3	2	5	15	1	3	3	0	6
Mitch Richmond, Sacramento	22	10-13	3-3	0-0	3	1	4	2	0	0	0	0	23
David Robinson, San Antonio	14	3-5	0-0	4-6	0	3	3	2	2	2	1	1	10
Detlef Schrempf, Seattle	18	4-11	1-4	0-0	0	4	4	5	2	0	0	0	9
Dikembe Mutombo, Denver	20	6-8	0-0	0-0	3	5	8	1	3	0	0	4	12
Karl Malone, Utah	16	6-6	0-0	3-4	0	3	3	1	0	0	1	0	15
John Stockton, Utah	14	2-6	0-3	0-0	1	0	1	6	0	2	0	0	4
Cedric Ceballos, L.A. Lakers *(Selected but did not play due to injury.)*													
TOTALS	240	59-111	8-27	13-19	22	37	59	44	17	15	15	7	139

SCORE BY PERIODS:	1	2	3	4	FINAL
EAST	28	28	25	31	112
WEST	31	41	32	35	139

GAME 44: February 13, 1994

LOCATION	EAST COACH	WEST COACH	MOST VALUABLE PLAYER	OFFICIALS	ATTENDANCE
Minneapolis	Lenny Wilkens, Atlanta	George Karl, Seattle	Scottie Pippen, Chicago	Jack Madden, Jess Kersey, Dan Crawford	17,096

East (127)

PLAYER	MIN	FGM-FGA	3PM-3PT	FT	REBOUNDS OFF	DEF	TOT	AST	PF	ST	TO	BS	PTS
Scottie Pippen, Chicago	31	9-15	5-9	6-10	0	11	11	2	2	4	2	1	29
Derrick Coleman, New Jersey	18	1-6	0-0	0-0	1	2	3	1	3	1	0	0	2
Shaquille O'Neal, Orlando	26	2-12	0-0	4-11	4	6	10	0	2	1	1	4	8
Kenny Anderson, New Jersey	16	3-10	0-1	0-0	1	3	4	3	2	0	4	0	6
B.J. Armstrong, Chicago	22	5-9	1-2	0-0	1	0	1	4	1	0	1	0	11
John Starks, New York	20	4-9	1-3	0-0	1	2	3	3	1	1	2	0	9
Mark Price, Cleveland	22	8-10	2-3	2-2	0	2	2	5	1	1	0	1	20
Patrick Ewing, New York	24	7-15	0-0	6-7	4	4	8	1	2	0	1	0	20
Charles Oakley, New York	11	1-3	0-0	0-0	1	2	3	3	3	0	0	0	2
Dominique Wilkins, Atlanta	17	4-9	0-2	3-6	2	0	2	4	1	0	0	0	11
Mookie Blaylock, Atlanta	16	2-5	1-2	0-0	0	1	1	2	3	2	1	0	5
Horace Grant, Chicago	17	2-8	0-0	0-0	6	2	8	2	0	1	1	2	4
Alonzo Mourning, Charlotte *(Selected but did not play due to injury.)*													
TOTALS	240	48-111	10-22	21-36	21	35	56	30	21	11	13	8	127

West (118)

PLAYER	MIN	FGM-FGA	3PM-3PT	FT	REBOUNDS OFF	DEF	TOT	AST	PF	ST	TO	BS	PTS
Karl Malone, Utah	21	3-9	0-0	0-0	3	4	7	2	2	1	1	0	6
Shawn Kemp, Seattle	22	3-11	0-0	0-0	6	6	12	4	4	0	6	3	6
Hakeem Olajuwon, Houston	30	8-15	0-0	3-6	4	7	11	2	4	2	3	5	19
Mitch Richmond, Sacramento	24	5-16	0-0	0-0	0	2	2	3	0	0	2	0	10
Clyde Drexler, Portland	15	3-7	0-2	0-0	0	3	3	1	1	1	1	1	6
John Stockton, Utah	26	6-10	0-1	0-0	1	4	5	10	2	1	4	0	13
David Robinson, San Antonio	21	6-13	0-0	7-10	3	2	5	0	2	0	1	2	19
Kevin Johnson, Phoenix	14	3-6	0-0	0-1	0	1	1	2	1	1	2	0	6
Clifford Robinson, Portland	18	5-8	0-1	0-0	1	1	2	5	0	1	0	0	10
Danny Manning, L.A. Clippers	17	4-7	0-0	0-0	0	4	4	2	4	0	0	1	8
Gary Payton, Seattle	17	3-4	0-0	0-0	2	4	6	9	2	0	0	0	6
Latrell Sprewell, Golden State	15	3-8	0-2	3-7	4	3	7	1	1	0	2	0	9
Charles Barkley, Phoenix *(Selected but did not play due to injury.)*													
TOTALS	240	52-114	0-6	13-24	24	41	65	41	23	7	22	12	118

SCORE BY PERIODS:	1	2	3	4	FINAL
EAST	33	39	29	26	127
WEST	28	36	26	28	118

GAME 43: February 21, 1993

LOCATION	EAST COACH	WEST COACH	MOST VALUABLE PLAYER	OFFICIALS	ATTENDANCE
Salt Lake City	Pat Riley, New York	Paul Westphal, Phoenix	Karl Malone, Utah John Stockton, Utah	Jack Madden, Hue Hollins, Bennett Salvatore	19,459

East (132, OT)

PLAYER	MIN	FGM-FGA	3PM-3PT	FT	REBOUNDS OFF	DEF	TOT	AST	PF	ST	TO	BS	PTS
Larry Johnson, Charlotte	16	2-6	0-2	0-0	3	1	4	0	1	0	0	0	4
Scottie Pippen, Chicago	29	4-14	0-2	2-3	2	3	5	4	4	5	0	2	10
Shaquille O'Neal, Orlando	25	4-9	0-0	6-9	3	4	7	0	3	0	0	0	14
Isiah Thomas, Detroit	32	4-7	0-1	0-2	0	2	2	4	2	2	2	0	8
Michael Jordan, Chicago	36	10-24	1-2	9-13	3	1	4	5	5	4	6	0	30
Larry Nance, Cleveland	12	3-4	0-0	1-2	1	2	3	1	3	1	0	1	7
Patrick Ewing, New York	25	7-11	0-0	1-1	3	7	10	1	4	2	4	2	15
Joe Dumars, Detroit	17	2-8	1-4	0-0	0	2	2	4	1	0	1	0	5
Mark Price, Cleveland	23	6-11	6-9	1-2	0	1	1	4	5	1	3	0	19
Detlef Schrempf, Indiana	13	1-3	0-1	1-2	0	3	3	0	4	0	1	0	3
Brad Daugherty, Cleveland	19	3-4	0-0	2-4	1	6	7	0	0	0	0	0	8
Dominique Wilkins, Atlanta	18	2-11	1-3	4-4	4	3	7	0	2	1	1	0	9
TOTALS	265	48-112	9-24	27-42	20	35	55	23	34	16	18	5	132

West (135)

PLAYER	MIN	FGM-FGA	3PM-3PT	FT	REBOUNDS OFF	DEF	TOT	AST	PF	ST	TO	BS	PTS
Charles Barkley, Phoenix	34	5-11	1-2	5-7	0	4	4	7	3	4	4	0	16
Karl Malone, Utah	34	11-17	0-0	6-9	3	7	10	0	3	1	3	2	28
David Robinson, San Antonio	26	7-10	0-0	7-12	2	8	10	1	4	0	1	1	21
John Stockton, Utah	31	3-6	1-2	2-2	0	6	6	15	3	2	5	0	9
Clyde Drexler, Portland	11	1-3	0-1	0-0	1	2	1	1	3	0	2	0	2
Dan Majerle, Phoenix	26	6-11	3-6	3-4	2	5	7	3	2	1	0	2	18
Shawn Kemp, Seattle	9	0-2	0-0	0-0	2	0	2	0	3	0	0	0	0
Danny Manning, L.A. Clippers	18	2-2	0-0	0-0	1	3	4	1	1	0	0	0	10
Hakeem Olajuwon, Houston	21	1-5	0-0	1-2	2	5	7	1	3	2	3	2	3
Terry Porter, Portland	19	3-8	1-5	0-0	0	0	0	3	1	1	1	0	7
Sean Elliott, San Antonio	15	1-6	0-0	3-4	1	1	2	0	1	0	1	0	5
Tim Hardaway, Golden State	21	3-9	1-3	9-12	1	5	6	4	1	1	3	0	16
Chris Mullin, Golden State *(Selected but did not play due to injury.)*													
Mitch Richmond, Sacramento *(Selected but did not play due to injury.)*													
TOTALS	265	46-93	7-19	36-52	15	44	59	36	28	12	23	7	135

SCORE BY PERIODS:	1	2	3	4	OT	FINAL
EAST	26	26	32	35	13	132
WEST	27	30	29	33	16	135

GAME 42: February 9, 1992

LOCATION	EAST COACH	WEST COACH	MOST VALUABLE PLAYER	OFFICIALS	ATTENDANCE
Orlando	Phil Jackson, Chicago	Don Nelson, Golden State	Earvin Johnson, Los Angeles	Darell Garretson, Joe Crawford, Tommy Nunez	14,272

East (113)

PLAYER	MIN	FGM-FGA	3PM-3PT	FT	REBOUNDS OFF	DEF	TOT	AST	PF	ST	TO	BS	PTS
Scottie Pippen, Chicago	21	6-13	0-0	2-3	4	0	4	1	0	2	1	1	14
Charles Barkley, Philadelphia	28	6-14	0-2	0-0	2	7	9	1	3	0	3	0	12
Patrick Ewing, New York	17	4-7	0-0	2-5	2	2	4	0	3	2	2	1	10
Isiah Thomas, Detroit	28	7-14	1-3	0-0	0	1	1	5	0	3	3	0	15
Michael Jordan, Chicago	31	9-17	0-0	0-0	1	0	1	5	2	2	1	0	18
Mark Price, Cleveland	15	1-5	0-3	4-4	0	0	0	3	1	1	3	0	6
Brad Daugherty, Cleveland	15	3-11	0-0	0-0	3	3	6	1	0	1	3	0	6
Joe Dumars, Detroit	17	2-7	0-2	0-0	0	1	1	3	0	0	2	0	4
Dennis Rodman, Detroit	25	2-7	0-0	0-0	7	6	13	0	1	1	2	0	4
Reggie Lewis, Boston	15	3-7	0-0	1-2	4	0	4	2	3	0	1	1	7
Kevin Willis, Atlanta	14	4-10	0-0	0-0	4	0	4	0	1	0	0	0	8
Michael Adams, Washington	14	4-8	1-3	0-0	1	0	1	1	1	4	1	0	9
Larry Bird, Boston *(Selected but did not play due to injury.)*													
Dominique Wilkins, Atlanta *(Selected but did not play due to injury.)*													
TOTALS	240	51-117	2-13	9-14	28	20	48	22	15	16	22	3	113

West (153)

PLAYER	MIN	FGM-FGA	3PM-3PT	FT	REBOUNDS OFF	DEF	TOT	AST	PF	ST	TO	BS	PTS
Karl Malone, Utah	19	5-7	0-0	1-2	0	7	7	3	1	1	1	1	11
Chris Mullin, Golden State	24	6-7	1-1	0-0	0	1	1	3	0	0	1	0	13
David Robinson, San Antonio	18	7-9	0-0	5-8	1	4	5	2	3	3	0	1	19
Clyde Drexler, Portland	28	10-15	2-4	0-0	2	7	9	6	2	0	1	2	22
Earvin Johnson, L.A. Lakers	29	9-12	3-3	4-4	3	2	5	9	0	2	7	0	25
Tim Hardaway, Golden State	20	5-10	2-5	2-2	0	0	0	7	2	1	2	0	14
Hakeem Olajuwon, Houston	20	3-6	0-0	1-2	0	4	4	2	3	2	3	1	7
Jeff Hornacek, Phoenix	24	5-7	1-2	0-0	1	1	2	3	0	1	0	0	11
Otis Thorpe, Houston	4	1-1	0-0	0-0	0	0	0	0	0	0	0	0	2
James Worthy, L.A. Lakers	14	4-7	0-0	1-2	0	4	4	1	0	1	0	0	9
John Stockton, Utah	18	5-8	2-3	0-0	0	1	1	5	2	3	3	0	12
Dan Majerle, Phoenix	12	2-5	0-2	0-0	0	3	3	2	0	0	1	0	4
Dikembe Mutombo, Denver	10	2-4	0-0	0-0	1	1	2	1	0	1	2	0	4
TOTALS	240	64-98	11-20	14-20	8	35	43	44	13	15	21	5	153

SCORE BY PERIODS:	1	2	3	4	FINAL
WEST	44	35	36	38	153
EAST	31	24	28	30	113

GAME 41: February 10, 1991

LOCATION	EAST COACH	WEST COACH	MOST VALUABLE PLAYER	OFFICIALS	ATTENDANCE
Charlotte	Chris Ford, Boston	Rick Adelman, Portland	Charles Barkley, Philadelphia	Ed T. Rush, Mike Mathis, Lee Jones	23,530

East (116)

PLAYER	MIN	FGM-FGA	3PM-3PT	FT	REBOUNDS OFF	DEF	TOT	AST	PF	ST	TO	BS	PTS
Bernard King, Washington	26	2-8	0-0	4-4	2	1	3	3	1	0	1	1	8
Charles Barkley, Philadelphia	35	7-15	0-0	3-6	8	14	22	4	5	1	3	1	17
Patrick Ewing, New York	30	8-10	0-0	2-2	2	8	10	0	5	1	2	4	18
Joe Dumars, Detroit	15	1-4	0-1	0-0	1	1	2	1	1	0	4	0	2
Michael Jordan, Chicago	36	10-25	0-2	6-7	3	2	5	5	2	2	10	0	26
Alvin Robertson, Milwaukee	12	2-4	0-0	2-2	0	2	2	0	0	0	3	0	6
Dominique Wilkins, Atlanta	22	3-11	0-2	6-8	3	0	3	4	2	1	2	1	12
Robert Parish, Boston	5	1-2	0-0	0-0	1	3	4	0	2	0	1	0	2
Kevin McHale, Boston	14	0-3	0-1	2-2	1	2	3	2	2	1	0	0	2
Ricky Pierce, Milwaukee	19	4-8	0-0	1-1	0	2	2	2	2	0	2	0	9
Brad Daugherty, Cleveland	12	3-7	0-0	2-3	3	2	5	1	3	0	0	0	8
Hersey Hawkins, Philadelphia	14	3-5	0-1	0-0	0	0	0	1	1	0	1	0	6
Larry Bird, Boston *(Selected but did not play due to injury.)*													
TOTALS	240	44-102	0-7	28-35	24	37	61	23	26	6	29	7	116

West (114)

PLAYER	MIN	FGM-FGA	3PM-3PT	FT	REBOUNDS OFF	DEF	TOT	AST	PF	ST	TO	BS	PTS
Karl Malone, Utah	31	6-11	0-0	4-6	4	7	11	4	1	1	3	1	16
Chris Mullin, Golden State	24	4-8	1-1	4-4	0	2	2	2	2	2	2	0	13
David Robinson, San Antonio	18	6-13	0-0	4-5	3	3	6	0	5	2	2	3	16
Earvin Johnson, L.A. Lakers	28	7-16	2-5	0-0	1	3	4	3	1	0	3	0	16
Kevin Johnson, Phoenix	23	2-5	0-0	1-2	1	1	2	7	2	3	3	1	5
Kevin Duckworth, Portland	19	2-3	0-0	2-2	2	2	4	0	3	1	2	0	6
Clyde Drexler, Portland	19	4-9	0-0	4-4	2	2	4	2	3	1	0	1	12
James Worthy, L.A. Lakers	21	3-11	0-0	3-4	0	2	2	0	2	2	0	1	9
Terry Porter, Portland	15	2-6	0-2	0-0	1	2	3	4	2	2	3	1	4
Tom Chambers, Phoenix	18	4-11	0-1	0-0	2	2	4	1	3	1	4	0	8
John Stockton, Utah	12	1-6	0-1	2-4	0	1	1	2	2	0	0	0	4
Tim Hard.away, Golden State	12	2-7	1-2	0-0	2	1	3	4	1	2	0	0	5
TOTALS	240	43-106	4-12	24-31	18	28	46	29	27	17	22	8	114

SCORE BY PERIODS:	1	2	3	4	FINAL
WEST	23	35	34	22	114
EAST	22	45	27	22	116

GAME 40: February 11, 1990

LOCATION	EAST COACH	WEST COACH	MOST VALUABLE PLAYER	OFFICIALS	ATTENDANCE
Miami	Chuck Daly, Detroit	Pat Riley, L.A. Lakers	Earvin Johnson, L.A. Lakers	Earl Strom, Bill Oakes, Paul Mihalak	14,810

East (130)

		FGM-	3PM-		REBOUNDS								
PLAYER	MIN	FGA	3PT	FT	OFF	DEF	TOT	AST	PF	ST	TO	BS	PTS
Charles Barkley, Philadelphia	22	7-12	1-1	2-3	2	2	4	0	1	1	2	1	17
Larry Bird, Boston	23	3-8	0-1	2-2	2	6	8	3	1	3	3	0	8
Patrick Ewing, New York	27	5-9	0-0	2-2	1	9	10	1	5	1	5	5	12
Michael Jordan, Chicago	29	8-17	1-1	0-0	1	4	5	2	1	5	5	1	17
Isiah Thomas, Detroit	27	7-12	1-1	0-0	1	3	4	9	0	3	1	0	15
Kevin McHale, Boston	20	6-11	1-1	0-0	2	6	8	1	4	0	0	0	13
Joe Dumars, Detroit	18	3-4	2-2	1-2	0	1	1	5	0	0	3	0	9
Robert Parish, Boston	21	7-11	0-0	0-1	2	2	4	2	4	0	1	1	14
Reggie Miller, Indiana	14	2-3	0-1	0-0	0	1	1	3	1	1	0	0	4
Dominique Wilkins, Atlanta	16	5-10	1-1	2-2	0	0	0	4	1	1	0	0	13
Dennis Rodman, Detroit	11	2-4	0-0	0-0	3	1	4	1	1	0	2	1	4
Scottie Pippen, Chicago	12	2-4	0-1	0-0	0	1	1	0	1	1	1	1	4
TOTALS	240	57-105	7-10	9-12	14	36	50	31	20	16	23	10	130

West (113)

		FGM-	3PM-		REBOUNDS								
PLAYER	MIN	FGA	3PT	FT	OFF	DEF	TOT	AST	PF	ST	TO	BS	PTS
A. C. Green, L.A. Lakers	12	0-3	0-0	0-0	0	3	3	1	1	0	1	1	0
James Worthy, L.A. Lakers	19	1-11	0-0	0-0	3	1	4	0	1	1	1	0	2
Hakeem Olajuwon, Houston	31	2-14	0-0	4-10	9	7	16	2	1	1	4	1	8
Earvin Johnson, L.A. Lakers	25	9-15	4-6	0-0	1	5	6	4	1	0	3	1	22
John Stockton, Utah	15	1-4	0-1	0-0	0	0	0	6	1	1	3	1	2
Tom Chambers, Phoenix	21	8-12	0-1	5-7	2	1	3	1	0	1	3	0	21
Clyde Drexler, Portland	19	2-6	1-1	2-2	4	0	4	2	1	1	1	1	7
David Robinson, San Antonio	25	7-12	0-0	1-2	2	8	10	1	1	2	1	1	15
Chris Mullin, Golden State	16	1-5	0-0	1-2	1	2	3	1	0	2	1	1	3
Kevin Johnson, Phoenix	14	1-1	0-0	0-0	0	0	0	4	2	0	3	0	2
Rolando Blackman, Dallas	21	7-9	0-0	1-1	1	1	2	2	1	1	2	0	15
Lafayette Lever, Denver	22	7-13	0-2	2-2	0	3	3	2	0	2	0	0	16
Karl Malone, Utah *(Selected but did not play due to injury.)*													
TOTALS	240	46-105	5-11	16-26	23	31	54	26	10	12	23	7	113

SCORE BY PERIODS:	1	2	3	4	FINAL
WEST	23	29	31	30	113
EAST	40	25	35	30	130

GAME 39: February 12, 1989

LOCATION	EAST COACH	WEST COACH	MOST VALUABLE PLAYER	OFFICIALS	ATTENDANCE
Houston	Lenny Wilkens, Cleveland	Pat Riley, L.A. Lakers	Karl Malone, Utah	Hugh Evans, Dick Bavetta and Bill Saar	44,735

East (134)

		FGM-	3PM-		REBOUNDS								
PLAYER	MIN	FGA	3PT	FT	OFF	DEF	TOT	AST	PF	ST	TO	BS	PTS
Charles Barkley, Philadelphia	20	6-11	0-0	5-8	3	2	5	0	0	2	1	1	17
Dominique Wilkins, Atlanta	15	3-8	0-0	3-3	1	1	2	0	0	3	2	0	9
Moses Malone, Atlanta	19	3-9	0-0	3-3	4	4	8	0	1	1	1	1	9
Michael Jordan, Chicago	33	13-23	0-1	2-4	1	1	2	3	1	5	4	0	28
Isiah Thomas, Detroit	33	7-13	1-3	4-6	1	1	2	14	2	4	6	0	19
Patrick Ewing, New York	17	2-8	0-0	0-4	1	5	6	2	2	1	3	2	4
Terry Cummings, Milwaukee	19	4-9	0-0	2-2	2	3	5	1	4	3	0	1	10
Larry Nance, Cleveland	17	5-9	0-0	0-0	3	3	6	1	1	1	0	1	10
Mark Price, Cleveland	20	3-9	1-4	2-2	1	2	3	1	2	2	2	0	9
Mark Jackson, New York	16	3-5	1-1	2-4	1	1	2	4	1	1	2	1	9
Brad Daugherty, Cleveland	15	0-3	0-0	0-0	2	1	3	0	0	1	1	0	0
Kevin McHale, Boston	16	5-7	0-0	0-0	1	2	3	0	3	0	1	2	10
TOTALS	240	54-114	3-9	23-26	21	26	47	26	17	24	23	9	134

West (143)

		FGM-	3PM-		REBOUNDS								
PLAYER	MIN	FGA	3PT	FT	OFF	DEF	TOT	AST	PF	ST	TO	BS	PTS
Alex English, Denver	29	8-13	0-0	0-0	1	2	3	4	0	2	3	0	16
Karl Malone, Utah	26	12-17	0-0	4-6	4	5	9	3	3	2	2	0	28
Hakeem Olajuwon, Houston	25	5-12	0-0	2-3	4	3	7	3	2	3	3	2	12
Dale Ellis, Seattle	26	12-16	1-1	2-2	3	3	6	2	2	0	2	0	27
John Stockton, Utah	32	5-6	1-1	0-0	0	2	2	17	4	5	12	0	11
Kareem Abdul-Jabbar, L.A. Lakers	13	1-6	0-1	2-2	0	3	3	0	3	0	0	2	4
Clyde Drexler, Portland	25	7-19	0-0	0-0	6	6	12	4	3	2	6	0	14
Tom Chambers, Phoenix	16	4-8	0-0	6-6	2	3	5	1	3	0	2	0	14
Chris Mullin, Golden State	14	1-4	0-0	2-2	2	0	2	2	0	0	1	0	4
James Worthy, L.A. Lakers	18	4-7	0-1	0-0	0	2	2	2	0	2	0	0	8
Mark Eaton, Utah	9	0-0	0-0	0-0	0	5	5	0	1	0	0	2	0
Kevin Duckworth, Portland	7	2-5	0-0	1-2	1	0	1	0	2	0	0	0	5
Earvin Johnson, L.A. Lakers *(Selected but did not play due to injury.)*													
TOTALS	240	61-113	2-4	19-23	23	34	57	38	23	16	31	6	143

SCORE BY PERIODS:	1	2	3	4	FINAL
EAST	31	28	37	38	134
WEST	47	40	24	32	143

GAME 38: February 7, 1988

LOCATION	EAST COACH	WEST COACH	MOST VALUABLE PLAYER	OFFICIALS	ATTENDANCE
Chicago	Mike Fratello, Atlanta	Pat Riley, L.A. Lakers	Michael Jordan, Chicago	Darell Garretson and Jake O'Donnell	18,403

East (138)

		FGM-	3PM-		REBOUNDS								
PLAYER	MIN	FGA	3PT	FT	OFF	DEF	TOT	AST	PF	ST	TO	BS	PTS
Larry Bird, Boston	32	2-8	0-0	2-2	0	7	7	1	4	4	2	1	6
Dominique Wilkins, Atlanta	30	12-22	0-0	5-6	1	4	5	0	3	0	0	1	29
Moses Malone, Washington	22	2-6	0-0	3-6	5	4	9	2	2	0	2	0	7
Isiah Thomas, Detroit	28	4-10	0-0	0-0	1	1	2	15	1	1	6	0	8
Michael Jordan, Chicago	29	17-23	0-0	6-6	3	5	8	3	5	4	2	4	40
Patrick Ewing, New York	16	4-8	0-0	1-1	1	5	6	0	1	0	1	1	9
Glenn Rivers, Atlanta	16	2-4	0-0	5-11	0	3	3	6	3	0	3	0	9
Kevin McHale, Boston	14	0-1	0-0	2-2	0	1	1	1	2	0	2	2	2
Charles Barkley, Philadelphia	15	1-4	0-1	2-2	1	2	3	0	2	1	3	1	4
Danny Ainge, Boston	19	4-11	3-4	1-2	1	2	3	2	1	1	1	0	12
Brad Daugherty, Cleveland	15	6-7	0-0	0-0	0	3	3	1	4	0	0	1	12
Maurice Cheeks, Philadelphia	4	0-0	0-0	0-0	0	2	2	1	1	0	0	0	0
TOTALS	240	54-104	3-5	27-38	13	39	52	32	29	11	22	11	138

West (133)

		FGM-	3PM-		REBOUNDS								
PLAYER	MIN	FGA	3PT	FT	OFF	DEF	TOT	AST	PF	ST	TO	BS	PTS
Alex English, Denver	22	5-10	0-0	0-0	2	1	3	4	0	1	0	0	10
Karl Malone, Utah	33	9-19	0-0	4-5	4	6	10	2	4	2	3	0	22
Hakeem Olajuwon, Houston	28	8-13	0-0	5-7	7	2	9	2	3	2	4	2	21
Earvin Johnson, Lakers	39	4-15	0-1	9-9	1	5	6	19	2	2	8	2	17
Lafayette Lever, Denver	31	7-14	0-0	3-4	0	4	4	3	4	0	0	0	17
Mark Aguirre, Dallas	12	5-10	1-3	3-3	0	1	1	1	3	1	3	0	14
Kareem Abdul-Jabbar, Lakers	14	4-9	0-0	2-2	2	2	4	0	3	0	0	0	10
Alvin Robertson, San Antonio	12	1-3	0-0	0-0	0	0	0	1	1	2	2	0	2
Xavier McDaniel, Seattle	13	1-9	0-0	0-0	1	1	2	0	1	0	1	0	2
Clyde Drexler, Portland	15	3-5	0-1	6-6	2	3	5	0	3	1	1	0	12
James Worthy, Lakers	13	2-8	0-0	0-1	1	2	3	1	1	0	0	1	4
James Donaldson, Dallas	8	0-0	0-0	2-2	1	5	6	1	2	0	0	2	2
TOTALS	240	49-115	1-5	34-39	21	32	53	34	27	11	22	7	133

SCORE BY PERIODS:	1	2	3	4	FINAL
WEST	32	22	35	44	133
EAST	27	33	39	39	138

GAME 37: February 8, 1987

LOCATION	EAST COACH	WEST COACH	MOST VALUABLE PLAYER	OFFICIALS	ATTENDANCE
Seattle	K. C. Jones, Boston	Pat Riley, L.A. Lakers	Tom Chambers, Seattle	Jess Kersey and Hue Hollins	34,275

East (149, OT)

		FGM-	3PM-		REBOUNDS								
PLAYER	MIN	FGA	3PT	FT	OFF	DEF	TOT	AST	PF	ST	TO	BS	PTS
Larry Bird, Boston	35	7-18	0-3	4-4	2	4	6	5	5	2	2	0	18
Dominique Wilkins, Atlanta	24	3-9	0-0	4-7	3	2	5	1	2	0	2	1	10
Moses Malone, Washington	35	11-19	0-0	5-6	7	11	18	2	4	2	1	1	27
Julius Erving, Philadelphia	33	9-13	1-1	3-3	3	1	4	5	3	1	2	1	22
Michael Jordan, Chicago	28	5-12	0-1	1-2	0	0	0	4	2	2	5	0	11
Isiah Thomas, Detroit	24	4-6	0-0	8-9	2	1	3	9	3	0	5	0	16
Kevin McHale, Boston	30	7-11	0-0	2-2	4	3	7	2	5	0	0	4	16
Bill Laimbeer, Detroit	11	4-7	0-0	0-0	0	2	2	1	2	1	0	0	8
Jeff Malone, Washington	13	3-5	0-1	0-0	1	1	2	2	1	0	1	0	6
Charles Barkley, Philadelphia	16	2-6	0-2	3-6	1	3	4	1	2	1	0	0	7
Maurice Cheeks, Philadelphia	8	1-2	0-0	2-2	0	0	0	0	1	1	1	0	4
Robert Parish, Boston	8	2-3	0-0	0-0	0	3	3	0	1	0	0	1	4
TOTALS	265	58-111	1-8	32-41	23	31	54	32	31	10	19	8	149

West (154, OT)

		FGM-	3PM-		REBOUNDS								
PLAYER	MIN	FGA	3PT	FT	OFF	DEF	TOT	AST	PF	ST	TO	BS	PTS
Tom Chambers, Seattle	29	13-25	2-3	6-9	3	1	4	2	5	4	3	0	34
James Worthy, Lakers	29	10-14	0-0	2-2	6	2	8	3	3	1	2	0	22
Hakeem Olajuwon, Houston	26	2-6	0-0	6-8	4	9	13	2	6	0	1	3	10
Earvin Johnson, Lakers	34	4-10	0-0	1-2	1	6	7	13	2	4	1	0	9
Alvin Robertson, San Antonio	16	2-5	0-0	2-2	2	0	2	1	1	0	1	0	6
Mark Aguirre, Dallas	17	3-6	1-2	2-3	1	1	2	1	1	0	2	0	9
Kareem Abdul-Jabbar, Lakers	27	4-9	0-0	2-2	2	6	8	3	5	0	1	2	10
Walter Davis, Phoenix	15	3-12	1-1	0-0	2	0	2	1	0	0	0	0	7
Eric Floyd, Golden State	19	4-7	1-3	5-7	2	3	5	1	2	1	2	0	14
Joe Barry Carroll, Golden State	18	1-7	0-0	2-2	4	2	6	0	4	0	1	1	4
Rolando Blackman, Dallas	22	9-15	0-0	11-13	1	3	4	1	2	0	2	0	29
Alex English, Denver	13	0-6	0-0	0-0	0	0	0	1	1	0	2	0	0
Ralph Sampson, Houston *(Selected but did not play due to injury.)*													
TOTALS	265	55-122	5-9	39-50	28	33	61	29	32	10	18	6	154

SCORE BY PERIODS:	1	2	3	4	OT	FINAL
EAST	33	32	42	33	9	149
WEST	29	41	30	40	14	154

GAME 36: February 9, 1986

LOCATION	EAST COACH	WEST COACH	MOST VALUABLE PLAYER	OFFICIALS	ATTENDANCE
Dallas	K. C. Jones, Boston	Pat Riley, L.A. Lakers	Isiah Thomas, Detroit	Joe Crawford and Jack Madden	16,573

East (139)

PLAYER	MIN	FGM-FGA	3PM-3PT	FT	REBOUNDS OFF	REBOUNDS DEF	REBOUNDS TOT	AST	PF	ST	TO	BS	PTS
Julius Erving, Philadelphia	19	4-10	0-0	0-2	1	3	4	2	2	2	2	0	8
Larry Bird, Boston	35	8-18	2-4	5-6	2	6	8	5	5	7	4	0	23
Moses Malone, Philadelphia	34	5-12	0-0	6-9	5	8	13	0	4	1	1	0	16
Sidney Moncrief, Milwaukee	26	4-11	1-1	7-7	3	0	3	1	0	0	0	1	16
Isiah Thomas, Detroit	36	11-19	0-1	8-9	0	1	1	10	2	5	5	0	30
Buck Williams, New Jersey	20	5-8	0-0	3-5	3	4	7	4	0	0	1	0	13
Jeff Malone, Washington	12	3-5	0-0	0-0	0	1	1	4	0	1	0	0	6
Kevin McHale, Boston	20	3-8	0-0	2-2	3	7	10	2	4	0	0	4	8
Maurice Creeks, Philadelphia	14	3-6	0-0	0-0	0	0	0	2	0	2	3	0	6
Robert Parish, Boston	7	0-0	0-0	0-2	0	1	1	0	0	0	1	1	0
Dominique Wilkins, Atlanta	17	6-15	0-0	1-2	2	1	3	2	2	0	1	1	13
Patrick Ewing, New York *(Selected but did not play due to injury.)*													
Michael Jordan, Chicago *(Selected but did not play due to injury.)*													
TOTALS	240	52-112	3-6	32-44	19	32	51	32	19	18	18	7	139

West (132)

PLAYER	MIN	FGM-FGA	3PM-3PT	FT	REBOUNDS OFF	REBOUNDS DEF	REBOUNDS TOT	AST	PF	ST	TO	BS	PTS
James Worthy, Lakers	28	10-19	0-2	0-0	2	1	3	2	3	0	1	2	20
Ralph Sampson, Houston	21	7-11	0-0	2-2	1	3	4	1	4	0	2	0	16
Kareem Abdul-Jabbar, Lakers	32	9-15	0-0	3-4	2	5	7	2	4	2	5	2	21
Alvin Robertson, San Antonio	20	2-6	0-0	0-0	1	8	9	5	1	0	4	0	4
Earvin Johnson, Lakers	28	1-3	0-1	4-4	0	4	4	15	4	1	9	0	6
Rolando Blackman, Dallas	22	6-11	0-0	0-0	1	3	4	8	1	2	1	1	12
Artis Gilmore, San Antonio	13	3-4	0-0	4-4	1	1	2	1	4	2	0	0	10
Alex English, Denver	16	8-12	0-0	0-0	1	0	1	2	0	0	0	1	16
Adrian Dantley, Utah	17	3-8	0-0	2-2	1	6	7	3	1	1	0	0	8
Clyde Drexler, Portland	15	5-7	0-1	0-0	0	4	4	4	3	3	3	1	10
Hakeem Olajuwon, Houston	15	1-8	0-0	1-2	1	4	5	0	3	1	1	2	3
Marques Johnson, Clippers	13	3-6	0-0	0-0	2	1	3	2	3	0	1	0	6
TOTALS	240	58-110	0-4	16-18	13	40	53	45	31	12	27	9	132

SCORE BY PERIODS:	1	2	3	4	FINAL
EAST	34	35	31	39	139
WEST	36	30	36	30	132

GAME 35: February 10, 1985

LOCATION	EAST COACH	WEST COACH	MOST VALUABLE PLAYER	OFFICIALS	ATTENDANCE
Indiana	K. C. Jones, Boston	Pat Riley, L.A. Lakers	Ralph Sampson, Houston	Mike Mathis and Ed T. Rush	43,146

East (129)

PLAYER	MIN	FGM-FGA	3PM-3PT	FT	REBOUNDS OFF	REBOUNDS DEF	REBOUNDS TOT	AST	PF	ST	TO	BS	PTS
Julius Erving, Philadelphia	23	5-15	0-0	2-2	2	2	4	3	3	1	1	0	12
Larry Bird, Boston	31	8-16	0-1	5-6	5	3	8	2	3	0	4	1	21
Moses Malone, Philadelphia	33	2-10	0-0	3-6	5	7	12	1	4	0	3	0	7
Isiah Thomas, Detroit	25	9-14	3-4	1-1	1	1	2	5	2	2	1	0	22
Michael Jordan, Chicago	22	2-9	0-1	3-4	3	3	6	2	4	3	1	1	7
M. R. Richardson, New Jersey	13	2-8	0-2	1-2	2	0	2	1	3	2	2	0	5
Robert Parish, Boston	10	2-5	0-0	0-0	3	3	6	1	0	0	0	0	4
Bernard King, New York	22	6-10	0-0	1-2	4	3	7	1	5	0	1	0	13
Sidney Moncrief, Milwaukee	22	1-5	0-0	6-6	2	3	5	4	1	0	2	0	8
Terry Cummings, Milwaukee	16	7-17	0-0	3-4	4	3	7	0	1	0	0	1	17
Dennis Johnson, Boston	12	3-7	0-0	2-2	1	5	6	3	2	0	1	0	8
Bill Laimbeer, Detroit	11	2-4	0-0	1-2	1	2	3	1	1	0	0	0	5
TOTALS	240	49-120	3-7	28-37	33	35	68	24	29	8	16	3	129

West (140)

PLAYER	MIN	FGM-FGA	3PM-3PT	FT	REBOUNDS OFF	REBOUNDS DEF	REBOUNDS TOT	AST	PF	ST	TO	BS	PTS
Adrian Dantley, Utah	23	2-6	0-0	6-6	0	2	2	1	4	1	2	0	10
Ralph Sampson, Houston	29	10-15	0-0	4-6	3	7	10	1	5	0	1	1	24
Kareem Abdul-Jabbar, Lakers	23	5-10	0-0	1-2	0	6	6	1	5	1	1	1	11
Earvin Johnson, Lakers	31	7-14	0-0	7-8	2	3	5	15	2	1	3	0	21
George Gervin, San Antonio	25	10-12	0-0	3-4	0	3	3	1	2	3	4	1	23
Alex English, Denver	14	0-3	0-0	0-0	1	1	2	1	1	0	2	0	0
Norm Nixon, Clippers	19	5-7	0-0	1-2	0	2	2	8	0	1	1	0	11
Larry Nance, Phoenix	15	7-8	0-0	2-2	1	4	5	0	5	0	2	2	16
Rolando Blackman, Dallas	23	7-14	0-0	1-2	1	2	3	2	1	1	0	1	15
Jack Sikma, Seattle	12	0-2	0-0	0-0	0	2	2	0	1	0	0	1	0
Calvin Natt, Denver	11	1-3	0-0	1-2	0	3	3	1	1	0	1	0	3
Hakeem Olajuwon, Houston	15	2-2	0-0	2-6	2	3	5	1	1	0	0	2	6
TOTALS	240	56-96	0-0	28-40	10	38	48	32	28	8	17	9	140

SCORE BY PERIODS:	1	2	3	4	FINAL
WEST	40	28	29	43	140
EAST	35	33	24	37	129

GAME 34: January 29, 1984

LOCATION	EAST COACH	WEST COACH	MOST VALUABLE PLAYER	OFFICIALS	ATTENDANCE
Denver	K. C. Jones, Boston	Frank Layden, Utah	Isiah Thomas, Detroit	Earl Strom and John Vanak	17,500

East (154, OT)

PLAYER	MIN	FGM-FGA	3PM-3PT	FT	REBOUNDS OFF	REBOUNDS DEF	REBOUNDS TOT	AST	PF	ST	TO	BS	PTS
Julius Erving, Philadelphia	36	14-22	0-0	6-8	4	4	8	5	4	2	1	2	34
Larry Bird, Boston	33	6-18	0-0	4-4	1	6	7	3	1	2	2	0	16
Robert Parish, Boston	28	5-11	0-0	2-4	4	11	15	2	1	3	4	0	12
Sidney Moncrief, Milwaukee	26	3-6	0-0	2-2	1	4	5	2	3	5	4	0	8
Isiah Thomas, Detroit	39	9-17	0-2	3-3	2	3	5	15	4	4	6	0	21
Andrew Toney, Philadelphia	22	3-11	0-0	1-1	0	0	0	3	0	2	0	0	13
Jeff Rutland, Washington	13	2-3	0-0	2-2	1	3	4	2	2	1	2	0	6
Bernard King, New York	22	8-13	0-0	2-5	2	1	3	4	2	0	0	0	18
Otis Birdsong, New Jersey	12	1-5	0-0	0-0	2	1	3	1	1	0	0	0	2
Kevin McHale, Boston	11	3-7	0-0	4-6	2	3	5	0	1	0	2	0	10
Bill Laimbeer, Detroit	17	6-8	0-0	1-1	1	4	5	0	3	1	0	2	13
Kelly Tripucka, Detroit	6	0-0	0-0	1-2	0	0	0	2	1	1	2	0	1
TOTALS	265	63-121	0-2	28-38	20	40	60	39	23	21	23	4	154

West (145, OT)

PLAYER	MIN	FGM-FGA	3PM-3PT	FT	REBOUNDS OFF	REBOUNDS DEF	REBOUNDS TOT	AST	PF	ST	TO	BS	PTS
Alex English, Denver	19	6-8	0-0	1-1	0	0	0	2	2	1	3	1	13
Adrian Dantley, Utah	18	1-8	0-0	0-0	0	2	2	1	4	1	1	0	2
Kareem Abdul-Jabbar, Los Angeles	37	11-19	0-0	3-4	5	8	13	2	5	0	4	1	25
Earvin Johnson, Los Angeles	37	6-13	1-3	2-2	4	5	9	22	3	3	4	2	15
George Gervin, San Antonio	21	5-6	0-0	3-3	0	2	2	1	5	0	6	1	13
Kiki Vandeweghe, Denver	26	7-13	0-0	0-0	1	2	3	1	2	0	0	0	14
Jack Sikma, Seattle	30	5-12	0-0	5-6	5	7	12	1	4	3	2	0	15
Ralph Sampson, Houston	16	4-7	0-0	1-2	1	4	5	0	4	0	3	0	9
Walter Davis, Phoenix	15	5-9	0-0	0-0	0	2	2	1	0	1	0	0	10
Rickey Green, Utah	19	3-8	0-0	0-0	0	0	0	11	1	1	4	0	6
Mark Aguirre, Dallas	13	5-8	0-0	3-4	1	0	1	2	1	1	2	1	13
Jim Paxson, Portland	14	5-9	0-0	0-0	1	2	3	2	0	0	0	0	10
TOTALS	265	63-120	1-3	18-22	18	34	52	46	31	11	29	6	145

SCORE BY PERIODS:	1	2	3	4	OT	FINAL
EAST	32	30	37	33	22	154
WEST	40	36	31	25	13	145

GAME 33: February 13, 1983

LOCATION	EAST COACH	WEST COACH	MOST VALUABLE PLAYER	OFFICIALS	ATTENDANCE
Los Angeles	Billy Cunningham, Philadelphia	Pat Riley, Los Angeles	Julius Erving, Philadelphia	Hugh Evans and Jess Kersey	17,505

East (132)

PLAYER	MIN	FGM-FGA	3PM-3PT	FT	REBOUNDS OFF	REBOUNDS DEF	REBOUNDS TOT	AST	PF	ST	TO	BS	PTS
Larry Bird, Boston	29	7-14	0-1	0-0	3	10	13	7	4	2	5	0	14
Julius Erving, Philadelphia	28	11-19	0-0	3-3	3	3	6	3	1	1	2	2	25
Moses Malone, Philadelphia	24	3-8	0-0	4-6	2	6	8	3	1	0	1	1	10
Maurice Cheeks, Philadelphia	18	3-8	0-0	0-0	0	1	1	1	0	0	0	0	6
Isiah Thomas, Detroit	29	9-14	0-0	1-1	3	1	4	7	0	4	5	0	19
Sidney Moncrief, Milwaukee	28	8-14	0-0	4-5	3	2	5	4	1	6	1	1	20
Marques Johnson, Milwaukee	20	3-10	0-0	1-2	2	0	2	2	1	0	0	1	7
Robert Parish, Boston	18	5-6	0-0	3-4	0	3	3	0	2	1	1	1	13
Andrew Toney, Philadelphia	18	4-5	0-1	0-0	0	1	1	7	3	2	4	0	8
Buck Williams, New Jersey	19	3-4	0-0	2-4	3	4	7	1	0	1	0	0	8
Reggie Theus, Chicago	8	0-5	0-0	0-0	1	0	1	1	1	0	2	0	0
Bill Laimbeer, Detroit	6	1-1	0-0	0-0	1	0	1	0	1	0	1	0	2
TOTALS	240	57-108	0-2	18-25	21	31	52	36	15	17	22	6	132

West (123)

PLAYER	MIN	FGM-FGA	3PM-3PT	FT	REBOUNDS OFF	REBOUNDS DEF	REBOUNDS TOT	AST	PF	ST	TO	BS	PTS
Alex English, Denver	23	7-14	0-0	0-1	2	2	4	0	2	1	1	2	14
Maurice Lucas, Phoenix	27	3-8	0-0	0-1	1	6	7	1	1	0	1	0	6
Kareem Abdul-Jabbar, Los Angeles	32	9-12	0-0	2-3	2	4	6	5	1	1	1	4	20
Earvin Johnson, Los Angeles	33	7-16	0-1	3-4	3	2	5	16	2	5	7	0	17
David Thompson, Seattle	17	5-7	0-0	0-0	0	1	1	2	2	1	3	0	10
George Gervin, San Antonio	14	3-8	1-1	2-2	0	0	0	3	3	2	0	0	9
Jamaal Wilkes, Los Angeles	15	4-6	0-0	2-2	1	1	2	2	0	1	2	0	10
Jack Sikma, Seattle	17	4-6	0-0	0-0	1	2	3	1	2	1	1	1	8
Artis Gilmore, San Antonio	16	2-4	0-0	1-2	1	4	5	1	4	1	1	0	5
Gus Williams, Seattle	15	3-9	0-0	0-0	1	0	1	4	1	1	3	0	6
Jim Paxson, Portland	17	5-7	0-0	1-2	0	0	0	1	0	2	4	0	11
Kiki Vandeweghe, Denver	14	3-4	0-0	1-2	0	3	3	1	0	1	0	0	7
TOTALS	240	55-101	1-2	12-19	12	25	37	37	18	17	24	7	123

SCORE BY PERIODS:	1	2	3	4	FINAL
EAST	42	27	34	29	132
WEST	31	33	26	33	123

GAME 32: January 31, 1982

LOCATION	EAST COACH	WEST COACH	MOST VALUABLE PLAYER	OFFICIALS	ATTENDANCE
New Jersey	Bill Fitch, Boston	Pat Riley, Los Angeles	Larry Bird, Boston	Jake O'Donnell and Wally Rooney	20,149

East (120)

		FGM-	3PM-		REBOUNDS								
PLAYER	MIN	FGA	3PT	FT	OFF	DEF	TOT	AST	PF	ST	TO	BS	PTS
Julius Erving, Philadelphia	32	7-16	0-0	2-4	3	5	8	2	4	1	4	2	16
Larry Bird, Boston	28	7-12	0-0	5-8	0	12	12	5	3	1	4	1	19
Artis Gilmore, Chicago	16	3-6	0-0	1-1	1	2	3	2	4	0	2	1	7
Nate Archibald, Boston	23	2-5	0-0	2-2	1	1	2	7	3	1	2	0	6
Isiah Thomas, Detroit	17	5-7	0-0	2-4	1	0	1	4	1	3	1	0	12
Sidney Moncrief, Milwaukee	22	3-11	0-0	0-2	3	1	4	1	2	1	1	0	6
Bob Lanier, Milwaukee	11	3-7	0-0	2-2	2	1	3	0	3	0	1	1	8
M. Richardson, New York	20	5-10	0-0	0-0	0	2	2	4	1	2	1	0	10
Bobby Jones, Philadelphia	14	2-5	0-0	1-2	1	3	4	1	2	1	0	0	5
Buck Williams, New Jersey	22	2-7	0-0	0-2	1	9	10	1	3	0	3	2	4
Robert Parish, Boston	20	9-12	0-0	3-4	0	7	7	1	2	0	1	2	21
Kelly Tripucka, Detroit	15	3-7	0-0	0-0	0	1	1	2	0	0	1	0	6
Dan Roundfield, Atlanta *(Selected but did not play due to injury.)*													
TOTALS	240	51-105	0-0	18-31	13	44	57	30	28	10	21	9	120

West (118)

		FGM-	3PM-		REBOUNDS								
PLAYER	MIN	FGA	3PT	FT	OFF	DEF	TOT	AST	PF	ST	TO	BS	PTS
Adrian Dantley, Utah	21	66-8	0-0	0-1	1	1	2	0	2	0	1	0	12
Lonnie Shelton, Seattle	20	3-3	0-0	1-2	4	5	9	1	4	1	2	0	7
Kareem Abdul-Jabbar, Los Angeles	22	1-10	0-0	0-0	1	2	3	1	3	0	1	2	2
Gus Williams, Seattle	26	9-19	0-1	4-4	2	0	2	9	1	1	0	0	22
George Gervin, San Antonio	27	5-14	0-0	2-2	1	5	6	1	3	3	0	3	12
Bernard King, Golden State	14	2-7	0-0	2-2	0	4	4	1	2	3	2	1	6
Norm Nixon, Los Angeles	19	7-14	0-0	0-0	0	0	0	2	0	1	0	0	14
Earvin Johnson, Los Angeles	23	5-9	0-0	6-7	3	1	4	7	5	0	1	0	16
Moses Malone, Houston	20	5-11	0-0	2-6	5	6	11	0	2	1	3	1	12
Jack Sikma, Seattle	21	5-11	0-0	0-0	2	7	9	1	2	2	0	1	10
Alex English, Denver	12	2-6	0-0	0-0	2	3	5	1	2	1	1	0	4
Dennis Johnson, Phoenix	15	0-2	0-0	1-2	2	3	5	1	1	0	3	2	1
TOTALS	240	50-114	0-1	18-26	23	37	60	25	27	13	14	10	118

SCORE BY PERIODS:	1	2	3	4	FINAL
WEST	39	22	28	29	118
EAST	34	29	27	30	120

GAME 31: February 1, 1981

LOCATION	EAST COACH	WEST COACH	MOST VALUABLE PLAYER	OFFICIALS	ATTENDANCE
Cleveland	Billy Cunningham, Philadephia	John MacLeod, Phoenix	Nate Archibald, Boston	Paul Mihalak and Darell Garretson	20,239

East (123)

		FGM-							
PLAYER	MIN	FGA	FT	REB	AST	PF	TO	BS	PTS
Larry Bird, Boston	18	1-5	0-0	4	3	1	2	0	2
Julius Erving, Philadelphia	29	6-15	6-7	3	2	2	2	1	18
Artis Gilmore, Chicago	22	5-7	1-2	6	2	4	0	1	11
Eddie Johnson, Atlanta	28	7-12	2-3	2	2	1	3	0	16
Reggie Theus, Chicago	19	4-7	0-0	1	3	0	4	0	8
Nate Archibald, Boston	25	4-7	1-3	5	9	3	2	0	9
Robert Parish, Boston	25	5-18	6-6	10	2	3	1	2	16
Bobby Jones, Philadelphia	16	5-11	1-1	4	0	2	0	1	11
Marques Johnson, Milwaukee	19	1-2	5-6	4	2	2	0	0	7
M. Richardson, New York	24	5-8	1-2	5	3	3	2	0	11
Mike Mitchell, Cleveland	15	6-12	2-2	4	2	2	1	0	14
Dan Roundfield, Atlanta *(Selected but did not play due to injury.)*									
TOTALS	240	49-104	25-32	48	30	23	17	5	123

West (120)

		FGM-							
PLAYER	MIN	FGA	FT	REB	AST	PF	TO	BS	PTS
Walter Davis, Phoenix	22	5-9	2-2	7	1	2	1	0	12
Adrian Dantley, Utah	21	3-9	2-2	5	0	1	0	0	12
Kareem Abdul-Jabbar, Los Angeles	23	6-9	3-3	6	4	3	3	4	15
Paul Westphal, Seattle	25	8-12	3-3	4	3	3	4	0	19
George Gervin, San Antonio	24	5-9	1-2	3	0	3	2	1	11
Jamaal Wilkes, Los Angeles	25	6-12	3-3	8	3	3	2	0	15
Moses Malone, Houston	22	3-8	2-4	6	3	3	1	0	8
Leonard Robinson, Phoenix	21	3-6	0-0	5	2	4	4	0	6
Jack Sikma, Seattle	21	2-6	2-2	4	4	5	2	1	6
Dennis Johnson, Phoenix	24	5-8	9-10	2	1	1	2	0	19
Otis Birdsong, Kansas City	12	0-3	1-2	1	1	0	0	0	1
TOTALS	240	46-91	28-33	51	22	28	21	6	120

SCORE BY PERIODS:	1	2	3	4	FINAL
WEST	27	31	30	32	120
EAST	23	38	36	26	123

GAME 30: February 4, 1980

LOCATION	EAST COACH	WEST COACH	MOST VALUABLE PLAYER	OFFICIALS	ATTENDANCE
Landover, Md.	Billy Cunningham, Philadelphia	Lenny Wilkens, Seattle	George Gervin, San Antonio	Joe Gushue and Ed T. Rush	19,035

East (144, OT)

PLAYER, TEAM	MIN	FGM	FGA	FTM	FTA	REB	AST	PTS
John Drew, Atlanta	15	0	4	4	5	3	0	4
Julius Erving, Philadelphia	20	4	12	3	4	5	2	11
Moses Malone, Houston	31	7	12	6	12	12	2	20
George Gervin, San Antonio	40	14	26	6	9	10	3	34
Eddie Johnson, Atlanta	32	11	16	0	0	1	7	22
Dan Roundfield, Atlanta	27	7	15	4	9	13	0	18
Nate Archibald, Boston	21	0	8	2	3	3	6	2
Elvin Hayes, Washington	29	5	10	2	2	5	4	12
M. Richardson, New York	13	3	7	0	0	1	2	6
Bill Cartwright, New York	14	4	8	0	0	3	1	8
Larry Bird, Boston	23	3	6	0	0	6	7	7
TOTALS	265	58	124	27	44	62	34	144

West (136, OT)

PLAYER, TEAM	MIN	FGM	FGA	FTM	FTA	REB	AST	PTS
Adrian Dantley, Utah	30	8	15	7	8	5	2	23
Marques Johnson, Milwaukee	34	1	6	2	2	4	1	4
Kareem Abdul-Jabbar, Los Angeles	30	6	17	5	6	16	9	17
Lloyd Free, San Diego	21	7	13	0	1	3	5	14
Earvin Johnson, Los Angeles	24	5	8	2	2	2	4	12
Dennis Johnson, Seattle	20	7	13	5	6	4	1	19
Walter Davis, Phoenix	23	5	10	2	2	4	2	12
Jack Sikma, Seattle	28	4	10	0	0	8	4	8
Paul Westphal, Phoenix	27	8	14	5	6	1	5	21
Kermit Washington, Portland	14	1	6	2	4	8	1	4
Otis Birdsong, Kansas City	14	1	2	0	0	0	0	2
TOTALS	265	53	114	30	37	55	34	136

SCORE BY PERIODS:	1	2	3	4	FINAL
WEST	36	44	24	30	134
EAST	27	31	40	31	129

GAME 29: February 4, 1979

LOCATION	EAST COACH	WEST COACH	MOST VALUABLE PLAYER	OFFICIALS	ATTENDANCE
Detroit	Dick Motta, Washington	Lenny Wilkens, Seattle	David Thompson, Denver	John Vanak, Jack Madden, Hugh Evans	31,745

East (129)

PLAYER, TEAM	MIN	FGM	FGA	FTM	FTA	REB	AST	PTS
Julius Erving, Philadelphia	39	10	22	9	12	8	5	29
Rudy Tomjanovich, Houston	24	6	13	0	0	6	1	12
Moses Malone, Houston	17	2	2	4	5	7	1	8
Pete Maravich, New Orleans	14	5	8	0	0	2	2	10
George Gervin, San Antonio	34	8	16	10	11	6	2	26
Bob Dandridge, Washington	18	3	5	2	3	3	1	8
Elvin Hayes, Washington	28	5	11	3	5	13	0	13
Larry Kenon, San Antonio	7	1	3	1	2	2	1	3
Bob Lanier, Detroit	31	5	10	0	0	4	4	10
Calvin Murphy, Houston	15	3	5	0	0	1	5	6
Campy Russell, Cleveland	13	2	8	0	0	1	0	4
Doug Collins, Philadelphia (*Selected but did not play due to injury.*)								
TOTALS	240	50	103	29	38	53	22	129

West (134)

PLAYER, TEAM	MIN	FGM	FGA	FTM	FTA	REB	AST	PTS
Marques Johnson, Milwaukee	20	3	11	4	6	6	2	10
George McGinnis, Denver	25	5	12	6	11	6	3	16
Kareem Abdul-Jabbar, Los Angeles	28	5	12	1	2	8	3	11
David Thompson, Denver	34	11	17	3	7	5	2	25
Paul Westphal, Phoenix	21	8	12	1	2	1	5	17
Otis Birdsong, Kansas City	14	4	6	1	2	2	0	9
Walter Davis, Phoenix	19	4	9	0	0	4	4	8
Artis Gilmore, Chicago	15	3	4	2	2	1	2	8
Dennis Johnson, Seattle	27	5	7	2	2	1	3	12
Maurice Lucas, Portland	19	4	10	2	2	7	1	10
Jack Sikma, Seattle	18	4	5	0	0	4	0	8
TOTALS	240	56	105	22	36	45	25	134

SCORE BY PERIODS:	1	2	3	4	OT	FINAL
WEST	37	27	27	37	8	136
EAST	28	36	44	20	16	144

GAME 28: February 5, 1978

LOCATION	EAST COACH	WEST COACH	MOST VALUABLE PLAYER	OFFICIALS	ATTENDANCE
Atlanta	Billy Cunningham, Philadelphia	Jack Ramsay, Portland	Randy Smith, Buffalo	Jake O'Donnell and Jim Capers	15,491

East (133)

PLAYER, TEAM	MIN	FGM	FGA	FTM	FTA	REB	AST	PTS
Julius Erving, Philadelphia	27	3	14	10	12	8	3	16
Larry Kenon, San Antonio	20	8	15	0	0	4	0	16
Dave Cowens, Boston	28	7	9	0	0	14	5	14
George Gervin, San Antonio	18	4	11	1	3	2	1	9
John Havlicek, Boston	22	5	8	0	0	3	1	10
Doug Collins, Philadelphia	27	3	8	8	11	5	8	14
Truck Robinson, New Orleans	24	3	7	1	2	6	1	7
Bob McAdoo, New York	20	7	14	0	0	4	0	14
Randy Smith, Buffalo	29	11	14	5	6	7	6	27
Elvin Hayes, Washington	11	1	7	0	0	4	0	2
Moses Malone, Houston	14	1	1	2	4	4	1	4
Pete Maravich, New Orleans (*Selected but did not play due to injury.*)								
TOTALS	240	53	108	27	38	61	26	133

West (125)

PLAYER, TEAM	MIN	FGM	FGA	FTM	FTA	REB	AST	PTS
Rick Barry, Golden State	30	7	17	1	1	4	5	15
Maurice Lucas, Portland	33	6	13	0	0	13	4	12
Bill Walton, Portland	31	6	14	3	3	10	2	15
David Thompson, Denver	35	10	16	2	4	3	3	22
Paul Westphal, Phoenix	24	9	14	2	5	0	5	20
Walter Davis, Phoenix	15	3	6	4	4	1	6	10
Artis Gilmore, Chicago	13	2	4	6	8	2	0	10
Lionel Hollins, Portland	23	3	8	4	5	0	8	10
Bobby Jones, Denver	18	1	3	0	0	6	2	2
Brian Winters, Milwaukee	14	4	7	0	0	4	1	8
Bob Lanier, Detroit	4	0	0	1	2	2	0	1
TOTALS	240	51	102	23	32	45	36	125

SCORE BY PERIODS:	1	2	3	4	FINAL
WEST	23	35	39	28	125
EAST	34	34	21	35	124

GAME 27: February 13, 1977

LOCATION	EAST COACH	WEST COACH	MOST VALUABLE PLAYER	OFFICIALS	ATTENDANCE
Milwaukee	Gene Shue, Philadelphia	Larry Brown, Denver	Julius Erving, Philadelphia	Earl Strom and Lee Jones	10,938

East (124)

PLAYER, TEAM	MIN	FGM	FGA	FTM	FTA	REB	AST	PTS
Julius Erving, Philadelphia	30	12	20	6	6	12	3	30
George McGinnis, Philadelphia	26	2	9	0	2	7	2	4
Bob McAdoo, Buffalo	38	13	23	4	4	10	2	30
Doug Collins, Philadelphia	21	3	6	2	2	2	6	8
Pete Maravich, New Orleans	21	5	13	0	0	0	4	10
John Havlicek, Boston	17	2	5	0	0	1	1	4
Earl Monroe, N.Y. Knicks	15	2	7	0	0	0	3	4
Jo Jo White, Boston	15	5	7	0	0	1	2	10
Elvin Hayes, Washington	11	6	6	0	0	2	1	12
Rudy Tomjanovich, Houston	22	3	9	0	0	10	1	6
Phil Chenier, Washington	12	3	6	0	0	1	1	6
George Gervin, San Antonio	12	0	6	0	0	1	0	0
Dave Cowens, Boston (*Selected but did not play due to injury.*)								
TOTALS	240	56	117	12	14	47	26	124

West (125)

PLAYER, TEAM	MIN	FGM	FGA	FTM	FTA	REB	AST	PTS
Bobby Jones, Denver	14	1	4	0	0	0	3	2
David Thompson, Denver	29	7	9	4	6	7	3	18
Dan Issel, Denver	10	0	3	0	0	1	0	0
Paul Westphal, Phoenix	31	10	16	0	0	1	6	20
Norm Van Lier, Chicago	14	1	3	0	0	1	1	2
Kareem Abdul-Jabbar, Los Angeles	23	8	14	5	6	4	2	21
Rick Barry, Golden State	29	7	16	4	4	4	8	18
Phil Smith, Golden State	28	6	13	1	2	6	8	13
Don Buse, Indiana	19	2	4	0	0	2	5	4
Billy Knight, Indiana	12	1	5	2	2	5	0	4
Bob Lanier, Detroit	20	7	8	3	3	10	4	17
Maurice Lucas, Portland	11	3	9	0	0	4	2	6
Bill Walton, Portland (*Selected but did not play due to injury.*)								
TOTALS	240	53	104	19	23	45	42	125

SCORE BY PERIODS:	1	2	3	4	FINAL
EAST	34	34	21	35	124
WEST	23	35	39	22	125

GAME 26: February 3, 1976

LOCATION	EAST COACH	WEST COACH	MOST VALUABLE PLAYER	OFFICIALS	ATTENDANCE
Philadelphia	Tom Heinsohn, Boston	Al Attles, Golden State	Dave Bing, Washington	Paul Mihalak and Darell Garretson	17,511

East (123)

PLAYER, TEAM	MIN	FGM	FGA	FTM	FTA	REB	AST	PTS
John Havlicek, Boston	21	3	10	3	3	2	2	9
Elvin Hayes, Washington	31	6	14	0	2	10	1	12
Bob McAdoo, Buffalo	29	10	14	2	4	7	1	22
Walt Frazier, New York	19	2	7	4	4	2	3	8
Dave Bing, Washington	26	7	11	2	2	3	4	16
Dave Cowens, Boston	23	6	13	4	5	16	1	16
George McGinnis, Philadelphia	19	4	9	2	4	7	2	10
Rudy Tomjanovich, Houston	12	1	2	0	0	3	0	2
John Drew, Atlanta	9	1	3	0	0	3	0	2
Jo Jo White, Boston	16	3	7	0	0	1	1	6
Doug Collins, Philadelphia	20	5	10	2	2	6	3	12
Randy Smith, Buffalo	15	4	7	0	0	1	3	8
TOTALS	240	52	107	19	26	61	21	123

West (109)

PLAYER, TEAM	MIN	FGM	FGA	FTM	FTA	REB	AST	PTS
Rick Barry, Golden State	28	6	15	5	5	4	2	17
Bob Dandridge, Milwaukee	27	5	10	0	0	6	0	10
Kareem Abdul-Jabbar, Los Angeles	36	9	16	4	4	15	3	22
Nate Archibald, Kansas City	30	5	13	3	3	5	7	13
Brian Winters, Milwaukee	16	1	5	0	0	2	1	2
Alvan Adams, Phoenix	11	2	4	0	0	3	0	4
Jamaal Wilkes, Golden State	14	3	9	2	2	4	2	8
Curtis Rowe, Detroit	8	0	2	1	2	2	0	1
Scott Wedman, Kansas City	20	4	5	0	0	6	2	8
Norm Van Lier, Chicago	14	1	4	1	2	1	0	3
Fred Brown, Seattle	24	7	13	0	0	0	1	14
Phil Smith, Golden State	12	3	7	1	4	1	0	7
TOTALS	240	46	103	17	22	49	18	109

SCORE BY PERIODS:	1	2	3	4	FINAL
WEST	23	27	30	29	109
EAST	28	17	38	40	123

GAME 25: January 14, 1975

LOCATION	EAST COACH	WEST COACH	MOST VALUABLE PLAYER	OFFICIALS	ATTENDANCE
Phoenix	K.C. Jones, Washington	Al Attles, Golden State	Walt Frazier, New York	Mendy Rudolph and Jerry Loeber	12,885

East (108)

PLAYER, TEAM	MIN	FGM	FGA	FTM	FTA	REB	AST	PTS
John Havlicek, Boston	31	7	12	2	2	6	1	16
Elvin Hayes, Washington	17	2	6	0	0	5	2	4
Bob McAdoo, Buffalo	26	4	9	3	3	6	2	11
Walt Frazier, New York	35	10	17	10	11	5	2	30
Earl Monroe, New York	25	3	8	3	5	3	2	9
Rudy Tomjanovich, Houston	14	0	3	0	0	3	0	0
Wes Unseld, Washington	15	2	3	2	2	6	1	6
Phil Chenier, Washington	23	4	8	1	2	2	1	9
Dave Cowens, Boston	15	3	7	0	0	6	3	6
Steve Mix, Philadelphia	11	2	5	0	0	2	0	4
Jo Jo White, Boston	13	1	2	5	6	1	4	7
Paul Silas, Boston	15	2	4	2	2	2	2	6
TOTALS	240	40	84	28	33	47	20	108

West (102)

PLAYER, TEAM	MIN	FGM	FGA	FTM	FTA	REB	AST	PTS
Rick Barry, Golden State	38	11	20	0	0	5	8	22
Spencer Haywood, Seattle	17	1	9	0	0	3	0	2
Kareem Abdul-Jabbar, Milwaukee	19	3	10	1	2	10	3	7
Nate Archibald, K.C.-Omaha	36	10	15	7	8	2	6	27
Gail Goodrich, Los Angeles	15	2	4	0	0	1	4	4
Sidney Wicks, Portland	23	7	19	2	3	9	1	16
Bob Lanier, Detroit	12	1	4	0	0	7	2	2
Charlie Scott, Phoenix	16	1	6	0	0	2	1	2
Dave Bing, Detroit	12	0	2	2	2	0	1	2
Bob Dandridge, Milwaukee	18	2	6	0	0	2	1	4
Sam Lacey, K.C.-Omaha	17	2	6	2	2	7	1	6
Jim Price, Milwaukee	17	3	9	2	2	2	0	8
TOTALS	240	43	110	16	19	50	28	102

SCORE BY PERIODS:	1	2	3	4	FINAL
EAST	29	22	32	25	108
WEST	29	17	27	29	102

GAME 24: January 15, 1974

LOCATION	EAST COACH	WEST COACH	MOST VALUABLE PLAYER	OFFICIALS	ATTENDANCE
Seattle	Tom Heinsohn, Boston	Larry Costello, Milwaukee	Bob Lanier, Detroit	Don Murphy and Bob Rakel	14,360

East (123)

PLAYER, TEAM	MIN	FGM	FGA	FTM	FTA	REB	AST	PTS
John Havlicek, Boston	18	5	10	0	2	0	2	10
Lou Hudson, Atlanta	17	5	8	2	2	3	1	12
Dave Cowens, Boston	26	5	10	1	3	12	1	11
Walt Frazier, New York	28	5	12	2	2	2	5	12
Pete Maravich, Atlanta	22	4	15	7	9	3	4	15
Elvin Hayes, Capital	35	5	13	2	3	15	6	12
Bob McAdoo, Buffalo	13	3	4	5	8	3	1	11
Jo Jo White, Boston	22	6	12	1	3	6	4	13
Dave DeBusschere, New York	24	8	14	0	0	3	3	16
Phil Chenier, Capital	13	3	6	1	2	2	1	7
Rudy Tomjanovich, Houston	17	2	5	0	0	5	0	4
Austin Carr, Cleveland	5	0	4	0	0	1	0	0
TOTALS	240	51	113	21	34	55	28	123

West (134)

PLAYER, TEAM	MIN	FGM	FGA	FTM	FTA	REB	AST	PTS
Rick Barry, Golden State	19	3	6	2	2	4	3	8
Chet Walker, Chicago	14	4	5	4	4	2	1	12
Kareem Abdul-Jabbar, Milwaukee	23	7	11	0	0	8	6	14
Gail Goodrich, Los Angeles	26	9	16	0	0	4	6	18
Geoff Petrie, Portland	26	3	11	2	2	2	4	8
Sidney Wicks, Portland	24	5	6	6	10	1	1	16
Charlie Scott, Phoenix	19	0	4	2	2	1	4	2
Bob Lanier, Detroit	26	11	15	2	2	10	2	24
Spencer Haywood, Seattle	33	10	17	3	3	11	5	23
Dave Bing, Detroit	16	2	9	1	1	6	2	5
Norm Van Lier, Chicago	9	0	0	0	0	1	2	0
Nate Thurmond, Golden State	5	2	4	0	1	3	0	4
TOTALS	240	56	104	22	27	53	36	134

SCORE BY PERIODS:	1	2	3	4	FINAL
EAST	29	18	38	38	123
WEST	39	27	35	33	134

GAME 23: January 23, 1973

LOCATION	EAST COACH	WEST COACH	MOST VALUABLE PLAYER	OFFICIALS	ATTENDANCE
Chicago	Tom Heinsohn, Boston	Bill Sharman, Los Angeles	Dave Cowens, Boston	Richie Powers and Jake O'Donnell	17,527

East (104)

PLAYER, TEAM	MIN	FGM	FGA	FTM	FTA	REB	AST	PTS
John Havlicek, Boston	22	6	10	2	5	3	5	14
Dave DeBusschere, New York	25	4	8	1	2	7	2	9
Dave Cowens, Boston	30	7	15	1	1	13	1	15
Pete Maravich, Atlanta	22	4	8	0	0	3	5	8
Walt Frazier, New York	26	5	15	0	0	6	2	10
Elvin Hayes, Baltimore	16	4	13	2	2	12	0	10
Lou Hudson, Atlanta	9	2	8	2	2	2	0	6
Bob Kauffman, Buffalo	9	1	2	1	2	1	1	3
John Block, Philadelphia	5	2	4	0	0	2	0	4
Bill Bradley, New York	12	2	5	0	0	1	0	4
Jack Marin, Houston	11	2	6	0	0	4	1	4
Wes Unseld, Baltimore	11	2	4	0	0	5	1	4
Jo Jo White, Boston	18	3	7	0	0	5	5	6
Lenny Wilkens, Cleveland	24	3	8	1	2	2	1	7
TOTALS	240	47	113	10	16	66	24	104

West (84)

PLAYER, TEAM	MIN	FGM	FGA	FTM	FTA	REB	AST	PTS
Spencer Haywood, Seattle	22	5	10	2	2	10	0	12
Sidney Wicks, Portland	24	4	10	5	5	5	1	13
Wilt Chamberlain, Los Angeles	22	1	2	0	0	7	3	2
Nate Archibald, K.C.-Omaha	27	6	12	5	5	1	5	17
Jerry West, Los Angeles	20	3	6	0	0	4	3	6
Dave Bing, Detroit	19	0	4	2	2	3	0	2
Bob Lanier, Detroit	12	5	9	0	0	6	0	10
Bob Love, Chicago	12	2	4	2	2	3	0	6
Charlie Scott, Phoenix	14	0	5	0	0	2	2	0
Nate Thurmond, Golden State	14	2	5	0	0	4	1	4
Chet Walker, Chicago	16	1	5	2	2	1	0	4
Bob Dandridge, Milwaukee	11	2	4	0	0	3	0	4
Gail Goodrich, Los Angeles	16	1	7	0	0	2	1	2
Connie Hawkins, Phoenix	11	1	5	0	0	2	3	2
Kareem Abdul-Jabbar, Milwaukee *(Selected but did not play due to injury.)*								
Rick Barry, Golden State *(Selected but did not play due to injury.)*								
TOTALS	240	33	88	18	18	53	19	84

SCORE BY PERIODS:	1	2	3	4	FINAL
WEST	27	18	20	19	84
EAST	27	23	26	28	104

GAME 22: January 18, 1972

LOCATION	EAST COACH	WEST COACH	MOST VALUABLE PLAYER	OFFICIALS	ATTENDANCE
Los Angeles	Tom Heinsohn, Boston	Bill Sharman, Los Angeles	Jerry West, Los Angeles	Darell Garretson and Manny Sokol	17,214

East (110)

PLAYER, TEAM	MIN	FGM	FGA	FTM	FTA	REB	AST	PTS
John Havlicek, Boston	24	5	13	5	5	3	5	15
Billy Cunningham, Philadelphia	24	4	13	6	8	10	3	14
Dave Cowens, Boston	32	5	12	4	5	20	1	14
Lou Hudson, Atlanta	18	2	7	2	2	3	3	6
Walt Frazier, New York	25	7	11	1	2	3	5	15
John Johnson, Cleveland	3	0	2	0	0	1	0	0
Bob Kauffman, Buffalo	7	1	1	0	0	1	1	2
Jack Marin, Baltimore	15	5	8	1	1	0	1	11
Wes Unseld, Baltimore	16	1	5	0	0	7	1	2
Tom Van Arsdale, Cincinnati	4	0	1	0	0	1	0	0
Jo Jo White, Boston	18	6	15	0	2	4	3	12
Butch Beard, Cleveland	7	1	4	1	1	1	0	3
Archie Clark, Baltimore	21	2	5	4	4	1	6	8
Dave DeBusschere, New York	26	4	8	0	0	11	0	8
TOTALS	240	43	105	24	30	66	26	110

West (112)

PLAYER, TEAM	MIN	FGM	FGA	FTM	FTA	REB	AST	PTS
Bob Love, Chicago	16	4	11	0	2	6	0	8
Spencer Haywood, Seattle	25	4	10	3	4	7	1	11
Kareem Abdul-Jabbar, Milwaukee	19	5	10	2	2	7	2	12
Gail Goodrich, Los Angeles	14	2	7	0	0	1	2	4
Jerry West, Los Angeles	27	6	9	1	2	6	5	13
Oscar Robertson, Milwaukee	24	3	9	5	10	3	3	11
Cazzie Russell, Golden State	20	4	13	2	2	1	0	10
Paul Silas, Phoenix	15	0	6	2	3	9	1	2
Jimmy Walker, Detroit	16	4	9	2	5	2	1	10
Connie Hawkins, Phoenix	14	5	7	3	4	4	0	13
Elvin Hayes, Houston	11	1	6	2	2	2	0	4
Wilt Chamberlain, Los Angeles	24	3	3	2	8	10	3	8
Bob Lanier, Detroit	5	0	2	2	3	3	0	2
Sidney Wicks, Portland	10	2	5	0	0	2	0	4
TOTALS	240	43	107	26	47	63	18	112

SCORE BY PERIODS:	1	2	3	4	FINAL
EAST	33	31	20	26	110
WEST	27	27	33	25	112

GAME 21: January 12, 1971

LOCATION	EAST COACH	WEST COACH	MOST VALUABLE PLAYER	OFFICIALS	ATTENDANCE
San Diego	Red Holzman, New York	Larry Costello, Milwaukee	Lenny Wilkens, Seattle	Mendy Rudolph and Ed T. Rush	14,378

East (107)

PLAYER, TEAM	MIN	FGM	FGA	FTM	FTA	REB	AST	PTS
Billy Cunningham, Philadelphia	19	2	8	1	2	4	3	5
John Havlicek, Boston	24	6	12	0	2	3	2	12
Willis Reed, New York	27	5	16	4	6	13	1	14
Earl Monroe, Baltimore	18	3	9	0	0	5	2	6
Walt Frazier, New York	26	3	9	0	0	6	5	6
Johnny Green, Cincinnati	7	2	3	0	1	2	0	4
Dave DeBusschere, New York	19	4	7	0	0	7	3	8
Lou Hudson, Atlanta	17	6	13	2	3	3	1	14
Gus Johnson, Baltimore	23	5	12	2	2	4	2	12
John Johnson, Cleveland	2	0	0	0	0	0	1	0
Bob Kauffman, Buffalo	4	0	2	0	0	0	0	0
Wes Unseld, Baltimore	21	4	9	0	0	10	2	8
Tom Van Arsdale, Cincinnati	11	4	8	0	2	2	1	8
Jo Jo White, Boston	22	5	10	0	0	9	2	10
Totals	240	49	118	9	18	68	25	107

West (108)

PLAYER, TEAM	MIN	FGM	FGA	FTM	FTA	REB	AST	PTS
Connie Hawkins, Phoenix	1	0	0	0	0	0	0	0
Jerry Lucas, San Francisco	29	5	9	2	2	9	4	12
Kareem Abdul-Jabbar, Milwaukee	30	8	16	3	4	14	1	19
Dave Bing, Detroit	19	2	7	0	0	2	2	4
Jerry West, Los Angeles	20	2	4	1	3	1	9	5
Elvin Hayes, San Diego	19	4	13	2	3	4	2	10
Bob Love, Chicago	21	6	12	4	5	4	0	16
Wilt Chamberlain, Los Angeles	18	1	1	0	0	8	5	2
Jeff Mullins, San Francisco	3	0	0	0	0	0	0	0
Geoff Petrie, Portland	5	0	3	0	0	0	1	0
Oscar Robertson, Milwaukee	24	2	6	1	3	2	2	5
Dick Van Arsdale, Phoenix	12	2	4	0	1	5	3	4
Chet Walker, Chicago	19	3	9	4	5	3	1	10
Lenny Wilkens, Seattle	20	8	11	5	5	1	1	21
TOTALS	240	43	95	22	31	53	31	108

SCORE BY PERIODS:	1	2	3	4	FINAL
EAST	26	34	23	24	107
WEST	30	32	20	26	108

GAME 20: January 20, 1970

LOCATION	EAST COACH	WEST COACH	MOST VALUABLE PLAYER	OFFICIALS	ATTENDANCE
Philadelphia	Red Holzman, New York	Richie Guerin, Atlanta	Willis Reed, New York	Richie Powers and Jack Madden	15,244

East (142)

PLAYER, TEAM	MIN	FGM	FGA	FTM	FTA	REB	AST	PTS
Billy Cunningham, Philadelphia	28	7	13	5	5	4	2	19
John Havlicek, Boston	29	7	15	3	3	5	7	17
Willis Reed, New York	30	9	18	3	3	11	0	21
Oscar Robertson, Cincinnati	29	9	11	3	4	6	4	21
Walt Frazier, New York	24	3	7	1	2	3	4	7
Hal Greer, Philadelphia	21	7	11	1	1	4	3	15
Dave DeBusschere, New York	14	5	10	0	0	7	2	10
Kareem Abdul-Jabbar, Milwaukee	18	4	8	2	2	11	4	10
Gus Johnson, Baltimore	17	5	12	0	0	7	1	10
Tom Van Arsdale, Cincinnati	8	2	7	1	1	0	1	5
Jimmy Walker, Detroit	14	0	3	1	1	1	0	1
Flynn Robinson, Milwaukee	8	3	4	0	0	1	2	6
TOTALS	240	61	119	20	22	60	30	142

West (135)

PLAYER, TEAM	MIN	FGM	FGA	FTM	FTA	REB	AST	PTS
Elgin Baylor, Los Angeles	26	2	9	5	7	7	3	9
Connie Hawkins, Phoenix	19	2	4	6	6	4	2	10
Elvin Hayes, San Diego	35	9	21	6	12	15	1	24
Lou Hudson, Atlanta	18	5	12	5	5	1	0	15
Jerry West, Los Angeles	31	7	12	8	12	5	5	22
Jeff Mullins, San Francisco	14	4	6	0	0	1	1	8
Bob Rule, Seattle	13	2	6	1	1	4	0	5
Joe Caldwell, Atlanta	19	5	11	3	4	7	1	13
Chet Walker, Chicago	17	1	3	2	2	2	1	4
Bill Bridges, Atlanta	15	2	2	1	5	4	2	5
Dick Van Arsdale, Phoenix	16	4	8	0	0	2	2	8
Lenny Wilkens, Seattle	17	5	7	2	3	2	4	12
Nate Thurmond, San Francisco (*Selected but did not play due to injury.*)								
TOTALS	240	48	101	39	57	54	22	135

SCORE BY PERIODS:	1	2	3	4	FINAL
WEST	21	38	26	50	135
EAST	36	35	35	36	142

GAME 19: January 14, 1969

LOCATION	EAST COACH	WEST COACH	MOST VALUABLE PLAYER	OFFICIALS	ATTENDANCE
Baltimore	Gene Shue, Baltimore	Richie Guerin, Atlanta	Oscar Robertson, Cincinnati	Joe Gushue and Norm Drucker	12,348

East (123)

PLAYER, TEAM	MIN	FGM	FGA	FTM	FTA	REB	AST	PTS
John Havlicek, Boston	31	6	14	2	2	7	2	14
Jerry Lucas, Cincinnati	17	2	5	4	5	6	1	8
Bill Russell, Boston	28	1	4	1	2	6	3	3
Oscar Robertson, Cincinnati	32	8	16	8	8	6	5	24
Earl Monroe, Baltimore	27	6	15	9	12	4	4	21
Gus Johnson, Baltimore	18	4	10	5	8	10	0	13
Dave Bing, Detroit	13	1	3	1	1	0	3	3
Billy Cunningham, Philadelphia	22	5	10	0	0	5	1	10
Willis Reed, New York	14	5	8	0	0	4	2	10
Wes Unseld, Baltimore	14	5	7	1	3	8	1	11
Hal Greer, Philadelphia	17	0	1	4	5	3	2	4
Jon McGlocklin, Milwaukee	7	1	2	0	0	1	0	2
TOTALS	240	44	95	35	46	60	24	123

West (112)

PLAYER, TEAM	MIN	FGM	FGA	FTM	FTA	REB	AST	PTS
Elgin Baylor, Los Angeles	32	5	13	11	12	9	5	21
Don Kojis, San Diego	16	2	7	4	5	5	3	8
Elvin Hayes, San Diego	21	4	9	3	3	5	0	11
Jerry Sloan, Chicago	18	2	8	0	1	3	0	4
Len Wilkens, Seattle	24	3	15	4	5	7	5	10
Jeff Mullins, San Francisco	25	7	14	0	0	4	5	14
Wilt Chamberlain, Los Angeles	27	2	3	0	1	12	2	4
Rudy LaRusso, San Francisco	18	3	6	0	0	6	2	6
Dick Van Arsdale, Phoenix	10	2	4	0	0	1	0	4
Lou Hudson, Atlanta	20	6	13	1	1	1	1	13
Joe Caldwell, Atlanta	23	6	9	0	1	4	3	12
Gail Goodrich, Phoenix	6	2	4	1	2	1	1	5
Jerry West, Los Angeles (*Selected but did not play due to injury.*)								
TOTALS	240	44	105	24	31	58	27	112

SCORE BY PERIODS:	1	2	3	4	FINAL
WEST	19	34	30	29	112
EAST	35	25	26	37	123

GAME 18: January 23, 1968

LOCATION	EAST COACH	WEST COACH	MOST VALUABLE PLAYER	OFFICIALS	ATTENDANCE
New York	Alex Hannum, Philadelphia	Bill Sharman, Los Angeles	Hal Greer, Philadelphia	Mendy Rudolph and Don Murphy	18,422

East (144)

PLAYER, TEAM	MIN	FGM	FGA	FTM	FTA	REB	AST	PTS
Jerry Lucas, Cincinnati	21	6	9	4	4	5	4	16
Willis Reed, New York	25	7	14	2	3	8	1	16
Wilt Chamberlain, Philadelphia	25	3	4	1	4	7	6	7
Dave Bing, Detroit	20	4	7	1	1	2	4	9
Oscar Robertson, Cincinnati	22	7	9	4	7	1	5	18
Dick Barnett, New York	22	7	12	1	2	1	0	15
Dave DeBusschere, Detroit	12	0	3	0	0	4	0	0
John Havlicek, Boston	22	9	15	8	11	5	4	26
Bill Russell, Boston	23	2	4	0	0	9	8	4
Gus Johnson, Baltimore	16	3	9	1	2	6	1	7
Sam Jones, Boston	15	2	5	1	1	2	4	5
Hal Greer, Philadelphia	17	8	8	5	7	3	3	21
TOTALS	240	58	99	28	42	53	40	144

West (124)

PLAYER, TEAM	MIN	FGM	FGA	FTM	FTA	REB	AST	PTS
Bob Boozer, Chicago	19	2	5	0	0	5	0	4
Elgin Baylor, Los Angeles	27	8	13	6	7	6	1	22
Zelmo Beaty, St. Louis	30	2	11	2	2	10	1	6
Len Wilkens, St. Louis	22	4	10	6	8	3	3	14
Jerry West, Los Angeles	32	7	17	3	4	6	6	17
Bill Bridges, St. Louis	21	7	9	1	4	7	1	15
Rudy LaRusso, San Francisco	19	3	8	0	2	7	0	6
Don Kojis, San Diego	10	2	5	0	0	2	1	4
Archie Clark, Los Angeles	15	5	8	7	7	0	3	17
Clyde Lee, San Francisco	18	2	8	2	4	11	2	6
Walt Hazzard, Seattle	20	4	12	1	1	3	3	9
Jim King, San Francisco	7	1	4	2	3	1	2	4
Nate Thurmond (*Selected but did not play due to injury.*)								
TOTALS	240	47	110	30	42	61	23	124

SCORE BY PERIODS:	1	2	3	4	FINAL
WEST	25	34	32	33	124
EAST	37	27	37	43	144

GAME 17: January 10, 1967

LOCATION	EAST COACH	WEST COACH	MOST VALUABLE PLAYER	OFFICIALS	ATTENDANCE
San Francisco	Red Auerbach, Boston	Fred Schaus, Los Angeles	Rick Barry, San Francisco	Willie Smith and Earl Strom	13,972

East (120)

PLAYER, TEAM	MIN	FGM	FGA	FTM	FTA	REB	AST	PTS
Bailey Howell, Boston	14	1	4	2	2	2	1	4
Willis Reed, New York	17	2	6	0	0	9	1	4
Wilt Chamberlain, Philadelphia	39	6	7	2	5	22	4	14
Oscar Robertson, Cincinnati	34	9	20	8	10	2	5	26
Hal Greer, Philadelphia	31	5	16	7	8	4	1	17
John Havlicek, Boston	17	7	14	0	0	2	1	14
Don Ohl, Baltimore	22	5	13	7	7	1	2	17
Bill Russell, Boston	22	1	2	0	0	5	5	2
Chet Walker, Philadelphia	22	6	9	3	4	4	2	15
Jerry Lucas, Cincinnati	22	3	5	1	1	7	2	7
TOTALS	240	45	96	30	37	58	24	120

West (135)

PLAYER, TEAM	MIN	FGM	FGA	FTM	FTA	REB	AST	PTS
Rick Barry, San Francisco	34	16	27	6	8	6	3	38
Elgin Baylor, Los Angeles	20	8	14	4	4	5	5	20
Nate Thurmond, San Francisco	42	7	16	2	4	18	0	16
Guy Rodgers, Chicago	28	0	4	1	1	2	8	1
Jerry West, Los Angeles	30	6	11	4	4	3	6	16
Darrall Imhoff, Los Angeles	6	0	7	0	0	7	1	0
Jerry Sloan, Chicago	22	4	9	0	0	4	4	8
Dave DeBusschere, Detroit	25	11	17	0	0	6	0	22
Bill Bridges, St. Louis	17	4	5	0	2	3	3	8
Len Wilkens, St. Louis	16	2	6	2	3	2	6	6
TOTALS	240	58	116	19	26	56	36	135

SCORE BY PERIODS:	1	2	3	4	FINAL
EAST	33	34	28	35	120
WEST	39	38	27	31	135

GAME 16: January 11, 1966

LOCATION	EAST COACH	WEST COACH	MOST VALUABLE PLAYER	OFFICIALS	ATTENDANCE
Cincinnati	Red Auerbach, Boston	Fred Schaus, Los Angeles	Adrian Smith, Cincinnati	Norm Drucker and John Vanak	13,653

East (137)

PLAYER, TEAM	MIN	FGM	FGA	FTM	FTA	REB	AST	PTS
Jerry Lucas, Cincinnati	23	4	11	2	2	19	0	10
John Havlicek, Boston	25	6	16	6	6	6	1	18
Wilt Chamberlain, Philadelphia	25	8	11	5	9	9	3	21
Oscar Robertson, Cincinnati	25	6	12	5	6	10	8	17
Sam Jones, Boston	22	5	11	2	2	2	5	12
Chet Walker, Philadelphia	25	3	10	2	3	6	4	8
Willis Reed, New York	23	7	11	2	2	8	1	16
Bill Russell, Boston	23	1	6	0	0	10	2	2
Hal Greer, Philadelphia	23	4	13	1	1	5	1	9
Adrian Smith, Cincinnati	26	9	18	6	6	8	3	24
TOTALS	240	53	118	31	37	83	28	137

West (94)

PLAYER, TEAM	MIN	FGM	FGA	FTM	FTA	REB	AST	PTS
Rick Barry, San Francisco	17	4	10	2	4	2	2	10
Bailey Howell, Baltimore	26	3	11	1	2	2	2	7
Nate Thurmond, San Francisco	33	3	16	1	3	16	1	7
Guy Rodgers, San Francisco	34	3	11	0	0	7	11	8
Jerry West, Los Angeles	11	1	5	2	2	1	0	4
Dave DeBusschere, Detroit	22	1	14	2	2	6	1	4
Eddie Miles, Detroit	28	8	16	1	5	1	0	17
Zelmo Beaty, St. Louis	24	0	11	10	13	18	1	10
Rudy LaRusso, Los Angeles	22	4	10	3	7	3	2	11
Don Ohl, Baltimore	23	7	16	2	3	4	2	16
TOTALS	240	35	120	24	41	60	22	94

SCORE BY PERIODS:	1	2	3	4	FINAL
WEST	18	18	32	26	94
EAST	33	30	38	36	137

GAME 15: January 13, 1965

LOCATION	EAST COACH	WEST COACH	MOST VALUABLE PLAYER	OFFICIALS	ATTENDANCE
St. Louis	Red Auerbach, Boston	Alex Hannum, San Francisco	Jerry Lucas,Cincinnati	Mendy Rudolph and Joe Gushue	16,713

East (124)

PLAYER, TEAM	MIN	FGM	FGA	FTM	FTA	REB	AST	PTS
Jerry Lucas, Cincinnati	35	12	19	1	1	10	1	25
Lucious Jackson, Philadelphia	15	2	5	1	2	1	1	5
Bill Russell, Boston	33	7	12	3	9	13	5	17
Sam Jones, Boston	24	2	12	2	2	5	3	6
Oscar Robertson, Cincinnati	40	8	18	12	13	6	8	28
Wayne Embry, Cincinnati	19	5	10	1	1	4	0	11
John Green, New York	17	3	4	2	3	0	0	8
Willis Reed, New York	25	3	11	1	2	5	1	7
Hal Greer, Philadelphia	21	5	11	3	4	4	1	13
Larry Costello, Philadelphia	11	2	7	0	0	1	2	4
Tom Heinsohn, Boston (*Selected but did not play due to injury.*)								
Totals	240	49	109	26	37	49	22	124

West (123)

PLAYER, TEAM	MIN	FGM	FGA	FTM	FTA	REB	AST	PTS
Elgin Baylor, Los Angeles	27	5	13	8	8	7	0	18
Bob Pettit, St. Louis	34	5	14	3	5	12	0	13
Wilt Chamberlain, San Francisco	31	9	15	2	8	16	1	20
Len Wilkens, St. Louis	20	2	6	4	4	3	3	8
Jerry West, Los Angeles	40	8	16	4	6	5	6	20
Nate Thurmond, San Francisco	10	0	2	0	0	3	0	0
Walt Bellamy, Baltimore	17	4	5	4	4	5	1	12
Don Ohl, Baltimore	12	0	1	2	2	2	1	2
Gus Johnson, Baltimore	25	7	13	11	13	8	2	25
Terry Dischinger, Detroit	24	2	8	1	2	5	1	5
Totals	240	42	93	39	52	66	15	123

SCORE BY PERIODS:	1	2	3	4	FINAL
EAST	36	39	32	17	124
WEST	27	34	30	32	123

GAME 14: January 14, 1964

LOCATION	EAST COACH	WEST COACH	MOST VALUABLE PLAYER	OFFICIALS	ATTENDANCE
Boston	Red Auerbach, Boston	Fred Schaus, Los Angeles	Oscar Robertson, Cincinnati	Sid Borgia and Mendy Rudolph	13,464

East (111)

PLAYER, TEAM	MIN	FGM	FGA	FTM	FTA	REB	AST	PTS
Jerry Lucas, Cincinnati	36	3	6	5	6	8	0	11
Tom Heinsohn, Boston	21	5	12	0	0	3	0	10
Bill Russell, Boston	42	6	13	1	2	21	2	13
Oscar Robertson, Cincinnati	42	10	23	6	10	14	8	26
Hal Greer, Philadelphia	20	5	10	3	4	3	4	13
Tom Gola, New York	7	0	0	1	2	0	1	1
Chet Walker, Philadelphia	12	2	5	0	0	0	0	4
Len Chappell, New York	12	1	5	2	2	1	2	4
Wayne Embry, Cincinnati	21	6	14	1	1	7	1	13
Sam Jones, Boston	27	8	20	0	0	4	3	16
TOTALS	240	46	108	19	27	61	21	111

West (107)

PLAYER, TEAM	MIN	FGM	FGA	FTM	FTA	REB	AST	PTS
Bob Pettit, St. Louis	36	6	15	7	9	17	2	19
Elgin Baylor, Los Angeles	29	5	15	5	11	8	5	15
Walt Bellamy, Baltimore	23	4	11	3	5	7	0	11
Guy Rodgers, San Francisco	22	3	6	0	0	2	2	6
Jerry West, Los Angeles	42	8	20	1	1	4	5	17
Wilt Chamberlain, San Francisco	37	4	14	11	14	20	1	19
Terry Dischinger, Baltimore	13	2	4	3	3	2	1	7
Bailey Howell, Detroit	6	1	3	0	0	2	0	2
Don Ohl, Detroit	18	3	9	2	2	2	0	8
Len Wilkens, St. Louis	14	1	5	1	1	0	0	3
TOTALS	240	37	102	33	46	64	16	107

SCORE BY PERIODS:	1	2	3	4	FINAL
WEST	22	27	28	30	107
EAST	25	34	27	25	111

GAME 13: January 16, 1963

LOCATION	EAST COACH	WEST COACH	MOST VALUABLE PLAYER	OFFICIALS	ATTENDANCE
Los Angeles	Red Auerbach, Boston	Fred Schaus, Los Angeles	Bill Russell, Boston	Sid Borgia and Earl Strom	14,838

East (115)

PLAYER, TEAM	MIN	FGM	FGA	FTM	FTA	REB	AST	PTS
Jack Twyman, Cincinnati	16	6	12	0	0	4	1	12
Tom Heinsohn, Boston	21	6	11	3	4	2	1	15
Bill Russell, Boston	37	8	14	3	4	24	5	19
Oscar Robertson, Cincinnati	37	9	15	3	4	3	6	21
Bob Cousy, Boston	25	4	11	0	0	4	6	8
John Kerr, Syracuse	11	0	4	2	2	2	1	2
Lee Shaffer, Syracuse	19	6	13	0	0	1	1	12
John Green, New York	27	6	8	1	1	5	0	13
Tom Gola, New York	18	1	3	0	0	2	1	2
Hal Greer, Syracuse	15	3	7	0	0	3	2	6
Richie Guerin, New York	14	2	3	1	3	1	1	5
Wayne Embry, Cincinnati (*Selected but did not play due to injury.*)								
TOTALS	240	51	101	13	18	51	25	115

West (108)

PLAYER, TEAM	MIN	FGM	FGA	FTM	FTA	REB	AST	PTS
Walt Bellamy, Chicago	14	1	4	0	2	1	2	2
Bob Pettit, St. Louis	32	7	16	11	12	13	0	25
Wilt Chamberlain, San Francisco	35	7	11	3	7	19	0	17
Jerry West, Los Angeles	32	5	15	3	4	7	5	13
Elgin Baylor, Los Angeles	36	4	15	9	13	14	7	17
Tom Meschery, San Francisco	8	1	3	1	2	1	1	3
Don Ohl, Detroit	12	1	4	1	1	0	2	3
Len Wilkens, St. Louis	25	2	7	0	1	2	3	4
Bailey Howell, Detroit	11	2	3	0	0	1	1	4
Rudy LaRusso, Los Angeles	11	3	3	0	0	1	2	6
Terry Dischinger, Chicago	7	3	3	1	1	1	0	7
Guy Rodgers, San Francisco	17	3	6	1	2	2	4	7
TOTALS	240	39	90	30	45	62	27	108

SCORE BY PERIODS:	1	2	3	4	FINAL
EAST	32	24	24	35	115
WEST	25	25	23	35	108

GAME 12: January 16, 1962

LOCATION	EAST COACH	WEST COACH	MOST VALUABLE PLAYER	OFFICIALS	ATTENDANCE
St. Louis	Red Auerbach, Boston	Fred Schaus, Los Angeles	Bob Pettit, St. Louis	Sid Borgia and Willie Smith	15,112

East (130)

PLAYER, TEAM	MIN	FGM	FGA	FTM	FTA	REB	AST	PTS
Dolph Schayes, Syracuse	4	0	0	0	0	1	0	0
Tom Heinsohn, Boston	13	4	11	2	2	2	1	10
Wilt Chamberlain, Philadelphia	37	17	23	8	16	24	1	42
Bob Cousy, Boston	31	4	13	3	4	6	8	11
Richie Guerin, New York	27	10	17	3	6	3	1	23
Bill Russell, Boston	27	5	12	2	3	12	2	12
John Green, New York	21	2	4	3	3	2	0	7
Willie Naulls, New York	21	5	16	1	1	7	0	11
Hal Greer, Syracuse	24	3	14	2	7	10	9	8
Paul Arizin, Philadelphia	21	2	12	0	0	2	0	4
Sam Jones, Boston	14	1	8	0	1	1	0	2
Tom Gola, Philadelphia (*Selected but did not play due to injury.*)								
Larry Costello, Syracuse (*Selected but did not play due to injury.*)								
TOTALS	240	53	130	24	43	70	22	130

West (150)

PLAYER, TEAM	MIN	FGM	FGA	FTM	FTA	REB	AST	PTS
Elgin Baylor, Los Angeles	37	10	23	12	14	9	4	32
Bob Pettit, St. Louis	37	10	20	5	5	27	2	25
Walt Bellamy, Chicago	29	10	18	3	8	17	1	23
Oscar Robertson, Cincinnati	37	9	20	8	14	7	13	26
Jerry West, Los Angeles	31	7	14	4	6	3	1	18
Wayne Embry, Cincinnati	16	2	6	0	0	4	1	4
Bailey Howell, Detroit	8	1	2	0	0	0	1	2
Jack Twyman, Cincinnati	8	4	6	3	3	1	2	11
Cliff Hagan, St. Louis	9	1	3	0	0	2	1	2
Frank Selvy, Los Angeles	11	0	3	0	0	4	1	0
Gene Shue, Detroit	17	3	6	1	1	5	4	7
Rudy LaRusso, Los Angeles (*Selected but did not play due to injury.*).								
TOTALS	240	57	121	36	51	79	31	150

SCORE BY PERIODS:	1	2	3	4	FINAL
EAST	32	28	34	36	130
WEST	35	29	41	45	150

GAME 11: January 17, 1961

LOCATION	EAST COACH	WEST COACH	MOST VALUABLE PLAYER	OFFICIALS	ATTENDANCE
Syracuse	Red Auerbach, Boston	Paul Seymour, St. Louis	Oscar Robertson, Cincinnati	Norm Drucker and Richie Powers	8,016

East (131)

PLAYER, TEAM	MIN	FGM	FGA	FTM	FTA	REB	AST	PTS
Tom Heinsohn, Boston	19	2	16	0	0	6	1	4
Dolph Schayes, Syracuse	27	7	15	7	7	6	3	21
Wilt Chamberlain, Philadelphia	38	2	8	8	15	18	5	12
Bob Cousy, Boston	33	2	11	0	0	3	8	4
Richie Guerin, New York	15	3	8	5	6	0	2	14
Paul Arizin, Philadelphia	17	6	12	5	6	2	1	17
Willie Naulls, New York	16	4	6	0	1	6	2	8
Larry Costello, Syracuse	5	1	2	0	0	0	0	2
Bill Russell, Boston	28	9	15	6	8	11	1	24
Tom Gola, Philadelphia	25	6	13	2	4	5	3	14
Hal Greer, Syracuse	18	7	11	0	0	6	2	14
TOTALS	204	49	117	33	47	63	28	131

West (153)

PLAYER, TEAM	MIN	FGM	FGA	FTM	FTA	REB	AST	PTS
Elgin Baylor, Los Angeles	27	3	11	9	10	10	4	15
Clyde Lovellette, St. Louis	31	10	19	1	1	10	3	21
Bob Pettit, St. Louis	32	13	22	3	7	9	0	29
Gene Shue, Detroit	23	6	10	3	4	3	6	15
Oscar Robertson, Cincinnati	34	8	13	7	9	9	14	23
Wayne Embry, Cincinnati	8	2	4	0	0	3	0	4
Walt Dukes, Detroit	17	3	6	2	2	4	1	8
Bailey Howell, Detroit	16	5	10	3	4	3	3	13
Cliff Hagan, St. Louis	13	0	2	2	2	2	0	2
Jerry West, Los Angeles	25	2	8	5	6	2	4	9
Rod Hundley, Los Angeles	14	6	10	2	2	0	2	14
TOTALS	240	58	115	37	47	55	37	153

SCORE BY PERIODS:	1	2	3	4	FINAL
WEST	47	37	31	38	153
EAST	19	43	35	34	131

GAME 10: January 22, 1960

LOCATION	EAST COACH	WEST COACH	MOST VALUABLE PLAYER	OFFICIALS	ATTENDANCE
Philadelphia	Red Auerbach, Boston	Ed Macauley, St. Louis	Wilt Chamberlain, Philadelphia	Arnie Heft and Sid Borgia	10,421

East (125)

PLAYER, TEAM	MIN	FGM	FGA	FTM	FTA	REB	AST	PTS
Dolph Schayes, Syracuse	27	8	19	3	3	10	0	19
Bill Russell, Boston	27	3	7	0	2	8	3	6
Wilt Chamberlain, Philadelphia	30	9	20	5	7	25	2	23
Bob Cousy, Boston	26	1	7	0	0	5	8	2
Richie Guerin, New York	22	5	11	2	2	4	4	12
George Yardley, Syracuse	16	5	9	1	2	3	0	11
Tom Gola, Philadelphia	20	5	13	2	3	4	2	12
Willie Naulls, New York	26	5	19	3	4	10	0	13
Bill Sharman, Boston	26	8	21	1	1	6	2	17
Larry Costello, Syracuse	20	5	9	0	0	4	2	10
Paul Arizin, Philadelphia (*Selected but did not play due to injury.*)								
TOTALS	240	54	135	17	24	79	23	125

West (115)

PLAYER, TEAM	MIN	FGM	FGA	FTM	FTA	REB	AST	PTS
Bob Pettit, St. Louis	28	4	15	3	6	14	2	11
Jack Twyman, Cincinnati	28	11	17	5	8	5	1	27
Walter Dukes, Detroit	26	2	10	0	1	15	1	4
Gene Shue, Detroit	34	6	13	1	2	6	6	13
Elgin Baylor, Minneapolis	28	10	18	5	7	13	3	25
Cliff Hagan, St. Louis	21	1	9	0	0	3	2	1
Chuck Noble, Detroit	11	0	5	0	0	1	3	0
Clyde Lovellette, St. Louis	18	6	11	0	0	8	1	12
Rod Hundley, Minneapolis	23	5	12	0	0	3	2	10
Dick Garmaker, Minneapolis	23	5	11	1	2	4	3	11
TOTALS	240	50	121	15	26	72	24	115

SCORE BY PERIODS:	1	2	3	4	FINAL
WEST	26	25	30	34	115
EAST	25	33	33	34	125

GAME 9: January 23, 1959

LOCATION	EAST COACH	WEST COACH	MOST VALUABLE PLAYER	OFFICIALS	ATTENDANCE
Detroit	Red Auerbach, Boston	Ed Macauley, St. Louis	Elgin Baylor, Minneapolis Bob Pettit, St. Louis	Jim Duffy and Mendy Rudolph	10,541

East (108)

PLAYER, TEAM	MIN	FGM	FGA	FTM	FTA	REB	AST	PTS
Ken Sears, New York	26	5	9	5	5	8	1	15
Paul Arizin, Philadelphia	30	4	15	8	9	8	0	16
Bill Russell, Boston	27	3	10	1	1	9	1	7
Bill Sharman, Boston	24	3	12	5	6	2	0	11
Bob Cousy, Boston	32	4	8	5	6	5	4	13
Dolph Schayes, Syracuse	22	3	11	7	8	13	1	13
Woody Sauldsberry, Philadelphia	18	5	11	4	4	2	3	14
John Kerr, Syracuse	21	3	14	1	2	9	2	7
Larry Costello, Syracuse	18	3	8	1	1	3	3	7
Richie Guerin, New York	22	1	7	3	5	3	3	5
TOTALS	240	34	108	40	47	62	18	108

West (124)

PLAYER, TEAM	MIN	FGM	FGA	FTM	FTA	REB	AST	PTS
Cliff Hagan, St. Louis	22	6	12	3	3	8	3	15
Elgin Baylor, Minneapolis	32	10	20	4	5	11	1	24
Bob Pettit, St. Louis	34	8	21	9	9	16	5	25
Gene Shue, Detroit	31	6	11	1	2	4	3	13
Slater Martin, St. Louis	22	2	6	1	2	6	1	5
George Yardley, Detroit	17	2	8	2	2	4	0	6
Jack Twyman, Cincinnati	23	8	12	2	4	8	3	18
Larry Foust, Minneapolis	16	3	9	2	2	9	0	8
Dick McGuire, Detroit	24	2	7	1	2	3	3	5
Dick Garmaker, Minneapolis	19	2	6	1	1	2	1	5
TOTALS	240	49	112	26	32	71	20	124

SCORE BY PERIODS:	1	2	3	4	FINAL
WEST	27	34	30	33	124
EAST	31	21	32	24	108

GAME 8: January 21, 1958

LOCATION	EAST COACH	WEST COACH	MOST VALUABLE PLAYER	OFFICIALS	ATTENDANCE
St. Louis	Red Auerbach, Boston	Alex Hannum, St. Louis	Bob Pettit, St. Louis	Jim Duffy and Arnie Heft	12,854

East (130)

PLAYER, TEAM	MIN	FGM	FGA	FTM	FTA	REB	AST	PTS
Dolph Schayes, Syracuse	39	6	15	6	6	9	2	18
Willie Naulis, New York	15	3	9	2	2	3	0	8
Bill Russell, Boston	26	5	12	1	3	11	2	11
Bob Cousy, Boston	31	8	20	4	6	5	10	20
Bill Sharman, Boston	25	6	19	3	3	4	3	15
Ken Sears, New York	14	4	8	4	5	1	0	12
Paul Arizin, Philadelphia	29	11	17	2	2	8	2	24
Neil Johnston, Philadelphia	22	6	13	2	2	8	1	14
Richie Guerin, New York	22	2	10	3	4	8	7	7
Larry Costello, Syracuse	17	0	6	1	1	1	4	1
TOTALS	240	51	129	28	34	58	31	130

West (118)

PLAYER, TEAM	MIN	FGM	FGA	FTM	FTA	REB	AST	PTS
George Yardley, Detroit	32	8	15	3	5	9	1	19
Jack Twyman, Cincinnati	25	8	13	2	2	3	0	18
Bob Pettit, St. Louis	38	10	21	8	10	26	1	28
Slater Martin, St. Louis	26	2	9	2	4	2	8	6
Dick Garmaker, Minneapolis	13	1	9	3	3	6	1	5
Maurice Stokes, Cincinnati	36	3	13	4	7	14	3	10
Larry Foust, Minneapolis	13	1	4	8	8	3	0	10
Gene Shue, Detroit	25	8	11	2	3	2	0	18
Dick McGuire, Detroit	31	2	4	0	0	7	10	4
Cliff Hagan, St. Louis (*Selected but did not play due to injury.*)								
TOTALS	240	43	99	32	42	72	24	118

SCORE BY PERIODS:	1	2	3	4	FINAL
EAST	30	31	31	38	130
WEST	31	35	25	27	118

GAME 7: January 15, 1957

LOCATION	EAST COACH	WEST COACH	MOST VALUABLE PLAYER	OFFICIALS	ATTENDANCE
Boston	Red Auerbach, Boston	Bobby Wanzer, Rochester	Bob Cousy, Boston	Mendy Rudolph and Sid Borgia	11,178

East (109)

PLAYER, TEAM	MIN	FGM	FGA	FTM	FTA	REB	AST	PTS
Paul Arizin, Philadelphia	26	6	13	1	2	5	0	13
Tom Heinsohn, Boston	23	5	17	2	2	7	0	12
Harry Gallatin, New York	24	4	7	0	2	11	1	8
Bob Cousy, Boston	28	4	14	2	2	5	7	10
Bill Sharman, Boston	23	5	17	2	2	6	5	12
Dolph Schayes, Syracuse	25	4	6	1	1	10	1	9
Neil Johnston, Philadelphia	23	8	12	3	3	9	1	19
Nat Clifton, New York	23	4	11	0	0	11	3	8
Jack George, Philadelphia	21	3	6	2	2	1	5	8
Carl Braun, New York	24	4	9	2	2	3	2	10
TOTALS	240	47	112	15	18	68	25	109

West (97)

PLAYER, TEAM	MIN	FGM	FGA	FTM	FTA	REB	AST	PTS
George Yardley, Fort Wayne	25	4	10	1	1	9	0	9
Bob Pettit, St. Louis	31	8	18	5	6	11	2	21
Maurice Stokes, Rochester	31	8	19	3	3	12	7	19
Slater Martin, St. Louis	31	4	11	0	0	2	3	8
Dick Garmaker, Minneapolis	18	5	10	0	0	7	1	10
Ed Macauley, St. Louis	19	3	6	1	2	5	3	7
Jack Twyman, Rochester	17	1	8	1	3	0	1	3
Mel Hutchins, Fort Wayne	26	4	12	2	3	7	0	10
Vern Mikkelsen, Minneapolis	21	3	10	0	4	9	1	6
Richie Regan, Rochester	21	2	7	0	0	4	1	4
TOTALS	240	42	111	13	22	66	19	97

SCORE BY PERIODS:	1	2	3	4	FINAL
EAST	18	23	33	35	109
WEST	26	17	23	31	97

GAME 6: January 24, 1956

LOCATION	EAST COACH	WEST COACH	MOST VALUABLE PLAYER	OFFICIALS	ATTENDANCE
Rochester	George Senesky, Philadelphia	Charley Eckman, Fort Wayne	Bob Pettit, St Louis	Arnie Heft and Lou Eisenstein	8,517

East (94)

PLAYER, TEAM	MIN	FGM	FGA	FTM	FTA	REB	AST	PTS
Paul Arizin, Philadelphia	28	5	13	3	5	7	1	13
Dolph Schayes, Syracuse	25	4	8	6	10	4	2	14
Neil Johnston, Philadelphia	25	5	9	7	11	10	1	17
Bob Cousy, Boston	24	2	8	3	4	7	2	7
Dick McGuire, New York	29	2	9	2	5	0	3	6
John Kerr, Syracuse	16	2	4	0	1	8	0	4
Harry Gallatin, New York	30	5	12	6	7	5	2	16
Ed Macauley, Boston	20	1	9	2	4	2	3	4
Jack George, Philadelphia	21	2	7	2	2	3	2	6
Bill Sharman, Boston	24	2	8	3	4	7	2	7
Carl Braun, New York (*Selected but did not play due to injury.*)								
TOTALS	240	30	87	34	53	53	18	94

West (108)

PLAYER, TEAM	MIN	FGM	FGA	FTM	FTA	REB	AST	PTS
Mel Hutchins, Fort Wayne	27	5	11	1	2	4	0	11
George Yardley, Fort Wayne	19	3	7	2	3	6	1	8
Larry Foust, Fort Wayne	20	3	9	3	4	4	0	9
Slater Martin, Minneapolis	29	3	7	3	3	1	7	9
Bobby Wanzer, Rochester	25	4	8	5	6	5	2	13
Maurice Stokes, Rochester	20	4	11	2	5	16	2	10
Bob Pettit, St. Louis	31	7	17	6	7	24	7	20
Vern Mikkelsen, Minneapolis	22	5	13	6	7	9	2	16
Clyde Lovellette, Minneapolis	20	3	10	1	3	10	0	7
Bob Harrison, St. Louis	25	2	7	1	2	0	1	5
TOTALS	240	39	100	30	42	79	22	108

SCORE BY PERIODS:	1	2	3	4	FINAL
WEST	17	26	41	24	108
EAST	24	16	24	30	94

GAME 5: January 18, 1955

LOCATION	EAST COACH	WEST COACH	MOST VALUABLE PLAYER	OFFICIALS	ATTENDANCE
New York	Al Cervi, Syracuse	Charley Eckman,Fort Wayne	Bill Sharman, Boston	Phil Fox and Joe Serafin	15,564

East (100)

PLAYER, TEAM	MIN	FGM	FGA	FTM	FTA	REB	AST	PTS
Harry Gallatin, New York	36	4	7	5	5	14	3	13
Dolph Schayes, Syracuse	29	6	12	3	3	13	1	15
Ed Macauley, Boston	27	1	5	4	5	4	2	6
Bob Cousy, Boston	35	7	14	6	7	9	5	20
Paul Seymour, Syracuse	16	3	8	2	2	3	1	8
Paul Arizin, Philadelphia	23	4	9	1	2	2	2	9
Carl Braun, New York	16	4	6	0	0	2	2	8
Neil Johnston, Philadelphia	15	1	7	1	1	6	1	3
Dick McGuire, New York	25	1	2	1	2	3	6	3
Bill Sharman, Boston	18	5	10	5	5	4	2	15
TOTALS	240	36	80	28	32	60	25	100

West (91)

PLAYER, TEAM	MIN	FGM	FGA	FTM	FTA	REB	AST	PTS
Jim Pollard, Minneapolis	27	7	19	3	3	4	0	17
George Yardley, Fort Wayne	22	4	11	3	4	4	2	11
Larry Foust, Fort Wayne	24	3	10	1	1	7	1	7
Andy Phillip, Fort Wayne	28	3	4	0	0	3	6	6
Bobby Wanzer, Rochester	26	3	7	2	2	3	2	8
Bob Pettit, Milwaukee	27	3	14	2	4	9	2	8
Jack Coleman, Rochester	19	2	8	2	3	6	1	6
Vern Mikkelsen, Minneapolis	25	7	15	2	3	9	1	16
Slater Martin, Minneapolis	23	2	5	1	2	2	5	5
Frank Selvy, Milwaukee	19	2	7	3	4	3	1	7
Arnie Risen, Rochester (*Selected but did not play due to injury.*)								
TOTALS	240	36	100	19	26	50	21	91

SCORE BY PERIODS:	1	2	3	4	FINAL
WEST	21	29	21	20	91
EAST	21	28	21	30	100

GAME 4: January 21, 1954

LOCATION	EAST COACH	WEST COACH	MOST VALUABLE PLAYER	OFFICIALS	ATTENDANCE
New York	Joe Lapchick, New York	John Kundla, Minneapolis	Bob Cousy, Boston	Mendy Rudolph and Sid Borgia	16,487

East (98, OT)

PLAYER, TEAM	MIN	FGM	FGA	FTM	FTA	REB	AST	PTS
Dolph Schayes, Syracuse	24	1	3	4	6	12	1	6
Carl Braun, New York	29	4	8	1	1	4	2	9
Ed Macauley, Boston	25	4	11	5	6	1	3	13
Harry Gallatin, New York	28	0	2	5	6	18	3	5
Ray Felix, Baltimore	32	4	8	5	5	11	1	13
Neil Johnston, Philadelphia	20	2	9	2	4	7	2	6
Bob Cousy, Boston	34	6	15	8	8	11	4	20
Bill Sharman, Boston	30	6	9	2	4	2	3	14
Dick McGuire, New York	24	2	5	0	0	4	2	4
Paul Seymour, Syracuse	19	2	6	4	4	1	3	8
TOTALS	265	31	76	36	44	71	24	98

West (93, OT)

PLAYER, TEAM	MIN	FGM	FGA	FTM	FTA	REB	AST	PTS
Mel Hutchins, Milwaukee	31	1	8	1	2	4	2	3
Jim Pollard, Minneapolis	41	10	22	3	5	3	3	23
George Mikan, Minneapolis	31	6	18	6	8	9	1	18
Slater Martin, Minneapolis	23	1	5	0	0	0	3	2
Bobby Wanzer, Rochester	36	5	13	2	3	2	6	12
Arnie Risen, Rochester	20	4	10	0	1	7	0	8
Bobby Davies, Rochester	31	8	16	2	3	5	5	18
Don Sunderlage, Milwaukee	6	1	2	2	2	0	1	4
Larry Foust, Fort Wayne	27	1	9	1	1	15	0	3
Andy Phillip, Fort Wayne	19	1	4	0	1	3	3	2
TOTALS	265	38	107	17	26	48	24	93

SCORE BY PERIODS:	1	2	3	4	OT	FINAL
EAST	28	20	17	19	14	98
WEST	25	19	23	17	9	93

GAME 3: January 13, 1953

LOCATION	EAST COACH	WEST COACH	MOST VALUABLE PLAYER	OFFICIALS	ATTENDANCE
Fort Wayne	Joe Lapchick, New York	John Kundla, Minneapolis	George Mikan, Minneapolis	Sid Borgia and Bud Lowell	10,322

East (75)

PLAYER, TEAM	MIN	FGM	FGA	FTM	FTA	REB	AST	PTS
Harry Gallatin, New York	19	1	4	1	2	3	2	3
Dolph Schayes, Syracuse	26	2	7	4	4	13	3	8
Ed Macauley, Boston	35	5	12	8	8	7	3	18
Bob Cousy, Boston	36	4	11	7	7	5	3	15
Bill Sharman, Boston	26	5	8	1	1	4	0	11
Don Barksdale, Boston	11	0	1	1	3	3	2	1
Carl Braun, New York	21	1	4	1	1	3	2	3
Neil Johnston, Philadelphia	27	5	13	1	2	12	0	11
Paul Seymour, Syracuse	14	2	3	1	2	3	2	5
Billy Gabor, Syracuse	25	0	3	0	1	5	2	0
Fred Scolari, Baltimore *(Selected but did not play due to injury.)*								
TOTALS	240	25	66	25	31	58	19	75

West (79)

PLAYER, TEAM	MIN	FGM	FGA	FTM	FTA	REB	AST	PTS
Mel Hutchins, Milwaukee	30	1	8	0	1	6	5	2
Vern Mikkelsen, Minneapolis	19	3	13	0	0	6	3	6
George Mikan, Minneapolis	40	9	26	4	4	16	2	22
Andy Phillip, Fort Wayne	36	4	9	1	1	6	8	9
Bob Wanzer, Rochester	22	4	7	1	1	2	2	9
Leo Barnhorst, Indianapolis	13	1	2	0	1	3	2	2
Larry Foust, Fort Wayne	18	5	7	0	0	6	0	10
Arnie Risen, Rochester	19	2	7	1	3	9	2	5
Bob Davies, Rochester	17	3	7	3	6	3	2	9
Slater Martin, Minneapolis	26	2	10	1	1	2	1	5
TOTALS	240	34	97	11	18	59	26	79

SCORE BY PERIODS:	1	2	3	4	FINAL
EAST	20	14	21	20	75
WEST	20	15	22	22	79

GAME 2: February 11, 1952

LOCATION	EAST COACH	WEST COACH	MOST VALUABLE PLAYER	OFFICIALS	ATTENDANCE
Boston	Al Cervi, Syracuse	John Kundla, Minneapolis	Paul Arizin, Philadelphia	Sid Borgia and Stan Stutz	10,211

East (108)

PLAYER, TEAM	MIN	FGM	FGA	FTM	FTA	REB	AST	PTS
Paul Arizin, Philadelphia	32	9	13	8	8	6	0	26
Harry Gallatin, New York	22	3	5	1	4	9	3	7
Ed Macauley, Boston	28	3	7	9	9	7	3	15
Bob Cousy, Boston	33	4	14	1	2	4	13	9
Andy Phillip, Philadelphia	30	4	6	3	3	3	6	11
Joe Fulks, Philadelphia	9	3	7	0	1	5	2	6
Red Rocha, Syracuse	28	5	11	2	2	5	2	12
Max Zaslofsky, New York	25	3	7	5	5	4	2	11
Dick McGuire, New York	18	0	0	1	3	1	4	1
Fred Scolari, Baltimore	15	5	9	0	0	0	2	10
Dolph Schayes, Syracuse *(Selected but did not play due to injury.)*								
TOTALS	240	39	79	30	37	44	37	108

West (91)

PLAYER, TEAM	MIN	FGM	FGA	FTM	FTA	REB	AST	PTS
Jim Pollard, Minneapolis	29	2	17	0	0	11	5	4
Leo Barnhorst, Indianapolis	23	7	16	0	1	2	2	14
George Mikan, Minneapolis	29	9	19	8	9	15	1	26
Bobby Davis, Rochester	27	4	11	0	0	0	5	8
Bobby Wanzer, Rochester	22	1	8	2	2	5	5	4
Frank Brian, Fort Wayne	25	4	10	5	6	7	4	13
Vern Mikkelsen, Minneapolis	23	5	8	2	2	10	0	12
Dike Eddleman, Milwaukee	26	1	3	0	0	2	2	2
Arnie Risen, Rochester	19	3	7	0	1	5	1	6
Paul Walther, Indianapolis	17	1	4	0	0	2	2	2
Larry Foust, Fort Wayne *(Selected but did not play due to injury.)*								
TOTALS	240	37	103	17	21	59	27	91

SCORE BY PERIODS:	1	2	3	4	FINAL
WEST	22	22	27	20	91
EAST	26	23	33	26	108

GAME 1: March 2, 1951

LOCATION	EAST COACH	WEST COACH	MOST VALUABLE PLAYER	OFFICIALS	ATTENDANCE
Boston	Joe Lapchick, New York	John Kundla, Minneapolis	Ed Macauley, Boston	Pat Kennedy and Charley Eckman	10,094

East (111)

PLAYER, TEAM	FGM	FGA	FTM	FTA	REB	AST	PTS
Joe Fulks, Philadelphia	6	15	7	9	7	3	19
Dolph Schayes, Syracuse	7	10	1	2	14	3	15
Ed Macauley, Boston	7	12	6	7	6	1	20
Bob Cousy, Boston	2	12	4	5	9	8	8
Andy Phillip, Philadelphia	3	8	0	0	10	8	6
Paul Arizin, Philadelphia	7	12	1	2	7	0	15
Vince Boryla, New York	4	6	1	1	2	2	9
Harry Gallatin, New York	2	4	1	1	5	2	5
Red Rocha, Baltimore	2	10	4	4	2	3	8
Dick McGuire, New York	3	4	0	0	5	10	6
TOTALS	43	93	25	31	67	40	111

West (94)

PLAYER, TEAM	FGM	FGA	FTM	FTA	REB	AST	PTS
Alex Groza, Indianapolis	8	16	1	1	13	1	17
Jim Pollard, Minneapolis	2	11	0	0	4	5	4
George Mikan, Minneapolis	4	17	4	6	11	3	12
Bob Davies, Rochester	4	6	5	5	5	5	13
Ralph Beard, Indianapolis	3	8	0	3	3	2	6
Dike Eddleman, Tri-Cities	2	9	3	5	0	3	7
Vern Mikkelsen, Minneapolis	4	11	3	4	9	1	11
Larry Foust, Fort Wayne	1	6	0	0	5	2	2
Frank Brian, Tri-Cities	5	14	4	5	6	3	14
Fred Schaus, Fort Wayne	2	9	4	4	4	2	8
TOTALS	35	107	24	33	60	27	94

SCORE BY PERIODS:	1	2	3	4	FINAL
WEST	22	20	22	30	94
EAST	31	22	30	28	111

CHAPTER 23

USA BASKETBALL

By Rita Sullivan

USA Basketball catapulted into the spotlight in 1992 when the first Dream Team mesmerized the world with its performance at the Olympics in Barcelona. Although 11 of the 12 players were from NBA teams, the Dream Team was created under the auspices of USA Basketball, which is the governing body for teams representing the United States in international play. The Dream Team obviously generated worldwide interest, but overseeing that team is only a small part of what USA Basketball does.

"Many people think of USA Basketball and they think of the Olympics," said NBA Deputy Commissioner Russ Granik, who recently completed a four-year term as the president of USA Basketball. "But that's just an event every four years, and in fact there are dozens of other events where American players compete against international players, at all different levels."

As the governing body for basketball in the United States, USA Basketball is responsible for putting together the men's and women's teams that compete in international competi-

THE 1996 U.S. MEN'S OLYMPIC TEAM, COACHED BY LENNY WILKENS, WON THE SECOND CONSECUTIVE OLYMPIC GOLD MEDAL WHILE BEING REPRESENTED BY NBA PLAYERS. THE TEAM DOMINATED THE COMPETITION, WINNING THE EIGHT GAMES IN THE OLYMPICS BY AN AVERAGE OF 31.8 POINTS PER GAME.

tion at all levels, from high schools to World Championship competitors. The organization has been around for more than 35 years, but until 1989, its jurisdiction did not include U.S. professional players. When FIBA, the governing body for international basketball, voted to allow NBA players to play in international competition, USA basketball's role expanded, and its reach grew.

"It's a whole new situation," said USA Basketball Executive Director Warren Brown. "It got us into a whole area of corporate sponsorship and marketing that we never really did before."

NBA Deputy Commissioner Russ Granik played a key role when NBA players became eligible for international play. Granik is the first NBA official to serve as President of USA Basketball, a position he held from 1996-2000, and also served as a USA Basketball Vice President from 1989-96. Granik joined the NBA in 1976 as a staff attorney and held several positions before being promoted to Deputy Commissioner in 1990.

The evolution of USA Basketball began in 1964 with the creation of the Basketball Federation of the USA (BFUSA). A new organization was created in 1974, the Amateur Basketball Association of the USA (ABAUSA), containing representatives from every amateur U.S. basketball organization. In 1989, FIBA modified its rules to allow professionals to compete, thus clearing the way for NBA stars from all countries to participate. ABAUSA changed its name to USA Basketball and the NBA was welcomed as an active member with many of its executives serving on committees.

Through all the changes, the goal of USA Basketball has remained the same, and that is to bring home gold medals. While that had never been a problem for the NBA's finest players, it has taken an extra effort in other areas.

The U.S. Women's Olympic team toured the world for a year in preparation for the 1996 Olympics, and their preparation resulted in a gold medal.

For the 1996 Olympics, USA Basketball used its resources to allow the U.S. Women's National Team to train together for a year, a commitment to the women's game that paid off in the form of a gold medal in Atlanta and unprecedented exposure for women's basketball.

The overwhelming success of the Men's Senior program and the emerging prominence of the U.S. Women's National Team have had an impact on junior programs.

Each year, top high school prospects are invited to camps, a vehicle for the eventual selection of teams that compete at various competitions, such as the World Championship for Young Men, the 21-years-old or younger competition; the Pan American Games; the World University Games; the Junior National Teams; the annual Youth Development Festival; and USA Basketball Select Teams, to name a few.

No matter the age or the level, the ultimate thrill of donning a USA jersey and representing the United States never diminishes.

CHAPTER 24

THE DREAM TEAM

A Global Explosion

By Jan Hubbard

When the roster was announced for the first team of NBA players to represent the United States in the Olympics, USA Basketball selection committee members knew they had something special.

They did not know they had landed on the moon.

Given the reaction of the sporting world, it at least seemed that way. For 15 days in Barcelona in 1992, a group of players accurately referred to as the Dream Team was the focal point at the Olympics. The only way the players could have been more popular would have been to arrive at games in the lunar lander.

MANY HAVE SAID IT IS THE GREATEST TEAM EVER ASSEMBLED, AND WHO CAN ARGUE? THE 1992 U.S. OLYMPIC TEAM WAS A DREAM COME TRUE.

"It was an out of this world experience," said Dream Team Coach Chuck Daly. "Dream Team is a lot of name to live up to. But if anything, the 1992 U.S. Olympic men's basketball team exceeded all hopes and expectations."

There was little doubt that much of the excitement was because of the presence of Michael Jordan, Magic Johnson and Larry Bird on the same team. The rivalry between Bird and Magic dominated the '80s, and Jordan was the most exciting, prolific player in the game. When they became one team united against the world, the fascination reached stratospheric levels. Comparisons with the Beatles and Elvis became popular, but perhaps it was Lithuanian forward Arturas Karnisovas who summarized it best by saying: "These are the stars from the stars."

"I don't think you'll see another team quite like this," Daly said. "This team had a mystique and a quality that had been building for 15 years with Magic and Bird and now Jordan. This was a majestic team."

It did not stop with the three legends. The forwards were Charles Barkley, Karl Malone, Scottie Pippen and

OLYMPIC COACH CHUCK DALY SAID THE DREAM TEAM HAD A SPECIAL MYSTIQUE BECAUSE OF THE THREE LEGENDS — MICHAEL JORDAN, LARRY BIRD AND MAGIC JOHNSON (LEFT TO RIGHT). JOHNSON HAD NOT PLAYED DURING THE 1991-92 SEASON AFTER RETIRING BECAUSE HE HAD THE HUMAN IMMUNODEFICIENCY VIRUS (HIV). BUT HE RECEIVED CLEARANCE TO PLAY IN THE OLYMPICS. BIRD HAD BEEN PLAGUED BY BACK PROBLEMS AND WOULD RETIRE AFTER THE OLYMPICS. SO IT WAS A ONCE-IN-A-LIFETIME OPPORTUNITY, AND AS MUCH AS THE BASKETBALL WORLD ENJOYED IT, THE THREE LEGENDS ENJOYED IT EVEN MORE.

Chris Mullin. The centers were David Robinson and Patrick Ewing. The guards were John Stockton and Clyde Drexler. And Christian Laettner was the college representative from Duke.

The team accomplished something that no team before, nor any team since, has accomplished. The players were so popular that opponents enjoyed losing to them. Whether it was at the Tournament of the Americas (the Olympic qualifying tournament held in Portland) or the Olympics, players simply enjoyed being on the same floor as the Dream Team. They enjoyed it so much, in fact, that at times it was comical.

In Portland, an Argentinean guard named Marcelo Milanesio asked Magic for his jersey before the game. Johnson said he could not give it away and thought that was the end of it. But during the game, Milanesio was guarding Johnson and said, "I must have your jersey, I must have your jersey," which, of course, he didn't get.

A number of players, including Milanesio and Karnisovas, had teammates snap photos of them while they were guarding a player during the game. "When I was playing, I told our manager to take a few pictures of me guarding Barkley," Karnisovas said. "Then, when I was on the bench, I decided to take a few more shots."

It was hero worship at its purest. For the international players, playing on the same court with the NBA stars was the equivalent of a struggling writer being asked to pen a chapter in an Ernest Hemingway book.

"They knew they were playing the best in the world," Daly said. "They'll go home and for the rest of their lives be able to tell their kids, 'I played against Michael Jordan and Magic Johnson and Larry Bird.'"

The games were no contest. In Portland, the average margin of victory was 51.5 points per game. In Barcelona, it was 43.8 points a game. But the international players didn't care.

"It has been great," said Brazilian guard Marcel de Souza after a 44-point loss to the U.S.

"I am so overwhelmed with joy," said Milanesio after Argentina's 41-point loss in Portland.

If the Dream Team was worshiped by the others players, it is easy to deduce that it was even more cherished by international fans. Indeed one of the results of the popularity of the team is that it increased interest in basketball all over the world.

"We knew it was going to be received well," said Russ Granik, the NBA Deputy Commissioner who also served a term as President of USA Basketball. "But we were surprised at the extraordinary level of interest. That certainly accelerated our popularity on a global basis."

The most memorable part of the basketball experience

IN THE GOLD MEDAL GAME, CROATIA WAS LED BY NBA PLAYERS DINO RADJA (14) AND DRAZEN PETROVIC (FAR RIGHT IN WHITE) AND PUT UP A GOOD BATTLE IN THE FIRST HALF. IN THE SECOND HALF, HOWEVER, THE DREAM TEAM DOMINATED TO WIN THE GOLD. THE U.S. PLAYERS (LEFT TO RIGHT) ARE LARRY BIRD, CLYDE DREXLER AND KARL MALONE.

actually occurred in Monte Carlo, where the team trained for a week. The daily scrimmages were the most spirited games, especially one that has become almost mythical. A closed, 20-minute intrasquad scrimmage was played with referees, a scoreboard and a clock to simulate game conditions. Jordan and Pippen, teammates on the Bulls, were on one team with Robinson, Malone and Laettner; Johnson and Bird, longtime rivals, headed the other team along with Ewing, Barkley and Mullin. Stockton and Drexler were nursing injuries.

"We were leading 14-2 and I let Michael know about it," said Johnson. "I told him he'd better get into the show or it's all over. I don't know why I said that. All of a sudden he said, 'I'm bringing us back,' and he did. Single-handedly. I pushed him to his level, the highest that he can go. I didn't like it at the time, but at the same time, I did enjoy it. It was really something. Your mind says you want to stop him, but the other side of it says you have no chance. He just starts jumping over you. Every time I looked up, he had his shoes on my No. 15! It was as good a demonstration of basketball as I've ever seen in my life, everything a basketball player could want."

Jordan's team came back to win 40-36 and after the game, Jordan, mimicking one of his commercials, grabbed a drink out of a cooler, ran around the court, and yelled: "Sometimes I dream ..."

The only brief scare for the U.S. during the Olympics

came in the gold medal game when Croatia, led by New Jersey Nets guard Drazen Petrovic, led 25-23. But the Dream Team regrouped and roared to a 117-85 victory, along the way preserving Daly's private goal of never calling a timeout.

Perhaps the most impressive aspect of the Dream Team's run was the way the players came together as a team. Because of the star status of the players, there was some concern early on whether they would be willing to share the ball. But at one of the first workouts, players were so intent on passing that Daly finally screamed out: "Will somebody shoot!"

"I think we took care of all those worries," said Jordan, who in particular made an effort to blend in with his teammates and not to stand out. "I don't think you had any ego problems, any animosity. No ball hogging — only Charles Barkley every now and then."

But Jordan quickly smiled.

"This was smooth sailing," he said. "Every player got along with every player. Even we were a little concerned when we started reading about problems that there might be. Everyone made a conscious effort to mingle and form a part of the chemistry. It happened, and it happened so easily. We didn't have any problems, and I think that's why the trip was so good and so much fun for everybody."

It was fun, unforgettable and momentous — a once in a lifetime, out of this world experience.

1992 USA RESULTS 8-0

USA	116	Angola	48
USA	103	Croatia	70
USA	111	Germany	68
USA	127	Brazil	83
USA	122	Spain	81
USA	115	Puerto Rico	77
USA	127	Lithuania	76
USA	117	Croatia	85

1992 OLYMPIC GAMES FINAL STANDINGS

1. United States (8-0)
2. Croatia (6-2)
3. Lithuania (6-2)
4. Com. of Ind. States (5-3)
5. Brazil (4-4)
6. Australia (4-4)
7. Germany (3-5)
8. Puerto Rico (3-5)
9. Spain (3-4)
10. Angola (2-5)
11. Venezuela (2-5)
12. China (0-7)

1992 USA MEN'S OLYMPIC GAMES CUMULATIVE STATISTICS

PLAYER	G	GS	FGM	FGA	PCT	3PM	3PA	PCT	FTM	FTA	PCT	REB	AVG	PTS	AVG	AST	BLK	STL
C. BARKLEY	8	4	59	83	.711	7	8	.875	19	26	.731	33	4.1	144	18.0	19	1	2
M. JORDAN	8	8	51	113	.451	4	19	.211	13	19	.684	19	2.4	119	14.9	38	4	37
K. MALONE	8	4	40	62	.645	0	0	.000	24	32	.750	42	5.3	104	13.0	9	5	12
C. MULLIN	8	2	39	63	.619	14	26	.538	11	14	.786	13	1.6	103	12.9	29	2	14
K. DREXLER	8	3	37	64	.578	6	21	.286	4	10	.400	24	3.0	84	10.5	29	2	19
P. EWING	8	4	33	53	.623	0	0	.000	10	16	.625	42	5.3	76	9.5	3	15	7
S. PIPPEN	8	3	28	47	.596	5	13	.385	11	15	.733	17	2.1	72	9.0	47	1	23
D. ROBINSON	8	4	27	47	.574	0	0	.000	18	26	.692	33	4.1	72	9.0	7	12	14
L. BIRD	8	3	25	48	.521	9	27	.333	8	10	.800	30	3.8	67	8.4	14	2	14
E. JOHNSON	6	5	17	30	.567	6	13	.462	8	10	.800	14	2.3	48	8.0	33	0	8
C. LAETTNER	8	0	9	20	.450	2	6	.333	18	20	.900	20	2.5	38	4.8	3	3	8
J. STOCKTON	4	0	4	8	.500	1	2	.500	2	3	.667	1	0.3	11	2.8	8	0	0
USA	8	40	369	638	.578	54	135	.400	146	201	.726	288	36.0	938	117.3	239	47	177
OPP.	8	40	214	586	.365	57	187	.305	103	151	.682	180	22.5	588	73.5	109	13	104

Head Coach: Chuck Daly **Assistant Coaches:** Lenny Wilkens, P.J. Carlesimo, Mike Krzyzewski.

1996 SUMMER OLYMPIC GAMES, ATLANTA

Playing in front of the largely American home crowd in Atlanta, expectations were high for Team USA to live up to past successes. As it turned out, the squad — once again comprised of the NBA elite — would fulfill those expectations rather easily, as it defeated the opposition by an average of 31.8 on the way to an 8-0 record and another gold medal. Along the way, Team USA reinforced the idea — originated by the original "Dream Team" in 1992 — that on the world basketball stage, the United States truly is in a league of its own.

In its opener, Team USA started slowly against Argentina, but was lifted by David Robinson's 18 points on the way to an eventual 96-68 triumph. The squad then began to build momentum with an 87-54 defeat of Angola and a 104-82 triumph over highly-regarded Lithuania. Team USA then set a record for most points scored in an Olympic basketball game, as Scottie Pippen scored 24 points and Reggie Miller hit a record five three-pointers in a 133-70 victory over China. That preceded a 102-71 conquest of Croatia.

Brazil and its prolific scorer, Oscar Schmidt, waited in the quarterfinals, but Anfernee Hardaway and Shaquille O'Neal combined for 25 points as Team USA advanced with a 98-75 victory. Only Australia stood between Lenny Wilkens' club and the gold medal game, and Team USA responded with a 101-73 triumph.

Team USA faced Yugoslavia for the gold medal, and the Olympic men's basketball record crowd of 34,600 at the Georgia Dome would not be disappointed, as Robinson netted 28 points, Miller had 20 and Hardaway 17 in a 95-69 victory that forged yet another golden moment for USA Basketball.

1996 USA RESULTS 8-0

USA	96	Argentina	68
USA	87	Angola	54
USA	104	Lithuania	82
USA	133	China	70
USA	102	Croatia	71
USA	98	Brazil	75
USA	101	Australia	73
USA	95	Yugoslavia	69

1996 OLYMPIC GAMES FINAL STANDINGS

1. United States (8-0)
2. Yugoslavia (7-1)
3. Lithuania (5-3)
4. Australia (5-3)
5. Greece (5-3)
6. Brazil (3-5)
7. Croatia (4-4)
8. China (2-6)
9. Argentina (3-4)
10. Puerto Rico (2-5)
11. Angola (1-6)
12. South Korea (0-7)

1996 USA MEN'S OLYMPIC GAMES CUMULATIVE STATISTICS

PLAYER	G	GS	FGM	FGA	PCT	3PM	3PA	PCT	FTM	FTA	PCT	REB	AVG	PTS	AVG	AST	BLK	STL
D. ROBINSON	8	3	34	50	.680	0	0	.000	28	40	.700	37	4.6	96	12.0	0	3	5
R. MILLER	8	5	33	64	.516	17	41	.415	8	9	.889	8	1.0	91	11.4	17	0	8
S. PIPPEN	8	7	37	71	.521	8	23	.348	6	11	.545	31	3.9	88	11.0	26	4	13
C. BARKLEY	7	4	31	38	.816	2	4	.500	23	32	.719	46	6.6	87	12.4	17	1	6
M. RICHMOND	8	3	25	54	.463	11	26	.423	16	19	.842	13	1.6	77	9.6	10	0	10
S. O'NEAL	8	3	31	50	.620	0	0	.000	12	23	.522	42	5.3	74	9.3	7	8	5
P. HARDAWAY	8	1	25	44	.568	4	13	.308	18	25	.720	22	2.8	72	9.0	35	1	11
K. MALONE	8	4	29	51	.569	0	0	.000	9	17	.529	36	4.5	67	8.4	11	1	8
G. HILL	6	1	22	36	.611	2	6	.333	12	16	.750	17	2.8	58	9.7	21	1	18
G. PAYTON	8	6	14	37	.378	3	7	.429	10	19	.526	25	3.1	41	5.1	36	0	6
H. OLAJUWON	7	2	13	29	.448	0	0	.000	9	13	.692	22	3.1	35	5.0	8	3	6
J. STOCKTON	8	1	10	19	.526	1	2	.500	9	11	.818	6	0.8	30	3.8	22	0	13
USA	8	304	54	3	.560	48	122	.393	160	235	.681	305	38.1	816	102.0	210	22	109
OPP.	8	190	45	2	.420	61	161	.379	121	174	.695	201	25.1	562	70.3	119	9	51

Head Coach: Lenny Wilkens **Assistant Coaches:** Jerry Sloan, Bobby Cremins, Clem Haskins.

1994 WORLD CHAMPIONSHIP, TORONTO, CANADA

After a stellar performance at the 1992 Summer Olympics in Barcelona, Spain, NBA players again represented the USA in men's basketball at the World Championships in Toronto two years later.

Coached by Don Nelson, Team USA got off to an inauspicious start, trailing at halftime in its opener against Spain. But led by Joe Dumars' 21 points, the team wound up on the long end of a 115-100 victory. That was followed by a 132-77 victory over China and a 105-82 conquest of Brazil, which vaulted Team USA into the first playoff round, where it notched a 130-74 triumph over Australia and a 134-83 defeat of Puerto Rico.

That put Team USA in the quarterfinals against Russia, a traditionally powerful team in global competition. The game, held before 27,083 fans at SkyDome, was close much of the way. Russia's tight defense helped close its deficit to two points midway through the first half. Again, Team USA responded to the challenge, as Dumars and Shaquille O'Neal finished the game combining for 41 points in a 111-94 victory. The semifinal matchup against Greece was not nearly as dramatic; behind 14 points each by Mark Price and Reggie Miller, Team USA won 97-58, and claimed a berth in the gold medal game and a rematch against Russia.

The gold medal victory was impressive; Team USA made 16 of its first 17 shots, scored 73 first-half points and finished with 19 three-pointers. Dominique Wilkins led the way with 20 points, and Team USA captured the title with a 137-91 triumph, marking the second-most points scored by the Americans in World Championship competition.

1994 USA RESULTS 8-0

USA	115	Spain	100
USA	132	China	77
USA	105	Brazil	82
USA	130	Australia	74
USA	134	Puerto Rico	83
USA	111	Russia	94
USA	97	Greece	58
USA	137	Russia	91

1994 WORLD CHAMPIONSHIP FINAL STANDINGS

1. USA (8-0)
2. Russia (6-2)
3. Croatia (7-1)
4. Greece (4-4)
5. Australia (5-3)
6. Puerto Rico (3-5)
7. Canada (4-4)
8. China (2-6)
9. Argentina (5-3)
10. Spain (5-3)
11. Brazil (2-6)
12. Germany (5-3)
13. South Korea (3-5)
14. Egypt (1-7)
15. Cuba (3-5)
16. Angola (1-7)

1994 USA MEN'S WORLD CHAMPIONSHIP CUMULATIVE STATISTICS

PLAYER	G	FGM	FGA	PCT	3PM	3PA	PCT	FTM	FTA	PCT	REB	AVG	PTS	AVG	AST	BLK	STL
S. O'NEAL	8	62	87	.713	0	4	.000	20	38	.526	68	8.5	144	18.0	4	15	9
R. MILLER	8	44	73	.603	30	57	.526	19	20	.950	13	1.6	137	17.1	18	0	9
D. WILKINS	8	38	67	.567	8	21	.381	17	22	.773	26	3.3	101	12.6	8	1	6
J. DUMARS	7	33	57	.579	16	31	.516	6	6	1.000	10	1.4	88	12.6	20	0	6
A. MOURNING	8	37	54	.685	1	3	.333	12	17	.706	41	5.1	87	10.9	5	9	7
M. PRICE	8	25	62	.403	19	45	.422	8	10	.800	20	2.5	77	9.6	29	1	12
S. KEMP	8	31	45	.689	0	1	.000	13	26	.500	54	6.8	75	9.4	12	9	8
D. MAJERLE	8	23	51	.451	15	33	.455	9	13	.692	18	2.3	70	8.8	13	1	6
D. COLEMAN	8	26	38	.684	6	10	.600	11	13	.846	31	3.9	69/	8.6	6	4	11
K. JOHNSON	8	20	40	.500	2	21	.000	7	11	.636	41	5.1	49	6.1	7	2	2
L. JOHNSON	8	16	34	.471	0	2	.000	8	9	.889	14	1.8	40	5.0	31	1	8
S. SMITH	8	7	20	.350	6	13	.462	4	8	.500	10	1.3	24	3.0	14	1	4
USA	8	362	628	.576	103	222	.464	134	193	.694	346	43.3	961	120.1	167	44	88
OPP.	8	237	541	.438	55	147	.374	130	175	.743	225	28.1	659	82.4	99	17	43

Head Coach: Don Nelson **Assistant Coaches:** Don Chaney, Pete Gillen, Rick Majerus.

CHAPTER 25

THE INTERNATIONAL PLAYER

A Growing Influence

By Mary Schmitt Boyer

Zydrunas Ilgauskas was 13 years old when the NBA came to town. In July 1988, the Atlanta Hawks played an exhibition game against the Soviet National Team in Vilnius, Lithuania, not far from Ilgauskas' hometown of Kaunas. His father took him to the game, and the two sat in wonderment as Dominique Wilkins flew through the air with the greatest of ease.

It was like nothing they'd ever seen before.

Little did they realize that about a year later, several of the stars from the Soviet team would join Wilkins in the NBA and in only eight years, Ilgauskas would follow in their footsteps.

But on that glorious afternoon, no one had any idea things would change so soon or that by the turn of the century there would be 36 international players from 24 countries and territories on NBA rosters.

Actually, NBA Commissioner David Stern set the wheels in motion during a 1984 meeting with Boris Stankovic, Secretary General of the Federation Internationale de Basketball, or FIBA, the world governing body for basketball. Three years later, the NBA invited the Soviet National Team and Tracer Milan of Italy to take part in the first

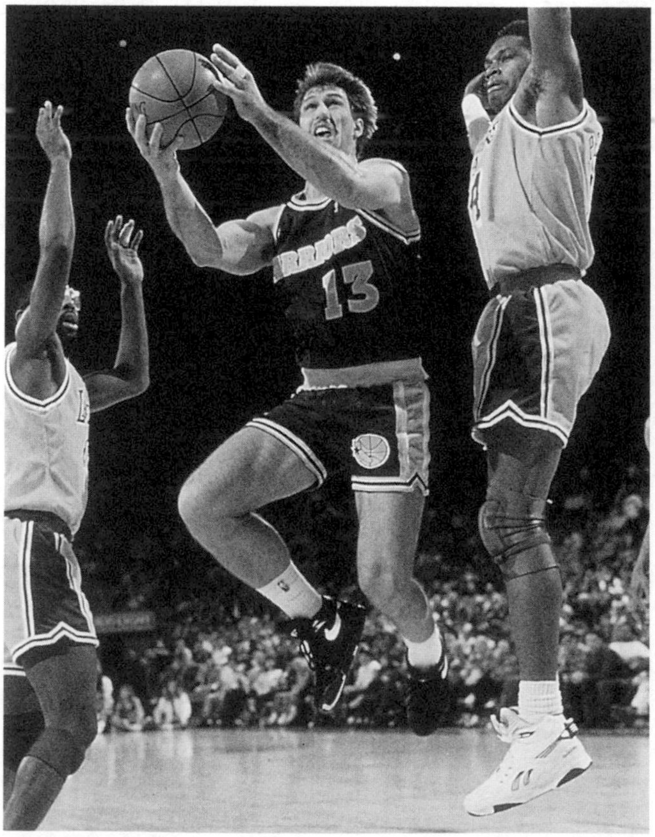

LITHUANIA'S SARUNAS MARCIULIONIS WAS THE FIRST PLAYER FROM THE FORMER SOVIET UNION TO SIGN A PRO CONTRACT, BEGINNING HIS CAREER IN GOLDEN STATE.

McDonald's Open tournament hosted by the Milwaukee Bucks. The next year, the McDonald's Open was held in Madrid, Spain a couple of months after the Hawks made their historic trip to the Soviet Union — the first NBA team to do so.

Sarunas Marciulionis was one of the stars of the Soviet team, a flashy guard whose skills would have allowed him to blend in on any playground or CYO league in the U.S. Like his countryman Ilgauskas, he knew little about the NBA. In those days before widespread use of satellite dishes or the Internet, he'd seen only one fantastic highlight or another.

"They looked like magicians," he said of his first glimpse of NBA players.

Even then, Marciulionis had no idea he'd get a chance to play in the NBA years later. First, the Soviets won the gold medal in the 1988 Summer Olympics in Seoul, South Korea where the U.S. collegians finished third. Coincidentally, on April 8, 1989, FIBA voted to eliminate the distinction between amateurs and professionals, making all players eligible for FIBA competitions, including the Olympics.

The late Drazen Petrovic was perhaps the best international player who never played in a U.S. college. Petrovic was an All-NBA Third Team selection before his tragic death in a 1993 automobile accident.

Although drafted in 1986 by Portland, Arvydas Sabonis continued to play in Europe, finally joining the Blazers in 1995.

While this allowed the formation of the Dream Team of NBA players to compete in the 1992 Summer Games in Barcelona, the key for Marciulionis and other international players was that playing in the NBA would no longer disqualify them from representing their countries in the Olympics.

With that obstacle out of the way, Marciulionis led the parade across the Atlantic. For the 1989-90 season, he joined the Golden State Warriors. Alexander Volkov joined the Hawks. Drazen Petrovic of Croatia joined the Portland Trail Blazers. Zarko Paspalj of Yugoslavia joined the San Antonio Spurs.

But they were not the first international players in the league. In the first game of the 1946-47 season, Hank Arcado Biasatti, an Italian-Canadian, played for the Toronto Huskies in a 68-66 loss to the New York Knickerbockers in Maple Leaf Gardens. Throughout the years, many international players came to the United States to attend college and then get drafted to play in the NBA. Among them were Jamaica's Patrick Ewing (Georgetown), Germany's Detlef Schrempf (University of Washington), Holland's Rik Smits (Marist), Nigeria's Hakeem Olajuwon (University of Houston), Australia's

Hakeem Olajuwon, a native of Nigeria, has played his entire career in Houston, first in college at the University of Houston and then with the Rockets.

Luc Longley (University of New Mexico) and Congo's Dikembe Mutombo (Georgetown).

That was the normal route to the league for most players born outside the U.S., but in 1970, the Atlanta Hawks under General Manager Marty Blake and his top scout Richard Kaner began looking in non-traditional places for players and drafted Italy's Dino Meneghin in the 11th round. In 1985, they selected 20-year-old Arvydas Sabonis, who was a star for the former U.S.S.R. team, in the fourth round. Meneghin never played in the league, and the selection of Sabonis was voided because he had not reached his 21st birthday.

"We were pioneers," said Mike Fratello, who coached the Hawks from 1983-90, including that summer trip to Vilnius. "We had a general manager, Stan Kasten, who had really great foresight. Stan was very perceptive in understanding there was a lot of talent in other countries we needed to start paying attention to."

Because Sabonis couldn't sign with the Hawks, they lost his rights and he was eligible in the next NBA Draft. The rules were changed the next season and teams retained the rights of players they drafted even when they didn't sign. That's what allowed the Portland Trail Blazers to draft Sabonis in the first round in 1986 and hold onto his draft rights until he finally decided to come to the U.S. for the 1995-96 season.

But the Hawks were undeterred. In 1986, they drafted Italian Augusto Binelli in the second round and the U.S.S.R.'s Volkov and forward Valery Tikhonenko in the sixth and seventh rounds, respectively. In 1987, they drafted China's Song Tao in the third round, Greece's Theo Christodoulou in the fourth round, Spain's Jose-Antonio Montero in the fifth round, Italy's Ricardo Morandoti in the sixth round and

The two best players in German basketball history are Detlef Schrempf (left) and Dirk Nowitzki (41). Schrempf went to high school and college in the U.S., but Nowitzki did not.

Yugoslavia's Franjo Arapovic in the seventh round. In 1988, they took Argentina's Jorge Gonzalez in the third round.

All of which made their summer league teams more like a United Nations assembly. But Fratello said there was no communication problem.

GEORGI GLOUCHKOV OF BULGARIA WAS THE FIRST PLAYER FROM AN EASTERN BLOC COUNTRY, PLAYING FOR THE SUNS IN 1985-86.

"I'm Italian, I talk with my hands anyway," he laughed. "They just followed what I said with my hands."

In the middle of all this, Bulgarian Georgi Nikolov Glouchkov became the first player from the former Eastern Bloc countries to join the league when he signed with the Phoenix Suns in 1985-86. Much like the Hawks' Kaner, the Suns also had a scout in Europe, Dick Percudani, a former coach in the Italian League who still works for the team. He first spotted the 6-8, 235-pound Glouchkov, and Jerry Colangelo, then the Suns general manager, went to Sofia, Bulgaria, to negotiate with the Bulgarians and left with Glouchkov signed.

The Suns public relations department played all this up to the hilt, putting out a special press kit that included the history of the Ottoman Empire as well as other background information on Bulgaria, a map and a Bulgarian glossary of basketball terms. Unfortunately, the glossary wasn't extensive enough either. Despite the fact that Glouchkov was accompanied by 65-year-old Bozhidar Takev, nicknamed "Bo" and described as the Mr. Basketball of Bulgaria, communication was a serious problem, recalled John MacLeod, coach of the Suns at the time.

"Bo was hard of hearing, so by the time I'd repeat what I needed him to interpret for Georgi during a timeout, we'd have to be back on the floor," MacLeod said.

Although Glouchkov averaged 4.9 points and 3.3 rebounds in 49 games, when he showed up the next season 25 pounds lighter, the Suns sent him back to Europe.

Much has changed since then, according to Herb Rudoy, an agent who represents Ilgauskas, Sabonis and many other international players.

"The big change is that the Russians, Serbians and Croatians are MTV babies and no longer the typical Iron Curtain non-athletes of the 1960s and '70s," Rudoy said. "They are athletic and completely comfortable with the NBA and the lifestyle in the United States."

And, according to Marciulionis, anybody who can play wants to play in the NBA.

"All of them have dreams," he said.

That is not limited to European players. By the 1999-2000 season, the league had welcomed its first Mexican (Phoenix's Horacio Llamas) and New Zealander (Toronto's Sean Marks) while teams still held rights to players from China (Wang Zhi Zhi), Argentina (Marcelo Nicola and Emanuel Ginobili) and Israel (Doron Sheffer.)

For players worldwide, the NBA remains a goal, a dream. But these days, the chances of reaching that goal and fulfilling that dream are much more real than they were for a starry-eyed young Lithuanian one memorable summer afternoon barely more than a decade ago.

ALL-TIME LIST OF NBA PLAYERS FROM AROUND THE WORLD

(Active players in bold: 36 players from 24 countries)

COUNTRY	PLAYER	TEAM AND YEARS PLAYED
AUSTRALIA	**Chris Anstey**	Dallas 97-98 to 98-99
		Chicago 99-00
	Luc Longley	Minnesota 91-92 to 93-94
		Chicago 93-94 to 97-98
		Phoenix 98-99 to present
	Mark Bradtke	Philadelphia 96-97
	Andrew Gaze	Washington 93-94
		San Antonio 98-99
	Shane Heal	Minnesota 96-97
BELIZE	**Milt Palacio**	Vancouver 99-00
BAHAMAS	Dexter Cambridge	Dallas 92-93
	Ian Lockhart	Phoenix 90-91
	Mychal Thompson	Portland 78-79 to 85-86
		San Antonio, Lakers 86-87
		Lakers 87-88 to 90-91
BRAZIL	Joao Vianna	Dallas 91-92
	Rolando Ferreira	Portland 88-89
BULGARIA	Georgi Glouchkov	Phoenix 85-86
CANADA	Norm Baker	Chicago 46-47
	Ron Crevier	Golden State, Detroit 85-86
	Rick Fox	Boston 91-92 to 96-97
		Lakers 97-98 to present
	Stewart Granger	Cleveland 83-84
		Atlanta 84-85
		New York 86-87
	Bob Houbregs	Milwaukee and Baltimore 53-54
		Baltimore-Boston-Fort Wayne 54-55
		Fort Wayne/Detroit 55-56 to 57-58
	Steve Nash	Phoenix 96-97 to 97-98
		Dallas 98-99 to present
	Leo Rautins	Philadelphia 83-84
		Atlanta 84-85
	Mike Smrek	Chicago 85-86
		Lakers 86-87 to 87-88
		San Antonio 88-89
		Golden State 89-90
		Golden State, Clippers 90-91
		Golden State 91-92
	Gino Sovran	Toronto 46-47
	Ernie Vandeweghe	New York 49-50 to 53-54 & 55-56
	Bill Wennington	Dallas 85-86 to 89-90
		Sacramento 90-91
		Chicago 93-94 to 98-99
		Sacramento 99-00
	Jim Zoet	Detroit 82-83
	Todd MacCulloch	Philadelphia 76ers 99-00 to present
CONGO (ZAIRE)	**Dikembe Mutombo**	Denver 91-92 to 95-96
		Atlanta 96-97 to present
CROATIA	**Toni Kukoc**	Chicago 93-94 to 99-00
		Philadelphia 99-00 to present
	Drazen Petrovic	Portland 89-90 to 90-91
		New Jersey 90-91 to 92-93

COUNTRY	PLAYER	TEAM AND YEARS PLAYED
	Dino Radja	Boston 93-94 to 96-97
	Bruno Sundov	Dallas 98-99 to present
	Zan Tabak	Houston 94-95
		Toronto 95-96 to 96-97
		Toronto, Boston 97-98
		Indiana 99-00 to present
	Stojko Vrankovic	Boston 90-91 to 91-92
		Minnesota 96-97
		Minnesota, Clippers 97-98 to 99-98
CUBA	Andres Guibert	Minnesota 93-94 to 94-95
	Lazaro Borrell	Seattle 99-00 to present
CZECH REPUBLIC	George Zidek	Charlotte 95-96 to 96-97
		Denver 96-97
		Denver, Seattle 97-98 to 98-99
DENMARK	Lars Hansen	Seattle 78-79
DOMINICAN REPUBLIC	Tito Horford	Milwaukee 88-89 to 89-90
		Washington 93-94
	Felipe Lopez	Vancouver 98-99 to present
EGYPT	Alaa Abdelnaby	Portland 90-91 to 91-92
		Milwaukee 92-93
		Boston 92-93 to 93-94
		Sacramento, Philadelphia 94-95
ESTONIA	Martin Muursepp	Miami, Dallas 96-97 to 98-99
FRANCE	**Tariq Abdul-Wahad**	Sacramento 97-98 to 98-99
		Orlando , Denver 99-00 to present
GERMANY	Uwe Blab	Dallas 85-86 to 88-89
		Golden State, San Antonio 89-90
	John Brown	Atlanta 73-74 to 77-78
		Chicago 78-79
		Utah, Atlanta 79-80
	Frido Frey	New York 46-47
	Detlef Schrempf	Dallas 85-86 to 88-89
		Indiana 88-89 to 92-93
		Seattle 93-94 to 98-99
		Portland 99-00 to present
	Kiki Vandeweghe	Denver 80-81 to 83-84
		Portland 84-85 to 88-89
		New York 88-89 to 91-92
		LA Clippers 92-93
	Christian Welp	Philadelphia 87-88 to 88-89
		San Antonio, Golden State 89-90
	Dirk Nowitzki	Dallas 98-99 to present
GEORGIA	**Vladimir Stepania**	Seattle 98-99 to present
GRENADINES	**Adonal Foyle**	Golden State 97-98 to present
HAITI	**Olden Polynice**	Seattle 87-88 to 90-91
		LA Clippers 90-91 to 91-92
		Detroit 92-93 to 93-94
		Sacramento 93-94 to 98-99
		Seattle 98-99, Utah 99-00 to present
	Yvon Joseph	New Jersey 85-86

COUNTRY	PLAYER	TEAM AND YEARS PLAYED
HOLLAND	Hank Beenders	Providence 46-47
		Providence-Philadelphia 47-48
		Boston 48-49
	Geert Hammink	Orlando 93-94 to 95-96
	Rik Smits	Indiana 88-89 to present
	Swen Nater	Milwaukee 76-77, Buffalo 77-78
		San Diego 78-79 to 82-83
		LA Clippers 83-84
	Serge Zwikker	Houston 97-98
HUNGARY	Kornel David	Chicago, Cleveland 98-99 to 99-00
ICELAND	Petur Gudmundsson	Portland 81-82
		LA Lakers 85-86
		San Antonio 87-88 to 88-89
ITALY	Hank Biasatti	Toronto 46-47
	Vincenzo Esposito	Toronto 95-96
	Stefano Rusconi	Phoenix 95-96
JAMAICA	**Patrick Ewing**	New York 85-86 to present
	Rumeal Robinson	Atlanta 90-91 to 91-92
		New Jersey 92-93
		New Jersey, Charlotte 93-94
		Portland 95-96
		LAL-Pho-Por 96-97
	Wayne Sappleton	New Jersey 84-85
	Gary Voce	Cleveland 89-90
LATVIA	Gundars Vetra	Minnesota 92-93
LEBANON	Rony Seikaly	Miami 88-89 to 93-94
		Golden State 94-95 95-96
		Orlando 96-97 to 97-98
		Orlando, New Jersey 97-98 to 98-99
LITHUANIA	Sarunas Marciulionis	Golden State 89-90 to 93-94
		Seattle 94-95
		Sacramento 95-96
		Denver 96-97
	Zydrunas Ilgauskas	Cleveland 96-97 to present
	Virginius Praskevicius	Minnesota 96-97
	Arvydas Sabonis	Portland 95-96 to present
MEXICO	Horacio Llamas	Phoenix 96-97 to 98-99
MONTENEGRO	Zarko Paspalj	San Antonio 89-90
MOROCCO	Mike Flynn	ABA/NBA Indiana 75-76 to 77-78
NEW ZEALAND	**Sean Marks**	Toronto 98-99 to 99-00
NIGERIA	Yinka Dare	New Jersey 94-95 to 97-98
	Julius Nwosu	San Antonio 94-95
	Hakeem Olajuwon	Houston 84-85 to present
	Michael Olowokandi	LA Clippers 98 to present
	Obinna Ekezie	Vancouver 99-00 to present
NORWAY	Torgeir Bryn	LA Clippers 89-90
PANAMA	Rolando Blackman	Dallas 81-82 to 91-92
		New York 92-93 to 93-94
		Atlanta 96-97 to present
PANAMA CANAL ZONE	Stuart Gray	Indiana 84-85 to 88-89
		Charlotte, New York 89-90
		New York 89 -90 to 90-91
PUERTO RICO	Butch Lee	Atlanta, Cleveland 78-79
		Cleveland, LA Lakers 79-80
	Jose Ortiz	Utah 88-89 to 89-90
	Ramon Rivas	Boston 88-89
ROMANIA	Ernie Grunfeld	Milwaukee 77-78 to 78-79
		Kansas City 79-80 to 81-82
		New York 82-83 to 85-86
	Gheorghe Muresan	Washington 93-94 to 97-98
		New Jersey 98-99 to present
RUSSIA	Sergei Bazarevich	Atlanta 94-95
SENEGAL	Makhtar Ndiaye	Vancouver 98-99
SLOVENIA	Marko Milic	Philadelphia, Phoenix 97-98 to 98-99
	Radoslav Nesterovic	Minnesota 98 to present
SPAIN	Fernando Martin	Portland 86-87
	Wallace Bryant	Chicago 83-84
		Dallas 84-85
		Dallas, LA Clippers 85-86
SUDAN	Manute Bol	Washington 85-86 to 87-88
		Golden State 88-89 to 89-90
		Philadelphia 90-91 to 92-93
		Miami, Washington, Phil. 93-94
		Golden State 94-95
TRINIDAD	Ken Charles	Buffalo 73-74 to 75-76
		Atlanta 76-77 to 77-78
TURKEY	**Mirsad Turkcan**	New York 98-00
		Houston 98-99
		Milwaukee 99-00
UKRAINE	Alexander Volkov	Atlanta 89-90, 91-92
	Vitaly Potapenko	Cleveland 96-97 to 98-99
		Boston 99-00 to present
UNITED KINGDOM	**John Amaechi**	Cleveland 95-96
		Orlando 99-00 to present
	Steve Bucknall	Lakers 89-90
	Chris Harris	St.Louis-Rochester 55-56
	Andrew Betts	Charlotte 98-99
U.S. VIRGIN ISLANDS	**Tim Duncan**	San Antonio 97-98 to present
VENEZUELA	Carl Herrera	Houston 91-92 to 94-95
YUGOSLAVIA	Milos Babic	Cleveland 90-91
		Miami 91-92
	Radisav Curcic	Dallas 92-93
	Rastko Cvetkovic	Denver 95-96
	Predrag Danilovic	Miami 95-96 to 96-97, Dallas 96-97
	Vlade Divac	LA Lakers 89-90 to 95-96
		Charlotte 96-97 to 97-98
		Sacramento 98-99 to present
	Aleksandar Djordjevic	Portland 96-97
	Predrag Stojakovic	Sacramento 98 to present
	Aleksandar Radojevic	Toronto Raptors 99-00 to present

CHAPTER 26

AROUND THE WORLD

NBA Goes Global

By Rob Reheuser

More than 32,000 fans were on hand to watch the regular-season NBA action, and as usual, signs of support and adulation dotted the stands. Kids were wearing NBA authentic jerseys with the names and numbers of Chris Webber and Kevin Garnett on the back, just as you'd expect when the Sacramento Kings play the Minnesota Timberwolves.

But the remarkable part of the scene was that it was taking place in the Tokyo Dome, where the Wolves and Kings opened the 1999-2000 season playing a two-game set before more than 66,000 fans. It marked the fifth time in the 1990s that two NBA teams had played regular-season games in Japan. Each time, the players were stunned not only by the enthusiasm of the fans at the games, but also by the reception they received from the general populace during the week the two teams spent in Tokyo.

"It was like being a rock star," Garnett said of the experience. "The people here are so into the NBA game and they know all about us." Echoed Webber, "What sticks out in my mind first about Japan is the people, just how much respect they showed us and how much hospitality we received here. They welcomed us with open arms."

Magic Johnson and the Lakers were a towering presence in Paris at the McDonald's Championship in 1991.

KEVIN GARNETT OF THE MINNESOTA TIMBERWOLVES AND CHRIS WEBBER OF THE SACRAMENTO KINGS TIP OFF BEFORE MORE THAN 32,000 FANS AT THE TOKYO DOME IN THE 1999 JAPAN GAMES.

The NBA became the first major American sports league to play regular-season games outside of North America when the Phoenix Suns and Utah Jazz opened the 1990-91 season with a pair of games in Tokyo's Metropolitan Gym. NBA teams also played regular-season games in Japan in 1992, 1994 and 1996, as well as 1999.

"The Japan Games are part of the continuing globalization of basketball," said NBA Commissioner David Stern, noting that the two games were broadcast to 131 countries in 13 different languages. NBA games in the 1999-2000 season were broadcast to 205 countries in 42 languages.

There is little doubt that the NBA's global popularity got a huge boost from the Dream Team that won the gold medal at the 1992 Olympics in Barcelona. That said, the league's plan to not only televise but also play games all over the world was launched during the early 1980s.

A major element of this plan has been the McDonald's Championship. NBA teams players and coaches have been playing exhibition games and giving clinics overseas for decades, but the McDonald's Championship in 1987 marked the first time an NBA team competed against international clubs in a competition sanctioned by FIBA, basketball's world governing body.

The inaugural McDonald's Championship was hosted by the Milwaukee Bucks and included the Soviet National Team and Tracer Milan, a prominent Italian pro team, in a round-robin competition. The Bucks won both their games to start a streak of NBA dominance — no NBA team has lost in the McDonald's Championship, although a number of games have been close and even gone into overtime.

The McDonald's Championship was held annually through 1991, with the Boston Celtics winning in 1988 in Madrid, the Denver Nuggets in 1989 in Rome, the New York Knicks in 1990 in Barcelona and the Los Angeles Lakers in 1991 in Paris. The NBA and FIBA then decided to hold the event every other year when Olympics and World Championships were not being staged. In 1993 the Phoenix Suns won in Munich as the field was expanded to six teams including All-Star Franca of Brazil, the first international entrant from outside Europe.

The McDonald's Championship received a boost in 1995 when the NBA committed to having its reigning champion compete against five other championship clubs from around the world. The Houston Rockets won the event that year in London, when the field included teams from Australia and Israel as well as Europe. Two years later, Michael Jordan and the Chicago Bulls won in Paris, and in 1999 the San Antonio Spurs won in Milan.

The MVP of the McDonald's Championship receives the Drazen Petrovic Trophy, named in honor of the Croatian-born star who won acclaim in Europe as well as the NBA before dying in an automobile accident in 1993. "Drazen was a pioneer in our sport, having been a star in European basketball, the NBA and the Olympics," said Stern. "He demon-

THEY MAY BE HALF A WORLD AWAY, BUT FANS IN JAPAN ARE AS ENTHUSIASTIC AS NBA FANS ANYWHERE. IN 1996, FANS TURNED OUT EN MASSE FOR GAMES BETWEEN ORLANDO AND NEW JERSEY AND SUPPORTED THEIR FAVORITE TEAM, BUT THEY WOULDN'T MIND HAVING A TEAM OF THEIR OWN.

SHAQUILLE O'NEAL REFERS TO HIMSELF AS "THE BIG ARISTOTLE," AND OTHER PHRASES PRECEDED BY "BIG." MAYBE HE GOT THE IDEA IN 1995 WHEN HE WAS WITH THE MAGIC AND THEY PLAYED IN LONDON.

strated that basketball is truly a global sport, and through his skills and character was a hero to fans around the world."

The NBA has staged games in Mexico seven times in the past 10 years, including a preseason matchup between the Golden State Warriors and the New Jersey Nets in 1999. Two years earlier, in a regular-season game, the Houston Rockets defeated the Dallas Mavericks 108-106 in front of a crowd of 20,635 at the Palacio de los Deportes in Mexico City, a record attendance for a basketball game in Mexico.

The NBA also stages exhibition games at other venues around the globe. The Atlanta Hawks and Orlando Magic played two games in London in 1993. The following year the Golden State Warriors and Charlotte Hornets played each other in Paris, then played local teams in Barcelona and Bologna, respectively. In 1996, the Seattle SuperSonics and Indiana Pacers played exhibition games in Berlin, Germany, and Seville, Spain. In 1999 the Miami Heat traveled to Tel Aviv and played perennial Israeli champion Maccabi Tel Aviv.

This global exposure is fitting for the NBA. After all, the first game in league history was played not in the United States but in Toronto, Canada, the New York Knicks defeating the Toronto Huskies 68-66 at Maple Leaf Gardens. That Toronto franchise folded after one season, but the Toronto Raptors along with the Vancouver Grizzlies joined the league in 1995, furthering the NBA's global reach.

CHAPTER 27

THE WNBA
A League of Their Own

By Jeanne Tang

For many years, the NBA had been aware of an elite group of basketball players who were the very best at what they did. They could not play in the NBA for the simple reason that they were women. Nonetheless, they were exceptionally talented and needed only one thing: a league of their own.

Shortly after James Naismith invented the game, Senda Berenson (holding the ball) at Smith College adapted the rules for women.

So, in 1996, the 29 NBA teams created the WNBA with great hopes but also with caution. More than a dozen failed women's leagues littered the American sports scene, and many wondered whether acceptance by a national audience was a realistic goal. Thus, the WNBA began modestly with eight teams for the 1997 season.

Behind the scenes, the NBA was confident. The 1996 U.S. Olympic team had won the gold medal. There was a large pool of domestic and international talent, with many players coveting an association with a league sponsored by the NBA. The league also decided to play in the summer when the sports schedule was not as crowded and prime television time was available. And the league was confident that the idea of an elite women's league would be attractive to advertisers, whose financial support was vital.

The rest, as they say, is history, although it is a short one. Still, in only three years, the WNBA has doubled in size to 16 teams and the excitement generated by the greatest women players in the world has appealed to a huge audience, both in the United States and throughout the world.

NBA Commissioner David Stern had first considered starting a women's league in the mid '80s. Around that time, several former women players joined the NBA in various capacities. Among the new female NBA executives was a young lawyer and a former four-year starter at the University of Virginia named Val Ackerman, who soon took the lead in studying the viability of a new

VAL ACKERMAN, WHO PLAYED AT THE UNIVERSITY OF VIRGINIA, HAS BEEN THE WNBA PRESIDENT SINCE ITS INCEPTION.

league. All of the careful planning paid off in 1996. On the heels of a wildly successful, NBA-sponsored year-long tour of the 1995-96 USA Basketball Women's National team, which would go on to secure the gold medal at the Atlanta Olympics, the NBA Board of Governors approved the concept of the WNBA on April 24, 1996.

"We Got Next" was the rallying cry as the concept turned into reality. The league, in short order, announced broadcast partnerships with NBC, ESPN and Lifetime. During the inaugural season, the WNBA attracted 50 million viewers. By 1999, 37 broadcasters telecast WNBA games to more than 125 countries in 17 languages.

"We would not have been able to move forward without television," said Ackerman, who would become the new league's president. "It was always the first step. We didn't

WNBA.COM FACT

The Los Angeles Sparks' Lisa Leslie took home the inaugural WNBA All-Star Game MVP when she led the West team to a 79-61 victory over the East at Madison Square Garden on July 14, 1999.

WNBA.COM FACT

Penny Toler of the Los Angeles Sparks scored the first basket in WNBA history. It came at the 19:01 mark in the first half of the New York Liberty at Los Angeles game on June 21, 1997.

sign sponsors and we didn't sign players until we had the TV deals in place."

With the TV deals negotiated, the WNBA began to identify prospective players. Three stars from the national team — Sheryl Swoopes, Lisa Leslie and Rebecca Lobo — were naturals. The three became the public face of the budding league.

"It was a bit overwhelming because there was so much promotional activity and only three of us were signed," Lobo said. "We didn't even have enough players to play three-on-three. It was fun when the league started to come together because you can only answer so many questions like, 'So who do you have on your team?' We didn't have a team."

She would soon have a team as the league decided to open

WITH A SLOGAN OF "WE GOT NEXT," SHERYL SWOOPES, LISA LESLIE AND REBECCA LOBO (LEFT TO RIGHT) LAUNCHED THE WNBA.

After 11 years overseas, Cynthia Cooper returned to the U.S. and was the dominant player in the WNBA's first three years, winning two regular season MVP awards and three MVPs in the WNBA Championship.

its inaugural season with eight squads: the Charlotte Sting, Cleveland Rockers, New York Liberty, Houston Comets, Los Angeles Sparks, Phoenix Mercury, Sacramento Monarchs and Utah Starzz. But three players and eight teams do not a league make.

The WNBA welcomed talent from around the world, signing international players such as Australian Olympian Michele Timms, Chinese star Haixia Zheng and Russian standout Elena Baranova. The league also put out the call for American players forced to play overseas because of the lack of post-collegiate opportunities in the States. One of them was a well-regarded but almost-forgotten player named Cynthia Cooper. Afraid she was out of sight and out of mind, Cooper, who was playing in the Italian League at the time, called the WNBA office to lobby for a place in the league.

Cooper would turn out to be the WNBA's first superstar, leading her Comets to championships in each of the league's first three seasons. Along the way, she took home two league MVP and three Championship MVP Awards. "Give the ball to Cooper and let her work her magic, then sit back and reap the rewards," is how Houston coach Van Chancellor described his philosophy. "That's what I do best as a coach."

Cooper unquestionably dominated the WNBA in its first two seasons, but in the third season, she and the league welcomed a spectacular class of players that would elevate the WNBA to new heights. By then, the league had grown to 12 teams, adding the Detroit Shock and Washington Mystics in 1998 and the Orlando Miracle and Minnesota Lynx in 1999.

Another women's league that had launched following the 1996 Olympics, the American Basketball League, had ceased operating in late 1998, freeing its stars to join the WNBA.

WNBA.COM FACT

Cynthia Cooper of the Houston Comets became the first player in WNBA history to score 2,000 points when she hit for 19 points in the first game of the 2000 season against the New York Liberty. Cooper, the league's first superstar, also won the WNBA's first two MVP awards and the first three Championship MVP trophies.

Chamique Holdsclaw, one of the greatest players in college basketball history, brought her considerable talents to the Washington Mystics in 1999.

Former ABL standouts such as Sacramento's Yolanda Griffith, who would dethrone Cooper as the MVP in 1999; Los Angeles' DeLisha Milton; and Utah's Natalie Williams, transformed their teams into contenders. And the most celebrated college player of her generation, Chamique Holdsclaw, was selected from Tennessee by Washington with the first overall pick in the 1999 draft. With this impressive roster of talent, the WNBA held its inaugural All-Star Game on July 14, 1999, at New York's Madison Square Garden.

Television beams WNBA games around the world, and its great athletes display their grace and skill on the court, but the glue that holds the league together and will sustain it in the future is the enthusiasm of its fans. Not having much history to draw upon, the WNBA projected an attendance figure of 4,000 per game in its inaugural season. The first game in league history, between the Liberty and the Sparks on June 21, 1997, attracted a crowd of 14,284. By August 22 of that year, the one millionth fan had passed through the turnstiles. The league averaged an astounding 9,669 spectators that first season and topped 10,000 in the next two. More than four million fans attended WNBA games in its first three seasons.

WNBA.COM FACT

The most famous shot in WNBA history is Teresa Weatherspoon's Hail Mary from beyond mid-court at the end of Game 2 of the 1999 WNBA Championship. The New York Liberty won the game 68-67, but lost the series to the Houston Comets in three games.

"I had players tell me that when they walked out for the first games with 15,000 people in the stands, they just froze because they'd never played in front of so many people," Ackerman said.

The players, grateful for the devotion of the faithful, connect with fans at a level unprecedented in professional athletics. Players and coaches make countless community service appearances, sign autographs with a smile and share their triumphs and setbacks openly with their fans.

"The fans have really been the success of the league, people just coming out and really supporting us," Leslie said.

"It's kind of like we were instant superstars," said Houston's Tina Thompson. "There was no one before us to make a path. But I believe all the WNBA players have been great role models."

Indeed, not only the players have been great role models. The league, which added the Indiana Fever, Miami Sol, Portland Fire and Seattle Storm in 2000 to expand to 16 teams, is a model for future professional sports leagues to emulate.

The WNBA has enjoyed enthusiastic fan support in all of its four years, expanding from eight to 16 teams during that time.

CHAPTER 28

THE DRAFT

By Chris Ekstrand

There isn't much about the NBA Draft that has escaped Marty Blake's notice. One of the NBA's most colorful figures, Blake has been involved with the draft for nearly five decades, first as general manager of the St. Louis and Atlanta Hawks in the 1950s and '60s, and for the past 30 years as the NBA's Director of Scouting. You need to know something about the draft? Ask Marty.

So what light can the "Godfather of the NBA Draft" shed on this annual rite of passage for top amateur players?

"The NBA Draft," Blake said with a wry smile, "is an inexact science."

He isn't kidding. For every obvious No. 1 overall pick — for every Kareem Abdul-Jabbar, Patrick Ewing or Shaquille O'Neal — there is a great player who didn't seem so obvious on draft day.

Willis Reed, NBA icon for the ages, was a second round pick. So was Nate "Tiny" Archibald, another Hall of Famer. Other second round picks who went on to stardom include Bill Sharman, Hal Greer, Calvin Murphy, Chet Walker, Gus Johnson, Dennis Johnson, Mark Price and Jeff Hornacek.

Even with today's 29-pick first round, second round picks like Nick Van Exel, P.J. Brown, Shandon Anderson and Antonio Davis are thriving in the NBA.

Kenyon Martin of the University of Cincinnati confirms what the New Jersey Nets made public to the world at NBA Draft 2000 — he is No. 1.

FOR THE LAST 30 YEARS, MARTY BLAKE HAS BEEN IDENTIFYING TOP COLLEGE AND INTERNATIONAL TALENT AS THE NBA'S DIRECTOR OF SCOUTING.

The NBA Draft has repeatedly changed shape and scope over the years. What began as a marathon coast-to-coast conference call of general managers grew into a fraternal meeting in a smoky New York City hotel ballroom, then metamorphosed into a global live television event watched by millions. But the one characteristic that has remained constant is the draft's ability to leave basketball experts redfaced. Even today — when promising players from smaller schools are identified by Blake and his network of scouts, college coaches and former players, and NBA teams spend hundreds of thousands of dollars combing every continent for talent — it isn't always obvious which players will ultimately succeed in the NBA.

"In 1985, I had 20 NBA guys come and see Karl Malone [of Louisiana Tech] play against Joe Dumars [of McNeese State]," Blake recalled. "Even after that, 12 teams bypassed Karl and 17 didn't draft Joe. But my job is to make sure all the teams see everyone who is a legitimate prospect, no matter where the guy is playing."

"If we could look inside of a player, and see what was in there, then we wouldn't make as many mistakes as we make," said Cotton Fitzsimmons, Senior Executive Vice President of the Phoenix Suns and a respected player personnel man. "In evaluating players, we are all looking for guys who have a little more flash, a little more jumping ability, a little more speed, because you really can't coach speed and quickness. But inside, you don't really know about what's inside."

In the early days, the draft used to last as long as teams desired, with the proceedings ending only when every team tired of calling out names. As late as 1973, the draft lasted an amazing 20 rounds (at least it did for the fledgling Buffalo Braves, who needed all the players they could get after winning 21 games the season before).

In 1974, the league adopted a 10-round draft, a format that stayed in place until 1985 when it was scaled back to seven rounds. After three years of seven-round drafts, the draft was shaved to three rounds in 1988 and to its current length of two rounds in 1989.

But the capacity to draft fewer players doesn't mean less scouting; it means more scouting than ever. Teams used to feel secure if they had the major conferences in the NCAA covered. Today some of the best basketball players in the world are found outside the borders of the United States. A contemporary NBA general manager who doesn't prepare for draft day by compiling intelligence on the best international players is asking for embarrassment. Players like Arvydas Sabonis, Sarunas Marciulionis, the late Drazen Petrovic and Toni Kukoc have become NBA stars without ever playing at a U.S. college.

"When I came into the league, nobody ever scouted overseas," said Blake, who as Hawks' GM expanded the scope of NBA scouting by using late-round picks in 1970 on Italian legend Dino Meneghin and Mexican National Team star Manuel Raga. "Now it's standard operating procedure for every team. The league has progressed to the point where there is enough money to scout worldwide."

But drafting players for the NBA wasn't always the sophisticated process it is today. Red Auerbach, the legendary Boston Celtics coach and general manager, drafted

WHEN THE NBA HELD THE FIRST LOTTERY IN 1985, KNICKS GM DAVE DEBUSSCHERE GOT LUCKY AND THE PRIZE WAS PATRICK EWING.

Hall of Famer Sam Jones out of tiny North Carolina Central in 1957 on the strength of some sage advice from one of his former players, Bones McKinney.

"It was worth a shot, so I took him," said Auerbach, who fashioned the NBA's most revered dynasty with savvy personnel moves of that sort. Jones went on to win 10 championship rings in 12 seasons with the Celtics, many as the team's top offensive weapon.

Even today, when NBA talent evaluators watch top prospects play at events like the Portsmouth Invitational Tournament, the Nike Desert Classic and the NBA Pre-Draft Camp and watch thousands of hours of videotape, drafting remains an inexact science. Sometimes, a crushing injury to a top player (like Sam Bowie) or the unexpected development of a late bloomer (Jeff Hornacek) can make wise personnel men shake their heads. Sometimes, a little luck is all that's needed to look like a genius.

In 1998, Boston general manager Chris Wallace and coach Rick Pitino held the 10th pick in the draft, and expected talented Kansas forward Paul Pierce to be gone by then. But with several teams drafting based on perceived needs rather than on the "best player available" theory, Pierce was still on the board when Boston's selection came around.

"With Paul, we didn't have a chance to outsmart ourselves," said Wallace with a laugh. "Sometimes we overdo this. We did not have him in for a visit. He did not receive a psychological test from this organization. Hey, we knew who he was from scouting college basketball. And there was no doubt in my mind that he was the player to take at that spot."

If only it were always that easy.

THE NBA DRAFT OVERVIEW

by Alex Sachare

In its evolution over the past half-century, the NBA Draft has become much more — and much less — than it was when it first began.

Once held in small meeting rooms or by conference call from NBA headquarters in New York, the NBA Draft has become a traveling road show that now plays in sold-out arenas all around North America. What used to be an internal process for the allocation of available players, most of whom were barely known outside their immediate families, has become a highly anticipated media event that is the culmination of months of speculation regarding the futures of athletes of national and even global renown.

On the other hand, what was once a two-day marathon has been streamlined to one fast-paced evening of prime time national television programming.

One thing that hasn't changed is that a team that strikes it rich on draft day can change the course of its destiny for years to come:

• In 1956 Boston traded for the draft rights to Bill Russell and also selected Tom Heinsohn and K.C. Jones, all of whom would play key roles in the Celtics dynasty that won 11 championships in 13 seasons. (Jones would not join the team for two years because of a military commitment.)

• In 1984 Chicago drafted a junior from North Carolina named Michael Jordan, and by the time he retired (for the second time), the Bulls had raised six championship banners.

• In 1997 San Antonio opened the draft by selecting Tim Duncan, and the Spurs teamed him with David Robinson in a Twin Towers alignment that would win the league title in 1999.

Basketball's global growth in popularity has translated into few if any "sleepers" at the NBA Draft. If a prospect can play, everybody finds out about it very quickly. Teams operate their drafts from "war rooms" dominated by sophisticated computers and boards listing the top players. Teams select players in inverse order of their regular season records. In 1985, a draft lottery was introduced for all teams not qualifying for the playoffs, in order to erase any incentive for losing late-season games. As the league expanded in the late 1980s, the lottery field grew and a weighted system was introduced, giving teams with poorer records better chances — but no guarantees — at the top pick. The system has been modified so the lottery now determines the order of selection for the first three choices only; remaining teams are listed in inverse order of their records so the team with the worst record in the league is assured at least the fourth selection.

In the league's early years, when teams were struggling to build fan bases, the draft included territorial picks. Before the start of the draft, a team could forfeit its first-round pick and instead select a player from its immediate area, presumably with a strong local following. For example, the Cincinnati Royals selected Jerry Lucas from Ohio State as a territorial pick in 1962.

Territorial picks were eliminated after 1965. In 1966 the league adopted a coin flip between the last-place finishers in each of its two divisions to determine which club would open the draft, a system that remained in place until the first lottery in 1985.

In the early years of the draft, teams would select players until they ran out of prospects. By agreement with the National Basketball Players Association, today's draft is limited to two rounds, which gives undrafted players the chance to try out for any team.

Any player who has completed his college eligibility, or any international player who is in the calendar year of his 22nd birthday, is eligible for the draft. Anyone else may declare himself eligible by notifying the league at least 45 days before the draft.

History of the NBA Draft Lottery

Beginning in 1985, a lottery was held among teams that failed to qualify for the playoffs to determine their order of selection. The lottery was later modified to determine only the order of selection for the first three picks, after which teams were listed in inverse order of their records. Also, the lottery was weighted to give teams with worse records a better chance at the top picks.

2000

NO.	NAME	COLLEGE/HS	TEAM
1	Kenyon Martin	Cincinnati	New Jersey Nets
2	Stromile Swift	LSU	Vancouver Grizzlies
3	Darius Miles	East St. Louis HS (Ill.)	Los Angeles Clippers
4	Marcus Fizer	Iowa State	Chicago Bulls
5	Mike Miller	Florida	Orlando Magic
6	DerMarr Johnson	Cincinnati	Atlanta Hawks
7	Chris Mihm	Texas	Chicago Bulls
8	Jamal Crawford	Michigan	Cleveland Cavaliers
9	Joel Przybilla	Minnesota	Houston Rockets
10	Keyon Dooling	Missouri	Orlando Magic
11	Jerome Moiso	UCLA	Boston Celtics
12	Etan Thomas	Syracuse	Dallas Mavericks
13	Courtney Alexander	Fresno State	Orlando Magic

1999

NO.	NAME	COLLEGE/HS	TEAM
1	Elton Brand	Duke	Chicago
2	Steve Francis	Maryland	Vancouver
3	Baron Davis	UCLA	Charlotte
4	Lamar Odom	Rhode Island	L.A. Clippers
5	Jonathan Bender	Picayune HS (Miss.)	Toronto
6	Wally Szczerbiak	Miami (Ohio)	Minnesota
7	Richard Hamilton	Connecticut	Washington
8	Andre Miller	Utah	Cleveland
9	Shawn Marion	UNLV	Phoenix
10	Jason Terry	Arizona	Atlanta
11	Trajan Langdon	Duke	Cleveland
12	Aleksandar Radojevic	Barton CC (Kan.)	Toronto
13	Corey Maggette	Duke	Seattle

1998

NO.	NAME	COLLEGE/HS	TEAM
1	Michael Olowokandi	Pacific	L.A. Clippers
2	Mike Bibby	Arizona	Vancouver
3	Raef LaFrentz	Kansas	Denver
4	Antawn Jamison	North Carolina	Toronto
5	Vince Carter	North Carolina	Golden State
6	Robert Traylor	Michigan	Dallas
7	Jason Williams	Florida	Sacramento
8	Larry Hughes	Saint Louis	Philadelphia
9	Dirk Nowitzki	DJK Wurzburg (Germany)	Milwaukee
10	Paul Pierce	Kansas	Boston
11	Bonzi Wells	Ball State	Detroit
12	Michael Doleac	Utah	Orlando
13	Keon Clark	UNLV	Orlando

1997

NO.	NAME	COLLEGE/HS	TEAM
1	Tim Duncan	Wake Forest	San Antonio
2	Keith Van Horn	Utah	Philadelphia
3	Chauncey Billups	Colorado	Boston
4	Antonio Daniels	Bowling Green	Vancouver
5	Tony Battie	Texas Tech	Denver
6	Ron Mercer	Kentucky	Boston
7	Tim Thomas	Villanova	New Jersey
8	Adonal Foyle	Colgate	Golden State
9	Tracy McGrady	Mt. Zion Academy (H.S.)	Toronto
10	Danny Fortson	Cincinnati	Milwaukee
11	Olivier Saint-Jean	San Jose State	Sacramento
12	Austin Croshere	Providence	Indiana
13	Derek Anderson	Kentucky	Cleveland

1996

NO.	NAME	COLLEGE/HS	TEAM
1	Allen Iverson	Georgetown	Philadelphia
2	Marcus Camby	Massachusetts	Toronto
3	Shareef Abdur-Rahim	California	Vancouver
4	Stephon Marbury	Georgia Tech	Milwaukee
5	Ray Allen	Connecticut	Minnesota
6	Antoine Walker	Kentucky	Boston
7	Lorenzen Wright	Memphis	L.A. Clippers
8	Kerry Kittles	Villanova	New Jersey
9	Samaki Walker	Louisville	Dallas
10	Erick Dampier	Mississippi State	Indiana
11	Todd Fuller	N.C. State	Golden State
12	Vitaly Potapenko	Wright State	Cleveland
13	Kobe Bryant	Lower Merion HS (Pa.)	Charlotte

1995

NO.	NAME	COLLEGE/HS	TEAM
1	Joe Smith	Maryland	Golden State
2	Antonio McDyess	Alabama	L.A. Clippers
3	Jerry Stackhouse	North Carolina	Philadelphia
4	Rasheed Wallace	North Carolina	Washington
5	Kevin Garnett	Farragut Academy	Minnesota
6	Bryant Reeves	Oklahoma State	Vancouver
7	Damon Stoudamire	Arizona	Toronto
8	Shawn Respert	Michigan State	Portland
9	Ed O'Bannon	UCLA	New Jersey
10	Kurt Thomas	Texas Christian	Miami
11	Gary Trent	Ohio	Milwaukee
12	Cherokee Parks	Duke	Dallas
13	Corliss Williamson	Arkansas	Sacramento

1994

NO.	NAME	COLLEGE/HS	TEAM
1	Glenn Robinson	Purdue	Milwaukee
2	Jason Kidd	California	Dallas
3	Grant Hill	Duke	Detroit
4	Donyell Marshall	Connecticut	Minnesota
5	Juwan Howard	Michigan	Washington
6	Sharone Wright	Clemson	Philadelphia
7	Lamond Murray	California	L.A. Clippers
8	Brian Grant	Xavier (Ohio)	Sacramento
9	Eric Montross	North Carolina	Boston
10	Eddie Jones	Temple	L.A. Lakers
11	Carlos Rogers	Tennessee St.	Seattle

1993

NO.	NAME	COLLEGE/HS	TEAM
1	Chris Webber	Michigan	Orlando
2	Shawn Bradley	Brigham Young	Philadelphia
3	Anfernee Hardaway	Memphis	Golden State
4	Jamal Mashburn	Kentucky	Dallas
5	Isaiah (J.R.) Rider	UNLV	Minnesota
6	Calbert Cheaney	Indiana	Washington
7	Bobby Hurley	Duke	Sacramento
8	Vin Baker	Hartford	Milwaukee
9	Rodney Rogers	Wake Forest	Denver
10	Lindsey Hunter	Jackson State	Detroit
11	Allan Houston	Tennessee	Detroit

1992

NO.	NAME	COLLEGE/HS	TEAM
1	Shaquille O'Neal	Louisiana St.	Orlando
2	Alonzo Mourning	Georgetown	Charlotte
3	Christian Laettner	Duke	Minnesota
4	Jimmy Jackson	Ohio State	Dallas
5	LaPhonso Ellis	Notre Dame	Denver

NO.	NAME	COLLEGE/HS	TEAM
6	Tom Gugliotta	North Carolina St.	Washington
7	Walt Williams	Maryland	Sacramento
8	Todd Day	Arkansas	Milwaukee
9	Clarence Weatherspoon	So. Mississippi	Philadelphia
10	Adam Keefe	Stanford	Atlanta
11	Robert Horry	Alabama	Houston
1991			
1	Larry Johnson	UNLV	Charlotte
2	Kenny Anderson	Georgia Tech	New Jersey
3	Billy Owens	Syracuse	Sacramento
4	Dikembe Mutombo	Georgetown	Denver
5	Steve Smith	Michigan State	Miami
6	Doug Smith	Missouri	Dallas
7	Luc Longley	New Mexico	Minnesota
8	Mark Macon	Temple	Denver
9	Stacey Augmon	UNLV	Atlanta
10	Brian Williams	Arizona	Orlando
11	Terrell Brandon	Oregon	Cleveland
1990			
1	Derrick Coleman	Syracuse	New Jersey
2	Gary Payton	Oregon State	Seattle
3	Chris Jackson	LSU	Denver
4	Dennis Scott	Georgia Tech	Orlando
5	Kendall Gill	Illinois	Charlotte
6	Felton Spencer	Louisville	Minnesota
7	Lionel Simmons	La Salle	Sacramento
8	Bo Kimble	Loyola Marymount	L.A. Clippers
9	Willie Burton	Minnesota	Miami
10	Rumeal Robinson	Michigan	Atlanta
11	Tyrone Hill	Xavier (Ohio)	Golden State
1989			
1	Pervis Ellison	Louisville	Sacramento
2	Danny Ferry	Duke	L.A. Clippers
3	Sean Elliott	Arizona	San Antonio
4	Glen Rice	Michigan	Miami
5	J.R. Reid	North Carolina	Charlotte
6	Stacey King	Oklahoma	Chicago
7	George McCloud	Florida State	Indiana
8	Randy White	Louisiana Tech	Dallas
9	Tom Hammonds	Georgia Tech	Washington
1988			
1	Danny Manning	Kansas	L.A. Clippers
2	Rik Smits	Marist	Indiana
3	Charles Smith	Pittsburgh	Philadelphia
4	Chris Morris	Auburn	New Jersey
5	Mitch Richmond	Kansas State	Golden State
6	Hersey Hawkins	Bradley	L.A. Clippers
7	Tim Perry	Temple	Phoenix
1987			
1	David Robinson	Navy	San Antonio
2	Armon Gilliam	UNLV	Phoenix
3	Dennis Hopson	Ohio State	New Jersey
4	Reggie Williams	Georgetown	L.A. Clippers
5	Scottie Pippen	Central Arkansas	Seattle
6	Kenny Smith	North Carolina	Sacramento
7	Kevin Johnson	California	Cleveland
1986			
1	Brad Daugherty	North Carolina	Cleveland
2	Len Bias	Maryland	Boston
3	Chris Washburn	N.C. State	Golden State
4	Chuck Person	Auburn	Indiana
5	Kenny Walker	Kentucky	New York
6	William Bedford	Memphis State	Phoenix
7	Roy Tarpley	Michigan	Dallas
1985			
1	Patrick Ewing	Georgetown	New York
2	Wayman Tisdale	Oklahoma	Indiana
3	Benoit Benjamin	Creighton	L.A. Clippers
4	Xavier McDaniel	Wichita State	Seattle
5	Jon Koncak	Southern Methodist	Atlanta
6	Joe Kleine	Arkansas	Sacramento
7	Chris Mullin	St. John's	Golden State

History of the NBA Coin Flip

Beginning in 1966, a coin flip was held between the teams with the worst records in each division to determine which team would select first overall in the draft. This coin flip was in effect through 1984.

YEAR	FLIP CALL	RESULT	FIRST TWO PICKS
1984	Portland – Tails	Heads	Houston – Hakeem Olajuwon Portland – Sam Bowie (from Indiana)
1983	Houston – Heads	Heads	Houston – Ralph Sampson Indiana – Steve Stipanovich
1982	LA Lakers – Heads	Heads	LA Lakers – James Worthy (from Cleveland) San Diego—Terry Cummings
1981	Detroit – Heads	Tails	Dallas – Mark Aguirre Detroit – Isiah Thomas
1980	Utah – Heads	Tails	Golden State – Joe Barry Carroll (from Detroit via Boston) Utah – Darrell Griffith
1979	Chicago – Heads	Tails	LA Lakers – Magic Johnson (from New Orleans) Chicago – David Greenwood
1978	Kansas City – Heads	Tails	Portland – Mychal Thompson (from Indiana) Kansas City – Phil Ford (from New Jersey)
1977	Kansas City – Heads	Tails	Milwaukee – Kent Benson Kansas City – Otis Birdsong (from New Jersey)
1976	Houston – Heads	Heads	Houston – John Lucas (from Atlanta) Chicago – Scott May
1975	Atlanta – Tails	Tails	Atlanta – David Thompson LA Lakers – David Meyers
1974	Philadelphia – Heads	Tails	Portland – Bill Walton Philadelphia – Marvin Barnes
1973	Philadelphia – Tails	Tails	Philadelphia – Doug Collins Cleveland – Jim Brewer (from Portland)
1972	Portland – Tails	Tails	Portland – LaRue Martin Buffalo – Bob McAdoo
1971	Portland – Heads	Tails	Cleveland – Austin Carr Portland – Sidney Wicks
1970	San Diego – Heads	Tails	Detroit – Bob Lanier San Diego – Rudy Tomjanovich
1969	Phoenix – Heads	Tails	Milwaukee – Kareem Abdul-Jabbar Phoenix – Neal Walk
1968	San Diego – Heads	Heads	San Diego – Elvin Hayes Baltimore – Wes Unseld
1967	Baltimore – Tails	Heads	Detroit – Jimmy Walker Baltimore – Earl Monroe
1966	Detroit – Tails	Heads	New York – Cazzie Russell Detroit – Dave Bing

The Draft

2000

Round		Name	Team	College	# Overall
FIRST ROUND	1	Kenyon Martin	New Jersey Nets	Cincinnati	1
	2	Stromile Swift	Vancouver Grizzlies	LSU	2
	3	Darius Miles	Los Angeles Clippers	East St. Louis H.S.	3
	4	Marcus Fizer	Chicago Bulls	Iowa State	4
	5	Mike Miller	Orlando Magic	Florida	5
	6	DerMarr Johnson	Atlanta Hawks	Cincinnati	6
	7	Chris Mihm	Chicago Bulls	Texas	7
	8	Jamal Crawford	Cleveland Cavaliers	Michigan	8
	9	Joel Przybilla	Houston Rockets	Minnesota	9
	10	Keyon Dooling	Orlando Magic	Missouri	10
	11	Jerome Moiso	Boston Celtics	UCLA	11
	12	Etan Thomas	Dallas Mavericks	Syracuse	12
	13	Courtney Alexander	Orlando Magic	Fresno State	13
	14	Mateen Cleaves	Detroit Pistons	Michigan State	14
	15	Jason Collier	Milwaukee Bucks	Georgia Tech	15
	16	Hidayet Turkoglu	Sacramento Kings	Efes Pilsen (Turkey)	16
	17	Desmond Mason	Seattle SuperSonics	Oklahoma State	17
	18	Quentin Richardson	Denver Nuggets	DePaul	18
	19	Jamaal Magloire	Charlotte Hornets	Kentucky	19
	20	Speedy Claxton	Philadelphia 76ers	Hofstra	20
	21	Morris Peterson	Toronto Raptors	Michigan State	21
	22	Donnell Harvey	New York Knicks	Florida	22
	23	DeShawn Stevenson	Utah Jazz	Washington Union H.S.	23
	24	Dalibor Bagaric	Chicago Bulls	Benston Zagreb (Croatia)	24
	25	Iakovos Tsakalidis	Phoenix Suns	AEK (Greece)	25
	26	Mamadou N'diaye	Denver Nuggets	Auburn	26
	27	Primoz Brezec	Indiana Pacers	Olympija Ljubljiana (Slovenia)	27
	28	Erick Barkley	Portland Trail Blazers	St. John's	28
	29	Mark Madsen	Los Angeles Lakers	Stanford	29
SECOND ROUND	1	Marko Jaric	Los Angeles Clippers	Fortitudo Bologna (Italy)	30
	2	Dan Langhi	Dallas Mavericks	Vanderbilt	31
	3	A.J. Guyton	Chicago Bulls	Indiana	32
	4	Jake Voskuhl	Chicago Bulls	Connecticut	33
	5	Khalid El-Amin	Chicago Bulls	Connecticut	34
	6	Mike Smith	Washington Wizards	Louisiana-Monroe	35
	7	Soumaila Samake	New Jersey Nets	Mali	36
	8	Eddie House	Miami Heat	Arizona State	37
	9	Eduardo Najera	Houston Rockets	Oklahoma	38
	10	Lavor Postell	New York Knicks	St. John's	39
	11	Hanno Möttölä	Atlanta Hawks	Utah	40
	12	Chris Carrawell	San Antonio Spurs	Duke	41
	13	Olumide Oyedeji	Seattle SuperSonics	DJK Wurzburg	42
	14	Michael Redd	Milwaukee Bucks	Ohio State	43
	15	Brian Cardinal	Detroit Pistons	Purdue	44
	16	Jabari Smith	Sacramento Kings	LSU	45
	17	DeeAndre Hulett	Toronto Raptors	Las Vegas (IBL)	46
	18	Josip Sesar	Seattle SuperSonics	Cibona Zagreb (Croatia)	47
	19	Mark Karcher	Philadelphia 76ers	Temple	48
	20	Jason Hart	Milwaukee Bucks	Syracuse	49
	21	Kaniel Dickens	Utah Jazz	Idaho	50
	22	Igor Rakocevic	Minnesota Timberwolves	Red Star Belgrade	51
	23	Ernest Brown	Miami Heat	Indian Hills CC	52
	24	Daniel McClintock	Denver Nuggets	Northern Arizona	53
	25	Corey Hightower	San Antonio Spurs	Indian Hills CC	54
	26	Chris Porter	Golden State Warriors	Auburn	55
	27	Jacquay Wells	Indiana Pacers	Colorado	56
	28	Scoonie Penn	Atlanta Hawks	Ohio State	57
	29	Pete Mickeal	Dallas Mavericks	Cincinnati	58

1999

Round		Name	Team	College	# Overall
FIRST ROUND	1	Elton Brand	Chicago Bulls	Duke	1
	2	Steve Francis	Vancouver Grizzlies	Maryland	2
	3	Baron Davis	Charlotte Hornets	UCLA	3
	4	Lamar Odom	Los Angeles Clippers	Rhode Island	4
	5	Jonathan Bender	Toronto Raptors	Picayune (Miss.) H.S.	5
	6	Wally Szczerbiak	Minnesota Timberwolves	Miami (Ohio)	6
	7	Richard Hamilton	Washington Wizards	UConn	7
	8	Andre Miller	Cleveland Cavaliers	Utah	8
	9	Shawn Marion	Phoenix Suns	UNLV	9
	10	Jason Terry	Atlanta Hawks	Arizona	10
	11	Trajan Langdon	Cleveland Cavaliers	Duke	11
	12	Aleksandar Radojevic	Toronto Raptors	Barton County C.C.	12
	13	Corey Maggette	Seattle SuperSonics	Duke	13
	14	William Avery	Minnesota Timberwolves	Duke	14
	15	Frederic Weis	New York Knicks	Limoges (France)	15
	16	Ron Artest	Chicago Bulls	St. John's	16
	17	Cal Bowdler	Atlanta Hawks	Old Dominion	17
	18	James Posey	Denver Nuggets	Xavier	18
	19	Quincy Lewis	Utah Jazz	Minnesota	19
	20	Dion Glover	Atlanta Hawks	Georgia Tech	20
	21	Jeff Foster	Golden State Warriors	SW Texas State	21
	22	Kenny Thomas	Houston Rockets	New Mexico	22
	23	Devean George	Los Angeles Lakers	Augsburg (Minn.)	23
	24	Andrei Kirilenko	Utah Jazz	CSKA (Russia)	24
	25	Tim James	Miami Heat	Miami	25
	26	Vonteego Cummings	Indiana Pacers	Pittsburgh	26
	27	Jumaine Jones	Atlanta Hawks	Georgia	27
	28	Scott Padgett	Utah Jazz	Kentucky	28
	29	Leon Smith	San Antonio Spurs	MLK H.S. (Chicago)	29
SECOND ROUND	1	John Celestand	Los Angeles Lakers	Villanova	30
	2	Rico Hill	Los Angeles Clippers	Illinois State	31
	3	Michael Ruffin	Chicago Bulls	Tulsa	32
	4	Chris Herren	Denver Nuggets	Fresno State	33
	5	Evan Eschmeyer	New Jersey Nets	Northwestern	34
	6	Calvin Booth	Washington Wizards	Penn State	35
	7	Wang Zhi-Zhi	Dallas Mavericks	(China)	36
	8	Obinna Ekezie	Vancouver Grizzlies	Maryland	37
	9	Laron Profit	Orlando Magic	Maryland	38
	10	A.J. Bramlett	Cleveland Cavaliers	Arizona	39
	11	Gordan Giricek	Dallas Mavericks	Zagreb-Croatia	40
	12	Francisco Elson	Denver Nuggets	California	41
	13	Louis Bullock	Minnesota Timberwolves	Michigan	42
	14	Lee Nailon	Charlotte Hornets	TCU	43
	15	Tyrone Washington	Houston Rockets	Mississippi State	44
	16	Ryan Robertson	Sacramento Kings	Kansas	45
	17	J.R. Koch	New York Knicks	Iowa	46
	18	Todd MacCulloch	Philadelphia 76ers	Washington	47
	19	Galen Young	Milwaukee Bucks	UNC-Charlotte	48
	20	Lari Ketner	Chicago Bulls	UMass	49
	21	Venson Hamilton	Houston Rockets	Nebraska	50
	22	Antwain Smith	Vancouver Grizzlies	St. Paul's College	51
	23	Roberto Bergersen	Atlanta Hawks	Boise State	52

	NAME	TEAM	COLLEGE	# OVERALL
24	Rodney Buford	Miami Heat	Creighton	53
25	Melvin Levett	Detroit Pistons	Cincinnati	54
26	Kris Clack	Boston Celtics	Texas	55
27	Tim Young	Golden State Warriors	Stanford	56
28	Emanuel Ginobili	San Antonio Spurs	Reggio Calabria (Italy)	57
29	Eddie Lucas	Utah Jazz	Virginia Tech	58

1998

ROUND		NAME	TEAM	COLLEGE	# OVERALL
FIRST ROUND	1	Michael Olowokandi	Los Angeles Clippers	Pacific	1
	2	Mike Bibby	Vancouver Grizzlies	Arizona	2
	3	Raef LaFrentz	Denver Nuggets	Kansas	3
	4	Antawn Jamison	Toronto Raptors	North Carolina	4
	5	Vince Carter	Golden State Warriors	North Carolina	5
	6	Robert Traylor	Dallas Mavericks	Michigan	6
	7	Jason Williams	Sacramento Kings	Florida	7
	8	Larry Hughes	Philadelphia 76ers	Saint Louis	8
	9	Dirk Nowitzki	Milwaukee Bucks	DJK Wurzburg (Germany)	9
	10	Paul Pierce	Boston Celtics	Kansas	10
	11	Bonzi Wells	Detroit Pistons	Ball State	11
	12	Michael Doleac	Orlando Magic	Utah	12
	13	Keon Clark	Orlando Magic	UNLV	13
	14	Michael Dickerson	Houston Rockets	Arizona	14
	15	Matt Harpring	Orlando Magic	Georgia Tech	15
	16	Bryce Drew	Houston Rockets	Valparaiso	16
	17	Radoslav Nesterovic	Minnesota Timberwolves	Kinder Bologna (Italy)	17
	18	Mirsad Tuckcan	Houston Rockets	Efes Pilsen (Turkey)	18
	19	Pat Garrity	Milwaukee Bucks	Notre Dame	19
	20	Roshown McLeod	Atlanta Hawks	Duke	20
	21	Ricky Davis	Charlotte Hornets	Iowa	21
	22	Brian Skinner	Los Angeles Clippers	Baylor	22
	23	Tyronn Lue	Denver Nuggets	Nebraska	23
	24	Felipe Lopez	San Antonio Spurs	St. John's	24
	25	Al Harrington	Indiana Pacers	St. Patrick's HS	25
	26	Sam Jacobson	Los Angeles Lakers	Minnesota	26
	27	Vladimir Stepania	Seattle SuperSonics	Olympija (Ljubljana)	27
	28	Corey Benjamin	Chicago Bulls	Oregon State	28
	29	Nazr Mohammed	Utah Jazz	Kentucky	29
SECOND ROUND	1	Ansu Sesay	Dallas Mavericks	Mississippi	30
	2	Ruben Patterson	Los Angeles Lakers	Cincinnati	31
	3	Rashard Lewis	Seattle SuperSonics	Alief Elsik HS (Texas)	32
	4	Jelani McCoy	Seattle SuperSonics	UCLA	33
	5	Shammond Williams	Chicago Bulls	North Carolina	34
	6	Bruno Sundov	Dallas Mavericks	Split (Croatia)	35
	7	Jerome James	Sacramento Kings	Florida A&M	36
	8	Casey Shaw	Philadelphia 76ers	Toledo	37
	9	DeMarco Johnson	New York Knicks	UNC-Charlotte	38
	10	Rafer Alston	Milwaukee Bucks	Fresno State	39
	11	Korleone Young	Detroit Pistons	Hargrave Military Acad.	40
	12	Cuttino Mobley	Houston Rockets	Rhode Island	41
	13	Miles Simon	Orlando Magic	Arizona	42
	14	Jahidi White	Washington Wizards	Georgetown	43
	15	Sean Marks	New York Knicks	California	44
	16	Toby Bailey	Los Angeles Lakers	UCLA	45
	17	Andrae Patterson	Minnesota Timberwolves	Indiana	46
	18	Tyson Wheeler	Toronto Raptors	Rhode Island	47
	19	Ryan Stack	Cleveland Cavaliers	South Carolina	48
	20	Cory Carr	Atlanta Hawks	Texas Tech	49
	21	Andrew Betts	Charlotte Hornets	Long Beach State	50
	22	Corey Brewer	Miami Heat	Oklahoma	51
	23	Derrick Dial	San Antonio Spurs	Eastern Michigan	52
	24	Greg Buckner	Dallas Mavericks	Clemson	53
	25	Tremaine Fowlkes	Denver Nuggets	Fresno State	54
	26	Ryan Bowen	Denver Nuggets	Iowa	55
	27	J.R. Henderson	Vancouver Grizzlies	UCLA	56
	28	Torraye Braggs	Utah Jazz	Xavier	57
	29	Maceo Baston	Chicago Bulls	Michigan	58

1997

ROUND		NAME	TEAM	COLLEGE	# OVERALL
FIRST ROUND	1	Tim Duncan	San Antonio Spurs	Wake Forest	1
	2	Keith Van Horn	Philadelphia 76ers	Utah	2
	3	Chauncey Billups	Boston Celtics	Colorado	3
	4	Antonio Daniels	Vancouver Grizzlies	Bowling Green	4
	5	Tony Battie	Denver Nuggets	Texas Tech	5
	6	Ron Mercer	Boston Celtics	Kentucky	6
	7	Tim Thomas	New Jersey Nets	Villanova	7
	8	Adonal Foyle	Golden State Warriors	Colgate	8
	9	Tracy McGrady	Toronto Raptors	Mt. Zion Academy (HS)	9
	10	Danny Fortson	Milwaukee Bucks	Cincinnati	10
	11	Olivier Saint-Jean	Sacramento Kings	San Jose State	11
	12	Austin Croshere	Indiana Pacers	Providence	12
	13	Derek Anderson	Cleveland Cavaliers	Kentucky	13
	14	Maurice Taylor	Los Angeles Clippers	Michigan	14
	15	Kelvin Cato	Dallas Mavericks	Iowa State	15
	16	Brevin Knight	Cleveland Cavaliers	Stanford	16
	17	Johnny Taylor	Orlando Magic	Tennessee-Chattanooga	17
	18	Chris Anstey	Portland Trail Blazers	SE Melbourne (Australia)	18
	19	Scot Pollard	Detroit Pistons	Kansas	19
	20	Paul Grant	Minnesota Timberwolves	Wisconsin	20
	21	Anthony Parker	New Jersey Nets	Bradley	21
	22	Ed Gray	Atlanta Hawks	California	22
	23	Bobby Jackson	Seattle SuperSonics	Minnesota	23
	24	Rodrick Rhodes	Houston Rockets	USC	24
	25	John Thomas	New York Knicks	Minnesota	25
	26	Charles Smith	Miami Heat	New Mexico	26
	27	Jacque Vaughn	Utah Jazz	Kansas	27
	28	Keith Booth	Chicago Bulls	Maryland	28
SECOND ROUND	1	Serge Zwikker	Houston Rockets	North Carolina	30
	2	Mark Sanford	Miami Heat	Washington	31
	3	Charles O'Bannon	Detroit Pistons	UCLA	32
	4	James Cotton	Denver Nuggets	Long Beach State	33
	5	Marko Milic	Philadelphia 76ers	Smelt Olimpija (Slovenia)	34
	6	Bubba Wells	Dallas Mavericks	Austin Peay	35
	7	Kebu Stewart	Philadelphia 76ers	Cal State Bakersfield	36
	8	James Collins	Philadelphia 76ers	Florida State	37
	9	Marc Jackson	Golden State Warriors	Temple	38
	10	Jerald Honeycutt	Milwaukee Bucks	Tulane	39
	11	Anthony Johnson	Sacramento Kings	College of Charleston	40
	12	Ed Elisma	Seattle SuperSonics	Georgia Tech	41
	13	Jason Lawson	Denver Nuggets	Villanova	42
	14	Stephen Jackson	Phoenix Suns	Oak Hill (Va)	43
	15	Gordon Malone	Minnesota Timberwolves	West Virginia	44
	16	Cedric Henderson	Cleveland Cavaliers	Memphis	45
	17	God Shammgod	Washington Wizards	Providence	46
	18	Eric Washington	Orlando Magic	Alabama	47
	19	Alvin Williams	Portland Trail Blazers	Villanova	48
	20	Predrag Drobnjak	Washington Wizards	Partizan (Yugoslavia)	49
	21	Alain Digbeu	Atlanta Hawks	Villeurbanne (France)	50
	22	Chris Crawford	Atlanta Hawks	Marquette	51
	23	DeJuan Wheat	Los Angeles Lakers	Louisville	52
	24	C.J. Bruton	Vancouver Grizzlies	Indian Hills (Iowa) CC	53

Washington forfeited its 1997 first-round draft pick as compensation for re-signing free agent Juwan Howard in 1996. Washington would have had the 17th pick in the draft and the picks above (after the 16th pick) reflected that forfeiture.

		NAME	TEAM	COLLEGE	# OVERALL
	25	Paul Rogers	Los Angeles Lakers	Gonzaga	54
	26	Mark Blount	Seattle SuperSonics	Pittsburgh	55
	27	Ben Pepper	Boston Celtics	Newcastle Falcons (NBL)	56
	28	Nate Erdmann	Utah Jazz	Oklahoma	57
	29	Roberto Duenas	Chicago Bulls	FC Barcelona (Spain)	58

1996

		NAME	TEAM	COLLEGE	# OVERALL
FIRST ROUND	1	Allen Iverson	Philadelphia 76ers	Georgetown	1
	2	Marcus Camby	Toronto Raptors	Massachusetts	2
	3	Shareef Abdur-Rahim	Vancouver Grizzlies	California	3
	4	Stephon Marbury	Milwaukee Bucks	Georgia Tech	4
	5	Ray Allen	Minnesota Timberwolves	Connecticut	5
	6	Antoine Walker	Boston Celtics	Kentucky	6
	7	Lorenzen Wright	Los Angeles Clippers	Memphis	7
	8	Kerry Kittles	New Jersey Nets	Villanova	8
	9	Samaki Walker	Dallas Mavericks	Louisvile	9
	10	Erick Dampier	Indiana Pacers	Mississippi State	10
	11	Todd Fuller	Golden State Warriors	North Carolina State	11
	12	Vitaly Potapenko	Cleveland Cavaliers	Wright State	12
	13	Kobe Bryant	Charlotte Hornets	Lower Merion HS	13
	14	Predrag Stojakovic	Sacramento Kings	PAOK (Greece)	14
	15	Steve Nash	Phoenix Suns	Santa Clara	15
	16	Tony Delk	Charlotte Hornets	Kentucky	16
	17	Jermaine O'Neal	Portland Trail Blazers	Eau Claire HS	17
	18	John Wallace	New York Knicks	Syracuse	18
	19	Walter McCarty	New York Knicks	Kentucky	19
	20	Zydrunas Ilgauskas	Cleveland Cavaliers	Lithuania	20
	21	Dontae' Jones	New York Knicks	Mississippi State	21
	22	Roy Rogers	Vancouver Grizzlies	Alabama	22
	23	Efthimios Rentzias	Denver Nuggets	PAOK (Greece)	23
	24	Derek Fisher	Los Angeles Lakers	Arkansas-Little Rock	24
	25	Martin Muursepp	Utah Jazz	BC Kalev Tallinn	25
	26	Jerome Williams	Detroit Pistons	Georgetown	26
	27	Brian Evans	Orlando Magic	Indiana	27
	28	Priest Lauderdale	Atlanta Hawks	Peristeri (Greece)	28
	29	Travis Knight	Chicago Bulls	Connecticut	29
SECOND ROUND	1	Othella Harrington	Houston Rockets	Georgetown	30
	2	Mark Hendrickson	Philadelphia 76ers	Washington State	31
	3	Ryan Minor	Philadelphia 76ers	Oklahoma	32
	4	Moochie Norris	Milwaukee Bucks	West Florida	33
	5	Shawn Harvey	Dallas Mavericks	West Virginia State	34
	6	Joeseph Blair	Seattle SuperSonics	Arizona	35
	7	Doron Sheffer	Los Angeles Clippers	Connecticut	36
	8	Jeff McInnis	Denver Nuggets	North Carolina	37
	9	Steve Hamer	Boston Celtics	Tennessee	38
	10	Russ Millard	Phoenix Suns	Iowa	39
	11	Marcus Mann	Golden State Warriors	Mississippi Valley State	40
	12	Jason Sasser	Sacramento Kings	Texas Tech	41
	13	Randy Livingston	Houston Rockets	Louisiana State	42
	14	Ben Davis	Phoenix Suns	Arizona	43
	15	Malik Rose	Charlotte Hornets	Drexel	44
	16	Joe Vogel	Seattle SuperSonics	Colorado State	45
	17	Marcus Brown	Portland Trail Blazers	Murray State	46
	18	Ron Riley	Seattle SuperSonics	Arizona State	47
	19	Jamie Feick	Philadelphia 76ers	Michigan State	48
	20	Amal McCaskill	Orlando Magic	Marquette	49
	21	Terrell Bell	Houston Rockets	Georgia	50
	22	Chris Robinson	Vancouver Grizzlies	Western Kentucky	51
	23	Mark Pope	Indiana Pacers	Kentucky	52
	24	Jeff Nordgaard	Milwaukee Bucks	Wisconsin-Green Bay	53
	25	Shandon Anderson	Utah Jazz	Georgia	54

		NAME	TEAM	COLLEGE	# OVERALL
	26	Ronnie Henderson	Washington Bullets	Louisiana State	55
	27	Reggie Geary	Cleveland Cavaliers	Arizona	56
	28	Drew Barry	Seattle SuperSonics	Georgia Tech	57
	29	Darnell Robinson	Dallas Mavericks	Arkansas	58

1995

		NAME	TEAM	COLLEGE	# OVERALL
FIRST ROUND	1	Joe Smith	Golden State Warriors	Maryland	1
	2	Antonio McDyess	Los Angeles Clippers	Alabama	2
	3	Jerry Stackhouse	Philadelphia 76ers	North Carolina	3
	4	Rasheed Wallace	Washington Bullets	North Carolina	4
	5	Kevin Garnett	Minnesota Timberwolves	Farragut Academy (Ill.)	5
	6	Bryant Reeves	Vancouver Grizzlies	Oklahoma State	6
	7	Damon Stoudamire	Toronto Raptors	Arizona	7
	8	Shawn Respert	Portland Trail Blazers	Michigan State	8
	9	Ed O'Bannon	New Jersey Nets	UCLA	9
	10	Kurt Thomas	Miami Heat	Texas Christian	10
	11	Gary Trent	Milwaukee Bucks	Ohio University	11
	12	Cherokee Parks	Dallas Mavericks	Duke	12
	13	Corliss Williamson	Sacramento Kings	Arkansas	13
	14	Eric Williams	Boston Celtics	Providence	14
	15	Brent Barry	Denver Nuggets	Oregon State	15
	16	Alan Henderson	Atlanta Hawks	Indiana	16
	17	Bob Sura	Cleveland Cavaliers	Florida State	17
	18	Theo Ratliff	Detroit Pistons	Wyoming	18
	19	Randolph Childress	Detroit Pistons	Wake Forest	19
	20	Jason Caffey	Chicago Bulls	Alabama	20
	21	Michael Finley	Phoenix Suns	Wisconsin	21
	22	George Zidek	Charlotte Hornets	UCLA	22
	23	Travis Best	Indiana Pacers	Georgia Teach	23
	24	Loren Meyer	Dallas Mavericks	Iowa State	24
	25	David Vaughn	Orlando Magic	Memphis	25
	26	Sherell Ford	Seattle SuperSonics	Illinois-Chicago	26
	27	Mario Bennett	Phoenix Suns	Arizona State	27
	28	Greg Ostertag	Utah Jazz	Kansas	28
	29	Cory Alexander	San Antonio Spurs	Virginia	29
SECOND ROUND	1	Lou Roe	Detroit Pistons	Massachusetts	30
	2	Dragan Tarlac	Chicago Bulls	Olympiakos, Greece	31
	3	Terrence Rencher	Washington Bullets	Texas	32
	4	Junior Burrough	Boston Celtics	Virginia	33
	5	Andrew DeClercq	Golden State Warriors	Florida	34
	6	Jimmy King	Toronto Raptors	Michigan	35
	7	Lawrence Moten	Vancouver Grizzlies	Syracuse	36
	8	Frankie King	Los Angeles Lakers	Western Carolina	37
	9	Rashard Griffith	Milwaukee Bucks	Wisconsin	38
	10	Donny Marshall	Cleveland Cavaliers	Connecticut	39
	11	Dwayne Whitfield	Golden State Warriors	Jackson State	40
	12	Erik Meek	Houston Rockets	Duke	41
	13	Donnie Boyce	Atlanta Hawks	Colorado	42
	14	Eric Snow	Milwaukee Bucks	Michigan State	43
	15	Anthony Pelle	Denver Nuggets	Fresno State	44
	16	Troy Brown	Atlanta Hawks	Providence	45
	17	George Banks	Miami Heat	Texas-El Paso	46
	18	Tyus Edney	Sacramento Kings	UCLA	47
	19	Mark Davis	Minnesota Timberwolves	Texas Tech	48
	20	Jerome Allen	Minnesota Timberwolves	Pennsylvania	49
	21	Martin Lewis	Golden State Warriors	Seward County C.C.	50
	22	Dejan Bodiroga	Sacramento Kings	Italy	51
	23	Fred Hoiberg	Indiana Pacers	Iowa State	52
	24	Constantin Popa	Los Angeles Clippers	Miami	53
	25	Eurelijus Zukauskas	Seattle SuperSonics	Neptunas, Lithuania	54
	26	Michael McDonald	Golden State Warriors	New Orleans	55

	NAME	TEAM	COLLEGE	# OVERALL
27	Chris Carr	Phoenix Suns	Southern Illinois	56
28	Cuonzo Martin	Atlanta Hawks	Purdue	57
29	Don Reid	Detroit Pistons	Georgetown	58

1994

FIRST ROUND

	NAME	TEAM	COLLEGE	# OVERALL
1	Glenn Robinson	Milwaukee Bucks	Purdue	1
2	Jason Kidd	Dallas Mavericks	California	2
3	Grant Hill	Detroit Pistons	Duke	3
4	Donyell Marshall	Minnesota Timberwolves	Connecticut	4
5	Juwan Howard	Washington Bullets	Michigan	5
6	Sharone Wright	Philadelphia 76ers	Clemson	6
7	Lamond Murray	Los Angeles Clippers	California	7
8	Brian Grant	Sacramento Kings	Xavier (Ohio)	8
9	Eric Montross	Boston Celtics	North Carolina	9
10	Eddie Jones	Los Angeles Lakers	Temple	10
11	Carlos Rogers	Seattle SuperSonics	Tennessee State	11
12	Khalid Reeves	Miami Heat	Arizona	12
13	Jalen Rose	Denver Nuggets	Michigan	13
14	Yinka Dare	New Jersey Nets	George Washington	14
15	Eric Piatkowski	Indiana Pacers	Nebraska	15
16	Cliff Rozier	Golden State Warriors	Louisville	16
17	Aaron McKie	Portland Trail Blazers	Temple	17
18	Eric Mobley	Milwaukee Bucks	Pittsburgh	18
19	Tony Dumas	Dallas Mavericks	Missouri–Kansas City	19
20	B.J. Tyler	Philadelphia 76ers	Texas	20
21	Dickey Simpkins	Chicago Bulls	Providence	21
22	Bill Curley	San Antonio Spurs	Boston College	22
23	Wesley Person	Phoenix Suns	Auburn	23
24	Monty Williams	New York Knicks	Notre Dame	24
25	Greg Minor	Los Angeles Clippers	Louisville	25
26	Charlie Ward	New York Knicks	Florida State	26
27	Brooks Thompson	Orlando Magic	Oklahoma State	27

SECOND ROUND

	NAME	TEAM	COLLEGE	# OVERALL
1	Deon Thomas	Dallas Mavericks	Illinois	28
2	Antonio Lang	Phoenix Suns	Duke	29
3	Howard Eisley	Minnesota Timberwolves	Boston College	30
4	Rodney Dent	Orlando Magic	Kentucky	31
5	Jim McIlvaine	Washington Bullets	Marquette	32
6	Derrick Alston	Philadelphia 76ers	Duquesne	33
7	Gaylon Nickerson	Atlanta Hawks	NW Oklahoma State	34
8	Michael Smith	Sacramento Kings	Providence	35
9	Andrei Fetisov	Boston Celtics	Forum Valladolid (Spain)	36
10	Dontonio Wingfield	Seattle SuperSonics	Cincinnati	37
11	Darrin Hancock	Charlotte Hornets	Kansas	38
12	Anthony Miller	Golden State Warriors	Michigan State	39
13	Jeff Webster	Miami Heat	Oklahoma	40
14	William Njoku	Indiana Pacers	St. Mary's (Canada)	41
15	Gary Collier	Cleveland Cavaliers	Tulsa	42
16	Shawnelle Scott	Portland Trail Blazers	St. John's	43
17	Damon Bailey	Indiana Pacers	Indiana	44
18	Dwayne Morton	Golden State Warriors	Louisville	45
19	Voshon Lenard	Milwaukee Bucks	Minnesota	46
20	Jamie Watson	Utah Jazz	South Carolina	47
21	Jevon Crudup	Detroit Pistons	Missouri	48
22	Kris Bruton	Chicago Bulls	Benedict College	49
23	Charles Claxton	Phoenix Suns	Georgia	50
24	Lawrence Funderburke	Sacramento Kings	Ohio State	51
25	Anthony Goldwire	Phoenix Suns	Houston	52
26	Albert Burditt	Houston Rockets	Texas	53
27	Zeljko Rebraca	Seattle SuperSonics	Partizan Belgrade	54

1993

FIRST ROUND

	NAME	TEAM	COLLEGE	# OVERALL
1	Chris Webber	Orlando Magic	Michigan	1
2	Shawn Bradley	Philadelphia 76ers	Brigham Young	2
3	Anfernee Hardaway	Golden State Warriors	Memphis State	3
4	Jamal Mashburn	Dallas Mavericks	Kentucky	4
5	Isaiah Rider	Minnesota Timberwolves	Nevada–Las Vegas	5
6	Calbert Cheaney	Washington Bullets	Indiana	6
7	Bobby Hurley	Sacramento Kings	Duke	7
8	Vin Baker	Milwaukee Bucks	Hartford	8
9	Rodney Rogers	Denver Nuggets	Wake Forest	9
10	Lindsey Hunter	Detroit Pistons	Jackson State	10
11	Allan Houston	Detroit Pistons	Tennessee	11
12	George Lynch	Los Angeles Lakers	North Carolina	12
13	Terry Dehere	Los Angeles Clippers	Seton Hall	13
14	Scott Haskin	Indiana Pacers	Oregon State	14
15	Doug Edwards	Atlanta Hawks	Florida State	15
16	Rex Walters	New Jersey Nets	Kansas	16
17	Greg Graham	Charlotte Hornets	Indiana	17
18	Luther Wright	Utah Jazz	Seton Hall	18
19	Acie Earl	Boston Celtics	Iowa	19
20	Scott Burrell	Charlotte Hornets	Connecticut	20
21	James Robinson	Portland Trail Blazers	Alabama	21
22	Chris Mills	Cleveland Cavaliers	Arizona	22
23	Ervin Johnson	Seattle SuperSonics	New Orleans	23
24	Sam Cassell	Houston Rockets	Florida State	24
25	Corie Blount	Chicago Bulls	Cincinnati	25
26	Geert Hammink	Orlando Magic	Louisiana State	26
27	Malcolm Mackey	Phoenix Suns	Georgia Tech	27

SECOND ROUND

	NAME	TEAM	COLLEGE	# OVERALL
1	Lucious Harris	Dallas Mavericks	Long Beach State	28
2	Sherron Mills	Minnesota Timberwolves	Virginia Commonwealth	29
3	Gheorghe Muresan	Washington Bullets	Pau Orthez (France)	30
4	Evers Burns	Sacramento Kings	Maryland	31
5	Alphonso Ford	Philadelphia 76ers	Mississippi Valley State	32
6	Eric Riley	Dallas Mavericks	Michigan	33
7	Darnell Mee	Golden State Warriors	Western Kentucky	34
8	Ed Stokes	Miami Heat	Arizona	35
9	John Best	New Jersey Nets	Tennessee Tech	36
10	Nick Van Exel	Los Angeles Lakers	Cincinnati	37
11	Conrad McRae	Washington Bullets	Syracuse	38
12	Thomas Hill	Indiana Pacers	Duke	39
13	Richard Manning	Atlanta Hawks	Washington	40
14	Anthony Reed	Chicago Bulls	Tulane	41
15	Adonis Jordan	Seattle SuperSonics	Kansas	42
16	Josh Grant	Denver Nuggets	Utah	43
17	Alex Holcombe	Sacramento Kings	Baylor	44
18	Bryon Russell	Utah Jazz	Long Beach State	45
19	Richard Petruska	Houston Rockets	UCLA	46
20	Chris Whitney	San Antonio Spurs	Clemson	47
21	Kevin Thompson	Portland Trail Blazers	North Carolina State	48
22	Mark Buford	Phoenix Suns	Mississippi Valley State	49
23	Marcelo Nicola	Houston Rockets	Taugres (Spain)	50
24	Spencer Dunkley	Indiana Pacers	Delaware	51
25	Mike Peplowski	Sacramento Kings	Michigan State	52
26	Leonard White	Los Angeles Clippers	Southern	53
27	Byron Wilson	Phoenix Suns	Utah	54

1992

	NAME	TEAM	COLLEGE	# OVERALL
1	Shaquille O'Neal	Orlando Magic	Louisiana State	1
2	Alonzo Mourning	Charlotte Hornets	Georgetown	2

		NAME	TEAM	COLLEGE	# OVERALL
FIRST ROUND	3	Christian Laettner	Minnesota Timberwolves	Duke	3
	4	Jimmy Jackson	Dallas Mavericks	Ohio State	4
	5	LaPhonso Ellis	Denver Nuggets	Notre Dame	5
	6	Tom Gugliotta	Washington Bullets	North Carolina State	6
	7	Walt Williams	Sacramento Kings	Maryland	7
	8	Todd Day	Milwaukee Bucks	Arkansas	8
	9	Clarence Weatherspoon	Philadelphia 76ers	Southern Mississippi	9
	10	Adam Keefe	Atlanta Hawks	Stanford	10
	11	Robert Horry	Houston Rockets	Alabama	11
	12	Harold Miner	Miami Heat	USC	12
	13	Bryant Stith	Denver Nuggets	Virginia	13
	14	Malik Sealy	Indiana Pacers	St. John's	14
	15	Anthony Peeler	Los Angeles Lakers	Missouri	15
	16	Randy Woods	Los Angeles Clippers	La Salle	16
	17	Doug Christie	Seattle SuperSonics	Pepperdine	17
	18	Tracy Murray	San Antonio Spurs	UCLA	18
	19	Don MacLean	Detroit Pistons	UCLA	19
	20	Hubert Davis	New York Knicks	North Carolina	20
	21	Jon Barry	Boston Celtics	Georgia Tech	21
	22	Oliver Miller	Phoenix Suns	Arkansas	22
	23	Lee Mayberry	Milwaukee Bucks	Arkansas	23
	24	Latrell Sprewell	Golden State Warriors	Alabama	24
	25	Elmore Spencer	Los Angeles Clippers	Nevada–Las Vegas	25
	26	David Johnson	Portland Trail Blazers	Syracuse	26
	27	Byron Houston	Chicago Bulls	Oklahoma State	27
SECOND ROUND	1	Marlon Maxey	Minnesota Timberwolves	Texas–El Paso	28
	2	P.J. Brown	New Jersey Nets	Louisiana Tech	29
	3	Sean Rooks	Dallas Mavericks	Arizona	30
	4	Reggie Smith	Portland Trail Blazers	Texas Christian	31
	5	Brent Price	Washington Bullets	Oklahoma	32
	6	Corey Williams	Chicago Bulls	Oklahoma State	33
	7	Chris Smith	Minnesota Timberwolves	Connecticut	34
	8	Tony Bennett	Charlotte Hornets	Wisconsin–Green Bay	35
	9	Duane Cooper	Los Angeles Lakers	USC	36
	10	Isaiah Morris	Miami Heat	Arkansas	37
	11	Elmer Bennett	Atlanta Hawks	Notre Dame	38
	12	Litterial Green	Chicago Bulls	Georgia	39
	13	Steve Rogers	New Jersey Nets	Alabama State	40
	14	Ronald Jones	Houston Rockets	Murray State	41
	15	Matt Geiger	Miami Heat	Georgia Tech	42
	16	Predrag Danilovic	Golden State Warriors	Partizan Belgrade	43
	17	Henry Williams	San Antonio Spurs	North Carolina–Charlotte	44
	18	Chris King	Seattle SuperSonics	Wake Forest	45
	19	Robert Werdann	Denver Nuggets	St. John's	46
	20	Darren Morningstar	Boston Celtics	Pittsburgh	47
	21	Brian Davis	Phoenix Suns	Duke	48
	22	Ron Ellis	Phoenix Suns	Louisiana Tech	49
	23	Matt Fish	Golden State Warriors	North Carolina–Wilmington	50
	24	Tim Burroughs	Minnesota Timberwolves	Jacksonville	51
	25	Matt Steigenga	Chicago Bulls	Michigan State	52
	26	Curtis Blair	Houston Rockets	Richmond	53
	27	Brett Roberts	Sacramento Kings	Morehead State	54

1991

		NAME	TEAM	COLLEGE	# OVERALL
FIRST ROUND	1	Larry Johnson	Charlotte Hornets	Nevada–Las Vegas	1
	2	Kenny Anderson	New Jersey Nets	Georgia Tech	2
	3	Billy Owens	Sacramento Kings	Syracuse	3
	4	Dikembe Mutombo	Denver Nuggets	Georgetown	4
	5	Steve Smith	Miami Heat	Michigan State	5
	6	Doug Smith	Dallas Mavericks	Missouri	6
	7	Luc Longley	Minnesota Timberwolves	New Mexico	7
	8	Mark Macon	Denver Nuggets	Temple	8
	9	Stacey Augmon	Atlanta Hawks	Nevada–Las Vegas	9
	10	Brian Williams	Orlando Magic	Arizona	10
	11	Terrell Brandon	Cleveland Cavaliers	Oregon	11
	12	Greg Anthony	New York Knicks	Nevada–Las Vegas	12
	13	Dale Davis	Indiana Pacers	Clemson	13
	14	Rich King	Seattle SuperSonics	Nebraska	14
	15	Anthony Avent	Atlanta Hawks	Seton Hall	15
	16	Chris Gatling	Golden State Warriors	Old Dominion	16
	17	Victor Alexander	Golden State Warriors	Iowa State	17
	18	Kevin Brooks	Milwaukee Bucks	SW Louisiana	18
	19	LaBradford Smith	Washington Bullets	Louisville	19
	20	John Turner	Houston Rockets	Phillips	20
	21	Eric Murdock	Utah Jazz	Providence	21
	22	LeRon Ellis	Los Angeles Clippers	Syracuse	22
	23	Stanley Roberts	Orlando Magic	Louisiana State	23
	24	Rick Fox	Boston Celtics	North Carolina	24
	25	Shaun Vandiver	Golden State Warriors	Colorado	25
	26	Mark Randall	Chicago Bulls	Kansas	26
	27	Pete Chilcutt	Sacramento Kings	North Carolina	27
SECOND ROUND	1	Kevin Lynch	Charlotte Hornets	Minnesota	28
	2	George Ackles	Miami Heat	Nevada–Las Vegas	29
	3	Rodney Monroe	Atlanta Hawks	North Carolina State	30
	4	Randy Brown	Sacramento Kings	New Mexico State	31
	5	Chad Gallagher	Phoenix Suns	Creighton	32
	6	Donald Hodge	Dallas Mavericks	Temple	33
	7	Myron Brown	Minnesota Timberwolves	Slippery Rock	34
	8	Mike Iuzzolino	Dallas Mavericks	St. Francis (Pa.)	35
	9	Chris Corchiani	Orlando Magic	North Carolina State	36
	10	Elliot Perry	Los Angeles Clippers	Memphis State	37
	11	Joe Wylie	Los Angeles Clippers	Miami (Fla.)	38
	12	Jimmy Oliver	Cleveland Cavaliers	Purdue	39
	13	Doug Overton	Detroit Pistons	La Salle	40
	14	Sean Green	Indiana Pacers	Iona	41
	15	Steve Hood	Sacramento Kings	James Madison	42
	16	Lamont Strothers	Golden State Warriors	Christopher Newport	43
	17	Alvaro Teheran	Philadelphia 76ers	Houston	44
	18	Bobby Phills	Milwaukee Bucks	Southern	45
	19	Richard Dumas	Phoenix Suns	Oklahoma State	46
	20	Keith Hughes	Houston Rockets	Rutgers	47
	21	Isaac Austin	Utah Jazz	Arizona State	48
	22	Greg Sutton	San Antonio Spurs	Oral Roberts	49
	23	Joey Wright	Phoenix Suns	Texas	50
	24	Zan Tabak	Houston Rockets	Split (Croatia)	51
	25	Anthony Jones	Los Angeles Lakers	Oral Roberts	52
	26	Von McDade	New Jersey Nets	Wisconsin–Milwaukee	53
	27	Marcus Kennedy	Portland Trail Blazers	Eastern Michigan	54

1990

		NAME	TEAM	COLLEGE	# OVERALL
FIRST ROUND	1	Derrick Coleman	New Jersey Nets	Syracuse	1
	2	Gary Payton	Seattle SuperSonics	Oregon State	2
	3	Chris Jackson	Denver Nuggets	Louisiana State	3
	4	Dennis Scott	Orlando Magic	Georgia Tech	4
	5	Kendall Gill	Charlotte Hornets	Illinois	5
	6	Felton Spencer	Minnesota Timberwolves	Louisville	6
	7	Lionel Simmons	Sacramento Kings	La Salle	7
	8	Bo Kimble	Los Angeles Clippers	Loyola Marymount	8
	9	Willie Burton	Miami Heat	Minnesota	9
	10	Rumeal Robinson	Atlanta Hawks	Michigan	10
	11	Tyrone Hill	Golden State Warriors	Xavier (Ohio)	11
	12	Alec Kessler	Houston Rockets	Georgia	12

		NAME	TEAM	COLLEGE	# OVERALL
	13	Loy Vaught	Los Angeles Clippers	Michigan	13
	14	Travis Mays	Sacramento Kings	Texas	14
	15	Dave Jamerson	Miami Heat	Ohio	15
	16	Terry Mills	Milwaukee Bucks	Michigan	16
	17	Jerrod Mustaf	New York Knicks	Maryland	17
	18	Duane Causwell	Sacramento Kings	Temple	18
	19	Dee Brown	Boston Celtics	Jacksonville	19
	20	Gerald Glass	Minnesota Timberwolves	Mississippi	20
	21	Jayson Williams	Phoenix Suns	St. John's	21
	22	Tate George	New Jersey Nets	Connecticut	22
	23	Anthony Bonner	Sacramento Kings	St. Louis	23
	24	Dwayne Schintzius	San Antonio Spurs	Florida	24
	25	Alaa Abdelnaby	Portland Trail Blazers	Duke	25
	26	Lance Banks	Detroit Pistons	Texas	26
	27	Elden Campbell	Los Angeles Lakers	Clemson	27
SECOND ROUND	1	Les Jepsen	Golden State Warriors	Iowa	28
	2	Toni Kukoc	Chicago Bulls	Benetton Treviso (Italy)	29
	3	Carl Herrera	Miami Heat	Houston	30
	4	Negele Knight	Phoenix Suns	Dayton	31
	5	Brian Oliver	Philadelphia 76ers	Georgia Tech	32
	6	Walter Palmer	Utah Jazz	Dartmouth	33
	7	Kevin Pritchard	Golden State Warriors	Kansas	34
	8	Greg Foster	Washington Bullets	Texas–El Paso	35
	9	Trevor Wilson	Atlanta Hawks	UCLA	36
	10	A.J. English	Washington Bullets	Virginia Union	37
	11	Jud Buechler	Seattle SuperSonics	Arizona	38
	12	Steve Scheffler	Charlotte Hornets	Purdue	39
	13	Bimbo Coles	Sacramento Kings	Virginia Tech	40
	14	Steve Bardo	Atlanta Hawks	Illinois	41
	15	Marcus Liberty	Denver Nuggets	Illinois	42
	16	Tony Massenburg	San Antonio Spurs	Maryland	43
	17	Steve Henson	Milwaukee Bucks	Kansas State	44
	18	Antonio Davis	Indiana Pacers	Texas–El Paso	45
	19	Kenny Williams	Indiana Pacers	Elizabeth City State	46
	20	Derek Strong	Philadelphia 76ers	Xavier (Ohio)	47
	21	Cedric Ceballos	Phoenix Suns	Cal State–Fullerton	48
	22	Phil Henderson	Dallas Mavericks	Duke	49
	23	Milos Babic	Phoenix Suns	Tennessee Tech	50
	24	Tony Smith	Los Angeles Lakers	Marquette	51
	25	Stefano Rusconi	Cleveland Cavaliers	Varese (Italy)	52
	26	Abdul Shamsid-Deen	Seattle SuperSonics	Providence	53
	27	Sean Higgins	San Antonio Spurs	Michigan	54

1989

		NAME	TEAM	COLLEGE	# OVERALL
FIRST ROUND	1	Pervis Ellison	Sacramento Kings	Louisville	1
	2	Danny Ferry	Los Angeles Clippers	Duke	2
	3	Sean Elliott	San Antonio Spurs	Arizona	3
	4	Glen Rice	Miami Heat	Michigan	4
	5	J.R. Reid	Charlotte Hornets	North Carolina	5
	6	Stacey King	Chicago Bulls	Oklahoma	6
	7	George McCloud	Indiana Pacers	Florida State	7
	8	Randy White	Dallas Mavericks	Louisiana Tech	8
	9	Tom Hammonds	Washington Bullets	Georgia Tech	9
	10	Pooh Richardson	Minnesota Timberwolves	UCLA	10
	11	Nick Anderson	Orlando Magic	Illinois	11
	12	Mookie Blaylock	New Jersey Nets	Oklahoma	12
	13	Michael Smith	Boston Celtics	Brigham Young	13
	14	Tim Hardaway	Golden State Warriors	Texas–El Paso	14
	15	Todd Lichti	Denver Nuggets	Stanford	15
	16	Dana Barros	Seattle SuperSonics	Boston College	16
	17	Shawn Kemp	Seattle SuperSonics	Trinity Valley	17
	18	B.J. Armstrong	Chicago Bulls	Iowa	18
	19	Kenny Payne	Philadelphia 76ers	Louisville	19
	20	Jeff Sanders	Chicago Bulls	Georgia Southern	20
	21	Blue Edwards	Utah Jazz	East Carolina	21
	22	Byron Irvin	Portland Trail Blazers	Missouri	22
	23	Roy Marble	Atlanta Hawks	Iowa	23
	24	Anthony Cook	Phoenix Suns	Arizona	24
	25	John Morton	Cleveland Cavaliers	Seton Hall	25
	26	Vlade Divac	Los Angeles Lakers	Partizan Belgrade	26
	27	Kenny Battle	Detroit Pistons	Illinois	27
SECOND ROUND	1	Sherman Douglas	Miami Heat	Syracuse	28
	2	Dyron Nix	Charlotte Hornets	Tennesee	29
	3	Frank Kornet	Milwaukee Bucks	Vanderbilt	30
	4	Jeff Martin	Los Angeles Clippers	Murray State	31
	5	Stanley Brundy	New Jersey Nets	DePaul	32
	6	Jay Edwards	Los Angeles Clippers	Indiana	33
	7	Gary Leonard	Minnesota Timberwolves	Missouri	34
	8	Pat Durham	Dallas Mavericks	Colorado State	35
	9	Cliff Robinson	Portland Trail Blazers	Connecticut	36
	10	Michael Ansley	Orlando Magic	Alabama	37
	11	Doug West	Minnesota Timberwolves	Villanova	38
	12	Ed Horton	Washington Bullets	Iowa	39
	13	Dino Radja	Boston Celtics	Virtus Roma (Italy)	40
	14	Doug Roth	Washington Bullets	Tennessee	41
	15	Michael Cutright	Denver Nuggets	McNeese State	42
	16	Chucky Brown	Cleveland Cavaliers	North Carolina State	43
	17	Reggie Cross	Philadelphia 76ers	Hawaii	44
	18	Scott Haffner	Miami Heat	Evansville	45
	19	Ricky Blanton	Phoenix Suns	Louisiana State	46
	20	Reggie Turner	Denver Nuggets	Alabama–Birmingham	47
	21	Junie Lewis	Utah Jazz	South Alabama	48
	22	Haywoode Workman	Atlanta Hawks	Oral Roberts	49
	23	Brian Quinnett	New York Knicks	Washington State	50
	24	Mike Morrison	Phoenix Suns	Loyola (Md.)	51
	25	Greg Grant	Phoenix Suns	Trenton State	52
	26	Jeff Hodge	Dallas Mavericks	South Alabama	53
	27	Toney Mack	Philadelphia 76ers	Georgia	54

1988

		NAME	TEAM	COLLEGE	# OVERALL
FIRST ROUND	1	Danny Manning	Los Angeles Clippers	Kansas	1
	2	Rik Smits	Indiana Pacers	Marist	2
	3	Charles Smith	Philadelphia 76ers	Pittsburgh	3
	4	Chris Morris	New Jersey Nets	Auburn	4
	5	Mitch Richmond	Golden State Warriors	Kansas State	5
	6	Hersey Hawkins	Los Angeles Clippers	Bradley	6
	7	Tim Perry	Phoenix Suns	Temple	7
	8	Rex Chapman	Charlotte Hornets	Kentucky	8
	9	Rony Seikaly	Miami Heat	Syracuse	9
	10	Willie Anderson	San Antonio Spurs	Georgia	10
	11	Will Perdue	Chicago Bulls	Vanderbilt	11
	12	Harvey Grant	Washington Bullets	Oklahoma	12
	13	Jeff Grayer	Milwaukee Bucks	Iowa State	13
	14	Dan Majerle	Phoenix Suns	Central Michigan	14
	15	Gary Grant	Seattle SuperSonics	Michigan	15
	16	Derrick Chievous	Houston Rockets	Missouri	16
	17	Eric Leckner	Utah Jazz	Wyoming	17
	18	Rick Berry	Sacramento Kings	San Jose State	18
	19	Rod Strickland	New York Knicks	DePaul	19
	20	Kevin Edwards	Miami Heat	DePaul	20
	21	Mark Bryant	Portland Trail Blazers	Seton Hall	21
	22	Randolph Keys	Cleveland Cavaliers	Southern Mississippi	22

Round		NAME	TEAM	COLLEGE	#OVERALL
	23	Jerome Lane	Denver Nuggets	Pittsburgh	23
	24	Brian Shaw	Boston Celtics	UC Santa Barbara	24
	25	David Rivers	Los Angeles Lakers	Notre Dame	25
SECOND ROUND	1	Rolando Ferreira	Portland Trail Blazers	Houston	26
	2	Shelton Jones	San Antonio Spurs	St. John's	27
	3	Andrew Lang	Phoenix Suns	Arkansas	28
	4	Vinny Del Negro	Sacramento Kings	North Carolina State	29
	5	Fennis Dembo	Detroit Pistons	Wyoming	30
	6	Everette Stephens	Philadelphia 76ers	Purdue	31
	7	Charles Shackleford	New Jersey Nets	North Carolina State	32
	8	Grant Long	Miami Heat	Eastern Michigan	33
	9	Tom Tolbert	Charlotte Hornets	Arizona	34
	10	Sylvester Gray	Miami Heat	Memphis State	35
	11	Ledell Eackles	Washington Bullets	New Orleans	36
	12	Greg Butler	New York Knicks	Stanford	37
	13	Dean Garrett	Phoenix Suns	Indiana	38
	14	Tito Horford	Milwaukee Bucks	Miami (Fla.)	39
	15	Orlando Graham	Miami Heat	Auburn-Montgomery	40
	16	Keith Smart	Golden State Warriors	Indiana	41
	17	Jeff Moe	Utah Jazz	Iowa	42
	18	Todd Mitchell	Denver Nuggets	Purdue	43
	19	Anthony Taylor	Atlanta Hawks	Oregon	44
	20	Tom Garrick	Los Angeles Clippers	Rhode Island	45
	21	Morlon Wiley	Dallas Mavericks	Long Beach State	46
	22	Vernon Maxwell	Denver Nuggets	Florida	47
	23	Micheal Williams	Detroit Pistons	Baylor	48
	24	Jose Vargas	Dallas Mavericks	Louisiana State	49
	25	Steve Kerr	Phoenix Suns	Arizona	50
THIRD ROUND	1	Robert Lock	Los Angeles Clippers	Kentucky	51
	2	Derrick Hamilton	New Jersey Nets	Southern Mississippi	52
	3	Anthony Mason	Portland Trail Blazers	Tennessee State	53
	4	Jorge Gonzalez	Atlanta Hawks	Argentina	54
	5	Rodney Johns	Phoenix Suns	Grand Canyon	55
	6	Barry Sumpter	San Antonio Spurs	Austin Peay	56
	7	Hernan Montenegro	Philadelphia 76ers	Louisiana State	57
	8	Jeff Moore	Charlotte Hornets	Auburn	58
	9	Nate Johnston	Miami Heat	Tampa	59
	10	Ed Davender	Washington Bullets	Kentucky	60
	11	Herbert Crook	Indiana Pacers	Louisville	61
	12	Derrick Lewis	Chicago Bulls	Maryland	62
	13	Mike Jones	Milwaukee Bucks	Auburn	63
	14	Winston Bennett	Cleveland Cavaliers	Kentucky	64
	15	Corey Gaines	Seattle SuperSonics	Loyola Marymount	65
	16	Dwight Boyd	Denver Nuggets	Memphis State	66
	17	Ricky Grace	Utah Jazz	Oklahoma	67
	18	Darryl Middleton	Atlanta Hawks	Baylor	68
	19	Phil Stinnie	New York Knicks	Virginia Commonwealth	69
	20	Jerry Johnson	Dallas Mavericks	Florida Southern	70
	21	Craig Neal	Portland Trail Blazers	Georgia Tech	71
	22	Lee Johnson	Detroit Pistons	Norfolk State	72
	23	Michael Anderson	Indiana Pacers	Drexel	73
	24	Gerald Paddio	Boston Celtics	Nevada–Las Vegas	74
	25	Archie Marshall	San Antonio Spurs	Kansas	75

1987

Round		NAME	TEAM	COLLEGE	#OVERALL
FIRST ROUND	1	David Robinson	San Antonio Spurs	Navy	1
	2	Armon Gilliam	Phoenix Suns	Nevada–Las Vegas	2
	3	Dennis Hopson	New Jersey Nets	Ohio State	3
	4	Reggie Williams	Los Angeles Clippers	Georgetown	4
	5	Scottie Pippen	Seattle SuperSonics	Central Arkansas	5
	6	Kenny Smith	Sacramento Kings	North Carolina	6
	7	Kevin Johnson	Cleveland Cavaliers	California	7
	8	Olden Polynice	Chicago Bulls	Virginia	8
	9	Derrick McKey	Seattle SuperSonics	Alabama	9
	10	Horace Grant	Chicago Bulls	Clemson	10
	11	Reggie Miller	Indiana Pacers	UCLA	11
	12	Tyrone Bogues	Washington Bullets	Wake Forest	12
	13	Joe Wolf	Los Angeles Clippers	North Carolina	13
	14	Tellis Frank	Golden State Warriors	Western Kentucky	14
	15	Jose Ortiz	Utah Jazz	Oregon State	15
	16	Christian Welp	Philadelphia 76ers	Washington	16
	17	Ronnie Murphy	Portland Trail Blazers	Jacksonville	17
	18	Mark Jackson	New York Knicks	St. John's	18
	19	Ken Norman	Los Angeles Clippers	Illinois	19
	20	Jim Farmer	Dallas Mavericks	Alabama	20
	21	Dallas Comegys	Atlanta Hawks	DePaul	21
	22	Reggie Lewis	Boston Celtics	Northeastern	22
	23	Greg Anderson	San Antonio Spurs	Houston	23
SECOND ROUND	1	Fred Banks	Detroit Pistons	Nevada–Las Vegas	24
	2	Ron Moore	New York Knicks	West Virginia State	25
	3	Steve Alford	Dallas Mavericks	Indiana	26
	4	Nate Blackwell	San Antonio Spurs	Temple	27
	5	Rickie Winslow	Chicago Bulls	Houston	28
	6	Lester Fonville	Portland Trail Blazers	Jackson State	29
	7	Nikita Wilson	Portland Trail Blazers	Louisiana State	30
	8	Andre Moore	Denver Nuggets	Loyola (Ill.)	31
	9	Bob McCann	Milwaukee Bucks	Morehead State	32
	10	Tony White	Chicago Bulls	Tennessee	33
	11	Brian Rowsom	Indiana Pacers	North Carolina–Wilmington	34
	12	Doug Lee	Houston Rockets	Purdue	35
	13	Duane Washington	Washington Bullets	Middle Tennessee	36
	14	Derrick Dowell	Washington Bullets	USC	37
	15	Norris Coleman	Los Angeles Clippers	Kansas State	38
	16	Vincent Askew	Philadelphia 76ers	Memphis State	39
	17	Winston Garland	Milwaukee Bucks	SW Missouri State	40
	18	Kannard Johnson	Cleveland Cavaliers	Western Kentucky	41
	19	Terence Bailey	Atlanta Hawks	Wagner	42
	20	Andrew Kennedy	Philadelphia 76ers	Virginia	43
	21	Terry Coner	Atlanta Hawks	Alabama	44
	22	Brad Lohaus	Boston Celtics	Iowa	45
	23	Bruce Dalrymple	Phoenix Suns	Georgia Tech	46
THIRD ROUND	1	Tim McCalister	Los Angeles Clippers	Oklahoma	47
	2	Jamie Waller	New Jersey Nets	Virginia Union	48
	3	Jerome Batiste	New York Knicks	McNeese State	49
	4	Phil Zevenbergen	San Antonio Spurs	Washington	50
	5	Sven Meyer	Sacramento Kings	Oregon	51
	6	Donald Royal	Cleveland Cavaliers	Notre Dame	52
	7	Winston Crite	Phoenix Suns	Texas A&M	53
	8	Tom Schafer	Denver Nuggets	Iowa State	54
	9	Tommy Amaker	Seattle SuperSonics	Duke	55
	10	John Fox	Chicago Bulls	Millersville State	56
	11	Hansi Gnad	Philadelphia 76ers	Alaska-Anchorage	57
	12	Darryl Johnson	Golden State Warriors	Michigan State	58
	13	Danny Pearson	Washington Bullets	Jacksonville	59
	14	Sean Couch	Indiana Pacers	Columbia	60
	15	Clarence Martin	Utah Jazz	Western Kentucky	61
	16	Eric Riggins	Philadelphia 76ers	Rutgers	62
	17	Kevin Gamble	Portland Trail Blazers	Iowa	63
	18	J.J. Weber	Milwaukee Bucks	Wisconsin	64
	19	Eric White	Detroit Pistons	Pepperdine	65
	20	Mike Richmond	Dallas Mavericks	Texas El–Paso	66
	21	Song Tao	Atlanta Hawks	(China)	67
	22	Billy Donovan	Utah Jazz	Providence	68

Round		NAME	TEAM	COLLEGE	# OVERALL
	23	Willie Glass	Los Angeles Lakers	St. John's	69
FOURTH ROUND	1	Tom Sheehey	Boston Celtics	Virginia	70
	2	Mike Morgan	New York Knicks	Drake	71
	3	Andrew Moten	New Jersey Nets	Florida	72
	4	Todd May	San Antonio Spurs	Pikeville	73
	5	Joe Arlauckas	Sacramento Kings	Niagara	74
	6	Chris Dudley	Cleveland Cavaliers	Yale	75
	7	Steve Beck	Phoenix Suns	Arizona State	76
	8	David Boone	Denver Nuggets	Marquette	77
	9	Todd Linder	Seattle SuperSonics	Tampa	78
	10	Jack Haley	Chicago Bulls	UCLA	79
	11	Carven Holcomb	Cleveland Cavaliers	Texas Christian	80
	12	Scott Thompson	Washington Bullets	San Diego	81
	13	Joe Niego	Houston Rockets	Lewis (Ill.)	82
	14	Benny Bolton	Golden State Warriors	North Carolina State	83
	15	Reuben Holmes	Utah Jazz	Alabama State	84
	16	Brian Rahilly	Philadelphia 76ers	Tulsa	85
	17	Norwood Barber	Portland Trail Blazers	Florida State	86
	18	Darryl Bedford	Milwaukee Bucks	Austin Peay	87
	19	Dave Popson	Detroit Pistons	North Carolina	88
	20	David Johnson	Dallas Mavericks	Oklahoma	89
	21	Fanis Christodoulou	Atlanta Hawks	(Greece)	90
	22	Darryl Kennedy	Boston Celtics	Oklahoma	91
	23	Ralph Tally	Los Angeles Lakers	Norfolk State	92
FIFTH ROUND	1	Chad Kessler	Los Angeles Clippers	Georgia	93
	2	James Blackmon	New Jersey Nets	Kentucky	94
	3	Glenn Clem	New York Knicks	Vanderbilt	95
	4	Dennis Williams	San Antonio Spurs	Georgia	96
	5	Vernon Carr	Sacramento Kings	Michigan State	97
	6	Carl Lott	Cleveland Cavaliers	Texas Christian	98
	7	Brent Counts	Phoenix Suns	Pacific	99
	8	Ron Grandison	Denver Nuggets	New Orleans	100
	9	Michael Tait	Seattle SuperSonics	Clemson	101
	10	Anthony Wilson	Chicago Bulls	Louisiana State	102
	11	Mike Milling	Indiana Pacers	North Carolina–Charlotte	103
	12	Andre LaFleur	Houston Rockets	Northeastern	104
	13	Terry Williams	Golden State Warriors	Southern Methodist	105
	14	Patrick Fairs	Washington Bullets	Texas	106
	15	Bart Kofoed	Utah Jazz	Kearney State	107
	16	Frank Ross	Philadelphia 76ers	American	108
	17	David Moss	Portland Trail Blazers	Tulsa	109
	18	Brian Vaughns	Milwaukee Bucks	UC Santa Barbara	110
	19	Gerry Wright	Detroit Pistons	Iowa	111
	20	Sam Hill	Dallas Mavericks	Iowa State	112
	21	Jose Antonio Montero	Atlanta Hawks	Barcelona (Spain)	113
	22	Dave Butler	Boston Celtics	California	114
SIXTH ROUND	1	Kenny Travis	Los Angeles Lakers	New Mexico State	115
	2	Martin Nessley	Los Angeles Clippers	Duke	116
	3	Howard Triche	New York Knicks	Syracuse	117
	4	Perry Bromwell	New Jersey Nets	Penn	118
	5	Ricky Brown	San Antonio Spurs	South Alabama	119
	6	Darryl Thomas	Sacramento Kings	Indiana	120
	7	Harold Jensen	Cleveland Cavaliers	Villanova	121
	8	Marcel Boyce	Phoenix Suns	Akron	122
	9	Kelvin Scarborough	Denver Nuggets	New Mexico	123
	10	Tom Gneiting	Seattle SuperSonics	Brigham Young	124
	11	Doug Altenberger	Chicago Bulls	Illinois	125
	12	Gary Graham	Indiana Pacers	Nevada–Las Vegas	126
	13	Sarunas Marciulionis	Golden State Warriors	Vilnius Lithuania (USSR)	127
	14	Dwayne Scholten	Washington Bullets	Washington State	128
	15	Fred Jenkins	Houston Rockets	Tennessee	129
	16	Art Sabb	Utah Jazz	Bloomfield (N.J.)	130
	17	Tracy Foster	Philadelphia 76ers	Alabama–Birmingham	131
	18	Bernard Johnson	Portland Trail Blazers	Loyola (Ill.)	132
	19	Gay Elmore	Milwaukee Bucks	Virginia Military Institute	133
	20	Antoine Joubert	Detroit Pistons	Michigan	134
	21	Quintan Gates	Dallas Mavericks	Texas–El Paso	135
	22	Riccardo Morandoti	Atlanta Hawks	Turino (Italy)	136
	23	Tim Naegeli	Boston Celtics	Wisconsin–Stevens Point	137
	24	Frank Ford	Los Angeles Lakers	Auburn	138
SEVENTH ROUND	1	Henry Carr	Los Angeles Clippers	Wichita State	139
	2	Frank Booker	New Jersey Nets	Bowling Green	140
	3	Wayne Williams	New York Knicks	St. Joseph's	141
	4	Raynard Davis	San Antonio Spurs	Texas	142
	5	Scott Adubato	Sacramento Kings	Upsala	143
	6	Michael Foster	Cleveland Cavaliers	South Carolina	144
	7	Ron Singleton	Phoenix Suns	Grand Canyon	145
	8	Rowan Gomes	Denver Nuggets	Hampton Institute	146
	9	Mike Giomi	Seattle SuperSonics	North Carolina State	147
	10	Earvin Leavy	Chicago Bulls	Central Michigan	148
	11	Montel Hatcher	Indiana Pacers	UCLA	149
	12	Jamie Dixon	Washington Bullets	Texas Christian	150
	13	Clarence Grier	Houston Rockets	Campbell	151
	14	Ronnie Leggette	Golden State Warriors	West Virginia State	152
	15	Keith Webster	Utah Jazz	Harvard	153
	16	Eric Semisch	Philadelphia 76ers	West Virginia	154
	17	Kenny Stone	Portland Trail Blazers	George Fox	155
	18	Curtis Hunter	Denver Nuggets	North Carolina	156
	19	Mark Gottfried	Detroit Pistons	Alabama	157
	20	Gerald White	Dallas Mavericks	Auburn	158
	21	Franjo Arapovic	Atlanta Hawks	Cibona Zagreb	159
	22	Jerry Corcoran	Boston Celtics	Northeastern	160
	23	Ron Vanderschaaf	Los Angeles Lakers	Central Washington	161

1986

Round		NAME	TEAM	COLLEGE	# OVERALL
FIRST ROUND	1	Brad Daugherty	Cleveland Cavaliers	North Carolina	1
	2	Len Bias	Boston Celtics	Maryland	2
	3	Chris Washburn	Golden State Warriors	North Carolina State	3
	4	Chuck Person	Indiana Pacers	Auburn	4
	5	Kenny Walker	New York Knicks	Kentucky	5
	6	William Bedford	Phoenix Suns	Memphis State	6
	7	Roy Tarpley	Dallas Mavericks	Michigan	7
	8	Ron Harper	Cleveland Cavaliers	Miami (Ohio)	8
	9	Brad Sellers	Chicago Bulls	Ohio State	9
	10	Johnny Dawkins	San Antonio Spurs	Duke	10
	11	John Salley	Detroit Pistons	Georgia Tech	11
	12	John Williams	Washington Bullets	Louisiana State	12
	13	Dwayne Washington	New Jersey Nets	Syracuse	13
	14	Walter Berry	Portland Trail Blazers	St. John's	14
	15	Dell Curry	Utah Jazz	Virginia Tech	15
	16	Mo Martin	Denver Nuggets	St. Joseph's	16
	17	Harold Pressley	Sacramento Kings	Villanova	17
	18	Mark Alarie	Denver Nuggets	Duke	18
	19	Billy Thompson	Atlanta Hawks	Louisville	19
	20	Buck Johnson	Houston Rockets	Alabama	20
	21	Anthony Jones	Washington Bullets	Nevada–Las Vegas	21
	22	Scott Skiles	Milwaukee Bucks	Michigan State	22
	23	Ken Barlow	Los Angeles Lakers	Notre Dame	23
	24	Arvydas Sabonis	Portland Trail Blazers	Zalgiris Kaunas	24
SECOND ROUND	1	Mark Price	Dallas Mavericks	Georgia Tech	25
	2	Greg Dreiling	Indiana Pacers	Kansas	26
	3	Dennis Rodman	Detroit Pistons	SE Oklahoma	27
	4	Larry Krystkowiak	Chicago Bulls	Montana	28

Round		NAME	TEAM	COLLEGE	# OVERALL
	5	Johnny Newman	Cleveland Cavaliers	Richmond	29
	6	Nate McMillan	Seattle SuperSonics	North Carolina State	30
	7	Joe Ward	Phoenix Suns	Georgia	31
	8	Cedric Henderson	Atlanta Hawks	Georgia	32
	9	Kevin Duckworth	San Antonio Spurs	Eastern Illinois	33
	10	Johnny Rogers	Sacramento Kings	California–Irvine	34
	11	Milt Wagner	Dallas Mavericks	Louisville	35
	12	Steve Mitchell	Washington Bullets	Alabama–Birmingham	36
	13	Panayiotis Fassoulas	Portland Trail Blazers	North Carolina State	37
	14	Lemone Lampley	Seattle SuperSonics	DePaul	38
	15	Rafael Addison	Phoenix Suns	Syracuse	39
	16	Augusto Binelli	Atlanta Hawks	(Italy)	40
	17	Otis Smith	Denver Nuggets	Jacksonville	41
	18	Ron Kellogg	Atlanta Hawks	Kansas	42
	19	Dave Feitl	Houston Rockets	Texas–El Paso	43
	20	David Wingate	Philadelphia 76ers	Georgetown	44
	21	Keith Smith	Milwaukee Bucks	Loyola Marymount	45
	22	Jeff Hornacek	Phoenix Suns	Iowa State	46
	23	Michael Jackson	New York Knicks	Georgetown	47
THIRD ROUND	1	Forrest McKenzie	San Antonio Spurs	Loyola Marymount	48
	2	Juden Smith	Portland Trail Blazers	Texas–El Paso	49
	3	Kevin Henderson	Cleveland Cavaliers	Cal State–Fullerton	50
	4	Mike Williams	Golden State Warriors	Bradley	51
	5	Ricky Wilson	Chicago Bulls	George Mason	52
	6	Tod Murphy	Seattle SuperSonics	California–Irvine	53
	7	Dwayne Polee	Los Angeles Clippers	Pepperdine	54
	8	Ken Gattison	Phoenix Suns	Old Dominion	55
	9	Keith Colbert	Philadelphia 76ers	Virginia Tech	56
	10	Bruce Douglas	Sacramento Kings	Illinois	57
	11	David Henderson	Washington Bullets	Duke	58
	12	Wendell Alexis	Golden State Warriors	Syracuse	59
	13	Drazen Petrovic	Portland Trail Blazers	Zagreb (Yugoslavia)	60
	14	John Shasky	Utah Jazz	Minnesota	61
	15	Anthony Welch	Dallas Mavericks	Illinois	62
	16	Bill Breeding	Utah Jazz	Rocky Mountain	63
	17	Don Redden	Denver Nuggets	Louisiana State	64
	18	Dave Hoppen	Atlanta Hawks	Nebraska	65
	19	Anthony Bowie	Houston Rockets	Oklahoma	66
	20	Ron Rowan	Philadelphia 76ers	St. John's	67
	21	Baskerville Holmes	Milwaukee Bucks	Memphis	68
	22	Andre Turner	Los Angeles Lakers	Memphis	69
	23	Jim Les	Atlanta Hawks	Bradley	70
FOURTH ROUND	1	Calvin Thompson	New York Knicks	Kansas	71
	2	Derrick Taylor	Indiana Pacers	Louisiana State	72
	3	Warren Martin	Cleveland Cavaliers	North Carolina	73
	4	Scott Meents	Chicago Bulls	Illinois	74
	5	Dan Bingenheimer	Golden State Warriors	Missouri	75
	6	Michael Graham	Seattle SuperSonics	Georgetown	76
	7	Grant Gondrezick	Phoenix Suns	Pepperdine	77
	8	John Brownlee	Los Angeles Clippers	Texas	78
	9	Carlos Briggs	San Antonio Spurs	Baylor	79
	10	Alvin Franklin	Sacramento Kings	Houston	80
	11	Steve Hale	New Jersey Nets	North Carolina	81
	12	Barry Mungar	Washington Bullets	St. Bonaventure	82
	13	David Shaffer	Portland Trail Blazers	Florida State	83
	14	Marty Embry	Utah Jazz	DePaul	84
	15	Myron Jackson	Dallas Mavericks	Arkansas–Little Rock	85
	16	Chauncey Robinson	Detroit Pistons	Mississippi State	86
	17	Anthony Watson	Denver Nuggets	San Diego State	87
	18	Efrem Winters	Atlanta Hawks	Illinois	88
	19	Conner Henry	Houston Rockets	UC Santa Barbara	89
	20	Wes Stallings	Philadelphia 76ers	East Tennessee State	90
	21	Bob Beecher	Sacramento Kings	Virginia Tech	91
	22	Dale Blaney	Los Angeles Lakers	West Virginia	92
	23	Tony Benford	Boston Celtics	Texas Tech	93
FIFTH ROUND	1	Jerome Mincey	New York Knicks	Alabama–Birmingham	94
	2	Richard Rellford	Indiana Pacers	Michigan	95
	3	Ben Davis	Cleveland Cavaliers	Gardner-Webb	96
	4	Clinton Smith	Golden State Warriors	Cleveland State	97
	5	Jimmy Gilbert	Chicago Bulls	Texas A&M	98
	6	Dominic Pressley	Seattle SuperSonics	Boston College	99
	7	Steffond Johnson	Los Angeles Clippers	San Diego State	100
	8	Greg Spurling	Phoenix Suns	Carson-Newman	101
	9	Earl Kelley	San Antonio Spurs	Connecticut	102
	10	Keith Morrison	Sacramento Kings	Washington State	103
	11	Paul Fortier	Washington Bullets	Washington	104
	12	Archie Johnson	New Jersey Nets	Alabama–Birmingham	105
	13	Jerry Adams	Portland Trail Blazers	Oregon	106
	14	Kerry Boagni	Utah Jazz	Cal State–Fullerton	107
	15	Jay Bilas	Dallas Mavericks	Duke	108
	16	Clarence Hanley	Detroit Pistons	Old Dominion	109
	17	Jon Collins	Denver Nuggets	Eastern Illinois	110
	18	Nicky Jones	Atlanta Hawks	Virginia Commonwealth	111
	19	Andre Banks	Houston Rockets	Iowa	112
	20	Kevin Holmes	Philadelphia 76ers	DePaul	113
	21	Bobby Deaton	Milwaukee Bucks	Southwestern (Tex.)	114
	22	Roger Harden	Los Angeles Lakers	Kentucky	115
	23	Dave Colbert	Boston Celtics	Dayton	116
SIXTH ROUND	1	Butch Wade	New York Knicks	Michigan	117
	2	Jeff Hall	Indiana Pacers	Louisville	118
	3	Gilbert Wilburn	Cleveland Cavaliers	New Mexico State	119
	4	Pete Myers	Chicago Bulls	Arkansas–Little Rock	120
	5	Bobby Lee Hurt	Golden State Warriors	Alabama	121
	6	Curtis Kitchen	Seattle SuperSonics	South Florida	122
	7	Jim McCaffrey	Phoenix Suns	Holy Cross	123
	8	Tim Kempton	Los Angeles Clippers	Notre Dame	124
	9	Kevin Lewis	San Antonio Spurs	Southern Methodist	125
	10	John Flowers	Sacramento Kings	Nevada–Las Vegas	126
	11	Troy Webster	New Jersey Nets	George Washington	127
	12	Lorenzo Duncan	Washington Bullets	Sam Houston State	128
	13	Tony Hampton	Portland Trail Blazers	Montana State	129
	14	Chuck Everson	Utah Jazz	Villanova	130
	15	Greg Anderson	Dallas Mavericks	Lamar	131
	16	Greg Grant	Detroit Pistons	Utah State	132
	17	Anthony Frederick	Denver Nuggets	Pepperdine	133
	18	Aleksandr Volkov	Atlanta Hawks	Kiev Institute (USSR)	134
	19	Robert Worthy	Houston Rockets	Dyke (Ohio)	135
	20	Andre McCloud	Philadelphia 76ers	Seton Hall	136
	21	John Kimbrell	Milwaukee Bucks	David Lipscomb (Tenn.)	137
	22	Walter Downing	Los Angeles Lakers	Marquette	138
	23	Greg Wendt	Boston Celtics	Detroit	139
SEVENTH ROUND	1	Duane Kendall	New York Knicks	South Carolina	140
	2	Steve Woodside	Indiana Pacers	Oregon State	141
	3	Ralph Dalton	Cleveland Cavaliers	Georgetown	142
	4	Steve Kenilvort	Golden State Warriors	Santa Clara	143
	5	Robert Henderson	Chicago Bulls	Michigan	144
	6	Glen McCants	Seattle SuperSonics	Clemson	145
	7	Johnny Brown	Los Angeles Clippers	New Mexico	146
	8	Damon Goodwin	Phoenix Suns	Dayton	147
	9	Michael Anderson	San Antonio Spurs	Pan American	148
	10	Ron Rankin	Sacramento Kings	SE Missouri State	149
	11	Joe Price	Washington Bullets	Notre Dame	150
	12	Jim Dolan	New Jersey Nets	Notre Dame	151
	13	Randy Schiff	Portland Trail Blazers	Linfield	152

		NAME	TEAM	COLLEGE	# OVERALL
	14	Mark Mitchell	Utah Jazz	Hartford	153
	15	Kim Cooksey	Dallas Mavericks	Middle Tennessee	154
	16	Larry Polec	Detroit Pistons	Michigan State	155
	17	Mike Marshall	Denver Nuggets	McNeese State	156
	18	Valerie Tikhonenko	Atlanta Hawks	(Soviet Union)	157
	19	Rick Olson	Houston Rockets	Wisconsin	158
	20	Dan Palombizio	Philadelphia 76ers	Ball State	159
	21	Jeff Strong	Milwaukee Bucks	Missouri	160
	22	Mark Coleman	Los Angeles Lakers	Mississippi Valley State	161
	23	Tom Ivey	Boston Celtics	Boston Univ.	162

1985

		NAME	TEAM	COLLEGE	# OVERALL
FIRST ROUND	1	Patrick Ewing	New York Knicks	Georgetown	1
	2	Wayman Tisdale	Indiana Pacers	Oklahoma	2
	3	Benoit Benjamin	Los Angeles Clippers	Creighton	3
	4	Xavier McDaniel	Seattle SuperSonics	Wichita State	4
	5	Jon Koncak	Atlanta Hawks	Southern Methodist	5
	6	Joe Kleine	Sacramento Kings	Arkansas	6
	7	Chris Mullin	Golden State Warriors	St. John's	7
	8	Detlef Schrempf	Dallas Mavericks	Washington	8
	9	Charles Oakley	Cleveland Cavaliers	Virginia Union	9
	10	Ed Pinckney	Phoenix Suns	Villanova	10
	11	Keith Lee	Chicago Bulls	Memphis State	11
	12	Kenny Green	Washington Bullets	Wake Forest	12
	13	Karl Malone	Utah Jazz	Louisiana Tech	13
	14	Alfredrick Hughes	San Antonio Spurs	Loyola (Ill.)	14
	15	Blair Rasmussen	Denver Nuggets	Oregon	15
	16	Bill Wennington	Dallas Mavericks	St. John's	16
	17	Uwe Blab	Dallas Mavericks	Indiana	17
	18	Joe Dumars	Detroit Pistons	McNeese State	18
	19	Steve Harris	Houston Rockets	Tulsa	19
	20	Sam Vincent	Boston Celtics	Michigan State	20
	21	Terry Catledge	Philadelphia 76ers	South Alabama	21
	22	Jerry Reynolds	Milwaukee Bucks	Louisiana State	22
	23	A.C. Green	Los Angeles Lakers	Oregon State	23
	24	Terry Porter	Portland Trail Blazers	Wisconsin–Stevens Point	24
SECOND ROUND	1	Mike Smrek	Portland Trail Blazers	Canisius	25
	2	Bill Martin	Indiana Pacers	Georgetown	26
	3	Dwayne McClain	Indiana Pacers	Villanova	27
	4	Ken Johnson	Chicago Bulls	Michigan State	28
	5	Mike Brittain	San Antonio Spurs	South Carolina	29
	6	Calvin Duncan	Cleveland Cavaliers	Virginia Commonwealth	30
	7	Manute Bol	Washington Bullets	Bridgeport	31
	8	Nick Vanos	Phoenix Suns	Santa Clara	32
	9	Greg Stokes	Philadelphia 76ers	Iowa	33
	10	Aubrey Sherrod	Chicago Bulls	Wichita State	34
	11	Tyrone Corbin	San Antonio Spurs	DePaul	35
	12	Yvon Joseph	New Jersey Nets	Georgia Tech	36
	13	Carey Scurry	Utah Jazz	Long Island	37
	14	Fernando Martin	New Jersey Nets	Madrid (Spain)	38
	15	George Montgomery	Portland Trail Blazers	Illinois	39
	16	Mark Acres	Dallas Mavericks	Oral Roberts	40
	17	Lorenzo Charles	Atlanta Hawks	North Carolina State	41
	18	Bobby Lee Hurt	Golden State Warriors	Alabama	42
	19	Barry Stevens	Denver Nuggets	Iowa State	43
	20	Voise Winters	Philadelphia 76ers	Bradley	44
	21	John Williams	Cleveland Cavaliers	Tulane	45
	22	Adrian Branch	Chicago Bulls	Maryland	46
	23	Gerald Wilkins	New York Knicks	Tennessee–Chattanooga	47
THIRD ROUND	1	Kenny Patterson	Indiana Pacers	DePaul	48
	2	Brad Wright	Golden State Warriors	UCLA	49
	3	Leonard Allen	Dallas Mavericks	San Diego State	50
	4	Charles Bradley	Sacramento Kings	South Florida	51
	5	Anicet Lavodrama	Los Angeles Clippers	Houston Baptist	52
	6	Rolando Lamb	Seattle SuperSonics	Virginia Commonwealth	53
	7	Sam Mitchell	Houston Rockets	Mercer	54
	8	Herb Johnson	Cleveland Cavaliers	Tulsa	55
	9	Jerry Everett	Phoenix Suns	Lamar	56
	10	Michael Payne	Houston Rockets	Iowa	57
	11	Vernon Moore	Washington Bullets	Creighton	58
	12	Sedric Toney	Atlanta Hawks	Dayton	59
	13	Andre Goode	Detroit Pistons	Northwestern	60
	14	Perry Young	Portland Trail Blazers	Virginia Tech	61
	15	Nigel Manuel	New Jersey Nets	UCLA	62
	16	Harold Keeling	Dallas Mavericks	Santa Clara	63
	17	Richie Johnson	Detroit Pistons	Evansville	64
	18	Ken Perry	Washington Bullets	Southern Illinois	65
	19	Michael Adams	Sacramento Kings	Boston College	66
	20	Steve Black	Philadelphia 76ers	La Salle	67
	21	Eugene McDowell	Milwaukee Bucks	Florida	68
	22	Mike Brown	Chicago Bulls	George Washington	69
	23	Andre Battle	Boston Celtics	Loyola (Ill.)	70
FOURTH ROUND	1	Luster Goodwin	Golden State Warriors	Texas–El Paso	71
	2	Vince Hamilton	Indiana Pacers	Clemson	72
	3	Fred Cofield	New York Knicks	Eastern Michigan	73
	4	Jim Deines	Los Angeles Clippers	Arizona State	74
	5	Alex Stivrins	Seattle SuperSonics	Colorado	75
	6	Willie Simmons	Sacramento Kings	Louisiana Tech	76
	7	Arvydas Sabonis*	Atlanta Hawks	(Soviet Union)	77
	8	Granger Hall	Phoenix Suns	Temple	78
	9	Mark Davis	Cleveland Cavaliers	Old Dominion	79
	10	Craig Beard	Chicago Bulls	Samford	80
	11	Richie Adams	Washington Bullets	Nevada–Las Vegas	81
	12	Scott Roth	San Antonio Spurs	Wisconsin	82
	13	Delaney Rudd	Utah Jazz	Wake Forest	83
	14	John Battle	Atlanta Hawks	Rutgers	84
	15	Joe Atkinson	Portland Trail Blazers	Oklahoma State	85
	16	Bubba Jennings	Dallas Mavericks	Texas Tech	86
	17	Spud Webb	Detroit Pistons	North Carolina State	87
	18	Mike Brooks	Houston Rockets	Tennessee	88
	19	Pete Williams	Denver Nuggets	Arizona	89
	20	Derrick Gervin	Philadelphia 76ers	Texas–San Antonio	90
	21	Cozell McQueen	Milwaukee Bucks	North Carolina State	91
	22	Dexter Shouse	Los Angeles Lakers	South Alabama	92
	23	Cliff Weber	Boston Celtics	Liberty Baptist	93

*declared ineligible; drafted in 1986 by Portland

		NAME	TEAM	COLLEGE	# OVERALL
FIFTH ROUND	1	Kelvin Johnson	Indiana Pacers	Richmond	94
	2	Greg Cavener	Golden State Warriors	Missouri	95
	3	Mike Schlegel	New York Knicks	Virginia Commonwealth	96
	4	Lou Stefanovic	Seattle SuperSonics	Illinois State	97
	5	Bob Lojewski	Sacramento Kings	St. Joseph's	98
	6	Wayne Carlander	Los Angeles Clippers	USC	99
	7	Larry Hampton	Atlanta Hawks	Fairleign Dickinson	100
	8	Gunther Behnke	Cleveland Cavaliers	(West Germany)	101
	9	Shawn Campbell	Phoenix Suns	Weber State	102
	10	Reid Gettys	Chicago Bulls	Houston	103
	11	Dean Shaffer	Washington Bullets	Florida State	104
	12	Ray Hall	Utah Jazz	Canisius	105
	13	Clayton Olivier	San Antonio Spurs	USC	106
	14	James Anderson	Portland Trail Blazers	Union (Ky.)	107
	15	Kelly Blaine	New Jersey Nets	South Alabama	108
	16	Tommy Davis	Dallas Mavericks	Minnesota	109
	17	Mike Lahm	Detroit Pistons	Murray State	110

		NAME	TEAM	COLLEGE	# OVERALL
	18	Ivan Daniels	Indiana Pacers	Illinois–Chicago	111
	19	Kenny Brown	Denver Nuggets	Texas A&M	112
	20	Carl Wright	Philadelphia 76ers	Southern Methodist	113
	21	Ray Knight	Milwaukee Bucks	Providence	114
	22	Timo Saarelainen	Los Angeles Lakers	Brigham Young	115
	23	Albert Butts	Boston Celtics	La Salle	116
SIXTH ROUND	1	Gerald Crosby	Golden State Warriors	Georgia	117
	2	Stu Primus	Indiana Pacers	Boston College	118
	3	Kent Lockhart	New York Knicks	Texas–El Paso	119
	4	Charles Balentine	Sacramento Kings	Arkansas	120
	5	Malcolm Thomas	Los Angeles Clippers	Missouri	121
	6	Earl Walker	Seattle SuperSonics	Mercer	122
	7	Tony Duckett	Atlanta Hawks	Lafayette	123
	8	Charles Rayne	Phoenix Suns	Temple	124
	9	Ricky Johnson	Cleveland Cavaliers	Illinois State	125
	10	Dan Meagher	Chicago Bulls	Duke	126
	11	Matt England	Washington Bullets	Houston Baptist	127
	12	Chris Harper	San Antonio Spurs	Oregon	128
	13	Jim Miller	Utah Jazz	Virginia	129
	14	George Almones	New Jersey Nets	SW Louisiana	130
	15	Curtis Moore	Portland Trail Blazers	Nebraska	131
	16	Carlton Cooper	Dallas Mavericks	Texas	132
	17	Vincent Giles	Detroit Pistons	Eastern Michigan	133
	18	Sam Potter	Houston Rockets	Oral Roberts	134
	19	Joe Carrabino	Denver Nuggets	Harvard	135
	20	Daryl Lloyd	Philadelphia 76ers	Drake	136
	21	Quentin Anderson	Milwaukee Bucks	Texas Tech	137
	22	Tony Neal	Los Angeles Lakers	Cal State–Fullerton	138
	23	Ralph Lewis	Boston Celtics	La Salle	139
SEVENTH ROUND	1	Jeff Acres	Indiana Pacers	Oral Roberts	140
	2	Eric Boyd	Golden State Warriors	North Carolina A&T	141
	3	Ken Bantum	New York Knicks	Cornell	142
	4	Gary Maloncon	Los Angeles Clippers	UCLA	143
	5	Michael Phelps	Seattle SuperSonics	Alcorn State	144
	6	Alton Lee Gipson	Sacramento Kings	Florida State	145
	7	Bob Ferry Jr.	Atlanta Hawks	Harvard	146
	8	Buzz Peterson	Cleveland Cavaliers	North Carolina	147
	9	Georgi Glouchkov	Phoenix Suns	Akademik Varna (Bulgaria)	148
	10	Jeff Adkins	Chicago Bulls	Maryland	149
	11	Keith Gray	Washington Bullets	Detroit	150
	12	Mike Wacker	Utah Jazz	Texas–San Antonio	151
	13	Al Young	San Antonio Spurs	Virginia Tech	152
	14	Mark Owen	Portland Trail Blazers	College of Idaho	153
	15	Gary McLain	New Jersey Nets	Villanova	154
	16	Ed Catchings	Dallas Mavericks	Nevada–Las Vegas	155
	17	Frank James	Detroit Pistons	Nevada–Las Vegas	156
	18	Don Turney	Houston Rockets	Marshall	157
	19	Eddie Smith	Denver Nuggets	Arizona	158
	20	Jaye Andrews	Philadelphia 76ers	Bucknell	159
	21	Mario Elie	Milwaukee Bucks	American International	160
	22	Keith Cieplicki	Los Angeles Lakers	William & Mary	161
	23	Chris Remly	Boston Celtics	Rutgers	162

1984

		NAME	TEAM	COLLEGE	# OVERALL
FIRST ROUND	1	Akeem Olajuwon	Houston Rockets	Houston	1
	2	Sam Bowie	Portland Trail Blazers	Kentucky	2
	3	Michael Jordan	Chicago Bulls	North Carolina	3
	4	Sam Perkins	Dallas Mavericks	North Carolina	4
	5	Charles Barkley	Philadelphia 76ers	Auburn	5
	6	Mel Turpin	Washington Bullets	Kentucky	6
	7	Alvin Robertson	San Antonio Spurs	Arkansas	7
	8	Lancaster Gordon	Los Angeles Clippers	Louisville	8
	9	Otis Thorpe	Kansas City Kings	Providence	9
	10	Leon Wood	Philadelphia 76ers	Cal State–Fullerton	10
	11	Kevin Willis	Atlanta Hawks	Michigan State	11
	12	Tim McCormick	Cleveland Cavaliers	Michigan	12
	13	Jay Humphries	Phoenix Suns	Colorado	13
	14	Michael Cage	Los Angeles Clippers	San Diego State	14
	15	Terence Stansbury	Dallas Mavericks	Temple	15
	16	John Stockton	Utah Jazz	Gonzaga	16
	17	Jeff Turner	New Jersey Nets	Vanderbilt	17
	18	Vern Fleming	Indiana Pacers	Georgia	18
	19	Bernard Thompson	Portland Trail Blazers	Fresno State	19
	20	Tony Campbell	Detroit Pistons	Ohio State	20
	21	Kenny Fields	Milwaukee Bucks	UCLA	21
	22	Tom Sewell	Philadelphia 76ers	Lamar	22
	23	Earl Jones	Los Angeles Lakers	District of Columbia	23
	24	Michael Young	Boston Celtics	Houston	24
SECOND ROUND	1	Devin Durrant	Indiana Pacers	Brigham Young	25
	2	Victor Fleming	Portland Trail Blazers	Xavier (Ohio)	26
	3	Ron Anderson	Cleveland Cavaliers	Fresno State	27
	4	Cory Blackwell	Seattle SuperSonics	Wisconsin	28
	5	Stuart Gray	Indiana Pacers	UCLA	29
	6	Steve Burtt	Golden State Warriors	Iona	30
	7	Jay Murphy	Golden State Warriors	Boston College	31
	8	Eric Turner	Detroit Pistons	Michigan	32
	9	Steve Colter	Portland Trail Blazers	New Mexico State	33
	10	Tony Costner	Washington Bullets	St. Joseph's	34
	11	Othell Wilson	Golden State Warriors	Virginia	35
	12	Charles Jones	Phoenix Suns	Louisville	36
	13	Ben Coleman	Chicago Bulls	Maryland	37
	14	Charles Sitton	Dallas Mavericks	Oregon State	38
	15	Danny Young	Seattle SuperSonics	Wake Forest	39
	16	Anthony Teachey	Dallas Mavericks	Wake Forest	40
	17	Tom Sluby	Dallas Mavericks	Notre Dame	41
	18	Willie White	Denver Nuggets	Tennessee–Chattanooga	42
	19	Greg Wiltjer	Chicago Bulls	Victoria (Canada)	43
	20	Fred Raynolds	Washington Bullets	Texas–El Paso	44
	21	Gary Plummer	Golden State Warriors	Boston Univ.	45
	22	Jerome Kersey	Portland Trail Blazers	Longwood (Va.)	46
	23	Ronnie Williams	Boston Celtics	Florida	47
THIRD ROUND	1	James Banks	Philadelphia 76ers	Georgia	48
	2	Tim Dillon	Chicago Bulls	Northern Illinois	49
	3	Ben McDonald	Cleveland Cavaliers	California–Irvine	50
	4	Jim Petersen	Houston Rockets	Minnesota	51
	5	Terry Williams	Seattle SuperSonics	Alabama	52
	6	Ricky Ross	Washington Bullets	Tulsa	53
	7	Roosevelt Chapman	Kansas City Kings	Dayton	54
	8	Lewis Jackson	Golden State Warriors	Alabama State	55
	9	Jeff Allen	Kansas City Kings	St. John's	56
	10	Joe Binion	San Antonio Spurs	North Carolina A&T	57
	11	Bobby Parks	Atlanta Hawks	Memphis State	58
	12	Murray Jarman	Phoenix Suns	Clemson	59
	13	Leonard Mitchell	Cleveland Cavaliers	Louisiana State	60
	14	Jeff Cross	Dallas Mavericks	Maine	61
	15	David Pope	Utah Jazz	Norfolk State	62
	16	Yommy Sangodeyi	New Jersey Nets	Sam Houston State	63
	17	Curtis Green	New York Knicks	Southern Mississippi	64
	18	Tim Kearney	Portland Trail Blazers	West Virginia	65
	19	Kevin Springman	Detroit Pistons	St. Joseph's	66
	20	Vernon Delancy	Milwaukee Bucks	Florida	67
	21	Butch Graves	Philadelphia 76ers	Yale	68
	22	George Singleton	Los Angeles Lakers	Furman	69

		NAME	TEAM	COLLEGE	# OVERALL
	23	Rick Carlisle	Boston Celtics	Virginia	70
FOURTH ROUND	1	Ralph Jackson	Indiana Pacers	UCLA	71
	2	Melvin Johnson	Chicago Bulls	North Carolina–Charlotte	72
	3	Art Aaron	Cleveland Cavaliers	Northwestern	73
	4	Willie Jackson	Houston Rockets	Centenary	74
	5	Marc Glass	Los Angeles Clippers	Montana	75
	6	Jim Grandholm	Washington Bullets	South Florida	76
	7	Mark Halsel	Chicago Bulls	Northeastern	77
	8	John Devereaux	San Antonio Spurs	Ohio	78
	9	Karl Tilleman	Denver Nuggets	Calgary (Canada)	79
	10	Carl Henry	Kansas City Kings	Kansas	80
	11	Dickie Beal	Atlanta Hawks	Kentucky	81
	12	Jeff Collins	Phoenix Suns	Nevada–Las Vegas	82
	13	Jeff Jenkins	Seattle SuperSonics	Xavier (Ohio)	83
	14	John Horrocks	Dallas Mavericks	North Texas State	84
	15	Hank Cornley	New Jersey Nets	Illinois State	85
	16	Jim Rowinski	Utah Jazz	Purdue	86
	17	Bob Thornton	New York Knicks	California–Irvine	87
	18	Brett Applegate	Portland Trail Blazers	Brigham Young	88
	19	Phillip Smith	Detroit Pistons	New Mexico	89
	20	Ozell Jones	San Antonio Spurs	Cal State–Fullerton	90
	21	Earl Harrison	Philadelphia 76ers	Morehead State	91
	22	John Revelli	Los Angeles Lakers	Stanford	92
	23	Kevin Mullin	Boston Celtics	Princeton	93
FIFTH ROUND	1	Gene Smith	Indiana Pacers	Georgetown	94
	2	Lamont Robinson	Chicago Bulls	Lamar	95
	3	Vince Hinchen	Cleveland Cavaliers	Boise State	96
	4	Al McClain	Houston Rockets	New Hampshire	97
	5	Alonza Allen	Los Angeles Clippers	SW Louisiana	98
	6	Colin Irish	Washington Bullets	Bowling Green	99
	7	Eric Richardson	San Antonio Spurs	Alabama	100
	8	Steve Bartek	Golden State Warriors	Doane	101
	9	Jim Foster	Kansas City Kings	South Carolina	102
	10	Prince Bridges	Denver Nuggets	Missouri	103
	11	Terry Martin	Atlanta Hawks	NE Louisiana	104
	12	Bill Flye	Phoenix Suns	Richmond	105
	13	Elv Parsquale	Seattle SuperSonics	Victoria (Canada)	106
	14	Dave Williams	Dallas Mavericks	Illinois–Chicago	107
	15	Marcus Gaither	Utah Jazz	Fairleigh Dickinson	108
	16	Michael Gerren	New Jersey Nets	South Alabama	109
	17	Scott McCollum	Golden State Warriors	Pepperdine	110
	18	Mike Whitmarsh	Portland Trail Blazers	San Diego	111
	19	Rick Doyle	Detroit Pistons	Texas–San Antonio	112
	20	Ernie Floyd	Milwaukee Bucks	Holy Cross	113
	21	Dan Federman	Philadelphia 76ers	Tennessee	114
	22	Lance Berwald	Los Angeles Lakers	North Dakota State	115
	23	Todd Orlando	Boston Celtics	Bentley	116
SIXTH ROUND	1	Clyde Vaughan	Indiana Pacers	Pittsburgh	117
	2	Jeff Tipton	Chicago Bulls	Morehead State	118
	3	Matt Doherty	Cleveland Cavaliers	North Carolina	119
	4	McKinley Singleton	Milwaukee Bucks	Alabama–Birmingham	120
	5	Phillip Haynes	Los Angeles Clippers	Memphis State	121
	6	Blaise Bugajeski	Washington Bullets	Illinois Wesleyan	122
	7	Tony Martin	Golden State Warriors	Wyoming	123
	8	Dion Brown	San Antonio Spurs	SW Louisiana	124
	9	Willie Burton	Denver Nuggets	Tennessee	125
	10	Bruce Vanley	Kansas City Kings	Tulsa	126
	11	Jim Master	Atlanta Hawks	Kentucky	127
	12	Herman Veal	Phoenix Suns	Maryland	128
	13	Graylin Warner	Seattle SuperSonics	SW Louisiana	129
	14	LaVerne Evans	Dallas Mavericks	Marshall	130
	15	Oscar Schmidt	New Jersey Nets	(Brazil)	131
	16	Chris Harrison	Utah Jazz	West Virginia Wesleyan	132
	17	Eddie Lee Wilkins	New York Knicks	Gardner-Webb	133
	18	Lance Ball	Portland Trail Blazers	Western Oregon	134
	19	Rennie Bailey	Detroit Pistons	Louisiana Tech	135
	20	Mike Reddick	Milwaukee Bucks	Stetson	136
	21	Gary Springer	Philadelphia 76ers	Iona	137
	22	Keith Jones	Los Angeles Lakers	Stanford	138
	23	Steve Carfino	Boston Celtics	Iowa	139
SEVENTH ROUND	1	Kenton Edelin	Indiana Pacers	Virginia	140
	2	Butch Hays	Chicago Bulls	California	141
	3	Joe Jakubick	Cleveland Cavaliers	Akron	142
	4	Joedy Gardner	Houston Rockets	Cal State–Long Beach	143
	5	David Brantley	Los Angeles Clippers	Oregon	144
	6	Tim Garrett	Washington Bullets	New Mexico	145
	7	Michael Pitts	San Antonio Spurs	California	146
	8	Cliff Higgins	Golden State Warriors	Cal State–Northridge	147
	9	Chip Harris	Kansas City Kings	Robert Morris	148
	10	Mark Simpson	Denver Nuggets	Catawba	149
	11	Vince Martello	Atlanta Hawks	Florida State	150
	12	Raymond Crenshaw	Phoenix Suns	Oklahoma State	151
	13	Gary Gatewood	Seattle SuperSonics	Oregon	152
	14	George Turner	Dallas Mavericks	California–Irvine	153
	15	Bob Evans	Utah Jazz	Southern Utah State	154
	16	Sean Kerins	New Jersey Nets	Syracuse	155
	17	Ken Bannister	New York Knicks	St. Augustine	156
	18	Victor Anger	Portland Trail Blazers	Pepperdine	157
	19	Barry Francisco	Detroit Pistons	Bloomsburg State	158
	20	Tony William	Milwaukee Bucks	Florida State	159
	21	Rich Congo	Philadelphia 76ers	Drexel	160
	22	Richard Haenisch	Los Angeles Lakers	Chaminade	161
	23	Mark Van Valkenburg	Boston Celtics	Framingham State	162
EIGHTH ROUND	1	Tom Heitz	Indiana Pacers	Kentucky	163
	2	Brett Crawford	Chicago Bulls	U.S. International	164
	3	Elliot Beard	Cleveland Cavaliers	Oberlin	165
	4	Greg Wolff	Houston Rockets	Angelo State	166
	5	Jim McLoughlin	Los Angeles Clippers	Temple	167
	6	Darryl Odom	Washington Bullets	West Virginia Wesleyan	168
	7	Paul Brozovich	Golden State Warriors	Nevada–Las Vegas	169
	8	Dan Tarkanian	San Antonio Spurs	Nevada–Las Vegas	170
	9	Bill Wendlandt	Denver Nuggets	Texas	171
	10	Nate Rollins	Kansas City Kings	Fort Hays State	172
	11	Robert Brown	Atlanta Hawks	Long Island	173
	12	Mark Fothergill	Phoenix Suns	Maryland	174
	13	Jerry McMillan	Seattle SuperSonics	DePaul	175
	14	Leroy Sutton	Dallas Mavericks	Arkansas	176
	15	Chris Winans	New Jersey Nets	Utah	177
	16	Eric Booker	Utah Jazz	Nevada–Las Vegas	178
	17	Ricky Tunstall	New York Knicks	Youngstown State	179
	18	Steve Flint	Portland Trail Blazers	California–San Diego	180
	19	Dale Roberts	Detroit Pistons	Appalachian State	181
	20	Brad Jergenson	Milwaukee Bucks	South Carolina	182
	21	Frank Dobbs	Philadelphia 76ers	Villanova	183
	22	Champ Godboldt	Boston Celtics	Holy Cross	184
NINTH ROUND	1	Brian Martin	Indiana Pacers	Kansas	185
	2	Calvin Pierce	Chicago Bulls	Oklahoma	186
	3	John Shimko	Cleveland Cavaliers	Xavier (Ohio)	187
	4	Bill Coon	Houston Rockets	Presbyterian	188
	5	Dave Schultz	Los Angeles Clippers	Westmont	189
	6	Mike Emanuel	Washington Bullets	Pembroke State	190
	7	Melvin Roseboro	San Antonio Spurs	St. Mary's (Tex.)	191
	8	Mitch Arnold	Golden State Warriors	Fresno State	192
	9	Greg Turner	Kansas City Kings	Auburn	193

		NAME	TEAM	COLLEGE	# OVERALL
	10	Cecil Exum	Denver Nuggets	North Carolina	194
	11	Fred Brown	Atlanta Hawks	Georgetown	195
	12	Buddy Cox	Phoenix Suns	Bellarmine	196
	13	Mike Williams	Seattle SuperSonics	Idaho State	197
	14	John Tudor	Dallas Mavericks	Louisiana State	198
	15	Kelly Knight	Utah Jazz	Kansas	199
	16	Billy Ryan	New Jersey Nets	Princeton	200
	17	Marc Marotta	New York Knicks	Marquette	201
	18	Dennis Black	Portland Trail Blazers	Portland	202
	19	Ben Tower	Detroit Pistons	Michigan State	203
	20	Edwin Green	Milwaukee Bucks	Massachusetts	204
	21	Michael Mitchell	Philadelphia 76ers	Drexel	205
	22	Joe Dixon	Boston Celtics	Merrimack	206
TENTH ROUND	1	Gary Carver	Indiana Pacers	Western Kentucky	207
	2	Carl Lewis	Chicago Bulls	Houston	208
	3	Darrell Space	Cleveland Cavaliers	NE Illinois	209
	4	Robert Turner	Houston Rockets	Canisius	210
	5	Dick Mumma	Los Angeles Clippers	Penn State	211
	6	Glynn Myrick	Washington Bullets	Stetson	212
	7	Tim Bell	Golden State Warriors	California–Riverside	213
	8	Frank Rodriguez	San Antonio Spurs	New Mexico State	214
	9	Dexter Bailey	Denver Nuggets	Xavier (Ohio)	215
	10	Victor Coleman	Kansas City Kings	NW Missouri State	216
	11	Doug Mills	Atlanta Hawks	Hofstra	217
	12	Ezra Hill	Phoenix Suns	Liberty Baptist	218
	13	Greg Brandon	Seattle SuperSonics	Creighton	219
	14	Napoleon Johnson	Dallas Mavericks	Grambling	220
	15	Phil Jamison	New Jersey Nets	St. Peter's	221
	16	Mike Curran	Utah Jazz	Niagara	222
	17	Mike Henderson	New York Knicks	C.W. Post	223
	18	Randy Dunn	Portland Trail Blazers	George Fox	224
	19	Dan Pelekoudas	Detroit Pistons	Michigan	225
	20	Mike Toomer	Milwaukee Bucks	Florida A&M	226
	21	Martin Clark	Philadelphia 76ers	Boston College	227
	22	Dan Trant	Boston Celtics	Clark	228

1983

		NAME	TEAM	COLLEGE	# OVERALL
FIRST ROUND	1	Ralph Sampson	Houston Rockets	Virginia	1
	2	Steve Stipanovich	Indiana Pacers	Missouri	2
	3	Rodney McCray	Houston Rockets	Louisville	3
	4	Byron Scott	San Diego Clippers	Arizona State	4
	5	Sidney Green	Chicago Bulls	Nevada–Las Vegas	5
	6	Russell Cross	Golden State Warriors	Purdue	6
	7	Thurl Bailey	Utah Jazz	North Carolina State	7
	8	Antoine Carr	Detroit Pistons	Wichita State	8
	9	Dale Ellis	Dallas Mavericks	Tennessee	9
	10	Jeff Malone	Washington Bullets	Mississippi State	10
	11	Derek Harper	Dallas Mavericks	Illinois	11
	12	Darrell Walker	New York Knicks	Arkansas	12
	13	Ennis Whatley	Kansas City Kings	Alabama	13
	14	Clyde Drexler	Portland Trail Blazers	Houston	14
	15	Howard Carter	Denver Nuggets	Louisiana State	15
	16	Jon Sundvold	Seattle SuperSonics	Missouri	16
	17	Leo Rautins	Philadelphia 76ers	Syracuse	17
	18	Randy Breuer	Milwaukee Bucks	Minnesota	18
	19	John Paxson	San Antonio Spurs	Notre Dame	19
	20	Roy Hinson	Cleveland Cavaliers	Rutgers	20
	21	Greg Kite	Boston Celtics	Brigham Young	21
	22	Randy Wittman	Washington Bullets	Indiana	22
	23	Mitchell Wiggins	Indiana Pacers	Florida State	23
	24	Stewart Granger	Cleveland Cavaliers	Villanova	24
SECOND ROUND	1	Sidney Lowe	Chicago Bulls	North Carolina State	25
	2	Leroy Combs	Indiana Pacers	Oklahoma State	26
	3	John Garris	Cleveland Cavaliers	Boston College	27
	4	Rod Foster	Phoenix Suns	UCLA	28
	5	Larry Micheaux	Chicago Bulls	Houston	29
	6	Mark West	Dallas Mavericks	Old Dominion	30
	7	Glenn Rivers	Atlanta Hawks	Marquette	31
	8	Michael Britt	Washington Bullets	District of Columbia	32
	9	Dirk Minniefield	Dallas Mavericks	Kentucky	33
	10	Guy Williams	Washington Bullets	Washington State	34
	11	Darrell Lockhart	San Antonio Spurs	Auburn	35
	12	Scooter McCray	Seattle SuperSonics	Louisville	36
	13	David Russell	Denver Nuggets	St. John's	37
	14	Chris McNealy	Kansas City Kings	San Jose State	38
	15	Granville Waiters	Portland Trail Blazers	Ohio State	39
	16	James Thomas	Indiana Pacers	Indiana	40
	17	Ted Kitchel	Milwaukee Bucks	Indiana	41
	18	Mike Davis	Milwaukee Bucks	Alabama	42
	19	Pace Mannion	Golden State Warriors	Utah	43
	20	Horace Owens	New Jersey Nets	Rhode Island	44
	21	Paul Williams	Phoenix Suns	Arizona State	45
	22	Kevin Williams	San Antonio Spurs	St. John's	46
	23	Ken Lyons	Philadelphia 76ers	North Texas State	47
THIRD ROUND	1	Craig Ehlo	Houston Rockets	Washington State	48
	2	Greg Jones	Indiana Pacers	West Virginia	49
	3	Paul Thompson	Cleveland Cavaliers	Tulane	50
	4	Derek Whittenburg	Phoenix Suns	North Carolina State	51
	5	Winfred King	Boston Celtics	East Tennessee	52
	6	Michael Holton	Golden State Warriors	UCLA	53
	7	Robert Hansen	Utah Jazz	Iowa	54
	8	Erich Santifer	Detroit Pistons	Syracuse	55
	9	Larry Anderson	Cleveland Cavaliers	Nevada–Las Vegas	56
	10	Darren Daye	Washington Bullets	UCLA	57
	11	John Pinone	Atlanta Hawks	Villanova	58
	12	Bruce Kuczenski	New Jersey Nets	Connecticut	59
	13	Steve Harriel	Kansas City Kings	Washington State	60
	14	David Little	Denver Nuggets	Oklahoma	61
	15	Tom Piotrowski	Portland Trail Blazers	La Salle	62
	16	Frank Burnell	Seattle SuperSonics	Stetson	63
	17	Claude Riley	Philadelphia 76ers	Texas A&M	64
	18	Billy Goodwin	Milwaukee Bucks	St. John's	65
	19	Les Craft	Cleveland Cavaliers	Kansas State	66
	20	Derrick Hord	Cleveland Cavaliers	Kentucky	67
	21	Craig Robinson	Boston Celtics	Virginia	68
	22	Orlando Phillips	Los Angeles Lakers	Pepperdine	69
	23	Dan Ruland	Philadelphia 76ers	James Madison	70
FOURTH ROUND	1	Darrell Browder	Houston Rockets	Texas Christian	71
	2	Terry Fair	Indiana Pacers	Georgia	72
	3	Dwight Jones	Cleveland Cavaliers	Cincinnati	73
	4	Kalpatrick Wells	Philadelphia 76ers	Mississippi State	74
	5	Ron Crevier	Chicago Bulls	Boston College	75
	6	Doug Arnold	Utah Jazz	Texas Christian	76
	7	Pete Thibeaux	Golden State Warriors	St. Mary's (Cal.)	77
	8	Steve Bouchie	Detroit Pistons	Indiana	78
	9	Johnny Martin	Dallas Mavericks	NW Louisiana	79
	10	Dan Gay	Washington Bullets	SW Louisiana	80
	11	Harry Kelley	Atlanta Hawks	Texas Southern	81
	12	Mark Jones	New York Knicks	St. Bonaventure	82
	13	York Gross	Denver Nuggets	UC Santa Barbara	83
	14	Mike Jackson	Kansas City Kings	Wyoming	84
	15	Tim Dunham	Portland Trail Blazers	Chaminade	85
	16	Pete DeBisschop	Seattle SuperSonics	Fairfield	86

Round	#	NAME	TEAM	COLLEGE	# OVERALL
	17	Barney Mines	New Jersey Nets	Bradley	87
	18	Mark Nickens	Milwaukee Bucks	American	88
	19	Sam Mosley	Phoenix Suns	Nevada–Reno	89
	20	Brant Weidner	San Antonio Spurs	William & Mary	90
	21	Carlos Clark	Boston Celtics	Mississippi	91
	22	Terry Lewis	Los Angeles Lakers	Mississippi State	92
	23	Craig Robinson	Philadelphia 76ers	Princeton	93
FIFTH ROUND	1	Chuck Barnett	Houston Rockets	Oklahoma	94
	2	Roger Stieg	Indiana Pacers	Mississippi	95
	3	Chris Logan	Cleveland Cavaliers	Holy Cross	96
	4	Manute Bol	San Diego Clippers	(Sudan)	97
	5	Tim Andree	Chicago Bulls	Notre Dame	98
	6	Greg Hines	Golden State Warriors	Hampton Institute	99
	7	Mark Clark	Utah Jazz	Oklahoma	100
	8	Ken Austin	Detroit Pistons	Rice	101
	9	Jim Lampley	Dallas Mavericks	Arkansas-Little Rock	102
	10	Robin Dixon	Washington Bullets	New Hampshire	103
	11	Charles Jones	Atlanta Hawks	Oklahoma	104
	12	Troy Lee Mikell	New York Knicks	East Tennessee	105
	13	Lorenza Andrews	Kansas City Kings	Oklahoma State	106
	14	James Braddock	Denver Nuggets	North Carolina	107
	15	Gary Monroe	Portland Trail Blazers	Wright State	108
	16	Brad Watson	Seattle SuperSonics	Washington	109
	17	Tyren Naulls	New Jersey Nets	Texas A&M	110
	18	Mark Petteway	Milwaukee Bucks	New Orleans	111
	19	Jeff Pehl	San Antonio Spurs	Richmond	112
	20	Rick Lamb	Phoenix Suns	Illinois State	113
	21	Bob Reitz	Boston Celtics	Stonehill	114
	22	Danny Dixon	Los Angeles Lakers	Alabama A&M	115
	23	Mike Milligan	Philadelphia 76ers	Tennessee State	116
SIXTH ROUND	1	Jim Stack	Houston Rockets	Northwestern	117
	2	Cliff Pruitt	Indiana Pacers	Alabama–Birmingham	118
	3	Mel McLaughlin	Cleveland Cavaliers	Central Michigan	119
	4	Russell Todd	Milwaukee Bucks	West Virginia	120
	5	Ernest Patterson	Chicago Bulls	New Mexico State	121
	6	Fred Gilliam	Utah Jazz	Clemson	122
	7	Tom Heywood	Golden State Warriors	Weber State	123
	8	Derek Perry	Detroit Pistons	Michigan State	124
	9	Billy Allen	Dallas Mavericks	Nevada–Reno	125
	10	Donald Carroll	Washington Bullets	St. Augustine's	126
	11	Tom Bethea	Atlanta Hawks	Richmond	127
	12	Tony Simms	New York Knicks	Boston Univ.	128
	13	Glenn Green	Denver Nuggets	Murray State	129
	14	Alvis Rogers	Kansas City Kings	Wake Forest	130
	15	Derrick Pope	Portland Trail Blazers	Montana	131
	16	Tony Wilson	Seattle SuperSonics	Western Kentucky	132
	17	Oscar Taylor	New Jersey Nets	New Orleans	133
	18	Charles Hurt	Milwaukee Bucks	Kentucky	134
	19	Edward Bona	Phoenix Suns	Fordham	135
	20	Ricky Hooker	San Antonio Spurs	St. Mary's (Tex.)	136
	21	Paul Atkins	Boston Celtics	Dallas Baptist	137
	22	Mark Steele	Los Angeles Lakers	Colorado State	138
	23	Sedale Threatt	Philadelphia 76ers	West Virginia Tech	139
SEVENTH ROUND	1	Brian Kellerman	Houston Rockets	Idaho	140
	2	Tony Brown	Indiana Pacers	Indiana	141
	3	John Columbo	Cleveland Cavaliers	John Carroll	142
	4	Dan Evans	San Diego Clippers	Oregon State	143
	5	Jacque Hill	Chicago Bulls	USC	144
	6	Peter Williams	Golden State Warriors	Utah	145
	7	Joe Kazanowski	Utah Jazz	Victoria (Canada)	146
	8	Rob Gonzalez	Detroit Pistons	Colorado	147
	9	Terrell Schlundt	Dallas Mavericks	Marquette	148
	10	Danny Womack	Washington Bullets	Winston-Salem	149
	11	Lex Drum	Atlanta Hawks	Alabama–Birmingham	150
	12	Desi Barmore	New York Knicks	Fresno State	151
	13	Dane Suttle	Kansas City Kings	Pepperdine	152
	14	Maurice McDaniel	Denver Nuggets	Catawba	153
	15	Paul Little	Portland Trail Blazers	Penn	154
	16	Tony Gattis	Seattle SuperSonics	Mercer	155
	17	Keith Bennett	New Jersey Nets	Sacred Heart	156
	18	Anthony Hicks	Milwaukee Bucks	Xavier (Ohio)	157
	19	Keith Williams	San Antonio Spurs	Panhandle State	158
	20	Fred Brown	Phoenix Suns	Virginia Commonwealth	159
	21	Roy Jackson	Boston Celtics	Providence	160
	22	Ricky Mixon	Los Angeles Lakers	Cal State–Fullerton	161
	23	Tony Bruin	Philadelphia 76ers	Syracuse	162
EIGHTH ROUND	1	Jeff Bolding	Houston Rockets	Arkansas State	163
	2	Ray McCallum	Indiana Pacers	Ball State	164
	3	Larry Tucker	Cleveland Cavaliers	Lewis (Ill.)	165
	4	Mark Gannon	San Diego Clippers	Iowa	166
	5	Terry Bradley	Chicago Bulls	Chicago State	167
	6	Michael McCombs	Utah Jazz	Santa Fe	168
	7	Doug Harris	Golden State Warriors	Central Washington	169
	8	George Wenzel	Detroit Pistons	Augustana (IL)	170
	9	Bill Sadler	Dallas Mavericks	Pepperdine	171
	10	Bernard Perry	Washington Bullets	Howard	172
	11	George Thomas	Atlanta Hawks	Georgia Tech	173
	12	Mike Lang	New York Knicks	Penn State	174
	13	Cliff Tribus	Denver Nuggets	Davidson	175
	14	Preston Neumayr	Kansas City Kings	Cal–Davis	176
	15	Frank Smith	Portland Trail Blazers	Arizona	177
	16	Ray Smith	Seattle SuperSonics	Armstrong State	178
	17	Joe Myers	New Jersey Nets	Duquesne	179
	18	Brett Burkholder	Milwaukee Bucks	DePaul	180
	19	Mike Mulquin	Phoenix Suns	Villanova	181
	20	Norville Brown	San Antonio Spurs	Oklahoma Christian	182
	21	Trent Johnson	Boston Celtics	Pittsburgh	183
	22	Gordon Austin	Philadelphia 76ers	American	184
NINTH ROUND	1	James Campbell	Houston Rockets	Oklahoma City	185
	2	Lynn Mitchem	Indiana Pacers	Butler	186
	3	Joe Brown	Cleveland Cavaliers	Georgia State	187
	4	David Maxwell	San Diego Clippers	Fordham	188
	5	Ray Orange	Chicago Bulls	Oklahoma Christian	189
	6	Greg Goorjia	Golden State Warriors	Loyola Marymount	190
	7	Ron Webb	Utah Jazz	Oklahoma Christian	191
	8	Marlow McLain	Detroit Pistons	Eastern Michigan	192
	9	Sherrod Arnold	Dallas Mavericks	Chicago State	193
	10	Ricky Moreland	Washington Bullets	Maryland–Baltimore	194
	11	Wil Kotchery	Atlanta Hawks	Livingston State	195
	12	Charles Jones	New York Knicks	Marshall	196
	13	Bernard Hill	Kansas City Kings	Panhandle State	197
	14	Bobby Van Noy	Denver Nuggets	Catawba	198
	15	Phil Hopson	Portland Trail Blazers	Idaho	199
	16	Tony Washington	Seattle SuperSonics	Hampton Institute	200
	17	Kevin Black	New Jersey Nets	Rutgers	201
	18	Bill Varner	Milwaukee Bucks	Notre Dame	202
	19	Gary Gaspard	San Antonio Spurs	St. Mary's (Tex.)	203
	20	Joe Dykstra	Phoenix Suns	Western Illinois	204
	21	John Rice	Boston Celtics	Massachusetts–Boston	205
	22	Charles Fisher	Philadelphia 76ers	James Madison	206
TENTH ROUND	1	Mark Smed	Indiana Pacers	Augustana (S.D.)	207
	2	Jon Hanley	Cleveland Cavaliers	Xavier (Ohio)	208
	3	Keith Smith	San Diego Clippers	San Diego State	209

		NAME	TEAM	COLLEGE	# OVERALL
	4	Tom Emma	Chicago Bulls	Duke	210
	5	Odell Mosteller	Utah Jazz	Auburn	211
	6	Michael Zeno	Golden State Warriors	Long Beach State	212
	7	Ike Person	Detroit Pistons	Michigan	213
	8	Clyde Corley	Dallas Mavericks	Florida International	214
	9	Isiah Singletary	Washington Bullets	St. Louis	215
	10	Ronnie Carr	Atlanta Hawks	Western Carolina	216
	11	Bernard Randolph	New York Knicks	DePaul	217
	12	Cleveland McCrae	Denver Nuggets	Catawba	218
	13	Aaron Haskins	Kansas City Kings	Washington State	219
	14	Russ Christianson	Portland Trail Blazers	East Oregon State	220
	15	David Binion	Seattle SuperSonics	North Carolina Central	221
	16	Rich Simkus	New Jersey Nets	Princeton	222
	17	Bob Kelly	Milwaukee Bucks	St. John's	223
	18	Bo Overton	Phoenix Suns	Oklahoma	224
	19	Lamar Heard	San Antonio Spurs	Georgia	225
	20	Andy Kupec	Boston Celtics	Bentley	226

1982

		NAME	TEAM	COLLEGE	# OVERALL
FIRST ROUND	1	James Worthy	Los Angeles Lakers	North Carolina	1
	2	Terry Cummings	San Diego Clippers	DePaul	2
	3	Dominique Wilkins	Utah Jazz	Georgia	3
	4	Bill Garnett	Dallas Mavericks	Wyoming	4
	5	LaSalle Thompson	Kansas City Kings	Texas	5
	6	Trent Tucker	New York Knicks	Minnesota	6
	7	Quintin Dailey	Chicago Bulls	San Francisco	7
	8	Clark Kellogg	Indiana Pacers	Ohio State	8
	9	Cliff Levingston	Detroit Pistons	Wichita State	9
	10	Keith Edmonson	Atlanta Hawks	Purdue	10
	11	Lafayette Lever	Portland Trail Blazers	Arizona State	11
	12	John Bagley	Cleveland Cavaliers	Boston College	12
	13	Eric Floyd	New Jersey Nets	Georgetown	13
	14	Lester Conner	Golden State Warriors	Oregon State	14
	15	David Thirdkill	Phoenix Suns	Bradley	15
	16	Terry Teagle	Houston Rockets	Baylor	16
	17	Brook Steppe	Kansas City Kings	Georgia Tech	17
	18	Ricky Pierce	Detroit Pistons	Rice	18
	19	Rob Williams	Denver Nuggets	Houston	19
	20	Paul Pressey	Milwaukee Bucks	Tulsa	20
	21	Eddie Phillips	New Jersey Nets	Alabama	21
	22	Mark McNamara	Philadelphia 76ers	California	22
	23	Darren Tillis	Boston Celtics	Cleveland State	23
SECOND ROUND	1	Oliver Robinson	San Antonio Spurs	Alabama–Birmingham	24
	2	Bryan Warrick	Washington Bullets	St. Joseph's	25
	3	Ricky Frazier	Chicago Bulls	Missouri	26
	4	Fred Roberts	Milwaukee Bucks	Brigham Young	27
	5	David Magley	Cleveland Cavaliers	Kansas	28
	6	Scott Hastings	New York Knicks	Arkansas	29
	7	Wallace Bryant	Chicago Bulls	San Francisco	30
	8	Rod Higgins	Chicago Bulls	Fresno State	31
	9	Richard Anderson	San Diego Clippers	UC Santa Barbara	32
	10	Linton Townes	Portland Trail Blazers	James Madison	33
	11	Vince Taylor	New York Knicks	Duke	34
	12	Derek Smith	Golden State Warriors	Louisville	35
	13	Mitchell Anderson	Philadelphia 76ers	Bradley	36
	14	Audie Norris	Portland Trail Blazers	Jackson State	37
	15	Wayne Sappleton	Golden State Warriors	Loyola (Ill.)	38
	16	Kevin Magee	Phoenix Suns	California–Irvine	39
	17	Guy Morgan	Indiana Pacers	Wake Forest	40
	18	Dwight Anderson	Washington Bullets	USC	41
	19	Jeff Taylor	Houston Rockets	Texas Tech	42
	20	Jose Slaughter	Indiana Pacers	Portland	43
	21	Mike Gibson	Washington Bullets	S. Carolina–Spartanburg	44
	22	Russ Schoene	Philadelphia 76ers	Tennessee–Chattanooga	45
	23	Tony Guy	Boston Celtics	Kansas	46
THIRD ROUND	1	Michael Wilson	Cleveland Cavaliers	Marquette	47
	2	Craig Hodges	San Diego Clippers	Long Beach State	48
	3	Steve Trumbo	Utah Jazz	Brigham Young	49
	4	Corny Thompson	Dallas Mavericks	Connecticut	50
	5	Jim Johnstone	Kansas City Kings	Wake Forest	51
	6	Dan Caldwell	New York Knicks	Washington	52
	7	Tyrone Adams	Chicago Bulls	Kansas State	53
	8	Willie Jones	Los Angeles Lakers	Vanderbilt	54
	9	Jerry Eaves	Utah Jazz	Louisville	55
	10	Joe Kopicki	Atlanta Hawks	Detroit	56
	11	Craig Tucker	New York Knicks	Illinois	57
	12	Mike Largey	Washington Bullets	Upsala	58
	13	Jimmy Black	New Jersey Nets	North Carolina	59
	14	Chris Engler	Golden State Warriors	Wyoming	60
	15	Charles Pittman	Phoenix Suns	Maryland	61
	16	Roylin Bond	Denver Nuggets	Pepperdine	62
	17	Chuck Nevitt	Houston Rockets	North Carolina State	63
	18	Willie Redden	San Antonio Spurs	South Florida	64
	19	John Greig	Seattle SuperSonics	Oregon	65
	20	Phillip Lockett	Portland Trail Blazers	Alabama	66
	21	Mike Hackett	Los Angeles Lakers	Jacksonville	67
	22	Dale Solomon	Philadelphia 76ers	Virginia Tech	68
	23	Perry Moss	Boston Celtics	Northeastern	69
FOURTH ROUND	1	Reggie Hannah	Cleveland Cavaliers	South Alabama	70
	2	Darius Clemons	San Diego Clippers	Loyola (Ill.)	71
	3	Mark Eaton	Utah Jazz	UCLA	72
	4	Rudy Woods	Dallas Mavericks	Texas A&M	73
	5	Mike Sanders	Kansas City Kings	UCLA	74
	6	Norm Anchrum	New York Knicks	Alabama–Birmingham	75
	7	Chuck Aleksinas	Chicago Bulls	Connecticut	76
	8	Jeff Jones	Indiana Pacers	Virginia	77
	9	Walker Russell	Detroit Pistons	Western Michigan	78
	10	Eric Smith	Portland Trail Blazers	Georgetown	79
	11	James Griffin	New Jersey Nets	Illinois	80
	12	Dino Gregory	Washington Bullets	Long Beach State	81
	13	Tony Brown	New Jersey Nets	Arkansas	82
	14	Ken Stancell	Golden State Warriors	Virginia Commonwealth	83
	15	Alford Turner	Denver Nuggets	SW Louisiana	84
	16	Andre Gaddy	Houston Rockets	George Mason	85
	17	Rory White	Phoenix Suns	South Alabama	86
	18	Tony Grier	San Antonio Spurs	South Florida	87
	19	Ken Owens	Seattle SuperSonics	Idaho	88
	20	Jerry Beck	Milwaukee Bucks	Middle Tennessee	89
	21	Craig McCormick	Los Angeles Lakers	Western Kentucky	90
	22	Bruce Atkins	Philadelphia 76ers	Duquesne	91
	23	Greg Stewart	Boston Celtics	Tulsa	92
FIFTH ROUND	1	Terry White	Cleveland Cavaliers	Texas–El Paso	93
	2	Gary Carter	San Diego Clippers	Tennessee	94
	3	Mike McKay	Utah Jazz	Connecticut	95
	4	Ken Arnold	Dallas Mavericks	Iowa	96
	5	Ken Simpson	Kansas City Kings	Grambling	97
	6	Aaron Howard	New York Knicks	Villanova	98
	7	Rubin Jackson	Chicago Bulls	Oklahoma City	99
	8	Rich DiBenedetto	Indiana Pacers	Wisconsin–Eau Claire	100
	9	John Ebeling	Detroit Pistons	Florida Southern	101
	10	Mark Hall	Atlanta Hawks	Minnesota	102
	11	Cherokee Rhone	Portland Trail Blazers	Centenary	103
	12	Clarence Dickerson	Washington Bullets	Hawaii	104

		NAME	TEAM	COLLEGE	# OVERALL
	13	Chris Giles	New Jersey Nets	Alabama–Birmingham	105
	14	Albert Irving	Golden State Warriors	Alcorn State	106
	15	Jeff Schneider	Houston Rockets	Virginia Tech	107
	16	Marvin McCrary	Phoenix Suns	Missouri	108
	17	Bill Duffy	Denver Nuggets	Santa Clara	109
	18	Clarence Swannegan	San Antonio Spurs	Texas Tech	110
	19	Rod Camp	Seattle SuperSonics	Southern Illinois	111
	20	Jerry Davis	Washington Bullets	Detroit	112
	21	Howard McNeill	Los Angeles Lakers	Seton Hall	113
	22	Donald Mason	Philadelphia 76ers	Fresno State	114
	23	William Brown	Boston Celtics	St. Peter's	115
SIXTH ROUND	1	Vince Reynolds	Cleveland Cavaliers	South Florida	116
	2	Eric Marbury	San Diego Clippers	Georgia	117
	3	Alvin Jackson	Utah Jazz	Southern	118
	4	Wayne Waggoner	Dallas Mavericks	NW Louisiana	119
	5	Poncho Wright	Kansas City Kings	Louisville	120
	6	Mike Kanieski	New York Knicks	Dayton	121
	7	B.B. Fontenet	Chicago Bulls	Nevada–Reno	122
	8	Jeff Clark	Indiana Pacers	St. Joseph's	123
	9	Gary Holmes	Detroit Pistons	Minnesota	124
	10	Leo Cunningham	Portland Trail Blazers	Utah State	125
	11	Jay Bruchak	Atlanta Hawks	Mount St. Mary's	126
	12	Byron Williams	Washington Bullets	Idaho State	127
	13	Mel Daniel	New Jersey Nets	Furman	128
	14	David Vann	Golden State Warriors	St. Mary's (Cal.)	129
	15	Jake Bethany	Phoenix Suns	Hardin-Simmons	130
	16	Chris Brust	Denver Nuggets	North Carolina	131
	17	Don Wilson	Houston Rockets	NE Louisiana	132
	18	Jaime Pena	San Antonio Spurs	New Mexico State	133
	19	Bobby Potts	Seattle SuperSonics	North Carolina–Charlotte	134
	20	Tony Carr	Milwaukee Bucks	Wisconsin–Eau Claire	135
	21	Lynden Rose	Los Angeles Lakers	Houston	136
	22	Kevin Boyle	Philadelphia 76ers	Iowa	137
	23	John Schweitz	Boston Celtics	Richmond	138
SEVENTH ROUND	1	Randy Reed	Cleveland Cavaliers	Kansas State	139
	2	Ed Hughes	San Diego Clippers	Colorado State	140
	3	Thad Gardner	Utah Jazz	Michigan	141
	4	Bob Grady	Dallas Mavericks	Northwestern	142
	5	Perry Range	Kansas City Kings	Illinois	143
	6	Phil Seymore	New York Knicks	Canisius	144
	7	Chuck Verderber	Chicago Bulls	Kentucky	145
	8	Brad Leaf	Indiana Pacers	Evansville	146
	9	Dean Marquardt	Detroit Pistons	Marquette	147
	10	Horace Wyatt	Atlanta Hawks	Clemson	148
	11	Terry Long	Portland Trail Blazers	Lamar	149
	12	Wendell Gibson	Washington Bullets	Spartanburg South Carolina	150
	13	Tony Anderson	New Jersey Nets	UCLA	151
	14	Matt Waldron	Golden State Warriors	Pacific	152
	15	Jeb Barlow	Denver Nuggets	North Carolina	153
	16	Mike Helms	Houston Rockets	Wake Forest	154
	17	Phil Ward	Phoenix Suns	North Carolina–Charlotte	155
	18	Delonte Taylor	San Antonio Spurs	North Texas State	156
	19	Allen Rayhorn	Seattle SuperSonics	Northern Illinois	157
	20	Bobby Austin	Milwaukee Bucks	Cincinnati	158
	21	Maurice Williams	Los Angeles Lakers	USC	159
	22	Keith Hilliard	Philadelphia 76ers	SW Missouri State	160
	23	Phil Collins	Boston Celtics	West Virginia	161
EIGHTH ROUND	1	Monty Knight	Cleveland Cavaliers	Virginia Commonwealth	162
	2	Jacques Tuz	San Diego Clippers	Colorado	163
	3	Rick Campbell	Utah Jazz	Middle Tennessee	164
	4	Keith Peterson	Dallas Mavericks	Arkansas	165
	5	Ed Nealy	Kansas City Kings	Kansas State	166

		NAME	TEAM	COLLEGE	# OVERALL
	6	Dan Terwilliger	New York Knicks	Siena	167
	7	Mike Burns	Chicago Bulls	Nevada–Las Vegas	168
	8	Donald Reese	Indiana Pacers	Bradley	169
	9	Brian Nyenhuis	Detroit Pistons	Marquette	170
	10	Dave Porter	Portland Trail Blazers	Western Oregon	171
	11	James Ratiff	Atlanta Hawks	Howard	172
	12	Ken Luck	Washington Bullets	Delaware	173
	13	Otis Jackson	New Jersey Nets	Memphis State	174
	14	Mark King	Golden State Warriors	Florida Southern	175
	15	Dan Callandrillo	Houston Rockets	Seton Hall	176
	16	Rick Elrod	Phoenlx Suns	Georgetown (Ky.)	177
	17	Donny Speer	Denver Nuggets	Alabama–Birmingham	178
	18	Chris Faggi	San Antonio Spurs	Memphis State	179
	19	Steve Burks	Seattle SuperSonics	Washington	180
	20	Bryan Leonard	Milwaukee Bucks	Illinois	181
	21	Micah Blunt	Los Angeles Lakers	Tulane	182
	22	Donald Seals	Philadelphia 76ers	Jackson State	183
	23	Ed Spriggs	Boston Celtics	Georgetown	184
NINTH ROUND	1	Tony Hafley	Cleveland Cavaliers	South Alabama	185
	2	John Hegwood	San Diego Clippers	San Francisco	186
	3	Riley Clarida	Utah Jazz	Long Island	187
	4	Ralph McPherson	Dallas Mavericks	Texas–Arlington	188
	5	Jack Moore	Kansas City Kings	Nebraska	189
	6	Merle Scott	New York Knicks	South Carolina State	190
	7	Skip Dillard	Chicago Bulls	DePaul	191
	8	Mike Scearce	Indiana Pacers	Purdue	192
	9	Kevin Smith	Detroit Pistons	Michigan State	193
	10	Pierre Bland	Atlanta Hawks	Elizabeth City State	194
	11	Mark Dearborn	Portland Trail Blazers	St. Joseph's	195
	12	James Terry	Washington Bullets	Howard	196
	13	Gary Johnson	New Jersey Nets	Oral Roberts	197
	14	Nick Morken	Golden State Warriors	Tennessee	198
	15	Ken Lyles	Phoenix Suns	Washington	199
	16	Dean Sears	Denver Nuggets	UCLA	200
	17	Harry O'Brien	San Antonio Spurs	St. Mary's (Tex.)	201
	18	Robert Tate	Milwaukee Bucks	Idaho State	202
	19	Tim Byrne	Los Angeles Lakers	Rutgers	203
	20	George Melton	Philadelphia 76ers	Cheyney State	204
	21	Panayoti Giannakis	Boston Celtics	Hellenic	205
TENTH ROUND	1	Durand Walker	Cleveland Cavaliers	Marion	206
	2	Daryl Stovall	San Diego Clippers	Creighton	207
	3	Michael Edwards	Utah Jazz	New Orleans	208
	4	Albert Culton	Dallas Mavericks	Texas–Arlington	209
	5	Robert Estes	Kansas City Kings	Iowa State	210
	6	John Leonard	New York Knicks	Manhattan	211
	7	Tony Britto	Chicago Bulls	Campbell	212
	8	Craig Summers	Indiana Pacers	Wisconsin–Stout	213
	9	David Coulthard	Detroit Pistons	York (Canada)	214
	10	Grant Taylor	Portland Trail Blazers	California–Irvine	215
	11	Ronnie McAdoo	Atlanta Hawks	Old Dominion	216
	12	Donald Sinclair	Washington Bullets	North Carolina Central	217
	13	Sean Tuohy	New Jersey Nets	Mississippi	218
	14	Randy Whieldon	Golden State Warriors	California–Irvine	219
	15	Mike Phillips	Denver Nuggets	Niagara	220
	16	Dale Wilkinson	Phoenix Suns	Idaho State	221
	17	Keith White	San Antonio Spurs	McMurray	222
	18	Bob Coenen	Milwaukee Bucks	Wisconsin–Eau Claire	223
	20	Randy Burkert	Philadelphia 76ers	Drexel	224
	21	Landon Turner	Boston Celtics	Indiana	225

1981

ROUND		NAME	TEAM	COLLEGE	# OVERALL
FIRST ROUND	1	Mark Aguirre	Dallas Mavericks	DePaul	1
	2	Isiah Thomas	Detroit Pistons	Indiana	2
	3	Buck Williams	New Jersey Nets	Maryland	3
	4	Al Wood	Atlanta Hawks	North Carolina	4
	5	Danny Vranes	Seattle SuperSonics	Utah	5
	6	Orlando Woolridge	Chicago Bulls	Notre Dame	6
	7	Steve Johnson	Kansas City Kings	Oregon State	7
	8	Tom Chambers	San Diego Clippers	Utah	8
	9	Rolando Blackman	Dallas Mavericks	Kansas State	9
	10	Albert King	New Jersey Nets	Maryland	10
	11	Frank Johnson	Washington Bullets	Wake Forest	11
	12	Kelly Tripucka	Detroit Pistons	Notre Dame	12
	13	Danny Schayes	Utah Jazz	Syracuse	13
	14	Herb Williams	Indiana Pacers	Ohio State	14
	15	Jeff Lamp	Portland Trail Blazers	Virginia	15
	16	Darnell Valentine	Portland Trail Blazers	Kansas	16
	17	Kevin Loder	Kansas City Kings	Alabama State	17
	18	Ray Tolbert	New Jersey Nets	Indiana	18
	19	Mike McGee	Los Angeles Lakers	Michigan	19
	20	Larry Nance	Phoenix Suns	Clemson	20
	21	Alton Lister	Milwaukee Bucks	Arizona State	21
	22	Franklin Edwards	Philadelphia 76ers	Cleveland State	22
	23	Charles Bradley	Boston Celtics	Wyoming	23
SECOND ROUND	1	Jay Vincent	Dallas Mavericks	Michigan State	24
	2	Tracy Jackson	Boston Celtics	Notre Dame	25
	3	Brian Jackson	Portland Trail Blazers	Utah State	26
	4	Howard Wood	Utah Jazz	Tennessee	27
	5	Gene Banks	San Antonio Spurs	Duke	28
	6	Eddie Johnson	Kansas City Kings	Illinois	29
	7	Ed Rains	San Antonio Spurs	South Alabama	30
	8	Danny Ainge	Boston Celtics	Brigham Young	31
	9	Mike Olliver	Chicago Bulls	Lamar	32
	10	Sam Williams	Golden State Warriors	Arizona State	33
	11	Kenneth Green	Denver Nuggets	Pan American	34
	12	Charles Davis	Washington Bullets	Vanderbilt	35
	13	Ray Blume	Indiana Pacers	Oregon State	36
	14	Al Leslie	Indiana Pacers	Bucknell	37
	15	Clyde Bradshaw	Atlanta Hawks	DePaul	38
	16	Harvey Knuckles	Los Angeles Lakers	Toledo	39
	17	Greg Cook	New York Knicks	Louisiana State	40
	18	Claude Gregory	Washington Bullets	Wisconsin	41
	19	Elvis Rolle	Los Angeles Lakers	Florida State	42
	20	Elston Turner	Dallas Mavericks	Mississippi	43
	21	Steve Lingenfelter	Washington Bullets	South Dakota State	44
	22	Ed Turner	Houston Rockets	Texas A&I	45
	23	Vernon Smith	Philadelphia 76ers	Texas A&M	46
THIRD ROUND	1	Art Housey	Dallas Mavericks	Kansas	47
	2	Mike Ferrara	Washington Bullets	Colgate	48
	3	David Burns	New Jersey Nets	St. Louis	49
	4	Derek Holcomb	Portland Trail Blazers	Illinois	50
	5	Zam Fredrick	Los Angeles Lakers	South Carolina	51
	6	Rudy Macklin	Atlanta Hawks	Louisiana State	52
	7	Mark Radford	Seattle SuperSonics	Oregon State	53
	8	Jim Smith	San Diego Clippers	Ohio State	54
	9	Mickey Dillard	Cleveland Cavaliers	Florida State	55
	10	Carlton Neverson	Golden State Warriors	Pittsburgh	56
	11	Frank Brickowski	New York Knicks	Penn State	57
	12	Curtis Berry	Kansas City Kings	Missouri	58
	13	Russell Bowers	Cleveland Cavaliers	American	59
	14	Purvis Miller	Indiana Pacers	USC	60
	15	Petur Gudmundsson	Portland Trail Blazers	Washington	61
	16	Sam Clancy	Phoenix Suns	Pittsburgh	62
	17	Wayne McKoy	New York Knicks	St. John's	63
	18	Tom Baker	San Antonio Spurs	Eastern Kentucky	64
	19	Ron Cornelius	Los Angeles Lakers	Pacific	65
	20	Craig Dykema	Phoenix Suns	Long Beach State	66
	21	Mark Smith	Milwaukee Bucks	Illinois	67
	22	Ernest Graham	Philadelphia 76ers	Maryland	68
	23	John Johnson	Boston Celtics	Michigan	69
FOURTH ROUND	1	Eddie Moss	Dallas Mavericks	Syracuse	70
	2	John May	Detroit Pistons	South Alabama	71
	3	Edmund Sherod	New Jersey Nets	Virginia Commonwealth	72
	4	George Torres	Utah Jazz	Bethany Nazarene	73
	5	Ethan Martin	Cleveland Cavaliers	Louisiana State	74
	6	Kevin Figaro	Atlanta Hawks	SW Louisiana	75
	7	Lewis Lloyd	Golden State Warriors	Drake	76
	8	Lee Raker	San Diego Clippers	Virginia	77
	9	Kenny Dennard	Kansas City Kings	Duke	78
	10	Ron Davis	Washington Bullets	Arizona	79
	11	Terry Adolph	Golden State Warriors	West Texas State	80
	12	Larry Spriggs	Houston Rockets	Howard	81
	13	B.B. Davis	Kansas City Kings	Lamar	82
	14	Rolando Frazier	Indiana Pacers	Briar Cliff	83
	15	Oliver Lee	Chicago Bulls	Marquette	84
	16	Peter Verhoeven	Portland Trail Blazers	Fresno State	85
	17	Alex Bradley	New York Knicks	Villanova	86
	18	Earl Belcher	San Antonio Spurs	St. Bonaventure	87
	19	Kevin McKenna	Los Angeles Lakers	Creighton	88
	20	Don Koonce	Detroit Pistons	North Carolina–Charlotte	89
	21	Kris Anderson	Milwaukee Bucks	Florida State	90
	22	Stanley Williams	Boston Celtics	La Salle	91
	23	Rynn Wright	Philadelphia 76ers	Texas A&M	92
FIFTH ROUND	1	Pete Budko	Dallas Mavericks	North Carolina	93
	2	George DeVone	Detroit Pistons	North Carolina–Charlotte	94
	3	Joe Cooper	New Jersey Nets	Colorado	95
	4	Ken Page	Cleveland Cavaliers	New Mexico	96
	5	Mike Clark	Utah Jazz	Oregon	97
	6	Steve Krafcisin	Atlanta Hawks	Iowa	98
	7	Andra Griffin	Seattle SuperSonics	Washington	99
	8	Dennis Isbell	San Diego Clippers	Memphis State	100
	9	Willie Sims	Denver Nuggets	Louisiana State	101
	10	Hank McDowell	Golden State Warriors	Memphis State	102
	11	Garry Witts	Washington Bullets	Holy Cross	103
	12	U.S. Reed	Kansas City Kings	Arkansas	104
	13	Hasan Houston	Houston Rockets	Bradley	105
	14	George Peterson	Indiana Pacers	Jersey City State	106
	15	Herb Andrew	Portland Trail Blazers	South Alabama	107
	16	Johnny Nash	Chicago Bulls	Arizona State	108
	17	Jim Wright	New York Knicks	Rhode Island	109
	18	Mike Rhodes	San Antonio Spurs	Vanderbilt	110
	19	Craig Watts	Los Angeles Lakers	North Carolina State	111
	20	Paul Heuerman	Phoenix Suns	Michigan	112
	21	Kelvin Troy	Milwaukee Bucks	Rutgers	113
	22	Steve Craig	Philadelphia 76ers	Brigham Young	114
	23	Glen Grunwald	Boston Celtics	Indiana	115
SIXTH ROUND	1	Karl Bakowski	Dallas Mavericks	Utah	116
	2	Vince Brookins	Detroit Pistons	Iowa	117
	3	Kevin Lynam	New Jersey Nets	La Salle	118
	4	Kevin Sprewer	Utah Jazz	Loyola (Ill.)	119
	5	Aaron Strayhorn	Cleveland Cavaliers	Hawaii	120
	6	Darryl Warwick	Atlanta Hawks	Hampton Institute	121

ROUND		NAME	TEAM	COLLEGE	# OVERALL
	7	Earl Banks	Seattle SuperSonics	Auburn	122
	8	Mike Pepper	San Diego Clippers	North Carolina	123
	9	Alonzo Weatherley	Denver Nuggets	Denver	124
	10	Robert Williams	Washington Bullets	Grambling	125
	11	Carter Scott	Golden State Warriors	Ohio State	126
	12	Fred Cowan	Houston Rockets	Kentucky	127
	13	Brian Walker	Kansas City Kings	Purdue	128
	14	Robert Fronk	Indiana Pacers	Washington	129
	15	Roger Burkman	Chicago Bulls	Louisville	130
	16	Roshern Amie	Portland Trail Blazers	Texas–El Paso	131
	17	John Blair	New York Knicks	Monmouth	132
	18	Norman Shavers	San Antonio Spurs	Jackson State	133
	19	Kevin Singleton	Los Angeles Lakers	California	134
	20	Pete Harris	Phoenix Suns	Northeastern	135
	21	Jo Jo Hunter	Milwaukee Bucks	Colorado	136
	22	Steve Waite	Boston Celtics	Iowa	137
	23	Michael Thomas	Philadelphia 76ers	North Park	138
SEVENTH ROUND	1	Danny Davis	Dallas Mavericks	North Carolina–Wilmington	139
	2	Greg Nance	Detroit Pistons	West Virginia	140
	3	Rod Robertson	New Jersey Nets	Northwestern	141
	4	Andre Smith	Cleveland Cavaliers	Nebraska	142
	5	Mike Robinson	Utah Jazz	Central Michigan	143
	6	Kevin Vesey	Atlanta Hawks	Iona	144
	7	Tom Sienkiewicz	Seattle SuperSonics	Villanova	145
	8	Randy Johnson	San Diego Clippers	Southern Colorado	146
	9	Greg Manning	Denver Nuggets	Maryland	147
	10	Robby Dosty	Golden State Warriors	Arizona	148
	11	Randy Martell	Washington Bullets	Houston Baptist	149
	12	Clinton Wheeler	Kansas City Kings	William Paterson	150
	13	Joe Faine	Houston Rockets	Bowling Green	151
	14	Larry McKinney	Indiana Pacers	Boise State	152
	15	Julius Wayne	Portland Trail Blazers	Texas–El Paso	153
	16	Scott Williams	Chicago Bulls	South Alabama	154
	17	Terry Cramer	New York Knicks	Ripon	155
	18	Mark Mindeman	San Antonio Spurs	Northern Michigan	156
	19	Larry Petty	Los Angeles Lakers	Wisconsin	157
	20	David Williams	Phoenix Suns	Southern	158
	21	Lewis Latimore	Milwaukee Bucks	Virginia	159
	22	John Crawford	Philadelphia 76ers	Kansas	160
	23	Tom Seaman	Boston Celtics	Holy Cross	161
EIGHTH ROUND	1	David Kennedy	Dallas Mavericks	Cincinnati	162
	2	Joe Schoen	Detroit Pistons	St. Francis (Pa.)	163
	3	Ken Webb	New Jersey Nets	Fairleigh Dickinson	164
	4	Bob Cattage	Utah Jazz	Auburn	165
	5	Glen Marcus	Cleveland Cavaliers	Alabama–Birmingham	166
	6	Gilbert Salinas	Atlanta Hawks	Notre Dame	167
	7	Todd Haynes	San Diego Clippers	Davidson	168
	8	Curtis Redding	Denver Nuggets	St. John's	169
	9	Mike Howard	Washington Bullets	Wofford	170
	10	Yasutaka Okayama	Golden State Warriors	Osaka (Japan)	171
	11	Stanley Brewer	Houston Rockets	Western Georgia	172
	12	Randy Smithson	Kansas City Kings	Wichita State	173
	13	Len Hatzenbeller	Indiana Pacers	Drexel	174
	14	Ben Mitchell	Chicago Bulls	Alabama–Huntsville	175
	15	John Smith	Portland Trail Blazers	St. Joseph's	176
	16	Brian O'Connor	New York Knicks	Thomas More (Ky.)	177
	17	Bob Bartholomew	San Antonio Spurs	San Diego	178
	18	Jay Triano	Los Angeles Lakers	Simon Fraser (Canada)	179
	19	Steve Risley	Phoenix Suns	Indiana	180
	20	Mike Brkovich	Milwaukee Bucks	Michigan State	181
	21	George Morrow	Boston Celtics	Creighton	182
	22	Frank Gilroy	Philadelphia 76ers	St. John's	183
NINTH ROUND	1	John Hollinden	Dallas Mavericks	Indiana State–Evansville	184
	2	Eddie Baker	Detroit Pistons	Alcorn State	185
	3	Rudy Williams	New Jersey Nets	Providence	186
	4	Paul Roba	Cleveland Cavaliers	Cleveland State	187
	5	Ken Ollie	Utah Jazz	Wyoming	188
	6	Howard Thompkins	Atlanta Hawks	Wagner	189
	7	Art Jones	San Diego Clippers	North Carolina State	190
	8	Andrew Burton	Denver Nuggets	Austin Peay	191
	9	Doug Murrey	Golden State Warriors	San Jose State	192
	10	Eddie Brown	Washington Bullets	Valdosta State	193
	11	Mike Perry	Kansas City Kings	Richmond	194
	12	Scott Whitley	Indiana Pacers	William & Mary	195
	13	Sid Williams	Portland Trail Blazers	San Jose State	196
	14	Terry Martin	Chicago Bulls	Lambuth (Tenn.)	197
	15	Marty Headd	New York Knicks	Syracuse	198
	16	Leonel Marquetti	San Antonio Spurs	Hampton Institute	199
	17	Brian Johnson	Phoenix Suns	Colorado	200
	18	Chip Rucker	Milwaukee Bucks	Northeastern	201
	19	Ron Wister	Philadelphia 76ers	Temple	202
	20	Greg McCray	Boston Celtics	Virginia Commonwealth	203
TENTH ROUND	1	Scott Bosanko	Dallas Mavericks	Northern State College	204
	2	Melvin Maxwell	Detroit Pistons	Western Michigan	205
	3	Vic Sison	New Jersey Nets	UCLA	206
	4	Joe Merten	Utah Jazz	Wisconsin–Eau Claire	207
	5	Greg Boone	Cleveland Cavaliers	Augsburg	208
	6	Mike Frazier	Atlanta Hawks	Georgetown	209
	7	Tony Gwynn	San Diego Clippers	San Diego State	210
	8	Derrick Rowland	Denver Nuggets	Potsdam State	211
	9	Ralton Way	Washington Bullets	Houston Baptist	212
	10	Barry Brooks	Golden State Warriors	USC	213
	12	Mark Wilson	Kansas City Kings	Fort Hays State	214
	13	Rodney Benson	Indiana Pacers	Wright State	215
	14	Kenny Easley	Chicago Bulls	UCLA	216
	15	Steve Cochran	Portland Trail Blazers	Lewis & Clark	217
	16	Kevin Rogers	New York Knicks	St. Peter's	218
	17	Alvin Brooks	San Antonio Spurs	Lamar	219
	19	Felton Sealey	Phoenix Suns	Oregon	220
	20	Artie Green	Milwaukee Bucks	Marquette	221
	21	Ken Matthews	Boston Celtics	North Carolina State	222
	22	Pete Mullenberg	Philadelphia 76ers	Delaware	223

1980

ROUND		NAME	TEAM	COLLEGE	# OVERALL
FIRST ROUND	1	Joe Barry Carroll	Golden State Warriors	Purdue	1
	2	Darrell Griffith	Utah Jazz	Louisville	2
	3	Kevin McHale	Boston Celtics	Minnesota	3
	4	Kelvin Ransey	Chicago Bulls	Ohio State	4
	5	James Ray	Denver Nuggets	Jacksonville	5
	6	Mike O'Koren	New Jersey Nets	North Carolina	6
	7	Mike Gminski	New Jersey Nets	Duke	7
	8	Andrew Toney	Philadelphia 76ers	SW Louisiana	8
	9	Michael Brooks	San Diego Clippers	La Salle	9
	10	Ronnie Lester	Portland Trail Blazers	Iowa	10
	11	Kiki Vandeweghe	Dallas Mavericks	UCLA	11
	12	Mike Woodson	New York Knicks	Indiana	12
	13	Rickey Brown	Golden State Warriors	Mississippi State	13
	14	Wes Matthews	Washington Bullets	Wisconsin	14
	15	Reggie Johnson	San Antonio Spurs	Tennessee	15
	16	Hawkeye Whitney	Kansas City Kings	North Carolina State	16
	17	Larry Drew	Detroit Pistons	Missouri	17
	18	Don Collins	Atlanta Hawks	Washington State	18
	19	John Duren	Utah Jazz	Georgetown	19

		NAME	TEAM	COLLEGE	#OVERALL
	20	Bill Hanzlik	Seattle SuperSonics	Notre Dame	20
	21	Monti Davis	Philadelphia 76ers	Tennessee State	21
	22	Chad Kinch	Cleveland Cavaliers	North Carolina–Charlotte	22
	23	Carl Nicks	Denver Nuggets	Indiana State	23
SECOND ROUND	1	Larry Smith	Golden State Warriors	Alcorn State	24
	2	Jeff Ruland	Golden State Warriors	Iona	25
	3	Sam Worthen	Chicago Bulls	Marquette	26
	4	John Stroud	Houston Rockets	Mississippi	27
	5	Craig Shelton	Atlanta Hawks	Georgetown	28
	6	Louis Orr	Indiana Pacers	Syracuse	29
	7	Kenny Natt	Indiana Pacers	NE Louisiana	30
	8	Wayne Robinson	Los Angeles Lakers	Virginia Tech	31
	9	David Lawrence	Portland Trail Blazers	McNeese State	32
	10	Bruce Collins	Portland Trail Blazers	Weber State	33
	11	Roosevelt Bouie	Dallas Mavericks	Syracuse	34
	12	Ricky Mahorn	Washington Bullets	Hampton Institute	35
	13	DeWayne Scales	New York Knicks	Louisiana State	36
	14	Butch Carter	Los Angeles Lakers	Indiana	37
	15	Terry Stotts	Houston Rockets	Oklahoma	38
	16	Michael Wiley	San Antonio Spurs	Long Beach State	39
	17	Dick Miller	Indiana Pacers	Toledo	40
	18	Jawann Oldham	Denver Nuggets	Seattle	41
	19	Kimberly Belton	Phoenix Suns	Stanford	42
	20	Billy Williams	Houston Rockets	Clemson	43
	21	Clyde Austin	Philadelphia 76ers	North Carolina State	44
	22	Brad Branson	Detroit Pistons	Southern Methodist	45
	23	Arnette Hallman	Boston Celtics	Purdue	46
THIRD ROUND	1	Kurt Nimphius	Denver Nuggets	Arizona State	47
	2	Eddie Lee	Denver Nuggets	Cincinnati	48
	3	John Virgil	Golden State Warriors	North Carolina	49
	4	James Wilkes	Chicago Bulls	UCLA	50
	5	Ron Valentine	Denver Nuggets	Old Dominion	51
	6	Lowes Moore	New Jersey Nets	West Virginia	52
	7	Stuart House	Cleveland Cavaliers	Washington State	53
	8	Ron Perry	Boston Celtics	Holy Cross	54
	9	Wayne Abrams	Cleveland Cavaliers	Southern Illinois	55
	10	Mike Harper	Portland Trail Blazers	North Park	56
	11	Dave Britton	Dallas Mavericks	Texas A&M	57
	12	Kurt Rambis	New York Knicks	Santa Clara	58
	13	John Campbell	Phoenix Suns	Clemson	59
	14	Lavon Mercer	San Antonio Spurs	Georgia	60
	15	Rich Yonakor	San Antonio Spurs	North Carolina	61
	16	Tony Murphy	Kansas City Kings	Southern	62
	17	Al Beal	Milwaukee Bucks	Oklahoma	63
	18	Jonathan Moore	Detroit Pistons	Furman	64
	19	Doug True	Phoenix Suns	California	65
	20	Carl Bailey	Seattle SuperSonics	Tuskegee	66
	21	Reggie Gaines	Philadelphia 76ers	Winston-Salem	67
	22	Ron Jones	Cleveland Cavaliers	Illinois State	68
	23	Donald Newman	Boston Celtics	Idaho	69
FOURTH ROUND	1	Darwin Cook	Detroit Pistons	Portland	70
	2	Robert Scott	Golden State Warriors	Alabama	71
	3	Alan Taylor	Utah Jazz	Brigham Young	72
	4	Sammie Ellis	Denver Nuggets	Pittsburgh	73
	5	Ron Charles	Chicago Bulls	Michigan State	74
	6	Rory Sparrow	New Jersey Nets	Villanova	75
	7	Ed Odom	San Diego Clippers	Oklahoma State	76
	8	Murray Brown	Cleveland Cavaliers	Florida State	77
	9	Rich Branning	Indiana Pacers	Notre Dame	78
	10	Kelvin Henderson	Portland Trail Blazers	St. Louis	79
	11	David Johnson	Dallas Mavericks	Weber State	80
	12	Francois Wise	Washington Bullets	Long Beach State	81

		NAME	TEAM	COLLEGE	#OVERALL
	13	Joseph Chrnelich	New York Knicks	Wisconsin	82
	14	Calvin Roberts	San Antonio Spurs	Cal State–Fullerton	83
	15	Dean Hunger	Houston Rockets	Utah State	84
	16	Billy Bryant	Philadelphia 76ers	Western Kentucky	85
	17	Jeff Wolf	Milwaukee Bucks	North Carolina	86
	18	Tony Jackson	Los Angeles Lakers	Florida State	87
	19	Leroy Stampley	Phoenix Suns	Loyola (Ill.)	88
	20	Gary Ray Hooker	Seattle SuperSonics	Murray State	89
	21	Harold Hubbard	Philadelphia 76ers	Savannah State	90
	22	Ron Baxter	Los Angeles Lakers	Texas	91
	23	Kevin Hamilton	Boston Celtics	Iona	92
FIFTH ROUND	1	Tony Fuller	Detroit Pistons	Pepperdine	93
	2	Wally West	Utah Jazz	Boston Univ.	94
	3	Don Carlino	Golden State Warriors	USC	95
	4	Mike Campbell	Chicago Bulls	Northwestern	96
	5	James Patrick	Denver Nuggets	SW Texas State	97
	6	Aaron Curry	New Jersey Nets	Oklahoma	98
	7	Wally Rank	San Diego Clippers	San Jose State	99
	8	Joe Galvin	Indiana Pacers	Illinois State	100
	9	LaVon Williams	Cleveland Cavaliers	Kentucky	101
	10	Larry Belin	Portland Trail Blazers	New Mexico	102
	11	Darrell Allums	Dallas Mavericks	UCLA	103
	12	William Carey	New York Knicks	Albright	104
	13	Daryl Strickland	Washington Bullets	Rutgers	105
	14	Albert Jones	Houston Rockets	New Mexico State	106
	15	Gib Hinz	San Antonio Spurs	Wisconsin–Eau Claire	107
	16	Kevin Blakley	Kansas City Kings	Eastern Michigan	108
	17	Ken Jones	Milwaukee Bucks	Virginia Commonwealth	109
	18	Mike Doyle	Atlanta Hawks	South Carolina	110
	19	Mark Stevens	Phoenix Suns	Northern Arizona	111
	20	Lenny Horton	Seattle SuperSonics	Georgia Tech	112
	21	Jim Swaney	Philadelphia 76ers	Toledo	113
	22	Rick Raivio	Los Angeles Lakers	Portland	114
	23	Rufus Harris	Boston Celtics	Maine	115
SIXTH ROUND	1	Tony Turner	Detroit Pistons	Alaska-Anchorage	116
	2	Neil Bresnahan	Golden State Warriors	Illinois	117
	3	Ken Cunningham	Utah Jazz	Western Michigan	118
	4	Ernie Hill	Denver Nuggets	Oklahoma City	119
	5	Bernard Rencher	Chicago Bulls	St. John's	120
	6	Rick Mattick	New Jersey Nets	Louisiana State	121
	7	Londale Theus	San Diego Clippers	Santa Clara	122
	8	Antonio Martin	Cleveland Cavaliers	Oral Roberts	123
	9	Randy Owens	Indiana Pacers	Philadelphia Textile	124
	10	Perry Mirkovich	Portland Trail Blazers	Lethbridge (Canada)	125
	11	Leroy Jackson	Dallas Mavericks	Cameron	126
	12	Ken Dancy	Washington Bullets	Chicago State	127
	13	Kelvin Hicks	New York Knicks	New York Tech	128
	14	Dean Uthoff	San Antonio Spurs	Iowa State	129
	15	Everette Jefferson	Houston Rockets	New Mexico	130
	16	Kent Grooms	Kansas City Kings	Kent State	131
	17	Alex Gilbert	Milwaukee Bucks	Indiana State	132
	18	Mike Zagardo	Atlanta Hawks	George Washington	133
	19	Coby Leavitt	Phoenix Suns	Utah	134
	20	Jim Strickland	Seattle SuperSonics	South Carolina	135
	21	Donald Cooper	Philadelphia 76ers	St. Augustine	136
	22	Odis Boddie	Los Angeles Lakers	North Alabama	137
	23	Kenny Evans	Boston Celtics	Norfolk State	138
SEVENTH ROUND	1	Carl Pierce	Detroit Pistons	Gonzaga	139
	2	Dave Colescott	Utah Jazz	North Carolina	140
	3	Lorenzo Romar	Golden State Warriors	Washington	141
	4	Robert Byrd	Chicago Bulls	Marquette	142
	5	Tommy Springer	Denver Nuggets	Vanderbilt	143

ROUND		NAME	TEAM	COLLEGE	# OVERALL
	6	Larry Spicer	New Jersey Nets	Alabama–Birmingham	144
	7	Paul Anderson	San Diego Clippers	USC	145
	8	Charles Naddaff	Indiana Pacers	Lafayette	146
	9	Leroy Berry	Cleveland Cavaliers	Wilmington (Ohio)	147
	10	Gig Sims	Portland Trail Blazers	UCLA	148
	11	Tony Forch	Dallas Mavericks	Midwestern	149
	12	Bobby Turner	New York Knicks	Louisville	150
	13	Karl Godine	Washington Bullets	Stephen F. Austin	151
	14	Joe Nehls	Houston Rockets	Arizona	152
	15	Allan Zahn	San Antonio Spurs	Arkansas	153
	16	Arnold McDowell	Kansas City Kings	Montana State	154
	17	Ron White	Milwaukee Bucks	Furman	155
	18	Charles Hightower	Atlanta Hawks	Dillard	156
	19	Ron Williams	Phoenix Suns	Western Montana	157
	20	Carl Ervin	Seattle SuperSonics	Seattle	158
	21	Richard Smith	Philadelphia 76ers	Weber State	159
	22	Les Henson	Boston Celtics	Virginia Tech	160
EIGHTH ROUND	1	Leroy Loggins	Detroit Pistons	Fairmont State	161
	2	Kurt Kanaskie	Golden State Warriors	La Salle	162
	3	Jim Brandon	Utah Jazz	St. Peter's	163
	4	Modzel Greer	Chicago Bulls	North Park	164
	5	Lloyd Terry	New Jersey Nets	New Orleans	165
	6	Jim Ellinghausen	Cleveland Cavaliers	Ohio State	166
	7	Steve Stielper	Indiana Pacers	James Madison	167
	8	John Stroeder	Portland Trail Blazers	Montana	168
	9	Clarence Kea	Dallas Mavericks	Lamar	169
	10	Rich Valavicius	Washington Bullets	Auburn	170
	11	James Salters	New York Knicks	Penn	171
	12	Bill Bailey	San Antonio Spurs	Pan American	172
	13	Rosie Barnes	Houston Rockets	Bowling Green	173
	14	Keith Valentine	Milwaukee Bucks	Virginia Union	174
	15	Jim Connolly	Phoenix Suns	La Salle	175
	16	Al Dutch	Seattle SuperSonics	Georgetown	176
	17	Martin Lemelle	Philadelphia 76ers	Grambling	177
	18	Melvin Hooker	Los Angeles Lakers	Edinboro State	178
	19	Steve Wright	Boston Celtics	Boston Univ.	179
NINTH ROUND	1	Terry Dupris	Detroit Pistons	Huron	180
	2	Paul Renfro	Utah Jazz	Texas–Arlington	181
	3	Billy Reid	Golden State Warriors	San Francisco	182
	4	Jay Shidler	Chicago Bulls	Kentucky	183
	5	Jim Graziano	Denver Nuggets	South Carolina	184
	6	Barry Young	New Jersey Nets	Colorado State	185
	7	Scott Rogers	Indiana Pacers	Kenyon	186
	8	Melvin Crafter	Cleveland Cavaliers	Central State (Ohio)	187
	9	Rich Boucher	Portland Trail Blazers	Maine	188
	10	Ken Williams	Dallas Mavericks	Houston	189
	11	Don Wiley	New York Knicks	Monmouth	190
	12	Clinton Wyatt	Washington Bullets	Alcorn State	191
	13	Al Williams	San Antonio Spurs	North Texas State	192
	14	Charley Cole	Kansas City Kings	Delta State	193
	15	Del Yarbrough	Milwaukee Bucks	Illinois State	194
	16	Stanley Lamb	Atlanta Hawks	Steubenville	195
	17	Keith French	Phoenix Suns	North Park	196
	18	Jim Tillman	Seattle SuperSonics	Eastern Kentucky	197
	19	Luke Griffin	Philadelphia 76ers	St. Joseph's	198
	20	Brian Jung	Boston Celtics	Northwestern	199
TENTH ROUND	1	Tim Higgins	Golden State Warriors	Kearney State	200
	2	Leroy Coleman	Utah Jazz	Middle Tennessee	201
	3	Earl Sango	Denver Nuggets	Regis	202
	4	Billy Foster	Chicago Bulls	Eastern Montana	203
	5	John Bates	Indiana Pacers	West Virginia Wesleyan	204
	6	Dave Kufeld	Portland Trail Blazers	Yeshiva	205
	7	Tom Morgan	Dallas Mavericks	Cal State–Fullerton	206
	8	Don Youman	Washington Bullets	Oklahoma State	207
	9	Gerald Ross	New York Knicks	Grand Canyon	208
	10	Steve Schall	San Antonio Spurs	Arkansas	209
	11	Melvin Crayton	Milwaukee Bucks	Alabama State	210
	12	Randy Carroll	Phoenix Suns	Kansas	211
	13	Kent Williams	Seattle SuperSonics	Texas Tech	212
	14	Joe Hand	Philadelphia 76ers	Kings (Pa.)	213
	15	John Nolan	Boston Celtics	Providence	214

1979

ROUND		NAME	TEAM	COLLEGE	# OVERALL
FIRST ROUND	1	Earvin Johnson	Los Angeles Lakers	Michigan State	1
	2	David Greenwood	Chicago Bulls	UCLA	2
	3	Bill Cartwright	New York Knicks	San Francisco	3
	4	Greg Kelser	Detroit Pistons	Michigan State	4
	5	Sidney Moncrief	Milwaukee Bucks	Arkansas	5
	6	James Bailey	Seattle SuperSonics	Rutgers	6
	7	Vinnie Johnson	Seattle SuperSonics	Baylor	7
	8	Calvin Natt	New Jersey Nets	NE Louisiana	8
	9	Larry Demic	New York Knicks	Arizona	9
	10	Roy Hamilton	Detroit Pistons	UCLA	10
	11	Cliff Robinson	New Jersey Nets	USC	11
	12	Jim Paxson	Portland Trail Blazers	Dayton	12
	13	Dudley Bradley	Indiana Pacers	North Carolina	13
	14	Brad Holland	Los Angeles Lakers	UCLA	14
	15	Phil Hubbard	Detroit Pistons	Michigan	15
	16	Jim Spanarkel	Philadelphia 76ers	Duke	16
	17	Lee Johnson	Houston Rockets	East Texas State	17
	18	Reggie King	Kansas City Kings	Alabama	18
	19	Wiley Peck	San Antonio Spurs	Mississippi State	19
	20	Larry Knight	Utah Jazz	Loyola (Ill.)	20
	21	Sylvester Williams	New York Knicks	Rhode Island	21
	22	Kyle Macy	Phoenix Suns	Kentucky	22
SECOND ROUND	1	Tico Brown	Utah Jazz	Georgia Tech	23
	2	Johnny High	Phoenix Suns	Nevada–Reno	24
	3	Oliver Mack	Los Angeles Lakers	East Carolina	25
	4	Bruce Flowers	Cleveland Cavaliers	Notre Dame	26
	5	Reggie Carter	New York Knicks	St. John's	27
	6	Danny Salisbury	Golden State Warriors	Pan American	28
	7	Tony Price	Detroit Pistons	Penn	29
	8	Gary Garland	Denver Nuggets	DePaul	30
	9	Edgar Jones	Milwaukee Bucks	Nevada–Reno	31
	10	Tony Zeno	Indiana Pacers	Arizona State	32
	11	Lawrence Butler	Chicago Bulls	Idaho State	33
	12	Kim Goetz	New York Knicks	San Diego State	34
	13	James Bradley	Atlanta Hawks	Memphis State	35
	14	Clint Richardson	Philadelphia 76ers	Seattle	36
	15	Bernard Toone	Philadelphia 76ers	Marquette	37
	16	Larry Wilson	Atlanta Hawks	Nicholls State	38
	17	Victor King	Los Angeles Lakers	Louisiana Tech	39
	18	Andrew Fields	Portland Trail Blazers	Cheyney State	40
	19	Mark Young	Los Angeles Lakers	Fairfield	41
	20	Paul Mokeski	Houston Rockets	Kansas	42
	21	John Moore	Seattle SuperSonics	Texas	43
	22	Joe DeSantis	Washington Bullets	Fairfield	44
THIRD ROUND	1	Arvid Kramer	Utah Jazz	Augustana (S.D.)	45
	2	Andrew Parker	Washington Bullets	Iowa State	46
	3	Calvin Garrett	Chicago Bulls	Oral Roberts	47
	4	Terry Duerod	Detroit Pistons	Detroit	48
	5	Cedric Hordges	Chicago Bulls	South Carolina	49
	6	Geoff Huston	New York Knicks	Texas Tech	50

Round		NAME	TEAM	COLLEGE	# OVERALL
	7	John Gerdy	New Jersey Nets	Davidson	51
	8	Larry Gibson	Milwaukee Bucks	Maryland	52
	9	Wayne Kreklow	Boston Celtics	Drake	53
	10	Lynbert Johnson	Golden State Warriors	Wichita State	54
	11	Tom Channel	San Diego Clippers	Boston Univ.	55
	12	Mickey Fox	Portland Trail Blazers	St. Mary's (Canada)	56
	13	Don March	Atlanta Hawks	Franklin & Marshall	57
	14	Earl Cureton	Philadelphia 76ers	Detroit	58
	15	Ricardo Brown	Houston Rockets	Pepperdine	59
	16	Walter Daniels	Los Angeles Lakers	Georgia	60
	17	Ernesto Malcolm	Boston Celtics	Briarcliff	61
	18	Terry Crosby	Kansas City Kings	Tennessee	62
	19	Sylvester Norris	San Antonio Spurs	Jackson State	63
	20	Al Green	Phoenix Suns	Louisiana State	64
	21	Bill Laimbeer	Cleveland Cavaliers	Notre Dame	65
	22	Charles Floyd	Washington Bullets	High Point	66
FOURTH ROUND	1	Greg Deane	Utah Jazz	Utah	67
	2	Nick Galis	Boston Celtics	Seton Hall	68
	3	Eugene Robinson	Milwaukee Bucks	NE Louisiana	69
	4	Rick Swing	Cleveland Cavaliers	Citadel	70
	5	Larry Rogers	New York Knicks	SE Missouri State	71
	6	George Maynor	Chicago Bulls	East Carolina	72
	7	James Donaldson	Seattle SuperSonics	Washington State	73
	8	Don Newman	Indiana Pacers	Idaho	74
	9	Ron Ripley	Golden State Warriors	Wisconsin–Green Bay	75
	10	Sammy Drummer	Houston Rockets	Georgia Tech	76
	11	Lionel Garrett	San Diego Clippers	Southern	77
	12	Daryll Robinson	Portland Trail Blazers	Appalachian State	78
	13	Ray White	Los Angeles Lakers	Mississippi State	79
	14	Lionel Green	Houston Rockets	Louisiana State	80
	15	Ricky Reed	Los Angeles Lakers	Temple	81
	16	Jerry Sichting	Golden State Warriors	Purdue	82
	17	Mike Niles	Philadelphia 76ers	Cal State–Fullerton	83
	18	Al Daniel	San Antonio Spurs	Furman	84
	19	John McCullough	Kansas City Kings	Oklahoma	85
	20	Malcolm Cesare	Phoenix Suns	Florida	86
	21	Richie Allen	Seattle SuperSonics	Cal State–Dominguez Hills	87
	22	Lamont Reid	Washington Bullets	Oral Roberts	88
FIFTH ROUND	1	Perry Wolfe	Utah Jazz	Stanford	89
	2	Jimmy Allen	Boston Celtics	New Haven	90
	3	Matt Simpkins	Cleveland Cavaliers	Georgia Southern	91
	4	Flintie Ray Williams	Detroit Pistons	Nevada–Las Vegas	92
	5	Larry Washington	Chicago Bulls	Drury (Mo.)	93
	6	Johnny Green	New York Knicks	California–Riverside	94
	7	Joe Abramaitis	New Jersey Nets	Connecticut	95
	8	George Lett	Golden State Warriors	Centenary	96
	9	Jim Tillman	Milwaukee Bucks	Eastern Kentucky	97
	10	Billy Reid	Indiana Pacers	San Francisco	98
	11	Greg Joyner	San Diego Clippers	Middle Tennessee State	99
	12	Matt White	Portland Trail Blazers	Penn	100
	13	Tiny Pinder	Atlanta Hawks	North Carolina State	101
	14	Larry Williams	Denver Nuggets	Louisville	102
	15	Carl McPipe	Philadelphia 76ers	Nebraska	103
	16	Allen Leavell	Houston Rockets	Oklahoma City	104
	17	Curtis Watkins	Kansas City Kings	DePaul	105
	18	Steve Schall	San Antonio Spurs	Arkansas	106
	19	Mark Eaton	Phoenix Suns	Cypress JC	107
	20	Marshall Ashford	Washington Bullets	Virginia Tech	108
SIXTH ROUND	1	Ernie Cobb	Utah Jazz	Boston Univ.	109
	2	Marvin Delph	Boston Celtics	Arkansas	110
	3	Truman Clayton	Detroit Pistons	Kentucky	111
	4	Joe Manning	Cleveland Cavaliers	North Texas State	112
	5	Phil Abney	New York Knicks	New Mexico	113
	6	Steve Smith	Chicago Bulls	USC	114
	7	Tony Smith	New Jersey Nets	Nevada–Las Vegas	115
	8	Derrick Mayes	Milwaukee Bucks	Illinois State	116
	9	Greg Guye	Indiana Pacers	Stetson	117
	10	Jim Mitchem	Golden State Warriors	DePaul	118
	11	Bob Bender	San Diego Clippers	Duke	119
	12	Ray Ellis	Portland Trail Blazers	Pepperdine	120
	13	Dwight Williams	Atlanta Hawks	Gardner-Webb	121
	14	Odell Ball	Denver Nuggets	Marquette	122
	15	Dan Hartshorne	Philadelphia 76ers	Oregon	123
	16	Collie Davis	Houston Rockets	Southern	124
	17	Terry Knight	San Antonio Spurs	Pittsburgh	125
	18	Bob Roma	Kansas City Kings	Princeton	126
	19	Dale Shackelford	Phoenix Suns	Syracuse	127
	20	Garcia Hopkins	Washington Bullets	Morgan State	128
SEVENTH ROUND	1	Paul Poe	Utah Jazz	Louisiana	129
	2	Steve Castellan	Boston Celtics	Virginia	130
	3	Steve Skaggs	Cleveland Cavaliers	Ohio	131
	4	Ken Jones	Detroit Pistons	St. Mary's (Cal.)	132
	5	Mike Eversley	Chicago Bulls	Chicago State	133
	6	Marc Coleman	New York Knicks	Seton Hall	134
	7	Jim Strickland	New Jersey Nets	South Carolina	135
	8	Dirk Ewing	Indiana Pacers	Stetson	136
	9	Ren Watson	Golden State Warriors	Virginia Commonwealth	137
	10	Stan Ray	Milwaukee Bucks	Cal State–Fullerston	138
	11	Jene Grey	San Diego Clippers	LeMoyne	139
	12	Jeff Tropf	Portland Trail Blazers	Central Michigan	140
	13	Tim Waterman	Atlanta Hawks	St. Bonaventure	141
	14	Bobby Willis	Philadelphia 76ers	Penn	142
	15	Rich Valavicius	Houston Rockets	Auburn	143
	16	John Johnson	Denver Nuggets	Creighton	144
	17	Nick Daniels	Kansas City Kings	Xavier (Ohio)	145
	18	Tyrone Branyan	San Antonio Spurs	Texas	146
	19	Ollie Matson	Phoenix Suns	Pepperdine	147
EIGHTH ROUND	1	Keith McDonald	Utah Jazz	Utah State	148
	2	Glenn Sudhop	Boston Celtics	North Carolina State	149
	3	Rodney Lee	Detroit Pistons	Memphis State	150
	4	Mark Haymore	Cleveland Cavaliers	Massachusetts	151
	5	Billy Tucker	New York Knicks	Tennessee State	152
	6	Tony Warren	Chicago Bulls	North Carolina State	153
	7	Henry Hollingsworth	New Jersey Nets	Hofstra	154
	8	Mario Butler	Golden State Warriors	Briarcliff	155
	9	Larry Spicer	Milwaukee Bucks	Alabama–Birmingham	156
	10	Brian Magid	Indiana Pacers	George Washington	157
	11	Renaldo Lawrence	San Diego Clippers	Appalachian State	158
	12	Willie Pounds	Portland Trail Blazers	Chaminade	159
	13	John Goedeke	Atlanta Hawks	Maryland–Baltimore County	160
	14	Delbert Watson	Houston Rockets	East Tennessee State	161
	15	Matt Teahan	Denver Nuggets	Denver	162
	16	Rick Raivio	Philadelphia 76ers	Portland	163
	17	Tony Vann	Kansas City Kings	Alabama–Huntsville	164
	18	Charles Jones	Phoenix Suns	Albany State	165
	19	Jo Jo Walters	Washington Bullets	Manhattan	166
NINTH ROUND	1	Milt Huggins	Utah Jazz	Southern Illinois	167
	2	Kevin Sinnett	Boston Celtics	Navy	168
	3	Tim Joyce	Cleveland Cavaliers	Ohio	169
	4	Val Bracey	Detroit Pistons	Central Michigan	170
	5	James Jackson	Chicago Bulls	Minnesota	171
	6	Brett Wyatt	New York Knicks	Jersey City State	172
	7	Ricky Free	New Jersey Nets	Columbia	173
	8	Roger Lapham	Milwaukee Bucks	Maine	174

		NAME	TEAM	COLLEGE	# OVERALL
	9	Gene Ransom	Golden State Warriors	California	175
	10	Mike Dodd	San Diego Clippers	San Diego State	176
	11	Stan Eckwood	Portland Trail Blazers	Harding (Ark.)	177
	12	Cedric Oliver	Atlanta Hawks	Hamilton	178
	13	Emmett Lewis	Denver Nuggets	Colorado	179
	14	Coby Leavitt	Philadelphia 76ers	Utah	180
	15	Gary Wilson	Kansas City Kings	Southern Illinois	181
	16	Eddie McLeod	San Antonio Spurs	Nevada–Las Vegas	182
	17	Hosea Champine	Phoenix Suns	Robert Morris	183
	18	Ray Hooker	Washington Bullets	Murray State	184
TENTH ROUND	1	Paul Dawkins	Utah Jazz	Northern Illinois	185
	2	Alton Byrd	Boston Celtics	Columbia	186
	3	Willie Polk	Detroit Pistons	Grand Canyon	187
	4	Terry Peavy	Cleveland Cavaliers	Point Park	188
	5	Gordon Thomas	New York Knicks	St. John's	189
	6	Marvin Thoms	Chicago Bulls	UCLA	190
	7	Eric Fleisher	New Jersey Nets	Tulane	191
	8	Kevin Heenan	Golden State Warriors	Cal State–Fullerton	192
	9	Chris Fahrbach	Milwaukee Bucks	North Dakota	193
	10	Greg Hunter	San Diego Clippers	Loyola Marymount	194
	11	Kelvin Small	Portland Trail Blazers	Oregon	195
	12	Chad Nelson	Atlanta Hawks	Drake	196
	13	Cortez Collins	Chicago Bulls	Indiana State–Evansville	197
	14	Keith McCord	Philadelphia 76ers	Alabama–Birmingham	198
	15	Glen Fine	San Antonio Spurs	Harvard	199
	16	Russell Saunders	Kansas City Kings	New Mexico	200
	17	Korky Nelson	Phoenix Suns	Santa Clara	201
	18	Steve Martin	Washington Bullets	Georgetown	202

1978

		NAME	TEAM	COLLEGE	# OVERALL
FIRST ROUND	1	Mychal Thompson	Portland Trail Blazers	Minnesota	1
	2	Phil Ford	Kansas City Kings	North Carolina	2
	3	Rick Robey	Indiana Pacers	Kentucky	3
	4	Micheal Ray Richardson	New York Knicks	Montana	4
	5	Purvis Short	Golden State Warriors	Jackson State	5
	6	Larry Bird	Boston Celtics	Indiana State	6
	7	Ron Brewer	Portland Trail Blazers	Arkansas	7
	8	Freeman Williams	Boston Celtics	Portland State	8
	9	Reggie Theus	Chicago Bulls	Nevada–Las Vegas	9
	10	Butch Lee	Atlanta Hawks	Marquette	10
	11	James Hardy	New Orleans Jazz	San Francisco	11
	12	George Johnson	Milwaukee Bucks	St. John's	12
	13	Winford Boynes	New Jersey Nets	San Francisco	13
	14	Roger Phegley	Washington Bullets	Bradley	14
	15	Mike Mitchell	Cleveland Cavaliers	Auburn	15
	16	Jack Givens	Atlanta Hawks	Kentucky	16
	17	Rod Griffin	Denver Nuggets	Wake Forest	17
	18	Dave Corzine	Washington Bullets	DePaul	18
	19	Marty Byrnes	Phoenix Suns	Syracuse	19
	20	Frank Sanders	San Antonio Spurs	Southern	20
	21	Mike Evans	Denver Nuggets	Kansas State	21
	22	Ray Townsend	Golden State Warriors	UCLA	22
SECOND ROUND	1	Terry Tyler	Detroit Pistons	Detroit	23
	2	Keith Herron	Portland Trail Blazers	Villanova	24
	3	Rick Wilson	Atlanta Hawks	Louisville	25
	4	Ron Carter	Los Angeles Lakers	Virginia Military Institute	26
	5	Wayne Radford	Indiana Pacers	Indiana	27
	6	Buster Matheney	Houston Rockets	Utah	28
	7	John Long	Detroit Pistons	Detroit	29
	8	Jeff Judkins	Boston Celtics	Utah	30
	9	Marvin Johnson	Chicago Bulls	New Mexico	31
	10	John Rudd	New York Knicks	McNeese State	32
	11	Harry Davis	Cleveland Cavaliers	Florida State	33
	12	Greg Bunch	New York Knicks	Cal State–Fullerton	34
	13	Tom Green	New Orleans Jazz	Southern	35
	14	Maurice Cheeks	Philadelphia 76ers	West Texas State	36
	15	Terry Sykes	Washington Bullets	Grambling	37
	16	Lew Massey	Los Angeles Lakers	North Carolina–Charlotte	38
	17	James Lee	Seattle SuperSonics	Kentucky	39
	18	Wayne Cooper	Golden State Warriors	New Orleans	40
	19	Jerome Whitehead	Buffalo Braves	Marquette	41
	20	Kevin McDonald	Seattle SuperSonics	Penn	42
	21	Glenn Hagan	Philadelphia 76ers	St. Bonaventure	43
	22	Clemon Johnson	Portland Trail Blazers	Florida A&M	44
THIRD ROUND	1	Mike Phillips	New Jersey Nets	Kentucky	45
	2	Hollis Copeland	Denver Nuggets	Rutgers	46
	3	Billy Ray Bates	Houston Rockets	Kentucky State	47
	4	Mike Santos	Buffalo Braves	Utah State	48
	5	Jeff Cook	Kansas City Kings	Idaho State	49
	6	Dana Skinner	Boston Celtics	Merrimack	50
	7	Ricky Gallon	Buffalo Braves	Louisville	51
	8	Mike Russell	Kansas City Kings	Texas Tech	52
	9	Randy Ayers	Chicago Bulls	Miami (Ohio)	53
	10	Steve Grant	Atlanta Hawks	Manhattan	54
	11	Marc Iavaroni	New York Knicks	Virginia	55
	12	Steve Neff	Golden State Warriors	Bethany Nazarene	56
	13	Ken Higgs	Cleveland Cavaliers	Louisiana State	57
	14	Rick Apke	Washington Bullets	Creighton	58
	15	Pat Cummings	Milwaukee Bucks	Cincinnati	59
	16	Michael Cooper	Los Angeles Lakers	New Mexico	60
	17	Dave Baxter	Seattle SuperSonics	Michigan	61
	18	Dave Batton	New Jersey Nets	Notre Dame	62
	19	Joel Kramer	Phoenix Suns	San Diego State	63
	20	Gerald Henderson	San Antonio Spurs	Virginia Commonwealth	64
	21	Marvin Delph	Buffalo Braves	Arkansas	65
	22	Sterling Edmunds	Portland Trail Blazers	Dartmouth	66
FOURTH ROUND	1	Jackie Robinson	Houston Rockets	Nevada–Las Vegas	67
	2	Jim Boylan	Buffalo Braves	Marquette	68
	3	Joel Thompson	Houston Rockets	Michigan	69
	4	Geoff Crompton	Kansas City Kings	North Carolina	70
	5	Ricky Lee	Indiana Pacers	Oregon State	71
	6	Dave Nelson	Boston Celtics	Bloomfield (N.J.)	72
	7	Larry Harris	Buffalo Braves	Pittsburgh	73
	8	Mel Davis	New Orleans Jazz	North Texas State	74
	9	Jeff Covington	New Orleans Jazz	Youngstown State	75
	10	Leroy McDonald	Buffalo Braves	Wake Forest	76
	11	Derrick Jackson	Golden State Warriors	Georgetown	77
	12	Stan Rome	Cleveland Cavaliers	Clemson	78
	13	Erving Giddings	New York Knicks	Dayton	79
	14	Otis Howard	Milwaukee Bucks	Austin Peay	80
	15	Larry Boston	Washington Bullets	Maryland	81
	16	Harold Robertson	Los Angeles Lakers	Lincoln	82
	17	Billy Lewis	Seattle SuperSonics	Illinois State	83
	18	Walter Jordan	New Jersey Nets	Purdue	84
	19	Bob Miller	Phoenix Suns	Cincinnati	85
	20	Rich Adams	San Antonio Spurs	Illinois	86
	21	Brett Vroman	Philadelphia 76ers	Nevada–Las Vegas	87
	22	Wayne Smith	Phoenix Suns	California–Irvine	88
FIFTH ROUND	1	Cecile Rose	New Jersey Nets	Houston	89
	2	David Thompson	Buffalo Braves	Florida State	90
	3	Gary Goodner	Houston Rockets	Texas	91
	4	James Sparrow	Indiana Pacers	North Carolina A&T	92
	5	Derick Clairborne	Kansas City Kings	Massachusetts	93

ROUND		NAME	TEAM	COLLEGE	# OVERALL
	6	Greg Tynes	Boston Celtics	Seton Hall	94
	7	Dave Caligaris	Detroit Pistons	Northeastern	95
	8	Donald Williams	New Orleans Jazz	Notre Dame	96
	9	Ron Anthony	Chicago Bulls	Jacksonville	97
	10	Chris Potter	Atlanta Hawks	Holy Cross	98
	11	Ken Koenigs	Cleveland Cavaliers	Kansas	99
	12	Greg Green	New York Knicks	Southern	100
	13	Bubba Wilson	Golden State Warriors	Western Carolina	101
	14	Roger Dickens	Washington Bullets	Towson State	102
	15	Russ Coleman	Milwaukee Bucks	Pacific	103
	16	Carlos Terry	Los Angeles Lakers	Winston-Salem	104
	17	Ralph Drollinger	Seattle SuperSonics	UCLA	105
	18	Michael Edwards	Denver Nuggets	Pan American	106
	19	Andre Wakefield	Phoenix Suns	Loyola (Ill.)	107
	20	Eugene Parker	San Antonio Spurs	Purdue	108
	21	Mark Haymoore	Philadelphia 76ers	Massachusetts	109
	22	Clay Johnson	Portland Trail Blazers	Missouri	110
SIXTH ROUND	1	Golie Augustus	New Jersey Nets	South Carolina	111
	2	Bob Misevicius	Buffalo Braves	Providence	112
	3	Eddie Joe Chavez	Houston Rockets	Santa Clara	113
	4	Jim Krivacs	Kansas City Kings	Texas	114
	5	Sherman Dillard	Indiana Pacers	James Madison	115
	6	Dave Winey	Boston Celtics	Minnesota	116
	7	Audie Matthews	Detroit Pistons	Illinois	117
	8	John Douglas	New Orleans Jazz	Kansas	118
	9	John Shoemaker	Chicago Bulls	Miami (Ohio)	119
	10	Gerald Glover	Atlanta Hawks	Howard	120
	11	Ed Warren	New York Knicks	Briarcliff	121
	12	Buzz Hartnett	Golden State Warriors	San Diego	122
	13	Ron Bell	Cleveland Cavaliers	Virginia Tech	123
	14	Dave Kyle	Milwaukee Bucks	Cleveland State	124
	15	Archie Aldridge	Washington Bullets	Miami (Ohio)	125
	16	Kim Stewart	Los Angeles Lakers	Washington	126
	17	Robert Heard	Denver Nuggets	Columbus (Ga.)	127
	18	Charles Thompson	Phoenix Suns	Houston	128
	19	Harry Morgan	San Antonio Spurs	Indiana State	129
	20	Osborne Lockhart	Philadelphia 76ers	Minnesota	130
	21	Tim Evans	Portland Trail Blazers	Puget Sound	131
SEVENTH ROUND	1	Doug Jemison	New Jersey Nets	San Francisco	132
	2	Stan Pietkiewicz	Buffalo Braves	Auburn	133
	3	Stan Stewart	Houston Rockets	Loyola Marymount	134
	4	Ollie Matson Jr.	Indiana Pacers	Pepperdine	135
	5	Charles McMillian	Kansas City Kings	North Texas State	136
	6	Steve Balkun	Boston Celtics	Fairfield	137
	7	Herb Entzminger	Detroit Pistons	J.C. Smith	138
	8	Willie Howard	New Orleans Jazz	New Mexico	139
	9	Jarvis Reynolds	Chicago Bulls	West Georgia	140
	10	Jim DeWeese	Atlanta Hawks	Gonzaga	141
	11	Rick Bernard	Golden State Warriors	St. Mary's (Cal.)	142
	12	Tony Smith	Cleveland Cavaliers	Nevada–Las Vegas	143
	13	Gary Pember	New York Knicks	Nasson	144
	14	Ed Hopkins	Washington Bullets	Georgetown	145
	15	Kim Anderson	Milwaukee Bucks	Missouri	146
	16	Larry Paige	Los Angeles Lakers	Colorado State	147
	17	Jack Gilloon	Denver Nuggets	South Carolina	148
	18	Steve Malovic	Phoenix Suns	San Diego State	149
	19	Hector Olivencia	San Antonio Spurs	Sacred Heart	150
	20	Anthony Murray	Philadelphia 76ers	Alabama	151
	21	Walter Reason	Portland Trail Blazers	Pacific	152
	1	Bruce Campbell	New Jersey Nets	Providence	153
	2	Felton Young	Buffalo Braves	Jacksonville	154
	3	Ron Hammye	Kansas City Kings	Bowling Green	155

ROUND		NAME	TEAM	COLLEGE	# OVERALL
EIGHTH ROUND	4	Kim Fisher	Boston Celtics	Fairfield	156
	5	Earl Evans	Detroit Pistons	Nevada–Las Vegas	157
	6	Carl Kilpatrick	New Orleans Jazz	NE Louisiana	158
	7	Chubby Cox	Chicago Bulls	San Francisco	159
	8	Ed Murphy	Atlanta Hawks	Merrimack	160
	9	Roland Martin	Cleveland Cavaliers	Missouri Southern	161
	10	Greg Sanders	New York Knicks	St. Bonaventure	162
	11	Tony Searcy	Golden State Warriors	Appalachian State	163
	12	Tom Zaligaris	Milwaukee Bucks	North Carolina	164
	13	Nestor Cora	Washington Bullets	St. Francis (N.Y.)	165
	14	Larry Vaculik	Denver Nuggets	Colorado	166
	15	George Fowler	Phoenix Suns	Pacific	167
	16	Henry Taylor	San Antonio Spurs	Pan American	168
	17	Alan Cunningham	Philadelphia 76ers	Colorado State	169
	18	Mark Wickman	Portland Trail Blazers	Linfield	170
NINTH ROUND	1	Frank Sowinski	New Jersey Nets	Princeton	171
	2	Bobby White	Buffalo Braves	Centenary	172
	3	Les Anderson	Boston Celtics	George Washington	173
	4	Ulice Payne	Detroit Pistons	Marquette	174
	5	Chad Nelson	New Orleans Jazz	Drake	175
	6	Joe Ponsetto	Chicago Bulls	DePaul	176
	7	Maurice Robinson	Atlanta Hawks	West Virginia	177
	8	Danny Fields	New York Knicks	North Carolina–Wilmington	178
	9	Bobby Humbles	Golden State Warriors	Bradley	179
	10	Steve Bayless	Cleveland Cavaliers	Central State (Ohio)	180
	11	Tim Claxton	Washington Bullets	Temple	181
	12	Gary Rosenberger	Milwaukee Bucks	Marquette	182
	13	Tom Schneeberger	Denver Nuggets	Air Force	183
	14	Nate Stokes	Phoenix Suns	Grand Canyon	184
	15	Rick Taylor	San Antonio Spurs	Arizona State	185
	16	Paul Cozens	Portland Trail Blazers	George Fox	186
TENTH ROUND	1	Michael Vicens	New Jersey Nets	Holy Cross	187
	2	Walter Harrigan	Boston Celtics	Brandeis	188
	3	Dave Grauzer	Detroit Pistons	Central Michigan	189
	4	Rickey Williams	New Orleans Jazz	Long Beach State	190
	5	Mark Tucker	Chicago Bulls	Oklahoma	191
	6	Marshall Lester	Atlanta Hawks	Florida Southern	192
	7	Mike Muff	Golden State Warriors	Murray State	193
	8	Gary Winston	Cleveland Cavaliers	Army	194
	9	Ernest Simons	New York Knicks	Pace	195
	10	Tom Anderson	Milwaukee Bucks	Wisconsin–Green Bay	196
	11	Steve Connor	Washington Bullets	Boise State	197
	12	Phil Taylor	Denver Nuggets	Arizona	198
	13	Lewis Cohen	Phoenix Suns	Cal Poly–San Luis Obispo	199
	14	Larry Brewster	San Antonio Spurs	Florida	200
	15	Dennis James	Philadelphia 76ers	Widener	201
	16	Tim Workington	Portland Trail Blazers	Biola	202

1977

ROUND		NAME	TEAM	COLLEGE	# OVERALL
FIRST ROUND	1	Kent Benson	Milwaukee Bucks	Indiana	1
	2	Otis Birdsong	Kansas City Kings	Houston	2
	3	Marques Johnson	Milwaukee Bucks	UCLA	3
	4	Greg Ballard	Washington Bullets	Oregon	4
	5	Walter Davis	Phoenix Suns	North Carolina	5
	6	Kenny Carr	Los Angeles Lakers	North Carolina State	6
	7	Bernard King	New York Nets	Tennessee	7
	8	Jack Sikma	Seattle SuperSonics	Illinois Wesleyan	8
	9	Tom LaGarde	Denver Nuggets	North Carolina	9
	10	Ray Williams	New York Knicks	Minnesota	10
	11	Ernie Grunfeld	Milwaukee Bucks	Tennessee	11
	12	Cedric Maxwell	Boston Celtics	North Carolina–Charlotte	12

Round		NAME	TEAM	COLLEGE	# OVERALL
	13	Tate Armstrong	Chicago Bulls	Duke	13
	14	Tree Rollins	Atlanta Hawks	Clemson	14
	15	Brad Davis	Los Angeles Lakers	Maryland	15
	16	Rickey Green	Golden State Warriors	Michigan	16
	17	Bo Ellis	Washington Bullets	Marquette	17
	18	Wesley Cox	Golden State Warriors	Louisville	18
	19	Rich Laurel	Portland Trail Blazers	Hofstra	19
	20	Glenn Mosley	Philadelphia 76ers	Seton Hall	20
	21	Anthony Roberts	Denver Nuggets	Oral Roberts	21
	22	Norm Nixon	Los Angeles Lakers	Duquesne	22
SECOND ROUND	1	Mike Glenn	Chicago Bulls	Southern Illinois	23
	2	Larry Johnson	Buffalo Braves	Kentucky	24
	3	Wilson Washington	Philadelphia 76ers	Old Dominion	25
	4	Glen Gondrezick	New York Knicks	Nevada–Las Vegas	26
	5	Glenn Williams	Milwaukee Bucks	St. John's	27
	6	Kim Anderson	Portland Trail Blazers	Missouri	28
	7	Alonzo Bradley	Indiana Pacers	Texas Southern	29
	8	Steve Sheppard	Chicago Bulls	Maryland	30
	9	Eddie Owens	Kansas City Kings	Nevada–Las Vegas	31
	10	Toby Knight	New York Knicks	Notre Dame	32
	11	Ed Jordan	Cleveland Cavaliers	Rutgers	33
	12	Larry Moffett	Houston Rockets	Nevada–Las Vegas	34
	13	Mark Landsberger	Chicago Bulls	Arizona State	35
	14	Ben Poquette	Detroit Pistons	Central Michigan	36
	15	Jeff Wilkins	San Antonio Spurs	Illinois State	37
	16	Ricky Love	Golden State Warriors	Alabama–Huntsville	38
	17	Phil Walker	Washington Bullets	Millersville	39
	18	Robert Reid	Houston Rockets	St. Mary's (Tex.)	40
	19	T.R. Dunn	Portland Trail Blazers	Alabama	41
	20	Bob Elliott	Philadelphia 76ers	Arizona	42
	21	Herm Harris	Philadelphia 76ers	Arizona	43
	22	Essie Hollis	New Orleans Jazz	St. Bonaventure	44
THIRD ROUND	1	Bill Paterno	Kansas City Kings	Notre Dame	45
	2	James Edwards	Los Angeles Lakers	Washington	46
	3	Gary Yoder	Milwaukee Bucks	Cincinnati	47
	4	Sam Smith	Atlanta Hawks	Nevada–Las Vegas	48
	5	Eddie Johnson	Atlanta Hawks	Auburn	49
	6	Tony Hansen	New Orleans Jazz	Connecticut	50
	7	Stan Mayhew	Indiana Pacers	Weber State	51
	8	Joe Hassett	Seattle SuperSonics	Providence	52
	9	John Kuester	Kansas City Kings	North Carolina	53
	10	Lloyd McMillian	New York Knicks	Long Beach State	54
	11	Steve Grote	Cleveland Cavaliers	Michigan	55
	12	Skip Brown	Boston Celtics	Wake Forest	56
	13	Steve Puidokas	Washington Bullets	Washington State	57
	14	John Irving	Detroit Pistons	Hofstra	58
	15	Dan Henderson	San Antonio Spurs	Arkansas State	59
	16	Marlon Redmond	Golden State Warriors	San Francisco	60
	17	Jerry Schellenberg	Washington Bullets	Wake Forest	61
	18	Phil Bond	Houston Rockets	Louisville	62
	19	Ricky Brown	Portland Trail Blazers	Alabama	63
	20	Arnold Dugger	Philadelphia 76ers	Oral Roberts	64
	21	Robert Smith	Denver Nuggets	Nevada–Las Vegas	65
	22	Mike Bratz	Phoenix Suns	Stanford	66
FOURTH ROUND	1	Bob Elmore	New York Nets	Wichita State	67
	2	Melvin Watkins	Buffalo Braves	North Carolina–Charlotte	68
	3	Lewis Brown	Milwaukee Bucks	Nevada–Las Vegas	69
	4	Dave Bormann	Atlanta Hawks	Gardner-Webb	70
	5	Greg Griffin	Phoenix Suns	Idaho State	71
	6	Dennis Boyd	New Orleans Jazz	Detroit	72
	7	George Pendleton	Indiana Pacers	Georgia State	73
	8	Jim Cooper	Seattle SuperSonics	Alabama State	74
	9	Larry Williams	Kansas City Kings	Texas Southern	75
	10	Steve Hayes	New York Knicks	Idaho State	76
	11	Melvin Jones	Cleveland Cavaliers	West Texas State	77
	12	Jeff Cummings	Boston Celtics	Tulane	78
	13	Mike McConalthy	Chicago Bulls	Louisiana Tech	79
	14	Bruce King	Detroit Pistons	Iowa	80
	15	Matt Hicks	San Antonio Spurs	Northern Illinois	81
	16	Roy Smith	Golden State Warriors	Kentucky State	82
	17	David Reavis	Washington Bullets	Georgia	83
	18	Rocky Smith	Houston Rockets	Oregon State	84
	19	Greg White	Portland Trail Blazers	USC	85
	20	Jack Jones	Philadelphia 76ers	Utah	86
	21	Leartha Scott	Golden State Warriors	Wisconsin–Parkside	87
	22	Tony Robertson	Los Angeles Lakers	West Virginia	88
FIFTH ROUND	1	Gerald Cunningham	New York Nets	Kentucky State	89
	2	Mike Hanley	Buffalo Braves	Niagara	90
	3	Ron Norwood	Milwaukee Bucks	DePaul	91
	4	Bill Gordon	Atlanta Hawks	Tennessee–Chattanooga	92
	5	Cecil Rellford	Phoenix Suns	St. John's	93
	6	Jim Grady	New Orleans Jazz	Gonzaga	94
	7	Marvin Jackson	Indiana Pacers	Prairie View A&M	95
	8	Dale Haverman	Seattle SuperSonics	McKendree	96
	9	Bob Chapman	Kansas City Kings	Michigan State	97
	10	Bill Terry	New York Knicks	Monmouth	98
	11	Al Smith	Cleveland Cavaliers	Jackson State	99
	12	Bill Langloh	Boston Celtics	Virginia	100
	13	Nate Davis	Chicago Bulls	South Carolina	101
	14	Jim Kennedy	Detroit Pistons	Missouri	102
	15	Scott Sims	San Antonio Spurs	Missouri	103
	16	Ray Epps	Golden State Warriors	Norfolk State	104
	17	Bruce Parkinson	Washington Bullets	Purdue	105
	18	Ed Thompson	Houston Rockets	Idaho State	106
	19	Donn Wilber	Portland Trail Blazers	La Salle	107
	20	Teko Wynder	Philadelphia 76ers	Tulsa	108
	21	John Billups	Denver Nuggets	Mississippi	109
	22	John Robinson	Los Angeles Lakers	Michigan	110
SIXTH ROUND	1	Mark Crow	New York Nets	Duke	111
	2	Curvan Lewis	Buffalo Braves	Virginia Union	112
	3	Chuck Goodyear	Milwaukee Bucks	Miami (Ohio)	113
	4	Calvin Crews	Atlanta Hawks	SW Louisiana	114
	5	Billy McKinney	Phoenix Suns	Northwestern	115
	6	Wayne Golden	New Orleans Jazz	Tennessee–Chattanooga	116
	7	Tom Scheffler	Indiana Pacers	Purdue	117
	8	Bucky O'Brien	Seattle SuperSonics	Seattle	118
	9	Bob Cooper	Kansas City Kings	Providence	119
	10	Jerry Graycraft	New York Knicks	Milligan	120
	11	Ron Cox	Cleveland Cavaliers	East Washington State	121
	12	Roy Pace	Boston Celtics	Rutgers-Camden	122
	13	Jay Chessman	Chicago Bulls	Brigham Young	123
	14	Herb Nobles	Detroit Pistons	Kansas	124
	15	Bruce Buckley	San Antonio Spurs	North Carolina	125
	16	Jack Phelan	Golden State Warriors	St. Francis (Pa.)	126
	17	Ernie Wansley	Washington Bullets	Virginia Tech	127
	18	Myron Jordan	Portland Trail Blazers	Pacific	128
	19	George Gibson	Philadelphia 76ers	Winston-Salem	129
	20	Jim Town	Denver Nuggets	Massachusetts	130
	21	Grover Woolard	Los Angeles Lakers	Murray State	131
SEVENTH ROUND	1	Scott Conant	New York Nets	Newberry	132
	2	Mike Jackson	Buffalo Braves	Tennessee	133
	3	Ron Bostic	Milwaukee Bucks	Detroit	134
	4	James Holliman	Atlanta Hawks	Arizona State	135
	5	Alvin Scott	Phoenix Suns	Oral Roberts	136

		NAME	TEAM	COLLEGE	# OVERALL
	6	Lusia Harris	New Orleans Jazz	Delta State	137
	7	Billy Reynolds	Seattle SuperSonics	NW Louisiana	138
	8	Bruce Jenner	Kansas City Kings	Graceland	139
	9	Tom Weadock	New York Knicks	St. John's	140
	10	Bob Riddle	Cleveland Cavaliers	Eastern Michigan	141
	11	Dave Kyle	Boston Celtics	Cleveland State	142
	12	Mike Smith	Chicago Bulls	Evansville	143
	13	Robert Lewis	Detroit Pistons	Johnson C. Smith	144
	14	Richard Robinson	San Antonio Spurs	New Mexico State	145
	15	Jerry Thurston	Golden State Warriors	Mercer	146
	16	Calvin Brown	Washington Bullets	American	147
	17	Don Smith	Portland Trail Blazers	Oregon State	148
	18	Dennis Forest	Philadelphia 76ers	Nebraska–Omaha	149
	19	Willie High	Denver Nuggets	Alabama State	150
	20	Lars Hansen	Los Angeles Lakers	Washington	151
EIGHTH ROUND	1	Ralph Drollinger	New York Nets	UCLA	152
	2	Emery Sammons	Buffalo Braves	Philadelphia Textile	153
	3	Larry Pikes	Milwaukee Bucks	Wisconsin–Milwaukee	154
	4	Vern Thompson	Atlanta Hawks	Brigham Young	155
	5	Alvin Joseph	Phoenix Suns	California–Riverside	156
	6	Dave Speicher	New Orleans Jazz	Toledo	157
	8	Jeff Frey	Seattle SuperSonics	Evansville	158
	10	Ken Slappy	New York Knicks	St. Peter's	159
	11	Tom Cutter	Cleveland Cavaliers	Western Michigan	160
	12	Tom Harris	Boston Celtics	Bowling Green	161
	13	Rich Rhodes	Chicago Bulls	Eastern Illinois	162
	14	Tim Appleton	Detroit Pistons	Kenyon	163
	15	Jerome Gladney	San Antonio Spurs	Arizona	164
	16	Ricky March	Golden State Warriors	Manhattan	165
	17	Pat McKinley	Washington Bullets	Towson State	166
	19	Harold Rhodes	Portland Trail Blazers	Washington	167
	20	John Olive	Philadelphia 76ers	Villanova	168
	21	Len Saunders	Denver Nuggets	Florida	169
	22	Art Allen	Los Angeles Lakers	Pepperdine	170

1976

		NAME	TEAM	COLLEGE	# OVERALL
FIRST ROUND	1	John Lucas	Houston Rockets	Maryland	1
	2	Scott May	Chicago Bulls	Indiana	2
	3	Richard Washington	Kansas City Kings	UCLA	3
	4	Leon Douglas	Detroit Pistons	Alabama	4
	5	Wally Walker	Portland Trail Blazers	Virginia	5
	6	Adrian Dantley	Buffalo Braves	Notre Dame	6
	7	Quinn Buckner	Milwaukee Bucks	Indiana	7
	8	Robert Parish	Golden State Warriors	Centenary	8
	9	Armond Hill	Atlanta Hawks	Princeton	9
	10	Ron Lee	Phoenix Suns	Oregon	10
	11	Bob Wilkerson	Seattle SuperSonics	Indiana	11
	12	Terry Furlow	Philadelphia 76ers	Michigan State	12
	13	Mitch Kupchak	Washington Bullets	North Carolina	13
	14	Larry Wright	Washington Bullets	Grambling	14
	15	Chuckie Williams	Cleveland Cavaliers	Kansas State	15
	16	Norman Cook	Boston Celtics	Kansas	16
	17	Sonny Parker	Golden State Warriors	Texas A&M	17
SECOND ROUND	1	Willie Smith	Chicago Bulls	Missouri	18
	2	Bayard Forrest	Seattle SuperSonics	Grand Canyon	19
	3	Major Jones	Portland Trail Blazers	Albany State (Ga.)	20
	4	Earl Tatum	Los Angeles Lakers	Marquette	21
	5	John Davis	Portland Trail Blazers	Dayton	22
	6	Alex English	Milwaukee Bucks	South Carolina	23
	7	Scott Lloyd	Milwaukee Bucks	Arizona State	24
	8	Lonnie Shelton	New York Knicks	Oregon State	25
	9	Jacky Dorsey	New Orleans Jazz	Georgia	26
	10	Phil Hicks	Houston Rockets	Tulane	27
	11	Bob Carrington	Atlanta Hawks	Boston College	28
	12	Dennis Johnson	Seattle SuperSonics	Pepperdine	29
	13	Al Fleming	Phoenix Suns	Arizona	30
	14	Joe Pace	Washington Bullets	Coppin State	31
	15	Mo Howard	Cleveland Cavaliers	Maryland	32
	16	Butch Feher	Phoenix Suns	Vanderbilt	33
	17	Marshall Rogers	Golden State Warriors	Pan American	34
THIRD ROUND	1	Dallas Smith	Chicago Bulls	West Texas State	35
	2	Mike Dabney	Los Angeles Lakers	Rutgers	36
	3	Lars Hansen	Chicago Bulls	Washington	37
	4	Phil Sellers	Detroit Pistons	Rutgers	38
	5	Jeff Tyson	Portland Trail Blazers	Western Michigan	39
	6	Lloyd Walton	Milwaukee Bucks	Marquette	40
	7	John McGill	New York Knicks	Alcorn State	41
	8	Steve Copp	New Orleans Jazz	San Diego State	42
	9	Tom Abernethy	Los Angeles Lakers	Indiana	43
	10	Barnes Hauptfuhrer	Houston Rockets	Princeton	44
	11	Ira Terrell	Phoenix Suns	Southern Methodist	45
	12	Larry Cooke	Atlanta Hawks	Virginia Tech	46
	13	Ron Norwood	Philadelphia 76ers	DePaul	47
	14	Gary Brewster	Buffalo Braves	Texas–El Paso	48
	15	Bill Cook	Washington Bullets	Memphis State	49
	16	Gary Cole	Cleveland Cavaliers	Wisconsin–Parkside	50
	17	Jerry Fort	Boston Celtics	Nebraska	51
FOURTH ROUND	1	Keith Starr	Chicago Bulls	Pittsburgh	52
	2	Tom Barker	Atlanta Hawks	Hawaii	53
	3	Clarence Ramsey	Kansas City Kings	Washington	54
	4	Scott Thompson	Detroit Pistons	Iowa	55
	5	David Everett	Portland Trail Blazers	Grand Canyon	56
	6	Rick Bullock	New York Knicks	Texas Tech	57
	7	John Service	New Orleans Jazz	UC Santa Barbara	58
	8	Dan Frost	Milwaukee Bucks	Iowa	59
	9	Wayman Britt	Los Angeles Lakers	Michigan	60
	10	Hercle Ivy	Houston Rockets	Iowa State	61
	11	Paul Miller	Phoenix Suns	Oregon State	62
	12	Willie Parr	Seattle SuperSonics	LeMoyne-Owen	63
	13	Freeman Blade	Philadelphia 76ers	Eastern Montana	64
	14	Marion Hillard	Washington Bullets	Memphis State	65
	15	John Engles	Cleveland Cavaliers	Penn	66
	16	Lewis Linder	Boston Celtics	Kentucky State	67
	17	Jeff Fosnes	Golden State Warriors	Vanderbilt	68
FIFTH ROUND	1	Nate Williams	Chicago Bulls	Illinois	69
	2	Ron Davis	Atlanta Hawks	Washington State	70
	3	Willie Hodge	Kansas City Kings	Duke	71
	4	Jim Hearns	Detroit Pistons	Marymount	72
	5	Gary Reddings	Portland Trail Blazers	Auburn	73
	6	Paul Griffin	New Orleans Jazz	Western Michigan	74
	7	Tom Lockhart	Milwaukee Bucks	Manhattan	75
	8	Beaver Smith	New York Knicks	St. John's	76
	9	James Rappis	Milwaukee Bucks	Arizona	77
	10	Dave Marrs	Houston Rockets	Houston	78
	11	Ralph Walker	Phoenix Suns	St. Mary's (Cal.)	79
	12	Robert Gray	Seattle SuperSonics	Wichita State	80
	13	Jeff Browne	Philadelphia 76ers	Missouri Western	81
	14	Connie White	Atlanta Hawks	California	82
	15	L.C. Mason	Washington Bullets	Alabama State	83
	16	Ed Lawrence	Cleveland Cavaliers	McNeese State	84
	17	Lewis McKinney	Boston Celtics	St. Louis	85
	18	Carl Bird	Golden State Warriors	California	86
	1	Tom Paulin	Chicago Bulls	Winston-Salem	87

		NAME	TEAM	COLLEGE	#OVERALL
SIXTH ROUND	2	Pete Padgett	Atlanta Hawks	Nevada–Reno	88
	3	Andre McCarter	Kansas City Kings	UCLA	89
	4	Russell Davis	Detroit Pistons	Virginia Tech	90
	5	Duane Barnett	Golden State Warriors	Stanford	91
	6	Phil Spence	Milwaukee Bucks	North Carolina State	92
	7	Joe Jones	New York Knicks	Grambling	93
	8	Bernard Tomlin	New Orleans Jazz	Hofstra	94
	9	Ed Schweitzer	Los Angeles Lakers	Stanford	95
	10	Robert Paige	Houston Rockets	Houston Baptist	96
	11	Carl Brown	Phoenix Suns	Eastern Kentucky	97
	12	Daryl Peterson	Seattle SuperSonics	Wake Forest	98
	13	Mike Dunleavy	Philadelphia 76ers	South Carolina	99
	14	Danny Odums	Buffalo Braves	Fairfield	100
	15	Pat Tallent	Washington Bullets	George Washington	101
	16	Harry Davis	Cleveland Cavaliers	Morris Brown	102
	17	Art Collins	Boston Celtics	Biscayne	103
	18	Gene Cunningham	Golden State Warriors	Norfolk State	104
SEVENTH ROUND	1	Barry McLeod	Chicago Bulls	Centenary	105
	2	Carl Gerlach	Atlanta Hawks	Kansas State	106
	3	Craig Prosser	Kansas City Kings	Canisius	107
	4	Curt Peterson	Detroit Pistons	Puget Sound	108
	5	Al DeWitt	Portland Trail Blazers	Weber State	109
	6	Boyd Batts	New York Knicks	Nevada–Las Vegas	110
	7	Andy Walker	New Orleans Jazz	Niagara	111
	8	Ron Barrow	Milwaukee Bucks	Southern	112
	9	Tommie Lipsey	Los Angeles Lakers	Cal State–Los Angeles	113
	10	Barry Davis	Houston Rockets	Texas A&M	114
	11	Brad Warble	Phoenix Suns	East Illinois	115
	12	Mark Klein	Seattle SuperSonics	Malone	116
	13	Phil Walker	Philadelphia 76ers	Millersville	117
	14	Frank Jones	Buffalo Braves	Tennessee Tech	118
	15	Ralph Vallott	Washington Bullets	Loyola (Ill.)	119
	16	Johnny Britt	Cleveland Cavaliers	Western Kentucky	120
	17	Ralph Drollinger	Boston Celtics	UCLA	121
	18	Jesse Campbell	Golden State Warriors	Mercyhurst	122
EIGHTH ROUND	1	Dave Koehler	Cleveland Cavaliers	Wisconsin	123
	2	Doug Terry	Atlanta Hawks	Utah	124
	3	Mike Davis	Kansas City Kings	Bradley	125
	4	Randy Heany	Detroit Pistons	Illinois State	126
	5	Brant Gibbler	Portland Trail Blazers	Puget Sound	127
	6	Richard Bryant	New Orleans Jazz	SW Texas State	128
	7	Bob Warner	Milwaukee Bucks	Maine	129
	8	Rick McCutcheon	New York Knicks	Arizona State	130
	9	Ed Gregg	Los Angeles Lakers	Utah State	131
	10	Dan Kruger	Houston Rockets	Texas	132
	11	Tom DeBerry	Phoenix Suns	Northern Arizona	133
	12	Norton Barnhill	Seattle SuperSonics	Washington State	134
	13	Lee Dixon	Philadelphia 76ers	Hardin-Simmons	135
	14	Mark McAndrew	Buffalo Braves	Providence	136
	15	Merlin Wilson	Washington Bullets	Georgetown	137
	16	Tim Sisneros	Cleveland Cavaliers	Middle Tennessee	138
	17	John Clark	Boston Celtics	Northeastern	139
	18	Stan Boskovich	Golden State Warriors	West Virginia	140
NINTH ROUND	1	John Thomas	Chicago Bulls	Connecticut	141
	2	Bob Kovach	Atlanta Hawks	San Diego State	142
	3	Dave Logan	Kansas City Kings	Colorado	143
	4	Bill Martin	Detroit Pistons	Hartwick	144
	5	Rob Torresdal	Portland Trail Blazers	Linfield	145
	6	Benny Shaw	Milwaukee Bucks	Florida Tech	146
	7	Archie Talley	New York Knicks	Salem (W.Va.)	147
	8	Calvin Robinson	New Orleans Jazz	Mississippi Valley	148
	9	David Pickett	Los Angeles Lakers	NE Louisiana	149
TENTH ROUND	10	John Irving	Phoenix Suns	Hofstra	150
	11	Ron Johnson	Seattle SuperSonics	North Carolina A&T	151
	12	Fly Williams	Philadelphia 76ers	Austin Peay	152
	13	Bob Rozyczko	Buffalo Braves	St. Bonaventure	153
	14	Clyde Agnew	Washington Bullets	Newberry	154
	15	Bruce Parkinson	Cleveland Cavaliers	Purdue	155
	16	Bill Collins	Boston Celtics	Boston College	156
	17	Howard Smith	Golden State Warriors	San Francisco	157
	1	John Hudson	Chicago Bulls	Concord	158
	2	Mike Dickerson	Atlanta Hawks	South Florida	159
	3	Harry Bailey	Kansas City Kings	North Texas State	160
	4	Bob Johnson	Detroit Pistons	Wisconsin	161
	5	Marcus Leite	Portland Trail Blazers	Pepperdine	162
	6	Eugene Shy	New York Knicks	Florida	163
	7	Art Johnson	New Orleans Jazz	Iowa State	164
	8	Hugo Cabrera	Milwaukee Bucks	East Texas State	165
	9	Gary Jackson	Phoenix Suns	Arizona State	166
	10	Ricky Lewis	Seattle SuperSonics	Alcorn State	167
	11	Ed Stefanski	Philadelphia 76ers	Penn	168
	12	Tim Stokes	Buffalo Braves	Canisius	169
	13	Mike Beuscher	Washington Bullets	Seton Hall	170
	14	Elisha McSweeney	Cleveland Cavaliers	Mankato State	171
	15	Otho Tucker	Boston Celtics	Illinois	172
	16	Ken Smith	Golden State Warriors	San Diego State	173

1975

		NAME	TEAM	COLLEGE	#OVERALL
FIRST ROUND	1	David Thompson	Atlanta Hawks	North Carolina State	1
	2	David Meyers	Los Angeles Lakers	UCLA	2
	3	Marvin Webster	Atlanta Hawks	Morgan State	3
	4	Alvan Adams	Phoenix Suns	Oklahoma	4
	5	Darryl Dawkins	Philadelphia 76ers	Maynard Evans H.S.	5
	6	Lionel Hollins	Portland Trail Blazers	Arizona State	6
	7	Rich Kelley	New Orleans Jazz	Stanford	7
	8	Junior Bridgeman	Los Angeles Lakers	Louisville	8
	9	Eugene Short	New York Knicks	Jackson State	9
	10	Bill Robinzine	KC-Omaha Kings	DePaul	10
	11	Joe Meriweather	Houston Rockets	Southern Illinois	11
	12	Frank Oleynick	Seattle SuperSonics	Seattle	12
	13	Bob Bigelow	KC-Omaha Kings	Penn	13
	14	Joe Bryant	Golden State Warriors	La Salle	14
	15	John Lambert	Cleveland Cavaliers	USC	15
	16	Ricky Sobers	Phoenix Suns	Nevada–Las Vegas	16
	17	Tom Boswell	Boston Celtics	South Carolina	17
	18	Kevin Grevey	Washington Bullets	Kentucky	18
SECOND ROUND	1	Bill Willoughby	Atlanta Hawks	Dwight Morrow H.S.	19
	2	Gus Williams	Golden State Warriors	USC	20
	3	Bruce Seals	Seattle SuperSonics	Xavier (La.)	21
	4	Clyde Mayes	Milwaukee Bucks	Furman	22
	5	Lloyd Free	Philadelphia 76ers	Guilford	23
	6	Cornelius Cash	Milwaukee Bucks	Bowling Green	24
	7	Bob Gross	Portland Trail Blazers	Long Beach State	25
	8	Luther Burden	New York Knicks	Utah	26
	9	Walter Luckett	Detroit Pistons	Ohio	27
	10	Dan Roundfield	Cleveland Cavaliers	Central Michigan	28
	11	Jim Blanks	Houston Rockets	Gardner-Webb	29
	12	Steve Green	Chicago Bulls	Indiana	30
	13	Glenn Hansen	KC-Omaha Kings	Louisiana State	31
	14	John Laskowski	Chicago Bulls	Indiana	32
	15	Mel Utley	Cleveland Cavaliers	St. John's	33
	16	Larry Fogle	New York Knicks	Canisius	34
	17	Allen Murphy	Phoenix Suns	Louisville	35

Round		NAME	TEAM	COLLEGE	# OVERALL
	18	Jimmy Dan Conner	Phoenix Suns	Kentucky	36
THIRD ROUND	1	Rudy Hackett	New Orleans Jazz	Syracuse	37
	2	Jim McElroy	New Orleans Jazz	Central Michigan	38
	3	Jim Baker	Philadelphia 76ers	Hawaii	39
	4	Otis Johnson	Golden State Warriors	Stetson	40
	5	Charles Cleveland	Philadelphia 76ers	Alabama	41
	6	Tom Roy	Portland Trail Blazers	Maryland	42
	7	Brian Hammel	Milwaukee Bucks	Bentley	43
	8	Pete Trgovich	Detroit Pistons	UCLA	44
	9	Ted Hathaway	Cleveland Cavaliers	Cleveland State	45
	10	John Ramsey	New York Knicks	Seton Hall	46
	11	Rudy White	Houston Rockets	Arizona State	47
	12	Tom Kropp	Washington Bullets	Kearney State	48
	13	Bob Guyette	KC-Omaha Kings	Kentucky	49
	14	Gus Gerard	Portland Trail Blazers	Virginia	50
	15	Robert Hawkins	Golden State Warriors	Illinois State	51
	16	George Bucci	Buffalo Braves	Manhattan	52
	17	Jerome Anderson	Boston Celtics	West Virginia	53
	18	Bayard Forrest	Phoenix Suns	Grand Canyon	54
FOURTH ROUND	1	Mack Coleman	New Orleans Jazz	Houston Baptist	55
	2	C.J. Kupec	Los Angeles Lakers	Michigan	56
	3	Monte Towe	Atlanta Hawks	North Carolina State	57
	4	Sam McCants	Phoenix Suns	Oral Roberts	58
	5	Louis Dunbar	Philadelphia 76ers	Houston	59
	6	Bill Campion	Milwaukee Bucks	Manhattan	60
	7	Phil Hicks	Portland Trail Blazers	Tulane	61
	8	Eric Fernsten	Cleveland Cavaliers	San Francisco	62
	9	David Vaughn	New York Knicks	Oral Roberts	63
	10	Lindsay Hairston	Detroit Pistons	Michigan State	64
	11	Ken Smith	Houston Rockets	Tulsa	65
	12	Jim Moore	Seattle SuperSonics	Utah State	66
	13	Kevin Cleuss	KC-Omaha Kings	St. John's	67
	14	Ron Haigler	Chicago Bulls	Penn	68
	15	Billy Taylor	Golden State Warriors	La Salle	69
	16	Bob Fleischer	Buffalo Braves	Duke	70
	17	Fessor Leonard	Washington Bullets	Furman	71
	18	Cyrus Mann	Boston Celtics	Illinois State	72
FIFTH ROUND	1	Andre Hampton	New Orleans Jazz	Kentucky State	73
	2	Charles Russell	Los Angeles Lakers	Alabama	74
	3	Wilbur Holland	Atlanta Hawks	New Orleans	75
	4	Joe Pace	Phoenix Suns	Coppin State	76
	5	Ken Tyler	Philadelphia 76ers	Gonzaga	77
	6	Maurice Presley	Portland Trail Blazers	Houston	78
	7	Jim Lee	Cleveland Cavaliers	Syracuse	79
	8	Don Washington	New York Knicks	North Carolina	80
	9	Cliff Pratt	Detroit Pistons	Shaw	81
	10	Mike Odems	Cleveland Cavaliers	Western Kentucky	82
	11	Rick Whitlow	Houston Rockets	Illinois State	83
	12	Dwain Govan	Seattle SuperSonics	Bishop (Tex.)	84
	13	Ed Stahl	KC-Omaha Kings	North Carolina	85
	14	Bob Iverson	Chicago Bulls	North Texas State	86
	15	Larry Pounds	Golden State Warriors	Washington	87
	16	Sam Berry	Buffalo Braves	Armstrong State	88
	17	Darryl Brown	Boston Celtics	Fordham	89
	18	Rich Jones	Washington Bullets	Virginia Commonwealth	90
SIXTH ROUND	1	Rich Schmidt	New Orleans Jazz	Illinois	91
	2	Don Ford	Los Angeles Lakers	UC Santa Barbara	92
	3	Danny Williams	Atlanta Hawks	Mississippi	93
	4	Buff Burrell	Phoenix Suns	USC	94
	5	Ken Alston	Philadelphia 76ers	Valdosta State	95
	6	Oliver Purnell	Milwaukee Bucks	Old Dominion	96
	7	Gerald Willett	Portland Trail Blazers	Oregon	97

Round		NAME	TEAM	COLLEGE	# OVERALL
	8	Allen Spruill	Detroit Pistons	North Carolina A&T	98
	9	Henry Ward	Cleveland Cavaliers	Jackson State	99
	10	Henry Williams	New York Knicks	Jacksonville	100
	11	William Johnson	Houston Rockets	Texas Tech	101
	12	Larry Smith	Seattle SuperSonics	North Carolina A&T	102
	13	Clint Chapman	KC-Omaha Kings	USC	103
	14	Bill Andreas	Chicago Bulls	Ohio State	104
	15	Tony Styles	Golden State Warriors	San Francisco	105
	16	Larry Jackson	Buffalo Braves	North Carolina–Charlotte	106
	17	John Garrett	Washington Bullets	Purdue	107
	18	Rick Coleman	Boston Celtics	Jacksonville	108
SEVENTH ROUND	1	Bill Higgins	New Orleans Jazz	Ashland	109
	2	Rick Suttle	Los Angeles Lakers	Kansas	110
	3	Gus Johnson	Atlanta Hawks	Winona State	111
	4	Dave Edmunds	Phoenix Suns	Western Georgia	112
	5	Mike Flynn	Philadelphia 76ers	Kentucky	113
	6	Steve Fields	Portland Trail Blazers	Miami (Ohio)	114
	7	Wilbur Thomas	Milwaukee Bucks	American	115
	8	Shawn Leftwick	Cleveland Cavaliers	Jacksonville	116
	9	Peter Davis	New York Knicks	Michigan State	117
	10	Ike Williams	Detroit Pistons	Armstrong State	118
	11	Nate Barnett	Houston Rockets	Akron	119
	12	Hollis Miller	Seattle SuperSonics	Drury (Mo.)	120
	13	Wayne Croft	KC-Omaha Kings	Clemson	121
	14	John Grochowalski	Chicago Bulls	Assumption	122
	15	Stan Boyer	Golden State Warriors	Wyoming	123
	16	Mike Franklin	Buffalo Braves	Cincinnati	124
	17	Al Boswell	Boston Celtics	Oral Roberts	125
	18	Fletcher Johnson	Washington Bullets	Randolph-Macon	126
EIGHTH ROUND	1	Harvey Carmichael	New Orleans Jazz	Kentucky State	127
	2	Mike Cashman	Los Angeles Lakers	Willamette	128
	3	Oscar Jackson	Atlanta Hawks	Duquesne	129
	4	Jack Schrader	Phoenix Suns	Arizona State	130
	5	Freeman Blade	Philadelphia 76ers	Eastern Montana	131
	6	Bob McCurdy	Milwaukee Bucks	Richmond	132
	7	Charley Neal	Portland Trail Blazers	Oregon State	133
	8	Jerry Homan	New York Knicks	Marquette	134
	9	John Kelley	Detroit Pistons	Dillard	135
	10	Andre McCarter	Cleveland Cavaliers	UCLA	136
	11	Leon Johnson	Houston Rockets	Centenary	137
	12	Ken McKenzie	Seattle SuperSonics	Montana	138
	13	Jim Bostic	KC-Omaha Kings	New Mexico State	139
	14	John Murphy	Chicago Bulls	Massachusetts	140
	15	Mike Rozenski	Golden State Warriors	St. Mary's (Cal.)	141
	16	Allen Jones	Buffalo Braves	Pepperdine	142
	17	Bruce Hamming	Washington Bullets	Augustana (IL)	143
	18	Roger Morningstar	Boston Celtics	Kansas	144
NINTH ROUND	1	Fred Stokes	New Orleans Jazz	Barber Scotia	145
	2	Dave Schlesser	Atlanta Hawks	Morningside	146
	3	Owen Brown	Phoenix Suns	Maryland	147
	4	Larry Harralson	Philadelphia 76ers	Drake	148
	5	Quintin Braxton	Portland Trail Blazers	Portland	149
	6	Eric Hays	Milwaukee Bucks	Montana	150
	7	Terry Thomas	Detroit Pistons	Detroit	151
	8	Skip Howard	Cleveland Cavaliers	Bowling Green	152
	9	Tim van Blommesteyn	New York Knicks	Princeton	153
	10	Steve Storther	Houston Rockets	Providence	154
	11	Rich Haws	Seattle SuperSonics	Utah State	155
	12	Gary Tomaszewski	Chicago Bulls	St. Mary's (Tex.)	156
	13	Scott Trobbe	Golden State Warriors	Stanford	157
	14	George Rautins	Buffalo Braves	Niagara	158
	15	Robert Rhodes	Boston Celtics	Albany State (Ga.)	159

		NAME	TEAM	COLLEGE	# OVERALL
	16	Doug Brookins	Washington Bullets	Creighton	160
TENTH ROUND	1	Aleksander Belov	New Orleans Jazz	Soviet Union	161
	2	Vic Kelly	Atlanta Hawks	Hawaii	162
	3	Mike Moon	Phoenix Suns	Arizona State	163
	4	Rick Reed	Philadelphia 76ers	Azusa Pacific	164
	5	Romy Thomas	Milwaukee Bucks	Eau Claire	165
	6	Tyree Foster	Portland Trail Blazers	Portland	166
	7	Eric Anderson	Cleveland Cavaliers	McAlister	167
	8	Mo Rivers	New York Knicks	North Carolina State	168
	9	Mickey Fox	Detroit Pistons	St. Mary's (N.S.)	169
	10	Jerry Bellotti	Seattle SuperSonics	Santa Clara	170
	11	Maurice Harper	Golden State Warriors	St. Mary's (Cal.)	171
	12	Art Allen	Buffalo Braves	Pepperdine	172
	13	Mike Fahey	Washington Bullets	Brandeis	173
	14	Bill Endicott	Boston Celtics	Massachusetts	174

1974

		NAME	TEAM	COLLEGE	# OVERALL
FIRST ROUND	1	Bill Walton	Portland Trail Blazers	UCLA	1
	2	Marvin Barnes	Philadelphia 76ers	Providence	2
	3	Tom Burleson	Seattle SuperSonics	North Carolina State	3
	4	John Shumate	Phoenix Suns	Notre Dame	4
	5	Bobby Jones	Houston Rockets	North Carolina	5
	6	Scott Wedman	KC-Omaha Kings	Colorado	6
	7	Tom Henderson	Atlanta Hawks	Hawaii	7
	8	Campy Russell	Cleveland Cavaliers	Michigan	8
	9	Tom McMillen	Buffalo Braves	Maryland	9
	10	Mike Sojourner	Atlanta Hawks	Utah	10
	11	Keith Wilkes	Golden State Warriors	UCLA	11
	12	Brian Winters	Los Angeles Lakers	South Carolina	12
	13	Len Elmore	Washington Bullets	Maryland	13
	14	Maurice Lucas	Chicago Bulls	Marquette	14
	15	Al Eberhard	Detroit Pistons	Missouri	15
	16	Cliff Pondexter	Chicago Bulls	Long Beach State	16
	17	Glenn McDonald	Boston Celtics	Long Beach State	17
	18	Gary Brokaw	Milwaukee Bucks	Notre Dame	18
SECOND ROUND	1	Don Smith	Philadelphia 76ers	Dayton	19
	2	Jan van Breda Kolff	Portland Trail Blazers	Vanderbilt	20
	3	Billy Knight	Los Angeles Lakers	Pittsburgh	21
	4	Leonard Robinson	Washington Bullets	Tennessee State	22
	5	Gus Bailey	Houston Rockets	Texas–El Paso	23
	6	Len Kosmalski	KC-Omaha Kings	Tennessee	24
	7	John Drew	Atlanta Hawks	Gardner-Webb	25
	8	Leonard Gray	Seattle SuperSonics	Long Beach State	26
	9	Leon Benbow	Chicago Bulls	Jacksonville	27
	10	Aaron James	New Orleans Jazz	Grambling	28
	11	Phil Smith	Golden State Warriors	San Francisco	29
	12	Dennis DuVal	Washington Bullets	Syracuse	30
	13	Fred Saunders	Phoenix Suns	Syracuse	31
	14	Jesse Dark	New York Knicks	Virginia Commonwealth	32
	15	Eric Money	Detroit Pistons	Arizona	33
	16	Phil Lumpkin	Portland Trail Blazers	Miami (Ohio)	34
	17	Kevin Stacom	Boston Celtics	Providence	35
	18	Rubin Collins	Portland Trail Blazers	Maryland–Eastern Shore	36
THIRD ROUND	1	Coniel Norman	Philadelphia 76ers	Arizona	37
	2	Clarence Walker	Cleveland Cavaliers	West Georgia	38
	3	Kevin Restani	Cleveland Cavaliers	San Francisco	39
	4	George Gervin	Phoenix Suns	Eastern Michigan	40
	5	Robert Wilson	Houston Rockets	Iowa State	41
	6	Harvey Catchings	Philadelphia 76ers	Hardin-Simmons	42
	7	Darrell Elston	Atlanta Hawks	North Carolina	43
	8	Talvin Skinner	Seattle SuperSonics	Maryland–Eastern Shore	44

		NAME	TEAM	COLLEGE	# OVERALL
	9	Kim Hughes	Buffalo Braves	Wisconsin	45
	10	Bruce King	New Orleans Jazz	Pan American	46
	11	Frank Kendrick	Golden State Warriors	Purdue	47
	12	Jim Bradley	Los Angeles Lakers	Northern Illinois	48
	13	Earl Williams	Phoenix Suns	Winston-Salem	49
	14	Rudy Jackson	New York Knicks	Hutchinson JC	50
	15	Roland Grant	Detroit Pistons	New Mexico State	51
	16	Bobby Wilson	Chicago Bulls	Wichita State	52
	17	Roscoe Pondexter	Boston Celtics	Long Beach State	53
	18	Greg McDougald	Milwaukee Bucks	Oral Roberts	54
FOURTH ROUND	1	Butch Taylor	Philadelphia 76ers	Jacksonville	55
	2	Mickey Johnson	Portland Trail Blazers	Aurora	56
	3	Jim Foster	Cleveland Cavaliers	Connecticut	57
	4	Randy Allen	Phoenix Suns	Indiana (Pa.)	58
	5	Larry Robinson	Houston Rockets	Texas	59
	6	Lloyd Batts	KC-Omaha Kings	Cincinnati	60
	7	Ed Palubinskas	Atlanta Hawks	Louisiana State	61
	8	William Gordon	Seattle SuperSonics	Maryland–Eastern Shore	62
	9	Bernard Harris	Buffalo Braves	Virginia Commonwealth	63
	10	Ray Price	New Orleans Jazz	Washington	64
	11	Willie Biles	Golden State Warriors	Tulsa	65
	12	Stan Washington	Washington Bullets	San Diego	66
	13	Ron de Vries	Los Angeles Lakers	Illinois State	67
	14	Roy Ebron	New York Knicks	SW Louisiana	68
	15	Mickey Martin	Detroit Pistons	Pittsburgh	69
	16	Jim Forbes	Chicago Bulls	Texas–El Paso	70
	17	Lerman Battle	Boston Celtics	Fairmont State	71
	18	Lionel Billingy	Milwaukee Bucks	Duquesne	72
FIFTH ROUND	1	Gary Crowthers	Philadelphia 76ers	Hardin-Simmons	73
	2	Bernard Hardin	Portland Trail Blazers	New Mexico	74
	3	Gary Novak	Cleveland Cavaliers	Notre Dame	75
	4	Ralph Bobik	Phoenix Suns	Creighton	76
	5	Owen Wells	Houston Rockets	Detroit	77
	6	Terry Compton	KC-Omaha Kings	Vanderbilt	78
	7	Tyrone Medley	Atlanta Hawks	Utah	79
	8	Dean Tolson	Seattle SuperSonics	Arkansas	80
	9	Tony Byers	Buffalo Braves	Wake Forest	81
	10	Ed Searcy	New Orleans Jazz	St. John's	82
	11	Steve Erickson	Golden State Warriors	Oregon	83
	12	Seymour Reed	Los Angeles Lakers	Bradley	84
	13	Gary Anderson	Washington Bullets	Wisconsin	85
	14	Greg Jackson	New York Knicks	Guilford	86
	15	Joe Newman	Detroit Pistons	Temple	87
	16	Randy Knowles	Chicago Bulls	Texas A&M	88
	17	Ben Clyde	Boston Celtics	Florida State	89
	18	John Johnson	Milwaukee Bucks	Denver	90
SIXTH ROUND	1	Mark Westra	Philadelphia 76ers	USC	91
	2	Dan Anderson	Portland Trail Blazers	USC	92
	3	Aron Stewart	Cleveland Cavaliers	Richmond	93
	4	Collis Temple	Phoenix Suns	Louisiana State	94
	5	Lawrence Johnson	Houston Rockets	Prairie View	95
	6	Ron Kennedy	KC-Omaha Kings	Arizona	96
	7	Sam Hervey	Atlanta Hawks	Southern Methodist	97
	8	Wardell Jackson	Seattle SuperSonics	Ohio State	98
	9	Gary Link	Buffalo Braves	Missouri	99
	10	Lawrence McCray	New Orleans Jazz	Florida State	100
	11	John Errecart	Golden State Warriors	Pacific	101
	12	Roy McPipe	Washington Bullets	Eastern Montana	102
	13	Billy Morris	Los Angeles Lakers	St. Louis	103
	14	Terry Mikan	New York Knicks	St. Thomas	104
	15	Mike Sylvester	Detroit Pistons	Dayton	105
	16	Robert Rosier	Chicago Bulls	St. Thomas	106

Round		NAME	TEAM	COLLEGE	# OVERALL
	17	Gene Harmon	Boston Celtics	Creighton	107
	18	Larry Williams	Milwaukee Bucks	Kansas State	108
SEVENTH ROUND	1	Dave Stoczynski	Philadelphia 76ers	Gannon	109
	2	Doug Richards	Portland Trail Blazers	Brigham Young	110
	3	Mike Robinson	Cleveland Cavaliers	Michigan State	111
	4	Clyde Dickey	Phoenix Suns	Boise State	112
	5	Kevin Fitzgerald	Houston Rockets	Oklahoma	113
	6	Mark Browne	KC-Omaha Kings	Missouri	114
	7	Greg Lee	Atlanta Hawks	UCLA	115
	8	Jerry Faulkner	Seattle SuperSonics	Western Georgia	116
	9	Tommy Curtis	Buffalo Braves	UCLA	117
	10	Joel Copeland	New Orleans Jazz	Old Dominion	118
	11	Brady Allen	Golden State Warriors	California	119
	12	Dennis Van Zant	Los Angeles Lakers	Azusa Pacific	120
	13	Tom Turner	Washington Bullets	Western Georgia	121
	14	Billy Smith	New York Knicks	Mercer	122
	15	Sammy High	Detroit Pistons	Tulsa	123
	16	Geoff Roberts	Chicago Bulls	Missouri	124
	17	Ron Brown	Boston Celtics	Penn State	125
	18	Bob Hornstein	Milwaukee Bucks	West Virginia	126
EIGHTH ROUND	1	Jimmy Powell	Philadelphia 76ers	Middle Tennessee	127
	2	Eldridge Broussard	Portland Trail Blazers	Pacific (Ore.)	128
	3	Kerry Hughes	Cleveland Cavaliers	Wisconsin	129
	4	Tom Holland	Phoenix Suns	Oklahoma	130
	5	Steve Brooks	Houston Rockets	Arkansas State	131
	6	Richie O'Connor	KC-Omaha Kings	Fairfield	132
	7	Bill Butler	Atlanta Hawks	Louisville	133
	8	Leonard Coulter	Seattle SuperSonics	Morehead State	134
	9	Glenn Price	Buffalo Braves	St. Bonaventure	135
	10	Jay Piccola	New Orleans Jazz	Roanoke	136
	11	Clarence Allen	Golden State Warriors	UC Santa Barbara	137
	12	Steve Platt	Washington Bullets	Huntington (Ind.)	138
	13	Bob Florence	Los Angeles Lakers	Nevada–Las Vegas	139
	14	Dennis McDermott	New York Knicks	St. Francis	140
	15	Greg Newman	Detroit Pistons	Drexel	141
	16	Sam McCants	Chicago Bulls	Oral Roberts	142
	17	Richard Wallace	Boston Celtics	Georgia Southern	143
	18	Ralph Palamar	Milwaukee Bucks	Cameron	144
NINTH ROUND	1	Perry Warbington	Philadelphia 76ers	Georgia Southern	145
	2	Lee Haven	Portland Trail Blazers	Colorado	146
	3	Jim Buskofsky	Cleveland Cavaliers	Upper Iowa	147
	4	Ted Evans	Phoenix Suns	Oklahoma	148
	5	Ken Stalling	Houston Rockets	Missouri–Rolla	149
	6	Jeff Dawson	KC-Omaha Kings	Illinois	150
	7	Lon Kruger	Atlanta Hawks	Kansas State	151
	8	Bertrand du Pont	Seattle SuperSonics	Dillard	152
	9	John Falconi	Buffalo Braves	Davidson	153
	10	Ken Boyd	New Orleans Jazz	Boston Univ.	154
	11	Carl Meier	Golden State Warriors	California	155
	12	Mark Raterink	Washington Bullets	Boston College	156
	13	Earl Brown	New York Knicks	Lafayette	157
	14	Gary Deitelhoff	Detroit Pistons	Millikin	158
	15	Jerry Davenport	Chicago Bulls	Cameron	159
	16	Al Skinner	Boston Celtics	Massachusetts	160
	17	Mike Deane	Milwaukee Bucks	Potsdam State	161
TENTH ROUND	1	Larry Witherspoon	Philadelphia 76ers	Towson State	162
	2	Ron Jones	Portland Trail Blazers	Oregon State	163
	3	Jim Kelly	Cleveland Cavaliers	Loras	164
	4	Mark Wasley	Phoenix Suns	Arizona State	165
	5	Marcus Washington	Houston Rockets	Marquette	166
	6	Dennis White	KC-Omaha Kings	Arkansas	167
	7	Brendy Lee	Atlanta Hawks	Nebraska	168
	8	Rod Derline	Seattle SuperSonics	Seattle	169
	9	Andy Rimol	Buffalo Braves	Princeton	170
	10	Walt McGary	New Orleans Jazz	Chattanooga	171
	11	Marvin Buckley	Golden State Warriors	Nevada–Reno	172
	13	Pete Collins	Washington Bullets	High Point	173
	14	John O'Connell	New York Knicks	North Carolina	174
	15	Bill Ligon	Detroit Pistons	Vanderbilt	175
	16	Rick Hockenos	Chicago Bulls	St. Francis (Pa.)	176
	17	Phil Rogers	Boston Celtics	Fairfield	177
	18	Bruce Featherston	Milwaukee Bucks	SW Texas State	178

1973

Round		NAME	TEAM	COLLEGE	# OVERALL
FIRST ROUND	1	Doug Collins	Philadelphia 76ers	Illinois State	1
	2	Jim Brewer	Cleveland Cavaliers	Minnesota	2
	3	Ernie DiGregorio	Buffalo Braves	Providence	3
	4	Mike Green	Seattle SuperSonics	Louisiana Tech	4
	5	Kermit Washington	Los Angeles Lakers	American	5
	6	Ed Ratleff	Houston Rockets	Long Beach State	6
	7	Ron Behagen	KC-Omaha Kings	MInnesota	7
	8	Mike Bantom	Phoenix Suns	St. Joseph's	8
	9	Dwight Jones	Atlanta Hawks	Houston	9
	10	John Brown	Atlanta Hawks	Missouri	10
	11	Kevin Joyce	Golden State Warriors	South Carolina	11
	12	Kevin Kunnert	Chicago Bulls	Iowa	12
	13	Nick Weatherspoon	Capital Bullets	Illinois	13
	14	Mel Davis	New York Knicks	St. John's	14
	15	Barry Parkhill	Portland Trail Blazers	Virginia	15
	16	Swen Nater	Milwaukee Bucks	UCLA	16
	17	Steve Downing	Boston Celtics	Indiana	17
	18	Raymond Lewis	Philadelphia 76ers	Cal State–Los Angeles	18
SECOND ROUND	1	Louis Nelson	Capital Bullets	Washington	19
	2	Mike D'Antoni	KC-Omaha Kings	Marshall	20
	3	Allan Bristow	Philadelphia 76ers	Virginia Tech	21
	4	George McGinnis	Philadelphia 76ers	Indiana	22
	5	Bill Schaeffer	Los Angeles Lakers	St. John's	23
	6	Kevin Stacom	Chicago Bulls	Providence	24
	7	Larry McNeill	KC-Omaha Kings	Marquette	25
	8	Allan Hornyak	Cleveland Cavaliers	Ohio State	26
	9	Tom Inglesby	Atlanta Hawks	Villanova	27
	10	Pat McFarland	New York Knicks	St. Joseph's	28
	11	Derrek Dickey	Golden State Warriors	Cincinnati	29
	12	Wendell Hudson	Chicago Bulls	Alabama	30
	13	Jim Chones	Los Angeles Lakers	Marquette	31
	14	Caldwell Jones	Philadelphia 76ers	Albany State (Ga.)	32
	15	Gary Melchionni	Phoenix Suns	Duke	33
	16	John Perry	Los Angeles Lakers	Pan American	34
	17	Phil Hankinson	Boston Celtics	Penn	35
THIRD ROUND	1	Ted Manakas	Atlanta Hawks	Princeton	36
	2	Jim O'Brien	Portland Trail Blazers	Maryland	37
	3	Ken Charles	Buffalo Braves	Fordham	38
	4	Martin Terry	Chicago Bulls	Arkansas	39
	5	Ozzie Edwards	Cleveland Cavaliers	Oklahoma City	40
	6	James Lister	Cleveland Cavaliers	Sam Houston	41
	7	Joe Reaves	Phoenix Suns	Bethel (Tenn.)	42
	8	Steve Mitchell	Phoenix Suns	Kansas State	43
	9	Dwight Lamar	Detroit Pistons	SW Louisiana	44
	10	Leonard Gray	Atlanta Hawks	Long Beach State	45
	11	Jim Retseck	Golden State Warriors	Auburn	46
	12	Steve Newsome	Chicago Bulls	Houston	47
	13	Tom Kozelko	Capital Bullets	Toledo	48
	14	Allie McGuire	New York Knicks	Marquette	49

ROUND		NAME	TEAM	COLLEGE	# OVERALL
	15	Larry Kenon	Detroit Pistons	Memphis State	50
	16	E.C. Coleman	Houston Rockets	Houston Baptist	51
	17	Martinez Denmon	Boston Celtics	Iowa State	52
FOURTH ROUND	1	Darrel Minniefield	Philadelphia 76ers	New Mexico	53
	2	Doug Little	Buffalo Braves	Oregon	54
	3	William Averitt	Portland Trail Blazers	Pepperdine	55
	4	William Harris	Seattle SuperSonics	North Carolina A&T	56
	5	Luke Witte	Cleveland Cavaliers	Ohio State	57
	6	Lee Colburn	Houston Rockets	South Dakota State	58
	7	Clyde Turner	Milwaukee Bucks	Minnesota	59
	8	Ron Robinson	Phoenix Suns	Memphis State	60
	9	Ken Brady	Detroit Pistons	Michigan	61
	10	James Brown	Atlanta Hawks	Harvard	62
	11	Ron King	Golden State Warriors	Florida State	63
	12	Mark Sibley	Chicago Bulls	Northwestern	64
	13	Aaron Stewart	Capital Bullets	Richmond	65
	14	George Karl	New York Knicks	North Carolina	66
	15	Harry Rogers	Milwaukee Bucks	St. Louis	67
	16	Larry Finch	Los Angeles Lakers	Memphis State	68
	17	Richie Fuqua	Boston Celtics	Oral Roberts	69
FIFTH ROUND	1	Reggie Royals	Philadelphia 76ers	Florida State	70
	2	Fran Costello	Portland Trail Blazers	Providence	71
	3	Randy Knoll	Buffalo Braves	Marshall	72
	4	Chuck Iverson	Seattle SuperSonics	South Dakota	73
	5	John Coughran	Cleveland Cavaliers	California	74
	6	Gary Rhoades	Houston Rockets	Colorado State	75
	7	M.L. Carr	KC-Omaha Kings	Guilford	76
	8	Clinton Harris	Phoenix Suns	Iowa State	77
	9	Henry Wilmore	Detroit Pistons	Michigan	78
	10	Dave Winfield	Atlanta Hawks	Minnesota	79
	11	Nate Stephens	Golden State Warriors	Long Beach State	80
	12	Ray Simpson	Chicago Bulls	Furman	81
	13	Danny Traylor	Capital Bullets	South Carolina	82
	14	Dennis Bell	New York Knicks	Drake	83
	15	Kresimir Cosic	Los Angeles Lakers	Brigham Young	84
	16	Larry Jackson	Milwaukee Bucks	Northern Illinois	85
	17	Byron Jones	Boston Celtics	San Francisco	86
SIXTH ROUND	1	Sterling Wright	Philadelphia 76ers	Lincoln	87
	2	Mike Macaluso	Buffalo Braves	Canisius	88
	3	Neal Jurgensen	Portland Trail Blazers	Oregon State	89
	4	Bill McCoy	Seattle SuperSonics	Northern Iowa	90
	5	Willie Calvert	Cleveland Cavaliers	Abilene Christian	91
	6	Tom Peck	Houston Rockets	Eau Claire	92
	7	Mike Quick	KC-Omaha Kings	San Francisco	93
	8	Gene Doyle	Phoenix Suns	Holy Cross	94
	9	Dennis Johnson	Detroit Pistons	Ferris State	95
	10	John Williamson	Atlanta Hawks	New Mexico State	96
	11	Bob Lauriski	Golden State Warriors	Utah State	97
	12	John Neumann	Chicago Bulls	Mississippi	98
	13	Mike Allocco	Capital Bullets	Stonehill	99
	14	Lawrence Lilly	New York Knicks	Alabama State	100
	15	James Floyd	Milwaukee Bucks	Shaw	101
	16	David Brent	Los Angeles Lakers	Jacksonville	102
	17	Joe Cafferty	Boston Celtics	North Carolina State	103
SEVENTH ROUND	1	James Greene	Philadelphia 76ers	Kentucky Wesleyan	104
	2	Larry Hollyfield	Portland Trail Blazers	UCLA	105
	3	Tim Bassett	Buffalo Braves	Georgia	106
	4	Jim Andrews	Seattle SuperSonics	Kentucky	107
	5	Larry Farmer	Cleveland Cavaliers	UCLA	108
	6	Fred DeVaughn	Houston Rockets	Westmont	109
	7	Mike Jeffries	KC-Omaha Kings	Missouri	110
	8	Jerry Bisbano	Phoenix Suns	SW Louisiana	111
	9	Fred Smiley	Detroit Pistons	Northwood Mich.	112
	10	Pete Harris	Atlanta Hawks	Stephen F. Austin	113
	11	Steve Smith	Golden State Warriors	Loyola (Cal.)	114
	12	Billy Harris	Chicago Bulls	Northern Illinois	115
	13	Rod Hogue	Capital Bullets	Georgia	116
	14	Mike Moore	New York Knicks	Manhattan	117
	15	Nate Hawthorne	Los Angeles Lakers	Southern Illinois	118
	16	Eddie Childress	Milwaukee Bucks	Austin Peay	119
	17	Mike Stewart	Boston Celtics	Santa Clara	120
EIGHTH ROUND	1	Dave Langston	Philadelphia 76ers	Drake	121
	2	Carl Jackson	Buffalo Braves	St. Bonaventure	122
	3	Lindell Resson	Portland Trail Blazers	Eastern Michigan	123
	4	Wardell Jeffries	Seattle SuperSonics	Oklahoma Baptist	124
	5	John Ritter	Cleveland Cavaliers	Indiana	125
	6	John Thomas	Houston Rockets	Missouri Southern	126
	7	Mike Williams	KC-Omaha Kings	Kentucky Wesleyan	127
	8	Jim Owens	Phoenix Suns	Oregon State	128
	9	Ben Kelso	Detroit Pistons	Central Michigan	129
	10	Tim Dominey	Atlanta Hawks	Valdosta State	130
	11	Jeff Dawson	Golden State Warriors	Illinois	131
	12	J.G. Brosterhos	Chicago Bulls	Texas	132
	13	Mark Jellison	Capital Bullets	Northeastern	133
	14	Steve Rowell	New York Knicks	Rhode Island	134
	15	Walt McGrary	Milwaukee Bucks	Tennessee–Chattanooga	135
	16	Roy McPipe	Los Angeles Lakers	Eastern Montana	136
	17	Robert White	Boston Celtics	Sam Houston State	137
NINTH ROUND	1	Harvey Catchings	Philadelphia 76ers	Hardin-Simmons	138
	2	Mike Contreras	Portland Trail Blazers	Arizona State	139
	3	Bob Fullerton	Buffalo Braves	Xavier (Ohio)	140
	4	Greg Williams	Seattle SuperSonics	Seattle	141
	5	Les Taylor	Cleveland Cavaliers	Murray State	142
	6	James Brown	KC-Omaha Kings	Dartmouth	143
	7	Sandy Smith	Phoenix Suns	Winston-Salem	144
	8	Bill Kelgore	Detroit Pistons	Michigan State	145
	9	Everett Fopma	Golden State Warriors	Idaho State	146
	10	Rubin Montanez	Chicago Bulls	Duquesne	147
	11	Mike Boylan	Capital Bullets	Assumption	148
	12	Joe Wise	New York Knicks	Bridgewater State	149
	13	Bob Bocca	Milwaukee Bucks	Quinnipiac	150
	14	Corky Taylor	Boston Celtics	Minnesota	151
TENTH ROUND	1	Abe Steward	Philadelphia 76ers	Jacksonville	152
	2	Nick Connor	Buffalo Braves	Illinois	153
	3	Sam Whitehead	Portland Trail Blazers	Oregon State	154
	4	Bob Bodell	Seattle SuperSonics	Maryland	155
	5	Dean Martin	Cleveland Cavaliers	Baldwin-Wallace	156
	6	Ernie Kusyner	KC-Omaha Kings	Kansas State	157
	7	Claude White	Phoenix Suns	Elmhurst	158
	8	Bob Solomon	Detroit Pistons	Wayne State	159
	9	Fred Lavoroni	Golden State Warriors	Santa Clara	160
	10	Russ Hunt	Chicago Bulls	Furman	161
	11	Dick Kelly	Capital Bullets	Bay College	162
	12	Ed Fields	New York Knicks	C.W. Post	163
	13	Ron Battle	Milwaukee Bucks	Sam Houston State	164
	14	Steve Turner	Boston Celtics	Vanderbilt	165
ELEVENTH ROUND	1	Rod Freeman	Philadelphia 76ers	Vanderbilt	166
	2	Ed Payne	Portland Trail Blazers	Wake Forest	167
	3	Mike Lee	Buffalo Braves	Syracuse	168
	4	Floyd Lewis	Cleveland Cavaliers	Harvard	169
	5	Lynn Greer	Phoenix Suns	Virginia State	170
	6	Len Paul	Detroit Pistons	Akron	171
	7	Dale Adams	Capital Bullets	St. Mary's (Md.)	172
	8	Charles Edge	New York Knicks	LeMoyne-Owen	173

		NAME	TEAM	COLLEGE	# OVERALL
	9	Ed Hastings	Boston Celtics	Villanova	174
TWELTH ROUND	1	Connie Warren	Philadelphia 76ers	Xavier (Ohio)	175
	2	Aaron Covington	Buffalo Braves	Canisius	176
	3	Rick Holdt	Portland Trail Blazers	North Carolina State	177
	4	Chris McMurray	Cleveland Cavaliers	San Diego State	178
	5	Lyman Williamson	Phoenix Suns	Samford	179
	6	Clarence Carlisle	Detroit Pistons	Ferris State	180
	7	Mike Battle	Capital Bullets	George Washington	181
	8	Bruce Winkler	Boston Celtics	Santa Clara	182
THIRTEENTH ROUND	1	Jim Crawford	Philadelphia 76ers	La Salle	183
	2	Bob Vartanian	Buffalo Braves	Buffalo	184
	3	John Pennebacker	Cleveland Cavaliers	Hawaii	185
	4	Kalevi Sarkalahti	Phoenix Suns	Brigham Young	186
	5	Chester Davis	Capital Bullets	Morgan State	187
	6	Scott Koelzer	Boston Celtics	Montana State	188
FOURTEENTH ROUND	1	Ernie Johnson	Philadelphia 76ers	Michigan	189
	2	Ron Gilliam	Buffalo Braves	Brockport State	190
	3	Charles Mitchell	Cleveland Cavaliers	Eastern Kentucky	191
	4	Howard White	Capital Bullets	Maryland	192
	5	Rick Williams	Boston Celtics	Iowa	193
FIFTEENTH ROUND	1	Lionel Harris	Philadelphia 76ers	Cincinnati	194
	2	John Fraley	Buffalo Braves	Georgia	195
	3	Reese Stovall	Cleveland Cavaliers	Pan American	196
	4	W. Shorty Simmons	Capital Bullets	St. Mary's (Md.)	197
	5	James Gilchrist	Boston Celtics	Florida Southern	198
SIXTEENTH RD	1	Larry Robinson	Philadelphia 76ers	Tennessee	199
	2	John Green	Buffalo Braves	Oregon	200
	3	Tom O'Connor	Cleveland Cavaliers	Iowa	201
	4	Sam Barber	Boston Celtics	Bethune-Cookman	202
17 RD	1	Tony Prince	Philadelphia 76ers	St. John's	203
	2	James Garvin	Buffalo Braves	Boston Univ.	204
	3	Phil Elderkin	Cleveland Cavaliers	Boston Univ.	205
	4	Lamont King	Boston Celtics	Long Beach State	206
18 RD	1	Don Johnston	Buffalo Braves	North Carolina	207
	2	Peter Gavitt	Boston Celtics	Maine	208
19 RD	1	Ron Thornson	Buffalo Braves	British Columbia	209
	2	Tom Austin	Boston Celtics	Massachusetts	210
20	1	Phil Tollestrop	Buffalo Braves	Brigham Young	211

1972

		NAME	TEAM	COLLEGE	# OVERALL
FIRST ROUND	1	LaRue Martin	Portland Trail Blazers	Loyola (Ill.)	1
	2	Bob McAdoo	Buffalo Braves	North Carolina	2
	3	Dwight Davis	Cleveland Cavaliers	Houston	3
	4	Corky Calhoun	Phoenix Suns	Penn	4
	5	Fred Boyd	Philadelphia 76ers	Oregon State	5
	6	Russell Lee	Milwaukee Bucks	Marshall	6
	7	Bud Stallworth	Seattle SuperSonics	Kansas	7
	8	Tom Riker	New York Knicks	South Carolina	8
	9	Bob Nash	Detroit Pistons	Hawaii	9
	10	Paul Westphal	Boston Celtics	USC	10
	11	Ralph Simpson	Chicago Bulls	Michigan State	11
	12	Julius Erving	Milwaukee Bucks	Massachusetts	12
	13	Travis Grant	Los Angeles Lakers	Kentucky State	13
SECOND ROUND	1	Bob Davis	Portland Trail Blazers	Weber State	14
	2	Harold Fox	Buffalo Braves	Jacksonville	15
	3	Jim Price	Los Angeles Lakers	Louisville	16
	4	Chris Ford	Detroit Pistons	Villanova	17
	5	Joby Wright	Seattle SuperSonics	Indiana	18
	6	Sam Sibert	Cincinnati Royals	Kentucky State	19
	7	John Gianelli	Houston Rockets	Pacific	20
	8	Steve Bracey	Atlanta Hawks	Tulsa	21
	9	Paul Stovall	Los Angeles Lakers	Arizona State	22
	10	Brian Taylor	Seattle SuperSonics	Princeton	23
	11	Steve Hawes	Cleveland Cavaliers	Washington	24
	12	Tom Patterson	Baltimore Bullets	Ouachita Baptist	25
	13	Dave Twardzik	Portland Trail Blazers	Old Dominion	26
	14	Dennis Wuycik	Boston Celtics	North Carolina	27
	15	Mike Ratliff	Cincinnati Royals	Eau Claire State	28
	16	Chuck Terry	Milwaukee Bucks	Long Beach State	29
	17	Ollie Johnson	Portland Trail Blazers	Temple	30
THIRD ROUND	1	Lloyd Neal	Portland Trail Blazers	Tennessee State	31
	2	Bob Morse	Buffalo Braves	Penn	32
	3	Scott English	Phoenix Suns	Texas–El Paso	33
	4	Don Buse	Phoenix Suns	Evansville	34
	5	Frank Russell	Chicago Bulls	Detroit	35
	6	Charlie Tharpe	Philadelphia 76ers	Belhaven	36
	7	Eric McWilliams	Houston Rockets	Long Beach State	37
	8	Ron Riley	Cincinnati Royals	USC	38
	9	Kevin Porter	Baltimore Bullets	St. Francis (Pa.)	39
	10	Jim Creighton	Seattle SuperSonics	Colorado	40
	11	Ansley Truitt	New York Knicks	California	41
	12	Claude Terry	Phoenix Suns	Stanford	42
	13	Bill Chamberlain	Golden State Warriors	North Carolina	43
	14	Wayne Grabiec	Boston Celtics	Michigan	44
	15	Chuck Jura	Chicago Bulls	Nebraska	45
	16	George Adams	Milwaukee Bucks	Gardner-Webb	46
	17	Gregg Northington	Los Angeles Lakers	Alabama State	47
FOURTH ROUND	1	Gary Stewart	Portland Trail Blazers	Canisius	48
	2	George Bryant	Buffalo Braves	Eastern Kentucky State	49
	3	Hank Siemiontkowski	Cleveland Cavaliers	Villanova	50
	4	Ernie Fleming	Detroit Pistons	Jacksonville	51
	5	Marshall Wingate	Philadelphia 76ers	Niagara	52
	6	Frank Schade	Cincinnati Royals	Eau Claire State	53
	7	Wil Robinson	Houston Rockets	West Virginia	54
	8	Reggie Bird	Atlanta Hawks	Princeton	55
	9	Al Saunders	Baltimore Bullets	Louisiana State	56
	10	Joe Mackey	Seattle SuperSonics	USC	57
	11	Henry Bibby	New York Knicks	UCLA	58
	12	Matt Gantt	Phoenix Suns	St. Bonaventure	59
	13	John Tschogl	Golden State Warriors	UC Santa Barbara	60
	14	Nate Stephens	Boston Celtics	Long Beach State	61
	15	Ted Martiniuk	Chicago Bulls	St. Peter's	62
	16	Art White	Milwaukee Bucks	Georgetown	63
FIFTH ROUND	1	Mike Reid	Portland Trail Blazers	California–Riverside	64
	2	Arnie Berman	Buffalo Braves	Brown	65
	3	Sam Cash	Cleveland Cavaliers	California–Riverside	66
	4	Ernest Pettis	Detroit Pistons	Western Michigan	67
	5	Dave Bustion	Cincinnati Royals	Denver	68
	6	Joe Bynes	Philadelphia 76ers	Arkansas AM&N	69
	7	James Silas	Houston Rockets	Stephen F. Austin	70
	8	Bob Lackey	Atlanta Hawks	Marquette	71
	9	Walter Jones	Baltimore Bullets	Long Island	72
	10	Gary Ladd	Seattle SuperSonics	Seattle	73
	11	Bob Ford	New York Knicks	Purdue	74
	12	Wardell Dyson	Phoenix Suns	Shaw	75
	13	Charles Dudley	Golden State Warriors	Washington	76
	14	Bryan Adrian	Boston Celtics	Davidson	77
	15	Rowland Garrett	Chicago Bulls	Florida State	78
	16	Ron Harris	Milwaukee Bucks	Wichita State	79
	17	Glen Summors	Los Angeles Lakers	Gannon	80
SIXTH ROUND	1	Joe Gaines	Portland Trail Blazers	Belmont	81
	2	Ed Czernota	Buffalo Braves	Sacred Heart	82
	3	Tom Parker	Cleveland Cavaliers	Kentucky	83

		NAME	TEAM	COLLEGE	# OVERALL
	4	Terry Benton	Detroit Pistons	Wichita State	84
	5	John Glover	Philadelphia 76ers	Wiley	85
	6	Jerry Crocker	Cincinnati Royals	Guilford	86
	7	Mike Collins	Houston Rockets	Seattle	87
	8	Randy Knoll	Atlanta Hawks	Marshall	88
	9	Wayne Dillard	Baltimore Bullets	Eastern Michigan	89
	10	Ron Thomas	Seattle SuperSonics	Louisville	90
	11	Greg Cleuss	New York Knicks	St. John's	91
	12	Charles Edge	Phoenix Suns	LeMoyne-Owen	92
	13	Henry Bacon	Golden State Warriors	Louisville	93
	14	Doug Holcomb	Boston Celtics	Memphis	94
	15	Mike Stewart	Chicago Bulls	Santa Clara	95
	16	Wally Wright	Boston Celtics	PMC Colleges	96
	17	Sam Simmons	Los Angeles Lakers	Bradley	97
SEVENTH ROUND	1	Bob Lynn	Portland Trail Blazers	Long Beach State	98
	2	Greg Kohls	Buffalo Braves	Syracuse	99
	3	Steve Davidson	Cleveland Cavaliers	West Texas State	100
	4	Bruce Anderson	Detroit Pistons	Arizona	101
	5	Mike Sneed	Cincinnati Royals	Fayetteville	102
	6	Curtis Pritchett	Philadelphia 76ers	St. Augustine	103
	7	Mike Jackson	Houston Rockets	Cal State–Los Angeles	104
	8	Billy Pleas	Atlanta Hawks	Detroit	105
	9	Marvin Brown	Baltimore Bullets	Jackson State	106
	10	Jerry Dunn	Seattle SuperSonics	Western Kentucky	107
	11	Tracy Tripucka	New York Knicks	Lafayette	108
	12	Bernie Fryer	Phoenix Suns	Brigham Young	109
	13	William Franklin	Golden State Warriors	Purdue	110
	14	Steve Previs	Boston Celtics	North Carolina	111
	15	Jerry Pender	Chicago Bulls	Fresno State	112
	16	Mickey Davis	Milwaukee Bucks	Duquesne	113
EIGHTH ROUND	1	Ruben Vance	Portland Trail Blazers	Kent State	114
	2	Andy Denny	Buffalo Braves	South Alabama State	115
	3	Roger Evans	Cleveland Cavaliers	Kent State	116
	4	Ben Kelso	Detroit Pistons	Central Michigan	117
	5	Jim Kopp	Philadelphia 76ers	Rockhurst (Mo.)	118
	6	Jerry Clack	Cincinnati Royals	Oklahoma	119
	7	Henry Harris	Houston Rockets	Auburn	120
	8	Oscar Evans	Atlanta Hawks	Butler	121
	9	Jim Floyd	Baltimore Bullets	Shaw	122
	10	Willy Stoudamire	Seattle SuperSonics	Portland State	123
	11	Tom Corde	New York Knicks	Ohio	124
	12	Russell Golden	Phoenix Suns	Jackson State	125
	13	John Burks	Golden State Warriors	San Francisco	126
	14	Sam McCarney	Boston Celtics	Oral Roberts	127
	15	Cavin Anderson	Chicago Bulls	Valley City	128
	16	Charles Kirkland	Milwaukee Bucks	Cheyney State	129
NINTH ROUND	1	Scott McCandlish	Portland Trail Blazers	Virginia	130
	2	John Collins	Buffalo Braves	Brockport State	131
	3	Greg Starrick	Cleveland Cavaliers	Southern Illinois	132
	4	Kessie Mangam	Detroit Pistons	Ferris State	133
	5	Steve McMahon	Cincinnati Royals	Merrimack	134
	6	Rod Murray	Philadelphia 76ers	Cal State–Los Angeles	135
	7	Larry Strozier	Atlanta Hawks	Morehouse	136
	8	Ruppert Breedlove	Baltimore Bullets	Oglethorpe	137
	9	Dwight Holliday	Seattle SuperSonics	Hawaii	138
	10	Tom Sullivan	New York Knicks	Fordham	139
	11	Bill Kennedy	Phoenix Suns	Arizona	140
	12	Bill Duey	Golden State Warriors	California	141
	13	Ralph Houston	Chicago Bulls	West Texas State	142
	14	Jim Regenold	Milwaukee Bucks	Ball State	143
	1	Kresimir Cosic	Portland Trail Blazers	Brigham Young	144
	2	Kent Martens	Cleveland Cavaliers	Abilene Christian	145

		NAME	TEAM	COLLEGE	# OVERALL
TENTH ROUND	3	Kent Hollenbeck	Detroit Pistons	Kentucky	146
	4	Gary Watson	Philadelphia 76ers	Wisconsin	147
	5	David Hall	Cincinnati Royals	Kansas State	148
	6	Jim Clesson	Atlanta Hawks	Tulsa	149
	7	Will Loftin	Baltimore Bullets	SW Louisiana	150
	8	Dan Stewart	Seattle SuperSonics	Washington State	151
	9	Richie Garner	New York Knicks	Manhattan	152
	10	Al Vilcheck	Phoenix Suns	Louisville	153
	11	Marty Hunt	Boston Celtics	Kenyon	154
	12	Chuck Taylor	Chicago Bulls	West Liberty State	155
	13	Jolly Spight	Milwaukee Bucks	Santa Clara	156
ELEVENTH ROUND	1	Jimmy Wilkins	Portland Trail Blazers	San Diego State	157
	2	Jim Prokell	Buffalo Braves	Edinboro State	158
	3	Floyd Mathew	Cincinnati Royals	Northern Arizona	159
	4	Charles Allen	Atlanta Hawks	Texas Southern	160
	5	Marvin Watkins	Baltimore Bullets	Jackson State	161
	6	Steve Turner	Seattle SuperSonics	Vanderbilt	162
	7	Chic Downing	New York Knicks	Benedictine	163
	8	John Belcher	Phoenix Suns	Arkansas State	164
	9	Mark Minor	Boston Celtics	Ohio State	165
	10	Jackie Young	Chicago Bulls	Rocky Mountain	166
TWELTH ROUND	1	Frank Dewitt	Buffalo Braves	Virginia	167
	2	Len Baltimore	Cincinnati Royals	George Washington	168
	3	James Green	Atlanta Hawks	Paine College	169
	4	Lloyd Adams	Baltimore Bullets	Rhode Island	170
	5	Gregg Daust	Seattle SuperSonics	Missouri-St. Louis	171
	6	Mark Soderberg	Phoenix Suns	Utah	172
	7	Phil Stephens	Boston Celtics	S. Carolina State	173
	8	Al Cotler	Chicago Bulls	Penn.	174
THIRTEENTH ROUND	1	Larry Morris	Portland Trail Blazers	Tulsa	175
	2	Kim Huband	Buffalo Braves	North Carolina	176
	3	Kent Scott	Cincinnati Royals	Pittsburgh	177
	4	Mike Krawzyk	Baltimore Bullets	Loyola (Md.)	178
	5	Kelly Utley	Phoenix Suns	Shaw	179
	6	Mike Barr	Chicago Bulls	Duquesne	180
FOURTEENTH ROUND	1	Paul Kelly	Portland Trail Blazers	Shaw	181
	2	Greg Corson	Buffalo Braves	North Carolina	182
	3	Bob Allan	Cincinnati Royals	Missouri	183
	4	Aubrey Nash	Baltimore Bullets	Kansas	184
	5	Cleveland Hill	Seattle SuperSonics	Nicholas State	185
	6	Ray Golson	Phoenix Suns	West Texas State	186
	7	Andrew Pettes	Chicago Bulls	Oklahoma	187
FIFTEENTH ROUND	1	Rich Haubeggar	Portland Trail Blazers	Wake Forest	188
	2	Paul Hoffman	Buffalo Braves	St. Bonaventure	189
	3	Mike Jefferies	Cincinnati Royals	Oklahoma State	190
	4	Gary Handelman	Baltimore Bullets	Hopkins	191
	5	Greg Lowery	Chicago Bulls	Texas Tech.	192
16 RD	1	Mose Adolph	Portland Trail Blazers	Los Angeles State	193
	2	Norman Bounds	Buffalo Braves	Brockport State	194
	3	Mike Peterson	Cincinnati Royals	None	195
	4	Charles Hall	Chicago Bulls	West Montana	196
17	1	John Thornton	Chicago Bulls	S. Carolina State	197
18	1	Ron Manning	Chicago Bulls	Manhattan	198

1971

		NAME	TEAM	COLLEGE	# OVERALL
FIRST ROUND	1	Austin Carr	Cleveland Cavaliers	Notre Dame	1
	2	Sidney Wicks	Portland Trail Blazers	UCLA	2
	3	Elmore Smith	Buffalo Braves	Kentucky State	3
	4	Ken Durrett	Cincinnati Royals	La Salle	4
	5	George Trapp	Atlanta Hawks	Long Beach State	5
	6	Fred Brown	Seattle SuperSonics	Iowa	6

ROUND		NAME	TEAM	COLLEGE	# OVERALL
	7	Cliff Meely	San Diego Rockets	Colorado	7
	8	Darnell Hillman	San Francisco Warriors	San Jose State	8
	9	Stan Love	Baltimore Bullets	Oregon	9
	10	Clarence Glover	Boston Celtics	Western Kentucky	10
	11	Curtis Rowe	Detroit Pistons	UCLA	11
	12	Dana Lewis	Philadelphia 76ers	Tulsa	12
	13	Jim Cleamons	Los Angeles Lakers	Ohio State	13
	14	John Roche	Phoenix Suns	South Carolina	14
	15	Kennedy McIntosh	Chicago Bulls	Eastern Michigan	15
	16	Dean Meminger	New York Knicks	Marquette	16
	17	Collis Jones	Milwaukee Bucks	Notre Dame	17
SECOND ROUND	1	Steve Patterson	Cleveland Cavaliers	UCLA	18
	2	Fred Hilton	Buffalo Braves	Grambling	19
	3	Willie Sojourner	Chicago Bulls	Weber State	20
	4	John Mengelt	Cincinnati Royals	Auburn	21
	5	Ted McClain	Atlanta Hawks	Tennessee State	22
	6	Jim McDaniels	Seattle SuperSonics	Western Kentucky	23
	7	Mike Newlin	San Diego Rockets	Utah	24
	8	Charles Yelverton	Portland Trail Blazers	Fordham	25
	9	Amos Thomas	Buffalo Braves	SW Oklahoma State	26
	10	Rick Fisher	Portland Trail Blazers	Colorado State	27
	11	Jim Rose	Boston Celtics	Western Kentucky	28
	12	Isaiah Wilson	Detroit Pistons	Baltimore	29
	13	Spencer Haywood	Buffalo Braves	Detroit	30
	14	Joe Bergman	Cincinnati Royals	Creighton	31
	15	Howard Porter	Chicago Bulls	Villanova	32
	16	Marvin Stewart	Philadelphia 76ers	Nebraska	33
	17	Gregg Northington	New York Knicks	Alabama State	34
	18	Willie Long	Cleveland Cavaliers	New Mexico	35
THIRD ROUND	1	Gerald Lockett	Cleveland Cavaliers	Arkansas AM&N	36
	2	Larry Steele	Portland Trail Blazers	Kentucky	37
	3	Rich Yunkus	Cincinnati Royals	Georgia Tech	38
	4	Jeff Halliburton	Atlanta Hawks	Drake	39
	5	Clifford Ray	Chicago Bulls	Oklahoma	40
	6	Jackie Ridgle	Cleveland Cavaliers	California	41
	7	Bill Smith	Portland Trail Blazers	Syracuse	42
	8	Rich Rinaldi	Baltimore Bullets	St. Peter's	43
	9	Dave Robisch	Boston Celtics	Kansas	44
	10	Marv Roberts	Detroit Pistons	Utah State	45
	11	Dave Wohl	Philadelphia 76ers	Penn	46
	12	Mike Gale	Chicago Bulls	Elizabeth City State	47
	13	Dennis Layton	Phoenix Suns	USC	48
	14	Dick Gibbs	Chicago Bulls	Texas–El Paso	49
	15	Ken Mayfield	New York Knicks	Tuskegee	50
	16	Gary Brell	Milwaukee Bucks	Marquette	51
FOURTH ROUND	1	Cliff Harris	Cleveland Cavaliers	Hardin-Simmons	52
	2	Jim O'Brien	Buffalo Braves	Boston College	53
	3	Bobby Fields	Portland Trail Blazers	La Salle	54
	4	Sid Catlett	Cincinnati Royals	Notre Dame	55
	5	Jim Welch	Atlanta Hawks	Houston	56
	6	Pembroke Burrows	Seattle SuperSonics	Jacksonville	57
	7	Tom Owens	San Diego Rockets	South Carolina	58
	8	Greg Gary	San Francisco Warriors	St. Bonaventure	59
	9	Willie Allen	Baltimore Bullets	Miami (Fla.)	60
	10	Randy Denton	Boston Celtics	Duke	61
	11	Jarrett Durham	Detroit Pistons	Duquesne	62
	12	Erwin Johnson	Philadelphia 76ers	Augusta	63
	13	Roger Brown	Los Angeles Lakers	Kansas	64
	14	Walt Szczerbiak	Phoenix Suns	George Washington	65
	15	Jim Irving	Chicago Bulls	St. Louis	66
	16	Steve Niles	New York Knicks	Texas A&M	67
	17	Henry Smith	Milwaukee Bucks	Missouri	68

ROUND		NAME	TEAM	COLLEGE	# OVERALL
FIFTH ROUND	1	Brian Mahoney	Cleveland Cavaliers	Manhattan	69
	2	Garry Nelson	Buffalo Braves	Duquesne	70
	3	Hector Blondet	Portland Trail Blazers	Murray State	71
	4	Jim Guymond	Cincinnati Royals	Eastern New Mexico	72
	5	Tyrone Marioneaux	Cincinnati Royals	Loyola (La.)	73
	6	Jeff Smith	Seattle SuperSonics	New Mexico State	74
	7	Rudy Benjamin	San Diego Rockets	Michigan State	75
	8	Odis Allison	San Francisco Warriors	Nevada–Las Vegas	76
	9	Don Johnson	Baltimore Bullets	Tennessee	77
	10	Greg Nelson	San Diego Rockets	Jacksonville	78
	11	Vincent White	Detroit Pistons	Savannah State	79
	12	Richard Hood	Philadelphia 76ers	Phillips	80
	13	Lee Dedmon	Los Angeles Lakers	North Carolina	81
	14	Ken Gardner	Phoenix Suns	Utah	82
	15	Larry Weatherford	Chicago Bulls	Purdue	83
	16	Bob Kissane	Phoenix Suns	Holy Cross	84
	17	Barry Nelson	Milwaukee Bucks	Duquesne	85
SIXTH ROUND	1	Mike Childress	Cleveland Cavaliers	Colorado State	86
	2	Glen Summors	Buffalo Braves	Gannon	87
	3	Jim Day	Portland Trail Blazers	Morehead State	88
	4	Gil McGregor	Cincinnati Royals	Wake Forest	89
	5	Willie Humes	Atlanta Hawks	Idaho State	90
	6	Mike Necaise	Seattle SuperSonics	William Carey	91
	7	Garry Reist	San Diego Rockets	Rice	92
	8	Charlie Johnson	San Francisco Warriors	California	93
	9	John Novey	Baltimore Bullets	Mount St. Mary's	94
	10	Thorpe Weber	Boston Celtics	Vanderbilt	95
	11	Jim Larranaga	Detroit Pistons	Providence	96
	12	Jake Jones	Philadelphia 76ers	Assumption	97
	13	Bill Brickhouse	Los Angeles Lakers	Montana State	98
	14	William Graham	Phoenix Suns	Kentucky State	99
	15	Jim England	Chicago Bulls	Tennessee	100
	16	Bill Mainor	New York Knicks	Fordham	101
	17	Ed Kemp	Milwaukee Bucks	Adams State	102
SEVENTH ROUND	1	Tom Bush	Cleveland Cavaliers	Drake	103
	2	Randy Smith	Buffalo Braves	Buffalo State	104
	3	Gene Knolle	Portland Trail Blazers	Texas Tech	105
	4	Ollie Shannon	Cincinnati Royals	Minnesota	106
	5	Mike Jordan	Atlanta Hawks	Savannah State	107
	6	John Duncan	Seattle SuperSonics	Kentucky Wesleyan	108
	7	Eric Hill	San Diego Rockets	Minnesota	109
	8	Ken May	San Francisco Warriors	Dayton	110
	9	Dennis Hogg	Baltimore Bullets	Washington State	111
	10	Skip Young	Boston Celtics	Florida State	112
	11	Steve Kelly	Detroit Pistons	Brigham Young	113
	12	Curtis Ford	Philadelphia 76ers	NE Oklahoma State	114
	13	Gene Gathers	Los Angeles Lakers	Bradley	115
	14	Ralph Brateris	Phoenix Suns	Trenton State	116
	15	Artis Gilmore	Chicago Bulls	Jacksonville	117
	16	Danny Davis	New York Knicks	Henderson State	118
	17	Gene Phillips	Milwaukee Bucks	Southern Methodist	119
EIGHTH ROUND	1	Charlie Davis	Cleveland Cavaliers	Wake Forest	120
	2	Craig Love	Buffalo Braves	Ohio	121
	3	John Sutter	Portland Trail Blazers	Tulane	122
	4	Frank Fitzgerald	Cincinnati Royals	Boston College	123
	5	Jim Smith	Atlanta Hawks	Kentucky Wesleyan	124
	6	Chuck Lowery	Seattle SuperSonics	Puget Sound	125
	7	Rich Katherman	San Diego Rockets	Duke	126
	8	Jim Haderlein	San Francisco Warriors	Loyola (Cal.)	127
	9	Russell Golden	Baltimore Bullets	Jackson State	128
	10	John Ribock	Boston Celtics	South Carolina	129
	11	Wayne Jones	Detroit Pistons	Niagara	130

ROUND		NAME	TEAM	COLLEGE	# OVERALL
	12	Barry Yates	Philadelphia 76ers	Maryland	131
	13	Luke Adams	Los Angeles Lakers	Lamar Tech	132
	14	Vernell Ellzy	Phoenix Suns	Florida State	133
	15	Clarence Sherrod	Chicago Bulls	Wisconsin	134
	16	Leroy Eldridge	New York Knicks	Cheyney State	135
	17	Felix Thurston	Milwaukee Bucks	Trinity (Tex.)	136
NINTH ROUND	1	Rich Walker	Cleveland Cavaliers	Bowling Green	137
	2	Gary Stewart	Buffalo Braves	Canisius	138
	3	Gene Kennedy	Portland Trail Blazers	Texas Christian	139
	4	Ernie Fleming	Atlanta Hawks	Jacksonville	140
	5	Larry Holliday	Seattle SuperSonics	Oregon	141
	6	Willie Kerry	San Diego Rockets	Denver	142
	7	Clarence Smith	San Francisco Warriors	Villanova	143
	8	Ron Johnston	Baltimore Bullets	Murray State	144
	9	Ray Green	Boston Celtics	Cal State (Pa.)	145
	10	Paul Botts	Detroit Pistons	Central Michigan	146
	11	Tom Lee	Philadelphia 76ers	Arizona	147
	12	Bob Cheeks	Los Angeles Lakers	Whittier	148
	13	Mike Johnson	Phoenix Suns	Kansas State	149
	14	Jackie Dinkins	Chicago Bulls	Voorhees State	150
	15	Mike O'Brien	New York Knicks	St. Leo's	151
	16	Rick Howat	Milwaukee Bucks	Illinois	152
TENTH ROUND	1	Jim Meredith	Cleveland Cavaliers	Washington State	153
	2	Don Ward	Buffalo Braves	Colgate	154
	3	Greg Starrick	Portland Trail Blazers	Southern Illinois	155
	4	Ron Rippicoe	Atlanta Hawks	David Lipscomb (Tenn.)	156
	5	Ed Huston	Seattle SuperSonics	Puget Sound	157
	6	Calvin Oliver	San Diego Rockets	Pan American	158
	7	Bill Drosdiak	San Francisco Warriors	Oregon	159
	8	Eddie Myers	Baltimore Bullets	Arizona	160
	9	Dale Dover	Boston Celtics	Harvard	161
	10	Steve Butcher	Detroit Pistons	Pikeville	162
	11	Jim Dinwiddie	Philadelphia 76ers	Kentucky	163
	12	Cliff Mosely	Los Angeles Lakers	Quinnipiac	164
	13	Tom Newell	Phoenix Suns	Hawaii	165
	14	David Withers	Chicago Bulls	Delaware State	166
	15	Andy Toth	New York Knicks	Cheyney State	167
	16	Dan Fife	Milwaukee Bucks	Michigan	168
ELEVENTH ROUND	1	Mike Casey	Cleveland Cavaliers	Kentucky	169
	2	Bill Warner	Buffalo Braves	Arizona	170
	3	Howard Burford	Portland Trail Blazers	Gonzaga	171
	4	Levi Wyatt	Atlanta Hawks	Alcorn A&M	172
	5	Jerome Perry	Seattle SuperSonics	Western Kentucky	173
	6	Doug Rex	San Diego Rockets	UC Santa Barbara	174
	7	Chuck Olowski	Baltimore Bullets	Baltimore	175
	8	Reggie Brooks	Boston Celtics	New Hampshire College	176
	9	Larry Saunders	Detroit Pistons	Duke	177
	10	Dana Pagett	Philadelphia 76ers	USC	178
	11	Paul Leitz	Phoenix Suns	Western Carolina	179
	12	Al Smith	Chicago Bulls	Bradley	180
	13	Ken Davis	New York Knicks	Georgetown	181
	14	Blaine Henry	Milwaukee Bucks	Marshall	182
TWELTH ROUND	1	Doug Hess	Cleveland Cavaliers	Toledo	183
	2	Butch Webster	Buffalo Braves	LSU/New Orleans	184
	3	Don Sechler	Portland Trail Blazers	Delaware Valley	185
	4	Roger Moore	Atlanta Hawks	Columbus College	186
	5	Chris Schrobilgen	San Diego Rockets	USC	187
	6	Bob Connor	Baltimore Bullets	Loyola (Md.)	188
	7	John Dalton	Boston Celtics	Suffolk	189
	8	Bob Horn	Detroit Pistons	Drake	190
	9	Ken Kowall	Philadelphia 76ers	Ohio	191
	10	Floyd Mason	Phoenix Suns	Alcorn A&M	192

ROUND		NAME	TEAM	COLLEGE	# OVERALL
	11	Ken Riley	Chicago Bulls	Middle Tennessee	193
	12	Carl Greenfield	New York Knicks	Eastern Kentucky	194
	13	Gene Mumford	Milwaukee Bucks	Scranton	195
THIRTEENTH ROUND	1	Bobby Jones	Cleveland Cavaliers	Drake	196
	2	Pete Smith	Buffalo Braves	Valdosta State	197
	3	Ed Jenkins	Atlanta Hawks	Michigan Lutheran	198
	4	Lee McCollough	San Diego Rockets	Indiana	199
	5	Ron Crosswhite	Baltimore Bullets	Dayton	200
	6	Leroy Chalk	Boston Celtics	Nebraska	201
	7	Willie Roberson	Detroit Pistons	Wyoming	202
	8	Hank Commodore	Philadelphia 76ers	NW Oklahoma	203
	9	Ron Dorsey	Phoenix Suns	Tennessee State	204
	10	Ed Goode	Chicago Bulls	DePaul	205
	11	Larry Duckworth	New York Knicks	Henderson State	206
	12	Pierre Russell	Milwaukee Bucks	Kansas	207
FOURTEENTH ROUND	1	Bubbles Harris	Cleveland Cavaliers	Indiana	208
	2	Ray Lavender	Buffalo Braves	Drury (Mo.)	209
	3	Gene Roberson	San Diego Rockets	Canisius	210
	4	Rudolph Peele	Baltimore Bullets	Norfolk State	211
	5	Art Davis	Detroit Pistons	J.C. Smith	212
	6	Ken Booker	Phoenix Suns	UCLA	213
	7	Richard Dixon	Chicago Bulls	Loyola (La.)	214
	8	Jack O'Connor	New York Knicks	Grant Falls	215
	9	George Jackson	Milwaukee Bucks	Dayton	216
FIFTEENTH ROUND	1	Larry Baker	Cleveland Cavaliers	Wittenberg	217
	2	William Chatmon	Buffalo Braves	Baylor	218
	3	Terry Guigg	San Diego Rockets	Gonzaga	219
	4	James Morrell	Baltimore Bullets	Norfolk State	220
	5	James Fleming	Detroit Pistons	Alcorn A&M	221
	6	Curtis Carter	Phoenix Suns	Bishop	222
	7	Liscio Thomas	Chicago Bulls	Furman	223
	8	Loyd King	Milwaukee Bucks	Virginia Tech	224
SIXTEENTH ROUND	1	Vance Tyree	Cleveland Cavaliers	Wisconsin State	225
	2	James Douglas	Buffalo Braves	Memphis	226
	3	Leonard Jackson	San Diego Rockets	Oregon	227
	4	Fred Smiley	Detroit Pistons	Detroit	228
	5	Bob Bissant	Chicago Bulls	Loyola (La.)	229
17 ROUND	1	Nelson Isley	Buffalo Braves	Louisiana State	230
	2	Steve Sims	San Diego Rockets	Pepperdine	231
	3	Leroy Jenkins	Detroit Pistons	Detroit	232
18 ROUND	1	Joey Meyer	Buffalo Braves	DePaul	233
	2	Carlos Quintar	San Diego Rockets	Mexico City	234
	3	Ike Bundy	Detroit Pistons	Detroit Tech	235
19 RD	1	Gary Schneider	San Diego Rockets	San Diego State	236
	2	Ed Jenkins	Detroit Pistons	Shaw	237

1970

ROUND		NAME	TEAM	COLLEGE	# OVERALL
FIRST ROUND	1	Bob Lanier	Detroit Pistons	St. Bonaventure	1
	2	Rudy Tomjanovich	San Diego Rockets	Michigan	2
	3	Pete Maravich	Atlanta Hawks	Louisiana State	3
	4	Dave Cowens	Boston Celtics	Florida State	4
	5	Sam Lacey	Cincinnati Royals	New Mexico State	5
	6	Jim Ard	Seattle SuperSonics	Cincinnati	6
	7	John Johnson	Cleveland Cavaliers	Iowa	7
	8	Geoff Petrie	Portland Trail Blazers	Princeton	8
	9	George Johnson	Baltimore Bullets	Stephen F. Austin	9
	10	Greg Howard	Phoenix Suns	New Mexico	10
	11	Jimmy Collins	Chicago Bulls	New Mexico State	11
	12	Al Henry	Philadelphia 76ers	Wisconsin	12
	13	Jim McMillian	Los Angeles Lakers	Columbia	13
	14	John Vallely	Atlanta Hawks	UCLA	14

Round		NAME	TEAM	COLLEGE	# OVERALL
	15	John Hummer	Buffalo Braves	Princeton	15
	16	Gary Freeman	Milwaukee Bucks	Oregon State	16
	17	Mike Price	New York Knicks	Illinois	17
SECOND ROUND	1	Calvin Murphy	San Diego Rockets	Niagara	18
	2	Nate Archibald	Cincinnati Royals	Texas–El Paso	19
	3	Jake Ford	Seattle SuperSonics	Maryland State	20
	4	Rex Morgan	Boston Celtics	Jacksonville	21
	5	Doug Cook	Cincinnati Royals	Davidson	22
	6	Pete Cross	Seattle SuperSonics	San Francisco	23
	7	Cornell Warner	Buffalo Braves	Jackson State	24
	8	Walt Gilmore	Portland Trail Blazers	Fort Valley State	25
	9	Dave Sorenson	Cleveland Cavaliers	Ohio State	26
	10	Fred Taylor	Phoenix Suns	Pan American	27
	11	Paul Ruffner	Chicago Bulls	Brigham Young	28
	12	Joe DePre	Phoenix Suns	St. John's	29
	13	Earnest Killum	Los Angeles Lakers	Stetson	30
	14	Dan Hester	Atlanta Hawks	Louisiana State	31
	15	Ken Warzynski	Detroit Pistons	DePaul	32
	16	Bill Zopf	Milwaukee Bucks	Duquesne	33
	17	Howie Wright	New York Knicks	Austin Peay	34
THIRD ROUND	1	Curtis Perry	San Diego Rockets	SW Missouri	35
	2	Earl Higgins	San Francisco Warriors	Eastern Michigan	36
	3	Bob St. Pierre	Detroit Pistons	Hanover	37
	4	Willie Williams	Boston Celtics	Florida State	38
	5	Greg Hyder	Cincinnati Royals	Eastern New Mexico	39
	6	Garfield Heard	Seattle SuperSonics	Oklahoma	40
	7	Surry Oliver	Cleveland Cavaliers	Stephen F. Austin	41
	8	Bill Cain	Portland Trail Blazers	Iowa State	42
	9	Chip Case	Buffalo Braves	Virginia	43
	10	Greg McDivitt	Phoenix Suns	Ohio	44
	11	Lou Herndon	Chicago Bulls	Jackson State	45
	12	Dennis Awtrey	Philadelphia 76ers	Santa Clara	46
	13	Jim Hayes	Detroit Pistons	Boston Univ.	47
	14	Vann Williford	Phoenix Suns	North Carolina State	48
	15	Seaburn Hill	Baltimore Bullets	Arizona State	49
	16	Marvin Winkler	Milwaukee Bucks	SW Louisiana	50
	17	Al Williams	New York Knicks	Drake	51
FOURTH ROUND	1	Jody Finney	San Diego Rockets	Ohio State	52
	2	Ralph Ogden	San Francisco Warriors	Santa Clara	53
	3	Bill Stricker	Baltimore Bullets	Pacific	54
	4	Jon McKinney	Boston Celtics	Norfolk State	55
	5	Wade Fuller	Cincinnati Royals	Loyola (Ill.)	56
	6	John Davis	Chicago Bulls	Alabama State	57
	7	Erwin Polnick	Buffalo Braves	Stephen F. Austin	58
	8	Jim Penix	Portland Trail Blazers	Bowling Green	59
	9	Glen Vidnovic	Cleveland Cavaliers	Iowa	60
	10	Bob Lienhard	Phoenix Suns	Georgia	61
	11	Jimmy Wilson	Chicago Bulls	Cheyney State	62
	12	Dan Crenshaw	Philadelphia 76ers	Alabama State	63
	13	Larry Mikan	Los Angeles Lakers	Minnesota	64
	14	Fred Davis	Atlanta Hawks	Howard Payne	65
	15	Billy Jones	Baltimore Bullets	Louisiana College	66
	16	Virgle Fredricks	Milwaukee Bucks	Drury (Mo.)	67
	17	John Warren	New York Knicks	Manhattan	68
FIFTH ROUND	1	James Gilbert	San Diego Rockets	Adams State	69
	2	Levi Fontaine	San Francisco Warriors	Maryland State	70
	3	Bill Jankans	Detroit Pistons	Long Beach State	71
	4	Tom Carter	Boston Celtics	Paul Quinn	72
	5	Uluss Thompson	Cincinnati Royals	Wiley	73
	6	Boyd Lynch	Seattle SuperSonics	Eastern Kentucky	74
	7	Wayne Sokolowski	Cleveland Cavaliers	Ashland	75
	8	Ron Knight	Portland Trail Blazers	Cal State–Los Angeles	76
	9	Robert Moore	Buffalo Braves	Central State (Ohio)	77
	10	John Canine	Phoenix Suns	Ohio	78
	11	George Johnson	Chicago Bulls	Dillard	79
	12	Perry Wallace	Philadelphia 76ers	Vanderbilt	80
	13	John Fultz	Los Angeles Lakers	Rhode Island	81
	14	Bob Riley	Atlanta Hawks	Mount St. Mary's	82
	15	Gary Zeller	Baltimore Bullets	Drake	83
	16	Mike Grosso	Milwaukee Bucks	Louisville	84
	17	Jim Oxley	New York Knicks	Army	85
SIXTH ROUND	1	Mike Kretzer	San Diego Rockets	East Tennessee	86
	2	Vic Bartolome	San Francisco Warriors	Oregon State	87
	3	Sevira Brown	Detroit Pistons	DePaul	88
	4	Rod McIntyre	Boston Celtics	Jacksonville	89
	5	Charles Bishop	Cincinnati Royals	Louisiana Tech	90
	6	Sam Robinson	Seattle SuperSonics	Long Beach State	91
	7	Doug Hess	Buffalo Braves	Toledo	92
	8	George Janky	Portland Trail Blazers	Dayton	93
	9	Joe Cooke	Cleveland Cavaliers	Indiana	94
	10	Joe Thomas	Phoenix Suns	Marquette	95
	11	Lonnie Kluttz	Chicago Bulls	North Carolina A&T	96
	12	Jerry Venable	Philadelphia 76ers	Kansas State	97
	13	Jerry Kroll	Los Angeles Lakers	Davidson	98
	14	Dave Parker	Atlanta Hawks	Windham	99
	15	Marvin Polnick	Baltimore Bullets	Stephen F. Austin	100
	16	Willy Watson	Milwaukee Bucks	Oklahoma City	101
	17	Jim Signorile	New York Knicks	New York University	102
SEVENTH ROUND	1	Bill Paultz	San Diego Rockets	St. John's	103
	2	Joe Bergman	San Francisco Warriors	Creighton	104
	3	Marv Copeland	Detroit Pistons	Michigan Lutheran	105
	4	Charlie Scott	Boston Celtics	North Carolina	106
	5	Mike Bernard	Cincinnati Royals	Kentucky State	107
	6	James Morgan	Seattle SuperSonics	Maryland State	108
	7	Narvis Anderson	Cleveland Cavaliers	Stephen F. Austin	109
	8	Claude English	Portland Trail Blazers	Rhode Island	110
	9	Cliff Shegogg	Buffalo Braves	Colorado State	111
	10	Heyward Dotson	Phoenix Suns	Columbia	112
	11	Lou West	Chicago Bulls	Seattle	113
	12	Carlton Poole	Philadelphia 76ers	Philadelphia Textile	114
	13	Willie Woods	Los Angeles Lakers	Eastern Kentucky	115
	14	John Shinall	Atlanta Hawks	Jackson State	116
	15	Charlie Wallace	Baltimore Bullets	Oklahoma City	117
	16	John Rinka	Milwaukee Bucks	Kenyon	118
	17	Ray Hodge	New York Knicks	Wagner	119
EIGHTH ROUND	1	Don Adams	San Diego Rockets	Northwestern	120
	2	Jeff Sewell	San Francisco Warriors	Marquette	121
	3	Dan Issel	Detroit Pistons	Kentucky	122
	4	Bob Croft	Boston Celtics	Tennessee	123
	5	Joel McBride	Cincinnati Royals	Augusta	124
	6	George Irvine	Seattle SuperSonics	Washington	125
	7	Larry Woods	Buffalo Braves	West Virginia	126
	8	Doug Boyd	Portland Trail Blazers	Texas Christian	127
	9	Walter Robertson	Cleveland Cavaliers	Loyola (Ill.)	128
	10	Steve Patterson	Phoenix Suns	UCLA	129
	11	Mike Casey	Chicago Bulls	Kentucky	130
	12	Fran O'Hanlon	Philadelphia 76ers	Villanova	131
	13	Rick Mount	Los Angeles Lakers	Purdue	132
	14	Herb White	Atlanta Hawks	Georgia	133
	15	Tom Dyksera	Baltimore Bullets	Wheaton	134
	16	Jim Sarno	Milwaukee Bucks	Northwestern	135
	17	Greg Fillmore	New York Knicks	Cheyney State	136
	1	Jim Gottschall	San Diego Rockets	Dayton	137
	2	Lou Small	San Francisco Warriors	Nevada	138

		NAME	TEAM	COLLEGE	# OVERALL
NINTH ROUND	3	Alex Wynn	Detroit Pistons	Dartmouth	139
	4	Tom Little	Boston Celtics	Seattle	140
	5	Bob Mabry	Cincinnati Royals	Rio Grande	141
	6	Claude Virden	Seattle SuperSonics	Murray State	142
	7	Tom Lagodich	Cleveland Cavaliers	Kent State	143
	8	Billy Gaskins	Portland Trail Blazers	Oregon	144
	9	Larry Duckworth	Buffalo Braves	Henderson State	145
	10	Carl Ashley	Phoenix Suns	Wyoming	146
	11	Glen Johnson	Chicago Bulls	Jackson State	147
	12	Mike Hauer	Philadelphia 76ers	St. Joseph's	148
	13	Bobby Sands	Los Angeles Lakers	Pepperdine	149
	14	Larry Jackson	Atlanta Hawks	Sul Ross	150
	15	Will Hetzel	Baltimore Bullets	Maryland	151
	16	Joe Hamilton	Milwaukee Bucks	North Texas State	152
	17	Walker Banks	New York Knicks	Western Kentucky	153
TENTH ROUND	1	Toke Coleman	San Diego Rockets	Eastern Kentucky	154
	2	Coby Dietrick	San Francisco Warriors	San Jose State	155
	3	Bruce Chapman	Detroit Pistons	Nevada	156
	4	Mike Maloy	Boston Celtics	Davidson	157
	5	Carl Johnson	Cincinnati Royals	Gustavus Adolphus	158
	6	Chuck Lloyd	Seattle SuperSonics	Yankton	159
	7	Joe Taylor	Buffalo Braves	Dillard	160
	8	Israel Oliver	Portland Trail Blazers	Elizabeth City State	161
	9	Ken Johnson	Cleveland Cavaliers	Indiana	162
	10	Gerhardus Schreur	Phoenix Suns	Arizona State	163
	11	Dale Blaut	Chicago Bulls	West Texas State	164
	12	Gordon Stiles	Philadelphia 76ers	American	165
	13	Kindell Stephens	Los Angeles Lakers	Fisk	166
	14	Manuel Raga	Atlanta Hawks	(Mexico)	167
	15	Ron Becker	Baltimore Bullets	New Mexico	168
	16	Bob Seemer	Milwaukee Bucks	Georgia Tech	169
	17	Don Curnutt	New York Knicks	Miami (Fla.)	170
ELEVENTH ROUND	1	Ron Belton	San Diego Rockets	Bellarmine	171
	2	Rick Anheuser	Detroit Pistons	North Carolina State	172
	3	Ted Hillary	Cincinnati Royals	St. Joseph's (Ind.)	173
	4	Andy Owens	Seattle SuperSonics	Florida	174
	5	Dave Schneider	Cleveland Cavaliers	Wayne State	175
	6	Don McClemore	Portland Trail Blazers	Bowling Green	176
	7	Dick Walker	Buffalo Braves	Wake Forest	177
	8	Jim Walls	Phoenix Suns	Clark	178
	9	Doug Howard	Chicago Bulls	Brigham Young	179
	10	David Whitley	Philadelphia 76ers	Tufts	180
	11	Bob Dukiet	Los Angeles Lakers	Boston College	181
	12	Dino Meneghin	Atlanta Hawks	(Italy)	182
	13	Mel Bell	Baltimore Bullets	Houston	183
TWELFTH ROUND	1	Jim Brooks	San Diego Rockets	Nebraska	184
	2	Don Ogletree	Detroit Pistons	Cincinnati	185
	3	Reggie Roach	Cincinnati Royals	Virginia State	186
	4	John Brunson	Seattle SuperSonics	Furman	187
	5	Paul Adams	Portland Trail Blazers	Central Washington	188
	6	Ollie Taylor	Cleveland Cavaliers	Houston	189
	7	Ric Cobb	Phoenix Suns	Marquette	190
	8	Booker Brown	Chicago Bulls	Middle Tennessee	191
	9	Dewey Varner	Los Angeles Lakers	Tuskegee	192
	10	Ben McGilmer	Baltimore Bullets	Iowa	193
THIRTEENTH ROUND	1	Harry Lozon	San Diego Rockets	Old Dominion	194
	2	Ernest Hardy	Detroit Pistons	Harvard	195
	3	Larry Gray	Cincinnati Royals	Huston-Pillotson	196
	4	Allen McManus	Seattle SuperSonics	Winston-Salem	197
	5	Kevin Wilson	Cleveland Cavaliers	Ashland	198
	6	Alex Boyd	Portland Trail Blazers	Nevada–Reno	199
	7	Fred Carpenter	Phoenix Suns	Hawaii	200
	8	Charles Bloodworth	Chicago Bulls	NW Louisiana	201
	9	Garry Elliott	Los Angeles Lakers	Washington	202
	10	Dan Debardabi	Baltimore Bullets	Northern Arizona	203
FOURTEENTH ROUND	1	Clyde Oatis	San Diego Rockets	Aurora	204
	2	Randy Smith	Detroit Pistons	Buffalo State	205
	3	Andy Jennings	Cincinnati Royals	Alderson-Broaddus	206
	4	Don Beenson	Seattle SuperSonics	Linfield	207
	5	Frank Loteridge	Portland Trail Blazers	Pan American	208
	6	Don Tomilson	Cleveland Cavaliers	Missouri	209
	7	Chad Calabria	Phoenix Suns	Iowa	210
	8	Paul Funkhouser	Chicago Bulls	McKendree	211
	9	Ron Sanford	Los Angeles Lakers	New Mexico State	212
	10	Mike Williams	Baltimore Bullets	Northern Arizona	213
FIFTEENTH ROUND	1	Jay Bond	San Diego Rockets	Washington	214
	2	Dennis Clark	Detroit Pistons	Springfield (Mass.)	215
	3	Mike Neer	Cincinnati Royals	Washington & Lee	216
	4	Steve Wannamaker	Cleveland Cavaliers	Drake	217
	5	John Canady	Portland Trail Blazers	Miami (Fla.)	218
	6	Walt Williams	Phoenix Suns	Miami (Ohio)	219
	7	Paul Otay	Chicago Bulls	Boise State	220
	8	Will Teague	Los Angeles Lakers	Youngstown	221
	9	Ted Rose	Baltimore Bullets	Northern Michigan	222
SIXTEENTH ROUND	1	Dean Olofson	San Diego Rockets	Wayne State	223
	2	Harvey Marlatt	Detroit Pistons	Eastern Michigan	224
	3	Paul Favorite	Cincinnati Royals	Georgetown	225
	4	Doug Williams	Portland Trail Blazers	St. Mary's (Tex.)	226
	5	Steve Wilson	Cleveland Cavaliers	Hanover	227
	6	Pete Walthour	Los Angeles Lakers	Fort Valley	228
	7	Don Rather	Baltimore Bullets	Northern Arizona	229
17 ROUND	1	Dennis Dickens	San Diego Rockets	Azusa Pacific	230
	2	Bob Peterson	Cleveland Cavaliers	Concordia	231
	3	Bob Thate	Los Angeles Lakers	Occidental	232
	4	Vince Fritz	Baltimore Bullets	Oregon State	233
18 ROUND	1	Jeff Cunningham	San Diego Rockets	California–Irvine	234
	2	Bruce Butchko	Portland Trail Blazers	Southern Illinois	235
	3	John Cannon	Cleveland Cavaliers	Grambling	236
19 ROUND	1	Rick Erickson	San Diego Rockets	Washington State	237
	2	Allen Waller	Cleveland Cavaliers	St. Mary's (Kansas)	238
	3	Mark Gabriel	Portland Trail Blazers	Hanover	239

1969

		NAME	TEAM	COLLEGE	# OVERALL
FIRST ROUND	1	Lew Alcindor	Milwaukee Bucks	UCLA	1
	2	Neal Walk	Phoenix Suns	Florida	2
	3	Lucius Allen	Seattle SuperSonics	UCLA	3
	4	Terry Driscoll	Detroit Pistons	Boston College	4
	5	Larry Cannon	Chicago Bulls	La Salle	5
	6	Bobby Smith	San Diego Rockets	Tulsa	6
	7	Bob Portman	San Francisco Warriors	Creighton	7
	8	Herm Gilliam	Cincinnati Royals	Purdue	8
	9	Jo Jo White	Boston Celtics	Kansas	9
	10	Butch Beard	Atlanta Hawks	Louisville	10
	11	John Warren	New York Knicks	St. John's	11
	12	Willie McCarter	Los Angeles Lakers	Drake	12
	13	Bud Ogden	Philadelphia 76ers	Santa Clara	13
	14	Mike Davis	Baltimore Bullets	Virginia Union	14
	15	Rick Roberson	Los Angeles Lakers	Cincinnati	15
SECOND ROUND	1	Simmie Hill	Chicago Bulls	West Texas State	16
	2	Bob Greacen	Milwaukee Bucks	Rutgers	17
	3	Ron Taylor	Seattle SuperSonics	USC	18
	4	Willie Norwood	Detroit Pistons	Alcorn A&M	19
	5	Kenny Spain	Chicago Bulls	Houston	20

		NAME	TEAM	COLLEGE	# OVERALL
	6	Bernie Williams	San Diego Rockets	La Salle	21
	7	Ed Siudet	San Francisco Warriors	Holy Cross	22
	8	John Baum	Chicago Bulls	Temple	23
	9	Gene Williams	Phoenix Suns	Kansas State	24
	10	Wally Anderzunas	Atlanta Hawks	Creighton	25
	11	Bill Bunting	New York Knicks	North Carolina	26
	12	Eldo Garrett	Los Angeles Lakers	Southern Illinois	27
	13	Willie Taylor	Philadelphia 76ers	LeMoyne	28
	14	Willie Scott	Baltimore Bullets	Alabama State	29
THIRD ROUND	1	Floyd Kerr	Phoenix Suns	Colorado State	30
	2	Harley Swift	Milwaukee Bucks	East Tennessee State	31
	3	Leroy Winfield	Seattle SuperSonics	North Texas State	32
	4	Lamar Green	Phoenix Suns	Morehead State	33
	5	Norm Van Lier	Chicago Bulls	St. Francis (Pa.)	34
	6	Charles Bonaparte	San Diego Rockets	Norfolk State	35
	7	Tom Hagan	San Francisco Warriors	Vanderbilt	36
	8	Luther Rackley	Cincinnati Royals	Xavier (Ohio)	37
	9	Julius Keye	Boston Celtics	Alcorn A&M	38
	10	Lloyd Kerr	Phoenix Suns	Colorado State	39
	11	Ed Mast	New York Knicks	Temple	40
	12	Luther Green	Cincinnati Royals	Long Island	41
	13	Mike Grosso	Philadelphia 76ers	Louisville	42
	14	Fred Carter	Baltimore Bullets	Mount St. Mary's	43
FOURTH ROUND	1	Dennis Stewart	Phoenix Suns	Michigan	44
	2	Bob Dandridge	Milwaukee Bucks	Norfolk State	45
	3	Hal Booker	Seattle SuperSonics	Cheyney State	46
	4	Ted Wierman	Detroit Pistons	Washington State	47
	5	Dave Nash	Chicago Bulls	Kansas	48
	6	Johnny Allen	San Diego Rockets	Bethune-Cookman	49
	7	Lee Lafayette	San Francisco Warriors	Michigan State	50
	8	Ron Sanford	Cincinnati Royals	New Mexico	51
	9	Steve Kuberski	Boston Celtics	Bradley	52
	10	Billy Hann	Atlanta Hawks	Tennessee	53
	11	Elnardo Webster	New York Knicks	St. Peter's	54
	12	Don Griffin	Atlanta Hawks	Stanford	55
	13	Dave Scholz	Philadelphia 76ers	Illinois	56
	14	Gene Ford	Baltimore Bullets	Western Michigan	57
FIFTH ROUND	1	Rich Jones	Phoenix Suns	Memphis State	58
	2	Ken Heitz	Milwaukee Bucks	UCLA	59
	3	Jerry King	Seattle SuperSonics	Louisville	60
	4	Steve Mix	Detroit Pistons	Toledo	61
	5	Chris Ellis	Chicago Bulls	Virginia Tech	62
	6	Charles Hentz	San Diego Rockets	Arkansas A&M	63
	7	Willie Wise	San Francisco Warriors	Drake	64
	8	Jake Ford	Cincinnati Royals	Maryland State	65
	9	George Thompson	Boston Celtics	Marquette	66
	10	Mike Mitchell	Atlanta Hawks	West Texas State	67
	11	Gene Littles	New York Knicks	High Point	68
	12	Wilbert Jones	Los Angeles Lakers	Albany State	69
	13	Joe Cromer	Philadelphia 76ers	Temple	70
	14	Willie Jackson	Baltimore Bullets	Morehead State	71
SIXTH ROUND	1	Dan Sadlier	Phoenix Suns	Dayton	72
	2	John Arthurs	Milwaukee Bucks	Tulane	73
	3	Ben McGilmer	Seattle SuperSonics	Iowa	74
	4	Larry Jeffries	Detroit Pistons	Trinity	75
	5	George Tinsley	Chicago Bulls	Kentucky Wesleyan	76
	6	Bob Tallent	San Diego Rockets	George Washington	77
	7	Dan Obravak	San Francisco Warriors	Dayton	78
	8	Mel Coleman	Cincinnati Royals	Stout State	79
	9	Dolph Pulliam	Boston Celtics	Drake	80
	10	Guy Mackner	Atlanta Hawks	South Dakota	81
	11	Dwight Durante	New York Knicks	Catawba	82

		NAME	TEAM	COLLEGE	# OVERALL
	12	Dick Grubar	Los Angeles Lakers	North Carolina	83
	13	John Jones	Philadelphia 76ers	Villanova	84
	14	Paul Loveday	Baltimore Bullets	California	85
SEVENTH ROUND	1	Bill Sweet	Phoenix Suns	UCLA	86
	2	Bill Keller	Milwaukee Bucks	Purdue	87
	3	Greg Wittman	Seattle SuperSonics	Western Carolina	88
	4	Steve Vandenberg	Detroit Pistons	Duke	89
	5	Frank Judge	Chicago Bulls	Houston Tillotson	90
	6	Lynn Shackelford	San Diego Rockets	UCLA	91
	7	Pat Foley	San Francisco Warriors	Pacific	92
	8	L.C. Bowen	Cincinnati Royals	Bradley	93
	9	Jim Johnson	Boston Celtics	Wisconsin	94
	10	Bob Bundy	Atlanta Hawks	Vanderbilt	95
	11	Chris Thomforde	New York Knicks	Princeton	96
	12	Kari Liimbo	Los Angeles Lakers	Brigham Young	97
	13	Dave Hamilton	Philadelphia 76ers	West Virginia State	98
	14	Jeff Claypool	Baltimore Bullets	Grove City	99
EIGHTH ROUND	1	Bob Edwards	Phoenix Suns	Arizona State	100
	2	John Schell	Milwaukee Bucks	Wisconsin	101
	3	Theartis Wallace	Seattle SuperSonics	Central Washington	102
	4	Bob Arnzen	Detroit Pistons	Notre Dame	103
	5	Roger Moller	Chicago Bulls	Westmar	104
	6	Bill DeHeer	San Diego Rockets	Indiana	105
	7	Steve Rippe	San Francisco Warriors	Santa Barbara	106
	8	Merton Bancroft	Cincinnati Royals	SW Missouri State	107
	9	Bob Whitmore	Boston Celtics	Notre Dame	108
	10	Bob Christian	Atlanta Hawks	Grambling	109
	11	Jim Healey	New York Knicks	Rockhurst (Mo.)	110
	12	Joe Smith	Los Angeles Lakers	Oklahoma State	111
	13	Jim Bowles	Philadelphia 76ers	Trinity (Tex.)	112
	14	Barry White	Baltimore Bullets	Hofstra	113
NINTH ROUND	1	Steve Jennings	Phoenix Suns	USC	114
	2	Jim Satalin	Milwaukee Bucks	St. Bonaventure	115
	3	Vince Fritz	Seattle SuperSonics	Oregon State	116
	4	George Reynolds	Detroit Pistons	Houston	117
	5	Sterling Burke	Chicago Bulls	Northwestern	118
	6	Larry Cheatham	San Diego Rockets	Tulsa	119
	7	Greg Reed	San Francisco Warriors	Sacramento State	120
	8	James Hurley	Cincinnati Royals	Transylvania	121
	9	Gordon Smith	Boston Celtics	Cincinnati	122
	10	Pete Gayeska	Atlanta Hawks	Massachusetts	123
	11	Roger Walaszak	New York Knicks	Columbia	124
	12	Jim Smith	Los Angeles Lakers	Northern Illinois	125
	13	Larry Lewis	Philadelphia 76ers	St. Francis (Pa.)	126
	14	Gary Major	Baltimore Bullets	Duquesne	127
TENTH ROUND	1	Rich Abrahamson	Phoenix Suns	Oregon	128
	2	Willie Brown	Milwaukee Bucks	Middle Tennessee	129
	3	Al Cueto	Seattle SuperSonics	Tulsa	130
	4	Bill English	Detroit Pistons	Winston-Salem	131
	5	Al Smith	Chicago Bulls	Bradley	132
	6	Lee Sims	San Diego Rockets	Ashland	133
	7	Dick Chapman	San Francisco Warriors	San Francisco State	134
	8	Bill Bowes	Cincinnati Royals	Elon	135
	9	Jim Picka	Boston Celtics	High Point	136
	10	Dick Stewart	Atlanta Hawks	Rutgers	137
	11	Frank McLaughlin	New York Knicks	Fordham	138
	12	Phil Argento	Los Angeles Lakers	Kentucky	139
	13	Bill Justus	Philadelphia 76ers	Tennessee	140
	14	Frank Bartleson	Baltimore Bullets	Tennessee Tech	141
	1	Fred Lind	Phoenix Suns	Duke	142
	2	Bob Presley	Milwaukee Bucks	California	143
	3	Jim Connolly	Seattle SuperSonics	Bowling Green	144

		NAME	TEAM	COLLEGE	# OVERALL
ELEVENTH ROUND	4	Rusty Clark	Detroit Pistons	North Carolina	145
	5	Larry Bergh	Chicago Bulls	Weber State	146
	6	Justus Thigpen	San Diego Rockets	Weber State	147
	7	Rich Holmberg	San Francisco Warriors	St. Mary's	148
	8	Jim Supple	Cincinnati Royals	Georgetown	149
	9	Larry Frinston	Boston Celtics	Kenyon	150
	10	Loran Bracci	Atlanta Hawks	San Fernando Valley State	151
	11	Marvin Lewis	New York Knicks	Southampton	152
	12	Ron Peret	Los Angeles Lakers	Texas A&M	153
	13	Bruce Sloan	Philadelphia 76ers	Kansas	154
	14	Gerald McKee	Baltimore Bullets	Ohio	155
TWELFTH ROUND	1	Bob Miller	Phoenix Suns	Toledo	156
	2	Jack Lutz	Milwaukee Bucks	Carthage	157
	3	John Smith	Seattle SuperSonics	Puget Sound	158
	4	Harry Hall	Chicago Bulls	Wyoming	159
	5	Raul Duarte	San Diego Rockets	South Dakota State	160
	6	Joe Callahan	San Francisco Warriors	San Francisco State	161
	7	Mike Davis	Cincinnati Royals	Colorado State	162
	8	Rod Forbes	Boston Celtics	Boston State	163
	9	Dave Jones	Atlanta Hawks	LaVerne	164
	10	Bill O'Rourke	New York Knicks	St. John Fisher	165
	11	Jack Gillespie	Los Angeles Lakers	Montana State	166
	12	Roland Taylor	Philadelphia 76ers	La Salle	167
	13	Bob Washington	Baltimore Bullets	Tulsa	168
THIRTEENTH ROUND	1	Andy White	Phoenix Suns	Texas–El Paso	169
	2	Lee Osgood	Milwaukee Bucks	Northeastern	170
	3	Bob Burrow	Seattle SuperSonics	Seattle Pacific	171
	4	Rick Kirkland	Chicago Bulls	Norfolk State	172
	5	Joe McBride	San Diego Rockets	Augusta	173
	6	Ted Johnson	Cincinnati Royals	Baldwin-Wallace	174
	7	Billy Evans	Boston Celtics	Boston College	175
	8	Dick Barton	Atlanta Hawks	Riverside	176
	9	James Wyatt	New York Knicks	NW Louisiana	177
	10	Mallory Chestnutt	Los Angeles Lakers	Tuskegee	178
	11	Bill Thompson	Baltimore Bullets	Shephard	179
FOURTEENTH ROUND	1	Marv Schmitt	Phoenix Suns	West Mexico	180
	2	Laymon Stewart	Milwaukee Bucks	Lakeland	181
	3	Jerry Conley	Seattle SuperSonics	Morehead State	182
	4	Bill Voight	Chicago Bulls	Southern Methodist	183
	5	Mike Heckman	San Diego Rockets	California–Irvine	184
	6	Mike Dahl	Atlanta Hawks	Oglethorpe	185
	7	Rich Travis	New York Knicks	Oklahoma City	186
	8	Mack Calvin	Los Angeles Lakers	USC	187
	9	Perry Johnson	Baltimore Bullets	Robert Morris JC	188
FIFTEENTH ROUND	1	Bob Beamon	Phoenix Suns	Texas–El Paso	189
	2	Stan Wiodarszek	Milwaukee Bucks	La Salle	190
	3	Ernie Powell	Seattle SuperSonics	USC	191
	4	Jerry Nickens	San Diego Rockets	Tougaloo	192
	5	Norm Carmichael	Atlanta Hawks	Virginia	193
	6	Jodie Harrison	Baltimore Bullets	Illinois	194
SIXTEENTH ROUND	1	Wayne Huckel	Phoenix Suns	Davidson	195
	2	Bill Voight	Milwaukee Bucks	Southern Methodist	196
	3	Danny Cornett	Seattle SuperSonics	Morehead State	197
	4	Dick Groves	San Diego Rockets	San Jose State	198
	5	Buddy Cornelius	Atlanta Hawks	Jacksonville (Ala.)	199
	6	Phil Harris	Baltimore Bullets	Texas A&M	200
SEVENTEENTH ROUND	1	Howie Dickenman	Phoenix Suns	Central Connecticut	201
	2	Lynn Phillips	Milwaukee Bucks	Southern Methodist	202
	3	Steve Honeycutt	Seattle SuperSonics	Kansas State	203
	4	Steve Howell	San Diego Rockets	Ohio State	204
	5	John Tolmie	Atlanta Hawks	Navy	205
	6	Tom Haggart	Baltimore Bullets	Brandeis	206
EIGHTEENTH ROUND	1	Al Nuness	Phoenix Suns	Minnesota	207
	2	Ken Hall	Milwaukee Bucks	Westminster	208
	3	Joe Pridgen	San Diego Rockets	North Carolina College	209
	4	Cliff Parsons	Atlanta Hawks	Air Force	210
	5	Chip Case	Baltimore Bullets	Virginia	211
19 ROUND	1	Solomon Davis	Phoenix Suns	Kentucky State	212
	2	Blaine Royer	San Diego Rockets	Illinois State	213
	3	Grady O'Malley	Atlanta Hawks	Manhattan	214
	4	Brian Heaney	Baltimore Bullets	Acadia	215
20 ROUND	1	Jim Plump	Phoenix Suns	Northern Arizona	216
	2	Carl Rodwell	Atlanta Hawks	California–Riverside	217
	3	Stan McKain	Baltimore Bullets	Southern	218

1968

		NAME	TEAM	COLLEGE	# OVERALL
FIRST ROUND	1	Elvin Hayes	San Diego Rockets	Houston	1
	2	Wes Unseld	Baltimore Bullets	Louisville	2
	3	Bob Kauffman	Seattle SuperSonics	Guilford	3
	4	Tom Boerwinkle	Chicago Bulls	Tennessee	4
	5	Don Smith	Cincinnati Royals	Iowa State	5
	6	Otto Moore	Detroit Pistons	Pan American	6
	7	Charles Paulk	Milwaukee Bucks	NE Oklahoma	7
	8	Gary Gregor	Phoenix Suns	South Carolina	8
	9	Ron Williams	San Francisco Warriors	West Virginia	9
	10	Bill Hosket	New York Knicks	Ohio State	10
	11	Bill Hewitt	Los Angeles Lakers	USC	11
	12	Don Chaney	Boston Celtics	Houston	12
	13	Skip Harlicka	Atlanta Hawks	South Carolina	13
	14	Shaler Halimon	Philadelphia 76ers	Utah State	14
SECOND ROUND	1	John Trapp	San Diego Rockets	Nevada–Las Vegas	15
	2	Art Harris	Seattle SuperSonics	Stanford	16
	3	Loy Petersen	Chicago Bulls	Oregon State	17
	4	Bob Quick	Baltimore Bullets	Xavier (Ohio)	18
	5	Ron Dunlap	Chicago Bulls	Illinois	19
	6	Manny Leaks	Detroit Pistons	Niagara	20
	7	Dick Cunningham	Phoenix Suns	Murray State	21
	8	Eugene Moore	Milwaukee Bucks	St. Louis	22
THIRD ROUND	1	Stu Lantz	San Diego Rockets	Nebraska	23
	2	Jeff Ockel	Seattle SuperSonics	Utah	24
	3	Don Dee	Detroit Pistons	St. Mary of the Plains	25
	4	Ron Nelson	Baltimore Bullets	New Mexico	26
	5	Pat Frink	Cincinnati Royals	Colorado	27
	6	Fred Foster	Cincinnati Royals	Miami (Ohio)	28
	7	Don Sidle	San Francisco Warriors	Oklahoma	29
	8	Don May	New York Knicks	Dayton	30
	9	Dave Newmark	Chicago Bulls	Columbia	31
	10	Garfield Smith	Boston Celtics	Eastern Kentucky	32
	11	Jack Thompson	Baltimore Bullets	South Carolina	33
	12	Ed Johnson	Seattle SuperSonics	Tennessee State	34
	13	Sam Williams	Milwaukee Bucks	Iowa	35
	14	Art Beatty	Phoenix Suns	American	36
FOURTH ROUND	1	Harry Barnes	San Diego Rockets	Northeastern	37
	2	Henry Logan	Seattle SuperSonics	Western Carolina	38
	3	Mike Lynn	Chicago Bulls	UCLA	39
	4	Dallas Thornton	Baltimore Bullets	Kentucky Wesleyan	40
	5	Dan Sparks	Cincinnati Royals	Weber State	41
	6	Rich Niemann	Detroit Pistons	St. Louis	42
	7	Edgar Lacy	San Francisco Warriors	UCLA	43
	8	Warren Armstrong	New York Knicks	Wichita State	44
	9	Ed Biedenbach	Los Angeles Lakers	North Carolina State	45
	10	Rich Johnson	Boston Celtics	Grambling	46
	11	Bob Warren	Atlanta Hawks	Vanderbilt	47

		NAME	TEAM	COLLEGE	#OVERALL
	12	Darryl Jones	San Diego Rockets	St. Benedict's	48
	13	Rich Jones	Phoenix Suns	Memphis State	49
	14	Greg Smith	Milwaukee Bucks	Western Kentucky	50
FIFTH ROUND	1	Glen Combs	San Diego Rockets	Virginia Tech	51
	2	Al Hairston	Seattle SuperSonics	Bowling Green	52
	3	Jim Tillman	Chicago Bulls	Loyola (Ill.)	53
	4	Ed Chaplin	Baltimore Bullets	Voorhees	54
	5	Jim Kissane	Cincinnati Royals	Boston College	55
	6	Carl Fuller	Detroit Pistons	Bethune-Cookman	56
	7	Jim Eakins	San Francisco Warriors	Brigham Young	57
	8	Hal Booker	New York Knicks	Cheyney State	58
	9	Lou Shepherd	Los Angeles Lakers	SW Missouri State	59
	10	Thad Jaracz	Boston Celtics	Kentucky	60
	11	Rusty Parker	Atlanta Hawks	Miami (Fla.)	61
	12	Larry Miller	Philadelphia 76ers	North Carolina	62
	13	Joe Franklin	Milwaukee Bucks	Wisconsin	63
	14	Harry Hollines	Phoenix Suns	Denver	64
SIXTH ROUND	1	Eldridge Webb	San Diego Rockets	Tulsa	65
	2	Ron Guziak	Seattle SuperSonics	Duquesne	66
	3	Ken Barnett	Chicago Bulls	Delaware	67
	4	Joe Heiser	Baltimore Bullets	Princeton	68
	5	Calvin Martin	Cincinnati Royals	Texas Southern	69
	6	Wally Anderzunas	Detroit Pistons	Creighton	70
	7	Bob Allen	San Francisco Warriors	Marshall	71
	8	Brian Brunkhorst	New York Knicks	Marquette	72
	9	Nick Pino	Los Angeles Lakers	Kansas State	73
	10	Jerry Newsom	Boston Celtics	Indiana State	74
	11	Phil Wagner	Atlanta Hawks	Georgia Tech	75
	12	Chuck Williams	Philadelphia 76ers	Colorado	76
	13	Rodney Knowles	Phoenix Suns	Davidson	77
	14	Fred Smith	Milwaukee Bucks	Hawaii	78
SEVENTH ROUND	1	Rick Adelman	San Diego Rockets	Loyola (Cal.)	79
	2	Jim McKean	Seattle SuperSonics	Washington State	80
	3	Willie Davis	Chicago Bulls	North Texas State	81
	4	Jasper Wilson	Baltimore Bullets	Southern	82
	5	Rich Dumas	Cincinnati Royals	NE Oklahoma	83
	6	Larry Newbold	Detroit Pistons	Long Island	84
	7	Dave Reasor	San Francisco Warriors	West Virginia	85
	8	Bob Waldal	New York Knicks	Dickinson State	86
	9	Dennis Hrcka	Los Angeles Lakers	Hillsdale	87
	10	Mike Lewis	Boston Celtics	Duke	88
	11	Oscar Smith	Atlanta Hawks	Elizabeth City State	89
	12	Bill Jones	Philadelphia 76ers	Fairfield	90
	13	Tom Kondla	Milwaukee Bucks	Minnesota	91
	14	Charles Parks	Phoenix Suns	Idaho State	92
EIGHTH ROUND	1	Aaron Sellers	San Diego Rockets	Jackson State	93
	2	Willie Rodgers	Seattle SuperSonics	Oklahoma	94
	3	Lloyd Higgins	Chicago Bulls	Pasadena College	95
	4	Barry Orms	Baltimore Bullets	St. Louis	96
	5	Dave Williams	Cincinnati Royals	Mississippi State	97
	6	Harry Laurie	Detroit Pistons	St. Peter's	98
	7	Walt Piatkowski	San Francisco Warriors	Bowling Green	99
	8	Bob Hooper	New York Knicks	Dayton	100
	9	John Smith	Los Angeles Lakers	Southern Colorado	101
	10	Julius Keye	Boston Celtics	Alcorn State	102
	11	Martin Baietti	Atlanta Hawks	Manhattan	103
	12	Melvin Jones	Philadelphia 76ers	Albany State	104
	13	Brian Clare	Phoenix Suns	Denver	105
	14	Elbert Miller	Milwaukee Bucks	UNLV	106
NINTH ROUND	1	John Schetzsle	San Diego Rockets	Ashland	107
	2	Jimmy Smith	Seattle SuperSonics	Utah State	108
	3	Corky Bell	Chicago Bulls	Loyola (Ill.)	109

		NAME	TEAM	COLLEGE	#OVERALL
	4	Wayne Chapman	Baltimore Bullets	Western Kentucky	110
	5	Butch Joyner	Cincinnati Royals	Indiana	111
	6	Vaughn Harper	Detroit Pistons	Syracuse	112
	7	Art Wilmore	San Francisco Warriors	San Francisco	113
	8	Roger Bohnenstiel	New York Knicks	Kansas	114
	9	George Stone	Los Angeles Lakers	Marshall	115
	10	Bill Butler	Boston Celtics	St. Bonaventure	116
	11	Mack Daughtry	Atlanta Hawks	Albany State	117
	12	Clarence Brookins	Philadelphia 76ers	Temple	118
	13	Cliff Berger	Milwaukee Bucks	Kentucky	119
	14	Merv Jackson	Phoenix Suns	Utah	120
TENTH ROUND	1	Mike Butler	San Diego Rockets	Memphis State	121
	2	Joe Kennedy	Seattle SuperSonics	Duke	122
	3	Mike Weaver	Chicago Bulls	Northwestern	123
	4	Steve Adelman	Baltimore Bullets	Boston College	124
	5	Robert Wyendanet	Cincinnati Royals	Vanderbilt	125
	6	Tom Baack	Detroit Pistons	Nebraska	126
	7	Bob Heaney	San Francisco Warriors	Santa Clara	127
	8	Sylvester Adams	New York Knicks	North Carolina A&T	128
	9	Charles Alford	Los Angeles Lakers	East Carolina	129
	10	Ivan Leschinsky	Boston Celtics	Long Island	130
	11	Dwight Waller	Atlanta Hawks	Tennessee State	131
	12	Greg Cisson	Philadelphia 76ers	Rider	132
	13	Lee Davis	Phoenix Suns	North Carolina College	133
	14	Eugene Jones	Milwaukee Bucks	Missouri	134
ELEVENTH ROUND	1	Leonardo Epps	San Diego Rockets	Clark	135
	2	Jim Marsh	Seattle SuperSonics	USC	136
	3	Jim McGonigle	Chicago Bulls	Iowa State	137
	4	Al Dixon	Baltimore Bullets	Bowling Green	138
	5	James Robinson	Cincinnati Royals	Rochester Institute	139
	6	Jerry Chandler	San Francisco Warriors	UNLV	140
	7	Bob Redd	New York Knicks	Marshall	141
	8	Harry Singletary	Los Angeles Lakers	Presbyterian	142
	9	Tom Neimeir	Boston Celtics	Evansville	143
	10	Henry Watkins	Atlanta Hawks	Tennessee State	144
	11	Bill Soens	Philadelphia 76ers	Miami (Fla.)	145
	12	Brad Luchini	Milwaukee Bucks	Marquette	146
	13	Ron Boone	Phoenix Suns	Idaho State	147
TWELFTH ROUND	1	Roy Manning	San Diego Rockets	Lane	148
	2	Walt Simon	Seattle SuperSonics	Utah	149
	3	John Lallensack	Chicago Bulls	Oshkosh State	150
	4	Willie Cager	Baltimore Bullets	Texas Western	151
	5	Glynn Saulters	Cincinnati Royals	Western Louisiana	152
	6	Bob Wolfe	San Francisco Warriors	California	153
	7	Pat Moriarty	New York Knicks	Guilford	154
	8	Reggie Lacefield	Los Angeles Lakers	Western Michigan	155
	9	Bill Langheld	Boston Celtics	Fordham	156
	10	Bill Harris	Atlanta Hawks	Texas Western	157
	11	Ted Campbell	Philadelphia 76ers	North Carolina A&T	158
	12	Dave Miller	Milwaukee Bucks	Florida	159
	13	Bill Davis	Phoenix Suns	Arizona	160
	1	Marshall Evans	San Diego Rockets	Lincoln	161
	2	Bud Ogden	Seattle SuperSonics	Santa Clara	162
	3	Herm Gilliam	Chicago Bulls	Purdue	163
	4	Rudy Bogad	Baltimore Bullets	St. John's	164
	5	Jim Tindell	Cincinnati Royals	Massachusetts	165
	6	Ken Morehead	New York Knicks	Hillside	166
	7	Harvey Mumford	Los Angeles Lakers	Montana State	167
	8	Art Stephenson	Boston Celtics	Rhode Island	168
	9	Frank Standard	Atlanta Hawks	South Carolina	169
	10	Earl Seyfert	Philadelphia 76ers	Kansas State	170
	11	Pat Hobard	Phoenix Suns	Cal State	171

		NAME	TEAM	COLLEGE	# OVERALL
THIRTEENTH ROUND	1	Bobby Lewis	San Diego Rockets	North Carolina State	172
	2	Mike Warren	Seattle SuperSonics	UCLA	173
	3	Dave Carr	Chicago Bulls	Washington	174
	4	Ernest Sims	Baltimore Bullets	East Tennessee	175
	5	Charles Core	Cincinnati Royals	SE Louisiana	176
	6	John Haarlow	New York Knicks	Princeton	177
	7	John Godfrey	Los Angeles Lakers	Abilene Christian	178
	8	Keith Hockstein	Boston Celtics	Holy Cross	179
	9	George Hicker	Atlanta Hawks	Syracuse	180
	10	Tom Youngdale	Philadelphia 76ers	Davidson	181
FOURTEENTH ROUND	1	Bill Gaines	San Diego Rockets	East Texas State	182
	2	Mickey McCarthy	Chicago Bulls	Texas Christian	183
	3	Joe Allen	Baltimore Bullets	Bradley	184
	4	Mike Drepling	Cincinnati Royals	Westminster	185
	5	Ed Fellers	New York Knicks	Guilford	186
	6	John Baum	Los Angeles Lakers	Temple	187
	7	Bernie Foster	Atlanta Hawks	Pasadena	188
	8	George Mack	Philadelphia 76ers	North Carolina A&T	189
FIFTEENTH ROUND	1	Chuck Caldwell	San Diego Rockets	Missouri–St. Louis	190
	2	Fred Holden	Chicago Bulls	Louisville	191
	3	Dennis Blace	Baltimore Bullets	San Francisco	192
	4	Dick Harris	Cincinnati Royals	None	193
	5	Bob Ferguson	New York Knicks	Tennessee Wesleyan	194
	6	Mike Eberle	Los Angeles Lakers	Wyoming	195
	7	Terry Allerton	Atlanta Hawks	Baldwin-Wallace	196
	8	Joe Crews	Philadelphia 76ers	Villanova	197
SIXTEENTH ROUND	1	Dave Miller	San Diego Rockets	South Dakota State	198
	2	Tom Benedict	Chicago Bulls	Central Washington State	199
	3	Greg Morris	Baltimore Bullets	Cornell	200
	4	John Howard	Cincinnati Royals	Cincinnati	201
	5	Milt Williams	New York Knicks	Lincoln	202
	6	Nate Ware	Philadelphia 76ers	Tennessee State	203
17 ROUND	1	Harold Grant	San Diego Rockets	Pepperdine	204
	2	Bob Zoretich	Chicago Bulls	DePaul	205
	3	Art Kenny	Baltimore Bullets	Fairfield	206
	4	Larry Humes	Cincinnati Royals	Evansville	207
18 ROUND	1	Bill Corley	San Diego Rockets	Connecticut	208
	2	Rich Mason	Chicago Bulls	Indiana State	209
	3	Jim LaCour	Baltimore Bullets	Seattle	210
	4	Jay Reffords	Cincinnati Royals	None	211
19 RD	1	Rich Rirkendal	Chicago Bulls	Norfolk State	212
	2	Ron Woodruff	Baltimore Bullets	Midwestern	213
20	1	Willie Horton	Chicago Bulls	Delaware	214

1967

		NAME	TEAM	COLLEGE	# OVERALL
FIRST ROUND	1	Jimmy Walker	Detroit Pistons	Providence	1
	2	Earl Monroe	Baltimore Bullets	Winston-Salem	2
	3	Clem Haskins	Chicago Bulls	Western Kentucky	3
	4	Sonny Dove	Detroit Pistons	St. John's	4
	5	Walt Frazier	New York Knicks	Southern Illinois	5
	6	Al Tucker	Seattle SuperSonics	Oklahoma Baptist	6
	7	Pat Riley	San Diego Rockets	Kentucky	7
	8	Tom Workman	St. Louis Hawks	Seattle	8
	9	Mel Daniels	Cincinnati Royals	New Mexico	9
	10	Dave Lattin	San Francisco Warriors	Texas–El Paso	10
	11	Mal Graham	Boston Celtics	New York University	11
	12	Craig Raymond	Philadelphia 76ers	Brigham Young	12
SECOND ROUND	1	James Jones	Baltimore Bullets	Grambling	13
	2	Steve Sullivan	Detroit Pistons	Georgetown	14
	3	Byron Beck	Chicago Bulls	Denver	15
	4	Randy Mahaffey	Los Angeles Lakers	Clemson	16
	5	Phil Jackson	New York Knicks	North Dakota	17
	6	Bob Netolicky	San Diego Rockets	Drake	18
	7	Bob Rule	Seattle SuperSonics	Colorado State	19
THIRD ROUND	1	Malkin Strong	Baltimore Bullets	Seattle	20
	2	Darrell Hardy	Detroit Pistons	Baylor	21
	3	John Dickson	Chicago Bulls	Arkansas State	22
	4	Dwight Smith	Los Angeles Lakers	Western Kentucky	23
	5	Gary Gregor	New York Knicks	South Carolina	24
	6	Bob Verga	St. Louis Hawks	Duke	25
	7	Gary Gray	Cincinnati Royals	Oklahoma City	26
	8	Bill Turner	San Francisco Warriors	Akron	27
	9	Sam Smith	Cincinnati Royals	Kentucky Wesleyan	28
	10	Richie Moore	San Diego Rockets	Hiram Scott	29
	11	Sam Singleton	Seattle SuperSonics	Omaha	30
	12	Nick Jones	San Diego Rockets	Oregon	31
FOURTH ROUND	1	Al Salvadori	Baltimore Bullets	South Carolina	32
	2	Ron Franz	Detroit Pistons	Kansas	33
	3	Jim Burns	Chicago Bulls	Northwestern	34
	4	Cliff Anderson	Los Angeles Lakers	St. Joseph's	35
	5	Keith Swagerty	New York Knicks	Pacific	36
	6	Wes Bialosuknia	St. Louis Hawks	Connecticut	37
	7	Louie Dampier	Cincinnati Royals	Kentucky	38
	8	Bob Lewis	San Francisco Warriors	North Carolina	39
	9	Neville Shedd	Boston Celtics	Texas Western	40
	10	Ron Kozlicki	San Diego Rockets	Northwestern	41
	11	Craig Dill	San Diego Rockets	Michigan	42
	12	Larry Bunce	Seattle SuperSonics	Utah State	43
FIFTH ROUND	1	Dexter Westbrook	Baltimore Bullets	Providence	44
	2	Paul Long	Detroit Pistons	Wake Forest	45
	3	Dick Pruet	Chicago Bulls	Jacksonville	46
	4	Joe Allen	Los Angeles Lakers	Bradley	47
	5	Barry Leibowitz	New York Knicks	Long Island	48
	6	Mike Wittman	St. Louis Hawks	Miami (Fla.)	49
	7	Tom Washington	Cincinnati Royals	Cheyney State	50
	8	Mike Lynn	San Francisco Warriors	UCLA	51
	9	Mike Redd	Boston Celtics	Kentucky Wesleyan	52
	10	James Reid	Philadelphia 76ers	Winston-Salem	53
	11	Plummer Lott	Seattle SuperSonics	Seattle	54
	12	Herb McPherson	San Diego Rockets	Murray State	55
SIXTH ROUND	1	Bob Reidy	Baltimore Bullets	Duke	56
	2	Vaughn Harper	Detroit Pistons	Syracuse	57
	3	Mal Pradd	Chicago Bulls	Dillard	58
	4	Gary Keller	Los Angeles Lakers	Florida	59
	5	Bob Benfield	New York Knicks	West Virginia	60
	6	John Morrison	St. Louis Hawks	Canisius	61
	7	Frank Stronczek	Cincinnati Royals	American International	62
	8	Dale Schlueter	San Francisco Warriors	Colorado State	63
	9	Ed Hummer	Boston Celtics	Princeton	64
	10	Tim Powers	Philadelphia 76ers	Creighton	65
	11	Robert Cole	San Diego Rockets	St. Louis	66
	12	Gordon Harris	Seattle SuperSonics	Washington	67
SEVENTH ROUND	1	Ron Perry	Baltimore Bullets	VPI	68
	2	Bob Lloyd	Detroit Pistons	Rutgers	69
	3	Bob Wolf	Chicago Bulls	Marquette	70
	4	Jamie Thompson	Los Angeles Lakers	Wichita State	71
	5	Butch Wade	New York Knicks	Indiana State	72
	6	Carl Fuller	St. Louis Hawks	Bethune-Cookman	73
	7	Charles Beasley	Cincinnati Royals	Southern Methodist	74
	8	Sonny Bustion	San Francisco Warriors	Colorado State	75
	9	Edgar Lacy	Boston Celtics	UCLA	76
	10	Frank Card	Philadelphia 76ers	South Carolina State	77
	11	Dick Kolbert	Seattle SuperSonics	Santa Barbara	78

Round		Name	Team	College	# Overall
	12	Elbert Miller	San Diego Rockets	Nevade Southern	79
Eighth Round	1	Ed Manning	Baltimore Bullets	Jackson State Teachers	80
	2	George Carter	Detroit Pistons	St. Bonaventure	81
	3	Leon Simon	Chicago Bulls	Santa Fe	82
	4	Don Carlos	Los Angeles Lakers	Otherbein	83
	5	Gil Radday	New York Knicks	St. Francis	84
	6	Arvesta Kelly	St. Louis Hawks	Lincoln (Mo.)	85
	7	Frank Holloendoner	Cincinnati Royals	Georgetown	86
	8	Bob Krulish	San Francisco Warriors	Pacific	87
	9	Andy Anderson	Boston Celtics	Canisius	88
	10	Jim Conley	Philadelphia 76ers	Virginia	89
	11	Al Grundy	San Diego Rockets	St. Joseph's	90
	12	Willie Wolters	Seattle SuperSonics	Boston College	91
Ninth Round	1	Robert Allen	Baltimore Bullets	Arkansas A&M	92
	2	Ernie Laurent	Chicago Bulls	Albuquerque	93
	3	Jay McMillon	Los Angeles Lakers	Maryland	94
	4	Ray Smith	New York Knicks	Kansas State	95
	5	Ed Biedenbach	St. Louis Hawks	North Carolina State	96
	6	Ron Sepic	Cincinnati Royals	Ohio State	97
	7	Richard Dean	San Francisco Warriors	Syracuse	98
	8	Henry Brown	Boston Celtics	Lowell Tech	99
	9	Ron Filipek	Philadelphia 76ers	Tennessee Tech	100
	10	Rod McDonald	Seattle SuperSonics	Whitworth	101
	11	Ron Coleman	San Diego Rockets	Missouri	102
Tenth Round	1	Bill Gillespie	Baltimore Bullets	Montana State	103
	2	Jim Boshart	Chicago Bulls	Wake Forest	104
	3	Don Kruze	Los Angeles Lakers	Houston	105
	4	Bruce Kaplan	New York Knicks	New York University	106
	5	Rich Falkenbrush	St. Louis Hawks	St. Michael's (Vt.)	107
	6	Willie Davis	Cincinnati Royals	North Texas State	108
	7	Joe Galbo	San Francisco Warriors	San Francisco State	109
	8	Rick Weitzman	Boston Celtics	Northeastern	110
	9	Butch Ervin	Philadelphia 76ers	Niagara	111
	10	John Duncan	San Diego Rockets	Murray State	112
	11	Gary Lechman	Seattle SuperSonics	Gonzaga	113
Eleventh Round	1	Bubba Smith	Baltimore Bullets	Michigan State	114
	2	Jim Andros	Chicago Bulls	New Haven	115
	3	Nick Pino	Los Angeles Lakers	Kansas State	116
	4	Mark Merkin	New York Knicks	North Carolina	117
	5	Ken Callaway	Cincinnati Royals	Cincinnati	118
	6	Bill Morgan	San Francisco Warriors	New Mexico	119
	7	Joe Harrington	Boston Celtics	Maryland	120
	8	Ted Campbell	Philadelphia 76ers	North Carolina A&T	121
	9	Randy Matson	Seattle SuperSonics	Texas A&M	122
	10	Al Razutis	San Diego Rockets	California Western	123
Twelth Round	1	Tony Eatmon	Baltimore Bullets	Pan American	124
	2	George Dalzell	Detroit Pistons	Colgate College	125
	3	Ron Widby	Chicago Bulls	Tennessee	126
	4	Ben Monroe	Los Angeles Lakers	New Mexico	127
	5	Mike Riordan	New York Knicks	Providence	128
	6	Frank Gadjunas	Cincinnati Royals	Villanova	129
	7	David Fox	San Francisco Warriors	Pacific	130
	8	Hubie Marshall	Philadelphia 76ers	La Salle	131
	9	Martin Navia	San Diego Rockets	New Mexico Highlands	132
	10	Rubin Russell	Seattle SuperSonics	North Texas State	133
Thirteenth Round	1	Lyn Burkholder	Baltimore Bullets	South Carolina	134
	2	Matthew Aitch	Detroit Pistons	Michigan State	135
	3	Tom Storm	Chicago Bulls	Montana State	136
	4	Gary Jones	Los Angeles Lakers	Iowa	137
	5	John Moates	Cincinnati Royals	Richmond	138
	6	George Mack	Philadelphia 76ers	North Carolina A&T	139
	7	John Schroeder	Seattle SuperSonics	Ohio	140
	8	Bob Chlupsa	San Diego Rockets	Manhattan	141
Fourteenth Round	1	Paul Mickey	Baltimore Bullets	Penn State	142
	2	Don Whitehead	Chicago Bulls	Erskine	143
	3	Jerry Pettway	Cincinnati Royals	Northwood Institute	144
	4	Wayne Brabender	Philadelphia 76ers	Minnesota–Morris	145
	5	John Toldar	San Diego Rockets	S. Carolina Trade School	146
	6	Jim Sutherland	Seattle SuperSonics	Wake Forest	147
15 Round	1	Rich Peek	Baltimore Bullets	Louisiana Tech	148
	2	Jim Garza	Chicago Bulls	Detroit Tech	149
	3	Earl Beechum	Cincinnati Royals	Midwestern	150
	4	Sherman Dillard	Philadelphia 76ers	Tulsa	151
	5	Willie Campbell	Seattle SuperSonics	Nebraska	152
16 Round	1	Gary Williams	Baltimore Bullets	Oklahoma	153
	2	Jim Dawson	Chicago Bulls	Illinois	154
	3	John Vermelyea	Cincinnati Royals	Morningside	155
	4	Wayne Chapman	Philadelphia 76ers	Western Kentucky	156
17 Round	1	Loy Peterson	Baltimore Bullets	Oregon State	157
	2	Darryll Meachem	Cincinnati Royals	Edinboro State	158
	3	Gary Paulk	Philadelphia 76ers	Oklahoma State	159
18	1	Jerry Southwood	Baltimore Bullets	Vanderbilt	160
19	1	George Spencer	Baltimore Bullets	Washington	161
20	1	Roland West	Baltimore Bullets	Cincinnati	162

1966

Round		Name	Team	College	# Overall
First Round	1	Cazzie Russell	New York Knicks	Michigan	1
	2	Dave Bing	Detroit Pistons	Syracuse	2
	3	Clyde Lee	San Francisco Warriors	Vanderbilt	3
	4	Lou Hudson	St. Louis Hawks	Minnesota	4
	5	Jack Marin	Baltimore Bullets	Duke	5
	6	Walt Wesley	Cincinnati Royals	Kansas	6
	7	Jerry Chambers	Los Angeles Lakers	Utah	7
	8	Jim Barnett	Boston Celtics	Oregon	8
	9	Matt Guokas	Philadelphia 76ers	St. Joseph's (Pa.)	9
	10	Dave Schellhase	Chicago Bulls	Purdue	10
Second Round	1	Henry Akin	New York Knicks	Morehead State	11
	2	Dorie Murrey	Detroit Pistons	Detroit	12
	3	Joe Ellis	San Francisco Warriors	San Francisco	13
	4	Dick Snyder	St. Louis Hawks	Davidson	14
	5	Neil Johnson	Baltimore Bullets	Creighton	15
	6	Jerry Lee Wells	Cincinnati Royals	Oklahoma City	16
	7	Henry Finkel	Los Angeles Lakers	Dayton	17
	8	Leon Clark	Boston Celtics	Wyoming	18
	9	Bill Melchionni	Philadelphia 76ers	Villanova	19
	10	Erwin Mueller	Chicago Bulls	San Francisco	20
Third Round	1	Stewart Johnson	New York Knicks	Murray State	21
	2	Oliver Darden	Detroit Pistons	Michigan	22
	3	Steve Chubin	San Francisco Warriors	Rhode Island	23
	4	Tommy Kron	St. Louis Hawks	Kentucky	24
	5	Dave Wagnon	Baltimore Bullets	Idaho State	25
	6	James Ware	Cincinnati Royals	Oklahoma City	26
	7	John Block	Los Angeles Lakers	USC	27
	8	Gary Turner	Boston Celtics	Texas Christian	28
	9	Don Freeman	Philadelphia 76ers	Illinois	29
	10	Ed Bodkin	Chicago Bulls	Eastern Kentucky	30
Fourth Round	1	Lee DeFore	New York Knicks	Auburn	31
	2	Jeff Congdon	Detroit Pistons	Brigham Young	32
	3	Steve Vacendak	San Francisco Warriors	Duke	33
	4	Bob McIntyre	St. Louis Hawks	St. John's	34
	5	George Peeples	Baltimore Bullets	Iowa	35
	6	Charles Schmaus	Cincinnati Royals	Virginia Military Institute	36
	7	Archie Clark	Los Angeles Lakers	Minnesota	37

		NAME	TEAM	COLLEGE	# OVERALL
	8	John Austin	Boston Celtics	Boston College	38
	9	Ken Wilburn	Philadelphia 76ers	Central State (Ohio)	39
	10	Jim Williams	Chicago Bulls	Temple	40
FIFTH ROUND	1	Ron Jackson	New York Knicks	Clark	41
	2	William Pickens	Detroit Pistons	Georgia Southern	42
	3	Tom Kerwin	San Francisco Warriors	Centenary	43
	4	Dick Nemelka	St. Louis Hawks	Brigham Young	44
	5	John Beasley	Baltimore Bullets	Texas A&M	45
	6	John Jones	Baltimore Bullets	Louisiana State	46
	7	Rick Parks	Cincinnati Royals	St. Louis	47
	8	Stan Washington	Los Angeles Lakers	Michigan State	48
	9	Tom Duff	Philadelphia 76ers	St. Joseph's (Pa.)	49
	10	Larry Humes	Chicago Bulls	Evansville	50
SIXTH ROUND	1	George Fisher	New York Knicks	Utah	51
	2	Carroll Hooser	Detroit Pistons	Southern Methodist	52
	3	Jim Pitts	San Francisco Warriors	Northwestern	53
	4	Lonnie Wright	St. Louis Hawks	Colorado State	54
	5	Jeff Newman	Baltimore Bullets	Penn	55
	6	Steve Cunningham	Cincinnati Royals	Western Kentucky	56
	7	Keith Thomas	Los Angeles Lakers	Vanderbilt	57
	8	Charlie Hunter	Boston Celtics	Oklahoma City	58
	9	Red Robbins	Philadelphia 76ers	Tennessee	59
SEVENTH ROUND	1	Mike Dabich	New York Knicks	New Mexico State	60
	2	Ted Manning	Detroit Pistons	North Carolina College	61
	3	Lon Hughey	San Francisco Warriors	Fresno State	62
	4	Jay Neary	St. Louis Hawks	North Carolina–Wilmington	63
	5	Dave Mills	Baltimore Bullets	DePaul	64
	6	Gary Schull	Cincinnati Royals	Florida State	65
	7	Tab Jackson	Los Angeles Lakers	Idaho College	66
	8	Jerry Ward	Boston Celtics	Maryland	67
	9	John Comeaux	Chicago Bulls	Grambling	68
EIGHTH ROUND	1	Mike Silliman	New York Knicks	Army	69
	2	George McNeil	Detroit Pistons	Southern Illinois	70
	3	Ken Washington	San Francisco Warriors	UCLA	71
	4	Brian Williams	St. Louis Hawks	Xavier (Ohio)	72
	5	Roland West	Baltimore Bullets	Cincinnati	73
	6	Ron Krick	Cincinnati Royals	Cincinnati	74
	7	John Wetzel	Los Angeles Lakers	Virginia Tech	75
	8	Russ Gumina	Boston Celtics	San Francisco	76
	9	Stan Curtis	Chicago Bulls	Northern Michigan	77
NINTH ROUND	1	Bill Turner	New York Knicks	Akron	78
	2	Al Grant	St. Louis Hawks	Long Island	79
	3	Chuck Gardner	Baltimore Bullets	Colorado	80
	4	Billy Smith	Cincinnati Royals	Loyola (Ill.)	81
	5	Julian Hammond	Los Angeles Lakers	Tulsa	82
	6	Pat Caldwell	Philadelphia 76ers	Rockhurst (Mo.)	83
	7	Gene Summers	Chicago Bulls	Northern Michigan	84
TENTH ROUND	1	Rich Moore	New York Knicks	Hiram Scott	85
	2	Don Yates	St. Louis Hawks	Minnesota	86
	3	Guy Manning	Baltimore Bullets	Prairie View	87
	4	Freddie Lewis	Cincinnati Royals	Arizona State	88
	5	Mike Rooney	Los Angeles Lakers	Oklahoma	89
	6	Bob Bedell	Philadelphia 76ers	Stanford	90
	7	Don Swanson	Chicago Bulls	DePaul	91
ELEVENTH ROUND	1	Rich Dyer	New York Knicks	New York University	92
	2	Curt Gammell	St. Louis Hawks	Pacific Lutheran	93
	3	Stan McKenzie	Baltimore Bullets	New York University	94
	4	R.B. Lynam	Cincinnati Royals	Oklahoma Baptist	95
	5	George Grams	Los Angeles Lakers	Purdue	96
	6	Carver Clinton	Chicago Bulls	Penn State	97
12 RD	1	Dave Deutsch	New York Knicks	Rochester	98
	2	Lonnie Lynn	St. Louis Hawks	Wilberforce	99
	3	Grant Simmons	Baltimore Bullets	Nebraska	100
13 ROUND	1	Bob Bennett	New York Knicks	North Carolina	101
	2	Nick Aloi	St. Louis Hawks	Bowling Green	102
	3	Al Lopes	Baltimore Bullets	Kansas	103
14 RD	1	Ollie Carter	St. Louis Hawks	San Francisco	104
	2	Jim Harter	Baltimore Bullets	Pan America	105
15 RD	1	Paul Long	St. Louis Hawks	Wake Forest	106
	2	Howard Bayne	Baltimore Bullets	Tennessee	107
16 RD	1	Eddie Jackson	St. Louis Hawks	Bradley	108
	2	Ken Barnes	Baltimore Bullets	Wisconsin	109
17	1	Chris Pervall	Baltimore Bullets	Iowa	110
18	1	Jerry Trice	Baltimore Bullets	Weber State	111
19	1	Gene Visscher	Baltimore Bullets	Weber State	112

TERRITORIAL DRAFT

To enable teams to take advantage of the regional popularity of college stars, they were given the option of forfeiting their first-round pick and instead selecting, before the start of the draft, a player from the franchise's immediate geographical area. These "territorial picks," as they were known, are listed at the start of each year's draft. The territorial option was in effect through 1965.

1965

		NAME	TEAM	COLLEGE	# OVERALL
TERRIT.	1	Bill Bradley	New York Knicks	Princeton	
	2	Bill Buntin	Detroit Pistons	Michigan	
	3	Gail Goodrich	Los Angeles Lakers	UCLA	
FIRST ROUND	1	Fred Hetzel	San Francisco Warriors	Davidson	1
	2	Rick Barry	San Francisco Warriors	Miami (Fla.)	2
	3	Dave Stallworth	New York Knicks	Wichita State	3
	4	Bill Cunningham	Philadelphia 76ers	North Carolina	4
	5	Jim Washington	St. Louis Hawks	Villanova	5
	6	Nate Bowman	Cincinnati Royals	Wichita State	6
	7	Ollie Johnson	Boston Celtics	San Francisco	7
SECOND ROUND	1	Jerry Sloan	Baltimore Bullets	Evansville	8
	2	Jesse Branson	Philadelphia 76ers	Elon	9
	3	Hal Blevins	New York Knicks	Arkansas A&M	10
	4	Flynn Robinson	Cincinnati Royals	Wyoming	11
	5	John Fairchild	Los Angeles Lakers	Brigham Young	12
	6	Ronnie Watts	Boston Celtics	Wake Forest	13
THIRD ROUND	1	Wilbert Frazier	San Francisco Warriors	Grambling	14
	2	Dick Van Arsdale	New York Knicks	Indiana	15
	3	Tom Van Arsdale	Detroit Pistons	Indiana	16
	4	Tal Brody	Baltimore Bullets	Illinois	17
	5	Bob Weiss	Philadelphia 76ers	Penn State	18
	6	Ken McIntyre	St. Louis Hawks	St. John's	19
	7	Jon McGlocklin	Cincinnati Royals	Indiana	20
	8	Jim Caldwell	Los Angeles Lakers	Georgia Tech	21
	9	Toby Kimball	Boston Celtics	Connecticut	22
FOURTH ROUND	1	Keith Erickson	San Francisco Warriors	UCLA	23
	2	Barry Clemens	New York Knicks	Ohio Wesleyan	24
	3	Ron Reed	Detroit Pistons	Notre Dame	25
	4	Joe Newton	Baltimore Bullets	Auburn	26
	5	Henry Finkel	Philadelphia 76ers	Dayton	27
	6	Lynn Nance	St. Louis Hawks	Washington	28
	7	Bob Love	Cincinnati Royals	Southern	29
	8	Brooks Henderson	Los Angeles Lakers	Florida	30
	9	Richie Tarrant	Boston Celtics	St. Michael's (Vt.)	31
	1	Warren Rustand	San Francisco Warriors	Arizona	32

		NAME	TEAM	COLLEGE	# OVERALL
FIFTH ROUND	2	Larry Lembo	New York Knicks	Manhattan	33
	3	Jim King	Detroit Pistons	Oklahoma State	34
	4	Skip Thoren	Baltimore Bullets	Illinois	35
	5	Richie Moore	Philadelphia 76ers	Villanova	36
	6	Theodore Werner	St. Louis Hawks	Washington State	37
	7	Warren Isaac	Cincinnati Royals	Iona	38
	8	A.W. Davis	Los Angeles Lakers	Tennessee	39
	9	Don Davidson	Boston Celtics	Davidson	40
SIXTH ROUND	1	Eddie Jackson	San Francisco Warriors	Oklahoma City	41
	2	Steve Nisenson	New York Knicks	Hofstra	42
	3	Ted Manning	Detroit Pistons	North Carolina College	43
	4	Charles Dinkens	Baltimore Bullets	Miami (Oh.)	44
	5	Mitch Edwards	Philadelphia 76ers	Pan American	45
	6	John Rambo	St. Louis Hawks	Long Beach College	46
	7	Leon Clements	Cincinnati Royals	Ouachita Baptist	47
	8	Theo Cruz	Los Angeles Lakers	Seattle	48
	9	Haskell Tison	Boston Celtics	Duke	49
SEVENTH ROUND	1	Jim Jarvis	San Francisco Warriors	Oregon State	50
	2	Warren Davis	New York Knicks	North Carolina A&T	51
	3	Barry Smith	Detroit Pistons	High Point	52
	4	Lavonne LeFlore	Baltimore Bullets	Jackson State	53
	5	John Young	Philadelphia 76ers	Midwestern (Tex.)	54
	6	Terry Kunze	St. Louis Hawks	Minnesota	55
	7	Jeff Gehring	Cincinnati Royals	Miami (Ohio)	56
	8	Dwayne Cruze	Los Angeles Lakers	Idaho State	57
	9	George Deehan	Boston Celtics	Lenoir Rhyne	58
EIGHTH ROUND	1	Dan Wolters	San Francisco Warriors	California	59
	2	Dale Neel	New York Knicks	High Point	60
	3	Willie Somerset	Baltimore Bullets	Duquesne	61
	4	Bob Barnek	Philadelphia 76ers	St. Bonaventure	62
	5	Cincy Powell	St. Louis Hawks	Portland	63
	6	Jim Fox	Cincinnati Royals	South Carolina	64
	7	George Unseld	Los Angeles Lakers	Kansas	65
NINTH ROUND	1	Willie Cotton	San Francisco Warriors	Central State	66
	2	Frank Granat	New York Knicks	Alliance	67
	3	Jim Murphy	Baltimore Bullets	DePaul	68
	4	Gene West	Philadelphia 76ers	Drake	69
	5	Leroy Walker	St. Louis Hawks	Utah State	70
	6	Ron Krick	Cincinnati Royals	Cincinnati	71
	7	Marlbert Pradd	Los Angeles Lakers	Dillard	72
TENTH ROUND	1	Jay Neary	New York Knicks	North Carolina–Wilmington	73
	2	John Wendelkin	Baltimore Bullets	Holy Cross	74
	3	Dean Church	Philadelphia 76ers	SW Louisiana	75
	4	Spencer Carlson	St. Louis Hawks	Baylor	76
	5	Richie Dec	Cincinnati Royals	Seton Hall	77
	6	Don Rae	Los Angeles Lakers	Montana State	78
ELEVENTH ROUND	1	Wayne Molis	New York Knicks	Lewis	79
	2	Bogie Redmon	Baltimore Bullets	Illinois	80
	3	Curt Fromal	Philadelphia 76ers	La Salle	81
	4	Weldon Kytle	St. Louis Hawks	Fenn	82
	5	Dick Maile	Cincinnati Royals	Louisiana State	83
	6	Bob Andrews	Los Angeles Lakers	Alabama	84
TWELTH ROUND	1	Bill Meyer	New York Knicks	Hirum Scott	85
	2	Thales McReynolds	Baltimore Bullets	Miles	86
	3	Dan Anderson	Philadelphia 76ers	Augsburg	87
	4	Elton McGriff	St. Louis Hawks	Creighton	88
	5	Robert McCollough	Cincinnati Royals	Benedict	89
THIRTEENTH ROUND	1	Steve Trupin	New York Knicks	Yale	90
	2	Walt Sahm	Baltimore Bullets	Notre Dame	91
	3	Rich Parks	Philadelphia 76ers	Tulsa	92
	4	Mel Northway	St. Louis Hawks	Minnesota	93
	5	Oliver Jones	Cincinnati Royals	Albany State (Ga.)	94
FOURTEENTH ROUND	1	Dennis McGovern	New York Knicks	Rhode Island	95
	2	Joe Ramsey	Baltimore Bullets	Southern Illinois	96
	3	Jack Morgenthal	Philadelphia 76ers	Houston	97
	4	Terry Page	St. Louis Hawks	Detroit	98
	5	Larry Franks	Cincinnati Royals	Texas	99
15 ROUND	1	Jerry Rook	Baltimore Bullets	Arkansas State	100
	2	James Pitts	Philadelphia 76ers	Georgia	101
	3	George Pomey	St. Louis Hawks	Michigan	102
	4	Ronald Scharf	Cincinnati Royals	Georgia Tech	103
16 ROUND	1	Dave Hicks	Baltimore Bullets	New Haven H.S.	104
	2	Larry Rafferty	Philadelphia 76ers	Fairchild	105
	3	Bob Tolan	St. Louis Hawks	Eastern Kentucky	106
	4	Willie Porter	Cincinnati Royals	Tennessee State	107
17	1	Bunk Adams	Baltimore Bullets	Ohio	108
18	1	Roger Taylor	Baltimore Bullets	Illinois	109

1964

		NAME	TEAM	COLLEGE	# OVERALL
TERRIT.	1	George Wilson	Cincinnati Royals	Cincinnati	
	2	Walt Hazzard	Los Angeles Lakers	UCLA	
FIRST ROUND	1	Jim Barnes	New York Knicks	Texas Western	1
	2	Joe Caldwell	Detroit Pistons	Arizona State	2
	3	Gary Bradds	Baltimore Bullets	Ohio State	3
	4	Lucious Jackson	Philadelphia 76ers	Pan American	4
	5	Jeff Mullins	St. Louis Hawks	Duke	5
	6	Barry Kramer	San Francisco Warriors	New York University	6
	7	Mel Counts	Boston Celtics	Oregon State	7
SECOND ROUND	1	Willis Reed	New York Knicks	Grambling	8
	2	Les Hunter	Detroit Pistons	Loyola (Ill.)	9
	3	Paul Silas	St. Louis Hawks	Creighton	10
	4	Ira Harge	Philadelphia 76ers	New Mexico	11
	5	Cotton Nash	Los Angeles Lakers	Kentucky	12
	6	Howard Komives	New York Knicks	Bowling Green	13
	7	Bud Koper	San Francisco Warriors	Oklahoma City	14
	8	Bill Chmielewski	Cincinnati Royals	Dayton	15
	9	Ron Bonham	Boston Celtics	Cincinnati	16
THIRD ROUND	1	Brian Generalovich	New York Knicks	Pittsburgh	17
	2	Wally Jones	Detroit Pistons	Villanova	18
	3	Jerry Sloan	Baltimore Bullets	Evansville	19
	4	Larry Jones	Philadelphia 76ers	Toledo	20
	5	Tom Dose	Los Angeles Lakers	Stanford	21
	6	Art Becker	St. Louis Hawks	Arizona State	22
	7	McCoy McLemore	San Francisco Warriors	Drake	23
	8	Steve Courtin	Cincinnati Royals	St. Joseph's (Pa.)	24
	9	John Thompson	Boston Celtics	Providence	25
FOURTH ROUND	1	Fred Crawford	New York Knicks	St. Bonaventure	26
	2	Jim Davis	Detroit Pistons	Colorado	27
	3	Pete Spoden	Baltimore Bullets	State College of Iowa	28
	4	Frank Corace	Philadelphia 76ers	La Salle	29
	5	Henry Finkel	Los Angeles Lakers	Dayton	30
	6	Willie Murrell	St. Louis Hawks	Kansas State	31
	7	Gene Elmore	San Francisco Warriors	Southern Methodist	32
	8	Happy Hairston	Cincinnati Royals	New York University	33
	9	Joe Strawder	Boston Celtics	Bradley	34
FIFTH ROUND	1	Tony Gennari	New York Knicks	Canisius	35
	2	Ray Wolford	Detroit Pistons	Toledo	36
	3	Bennie Lennox	Baltimore Bullets	Texas A&M	37
	4	Lou Skurcenski	Philadelphia 76ers	Westminster	38
	5	John Savage	Los Angeles Lakers	North Texas State	39
	6	John Tresvant	St. Louis Hawks	Seattle	40
	7	Roger Suttner	San Francisco Warriors	Kansas State	41
	8	George Kirk	Cincinnati Royals	Memphis State	42

Round	#	Name	Team	College	# Overall
	9	Nick Werkman	Boston Celtics	Seton Hall	43
SIXTH ROUND	1	Tom Lavelle	New York Knicks	Western Carolina	44
	2	Larry Phillips	Detroit Pistons	Rice	45
	3	Bobby Joe Edmonds	Baltimore Bullets	Tennessee State	46
	4	Ricky Kaminsky	Philadelphia 76ers	Yale	47
	5	Troy Collier	Los Angeles Lakers	Utah State	48
	6	Ernest Brock	St. Louis Hawks	Virginia State	49
	7	Ray Carey	San Francisco Warriors	Missouri	50
	8	Al Thresher	Cincinnati Royals	Wittenberg	51
	9	Levern Tart	Boston Celtics	Bradley	52
SEVENTH ROUND	1	Emmette Bryant	New York Knicks	DePaul	53
	2	Jerry Jackson	Detroit Pistons	Ohio	54
	3	Ron Miller	Baltimore Bullets	Loyola (Ill.)	55
	4	Gordon Hatton	Philadelphia 76ers	Dayton	56
	5	Steve Anstett	Los Angeles Lakers	Portland	57
	6	Maurice McHartley	St. Louis Hawks	North Carolina A&T	58
	7	Dave Lee	San Francisco Warriors	San Francisco	59
	8	Vic Rouse	Cincinnati Royals	Loyola (Ill.)	60
	9	Rich Falk	Boston Celtics	Northwestern	61
EIGHTH ROUND	1	Jim Boutin	New York Knicks	Lewis & Clark	62
	2	Ralph Telken	Detroit Pistons	Rockhurst (Mo.)	63
	3	Danny Schultz	Baltimore Bullets	Tennessee	64
	4	Bob Pelkington	Philadelphia 76ers	Xavier (Ohio)	65
	5	Jay Buckley	Los Angeles Lakers	Duke	66
	6	Kendall Rhine	St. Louis Hawks	Rice	67
	7	Bob Garibaldi	San Francisco Warriors	Santa Clara	68
	8	Joe Gieger	Cincinnati Royals	Xavier (Ohio)	69
	9	Jeff Blue	Boston Celtics	Butler	70
NINTH ROUND	1	Jack Brens	New York Knicks	Wisconsin	71
	2	Tom Black	Baltimore Bullets	South Dakota State	72
	3	Jim Brennan	Philadelphia 76ers	Clemson	73
	4	Darel Carrier	St. Louis Hawks	Western Kentucky	74
	5	Camden Wail	San Francisco Warriors	California	75
	6	Scotty Pierce	Cincinnati Royals	West Texas State	76
	7	Charles Kelley	Boston Celtics	West Virginia Tech	77
TENTH ROUND	1	Jim Christie	New York Knicks	Georgetown	78
	2	Bill Kusleika	Baltimore Bullets	Tulsa	79
	3	Wally Briggs	Philadelphia 76ers	North Carolina A&M	80
	4	Frank Stephens	St. Louis Hawks	Virginia State	81
	5	Jeff Cartwright	San Francisco Warriors	Chapman	82
	6	Bob Neumann	Cincinnati Royals	Memphis State	83
	7	Duane Corribeau	Boston Celtics	Clark	84
ELEVENTH ROUND	1	Dennis Lynch	New York Knicks	Yale	85
	2	Fred Glover	Baltimore Bullets	Winston-Salem	86
	3	Thomas Lowry	Philadelphia 76ers	West Virginia	87
	4	Gerry Goran	St. Louis Hawks	St. Mary of the Plains	88
	5	Jim Reynolds	Cincinnati Royals	Abilene Christian	89
12 ROUND	1	Frank Kamiaski	Baltimore Bullets	Randolph-Macon	90
	2	Julius Myers	Philadelphia 76ers	Morris Brown	91
	3	Warren Sutton	St. Louis Hawks	George Williams	92
	4	Fred Jones	Cincinnati Royals	Youngstown	93
13 RD	1	Doug Moon	Baltimore Bullets	Utah	94
	2	Cecil Tuttle	St. Louis Hawks	Georgetown (Ky.)	95
14 RD	1	Pete Gent	Baltimore Bullets	Michigan State	96
	2	Bill Blair	St. Louis Hawks	Virginia Military Institute	97
15 RD	1	Sandy Williams	Baltimore Bullets	St. Francis (Pa.)	98
	2	Al Cech	St. Louis Hawks	Detroit	99

1963

Round	#	Name	Team	College	# Overall
TER.	1	Tom Thacker	Cincinnati Royals	Cincinnati	
1 RD	1	Art Heyman	New York Knicks	Duke	1
	2	Rod Thorn	Baltimore Bullets	West Virginia	2
	3	Nate Thurmond	San Francisco Warriors	Bowling Green	3
	4	Ed Miles	Detroit Pistons	Seattle	4
	5	Gerry Ward	St. Louis Hawks	Boston College	5
	6	Tom Hoover	Syracuse Nationals	Villanova	6
	7	Roger Strickland	Los Angeles Lakers	Jacksonville	7
	8	Bill Green	Boston Celtics	Colorado State	8
SECOND ROUND	1	Jerry Harkness	New York Knicks	Loyola (Ill.)	9
	2	Gus Johnson	Baltimore Bullets	Idaho	10
	3	Gary Hill	San Francisco Warriors	Oklahoma City	11
	4	Jerry Smith	Detroit Pistons	Furman	12
	5	Jim King	Los Angeles Lakers	Tulsa	13
	6	Leland Mitchell	St. Louis Hawks	Mississippi State	14
	7	Hershell West	Syracuse Nationals	Grambling	15
	8	Mel Gibson	Los Angeles Lakers	Western Carolina	16
	9	Ken Saylors	St. Louis Hawks	Arkansas Tech	17
THIRD ROUND	1	Bill O'Connor	New York Knicks	Canisius	18
	2	Tom Bolyard	Baltimore Bullets	Indiana	19
	3	Steve Gray	San Francisco Warriors	St. Mary's (Cal.)	20
	4	Mike McCoy	Detroit Pistons	Miami (Fla.)	21
	5	Jimmy Rayl	Cincinnati Royals	Indiana	22
	6	Bill Burwell	St. Louis Hawks	Illinois	23
	7	Jerry Greenspan	Syracuse Nationals	Maryland	24
	8	Lyle Harger	Los Angeles Lakers	Houston	25
	9	Chuck Kriston	Boston Celtics	Valparaiso	26
FOURTH ROUND	1	Nate Cloud	New York Knicks	Delaware	27
	2	Nolen Ellison	Baltimore Bullets	Kansas	28
	3	Dave Downey	San Francisco Warriors	Illinois	29
	4	Dave Erickson	Detroit Pistons	Marquette	30
	5	Ken Charlton	Cincinnati Royals	Colorado	31
	6	Waite Bellamy	St. Louis Hawks	Florida A&M	32
	7	Ray Flynn	Syracuse Nationals	Providence	33
	8	Layton Johns	Los Angeles Lakers	Auburn	34
	9	Connie McGuire	Boston Celtics	SE Oklahoma	35
FIFTH ROUND	1	Joe McDermott	New York Knicks	Belmont Abbey	36
	2	Ron Glaser	Baltimore Bullets	Marquette	37
	3	Don Turner	San Francisco Warriors	SW Kansas	38
	4	Bill Small	Detroit Pistons	Illinois	39
	5	Mac Herndon	Cincinnati Royals	Bradley	40
	6	Tony Yates	St. Louis Hawks	Cincinnati	41
	7	Tony Cerkvenik	Syracuse Nationals	Arizona State	42
	8	Larry Jones	Los Angeles Lakers	Toledo	43
	9	W.D. Stroud	Boston Celtics	Mississippi State	44
SIXTH ROUND	1	Jim Kerwin	New York Knicks	Tulane	45
	2	Ken Siebel	Baltimore Bullets	Wisconsin	46
	3	Gene Shields	San Francisco Warriors	Santa Clara	47
	4	Reggie Harding	Detroit Pistons	Detroit Eastern H.S.	48
	5	Jim McCormack	Cincinnati Royals	West Virginia	49
	6	Al Santio	St. Louis Hawks	Maryland State	50
	7	Vince Brewer	Syracuse Nationals	Iowa State	51
	8	Warren Salade	Los Angeles Lakers	Westminster	52
	9	Vinnie Ernst	Boston Celtics	Providence	53
SEVENTH ROUND	1	Bob Woollard	New York Knicks	Wake Forest	54
	2	Larry Brown	Baltimore Bullets	North Carolina	55
	3	Don Clemetson	San Francisco Warriors	Stanford	56
	4	Ira Harge	Detroit Pistons	New Mexico	57
	5	Hunter Beckman	Cincinnati Royals	Memphis State	58
	6	Ken Rohloff	St. Louis Hawks	North Carolina State	59
	7	Bill Brown	Syracuse Nationals	Howard Payne	60
	8	Gordie Martin	Los Angeles Lakers	USC	61
	9	Herb Magee	Boston Celtics	Philadelphia Textile	62
	1	Fred Crawford	New York Knicks	St. Bonaventure	63

ROUND		NAME	TEAM	COLLEGE	# OVERALL
EIGHTH ROUND	2	Dick Riesback	Baltimore Bullets	Iowa State	64
	3	Harry Dinnell	San Francisco Warriors	Pepperdine	65
	4	Gary Silc	Detroit Pistons	Northern Michigan	66
	5	Harold Strothers	St. Louis Hawks	Texas A&M	67
NINTH ROUND	1	Ray Cronk	New York Knicks	Lakeland	68
	2	Ron Jackson	Baltimore Bullets	Wisconsin	69
	3	Chuck White	San Francisco Warriors	Idaho	70
	4	Ernie Durston	Detroit Pistons	Seattle	71
	5	Frank Davis	St. Louis Hawks	Oklahoma Christian	72
10 RD	1	Gerald Glur	New York Knicks	Furman	73
	2	M.C. Thompson	Baltimore Bullets	DePaul	74
	3	Carl Ritter	St. Louis Hawks	SE Missouri State	75
11 RD	1	Orb Bowling	New York Knicks	Tennessee	76
	2	Marv Straw	St. Louis Hawks	Iowa State	77
12 RD	1	Bob Walters	New York Knicks	Baldwin-Wallace	78
	2	Hugh Evans	St. Louis Hawks	North Carolina A&T	79
13 RD	1	Jerry Szachara	New York Knicks	Cornell	80
	2	Gary McFarland	St. Louis Hawks	Central Missouri State	81
14	1	Bill Raftery	New York Knicks	La Salle	82
15	1	Ron Pickett	New York Knicks	Eastern Kentucky	83

1962

ROUND		NAME	TEAM	COLLEGE	# OVERALL
TERRIT.	1	Dave DeBusschere	Detroit Pistons	Detroit	
	2	Jerry Lucas	Cincinnati Royals	Ohio State	
FIRST ROUND	1	Bill McGill	Chicago Zephyrs	Utah	1
	2	Paul Hogue	New York Knicks	Cincinnati	2
	3	Zelmo Beaty	St. Louis Hawks	Prairie View	3
	4	Len Chappell	Syracuse Nationals	Wake Forest	4
	5	Wayne Hightower	Philadelphia Warriors	Kansas	5
	6	Leroy Ellis	Los Angeles Lakers	St. John's	6
	7	John Havlicek	Boston Celtics	Ohio State	7
SECOND ROUND	1	Terry Dischinger	Chicago Zephyrs	Purdue	8
	2	John Rudometkin	New York Knicks	USC	9
	3	Bob Duffy	St. Louis Hawks	Colgate	10
	4	Kevin Loughery	Detroit Pistons	St. John's	11
	5	Chet Walker	Syracuse Nationals	Bradley	12
	6	Bud Olsen	Cincinnati Royals	Louisville	13
	7	Hubie White	Philadelphia Warriors	Villanova	14
	8	Gene Wiley	Los Angeles Lakers	Wichita State	15
	9	Jack Foley	Boston Celtics	Holy Cross	16
THIRD ROUND	1	Don Nelson	Chicago Zephyrs	Iowa	17
	2	Bobby Rascoe	New York Knicks	Western Kentucky	18
	3	Charles Hardnett	St. Louis Hawks	Grambling	19
	4	Harold Hudgens	Detroit Pistons	Texas Tech	20
	5	Porter Meriwether	Syracuse Nationals	Tennessee State	21
	6	Chris Appel	Cincinnati Royals	USC	22
	7	Dave Fedor	Philadelphia Warriors	Florida State	23
	8	John Green	Los Angeles Lakers	UCLA	24
	9	Jim Hadnot	Boston Celtics	Providence	25
FOURTH ROUND	1	Charles Vaughn	St. Louis Hawks	Southern Illinois	26
	2	Cliff Luyk	New York Knicks	Florida	27
	3	Jerry Grote	St. Louis Hawks	Loyola (Cal.)	28
	4	Reggie Harding	Detroit Pistons	Detroit Eastern H.S.	29
	5	Bob McCully	Syracuse Nationals	St. Bonaventure	30
	6	Jack Thobe	Cincinnati Royals	Xavier (Ohio)	31
	7	Garry Roggenburk	Philadelphia Warriors	Dayton	32
	8	Jan Loudermilk	Los Angeles Lakers	Southern Methodist	33
	9	Roger Strickland	Boston Celtics	Jacksonville	34
FIFTH ROUND	1	Cornell Green	Chicago Zephyrs	Utah State	35
	2	Bob Burgess	New York Knicks	Marshall	36
	3	Tom Hatton	St. Louis Hawks	Dayton	37
	4	Lindbergh Moody	Detroit Pistons	South Carolina	38
	5	John Windsor	Syracuse Nationals	Stanford	39
	6	Mike Wroblewski	Cincinnati Royals	Kansas State	40
	7	Jack Jackson	Philadelphia Warriors	Virginia Union	41
	8	Art Whisnant	Los Angeles Lakers	South Carolina	42
	9	Gary Daniels	Boston Celtics	Citadel	43
SIXTH ROUND	1	Bill Hanson	Chicago Zephyrs	Washington	44
	2	Ken Stanley	New York Knicks	Pacific	45
	3	Jay Carty	St. Louis Hawks	Oregon State	46
	4	Ed Noe	Detroit Pistons	Morehead State	47
	5	Larry Van Eman	Syracuse Nationals	Wichita State	48
	6	Jerry Foster	Cincinnati Royals	Drake	49
	7	Jim Hudock	Philadelphia Warriors	North Carolina	50
	8	Bucky Keller	Los Angeles Lakers	Virginia Tech	51
	9	Jim Hooley	Boston Celtics	Boston College	52
SEVENTH ROUND	1	Jack Ardon	Chicago Zephyrs	Tulane	53
	2	Richie Swartz	New York Knicks	Hofstra	54
	3	Bob McAteer	St. Louis Hawks	La Salle	55
	4	John Bradley	Detroit Pistons	Lawrence Tech.	56
	5	Bob Sharpenter	Syracuse Nationals	Georgetown	57
	6	Gary Cunningham	Cincinnati Royals	UCLA	58
	7	Howard Montgomery	Philadelphia Warriors	Pan American	59
	8	Clyde Arnold	Boston Celtics	Duquesne	60
EIGHTH ROUND	1	Larry Pursiful	Chicago Zephyrs	Kentucky	61
	2	Warren Fouts	New York Knicks	Oklahoma	62
	3	Terry Ball	St. Louis Hawks	Washington State	63
	4	Mike Rice	Detroit Pistons	Duquesne	64
	5	Jerry Harkness	Syracuse Nationals	Loyola (Ill.)	65
	6	Ed Bento	Cincinnati Royals	Loyola (Cal.)	66
	7	Bill Kirvin	Philadelphia Warriors	Xavier (Ohio)	67
	8	Bill Garner	Los Angeles Lakers	Portland	68
	9	Chuck Chevalier	Boston Celtics	Boston College	69
NINTH ROUND	1	Carroll Broussard	Chicago Zephyrs	Texas A&M	70
	2	Paul Benec	New York Knicks	Duquesne	71
	3	Marvin Trotman	St. Louis Hawks	Elizabeth City State	72
	4	Bill Nelson	Detroit Pistons	Hamline	73
	5	Vince Brewer	Syracuse Nationals	Iowa State	74
	6	Chris Jones	Cincinnati Royals	Carson-Newman	75
	7	Tom Kiefer	Philadelphia Warriors	St. Louis	76
	8	Bill Matson	Los Angeles Lakers	Minnesota	77
	9	Mike Cingiser	Boston Celtics	Brown	78
TENTH ROUND	1	Pete Campbell	Chicago Zephyrs	Princeton	79
	2	Ralph Richardson	New York Knicks	Eastern Kentucky	80
	3	Charlie Sells	St. Louis Hawks	Washington State	81
	4	Glenn Moore	Detroit Pistons	Oregon	82
	5	George Knighton	Cincinnati Royals	New Mexico State	83
	6	Ken McComb	Philadelphia Warriors	North Carolina	84
ELEVENTH ROUND	1	Jeff Slade	Chicago Zephyrs	Kenyon	85
	2	Ed Mazria	New York Knicks	Pratt	86
	3	Tom Chappelle	St. Louis Hawks	Maine	87
	4	Frank Pinchback	Cincinnati Royals	Xavier (Ohio)	88
	5	Donnie Walsh	Philadelphia Warriors	North Carolina	89
12 ROUND	1	Mel Nowell	Chicago Zephyrs	Ohio State	90
	2	John Caveny	St. Louis Hawks	LeMoyne	91
	3	Charles Warren	Philadelphia Warriors	Oregon	92
13 RD	1	Tom Kennedy	Chicago Zephyrs	Lewis	93
	2	Jerry Carlton	St. Louis Hawks	Arkansas	94
14 RD	1	Bob Mahland	Chicago Zephyrs	Williams	95
	2	Wilky Gilmore	St. Louis Hawks	Colorado	96
15 RD	1	Pat McKenzie	Chicago Zephyrs	Kansas State	97
	2	Dave Ricerto	St. Louis Hawks	Rhode Island	98
16 RD	1	Norman Majors	Chicago Zephyrs	Rockhurst (Mo.)	99

Round		NAME	TEAM	COLLEGE	# OVERALL
	2	Wally Roundsville	St. Louis Hawks	California Tech	100

1961

Round		NAME	TEAM	COLLEGE	# OVERALL
FIRST ROUND	1	Walt Bellamy	Chicago Packers	Indiana	1
	2	Tom Stith	New York Knicks	St. Bonaventure	2
	3	Larry Siegfried	Cincinnati Royals	Ohio State	3
	4	Ray Scott	Detroit Pistons	Portland	4
	5	Wayne Yates	Los Angeles Lakers	Memphis State	5
	6	Ben Warley	Syracuse Nationals	Tennessee State	6
	7	Tom Meschery	Philadelphia Warriors	St. Mary's (Cal.)	7
	8	Cleo Hill	St. Louis Hawks	Winston-Salem	8
	9	Gary Phillips	Boston Celtics	Houston	9
SECOND ROUND	1	Ronald Martin	New York Knicks	St. Bonaventure	10
	2	Bob Wiesenhahn	Cincinnati Royals	Cincinnati	11
	3	Johnny Egan	Detroit Pistons	Providence	12
	4	Fred Sawyer	Los Angeles Lakers	Louisville	13
	5	Chris Smith	Syracuse Nationals	Virginia Tech	14
	6	Ted Luckenbill	Philadelphia Warriors	Houston	15
	7	Ron Horn	St. Louis Hawks	Indiana	16
	8	Al Butler	Boston Celtics	Niagara	17
	9	John Turner	Chicago Packers	Louisville	18
	10	Jerry Graves	Chicago Packers	Mississippi State	19
	11	York Larese	Chicago Packers	North Carolina	20
	12	Don Kojis	Chicago Packers	Marquette	21
	13	Doug Moe	Chicago Packers	North Carolina	22
	14	Jeff Cohen	Chicago Packers	William & Mary	23
THIRD ROUND	1	Tony Jackson	New York Knicks	St. John's	24
	2	Bob Nordmann	Cincinnati Royals	St. Louis	25
	3	Doug Kistler	Detroit Pistons	Duke	26
	4	Frank Burgess	Los Angeles Lakers	Gonzaga	27
	5	Charles Osborne	Syracuse Nationals	Western Kentucky	28
	6	Jack Egan	Philadelphia Warriors	St. Joseph's (Pa.)	29
	7	Tom Chilton	St. Louis Hawks	East Tennessee	30
	8	Bill Depp	Boston Celtics	Vanderbilt	31
	9	Bill Bridges	Chicago Packers	Kansas	32
FOURTH ROUND	1	George Blaney	New York Knicks	Holy Cross	33
	2	Lowery Kirk	Cincinnati Royals	Memphis State	34
	3	George Finley	Detroit Pistons	Tennessee A&I	35
	4	Charles Henke	Los Angeles Lakers	Missouri	36
	5	Henry Whitney	Syracuse Nationals	Iowa State	37
	6	John Tidwell	Philadelphia Warriors	Michigan	38
	7	Gus Guydon	St. Louis Hawks	Drake	39
	8	Carl Cole	Boston Celtics	Eastern Kentucky	40
	9	Roger Kaiser	Chicago Packers	Georgia Tech	41
FIFTH ROUND	1	Bill Smith	New York Knicks	St. Peter's	42
	2	Rossie Johnson	Cincinnati Royals	Tennessee A&I	43
	3	Dan Doyle	Detroit Pistons	Belmont Abbey	44
	4	Bill Lickert	Los Angeles Lakers	Kentucky	45
	5	Don Jacobson	Syracuse Nationals	South Dakota	46
	6	Bruce Spraggins	Philadelphia Warriors	Virginia Union	47
	7	John Berberich	St. Louis Hawks	UCLA	48
	8	Bob DiStefano	Boston Celtics	North Carolina State	49
	9	Howie Carl	Chicago Packers	DePaul	50
SIXTH ROUND	1	Cleveland Buckner	New York Knicks	Jackson State	51
	2	Bob Slobodnik	Cincinnati Royals	Duquesne	52
	3	Lee Patrone	Detroit Pistons	West Virginia	53
	4	Bill McClintock	Los Angeles Lakers	California	54
	5	Billy Joe Price	Syracuse Nationals	New Mexico State	55
	6	Dick Goldberg	Philadelphia Warriors	Mississippi Southern	56
	7	Bob McDonald	St. Louis Hawks	Maryland	57
	8	Ned Twyman	Boston Celtics	Duquesne	58
	9	Dave Voss	Chicago Packers	Tulsa	59
SEVENTH ROUND	1	Donnis Butcher	New York Knicks	Pikeville	60
	2	Dave Zeller	Cincinnati Royals	Miami (Ohio)	61
	3	Burt Price	Detroit Pistons	Wittenberg	62
	4	Albert Alamanza	Los Angeles Lakers	Texas	63
	5	Roger Newman	Syracuse Nationals	Kentucky	64
	6	Charles McNeil	Philadelphia Warriors	Maryland	65
	7	Charles Riley	St. Louis Hawks	Winston-Salem	66
	8	Mel Klein	Boston Celtics	Aberdeen	67
	9	Ron Heller	Chicago Packers	Wichita	68
EIGHTH ROUND	1	Cedrick Price	New York Knicks	Kansas State	69
	2	Jerry Thelen	Cincinnati Royals	Villa Madonna	70
	3	Walter Ward	Detroit Pistons	Hampton Institute	71
	4	Bill Ellis	Los Angeles Lakers	UCLA	72
	5	Dave Mills	Syracuse Nationals	Seattle	73
	6	Larry Swift	Philadelphia Warriors	NE Missouri State	74
	7	Gene Velloff	St. Louis Hawks	Doane	75
	8	John Wessels	Chicago Packers	Illinois	76
NINTH ROUND	1	Charles Bowman	New York Knicks	Wabash	77
	2	Larry Krueger	Cincinnati Royals	Ohio	78
	3	Peter Baltic	Detroit Pistons	Penn State	79
	4	Carl Anderson	Los Angeles Lakers	Oregon State	80
	5	Rex Tippitt	Syracuse Nationals	Grambling	81
	6	Herbert Gray	St. Louis Hawks	North Carolina A&T	82
	7	Steve Strange	Chicago Packers	Southern Methodist	83
TENTH ROUND	1	Ron Debillous	New York Knicks	Wisconsin State Teachers	84
	2	Jack Waters	Cincinnati Royals	Mississippi	85
	3	Wayne Monson	Detroit Pistons	Northern Michigan	86
	4	Robert Williams	Los Angeles Lakers	Hancock	87
	5	Pete Chudy	Syracuse Nationals	Syracuse	88
	6	Leo Hill	Philadelphia Warriors	Cal State–Los Angeles	89
	7	Tom Faszholz	St. Louis Hawks	Concordia (Mo.)	90
	8	Larry Comley	Chicago Packers	Kansas State	91
ELEVENTH ROUND	1	Kevin Loughery	New York Knicks	St. John's	92
	2	Carl Short	Cincinnati Royals	Newberry	93
	3	Richard Kraft	Detroit Pistons	Brockport	94
	4	Howard Hunt	Los Angeles Lakers	Duke	95
	5	Dick Sammons	Syracuse Nationals	LeMoyne	96
	6	Corky Whitrow	Philadelphia Warriors	Georgetown (Ky.)	97
	7	Dick Kepley	St. Louis Hawks	North Carolina	98
12 RD	1	Earl Shultz	New York Knicks	California	99
	2	George Patterson	Cincinnati Royals	Toledo	100
	3	Jackie Crawford	St. Louis Hawks	Centenary	101
13 RD	1	Ned Jennings	New York Knicks	Kentucky	102
	2	Clair McRoberts	Cincinnati Royals	Monmouth	103
	3	Howard Stacy	St. Louis Hawks	Louisville	104
14 RD	1	Bill Engressor	New York Knicks	Louisiana State	105
	2	Carl Bouldin	Cincinnati Royals	Cincinnati	106
15	1	Vince Kempton	New York Knicks	St. Joseph's (Pa.)	107

1960

Round		NAME	TEAM	COLLEGE	# OVERALL
FIRST ROUND	1	Oscar Robertson	Cincinnati Royals	Cincinnati	1
	2	Jerry West	Minneapolis Lakers	West Virginia	2
	3	Darrall Imhoff	New York Knicks	California	3
	4	Jack Moreland	Detroit Pistons	Louisiana Tech	4
	5	Lee Shaffer	Syracuse Nationals	North Carolina	5
	6	Lenny Wilkens	St. Louis Hawks	Providence	6
	7	Al Bunge	Philadelphia Warriors	Maryland	7
	8	Tom Sanders	Boston Celtics	New York University	8
	1	Jay Arnette	Cincinnati Royals	Texas	9
	2	Dave Budd	New York Knicks	Wake Forest	10

		NAME	TEAM	COLLEGE	# OVERALL
SECOND ROUND	3	Kelly Coleman	New York Knicks	Kentucky Wesleyan	11
	4	Ron Johnson	Detroit Pistons	Minnesota	12
	5	Wilbur Trosch	Syracuse Nationals	St. Francis (Pa.)	13
	6	Frank Radovich	St. Louis Hawks	Indiana	14
	7	Bill Kennedy	Philadelphia Warriors	Temple	15
	8	Leroy Wright	Boston Celtics	College of Pacific	16
THIRD ROUND	1	Ralph Davis	Cincinnati Royals	Cincinnati	17
	2	Jim Hagan	Minneapolis Lakers	Tennessee Tech	18
	3	Bob McNeill	New York Knicks	St. Joseph's (Pa.)	19
	4	Frank Case	Detroit Pistons	Dayton	20
	5	Joe Roberts	Syracuse Nationals	Ohio State	21
	6	Fred LaLour	St. Louis Hawks	San Francisco	22
	7	Bob Mealy	Philadelphia Warriors	Manhattan	23
	8	Mike Graney	Boston Celtics	Notre Dame	24
FOURTH ROUND	1	Dalen Showalter	Cincinnati Royals	Tennessee	25
	2	Wally Frank	Minneapolis Lakers	Kansas State	26
	3	Ben Warley	Minneapolis Lakers	Tennessee A&I	27
	4	Ken Remley	Detroit Pistons	West Virginia Wesleyan	28
	5	Carl Cole	Syracuse Nationals	Eastern Kentucky	29
	6	Horace Walker	St. Louis Hawks	Michigan State	30
	7	Charley Sharp	Philadelphia Warriors	Southwest Texas	31
	8	Sid Cohen	Boston Celtics	Kentucky	32
FIFTH ROUND	1	Don Ogorek	Cincinnati Royals	Seattle	33
	2	George Farley	Minneapolis Lakers	Cornell	34
	3	Charley McNeil	New York Knicks	Maryland	35
	4	Willie Jones	Detroit Pistons	Northwestern	36
	5	Jim Mudd	Syracuse Nationals	North Texas State	37
	6	Jim Darrow	St. Louis Hawks	Bowling Green	38
	7	Al Attles	Philadelphia Warriors	North Carolina A&T	39
	8	Wayne Lawrence	Boston Celtics	Texas A&M	40
SIXTH ROUND	1	Bobby Joe Mason	Cincinnati Royals	Bradley	41
	2	Bobby Goodall	Minneapolis Lakers	Tulsa	42
	3	David Denton	New York Knicks	Georgia Tech	43
	4	Bill Lowry	Detroit Pistons	Christian Brothers	44
	5	Herschell Turner	Syracuse Nationals	Nebraska	45
	6	York Larese	St. Louis Hawks	North Carolina	46
	7	Jim Brangan	Philadelphia Warriors	Princeton	47
	8	George Newman	Boston Celtics	Kentucky	48
SEVENTH ROUND	1	Fred Sobrero	Cincinnati Royals	Santa Clara	49
	2	Howard Jolliff	Minneapolis Lakers	Ohio	50
	3	Dick Doughty	New York Knicks	California	51
	4	Doug Moe	Detroit Pistons	North Carolina	52
	5	Bernie Kauffman	Syracuse Nationals	Kentucky	53
	6	Bob Sims	St. Louis Hawks	Pepperdine	54
	7	Bob Clarke	Philadelphia Warriors	St. Joseph's (Pa.)	55
EIGHTH ROUND	1	Sam Stith	Cincinnati Royals	St. Bonaventure	56
	2	John Werhas	Minneapolis Lakers	USC	57
	3	George Price	New York Knicks	Memphis State	58
	4	Mike Yugovich	Detroit Pistons	Youngstown State	59
	5	Don Lynch	Syracuse Nationals	LeMoyne	60
	6	Don Cury	St. Louis Hawks	Mississippi Southern	61
	7	George Raveling	Philadelphia Warriors	Villanova	62
NINTH ROUND	1	Al Nealey	Cincinnati Royals	Arizona State	63
	2	Claude Lefevre	Minneapolis Lakers	Gonzaga	64
	3	Tony Davis	New York Knicks	Hawaii	65
	4	Martin Holland	Detroit Pistons	Kentucky Wesleyan	66
	5	Bernie Findlay	Syracuse Nationals	San Diego State	67
	6	Bob Castanada	St. Louis Hawks	Rockhurst	68
	7	Joe Gallo	Philadelphia Warriors	St. Josephs	
TENTH RD	1	Lon Sizemore	Cincinnati Royals	West Virginia Tech	69
	2	Dick Harvey	Minneapolis Lakers	Creighton	70
	3	Walter Mangham	New York Knicks	Marquette	71
	4	Joe Kennelly	Detroit Pistons	Dayton	72
	5	Americas John-Lewis	St. Louis Hawks	Iowa	73
ELEVENTH ROUND	1	Dennis Boone	Cincinnati Royals	Regis	74
	2	Sterling Forbes	Minneapolis Lakers	Pepperdine	75
	3	Howard Willis	New York Knicks	Grambling	76
	4	Mel Peterson	Detroit Pistons	Wheaton	77
	5	Dick Davies		Louisiana St.	
12 ROUND	1	Ron Altenberg	Cincinnati Royals	Cornell (Iowa)	78
	2	Will Jones	Minneapolis Lakers	American	79
	3	Henry Hart	New York Knicks	Auburn	80
	4	Don Dobbert	Detroit Pistons	Wheaton	81
	5	Bob Wilkinson	St. Louis Hawks	Indiana	
13 RD	1	John Milhoan	Cincinnati Royals	Marshall	82
	2	Dick Furry	New York Knicks	Ohio State	83
14 RD	1	Larry Chaney	Cincinnati Royals	Montana State	84
	2	Jim Hanna	New York Knicks	USC	85
15 RD	1	Ducky Potter	Cincinnati Royals	Moravian	86
	2	Jerry Bechtal	New York Knicks	Maryland	87
16 RD	1	Gene Jordan	Cincinnati Royals	NW Missouri	88
	2	Jerry Schofield	New York Knicks	Utah State	89
17 RD	1	Ernie McCray	Cincinnati Royals	Arizona	90
	2	Tandy Gillis	New York Knicks	California	91
18 RD	1	Don Mills	Cincinnati Royals	Kentucky	92
	2	George Krajack	New York Knicks	Clemson	93
19	1	Larry Willey	Cincinnati Royals	Cincinnati	94
20	1	Tony Wilcox	Cincinnati Royals	Wittenberg	95
21	1	Jim McDonald	Cincinnati Royals	West Virginia Wesleyan	96

1959

		NAME	TEAM	COLLEGE	# OVERALL
TERRIT.	1	Wilt Chamberlain	Philadelphia Warriors	Kansas	
	2	Bob Ferry	St. Louis Hawks	St. Louis	
FIRST ROUND	1	Bob Boozer	Cincinnati Royals	Kansas State	1
	2	Bailey Howell	Detroit Pistons	Mississippi State	2
	3	Tom Hawkins	Minneapolis Lakers	Notre Dame	3
	4	Dick Barnett	Syracuse Nationals	Tennessee State	4
	5	Johnny Green	New York Knicks	Michigan State	5
	6	John Richter	Boston Celtics	North Carolina State	6
SECOND ROUND	1	Tom Robitaille	Detroit Pistons	Rice	7
	2	Don Goldstein	Detroit Pistons	Louisville	8
	3	Joe Ruklick	Philadelphia Warriors	Northwestern	9
	4	Rudy LaRusso	Minneapolis Lakers	Dartmouth	10
	5	Gene Tormohlen	Syracuse Nationals	Tennessee	11
	6	Alan Seiden	St. Louis Hawks	St. John's	12
	7	Cal Ramsey	St. Louis Hawks	New York University	13
	8	Gene Guarilia	Boston Celtics	George Washington	14
THIRD ROUND	1	Mike Mendenhall	Cincinnati Royals	Cincinnati	15
	2	Gary Alcorn	Detroit Pistons	Fresno State	16
	3	Jim Hickaday	Philadelphia Warriors	Memphis State	17
	4	Bob Smith	Minneapolis Lakers	West Virginia	18
	5	Jon Cincebox	Syracuse Nationals	Syracuse	19
	6	Bob Anderegg	New York Knicks	Michigan State	20
	7	Hank Stein	St. Louis Hawks	Xavier (Ohio)	21
	8	Ralph Croswaite	Boston Celtics	Western Kentucky	22
FOURTH ROUND	1	Leo Byrd	Cincinnati Royals	Marshall	23
	2	George Lee	Detroit Pistons	Michigan	24
	3	Ron Stevenson	Philadelphia Warriors	Texas Christian	25
	4	Wilson Eison	Minneapolis Lakers	Purdue	26
	5	Paul Neumann	Syracuse Nationals	Stanford	27
	6	John Cox	New York Knicks	Kentucky	28
	7	Lee Harman	St. Louis Hawks	Oregon State	29
	8	Ed Kazakavich	Boston Celtics	Stanford	30

Round		Name	Team	College	# Overall
Fifth Round	1	Harry Kirchner	Cincinnati Royals	Texas Christian	31
	2	Tony Windis	Detroit Pistons	Wyoming	32
	3	Bill Telasky	Philadelphia Warriors	George Washington	33
	4	Bobby Joe Mason	Minneapolis Lakers	Bradley	34
	5	Roger Taylor	Syracuse Nationals	Illinois	35
	6	Herb Busch	New York Knicks	Virginia	36
	7	Nick Mantis	St. Louis Hawks	Northwestern	37
	8	Don Lange	Boston Celtics	William & Mary	38
Sixth Round	1	Don Hennon	Cincinnati Royals	Pittsburgh	39
	2	Lou Jordan	Detroit Pistons	Cornell	40
	3	Joe Spratt	Philadelphia Warriors	St. Joseph's (Pa.)	41
	4	Jim Henry	Minneapolis Lakers	Vanderbilt	42
	5	Bob Dalton	Syracuse Nationals	California	43
	6	Bucky McDonald	New York Knicks	George Washington	44
	7	Mike Moran	St. Louis Hawks	Marquette	45
	8	Bob Cumings	Boston Celtics	Boston Univ.	46
Seventh Round	1	Dale Moore	Cincinnati Royals	Eastern Kentucky	47
	2	Doug Smart	Detroit Pistons	Washington	48
	3	Joe Ryan	Philadelphia Warriors	Villanova	49
	4	Charley Grote	Minneapolis Lakers	Georgetown (Ky.)	50
	5	Darnell Haney	Syracuse Nationals	Navy	51
	6	Russ Robinson	New York Knicks	SW Missouri	52
	7	Orby Arnold	St. Louis Hawks	Memphis State	53
Eighth Round	1	Don Matuszak	Cincinnati Royals	Kansas State	54
	2	Chuck Curtis	Detroit Pistons	Pacific Lutheran	55
	3	Dave Gunther	Philadelphia Warriors	Iowa	56
	4	Leon Hill	Minneapolis Lakers	Texas Tech	57
	5	Walt Torrence	New York Knicks	UCLA	58
	6	Willie Merriwether	St. Louis Hawks	Purdue	59
Ninth Round	1	Joe Billy McDade	Cincinnati Royals	Bradley	60
	2	Doyle Edmiston	Detroit Pistons	Hardin-Simmons	61
	3	Carl Belz	Philadelphia Warriors	Princeton	62
	4	Jim Mudd	Minneapolis Lakers	North Texas State	63
	5	Jerry Shipp	New York Knicks	SE Oklahoma	64
	6	Lou Pucillo	St. Louis Hawks	North Carolina State	65
Tenth Round	1	Joe Viviano	Cincinnati Royals	Xavier (Ohio)	66
	2	Bruno Boin	Detroit Pistons	Washington	67
	3	Tony Sellari	Philadelphia Warriors	Lenoir Rhyne	68
	4	Roger Johnson	Minneapolis Lakers	Minnesota	69
	5	Paul Wilcox	New York Knicks	Davis & Elkins	70
	6	Ron Loneski	St. Louis Hawks	Kansas	71
Eleventh Round	1	Charley Brown	Cincinnati Royals	Seattle	72
	2	M.C. Burton	Detroit Pistons	Michigan	73
	3	Phil Warren	Philadelphia Warriors	Northwestern	74
	4	Jack Evans	Minneapolis Lakers	Superior State	75
	5	Paul Benes	New York Knicks	Hope	76
	6	John Barnhill	St. Louis Hawks	Tennessee State	77
12 Rd	1	Roger Wendel	Cincinnati Royals	Tulsa	78
	2	Vern Baggenstoss	Minneapolis Lakers	St. Cloud State	79
	3	Ed Blair	New York Knicks	Western Michigan	80
13 Rd	1	Dwayne Smith	Minneapolis Lakers	Gustavus Adolphus	81
	2	John Nicoll	New York Knicks	Brigham Young	82
14	1	Jack Israel	New York Knicks	SW Missouri	83

1958

Round		Name	Team	College	# Overall
First Round	1	Elgin Baylor	Minneapolis Lakers	Seattle	1
	2	Archie Dees	Cincinnati Royals	Indiana	2
	3	Mike Farmer	New York Knicks	San Francisco	3
	4	Pete Brennan	New York Knicks	North Carolina	4
	5	Guy Rodgers	Philadelphia Warriors	Temple	5
	6	Connie Dierking	Syracuse Nationals	Cincinnati	6
	7	Dave Gambee	St. Louis Hawks	Oregon State	7
	8	Ben Swain	Boston Celtics	Texas Southern	8
Second Round	1	Steve Hamilton	Minneapolis Lakers	Morehead State	9
	2	Vern Hatton	Cincinnati Royals	Kentucky	10
	3	Barney Cable	Detroit Pistons	Bradley	11
	4	Joe Quigg	New York Knicks	North Carolina	12
	5	Lamar Sharrar	Philadelphia Warriors	West Virginia	13
	6	Hal Greer	Syracuse Nationals	Marshall	14
	7	Jimmy Smith	Boston Celtics	Steubenville	15
Third Round	1	Alex Ellis	Minneapolis Lakers	Niagara	16
	2	Arlen Bockhorn	Cincinnati Royals	Dayton	17
	3	Roy DeWitz	Detroit Pistons	Kansas State	18
	4	John Lee	New York Knicks	Yale	19
	5	Frank Howard	Philadelphia Warriors	Ohio State	20
	6	John Nacincik	Syracuse Nationals	Maryland	21
	7	Hub Reed	St. Louis Hawks	Oklahoma City	22
	8	Jim Cunningham	Boston Celtics	Fordham	23
Fourth Round	1	George Kline	Minneapolis Lakers	Minnesota	24
	2	Phil Murrell	Cincinnati Royals	Drake	25
	3	Ralph Croswaite	Detroit Pistons	Western Kentucky	26
	4	John Cox	New York Knicks	Kentucky	27
	5	Temple Tucker	Philadelphia Warriors	Rice	28
	6	Tommy Kearns	Syracuse Nationals	North Carolina	29
	7	Wayne Embry	St. Louis Hawks	Miami (Ohio)	30
	8	Don Flora	Boston Celtics	Washington & Lee	31
Fifth Round	1	Quitman Sullins	Minneapolis Lakers	Murray State	32
	2	Jim Fulmer	Cincinnati Royals	Alabama	33
	3	Hank Morano	Detroit Pistons	St. Peter's	34
	4	Don Lane	New York Knicks	Dayton	35
	5	Don Ohl	Philadelphia Warriors	Illinois	36
	6	Fred Grim	Syracuse Nationals	Arkansas	37
	7	Julius Peques	St. Louis Hawks	Pittsburgh	38
	8	Gene Brown	Boston Celtics	San Francisco	39
Sixth Round	1	Al Inniss	Minneapolis Lakers	St. Francis (N.Y.)	40
	2	Jim McClennan	Cincinnati Royals	St. Francis (Pa.)	41
	3	Shellie McMillon	Detroit Pistons	Bradley	42
	4	Joe King	New York Knicks	Oklahoma	43
	5	Bucky Allen	Philadelphia Warriors	Duke	44
	6	Jack Mimitz	Syracuse Nationals	St. Louis	45
	7	Rick Herrscher	St. Louis Hawks	Southern Methodist	46
	8	Dave Keleher	Boston Celtics	Morehead State	47
Seventh Round	1	Jim Bond	Minneapolis Lakers	Pasadena	48
	2	Wayne Stevens	Cincinnati Royals	Cincinnati	49
	3	Ed Blair	Detroit Pistons	Western Michigan	50
	4	Owen Lawson	New York Knicks	Western Kentucky	51
	5	Jay Norman	Philadelphia Warriors	Temple	52
	6	Pete Tillotson	Syracuse Nationals	Michigan	53
	7	John Crawford	St. Louis Hawks	Iowa State	54
	8	Rudy Fenderson	Boston Celtics	Brandeis	55
Eighth Round	1	Ed Brinkley	Minneapolis Lakers	Clemson	56
	2	Bob Mantz	Cincinnati Royals	Lafayette	57
	3	Jack Quiggle	Detroit Pistons	Michigan State	58
	4	Milt Kane	New York Knicks	Utah	59
	5	Tom Brennan	Philadelphia Warriors	Villanova	60
	6	Ruel Tucker	Syracuse Nationals	Rockhurst (Mo.)	61
	7	Ken Sidle	St. Louis Hawks	Ohio State	62
Ninth Round	1	Joe Hobbs	Minneapolis Lakers	Florida	63
	2	Larry Staverman	Cincinnati Royals	Villa Madonna	64
	3	Harry Marske	Detroit Pistons	North Dakota State	65
	4	John McCarthy	New York Knicks	Notre Dame	66
	5	Nick Davis	Philadelphia Warriors	Maryland	67
	6	Bruno Boin	St. Louis Hawks	Washington	68

Round	Pick	Player	Team	College	Overall
TENTH ROUND	1	Shorty Patterson	Minneapolis Lakers	Gustavus Adolphus	69
	2	Jack Parr	Cincinnati Royals	Kansas State	70
	3	Pete Gaudin	Detroit Pistons	Loyola (La.)	71
	4	Larry Hedden	Philadelphia Warriors	Michigan State	72
	5	Tink Van Patton	St. Louis Hawks	Temple	73
11 ROUND	1	Hal Duffy	Minneapolis Lakers	Oregon	74
	2	Frank Tartaton	Cincinnati Royals	Xavier (Ohio)	75
	3	Herb Merritt	Detroit Pistons	Tennessee Tech	76
	4	James Purcell	St. Louis Hawks	Coe	77
12 ROUND	1	Gary Simmons	Minneapolis Lakers	Idaho	78
	2	Don Medsker	Cincinnati Royals	Iowa State	79
	3	Jim Dew	Detroit Pistons	Alabama State	80
	4	Don Klein	St. Louis Hawks	Rockhurst (Mo.)	81
13 RD	1	Jerry Alcom	Minneapolis Lakers	Fresno State	82
	2	Jerry DuPont	Cincinnati Royals	Louisville	83
	3	Joe Buckhalter	St. Louis Hawks	Tennessee State	84
14	1	Jim Newcomb	Cincinnati Royals	Duke	85
15	1	Bill Smith	Cincinnati Royals	Kentucky	86
16	1	Jack McCarthy	Cincinnati Royals	Dayton	87
17	1	John Powell	Cincinnati Royals	Miami (Ohio)	88

Beginning in 1957, the draft is recorded round-by-round.

1957

Round	Pick	Player	Team	College	Overall
FIRST ROUND	1	Rod Hundley	Cincinnati Royals	West Virginia	1
	2	Charles Tyra	Detroit Pistons	Louisville	2
	3	Jim Krebs	Minneapolis Lakers	Southern Methodist	3
	4	Win Wilfong	St. Louis Hawks	Memphis State	4
	5	Brendan McCann	New York Knicks	St. Bonaventure	5
	6	Leonard Rosenbluth	Philadelphia Warriors	North Carolina	6
	7	George Bon Salle	Syracuse Nationals	Illinois	7
	8	Sam Jones	Boston Celtics	North Carolina Central	8
SECOND ROUND	1	Dick Duckett	Cincinnati Royals	St. John's	9
	2	Bob McCoy	Detroit Pistons	Grambling	10
	3	Harvey Schmidt	Minneapolis Lakers	Illinois	11
	4	Jim Palmer	St. Louis Hawks	Dayton	12
	5	Larry Friend	New York Knicks	California	13
	6	Jack Sullivan	Philadelphia Warriors	Mount St. Mary's	14
	7	Jim Morgan	Syracuse Nationals	Louisville	15
	8	Dick O'Neal	Boston Celtics	Texas Christian	16
THIRD ROUND	1	Jerry Paulson	Cincinnati Royals	Manhattan	17
	2	Bill Ebben	Detroit Pistons	Detroit	18
	3	Jim Spivey	Minneapolis Lakers	SE Oklahoma	19
	4	John Smyth	St. Louis Hawks	Notre Dame	20
	5	Gary Clark	New York Knicks	Syracuse	21
	6	Angelo Lombardo	Philadelphia Warriors	Manhattan	22
	7	Vince Cohen	Syracuse Nationals	Syracuse	23
	8	Chuck Schramm	Boston Celtics	Western Illinois	24
FOURTH ROUND	1	Jed Dormeyer	Cincinnati Royals	Minnesota	25
	2	Kurt Englebert	Detroit Pistons	St. Joseph's (Pa.)	26
	3	George Brown	Minneapolis Lakers	Wayne State	27
	4	Hank Nowak	St. Louis Hawks	Canisius	28
	5	Rayford Wells	New York Knicks	Lenoir Rhyne	29
	6	Ray Radziszewski	Philadelphia Warriors	St. Joseph's (Pa.)	30
	7	Jerry Mallett	Syracuse Nationals	Baylor	31
	8	Jim Ashmore	Boston Celtics	Mississippi State	32
FIFTH ROUND	1	Stewart Murray	Cincinnati Royals	Lafayette	33
	2	Ron Kramer	Detroit Pistons	Michigan	34
	3	Gary Thompson	Minneapolis Lakers	Iowa State	35
	4	Al Rochelle	St. Louis Hawks	Vanderbilt	36
	5	Lee Marshall	New York Knicks	Washington & Lee	37
	6	Jim Radcliffe	Philadelphia Warriors	Lafayette	38
	7	Frank Nimmo	Syracuse Nationals	Cincinnati	39
	8	Grady Wallace	Boston Celtics	South Carolina	40
SIXTH ROUND	1	John Maglio	Cincinnati Royals	North Carolina State	41
	2	Walt Adamushko	Detroit Pistons	St. Francis (N.Y.)	42
	3	Phil Murrell	Minneapolis Lakers	Drake	43
	4	Raymond Downs	St. Louis Hawks	Texas	44
	5	Jim Humphreys	New York Knicks	St. Michael's (Vt.)	45
	6	Alonzo Lewis	Philadelphia Warriors	La Salle	46
	7	Lyndon Lee	Syracuse Nationals	Oklahoma City	47
	8	Maurice King	Boston Celtics	Kansas	48
SEVENTH ROUND	1	Chet Forte	Cincinnati Royals	Columbia	49
	2	Carl Boldt	Detroit Pistons	San Francisco	50
	3	George Ferguson	Minneapolis Lakers	Michigan	51
	4	Mason Pope	St. Louis Hawks	Kentucky Wesleyan	52
	5	Max Jameson	Philadelphia Warriors	Kentucky State	53
	6	Dick Gaines	Syracuse Nationals	Seton Hall	54
	7	Dick Brott	Boston Celtics	Denver	55
EIGHTH ROUND	1	Bob Daniels	Cincinnati Royals	Western Kentucky	56
	2	Doug Bolstorff	Detroit Pistons	Minnesota	57
	3	John Haaven	Minneapolis Lakers	North Dakota	58
	4	Bill Darragh	St. Louis Hawks	Louisville	59
	5	Woody Sauldsberry	Philadelphia Warriors	Texas Southern	60
	6	Cebe Prince	Syracuse Nationals	Marshall	61
	7	Bill Von Weyhe	Boston Celtics	Rhode Island	62
NINTH ROUND	1	Dick Heise	Cincinnati Royals	DePaul	63
	2	Bob Lazor	Detroit Pistons	Pittsburgh	64
	3	Jim Sutton	Minneapolis Lakers	North Dakota State	65
	4	Calvin Grosscup	St. Louis Hawks	Tulane	66
	5	Steve Hamilton	Philadelphia Warriors	Morehead State	67
	6	Jim Brown	Syracuse Nationals	Syracuse	68
	7	Joe Gibbon	Boston Celtics	Mississippi	69
TENTH ROUND	1	Mel Wright	Cincinnati Royals	Oklahoma A&M	70
	2	Gordon Fosness	Minneapolis Lakers	Dakota Wesleyan	71
	3	Bobby Mills	St. Louis Hawks	Southern Methodist	72
	4	Jerry Calvert	Philadelphia Warriors	Kentucky	73
	5	Jack Nichols	Syracuse Nationals	Colgate	74
	6	Jack Butcher	Boston Celtics	Memphis State	75
11 ROUND	1	Cliff Hafer	Cincinnati Royals	North Carolina State	76
	2	Gerald Dreier	St. Louis Hawks	Macalaster	77
	3	Dick Neal	Boston Celtics	Indiana	78
12 ROUND	1	Jim Boothe	Cincinnati Royals	Xavier (Ohio)	79
	2	Bob Seitz	St. Louis Hawks	North Carolina State	80
	3	Jim Weeks	Syracuse Nationals	New York Tech	81
13	1	Ed Romanoff	St. Louis Hawks	None	82
14	1	Lavelle Langston	St. Louis Hawks	Northwestern State	83

1956

Early draft records are incomplete, so until 1956 players are listed in the order in which they were selected by each team.

TERRITORIAL CHOICE

Boston – Tom Heinsohn, Holy Cross.

BOSTON

K.C. Jones, San Francisco; George Linn, Alabama; Dan Swartz, Morehead State; Bill Logan, Iowa; Don Boldebuck, Houston; O'Neal Weaver, Midwestern (Tex.); Vic Molodet, North Carolina State; Jim Houston, Brandeis; Theophileus Lloyd, Maryland State.

FORT WAYNE
Ron Sobieszczyk, DePaul; Bob Kessler, Maryland; Bill Thieben, Hofstra; Charles Slack, Marshall; Joe Lieber, Holy Cross; John Schlimm, John Carroll; Bruce Harris, Tennessee Tech.

MINNEAPOLIS
Elgin Baylor, Seattle; Jim Paxson, Dayton; Terry Rand, Marquette; Jerry Bird, Kentucky; Lloyd Aubrey, Notre Dame; Bill Reigel, McNeese State; Phil Jordon, Whitworth; John Barber, Cal State–Los Angeles; Sam Jones, North Carolina College; Jim Springer, Gustavus Adolphus; Phil Grawmeyer, Kentucky; Robert Hodgson, Wichita; Carl Widseth, Tennessee; John Patzwald, Gustavus Adolphus.

NEW YORK
Ronnie Shavlik, North Carolina State; Gary Bergen, Utah; Jerry Harper, Alabama, Ronnie Mayer, Duke; Joe Sexton, Purdue; Pat Dunn, Utah State; Jack Adams, Eastern Kentucky; Art Bunte, Utah; Dick Miller, Wisconsin; Howard Crittendon, Murray State; Dick Miani, Miami (Fla.); Ed Petrie, Seton Hall; Tony Roybal, New Mexico.

PHILADELPHIA
Hal Lear, Temple; Phil Rollins, Louisville; Bevo Francis, Rio Grande; Phil Wheeler, Cincinnati; Joe Belmont, Duke; Mickey Winograd, Duquesne; John Fannon, Notre Dame; Max Anderson, Oregon; Ronald Clark, Springfield.

ROCHESTER
Sihugo, Duquesne; Bob Burrow, Kentucky; Dave Piontek, Xavier (Ohio); John McCarthy, Canisius; Bill Uhl, Dayton; Kevin Thomas, Boston; Carl Cain, Iowa; Clayton Carter, Oklahoma A&M; Dan Mannix, St. Francis (N.Y.); Jerry Moreman, Louisville; Gene Carpenter, Texas Tech.

ST. LOUIS
Bill Russell, San Francisco; Willie Naulls, UCLA; Darrell Floyd, Furman; Robin Freeman, Ohio State; Norman Stewart, Missouri; Dave Plunkett, Cincinnati; Julius McCoy, Michigan State; Morris Taft, UCLA; Jim Reed, Texas Tech; Hershel Pederson, Brigham Young; Wally Choice, Indiana; Ed Huse, Wyoming; Arthur Helms, Houston; Junior Morgan, Duke.

SYRACUSE
Joe Holup, George Washington; Paul Judson, Illinois; Forest Able, Western Kentucky; Wade Halbrook, Oregon State; Jim Ray, Toledo; Jim McLaughlin, St. Louis; Jess Roh, Idaho State; Chester Webb, Georgia State; Dick Julio, New Bedford State; Bob Hopkins, Grambling, Willie Bergines,West Virginia; Dick Kenyon, LeMoyne; Milt Graham, Colgate; Chuck Rolles, Cornell.

1955

BOSTON
Jim Ahearn, Connecticut; Mark Davis, Marietta; Henry Dooley, Wiley; Carl Hartman, Alderson-Broaddus; Dick Hemric, Wake Forest; Bart Leach, Penn; Jim Loscutoff, Oregon; John Mahoney, William & Mary; John Moore, UCLA; Bob Patterson, Tulsa; Dean Parsons; Washington; Nick Romanoff, College of Pacific; Bob Scuddelari, Cooper Union; Buzz Wilkinson, Virginia.

FORT WAYNE
Jesse Arnelle, Penn State; Don Belcher, Louisiana State; Ron Bennink, Washington State; Tom Harrold, Colorado; John Horan, Dayton; Dick Howard, Western Reserve; Cleo Littleton, Wichita State; Happy Mahfouz, Spring Hill; Tom Mock, Colorado; Tom Mixon, Mercer; Bob Reiter, Missouri; Ray Warren, Texas Christian.

MILWAUKEE
Harvey Babetch, Bradley; Dick Cable, Wisconsin; Lynn Cole, Creighton; Al Ferrari, Michigan State; Joe Fitt, Burdette Haldorson (Col.); Charles Hoxie, Niagara; Ed O'Connor, Manhattan; Bill Reigel, McNeese; Dick Ricketts, Duquesne; Jack Stephens, Notre Dame; Dick Welsh, USC.

MINNEAPOLIS
Bill Banks, SW Texas; Don Boldebuck, Houston; Dick Boushka, St. Louis; Don Bragg, UCLA; Dick Garmaker, Minnesota; K.C. Jones, San Francisco; Chuck Mencel, Minnesota; John Miller, Ohio State; Jim Scott, West Texas; Bill Warden, North Central (Ill.); O'Neal Weaver, Midwestern (Tex.).

NEW YORK
Joe Beck, NW Missouri; Denver Brackeen, Mississippi; Ed Cole, Creighton; Joe Fay, St. Ambrose; Mickey Harrington, Southern Mississippi; Wally McCarvill, Iona; Jerry Mullen, San Francisco; Don Payne, Adelphi; Ken Sears, Santa Clara; Howard Sessums, Mississippi College; Guy Sparrow, Detroit; Charles Stickels, Hastings.

PHILADELPHIA
Jack Devine, Villanova; Walt Devlin, George Washington; Al Didriksen, Temple; Tom Gola, La Salle; Jerry Koch, St. Louis; Lester Lane, Oklahoma; Bob Schafer, Villanova; Harry Silcox, Temple; George Swyers, West Virginia Tech; Ed Wiener, Tennessee.

ROCHESTER
Jack Twyman, Cincinnati; Bob Armstrong, Michigan State; Bill Evans, Kentucky; Ed Fleming, Niagara; Harry Jorgensen, Wyoming; Jerry Jung, Kansas State; Jim McConnell, Niagara; Bob McKeen, California; John Prudhoe, Louisville; Art Quimby, Connecticut; Maurice Stokes, St. Francis (Pa.); Tony Vlastelica, Oregon State.

SYRACUSE
Ed Conlin, Fordham; Mal Duffy, St. Bonaventure; Frank Ehmann, Northwestern; Cliff Dwyer, North Carolina State; Ed Galvin, Loyola (La.); Stan Glowaski, Seattle; Russ Lawler, Stanford; Jack Sallee, Dayton; Don Schlundt, Indiana; Marty Satalino, St. John's; Ron Tomsic, Stanford.

1954

BALTIMORE
Frank Selvy, Furman; Bob Leonard, Indiana; Werner Killen, Lawrence; Burt Spice, Toledo; Lou Scott, Indiana; Bob Heim, Xavier (Ohio); Joe Pehanick, Seattle; Harry Brooks, Seton Hall; Ron Goerrs, Concordia (Mo.); Don Shivers, Houston; Elliott Karver, George Washington.

BOSTON
Togo Palazzi, Holy Cross; Dwight Morrison, Idaho; Henry Daubenschmidt, St. Francis (N.Y.); Ron Perry, Holy Cross; Troy Burris, West Texas; Otto Krieghauser, Washington (Mo.); Paul Estergaard, Bradley; Jim Young, Santa Clara; Tony Daukas, Boston College; Bill Johnson, Nebraska.

FORT WAYNE
DicK Rosenthal, Notre Dame; Arnold Short, Oklahoma City; B.H. Born, Kansas; Mel Thompson, North Carolina State; Dutch Burch, Pittsburgh; Charles Kraak, Indiana; Bernie Janicki, Duke; Don Bielke, Valparaiso; Joel Hittleman, Loyola (Md.); Phil Larson, Brigham Young; Forrest Jackson, Taylor.

MILWAUKEE

Bob Pettit, Louisiana State; Bob Mattick, Oklahoma State; Walt Walowac, Marshall; Phil Martin, Toledo; Paul Ebert, Ohio State; Bob Carney, Bradley; Alan Kelley, Kansas; Dick Nunneley, Tulsa; Hal Cervini, Tulane; Joe Bertrand, Notre Dame; Jerry Domerschick, CCNY; Ron Weisner, Wisconsin.

MINNEAPOLIS

Ed Kalafat, Minnesota; Al Bianchi, Bowling Green; Don Lance, Rice; Gene Schwinger, Rice; Buzz Bennett, Minnesota; Nick Revon, Mississippi Southern; Dan Finch, Vanderbilt; Bob Hopkins, Pasadena; Dick Garmaker, Minnesota; John Blever, Northwestern.

NEW YORK

Jack Turner, Western Kentucky; Richie Guerin, Iona; Don Anielak, SW Missouri; Don Lange, Navy; Jesse Priscock., Kansas State; Ron Rivers, Wyoming; Solly Walker, St. John's; Cob Jarvis, Mississippi State; Henry Duckham, Brooklyn Polytechnic; John Clune, Navy; Bob Walter, Oklahoma; Bill Stickel, Hastings.

PHILADELPHIA

Gene Shue, Maryland; Larry Costello, Niagara; Ben Peters, St. Benedict; Chuck Noble, Louisville; Rudy D'Emilio, Duke; Len Winogard, Brandeis; Bob Brady, San Diego State; Bob Hodges, East Carolina; Vince Leta, Lycoming; Bill Sullivan, Notre Dame; Frank O'Hara, La Salle; John Glinski; John Holup, George Washington.

ROCHESTER

Tom Marshall, Western Kentucky; Boris Nachamkin, New York University; Lee Morton, Cornell; Art Spoelstra, Western Kentucky; Bo Erias, Niagara; Jim Davis, St. John's; Bill Hull, Utah State; Paul Morrow, Wisconsin; Roy Irvin, USC; Ed Parchinski, Fordham; John Paxson, Dayton.

SYRACUSE

John Kerr, Illinois; Dick Farley, Indiana; Jim Tucker, Duquesne; Don McLane, Duquesne; Paul Pottenburgh, Siena; Norman Pott, Wheaton; Gus Levett, Franklin & Marshall; Mel Besdin, Syracuse; Fletcher Johnson, Duquesne; Jack Davidson, UCLA.

1953

BALTIMORE

Ray Felix, Long Island; Bob Speight, North Carolina State; Bob Peterson, Oregon; Bill Schyman, DePaul; Paul Nolen, Texas Tech; Elmer Tolson, Eastern Kentucky; Herman Sledzik, Penn State; Connie Rea, Centenary; Dennis Murphy, Georgetown; Jack Carby, Kansas State; Bob Emmerick, Clarion State; Russ Johnson; Don Stemmerich; Bob Kraback; Joe Piorkowski; Edward Walsh.

BOSTON

Frank Ramsey, Kentucky; Chet Noe, Oregon; Cliff Hagan, Kentucky; Earle Markey, Holy Cross; John Holup, George Washington; Vernon Stokes, St. Francis (N.Y.); Lou Tsioropoulos, Kentucky; Ted Lallier, Colby; Lewis Gilcrease, SW Texas; Tom Lillis, St. Louis; Gil Reich, Kansas; Jim Dogerty, Whitworth.

FORT WAYNE

Jack Molinas, Columbia; George Glasgow, Fairleigh Dickinson; Jim Bredar, Illinois; Jim Bingham, Eastern Kentucky; Mike Bodnar, St. Bonaventure; Norb Lewinski, Notre Dame; William Hagan, Siena; Dean Kelley, Kansas; Dick White, Eastern Kentucky.

MILWAUKEE

Bob Houbregs, Washington; Bill Bolger, Georgetown; Irv Bemoras, Illinois; Gene Dyker, DePaul; Joe Cipriano, Washington; John O'Brien, Seattle; Eddie O'Brien, Seattle; Darrell Tucker, Utah State; Paul Brandt, Columbia; Bob Rousey, Kansas State.

MINNEAPOLIS

Jim Fritsche, Hamline; Ron Feiereisel, DePaul; HartlyKruger, Idaho; Ken Flowers, USC; Zippy Morroco, Georgia; Pete Silas, Georgia Tech; Lloyd Olmstead, Cornell (Iowa); Joe Richey, Brigham Young; Hank Budde, Xavier (Ohio); Walt Kearns, Arkansas; Bill Chambers, William & Mary; Harold Christensen, Brigham Young; Bob Gelle, Minnesota; Lloyd Thorgaard, Hamline; Bob Gussner, Hamline; Chuck Wolfe, North Dakota; Doug Atkins; Tennessee; Roger Kuss, River Falls State.

NEW YORK

Walter Dukes, Seton Hall; Buddy Ackerman, Long Island; Neil Gordon, Furman; Joe Smyth, Niagara; Allan Schutts, Springfield; Richard Atha, Indiana State; Forrest Hamilton, SW Missouri State; Robert Santini, Iona; Thomas Bishop, Mississippi Southern; Richard Prater, Kentucky, Bob Matheny, California; Larry O'Connor, Canisius; Delmar Diercks, Iowa State.

PHILADELPHIA

Ernie Beck, Penn; Larry Hennessy, Villanova; Norm Grekin, La Salle; Fred Iehle, La Salle; Eddie Solomon, West Virginia Tech; Don Eby, USC; Bob Marske, South Dakota; Bill Dodd,Colgate; Bob Sassone, St. Bonaventure; Toar Hester, Centenary; John Doogan, St. Joseph's (Pa.); Charles Duffley, St. Anselm's.

ROCHESTER

Richie Regan, Seton Hall; Norman Swanson, Detroit; Frank Reddout, Syracuse; Will Walls, Miami (Ohio); Hugh Beins, Georgetown; Kendall Sheets, Oklahoma A&M; Jim Scottile, West Virginia; Dick Gross, Wheaton; Jim Gerber, Bowling Green; Will Bales, Eastern Kentucky; Bill Edwards, St. Bonaventure; Bob Goss, North Carolina State; Paul Smaagard, Hamline; Ken Sears, Santa Clara; John Kurz, Loyola (Cal.); Ed Kohl, Regis; Gene Lambert Jr., Arkansas; Tex Silverman; Nick McGuire.

SYRACUSE

James Neal, Wofford; Dick Knostman, Kansas State; Bill Kenville, St. Bonaventure; Andy McGowan, Manhattan; Warren Shackelford, Tulsa; Bill Jenkins, LeMoyne; Bill Hull, Utah State; Joe Hughes, Denver; Gerald Nappy, Georgetown; Al Bailey, Duquesne; Glen Dille, Tulsa; Garrett Beshear, Murray State.

1952

BALTIMORE

Jim Baechtold, Eastern Kentucky; Blaine Denning, Lawrence Tech.; Chuck Grigsby, Dayton; Frank Guisness, Washington; Bill Lea, SW Missouri; Art Press, Western Maryland; Bob Priddy, New Mexico A&M; Benny Purcell, Murray State; Bud Penwell, Oklahoma City; Mike Magula, Youngstown; Bob Peterson, Oregon; Jim Walsh, Stanford.

BOSTON

Bill Stauffer, Missouri; Jim Iverson, Kansas State; J.C. Maze, SW Texas; Herm Hedderick, Canisius; Don Johnson, Oklahoma State; Jim Buchanan, Nebraska; Fred Eydt, Cornell; Gordon Mungier, Spring Hill; Jim Dilling, Holy Cross; Gene Conley, Washington State.

FORT WAYNE

Bill Carlson, Fordham; Hal Cerra, Duquesne; Bob Clifton, Iowa; Leo Corkery, St. Bonaventure; Dick Groat, Duke; Don Meineke, Dayton; Lee Terrill, North Carolina State; Jim Ramstead, Stanford.

INDIANAPOLIS

Joe Dean, Louisiana State; Jay Handlan, Washington & Lee; Bill Harrell, Siena; Jim Hoverder, Central Missouri State; Gene Rhodes, Western Kentucky; Dale Toft, Denver; Lucian Whitaker, Kentucky; Bob Zawoluk, St. John's; Gordon Stauffer, Michigan State.

MILWAUKEE

Pete Brewster, Purdue; Roger Johnson, Arizona; Ed Miller, Syracuse; George McLeod, Texas Christian; Ab Nicholas, Wisconsin; Dick Retherford, Baldwin-Wallace; John Snee, Clemson; Jim Tackett, New Mexico; Coyt Vance, Mississippi State; Bob Watson, Kentucky; Mark Workman, West Virginia.

MINNEAPOLIS

Tom Ackerman, West Liberty; Jim Bishop, Mississippi Southern; Rod Fletcher, Illinois; Cliff Haag, Wyoming; Jim Holstein, Cincinnati; Bob Holt, Tulane; Tom Katsimpalis, Eastern Illinois; Clyde Lovellette, Kansas; Dick Means, Minnesota; Dwight Morrison, USC; Carl McNulty, Purdue; Ed Ramiraz, Centenary; Don Schneider, Arizona; Gene Smith, Xavier (Ohio); Gene Smith, Huron; Homer Spain, Union (Tenn.); John Wallesea, Memphis State.

NEW YORK

Roy Belliveau, Seton Hall; Dick Bunt, New York University; Bert Cook, Utah State; Ben Gibson, St. Mary's (Cal.); Bud Julian, SW Missouri State; Ralph Polson, Whitworth; Paul Sullivan, Alabama; Dick Surhoff, Long Island.

PHILADELPHIA

Tom Brennan, Villanova; Bob Brown, Louisville; Burr Carlson, Connecticut; Walter Davis, Texas A&M; Nick Kladis, Loyola (Ill.); Bill Mlkvy, Temple; Newt Jones, La Salle; Moe Radovich, Wyoming; Don Scanlon, Penn; Glenn Smith, Utah; Ben Stewart, Villanova.

ROCHESTER

Chuck Darling, Iowa; Bryant Ivey, Alabama; Leroy Leslie, Notre Dame; Ronnie MacGilvray, St. John's; Jewell McDowell, Texas A&M; Jack McMahon, St. John's; Sam Miranda, Indiana; Jerry Romney, Brigham Young; Ray Royce, Houston; Arnold Smith,CCNY; Ray Sonnenberg, St. Louis; Ray Steiner, St. Louis; Bob Whitmer, Florida State.

SYRACUSE

Jim Brasco, New York University; Bud Donnelly, La Salle; Jim Kennedy, Duquesne; Bob Lochmueller, Lousiville; Ken McBride, Maryland State; Harry Moore, West Virginia; Bob Roche, Syracuse.

1951

BALTIMORE

Gene Melchiorre, Bradley; Jack Stone, Kansas State; Bill Mann, Bradley; Bill Hagler, California; Leroy Ishman, American; Glen Duggins, Utah; Tom Riach, USC; Bill Harper, Oregon State; Bob Crowe, San Jose State; Dan Torrey, Oregon State; Clem Pavilonis, DePaul, John Burke, Springfield (Mass.).

BOSTON

Ernie Barrett, Kansas State; Bill Garrett, Indiana; John Furlong, Pepperdine; Bob Barnett, Evansville; Rip Gish, Western Kentucky; Jim Luisi, St. Francis (N.Y.); John Azary, Columbia; Hugo Kappler, North Carolina State.

FORT WAYNE

Zeke Sinicola, Niagara; Jack Kiley, Syracuse; Jake Fendley, Northwestern; Herb Hargett, Mississippi State; Leo Johnson, Arizona; Frank Clasbeek, Iowa; Jim Ramstead, Stanford; John Manning, Duquesne.

INDIANAPOLIS

Marcus Freiberger, Oklahoma; Scotty Steagall, Millikin; Glenn Kammeyer, Central Missouri State; Bill Tosheff, Indiana; Bob Pierce, Nebraska; Marv Johnson, Wheaton; Ted Beach, Illinois; George Kelly, Vanderbilt.

MINNEAPOLIS

Whitey Skoog, Minnesota; Lew Hitch, Kansas State; Bob Payne, Oregon State; Gale McArthur, Oklahoma A&M; Leo Vander Kuy, Michigan; Deward Dopson, Arkansas Polytechnic; Ed Head, Kansas State.

NEW YORK

Ed Smith, Harvard; Roland Minson, Brigham Young; Joe Luchi, Cincinnati; Lloyd Sandstrom, St. Thomas; Tom Smith, St. Peter's; Al McGuire, St. John's; Sid Ryen, Denver.

PHILADELPHIA

Don Sunderlage, Illinois; Mel Payton, Tulane; Bob Schloss, Georgia; Jud Milhon, Ohio Wesleyan; Mike Kearns, Princeton; Bob Swalls, Indiana Central; George Dempsey, King's; Jim Phelan, La Salle; Hugh Faulkner, Pepperdine; Paul Gerwin, Cornell.

ROCHESTER

Sam Ranzino, North Carolina State; Ray Ragelis, Northwestern; Fred Diute, St. Bonaventure; Elmer Behnke, Bradley; Dan Bagley, Notre Dame; Jim Ove, Valparaiso; John Brown, Southern Methodist; George Davidson, Lafayette.

SYRACUSE

John McConathy, NW Louisiana; Don Savage, LeMoyne; Bato Govedarica, DePaul; Paul Horvath, North Carolina State; Glen Anderson, Colorado A&M; Bob Wheeler, Idaho; Roy Reardon, St. Francis (N.Y.); Tom Jockle, Syracuse; Ray Kirkwasser, Ithaca.

TRI-CITIES

Mel Hutchins, Brigham Young; Bill Gossett, Colorado A&M; Ron Bontemps, Beloit; Jim Slaughter, South Carolina; Bob Sakel, Evansville; John Rennicke, Drake; Bob Ambler, Arkansas; Aaron Pierce, Bradley; Wayne Tucker, Colorado; John DeWitt, Texas A&M.

1950

BALTIMORE

Don Rehfeldt, Wisconsin; John Pilch, Wyoming; Dick Dickey, North Carolina State; Jerry Reed, Wyoming; Norm Mager, CCNY; Rick Harman, Kansas State; Frank Comerford, La Salle; George Bush, Toledo; Jack Laub, Cincinnati; Mike Zedalis, Loyola (Md.).

BOSTON

Charlie Share, Bowling Green; Chuck Cooper, Duquesne; Bob Donham, Ohio State; Ken Reeves, Louisville; Jack Shelton, Oklahoma A&M; Fran Mahoney, Brown; Dale Barnstable, Kentucky; Frank Oftring, Holy Cross; Bob Cope, Montana State; Matt Forman, Holy Cross.

CHICAGO

Larry Foust, La Salle; Wally Osterkorn, Illinois; Lou Watson, Indiana; Ken Murray, St. Bonaventure; Don Stroot, Missouri; Stu Inman, San Jose State; Milt Whitehead, Nebraska; George King, Morris Harvey; John Brown, Georgetown; Bud Schaeffer, Wheaton.

FORT WAYNE

George Yardley, Stanford; Jim Riffey, Tulane; Art Burris, Tennessee; Len Rzewszewski, Indiana State; Ed Thompson, Kent State; Bob Metcalf, Valparaiso; Ed Jones, Tennessee; Billy Joe Adcock, Vanderbilt; Al Henningsen, NW Missouri.

INDIANAPOLIS

Bob Lavoy, Western Kentucky; Paul Unruh, Bradley; Charles Mrazovich, Eastern Kentucky; Jim Line, Kentucky; Sonny Allen, Morehead State; Ralph O'Brien, Butler; Leon Blevins, Arizona; Jerry Stuteville, Indiana; Colin Anderson, Georgia Tech; Gene Schmidt, Texas Christian; Jimmy Doyle, Butler.

MINNEAPOLIS

Kevin O'Shea, Notre Dame; Hal Haskins, Hamline; Howie Williams, Purdue; Bud Grant, Minnesota; Ed Beach, West Virginia; Wayne Glasgow, Oklahoma; Joe Hutton Jr., Hamline; Newt Benson, River Falls Teachers; Jim Reilly, Swarthmore; Andy Butchko, Purdue.

NEW YORK

Irwin Dambrot, CCNY; Herb Scherer, Long Island; Stan Weber, Bowling Green; Joe Ossola, St. Louis; Dick Barnes, San Diego State; Don Parsons, Rutgers; Dan Bagley, Notre Dame; Charles Hope, Appalachian; Don Heathington, Baylor.

PHILADELPHIA

Paul Arizin, Villanova; Ed Dahler, Duquesne; Buddy Cate, Western Kentucky; Paul Senesky, St. Joseph's (Pa.); Ike Borsavage, Temple; Dick Dallmer, Cincinnati; Charles Northrup, Siena; Brooks Ricca, Villanova; Joe Kaufman, New York University; Bernie Adams, Princeton; Leo Wolfe, Villanova; Ed Montgomery, Tennessee.

ROCHESTER

Joe McNamee, San Francisco; George Stanich, UCLA; Bob Roper, John Carroll; Chet Giermak, William & Mary; Joe Nelson, Brigham Young; John Givens, Western Kentucky; Dan Kahler, Southwestern (Kan.); Carl Kraushaar, UCLA; Warren Switzer, Rice; Harry Foley, Niagara.

SYRACUSE

Don Lofgran, San Francisco; Gerry Calabrese, St. John's; Stan Christie, USC; Paul Merchant, Oklahoma; Paul Hickey, Denver; Mack Suprunowicz, Michigan; Lou Arko, Akron; Bob Healey, Georgia; Bob Savage, Syracuse; Glenn Wilkes, Mercer.

TRI-CITIES

Bob Cousy, Holy Cross; Ed Gayda, Washington State; Clarence Brannum, Kansas State; Paul Hicks, Eastern Kentucky; Cal Christensen, Toledo; Bob Anderson, Loyola (Md.); Bill Erickson, Illinois; Loy Doty, Wyoming; Nate DeLong River Falls Teachers; Keith Bloom, Wyoming.

WASHINGTON

Dick Schnittker, Ohio State; Bill Sharman, USC; Alan Sawyer, UCLA; Tom O'Keefe, Georgetown; Claude Overton, East Central Oklahoma; Warren Cartier, North Carolina State; Jim Cathcart, Arkansas; Joe Greenbach, Santa Clara; Earl Lloyd, West Virginia State; Joe Noertker, Virginia.

1949

BALTIMORE

Ron Livingston, Wyoming; Roger Wiley, Oregon.

BOSTON

Tony Lavelli, Yale; Joe Mullaney, Holy Cross; Bill Tom, Rice; Ed Little, Denver JC; Jim Simpson, Bates; Bill Vandenburgh, Washington; Duane Klueh, Indiana State; Emerson Speicher, Bowling Green; Bill Weight, Brigham Young; Russ Washburn, Colby.

CHICAGO

Ralph Beard, Kentucky; Jack Kerris, Loyola (Ill.).

FORT WAYNE

Bob Harris, Oklahoma A&M; John Oldham, Western Kentucky.

INDIANAPOLIS

Alex Groza, Kentucky; Leo Barnhorst, Notre Dame; Mac Otten, Bowling Green; Bob Evans, Butler; Charlie Maas, Butler; Don Boven, Western Michigan; Jim O'Halloran, Notre Dame; J.L. Parks, Oklahoma A&M.

MINNEAPOLIS

Vern Mikkelsen, Hamline; Bob Harrison, Michigan.

NEW YORK

Dick McGuire, St. John's; Harry Donovan, Muhlenberg; Ernie Vandeweghe, Colgate; Bill Kleine, Missouri Valley; Don Bagley, Notre Dame; Bob Prewitt, Southern Methodist; Ken Kearns, Arkansas; Bill Litchfield, Emporia State.

PHILADELPHIA

Vern Gardner, Utah; Jim Nolan, Georgia Tech.

PROVIDENCE

Paul Courty, Oklahoma; Howie Shannon, Kansas State.

ROCHESTER

Frank Saul, Seton Hall; Jack Coleman, Louisville.

ST. LOUIS

Ed Macauley, St. Louis; John Orr, Beloit; Marv Schatzman, St. Louis; Preston Ward, Soutwest Missouri; Earl Dodd, NE Missouri State; Jack Davidson, Stanford; John Pritchard, Drake; Bob Retherford, Nebraska; Joe Crandall, Oregon State; Eddie Van Zant, NW Oklahoma.

WASHINGTON

Wallace Jones, Kentucky; Jim Owens, Baylor.

1948

BALTIMORE

Jim Black, Occidental; Darrell Brown, Humboldt State; Walter Budko, Columbia; Robert Carroll, West Virginia; Jake Carter, East Texas State; Marvin English, Newberry; Gene Fellmoth, Whittenberg; J.W. Fullerton, Arkansas State; Marshall Gemberling, Lebanon Valley; Vince Hansen, Washington State;

Joe Holland, Kentucky; Dan Kraus, Georgetown; Wayne Jones, American International; Herbert Krautblatt, Rider; Paul Marcincin, Moravian.

BOSTON

John Bach, Fordham; Norman Carey, Oregon State; Bob Curran, Holy Cross; Neil Dooley, Colgate; George Hauptfuhrer, Harvard; Jack Hauser, Denver; Marshall Hawkins, Tennessee; Tom Kelly, New York University; Murray Mitchell, Sam Houston State; Guinn Phillips, Texas Wesleyan; Ray Wehde, Iowa State.

CHICAGO

John Dillon, North Carolina; Ed Kachan, DePaul; Mickey Marty, Loras; Ed Mikan, DePaul; Ed Mills, Wisconsin; Don Reagan, Murray State; Joe Shafer, Wheaton; Odie Spears; Western Kentucky; Fred Weber, Siena.

FORT WAYNE

Bobby Cook, Wisconsin; Link Richmond, Arizona; Ken Rollins, Kentucky; Murray Wier, Iowa; Ward Williams; Indiana.

INDIANAPOLIS

Reede Berg, Oregon; Jack Coleman, Louisiana State; Alex Hannum, USC; Norman Kohler, North Carolina; George Kok, Arkansas; Andy Kostecka, Georgetown; Ray Lumpp, New York University; Bob Paxton, North Carolina; Jack Phoenix, Idaho; Dick Wehr, Rice.

MINNEAPOLIS

Cliff Crandall, Oregon State; Arnold Ferrin, Utah; Earl Gardner, DePauw; Dee Gibson, Western Kentucky; Chuck Hanger, California; Ken Jastrow, Denver; Bob Lowther, Louisiana State; Junior Skogland, Gustavus Adolphus; Quentin Stinson, Southern Illinois; Johnny Orr, Beloit.

NEW YORK

Gene Berce, Marquette; Leland Byrd, West Virginia; Harry Gallatin, NE Missouri State; Keith Grimes, East Central State; Melvin McGaha, Arkansas; Ed Peterson, Cornell; Gobel Ritter, Western Kentucky; Adolph Schayes, New York University; Richard Shrider, Ohio; John Stanisch, UCLA.

PHILADELPHIA

William Brown, Maryland; Hugh Compton, Louisville; Joe Nelson, Brigham Young; Clint Pace, Pepperdine; Roy Pugh, Southern Methodist; Don Ray, Western Kentucky; Tom Short, Kansas Wesleyan; Joe Wahl, Akron; Andy Wolfe, California.

PROVIDENCE

A.L. Bennett, Oklahoma A&M; Jack Coleman, Louisville; Ed Faber, Trinity; Verl Heap, Arizona State; Otto Snellbacher, Kansas; Andy Tonkovich, Marshall; Brady Walker, Brigham Young.

ROCHESTER

Bill Gabor, Syracuse; Ed Keim, Niagara; Leo Kubiak, Bowling Green; Hank O'Keefe, Canisius; Johnny Macknowski, Seton Hall; Lionel Malamed, CCNY; Warren Stickel, Syracuse; Robert Wanzer, Seton Hall; Paul Yesavi, Niagara; Alex Athas, Tulane.

ST. LOUIS

Jack Burmaster, Illinois; Gordon Flick, Drake; Robert Gale, Cornell; John Hoppin, Dickinson; Dan London, Washington U. (St. Louis); D. Miller, St. Louis; Easy Parham, Texas Wesleyan; D.C. Wilcutt, St. Louis.

WASHINGTON

Fred Bartell, Oregon; Ed Hughes, San Jose State; Thorton Jenkins, Missouri; Leo Katkaveck, North Carolina State; Jack Nichols, Washington; C.T. Parker, Louisiana Tech; John Parkinson, Kentucky; Don Walker, Sam Houston State; Al Williams, Arkansas.

1947

BALTIMORE

Larry Killick, Vermont; Bob Jake, Vermont; John Rusinko, Penn State; Chick Gallatin, Missouri State Teachers; Charles Raynor, Houston.

Negotiation list: Elmer Gainer, Scotty Hamilton, Hugh Hampton, Chick Reiser, Robert Belyard.

BOSTON

Ed Ehlers, Purdue; Hank Biasetti, Long Island; Gene Stump, DePaul; George Felt, Northwestern.

Negotiation list: Bob Alemeida, George Petrovick, John Ezersky, Jack Hewson, John Kelly.

CHICAGO

Paul Huston, Ohio State; Ben Shadler, Northwestern; Hank Decker, West Texas State; Gene Vance, Illinois; Andy Phillip, Illinois.

Negotiation list: Ralph Bishop, Jim Darden, Jim Pollard, Don Smith, Jack Stone.

NEW YORK

Dick Holub, Long Island; Tom Tomlinson, Southern Methodist; Garland Head, Texas Tech; Carl Reichert, Findlay; Ray Evans, Kansas.

Negotiation list: Andy Duncan, Ed Golub, Ron Livingston, Dan Miller, Wat Misaka.

PHILADELPHIA

Francis Crossin, Penn; Ed Koffenberger, Duke; Norman Butz, St. Joseph's (Pa.); Jim Kaeding, York.

Negotiation list: Jim Pollard.

PIITSBURGH

Clifton McNeeley, Texas Western; Bob Alamo, Santa Clara; Herman Knoche, Washington & Jefferson; Dick Ives, Iowa; Jack Walton, DePauw.
Negotiation list: Fritz Nagy, George Brown.

PROVIDENCE

Walt Dropo, Connecticut; Roy Lipscomb, St. Mary's; John Mills, Hofstra; Al Nichols, Rhode Island State. Dick Furey, Robert Hubbard, Joe Barry, Bob Joyce.

ST. LOUIS

Jack Underman, Ohio State; Herb Wilkinson, Iowa; Jack Knopf, Louisville.

Negotiation list: Bob Kurland, Paul Napolitano, Jim Pollard, Bill Strannigan.

TORONTO

Glen Selbo, Wisconsin; Red Rocha, Oregon State; Frank Broyles, Georgia Tech; Wimpy Quinn, Oregon; Paul Hoffman, Purdue. Negotiation list: None

WASHINGTON

Dick O'Keefe, Santa Clara; Jack Tingle, Kentucky; Bill Burke, St. Mary's; Abel Rodriguez, San Francisco. Negotiation list: Paul Cloyd, Nat Zunic, John Mandic, Irwin Rothenberg, Saul Mariaschin.

CHAPTER 29

ALL-TIME PLAYER DIRECTORY

The summaries and year-by-year records are listed for every player who played in the National Basketball Association, Basketball Association of America and American Basketball Association. Also included are statistics for National Basketball League players who appeared in the BAA or NBA.

The NBA began keeping statistics for blocked shots, steals and offensive and defensive rebounds in 1973-74 and for turnovers in 1977-78. The ABA had the three-point shot during its nine-year history, but the NBA did not adopt the three-pointer until 1979-80, therefore, ABA players have three-point statistics for the ABA years, but not for their first three years in the NBA. The NBA began keeping statistics for games started in the 1981-82 season, so any games started before that season are not reflected in the totals. Dashes indicate that no records were available or that records were not yet kept for some of the categories.

The letters HOF means the player has been enshrined in the Naismith Memorial Basketball Hall of Fame. The letter "A" next to a team name refers to the American Basketball Association. The letter "N" refers to the National Basketball League.

Additional statistics and historical information are available on NBA.com.

FROM A . . .

Paul Arizin

. . . TO Z

Max Zaslofsky

Abdelnaby, Alaa b. June 24, 1968 Ht. 6-10 Wt. 240 College: Duke

SEASON–TEAM	G	GS	MIN	FGM	FGA	PCT	3FGM	3FGA	PCT	FTM	FTA	PCT	O-RB	D-RB	TOT	AST	PF	DQ	STL	TO	BLK	PTS	RPG	APG	PPG
90-91–Portland	43	0	290	55	116	.474	0	0	–	25	44	.568	27	62	89	12	39	0	4	22	12	135	2.1	0.3	3.1
91-92–Portland	71	1	934	178	361	.493	0	0	–	76	101	.752	81	179	260	30	132	1	25	66	16	432	3.7	0.4	6.1
92-93–Milw.-Boston	75	52	1311	245	473	.518	0	1	.000	88	116	.759	126	211	337	27	189	0	25	97	26	578	4.5	0.4	7.7
93-94–Boston	13	0	159	24	55	.436	0	0	–	16	25	.640	12	34	46	3	20	0	2	17	3	64	3.5	0.2	4.9
94-95–Sac.-Phil.	54	0	506	118	231	.511	0	2	.000	20	35	.571	37	77	114	13	104	1	15	45	12	256	2.1	0.2	4.7
Reg. Season Totals	256	53	3200	620	1236	.502	0	3	.000	225	321	.701	283	563	846	85	484	2	71	247	69	1465	3.3	0.3	5.7
Playoff Totals	17	4	106	18	40	.450	0	0	–	2	4	.500	3	17	20	3	11	0	0	11	1	38	1.2	0.2	2.2

Abdul-Aziz, Zaid (formerly Donald A. Smith) b. April 7, 1946 Ht. 6-9 Wt. 235 College: Iowa State

SEASON–TEAM	G	GS	MIN	FGM	FGA	PCT	3FGM	3FGA	PCT	FTM	FTA	PCT	O-RB	D-RB	TOT	AST	PF	DQ	STL	TO	BLK	PTS	RPG	APG	PPG
68-69–Cin.-Milw.	49	–	945	144	390	.369	–	–	–	70	113	.619	–	–	409	37	115	3	–	–	–	358	8.3	0.8	7.3
69-70–Milwaukee	80	–	1637	237	546	.434	–	–	–	119	185	.643	–	–	603	62	167	2	–	–	–	593	7.5	0.8	7.4
70-71–Seattle	61	–	1276	263	597	.441	–	–	–	139	188	.739	–	–	468	42	118	0	–	–	–	665	7.7	0.7	10.9
71-72–Seattle	58	–	1780	322	751	.429	–	–	–	154	214	.720	–	–	654	124	178	1	–	–	–	798	11.3	2.1	13.8
72-73–Houston	48	–	900	149	375	.397	–	–	–	119	162	.735	–	–	304	53	108	2	–	–	–	417	6.3	1.1	8.7
73-74–Houston	79	–	2459	336	732	.459	–	–	–	193	240	.804	259	664	923	166	227	3	80	–	104	865	11.7	2.1	10.9
74-75–Houston	65	–	1450	235	538	.437	–	–	–	159	203	.783	154	334	488	84	128	1	37	–	74	629	7.5	1.3	9.7
75-76–Seattle	27	–	223	35	75	.467	–	–	–	16	29	.552	30	46	76	16	29	0	8	–	15	86	2.8	0.6	3.2
76-77–Buffalo	22	–	195	25	74	.338	–	–	–	33	43	.767	41	49	90	7	21	0	3	–	9	83	4.1	0.3	3.8
77-78–Boston-Hou.	16	–	158	23	60	.383	–	–	–	17	23	.739	19	31	50	10	29	0	3	11	3	63	3.1	0.6	3.9
Reg. Season Totals	505	–	11023	1769	4138	.428	–	–	–	1019	1400	.728	503	1124	4065	601	1120	12	131	11	205	4557	8.0	1.2	9.0
Playoff Totals	18	–	210	37	70	.529	–	–	–	18	26	.692	11	27	64	9	12	0	1	–	8	92	3.6	0.5	5.1

Abdul-Jabbar, Kareem (formerly Ferdinand Lewis Alcindor Jr.) b. April 16, 1947 Ht. 7-2 Wt. 267 College: UCLA HOF: 1995

SEASON–TEAM	G	GS	MIN	FGM	FGA	PCT	3FGM	3FGA	PCT	FTM	FTA	PCT	O-RB	D-RB	TOT	AST	PF	DQ	STL	TO	BLK	PTS	RPG	APG	PPG
69-70–Milwaukee	82	–	3534	938	1810	.518	–	–	–	485	743	.653	–	–	1190	337	283	8	–	–	–	2361	14.5	4.1	28.8
70-71–Milwaukee	82	–	3288	1063	1843	.577	–	–	–	470	681	.690	–	–	1311	272	264	4	–	–	–	2596	16.0	3.3	31.7
71-72–Milwaukee	81	–	3583	1159	2019	.574	–	–	–	504	732	.689	–	–	1346	370	235	1	–	–	–	2822	16.6	4.6	34.8
72-73–Milwaukee	76	–	3254	982	1772	.554	–	–	–	328	460	.713	–	–	1224	379	208	0	–	–	–	2292	16.1	5.0	30.2
73-74–Milwaukee	81	–	3548	948	1759	.539	–	–	–	295	420	.702	287	891	1178	386	238	2	112	–	283	2191	14.5	4.8	27.0
74-75–Milwaukee	65	–	2747	812	1584	.513	–	–	–	325	426	.763	194	718	912	264	205	2	65	–	212	1949	14.0	4.1	30.0
75-76–Los Angeles	82	–	3379	914	1728	.529	–	–	–	447	636	.703	272	1111	1383	413	292	6	119	–	338	2275	16.9	5.0	27.7
76-77–Los Angeles	82	–	3016	888	1533	.579	–	–	–	376	536	.701	266	824	1090	319	262	4	101	–	261	2152	13.3	3.9	26.2
77-78–Los Angeles	62	–	2265	663	1205	.550	–	–	–	274	350	.783	186	615	801	269	182	1	103	208	185	1600	12.9	4.3	25.8
78-79–Los Angeles	80	–	3157	777	1347	.577	–	–	–	349	474	.736	207	818	1025	431	230	3	76	282	316	1903	12.8	5.4	23.8
79-80–Los Angeles	82	–	3143	835	1383	.604	0	1	.000	364	476	.765	190	696	886	371	216	2	81	297	280	2034	10.8	4.5	24.8
80-81–Los Angeles	80	–	2976	836	1457	.574	0	1	.000	423	552	.766	197	624	821	272	244	4	59	249	228	2095	10.3	3.4	26.2
81-82–Los Angeles	76	76	2677	753	1301	.579	0	3	.000	312	442	.706	172	487	659	225	224	0	63	230	207	1818	8.7	3.0	23.9
82-83–Los Angeles	79	79	2554	722	1228	.588	0	2	.000	278	371	.749	167	425	592	200	220	1	61	200	170	1722	7.5	2.5	21.8
83-84–Los Angeles	80	80	2622	716	1238	.578	0	1	.000	285	394	.723	169	418	587	211	211	1	55	221	143	1717	7.3	2.6	21.5
84-85–L.A. Lakers	79	79	2630	723	1207	.599	0	1	.000	289	395	.732	162	460	622	249	238	3	63	197	162	1735	7.9	3.2	22.0
85-86–L.A. Lakers	79	79	2629	755	1338	.564	0	2	.000	336	439	.765	133	345	478	280	248	2	67	203	130	1846	6.1	3.5	23.4
86-87–L.A. Lakers	78	78	2441	560	993	.564	1	3	.333	245	343	.714	152	371	523	203	245	2	49	186	97	1366	6.7	2.6	17.5
87-88–L.A. Lakers	80	80	2308	480	903	.532	0	1	.000	205	269	.762	118	360	478	135	216	1	48	159	92	1165	6.0	1.7	14.6
88-89–L.A. Lakers	74	74	1695	313	659	.475	0	3	.000	122	165	.739	103	231	334	74	196	1	38	95	85	748	4.5	1.0	10.1
Reg. Season Totals	1560	625	57446	15837	28307	.559	1	18	.056	6712	9304	.721	2975	9394	17440	5660	4657	48	1160	2527	3189	38387	11.2	3.6	24.6
Playoff Totals	237	140	8851	2356	4422	.533	0	4	.000	1050	1419	.740	505	1273	2481	767	797	7	189	447	476	5762	10.5	3.2	24.3
All-Star Totals	18	13	449	105	213	.493	0	1	.000	41	50	.820	33	84	149	51	57	1	6	28	31	251	8.3	2.8	13.9

Abdul-Rahman, Mahdi (see Walter Raphael Hazzard Jr.)

Abdul-Rauf, Mahmoud (formerly Chris Wayne Jackson) b. March 9, 1969 Ht. 6-1 Wt. 162 College: Louisiana State

SEASON–TEAM	G	GS	MIN	FGM	FGA	PCT	3FGM	3FGA	PCT	FTM	FTA	PCT	O-RB	D-RB	TOT	AST	PF	DQ	STL	TO	BLK	PTS	RPG	APG	PPG
90-91–Denver	67	19	1505	417	1009	.413	24	100	.240	84	98	.857	34	87	121	206	149	2	55	110	4	942	1.8	3.1	14.1
91-92–Denver	81	11	1538	356	845	.421	31	94	.330	94	108	.870	22	92	114	192	130	0	44	117	4	837	1.4	2.4	10.3
92-93–Denver	81	81	2710	633	1407	.450	70	197	.355	217	232	.935	51	174	225	344	179	0	84	187	8	1553	2.8	4.2	19.2
93-94–Denver	80	78	2617	588	1279	.460	42	133	.316	219	229	.956	27	141	168	362	150	1	82	151	10	1437	2.1	4.5	18.0
94-95–Denver	73	43	2082	472	1005	.470	83	215	.386	138	156	.885	32	105	137	263	126	0	77	119	9	1165	1.9	3.6	16.0
95-96–Denver	57	53	2029	414	955	.434	121	309	.392	146	157	.930	26	112	138	389	117	0	64	115	3	1095	2.4	6.8	19.2
96-97–Sacramento	75	51	2131	411	924	.445	94	246	.382	115	136	.846	16	106	122	189	174	3	56	119	6	1031	1.6	2.5	13.7
97-98–Sacramento	31	0	530	103	273	.377	5	31	.161	16	16	1.000	6	31	37	58	31	0	16	19	1	227	1.2	1.9	7.3
Reg. Season Totals	545	336	15142	3394	7697	.441	470	1325	.355	1029	1132	.909	214	848	1062	2003	1056	6	478	937	45	8287	1.9	3.7	15.2
Playoff Totals	15	14	415	69	187	.369	14	49	.286	43	45	.956	5	18	23	35	37	0	7	22	1	195	1.5	2.3	13.0

Abdul-Wahad, Tariq (formerly Olivier Saint-Jean) b. November 3, 1974 Ht. 6-6 Wt. 223 College: Michigan; San Jose State

SEASON–TEAM	G	GS	MIN	FGM	FGA	PCT	3FGM	3FGA	PCT	FTM	FTA	PCT	O-RB	D-RB	TOT	AST	PF	DQ	STL	TO	BLK	PTS	RPG	APG	PPG
97-98–Sacramento	59	16	959	144	357	.403	4	19	.211	84	125	.672	44	72	116	51	81	0	35	65	13	376	2.0	0.9	6.4
98-99–Sacramento	49	49	1205	177	407	.435	6	21	.286	94	136	.691	72	114	186	50	121	0	50	70	16	454	3.8	1.0	9.3
99-00–Orlando-Denver	61	56	1578	274	646	.424	3	23	.130	146	193	.756	101	190	291	98	147	1	59	106	28	697	4.8	1.6	11.4
Reg. Season Totals	169	121	3742	595	1410	.422	13	63	.206	324	454	.714	217	376	593	199	349	1	144	241	57	1527	3.5	1.2	9.0
Playoff Totals	5	5	99	15	33	.455	0	1	.000	13	16	.813	6	13	19	4	8	0	4	3	4	43	3.8	0.8	8.6

Abdur-Rahim, Julius Shareef (Shareef) b. December 11, 1976 Ht. 6-9 Wt. 230 College: California

SEASON–TEAM	G	GS	MIN	FGM	FGA	PCT	3FGM	3FGA	PCT	FTM	FTA	PCT	O-RB	D-RB	TOT	AST	PF	DQ	STL	TO	BLK	PTS	RPG	APG	PPG
96-97–Vancouver	80	71	2802	550	1214	.453	7	27	.259	387	519	.746	216	339	555	175	199	0	79	225	79	1494	6.9	2.2	18.7
97-98–Vancouver	82	82	2950	653	1347	.485	21	51	.412	502	640	.784	227	354	581	213	201	0	89	257	76	1829	7.1	2.6	22.3
98-99–Vancouver	50	50	2021	386	893	.432	11	36	.306	369	439	.841	114	260	374	172	137	1	69	186	55	1152	7.5	3.4	23.0
99-00–Vancouver	82	82	3223	594	1277	.465	29	96	.302	446	551	.809	218	607	825	271	244	3	89	249	87	1663	10.1	3.3	20.3
Reg. Season Totals	294	285	10996	2183	4731	.461	68	210	.324	1704	2149	.793	775	1560	2335	831	781	4	326	917	297	6138	7.9	2.8	20.9

Abernethy, Thomas Craig (Tom) b. May 6, 1954 Ht. 6-7 Wt. 220 College: Indiana

SEASON–TEAM	G	GS	MIN	FGM	FGA	PCT	3FGM	3FGA	PCT	FTM	FTA	PCT	O-RB	D-RB	TOT	AST	PF	DQ	STL	TO	BLK	PTS	RPG	APG	PPG
76-77–Los Angeles	70	–	1378	169	349	.484	–	–	–	101	134	.754	113	178	291	98	118	1	49	–	10	439	4.2	1.4	6.3
77-78–Los Angeles	73	–	1317	201	404	.498	–	–	–	91	111	.820	105	160	265	101	122	1	55	50	22	493	3.6	1.4	6.8
78-79–Golden State	70	–	1219	176	342	.515	–	–	–	70	94	.745	74	142	216	79	133	1	39	32	13	422	3.1	1.1	6.0
79-80–Golden State	67	–	1222	153	318	.481	0	1	.000	56	82	.683	62	129	191	87	118	0	35	39	12	362	2.9	1.3	5.4
80-81–G.S.-Indiana	39	–	298	25	59	.424	0	1	.000	13	22	.591	20	28	48	19	34	0	7	8	3	63	1.2	0.5	1.6
Reg. Season Totals	319	–	5434	724	1472	.492	0	2	.000	331	443	.747	374	637	1011	384	525	3	185	129	60	1779	3.2	1.2	5.6
Playoff Totals	13	–	226	22	54	.407	0	0	–	24	29	.828	14	28	42	23	18	0	7	0	2	68	3.2	1.8	5.2

Able, Forest Edward (Frosty) b. July 27, 1932 Ht. 6-3 Wt. 180 College: Western Kentucky; Louisville

SEASON–TEAM	G	GS	MIN	FGM	FGA	PCT	3FGM	3FGA	PCT	FTM	FTA	PCT	O-RB	D-RB	TOT	AST	PF	DQ	STL	TO	BLK	PTS	RPG	APG	PPG
56-57–Syracuse	1	–	1	0	2	.000	–	–	–	0	0	–	–	–	1	1	1	0	–	–	–	0	1.0	1.0	0.0
Reg. Season Totals	1	–	1	0	2	.000	–	–	–	0	0	–	–	–	1	1	1	0	–	–	–	0	1.0	1.0	0.0

Abramovic, John Jr. (Brooms) b. February 9, 1919 Ht. 6-3 Wt. 195 College: Salem (N.C.)

SEASON–TEAM	G	GS	MIN	FGM	FGA	PCT	3FGM	3FGA	PCT	FTM	FTA	PCT	O-RB	D-RB	TOT	AST	PF	DQ	STL	TO	BLK	PTS	RPG	APG	PPG
46-47–Pittsburgh	47	–	–	202	834	.242	–	–	–	123	178	.691	–	–	–	35	161	–	–	–	–	527	–	0.7	11.2
47-48–St. Louis-Balt.	9	–	–	1	21	.048	–	–	–	4	7	.571	–	–	–	2	10	–	–	–	–	6	–	0.2	0.7
47-48–Syracuse (N)	35	–	–	72	–	–	–	–	–	42	54	.778	–	–	–	–	96	–	–	–	–	186	–	–	5.3
Reg. NBA Totals	56	–	–	203	855	.237	–	–	–	127	185	.686	–	–	–	37	171	–	–	–	–	533	–	0.7	9.5
Reg. NBL Totals	35	–	–	72	–	–	–	–	–	42	54	.778	–	–	–	–	96	–	–	–	–	186	–	–	5.3
NBL Playoff Totals	3	–	–	5	–	–	–	–	–	2	3	.667	–	–	–	–	8	–	–	–	–	12	–	–	4.0

Ackerman, Donald D. (Buddy) b. September 4, 1930 Ht. 6-0 Wt. 185 College: Long Island University

SEASON–TEAM	G	GS	MIN	FGM	FGA	PCT	3FGM	3FGA	PCT	FTM	FTA	PCT	O-RB	D-RB	TOT	AST	PF	DQ	STL	TO	BLK	PTS	RPG	APG	PPG
53-54–New York	28	–	220	14	63	.222	–	–	–	15	28	.536	–	–	15	23	43	0	–	–	–	43	0.5	0.8	1.5
Reg. Season Totals	28	–	220	14	63	.222	–	–	–	15	28	.536	–	–	15	23	43	0	–	–	–	43	0.5	0.8	1.5
Playoff Totals	4	–	20	1	3	.333	–	–	–	0	0	–	–	–	4	1	7	0	–	–	–	2	1.3	0.3	0.5

Acres, Mark Richard b. November 15, 1962 Ht. 6-11 Wt. 220 College: Oral Roberts

SEASON–TEAM	G	GS	MIN	FGM	FGA	PCT	3FGM	3FGA	PCT	FTM	FTA	PCT	O-RB	D-RB	TOT	AST	PF	DQ	STL	TO	BLK	PTS	RPG	APG	PPG
87-88–Boston	79	5	1151	108	203	.532	0	0	–	71	111	.640	105	165	270	42	198	2	29	54	27	287	3.4	0.5	3.6
88-89–Boston	62	0	632	55	114	.482	1	1	1.000	26	48	.542	59	87	146	19	94	0	19	23	6	137	2.4	0.3	2.2
89-90–Orlando	80	50	1691	138	285	.484	3	4	.750	83	120	.692	154	277	431	67	248	4	36	70	25	362	5.4	0.8	4.5
90-91–Orlando	68	0	1313	109	214	.509	1	3	.333	66	101	.653	140	219	359	25	218	4	25	42	25	285	5.3	0.4	4.2
91-92–Orlando	68	6	926	78	151	.517	1	3	.333	51	67	.761	97	155	252	22	140	1	25	33	15	208	3.7	0.3	3.1
92-93–Hou.-Chi.-Wash.	18	7	269	26	49	.531	1	2	.500	11	16	.688	26	41	67	5	34	0	3	13	6	64	3.7	0.3	3.6
Reg. Season Totals	375	68	5982	514	1016	.506	7	13	.538	308	463	.665	581	944	1525	180	932	11	137	235	104	1343	4.1	0.5	3.6
Playoff Totals	19	0	160	14	27	.519	0	1	.000	9	18	.500	14	23	37	2	33	0	1	6	1	37	1.9	0.1	1.9

Acton, Charles R. (Bud) b. January 11, 1942 Ht. 6-6 Wt. 210 College: Alma; Hillsdale

SEASON–TEAM	G	GS	MIN	FGM	FGA	PCT	3FGM	3FGA	PCT	FTM	FTA	PCT	O-RB	D-RB	TOT	AST	PF	DQ	STL	TO	BLK	PTS	RPG	APG	PPG
67-68–San Diego	23	–	195	29	74	.392	–	–	–	19	29	.655	–	–	47	11	35	0	–	–	–	77	2.0	0.5	3.3
Reg. Season Totals	23	–	195	29	74	.392	–	–	–	19	29	.655	–	–	47	11	35	0	–	–	–	77	2.0	0.5	3.3

Adams, Alvan Leigh (Double A) b. July 19, 1954 Ht. 6-9 Wt. 220 College: Oklahoma

SEASON–TEAM	G	GS	MIN	FGM	FGA	PCT	3FGM	3FGA	PCT	FTM	FTA	PCT	O-RB	D-RB	TOT	AST	PF	DQ	STL	TO	BLK	PTS	RPG	APG	PPG
75-76–Phoenix	80	–	2656	629	1341	.469	–	–	–	261	355	.735	215	512	727	450	274	6	121	–	116	1519	9.1	5.6	19.0
76-77–Phoenix	72	–	2278	522	1102	.474	–	–	–	252	334	.754	180	472	652	322	260	4	95	–	87	1296	9.1	4.5	18.0
77-78–Phoenix	70	–	1914	434	895	.485	–	–	–	214	293	.730	158	407	565	225	242	8	86	234	63	1082	8.1	3.2	15.5
78-79–Phoenix	77	–	2364	569	1073	.530	–	–	–	231	289	.799	220	485	705	360	246	4	110	279	63	1369	9.2	4.7	17.8
79-80–Phoenix	75	–	2168	465	875	.531	0	2	.000	188	236	.797	158	451	609	322	237	4	108	218	55	1118	8.1	4.3	14.9
80-81–Phoenix	75	–	2054	458	870	.526	0	0	–	199	259	.768	157	389	546	344	226	2	106	226	69	1115	7.3	4.6	14.9
81-82–Phoenix	79	75	2393	507	1027	.494	0	1	.000	182	233	.781	138	448	586	356	269	7	114	196	78	1196	7.4	4.5	15.1
82-83–Phoenix	80	75	2447	477	981	.486	1	3	.333	180	217	.829	161	387	548	376	287	7	114	242	74	1135	6.9	4.7	14.2
83-84–Phoenix	70	13	1452	269	582	.462	0	4	.000	132	160	.825	118	201	319	219	195	1	73	117	31	670	4.6	3.1	9.6
84-85–Phoenix	82	69	2136	476	915	.520	0	0	–	250	283	.883	153	347	500	308	254	2	115	197	48	1202	6.1	3.8	14.7
85-86–Phoenix	78	45	2005	341	679	.502	0	2	.000	159	203	.783	148	329	477	324	272	7	103	206	46	841	6.1	4.2	10.8
86-87–Phoenix	68	40	1690	311	618	.503	0	1	.000	134	170	.788	91	247	338	223	207	3	62	139	37	756	5.0	3.3	11.1
87-88–Phoenix	82	25	1646	251	506	.496	1	2	.500	108	128	.844	118	247	365	183	245	3	82	140	41	611	4.5	2.2	7.5
Reg. Season Totals	988	342	27203	5709	11464	.498	2	15	.133	2490	3160	.788	2015	4922	6937	4012	3214	58	1289	2194	808	13910	7.0	4.1	14.1
Playoff Totals	78	13	2288	440	930	.473	0	0	–	196	256	.766	169	419	588	320	251	3	88	154	71	1076	7.5	4.1	13.8
All-Star Totals	1	0	11	2	4	.500	0	0	–	0	0	–	2	1	3	0	1	0	0	–	0	4	3.0	0.0	4.0

Adams, Donald L. (Don) b. November 27, 1947 Ht. 6-7 Wt. 210 College: Northwestern

SEASON–TEAM	G	GS	MIN	FGM	FGA	PCT	3FGM	3FGA	PCT	FTM	FTA	PCT	O-RB	D-RB	TOT	AST	PF	DQ	STL	TO	BLK	PTS	RPG	APG	PPG
70-71–San Diego	82	–	2374	391	957	.409	–	–	–	155	212	.731	–	–	581	173	344	11	–	–	–	937	7.1	2.1	11.4
71-72–Hou.-Atlanta	73	–	2071	313	798	.392	–	–	–	205	275	.745	–	–	502	140	266	6	–	–	–	831	6.9	1.9	11.4
72-73–Atlanta-Detroit	74	–	1874	265	678	.391	–	–	–	145	184	.788	–	–	441	117	231	2	–	–	–	675	6.0	1.6	9.1
73-74–Detroit	74	–	2298	303	742	.408	–	–	–	153	201	.761	133	315	448	141	242	2	110	–	12	759	6.1	1.9	10.3
74-75–Detroit	51	–	1376	127	315	.403	–	–	–	45	78	.577	63	181	244	75	179	1	69	–	20	299	4.8	1.5	5.9
74-75–St. Louis (A)	16	–	342	42	98	.429	0	1	.000	17	22	.773	21	47	68	54	38	–	13	27	2	101	4.3	3.4	6.3
75-76–Buffalo	56	–	704	67	170	.394	–	–	–	40	57	.702	38	107	145	73	128	1	30	–	7	174	2.6	1.3	3.1
75-76–St. Louis (A)	20	–	725	99	251	.394	0	2	.000	63	83	.759	44	72	116	88	80	–	38	52	7	261	5.8	4.4	13.1
76-77–Buffalo	77	–	1710	216	526	.411	–	–	–	129	173	.746	130	241	371	150	201	0	74	–	16	561	4.8	1.9	7.3
Reg. NBA Totals	487	–	12407	1682	4186	.402	–	–	–	872	1180	.739	364	844	2732	869	1591	23	283	–	55	4236	5.6	1.8	8.7
Reg. ABA Totals	36	–	1067	141	349	.404	0	3	.000	80	105	.762	65	119	184	142	118	–	51	79	9	362	5.1	3.9	10.1
NBA Playoff Totals	22	–	566	63	165	.382	–	–	–	30	44	.682	25	53	116	45	74	1	8	–	1	156	5.3	2.0	7.1
ABA Playoff Totals	10	–	301	35	82	.427	0	0	–	20	28	.714	12	35	47	46	32	–	17	28	11	90	4.7	4.6	9.0

Adams, George b. May 15, 1949 Ht. 6-6 Wt. 210 College: Gardner-Webb

SEASON–TEAM	G	GS	MIN	FGM	FGA	PCT	3FGM	3FGA	PCT	FTM	FTA	PCT	O-RB	D-RB	TOT	AST	PF	DQ	STL	TO	BLK	PTS	RPG	APG	PPG
72-73–San Diego (A)	60	–	865	153	312	.490	2	7	.286	65	83	.783	75	130	205	64	97	0	–	67	–	373	3.4	1.1	6.2
73-74–San Diego (A)	80	–	1433	253	506	.500	1	7	.143	78	103	.757	124	217	341	127	111	–	44	119	23	585	4.3	1.6	7.3
74-75–San Diego (A)	75	–	1605	310	622	.498	1	3	.333	73	86	.849	114	213	327	126	164	–	44	106	36	694	4.4	1.7	9.3
Reg. ABA Totals	215	–	3903	716	1440	.497	4	17	.235	216	272	.794	313	560	873	317	372	0	88	292	59	1652	4.1	1.5	7.7
ABA Playoff Totals	9	–	184	34	66	.515	0	1	.000	12	16	.750	13	15	34	15	14	0	4	16	4	80	3.8	1.7	8.9

Adams, Michael b. January 19, 1963 Ht. 5-10 Wt. 165 College: Boston College

SEASON–TEAM	G	GS	MIN	FGM	FGA	PCT	3FGM	3FGA	PCT	FTM	FTA	PCT	O-RB	D-RB	TOT	AST	PF	DQ	STL	TO	BLK	PTS	RPG	APG	PPG
85-86–Sacramento	18	0	139	16	44	.364	0	3	.000	8	12	.667	2	4	6	22	9	0	9	11	1	40	0.3	1.2	2.2
86-87–Washington	63	0	1303	160	393	.407	28	102	.275	105	124	.847	38	85	123	244	88	0	85	81	6	453	2.0	3.9	7.2
87-88–Denver	82	75	2778	416	927	.449	139	379	.367	166	199	.834	40	183	223	503	138	0	168	144	16	1137	2.7	6.1	13.9
88-89–Denver	77	77	2787	468	1082	.433	166	466	.356	322	393	.819	71	212	283	490	149	0	166	180	11	1424	3.7	6.4	18.5
89-90–Denver	79	74	2690	398	989	.402	158	432	.366	267	314	.850	49	176	225	495	133	0	121	141	3	1221	2.8	6.3	15.5
90-91–Denver	66	66	2346	560	1421	.394	167	564	.296	465	529	.879	58	198	256	693	162	1	147	240	6	1752	3.9	10.5	26.5
91-92–Washington	78	78	2795	485	1233	.393	125	386	.324	313	360	.869	58	252	310	594	162	1	145	212	9	1408	4.0	7.6	18.1
92-93–Washington	70	70	2499	365	831	.439	68	212	.321	237	277	.856	52	188	240	526	146	0	100	175	4	1035	3.4	7.5	14.8
93-94–Washington	70	67	2337	285	698	.408	55	191	.288	224	270	.830	37	146	183	480	140	0	96	167	6	849	2.6	6.9	12.1
94-95–Charlotte	29	0	443	67	148	.453	29	81	.358	25	30	.833	6	23	29	95	41	0	23	26	1	188	1.0	3.3	6.5
95-96–Charlotte	21	3	329	37	83	.446	14	41	.341	26	35	.743	5	17	22	67	25	0	21	25	4	114	1.0	3.2	5.4
Reg. Season Totals	653	510	20446	3257	7849	.415	949	2857	.332	2158	2543	.849	416	1484	1900	4209	1193	2	1081	1402	67	9621	2.9	6.4	14.7
Playoff Totals	20	16	679	85	230	.370	35	107	.327	51	60	.850	14	53	67	103	41	0	32	44	2	256	3.4	5.2	12.8
All-Star Totals	1	0	14	4	8	.500	1	3	.333	0	0	–	1	0	1	1	1	0	4	1	0	9	1.0	1.0	9.0

Addison, Rafael b. July 22, 1964 Ht. 6-8 Wt. 241 College: Syracuse

SEASON–TEAM	G	GS	MIN	FGM	FGA	PCT	3FGM	3FGA	PCT	FTM	FTA	PCT	O-RB	D-RB	TOT	AST	PF	DQ	STL	TO	BLK	PTS	RPG	APG	PPG
86-87–Phoenix	62	12	711	146	331	.441	16	50	.320	51	64	.797	41	65	106	45	75	1	27	54	7	359	1.7	0.7	5.8
91-92–New Jersey	76	8	1175	187	432	.433	14	49	.286	56	76	.737	65	100	165	68	109	1	28	46	28	444	2.2	0.9	5.8
92-93–New Jersey	68	15	1164	182	411	.443	7	34	.206	57	70	.814	45	87	132	53	125	0	23	64	11	428	1.9	0.8	6.3
94-95–Detroit	79	16	1776	279	586	.476	24	83	.289	74	99	.747	67	175	242	109	236	2	53	76	25	656	3.1	1.4	8.3
95-96–Charlotte	53	0	516	77	165	.467	0	9	.000	17	22	.773	25	65	90	30	74	0	9	27	9	171	1.7	0.6	3.2
96-97–Charlotte	41	3	355	49	122	.402	8	20	.400	22	28	.786	19	26	45	34	52	0	8	17	3	128	1.1	0.8	3.1
Reg. Season Totals	379	54	5697	920	2047	.449	69	245	.282	277	359	.772	262	518	780	339	671	4	148	284	83	2186	2.1	0.9	5.8
Playoff Totals	6	0	62	9	28	.321	1	2	.500	3	3	1.000	3	3	6	6	3	0	3	3	0	22	1.0	1.0	3.7

Adelman, Richard Leonard (Rick) b. June 16, 1946 Ht. 6-2 Wt. 180 College: Loyola Marymount

SEASON–TEAM	G	GS	MIN	FGM	FGA	PCT	3FGM	3FGA	PCT	FTM	FTA	PCT	O-RB	D-RB	TOT	AST	PF	DQ	STL	TO	BLK	PTS	RPG	APG	PPG
68-69–San Diego	77	–	1448	177	449	.394	–	–	–	131	204	.642	–	–	216	238	158	1	–	–	–	485	2.8	3.1	6.3
69-70–San Diego	35	–	717	96	247	.389	–	–	–	68	91	.747	–	–	81	113	90	0	–	–	–	260	2.3	3.2	7.4
70-71–Portland	81	–	2303	378	895	.422	–	–	–	267	369	.724	–	–	282	380	214	2	–	–	–	1023	3.5	4.7	12.6
71-72–Portland	80	–	2445	329	753	.437	–	–	–	151	201	.751	–	–	229	413	209	2	–	–	–	809	2.9	5.2	10.1
72-73–Portland	76	–	1822	214	525	.408	–	–	–	73	102	.716	–	–	157	294	155	2	–	–	–	501	2.1	3.9	6.6
73-74–Chicago	55	–	618	64	170	.376	–	–	–	54	76	.711	16	53	69	56	63	0	36	–	1	182	1.3	1.0	3.3
74-75–Chi.-N.O.-K.C.-Omaha	58	–	1074	123	291	.423	–	–	–	73	103	.709	25	70	95	112	101	1	70	–	8	319	1.6	1.9	5.5
Reg. Season Totals	462	–	10427	1381	3330	.415	–	–	–	817	1146	.713	41	123	1129	1606	990	8	106	–	9	3579	2.4	3.5	7.7
Playoff Totals	21	–	329	43	96	.448	–	–	–	35	56	.625	2	10	27	39	32	0	8	–	0	121	1.3	1.9	5.8

Aguirre, Mark Anthony b. December 10, 1959 Ht. 6-6 Wt. 235 College: DePaul

SEASON–TEAM	G	GS	MIN	FGM	FGA	PCT	3FGM	3FGA	PCT	FTM	FTA	PCT	O-RB	D-RB	TOT	AST	PF	DQ	STL	TO	BLK	PTS	RPG	APG	PPG
81-82–Dallas	51	20	1468	381	820	.465	25	71	.352	168	247	.680	89	160	249	164	152	0	37	135	22	955	4.9	3.2	18.7
82-83–Dallas	81	75	2784	767	1589	.483	16	76	.211	429	589	.728	191	317	508	332	247	5	80	261	26	1979	6.3	4.1	24.4
83-84–Dallas	79	79	2900	925	1765	.524	15	56	.268	465	621	.749	161	308	469	358	246	5	80	285	22	2330	5.9	4.5	29.5
84-85–Dallas	80	79	2699	794	1569	.506	27	85	.318	440	580	.759	188	289	477	249	250	3	60	253	24	2055	6.0	3.1	25.7
85-86–Dallas	74	73	2501	668	1327	.503	16	56	.286	318	451	.705	177	268	445	339	229	6	62	252	14	1670	6.0	4.6	22.6
86-87–Dallas	80	80	2663	787	1590	.495	53	150	.353	429	557	.770	181	246	427	254	243	4	84	217	30	2056	5.3	3.2	25.7
87-88–Dallas	77	77	2610	746	1571	.475	52	172	.302	388	504	.770	182	252	434	278	223	1	70	203	57	1932	5.6	3.6	25.1
88-89–Dallas-Detroit	80	76	2597	586	1270	.461	51	174	.293	288	393	.733	146	240	386	278	229	2	45	208	36	1511	4.8	3.5	18.9
89-90–Detroit	78	40	2005	438	898	.488	31	93	.333	192	254	.756	117	188	305	145	201	2	34	121	19	1099	3.9	1.9	14.1
90-91–Detroit	78	13	2006	420	909	.462	24	78	.308	240	317	.757	134	240	374	139	209	2	47	128	20	1104	4.8	1.8	14.2
91-92–Detroit	75	12	1582	339	787	.431	15	71	.211	158	230	.687	67	169	236	126	171	0	51	105	11	851	3.1	1.7	11.3
92-93–Detroit	51	15	1056	187	422	.443	30	83	.361	99	129	.767	43	109	152	105	101	1	16	68	7	503	3.0	2.1	9.9
93-94–L.A. Clippers	39	0	859	163	348	.468	37	93	.398	50	72	.694	28	88	116	104	98	2	21	70	8	413	3.0	2.7	10.6
Reg. Season Totals	923	639	27730	7201	14865	.484	392	1258	.312	3664	4944	.741	1704	2874	4578	2871	2599	33	687	2306	296	18458	5.0	3.1	20.0
Playoff Totals	102	66	2958	696	1435	.485	45	142	.317	310	417	.743	181	356	537	262	281	5	71	198	22	1747	5.3	2.6	17.1
All-Star Totals	3	0	42	13	24	.542	2	5	.400	8	10	.800	2	2	4	4	5	0	2	7	1	36	1.3	1.3	12.0

Ainge, Daniel Rae (Danny) b. March 17, 1959 Ht. 6-5 Wt. 185 College: Brigham Young

SEASON–TEAM	G	GS	MIN	FGM	FGA	PCT	3FGM	3FGA	PCT	FTM	FTA	PCT	O-RB	D-RB	TOT	AST	PF	DQ	STL	TO	BLK	PTS	RPG	APG	PPG
81-82–Boston	53	1	564	79	221	.357	5	17	.294	56	65	.862	25	31	56	87	86	1	37	53	3	219	1.1	1.6	4.1
82-83–Boston	80	76	2048	357	720	.496	5	29	.172	72	97	.742	83	131	214	251	259	2	109	98	6	791	2.7	3.1	9.9
83-84–Boston	71	3	1154	166	361	.460	6	22	.273	46	56	.821	29	87	116	162	143	2	41	70	4	384	1.6	2.3	5.4
84-85–Boston	75	73	2564	419	792	.529	15	56	.268	118	136	.868	76	192	268	399	228	4	122	149	6	971	3.6	5.3	12.9
85-86–Boston	80	78	2407	353	701	.504	26	73	.356	123	136	.904	47	188	235	405	204	4	94	129	7	855	2.9	5.1	10.7
86-87–Boston	71	66	2499	410	844	.486	85	192	.443	148	165	.897	49	193	242	400	189	3	101	141	14	1053	3.4	5.6	14.8
87-88–Boston	81	81	3018	482	982	.491	148	357	.415	158	180	.878	59	190	249	503	203	1	115	153	17	1270	3.1	6.2	15.7
88-89–Boston-Sac.	73	54	2377	480	1051	.457	116	305	.380	205	240	.854	71	184	255	402	186	1	93	145	8	1281	3.5	5.5	17.5
89-90–Sacramento	75	68	2727	506	1154	.438	108	289	.374	222	267	.831	69	257	326	453	238	2	113	185	18	1342	4.3	6.0	17.9
90-91–Portland	80	0	1710	337	714	.472	102	251	.406	114	138	.826	45	160	205	285	195	2	63	100	13	890	2.6	3.6	11.1
91-92–Portland	81	6	1595	299	676	.442	78	230	.339	108	131	.824	40	108	148	202	148	0	73	70	13	784	1.8	2.5	9.7
92-93–Phoenix	80	0	2163	337	730	.462	150	372	.403	123	145	.848	49	165	214	260	175	3	69	113	8	947	2.7	3.3	11.8
93-94–Phoenix	68	1	1555	224	537	.417	80	244	.328	78	94	.830	28	103	131	180	140	0	57	81	8	606	1.9	2.6	8.9
94-95–Phoenix	74	1	1374	194	422	.460	78	214	.364	105	130	.808	25	84	109	210	155	1	46	79	7	571	1.5	2.8	7.7
Reg. Season Totals	1042	508	27755	4643	9905	.469	1002	2651	.378	1676	1980	.846	695	2073	2768	4199	2549	26	1133	1566	132	11964	2.7	4.0	11.5
Playoff Totals	193	82	5038	717	1571	.456	172	433	.397	296	357	.829	120	323	443	656	533	4	172	257	19	1902	2.3	3.4	9.9
All-Star Totals	1	0	19	4	11	.364	3	4	.750	1	2	.500	1	2	3	2	1	0	1	1	0	12	3.0	2.0	12.0

Aitch, Matthew Alexander (Matt) b. September 21, 1944 Ht. 6-7 Wt. 230 College: Moberly Area (Mo.) J.C.; Michigan State

SEASON–TEAM	G	GS	MIN	FGM	FGA	PCT	3FGM	3FGA	PCT	FTM	FTA	PCT	O-RB	D-RB	TOT	AST	PF	DQ	STL	TO	BLK	PTS	RPG	APG	PPG
67-68–Indiana (A)	45	–	637	100	247	.405	0	2	.000	52	77	.675	–	–	160	18	69	1	–	37	–	252	3.6	0.4	5.6
Reg. ABA Totals	45	–	637	100	247	.405	0	2	.000	52	77	.675	–	–	160	18	69	1	–	37	–	252	3.6	0.4	5.6
ABA Playoff Totals	2	–	4	2	4	.500	0	0	–	0	0	–	–	–	–	0	0	0	–	1	–	4	0.0	0.0	2.0

Akin, Henry T. b. July 31, 1944 Ht. 6-10 Wt. 235 College: William Carey; Morehead State

SEASON–TEAM	G	GS	MIN	FGM	FGA	PCT	3FGM	3FGA	PCT	FTM	FTA	PCT	O-RB	D-RB	TOT	AST	PF	DQ	STL	TO	BLK	PTS	RPG	APG	PPG
66-67–New York	50	–	453	83	230	.361	–	–	–	26	37	.703	–	–	120	25	82	0	–	–	–	192	2.4	0.5	3.8
67-68–Seattle	36	–	259	46	137	.336	–	–	–	20	31	.645	–	–	57	14	48	1	–	–	–	112	1.6	0.4	3.1
68-69–Kentucky (A)	2	–	25	1	4	.250	0	2	.000	2	3	.667	–	–	4	1	0	0	–	4	–	4	2.0	0.5	2.0
Reg. NBA Totals	86	–	712	129	367	.351	–	–	–	46	68	.676	–	–	177	39	130	1	–	–	–	304	2.1	0.5	3.5
Reg. ABA Totals	2	–	25	1	4	.250	0	2	.000	2	3	.667	–	–	4	1	0	0	–	4	–	4	2.0	0.5	2.0
NBA Playoff Totals	2	–	16	1	7	.143	–	–	–	1	2	.500	–	–	8	–	3	0	–	–	–	3	4.0	0.0	1.5

A

Alarie, Mark Steven b. December 11, 1963 Ht. 6-8 Wt. 220 College: Duke

SEASON–TEAM	G	GS	MIN	FGM	FGA	PCT	3FGM	3FGA	PCT	FTM	FTA	PCT	O-RB	D-RB	TOT	AST	PF	DQ	STL	TO	BLK	PTS	RPG	APG	PPG
86-87–Denver	64	25	1110	217	443	.490	2	9	.222	67	101	.663	73	141	214	74	138	1	22	56	28	503	3.3	1.2	7.9
87-88–Washington	63	0	769	144	300	.480	4	18	.222	35	49	.714	70	90	160	39	107	1	10	50	12	327	2.5	0.6	5.2
88-89–Washington	74	5	1141	206	431	.478	13	38	.342	73	87	.839	103	152	255	63	160	1	25	62	22	498	3.4	0.9	6.7
89-90–Washington	82	10	1893	371	785	.473	10	49	.204	108	133	.812	151	223	374	142	219	2	60	101	39	860	4.6	1.7	10.5
90-91–Washington	42	1	587	99	225	.440	5	21	.238	41	48	.854	41	76	117	45	88	1	15	40	8	244	2.8	1.1	5.8
Reg. Season Totals	325	41	5500	1037	2184	.475	34	135	.252	324	418	.775	438	682	1120	363	712	6	132	309	109	2432	3.4	1.1	7.5
Playoff Totals	4	0	45	10	17	.588	1	2	.500	2	2	1.000	0	6	6	1	9	0	2	4	2	23	1.5	0.3	5.8

Alcindor, Ferdinand Lewis Jr. (Lew, see Kareem Abdul-Jabbar)

Alcorn, Gary R. b. October 8, 1936 Ht. 6-9 Wt. 225 College: Fresno City (Calif.) Coll.; Fresno State

SEASON–TEAM	G	GS	MIN	FGM	FGA	PCT	3FGM	3FGA	PCT	FTM	FTA	PCT	O-RB	D-RB	TOT	AST	PF	DQ	STL	TO	BLK	PTS	RPG	APG	PPG
59-60–Detroit	58	–	670	91	312	.292	–	–	–	48	84	.571	–	–	279	22	123	4	–	–	–	230	4.8	0.4	4.0
60-61–Los Angeles	20	–	174	12	40	.300	–	–	–	7	8	.875	–	–	50	2	47	1	–	–	–	31	2.5	0.1	1.6
Reg. Season Totals	78	–	844	103	352	.293	–	–	–	55	92	.598	–	–	329	24	170	5	–	–	–	261	4.2	0.3	3.3

Aleksinas, Charles (Chuck) b. February 26, 1959 Ht. 6-11 Wt. 260 College: Kentucky; Connecticut

SEASON–TEAM	G	GS	MIN	FGM	FGA	PCT	3FGM	3FGA	PCT	FTM	FTA	PCT	O-RB	D-RB	TOT	AST	PF	DQ	STL	TO	BLK	PTS	RPG	APG	PPG
84-85–Golden State	74	4	1114	161	337	.478	0	1	.000	55	75	.733	87	183	270	36	171	1	15	72	15	377	3.6	0.5	5.1
Reg. Season Totals	74	4	1114	161	337	.478	0	1	.000	55	75	.733	87	183	270	36	171	1	15	72	15	377	3.6	0.5	5.1

Alexander, Cory Lynn b. June 22, 1973 Ht. 6-1 Wt. 190 College: Virginia

SEASON–TEAM	G	GS	MIN	FGM	FGA	PCT	3FGM	3FGA	PCT	FTM	FTA	PCT	O-RB	D-RB	TOT	AST	PF	DQ	STL	TO	BLK	PTS	RPG	APG	PPG
95-96–San Antonio	60	0	560	63	155	.406	26	66	.394	16	25	.640	9	33	42	121	94	0	27	68	2	168	0.7	2.0	2.8
96-97–San Antonio	80	6	1454	194	490	.396	94	252	.373	95	129	.736	29	94	123	254	148	0	82	146	16	577	1.5	3.2	7.2
97-98–S.A.-Denver	60	22	1298	171	400	.428	66	176	.375	80	102	.784	17	129	146	209	98	2	70	112	11	488	2.4	3.5	8.1
98-99–Denver	36	4	778	97	260	.373	30	105	.286	37	44	.841	7	67	74	119	77	0	35	69	5	261	2.1	3.3	7.3
99-00–Denver	29	2	329	28	98	.286	9	35	.257	17	22	.773	8	34	42	58	39	0	24	28	2	82	1.4	2.0	2.8
Reg. Season Totals	265	34	4419	553	1403	.394	225	634	.355	245	322	.761	70	357	427	761	456	2	238	423	36	1576	1.6	2.9	5.9
Playoff Totals	9	0	70	10	24	.417	1	5	.200	5	7	.714	4	5	9	9	8	0	2	6	0	26	1.0	1.0	2.9

Alexander, Gary b. November 1, 1969 Ht. 6-7 Wt. 240 College: South Florida

SEASON–TEAM	G	GS	MIN	FGM	FGA	PCT	3FGM	3FGA	PCT	FTM	FTA	PCT	O-RB	D-RB	TOT	AST	PF	DQ	STL	TO	BLK	PTS	RPG	APG	PPG
93-94–Miami-Clev.	11	0	55	8	14	.571	0	0	–	3	9	.333	7	8	15	2	10	0	3	8	0	19	1.4	0.2	1.7
Reg. Season Totals	11	0	55	8	14	.571	0	0	–	3	9	.333	7	8	15	2	10	0	3	8	0	19	1.4	0.2	1.7

Alexander, Victor Joe b. August 31, 1969 Ht. 6-10 Wt. 265 College: Iowa State

SEASON–TEAM	G	GS	MIN	FGM	FGA	PCT	3FGM	3FGA	PCT	FTM	FTA	PCT	O-RB	D-RB	TOT	AST	PF	DQ	STL	TO	BLK	PTS	RPG	APG	PPG
91-92–Golden State	80	28	1350	243	459	.529	0	1	.000	103	149	.691	106	230	336	32	176	0	45	91	62	589	4.2	0.4	7.4
92-93–Golden State	72	59	1753	344	667	.516	10	22	.455	111	162	.685	132	288	420	93	218	2	34	120	53	809	5.8	1.3	11.2
93-94–Golden State	69	39	1318	266	502	.530	2	13	.154	68	129	.527	114	194	308	66	168	0	28	86	32	602	4.5	1.0	8.7
94-95–Golden State	50	29	1237	230	447	.515	6	25	.240	36	60	.600	87	204	291	60	145	2	28	76	29	502	5.8	1.2	10.0
Reg. Season Totals	271	155	5658	1083	2075	.522	18	61	.295	318	500	.636	439	916	1355	251	707	4	135	373	176	2502	5.0	0.9	9.2
Playoff Totals	4	0	24	3	5	.600	0	0	–	1	1	1.000	1	5	6	1	8	0	2	2	0	7	1.5	0.3	1.8

Alford, Stephen Todd (Steve) b. November 23, 1964 Ht. 6-2 Wt. 185 College: Indiana

SEASON–TEAM	G	GS	MIN	FGM	FGA	PCT	3FGM	3FGA	PCT	FTM	FTA	PCT	O-RB	D-RB	TOT	AST	PF	DQ	STL	TO	BLK	PTS	RPG	APG	PPG
87-88–Dallas	28	0	197	21	55	.382	1	8	.125	16	17	.941	3	20	23	23	23	0	17	12	3	59	0.8	0.8	2.1
88-89–Dallas-G.S.	66	3	906	148	324	.457	20	55	.364	50	61	.820	10	62	72	92	57	0	45	45	3	366	1.1	1.4	5.5
89-90–Dallas	41	0	302	63	138	.457	7	22	.318	35	37	.946	2	23	25	39	22	0	15	16	3	168	0.6	1.0	4.1
90-91–Dallas	34	0	236	59	117	.504	7	23	.304	26	31	.839	10	14	24	22	11	0	8	16	1	151	0.7	0.6	4.4
Reg. Season Totals	169	3	1641	291	634	.459	35	108	.324	127	146	.870	25	119	144	176	113	0	85	89	10	744	0.9	1.0	4.4
Playoff Totals	13	0	106	20	48	.417	6	17	.353	8	9	.889	4	5	9	15	11	0	3	5	0	54	0.7	1.2	4.2

Allen, Bill b. 1945 Ht. 6-8 Wt. 205 College: New Mexico State

SEASON–TEAM	G	GS	MIN	FGM	FGA	PCT	3FGM	3FGA	PCT	FTM	FTA	PCT	O-RB	D-RB	TOT	AST	PF	DQ	STL	TO	BLK	PTS	RPG	APG	PPG
67-68–Anaheim (A)	38	–	857	120	280	.429	2	2	1.000	58	99	.586	–	–	269	23	121	5	–	38	–	300	7.1	0.6	7.9
Reg. ABA Totals	38	–	857	120	280	.429	2	2	1.000	58	99	.586	–	–	269	23	121	5	–	38	–	300	7.1	0.6	7.9

Allen, James Randall (Randy) b. January 26, 1965 Ht. 6-8 Wt. 220 College: Florida State

SEASON–TEAM	G	GS	MIN	FGM	FGA	PCT	3FGM	3FGA	PCT	FTM	FTA	PCT	O-RB	D-RB	TOT	AST	PF	DQ	STL	TO	BLK	PTS	RPG	APG	PPG
88-89–Sacramento	7	0	43	8	19	.421	0	1	.000	1	2	.500	3	4	7	0	7	0	1	2	1	17	1.0	0.0	2.4
89-90–Sacramento	63	6	746	106	239	.444	0	7	.000	23	43	.535	49	89	138	23	102	0	16	28	19	235	2.2	0.4	3.7
Reg. Season Totals	70	6	789	114	258	.442	0	8	.000	24	45	.533	52	93	145	23	109	0	17	30	20	252	2.1	0.3	3.6

Allen, Jerome Byron b. January 28, 1973 Ht. 6-4 Wt. 184 College: Pennsylvania

SEASON–TEAM	G	GS	MIN	FGM	FGA	PCT	3FGM	3FGA	PCT	FTM	FTA	PCT	O-RB	D-RB	TOT	AST	PF	DQ	STL	TO	BLK	PTS	RPG	APG	PPG
95-96–Minnesota	41	0	362	36	105	.343	10	33	.303	26	36	.722	5	20	25	49	42	0	21	34	5	108	0.6	1.2	2.6
96-97–Ind.-Denver	76	1	943	78	221	.353	30	93	.323	42	72	.583	25	73	98	152	84	0	31	69	4	228	1.3	2.0	3.0
Reg. Season Totals	117	1	1305	114	326	.350	40	126	.317	68	108	.630	30	93	123	201	126	0	52	103	9	336	1.1	1.7	2.9

Allen, Lucius Oliver Jr. b. September 26, 1947 Ht. 6-2 Wt. 175 College: UCLA

SEASON–TEAM	G	GS	MIN	FGM	FGA	PCT	3FGM	3FGA	PCT	FTM	FTA	PCT	O-RB	D-RB	TOT	AST	PF	DQ	STL	TO	BLK	PTS	RPG	APG	PPG
69-70–Seattle	81	–	1817	306	692	.442	–	–	–	182	249	.731	–	–	211	342	201	0	–	–	–	794	2.6	4.2	9.8
70-71–Milwaukee	61	–	1162	178	398	.447	–	–	–	77	110	.700	–	–	152	161	108	0	–	–	–	433	2.5	2.6	7.1
71-72–Milwaukee	80	–	2316	441	874	.505	–	–	–	198	259	.764	–	–	254	333	214	2	–	–	–	1080	3.2	4.2	13.5
72-73–Milwaukee	80	–	2693	547	1130	.484	–	–	–	143	200	.715	–	–	279	426	188	1	–	–	–	1237	3.5	5.3	15.5
73-74–Milwaukee	72	–	2388	526	1062	.495	–	–	–	216	274	.788	89	202	291	374	215	2	137	–	22	1268	4.0	5.2	17.6
74-75–Milw.-L.A.	66	–	2353	511	1170	.437	–	–	–	238	306	.778	90	188	278	372	217	4	136	–	29	1260	4.2	5.6	19.1
75-76–Los Angeles	76	–	2388	461	1004	.459	–	–	–	197	254	.776	64	150	214	357	241	2	101	–	20	1119	2.8	4.7	14.7
76-77–Los Angeles	78	–	2482	472	1035	.456	–	–	–	195	252	.774	58	193	251	405	183	0	116	–	19	1139	3.2	5.2	14.6
77-78–Kansas City	77	–	2147	373	846	.441	–	–	–	174	220	.791	66	163	229	360	180	0	93	217	28	920	3.0	4.7	11.9
78-79–Kansas City	31	–	413	69	174	.397	–	–	–	19	33	.576	14	32	46	44	52	0	21	30	6	157	1.5	1.4	5.1
Reg. Season Totals	702	–	20159	3884	8385	.463	–	–	–	1639	2157	.760	381	928	2205	3174	1799	11	604	247	124	9407	3.1	4.5	13.4
Playoff Totals	43	–	1160	202	450	.449	–	–	–	102	135	.756	9	30	133	142	100	0	13	5	4	506	3.1	3.3	11.8

Allen, Robert J. (Bob) b. July 17, 1946 Ht. 6-9 Wt. 205 College: Marshall

SEASON–TEAM	G	GS	MIN	FGM	FGA	PCT	3FGM	3FGA	PCT	FTM	FTA	PCT	O-RB	D-RB	TOT	AST	PF	DQ	STL	TO	BLK	PTS	RPG	APG	PPG
68-69–San Francisco	27	–	232	14	43	.326	–	–	–	20	36	.556	–	–	56	10	27	0	–	–	–	48	2.1	0.4	1.8
Reg. Season Totals	27	–	232	14	43	.326	–	–	–	20	36	.556	–	–	56	10	27	0	–	–	–	48	2.1	0.4	1.8
Playoff Totals	3	–	19	0	4	.000	–	–	–	4	7	.571	–	–	6	–	2	0	–	–	–	4	2.0	0.0	1.3

Allen, Walter Ray (Ray) b. July 20, 1975 Ht. 6-5 Wt. 205 College: Connecticut

SEASON–TEAM	G	GS	MIN	FGM	FGA	PCT	3FGM	3FGA	PCT	FTM	FTA	PCT	O-RB	D-RB	TOT	AST	PF	DQ	STL	TO	BLK	PTS	RPG	APG	PPG
96-97–Milwaukee	82	81	2532	390	908	.430	117	298	.393	205	249	.823	97	229	326	210	218	0	75	149	10	1102	4.0	2.6	13.4
97-98–Milwaukee	82	82	3287	563	1315	.428	134	368	.364	342	391	.875	127	278	405	356	244	2	111	263	12	1602	4.9	4.3	19.5
98-99–Milwaukee	50	50	1719	303	673	.450	74	208	.356	176	195	.903	57	155	212	178	117	0	53	122	7	856	4.2	3.6	17.1
99-00–Milwaukee	82	82	3070	642	1411	.455	172	407	.423	353	398	.887	83	276	359	308	187	1	110	183	19	1809	4.4	3.8	22.1
Reg. Season Totals	296	295	10608	1898	4307	.441	497	1281	.388	1076	1233	.873	364	938	1302	1052	766	3	349	717	48	5369	4.4	3.6	18.1
Playoff Totals	8	8	306	65	137	.474	19	45	.422	28	35	.800	18	37	55	26	19	0	11	20	1	177	6.9	3.3	22.1
All-Star Totals	1	0	17	4	13	.308	1	6	.167	5	6	.833	1	0	1	2	2	0	3	3	1	14	1.0	2.0	14.0

Allen, Willie b. February 8, 1949 Ht. 6-6 Wt. 230 College: Miami (Fla.)

SEASON–TEAM	G	GS	MIN	FGM	FGA	PCT	3FGM	3FGA	PCT	FTM	FTA	PCT	O-RB	D-RB	TOT	AST	PF	DQ	STL	TO	BLK	PTS	RPG	APG	PPG
71-72–Floridians (A)	7	–	30	4	13	.308	0	0	–	5	6	.833	–	–	14	4	11	–	–	6	–	13	2.0	0.6	1.9
Reg. ABA Totals	7	–	30	4	13	.308	0	0	–	5	6	.833	–	–	14	4	11	–	–	6	–	13	2.0	0.6	1.9

Allison, Odis Jr. b. October 2, 1949 Ht. 6-6 Wt. 195 College: Laney (Calif.) Coll.; Nevada-Las Vegas

SEASON–TEAM	G	GS	MIN	FGM	FGA	PCT	3FGM	3FGA	PCT	FTM	FTA	PCT	O-RB	D-RB	TOT	AST	PF	DQ	STL	TO	BLK	PTS	RPG	APG	PPG
71-72–Golden State	36	–	166	17	78	.218	–	–	–	33	61	.541	–	–	45	10	34	0	–	–	–	67	1.3	0.3	1.9
Reg. Season Totals	36	–	166	17	78	.218	–	–	–	33	61	.541	–	–	45	10	34	0	–	–	–	67	1.3	0.3	1.9

Allums, Darrell Wilbert Jr. b. September 12, 1958 Ht. 6-9 Wt. 225 College: UCLA

SEASON–TEAM	G	GS	MIN	FGM	FGA	PCT	3FGM	3FGA	PCT	FTM	FTA	PCT	O-RB	D-RB	TOT	AST	PF	DQ	STL	TO	BLK	PTS	RPG	APG	PPG
80-81–Dallas	22	–	276	23	67	.343	0	1	.000	13	22	.591	19	46	65	25	51	2	5	23	8	59	3.0	1.1	2.7
Reg. Season Totals	22	–	276	23	67	.343	0	1	.000	13	22	.591	19	46	65	25	51	2	5	23	8	59	3.0	1.1	2.7

Alston, Derrick Samuel b. August 20, 1972 Ht. 6-11 Wt. 225 College: Duquesne

SEASON–TEAM	G	GS	MIN	FGM	FGA	PCT	3FGM	3FGA	PCT	FTM	FTA	PCT	O-RB	D-RB	TOT	AST	PF	DQ	STL	TO	BLK	PTS	RPG	APG	PPG
94-95–Philadelphia	64	1	1032	120	258	.465	0	4	.000	59	120	.492	98	121	219	33	107	1	39	53	35	299	3.4	0.5	4.7
95-96–Philadelphia	73	41	1614	198	387	.512	1	3	.333	55	112	.491	127	175	302	61	191	1	56	59	52	452	4.1	0.8	6.2
96-97–Atlanta	2	0	11	0	5	.000	0	0	–	0	2	.000	3	1	4	0	0	0	0	0	0	0	2.0	0.0	0.0
Reg. Season Totals	139	42	2657	318	650	.489	1	7	.143	114	234	.487	228	297	525	94	298	2	95	112	87	751	3.8	0.7	5.4

Alston, Rafer b. July 24, 1976 Ht. 6-2 Wt. 171 College: Fresno State

SEASON–TEAM	G	GS	MIN	FGM	FGA	PCT	3FGM	3FGA	PCT	FTM	FTA	PCT	O-RB	D-RB	TOT	AST	PF	DQ	STL	TO	BLK	PTS	RPG	APG	PPG
99-00–Milwaukee	27	0	361	27	95	.284	3	14	.214	3	4	.750	5	18	23	70	29	0	12	29	0	60	0.9	2.6	2.2
Reg. Season Totals	27	0	361	27	95	.284	3	14	.214	3	4	.750	5	18	23	70	29	0	12	29	0	60	0.9	2.6	2.2
Playoff Totals	4	0	16	0	3	.000	0	1	.000	0	2	.000	0	0	0	1	0	0	0	1	0	0	0.0	0.3	0.0

Aluma, Peter b. April 26, 1973 Ht. 6-10 Wt. 260 College: Liberty

SEASON–TEAM	G	GS	MIN	FGM	FGA	PCT	3FGM	3FGA	PCT	FTM	FTA	PCT	O-RB	D-RB	TOT	AST	PF	DQ	STL	TO	BLK	PTS	RPG	APG	PPG
98-99–Sacramento	2	0	5	1	2	.500	0	0	–	0	0	–	1	1	2	0	4	0	1	2	1	2	1.0	0.0	1.0
Reg. Season Totals	2	0	5	1	2	.500	0	0	–	0	0	–	1	1	2	0	4	0	1	2	1	2	1.0	0.0	1.0

Amaechi, John b. November 26, 1970 Ht. 6-10 Wt. 270 College: Penn State

SEASON–TEAM	G	GS	MIN	FGM	FGA	PCT	3FGM	3FGA	PCT	FTM	FTA	PCT	O-RB	D-RB	TOT	AST	PF	DQ	STL	TO	BLK	PTS	RPG	APG	PPG
95-96–Cleveland	28	3	357	29	70	.414	0	0	–	19	33	.576	13	39	52	9	49	1	6	34	11	77	1.9	0.3	2.8
99-00–Orlando	80	53	1684	306	700	.437	1	6	.167	223	291	.766	62	204	266	95	161	1	35	139	37	836	3.3	1.2	10.5
Reg. Season Totals	108	56	2041	335	770	.435	1	6	.167	242	324	.747	75	243	318	104	210	2	41	173	48	913	2.9	1.0	8.5
Playoff Totals	1	0	2	0	1	.000	0	0	–	0	0	–	0	0	0	–	0	0	0	0	0	0	0.0	0.0	0.0

Amaya, Ashraf b. November 23, 1971 Ht. 6-7 Wt. 250 College: Southern Illinois

SEASON–TEAM	G	GS	MIN	FGM	FGA	PCT	3FGM	3FGA	PCT	FTM	FTA	PCT	O-RB	D-RB	TOT	AST	PF	DQ	STL	TO	BLK	PTS	RPG	APG	PPG
95-96–Vancouver	54	34	1104	121	252	.480	0	1	.000	97	149	.651	114	189	303	33	151	3	22	57	10	339	5.6	0.6	6.3
96-97–Washington	31	0	144	12	40	.300	1	1	1.000	15	28	.536	19	33	52	3	29	0	7	10	3	40	1.7	0.1	1.3
Reg. Season Totals	85	34	1248	133	292	.455	1	2	.500	112	177	.633	133	222	355	36	180	3	29	67	13	379	4.2	0.4	4.5

Anderegg, Robert H. **(Bob)** b. August 24, 1937 Ht. 6-3 Wt. 200 College: Michigan State

SEASON–TEAM	G	GS	MIN	FGM	FGA	PCT	3FGM	3FGA	PCT	FTM	FTA	PCT	O-RB	D-RB	TOT	AST	PF	DQ	STL	TO	BLK	PTS	RPG	APG	PPG
59-60–New York	33	–	373	55	143	.385	–	–	–	23	42	.548	–	–	69	29	32	0	–	–	–	133	2.1	0.9	4.0
Reg. Season Totals	33	–	373	55	143	.385	–	–	–	23	42	.548	–	–	69	29	32	0	–	–	–	133	2.1	0.9	4.0

Anderson, Andrew Emil **(Andy)** b. July 6, 1945 Ht. 6-2 Wt. 185 College: Canisius

SEASON–TEAM	G	GS	MIN	FGM	FGA	PCT	3FGM	3FGA	PCT	FTM	FTA	PCT	O-RB	D-RB	TOT	AST	PF	DQ	STL	TO	BLK	PTS	RPG	APG	PPG
67-68–Oakland (A)	77	–	1894	279	756	.369	9	44	.205	163	225	.724	–	–	167	118	190	1	–	120	–	730	2.2	1.5	9.5
68-69–Oak.-Miami (A)	36	–	742	123	272	.452	0	6	.000	98	123	.797	–	–	105	45	76	1	–	53	–	344	2.9	1.3	9.6
69-70–Miami-L.A. (A)	81	–	2150	401	930	.431	1	13	.077	204	268	.761	–	–	255	164	196	1	–	–	–	1007	3.1	2.0	12.4
Reg. ABA Totals	194	–	4786	803	1958	.410	10	63	.159	465	616	.755	–	–	527	327	462	3	–	173	–	2081	2.7	1.7	10.7
ABA Playoff Totals	28	–	551	85	215	.395	1	5	.200	54	66	.818	–	–	60	42	59	1	–	–	–	225	2.1	1.5	8.0

Anderson, Clifford V. **(Cliff)** b. September 7, 1944 Ht. 6-5 Wt. 200 College: St. Joseph's (Pa.)

SEASON–TEAM	G	GS	MIN	FGM	FGA	PCT	3FGM	3FGA	PCT	FTM	FTA	PCT	O-RB	D-RB	TOT	AST	PF	DQ	STL	TO	BLK	PTS	RPG	APG	PPG
67-68–Los Angeles	18	–	94	7	29	.241	–	–	–	12	28	.429	–	–	11	17	18	1	–	–	–	26	0.6	0.9	1.4
68-69–Los Angeles	35	–	289	44	108	.407	–	–	–	47	82	.573	–	–	44	31	58	0	–	–	–	135	1.3	0.9	3.9
69-70–Denver (A)	3	–	22	2	4	.500	0	0	–	2	6	.333	–	–	4	4	3	0	–	–	–	6	1.3	1.3	2.0
70-71–Clev.-Phil.	28	–	198	20	65	.308	–	–	–	46	67	.687	–	–	48	20	29	1	–	–	–	86	1.7	0.7	3.1
Reg. NBA Totals	81	–	581	71	202	.351	–	–	–	105	177	.593	–	–	103	68	105	2	–	–	–	247	1.3	0.8	3.0
Reg. ABA Totals	3	–	22	2	4	.500	0	0	–	2	6	.333	–	–	4	4	3	0	–	–	–	6	1.3	1.3	2.0
NBA Playoff Totals	3	–	10	2	5	.400	–	–	–	0	0	–	–	–	1	–	1	0	–	–	–	4	0.3	0.0	1.3

Anderson, Daniel Edward b. January 1, 1951 Ht. 6-2 Wt. 185 College: USC

SEASON–TEAM	G	GS	MIN	FGM	FGA	PCT	3FGM	3FGA	PCT	FTM	FTA	PCT	O-RB	D-RB	TOT	AST	PF	DQ	STL	TO	BLK	PTS	RPG	APG	PPG
74-75–Portland	43	–	453	47	105	.448	–	–	–	26	30	.867	8	21	29	81	44	0	16	–	1	120	0.7	1.9	2.8
75-76–Portland	52	–	614	88	181	.486	–	–	–	51	61	.836	15	47	62	85	58	0	20	–	2	227	1.2	1.6	4.4
Reg. Season Totals	95	–	1067	135	286	.472	–	–	–	77	91	.846	23	68	91	166	102	0	36	–	3	347	1.0	1.7	3.7

Anderson, Daniel W. b. February 15, 1943 Ht. 6-10 Wt. 230 College: Augsburg

SEASON–TEAM	G	GS	MIN	FGM	FGA	PCT	3FGM	3FGA	PCT	FTM	FTA	PCT	O-RB	D-RB	TOT	AST	PF	DQ	STL	TO	BLK	PTS	RPG	APG	PPG
67-68–New Jersey (A)	78	–	2626	463	938	.494	0	0	–	223	320	.697	303	553	856	92	329	10	–	131	–	1149	11.0	1.2	14.7
68-69–N.Y.-Ken.-Minn. (A)	62	–	1399	220	483	.455	0	0	–	118	149	.792	–	–	460	66	174	9	–	81	–	558	7.4	1.1	9.0
Reg. ABA Totals	140	–	4025	683	1421	.481	0	0	–	341	469	.727	303	553	1316	158	503	19	–	212	–	1707	9.4	1.1	12.2
ABA Playoff Totals	5	–	38	6	13	.462	0	0	–	3	4	.750	–	–	10	5	8	0	–	–	–	15	2.0	1.0	3.0

Anderson, Derek Lamont b. July 18, 1974 Ht. 6-5 Wt. 195 College: Ohio State; Kentucky

SEASON–TEAM	G	GS	MIN	FGM	FGA	PCT	3FGM	3FGA	PCT	FTM	FTA	PCT	O-RB	D-RB	TOT	AST	PF	DQ	STL	TO	BLK	PTS	RPG	APG	PPG
97-98–Cleveland	66	13	1839	239	586	.408	17	84	.202	275	315	.873	55	132	187	227	136	0	86	128	13	770	2.8	3.4	11.7
98-99–Cleveland	38	13	978	125	314	.398	21	69	.304	138	165	.836	20	89	109	145	73	0	48	82	4	409	2.9	3.8	10.8
99-00–L.A. Clippers	64	58	2201	377	860	.438	55	178	.309	271	309	.877	80	178	258	220	149	2	90	167	11	1080	4.0	3.4	16.9
Reg. Season Totals	168	84	5018	741	1760	.421	93	331	.281	684	789	.867	155	399	554	592	358	2	224	377	28	2259	3.3	3.5	13.4
Playoff Totals	4	0	103	10	22	.455	0	0	–	23	26	.885	0	9	9	11	10	0	5	12	1	43	2.3	2.8	10.8

Anderson, Dwight Anthony b. December 28, 1960 Ht. 6-3 Wt. 185 College: Kentucky; USC

SEASON–TEAM	G	GS	MIN	FGM	FGA	PCT	3FGM	3FGA	PCT	FTM	FTA	PCT	O-RB	D-RB	TOT	AST	PF	DQ	STL	TO	BLK	PTS	RPG	APG	PPG
82-83–Denver	5	0	33	7	14	.500	0	0	–	7	10	.700	0	2	2	3	7	0	1	5	0	21	0.4	0.6	4.2
Reg. Season Totals	5	0	33	7	14	.500	0	0	–	7	10	.700	0	2	2	3	7	0	1	5	0	21	0.4	0.6	4.2

Anderson, Eric Walfred b. May 26, 1970 Ht. 6-9 Wt. 230 College: Indiana

SEASON–TEAM	G	GS	MIN	FGM	FGA	PCT	3FGM	3FGA	PCT	FTM	FTA	PCT	O-RB	D-RB	TOT	AST	PF	DQ	STL	TO	BLK	PTS	RPG	APG	PPG
92-93–New York	16	0	44	5	18	.278	0	0	–	11	13	.846	6	8	14	3	14	0	3	5	1	21	0.9	0.2	1.3
93-94–New York	11	0	39	7	17	.412	2	2	1.000	5	14	.357	6	11	17	2	9	0	0	2	1	21	1.5	0.2	1.9
Reg. Season Totals	27	0	83	12	35	.343	2	2	1.000	16	27	.593	12	19	31	5	23	0	3	7	2	42	1.1	0.2	1.6
Playoff Totals	2	0	6	1	2	.500	0	0	–	0	0	–	0	1	1	–	2	0	0	1	0	2	0.5	0.0	1.0

Anderson, Gregory Wayne (Greg, Cadillac) b. June 22, 1964 Ht. 6-10 Wt. 250 College: Houston

SEASON–TEAM	G	GS	MIN	FGM	FGA	PCT	3FGM	3FGA	PCT	FTM	FTA	PCT	O-RB	D-RB	TOT	AST	PF	DQ	STL	TO	BLK	PTS	RPG	APG	PPG
87-88–San Antonio	82	45	1984	379	756	.501	1	5	.200	198	328	.604	161	352	513	79	228	1	54	143	122	957	6.3	1.0	11.7
88-89–San Antonio	82	56	2401	460	914	.503	0	3	.000	207	403	.514	255	421	676	61	221	2	102	180	103	1127	8.2	0.7	13.7
89-90–Milwaukee	60	28	1291	219	432	.507	0	0	–	91	170	.535	112	261	373	24	176	3	32	80	54	529	6.2	0.4	8.8
90-91–Milw.-N.J.-Den.	68	2	924	116	270	.430	0	1	.000	60	115	.522	97	221	318	16	140	3	35	84	45	292	4.7	0.2	4.3
91-92–Denver	82	82	2793	389	854	.456	0	4	.000	167	268	.623	337	604	941	78	263	3	88	201	65	945	11.5	1.0	11.5
93-94–Detroit	77	47	1624	201	370	.543	1	3	.333	88	154	.571	183	388	571	51	234	4	55	94	68	491	7.4	0.7	6.4
94-95–Atlanta	51	0	622	57	104	.548	0	0	–	34	71	.479	62	126	188	17	103	0	23	32	32	148	3.7	0.3	2.9
95-96–San Antonio	46	7	344	24	47	.511	0	1	.000	6	25	.240	29	71	100	10	66	0	9	22	24	54	2.2	0.2	1.2
96-97–San Antonio	82	48	1659	130	262	.496	0	1	.000	62	93	.667	157	291	448	34	225	2	63	73	67	322	5.5	0.4	3.9
97-98–Atlanta	50	0	398	36	81	.444	0	5	.000	16	41	.390	39	79	118	15	85	0	19	17	10	88	2.4	0.3	1.8
Reg. Season Totals	680	315	14040	2011	4090	.492	2	23	.087	929	1668	.557	1432	2814	4246	385	1741	18	480	926	590	4953	6.2	0.6	7.3
Playoff Totals	17	3	273	31	65	.477	0	0	–	15	31	.484	15	54	69	5	44	3	7	19	12	77	4.1	0.3	4.5

Anderson, Jerome b. October 9, 1953 Ht. 6-5 Wt. 195 College: West Virginia

SEASON–TEAM	G	GS	MIN	FGM	FGA	PCT	3FGM	3FGA	PCT	FTM	FTA	PCT	O-RB	D-RB	TOT	AST	PF	DQ	STL	TO	BLK	PTS	RPG	APG	PPG
75-76–Boston	22	–	126	25	45	.556	–	–	–	11	16	.688	4	9	13	6	25	0	3	–	3	61	0.6	0.3	2.8
76-77–Indiana	27	–	164	26	59	.441	–	–	–	14	20	.700	9	3	12	10	26	0	6	–	2	66	0.4	0.4	2.4
Reg. Season Totals	49	–	290	51	104	.490	–	–	–	25	36	.694	13	12	25	16	51	0	9	–	5	127	0.5	0.3	2.6
Playoff Totals	4	–	5	1	3	.333	–	–	–	0	0	–	1	0	1	1	1	0	0	–	0	2	0.3	0.3	0.5

Anderson, Keith Kim (Kim) b. May 12, 1955 Ht. 6-7 Wt. 200 College: Missouri

SEASON–TEAM	G	GS	MIN	FGM	FGA	PCT	3FGM	3FGA	PCT	FTM	FTA	PCT	O-RB	D-RB	TOT	AST	PF	DQ	STL	TO	BLK	PTS	RPG	APG	PPG
78-79–Portland	21	–	224	24	77	.312	–	–	–	15	28	.536	17	28	45	15	42	0	4	22	5	63	2.1	0.7	3.0
Reg. Season Totals	21	–	224	24	77	.312	–	–	–	15	28	.536	17	28	45	15	42	0	4	22	5	63	2.1	0.7	3.0

Anderson, Kenneth (Kenny) b. October 9, 1970 Ht. 6-1 Wt. 168 College: Georgia Tech

SEASON–TEAM	G	GS	MIN	FGM	FGA	PCT	3FGM	3FGA	PCT	FTM	FTA	PCT	O-RB	D-RB	TOT	AST	PF	DQ	STL	TO	BLK	PTS	RPG	APG	PPG
91-92–New Jersey	64	13	1086	187	480	.390	3	13	.231	73	98	.745	38	89	127	203	68	0	67	97	9	450	2.0	3.2	7.0
92-93–New Jersey	55	55	2010	370	850	.435	7	25	.280	180	232	.776	51	175	226	449	140	1	96	153	11	927	4.1	8.2	16.9
93-94–New Jersey	82	82	3135	576	1381	.417	40	132	.303	346	423	.818	89	233	322	784	201	0	158	266	15	1538	3.9	9.6	18.8
94-95–New Jersey	72	70	2689	411	1031	.399	97	294	.330	348	414	.841	73	177	250	680	184	1	103	225	14	1267	3.5	9.4	17.6
95-96–N.J.-Cha.	69	64	2344	349	834	.418	92	256	.359	260	338	.769	63	140	203	575	178	1	111	146	14	1050	2.9	8.3	15.2
96-97–Portland	82	81	3081	485	1137	.427	132	366	.361	334	435	.768	91	272	363	584	222	2	162	193	15	1436	4.4	7.1	17.5
97-98–Port.-Boston	61	56	1858	268	674	.398	57	160	.356	153	194	.789	39	134	173	345	135	1	87	143	1	746	2.8	5.7	12.2
98-99–Boston	34	33	1010	161	357	.451	6	24	.250	84	101	.832	24	79	103	193	78	1	33	71	2	412	3.0	5.7	12.1
99-00–Boston	82	82	2593	434	986	.440	85	220	.386	196	253	.775	55	170	225	420	230	4	139	130	8	1149	2.7	5.1	14.0
Reg. Season Totals	601	536	19806	3241	7730	.419	519	1490	.348	1974	2488	.793	523	1469	1992	4233	1436	11	956	1424	89	8975	3.3	7.0	14.9
Playoff Totals	11	8	374	44	109	.404	8	29	.276	43	55	.782	5	27	32	49	22	0	17	21	1	139	2.9	4.5	12.6
All-Star Totals	1	1	16	3	10	.300	0	1	.000	0	0	–	1	3	4	3	2	0	0	4	0	6	4.0	3.0	6.0

Anderson, Michael Levin b. March 23, 1966 Ht. 5-11 Wt. 185 College: Drexel

SEASON–TEAM	G	GS	MIN	FGM	FGA	PCT	3FGM	3FGA	PCT	FTM	FTA	PCT	O-RB	D-RB	TOT	AST	PF	DQ	STL	TO	BLK	PTS	RPG	APG	PPG
88-89–San Antonio	36	12	730	73	175	.417	1	7	.143	57	82	.695	44	45	89	153	64	0	44	84	3	204	2.5	4.3	5.7
Reg. Season Totals	36	12	730	73	175	.417	1	7	.143	57	82	.695	44	45	89	153	64	0	44	84	3	204	2.5	4.3	5.7

Anderson, Mitchell Keith (J.J.) b. September 23, 1960 Ht. 6-8 Wt. 195 College: Bradley

SEASON–TEAM	G	GS	MIN	FGM	FGA	PCT	3FGM	3FGA	PCT	FTM	FTA	PCT	O-RB	D-RB	TOT	AST	PF	DQ	STL	TO	BLK	PTS	RPG	APG	PPG
82-83–Phil.-Utah	65	2	1202	190	379	.501	0	4	.000	100	175	.571	119	175	294	67	153	1	63	79	21	480	4.5	1.0	7.4
83-84–Utah	48	0	311	55	130	.423	0	3	.000	12	29	.414	38	25	63	22	28	0	15	20	9	122	1.3	0.5	2.5
84-85–Utah	44	0	457	61	149	.409	0	2	.000	27	45	.600	29	53	82	21	70	0	29	32	9	149	1.9	0.5	3.4
Reg. Season Totals	157	2	1970	306	658	.465	0	9	.000	139	249	.558	186	253	439	110	251	1	107	131	39	751	2.8	0.7	4.8
Playoff Totals	5	0	13	5	8	.625	1	1	1.000	0	0	–	3	1	4	–	2	0	0	0	1	11	0.8	0.0	2.2

Anderson, Nelison (Nick) b. January 20, 1968 Ht. 6-6 Wt. 228 College: Illinois

SEASON–TEAM	G	GS	MIN	FGM	FGA	PCT	3FGM	3FGA	PCT	FTM	FTA	PCT	O-RB	D-RB	TOT	AST	PF	DQ	STL	TO	BLK	PTS	RPG	APG	PPG
89-90–Orlando	81	9	1785	372	753	.494	1	17	.059	186	264	.705	107	209	316	124	140	0	69	138	34	931	3.9	1.5	11.5
90-91–Orlando	70	42	1971	400	857	.467	17	58	.293	173	259	.668	92	294	386	106	145	0	74	113	44	990	5.5	1.5	14.1
91-92–Orlando	60	59	2203	482	1042	.463	30	85	.353	202	303	.667	98	286	384	163	132	0	97	126	33	1196	6.4	2.7	19.9
92-93–Orlando	79	76	2920	594	1324	.449	88	249	.353	298	402	.741	122	355	477	265	200	1	128	164	56	1574	6.0	3.4	19.9
93-94–Orlando	81	81	2811	504	1054	.478	101	314	.322	168	250	.672	113	363	476	294	148	1	134	165	33	1277	5.9	3.6	15.8
94-95–Orlando	76	76	2588	439	923	.476	179	431	.415	143	203	.704	85	250	335	314	124	0	125	141	22	1200	4.4	4.1	15.8
95-96–Orlando	77	77	2717	400	904	.442	168	430	.391	166	240	.692	92	323	415	279	135	0	121	141	46	1134	5.4	3.6	14.7
96-97–Orlando	63	61	2163	288	725	.397	143	405	.353	38	94	.404	66	238	304	182	160	1	120	86	32	757	4.8	2.9	12.0
97-98–Orlando	58	44	1701	343	754	.455	77	214	.360	127	199	.638	98	199	297	119	98	1	72	85	23	890	5.1	2.1	15.3
98-99–Orlando	47	39	1581	253	640	.395	96	277	.347	99	162	.611	51	226	277	91	72	0	64	83	15	701	5.9	1.9	14.9
99-00–Sacramento	72	72	2094	306	782	.391	132	397	.332	37	76	.487	83	256	339	123	118	0	94	95	16	781	4.7	1.7	10.8
Reg. Season Totals	764	636	24534	4381	9758	.449	1032	2877	.359	1637	2452	.668	1007	2999	4006	2060	1472	4	1098	1337	354	11431	5.2	2.7	15.0
Playoff Totals	49	49	1766	227	549	.413	89	267	.333	101	149	.678	53	185	238	110	108	1	72	76	29	644	4.9	2.2	13.1

Anderson, Richard Andrew b. November 19, 1960 Ht. 6-10 Wt. 240 College: California-Santa Barbara

SEASON–TEAM	G	GS	MIN	FGM	FGA	PCT	3FGM	3FGA	PCT	FTM	FTA	PCT	O-RB	D-RB	TOT	AST	PF	DQ	STL	TO	BLK	PTS	RPG	APG	PPG
82-83–San Diego	78	5	1274	174	431	.404	7	19	.368	48	69	.696	111	161	272	120	170	2	57	93	26	403	3.5	1.5	5.2
83-84–Denver	78	17	1380	272	638	.426	3	19	.158	116	150	.773	136	270	406	193	183	0	46	109	28	663	5.2	2.5	8.5
86-87–Houston	51	0	312	59	139	.424	4	16	.250	22	29	.759	24	55	79	33	37	0	7	19	3	144	1.5	0.6	2.8
87-88–Houston-Port.	74	3	1350	171	439	.390	48	150	.320	58	77	.753	91	212	303	112	137	1	51	61	16	448	4.1	1.5	6.1
88-89–Portland	72	3	1082	145	348	.417	49	141	.348	32	38	.842	62	169	231	98	100	1	44	54	12	371	3.2	1.4	5.2
89-90–Charlotte	54	2	604	88	211	.417	37	100	.370	18	23	.783	33	94	127	55	64	0	20	26	9	231	2.4	1.0	4.3
Reg. Season Totals	407	30	6002	909	2206	.412	148	445	.333	294	386	.762	457	961	1418	611	691	4	225	362	94	2260	3.5	1.5	5.6
Playoff Totals	15	0	140	20	48	.417	8	21	.381	10	12	.833	7	19	26	10	20	0	2	4	3	58	1.7	0.7	3.9

Anderson, Ronald Gene (Ron) b. October 15, 1958 Ht. 6-7 Wt. 215 College: Fresno State

SEASON–TEAM	G	GS	MIN	FGM	FGA	PCT	3FGM	3FGA	PCT	FTM	FTA	PCT	O-RB	D-RB	TOT	AST	PF	DQ	STL	TO	BLK	PTS	RPG	APG	PPG
84-85–Cleveland	36	7	520	84	195	.431	1	2	.500	41	50	.820	39	49	88	34	40	0	9	34	7	210	2.4	0.9	5.8
85-86–Clev.-Indiana	77	30	1676	310	628	.494	2	9	.222	85	127	.669	130	144	274	144	125	0	56	82	6	707	3.6	1.9	9.2
86-87–Indiana	63	0	721	139	294	.473	0	5	.000	85	108	.787	73	78	151	54	65	0	31	55	3	363	2.4	0.9	5.8
87-88–Indiana	74	1	1097	217	436	.498	0	2	.000	108	141	.766	89	127	216	78	98	0	41	73	6	542	2.9	1.1	7.3
88-89–Philadelphia	82	12	2618	566	1152	.491	2	11	.182	196	229	.856	167	239	406	139	166	1	71	126	23	1330	5.0	1.7	16.2
89-90–Philadelphia	78	3	2089	379	841	.451	3	21	.143	165	197	.838	81	214	295	143	143	0	72	78	13	926	3.8	1.8	11.9
90-91–Philadelphia	82	13	2340	512	1055	.485	9	43	.209	165	198	.833	103	264	367	115	163	1	65	100	13	1198	4.5	1.4	14.6
91-92–Philadelphia	82	11	2432	469	1008	.465	42	127	.331	143	163	.877	96	182	278	135	128	0	86	109	11	1123	3.4	1.6	13.7
92-93–Philadelphia	69	0	1263	225	544	.414	39	120	.325	72	89	.809	62	122	184	93	75	0	31	63	5	561	2.7	1.3	8.1
93-94–N.J.-Wash.	21	2	356	35	86	.407	7	26	.269	19	23	.826	16	37	53	17	16	0	8	10	3	96	2.5	0.8	4.6
Reg. Season Totals	664	79	15112	2936	6239	.471	105	366	.287	1079	1325	.814	856	1456	2312	952	1019	2	470	730	90	7056	3.5	1.4	10.6
Playoff Totals	27	0	621	106	239	.444	4	11	.364	50	54	.926	25	55	80	46	58	0	11	29	2	266	3.0	1.7	9.9

Anderson, Shandon Rodriguez (Rod) b. December 13, 1973 Ht. 6-6 Wt. 210 College: Georgia

SEASON–TEAM	G	GS	MIN	FGM	FGA	PCT	3FGM	3FGA	PCT	FTM	FTA	PCT	O-RB	D-RB	TOT	AST	PF	DQ	STL	TO	BLK	PTS	RPG	APG	PPG
96-97–Utah	65	0	1066	147	318	.462	24	47	.511	68	99	.687	52	127	179	49	113	0	27	73	8	386	2.8	0.8	5.9
97-98–Utah	82	2	1602	269	500	.538	7	32	.219	136	185	.735	86	141	227	89	145	0	66	91	18	681	2.8	1.1	8.3
98-99–Utah	50	2	1072	162	363	.446	14	41	.341	89	125	.712	49	83	132	56	89	0	39	66	10	427	2.6	1.1	8.5
99-00–Houston	82	82	2700	368	778	.473	79	225	.351	194	253	.767	91	293	384	239	182	0	96	194	32	1009	4.7	2.9	12.3
Reg. Season Totals	279	86	6440	946	1959	.483	124	345	.359	487	662	.736	278	644	922	433	529	0	228	424	68	2503	3.3	1.6	9.0
Playoff Totals	49	0	971	119	246	.484	14	37	.378	69	99	.697	54	98	152	45	92	2	22	57	5	321	3.1	0.9	6.6

Anderson, Willie Lloyd Jr. (Chill) b. January 8, 1967 Ht. 6-8 Wt. 200 College: Georgia

SEASON–TEAM	G	GS	MIN	FGM	FGA	PCT	3FGM	3FGA	PCT	FTM	FTA	PCT	O-RB	D-RB	TOT	AST	PF	DQ	STL	TO	BLK	PTS	RPG	APG	PPG
88-89–San Antonio	81	79	2738	640	1285	.498	4	21	.190	224	289	.775	152	265	417	372	295	8	150	261	62	1508	5.1	4.6	18.6
89-90–San Antonio	82	81	2788	532	1082	.492	7	26	.269	217	290	.748	115	257	372	364	252	3	111	198	58	1288	4.5	4.4	15.7
90-91–San Antonio	75	75	2592	453	991	.457	7	35	.200	170	213	.798	68	283	351	358	226	4	79	167	46	1083	4.7	4.8	14.4
91-92–San Antonio	57	55	1889	312	685	.455	13	56	.232	107	138	.775	62	238	300	302	151	2	54	140	51	744	5.3	5.3	13.1
92-93–San Antonio	38	7	560	80	186	.430	1	8	.125	22	28	.786	7	50	57	79	52	0	14	44	6	183	1.5	2.1	4.8
93-94–San Antonio	80	79	2488	394	837	.471	22	68	.324	145	171	.848	68	174	242	347	187	1	71	153	46	955	3.0	4.3	11.9
94-95–San Antonio	38	11	556	76	162	.469	3	19	.158	30	41	.732	15	40	55	52	71	1	26	38	10	185	1.4	1.4	4.9
95-96–Toronto-N.Y.	76	44	2060	288	660	.436	34	120	.283	132	163	.810	48	198	246	197	230	5	75	143	59	742	3.2	2.6	9.8
96-97–Miami	28	1	303	29	64	.453	8	19	.421	17	20	.850	15	27	42	34	36	0	14	19	4	83	1.5	1.2	3.0
Reg. Season Totals	555	432	15974	2804	5952	.471	99	372	.266	1064	1353	.786	550	1532	2082	2105	1500	24	594	1163	342	6771	3.8	3.8	12.2
Playoff Totals	52	18	1140	198	427	.464	14	42	.333	73	93	.785	34	108	142	127	128	2	42	81	12	483	2.7	2.4	9.3

Anderzunas, Walter Charles (Wally) b. January 11, 1946 d. May 28, 1989 Ht. 6-7 Wt. 220 College: Creighton

SEASON–TEAM	G	GS	MIN	FGM	FGA	PCT	3FGM	3FGA	PCT	FTM	FTA	PCT	O-RB	D-RB	TOT	AST	PF	DQ	STL	TO	BLK	PTS	RPG	APG	PPG
69-70–Cincinnati	44	–	370	65	166	.392	–	–	–	29	46	.630	–	–	82	9	47	1	–	–	–	159	1.9	0.2	3.6
Reg. Season Totals	44	–	370	65	166	.392	–	–	–	29	46	.630	–	–	82	9	47	1	–	–	–	159	1.9	0.2	3.6

A

Anielak, Donald Robert (Don) b. November 1, 1930 Ht. 6-7 Wt. 190 College: Southwest Missouri State; Bradley

SEASON–TEAM	G	GS	MIN	FGM	FGA	PCT	3FGM	3FGA	PCT	FTM	FTA	PCT	O-RB	D-RB	TOT	AST	PF	DQ	STL	TO	BLK	PTS	RPG	APG	PPG
54-55–New York	1	–	10	0	4	.000	–	–	–	3	4	.750	–	–	2	0	0	0	–	–	–	3	2.0	0.0	3.0
Reg. Season Totals	1	–	10	0	4	.000	–	–	–	3	4	.750	–	–	2	0	0	0	–	–	–	3	2.0	0.0	3.0

Ansley, Michael Antonio b. February 8, 1967 Ht. 6-7 Wt. 225 College: Alabama

SEASON–TEAM	G	GS	MIN	FGM	FGA	PCT	3FGM	3FGA	PCT	FTM	FTA	PCT	O-RB	D-RB	TOT	AST	PF	DQ	STL	TO	BLK	PTS	RPG	APG	PPG
89-90–Orlando	72	5	1221	231	465	.497	0	0	–	164	227	.722	187	175	362	40	152	0	24	50	17	626	5.0	0.6	8.7
90-91–Orlando	67	1	877	144	263	.548	0	0	–	91	127	.717	122	131	253	25	125	0	27	32	7	379	3.8	0.4	5.7
91-92–Phil.-Cha.	10	0	45	8	18	.444	0	0	–	5	6	.833	2	4	6	2	7	0	0	3	0	21	0.6	0.2	2.1
Reg. Season Totals	149	6	2143	383	746	.513	0	0	–	260	360	.722	311	310	621	67	284	0	51	85	24	1026	4.2	0.4	6.9

Anstey, Christopher John (Chris) b. January 1, 1975 Ht. 7-0 Wt. 249 High School: Catholic Regional, Melbourne, Australia

SEASON–TEAM	G	GS	MIN	FGM	FGA	PCT	3FGM	3FGA	PCT	FTM	FTA	PCT	O-RB	D-RB	TOT	AST	PF	DQ	STL	TO	BLK	PTS	RPG	APG	PPG
97-98–Dallas	41	8	680	92	231	.398	3	16	.188	53	74	.716	53	104	157	35	95	1	31	41	27	240	3.8	0.9	5.9
98-99–Dallas	41	4	470	50	139	.360	0	7	.000	34	48	.708	35	62	97	27	98	1	18	26	13	134	2.4	0.7	3.3
99-00–Chicago	73	11	1007	161	364	.442	1	6	.167	116	147	.789	90	190	280	65	180	4	29	80	25	439	3.8	0.9	6.0
Reg. Season Totals	155	23	2157	303	734	.413	4	29	.138	203	269	.755	178	356	534	127	373	6	78	147	65	813	3.4	0.8	5.2

Anthony, Gregory C. (Greg) b. November 15, 1967 Ht. 6-1 Wt. 180 College: Nevada-Las Vegas

SEASON–TEAM	G	GS	MIN	FGM	FGA	PCT	3FGM	3FGA	PCT	FTM	FTA	PCT	O-RB	D-RB	TOT	AST	PF	DQ	STL	TO	BLK	PTS	RPG	APG	PPG
91-92–New York	82	1	1510	161	435	.370	8	55	.145	117	158	.741	33	103	136	314	170	0	59	98	9	447	1.7	3.8	5.5
92-93–New York	70	35	1699	174	419	.415	4	30	.133	107	159	.673	42	128	170	398	141	0	113	104	12	459	2.4	5.7	6.6
93-94–New York	80	36	1994	225	571	.394	48	160	.300	130	168	.774	43	146	189	365	163	1	114	127	13	628	2.4	4.6	7.9
94-95–New York	61	2	943	128	293	.437	56	155	.361	60	76	.789	7	57	64	160	99	1	50	57	7	372	1.0	2.6	6.1
95-96–Vancouver	69	68	2096	324	781	.415	90	271	.332	229	297	.771	29	145	174	476	137	1	116	160	11	967	2.5	6.9	14.0
96-97–Vancouver	65	44	1863	199	507	.393	88	238	.370	130	178	.730	25	159	184	407	122	0	129	129	4	616	2.8	6.3	9.5
97-98–Seattle	80	0	1021	150	349	.430	66	159	.415	53	80	.663	18	93	111	205	97	0	64	91	3	419	1.4	2.6	5.2
98-99–Portland	50	0	806	104	251	.414	49	125	.392	62	89	.697	14	49	63	100	75	0	66	55	3	319	1.3	2.0	6.4
99-00–Portland	82	3	1548	169	416	.406	88	233	.378	88	114	.772	17	116	133	208	143	0	59	85	9	514	1.6	2.5	6.3
Reg. Season Totals	639	189	13480	1634	4022	.406	497	1426	.349	976	1319	.740	228	996	1224	2633	1147	3	770	906	71	4741	1.9	4.1	7.4
Playoff Totals	100	3	1580	152	419	.363	56	191	.293	90	140	.643	28	96	124	234	205	1	81	93	18	450	1.2	2.3	4.5

Arceneaux, Stacey (formerly Robert L. Stacey) b. February 17, 1936 Ht. 6-4 Wt. 220 College: Iowa State

SEASON–TEAM	G	GS	MIN	FGM	FGA	PCT	3FGM	3FGA	PCT	FTM	FTA	PCT	O-RB	D-RB	TOT	AST	PF	DQ	STL	TO	BLK	PTS	RPG	APG	PPG
61-62–St. Louis	7	–	110	22	56	.393	–	–	–	6	13	.462	–	–	32	4	10	0	–	–	–	50	4.6	0.6	7.1
Reg. Season Totals	7	–	110	22	56	.393	–	–	–	6	13	.462	–	–	32	4	10	0	–	–	–	50	4.6	0.6	7.1

Archibald, Nathaniel (Nate, Tiny) b. September 2, 1948 Ht. 6-1 Wt. 160 College: Arizona Western Coll. (J.C.); Texas-El Paso HOF: 1990

SEASON–TEAM	G	GS	MIN	FGM	FGA	PCT	3FGM	3FGA	PCT	FTM	FTA	PCT	O-RB	D-RB	TOT	AST	PF	DQ	STL	TO	BLK	PTS	RPG	APG	PPG
70-71–Cincinnati	82	–	2867	486	1095	.444	–	–	–	336	444	.757	–	–	242	450	218	2	–	–	–	1308	3.0	5.5	16.0
71-72–Cincinnati	76	–	3272	734	1511	.486	–	–	–	677	824	.822	–	–	222	701	198	3	–	–	–	2145	2.9	9.2	28.2
72-73–K.C.-Omaha	80	–	3681	1028	2106	.488	–	–	–	663	783	.847	–	–	223	910	207	2	–	–	–	2719	2.8	11.4	34.0
73-74–K.C.-Omaha	35	–	1272	222	492	.451	–	–	–	173	211	.820	21	64	85	266	76	0	56	–	7	617	2.4	7.6	17.6
74-75–K.C.-Omaha	82	–	3244	759	1664	.456	–	–	–	652	748	.872	48	174	222	557	187	0	119	–	7	2170	2.7	6.8	26.5
75-76–Kansas City	78	–	3184	717	1583	.453	–	–	–	501	625	.802	67	146	213	615	169	0	126	–	15	1935	2.7	7.9	24.8
76-77–N.Y. Nets	34	–	1277	250	560	.446	–	–	–	197	251	.785	22	58	80	254	77	1	59	–	11	697	2.4	7.5	20.5
78-79–Boston	69	–	1662	259	573	.452	–	–	–	242	307	.788	25	78	103	324	132	2	55	197	6	760	1.5	4.7	11.0
79-80–Boston	80	–	2864	383	794	.482	4	18	.222	361	435	.830	59	138	197	671	218	2	106	242	10	1131	2.5	8.4	14.1
80-81–Boston	80	–	2820	382	766	.499	0	9	.000	342	419	.816	36	140	176	618	201	1	75	265	18	1106	2.2	7.7	13.8
81-82–Boston	68	51	2167	308	652	.472	6	16	.375	236	316	.747	25	91	116	541	131	1	52	178	3	858	1.7	8.0	12.6
82-83–Boston	66	18	1811	235	553	.425	5	24	.208	220	296	.743	25	66	91	409	110	1	38	163	4	695	1.4	6.2	10.5
83-84–Milwaukee	46	46	1038	136	279	.487	4	18	.222	64	101	.634	16	60	76	160	78	0	33	78	0	340	1.7	3.5	7.4
Reg. Season Totals	876	115	31159	5899	12628	.467	19	85	.224	4664	5760	.810	344	1015	2046	6476	2002	15	719	1123	81	16481	2.3	7.4	18.8
Playoff Totals	47	8	1642	235	556	.423	2	17	.118	195	236	.826	15	62	77	306	118	1	34	122	2	667	1.6	6.5	14.2
All-Star Totals	6	4	162	27	60	.450	0	0	–	20	24	.833	5	12	18	40	10	0	11	6	1	74	3.0	6.7	12.3

Ard, Jimmie Lee (Jim) b. September 19, 1948 Ht. 6-9 Wt. 220 College: Cincinnati

SEASON–TEAM	G	GS	MIN	FGM	FGA	PCT	3FGM	3FGA	PCT	FTM	FTA	PCT	O-RB	D-RB	TOT	AST	PF	DQ	STL	TO	BLK	PTS	RPG	APG	PPG
70-71–New York (A)	73	–	1027	174	382	.455	0	3	.000	79	132	.598	–	–	337	40	119	–	–	–	–	427	4.6	0.5	5.8
71-72–New York (A)	71	–	1145	159	353	.450	2	8	.250	77	127	.606	–	–	368	34	150	–	–	98	–	397	5.2	0.5	5.6
72-73–New York (A)	42	–	426	53	140	.379	0	4	.000	34	50	.680	48	100	148	14	50	0	–	29	–	140	3.5	0.3	3.3
73-74–Memphis (A)	27	–	502	66	164	.402	2	2	1.000	40	51	.784	48	111	159	41	44	–	16	42	25	174	5.9	1.5	6.4
74-75–Boston	59	–	719	89	266	.335	–	–	–	48	65	.738	59	140	199	40	96	2	13	–	32	226	3.4	0.7	3.8
75-76–Boston	81	–	853	107	294	.364	–	–	–	71	100	.710	96	193	289	48	141	2	12	–	36	285	3.6	0.6	3.5
76-77–Boston	63	–	969	96	254	.378	–	–	–	49	76	.645	77	219	296	53	128	1	18	–	28	241	4.7	0.8	3.8
77-78–Boston-Chi.	15	–	125	8	17	.471	–	–	–	3	5	.600	9	27	36	8	19	0	0	14	0	19	2.4	0.5	1.3
Reg. NBA Totals	218	–	2666	300	831	.361	–	–	–	171	246	.695	241	579	820	149	384	5	43	14	96	771	3.8	0.7	3.5
Reg. ABA Totals	213	–	3100	452	1039	.435	4	17	.235	230	360	.639	96	211	1012	129	363	0	16	169	25	1138	4.8	0.6	5.3
NBA Playoff Totals	21	–	124	14	37	.378	–	–	–	11	14	.786	12	16	28	9	34	0	1	–	4	39	1.3	0.4	1.9
ABA Playoff Totals	19	–	215	30	61	.492	0	2	.000	18	32	.563	0	0	57	7	34	0	0	6	0	78	3.0	0.4	4.1

Arizin, Paul Joseph (Pitchin' Paul) b. April 9, 1928 Ht. 6-4 Wt. 200 College: Villanova HOF: 1977

SEASON–TEAM	G	GS	MIN	FGM	FGA	PCT	3FGM	3FGA	PCT	FTM	FTA	PCT	O-RB	D-RB	TOT	AST	PF	DQ	STL	TO	BLK	PTS	RPG	APG	PPG
50-51–Philadelphia	65	–	–	352	864	.407	–	–	–	417	526	.793	–	–	640	138	284	18	–	–	–	1121	9.8	2.1	17.2
51-52–Philadelphia	66	–	2939	548	1222	.448	–	–	–	578	707	.818	–	–	745	170	250	5	–	–	–	1674	11.3	2.6	25.4
54-55–Philadelphia	72	–	2953	529	1325	.399	–	–	–	454	585	.776	–	–	675	210	270	5	–	–	–	1512	9.4	2.9	21.0
55-56–Philadelphia	72	–	2724	617	1378	.448	–	–	–	507	626	.810	–	–	539	189	282	11	–	–	–	1741	7.5	2.6	24.2
56-57–Philadelphia	71	–	2767	613	1451	.422	–	–	–	591	713	.829	–	–	561	150	274	13	–	–	–	1817	7.9	2.1	25.6
57-58–Philadelphia	68	–	2377	483	1229	.393	–	–	–	440	544	.809	–	–	503	135	235	7	–	–	–	1406	7.4	2.0	20.7
58-59–Philadelphia	70	–	2799	632	1466	.431	–	–	–	587	722	.813	–	–	637	119	264	7	–	–	–	1851	9.1	1.7	26.4
59-60–Philadelphia	72	–	2618	593	1400	.424	–	–	–	420	526	.798	–	–	621	165	263	6	–	–	–	1606	8.6	2.3	22.3
60-61–Philadelphia	79	–	2935	650	1529	.425	–	–	–	532	639	.833	–	–	681	188	335	11	–	–	–	1832	8.6	2.4	23.2
61-62–Philadelphia	78	–	2785	611	1490	.410	–	–	–	484	601	.805	–	–	527	201	307	18	–	–	–	1706	6.8	2.6	21.9
Reg. Season Totals	713	–	24897	5628	13354	.421	–	–	–	5010	6189	.810	–	–	6129	1665	2764	101	–	–	–	16266	8.6	2.3	22.8
Playoff Totals	49	–	1935	411	1001	.411	–	–	–	364	439	.829	–	–	404	128	177	8	–	–	–	1186	8.2	2.6	24.2
All-Star Totals	9	–	206	54	116	.466	–	–	–	29	36	.806	–	–	47	6	29	1	–	–	–	137	5.2	0.7	15.2

Arlauckas, Joseph (Joe) b. July 20, 1965 Ht. 6-9 Wt. 230 College: Niagara

SEASON–TEAM	G	GS	MIN	FGM	FGA	PCT	3FGM	3FGA	PCT	FTM	FTA	PCT	O-RB	D-RB	TOT	AST	PF	DQ	STL	TO	BLK	PTS	RPG	APG	PPG
87-88–Sacramento	9	0	85	14	43	.326	0	0	–	6	8	.750	6	7	13	8	16	0	3	4	4	34	1.4	0.9	3.8
Reg. Season Totals	9	0	85	14	43	.326	0	0	–	6	8	.750	6	7	13	8	16	0	3	4	4	34	1.4	0.9	3.8

Armstrong, Benjamin Roy Jr. (B.J.) b. September 9, 1967 Ht. 6-2 Wt. 185 College: Iowa

SEASON–TEAM	G	GS	MIN	FGM	FGA	PCT	3FGM	3FGA	PCT	FTM	FTA	PCT	O-RB	D-RB	TOT	AST	PF	DQ	STL	TO	BLK	PTS	RPG	APG	PPG
89-90–Chicago	81	0	1291	190	392	.485	3	6	.500	69	78	.885	19	83	102	199	105	0	46	83	6	452	1.3	2.5	5.6
90-91–Chicago	82	0	1731	304	632	.481	15	30	.500	97	111	.874	25	124	149	301	118	0	70	107	4	720	1.8	3.7	8.8
91-92–Chicago	82	3	1875	335	697	.481	35	87	.402	104	129	.806	19	126	145	266	88	0	46	94	5	809	1.8	3.2	9.9
92-93–Chicago	82	74	2492	408	818	.499	63	139	.453	130	151	.861	27	122	149	330	169	0	66	83	6	1009	1.8	4.0	12.3
93-94–Chicago	82	82	2770	479	1007	.476	60	135	.444	194	227	.855	28	142	170	323	147	1	80	131	9	1212	2.1	3.9	14.8
94-95–Chicago	82	82	2577	418	894	.468	108	253	.427	206	233	.884	25	161	186	244	159	0	84	103	8	1150	2.3	3.0	14.0
95-96–Golden State	82	64	2262	340	727	.468	98	207	.473	234	279	.839	22	162	184	401	147	0	68	128	6	1012	2.2	4.9	12.3
96-97–Golden State	49	17	1020	148	327	.453	25	90	.278	68	79	.861	7	67	74	126	56	0	25	53	2	389	1.5	2.6	7.9
97-98–G.S.-Cha.	66	0	831	105	213	.493	9	35	.257	42	50	.840	16	60	76	150	74	0	29	42	0	261	1.2	2.3	4.0
98-99–Cha.-Orlando	32	1	358	40	88	.455	7	15	.467	18	21	.857	2	37	39	61	31	0	12	25	0	105	1.2	1.9	3.3
99-00–Chicago	27	18	583	83	186	.446	13	29	.448	22	25	.880	2	45	47	78	34	0	7	40	1	201	1.7	2.9	7.4
Reg. Season Totals	747	341	17790	2850	5981	.477	436	1026	.425	1184	1383	.856	192	1129	1321	2479	1128	1	533	889	47	7320	1.8	3.3	9.8
Playoff Totals	105	39	2364	314	667	.471	51	113	.451	149	179	.832	24	127	151	252	171	0	82	79	3	828	1.4	2.4	7.9
All-Star Totals	1	1	22	5	9	.556	1	2	.500	0	0	–	1	0	1	4	1	0	0	1	0	11	1.0	4.0	11.0

Armstrong, Darrell Eugene b. June 22, 1968 Ht. 6-1 Wt. 180 College: Fayetteville State

SEASON–TEAM	G	GS	MIN	FGM	FGA	PCT	3FGM	3FGA	PCT	FTM	FTA	PCT	O-RB	D-RB	TOT	AST	PF	DQ	STL	TO	BLK	PTS	RPG	APG	PPG
94-95–Orlando	3	0	8	3	8	.375	2	6	.333	2	2	1.000	1	0	1	3	3	0	1	1	0	10	0.3	1.0	3.3
95-96–Orlando	13	0	41	16	32	.500	6	12	.500	4	4	1.000	0	2	2	5	4	0	6	6	0	42	0.2	0.4	3.2
96-97–Orlando	67	0	1010	132	345	.383	55	181	.304	92	106	.868	35	41	76	175	114	1	61	99	9	411	1.1	2.6	6.1
97-98–Orlando	48	17	1236	156	380	.411	25	68	.368	105	123	.854	65	94	159	236	96	1	58	112	5	442	3.3	4.9	9.2
98-99–Orlando	50	15	1502	230	522	.441	69	189	.365	161	178	.904	53	127	180	335	90	0	108	158	4	690	3.6	6.7	13.8
99-00–Orlando	82	82	2590	484	1119	.433	137	403	.340	225	247	.911	65	205	270	501	137	0	169	248	9	1330	3.3	6.1	16.2
Reg. Season Totals	263	114	6387	1021	2406	.424	294	859	.342	589	660	.892	219	469	688	1255	444	2	403	624	27	2925	2.6	4.8	11.1
Playoff Totals	9	4	306	37	88	.420	15	42	.357	27	29	.931	9	32	41	42	22	1	17	32	1	116	4.6	4.7	12.9

Armstrong, Michael Taylor (Tate) b. October 5, 1955 Ht. 6-3 Wt. 175 College: Duke

SEASON–TEAM	G	GS	MIN	FGM	FGA	PCT	3FGM	3FGA	PCT	FTM	FTA	PCT	O-RB	D-RB	TOT	AST	PF	DQ	STL	TO	BLK	PTS	RPG	APG	PPG
77-78–Chicago	66	–	716	131	280	.468	–	–	–	22	27	.815	24	44	68	74	42	0	23	58	0	284	1.0	1.1	4.3
78-79–Chicago	26	–	259	28	70	.400	–	–	–	10	13	.769	7	13	20	31	22	0	10	21	0	66	0.8	1.2	2.5
Reg. Season Totals	92	–	975	159	350	.454	–	–	–	32	40	.800	31	57	88	105	64	0	33	79	0	350	1.0	1.1	3.8

Armstrong, Paul Carlyle (Curly) b. November 1, 1918 d. June 6, 1983 Ht. 5-11 Wt. 170 College: Indiana

SEASON–TEAM	G	GS	MIN	FGM	FGA	PCT	3FGM	3FGA	PCT	FTM	FTA	PCT	O-RB	D-RB	TOT	AST	PF	DQ	STL	TO	BLK	PTS	RPG	APG	PPG
41-42–Fort Wayne (N)	24	–	–	69	–	–	–	–	–	60	–	–	–	–	–	–	–	–	–	–	–	198	–	–	8.3
42-43–Fort Wayne (N)	23	–	–	67	–	–	–	–	–	49	–	–	–	–	–	–	61	–	–	–	–	183	–	–	8.0
45-46–Fort Wayne (N)	6	–	–	3	–	–	–	–	–	1	–	–	–	–	–	–	–	–	–	–	–	7	–	–	1.2
46-47–Fort Wayne (N)	44	–	–	127	–	–	–	–	–	134	195	.687	–	–	–	–	145	–	–	–	–	388	–	–	8.8
47-48–Fort Wayne (N)	53	–	–	148	–	–	–	–	–	139	206	.675	–	–	–	–	180	–	–	–	–	435	–	–	8.2
48-49–Fort Wayne	52	–	–	131	428	.306	–	–	–	118	169	.698	–	–	–	105	152	–	–	–	–	380	–	2.0	7.3
49-50–Fort Wayne	63	–	–	144	516	.279	–	–	–	170	241	.705	–	–	–	176	217	–	–	–	–	458	–	2.8	7.3
50-51–Fort Wayne	38	–	–	72	232	.310	–	–	–	58	90	.644	–	–	89	77	87	2	–	–	–	202	2.3	2.0	5.3
Reg. NBA Totals	153	–	–	347	1176	.295	–	–	–	346	500	.692	–	–	89	358	456	2	–	–	–	1040	2.3	2.3	6.8
Reg. NBL Totals	150	–	–	414	–	–	–	–	–	383	401	.681	–	–	–	–	386	–	–	–	–	1211	–	–	8.1
NBA Playoff Totals	6	–	–	11	63	.238	–	–	–	2	5	.400	–	–	7	17	12	0	–	–	–	24	2.3	1.9	4.0
NBL Playoff Totals	27	–	–	87	–	–	–	–	–	75	49	.714	–	–	–	–	71	–	–	–	–	249	–	–	9.2

Armstrong, T. Robert (Bob) b. June 17, 1933 Ht. 6-8 Wt. 220 College: Michigan State

SEASON–TEAM	G	GS	MIN	FGM	FGA	PCT	3FGM	3FGA	PCT	FTM	FTA	PCT	O-RB	D-RB	TOT	AST	PF	DQ	STL	TO	BLK	PTS	RPG	APG	PPG
56-57–Philadelphia	19	–	110	11	37	.297	–	–	–	6	12	.500	–	–	39	3	13	0	–	–	–	28	2.1	0.2	1.5
Reg. Season Totals	19	–	110	11	37	.297	–	–	–	6	12	.500	–	–	39	3	13	0	–	–	–	28	2.1	0.2	1.5

Armstrong, Warren Edward (see Warren Jabali)

Arnelle, Hugh Jesse (Jesse) b. December 30, 1933 Ht. 6-5 Wt. 225 College: Penn State

SEASON–TEAM	G	GS	MIN	FGM	FGA	PCT	3FGM	3FGA	PCT	FTM	FTA	PCT	O-RB	D-RB	TOT	AST	PF	DQ	STL	TO	BLK	PTS	RPG	APG	PPG
55-56–Fort Wayne	31	–	409	52	164	.317	–	–	–	43	69	.623	–	–	170	18	60	0	–	–	–	147	5.5	0.6	4.7
Reg. Season Totals	31	–	409	52	164	.317	–	–	–	43	69	.623	–	–	170	18	60	0	–	–	–	147	5.5	0.6	4.7

Arnette, Jay Hoyland b. December 19, 1938 Ht. 6-2 Wt. 175 College: Texas

SEASON–TEAM	G	GS	MIN	FGM	FGA	PCT	3FGM	3FGA	PCT	FTM	FTA	PCT	O-RB	D-RB	TOT	AST	PF	DQ	STL	TO	BLK	PTS	RPG	APG	PPG
63-64–Cincinnati	48	–	501	71	196	.362	–	–	–	42	54	.778	–	–	54	71	105	2	–	–	–	184	1.1	1.5	3.8
64-65–Cincinnati	63	–	662	91	245	.371	–	–	–	56	75	.747	–	–	62	68	125	1	–	–	–	238	1.0	1.1	3.8
65-66–Cincinnati	3	–	14	1	6	.167	–	–	–	0	0	–	–	–	0	0	3	0	–	–	–	2	0.0	0.0	0.7
Reg. Season Totals	114	–	1177	163	447	.365	–	–	–	98	129	.760	–	–	116	139	233	3	–	–	–	424	1.0	1.2	3.7
Playoff Totals	9	–	81	11	32	.344	–	–	–	7	8	.875	–	–	10	10	22	1	–	–	–	29	1.1	1.1	3.2

Arnzen, Robert Louis (Bob) b. November 3, 1947 Ht. 6-6 Wt. 210 College: Notre Dame

SEASON–TEAM	G	GS	MIN	FGM	FGA	PCT	3FGM	3FGA	PCT	FTM	FTA	PCT	O-RB	D-RB	TOT	AST	PF	DQ	STL	TO	BLK	PTS	RPG	APG	PPG
69-70–New York (A)	13	–	98	19	48	.396	0	1	.000	2	6	.333	–	–	22	5	11	0	–	–	–	40	1.7	0.4	3.1
70-71–Cincinnati	55	–	594	128	277	.462	–	–	–	45	52	.865	–	–	152	24	54	0	–	–	–	301	2.8	0.4	5.5
72-73–Indiana (A)	23	–	111	20	38	.526	0	3	.000	6	8	.750	11	12	23	3	12	0	–	0	–	46	1.0	0.1	2.0
73-74–Indiana (A)	20	–	149	24	48	.500	1	1	1.000	7	9	.778	10	10	20	3	11	–	3	8	2	56	1.0	0.2	2.8
Reg. NBA Totals	55	–	594	128	277	.462	–	–	–	45	52	.865	–	–	152	24	54	0	–	–	–	301	2.8	0.4	5.5
Reg. ABA Totals	56	–	358	63	134	.470	1	5	.200	15	23	.652	21	22	65	11	34	0	3	8	2	142	1.2	0.2	2.5
ABA Playoff Totals	7	–	13	3	6	.500	0	2	.000	1	1	1.000	0	0	0	0	1	0	0	0	0	7	0.0	0.0	1.0

Artest, Ronald (Ron) b. November 13, 1979 Ht. 6-6 Wt. 244 College: St. John's (N.Y.)

SEASON–TEAM	G	GS	MIN	FGM	FGA	PCT	3FGM	3FGA	PCT	FTM	FTA	PCT	O-RB	D-RB	TOT	AST	PF	DQ	STL	TO	BLK	PTS	RPG	APG	PPG
99-00–Chicago	72	63	2238	309	759	.407	60	191	.314	188	279	.674	62	246	308	202	159	0	119	166	39	866	4.3	2.8	12.0
Reg. Season Totals	72	63	2238	309	759	.407	60	191	.314	188	279	.674	62	246	308	202	159	0	119	166	39	866	4.3	2.8	12.0

Arthurs, John Charles b. August 15, 1947 Ht. 6-4 Wt. 185 College: Tulane

SEASON–TEAM	G	GS	MIN	FGM	FGA	PCT	3FGM	3FGA	PCT	FTM	FTA	PCT	O-RB	D-RB	TOT	AST	PF	DQ	STL	TO	BLK	PTS	RPG	APG	PPG
69-70–Milwaukee	11	–	86	12	35	.343	–	–	–	11	15	.733	–	–	14	17	15	0	–	–	–	35	1.3	1.5	3.2
Reg. Season Totals	11	–	86	12	35	.343	–	–	–	11	15	.733	–	–	14	17	15	0	–	–	–	35	1.3	1.5	3.2

Askew, Vincent Jerome b. February 28, 1966 Ht. 6-6 Wt. 235 College: Memphis State

SEASON–TEAM	G	GS	MIN	FGM	FGA	PCT	3FGM	3FGA	PCT	FTM	FTA	PCT	O-RB	D-RB	TOT	AST	PF	DQ	STL	TO	BLK	PTS	RPG	APG	PPG
87-88–Philadelphia	14	2	234	22	74	.297	0	0	–	8	11	.727	6	16	22	33	12	0	10	12	6	52	1.6	2.4	3.7
90-91–Golden State	7	0	85	12	25	.480	0	0	–	9	11	.818	7	4	11	13	21	1	2	6	0	33	1.6	1.9	4.7
91-92–Golden State	80	10	1496	193	379	.509	1	10	.100	111	160	.694	89	144	233	188	128	1	47	84	23	498	2.9	2.4	6.2
92-93–Sac.-Seattle	73	4	1129	152	309	.492	2	6	.333	105	149	.705	62	99	161	122	135	2	40	69	19	411	2.2	1.7	5.6
93-94–Seattle	80	3	1690	273	567	.481	6	31	.194	175	211	.829	60	124	184	194	145	0	73	70	19	727	2.3	2.4	9.1
94-95–Seattle	71	1	1721	248	504	.492	31	94	.330	176	238	.739	65	116	181	176	191	1	49	85	13	703	2.5	2.5	9.9
95-96–Seattle	69	2	1725	215	436	.493	29	86	.337	123	161	.764	65	153	218	163	178	0	47	96	15	582	3.2	2.4	8.4
96-97–N.J.-Ind.-Den.	43	0	838	81	186	.435	7	24	.292	70	88	.795	25	73	98	90	123	5	17	46	6	239	2.3	2.1	5.6
97-98–Portland	30	5	443	19	54	.352	0	2	.000	28	39	.718	21	47	68	38	39	0	19	35	5	66	2.3	1.3	2.2
Reg. Season Totals	467	27	9361	1215	2534	.479	76	253	.300	805	1068	.754	400	776	1176	1017	972	10	304	503	106	3311	2.5	2.2	7.1
Playoff Totals	50	0	707	76	191	.398	10	29	.345	54	79	.684	36	60	96	59	95	1	21	42	9	216	1.9	1.2	4.3

Askins, Keith Bernard b. December 15, 1967 Ht. 6-8 Wt. 215 College: Alabama

SEASON–TEAM	G	GS	MIN	FGM	FGA	PCT	3FGM	3FGA	PCT	FTM	FTA	PCT	O-RB	D-RB	TOT	AST	PF	DQ	STL	TO	BLK	PTS	RPG	APG	PPG
90-91–Miami	39	1	266	34	81	.420	6	25	.240	12	25	.480	30	38	68	19	46	0	16	11	13	86	1.7	0.5	2.2
91-92–Miami	59	4	843	84	205	.410	25	73	.342	26	37	.703	65	77	142	38	109	0	40	47	15	219	2.4	0.6	3.7
92-93–Miami	69	1	935	88	213	.413	22	65	.338	29	40	.725	74	124	198	31	141	2	31	37	29	227	2.9	0.4	3.3
93-94–Miami	37	0	319	36	88	.409	4	21	.190	9	10	.900	33	49	82	13	57	0	11	21	1	85	2.2	0.4	2.3
94-95–Miami	50	5	854	81	207	.391	21	78	.269	46	57	.807	86	112	198	39	109	0	35	25	17	229	4.0	0.8	4.6
95-96–Miami	75	14	1897	157	391	.402	99	237	.418	45	57	.789	113	211	324	121	271	6	48	82	61	458	4.3	1.6	6.1
96-97–Miami	78	30	1773	138	319	.433	69	172	.401	39	58	.672	86	185	271	75	196	4	53	59	19	384	3.5	1.0	4.9
97-98–Miami	46	12	681	39	122	.320	21	74	.284	12	19	.632	28	73	101	29	107	3	27	26	12	111	2.2	0.6	2.4
98-99–Miami	33	13	415	20	62	.323	8	29	.276	5	8	.625	10	34	44	10	58	0	17	13	3	53	1.3	0.3	1.6
Reg. Season Totals	486	80	7983	677	1688	.401	275	774	.355	223	311	.717	525	903	1428	375	1094	15	278	321	170	1852	2.9	0.8	3.8
Playoff Totals	27	0	333	21	57	.368	12	31	.387	7	9	.778	22	35	57	13	56	0	9	11	3	61	2.1	0.5	2.3

Asmonga, Donald A. (Don) b. February 15, 1928 Ht. 6-2 Wt. 185 College: California (Pa.); Alliance

SEASON–TEAM	G	GS	MIN	FGM	FGA	PCT	3FGM	3FGA	PCT	FTM	FTA	PCT	O-RB	D-RB	TOT	AST	PF	DQ	STL	TO	BLK	PTS	RPG	APG	PPG
53-54–Baltimore	7	–	46	2	15	.133	–	–	–	1	1	1.000	–	–	1	5	12	1	–	–	–	5	0.1	0.7	0.7
Reg. Season Totals	7	–	46	2	15	.133	–	–	–	1	1	1.000	–	–	1	5	12	1	–	–	–	5	0.1	0.7	0.7

Atha, Richard E. (Dick) b. September 21, 1931 Ht. 6-2 Wt. 195 College: Indiana State

SEASON–TEAM	G	GS	MIN	FGM	FGA	PCT	3FGM	3FGA	PCT	FTM	FTA	PCT	O-RB	D-RB	TOT	AST	PF	DQ	STL	TO	BLK	PTS	RPG	APG	PPG
55-56–New York	25	–	288	36	88	.409	–	–	–	21	27	.778	–	–	42	32	39	0	–	–	–	93	1.7	1.3	3.7
57-58–Detroit	18	–	160	17	47	.362	–	–	–	10	12	.833	–	–	24	19	24	0	–	–	–	44	1.3	1.1	2.4
Reg. Season Totals	43	–	448	53	135	.393	–	–	–	31	39	.795	–	–	66	51	63	0	–	–	–	137	1.5	1.2	3.2

Atkins, Chucky b. August 14, 1974 Ht. 5-11 Wt. 160 College: South Florida

SEASON–TEAM	G	GS	MIN	FGM	FGA	PCT	3FGM	3FGA	PCT	FTM	FTA	PCT	O-RB	D-RB	TOT	AST	PF	DQ	STL	TO	BLK	PTS	RPG	APG	PPG
99-00–Orlando	82	0	1626	314	741	.424	57	163	.350	97	133	.729	20	106	126	306	137	1	52	142	3	782	1.5	3.7	9.5
Reg. Season Totals	82	0	1626	314	741	.424	57	163	.350	97	133	.729	20	106	126	306	137	1	52	142	3	782	1.5	3.7	9.5

Attles, Alvin A. Jr. (Al) b. November 7, 1936 Ht. 6-1 Wt. 180 College: North Carolina A&T

SEASON–TEAM	G	GS	MIN	FGM	FGA	PCT	3FGM	3FGA	PCT	FTM	FTA	PCT	O-RB	D-RB	TOT	AST	PF	DQ	STL	TO	BLK	PTS	RPG	APG	PPG
60-61–Philadelphia	77	–	1544	222	543	.409	–	–	–	97	162	.599	–	–	214	174	235	5	–	–	–	541	2.8	2.3	7.0
61-62–Philadelphia	75	–	2468	343	724	.474	–	–	–	158	267	.592	–	–	355	333	279	8	–	–	–	844	4.7	4.4	11.3
62-63–San Francisco	71	–	1876	301	630	.478	–	–	–	133	206	.646	–	–	205	184	253	7	–	–	–	735	2.9	2.6	10.4
63-64–San Francisco	70	–	1883	289	640	.452	–	–	–	185	275	.673	–	–	236	197	249	4	–	–	–	763	3.4	2.8	10.9
64-65–San Francisco	73	–	1733	254	662	.384	–	–	–	171	274	.624	–	–	239	205	242	7	–	–	–	679	3.3	2.8	9.3
65-66–San Francisco	79	–	2053	364	724	.503	–	–	–	154	252	.611	–	–	322	225	265	7	–	–	–	882	4.1	2.8	11.2
66-67–San Francisco	69	–	1764	212	467	.454	–	–	–	88	151	.583	–	–	321	269	265	13	–	–	–	512	4.7	3.9	7.4
67-68–San Francisco	67	–	1992	252	540	.467	–	–	–	150	216	.694	–	–	276	390	284	9	–	–	–	654	4.1	5.8	9.8
68-69–San Francisco	51	–	1516	162	359	.451	–	–	–	95	149	.638	–	–	181	306	183	3	–	–	–	419	3.5	6.0	8.2
69-70–San Francisco	45	–	676	78	202	.386	–	–	–	75	113	.664	–	–	74	142	103	0	–	–	–	231	1.6	3.2	5.1
70-71–San Francisco	34	–	321	22	54	.407	–	–	–	24	41	.585	–	–	40	58	59	2	–	–	–	68	1.2	1.7	2.0
Reg. Season Totals	711	–	17826	2499	5545	.451	–	–	–	1330	2106	.632	–	–	2463	2483	2417	65	–	–	–	6328	3.5	3.5	8.9
Playoff Totals	62	–	1504	154	382	.403	–	–	–	86	158	.544	–	–	245	206	246	12	–	–	–	394	4.0	3.3	6.4

Aubuchon, Chester J. Jr. (Chet) b. May 8, 1916 Ht. 5-10 Wt. 145 College: Michigan State

SEASON–TEAM	G	GS	MIN	FGM	FGA	PCT	3FGM	3FGA	PCT	FTM	FTA	PCT	O-RB	D-RB	TOT	AST	PF	DQ	STL	TO	BLK	PTS	RPG	APG	PPG
46-47–Detroit	30	–	–	23	91	.253	–	–	–	19	35	.543	–	–	–	20	46	–	–	–	–	65	–	0.7	2.2
Reg. Season Totals	30	–	–	23	91	.253	–	–	–	19	35	.543	–	–	–	20	46	–	–	–	–	65	–	0.7	2.2

Augmon, Stacey Orlando (Plastic Man) b. August 1, 1968 Ht. 6-8 Wt. 205 College: Nevada-Las Vegas

SEASON–TEAM	G	GS	MIN	FGM	FGA	PCT	3FGM	3FGA	PCT	FTM	FTA	PCT	O-RB	D-RB	TOT	AST	PF	DQ	STL	TO	BLK	PTS	RPG	APG	PPG
91-92–Atlanta	82	82	2505	440	899	.489	1	6	.167	213	320	.666	191	229	420	201	161	0	124	181	27	1094	5.1	2.5	13.3
92-93–Atlanta	73	66	2112	397	792	.501	0	4	.000	227	307	.739	141	146	287	170	141	1	91	157	18	1021	3.9	2.3	14.0
93-94–Atlanta	82	82	2605	439	861	.510	1	7	.143	333	436	.764	178	216	394	187	179	0	149	147	45	1212	4.8	2.3	14.8
94-95–Atlanta	76	76	2362	397	876	.453	7	26	.269	252	346	.728	157	211	368	197	163	0	100	152	47	1053	4.8	2.6	13.9
95-96–Atlanta	77	49	2294	362	738	.491	1	4	.250	251	317	.792	137	167	304	137	188	1	106	138	31	976	3.9	1.8	12.7
96-97–Detroit-Port.	60	10	942	105	220	.477	0	0	–	69	97	.711	47	91	138	56	87	0	42	64	17	279	2.3	0.9	4.7
97-98–Portland	71	23	1445	154	372	.414	1	7	.143	94	156	.603	104	131	235	88	144	0	57	81	32	403	3.3	1.2	5.7
98-99–Portland	48	21	874	78	174	.448	0	2	.000	52	76	.684	47	78	125	58	81	0	57	30	18	208	2.6	1.2	4.3
99-00–Portland	59	0	692	83	175	.474	0	2	.000	37	55	.673	42	74	116	53	69	0	27	38	11	203	2.0	0.9	3.4
Reg. Season Totals	628	409	15831	2455	5107	.481	11	58	.190	1528	2110	.724	1044	1343	2387	1147	1213	2	753	988	246	6449	3.8	1.8	10.3
Playoff Totals	55	25	1056	119	256	.465	0	2	.000	97	128	.758	40	79	119	74	96	0	36	44	12	335	2.2	1.3	6.1

Austin, Isaac Edward (Ike) b. August 18, 1969 Ht. 6-10 Wt. 270 College: Kings River (Calif.) Coll.; Arizona State

SEASON–TEAM	G	GS	MIN	FGM	FGA	PCT	3FGM	3FGA	PCT	FTM	FTA	PCT	O-RB	D-RB	TOT	AST	PF	DQ	STL	TO	BLK	PTS	RPG	APG	PPG
91-92–Utah	31	0	112	21	46	.457	0	0	–	19	30	.633	11	24	35	5	20	0	2	8	2	61	1.1	0.2	2.0
92-93–Utah	46	3	306	50	112	.446	0	1	.000	29	44	.659	38	41	79	6	60	1	8	23	14	129	1.7	0.1	2.8
93-94–Philadelphia	14	0	201	29	66	.439	0	1	.000	14	23	.609	25	44	69	17	29	0	5	17	10	72	4.9	1.2	5.1
96-97–Miami	82	17	1881	321	639	.502	0	3	.000	150	226	.664	136	342	478	101	244	4	45	161	43	792	5.8	1.2	9.7
97-98–Miami-LAClips	78	50	2266	406	871	.466	0	8	.000	243	363	.669	199	358	557	175	231	5	61	206	56	1055	7.1	2.2	13.5
98-99–Orlando	49	49	1259	185	453	.408	2	7	.286	105	157	.669	83	154	237	89	125	1	47	114	35	477	4.8	1.8	9.7
99-00–Washington	59	23	1173	151	352	.429	1	4	.250	94	137	.686	64	218	282	74	128	0	17	107	38	397	4.8	1.3	6.7
Reg. Season Totals	359	142	7198	1163	2539	.458	3	24	.125	654	980	.667	556	1181	1737	467	837	11	185	636	198	2983	4.8	1.3	8.3
Playoff Totals	20	4	402	46	106	.434	1	6	.167	33	43	.767	23	60	83	14	50	0	10	30	11	126	4.2	0.7	6.3

Austin, John W. (Johnny) b. August 31, 1944 Ht. 6-0 Wt. 175 College: Boston College

SEASON–TEAM	G	GS	MIN	FGM	FGA	PCT	3FGM	3FGA	PCT	FTM	FTA	PCT	O-RB	D-RB	TOT	AST	PF	DQ	STL	TO	BLK	PTS	RPG	APG	PPG
66-67–Baltimore	4	–	61	5	22	.227	–	–	–	13	16	.813	–	–	7	4	12	0	–	–	–	23	1.8	1.0	5.8
67-68–New Jersey (A)	41	–	692	108	279	.387	0	11	.000	101	140	.721	–	–	64	58	110	0	–	57	–	317	1.6	1.4	7.7
Reg. NBA Totals	4	–	61	5	22	.227	–	–	–	13	16	.813	–	–	7	4	12	0	–	–	–	23	1.8	1.0	5.8
Reg. ABA Totals	41	–	692	108	279	.387	0	11	.000	101	140	.721	–	–	64	58	110	0	–	57	–	317	1.6	1.4	7.7

Austin, Ken b. July 15, 1961 Ht. 6-9 Wt. 205 College: Rice

SEASON–TEAM	G	GS	MIN	FGM	FGA	PCT	3FGM	3FGA	PCT	FTM	FTA	PCT	O-RB	D-RB	TOT	AST	PF	DQ	STL	TO	BLK	PTS	RPG	APG	PPG
83-84–Detroit	7	0	28	6	13	.462	0	0	–	0	0	–	2	1	3	1	7	0	1	3	1	12	0.4	0.1	1.7
Reg. Season Totals	7	0	28	6	13	.462	0	0	–	0	0	–	2	1	3	1	7	0	1	3	1	12	0.4	0.1	1.7

Avent, Anthony b. October 18, 1969 Ht. 6-9 Wt. 240 College: Seton Hall

SEASON–TEAM	G	GS	MIN	FGM	FGA	PCT	3FGM	3FGA	PCT	FTM	FTA	PCT	O-RB	D-RB	TOT	AST	PF	DQ	STL	TO	BLK	PTS	RPG	APG	PPG
92-93–Milwaukee	82	78	2285	347	802	.433	0	2	.000	112	172	.651	180	332	512	91	237	0	57	140	73	806	6.2	1.1	9.8
93-94–Milw.-Orlando	74	40	1371	150	398	.377	0	0	–	89	123	.724	144	194	338	65	147	0	33	85	31	389	4.6	0.9	5.3
94-95–Orlando	71	3	1066	105	244	.430	0	0	–	48	75	.640	97	196	293	41	170	1	28	53	50	258	4.1	0.6	3.6
95-96–Vancouver	71	32	1586	179	466	.384	0	0	–	57	77	.740	108	247	355	69	202	3	30	107	42	415	5.0	1.0	5.8
98-99–Utah	5	0	44	4	13	.308	0	0	–	1	2	.500	8	4	12	1	6	0	2	7	0	9	2.4	0.2	1.8
99-00–L.A. Clippers	49	3	377	29	96	.302	0	0	–	23	32	.719	23	51	74	11	62	1	16	24	15	81	1.5	0.2	1.7
Reg. Season Totals	352	156	6729	814	2019	.403	0	2	.000	330	481	.686	560	1024	1584	278	824	5	166	416	211	1958	4.5	0.8	5.6
Playoff Totals	9	0	80	9	20	.450	0	1	.000	10	12	.833	12	7	19	1	13	0	0	3	1	28	2.1	0.1	3.1

Averitt, William Rodney (Bird) b. July 22, 1952 Ht. 6-2 Wt. 175 College: Pepperdine

SEASON–TEAM	G	GS	MIN	FGM	FGA	PCT	3FGM	3FGA	PCT	FTM	FTA	PCT	O-RB	D-RB	TOT	AST	PF	DQ	STL	TO	BLK	PTS	RPG	APG	PPG
73-74–San Antonio (A)	74	–	1639	343	912	.376	9	50	.180	156	224	.696	44	77	121	132	166	–	63	137	6	851	1.6	1.8	11.5
74-75–Kentucky (A)	84	–	2031	422	1014	.416	7	47	.149	249	320	.778	51	134	185	319	212	–	87	232	13	1100	2.2	3.8	13.1
75-76–Kentucky (A)	78	–	2272	546	1274	.429	40	128	.313	266	346	.769	55	158	213	297	208	–	106	221	22	1398	2.7	3.8	17.9
76-77–Buffalo	75	–	1136	234	619	.378	–	–	–	121	169	.716	20	58	78	134	127	2	30	–	5	589	1.0	1.8	7.9
77-78–N.J.-Buffalo	55	–	1085	198	484	.409	–	–	–	100	141	.709	17	66	83	196	123	3	39	143	9	496	1.5	3.6	9.0
Reg. NBA Totals	130	–	2221	432	1103	.392	–	–	–	221	310	.713	37	124	161	330	250	5	69	143	14	1085	1.2	2.5	8.3
Reg. ABA Totals	236	–	5942	1311	3200	.410	56	225	.249	671	890	.754	150	369	519	748	586	0	256	590	41	3349	2.2	3.2	14.2
ABA Playoff Totals	30	–	727	155	403	.385	3	21	.143	77	92	.837	12	43	55	93	74	0	20	63	6	390	1.8	3.1	13.0

Avery, William b. August 8, 1979 Ht. 6-2 Wt. 180 College: Duke

SEASON–TEAM	G	GS	MIN	FGM	FGA	PCT	3FGM	3FGA	PCT	FTM	FTA	PCT	O-RB	D-RB	TOT	AST	PF	DQ	STL	TO	BLK	PTS	RPG	APG	PPG
99-00–Minnesota	59	1	484	56	181	.309	18	63	.286	24	36	.667	8	32	40	88	60	0	14	42	2	154	0.7	1.5	2.6
Reg. Season Totals	59	1	484	56	181	.309	18	63	.286	24	36	.667	8	32	40	88	60	0	14	42	2	154	0.7	1.5	2.6

Awtrey, Dennis Wade b. February 22, 1948 Ht. 6-10 Wt. 250 College: Santa Clara

SEASON–TEAM	G	GS	MIN	FGM	FGA	PCT	3FGM	3FGA	PCT	FTM	FTA	PCT	O-RB	D-RB	TOT	AST	PF	DQ	STL	TO	BLK	PTS	RPG	APG	PPG
70-71–Philadelphia	70	–	1292	200	421	.475	–	–	–	104	157	.662	–	–	430	89	211	7	–	–	–	504	6.1	1.3	7.2
71-72–Philadelphia	58	–	794	98	222	.441	–	–	–	49	76	.645	–	–	248	51	141	3	–	–	–	245	4.3	0.9	4.2
72-73–Phil.-Chicago	82	–	1687	146	305	.479	–	–	–	86	153	.562	–	–	447	224	234	6	–	–	–	378	5.5	2.7	4.6
73-74–Chicago	68	–	756	65	123	.528	–	–	–	54	94	.574	49	125	174	86	128	3	22	–	14	184	2.6	1.3	2.7
74-75–Phoenix	82	–	2837	339	722	.470	–	–	–	132	195	.677	242	462	704	342	227	2	60	–	52	810	8.6	4.2	9.9
75-76–Phoenix	74	–	1376	142	304	.467	–	–	–	75	109	.688	93	200	293	159	153	1	21	–	22	359	4.0	2.1	4.9
76-77–Phoenix	72	–	1760	160	373	.429	–	–	–	91	126	.722	111	245	356	182	170	1	23	–	31	411	4.9	2.5	5.7
77-78–Phoenix	81	–	1623	112	264	.424	–	–	–	69	109	.633	97	205	302	163	153	0	19	127	25	293	3.7	2.0	3.6
78-79–Boston-Seattle	63	–	746	44	107	.411	–	–	–	41	56	.732	42	109	151	69	106	0	16	52	13	129	2.4	1.1	2.0
79-80–Chicago	26	–	560	27	60	.450	0	0	–	32	50	.640	29	86	115	40	66	0	12	27	15	86	4.4	1.5	3.3
80-81–Seattle	47	–	607	44	93	.473	0	0	–	14	20	.700	33	75	108	54	85	0	12	33	8	102	2.3	1.1	2.2
81-82–Portland	10	3	121	5	15	.333	0	0	–	5	9	.556	7	7	14	8	28	1	1	6	2	15	1.4	0.8	1.5
Reg. Season Totals	733	3	14159	1382	3009	.459	0	0	–	752	1154	.652	703	1514	3342	1467	1702	24	186	245	182	3516	4.6	2.0	4.8
Playoff Totals	61	0	1033	91	177	.514	0	0	–	55	94	.585	45	102	251	88	144	3	17	10	15	237	4.1	1.4	3.9

Babic, Milos b. November 23, 1968 Ht. 7-0 Wt. 240 College: Tennessee Tech

SEASON–TEAM	G	GS	MIN	FGM	FGA	PCT	3FGM	3FGA	PCT	FTM	FTA	PCT	O-RB	D-RB	TOT	AST	PF	DQ	STL	TO	BLK	PTS	RPG	APG	PPG
90-91–Cleveland	12	0	52	6	19	.316	0	0	–	7	12	.583	6	3	9	4	7	0	1	5	1	19	0.8	0.3	1.6
91-92–Miami	9	0	35	6	13	.462	0	0	–	6	8	.750	2	9	11	6	0	0	1	5	0	18	1.2	0.7	2.0
Reg. Season Totals	21	0	87	12	32	.375	0	0	–	13	20	.650	8	12	20	10	7	0	2	10	1	37	1.0	0.5	1.8

Bach, John William (Johnny) b. July 10, 1924 Ht. 6-2 Wt. 180 College: Rochester; Fordham; Brown

SEASON–TEAM	G	GS	MIN	FGM	FGA	PCT	3FGM	3FGA	PCT	FTM	FTA	PCT	O-RB	D-RB	TOT	AST	PF	DQ	STL	TO	BLK	PTS	RPG	APG	PPG
48-49–Boston	34	–	–	34	119	.286	–	–	–	51	75	.680	–	–	–	25	24	–	–	–	–	119	–	0.7	3.5
Reg. Season Totals	34	–	–	34	119	.286	–	–	–	51	75	.680	–	–	–	25	24	–	–	–	–	119	–	0.7	3.5

Bacon, William Henry (Henry) b. July 5, 1948 Ht. 6-3 Wt. 205 College: Louisville

SEASON–TEAM	G	GS	MIN	FGM	FGA	PCT	3FGM	3FGA	PCT	FTM	FTA	PCT	O-RB	D-RB	TOT	AST	PF	DQ	STL	TO	BLK	PTS	RPG	APG	PPG
72-73–San Diego (A)	47	–	425	60	164	.366	2	10	.200	44	73	.603	40	42	82	38	72	1	–	64	–	166	1.7	0.8	3.5
Reg. ABA Totals	47	–	425	60	164	.366	2	10	.200	44	73	.603	40	42	82	38	72	1	–	64	–	166	1.7	0.8	3.5
ABA Playoff Totals	2	–	16	4	9	.444	2	3	.667	0	2	.000	–	–	6	1	0	0	–	2	–	10	3.0	0.5	5.0

Baechtold, James E. (Jim) b. December 9, 1927 Ht. 6-4 Wt. 205 College: Eastern Kentucky

SEASON–TEAM	G	GS	MIN	FGM	FGA	PCT	3FGM	3FGA	PCT	FTM	FTA	PCT	O-RB	D-RB	TOT	AST	PF	DQ	STL	TO	BLK	PTS	RPG	APG	PPG
52-53–Baltimore	64	–	1893	242	621	.390	–	–	–	177	240	.738	–	–	219	154	203	8	–	–	–	661	3.4	2.4	10.3
53-54–New York	70	–	1627	170	465	.366	–	–	–	134	177	.757	–	–	183	117	195	5	–	–	–	474	2.6	1.7	6.8
54-55–New York	72	–	2536	362	898	.403	–	–	–	279	339	.823	–	–	307	218	202	0	–	–	–	1003	4.3	3.0	13.9
55-56–New York	70	–	1738	268	695	.386	–	–	–	233	291	.801	–	–	220	163	156	2	–	–	–	769	3.1	2.3	11.0
56-57–New York	45	–	462	75	197	.381	–	–	–	66	88	.750	–	–	80	33	39	0	–	–	–	216	1.8	0.7	4.8
Reg. Season Totals	321	–	8256	1117	2876	.388	–	–	–	889	1135	.783	–	–	1009	685	795	15	–	–	–	3123	3.1	2.1	9.7
Playoff Totals	9	–	307	45	104	.433	–	–	–	31	38	.816	–	–	33	36	41	1	–	–	–	121	3.3	4.0	13.4

Bagley, John Edward (Bags) b. April 23, 1960 Ht. 6-0 Wt. 195 College: Boston College

SEASON–TEAM	G	GS	MIN	FGM	FGA	PCT	3FGM	3FGA	PCT	FTM	FTA	PCT	O-RB	D-RB	TOT	AST	PF	DQ	STL	TO	BLK	PTS	RPG	APG	PPG
82-83–Cleveland	68	3	990	161	373	.432	0	14	.000	64	84	.762	17	79	96	167	74	0	54	118	5	386	1.4	2.5	5.7
83-84–Cleveland	76	19	1712	257	607	.423	2	17	.118	157	198	.793	49	107	156	333	113	1	78	170	4	673	2.1	4.4	8.9
84-85–Cleveland	81	65	2401	338	693	.488	3	26	.115	125	167	.749	54	237	291	697	132	0	129	207	5	804	3.6	8.6	9.9
85-86–Cleveland	78	77	2472	366	865	.423	9	37	.243	170	215	.791	76	199	275	735	165	1	122	239	10	911	3.5	9.4	11.7
86-87–Cleveland	72	67	2182	312	732	.426	31	103	.301	113	136	.831	55	197	252	379	114	0	91	163	7	768	3.5	5.3	10.7
87-88–New Jersey	82	74	2774	393	896	.439	47	161	.292	148	180	.822	61	196	257	479	162	0	110	201	10	981	3.1	5.8	12.0
88-89–New Jersey	68	20	1642	200	481	.416	11	54	.204	89	123	.724	36	108	144	391	117	0	72	159	5	500	2.1	5.8	7.4
89-90–Boston	54	17	1095	100	218	.459	1	18	.056	29	39	.744	26	63	89	296	77	0	40	90	4	230	1.6	5.5	4.3
91-92–Boston	73	59	1742	223	506	.441	10	42	.238	68	95	.716	38	123	161	480	123	1	57	148	4	524	2.2	6.6	7.2
92-93–Boston	10	0	97	9	25	.360	0	1	.000	5	6	.833	1	6	7	20	11	0	2	17	0	23	0.7	2.0	2.3
93-94–Atlanta	3	0	13	0	2	.000	0	0	–	2	2	1.000	0	1	1	3	2	0	0	0	0	2	0.3	1.0	0.7
Reg. Season Totals	665	401	17120	2359	5398	.437	114	473	.241	970	1245	.779	413	1316	1729	3980	1090	3	755	1512	54	5802	2.6	6.0	8.7
Playoff Totals	19	14	546	72	166	.434	1	8	.125	36	51	.706	12	35	47	142	33	0	23	61	2	181	2.5	7.5	9.5

Bailey, Augustus (Gus) b. February 18, 1951 d. November 28, 1988 Ht. 6-5 Wt. 185 College: Texas-El Paso

SEASON–TEAM	G	GS	MIN	FGM	FGA	PCT	3FGM	3FGA	PCT	FTM	FTA	PCT	O-RB	D-RB	TOT	AST	PF	DQ	STL	TO	BLK	PTS	RPG	APG	PPG
74-75–Houston	47	–	446	51	126	.405	–	–	–	20	41	.488	23	59	82	59	52	0	17	–	16	122	1.7	1.3	2.6
75-76–Houston	30	–	262	28	77	.364	–	–	–	14	28	.500	20	30	50	41	33	1	14	–	8	70	1.7	1.4	2.3
77-78–New Orleans	48	–	449	59	139	.424	–	–	–	37	67	.552	44	38	82	40	46	0	18	33	15	155	1.7	0.8	3.2
78-79–New Orleans	2	–	9	2	7	.286	–	–	–	0	0	–	2	0	2	2	1	0	0	1	0	4	1.0	1.0	2.0
79-80–Washington	20	–	180	16	35	.457	1	1	1.000	5	13	.385	6	22	28	26	18	0	7	11	4	38	1.4	1.3	1.9
Reg. Season Totals	147	–	1346	156	384	.406	1	1	1.000	76	149	.510	95	149	244	168	150	1	56	45	43	389	1.7	1.1	2.6
Playoff Totals	8	–	116	18	36	.500	0	0	–	9	10	.900	6	13	19	16	12	0	6	–	2	45	2.4	2.0	5.6

Bailey, Carl b. April 23, 1958 Ht. 7-0 Wt. 210 College: Tuskegee

SEASON–TEAM	G	GS	MIN	FGM	FGA	PCT	3FGM	3FGA	PCT	FTM	FTA	PCT	O-RB	D-RB	TOT	AST	PF	DQ	STL	TO	BLK	PTS	RPG	APG	PPG
81-82–Portland	1	0	7	1	1	1.000	0	0	–	0	0	–	0	0	0	0	2	0	0	2	0	2	0.0	0.0	2.0
Reg. Season Totals	1	0	7	1	1	1.000	0	0	–	0	0	–	0	0	0	0	2	0	0	2	0	2	0.0	0.0	2.0

Bailey, James L. b. May 21, 1957 Ht. 6-9 Wt. 220 College: Rutgers

SEASON–TEAM	G	GS	MIN	FGM	FGA	PCT	3FGM	3FGA	PCT	FTM	FTA	PCT	O-RB	D-RB	TOT	AST	PF	DQ	STL	TO	BLK	PTS	RPG	APG	PPG
79-80–Seattle	67	–	726	122	271	.450	0	0	–	68	101	.673	71	126	197	28	116	1	21	79	54	312	2.9	0.4	4.7
80-81–Seattle	82	–	2539	444	889	.499	1	2	.500	256	361	.709	192	415	607	98	332	11	74	219	143	1145	7.4	1.2	14.0
81-82–Seattle-N.J.	77	0	1468	261	505	.517	0	0	–	137	224	.612	127	264	391	65	270	5	42	139	83	659	5.1	0.8	8.6
82-83–N.J.-Houston	75	39	1765	385	774	.497	0	1	.000	226	322	.702	171	303	474	67	271	7	43	196	60	996	6.3	0.9	13.3
83-84–Houston	73	0	1174	254	517	.491	0	1	.000	138	192	.719	104	190	294	79	197	8	33	101	40	646	4.0	1.1	8.8
84-85–New York	74	28	1297	156	349	.447	0	1	.000	73	108	.676	122	222	344	39	286	10	30	100	50	385	4.6	0.5	5.2
85-86–New York	48	36	1245	202	443	.456	0	4	.000	129	167	.772	102	232	334	50	207	12	33	99	40	533	7.0	1.0	11.1
86-87–New Jersey	34	2	542	112	239	.469	0	0	–	58	80	.725	48	89	137	20	119	5	12	54	23	282	4.0	0.6	8.3
87-88–Phoenix	65	0	869	109	241	.452	0	4	.000	70	89	.787	73	137	210	42	180	1	17	70	28	288	3.2	0.6	4.4
Reg. Season Totals	595	105	11625	2045	4228	.484	1	13	.077	1155	1644	.703	1010	1978	2988	488	1978	60	305	1057	521	5246	5.0	0.8	8.8
Playoff Totals	14	0	164	22	47	.468	0	0	–	15	22	.682	10	21	31	6	27	0	11	12	10	59	2.2	0.4	4.2

Bailey, John Garfield Jr. (Toby) b. November 19, 1975 Ht. 6-6 Wt. 213 College: UCLA

SEASON–TEAM	G	GS	MIN	FGM	FGA	PCT	3FGM	3FGA	PCT	FTM	FTA	PCT	O-RB	D-RB	TOT	AST	PF	DQ	STL	TO	BLK	PTS	RPG	APG	PPG
98-99–Phoenix	27	10	249	34	86	.395	1	5	.200	9	13	.692	24	30	54	13	24	0	9	11	2	78	2.0	0.5	2.9
99-00–Phoenix	46	2	449	58	140	.414	2	10	.200	45	65	.692	26	46	72	30	55	0	13	24	4	163	1.6	0.7	3.5
Reg. Season Totals	73	12	698	92	226	.407	3	15	.200	54	78	.692	50	76	126	43	79	0	22	35	6	241	1.7	0.6	3.3
Playoff Totals	5	0	15	1	4	.250	0	0	–	2	4	.500	1	1	2	2	1	0	0	0	0	4	0.4	0.4	0.8

Bailey, Thurl Lee (Big T) b. April 7, 1961 Ht. 6-11 Wt. 247 College: North Carolina State

SEASON–TEAM	G	GS	MIN	FGM	FGA	PCT	3FGM	3FGA	PCT	FTM	FTA	PCT	O-RB	D-RB	TOT	AST	PF	DQ	STL	TO	BLK	PTS	RPG	APG	PPG
83-84–Utah	81	54	2009	302	590	.512	0	0	–	88	117	.752	115	349	464	129	193	1	38	105	122	692	5.7	1.6	8.5
84-85–Utah	80	68	2481	507	1034	.490	1	1	1.000	197	234	.842	153	372	525	138	215	2	51	152	105	1212	6.6	1.7	15.2
85-86–Utah	82	13	2358	483	1077	.448	0	7	.000	230	277	.830	148	345	493	153	160	0	42	144	114	1196	6.0	1.9	14.6
86-87–Utah	81	2	2155	463	1036	.447	0	2	.000	190	236	.805	145	287	432	102	150	0	38	123	88	1116	5.3	1.3	13.8
87-88–Utah	82	10	2804	633	1286	.492	1	3	.333	337	408	.826	134	397	531	158	186	1	49	190	125	1604	6.5	1.9	19.6
88-89–Utah	82	3	2777	615	1272	.483	2	5	.400	363	440	.825	115	332	447	138	185	0	48	208	91	1595	5.5	1.7	19.5
89-90–Utah	82	33	2583	470	977	.481	0	8	.000	222	285	.779	116	294	410	137	175	2	32	139	100	1162	5.0	1.7	14.2
90-91–Utah	82	22	2486	399	872	.458	0	3	.000	219	271	.808	101	306	407	124	160	0	53	130	91	1017	5.0	1.5	12.4
91-92–Utah-Minn.	84	18	2104	368	836	.440	0	2	.000	215	270	.796	122	363	485	78	160	1	35	108	117	951	5.8	0.9	11.3
92-93–Minnesota	70	3	1276	203	446	.455	0	0	–	119	142	.838	53	162	215	61	88	0	20	60	47	525	3.1	0.9	7.5
93-94–Minnesota	79	3	1297	232	455	.510	0	2	.000	119	149	.799	66	149	215	54	93	0	20	58	58	583	2.7	0.7	7.4
98-99–Utah	43	0	543	78	175	.446	0	2	.000	25	34	.735	36	58	94	26	78	0	9	27	28	181	2.2	0.6	4.2
Reg. Season Totals	928	229	24873	4753	10056	.473	4	35	.114	2324	2863	.812	1304	3414	4718	1298	1843	7	435	1444	1086	11834	5.1	1.4	12.8
Playoff Totals	69	31	2117	364	811	.449	0	4	.000	201	241	.834	116	266	382	98	196	3	30	109	82	929	5.5	1.4	13.5

Baker, Jimmie Jr. b. December 25, 1953 Ht. 6-9 Wt. 220 College: Nevada-Las Vegas; Hawaii

SEASON–TEAM	G	GS	MIN	FGM	FGA	PCT	3FGM	3FGA	PCT	FTM	FTA	PCT	O-RB	D-RB	TOT	AST	PF	DQ	STL	TO	BLK	PTS	RPG	APG	PPG
75-76–Kentucky (A)	5	–	40	3	15	.200	0	0	–	0	2	.000	4	10	14	4	11	–	0	6	3	6	2.8	0.8	1.2
Reg. ABA Totals	5	–	40	3	15	.200	0	0	–	0	2	.000	4	10	14	4	11	–	0	6	3	6	2.8	0.8	1.2

Baker, Mark b. November 11, 1969 Ht. 6-1 Wt. 187 College: Ohio State

SEASON–TEAM	G	GS	MIN	FGM	FGA	PCT	3FGM	3FGA	PCT	FTM	FTA	PCT	O-RB	D-RB	TOT	AST	PF	DQ	STL	TO	BLK	PTS	RPG	APG	PPG
98-99–Toronto	1	0	2	0	1	.000	0	0	–	0	0	–	0	0	0	0	0	0	0	1	0	0	0.0	0.0	0.0
Reg. Season Totals	1	0	2	0	1	.000	0	0	–	0	0	–	0	0	0	0	0	0	0	1	0	0	0.0	0.0	0.0

Baker, Norman Henry (Norm) b. February 17, 1923 Ht. 6-0 Wt. 180

SEASON–TEAM	G	GS	MIN	FGM	FGA	PCT	3FGM	3FGA	PCT	FTM	FTA	PCT	O-RB	D-RB	TOT	AST	PF	DQ	STL	TO	BLK	PTS	RPG	APG	PPG
46-47–Chicago	4	–	–	0	1	.000	–	–	–	0	0	–	–	–	–	0	0	–	–	–	–	0	–	0.0	0.0
Reg. Season Totals	4	–	–	0	1	.000	–	–	–	0	0	–	–	–	–	0	0	–	–	–	–	0	–	0.0	0.0

Baker, Vincent Lamont (Vin) b. November 23, 1971 Ht. 6-11 Wt. 250 College: Hartford

SEASON–TEAM	G	GS	MIN	FGM	FGA	PCT	3FGM	3FGA	PCT	FTM	FTA	PCT	O-RB	D-RB	TOT	AST	PF	DQ	STL	TO	BLK	PTS	RPG	APG	PPG
93-94–Milwaukee	82	63	2560	435	869	.501	1	5	.200	234	411	.569	277	344	621	163	231	3	60	162	114	1105	7.6	2.0	13.5
94-95–Milwaukee	82	82	3361	594	1229	.483	7	24	.292	256	432	.593	289	557	846	296	277	5	86	221	116	1451	10.3	3.6	17.7
95-96–Milwaukee	82	82	3319	699	1429	.489	10	48	.208	321	479	.670	263	545	808	212	272	3	68	216	91	1729	9.9	2.6	21.1
96-97–Milwaukee	78	78	3159	632	1251	.505	15	54	.278	358	521	.687	267	537	804	211	275	8	81	245	112	1637	10.3	2.7	21.0
97-98–Seattle	82	82	2944	631	1164	.542	1	7	.143	311	526	.591	286	370	656	152	278	7	91	174	86	1574	8.0	1.9	19.2
98-99–Seattle	34	31	1162	198	437	.453	0	3	.000	72	160	.450	86	125	211	56	121	2	32	76	34	468	6.2	1.6	13.8
99-00–Seattle	79	75	2849	514	1129	.455	2	8	.250	281	412	.682	227	378	605	148	288	6	47	213	66	1311	7.7	1.9	16.6
Reg. Season Totals	519	493	19354	3703	7508	.493	36	149	.242	1833	2941	.623	1695	2856	4551	1238	1742	34	465	1307	619	9275	8.8	2.4	17.9
Playoff Totals	15	14	548	101	209	.483	0	1	.000	26	55	.473	57	75	132	28	57	1	23	38	17	228	8.8	1.9	15.2
All-Star Totals	4	0	70	13	31	.419	0	0	–	9	12	.750	16	8	24	3	8	0	2	1	1	35	6.0	0.8	8.8

Ball, Cedric Glenn b. April 16, 1968 Ht. 6-8 Wt. 210 College: North Carolina-Charlotte

SEASON–TEAM	G	GS	MIN	FGM	FGA	PCT	3FGM	3FGA	PCT	FTM	FTA	PCT	O-RB	D-RB	TOT	AST	PF	DQ	STL	TO	BLK	PTS	RPG	APG	PPG
90-91–L.A. Clippers	7	0	26	3	8	.375	0	0	–	2	2	1.000	5	6	11	0	5	0	0	2	2	8	1.6	0.0	1.1
Reg. Season Totals	7	0	26	3	8	.375	0	0	–	2	2	1.000	5	6	11	0	5	0	0	2	2	8	1.6	0.0	1.1

Ballard, Gregory (Greg) b. January 29, 1955 Ht. 6-7 Wt. 215 College: Shasta (Calif.) Coll.; Oregon

SEASON–TEAM	G	GS	MIN	FGM	FGA	PCT	3FGM	3FGA	PCT	FTM	FTA	PCT	O-RB	D-RB	TOT	AST	PF	DQ	STL	TO	BLK	PTS	RPG	APG	PPG
77-78–Washington	76	–	936	142	334	.425	–	–	–	88	114	.772	102	164	266	62	90	1	30	64	13	372	3.5	0.8	4.9
78-79–Washington	82	–	1552	260	559	.465	–	–	–	119	172	.692	143	307	450	116	166	3	58	97	30	639	5.5	1.4	7.8
79-80–Washington	82	–	2438	545	1101	.495	16	47	.340	171	227	.753	240	398	638	159	197	2	90	133	36	1277	7.8	1.9	15.6
80-81–Washington	82	–	2610	549	1186	.463	7	32	.219	166	196	.847	167	413	580	195	194	1	118	117	39	1271	7.1	2.4	15.5
81-82–Washington	79	79	2946	621	1307	.475	9	22	.409	235	283	.830	136	497	633	250	204	0	137	119	22	1486	8.0	3.2	18.8
82-83–Washington	78	78	2840	603	1274	.473	13	37	.351	182	233	.781	123	385	508	262	176	2	135	157	25	1401	6.5	3.4	18.0
83-84–Washington	82	82	2701	510	1061	.481	2	15	.133	166	208	.798	140	348	488	290	214	1	94	142	35	1188	6.0	3.5	14.5
84-85–Washington	82	77	2664	469	978	.480	14	46	.304	120	151	.795	150	381	531	208	221	0	100	106	33	1072	6.5	2.5	13.1
85-86–Golden State	75	14	1792	272	570	.477	17	35	.486	101	126	.802	132	285	417	83	174	0	65	54	8	662	5.6	1.1	8.8
86-87–Golden State	82	7	1579	248	564	.440	15	40	.375	68	91	.747	99	241	340	108	167	0	50	70	15	579	4.1	1.3	7.1
88-89–Seattle	2	0	15	1	8	.125	0	1	.000	4	4	1.000	2	5	7	0	3	0	0	0	0	6	3.5	0.0	3.0
Reg. Season Totals	802	337	22073	4220	8942	.472	93	275	.338	1420	1805	.787	1434	3424	4858	1733	1806	10	877	1059	256	9953	6.1	2.2	12.4
Playoff Totals	65	11	1308	183	423	.433	4	13	.308	111	140	.793	114	212	326	103	120	1	51	76	16	481	5.0	1.6	7.4

Baltimore, Herschel David (Herk) b. June 21, 1921 d. January 1, 1968 Ht. 6-4 Wt. 195 College: Penn State

SEASON–TEAM	G	GS	MIN	FGM	FGA	PCT	3FGM	3FGA	PCT	FTM	FTA	PCT	O-RB	D-RB	TOT	AST	PF	DQ	STL	TO	BLK	PTS	RPG	APG	PPG
46-47–St. Louis	58	–	–	53	263	.202	–	–	–	32	69	.464	–	–	–	16	98	–	–	–	–	138	–	0.3	2.4
Reg. Season Totals	58	–	–	53	263	.202	–	–	–	32	69	.464	–	–	–	16	98	–	–	–	–	138	–	0.3	2.4
Playoff Totals	3	–	–	2	20	.200	–	–	–	0	1	.000	–	–	–	–	3	–	–	–	–	4	–	0.0	1.3

Banks, Eugene Lavon (Gene) b. May 15, 1959 Ht. 6-7 Wt. 215 College: Duke

SEASON–TEAM	G	GS	MIN	FGM	FGA	PCT	3FGM	3FGA	PCT	FTM	FTA	PCT	O-RB	D-RB	TOT	AST	PF	DQ	STL	TO	BLK	PTS	RPG	APG	PPG
81-82–San Antonio	80	4	1700	311	652	.477	0	8	.000	145	212	.684	157	254	411	147	199	2	55	106	17	767	5.1	1.8	9.6
82-83–San Antonio	81	81	2722	505	919	.550	0	5	.000	196	278	.705	222	390	612	279	229	3	78	171	21	1206	7.6	3.4	14.9
83-84–San Antonio	80	66	2600	424	747	.568	1	6	.167	200	270	.741	204	378	582	254	256	5	105	166	23	1049	7.3	3.2	13.1
84-85–San Antonio	82	41	2091	289	493	.586	1	3	.333	199	257	.774	133	312	445	234	220	3	65	140	13	778	5.4	2.9	9.5
85-86–Chicago	82	33	2139	356	688	.517	0	19	.000	183	255	.718	178	182	360	251	212	4	81	139	10	895	4.4	3.1	10.9
86-87–Chicago	63	39	1822	249	462	.539	0	5	.000	112	146	.767	115	193	308	170	173	3	52	113	17	610	4.9	2.7	9.7
Reg. Season Totals	468	264	13074	2134	3961	.539	2	46	.043	1035	1418	.730	1009	1709	2718	1335	1289	20	436	835	101	5305	5.8	2.9	11.3
Playoff Totals	27	14	702	129	256	.504	0	3	.000	34	57	.596	55	82	137	67	63	2	16	35	4	292	5.1	2.5	10.8

Banks, Walker Burrell Jr. b. August 26, 1947 Ht. 6-10 Wt. 205 College: Western Kentucky

SEASON–TEAM	G	GS	MIN	FGM	FGA	PCT	3FGM	3FGA	PCT	FTM	FTA	PCT	O-RB	D-RB	TOT	AST	PF	DQ	STL	TO	BLK	PTS	RPG	APG	PPG
70-71–Pittsburgh (A)	16	–	154	17	34	.500	0	0	–	7	17	.412	–	–	49	8	34	–	–	–	–	41	3.1	0.5	2.6
Reg. ABA Totals	16	–	154	17	34	.500	0	0	–	7	17	.412	–	–	49	8	34	–	–	–	–	41	3.1	0.5	2.6

Bannister, Kenneth (Ken, The Animal) b. April 1, 1960 Ht. 6-9 Wt. 235 College: Trinidad State (Colo.) J.C.; Indiana State; Saint Augustine College

SEASON–TEAM	G	GS	MIN	FGM	FGA	PCT	3FGM	3FGA	PCT	FTM	FTA	PCT	O-RB	D-RB	TOT	AST	PF	DQ	STL	TO	BLK	PTS	RPG	APG	PPG
84-85–New York	75	50	1404	209	445	.470	0	0	–	91	192	.474	108	222	330	39	279	16	38	141	40	509	4.4	0.5	6.8
85-86–New York	70	15	1405	235	479	.491	0	1	.000	131	249	.526	89	233	322	42	208	5	42	129	24	601	4.6	0.6	8.6
88-89–L.A. Clippers	9	2	130	22	36	.611	0	1	.000	30	53	.566	6	27	33	3	17	0	7	8	2	74	3.7	0.3	8.2
89-90–L.A. Clippers	52	1	589	77	161	.478	0	1	.000	52	110	.473	39	73	112	18	92	1	17	44	7	206	2.2	0.3	4.0
90-91–L.A. Clippers	47	3	339	43	81	.531	0	1	.000	25	65	.385	34	62	96	9	73	0	5	25	7	111	2.0	0.2	2.4
Reg. Season Totals	253	71	3867	586	1202	.488	0	4	.000	329	669	.492	276	617	893	111	669	22	109	347	80	1501	3.5	0.4	5.9

Bantom, Michael Allen (Mike) b. December 3, 1951 Ht. 6-9 Wt. 200 College: St. Joseph's (Pa.)

SEASON–TEAM	G	GS	MIN	FGM	FGA	PCT	3FGM	3FGA	PCT	FTM	FTA	PCT	O-RB	D-RB	TOT	AST	PF	DQ	STL	TO	BLK	PTS	RPG	APG	PPG
73-74–Phoenix	76	–	1982	314	787	.399	–	–	–	141	213	.662	172	347	519	163	289	15	50	–	47	769	6.8	2.1	10.1
74-75–Phoenix	82	–	2239	418	907	.461	–	–	–	185	259	.714	211	342	553	159	273	8	62	–	47	1021	6.7	1.9	12.5
75-76–Phoenix-Seattle	73	–	1571	220	476	.462	–	–	–	136	199	.683	140	251	391	105	221	4	28	–	28	576	5.4	1.4	7.9
76-77–Seattle-N.Y.	77	–	1909	361	755	.478	–	–	–	224	310	.723	184	287	471	102	233	7	63	–	49	946	6.1	1.3	12.3
77-78–Indiana	82	–	2775	502	1047	.479	–	–	–	254	342	.743	184	426	610	238	333	13	100	218	50	1258	7.4	2.9	15.3
78-79–Indiana	81	–	2528	482	1036	.465	–	–	–	227	338	.672	225	425	650	223	316	8	99	193	62	1191	8.0	2.8	14.7
79-80–Indiana	77	–	2330	384	760	.505	1	3	.333	139	209	.665	192	264	456	279	268	7	85	189	49	908	5.9	3.6	11.8
80-81–Indiana	76	–	2375	431	882	.489	0	6	.000	199	281	.708	150	277	427	240	284	9	80	197	85	1061	5.6	3.2	14.0
81-82–Indiana-Phil.	82	38	2016	334	712	.469	2	6	.333	168	267	.629	174	266	440	114	272	5	63	149	61	838	5.4	1.4	10.2
Reg. Season Totals	706	38	19725	3446	7362	.468	3	15	.200	1673	2418	.692	1632	2885	4517	1623	2489	76	630	946	478	8568	6.4	2.3	12.1
Playoff Totals	29	0	564	70	145	.483	0	0	–	38	69	.551	53	55	108	33	97	2	20	30	12	178	3.7	1.1	6.1

Barber, John b. June 27, 1927 Ht. 6-6 Wt. 210 College: Los Angeles State

SEASON–TEAM	G	GS	MIN	FGM	FGA	PCT	3FGM	3FGA	PCT	FTM	FTA	PCT	O-RB	D-RB	TOT	AST	PF	DQ	STL	TO	BLK	PTS	RPG	APG	PPG
56-57–St. Louis	5	–	5	2	8	.250	–	–	–	3	6	.500	–	–	6	0	4	0	–	–	–	7	1.2	0.0	1.4
Reg. Season Totals	5	–	5	2	8	.250	–	–	–	3	6	.500	–	–	6	0	4	0	–	–	–	7	1.2	0.0	1.4

Bardo, Stephen Dean b. April 5, 1968 Ht. 6-5 Wt. 190 College: Illinois

SEASON–TEAM	G	GS	MIN	FGM	FGA	PCT	3FGM	3FGA	PCT	FTM	FTA	PCT	O-RB	D-RB	TOT	AST	PF	DQ	STL	TO	BLK	PTS	RPG	APG	PPG
91-92–San Antonio	1	0	1	0	0	–	0	0	–	0	0	–	1	0	1	0	0	0	0	0	0	0	1.0	0.0	0.0
92-93–Dallas	23	0	175	19	62	.306	1	6	.167	12	17	.706	10	27	37	29	28	0	8	17	3	51	1.6	1.3	2.2
95-96–Detroit	9	0	123	9	23	.391	0	4	.000	4	6	.667	2	20	22	15	17	1	4	5	1	22	2.4	1.7	2.4
Reg. Season Totals	33	0	299	28	85	.329	1	10	.100	16	23	.696	13	47	60	44	45	1	12	22	4	73	1.8	1.3	2.2

Barker, Clifford E. b. January 15, 1921 d. March 17, 1998 Ht. 6-2 Wt. 185 College: Kentucky

SEASON–TEAM	G	GS	MIN	FGM	FGA	PCT	3FGM	3FGA	PCT	FTM	FTA	PCT	O-RB	D-RB	TOT	AST	PF	DQ	STL	TO	BLK	PTS	RPG	APG	PPG
49-50–Indianapolis	49	–	–	102	274	.372	–	–	–	75	106	.708	–	–	–	109	99	–	–	–	–	279	–	2.2	5.7
50-51–Indianapolis	56	–	–	51	202	.252	–	–	–	50	77	.649	–	–	100	115	98	0	–	–	–	152	1.8	2.1	2.7
51-52–Indianapolis	44	–	494	48	161	.298	–	–	–	30	51	.588	–	–	81	70	56	0	–	–	–	126	1.8	1.6	2.9
Reg. Season Totals	149	–	494	201	637	.316	–	–	–	155	234	.662	–	–	181	294	253	0	–	–	–	557	1.8	2.0	3.7
Playoff Totals	9	–	0	16	81	.346	–	–	–	10	18	.556	–	–	15	36	20	0	–	–	–	42	5.0	2.4	4.7

Barker, Thomas Kevin (Tom) b. March 11, 1955 Ht. 6-11 Wt. 225 College: Minnesota; Coll. of Southern Idaho; Hawaii

SEASON–TEAM	G	GS	MIN	FGM	FGA	PCT	3FGM	3FGA	PCT	FTM	FTA	PCT	O-RB	D-RB	TOT	AST	PF	DQ	STL	TO	BLK	PTS	RPG	APG	PPG
76-77–Atlanta	59	–	1354	182	436	.417	–	–	–	112	164	.683	111	290	401	60	223	11	33	–	41	476	6.8	1.0	8.1
78-79–Hou.-Bos.-N.Y.	39	–	476	68	156	.436	–	–	–	27	37	.730	45	74	119	15	76	0	10	34	11	163	3.1	0.4	4.2
Reg. Season Totals	98	–	1830	250	592	.422	–	–	–	139	201	.692	156	364	520	75	299	11	43	34	52	639	5.3	0.8	6.5

Barkley, Charles Wade (Sir Charles, Round Mound of Rebound) b. February 20, 1963 Ht. 6-6 Wt. 252 College: Auburn

SEASON–TEAM	G	GS	MIN	FGM	FGA	PCT	3FGM	3FGA	PCT	FTM	FTA	PCT	O-RB	D-RB	TOT	AST	PF	DQ	STL	TO	BLK	PTS	RPG	APG	PPG
84-85–Philadelphia	82	60	2347	427	783	.545	1	6	.167	293	400	.733	266	437	703	155	301	5	95	209	80	1148	8.6	1.9	14.0
85-86–Philadelphia	80	80	2952	595	1041	.572	17	75	.227	396	578	.685	354	672	1026	312	333	8	173	350	125	1603	12.8	3.9	20.0
86-87–Philadelphia	68	62	2740	557	937	.594	21	104	.202	429	564	.761	390	604	994	331	252	5	119	322	104	1564	14.6	4.9	23.0
87-88–Philadelphia	80	80	3170	753	1283	.587	44	157	.280	714	951	.751	385	566	951	254	278	6	100	304	103	2264	11.9	3.2	28.3
88-89–Philadelphia	79	79	3088	700	1208	.579	35	162	.216	602	799	.753	403	583	986	325	262	3	126	254	67	2037	12.5	4.1	25.8
89-90–Philadelphia	79	79	3085	706	1177	.600	20	92	.217	557	744	.749	361	548	909	307	250	2	148	243	50	1989	11.5	3.9	25.2
90-91–Philadelphia	67	67	2498	665	1167	.570	44	155	.284	475	658	.722	258	422	680	284	173	2	110	210	33	1849	10.1	4.2	27.6
91-92–Philadelphia	75	75	2881	622	1126	.552	32	137	.234	454	653	.695	271	559	830	308	196	2	136	235	44	1730	11.1	4.1	23.1
92-93–Phoenix	76	76	2859	716	1376	.520	67	220	.305	445	582	.765	237	691	928	385	196	0	119	233	74	1944	12.2	5.1	25.6
93-94–Phoenix	65	65	2298	518	1046	.495	48	178	.270	318	452	.704	198	529	727	296	160	1	101	206	37	1402	11.2	4.6	21.6
94-95–Phoenix	68	66	2382	554	1141	.486	74	219	.338	379	507	.748	203	553	756	276	201	3	110	150	45	1561	11.1	4.1	23.0
95-96–Phoenix	71	71	2632	580	1160	.500	49	175	.280	440	566	.777	243	578	821	262	208	3	114	218	56	1649	11.6	3.7	23.2
96-97–Houston	53	53	2009	335	692	.484	58	205	.283	288	415	.694	212	504	716	248	153	2	69	151	25	1016	13.5	4.7	19.2
97-98–Houston	68	41	2243	361	744	.485	18	84	.214	296	397	.746	241	553	794	217	187	2	71	147	28	1036	11.7	3.2	15.2
98-99–Houston	42	40	1526	240	502	.478	4	25	.160	192	267	.719	167	349	516	192	89	0	43	100	13	676	12.3	4.6	16.1
99-00–Houston	20	18	620	106	222	.477	6	26	.231	71	110	.645	71	138	209	63	48	0	14	44	4	289	10.5	3.2	14.5
Reg. Season Totals	1073	1012	39330	8435	15605	.541	538	2020	.266	6349	8643	.735	4260	8286	12546	4215	3287	44	1648	3376	888	23757	11.7	3.9	22.1
Playoff Totals	123	108	4849	1009	1965	.513	64	251	.255	751	1048	.717	510	1072	1582	482	408	4	193	353	108	2833	12.9	3.9	23.0
All-Star Totals	9	7	209	45	91	.495	3	12	.250	20	32	.625	22	38	60	16	18	0	12	20	4	113	6.7	1.8	12.6

Barksdale, Don Angelo b. March 31, 1923 d. March 8, 1993 Ht. 6-6 Wt. 200 College: Marin (Calif.) C.C.; UCLA

SEASON–TEAM	G	GS	MIN	FGM	FGA	PCT	3FGM	3FGA	PCT	FTM	FTA	PCT	O-RB	D-RB	TOT	AST	PF	DQ	STL	TO	BLK	PTS	RPG	APG	PPG
51-52–Baltimore	62	–	2014	272	804	.338	–	–	–	237	343	.691	–	–	601	137	230	13	–	–	–	781	9.7	2.2	12.6
52-53–Baltimore	65	–	2298	321	829	.387	–	–	–	257	401	.641	–	–	597	166	273	13	–	–	–	899	9.2	2.6	13.8
53-54–Boston	63	–	1358	156	415	.376	–	–	–	149	225	.662	–	–	345	117	213	4	–	–	–	461	5.5	1.9	7.3
54-55–Boston	72	–	1790	267	699	.382	–	–	–	220	338	.651	–	–	545	129	225	7	–	–	–	754	7.6	1.8	10.5
Reg. Season Totals	262	–	7460	1016	2747	.370	–	–	–	863	1307	.660	–	–	2088	549	941	37	–	–	–	2895	8.0	2.1	11.0
Playoff Totals	13	–	236	29	76	.382	–	–	–	26	31	.839	–	–	89	17	40	3	–	–	–	84	4.9	1.3	6.5
All-Star Totals	1	–	11	0	1	.000	–	–	–	1	3	.333	–	–	3	2	0	0	–	–	–	1	3.0	2.0	1.0

Barnes, Harry J. b. July 25, 1945 Ht. 6-3 Wt. 205 College: Northeastern

SEASON–TEAM	G	GS	MIN	FGM	FGA	PCT	3FGM	3FGA	PCT	FTM	FTA	PCT	O-RB	D-RB	TOT	AST	PF	DQ	STL	TO	BLK	PTS	RPG	APG	PPG
68-69–San Diego	22	–	126	18	64	.281	–	–	–	7	13	.538	–	–	26	5	25	0	–	–	–	43	1.2	0.2	2.0
Reg. Season Totals	22	–	126	18	64	.281	–	–	–	7	13	.538	–	–	26	5	25	0	–	–	–	43	1.2	0.2	2.0

Barnes, Marvin Jerome b. July 27, 1952 Ht. 6-9 Wt. 225 College: Providence

SEASON–TEAM	G	GS	MIN	FGM	FGA	PCT	3FGM	3FGA	PCT	FTM	FTA	PCT	O-RB	D-RB	TOT	AST	PF	DQ	STL	TO	BLK	PTS	RPG	APG	PPG
74-75–St. Louis (A)	77	–	3076	777	1561	.498	0	3	.000	295	440	.670	419	783	1202	250	328	–	96	307	137	1849	15.6	3.2	24.0
75-76–St. Louis (A)	67	–	2487	681	1355	.503	3	11	.273	251	339	.740	263	462	725	149	273	–	124	230	134	1616	10.8	2.2	24.1
76-77–Detroit	53	–	989	202	452	.447	–	–	–	106	156	.679	69	184	253	45	139	1	38	–	33	510	4.8	0.8	9.6
77-78–Detroit-Buffalo	60	–	1646	279	661	.422	–	–	–	128	182	.703	135	304	439	136	241	9	64	136	83	686	7.3	2.3	11.4
78-79–Boston	38	–	796	133	271	.491	–	–	–	43	66	.652	57	120	177	53	144	3	38	68	39	309	4.7	1.4	8.1
79-80–San Diego	20	–	287	24	60	.400	0	0	–	16	32	.500	34	43	77	18	52	0	5	18	12	64	3.9	0.9	3.2
Reg. NBA Totals	171	–	3718	638	1444	.442	0	0	–	293	436	.672	295	651	946	252	576	13	145	222	167	1569	5.5	1.5	9.2
Reg. ABA Totals	144	–	5563	1458	2916	.500	3	14	.214	546	779	.701	682	1245	1927	399	601	–	220	537	271	3465	13.4	2.8	24.1
ABA Playoff Totals	10	–	444	124	249	.498	0	1	.000	60	77	.779	53	88	141	16	45	–	20	38	19	308	14.1	1.6	30.8

Barnes, V. James (Jim, Bad News) b. April 13, 1941 Ht. 6-8 Wt. 240 College: Cameron; Texas-El Paso

SEASON–TEAM	G	GS	MIN	FGM	FGA	PCT	3FGM	3FGA	PCT	FTM	FTA	PCT	O-RB	D-RB	TOT	AST	PF	DQ	STL	TO	BLK	PTS	RPG	APG	PPG
64-65–New York	75	–	2586	454	1070	.424	–	–	–	251	379	.662	–	–	729	93	312	8	–	–	–	1159	9.7	1.2	15.5
65-66–N.Y.-Balt.	73	–	2191	348	818	.425	–	–	–	212	310	.684	–	–	755	94	283	10	–	–	–	908	10.3	1.3	12.4
66-67–Los Angeles	80	–	1398	217	497	.437	–	–	–	128	187	.684	–	–	450	47	266	5	–	–	–	562	5.6	0.6	7.0
67-68–L.A.-Chicago	79	–	1425	221	499	.443	–	–	–	133	191	.696	–	–	415	55	262	7	–	–	–	575	5.3	0.7	7.3
68-69–Chi.-Boston	59	–	706	115	261	.441	–	–	–	75	111	.676	–	–	224	28	122	2	–	–	–	305	3.8	0.5	5.2
69-70–Boston	77	–	1049	178	434	.410	–	–	–	95	128	.742	–	–	350	52	229	4	–	–	–	451	4.5	0.7	5.9
70-71–Baltimore	11	–	100	15	28	.536	–	–	–	7	11	.636	–	–	16	8	23	0	–	–	–	37	1.5	0.7	3.4
Reg. Season Totals	454	–	9455	1548	3607	.429	–	–	–	901	1317	.684	–	–	2939	377	1497	36	–	–	–	3997	6.5	0.8	8.8
Playoff Totals	11	–	200	26	63	.413	–	–	–	12	18	.667	–	–	61	6	35	2	–	–	–	64	5.5	0.5	5.8

Barnett, James Franklin (Jim) b. July 7, 1944 Ht. 6-4 Wt. 180 College: Oregon

SEASON–TEAM	G	GS	MIN	FGM	FGA	PCT	3FGM	3FGA	PCT	FTM	FTA	PCT	O-RB	D-RB	TOT	AST	PF	DQ	STL	TO	BLK	PTS	RPG	APG	PPG
66-67–Boston	48	–	383	78	211	.370	–	–	–	42	62	.677	–	–	53	41	61	0	–	–	–	198	1.1	0.9	4.1
67-68–San Diego	47	–	1068	179	456	.393	–	–	–	84	118	.712	–	–	155	134	101	0	–	–	–	442	3.3	2.9	9.4
68-69–San Diego	80	–	2346	465	1093	.425	–	–	–	233	310	.752	–	–	362	339	240	2	–	–	–	1163	4.5	4.2	14.5
69-70–San Diego	80	–	2105	450	998	.451	–	–	–	289	366	.790	–	–	305	287	222	3	–	–	–	1189	3.8	3.6	14.9
70-71–Portland	78	–	2371	559	1283	.436	–	–	–	326	402	.811	–	–	376	323	190	1	–	–	–	1444	4.8	4.1	18.5
71-72–Golden State	80	–	2200	374	915	.409	–	–	–	244	292	.836	–	–	250	309	189	0	–	–	–	992	3.1	3.9	12.4
72-73–Golden State	82	–	2215	394	844	.467	–	–	–	183	217	.843	–	–	255	301	150	1	–	–	–	971	3.1	3.7	11.8
73-74–Golden State	77	–	1689	350	755	.464	–	–	–	184	226	.814	76	146	222	209	146	1	56	–	11	884	2.9	2.7	11.5
74-75–N.O.-N.Y.	73	–	1776	285	652	.437	–	–	–	199	238	.836	60	119	179	176	160	1	47	–	16	769	2.5	2.4	10.5
75-76–New York	71	–	1026	164	371	.442	–	–	–	90	114	.789	48	40	88	90	86	0	24	–	3	418	1.2	1.3	5.9
76-77–Philadelphia	16	–	231	28	64	.438	–	–	–	10	18	.556	7	7	14	23	28	0	4	–	0	66	0.9	1.4	4.1
Reg. Season Totals	732	–	17410	3326	7642	.435	–	–	–	1884	2363	.797	191	312	2259	2232	1573	9	131	–	30	8536	3.1	3.0	11.7
Playoff Totals	30	–	669	127	303	.419	–	–	–	67	83	.807	5	3	74	78	64	0	1	–	1	321	2.5	2.6	10.7

Barnett, Nathaniel Jr. (Nate) b. January 29, 1953 Ht. 6-4 Wt. 180 College: Akron

SEASON–TEAM	G	GS	MIN	FGM	FGA	PCT	3FGM	3FGA	PCT	FTM	FTA	PCT	O-RB	D-RB	TOT	AST	PF	DQ	STL	TO	BLK	PTS	RPG	APG	PPG
75-76–Indiana (A)	12	–	73	12	26	.462	0	1	.000	3	8	.375	3	5	8	8	22	–	3	8	1	27	0.7	0.7	2.3
Reg. ABA Totals	12	–	73	12	26	.462	0	1	.000	3	8	.375	3	5	8	8	22	–	3	8	1	27	0.7	0.7	2.3

Barnett, Richard (Dick) b. October 2, 1936 Ht. 6-4 Wt. 190 College: Tennessee State

SEASON–TEAM	G	GS	MIN	FGM	FGA	PCT	3FGM	3FGA	PCT	FTM	FTA	PCT	O-RB	D-RB	TOT	AST	PF	DQ	STL	TO	BLK	PTS	RPG	APG	PPG
59-60–Syracuse	57	–	1235	289	701	.412	–	–	–	128	180	.711	–	–	155	160	98	0	–	–	–	706	2.7	2.8	12.4
60-61–Syracuse	78	–	2070	540	1194	.452	–	–	–	240	337	.712	–	–	283	218	169	0	–	–	–	1320	3.6	2.8	16.9
62-63–Los Angeles	80	–	2544	547	1162	.471	–	–	–	343	421	.815	–	–	242	224	189	3	–	–	–	1437	3.0	2.8	18.0
63-64–Los Angeles	78	–	2620	541	1197	.452	–	–	–	351	454	.773	–	–	250	238	233	3	–	–	–	1433	3.2	3.1	18.4
64-65–Los Angeles	74	–	2026	375	908	.413	–	–	–	270	338	.799	–	–	200	159	209	1	–	–	–	1020	2.7	2.1	13.8
65-66–New York	75	–	2589	631	1344	.469	–	–	–	467	605	.772	–	–	310	259	235	6	–	–	–	1729	4.1	3.5	23.1
66-67–New York	67	–	1969	454	949	.478	–	–	–	231	295	.783	–	–	226	161	185	2	–	–	–	1139	3.4	2.4	17.0
67-68–New York	81	–	2488	559	1159	.482	–	–	–	343	440	.780	–	–	238	242	222	0	–	–	–	1461	2.9	3.0	18.0
68-69–New York	82	–	2953	565	1220	.463	–	–	–	312	403	.774	–	–	251	291	239	4	–	–	–	1442	3.1	3.5	17.6
69-70–New York	82	–	2772	494	1039	.475	–	–	–	232	325	.714	–	–	221	298	220	0	–	–	–	1220	2.7	3.6	14.9
70-71–New York	82	–	2843	540	1184	.456	–	–	–	193	278	.694	–	–	238	225	232	1	–	–	–	1273	2.9	2.7	15.5
71-72–New York	79	–	2256	401	918	.437	–	–	–	162	215	.753	–	–	153	198	229	4	–	–	–	964	1.9	2.5	12.2
72-73–New York	51	–	514	88	226	.389	–	–	–	16	30	.533	–	–	41	50	52	0	–	–	–	192	0.8	1.0	3.8
73-74–New York	5	–	58	10	26	.385	–	–	–	2	3	.667	1	3	4	6	2	0	1	–	0	22	0.8	1.2	4.4
Reg. Season Totals	971	–	28937	6034	13227	.456	–	–	–	3290	4324	.761	1	3	2812	2729	2514	24	1	–	0	15358	2.9	2.8	15.8
Playoff Totals	102	–	3027	603	1317	.458	–	–	–	333	445	.748	0	0	273	247	282	1	0	–	0	1539	2.7	2.4	15.1
All-Star Totals	1	–	22	7	12	.583	–	–	–	1	2	.500	0	0	1	0	2	0	0	–	0	15	1.0	0.0	15.0

Barnhill, John Anthony (Rabbit) b. March 20, 1938 Ht. 6-1 Wt. 180 College: Tennessee State

SEASON–TEAM	G	GS	MIN	FGM	FGA	PCT	3FGM	3FGA	PCT	FTM	FTA	PCT	O-RB	D-RB	TOT	AST	PF	DQ	STL	TO	BLK	PTS	RPG	APG	PPG
62-63–St. Louis	77	–	2692	360	838	.430	–	–	–	181	255	.710	–	–	359	322	168	0	–	–	–	901	4.7	4.2	11.7
63-64–St. Louis	74	–	1367	208	505	.412	–	–	–	70	115	.609	–	–	157	145	107	0	–	–	–	486	2.1	2.0	6.6
64-65–St. Louis	41	–	777	121	312	.388	–	–	–	45	70	.643	–	–	91	76	56	0	–	–	–	287	2.2	1.9	7.0
65-66–St. Louis-Detroit	76	–	1617	243	606	.401	–	–	–	113	184	.614	–	–	203	196	134	0	–	–	–	599	2.7	2.6	7.9
66-67–Baltimore	53	–	1214	187	447	.418	–	–	–	66	103	.641	–	–	157	136	80	0	–	–	–	440	3.0	2.6	8.3
67-68–San Diego	75	–	1883	295	700	.421	–	–	–	154	234	.658	–	–	173	259	143	1	–	–	–	744	2.3	3.5	9.9
68-69–Baltimore	30	–	504	76	175	.434	–	–	–	39	65	.600	–	–	53	71	63	0	–	–	–	191	1.8	2.4	6.4
69-70–Indiana (A)	77	–	2374	325	824	.394	71	272	.261	158	238	.664	–	–	173	312	196	2	–	–	–	879	2.2	4.1	11.4
70-71–Ind.-Denver (A)	67	–	1303	181	496	.365	32	147	.218	96	134	.716	–	–	116	160	106	–	–	–	–	490	1.7	2.4	7.3
71-72–Indiana (A)	19	–	194	28	87	.322	4	35	.114	8	15	.533	–	–	19	16	16	–	–	12	–	68	1.0	0.8	3.6
Reg. NBA Totals	426	–	10054	1490	3583	.416	–	–	–	668	1026	.651	–	–	1193	1205	751	1	–	–	–	3648	2.8	2.8	8.6
Reg. ABA Totals	163	–	3871	534	1407	.380	107	454	.236	262	387	.677	–	–	308	488	318	2	–	12	–	1437	1.9	3.0	8.8
NBA Playoff Totals	21	–	421	46	113	.407	–	–	–	19	31	.613	–	–	41	44	42	0	–	–	–	111	2.0	2.1	5.3
ABA Playoff Totals	14	–	317	28	88	.318	8	35	.229	21	41	.512	–	–	33	25	41	0	–	–	–	85	2.4	1.8	6.1

Barnhill, Norton b. July 15, 1953 Ht. 6-4 Wt. 205 College: Washington State

SEASON–TEAM	G	GS	MIN	FGM	FGA	PCT	3FGM	3FGA	PCT	FTM	FTA	PCT	O-RB	D-RB	TOT	AST	PF	DQ	STL	TO	BLK	PTS	RPG	APG	PPG
76-77–Seattle	4	–	10	2	6	.333	–	–	–	0	0	–	2	1	3	1	5	0	0	–	0	4	0.8	0.3	1.0
Reg. Season Totals	4	–	10	2	6	.333	–	–	–	0	0	–	2	1	3	1	5	0	0	–	0	4	0.8	0.3	1.0

Barnhorst, Leo A. (Barney) b. May 11, 1924 Ht. 6-4 Wt. 195 College: Notre Dame

SEASON–TEAM	G	GS	MIN	FGM	FGA	PCT	3FGM	3FGA	PCT	FTM	FTA	PCT	O-RB	D-RB	TOT	AST	PF	DQ	STL	TO	BLK	PTS	RPG	APG	PPG
49-50–Chicago	67	–	–	174	499	.349	–	–	–	90	129	.698	–	–	–	140	192	–	–	–	–	438	–	2.1	6.5
50-51–Indianapolis	68	–	–	232	671	.346	–	–	–	82	119	.689	–	–	296	218	197	1	–	–	–	546	4.4	3.2	8.0
51-52–Indianapolis	66	–	2344	349	897	.389	–	–	–	122	187	.652	–	–	430	255	196	3	–	–	–	820	6.5	3.9	12.4
52-53–Indianapolis	71	–	2871	402	1034	.389	–	–	–	163	259	.629	–	–	483	277	245	8	–	–	–	967	6.8	3.9	13.6
53-54–Balt.-FtWayne	72	–	2064	199	588	.338	–	–	–	63	88	.716	–	–	297	226	203	4	–	–	–	461	4.1	3.1	6.4
Reg. Season Totals	344	–	7279	1356	3689	.368	–	–	–	520	782	.665	–	–	1506	1116	1033	16	–	–	–	3232	5.4	3.2	9.4
Playoff Totals	13	–	309	57	171	.380	–	–	–	26	38	.684	–	–	54	47	44	1	–	–	–	140	4.2	2.8	10.8
All-Star Totals	2	–	36	8	18	.444	–	–	–	0	2	.000	–	–	5	3	6	0	–	–	–	16	2.5	1.5	8.0

Barr, John E. b. August 18, 1918 Ht. 6-3 Wt. 205 College: Penn State

SEASON–TEAM	G	GS	MIN	FGM	FGA	PCT	3FGM	3FGA	PCT	FTM	FTA	PCT	O-RB	D-RB	TOT	AST	PF	DQ	STL	TO	BLK	PTS	RPG	APG	PPG
46-47–St. Louis	58	–	–	124	438	.283	–	–	–	47	79	.595	–	–	–	54	164	–	–	–	–	295	–	0.9	5.1
Reg. Season Totals	58	–	–	124	438	.283	–	–	–	47	79	.595	–	–	–	54	164	–	–	–	–	295	–	0.9	5.1

Barr, Michael J. (Mike) b. October 19, 1950 Ht. 6-3 Wt. 180 College: Duquesne

SEASON–TEAM	G	GS	MIN	FGM	FGA	PCT	3FGM	3FGA	PCT	FTM	FTA	PCT	O-RB	D-RB	TOT	AST	PF	DQ	STL	TO	BLK	PTS	RPG	APG	PPG
72-73–Virginia (A)	79	–	2076	289	612	.472	1	4	.250	141	188	.750	–	–	227	254	220	0	–	185	–	720	2.9	3.2	9.1
73-74–Virginia (A)	45	–	652	82	171	.480	2	5	.400	33	43	.767	22	49	71	82	80	–	27	60	4	199	1.6	1.8	4.4
74-75–St. Louis (A)	54	–	1341	136	269	.506	0	2	.000	28	41	.683	20	75	95	176	117	–	67	100	14	300	1.8	3.3	5.6
75-76–St. Louis (A)	56	–	1048	124	240	.517	6	16	.375	46	55	.836	29	80	109	174	76	–	64	83	7	300	1.9	3.1	5.4
76-77–Kansas City	73	–	1224	122	279	.437	–	–	–	41	57	.719	33	97	130	175	96	0	52	–	18	285	1.8	2.4	3.9
Reg. NBA Totals	73	–	1224	122	279	.437	–	–	–	41	57	.719	33	97	130	175	96	0	52	–	18	285	1.8	2.4	3.9
Reg. ABA Totals	234	–	5117	631	1292	.488	9	27	.333	248	327	.758	71	204	502	686	493	0	158	428	25	1519	2.1	2.9	6.5
ABA Playoff Totals	20	–	639	58	128	.453	1	1	1.000	19	24	.792	15	44	65	72	62	0	25	37	5	136	3.3	3.6	6.8

Barr, Thomas L. (Moe) b. June 19, 1944 Ht. 6-4 Wt. 195 College: Duquesne

SEASON–TEAM	G	GS	MIN	FGM	FGA	PCT	3FGM	3FGA	PCT	FTM	FTA	PCT	O-RB	D-RB	TOT	AST	PF	DQ	STL	TO	BLK	PTS	RPG	APG	PPG
70-71–Cincinnati	31	–	145	25	62	.403	–	–	–	11	13	.846	–	–	20	28	27	0	–	–	–	61	0.6	0.9	2.0
Reg. Season Totals	31	–	145	25	62	.403	–	–	–	11	13	.846	–	–	20	28	27	0	–	–	–	61	0.6	0.9	2.0

Barrett, Ernie Drew b. August 27, 1929 Ht. 6-3 Wt. 180 College: Kansas State

SEASON–TEAM	G	GS	MIN	FGM	FGA	PCT	3FGM	3FGA	PCT	FTM	FTA	PCT	O-RB	D-RB	TOT	AST	PF	DQ	STL	TO	BLK	PTS	RPG	APG	PPG
53-54–Boston	59	–	641	60	191	.314	–	–	–	14	25	.560	–	–	100	55	116	2	–	–	–	134	1.7	0.9	2.3
55-56–Boston	72	–	1451	207	533	.388	–	–	–	93	118	.788	–	–	243	174	184	4	–	–	–	507	3.4	2.4	7.0
Reg. Season Totals	131	–	2092	267	724	.369	–	–	–	107	143	.748	–	–	343	229	300	6	–	–	–	641	2.6	1.7	4.9
Playoff Totals	9	–	106	7	42	.167	–	–	–	5	5	1.000	–	–	17	8	18	0	–	–	–	19	1.2	0.9	2.1

Barrett, Michael Thomas (Mike, Bird Man) b. September 5, 1943 Ht. 6-2 Wt. 160 College: West Virginia Tech

SEASON–TEAM	G	GS	MIN	FGM	FGA	PCT	3FGM	3FGA	PCT	FTM	FTA	PCT	O-RB	D-RB	TOT	AST	PF	DQ	STL	TO	BLK	PTS	RPG	APG	PPG
69-70–Washington (A)	84	–	2262	479	1126	.425	62	180	.344	232	305	.761	–	–	296	259	243	2	–	–	–	1252	3.5	3.1	14.9
70-71–Virginia (A)	84	–	2754	458	988	.464	28	103	.272	208	274	.759	–	–	272	425	202	–	–	–	–	1152	3.2	5.1	13.7
72-73–San Diego (A)	19	–	284	37	101	.366	4	20	.200	18	35	.514	8	16	24	46	28	0	–	39	–	96	1.3	2.4	5.1
Reg. ABA Totals	187	–	5300	974	2215	.440	94	303	.310	458	614	.746	8	16	592	730	473	2	–	39	–	2500	3.2	3.9	13.4
ABA Playoff Totals	20	–	727	143	328	.436	24	76	.316	77	92	.837	–	–	49	74	52	0	–	–	–	387	2.5	3.7	19.4

Barros, Dana Bruce b. April 13, 1967 Ht. 5-11 Wt. 163 College: Boston College

SEASON–TEAM	G	GS	MIN	FGM	FGA	PCT	3FGM	3FGA	PCT	FTM	FTA	PCT	O-RB	D-RB	TOT	AST	PF	DQ	STL	TO	BLK	PTS	RPG	APG	PPG
89-90–Seattle	81	25	1630	299	738	.405	95	238	.399	89	110	.809	35	97	132	205	97	0	53	123	1	782	1.6	2.5	9.7
90-91–Seattle	66	0	750	154	311	.495	32	81	.395	78	85	.918	17	54	71	111	40	0	23	54	1	418	1.1	1.7	6.3
91-92–Seattle	75	1	1331	238	493	.483	83	186	.446	60	79	.759	17	64	81	125	84	0	51	56	4	619	1.1	1.7	8.3
92-93–Seattle	69	2	1243	214	474	.451	64	169	.379	49	59	.831	18	89	107	151	78	0	63	58	3	541	1.6	2.2	7.8
93-94–Philadelphia	81	70	2519	412	878	.469	135	354	.381	116	145	.800	28	168	196	424	96	0	107	167	5	1075	2.4	5.2	13.3
94-95–Philadelphia	82	82	3318	571	1165	.490	197	425	.464	347	386	.899	27	247	274	619	159	1	149	242	4	1686	3.3	7.5	20.6
95-96–Boston	80	25	2328	379	806	.470	150	368	.408	130	147	.884	21	171	192	306	116	1	58	120	3	1038	2.4	3.8	13.0
96-97–Boston	24	8	708	110	253	.435	43	105	.410	37	43	.860	5	43	48	81	34	0	26	39	6	300	2.0	3.4	12.5
97-98–Boston	80	15	1686	281	609	.461	100	246	.407	122	144	.847	28	125	153	286	124	0	83	107	6	784	1.9	3.6	9.8
98-99–Boston	50	16	1156	168	371	.453	64	160	.400	64	73	.877	16	89	105	208	64	1	52	88	5	464	2.1	4.2	9.3
99-00–Boston	72	0	1139	196	435	.451	59	144	.410	66	76	.868	13	86	99	133	80	0	31	66	4	517	1.4	1.8	7.2
Reg. Season Totals	760	244	17808	3022	6533	.463	1022	2476	.413	1158	1347	.860	225	1233	1458	2649	972	3	696	1120	42	8224	1.9	3.5	10.8
Playoff Totals	26	0	257	52	100	.520	17	38	.447	9	12	.750	2	21	23	25	18	0	12	17	0	130	0.9	1.0	5.0
All-Star Totals	1	0	11	2	5	.400	1	3	.333	0	0	–	0	1	1	3	0	0	0	0	0	5	1.0	3.0	5.0

Barry, Brent Robert b. December 31, 1971 Ht. 6-6 Wt. 195 College: Oregon State

SEASON–TEAM	G	GS	MIN	FGM	FGA	PCT	3FGM	3FGA	PCT	FTM	FTA	PCT	O-RB	D-RB	TOT	AST	PF	DQ	STL	TO	BLK	PTS	RPG	APG	PPG
95-96–L.A. Clippers	79	44	1898	283	597	.474	123	296	.416	111	137	.810	38	130	168	230	196	2	95	120	22	800	2.1	2.9	10.1
96-97–L.A. Clippers	59	0	1094	155	379	.409	56	173	.324	76	93	.817	30	80	110	154	88	1	51	76	15	442	1.9	2.6	7.5
97-98–LAClips-Miami	58	36	1600	213	506	.421	90	229	.393	115	134	.858	29	142	171	153	118	0	64	104	27	631	2.9	2.6	10.9
98-99–Chicago	37	30	1181	141	356	.396	52	172	.302	78	101	.772	39	105	144	116	98	2	42	72	11	412	3.9	3.1	11.1
99-00–Seattle	80	74	2726	327	707	.463	164	399	.411	127	157	.809	50	322	372	291	228	4	103	142	31	945	4.7	3.6	11.8
Reg. Season Totals	313	184	8499	1119	2545	.440	485	1269	.382	507	622	.815	186	779	965	944	728	9	355	514	106	3230	3.1	3.0	10.3
Playoff Totals	8	3	239	23	60	.383	13	31	.419	18	23	.783	4	16	20	25	30	2	7	11	3	77	2.5	3.1	9.6

Barry, Drew William b. February 17, 1973 Ht. 6-5 Wt. 191 College: Georgia Tech

SEASON–TEAM	G	GS	MIN	FGM	FGA	PCT	3FGM	3FGA	PCT	FTM	FTA	PCT	O-RB	D-RB	TOT	AST	PF	DQ	STL	TO	BLK	PTS	RPG	APG	PPG
97-98–Atlanta	27	0	256	18	38	.474	9	21	.429	11	13	.846	5	30	35	49	28	0	10	30	1	56	1.3	1.8	2.1
98-99–Seattle	17	0	183	10	32	.313	8	24	.333	9	13	.692	3	17	20	29	24	0	7	12	1	37	1.2	1.7	2.2
99-00–G.S.-Atlanta	16	0	159	15	33	.455	7	18	.389	4	5	.800	0	12	12	33	23	0	2	13	0	41	0.8	2.1	2.6
Reg. Season Totals	60	0	598	43	103	.417	24	63	.381	24	31	.774	8	59	67	111	75	0	19	55	2	134	1.1	1.9	2.2
Playoff Totals	2	0	5	0	1	.000	0	1	.000	0	0	–	0	1	1	–	0	0	0	0	0	0	0.5	0.0	0.0

Barry, Jon Alan b. July 25, 1969 Ht. 6-5 Wt. 210 College: U. of Pacific; Paris (Texas) J.C.; Georgia Tech

SEASON–TEAM	G	GS	MIN	FGM	FGA	PCT	3FGM	3FGA	PCT	FTM	FTA	PCT	O-RB	D-RB	TOT	AST	PF	DQ	STL	TO	BLK	PTS	RPG	APG	PPG
92-93–Milwaukee	47	0	552	76	206	.369	21	63	.333	33	49	.673	10	33	43	68	57	0	35	42	3	206	0.9	1.4	4.4
93-94–Milwaukee	72	7	1242	158	382	.414	32	115	.278	97	122	.795	36	110	146	168	110	0	102	83	17	445	2.0	2.3	6.2
94-95–Milwaukee	52	0	602	57	134	.425	16	48	.333	61	80	.763	15	34	49	85	54	0	30	41	4	191	0.9	1.6	3.7
95-96–Golden State	68	0	712	91	185	.492	44	93	.473	31	37	.838	17	46	63	85	51	1	33	42	11	257	0.9	1.3	3.8
96-97–Atlanta	58	8	965	100	246	.407	48	124	.387	37	46	.804	26	73	99	115	56	0	55	59	3	285	1.7	2.0	4.9
97-98–L.A. Lakers	49	1	374	38	104	.365	18	61	.295	27	29	.931	8	29	37	51	33	0	24	22	3	121	0.8	1.0	2.5
98-99–Sacramento	43	0	736	59	138	.428	24	79	.304	71	84	.845	25	71	96	112	61	1	53	47	5	213	2.2	2.6	5.0
99-00–Sacramento	62	1	1281	161	346	.465	66	154	.429	107	116	.922	38	121	159	150	104	1	75	85	7	495	2.6	2.4	8.0
Reg. Season Totals	451	17	6464	740	1741	.425	269	737	.365	464	563	.824	175	517	692	834	526	3	407	421	53	2213	1.5	1.8	4.9
Playoff Totals	19	0	241	21	66	.318	12	39	.308	25	28	.893	5	19	24	21	17	0	10	13	1	79	1.3	1.1	4.2

Barry, Richard Francis Dennis III (Rick) b. March 28, 1944 Ht. 6-7 Wt. 205 College: Miami (Fla.) HOF: 1986

SEASON–TEAM	G	GS	MIN	FGM	FGA	PCT	3FGM	3FGA	PCT	FTM	FTA	PCT	O-RB	D-RB	TOT	AST	PF	DQ	STL	TO	BLK	PTS	RPG	APG	PPG
65-66–San Francisco	80	–	2990	745	1698	.439	–	–	–	569	660	.862	–	–	850	173	297	2	–	–	–	2059	10.6	2.2	25.7
66-67–San Francisco	78	–	3175	1011	2240	.451	–	–	–	753	852	.884	–	–	714	282	258	1	–	–	–	2775	9.2	3.6	35.6
68-69–Oakland (A)	35	–	1361	392	767	.511	3	10	.300	403	454	.888	–	–	329	136	124	1	–	141	–	1190	9.4	3.9	34.0
69-70–Washington (A)	52	–	1849	517	1036	.499	8	39	.205	400	463	.864	–	–	363	178	174	1	–	–	–	1442	7.0	3.4	27.7
70-71–New York (A)	59	–	2502	632	1348	.469	19	86	.221	451	507	.890	–	–	401	294	205	–	–	–	–	1734	6.8	5.0	29.4
71-72–New York (A)	80	–	3616	902	1969	.458	73	237	.308	641	730	.878	–	–	602	327	261	–	–	263	–	2518	7.5	4.1	31.5
72-73–Golden State	82	–	3075	737	1630	.452	–	–	–	358	397	.902	–	–	728	399	245	2	–	–	–	1832	8.9	4.9	22.3
73-74–Golden State	80	–	2918	796	1746	.456	–	–	–	417	464	.899	103	437	540	484	265	4	169	–	40	2009	6.8	6.1	25.1
74-75–Golden State	80	–	3235	1028	2217	.464	–	–	–	394	436	.904	92	364	456	492	225	0	228	–	33	2450	5.7	6.2	30.6
75-76–Golden State	81	–	3122	707	1624	.435	–	–	–	287	311	.923	74	422	496	496	215	1	202	–	27	1701	6.1	6.1	21.0
76-77–Golden State	79	–	2904	682	1551	.440	–	–	–	359	392	.916	73	349	422	475	194	2	172	–	58	1723	5.3	6.0	21.8
77-78–Golden State	82	–	3024	760	1686	.451	–	–	–	378	409	.924	75	374	449	446	188	1	158	224	45	1898	5.5	5.4	23.1
78-79–Houston	80	–	2566	461	1000	.461	–	–	–	160	169	.947	40	237	277	502	195	0	95	198	38	1082	3.5	6.3	13.5
79-80–Houston	72	–	1816	325	771	.422	73	221	.330	143	153	.935	53	183	236	268	182	0	80	152	28	866	3.3	3.7	12.0
Reg. NBA Totals	794	–	28825	7252	16163	.449	73	221	.330	3818	4243	.900	510	2366	5168	4017	2264	13	1104	574	269	18395	6.5	5.1	23.2
Reg. ABA Totals	226	–	9328	2443	5120	.477	103	372	.277	1895	2154	.880	–	–	1695	935	764	2	–	404	–	6884	7.5	4.1	30.5
NBA Playoff Totals	74	–	2723	719	1688	.426	3	12	.250	392	448	.875	69	182	418	340	232	3	106	12	39	1833	5.6	4.6	24.8
ABA Playoff Totals	31	–	1338	381	767	.497	40	97	.412	235	273	.861	17	53	257	116	118	0	–	61	–	1037	8.3	3.7	33.5
NBA All-Star Totals	7	–	195	54	111	.486	0	0	–	20	24	.833	7	14	29	31	30	2	16	5	1	128	4.1	4.4	18.3

Bartels, Edward John (Ed) b. October 8, 1925 Ht. 6-5 Wt. 195 College: North Carolina State

SEASON–TEAM	G	GS	MIN	FGM	FGA	PCT	3FGM	3FGA	PCT	FTM	FTA	PCT	O-RB	D-RB	TOT	AST	PF	DQ	STL	TO	BLK	PTS	RPG	APG	PPG
49-50–Denver-N.Y.	15	–	–	22	86	.256	–	–	–	19	34	.559	–	–	–	20	29	–	–	–	–	63	–	1.3	4.2
50-51–Washington	17	–	–	24	97	.247	–	–	–	24	46	.522	–	–	84	12	54	0	–	–	–	72	4.9	0.7	4.2
Reg. Season Totals	32	–	–	46	183	.251	–	–	–	43	80	.538	–	–	84	32	83	0	–	–	–	135	4.9	1.0	4.2

Bartolome, Victor (Vic) b. September 29, 1948 Ht. 7-0 Wt. 230 College: Oregon State

SEASON–TEAM	G	GS	MIN	FGM	FGA	PCT	3FGM	3FGA	PCT	FTM	FTA	PCT	O-RB	D-RB	TOT	AST	PF	DQ	STL	TO	BLK	PTS	RPG	APG	PPG
71-72–Golden State	38	–	165	15	59	.254	–	–	–	4	5	.800	–	–	60	3	22	0	–	–	–	34	1.6	0.1	0.9
Reg. Season Totals	38	–	165	15	59	.254	–	–	–	4	5	.800	–	–	60	3	22	0	–	–	–	34	1.6	0.1	0.9

Baskerville, Jerry W. b. November 10, 1951 Ht. 6-7 Wt. 190 College: Temple; Nevada-Las Vegas

SEASON–TEAM	G	GS	MIN	FGM	FGA	PCT	3FGM	3FGA	PCT	FTM	FTA	PCT	O-RB	D-RB	TOT	AST	PF	DQ	STL	TO	BLK	PTS	RPG	APG	PPG
75-76–Philadelphia	21	–	105	8	26	.308	–	–	–	10	16	.625	13	15	28	3	32	0	6	–	5	26	1.3	0.1	1.2
Reg. Season Totals	21	–	105	8	26	.308	–	–	–	10	16	.625	13	15	28	3	32	0	6	–	5	26	1.3	0.1	1.2

Bassett, Eugene Timothy (Tim) b. April 1, 1951 Ht. 6-8 Wt. 225 College: Coll. of Southern Idaho; Georgia

SEASON–TEAM	G	GS	MIN	FGM	FGA	PCT	3FGM	3FGA	PCT	FTM	FTA	PCT	O-RB	D-RB	TOT	AST	PF	DQ	STL	TO	BLK	PTS	RPG	APG	PPG
73-74–San Diego (A)	82	–	1854	233	499	.467	0	4	.000	99	167	.593	252	343	595	109	185	–	57	87	35	565	7.3	1.3	6.9
74-75–San Diego (A)	72	–	1998	244	518	.471	3	4	.750	82	146	.562	210	316	526	117	159	–	45	97	36	573	7.3	1.6	8.0
75-76–New York (A)	84	–	1790	173	396	.437	1	6	.167	58	98	.592	185	346	531	65	247	–	47	97	41	405	6.3	0.8	4.8
76-77–New York Nets	76	–	2442	293	739	.396	–	–	–	101	177	.571	175	466	641	109	246	10	95	–	53	687	8.4	1.4	9.0
77-78–New Jersey	65	–	1474	149	384	.388	–	–	–	50	97	.515	142	262	404	63	181	5	62	80	33	348	6.2	1.0	5.4
78-79–New Jersey	82	–	1508	116	313	.371	–	–	–	89	131	.679	174	244	418	99	219	1	44	103	29	321	5.1	1.2	3.9
79-80–N.J.-S.A.	12	–	164	12	34	.353	0	0	–	10	15	.667	11	22	33	14	27	0	8	9	0	34	2.8	1.2	2.8
Reg. NBA Totals	235	–	5588	570	1470	.388	0	0	–	250	420	.595	502	994	1496	285	673	16	209	192	115	1390	6.4	1.2	5.9
Reg. ABA Totals	238	–	5642	650	1413	.460	4	14	.286	239	411	.582	647	1005	1652	291	591	0	149	281	112	1543	6.9	1.2	6.5
NBA Playoff Totals	5	–	36	3	7	.429	0	0	–	2	2	1.000	3	0	3	–	11	0	0	2	0	8	0.6	0.0	1.6
ABA Playoff Totals	19	–	556	77	158	.487	0	1	.000	16	23	.696	85	97	182	29	64	0	9	24	14	170	9.6	1.5	8.9

Bates, Billy Ray (Dunk) b. May 31, 1956 Ht. 6-4 Wt. 210 College: Kentucky State

SEASON–TEAM	G	GS	MIN	FGM	FGA	PCT	3FGM	3FGA	PCT	FTM	FTA	PCT	O-RB	D-RB	TOT	AST	PF	DQ	STL	TO	BLK	PTS	RPG	APG	PPG
79-80–Portland	16	–	235	72	146	.493	8	19	.421	28	39	.718	13	16	29	31	26	0	14	20	2	180	1.8	1.9	11.3
80-81–Portland	77	–	1560	439	902	.487	14	54	.259	170	199	.854	71	86	157	196	120	0	82	149	6	1062	2.0	2.5	13.8
81-82–Portland	75	0	1229	327	692	.473	12	41	.293	166	211	.787	53	55	108	111	100	0	41	93	5	832	1.4	1.5	11.1
82-83–Wash.-L.A.	19	3	304	55	145	.379	2	5	.400	11	22	.500	11	8	19	14	19	0	14	12	3	123	1.0	0.7	6.5
Reg. Season Totals	187	3	3328	893	1885	.474	36	119	.303	375	471	.796	148	165	313	352	265	0	151	274	16	2197	1.7	1.9	11.7
Playoff Totals	6	0	219	66	121	.545	3	8	.375	25	31	.806	5	12	17	25	24	0	10	26	2	160	2.8	4.2	26.7

Battie, Demetrius Antonio (Tony) b. February 11, 1976 Ht. 6-11 Wt. 240 College: Texas Tech

SEASON–TEAM	G	GS	MIN	FGM	FGA	PCT	3FGM	3FGA	PCT	FTM	FTA	PCT	O-RB	D-RB	TOT	AST	PF	DQ	STL	TO	BLK	PTS	RPG	APG	PPG
97-98–Denver	65	49	1506	234	525	.446	3	14	.214	73	104	.702	138	213	351	60	199	6	54	98	69	544	5.4	0.9	8.4
98-99–Boston	50	15	1121	147	283	.519	0	3	.000	41	61	.672	96	204	300	53	159	1	29	45	71	335	6.0	1.1	6.7
99-00–Boston	82	4	1505	219	459	.477	1	8	.125	102	151	.675	152	258	410	63	249	4	47	67	70	541	5.0	0.8	6.6
Reg. Season Totals	197	68	4132	600	1267	.474	4	25	.160	216	316	.684	386	675	1061	176	607	11	130	210	210	1420	5.4	0.9	7.2

Battle, John Sidney (Cricket, Pickle) b. November 9, 1962 Ht. 6-2 Wt. 190 College: Rutgers

SEASON–TEAM	G	GS	MIN	FGM	FGA	PCT	3FGM	3FGA	PCT	FTM	FTA	PCT	O-RB	D-RB	TOT	AST	PF	DQ	STL	TO	BLK	PTS	RPG	APG	PPG
85-86–Atlanta	64	0	639	101	222	.455	0	7	.000	75	103	.728	12	50	62	74	80	0	23	47	3	277	1.0	1.2	4.3
86-87–Atlanta	64	8	804	144	315	.457	0	10	.000	93	126	.738	16	44	60	124	76	0	29	60	5	381	0.9	1.9	6.0
87-88–Atlanta	67	1	1227	278	613	.454	16	41	.390	141	188	.750	26	87	113	158	84	0	31	75	5	713	1.7	2.4	10.6
88-89–Atlanta	82	0	1672	287	628	.457	11	34	.324	194	238	.815	30	110	140	197	125	0	42	104	9	779	1.7	2.4	9.5
89-90–Atlanta	60	48	1477	275	544	.506	2	13	.154	102	135	.756	27	72	99	154	115	0	28	89	3	654	1.7	2.6	10.9
90-91–Atlanta	79	2	1863	397	862	.461	14	49	.286	270	316	.854	34	125	159	217	145	0	45	113	6	1078	2.0	2.7	13.6
91-92–Cleveland	76	2	1637	316	659	.480	2	17	.118	145	171	.848	19	93	112	159	116	0	36	91	5	779	1.5	2.1	10.3
92-93–Cleveland	41	0	497	83	200	.415	1	6	.167	56	72	.778	4	25	29	54	39	0	9	22	5	223	0.7	1.3	5.4
93-94–Cleveland	51	1	814	130	273	.476	5	19	.263	73	97	.753	7	32	39	83	66	0	22	41	1	338	0.8	1.6	6.6
94-95–Cleveland	28	0	280	43	114	.377	11	31	.355	19	26	.731	3	8	11	37	28	0	8	17	1	116	0.4	1.3	4.1
Reg. Season Totals	612	62	10910	2054	4430	.464	62	227	.273	1168	1472	.793	178	646	824	1257	874	0	273	659	43	5338	1.3	2.1	8.7
Playoff Totals	55	0	719	124	289	.429	4	22	.182	95	112	.848	17	55	72	80	70	0	13	55	1	347	1.3	1.5	6.3

Battle, Kenneth R. (Kenny) b. October 10, 1964 Ht. 6-6 Wt. 210 College: Northern Illinois; Illinois

SEASON–TEAM	G	GS	MIN	FGM	FGA	PCT	3FGM	3FGA	PCT	FTM	FTA	PCT	O-RB	D-RB	TOT	AST	PF	DQ	STL	TO	BLK	PTS	RPG	APG	PPG
89-90–Phoenix	59	8	729	93	170	.547	1	4	.250	55	82	.671	44	80	124	38	94	2	35	32	11	242	2.1	0.6	4.1
90-91–Phoenix-Denver	56	8	945	133	282	.472	3	24	.125	70	93	.753	83	93	176	62	108	0	60	53	18	339	3.1	1.1	6.1
91-92–Boston-G.S.	16	0	92	11	17	.647	0	1	.000	10	12	.833	4	12	16	4	10	0	2	4	2	32	1.0	0.3	2.0
92-93–Boston	3	1	29	6	13	.462	0	1	.000	2	2	1.000	7	4	11	2	2	0	1	2	0	14	3.7	0.7	4.7
Reg. Season Totals	134	17	1795	243	482	.504	4	30	.133	137	189	.725	138	189	327	106	214	2	98	91	31	627	2.4	0.8	4.7
Playoff Totals	8	0	34	4	13	.308	0	0	–	1	1	1.000	1	4	5	–	5	0	0	2	0	9	0.6	0.0	1.1

Batton, David Robert (Dave) b. March 26, 1956 Ht. 6-10 Wt. 240 College: Notre Dame

SEASON–TEAM	G	GS	MIN	FGM	FGA	PCT	3FGM	3FGA	PCT	FTM	FTA	PCT	O-RB	D-RB	TOT	AST	PF	DQ	STL	TO	BLK	PTS	RPG	APG	PPG
82-83–Washington	54	5	558	85	191	.445	0	3	.000	8	17	.471	45	74	119	29	56	0	15	28	13	178	2.2	0.5	3.3
83-84–San Antonio	4	0	31	5	10	.500	0	0	–	0	0	–	1	3	4	3	5	0	0	4	3	10	1.0	0.8	2.5
Reg. Season Totals	58	5	589	90	201	.448	0	3	.000	8	17	.471	46	77	123	32	61	0	15	32	16	188	2.1	0.6	3.2

Batts, Lloyd b. May 9, 1951 Ht. 6-4 Wt. 185 College: Cincinnati

SEASON–TEAM	G	GS	MIN	FGM	FGA	PCT	3FGM	3FGA	PCT	FTM	FTA	PCT	O-RB	D-RB	TOT	AST	PF	DQ	STL	TO	BLK	PTS	RPG	APG	PPG
74-75–Virginia (A)	58	–	1317	249	680	.366	42	147	.286	58	94	.617	71	126	197	106	104	–	73	89	6	598	3.4	1.8	10.3
Reg. ABA Totals	58	–	1317	249	680	.366	42	147	.286	58	94	.617	71	126	197	106	104	–	73	89	6	598	3.4	1.8	10.3

Baum, John (Johnny) b. June 17, 1946 Ht. 6-5 Wt. 200 College: Pierce (Pa.) Coll.; Temple

SEASON–TEAM	G	GS	MIN	FGM	FGA	PCT	3FGM	3FGA	PCT	FTM	FTA	PCT	O-RB	D-RB	TOT	AST	PF	DQ	STL	TO	BLK	PTS	RPG	APG	PPG
69-70–Chicago	3	–	13	3	11	.273	–	–	–	0	0	–	–	–	4	0	1	0	–	–	–	6	1.3	0.0	2.0
70-71–Chicago	62	–	543	123	293	.420	–	–	–	40	58	.690	–	–	125	31	55	0	–	–	–	286	2.0	0.5	4.6
71-72–New York (A)	44	–	551	103	170	.606	0	0	–	41	52	.788	–	–	135	17	75	–	–	24	–	247	3.1	0.4	5.6
72-73–New York (A)	75	–	1071	221	438	.505	0	2	.000	107	143	.748	75	126	201	31	99	0	–	76	–	549	2.7	0.4	7.3
73-74–Memphis-Ind. (A)	60	–	1219	180	400	.450	0	0	–	50	61	.820	81	120	201	62	101	–	36	47	16	410	3.4	1.0	6.8
Reg. NBA Totals	65	–	556	126	304	.414	–	–	–	40	58	.690	–	–	129	31	56	0	–	–	–	292	2.0	0.5	4.5
Reg. ABA Totals	179	–	2841	504	1008	.500	0	2	.000	198	256	.773	156	246	537	110	275	0	36	147	16	1206	3.0	0.6	6.7
NBA Playoff Totals	2	–	5	0	0	–	–	–	–	0	0	–	–	–	1	–	2	0	–	–	–	0	0.5	0.0	0.0
ABA Playoff Totals	33	–	600	117	217	.539	0	0	–	28	39	.718	8	12	113	13	66	0	5	34	1	262	3.4	0.4	7.9

Baumholtz, Frank Conrad (Frankie) b. October 7, 1918 d. December 14, 1997 Ht. 5-11 Wt. 170 College: Ohio U.

SEASON–TEAM	G	GS	MIN	FGM	FGA	PCT	3FGM	3FGA	PCT	FTM	FTA	PCT	O-RB	D-RB	TOT	AST	PF	DQ	STL	TO	BLK	PTS	RPG	APG	PPG
45-46–Youngstown (N)	26	–	–	99	–	–	–	–	–	76	107	.710	–	–	–	–	28	–	–	–	–	274	–	–	10.5
46-47–Cleveland	45	–	–	255	856	.298	–	–	–	121	156	.776	–	–	–	54	93	–	–	–	–	631	–	1.2	14.0
Reg. NBA Totals	45	–	–	255	856	.298	–	–	–	121	156	.776	–	–	–	54	93	–	–	–	–	631	–	1.2	14.0
Reg. NBL Totals	26	–	–	99	–	–	–	–	–	76	107	.710	–	–	–	–	28	–	–	–	–	274	–	–	10.5

Baylor, Elgin Gay b. September 16, 1934 Ht. 6-5 Wt. 225 College: Coll. of Idaho; Seattle HOF: 1976

SEASON–TEAM	G	GS	MIN	FGM	FGA	PCT	3FGM	3FGA	PCT	FTM	FTA	PCT	O-RB	D-RB	TOT	AST	PF	DQ	STL	TO	BLK	PTS	RPG	APG	PPG
58-59–Minneapolis	70	–	2855	605	1482	.408	–	–	–	532	685	.777	–	–	1050	287	270	4	–	–	–	1742	15.0	4.1	24.9
59-60–Minneapolis	70	–	2873	755	1781	.424	–	–	–	564	770	.732	–	–	1150	243	234	2	–	–	–	2074	16.4	3.5	29.6
60-61–Los Angeles	73	–	3133	931	2166	.430	–	–	–	676	863	.783	–	–	1447	371	279	3	–	–	–	2538	19.8	5.1	34.8
61-62–Los Angeles	48	–	2129	680	1588	.428	–	–	–	476	631	.754	–	–	892	222	155	1	–	–	–	1836	18.6	4.6	38.3
62-63–Los Angeles	80	–	3370	1029	2273	.453	–	–	–	661	790	.837	–	–	1146	386	226	1	–	–	–	2719	14.3	4.8	34.0
63-64–Los Angeles	78	–	3164	756	1778	.425	–	–	–	471	586	.804	–	–	936	347	235	1	–	–	–	1983	12.0	4.4	25.4
64-65–Los Angeles	74	–	3056	763	1903	.401	–	–	–	483	610	.792	–	–	950	280	235	0	–	–	–	2009	12.8	3.8	27.1
65-66–Los Angeles	65	–	1975	415	1034	.401	–	–	–	249	337	.739	–	–	621	224	157	0	–	–	–	1079	9.6	3.4	16.6
66-67–Los Angeles	70	–	2706	711	1658	.429	–	–	–	440	541	.813	–	–	898	215	211	1	–	–	–	1862	12.8	3.1	26.6
67-68–Los Angeles	77	–	3029	757	1709	.443	–	–	–	488	621	.786	–	–	941	355	232	0	–	–	–	2002	12.2	4.6	26.0
68-69–Los Angeles	76	–	3064	730	1632	.447	–	–	–	421	567	.743	–	–	805	408	204	0	–	–	–	1881	10.6	5.4	24.8
69-70–Los Angeles	54	–	2213	511	1051	.486	–	–	–	276	357	.773	–	–	559	292	132	1	–	–	–	1298	10.4	5.4	24.0
70-71–Los Angeles	2	–	57	8	19	.421	–	–	–	4	6	.667	–	–	11	2	6	0	–	–	–	20	5.5	1.0	10.0
71-72–Los Angeles	9	–	239	42	97	.433	–	–	–	22	27	.815	–	–	57	18	20	0	–	–	–	106	6.3	2.0	11.8
Reg. Season Totals	846	–	33863	8693	20171	.431	–	–	–	5763	7391	.780	–	–	11463	3650	2596	14	–	–	–	23149	13.5	4.3	27.4
Playoff Totals	134	–	5510	1388	3161	.439	–	–	–	847	1098	.771	–	–	1724	541	435	3	–	–	–	3623	12.9	4.0	27.0
All-Star Totals	11	–	321	70	164	.427	–	–	–	78	98	.796	–	–	99	38	31	0	–	–	–	218	9.0	3.5	19.8

Bayne, Howard Edgar b. July 28, 1942 Ht. 6-7 Wt. 235 College: Tennessee

SEASON–TEAM	G	GS	MIN	FGM	FGA	PCT	3FGM	3FGA	PCT	FTM	FTA	PCT	O-RB	D-RB	TOT	AST	PF	DQ	STL	TO	BLK	PTS	RPG	APG	PPG
67-68–Kentucky (A)	69	–	1181	130	361	.360	1	7	.143	77	143	.538	–	–	456	71	199	6	–	117	–	338	6.6	1.0	4.9
Reg. ABA Totals	69	–	1181	130	361	.360	1	7	.143	77	143	.538	–	–	456	71	199	6	–	117	–	338	6.6	1.0	4.9
ABA Playoff Totals	5	–	85	3	19	.158	0	1	.000	6	11	.545	–	–	23	5	12	0	–	7	–	12	4.6	1.0	2.4

Bazarevich, Sergei b. March 15, 1965 Ht. 6-2 Wt. 162 Country:Russia

SEASON–TEAM	G	GS	MIN	FGM	FGA	PCT	3FGM	3FGA	PCT	FTM	FTA	PCT	O-RB	D-RB	TOT	AST	PF	DQ	STL	TO	BLK	PTS	RPG	APG	PPG
94-95–Atlanta	10	0	74	11	22	.500	1	6	.167	7	9	.778	1	6	7	14	10	0	1	7	1	30	0.7	1.4	3.0
Reg. Season Totals	10	0	74	11	22	.500	1	6	.167	7	9	.778	1	6	7	14	10	0	1	7	1	30	0.7	1.4	3.0

Beach, Edward Leon Jr. (Ed) b. January 25, 1929 Ht. 6-3 Wt. 200 College: West Virginia

SEASON–TEAM	G	GS	MIN	FGM	FGA	PCT	3FGM	3FGA	PCT	FTM	FTA	PCT	O-RB	D-RB	TOT	AST	PF	DQ	STL	TO	BLK	PTS	RPG	APG	PPG
50-51–Minn.-Tri-Cit	12	–	–	8	38	.211	–	–	–	6	9	.667	–	–	25	3	14	0	–	–	–	22	2.1	0.3	1.8
Reg. Season Totals	12	–	–	8	38	.211	–	–	–	6	9	.667	–	–	25	3	14	0	–	–	–	22	2.1	0.3	1.8

Beard, Albert (Al) b. April 27, 1942 Ht. 6-10 Wt. 200 College: Norfolk State

SEASON–TEAM	G	GS	MIN	FGM	FGA	PCT	3FGM	3FGA	PCT	FTM	FTA	PCT	O-RB	D-RB	TOT	AST	PF	DQ	STL	TO	BLK	PTS	RPG	APG	PPG
67-68–New Jersey (A)	12	–	118	12	23	.522	0	0	–	6	11	.545	–	–	46	0	39	1	–	12	–	30	3.8	0.0	2.5
Reg. ABA Totals	12	–	118	12	23	.522	0	0	–	6	11	.545	–	–	46	0	39	1	–	12	–	30	3.8	0.0	2.5

Beard, Alfred Jr. (Butch) b. May 4, 1947 Ht. 6-3 Wt. 185 College: Louisville

SEASON–TEAM	G	GS	MIN	FGM	FGA	PCT	3FGM	3FGA	PCT	FTM	FTA	PCT	O-RB	D-RB	TOT	AST	PF	DQ	STL	TO	BLK	PTS	RPG	APG	PPG
69-70–Atlanta	72	–	941	183	392	.467	–	–	–	135	163	.828	–	–	140	121	124	0	–	–	–	501	1.9	1.7	7.0
71-72–Cleveland	68	–	2434	394	849	.464	–	–	–	260	342	.760	–	–	276	456	213	2	–	–	–	1048	4.1	6.7	15.4
72-73–Seattle	73	–	1403	191	435	.439	–	–	–	100	140	.714	–	–	174	247	139	0	–	–	–	482	2.4	3.4	6.6
73-74–Golden State	79	–	2134	316	617	.512	–	–	–	173	234	.739	136	253	389	300	241	11	105	–	9	805	4.9	3.8	10.2
74-75–Golden State	82	–	2521	408	773	.528	–	–	–	232	279	.832	116	200	316	345	297	9	132	–	11	1048	3.9	4.2	12.8
75-76–Clev.-N.Y.	75	–	1704	228	496	.460	–	–	–	144	192	.750	103	207	310	218	216	2	81	–	8	600	4.1	2.9	8.0
76-77–N.Y. Knicks	70	–	1082	148	293	.505	–	–	–	75	109	.688	50	113	163	144	137	0	57	–	5	371	2.3	2.1	5.3
77-78–New York	79	–	1979	308	614	.502	–	–	–	129	160	.806	76	188	264	339	201	2	117	154	3	745	3.3	4.3	9.4
78-79–New York	7	–	85	11	26	.423	–	–	–	0	0	–	1	9	10	19	13	0	7	10	0	22	1.4	2.7	3.1
Reg. Season Totals	605	–	14283	2187	4495	.487	–	–	–	1248	1619	.771	482	970	2042	2189	1581	26	499	164	36	5622	3.4	3.6	9.3
Playoff Totals	32	–	754	115	259	.444	–	–	–	59	89	.663	30	63	119	88	105	1	34	11	4	289	3.7	2.8	9.0
All-Star Totals	1	–	7	1	4	.250	–	–	–	1	1	1.000	0	0	1	0	0	0	0	–	0	3	1.0	0.0	3.0

Beard, Ralph Milton Jr. b. December 2, 1927 Ht. 5-10 Wt. 175 College: Kentucky

SEASON–TEAM	G	GS	MIN	FGM	FGA	PCT	3FGM	3FGA	PCT	FTM	FTA	PCT	O-RB	D-RB	TOT	AST	PF	DQ	STL	TO	BLK	PTS	RPG	APG	PPG
49-50–Indianapolis	60	–	–	340	936	.363	–	–	–	215	282	.762	–	–	–	233	132	–	–	–	–	895	–	3.9	14.9
50-51–Indianapolis	66	–	–	409	1110	.368	–	–	–	293	378	.775	–	–	251	318	96	0	–	–	–	1111	3.8	4.8	16.8
Reg. Season Totals	126	–	–	749	2046	.366	–	–	–	508	660	.770	–	–	251	551	228	0	–	–	–	2006	3.8	4.4	15.9
Playoff Totals	8	–	–	49	201	.353	–	–	–	33	44	.750	–	–	12	57	17	0	–	–	–	131	4.0	4.4	16.4
All-Star Totals	1	–	–	3	8	.375	–	–	–	0	3	.000	–	–	3	2	1	0	–	–	–	6	3.0	2.0	6.0

Beasley, Charles P. (Charlie) b. September 23, 1945 Ht. 6-5 Wt. 190 College: Southern Methodist

SEASON–TEAM	G	GS	MIN	FGM	FGA	PCT	3FGM	3FGA	PCT	FTM	FTA	PCT	O-RB	D-RB	TOT	AST	PF	DQ	STL	TO	BLK	PTS	RPG	APG	PPG
67-68–Dallas (A)	78	–	2969	374	758	.493	3	13	.231	285	327	.872	–	–	295	290	202	3	–	189	–	1036	3.8	3.7	13.3
68-69–Dallas (A)	75	–	1719	220	506	.435	1	15	.067	161	192	.839	–	–	158	208	158	0	–	129	–	602	2.1	2.8	8.0
69-70–Dallas (A)	80	–	2150	292	667	.438	19	72	.264	231	262	.882	–	–	205	280	222	2	–	–	–	834	2.6	3.5	10.4
70-71–Fla.-Texas (A)	48	–	509	57	136	.419	7	26	.269	40	49	.816	–	–	46	82	69	–	–	–	–	161	1.0	1.7	3.4
Reg. ABA Totals	281	–	7347	943	2067	.456	30	126	.238	717	830	.864	–	–	704	860	651	5	–	318	–	2633	2.5	3.1	9.4
ABA Playoff Totals	23	–	698	99	218	.454	3	18	.167	63	78	.808	–	–	50	80	66	1	–	24	–	264	2.2	3.5	11.5

Beasley, John Michael b. February 5, 1944 Ht. 6-9 Wt. 225 College: Texas A&M

SEASON–TEAM	G	GS	MIN	FGM	FGA	PCT	3FGM	3FGA	PCT	FTM	FTA	PCT	O-RB	D-RB	TOT	AST	PF	DQ	STL	TO	BLK	PTS	RPG	APG	PPG
67-68–Dallas (A)	77	–	2840	622	1264	.492	0	2	.000	271	322	.842	278	704	982	112	245	3	–	107	–	1515	12.8	1.5	19.7
68-69–Dallas (A)	78	–	3050	585	1200	.488	3	10	.300	332	402	.826	248	582	830	110	259	5	–	136	–	1505	10.6	1.4	19.3
69-70–Dallas (A)	84	–	3066	626	1254	.499	3	8	.375	284	347	.818	303	703	1006	132	278	4	–	–	–	1539	12.0	1.6	18.3
70-71–Texas (A)	83	–	2691	532	1070	.497	16	58	.276	236	285	.828	–	–	765	147	206	–	–	–	–	1316	9.2	1.8	15.9
71-72–Dallas-Utah (A)	70	–	885	132	284	.465	8	25	.320	61	75	.813	–	–	290	39	107	–	–	36	–	333	4.1	0.6	4.8
72-73–Utah (A)	71	–	934	214	417	.513	29	89	.326	62	70	.886	82	182	264	43	142	0	–	39	–	519	3.7	0.6	7.3
73-74–Utah (A)	43	–	481	75	181	.414	22	64	.344	10	11	.909	45	75	120	19	57	–	7	21	10	182	2.8	0.4	4.2
Reg. ABA Totals	506	–	13947	2786	5670	.491	81	256	.316	1256	1512	.831	956	2246	4257	602	1294	12	7	339	10	6909	8.4	1.2	13.7
ABA Playoff Totals	51	–	1274	228	465	.490	8	36	.222	96	112	.857	43	84	376	62	126	1	0	24	2	560	7.4	1.2	11.0

Beaty, Zelmo Jr. (Big Z) b. October 25, 1939 Ht. 6-9 Wt. 235 College: Prairie View A&M

SEASON–TEAM	G	GS	MIN	FGM	FGA	PCT	3FGM	3FGA	PCT	FTM	FTA	PCT	O-RB	D-RB	TOT	AST	PF	DQ	STL	TO	BLK	PTS	RPG	APG	PPG
62-63–St. Louis	80	–	1918	297	677	.439	–	–	–	220	307	.717	–	–	665	85	312	12	–	–	–	814	8.3	1.1	10.2
63-64–St. Louis	59	–	1922	287	647	.444	–	–	–	200	270	.741	–	–	633	79	262	11	–	–	–	774	10.7	1.3	13.1
64-65–St. Louis	80	–	2916	505	1047	.482	–	–	–	341	477	.715	–	–	966	111	328	11	–	–	–	1351	12.1	1.4	16.9
65-66–St. Louis	80	–	3072	616	1301	.473	–	–	–	424	559	.758	–	–	1086	125	344	15	–	–	–	1656	13.6	1.6	20.7
66-67–St. Louis	48	–	1661	328	694	.473	–	–	–	197	260	.758	–	–	515	60	189	3	–	–	–	853	10.7	1.3	17.8
67-68–St. Louis	82	–	3068	639	1310	.488	–	–	–	455	573	.794	–	–	959	174	295	6	–	–	–	1733	11.7	2.1	21.1
68-69–Atlanta	72	–	2578	588	1251	.470	–	–	–	370	506	.731	–	–	798	131	272	7	–	–	–	1546	11.1	1.8	21.5
70-71–Utah (A)	76	–	2915	661	1192	.555	2	4	.500	420	531	.791	407	783	1190	148	299	–	–	–	–	1744	15.7	1.9	22.9
71-72–Utah (A)	84	–	3133	729	1353	.539	0	7	.000	522	630	.829	355	755	1110	125	315	–	–	223	–	1980	13.2	1.5	23.6
72-73–Utah (A)	82	–	2804	521	1002	.520	0	1	.000	306	381	.803	261	540	801	125	269	3	–	197	79	1348	9.8	1.5	16.4
73-74–Utah (A)	77	–	2476	417	796	.524	0	1	.000	194	244	.795	170	445	615	128	229	–	62	110	64	1028	8.0	1.7	13.4
74-75–Los Angeles	69	–	1213	136	310	.439	–	–	–	108	135	.800	93	234	327	74	130	1	45	–	29	380	4.7	1.1	5.5
Reg. NBA Totals	570	–	18348	3396	7237	.469	–	–	–	2315	3087	.750	93	234	5949	839	2132	66	45	–	29	9107	10.4	1.5	16.0
Reg. ABA Totals	319	–	11328	2328	4343	.536	2	13	.154	1442	1786	.807	1193	2523	3716	526	1112	3	62	530	143	6100	11.6	1.6	19.1
NBA Playoff Totals	63	–	2345	399	857	.466	–	–	–	273	370	.738	0	0	696	98	267	7	0	–	0	1071	11.0	1.6	17.0
ABA Playoff Totals	52	–	2000	369	691	.534	0	0	–	253	303	.835	224	450	674	102	192	0	18	82	12	991	13.0	2.0	19.1
NBA All-Star Totals	2	–	54	2	22	.091	–	–	–	12	15	.800	0	0	28	2	6	0	0	–	0	16	14.0	1.0	8.0

B

Beck, A. Byron (Byron) b. January 25, 1945 Ht. 6-9 Wt. 235 College: Columbia Basin (Wash.) C.C.; Denver

SEASON–TEAM	G	GS	MIN	FGM	FGA	PCT	3FGM	3FGA	PCT	FTM	FTA	PCT	O-RB	D-RB	TOT	AST	PF	DQ	STL	TO	BLK	PTS	RPG	APG	PPG
67-68–Denver (A)	71	–	1623	275	570	.482	0	2	.000	119	159	.748	–	–	559	38	219	6	–	72	–	669	7.9	0.5	9.4
68-69–Denver (A)	71	–	2289	423	843	.502	2	3	.667	182	238	.765	272	507	779	77	248	9	–	92	–	1030	11.0	1.1	14.5
69-70–Denver (A)	79	–	2454	440	841	.523	0	2	.000	137	174	.787	–	–	764	112	293	12	–	–	–	1017	9.7	1.4	12.9
70-71–Denver (A)	84	–	2849	490	1033	.474	4	14	.286	158	182	.868	280	604	884	177	273	–	–	–	–	1142	10.5	2.1	13.6
71-72–Denver (A)	66	–	1816	337	669	.504	0	3	.000	140	166	.843	–	–	528	136	213	–	–	96	–	814	8.0	2.1	12.3
72-73–Denver (A)	77	–	2303	466	879	.530	2	7	.286	158	198	.798	203	334	537	107	267	9	–	126	–	1092	7.0	1.4	14.2
73-74–Denver (A)	82	–	1979	425	823	.516	0	1	.000	120	141	.851	164	253	417	76	233	–	48	83	8	970	5.1	0.9	11.8
74-75–Denver (A)	84	–	1818	384	745	.515	0	1	.000	81	97	.835	127	216	343	106	270	–	59	76	14	849	4.1	1.3	10.1
75-76–Denver (A)	80	–	1586	334	646	.517	5	11	.455	97	116	.836	123	231	354	116	192	–	48	91	20	770	4.4	1.5	9.6
76-77–Denver	53	–	480	107	246	.435	–	–	–	36	44	.818	45	51	96	33	59	1	15	–	1	250	1.8	0.6	4.7
Reg. NBA Totals	53	–	480	107	246	.435	–	–	–	36	44	.818	45	51	96	33	59	1	15	–	1	250	1.8	0.6	4.7
Reg. ABA Totals	694	–	18717	3574	7049	.507	13	44	.295	1192	1471	.810	1169	2145	5165	945	2208	36	155	636	42	8353	7.4	1.4	12.0
NBA Playoff Totals	5	–	29	3	9	.333	–	–	–	2	2	1.000	2	4	6	1	5	0	0	–	0	8	1.2	0.2	1.6
ABA Playoff Totals	61	–	1761	343	728	.471	2	10	.200	152	186	.817	104	218	479	81	215	1	8	68	4	840	7.9	1.3	13.8

Beck, Corey Laveon b. May 27, 1971 Ht. 6-3 Wt. 200 College: Arkansas

SEASON–TEAM	G	GS	MIN	FGM	FGA	PCT	3FGM	3FGA	PCT	FTM	FTA	PCT	O-RB	D-RB	TOT	AST	PF	DQ	STL	TO	BLK	PTS	RPG	APG	PPG
95-96–Charlotte	5	0	33	2	8	.250	0	0	–	1	2	.500	3	4	7	5	8	0	1	4	0	5	1.4	1.0	1.0
97-98–Charlotte	59	14	738	73	159	.459	2	4	.500	43	59	.729	27	63	90	98	100	0	33	70	7	191	1.5	1.7	3.2
98-99–Detroit-Cha.	24	0	180	18	39	.462	1	1	1.000	8	15	.533	6	22	28	20	26	0	9	13	2	45	1.2	0.8	1.9
Reg. Season Totals	88	14	951	93	206	.451	3	5	.600	52	76	.684	36	89	125	123	134	0	43	87	9	241	1.4	1.4	2.7
Playoff Totals	6	0	26	6	12	.500	1	2	.500	2	2	1.000	1	0	1	–	4	0	4	3	0	15	0.2	0.0	2.5

Beck, Ernest Joseph (Ernie) b. December 11, 1931 Ht. 6-4 Wt. 190 College: Pennsylvania

SEASON–TEAM	G	GS	MIN	FGM	FGA	PCT	3FGM	3FGA	PCT	FTM	FTA	PCT	O-RB	D-RB	TOT	AST	PF	DQ	STL	TO	BLK	PTS	RPG	APG	PPG
53-54–Philadelphia	15	–	422	39	142	.275	–	–	–	34	43	.791	–	–	50	34	29	0	–	–	–	112	3.3	2.3	7.5
55-56–Philadelphia	67	–	1007	136	351	.387	–	–	–	76	106	.717	–	–	196	79	86	0	–	–	–	348	2.9	1.2	5.2
56-57–Philadelphia	72	–	1743	195	508	.384	–	–	–	111	157	.707	–	–	312	190	155	1	–	–	–	501	4.3	2.6	7.0
57-58–Philadelphia	71	–	1974	272	683	.398	–	–	–	170	203	.837	–	–	307	190	173	2	–	–	–	714	4.3	2.7	10.1
58-59–Philadelphia	70	–	1017	163	418	.390	–	–	–	43	65	.662	–	–	176	89	124	0	–	–	–	369	2.5	1.3	5.3
59-60–Philadelphia	66	–	809	114	294	.388	–	–	–	27	32	.844	–	–	127	72	90	0	–	–	–	255	1.9	1.1	3.9
60-61–St. Louis-Syr.	10	–	82	10	29	.345	–	–	–	6	7	.857	–	–	23	15	10	0	–	–	–	26	2.3	1.5	2.6
Reg. Season Totals	371	–	7054	929	2425	.383	–	–	–	467	613	.762	–	–	1191	669	667	3	–	–	–	2325	3.2	1.8	6.3
Playoff Totals	24	–	517	72	180	.400	–	–	–	31	44	.705	–	–	99	43	53	1	–	–	–	175	4.1	1.8	7.3

Becker, Arthur C. (Art) b. January 12, 1942 Ht. 6-9 Wt. 210 College: Arizona State

SEASON–TEAM	G	GS	MIN	FGM	FGA	PCT	3FGM	3FGA	PCT	FTM	FTA	PCT	O-RB	D-RB	TOT	AST	PF	DQ	STL	TO	BLK	PTS	RPG	APG	PPG
67-68–Houston (A)	76	–	2689	563	1204	.468	4	12	.333	297	362	.820	252	461	713	95	321	12	–	154	–	1427	9.4	1.3	18.8
68-69–Houston (A)	78	–	2429	423	888	.476	0	3	.000	200	240	.833	–	–	597	103	304	9	–	156	–	1046	7.7	1.3	13.4
69-70–Indiana (A)	82	–	1504	309	593	.521	0	1	.000	111	137	.810	–	–	379	45	249	8	–	–	–	729	4.6	0.5	8.9
70-71–Ind.-Denver (A)	80	–	1643	370	741	.499	5	8	.625	135	156	.865	–	–	426	53	260	–	–	–	–	880	5.3	0.7	11.0
71-72–Denver (A)	84	–	2193	435	954	.456	0	3	.000	165	195	.846	–	–	471	113	271	–	–	132	–	1035	5.6	1.3	12.3
72-73–N.Y.-Dallas (A)	14	–	96	16	28	.571	0	1	.000	11	11	1.000	5	13	18	1	6	0	–	5	–	43	1.3	0.1	3.1
Reg. ABA Totals	414	–	10554	2116	4408	.480	9	28	.321	919	1101	.835	257	474	2604	410	1411	29	–	447	–	5160	6.3	1.0	12.5
ABA Playoff Totals	25	–	415	68	143	.476	0	1	.000	42	51	.824	–	–	86	14	64	1	–	9	–	178	3.4	0.6	7.1

Becker, Morris R. (Moe) b. February 24, 1917 d. January 9, 1996 Ht. 6-1 Wt. 185 College: Duquesne

SEASON–TEAM	G	GS	MIN	FGM	FGA	PCT	3FGM	3FGA	PCT	FTM	FTA	PCT	O-RB	D-RB	TOT	AST	PF	DQ	STL	TO	BLK	PTS	RPG	APG	PPG
45-46–Youngstown (N)	30	–	–	115	–	–	–	–	–	40	69	.580	–	–	–	–	114	–	–	–	–	270	–	–	9.0
46-47–Pitt.-Boston-DetFalc	43	–	–	70	358	.196	–	–	–	22	44	.500	–	–	–	30	98	–	–	–	–	162	–	0.7	3.8
Reg. NBA Totals	43	–	–	70	358	.196	–	–	–	22	44	.500	–	–	–	30	98	–	–	–	–	162	–	0.7	3.8
Reg. NBL Totals	30	–	–	115	–	–	–	–	–	40	69	.580	–	–	–	–	114	–	–	–	–	270	–	–	9.0

Bedell, Robert George (Bob) b. June 26, 1944 Ht. 6-8 Wt. 205 College: Stanford

SEASON–TEAM	G	GS	MIN	FGM	FGA	PCT	3FGM	3FGA	PCT	FTM	FTA	PCT	O-RB	D-RB	TOT	AST	PF	DQ	STL	TO	BLK	PTS	RPG	APG	PPG
67-68–Anaheim (A)	76	–	1492	325	736	.442	0	4	.000	142	190	.747	–	–	506	79	203	5	–	111	–	792	6.7	1.0	10.4
68-69–Dallas (A)	42	–	479	92	221	.416	0	2	.000	48	84	.571	–	–	116	30	76	1	–	35	–	232	2.8	0.7	5.5
69-70–Dallas (A)	80	–	1536	285	677	.421	2	10	.200	207	246	.841	–	–	454	126	192	3	–	–	–	779	5.7	1.6	9.7
70-71–Texas (A)	71	–	970	176	441	.399	9	42	.214	93	113	.823	–	–	310	85	124	–	–	–	–	454	4.4	1.2	6.4
Reg. ABA Totals	269	–	4477	878	2075	.423	11	58	.190	490	633	.774	–	–	1386	320	595	9	–	146	–	2257	5.2	1.2	8.4
ABA Playoff Totals	16	–	250	50	114	.439	0	9	.000	25	32	.781	–	–	78	15	34	1	–	–	–	125	4.9	0.9	7.8

Bedford, William b. December 14, 1963 Ht. 7-0 Wt. 235 College: Memphis State

SEASON–TEAM	G	GS	MIN	FGM	FGA	PCT	3FGM	3FGA	PCT	FTM	FTA	PCT	O-RB	D-RB	TOT	AST	PF	DQ	STL	TO	BLK	PTS	RPG	APG	PPG
86-87–Phoenix	50	18	979	142	358	.397	0	1	.000	50	86	.581	79	167	246	57	125	1	18	85	37	334	4.9	1.1	6.7
87-88–Detroit	38	0	298	44	101	.436	0	0	–	13	23	.565	27	38	65	4	47	0	8	19	17	101	1.7	0.1	2.7
89-90–Detroit	42	0	246	54	125	.432	1	6	.167	9	22	.409	15	43	58	4	39	0	3	21	17	118	1.4	0.1	2.8
90-91–Detroit	60	4	562	106	242	.438	5	13	.385	55	78	.705	55	76	131	32	76	0	2	32	36	272	2.2	0.5	4.5
91-92–Detroit	32	8	363	50	121	.413	0	1	.000	14	22	.636	24	39	63	12	56	0	6	15	18	114	2.0	0.4	3.6
92-93–San Antonio	16	0	66	9	27	.333	1	1	1.000	6	12	.500	1	9	10	0	15	0	0	1	1	25	0.6	0.0	1.6
Reg. Season Totals	238	30	2514	405	974	.416	7	22	.318	147	243	.605	201	372	573	109	358	1	37	173	126	964	2.4	0.5	4.1
Playoff Totals	14	3	93	9	36	.250	0	2	.000	11	16	.688	9	17	26	4	19	0	3	4	5	29	1.9	0.3	2.1

Beenders, Henry G. (Hank) b. June 2, 1916 Ht. 6-6 Wt. 185 College: Long Island University

SEASON–TEAM	G	GS	MIN	FGM	FGA	PCT	3FGM	3FGA	PCT	FTM	FTA	PCT	O-RB	D-RB	TOT	AST	PF	DQ	STL	TO	BLK	PTS	RPG	APG	PPG
46-47–Providence	58	–	–	266	1016	.262	–	–	–	181	257	.704	–	–	–	37	196	–	–	–	–	713	–	0.6	12.3
47-48–Prov.-Phil.	45	–	–	76	269	.283	–	–	–	51	82	.622	–	–	–	13	99	–	–	–	–	203	–	0.3	4.5
48-49–Boston	8	–	–	6	28	.214	–	–	–	7	9	.778	–	–	–	3	9	–	–	–	–	19	–	0.4	2.4
Reg. Season Totals	111	–	–	348	1313	.265	–	–	–	239	348	.687	–	–	–	53	304	–	–	–	–	935	–	0.5	8.4
Playoff Totals	12	–	–	8	35	.229	–	–	–	7	13	.538	–	–	–	4	15	–	–	–	–	23	–	0.3	1.9

Behagen, Ronald Michael (Ron) b. January 14, 1951 Ht. 6-9 Wt. 185 College: Coll. of Southern Idaho; Minnesota

SEASON–TEAM	G	GS	MIN	FGM	FGA	PCT	3FGM	3FGA	PCT	FTM	FTA	PCT	O-RB	D-RB	TOT	AST	PF	DQ	STL	TO	BLK	PTS	RPG	APG	PPG
73-74–K.C.-Omaha	80	–	2059	357	827	.432	–	–	–	162	212	.764	188	379	567	134	291	9	56	–	37	876	7.1	1.7	11.0
74-75–K.C.-Omaha	81	–	2205	333	834	.399	–	–	–	199	264	.754	146	446	592	153	301	8	60	–	42	865	7.3	1.9	10.7
75-76–New Orleans	66	–	1733	308	691	.446	–	–	–	144	179	.804	190	363	553	139	222	6	67	–	26	760	8.4	2.1	11.5
76-77–New Orleans	60	–	1170	213	509	.418	–	–	–	90	126	.714	144	287	431	83	166	1	41	–	19	516	7.2	1.4	8.6
77-78–Atlanta-Hou.-Ind.	80	–	1735	346	804	.430	–	–	–	179	247	.725	201	312	513	101	263	4	62	174	31	871	6.4	1.3	10.9
78-79–Detroit-N.Y.-K.C.	15	–	165	28	62	.452	–	–	–	10	13	.769	13	29	42	7	36	0	4	11	1	66	2.8	0.5	4.4
79-80–Washington	6	–	64	9	23	.391	0	0	–	5	6	.833	6	8	14	7	14	0	0	4	4	23	2.3	1.2	3.8
Reg. Season Totals	388	–	9131	1594	3750	.425	0	0	–	789	1047	.754	888	1824	2712	624	1293	28	290	189	160	3977	7.0	1.6	10.3
Playoff Totals	8	–	122	24	50	.480	0	0	–	3	3	1.000	5	26	31	9	32	2	1	1	2	51	3.9	1.1	6.4

Behnke, Elmer H. b. February 3, 1929 Ht. 6-7 Wt. 210 College: Bradley

SEASON–TEAM	G	GS	MIN	FGM	FGA	PCT	3FGM	3FGA	PCT	FTM	FTA	PCT	O-RB	D-RB	TOT	AST	PF	DQ	STL	TO	BLK	PTS	RPG	APG	PPG
51-52–Milwaukee	4	–	55	6	22	.273	–	–	–	4	7	.571	–	–	17	4	13	1	–	–	–	16	4.3	1.0	4.0
Reg. Season Totals	4	–	55	6	22	.273	–	–	–	4	7	.571	–	–	17	4	13	1	–	–	–	16	4.3	1.0	4.0

Bell, Dennis R. b. June 2, 1951 Ht. 6-5 Wt. 210 College: Gulf Coast (Fla.) C.C.; Drake

SEASON–TEAM	G	GS	MIN	FGM	FGA	PCT	3FGM	3FGA	PCT	FTM	FTA	PCT	O-RB	D-RB	TOT	AST	PF	DQ	STL	TO	BLK	PTS	RPG	APG	PPG
73-74–New York	1	–	4	0	1	.000	–	–	–	0	0	–	0	0	0	0	0	0	0	–	0	0	0.0	0.0	0.0
74-75–New York	52	–	465	68	181	.376	–	–	–	20	36	.556	48	57	105	25	54	0	22	–	9	156	2.0	0.5	3.0
75-76–New York	10	–	76	8	21	.381	–	–	–	3	7	.429	4	10	14	3	11	0	6	–	1	19	1.4	0.3	1.9
Reg. Season Totals	63	–	545	76	203	.374	–	–	–	23	43	.535	52	67	119	28	65	0	28	–	10	175	1.9	0.4	2.8
Playoff Totals	3	–	27	1	8	.125	–	–	–	0	5	.000	0	4	4	–	6	0	0	–	0	2	1.3	0.0	0.7

Bell, William Hoyet (Whitey) b. September 13, 1932 Ht. 6-0 Wt. 180 College: North Carolina State

SEASON–TEAM	G	GS	MIN	FGM	FGA	PCT	3FGM	3FGA	PCT	FTM	FTA	PCT	O-RB	D-RB	TOT	AST	PF	DQ	STL	TO	BLK	PTS	RPG	APG	PPG
59-60–New York	31	–	449	70	185	.378	–	–	–	28	43	.651	–	–	87	55	59	0	–	–	–	168	2.8	1.8	5.4
60-61–New York	5	–	45	7	18	.389	–	–	–	1	3	.333	–	–	7	1	7	0	–	–	–	15	1.4	0.2	3.0
Reg. Season Totals	36	–	494	77	203	.379	–	–	–	29	46	.630	–	–	94	56	66	0	–	–	–	183	2.6	1.6	5.1

Bellamy, Walter Jones (Walt, Bells) b. July 24, 1939 Ht. 6-11 Wt. 245 College: Indiana HOF: 1993

SEASON–TEAM	G	GS	MIN	FGM	FGA	PCT	3FGM	3FGA	PCT	FTM	FTA	PCT	O-RB	D-RB	TOT	AST	PF	DQ	STL	TO	BLK	PTS	RPG	APG	PPG
61-62–Chicago	79	–	3344	973	1875	.519	–	–	–	549	853	.644	–	–	1500	210	281	6	–	–	–	2495	19.0	2.7	31.6
62-63–Chicago	80	–	3306	840	1595	.527	–	–	–	553	821	.674	–	–	1309	233	283	7	–	–	–	2233	16.4	2.9	27.9
63-64–Baltimore	80	–	3394	811	1582	.513	–	–	–	537	825	.651	–	–	1361	126	300	7	–	–	–	2159	17.0	1.6	27.0
64-65–Baltimore	80	–	3301	733	1441	.509	–	–	–	515	752	.685	–	–	1166	191	260	2	–	–	–	1981	14.6	2.4	24.8
65-66–Balt.-N.Y.	80	–	3352	695	1373	.506	–	–	–	430	689	.624	–	–	1254	235	294	9	–	–	–	1820	15.7	2.9	22.8
66-67–New York	79	–	3010	565	1084	.521	–	–	–	369	580	.636	–	–	1064	206	275	5	–	–	–	1499	13.5	2.6	19.0
67-68–New York	82	–	2695	511	944	.541	–	–	–	350	529	.662	–	–	961	164	259	3	–	–	–	1372	11.7	2.0	16.7
68-69–N.Y.-Detroit	88	–	3159	563	1103	.510	–	–	–	401	618	.649	–	–	1101	176	320	5	–	–	–	1527	12.5	2.0	17.4
69-70–Detroit-Atlanta	79	–	2028	351	671	.523	–	–	–	215	373	.576	–	–	707	143	260	5	–	–	–	917	8.9	1.8	11.6
70-71–Atlanta	82	–	2908	433	879	.493	–	–	–	336	556	.604	–	–	1060	230	271	4	–	–	–	1202	12.9	2.8	14.7
71-72–Atlanta	82	–	3187	593	1089	.545	–	–	–	340	581	.585	–	–	1049	262	255	2	–	–	–	1526	12.8	3.2	18.6
72-73–Atlanta	74	–	2802	455	901	.505	–	–	–	283	526	.538	–	–	964	179	244	1	–	–	–	1193	13.0	2.4	16.1
73-74–Atlanta	77	–	2440	389	801	.486	–	–	–	233	383	.608	264	476	740	189	232	2	52	–	48	1011	9.6	2.5	13.1
74-75–New Orleans	1	–	14	2	2	1.000	–	–	–	2	2	1.000	0	5	5	0	2	0	0	–	0	6	5.0	0.0	6.0
Reg. Season Totals	1043	–	38940	7914	15340	.516	–	–	–	5113	8088	.632	264	481	14241	2544	3536	58	52	–	48	20941	13.7	2.4	20.1
Playoff Totals	46	–	1939	323	686	.471	–	–	–	204	318	.642	0	0	680	136	160	0	0	–	0	850	14.8	3.0	18.5
All-Star Totals	4	–	83	19	38	.500	–	–	–	10	19	.526	0	0	30	4	15	1	0	–	0	48	7.5	1.0	12.0

B

Bemoras, Irving **(Irv)** b. November 18, 1930 Ht. 6-3 Wt. 185 College: Illinois

SEASON–TEAM	G	GS	MIN	FGM	FGA	PCT	3FGM	3FGA	PCT	FTM	FTA	PCT	O-RB	D-RB	TOT	AST	PF	DQ	STL	TO	BLK	PTS	RPG	APG	PPG
53-54–Milwaukee	69	–	1496	185	505	.366	–	–	–	139	208	.668	–	–	214	79	152	2	–	–	–	509	3.1	1.1	7.4
56-57–St. Louis	62	–	983	124	385	.322	–	–	–	70	103	.680	–	–	127	46	76	0	–	–	–	318	2.0	0.7	5.1
Reg. Season Totals	131	–	2479	309	890	.347	–	–	–	209	311	.672	–	–	341	125	228	2	–	–	–	827	2.6	1.0	6.3
Playoff Totals	3	–	20	3	8	.375	–	–	–	3	3	1.000	–	–	6	1	4	0	–	–	–	9	2.0	0.3	3.0

Benbow, Leon b. July 23, 1949 Ht. 6-4 Wt. 185 College: Jacksonville

SEASON–TEAM	G	GS	MIN	FGM	FGA	PCT	3FGM	3FGA	PCT	FTM	FTA	PCT	O-RB	D-RB	TOT	AST	PF	DQ	STL	TO	BLK	PTS	RPG	APG	PPG
74-75–Chicago	39	–	252	35	94	.372	–	–	–	15	18	.833	14	24	38	25	41	0	11	–	6	85	1.0	0.6	2.2
75-76–Chicago	76	–	1586	219	551	.397	–	–	–	105	140	.750	65	111	176	158	186	1	62	–	11	543	2.3	2.1	7.1
Reg. Season Totals	115	–	1838	254	645	.394	–	–	–	120	158	.759	79	135	214	183	227	1	73	–	17	628	1.9	1.6	5.5
Playoff Totals	2	–	5	2	4	.500	–	–	–	1	2	.500	1	0	1	2	0	0	0	–	0	5	0.5	1.0	2.5

Bender, Jonathan Rene b. January 30, 1981 Ht. 6-11 Wt. 202 High School: Picayune Memorial (Miss.)

SEASON–TEAM	G	GS	MIN	FGM	FGA	PCT	3FGM	3FGA	PCT	FTM	FTA	PCT	O-RB	D-RB	TOT	AST	PF	DQ	STL	TO	BLK	PTS	RPG	APG	PPG
99-00–Indiana	24	1	130	23	70	.329	2	12	.167	16	24	.667	4	17	21	3	18	0	1	7	5	64	0.9	0.1	2.7
Reg. Season Totals	24	1	130	23	70	.329	2	12	.167	16	24	.667	4	17	21	3	18	0	1	7	5	64	0.9	0.1	2.7
Playoff Totals	9	0	21	4	6	.667	1	1	1.000	3	6	.500	0	3	3	–	2	0	1	0	0	12	0.3	0.0	1.3

Benjamin, Corey b. February 24, 1978 Ht. 6-6 Wt. 205 College: Oregon State

SEASON–TEAM	G	GS	MIN	FGM	FGA	PCT	3FGM	3FGA	PCT	FTM	FTA	PCT	O-RB	D-RB	TOT	AST	PF	DQ	STL	TO	BLK	PTS	RPG	APG	PPG
98-99–Chicago	31	1	320	44	117	.376	3	14	.214	27	40	.675	15	25	40	10	46	0	11	21	8	118	1.3	0.3	3.8
99-00–Chicago	48	10	862	145	350	.414	31	89	.348	49	82	.598	21	67	88	54	122	2	31	74	22	370	1.8	1.1	7.7
Reg. Season Totals	79	11	1182	189	467	.405	34	103	.330	76	122	.623	36	92	128	64	168	2	42	95	30	488	1.6	0.8	6.2

Benjamin, Lenard Benoit **(Benoit, Big Ben)** b. November 22, 1964 Ht. 7-0 Wt. 265 College: Creighton

SEASON–TEAM	G	GS	MIN	FGM	FGA	PCT	3FGM	3FGA	PCT	FTM	FTA	PCT	O-RB	D-RB	TOT	AST	PF	DQ	STL	TO	BLK	PTS	RPG	APG	PPG
85-86–L.A. Clippers	79	37	2088	324	661	.490	1	3	.333	229	307	.746	161	439	600	79	286	5	64	145	206	878	7.6	1.0	11.1
86-87–L.A. Clippers	72	61	2230	320	713	.449	0	2	.000	188	263	.715	134	452	586	135	251	7	60	184	187	828	8.1	1.9	11.5
87-88–L.A. Clippers	66	59	2171	340	693	.491	0	8	.000	180	255	.706	112	418	530	172	203	2	50	223	225	860	8.0	2.6	13.0
88-89–L.A. Clippers	79	62	2585	491	907	.541	0	2	.000	317	426	.744	164	532	696	157	221	4	57	237	221	1299	8.8	2.0	16.4
89-90–L.A. Clippers	71	58	2313	362	688	.526	0	1	.000	235	321	.732	156	501	657	159	217	3	59	187	187	959	9.3	2.2	13.5
90-91–LAClips-Seattle	70	65	2236	386	778	.496	0	0	–	210	295	.712	157	566	723	119	184	1	54	235	145	982	10.3	1.7	14.0
91-92–Seattle	63	61	1941	354	740	.478	0	2	.000	171	249	.687	130	383	513	76	185	1	39	175	118	879	8.1	1.2	14.0
92-93–Seattle-Lakers	59	6	754	133	271	.491	0	0	–	69	104	.663	51	158	209	22	134	0	31	78	48	335	3.5	0.4	5.7
93-94–New Jersey	77	74	1817	283	589	.480	0	0	–	152	214	.710	135	364	499	44	198	0	35	97	90	718	6.5	0.6	9.3
94-95–New Jersey	61	57	1598	271	531	.510	0	0	–	133	175	.760	94	346	440	38	151	3	23	125	64	675	7.2	0.6	11.1
95-96–Vanc.-Milw.	83	71	1896	294	590	.498	0	3	.000	140	194	.722	141	398	539	64	224	1	45	144	85	728	6.5	0.8	8.8
96-97–Toronto	4	3	44	5	12	.417	0	0	–	3	4	.750	3	6	9	1	5	0	1	2	0	13	2.3	0.3	3.3
97-98–Philadelphia	14	0	197	22	41	.537	0	0	–	19	30	.633	18	35	53	3	26	0	4	12	4	63	3.8	0.2	4.5
98-99–Philadelphia	6	0	33	2	7	.286	0	0	–	0	0	–	3	5	8	1	6	0	0	3	0	4	1.3	0.2	0.7
99-00–Cleveland	3	0	8	1	3	.333	0	0	–	0	0	–	0	1	1	0	1	0	0	0	1	2	0.3	0.0	0.7
Reg. Season Totals	807	614	21911	3588	7224	.497	1	21	.048	2046	2837	.721	1459	4604	6063	1070	2292	27	522	1847	1581	9223	7.5	1.3	11.4
Playoff Totals	18	13	432	50	99	.505	0	1	.000	45	58	.776	22	78	100	7	53	1	10	24	34	145	5.6	0.4	8.1

Bennett, Anthony Guy **(Tony)** b. June 1, 1969 Ht. 6-0 Wt. 186 College: Wisconsin-Green Bay

SEASON–TEAM	G	GS	MIN	FGM	FGA	PCT	3FGM	3FGA	PCT	FTM	FTA	PCT	O-RB	D-RB	TOT	AST	PF	DQ	STL	TO	BLK	PTS	RPG	APG	PPG
92-93–Charlotte	75	2	857	110	260	.423	26	80	.325	30	41	.732	12	51	63	136	110	0	30	50	0	276	0.8	1.8	3.7
93-94–Charlotte	74	5	983	105	263	.399	27	75	.360	11	15	.733	16	74	90	163	84	0	39	40	1	248	1.2	2.2	3.4
94-95–Charlotte	3	0	46	6	13	.462	2	9	.222	0	0	–	0	2	2	4	6	0	0	3	0	14	0.7	1.3	4.7
Reg. Season Totals	152	7	1886	221	536	.412	55	164	.335	41	56	.732	28	127	155	303	200	0	69	93	1	538	1.0	2.0	3.5
Playoff Totals	8	0	86	12	25	.480	4	8	.500	2	2	1.000	1	8	9	13	8	0	2	5	1	30	1.1	1.6	3.8

Bennett, Elmer James b. February 13, 1970 Ht. 6-0 Wt. 171 College: Notre Dame

SEASON–TEAM	G	GS	MIN	FGM	FGA	PCT	3FGM	3FGA	PCT	FTM	FTA	PCT	O-RB	D-RB	TOT	AST	PF	DQ	STL	TO	BLK	PTS	RPG	APG	PPG
94-95–Cleveland	4	0	18	6	11	.545	0	2	.000	3	4	.750	0	1	1	3	3	0	4	3	0	15	0.3	0.8	3.8
95-96–Philadelphia	8	0	66	4	17	.235	0	0	–	3	4	.750	1	4	5	8	6	0	1	7	1	11	0.6	1.0	1.4
96-97–Houston-Denver	9	0	75	6	19	.316	3	9	.333	7	10	.700	0	4	4	11	7	0	4	10	0	22	0.4	1.2	2.4
Reg. Season Totals	21	0	159	16	47	.340	3	11	.273	13	18	.722	1	9	10	22	16	0	9	20	1	48	0.5	1.0	2.3

Bennett, Mario Marcell b. August 1, 1973 Ht. 6-9 Wt. 220 College: Arizona State

SEASON–TEAM	G	GS	MIN	FGM	FGA	PCT	3FGM	3FGA	PCT	FTM	FTA	PCT	O-RB	D-RB	TOT	AST	PF	DQ	STL	TO	BLK	PTS	RPG	APG	PPG
95-96–Phoenix	19	14	230	29	64	.453	0	1	.000	27	42	.643	21	28	49	6	46	0	11	11	11	85	2.6	0.3	4.5
97-98–L.A. Lakers	45	4	354	80	135	.593	1	2	.500	16	44	.364	60	66	126	18	61	0	19	21	11	177	2.8	0.4	3.9
98-99–Chicago	3	0	19	2	6	.333	0	0	–	3	4	.750	2	3	5	0	4	0	1	1	0	7	1.7	0.0	2.3
99-00–L.A. Clippers	1	0	3	0	3	.000	0	0	–	0	0	–	1	1	2	0	1	0	0	0	0	0	2.0	0.0	0.0
Reg. Season Totals	68	18	606	111	208	.534	1	3	.333	46	90	.511	84	98	182	24	112	0	31	33	22	269	2.7	0.4	4.0
Playoff Totals	6	0	18	3	6	.500	0	0	–	2	2	1.000	4	5	9	–	2	0	0	2	1	8	1.5	0.0	1.3

Bennett, Melvin P. **(Mel)** b. January 4, 1955 d. 1981 Ht. 6-7 Wt. 215 College: Pittsburgh

SEASON–TEAM	G	GS	MIN	FGM	FGA	PCT	3FGM	3FGA	PCT	FTM	FTA	PCT	O-RB	D-RB	TOT	AST	PF	DQ	STL	TO	BLK	PTS	RPG	APG	PPG
75-76–Virginia (A)	75	–	2193	329	819	.402	0	2	.000	246	403	.610	249	277	526	97	266	–	77	176	47	904	7.0	1.3	12.1
76-77–Indiana	67	–	911	101	294	.344	–	–	–	112	187	.599	110	127	237	70	155	0	37	–	33	314	3.5	1.0	4.7
77-78–Indiana	31	–	285	23	81	.284	–	–	–	28	45	.622	49	44	93	22	54	1	11	30	7	74	3.0	0.7	2.4
80-81–Utah	28	–	313	26	60	.433	0	2	.000	53	81	.654	33	60	93	15	56	0	3	31	11	105	3.3	0.5	3.8
81-82–Cleveland	3	0	23	2	4	.500	0	0	–	1	6	.167	1	2	3	0	2	0	1	4	0	5	1.0	0.0	1.7
Reg. NBA Totals	129	0	1532	152	439	.346	0	2	.000	194	319	.608	193	233	426	107	267	1	52	65	51	498	3.3	0.8	3.9
Reg. ABA Totals	75	–	2193	329	819	.402	0	2	.000	246	403	.610	249	277	526	97	266	–	77	176	47	904	7.0	1.3	12.1

Bennett, Willis **(Spider)** b. August 4, 1943 Ht. 6-3 Wt. 190 College: Winston-Salem State

SEASON–TEAM	G	GS	MIN	FGM	FGA	PCT	3FGM	3FGA	PCT	FTM	FTA	PCT	O-RB	D-RB	TOT	AST	PF	DQ	STL	TO	BLK	PTS	RPG	APG	PPG
68-69–Dallas-Houston (A)	59	–	993	147	385	.382	6	25	.240	140	216	.648	–	–	147	84	165	9	–	145	–	440	2.5	1.4	7.5
Reg. ABA Totals	59	–	993	147	385	.382	6	25	.240	140	216	.648	–	–	147	84	165	9	–	145	–	440	2.5	1.4	7.5

Bennett, Winston George III **(Steady Bee)** b. February 9, 1965 Ht. 6-7 Wt. 220 College: Kentucky

SEASON–TEAM	G	GS	MIN	FGM	FGA	PCT	3FGM	3FGA	PCT	FTM	FTA	PCT	O-RB	D-RB	TOT	AST	PF	DQ	STL	TO	BLK	PTS	RPG	APG	PPG
89-90–Cleveland	55	34	990	137	286	.479	0	0	–	64	96	.667	84	104	188	54	133	1	23	62	10	338	3.4	1.0	6.1
90-91–Cleveland	27	13	334	40	107	.374	0	0	–	35	47	.745	30	34	64	28	50	0	8	20	2	115	2.4	1.0	4.3
91-92–Clev.-Miami	54	45	833	80	211	.379	0	1	.000	35	50	.700	63	99	162	38	122	1	19	33	9	195	3.0	0.7	3.6
Reg. Season Totals	136	92	2157	257	604	.425	0	1	.000	134	193	.694	177	237	414	120	305	2	50	115	21	648	3.0	0.9	4.8
Playoff Totals	5	5	135	23	47	.489	0	0	–	4	6	.667	14	7	21	5	11	0	3	4	1	50	4.2	1.0	10.0

Benoit, David b. May 9, 1968 Ht. 6-8 Wt. 220 College: Tyler (Texas) J.C.; Alabama

SEASON–TEAM	G	GS	MIN	FGM	FGA	PCT	3FGM	3FGA	PCT	FTM	FTA	PCT	O-RB	D-RB	TOT	AST	PF	DQ	STL	TO	BLK	PTS	RPG	APG	PPG
91-92–Utah	77	2	1161	175	375	.467	3	14	.214	81	100	.810	105	191	296	34	124	0	19	71	44	434	3.8	0.4	5.6
92-93–Utah	82	27	1712	258	592	.436	34	98	.347	114	152	.750	116	276	392	43	201	2	45	90	43	664	4.8	0.5	8.1
93-94–Utah	55	18	1070	139	361	.385	12	59	.203	68	88	.773	89	171	260	23	115	0	23	37	37	358	4.7	0.4	6.5
94-95–Utah	71	67	1841	285	587	.486	38	115	.330	132	157	.841	96	272	368	58	183	1	45	75	47	740	5.2	0.8	10.4
95-96–Utah	81	63	1961	255	581	.439	64	192	.333	87	112	.777	90	293	383	82	166	2	43	71	49	661	4.7	1.0	8.2
97-98–N.J.-Orlando	77	0	1123	152	408	.373	55	170	.324	61	74	.824	60	143	203	25	157	0	35	52	20	420	2.6	0.3	5.5
Reg. Season Totals	443	177	8868	1264	2904	.435	206	648	.318	543	683	.795	556	1346	1902	265	946	5	210	396	240	3277	4.3	0.6	7.4
Playoff Totals	53	29	1176	151	362	.417	36	91	.396	49	67	.731	61	145	206	32	105	0	19	52	29	387	3.9	0.6	7.3

Benson, Michael Kent **(Kent)** b. December 27, 1954 Ht. 6-11 Wt. 245 College: Indiana

SEASON–TEAM	G	GS	MIN	FGM	FGA	PCT	3FGM	3FGA	PCT	FTM	FTA	PCT	O-RB	D-RB	TOT	AST	PF	DQ	STL	TO	BLK	PTS	RPG	APG	PPG
77-78–Milwaukee	69	–	1288	220	473	.465	–	–	–	92	141	.652	89	206	295	99	177	1	69	119	54	532	4.3	1.4	7.7
78-79–Milwaukee	82	–	2132	413	798	.518	–	–	–	180	245	.735	187	397	584	204	280	4	89	156	81	1006	7.1	2.5	12.3
79-80–Milw.-Detroit	73	–	1891	299	618	.484	1	5	.200	99	141	.702	126	327	453	178	246	4	73	157	92	698	6.2	2.4	9.6
80-81–Detroit	59	–	1956	364	770	.473	0	4	.000	196	254	.772	124	276	400	172	184	1	72	190	67	924	6.8	2.9	15.7
81-82–Detroit	75	72	2467	405	802	.505	3	11	.273	127	158	.804	219	434	653	159	214	2	66	160	98	940	8.7	2.1	12.5
82-83–Detroit	21	15	599	85	182	.467	0	1	.000	38	50	.760	53	102	155	49	61	0	14	35	17	208	7.4	2.3	9.9
83-84–Detroit	82	58	1734	248	451	.550	0	1	.000	83	101	.822	117	292	409	130	230	4	71	79	53	579	5.0	1.6	7.1
84-85–Detroit	72	35	1401	201	397	.506	0	3	.000	76	94	.809	103	221	324	93	207	4	53	68	44	478	4.5	1.3	6.6
85-86–Detroit	72	51	1344	201	415	.484	1	2	.500	66	83	.795	118	258	376	80	196	3	58	58	51	469	5.2	1.1	6.5
86-87–Utah	73	2	895	140	316	.443	2	7	.286	47	58	.810	80	151	231	39	138	0	39	45	28	329	3.2	0.5	4.5
87-88–Cleveland	2	0	12	2	2	1.000	0	0	–	1	2	.500	0	1	1	0	2	0	1	2	1	5	0.5	0.0	2.5
Reg. Season Totals	680	233	15719	2578	5224	.493	7	34	.206	1005	1327	.757	1216	2665	3881	1203	1935	23	605	1069	586	6168	5.7	1.8	9.1
Playoff Totals	29	6	432	56	116	.483	0	0	–	25	36	.694	26	68	94	14	72	0	18	17	14	137	3.2	0.5	4.7

Berce, Eugene D. **(Gene)** b. November 22, 1926 Ht. 5-11 Wt. 175 College: Cornell; Marquette

SEASON–TEAM	G	GS	MIN	FGM	FGA	PCT	3FGM	3FGA	PCT	FTM	FTA	PCT	O-RB	D-RB	TOT	AST	PF	DQ	STL	TO	BLK	PTS	RPG	APG	PPG
48-49–Oshkosh (N)	58	–	–	120	–	–	–	–	–	101	153	.660	–	–	–	–	137	–	–	–	–	341	–	–	5.9
49-50–Tri-Cities	3	–	–	5	16	.313	–	–	–	0	5	.000	–	–	–	2	6	–	–	–	–	10	–	0.7	3.3
Reg. NBA Totals	3	–	–	5	16	.313	–	–	–	0	5	.000	–	–	–	2	6	–	–	–	–	10	–	0.7	3.3
Reg. NBL Totals	58	–	–	120	–	–	–	–	–	101	153	.660	–	–	–	–	137	–	–	–	–	341	–	–	5.9
NBL Playoff Totals	7	–	–	8	–	–	–	–	–	32	39	.821	–	–	–	–	17	–	–	–	–	48	–	–	6.9

Bergen, Gary Dean b. July 16, 1932 Ht. 6-8 Wt. 210 College: Utah; Kansas State

SEASON–TEAM	G	GS	MIN	FGM	FGA	PCT	3FGM	3FGA	PCT	FTM	FTA	PCT	O-RB	D-RB	TOT	AST	PF	DQ	STL	TO	BLK	PTS	RPG	APG	PPG
56-57–New York	6	–	40	3	11	.273	–	–	–	2	2	1.000	–	–	8	1	4	0	–	–	–	8	1.3	0.2	1.3
Reg. Season Totals	6	–	40	3	11	.273	–	–	–	2	2	1.000	–	–	8	1	4	0	–	–	–	8	1.3	0.2	1.3

Bergh, Larry Clifford b. April 2, 1945 Ht. 6-8 Wt. 210 College: Tuskegee; Weber State

SEASON–TEAM	G	GS	MIN	FGM	FGA	PCT	3FGM	3FGA	PCT	FTM	FTA	PCT	O-RB	D-RB	TOT	AST	PF	DQ	STL	TO	BLK	PTS	RPG	APG	PPG
69-70–Pittsburgh (A)	20	–	255	49	120	.408	0	1	.000	23	33	.697	–	–	85	18	52	2	–	–	–	121	4.3	0.9	6.1
Reg. ABA Totals	20	–	255	49	120	.408	0	1	.000	23	33	.697	–	–	85	18	52	2	–	–	–	121	4.3	0.9	6.1

Berry, Ricky Alan b. October 6, 1964 d. August 14, 1989 Ht. 6-8 Wt. 205 College: Oregon State; San Jose State

SEASON–TEAM	G	GS	MIN	FGM	FGA	PCT	3FGM	3FGA	PCT	FTM	FTA	PCT	O-RB	D-RB	TOT	AST	PF	DQ	STL	TO	BLK	PTS	RPG	APG	PPG
88-89–Sacramento	64	21	1406	255	567	.450	65	160	.406	131	166	.789	57	140	197	80	197	4	37	82	22	706	3.1	1.3	11.0
Reg. Season Totals	64	21	1406	255	567	.450	65	160	.406	131	166	.789	57	140	197	80	197	4	37	82	22	706	3.1	1.3	11.0

Berry, Walter b. May 14, 1964 Ht. 6-8 Wt. 215 College: San Jacinto (Texas) Coll.; St. John's (N.Y.)

SEASON–TEAM	G	GS	MIN	FGM	FGA	PCT	3FGM	3FGA	PCT	FTM	FTA	PCT	O-RB	D-RB	TOT	AST	PF	DQ	STL	TO	BLK	PTS	RPG	APG	PPG
86-87–Port.-S.A.	63	45	1586	407	766	.531	0	3	.000	187	288	.649	136	173	309	105	196	2	38	153	40	1001	4.9	1.7	15.9
87-88–San Antonio	73	56	1922	540	960	.563	0	0	–	192	320	.600	176	219	395	110	207	2	55	162	63	1272	5.4	1.5	17.4
88-89–N.J.-Houston	69	31	1355	254	501	.507	1	2	.500	100	143	.699	86	181	267	77	183	1	29	89	48	609	3.9	1.1	8.8
Reg. Season Totals	205	132	4863	1201	2227	.539	1	5	.200	479	751	.638	398	573	971	292	586	5	122	404	151	2882	4.7	1.4	14.1
Playoff Totals	7	0	151	40	76	.526	0	1	.000	19	23	.826	16	14	30	11	18	0	7	17	3	99	4.3	1.6	14.1

Beshore, Delmer (Del) b. November 29, 1956 Ht. 6-0 Wt. 170 College: California (Pa.)

SEASON–TEAM	G	GS	MIN	FGM	FGA	PCT	3FGM	3FGA	PCT	FTM	FTA	PCT	O-RB	D-RB	TOT	AST	PF	DQ	STL	TO	BLK	PTS	RPG	APG	PPG
78-79–Milwaukee	1	–	1	0	0	–	–	–	–	0	0	–	0	0	0	0	0	0	0	0	0	0	0.0	0.0	0.0
79-80–Chicago	68	–	869	88	250	.352	10	26	.385	58	87	.667	16	47	63	139	105	0	58	104	5	244	0.9	2.0	3.6
Reg. Season Totals	69	–	870	88	250	.352	10	26	.385	58	87	.667	16	47	63	139	105	0	58	104	5	244	0.9	2.0	3.5

Best, Travis Eric b. July 12, 1972 Ht. 5-11 Wt. 182 College: Georgia Tech

SEASON–TEAM	G	GS	MIN	FGM	FGA	PCT	3FGM	3FGA	PCT	FTM	FTA	PCT	O-RB	D-RB	TOT	AST	PF	DQ	STL	TO	BLK	PTS	RPG	APG	PPG
95-96–Indiana	59	1	571	69	163	.423	8	25	.320	75	90	.833	11	33	44	97	80	0	20	63	3	221	0.7	1.6	3.7
96-97–Indiana	76	46	2064	274	620	.442	57	155	.368	149	197	.756	36	130	166	318	221	3	98	153	5	754	2.2	4.2	9.9
97-98–Indiana	82	0	1547	201	480	.419	21	70	.300	112	131	.855	28	94	122	281	193	3	85	111	5	535	1.5	3.4	6.5
98-99–Indiana	49	0	1043	127	305	.416	22	59	.373	70	83	.843	19	61	80	169	111	2	42	62	4	346	1.6	3.4	7.1
99-00–Indiana	82	0	1691	271	561	.483	35	93	.376	156	190	.821	16	126	142	272	204	1	76	107	5	733	1.7	3.3	8.9
Reg. Season Totals	348	47	6916	942	2129	.442	143	402	.356	562	691	.813	110	444	554	1137	809	9	321	496	22	2589	1.6	3.3	7.4
Playoff Totals	55	0	977	131	319	.411	21	64	.328	93	107	.869	26	75	101	127	141	2	40	68	8	376	1.8	2.3	6.8

Bialosuknia, Wesley John (Wes) b. June 8, 1945 Ht. 6-2 Wt. 185 College: Connecticut

SEASON–TEAM	G	GS	MIN	FGM	FGA	PCT	3FGM	3FGA	PCT	FTM	FTA	PCT	O-RB	D-RB	TOT	AST	PF	DQ	STL	TO	BLK	PTS	RPG	APG	PPG
67-68–Oakland (A)	70	–	1224	238	570	.418	29	73	.397	103	132	.780	–	–	89	57	101	1	–	62	–	608	1.3	0.8	8.7
Reg. ABA Totals	70	–	1224	238	570	.418	29	73	.397	103	132	.780	–	–	89	57	101	1	–	62	–	608	1.3	0.8	8.7

Bianchi, Alfred A. (Al) b. March 26, 1932 Ht. 6-3 Wt. 185 College: Bowling Green State

SEASON–TEAM	G	GS	MIN	FGM	FGA	PCT	3FGM	3FGA	PCT	FTM	FTA	PCT	O-RB	D-RB	TOT	AST	PF	DQ	STL	TO	BLK	PTS	RPG	APG	PPG
56-57–Syracuse	68	–	1577	199	567	.351	–	–	–	165	239	.690	–	–	227	106	198	5	–	–	–	563	3.3	1.6	8.3
57-58–Syracuse	69	–	1421	215	625	.344	–	–	–	140	205	.683	–	–	221	114	188	4	–	–	–	570	3.2	1.7	8.3
58-59–Syracuse	72	–	1779	285	756	.377	–	–	–	149	206	.723	–	–	199	159	260	8	–	–	–	719	2.8	2.2	10.0
59-60–Syracuse	69	–	1256	211	576	.366	–	–	–	109	155	.703	–	–	179	169	231	5	–	–	–	531	2.6	2.4	7.7
60-61–Syracuse	52	–	667	118	342	.345	–	–	–	60	87	.690	–	–	105	93	137	5	–	–	–	296	2.0	1.8	5.7
61-62–Syracuse	80	–	1925	336	847	.397	–	–	–	154	221	.697	–	–	281	263	232	5	–	–	–	826	3.5	3.3	10.3
62-63–Syracuse	61	–	1159	202	476	.424	–	–	–	120	164	.732	–	–	134	170	165	2	–	–	–	524	2.2	2.8	8.6
63-64–Philadelphia	78	–	1437	257	684	.376	–	–	–	109	141	.773	–	–	147	149	248	6	–	–	–	623	1.9	1.9	8.0
64-65–Philadelphia	60	–	1116	175	486	.360	–	–	–	54	76	.711	–	–	95	140	178	10	–	–	–	404	1.6	2.3	6.7
65-66–Philadelphia	78	–	1312	214	560	.382	–	–	–	66	98	.673	–	–	134	134	232	4	–	–	–	494	1.7	1.7	6.3
Reg. Season Totals	687	–	13649	2212	5919	.374	–	–	–	1126	1592	.707	–	–	1722	1497	2069	54	–	–	–	5550	2.5	2.2	8.1
Playoff Totals	56	–	1135	184	471	.391	–	–	–	80	115	.696	–	–	125	101	193	9	–	–	–	448	2.2	1.8	8.0

Biasatti, Henry Arcado (Hank) b. January 14, 1922 d. 1996 Ht. 6-0 Wt. 180 College: Assumption

SEASON–TEAM	G	GS	MIN	FGM	FGA	PCT	3FGM	3FGA	PCT	FTM	FTA	PCT	O-RB	D-RB	TOT	AST	PF	DQ	STL	TO	BLK	PTS	RPG	APG	PPG
46-47–Toronto	6	–	–	2	5	.400	–	–	–	2	4	.500	–	–	–	0	3	–	–	–	–	6	–	0.0	1.0
Reg. Season Totals	6	–	–	2	5	.400	–	–	–	2	4	.500	–	–	–	0	3	–	–	–	–	6	–	0.0	1.0

Bibby, Charles Henry (Henry) b. November 24, 1949 Ht. 6-1 Wt. 185 College: UCLA

SEASON–TEAM	G	GS	MIN	FGM	FGA	PCT	3FGM	3FGA	PCT	FTM	FTA	PCT	O-RB	D-RB	TOT	AST	PF	DQ	STL	TO	BLK	PTS	RPG	APG	PPG
72-73–New York	55	–	475	78	205	.380	–	–	–	73	86	.849	–	–	82	64	67	0	–	–	–	229	1.5	1.2	4.2
73-74–New York	66	–	986	210	465	.452	–	–	–	73	88	.830	48	85	133	91	123	0	65	–	2	493	2.0	1.4	7.5
74-75–N.Y.-N.O.	75	–	1400	270	619	.436	–	–	–	137	189	.725	47	90	137	181	157	0	54	–	3	677	1.8	2.4	9.0
75-76–New Orleans	79	–	1772	266	622	.428	–	–	–	200	251	.797	58	121	179	225	165	0	62	–	3	732	2.3	2.8	9.3
76-77–Philadelphia	81	–	2639	302	702	.430	–	–	–	221	282	.784	86	187	273	356	200	2	108	–	5	825	3.4	4.4	10.2
77-78–Philadelphia	82	–	2518	286	659	.434	–	–	–	171	219	.781	62	189	251	464	207	0	91	153	6	743	3.1	5.7	9.1
78-79–Philadelphia	82	–	2538	368	869	.423	–	–	–	266	335	.794	72	172	244	371	199	0	72	197	7	1002	3.0	4.5	12.2
79-80–Philadelphia	82	–	2035	251	626	.401	11	52	.212	226	286	.790	65	143	208	307	161	0	62	147	6	739	2.5	3.7	9.0
80-81–San Diego	73	–	1112	118	306	.386	32	95	.337	67	98	.684	25	49	74	200	85	0	47	76	2	335	1.0	2.7	4.6
Reg. Season Totals	675	–	15475	2149	5073	.424	43	147	.293	1434	1834	.782	463	1036	1581	2259	1364	2	561	573	34	5775	2.3	3.3	8.6
Playoff Totals	72	–	1743	211	533	.396	5	13	.385	139	181	.768	65	109	176	231	165	0	50	71	2	566	2.4	3.2	7.9

Bibby, Michael (Mike) b. May 13, 1978 Ht. 6-2 Wt. 190 College: Arizona

SEASON–TEAM	G	GS	MIN	FGM	FGA	PCT	3FGM	3FGA	PCT	FTM	FTA	PCT	O-RB	D-RB	TOT	AST	PF	DQ	STL	TO	BLK	PTS	RPG	APG	PPG
98-99–Vancouver	50	50	1758	260	605	.430	15	74	.203	127	169	.751	30	106	136	325	122	0	78	146	5	662	2.7	6.5	13.2
99-00–Vancouver	82	82	3155	459	1031	.445	77	212	.363	195	250	.780	73	233	306	665	171	1	132	247	15	1190	3.7	8.1	14.5
Reg. Season Totals	132	132	4913	719	1636	.439	92	286	.322	322	419	.768	103	339	442	990	293	1	210	393	20	1852	3.3	7.5	14.0

Biedenbach, Edward Joseph (Ed) b. August 12, 1945 Ht. 6-1 Wt. 175 College: North Carolina State

SEASON–TEAM	G	GS	MIN	FGM	FGA	PCT	3FGM	3FGA	PCT	FTM	FTA	PCT	O-RB	D-RB	TOT	AST	PF	DQ	STL	TO	BLK	PTS	RPG	APG	PPG
68-69–Phoenix	7	–	18	0	6	.000	–	–	–	4	6	.667	–	–	2	3	1	0	–	–	–	4	0.3	0.4	0.6
Reg. Season Totals	7	–	18	0	6	.000	–	–	–	4	6	.667	–	–	2	3	1	0	–	–	–	4	0.3	0.4	0.6

Bielke, Donald P. (Don) Ht. 6-7 Wt. 240 College: Valparaiso

SEASON–TEAM	G	GS	MIN	FGM	FGA	PCT	3FGM	3FGA	PCT	FTM	FTA	PCT	O-RB	D-RB	TOT	AST	PF	DQ	STL	TO	BLK	PTS	RPG	APG	PPG
55-56–Fort Wayne	7	–	38	5	9	.556	–	–	–	4	7	.571	–	–	9	1	9	0	–	–	–	14	1.3	0.1	2.0
Reg. Season Totals	7	–	38	5	9	.556	–	–	–	4	7	.571	–	–	9	1	9	0	–	–	–	14	1.3	0.1	2.0

Bigelow, Robert S. (Bob) b. December 26, 1953 Ht. 6-7 Wt. 215 College: Pennsylvania

SEASON–TEAM	G	GS	MIN	FGM	FGA	PCT	3FGM	3FGA	PCT	FTM	FTA	PCT	O-RB	D-RB	TOT	AST	PF	DQ	STL	TO	BLK	PTS	RPG	APG	PPG
75-76–Kansas City	31	–	163	16	47	.340	–	–	–	24	33	.727	9	20	29	9	18	0	4	–	1	56	0.9	0.3	1.8
76-77–Kansas City	29	–	162	35	70	.500	–	–	–	15	17	.882	8	19	27	8	17	0	3	–	1	85	0.9	0.3	2.9
77-78–K.C.-Boston	5	–	24	4	13	.308	–	–	–	0	0	–	3	6	9	0	3	0	0	0	0	8	1.8	0.0	1.6
78-79–San Diego	29	–	413	36	90	.400	–	–	–	13	21	.619	15	31	46	25	37	0	12	18	2	85	1.6	0.9	2.9
Reg. Season Totals	94	–	762	91	220	.414	–	–	–	52	71	.732	35	76	111	42	75	0	19	18	4	234	1.2	0.4	2.5

Billingy, Lionel b. 1952 Ht. 6-9 Wt. 215 College: Duquesne

SEASON–TEAM	G	GS	MIN	FGM	FGA	PCT	3FGM	3FGA	PCT	FTM	FTA	PCT	O-RB	D-RB	TOT	AST	PF	DQ	STL	TO	BLK	PTS	RPG	APG	PPG
74-75–Virginia (A)	46	–	1022	150	351	.427	0	2	.000	93	143	.650	107	173	280	49	112	–	40	122	10	393	6.1	1.1	8.5
Reg. ABA Totals	46	–	1022	150	351	.427	0	2	.000	93	143	.650	107	173	280	49	112	–	40	122	10	393	6.1	1.1	8.5

Billups, Chauncey Ray b. September 25, 1976 Ht. 6-3 Wt. 202 College: Colorado

SEASON–TEAM	G	GS	MIN	FGM	FGA	PCT	3FGM	3FGA	PCT	FTM	FTA	PCT	O-RB	D-RB	TOT	AST	PF	DQ	STL	TO	BLK	PTS	RPG	APG	PPG
97-98–Boston-Toronto	80	70	2216	280	749	.374	107	325	.329	226	266	.850	62	128	190	314	172	2	107	174	4	893	2.4	3.9	11.2
98-99–Denver	45	41	1488	191	495	.386	85	235	.362	157	172	.913	24	72	96	173	115	0	58	98	14	624	2.1	3.8	13.9
99-00–Denver-Orlando	13	5	305	34	101	.337	7	41	.171	37	44	.841	8	26	34	39	27	0	10	24	2	112	2.6	3.0	8.6
Reg. Season Totals	138	116	4009	505	1345	.375	199	601	.331	420	482	.871	94	226	320	526	314	2	175	296	20	1629	2.3	3.8	11.8

Bing, David (Dave) b. November 24, 1943 Ht. 6-3 Wt. 180 College: Syracuse HOF: 1989

SEASON–TEAM	G	GS	MIN	FGM	FGA	PCT	3FGM	3FGA	PCT	FTM	FTA	PCT	O-RB	D-RB	TOT	AST	PF	DQ	STL	TO	BLK	PTS	RPG	APG	PPG
66-67–Detroit	80	–	2762	664	1522	.436	–	–	–	273	370	.738	–	–	359	330	217	2	–	–	–	1601	4.5	4.1	20.0
67-68–Detroit	79	–	3209	835	1893	.441	–	–	–	472	668	.707	–	–	373	509	254	2	–	–	–	2142	4.7	6.4	27.1
68-69–Detroit	77	–	3039	678	1594	.425	–	–	–	444	623	.713	–	–	382	546	256	3	–	–	–	1800	5.0	7.1	23.4
69-70–Detroit	70	–	2334	575	1295	.444	–	–	–	454	580	.783	–	–	299	418	196	0	–	–	–	1604	4.3	6.0	22.9
70-71–Detroit	82	–	3065	799	1710	.467	–	–	–	615	772	.797	–	–	364	408	228	4	–	–	–	2213	4.4	5.0	27.0
71-72–Detroit	45	–	1936	369	891	.414	–	–	–	278	354	.785	–	–	186	317	138	3	–	–	–	1016	4.1	7.0	22.6
72-73–Detroit	82	–	3361	692	1545	.448	–	–	–	456	560	.814	–	–	298	637	229	1	–	–	–	1840	3.6	7.8	22.4
73-74–Detroit	81	–	3124	582	1336	.436	–	–	–	356	438	.813	108	173	281	555	216	1	109	–	17	1520	3.5	6.9	18.8
74-75–Detroit	79	–	3222	578	1333	.434	–	–	–	343	424	.809	86	200	286	610	222	3	116	–	26	1499	3.6	7.7	19.0
75-76–Washington	82	–	2945	497	1113	.447	–	–	–	332	422	.787	94	143	237	492	262	0	118	–	23	1326	2.9	6.0	16.2
76-77–Washington	64	–	1516	271	597	.454	–	–	–	136	176	.773	54	89	143	275	150	1	61	–	5	678	2.2	4.3	10.6
77-78–Boston	80	–	2256	422	940	.449	–	–	–	244	296	.824	76	136	212	300	247	2	79	216	18	1088	2.7	3.8	13.6
Reg. Season Totals	901	–	32769	6962	15769	.441	–	–	–	4403	5683	.775	418	741	3420	5397	2615	22	483	216	89	18327	3.8	6.0	20.3
Playoff Totals	31	–	964	191	452	.423	–	–	–	95	127	.748	18	43	85	133	76	0	15	–	4	477	2.7	4.3	15.4
All-Star Totals	7	–	125	16	43	.372	–	–	–	9	9	1.000	2	7	16	16	7	0	0	–	0	41	2.3	2.3	5.9

Binion, Joe b. March 26, 1961 Ht. 6-8 Wt. 235 College: North Carolina A&T

SEASON–TEAM	G	GS	MIN	FGM	FGA	PCT	3FGM	3FGA	PCT	FTM	FTA	PCT	O-RB	D-RB	TOT	AST	PF	DQ	STL	TO	BLK	PTS	RPG	APG	PPG
86-87–Portland	11	0	51	4	10	.400	0	0	–	6	10	.600	8	10	18	1	5	0	2	3	2	14	1.6	0.1	1.3
Reg. Season Totals	11	0	51	4	10	.400	0	0	–	6	10	.600	8	10	18	1	5	0	2	3	2	14	1.6	0.1	1.3

Bird, Jerry Lee b. February 2, 1935 Ht. 6-6 Wt. 215 College: Kentucky

SEASON–TEAM	G	GS	MIN	FGM	FGA	PCT	3FGM	3FGA	PCT	FTM	FTA	PCT	O-RB	D-RB	TOT	AST	PF	DQ	STL	TO	BLK	PTS	RPG	APG	PPG
58-59–New York	11	–	45	12	32	.375	–	–	–	1	1	1.000	–	–	12	4	7	0	–	–	–	25	1.1	0.4	2.3
Reg. Season Totals	11	–	45	12	32	.375	–	–	–	1	1	1.000	–	–	12	4	7	0	–	–	–	25	1.1	0.4	2.3

Bird, Larry Joe b. December 7, 1956 Ht. 6-9 Wt. 220 College: Indiana; Northwood; Indiana State HOF: 1998

SEASON–TEAM	G	GS	MIN	FGM	FGA	PCT	3FGM	3FGA	PCT	FTM	FTA	PCT	O-RB	D-RB	TOT	AST	PF	DQ	STL	TO	BLK	PTS	RPG	APG	PPG
79-80–Boston	82	–	2955	693	1463	.474	58	143	.406	301	360	.836	216	636	852	370	279	4	143	263	53	1745	10.4	4.5	21.3
80-81–Boston	82	–	3239	719	1503	.478	20	74	.270	283	328	.863	191	704	895	451	239	2	161	289	63	1741	10.9	5.5	21.2
81-82–Boston	77	58	2923	711	1414	.503	11	52	.212	328	380	.863	200	637	837	447	244	0	143	254	66	1761	10.9	5.8	22.9
82-83–Boston	79	79	2982	747	1481	.504	22	77	.286	351	418	.840	193	677	870	458	197	0	148	240	71	1867	11.0	5.8	23.6
83-84–Boston	79	77	3028	758	1542	.492	18	73	.247	374	421	.888	181	615	796	520	197	0	144	237	69	1908	10.1	6.6	24.2
84-85–Boston	80	77	3161	918	1760	.522	56	131	.427	403	457	.882	164	678	842	531	208	0	129	248	98	2295	10.5	6.6	28.7
85-86–Boston	82	81	3113	796	1606	.496	82	194	.423	441	492	.896	190	615	805	557	182	0	166	266	51	2115	9.8	6.8	25.8
86-87–Boston	74	73	3005	786	1497	.525	90	225	.400	414	455	.910	124	558	682	566	185	3	135	240	70	2076	9.2	7.6	28.1
87-88–Boston	76	75	2965	881	1672	.527	98	237	.414	415	453	.916	108	595	703	467	157	0	125	213	57	2275	9.3	6.1	29.9
88-89–Boston	6	6	189	49	104	.471	0	0	–	18	19	.947	1	36	37	29	18	0	6	11	5	116	6.2	4.8	19.3
89-90–Boston	75	75	2944	718	1517	.473	65	195	.333	319	343	.930	90	622	712	562	173	2	106	243	61	1820	9.5	7.5	24.3
90-91–Boston	60	60	2277	462	1017	.454	77	198	.389	163	183	.891	53	456	509	431	118	0	108	187	58	1164	8.5	7.2	19.4
91-92–Boston	45	45	1662	353	758	.466	52	128	.406	150	162	.926	46	388	434	306	82	0	42	125	33	908	9.6	6.8	20.2
Reg. Season Totals	897	706	34443	8591	17334	.496	649	1727	.376	3960	4471	.886	1757	7217	8974	5695	2279	11	1556	2816	755	21791	10.0	6.3	24.3
Playoff Totals	164	136	6886	1458	3090	.472	80	249	.321	901	1012	.890	360	1323	1683	1062	466	1	296	506	145	3897	10.3	6.5	23.8
All-Star Totals	10	9	287	52	123	.423	3	13	.231	27	32	.844	19	60	79	41	28	0	23	31	3	134	7.9	4.1	13.4

Birdsong, Otis Lee b. December 9, 1955 Ht. 6-4 Wt. 195 College: Houston

SEASON–TEAM	G	GS	MIN	FGM	FGA	PCT	3FGM	3FGA	PCT	FTM	FTA	PCT	O-RB	D-RB	TOT	AST	PF	DQ	STL	TO	BLK	PTS	RPG	APG	PPG
77-78–Kansas City	73	–	1878	470	955	.492	–	–	–	216	310	.697	70	105	175	174	179	1	74	145	12	1156	2.4	2.4	15.8
78-79–Kansas City	82	–	2839	741	1456	.509	–	–	–	296	408	.725	176	178	354	281	255	2	125	200	17	1778	4.3	3.4	21.7
79-80–Kansas City	82	–	2885	781	1546	.505	10	36	.278	286	412	.694	170	161	331	202	226	2	136	179	22	1858	4.0	2.5	22.7
80-81–Kansas City	71	–	2593	710	1306	.544	10	35	.286	317	455	.697	119	139	258	233	172	2	93	173	18	1747	3.6	3.3	24.6
81-82–New Jersey	37	22	1025	225	480	.469	0	10	.000	74	127	.583	30	67	97	124	74	0	30	64	5	524	2.6	3.4	14.2
82-83–New Jersey	62	54	1885	426	834	.511	2	6	.333	82	145	.566	53	97	150	239	155	0	85	114	16	936	2.4	3.9	15.1
83-84–New Jersey	69	57	2168	583	1147	.508	5	20	.250	194	319	.608	74	96	170	266	180	2	86	170	17	1365	2.5	3.9	19.8
84-85–New Jersey	56	45	1842	495	968	.511	4	21	.190	161	259	.622	60	88	148	232	145	1	84	117	7	1155	2.6	4.1	20.6
85-86–New Jersey	77	74	2395	542	1056	.513	8	22	.364	122	210	.581	88	114	202	261	228	8	85	179	17	1214	2.6	3.4	15.8
86-87–New Jersey	7	6	127	19	42	.452	0	1	.000	6	9	.667	3	4	7	17	16	0	3	9	0	44	1.0	2.4	6.3
87-88–New Jersey	67	59	1882	337	736	.458	9	25	.360	47	92	.511	73	94	167	222	143	2	54	129	11	730	2.5	3.3	10.9
88-89–Boston	13	0	108	18	36	.500	1	3	.333	0	2	.000	4	9	13	9	10	0	3	12	1	37	1.0	0.7	2.8
Reg. Season Totals	696	317	21627	5347	10562	.506	49	179	.274	1801	2748	.655	920	1152	2072	2260	1783	20	858	1491	143	12544	3.0	3.2	18.0
Playoff Totals	35	15	1090	232	483	.480	1	11	.091	81	139	.583	40	64	104	104	89	1	56	71	5	546	3.0	3.0	15.6
All-Star Totals	4	0	52	6	16	.375	0	0	–	2	4	.500	4	2	6	2	3	0	3	3	0	14	1.5	0.5	3.5

Bishop, Gale b. June 4, 1922 Ht. 6-3 Wt. 195 College: Washington State

SEASON–TEAM	G	GS	MIN	FGM	FGA	PCT	3FGM	3FGA	PCT	FTM	FTA	PCT	O-RB	D-RB	TOT	AST	PF	DQ	STL	TO	BLK	PTS	RPG	APG	PPG
48-49–Philadelphia	56	–	–	170	523	.325	–	–	–	127	195	.651	–	–	–	92	137	–	–	–	–	467	–	1.6	8.3
Reg. Season Totals	56	–	–	170	523	.325	–	–	–	127	195	.651	–	–	–	92	137	–	–	–	–	467	–	1.6	8.3
Playoff Totals	2	–	–	7	26	.269	–	–	–	4	8	.500	–	–	–	2	3	–	–	–	–	18	–	1.0	9.0

Blab, Uwe Konstantine b. March 26, 1962 Ht. 7-1 Wt. 255 College: Indiana

SEASON–TEAM	G	GS	MIN	FGM	FGA	PCT	3FGM	3FGA	PCT	FTM	FTA	PCT	O-RB	D-RB	TOT	AST	PF	DQ	STL	TO	BLK	PTS	RPG	APG	PPG
85-86–Dallas	48	0	409	44	94	.468	0	0	–	36	67	.537	25	66	91	17	65	0	3	28	12	124	1.9	0.4	2.6
86-87–Dallas	30	0	160	20	51	.392	0	0	–	13	28	.464	11	25	36	13	33	0	4	15	9	53	1.2	0.4	1.8
87-88–Dallas	73	1	658	58	132	.439	0	0	–	46	65	.708	52	82	134	35	108	1	8	49	29	162	1.8	0.5	2.2
88-89–Dallas	37	0	208	24	52	.462	0	0	–	20	25	.800	11	33	44	12	36	0	3	14	13	68	1.2	0.3	1.8
89-90–G.S.-S.A.	47	33	531	39	98	.398	0	0	–	20	37	.541	29	79	108	25	102	0	1	35	22	98	2.3	0.5	2.1
Reg. Season Totals	235	34	1966	185	427	.433	0	0	–	135	222	.608	128	285	413	102	344	1	19	141	85	505	1.8	0.4	2.1
Playoff Totals	7	0	29	3	7	.429	0	0	–	6	12	.500	2	5	7	1	6	0	1	3	1	12	1.0	0.1	1.7

Black, Charles Bradford Jr. (Charlie, Hawk) b. June 15, 1921 d. December 22, 1992 Ht. 6-5 Wt. 200 College: Kansas

SEASON–TEAM	G	GS	MIN	FGM	FGA	PCT	3FGM	3FGA	PCT	FTM	FTA	PCT	O-RB	D-RB	TOT	AST	PF	DQ	STL	TO	BLK	PTS	RPG	APG	PPG
47-48–Anderson (N)	58	–	–	148	–	–	–	–	–	149	249	.598	–	–	–	–	196	–	–	–	–	445	–	–	7.7
48-49–Ind.-FtWayne	58	–	–	203	691	.294	–	–	–	161	291	.553	–	–	–	140	247	–	–	–	–	567	–	2.4	9.8
49-50–FtWayne-And.	65	–	–	226	813	.278	–	–	–	209	321	.651	–	–	–	163	273	–	–	–	–	661	–	2.5	10.2
51-52–Milwaukee	13	–	117	6	31	.194	–	–	–	5	12	.417	–	–	31	9	31	2	–	–	–	17	2.4	0.7	1.3
Reg. NBA Totals	136	–	117	435	1535	.283	–	–	–	375	624	.601	–	–	31	312	551	2	–	–	–	1245	2.4	2.3	9.2
Reg. NBL Totals	58	–	–	148	–	–	–	–	–	149	249	.598	–	–	–	–	196	–	–	–	–	445	–	–	7.7
NBA Playoff Totals	8	–	0	18	61	.295	–	–	–	21	29	.724	–	–	–	17	38	4	–	–	–	57	–	2.1	7.1
NBL Playoff Totals	6	–	–	28	–	–	–	–	–	10	22	.455	–	–	–	–	18	–	–	–	–	66	–	–	11.0

Black, Norman Augustus b. November 12, 1957 Ht. 6-5 Wt. 190 College: St. Joseph's (Pa.)

SEASON–TEAM	G	GS	MIN	FGM	FGA	PCT	3FGM	3FGA	PCT	FTM	FTA	PCT	O-RB	D-RB	TOT	AST	PF	DQ	STL	TO	BLK	PTS	RPG	APG	PPG
80-81–Detroit	3	–	28	3	10	.300	0	0	–	2	8	.250	0	2	2	2	2	0	1	1	0	8	0.7	0.7	2.7
Reg. Season Totals	3	–	28	3	10	.300	0	0	–	2	8	.250	0	2	2	2	2	0	1	1	0	8	0.7	0.7	2.7

Black, Thomas Donald (Tom) b. July 9, 1941 Ht. 6-11 Wt. 240 College: Wisconsin; South Dakota State

SEASON–TEAM	G	GS	MIN	FGM	FGA	PCT	3FGM	3FGA	PCT	FTM	FTA	PCT	O-RB	D-RB	TOT	AST	PF	DQ	STL	TO	BLK	PTS	RPG	APG	PPG
70-71–Seattle-Cin.	71	–	873	121	301	.402	–	–	–	57	88	.648	–	–	259	44	136	1	–	–	–	299	3.6	0.6	4.2
Reg. Season Totals	71	–	873	121	301	.402	–	–	–	57	88	.648	–	–	259	44	136	1	–	–	–	299	3.6	0.6	4.2

Blackman, Rolando Antonio (Ro) b. February 26, 1959 Ht. 6-6 Wt. 205 College: Kansas State

SEASON–TEAM	G	GS	MIN	FGM	FGA	PCT	3FGM	3FGA	PCT	FTM	FTA	PCT	O-RB	D-RB	TOT	AST	PF	DQ	STL	TO	BLK	PTS	RPG	APG	PPG
81-82–Dallas	82	16	1979	439	855	.513	1	4	.250	212	276	.768	97	157	254	105	122	0	46	113	30	1091	3.1	1.3	13.3
82-83–Dallas	75	62	2349	513	1042	.492	3	15	.200	297	381	.780	108	185	293	185	116	0	37	118	29	1326	3.9	2.5	17.7
83-84–Dallas	81	81	3025	721	1320	.546	1	11	.091	372	458	.812	124	249	373	288	127	0	56	169	37	1815	4.6	3.6	22.4
84-85–Dallas	81	80	2834	625	1230	.508	6	20	.300	342	413	.828	107	193	300	289	96	0	61	162	16	1598	3.7	3.6	19.7
85-86–Dallas	82	81	2787	677	1318	.514	4	29	.138	404	483	.836	88	203	291	271	138	0	79	189	25	1762	3.5	3.3	21.5
86-87–Dallas	80	80	2758	626	1264	.495	5	15	.333	419	474	.884	96	182	278	266	142	0	64	174	21	1676	3.5	3.3	21.0
87-88–Dallas	71	69	2580	497	1050	.473	0	5	.000	331	379	.873	82	164	246	262	112	0	64	144	18	1325	3.5	3.7	18.7
88-89–Dallas	78	78	2946	594	1249	.476	30	85	.353	316	370	.854	70	203	273	288	137	0	65	165	20	1534	3.5	3.7	19.7
89-90–Dallas	80	80	2934	626	1256	.498	13	43	.302	287	340	.844	88	192	280	289	128	0	77	174	21	1552	3.5	3.6	19.4
90-91–Dallas	80	80	2965	634	1316	.482	40	114	.351	282	326	.865	63	193	256	301	153	0	69	159	19	1590	3.2	3.8	19.9
91-92–Dallas	75	74	2527	535	1161	.461	65	169	.385	239	266	.898	78	161	239	204	134	0	50	153	22	1374	3.2	2.7	18.3
92-93–New York	60	33	1434	239	539	.443	31	73	.425	71	90	.789	23	79	102	157	129	1	22	65	10	580	1.7	2.6	9.7
93-94–New York	55	1	969	161	369	.436	30	84	.357	48	53	.906	23	70	93	76	100	0	25	44	6	400	1.7	1.4	7.3
Reg. Season Totals	980	815	32087	6887	13969	.493	229	667	.343	3620	4309	.840	1047	2231	3278	2981	1634	1	715	1829	274	17623	3.3	3.0	18.0
Playoff Totals	69	48	2137	434	897	.484	9	31	.290	233	268	.869	78	122	200	217	119	1	42	126	14	1110	2.9	3.1	16.1
All-Star Totals	4	0	88	29	49	.592	0	0	–	13	16	.813	4	9	13	13	5	0	5	5	2	71	3.3	3.3	17.8

Blackwell, Cory b. March 27, 1963 Ht. 6-6 Wt. 210 College: Wisconsin

SEASON–TEAM	G	GS	MIN	FGM	FGA	PCT	3FGM	3FGA	PCT	FTM	FTA	PCT	O-RB	D-RB	TOT	AST	PF	DQ	STL	TO	BLK	PTS	RPG	APG	PPG
84-85–Seattle	60	0	551	87	237	.367	0	2	.000	28	55	.509	42	54	96	26	55	0	25	44	3	202	1.6	0.4	3.4
Reg. Season Totals	60	0	551	87	237	.367	0	2	.000	28	55	.509	42	54	96	26	55	0	25	44	3	202	1.6	0.4	3.4

Blackwell, James b. February 25, 1968 Ht. 6-0 Wt. 190 College: Dartmouth

SEASON–TEAM	G	GS	MIN	FGM	FGA	PCT	3FGM	3FGA	PCT	FTM	FTA	PCT	O-RB	D-RB	TOT	AST	PF	DQ	STL	TO	BLK	PTS	RPG	APG	PPG
94-95–Cha.-Boston	13	0	80	8	13	.615	0	0	–	2	3	.667	2	9	11	11	8	0	4	5	0	18	0.8	0.8	1.4
Reg. Season Totals	13	0	80	8	13	.615	0	0	–	2	3	.667	2	9	11	11	8	0	4	5	0	18	0.8	0.8	1.4

Blackwell, Nathaniel (Nate) b. February 15, 1965 Ht. 6-4 Wt. 170 College: Temple

SEASON–TEAM	G	GS	MIN	FGM	FGA	PCT	3FGM	3FGA	PCT	FTM	FTA	PCT	O-RB	D-RB	TOT	AST	PF	DQ	STL	TO	BLK	PTS	RPG	APG	PPG
87-88–San Antonio	10	0	112	15	41	.366	2	11	.182	5	6	.833	2	4	6	18	16	0	3	8	0	37	0.6	1.8	3.7
Reg. Season Totals	10	0	112	15	41	.366	2	11	.182	5	6	.833	2	4	6	18	16	0	3	8	0	37	0.6	1.8	3.7

Blackwell, Robert Alexander (Alex) b. June 27, 1970 Ht. 6-6 Wt. 255 College: Monmouth

SEASON–TEAM	G	GS	MIN	FGM	FGA	PCT	3FGM	3FGA	PCT	FTM	FTA	PCT	O-RB	D-RB	TOT	AST	PF	DQ	STL	TO	BLK	PTS	RPG	APG	PPG
92-93–L.A. Lakers	27	0	109	14	42	.333	0	3	.000	6	8	.750	10	13	23	7	14	0	4	5	2	34	0.9	0.3	1.3
Reg. Season Totals	27	0	109	14	42	.333	0	3	.000	6	8	.750	10	13	23	7	14	0	4	5	2	34	0.9	0.3	1.3

Blaney, George R. b. November 12, 1939 Ht. 6-1 Wt. 175 College: Holy Cross

SEASON–TEAM	G	GS	MIN	FGM	FGA	PCT	3FGM	3FGA	PCT	FTM	FTA	PCT	O-RB	D-RB	TOT	AST	PF	DQ	STL	TO	BLK	PTS	RPG	APG	PPG
61-62–New York	36	–	363	54	142	.380	–	–	–	9	17	.529	–	–	36	45	34	0	–	–	–	117	1.0	1.3	3.3
Reg. Season Totals	36	–	363	54	142	.380	–	–	–	9	17	.529	–	–	36	45	34	0	–	–	–	117	1.0	1.3	3.3

Blanks, Lance b. September 9, 1966 Ht. 6-4 Wt. 195 College: Virginia; Texas

SEASON–TEAM	G	GS	MIN	FGM	FGA	PCT	3FGM	3FGA	PCT	FTM	FTA	PCT	O-RB	D-RB	TOT	AST	PF	DQ	STL	TO	BLK	PTS	RPG	APG	PPG
90-91–Detroit	38	0	214	26	61	.426	2	16	.125	10	14	.714	4	16	20	26	35	0	9	18	2	64	0.5	0.7	1.7
91-92–Detroit	43	0	189	25	55	.455	6	16	.375	8	11	.727	9	13	22	19	26	0	14	14	1	64	0.5	0.4	1.5
92-93–Minnesota	61	2	642	65	150	.433	11	43	.256	20	32	.625	18	50	68	72	61	1	16	31	5	161	1.1	1.2	2.6
Reg. Season Totals	142	2	1045	116	266	.436	19	75	.253	38	57	.667	31	79	110	117	122	1	39	63	8	289	0.8	0.8	2.0
Playoff Totals	1	0	10	1	2	.500	0	0	–	0	0	–	0	1	1	3	2	0	3	1	0	2	1.0	3.0	2.0

Blanton, Ricky Wayne b. April 21, 1966 Ht. 6-7 Wt. 215 College: Louisiana State

SEASON–TEAM	G	GS	MIN	FGM	FGA	PCT	3FGM	3FGA	PCT	FTM	FTA	PCT	O-RB	D-RB	TOT	AST	PF	DQ	STL	TO	BLK	PTS	RPG	APG	PPG
92-93–Chicago	2	0	13	3	7	.429	0	0	–	0	0	–	2	1	3	1	1	0	2	1	0	6	1.5	0.5	3.0
Reg. Season Totals	2	0	13	3	7	.429	0	0	–	0	0	–	2	1	3	1	1	0	2	1	0	6	1.5	0.5	3.0

B

Blaylock, Daron Oshay (Mookie) b. March 20, 1967 Ht. 6-1 Wt. 185 College: Midland (Texa) Coll.; Oklahoma

SEASON–TEAM	G	GS	MIN	FGM	FGA	PCT	3FGM	3FGA	PCT	FTM	FTA	PCT	O-RB	D-RB	TOT	AST	PF	DQ	STL	TO	BLK	PTS	RPG	APG	PPG
89-90–New Jersey	50	17	1267	212	571	.371	18	80	.225	63	81	.778	42	98	140	210	110	0	82	111	14	505	2.8	4.2	10.1
90-91–New Jersey	72	70	2585	432	1039	.416	14	91	.154	139	176	.790	67	182	249	441	180	0	169	207	40	1017	3.5	6.1	14.1
91-92–New Jersey	72	67	2548	429	993	.432	12	54	.222	126	177	.712	101	168	269	492	182	1	170	152	40	996	3.7	6.8	13.8
92-93–Atlanta	80	78	2820	414	964	.429	118	315	.375	123	169	.728	89	191	280	671	156	0	203	187	23	1069	3.5	8.4	13.4
93-94–Atlanta	81	81	2915	444	1079	.411	114	341	.334	116	159	.730	117	307	424	789	144	0	212	196	44	1118	5.2	9.7	13.8
94-95–Atlanta	80	80	3069	509	1198	.425	199	555	.359	156	214	.729	117	276	393	616	164	3	200	242	26	1373	4.9	7.7	17.2
95-96–Atlanta	81	81	2893	455	1123	.405	231	623	.371	127	170	.747	110	222	332	478	151	1	212	188	17	1268	4.1	5.9	15.7
96-97–Atlanta	78	78	3056	501	1159	.432	221	604	.366	131	174	.753	114	299	413	463	141	0	212	185	20	1354	5.3	5.9	17.4
97-98–Atlanta	70	69	2700	368	938	.392	90	334	.269	95	134	.709	81	260	341	469	122	0	183	176	21	921	4.9	6.7	13.2
98-99–Atlanta	48	48	1763	247	651	.379	77	251	.307	69	91	.758	45	179	224	278	61	0	99	115	9	640	4.7	5.8	13.3
99-00–Golden State	73	72	2459	327	837	.391	101	301	.336	67	95	.705	55	215	270	489	122	0	146	143	22	822	3.7	6.7	11.3
Reg. Season Totals	785	741	28075	4338	10552	.411	1195	3549	.337	1212	1640	.739	938	2397	3335	5396	1533	5	1888	1902	276	11083	4.2	6.9	14.1
Playoff Totals	54	54	2161	280	757	.370	125	357	.350	84	123	.683	67	199	266	357	102	0	116	162	24	769	4.9	6.6	14.2
All-Star Totals	1	0	16	2	5	.400	1	2	.500	0	0	–	0	1	1	2	3	0	2	1	0	5	1.0	2.0	5.0

Blevins, Leon Gravette b. June 25, 1926 Ht. 6-2 Wt. 160 College: Phoenix (Ariz.) Coll.; Arizona

SEASON–TEAM	G	GS	MIN	FGM	FGA	PCT	3FGM	3FGA	PCT	FTM	FTA	PCT	O-RB	D-RB	TOT	AST	PF	DQ	STL	TO	BLK	PTS	RPG	APG	PPG
50-51–Indianapolis	3	–	–	1	4	.250	–	–	–	0	1	.000	–	–	2	1	3	0	–	–	–	2	0.7	0.3	0.7
Reg. Season Totals	3	–	–	1	4	.250	–	–	–	0	1	.000	–	–	2	1	3	0	–	–	–	2	0.7	0.3	0.7

Block, John William Jr. b. April 16, 1944 Ht. 6-10 Wt. 210 College: USC

SEASON–TEAM	G	GS	MIN	FGM	FGA	PCT	3FGM	3FGA	PCT	FTM	FTA	PCT	O-RB	D-RB	TOT	AST	PF	DQ	STL	TO	BLK	PTS	RPG	APG	PPG
66-67–Los Angeles	22	–	118	20	52	.385	–	–	–	24	34	.706	–	–	45	5	20	0	–	–	–	64	2.0	0.2	2.9
67-68–San Diego	52	–	1805	366	865	.423	–	–	–	316	394	.802	–	–	571	71	189	3	–	–	–	1048	11.0	1.4	20.2
68-69–San Diego	78	–	2489	448	1061	.422	–	–	–	299	400	.748	–	–	703	141	249	0	–	–	–	1195	9.0	1.8	15.3
69-70–San Diego	82	–	2152	453	1025	.442	–	–	–	287	367	.782	–	–	609	137	275	2	–	–	–	1193	7.4	1.7	14.5
70-71–San Diego	73	–	1464	245	584	.420	–	–	–	212	270	.785	–	–	442	98	193	2	–	–	–	702	6.1	1.3	9.6
71-72–Milwaukee	79	–	1524	233	530	.440	–	–	–	206	275	.749	–	–	410	95	213	4	–	–	–	672	5.2	1.2	8.5
72-73–Phil.-K.C.-Omaha	73	–	2041	391	886	.441	–	–	–	300	378	.794	–	–	562	113	242	5	–	–	–	1082	7.7	1.5	14.8
73-74–K.C.-Omaha	82	–	1777	275	634	.434	–	–	–	164	206	.796	129	260	389	94	229	2	68	–	35	714	4.7	1.1	8.7
74-75–N.O.-Chicago	54	–	939	159	346	.460	–	–	–	114	144	.792	69	163	232	51	121	0	42	–	32	432	4.3	0.9	8.0
75-76–Chicago	2	–	7	2	4	.500	–	–	–	0	2	.000	0	2	2	0	2	0	1	–	0	4	1.0	0.0	2.0
Reg. Season Totals	597	–	14316	2592	5987	.433	–	–	–	1922	2470	.778	198	425	3965	805	1733	18	111	–	67	7106	6.6	1.3	11.9
Playoff Totals	21	–	288	50	112	.446	–	–	–	30	39	.769	2	4	75	9	38	0	4	–	0	130	3.6	0.4	6.2
All-Star Totals	1	–	5	2	4	.500	–	–	–	0	0	–	0	0	2	0	1	0	0	–	0	4	2.0	0.0	4.0

Bloom, Meyer (Mike) b. January 14, 1915 d. 1993 Ht. 6-6 Wt. 190 College: Temple

SEASON–TEAM	G	GS	MIN	FGM	FGA	PCT	3FGM	3FGA	PCT	FTM	FTA	PCT	O-RB	D-RB	TOT	AST	PF	DQ	STL	TO	BLK	PTS	RPG	APG	PPG
47-48–Balt.-Boston	48	–	–	174	640	.272	–	–	–	160	229	.699	–	–	–	38	116	–	–	–	–	508	–	0.8	10.6
48-49–Minn.-Chicago	45	–	–	35	181	.193	–	–	–	56	74	.757	–	–	–	32	53	–	–	–	–	126	–	0.7	2.8
Reg. Season Totals	93	–	–	209	821	.255	–	–	–	216	303	.713	–	–	–	70	169	–	–	–	–	634	–	0.8	6.8
Playoff Totals	4	–	–	11	48	.229	–	–	–	16	21	.762	–	–	–	2	10	–	–	–	–	38	–	0.5	9.5

Blount, Corie Kasoun b. January 4, 1969 Ht. 6-10 Wt. 242 College: Rancho Santiago (Calif.) Coll.; Cincinnati

SEASON–TEAM	G	GS	MIN	FGM	FGA	PCT	3FGM	3FGA	PCT	FTM	FTA	PCT	O-RB	D-RB	TOT	AST	PF	DQ	STL	TO	BLK	PTS	RPG	APG	PPG
93-94–Chicago	67	8	690	76	174	.437	0	0	–	46	75	.613	76	118	194	56	93	0	19	52	33	198	2.9	0.8	3.0
94-95–Chicago	68	9	889	100	210	.476	0	2	.000	38	67	.567	107	133	240	60	146	0	26	59	33	238	3.5	0.9	3.5
95-96–L.A. Lakers	57	2	715	79	167	.473	0	2	.000	25	44	.568	69	101	170	42	109	2	25	47	35	183	3.0	0.7	3.2
96-97–L.A. Lakers	58	18	1009	92	179	.514	1	3	.333	56	83	.675	113	163	276	35	121	2	22	50	26	241	4.8	0.6	4.2
97-98–L.A. Lakers	70	3	1029	107	187	.572	0	4	.000	39	78	.500	114	184	298	37	157	2	29	51	25	253	4.3	0.5	3.6
98-99–Lakers-Clev.	34	3	530	36	100	.360	0	1	.000	28	54	.519	58	93	151	12	74	0	19	21	16	100	4.4	0.4	2.9
99-00–Phoenix	38	1	446	44	89	.494	0	2	.000	19	33	.576	52	61	113	10	78	0	15	28	7	107	3.0	0.3	2.8
Reg. Season Totals	392	44	5308	534	1106	.483	1	14	.071	251	434	.578	589	853	1442	252	778	6	155	308	175	1320	3.7	0.6	3.4
Playoff Totals	32	0	399	30	59	.508	0	1	.000	18	31	.581	50	77	127	11	70	1	12	17	10	78	4.0	0.3	2.4

Blume, Bernard Ray (Ray) b. September 23, 1958 Ht. 6-4 Wt. 185 College: Oregon State

SEASON–TEAM	G	GS	MIN	FGM	FGA	PCT	3FGM	3FGA	PCT	FTM	FTA	PCT	O-RB	D-RB	TOT	AST	PF	DQ	STL	TO	BLK	PTS	RPG	APG	PPG
81-82–Chicago	49	2	546	102	222	.459	4	18	.222	18	28	.643	14	27	41	68	57	0	23	54	2	226	0.8	1.4	4.6
Reg. Season Totals	49	2	546	102	222	.459	4	18	.222	18	28	.643	14	27	41	68	57	0	23	54	2	226	0.8	1.4	4.6

Bobb, Nelson b. February 25, 1924 Ht. 6-0 Wt. 170 College: Temple

SEASON–TEAM	G	GS	MIN	FGM	FGA	PCT	3FGM	3FGA	PCT	FTM	FTA	PCT	O-RB	D-RB	TOT	AST	PF	DQ	STL	TO	BLK	PTS	RPG	APG	PPG
49-50–Philadelphia	57	–	–	80	248	.323	–	–	–	82	131	.626	–	–	–	46	97	–	–	–	–	242	–	0.8	4.2
50-51–Philadelphia	53	–	–	52	158	.329	–	–	–	44	79	.557	–	–	101	82	83	1	–	–	–	148	1.9	1.5	2.8
51-52–Philadelphia	62	–	1182	110	306	.359	–	–	–	99	167	.593	–	–	147	168	182	9	–	–	–	319	2.4	2.7	5.1
52-53–Philadelphia	55	–	1286	119	318	.374	–	–	–	105	162	.648	–	–	157	192	161	7	–	–	–	343	2.9	3.5	6.2
Reg. Season Totals	227	–	2468	361	1030	.350	–	–	–	330	539	.612	–	–	405	488	523	17	–	–	–	1052	2.4	2.1	4.6
Playoff Totals	6	–	58	2	6	.333	–	–	–	2	5	.400	–	–	2	4	9	0	–	–	–	6	0.5	0.7	1.0

Bockhorn, Arlen Dale (Bucky) b. July 8, 1933 Ht. 6-4 Wt. 200 College: Dayton

SEASON–TEAM	G	GS	MIN	FGM	FGA	PCT	3FGM	3FGA	PCT	FTM	FTA	PCT	O-RB	D-RB	TOT	AST	PF	DQ	STL	TO	BLK	PTS	RPG	APG	PPG
58-59–Cincinnati	71	–	2251	294	771	.381	–	–	–	138	196	.704	–	–	460	206	215	6	–	–	–	726	6.5	2.9	10.2
59-60–Cincinnati	75	–	2103	323	812	.398	–	–	–	145	194	.747	–	–	382	256	249	8	–	–	–	791	5.1	3.4	10.5
60-61–Cincinnati	79	–	2669	420	1059	.397	–	–	–	152	208	.731	–	–	434	338	282	9	–	–	–	992	5.5	4.3	12.6
61-62–Cincinnati	80	–	3062	531	1234	.430	–	–	–	198	251	.789	–	–	376	366	280	5	–	–	–	1260	4.7	4.6	15.8
62-63–Cincinnati	80	–	2612	375	954	.393	–	–	–	183	242	.756	–	–	322	261	260	6	–	–	–	933	4.0	3.3	11.7
63-64–Cincinnati	70	–	1670	242	587	.412	–	–	–	96	126	.762	–	–	205	173	227	4	–	–	–	580	2.9	2.5	8.3
64-65–Cincinnati	19	–	424	60	157	.382	–	–	–	28	39	.718	–	–	55	45	52	1	–	–	–	148	2.9	2.4	7.8
Reg. Season Totals	474	–	14791	2245	5574	.403	–	–	–	940	1256	.748	–	–	2234	1645	1565	39	–	–	–	5430	4.7	3.5	11.5
Playoff Totals	26	–	865	124	305	.407	–	–	–	52	67	.776	–	–	103	98	95	2	–	–	–	300	4.0	3.8	11.5

Boerwinkle, Thomas F. (Tom) b. August 23, 1945 Ht. 7-0 Wt. 265 College: Tennessee

SEASON–TEAM	G	GS	MIN	FGM	FGA	PCT	3FGM	3FGA	PCT	FTM	FTA	PCT	O-RB	D-RB	TOT	AST	PF	DQ	STL	TO	BLK	PTS	RPG	APG	PPG
68-69–Chicago	80	–	2365	318	831	.383	–	–	–	145	222	.653	–	–	889	178	317	11	–	–	–	781	11.1	2.2	9.8
69-70–Chicago	81	–	2335	348	775	.449	–	–	–	150	226	.664	–	–	1016	229	255	4	–	–	–	846	12.5	2.8	10.4
70-71–Chicago	82	–	2370	357	736	.485	–	–	–	168	232	.724	–	–	1133	397	275	3	–	–	–	882	13.8	4.8	10.8
71-72–Chicago	80	–	2022	219	500	.438	–	–	–	118	180	.656	–	–	897	281	253	4	–	–	–	556	11.2	3.5	7.0
72-73–Chicago	8	–	176	9	24	.375	–	–	–	12	20	.600	–	–	54	40	22	0	–	–	–	30	6.8	5.0	3.8
73-74–Chicago	46	–	602	58	119	.487	–	–	–	42	60	.700	53	160	213	94	80	0	16	–	18	158	4.6	2.0	3.4
74-75–Chicago	80	–	1175	132	271	.487	–	–	–	73	95	.768	105	275	380	272	163	0	25	–	45	337	4.8	3.4	4.2
75-76–Chicago	74	–	2045	265	530	.500	–	–	–	118	177	.667	263	529	792	283	263	9	47	–	52	648	10.7	3.8	8.8
76-77–Chicago	82	–	1070	134	273	.491	–	–	–	34	63	.540	101	211	312	189	147	0	19	–	19	302	3.8	2.3	3.7
77-78–Chicago	22	–	227	23	50	.460	–	–	–	10	13	.769	14	45	59	44	36	0	3	26	4	56	2.7	2.0	2.5
Reg. Season Totals	635	–	14387	1863	4109	.453	–	–	–	870	1288	.675	536	1220	5745	2007	1811	31	110	26	138	4596	9.0	3.2	7.2
Playoff Totals	35	–	785	107	233	.459	–	–	–	36	48	.750	58	118	330	123	94	2	4	–	11	250	9.4	3.5	7.1

Bogues, Tyrone Curtis (Muggsy) b. January 9, 1965 Ht. 5-3 Wt. 141 College: Wake Forest

SEASON–TEAM	G	GS	MIN	FGM	FGA	PCT	3FGM	3FGA	PCT	FTM	FTA	PCT	O-RB	D-RB	TOT	AST	PF	DQ	STL	TO	BLK	PTS	RPG	APG	PPG
87-88–Washington	79	14	1628	166	426	.390	3	16	.188	58	74	.784	35	101	136	404	138	1	127	101	3	393	1.7	5.1	5.0
88-89–Charlotte	79	21	1755	178	418	.426	1	13	.077	66	88	.750	53	112	165	620	141	1	111	124	7	423	2.1	7.8	5.4
89-90–Charlotte	81	65	2743	326	664	.491	5	26	.192	106	134	.791	48	159	207	867	168	1	166	146	3	763	2.6	10.7	9.4
90-91–Charlotte	81	46	2299	241	524	.460	0	12	.000	86	108	.796	58	158	216	669	160	2	137	120	3	568	2.7	8.3	7.0
91-92–Charlotte	82	69	2790	317	671	.472	2	27	.074	94	120	.783	58	177	235	743	156	0	170	156	6	730	2.9	9.1	8.9
92-93–Charlotte	81	80	2833	331	730	.453	6	26	.231	140	168	.833	51	247	298	711	179	0	161	154	5	808	3.7	8.8	10.0
93-94–Charlotte	77	77	2746	354	751	.471	2	12	.167	125	155	.806	78	235	313	780	147	1	133	171	2	835	4.1	10.1	10.8
94-95–Charlotte	78	78	2629	348	730	.477	6	30	.200	160	180	.889	51	206	257	675	151	0	103	132	0	862	3.3	8.7	11.1
95-96–Charlotte	6	0	77	6	16	.375	0	1	.000	2	2	1.000	6	1	7	19	4	0	2	6	0	14	1.2	3.2	2.3
96-97–Charlotte	65	65	1880	204	443	.460	60	144	.417	54	64	.844	25	116	141	469	114	0	82	108	2	522	2.2	7.2	8.0
97-98–Cha.-G.S.	61	31	1570	141	323	.437	4	16	.250	61	68	.897	30	102	132	331	58	0	67	105	3	347	2.2	5.4	5.7
98-99–Golden State	36	5	714	76	154	.494	0	6	.000	31	36	.861	16	57	73	134	44	0	43	47	1	183	2.0	3.7	5.1
99-00–Toronto	80	5	1731	157	358	.439	17	51	.333	79	87	.908	25	110	135	299	119	0	65	59	4	410	1.7	3.7	5.1
Reg. Season Totals	886	556	25395	2845	6208	.458	106	380	.279	1062	1284	.827	534	1781	2315	6721	1579	6	1367	1429	39	6858	2.6	7.6	7.7
Playoff Totals	19	17	638	70	167	.419	10	21	.476	20	26	.769	13	38	51	107	36	0	33	37	0	170	2.7	5.6	8.9

Bohannon, Etdrick b. May 29, 1973 Ht. 6-9 Wt. 235 College: Auburn-Montgomery

SEASON–TEAM	G	GS	MIN	FGM	FGA	PCT	3FGM	3FGA	PCT	FTM	FTA	PCT	O-RB	D-RB	TOT	AST	PF	DQ	STL	TO	BLK	PTS	RPG	APG	PPG
97-98–Indiana	5	0	11	0	4	.000	0	0	–	0	0	–	2	4	6	1	3	0	0	3	2	0	1.2	0.2	0.0
98-99–Washington	2	0	4	0	0	–	0	0	–	0	0	–	0	0	0	0	0	0	0	0	0	0	0.0	0.0	0.0
99-00–N.Y.-LAClips	13	0	118	7	13	.538	0	0	–	15	24	.625	13	18	31	5	25	0	2	10	6	29	2.4	0.4	2.2
Reg. Season Totals	20	0	133	7	17	.412	0	0	–	15	24	.625	15	22	37	6	28	0	2	13	8	29	1.9	0.3	1.5

Bol, Manute b. October 16, 1962 Ht. 7-7 Wt. 225 College: Bridgeport

SEASON–TEAM	G	GS	MIN	FGM	FGA	PCT	3FGM	3FGA	PCT	FTM	FTA	PCT	O-RB	D-RB	TOT	AST	PF	DQ	STL	TO	BLK	PTS	RPG	APG	PPG
85-86–Washington	80	60	2090	128	278	.460	0	1	.000	42	86	.488	123	354	477	23	255	5	28	65	397	298	6.0	0.3	3.7
86-87–Washington	82	12	1552	103	231	.446	0	1	.000	45	67	.672	84	278	362	11	189	1	20	61	302	251	4.4	0.1	3.1
87-88–Washington	77	4	1136	75	165	.455	0	1	.000	26	49	.531	72	203	275	13	160	0	11	35	208	176	3.6	0.2	2.3
88-89–Golden State	80	4	1769	127	344	.369	20	91	.220	40	66	.606	116	346	462	27	226	2	11	79	345	314	5.8	0.3	3.9
89-90–Golden State	75	20	1310	56	169	.331	9	48	.188	25	49	.510	33	243	276	36	194	3	13	51	238	146	3.7	0.5	1.9
90-91–Philadelphia	82	6	1522	65	164	.396	1	14	.071	24	41	.585	66	284	350	20	184	0	16	63	247	155	4.3	0.2	1.9
91-92–Philadelphia	71	2	1267	49	128	.383	0	9	.000	12	26	.462	54	168	222	22	139	1	11	41	205	110	3.1	0.3	1.5
92-93–Philadelphia	58	23	855	52	127	.409	10	32	.313	12	19	.632	44	149	193	18	87	0	14	50	119	126	3.3	0.3	2.2
93-94–Miami-Wash.-Phil.	14	0	116	4	19	.211	0	3	.000	0	0	–	3	15	18	1	13	0	2	5	16	8	1.3	0.1	0.6
94-95–Golden State	5	2	81	6	10	.600	3	5	.600	0	0	–	1	11	12	0	10	0	0	1	9	15	2.4	0.0	3.0
Reg. Season Totals	624	133	11698	665	1635	.407	43	205	.210	226	403	.561	596	2051	2647	171	1457	12	126	451	2086	1599	4.2	0.3	2.6
Playoff Totals	29	5	496	34	88	.386	2	23	.087	12	27	.444	37	72	109	3	61	0	6	13	77	82	3.8	0.1	2.8

Bolger, William J. (Bill) b. August 21, 1931 Ht. 6-5 Wt. 205 College: Georgetown

SEASON–TEAM	G	GS	MIN	FGM	FGA	PCT	3FGM	3FGA	PCT	FTM	FTA	PCT	O-RB	D-RB	TOT	AST	PF	DQ	STL	TO	BLK	PTS	RPG	APG	PPG
53-54–Baltimore	20	–	202	24	59	.407	–	–	–	8	13	.615	–	–	36	11	27	0	–	–	–	56	1.8	0.6	2.8
Reg. Season Totals	20	–	202	24	59	.407	–	–	–	8	13	.615	–	–	36	11	27	0	–	–	–	56	1.8	0.6	2.8

Bolstorff, F. Douglas (Doug) b. October 29, 1931 Ht. 6-4 Wt. 195 College: Minnesota

SEASON–TEAM	G	GS	MIN	FGM	FGA	PCT	3FGM	3FGA	PCT	FTM	FTA	PCT	O-RB	D-RB	TOT	AST	PF	DQ	STL	TO	BLK	PTS	RPG	APG	PPG
57-58–Detroit	3	–	21	2	5	.400	–	–	–	0	0	–	–	–	0	0	1	0	–	–	–	4	0.0	0.0	1.3
Reg. Season Totals	3	–	21	2	5	.400	–	–	–	0	0	–	–	–	0	0	1	0	–	–	–	4	0.0	0.0	1.3

Bon Salle, George H. b. July 1, 1935 Ht. 6-8 Wt. 230 College: Illinois

SEASON–TEAM	G	GS	MIN	FGM	FGA	PCT	3FGM	3FGA	PCT	FTM	FTA	PCT	O-RB	D-RB	TOT	AST	PF	DQ	STL	TO	BLK	PTS	RPG	APG	PPG
61-62–Chicago	3	–	9	2	8	.250	–	–	–	0	0	–	–	–	2	0	0	0	–	–	–	4	0.7	0.0	1.3
Reg. Season Totals	3	–	9	2	8	.250	–	–	–	0	0	–	–	–	2	0	0	0	–	–	–	4	0.7	0.0	1.3

Bond, Phillip Damone (Phil) b. July 27, 1954 Ht. 6-2 Wt. 175 College: Louisville

SEASON–TEAM	G	GS	MIN	FGM	FGA	PCT	3FGM	3FGA	PCT	FTM	FTA	PCT	O-RB	D-RB	TOT	AST	PF	DQ	STL	TO	BLK	PTS	RPG	APG	PPG
77-78–Houston	7	–	21	2	6	.333	–	–	–	0	0	–	1	3	4	2	1	0	1	2	0	4	0.6	0.3	0.6
Reg. Season Totals	7	–	21	2	6	.333	–	–	–	0	0	–	1	3	4	2	1	0	1	2	0	4	0.6	0.3	0.6

Bond, Walter b. February 1, 1969 Ht. 6-5 Wt. 200 College: Minnesota

SEASON–TEAM	G	GS	MIN	FGM	FGA	PCT	3FGM	3FGA	PCT	FTM	FTA	PCT	O-RB	D-RB	TOT	AST	PF	DQ	STL	TO	BLK	PTS	RPG	APG	PPG
92-93–Dallas	74	38	1578	227	565	.402	7	42	.167	129	167	.772	52	144	196	122	223	3	75	112	18	590	2.6	1.6	8.0
93-94–Utah	56	4	559	63	156	.404	19	54	.352	31	40	.775	20	41	61	31	90	1	16	17	12	176	1.1	0.6	3.1
94-95–Detroit-Utah	23	0	290	39	84	.464	15	41	.366	14	20	.700	8	24	32	24	47	0	6	17	4	107	1.4	1.0	4.7
Reg. Season Totals	153	42	2427	329	805	.409	41	137	.299	174	227	.767	80	209	289	177	360	4	97	146	34	873	1.9	1.2	5.7
Playoff Totals	4	0	13	0	2	.000	0	1	.000	1	2	.500	0	1	1	–	4	0	1	0	0	1	0.3	0.0	0.3

Boney, Dexter b. April 27, 1970 Ht. 6-4 Wt. 220 College: Nevada-Las Vegas

SEASON–TEAM	G	GS	MIN	FGM	FGA	PCT	3FGM	3FGA	PCT	FTM	FTA	PCT	O-RB	D-RB	TOT	AST	PF	DQ	STL	TO	BLK	PTS	RPG	APG	PPG
96-97–Phoenix	8	0	48	6	19	.316	1	6	.167	6	8	.750	3	3	6	0	3	0	2	1	1	19	0.8	0.0	2.4
Reg. Season Totals	8	0	48	6	19	.316	1	6	.167	6	8	.750	3	3	6	0	3	0	2	1	1	19	0.8	0.0	2.4

Bonham, Ronald D. (Ron) b. May 31, 1942 Ht. 6-5 Wt. 195 College: Cincinnati

SEASON–TEAM	G	GS	MIN	FGM	FGA	PCT	3FGM	3FGA	PCT	FTM	FTA	PCT	O-RB	D-RB	TOT	AST	PF	DQ	STL	TO	BLK	PTS	RPG	APG	PPG
64-65–Boston	37	–	369	91	220	.414	–	–	–	92	112	.821	–	–	78	19	33	0	–	–	–	274	2.1	0.5	7.4
65-66–Boston	39	–	312	76	207	.367	–	–	–	52	61	.852	–	–	35	11	29	0	–	–	–	204	0.9	0.3	5.2
67-68–Indiana (A)	42	–	426	80	210	.381	0	2	.000	85	105	.810	–	–	57	14	36	0	–	32	–	245	1.4	0.3	5.8
Reg. NBA Totals	76	–	681	167	427	.391	–	–	–	144	173	.832	–	–	113	30	62	0	–	–	–	478	1.5	0.4	6.3
Reg. ABA Totals	42	–	426	80	210	.381	0	2	.000	85	105	.810	–	–	57	14	36	0	–	32	–	245	1.4	0.3	5.8
NBA Playoff Totals	9	–	29	12	23	.522	–	–	–	7	14	.500	–	–	4	–	3	0	–	–	–	31	0.4	0.0	3.4
ABA Playoff Totals	3	–	30	4	15	.267	0	0	–	5	6	.833	–	–	6	3	4	0	–	2	–	13	2.0	1.0	4.3

Bonner, Anthony b. June 8, 1968 Ht. 6-8 Wt. 225 College: St. Louis

SEASON–TEAM	G	GS	MIN	FGM	FGA	PCT	3FGM	3FGA	PCT	FTM	FTA	PCT	O-RB	D-RB	TOT	AST	PF	DQ	STL	TO	BLK	PTS	RPG	APG	PPG
90-91–Sacramento	34	6	750	103	230	.448	0	0	–	44	76	.579	59	102	161	49	62	0	39	41	5	250	4.7	1.4	7.4
91-92–Sacramento	79	18	2287	294	658	.447	1	4	.250	151	241	.627	192	293	485	125	194	0	94	133	26	740	6.1	1.6	9.4
92-93–Sacramento	70	35	1764	229	497	.461	0	7	.000	143	241	.593	188	267	455	96	183	1	86	105	17	601	6.5	1.4	8.6
93-94–New York	73	38	1402	162	288	.563	0	0	–	50	105	.476	150	194	344	88	175	3	76	89	13	374	4.7	1.2	5.1
94-95–New York	58	23	1126	88	193	.456	1	5	.200	44	67	.657	113	149	262	80	159	0	48	79	23	221	4.5	1.4	3.8
95-96–Orlando	4	0	43	5	15	.333	0	0	–	3	7	.429	6	13	19	4	11	0	3	3	0	13	4.8	1.0	3.3
Reg. Season Totals	318	120	7372	881	1881	.468	2	16	.125	435	737	.590	708	1018	1726	442	784	4	346	450	84	2199	5.4	1.4	6.9
Playoff Totals	23	7	172	17	36	.472	0	1	.000	11	21	.524	21	17	38	5	31	0	6	16	1	45	1.7	0.2	2.0

Booker, Harold (Butch) b. July 20, 1945 Ht. 6-10 Wt. 230 College: Cheyney State

SEASON–TEAM	G	GS	MIN	FGM	FGA	PCT	3FGM	3FGA	PCT	FTM	FTA	PCT	O-RB	D-RB	TOT	AST	PF	DQ	STL	TO	BLK	PTS	RPG	APG	PPG
69-70–Miami (A)	12	–	221	30	61	.492	0	1	.000	10	18	.556	–	–	91	6	23	0	–	–	–	70	7.6	0.5	5.8
Reg. ABA Totals	12	–	221	30	61	.492	0	1	.000	10	18	.556	–	–	91	6	23	0	–	–	–	70	7.6	0.5	5.8

Booker, Melvin b. August 20, 1972 Ht. 6-2 Wt. 185 College: Missouri

SEASON–TEAM	G	GS	MIN	FGM	FGA	PCT	3FGM	3FGA	PCT	FTM	FTA	PCT	O-RB	D-RB	TOT	AST	PF	DQ	STL	TO	BLK	PTS	RPG	APG	PPG
95-96–Houston	11	0	131	16	50	.320	3	19	.158	9	11	.818	1	8	9	21	18	0	5	12	1	44	0.8	1.9	4.0
96-97–Denver-G.S.	21	4	430	46	105	.438	12	37	.324	18	20	.900	7	22	29	53	28	0	3	27	2	122	1.4	2.5	5.8
Reg. Season Totals	32	4	561	62	155	.400	15	56	.268	27	31	.871	8	30	38	74	46	0	8	39	3	166	1.2	2.3	5.2

Boone, Ronald Bruce (Ron) b. September 6, 1946 Ht. 6-2 Wt. 200 College: Idaho Western C.C.; Baylor; Idaho State

SEASON–TEAM	G	GS	MIN	FGM	FGA	PCT	3FGM	3FGA	PCT	FTM	FTA	PCT	O-RB	D-RB	TOT	AST	PF	DQ	STL	TO	BLK	PTS	RPG	APG	PPG
68-69–Dallas (A)	78	–	2682	520	1197	.434	2	15	.133	436	537	.812	–	–	394	279	303	8	–	355	–	1478	5.1	3.6	18.9
69-70–Dallas (A)	84	–	2340	423	980	.432	17	55	.309	300	382	.785	–	–	366	272	265	5	–	–	–	1163	4.4	3.2	13.8
70-71–Texas-Utah (A)	86	–	2476	610	1395	.437	49	138	.355	278	357	.779	–	–	564	256	298	–	–	–	–	1547	6.6	3.0	18.0
71-72–Utah (A)	84	–	2040	404	962	.420	13	65	.200	271	341	.795	–	–	393	233	274	–	–	215	–	1092	4.7	2.8	13.0
72-73–Utah (A)	84	–	2585	566	1136	.498	10	40	.250	415	479	.866	173	252	425	353	308	0	–	276	–	1557	5.1	4.2	18.5
73-74–Utah (A)	84	–	3098	587	1188	.494	6	26	.231	300	343	.875	157	278	435	417	289	–	123	316	22	1480	5.2	5.0	17.6
74-75–Utah (A)	84	–	3414	872	1776	.491	10	33	.303	363	422	.860	141	265	406	372	265	–	126	335	34	2117	4.8	4.4	25.2
75-76–Utah-St. L. (A)	78	–	2961	713	1467	.486	16	43	.372	277	318	.871	115	204	319	387	243	–	154	276	15	1719	4.1	5.0	22.0
76-77–Kansas City	82	–	3021	747	1577	.474	–	–	–	324	384	.844	128	193	321	338	258	1	119	–	19	1818	3.9	4.1	22.2
77-78–Kansas City	82	–	2653	563	1271	.443	–	–	–	322	377	.854	112	157	269	311	233	3	105	303	11	1448	3.3	3.8	17.7
78-79–Los Angeles	82	–	1583	259	569	.455	–	–	–	90	104	.865	53	92	145	154	171	1	66	147	11	608	1.8	1.9	7.4
79-80–L.A.-Utah	81	–	2392	405	915	.443	19	50	.380	175	196	.893	54	173	227	309	232	3	97	197	3	1004	2.8	3.8	12.4
80-81–Utah	52	–	1146	160	371	.431	11	39	.282	75	94	.798	17	67	84	161	126	0	33	111	8	406	1.6	3.1	7.8
Reg. NBA Totals	379	–	10795	2134	4703	.454	30	89	.337	986	1155	.854	364	682	1046	1273	1020	8	420	758	52	5284	2.8	3.4	13.9
Reg. ABA Totals	662	–	21596	4695	10101	.465	123	415	.296	2640	3179	.830	586	999	3302	2569	2245	13	403	1773	71	12153	5.0	3.9	18.4
NBA Playoff Totals	8	–	226	37	77	.481	0	0	–	20	21	.952	7	8	15	14	28	0	9	14	0	94	1.9	1.8	11.8
ABA Playoff Totals	76	–	2493	506	1094	.463	13	54	.241	236	270	.874	57	75	358	371	243	1	44	137	10	1261	4.7	4.9	16.6

Booth, Calvin L. b. May 7, 1976 Ht. 6-11 Wt. 241 College: Penn State

SEASON–TEAM	G	GS	MIN	FGM	FGA	PCT	3FGM	3FGA	PCT	FTM	FTA	PCT	O-RB	D-RB	TOT	AST	PF	DQ	STL	TO	BLK	PTS	RPG	APG	PPG
99-00–Washington	11	0	143	16	46	.348	0	0	–	10	14	.714	15	17	32	7	23	0	3	6	14	42	2.9	0.6	3.8
Reg. Season Totals	11	0	143	16	46	.348	0	0	–	10	14	.714	15	17	32	7	23	0	3	6	14	42	2.9	0.6	3.8

Booth, Keith Eugene b. October 9, 1974 Ht. 6-6 Wt. 235 College: Maryland

SEASON–TEAM	G	GS	MIN	FGM	FGA	PCT	3FGM	3FGA	PCT	FTM	FTA	PCT	O-RB	D-RB	TOT	AST	PF	DQ	STL	TO	BLK	PTS	RPG	APG	PPG
97-98–Chicago	6	0	17	2	6	.333	0	1	.000	6	6	1.000	2	2	4	1	3	0	0	3	0	10	0.7	0.2	1.7
98-99–Chicago	39	4	432	49	151	.325	1	10	.100	21	42	.500	25	68	93	38	60	0	22	39	11	120	2.4	1.0	3.1
Reg. Season Totals	45	4	449	51	157	.325	1	11	.091	27	48	.563	27	70	97	39	63	0	22	42	11	130	2.2	0.9	2.9

Boozer, Robert Lewis (Bob, Bullet Bob) b. April 26, 1937 Ht. 6-8 Wt. 220 College: Kansas State

SEASON–TEAM	G	GS	MIN	FGM	FGA	PCT	3FGM	3FGA	PCT	FTM	FTA	PCT	O-RB	D-RB	TOT	AST	PF	DQ	STL	TO	BLK	PTS	RPG	APG	PPG
60-61–Cincinnati	79	–	1573	250	603	.415	–	–	–	166	247	.672	–	–	488	109	193	1	–	–	–	666	6.2	1.4	8.4
61-62–Cincinnati	79	–	2488	410	936	.438	–	–	–	263	372	.707	–	–	804	130	275	3	–	–	–	1083	10.2	1.6	13.7
62-63–Cincinnati	79	–	2488	440	992	.444	–	–	–	252	353	.714	–	–	878	102	299	8	–	–	–	1132	11.1	1.3	14.3
63-64–Cin.-N.Y.	81	–	2379	468	1096	.427	–	–	–	272	376	.723	–	–	596	96	231	1	–	–	–	1208	7.4	1.2	14.9
64-65–New York	80	–	2139	424	963	.440	–	–	–	288	375	.768	–	–	604	108	183	0	–	–	–	1136	7.6	1.4	14.2
65-66–Los Angeles	78	–	1847	365	754	.484	–	–	–	225	289	.779	–	–	548	87	196	0	–	–	–	955	7.0	1.1	12.2
66-67–Chicago	80	–	2451	538	1104	.487	–	–	–	360	461	.781	–	–	679	90	212	0	–	–	–	1436	8.5	1.1	18.0
67-68–Chicago	77	–	2988	622	1265	.492	–	–	–	411	535	.768	–	–	756	121	229	1	–	–	–	1655	9.8	1.6	21.5
68-69–Chicago	79	–	2872	661	1375	.481	–	–	–	394	489	.806	–	–	614	156	218	2	–	–	–	1716	7.8	2.0	21.7
69-70–Seattle	82	–	2549	493	1005	.491	–	–	–	263	320	.822	–	–	717	110	237	2	–	–	–	1249	8.7	1.3	15.2
70-71–Milwaukee	80	–	1775	290	645	.450	–	–	–	148	181	.818	–	–	435	128	216	0	–	–	–	728	5.4	1.6	9.1
Reg. Season Totals	874	–	25549	4961	10738	.462	–	–	–	3042	3998	.761	–	–	7119	1237	2489	18	–	–	–	12964	8.1	1.4	14.8
Playoff Totals	48	–	1283	213	456	.467	–	–	–	130	176	.739	–	–	341	58	136	0	–	–	–	556	7.1	1.2	11.6
All-Star Totals	1	–	19	2	5	.400	–	–	–	0	0	–	–	–	5	0	0	0	–	–	–	4	5.0	0.0	4.0

Bornheimer, Jacob (Jake) b. June 29, 1927 d. September 10, 1986 Ht. 6-5 Wt. 205 College: Muhlenberg

SEASON–TEAM	G	GS	MIN	FGM	FGA	PCT	3FGM	3FGA	PCT	FTM	FTA	PCT	O-RB	D-RB	TOT	AST	PF	DQ	STL	TO	BLK	PTS	RPG	APG	PPG
48-49–Philadelphia	15	–	–	34	109	.312	–	–	–	20	29	.690	–	–	–	13	47	–	–	–	–	88	–	0.9	5.9
49-50–Philadelphia	60	–	–	88	305	.289	–	–	–	78	117	.667	–	–	–	40	111	–	–	–	–	254	–	0.7	4.2
Reg. Season Totals	75	–	–	122	414	.295	–	–	–	98	146	.671	–	–	–	53	158	–	–	–	–	342	–	0.7	4.6
Playoff Totals	4	–	–	8	20	.400	–	–	–	6	9	.667	–	–	–	2	13	1	–	–	–	22	–	0.5	5.5

Borrell, Lazaro b. September 20, 1972 Ht. 6-8 Wt. 220 Country: Cuba

SEASON–TEAM	G	GS	MIN	FGM	FGA	PCT	3FGM	3FGA	PCT	FTM	FTA	PCT	O-RB	D-RB	TOT	AST	PF	DQ	STL	TO	BLK	PTS	RPG	APG	PPG
99-00–Seattle	17	6	167	28	63	.444	0	3	.000	6	11	.545	14	26	40	10	9	0	6	6	3	62	2.4	0.6	3.6
Reg. Season Totals	17	6	167	28	63	.444	0	3	.000	6	11	.545	14	26	40	10	9	0	6	6	3	62	2.4	0.6	3.6
Playoff Totals	2	1	26	4	7	.571	0	0	–	2	4	.500	3	8	11	1	2	0	0	1	0	10	5.5	0.5	5.0

Borsavage, Costic F. (Ike) b. July 25, 1924 Ht. 6-8 Wt. 220 College: Temple

SEASON–TEAM	G	GS	MIN	FGM	FGA	PCT	3FGM	3FGA	PCT	FTM	FTA	PCT	O-RB	D-RB	TOT	AST	PF	DQ	STL	TO	BLK	PTS	RPG	APG	PPG
50-51–Philadelphia	24	–	–	26	74	.351	–	–	–	12	18	.667	–	–	24	4	34	1	–	–	–	64	1.0	0.2	2.7
Reg. Season Totals	24	–	–	26	74	.351	–	–	–	12	18	.667	–	–	24	4	34	1	–	–	–	64	1.0	0.2	2.7

Boryla, Vincent J. (Vince, Moose) b. March 11, 1927 Ht. 6-5 Wt. 210 College: Notre Dame; Denver

SEASON–TEAM	G	GS	MIN	FGM	FGA	PCT	3FGM	3FGA	PCT	FTM	FTA	PCT	O-RB	D-RB	TOT	AST	PF	DQ	STL	TO	BLK	PTS	RPG	APG	PPG
49-50–New York	59	–	–	204	600	.340	–	–	–	204	267	.764	–	–	–	95	203	–	–	–	–	612	–	1.6	10.4
50-51–New York	66	–	–	352	867	.406	–	–	–	278	332	.837	–	–	249	182	244	6	–	–	–	982	3.8	2.8	14.9
51-52–New York	42	–	1440	202	522	.387	–	–	–	96	115	.835	–	–	219	90	121	2	–	–	–	500	5.2	2.1	11.9
52-53–New York	66	–	2200	254	686	.370	–	–	–	165	201	.821	–	–	233	166	226	8	–	–	–	673	3.5	2.5	10.2
53-54–New York	52	–	1522	175	525	.333	–	–	–	70	81	.864	–	–	130	77	128	0	–	–	–	420	2.5	1.5	8.1
Reg. Season Totals	285	–	5162	1187	3200	.371	–	–	–	813	996	.816	–	–	831	610	922	16	–	–	–	3187	3.7	2.1	11.2
Playoff Totals	33	–	463	158	380	.421	–	–	–	120	135	.889	–	–	91	67	114	5	–	–	–	436	3.1	2.0	13.2
All-Star Totals	1	–	0	4	6	.667	–	–	–	1	1	1.000	–	–	2	2	3	0	–	–	–	9	2.0	2.0	9.0

Bostic, James (Jim) b. January 28, 1953 Ht. 6-7 Wt. 225 College: New Mexico State

SEASON–TEAM	G	GS	MIN	FGM	FGA	PCT	3FGM	3FGA	PCT	FTM	FTA	PCT	O-RB	D-RB	TOT	AST	PF	DQ	STL	TO	BLK	PTS	RPG	APG	PPG
77-78–Detroit	4	–	48	12	22	.545	–	–	–	2	5	.400	8	8	16	3	5	0	0	3	0	26	4.0	0.8	6.5
Reg. Season Totals	4	–	48	12	22	.545	–	–	–	2	5	.400	8	8	16	3	5	0	0	3	0	26	4.0	0.8	6.5

Boston, Lawrence D. (Larry) b. May 18, 1956 Ht. 6-9 Wt. 225 College: Vincennes (Ind.); Maryland

SEASON–TEAM	G	GS	MIN	FGM	FGA	PCT	3FGM	3FGA	PCT	FTM	FTA	PCT	O-RB	D-RB	TOT	AST	PF	DQ	STL	TO	BLK	PTS	RPG	APG	PPG
79-80–Washington	13	–	125	24	52	.462	0	0	–	8	13	.615	19	20	39	2	25	0	4	8	2	56	3.0	0.2	4.3
Reg. Season Totals	13	–	125	24	52	.462	0	0	–	8	13	.615	19	20	39	2	25	0	4	8	2	56	3.0	0.2	4.3

Boswell, Tommy G. (Tom) b. October 2, 1953 Ht. 6-7 Wt. 220 College: South Carolina State; South Carolina

SEASON–TEAM	G	GS	MIN	FGM	FGA	PCT	3FGM	3FGA	PCT	FTM	FTA	PCT	O-RB	D-RB	TOT	AST	PF	DQ	STL	TO	BLK	PTS	RPG	APG	PPG
75-76–Boston	35	–	275	41	93	.441	–	–	–	14	24	.583	26	45	71	16	70	1	2	–	1	96	2.0	0.5	2.7
76-77–Boston	70	–	1083	175	340	.515	–	–	–	96	135	.711	111	195	306	85	237	9	27	–	8	446	4.4	1.2	6.4
77-78–Boston	65	–	1149	185	357	.518	–	–	–	93	123	.756	117	171	288	71	204	5	25	95	14	463	4.4	1.1	7.1
78-79–Denver	79	–	2201	321	603	.532	–	–	–	198	284	.697	248	290	538	242	263	4	50	185	51	840	6.8	3.1	10.6
79-80–Denver-Utah	79	–	2077	346	613	.564	5	10	.500	206	273	.755	146	296	442	161	270	9	29	181	37	903	5.6	2.0	11.4
83-84–Utah	38	0	261	28	52	.538	1	1	1.000	16	21	.762	28	36	64	16	58	1	9	13	0	73	1.7	0.4	1.9
Reg. Season Totals	366	0	7046	1096	2058	.533	6	11	.545	623	860	.724	676	1033	1709	591	1102	29	142	474	111	2821	4.7	1.6	7.7
Playoff Totals	20	0	259	33	59	.559	0	0	–	16	24	.667	26	28	54	25	42	0	4	10	6	82	2.7	1.3	4.1

Boven, Donald E. (Don) b. March 6, 1925 Ht. 6-4 Wt. 210 College: Western Michigan

SEASON–TEAM	G	GS	MIN	FGM	FGA	PCT	3FGM	3FGA	PCT	FTM	FTA	PCT	O-RB	D-RB	TOT	AST	PF	DQ	STL	TO	BLK	PTS	RPG	APG	PPG
49-50–Waterloo	62	–	–	208	558	.373	–	–	–	240	349	.688	–	–	–	137	255	–	–	–	–	656	–	2.2	10.6
51-52–Milwaukee	66	–	1982	200	668	.299	–	–	–	256	350	.731	–	–	336	177	271	18	–	–	–	656	5.1	2.7	9.9
52-53–Milw.-Balt.-FtWayne	67	–	1373	153	427	.358	–	–	–	145	209	.694	–	–	217	79	227	13	–	–	–	451	3.2	1.2	6.7
Reg. Season Totals	195	–	3355	561	1653	.339	–	–	–	641	908	.706	–	–	553	393	753	31	–	–	–	1763	4.2	2.0	9.0
Playoff Totals	8	–	111	7	28	.250	–	–	–	9	16	.563	–	–	16	2	22	0	–	–	–	23	2.0	0.3	2.9

Bowdler, James Calloway II (Cal) b. March 31, 1977 Ht. 6-10 Wt. 245 College: Old Dominion

SEASON–TEAM	G	GS	MIN	FGM	FGA	PCT	3FGM	3FGA	PCT	FTM	FTA	PCT	O-RB	D-RB	TOT	AST	PF	DQ	STL	TO	BLK	PTS	RPG	APG	PPG
99-00–Atlanta	46	0	423	49	115	.426	0	1	.000	24	38	.632	22	63	85	14	46	1	14	21	9	122	1.8	0.3	2.7
Reg. Season Totals	46	0	423	49	115	.426	0	1	.000	24	38	.632	22	63	85	14	46	1	14	21	9	122	1.8	0.3	2.7

Bowen, Bruce b. June 14, 1971 Ht. 6-7 Wt. 200 College: Cal State-Fullerton

SEASON–TEAM	G	GS	MIN	FGM	FGA	PCT	3FGM	3FGA	PCT	FTM	FTA	PCT	O-RB	D-RB	TOT	AST	PF	DQ	STL	TO	BLK	PTS	RPG	APG	PPG
96-97–Miami	1	0	1	0	0	–	0	0	–	0	0	–	0	0	0	0	0	0	0	0	1	0	0.0	0.0	0.0
97-98–Boston	61	9	1305	122	298	.409	20	59	.339	76	122	.623	79	95	174	81	174	0	87	52	29	340	2.9	1.3	5.6
98-99–Boston	30	1	494	26	93	.280	7	26	.269	11	24	.458	15	37	52	28	51	2	21	13	9	70	1.7	0.9	2.3
99-00–Phil.-Miami	69	2	878	72	194	.371	27	58	.466	25	43	.581	27	69	96	34	118	0	23	19	15	196	1.4	0.5	2.8
Reg. Season Totals	161	12	2678	220	585	.376	54	143	.378	112	189	.593	121	201	322	143	343	2	131	84	54	606	2.0	0.9	3.8
Playoff Totals	10	0	157	10	27	.370	5	22	.227	10	16	.625	1	9	10	8	27	1	7	6	4	35	1.0	0.8	3.5

Bowen, Ryan Cleo b. November 20, 1975 Ht. 6-7 Wt. 215 College: Iowa

SEASON–TEAM	G	GS	MIN	FGM	FGA	PCT	3FGM	3FGA	PCT	FTM	FTA	PCT	O-RB	D-RB	TOT	AST	PF	DQ	STL	TO	BLK	PTS	RPG	APG	PPG
99-00–Denver	52	0	589	46	117	.393	1	9	.111	38	53	.717	75	39	114	20	95	0	39	14	13	131	2.2	0.4	2.5
Reg. Season Totals	52	0	589	46	117	.393	1	9	.111	38	53	.717	75	39	114	20	95	0	39	14	13	131	2.2	0.4	2.5

Bowens, Tommie Lee Jr. (Tom) b. July 7, 1940 Ht. 6-8 Wt. 220 College: Grambling State

SEASON–TEAM	G	GS	MIN	FGM	FGA	PCT	3FGM	3FGA	PCT	FTM	FTA	PCT	O-RB	D-RB	TOT	AST	PF	DQ	STL	TO	BLK	PTS	RPG	APG	PPG
67-68–Denver (A)	67	–	1287	177	453	.391	1	2	.500	55	90	.611	–	–	374	41	159	3	–	83	–	410	5.6	0.6	6.1
68-69–New York (A)	76	–	1550	186	453	.411	0	3	.000	83	128	.648	–	–	455	52	236	6	–	111	–	455	6.0	0.7	6.0
69-70–New Orleans (A)	68	–	753	110	251	.438	0	0	–	47	62	.758	–	–	178	41	147	2	–	–	–	267	2.6	0.6	3.9
Reg. ABA Totals	211	–	3590	473	1157	.409	1	5	.200	185	280	.661	–	–	1007	134	542	11	–	194	–	1132	4.8	0.6	5.4
ABA Playoff Totals	5	–	94	14	31	.452	0	1	.000	2	2	1.000	–	–	25	5	17	1	–	6	–	30	5.0	1.0	6.0

Bowie, Anthony Lee b. November 9, 1963 Ht. 6-6 Wt. 200 College: Oklahoma

SEASON–TEAM	G	GS	MIN	FGM	FGA	PCT	3FGM	3FGA	PCT	FTM	FTA	PCT	O-RB	D-RB	TOT	AST	PF	DQ	STL	TO	BLK	PTS	RPG	APG	PPG
88-89–San Antonio	18	5	438	72	144	.500	1	5	.200	10	15	.667	25	31	56	29	43	1	18	22	4	155	3.1	1.6	8.6
89-90–Houston	66	0	918	119	293	.406	6	21	.286	40	54	.741	36	82	118	96	80	0	42	59	5	284	1.8	1.5	4.3
91-92–Orlando	52	26	1721	312	633	.493	17	44	.386	117	136	.860	70	175	245	163	101	1	55	107	38	758	4.7	3.1	14.6
92-93–Orlando	77	45	1761	268	569	.471	15	48	.313	67	84	.798	36	158	194	175	131	0	54	84	14	618	2.5	2.3	8.0
93-94–Orlando	70	0	948	139	289	.481	1	18	.056	41	49	.837	29	91	120	102	81	0	32	58	12	320	1.7	1.5	4.6
94-95–Orlando	77	4	1261	177	369	.480	12	40	.300	61	73	.836	54	85	139	159	138	1	47	86	21	427	1.8	2.1	5.5
95-96–Orlando	74	4	1078	128	272	.471	12	31	.387	40	46	.870	40	83	123	105	112	0	34	55	10	308	1.7	1.4	4.2
97-98–New York	27	3	224	32	59	.542	3	4	.750	8	9	.889	9	17	26	11	25	1	6	7	2	75	1.0	0.4	2.8
Reg. Season Totals	461	87	8349	1247	2628	.475	67	211	.318	384	466	.824	299	722	1021	840	711	4	288	478	106	2945	2.2	1.8	6.4
Playoff Totals	40	1	310	36	75	.480	5	7	.714	12	13	.923	7	22	29	33	47	0	5	14	3	89	0.7	0.8	2.2

Bowie, Samuel Paul (Sam) b. March 17, 1961 Ht. 7-1 Wt. 263 College: Kentucky

SEASON–TEAM	G	GS	MIN	FGM	FGA	PCT	3FGM	3FGA	PCT	FTM	FTA	PCT	O-RB	D-RB	TOT	AST	PF	DQ	STL	TO	BLK	PTS	RPG	APG	PPG
84-85–Portland	76	62	2216	299	557	.537	0	0	–	160	225	.711	207	449	656	215	278	9	55	172	203	758	8.6	2.8	10.0
85-86–Portland	38	34	1132	167	345	.484	0	0	–	114	161	.708	93	234	327	99	142	4	21	88	96	448	8.6	2.6	11.8
86-87–Portland	5	5	163	30	66	.455	0	0	–	20	30	.667	14	19	33	9	19	0	1	15	10	80	6.6	1.8	16.0
88-89–Portland	20	0	412	69	153	.451	5	7	.714	28	49	.571	36	70	106	36	43	0	7	33	33	171	5.3	1.8	8.6
89-90–New Jersey	68	54	2207	347	834	.416	10	31	.323	294	379	.776	206	484	690	91	211	5	38	125	121	998	10.1	1.3	14.7
90-91–New Jersey	62	51	1916	314	723	.434	4	22	.182	169	231	.732	176	304	480	147	175	4	43	141	90	801	7.7	2.4	12.9
91-92–New Jersey	71	61	2179	421	947	.445	8	25	.320	212	280	.757	203	375	578	186	212	2	41	150	120	1062	8.1	2.6	15.0
92-93–New Jersey	79	65	2092	287	638	.450	2	6	.333	141	181	.779	158	398	556	127	226	3	32	120	128	717	7.0	1.6	9.1
93-94–L.A. Lakers	25	7	556	75	172	.436	1	4	.250	72	83	.867	27	104	131	47	65	0	4	43	28	223	5.2	1.9	8.9
94-95–L.A. Lakers	67	10	1225	118	267	.442	2	11	.182	68	89	.764	72	216	288	118	182	4	21	91	80	306	4.3	1.8	4.6
Reg. Season Totals	511	349	14098	2127	4702	.452	32	106	.302	1278	1708	.748	1192	2653	3845	1075	1553	31	263	978	909	5564	7.5	2.1	10.9
Playoff Totals	29	17	644	64	159	.403	2	4	.500	35	52	.673	49	111	160	38	97	2	14	30	41	165	5.5	1.3	5.7

Bowling, Orbie Lee (Orb) b. March 21, 1939 Ht. 6-10 Wt. 215 College: Tennessee

SEASON–TEAM	G	GS	MIN	FGM	FGA	PCT	3FGM	3FGA	PCT	FTM	FTA	PCT	O-RB	D-RB	TOT	AST	PF	DQ	STL	TO	BLK	PTS	RPG	APG	PPG
67-68–Kentucky (A)	11	–	90	9	28	.321	0	0	–	3	12	.250	–	–	29	1	16	0	–	6	–	21	2.6	0.1	1.9
Reg. ABA Totals	11	–	90	9	28	.321	0	0	–	3	12	.250	–	–	29	1	16	0	–	6	–	21	2.6	0.1	1.9

Bowman, Ira b. June 11, 1973 Ht. 6-5 Wt. 195 College: Pennsylvania

SEASON–TEAM	G	GS	MIN	FGM	FGA	PCT	3FGM	3FGA	PCT	FTM	FTA	PCT	O-RB	D-RB	TOT	AST	PF	DQ	STL	TO	BLK	PTS	RPG	APG	PPG
99-00–Philadelphia	11	0	20	2	2	1.000	0	0	–	1	2	.500	0	2	2	1	0	0	1	1	0	5	0.2	0.1	0.5
Reg. Season Totals	11	0	20	2	2	1.000	0	0	–	1	2	.500	0	2	2	1	0	0	1	1	0	5	0.2	0.1	0.5
Playoff Totals	7	0	11	0	2	.000	0	1	.000	0	2	.000	0	0	0	2	0	0	0	0	0	0	0.0	0.3	0.0

Bowman, Nathaniel (Nate, Nate the Skate) b. March 19, 1943 d. December 11, 1984 Ht. 6-10 Wt. 230 College: Wichita State

SEASON–TEAM	G	GS	MIN	FGM	FGA	PCT	3FGM	3FGA	PCT	FTM	FTA	PCT	O-RB	D-RB	TOT	AST	PF	DQ	STL	TO	BLK	PTS	RPG	APG	PPG
66-67–Chicago	9	–	65	8	21	.381	–	–	–	6	8	.750	–	–	28	2	18	0	–	–	–	22	3.1	0.2	2.4
67-68–New York	42	–	272	52	134	.388	–	–	–	10	15	.667	–	–	113	20	69	0	–	–	–	114	2.7	0.5	2.7
68-69–New York	67	–	607	82	226	.363	–	–	–	29	61	.475	–	–	220	53	142	4	–	–	–	193	3.3	0.8	2.9
69-70–New York	81	–	744	98	235	.417	–	–	–	41	79	.519	–	–	257	46	189	2	–	–	–	237	3.2	0.6	2.9
70-71–Buffalo	44	–	483	58	148	.392	–	–	–	20	38	.526	–	–	173	41	91	2	–	–	–	136	3.9	0.9	3.1
71-72–Pittsburgh (A)	18	–	217	19	53	.358	0	1	.000	5	9	.556	–	–	87	13	48	–	–	17	–	43	4.8	0.7	2.4
Reg. NBA Totals	243	–	2171	298	764	.390	–	–	–	106	201	.527	–	–	791	162	509	8	–	–	–	702	3.3	0.7	2.9
Reg. ABA Totals	18	–	217	19	53	.358	0	1	.000	5	9	.556	–	–	87	13	48	–	–	17	–	43	4.8	0.7	2.4
NBA Playoff Totals	29	–	196	22	66	.333	–	–	–	10	13	.769	–	–	79	9	51	0	–	–	–	54	2.7	0.3	1.9

Boyce, Donald Nathaniel (Donnie) b. September 2, 1973 Ht. 6-5 Wt. 195 College: Colorado

SEASON–TEAM	G	GS	MIN	FGM	FGA	PCT	3FGM	3FGA	PCT	FTM	FTA	PCT	O-RB	D-RB	TOT	AST	PF	DQ	STL	TO	BLK	PTS	RPG	APG	PPG
95-96–Atlanta	8	0	41	9	23	.391	4	8	.500	2	4	.500	5	5	10	3	2	0	3	6	1	24	1.3	0.4	3.0
96-97–Atlanta	22	2	154	21	63	.333	2	16	.125	11	22	.500	7	8	15	13	17	0	10	16	4	55	0.7	0.6	2.5
Reg. Season Totals	30	2	195	30	86	.349	6	24	.250	13	26	.500	12	13	25	16	19	0	13	22	5	79	0.8	0.5	2.6
Playoff Totals	1	0	2	0	2	.000	0	2	.000	0	0	–	0	0	0	–	0	0	0	0	0	0	0.0	0.0	0.0

Boyd, Dennis b. May 21, 1954 Ht. 6-1 Wt. 175 College: Detroit Mercy

SEASON–TEAM	G	GS	MIN	FGM	FGA	PCT	3FGM	3FGA	PCT	FTM	FTA	PCT	O-RB	D-RB	TOT	AST	PF	DQ	STL	TO	BLK	PTS	RPG	APG	PPG
78-79–Detroit	5	–	40	3	12	.250	–	–	–	0	0	–	0	2	2	7	5	0	0	6	0	6	0.4	1.4	1.2
Reg. Season Totals	5	–	40	3	12	.250	–	–	–	0	0	–	0	2	2	7	5	0	0	6	0	6	0.4	1.4	1.2

Boyd, Fred L. (Freddie) b. June 13, 1950 Ht. 6-2 Wt. 180 College: Oregon State

SEASON–TEAM	G	GS	MIN	FGM	FGA	PCT	3FGM	3FGA	PCT	FTM	FTA	PCT	O-RB	D-RB	TOT	AST	PF	DQ	STL	TO	BLK	PTS	RPG	APG	PPG
72-73–Philadelphia	82	–	2351	362	923	.392	–	–	–	136	200	.680	–	–	210	301	184	1	–	–	–	860	2.6	3.7	10.5
73-74–Philadelphia	75	–	1818	286	712	.402	–	–	–	141	195	.723	16	77	93	249	173	1	60	–	9	713	1.2	3.3	9.5
74-75–Philadelphia	66	–	1362	205	495	.414	–	–	–	55	115	.478	16	73	89	161	134	0	43	–	4	465	1.3	2.4	7.0
75-76–Phil.-N.O.	36	–	617	74	171	.433	–	–	–	29	51	.569	4	28	32	80	59	0	28	–	7	177	0.9	2.2	4.9
76-77–New Orleans	47	–	1212	194	406	.478	–	–	–	79	98	.806	19	71	90	147	78	0	44	–	6	467	1.9	3.1	9.9
77-78–New Orleans	21	–	363	44	110	.400	–	–	–	14	22	.636	2	17	19	48	23	0	9	20	3	102	0.9	2.3	4.9
Reg. Season Totals	327	–	7723	1165	2817	.414	–	–	–	454	681	.667	57	266	533	986	651	2	184	20	29	2784	1.6	3.0	8.5

Boyd, Ken b. March 25, 1952 Ht. 6-5 Wt. 195 College: Boston University

SEASON–TEAM	G	GS	MIN	FGM	FGA	PCT	3FGM	3FGA	PCT	FTM	FTA	PCT	O-RB	D-RB	TOT	AST	PF	DQ	STL	TO	BLK	PTS	RPG	APG	PPG
74-75–New Orleans	6	–	25	7	13	.538	–	–	–	5	11	.455	3	2	5	2	2	0	3	–	0	19	0.8	0.3	3.2
Reg. Season Totals	6	–	25	7	13	.538	–	–	–	5	11	.455	3	2	5	2	2	0	3	–	0	19	0.8	0.3	3.2

Boykins, Earl b. June 2, 1976 Ht. 5-5 Wt. 133 College: Eastern Michigan

SEASON–TEAM	G	GS	MIN	FGM	FGA	PCT	3FGM	3FGA	PCT	FTM	FTA	PCT	O-RB	D-RB	TOT	AST	PF	DQ	STL	TO	BLK	PTS	RPG	APG	PPG
98-99–N.J.-Clev.	22	0	221	30	79	.380	3	18	.167	2	3	.667	7	10	17	33	20	0	6	20	0	65	0.8	1.5	3.0
99-00–Orlando-Clev.	26	0	261	56	116	.483	8	20	.400	18	23	.783	12	14	26	48	23	0	12	17	1	138	1.0	1.8	5.3
Reg. Season Totals	48	0	482	86	195	.441	11	38	.289	20	26	.769	19	24	43	81	43	0	18	37	1	203	0.9	1.7	4.2

Boykoff, Harry J. (Big Hesh) b. July 24, 1922 Ht. 6-10 Wt. 225 College: St. John's (N.Y.)

SEASON–TEAM	G	GS	MIN	FGM	FGA	PCT	3FGM	3FGA	PCT	FTM	FTA	PCT	O-RB	D-RB	TOT	AST	PF	DQ	STL	TO	BLK	PTS	RPG	APG	PPG
47-48–Toledo (N)	59	–	–	225	–	–	–	–	–	124	161	.770	–	–	–	–	219	–	–	–	–	574	–	–	9.7
48-49–Waterloo (N)	61	–	–	293	–	–	–	–	–	191	265	.721	–	–	–	–	237	28	–	–	–	777	–	–	12.7
49-50–Waterloo	61	–	–	288	698	.413	–	–	–	203	262	.775	–	–	–	149	229	–	–	–	–	779	–	2.4	12.8
50-51–Boston-Tri-Cit	48	–	–	126	336	.375	–	–	–	74	100	.740	–	–	220	60	197	12	–	–	–	326	4.6	1.3	6.8
Reg. NBA Totals	109	–	–	414	1034	.400	–	–	–	277	362	.765	–	–	220	209	426	12	–	–	–	1105	4.6	1.9	10.1
Reg. NBL Totals	120	–	–	518	–	–	–	–	–	315	426	.739	–	–	–	–	456	28	–	–	–	1351	–	–	11.3

Boynes, Winford Gladstone III b. May 17, 1957 Ht. 6-6 Wt. 185 College: San Francisco

SEASON–TEAM	G	GS	MIN	FGM	FGA	PCT	3FGM	3FGA	PCT	FTM	FTA	PCT	O-RB	D-RB	TOT	AST	PF	DQ	STL	TO	BLK	PTS	RPG	APG	PPG
78-79–New Jersey	69	–	1176	256	595	.430	–	–	–	133	169	.787	60	95	155	75	117	1	43	119	7	645	2.2	1.1	9.3
79-80–New Jersey	64	–	1102	221	467	.473	0	4	.000	104	136	.765	51	82	133	95	132	1	59	96	19	546	2.1	1.5	8.5
80-81–Dallas	44	–	757	121	313	.387	0	0	–	45	55	.818	24	51	75	37	79	1	23	69	16	287	1.7	0.8	6.5
Reg. Season Totals	177	–	3035	598	1375	.435	0	4	.000	282	360	.783	135	228	363	207	328	3	125	284	42	1478	2.1	1.2	8.4

Bracey, Stephen Henry (Steve) b. August 1, 1950 Ht. 6-1 Wt. 185 College: Kilgore (Texas) Coll.; Tulsa

SEASON–TEAM	G	GS	MIN	FGM	FGA	PCT	3FGM	3FGA	PCT	FTM	FTA	PCT	O-RB	D-RB	TOT	AST	PF	DQ	STL	TO	BLK	PTS	RPG	APG	PPG
72-73–Atlanta	70	–	1050	192	395	.486	–	–	–	73	110	.664	–	–	107	125	125	0	–	–	–	457	1.5	1.8	6.5
73-74–Atlanta	75	–	1463	241	520	.463	–	–	–	69	96	.719	26	120	146	231	157	0	60	–	5	551	1.9	3.1	7.3
74-75–Golden State	42	–	340	54	130	.415	–	–	–	25	38	.658	10	28	38	52	41	0	14	–	1	133	0.9	1.2	3.2
Reg. Season Totals	187	–	2853	487	1045	.466	–	–	–	167	244	.684	36	148	291	408	323	0	74	–	6	1141	1.6	2.2	6.1
Playoff Totals	10	–	137	27	54	.500	–	–	–	15	20	.750	0	1	14	23	14	0	3	–	0	69	1.4	2.3	6.9

Bradds, Gary Lee (Tex) b. July 26, 1942 d. July 15, 1983 Ht. 6-8 Wt. 220 College: Ohio State

SEASON–TEAM	G	GS	MIN	FGM	FGA	PCT	3FGM	3FGA	PCT	FTM	FTA	PCT	O-RB	D-RB	TOT	AST	PF	DQ	STL	TO	BLK	PTS	RPG	APG	PPG
64-65–Baltimore	41	–	335	46	111	.414	–	–	–	45	63	.714	–	–	84	19	36	0	–	–	–	137	2.0	0.5	3.3
65-66–Baltimore	3	–	15	2	6	.333	–	–	–	3	4	.750	–	–	8	1	1	0	–	–	–	7	2.7	0.3	2.3
67-68–Oakland (A)	49	–	1052	199	440	.452	0	4	.000	221	283	.781	–	–	289	51	131	1	–	81	–	619	5.9	1.0	12.6
68-69–Oakland (A)	75	–	2249	517	1041	.497	1	7	.143	364	444	.820	–	–	577	88	244	6	–	175	–	1399	7.7	1.2	18.7
69-70–Washington (A)	60	–	1239	292	608	.480	0	5	.000	217	262	.828	–	–	336	54	181	1	–	–	–	801	5.6	0.9	13.4
70-71–Car.-Texas (A)	26	–	321	52	127	.409	0	2	.000	39	58	.672	–	–	104	14	41	–	–	–	–	143	4.0	0.5	5.5
Reg. NBA Totals	44	–	350	48	117	.410	–	–	–	48	67	.716	–	–	92	20	37	0	–	–	–	144	2.1	0.5	3.3
Reg. ABA Totals	210	–	4861	1060	2216	.478	1	18	.056	841	1047	.803	–	–	1306	207	597	8	–	256	–	2962	6.2	1.0	14.1
NBA Playoff Totals	1	–	5	2	3	.667	–	–	–	2	2	1.000	–	–	2	–	0	0	–	–	–	6	2.0	0.0	6.0
ABA Playoff Totals	22	–	633	146	314	.465	1	1	1.000	92	115	.800	–	–	179	18	83	1	–	–	–	385	8.1	0.8	17.5

Bradley, Alex III b. October 30, 1959 Ht. 6-7 Wt. 215 College: Villanova

SEASON–TEAM	G	GS	MIN	FGM	FGA	PCT	3FGM	3FGA	PCT	FTM	FTA	PCT	O-RB	D-RB	TOT	AST	PF	DQ	STL	TO	BLK	PTS	RPG	APG	PPG
81-82–New York	39	0	331	54	103	.524	0	1	.000	29	48	.604	31	34	65	11	37	0	12	28	5	137	1.7	0.3	3.5
Reg. Season Totals	39	0	331	54	103	.524	0	1	.000	29	48	.604	31	34	65	11	37	0	12	28	5	137	1.7	0.3	3.5

Bradley, Alonzo b. October 16, 1953 Ht. 6-6 Wt. 195 College: Utica (Miss.) J.C.; Texas Southern

SEASON–TEAM	G	GS	MIN	FGM	FGA	PCT	3FGM	3FGA	PCT	FTM	FTA	PCT	O-RB	D-RB	TOT	AST	PF	DQ	STL	TO	BLK	PTS	RPG	APG	PPG
77-78–Houston	43	–	798	130	304	.428	–	–	–	43	59	.729	24	75	99	54	83	1	16	55	6	303	2.3	1.3	7.0
78-79–Houston	34	–	245	37	88	.420	–	–	–	22	33	.667	13	33	46	17	33	0	5	17	1	96	1.4	0.5	2.8
79-80–Houston	22	–	96	17	48	.354	1	1	1.000	6	9	.667	2	4	6	3	9	0	3	8	0	41	0.3	0.1	1.9
Reg. Season Totals	99	–	1139	184	440	.418	1	1	1.000	71	101	.703	39	112	151	74	125	1	24	80	7	440	1.5	0.7	4.4
Playoff Totals	5	–	16	6	9	.667	1	1	1.000	3	5	.600	1	2	3	1	2	0	1	0	0	16	0.6	0.2	3.2

Bradley, Bill b. 1941 Ht. 5-11 Wt. 165 College: Tennessee State

SEASON–TEAM	G	GS	MIN	FGM	FGA	PCT	3FGM	3FGA	PCT	FTM	FTA	PCT	O-RB	D-RB	TOT	AST	PF	DQ	STL	TO	BLK	PTS	RPG	APG	PPG
67-68–Kentucky (A)	58	–	521	82	258	.318	3	18	.167	51	56	.911	–	–	47	54	40	0	–	50	–	218	0.8	0.9	3.8
Reg. ABA Totals	58	–	521	82	258	.318	3	18	.167	51	56	.911	–	–	47	54	40	0	–	50	–	218	0.8	0.9	3.8
ABA Playoff Totals	2	–	9	2	2	1.000	0	0	–	2	2	1.000	–	–	1	1	3	0	–	–	–	6	0.5	0.5	3.0

Bradley, Charles Warnell b. May 16, 1959 Ht. 6-5 Wt. 215 College: Wyoming

SEASON–TEAM	G	GS	MIN	FGM	FGA	PCT	3FGM	3FGA	PCT	FTM	FTA	PCT	O-RB	D-RB	TOT	AST	PF	DQ	STL	TO	BLK	PTS	RPG	APG	PPG
81-82–Boston	51	1	339	55	122	.451	0	1	.000	42	62	.677	12	26	38	22	61	0	14	37	6	152	0.7	0.4	3.0
82-83–Boston	51	5	532	69	176	.392	0	3	.000	46	90	.511	30	48	78	28	84	0	32	42	27	184	1.5	0.5	3.6
83-84–Seattle	8	0	39	3	7	.429	0	0	–	5	7	.714	0	3	3	5	6	0	0	8	1	11	0.4	0.6	1.4
Reg. Season Totals	110	6	910	127	305	.416	0	4	.000	93	159	.585	42	77	119	55	151	0	46	87	34	347	1.1	0.5	3.2
Playoff Totals	9	0	22	2	8	.250	0	0	–	0	2	.000	1	4	5	1	6	0	1	4	0	4	0.6	0.1	0.4

Bradley, Dudley Leroy b. March 19, 1957 Ht. 6-6 Wt. 195 College: North Carolina

SEASON–TEAM	G	GS	MIN	FGM	FGA	PCT	3FGM	3FGA	PCT	FTM	FTA	PCT	O-RB	D-RB	TOT	AST	PF	DQ	STL	TO	BLK	PTS	RPG	APG	PPG
79-80–Indiana	82	–	2027	275	609	.452	2	5	.400	136	174	.782	69	154	223	252	194	1	211	166	48	688	2.7	3.1	8.4
80-81–Indiana	82	–	1867	265	559	.474	2	16	.125	125	178	.702	70	123	193	188	236	2	186	122	37	657	2.4	2.3	8.0
81-82–Phoenix	64	3	937	125	281	.445	1	4	.250	74	100	.740	30	57	87	80	115	0	78	71	10	325	1.4	1.3	5.1
82-83–Chicago	58	11	683	82	159	.516	1	5	.200	36	45	.800	27	78	105	106	91	0	49	59	10	201	1.8	1.8	3.5
84-85–Washington	73	24	1232	142	299	.475	20	65	.308	54	79	.684	34	100	134	173	152	0	96	84	21	358	1.8	2.4	4.9
85-86–Washington	70	7	842	73	209	.349	17	68	.250	32	56	.571	24	71	95	107	101	0	85	44	3	195	1.4	1.5	2.8
86-87–Milwaukee	68	2	900	76	213	.357	13	50	.260	47	58	.810	31	71	102	66	118	2	105	34	8	212	1.5	1.0	3.1
87-88–Milw.-N.J.	65	15	1437	156	365	.427	37	102	.363	74	97	.763	25	102	127	151	172	1	114	88	43	423	2.0	2.3	6.5
88-89–Atlanta	38	0	267	28	86	.326	8	31	.258	8	16	.500	7	25	32	24	41	0	16	14	2	72	0.8	0.6	1.9
Reg. Season Totals	600	62	10192	1222	2780	.440	101	346	.292	586	803	.730	317	781	1098	1147	1220	6	940	682	182	3131	1.8	1.9	5.2
Playoff Totals	30	0	212	26	66	.394	5	22	.227	13	18	.722	5	9	14	22	35	0	13	23	1	70	0.5	0.7	2.3

Bradley, James Arthur (Jim) b. March 16, 1952 d. February 20, 1982 Ht. 6-8 Wt. 225 College: Northern Illinois

SEASON–TEAM	G	GS	MIN	FGM	FGA	PCT	3FGM	3FGA	PCT	FTM	FTA	PCT	O-RB	D-RB	TOT	AST	PF	DQ	STL	TO	BLK	PTS	RPG	APG	PPG
73-74–Kentucky (A)	35	–	884	130	309	.421	0	2	.000	31	44	.705	67	147	214	49	106	–	37	55	27	291	6.1	1.4	8.3
74-75–Kentucky (A)	56	–	922	144	327	.440	0	4	.000	76	103	.738	101	183	284	68	112	–	27	73	30	364	5.1	1.2	6.5
75-76–Denver (A)	7	–	107	15	38	.395	0	0	–	2	3	.667	4	26	30	11	26	–	5	5	5	32	4.3	1.6	4.6
Reg. ABA Totals	98	–	1913	289	674	.429	0	6	.000	109	150	.727	172	356	528	128	244	0	69	133	62	687	5.4	1.3	7.0
ABA Playoff Totals	12	–	182	27	76	.355	0	0	–	7	13	.538	13	33	46	11	24	0	4	15	5	61	3.8	0.9	5.1

Bradley, Joseph L. (Joe) b. September 24, 1928 d. June 5, 1987 Ht. 6-3 Wt. 175 College: Oklahoma State

SEASON–TEAM	G	GS	MIN	FGM	FGA	PCT	3FGM	3FGA	PCT	FTM	FTA	PCT	O-RB	D-RB	TOT	AST	PF	DQ	STL	TO	BLK	PTS	RPG	APG	PPG
49-50–Chicago	46	–	–	36	134	.269	–	–	–	15	38	.395	–	–	–	36	51	–	–	–	–	87	–	0.8	1.9
Reg. Season Totals	46	–	–	36	134	.269	–	–	–	15	38	.395	–	–	–	36	51	–	–	–	–	87	–	0.8	1.9

Bradley, Shawn Paul b. March 22, 1972 Ht. 7-6 Wt. 263 College: Brigham Young

SEASON–TEAM	G	GS	MIN	FGM	FGA	PCT	3FGM	3FGA	PCT	FTM	FTA	PCT	O-RB	D-RB	TOT	AST	PF	DQ	STL	TO	BLK	PTS	RPG	APG	PPG
93-94–Philadelphia	49	45	1385	201	491	.409	0	3	.000	102	168	.607	98	208	306	98	170	3	45	148	147	504	6.2	2.0	10.3
94-95–Philadelphia	82	59	2365	315	693	.455	0	3	.000	148	232	.638	243	416	659	53	338	18	54	142	274	778	8.0	0.6	9.5
95-96–Phil.-N.J.	79	68	2329	387	873	.443	1	4	.250	169	246	.687	221	417	638	63	286	5	49	179	288	944	8.1	0.8	11.9
96-97–N.J.-Dallas	73	70	2288	406	905	.449	0	8	.000	149	228	.654	221	390	611	52	237	7	40	134	248	961	8.4	0.7	13.2
97-98–Dallas	64	46	1822	300	711	.422	1	3	.333	130	180	.722	164	354	518	60	214	9	51	96	214	731	8.1	0.9	11.4
98-99–Dallas	49	33	1294	167	348	.480	0	4	.000	86	115	.748	130	262	392	40	153	2	35	56	159	420	8.0	0.8	8.6
99-00–Dallas	77	54	1901	266	555	.479	1	5	.200	114	149	.765	160	337	497	60	260	7	71	74	190	647	6.5	0.8	8.4
Reg. Season Totals	473	375	13384	2042	4576	.446	3	30	.100	898	1318	.681	1237	2384	3621	426	1658	51	345	829	1520	4985	7.7	0.9	10.5

Bradley, William Warren (Bill, Dollar Bill) b. July 28, 1943 Ht. 6-5 Wt. 205 College: Princeton HOF: 1982

SEASON–TEAM	G	GS	MIN	FGM	FGA	PCT	3FGM	3FGA	PCT	FTM	FTA	PCT	O-RB	D-RB	TOT	AST	PF	DQ	STL	TO	BLK	PTS	RPG	APG	PPG
67-68–New York	45	–	874	142	341	.416	–	–	–	76	104	.731	–	–	113	137	138	2	–	–	–	360	2.5	3.0	8.0
68-69–New York	82	–	2413	407	948	.429	–	–	–	206	253	.814	–	–	350	302	295	4	–	–	–	1020	4.3	3.7	12.4
69-70–New York	67	–	2098	413	897	.460	–	–	–	145	176	.824	–	–	239	268	219	0	–	–	–	971	3.6	4.0	14.5
70-71–New York	78	–	2300	413	912	.453	–	–	–	144	175	.823	–	–	260	280	245	3	–	–	–	970	3.3	3.6	12.4
71-72–New York	78	–	2780	504	1085	.465	–	–	–	169	199	.849	–	–	250	315	254	4	–	–	–	1177	3.2	4.0	15.1
72-73–New York	82	–	2998	575	1252	.459	–	–	–	169	194	.871	–	–	301	367	273	5	–	–	–	1319	3.7	4.5	16.1
73-74–New York	82	–	2813	502	1112	.451	–	–	–	146	167	.874	59	194	253	242	278	2	42	–	21	1150	3.1	3.0	14.0
74-75–New York	79	–	2787	452	1036	.436	–	–	–	144	165	.873	65	186	251	247	283	5	74	–	18	1048	3.2	3.1	13.3
75-76–New York	82	–	2709	392	906	.433	–	–	–	130	148	.878	47	187	234	247	256	2	68	–	18	914	2.9	3.0	11.1
76-77–N.Y. Knicks	67	–	1027	127	274	.464	–	–	–	34	42	.810	27	76	103	128	122	0	25	–	8	288	1.5	1.9	4.3
Reg. Season Totals	742	–	22799	3927	8763	.448	–	–	–	1363	1623	.840	198	643	2354	2533	2363	27	209	–	65	9217	3.2	3.4	12.4
Playoff Totals	95	–	3161	510	1165	.438	–	–	–	202	251	.805	12	25	333	263	313	5	9	–	3	1222	3.5	2.8	12.9
All-Star Totals	1	–	12	2	5	.400	–	–	–	0	0	–	0	0	1	0	2	0	0	–	0	4	1.0	0.0	4.0

Bradtke, Mark b. September 27, 1968 Ht. 6-10 Wt. 265 High School: Redcliffe (Australia)

SEASON–TEAM	G	GS	MIN	FGM	FGA	PCT	3FGM	3FGA	PCT	FTM	FTA	PCT	O-RB	D-RB	TOT	AST	PF	DQ	STL	TO	BLK	PTS	RPG	APG	PPG
96-97–Philadelphia	36	0	251	25	58	.431	0	0	–	9	13	.692	26	42	68	7	34	0	5	9	5	59	1.9	0.2	1.6
Reg. Season Totals	36	0	251	25	58	.431	0	0	–	9	13	.692	26	42	68	7	34	0	5	9	5	59	1.9	0.2	1.6

Bragg, Marques b. March 24, 1970 Ht. 6-8 Wt. 230 College: Providence

SEASON–TEAM	G	GS	MIN	FGM	FGA	PCT	3FGM	3FGA	PCT	FTM	FTA	PCT	O-RB	D-RB	TOT	AST	PF	DQ	STL	TO	BLK	PTS	RPG	APG	PPG
95-96–Minnesota	53	0	369	54	120	.450	0	0	–	23	41	.561	38	41	79	8	71	0	17	26	8	131	1.5	0.2	2.5
Reg. Season Totals	53	0	369	54	120	.450	0	0	–	23	41	.561	38	41	79	8	71	0	17	26	8	131	1.5	0.2	2.5

Bramlett, Aaron Jordan (A.J.) b. January 10, 1977 Ht. 6-10 Wt. 227 College: Arizona

SEASON–TEAM	G	GS	MIN	FGM	FGA	PCT	3FGM	3FGA	PCT	FTM	FTA	PCT	O-RB	D-RB	TOT	AST	PF	DQ	STL	TO	BLK	PTS	RPG	APG	PPG
99-00–Cleveland	8	0	61	4	21	.190	0	0	–	0	0	–	12	10	22	0	13	0	1	3	0	8	2.8	0.0	1.0
Reg. Season Totals	8	0	61	4	21	.190	0	0	–	0	0	–	12	10	22	0	13	0	1	3	0	8	2.8	0.0	1.0

Branch, Adrian Francis b. November 17, 1963 Ht. 6-8 Wt. 185 College: Maryland

SEASON–TEAM	G	GS	MIN	FGM	FGA	PCT	3FGM	3FGA	PCT	FTM	FTA	PCT	O-RB	D-RB	TOT	AST	PF	DQ	STL	TO	BLK	PTS	RPG	APG	PPG
86-87–L.A. Lakers	32	0	219	48	96	.500	0	2	.000	42	54	.778	23	30	53	16	39	0	16	24	3	138	1.7	0.5	4.3
87-88–New Jersey	20	3	308	56	134	.418	1	5	.200	20	23	.870	20	28	48	16	41	1	16	29	11	133	2.4	0.8	6.7
88-89–Portland	67	4	811	202	436	.463	7	31	.226	87	120	.725	63	69	132	60	99	0	45	64	3	498	2.0	0.9	7.4
89-90–Minnesota	11	0	91	25	61	.410	1	1	1.000	14	22	.636	8	12	20	4	14	0	6	8	0	65	1.8	0.4	5.9
Reg. Season Totals	130	7	1429	331	727	.455	9	39	.231	163	219	.744	114	139	253	96	193	1	83	125	17	834	1.9	0.7	6.4
Playoff Totals	12	0	47	4	24	.167	0	1	.000	8	14	.571	3	8	11	7	10	0	2	5	0	16	0.9	0.6	1.3

Brand, Elton Tyron b. March 11, 1979 Ht. 6-8 Wt. 260 College: Duke

SEASON–TEAM	G	GS	MIN	FGM	FGA	PCT	3FGM	3FGA	PCT	FTM	FTA	PCT	O-RB	D-RB	TOT	AST	PF	DQ	STL	TO	BLK	PTS	RPG	APG	PPG
99-00–Chicago	81	80	2999	630	1306	.482	0	2	.000	367	536	.685	348	462	810	155	259	3	66	228	132	1627	10.0	1.9	20.1
Reg. Season Totals	81	80	2999	630	1306	.482	0	2	.000	367	536	.685	348	462	810	155	259	3	66	228	132	1627	10.0	1.9	20.1

Brandon, Thomas Terrell (Terrell) b. May 20, 1970 Ht. 5-11 Wt. 173 College: Oregon

SEASON–TEAM	G	GS	MIN	FGM	FGA	PCT	3FGM	3FGA	PCT	FTM	FTA	PCT	O-RB	D-RB	TOT	AST	PF	DQ	STL	TO	BLK	PTS	RPG	APG	PPG
91-92–Cleveland	82	9	1605	252	601	.419	1	23	.043	100	124	.806	49	113	162	316	107	0	81	136	22	605	2.0	3.9	7.4
92-93–Cleveland	82	8	1622	297	621	.478	13	42	.310	118	143	.825	37	142	179	302	122	1	79	107	27	725	2.2	3.7	8.8
93-94–Cleveland	73	10	1548	230	548	.420	7	32	.219	139	162	.858	38	121	159	277	108	0	84	111	16	606	2.2	3.8	8.3
94-95–Cleveland	67	41	1961	341	762	.448	48	121	.397	159	186	.855	35	151	186	363	118	0	107	144	14	889	2.8	5.4	13.3
95-96–Cleveland	75	75	2570	510	1096	.465	91	235	.387	338	381	.887	47	201	248	487	146	1	132	142	33	1449	3.3	6.5	19.3
96-97–Cleveland	78	78	2868	575	1313	.438	101	271	.373	268	297	.902	48	253	301	490	177	1	138	178	30	1519	3.9	6.3	19.5
97-98–Milwaukee	50	48	1784	339	731	.464	31	93	.333	132	156	.846	23	153	176	387	120	1	111	145	17	841	3.5	7.7	16.8
98-99–Milw.-Minn.	36	34	1217	212	507	.418	12	47	.255	65	78	.833	27	107	134	309	82	0	63	74	10	501	3.7	8.6	13.9
99-00–Minnesota	71	71	2587	486	1042	.466	53	132	.402	187	208	.899	44	194	238	629	158	1	134	184	30	1212	3.4	8.9	17.1
Reg. Season Totals	614	374	17762	3242	7221	.449	357	996	.358	1506	1735	.868	348	1435	1783	3560	1138	5	929	1221	199	8347	2.9	5.8	13.6
Playoff Totals	34	11	793	138	299	.462	12	33	.364	49	55	.891	16	89	105	138	56	0	27	59	7	337	3.1	4.1	9.9
All-Star Totals	2	0	37	8	21	.381	3	8	.375	2	2	1.000	2	2	4	11	3	0	3	3	1	21	2.0	5.5	10.5

Brannum, Robert Warren (Bob, Beeb) b. May 28, 1925 Ht. 6-6 Wt. 215 College: Kentucky; Michigan State

SEASON–TEAM	G	GS	MIN	FGM	FGA	PCT	3FGM	3FGA	PCT	FTM	FTA	PCT	O-RB	D-RB	TOT	AST	PF	DQ	STL	TO	BLK	PTS	RPG	APG	PPG
48-49–Sheboygan (N)	64	–	–	169	–	–	–	–	–	169	261	.648	–	–	–	–	232	–	–	–	–	507	–	–	7.9
49-50–Sheboygan	59	–	–	234	718	.326	–	–	–	245	355	.690	–	–	–	205	279	–	–	–	–	713	–	3.5	12.1
51-52–Boston	66	–	1324	149	404	.369	–	–	–	107	171	.626	–	–	406	76	235	9	–	–	–	405	6.2	1.2	6.1
52-53–Boston	71	–	1900	188	541	.348	–	–	–	110	185	.595	–	–	537	147	287	17	–	–	–	486	7.6	2.1	6.8
53-54–Boston	71	–	1729	140	453	.309	–	–	–	129	206	.626	–	–	509	144	280	10	–	–	–	409	7.2	2.0	5.8
54-55–Boston	71	–	1623	176	465	.378	–	–	–	90	127	.709	–	–	492	127	232	6	–	–	–	442	6.9	1.8	6.2
Reg. NBA Totals	338	–	6576	887	2581	.344	–	–	–	681	1044	.652	–	–	1944	699	1313	42	–	–	–	2455	7.0	2.1	7.3
Reg. NBL Totals	64	–	–	169	–	–	–	–	–	169	261	.648	–	–	–	–	232	–	–	–	–	507	–	–	7.9
NBA Playoff Totals	25	–	492	68	220	.377	–	–	–	38	67	.567	–	–	191	58	116	10	–	–	–	174	7.1	2.1	7.0
NBL Playoff Totals	2	–	–	7	–	–	–	–	–	2	3	.667	–	–	–	–	10	–	–	–	–	16	–	–	8.0

Branson, Bradley Alexander (Brad) b. September 24, 1958 Ht. 6-10 Wt. 220 College: Edison (Fla.) C.C.; Southern Methodist

SEASON–TEAM	G	GS	MIN	FGM	FGA	PCT	3FGM	3FGA	PCT	FTM	FTA	PCT	O-RB	D-RB	TOT	AST	PF	DQ	STL	TO	BLK	PTS	RPG	APG	PPG
81-82–Cleveland	10	3	176	21	52	.404	0	0	–	11	12	.917	14	19	33	6	17	0	5	13	4	53	3.3	0.6	5.3
82-83–Indiana	62	2	680	131	308	.425	0	1	.000	76	108	.704	73	100	173	46	81	0	27	45	26	338	2.8	0.7	5.5
Reg. Season Totals	72	5	856	152	360	.422	0	1	.000	87	120	.725	87	119	206	52	98	0	32	58	30	391	2.9	0.7	5.4

Branson, Herman Jesse (Jesse) b. January 7, 1942 Ht. 6-7 Wt. 200 College: Elon

SEASON–TEAM	G	GS	MIN	FGM	FGA	PCT	3FGM	3FGA	PCT	FTM	FTA	PCT	O-RB	D-RB	TOT	AST	PF	DQ	STL	TO	BLK	PTS	RPG	APG	PPG
65-66–Philadelphia	5	–	14	1	6	.167	–	–	–	3	4	.750	–	–	9	1	4	0	–	–	–	5	1.8	0.2	1.0
67-68–New Orleans (A)	78	–	1892	376	877	.429	2	9	.222	332	473	.702	–	–	541	67	248	3	–	115	–	1086	6.9	0.9	13.9
Reg. NBA Totals	5	–	14	1	6	.167	–	–	–	3	4	.750	–	–	9	1	4	0	–	–	–	5	1.8	0.2	1.0
Reg. ABA Totals	78	–	1892	376	877	.429	2	9	.222	332	473	.702	–	–	541	67	248	3	–	115	–	1086	6.9	0.9	13.9
ABA Playoff Totals	17	–	402	61	155	.394	0	3	.000	71	87	.816	–	–	102	20	62	0	–	31	–	193	6.0	1.2	11.4

Brasco, James J. (Jim) b. February 3, 1931 Ht. 6-1 Wt. 170 College: New York U.

SEASON–TEAM	G	GS	MIN	FGM	FGA	PCT	3FGM	3FGA	PCT	FTM	FTA	PCT	O-RB	D-RB	TOT	AST	PF	DQ	STL	TO	BLK	PTS	RPG	APG	PPG
52-53–Syr.-Milw.	30	–	359	36	142	.254	–	–	–	38	48	.792	–	–	39	33	48	3	–	–	–	110	1.3	1.1	3.7
Reg. Season Totals	30	–	359	36	142	.254	–	–	–	38	48	.792	–	–	39	33	48	3	–	–	–	110	1.3	1.1	3.7

Bratz, Michael Louis (Mike) b. October 17, 1955 Ht. 6-2 Wt. 185 College: Allan Hancock (Calif.) Coll.; Stanford

SEASON–TEAM	G	GS	MIN	FGM	FGA	PCT	3FGM	3FGA	PCT	FTM	FTA	PCT	O-RB	D-RB	TOT	AST	PF	DQ	STL	TO	BLK	PTS	RPG	APG	PPG
77-78–Phoenix	80	–	933	159	395	.403	–	–	–	56	68	.824	42	73	115	123	104	1	39	89	5	374	1.4	1.5	4.7
78-79–Phoenix	77	–	1297	242	533	.454	–	–	–	139	170	.818	55	86	141	179	151	0	64	135	7	623	1.8	2.3	8.1
79-80–Phoenix	82	–	1589	269	687	.392	21	86	.244	141	162	.870	50	117	167	223	165	0	93	135	9	700	2.0	2.7	8.5
80-81–Cleveland	80	–	2595	319	817	.390	57	169	.337	107	132	.811	66	132	198	452	194	1	136	162	17	802	2.5	5.7	10.0
81-82–San Antonio	81	3	1616	230	565	.407	46	138	.333	119	152	.783	40	126	166	438	183	0	65	139	11	625	2.0	5.4	7.7
82-83–Chicago	15	0	140	14	42	.333	1	8	.125	10	13	.769	3	16	19	23	20	0	7	14	0	39	1.3	1.5	2.6
83-84–Golden State	82	0	1428	213	521	.409	15	51	.294	120	137	.876	41	102	143	252	155	0	84	109	6	561	1.7	3.1	6.8
84-85–Golden State	56	6	746	106	250	.424	6	26	.231	69	82	.841	11	47	58	122	76	1	47	54	4	287	1.0	2.2	5.1
85-86–Sacramento	33	0	269	26	70	.371	4	14	.286	14	18	.778	2	21	23	39	43	0	13	17	0	70	0.7	1.2	2.1
Reg. Season Totals	586	9	10613	1578	3880	.407	150	492	.305	775	934	.830	310	720	1030	1851	1091	3	548	854	59	4081	1.8	3.2	7.0
Playoff Totals	37	0	666	119	262	.454	14	41	.341	63	80	.788	20	39	59	96	82	0	33	56	3	315	1.6	2.6	8.5

Braun, Carl August b. September 25, 1927 Ht. 6-5 Wt. 180 College: Colgate

SEASON–TEAM	G	GS	MIN	FGM	FGA	PCT	3FGM	3FGA	PCT	FTM	FTA	PCT	O-RB	D-RB	TOT	AST	PF	DQ	STL	TO	BLK	PTS	RPG	APG	PPG
47-48–New York	47	–	–	276	854	.323	–	–	–	119	183	.650	–	–	–	61	102	–	–	–	–	671	–	1.3	14.3
48-49–New York	57	–	–	299	906	.330	–	–	–	212	279	.760	–	–	–	173	144	–	–	–	–	810	–	3.0	14.2
49-50–New York	67	–	–	373	1024	.364	–	–	–	285	374	.762	–	–	–	247	188	–	–	–	–	1031	–	3.7	15.4
52-53–New York	70	–	2316	323	807	.400	–	–	–	331	401	.825	–	–	233	243	287	14	–	–	–	977	3.3	3.5	14.0
53-54–New York	72	–	2373	354	884	.400	–	–	–	354	429	.825	–	–	246	209	259	6	–	–	–	1062	3.4	2.9	14.8
54-55–New York	71	–	2479	400	1032	.388	–	–	–	274	342	.801	–	–	295	274	208	3	–	–	–	1074	4.2	3.9	15.1
55-56–New York	72	–	2316	396	1064	.372	–	–	–	320	382	.838	–	–	259	298	215	3	–	–	–	1112	3.6	4.1	15.4
56-57–New York	72	–	2345	378	993	.381	–	–	–	245	303	.809	–	–	259	256	195	1	–	–	–	1001	3.6	3.6	13.9
57-58–New York	71	–	2475	426	1018	.418	–	–	–	321	378	.849	–	–	330	393	183	2	–	–	–	1173	4.6	5.5	16.5
58-59–New York	72	–	1959	287	684	.420	–	–	–	180	218	.826	–	–	251	349	178	3	–	–	–	754	3.5	4.8	10.5
59-60–New York	54	–	1514	285	659	.432	–	–	–	129	154	.838	–	–	168	270	127	2	–	–	–	699	3.1	5.0	12.9
60-61–New York	15	–	218	37	79	.468	–	–	–	11	14	.786	–	–	31	48	29	0	–	–	–	85	2.1	3.2	5.7
61-62–Boston	48	–	414	78	207	.377	–	–	–	20	27	.741	–	–	50	71	49	0	–	–	–	176	1.0	1.5	3.7
Reg. Season Totals	788	–	18409	3912	10211	.383	–	–	–	2801	3484	.804	–	–	2122	2892	2164	34	–	–	–	10625	3.4	3.7	13.5
Playoff Totals	40	–	706	179	551	.348	–	–	–	203	258	.810	–	–	82	117	138	6	–	–	–	561	3.0	2.7	14.0
All-Star Totals	4	–	90	13	27	.481	–	–	–	4	4	1.000	–	–	12	8	9	0	–	–	–	30	3.0	2.0	7.5

B

Breaux, Tim b. September 19, 1970 Ht. 6-6 Wt. 216 College: Wyoming

SEASON–TEAM	G	GS	MIN	FGM	FGA	PCT	3FGM	3FGA	PCT	FTM	FTA	PCT	O-RB	D-RB	TOT	AST	PF	DQ	STL	TO	BLK	PTS	RPG	APG	PPG
94-95–Houston	42	2	340	45	121	.372	6	25	.240	32	49	.653	16	18	34	15	25	0	11	16	4	128	0.8	0.4	3.0
95-96–Houston	54	4	570	59	161	.366	15	46	.326	28	45	.622	22	38	60	24	42	0	11	30	8	161	1.1	0.4	3.0
97-98–Milwaukee	6	0	30	4	11	.364	1	3	.333	1	2	.500	0	2	2	2	1	0	2	1	1	10	0.3	0.3	1.7
Reg. Season Totals	102	6	940	108	293	.369	22	74	.297	61	96	.635	38	58	96	41	68	0	24	47	13	299	0.9	0.4	2.9

Brennan, Peter Joseph (Pete) b. September 23, 1936 Ht. 6-6 Wt. 205 College: North Carolina

SEASON–TEAM	G	GS	MIN	FGM	FGA	PCT	3FGM	3FGA	PCT	FTM	FTA	PCT	O-RB	D-RB	TOT	AST	PF	DQ	STL	TO	BLK	PTS	RPG	APG	PPG
58-59–New York	16	–	136	13	43	.302	–	–	–	14	25	.560	–	–	31	6	15	0	–	–	–	40	1.9	0.4	2.5
Reg. Season Totals	16	–	136	13	43	.302	–	–	–	14	25	.560	–	–	31	6	15	0	–	–	–	40	1.9	0.4	2.5
Playoff Totals	2	–	6	2	7	.286	–	–	–	0	1	.000	–	–	5	–	4	0	–	–	–	4	2.5	0.0	2.0

Brennan, Thomas F. (Tom) b. August 6, 1930 d. Deceased Ht. 6-4 Wt. 200 College: Villanova

SEASON–TEAM	G	GS	MIN	FGM	FGA	PCT	3FGM	3FGA	PCT	FTM	FTA	PCT	O-RB	D-RB	TOT	AST	PF	DQ	STL	TO	BLK	PTS	RPG	APG	PPG
54-55–Philadelphia	11	–	52	5	11	.455	–	–	–	0	0	–	–	–	5	2	5	0	–	–	–	10	0.5	0.2	0.9
Reg. Season Totals	11	–	52	5	11	.455	–	–	–	0	0	–	–	–	5	2	5	0	–	–	–	10	0.5	0.2	0.9

Breuer, Randall W. (Randy) b. October 11, 1960 Ht. 7-3 Wt. 260 College: Minnesota

SEASON–TEAM	G	GS	MIN	FGM	FGA	PCT	3FGM	3FGA	PCT	FTM	FTA	PCT	O-RB	D-RB	TOT	AST	PF	DQ	STL	TO	BLK	PTS	RPG	APG	PPG
83-84–Milwaukee	57	8	472	68	177	.384	0	0	–	32	46	.696	48	61	109	17	98	1	11	35	38	168	1.9	0.3	2.9
84-85–Milwaukee	78	0	1083	162	317	.511	0	0	–	89	127	.701	92	164	256	40	179	4	21	63	82	413	3.3	0.5	5.3
85-86–Milwaukee	82	63	1792	272	570	.477	0	1	.000	141	198	.712	159	299	458	114	214	2	50	122	116	685	5.6	1.4	8.4
86-87–Milwaukee	76	10	1467	241	497	.485	0	0	–	118	202	.584	129	221	350	47	229	9	56	100	61	600	4.6	0.6	7.9
87-88–Milwaukee	81	73	2258	390	788	.495	0	0	–	188	286	.657	191	360	551	103	198	3	46	107	107	968	6.8	1.3	12.0
88-89–Milwaukee	48	4	513	86	179	.480	0	0	–	28	51	.549	51	84	135	22	59	0	9	29	37	200	2.8	0.5	4.2
89-90–Milw.-Minn.	81	55	1879	298	696	.428	0	1	.000	126	193	.653	154	263	417	97	196	2	42	96	108	722	5.1	1.2	8.9
90-91–Minnesota	73	44	1505	197	435	.453	0	0	–	35	79	.443	114	231	345	73	132	1	35	69	80	429	4.7	1.0	5.9
91-92–Minnesota	67	25	1176	161	344	.468	0	1	.000	41	77	.532	98	183	281	89	117	0	27	41	99	363	4.2	1.3	5.4
92-93–Atlanta	12	0	107	15	31	.484	0	0	–	2	5	.400	10	18	28	6	12	0	2	5	3	32	2.3	0.5	2.7
93-94–Sacramento	26	3	247	8	26	.308	0	1	.000	3	14	.214	15	41	56	8	30	0	6	9	19	19	2.2	0.3	0.7
Reg. Season Totals	681	285	12499	1898	4060	.467	0	4	.000	803	1278	.628	1061	1925	2986	616	1464	22	305	676	750	4599	4.4	0.9	6.8
Playoff Totals	60	17	870	115	223	.516	0	0	–	57	95	.600	56	130	186	26	129	2	23	30	44	287	3.1	0.4	4.8

Brewer, James Turner (Jim, Brew) b. December 3, 1951 Ht. 6-9 Wt. 220 College: Minnesota

SEASON–TEAM	G	GS	MIN	FGM	FGA	PCT	3FGM	3FGA	PCT	FTM	FTA	PCT	O-RB	D-RB	TOT	AST	PF	DQ	STL	TO	BLK	PTS	RPG	APG	PPG
73-74–Cleveland	82	–	1862	210	548	.383	–	–	–	80	123	.650	207	317	524	149	192	1	46	–	35	500	6.4	1.8	6.1
74-75–Cleveland	82	–	1991	291	639	.455	–	–	–	103	159	.648	205	304	509	128	150	2	77	–	43	685	6.2	1.6	8.4
75-76–Cleveland	82	–	2913	400	874	.458	–	–	–	140	214	.654	298	593	891	209	214	0	94	–	89	940	10.9	2.5	11.5
76-77–Cleveland	81	–	2672	296	657	.451	–	–	–	97	178	.545	275	487	762	195	214	3	94	–	82	689	9.4	2.4	8.5
77-78–Cleveland	80	–	1798	175	390	.449	–	–	–	46	100	.460	182	313	495	98	178	1	60	103	48	396	6.2	1.2	5.0
78-79–Clev.-Detroit	80	–	1611	141	319	.442	–	–	–	26	63	.413	159	316	475	87	174	2	61	97	66	308	5.9	1.1	3.9
79-80–Portland	67	–	1016	90	184	.489	0	5	.000	14	29	.483	101	156	257	75	129	2	42	47	43	194	3.8	1.1	2.9
80-81–Los Angeles	78	–	1107	101	197	.513	0	2	.000	15	40	.375	127	154	281	55	158	2	43	48	58	217	3.6	0.7	2.8
81-82–Los Angeles	71	9	966	81	175	.463	1	6	.167	7	19	.368	106	158	264	42	127	1	39	37	46	170	3.7	0.6	2.4
Reg. Season Totals	703	9	15936	1785	3983	.448	1	13	.077	528	925	.571	1660	2798	4458	1038	1536	14	556	332	510	4099	6.3	1.5	5.8
Playoff Totals	31	0	742	68	145	.469	0	0	–	28	54	.519	61	143	204	49	59	0	24	5	24	164	6.6	1.6	5.3

Brewer, Ronald Charles (Ron) b. September 16, 1955 Ht. 6-4 Wt. 180 College: Westark (Ark.) C.C.; Arkansas

SEASON–TEAM	G	GS	MIN	FGM	FGA	PCT	3FGM	3FGA	PCT	FTM	FTA	PCT	O-RB	D-RB	TOT	AST	PF	DQ	STL	TO	BLK	PTS	RPG	APG	PPG
78-79–Portland	81	–	2454	434	878	.494	–	–	–	210	256	.820	88	141	229	165	181	3	102	153	79	1078	2.8	2.0	13.3
79-80–Portland	82	–	2815	548	1182	.464	6	32	.188	184	219	.840	54	160	214	216	154	0	98	167	48	1286	2.6	2.6	15.7
80-81–Port.-S.A.	75	–	1452	275	631	.436	1	7	.143	91	114	.798	34	52	86	148	95	0	61	92	34	642	1.1	2.0	8.6
81-82–S.A.-Clev.	72	45	2319	569	1194	.477	8	31	.258	211	260	.812	55	106	161	188	151	0	82	125	30	1357	2.2	2.6	18.8
82-83–Clev.-G.S.	74	52	1964	344	807	.426	7	18	.389	142	170	.835	59	85	144	96	123	0	90	97	25	837	1.9	1.3	11.3
83-84–G.S.-S.A.	53	8	992	179	403	.444	3	14	.214	52	67	.776	22	41	63	50	64	0	24	40	21	413	1.2	0.9	7.8
84-85–S.A.-N.J.	20	0	326	62	118	.525	0	2	.000	23	25	.920	9	12	21	17	23	0	6	9	6	147	1.1	0.9	7.4
85-86–Chicago-Clev.	44	3	570	86	224	.384	5	17	.294	34	38	.895	14	39	53	40	44	0	17	23	6	211	1.2	0.9	4.8
Reg. Season Totals	501	108	12892	2497	5437	.459	30	121	.248	947	1149	.824	335	636	971	920	835	3	480	706	249	5971	1.9	1.8	11.9
Playoff Totals	16	0	411	92	191	.482	1	7	.143	41	59	.695	6	18	24	32	30	0	8	21	16	226	1.5	2.0	14.1

Brian, Frank Sands (Flash) b. May 1, 1923 Ht. 6-1 Wt. 180 College: Louisiana State

SEASON–TEAM	G	GS	MIN	FGM	FGA	PCT	3FGM	3FGA	PCT	FTM	FTA	PCT	O-RB	D-RB	TOT	AST	PF	DQ	STL	TO	BLK	PTS	RPG	APG	PPG
47-48–Anderson (N)	59	–	–	248	–	–	–	–	–	155	210	.738	–	–	–	–	–	–	–	–	–	651	–	–	11.0
48-49–Anderson (N)	64	–	–	216	–	–	–	–	–	201	256	.785	–	–	–	–	–	–	–	–	–	633	–	–	9.9
49-50–Anderson	64	–	–	368	1156	.318	–	–	–	402	488	.824	–	–	–	189	192	–	–	–	–	1138	–	3.0	17.8
50-51–Tri-Cities	68	–	–	363	1127	.322	–	–	–	418	508	.823	–	–	244	266	215	4	–	–	–	1144	3.6	3.9	16.8
51-52–Fort Wayne	66	–	2672	342	972	.352	–	–	–	367	433	.848	–	–	232	233	220	6	–	–	–	1051	3.5	3.5	15.9
52-53–Fort Wayne	68	–	1910	245	699	.351	–	–	–	236	297	.795	–	–	133	142	205	8	–	–	–	726	2.0	2.1	10.7
53-54–Fort Wayne	64	–	973	132	352	.375	–	–	–	137	182	.753	–	–	79	92	100	2	–	–	–	401	1.2	1.4	6.3
54-55–Fort Wayne	71	–	1381	237	623	.380	–	–	–	217	255	.851	–	–	127	142	133	0	–	–	–	691	1.8	2.0	9.7
55-56–Fort Wayne	37	–	680	78	263	.297	–	–	–	72	88	.818	–	–	88	74	62	0	–	–	–	228	2.4	2.0	6.2
Reg. NBA Totals	438	–	7616	1765	5192	.340	–	–	–	1849	2251	.821	–	–	903	1138	1127	20	–	–	–	5379	2.4	2.6	12.3
Reg. NBL Totals	123	–	–	464	–	–	–	–	–	356	466	.764	–	–	–	–	–	–	–	–	–	1284	–	–	10.4
NBA Playoff Totals	43	–	955	134	523	.340	–	–	–	126	154	.818	–	–	79	131	106	1	–	–	–	394	1.9	2.3	9.2
NBL Playoff Totals	13	–	–	44	–	–	–	–	–	38	48	.792	–	–	–	–	35	–	–	–	–	126	–	–	9.7
NBA All-Star Totals	2	–	25	9	24	.375	–	–	–	9	11	.818	–	–	13	7	4	0	–	–	–	27	6.5	3.5	13.5

Brickowski, Francis Anthony (Frank, Brick) b. August 14, 1959 Ht. 6-9 Wt. 248 College: Penn State

SEASON–TEAM	G	GS	MIN	FGM	FGA	PCT	3FGM	3FGA	PCT	FTM	FTA	PCT	O-RB	D-RB	TOT	AST	PF	DQ	STL	TO	BLK	PTS	RPG	APG	PPG
84-85–Seattle	78	9	1115	150	305	.492	0	4	.000	85	127	.669	76	184	260	100	171	1	34	100	15	385	3.3	1.3	4.9
85-86–Seattle	40	2	311	30	58	.517	0	0	–	18	27	.667	16	38	54	21	74	2	11	23	7	78	1.4	0.5	2.0
86-87–Lakers-S.A.	44	0	487	63	124	.508	0	4	.000	50	70	.714	48	68	116	17	118	4	20	32	6	176	2.6	0.4	4.0
87-88–San Antonio	70	68	2227	425	805	.528	1	5	.200	268	349	.768	167	316	483	266	275	11	74	207	36	1119	6.9	3.8	16.0
88-89–San Antonio	64	60	1822	337	654	.515	0	2	.000	201	281	.715	148	258	406	131	252	10	102	165	35	875	6.3	2.0	13.7
89-90–San Antonio	78	12	1438	211	387	.545	0	2	.000	95	141	.674	89	238	327	105	226	4	66	93	37	517	4.2	1.3	6.6
90-91–Milwaukee	75	73	1912	372	706	.527	0	2	.000	198	248	.798	129	297	426	131	255	4	86	160	43	942	5.7	1.7	12.6
91-92–Milwaukee	65	60	1556	306	584	.524	3	6	.500	125	163	.767	97	247	344	122	223	11	60	112	23	740	5.3	1.9	11.4
92-93–Milwaukee	66	64	2075	456	836	.545	8	26	.308	195	268	.728	120	285	405	196	235	8	80	202	44	1115	6.1	3.0	16.9
93-94–Milw.-Cha.	71	46	2094	368	754	.488	4	20	.200	195	254	.768	85	319	404	222	242	6	80	181	27	935	5.7	3.1	13.2
95-96–Seattle	63	8	986	123	252	.488	32	79	.405	61	86	.709	26	125	151	58	185	4	26	78	8	339	2.4	0.9	5.4
96-97–Boston	17	2	255	32	73	.438	7	20	.350	10	14	.714	6	28	34	15	42	1	5	19	4	81	2.0	0.9	4.8
Reg. Season Totals	731	404	16278	2873	5538	.519	55	170	.324	1501	2028	.740	1007	2403	3410	1384	2298	66	644	1372	285	7302	4.7	1.9	10.0
Playoff Totals	37	9	590	93	181	.514	7	25	.280	40	63	.635	30	92	122	39	114	2	22	50	10	233	3.3	1.1	6.3

Bridgeman, Ulysses Lee (Junior) b. September 17, 1953 Ht. 6-5 Wt. 210 College: Louisville

SEASON–TEAM	G	GS	MIN	FGM	FGA	PCT	3FGM	3FGA	PCT	FTM	FTA	PCT	O-RB	D-RB	TOT	AST	PF	DQ	STL	TO	BLK	PTS	RPG	APG	PPG
75-76–Milwaukee	81	–	1646	286	651	.439	–	–	–	128	161	.795	113	181	294	157	235	3	52	–	21	700	3.6	1.9	8.6
76-77–Milwaukee	82	–	2410	491	1094	.449	–	–	–	197	228	.864	129	287	416	205	221	3	82	–	26	1179	5.1	2.5	14.4
77-78–Milwaukee	82	–	1876	476	947	.503	–	–	–	166	205	.810	114	176	290	175	202	1	72	176	30	1118	3.5	2.1	13.6
78-79–Milwaukee	82	–	1963	540	1067	.506	–	–	–	189	228	.829	113	184	297	163	184	2	88	138	41	1269	3.6	2.0	15.5
79-80–Milwaukee	81	–	2316	594	1243	.478	5	27	.185	230	266	.865	104	197	301	237	216	3	94	172	20	1423	3.7	2.9	17.6
80-81–Milwaukee	77	–	2215	537	1102	.487	3	21	.143	213	241	.884	78	211	289	234	182	2	88	150	28	1290	3.8	3.0	16.8
81-82–Milwaukee	41	4	924	209	433	.483	4	9	.444	89	103	.864	37	88	125	109	91	0	28	64	3	511	3.0	2.7	12.5
82-83–Milwaukee	70	5	1855	421	856	.492	1	13	.077	164	196	.837	44	202	246	207	155	0	40	122	9	1007	3.5	3.0	14.4
83-84–Milwaukee	81	10	2431	509	1094	.465	6	31	.194	196	243	.807	80	252	332	265	224	2	53	148	14	1220	4.1	3.3	15.1
84-85–L.A. Clippers	80	15	2042	460	990	.465	14	39	.359	181	206	.879	55	175	230	171	128	0	47	116	18	1115	2.9	2.1	13.9
85-86–L.A. Clippers	58	14	1161	199	451	.441	6	18	.333	106	119	.891	29	94	123	108	81	1	31	68	8	510	2.1	1.9	8.8
86-87–Milwaukee	34	4	418	79	171	.462	1	6	.167	16	20	.800	14	38	52	35	50	0	10	15	2	175	1.5	1.0	5.1
Reg. Season Totals	849	52	21257	4801	10099	.475	40	164	.244	1875	2216	.846	910	2085	2995	2066	1969	17	685	1169	220	11517	3.5	2.4	13.6
Playoff Totals	49	8	1359	264	581	.454	4	16	.250	118	145	.814	53	119	172	128	148	2	37	74	11	650	3.5	2.6	13.3

Bridges, William C. (Bill) b. April 4, 1939 Ht. 6-6 Wt. 230 College: Kansas

SEASON–TEAM	G	GS	MIN	FGM	FGA	PCT	3FGM	3FGA	PCT	FTM	FTA	PCT	O-RB	D-RB	TOT	AST	PF	DQ	STL	TO	BLK	PTS	RPG	APG	PPG
62-63–St. Louis	27	–	374	66	160	.413	–	–	–	32	51	.627	–	–	144	23	58	0	–	–	–	164	5.3	0.9	6.1
63-64–St. Louis	80	–	1949	268	675	.397	–	–	–	146	224	.652	–	–	680	181	269	6	–	–	–	682	8.5	2.3	8.5
64-65–St. Louis	79	–	2362	362	938	.386	–	–	–	186	275	.676	–	–	853	187	276	3	–	–	–	910	10.8	2.4	11.5
65-66–St. Louis	78	–	2677	377	927	.407	–	–	–	257	364	.706	–	–	951	208	333	11	–	–	–	1011	12.2	2.7	13.0
66-67–St. Louis	79	–	3130	503	1106	.455	–	–	–	367	523	.702	–	–	1190	222	325	12	–	–	–	1373	15.1	2.8	17.4
67-68–St. Louis	82	–	3197	466	1009	.462	–	–	–	347	484	.717	–	–	1102	253	366	12	–	–	–	1279	13.4	3.1	15.6
68-69–Atlanta	80	–	2930	351	775	.453	–	–	–	239	353	.677	–	–	1132	298	290	3	–	–	–	941	14.2	3.7	11.8
69-70–Atlanta	82	–	3269	443	932	.475	–	–	–	331	451	.734	–	–	1181	345	292	6	–	–	–	1217	14.4	4.2	14.8
70-71–Atlanta	82	–	3140	382	834	.458	–	–	–	211	330	.639	–	–	1233	240	317	7	–	–	–	975	15.0	2.9	11.9
71-72–Atlanta-Phil.	78	–	2756	379	779	.487	–	–	–	222	316	.703	–	–	1051	198	269	6	–	–	–	980	13.5	2.5	12.6
72-73–Phil.-L.A.	82	–	2867	333	722	.461	–	–	–	179	255	.702	–	–	904	219	296	3	–	–	–	845	11.0	2.7	10.3
73-74–Los Angeles	65	–	1812	216	513	.421	–	–	–	116	164	.707	193	306	499	148	219	3	58	–	31	548	7.7	2.3	8.4
74-75–L.A.-G.S.	32	–	415	35	93	.376	–	–	–	17	34	.500	64	70	134	31	65	1	11	–	5	87	4.2	1.0	2.7
Reg. Season Totals	926	–	30878	4181	9463	.442	–	–	–	2650	3824	.693	257	376	11054	2553	3375	73	69	–	36	11012	11.9	2.8	11.9
Playoff Totals	113	–	3521	475	1135	.419	–	–	–	235	349	.673	27	52	1305	219	408	10	16	–	4	1185	11.5	1.9	10.5
All-Star Totals	3	–	53	13	16	.813	–	–	–	2	11	.182	0	0	14	6	6	0	0	–	0	28	4.7	2.0	9.3

Brightman, Horace Albert (Al) b. September 22, 1923 d. June 10, 1992 Ht. 6-2 Wt. 195 College: Charleston (W.Va.); Long Beach State

SEASON–TEAM	G	GS	MIN	FGM	FGA	PCT	3FGM	3FGA	PCT	FTM	FTA	PCT	O-RB	D-RB	TOT	AST	PF	DQ	STL	TO	BLK	PTS	RPG	APG	PPG
46-47–Boston	58	–	–	223	870	.256	–	–	–	121	193	.627	–	–	–	60	115	–	–	–	–	567	–	1.0	9.8
Reg. Season Totals	58	–	–	223	870	.256	–	–	–	121	193	.627	–	–	–	60	115	–	–	–	–	567	–	1.0	9.8

Brindley, Audley (Aud) b. December 31, 1923 d. November 19, 1958 Ht. 6-4 Wt. 175 College: Dartmouth

SEASON–TEAM	G	GS	MIN	FGM	FGA	PCT	3FGM	3FGA	PCT	FTM	FTA	PCT	O-RB	D-RB	TOT	AST	PF	DQ	STL	TO	BLK	PTS	RPG	APG	PPG
46-47–New York	12	–	–	14	49	.286	–	–	–	6	7	.857	–	–	–	1	16	–	–	–	–	34	–	0.1	2.8
Reg. Season Totals	12	–	–	14	49	.286	–	–	–	6	7	.857	–	–	–	1	16	–	–	–	–	34	–	0.1	2.8
Playoff Totals	3	–	–	3	6	.500	–	–	–	4	6	.667	–	–	–	–	4	–	–	–	–	10	–	0.0	3.3

Brisker, John b. June 15, 1947 d. April 1978 Ht. 6-5 Wt. 210 College: Toledo

SEASON–TEAM	G	GS	MIN	FGM	FGA	PCT	3FGM	3FGA	PCT	FTM	FTA	PCT	O-RB	D-RB	TOT	AST	PF	DQ	STL	TO	BLK	PTS	RPG	APG	PPG
69-70–Pittsburgh (A)	77	–	2173	627	1361	.461	34	116	.293	329	398	.827	–	–	441	133	236	4	–	–	–	1617	5.7	1.7	21.0
70-71–Pittsburgh (A)	79	–	3089	898	1972	.455	89	264	.337	430	519	.829	–	–	766	226	273	–	–	–	–	2315	9.7	2.9	29.3
71-72–Pittsburgh (A)	49	–	2065	563	1228	.458	43	137	.314	248	286	.867	–	–	447	203	156	–	–	210	–	1417	9.1	4.1	28.9
72-73–Seattle	70	–	1633	352	809	.435	–	–	–	194	236	.822	–	–	319	150	169	1	–	–	–	898	4.6	2.1	12.8
73-74–Seattle	35	–	717	178	396	.449	–	–	–	82	100	.820	59	87	146	56	70	0	28	–	6	438	4.2	1.6	12.5
74-75–Seattle	21	–	276	60	141	.426	–	–	–	42	49	.857	15	18	33	19	33	0	7	–	3	162	1.6	0.9	7.7
Reg. NBA Totals	126	–	2626	590	1346	.438	–	–	–	318	385	.826	74	105	498	225	272	1	35	–	9	1498	4.0	1.8	11.9
Reg. ABA Totals	205	–	7327	2088	4561	.458	166	517	.321	1007	1203	.837	–	–	1654	562	665	4	–	210	–	5349	8.1	2.7	26.1

Bristow, Allan Mercer Jr. b. August 23, 1951 Ht. 6-7 Wt. 220 College: Toledo; Virginia Tech

SEASON–TEAM	G	GS	MIN	FGM	FGA	PCT	3FGM	3FGA	PCT	FTM	FTA	PCT	O-RB	D-RB	TOT	AST	PF	DQ	STL	TO	BLK	PTS	RPG	APG	PPG
73-74–Philadelphia	55	–	643	108	270	.400	–	–	–	42	57	.737	68	99	167	92	68	1	29	–	1	258	3.0	1.7	4.7
74-75–Philadelphia	72	–	1101	163	393	.415	–	–	–	121	153	.791	111	143	254	99	101	0	25	–	2	447	3.5	1.4	6.2
75-76–San Antonio (A)	47	–	882	125	271	.461	0	1	.000	78	92	.848	68	106	174	121	81	–	24	63	2	328	3.7	2.6	7.0
76-77–San Antonio	82	–	2017	365	747	.489	–	–	–	206	258	.798	119	229	348	240	195	1	89	–	2	936	4.2	2.9	11.4
77-78–San Antonio	82	–	1481	257	538	.478	–	–	–	152	208	.731	99	158	257	194	150	0	69	146	4	666	3.1	2.4	8.1
78-79–San Antonio	74	–	1324	174	354	.492	–	–	–	124	149	.832	80	167	247	231	154	0	56	108	15	472	3.3	3.1	6.4
79-80–Utah	82	–	2304	377	785	.480	2	7	.286	197	243	.811	170	342	512	341	211	2	88	179	6	953	6.2	4.2	11.6
80-81–Utah	82	–	2001	271	611	.444	5	18	.278	166	198	.838	103	327	430	383	190	1	63	171	3	713	5.2	4.7	8.7
81-82–Dallas	82	54	2035	218	499	.437	3	18	.167	134	164	.817	119	220	339	448	222	2	65	165	6	573	4.1	5.5	7.0
82-83–Dallas	37	0	371	44	99	.444	6	13	.462	10	14	.714	24	35	59	70	46	0	6	31	1	104	1.6	1.9	2.8
Reg. NBA Totals	648	54	13277	1977	4296	.460	16	56	.286	1152	1444	.798	893	1720	2613	2098	1337	7	490	800	40	5122	4.0	3.2	7.9
Reg. ABA Totals	47	–	882	125	271	.461	0	1	.000	78	92	.848	68	106	174	121	81	–	24	63	2	328	3.7	2.6	7.0
NBA Playoff Totals	20	0	242	32	73	.438	0	0	–	22	36	.611	19	23	42	42	33	0	13	16	5	86	2.1	2.1	4.3
ABA Playoff Totals	7	–	97	13	35	.371	0	1	.000	19	24	.792	9	5	14	12	14	–	5	8	0	45	2.0	1.7	6.4

Britt, Tyrone b. April 18, 1944 Ht. 6-4 Wt. 195 College: North Carolina Central; Johnson C. Smith

SEASON–TEAM	G	GS	MIN	FGM	FGA	PCT	3FGM	3FGA	PCT	FTM	FTA	PCT	O-RB	D-RB	TOT	AST	PF	DQ	STL	TO	BLK	PTS	RPG	APG	PPG
67-68–San Diego	11	–	84	13	34	.382	–	–	–	2	3	.667	–	–	15	12	10	0	–	–	–	28	1.4	1.1	2.5
Reg. Season Totals	11	–	84	13	34	.382	–	–	–	2	3	.667	–	–	15	12	10	0	–	–	–	28	1.4	1.1	2.5

Britt, Wayman P. b. August 31, 1952 Ht. 6-2 Wt. 185 College: Michigan

SEASON–TEAM	G	GS	MIN	FGM	FGA	PCT	3FGM	3FGA	PCT	FTM	FTA	PCT	O-RB	D-RB	TOT	AST	PF	DQ	STL	TO	BLK	PTS	RPG	APG	PPG
77-78–Detroit	7	–	16	3	10	.300	–	–	–	3	4	.750	1	3	4	2	3	0	1	1	0	9	0.6	0.3	1.3
Reg. Season Totals	7	–	16	3	10	.300	–	–	–	3	4	.750	1	3	4	2	3	0	1	1	0	9	0.6	0.3	1.3

Brittain, Michael James (Mike) b. June 21, 1963 Ht. 7-1 Wt. 235 College: South Carolina

SEASON–TEAM	G	GS	MIN	FGM	FGA	PCT	3FGM	3FGA	PCT	FTM	FTA	PCT	O-RB	D-RB	TOT	AST	PF	DQ	STL	TO	BLK	PTS	RPG	APG	PPG
85-86–San Antonio	32	2	219	22	43	.512	0	0	–	10	19	.526	10	39	49	5	54	1	3	20	12	54	1.5	0.2	1.7
86-87–San Antonio	6	0	29	4	9	.444	0	0	–	1	2	.500	2	2	4	2	3	0	1	2	0	9	0.7	0.3	1.5
Reg. Season Totals	38	2	248	26	52	.500	0	0	–	11	21	.524	12	41	53	7	57	1	4	22	12	63	1.4	0.2	1.7
Playoff Totals	1	0	2	1	2	.500	0	0	–	0	0	–	1	0	1	–	0	0	0	0	1	2	1.0	0.0	2.0

Britton, David b. August 29, 1958 Ht. 6-4 Wt. 190 College: Potomac State (W.Va.) Coll.; Texas A&M

SEASON–TEAM	G	GS	MIN	FGM	FGA	PCT	3FGM	3FGA	PCT	FTM	FTA	PCT	O-RB	D-RB	TOT	AST	PF	DQ	STL	TO	BLK	PTS	RPG	APG	PPG
80-81–Washington	2	–	9	2	3	.667	0	0	–	0	0	–	0	2	2	3	2	0	1	2	0	4	1.0	1.5	2.0
Reg. Season Totals	2	–	9	2	3	.667	0	0	–	0	0	–	0	2	2	3	2	0	1	2	0	4	1.0	1.5	2.0

Brogan, James Riley (Jim) b. February 24, 1958 Ht. 6-4 Wt. 185 College: West Virginia Wesleyan

SEASON–TEAM	G	GS	MIN	FGM	FGA	PCT	3FGM	3FGA	PCT	FTM	FTA	PCT	O-RB	D-RB	TOT	AST	PF	DQ	STL	TO	BLK	PTS	RPG	APG	PPG
81-82–San Diego	63	19	1027	165	364	.453	9	32	.281	61	84	.726	61	59	120	156	123	2	49	83	13	400	1.9	2.5	6.3
82-83–San Diego	58	0	466	91	213	.427	3	13	.231	34	43	.791	33	29	62	66	79	0	26	43	9	219	1.1	1.1	3.8
Reg. Season Totals	121	19	1493	256	577	.444	12	45	.267	95	127	.748	94	88	182	222	202	2	75	126	22	619	1.5	1.8	5.1

Brokaw, Gary George b. January 11, 1954 Ht. 6-4 Wt. 180 College: Notre Dame

SEASON–TEAM	G	GS	MIN	FGM	FGA	PCT	3FGM	3FGA	PCT	FTM	FTA	PCT	O-RB	D-RB	TOT	AST	PF	DQ	STL	TO	BLK	PTS	RPG	APG	PPG
74-75–Milwaukee	73	–	1639	234	514	.455	–	–	–	126	184	.685	36	111	147	221	176	3	31	–	18	594	2.0	3.0	8.1
75-76–Milwaukee	75	–	1468	237	519	.457	–	–	–	159	227	.700	26	99	125	246	138	1	37	–	17	633	1.7	3.3	8.4
76-77–Milw.-Clev.	80	–	1487	242	564	.429	–	–	–	163	219	.744	22	101	123	228	164	2	36	–	36	647	1.5	2.9	8.1
77-78–Buffalo	13	–	130	18	43	.419	–	–	–	18	24	.750	3	9	12	20	11	0	3	12	5	54	0.9	1.5	4.2
Reg. Season Totals	241	–	4724	731	1640	.446	–	–	–	466	654	.713	87	320	407	715	489	6	107	12	76	1928	1.7	3.0	8.0
Playoff Totals	6	–	152	32	56	.571	–	–	–	19	24	.792	3	12	15	36	17	0	5	–	4	83	2.5	6.0	13.8

Brookfield, Emery Price (Price) b. May 11, 1920 Ht. 6-4 Wt. 185 College: West Texas A&M; Iowa State

SEASON–TEAM	G	GS	MIN	FGM	FGA	PCT	3FGM	3FGA	PCT	FTM	FTA	PCT	O-RB	D-RB	TOT	AST	PF	DQ	STL	TO	BLK	PTS	RPG	APG	PPG
46-47–Chicago (N)	42	–	–	82	–	–	–	–	–	24	33	.727	–	–	–	–	53	–	–	–	–	188	–	–	4.5
47-48–Anderson (N)	49	–	–	82	–	–	–	–	–	27	40	.675	–	–	–	–	56	–	–	–	–	191	–	–	3.9
48-49–Indianapolis	54	–	–	176	638	.276	–	–	–	90	125	.720	–	–	–	136	145	–	–	–	–	442	–	2.5	8.2
49-50–Rochester	7	–	–	11	23	.478	–	–	–	12	13	.923	–	–	–	1	7	–	–	–	–	34	–	0.1	4.9
Reg. NBA Totals	61	–	–	187	661	.283	–	–	–	102	138	.739	–	–	–	137	152	–	–	–	–	476	–	2.2	7.8
Reg. NBL Totals	91	–	–	164	–	–	–	–	–	51	73	.699	–	–	–	–	109	–	–	–	–	379	–	–	4.2
NBL Playoff Totals	17	–	–	46	–	–	–	–	–	12	19	.632	–	–	–	–	38	–	–	–	–	104	–	–	6.1

Brookins, Clarence b. 1946 Ht. 6-4 Wt. 190 College: Temple

SEASON–TEAM	G	GS	MIN	FGM	FGA	PCT	3FGM	3FGA	PCT	FTM	FTA	PCT	O-RB	D-RB	TOT	AST	PF	DQ	STL	TO	BLK	PTS	RPG	APG	PPG
70-71–Floridians (A)	8	–	59	8	26	.308	0	1	.000	5	12	.417	–	–	12	1	5	–	–	–	–	21	1.5	0.1	2.6
Reg. ABA Totals	8	–	59	8	26	.308	0	1	.000	5	12	.417	–	–	12	1	5	–	–	–	–	21	1.5	0.1	2.6

Brooks, Kevin b. October 12, 1969 Ht. 6-8 Wt. 200 College: Louisiana-Lafayette

SEASON–TEAM	G	GS	MIN	FGM	FGA	PCT	3FGM	3FGA	PCT	FTM	FTA	PCT	O-RB	D-RB	TOT	AST	PF	DQ	STL	TO	BLK	PTS	RPG	APG	PPG
91-92–Denver	37	0	270	43	97	.443	2	11	.182	17	21	.810	13	26	39	11	19	0	8	18	2	105	1.1	0.3	2.8
92-93–Denver	55	2	571	93	233	.399	6	26	.231	35	40	.875	22	59	81	34	46	0	10	39	2	227	1.5	0.6	4.1
93-94–Denver	34	0	190	36	99	.364	4	23	.174	9	10	.900	5	16	21	3	19	0	0	12	2	85	0.6	0.1	2.5
Reg. Season Totals	126	2	1031	172	429	.401	12	60	.200	61	71	.859	40	101	141	48	84	0	18	69	6	417	1.1	0.4	3.3
Playoff Totals	2	0	5	2	7	.286	0	1	.000	1	2	.500	1	1	2	–	0	0	0	0	0	5	1.0	0.0	2.5

Brooks, Michael Anthony b. August 17, 1958 Ht. 6-7 Wt. 220 College: La Salle

SEASON–TEAM	G	GS	MIN	FGM	FGA	PCT	3FGM	3FGA	PCT	FTM	FTA	PCT	O-RB	D-RB	TOT	AST	PF	DQ	STL	TO	BLK	PTS	RPG	APG	PPG
80-81–San Diego	82	–	2479	488	1018	.479	0	6	.000	226	320	.706	210	232	442	208	234	2	99	163	31	1202	5.4	2.5	14.7
81-82–San Diego	82	73	2750	537	1066	.504	0	7	.000	202	267	.757	207	417	624	236	285	7	113	197	39	1276	7.6	2.9	15.6
82-83–San Diego	82	26	2457	402	830	.484	5	15	.333	193	277	.697	239	282	521	262	297	6	112	177	39	1002	6.4	3.2	12.2
83-84–San Diego	47	30	1405	213	445	.479	0	5	.000	104	151	.689	142	200	342	88	125	1	50	78	14	530	7.3	1.9	11.3
86-87–Indiana	10	0	148	13	37	.351	0	0	–	7	10	.700	9	19	28	11	19	0	9	11	0	33	2.8	1.1	3.3
87-88–Denver	16	0	133	20	49	.408	0	0	–	3	4	.750	19	25	44	13	21	1	4	12	1	43	2.8	0.8	2.7
Reg. Season Totals	319	129	9372	1673	3445	.486	5	33	.152	735	1029	.714	826	1175	2001	818	981	17	387	638	124	4086	6.3	2.6	12.8
Playoff Totals	4	0	11	1	3	.333	1	2	.500	0	0	–	1	3	4	2	1	0	0	0	0	3	1.0	0.5	0.8

Brooks, Scott William b. July 31, 1965 Ht. 5-11 Wt. 165 College: California-Irvine

SEASON–TEAM	G	GS	MIN	FGM	FGA	PCT	3FGM	3FGA	PCT	FTM	FTA	PCT	O-RB	D-RB	TOT	AST	PF	DQ	STL	TO	BLK	PTS	RPG	APG	PPG
88-89–Philadelphia	82	6	1372	156	371	.420	55	153	.359	61	69	.884	19	75	94	306	116	0	69	65	3	428	1.1	3.7	5.2
89-90–Philadelphia	72	1	975	119	276	.431	31	79	.392	50	57	.877	15	49	64	207	105	0	47	38	0	319	0.9	2.9	4.4
90-91–Minnesota	80	0	980	159	370	.430	45	135	.333	61	72	.847	28	44	72	204	122	1	53	51	5	424	0.9	2.6	5.3
91-92–Minnesota	82	0	1082	167	374	.447	32	90	.356	51	63	.810	27	72	99	205	82	0	66	51	7	417	1.2	2.5	5.1
92-93–Houston	82	0	1516	183	385	.475	41	99	.414	112	135	.830	22	77	99	243	136	0	79	72	3	519	1.2	3.0	6.3
93-94–Houston	73	0	1225	142	289	.491	23	61	.377	74	85	.871	10	92	102	149	98	0	51	55	2	381	1.4	2.0	5.2
94-95–Hou.-Dallas	59	0	808	126	275	.458	25	69	.362	64	79	.810	14	52	66	116	56	0	34	47	4	341	1.1	2.0	5.8
95-96–Dallas	69	0	716	134	293	.457	25	62	.403	59	69	.855	11	30	41	100	53	0	42	43	3	352	0.6	1.4	5.1
96-97–New York	38	0	251	19	39	.487	5	12	.417	14	15	.933	6	12	18	29	35	1	21	17	0	57	0.5	0.8	1.5
97-98–Cleveland	43	0	312	28	66	.424	5	11	.455	18	20	.900	6	24	30	49	25	0	18	12	3	79	0.7	1.1	1.8
Reg. Season Totals	680	7	9237	1233	2738	.450	287	771	.372	564	664	.849	158	527	685	1608	828	2	480	451	30	3317	1.0	2.4	4.9
Playoff Totals	34	0	355	29	76	.382	10	23	.435	21	28	.750	4	20	24	57	42	0	12	21	0	89	0.7	1.7	2.6

Brown, Anthony William (Tony) b. July 29, 1960 Ht. 6-6 Wt. 200 College: Arkansas

SEASON–TEAM	G	GS	MIN	FGM	FGA	PCT	3FGM	3FGA	PCT	FTM	FTA	PCT	O-RB	D-RB	TOT	AST	PF	DQ	STL	TO	BLK	PTS	RPG	APG	PPG
84-85–Indiana	82	26	1586	214	465	.460	0	6	.000	116	171	.678	146	142	288	159	212	3	59	116	12	544	3.5	1.9	6.6
85-86–Chicago	10	0	132	18	41	.439	0	2	.000	9	13	.692	5	11	16	14	16	0	5	4	1	45	1.6	1.4	4.5
86-87–New Jersey	77	67	2339	358	810	.442	5	20	.250	152	206	.738	84	135	219	259	273	12	89	153	14	873	2.8	3.4	11.3
88-89–Houston-Milw.	43	0	365	50	118	.424	4	16	.250	24	31	.774	22	22	44	26	42	0	15	17	4	128	1.0	0.6	3.0
89-90–Milwaukee	61	10	635	88	206	.427	5	20	.250	38	56	.679	39	33	72	41	79	0	32	51	4	219	1.2	0.7	3.6
90-91–Lakers-Utah	30	0	294	30	80	.375	3	12	.250	20	23	.870	24	19	43	16	47	0	4	16	0	83	1.4	0.5	2.8
91-92–LAClips-Seattle	56	2	654	102	249	.410	19	63	.302	48	66	.727	32	52	84	48	82	0	30	35	5	271	1.5	0.9	4.8
Reg. Season Totals	359	105	6005	860	1969	.437	36	139	.259	407	566	.719	352	414	766	563	751	15	234	392	40	2163	2.1	1.6	6.0
Playoff Totals	17	0	133	11	28	.393	3	8	.375	7	11	.636	4	8	12	9	17	1	4	2	0	32	0.7	0.5	1.9

Brown, Clarence (Chucky, Wild Thing) b. February 29, 1968 Ht. 6-8 Wt. 215 College: North Carolina State

SEASON–TEAM	G	GS	MIN	FGM	FGA	PCT	3FGM	3FGA	PCT	FTM	FTA	PCT	O-RB	D-RB	TOT	AST	PF	DQ	STL	TO	BLK	PTS	RPG	APG	PPG
89-90–Cleveland	75	35	1339	210	447	.470	0	7	.000	125	164	.762	83	148	231	50	148	0	33	69	26	545	3.1	0.7	7.3
90-91–Cleveland	74	51	1485	263	502	.524	0	4	.000	101	144	.701	78	135	213	80	130	0	26	94	24	627	2.9	1.1	8.5
91-92–Clev.-Lakers	42	2	431	60	128	.469	0	3	.000	30	49	.612	31	51	82	26	48	0	12	29	7	150	2.0	0.6	3.6
92-93–New Jersey	77	20	1186	160	331	.483	0	5	.000	71	98	.724	88	144	232	51	112	0	20	56	24	391	3.0	0.7	5.1
93-94–Dallas	1	0	10	1	1	1.000	0	0	–	1	1	1.000	0	1	1	0	2	0	0	0	0	3	1.0	0.0	3.0
94-95–Houston	41	14	814	105	174	.603	1	3	.333	38	62	.613	64	125	189	30	105	0	11	29	14	249	4.6	0.7	6.1
95-96–Houston	82	82	2019	300	555	.541	1	8	.125	104	150	.693	134	307	441	89	163	0	47	94	38	705	5.4	1.1	8.6
96-97–Phoenix-Milw.	70	1	757	78	154	.506	1	6	.167	47	70	.671	41	107	148	28	100	1	9	19	22	204	2.1	0.4	2.9
97-98–Atlanta	77	8	1202	161	372	.433	2	8	.250	63	87	.724	57	126	183	55	100	0	23	51	13	387	2.4	0.7	5.0
98-99–Charlotte	48	21	1192	176	373	.472	15	40	.375	40	59	.678	36	138	174	57	106	0	16	38	19	407	3.6	1.2	8.5
99-00–S.A.-Cha.	63	29	1096	148	328	.451	2	10	.200	36	52	.692	35	132	167	66	114	1	20	45	18	334	2.7	1.0	5.3
Reg. Season Totals	650	263	11531	1662	3365	.494	22	94	.234	656	936	.701	647	1414	2061	532	1128	2	217	524	205	4002	3.2	0.8	6.2
Playoff Totals	40	9	650	83	177	.469	2	5	.400	50	70	.714	33	82	115	19	73	2	15	21	7	218	2.9	0.5	5.5

Brown, Collier Jr. (P.J.) b. October 14, 1969 Ht. 6-11 Wt. 240 College: Louisiana Tech

SEASON–TEAM	G	GS	MIN	FGM	FGA	PCT	3FGM	3FGA	PCT	FTM	FTA	PCT	O-RB	D-RB	TOT	AST	PF	DQ	STL	TO	BLK	PTS	RPG	APG	PPG
93-94–New Jersey	79	54	1950	167	402	.415	1	6	.167	115	152	.757	188	305	493	93	177	1	71	72	93	450	6.2	1.2	5.7
94-95–New Jersey	80	63	2466	254	570	.446	4	24	.167	139	207	.671	178	309	487	135	262	8	69	80	135	651	6.1	1.7	8.1
95-96–New Jersey	81	81	2942	354	798	.444	3	15	.200	204	265	.770	215	345	560	165	249	5	79	133	100	915	6.9	2.0	11.3
96-97–Miami	80	71	2592	300	656	.457	0	2	.000	161	220	.732	239	431	670	92	283	7	85	113	98	761	8.4	1.2	9.5
97-98–Miami	74	74	2362	278	590	.471	0	0	–	151	197	.766	235	400	635	103	264	9	66	97	98	707	8.6	1.4	9.6
98-99–Miami	50	50	1611	229	477	.480	0	0	–	113	146	.774	115	231	346	66	166	2	46	69	48	571	6.9	1.3	11.4
99-00–Miami	80	80	2302	322	671	.480	0	1	.000	120	159	.755	216	384	600	145	264	4	65	100	61	764	7.5	1.8	9.6
Reg. Season Totals	524	473	16225	1904	4164	.457	8	48	.167	1003	1346	.745	1386	2405	3791	799	1665	36	481	664	633	4819	7.2	1.5	9.2
Playoff Totals	39	36	1149	119	276	.431	0	1	.000	68	99	.687	107	187	294	33	134	4	26	39	31	306	7.5	0.8	7.8

Brown, Darrell H. b. March 14, 1923 Ht. 6-2 Wt. 175 College: Humboldt State; U. of Pacific

SEASON–TEAM	G	GS	MIN	FGM	FGA	PCT	3FGM	3FGA	PCT	FTM	FTA	PCT	O-RB	D-RB	TOT	AST	PF	DQ	STL	TO	BLK	PTS	RPG	APG	PPG
48-49–Baltimore	3	–	–	2	6	.333	–	–	–	0	2	.000	–	–	–	0	3	–	–	–	–	4	–	0.0	1.3
Reg. Season Totals	3	–	–	2	6	.333	–	–	–	0	2	.000	–	–	–	0	3	–	–	–	–	4	–	0.0	1.3

Brown, DeCovan Kadell (Dee, Dee-lightful) b. November 29, 1968 Ht. 6-2 Wt. 205 College: Jacksonville

SEASON–TEAM	G	GS	MIN	FGM	FGA	PCT	3FGM	3FGA	PCT	FTM	FTA	PCT	O-RB	D-RB	TOT	AST	PF	DQ	STL	TO	BLK	PTS	RPG	APG	PPG
90-91–Boston	82	5	1945	284	612	.464	7	34	.206	137	157	.873	41	141	182	344	161	0	83	137	14	712	2.2	4.2	8.7
91-92–Boston	31	20	883	149	350	.426	5	22	.227	60	78	.769	15	64	79	164	74	0	33	59	7	363	2.5	5.3	11.7
92-93–Boston	80	48	2254	328	701	.468	26	82	.317	192	242	.793	45	201	246	461	203	2	138	136	32	874	3.1	5.8	10.9
93-94–Boston	77	76	2867	490	1021	.480	30	96	.313	182	219	.831	63	237	300	347	207	3	156	126	47	1192	3.9	4.5	15.5
94-95–Boston	79	69	2792	437	977	.447	126	327	.385	236	277	.852	63	186	249	301	181	0	110	146	49	1236	3.2	3.8	15.6
95-96–Boston	65	23	1591	246	616	.399	68	220	.309	135	158	.854	36	100	136	146	119	0	80	74	12	695	2.1	2.2	10.7
96-97–Boston	21	2	522	61	166	.367	20	65	.308	18	22	.818	8	40	48	67	45	0	31	24	7	160	2.3	3.2	7.6
97-98–Boston-Toronto	72	12	1719	246	562	.438	108	271	.399	58	71	.817	24	128	152	154	123	1	82	73	23	658	2.1	2.1	9.1
98-99–Toronto	49	0	1377	187	495	.378	135	349	.387	40	55	.727	15	88	103	143	75	0	56	80	8	549	2.1	2.9	11.2
99-00–Toronto	38	12	673	93	258	.360	67	187	.358	11	16	.688	9	45	54	86	62	1	24	39	5	264	1.4	2.3	6.9
Reg. Season Totals	594	267	16623	2521	5758	.438	592	1653	.358	1069	1295	.825	319	1230	1549	2213	1250	7	793	894	204	6703	2.6	3.7	11.3
Playoff Totals	28	7	728	116	259	.448	10	44	.227	60	70	.857	20	65	85	108	76	3	21	43	15	302	3.0	3.9	10.8

Brown, Fred (Downtown) b. August 7, 1948 Ht. 6-3 Wt. 185 College: Southeastern (Iowa) C.C.; Iowa

SEASON–TEAM	G	GS	MIN	FGM	FGA	PCT	3FGM	3FGA	PCT	FTM	FTA	PCT	O-RB	D-RB	TOT	AST	PF	DQ	STL	TO	BLK	PTS	RPG	APG	PPG
71-72–Seattle	33	–	359	59	180	.328	–	–	–	22	29	.759	–	–	37	60	44	0	–	–	–	140	1.1	1.8	4.2
72-73–Seattle	79	–	2320	471	1035	.455	–	–	–	121	148	.818	–	–	318	438	226	5	–	–	–	1063	4.0	5.5	13.5
73-74–Seattle	82	–	2501	578	1226	.471	–	–	–	195	226	.863	114	287	401	414	276	6	136	–	18	1351	4.9	5.0	16.5
74-75–Seattle	81	–	2669	737	1537	.480	–	–	–	226	272	.831	113	230	343	284	227	2	187	–	14	1700	4.2	3.5	21.0
75-76–Seattle	76	–	2516	742	1522	.488	–	–	–	273	314	.869	111	206	317	207	186	0	143	–	18	1757	4.2	2.7	23.1
76-77–Seattle	72	–	2098	534	1114	.479	–	–	–	168	190	.884	68	164	232	176	140	1	124	–	19	1236	3.2	2.4	17.2
77-78–Seattle	72	–	1965	508	1042	.488	–	–	–	176	196	.898	61	127	188	240	145	0	110	164	25	1192	2.6	3.3	16.6
78-79–Seattle	77	–	1961	446	951	.469	–	–	–	183	206	.888	38	134	172	260	142	0	119	164	23	1075	2.2	3.4	14.0
79-80–Seattle	80	–	1701	404	843	.479	39	88	.443	113	135	.837	35	120	155	174	117	0	65	105	17	960	1.9	2.2	12.0
80-81–Seattle	78	–	1986	505	1035	.488	23	64	.359	173	208	.832	53	122	175	233	141	0	88	131	13	1206	2.2	3.0	15.5
81-82–Seattle	82	2	1785	393	863	.455	25	77	.325	111	129	.860	42	98	140	238	111	0	69	96	4	922	1.7	2.9	11.2
82-83–Seattle	80	1	1432	371	714	.520	14	32	.438	58	72	.806	32	65	97	242	98	0	59	110	13	814	1.2	3.0	10.2
83-84–Seattle	71	1	1129	258	506	.510	9	34	.265	77	86	.895	14	48	62	194	84	0	49	70	2	602	0.9	2.7	8.5
Reg. Season Totals	963	4	24422	6006	12568	.478	110	295	.373	1896	2211	.858	681	1601	2637	3160	1937	14	1149	840	166	14018	2.7	3.3	14.6
Playoff Totals	83	0	1900	499	1082	.461	13	42	.310	186	227	.819	72	124	196	193	144	0	74	82	8	1197	2.4	2.3	14.4
All-Star Totals	1	0	24	7	13	.538	0	0	–	0	0	–	0	0	0	1	3	0	5	–	0	14	0.0	1.0	14.0

Brown, George Raff b. October 30, 1935 Ht. 6-6 Wt. 190 College: Wayne State (Mich.)

SEASON–TEAM	G	GS	MIN	FGM	FGA	PCT	3FGM	3FGA	PCT	FTM	FTA	PCT	O-RB	D-RB	TOT	AST	PF	DQ	STL	TO	BLK	PTS	RPG	APG	PPG
57-58–Minneapolis	1	–	6	0	2	.000	–	–	–	1	2	.500	–	–	1	0	1	0	–	–	–	1	1.0	0.0	1.0
Reg. Season Totals	1	–	6	0	2	.000	–	–	–	1	2	.500	–	–	1	0	1	0	–	–	–	1	1.0	0.0	1.0

Brown, Gerald b. July 28, 1975 Ht. 6-4 Wt. 210 College: Pepperdine

SEASON–TEAM	G	GS	MIN	FGM	FGA	PCT	3FGM	3FGA	PCT	FTM	FTA	PCT	O-RB	D-RB	TOT	AST	PF	DQ	STL	TO	BLK	PTS	RPG	APG	PPG
98-99–Phoenix	33	0	236	33	89	.371	3	10	.300	11	14	.786	5	17	22	31	21	0	5	22	1	80	0.7	0.9	2.4
Reg. Season Totals	33	0	236	33	89	.371	3	10	.300	11	14	.786	5	17	22	31	21	0	5	22	1	80	0.7	0.9	2.4
Playoff Totals	1	0	1	1	1	1.000	0	0	–	0	0	–	0	0	0	–	0	0	0	0	0	2	0.0	0.0	2.0

Brown, Harold V. (Brownie) b. October 2, 1923 d. September 1980 Ht. 6-0 Wt. 155 College: Evansville

SEASON–TEAM	G	GS	MIN	FGM	FGA	PCT	3FGM	3FGA	PCT	FTM	FTA	PCT	O-RB	D-RB	TOT	AST	PF	DQ	STL	TO	BLK	PTS	RPG	APG	PPG
46-47–Detroit	54	–	–	95	383	.248	–	–	–	74	117	.632	–	–	–	39	122	–	–	–	–	264	–	0.7	4.9
Reg. Season Totals	54	–	–	95	383	.248	–	–	–	74	117	.632	–	–	–	39	122	–	–	–	–	264	–	0.7	4.9

Brown, John Young b. December 14, 1951 Ht. 6-7 Wt. 220 College: Missouri

SEASON–TEAM	G	GS	MIN	FGM	FGA	PCT	3FGM	3FGA	PCT	FTM	FTA	PCT	O-RB	D-RB	TOT	AST	PF	DQ	STL	TO	BLK	PTS	RPG	APG	PPG
73-74–Atlanta	77	–	1715	277	632	.438	–	–	–	163	217	.751	177	264	441	114	239	10	29	–	16	717	5.7	1.5	9.3
74-75–Atlanta	73	–	1986	315	684	.461	–	–	–	185	250	.740	180	254	434	133	228	7	54	–	15	815	5.9	1.8	11.2
75-76–Atlanta	75	–	1758	215	486	.442	–	–	–	162	209	.775	146	257	403	126	235	7	45	–	16	592	5.4	1.7	7.9
76-77–Atlanta	77	–	1405	160	350	.457	–	–	–	121	150	.807	75	161	236	103	217	7	46	–	7	441	3.1	1.3	5.7
77-78–Atlanta	75	–	1594	192	405	.474	–	–	–	165	200	.825	137	166	303	105	280	18	55	116	8	549	4.0	1.4	7.3
78-79–Chicago	77	–	1265	152	317	.479	–	–	–	84	98	.857	83	155	238	104	180	5	18	89	10	388	3.1	1.4	5.0
79-80–Utah-Atlanta	32	–	385	37	105	.352	0	0	–	38	48	.792	26	45	71	18	70	0	3	29	4	112	2.2	0.6	3.5
Reg. Season Totals	486	–	10108	1348	2979	.453	0	0	–	918	1172	.783	824	1302	2126	703	1449	54	250	234	76	3614	4.4	1.4	7.4
Playoff Totals	7	–	64	4	13	.308	0	1	.000	2	2	1.000	2	8	10	1	10	0	1	7	1	10	1.4	0.1	1.4

Brown, Julian Myron (Myron) b. November 3, 1969 Ht. 6-3 Wt. 180 College: Slippery Rock

SEASON–TEAM	G	GS	MIN	FGM	FGA	PCT	3FGM	3FGA	PCT	FTM	FTA	PCT	O-RB	D-RB	TOT	AST	PF	DQ	STL	TO	BLK	PTS	RPG	APG	PPG
91-92–Minnesota	4	0	23	4	6	.667	1	3	.333	0	0	–	0	3	3	6	2	0	1	4	0	9	0.8	1.5	2.3
Reg. Season Totals	4	0	23	4	6	.667	1	3	.333	0	0	–	0	3	3	6	2	0	1	4	0	9	0.8	1.5	2.3

Brown, Lawrence Harvey (Larry) b. September 14, 1940 Ht. 5-9 Wt. 160 College: North Carolina

SEASON–TEAM	G	GS	MIN	FGM	FGA	PCT	3FGM	3FGA	PCT	FTM	FTA	PCT	O-RB	D-RB	TOT	AST	PF	DQ	STL	TO	BLK	PTS	RPG	APG	PPG
67-68–New Orleans (A)	78	–	2807	330	901	.366	19	89	.213	366	450	.813	–	–	249	506	220	1	–	355	–	1045	3.2	6.5	13.4
68-69–Oakland (A)	77	–	2381	308	706	.436	8	35	.229	301	379	.794	–	–	235	544	230	6	–	331	–	925	3.1	7.1	12.0
69-70–Wash. (A)	82	–	2766	376	854	.440	10	39	.256	362	439	.825	–	–	246	580	257	4	–	–	–	1124	3.0	7.1	13.7
70-71–Vir.-Denver (A)	63	–	1343	127	340	.374	6	21	.286	186	225	.827	–	–	109	330	145	–	–	–	–	446	1.7	5.2	7.1
71-72–Denver (A)	76	–	2012	243	556	.437	5	25	.200	198	244	.811	–	–	166	549	207	–	–	217	–	689	2.2	7.2	9.1
Reg. ABA Totals	376	–	11309	1384	3357	.412	48	209	.230	1413	1737	.813	–	–	1005	2509	1059	11	–	903	–	4229	2.7	6.7	11.2
ABA Playoff Totals	47	–	1710	218	508	.429	5	29	.172	229	270	.848	–	–	156	320	158	1	–	91	–	670	3.3	6.8	14.3

Brown, Leon (Stretch) b. October 12, 1919 Ht. 6-3 Wt. 190 College: Wyoming

SEASON–TEAM	G	GS	MIN	FGM	FGA	PCT	3FGM	3FGA	PCT	FTM	FTA	PCT	O-RB	D-RB	TOT	AST	PF	DQ	STL	TO	BLK	PTS	RPG	APG	PPG
46-47–Cleveland	5	–	–	0	3	.000	–	–	–	0	0	–	–	–	–	0	2	–	–	–	–	0	–	0.0	0.0
Reg. Season Totals	5	–	–	0	3	.000	–	–	–	0	0	–	–	–	–	0	2	–	–	–	–	0	–	0.0	0.0

Brown, Lewis b. February 19, 1955 Ht. 6-11 Wt. 230 College: Nevada-Las Vegas

SEASON–TEAM	G	GS	MIN	FGM	FGA	PCT	3FGM	3FGA	PCT	FTM	FTA	PCT	O-RB	D-RB	TOT	AST	PF	DQ	STL	TO	BLK	PTS	RPG	APG	PPG
80-81–Washington	2	–	5	0	3	.000	0	0	–	2	5	.400	1	1	2	0	2	0	0	1	0	2	1.0	0.0	1.0
Reg. Season Totals	2	–	5	0	3	.000	0	0	–	2	5	.400	1	1	2	0	2	0	0	1	0	2	1.0	0.0	1.0

Brown, Marcus James b. April 3, 1974 Ht. 6-3 Wt. 185 College: Murray State

SEASON–TEAM	G	GS	MIN	FGM	FGA	PCT	3FGM	3FGA	PCT	FTM	FTA	PCT	O-RB	D-RB	TOT	AST	PF	DQ	STL	TO	BLK	PTS	RPG	APG	PPG
96-97–Portland	21	0	184	28	70	.400	13	32	.406	13	19	.684	4	11	15	20	26	0	8	13	2	82	0.7	1.0	3.9
99-00–Detroit	6	0	45	4	14	.286	0	7	.000	2	2	1.000	3	4	7	3	8	0	0	3	0	10	1.2	0.5	1.7
Reg. Season Totals	27	0	229	32	84	.381	13	39	.333	15	21	.714	7	15	22	23	34	0	8	16	2	92	0.8	0.9	3.4

Brown, Michael (Mike) b. July 19, 1963 Ht. 6-10 Wt. 260 College: George Washington

SEASON–TEAM	G	GS	MIN	FGM	FGA	PCT	3FGM	3FGA	PCT	FTM	FTA	PCT	O-RB	D-RB	TOT	AST	PF	DQ	STL	TO	BLK	PTS	RPG	APG	PPG
86-87–Chicago	62	3	818	106	201	.527	0	0	–	46	72	.639	71	143	214	24	129	2	20	59	7	258	3.5	0.4	4.2
87-88–Chicago	46	27	591	78	174	.448	0	1	.000	41	71	.577	66	93	159	28	85	0	11	38	4	197	3.5	0.6	4.3
88-89–Utah	66	16	1051	104	248	.419	0	0	–	92	130	.708	92	166	258	41	133	0	25	77	17	300	3.9	0.6	4.5
89-90–Utah	82	0	1397	177	344	.515	1	2	.500	157	199	.789	111	262	373	47	187	0	32	88	28	512	4.5	0.6	6.2
90-91–Utah	82	2	1391	129	284	.454	0	0	–	132	178	.742	109	228	337	49	166	0	29	82	24	390	4.1	0.6	4.8
91-92–Utah	82	1	1783	221	488	.453	0	1	.000	190	285	.667	187	289	476	81	196	1	42	105	34	632	5.8	1.0	7.7
92-93–Utah	82	21	1551	176	409	.430	0	1	.000	113	164	.689	147	244	391	64	190	1	32	95	23	465	4.8	0.8	5.7
93-94–Minnesota	82	40	1921	111	260	.427	0	2	.000	77	118	.653	119	328	447	72	218	4	51	75	29	299	5.5	0.9	3.6
94-95–Minnesota	27	0	213	10	40	.250	0	1	.000	15	27	.556	9	36	45	10	35	0	7	16	0	35	1.7	0.4	1.3
95-96–Philadelphia	9	1	162	9	16	.563	0	0	–	8	17	.471	14	23	37	3	24	1	3	6	2	26	4.1	0.3	2.9
96-97–Phoenix	6	1	83	5	12	.417	0	0	–	6	10	.600	9	16	25	5	9	0	1	2	1	16	4.2	0.8	2.7
Reg. Season Totals	626	112	10961	1126	2476	.455	1	8	.125	877	1271	.690	934	1828	2762	424	1372	9	253	643	169	3130	4.4	0.7	5.0
Playoff Totals	44	1	703	79	179	.441	0	0	–	83	105	.790	53	110	163	23	109	1	8	40	5	241	3.7	0.5	5.5

Brown, Randy
b. May 22, 1968 Ht. 6-2 Wt. 191 College: Houston; Howard (Texas) Coll.; New Mexico State

SEASON–TEAM	G	GS	MIN	FGM	FGA	PCT	3FGM	3FGA	PCT	FTM	FTA	PCT	O-RB	D-RB	TOT	AST	PF	DQ	STL	TO	BLK	PTS	RPG	APG	PPG
91-92–Sacramento	56	0	535	77	169	.456	0	6	.000	38	58	.655	26	43	69	59	68	0	35	42	12	192	1.2	1.1	3.4
92-93–Sacramento	75	34	1726	225	486	.463	2	6	.333	115	157	.732	75	137	212	196	206	4	108	120	34	567	2.8	2.6	7.6
93-94–Sacramento	61	2	1041	110	251	.438	0	4	.000	53	87	.609	40	72	112	133	132	2	63	75	14	273	1.8	2.2	4.5
94-95–Sacramento	67	2	1086	124	287	.432	14	47	.298	55	82	.671	24	84	108	133	153	0	99	78	19	317	1.6	2.0	4.7
95-96–Chicago	68	0	671	78	192	.406	1	11	.091	28	46	.609	17	49	66	73	88	0	57	31	12	185	1.0	1.1	2.7
96-97–Chicago	72	3	1057	140	333	.420	4	22	.182	57	84	.679	34	77	111	133	116	0	81	58	17	341	1.5	1.8	4.7
97-98–Chicago	71	6	1147	116	302	.384	0	5	.000	56	78	.718	34	60	94	151	118	0	71	63	12	288	1.3	2.1	4.1
98-99–Chicago	39	32	1139	132	319	.414	0	10	.000	78	103	.757	27	105	132	149	93	1	68	80	8	342	3.4	3.8	8.8
99-00–Chicago	59	55	1625	157	435	.361	3	6	.500	62	84	.738	23	121	144	202	120	1	61	105	15	379	2.4	3.4	6.4
Reg. Season Totals	568	134	10027	1159	2774	.418	24	117	.205	542	779	.696	300	748	1048	1229	1094	8	643	652	143	2884	1.8	2.2	5.1
Playoff Totals	47	0	281	27	70	.386	3	6	.500	17	23	.739	9	20	29	22	46	0	15	18	3	74	0.6	0.5	1.6

Brown, Raymond
b. July 5, 1965 Ht. 6-8 Wt. 220 College: Mississippi State; Idaho

SEASON–TEAM	G	GS	MIN	FGM	FGA	PCT	3FGM	3FGA	PCT	FTM	FTA	PCT	O-RB	D-RB	TOT	AST	PF	DQ	STL	TO	BLK	PTS	RPG	APG	PPG
89-90–Utah	16	0	56	8	28	.286	0	0	–	0	2	.000	10	5	15	4	11	0	0	6	0	16	0.9	0.3	1.0
Reg. Season Totals	16	0	56	8	28	.286	0	0	–	0	2	.000	10	5	15	4	11	0	0	6	0	16	0.9	0.3	1.0
Playoff Totals	3	0	6	0	0	–	0	0	–	0	0	–	0	0	0	–	2	0	0	0	0	0	0.0	0.0	0.0

Brown, Rickey Darnell
b. August 20, 1958 Ht. 6-10 Wt. 220 College: Mississippi State

SEASON–TEAM	G	GS	MIN	FGM	FGA	PCT	3FGM	3FGA	PCT	FTM	FTA	PCT	O-RB	D-RB	TOT	AST	PF	DQ	STL	TO	BLK	PTS	RPG	APG	PPG
80-81–Golden State	45	–	580	83	162	.512	0	0	–	16	21	.762	52	114	166	21	103	4	9	31	14	182	3.7	0.5	4.0
81-82–Golden State	82	11	1260	192	418	.459	0	0	–	86	122	.705	136	228	364	19	243	4	36	84	29	470	4.4	0.2	5.7
82-83–G.S.-Atlanta	76	7	1048	167	349	.479	0	3	.000	65	105	.619	91	175	266	25	172	1	13	82	26	399	3.5	0.3	5.3
83-84–Atlanta	68	3	785	94	201	.468	0	0	–	48	65	.738	67	114	181	29	161	4	18	53	23	236	2.7	0.4	3.5
84-85–Atlanta	69	5	814	78	192	.406	0	0	–	39	68	.574	76	147	223	25	117	0	19	51	22	195	3.2	0.4	2.8
Reg. Season Totals	340	26	4487	614	1322	.464	0	3	.000	254	381	.667	422	778	1200	119	796	13	95	301	114	1482	3.5	0.4	4.4
Playoff Totals	7	0	98	11	24	.458	0	0	–	11	14	.786	5	17	22	2	22	0	0	5	1	33	3.1	0.3	4.7

Brown, Robert Edward (Bob)
b. November 12, 1923 Ht. 6-4 Wt. 205 College: Miami (Ohio)

SEASON–TEAM	G	GS	MIN	FGM	FGA	PCT	3FGM	3FGA	PCT	FTM	FTA	PCT	O-RB	D-RB	TOT	AST	PF	DQ	STL	TO	BLK	PTS	RPG	APG	PPG
48-49–Providence	20	–	–	37	111	.333	–	–	–	34	47	.723	–	–	–	14	67	–	–	–	–	108	–	0.7	5.4
49-50–Denver	62	–	–	276	764	.361	–	–	–	172	252	.683	–	–	–	101	269	–	–	–	–	724	–	1.6	11.7
Reg. Season Totals	82	–	–	313	875	.358	–	–	–	206	299	.689	–	–	–	115	336	–	–	–	–	832	–	1.4	10.1

Brown, Roger A.
b. May 22, 1942 d. March 4, 1997 Ht. 6-5 Wt. 205 College: Dayton

SEASON–TEAM	G	GS	MIN	FGM	FGA	PCT	3FGM	3FGA	PCT	FTM	FTA	PCT	O-RB	D-RB	TOT	AST	PF	DQ	STL	TO	BLK	PTS	RPG	APG	PPG
67-68–Indiana (A)	76	–	2974	544	1286	.423	14	54	.259	390	517	.754	–	–	647	327	296	10	–	265	–	1492	8.5	4.3	19.6
68-69–Indiana (A)	75	–	2658	563	1169	.482	5	16	.313	442	563	.785	–	–	510	345	281	11	–	215	–	1573	6.8	4.6	21.0
69-70–Indiana (A)	84	–	3495	719	1444	.498	40	120	.333	457	562	.813	–	–	620	392	308	3	–	–	–	1935	7.4	4.7	23.0
70-71–Indiana (A)	82	–	3364	610	1266	.482	63	223	.283	407	512	.795	–	–	569	395	289	–	–	–	–	1690	6.9	4.8	20.6
71-72–Indiana (A)	78	–	2987	532	1112	.478	57	185	.308	323	401	.805	–	–	502	306	227	–	–	214	–	1444	6.4	3.9	18.5
72-73–Indiana (A)	72	–	2177	332	700	.474	42	118	.356	203	247	.822	111	237	348	204	181	0	–	120	–	909	4.8	2.8	12.6
73-74–Indiana (A)	82	–	2527	379	829	.457	56	155	.361	155	200	.775	112	278	390	232	248	–	56	125	60	969	4.8	2.8	11.8
74-75–Mem.-Utah-Ind. (A)	56	–	1272	181	421	.430	35	100	.350	89	114	.781	56	116	172	114	99	–	47	94	21	486	3.1	2.0	8.7
Reg. ABA Totals	605	–	21454	3860	8227	.469	312	971	.321	2466	3116	.791	279	631	3758	2315	1929	24	103	1033	81	10498	6.2	3.8	17.4
ABA Playoff Totals	110	–	4030	765	1590	.481	68	190	.358	462	583	.792	72	180	705	405	391	8	13	88	35	2060	6.4	3.7	18.7

Brown, Stanley (Stan)
b. June 27, 1929 Ht. 6-3 Wt. 200 College: None

SEASON–TEAM	G	GS	MIN	FGM	FGA	PCT	3FGM	3FGA	PCT	FTM	FTA	PCT	O-RB	D-RB	TOT	AST	PF	DQ	STL	TO	BLK	PTS	RPG	APG	PPG
47-48–Philadelphia	19	–	–	19	71	.268	–	–	–	12	19	.632	–	–	–	1	16	–	–	–	–	50	–	0.1	2.6
51-52–Philadelphia	15	–	141	22	63	.349	–	–	–	10	18	.556	–	–	17	9	32	0	–	–	–	54	1.1	0.6	3.6
Reg. Season Totals	34	–	141	41	134	.306	–	–	–	22	37	.595	–	–	17	10	48	0	–	–	–	104	1.1	0.3	3.1

Brown, W. Roger (Roger)
b. February 23, 1950 Ht. 6-11 Wt. 230 College: Kansas

SEASON–TEAM	G	GS	MIN	FGM	FGA	PCT	3FGM	3FGA	PCT	FTM	FTA	PCT	O-RB	D-RB	TOT	AST	PF	DQ	STL	TO	BLK	PTS	RPG	APG	PPG
72-73–Los Angeles	1	–	5	0	0	–	–	–	–	1	3	.333	–	–	0	0	1	0	–	–	–	1	0.0	0.0	1.0
72-73–Carolina (A)	62	–	579	59	129	.457	0	0	–	28	51	.549	62	116	178	25	120	2	–	46	–	146	2.9	0.4	2.4
73-74–S.A.-Vir. (A)	63	–	990	98	260	.377	0	0	–	34	56	.607	145	207	352	46	129	–	23	80	62	230	5.6	0.7	3.7
75-76–Detroit	29	–	454	29	72	.403	–	–	–	14	18	.778	47	83	130	12	76	1	6	–	25	72	4.5	0.4	2.5
75-76–Denver (A)	37	–	291	28	61	.459	2	2	1.000	16	24	.667	25	50	75	22	63	–	8	17	22	74	2.0	0.6	2.0
76-77–Detroit	43	–	322	21	56	.375	–	–	–	18	26	.692	31	59	90	12	68	4	15	–	18	60	2.1	0.3	1.4
79-80–Chicago	4	–	37	1	3	.333	0	0	–	0	0	–	2	8	10	1	4	0	0	0	3	2	2.5	0.3	0.5
Reg. NBA Totals	77	–	818	51	131	.389	0	0	–	33	47	.702	80	150	230	25	149	5	21	0	46	135	3.0	0.3	1.8
Reg. ABA Totals	162	–	1860	185	450	.411	2	2	1.000	78	131	.595	232	373	605	93	312	2	31	143	84	450	3.7	0.6	2.8
NBA Playoff Totals	11	–	56	4	10	.400	0	0	–	2	4	.500	7	7	14	2	10	0	0	–	2	10	1.3	0.2	0.9
ABA Playoff Totals	12	–	90	14	26	.538	0	0	–	3	4	.750	8	6	25	3	12	0	0	4	2	31	2.1	0.3	2.6

Browne, James (Jim) b. January 1, 1930 Ht. 6-10 Wt. 235 College: None

SEASON–TEAM	G	GS	MIN	FGM	FGA	PCT	3FGM	3FGA	PCT	FTM	FTA	PCT	O-RB	D-RB	TOT	AST	PF	DQ	STL	TO	BLK	PTS	RPG	APG	PPG
48-49–Chicago	4	–	–	1	2	.500	–	–	–	1	2	.500	–	–	–	0	4	–	–	–	–	3	–	0.0	0.8
49-50–Denver	31	–	–	17	48	.354	–	–	–	13	27	.481	–	–	–	8	16	–	–	–	–	47	–	0.3	1.5
Reg. Season Totals	35	–	–	18	50	.360	–	–	–	14	29	.483	–	–	–	8	20	–	–	–	–	50	–	0.2	1.4

Brundy, Stanley Dwayne (Stan) b. November 13, 1967 Ht. 6-6 Wt. 210 College: DePaul

SEASON–TEAM	G	GS	MIN	FGM	FGA	PCT	3FGM	3FGA	PCT	FTM	FTA	PCT	O-RB	D-RB	TOT	AST	PF	DQ	STL	TO	BLK	PTS	RPG	APG	PPG
89-90–New Jersey	16	0	128	15	30	.500	0	0	–	7	18	.389	15	11	26	3	24	0	6	6	5	37	1.6	0.2	2.3
Reg. Season Totals	16	0	128	15	30	.500	0	0	–	7	18	.389	15	11	26	3	24	0	6	6	5	37	1.6	0.2	2.3

Brunkhorst, Brian J. (Bronk) b. June 12, 1945 Ht. 6-6 Wt. 210 College: Marquette

SEASON–TEAM	G	GS	MIN	FGM	FGA	PCT	3FGM	3FGA	PCT	FTM	FTA	PCT	O-RB	D-RB	TOT	AST	PF	DQ	STL	TO	BLK	PTS	RPG	APG	PPG
68-69–Los Angeles (A)	3	–	56	6	11	.545	0	0	–	13	17	.765	–	–	13	3	8	0	–	5	–	25	4.3	1.0	8.3
Reg. ABA Totals	3	–	56	6	11	.545	0	0	–	13	17	.765	–	–	13	3	8	0	–	5	–	25	4.3	1.0	8.3

Bruns, George William b. August 30, 1946 Ht. 6-0 Wt. 160 College: Manhattan

SEASON–TEAM	G	GS	MIN	FGM	FGA	PCT	3FGM	3FGA	PCT	FTM	FTA	PCT	O-RB	D-RB	TOT	AST	PF	DQ	STL	TO	BLK	PTS	RPG	APG	PPG
72-73–New York (A)	13	–	236	31	66	.470	2	4	.500	22	27	.815	1	7	8	36	26	0	–	20	–	86	0.6	2.8	6.6
Reg. ABA Totals	13	–	236	31	66	.470	2	4	.500	22	27	.815	1	7	8	36	26	0	–	20	–	86	0.6	2.8	6.6
ABA Playoff Totals	2	–	7	0	1	.000	0	0	–	1	2	.500	–	–	–	1	3	0	–	2	–	1	0.0	0.5	0.5

Brunson, Rick Daniel b. June 14, 1972 Ht. 6-4 Wt. 190 College: Temple

SEASON–TEAM	G	GS	MIN	FGM	FGA	PCT	3FGM	3FGA	PCT	FTM	FTA	PCT	O-RB	D-RB	TOT	AST	PF	DQ	STL	TO	BLK	PTS	RPG	APG	PPG
97-98–Portland	38	10	622	49	141	.348	22	61	.361	42	62	.677	14	42	56	100	55	0	25	52	3	162	1.5	2.6	4.3
98-99–New York	17	0	95	6	21	.286	0	5	.000	5	18	.278	3	7	10	19	8	0	9	12	0	17	0.6	1.1	1.0
99-00–New York	37	0	289	29	70	.414	2	13	.154	11	18	.611	3	24	27	49	35	0	9	31	1	71	0.7	1.3	1.9
Reg. Season Totals	92	10	1006	84	232	.362	24	79	.304	58	98	.592	20	73	93	168	98	0	43	95	4	250	1.0	1.8	2.7
Playoff Totals	12	0	22	2	6	.333	0	0	–	2	2	1.000	1	0	1	3	5	0	1	4	0	6	0.1	0.3	0.5

Bryant, Emmette b. November 4, 1938 Ht. 6-1 Wt. 175 College: DePaul

SEASON–TEAM	G	GS	MIN	FGM	FGA	PCT	3FGM	3FGA	PCT	FTM	FTA	PCT	O-RB	D-RB	TOT	AST	PF	DQ	STL	TO	BLK	PTS	RPG	APG	PPG
64-65–New York	77	–	1332	145	436	.333	–	–	–	87	133	.654	–	–	167	167	212	3	–	–	–	377	2.2	2.2	4.9
65-66–New York	71	–	1193	212	449	.472	–	–	–	74	101	.733	–	–	170	216	215	4	–	–	–	498	2.4	3.0	7.0
66-67–New York	63	–	1593	236	577	.409	–	–	–	74	114	.649	–	–	273	218	231	4	–	–	–	546	4.3	3.5	8.7
67-68–New York	77	–	968	112	291	.385	–	–	–	59	86	.686	–	–	133	134	173	0	–	–	–	283	1.7	1.7	3.7
68-69–Boston	80	–	1388	197	488	.404	–	–	–	65	100	.650	–	–	192	176	264	9	–	–	–	459	2.4	2.2	5.7
69-70–Boston	71	–	1617	210	520	.404	–	–	–	135	181	.746	–	–	269	231	201	5	–	–	–	555	3.8	3.3	7.8
70-71–Buffalo	73	–	2137	288	684	.421	–	–	–	151	203	.744	–	–	262	352	266	7	–	–	–	727	3.6	4.8	10.0
71-72–Buffalo	54	–	1223	101	220	.459	–	–	–	75	125	.600	–	–	127	206	167	5	–	–	–	277	2.4	3.8	5.1
Reg. Season Totals	566	–	11451	1501	3665	.410	–	–	–	720	1043	.690	–	–	1593	1700	1729	37	–	–	–	3722	2.8	3.0	6.6
Playoff Totals	27	–	758	88	227	.388	–	–	–	55	69	.797	–	–	111	70	104	0	–	–	–	231	4.1	2.6	8.6

Bryant, Joseph Washington (Joe, Jelly Bean) b. October 19, 1954 Ht. 6-10 Wt. 200 College: La Salle

SEASON–TEAM	G	GS	MIN	FGM	FGA	PCT	3FGM	3FGA	PCT	FTM	FTA	PCT	O-RB	D-RB	TOT	AST	PF	DQ	STL	TO	BLK	PTS	RPG	APG	PPG
75-76–Philadelphia	75	–	1203	233	552	.422	–	–	–	92	147	.626	97	181	278	61	165	0	44	–	23	558	3.7	0.8	7.4
76-77–Philadelphia	61	–	612	107	240	.446	–	–	–	53	70	.757	45	72	117	48	84	1	36	–	13	267	1.9	0.8	4.4
77-78–Philadelphia	81	–	1236	190	436	.436	–	–	–	111	144	.771	103	177	280	129	185	1	56	115	24	491	3.5	1.6	6.1
78-79–Philadelphia	70	–	1064	205	478	.429	–	–	–	123	170	.724	96	163	259	103	171	1	49	114	9	533	3.7	1.5	7.6
79-80–San Diego	81	–	2328	294	682	.431	5	34	.147	161	217	.742	171	345	516	144	258	4	102	170	39	754	6.4	1.8	9.3
80-81–San Diego	82	–	2359	379	791	.479	2	15	.133	193	244	.791	146	294	440	189	264	4	72	176	34	953	5.4	2.3	11.6
81-82–San Diego	75	49	1988	341	701	.486	8	30	.267	194	247	.785	79	195	274	189	250	1	78	183	29	884	3.7	2.5	11.8
82-83–Houston	81	56	2055	344	768	.448	8	36	.222	116	165	.703	88	189	277	186	258	4	82	177	30	812	3.4	2.3	10.0
Reg. Season Totals	606	105	12845	2093	4648	.450	23	115	.200	1043	1404	.743	825	1616	2441	1049	1635	16	519	935	201	5252	4.0	1.7	8.7
Playoff Totals	30	0	274	52	116	.448	0	0	–	19	28	.679	12	42	54	21	54	1	14	7	4	123	1.8	0.7	4.1

Bryant, Kobe B. b. August 23, 1978 Ht. 6-7 Wt. 210 High School: Lower Merion (Pa.)

SEASON–TEAM	G	GS	MIN	FGM	FGA	PCT	3FGM	3FGA	PCT	FTM	FTA	PCT	O-RB	D-RB	TOT	AST	PF	DQ	STL	TO	BLK	PTS	RPG	APG	PPG
96-97–L.A. Lakers	71	6	1103	176	422	.417	51	136	.375	136	166	.819	47	85	132	91	102	0	49	112	23	539	1.9	1.3	7.6
97-98–L.A. Lakers	79	1	2056	391	913	.428	75	220	.341	363	457	.794	79	163	242	199	180	1	74	157	40	1220	3.1	2.5	15.4
98-99–L.A. Lakers	50	50	1896	362	779	.465	27	101	.267	245	292	.839	53	211	264	190	153	3	72	157	50	996	5.3	3.8	19.9
99-00–L.A. Lakers	66	62	2524	554	1183	.468	46	144	.319	331	403	.821	108	308	416	323	220	4	106	182	62	1485	6.3	4.9	22.5
Reg. Season Totals	266	119	7579	1483	3297	.450	199	601	.331	1075	1318	.816	287	767	1054	803	655	8	301	608	175	4240	4.0	3.0	15.9
Playoff Totals	50	30	1525	287	667	.430	39	124	.315	180	236	.763	47	138	185	161	164	2	53	111	52	793	3.7	3.2	15.9
All-Star Totals	2	2	50	14	32	.438	3	7	.429	2	2	1.000	3	4	7	4	4	0	4	2	0	33	3.5	2.0	16.5

Bryant, Mark Craig b. April 25, 1965 Ht. 6-9 Wt. 245 College: Seton Hall

SEASON–TEAM	G	GS	MIN	FGM	FGA	PCT	3FGM	3FGA	PCT	FTM	FTA	PCT	O-RB	D-RB	TOT	AST	PF	DQ	STL	TO	BLK	PTS	RPG	APG	PPG
88-89–Portland	56	32	803	120	247	.486	0	0	–	40	69	.580	65	114	179	33	144	3	20	41	7	280	3.2	0.6	5.0
89-90–Portland	58	0	562	70	153	.458	0	0	–	28	50	.560	54	92	146	13	93	0	18	25	9	168	2.5	0.2	2.9
90-91–Portland	53	0	781	99	203	.488	0	1	.000	74	101	.733	65	125	190	27	120	0	15	33	12	272	3.6	0.5	5.1
91-92–Portland	56	0	800	95	198	.480	0	3	.000	40	60	.667	87	114	201	41	105	0	26	30	8	230	3.6	0.7	4.1
92-93–Portland	80	24	1396	186	370	.503	0	1	.000	104	148	.703	132	192	324	41	226	1	37	65	23	476	4.1	0.5	6.0
93-94–Portland	79	10	1441	185	384	.482	0	1	.000	72	104	.692	117	198	315	37	187	0	32	66	29	442	4.0	0.5	5.6
94-95–Portland	49	0	658	101	192	.526	1	2	.500	41	63	.651	55	106	161	28	109	1	19	39	16	244	3.3	0.6	5.0
95-96–Houston	71	9	1587	242	446	.543	0	2	.000	127	177	.718	131	220	351	52	234	4	31	85	19	611	4.9	0.7	8.6
96-97–Phoenix	41	18	1018	152	275	.553	0	0	–	76	108	.704	67	145	212	47	136	4	22	46	5	380	5.2	1.1	9.3
97-98–Phoenix	70	22	1110	109	225	.484	0	1	.000	73	95	.768	92	152	244	46	180	3	36	58	15	291	3.5	0.7	4.2
98-99–Chicago	45	29	1204	168	348	.483	0	1	.000	71	110	.645	92	140	232	48	149	2	34	68	16	407	5.2	1.1	9.0
99-00–Cleveland	75	50	1712	174	346	.503	0	0	–	76	94	.809	126	226	352	61	250	5	31	87	31	424	4.7	0.8	5.7
Reg. Season Totals	733	194	13072	1701	3387	.502	1	12	.083	822	1179	.697	1083	1824	2907	474	1933	23	321	643	190	4225	4.0	0.6	5.8
Playoff Totals	65	6	840	103	219	.470	0	2	.000	49	65	.754	68	108	176	13	137	2	15	42	12	255	2.7	0.2	3.9

Bryant, Wallace Gordon Jr. b. July 14, 1959 Ht. 7-0 Wt. 245 College: San Francisco

SEASON–TEAM	G	GS	MIN	FGM	FGA	PCT	3FGM	3FGA	PCT	FTM	FTA	PCT	O-RB	D-RB	TOT	AST	PF	DQ	STL	TO	BLK	PTS	RPG	APG	PPG
83-84–Chicago	29	0	317	52	133	.391	0	0	–	14	33	.424	37	43	80	13	48	0	9	16	11	118	2.8	0.4	4.1
84-85–Dallas	56	35	860	67	148	.453	0	0	–	30	44	.682	74	167	241	84	110	1	21	46	24	164	4.3	1.5	2.9
85-86–Dallas-LAC	17	8	218	15	48	.313	0	0	–	11	19	.579	17	36	53	15	38	2	5	9	5	41	3.1	0.9	2.4
Reg. Season Totals	102	43	1395	134	329	.407	0	0	–	55	96	.573	128	246	374	112	196	3	35	71	40	323	3.7	1.1	3.2
Playoff Totals	2	1	36	0	1	.000	0	0	–	2	2	1.000	1	6	7	1	5	0	1	2	1	2	3.5	0.5	1.0

Bryn, Torgeir b. August 8, 1964 Ht. 6-9 Wt. 250 College: Mira Costa (Calif.) Coll.; Southwest Texas State

SEASON–TEAM	G	GS	MIN	FGM	FGA	PCT	3FGM	3FGA	PCT	FTM	FTA	PCT	O-RB	D-RB	TOT	AST	PF	DQ	STL	TO	BLK	PTS	RPG	APG	PPG
89-90–L.A. Clippers	3	0	10	0	2	.000	0	0	–	4	6	.667	0	2	2	0	5	0	2	1	1	4	0.7	0.0	1.3
Reg. Season Totals	3	0	10	0	2	.000	0	0	–	4	6	.667	0	2	2	0	5	0	2	1	1	4	0.7	0.0	1.3

Bucci, George P. Jr. b. July 9, 1953 Ht. 6-3 Wt. 200 College: Manhattan

SEASON–TEAM	G	GS	MIN	FGM	FGA	PCT	3FGM	3FGA	PCT	FTM	FTA	PCT	O-RB	D-RB	TOT	AST	PF	DQ	STL	TO	BLK	PTS	RPG	APG	PPG
75-76–New York (A)	33	–	237	50	124	.403	0	4	.000	28	41	.683	15	22	37	15	19	–	12	22	3	128	1.1	0.5	3.9
Reg. ABA Totals	33	–	237	50	124	.403	0	4	.000	28	41	.683	15	22	37	15	19	–	12	22	3	128	1.1	0.5	3.9
ABA Playoff Totals	2	–	9	3	7	.429	1	1	1.000	1	2	.500	0	0	–	0	2	–	0	0	0	8	0.0	0.0	4.0

Buckhalter, Joseph (Joe) b. August 1, 1937 Ht. 6-7 Wt. 210 College: Tennessee State

SEASON–TEAM	G	GS	MIN	FGM	FGA	PCT	3FGM	3FGA	PCT	FTM	FTA	PCT	O-RB	D-RB	TOT	AST	PF	DQ	STL	TO	BLK	PTS	RPG	APG	PPG
61-62–Cincinnati	63	–	728	153	334	.458	–	–	–	67	108	.620	–	–	262	43	123	1	–	–	–	373	4.2	0.7	5.9
62-63–Cincinnati	2	–	12	0	5	.000	–	–	–	2	2	1.000	–	–	3	0	1	0	–	–	–	2	1.5	0.0	1.0
Reg. Season Totals	65	–	740	153	339	.451	–	–	–	69	110	.627	–	–	265	43	124	1	–	–	–	375	4.1	0.7	5.8
Playoff Totals	4	–	60	16	38	.421	–	–	–	2	3	.667	–	–	22	4	14	0	–	–	–	34	5.5	1.0	8.5

Bucknall, Steven Lee (Steve) b. March 17, 1966 Ht. 6-6 Wt. 215 College: North Carolina

SEASON–TEAM	G	GS	MIN	FGM	FGA	PCT	3FGM	3FGA	PCT	FTM	FTA	PCT	O-RB	D-RB	TOT	AST	PF	DQ	STL	TO	BLK	PTS	RPG	APG	PPG
89-90–L.A. Lakers	18	0	75	9	33	.273	0	1	.000	5	6	.833	5	2	7	10	10	0	2	11	1	23	0.4	0.6	1.3
Reg. Season Totals	18	0	75	9	33	.273	0	1	.000	5	6	.833	5	2	7	10	10	0	2	11	1	23	0.4	0.6	1.3

Buckner, Cleveland b. August 17, 1938 Ht. 6-9 Wt. 210 College: Jackson State

SEASON–TEAM	G	GS	MIN	FGM	FGA	PCT	3FGM	3FGA	PCT	FTM	FTA	PCT	O-RB	D-RB	TOT	AST	PF	DQ	STL	TO	BLK	PTS	RPG	APG	PPG
61-62–New York	62	–	696	158	367	.431	–	–	–	83	133	.624	–	–	236	39	114	1	–	–	–	399	3.8	0.6	6.4
62-63–New York	6	–	27	5	10	.500	–	–	–	2	4	.500	–	–	4	5	6	0	–	–	–	12	0.7	0.8	2.0
Reg. Season Totals	68	–	723	163	377	.432	–	–	–	85	137	.620	–	–	240	44	120	1	–	–	–	411	3.5	0.6	6.0

Buckner, Gregory Derayle (Greg) b. September 16, 1976 Ht. 6-4 Wt. 210 College: Clemson

SEASON–TEAM	G	GS	MIN	FGM	FGA	PCT	3FGM	3FGA	PCT	FTM	FTA	PCT	O-RB	D-RB	TOT	AST	PF	DQ	STL	TO	BLK	PTS	RPG	APG	PPG
99-00–Dallas	48	1	923	111	233	.476	10	26	.385	43	63	.683	56	118	174	55	148	1	38	36	20	275	3.6	1.1	5.7
Reg. Season Totals	48	1	923	111	233	.476	10	26	.385	43	63	.683	56	118	174	55	148	1	38	36	20	275	3.6	1.1	5.7

Buckner, William Quinn (Quinn) b. August 20, 1954 Ht. 6-3 Wt. 205 College: Indiana

SEASON–TEAM	G	GS	MIN	FGM	FGA	PCT	3FGM	3FGA	PCT	FTM	FTA	PCT	O-RB	D-RB	TOT	AST	PF	DQ	STL	TO	BLK	PTS	RPG	APG	PPG
76-77–Milwaukee	79	–	2095	299	689	.434	–	–	–	83	154	.539	91	173	264	372	291	5	192	–	21	681	3.3	4.7	8.6
77-78–Milwaukee	82	–	2072	314	671	.468	–	–	–	131	203	.645	78	169	247	456	287	6	188	228	19	759	3.0	5.6	9.3
78-79–Milwaukee	81	–	1757	251	553	.454	–	–	–	79	125	.632	57	153	210	468	224	1	156	208	17	581	2.6	5.8	7.2
79-80–Milwaukee	67	–	1690	306	655	.467	2	5	.400	105	143	.734	69	169	238	383	202	1	135	149	4	719	3.6	5.7	10.7
80-81–Milwaukee	82	–	2384	471	956	.493	1	6	.167	149	203	.734	88	210	298	384	271	3	197	236	3	1092	3.6	4.7	13.3
81-82–Milwaukee	70	70	2156	396	822	.482	4	15	.267	110	168	.655	77	173	250	328	218	2	174	180	3	906	3.6	4.7	12.9
82-83–Boston	72	56	1565	248	561	.442	0	4	.000	74	117	.632	62	125	187	275	195	2	108	159	5	570	2.6	3.8	7.9
83-84–Boston	79	0	1249	138	323	.427	0	6	.000	48	74	.649	41	96	137	214	187	0	84	100	3	324	1.7	2.7	4.1
84-85–Boston	75	6	858	74	193	.383	0	1	.000	32	50	.640	26	61	87	148	142	0	63	67	2	180	1.2	2.0	2.4
85-86–Indiana	32	3	419	49	104	.471	0	1	.000	19	27	.704	9	42	51	86	80	0	40	55	3	117	1.6	2.7	3.7
Reg. Season Totals	719	135	16245	2546	5527	.461	7	38	.184	830	1264	.657	598	1371	1969	3114	2097	20	1337	1382	80	5929	2.7	4.3	8.2
Playoff Totals	68	0	1057	148	337	.439	0	4	.000	50	82	.610	29	86	115	170	170	2	64	95	1	346	1.7	2.5	5.1

Budd, David L. (Dave) b. October 28, 1938 Ht. 6-6 Wt. 210 College: Wake Forest

SEASON–TEAM	G	GS	MIN	FGM	FGA	PCT	3FGM	3FGA	PCT	FTM	FTA	PCT	O-RB	D-RB	TOT	AST	PF	DQ	STL	TO	BLK	PTS	RPG	APG	PPG
60-61–New York	61	–	1075	156	361	.432	–	–	–	87	134	.649	–	–	297	45	171	2	–	–	–	399	4.9	0.7	6.5
61-62–New York	79	–	1370	188	431	.436	–	–	–	138	231	.597	–	–	345	86	162	4	–	–	–	514	4.4	1.1	6.5
62-63–New York	78	–	1725	294	596	.493	–	–	–	151	202	.748	–	–	395	87	204	3	–	–	–	739	5.1	1.1	9.5
63-64–New York	73	–	1031	128	297	.431	–	–	–	84	115	.730	–	–	276	57	130	1	–	–	–	340	3.8	0.8	4.7
64-65–New York	62	–	1188	196	407	.482	–	–	–	121	170	.712	–	–	310	62	147	1	–	–	–	513	5.0	1.0	8.3
Reg. Season Totals	353	–	6389	962	2092	.460	–	–	–	581	852	.682	–	–	1623	337	814	11	–	–	–	2505	4.6	1.0	7.1

Budko, Walter Jr. (Walt) b. June 30, 1925 Ht. 6-5 Wt. 220 College: Columbia

SEASON–TEAM	G	GS	MIN	FGM	FGA	PCT	3FGM	3FGA	PCT	FTM	FTA	PCT	O-RB	D-RB	TOT	AST	PF	DQ	STL	TO	BLK	PTS	RPG	APG	PPG
48-49–Baltimore	60	–	–	224	644	.348	–	–	–	244	309	.790	–	–	–	99	201	–	–	–	–	692	–	1.7	11.5
49-50–Baltimore	66	–	–	198	652	.304	–	–	–	199	263	.757	–	–	–	146	259	–	–	–	–	595	–	2.2	9.0
50-51–Baltimore	64	–	–	165	464	.356	–	–	–	166	223	.744	–	–	452	135	203	7	–	–	–	496	7.1	2.1	7.8
51-52–Philadelphia	63	–	1126	97	240	.404	–	–	–	60	89	.674	–	–	232	91	196	10	–	–	–	254	3.7	1.4	4.0
Reg. Season Totals	253	–	1126	684	2000	.342	–	–	–	669	884	.757	–	–	684	471	859	17	–	–	–	2037	5.4	1.9	8.1
Playoff Totals	6	–	116	17	40	.425	–	–	–	19	26	.731	–	–	12	9	27	2	–	–	–	53	4.0	1.5	8.8

Buechler, Judson Donald (Jud) b. June 19, 1968 Ht. 6-6 Wt. 228 College: Arizona

SEASON–TEAM	G	GS	MIN	FGM	FGA	PCT	3FGM	3FGA	PCT	FTM	FTA	PCT	O-RB	D-RB	TOT	AST	PF	DQ	STL	TO	BLK	PTS	RPG	APG	PPG
90-91–New Jersey	74	10	859	94	226	.416	1	4	.250	43	66	.652	61	80	141	51	79	0	33	26	15	232	1.9	0.7	3.1
91-92–N.J.-S.A.-G.S.	28	0	290	29	71	.408	0	1	.000	12	21	.571	18	34	52	23	31	0	19	13	7	70	1.9	0.8	2.5
92-93–Golden State	70	9	1287	176	403	.437	20	59	.339	65	87	.747	81	114	195	94	98	0	47	55	19	437	2.8	1.3	6.2
93-94–Golden State	36	0	218	42	84	.500	12	29	.414	10	20	.500	13	19	32	16	24	0	8	12	1	106	0.9	0.4	2.9
94-95–Chicago	57	0	605	90	183	.492	15	48	.313	22	39	.564	36	62	98	50	64	0	24	30	12	217	1.7	0.9	3.8
95-96–Chicago	74	0	740	112	242	.463	40	90	.444	14	22	.636	45	66	111	56	70	0	34	39	7	278	1.5	0.8	3.8
96-97–Chicago	76	0	703	58	158	.367	18	54	.333	5	14	.357	45	81	126	60	50	0	23	27	21	139	1.7	0.8	1.8
97-98–Chicago	74	0	608	85	176	.483	25	65	.385	3	6	.500	24	53	77	49	47	0	22	21	15	198	1.0	0.7	2.7
98-99–Detroit	50	0	1056	100	240	.417	61	148	.412	13	18	.722	29	104	133	57	83	0	37	21	13	274	2.7	1.1	5.5
99-00–Detroit	58	5	657	55	156	.353	18	83	.217	2	7	.286	30	61	91	33	50	1	25	13	16	130	1.6	0.6	2.2
Reg. Season Totals	597	24	7023	841	1939	.434	210	581	.361	189	300	.630	382	674	1056	489	596	1	272	257	126	2081	1.8	0.8	3.5
Playoff Totals	69	0	551	49	123	.398	19	53	.358	7	13	.538	30	51	81	23	60	0	20	16	7	124	1.2	0.3	1.8

Buford, Rodney Alan b. November 2, 1977 Ht. 6-5 Wt. 189 College: Creighton

SEASON–TEAM	G	GS	MIN	FGM	FGA	PCT	3FGM	3FGA	PCT	FTM	FTA	PCT	O-RB	D-RB	TOT	AST	PF	DQ	STL	TO	BLK	PTS	RPG	APG	PPG
99-00–Miami	34	0	386	62	151	.411	7	29	.241	16	22	.727	10	38	48	21	44	0	10	9	8	147	1.4	0.6	4.3
Reg. Season Totals	34	0	386	62	151	.411	7	29	.241	16	22	.727	10	38	48	21	44	0	10	9	8	147	1.4	0.6	4.3
Playoff Totals	1	0	16	4	8	.500	1	2	.500	2	2	1.000	0	1	1	1	3	0	0	0	0	11	1.0	1.0	11.0

Bullard, Matthew Gordon (Matt) b. June 5, 1967 Ht. 6-10 Wt. 235 College: Colorado; Iowa

SEASON–TEAM	G	GS	MIN	FGM	FGA	PCT	3FGM	3FGA	PCT	FTM	FTA	PCT	O-RB	D-RB	TOT	AST	PF	DQ	STL	TO	BLK	PTS	RPG	APG	PPG
90-91–Houston	18	0	63	14	31	.452	0	3	.000	11	17	.647	6	8	14	2	10	0	3	3	0	39	0.8	0.1	2.2
91-92–Houston	80	7	1278	205	447	.459	64	166	.386	38	50	.760	73	150	223	75	129	1	26	56	21	512	2.8	0.9	6.4
92-93–Houston	79	4	1356	213	494	.431	91	243	.374	58	74	.784	66	156	222	110	129	0	30	57	11	575	2.8	1.4	7.3
93-94–Houston	65	0	725	78	226	.345	50	154	.325	20	26	.769	23	61	84	64	67	0	14	28	6	226	1.3	1.0	3.5
95-96–Atlanta	46	0	460	66	162	.407	26	72	.361	16	20	.800	18	42	60	18	50	0	17	24	11	174	1.3	0.4	3.8
96-97–Houston	71	12	1025	114	284	.401	67	183	.366	25	34	.735	13	104	117	67	68	0	21	38	18	320	1.6	0.9	4.5
97-98–Houston	67	24	1190	175	389	.450	96	231	.416	20	27	.741	25	121	146	60	104	0	31	39	24	466	2.2	0.9	7.0
98-99–Houston	41	0	413	43	114	.377	24	62	.387	7	10	.700	9	33	42	18	28	0	13	14	4	117	1.0	0.4	2.9
99-00–Houston	56	27	1024	139	340	.409	79	177	.446	25	30	.833	13	125	138	63	85	0	19	36	13	382	2.5	1.1	6.8
Reg. Season Totals	523	74	7534	1047	2487	.421	497	1291	.385	220	288	.764	246	800	1046	477	670	1	174	295	108	2811	2.0	0.9	5.4
Playoff Totals	35	4	360	38	95	.400	27	59	.458	18	22	.818	10	39	49	19	29	0	6	11	9	121	1.4	0.5	3.5

Bunce, Lawrence Melvin (Larry) b. July 29, 1945 Ht. 7-0 Wt. 245 College: Texas-El Paso; Riverside (Calif) C.C.; Utah State

SEASON–TEAM	G	GS	MIN	FGM	FGA	PCT	3FGM	3FGA	PCT	FTM	FTA	PCT	O-RB	D-RB	TOT	AST	PF	DQ	STL	TO	BLK	PTS	RPG	APG	PPG
67-68–Anaheim (A)	71	–	2266	300	716	.419	0	1	.000	256	352	.727	–	–	589	75	189	8	–	132	–	856	8.3	1.1	12.1
68-69–Den.-Dallas-Hou. (A)	58	–	804	86	203	.424	0	0	–	114	165	.691	–	–	232	19	128	3	–	60	–	286	4.0	0.3	4.9
Reg. ABA Totals	129	–	3070	386	919	.420	0	1	.000	370	517	.716	–	–	821	94	317	11	–	192	–	1142	6.4	0.7	8.9

Bunch, Darnell Greg (Greg) b. May 15, 1956 Ht. 6-6 Wt. 190 College: Cal State-Fullerton

SEASON–TEAM	G	GS	MIN	FGM	FGA	PCT	3FGM	3FGA	PCT	FTM	FTA	PCT	O-RB	D-RB	TOT	AST	PF	DQ	STL	TO	BLK	PTS	RPG	APG	PPG
78-79–New York	12	–	97	9	26	.346	–	–	–	10	12	.833	9	8	17	4	10	0	3	5	3	28	1.4	0.3	2.3
Reg. Season Totals	12	–	97	9	26	.346	–	–	–	10	12	.833	9	8	17	4	10	0	3	5	3	28	1.4	0.3	2.3

Bunt, Richard J. (Dick) b. July 13, 1930 Ht. 6-0 Wt. 170 College: New York U.

SEASON–TEAM	G	GS	MIN	FGM	FGA	PCT	3FGM	3FGA	PCT	FTM	FTA	PCT	O-RB	D-RB	TOT	AST	PF	DQ	STL	TO	BLK	PTS	RPG	APG	PPG
52-53–N.Y.-Balt.	26	–	271	29	107	.271	–	–	–	34	48	.708	–	–	28	17	40	0	–	–	–	92	1.1	0.7	3.5
Reg. Season Totals	26	–	271	29	107	.271	–	–	–	34	48	.708	–	–	28	17	40	0	–	–	–	92	1.1	0.7	3.5
Playoff Totals	1	–	1	0	0	–	–	–	–	0	0	–	–	–	0	1	0	0	–	–	–	0	0.0	1.0	0.0

Buntin, William L. (Bill) b. May 5, 1942 d. May 9, 1968 Ht. 6-7 Wt. 250 College: Michigan

SEASON–TEAM	G	GS	MIN	FGM	FGA	PCT	3FGM	3FGA	PCT	FTM	FTA	PCT	O-RB	D-RB	TOT	AST	PF	DQ	STL	TO	BLK	PTS	RPG	APG	PPG
65-66–Detroit	42	–	713	118	299	.395	–	–	–	88	143	.615	–	–	252	36	119	4	–	–	–	324	6.0	0.9	7.7
Reg. Season Totals	42	–	713	118	299	.395	–	–	–	88	143	.615	–	–	252	36	119	4	–	–	–	324	6.0	0.9	7.7

Bunting, William Carl (Bill) b. August 26, 1947 Ht. 6-8 Wt. 200 College: North Carolina

SEASON–TEAM	G	GS	MIN	FGM	FGA	PCT	3FGM	3FGA	PCT	FTM	FTA	PCT	O-RB	D-RB	TOT	AST	PF	DQ	STL	TO	BLK	PTS	RPG	APG	PPG
69-70–Carolina (A)	57	–	701	96	248	.387	0	0	–	79	106	.745	–	–	169	34	106	3	–	–	–	271	3.0	0.6	4.8
70-71–N.Y.-Vir. (A)	72	–	1123	114	245	.465	0	0	–	104	124	.839	–	–	233	58	157	–	–	–	–	332	3.2	0.8	4.6
71-72–Virginia (A)	16	–	115	4	15	.267	0	1	.000	12	17	.706	–	–	15	3	11	–	–	5	–	20	0.9	0.2	1.3
Reg. ABA Totals	145	–	1939	214	508	.421	0	1	.000	195	247	.789	–	–	417	95	274	3	–	5	–	623	2.9	0.7	4.3
ABA Playoff Totals	6	–	35	5	10	.500	0	0	–	8	12	.667	–	–	6	1	4	0	–	–	–	18	1.0	0.2	3.0

Burden, Luther D. (Ticky) b. February 28, 1953 Ht. 6-2 Wt. 190 College: Utah

SEASON–TEAM	G	GS	MIN	FGM	FGA	PCT	3FGM	3FGA	PCT	FTM	FTA	PCT	O-RB	D-RB	TOT	AST	PF	DQ	STL	TO	BLK	PTS	RPG	APG	PPG
75-76–Virginia (A)	71	–	2181	561	1247	.450	8	36	.222	283	369	.767	108	94	202	131	188	–	103	181	9	1413	2.8	1.8	19.9
76-77–N.Y. Knicks	61	–	608	148	352	.420	–	–	–	51	85	.600	26	40	66	62	88	0	47	–	1	347	1.1	1.0	5.7
77-78–New York	2	–	15	1	2	.500	–	–	–	0	0	–	0	0	0	1	1	0	1	0	0	2	0.0	0.5	1.0
Reg. NBA Totals	63	–	623	149	354	.421	–	–	–	51	85	.600	26	40	66	63	89	0	48	0	1	349	1.0	1.0	5.5
Reg. ABA Totals	71	–	2181	561	1247	.450	8	36	.222	283	369	.767	108	94	202	131	188	–	103	181	9	1413	2.8	1.8	19.9

Burkman, Roger Allen b. May 22, 1958 Ht. 6-5 Wt. 175 College: Louisville

SEASON–TEAM	G	GS	MIN	FGM	FGA	PCT	3FGM	3FGA	PCT	FTM	FTA	PCT	O-RB	D-RB	TOT	AST	PF	DQ	STL	TO	BLK	PTS	RPG	APG	PPG
81-82–Chicago	6	0	30	0	4	.000	0	1	.000	5	6	.833	2	4	6	5	6	0	6	3	2	5	1.0	0.8	0.8
Reg. Season Totals	6	0	30	0	4	.000	0	1	.000	5	6	.833	2	4	6	5	6	0	6	3	2	5	1.0	0.8	0.8

Burleson, Thomas L. (Tom) b. February 24, 1952 Ht. 7-2 Wt. 230 College: North Carolina State

SEASON–TEAM	G	GS	MIN	FGM	FGA	PCT	3FGM	3FGA	PCT	FTM	FTA	PCT	O-RB	D-RB	TOT	AST	PF	DQ	STL	TO	BLK	PTS	RPG	APG	PPG
74-75–Seattle	82	–	1888	322	772	.417	–	–	–	182	265	.687	155	417	572	115	221	1	64	–	153	826	7.0	1.4	10.1
75-76–Seattle	82	–	2647	496	1032	.481	–	–	–	291	388	.750	258	484	742	180	273	1	70	–	150	1283	9.0	2.2	15.6
76-77–Seattle	82	–	1803	288	652	.442	–	–	–	220	301	.731	184	367	551	93	259	1	74	–	117	796	6.7	1.1	9.7
77-78–Kansas City	76	–	1525	228	525	.434	–	–	–	197	248	.794	170	312	482	131	259	6	62	123	81	653	6.3	1.7	8.6
78-79–Kansas City	56	–	927	157	342	.459	–	–	–	121	169	.716	84	197	281	50	183	3	26	64	58	435	5.0	0.9	7.8
79-80–Kansas City	37	–	272	36	104	.346	0	3	.000	23	40	.575	23	49	72	20	49	0	8	25	13	95	1.9	0.5	2.6
80-81–Atlanta	31	–	363	41	99	.414	0	0	–	20	41	.488	44	50	94	12	73	2	8	24	19	102	3.0	0.4	3.3
Reg. Season Totals	446	–	9425	1568	3526	.445	0	3	.000	1054	1452	.726	918	1876	2794	601	1317	14	312	236	591	4190	6.3	1.3	9.4
Playoff Totals	15	–	572	123	227	.542	0	0	–	65	86	.756	45	108	153	23	54	1	13	–	26	311	10.2	1.5	20.7

Burmaster, John H. (Jack) b. December 23, 1926 Ht. 6-3 Wt. 190 College: Illinois

SEASON–TEAM	G	GS	MIN	FGM	FGA	PCT	3FGM	3FGA	PCT	FTM	FTA	PCT	O-RB	D-RB	TOT	AST	PF	DQ	STL	TO	BLK	PTS	RPG	APG	PPG
48-49–Oshkosh (N)	64	–	–	140	–	–	–	–	–	80	128	.625	–	–	–	–	168	–	–	–	–	360	–	–	5.6
49-50–Sheboygan	61	–	–	237	711	.333	–	–	–	124	182	.681	–	–	–	179	237	–	–	–	–	598	–	2.9	9.8
Reg. NBA Totals	61	–	–	237	711	.333	–	–	–	124	182	.681	–	–	–	179	237	–	–	–	–	598	–	2.9	9.8
Reg. NBL Totals	64	–	–	140	–	–	–	–	–	80	128	.625	–	–	–	–	168	–	–	–	–	360	–	–	5.6
NBA Playoff Totals	3	–	–	16	62	.516	–	–	–	4	4	1.000	–	–	–	16	7	–	–	–	–	36	–	2.7	12.0
NBL Playoff Totals	7	–	–	14	–	–	–	–	–	16	22	.727	–	–	–	–	21	–	–	–	–	44	–	–	6.3

Burns, David Earl b. July 3, 1958 Ht. 6-2 Wt. 180 College: Navarro (Texas) Coll.; St. Louis

SEASON–TEAM	G	GS	MIN	FGM	FGA	PCT	3FGM	3FGA	PCT	FTM	FTA	PCT	O-RB	D-RB	TOT	AST	PF	DQ	STL	TO	BLK	PTS	RPG	APG	PPG
81-82–N.J.-Denver	9	1	87	7	16	.438	0	0	–	9	15	.600	1	4	5	15	17	0	3	13	0	23	0.6	1.7	2.6
Reg. Season Totals	9	1	87	7	16	.438	0	0	–	9	15	.600	1	4	5	15	17	0	3	13	0	23	0.6	1.7	2.6

Burns, Evers Allen b. August 24, 1971 Ht. 6-8 Wt. 260 College: Maryland

SEASON–TEAM	G	GS	MIN	FGM	FGA	PCT	3FGM	3FGA	PCT	FTM	FTA	PCT	O-RB	D-RB	TOT	AST	PF	DQ	STL	TO	BLK	PTS	RPG	APG	PPG
93-94–Sacramento	23	0	143	22	55	.400	0	0	–	12	23	.522	13	17	30	9	33	0	6	7	3	56	1.3	0.4	2.4
Reg. Season Totals	23	0	143	22	55	.400	0	0	–	12	23	.522	13	17	30	9	33	0	6	7	3	56	1.3	0.4	2.4

Burns, James B. (Jim) b. September 21, 1945 Ht. 6-3 Wt. 195 College: Northwestern

SEASON–TEAM	G	GS	MIN	FGM	FGA	PCT	3FGM	3FGA	PCT	FTM	FTA	PCT	O-RB	D-RB	TOT	AST	PF	DQ	STL	TO	BLK	PTS	RPG	APG	PPG
67-68–Chicago	3	–	11	2	7	.286	–	–	–	0	0	–	–	–	2	1	1	0	–	–	–	4	0.7	0.3	1.3
67-68–Dallas (A)	33	–	392	52	137	.380	0	2	.000	51	89	.573	–	–	60	24	52	0	–	42	–	155	1.8	0.7	4.7
Reg. NBA Totals	3	–	11	2	7	.286	–	–	–	0	0	–	–	–	2	1	1	0	–	–	–	4	0.7	0.3	1.3
Reg. ABA Totals	33	–	392	52	137	.380	0	2	.000	51	89	.573	–	–	60	24	52	0	–	42	–	155	1.8	0.7	4.7

Burrell, Scott David b. January 12, 1971 Ht. 6-7 Wt. 218 College: Connecticut

SEASON–TEAM	G	GS	MIN	FGM	FGA	PCT	3FGM	3FGA	PCT	FTM	FTA	PCT	O-RB	D-RB	TOT	AST	PF	DQ	STL	TO	BLK	PTS	RPG	APG	PPG
93-94–Charlotte	51	16	767	98	234	.419	2	6	.333	46	70	.657	46	86	132	62	88	0	37	45	16	244	2.6	1.2	4.8
94-95–Charlotte	65	62	2014	277	593	.467	96	235	.409	100	144	.694	96	272	368	161	187	1	75	85	40	750	5.7	2.5	11.5
95-96–Charlotte	20	20	693	92	206	.447	37	98	.378	42	56	.750	26	72	98	47	76	2	27	43	13	263	4.9	2.4	13.2
96-97–Charlotte-G.S.	57	2	939	98	271	.362	41	116	.353	57	76	.750	49	109	158	74	120	0	28	53	19	294	2.8	1.3	5.2
97-98–Chicago	80	3	1096	159	375	.424	51	144	.354	47	64	.734	80	118	198	65	131	1	64	50	37	416	2.5	0.8	5.2
98-99–New Jersey	32	10	706	75	208	.361	28	72	.389	34	42	.810	32	87	119	45	82	2	40	23	11	212	3.7	1.4	6.6
99-00–New Jersey	74	9	1336	165	419	.394	82	232	.353	39	50	.780	65	191	256	72	173	1	67	38	44	451	3.5	1.0	6.1
Reg. Season Totals	379	122	7551	964	2306	.418	337	903	.373	365	502	.727	394	935	1329	526	857	7	338	337	180	2630	3.5	1.4	6.9
Playoff Totals	21	0	261	32	73	.438	6	20	.300	10	11	.909	11	32	43	10	33	0	19	11	3	80	2.0	0.5	3.8

Burris, Arthur C. (Art) b. April 7, 1924 Ht. 6-5 Wt. 225 College: Tennessee

SEASON–TEAM	G	GS	MIN	FGM	FGA	PCT	3FGM	3FGA	PCT	FTM	FTA	PCT	O-RB	D-RB	TOT	AST	PF	DQ	STL	TO	BLK	PTS	RPG	APG	PPG
50-51–Fort Wayne	33	–	–	28	113	.248	–	–	–	21	36	.583	–	–	106	27	51	0	–	–	–	77	3.2	0.8	2.3
51-52–FtWayne-Milw.	41	–	514	42	156	.269	–	–	–	26	39	.667	–	–	99	27	49	3	–	–	–	110	2.4	0.7	2.7
Reg. Season Totals	74	–	514	70	269	.260	–	–	–	47	75	.627	–	–	205	54	100	3	–	–	–	187	2.8	0.7	2.5

Burrough, Thomas Harold (Junior) b. January 18, 1973 Ht. 6-8 Wt. 242 College: Virginia

SEASON–TEAM	G	GS	MIN	FGM	FGA	PCT	3FGM	3FGA	PCT	FTM	FTA	PCT	O-RB	D-RB	TOT	AST	PF	DQ	STL	TO	BLK	PTS	RPG	APG	PPG
95-96–Boston	61	3	495	64	170	.376	0	0	–	61	93	.656	45	64	109	15	74	0	15	40	10	189	1.8	0.2	3.1
Reg. Season Totals	61	3	495	64	170	.376	0	0	–	61	93	.656	45	64	109	15	74	0	15	40	10	189	1.8	0.2	3.1

Burrow, Robert Brantley (Bob) b. June 29, 1934 Ht. 6-7 Wt. 230 College: Lon Morris (Texas) Coll.; Kentucky

SEASON–TEAM	G	GS	MIN	FGM	FGA	PCT	3FGM	3FGA	PCT	FTM	FTA	PCT	O-RB	D-RB	TOT	AST	PF	DQ	STL	TO	BLK	PTS	RPG	APG	PPG
56-57–Rochester	67	–	1028	137	366	.374	–	–	–	130	211	.616	–	–	293	41	165	2	–	–	–	404	4.4	0.6	6.0
57-58–Minneapolis	14	–	171	22	70	.314	–	–	–	11	33	.333	–	–	64	6	15	0	–	–	–	55	4.6	0.4	3.9
Reg. Season Totals	81	–	1199	159	436	.365	–	–	–	141	244	.578	–	–	357	47	180	2	–	–	–	459	4.4	0.6	5.7

Burton, Edward (Ed) b. August 13, 1939 Ht. 6-6 Wt. 225 College: Michigan State

SEASON–TEAM	G	GS	MIN	FGM	FGA	PCT	3FGM	3FGA	PCT	FTM	FTA	PCT	O-RB	D-RB	TOT	AST	PF	DQ	STL	TO	BLK	PTS	RPG	APG	PPG
61-62–New York	8	–	28	7	14	.500	–	–	–	1	4	.250	–	–	5	1	3	0	–	–	–	15	0.6	0.1	1.9
64-65–St. Louis	7	–	42	7	20	.350	–	–	–	4	7	.571	–	–	13	2	13	0	–	–	–	18	1.9	0.3	2.6
Reg. Season Totals	15	–	70	14	34	.412	–	–	–	5	11	.455	–	–	18	3	16	0	–	–	–	33	1.2	0.2	2.2

Burton, Willie Ricardo b. May 26, 1968 Ht. 6-8 Wt. 219 College: Minnesota

SEASON–TEAM	G	GS	MIN	FGM	FGA	PCT	3FGM	3FGA	PCT	FTM	FTA	PCT	O-RB	D-RB	TOT	AST	PF	DQ	STL	TO	BLK	PTS	RPG	APG	PPG
90-91–Miami	76	26	1928	341	773	.441	4	30	.133	229	293	.782	111	151	262	107	275	6	72	144	24	915	3.4	1.4	12.0
91-92–Miami	68	50	1585	280	622	.450	6	15	.400	196	245	.800	76	168	244	123	186	2	46	119	37	762	3.6	1.8	11.2
92-93–Miami	26	8	451	54	141	.383	5	15	.333	91	127	.717	22	48	70	16	58	0	13	50	16	204	2.7	0.6	7.8
93-94–Miami	53	1	697	124	283	.438	3	15	.200	120	158	.759	50	86	136	39	96	0	18	54	20	371	2.6	0.7	7.0
94-95–Philadelphia	53	31	1564	243	606	.401	106	275	.385	220	267	.824	49	115	164	96	167	3	32	122	19	812	3.1	1.8	15.3
96-97–Atlanta	24	2	380	39	116	.336	13	46	.283	57	68	.838	11	30	41	11	55	0	8	26	3	148	1.7	0.5	6.2
97-98–San Antonio	13	0	43	8	21	.381	3	9	.333	8	12	.667	3	6	9	1	7	0	2	1	2	27	0.7	0.1	2.1
98-99–Charlotte	3	0	18	1	7	.143	0	1	.000	2	4	.500	4	2	6	0	2	0	0	1	0	4	2.0	0.0	1.3
Reg. Season Totals	316	118	6666	1090	2569	.424	140	406	.345	923	1174	.786	326	606	932	393	846	11	191	517	121	3243	2.9	1.2	10.3
Playoff Totals	2	0	11	1	4	.250	0	2	.000	0	0	–	0	0	0	–	3	0	0	1	0	2	0.0	0.0	1.0

Burtt, Steven Dwayne (Steve) b. November 5, 1962 Ht. 6-2 Wt. 185 College: Iona

SEASON–TEAM	G	GS	MIN	FGM	FGA	PCT	3FGM	3FGA	PCT	FTM	FTA	PCT	O-RB	D-RB	TOT	AST	PF	DQ	STL	TO	BLK	PTS	RPG	APG	PPG
84-85–Golden State	47	0	418	72	188	.383	0	1	.000	53	77	.688	10	18	28	20	76	0	21	33	4	197	0.6	0.4	4.2
87-88–L.A. Clippers	19	0	312	62	138	.449	0	4	.000	47	69	.681	6	21	27	38	56	0	10	40	5	171	1.4	2.0	9.0
91-92–Phoenix	31	2	356	74	160	.463	1	6	.167	38	54	.704	10	24	34	59	58	0	16	33	4	187	1.1	1.9	6.0
92-93–Washington	4	0	35	10	26	.385	1	3	.333	8	10	.800	2	1	3	6	5	0	2	4	0	29	0.8	1.5	7.3
Reg. Season Totals	101	2	1121	218	512	.426	2	14	.143	146	210	.695	28	64	92	123	195	0	49	110	13	584	0.9	1.2	5.8
Playoff Totals	8	0	104	16	38	.421	0	2	.000	18	21	.857	3	9	12	14	18	0	5	8	0	50	1.5	1.8	6.3

Buse, Donald R. (Don, Boo) b. August 10, 1950 Ht. 6-4 Wt. 195 College: Evansville

SEASON–TEAM	G	GS	MIN	FGM	FGA	PCT	3FGM	3FGA	PCT	FTM	FTA	PCT	O-RB	D-RB	TOT	AST	PF	DQ	STL	TO	BLK	PTS	RPG	APG	PPG
72-73–Indiana (A)	77	–	1484	163	360	.453	5	24	.208	82	109	.752	96	114	210	223	143	0	–	66	–	413	2.7	2.9	5.4
73-74–Indiana (A)	77	–	1877	170	427	.398	36	107	.336	48	70	.686	85	169	254	258	109	–	146	75	20	424	3.3	3.4	5.5
74-75–Indiana (A)	80	–	2369	216	500	.432	38	123	.309	47	59	.797	84	188	272	335	149	–	166	95	15	517	3.4	4.2	6.5
75-76–Indiana (A)	84	–	3380	400	887	.451	72	208	.346	179	220	.814	90	232	322	689	194	–	346	159	31	1051	3.8	8.2	12.5
76-77–Indiana	81	–	2947	266	639	.416	–	–	–	114	145	.786	66	204	270	685	129	0	281	–	16	646	3.3	8.5	8.0
77-78–Phoenix	82	–	2547	287	626	.458	–	–	–	112	136	.824	59	190	249	391	144	0	185	124	14	686	3.0	4.8	8.4
78-79–Phoenix	82	–	2544	285	576	.495	–	–	–	70	91	.769	44	173	217	356	149	0	156	96	18	640	2.6	4.3	7.8
79-80–Phoenix	81	–	2499	261	589	.443	19	79	.241	85	128	.664	70	163	233	320	111	0	132	91	10	626	2.9	4.0	7.7
80-81–Indiana	58	–	1095	114	287	.397	19	58	.328	50	65	.769	19	65	84	140	61	0	74	38	8	297	1.4	2.4	5.1
81-82–Indiana	82	78	2529	312	685	.455	73	189	.386	100	123	.813	46	177	223	407	176	0	164	95	27	797	2.7	5.0	9.7
82-83–Portland	41	1	643	72	182	.396	9	35	.257	41	46	.891	19	35	54	115	60	0	44	25	2	194	1.3	2.8	4.7
83-84–Kansas City	76	10	1327	150	352	.426	18	59	.305	63	80	.788	29	87	116	303	62	0	86	87	1	381	1.5	4.0	5.0
84-85–Kansas City	65	14	939	82	203	.404	31	87	.356	23	30	.767	21	40	61	203	75	0	38	45	1	218	0.9	3.1	3.4
Reg. NBA Totals	648	103	17070	1829	4139	.442	169	507	.333	658	844	.780	373	1134	1507	2920	967	0	1160	601	97	4485	2.3	4.5	6.9
Reg. ABA Totals	318	–	9110	949	2174	.437	151	462	.327	356	458	.777	355	703	1058	1505	595	0	658	395	66	2405	3.3	4.7	7.6
NBA Playoff Totals	35	0	940	89	223	.399	9	23	.391	40	56	.714	25	66	91	125	60	0	37	36	6	227	2.6	3.6	6.5
ABA Playoff Totals	49	–	1208	100	249	.402	16	64	.250	39	64	.609	36	73	134	159	100	0	82	46	6	255	2.7	3.2	5.2
NBA All-Star Totals	1	0	19	2	4	.500	0	0	–	0	0	–	0	2	2	5	0	0	4	–	0	4	2.0	5.0	4.0

Bustion, David C. (Dave) b. August 30, 1949 Ht. 6-8 Wt. 215 College: Northeastern Christian (Pa.) J.C.; Denver

SEASON–TEAM	G	GS	MIN	FGM	FGA	PCT	3FGM	3FGA	PCT	FTM	FTA	PCT	O-RB	D-RB	TOT	AST	PF	DQ	STL	TO	BLK	PTS	RPG	APG	PPG
72-73–Denver (A)	47	–	355	58	133	.436	0	0	–	42	59	.712	39	62	101	21	82	0	–	54	–	158	2.1	0.4	3.4
Reg. ABA Totals	47	–	355	58	133	.436	0	0	–	42	59	.712	39	62	101	21	82	0	–	54	–	158	2.1	0.4	3.4
ABA Playoff Totals	1	–	11	2	7	.286	0	0	–	6	7	.857	–	–	1	1	3	0	–	1	–	10	1.0	1.0	10.0

Butcher, Donnis (Donnie) b. February 8, 1936 Ht. 6-3 Wt. 200 College: Pikeville

SEASON–TEAM	G	GS	MIN	FGM	FGA	PCT	3FGM	3FGA	PCT	FTM	FTA	PCT	O-RB	D-RB	TOT	AST	PF	DQ	STL	TO	BLK	PTS	RPG	APG	PPG
61-62–New York	47	–	479	48	155	.310	–	–	–	42	69	.609	–	–	79	51	63	0	–	–	–	138	1.7	1.1	2.9
62-63–New York	68	–	1193	172	424	.406	–	–	–	131	194	.675	–	–	180	138	164	1	–	–	–	475	2.6	2.0	7.0
63-64–N.Y.-Detroit	78	–	1971	202	507	.398	–	–	–	159	256	.621	–	–	329	244	249	4	–	–	–	563	4.2	3.1	7.2
64-65–Detroit	71	–	1157	143	353	.405	–	–	–	126	204	.618	–	–	200	122	183	4	–	–	–	412	2.8	1.7	5.8
65-66–Detroit	15	–	285	45	96	.469	–	–	–	18	34	.529	–	–	33	30	40	1	–	–	–	108	2.2	2.0	7.2
Reg. Season Totals	279	–	5085	610	1535	.397	–	–	–	476	757	.629	–	–	821	585	699	10	–	–	–	1696	2.9	2.1	6.1

Butler, Elbert J. (Al) b. July 9, 1938 Ht. 6-2 Wt. 175 College: Niagara

SEASON–TEAM	G	GS	MIN	FGM	FGA	PCT	3FGM	3FGA	PCT	FTM	FTA	PCT	O-RB	D-RB	TOT	AST	PF	DQ	STL	TO	BLK	PTS	RPG	APG	PPG
61-62–Boston-N.Y.	59	–	2016	349	754	.463	–	–	–	129	182	.709	–	–	337	205	156	0	–	–	–	827	5.7	3.5	14.0
62-63–New York	74	–	1488	297	676	.439	–	–	–	144	187	.770	–	–	170	156	145	3	–	–	–	738	2.3	2.1	10.0
63-64–New York	76	–	1379	260	616	.422	–	–	–	138	187	.738	–	–	168	157	167	3	–	–	–	658	2.2	2.1	8.7
64-65–Baltimore	25	–	172	24	73	.329	–	–	–	11	15	.733	–	–	21	12	25	0	–	–	–	59	0.8	0.5	2.4
Reg. Season Totals	234	–	5055	930	2119	.439	–	–	–	422	571	.739	–	–	696	530	493	6	–	–	–	2282	3.0	2.3	9.8

Butler, Gregory Edward (Greg) b. March 11, 1966 Ht. 6-11 Wt. 240 College: Stanford

SEASON–TEAM	G	GS	MIN	FGM	FGA	PCT	3FGM	3FGA	PCT	FTM	FTA	PCT	O-RB	D-RB	TOT	AST	PF	DQ	STL	TO	BLK	PTS	RPG	APG	PPG
88-89–New York	33	0	140	20	48	.417	0	3	.000	16	20	.800	9	19	28	2	28	0	1	17	2	56	0.8	0.1	1.7
89-90–New York	13	0	33	3	12	.250	0	0	–	0	2	.000	3	6	9	1	8	0	0	3	0	6	0.7	0.1	0.5
90-91–L.A. Clippers	9	0	37	5	19	.263	0	0	–	4	6	.667	8	8	16	1	9	0	0	4	0	14	1.8	0.1	1.6
Reg. Season Totals	55	0	210	28	79	.354	0	3	.000	20	28	.714	20	33	53	4	45	0	1	24	2	76	1.0	0.1	1.4

Butler, Michael Edward (Mike) b. October 22, 1946 Ht. 6-2 Wt. 175 College: Memphis State

SEASON–TEAM	G	GS	MIN	FGM	FGA	PCT	3FGM	3FGA	PCT	FTM	FTA	PCT	O-RB	D-RB	TOT	AST	PF	DQ	STL	TO	BLK	PTS	RPG	APG	PPG
68-69–New Orleans (A)	77	–	1315	207	528	.392	50	162	.309	112	133	.842	–	–	115	171	130	0	–	113	–	576	1.5	2.2	7.5
69-70–New Orleans (A)	83	–	1728	298	800	.373	87	300	.290	135	161	.839	–	–	119	134	193	1	–	–	–	818	1.4	1.6	9.9
70-71–Utah (A)	71	–	1414	271	646	.420	32	125	.256	153	168	.911	–	–	131	186	142	–	–	–	–	727	1.8	2.6	10.2
71-72–Utah (A)	14	–	97	14	36	.389	3	9	.333	6	7	.857	–	–	10	13	18	–	–	12	–	37	0.7	0.9	2.6
Reg. ABA Totals	245	–	4554	790	2010	.393	172	596	.289	406	469	.866	–	–	375	504	483	1	–	125	–	2158	1.5	2.1	8.8
ABA Playoff Totals	21	–	314	49	140	.350	16	61	.262	34	38	.895	–	–	40	23	34	0	–	–	–	148	1.9	1.1	7.0

Butler, Mitchell Leon b. December 15, 1970 Ht. 6-5 Wt. 210 College: UCLA

SEASON–TEAM	G	GS	MIN	FGM	FGA	PCT	3FGM	3FGA	PCT	FTM	FTA	PCT	O-RB	D-RB	TOT	AST	PF	DQ	STL	TO	BLK	PTS	RPG	APG	PPG
93-94–Washington	75	19	1321	207	418	.495	0	5	.000	104	180	.578	106	119	225	77	131	1	54	87	20	518	3.0	1.0	6.9
94-95–Washington	76	5	1554	214	508	.421	46	141	.326	123	185	.665	43	127	170	91	155	0	61	106	10	597	2.2	1.2	7.9
95-96–Washington	61	3	858	88	229	.384	13	60	.217	48	83	.578	29	89	118	67	104	0	41	67	12	237	1.9	1.1	3.9
96-97–Portland	49	1	465	52	125	.416	12	39	.308	32	50	.640	19	34	53	30	55	1	13	27	2	148	1.1	0.6	3.0
97-98–Cleveland	18	0	206	15	47	.319	1	6	.167	6	10	.600	6	16	22	18	26	0	8	8	0	37	1.2	1.0	2.1
98-99–Cleveland	31	1	418	67	139	.482	11	29	.379	23	32	.719	13	31	44	22	41	0	15	29	4	168	1.4	0.7	5.4
Reg. Season Totals	310	29	4822	643	1466	.439	83	280	.296	336	540	.622	216	416	632	305	512	2	192	324	48	1705	2.0	1.0	5.5
Playoff Totals	2	0	4	1	2	.500	0	0	–	0	0	–	0	1	1	–	0	0	0	0	0	2	0.5	0.0	1.0

Byrd, Walter (Walt) b. 1942 Ht. 6-7 Wt. 205 College: Temple

SEASON–TEAM	G	GS	MIN	FGM	FGA	PCT	3FGM	3FGA	PCT	FTM	FTA	PCT	O-RB	D-RB	TOT	AST	PF	DQ	STL	TO	BLK	PTS	RPG	APG	PPG
69-70–Miami (A)	22	–	109	14	43	.326	0	1	.000	5	17	.294	–	–	25	6	22	0	–	–	–	33	1.1	0.3	1.5
Reg. ABA Totals	22	–	109	14	43	.326	0	1	.000	5	17	.294	–	–	25	6	22	0	–	–	–	33	1.1	0.3	1.5

Byrnes, Martin William (Marty) b. April 30, 1956 Ht. 6-7 Wt. 220 College: Syracuse

SEASON–TEAM	G	GS	MIN	FGM	FGA	PCT	3FGM	3FGA	PCT	FTM	FTA	PCT	O-RB	D-RB	TOT	AST	PF	DQ	STL	TO	BLK	PTS	RPG	APG	PPG
78-79–Phoenix-N.O.	79	–	1264	187	389	.481	–	–	–	106	154	.688	90	101	191	104	111	0	27	119	10	480	2.4	1.3	6.1
79-80–Los Angeles	32	–	194	25	50	.500	0	0	–	13	15	.867	9	18	27	13	32	0	5	22	1	63	0.8	0.4	2.0
80-81–Dallas	72	–	1360	216	451	.479	9	20	.450	120	157	.764	74	103	177	113	126	0	29	61	17	561	2.5	1.6	7.8
82-83–Indiana	80	12	1436	157	374	.420	6	26	.231	71	95	.747	75	116	191	179	149	1	41	73	6	391	2.4	2.2	4.9
Reg. Season Totals	263	12	4254	585	1264	.463	15	46	.326	310	421	.736	248	338	586	409	418	1	102	275	34	1495	2.2	1.6	5.7
Playoff Totals	4	0	8	1	3	.333	0	0	–	4	6	.667	1	0	1	1	0	0	0	1	0	6	0.3	0.3	1.5

Byrnes, Thomas P. (Tommy) b. February 19, 1923 d. January 9, 1981 Ht. 6-3 Wt. 175 College: Seton Hall

SEASON–TEAM	G	GS	MIN	FGM	FGA	PCT	3FGM	3FGA	PCT	FTM	FTA	PCT	O-RB	D-RB	TOT	AST	PF	DQ	STL	TO	BLK	PTS	RPG	APG	PPG
46-47–New York	60	–	–	175	583	.300	–	–	–	103	160	.644	–	–	–	35	90	–	–	–	–	453	–	0.6	7.6
47-48–New York	47	–	–	117	410	.285	–	–	–	65	103	.631	–	–	–	17	56	–	–	–	–	299	–	0.4	6.4
48-49–N.Y.-Ind.	57	–	–	160	525	.305	–	–	–	92	149	.617	–	–	–	102	84	–	–	–	–	412	–	1.8	7.2
49-50–Baltimore	53	–	–	120	397	.302	–	–	–	87	124	.702	–	–	–	88	76	–	–	–	–	327	–	1.7	6.2
50-51–Balt.-Wash.-Tri-Cit	48	–	–	83	275	.302	–	–	–	55	84	.655	–	–	72	69	86	0	–	–	–	221	1.5	1.4	4.6
Reg. Season Totals	265	–	–	655	2190	.299	–	–	–	402	620	.648	–	–	72	311	392	0	–	–	–	1712	1.5	1.2	6.5
Playoff Totals	8	–	–	22	73	.301	–	–	–	6	24	.250	–	–	–	2	9	0	–	–	–	50	–	0.3	6.3

Bytzura, Michael John (Mike) b. June 18, 1922 d. January 24, 1989 Ht. 6-3 Wt. 175 College: Duquesne; Long Island University

SEASON–TEAM	G	GS	MIN	FGM	FGA	PCT	3FGM	3FGA	PCT	FTM	FTA	PCT	O-RB	D-RB	TOT	AST	PF	DQ	STL	TO	BLK	PTS	RPG	APG	PPG
44-45–Cleveland (N)	30	–	–	113	–	–	–	–	–	35	–	–	–	–	–	–	–	–	–	–	–	261	–	–	8.7
45-46–Cleveland (N)	33	–	–	78	–	–	–	–	–	35	65	.538	–	–	–	–	62	–	–	–	–	191	–	–	5.8
46-47–Pittsburgh	60	–	–	87	356	.244	–	–	–	36	72	.500	–	–	–	31	108	–	–	–	–	210	–	0.5	3.5
Reg. NBA Totals	60	–	–	87	356	.244	–	–	–	36	72	.500	–	–	–	31	108	–	–	–	–	210	–	0.5	3.5
Reg. NBL Totals	63	–	–	191	–	–	–	–	–	70	65	.538	–	–	–	–	62	–	–	–	–	452	–	–	7.2
NBL Playoff Totals	2	–	–	4	–	–	–	–	–	3	0	–	–	–	–	–	3	–	–	–	–	11	–	–	5.5

Cable, Byrum William (Barney) b. July 29, 1935 Ht. 6-7 Wt. 200 College: Bradley

SEASON–TEAM	G	GS	MIN	FGM	FGA	PCT	3FGM	3FGA	PCT	FTM	FTA	PCT	O-RB	D-RB	TOT	AST	PF	DQ	STL	TO	BLK	PTS	RPG	APG	PPG
58-59–Detroit	31	–	271	43	126	.341	–	–	–	23	29	.793	–	–	88	12	30	0	–	–	–	109	2.8	0.4	3.5
59-60–Detroit-Syr.	57	–	715	109	290	.376	–	–	–	44	67	.657	–	–	225	39	93	1	–	–	–	262	3.9	0.7	4.6
60-61–Syracuse	75	–	1642	266	574	.463	–	–	–	73	108	.676	–	–	469	85	246	1	–	–	–	605	6.3	1.1	8.1
61-62–Chicago-St. L.	67	–	1861	305	749	.407	–	–	–	118	181	.652	–	–	563	115	211	4	–	–	–	728	8.4	1.7	10.9
62-63–St. L.-Chicago	61	–	1200	173	380	.455	–	–	–	62	96	.646	–	–	242	82	136	0	–	–	–	408	4.0	1.3	6.7
63-64–Baltimore	71	–	1125	116	290	.400	–	–	–	28	42	.667	–	–	301	47	166	3	–	–	–	260	4.2	0.7	3.7
Reg. Season Totals	362	–	6814	1012	2409	.420	–	–	–	348	523	.665	–	–	1888	380	882	9	–	–	–	2372	5.2	1.0	6.6
Playoff Totals	11	–	248	31	79	.392	–	–	–	14	25	.560	–	–	89	8	41	1	–	–	–	76	8.1	0.7	6.9

Caffey, Jason Andre b. June 12, 1973 Ht. 6-8 Wt. 256 College: Alabama

SEASON–TEAM	G	GS	MIN	FGM	FGA	PCT	3FGM	3FGA	PCT	FTM	FTA	PCT	O-RB	D-RB	TOT	AST	PF	DQ	STL	TO	BLK	PTS	RPG	APG	PPG
95-96–Chicago	57	0	545	71	162	.438	0	1	.000	40	68	.588	51	60	111	24	91	3	12	48	7	182	1.9	0.4	3.2
96-97–Chicago	75	19	1405	205	385	.532	0	1	.000	139	211	.659	135	166	301	89	149	0	25	97	9	549	4.0	1.2	7.3
97-98–Chicago-G.S.	80	14	1423	226	466	.485	0	2	.000	131	200	.655	160	184	344	67	181	4	25	105	20	583	4.3	0.8	7.3
98-99–Golden State	35	32	876	123	277	.444	0	1	.000	62	98	.633	79	126	205	18	113	1	24	75	9	308	5.9	0.5	8.8
99-00–Golden State	71	56	2159	323	675	.479	0	2	.000	206	345	.597	189	293	482	119	269	11	62	170	20	852	6.8	1.7	12.0
Reg. Season Totals	318	121	6408	948	1965	.482	0	7	.000	578	922	.627	614	829	1443	317	803	19	148	495	65	2474	4.5	1.0	7.8
Playoff Totals	17	5	167	15	33	.455	0	0	–	11	14	.786	25	17	42	15	27	0	3	12	3	41	2.5	0.9	2.4

Cage, Michael Jerome (John Shaft) b. January 28, 1962 Ht. 6-9 Wt. 248 College: San Diego State

SEASON–TEAM	G	GS	MIN	FGM	FGA	PCT	3FGM	3FGA	PCT	FTM	FTA	PCT	O-RB	D-RB	TOT	AST	PF	DQ	STL	TO	BLK	PTS	RPG	APG	PPG
84-85–L.A. Clippers	75	41	1610	216	398	.543	0	0	–	101	137	.737	126	266	392	51	164	1	41	81	32	533	5.2	0.7	7.1
85-86–L.A. Clippers	78	12	1566	204	426	.479	0	3	.000	113	174	.649	168	249	417	81	176	1	62	106	34	521	5.3	1.0	6.7
86-87–L.A. Clippers	80	76	2922	457	878	.521	0	3	.000	341	467	.730	354	568	922	131	221	1	99	171	67	1255	11.5	1.6	15.7
87-88–L.A. Clippers	72	70	2660	360	766	.470	0	1	.000	326	474	.688	371	567	938	110	194	1	91	160	58	1046	13.0	1.5	14.5
88-89–Seattle	80	71	2536	314	630	.498	0	4	.000	197	265	.743	276	489	765	126	184	1	92	124	52	825	9.6	1.6	10.3
89-90–Seattle	82	82	2595	325	645	.504	0	0	–	148	212	.698	306	515	821	70	232	1	79	94	45	798	10.0	0.9	9.7
90-91–Seattle	82	55	2141	226	445	.508	0	3	.000	70	112	.625	177	381	558	89	194	0	85	83	58	522	6.8	1.1	6.4
91-92–Seattle	82	69	2461	307	542	.566	0	5	.000	106	171	.620	266	462	728	92	237	0	99	78	55	720	8.9	1.1	8.8
92-93–Seattle	82	66	2156	219	416	.526	0	1	.000	61	130	.469	268	391	659	69	183	0	76	59	46	499	8.0	0.8	6.1
93-94–Seattle	82	42	1708	171	314	.545	0	1	.000	36	74	.486	164	280	444	45	179	0	77	51	38	378	5.4	0.5	4.6
94-95–Cleveland	82	21	2040	177	340	.521	0	2	.000	53	88	.602	203	361	564	56	149	1	61	56	67	407	6.9	0.7	5.0
95-96–Cleveland	82	80	2631	220	396	.556	0	1	.000	50	92	.543	288	441	729	53	215	0	87	54	79	490	8.9	0.6	6.0
96-97–Philadelphia	82	24	1247	66	141	.468	0	0	–	19	41	.463	112	208	320	43	118	0	48	17	42	151	3.9	0.5	1.8
97-98–New Jersey	79	17	1201	43	84	.512	0	1	.000	20	36	.556	115	193	308	32	105	1	45	23	44	106	3.9	0.4	1.3
99-00–New Jersey	20	7	242	12	24	.500	0	0	–	3	3	1.000	33	48	81	9	30	0	8	4	8	27	4.1	0.5	1.4
Reg. Season Totals	1140	733	29716	3317	6445	.515	0	25	.000	1644	2476	.664	3227	5419	8646	1057	2581	8	1050	1161	725	8278	7.6	0.9	7.3
Playoff Totals	53	14	1105	113	216	.523	0	2	.000	35	71	.493	127	175	302	30	120	1	37	39	34	261	5.7	0.6	4.9

Calabrese, Gerald A. (Gerry) b. February 4, 1925 Ht. 6-1 Wt. 175 College: St. John's (N.Y.)

SEASON–TEAM	G	GS	MIN	FGM	FGA	PCT	3FGM	3FGA	PCT	FTM	FTA	PCT	O-RB	D-RB	TOT	AST	PF	DQ	STL	TO	BLK	PTS	RPG	APG	PPG
50-51–Syracuse	46	–	–	70	197	.355	–	–	–	61	88	.693	–	–	65	65	80	0	–	–	–	201	1.4	1.4	4.4
51-52–Syracuse	58	–	937	109	317	.344	–	–	–	73	103	.709	–	–	84	83	107	0	–	–	–	291	1.4	1.4	5.0
Reg. Season Totals	104	–	937	179	514	.348	–	–	–	134	191	.702	–	–	149	148	187	0	–	–	–	492	1.4	1.4	4.7
Playoff Totals	6	–	76	10	24	.417	–	–	–	4	4	1.000	–	–	8	4	18	0	–	–	–	24	1.3	0.7	4.0

Caldwell, Adrian Bernard b. July 4, 1966 Ht. 6-9 Wt. 265 College: Navarro (Texas) Coll.; Southern Methodist; Lamar

SEASON–TEAM	G	GS	MIN	FGM	FGA	PCT	3FGM	3FGA	PCT	FTM	FTA	PCT	O-RB	D-RB	TOT	AST	PF	DQ	STL	TO	BLK	PTS	RPG	APG	PPG
89-90–Houston	51	0	331	42	76	.553	0	0	–	13	28	.464	36	73	109	7	69	0	11	32	18	97	2.1	0.1	1.9
90-91–Houston	42	0	343	35	83	.422	0	1	.000	7	17	.412	43	57	100	8	35	0	19	30	10	77	2.4	0.2	1.8
94-95–Houston	7	0	30	1	4	.250	0	0	–	3	6	.500	1	9	10	0	6	0	1	1	0	5	1.4	0.0	0.7
95-96–Indiana	51	1	327	46	83	.554	0	0	–	18	36	.500	42	68	110	6	73	0	9	35	5	110	2.2	0.1	2.2
96-97–N.J.-Phil.	45	0	569	40	92	.435	0	2	.000	21	50	.420	58	109	167	12	87	1	16	28	8	101	3.7	0.3	2.2
97-98–Dallas	1	0	3	0	0	–	0	0	–	0	0	–	0	0	0	0	0	0	0	0	0	0	0.0	0.0	0.0
Reg. Season Totals	197	1	1603	164	338	.485	0	3	.000	62	137	.453	180	316	496	33	270	1	56	126	41	390	2.5	0.2	2.0
Playoff Totals	2	0	4	1	1	1.000	0	0	–	0	0	–	0	1	1	–	0	0	0	0	0	2	0.5	0.0	1.0

Caldwell, James W. Jr. (Jim) b. January 28, 1943 Ht. 6-10 Wt. 240 College: Georgia Tech

SEASON–TEAM	G	GS	MIN	FGM	FGA	PCT	3FGM	3FGA	PCT	FTM	FTA	PCT	O-RB	D-RB	TOT	AST	PF	DQ	STL	TO	BLK	PTS	RPG	APG	PPG
67-68–New York	2	–	7	0	1	.000	–	–	–	0	0	–	–	–	1	1	1	0	–	–	–	0	0.5	0.5	0.0
67-68–N.J.-Ken. (A)	70	–	1843	223	535	.417	1	6	.167	99	166	.596	–	–	628	147	234	10	–	121	–	546	9.0	2.1	7.8
68-69–Kentucky (A)	65	–	1235	167	381	.438	1	9	.111	87	129	.674	–	–	423	130	211	3	–	97	–	422	6.5	2.0	6.5
Reg. NBA Totals	2	–	7	0	1	.000	–	–	–	0	0	–	–	–	1	1	1	0	–	–	–	0	0.5	0.5	0.0
Reg. ABA Totals	135	–	3078	390	916	.426	2	15	.133	186	295	.631	–	–	1051	277	445	13	–	218	–	968	7.8	2.1	7.2
ABA Playoff Totals	12	–	238	26	66	.394	0	0	–	17	27	.630	–	–	80	19	36	0	–	12	–	69	6.7	1.6	5.8

Caldwell, Joe (Pogo) b. November 1, 1941 Ht. 6-5 Wt. 195 College: Arizona State

SEASON–TEAM	G	GS	MIN	FGM	FGA	PCT	3FGM	3FGA	PCT	FTM	FTA	PCT	O-RB	D-RB	TOT	AST	PF	DQ	STL	TO	BLK	PTS	RPG	APG	PPG
64-65–Detroit	66	–	1543	290	776	.374	–	–	–	129	210	.614	–	–	441	118	171	3	–	–	–	709	6.7	1.8	10.7
65-66–Detroit-St. L.	79	–	1857	411	938	.438	–	–	–	179	254	.705	–	–	436	126	203	3	–	–	–	1001	5.5	1.6	12.7
66-67–St. Louis	81	–	2256	458	1076	.426	–	–	–	200	308	.649	–	–	442	166	230	4	–	–	–	1116	5.5	2.0	13.8
67-68–St. Louis	79	–	2641	564	1219	.463	–	–	–	165	290	.569	–	–	338	240	208	1	–	–	–	1293	4.3	3.0	16.4
68-69–Atlanta	81	–	2720	561	1106	.507	–	–	–	159	296	.537	–	–	303	320	231	1	–	–	–	1281	3.7	4.0	15.8
69-70–Atlanta	82	–	2857	674	1329	.507	–	–	–	379	551	.688	–	–	407	287	255	3	–	–	–	1727	5.0	3.5	21.1
70-71–Carolina (A)	72	–	3008	685	1528	.448	6	30	.200	302	541	.558	–	–	489	301	237	–	–	–	–	1678	6.8	4.2	23.3
71-72–Carolina (A)	61	–	2145	434	922	.471	5	20	.250	159	318	.500	–	–	343	259	208	–	–	164	–	1032	5.6	4.2	16.9
72-73–Carolina (A)	77	–	2739	555	1118	.496	1	6	.167	172	405	.425	189	206	395	352	252	4	166	246	–	1283	5.1	4.6	16.7
73-74–Carolina (A)	79	–	2654	502	1027	.489	3	17	.176	128	258	.496	177	235	412	350	255	–	170	242	35	1135	5.2	4.4	14.4
74-75–St. Louis (A)	25	–	841	161	326	.494	3	7	.429	39	87	.448	44	67	111	128	78	–	49	74	10	364	4.4	5.1	14.6
Reg. NBA Totals	468	–	13874	2958	6444	.459	–	–	–	1211	1909	.634	–	–	2367	1257	1298	15	–	–	–	7127	5.1	2.7	15.2
Reg. ABA Totals	314	–	11387	2337	4921	.475	18	80	.225	800	1609	.497	410	508	1750	1390	1030	4	385	726	45	5492	5.6	4.4	17.5
NBA Playoff Totals	45	–	1477	293	652	.449	–	–	–	130	232	.560	–	–	215	119	140	3	–	–	–	716	4.8	2.6	15.9
ABA Playoff Totals	16	–	572	96	197	.487	3	10	.300	30	62	.484	18	9	95	53	49	0	31	56	0	225	5.9	3.3	14.1
NBA All-Star Totals	2	–	42	11	20	.550	–	–	–	3	5	.600	–	–	11	4	7	0	–	–	–	25	5.5	2.0	12.5

C

Calhoun, David L. (Corky) b. November 1, 1950 Ht. 6-7 Wt. 210 College: Pennsylvania

SEASON–TEAM	G	GS	MIN	FGM	FGA	PCT	3FGM	3FGA	PCT	FTM	FTA	PCT	O-RB	D-RB	TOT	AST	PF	DQ	STL	TO	BLK	PTS	RPG	APG	PPG
72-73–Phoenix	82	–	2025	211	450	.469	–	–	–	71	96	.740	–	–	338	76	214	2	–	–	–	493	4.1	0.9	6.0
73-74–Phoenix	77	–	2207	268	581	.461	–	–	–	98	129	.760	115	292	407	135	253	4	71	–	30	634	5.3	1.8	8.2
74-75–Phoenix-L.A.	70	–	1378	132	318	.415	–	–	–	58	77	.753	109	160	269	79	180	1	55	–	25	322	3.8	1.1	4.6
75-76–Los Angeles	76	–	1816	172	368	.467	–	–	–	65	83	.783	117	224	341	85	216	4	62	–	35	409	4.5	1.1	5.4
76-77–Portland	70	–	743	85	183	.464	–	–	–	66	85	.776	40	104	144	35	123	1	24	–	8	236	2.1	0.5	3.4
77-78–Portland	79	–	1370	175	365	.479	–	–	–	66	76	.868	73	142	215	87	141	3	42	64	15	416	2.7	1.1	5.3
78-79–Indiana	81	–	1332	153	335	.457	–	–	–	72	86	.837	64	174	238	104	189	1	37	56	19	378	2.9	1.3	4.7
79-80–Indiana	7	–	30	4	9	.444	0	0	–	0	2	.000	7	3	10	0	6	0	2	1	0	8	1.4	0.0	1.1
Reg. Season Totals	542	–	10901	1200	2609	.460	0	0	–	496	634	.782	525	1099	1962	601	1322	16	293	121	132	2896	3.6	1.1	5.3
Playoff Totals	18	–	203	28	54	.519	0	0	–	6	10	.600	12	16	28	7	22	0	6	3	3	62	1.6	0.4	3.4

Calhoun, William C. (Bill) b. November 4, 1927 Ht. 6-3 Wt. 180 College: San Francisco (Calif.) City Coll.

SEASON–TEAM	G	GS	MIN	FGM	FGA	PCT	3FGM	3FGA	PCT	FTM	FTA	PCT	O-RB	D-RB	TOT	AST	PF	DQ	STL	TO	BLK	PTS	RPG	APG	PPG
47-48–Rochester (N)	42	–	–	31	–	–	–	–	–	18	34	.529	–	–	–	–	32	–	–	–	–	80	–	–	1.9
48-49–Rochester	56	–	–	146	408	.358	–	–	–	75	131	.573	–	–	–	125	97	–	–	–	–	367	–	2.2	6.6
49-50–Rochester	62	–	–	207	549	.377	–	–	–	146	203	.719	–	–	–	115	100	–	–	–	–	560	–	1.9	9.0
50-51–Rochester	66	–	–	175	506	.346	–	–	–	161	228	.706	–	–	199	99	87	1	–	–	–	511	3.0	1.5	7.7
51-52–Baltimore	55	–	1594	129	409	.315	–	–	–	125	183	.683	–	–	252	117	84	0	–	–	–	383	4.6	2.1	7.0
52-53–Syr.-Milw.	62	–	2148	180	534	.337	–	–	–	211	292	.723	–	–	277	156	136	4	–	–	–	571	4.5	2.5	9.2
53-54–Milwaukee	72	–	2370	190	545	.349	–	–	–	214	292	.733	–	–	274	189	151	3	–	–	–	594	3.8	2.6	8.3
54-55–Milwaukee	69	–	2109	144	480	.300	–	–	–	166	236	.703	–	–	290	235	181	4	–	–	–	454	4.2	3.4	6.6
Reg. NBA Totals	442	–	8221	1171	3431	.341	–	–	–	1098	1565	.702	–	–	1292	1036	836	12	–	–	–	3440	4.0	2.3	7.8
Reg. NBL Totals	42	–	–	31	–	–	–	–	–	18	34	.529	–	–	–	–	32	–	–	–	–	80	–	–	1.9
NBA Playoff Totals	18	–	0	33	98	.439	–	–	–	34	46	.739	–	–	41	48	25	0	–	–	–	100	2.9	2.2	5.6
NBL Playoff Totals	8	–	–	11	–	–	–	–	–	2	3	.667	–	–	–	–	8	–	–	–	–	24	–	–	3.0

Calip, Demetrius b. November 18, 1969 Ht. 6-1 Wt. 165 College: Michigan

SEASON–TEAM	G	GS	MIN	FGM	FGA	PCT	3FGM	3FGA	PCT	FTM	FTA	PCT	O-RB	D-RB	TOT	AST	PF	DQ	STL	TO	BLK	PTS	RPG	APG	PPG
91-92–L.A. Lakers	7	0	58	4	18	.222	1	5	.200	2	3	.667	1	4	5	12	8	0	1	5	0	11	0.7	1.7	1.6
Reg. Season Totals	7	0	58	4	18	.222	1	5	.200	2	3	.667	1	4	5	12	8	0	1	5	0	11	0.7	1.7	1.6

Callahan, Thomas Francis (Tom) b. June 2, 1921 Ht. 6-1 Wt. 180 College: Notre Dame; Rockhurst

SEASON–TEAM	G	GS	MIN	FGM	FGA	PCT	3FGM	3FGA	PCT	FTM	FTA	PCT	O-RB	D-RB	TOT	AST	PF	DQ	STL	TO	BLK	PTS	RPG	APG	PPG
46-47–Providence	13	–	–	6	29	.207	–	–	–	5	12	.417	–	–	–	4	9	–	–	–	–	17	–	0.3	1.3
Reg. Season Totals	13	–	–	6	29	.207	–	–	–	5	12	.417	–	–	–	4	9	–	–	–	–	17	–	0.3	1.3

Calloway, Richard Marlon (Rick) b. October 12, 1966 Ht. 6-6 Wt. 190 College: Indiana; Kansas

SEASON–TEAM	G	GS	MIN	FGM	FGA	PCT	3FGM	3FGA	PCT	FTM	FTA	PCT	O-RB	D-RB	TOT	AST	PF	DQ	STL	TO	BLK	PTS	RPG	APG	PPG
90-91–Sacramento	64	0	678	75	192	.391	0	2	.000	55	79	.696	25	53	78	61	98	1	22	51	7	205	1.2	1.0	3.2
Reg. Season Totals	64	0	678	75	192	.391	0	2	.000	55	79	.696	25	53	78	61	98	1	22	51	7	205	1.2	1.0	3.2

Calverley, Ernest A. (Ernie) b. January 30, 1924 Ht. 5-10 Wt. 155 College: Rhode Island

SEASON–TEAM	G	GS	MIN	FGM	FGA	PCT	3FGM	3FGA	PCT	FTM	FTA	PCT	O-RB	D-RB	TOT	AST	PF	DQ	STL	TO	BLK	PTS	RPG	APG	PPG
46-47–Providence	59	–	–	323	1102	.293	–	–	–	199	283	.703	–	–	–	202	191	–	–	–	–	845	–	3.4	14.3
47-48–Providence	47	–	–	226	835	.271	–	–	–	107	161	.665	–	–	–	119	168	–	–	–	–	559	–	2.5	11.9
48-49–Providence	59	–	–	218	696	.313	–	–	–	121	160	.756	–	–	–	251	183	–	–	–	–	557	–	4.3	9.4
Reg. Season Totals	165	–	–	767	2633	.291	–	–	–	427	604	.707	–	–	–	572	542	–	–	–	–	1961	–	3.5	11.9

Calvin, Mack b. July 27, 1947 Ht. 6-0 Wt. 170 College: Long Beach (Calif.) CityColl.; USC

SEASON–TEAM	G	GS	MIN	FGM	FGA	PCT	3FGM	3FGA	PCT	FTM	FTA	PCT	O-RB	D-RB	TOT	AST	PF	DQ	STL	TO	BLK	PTS	RPG	APG	PPG
69-70–Los Angeles (A)	84	–	2955	441	1047	.421	3	25	.120	529	642	.824	–	–	294	478	289	6	–	–	–	1414	3.5	5.7	16.8
70-71–Floridians (A)	81	–	3394	744	1728	.431	17	59	.288	696	805	.865	–	–	283	619	263	–	–	–	–	2201	3.5	7.6	27.2
71-72–Floridians (A)	82	–	2977	552	1253	.441	11	48	.229	611	701	.872	–	–	274	481	270	–	–	261	–	1726	3.3	5.9	21.0
72-73–Carolina (A)	84	–	2228	478	944	.506	11	28	.393	500	582	.859	97	118	215	301	219	3	–	247	–	1467	2.6	3.6	17.5
73-74–Carolina (A)	83	–	2592	498	1078	.462	10	43	.233	490	560	.875	78	165	243	347	244	–	135	234	7	1496	2.9	4.2	18.0
74-75–Denver (A)	74	–	2463	483	996	.485	3	16	.188	475	530	.896	36	174	210	570	206	–	140	279	8	1444	2.8	7.7	19.5
75-76–Virginia (A)	45	–	1658	306	717	.427	7	26	.269	253	285	.888	38	90	128	271	122	–	71	192	1	872	2.8	6.0	19.4
76-77–L.A.-S.A.-Den.	76	–	1438	220	544	.404	–	–	–	287	338	.849	36	60	96	240	127	0	61	–	3	727	1.3	3.2	9.6
77-78–Denver	77	–	988	147	333	.441	–	–	–	173	206	.840	11	73	84	148	87	0	46	108	5	467	1.1	1.9	6.1
79-80–Utah	48	–	772	100	227	.441	1	11	.091	105	117	.897	13	71	84	134	72	0	27	57	0	306	1.8	2.8	6.4
80-81–Cleveland	21	–	128	13	39	.333	1	5	.200	25	35	.714	2	10	12	28	13	0	5	17	0	52	0.6	1.3	2.5
Reg. NBA Totals	222	–	3326	480	1143	.420	2	16	.125	590	696	.848	62	214	276	550	299	0	139	182	8	1552	1.2	2.5	7.0
Reg. ABA Totals	533	–	18267	3502	7763	.451	62	245	.253	3554	4105	.866	249	547	1647	3067	1613	9	346	1213	16	10620	3.1	5.8	19.9
NBA Playoff Totals	18	–	247	38	82	.463	0	0	–	51	58	.879	4	13	17	34	24	0	8	11	0	127	0.9	1.9	7.1
ABA Playoff Totals	56	–	1959	405	870	.466	12	35	.343	367	437	.840	14	46	189	297	179	0	28	98	1	1189	3.4	5.3	21.2

Cambridge, Dexter Ryan b. January 29, 1970 Ht. 6-7 Wt. 225 College: Lon Morris (Texas) Coll.; Texas

SEASON–TEAM	G	GS	MIN	FGM	FGA	PCT	3FGM	3FGA	PCT	FTM	FTA	PCT	O-RB	D-RB	TOT	AST	PF	DQ	STL	TO	BLK	PTS	RPG	APG	PPG
92-93–Dallas	53	13	885	151	312	.484	0	4	.000	68	99	.687	88	79	167	58	128	1	24	63	6	370	3.2	1.1	7.0
Reg. Season Totals	53	13	885	151	312	.484	0	4	.000	68	99	.687	88	79	167	58	128	1	24	63	6	370	3.2	1.1	7.0

Camby, Marcus D. b. March 22, 1974 Ht. 6-11 Wt. 225 College: Massachusetts

SEASON–TEAM	G	GS	MIN	FGM	FGA	PCT	3FGM	3FGA	PCT	FTM	FTA	PCT	O-RB	D-RB	TOT	AST	PF	DQ	STL	TO	BLK	PTS	RPG	APG	PPG
96-97–Toronto	63	38	1897	375	778	.482	2	14	.143	183	264	.693	131	263	394	97	214	7	66	134	130	935	6.3	1.5	14.8
97-98–Toronto	63	58	2002	308	747	.412	0	2	.000	149	244	.611	203	263	466	111	200	1	68	134	230	765	7.4	1.8	12.1
98-99–New York	46	0	945	136	261	.521	0	0	–	57	103	.553	102	151	253	12	131	2	29	39	74	329	5.5	0.3	7.2
99-00–New York	59	11	1548	226	471	.480	1	2	.500	148	221	.670	174	287	461	49	204	5	43	72	116	601	7.8	0.8	10.2
Reg. Season Totals	231	107	6392	1045	2257	.463	3	18	.167	537	832	.645	610	964	1574	269	749	15	206	379	550	2630	6.8	1.2	11.4
Playoff Totals	36	3	895	110	229	.480	0	2	.000	64	104	.615	86	179	265	12	127	3	32	27	61	284	7.4	0.3	7.9

Campbell, Anthony (Tony) b. May 7, 1962 Ht. 6-7 Wt. 215 College: Ohio State

SEASON–TEAM	G	GS	MIN	FGM	FGA	PCT	3FGM	3FGA	PCT	FTM	FTA	PCT	O-RB	D-RB	TOT	AST	PF	DQ	STL	TO	BLK	PTS	RPG	APG	PPG
84-85–Detroit	56	0	625	130	262	.496	0	1	.000	56	70	.800	41	48	89	24	107	1	28	69	3	316	1.6	0.4	5.6
85-86–Detroit	82	1	1292	294	608	.484	2	9	.222	58	73	.795	83	153	236	45	164	0	62	86	7	648	2.9	0.5	7.9
86-87–Detroit	40	0	332	57	145	.393	0	3	.000	24	39	.615	21	37	58	19	40	0	12	34	1	138	1.5	0.5	3.5
87-88–L.A. Lakers	13	1	242	57	101	.564	1	3	.333	28	39	.718	8	19	27	15	41	0	11	26	2	143	2.1	1.2	11.0
88-89–L.A. Lakers	63	2	787	158	345	.458	2	21	.095	70	83	.843	53	77	130	47	108	0	37	62	6	388	2.1	0.7	6.2
89-90–Minnesota	82	81	3164	723	1581	.457	9	54	.167	448	569	.787	209	242	451	213	260	7	111	251	31	1903	5.5	2.6	23.2
90-91–Minnesota	77	71	2893	652	1502	.434	16	61	.262	358	446	.803	161	185	346	214	204	0	121	190	48	1678	4.5	2.8	21.8
91-92–Minnesota	78	41	2441	527	1137	.464	13	37	.351	240	299	.803	141	145	286	229	206	1	84	165	31	1307	3.7	2.9	16.8
92-93–New York	58	13	1062	194	396	.490	2	5	.400	59	87	.678	59	96	155	62	150	0	34	51	5	449	2.7	1.1	7.7
93-94–N.Y.-Dallas	63	14	1214	227	512	.443	7	28	.250	94	120	.783	76	110	186	82	134	1	50	84	15	555	3.0	1.3	8.8
94-95–Cleveland	78	0	1128	161	392	.411	15	42	.357	132	159	.830	60	93	153	69	122	0	32	65	8	469	2.0	0.9	6.0
Reg. Season Totals	690	224	15180	3180	6981	.456	67	264	.254	1567	1984	.790	912	1205	2117	1019	1536	10	582	1083	157	7994	3.1	1.5	11.6
Playoff Totals	38	1	308	55	116	.474	4	9	.444	46	62	.742	11	26	37	15	59	1	8	21	1	160	1.0	0.4	4.2

Campbell, Elden Jerome (Big E) b. July 23, 1968 Ht. 7-0 Wt. 255 College: Clemson

SEASON–TEAM	G	GS	MIN	FGM	FGA	PCT	3FGM	3FGA	PCT	FTM	FTA	PCT	O-RB	D-RB	TOT	AST	PF	DQ	STL	TO	BLK	PTS	RPG	APG	PPG
90-91–L.A. Lakers	52	0	380	56	123	.455	0	0	–	32	49	.653	40	56	96	10	71	1	11	16	38	144	1.8	0.2	2.8
91-92–L.A. Lakers	81	47	1876	220	491	.448	0	2	.000	138	223	.619	155	268	423	59	203	1	53	73	159	578	5.2	0.7	7.1
92-93–L.A. Lakers	79	13	1551	238	520	.458	0	3	.000	130	204	.637	127	205	332	48	165	0	59	69	100	606	4.2	0.6	7.7
93-94–L.A. Lakers	76	74	2253	373	808	.462	0	2	.000	188	273	.689	167	352	519	86	241	2	64	98	146	934	6.8	1.1	12.3
94-95–L.A. Lakers	73	59	2076	360	785	.459	0	1	.000	193	290	.666	168	277	445	92	246	4	69	98	132	913	6.1	1.3	12.5
95-96–L.A. Lakers	82	82	2699	447	888	.503	0	5	.000	249	349	.713	162	461	623	181	300	4	88	137	212	1143	7.6	2.2	13.9
96-97–L.A. Lakers	77	77	2516	442	942	.469	1	4	.250	263	370	.711	207	408	615	126	276	6	46	130	117	1148	8.0	1.6	14.9
97-98–L.A. Lakers	81	28	1784	289	624	.463	1	2	.500	237	342	.693	143	312	455	78	209	1	35	115	102	816	5.6	1.0	10.1
98-99–Lakers-Cha.	49	33	1459	222	465	.477	0	1	.000	172	269	.639	126	271	397	69	159	3	39	80	73	616	8.1	1.4	12.6
99-00–Charlotte	78	77	2538	370	829	.446	0	6	.000	247	358	.690	168	422	590	129	269	6	56	127	150	987	7.6	1.7	12.7
Reg. Season Totals	728	490	19132	3017	6475	.466	2	26	.077	1849	2727	.678	1463	3032	4495	878	2139	28	520	943	1229	7885	6.2	1.2	10.8
Playoff Totals	63	34	1546	234	506	.462	1	3	.333	134	203	.660	103	215	318	61	186	4	32	82	94	603	5.0	1.0	9.6

Cannon, Lawrence T. (Larry) b. April 12, 1947 Ht. 6-5 Wt. 195 College: La Salle

SEASON–TEAM	G	GS	MIN	FGM	FGA	PCT	3FGM	3FGA	PCT	FTM	FTA	PCT	O-RB	D-RB	TOT	AST	PF	DQ	STL	TO	BLK	PTS	RPG	APG	PPG
69-70–Miami (A)	57	–	1503	253	660	.383	8	30	.267	158	232	.681	–	–	141	158	133	2	–	–	–	672	2.5	2.8	11.8
70-71–Denver (A)	80	–	3097	751	1722	.436	18	69	.261	606	763	.794	–	–	333	414	237	–	–	–	–	2126	4.2	5.2	26.6
71-72–Mem.-Ind. (A)	54	–	1171	228	610	.374	3	14	.214	164	221	.742	–	–	107	150	124	–	–	105	–	623	2.0	2.8	11.5
73-74–Indiana (A)	3	–	26	3	7	.429	0	0	–	1	3	.333	1	2	3	3	2	–	0	3	0	7	1.0	1.0	2.3
73-74–Philadelphia	19	–	335	49	127	.386	–	–	–	19	28	.679	16	20	36	52	48	0	7	–	4	117	1.9	2.7	6.2
Reg. NBA Totals	19	–	335	49	127	.386	–	–	–	19	28	.679	16	20	36	52	48	0	7	–	4	117	1.9	2.7	6.2
Reg. ABA Totals	194	–	5797	1235	2999	.412	29	113	.257	929	1219	.762	1	2	584	725	496	2	0	108	0	3428	3.0	3.7	17.7

Card, Frank Howard b. December 28, 1944 Ht. 6-7 Wt. 195 College: South Carolina State

SEASON–TEAM	G	GS	MIN	FGM	FGA	PCT	3FGM	3FGA	PCT	FTM	FTA	PCT	O-RB	D-RB	TOT	AST	PF	DQ	STL	TO	BLK	PTS	RPG	APG	PPG
68-69–Minnesota (A)	76	–	1596	222	537	.413	1	5	.200	146	244	.598	–	–	419	81	155	2	–	110	–	591	5.5	1.1	7.8
69-70–Washington (A)	74	–	1820	351	666	.527	1	5	.200	178	286	.622	–	–	480	92	216	3	–	–	–	881	6.5	1.2	11.9
70-71–Vir.-Car. (A)	70	–	1865	302	662	.456	1	5	.200	196	303	.647	–	–	457	113	216	–	–	–	–	801	6.5	1.6	11.4
71-72–Car.-Denver (A)	82	–	1584	235	543	.433	0	2	.000	130	197	.660	–	–	358	86	220	–	–	124	–	600	4.4	1.0	7.3
72-73–Denver (A)	4	–	36	6	15	.400	0	0	–	9	13	.692	4	3	7	0	4	0	–	3	–	21	1.8	0.0	5.3
Reg. ABA Totals	306	–	6901	1116	2423	.461	3	17	.176	659	1043	.632	4	3	1721	372	811	5	–	237	–	2894	5.6	1.2	9.5
ABA Playoff Totals	17	–	338	64	110	.582	0	1	.000	21	41	.512	–	–	84	22	56	2	–	1	–	149	4.9	1.3	8.8

Carl, Howard Hershey (Howie) b. June 7, 1938 Ht. 5-9 Wt. 160 College: Illinois; DePaul

SEASON–TEAM	G	GS	MIN	FGM	FGA	PCT	3FGM	3FGA	PCT	FTM	FTA	PCT	O-RB	D-RB	TOT	AST	PF	DQ	STL	TO	BLK	PTS	RPG	APG	PPG
61-62–Chicago	31	–	382	67	201	.333	–	–	–	36	51	.706	–	–	39	57	41	1	–	–	–	170	1.3	1.8	5.5
Reg. Season Totals	31	–	382	67	201	.333	–	–	–	36	51	.706	–	–	39	57	41	1	–	–	–	170	1.3	1.8	5.5

Carlisle, Chester G. (Chet) b. November 2, 1916 d. August 1988 Ht. 6-5 Wt. 195 College: California

SEASON–TEAM	G	GS	MIN	FGM	FGA	PCT	3FGM	3FGA	PCT	FTM	FTA	PCT	O-RB	D-RB	TOT	AST	PF	DQ	STL	TO	BLK	PTS	RPG	APG	PPG
46-47–Chicago	51	–	–	100	373	.268	–	–	–	56	92	.609	–	–	–	17	136	–	–	–	–	256	–	0.3	5.0
Reg. Season Totals	51	–	–	100	373	.268	–	–	–	56	92	.609	–	–	–	17	136	–	–	–	–	256	–	0.3	5.0
Playoff Totals	10	–	–	20	172	.227	–	–	–	16	27	.593	–	–	–	2	33	2	–	–	–	56	–	0.1	5.6

Carlisle, Richard Preston (Rick) b. October 27, 1959 Ht. 6-5 Wt. 210 College: Maine; Virginia

SEASON–TEAM	G	GS	MIN	FGM	FGA	PCT	3FGM	3FGA	PCT	FTM	FTA	PCT	O-RB	D-RB	TOT	AST	PF	DQ	STL	TO	BLK	PTS	RPG	APG	PPG
84-85–Boston	38	0	179	26	67	.388	0	2	.000	15	17	.882	8	13	21	25	21	0	3	19	0	67	0.6	0.7	1.8
85-86–Boston	77	1	760	92	189	.487	0	10	.000	15	23	.652	22	55	77	104	92	1	19	50	4	199	1.0	1.4	2.6
86-87–Boston	42	0	297	30	92	.326	5	16	.313	15	20	.750	8	22	30	35	28	0	8	25	0	80	0.7	0.8	1.9
87-88–New York	26	0	204	29	67	.433	6	17	.353	10	11	.909	6	7	13	32	39	1	11	22	4	74	0.5	1.2	2.8
89-90–New Jersey	5	0	21	1	7	.143	0	3	.000	0	0	–	0	0	0	5	7	0	1	4	1	2	0.0	1.0	0.4
Reg. Season Totals	188	1	1461	178	422	.422	11	48	.229	55	71	.775	44	97	141	201	187	2	42	120	9	422	0.8	1.1	2.2
Playoff Totals	12	0	62	9	19	.474	0	2	.000	3	4	.750	4	3	7	8	10	0	3	3	0	21	0.6	0.7	1.8

Carlos, Don A. b. March 3, 1944 Ht. 6-5 Wt. 210 College: Otterbein

SEASON–TEAM	G	GS	MIN	FGM	FGA	PCT	3FGM	3FGA	PCT	FTM	FTA	PCT	O-RB	D-RB	TOT	AST	PF	DQ	STL	TO	BLK	PTS	RPG	APG	PPG
68-69–Houston (A)	56	–	1527	207	505	.410	0	3	.000	214	283	.756	–	–	279	159	231	10	–	140	–	628	5.0	2.8	11.2
Reg. ABA Totals	56	–	1527	207	505	.410	0	3	.000	214	283	.756	–	–	279	159	231	10	–	140	–	628	5.0	2.8	11.2

Carlson, Alvin Harold b. September 17, 1951 Ht. 6-11 Wt. 235 College: USC; Oregon

SEASON–TEAM	G	GS	MIN	FGM	FGA	PCT	3FGM	3FGA	PCT	FTM	FTA	PCT	O-RB	D-RB	TOT	AST	PF	DQ	STL	TO	BLK	PTS	RPG	APG	PPG
75-76–Seattle	28	–	279	27	79	.342	–	–	–	18	29	.621	30	43	73	13	39	1	7	–	11	72	2.6	0.5	2.6
Reg. Season Totals	28	–	279	27	79	.342	–	–	–	18	29	.621	30	43	73	13	39	1	7	–	11	72	2.6	0.5	2.6

Carlson, Don Vernon (Swede) b. March 22, 1921 Ht. 6-0 Wt. 170 College: Minnesota

SEASON–TEAM	G	GS	MIN	FGM	FGA	PCT	3FGM	3FGA	PCT	FTM	FTA	PCT	O-RB	D-RB	TOT	AST	PF	DQ	STL	TO	BLK	PTS	RPG	APG	PPG
46-47–Chicago	59	–	–	272	845	.322	–	–	–	86	159	.541	–	–	–	59	182	–	–	–	–	630	–	1.0	10.7
47-48–Minneapolis (N)	58	–	–	205	–	–	–	–	–	65	109	.596	–	–	–	–	177	–	–	–	–	475	–	–	8.2
48-49–Minneapolis	55	–	–	211	632	.334	–	–	–	86	130	.662	–	–	–	170	180	–	–	–	–	508	–	3.1	9.2
49-50–Minneapolis	57	–	–	99	290	.341	–	–	–	69	95	.726	–	–	–	76	126	–	–	–	–	267	–	1.3	4.7
50-51–Washington	9	–	–	17	46	.370	–	–	–	8	16	.500	–	–	15	19	23	0	–	–	–	42	1.7	2.1	4.7
Reg. NBA Totals	180	–	–	599	1813	.330	–	–	–	249	400	.623	–	–	15	324	511	0	–	–	–	1447	1.7	1.8	8.0
Reg. NBL Totals	58	–	–	205	–	–	–	–	–	65	109	.596	–	–	–	–	177	–	–	–	–	475	–	–	8.2
NBA Playoff Totals	31	–	–	98	652	.294	–	–	–	53	84	.631	–	–	–	89	79	2	–	–	–	249	–	1.5	8.0
NBL Playoff Totals	9	–	–	17	–	–	–	–	–	4	10	.400	–	–	–	–	27	–	–	–	–	38	–	–	4.2

Carney, Robert Lee (Bob) b. August 3, 1932 Ht. 6-3 Wt. 170 College: Bradley

SEASON–TEAM	G	GS	MIN	FGM	FGA	PCT	3FGM	3FGA	PCT	FTM	FTA	PCT	O-RB	D-RB	TOT	AST	PF	DQ	STL	TO	BLK	PTS	RPG	APG	PPG
54-55–Minneapolis	19	–	244	24	64	.375	–	–	–	21	40	.525	–	–	45	16	36	0	–	–	–	69	2.4	0.8	3.6
Reg. Season Totals	19	–	244	24	64	.375	–	–	–	21	40	.525	–	–	45	16	36	0	–	–	–	69	2.4	0.8	3.6
Playoff Totals	7	–	41	1	8	.125	–	–	–	8	9	.889	–	–	5	3	7	0	–	–	–	10	0.7	0.4	1.4

Carpenter, Robert H. (Bob) b. November 6, 1917 d. April 18, 1997 Ht. 6-5 Wt. 200 College: Texas A&M-Commerce

SEASON–TEAM	G	GS	MIN	FGM	FGA	PCT	3FGM	3FGA	PCT	FTM	FTA	PCT	O-RB	D-RB	TOT	AST	PF	DQ	STL	TO	BLK	PTS	RPG	APG	PPG
40-41–Oshkosh (N)	24	–	–	40	–	–	–	–	–	41	–	–	–	–	–	–	37	–	–	–	–	121	–	–	5.0
45-46–Oshkosh (N)	34	–	–	186	–	–	–	–	–	101	144	.701	–	–	–	–	–	–	–	–	–	473	–	–	13.9
46-47–Oshkosh (N)	44	–	–	199	–	–	–	–	–	115	169	.680	–	–	–	–	–	–	–	–	–	513	–	–	11.7
47-48–Oshkosh (N)	60	–	–	211	–	–	–	–	–	160	213	.751	–	–	–	–	–	–	–	–	–	582	–	–	9.7
48-49–Hammond-Oshkosh (N)	47	–	–	160	–	–	–	–	–	131	180	.728	–	–	–	–	–	–	–	–	–	451	–	–	9.6
49-50–Fort Wayne	66	–	–	212	617	.344	–	–	–	190	256	.742	–	–	–	92	168	–	–	–	–	614	–	1.4	9.3
50-51–FtWayne-Tri-Cit	56	–	–	109	355	.307	–	–	–	105	128	.820	–	–	229	79	115	2	–	–	–	323	4.1	1.4	5.8
Reg. NBA Totals	122	–	–	321	972	.330	–	–	–	295	384	.768	–	–	229	171	283	2	–	–	–	937	4.1	1.4	7.7
Reg. NBL Totals	209	–	–	796	–	–	–	–	–	548	706	.718	–	–	–	–	37	–	–	–	–	2140	–	–	10.2
NBA Playoff Totals	4	–	–	11	60	.367	–	–	–	10	14	.714	–	–	–	4	6	0	–	–	–	32	–	0.5	8.0
NBL Playoff Totals	28	–	–	82	–	–	–	–	–	91	88	.682	–	–	–	–	58	–	–	–	–	255	–	–	9.1

Carr, Antoine Labotte (A.C.) b. July 23, 1961 Ht. 6-9 Wt. 270 College: Wichita State

SEASON–TEAM	G	GS	MIN	FGM	FGA	PCT	3FGM	3FGA	PCT	FTM	FTA	PCT	O-RB	D-RB	TOT	AST	PF	DQ	STL	TO	BLK	PTS	RPG	APG	PPG
84-85–Atlanta	62	15	1195	198	375	.528	2	6	.333	101	128	.789	79	153	232	80	219	4	29	108	78	499	3.7	1.3	8.0
85-86–Atlanta	17	0	258	49	93	.527	0	0	–	18	27	.667	16	36	52	14	51	1	7	14	15	116	3.1	0.8	6.8
86-87–Atlanta	65	2	695	134	265	.506	1	3	.333	73	103	.709	60	96	156	34	146	1	14	40	48	342	2.4	0.5	5.3
87-88–Atlanta	80	2	1483	281	517	.544	1	4	.250	142	182	.780	94	195	289	103	272	7	38	116	83	705	3.6	1.3	8.8
88-89–Atlanta	78	12	1488	226	471	.480	0	1	.000	130	152	.855	106	168	274	91	221	0	31	82	62	582	3.5	1.2	7.5
89-90–Atlanta-Sac.	77	4	1727	356	721	.494	0	7	.000	237	298	.795	115	207	322	119	247	6	30	125	68	949	4.2	1.5	12.3
90-91–Sacramento	77	48	2527	628	1228	.511	0	3	.000	295	389	.758	163	257	420	191	315	14	45	171	101	1551	5.5	2.5	20.1
91-92–San Antonio	81	27	1867	359	732	.490	1	5	.200	162	212	.764	128	218	346	63	264	5	32	114	96	881	4.3	0.8	10.9
92-93–San Antonio	71	46	1947	379	705	.538	0	5	.000	174	224	.777	107	281	388	97	264	5	35	96	87	932	5.5	1.4	13.1
93-94–San Antonio	34	0	465	78	160	.488	0	1	.000	42	58	.724	12	39	51	15	75	0	9	15	22	198	1.5	0.4	5.8
94-95–Utah	78	4	1677	290	546	.531	1	4	.250	165	201	.821	81	184	265	67	253	4	24	87	68	746	3.4	0.9	9.6
95-96–Utah	80	0	1532	233	510	.457	0	3	.000	114	144	.792	71	129	200	74	254	4	28	78	65	580	2.5	0.9	7.3
96-97–Utah	82	0	1460	252	522	.483	0	3	.000	99	127	.780	60	135	195	74	214	2	24	75	63	603	2.4	0.9	7.4
97-98–Utah	66	8	1086	151	325	.465	0	0	–	76	98	.776	42	89	131	48	195	3	11	48	53	378	2.0	0.7	5.7
98-99–Houston	18	0	152	21	52	.404	0	1	.000	5	7	.714	9	22	31	9	31	0	1	9	10	47	1.7	0.5	2.6
99-00–Vancouver	21	0	221	28	64	.438	0	0	–	11	14	.786	8	24	32	7	42	0	3	9	6	67	1.5	0.3	3.2
Reg. Season Totals	987	168	19780	3663	7286	.503	6	46	.130	1844	2364	.780	1151	2233	3384	1086	3063	56	361	1187	925	9176	3.4	1.1	9.3
Playoff Totals	107	11	1832	301	586	.514	1	3	.333	128	173	.740	94	181	275	103	383	12	27	86	92	731	2.6	1.0	6.8

Carr, Austin George b. March 10, 1948 Ht. 6-4 Wt. 200 College: Notre Dame

SEASON–TEAM	G	GS	MIN	FGM	FGA	PCT	3FGM	3FGA	PCT	FTM	FTA	PCT	O-RB	D-RB	TOT	AST	PF	DQ	STL	TO	BLK	PTS	RPG	APG	PPG
71-72–Cleveland	43	–	1539	381	894	.426	–	–	–	149	196	.760	–	–	150	148	99	0	–	–	–	911	3.5	3.4	21.2
72-73–Cleveland	82	–	3097	702	1575	.446	–	–	–	281	342	.822	–	–	369	279	185	1	–	–	–	1685	4.5	3.4	20.5
73-74–Cleveland	81	–	3100	748	1682	.445	–	–	–	279	326	.856	139	150	289	305	189	2	92	–	14	1775	3.6	3.8	21.9
74-75–Cleveland	41	–	1081	252	538	.468	–	–	–	89	106	.840	51	56	107	154	57	0	48	–	2	593	2.6	3.8	14.5
75-76–Cleveland	65	–	1282	276	625	.442	–	–	–	106	134	.791	67	65	132	122	92	0	37	–	2	658	2.0	1.9	10.1
76-77–Cleveland	82	–	2409	558	1221	.457	–	–	–	213	268	.795	120	120	240	220	221	3	57	–	10	1329	2.9	2.7	16.2
77-78–Cleveland	82	–	2186	414	945	.438	–	–	–	183	225	.813	76	111	187	225	168	1	68	146	19	1011	2.3	2.7	12.3
78-79–Cleveland	82	–	2714	551	1161	.475	–	–	–	292	358	.816	155	135	290	217	210	1	77	175	14	1394	3.5	2.6	17.0
79-80–Cleveland	77	–	1595	390	839	.465	2	6	.333	127	172	.738	81	84	165	150	120	0	39	108	3	909	2.1	1.9	11.8
80-81–Dallas-Wash.	47	–	657	87	234	.372	0	7	.000	34	54	.630	22	39	61	58	53	0	15	41	2	208	1.3	1.2	4.4
Reg. Season Totals	682	–	19660	4359	9714	.449	2	13	.154	1753	2181	.804	711	760	1990	1878	1394	8	433	470	66	10473	2.9	2.8	15.4
Playoff Totals	18	–	425	87	204	.426	0	0	–	38	55	.691	18	23	41	41	50	0	10	4	5	212	2.3	2.3	11.8
All-Star Totals	1	–	5	0	4	.000	0	0	–	0	0	–	0	1	1	0	1	0	0	–	0	0	1.0	0.0	0.0

Carr, Chris Dean b. March 12, 1974 Ht. 6-6 Wt. 220 College: Southern Illinois

SEASON–TEAM	G	GS	MIN	FGM	FGA	PCT	3FGM	3FGA	PCT	FTM	FTA	PCT	O-RB	D-RB	TOT	AST	PF	DQ	STL	TO	BLK	PTS	RPG	APG	PPG
95-96–Phoenix	60	10	590	90	217	.415	11	42	.262	49	60	.817	27	75	102	43	77	1	10	40	5	240	1.7	0.7	4.0
96-97–Minnesota	55	10	830	125	271	.461	31	88	.352	56	73	.767	31	82	113	48	93	0	24	37	10	337	2.1	0.9	6.1
97-98–Minnesota	51	40	1165	190	452	.420	40	127	.315	84	99	.848	43	112	155	85	129	1	17	69	11	504	3.0	1.7	9.9
98-99–Minn.-N.J.	39	4	445	76	205	.371	28	75	.373	27	40	.675	23	48	71	23	45	0	8	28	2	207	1.8	0.6	5.3
99-00–G.S.-Chicago	57	2	1166	196	496	.395	32	101	.317	107	125	.856	41	132	173	84	113	0	30	117	15	531	3.0	1.5	9.3
Reg. Season Totals	262	66	4196	677	1641	.413	142	433	.328	323	397	.814	165	449	614	283	457	2	89	291	43	1819	2.3	1.1	6.9
Playoff Totals	4	0	44	9	16	.563	2	5	.400	4	5	.800	3	6	9	5	6	0	2	5	1	24	2.3	1.3	6.0

Carr, Cory Jermaine b. December 5, 1975 Ht. 6-4 Wt. 215 College: Texas Tech

SEASON–TEAM	G	GS	MIN	FGM	FGA	PCT	3FGM	3FGA	PCT	FTM	FTA	PCT	O-RB	D-RB	TOT	AST	PF	DQ	STL	TO	BLK	PTS	RPG	APG	PPG
98-99–Chicago	42	7	624	71	216	.329	5	30	.167	24	32	.750	8	41	49	66	66	0	21	46	7	171	1.2	1.6	4.1
Reg. Season Totals	42	7	624	71	216	.329	5	30	.167	24	32	.750	8	41	49	66	66	0	21	46	7	171	1.2	1.6	4.1

Carr, Kenneth Alan (Kenny) b. August 15, 1955 Ht. 6-7 Wt. 220 College: North Carolina State

SEASON–TEAM	G	GS	MIN	FGM	FGA	PCT	3FGM	3FGA	PCT	FTM	FTA	PCT	O-RB	D-RB	TOT	AST	PF	DQ	STL	TO	BLK	PTS	RPG	APG	PPG
77-78–Los Angeles	52	–	733	134	302	.444	–	–	–	55	85	.647	53	155	208	26	127	0	18	89	14	323	4.0	0.5	6.2
78-79–Los Angeles	72	–	1149	225	450	.500	–	–	–	83	137	.606	70	222	292	60	152	0	38	116	31	533	4.1	0.8	7.4
79-80–L.A.-Clev.	79	–	1838	378	768	.492	0	4	.000	173	263	.658	199	389	588	77	246	3	66	154	52	929	7.4	1.0	11.8
80-81–Cleveland	81	–	2615	469	918	.511	0	4	.000	292	409	.714	260	575	835	192	296	3	76	231	42	1230	10.3	2.4	15.2
81-82–Clev.-Detroit	74	48	1926	348	692	.503	1	10	.100	198	302	.656	167	364	531	86	249	0	64	152	22	895	7.2	1.2	12.1
82-83–Portland	82	26	2331	362	717	.505	2	6	.333	255	366	.697	182	407	589	116	306	10	62	185	42	981	7.2	1.4	12.0
83-84–Portland	82	57	2455	518	923	.561	0	5	.000	247	367	.673	208	434	642	157	274	3	68	202	33	1283	7.8	1.9	15.6
84-85–Portland	48	30	1120	190	363	.523	0	3	.000	118	164	.720	90	233	323	56	141	0	25	100	17	498	6.7	1.2	10.4
85-86–Portland	55	31	1557	232	466	.498	0	4	.000	149	217	.687	146	346	492	70	203	5	38	106	30	613	8.9	1.3	11.1
86-87–Portland	49	43	1443	201	399	.504	0	2	.000	126	169	.746	131	368	499	83	159	1	29	103	13	528	10.2	1.7	10.8
Reg. Season Totals	674	235	17167	3057	5998	.510	3	38	.079	1696	2479	.684	1506	3493	4999	923	2153	25	484	1438	296	7813	7.4	1.4	11.6
Playoff Totals	35	18	893	153	299	.512	0	2	.000	62	85	.729	69	161	230	37	126	4	18	65	12	368	6.6	1.1	10.5

Carr, Michael Leon (M.L.) b. January 9, 1951 Ht. 6-6 Wt. 205 College: Guilford

SEASON–TEAM	G	GS	MIN	FGM	FGA	PCT	3FGM	3FGA	PCT	FTM	FTA	PCT	O-RB	D-RB	TOT	AST	PF	DQ	STL	TO	BLK	PTS	RPG	APG	PPG
75-76–St. Louis (A)	74	–	2174	380	786	.483	9	24	.375	137	206	.665	171	288	459	224	225	–	127	162	44	906	6.2	3.0	12.2
76-77–Detroit	82	–	2643	443	931	.476	–	–	–	205	279	.735	211	420	631	181	287	8	165	–	58	1091	7.7	2.2	13.3
77-78–Detroit	79	–	2556	390	857	.455	–	–	–	200	271	.738	202	355	557	185	243	4	147	210	27	980	7.1	2.3	12.4
78-79–Detroit	80	–	3207	587	1143	.514	–	–	–	323	435	.743	219	370	589	262	279	2	197	255	46	1497	7.4	3.3	18.7
79-80–Boston	82	–	1994	362	763	.474	12	41	.293	178	241	.739	106	224	330	156	214	1	120	143	36	914	4.0	1.9	11.1
80-81–Boston	41	–	655	97	216	.449	1	14	.071	53	67	.791	26	57	83	56	74	0	30	47	18	248	2.0	1.4	6.0
81-82–Boston	56	27	1296	184	409	.450	5	17	.294	82	116	.707	56	94	150	128	136	2	67	63	21	455	2.7	2.3	8.1
82-83–Boston	77	0	883	135	315	.429	3	19	.158	60	81	.741	51	86	137	71	140	0	48	79	10	333	1.8	0.9	4.3
83-84–Boston	60	1	585	70	171	.409	3	15	.200	42	48	.875	26	49	75	49	67	0	17	46	4	185	1.3	0.8	3.1
84-85–Boston	47	0	397	62	149	.416	9	23	.391	17	17	1.000	21	22	43	24	44	0	21	24	6	150	0.9	0.5	3.2
Reg. NBA Totals	604	28	14216	2330	4954	.470	33	129	.256	1160	1555	.746	918	1677	2595	1112	1484	17	812	867	226	5853	4.3	1.8	9.7
Reg. ABA Totals	74	–	2174	380	786	.483	9	24	.375	137	206	.665	171	288	459	224	225	–	127	162	44	906	6.2	3.0	12.2
NBA Playoff Totals	67	12	1005	142	372	.382	5	22	.227	65	91	.714	59	70	129	64	111	0	38	40	10	354	1.9	1.0	5.3

Carrier, James Darel (Darel) b. October 26, 1940 Ht. 6-3 Wt. 185 College: Western Kentucky

SEASON–TEAM	G	GS	MIN	FGM	FGA	PCT	3FGM	3FGA	PCT	FTM	FTA	PCT	O-RB	D-RB	TOT	AST	PF	DQ	STL	TO	BLK	PTS	RPG	APG	PPG
67-68–Kentucky (A)	77	–	3192	643	1545	.416	84	235	.357	395	479	.825	–	–	352	172	263	7	–	228	–	1765	4.6	2.2	22.9
68-69–Kentucky (A)	73	–	2858	559	1376	.406	125	330	.379	447	545	.820	–	–	283	214	227	1	–	213	–	1690	3.9	2.9	23.2
69-70–Kentucky (A)	77	–	2805	608	1458	.417	105	280	.375	454	509	.892	–	–	249	212	268	8	–	–	–	1775	3.2	2.8	23.1
70-71–Kentucky (A)	84	–	2664	495	1140	.434	63	161	.391	327	377	.867	–	–	232	244	229	–	–	–	–	1380	2.8	2.9	16.4
71-72–Kentucky (A)	23	–	629	117	288	.406	16	37	.432	76	88	.864	–	–	57	44	64	–	–	38	–	326	2.5	1.9	14.2
72-73–Memphis (A)	16	–	190	23	60	.383	5	12	.417	24	26	.923	2	12	14	10	21	0	–	15	–	75	0.9	0.6	4.7
Reg. ABA Totals	350	–	12338	2445	5867	.417	398	1055	.377	1723	2024	.851	2	12	1187	896	1072	16	–	494	–	7011	3.4	2.6	20.0
ABA Playoff Totals	45	–	1693	309	733	.422	57	146	.390	241	277	.870	–	–	151	131	156	2	–	15	–	916	3.4	2.9	20.4

Carrington, Robert Frederick (Bob) b. July 3, 1953 Ht. 6-6 Wt. 195 College: Boston College

SEASON–TEAM	G	GS	MIN	FGM	FGA	PCT	3FGM	3FGA	PCT	FTM	FTA	PCT	O-RB	D-RB	TOT	AST	PF	DQ	STL	TO	BLK	PTS	RPG	APG	PPG
77-78–N.J.-Indiana	72	–	1653	253	589	.430	–	–	–	130	171	.760	70	104	174	117	205	6	65	118	23	636	2.4	1.6	8.8
79-80–San Diego	10	–	134	15	37	.405	0	2	.000	6	8	.750	6	7	13	3	18	0	4	5	1	36	1.3	0.3	3.6
Reg. Season Totals	82	–	1787	268	626	.428	0	2	.000	136	179	.760	76	111	187	120	223	6	69	123	24	672	2.3	1.5	8.2

Carroll, Joe Barry (Joe Barry, J.B.) b. July 24, 1958 Ht. 7-0 Wt. 235 College: Purdue

SEASON–TEAM	G	GS	MIN	FGM	FGA	PCT	3FGM	3FGA	PCT	FTM	FTA	PCT	O-RB	D-RB	TOT	AST	PF	DQ	STL	TO	BLK	PTS	RPG	APG	PPG
80-81–Golden State	82	–	2919	616	1254	.491	0	2	.000	315	440	.716	274	485	759	117	313	10	50	243	121	1547	9.3	1.4	18.9
81-82–Golden State	76	75	2627	527	1016	.519	0	1	.000	235	323	.728	210	423	633	64	265	8	64	206	127	1289	8.3	0.8	17.0
82-83–Golden State	79	79	2988	785	1529	.513	0	3	.000	337	469	.719	220	468	688	169	260	7	108	285	155	1907	8.7	2.1	24.1
83-84–Golden State	80	80	2962	663	1390	.477	0	1	.000	313	433	.723	235	401	636	198	244	9	103	268	142	1639	8.0	2.5	20.5
85-86–Golden State	79	79	2801	650	1404	.463	0	2	.000	377	501	.752	193	477	670	176	277	13	101	275	144	1677	8.5	2.2	21.2
86-87–Golden State	81	81	2724	690	1461	.472	0	0	–	340	432	.787	173	416	589	214	255	2	92	226	123	1720	7.3	2.6	21.2
87-88–G.S.-Houston	77	30	2004	402	924	.435	0	2	.000	172	225	.764	131	358	489	113	195	1	50	164	106	976	6.4	1.5	12.7
88-89–New Jersey	64	62	1996	363	810	.448	0	0	–	176	220	.800	118	355	473	105	193	2	71	143	81	902	7.4	1.6	14.1
89-90–N.J.-Denver	76	47	1721	312	759	.411	0	2	.000	137	177	.774	133	310	443	97	192	4	47	142	115	761	5.8	1.3	10.0
90-91–Phoenix	11	0	96	13	36	.361	0	0	–	11	12	.917	3	21	24	11	18	0	1	12	8	37	2.2	1.0	3.4
Reg. Season Totals	705	533	22838	5021	10583	.474	0	13	.000	2413	3232	.747	1690	3714	5404	1264	2212	56	687	1964	1122	12455	7.7	1.8	17.7
Playoff Totals	19	17	511	105	234	.449	0	1	.000	51	64	.797	25	69	94	26	60	2	18	38	32	261	4.9	1.4	13.7
All-Star Totals	1	0	18	1	7	.143	0	0	–	2	2	1.000	4	2	6	0	4	0	0	1	1	4	6.0	0.0	4.0

Carruth, Jimmy Dawn b. November 4, 1969 Ht. 6-10 Wt. 265 College: Virginia Tech

SEASON–TEAM	G	GS	MIN	FGM	FGA	PCT	3FGM	3FGA	PCT	FTM	FTA	PCT	O-RB	D-RB	TOT	AST	PF	DQ	STL	TO	BLK	PTS	RPG	APG	PPG
96-97–Milwaukee	4	0	21	2	3	.667	0	0	–	1	1	1.000	0	4	4	0	4	0	0	1	2	5	1.0	0.0	1.3
Reg. Season Totals	4	0	21	2	3	.667	0	0	–	1	1	1.000	0	4	4	0	4	0	0	1	2	5	1.0	0.0	1.3

Carter, Anthony b. June 16, 1975 Ht. 6-1 Wt. 190 College: Hawaii

SEASON–TEAM	G	GS	MIN	FGM	FGA	PCT	3FGM	3FGA	PCT	FTM	FTA	PCT	O-RB	D-RB	TOT	AST	PF	DQ	STL	TO	BLK	PTS	RPG	APG	PPG
99-00–Miami	79	30	1859	201	509	.395	3	23	.130	93	124	.750	48	151	199	378	167	0	93	173	5	498	2.5	4.8	6.3
Reg. Season Totals	79	30	1859	201	509	.395	3	23	.130	93	124	.750	48	151	199	378	167	0	93	173	5	498	2.5	4.8	6.3
Playoff Totals	10	3	275	32	77	.416	1	6	.167	12	16	.750	8	32	40	56	23	0	12	24	2	77	4.0	5.6	7.7

Carter, Clarence Eugene Jr. (Butch) b. June 11, 1958 Ht. 6-5 Wt. 180 College: Indiana

SEASON–TEAM	G	GS	MIN	FGM	FGA	PCT	3FGM	3FGA	PCT	FTM	FTA	PCT	O-RB	D-RB	TOT	AST	PF	DQ	STL	TO	BLK	PTS	RPG	APG	PPG
80-81–Los Angeles	54	–	672	114	247	.462	3	10	.300	70	95	.737	34	31	65	52	99	0	23	50	1	301	1.2	1.0	5.6
81-82–Indiana	75	0	1035	188	402	.468	8	25	.320	58	70	.829	30	49	79	60	110	0	34	54	11	442	1.1	0.8	5.9
82-83–Indiana	81	28	1716	354	706	.501	17	51	.333	124	154	.805	62	88	150	194	207	5	78	118	13	849	1.9	2.4	10.5
83-84–Indiana	73	54	2045	413	862	.479	15	46	.326	136	178	.764	70	83	153	206	211	1	128	141	13	977	2.1	2.8	13.4
84-85–New York	69	11	1279	214	476	.450	11	43	.256	109	134	.813	36	59	95	167	151	1	57	109	5	548	1.4	2.4	7.9
85-86–N.Y.-Phil.	9	0	67	7	24	.292	0	1	.000	6	7	.857	2	2	4	4	14	0	1	7	0	20	0.4	0.4	2.2
Reg. Season Totals	361	93	6814	1290	2717	.475	54	176	.307	503	638	.788	234	312	546	683	792	7	321	479	43	3137	1.5	1.9	8.7

Carter, Frederick James **(Fred, Mad Dog)** b. February 14, 1945 Ht. 6-3 Wt. 185 College: Mount St. Mary's

SEASON–TEAM	G	GS	MIN	FGM	FGA	PCT	3FGM	3FGA	PCT	FTM	FTA	PCT	O-RB	D-RB	TOT	AST	PF	DQ	STL	TO	BLK	PTS	RPG	APG	PPG
69-70–Baltimore	76	–	1219	157	439	.358	–	–	–	80	116	.690	–	–	192	121	137	0	–	–	–	394	2.5	1.6	5.2
70-71–Baltimore	77	–	1707	340	815	.417	–	–	–	119	183	.650	–	–	251	165	165	0	–	–	–	799	3.3	2.1	10.4
71-72–Balt.-Phil.	79	–	2215	446	1018	.438	–	–	–	182	293	.621	–	–	326	211	242	4	–	–	–	1074	4.1	2.7	13.6
72-73–Philadelphia	81	–	2993	679	1614	.421	–	–	–	259	368	.704	–	–	485	349	252	8	–	–	–	1617	6.0	4.3	20.0
73-74–Philadelphia	78	–	3044	706	1641	.430	–	–	–	254	358	.709	82	289	371	443	276	4	113	–	23	1666	4.8	5.7	21.4
74-75–Philadelphia	77	–	3046	715	1598	.447	–	–	–	256	347	.738	73	267	340	336	257	5	82	–	20	1686	4.4	4.4	21.9
75-76–Philadelphia	82	–	2992	665	1594	.417	–	–	–	219	312	.702	113	186	299	372	286	5	137	–	13	1549	3.6	4.5	18.9
76-77–Phil.-Milw.	61	–	1112	209	500	.418	–	–	–	68	96	.708	55	62	117	125	125	0	39	–	9	486	1.9	2.0	8.0
Reg. Season Totals	611	–	18328	3917	9219	.425	–	–	–	1437	2073	.693	323	804	2381	2122	1740	26	371	–	65	9271	3.9	3.5	15.2
Playoff Totals	28	–	975	178	434	.410	–	–	–	90	131	.687	4	6	123	75	102	1	4	–	1	446	4.4	2.7	15.9

Carter, George b. January 10, 1944 Ht. 6-5 Wt. 220 College: St. Bonaventure

SEASON–TEAM	G	GS	MIN	FGM	FGA	PCT	3FGM	3FGA	PCT	FTM	FTA	PCT	O-RB	D-RB	TOT	AST	PF	DQ	STL	TO	BLK	PTS	RPG	APG	PPG
67-68–Detroit	1	–	5	1	2	.500	–	–	–	1	1	1.000	–	–	0	1	0	0	–	–	–	3	0.0	1.0	3.0
69-70–Washington (A)	67	–	1848	397	871	.456	7	13	.538	167	216	.773	–	–	425	94	203	1	–	–	–	968	6.3	1.4	14.4
70-71–Virginia (A)	81	–	2721	594	1255	.473	0	1	.000	346	437	.792	–	–	650	157	290	–	–	–	–	1534	8.0	1.9	18.9
71-72–Pitt.-Car. (A)	75	–	2623	538	1227	.438	0	10	.000	388	474	.819	–	–	506	128	220	–	–	190	–	1464	6.7	1.7	19.5
72-73–New York (A)	83	–	2976	569	1249	.456	0	9	.000	440	529	.832	205	310	515	173	308	7	–	255	–	1578	6.2	2.1	19.0
73-74–Virginia (A)	80	–	2815	561	1329	.422	32	93	.344	392	466	.841	189	346	535	136	308	–	67	229	12	1546	6.7	1.7	19.3
74-75–Memphis (A)	82	–	3066	590	1354	.436	10	37	.270	318	400	.795	232	349	581	255	276	–	92	198	33	1508	7.1	3.1	18.4
75-76–Utah (A)	10	–	180	25	65	.385	0	0	–	32	41	.780	11	20	31	15	27	–	5	16	3	82	3.1	1.5	8.2
Reg. NBA Totals	1	–	5	1	2	.500	–	–	–	1	1	1.000	–	–	0	1	0	0	–	–	–	3	0.0	1.0	3.0
Reg. ABA Totals	478	–	16229	3274	7350	.445	49	163	.301	2083	2563	.813	637	1025	3243	958	1632	8	164	888	48	8680	6.8	2.0	18.2
ABA Playoff Totals	30	–	1119	215	461	.466	2	14	.143	138	166	.831	49	71	246	60	123	0	5	63	3	570	8.2	2.0	19.0

Carter, Howard O'Neal b. October 26, 1961 Ht. 6-5 Wt. 215 College: Louisiana State

SEASON–TEAM	G	GS	MIN	FGM	FGA	PCT	3FGM	3FGA	PCT	FTM	FTA	PCT	O-RB	D-RB	TOT	AST	PF	DQ	STL	TO	BLK	PTS	RPG	APG	PPG
83-84–Denver	55	5	688	145	316	.459	5	19	.263	47	61	.770	38	48	86	71	81	0	19	42	4	342	1.6	1.3	6.2
84-85–Dallas	11	0	66	4	23	.174	0	3	.000	1	1	1.000	1	2	3	4	4	0	1	8	0	9	0.3	0.4	0.8
Reg. Season Totals	66	5	754	149	339	.440	5	22	.227	48	62	.774	39	50	89	75	85	0	20	50	4	351	1.3	1.1	5.3
Playoff Totals	5	0	60	7	22	.318	1	5	.200	0	0	–	1	4	5	5	3	0	4	5	1	15	1.0	1.0	3.0

Carter, John D. **(Jake)** b. July 25, 1924 Ht. 6-5 Wt. 195 College: Texas A&M-Commerce

SEASON–TEAM	G	GS	MIN	FGM	FGA	PCT	3FGM	3FGA	PCT	FTM	FTA	PCT	O-RB	D-RB	TOT	AST	PF	DQ	STL	TO	BLK	PTS	RPG	APG	PPG
48-49–Hammond (N)	62	–	–	133	–	–	–	–	–	188	267	.704	–	–	–	–	201	–	–	–	–	454	–	–	7.3
49-50–Denver-And.	24	–	–	23	75	.307	–	–	–	36	53	.679	–	–	–	24	59	–	–	–	–	82	–	1.0	3.4
Reg. NBA Totals	24	–	–	23	75	.307	–	–	–	36	53	.679	–	–	–	24	59	–	–	–	–	82	–	1.0	3.4
Reg. NBL Totals	62	–	–	133	–	–	–	–	–	188	267	.704	–	–	–	–	201	–	–	–	–	454	–	–	7.3
NBA Playoff Totals	8	–	–	3	21	.143	–	–	–	4	6	.667	–	–	–	3	12	–	–	–	–	10	–	0.4	1.3
NBL Playoff Totals	2	–	–	7	–	–	–	–	–	5	12	.417	–	–	–	–	5	–	–	–	–	19	–	–	9.5

Carter, Reginald **(Reggie)** b. October 10, 1957 d. December 24, 1999 Ht. 6-3 Wt. 175 College: Hawaii; St. John's (N.Y.)

SEASON–TEAM	G	GS	MIN	FGM	FGA	PCT	3FGM	3FGA	PCT	FTM	FTA	PCT	O-RB	D-RB	TOT	AST	PF	DQ	STL	TO	BLK	PTS	RPG	APG	PPG
80-81–New York	60	–	536	59	179	.330	0	3	.000	51	69	.739	30	39	69	76	68	0	22	38	2	169	1.2	1.3	2.8
81-82–New York	75	1	923	119	280	.425	0	0	–	64	80	.800	35	60	95	130	124	1	36	78	6	302	1.3	1.7	4.0
Reg. Season Totals	135	1	1459	178	459	.388	0	3	.000	115	149	.772	65	99	164	206	192	1	58	116	8	471	1.2	1.5	3.5
Playoff Totals	1	0	7	0	1	.000	0	0	–	0	0	–	1	1	2	–	4	0	0	1	0	0	2.0	0.0	0.0

Carter, Ronald Jr. **(Ron)** b. August 31, 1956 Ht. 6-5 Wt. 190 College: Virginia Military

SEASON–TEAM	G	GS	MIN	FGM	FGA	PCT	3FGM	3FGA	PCT	FTM	FTA	PCT	O-RB	D-RB	TOT	AST	PF	DQ	STL	TO	BLK	PTS	RPG	APG	PPG
78-79–Los Angeles	46	–	332	54	124	.435	–	–	–	36	54	.667	21	24	45	25	54	1	17	40	7	144	1.0	0.5	3.1
79-80–Indiana	13	–	117	15	37	.405	0	0	–	2	7	.286	5	14	19	9	19	0	2	10	3	32	1.5	0.7	2.5
Reg. Season Totals	59	–	449	69	161	.429	0	0	–	38	61	.623	26	38	64	34	73	1	19	50	10	176	1.1	0.6	3.0
Playoff Totals	2	–	2	0	1	.000	0	0	–	0	0	–	0	0	0	–	0	0	0	0	0	0	0.0	0.0	0.0

Carter, Vincent Lamar **(Vince, Air Canada)** b. January 26, 1977 Ht. 6-7 Wt. 215 College: North Carolina

SEASON–TEAM	G	GS	MIN	FGM	FGA	PCT	3FGM	3FGA	PCT	FTM	FTA	PCT	O-RB	D-RB	TOT	AST	PF	DQ	STL	TO	BLK	PTS	RPG	APG	PPG
98-99–Toronto	50	49	1760	345	766	.450	19	66	.288	204	268	.761	94	189	283	149	140	2	55	110	77	913	5.7	3.0	18.3
99-00–Toronto	82	82	3126	788	1696	.465	95	236	.403	436	551	.791	150	326	476	322	263	2	110	178	92	2107	5.8	3.9	25.7
Reg. Season Totals	132	131	4886	1133	2462	.460	114	302	.377	640	819	.781	244	515	759	471	403	4	165	288	169	3020	5.8	3.6	22.9
Playoff Totals	3	3	119	15	50	.300	1	10	.100	27	31	.871	9	9	18	19	12	0	3	8	4	58	6.0	6.3	19.3
All-Star Totals	1	1	28	6	11	.545	0	2	.000	0	0	–	2	2	4	2	0	0	2	2	0	12	4.0	2.0	12.0

Cartwright, James William (Bill, Mr. Bill) b. July 30, 1957 Ht. 7-1 Wt. 245 College: San Francisco

SEASON–TEAM	G	GS	MIN	FGM	FGA	PCT	3FGM	3FGA	PCT	FTM	FTA	PCT	O-RB	D-RB	TOT	AST	PF	DQ	STL	TO	BLK	PTS	RPG	APG	PPG
79-80–New York	82	–	3150	665	1215	.547	0	0	–	451	566	.797	194	532	726	165	279	2	48	222	101	1781	8.9	2.0	21.7
80-81–New York	82	–	2925	619	1118	.554	0	1	.000	408	518	.788	161	452	613	111	259	2	48	200	83	1646	7.5	1.4	20.1
81-82–New York	72	50	2060	390	694	.562	0	0	–	257	337	.763	116	305	421	87	208	2	48	166	65	1037	5.8	1.2	14.4
82-83–New York	82	82	2468	455	804	.566	0	0	–	380	511	.744	185	405	590	136	315	7	41	204	127	1290	7.2	1.7	15.7
83-84–New York	77	77	2487	453	808	.561	0	1	.000	404	502	.805	195	454	649	107	262	4	44	200	97	1310	8.4	1.4	17.0
85-86–New York	2	0	36	3	7	.429	0	0	–	6	10	.600	2	8	10	5	6	0	1	6	1	12	5.0	2.5	6.0
86-87–New York	58	50	1989	335	631	.531	0	0	–	346	438	.790	132	313	445	96	188	2	40	128	26	1016	7.7	1.7	17.5
87-88–New York	82	4	1676	287	528	.544	0	0	–	340	426	.798	127	257	384	85	234	4	43	135	43	914	4.7	1.0	11.1
88-89–Chicago	78	76	2333	365	768	.475	0	0	–	236	308	.766	152	369	521	90	234	2	21	190	41	966	6.7	1.2	12.4
89-90–Chicago	71	71	2160	292	598	.488	0	0	–	227	280	.811	137	328	465	145	243	6	38	123	34	811	6.5	2.0	11.4
90-91–Chicago	79	79	2273	318	649	.490	0	0	–	124	178	.697	167	319	486	126	167	0	32	113	15	760	6.2	1.6	9.6
91-92–Chicago	64	64	1471	208	445	.467	0	0	–	96	159	.604	93	231	324	87	131	0	22	75	14	512	5.1	1.4	8.0
92-93–Chicago	63	63	1253	141	343	.411	0	0	–	72	98	.735	83	150	233	83	154	1	20	62	10	354	3.7	1.3	5.6
93-94–Chicago	42	41	780	98	191	.513	0	0	–	39	57	.684	43	109	152	57	83	0	8	50	8	235	3.6	1.4	5.6
94-95–Seattle	29	19	430	27	69	.391	0	0	–	15	24	.625	25	62	87	10	70	0	6	18	3	69	3.0	0.3	2.4
Reg. Season Totals	963	676	27491	4656	8868	.525	0	2	.000	3401	4412	.771	1812	4294	6106	1390	2833	32	460	1892	668	12713	6.3	1.4	13.2
Playoff Totals	124	117	3496	417	866	.482	0	0	–	266	367	.725	207	461	668	162	412	3	54	192	57	1100	5.4	1.3	8.9
All-Star Totals	1	0	14	4	8	.500	0	0	–	0	0	–	1	2	3	1	1	0	0	2	0	8	3.0	1.0	8.0

Carty, Jay J. Jr. b. July 4, 1941 Ht. 6-8 Wt. 220 College: Oregon State

SEASON–TEAM	G	GS	MIN	FGM	FGA	PCT	3FGM	3FGA	PCT	FTM	FTA	PCT	O-RB	D-RB	TOT	AST	PF	DQ	STL	TO	BLK	PTS	RPG	APG	PPG
68-69–Los Angeles	28	–	192	34	89	.382	–	–	–	8	11	.727	–	–	58	11	31	0	–	–	–	76	2.1	0.4	2.7
Reg. Season Totals	28	–	192	34	89	.382	–	–	–	8	11	.727	–	–	58	11	31	0	–	–	–	76	2.1	0.4	2.7
Playoff Totals	3	–	10	0	2	.000	–	–	–	1	3	.333	–	–	2	1	3	0	–	–	–	1	0.7	0.3	0.3

Cash, Cornelius Jr. b. March 3, 1952 Ht. 6-8 Wt. 215 College: Bowling Green State

SEASON–TEAM	G	GS	MIN	FGM	FGA	PCT	3FGM	3FGA	PCT	FTM	FTA	PCT	O-RB	D-RB	TOT	AST	PF	DQ	STL	TO	BLK	PTS	RPG	APG	PPG
76-77–Detroit	6	–	49	9	23	.391	–	–	–	3	6	.500	8	8	16	1	8	0	2	–	1	21	2.7	0.2	3.5
Reg. Season Totals	6	–	49	9	23	.391	–	–	–	3	6	.500	8	8	16	1	8	0	2	–	1	21	2.7	0.2	3.5

Cash, Sam b. November 13, 1950 Ht. 6-8 Wt. 230 College: San Bernardino Valley (Calif.) Coll.; California-Riverside

SEASON–TEAM	G	GS	MIN	FGM	FGA	PCT	3FGM	3FGA	PCT	FTM	FTA	PCT	O-RB	D-RB	TOT	AST	PF	DQ	STL	TO	BLK	PTS	RPG	APG	PPG
72-73–Memphis (A)	7	–	52	4	18	.222	0	0	–	12	17	.706	9	10	19	0	11	0	–	5	–	20	2.7	0.0	2.9
Reg. ABA Totals	7	–	52	4	18	.222	0	0	–	12	17	.706	9	10	19	0	11	0	–	5	–	20	2.7	0.0	2.9

Cassell, Samuel James (Sam) b. November 18, 1969 Ht. 6-3 Wt. 185 College: San Jacinto (Texas) Coll.; Florida State

SEASON–TEAM	G	GS	MIN	FGM	FGA	PCT	3FGM	3FGA	PCT	FTM	FTA	PCT	O-RB	D-RB	TOT	AST	PF	DQ	STL	TO	BLK	PTS	RPG	APG	PPG
93-94–Houston	66	6	1122	162	388	.418	26	88	.295	90	107	.841	25	109	134	192	136	1	59	94	7	440	2.0	2.9	6.7
94-95–Houston	82	1	1882	253	593	.427	63	191	.330	214	254	.843	38	173	211	405	209	3	94	167	14	783	2.6	4.9	9.5
95-96–Houston	61	0	1682	289	658	.439	73	210	.348	235	285	.825	51	137	188	278	166	2	53	157	4	886	3.1	4.6	14.5
96-97–Phoenix-Dallas-N.J.	61	44	1714	337	783	.430	81	231	.351	212	251	.845	47	135	182	305	200	9	77	168	19	967	3.0	5.0	15.9
97-98–New Jersey	75	72	2606	510	1156	.441	15	80	.188	436	507	.860	73	155	228	603	262	5	121	269	20	1471	3.0	8.0	19.6
98-99–N.J.-Milw.	8	3	199	39	93	.419	2	10	.200	47	50	.940	5	10	15	36	22	1	9	20	0	127	1.9	4.5	15.9
99-00–Milwaukee	81	81	2899	545	1170	.466	26	90	.289	390	445	.876	69	232	301	729	255	5	102	267	8	1506	3.7	9.0	18.6
Reg. Season Totals	434	207	12104	2135	4841	.441	286	900	.318	1624	1899	.855	308	951	1259	2548	1250	26	515	1142	72	6180	2.9	5.9	14.2
Playoff Totals	63	9	1475	212	523	.405	50	140	.357	190	225	.844	29	115	144	292	188	4	55	116	9	664	2.3	4.6	10.5

Catchings, Harvey Lee b. September 2, 1951 Ht. 6-10 Wt. 220 College: Weatherford (Texas) Coll.; Hardin-Simmons

SEASON–TEAM	G	GS	MIN	FGM	FGA	PCT	3FGM	3FGA	PCT	FTM	FTA	PCT	O-RB	D-RB	TOT	AST	PF	DQ	STL	TO	BLK	PTS	RPG	APG	PPG
74-75–Philadelphia	37	–	528	41	74	.554	–	–	–	16	25	.640	49	104	153	21	82	1	10	–	60	98	4.1	0.6	2.6
75-76–Philadelphia	75	–	1731	103	242	.426	–	–	–	58	96	.604	191	329	520	63	262	6	21	–	164	264	6.9	0.8	3.5
76-77–Philadelphia	53	–	864	62	123	.504	–	–	–	33	47	.702	64	170	234	30	130	1	23	–	78	157	4.4	0.6	3.0
77-78–Philadelphia	61	–	748	70	178	.393	–	–	–	34	55	.618	105	145	250	34	124	1	20	44	67	174	4.1	0.6	2.9
78-79–Phil.-N.J.	56	–	948	102	243	.420	–	–	–	60	78	.769	101	201	302	48	132	3	23	88	91	264	5.4	0.8	4.7
79-80–Milwaukee	72	–	1366	97	244	.398	0	1	.000	39	62	.629	164	246	410	82	191	1	23	68	162	233	5.7	1.1	3.2
80-81–Milwaukee	77	–	1635	134	300	.447	0	0	–	59	92	.641	154	319	473	99	284	7	33	105	184	327	6.1	1.3	4.2
81-82–Milwaukee	80	9	1603	94	224	.420	0	0	–	41	69	.594	129	227	356	97	237	3	42	94	134	229	4.5	1.2	2.9
82-83–Milwaukee	74	33	1554	90	197	.457	0	0	–	62	92	.674	132	276	408	77	224	4	26	83	148	242	5.5	1.0	3.3
83-84–Milwaukee	69	3	1156	61	153	.399	0	1	.000	22	42	.524	89	182	271	43	172	3	25	57	81	144	3.9	0.6	2.1
84-85–L.A. Clippers	70	14	1049	72	149	.483	0	1	.000	59	89	.663	89	173	262	14	162	0	15	55	57	203	3.7	0.2	2.9
Reg. Season Totals	724	59	13182	926	2127	.435	0	3	.000	483	747	.647	1267	2372	3639	608	2000	30	261	594	1226	2335	5.0	0.8	3.2
Playoff Totals	53	0	556	31	78	.397	0	0	–	12	24	.500	60	94	154	23	99	0	3	18	49	74	2.9	0.4	1.4

Catledge, Terry DeWayne (Cat Man) b. August 22, 1963 Ht. 6-8 Wt. 230 College: Itawamba (Miss.) Coll.; South Alabama

SEASON–TEAM	G	GS	MIN	FGM	FGA	PCT	3FGM	3FGA	PCT	FTM	FTA	PCT	O-RB	D-RB	TOT	AST	PF	DQ	STL	TO	BLK	PTS	RPG	APG	PPG
85-86–Philadelphia	64	7	1092	202	431	.469	0	4	.000	90	139	.647	107	165	272	21	127	0	31	69	8	494	4.3	0.3	7.7
86-87–Washington	78	77	2149	413	835	.495	0	4	.000	199	335	.594	248	312	560	56	195	1	43	145	14	1025	7.2	0.7	13.1
87-88–Washington	70	40	1610	296	585	.506	0	2	.000	154	235	.655	180	217	397	63	172	0	33	101	9	746	5.7	0.9	10.7
88-89–Washington	79	77	2077	334	681	.490	1	5	.200	153	254	.602	230	342	572	75	250	5	46	120	25	822	7.2	0.9	10.4
89-90–Orlando	74	72	2462	546	1152	.474	2	8	.250	341	486	.702	271	292	563	72	201	0	36	181	17	1435	7.6	1.0	19.4
90-91–Orlando	51	38	1459	292	632	.462	0	5	.000	161	258	.624	168	187	355	58	113	2	34	107	9	745	7.0	1.1	14.6
91-92–Orlando	78	67	2430	457	922	.496	0	4	.000	240	346	.694	257	292	549	109	196	2	58	138	16	1154	7.0	1.4	14.8
92-93–Orlando	21	1	262	36	73	.493	0	0	–	27	34	.794	18	28	46	5	31	1	4	25	1	99	2.2	0.2	4.7
Reg. Season Totals	515	379	13541	2576	5311	.485	3	32	.094	1365	2087	.654	1479	1835	3314	459	1285	11	285	886	99	6520	6.4	0.9	12.7
Playoff Totals	19	13	436	73	169	.432	0	1	.000	34	59	.576	46	60	106	7	48	0	9	23	9	180	5.6	0.4	9.5

Catlett, Sidny Leon (Sid) b. April 18, 1948 Ht. 6-6 Wt. 230 College: Notre Dame

SEASON–TEAM	G	GS	MIN	FGM	FGA	PCT	3FGM	3FGA	PCT	FTM	FTA	PCT	O-RB	D-RB	TOT	AST	PF	DQ	STL	TO	BLK	PTS	RPG	APG	PPG
71-72–Cincinnati	9	–	40	2	9	.222	–	–	–	2	9	.222	–	–	4	1	3	0	–	–	–	6	0.4	0.1	0.7
Reg. Season Totals	9	–	40	2	9	.222	–	–	–	2	9	.222	–	–	4	1	3	0	–	–	–	6	0.4	0.1	0.7

Cato, Kelvin T. b. August 26, 1974 Ht. 6-11 Wt. 255 College: South Alabama; Iowa State

SEASON–TEAM	G	GS	MIN	FGM	FGA	PCT	3FGM	3FGA	PCT	FTM	FTA	PCT	O-RB	D-RB	TOT	AST	PF	DQ	STL	TO	BLK	PTS	RPG	APG	PPG
97-98–Portland	74	8	1007	98	229	.428	0	3	.000	86	125	.688	91	161	252	23	164	3	29	44	94	282	3.4	0.3	3.8
98-99–Portland	43	0	545	58	129	.450	1	1	1.000	34	67	.507	49	101	150	19	100	3	23	27	56	151	3.5	0.4	3.5
99-00–Houston	65	32	1581	216	402	.537	0	4	.000	135	208	.649	102	287	389	26	175	1	33	71	124	567	6.0	0.4	8.7
Reg. Season Totals	182	40	3133	372	760	.489	1	8	.125	255	400	.638	242	549	791	68	439	7	85	142	274	1000	4.3	0.4	5.5
Playoff Totals	12	0	101	10	26	.385	0	1	.000	12	21	.571	9	10	19	3	25	0	2	6	8	32	1.6	0.3	2.7

Cattage, Robert Lewis (Bobby) b. August 17, 1958 Ht. 6-9 Wt. 250 College: Auburn

SEASON–TEAM	G	GS	MIN	FGM	FGA	PCT	3FGM	3FGA	PCT	FTM	FTA	PCT	O-RB	D-RB	TOT	AST	PF	DQ	STL	TO	BLK	PTS	RPG	APG	PPG
81-82–Utah	49	0	337	60	135	.444	0	2	.000	30	41	.732	22	51	73	7	58	0	7	18	0	150	1.5	0.1	3.1
85-86–New Jersey	29	1	185	28	83	.337	1	5	.200	35	44	.795	15	19	34	4	23	0	6	13	0	92	1.2	0.1	3.2
Reg. Season Totals	78	1	522	88	218	.404	1	7	.143	65	85	.765	37	70	107	11	81	0	13	31	0	242	1.4	0.1	3.1

Causwell, Duane b. May 31, 1968 Ht. 7-0 Wt. 255 College: Temple

SEASON–TEAM	G	GS	MIN	FGM	FGA	PCT	3FGM	3FGA	PCT	FTM	FTA	PCT	O-RB	D-RB	TOT	AST	PF	DQ	STL	TO	BLK	PTS	RPG	APG	PPG
90-91–Sacramento	76	55	1719	210	413	.508	0	0	–	105	165	.636	141	250	391	69	225	4	49	96	148	525	5.1	0.9	6.9
91-92–Sacramento	80	77	2291	250	455	.549	0	1	.000	136	222	.613	196	384	580	59	281	4	47	124	215	636	7.3	0.7	8.0
92-93–Sacramento	55	45	1211	175	321	.545	0	1	.000	103	165	.624	112	191	303	35	192	7	32	58	87	453	5.5	0.6	8.2
93-94–Sacramento	41	8	674	71	137	.518	0	0	–	40	68	.588	68	118	186	11	109	2	19	33	49	182	4.5	0.3	4.4
94-95–Sacramento	58	24	820	76	147	.517	0	1	.000	57	98	.582	57	117	174	15	146	4	14	33	80	209	3.0	0.3	3.6
95-96–Sacramento	73	26	1044	90	216	.417	0	1	.000	70	96	.729	86	162	248	20	173	2	27	53	78	250	3.4	0.3	3.4
96-97–Sacramento	46	8	581	48	94	.511	2	3	.667	20	37	.541	57	70	127	20	131	5	15	34	38	118	2.8	0.4	2.6
97-98–Miami	37	2	363	37	89	.416	0	0	–	15	26	.577	29	70	99	5	73	0	7	18	27	89	2.7	0.1	2.4
98-99–Miami	19	1	137	20	35	.571	0	0	–	4	12	.333	14	21	35	2	32	1	0	18	11	44	1.8	0.1	2.3
99-00–Miami	25	2	185	20	37	.541	0	0	–	26	38	.684	11	36	47	2	42	0	2	10	16	66	1.9	0.1	2.6
Reg. Season Totals	510	248	9025	997	1944	.513	2	7	.286	576	927	.621	771	1419	2190	238	1404	29	212	477	749	2572	4.3	0.5	5.0
Playoff Totals	7	1	50	2	5	.400	0	1	.000	7	10	.700	1	8	9	2	5	0	1	3	0	11	1.3	0.3	1.6

Cavenall, Ronnie Goodall (Ron) b. April 30, 1959 Ht. 7-1 Wt. 230 College: Texas Southern

SEASON–TEAM	G	GS	MIN	FGM	FGA	PCT	3FGM	3FGA	PCT	FTM	FTA	PCT	O-RB	D-RB	TOT	AST	PF	DQ	STL	TO	BLK	PTS	RPG	APG	PPG
84-85–New York	53	2	653	28	86	.326	0	0	–	22	39	.564	53	113	166	19	123	2	12	45	42	78	3.1	0.4	1.5
88-89–New Jersey	5	0	16	2	3	.667	0	0	–	2	5	.400	0	2	2	0	2	0	0	2	2	6	0.4	0.0	1.2
Reg. Season Totals	58	2	669	30	89	.337	0	0	–	24	44	.545	53	115	168	19	125	2	12	47	44	84	2.9	0.3	1.4

Ceballos, Cedric Z. (Ice) b. August 2, 1969 Ht. 6-7 Wt. 220 College: Ventura (Calif.) Coll.; Cal State-Fullerton

SEASON–TEAM	G	GS	MIN	FGM	FGA	PCT	3FGM	3FGA	PCT	FTM	FTA	PCT	O-RB	D-RB	TOT	AST	PF	DQ	STL	TO	BLK	PTS	RPG	APG	PPG
90-91–Phoenix	63	0	730	204	419	.487	1	6	.167	110	166	.663	77	73	150	35	70	0	22	69	5	519	2.4	0.6	8.2
91-92–Phoenix	64	4	725	176	365	.482	1	6	.167	109	148	.736	60	92	152	50	52	0	16	71	11	462	2.4	0.8	7.2
92-93–Phoenix	74	46	1607	381	662	.576	0	2	.000	187	258	.725	172	236	408	77	103	1	54	106	28	949	5.5	1.0	12.8
93-94–Phoenix	53	43	1602	425	795	.535	0	9	.000	160	221	.724	153	191	344	91	124	0	59	93	23	1010	6.5	1.7	19.1
94-95–L.A. Lakers	58	54	2029	497	977	.509	58	146	.397	209	292	.716	169	295	464	105	131	1	60	143	19	1261	8.0	1.8	21.7
95-96–L.A. Lakers	78	71	2628	638	1203	.530	51	184	.277	329	409	.804	215	321	536	119	144	0	94	167	22	1656	6.9	1.5	21.2
96-97–Lakers-Phoenix	50	40	1426	282	617	.457	26	102	.255	139	186	.747	102	228	330	64	113	0	33	85	23	729	6.6	1.3	14.6
97-98–Phoenix-Dallas	47	25	990	204	415	.492	21	70	.300	107	145	.738	75	146	221	60	88	0	33	72	16	536	4.7	1.3	11.4
98-99–Dallas	13	5	352	59	140	.421	11	28	.393	34	49	.694	23	62	85	12	23	1	7	28	5	163	6.5	0.9	12.5
99-00–Dallas	69	25	2064	447	1002	.446	44	134	.328	209	248	.843	172	290	462	90	165	3	56	125	24	1147	6.7	1.3	16.6
Reg. Season Totals	569	313	14153	3313	6595	.502	213	687	.310	1593	2122	.751	1218	1934	3152	703	1013	6	434	959	176	8432	5.5	1.2	14.8
Playoff Totals	56	33	1198	223	476	.468	26	80	.325	100	134	.746	83	174	257	61	77	0	41	65	26	572	4.6	1.1	10.2

Celestand, John b. March 6, 1977 Ht. 6-4 Wt. 178 College: Villanova

SEASON–TEAM	G	GS	MIN	FGM	FGA	PCT	3FGM	3FGA	PCT	FTM	FTA	PCT	O-RB	D-RB	TOT	AST	PF	DQ	STL	TO	BLK	PTS	RPG	APG	PPG
99-00–L.A. Lakers	16	0	185	15	45	.333	2	9	.222	5	6	.833	1	10	11	20	22	0	7	16	0	37	0.7	1.3	2.3
Reg. Season Totals	16	0	185	15	45	.333	2	9	.222	5	6	.833	1	10	11	20	22	0	7	16	0	37	0.7	1.3	2.3

Cervi, Alfred Nicholas (Al, Digger) b. February 12, 1917 Ht. 5-11 Wt. 185 College: None HOF: 1984

SEASON–TEAM	G	GS	MIN	FGM	FGA	PCT	3FGM	3FGA	PCT	FTM	FTA	PCT	O-RB	D-RB	TOT	AST	PF	DQ	STL	TO	BLK	PTS	RPG	APG	PPG
37-38–Buffalo (N)	9	–	–	19	–	–	–	–	–	6	–	–	–	–	–	–	–	–	–	–	–	44	–	–	4.9
45-46–Rochester (N)	28	–	–	112	–	–	–	–	–	76	108	.704	–	–	–	–	21	–	–	–	–	300	–	–	10.7
46-47–Rochester (N)	44	–	–	228	–	–	–	–	–	176	236	.746	–	–	–	–	127	–	–	–	–	632	–	–	14.4
47-48–Rochester (N)	49	–	–	234	–	–	–	–	–	187	242	.773	–	–	–	–	118	–	–	–	–	655	–	–	13.4
48-49–Syracuse (N)	57	–	–	204	–	–	–	–	–	287	382	.751	–	–	–	–	170	–	–	–	–	695	–	–	12.2
49-50–Syracuse	56	–	–	143	431	.332	–	–	–	287	346	.829	–	–	–	264	223	–	–	–	–	573	–	4.7	10.2
50-51–Syracuse	53	–	–	132	346	.382	–	–	–	194	237	.819	–	–	152	208	180	9	–	–	–	458	2.9	3.9	8.6
51-52–Syracuse	55	–	850	99	280	.354	–	–	–	219	248	.883	–	–	87	148	176	7	–	–	–	417	1.6	2.7	7.6
52-53–Syracuse	38	–	301	31	71	.437	–	–	–	81	100	.810	–	–	22	28	90	2	–	–	–	143	0.6	0.7	3.8
Reg. NBA Totals	202	–	1151	405	1128	.359	–	–	–	781	931	.839	–	–	261	648	669	18	–	–	–	1591	1.8	3.2	7.9
Reg. NBL Totals	187	–	–	797	–	–	–	–	–	732	968	.750	–	–	–	–	436	–	–	–	–	2326	–	–	12.4
NBA Playoff Totals	27	–	193	50	197	.320	–	–	–	115	133	.865	–	–	43	142	102	6	–	–	–	215	2.7	4.2	8.0
NBL Playoff Totals	30	–	–	102	–	–	–	–	–	110	146	.753	–	–	–	–	98	–	–	–	–	314	–	–	10.5

Chamberlain, William Martin (Bill) b. December 16, 1949 Ht. 6-6 Wt. 195 College: North Carolina

SEASON–TEAM	G	GS	MIN	FGM	FGA	PCT	3FGM	3FGA	PCT	FTM	FTA	PCT	O-RB	D-RB	TOT	AST	PF	DQ	STL	TO	BLK	PTS	RPG	APG	PPG
72-73–Ken.-Mem. (A)	50	–	665	112	282	.397	2	8	.250	36	59	.610	61	57	118	76	98	1	–	58	–	262	2.4	1.5	5.2
73-74–Phoenix	28	–	367	57	130	.438	–	–	–	39	56	.696	33	47	80	37	74	2	20	–	12	153	2.9	1.3	5.5
Reg. NBA Totals	28	–	367	57	130	.438	–	–	–	39	56	.696	33	47	80	37	74	2	20	–	12	153	2.9	1.3	5.5
Reg. ABA Totals	50	–	665	112	282	.397	2	8	.250	36	59	.610	61	57	118	76	98	1	–	58	–	262	2.4	1.5	5.2

Chamberlain, Wilton Norman (Wilt, The Stilt, The Big Dipper) b. August 21, 1936 d. October 12, 1999 Ht. 7-1 Wt. 275 College: Kansas HOF: 1978

SEASON–TEAM	G	GS	MIN	FGM	FGA	PCT	3FGM	3FGA	PCT	FTM	FTA	PCT	O-RB	D-RB	TOT	AST	PF	DQ	STL	TO	BLK	PTS	RPG	APG	PPG
59-60–Philadelphia	72	–	3338	1065	2311	.461	–	–	–	577	991	.582	–	–	1941	168	150	0	–	–	–	2707	27.0	2.3	37.6
60-61–Philadelphia	79	–	3773	1251	2457	.509	–	–	–	531	1054	.504	–	–	2149	148	130	0	–	–	–	3033	27.2	1.9	38.4
61-62–Philadelphia	80	–	3882	1597	3159	.506	–	–	–	835	1363	.613	–	–	2052	192	123	0	–	–	–	4029	25.7	2.4	50.4
62-63–San Francisco	80	–	3806	1463	2770	.528	–	–	–	660	1113	.593	–	–	1946	275	136	0	–	–	–	3586	24.3	3.4	44.8
63-64–San Francisco	80	–	3689	1204	2298	.524	–	–	–	540	1016	.531	–	–	1787	403	182	0	–	–	–	2948	22.3	5.0	36.9
64-65–S.F.-Phil.	73	–	3301	1063	2083	.510	–	–	–	408	880	.464	–	–	1673	250	146	0	–	–	–	2534	22.9	3.4	34.7
65-66–Philadelphia	79	–	3737	1074	1990	.540	–	–	–	501	976	.513	–	–	1943	414	171	0	–	–	–	2649	24.6	5.2	33.5
66-67–Philadelphia	81	–	3682	785	1150	.683	–	–	–	386	875	.441	–	–	1957	630	143	0	–	–	–	1956	24.2	7.8	24.1
67-68–Philadelphia	82	–	3836	819	1377	.595	–	–	–	354	932	.380	–	–	1952	702	160	0	–	–	–	1992	23.8	8.6	24.3
68-69–Los Angeles	81	–	3669	641	1099	.583	–	–	–	382	857	.446	–	–	1712	366	142	0	–	–	–	1664	21.1	4.5	20.5
69-70–Los Angeles	12	–	505	129	227	.568	–	–	–	70	157	.446	–	–	221	49	31	0	–	–	–	328	18.4	4.1	27.3
70-71–Los Angeles	82	–	3630	668	1226	.545	–	–	–	360	669	.538	–	–	1493	352	174	0	–	–	–	1696	18.2	4.3	20.7
71-72–Los Angeles	82	–	3469	496	764	.649	–	–	–	221	524	.422	–	–	1572	329	196	0	–	–	–	1213	19.2	4.0	14.8
72-73–Los Angeles	82	–	3542	426	586	.727	–	–	–	232	455	.510	–	–	1526	365	191	0	–	–	–	1084	18.6	4.5	13.2
Reg. Season Totals	1045	–	47859	12681	23497	.540	–	–	–	6057	11862	.511	–	–	23924	4643	2075	0	–	–	–	31419	22.9	4.4	30.1
Playoff Totals	160	–	7559	1425	2728	.522	–	–	–	757	1627	.465	–	–	3913	673	412	0	–	–	–	3607	24.5	4.2	22.5
All-Star Totals	13	–	388	72	122	.590	–	–	–	47	94	.500	–	–	197	36	23	0	–	–	–	191	15.2	2.8	14.7

Chambers, Jerome Purcell (Jerry) b. July 18, 1943 Ht. 6-5 Wt. 185 College: Trinidad State (Colo.); Utah

SEASON–TEAM	G	GS	MIN	FGM	FGA	PCT	3FGM	3FGA	PCT	FTM	FTA	PCT	O-RB	D-RB	TOT	AST	PF	DQ	STL	TO	BLK	PTS	RPG	APG	PPG
66-67–Los Angeles	68	–	1015	224	496	.452	–	–	–	68	93	.731	–	–	208	44	143	0	–	–	–	516	3.1	0.6	7.6
69-70–Phoenix	79	–	1139	283	658	.430	–	–	–	91	125	.728	–	–	219	54	162	3	–	–	–	657	2.8	0.7	8.3
70-71–Atlanta	65	–	1168	237	526	.451	–	–	–	106	134	.791	–	–	245	61	119	0	–	–	–	580	3.8	0.9	8.9
71-72–Buffalo	26	–	369	78	180	.433	–	–	–	22	32	.688	–	–	67	23	39	0	–	–	–	178	2.6	0.9	6.8
72-73–San Diego (A)	43	–	885	199	468	.425	2	10	.200	112	130	.862	83	107	190	46	102	0	–	55	–	512	4.4	1.1	11.9
73-74–San Antonio (A)	38	–	579	94	206	.456	0	0	–	36	48	.750	37	66	103	42	74	–	11	28	3	224	2.7	1.1	5.9
Reg. NBA Totals	238	–	3691	822	1860	.442	–	–	–	287	384	.747	–	–	739	182	463	3	–	–	–	1931	3.1	0.8	8.1
Reg. ABA Totals	81	–	1464	293	674	.435	2	10	.200	148	178	.831	120	173	293	88	176	0	11	83	3	736	3.6	1.1	9.1
NBA Playoff Totals	14	–	139	29	69	.420	–	–	–	13	17	.765	–	–	30	8	17	0	–	–	–	71	2.1	0.6	5.1

Chambers, Thomas Doane (Tom) b. June 21, 1959 Ht. 6-10 Wt. 230 College: Utah

SEASON–TEAM	G	GS	MIN	FGM	FGA	PCT	3FGM	3FGA	PCT	FTM	FTA	PCT	O-RB	D-RB	TOT	AST	PF	DQ	STL	TO	BLK	PTS	RPG	APG	PPG
81-82–San Diego	81	58	2682	554	1056	.525	0	2	.000	284	458	.620	211	350	561	146	341	17	58	220	46	1392	6.9	1.8	17.2
82-83–San Diego	79	79	2665	519	1099	.472	0	8	.000	353	488	.723	218	301	519	192	333	15	79	234	57	1391	6.6	2.4	17.6
83-84–Seattle	82	44	2570	554	1110	.499	0	12	.000	375	469	.800	219	313	532	133	309	8	47	192	51	1483	6.5	1.6	18.1
84-85–Seattle	81	60	2923	629	1302	.483	6	22	.273	475	571	.832	164	415	579	209	312	4	70	260	57	1739	7.1	2.6	21.5
85-86–Seattle	66	26	2019	432	928	.466	13	48	.271	346	414	.836	126	305	431	132	248	6	55	194	37	1223	6.5	2.0	18.5
86-87–Seattle	82	82	3018	660	1446	.456	54	145	.372	535	630	.849	163	382	545	245	307	9	81	268	50	1909	6.6	3.0	23.3
87-88–Seattle	82	82	2680	611	1364	.448	33	109	.303	419	519	.807	135	355	490	212	297	4	87	209	53	1674	6.0	2.6	20.4
88-89–Phoenix	81	81	3002	774	1643	.471	28	86	.326	509	598	.851	143	541	684	231	271	2	87	231	55	2085	8.4	2.9	25.7
89-90–Phoenix	81	81	3046	810	1617	.501	24	86	.279	557	647	.861	121	450	571	190	260	1	88	218	47	2201	7.0	2.3	27.2
90-91–Phoenix	76	75	2475	556	1271	.437	20	73	.274	379	459	.826	104	386	490	194	235	3	65	177	52	1511	6.4	2.6	19.9
91-92–Phoenix	69	66	1948	426	989	.431	18	49	.367	258	311	.830	86	315	401	142	196	1	57	103	37	1128	5.8	2.1	16.3
92-93–Phoenix	73	0	1723	320	716	.447	11	28	.393	241	288	.837	96	249	345	101	212	2	43	92	23	892	4.7	1.4	12.2
93-94–Utah	80	0	1838	329	748	.440	14	45	.311	221	281	.786	87	239	326	79	232	2	40	89	32	893	4.1	1.0	11.2
94-95–Utah	81	4	1240	195	427	.457	4	24	.167	109	135	.807	66	147	213	73	173	1	25	52	30	503	2.6	0.9	6.2
96-97–Charlotte	12	5	83	7	31	.226	2	3	.667	3	4	.750	3	11	14	4	14	0	1	9	0	19	1.2	0.3	1.6
97-98–Philadelphia	1	0	10	2	2	1.000	0	0	–	2	2	1.000	0	2	2	0	2	0	2	1	0	6	2.0	0.0	6.0
Reg. Season Totals	1107	743	33922	7378	15749	.468	227	740	.307	5066	6274	.807	1942	4761	6703	2283	3742	75	885	2549	627	20049	6.1	2.1	18.1
Playoff Totals	108	57	3061	607	1380	.440	27	89	.303	421	509	.827	138	431	569	183	359	5	62	208	68	1662	5.3	1.7	15.4
All-Star Totals	4	1	84	29	56	.518	2	5	.400	17	22	.773	9	7	16	5	11	0	6	12	0	77	4.0	1.3	19.3

Champion, Mike O. b. April 5, 1964 Ht. 6-10 Wt. 230 College: Gonzaga

SEASON–TEAM	G	GS	MIN	FGM	FGA	PCT	3FGM	3FGA	PCT	FTM	FTA	PCT	O-RB	D-RB	TOT	AST	PF	DQ	STL	TO	BLK	PTS	RPG	APG	PPG
88-89–Seattle	2	0	4	0	3	.000	0	1	.000	0	0	–	0	0	0	0	2	0	0	1	0	0	0.0	0.0	0.0
Reg. Season Totals	2	0	4	0	3	.000	0	1	.000	0	0	–	0	0	0	0	2	0	0	1	0	0	0.0	0.0	0.0

Chaney, Donald R. (Don, Duck) b. March 22, 1946 Ht. 6-5 Wt. 210 College: Houston

SEASON–TEAM	G	GS	MIN	FGM	FGA	PCT	3FGM	3FGA	PCT	FTM	FTA	PCT	O-RB	D-RB	TOT	AST	PF	DQ	STL	TO	BLK	PTS	RPG	APG	PPG
68-69–Boston	20	–	209	36	113	.319	–	–	–	8	20	.400	–	–	46	19	32	0	–	–	–	80	2.3	1.0	4.0
69-70–Boston	63	–	839	115	320	.359	–	–	–	82	109	.752	–	–	152	72	118	0	–	–	–	312	2.4	1.1	5.0
70-71–Boston	81	–	2289	348	766	.454	–	–	–	234	313	.748	–	–	463	235	288	11	–	–	–	930	5.7	2.9	11.5
71-72–Boston	79	–	2275	373	786	.475	–	–	–	197	255	.773	–	–	395	202	295	7	–	–	–	943	5.0	2.6	11.9
72-73–Boston	79	–	2488	414	859	.482	–	–	–	210	267	.787	–	–	449	221	276	6	–	–	–	1038	5.7	2.8	13.1
73-74–Boston	81	–	2258	348	750	.464	–	–	–	149	180	.828	210	168	378	176	247	7	83	–	62	845	4.7	2.2	10.4
74-75–Boston	82	–	2208	321	750	.428	–	–	–	133	165	.806	171	199	370	181	244	5	122	–	66	775	4.5	2.2	9.5
75-76–St. Louis (A)	48	–	1475	191	457	.418	1	4	.250	64	82	.780	113	121	234	169	170	–	66	119	36	447	4.9	3.5	9.3
76-77–Los Angeles	81	–	2408	213	522	.408	–	–	–	70	94	.745	120	210	330	308	224	4	140	–	33	496	4.1	3.8	6.1
77-78–L.A.-Boston	51	–	835	104	269	.387	–	–	–	38	45	.844	40	76	116	66	107	0	44	61	13	246	2.3	1.3	4.8
78-79–Boston	65	–	1074	174	414	.420	–	–	–	36	42	.857	63	78	141	75	167	3	72	65	11	384	2.2	1.2	5.9
79-80–Boston	60	–	523	67	189	.354	1	6	.167	32	42	.762	31	42	73	38	80	1	31	33	11	167	1.2	0.6	2.8
Reg. NBA Totals	742	–	17406	2513	5738	.438	1	6	.167	1189	1532	.776	635	773	2913	1593	2078	44	492	159	196	6216	3.9	2.1	8.4
Reg. ABA Totals	48	–	1475	191	457	.418	1	4	.250	64	82	.780	113	121	234	169	170	–	66	119	36	447	4.9	3.5	9.3
NBA Playoff Totals	70	–	1835	230	511	.450	0	0	–	110	142	.775	85	82	250	156	229	3	66	–	17	570	3.6	2.2	8.1

Chaney, John Louie b. February 29, 1920 Ht. 6-3 Wt. 190 College: Louisiana State

SEASON–TEAM	G	GS	MIN	FGM	FGA	PCT	3FGM	3FGA	PCT	FTM	FTA	PCT	O-RB	D-RB	TOT	AST	PF	DQ	STL	TO	BLK	PTS	RPG	APG	PPG
46-47–Syracuse (N)	42	–	–	138	–	–	–	–	–	86	119	.723	–	–	–	–	119	–	–	–	–	362	–	–	8.6
47-48–Syracuse (N)	40	–	–	107	–	–	–	–	–	78	103	.757	–	–	–	–	112	–	–	–	–	292	–	–	7.3
48-49–Syracuse (N)	59	–	–	82	–	–	–	–	–	59	88	.670	–	–	–	–	84	–	–	–	–	223	–	–	3.8
49-50–Tri-Cit-She.	16	–	–	25	86	.291	–	–	–	20	29	.690	–	–	–	20	23	–	–	–	–	70	–	1.3	4.4
Reg. NBA Totals	16	–	–	25	86	.291	–	–	–	20	29	.690	–	–	–	20	23	–	–	–	–	70	–	1.3	4.4
Reg. NBL Totals	141	–	–	327	–	–	–	–	–	223	310	.719	–	–	–	–	315	–	–	–	–	877	–	–	6.2
NBL Playoff Totals	13	–	–	31	–	–	–	–	–	14	26	.538	–	–	–	–	31	–	–	–	–	76	–	–	5.8

Chapman, Rex Everett b. October 5, 1967 Ht. 6-4 Wt. 195 College: Kentucky

SEASON–TEAM	G	GS	MIN	FGM	FGA	PCT	3FGM	3FGA	PCT	FTM	FTA	PCT	O-RB	D-RB	TOT	AST	PF	DQ	STL	TO	BLK	PTS	RPG	APG	PPG
88-89–Charlotte	75	44	2219	526	1271	.414	60	191	.314	155	195	.795	74	113	187	176	167	1	70	113	25	1267	2.5	2.3	16.9
89-90–Charlotte	54	52	1762	377	924	.408	47	142	.331	144	192	.750	52	127	179	132	113	0	46	100	6	945	3.3	2.4	17.5
90-91–Charlotte	70	68	2100	410	922	.445	48	148	.324	234	282	.830	45	146	191	250	167	1	73	131	16	1102	2.7	3.6	15.7
91-92–Cha.-Wash.	22	11	567	113	252	.448	8	29	.276	36	53	.679	10	48	58	89	51	0	15	45	8	270	2.6	4.0	12.3
92-93–Washington	60	23	1300	287	602	.477	43	116	.371	132	163	.810	19	69	88	116	119	1	38	79	10	749	1.5	1.9	12.5
93-94–Washington	60	59	2025	431	865	.498	64	165	.388	168	206	.816	57	89	146	185	83	0	59	117	8	1094	2.4	3.1	18.2
94-95–Washington	45	29	1468	254	639	.397	86	274	.314	137	159	.862	23	90	113	128	85	0	67	62	15	731	2.5	2.8	16.2
95-96–Miami	56	50	1865	289	679	.426	125	337	.371	83	113	.735	22	123	145	166	117	0	45	79	10	786	2.6	3.0	14.0
96-97–Phoenix	65	33	1833	332	749	.443	110	314	.350	124	149	.832	25	156	181	182	108	1	52	96	7	898	2.8	2.8	13.8
97-98–Phoenix	68	67	2263	408	956	.427	120	311	.386	146	187	.781	30	143	173	203	102	0	71	116	14	1082	2.5	3.0	15.9
98-99–Phoenix	38	35	1183	165	459	.359	53	151	.351	76	91	.835	12	92	104	109	46	0	34	54	9	459	2.7	2.9	12.1
99-00–Phoenix	53	19	957	124	320	.388	41	123	.333	59	78	.756	10	70	80	62	70	0	22	38	1	348	1.5	1.2	6.6
Reg. Season Totals	666	490	19542	3716	8638	.430	805	2301	.350	1494	1868	.800	379	1266	1645	1798	1228	4	592	1030	129	9731	2.5	2.7	14.6
Playoff Totals	13	13	394	65	155	.419	27	72	.375	26	36	.722	4	24	28	28	30	1	8	22	0	183	2.2	2.2	14.1

Chapman, Wayne G. b. June 15, 1945 Ht. 6-6 Wt. 190 College: Western Kentucky

SEASON–TEAM	G	GS	MIN	FGM	FGA	PCT	3FGM	3FGA	PCT	FTM	FTA	PCT	O-RB	D-RB	TOT	AST	PF	DQ	STL	TO	BLK	PTS	RPG	APG	PPG
68-69–Kentucky (A)	48	–	458	68	202	.337	4	13	.308	54	72	.750	–	–	74	38	95	0	–	39	–	194	1.5	0.8	4.0
69-70–Kentucky (A)	82	–	1519	261	654	.399	8	37	.216	134	204	.657	–	–	252	139	250	7	–	–	–	664	3.1	1.7	8.1
70-71–Denver-Ind. (A)	69	–	1241	214	562	.381	15	57	.263	113	158	.715	–	–	174	128	158	–	–	–	–	556	2.5	1.9	8.1
71-72–Indiana (A)	7	–	76	7	18	.389	1	2	.500	3	6	.500	–	–	5	11	10	–	–	6	–	18	0.7	1.6	2.6
Reg. ABA Totals	206	–	3294	550	1436	.383	28	109	.257	304	440	.691	–	–	505	316	513	7	–	45	–	1432	2.5	1.5	7.0
ABA Playoff Totals	20	–	198	46	93	.495	2	9	.222	32	44	.727	–	–	33	16	40	0	–	–	–	126	1.7	0.8	6.3

Chappell, Leonard R. (Len) b. January 31, 1941 Ht. 6-8 Wt. 240 College: Wake Forest

SEASON–TEAM	G	GS	MIN	FGM	FGA	PCT	3FGM	3FGA	PCT	FTM	FTA	PCT	O-RB	D-RB	TOT	AST	PF	DQ	STL	TO	BLK	PTS	RPG	APG	PPG
62-63–Syracuse	80	–	1241	281	604	.465	–	–	–	148	238	.622	–	–	461	56	171	1	–	–	–	710	5.8	0.7	8.9
63-64–Phil.-N.Y.	79	–	2505	531	1185	.448	–	–	–	288	403	.715	–	–	771	83	214	1	–	–	–	1350	9.8	1.1	17.1
64-65–New York	43	–	655	145	367	.395	–	–	–	68	100	.680	–	–	140	15	73	0	–	–	–	358	3.3	0.3	8.3
65-66–New York	46	–	545	100	238	.420	–	–	–	46	78	.590	–	–	127	26	64	1	–	–	–	246	2.8	0.6	5.3
66-67–Chicago-Cin.	73	–	708	132	313	.422	–	–	–	53	81	.654	–	–	189	33	104	0	–	–	–	317	2.6	0.5	4.3
67-68–Cin.-Detroit	67	–	1064	235	458	.513	–	–	–	138	194	.711	–	–	361	53	119	1	–	–	–	608	5.4	0.8	9.1
68-69–Milwaukee	80	–	2207	459	1011	.454	–	–	–	250	339	.737	–	–	637	95	247	3	–	–	–	1168	8.0	1.2	14.6
69-70–Milwaukee	75	–	1134	243	523	.465	–	–	–	135	211	.640	–	–	276	56	127	1	–	–	–	621	3.7	0.7	8.3
70-71–Clev.-Atlanta	48	–	537	86	199	.432	–	–	–	71	88	.807	–	–	151	17	72	2	–	–	–	243	3.1	0.4	5.1
71-72–Dallas (A)	79	–	1403	231	511	.452	0	0	–	144	193	.746	–	–	318	69	158	–	–	63	–	606	4.0	0.9	7.7
Reg. NBA Totals	591	–	10596	2212	4898	.452	–	–	–	1197	1732	.691	–	–	3113	434	1191	10	–	–	–	5621	5.3	0.7	9.5
Reg. ABA Totals	79	–	1403	231	511	.452	0	0	–	144	193	.746	–	–	318	69	158	–	–	63	–	606	4.0	0.9	7.7
NBA Playoff Totals	22	–	273	44	105	.419	–	–	–	31	45	.689	–	–	69	17	34	0	–	–	–	119	3.1	0.8	5.4
ABA Playoff Totals	4	–	89	12	24	.500	0	0	–	5	8	.625	–	–	18	3	13	–	–	3	–	29	4.5	0.8	7.3

Charles, Kenneth M. (Ken) b. July 10, 1951 Ht. 6-3 Wt. 180 College: Fordham

SEASON–TEAM	G	GS	MIN	FGM	FGA	PCT	3FGM	3FGA	PCT	FTM	FTA	PCT	O-RB	D-RB	TOT	AST	PF	DQ	STL	TO	BLK	PTS	RPG	APG	PPG
73-74–Buffalo	59	–	693	88	185	.476	–	–	–	53	79	.671	25	40	65	54	91	0	31	–	10	229	1.1	0.9	3.9
74-75–Buffalo	79	–	1690	240	515	.466	–	–	–	120	146	.822	68	96	164	171	165	0	87	–	20	600	2.1	2.2	7.6
75-76–Buffalo	81	–	2247	328	719	.456	–	–	–	161	205	.785	58	161	219	204	257	5	123	–	48	817	2.7	2.5	10.1
76-77–Atlanta	82	–	2487	354	855	.414	–	–	–	205	256	.801	41	127	168	295	240	4	141	–	45	913	2.0	3.6	11.1
77-78–Atlanta	21	–	520	73	184	.397	–	–	–	42	50	.840	6	18	24	82	53	0	25	37	5	188	1.1	3.9	9.0
Reg. Season Totals	322	–	7637	1083	2458	.441	–	–	–	581	736	.789	198	442	640	806	806	9	407	37	128	2747	2.0	2.5	8.5
Playoff Totals	18	–	456	47	114	.412	–	–	–	17	24	.708	11	30	41	32	60	2	13	–	11	111	2.3	1.8	6.2

Charles, Lorenzo Emile b. November 25, 1963 Ht. 6-7 Wt. 225 College: North Carolina State

SEASON–TEAM	G	GS	MIN	FGM	FGA	PCT	3FGM	3FGA	PCT	FTM	FTA	PCT	O-RB	D-RB	TOT	AST	PF	DQ	STL	TO	BLK	PTS	RPG	APG	PPG
85-86–Atlanta	36	0	273	49	88	.557	0	0	–	24	36	.667	13	26	39	8	37	0	2	18	6	122	1.1	0.2	3.4
Reg. Season Totals	36	0	273	49	88	.557	0	0	–	24	36	.667	13	26	39	8	37	0	2	18	6	122	1.1	0.2	3.4
Playoff Totals	4	0	15	3	4	.750	0	0	–	1	1	1.000	0	2	2	2	1	0	0	0	0	7	0.5	0.5	1.8

Cheaney, Calbert Nathaniel b. July 17, 1971 Ht. 6-7 Wt. 215 College: Indiana

SEASON–TEAM	G	GS	MIN	FGM	FGA	PCT	3FGM	3FGA	PCT	FTM	FTA	PCT	O-RB	D-RB	TOT	AST	PF	DQ	STL	TO	BLK	PTS	RPG	APG	PPG
93-94–Washington	65	21	1604	327	696	.470	1	23	.043	124	161	.770	88	102	190	126	148	0	63	108	10	779	2.9	1.9	12.0
94-95–Washington	78	71	2651	512	1129	.453	96	283	.339	173	213	.812	105	216	321	177	215	0	80	151	21	1293	4.1	2.3	16.6
95-96–Washington	70	70	2324	426	905	.471	52	154	.338	151	214	.706	67	172	239	154	205	1	67	129	18	1055	3.4	2.2	15.1
96-97–Washington	79	79	2411	369	730	.505	4	30	.133	95	137	.693	70	198	268	114	226	3	77	94	18	837	3.4	1.4	10.6
97-98–Washington	82	82	2841	448	981	.457	15	53	.283	139	215	.647	82	242	324	173	264	4	96	104	36	1050	4.0	2.1	12.8
98-99–Washington	50	18	1266	172	415	.414	8	37	.216	33	67	.493	33	108	141	73	146	0	39	42	16	385	2.8	1.5	7.7
99-00–Boston	67	19	1309	120	273	.440	18	54	.333	9	21	.429	23	115	138	80	158	3	44	46	14	267	2.1	1.2	4.0
Reg. Season Totals	491	360	14406	2374	5129	.463	194	634	.306	724	1028	.704	468	1153	1621	897	1362	11	466	674	133	5666	3.3	1.8	11.5
Playoff Totals	3	3	120	18	41	.439	0	2	.000	9	12	.750	6	5	11	4	10	0	3	5	2	45	3.7	1.3	15.0

Cheeks, Maurice Edward (Mo) b. September 8, 1956 Ht. 6-1 Wt. 180 College: West Texas State

SEASON–TEAM	G	GS	MIN	FGM	FGA	PCT	3FGM	3FGA	PCT	FTM	FTA	PCT	O-RB	D-RB	TOT	AST	PF	DQ	STL	TO	BLK	PTS	RPG	APG	PPG
78-79–Philadelphia	82	–	2409	292	572	.510	–	–	–	101	140	.721	63	191	254	431	198	2	174	193	12	685	3.1	5.3	8.4
79-80–Philadelphia	79	–	2623	357	661	.540	4	9	.444	180	231	.779	75	199	274	556	197	1	183	216	32	898	3.5	7.0	11.4
80-81–Philadelphia	81	–	2415	310	581	.534	3	8	.375	140	178	.787	67	178	245	560	231	1	193	174	39	763	3.0	6.9	9.4
81-82–Philadelphia	79	79	2498	352	676	.521	6	22	.273	171	220	.777	51	197	248	667	247	0	209	184	33	881	3.1	8.4	11.2
82-83–Philadelphia	79	79	2465	404	745	.542	1	6	.167	181	240	.754	53	156	209	543	182	0	184	179	31	990	2.6	6.9	12.5
83-84–Philadelphia	75	75	2494	386	702	.550	8	20	.400	170	232	.733	44	161	205	478	196	1	171	182	20	950	2.7	6.4	12.7
84-85–Philadelphia	78	78	2616	422	741	.570	6	26	.231	175	199	.879	54	163	217	497	184	0	169	155	24	1025	2.8	6.4	13.1
85-86–Philadelphia	82	82	3270	490	913	.537	4	17	.235	282	335	.842	55	180	235	753	160	0	207	238	27	1266	2.9	9.2	15.4
86-87–Philadelphia	68	68	2624	415	788	.527	4	17	.235	227	292	.777	47	168	215	538	109	0	180	173	15	1061	3.2	7.9	15.6
87-88–Philadelphia	79	79	2871	428	865	.495	3	22	.136	227	275	.825	59	194	253	635	116	0	167	160	22	1086	3.2	8.0	13.7
88-89–Philadelphia	71	70	2298	336	696	.483	1	13	.077	151	195	.774	39	144	183	554	114	0	105	116	17	824	2.6	7.8	11.6
89-90–S.A.-N.Y.	81	62	2519	307	609	.504	4	16	.250	171	202	.847	50	190	240	453	78	0	124	121	10	789	3.0	5.6	9.7
90-91–New York	76	64	2147	241	483	.499	5	20	.250	105	129	.814	22	151	173	435	138	0	128	108	10	592	2.3	5.7	7.8
91-92–Atlanta	56	0	1086	115	249	.462	3	6	.500	26	43	.605	29	66	95	185	73	0	83	36	0	259	1.7	3.3	4.6
92-93–New Jersey	35	0	510	51	93	.548	0	2	.000	24	27	.889	5	37	42	107	35	0	33	33	2	126	1.2	3.1	3.6
Reg. Season Totals	1101	736	34845	4906	9374	.523	52	204	.255	2331	2938	.793	713	2375	3088	7392	2258	5	2310	2268	294	12195	2.8	6.7	11.1
Playoff Totals	133	85	4848	772	1509	.512	4	41	.098	362	466	.777	114	339	453	922	324	1	295	318	45	1910	3.4	6.9	14.4
All-Star Totals	4	1	44	7	16	.438	0	0	–	2	2	1.000	0	3	3	4	2	0	3	4	0	16	0.8	1.0	4.0

Chenier, Philip (Phil) b. October 30, 1950 Ht. 6-3 Wt. 180 College: California

SEASON–TEAM	G	GS	MIN	FGM	FGA	PCT	3FGM	3FGA	PCT	FTM	FTA	PCT	O-RB	D-RB	TOT	AST	PF	DQ	STL	TO	BLK	PTS	RPG	APG	PPG
71-72–Baltimore	81	–	2481	407	981	.415	–	–	–	182	247	.737	–	–	268	205	191	2	–	–	–	996	3.3	2.5	12.3
72-73–Baltimore	71	–	2776	602	1332	.452	–	–	–	194	244	.795	–	–	288	301	160	0	–	–	–	1398	4.1	4.2	19.7
73-74–Capital	76	–	2942	697	1607	.434	–	–	–	274	334	.820	114	274	388	239	135	0	155	–	67	1668	5.1	3.1	21.9
74-75–Washington	77	–	2869	690	1533	.450	–	–	–	301	365	.825	74	218	292	248	158	3	176	–	58	1681	3.8	3.2	21.8
75-76–Washington	80	–	2952	654	1355	.483	–	–	–	282	341	.827	84	236	320	255	186	2	158	–	45	1590	4.0	3.2	19.9
76-77–Washington	78	–	2842	654	1472	.444	–	–	–	270	321	.841	56	243	299	294	166	0	120	–	39	1578	3.8	3.8	20.2
77-78–Washington	36	–	937	200	451	.443	–	–	–	109	138	.790	15	87	102	73	54	0	36	67	9	509	2.8	2.0	14.1
78-79–Washington	27	–	385	69	158	.437	–	–	–	18	28	.643	3	17	20	31	28	0	4	31	5	156	0.7	1.1	5.8
79-80–Wash.-Indiana	43	–	850	136	349	.390	5	12	.417	49	67	.731	19	59	78	89	55	0	33	55	15	326	1.8	2.1	7.6
80-81–Golden State	9	–	82	11	33	.333	1	3	.333	6	6	1.000	1	7	8	7	10	0	0	4	0	29	0.9	0.8	3.2
Reg. Season Totals	578	–	19116	4120	9271	.444	6	15	.400	1685	2091	.806	366	1141	2063	1742	1143	7	682	157	238	9931	3.6	3.0	17.2
Playoff Totals	60	–	2088	438	974	.450	0	0	–	212	251	.845	41	152	230	131	152	1	59	6	26	1088	3.8	2.2	18.1
All-Star Totals	3	–	48	10	20	.500	0	0	–	2	4	.500	3	2	5	3	0	0	2	–	0	22	1.7	1.0	7.3

Chievous, Derrick Joseph (Band-Aid) b. July 3, 1967 Ht. 6-7 Wt. 195 College: Missouri

SEASON–TEAM	G	GS	MIN	FGM	FGA	PCT	3FGM	3FGA	PCT	FTM	FTA	PCT	O-RB	D-RB	TOT	AST	PF	DQ	STL	TO	BLK	PTS	RPG	APG	PPG
88-89–Houston	81	1	1539	277	634	.437	5	24	.208	191	244	.783	114	142	256	77	161	1	48	136	11	750	3.2	1.0	9.3
89-90–Houston-Clev.	55	0	591	105	220	.477	3	9	.333	80	111	.721	35	55	90	31	70	0	26	45	5	293	1.6	0.6	5.3
90-91–Cleveland	18	0	110	17	46	.370	0	0	–	9	16	.563	11	7	18	2	16	0	3	6	1	43	1.0	0.1	2.4
Reg. Season Totals	154	1	2240	399	900	.443	8	33	.242	280	371	.755	160	204	364	110	247	1	77	187	17	1086	2.4	0.7	7.1
Playoff Totals	7	0	68	11	27	.407	0	0	–	15	19	.789	7	2	9	4	9	0	2	6	1	37	1.3	0.6	5.3

Chilcutt, Peter Shawn (Pete) b. September 14, 1968 Ht. 6-10 Wt. 245 College: North Carolina

SEASON–TEAM	G	GS	MIN	FGM	FGA	PCT	3FGM	3FGA	PCT	FTM	FTA	PCT	O-RB	D-RB	TOT	AST	PF	DQ	STL	TO	BLK	PTS	RPG	APG	PPG
91-92–Sacramento	69	2	817	113	250	.452	2	2	1.000	23	28	.821	78	109	187	38	70	0	32	41	17	251	2.7	0.6	3.6
92-93–Sacramento	59	9	834	165	340	.485	0	0	–	32	46	.696	80	114	194	64	102	2	22	54	21	362	3.3	1.1	6.1
93-94–Sac.-Detroit	76	24	1365	203	448	.453	3	15	.200	41	65	.631	129	242	371	86	164	2	53	74	39	450	4.9	1.1	5.9
94-95–Houston	68	17	1347	146	328	.445	35	86	.407	31	42	.738	106	211	317	66	117	0	25	61	43	358	4.7	1.0	5.3
95-96–Houston	74	0	651	73	179	.408	37	98	.378	17	26	.654	51	105	156	26	65	0	19	22	14	200	2.1	0.4	2.7
96-97–Vancouver	54	1	662	72	165	.436	25	69	.362	13	22	.591	67	89	156	47	52	0	26	28	17	182	2.9	0.9	3.4
97-98–Vancouver	82	0	1420	156	359	.435	54	130	.415	39	59	.661	77	229	306	104	158	0	53	62	37	405	3.7	1.3	4.9
98-99–Vancouver	46	0	697	63	172	.366	26	68	.382	14	17	.824	29	88	117	30	52	0	22	28	12	166	2.5	0.7	3.6
99-00–Utah-Clev.-LAClips	56	2	601	53	127	.417	6	26	.231	8	8	1.000	46	85	131	27	73	2	15	20	10	120	2.3	0.5	2.1
Reg. Season Totals	584	55	8394	1044	2368	.441	188	494	.381	218	313	.696	663	1272	1935	488	853	6	267	390	210	2494	3.3	0.8	4.3
Playoff Totals	21	15	333	32	68	.471	14	37	.378	14	19	.737	17	44	61	18	39	0	7	12	4	92	2.9	0.9	4.4

Childress, Randolph b. September 21, 1972 Ht. 6-2 Wt. 188 College: Wake Forest

SEASON–TEAM	G	GS	MIN	FGM	FGA	PCT	3FGM	3FGA	PCT	FTM	FTA	PCT	O-RB	D-RB	TOT	AST	PF	DQ	STL	TO	BLK	PTS	RPG	APG	PPG
95-96–Portland	28	0	250	25	79	.316	13	47	.277	22	27	.815	1	18	19	32	22	0	8	28	1	85	0.7	1.1	3.0
96-97–Port.-Detroit	23	0	155	14	40	.350	5	19	.263	6	8	.750	1	5	6	17	16	0	9	18	0	39	0.3	0.7	1.7
Reg. Season Totals	51	0	405	39	119	.328	18	66	.273	28	35	.800	2	23	25	49	38	0	17	46	1	124	0.5	1.0	2.4

Childs, Chris b. November 20, 1967 Ht. 6-3 Wt. 195 College: Boise State

SEASON–TEAM	G	GS	MIN	FGM	FGA	PCT	3FGM	3FGA	PCT	FTM	FTA	PCT	O-RB	D-RB	TOT	AST	PF	DQ	STL	TO	BLK	PTS	RPG	APG	PPG
94-95–New Jersey	53	11	1021	106	279	.380	41	125	.328	55	73	.753	14	55	69	219	116	1	42	76	3	308	1.3	4.1	5.8
95-96–New Jersey	78	54	2408	324	778	.416	95	259	.367	259	304	.852	51	194	245	548	246	3	111	230	8	1002	3.1	7.0	12.8
96-97–New York	65	61	2076	211	510	.414	70	181	.387	113	149	.758	22	169	191	398	213	6	78	180	11	605	2.9	6.1	9.3
97-98–New York	68	0	1599	149	354	.421	27	87	.310	104	126	.825	29	133	162	268	179	2	56	103	6	429	2.4	3.9	6.3
98-99–New York	48	0	1297	114	267	.427	36	94	.383	64	78	.821	18	115	133	193	156	0	44	85	1	328	2.8	4.0	6.8
99-00–New York	71	2	1675	146	357	.409	37	104	.356	47	59	.797	17	130	147	285	240	4	36	105	4	376	2.1	4.0	5.3
Reg. Season Totals	383	128	10076	1050	2545	.413	306	850	.360	642	789	.814	151	796	947	1911	1150	16	367	779	33	3048	2.5	5.0	8.0
Playoff Totals	56	10	1410	122	308	.396	31	95	.326	73	92	.793	23	135	158	204	185	4	46	95	1	348	2.8	3.6	6.2

Chollet, Leroy Patrick b. March 5, 1925 Ht. 6-2 Wt. 190 College: Loyola (L.A.); Canisius

SEASON–TEAM	G	GS	MIN	FGM	FGA	PCT	3FGM	3FGA	PCT	FTM	FTA	PCT	O-RB	D-RB	TOT	AST	PF	DQ	STL	TO	BLK	PTS	RPG	APG	PPG
49-50–Syracuse	49	–	–	61	179	.341	–	–	–	35	56	.625	–	–	–	37	52	–	–	–	–	157	–	0.8	3.2
50-51–Syracuse	14	–	–	6	51	.118	–	–	–	12	19	.632	–	–	15	12	29	0	–	–	–	24	1.1	0.9	1.7
Reg. Season Totals	63	–	–	67	230	.291	–	–	–	47	75	.627	–	–	15	49	81	0	–	–	–	181	1.1	0.8	2.9
Playoff Totals	15	–	–	11	60	.233	–	–	–	10	21	.476	–	–	16	13	27	1	–	–	–	32	2.3	0.7	2.1

Chones, James Bernett (Jim) b. November 30, 1949 Ht. 6-11 Wt. 220 College: Marquette

SEASON–TEAM	G	GS	MIN	FGM	FGA	PCT	3FGM	3FGA	PCT	FTM	FTA	PCT	O-RB	D-RB	TOT	AST	PF	DQ	STL	TO	BLK	PTS	RPG	APG	PPG
72-73–New York (A)	82	–	2153	395	769	.514	0	1	.000	142	240	.592	143	443	586	95	291	7	–	213	–	932	7.1	1.2	11.4
73-74–Carolina (A)	83	–	2387	535	1017	.526	0	2	.000	155	252	.615	191	454	645	118	347	–	59	206	131	1225	7.8	1.4	14.8
74-75–Cleveland	72	–	2427	446	916	.487	–	–	–	152	224	.679	156	521	677	132	247	5	49	–	120	1044	9.4	1.8	14.5
75-76–Cleveland	82	–	2741	563	1258	.448	–	–	–	172	260	.662	197	542	739	163	241	2	42	–	93	1298	9.0	2.0	15.8
76-77–Cleveland	82	–	2378	450	972	.463	–	–	–	155	212	.731	208	480	688	104	258	3	32	–	77	1055	8.4	1.3	12.9
77-78–Cleveland	82	–	2906	525	1113	.472	–	–	–	180	250	.720	219	625	844	131	235	4	52	184	58	1230	10.3	1.6	15.0
78-79–Cleveland	82	–	2850	472	1073	.440	–	–	–	158	215	.735	260	582	842	181	278	4	47	187	102	1102	10.3	2.2	13.4
79-80–Los Angeles	82	–	2394	372	760	.489	0	2	.000	125	169	.740	143	421	564	151	271	5	56	175	65	869	6.9	1.8	10.6
80-81–Los Angeles	82	–	2562	378	751	.503	0	4	.000	126	193	.653	180	477	657	153	324	4	39	159	96	882	8.0	1.9	10.8
81-82–Washington	59	13	867	74	171	.433	0	0	–	36	46	.783	39	146	185	64	114	1	15	41	32	184	3.1	1.1	3.1
Reg. NBA Totals	623	13	19125	3280	7014	.468	0	6	.000	1104	1569	.704	1402	3794	5196	1079	1968	28	332	746	643	7664	8.3	1.7	12.3
Reg. ABA Totals	165	–	4540	930	1786	.521	0	3	.000	297	492	.604	334	897	1231	213	638	7	59	419	131	2157	7.5	1.3	13.1
NBA Playoff Totals	36	0	959	136	312	.436	0	0	–	50	78	.641	67	156	223	47	116	0	13	40	20	322	6.2	1.3	8.9
ABA Playoff Totals	9	–	170	29	70	.414	0	0	–	8	16	.500	6	18	51	8	25	0	2	8	4	66	5.7	0.9	7.3

Christ, Frederick L. (Fred) b. August 6, 1930 Ht. 6-4 Wt. 210 College: Fordham

SEASON–TEAM	G	GS	MIN	FGM	FGA	PCT	3FGM	3FGA	PCT	FTM	FTA	PCT	O-RB	D-RB	TOT	AST	PF	DQ	STL	TO	BLK	PTS	RPG	APG	PPG
54-55–New York	6	–	48	5	18	.278	–	–	–	10	11	.909	–	–	8	7	3	0	–	–	–	20	1.3	1.2	3.3
Reg. Season Totals	6	–	48	5	18	.278	–	–	–	10	11	.909	–	–	8	7	3	0	–	–	–	20	1.3	1.2	3.3

Christensen, Calvin L. (Cal) b. June 8, 1927 Ht. 6-5 Wt. 220 College: Toledo

SEASON–TEAM	G	GS	MIN	FGM	FGA	PCT	3FGM	3FGA	PCT	FTM	FTA	PCT	O-RB	D-RB	TOT	AST	PF	DQ	STL	TO	BLK	PTS	RPG	APG	PPG
50-51–Tri-Cities	67	–	–	134	445	.301	–	–	–	175	245	.714	–	–	523	161	266	19	–	–	–	443	7.8	2.4	6.6
51-52–Milwaukee	24	–	374	29	96	.302	–	–	–	30	57	.526	–	–	82	34	47	2	–	–	–	88	3.4	1.4	3.7
52-53–Rochester	59	–	777	72	230	.313	–	–	–	68	114	.596	–	–	199	54	148	6	–	–	–	212	3.4	0.9	3.6
53-54–Rochester	70	–	1654	137	395	.347	–	–	–	138	261	.529	–	–	395	107	196	1	–	–	–	412	5.6	1.5	5.9
54-55–Rochester	71	–	1204	114	305	.374	–	–	–	124	206	.602	–	–	388	104	174	2	–	–	–	352	5.5	1.5	5.0
Reg. Season Totals	291	–	4009	486	1471	.330	–	–	–	535	883	.606	–	–	1587	460	831	30	–	–	–	1507	5.5	1.6	5.2
Playoff Totals	11	–	317	12	54	.333	–	–	–	18	31	.581	–	–	80	31	21	1	–	–	–	42	4.7	1.8	3.8

Christian, Bob b. May 11, 1946 Ht. 7-0 Wt. 255 College: Grambling State

SEASON–TEAM	G	GS	MIN	FGM	FGA	PCT	3FGM	3FGA	PCT	FTM	FTA	PCT	O-RB	D-RB	TOT	AST	PF	DQ	STL	TO	BLK	PTS	RPG	APG	PPG
69-70–N.Y.-Dallas (A)	2	–	11	1	3	.333	0	0	–	0	0	–	–	–	3	0	3	0	–	–	–	2	1.5	0.0	1.0
70-71–Atlanta	54	–	524	55	127	.433	–	–	–	40	64	.625	–	–	177	30	118	0	–	–	–	150	3.3	0.6	2.8
71-72–Atlanta	56	–	485	66	142	.465	–	–	–	44	61	.721	–	–	181	28	77	0	–	–	–	176	3.2	0.5	3.1
72-73–Atlanta	55	–	759	85	155	.548	–	–	–	60	79	.759	–	–	305	47	111	2	–	–	–	230	5.5	0.9	4.2
73-74–Phoenix	81	–	1244	140	288	.486	–	–	–	106	151	.702	85	254	339	98	191	3	19	–	32	386	4.2	1.2	4.8
Reg. NBA Totals	246	–	3012	346	712	.486	–	–	–	250	355	.704	85	254	1002	203	497	5	19	–	32	942	4.1	0.8	3.8
Reg. ABA Totals	2	–	11	1	3	.333	0	0	–	0	0	–	–	–	3	0	3	0	–	–	–	2	1.5	0.0	1.0
NBA Playoff Totals	6	–	34	3	8	.375	–	–	–	1	1	1.000	0	0	7	–	10	0	0	–	0	7	1.2	0.0	1.2

Christie, Douglas Dale (Doug) b. May 9, 1970 Ht. 6-6 Wt. 205 College: Pepperdine

SEASON–TEAM	G	GS	MIN	FGM	FGA	PCT	3FGM	3FGA	PCT	FTM	FTA	PCT	O-RB	D-RB	TOT	AST	PF	DQ	STL	TO	BLK	PTS	RPG	APG	PPG
92-93–L.A. Lakers	23	0	332	45	106	.425	2	12	.167	50	66	.758	24	27	51	53	53	0	22	50	5	142	2.2	2.3	6.2
93-94–L.A. Lakers	65	34	1515	244	562	.434	39	119	.328	145	208	.697	93	142	235	136	186	2	89	140	28	672	3.6	2.1	10.3
94-95–New York	12	0	79	5	22	.227	1	7	.143	4	5	.800	3	10	13	8	18	1	2	13	1	15	1.1	0.7	1.3
95-96–N.Y.-Toronto	55	17	1036	150	337	.445	46	106	.434	69	93	.742	34	120	154	117	141	5	70	95	19	415	2.8	2.1	7.5
96-97–Toronto	81	81	3127	396	949	.417	147	383	.384	237	306	.775	85	347	432	315	245	6	201	200	45	1176	5.3	3.9	14.5
97-98–Toronto	78	78	2939	458	1071	.428	100	307	.326	271	327	.829	94	310	404	282	198	3	190	228	57	1287	5.2	3.6	16.5
98-99–Toronto	50	50	1768	252	650	.388	49	161	.304	207	246	.841	59	148	207	187	111	1	113	119	26	760	4.1	3.7	15.2
99-00–Toronto	73	73	2264	311	764	.407	99	275	.360	182	216	.843	63	222	285	321	167	1	102	144	43	903	3.9	4.4	12.4
Reg. Season Totals	437	333	13060	1861	4461	.417	483	1370	.353	1165	1467	.794	455	1326	1781	1419	1119	19	789	989	224	5370	4.1	3.2	12.3
Playoff Totals	10	1	106	7	28	.250	4	11	.364	3	6	.500	2	7	9	12	18	0	6	9	3	21	0.9	1.2	2.1

Chubin, Stephen (Steve, Chube) b. February 8, 1944 Ht. 6-2 Wt. 200 College: Rhode Island

SEASON–TEAM	G	GS	MIN	FGM	FGA	PCT	3FGM	3FGA	PCT	FTM	FTA	PCT	O-RB	D-RB	TOT	AST	PF	DQ	STL	TO	BLK	PTS	RPG	APG	PPG
67-68–Anaheim (A)	77	–	2441	439	1057	.415	2	10	.200	518	639	.811	–	–	433	364	292	10	–	310	–	1398	5.6	4.7	18.2
68-69–L.A.-Minn.-Ind.-N.Y. (A)	77	–	2097	344	875	.393	3	27	.111	386	472	.818	–	–	291	354	287	6	–	286	–	1077	3.8	4.6	14.0
69-70–N.Y.-Pitt.-Ind.-Ken.(A)	72	–	1058	127	352	.361	5	14	.357	170	199	.854	–	–	137	117	174	3	–	–	–	429	1.9	1.6	6.0
Reg. ABA Totals	226	–	5596	910	2284	.398	10	51	.196	1074	1310	.820	–	–	861	835	753	19	–	596	–	2904	3.8	3.7	12.8
ABA Playoff Totals	11	–	55	8	17	.471	0	4	.000	12	14	.857	–	–	3	0	0	0	–	–	–	28	0.3	0.0	2.5

Churchwell, Robert b. February 20, 1972 Ht. 6-6 Wt. 195 College: Georgetown

SEASON–TEAM	G	GS	MIN	FGM	FGA	PCT	3FGM	3FGA	PCT	FTM	FTA	PCT	O-RB	D-RB	TOT	AST	PF	DQ	STL	TO	BLK	PTS	RPG	APG	PPG
95-96–Golden State	4	0	20	3	8	.375	0	0	–	0	0	–	0	3	3	1	1	0	0	2	0	6	0.8	0.3	1.5
Reg. Season Totals	4	0	20	3	8	.375	0	0	–	0	0	–	0	3	3	1	1	0	0	2	0	6	0.8	0.3	1.5

Clark, Archie L. b. July 15, 1941 Ht. 6-2 Wt. 175 College: Minnesota

SEASON–TEAM	G	GS	MIN	FGM	FGA	PCT	3FGM	3FGA	PCT	FTM	FTA	PCT	O-RB	D-RB	TOT	AST	PF	DQ	STL	TO	BLK	PTS	RPG	APG	PPG
66-67–Los Angeles	76	–	1763	331	732	.452	–	–	–	136	192	.708	–	–	218	205	193	1	–	–	–	798	2.9	2.7	10.5
67-68–Los Angeles	81	–	3039	628	1309	.480	–	–	–	356	481	.740	–	–	342	353	235	3	–	–	–	1612	4.2	4.4	19.9
68-69–Philadelphia	82	–	2144	444	928	.478	–	–	–	219	314	.697	–	–	265	296	188	1	–	–	–	1107	3.2	3.6	13.5
69-70–Philadelphia	76	–	2772	594	1198	.496	–	–	–	311	396	.785	–	–	301	380	201	2	–	–	–	1499	4.0	5.0	19.7
70-71–Philadelphia	82	–	3245	662	1334	.496	–	–	–	422	536	.787	–	–	391	440	217	2	–	–	–	1746	4.8	5.4	21.3
71-72–Phil.-Balt.	77	–	3285	712	1516	.470	–	–	–	514	667	.771	–	–	268	613	194	0	–	–	–	1938	3.5	8.0	25.2
72-73–Baltimore	39	–	1477	302	596	.507	–	–	–	111	137	.810	–	–	129	275	111	1	–	–	–	715	3.3	7.1	18.3
73-74–Capital	56	–	1786	315	675	.467	–	–	–	103	131	.786	44	97	141	285	122	0	59	–	6	733	2.5	5.1	13.1
74-75–Seattle	77	–	2481	455	919	.495	–	–	–	161	193	.834	59	176	235	433	188	4	110	–	5	1071	3.1	5.6	13.9
75-76–Detroit	79	–	1589	250	577	.433	–	–	–	100	116	.862	27	110	137	218	157	0	62	–	4	600	1.7	2.8	7.6
Reg. Season Totals	725	–	23581	4693	9784	.480	–	–	–	2433	3163	.769	130	383	2427	3498	1806	14	231	–	15	11819	3.3	4.8	16.3
Playoff Totals	71	–	2387	444	977	.454	–	–	–	237	307	.772	12	54	229	297	197	2	17	–	1	1125	3.2	4.2	15.8
All-Star Totals	2	–	36	7	13	.538	–	–	–	11	11	1.000	0	0	1	9	3	0	0	–	0	25	0.5	4.5	12.5

Clark, Arian Keon (Keon) b. April 16, 1975 Ht. 6-11 Wt. 220 College: California-Irvine; Dixie (Utah) Coll.; Nevada-Las Vegas

SEASON–TEAM	G	GS	MIN	FGM	FGA	PCT	3FGM	3FGA	PCT	FTM	FTA	PCT	O-RB	D-RB	TOT	AST	PF	DQ	STL	TO	BLK	PTS	RPG	APG	PPG
98-99–Denver	28	0	409	36	80	.450	0	1	.000	21	37	.568	36	60	96	10	52	0	10	21	31	93	3.4	0.4	3.3
99-00–Denver	81	20	1850	286	528	.542	1	8	.125	121	176	.688	162	343	505	71	231	1	45	125	114	694	6.2	0.9	8.6
Reg. Season Totals	109	20	2259	322	608	.530	1	9	.111	142	213	.667	198	403	601	81	283	1	55	146	145	787	5.5	0.7	7.2

Clark, Carlos R. b. August 10, 1960 Ht. 6-4 Wt. 210 College: Mississippi

SEASON–TEAM	G	GS	MIN	FGM	FGA	PCT	3FGM	3FGA	PCT	FTM	FTA	PCT	O-RB	D-RB	TOT	AST	PF	DQ	STL	TO	BLK	PTS	RPG	APG	PPG
83-84–Boston	31	0	127	19	52	.365	0	2	.000	16	18	.889	7	10	17	17	13	0	8	12	1	54	0.5	0.5	1.7
84-85–Boston	62	3	562	64	152	.421	0	5	.000	41	53	.774	29	40	69	48	66	0	35	42	2	169	1.1	0.8	2.7
Reg. Season Totals	93	3	689	83	204	.407	0	7	.000	57	71	.803	36	50	86	65	79	0	43	54	3	223	0.9	0.7	2.4
Playoff Totals	11	0	31	7	15	.467	0	0	–	3	4	.750	3	0	3	4	5	0	2	1	2	17	0.3	0.4	1.5

Clark, Richard C. (Dick) b. January 5, 1944 Ht. 6-4 Wt. 195 College: Eastern Kentucky

SEASON–TEAM	G	GS	MIN	FGM	FGA	PCT	3FGM	3FGA	PCT	FTM	FTA	PCT	O-RB	D-RB	TOT	AST	PF	DQ	STL	TO	BLK	PTS	RPG	APG	PPG
67-68–Minnesota (A)	26	–	414	46	150	.307	0	10	.000	48	79	.608	–	–	52	33	49	0	–	33	–	140	2.0	1.3	5.4
68-69–Houston (A)	32	–	723	64	222	.288	1	8	.125	89	124	.718	–	–	88	68	99	0	–	73	–	218	2.8	2.1	6.8
Reg. ABA Totals	58	–	1137	110	372	.296	1	18	.056	137	203	.675	–	–	140	101	148	0	–	106	–	358	2.4	1.7	6.2
ABA Playoff Totals	10	–	231	17	65	.262	1	6	.167	21	28	.750	–	–	33	13	18	0	–	13	–	56	3.3	1.3	5.6

Clawson, John Richard b. May 15, 1944 Ht. 6-4 Wt. 200 College: Michigan

SEASON–TEAM	G	GS	MIN	FGM	FGA	PCT	3FGM	3FGA	PCT	FTM	FTA	PCT	O-RB	D-RB	TOT	AST	PF	DQ	STL	TO	BLK	PTS	RPG	APG	PPG
68-69–Oakland (A)	70	–	1067	147	309	.476	0	0	–	37	54	.685	–	–	195	51	187	1	–	73	–	331	2.8	0.7	4.7
Reg. ABA Totals	70	–	1067	147	309	.476	0	0	–	37	54	.685	–	–	195	51	187	1	–	73	–	331	2.8	0.7	4.7
ABA Playoff Totals	16	–	313	42	95	.442	1	3	.333	15	24	.625	–	–	54	14	60	2	–	–	–	100	3.4	0.9	6.3

Claxton, Charles b. December 13, 1970 Ht. 7-0 Wt. 265 College: Georgia

SEASON–TEAM	G	GS	MIN	FGM	FGA	PCT	3FGM	3FGA	PCT	FTM	FTA	PCT	O-RB	D-RB	TOT	AST	PF	DQ	STL	TO	BLK	PTS	RPG	APG	PPG
95-96–Boston	3	0	7	1	2	.500	0	0	–	0	2	.000	2	0	2	0	4	0	0	1	1	2	0.7	0.0	0.7
Reg. Season Totals	3	0	7	1	2	.500	0	0	–	0	2	.000	2	0	2	0	4	0	0	1	1	2	0.7	0.0	0.7

Cleamons, James Mitchell (Jim) b. September 13, 1949 Ht. 6-3 Wt. 185 College: Ohio State

SEASON–TEAM	G	GS	MIN	FGM	FGA	PCT	3FGM	3FGA	PCT	FTM	FTA	PCT	O-RB	D-RB	TOT	AST	PF	DQ	STL	TO	BLK	PTS	RPG	APG	PPG
71-72–Los Angeles	38	–	201	35	100	.350	–	–	–	28	36	.778	–	–	39	35	21	0	–	–	–	98	1.0	0.9	2.6
72-73–Cleveland	80	–	1399	192	421	.456	–	–	–	71	95	.747	–	–	173	206	111	0	–	–	–	455	2.2	2.6	5.7
73-74–Cleveland	81	–	1642	236	545	.433	–	–	–	93	133	.699	63	167	230	227	152	1	61	–	17	565	2.8	2.8	7.0
74-75–Cleveland	74	–	2691	369	768	.480	–	–	–	144	181	.796	97	232	329	381	194	0	84	–	21	882	4.4	5.1	11.9
75-76–Cleveland	82	–	2835	413	887	.466	–	–	–	174	218	.798	124	230	354	428	214	2	124	–	20	1000	4.3	5.2	12.2
76-77–Cleveland	60	–	2045	257	592	.434	–	–	–	112	148	.757	99	174	273	308	126	0	66	–	23	626	4.6	5.1	10.4
77-78–New York	79	–	2009	215	448	.480	–	–	–	81	103	.786	69	143	212	283	142	1	68	113	17	511	2.7	3.6	6.5
78-79–New York	79	–	2390	311	657	.473	–	–	–	130	171	.760	65	160	225	376	147	1	73	142	11	752	2.8	4.8	9.5
79-80–N.Y.-Wash.	79	–	1789	214	450	.476	7	31	.226	84	113	.743	53	99	152	288	133	0	57	109	11	519	1.9	3.6	6.6
Reg. Season Totals	652	–	17001	2242	4868	.461	7	31	.226	917	1198	.765	570	1205	1987	2532	1240	5	533	364	120	5408	3.0	3.9	8.3
Playoff Totals	27	–	667	91	230	.396	0	0	–	39	46	.848	28	57	89	89	50	0	12	9	3	221	3.3	3.3	8.2

Clemens, John Barry (Barry) b. May 1, 1943 Ht. 6-6 Wt. 215 College: Ohio Wesleyan

SEASON–TEAM	G	GS	MIN	FGM	FGA	PCT	3FGM	3FGA	PCT	FTM	FTA	PCT	O-RB	D-RB	TOT	AST	PF	DQ	STL	TO	BLK	PTS	RPG	APG	PPG
65-66–New York	70	–	877	161	391	.412	–	–	–	54	78	.692	–	–	183	67	113	0	–	–	–	376	2.6	1.0	5.4
66-67–Chicago	60	–	986	186	444	.419	–	–	–	68	90	.756	–	–	201	39	143	1	–	–	–	440	3.4	0.7	7.3
67-68–Chicago	78	–	1631	301	670	.449	–	–	–	123	170	.724	–	–	375	98	223	4	–	–	–	725	4.8	1.3	9.3
68-69–Chicago	75	–	1444	235	628	.374	–	–	–	82	125	.656	–	–	318	125	163	1	–	–	–	552	4.2	1.7	7.4
69-70–Seattle	78	–	1487	270	595	.454	–	–	–	111	140	.793	–	–	316	116	188	1	–	–	–	651	4.1	1.5	8.3
70-71–Seattle	78	–	1286	247	526	.470	–	–	–	83	114	.728	–	–	243	92	169	1	–	–	–	577	3.1	1.2	7.4
71-72–Seattle	82	–	1447	252	484	.521	–	–	–	76	90	.844	–	–	288	64	198	4	–	–	–	580	3.5	0.8	7.1
72-73–Cleveland	72	–	1112	209	407	.514	–	–	–	57	74	.770	–	–	205	114	133	0	–	–	–	475	2.8	1.6	6.6
73-74–Cleveland	71	–	913	163	346	.471	–	–	–	62	73	.849	42	124	166	80	136	2	36	–	2	388	2.3	1.1	5.5
74-75–Portland	77	–	952	168	355	.473	–	–	–	45	60	.750	33	128	161	76	139	0	68	–	2	381	2.1	1.0	4.9
75-76–Portland	49	–	443	70	143	.490	–	–	–	31	35	.886	27	43	70	33	57	0	27	–	7	171	1.4	0.7	3.5
Reg. Season Totals	790	–	12578	2262	4989	.453	–	–	–	792	1049	.755	102	295	2526	904	1662	14	131	–	11	5316	3.2	1.1	6.7
Playoff Totals	7	–	65	8	20	.400	–	–	–	10	11	.909	0	0	5	7	9	0	0	–	0	26	0.7	1.0	3.7

Clifton, Nathaniel (Nat, Sweetwater) b. October 13, 1922 d. August 31, 1990 Ht. 6-6 Wt. 235 College: Xavier (La.)

SEASON–TEAM	G	GS	MIN	FGM	FGA	PCT	3FGM	3FGA	PCT	FTM	FTA	PCT	O-RB	D-RB	TOT	AST	PF	DQ	STL	TO	BLK	PTS	RPG	APG	PPG
50-51–New York	65	–	–	211	656	.322	–	–	–	140	263	.532	–	–	491	162	269	13	–	–	–	562	7.6	2.5	8.6
51-52–New York	62	–	2101	244	729	.335	–	–	–	170	256	.664	–	–	731	209	227	8	–	–	–	658	11.8	3.4	10.6
52-53–New York	70	–	2496	272	794	.343	–	–	–	200	343	.583	–	–	761	231	274	6	–	–	–	744	10.9	3.3	10.6
53-54–New York	72	–	2179	257	699	.368	–	–	–	174	277	.628	–	–	528	176	215	0	–	–	–	688	7.3	2.4	9.6
54-55–New York	72	–	2390	360	932	.386	–	–	–	224	328	.683	–	–	612	198	221	2	–	–	–	944	8.5	2.8	13.1
55-56–New York	64	–	1537	213	541	.394	–	–	–	135	191	.707	–	–	386	151	189	4	–	–	–	561	6.0	2.4	8.8
56-57–New York	71	–	2231	308	818	.377	–	–	–	146	217	.673	–	–	557	164	243	5	–	–	–	762	7.8	2.3	10.7
57-58–Detroit	68	–	1435	217	597	.363	–	–	–	91	146	.623	–	–	403	76	202	3	–	–	–	525	5.9	1.1	7.7
Reg. Season Totals	544	–	14369	2082	5766	.361	–	–	–	1280	2021	.633	–	–	4469	1367	1840	41	–	–	–	5444	8.2	2.5	10.0
Playoff Totals	53	–	1304	170	489	.348	–	–	–	136	218	.624	–	–	501	142	215	9	–	–	–	476	9.3	2.7	9.0
All-Star Totals	1	–	23	4	11	.364	–	–	–	0	0	–	–	–	11	3	1	0	–	–	–	8	11.0	3.0	8.0

Closs, Keith Jr. b. April 3, 1976 Ht. 7-3 Wt. 212 College: Central Connecticut State

SEASON–TEAM	G	GS	MIN	FGM	FGA	PCT	3FGM	3FGA	PCT	FTM	FTA	PCT	O-RB	D-RB	TOT	AST	PF	DQ	STL	TO	BLK	PTS	RPG	APG	PPG
97-98–L.A. Clippers	58	1	740	93	207	.449	0	0	–	46	77	.597	63	105	168	19	73	0	12	38	81	232	2.9	0.3	4.0
98-99–L.A. Clippers	15	0	87	12	23	.522	0	1	.000	8	10	.800	5	20	25	0	14	1	3	6	9	32	1.7	0.0	2.1
99-00–L.A. Clippers	57	6	820	96	197	.487	0	3	.000	46	78	.590	65	114	179	25	80	0	13	34	73	238	3.1	0.4	4.2
Reg. Season Totals	130	7	1647	201	427	.471	0	4	.000	100	165	.606	133	239	372	44	167	1	28	78	163	502	2.9	0.3	3.9

Closs, William Thomas (Bill) b. January 8, 1922 Ht. 6-6 Wt. 205 College: Rice

SEASON–TEAM	G	GS	MIN	FGM	FGA	PCT	3FGM	3FGA	PCT	FTM	FTA	PCT	O-RB	D-RB	TOT	AST	PF	DQ	STL	TO	BLK	PTS	RPG	APG	PPG
46-47–Indianapolis (N)	44	–	–	119	–	–	–	–	–	34	63	.540	–	–	–	–	99	–	–	–	–	272	–	–	6.2
47-48–Indianapolis (N)	55	–	–	162	–	–	–	–	–	72	123	.585	–	–	–	–	139	–	–	–	–	396	–	–	7.2
48-49–Anderson (N)	64	–	–	203	–	–	–	–	–	110	166	.663	–	–	–	–	148	–	–	–	–	516	–	–	8.1
49-50–Anderson	64	–	–	283	898	.315	–	–	–	186	259	.718	–	–	–	160	190	–	–	–	–	752	–	2.5	11.8
50-51–Philadelphia	65	–	–	202	631	.320	–	–	–	166	223	.744	–	–	401	110	156	4	–	–	–	570	6.2	1.7	8.8
51-52–Fort Wayne	57	–	1120	120	389	.308	–	–	–	107	157	.682	–	–	204	76	125	2	–	–	–	347	3.6	1.3	6.1
Reg. NBA Totals	186	–	1120	605	1918	.315	–	–	–	459	639	.718	–	–	605	346	471	6	–	–	–	1669	5.0	1.9	9.0
Reg. NBL Totals	163	–	–	484	–	–	–	–	–	216	352	.614	–	–	–	–	386	–	–	–	–	1184	–	–	7.3
NBA Playoff Totals	11	–	42	36	238	.294	–	–	–	31	38	.816	–	–	24	41	29	2	–	–	–	103	6.0	2.1	9.4
NBL Playoff Totals	15	–	–	50	–	–	–	–	–	45	63	.698	–	–	–	–	41	–	–	–	–	145	–	–	9.7

Cloyd, Paul V. b. June 13, 1920 Ht. 6-2 Wt. 180 College: Wisconsin

SEASON–TEAM	G	GS	MIN	FGM	FGA	PCT	3FGM	3FGA	PCT	FTM	FTA	PCT	O-RB	D-RB	TOT	AST	PF	DQ	STL	TO	BLK	PTS	RPG	APG	PPG
47-48–Sheboygan (N)	60	–	–	213	–	–	–	–	–	129	181	.713	–	–	–	–	123	–	–	–	–	555	–	–	9.3
48-49–Sheboygan (N)	56	–	–	119	–	–	–	–	–	98	137	.715	–	–	–	–	75	–	–	–	–	336	–	–	6.0
49-50–Balt.-Wat.	7	–	–	7	26	.269	–	–	–	5	8	.625	–	–	–	2	5	–	–	–	–	19	–	0.3	2.7
Reg. NBA Totals	7	–	–	7	26	.269	–	–	–	5	8	.625	–	–	–	2	5	–	–	–	–	19	–	0.3	2.7
Reg. NBL Totals	116	–	–	332	–	–	–	–	–	227	318	.714	–	–	–	–	198	–	–	–	–	891	–	–	7.7
NBL Playoff Totals	2	–	–	3	–	–	–	–	–	2	3	.667	–	–	–	–	1	–	–	–	–	8	–	–	4.0

Cluggish, Marion R. (Bob) b. September 18, 1917 Ht. 6-10 Wt. 235 College: Kentucky

SEASON–TEAM	G	GS	MIN	FGM	FGA	PCT	3FGM	3FGA	PCT	FTM	FTA	PCT	O-RB	D-RB	TOT	AST	PF	DQ	STL	TO	BLK	PTS	RPG	APG	PPG
46-47–New York	54	–	–	93	356	.261	–	–	–	52	91	.571	–	–	–	22	113	–	–	–	–	238	–	0.4	4.4
Reg. Season Totals	54	–	–	93	356	.261	–	–	–	52	91	.571	–	–	–	22	113	–	–	–	–	238	–	0.4	4.4
Playoff Totals	5	–	–	4	27	.148	–	–	–	0	2	.000	–	–	–	–	12	1	–	–	–	8	–	0.0	1.6

Clyde, Bennie J. (Ben) b. June 10, 1951 Ht. 6-7 Wt. 200 College: Ellsworth (Iowa) C.C.; Florida State

SEASON–TEAM	G	GS	MIN	FGM	FGA	PCT	3FGM	3FGA	PCT	FTM	FTA	PCT	O-RB	D-RB	TOT	AST	PF	DQ	STL	TO	BLK	PTS	RPG	APG	PPG
74-75–Boston	25	–	157	31	72	.431	–	–	–	7	9	.778	15	26	41	5	34	1	5	–	3	69	1.6	0.2	2.8
Reg. Season Totals	25	–	157	31	72	.431	–	–	–	7	9	.778	15	26	41	5	34	1	5	–	3	69	1.6	0.2	2.8

Coffey, Richard Lee b. September 2, 1965 Ht. 6-6 Wt. 215 College: Minnesota

SEASON–TEAM	G	GS	MIN	FGM	FGA	PCT	3FGM	3FGA	PCT	FTM	FTA	PCT	O-RB	D-RB	TOT	AST	PF	DQ	STL	TO	BLK	PTS	RPG	APG	PPG
90-91–Minnesota	52	1	320	28	75	.373	0	1	.000	12	22	.545	42	37	79	3	45	0	6	5	4	68	1.5	0.1	1.3
Reg. Season Totals	52	1	320	28	75	.373	0	1	.000	12	22	.545	42	37	79	3	45	0	6	5	4	68	1.5	0.1	1.3

Cofield, Frederick (Fred) b. January 4, 1962 Ht. 6-3 Wt. 190 College: Oregon; Eastern Michigan

SEASON–TEAM	G	GS	MIN	FGM	FGA	PCT	3FGM	3FGA	PCT	FTM	FTA	PCT	O-RB	D-RB	TOT	AST	PF	DQ	STL	TO	BLK	PTS	RPG	APG	PPG
85-86–New York	45	1	469	75	184	.408	3	15	.200	12	20	.600	6	40	46	82	65	1	20	49	3	165	1.0	1.8	3.7
86-87–Chicago	5	0	27	2	11	.182	0	1	.000	0	0	–	1	4	5	4	1	0	2	1	0	4	1.0	0.8	0.8
Reg. Season Totals	50	1	496	77	195	.395	3	16	.188	12	20	.600	7	44	51	86	66	1	22	50	3	169	1.0	1.7	3.4

Coker, John Michael b. October 28, 1971 Ht. 7-0 Wt. 253 College: Boise State

SEASON–TEAM	G	GS	MIN	FGM	FGA	PCT	3FGM	3FGA	PCT	FTM	FTA	PCT	O-RB	D-RB	TOT	AST	PF	DQ	STL	TO	BLK	PTS	RPG	APG	PPG
95-96–Phoenix	5	0	11	4	5	.800	0	0	–	0	0	–	2	0	2	1	1	0	0	0	1	8	0.4	0.2	1.6
98-99–Houston-Wash.	14	0	98	13	31	.419	0	0	–	5	6	.833	7	15	22	0	17	0	1	2	2	31	1.6	0.0	2.2
Reg. Season Totals	19	0	109	17	36	.472	0	0	–	5	6	.833	9	15	24	1	18	0	1	2	3	39	1.3	0.1	2.1

Cole, Gary (see Abdul Qadir Jeelani)

Coleman, Benjamin (Ben, Big Ben) b. November 14, 1961 Ht. 6-9 Wt. 235 College: Minnesota; Maryland

SEASON–TEAM	G	GS	MIN	FGM	FGA	PCT	3FGM	3FGA	PCT	FTM	FTA	PCT	O-RB	D-RB	TOT	AST	PF	DQ	STL	TO	BLK	PTS	RPG	APG	PPG
86-87–New Jersey	68	7	1029	182	313	.581	0	1	.000	88	121	.727	99	189	288	37	200	7	32	94	31	452	4.2	0.5	6.6
87-88–N.J.-Phil.	70	24	1498	226	453	.499	0	3	.000	141	185	.762	116	234	350	62	230	5	43	127	41	593	5.0	0.9	8.5
88-89–Philadelphia	58	11	703	117	241	.485	0	0	–	61	77	.792	49	128	177	17	120	0	10	48	18	295	3.1	0.3	5.1
89-90–Milwaukee	22	0	305	46	97	.474	0	1	.000	34	41	.829	31	56	87	12	54	0	7	26	7	126	4.0	0.5	5.7
93-94–Detroit	9	0	77	12	25	.480	0	0	–	4	8	.500	10	16	26	0	9	0	2	7	2	28	2.9	0.0	3.1
Reg. Season Totals	227	42	3612	583	1129	.516	0	5	.000	328	432	.759	305	623	928	128	613	12	94	302	99	1494	4.1	0.6	6.6
Playoff Totals	3	0	23	6	8	.750	0	0	–	2	2	1.000	2	3	5	–	8	0	1	1	0	14	1.7	0.0	4.7

Coleman, Derrick D. (D.C.) b. June 21, 1967 Ht. 6-10 Wt. 270 College: Syracuse

SEASON–TEAM	G	GS	MIN	FGM	FGA	PCT	3FGM	3FGA	PCT	FTM	FTA	PCT	O-RB	D-RB	TOT	AST	PF	DQ	STL	TO	BLK	PTS	RPG	APG	PPG
90-91–New Jersey	74	68	2602	514	1100	.467	13	38	.342	323	442	.731	269	490	759	163	217	3	71	217	99	1364	10.3	2.2	18.4
91-92–New Jersey	65	58	2207	483	958	.504	23	76	.303	300	393	.763	203	415	618	205	168	2	54	248	98	1289	9.5	3.2	19.8
92-93–New Jersey	76	73	2759	564	1226	.460	23	99	.232	421	521	.808	247	605	852	276	210	1	92	243	126	1572	11.2	3.6	20.7
93-94–New Jersey	77	77	2778	541	1209	.447	38	121	.314	439	567	.774	262	608	870	262	209	2	68	208	142	1559	11.3	3.4	20.2
94-95–New Jersey	56	54	2103	371	875	.424	28	120	.233	376	490	.767	167	424	591	187	162	2	35	172	94	1146	10.6	3.3	20.5
95-96–Philadelphia	11	11	294	48	118	.407	7	21	.333	20	32	.625	13	59	72	31	30	0	4	28	10	123	6.5	2.8	11.2
96-97–Philadelphia	57	54	2102	364	836	.435	32	119	.269	272	365	.745	157	416	573	193	164	1	50	184	75	1032	10.1	3.4	18.1
97-98–Philadelphia	59	58	2135	356	867	.411	26	98	.265	302	391	.772	149	438	587	145	144	1	46	157	68	1040	9.9	2.5	17.6
98-99–Charlotte	37	29	1178	168	406	.414	7	33	.212	143	190	.753	76	252	328	78	96	1	24	90	42	486	8.9	2.1	13.1
99-00–Charlotte	74	64	2347	446	979	.456	51	141	.362	296	377	.785	124	508	632	175	195	2	34	173	130	1239	8.5	2.4	16.7
Reg. Season Totals	586	546	20505	3855	8574	.450	248	866	.286	2892	3768	.768	1667	4215	5882	1715	1595	15	478	1720	884	10850	10.0	2.9	18.5
Playoff Totals	17	17	729	140	293	.478	16	43	.372	106	135	.785	55	164	219	68	53	1	18	55	34	402	12.9	4.0	23.6
All-Star Totals	1	1	18	1	6	.167	0	2	.000	0	0	–	1	2	3	1	3	0	1	0	1	2	3.0	1.0	2.0

Coleman, E.C. Jr. b. September 25, 1950 Ht. 6-8 Wt. 225 College: Houston Baptist

SEASON–TEAM	G	GS	MIN	FGM	FGA	PCT	3FGM	3FGA	PCT	FTM	FTA	PCT	O-RB	D-RB	TOT	AST	PF	DQ	STL	TO	BLK	PTS	RPG	APG	PPG
73-74–Houston	58	–	1075	128	250	.512	–	–	–	47	74	.635	81	171	252	76	162	4	37	–	20	303	4.3	1.3	5.2
74-75–New Orleans	77	–	2176	253	568	.445	–	–	–	116	166	.699	189	360	549	105	277	10	82	–	37	622	7.1	1.4	8.1
75-76–New Orleans	67	–	1850	216	479	.451	–	–	–	59	89	.663	124	295	419	87	227	3	56	–	30	491	6.3	1.3	7.3
76-77–New Orleans	77	–	2369	290	628	.462	–	–	–	82	112	.732	149	399	548	103	280	9	62	–	32	662	7.1	1.3	8.6
77-78–Golden State	72	–	1801	212	446	.475	–	–	–	40	55	.727	117	259	376	100	253	4	66	95	23	464	5.2	1.4	6.4
78-79–Houston	6	–	39	5	7	.714	–	–	–	1	1	1.000	1	6	7	1	11	0	2	0	0	11	1.2	0.2	1.8
Reg. Season Totals	357	–	9310	1104	2378	.464	–	–	–	345	497	.694	661	1490	2151	472	1210	30	305	95	142	2553	6.0	1.3	7.2

Coleman, Jack L. b. May 23, 1924 d. December 8, 1997 Ht. 6-7 Wt. 230 College: Louisville

SEASON–TEAM	G	GS	MIN	FGM	FGA	PCT	3FGM	3FGA	PCT	FTM	FTA	PCT	O-RB	D-RB	TOT	AST	PF	DQ	STL	TO	BLK	PTS	RPG	APG	PPG
49-50–Rochester	68	–	–	250	663	.377	–	–	–	90	121	.744	–	–	–	153	223	–	–	–	–	590	–	2.3	8.7
50-51–Rochester	67	–	–	315	749	.421	–	–	–	134	172	.779	–	–	584	197	193	4	–	–	–	764	8.7	2.9	11.4
51-52–Rochester	66	–	2606	308	742	.415	–	–	–	120	169	.710	–	–	692	208	218	7	–	–	–	736	10.5	3.2	11.2
52-53–Rochester	70	–	2625	314	748	.420	–	–	–	135	208	.649	–	–	774	231	245	12	–	–	–	763	11.1	3.3	10.9
53-54–Rochester	71	–	2377	289	714	.405	–	–	–	108	181	.597	–	–	589	158	201	3	–	–	–	686	8.3	2.2	9.7
54-55–Rochester	72	–	2482	400	866	.462	–	–	–	124	183	.678	–	–	729	232	201	1	–	–	–	924	10.1	3.2	12.8
55-56–Roch.-St. Louis	75	–	2738	390	946	.412	–	–	–	177	249	.711	–	–	688	294	242	2	–	–	–	957	9.2	3.9	12.8
56-57–St. Louis	72	–	2145	316	775	.408	–	–	–	123	161	.764	–	–	645	159	235	7	–	–	–	755	9.0	2.2	10.5
57-58–St. Louis	72	–	1506	231	560	.413	–	–	–	84	131	.641	–	–	485	117	169	3	–	–	–	546	6.7	1.6	7.6
Reg. Season Totals	633	–	16479	2813	6763	.416	–	–	–	1095	1575	.695	–	–	5186	1749	1927	39	–	–	–	6721	9.2	2.8	10.6
Playoff Totals	63	–	2058	249	723	.393	–	–	–	133	209	.636	–	–	768	267	224	4	–	–	–	631	10.5	3.5	10.0
All-Star Totals	1	–	19	2	8	.250	–	–	–	2	3	.667	–	–	6	1	0	0	–	–	–	6	6.0	1.0	6.0

Coleman, Norris J. b. September 27, 1961 Ht. 6-8 Wt. 210 College: Kansas State

SEASON–TEAM	G	GS	MIN	FGM	FGA	PCT	3FGM	3FGA	PCT	FTM	FTA	PCT	O-RB	D-RB	TOT	AST	PF	DQ	STL	TO	BLK	PTS	RPG	APG	PPG
87-88–L.A. Clippers	29	11	431	66	191	.346	1	2	.500	20	36	.556	36	45	81	13	51	1	11	16	6	153	2.8	0.4	5.3
Reg. Season Totals	29	11	431	66	191	.346	1	2	.500	20	36	.556	36	45	81	13	51	1	11	16	6	153	2.8	0.4	5.3

Coles, Vernell Eufaye (Bimbo) b. April 22, 1968 Ht. 6-2 Wt. 182 College: Virginia Tech

SEASON–TEAM	G	GS	MIN	FGM	FGA	PCT	3FGM	3FGA	PCT	FTM	FTA	PCT	O-RB	D-RB	TOT	AST	PF	DQ	STL	TO	BLK	PTS	RPG	APG	PPG
90-91–Miami	82	9	1355	162	393	.412	6	34	.176	71	95	.747	56	97	153	232	149	0	65	98	12	401	1.9	2.8	4.9
91-92–Miami	81	28	1976	295	649	.455	10	52	.192	216	262	.824	69	120	189	366	151	3	73	167	13	816	2.3	4.5	10.1
92-93–Miami	81	37	2232	318	686	.464	42	137	.307	177	220	.805	58	108	166	373	199	4	80	108	11	855	2.0	4.6	10.6
93-94–Miami	76	4	1726	233	519	.449	20	99	.202	102	131	.779	50	109	159	263	132	0	75	107	12	588	2.1	3.5	7.7
94-95–Miami	68	65	2207	261	607	.430	16	76	.211	141	174	.810	46	145	191	416	185	1	99	156	13	679	2.8	6.1	10.0
95-96–Miami-G.S.	81	55	2615	318	777	.409	88	254	.346	168	211	.796	49	211	260	422	253	5	94	171	17	892	3.2	5.2	11.0
96-97–Golden State	51	13	1183	122	314	.389	30	102	.294	37	49	.755	39	79	118	149	96	0	35	59	7	311	2.3	2.9	6.1
97-98–Golden State	53	44	1471	166	438	.379	13	57	.228	78	88	.886	17	106	123	248	135	2	51	89	13	423	2.3	4.7	8.0
98-99–Golden State	48	32	1272	183	414	.442	6	25	.240	83	101	.822	21	96	117	222	113	2	45	82	11	455	2.4	4.6	9.5
99-00–Atlanta	80	54	1924	276	607	.455	8	39	.205	85	104	.817	30	142	172	290	178	1	58	103	11	645	2.2	3.6	8.1
Reg. Season Totals	701	341	17961	2334	5404	.432	239	875	.273	1158	1435	.807	435	1213	1648	2981	1591	18	675	1140	120	6065	2.4	4.3	8.7
Playoff Totals	8	0	185	32	57	.561	2	5	.400	26	33	.788	4	17	21	23	20	0	10	16	1	92	2.6	2.9	11.5

Collins, Arthur (Art) b. April 14, 1954 Ht. 6-4 Wt. 185 College: Biscayne

SEASON–TEAM	G	GS	MIN	FGM	FGA	PCT	3FGM	3FGA	PCT	FTM	FTA	PCT	O-RB	D-RB	TOT	AST	PF	DQ	STL	TO	BLK	PTS	RPG	APG	PPG
80-81–Atlanta	29	–	395	35	99	.354	0	2	.000	24	36	.667	19	22	41	25	35	0	11	32	1	94	1.4	0.9	3.2
Reg. Season Totals	29	–	395	35	99	.354	0	2	.000	24	36	.667	19	22	41	25	35	0	11	32	1	94	1.4	0.9	3.2

Collins, Donald (Don) b. November 28, 1958 Ht. 6-6 Wt. 190 College: Washington State

SEASON–TEAM	G	GS	MIN	FGM	FGA	PCT	3FGM	3FGA	PCT	FTM	FTA	PCT	O-RB	D-RB	TOT	AST	PF	DQ	STL	TO	BLK	PTS	RPG	APG	PPG
80-81–Atlanta-Wash.	81	–	1845	360	811	.444	0	6	.000	211	272	.776	129	139	268	190	259	6	104	174	25	931	3.3	2.3	11.5
81-82–Washington	79	18	1609	334	653	.511	1	12	.083	121	169	.716	101	95	196	148	195	3	89	135	24	790	2.5	1.9	10.0
82-83–Washington	65	21	1575	332	635	.523	0	6	.000	101	136	.743	116	94	210	132	166	1	87	146	30	765	3.2	2.0	11.8
83-84–Golden State	61	6	957	187	387	.483	1	5	.200	65	89	.730	62	67	129	67	119	1	43	80	14	440	2.1	1.1	7.2
84-85–Washington	11	0	91	12	34	.353	0	0	–	8	9	.889	10	9	19	7	5	0	7	8	4	32	1.7	0.6	2.9
86-87–Milwaukee	6	0	57	10	28	.357	0	0	–	5	7	.714	11	4	15	2	11	0	2	5	1	25	2.5	0.3	4.2
Reg. Season Totals	303	45	6134	1235	2548	.485	2	29	.069	511	682	.749	429	408	837	546	755	11	332	548	98	2983	2.8	1.8	9.8
Playoff Totals	8	6	151	19	44	.432	0	0	–	5	7	.714	9	13	22	6	25	1	4	11	1	43	2.8	0.8	5.4

Collins, James E. (Jimmy) b. November 24, 1946 Ht. 6-2 Wt. 175 College: New Mexico State

SEASON–TEAM	G	GS	MIN	FGM	FGA	PCT	3FGM	3FGA	PCT	FTM	FTA	PCT	O-RB	D-RB	TOT	AST	PF	DQ	STL	TO	BLK	PTS	RPG	APG	PPG
70-71–Chicago	55	–	478	92	214	.430	–	–	–	35	45	.778	–	–	54	60	43	0	–	–	–	219	1.0	1.1	4.0
71-72–Chicago	19	–	134	26	71	.366	–	–	–	10	11	.909	–	–	12	10	11	0	–	–	–	62	0.6	0.5	3.3
Reg. Season Totals	74	–	612	118	285	.414	–	–	–	45	56	.804	–	–	66	70	54	0	–	–	–	281	0.9	0.9	3.8
Playoff Totals	2	–	8	0	1	.000	–	–	–	3	3	1.000	–	–	1	–	1	0	–	–	–	3	0.5	0.0	1.5

Collins, James Edgar
b. November 5, 1973 Ht. 6-4 Wt. 196 College: Florida State

SEASON–TEAM	G	GS	MIN	FGM	FGA	PCT	3FGM	3FGA	PCT	FTM	FTA	PCT	O-RB	D-RB	TOT	AST	PF	DQ	STL	TO	BLK	PTS	RPG	APG	PPG
97-98–L.A. Clippers	23	0	103	21	55	.382	9	20	.450	8	14	.571	7	7	14	3	12	0	6	8	3	59	0.6	0.1	2.6
Reg. Season Totals	23	0	103	21	55	.382	9	20	.450	8	14	.571	7	7	14	3	12	0	6	8	3	59	0.6	0.1	2.6

Collins, Paul Douglas (Doug)
b. July 28, 1951 Ht. 6-6 Wt. 180 College: Illinois State

SEASON–TEAM	G	GS	MIN	FGM	FGA	PCT	3FGM	3FGA	PCT	FTM	FTA	PCT	O-RB	D-RB	TOT	AST	PF	DQ	STL	TO	BLK	PTS	RPG	APG	PPG
73-74–Philadelphia	25	–	436	72	194	.371	–	–	–	55	72	.764	7	39	46	40	65	1	13	–	2	199	1.8	1.6	8.0
74-75–Philadelphia	81	–	2820	561	1150	.488	–	–	–	331	392	.844	104	211	315	213	291	6	108	–	17	1453	3.9	2.6	17.9
75-76–Philadelphia	77	–	2995	614	1196	.513	–	–	–	372	445	.836	126	181	307	191	249	2	110	–	24	1600	4.0	2.5	20.8
76-77–Philadelphia	58	–	2037	426	823	.518	–	–	–	210	250	.840	64	131	195	271	174	2	70	–	15	1062	3.4	4.7	18.3
77-78–Philadelphia	79	–	2770	643	1223	.526	–	–	–	267	329	.812	87	143	230	320	228	2	128	250	25	1553	2.9	4.1	19.7
78-79–Philadelphia	47	–	1595	358	717	.499	–	–	–	201	247	.814	36	87	123	191	139	1	52	131	20	917	2.6	4.1	19.5
79-80–Philadelphia	36	–	963	191	410	.466	0	1	.000	113	124	.911	29	65	94	100	76	0	30	82	7	495	2.6	2.8	13.8
80-81–Philadelphia	12	–	329	62	126	.492	0	0	–	24	29	.828	6	23	29	42	23	0	7	22	4	148	2.4	3.5	12.3
Reg. Season Totals	415	–	13945	2927	5839	.501	0	1	.000	1573	1888	.833	459	880	1339	1368	1245	14	518	485	114	7427	3.2	3.3	17.9
Playoff Totals	32	–	1218	282	536	.526	0	0	–	123	159	.774	51	80	131	111	95	0	34	23	4	687	4.1	3.5	21.5
All-Star Totals	3	–	68	11	24	.458	0	0	–	12	15	.800	7	6	13	17	8	0	6	4	0	34	4.3	5.7	11.3

Colone, Joseph F. (Joe, Bells)
b. January 23, 1926 Ht. 6-5 Wt. 210 College: Bloomsburg

SEASON–TEAM	G	GS	MIN	FGM	FGA	PCT	3FGM	3FGA	PCT	FTM	FTA	PCT	O-RB	D-RB	TOT	AST	PF	DQ	STL	TO	BLK	PTS	RPG	APG	PPG
48-49–New York	15	–	–	35	113	.310	–	–	–	13	19	.684	–	–	–	9	25	–	–	–	–	83	–	0.6	5.5
Reg. Season Totals	15	–	–	35	113	.310	–	–	–	13	19	.684	–	–	–	9	25	–	–	–	–	83	–	0.6	5.5
Playoff Totals	4	–	–	7	43	.256	–	–	–	3	8	.500	–	–	–	4	17	–	–	–	–	17	–	0.7	4.3

Colter, Steve
b. July 24, 1962 Ht. 6-3 Wt. 175 College: New Mexico State

SEASON–TEAM	G	GS	MIN	FGM	FGA	PCT	3FGM	3FGA	PCT	FTM	FTA	PCT	O-RB	D-RB	TOT	AST	PF	DQ	STL	TO	BLK	PTS	RPG	APG	PPG
84-85–Portland	78	22	1462	216	477	.453	26	74	.351	98	130	.754	40	110	150	243	142	0	75	112	9	556	1.9	3.1	7.1
85-86–Portland	81	51	1868	272	597	.456	27	83	.325	135	164	.823	41	136	177	257	188	0	113	115	10	706	2.2	3.2	8.7
86-87–Chicago-Phil.	70	31	1322	169	397	.426	4	17	.235	82	107	.766	23	85	108	210	99	0	56	70	12	424	1.5	3.0	6.1
87-88–Phil.-Wash.	68	53	1513	203	441	.460	3	10	.300	75	95	.789	58	115	173	261	132	0	62	88	14	484	2.5	3.8	7.1
88-89–Washington	80	5	1425	203	457	.444	3	25	.120	125	167	.749	62	120	182	225	158	0	69	64	14	534	2.3	2.8	6.7
89-90–Washington	73	1	977	142	297	.478	0	5	.000	77	95	.811	55	121	176	148	98	0	47	38	10	361	2.4	2.0	4.9
90-91–Sacramento	19	0	251	23	56	.411	5	14	.357	7	10	.700	5	21	26	37	27	0	11	11	1	58	1.4	1.9	3.1
94-95–Cleveland	57	7	752	67	169	.396	8	35	.229	54	71	.761	13	46	59	101	53	0	30	36	6	196	1.0	1.8	3.4
Reg. Season Totals	526	170	9570	1295	2891	.448	76	263	.289	653	839	.778	297	754	1051	1482	897	0	463	534	76	3319	2.0	2.8	6.3
Playoff Totals	24	9	407	68	144	.472	3	13	.231	13	21	.619	13	34	47	77	49	1	14	21	4	152	2.0	3.2	6.3

Combs, Edwin Leroy (Leroy)
b. January 1, 1961 Ht. 6-8 Wt. 210 College: Oklahoma State

SEASON–TEAM	G	GS	MIN	FGM	FGA	PCT	3FGM	3FGA	PCT	FTM	FTA	PCT	O-RB	D-RB	TOT	AST	PF	DQ	STL	TO	BLK	PTS	RPG	APG	PPG
83-84–Indiana	48	0	446	81	163	.497	0	3	.000	56	91	.615	19	37	56	38	49	0	23	46	18	218	1.2	0.8	4.5
Reg. Season Totals	48	0	446	81	163	.497	0	3	.000	56	91	.615	19	37	56	38	49	0	23	46	18	218	1.2	0.8	4.5

Combs, Glen Courtney (The Kentucky Rifle)
b. October 30, 1946 Ht. 6-2 Wt. 185 College: Virginia Tech

SEASON–TEAM	G	GS	MIN	FGM	FGA	PCT	3FGM	3FGA	PCT	FTM	FTA	PCT	O-RB	D-RB	TOT	AST	PF	DQ	STL	TO	BLK	PTS	RPG	APG	PPG
68-69–Dallas (A)	72	–	2241	364	868	.419	84	233	.361	300	394	.761	–	–	195	165	218	3	–	158	–	1112	2.7	2.3	15.4
69-70–Dallas (A)	84	–	3260	640	1474	.434	130	370	.351	458	548	.836	–	–	289	342	265	2	–	–	–	1868	3.4	4.1	22.2
70-71–Texas-Utah (A)	86	–	3204	610	1372	.445	77	210	.367	448	546	.821	–	–	292	361	286	–	–	–	–	1745	3.4	4.2	20.3
71-72–Utah (A)	84	–	2906	483	1109	.436	103	254	.406	319	380	.839	–	–	215	306	255	–	–	191	–	1388	2.6	3.6	16.5
72-73–Utah (A)	50	–	1488	228	535	.426	51	134	.381	154	189	.815	21	63	84	138	142	1	–	90	–	661	1.7	2.8	13.2
73-74–Utah-Mem. (A)	76	–	1986	304	696	.437	52	147	.354	156	212	.736	46	98	144	304	154	–	52	146	11	816	1.9	4.0	10.7
74-75–Virginia (A)	13	–	190	23	67	.343	6	21	.286	24	27	.889	5	6	11	23	13	–	4	16	2	76	0.8	1.8	5.8
Reg. ABA Totals	465	–	15275	2652	6121	.433	503	1369	.367	1859	2296	.810	72	167	1230	1639	1333	6	56	601	13	7666	2.6	3.5	16.5
ABA Playoff Totals	51	–	1545	286	678	.422	34	121	.281	163	207	.787	0	0	141	144	154	0	0	30	0	769	2.8	2.8	15.1

Comeaux, John Roosevelt
b. September 15, 1943 Ht. 6-5 Wt. 195 College: Grambling State

SEASON–TEAM	G	GS	MIN	FGM	FGA	PCT	3FGM	3FGA	PCT	FTM	FTA	PCT	O-RB	D-RB	TOT	AST	PF	DQ	STL	TO	BLK	PTS	RPG	APG	PPG
67-68–New Orleans (A)	23	–	189	27	63	.429	0	0	–	23	32	.719	–	–	28	11	27	0	–	15	–	77	1.2	0.5	3.3
Reg. ABA Totals	23	–	189	27	63	.429	0	0	–	23	32	.719	–	–	28	11	27	0	–	15	–	77	1.2	0.5	3.3

Comegys, Dallas Alonzo
b. August 17, 1964 Ht. 6-9 Wt. 205 College: DePaul

SEASON–TEAM	G	GS	MIN	FGM	FGA	PCT	3FGM	3FGA	PCT	FTM	FTA	PCT	O-RB	D-RB	TOT	AST	PF	DQ	STL	TO	BLK	PTS	RPG	APG	PPG
87-88–New Jersey	75	17	1122	156	363	.430	0	1	.000	106	150	.707	54	164	218	65	175	3	36	116	70	418	2.9	0.9	5.6
88-89–San Antonio	67	10	1119	166	341	.487	0	2	.000	106	161	.658	112	122	234	30	160	2	42	85	63	438	3.5	0.4	6.5
Reg. Season Totals	142	27	2241	322	704	.457	0	3	.000	212	311	.682	166	286	452	95	335	5	78	201	133	856	3.2	0.7	6.0

C

Comley, Lawrence Robert (Larry) b. August 17, 1939 Ht. 6-5 Wt. 210 College: Kansas State

SEASON–TEAM	G	GS	MIN	FGM	FGA	PCT	3FGM	3FGA	PCT	FTM	FTA	PCT	O-RB	D-RB	TOT	AST	PF	DQ	STL	TO	BLK	PTS	RPG	APG	PPG
63-64–Baltimore	12	–	89	8	37	.216	–	–	–	9	16	.563	–	–	19	12	11	0	–	–	–	25	1.6	1.0	2.1
Reg. Season Totals	12	–	89	8	37	.216	–	–	–	9	16	.563	–	–	19	12	11	0	–	–	–	25	1.6	1.0	2.1

Congdon, Jeffrey D. (Jeff) b. October 17, 1943 Ht. 6-2 Wt. 180 College: Brigham Young

SEASON–TEAM	G	GS	MIN	FGM	FGA	PCT	3FGM	3FGA	PCT	FTM	FTA	PCT	O-RB	D-RB	TOT	AST	PF	DQ	STL	TO	BLK	PTS	RPG	APG	PPG
67-68–Anaheim-Denver (A)	64	–	1020	150	404	.371	13	54	.241	49	64	.766	–	–	106	133	84	1	–	119	–	362	1.7	2.1	5.7
68-69–Denver (A)	59	–	979	107	277	.386	5	31	.161	69	85	.812	–	–	93	135	104	1	–	97	–	288	1.6	2.3	4.9
69-70–Denver (A)	83	–	2461	299	775	.386	63	178	.354	151	192	.786	–	–	233	446	205	3	–	–	–	812	2.8	5.4	9.8
70-71–Utah-N.Y. (A)	80	–	1562	178	487	.366	18	88	.205	79	96	.823	–	–	143	252	126	–	–	–	–	453	1.8	3.2	5.7
71-72–Dallas (A)	20	–	261	30	86	.349	3	7	.429	17	20	.850	–	–	26	36	19	–	–	13	–	80	1.3	1.8	4.0
Reg. ABA Totals	306	–	6283	764	2029	.377	102	358	.285	365	457	.799	–	–	601	1002	538	5	–	229	–	1995	2.0	3.3	6.5
ABA Playoff Totals	26	–	607	78	202	.386	18	61	.295	54	66	.818	–	–	59	118	69	0	–	3	–	228	2.3	4.5	8.8

Conley, Donald Eugene (Gene) b. November 10, 1930 Ht. 6-8 Wt. 245 College: Washington State

SEASON–TEAM	G	GS	MIN	FGM	FGA	PCT	3FGM	3FGA	PCT	FTM	FTA	PCT	O-RB	D-RB	TOT	AST	PF	DQ	STL	TO	BLK	PTS	RPG	APG	PPG
52-53–Boston	39	–	461	35	108	.324	–	–	–	18	31	.581	–	–	171	19	74	1	–	–	–	88	4.4	0.5	2.3
58-59–Boston	50	–	663	86	262	.328	–	–	–	37	64	.578	–	–	276	19	117	2	–	–	–	209	5.5	0.4	4.2
59-60–Boston	71	–	1330	201	539	.373	–	–	–	76	114	.667	–	–	590	32	270	10	–	–	–	478	8.3	0.5	6.7
60-61–Boston	75	–	1242	183	495	.370	–	–	–	106	153	.693	–	–	550	40	275	15	–	–	–	472	7.3	0.5	6.3
62-63–New York	70	–	1544	254	651	.390	–	–	–	122	186	.656	–	–	469	70	263	10	–	–	–	630	6.7	1.0	9.0
63-64–New York	46	–	551	74	189	.392	–	–	–	44	65	.677	–	–	156	21	124	2	–	–	–	192	3.4	0.5	4.2
Reg. Season Totals	351	–	5791	833	2244	.371	–	–	–	403	613	.657	–	–	2212	201	1123	40	–	–	–	2069	6.3	0.6	5.9
Playoff Totals	33	–	482	70	187	.374	–	–	–	29	47	.617	–	–	222	11	119	4	–	–	–	169	6.7	0.3	5.1

Conley, George Larry (Larry) b. January 22, 1944 Ht. 6-3 Wt. 175 College: Kentucky

SEASON–TEAM	G	GS	MIN	FGM	FGA	PCT	3FGM	3FGA	PCT	FTM	FTA	PCT	O-RB	D-RB	TOT	AST	PF	DQ	STL	TO	BLK	PTS	RPG	APG	PPG
67-68–Kentucky (A)	1	–	18	1	4	.250	0	0	–	0	0	–	–	–	0	0	0	0	–	3	–	2	0.0	0.0	2.0
Reg. ABA Totals	1	–	18	1	4	.250	0	0	–	0	0	–	–	–	–	0	0	0	–	3	–	2	0.0	0.0	2.0

Conlin, Edward James (Ed) b. September 2, 1933 Ht. 6-6 Wt. 200 College: Fordham

SEASON–TEAM	G	GS	MIN	FGM	FGA	PCT	3FGM	3FGA	PCT	FTM	FTA	PCT	O-RB	D-RB	TOT	AST	PF	DQ	STL	TO	BLK	PTS	RPG	APG	PPG
55-56–Syracuse	66	–	1423	211	574	.368	–	–	–	121	178	.680	–	–	326	145	121	1	–	–	–	543	4.9	2.2	8.2
56-57–Syracuse	71	–	2250	335	896	.374	–	–	–	283	368	.769	–	–	430	205	170	0	–	–	–	953	6.1	2.9	13.4
57-58–Syracuse	60	–	1871	343	877	.391	–	–	–	215	270	.796	–	–	436	133	168	2	–	–	–	901	7.3	2.2	15.0
58-59–Syr.-Detroit	72	–	1955	329	891	.369	–	–	–	197	274	.719	–	–	394	132	188	6	–	–	–	855	5.5	1.8	11.9
59-60–Detroit	70	–	1636	300	831	.361	–	–	–	181	238	.761	–	–	346	126	158	2	–	–	–	781	4.9	1.8	11.2
60-61–Philadelphia	77	–	1294	216	599	.361	–	–	–	104	139	.748	–	–	262	123	153	1	–	–	–	536	3.4	1.6	7.0
61-62–Philadelphia	70	–	963	128	371	.345	–	–	–	66	89	.742	–	–	155	85	118	1	–	–	–	322	2.2	1.2	4.6
Reg. Season Totals	486	–	11392	1862	5039	.370	–	–	–	1167	1556	.750	–	–	2349	949	1076	13	–	–	–	4891	4.8	2.0	10.1
Playoff Totals	35	–	665	94	289	.325	–	–	–	65	96	.677	–	–	120	39	60	0	–	–	–	253	3.4	1.1	7.2

Conlon, Martin McBride (Marty) b. January 19, 1968 Ht. 6-11 Wt. 235 College: Providence

SEASON–TEAM	G	GS	MIN	FGM	FGA	PCT	3FGM	3FGA	PCT	FTM	FTA	PCT	O-RB	D-RB	TOT	AST	PF	DQ	STL	TO	BLK	PTS	RPG	APG	PPG
91-92–Seattle	45	1	381	48	101	.475	0	0	–	24	32	.750	33	36	69	12	40	0	9	27	7	120	1.5	0.3	2.7
92-93–Sacramento	46	0	467	81	171	.474	0	4	.000	57	81	.704	48	75	123	37	43	0	13	28	5	219	2.7	0.8	4.8
93-94–Cha.-Wash.	30	9	579	95	165	.576	0	2	.000	43	53	.811	53	86	139	34	69	1	9	33	8	233	4.6	1.1	7.8
94-95–Milwaukee	82	3	2064	344	647	.532	8	29	.276	119	194	.613	160	266	426	110	218	3	42	123	18	815	5.2	1.3	9.9
95-96–Milwaukee	74	1	958	153	327	.468	5	30	.167	84	110	.764	58	119	177	68	126	1	20	79	11	395	2.4	0.9	5.3
96-97–Boston	74	15	1614	214	454	.471	2	10	.200	144	171	.842	128	195	323	104	154	2	46	109	18	574	4.4	1.4	7.8
97-98–Miami	18	0	209	28	62	.452	0	0	–	32	44	.727	16	30	46	12	27	0	9	11	5	88	2.6	0.7	4.9
98-99–Miami	7	0	35	3	13	.231	0	0	–	2	2	1.000	1	4	5	1	6	0	0	3	1	8	0.7	0.1	1.1
99-00–Boston-LAClips	3	0	9	1	2	.500	0	0	–	0	0	–	1	1	2	0	1	0	0	0	0	2	0.7	0.0	0.7
Reg. Season Totals	379	29	6316	967	1942	.498	15	75	.200	505	687	.735	498	812	1310	378	684	7	148	413	73	2454	3.5	1.0	6.5
Playoff Totals	4	0	47	3	8	.375	0	0	–	3	4	.750	1	4	5	3	7	0	1	6	1	9	1.3	0.8	2.3

Conner, Jimmy Dan b. March 20, 1953 Ht. 6-4 Wt. 190 College: Kentucky

SEASON–TEAM	G	GS	MIN	FGM	FGA	PCT	3FGM	3FGA	PCT	FTM	FTA	PCT	O-RB	D-RB	TOT	AST	PF	DQ	STL	TO	BLK	PTS	RPG	APG	PPG
75-76–Kentucky (A)	24	–	240	42	86	.488	0	3	.000	22	29	.759	12	16	28	38	35	–	11	32	5	106	1.2	1.6	4.4
Reg. ABA Totals	24	–	240	42	86	.488	0	3	.000	22	29	.759	12	16	28	38	35	–	11	32	5	106	1.2	1.6	4.4

Conner, Lester Allen b. September 17, 1959 Ht. 6-4 Wt. 180 College: Oregon State

SEASON–TEAM	G	GS	MIN	FGM	FGA	PCT	3FGM	3FGA	PCT	FTM	FTA	PCT	O-RB	D-RB	TOT	AST	PF	DQ	STL	TO	BLK	PTS	RPG	APG	PPG
82-83–Golden State	75	10	1416	145	303	.479	0	4	.000	79	113	.699	69	152	221	253	141	1	116	99	7	369	2.9	3.4	4.9
83-84–Golden State	82	82	2573	360	730	.493	1	6	.167	186	259	.718	132	173	305	401	176	1	162	143	12	907	3.7	4.9	11.1
84-85–Golden State	79	49	2258	246	546	.451	4	20	.200	144	192	.750	87	159	246	369	136	1	161	138	13	640	3.1	4.7	8.1
85-86–Golden State	36	0	413	51	136	.375	2	7	.286	40	54	.741	25	37	62	43	23	0	24	15	1	144	1.7	1.2	4.0
87-88–Houston	52	3	399	50	108	.463	0	7	.000	32	41	.780	20	18	38	59	31	0	38	33	1	132	0.7	1.1	2.5
88-89–New Jersey	82	63	2532	309	676	.457	13	37	.351	212	269	.788	100	255	355	604	132	1	181	181	5	843	4.3	7.4	10.3
89-90–New Jersey	82	61	2355	237	573	.414	2	13	.154	172	214	.804	90	175	265	385	182	0	172	138	8	648	3.2	4.7	7.9
90-91–N.J.-Milw.	74	4	1008	96	207	.464	0	5	.000	68	94	.723	21	91	112	165	75	0	85	58	2	260	1.5	2.2	3.5
91-92–Milwaukee	81	9	1420	103	239	.431	0	7	.000	81	115	.704	63	121	184	294	86	0	97	79	10	287	2.3	3.6	3.5
92-93–L.A. Clippers	31	0	422	28	62	.452	0	0	–	18	19	.947	16	33	49	65	39	0	34	21	4	74	1.6	2.1	2.4
93-94–Indiana	11	0	169	14	38	.368	0	3	.000	3	6	.500	10	14	24	31	12	0	14	9	1	31	2.2	2.8	2.8
94-95–L.A. Lakers	2	0	5	0	0	–	0	0	–	2	2	1.000	0	0	0	0	3	0	1	0	0	2	0.0	0.0	1.0
Reg. Season Totals	687	281	14970	1639	3618	.453	22	109	.202	1037	1378	.753	633	1228	1861	2669	1036	4	1085	914	64	4337	2.7	3.9	6.3
Playoff Totals	13	0	94	12	18	.667	1	1	1.000	6	7	.857	5	8	13	13	8	0	5	1	1	31	1.0	1.0	2.4

Connors, Kevin Joseph Aloysius (Chuck, The Rifleman) b. April 10, 1921 d. November 10, 1992 Ht. 6-6 Wt. 205 College: Seton Hall

SEASON–TEAM	G	GS	MIN	FGM	FGA	PCT	3FGM	3FGA	PCT	FTM	FTA	PCT	O-RB	D-RB	TOT	AST	PF	DQ	STL	TO	BLK	PTS	RPG	APG	PPG
45-46–Rochester (N)	14	–	–	11	–	–	–	–	–	6	–	–	–	–	–	–	–	–	–	–	–	28	–	–	2.0
46-47–Boston	49	–	–	94	380	.247	–	–	–	39	84	.464	–	–	–	40	129	–	–	–	–	227	–	0.8	4.6
47-48–Boston	4	–	–	5	13	.385	–	–	–	2	3	.667	–	–	–	1	5	–	–	–	–	12	–	0.3	3.0
Reg. NBA Totals	53	–	–	99	393	.252	–	–	–	41	87	.471	–	–	–	41	134	–	–	–	–	239	–	0.8	4.5
Reg. NBL Totals	14	–	–	11	–	–	–	–	–	6	0	–	–	–	–	–	–	–	–	–	–	28	–	–	2.0

Cook, Anthony Lacquise b. March 19, 1967 Ht. 6-9 Wt. 240 College: Arizona

SEASON–TEAM	G	GS	MIN	FGM	FGA	PCT	3FGM	3FGA	PCT	FTM	FTA	PCT	O-RB	D-RB	TOT	AST	PF	DQ	STL	TO	BLK	PTS	RPG	APG	PPG
90-91–Denver	58	25	1121	118	283	.417	0	3	.000	71	129	.550	134	192	326	26	100	1	35	50	72	307	5.6	0.4	5.3
91-92–Denver	22	0	115	15	25	.600	0	0	–	4	6	.667	13	21	34	2	10	0	5	3	4	34	1.5	0.1	1.5
93-94–Orlando-Milw.	25	0	203	26	54	.481	0	1	.000	10	25	.400	20	36	56	4	22	0	3	12	14	62	2.2	0.2	2.5
95-96–Portland	11	0	60	7	16	.438	0	2	.000	1	4	.250	5	7	12	2	8	0	0	1	1	15	1.1	0.2	1.4
Reg. Season Totals	116	25	1499	166	378	.439	0	6	.000	86	164	.524	172	256	428	34	140	1	43	66	91	418	3.7	0.3	3.6

Cook, Bert E. b. April 26, 1929 Ht. 6-3 Wt. 185 College: Utah State

SEASON–TEAM	G	GS	MIN	FGM	FGA	PCT	3FGM	3FGA	PCT	FTM	FTA	PCT	O-RB	D-RB	TOT	AST	PF	DQ	STL	TO	BLK	PTS	RPG	APG	PPG
54-55–New York	37	–	424	42	133	.316	–	–	–	34	50	.680	–	–	72	33	39	0	–	–	–	118	1.9	0.9	3.2
Reg. Season Totals	37	–	424	42	133	.316	–	–	–	34	50	.680	–	–	72	33	39	0	–	–	–	118	1.9	0.9	3.2
Playoff Totals	1	–	20	4	6	.667	–	–	–	0	2	.000	–	–	0	2	3	0	–	–	–	8	0.0	2.0	8.0

Cook, Darwin Louis b. August 6, 1958 Ht. 6-3 Wt. 185 College: Portland

SEASON–TEAM	G	GS	MIN	FGM	FGA	PCT	3FGM	3FGA	PCT	FTM	FTA	PCT	O-RB	D-RB	TOT	AST	PF	DQ	STL	TO	BLK	PTS	RPG	APG	PPG
80-81–New Jersey	81	–	1980	383	819	.468	6	25	.240	132	180	.733	96	140	236	297	197	4	141	176	36	904	2.9	3.7	11.2
81-82–New Jersey	82	17	2090	387	803	.482	7	31	.226	118	162	.728	52	103	155	319	196	2	146	175	24	899	1.9	3.9	11.0
82-83–New Jersey	82	47	2625	443	986	.449	8	38	.211	186	242	.769	73	167	240	448	213	2	194	238	48	1080	2.9	5.5	13.2
83-84–New Jersey	82	31	1870	304	687	.443	11	46	.239	95	126	.754	51	105	156	356	184	3	164	142	36	714	1.9	4.3	8.7
84-85–New Jersey	58	9	1063	212	453	.468	2	23	.087	47	54	.870	21	71	92	160	96	0	74	75	10	473	1.6	2.8	8.2
85-86–New Jersey	79	33	1965	267	627	.426	11	53	.208	84	111	.757	51	126	177	390	172	0	156	132	22	629	2.2	4.9	8.0
86-87–Washington	82	2	1420	265	622	.426	2	23	.087	82	103	.796	46	99	145	151	136	0	98	96	17	614	1.8	1.8	7.5
88-89–S.A.-Denver	66	4	1143	218	478	.456	8	41	.195	63	78	.808	34	73	107	127	121	0	71	88	10	507	1.6	1.9	7.7
Reg. Season Totals	612	143	14156	2479	5475	.453	55	280	.196	807	1056	.764	424	884	1308	2248	1315	11	1044	1122	203	5820	2.1	3.7	9.5
Playoff Totals	25	7	525	86	223	.386	6	25	.240	30	46	.652	20	34	54	82	70	1	30	46	4	208	2.2	3.3	8.3

Cook, Jeffrey James (Jeff) b. October 21, 1956 Ht. 6-10 Wt. 215 College: Idaho State

SEASON–TEAM	G	GS	MIN	FGM	FGA	PCT	3FGM	3FGA	PCT	FTM	FTA	PCT	O-RB	D-RB	TOT	AST	PF	DQ	STL	TO	BLK	PTS	RPG	APG	PPG
79-80–Phoenix	66	–	904	129	275	.469	0	3	.000	104	129	.806	90	151	241	84	102	0	28	71	18	362	3.7	1.3	5.5
80-81–Phoenix	79	–	2192	286	616	.464	0	5	.000	100	155	.645	170	297	467	201	236	3	82	146	54	672	5.9	2.5	8.5
81-82–Phoenix	76	22	1298	151	358	.422	0	2	.000	89	134	.664	112	189	301	100	174	1	37	80	23	391	4.0	1.3	5.1
82-83–Phoenix-Clev.	75	22	1333	148	304	.487	0	3	.000	79	104	.760	119	216	335	102	181	3	39	105	31	375	4.5	1.4	5.0
83-84–Cleveland	81	21	1950	188	387	.486	1	2	.500	94	130	.723	174	310	484	123	282	7	68	91	47	471	6.0	1.5	5.8
84-85–Clev.-S.A.	72	5	1288	138	279	.495	0	1	.000	47	64	.734	122	192	314	62	203	2	30	48	23	323	4.4	0.9	4.5
85-86–S.A.-Utah	36	0	373	31	73	.425	0	1	.000	27	42	.643	33	53	86	21	65	0	13	14	11	89	2.4	0.6	2.5
87-88–Phoenix	33	0	359	14	59	.237	0	1	.000	23	28	.821	37	69	106	14	64	1	9	14	8	51	3.2	0.4	1.5
Reg. Season Totals	518	70	9697	1085	2351	.462	1	18	.056	563	786	.716	857	1477	2334	707	1307	17	306	569	215	2734	4.5	1.4	5.3
Playoff Totals	30	0	468	55	108	.509	1	2	.500	56	74	.757	35	76	111	31	71	1	12	23	10	167	3.7	1.0	5.6

Cook, Norman (Norm) b. March 21, 1955 Ht. 6-8 Wt. 210 College: Kansas

SEASON–TEAM	G	GS	MIN	FGM	FGA	PCT	3FGM	3FGA	PCT	FTM	FTA	PCT	O-RB	D-RB	TOT	AST	PF	DQ	STL	TO	BLK	PTS	RPG	APG	PPG
76-77–Boston	25	–	138	27	72	.375	–	–	–	9	17	.529	10	17	27	5	27	0	10	–	3	63	1.1	0.2	2.5
77-78–Denver	2	–	10	1	3	.333	–	–	–	0	0	–	1	2	3	1	4	0	0	0	0	2	1.5	0.5	1.0
Reg. Season Totals	27	–	148	28	75	.373	–	–	–	9	17	.529	11	19	30	6	31	0	10	0	3	65	1.1	0.2	2.4
Playoff Totals	1	–	3	2	2	1.000	–	–	–	0	0	–	0	0	0	–	0	0	0	–	0	4	0.0	0.0	4.0

Cook, Robert Bernard (Bobby, Cookie) b. April 1, 1923 Ht. 5-10 Wt. 155 College: Wisconsin

SEASON–TEAM	G	GS	MIN	FGM	FGA	PCT	3FGM	3FGA	PCT	FTM	FTA	PCT	O-RB	D-RB	TOT	AST	PF	DQ	STL	TO	BLK	PTS	RPG	APG	PPG
48-49–Sheboygan (N)	64	–	–	172	–	–	–	–	–	98	136	.721	–	–	–	–	111	–	–	–	–	442	–	–	6.9
49-50–Sheboygan	51	–	–	222	620	.358	–	–	–	143	181	.790	–	–	–	158	114	–	–	–	–	587	–	3.1	11.5
Reg. NBA Totals	51	–	–	222	620	.358	–	–	–	143	181	.790	–	–	–	158	114	–	–	–	–	587	–	3.1	11.5
Reg. NBL Totals	64	–	–	172	–	–	–	–	–	98	136	.721	–	–	–	–	111	–	–	–	–	442	–	–	6.9
NBA Playoff Totals	3	–	–	3	20	.300	–	–	–	3	6	.500	–	–	–	12	2	–	–	–	–	9	–	2.0	3.0
NBL Playoff Totals	2	–	–	5	–	–	–	–	–	9	10	.900	–	–	–	–	6	–	–	–	–	19	–	–	9.5

Cooke, David D. b. September 27, 1963 Ht. 6-8 Wt. 230 College: St. Mary's (Calif.)

SEASON–TEAM	G	GS	MIN	FGM	FGA	PCT	3FGM	3FGA	PCT	FTM	FTA	PCT	O-RB	D-RB	TOT	AST	PF	DQ	STL	TO	BLK	PTS	RPG	APG	PPG
85-86–Sacramento	6	0	38	2	11	.182	0	0	–	5	10	.500	5	5	10	1	5	0	4	2	0	9	1.7	0.2	1.5
Reg. Season Totals	6	0	38	2	11	.182	0	0	–	5	10	.500	5	5	10	1	5	0	4	2	0	9	1.7	0.2	1.5

Cooke, Joseph (Joe) b. August 14, 1948 Ht. 6-3 Wt. 175 College: Indiana

SEASON–TEAM	G	GS	MIN	FGM	FGA	PCT	3FGM	3FGA	PCT	FTM	FTA	PCT	O-RB	D-RB	TOT	AST	PF	DQ	STL	TO	BLK	PTS	RPG	APG	PPG
70-71–Cleveland	73	–	725	134	341	.393	–	–	–	48	59	.814	–	–	114	93	135	2	–	–	–	316	1.6	1.3	4.3
Reg. Season Totals	73	–	725	134	341	.393	–	–	–	48	59	.814	–	–	114	93	135	2	–	–	–	316	1.6	1.3	4.3

Cooper, Artis Wayne (Wayne, Coop) b. November 16, 1956 Ht. 6-10 Wt. 220 College: New Orleans

SEASON–TEAM	G	GS	MIN	FGM	FGA	PCT	3FGM	3FGA	PCT	FTM	FTA	PCT	O-RB	D-RB	TOT	AST	PF	DQ	STL	TO	BLK	PTS	RPG	APG	PPG
78-79–Golden State	65	–	795	128	293	.437	–	–	–	41	61	.672	90	190	280	21	118	0	7	52	44	297	4.3	0.3	4.6
79-80–Golden State	79	–	1781	367	750	.489	1	4	.250	136	181	.751	202	305	507	42	246	5	20	140	79	871	6.4	0.5	11.0
80-81–Utah	71	–	1420	213	471	.452	1	3	.333	62	90	.689	166	274	440	52	219	8	18	77	51	489	6.2	0.7	6.9
81-82–Dallas	76	38	1818	281	669	.420	1	8	.125	119	160	.744	200	350	550	115	285	10	37	88	106	682	7.2	1.5	9.0
82-83–Portland	80	60	2099	320	723	.443	0	5	.000	135	197	.685	214	397	611	116	318	5	27	162	136	775	7.6	1.5	9.7
83-84–Portland	81	38	1662	304	663	.459	0	7	.000	185	230	.804	176	300	476	76	247	2	26	110	106	793	5.9	0.9	9.8
84-85–Denver	80	78	2031	404	856	.472	0	2	.000	161	235	.685	229	402	631	86	304	2	28	149	197	969	7.9	1.1	12.1
85-86–Denver	78	78	2112	422	906	.466	3	7	.429	174	219	.795	190	420	610	81	315	6	42	117	227	1021	7.8	1.0	13.1
86-87–Denver	69	64	1561	235	524	.448	0	3	.000	79	109	.725	162	311	473	68	257	5	13	78	101	549	6.9	1.0	8.0
87-88–Denver	45	32	865	118	270	.437	0	1	.000	50	67	.746	98	172	270	30	145	3	12	59	94	286	6.0	0.7	6.4
88-89–Denver	79	72	1864	220	444	.495	1	4	.250	79	106	.745	212	407	619	78	302	7	36	73	211	520	7.8	1.0	6.6
89-90–Portland	79	0	1176	138	304	.454	0	3	.000	25	39	.641	118	221	339	44	211	2	18	39	95	301	4.3	0.6	3.8
90-91–Portland	67	1	746	57	145	.393	0	1	.000	33	42	.786	54	134	188	22	120	0	7	22	61	147	2.8	0.3	2.2
91-92–Portland	35	0	344	35	82	.427	0	0	–	7	11	.636	38	63	101	21	57	0	4	15	27	77	2.9	0.6	2.2
Reg. Season Totals	984	461	20274	3242	7100	.457	7	48	.146	1286	1747	.736	2149	3946	6095	852	3144	55	295	1181	1535	7777	6.2	0.9	7.9
Playoff Totals	74	28	1276	178	400	.445	0	1	.000	78	110	.709	133	223	356	56	214	5	22	64	96	434	4.8	0.8	5.9

Cooper, Charles H. (Chuck) b. September 29, 1926 d. February 5, 1984 Ht. 6-5 Wt. 215 College: West Virginia State; Duquesne

SEASON–TEAM	G	GS	MIN	FGM	FGA	PCT	3FGM	3FGA	PCT	FTM	FTA	PCT	O-RB	D-RB	TOT	AST	PF	DQ	STL	TO	BLK	PTS	RPG	APG	PPG
50-51–Boston	66	–	–	207	601	.344	–	–	–	201	267	.753	–	–	562	174	219	7	–	–	–	615	8.5	2.6	9.3
51-52–Boston	66	–	1976	197	545	.361	–	–	–	149	201	.741	–	–	502	134	219	8	–	–	–	543	7.6	2.0	8.2
52-53–Boston	70	–	1994	157	466	.337	–	–	–	144	190	.758	–	–	439	112	258	11	–	–	–	458	6.3	1.6	6.5
53-54–Boston	70	–	1101	78	261	.299	–	–	–	78	116	.672	–	–	304	74	150	1	–	–	–	234	4.3	1.1	3.3
54-55–Milwaukee	70	–	1749	193	569	.339	–	–	–	187	249	.751	–	–	385	151	210	8	–	–	–	573	5.5	2.2	8.2
55-56–St. L.-FtWayne	67	–	1144	101	308	.328	–	–	–	100	133	.752	–	–	239	89	140	0	–	–	–	302	3.6	1.3	4.5
Reg. Season Totals	409	–	7964	933	2750	.339	–	–	–	859	1156	.743	–	–	2431	734	1196	35	–	–	–	2725	5.9	1.8	6.7
Playoff Totals	26	–	489	44	126	.349	–	–	–	51	65	.785	–	–	138	27	78	5	–	–	–	139	4.5	1.0	5.3

Cooper, Joseph Edward (Joe) b. September 1, 1957 Ht. 6-10 Wt. 230 College: Howard (Texas) Coll.; Tulsa; Colorado

SEASON–TEAM	G	GS	MIN	FGM	FGA	PCT	3FGM	3FGA	PCT	FTM	FTA	PCT	O-RB	D-RB	TOT	AST	PF	DQ	STL	TO	BLK	PTS	RPG	APG	PPG
81-82–New Jersey	1	0	11	1	2	.500	0	0	–	0	0	–	1	1	2	0	2	0	0	1	0	2	2.0	0.0	2.0
82-83–L.A.-Wash.-S.D.	20	4	333	37	72	.514	0	0	–	16	29	.552	42	44	86	17	49	0	9	32	20	90	4.3	0.9	4.5
84-85–Seattle	3	1	45	7	15	.467	0	0	–	3	6	.500	3	6	9	2	7	1	2	0	1	17	3.0	0.7	5.7
Reg. Season Totals	24	5	389	45	89	.506	0	0	–	19	35	.543	46	51	97	19	58	1	11	33	21	109	4.0	0.8	4.5

Cooper, Michael Jerome b. April 15, 1956 Ht. 6-7 Wt. 170 College: Pasadena (Calif.) City Coll.; New Mexico

SEASON–TEAM	G	GS	MIN	FGM	FGA	PCT	3FGM	3FGA	PCT	FTM	FTA	PCT	O-RB	D-RB	TOT	AST	PF	DQ	STL	TO	BLK	PTS	RPG	APG	PPG
78-79–Los Angeles	3	–	7	3	6	.500	–	–	–	0	0	–	0	0	0	0	1	0	1	1	0	6	0.0	0.0	2.0
79-80–Los Angeles	82	–	1973	303	578	.524	5	20	.250	111	143	.776	101	128	229	221	215	3	86	142	38	722	2.8	2.7	8.8
80-81–Los Angeles	81	–	2625	321	654	.491	4	19	.211	117	149	.785	121	215	336	332	249	4	133	164	78	763	4.1	4.1	9.4
81-82–Los Angeles	76	14	2197	383	741	.517	2	17	.118	139	171	.813	84	185	269	230	216	1	120	151	61	907	3.5	3.0	11.9
82-83–Los Angeles	82	3	2148	266	497	.535	5	21	.238	102	130	.785	82	192	274	315	208	0	115	128	50	639	3.3	3.8	7.8
83-84–Los Angeles	82	9	2387	273	549	.497	38	121	.314	155	185	.838	53	209	262	482	267	3	113	148	67	739	3.2	5.9	9.0
84-85–L.A. Lakers	82	20	2189	276	593	.465	35	123	.285	115	133	.865	56	199	255	429	208	0	93	156	49	702	3.1	5.2	8.6
85-86–L.A. Lakers	82	15	2269	274	606	.452	63	163	.387	147	170	.865	44	200	244	466	238	2	89	151	43	758	3.0	5.7	9.2
86-87–L.A. Lakers	82	2	2253	322	736	.438	89	231	.385	126	148	.851	58	196	254	373	199	1	78	102	43	859	3.1	4.5	10.5
87-88–L.A. Lakers	61	8	1793	189	482	.392	57	178	.320	97	113	.858	50	178	228	289	136	1	66	101	26	532	3.7	4.7	8.7
88-89–L.A. Lakers	80	13	1943	213	494	.431	80	210	.381	81	93	.871	33	158	191	314	186	0	72	94	32	587	2.4	3.9	7.3
89-90–L.A. Lakers	80	10	1851	191	493	.387	50	157	.318	83	94	.883	59	168	227	215	206	1	67	91	36	515	2.8	2.7	6.4
Reg. Season Totals	873	94	23635	3014	6429	.469	428	1260	.340	1273	1529	.833	741	2028	2769	3666	2329	16	1033	1429	523	7729	3.2	4.2	8.9
Playoff Totals	168	26	4744	582	1244	.468	124	316	.392	293	355	.825	152	422	574	703	474	2	203	252	96	1581	3.4	4.2	9.4

Cooper, Samuel Duane (Duane) b. June 25, 1969 Ht. 6-1 Wt. 185 College: USC

SEASON–TEAM	G	GS	MIN	FGM	FGA	PCT	3FGM	3FGA	PCT	FTM	FTA	PCT	O-RB	D-RB	TOT	AST	PF	DQ	STL	TO	BLK	PTS	RPG	APG	PPG
92-93–L.A. Lakers	65	0	645	62	158	.392	7	30	.233	25	35	.714	13	37	50	150	66	0	18	69	2	156	0.8	2.3	2.4
93-94–Phoenix	23	2	136	18	41	.439	1	7	.143	11	15	.733	2	7	9	28	12	0	3	20	0	48	0.4	1.2	2.1
Reg. Season Totals	88	2	781	80	199	.402	8	37	.216	36	50	.720	15	44	59	178	78	0	21	89	2	204	0.7	2.0	2.3
Playoff Totals	2	0	4	0	6	.000	0	3	.000	0	0	–	2	0	2	1	0	0	0	0	0	0	1.0	0.5	0.0

Copa, Thomas James (Tom) b. October 30, 1964 Ht. 6-10 Wt. 275 College: Marquette

SEASON–TEAM	G	GS	MIN	FGM	FGA	PCT	3FGM	3FGA	PCT	FTM	FTA	PCT	O-RB	D-RB	TOT	AST	PF	DQ	STL	TO	BLK	PTS	RPG	APG	PPG
91-92–San Antonio	33	1	132	22	40	.550	0	0	–	4	13	.308	14	22	36	3	29	0	2	8	6	48	1.1	0.1	1.5
Reg. Season Totals	33	1	132	22	40	.550	0	0	–	4	13	.308	14	22	36	3	29	0	2	8	6	48	1.1	0.1	1.5

Copeland, Hollis Alphonso Jr. b. December 20, 1955 Ht. 6-6 Wt. 180 College: Rutgers

SEASON–TEAM	G	GS	MIN	FGM	FGA	PCT	3FGM	3FGA	PCT	FTM	FTA	PCT	O-RB	D-RB	TOT	AST	PF	DQ	STL	TO	BLK	PTS	RPG	APG	PPG
79-80–New York	75	–	1142	182	368	.495	0	2	.000	63	86	.733	70	86	156	80	154	0	61	84	25	427	2.1	1.1	5.7
81-82–New York	18	0	118	16	38	.421	0	0	–	5	6	.833	3	2	5	9	19	0	4	4	2	37	0.3	0.5	2.1
Reg. Season Totals	93	0	1260	198	406	.488	0	2	.000	68	92	.739	73	88	161	89	173	0	65	88	27	464	1.7	1.0	5.0

Copeland, Lanard b. July 16, 1965 Ht. 6-6 Wt. 210 College: Georgia State

SEASON–TEAM	G	GS	MIN	FGM	FGA	PCT	3FGM	3FGA	PCT	FTM	FTA	PCT	O-RB	D-RB	TOT	AST	PF	DQ	STL	TO	BLK	PTS	RPG	APG	PPG
89-90–Philadelphia	23	0	110	31	68	.456	1	5	.200	11	14	.786	4	6	10	9	12	0	1	19	1	74	0.4	0.4	3.2
91-92–L.A. Clippers	10	0	48	7	23	.304	0	2	.000	2	2	1.000	1	6	7	5	5	0	2	4	0	16	0.7	0.5	1.6
Reg. Season Totals	33	0	158	38	91	.418	1	7	.143	13	16	.813	5	12	17	14	17	0	3	23	1	90	0.5	0.4	2.7
Playoff Totals	4	0	9	2	6	.333	0	0	–	0	0	–	0	1	1	–	1	0	0	1	0	4	0.3	0.0	1.0

Corbin, Tyrone Kennedy b. December 31, 1962 Ht. 6-6 Wt. 225 College: DePaul

SEASON–TEAM	G	GS	MIN	FGM	FGA	PCT	3FGM	3FGA	PCT	FTM	FTA	PCT	O-RB	D-RB	TOT	AST	PF	DQ	STL	TO	BLK	PTS	RPG	APG	PPG
85-86–San Antonio	16	0	174	27	64	.422	0	1	.000	10	14	.714	11	14	25	11	21	0	11	12	2	64	1.6	0.7	4.0
86-87–S.A.-Clev.	63	15	1170	156	381	.409	1	4	.250	91	124	.734	88	127	215	97	129	0	55	66	5	404	3.4	1.5	6.4
87-88–Clev.-Phoenix	84	5	1739	257	525	.490	1	6	.167	110	138	.797	127	223	350	115	181	2	72	104	18	625	4.2	1.4	7.4
88-89–Phoenix	77	30	1655	245	454	.540	0	2	.000	141	179	.788	176	222	398	118	222	2	82	92	13	631	5.2	1.5	8.2
89-90–Minnesota	82	80	3011	521	1083	.481	0	11	.000	161	209	.770	219	385	604	216	288	5	175	143	41	1203	7.4	2.6	14.7
90-91–Minnesota	82	82	3196	587	1311	.448	2	10	.200	296	371	.798	185	404	589	347	257	3	162	209	53	1472	7.2	4.2	18.0
91-92–Minn.-Utah	80	9	2207	303	630	.481	0	4	.000	174	201	.866	163	309	472	140	193	1	82	97	20	780	5.9	1.8	9.8
92-93–Utah	82	58	2555	385	766	.503	0	5	.000	180	218	.826	194	325	519	173	252	3	108	108	32	950	6.3	2.1	11.6
93-94–Utah	82	17	2149	268	588	.456	6	29	.207	117	144	.813	150	239	389	122	212	0	99	92	24	659	4.7	1.5	8.0
94-95–Atlanta	81	4	1389	205	464	.442	14	56	.250	78	114	.684	98	164	262	67	161	1	55	74	16	502	3.2	0.8	6.2
95-96–Sac.-Miami	71	2	1284	155	351	.442	3	18	.167	100	120	.833	81	163	244	84	147	1	63	67	20	413	3.4	1.2	5.8
96-97–Atlanta	70	65	2305	253	600	.422	74	208	.356	86	108	.796	76	218	294	124	176	1	90	85	7	666	4.2	1.8	9.5
97-98–Atlanta	79	79	2699	328	747	.439	49	141	.348	101	128	.789	78	284	362	173	197	1	105	86	7	806	4.6	2.2	10.2
98-99–Atlanta	47	6	1066	131	335	.391	38	119	.319	52	80	.650	37	108	145	43	74	0	31	43	7	352	3.1	0.9	7.5
99-00–Sacramento	54	5	941	88	247	.356	10	44	.227	33	39	.846	40	125	165	60	99	2	36	29	5	219	3.1	1.1	4.1
Reg. Season Totals	1050	457	27540	3909	8546	.457	198	658	.301	1730	2187	.791	1723	3310	5033	1890	2609	22	1226	1307	270	9746	4.8	1.8	9.3
Playoff Totals	81	43	2226	273	608	.449	26	88	.295	109	138	.790	156	248	404	114	202	0	80	77	15	681	5.0	1.4	8.4

Corchiani, Christopher (Chris, Fire) b. March 28, 1968 Ht. 6-1 Wt. 185 College: North Carolina State

SEASON–TEAM	G	GS	MIN	FGM	FGA	PCT	3FGM	3FGA	PCT	FTM	FTA	PCT	O-RB	D-RB	TOT	AST	PF	DQ	STL	TO	BLK	PTS	RPG	APG	PPG
91-92–Orlando	51	1	741	77	193	.399	10	37	.270	91	104	.875	18	60	78	141	94	0	45	74	2	255	1.5	2.8	5.0
92-93–Orlando-Wash.	10	0	105	14	24	.583	0	3	.000	16	21	.762	1	6	7	16	18	0	6	8	0	44	0.7	1.6	4.4
93-94–Boston	51	0	467	40	94	.426	11	38	.289	26	38	.684	8	36	44	86	47	0	22	38	2	117	0.9	1.7	2.3
Reg. Season Totals	112	1	1313	131	311	.421	21	78	.269	133	163	.816	27	102	129	243	159	0	73	120	4	416	1.2	2.2	3.7

Corley, Kenneth (Ken) b. 1921 Ht. 6-8 Wt. 210 College: Oklahoma State

SEASON–TEAM	G	GS	MIN	FGM	FGA	PCT	3FGM	3FGA	PCT	FTM	FTA	PCT	O-RB	D-RB	TOT	AST	PF	DQ	STL	TO	BLK	PTS	RPG	APG	PPG
46-47–Cleveland	3	–	–	0	0	–	–	–	–	0	0	–	–	–	–	0	0	–	–	–	–	0	–	0.0	0.0
Reg. Season Totals	3	–	–	0	0	–	–	–	–	0	0	–	–	–	–	0	0	–	–	–	–	0	–	0.0	0.0

Corley, Raymond Charles (Ray) b. January 1, 1928 Ht. 6-0 Wt. 180 College: Notre Dame; Georgetown

SEASON–TEAM	G	GS	MIN	FGM	FGA	PCT	3FGM	3FGA	PCT	FTM	FTA	PCT	O-RB	D-RB	TOT	AST	PF	DQ	STL	TO	BLK	PTS	RPG	APG	PPG
49-50–Syracuse	60	–	–	117	370	.316	–	–	–	75	122	.615	–	–	–	109	81	–	–	–	–	309	–	1.8	5.2
50-51–Balt.-Tri-Cit	18	–	–	29	85	.341	–	–	–	16	29	.552	–	–	43	38	26	0	–	–	–	74	2.4	2.1	4.1
52-53–Fort Wayne	8	–	65	3	24	.125	–	–	–	5	6	.833	–	–	5	5	18	0	–	–	–	11	0.6	0.6	1.4
Reg. Season Totals	86	–	65	149	479	.311	–	–	–	96	157	.611	–	–	48	152	125	0	–	–	–	394	1.8	1.8	4.6
Playoff Totals	6	–	0	6	42	.143	–	–	–	5	11	.455	–	–	–	12	5	0	–	–	–	17	–	1.5	2.8

Corzine, David John (Dave) b. April 25, 1956 Ht. 6-11 Wt. 255 College: DePaul

SEASON–TEAM	G	GS	MIN	FGM	FGA	PCT	3FGM	3FGA	PCT	FTM	FTA	PCT	O-RB	D-RB	TOT	AST	PF	DQ	STL	TO	BLK	PTS	RPG	APG	PPG
78-79–Washington	59	–	532	63	118	.534	–	–	–	49	63	.778	52	95	147	49	67	0	10	53	14	175	2.5	0.8	3.0
79-80–Washington	78	–	826	90	216	.417	0	0	–	45	68	.662	104	166	270	63	120	1	9	60	31	225	3.5	0.8	2.9
80-81–San Antonio	82	–	1960	366	747	.490	0	3	.000	125	175	.714	228	408	636	117	212	0	42	131	99	857	7.8	1.4	10.5
81-82–San Antonio	82	21	2189	336	648	.519	1	4	.250	159	213	.746	211	418	629	130	235	3	33	139	126	832	7.7	1.6	10.1
82-83–Chicago	82	71	2496	457	920	.497	0	2	.000	232	322	.720	243	474	717	154	242	4	47	228	109	1146	8.7	1.9	14.0
83-84–Chicago	82	82	2674	385	824	.467	3	9	.333	231	275	.840	169	406	575	202	227	3	58	175	120	1004	7.0	2.5	12.2
84-85–Chicago	82	50	2062	276	568	.486	0	1	.000	149	200	.745	130	292	422	140	189	2	32	124	64	701	5.1	1.7	8.5
85-86–Chicago	67	4	1709	255	519	.491	3	12	.250	127	171	.743	132	301	433	150	133	0	28	104	53	640	6.5	2.2	9.6
86-87–Chicago	82	39	2287	294	619	.475	0	5	.000	95	129	.736	199	341	540	209	202	1	38	114	87	683	6.6	2.5	8.3
87-88–Chicago	80	32	2328	344	715	.481	1	9	.111	115	153	.752	170	357	527	154	149	1	36	109	95	804	6.6	1.9	10.1
88-89–Chicago	81	7	1483	203	440	.461	2	8	.250	71	96	.740	92	223	315	103	134	0	29	93	45	479	3.9	1.3	5.9
89-90–Orlando	6	3	79	11	29	.379	0	0	–	0	2	.000	7	11	18	2	7	0	2	8	0	22	3.0	0.3	3.7
90-91–Seattle	28	0	147	17	38	.447	0	0	–	13	22	.591	10	23	33	4	18	0	5	2	5	47	1.2	0.1	1.7
Reg. Season Totals	891	309	20772	3097	6401	.484	10	53	.189	1411	1889	.747	1747	3515	5262	1477	1935	15	369	1340	848	7615	5.9	1.7	8.5
Playoff Totals	68	20	1332	180	396	.455	0	0	–	70	99	.707	115	215	330	71	137	0	23	79	37	430	4.9	1.0	6.3

Costello, Lawrence Ronald (Larry) b. July 2, 1931 Ht. 6-1 Wt. 190 College: Niagara

SEASON–TEAM	G	GS	MIN	FGM	FGA	PCT	3FGM	3FGA	PCT	FTM	FTA	PCT	O-RB	D-RB	TOT	AST	PF	DQ	STL	TO	BLK	PTS	RPG	APG	PPG
54-55–Philadelphia	19	–	463	46	139	.331	–	–	–	26	32	.813	–	–	49	78	37	0	–	–	–	118	2.6	4.1	6.2
56-57–Philadelphia	72	–	2111	186	497	.374	–	–	–	175	222	.788	–	–	323	236	182	2	–	–	–	547	4.5	3.3	7.6
57-58–Syracuse	72	–	2746	378	888	.426	–	–	–	320	378	.847	–	–	378	317	246	3	–	–	–	1076	5.3	4.4	14.9
58-59–Syracuse	70	–	2750	414	948	.437	–	–	–	280	349	.802	–	–	365	379	263	7	–	–	–	1108	5.2	5.4	15.8
59-60–Syracuse	71	–	2469	372	822	.453	–	–	–	249	289	.862	–	–	388	449	234	4	–	–	–	993	5.5	6.3	14.0
60-61–Syracuse	75	–	2167	407	844	.482	–	–	–	270	338	.799	–	–	292	413	286	9	–	–	–	1084	3.9	5.5	14.5
61-62–Syracuse	63	–	1854	310	726	.427	–	–	–	247	295	.837	–	–	245	359	220	5	–	–	–	867	3.9	5.7	13.8
62-63–Syracuse	78	–	2066	285	660	.432	–	–	–	288	327	.881	–	–	237	334	263	4	–	–	–	858	3.0	4.3	11.0
63-64–Philadelphia	45	–	1137	191	408	.468	–	–	–	147	170	.865	–	–	105	167	150	3	–	–	–	529	2.3	3.7	11.8
64-65–Philadelphia	64	–	1967	309	695	.445	–	–	–	243	277	.877	–	–	169	275	242	10	–	–	–	861	2.6	4.3	13.5
66-67–Philadelphia	49	–	976	130	293	.444	–	–	–	120	133	.902	–	–	103	140	141	2	–	–	–	380	2.1	2.9	7.8
67-68–Philadelphia	28	–	492	67	148	.453	–	–	–	67	81	.827	–	–	51	68	62	0	–	–	–	201	1.8	2.4	7.2
Reg. Season Totals	706	–	21198	3095	7068	.438	–	–	–	2432	2891	.841	–	–	2705	3215	2326	49	–	–	–	8622	3.8	4.6	12.2
Playoff Totals	52	–	1471	198	476	.416	–	–	–	196	230	.852	–	–	171	218	210	11	–	–	–	592	3.3	4.2	11.4
All-Star Totals	5	–	71	11	32	.344	–	–	–	2	2	1.000	–	–	9	11	8	0	–	–	–	24	1.8	2.2	4.8

Cotton, James Wesley b. December 14, 1975 Ht. 6-5 Wt. 220 College: Long Beach State

SEASON–TEAM	G	GS	MIN	FGM	FGA	PCT	3FGM	3FGA	PCT	FTM	FTA	PCT	O-RB	D-RB	TOT	AST	PF	DQ	STL	TO	BLK	PTS	RPG	APG	PPG
97-98–Seattle	9	0	33	8	21	.381	0	4	.000	8	9	.889	2	4	6	0	3	0	1	6	1	24	0.7	0.0	2.7
98-99–Seattle	10	0	59	6	18	.333	0	3	.000	13	18	.722	2	8	10	0	6	0	3	3	0	25	1.0	0.0	2.5
Reg. Season Totals	19	0	92	14	39	.359	0	7	.000	21	27	.778	4	12	16	0	9	0	4	9	1	49	0.8	0.0	2.6

Cotton, John J. (Jack) b. October 15, 1924 Ht. 6-7 Wt. 205 College: Miles (Mont.) C.C.; Wyoming

SEASON–TEAM	G	GS	MIN	FGM	FGA	PCT	3FGM	3FGA	PCT	FTM	FTA	PCT	O-RB	D-RB	TOT	AST	PF	DQ	STL	TO	BLK	PTS	RPG	APG	PPG
48-49–Denver (N)	57	–	–	71	–	–	–	–	–	67	121	.554	–	–	–	–	110	–	–	–	–	209	–	–	3.7
49-50–Denver	54	–	–	97	332	.292	–	–	–	82	161	.509	–	–	–	65	184	–	–	–	–	276	–	1.2	5.1
Reg. NBA Totals	54	–	–	97	332	.292	–	–	–	82	161	.509	–	–	–	65	184	–	–	–	–	276	–	1.2	5.1
Reg. NBL Totals	57	–	–	71	–	–	–	–	–	67	121	.554	–	–	–	–	110	–	–	–	–	209	–	–	3.7

Coughran, John Douglas b. September 12, 1951 Ht. 6-7 Wt. 225 College: California

SEASON–TEAM	G	GS	MIN	FGM	FGA	PCT	3FGM	3FGA	PCT	FTM	FTA	PCT	O-RB	D-RB	TOT	AST	PF	DQ	STL	TO	BLK	PTS	RPG	APG	PPG
79-80–Golden State	24	–	160	29	81	.358	2	9	.222	8	14	.571	2	17	19	12	24	0	7	13	1	68	0.8	0.5	2.8
Reg. Season Totals	24	–	160	29	81	.358	2	9	.222	8	14	.571	2	17	19	12	24	0	7	13	1	68	0.8	0.5	2.8

Counts, Mel Grant (Goose) b. October 16, 1941 Ht. 7-0 Wt. 230 College: Oregon State

SEASON–TEAM	G	GS	MIN	FGM	FGA	PCT	3FGM	3FGA	PCT	FTM	FTA	PCT	O-RB	D-RB	TOT	AST	PF	DQ	STL	TO	BLK	PTS	RPG	APG	PPG
64-65–Boston	54	–	572	100	272	.368	–	–	–	58	74	.784	–	–	265	19	134	1	–	–	–	258	4.9	0.4	4.8
65-66–Boston	67	–	1021	221	549	.403	–	–	–	120	145	.828	–	–	432	50	207	5	–	–	–	562	6.4	0.7	8.4
66-67–Balt.-L.A.	56	–	860	177	419	.422	–	–	–	69	94	.734	–	–	344	52	183	6	–	–	–	423	6.1	0.9	7.6
67-68–Los Angeles	82	–	1739	384	808	.475	–	–	–	190	254	.748	–	–	732	139	309	6	–	–	–	958	8.9	1.7	11.7
68-69–Los Angeles	77	–	1866	390	867	.450	–	–	–	178	221	.805	–	–	600	109	223	5	–	–	–	958	7.8	1.4	12.4
69-70–Los Angeles	81	–	2193	434	1017	.427	–	–	–	156	201	.776	–	–	683	160	304	7	–	–	–	1024	8.4	2.0	12.6
70-71–Phoenix	80	–	1669	365	799	.457	–	–	–	149	198	.753	–	–	503	136	279	8	–	–	–	879	6.3	1.7	11.0
71-72–Phoenix	76	–	906	147	344	.427	–	–	–	101	140	.721	–	–	257	96	159	2	–	–	–	395	3.4	1.3	5.2
72-73–Phil.-L.A.	66	–	658	132	294	.449	–	–	–	39	58	.672	–	–	253	65	106	1	–	–	–	303	3.8	1.0	4.6
73-74–Los Angeles	45	–	499	61	167	.365	–	–	–	24	33	.727	56	90	146	54	85	2	20	–	23	146	3.2	1.2	3.2
74-75–New Orleans	75	–	1421	217	495	.438	–	–	–	86	113	.761	102	339	441	182	196	0	49	–	43	520	5.9	2.4	6.9
75-76–New Orleans	30	–	319	37	91	.407	–	–	–	16	21	.762	27	73	100	38	74	1	16	–	8	90	3.3	1.3	3.0
Reg. Season Totals	789	–	13723	2665	6122	.435	–	–	–	1186	1552	.764	185	502	4756	1100	2259	44	85	–	74	6516	6.0	1.4	8.3
Playoff Totals	85	–	1462	255	599	.426	–	–	–	138	178	.775	2	4	519	100	263	5	2	–	2	648	6.1	1.2	7.6

Courtin, Stephen Edward (Steve) b. September 21, 1942 Ht. 6-1 Wt. 190 College: St. Joseph's (Pa.)

SEASON–TEAM	G	GS	MIN	FGM	FGA	PCT	3FGM	3FGA	PCT	FTM	FTA	PCT	O-RB	D-RB	TOT	AST	PF	DQ	STL	TO	BLK	PTS	RPG	APG	PPG
64-65–Philadelphia	24	–	317	42	103	.408	–	–	–	17	21	.810	–	–	22	22	44	0	–	–	–	101	0.9	0.9	4.2
Reg. Season Totals	24	–	317	42	103	.408	–	–	–	17	21	.810	–	–	22	22	44	0	–	–	–	101	0.9	0.9	4.2

Courtney, Joseph Pierre (Joe) b. October 17, 1969 Ht. 6-9 Wt. 235 College: Mississippi State; Southern Mississippi

SEASON–TEAM	G	GS	MIN	FGM	FGA	PCT	3FGM	3FGA	PCT	FTM	FTA	PCT	O-RB	D-RB	TOT	AST	PF	DQ	STL	TO	BLK	PTS	RPG	APG	PPG
92-93–Chicago-G.S.	12	0	104	13	32	.406	0	0	–	7	9	.778	4	15	19	3	17	0	5	6	5	33	1.6	0.3	2.8
93-94–Phoenix-Milw.	52	1	345	67	148	.453	2	3	.667	32	47	.681	28	28	56	15	44	0	10	21	12	168	1.1	0.3	3.2
95-96–Cleveland	23	0	200	15	35	.429	0	0	–	8	18	.444	24	25	49	9	35	0	5	17	6	38	2.1	0.4	1.7
96-97–Phil.-S.A.	9	0	100	11	30	.367	0	0	–	3	5	.600	9	7	16	0	14	1	0	3	0	25	1.8	0.0	2.8
Reg. Season Totals	96	1	749	106	245	.433	2	3	.667	50	79	.633	65	75	140	27	110	1	20	47	23	264	1.5	0.3	2.8

Cousy, Robert Joseph (Bob, Cooz, Houdini of the Hardwood) b. August 9, 1928 Ht. 6-1 Wt. 175 College: Holy Cross HOF: 1970

SEASON–TEAM	G	GS	MIN	FGM	FGA	PCT	3FGM	3FGA	PCT	FTM	FTA	PCT	O-RB	D-RB	TOT	AST	PF	DQ	STL	TO	BLK	PTS	RPG	APG	PPG
50-51–Boston	69	–	–	401	1138	.352	–	–	–	276	365	.756	–	–	474	341	185	2	–	–	–	1078	6.9	4.9	15.6
51-52–Boston	66	–	2681	512	1388	.369	–	–	–	409	506	.808	–	–	421	441	190	5	–	–	–	1433	6.4	6.7	21.7
52-53–Boston	71	–	2945	464	1320	.352	–	–	–	479	587	.816	–	–	449	547	227	4	–	–	–	1407	6.3	7.7	19.8
53-54–Boston	72	–	2857	486	1262	.385	–	–	–	411	522	.787	–	–	394	518	201	3	–	–	–	1383	5.5	7.2	19.2
54-55–Boston	71	–	2747	522	1316	.397	–	–	–	460	570	.807	–	–	424	557	165	1	–	–	–	1504	6.0	7.8	21.2
55-56–Boston	72	–	2767	440	1223	.360	–	–	–	476	564	.844	–	–	492	642	206	2	–	–	–	1356	6.8	8.9	18.8
56-57–Boston	64	–	2364	478	1264	.378	–	–	–	363	442	.821	–	–	309	478	134	0	–	–	–	1319	4.8	7.5	20.6
57-58–Boston	65	–	2222	445	1262	.353	–	–	–	277	326	.850	–	–	322	463	136	1	–	–	–	1167	5.0	7.1	18.0
58-59–Boston	65	–	2403	484	1260	.384	–	–	–	329	385	.855	–	–	359	557	135	0	–	–	–	1297	5.5	8.6	20.0
59-60–Boston	75	–	2588	568	1481	.384	–	–	–	319	403	.792	–	–	352	715	146	2	–	–	–	1455	4.7	9.5	19.4
60-61–Boston	76	–	2468	513	1382	.371	–	–	–	352	452	.779	–	–	331	587	196	0	–	–	–	1378	4.4	7.7	18.1
61-62–Boston	75	–	2114	462	1181	.391	–	–	–	251	333	.754	–	–	261	584	135	0	–	–	–	1175	3.5	7.8	15.7
62-63–Boston	76	–	1975	392	988	.397	–	–	–	219	298	.735	–	–	193	515	175	0	–	–	–	1003	2.5	6.8	13.2
69-70–Cincinnati	7	–	34	1	3	.333	–	–	–	3	3	1.000	–	–	5	10	11	0	–	–	–	5	0.7	1.4	0.7
Reg. Season Totals	924	–	30165	6168	16468	.375	–	–	–	4624	5756	.803	–	–	4786	6955	2242	20	–	–	–	16960	5.2	7.5	18.4
Playoff Totals	109	–	4121	689	2016	.342	–	–	–	640	796	.804	–	–	570	937	314	4	–	–	–	2018	5.0	8.6	18.5
All-Star Totals	13	–	368	52	158	.329	–	–	–	43	51	.843	–	–	78	86	27	2	–	–	–	147	6.0	6.6	11.3

Cowens, David William (Dave, Big Red) b. October 25, 1948 Ht. 6-9 Wt. 230 College: Florida State HOF: 1990

SEASON–TEAM	G	GS	MIN	FGM	FGA	PCT	3FGM	3FGA	PCT	FTM	FTA	PCT	O-RB	D-RB	TOT	AST	PF	DQ	STL	TO	BLK	PTS	RPG	APG	PPG
70-71–Boston	81	–	3076	550	1302	.422	–	–	–	273	373	.732	–	–	1216	228	350	15	–	–	–	1373	15.0	2.8	17.0
71-72–Boston	79	–	3186	657	1357	.484	–	–	–	175	243	.720	–	–	1203	245	314	10	–	–	–	1489	15.2	3.1	18.8
72-73–Boston	82	–	3425	740	1637	.452	–	–	–	204	262	.779	–	–	1329	333	311	7	–	–	–	1684	16.2	4.1	20.5
73-74–Boston	80	–	3352	645	1475	.437	–	–	–	228	274	.832	264	993	1257	354	294	7	95	–	101	1518	15.7	4.4	19.0
74-75–Boston	65	–	2632	569	1199	.475	–	–	–	191	244	.783	229	729	958	296	243	7	87	–	73	1329	14.7	4.6	20.4
75-76–Boston	78	–	3101	611	1305	.468	–	–	–	257	340	.756	335	911	1246	325	314	10	94	–	71	1479	16.0	4.2	19.0
76-77–Boston	50	–	1888	328	756	.434	–	–	–	162	198	.818	147	550	697	248	181	7	46	–	49	818	13.9	5.0	16.4
77-78–Boston	77	–	3215	598	1220	.490	–	–	–	239	284	.842	248	830	1078	351	297	5	102	217	67	1435	14.0	4.6	18.6
78-79–Boston	68	–	2517	488	1010	.483	–	–	–	151	187	.807	152	500	652	242	263	16	76	174	51	1127	9.6	3.6	16.6
79-80–Boston	66	–	2159	422	932	.453	1	12	.083	95	122	.779	126	408	534	206	216	2	69	108	61	940	8.1	3.1	14.2
82-83–Milwaukee	40	34	1014	136	306	.444	0	2	.000	52	63	.825	73	201	274	82	137	4	30	44	15	324	6.9	2.1	8.1
Reg. Season Totals	766	34	29565	5744	12499	.460	1	14	.071	2027	2590	.783	1574	5122	10444	2910	2920	90	599	543	488	13516	13.6	3.8	17.6
Playoff Totals	89	0	3768	733	1627	.451	0	2	.000	218	293	.744	243	674	1285	333	398	15	78	8	56	1684	14.4	3.7	18.9
All-Star Totals	6	4	154	33	66	.500	0	0	–	10	14	.714	20	28	81	12	21	0	4	2	1	76	13.5	2.0	12.7

Cox, John Arthur III (Chubby) b. December 29, 1955 Ht. 6-2 Wt. 180 College: Villanova; San Francisco

SEASON–TEAM	G	GS	MIN	FGM	FGA	PCT	3FGM	3FGA	PCT	FTM	FTA	PCT	O-RB	D-RB	TOT	AST	PF	DQ	STL	TO	BLK	PTS	RPG	APG	PPG
82-83–Washington	7	0	78	13	37	.351	0	2	.000	3	6	.500	7	3	10	6	16	0	0	9	1	29	1.4	0.9	4.1
Reg. Season Totals	7	0	78	13	37	.351	0	2	.000	3	6	.500	7	3	10	6	16	0	0	9	1	29	1.4	0.9	4.1

Cox, Johnny W. b. November 1, 1936 Ht. 6-4 Wt. 180 College: Kentucky

SEASON–TEAM	G	GS	MIN	FGM	FGA	PCT	3FGM	3FGA	PCT	FTM	FTA	PCT	O-RB	D-RB	TOT	AST	PF	DQ	STL	TO	BLK	PTS	RPG	APG	PPG
62-63–Chicago	73	–	1685	239	568	.421	–	–	–	95	135	.704	–	–	280	142	149	4	–	–	–	573	3.8	1.9	7.8
Reg. Season Totals	73	–	1685	239	568	.421	–	–	–	95	135	.704	–	–	280	142	149	4	–	–	–	573	3.8	1.9	7.8

Cox, Wesley b. January 27, 1955 Ht. 6-6 Wt. 215 College: Louisville

SEASON–TEAM	G	GS	MIN	FGM	FGA	PCT	3FGM	3FGA	PCT	FTM	FTA	PCT	O-RB	D-RB	TOT	AST	PF	DQ	STL	TO	BLK	PTS	RPG	APG	PPG
77-78–Golden State	43	–	453	69	173	.399	–	–	–	58	100	.580	42	101	143	12	82	1	21	36	10	196	3.3	0.3	4.6
78-79–Golden State	31	–	360	53	123	.431	–	–	–	40	92	.435	18	45	63	11	68	0	13	44	5	146	2.0	0.4	4.7
Reg. Season Totals	74	–	813	122	296	.412	–	–	–	98	192	.510	60	146	206	23	150	1	34	80	15	342	2.8	0.3	4.6

Crawford, Christopher Lee (Chris) b. May 13, 1975 Ht. 6-9 Wt. 235 College: Marquette

SEASON–TEAM	G	GS	MIN	FGM	FGA	PCT	3FGM	3FGA	PCT	FTM	FTA	PCT	O-RB	D-RB	TOT	AST	PF	DQ	STL	TO	BLK	PTS	RPG	APG	PPG
97-98–Atlanta	40	0	256	46	110	.418	1	3	.333	57	68	.838	20	21	41	9	27	0	12	18	7	150	1.0	0.2	3.8
98-99–Atlanta	42	30	784	110	255	.431	11	33	.333	57	70	.814	37	53	90	24	106	1	10	48	13	288	2.1	0.6	6.9
99-00–Atlanta	55	11	668	91	229	.397	7	27	.259	63	81	.778	51	48	99	33	83	1	17	37	16	252	1.8	0.6	4.6
Reg. Season Totals	137	41	1708	247	594	.416	19	63	.302	177	219	.808	108	122	230	66	216	2	39	103	36	690	1.7	0.5	5.0
Playoff Totals	7	5	129	16	48	.333	4	14	.286	25	28	.893	7	14	21	5	21	2	1	8	2	61	3.0	0.7	8.7

Crawford, Frederick Russell Jr. (Freddie) b. December 23, 1940 Ht. 6-4 Wt. 195 College: St. Bonaventure

SEASON–TEAM	G	GS	MIN	FGM	FGA	PCT	3FGM	3FGA	PCT	FTM	FTA	PCT	O-RB	D-RB	TOT	AST	PF	DQ	STL	TO	BLK	PTS	RPG	APG	PPG
66-67–New York	19	–	192	44	116	.379	–	–	–	24	38	.632	–	–	48	12	39	0	–	–	–	112	2.5	0.6	5.9
67-68–N.Y.-L.A.	69	–	1182	224	507	.442	–	–	–	111	179	.620	–	–	195	141	171	1	–	–	–	559	2.8	2.0	8.1
68-69–Los Angeles	81	–	1690	211	454	.465	–	–	–	83	154	.539	–	–	215	154	224	1	–	–	–	505	2.7	1.9	6.2
69-70–Milwaukee	77	–	1331	243	506	.480	–	–	–	101	148	.682	–	–	184	225	181	1	–	–	–	587	2.4	2.9	7.6
70-71–Buffalo-Phil.	51	–	652	110	281	.391	–	–	–	48	98	.490	–	–	104	78	77	0	–	–	–	268	2.0	1.5	5.3
Reg. Season Totals	297	–	5047	832	1864	.446	–	–	–	367	617	.595	–	–	746	610	692	3	–	–	–	2031	2.5	2.1	6.8
Playoff Totals	35	–	606	105	252	.417	–	–	–	48	76	.632	–	–	97	73	89	2	–	–	–	258	2.8	2.1	7.4

Creighton, Jim b. April 18, 1950 Ht. 6-8 Wt. 200 College: Colorado

SEASON–TEAM	G	GS	MIN	FGM	FGA	PCT	3FGM	3FGA	PCT	FTM	FTA	PCT	O-RB	D-RB	TOT	AST	PF	DQ	STL	TO	BLK	PTS	RPG	APG	PPG
75-76–Atlanta	32	–	172	12	43	.279	–	–	–	7	16	.438	13	32	45	4	23	0	2	–	9	31	1.4	0.1	1.0
Reg. Season Totals	32	–	172	12	43	.279	–	–	–	7	16	.438	13	32	45	4	23	0	2	–	9	31	1.4	0.1	1.0

Crevier, Ronald Joseph Oscar Camille (Ron) b. August 14, 1958 Ht. 7-0 Wt. 235 College: Boston College

SEASON–TEAM	G	GS	MIN	FGM	FGA	PCT	3FGM	3FGA	PCT	FTM	FTA	PCT	O-RB	D-RB	TOT	AST	PF	DQ	STL	TO	BLK	PTS	RPG	APG	PPG
85-86–G.S.-Detroit	3	0	4	0	3	.000	0	0	–	0	2	.000	1	0	1	0	2	0	0	0	0	0	0.3	0.0	0.0
Reg. Season Totals	3	0	4	0	3	.000	0	0	–	0	2	.000	1	0	1	0	2	0	0	0	0	0	0.3	0.0	0.0

Crisler, Harold James (Hal) b. December 31, 1923 Ht. 6-3 Wt. 215 College: San Jose State; Iowa State

SEASON–TEAM	G	GS	MIN	FGM	FGA	PCT	3FGM	3FGA	PCT	FTM	FTA	PCT	O-RB	D-RB	TOT	AST	PF	DQ	STL	TO	BLK	PTS	RPG	APG	PPG
46-47–Boston	4	–	–	2	6	.333	–	–	–	2	2	1.000	–	–	–	0	6	–	–	–	–	6	–	0.0	1.5
Reg. Season Totals	4	–	–	2	6	.333	–	–	–	2	2	1.000	–	–	–	0	6	–	–	–	–	6	–	0.0	1.5

Criss, Charles Washington Jr. (Charlie) b. November 6, 1948 Ht. 5-8 Wt. 165 College: New Mexico J.C.; New Mexico State

SEASON–TEAM	G	GS	MIN	FGM	FGA	PCT	3FGM	3FGA	PCT	FTM	FTA	PCT	O-RB	D-RB	TOT	AST	PF	DQ	STL	TO	BLK	PTS	RPG	APG	PPG
77-78–Atlanta	77	–	1935	319	751	.425	–	–	–	236	296	.797	24	97	121	294	143	0	108	150	5	874	1.6	3.8	11.4
78-79–Atlanta	54	–	879	109	289	.377	–	–	–	67	86	.779	19	41	60	138	70	0	41	79	3	285	1.1	2.6	5.3
79-80–Atlanta	81	–	1794	249	578	.431	1	17	.059	172	212	.811	27	89	116	246	133	0	74	130	4	671	1.4	3.0	8.3
80-81–Atlanta	66	–	1708	220	485	.454	1	21	.048	185	214	.864	26	74	100	283	87	0	61	134	3	626	1.5	4.3	9.5
81-82–Atlanta-S.D.	55	20	1392	222	498	.446	10	29	.345	141	159	.887	13	69	82	187	96	0	44	82	6	595	1.5	3.4	10.8
82-83–Milwaukee	66	0	922	169	375	.451	6	31	.194	68	76	.895	14	65	79	127	44	0	27	44	0	412	1.2	1.9	6.2
83-84–Milw.-Atlanta	15	0	215	20	52	.385	1	6	.167	12	16	.750	5	15	20	38	11	0	8	10	0	53	1.3	2.5	3.5
84-85–Atlanta	4	2	115	7	17	.412	0	2	.000	4	6	.667	2	12	14	22	5	0	3	11	0	18	3.5	5.5	4.5
Reg. Season Totals	418	22	8960	1315	3045	.432	19	106	.179	885	1065	.831	130	462	592	1335	589	0	366	640	21	3534	1.4	3.2	8.5
Playoff Totals	25	0	432	66	146	.452	1	4	.250	44	49	.898	3	25	28	53	34	0	22	22	1	177	1.1	2.1	7.1

Critchfield, Russell Dean (Rusty) b. June 27, 1946 Ht. 5-10 Wt. 150 College: California

SEASON–TEAM	G	GS	MIN	FGM	FGA	PCT	3FGM	3FGA	PCT	FTM	FTA	PCT	O-RB	D-RB	TOT	AST	PF	DQ	STL	TO	BLK	PTS	RPG	APG	PPG
68-69–Oakland (A)	47	–	439	53	147	.361	0	3	.000	55	84	.655	–	–	29	54	41	0	–	33	–	161	0.6	1.1	3.4
Reg. ABA Totals	47	–	439	53	147	.361	0	3	.000	55	84	.655	–	–	29	54	41	0	–	33	–	161	0.6	1.1	3.4
ABA Playoff Totals	5	–	19	1	6	.167	0	0	–	2	6	.333	–	–	2	7	6	0	–	–	–	4	0.4	1.4	0.8

Crite, Winston Arnel b. June 20, 1965 Ht. 6-7 Wt. 235 College: Texas A&M

SEASON–TEAM	G	GS	MIN	FGM	FGA	PCT	3FGM	3FGA	PCT	FTM	FTA	PCT	O-RB	D-RB	TOT	AST	PF	DQ	STL	TO	BLK	PTS	RPG	APG	PPG
87-88–Phoenix	29	0	258	34	68	.500	0	0	–	19	25	.760	27	37	64	15	42	0	5	25	8	87	2.2	0.5	3.0
88-89–Phoenix	2	0	6	0	3	.000	0	0	–	0	0	–	1	0	1	0	1	0	0	1	0	0	0.5	0.0	0.0
Reg. Season Totals	31	0	264	34	71	.479	0	0	–	19	25	.760	28	37	65	15	43	0	5	26	8	87	2.1	0.5	2.8

Crocker, James Dillard (Dillard) b. January 19, 1925 Ht. 6-4 Wt. 205 College: Western Michigan

SEASON–TEAM	G	GS	MIN	FGM	FGA	PCT	3FGM	3FGA	PCT	FTM	FTA	PCT	O-RB	D-RB	TOT	AST	PF	DQ	STL	TO	BLK	PTS	RPG	APG	PPG
48-49–Detroit-And. (N)	51	–	–	101	–	–	–	–	–	95	131	.725	–	–	–	–	134	–	–	–	–	297	–	–	5.8
48-49–Fort Wayne	2	–	–	1	4	.250	–	–	–	4	6	.667	–	–	–	0	3	–	–	–	–	6	–	0.0	3.0
49-50–Denver	53	–	–	245	840	.292	–	–	–	233	317	.735	–	–	–	85	223	–	–	–	–	723	–	1.6	13.6
51-52–Ind.-Milw.	38	–	783	98	279	.351	–	–	–	97	145	.669	–	–	111	57	132	7	–	–	–	293	2.9	1.5	7.7
52-53–Milwaukee	61	–	776	100	284	.352	–	–	–	130	189	.688	–	–	104	63	199	11	–	–	–	330	1.7	1.0	5.4
Reg. NBA Totals	154	–	1559	444	1407	.316	–	–	–	464	657	.706	–	–	215	205	557	18	–	–	–	1352	2.2	1.3	8.8
Reg. NBL Totals	51	–	–	101	–	–	–	–	–	95	131	.725	–	–	–	–	134	–	–	–	–	297	–	–	5.8
NBL Playoff Totals	6	–	–	5	–	–	–	–	–	3	8	.375	–	–	–	–	10	–	–	–	–	13	–	–	2.2

Croft, Robert Alexander (Bobby) b. August 10, 1947 Ht. 6-10 Wt. 210 College: Tennessee

SEASON–TEAM	G	GS	MIN	FGM	FGA	PCT	3FGM	3FGA	PCT	FTM	FTA	PCT	O-RB	D-RB	TOT	AST	PF	DQ	STL	TO	BLK	PTS	RPG	APG	PPG
70-71–Ken.-Texas (A)	62	–	739	126	348	.362	0	2	.000	73	112	.652	–	–	206	41	137	–	–	–	–	325	3.3	0.7	5.2
Reg. ABA Totals	62	–	739	126	348	.362	0	2	.000	73	112	.652	–	–	206	41	137	–	–	–	–	325	3.3	0.7	5.2
ABA Playoff Totals	4	–	55	7	23	.304	1	1	1.000	5	7	.714	–	–	14	3	6	–	–	–	–	20	3.5	0.8	5.0

Crompton, Jeffrey (Geoff) b. July 4, 1955 Ht. 6-11 Wt. 280 College: North Carolina

SEASON–TEAM	G	GS	MIN	FGM	FGA	PCT	3FGM	3FGA	PCT	FTM	FTA	PCT	O-RB	D-RB	TOT	AST	PF	DQ	STL	TO	BLK	PTS	RPG	APG	PPG
78-79–Denver	20	–	88	10	26	.385	–	–	–	6	12	.500	6	17	23	5	19	0	0	12	3	26	1.2	0.3	1.3
80-81–Portland	6	–	33	4	8	.500	0	0	–	1	5	.200	7	11	18	2	4	0	0	5	2	9	3.0	0.3	1.5
81-82–Milwaukee	35	1	203	11	32	.344	0	0	–	6	15	.400	10	31	41	13	39	0	6	17	12	28	1.2	0.4	0.8
82-83–San Antonio	14	0	148	14	34	.412	0	0	–	3	5	.600	18	30	48	7	25	0	3	5	5	31	3.4	0.5	2.2
83-84–Cleveland	7	0	23	1	8	.125	0	0	–	3	6	.500	6	3	9	1	4	0	1	4	1	5	1.3	0.1	0.7
Reg. Season Totals	82	1	495	40	108	.370	0	0	–	19	43	.442	47	92	139	28	91	0	10	43	23	99	1.7	0.3	1.2

Crosby, Terry Dale b. January 4, 1957 Ht. 6-4 Wt. 195 College: Tennessee

SEASON–TEAM	G	GS	MIN	FGM	FGA	PCT	3FGM	3FGA	PCT	FTM	FTA	PCT	O-RB	D-RB	TOT	AST	PF	DQ	STL	TO	BLK	PTS	RPG	APG	PPG
79-80–Kansas City	4	–	28	2	4	.500	0	0	–	2	2	1.000	0	1	1	7	4	0	0	5	0	6	0.3	1.8	1.5
Reg. Season Totals	4	–	28	2	4	.500	0	0	–	2	2	1.000	0	1	1	7	4	0	0	5	0	6	0.3	1.8	1.5

Croshere, Austin Nathan b. May 1, 1975 Ht. 6-9 Wt. 235 College: Providence

SEASON–TEAM	G	GS	MIN	FGM	FGA	PCT	3FGM	3FGA	PCT	FTM	FTA	PCT	O-RB	D-RB	TOT	AST	PF	DQ	STL	TO	BLK	PTS	RPG	APG	PPG
97-98–Indiana	26	0	243	32	86	.372	4	13	.308	8	14	.571	10	35	45	8	32	1	9	13	5	76	1.7	0.3	2.9
98-99–Indiana	27	0	249	32	75	.427	8	29	.276	20	23	.870	16	29	45	10	32	0	7	23	8	92	1.7	0.4	3.4
99-00–Indiana	81	14	1885	288	653	.441	63	174	.362	196	231	.848	135	381	516	89	203	2	44	121	60	835	6.4	1.1	10.3
Reg. Season Totals	134	14	2377	352	814	.432	75	216	.347	224	268	.836	161	445	606	107	267	3	60	157	73	1003	4.5	0.8	7.5
Playoff Totals	24	2	491	64	154	.416	15	37	.405	75	89	.843	32	78	110	19	51	0	9	25	16	218	4.6	0.8	9.1

Cross, Jeffrey A. (Jeff) b. September 1, 1961 Ht. 6-10 Wt. 240 College: Maine

SEASON–TEAM	G	GS	MIN	FGM	FGA	PCT	3FGM	3FGA	PCT	FTM	FTA	PCT	O-RB	D-RB	TOT	AST	PF	DQ	STL	TO	BLK	PTS	RPG	APG	PPG
85-86–L.A. Clippers	21	0	128	6	24	.250	0	0	–	14	25	.560	9	21	30	1	38	0	2	6	3	26	1.4	0.0	1.2
Reg. Season Totals	21	0	128	6	24	.250	0	0	–	14	25	.560	9	21	30	1	38	0	2	6	3	26	1.4	0.0	1.2

Cross, Peter Michael (Pete) b. March 28, 1948 d. January 2, 1977 Ht. 6-9 Wt. 240 College: San Francisco

SEASON–TEAM	G	GS	MIN	FGM	FGA	PCT	3FGM	3FGA	PCT	FTM	FTA	PCT	O-RB	D-RB	TOT	AST	PF	DQ	STL	TO	BLK	PTS	RPG	APG	PPG
70-71–Seattle	79	–	2194	245	554	.442	–	–	–	140	203	.690	–	–	949	113	212	2	–	–	–	630	12.0	1.4	8.0
71-72–Seattle	74	–	1424	152	355	.428	–	–	–	103	140	.736	–	–	509	63	135	2	–	–	–	407	6.9	0.9	5.5
72-73–K.C.-Omaha-Seattle	29	–	157	6	25	.240	–	–	–	8	18	.444	–	–	61	11	29	0	–	–	–	20	2.1	0.4	0.7
Reg. Season Totals	182	–	3775	403	934	.431	–	–	–	251	361	.695	–	–	1519	187	376	4	–	–	–	1057	8.3	1.0	5.8

Cross, Russell Jr. b. September 5, 1961 Ht. 6-10 Wt. 215 College: Purdue

SEASON–TEAM	G	GS	MIN	FGM	FGA	PCT	3FGM	3FGA	PCT	FTM	FTA	PCT	O-RB	D-RB	TOT	AST	PF	DQ	STL	TO	BLK	PTS	RPG	APG	PPG
83-84–Golden State	45	0	354	64	112	.571	0	0	–	38	91	.418	35	47	82	22	58	0	12	19	7	166	1.8	0.5	3.7
Reg. Season Totals	45	0	354	64	112	.571	0	0	–	38	91	.418	35	47	82	22	58	0	12	19	7	166	1.8	0.5	3.7

Crossin, Francis P. b. July 4, 1924 d. January 10, 1981 Ht. 6-1 Wt. 165 College: Pennsylvania

SEASON–TEAM	G	GS	MIN	FGM	FGA	PCT	3FGM	3FGA	PCT	FTM	FTA	PCT	O-RB	D-RB	TOT	AST	PF	DQ	STL	TO	BLK	PTS	RPG	APG	PPG
47-48–Philadelphia	39	–	–	29	121	.240	–	–	–	13	23	.565	–	–	–	20	28	–	–	–	–	71	–	0.5	1.8
48-49–Philadelphia	44	–	–	74	212	.349	–	–	–	26	42	.619	–	–	–	55	53	–	–	–	–	174	–	1.3	4.0
49-50–Philadelphia	64	–	–	185	574	.322	–	–	–	79	101	.782	–	–	–	148	139	–	–	–	–	449	–	2.3	7.0
Reg. Season Totals	147	–	–	288	907	.318	–	–	–	118	166	.711	–	–	–	223	220	–	–	–	–	694	–	1.5	4.7
Playoff Totals	14	–	–	38	107	.355	–	–	–	21	25	.840	–	–	–	17	24	–	–	–	–	97	–	1.2	6.9

Crotty, John Kevin b. July 15, 1969 Ht. 6-2 Wt. 194 College: Virginia

SEASON–TEAM	G	GS	MIN	FGM	FGA	PCT	3FGM	3FGA	PCT	FTM	FTA	PCT	O-RB	D-RB	TOT	AST	PF	DQ	STL	TO	BLK	PTS	RPG	APG	PPG
92-93–Utah	40	0	243	37	72	.514	2	14	.143	26	38	.684	4	13	17	55	29	0	11	30	0	102	0.4	1.4	2.6
93-94–Utah	45	0	313	45	99	.455	11	24	.458	31	36	.861	11	20	31	77	36	0	15	27	1	132	0.7	1.7	2.9
94-95–Utah	80	0	1019	93	231	.403	11	36	.306	98	121	.810	27	70	97	205	105	0	39	70	6	295	1.2	2.6	3.7
95-96–Cleveland	58	4	617	51	114	.447	8	27	.296	62	72	.861	20	34	54	102	60	0	22	51	6	172	0.9	1.8	3.0
96-97–Miami	48	0	659	79	154	.513	20	49	.408	54	64	.844	15	32	47	102	79	0	18	42	0	232	1.0	2.1	4.8
97-98–Portland	26	2	379	29	90	.322	6	20	.300	32	34	.941	4	28	32	63	28	0	10	42	1	96	1.2	2.4	3.7
98-99–Port.-Seattle	27	0	382	51	124	.411	14	36	.389	43	50	.860	8	23	31	63	31	0	11	33	0	159	1.1	2.3	5.9
99-00–Detroit	69	0	937	106	251	.422	33	80	.413	80	93	.860	17	58	75	128	104	0	27	54	5	325	1.1	1.9	4.7
Reg. Season Totals	393	6	4549	491	1135	.433	105	286	.367	426	508	.839	106	278	384	795	472	0	153	349	19	1513	1.0	2.0	3.8
Playoff Totals	32	0	250	23	59	.390	7	17	.412	15	18	.833	7	13	20	32	27	0	8	20	2	68	0.6	1.0	2.1

Crow, Mark Harvey b. October 22, 1954 Ht. 6-7 Wt. 210 College: Duke

SEASON–TEAM	G	GS	MIN	FGM	FGA	PCT	3FGM	3FGA	PCT	FTM	FTA	PCT	O-RB	D-RB	TOT	AST	PF	DQ	STL	TO	BLK	PTS	RPG	APG	PPG
77-78–New Jersey	15	–	154	35	80	.438	–	–	–	14	20	.700	14	13	27	8	24	0	5	12	1	84	1.8	0.5	5.6
Reg. Season Totals	15	–	154	35	80	.438	–	–	–	14	20	.700	14	13	27	8	24	0	5	12	1	84	1.8	0.5	5.6

Crow, William R. (Bill) b. December 9, 1940 Ht. 6-1 Wt. 180 College: Westminster

SEASON–TEAM	G	GS	MIN	FGM	FGA	PCT	3FGM	3FGA	PCT	FTM	FTA	PCT	O-RB	D-RB	TOT	AST	PF	DQ	STL	TO	BLK	PTS	RPG	APG	PPG
67-68–Anaheim (A)	1	–	16	1	8	.125	0	0	–	1	4	.250	–	–	2	0	0	0	–	1	–	3	2.0	0.0	3.0
Reg. ABA Totals	1	–	16	1	8	.125	0	0	–	1	4	.250	–	–	2	0	0	0	–	1	–	3	2.0	0.0	3.0

Crowder, Jonathan Corey (Corey) b. April 13, 1969 Ht. 6-5 Wt. 215 College: Kentucky Wesleyan

SEASON–TEAM	G	GS	MIN	FGM	FGA	PCT	3FGM	3FGA	PCT	FTM	FTA	PCT	O-RB	D-RB	TOT	AST	PF	DQ	STL	TO	BLK	PTS	RPG	APG	PPG
91-92–Utah	51	0	328	43	112	.384	13	30	.433	15	18	.833	16	25	41	17	35	0	7	13	2	114	0.8	0.3	2.2
94-95–San Antonio	7	0	29	2	10	.200	0	4	.000	2	6	.333	1	2	3	1	1	0	1	2	0	6	0.4	0.1	0.9
Reg. Season Totals	58	0	357	45	122	.369	13	34	.382	17	24	.708	17	27	44	18	36	0	8	15	2	120	0.8	0.3	2.1
Playoff Totals	4	0	12	5	9	.556	0	2	.000	0	1	.000	1	1	2	1	1	0	1	2	0	10	0.5	0.3	2.5

Cueto, Alfonso Angel (Al) b. August 2, 1946 Ht. 6-8 Wt. 230 College: St. Gregory's (Okla.) Coll.; Tulsa

SEASON–TEAM	G	GS	MIN	FGM	FGA	PCT	3FGM	3FGA	PCT	FTM	FTA	PCT	O-RB	D-RB	TOT	AST	PF	DQ	STL	TO	BLK	PTS	RPG	APG	PPG
69-70–Miami (A)	78	–	1265	182	449	.405	5	16	.313	102	144	.708	–	–	452	58	257	12	–	–	–	471	5.8	0.7	6.0
70-71–Memphis (A)	71	–	974	134	333	.402	0	5	.000	55	77	.714	–	–	279	86	166	–	–	–	–	323	3.9	1.2	4.5
Reg. ABA Totals	149	–	2239	316	782	.404	5	21	.238	157	221	.710	–	–	731	144	423	12	–	–	–	794	4.9	1.0	5.3
ABA Playoff Totals	4	–	51	6	14	.429	0	0	–	2	3	.667	–	–	18	3	7	0	–	–	–	14	4.5	0.8	3.5

Cummings, Patrick Michael (Pat) b. July 11, 1956 Ht. 6-9 Wt. 235 College: Cincinnati

SEASON–TEAM	G	GS	MIN	FGM	FGA	PCT	3FGM	3FGA	PCT	FTM	FTA	PCT	O-RB	D-RB	TOT	AST	PF	DQ	STL	TO	BLK	PTS	RPG	APG	PPG
79-80–Milwaukee	71	–	900	187	370	.505	0	0	–	94	123	.764	81	157	238	53	141	0	22	74	17	468	3.4	0.7	6.6
80-81–Milwaukee	74	–	1084	248	460	.539	0	2	.000	99	140	.707	97	195	292	62	192	4	31	114	19	595	3.9	0.8	8.0
81-82–Milwaukee	78	7	1132	219	430	.509	0	2	.000	67	91	.736	61	184	245	99	227	6	22	108	9	505	3.1	1.3	6.5
82-83–Dallas	81	71	2317	433	878	.493	0	1	.000	148	196	.755	225	443	668	144	296	9	57	162	35	1014	8.2	1.8	12.5
83-84–Dallas	80	80	2492	452	915	.494	0	2	.000	141	190	.742	151	507	658	158	282	2	64	146	23	1045	8.2	2.0	13.1
84-85–New York	63	63	2069	410	797	.514	0	4	.000	177	227	.780	139	379	518	109	247	6	50	166	17	997	8.2	1.7	15.8
85-86–New York	31	30	1007	195	408	.478	0	2	.000	97	139	.698	92	188	280	47	136	7	27	87	12	487	9.0	1.5	15.7
86-87–New York	49	11	1056	172	382	.450	0	0	–	79	110	.718	123	189	312	38	145	2	26	85	7	423	6.4	0.8	8.6
87-88–New York	62	9	946	140	307	.456	0	1	.000	59	80	.738	82	153	235	37	143	0	20	65	10	339	3.8	0.6	5.5
88-89–Miami	53	28	1096	197	394	.500	0	2	.000	72	97	.742	84	197	281	47	160	3	29	111	18	466	5.3	0.9	8.8
89-90–Miami	37	1	391	77	159	.484	0	0	–	21	37	.568	28	65	93	13	60	1	12	32	4	175	2.5	0.4	4.7
90-91–Utah	4	0	26	4	6	.667	0	0	–	7	10	.700	3	2	5	0	8	0	0	2	0	15	1.3	0.0	3.8
Reg. Season Totals	683	300	14516	2734	5506	.497	0	16	.000	1061	1440	.737	1166	2659	3825	807	2037	40	360	1152	171	6529	5.6	1.2	9.6
Playoff Totals	30	10	454	67	159	.421	0	0	–	26	31	.839	38	74	112	22	59	0	6	22	4	160	3.7	0.7	5.3

C

Cummings, Robert Terrell (Terry) b. March 15, 1961 Ht. 6-9 Wt. 250 College: DePaul

SEASON–TEAM	G	GS	MIN	FGM	FGA	PCT	3FGM	3FGA	PCT	FTM	FTA	PCT	O-RB	D-RB	TOT	AST	PF	DQ	STL	TO	BLK	PTS	RPG	APG	PPG
82-83–San Diego	70	69	2531	684	1309	.523	0	1	.000	292	412	.709	303	441	744	177	294	10	129	204	62	1660	10.6	2.5	23.7
83-84–San Diego	81	80	2907	737	1491	.494	0	3	.000	380	528	.720	323	454	777	139	298	6	92	218	57	1854	9.6	1.7	22.9
84-85–Milwaukee	79	78	2722	759	1532	.495	0	1	.000	343	463	.741	244	472	716	228	264	4	117	190	67	1861	9.1	2.9	23.6
85-86–Milwaukee	82	82	2669	681	1438	.474	0	2	.000	265	404	.656	222	472	694	193	283	4	121	191	51	1627	8.5	2.4	19.8
86-87–Milwaukee	82	77	2770	729	1426	.511	0	3	.000	249	376	.662	214	486	700	229	296	3	129	172	81	1707	8.5	2.8	20.8
87-88–Milwaukee	76	76	2629	675	1392	.485	1	3	.333	270	406	.665	184	369	553	181	274	6	78	170	46	1621	7.3	2.4	21.3
88-89–Milwaukee	80	78	2824	730	1563	.467	7	15	.467	362	460	.787	281	369	650	198	265	5	106	201	72	1829	8.1	2.5	22.9
89-90–San Antonio	81	78	2821	728	1532	.475	19	59	.322	343	440	.780	226	451	677	219	286	1	110	202	52	1818	8.4	2.7	22.4
90-91–San Antonio	67	62	2195	503	1039	.484	7	33	.212	164	240	.683	194	327	521	157	225	5	61	131	30	1177	7.8	2.3	17.6
91-92–San Antonio	70	67	2149	514	1053	.488	5	13	.385	177	249	.711	247	384	631	102	210	4	58	115	34	1210	9.0	1.5	17.3
92-93–San Antonio	8	0	76	11	29	.379	0	0	–	5	10	.500	6	13	19	4	17	0	1	2	1	27	2.4	0.5	3.4
93-94–San Antonio	59	29	1133	183	428	.428	0	2	.000	63	107	.589	132	165	297	50	137	0	31	59	13	429	5.0	0.8	7.3
94-95–San Antonio	76	20	1273	224	464	.483	0	0	–	72	123	.585	138	240	378	59	188	1	36	95	19	520	5.0	0.8	6.8
95-96–Milwaukee	81	13	1777	270	584	.462	1	7	.143	104	160	.650	162	283	445	89	263	2	56	69	30	645	5.5	1.1	8.0
96-97–Seattle	45	3	828	155	319	.486	3	5	.600	57	82	.695	70	113	183	39	113	0	33	45	7	370	4.1	0.9	8.2
97-98–Phil.-N.Y.	74	3	1185	200	428	.467	0	1	.000	67	98	.684	97	186	283	47	181	1	38	51	10	467	3.8	0.6	6.3
98-99–Golden State	50	0	1011	186	424	.439	1	1	1.000	81	114	.711	95	160	255	58	168	4	46	58	10	454	5.1	1.2	9.1
99-00–Golden State	22	0	398	76	177	.429	0	0	–	32	39	.821	45	62	107	21	74	0	13	27	8	184	4.9	1.0	8.4
Reg. Season Totals	1183	815	33898	8045	16628	.484	44	149	.295	3326	4711	.706	3183	5447	8630	2190	3836	56	1255	2200	650	19460	7.3	1.9	16.4
Playoff Totals	110	68	2959	678	1351	.502	1	11	.091	307	435	.706	252	490	742	173	353	3	98	171	62	1664	6.7	1.6	15.1
All-Star Totals	2	0	35	11	26	.423	0	0	–	5	6	.833	6	6	12	1	5	0	3	0	2	27	6.0	0.5	13.5

Cummings, Vonteego Marfeek b. February 29, 1976 Ht. 6-3 Wt. 190 College: Pittsburgh

SEASON–TEAM	G	GS	MIN	FGM	FGA	PCT	3FGM	3FGA	PCT	FTM	FTA	PCT	O-RB	D-RB	TOT	AST	PF	DQ	STL	TO	BLK	PTS	RPG	APG	PPG
99-00–Golden State	75	11	1793	265	655	.405	49	151	.325	127	169	.751	57	127	184	247	174	4	91	132	13	706	2.5	3.3	9.4
Reg. Season Totals	75	11	1793	265	655	.405	49	151	.325	127	169	.751	57	127	184	247	174	4	91	132	13	706	2.5	3.3	9.4

Cunningham, Dick b. July 11, 1946 Ht. 6-10 Wt. 245 College: Murray State

SEASON–TEAM	G	GS	MIN	FGM	FGA	PCT	3FGM	3FGA	PCT	FTM	FTA	PCT	O-RB	D-RB	TOT	AST	PF	DQ	STL	TO	BLK	PTS	RPG	APG	PPG
68-69–Milwaukee	77	–	1236	141	332	.425	–	–	–	69	106	.651	–	–	438	58	166	2	–	–	–	351	5.7	0.8	4.6
69-70–Milwaukee	60	–	416	52	141	.369	–	–	–	22	33	.667	–	–	160	28	70	0	–	–	–	126	2.7	0.5	2.1
70-71–Milwaukee	76	–	675	81	195	.415	–	–	–	39	59	.661	–	–	257	43	90	1	–	–	–	201	3.4	0.6	2.6
71-72–Houston	63	–	720	67	174	.385	–	–	–	37	53	.698	–	–	243	57	76	0	–	–	–	171	3.9	0.9	2.7
72-73–Milwaukee	74	–	692	64	156	.410	–	–	–	29	50	.580	–	–	208	34	94	0	–	–	–	157	2.8	0.5	2.1
73-74–Milwaukee	8	–	45	3	6	.500	–	–	–	0	7	.000	1	15	16	0	5	0	2	–	2	6	2.0	0.0	0.8
74-75–Milwaukee	2	–	8	0	0	–	–	–	–	0	0	–	0	2	2	1	1	0	0	–	0	0	1.0	0.5	0.0
Reg. Season Totals	360	–	3792	408	1004	.406	–	–	–	196	308	.636	1	17	1324	221	502	3	2	–	2	1012	3.7	0.6	2.8
Playoff Totals	27	–	151	20	40	.500	–	–	–	7	11	.636	0	0	39	5	22	0	0	–	0	47	1.4	0.2	1.7

Cunningham, William b. March 25, 1974 Ht. 6-11 Wt. 240 College: Temple

SEASON–TEAM	G	GS	MIN	FGM	FGA	PCT	3FGM	3FGA	PCT	FTM	FTA	PCT	O-RB	D-RB	TOT	AST	PF	DQ	STL	TO	BLK	PTS	RPG	APG	PPG
97-98–Utah-Phil.	7	2	39	4	9	.444	0	0	–	0	0	–	4	6	10	1	10	0	2	0	0	8	1.4	0.1	1.1
98-99–Toronto-N.J.	16	6	162	3	18	.167	0	0	–	0	2	.000	13	15	28	1	30	0	1	5	11	6	1.8	0.1	0.4
Reg. Season Totals	23	8	201	7	27	.259	0	0	–	0	2	.000	17	21	38	2	40	0	3	5	11	14	1.7	0.1	0.6

Cunningham, William John (Billy, Kangaroo Kid) b. June 3, 1943 Ht. 6-6 Wt. 220 College: North Carolina HOF: 1986

SEASON–TEAM	G	GS	MIN	FGM	FGA	PCT	3FGM	3FGA	PCT	FTM	FTA	PCT	O-RB	D-RB	TOT	AST	PF	DQ	STL	TO	BLK	PTS	RPG	APG	PPG
65-66–Philadelphia	80	–	2134	431	1011	.426	–	–	–	281	443	.634	–	–	599	207	301	12	–	–	–	1143	7.5	2.6	14.3
66-67–Philadelphia	81	–	2168	556	1211	.459	–	–	–	383	558	.686	–	–	589	205	260	2	–	–	–	1495	7.3	2.5	18.5
67-68–Philadelphia	74	–	2076	516	1178	.438	–	–	–	368	509	.723	–	–	562	187	260	3	–	–	–	1400	7.6	2.5	18.9
68-69–Philadelphia	82	–	3345	739	1736	.426	–	–	–	556	754	.737	–	–	1050	287	329	10	–	–	–	2034	12.8	3.5	24.8
69-70–Philadelphia	81	–	3194	802	1710	.469	–	–	–	510	700	.729	–	–	1101	352	331	15	–	–	–	2114	13.6	4.3	26.1
70-71–Philadelphia	81	–	3090	702	1519	.462	–	–	–	455	620	.734	–	–	946	395	328	5	–	–	–	1859	11.7	4.9	23.0
71-72–Philadelphia	75	–	2900	658	1428	.461	–	–	–	428	601	.712	–	–	918	443	295	12	–	–	–	1744	12.2	5.9	23.3
72-73–Carolina (A)	84	–	3248	771	1583	.487	14	49	.286	472	598	.789	240	772	1012	530	309	6	216	381	–	2028	12.0	6.3	24.1
73-74–Carolina (A)	32	–	1190	253	537	.471	1	8	.125	149	187	.797	86	245	331	150	105	–	59	127	21	656	10.3	4.7	20.5
74-75–Philadelphia	80	–	2859	609	1423	.428	–	–	–	345	444	.777	130	596	726	442	270	4	91	–	35	1563	9.1	5.5	19.5
75-76–Philadelphia	20	–	640	103	251	.410	–	–	–	68	88	.773	29	118	147	107	57	1	24	–	10	274	7.4	5.4	13.7
Reg. NBA Totals	654	–	22406	5116	11467	.446	–	–	–	3394	4717	.720	159	714	6638	2625	2431	64	115	–	45	13626	10.1	4.0	20.8
Reg. ABA Totals	116	–	4438	1024	2120	.483	15	57	.263	621	785	.791	326	1017	1343	680	414	6	275	508	21	2684	11.6	5.9	23.1
NBA Playoff Totals	39	–	1217	289	677	.427	–	–	–	179	261	.686	0	0	356	125	151	3	0	–	0	757	9.1	3.2	19.4
ABA Playoff Totals	15	–	533	121	254	.476	1	6	.167	61	88	.693	39	119	158	67	57	0	22	56	0	304	10.5	4.5	20.3
NBA All-Star Totals	4	–	93	18	44	.409	–	–	–	12	15	.800	0	0	23	9	11	0	0	–	0	48	5.8	2.3	12.0

Curcic, Radisav b. September 26, 1965 Ht. 6-10 Wt. 275 College: None

SEASON–TEAM	G	GS	MIN	FGM	FGA	PCT	3FGM	3FGA	PCT	FTM	FTA	PCT	O-RB	D-RB	TOT	AST	PF	DQ	STL	TO	BLK	PTS	RPG	APG	PPG
92-93–Dallas	20	0	166	16	41	.390	0	0	–	26	36	.722	17	32	49	12	30	0	7	8	2	58	2.5	0.6	2.9
Reg. Season Totals	20	0	166	16	41	.390	0	0	–	26	36	.722	17	32	49	12	30	0	7	8	2	58	2.5	0.6	2.9

Cure, Armand Arthur b. August 1, 1919 Ht. 6-1 Wt. 200 College: Rhode Island

SEASON–TEAM	G	GS	MIN	FGM	FGA	PCT	3FGM	3FGA	PCT	FTM	FTA	PCT	O-RB	D-RB	TOT	AST	PF	DQ	STL	TO	BLK	PTS	RPG	APG	PPG
46-47–Providence	12	–	–	4	15	.267	–	–	–	2	3	.667	–	–	–	0	5	–	–	–	–	10	–	0.0	0.8
Reg. Season Totals	12	–	–	4	15	.267	–	–	–	2	3	.667	–	–	–	0	5	–	–	–	–	10	–	0.0	0.8

Cureton, Earl (The Twirl) b. September 3, 1957 Ht. 6-9 Wt. 210 College: Detroit Mercy

SEASON–TEAM	G	GS	MIN	FGM	FGA	PCT	3FGM	3FGA	PCT	FTM	FTA	PCT	O-RB	D-RB	TOT	AST	PF	DQ	STL	TO	BLK	PTS	RPG	APG	PPG
80-81–Philadelphia	52	–	528	93	205	.454	0	1	.000	33	64	.516	51	104	155	25	68	0	20	29	23	219	3.0	0.5	4.2
81-82–Philadelphia	66	8	956	149	306	.487	0	2	.000	51	94	.543	90	180	270	32	142	0	31	44	27	349	4.1	0.5	5.3
82-83–Philadelphia	73	3	987	108	258	.419	0	0	–	33	67	.493	84	185	269	43	144	1	37	76	24	249	3.7	0.6	3.4
83-84–Detroit	73	0	907	81	177	.458	0	1	.000	31	59	.525	86	201	287	36	143	3	24	55	31	193	3.9	0.5	2.6
84-85–Detroit	81	1	1642	207	428	.484	0	3	.000	82	144	.569	169	250	419	83	216	1	56	114	42	496	5.2	1.0	6.1
85-86–Detroit	80	19	2017	285	564	.505	0	2	.000	117	211	.555	198	306	504	137	239	3	58	150	58	687	6.3	1.7	8.6
86-87–Chi.-LAClips	78	47	1973	243	510	.476	0	2	.000	82	152	.539	212	240	452	122	188	2	33	80	56	568	5.8	1.6	7.3
87-88–L.A. Clippers	69	11	1128	133	310	.429	0	3	.000	33	63	.524	97	174	271	63	135	1	32	58	36	299	3.9	0.9	4.3
88-89–Charlotte	82	41	2047	233	465	.501	0	1	.000	66	123	.537	188	300	488	130	230	3	50	114	61	532	6.0	1.6	6.5
90-91–Charlotte	9	1	159	8	24	.333	0	1	.000	1	3	.333	6	30	36	3	16	0	0	6	3	17	4.0	0.3	1.9
93-94–Houston	2	0	30	2	8	.250	0	0	–	0	2	.000	4	8	12	0	4	0	0	1	0	4	6.0	0.0	2.0
96-97–Toronto	9	0	46	3	8	.375	0	0	–	1	3	.333	4	5	9	4	10	0	0	1	0	7	1.0	0.4	0.8
Reg. Season Totals	674	131	12420	1545	3263	.473	0	16	.000	530	985	.538	1189	1983	3172	678	1535	14	341	728	361	3620	4.7	1.0	5.4
Playoff Totals	54	4	588	76	169	.450	0	3	.000	17	36	.472	55	118	173	22	83	0	19	26	8	169	3.2	0.4	3.1

Curley, William Michael (Bill) b. May 29, 1972 Ht. 6-9 Wt. 245 College: Boston College

SEASON–TEAM	G	GS	MIN	FGM	FGA	PCT	3FGM	3FGA	PCT	FTM	FTA	PCT	O-RB	D-RB	TOT	AST	PF	DQ	STL	TO	BLK	PTS	RPG	APG	PPG
94-95–Detroit	53	1	595	58	134	.433	0	0	–	27	36	.750	54	70	124	25	128	3	21	25	21	143	2.3	0.5	2.7
97-98–Minnesota	11	1	146	16	33	.485	0	1	.000	2	3	.667	11	17	28	4	28	1	3	3	1	34	2.5	0.4	3.1
98-99–Minnesota	35	7	372	29	72	.403	1	5	.200	19	22	.864	20	31	51	14	83	1	17	10	9	78	1.5	0.4	2.2
99-00–Houston-G.S.	28	0	309	29	68	.426	0	1	.000	18	25	.720	18	32	50	14	61	2	13	21	4	76	1.8	0.5	2.7
Reg. Season Totals	127	9	1422	132	307	.430	1	7	.143	66	86	.767	103	150	253	57	300	7	54	59	35	331	2.0	0.4	2.6
Playoff Totals	2	0	7	0	0	–	0	0	–	0	0	–	0	0	0	–	0	0	0	0	0	0	0.0	0.0	0.0

Curran, Francis Hugh (Fran) b. September 19, 1925 Ht. 6-0 Wt. 175 College: Notre Dame

SEASON–TEAM	G	GS	MIN	FGM	FGA	PCT	3FGM	3FGA	PCT	FTM	FTA	PCT	O-RB	D-RB	TOT	AST	PF	DQ	STL	TO	BLK	PTS	RPG	APG	PPG
47-48–Toledo (N)	58	–	–	129	–	–	–	–	–	119	156	.763	–	–	–	–	145	–	–	–	–	377	–	–	6.5
48-49–Rochester	57	–	–	61	168	.363	–	–	–	85	126	.675	–	–	–	78	118	–	–	–	–	207	–	1.4	3.6
49-50–Rochester	66	–	–	98	235	.417	–	–	–	199	241	.826	–	–	–	71	113	–	–	–	–	395	–	1.1	6.0
Reg. NBA Totals	123	–	–	159	403	.395	–	–	–	284	367	.774	–	–	–	149	231	–	–	–	–	602	–	1.2	4.9
Reg. NBL Totals	58	–	–	129	–	–	–	–	–	119	156	.763	–	–	–	–	145	–	–	–	–	377	–	–	6.5
NBA Playoff Totals	6	–	–	3	23	.261	–	–	–	3	3	1.000	–	–	–	6	3	–	–	–	–	9	–	0.5	1.5

Curry, Michael b. August 22, 1968 Ht. 6-5 Wt. 227 College: Georgia Southern

SEASON–TEAM	G	GS	MIN	FGM	FGA	PCT	3FGM	3FGA	PCT	FTM	FTA	PCT	O-RB	D-RB	TOT	AST	PF	DQ	STL	TO	BLK	PTS	RPG	APG	PPG
93-94–Philadelphia	10	0	43	3	14	.214	0	2	.000	3	4	.750	0	1	1	1	6	0	1	3	0	9	0.1	0.1	0.9
95-96–Wash.-Detroit	46	1	783	73	161	.453	20	53	.377	45	62	.726	27	58	85	27	92	1	24	24	2	211	1.8	0.6	4.6
96-97–Detroit	81	2	1217	99	221	.448	23	77	.299	97	108	.898	23	96	119	43	128	0	31	28	12	318	1.5	0.5	3.9
97-98–Milwaukee	82	27	1978	196	418	.469	4	9	.444	147	176	.835	26	72	98	137	218	1	56	77	14	543	1.2	1.7	6.6
98-99–Milwaukee	50	4	1146	90	206	.437	1	15	.067	63	79	.797	19	89	108	78	135	0	42	37	7	244	2.2	1.6	4.9
99-00–Detroit	82	3	1611	182	379	.480	1	5	.200	141	168	.839	21	83	104	87	209	3	33	73	5	506	1.3	1.1	6.2
Reg. Season Totals	351	37	6778	643	1399	.460	49	161	.304	496	597	.831	116	399	515	373	788	5	187	242	40	1831	1.5	1.1	5.2
Playoff Totals	11	1	188	23	44	.523	0	2	.000	10	13	.769	2	9	11	7	19	0	4	4	3	56	1.0	0.6	5.1

Curry, Wardell Stephen (Dell) b. June 25, 1964 Ht. 6-5 Wt. 205 College: Virginia Tech

SEASON–TEAM	G	GS	MIN	FGM	FGA	PCT	3FGM	3FGA	PCT	FTM	FTA	PCT	O-RB	D-RB	TOT	AST	PF	DQ	STL	TO	BLK	PTS	RPG	APG	PPG
86-87–Utah	67	0	636	139	326	.426	17	60	.283	30	38	.789	30	48	78	58	86	0	27	44	4	325	1.2	0.9	4.9
87-88–Cleveland	79	8	1499	340	742	.458	28	81	.346	79	101	.782	43	123	166	149	128	0	94	108	22	787	2.1	1.9	10.0
88-89–Charlotte	48	0	813	256	521	.491	19	55	.345	40	46	.870	26	78	104	50	68	0	42	44	4	571	2.2	1.0	11.9
89-90–Charlotte	67	13	1860	461	990	.466	52	147	.354	96	104	.923	31	137	168	159	148	0	98	100	26	1070	2.5	2.4	16.0
90-91–Charlotte	76	14	1515	337	715	.471	32	86	.372	96	114	.842	47	152	199	166	125	0	75	80	25	802	2.6	2.2	10.6
91-92–Charlotte	77	0	2020	504	1038	.486	74	183	.404	127	152	.836	57	202	259	177	156	1	93	134	20	1209	3.4	2.3	15.7
92-93–Charlotte	80	0	2094	498	1102	.452	95	237	.401	136	157	.866	51	235	286	180	150	1	87	129	23	1227	3.6	2.3	15.3
93-94–Charlotte	82	0	2173	533	1171	.455	152	378	.402	117	134	.873	71	191	262	221	161	0	98	120	27	1335	3.2	2.7	16.3
94-95–Charlotte	69	0	1718	343	778	.441	154	361	.427	95	111	.856	41	127	168	113	144	1	55	98	18	935	2.4	1.6	13.6
95-96–Charlotte	82	29	2371	441	974	.453	164	406	.404	146	171	.854	68	196	264	176	173	2	108	130	25	1192	3.2	2.1	14.5
96-97–Charlotte	68	20	2078	384	836	.459	126	296	.426	114	142	.803	40	171	211	118	147	0	60	93	14	1008	3.1	1.7	14.8
97-98–Charlotte	52	1	971	194	434	.447	61	145	.421	41	52	.788	26	75	101	69	85	2	31	54	4	490	1.9	1.3	9.4
98-99–Milwaukee	42	0	864	163	336	.485	69	145	.476	28	34	.824	18	67	85	48	42	0	36	45	3	423	2.0	1.1	10.1
99-00–Toronto	67	9	1095	194	454	.427	95	242	.393	24	32	.750	11	89	100	89	66	0	32	40	9	507	1.5	1.3	7.6
Reg. Season Totals	956	94	21707	4787	10417	.460	1138	2822	.403	1169	1388	.842	560	1891	2451	1773	1679	7	936	1219	224	11881	2.6	1.9	12.4
Playoff Totals	35	1	650	89	226	.394	23	75	.307	33	38	.868	25	43	68	43	67	0	29	27	4	234	1.9	1.2	6.7

Cvetkovic, Rastko b. June 22, 1970 Ht. 7-1 Wt. 260 Country: Yugoslavia

SEASON–TEAM	G	GS	MIN	FGM	FGA	PCT	3FGM	3FGA	PCT	FTM	FTA	PCT	O-RB	D-RB	TOT	AST	PF	DQ	STL	TO	BLK	PTS	RPG	APG	PPG
95-96–Denver	14	0	48	5	16	.313	0	1	.000	0	4	.000	4	7	11	3	11	0	2	3	1	10	0.8	0.2	0.7
Reg. Season Totals	14	0	48	5	16	.313	0	1	.000	0	4	.000	4	7	11	3	11	0	2	3	1	10	0.8	0.2	0.7

Dabich, Michael Lee (Mike, Dabbo) b. December 27, 1942 Ht. 7-0 Wt. 255 College: New Mexico State

SEASON–TEAM	G	GS	MIN	FGM	FGA	PCT	3FGM	3FGA	PCT	FTM	FTA	PCT	O-RB	D-RB	TOT	AST	PF	DQ	STL	TO	BLK	PTS	RPG	APG	PPG
67-68–Oak.-Dallas (A)	10	–	49	8	12	.667	0	0	–	4	9	.444	–	–	13	2	12	0	–	5	–	20	1.3	0.2	2.0
Reg. ABA Totals	10	–	49	8	12	.667	0	0	–	4	9	.444	–	–	13	2	12	0	–	5	–	20	1.3	0.2	2.0

Dahler, Edward Jr. (Ed) b. January 31, 1926 Ht. 6-5 Wt. 190 College: Duquesne

SEASON–TEAM	G	GS	MIN	FGM	FGA	PCT	3FGM	3FGA	PCT	FTM	FTA	PCT	O-RB	D-RB	TOT	AST	PF	DQ	STL	TO	BLK	PTS	RPG	APG	PPG
51-52–Philadelphia	14	–	112	14	38	.368	–	–	–	7	7	1.000	–	–	22	5	16	0	–	–	–	35	1.6	0.4	2.5
Reg. Season Totals	14	–	112	14	38	.368	–	–	–	7	7	1.000	–	–	22	5	16	0	–	–	–	35	1.6	0.4	2.5

Dailey, Quintin (Q) b. January 22, 1961 Ht. 6-3 Wt. 180 College: San Francisco

SEASON–TEAM	G	GS	MIN	FGM	FGA	PCT	3FGM	3FGA	PCT	FTM	FTA	PCT	O-RB	D-RB	TOT	AST	PF	DQ	STL	TO	BLK	PTS	RPG	APG	PPG
82-83–Chicago	76	32	2081	470	1008	.466	5	25	.200	206	282	.730	87	173	260	280	248	7	72	205	10	1151	3.4	3.7	15.1
83-84–Chicago	82	42	2449	583	1229	.474	4	32	.125	321	396	.811	61	174	235	254	218	4	109	220	11	1491	2.9	3.1	18.2
84-85–Chicago	79	0	2101	525	1111	.473	7	30	.233	205	251	.817	57	151	208	191	192	0	71	154	5	1262	2.6	2.4	16.0
85-86–Chicago	35	0	723	203	470	.432	0	8	.000	163	198	.823	20	48	68	67	86	0	22	67	5	569	1.9	1.9	16.3
86-87–L.A. Clippers	49	5	924	200	491	.407	1	10	.100	119	155	.768	34	49	83	79	113	4	43	71	8	520	1.7	1.6	10.6
87-88–L.A. Clippers	67	7	1282	328	755	.434	2	12	.167	243	313	.776	62	92	154	109	128	1	69	123	4	901	2.3	1.6	13.4
88-89–L.A. Clippers	69	51	1722	448	964	.465	1	9	.111	217	286	.759	69	135	204	154	152	0	90	122	6	1114	3.0	2.2	16.1
89-90–Seattle	30	2	491	97	240	.404	1	5	.200	52	66	.788	18	33	51	34	63	0	12	34	0	247	1.7	1.1	8.2
90-91–Seattle	30	0	299	73	155	.471	0	1	.000	38	62	.613	11	21	32	16	25	0	7	19	1	184	1.1	0.5	6.1
91-92–Seattle	11	1	98	9	37	.243	0	1	.000	13	16	.813	2	10	12	4	6	0	5	10	1	31	1.1	0.4	2.8
Reg. Season Totals	528	140	12170	2936	6460	.454	21	133	.158	1577	2025	.779	421	886	1307	1188	1231	16	500	1025	51	7470	2.5	2.3	14.1
Playoff Totals	4	0	129	26	62	.419	1	7	.143	8	11	.727	5	8	13	11	9	0	4	5	0	61	3.3	2.8	15.3

Dallmar, Howard (Howie) b. May 24, 1922 d. December 19, 1991 Ht. 6-4 Wt. 200 College: Stanford; Pennsylvania

SEASON–TEAM	G	GS	MIN	FGM	FGA	PCT	3FGM	3FGA	PCT	FTM	FTA	PCT	O-RB	D-RB	TOT	AST	PF	DQ	STL	TO	BLK	PTS	RPG	APG	PPG
46-47–Philadelphia	60	–	–	199	710	.280	–	–	–	130	203	.640	–	–	–	104	141	–	–	–	–	528	–	1.7	8.8
47-48–Philadelphia	48	–	–	215	781	.275	–	–	–	157	211	.744	–	–	–	120	141	–	–	–	–	587	–	2.5	12.2
48-49–Philadelphia	38	–	–	105	342	.307	–	–	–	83	116	.716	–	–	–	116	104	–	–	–	–	293	–	3.1	7.7
Reg. Season Totals	146	–	–	519	1833	.283	–	–	–	370	530	.698	–	–	–	340	386	–	–	–	–	1408	–	2.3	9.6
Playoff Totals	25	–	–	68	371	.235	–	–	–	65	95	.684	–	–	–	67	92	7	–	–	–	201	–	2.1	8.0

Dampier, Erick Trevez b. July 14, 1974 Ht. 6-11 Wt. 265 College: Mississippi State

SEASON–TEAM	G	GS	MIN	FGM	FGA	PCT	3FGM	3FGA	PCT	FTM	FTA	PCT	O-RB	D-RB	TOT	AST	PF	DQ	STL	TO	BLK	PTS	RPG	APG	PPG
96-97–Indiana	72	21	1052	131	336	.390	1	1	1.000	107	168	.637	96	198	294	43	153	1	19	84	73	370	4.1	0.6	5.1
97-98–Golden State	82	82	2656	352	791	.445	0	2	.000	267	399	.669	272	443	715	94	281	6	39	175	139	971	8.7	1.1	11.8
98-99–Golden State	50	50	1414	161	414	.389	0	0	–	120	204	.588	164	218	382	54	165	2	26	92	58	442	7.6	1.1	8.8
99-00–Golden State	21	12	495	70	173	.405	0	0	–	27	51	.529	48	86	134	19	75	1	8	29	15	167	6.4	0.9	8.0
Reg. Season Totals	225	165	5617	714	1714	.417	1	3	.333	521	822	.634	580	945	1525	210	674	10	92	380	285	1950	6.8	0.9	8.7

Dampier, Louie (Lou) b. November 20, 1944 Ht. 6-0 Wt. 175 College: Kentucky

SEASON–TEAM	G	GS	MIN	FGM	FGA	PCT	3FGM	3FGA	PCT	FTM	FTA	PCT	O-RB	D-RB	TOT	AST	PF	DQ	STL	TO	BLK	PTS	RPG	APG	PPG
67-68–Kentucky (A)	72	–	2961	620	1473	.421	38	142	.268	209	254	.823	–	–	333	256	143	0	–	163	–	1487	4.6	3.6	20.7
68-69–Kentucky (A)	78	–	3326	713	1696	.420	199	552	.361	308	380	.811	–	–	299	456	156	1	–	251	–	1933	3.8	5.8	24.8
69-70–Kentucky (A)	82	–	3353	743	1864	.399	198	548	.361	447	538	.831	–	–	310	447	235	2	–	–	–	2131	3.8	5.5	26.0
70-71–Kentucky (A)	84	–	3221	566	1353	.418	103	280	.368	320	376	.851	–	–	297	460	213	–	–	–	–	1555	3.5	5.5	18.5
71-72–Kentucky (A)	83	–	3214	477	1078	.442	84	233	.361	281	336	.836	–	–	259	515	237	–	–	211	–	1319	3.1	6.2	15.9
72-73–Kentucky (A)	80	–	3039	515	1143	.451	54	155	.348	262	334	.784	55	158	213	521	216	0	–	188	–	1346	2.7	6.5	16.8
73-74–Kentucky (A)	84	–	2942	603	1296	.465	48	124	.387	238	286	.832	46	155	201	473	152	–	84	230	18	1492	2.4	5.6	17.8
74-75–Kentucky (A)	83	–	2879	598	1195	.500	38	96	.396	161	199	.809	42	169	211	449	140	–	92	146	53	1395	2.5	5.4	16.8
75-76–Kentucky (A)	82	–	2835	455	949	.479	32	87	.368	126	146	.863	35	124	159	467	141	–	60	148	46	1068	1.9	5.7	13.0
76-77–San Antonio	80	–	1634	233	507	.460	–	–	–	64	86	.744	22	54	76	234	93	0	49	–	15	530	1.0	2.9	6.6
77-78–San Antonio	82	–	2037	336	660	.509	–	–	–	76	101	.752	24	98	122	285	84	0	87	95	13	748	1.5	3.5	9.1
78-79–San Antonio	70	–	760	123	251	.490	–	–	–	29	39	.744	15	48	63	124	42	0	35	39	8	275	0.9	1.8	3.9
Reg. NBA Totals	232	–	4431	692	1418	.488	–	–	–	169	226	.748	61	200	261	643	219	0	171	134	36	1553	1.1	2.8	6.7
Reg. ABA Totals	728	–	27770	5290	12047	.439	794	2217	.358	2352	2849	.826	178	606	2282	4044	1633	3	236	1337	117	13726	3.1	5.6	18.9
NBA Playoff Totals	15	–	246	29	67	.433	–	–	–	9	15	.600	2	13	15	32	19	0	8	5	4	67	1.0	2.1	4.5
ABA Playoff Totals	94	–	3788	598	1371	.436	119	325	.366	269	341	.789	15	50	286	617	195	0	36	120	12	1584	3.0	6.6	16.9

Dandridge, Robert L. Jr. **(Bob)** b. November 15, 1947 Ht. 6-6 Wt. 195 College: Norfolk State

SEASON–TEAM	G	GS	MIN	FGM	FGA	PCT	3FGM	3FGA	PCT	FTM	FTA	PCT	O-RB	D-RB	TOT	AST	PF	DQ	STL	TO	BLK	PTS	RPG	APG	PPG
69-70–Milwaukee	81	–	2461	434	895	.485	–	–	–	199	264	.754	–	–	625	292	279	1	–	–	–	1067	7.7	3.6	13.2
70-71–Milwaukee	79	–	2862	594	1167	.509	–	–	–	264	376	.702	–	–	632	277	287	4	–	–	–	1452	8.0	3.5	18.4
71-72–Milwaukee	80	–	2957	630	1264	.498	–	–	–	215	291	.739	–	–	613	249	297	7	–	–	–	1475	7.7	3.1	18.4
72-73–Milwaukee	73	–	2852	638	1353	.472	–	–	–	198	251	.789	–	–	600	207	279	2	–	–	–	1474	8.2	2.8	20.2
73-74–Milwaukee	71	–	2521	583	1158	.503	–	–	–	175	214	.818	117	362	479	201	271	4	111	–	41	1341	6.7	2.8	18.9
74-75–Milwaukee	80	–	3031	691	1460	.473	–	–	–	211	262	.805	142	409	551	243	330	7	122	–	48	1593	6.9	3.0	19.9
75-76–Milwaukee	73	–	2735	650	1296	.502	–	–	–	271	329	.824	171	369	540	206	263	5	111	–	38	1571	7.4	2.8	21.5
76-77–Milwaukee	70	–	2501	585	1253	.467	–	–	–	283	367	.771	146	294	440	268	222	1	95	–	28	1453	6.3	3.8	20.8
77-78–Washington	75	–	2777	560	1190	.471	–	–	–	330	419	.788	137	305	442	287	262	6	101	241	44	1450	5.9	3.8	19.3
78-79–Washington	78	–	2629	629	1260	.499	–	–	–	331	401	.825	109	338	447	365	259	4	71	222	57	1589	5.7	4.7	20.4
79-80–Washington	45	–	1457	329	729	.451	2	11	.182	123	152	.809	63	183	246	178	112	1	29	123	36	783	5.5	4.0	17.4
80-81–Washington	23	–	545	101	237	.426	0	1	.000	28	39	.718	19	64	83	60	54	1	16	33	9	230	3.6	2.6	10.0
81-82–Milwaukee	11	0	174	21	55	.382	0	0	–	10	17	.588	4	13	17	13	25	0	5	11	2	52	1.5	1.2	4.7
Reg. Season Totals	839	0	29502	6445	13317	.484	2	12	.167	2638	3382	.780	908	2337	5715	2846	2940	43	661	630	303	15530	6.8	3.4	18.5
Playoff Totals	98	0	3882	823	1716	.480	0	0	–	321	422	.761	114	294	754	365	377	12	69	116	39	1967	7.7	3.7	20.1
All-Star Totals	4	1	74	12	25	.480	0	0	–	2	3	.667	8	3	14	2	9	0	5	1	0	26	3.5	0.5	6.5

Daniels, Antonio Robert b. March 19, 1975 Ht. 6-4 Wt. 205 College: Bowling Green

SEASON–TEAM	G	GS	MIN	FGM	FGA	PCT	3FGM	3FGA	PCT	FTM	FTA	PCT	O-RB	D-RB	TOT	AST	PF	DQ	STL	TO	BLK	PTS	RPG	APG	PPG
97-98–Vancouver	74	50	1956	228	548	.416	11	52	.212	112	170	.659	22	121	143	334	88	0	55	164	10	579	1.9	4.5	7.8
98-99–San Antonio	47	0	614	83	183	.454	5	17	.294	49	65	.754	13	41	54	106	39	0	30	44	6	220	1.1	2.3	4.7
99-00–San Antonio	68	1	1195	163	344	.474	22	66	.333	72	101	.713	16	70	86	177	73	0	55	58	5	420	1.3	2.6	6.2
Reg. Season Totals	189	51	3765	474	1075	.441	38	135	.281	233	336	.693	51	232	283	617	200	0	140	266	21	1219	1.5	3.3	6.4
Playoff Totals	19	0	188	18	44	.409	6	14	.429	14	19	.737	3	17	20	22	12	0	11	16	0	56	1.1	1.2	2.9

Daniels, Lloyd **(Sweet Pea)** b. September 4, 1967 Ht. 6-7 Wt. 205 College: Mount San Antonio (Calif.) Coll.

SEASON–TEAM	G	GS	MIN	FGM	FGA	PCT	3FGM	3FGA	PCT	FTM	FTA	PCT	O-RB	D-RB	TOT	AST	PF	DQ	STL	TO	BLK	PTS	RPG	APG	PPG
92-93–San Antonio	77	10	1573	285	644	.443	59	177	.333	72	99	.727	86	130	216	148	144	0	38	102	30	701	2.8	1.9	9.1
93-94–San Antonio	65	5	980	140	372	.376	44	125	.352	46	64	.719	45	66	111	94	69	0	29	60	16	370	1.7	1.4	5.7
94-95–Phil.-Lakers	30	14	604	80	209	.383	26	100	.260	22	27	.815	29	34	63	40	48	0	22	31	10	208	2.1	1.3	6.9
96-97–Sac.-N.J.	22	0	310	36	119	.303	21	70	.300	5	6	.833	19	24	43	26	33	0	10	14	3	98	2.0	1.2	4.5
97-98–Toronto-Atlanta	6	0	82	12	29	.414	2	9	.222	8	10	.800	4	3	7	4	4	0	3	4	2	34	1.2	0.7	5.7
Reg. Season Totals	200	29	3549	553	1373	.403	152	481	.316	153	206	.743	183	257	440	312	298	0	102	211	61	1411	2.2	1.6	7.1
Playoff Totals	12	0	140	19	50	.380	5	15	.333	7	8	.875	11	13	24	5	12	0	3	7	1	50	2.0	0.4	4.2

Daniels, Melvin Joe **(Mel)** b. July 20, 1944 Ht. 6-9 Wt. 225 College: New Mexico

SEASON–TEAM	G	GS	MIN	FGM	FGA	PCT	3FGM	3FGA	PCT	FTM	FTA	PCT	O-RB	D-RB	TOT	AST	PF	DQ	STL	TO	BLK	PTS	RPG	APG	PPG
67-68–Minnesota (A)	78	–	2938	669	1640	.408	1	5	.200	390	678	.575	502	711	1213	109	268	11	–	232	–	1729	15.6	1.4	22.2
68-69–Indiana (A)	76	–	2934	712	1496	.476	0	4	.000	400	662	.604	383	873	1256	116	276	8	–	272	–	1824	16.5	1.5	24.0
69-70–Indiana (A)	83	–	3039	613	1295	.473	0	2	.000	330	489	.675	423	1039	1462	131	309	7	–	–	–	1556	17.6	1.6	18.7
70-71–Indiana (A)	82	–	3170	698	1357	.514	1	13	.077	326	480	.679	394	1081	1475	178	292	–	–	–	–	1723	18.0	2.2	21.0
71-72–Indiana (A)	79	–	2971	598	1184	.505	0	6	.000	317	451	.703	383	914	1297	176	289	–	–	239	–	1513	16.4	2.2	19.2
72-73–Indiana (A)	81	–	3103	587	1217	.482	1	4	.250	322	446	.722	348	899	1247	177	315	8	–	275	157	1497	15.4	2.2	18.5
73-74–Indiana (A)	78	–	2539	492	1117	.440	0	0	–	217	287	.756	251	655	906	122	283	–	56	215	92	1201	11.6	1.6	15.4
74-75–Memphis (A)	71	–	1646	290	644	.450	0	0	–	116	183	.634	186	452	638	125	248	–	40	141	102	696	9.0	1.8	9.8
76-77–N.Y. Nets	11	–	126	13	35	.371	–	–	–	13	23	.565	10	24	34	6	29	0	3	–	11	39	3.1	0.5	3.5
Reg. NBA Totals	11	–	126	13	35	.371	–	–	–	13	23	.565	10	24	34	6	29	0	3	–	11	39	3.1	0.5	3.5
Reg. ABA Totals	628	–	22340	4659	9950	.468	3	34	.088	2418	3676	.658	2870	6624	9494	1134	2280	34	96	1374	351	11739	15.1	1.8	18.7
ABA Playoff Totals	109	–	3901	740	1648	.449	0	5	.000	421	616	.683	435	1012	1608	168	433	2	12	161	51	1901	14.8	1.5	17.4

Danilovic, Predrag **(Sasha)** b. February 26, 1970 Ht. 6-6 Wt. 200 Country: Serbia

SEASON–TEAM	G	GS	MIN	FGM	FGA	PCT	3FGM	3FGA	PCT	FTM	FTA	PCT	O-RB	D-RB	TOT	AST	PF	DQ	STL	TO	BLK	PTS	RPG	APG	PPG
95-96–Miami	19	18	542	83	184	.451	34	78	.436	55	72	.764	12	34	46	47	49	0	15	37	3	255	2.4	2.5	13.4
96-97–Miami-Dallas	56	42	1789	248	570	.435	85	236	.360	121	151	.801	29	107	136	102	160	2	54	116	9	702	2.4	1.8	12.5
Reg. Season Totals	75	60	2331	331	754	.439	119	314	.379	176	223	.789	41	141	182	149	209	2	69	153	12	957	2.4	2.0	12.8
Playoff Totals	3	0	60	9	18	.500	4	10	.400	3	3	1.000	1	0	1	4	8	0	1	3	0	25	0.3	1.3	8.3

Dantley, Adrian Delano (A.D) b. February 26, 1955 Ht. 6-5 Wt. 208 College: Notre Dame

SEASON–TEAM	G	GS	MIN	FGM	FGA	PCT	3FGM	3FGA	PCT	FTM	FTA	PCT	O-RB	D-RB	TOT	AST	PF	DQ	STL	TO	BLK	PTS	RPG	APG	PPG
76-77–Buffalo	77	–	2816	544	1046	.520	–	–	–	476	582	.818	251	336	587	144	215	2	91	–	15	1564	7.6	1.9	20.3
77-78–Indiana-L.A.	79	–	2933	578	1128	.512	–	–	–	541	680	.796	265	355	620	253	233	2	118	228	24	1697	7.8	3.2	21.5
78-79–Los Angeles	60	–	1775	374	733	.510	–	–	–	292	342	.854	131	211	342	138	162	0	63	155	12	1040	5.7	2.3	17.3
79-80–Utah	68	–	2674	730	1267	.576	0	2	.000	443	526	.842	183	333	516	191	211	2	96	233	14	1903	7.6	2.8	28.0
80-81–Utah	80	–	3417	909	1627	.559	2	7	.286	632	784	.806	192	317	509	322	245	1	109	282	18	2452	6.4	4.0	30.7
81-82–Utah	81	81	3222	904	1586	.570	1	3	.333	648	818	.792	231	283	514	324	252	1	95	299	14	2457	6.3	4.0	30.3
82-83–Utah	22	22	887	233	402	.580	0	0	–	210	248	.847	58	82	140	105	62	2	20	81	0	676	6.4	4.8	30.7
83-84–Utah	79	79	2984	802	1438	.558	1	4	.250	813	946	.859	179	269	448	310	201	0	61	263	4	2418	5.7	3.9	30.6
84-85–Utah	55	46	1971	512	964	.531	0	0	–	438	545	.804	148	175	323	186	133	0	57	171	8	1462	5.9	3.4	26.6
85-86–Utah	76	75	2744	818	1453	.563	1	11	.091	630	796	.791	178	217	395	264	206	2	64	231	4	2267	5.2	3.5	29.8
86-87–Detroit	81	81	2736	601	1126	.534	1	6	.167	539	664	.812	104	228	332	162	193	1	63	181	7	1742	4.1	2.0	21.5
87-88–Detroit	69	50	2144	444	863	.514	0	2	.000	492	572	.860	84	143	227	171	144	0	39	135	10	1380	3.3	2.5	20.0
88-89–Detroit-Dallas	73	67	2422	470	954	.493	0	1	.000	460	568	.810	117	200	317	171	186	1	43	163	13	1400	4.3	2.3	19.2
89-90–Dallas	45	45	1300	231	484	.477	0	2	.000	200	254	.787	78	94	172	80	99	0	20	75	7	662	3.8	1.8	14.7
90-91–Milwaukee	10	0	126	19	50	.380	1	3	.333	18	26	.692	8	5	13	9	8	0	5	6	0	57	1.3	0.9	5.7
Reg. Season Totals	955	546	34151	8169	15121	.540	7	41	.171	6832	8351	.818	2207	3248	5455	2830	2550	14	944	2503	150	23177	5.7	3.0	24.3
Playoff Totals	73	59	2515	531	1012	.525	0	3	.000	496	623	.796	149	246	395	169	188	1	69	185	6	1558	5.4	2.3	21.3
All-Star Totals	6	5	130	23	54	.426	0	0	–	17	19	.895	8	15	23	7	13	0	6	6	0	63	3.8	1.2	10.5

D'Antoni, Michael Andrew (Mike) b. May 8, 1951 Ht. 6-3 Wt. 190 College: Marshall

SEASON–TEAM	G	GS	MIN	FGM	FGA	PCT	3FGM	3FGA	PCT	FTM	FTA	PCT	O-RB	D-RB	TOT	AST	PF	DQ	STL	TO	BLK	PTS	RPG	APG	PPG
73-74–K.C.-Omaha	52	–	989	107	266	.402	–	–	–	33	47	.702	24	69	93	123	112	0	75	–	15	247	1.8	2.4	4.8
74-75–K.C.-Omaha	67	–	759	69	173	.399	–	–	–	28	36	.778	13	64	77	107	106	0	67	–	12	166	1.1	1.6	2.5
75-76–Kansas City	9	–	101	7	27	.259	–	–	–	2	2	1.000	4	10	14	16	18	0	10	–	0	16	1.6	1.8	1.8
75-76–St. Louis (A)	50	–	798	77	162	.475	0	4	.000	19	26	.731	16	60	76	115	134	–	63	47	14	173	1.5	2.3	3.5
76-77–San Antonio	2	–	9	1	3	.333	–	–	–	1	2	.500	0	2	2	2	3	0	0	–	0	3	1.0	1.0	1.5
Reg. NBA Totals	130	–	1858	184	469	.392	–	–	–	64	87	.736	41	145	186	248	239	0	152	–	27	432	1.4	1.9	3.3
Reg. ABA Totals	50	–	798	77	162	.475	0	4	.000	19	26	.731	16	60	76	115	134	–	63	47	14	173	1.5	2.3	3.5
NBA Playoff Totals	4	–	42	7	14	.500	–	–	–	4	4	1.000	2	5	7	1	6	0	4	–	1	18	1.8	0.3	4.5

Darcey, Henry J. (Pete) b. March 3, 1930 Ht. 6-9 Wt. 235 College: Oklahoma State

SEASON–TEAM	G	GS	MIN	FGM	FGA	PCT	3FGM	3FGA	PCT	FTM	FTA	PCT	O-RB	D-RB	TOT	AST	PF	DQ	STL	TO	BLK	PTS	RPG	APG	PPG
52-53–Milwaukee	12	–	90	3	18	.167	–	–	–	5	9	.556	–	–	10	2	29	2	–	–	–	11	0.8	0.2	0.9
Reg. Season Totals	12	–	90	3	18	.167	–	–	–	5	9	.556	–	–	10	2	29	2	–	–	–	11	0.8	0.2	0.9

Darden, James W. (Jimmy) b. June 19, 1922 d. April 29, 1994 Ht. 6-1 Wt. 170 College: Wyoming; Denver

SEASON–TEAM	G	GS	MIN	FGM	FGA	PCT	3FGM	3FGA	PCT	FTM	FTA	PCT	O-RB	D-RB	TOT	AST	PF	DQ	STL	TO	BLK	PTS	RPG	APG	PPG
48-49–Denver (N)	57	–	–	197	–	–	–	–	–	193	259	.745	–	–	–	–	149	–	–	–	–	587	–	–	10.3
49-50–Denver	26	–	–	78	243	.321	–	–	–	55	80	.688	–	–	–	67	67	–	–	–	–	211	–	2.6	8.1
Reg. NBA Totals	26	–	–	78	243	.321	–	–	–	55	80	.688	–	–	–	67	67	–	–	–	–	211	–	2.6	8.1
Reg. NBL Totals	57	–	–	197	–	–	–	–	–	193	259	.745	–	–	–	–	149	–	–	–	–	587	–	–	10.3

Darden, Oliver (Ollie) b. July 28, 1944 Ht. 6-7 Wt. 240 College: Michigan

SEASON–TEAM	G	GS	MIN	FGM	FGA	PCT	3FGM	3FGA	PCT	FTM	FTA	PCT	O-RB	D-RB	TOT	AST	PF	DQ	STL	TO	BLK	PTS	RPG	APG	PPG
67-68–Indiana (A)	77	–	2045	371	831	.446	0	1	.000	180	270	.667	–	–	527	69	277	2	–	140	–	922	6.8	0.9	12.0
68-69–N.Y.-Ken. (A)	77	–	1947	318	714	.445	1	5	.200	178	240	.742	–	–	594	104	274	5	–	138	–	815	7.7	1.4	10.6
69-70–Ken.-Indiana (A)	69	–	819	126	327	.385	1	5	.200	57	87	.655	–	–	260	46	142	1	–	–	–	310	3.8	0.7	4.5
Reg. ABA Totals	223	–	4811	815	1872	.435	2	11	.182	415	597	.695	–	–	1381	219	693	8	–	278	–	2047	6.2	1.0	9.2
ABA Playoff Totals	18	–	183	44	83	.530	1	2	.500	13	20	.650	–	–	62	12	35	0	–	4	–	102	3.4	0.7	5.7

Dare, Yinka b. October 10, 1972 Ht. 7-0 Wt. 265 College: George Washington

SEASON–TEAM	G	GS	MIN	FGM	FGA	PCT	3FGM	3FGA	PCT	FTM	FTA	PCT	O-RB	D-RB	TOT	AST	PF	DQ	STL	TO	BLK	PTS	RPG	APG	PPG
94-95–New Jersey	1	0	3	0	1	.000	0	0	–	0	0	–	0	1	1	0	2	0	0	1	0	0	1.0	0.0	0.0
95-96–New Jersey	58	23	626	63	144	.438	0	0	–	38	62	.613	56	125	181	0	117	3	8	72	40	164	3.1	0.0	2.8
96-97–New Jersey	41	2	313	19	54	.352	0	0	–	19	37	.514	35	47	82	3	51	0	4	21	28	57	2.0	0.1	1.4
97-98–New Jersey	10	0	60	4	18	.222	0	0	–	4	8	.500	10	7	17	1	9	0	0	2	2	12	1.7	0.1	1.2
Reg. Season Totals	110	25	1002	86	217	.396	0	0	–	61	107	.570	101	180	281	4	179	3	12	96	70	233	2.6	0.0	2.1

Dark, Jesse L. b. September 2, 1951 Ht. 6-5 Wt. 210 College: Virginia Commonwealth

SEASON–TEAM	G	GS	MIN	FGM	FGA	PCT	3FGM	3FGA	PCT	FTM	FTA	PCT	O-RB	D-RB	TOT	AST	PF	DQ	STL	TO	BLK	PTS	RPG	APG	PPG
74-75–New York	47	–	401	74	157	.471	–	–	–	22	40	.550	15	22	37	30	48	0	3	–	1	170	0.8	0.6	3.6
Reg. Season Totals	47	–	401	74	157	.471	–	–	–	22	40	.550	15	22	37	30	48	0	3	–	1	170	0.8	0.6	3.6
Playoff Totals	2	–	11	1	6	.167	–	–	–	5	5	1.000	1	0	1	1	2	0	0	–	0	7	0.5	0.5	3.5

Darnell, Rick b. January 1, 1953 Ht. 6-10 Wt. 215 College: San Jose State

SEASON–TEAM	G	GS	MIN	FGM	FGA	PCT	3FGM	3FGA	PCT	FTM	FTA	PCT	O-RB	D-RB	TOT	AST	PF	DQ	STL	TO	BLK	PTS	RPG	APG	PPG
75-76–Virginia (A)	11	–	120	11	30	.367	0	0	–	4	7	.571	12	24	36	9	30	–	5	14	3	26	3.3	0.8	2.4
Reg. ABA Totals	11	–	120	11	30	.367	0	0	–	4	7	.571	12	24	36	9	30	–	5	14	3	26	3.3	0.8	2.4

Darrow, James K. **(Jimmy)** b. September 25, 1937 d. June 8, 1987 Ht. 5-10 Wt. 170 College: Bowling Green State

SEASON–TEAM	G	GS	MIN	FGM	FGA	PCT	3FGM	3FGA	PCT	FTM	FTA	PCT	O-RB	D-RB	TOT	AST	PF	DQ	STL	TO	BLK	PTS	RPG	APG	PPG
61-62–St. Louis	5	–	34	3	15	.200	–	–	–	6	7	.857	–	–	7	6	9	0	–	–	–	12	1.4	1.2	2.4
Reg. Season Totals	5	–	34	3	15	.200	–	–	–	6	7	.857	–	–	7	6	9	0	–	–	–	12	1.4	1.2	2.4

Daugherty, Bradley Lee **(Brad, Big Dukie, Hooch)** b. October 19, 1965 Ht. 7-0 Wt. 269 College: North Carolina

SEASON–TEAM	G	GS	MIN	FGM	FGA	PCT	3FGM	3FGA	PCT	FTM	FTA	PCT	O-RB	D-RB	TOT	AST	PF	DQ	STL	TO	BLK	PTS	RPG	APG	PPG
86-87–Cleveland	80	80	2695	487	905	.538	0	0	–	279	401	.696	152	495	647	304	248	3	49	248	63	1253	8.1	3.8	15.7
87-88–Cleveland	79	78	2957	551	1081	.510	0	2	.000	378	528	.716	151	514	665	333	235	2	48	267	56	1480	8.4	4.2	18.7
88-89–Cleveland	78	78	2821	544	1012	.538	1	3	.333	386	524	.737	167	551	718	285	175	1	63	230	40	1475	9.2	3.7	18.9
89-90–Cleveland	41	40	1438	244	509	.479	0	2	.000	202	287	.704	77	296	373	130	108	1	29	110	22	690	9.1	3.2	16.8
90-91–Cleveland	76	76	2946	605	1155	.524	0	3	.000	435	579	.751	177	653	830	253	191	2	74	211	46	1645	10.9	3.3	21.6
91-92–Cleveland	73	73	2643	576	1010	.570	0	2	.000	414	533	.777	191	569	760	262	190	1	65	185	78	1566	10.4	3.6	21.5
92-93–Cleveland	71	71	2691	520	911	.571	1	2	.500	391	492	.795	164	562	726	312	174	0	53	150	56	1432	10.2	4.4	20.2
93-94–Cleveland	50	50	1838	296	606	.488	0	0	–	256	326	.785	128	380	508	149	145	1	41	110	36	848	10.2	3.0	17.0
Reg. Season Totals	548	546	20029	3823	7189	.532	2	14	.143	2741	3670	.747	1207	4020	5227	2028	1466	11	422	1511	397	10389	9.5	3.7	19.0
Playoff Totals	41	41	1600	275	530	.519	0	2	.000	232	307	.756	89	330	419	137	113	1	27	98	40	782	10.2	3.3	19.1
All-Star Totals	5	0	76	15	29	.517	0	0	–	4	7	.571	9	15	24	3	7	0	2	4	1	34	4.8	0.6	6.8

Daughtry, Mack b. 1947 Ht. 6-3 Wt. 175 College: Albany State (Ga.)

SEASON–TEAM	G	GS	MIN	FGM	FGA	PCT	3FGM	3FGA	PCT	FTM	FTA	PCT	O-RB	D-RB	TOT	AST	PF	DQ	STL	TO	BLK	PTS	RPG	APG	PPG
70-71–Carolina (A)	4	–	43	4	10	.400	0	0	–	5	5	1.000	–	–	5	3	4	–	–	–	–	13	1.3	0.8	3.3
Reg. ABA Totals	4	–	43	4	10	.400	0	0	–	5	5	1.000	–	–	5	3	4	–	–	–	–	13	1.3	0.8	3.3

David, Kornel b. October 22, 1971 Ht. 6-9 Wt. 230 Country: Hungary

SEASON–TEAM	G	GS	MIN	FGM	FGA	PCT	3FGM	3FGA	PCT	FTM	FTA	PCT	O-RB	D-RB	TOT	AST	PF	DQ	STL	TO	BLK	PTS	RPG	APG	PPG
98-99–Chicago	50	6	902	109	243	.449	0	1	.000	90	111	.811	70	103	173	40	88	0	23	48	17	308	3.5	0.8	6.2
99-00–Chicago-Clev.	32	5	474	67	157	.427	0	3	.000	45	56	.804	26	55	81	17	56	0	17	33	3	179	2.5	0.5	5.6
Reg. Season Totals	82	11	1376	176	400	.440	0	4	.000	135	167	.808	96	158	254	57	144	0	40	81	20	487	3.1	0.7	5.9

Davies, Robert Edris **(Bob, Harrisburg Houdini)** b. January 15, 1920 d. April 22, 1990 Ht. 6-1 Wt. 175 College: Franklin & Marshall; Seton Hall HOF: 1969

SEASON–TEAM	G	GS	MIN	FGM	FGA	PCT	3FGM	3FGA	PCT	FTM	FTA	PCT	O-RB	D-RB	TOT	AST	PF	DQ	STL	TO	BLK	PTS	RPG	APG	PPG
45-46–Rochester (N)	27	–	–	86	–	–	–	–	–	70	103	.680	–	–	–	–	85	–	–	–	–	242	–	–	9.0
46-47–Rochester (N)	32	–	–	166	–	–	–	–	–	130	166	.783	–	–	–	–	90	–	–	–	–	462	–	–	14.4
47-48–Rochester (N)	48	–	–	176	–	–	–	–	–	120	160	.750	–	–	–	–	111	–	–	–	–	472	–	–	9.8
48-49–Rochester	60	–	–	317	871	.364	–	–	–	270	348	.776	–	–	–	321	197	–	–	–	–	904	–	5.4	15.1
49-50–Rochester	64	–	–	317	887	.357	–	–	–	261	347	.752	–	–	–	294	187	–	–	–	–	895	–	4.6	14.0
50-51–Rochester	63	–	–	326	877	.372	–	–	–	303	381	.795	–	–	197	287	208	7	–	–	–	955	3.1	4.6	15.2
51-52–Rochester	65	–	2394	379	990	.383	–	–	–	294	379	.776	–	–	189	390	269	10	–	–	–	1052	2.9	6.0	16.2
52-53–Rochester	66	–	2216	339	880	.385	–	–	–	351	466	.753	–	–	195	280	261	7	–	–	–	1029	3.0	4.2	15.6
53-54–Rochester	72	–	2137	288	777	.371	–	–	–	311	433	.718	–	–	194	323	224	4	–	–	–	887	2.7	4.5	12.3
54-55–Rochester	72	–	1870	326	785	.415	–	–	–	220	293	.751	–	–	205	355	220	2	–	–	–	872	2.8	4.9	12.1
Reg. NBA Totals	462	–	8617	2292	6067	.378	–	–	–	2010	2647	.759	–	–	980	2250	1566	30	–	–	–	6594	2.9	4.9	14.3
Reg. NBL Totals	107	–	–	428	–	–	–	–	–	320	429	.746	–	–	–	–	286	–	–	–	–	1176	–	–	11.0
NBA Playoff Totals	38	–	976	173	643	.350	–	–	–	160	203	.788	–	–	103	226	125	2	–	–	–	506	2.3	4.0	13.3
NBL Playoff Totals	29	–	–	138	–	–	–	–	–	122	168	.726	–	–	–	–	71	–	–	–	–	398	–	–	13.7
NBA All-Star Totals	4	–	75	19	40	.475	–	–	–	10	14	.714	–	–	13	17	13	0	–	–	–	48	3.3	4.3	12.0

Davis, Antonio Lee b. October 31, 1968 Ht. 6-9 Wt. 230 College: Texas-El Paso

SEASON–TEAM	G	GS	MIN	FGM	FGA	PCT	3FGM	3FGA	PCT	FTM	FTA	PCT	O-RB	D-RB	TOT	AST	PF	DQ	STL	TO	BLK	PTS	RPG	APG	PPG
93-94–Indiana	81	4	1732	216	425	.508	0	1	.000	194	302	.642	190	315	505	55	189	1	45	107	84	626	6.2	0.7	7.7
94-95–Indiana	44	1	1030	109	245	.445	0	0	–	117	174	.672	105	175	280	25	134	2	19	64	29	335	6.4	0.6	7.6
95-96–Indiana	82	14	2092	236	482	.490	1	2	.500	246	345	.713	188	313	501	43	248	6	33	87	66	719	6.1	0.5	8.8
96-97–Indiana	82	28	2335	308	641	.480	1	14	.071	241	362	.666	190	408	598	65	260	4	42	141	84	858	7.3	0.8	10.5
97-98–Indiana	82	12	2191	254	528	.481	0	3	.000	277	398	.696	192	368	560	61	234	6	45	103	72	785	6.8	0.7	9.6
98-99–Indiana	49	1	1271	164	348	.471	0	0	–	135	192	.703	116	228	344	33	136	3	22	50	42	463	7.0	0.7	9.4
99-00–Toronto	79	78	2479	313	712	.440	0	0	–	284	371	.765	235	461	696	105	267	2	38	121	100	910	8.8	1.3	11.5
Reg. Season Totals	499	138	13130	1600	3381	.473	2	20	.100	1494	2144	.697	1216	2268	3484	387	1468	24	244	673	477	4696	7.0	0.8	9.4
Playoff Totals	70	3	1785	180	375	.480	1	1	1.000	202	310	.652	154	305	459	42	233	5	41	104	71	563	6.6	0.6	8.0

Davis, Aubrey D. b. March 28, 1921 Ht. 6-2 Wt. 175 College: Oklahoma Baptist

SEASON–TEAM	G	GS	MIN	FGM	FGA	PCT	3FGM	3FGA	PCT	FTM	FTA	PCT	O-RB	D-RB	TOT	AST	PF	DQ	STL	TO	BLK	PTS	RPG	APG	PPG
46-47–St. Louis	59	–	–	107	381	.281	–	–	–	73	115	.635	–	–	–	14	136	–	–	–	–	287	–	0.2	4.9
48-49–Hammond (N)	8	–	–	3	–	–	–	–	–	3	7	.429	–	–	–	–	5	–	–	–	–	9	–	–	1.1
Reg. NBA Totals	59	–	–	107	381	.281	–	–	–	73	115	.635	–	–	–	14	136	–	–	–	–	287	–	0.2	4.9
Reg. NBL Totals	8	–	–	3	–	–	–	–	–	3	7	.429	–	–	–	–	5	–	–	–	–	9	–	–	1.1
NBA Playoff Totals	3	–	–	2	12	.333	–	–	–	3	3	1.000	–	–	–	–	3	–	–	–	–	7	–	0.0	2.3

Davis, Baron b. April 13, 1979 Ht. 6-3 Wt. 210 College: UCLA

SEASON–TEAM	G	GS	MIN	FGM	FGA	PCT	3FGM	3FGA	PCT	FTM	FTA	PCT	O-RB	D-RB	TOT	AST	PF	DQ	STL	TO	BLK	PTS	RPG	APG	PPG
99-00–Charlotte	82	0	1523	182	433	.420	25	111	.225	97	153	.634	48	117	165	309	201	1	97	140	19	486	2.0	3.8	5.9
Reg. Season Totals	82	0	1523	182	433	.420	25	111	.225	97	153	.634	48	117	165	309	201	1	97	140	19	486	2.0	3.8	5.9
Playoff Totals	4	0	57	10	23	.435	1	6	.167	2	4	.500	3	3	6	6	6	0	4	3	0	23	1.5	1.5	5.8

Davis, Ben Jerome b. December 26, 1972 Ht. 6-9 Wt. 240 College: Arizona

SEASON–TEAM	G	GS	MIN	FGM	FGA	PCT	3FGM	3FGA	PCT	FTM	FTA	PCT	O-RB	D-RB	TOT	AST	PF	DQ	STL	TO	BLK	PTS	RPG	APG	PPG
96-97–Phoenix	20	0	98	10	26	.385	0	0	–	9	20	.450	12	15	27	0	16	0	4	3	1	29	1.4	0.0	1.5
97-98–New York	7	0	13	2	10	.200	0	0	–	0	0	–	6	0	6	0	3	0	1	0	0	4	0.9	0.0	0.6
98-99–New York	8	0	21	7	17	.412	0	0	–	3	6	.500	9	2	11	3	4	0	0	1	0	17	1.4	0.4	2.1
99-00–Phoenix	5	0	22	2	6	.333	0	0	–	0	0	–	3	6	9	2	2	0	1	3	1	4	1.8	0.4	0.8
Reg. Season Totals	40	0	154	21	59	.356	0	0	–	12	26	.462	30	23	53	5	25	0	6	7	2	54	1.3	0.1	1.4

Davis, Bradley Ernest (Brad) b. December 17, 1955 Ht. 6-3 Wt. 180 College: Maryland

SEASON–TEAM	G	GS	MIN	FGM	FGA	PCT	3FGM	3FGA	PCT	FTM	FTA	PCT	O-RB	D-RB	TOT	AST	PF	DQ	STL	TO	BLK	PTS	RPG	APG	PPG
77-78–Los Angeles	33	–	334	30	72	.417	–	–	–	22	29	.759	4	31	35	83	39	1	15	35	2	82	1.1	2.5	2.5
78-79–L.A.-Indiana	27	–	298	31	55	.564	–	–	–	16	23	.696	1	16	17	52	32	0	16	17	2	78	0.6	1.9	2.9
79-80–Indiana-Utah	18	–	268	35	63	.556	0	1	.000	13	16	.813	4	13	17	50	28	0	13	14	1	83	0.9	2.8	4.6
80-81–Dallas	56	–	1686	230	410	.561	3	17	.176	163	204	.799	29	122	151	385	156	2	52	123	11	626	2.7	6.9	11.2
81-82–Dallas	82	82	2614	397	771	.515	14	49	.286	185	230	.804	35	191	226	509	218	5	73	159	6	993	2.8	6.2	12.1
82-83–Dallas	79	78	2323	359	628	.572	11	43	.256	186	220	.845	34	164	198	565	176	2	80	143	11	915	2.5	7.2	11.6
83-84–Dallas	81	81	2665	345	651	.530	7	38	.184	199	238	.836	41	146	187	561	218	4	94	166	13	896	2.3	6.9	11.1
84-85–Dallas	82	82	2539	310	614	.505	47	115	.409	158	178	.888	39	154	193	581	219	1	91	123	10	825	2.4	7.1	10.1
85-86–Dallas	82	43	1971	267	502	.532	32	89	.360	198	228	.868	26	120	146	467	174	2	57	110	15	764	1.8	5.7	9.3
86-87–Dallas	82	6	1582	199	436	.456	32	106	.302	147	171	.860	27	87	114	373	159	0	63	114	10	577	1.4	4.5	7.0
87-88–Dallas	75	12	1480	208	415	.501	30	74	.405	91	108	.843	18	84	102	303	149	0	51	91	18	537	1.4	4.0	7.2
88-89–Dallas	78	4	1395	183	379	.483	32	102	.314	99	123	.805	14	94	108	242	151	0	48	92	18	497	1.4	3.1	6.4
89-90–Dallas	73	2	1292	179	365	.490	35	104	.337	77	100	.770	12	81	93	242	151	2	47	86	9	470	1.3	3.3	6.4
90-91–Dallas	80	6	1426	159	373	.426	22	85	.259	91	118	.771	13	105	118	230	212	1	45	77	17	431	1.5	2.9	5.4
91-92–Dallas	33	0	429	38	86	.442	5	18	.278	11	15	.733	4	29	33	66	57	0	11	27	3	92	1.0	2.0	2.8
Reg. Season Totals	961	396	22302	2970	5820	.510	270	841	.321	1656	2001	.828	301	1437	1738	4709	2139	20	756	1377	146	7866	1.8	4.9	8.2
Playoff Totals	45	14	950	125	236	.530	14	32	.438	77	91	.846	11	64	75	167	89	0	16	74	6	341	1.7	3.7	7.6

Davis, Brian Keith b. June 21, 1970 Ht. 6-7 Wt. 200 College: Duke

SEASON–TEAM	G	GS	MIN	FGM	FGA	PCT	3FGM	3FGA	PCT	FTM	FTA	PCT	O-RB	D-RB	TOT	AST	PF	DQ	STL	TO	BLK	PTS	RPG	APG	PPG
93-94–Minnesota	68	3	374	40	126	.317	1	3	.333	50	68	.735	21	34	55	22	34	0	16	19	4	131	0.8	0.3	1.9
Reg. Season Totals	68	3	374	40	126	.317	1	3	.333	50	68	.735	21	34	55	22	34	0	16	19	4	131	0.8	0.3	1.9

Davis, Charles Edward Jr. (Charlie) b. October 5, 1958 Ht. 6-7 Wt. 215 College: Vanderbilt

SEASON–TEAM	G	GS	MIN	FGM	FGA	PCT	3FGM	3FGA	PCT	FTM	FTA	PCT	O-RB	D-RB	TOT	AST	PF	DQ	STL	TO	BLK	PTS	RPG	APG	PPG
81-82–Washington	54	10	575	88	184	.478	0	2	.000	30	37	.811	54	79	133	31	89	0	10	43	13	206	2.5	0.6	3.8
82-83–Washington	74	10	1161	251	534	.470	2	10	.200	56	89	.629	83	130	213	73	122	0	32	91	22	560	2.9	1.0	7.6
83-84–Washington	46	0	467	103	218	.472	1	9	.111	24	39	.615	34	69	103	30	58	1	14	36	10	231	2.2	0.7	5.0
84-85–Wash.-Milw.	61	2	774	153	356	.430	1	10	.100	51	62	.823	59	94	153	51	113	1	22	54	5	358	2.5	0.8	5.9
85-86–Milwaukee	57	7	873	188	397	.474	3	24	.125	61	75	.813	60	110	170	55	113	1	26	50	7	440	3.0	1.0	7.7
87-88–Milw.-S.A.	21	0	226	48	115	.417	1	17	.059	7	10	.700	16	25	41	20	29	0	2	18	4	104	2.0	1.0	5.0
88-89–Chicago	49	3	545	81	190	.426	4	15	.267	19	26	.731	47	67	114	31	58	1	11	22	5	185	2.3	0.6	3.8
89-90–Chicago	53	0	429	58	158	.367	7	25	.280	7	8	.875	25	56	81	18	52	0	10	20	8	130	1.5	0.3	2.5
Reg. Season Totals	415	32	5050	970	2152	.451	19	112	.170	255	346	.737	378	630	1008	309	634	4	127	334	74	2214	2.4	0.7	5.3
Playoff Totals	49	0	476	64	161	.398	1	11	.091	30	35	.857	36	53	89	19	70	1	9	38	2	159	1.8	0.4	3.2

Davis, Charles Lawrence (Charlie) b. September 7, 1949 Ht. 6-2 Wt. 180 College: Wake Forest

SEASON–TEAM	G	GS	MIN	FGM	FGA	PCT	3FGM	3FGA	PCT	FTM	FTA	PCT	O-RB	D-RB	TOT	AST	PF	DQ	STL	TO	BLK	PTS	RPG	APG	PPG
71-72–Cleveland	61	–	1144	229	569	.402	–	–	–	142	169	.840	–	–	92	123	143	3	–	–	–	600	1.5	2.0	9.8
72-73–Clev.-Port.	75	–	1419	263	631	.417	–	–	–	130	168	.774	–	–	116	185	194	7	–	–	–	656	1.5	2.5	8.7
73-74–Portland	8	–	90	14	40	.350	–	–	–	3	4	.750	2	9	11	11	7	0	2	–	0	31	1.4	1.4	3.9
Reg. Season Totals	144	–	2653	506	1240	.408	–	–	–	275	341	.806	2	9	219	319	344	10	2	–	0	1287	1.5	2.2	8.9

Davis, Damon William (Monti) b. July 26, 1958 Ht. 6-7 Wt. 220 College: Tennessee State

SEASON–TEAM	G	GS	MIN	FGM	FGA	PCT	3FGM	3FGA	PCT	FTM	FTA	PCT	O-RB	D-RB	TOT	AST	PF	DQ	STL	TO	BLK	PTS	RPG	APG	PPG
80-81–Phil.-Dallas	2	–	10	1	5	.200	0	0	–	1	5	.200	2	2	4	0	0	0	0	0	1	3	2.0	0.0	1.5
Reg. Season Totals	2	–	10	1	5	.200	0	0	–	1	5	.200	2	2	4	0	0	0	0	0	1	3	2.0	0.0	1.5

Davis, Dwight E. (Double D) b. October 28, 1949 Ht. 6-8 Wt. 220 College: Houston

SEASON–TEAM	G	GS	MIN	FGM	FGA	PCT	3FGM	3FGA	PCT	FTM	FTA	PCT	O-RB	D-RB	TOT	AST	PF	DQ	STL	TO	BLK	PTS	RPG	APG	PPG
72-73–Cleveland	81	–	2151	293	748	.392	–	–	–	176	222	.793	–	–	563	118	297	5	–	–	–	762	7.0	1.5	9.4
73-74–Cleveland	76	–	2477	376	862	.436	–	–	–	197	274	.719	174	470	644	186	291	6	63	–	74	949	8.5	2.4	12.5
74-75–Cleveland	78	–	1964	295	666	.443	–	–	–	176	245	.718	108	356	464	150	254	3	45	–	39	766	5.9	1.9	9.8
75-76–Golden State	72	–	866	111	269	.413	–	–	–	78	113	.690	86	139	225	46	141	0	20	–	28	300	3.1	0.6	4.2
76-77–Golden State	33	–	552	55	124	.444	–	–	–	49	72	.681	34	61	95	29	93	1	11	–	8	159	2.9	0.9	4.8
Reg. Season Totals	340	–	8010	1130	2669	.423	–	–	–	676	926	.730	402	1026	1991	529	1076	15	139	–	149	2936	5.9	1.6	8.6
Playoff Totals	11	–	142	16	37	.432	–	–	–	18	22	.818	9	19	28	10	28	1	3	–	4	50	2.5	0.9	4.5

Davis, Edward J. (Mickey) b. June 16, 1950 Ht. 6-7 Wt. 205 College: Duquesne

SEASON–TEAM	G	GS	MIN	FGM	FGA	PCT	3FGM	3FGA	PCT	FTM	FTA	PCT	O-RB	D-RB	TOT	AST	PF	DQ	STL	TO	BLK	PTS	RPG	APG	PPG
71-72–Pittsburgh (A)	23	–	126	25	63	.397	0	2	.000	14	20	.700	–	–	41	9	23	–	–	17	–	64	1.8	0.4	2.8
72-73–Milwaukee	74	–	1046	152	347	.438	–	–	–	76	92	.826	–	–	226	72	119	0	–	–	–	380	3.1	1.0	5.1
73-74–Milwaukee	73	–	1012	169	335	.504	–	–	–	93	112	.830	78	146	224	87	94	0	27	–	5	431	3.1	1.2	5.9
74-75–Milwaukee	75	–	1077	174	363	.479	–	–	–	78	88	.886	68	169	237	79	103	0	30	–	5	426	3.2	1.1	5.7
75-76–Milwaukee	45	–	411	55	152	.362	–	–	–	50	63	.794	25	59	84	37	36	0	13	–	2	160	1.9	0.8	3.6
76-77–Milwaukee	19	–	165	29	68	.426	–	–	–	23	25	.920	11	18	29	20	11	0	6	–	4	81	1.5	1.1	4.3
Reg. NBA Totals	286	–	3711	579	1265	.458	–	–	–	320	380	.842	182	392	800	295	363	0	76	–	16	1478	2.8	1.0	5.2
Reg. ABA Totals	23	–	126	25	63	.397	0	2	.000	14	20	.700	–	–	41	9	23	–	–	17	–	64	1.8	0.4	2.8
NBA Playoff Totals	21	–	299	38	82	.463	–	–	–	24	26	.923	8	26	46	17	33	0	4	–	2	100	2.2	0.8	4.8

Davis, Elliott Lydell (Dale) b. March 25, 1969 Ht. 6-11 Wt. 230 College: Clemson

SEASON–TEAM	G	GS	MIN	FGM	FGA	PCT	3FGM	3FGA	PCT	FTM	FTA	PCT	O-RB	D-RB	TOT	AST	PF	DQ	STL	TO	BLK	PTS	RPG	APG	PPG
91-92–Indiana	64	23	1301	154	279	.552	0	1	.000	87	152	.572	158	252	410	30	191	2	27	49	74	395	6.4	0.5	6.2
92-93–Indiana	82	82	2264	304	535	.568	0	0	–	119	225	.529	291	432	723	69	274	5	63	79	148	727	8.8	0.8	8.9
93-94–Indiana	66	64	2292	308	582	.529	0	1	.000	155	294	.527	280	438	718	100	214	1	48	102	106	771	10.9	1.5	11.7
94-95–Indiana	74	70	2346	324	576	.563	0	1	.000	138	259	.533	259	437	696	58	222	2	72	124	116	786	9.4	0.8	10.6
95-96–Indiana	78	77	2617	334	599	.558	0	0	–	135	289	.467	252	457	709	76	238	0	56	119	112	803	9.1	1.0	10.3
96-97–Indiana	80	76	2589	370	688	.538	0	0	–	92	215	.428	301	471	772	59	233	3	60	108	77	832	9.7	0.7	10.4
97-98–Indiana	78	78	2174	273	498	.548	0	0	–	80	172	.465	233	378	611	70	209	1	51	73	87	626	7.8	0.9	8.0
98-99–Indiana	50	50	1374	161	302	.533	0	0	–	76	123	.618	155	261	416	22	115	0	20	43	57	398	8.3	0.4	8.0
99-00–Indiana	74	72	2127	302	602	.502	0	0	–	139	203	.685	256	473	729	64	203	1	52	91	94	743	9.9	0.9	10.0
Reg. Season Totals	646	592	19084	2530	4661	.543	0	3	.000	1021	1932	.528	2185	3599	5784	548	1899	15	449	788	871	6081	9.0	0.8	9.4
Playoff Totals	97	94	3012	320	578	.554	0	1	.000	128	271	.472	317	600	917	67	314	4	58	126	113	768	9.5	0.7	7.9
All-Star Totals	1	0	14	2	3	.667	0	0	–	0	0	–	3	5	8	1	0	0	0	0	0	4	8.0	1.0	4.0

Davis, Emanual b. August 27, 1968 Ht. 6-5 Wt. 195 College: Delaware State

SEASON–TEAM	G	GS	MIN	FGM	FGA	PCT	3FGM	3FGA	PCT	FTM	FTA	PCT	O-RB	D-RB	TOT	AST	PF	DQ	STL	TO	BLK	PTS	RPG	APG	PPG
96-97–Houston	13	0	230	24	54	.444	12	27	.444	5	8	.625	2	20	22	26	20	0	9	17	2	65	1.7	2.0	5.0
97-98–Houston	45	0	599	63	142	.444	27	72	.375	31	37	.838	10	37	47	59	55	0	17	52	3	184	1.0	1.3	4.1
99-00–Seattle	54	2	701	80	220	.364	31	103	.301	26	38	.684	15	85	100	70	72	0	38	44	5	217	1.9	1.3	4.0
Reg. Season Totals	112	2	1530	167	416	.401	70	202	.347	62	83	.747	27	142	169	155	147	0	64	113	10	466	1.5	1.4	4.2

Davis, Harry A. b. January 27, 1956 Ht. 6-7 Wt. 220 College: Florida State

SEASON–TEAM	G	GS	MIN	FGM	FGA	PCT	3FGM	3FGA	PCT	FTM	FTA	PCT	O-RB	D-RB	TOT	AST	PF	DQ	STL	TO	BLK	PTS	RPG	APG	PPG
78-79–Cleveland	40	–	394	66	153	.431	–	–	–	30	43	.698	27	39	66	16	66	1	13	23	8	162	1.7	0.4	4.1
79-80–San Antonio	4	–	30	6	12	.500	0	0	–	1	2	.500	2	4	6	0	8	0	1	3	0	13	1.5	0.0	3.3
Reg. Season Totals	44	–	424	72	165	.436	0	0	–	31	45	.689	29	43	72	16	74	1	14	26	8	175	1.6	0.4	4.0

Davis, Hubert Ira Jr. b. May 17, 1970 Ht. 6-5 Wt. 183 College: North Carolina

SEASON–TEAM	G	GS	MIN	FGM	FGA	PCT	3FGM	3FGA	PCT	FTM	FTA	PCT	O-RB	D-RB	TOT	AST	PF	DQ	STL	TO	BLK	PTS	RPG	APG	PPG
92-93–New York	50	2	815	110	251	.438	6	19	.316	43	54	.796	13	43	56	83	71	1	22	45	4	269	1.1	1.7	5.4
93-94–New York	56	27	1333	238	505	.471	53	132	.402	85	103	.825	23	44	67	165	118	0	40	76	4	614	1.2	2.9	11.0
94-95–New York	82	4	1697	296	617	.480	131	288	.455	97	120	.808	30	80	110	150	146	1	35	87	11	820	1.3	1.8	10.0
95-96–New York	74	14	1773	275	566	.486	127	267	.476	112	129	.868	35	88	123	103	120	1	31	63	8	789	1.7	1.4	10.7
96-97–Toronto	36	0	623	74	184	.402	16	70	.229	17	23	.739	11	29	40	34	40	0	11	21	2	181	1.1	0.9	5.0
97-98–Dallas	81	30	2378	350	767	.456	101	230	.439	97	116	.836	34	135	169	157	117	0	43	88	5	898	2.1	1.9	11.1
98-99–Dallas	50	21	1378	174	397	.438	65	144	.451	44	50	.880	3	83	86	89	76	0	21	57	3	457	1.7	1.8	9.1
99-00–Dallas	79	15	1817	217	464	.468	82	167	.491	67	77	.870	17	117	134	141	109	0	24	70	3	583	1.7	1.8	7.4
Reg. Season Totals	508	113	11814	1734	3751	.462	581	1317	.441	562	672	.836	166	619	785	922	797	3	227	507	40	4611	1.5	1.8	9.1
Playoff Totals	49	7	821	92	225	.409	31	83	.373	36	48	.750	10	36	46	44	83	0	12	48	8	251	0.9	0.9	5.1

Davis, James R. (Red) b. April 22, 1932 Ht. 6-7 Wt. 220 College: St. John's (N.Y.)

SEASON–TEAM	G	GS	MIN	FGM	FGA	PCT	3FGM	3FGA	PCT	FTM	FTA	PCT	O-RB	D-RB	TOT	AST	PF	DQ	STL	TO	BLK	PTS	RPG	APG	PPG
55-56–Rochester	3	–	16	0	6	.000	–	–	–	2	2	1.000	–	–	4	1	2	0	–	–	–	2	1.3	0.3	0.7
Reg. Season Totals	3	–	16	0	6	.000	–	–	–	2	2	1.000	–	–	4	1	2	0	–	–	–	2	1.3	0.3	0.7

Davis, James W. (Jim) b. December 18, 1941 Ht. 6-9 Wt. 230 College: Colorado

SEASON–TEAM	G	GS	MIN	FGM	FGA	PCT	3FGM	3FGA	PCT	FTM	FTA	PCT	O-RB	D-RB	TOT	AST	PF	DQ	STL	TO	BLK	PTS	RPG	APG	PPG
67-68–St. Louis	50	–	394	61	139	.439	–	–	–	25	64	.391	–	–	123	13	85	2	–	–	–	147	2.5	0.3	2.9
68-69–Atlanta	78	–	1367	265	568	.467	–	–	–	154	231	.667	–	–	529	97	239	6	–	–	–	684	6.8	1.2	8.8
69-70–Atlanta	82	–	2623	438	943	.464	–	–	–	240	318	.755	–	–	796	238	335	5	–	–	–	1116	9.7	2.9	13.6
70-71–Atlanta	82	–	1864	241	503	.479	–	–	–	195	288	.677	–	–	546	108	253	5	–	–	–	677	6.7	1.3	8.3
71-72–Atl.-Hou.-Det.	75	–	983	147	338	.435	–	–	–	100	154	.649	–	–	276	51	138	1	–	–	–	394	3.7	0.7	5.3
72-73–Detroit	73	–	771	131	257	.510	–	–	–	72	114	.632	–	–	261	56	126	2	–	–	–	334	3.6	0.8	4.6
73-74–Detroit	78	–	947	117	283	.413	–	–	–	90	139	.647	102	191	293	86	158	1	39	–	30	324	3.8	1.1	4.2
74-75–Detroit	79	–	1078	118	260	.454	–	–	–	85	117	.726	96	189	285	90	129	2	50	–	36	321	3.6	1.1	4.1
Reg. Season Totals	597	–	10027	1518	3291	.461	–	–	–	961	1425	.674	198	380	3109	739	1463	24	89	–	66	3997	5.2	1.2	6.7
Playoff Totals	33	–	382	49	114	.430	–	–	–	44	63	.698	6	14	92	16	62	2	3	–	1	142	2.8	0.5	4.3

Davis, Johnny Reginald (J.D.) b. October 21, 1955 Ht. 6-2 Wt. 170 College: Dayton

SEASON–TEAM	G	GS	MIN	FGM	FGA	PCT	3FGM	3FGA	PCT	FTM	FTA	PCT	O-RB	D-RB	TOT	AST	PF	DQ	STL	TO	BLK	PTS	RPG	APG	PPG
76-77–Portland	79	–	1451	234	531	.441	–	–	–	166	209	.794	62	64	126	148	128	1	41	–	11	634	1.6	1.9	8.0
77-78–Portland	82	–	2188	343	756	.454	–	–	–	188	227	.828	65	108	173	217	173	0	81	151	14	874	2.1	2.6	10.7
78-79–Indiana	79	–	2971	565	1240	.456	–	–	–	314	396	.793	70	121	191	453	177	1	95	214	22	1444	2.4	5.7	18.3
79-80–Indiana	82	–	2912	496	1159	.428	4	42	.095	304	352	.864	102	124	226	440	178	0	110	202	23	1300	2.8	5.4	15.9
80-81–Indiana	76	–	2536	426	917	.465	4	33	.121	238	299	.796	56	114	170	480	179	2	95	167	14	1094	2.2	6.3	14.4
81-82–Indiana	82	70	2664	538	1153	.467	5	27	.185	315	394	.799	72	106	178	346	176	1	76	186	11	1396	2.2	4.2	17.0
82-83–Atlanta	53	33	1465	258	567	.455	5	18	.278	164	206	.796	37	91	128	315	100	0	43	114	7	685	2.4	5.9	12.9
83-84–Atlanta	75	72	2079	354	800	.443	0	8	.000	217	256	.848	53	86	139	326	146	0	62	134	6	925	1.9	4.3	12.3
84-85–Cleveland	76	30	1920	337	791	.426	12	46	.261	255	300	.850	35	84	119	426	136	1	43	152	4	941	1.6	5.6	12.4
85-86–Clev.-Atlanta	66	7	1014	148	344	.430	3	13	.231	118	138	.855	8	47	55	217	76	0	37	78	4	417	0.8	3.3	6.3
Reg. Season Totals	750	212	21200	3699	8258	.448	33	187	.176	2279	2777	.821	560	945	1505	3368	1469	6	683	1398	116	9710	2.0	4.5	12.9
Playoff Totals	43	8	1070	178	392	.454	0	3	.000	89	114	.781	21	57	78	157	80	0	39	28	5	445	1.8	3.7	10.3

Davis, Lee Ommie b. October 11, 1945 Ht. 6-8 Wt. 235 College: North Carolina Central

SEASON–TEAM	G	GS	MIN	FGM	FGA	PCT	3FGM	3FGA	PCT	FTM	FTA	PCT	O-RB	D-RB	TOT	AST	PF	DQ	STL	TO	BLK	PTS	RPG	APG	PPG
68-69–New Orleans (A)	65	–	570	88	227	.388	1	4	.250	45	90	.500	–	–	202	18	87	1	–	31	–	222	3.1	0.3	3.4
69-70–New Orleans (A)	16	–	128	16	36	.444	0	0	–	8	15	.533	–	–	40	2	31	0	–	–	–	40	2.5	0.1	2.5
70-71–Memphis (A)	75	–	925	197	431	.457	0	2	.000	63	117	.538	–	–	251	62	169	–	–	–	–	457	3.3	0.8	6.1
71-72–Memphis (A)	58	–	550	101	231	.437	1	8	.125	25	43	.581	–	–	178	21	90	–	–	25	–	228	3.1	0.4	3.9
72-73–Memphis (A)	78	–	2111	453	871	.520	0	3	.000	131	209	.627	223	385	608	82	266	7	–	96	–	1037	7.8	1.1	13.3
73-74–Memphis (A)	79	–	1632	266	590	.451	1	4	.250	98	152	.645	139	280	419	139	237	–	28	104	40	631	5.3	1.8	8.0
74-75–San Diego (A)	75	–	1838	387	733	.528	4	16	.250	113	169	.669	178	314	492	110	179	–	40	92	40	891	6.6	1.5	11.9
75-76–San Diego (A)	7	–	51	2	11	.182	0	0	–	1	2	.500	0	5	5	1	12	–	0	1	0	5	0.7	0.1	0.7
Reg. ABA Totals	453	–	7805	1510	3130	.482	7	37	.189	484	797	.607	540	984	2195	435	1071	8	68	349	80	3511	4.8	1.0	7.8
ABA Playoff Totals	9	–	71	13	35	.371	0	1	.000	8	13	.615	0	0	33	6	14	0	0	0	0	34	3.7	0.7	3.8

Davis, Mark Anthony b. April 26, 1973 Ht. 6-7 Wt. 205 College: Texas Tech

SEASON–TEAM	G	GS	MIN	FGM	FGA	PCT	3FGM	3FGA	PCT	FTM	FTA	PCT	O-RB	D-RB	TOT	AST	PF	DQ	STL	TO	BLK	PTS	RPG	APG	PPG
95-96–Minnesota	57	0	571	55	149	.369	4	13	.308	74	116	.638	56	69	125	47	92	1	40	68	22	188	2.2	0.8	3.3
96-97–Philadelphia	75	17	1705	251	535	.469	24	93	.258	113	168	.673	138	185	323	135	230	7	85	118	31	639	4.3	1.8	8.5
97-98–Philadelphia	71	12	906	109	244	.447	0	6	.000	64	101	.634	64	94	158	73	95	1	49	91	18	282	2.2	1.0	4.0
98-99–Miami	4	1	35	2	6	.333	0	0	–	5	6	.833	2	5	7	1	12	1	1	7	0	9	1.8	0.3	2.3
99-00–Golden State	23	7	464	56	137	.409	0	2	.000	31	47	.660	31	53	84	38	52	0	25	40	4	143	3.7	1.7	6.2
Reg. Season Totals	230	37	3681	473	1071	.442	28	114	.246	287	438	.655	291	406	697	294	481	10	200	324	75	1261	3.0	1.3	5.5

Davis, Mark Giles b. June 8, 1963 Ht. 6-5 Wt. 195 College: Old Dominion

SEASON–TEAM	G	GS	MIN	FGM	FGA	PCT	3FGM	3FGA	PCT	FTM	FTA	PCT	O-RB	D-RB	TOT	AST	PF	DQ	STL	TO	BLK	PTS	RPG	APG	PPG
88-89–Milw.-Phoenix	33	0	258	49	102	.480	1	10	.100	28	34	.824	16	21	37	14	39	0	13	12	5	127	1.1	0.4	3.8
Reg. Season Totals	33	0	258	49	102	.480	1	10	.100	28	34	.824	16	21	37	14	39	0	13	12	5	127	1.1	0.4	3.8

Davis, Melvyn Jerome (Mel, Killer) b. November 9, 1950 Ht. 6-8 Wt. 220 College: St. John's (N.Y.)

SEASON–TEAM	G	GS	MIN	FGM	FGA	PCT	3FGM	3FGA	PCT	FTM	FTA	PCT	O-RB	D-RB	TOT	AST	PF	DQ	STL	TO	BLK	PTS	RPG	APG	PPG
73-74–New York	30	–	167	33	95	.347	–	–	–	12	16	.750	17	37	54	8	36	0	3	–	4	78	1.8	0.3	2.6
74-75–New York	62	–	903	154	395	.390	–	–	–	48	70	.686	70	251	321	54	105	0	16	–	8	356	5.2	0.9	5.7
75-76–New York	42	–	408	76	193	.394	–	–	–	22	29	.759	43	105	148	31	56	0	16	–	5	174	3.5	0.7	4.1
76-77–N.Y.K-N.Y.N	56	–	1094	168	464	.362	–	–	–	64	91	.703	98	195	293	71	130	0	31	–	5	400	5.2	1.3	7.1
Reg. Season Totals	190	–	2572	431	1147	.376	–	–	–	146	206	.709	228	588	816	164	327	0	66	–	22	1008	4.3	0.9	5.3
Playoff Totals	7	–	40	11	24	.458	–	–	–	2	2	1.000	2	7	9	2	3	0	0	–	0	24	1.3	0.3	3.4

Davis, Michael b. August 2, 1956 Ht. 6-10 Wt. 230 College: Mercer (N.S.) Co. C.C. ; Maryland

SEASON–TEAM	G	GS	MIN	FGM	FGA	PCT	3FGM	3FGA	PCT	FTM	FTA	PCT	O-RB	D-RB	TOT	AST	PF	DQ	STL	TO	BLK	PTS	RPG	APG	PPG
82-83–New York	8	0	28	4	10	.400	0	0	–	6	10	.600	3	7	10	0	4	0	0	0	4	14	1.3	0.0	1.8
Reg. Season Totals	8	0	28	4	10	.400	0	0	–	6	10	.600	3	7	10	0	4	0	0	0	4	14	1.3	0.0	1.8
Playoff Totals	1	0	1	0	0	–	0	0	–	0	0	–	0	0	0	–	0	0	0	0	0	0	0.0	0.0	0.0

Davis, Michael A. (Mike, Crusher) b. July 26, 1946 Ht. 6-3 Wt. 185 College: Virginia Union

SEASON–TEAM	G	GS	MIN	FGM	FGA	PCT	3FGM	3FGA	PCT	FTM	FTA	PCT	O-RB	D-RB	TOT	AST	PF	DQ	STL	TO	BLK	PTS	RPG	APG	PPG
69-70–Baltimore	56	–	1330	260	586	.444	–	–	–	149	192	.776	–	–	128	111	174	1	–	–	–	669	2.3	2.0	11.9
70-71–Buffalo	73	–	1617	317	774	.410	–	–	–	199	262	.760	–	–	187	153	220	7	–	–	–	833	2.6	2.1	11.4
71-72–Buffalo	62	–	1068	213	501	.425	–	–	–	138	180	.767	–	–	120	82	141	5	–	–	–	564	1.9	1.3	9.1
72-73–Baltimore	13	–	283	50	118	.424	–	–	–	23	25	.920	–	–	35	19	45	4	–	–	–	123	2.7	1.5	9.5
72-73–Memphis (A)	38	–	553	93	222	.419	6	23	.261	62	87	.713	21	20	41	47	87	2	–	36	–	254	1.1	1.2	6.7
Reg. NBA Totals	204	–	4298	840	1979	.424	–	–	–	509	659	.772	–	–	470	365	580	17	–	–	–	2189	2.3	1.8	10.7
Reg. ABA Totals	38	–	553	93	222	.419	6	23	.261	62	87	.713	21	20	41	47	87	2	–	36	–	254	1.1	1.2	6.7

Davis, Ralph E. b. September 7, 1938 Ht. 6-4 Wt. 180 College: Cincinnati

SEASON–TEAM	G	GS	MIN	FGM	FGA	PCT	3FGM	3FGA	PCT	FTM	FTA	PCT	O-RB	D-RB	TOT	AST	PF	DQ	STL	TO	BLK	PTS	RPG	APG	PPG
60-61–Cincinnati	73	–	1210	181	451	.401	–	–	–	34	52	.654	–	–	86	177	127	1	–	–	–	396	1.2	2.4	5.4
61-62–Chicago	77	–	1992	364	881	.413	–	–	–	71	103	.689	–	–	162	247	187	1	–	–	–	799	2.1	3.2	10.4
Reg. Season Totals	150	–	3202	545	1332	.409	–	–	–	105	155	.677	–	–	248	424	314	2	–	–	–	1195	1.7	2.8	8.0

Davis, Robert (Bob) b. April 2, 1950 Ht. 6-7 Wt. 215 College: Weber State

SEASON–TEAM	G	GS	MIN	FGM	FGA	PCT	3FGM	3FGA	PCT	FTM	FTA	PCT	O-RB	D-RB	TOT	AST	PF	DQ	STL	TO	BLK	PTS	RPG	APG	PPG
72-73–Portland	9	–	41	6	28	.214	–	–	–	4	6	.667	–	–	5	2	5	0	–	–	–	16	0.6	0.2	1.8
Reg. Season Totals	9	–	41	6	28	.214	–	–	–	4	6	.667	–	–	5	2	5	0	–	–	–	16	0.6	0.2	1.8

Davis, Ronald Howard (Ron) b. May 1, 1954 Ht. 6-6 Wt. 200 College: Glendale (Ariz.) C.C.; Washington State

SEASON–TEAM	G	GS	MIN	FGM	FGA	PCT	3FGM	3FGA	PCT	FTM	FTA	PCT	O-RB	D-RB	TOT	AST	PF	DQ	STL	TO	BLK	PTS	RPG	APG	PPG
76-77–Atlanta	7	–	67	8	35	.229	–	–	–	4	13	.308	2	5	7	2	9	0	7	–	0	20	1.0	0.3	2.9
80-81–San Diego	64	–	817	139	314	.443	2	8	.250	94	158	.595	47	72	119	47	98	0	36	61	11	374	1.9	0.7	5.8
81-82–San Diego	7	0	67	10	25	.400	0	0	–	3	6	.500	7	6	13	4	8	0	0	5	0	23	1.9	0.6	3.3
Reg. Season Totals	78	1	951	157	374	.420	2	8	.250	101	177	.571	56	83	139	53	115	0	43	66	11	417	1.8	0.7	5.3

Davis, Terry Raymond b. June 17, 1967 Ht. 6-10 Wt. 250 College: Virginia Union

SEASON–TEAM	G	GS	MIN	FGM	FGA	PCT	3FGM	3FGA	PCT	FTM	FTA	PCT	O-RB	D-RB	TOT	AST	PF	DQ	STL	TO	BLK	PTS	RPG	APG	PPG
89-90–Miami	63	9	884	122	262	.466	0	1	.000	54	87	.621	93	136	229	25	171	2	25	68	28	298	3.6	0.4	4.7
90-91–Miami	55	17	996	115	236	.487	1	2	.500	69	124	.556	107	159	266	39	129	2	18	36	28	300	4.8	0.7	5.5
91-92–Dallas	68	67	2149	256	531	.482	0	5	.000	181	285	.635	228	444	672	57	202	1	26	117	29	693	9.9	0.8	10.2
92-93–Dallas	75	74	2462	393	863	.455	2	8	.250	167	281	.594	259	442	701	68	199	3	36	160	28	955	9.3	0.9	12.7
93-94–Dallas	15	5	286	24	59	.407	0	0	–	8	12	.667	30	44	74	6	27	0	9	5	1	56	4.9	0.4	3.7
94-95–Dallas	46	2	580	49	113	.434	0	2	.000	42	66	.636	63	93	156	10	76	2	6	30	3	140	3.4	0.2	3.0
95-96–Dallas	28	0	501	55	108	.509	0	0	–	27	47	.574	43	74	117	21	66	2	10	25	4	137	4.2	0.8	4.9
97-98–Washington	74	66	1705	127	256	.496	0	1	.000	69	119	.580	209	271	480	30	193	4	41	56	24	323	6.5	0.4	4.4
98-99–Washington	37	34	578	49	92	.533	0	0	–	28	38	.737	50	89	139	10	79	0	11	16	3	126	3.8	0.3	3.4
Reg. Season Totals	461	274	10141	1190	2520	.472	3	19	.158	645	1059	.609	1082	1752	2834	266	1142	16	182	513	148	3028	6.1	0.6	6.6

Davis, Tyree Ricardo (Ricky) b. September 23, 1979 Ht. 6-7 Wt. 197 College: Iowa

SEASON–TEAM	G	GS	MIN	FGM	FGA	PCT	3FGM	3FGA	PCT	FTM	FTA	PCT	O-RB	D-RB	TOT	AST	PF	DQ	STL	TO	BLK	PTS	RPG	APG	PPG
98-99–Charlotte	46	1	557	81	200	.405	2	12	.167	45	59	.763	40	44	84	58	46	0	30	54	7	209	1.8	1.3	4.5
99-00–Charlotte	48	4	570	94	187	.503	0	4	.000	39	51	.765	29	54	83	62	39	0	30	46	8	227	1.7	1.3	4.7
Reg. Season Totals	94	5	1127	175	387	.452	2	16	.125	84	110	.764	69	98	167	120	85	0	60	100	15	436	1.8	1.3	4.6

Davis, Walter Francis (Walt, Buddy) b. January 5, 1931 Ht. 6-8 Wt. 205 College: Texas A&M

SEASON–TEAM	G	GS	MIN	FGM	FGA	PCT	3FGM	3FGA	PCT	FTM	FTA	PCT	O-RB	D-RB	TOT	AST	PF	DQ	STL	TO	BLK	PTS	RPG	APG	PPG
53-54–Philadelphia	68	–	1568	167	455	.367	–	–	–	65	101	.644	–	–	435	58	207	9	–	–	–	399	6.4	0.9	5.9
54-55–Philadelphia	61	–	766	70	182	.385	–	–	–	35	48	.729	–	–	206	36	100	0	–	–	–	175	3.4	0.6	2.9
55-56–Philadelphia	70	–	1097	123	333	.369	–	–	–	77	112	.688	–	–	276	56	230	7	–	–	–	323	3.9	0.8	4.6
56-57–Philadelphia	65	–	1250	178	437	.407	–	–	–	74	106	.698	–	–	306	52	235	9	–	–	–	430	4.7	0.8	6.6
57-58–Phil.-St. Louis	61	–	663	85	244	.348	–	–	–	61	82	.744	–	–	174	29	143	0	–	–	–	231	2.9	0.5	3.8
Reg. Season Totals	325	–	5344	623	1651	.377	–	–	–	312	449	.695	–	–	1397	231	915	25	–	–	–	1558	4.3	0.7	4.8
Playoff Totals	21	–	172	25	64	.391	–	–	–	17	22	.773	–	–	69	7	51	0	–	–	–	67	3.3	0.3	3.2

Davis, Walter Paul (Sweet D, Greyhound) b. September 9, 1954 Ht. 6-6 Wt. 193 College: North Carolina

SEASON–TEAM	G	GS	MIN	FGM	FGA	PCT	3FGM	3FGA	PCT	FTM	FTA	PCT	O-RB	D-RB	TOT	AST	PF	DQ	STL	TO	BLK	PTS	RPG	APG	PPG
77-78–Phoenix	81	–	2590	786	1494	.526	–	–	–	387	466	.830	158	326	484	273	242	2	113	283	20	1959	6.0	3.4	24.2
78-79–Phoenix	79	–	2437	764	1362	.561	–	–	–	340	409	.831	111	262	373	339	250	5	147	293	26	1868	4.7	4.3	23.6
79-80–Phoenix	75	–	2309	657	1166	.563	0	4	.000	299	365	.819	75	197	272	337	202	2	114	242	19	1613	3.6	4.5	21.5
80-81–Phoenix	78	–	2182	593	1101	.539	7	17	.412	209	250	.836	63	137	200	302	192	3	97	222	12	1402	2.6	3.9	18.0
81-82–Phoenix	55	12	1182	350	669	.523	3	16	.188	91	111	.820	21	82	103	162	104	1	46	112	3	794	1.9	2.9	14.4
82-83–Phoenix	80	79	2491	665	1289	.516	7	23	.304	184	225	.818	63	134	197	397	186	2	117	188	12	1521	2.5	5.0	19.0
83-84–Phoenix	78	70	2546	652	1274	.512	20	87	.230	233	270	.863	38	164	202	429	202	0	107	213	12	1557	2.6	5.5	20.0
84-85–Phoenix	23	9	570	139	309	.450	3	10	.300	64	73	.877	6	29	35	98	42	0	18	50	0	345	1.5	4.3	15.0
85-86–Phoenix	70	62	2239	624	1287	.485	18	76	.237	257	305	.843	54	149	203	361	153	1	99	219	3	1523	2.9	5.2	21.8
86-87–Phoenix	79	79	2646	779	1515	.514	21	81	.259	288	334	.862	90	154	244	364	184	1	96	226	5	1867	3.1	4.6	23.6
87-88–Phoenix	68	48	1951	488	1031	.473	36	96	.375	205	231	.887	32	127	159	278	131	0	86	126	3	1217	2.3	4.1	17.9
88-89–Denver	81	0	1857	536	1076	.498	20	69	.290	175	199	.879	41	110	151	190	187	1	72	132	5	1267	1.9	2.3	15.6
89-90–Denver	69	0	1635	497	1033	.481	6	46	.130	207	227	.912	46	133	179	155	160	1	59	102	9	1207	2.6	2.2	17.5
90-91–Denver-Port.	71	14	1483	403	862	.468	11	36	.306	107	117	.915	71	110	181	125	150	2	80	88	3	924	2.5	1.8	13.0
91-92–Denver	46	0	741	185	403	.459	5	16	.313	82	94	.872	20	50	70	68	69	0	29	45	1	457	1.5	1.5	9.9
Reg. Season Totals	1033	373	28859	8118	15871	.511	157	577	.272	3128	3676	.851	889	2164	3053	3878	2454	21	1280	2541	133	19521	3.0	3.8	18.9
Playoff Totals	78	20	2184	591	1192	.496	5	26	.192	263	317	.830	82	158	240	312	186	0	88	189	16	1450	3.1	4.0	18.6
All-Star Totals	6	1	109	25	55	.455	1	1	1.000	8	8	1.000	6	14	20	15	5	0	7	6	0	59	3.3	2.5	9.8

Davis, Warren Lee b. June 30, 1943 Ht. 6-6 Wt. 213 College: North Carolina A&T

SEASON–TEAM	G	GS	MIN	FGM	FGA	PCT	3FGM	3FGA	PCT	FTM	FTA	PCT	O-RB	D-RB	TOT	AST	PF	DQ	STL	TO	BLK	PTS	RPG	APG	PPG
67-68–Anaheim (A)	54	–	1816	343	758	.453	1	7	.143	229	353	.649	221	345	566	75	193	3	–	128	–	916	10.5	1.4	17.0
68-69–Los Angeles (A)	78	–	2406	356	711	.501	0	2	.000	282	433	.651	254	523	777	129	269	3	–	183	–	994	10.0	1.7	12.7
69-70–L.A.-Pitt. (A)	80	–	2647	428	861	.497	1	3	.333	304	418	.727	278	629	907	244	300	5	–	–	–	1161	11.3	3.1	14.5
70-71–Floridians (A)	76	–	1995	308	686	.449	0	2	.000	209	300	.697	–	–	639	170	254	–	–	–	–	825	8.4	2.2	10.9
71-72–Car.-Mem. (A)	86	–	2331	337	701	.481	0	2	.000	207	299	.692	–	–	693	180	279	–	–	187	–	881	8.1	2.1	10.2
72-73–Memphis (A)	73	–	1895	250	498	.502	0	0	–	172	227	.758	153	362	515	146	212	5	–	129	–	672	7.1	2.0	9.2
Reg. ABA Totals	447	–	13090	2022	4215	.480	2	16	.125	1403	2030	.691	906	1859	4097	944	1507	16	–	627	–	5449	9.2	2.1	12.2
ABA Playoff Totals	6	–	180	28	58	.483	0	0	–	22	29	.759	–	–	48	31	26	0	–	–	–	78	8.0	5.2	13.0

Davis, William F. (Bill) b. October 3, 1921 Ht. 6-3 Wt. 215 College: Notre Dame

SEASON–TEAM	G	GS	MIN	FGM	FGA	PCT	3FGM	3FGA	PCT	FTM	FTA	PCT	O-RB	D-RB	TOT	AST	PF	DQ	STL	TO	BLK	PTS	RPG	APG	PPG
46-47–Chicago	47	–	–	35	146	.240	–	–	–	14	41	.341	–	–	–	11	92	–	–	–	–	84	–	0.2	1.8
Reg. Season Totals	47	–	–	35	146	.240	–	–	–	14	41	.341	–	–	–	11	92	–	–	–	–	84	–	0.2	1.8
Playoff Totals	9	–	–	2	26	.154	–	–	–	2	5	.400	–	–	–	–	9	–	–	–	–	6	0.0	0.0	0.7

Davis, Willie Edward b. August 9, 1945 Ht. 6-8 Wt. 234 College: North Texas

SEASON–TEAM	G	GS	MIN	FGM	FGA	PCT	3FGM	3FGA	PCT	FTM	FTA	PCT	O-RB	D-RB	TOT	AST	PF	DQ	STL	TO	BLK	PTS	RPG	APG	PPG
70-71–Texas (A)	8	–	29	7	15	.467	0	0	–	4	8	.500	–	–	13	2	10	–	–	–	–	18	1.6	0.3	2.3
Reg. ABA Totals	8	–	29	7	15	.467	0	0	–	4	8	.500	–	–	13	2	10	–	–	–	–	18	1.6	0.3	2.3

Dawkins, Darryl (Chocolate Thunder, Double D) b. January 11, 1957 Ht. 6-11 Wt. 252 High School: Maynard Evans (Fla.)

SEASON–TEAM	G	GS	MIN	FGM	FGA	PCT	3FGM	3FGA	PCT	FTM	FTA	PCT	O-RB	D-RB	TOT	AST	PF	DQ	STL	TO	BLK	PTS	RPG	APG	PPG
75-76–Philadelphia	37	–	165	41	82	.500	–	–	–	8	24	.333	15	34	49	3	40	1	2	–	9	90	1.3	0.1	2.4
76-77–Philadelphia	59	–	684	135	215	.628	–	–	–	40	79	.506	59	171	230	24	129	1	12	–	49	310	3.9	0.4	5.3
77-78–Philadelphia	70	–	1722	332	577	.575	–	–	–	156	220	.709	117	438	555	85	268	5	34	123	125	820	7.9	1.2	11.7
78-79–Philadelphia	78	–	2035	430	831	.517	–	–	–	158	235	.672	123	508	631	128	295	5	32	197	143	1018	8.1	1.6	13.1
79-80–Philadelphia	80	–	2541	494	946	.522	0	6	.000	190	291	.653	197	496	693	149	328	8	49	230	142	1178	8.7	1.9	14.7
80-81–Philadelphia	76	–	2088	423	697	.607	0	0	–	219	304	.720	106	439	545	109	316	9	38	220	112	1065	7.2	1.4	14.0
81-82–Philadelphia	48	36	1124	207	367	.564	0	2	.000	114	164	.695	68	237	305	55	193	5	19	96	55	528	6.4	1.1	11.0
82-83–New Jersey	81	81	2093	401	669	.599	0	0	–	166	257	.646	127	293	420	114	379	23	67	281	152	968	5.2	1.4	12.0
83-84–New Jersey	81	80	2417	507	855	.593	2	5	.400	341	464	.735	159	382	541	123	386	22	60	231	136	1357	6.7	1.5	16.8
84-85–New Jersey	39	30	972	192	339	.566	0	1	.000	143	201	.711	55	126	181	45	171	11	14	93	35	527	4.6	1.2	13.5
85-86–New Jersey	51	3	1207	284	441	.644	0	1	.000	210	297	.707	85	166	251	77	227	10	16	124	59	778	4.9	1.5	15.3
86-87–New Jersey	6	2	106	20	32	.625	0	0	–	17	24	.708	9	10	19	2	25	0	2	15	3	57	3.2	0.3	9.5
87-88–Utah-Detroit	6	0	33	2	9	.222	0	0	–	6	15	.400	2	3	5	2	14	0	0	7	2	10	0.8	0.3	1.7
88-89–Detroit	14	0	48	9	19	.474	0	0	–	9	18	.500	3	4	7	1	13	0	0	4	1	27	0.5	0.1	1.9
Reg. Season Totals	726	232	17235	3477	6079	.572	2	15	.133	1777	2593	.685	1125	3307	4432	917	2784	100	345	1621	1023	8733	6.1	1.3	12.0
Playoff Totals	109	25	2734	542	992	.546	0	7	.000	291	414	.703	160	505	665	119	438	16	47	200	165	1375	6.1	1.1	12.6

Dawkins, Johnny Earl Jr. b. September 28, 1963 Ht. 6-2 Wt. 170 College: Duke

SEASON–TEAM	G	GS	MIN	FGM	FGA	PCT	3FGM	3FGA	PCT	FTM	FTA	PCT	O-RB	D-RB	TOT	AST	PF	DQ	STL	TO	BLK	PTS	RPG	APG	PPG
86-87–San Antonio	81	14	1682	334	764	.437	14	47	.298	153	191	.801	56	113	169	290	118	0	67	120	3	835	2.1	3.6	10.3
87-88–San Antonio	65	61	2179	405	835	.485	19	61	.311	198	221	.896	66	138	204	480	95	0	88	154	2	1027	3.1	7.4	15.8
88-89–San Antonio	32	30	1083	177	400	.443	0	4	.000	100	112	.893	32	69	101	224	64	0	55	111	0	454	3.2	7.0	14.2
89-90–Philadelphia	81	81	2865	465	950	.489	22	66	.333	210	244	.861	48	199	247	601	159	1	121	214	9	1162	3.0	7.4	14.3
90-91–Philadelphia	4	4	124	26	41	.634	1	4	.250	10	11	.909	0	16	16	28	4	0	3	8	0	63	4.0	7.0	15.8
91-92–Philadelphia	82	82	2815	394	902	.437	36	101	.356	164	186	.882	42	185	227	567	158	0	89	183	5	988	2.8	6.9	12.0
92-93–Philadelphia	74	10	1598	258	590	.437	26	84	.310	113	142	.796	33	103	136	339	91	0	80	121	4	655	1.8	4.6	8.9
93-94–Philadelphia	72	12	1343	177	423	.418	37	105	.352	84	100	.840	28	95	123	263	74	0	63	111	5	475	1.7	3.7	6.6
94-95–Detroit	50	9	1170	125	270	.463	25	73	.342	50	55	.909	28	85	113	205	74	1	52	86	1	325	2.3	4.1	6.5
Reg. Season Totals	541	303	14859	2361	5175	.456	180	545	.330	1082	1262	.857	333	1003	1336	2997	837	2	618	1108	29	5984	2.5	5.5	11.1
Playoff Totals	13	10	439	59	138	.428	0	9	.000	39	47	.830	6	19	25	98	24	0	19	30	2	157	1.9	7.5	12.1

Dawkins, Paul Lamar b. June 10, 1957 Ht. 6-5 Wt. 190 College: Northern Illinois

SEASON–TEAM	G	GS	MIN	FGM	FGA	PCT	3FGM	3FGA	PCT	FTM	FTA	PCT	O-RB	D-RB	TOT	AST	PF	DQ	STL	TO	BLK	PTS	RPG	APG	PPG
79-80–Utah	57	–	776	141	300	.470	1	5	.200	33	48	.688	42	83	125	77	112	0	33	76	9	316	2.2	1.4	5.5
Reg. Season Totals	57	–	776	141	300	.470	1	5	.200	33	48	.688	42	83	125	77	112	0	33	76	9	316	2.2	1.4	5.5

Dawson, James C. (Jimmy) b. April 18, 1945 Ht. 6-0 Wt. 175 College: Illinois

SEASON–TEAM	G	GS	MIN	FGM	FGA	PCT	3FGM	3FGA	PCT	FTM	FTA	PCT	O-RB	D-RB	TOT	AST	PF	DQ	STL	TO	BLK	PTS	RPG	APG	PPG
67-68–Indiana (A)	21	–	288	46	133	.346	1	7	.143	25	43	.581	–	–	21	32	16	0	–	16	–	118	1.0	1.5	5.6
Reg. ABA Totals	21	–	288	46	133	.346	1	7	.143	25	43	.581	–	–	21	32	16	0	–	16	–	118	1.0	1.5	5.6

Dawson, Tony b. August 25, 1967 Ht. 6-7 Wt. 215 College: Gulf Coast (Fla.) C.C.; Florida State

SEASON–TEAM	G	GS	MIN	FGM	FGA	PCT	3FGM	3FGA	PCT	FTM	FTA	PCT	O-RB	D-RB	TOT	AST	PF	DQ	STL	TO	BLK	PTS	RPG	APG	PPG
90-91–Sacramento	4	0	17	4	7	.571	1	1	1.000	0	0	–	2	0	2	0	0	0	0	1	0	9	0.5	0.0	2.3
94-95–Boston	2	0	13	3	8	.375	1	3	.333	1	1	1.000	0	3	3	1	4	0	0	2	0	8	1.5	0.5	4.0
Reg. Season Totals	6	0	30	7	15	.467	2	4	.500	1	1	1.000	2	3	5	1	4	0	0	3	0	17	0.8	0.2	2.8

Day, Todd Fitzgerald b. January 7, 1970 Ht. 6-6 Wt. 188 College: Arkansas

SEASON–TEAM	G	GS	MIN	FGM	FGA	PCT	3FGM	3FGA	PCT	FTM	FTA	PCT	O-RB	D-RB	TOT	AST	PF	DQ	STL	TO	BLK	PTS	RPG	APG	PPG
92-93–Milwaukee	71	37	1931	358	828	.432	54	184	.293	213	297	.717	144	147	291	117	222	1	75	118	48	983	4.1	1.6	13.8
93-94–Milwaukee	76	39	2127	351	845	.415	33	148	.223	231	331	.698	115	195	310	138	221	4	103	129	52	966	4.1	1.8	12.7
94-95–Milwaukee	82	81	2717	445	1049	.424	163	418	.390	257	341	.754	95	227	322	134	283	6	104	157	63	1310	3.9	1.6	16.0
95-96–Milw.-Boston	79	12	1807	299	817	.366	100	302	.331	224	287	.780	70	154	224	107	225	2	81	109	51	922	2.8	1.4	11.7
96-97–Boston	81	27	2277	398	999	.398	126	348	.362	256	331	.773	109	221	330	117	208	0	108	127	48	1178	4.1	1.4	14.5
97-98–Miami	5	0	69	11	31	.355	2	12	.167	6	9	.667	4	2	6	7	10	0	7	3	0	30	1.2	1.4	6.0
99-00–Phoenix	58	1	941	130	330	.394	64	165	.388	72	108	.667	31	98	129	65	127	1	44	50	22	396	2.2	1.1	6.8
Reg. Season Totals	452	197	11869	1992	4899	.407	542	1577	.344	1259	1704	.739	568	1044	1612	685	1296	14	522	693	284	5785	3.6	1.5	12.8
Playoff Totals	9	0	100	16	35	.457	5	16	.313	5	10	.500	6	4	10	4	24	0	4	4	1	42	1.1	0.4	4.7

Daye, Darren Keefe b. November 30, 1960 Ht. 6-8 Wt. 220 College: UCLA

SEASON–TEAM	G	GS	MIN	FGM	FGA	PCT	3FGM	3FGA	PCT	FTM	FTA	PCT	O-RB	D-RB	TOT	AST	PF	DQ	STL	TO	BLK	PTS	RPG	APG	PPG
83-84–Washington	75	0	1174	180	408	.441	0	6	.000	95	133	.714	90	98	188	176	154	0	38	96	12	455	2.5	2.3	6.1
84-85–Washington	80	8	1573	258	504	.512	1	7	.143	178	249	.715	93	179	272	240	164	1	53	134	19	695	3.4	3.0	8.7
85-86–Washington	64	4	1075	198	399	.496	1	3	.333	159	237	.671	71	112	183	109	121	0	46	98	11	556	2.9	1.7	8.7
86-87–Chicago-Boston	62	2	731	101	202	.500	0	0	–	34	65	.523	37	88	125	76	100	0	25	57	7	236	2.0	1.2	3.8
87-88–Boston	47	8	655	112	217	.516	0	1	.000	59	87	.678	30	46	76	71	68	0	29	44	4	283	1.6	1.5	6.0
Reg. Season Totals	328	22	5208	849	1730	.491	2	17	.118	525	771	.681	321	523	844	672	607	1	191	429	53	2225	2.6	2.0	6.8
Playoff Totals	34	5	372	64	119	.538	0	0	–	41	57	.719	20	32	52	28	46	1	12	30	4	169	1.5	0.8	5.0

Deane, Greg Steven b. December 6, 1957 Ht. 6-4 Wt. 190 College: Utah

SEASON–TEAM	G	GS	MIN	FGM	FGA	PCT	3FGM	3FGA	PCT	FTM	FTA	PCT	O-RB	D-RB	TOT	AST	PF	DQ	STL	TO	BLK	PTS	RPG	APG	PPG
79-80–Utah	7	–	48	2	11	.182	1	1	1.000	5	7	.714	2	4	6	6	3	0	0	3	0	10	0.9	0.9	1.4
Reg. Season Totals	7	–	48	2	11	.182	1	1	1.000	5	7	.714	2	4	6	6	3	0	0	3	0	10	0.9	0.9	1.4

Deangelis, William R. (Billy) b. October 5, 1946 Ht. 6-1 Wt. 180 College: St. Joseph's (Pa.)

SEASON–TEAM	G	GS	MIN	FGM	FGA	PCT	3FGM	3FGA	PCT	FTM	FTA	PCT	O-RB	D-RB	TOT	AST	PF	DQ	STL	TO	BLK	PTS	RPG	APG	PPG
70-71–New York (A)	8	–	47	3	6	.500	0	0	–	4	6	.667	–	–	6	8	16	–	–	–	–	10	0.8	1.0	1.3
Reg. ABA Totals	8	–	47	3	6	.500	0	0	–	4	6	.667	–	–	6	8	16	–	–	–	–	10	0.8	1.0	1.3

DeBusschere, David Albert (Dave) b. October 16, 1940 Ht. 6-6 Wt. 225 College: Detroit (Renamed Detroit Mercy) HOF: 1982

SEASON–TEAM	G	GS	MIN	FGM	FGA	PCT	3FGM	3FGA	PCT	FTM	FTA	PCT	O-RB	D-RB	TOT	AST	PF	DQ	STL	TO	BLK	PTS	RPG	APG	PPG
62-63–Detroit	80	–	2352	406	944	.430	–	–	–	206	287	.718	–	–	694	207	247	2	–	–	–	1018	8.7	2.6	12.7
63-64–Detroit	15	–	304	52	133	.391	–	–	–	25	43	.581	–	–	105	23	32	1	–	–	–	129	7.0	1.5	8.6
64-65–Detroit	79	–	2769	508	1196	.425	–	–	–	306	437	.700	–	–	874	253	242	5	–	–	–	1322	11.1	3.2	16.7
65-66–Detroit	79	–	2696	524	1284	.408	–	–	–	249	378	.659	–	–	916	209	252	5	–	–	–	1297	11.6	2.6	16.4
66-67–Detroit	78	–	2897	531	1278	.415	–	–	–	361	512	.705	–	–	924	216	297	7	–	–	–	1423	11.8	2.8	18.2
67-68–Detroit	80	–	3125	573	1295	.442	–	–	–	289	435	.664	–	–	1081	181	304	3	–	–	–	1435	13.5	2.3	17.9
68-69–Detroit-N.Y.	76	–	2943	506	1140	.444	–	–	–	229	328	.698	–	–	888	191	290	6	–	–	–	1241	11.7	2.5	16.3
69-70–New York	79	–	2627	488	1082	.451	–	–	–	176	256	.688	–	–	790	194	244	2	–	–	–	1152	10.0	2.5	14.6
70-71–New York	81	–	2891	523	1243	.421	–	–	–	217	312	.696	–	–	901	220	237	2	–	–	–	1263	11.1	2.7	15.6
71-72–New York	80	–	3072	520	1218	.427	–	–	–	193	265	.728	–	–	901	291	219	1	–	–	–	1233	11.3	3.6	15.4
72-73–New York	77	–	2827	532	1224	.435	–	–	–	194	260	.746	–	–	787	259	215	1	–	–	–	1258	10.2	3.4	16.3
73-74–New York	71	–	2699	559	1212	.461	–	–	–	164	217	.756	134	623	757	253	222	2	67	–	39	1282	10.7	3.6	18.1
Reg. Season Totals	875	–	31202	5722	13249	.432	–	–	–	2609	3730	.699	134	623	9618	2497	2801	37	67	–	39	14053	11.0	2.9	16.1
Playoff Totals	96	–	3682	634	1523	.416	–	–	–	268	384	.698	25	74	1155	253	327	5	7	–	4	1536	12.0	2.6	16.0
All-Star Totals	8	–	167	37	81	.457	–	–	–	3	4	.750	2	1	51	11	12	0	1	–	0	77	6.4	1.4	9.6

DeClercq, Andrew Donald (Drew) b. February 1, 1973 Ht. 6-10 Wt. 230 College: Florida

SEASON–TEAM	G	GS	MIN	FGM	FGA	PCT	3FGM	3FGA	PCT	FTM	FTA	PCT	O-RB	D-RB	TOT	AST	PF	DQ	STL	TO	BLK	PTS	RPG	APG	PPG
95-96–Golden State	22	1	203	24	50	.480	0	1	.000	11	19	.579	18	21	39	9	30	0	7	4	5	59	1.8	0.4	2.7
96-97–Golden State	71	1	1065	142	273	.520	0	0	–	91	151	.603	122	176	298	32	229	3	33	76	27	375	4.2	0.5	5.3
97-98–Boston	81	49	1523	169	340	.497	0	1	.000	101	168	.601	180	212	392	59	277	3	85	84	49	439	4.8	0.7	5.4
98-99–Boston-Clev.	47	32	1102	138	276	.500	0	0	–	95	141	.674	104	151	255	31	161	3	50	54	29	371	5.4	0.7	7.9
99-00–Cleveland	82	31	1831	225	443	.508	0	0	–	94	160	.588	156	283	439	58	275	6	63	108	66	544	5.4	0.7	6.6
Reg. Season Totals	303	114	5724	698	1382	.505	0	2	.000	392	639	.613	580	843	1423	189	972	15	238	326	176	1788	4.7	0.6	5.9

Dee, Donald M. (Don) b. August 9, 1943 Ht. 6-8 Wt. 210 College: St. Louis; St. Mary of the Plains

SEASON–TEAM	G	GS	MIN	FGM	FGA	PCT	3FGM	3FGA	PCT	FTM	FTA	PCT	O-RB	D-RB	TOT	AST	PF	DQ	STL	TO	BLK	PTS	RPG	APG	PPG
68-69–Indiana (A)	58	–	989	138	387	.357	0	1	.000	56	75	.747	–	–	292	33	179	9	–	72	–	332	5.0	0.6	5.7
Reg. ABA Totals	58	–	989	138	387	.357	0	1	.000	56	75	.747	–	–	292	33	179	9	–	72	–	332	5.0	0.6	5.7
ABA Playoff Totals	12	–	41	4	13	.308	0	0	–	0	0	–	–	–	10	1	10	0	–	–	–	8	0.8	0.1	0.7

Dees, Archie William b. February 22, 1936 Ht. 6-8 Wt. 205 College: Indiana

SEASON–TEAM	G	GS	MIN	FGM	FGA	PCT	3FGM	3FGA	PCT	FTM	FTA	PCT	O-RB	D-RB	TOT	AST	PF	DQ	STL	TO	BLK	PTS	RPG	APG	PPG
58-59–Cincinnati	68	–	1252	200	562	.356	–	–	–	159	204	.779	–	–	339	56	114	0	–	–	–	559	5.0	0.8	8.2
59-60–Detroit	73	–	1244	271	617	.439	–	–	–	165	204	.809	–	–	397	43	188	3	–	–	–	707	5.4	0.6	9.7
60-61–Detroit	28	–	308	53	135	.393	–	–	–	39	47	.830	–	–	94	17	50	0	–	–	–	145	3.4	0.6	5.2
61-62–Chicago-St. L.	21	–	288	51	115	.443	–	–	–	35	46	.761	–	–	77	16	33	0	–	–	–	137	3.7	0.8	6.5
Reg. Season Totals	190	–	3092	575	1429	.402	–	–	–	398	501	.794	–	–	907	132	385	3	–	–	–	1548	4.8	0.7	8.1
Playoff Totals	2	–	18	4	12	.333	–	–	–	3	3	1.000	–	–	4	2	2	0	–	–	–	11	2.0	1.0	5.5

Dehere, Lennox Dominique (Terry) b. September 12, 1971 Ht. 6-4 Wt. 190 College: Seton Hall

SEASON–TEAM	G	GS	MIN	FGM	FGA	PCT	3FGM	3FGA	PCT	FTM	FTA	PCT	O-RB	D-RB	TOT	AST	PF	DQ	STL	TO	BLK	PTS	RPG	APG	PPG
93-94–L.A. Clippers	64	6	759	129	342	.377	23	57	.404	61	81	.753	25	43	68	78	69	0	28	61	3	342	1.1	1.2	5.3
94-95–L.A. Clippers	80	28	1774	279	685	.407	48	163	.294	229	292	.784	35	117	152	225	200	0	45	157	7	835	1.9	2.8	10.4
95-96–L.A. Clippers	82	10	2018	315	686	.459	139	316	.440	247	327	.755	41	102	143	350	239	2	54	191	16	1016	1.7	4.3	12.4
96-97–L.A. Clippers	73	3	1053	148	383	.386	52	160	.325	122	148	.824	15	80	95	158	142	0	27	96	3	470	1.3	2.2	6.4
97-98–Sacramento	77	18	1410	180	451	.399	50	132	.379	79	99	.798	21	85	106	196	150	0	52	96	4	489	1.4	2.5	6.4
98-99–Sac.-Vanc.	26	0	291	31	85	.365	16	39	.410	5	7	.714	7	17	24	27	30	0	7	16	3	83	0.9	1.0	3.2
Reg. Season Totals	402	65	7305	1082	2632	.411	328	867	.378	743	954	.779	144	444	588	1034	830	2	213	617	36	3235	1.5	2.6	8.0
Playoff Totals	2	0	5	0	1	.000	0	1	.000	0	0	–	1	0	1	–	1	0	0	1	0	0	0.5	0.0	0.0

Dehnert, Henry G. (Red) b. 1924 Ht. 6-3 Wt. 175 College: Columbia

SEASON–TEAM	G	GS	MIN	FGM	FGA	PCT	3FGM	3FGA	PCT	FTM	FTA	PCT	O-RB	D-RB	TOT	AST	PF	DQ	STL	TO	BLK	PTS	RPG	APG	PPG
46-47–Providence	10	–	–	6	15	.400	–	–	–	2	6	.333	–	–	–	0	8	–	–	–	–	14	–	0.0	1.4
Reg. Season Totals	10	–	–	6	15	.400	–	–	–	2	6	.333	–	–	–	0	8	–	–	–	–	14	–	0.0	1.4

Dele, Bison (formerly Brian C. Williams) b. April 6, 1969 Ht. 6-11 Wt. 260 College: Maryland; Arizona

SEASON–TEAM	G	GS	MIN	FGM	FGA	PCT	3FGM	3FGA	PCT	FTM	FTA	PCT	O-RB	D-RB	TOT	AST	PF	DQ	STL	TO	BLK	PTS	RPG	APG	PPG
91-92–Orlando	48	2	905	171	324	.528	0	0	–	95	142	.669	115	157	272	33	139	2	41	86	53	437	5.7	0.7	9.1
92-93–Orlando	21	0	240	40	78	.513	0	1	.000	16	20	.800	24	32	56	5	48	2	14	25	17	96	2.7	0.2	4.6
93-94–Denver	80	1	1507	251	464	.541	0	3	.000	137	211	.649	138	308	446	50	221	3	49	104	87	639	5.6	0.6	8.0
94-95–Denver	63	10	1261	196	333	.589	0	0	–	106	162	.654	98	200	298	53	210	7	38	114	43	498	4.7	0.8	7.9
95-96–L.A. Clippers	65	65	2157	416	766	.543	1	6	.167	196	267	.734	149	343	492	122	226	5	70	190	55	1029	7.6	1.9	15.8
96-97–Chicago	9	0	138	26	63	.413	0	0	–	11	15	.733	14	19	33	12	20	0	3	11	5	63	3.7	1.3	7.0
97-98–Detroit	78	78	2619	531	1040	.511	1	3	.333	198	280	.707	223	472	695	94	252	4	67	181	55	1261	8.9	1.2	16.2
98-99–Detroit	49	48	1177	216	431	.501	0	1	.000	81	118	.686	92	180	272	71	181	3	38	111	40	513	5.6	1.4	10.5
Reg. Season Totals	413	204	10004	1847	3499	.528	2	14	.143	840	1215	.691	853	1711	2564	440	1297	26	320	822	355	4536	6.2	1.1	11.0
Playoff Totals	39	5	791	126	238	.529	0	0	–	52	85	.612	81	129	210	25	139	3	26	48	22	304	5.4	0.6	7.8

D

Delk, Tony Lorenzo b. January 28, 1974 Ht. 6-2 Wt. 192 College: Kentucky

SEASON–TEAM	G	GS	MIN	FGM	FGA	PCT	3FGM	3FGA	PCT	FTM	FTA	PCT	O-RB	D-RB	TOT	AST	PF	DQ	STL	TO	BLK	PTS	RPG	APG	PPG
96-97–Charlotte	61	1	867	119	256	.465	52	112	.464	42	51	.824	31	68	99	99	71	1	36	68	6	332	1.6	1.6	5.4
97-98–Cha.-G.S.	77	9	1681	314	798	.393	42	157	.268	111	151	.735	38	134	172	172	96	0	73	109	12	781	2.2	2.2	10.1
98-99–Golden State	36	13	630	92	253	.364	16	66	.242	46	71	.648	11	43	54	95	47	0	16	45	6	246	1.5	2.6	6.8
99-00–Sacramento	46	1	682	120	279	.430	9	40	.225	47	59	.797	36	52	88	55	58	0	35	32	5	296	1.9	1.2	6.4
Reg. Season Totals	220	24	3860	645	1586	.407	119	375	.317	246	332	.741	116	297	413	421	272	1	160	254	29	1655	1.9	1.9	7.5
Playoff Totals	8	1	186	31	72	.431	8	18	.444	17	23	.739	16	12	28	13	21	0	5	10	0	87	3.5	1.6	10.9

Del Negro, Vincent Joseph (Vinny) b. August 9, 1966 Ht. 6-4 Wt. 200 College: North Carolina State

SEASON–TEAM	G	GS	MIN	FGM	FGA	PCT	3FGM	3FGA	PCT	FTM	FTA	PCT	O-RB	D-RB	TOT	AST	PF	DQ	STL	TO	BLK	PTS	RPG	APG	PPG
88-89–Sacramento	80	2	1556	239	503	.475	6	20	.300	85	100	.850	48	123	171	206	160	2	65	77	14	569	2.1	2.6	7.1
89-90–Sacramento	76	29	1858	297	643	.462	10	32	.313	135	155	.871	39	159	198	250	182	2	64	111	10	739	2.6	3.3	9.7
92-93–San Antonio	73	31	1526	218	430	.507	6	24	.250	101	117	.863	19	144	163	291	146	0	44	92	1	543	2.2	4.0	7.4
93-94–San Antonio	77	56	1949	309	634	.487	15	43	.349	140	170	.824	27	134	161	320	168	0	64	102	1	773	2.1	4.2	10.0
94-95–San Antonio	75	71	2360	372	766	.486	66	162	.407	128	162	.790	28	164	192	226	179	0	61	56	14	938	2.6	3.0	12.5
95-96–San Antonio	82	82	2766	478	962	.497	57	150	.380	178	214	.832	36	236	272	315	166	0	85	100	6	1191	3.3	3.8	14.5
96-97–San Antonio	72	53	2243	365	781	.467	44	140	.314	112	129	.868	39	171	210	231	131	0	59	92	7	886	2.9	3.2	12.3
97-98–San Antonio	54	38	1721	211	479	.441	17	39	.436	74	93	.796	13	139	152	183	113	0	39	53	6	513	2.8	3.4	9.5
98-99–Milwaukee	48	7	1093	114	270	.422	13	30	.433	40	50	.800	14	88	102	174	62	0	33	55	3	281	2.1	3.6	5.9
99-00–Milwaukee	67	0	1211	153	325	.471	8	24	.333	35	39	.897	9	98	107	160	81	0	36	48	0	349	1.6	2.4	5.2
Reg. Season Totals	704	369	18283	2756	5793	.476	242	664	.364	1028	1229	.836	272	1456	1728	2356	1388	4	550	786	62	6782	2.5	3.3	9.6
Playoff Totals	51	32	1342	189	418	.452	31	72	.431	56	69	.812	17	99	116	146	95	0	34	47	6	465	2.3	2.9	9.1

DeLong, Nathan J. (Nate) b. January 5, 1926 Ht. 6-6 Wt. 220 College: Wisconsin-River Falls

SEASON–TEAM	G	GS	MIN	FGM	FGA	PCT	3FGM	3FGA	PCT	FTM	FTA	PCT	O-RB	D-RB	TOT	AST	PF	DQ	STL	TO	BLK	PTS	RPG	APG	PPG
51-52–Milwaukee	17	–	132	20	42	.476	–	–	–	24	35	.686	–	–	31	14	47	3	–	–	–	64	1.8	0.8	3.8
Reg. Season Totals	17	–	132	20	42	.476	–	–	–	24	35	.686	–	–	31	14	47	3	–	–	–	64	1.8	0.8	3.8

Dembo, Fennis Marx b. January 24, 1966 Ht. 6-6 Wt. 215 College: Wyoming

SEASON–TEAM	G	GS	MIN	FGM	FGA	PCT	3FGM	3FGA	PCT	FTM	FTA	PCT	O-RB	D-RB	TOT	AST	PF	DQ	STL	TO	BLK	PTS	RPG	APG	PPG
88-89–Detroit	31	0	74	14	42	.333	0	4	.000	8	10	.800	8	15	23	5	15	0	1	7	0	36	0.7	0.2	1.2
Reg. Season Totals	31	0	74	14	42	.333	0	4	.000	8	10	.800	8	15	23	5	15	0	1	7	0	36	0.7	0.2	1.2
Playoff Totals	2	0	4	1	1	1.000	0	0	–	0	0	–	0	0	0	–	1	0	0	1	0	2	0.0	0.0	1.0

Demic, Lawrence Curtis (Larry) b. June 27, 1957 Ht. 6-9 Wt. 225 College: Arizona

SEASON–TEAM	G	GS	MIN	FGM	FGA	PCT	3FGM	3FGA	PCT	FTM	FTA	PCT	O-RB	D-RB	TOT	AST	PF	DQ	STL	TO	BLK	PTS	RPG	APG	PPG
79-80–New York	82	–	1872	230	528	.436	0	0	–	110	183	.601	195	288	483	64	306	10	56	168	30	570	5.9	0.8	7.0
80-81–New York	76	–	964	128	254	.504	0	2	.000	58	92	.630	114	129	243	28	153	0	12	58	13	314	3.2	0.4	4.1
81-82–New York	48	0	356	39	83	.470	0	1	.000	14	39	.359	29	50	79	14	65	1	4	26	6	92	1.6	0.3	1.9
Reg. Season Totals	206	0	3192	397	865	.459	0	3	.000	182	314	.580	338	467	805	106	524	11	72	252	49	976	3.9	0.5	4.7
Playoff Totals	2	0	37	4	5	.800	0	0	–	1	2	.500	5	2	7	–	3	0	0	0	1	9	3.5	0.0	4.5

Demps, Dell b. February 12, 1970 Ht. 6-4 Wt. 210 College: U. of Pacific

SEASON–TEAM	G	GS	MIN	FGM	FGA	PCT	3FGM	3FGA	PCT	FTM	FTA	PCT	O-RB	D-RB	TOT	AST	PF	DQ	STL	TO	BLK	PTS	RPG	APG	PPG
93-94–Golden State	2	0	11	2	6	.333	0	0	–	0	2	.000	0	0	0	1	1	0	2	1	0	4	0.0	0.5	2.0
95-96–San Antonio	16	0	87	19	33	.576	1	2	.500	14	17	.824	2	7	9	8	10	0	3	12	1	53	0.6	0.5	3.3
96-97–Orlando	2	0	10	0	3	.000	0	1	.000	2	2	1.000	0	0	0	0	1	0	1	0	0	2	0.0	0.0	1.0
Reg. Season Totals	20	0	108	21	42	.500	1	3	.333	16	21	.762	2	7	9	9	12	0	6	13	1	59	0.5	0.5	3.0

Dempsey, George P. b. July 19, 1929 Ht. 6-3 Wt. 190 College: Kings College (Del.)

SEASON–TEAM	G	GS	MIN	FGM	FGA	PCT	3FGM	3FGA	PCT	FTM	FTA	PCT	O-RB	D-RB	TOT	AST	PF	DQ	STL	TO	BLK	PTS	RPG	APG	PPG
54-55–Philadelphia	48	–	1387	127	360	.353	–	–	–	98	141	.695	–	–	236	174	141	1	–	–	–	352	4.9	3.6	7.3
55-56–Philadelphia	72	–	1444	126	265	.475	–	–	–	88	139	.633	–	–	264	205	146	7	–	–	–	340	3.7	2.8	4.7
56-57–Philadelphia	71	–	1147	134	302	.444	–	–	–	55	102	.539	–	–	251	136	107	0	–	–	–	323	3.5	1.9	4.5
57-58–Philadelphia	67	–	1048	112	311	.360	–	–	–	70	105	.667	–	–	214	128	113	0	–	–	–	294	3.2	1.9	4.4
58-59–Phil.-Syr.	57	–	694	92	215	.428	–	–	–	81	106	.764	–	–	160	68	95	0	–	–	–	265	2.8	1.2	4.6
Reg. Season Totals	315	–	5720	591	1453	.407	–	–	–	392	593	.661	–	–	1125	711	602	8	–	–	–	1574	3.6	2.3	5.0
Playoff Totals	25	–	339	38	87	.437	–	–	–	29	49	.592	–	–	64	35	35	0	–	–	–	105	2.6	1.4	4.2

Dennard, Kenneth Stephen (Kenny) b. October 18, 1958 Ht. 6-8 Wt. 220 College: Duke

SEASON–TEAM	G	GS	MIN	FGM	FGA	PCT	3FGM	3FGA	PCT	FTM	FTA	PCT	O-RB	D-RB	TOT	AST	PF	DQ	STL	TO	BLK	PTS	RPG	APG	PPG
81-82–Kansas City	30	3	607	62	121	.512	0	0	–	26	40	.650	47	86	133	42	81	0	35	35	8	150	4.4	1.4	5.0
82-83–Kansas City	22	0	224	11	34	.324	0	0	–	6	9	.667	20	32	52	6	27	0	16	5	1	28	2.4	0.3	1.3
83-84–Denver	43	0	413	36	99	.364	3	10	.300	15	24	.625	37	64	101	45	83	0	23	29	8	90	2.3	1.0	2.1
Reg. Season Totals	95	3	1244	109	254	.429	3	10	.300	47	73	.644	104	182	286	93	191	0	74	69	17	268	3.0	1.0	2.8

Denning, Blaine b. September 19, 1930 Ht. 6-2 Wt. 175 College: Lawrence Tech

SEASON–TEAM	G	GS	MIN	FGM	FGA	PCT	3FGM	3FGA	PCT	FTM	FTA	PCT	O-RB	D-RB	TOT	AST	PF	DQ	STL	TO	BLK	PTS	RPG	APG	PPG
52-53–Baltimore	1	–	9	2	5	.400	–	–	–	1	1	1.000	–	–	4	0	3	0	–	–	–	5	4.0	0.0	5.0
Reg. Season Totals	1	–	9	2	5	.400	–	–	–	1	1	1.000	–	–	4	0	3	0	–	–	–	5	4.0	0.0	5.0

Denton, Randall Drew (Randy) b. February 18, 1949 Ht. 6-10 Wt. 245 College: Duke

SEASON–TEAM	G	GS	MIN	FGM	FGA	PCT	3FGM	3FGA	PCT	FTM	FTA	PCT	O-RB	D-RB	TOT	AST	PF	DQ	STL	TO	BLK	PTS	RPG	APG	PPG
71-72–Car.-Mem. (A)	81	–	2039	430	935	.460	0	2	.000	135	168	.804	–	–	740	66	180	–	–	111	–	995	9.1	0.8	12.3
72-73–Memphis (A)	66	–	2205	472	979	.482	3	8	.375	177	237	.747	276	544	820	98	197	2	–	124	–	1124	12.4	1.5	17.0
73-74–Memphis (A)	79	–	2218	447	902	.496	0	3	.000	156	197	.792	255	522	777	152	225	–	55	164	35	1050	9.8	1.9	13.3
74-75–Utah (A)	75	–	1482	300	597	.503	0	0	–	92	120	.767	154	319	473	90	176	–	29	99	43	692	6.3	1.2	9.2
75-76–Utah-St. L.(A)	67	–	1540	283	634	.446	0	1	.000	83	99	.838	156	363	519	89	180	–	37	83	32	649	7.7	1.3	9.7
76-77–Atlanta	45	–	700	103	256	.402	–	–	–	33	47	.702	81	137	218	33	100	1	14	–	16	239	4.8	0.7	5.3
Reg. NBA Totals	45	–	700	103	256	.402	–	–	–	33	47	.702	81	137	218	33	100	1	14	–	16	239	4.8	0.7	5.3
Reg. ABA Totals	368	–	9484	1932	4047	.477	3	14	.214	643	821	.783	841	1748	3329	495	958	2	121	581	110	4510	9.0	1.3	12.3
ABA Playoff Totals	6	–	236	49	92	.533	0	0	–	15	22	.682	28	52	80	11	18	0	4	15	2	113	13.3	1.8	18.8

DePre, Joe b. December 19, 1947 Ht. 6-3 Wt. 190 College: St. John's (N.Y.)

SEASON–TEAM	G	GS	MIN	FGM	FGA	PCT	3FGM	3FGA	PCT	FTM	FTA	PCT	O-RB	D-RB	TOT	AST	PF	DQ	STL	TO	BLK	PTS	RPG	APG	PPG
70-71–New York (A)	72	–	1707	250	488	.512	0	4	.000	132	172	.767	–	–	175	138	262	–	–	–	–	632	2.4	1.9	8.8
71-72–New York (A)	46	–	562	79	201	.393	2	6	.333	34	54	.630	–	–	49	45	80	–	–	66	–	194	1.1	1.0	4.2
72-73–New York (A)	1	–	12	2	5	.400	0	0	–	0	0	–	2	–	2	2	1	0	–	0	–	4	2.0	2.0	4.0
Reg. ABA Totals	119	–	2281	331	694	.477	2	10	.200	166	226	.735	2	–	226	185	343	0	–	66	–	830	1.9	1.6	7.0
ABA Playoff Totals	20	–	245	34	79	.430	1	3	.333	19	27	.704	–	–	26	19	45	0	–	6	–	88	1.3	1.0	4.4

Derline, Rodney G. (Rod) b. March 11, 1952 Ht. 6-0 Wt. 175 College: Seattle

SEASON–TEAM	G	GS	MIN	FGM	FGA	PCT	3FGM	3FGA	PCT	FTM	FTA	PCT	O-RB	D-RB	TOT	AST	PF	DQ	STL	TO	BLK	PTS	RPG	APG	PPG
74-75–Seattle	58	–	666	142	332	.428	–	–	–	43	56	.768	12	47	59	45	47	0	23	–	4	327	1.0	0.8	5.6
75-76–Seattle	49	–	339	73	181	.403	–	–	–	45	56	.804	8	19	27	26	22	0	11	–	1	191	0.6	0.5	3.9
Reg. Season Totals	107	–	1005	215	513	.419	–	–	–	88	112	.786	20	66	86	71	69	0	34	–	5	518	0.8	0.7	4.8
Playoff Totals	10	–	105	20	43	.465	–	–	–	8	9	.889	2	15	17	8	10	0	3	–	0	48	1.7	0.8	4.8

Deutsch, David (Dave) b. May 13, 1945 Ht. 6-1 Wt. 170 College: Rochester

SEASON–TEAM	G	GS	MIN	FGM	FGA	PCT	3FGM	3FGA	PCT	FTM	FTA	PCT	O-RB	D-RB	TOT	AST	PF	DQ	STL	TO	BLK	PTS	RPG	APG	PPG
66-67–New York	19	–	93	6	36	.167	–	–	–	9	20	.450	–	–	21	15	17	0	–	–	–	21	1.1	0.8	1.1
Reg. Season Totals	19	–	93	6	36	.167	–	–	–	9	20	.450	–	–	21	15	17	0	–	–	–	21	1.1	0.8	1.1
Playoff Totals	1	–	7	1	5	.200	–	–	–	0	0	–	–	–	3	1	0	0	–	–	–	2	3.0	1.0	2.0

Devlin, Walter James (Corky) b. December 21, 1931 d. April 28, 1995 Ht. 6-5 Wt. 195 College: George Washington

SEASON–TEAM	G	GS	MIN	FGM	FGA	PCT	3FGM	3FGA	PCT	FTM	FTA	PCT	O-RB	D-RB	TOT	AST	PF	DQ	STL	TO	BLK	PTS	RPG	APG	PPG
55-56–Fort Wayne	69	–	1535	200	541	.370	–	–	–	146	192	.760	–	–	171	138	119	0	–	–	–	546	2.5	2.0	7.9
56-57–Fort Wayne	71	–	1242	190	502	.378	–	–	–	97	143	.678	–	–	146	141	114	0	–	–	–	477	2.1	2.0	6.7
57-58–Minneapolis	70	–	1248	170	489	.348	–	–	–	133	172	.773	–	–	132	167	104	1	–	–	–	473	1.9	2.4	6.8
Reg. Season Totals	210	–	4025	560	1532	.366	–	–	–	376	507	.742	–	–	449	446	337	1	–	–	–	1496	2.1	2.1	7.1
Playoff Totals	11	–	300	47	109	.431	–	–	–	16	26	.615	–	–	26	28	26	0	–	–	–	110	2.4	2.5	10.0

DeZonie, Henry E. (Hank) b. February 12, 1922 Ht. 6-6 Wt. 215 College: Clark (Ga.)

SEASON–TEAM	G	GS	MIN	FGM	FGA	PCT	3FGM	3FGA	PCT	FTM	FTA	PCT	O-RB	D-RB	TOT	AST	PF	DQ	STL	TO	BLK	PTS	RPG	APG	PPG
48-49–Dayton (N)	18	–	–	90	–	–	–	–	–	44	59	.746	–	–	–	–	–	–	–	–	–	224	–	–	12.4
50-51–Tri-Cities	5	–	–	6	25	.240	–	–	–	5	7	.714	–	–	18	9	6	0	–	–	–	17	3.6	1.8	3.4
Reg. NBA Totals	5	–	–	6	25	.240	–	–	–	5	7	.714	–	–	18	9	6	0	–	–	–	17	3.6	1.8	3.4
Reg. NBL Totals	18	–	–	90	–	–	–	–	–	44	59	.746	–	–	–	–	–	–	–	–	–	224	–	–	12.4

Dial, Derrick Jonathon b. December 20, 1975 Ht. 6-4 Wt. 184 College: Eastern Michigan

SEASON–TEAM	G	GS	MIN	FGM	FGA	PCT	3FGM	3FGA	PCT	FTM	FTA	PCT	O-RB	D-RB	TOT	AST	PF	DQ	STL	TO	BLK	PTS	RPG	APG	PPG
99-00–San Antonio	8	0	95	17	46	.370	3	12	.250	3	5	.600	14	12	26	5	10	0	1	6	1	40	3.3	0.6	5.0
Reg. Season Totals	8	0	95	17	46	.370	3	12	.250	3	5	.600	14	12	26	5	10	0	1	6	1	40	3.3	0.6	5.0
Playoff Totals	2	0	8	2	4	.500	0	0	–	1	2	.500	2	0	2	–	1	0	0	0	0	5	1.0	0.0	2.5

Dickerson, Henry b. November 27, 1951 Ht. 6-4 Wt. 190 College: Charleston (W. Va)

SEASON–TEAM	G	GS	MIN	FGM	FGA	PCT	3FGM	3FGA	PCT	FTM	FTA	PCT	O-RB	D-RB	TOT	AST	PF	DQ	STL	TO	BLK	PTS	RPG	APG	PPG
75-76–Detroit	17	–	112	9	29	.310	–	–	–	10	16	.625	3	0	3	8	17	1	2	–	1	28	0.2	0.5	1.6
76-77–Atlanta	6	–	63	6	12	.500	–	–	–	5	8	.625	0	2	2	11	13	0	1	–	0	17	0.3	1.8	2.8
Reg. Season Totals	23	–	175	15	41	.366	–	–	–	15	24	.625	3	2	5	19	30	1	3	–	1	45	0.2	0.8	2.0
Playoff Totals	5	–	15	4	9	.444	–	–	–	1	2	.500	4	0	4	3	1	0	1	–	0	9	0.8	0.6	1.8

Dickerson, Michael b. June 25, 1975 Ht. 6-5 Wt. 190 College: Arizona

SEASON–TEAM	G	GS	MIN	FGM	FGA	PCT	3FGM	3FGA	PCT	FTM	FTA	PCT	O-RB	D-RB	TOT	AST	PF	DQ	STL	TO	BLK	PTS	RPG	APG	PPG
98-99–Houston	50	50	1558	215	462	.465	71	164	.433	46	72	.639	26	57	83	95	90	0	27	66	11	547	1.7	1.9	10.9
99-00–Vancouver	82	82	3103	554	1270	.436	119	291	.409	269	324	.830	78	201	279	208	226	0	116	165	45	1496	3.4	2.5	18.2
Reg. Season Totals	132	132	4661	769	1732	.444	190	455	.418	315	396	.795	104	258	362	303	316	0	143	231	56	2043	2.7	2.3	15.5
Playoff Totals	4	4	82	6	22	.273	3	8	.375	2	4	.500	2	2	4	3	8	0	2	2	3	17	1.0	0.8	4.3

Dickey, Clyde L. b. December 14, 1951 Ht. 6-3 Wt. 185 College: Cochise (Ariz.) Coll. (J.C.); Boston College; Boise State

SEASON–TEAM	G	GS	MIN	FGM	FGA	PCT	3FGM	3FGA	PCT	FTM	FTA	PCT	O-RB	D-RB	TOT	AST	PF	DQ	STL	TO	BLK	PTS	RPG	APG	PPG
74-75–Utah (A)	57	–	458	66	193	.342	2	15	.133	16	21	.762	12	42	54	46	45	–	14	45	0	150	0.9	0.8	2.6
Reg. ABA Totals	57	–	458	66	193	.342	2	15	.133	16	21	.762	12	42	54	46	45	–	14	45	0	150	0.9	0.8	2.6
ABA Playoff Totals	1	–	4	0	2	.000	0	0	–	0	0	–	0	1	1	0	0	–	0	1	0	0	1.0	0.0	0.0

Dickey, Derrek b. March 20, 1951 Ht. 6-7 Wt. 220 College: Cincinnati

SEASON–TEAM	G	GS	MIN	FGM	FGA	PCT	3FGM	3FGA	PCT	FTM	FTA	PCT	O-RB	D-RB	TOT	AST	PF	DQ	STL	TO	BLK	PTS	RPG	APG	PPG
73-74–Golden State	66	–	930	115	233	.494	–	–	–	51	66	.773	123	216	339	54	112	1	17	–	15	281	5.1	0.8	4.3
74-75–Golden State	80	–	1859	274	569	.482	–	–	–	66	99	.667	190	360	550	125	199	0	52	–	19	614	6.9	1.6	7.7
75-76–Golden State	79	–	1207	220	473	.465	–	–	–	62	79	.785	114	235	349	83	141	1	26	–	11	502	4.4	1.1	6.4
76-77–Golden State	49	–	856	158	345	.458	–	–	–	45	61	.738	100	140	240	63	101	1	20	–	11	361	4.9	1.3	7.4
77-78–G.S.-Chicago	47	–	493	87	198	.439	–	–	–	30	36	.833	36	61	97	21	56	0	14	40	4	204	2.1	0.4	4.3
Reg. Season Totals	321	–	5345	854	1818	.470	–	–	–	254	341	.745	563	1012	1575	346	609	3	129	40	60	1962	4.9	1.1	6.1
Playoff Totals	27	–	430	78	140	.557	–	–	–	23	33	.697	38	77	115	17	55	1	10	–	1	179	4.3	0.6	6.6

Dickey, Richard Lea (Dick) b. October 26, 1926 Ht. 6-1 Wt. 175 College: North Carolina State; DePauw; St. Mary's (Calif.)

SEASON–TEAM	G	GS	MIN	FGM	FGA	PCT	3FGM	3FGA	PCT	FTM	FTA	PCT	O-RB	D-RB	TOT	AST	PF	DQ	STL	TO	BLK	PTS	RPG	APG	PPG
51-52–Boston	45	–	440	40	136	.294	–	–	–	47	69	.681	–	–	81	50	79	2	–	–	–	127	1.8	1.1	2.8
Reg. Season Totals	45	–	440	40	136	.294	–	–	–	47	69	.681	–	–	81	50	79	2	–	–	–	127	1.8	1.1	2.8
Playoff Totals	3	–	31	1	8	.125	–	–	–	6	7	.857	–	–	3	5	7	0	–	–	–	8	1.0	1.7	2.7

Dickson, John b. November 18, 1945 Ht. 6-10 Wt. 240 College: Arkansas State

SEASON–TEAM	G	GS	MIN	FGM	FGA	PCT	3FGM	3FGA	PCT	FTM	FTA	PCT	O-RB	D-RB	TOT	AST	PF	DQ	STL	TO	BLK	PTS	RPG	APG	PPG
67-68–New Orleans (A)	21	–	100	14	39	.359	0	0	–	8	13	.615	–	–	33	3	11	0	–	10	–	36	1.6	0.1	1.7
Reg. ABA Totals	21	–	100	14	39	.359	0	0	–	8	13	.615	–	–	33	3	11	0	–	10	–	36	1.6	0.1	1.7
ABA Playoff Totals	1	–	3	0	4	.000	0	0	–	0	0	–	–	–	2	0	0	0	–	1	–	0	2.0	0.0	0.0

Dierking, Conrad William (Connie) b. October 2, 1936 Ht. 6-10 Wt. 230 College: Cincinnati

SEASON–TEAM	G	GS	MIN	FGM	FGA	PCT	3FGM	3FGA	PCT	FTM	FTA	PCT	O-RB	D-RB	TOT	AST	PF	DQ	STL	TO	BLK	PTS	RPG	APG	PPG
58-59–Syracuse	64	–	726	105	290	.362	–	–	–	83	140	.593	–	–	233	34	148	2	–	–	–	293	3.6	0.5	4.6
59-60–Syracuse	71	–	1119	192	526	.365	–	–	–	108	188	.574	–	–	456	54	168	4	–	–	–	492	6.4	0.8	6.9
63-64–Philadelphia	76	–	1286	191	514	.372	–	–	–	114	169	.675	–	–	422	50	221	3	–	–	–	496	5.6	0.7	6.5
64-65–Phil.-S.F.	68	–	1294	218	538	.405	–	–	–	100	168	.595	–	–	435	72	165	4	–	–	–	536	6.4	1.1	7.9
65-66–Cincinnati	57	–	782	134	322	.416	–	–	–	50	82	.610	–	–	245	43	113	0	–	–	–	318	4.3	0.8	5.6
66-67–Cincinnati	77	–	1905	291	729	.399	–	–	–	134	180	.744	–	–	603	158	251	7	–	–	–	716	7.8	2.1	9.3
67-68–Cincinnati	81	–	2637	544	1164	.467	–	–	–	237	310	.765	–	–	766	191	315	6	–	–	–	1325	9.5	2.4	16.4
68-69–Cincinnati	82	–	2540	546	1232	.443	–	–	–	243	319	.762	–	–	739	222	305	9	–	–	–	1335	9.0	2.7	16.3
69-70–Cincinnati	76	–	2448	521	1243	.419	–	–	–	230	306	.752	–	–	624	169	275	7	–	–	–	1272	8.2	2.2	16.7
70-71–Cin.-Phil.	54	–	737	125	322	.388	–	–	–	61	89	.685	–	–	234	60	114	1	–	–	–	311	4.3	1.1	5.8
Reg. Season Totals	706	–	15474	2867	6880	.417	–	–	–	1360	1951	.697	–	–	4757	1053	2075	43	–	–	–	7094	6.7	1.5	10.0
Playoff Totals	20	–	352	63	158	.399	–	–	–	27	35	.771	–	–	129	23	45	0	–	–	–	153	6.5	1.2	7.7

Dietrick, Coby Joseph b. July 23, 1948 Ht. 6-11 Wt. 230 College: San Jose State

SEASON–TEAM	G	GS	MIN	FGM	FGA	PCT	3FGM	3FGA	PCT	FTM	FTA	PCT	O-RB	D-RB	TOT	AST	PF	DQ	STL	TO	BLK	PTS	RPG	APG	PPG
70-71–Memphis (A)	37	–	357	61	160	.381	0	1	.000	21	34	.618	–	–	114	33	56	–	–	–	–	143	3.1	0.9	3.9
71-72–Memphis (A)	1	–	9	1	2	.500	0	0	–	0	2	.000	–	–	7	1	1	–	–	1	–	2	7.0	1.0	2.0
72-73–Dallas (A)	77	–	1347	205	489	.419	0	0	–	96	139	.691	133	244	377	136	224	5	–	93	88	506	4.9	1.8	6.6
73-74–San Antonio (A)	84	–	2142	251	569	.441	0	3	.000	81	114	.711	200	332	532	253	285	–	89	151	50	583	6.3	3.0	6.9
74-75–San Antonio (A)	82	–	1724	222	444	.500	2	4	.500	76	99	.768	191	333	524	168	266	–	82	117	55	522	6.4	2.0	6.4
75-76–San Antonio (A)	81	–	1467	200	403	.496	1	7	.143	68	82	.829	109	240	349	159	257	–	67	112	43	469	4.3	2.0	5.8
76-77–San Antonio	82	–	1772	285	620	.460	–	–	–	119	166	.717	111	261	372	148	267	8	88	–	57	689	4.5	1.8	8.4
77-78–San Antonio	79	–	1876	250	543	.460	–	–	–	89	114	.781	73	285	358	217	231	4	81	144	55	589	4.5	2.7	7.5
78-79–San Antonio	76	–	1487	209	400	.523	–	–	–	79	99	.798	88	227	315	198	206	7	72	92	38	497	4.1	2.6	6.5
79-80–Chicago	79	–	1830	227	500	.454	1	9	.111	90	118	.763	101	262	363	216	230	2	89	112	51	545	4.6	2.7	6.9
80-81–Chicago	82	–	1243	146	320	.456	2	6	.333	77	111	.694	79	186	265	118	176	1	48	88	53	371	3.2	1.4	4.5
81-82–Chicago	74	0	999	92	200	.460	0	1	.000	38	54	.704	63	125	188	87	131	1	49	44	30	222	2.5	1.2	3.0
82-83–San Antonio	8	0	34	1	5	.200	0	0	–	0	2	.000	2	6	8	6	6	0	1	1	0	2	1.0	0.8	0.3
Reg. NBA Totals	480	0	9241	1210	2588	.468	3	16	.188	492	664	.741	517	1352	1869	990	1247	23	428	481	284	2915	3.9	2.1	6.1
Reg. ABA Totals	362	–	7046	940	2067	.455	3	15	.200	342	470	.728	633	1149	1903	750	1089	5	238	474	236	2225	5.3	2.1	6.1
NBA Playoff Totals	28	0	522	73	164	.445	0	3	.000	10	20	.500	41	73	114	39	82	1	20	29	11	156	4.1	1.4	5.6
ABA Playoff Totals	22	–	534	71	133	.534	0	4	.000	27	38	.711	35	73	111	47	71	0	15	38	20	169	5.0	2.1	7.7

D

DiGregorio, Ernest (Ernie, Ernie D.) b. January 15, 1951 Ht. 6-0 Wt. 180 College: Providence

SEASON–TEAM	G	GS	MIN	FGM	FGA	PCT	3FGM	3FGA	PCT	FTM	FTA	PCT	O-RB	D-RB	TOT	AST	PF	DQ	STL	TO	BLK	PTS	RPG	APG	PPG
73-74–Buffalo	81	–	2910	530	1260	.421	–	–	–	174	193	.902	48	171	219	663	242	2	59	–	9	1234	2.7	8.2	15.2
74-75–Buffalo	31	–	712	103	234	.440	–	–	–	35	45	.778	6	39	45	151	62	0	19	–	0	241	1.5	4.9	7.8
75-76–Buffalo	67	–	1364	182	474	.384	–	–	–	86	94	.915	15	97	112	265	158	1	37	–	1	450	1.7	4.0	6.7
76-77–Buffalo	81	–	2267	365	875	.417	–	–	–	138	146	.945	52	132	184	378	150	1	57	–	3	868	2.3	4.7	10.7
77-78–L.A.-Boston	52	–	606	88	209	.421	–	–	–	28	33	.848	7	43	50	137	44	0	18	93	1	204	1.0	2.6	3.9
Reg. Season Totals	312	–	7859	1268	3052	.415	–	–	–	461	511	.902	128	482	610	1594	656	4	190	93	14	2997	2.0	5.1	9.6
Playoff Totals	15	–	457	67	148	.453	–	–	–	16	17	.941	4	25	29	97	43	2	6	–	2	150	1.9	6.5	10.0

Dill, Craig H. b. December 17, 1944 Ht. 6-11 Wt. 220 College: Michigan

SEASON–TEAM	G	GS	MIN	FGM	FGA	PCT	3FGM	3FGA	PCT	FTM	FTA	PCT	O-RB	D-RB	TOT	AST	PF	DQ	STL	TO	BLK	PTS	RPG	APG	PPG
67-68–Pittsburgh (A)	65	–	1354	187	488	.383	0	3	.000	71	106	.670	–	–	378	31	164	3	–	64	–	445	5.8	0.5	6.8
Reg. ABA Totals	65	–	1354	187	488	.383	0	3	.000	71	106	.670	–	–	378	31	164	3	–	64	–	445	5.8	0.5	6.8
ABA Playoff Totals	6	–	15	3	8	.375	0	0	–	1	1	1.000	–	–	6	2	5	0	–	3	–	7	1.0	0.3	1.2

Dillard, Dave College: None

SEASON–TEAM	G	GS	MIN	FGM	FGA	PCT	3FGM	3FGA	PCT	FTM	FTA	PCT	O-RB	D-RB	TOT	AST	PF	DQ	STL	TO	BLK	PTS	RPG	APG	PPG
75-76–Utah (A)	3	–	19	1	3	.333	0	0	–	2	2	1.000	2	7	9	2	7	–	2	5	2	4	3.0	0.7	1.3
Reg. ABA Totals	3	–	19	1	3	.333	0	0	–	2	2	1.000	2	7	9	2	7	–	2	5	2	4	3.0	0.7	1.3

Dillard, Mickey Anthony b. October 15, 1958 Ht. 6-3 Wt. 170 College: Florida State

SEASON–TEAM	G	GS	MIN	FGM	FGA	PCT	3FGM	3FGA	PCT	FTM	FTA	PCT	O-RB	D-RB	TOT	AST	PF	DQ	STL	TO	BLK	PTS	RPG	APG	PPG
81-82–Cleveland	33	0	221	29	79	.367	0	4	.000	15	23	.652	6	9	15	34	40	0	8	17	2	73	0.5	1.0	2.2
Reg. Season Totals	33	0	221	29	79	.367	0	4	.000	15	23	.652	6	9	15	34	40	0	8	17	2	73	0.5	1.0	2.2

Dille, Robert Orville (Bob, Oscar) b. July 2, 1917 Ht. 6-3 Wt. 200 College: Valparaiso

SEASON–TEAM	G	GS	MIN	FGM	FGA	PCT	3FGM	3FGA	PCT	FTM	FTA	PCT	O-RB	D-RB	TOT	AST	PF	DQ	STL	TO	BLK	PTS	RPG	APG	PPG
40-41–Hammond (N)	3	–	–	8	–	–	–	–	–	3	–	–	–	–	–	–	–	–	–	–	–	19	–	–	6.3
46-47–Detroit	57	–	–	111	563	.197	–	–	–	74	111	.667	–	–	–	40	92	–	–	–	–	296	–	0.7	5.2
Reg. NBA Totals	57	–	–	111	563	.197	–	–	–	74	111	.667	–	–	–	40	92	–	–	–	–	296	–	0.7	5.2
Reg. NBL Totals	3	–	–	8	–	–	–	–	–	3	–	–	–	–	–	–	–	–	–	–	–	19	–	–	6.3

Dillon, John Turley (Hooks) b. January 8, 1924 Ht. 6-3 Wt. 180 College: Kentucky; North Carolina

SEASON–TEAM	G	GS	MIN	FGM	FGA	PCT	3FGM	3FGA	PCT	FTM	FTA	PCT	O-RB	D-RB	TOT	AST	PF	DQ	STL	TO	BLK	PTS	RPG	APG	PPG
49-50–Washington	22	–	–	10	55	.182	–	–	–	16	22	.727	–	–	–	5	19	–	–	–	–	36	–	0.2	1.6
Reg. Season Totals	22	–	–	10	55	.182	–	–	–	16	22	.727	–	–	–	5	19	–	–	–	–	36	–	0.2	1.6
Playoff Totals	1	–	–	1	1	1.000	–	–	–	2	2	1.000	–	–	–	–	2	–	–	–	–	4	–	0.0	4.0

Dinkins, Byron Stewart b. June 15, 1967 Ht. 6-2 Wt. 170 College: North Carolina-Charlotte

SEASON–TEAM	G	GS	MIN	FGM	FGA	PCT	3FGM	3FGA	PCT	FTM	FTA	PCT	O-RB	D-RB	TOT	AST	PF	DQ	STL	TO	BLK	PTS	RPG	APG	PPG
89-90–Houston	33	0	362	44	109	.404	1	9	.111	26	30	.867	13	27	40	75	30	0	19	37	2	115	1.2	2.3	3.5
90-91–S.A.-Indiana	12	0	149	14	34	.412	0	0	–	8	9	.889	0	12	12	19	15	0	2	13	0	36	1.0	1.6	3.0
Reg. Season Totals	45	0	511	58	143	.406	1	9	.111	34	39	.872	13	39	52	94	45	0	21	50	2	151	1.2	2.1	3.4

Dinkins, Jackie b. January 22, 1950 d. March 1983 Ht. 6-5 Wt. 210 College: Voorhees

SEASON–TEAM	G	GS	MIN	FGM	FGA	PCT	3FGM	3FGA	PCT	FTM	FTA	PCT	O-RB	D-RB	TOT	AST	PF	DQ	STL	TO	BLK	PTS	RPG	APG	PPG
71-72–Chicago	18	–	89	17	41	.415	–	–	–	11	20	.550	–	–	20	7	10	0	–	–	–	45	1.1	0.4	2.5
Reg. Season Totals	18	–	89	17	41	.415	–	–	–	11	20	.550	–	–	20	7	10	0	–	–	–	45	1.1	0.4	2.5
Playoff Totals	1	–	1	1	1	1.000	–	–	–	0	0	–	–	–	0	–	0	0	–	–	–	2	0.0	0.0	2.0

Dinnel, Harry b. 1941 Ht. 6-4 Wt. 200 College: Pepperdine

SEASON–TEAM	G	GS	MIN	FGM	FGA	PCT	3FGM	3FGA	PCT	FTM	FTA	PCT	O-RB	D-RB	TOT	AST	PF	DQ	STL	TO	BLK	PTS	RPG	APG	PPG
67-68–Anaheim (A)	11	–	87	6	19	.316	0	0	–	7	8	.875	–	–	23	5	14	0	–	8	–	19	2.1	0.5	1.7
Reg. ABA Totals	11	–	87	6	19	.316	0	0	–	7	8	.875	–	–	23	5	14	0	–	8	–	19	2.1	0.5	1.7

Dinwiddie, William E. (Bill, Diamond Bill) b. July 15, 1943 Ht. 6-7 Wt. 220 College: New Mexico Highlands

SEASON–TEAM	G	GS	MIN	FGM	FGA	PCT	3FGM	3FGA	PCT	FTM	FTA	PCT	O-RB	D-RB	TOT	AST	PF	DQ	STL	TO	BLK	PTS	RPG	APG	PPG
67-68–Cincinnati	67	–	871	141	358	.394	–	–	–	62	102	.608	–	–	237	31	122	2	–	–	–	344	3.5	0.5	5.1
68-69–Cincinnati	69	–	1028	124	352	.352	–	–	–	45	87	.517	–	–	242	55	146	0	–	–	–	293	3.5	0.8	4.2
70-71–Boston	61	–	717	123	328	.375	–	–	–	54	74	.730	–	–	209	34	90	1	–	–	–	300	3.4	0.6	4.9
71-72–Milwaukee	23	–	144	16	57	.281	–	–	–	5	9	.556	–	–	32	9	23	0	–	–	–	37	1.4	0.4	1.6
Reg. Season Totals	220	–	2760	404	1095	.369	–	–	–	166	272	.610	–	–	720	129	381	3	–	–	–	974	3.3	0.6	4.4

Dischinger, Terry Gilbert b. November 21, 1940 Ht. 6-7 Wt. 200 College: Purdue

SEASON–TEAM	G	GS	MIN	FGM	FGA	PCT	3FGM	3FGA	PCT	FTM	FTA	PCT	O-RB	D-RB	TOT	AST	PF	DQ	STL	TO	BLK	PTS	RPG	APG	PPG
62-63–Chicago	57	–	2294	525	1026	.512	–	–	–	402	522	.770	–	–	458	175	188	2	–	–	–	1452	8.0	3.1	25.5
63-64–Baltimore	80	–	2816	604	1217	.496	–	–	–	454	585	.776	–	–	667	157	321	10	–	–	–	1662	8.3	2.0	20.8
64-65–Detroit	80	–	2698	568	1153	.493	–	–	–	320	424	.755	–	–	479	198	253	5	–	–	–	1456	6.0	2.5	18.2
67-68–Detroit	78	–	1936	394	797	.494	–	–	–	237	311	.762	–	–	483	114	247	6	–	–	–	1025	6.2	1.5	13.1
68-69–Detroit	75	–	1456	264	513	.515	–	–	–	130	178	.730	–	–	323	93	230	5	–	–	–	658	4.3	1.2	8.8
69-70–Detroit	75	–	1754	342	650	.526	–	–	–	174	241	.722	–	–	369	106	213	5	–	–	–	858	4.9	1.4	11.4
70-71–Detroit	65	–	1855	304	568	.535	–	–	–	161	211	.763	–	–	339	113	189	2	–	–	–	769	5.2	1.7	11.8
71-72–Detroit	79	–	2062	295	574	.514	–	–	–	156	200	.780	–	–	338	92	289	7	–	–	–	746	4.3	1.2	9.4
72-73–Portland	63	–	970	161	338	.476	–	–	–	64	96	.667	–	–	190	103	125	1	–	–	–	386	3.0	1.6	6.1
Reg. Season Totals	652	–	17841	3457	6836	.506	–	–	–	2098	2768	.758	–	–	3646	1151	2055	43	–	–	–	9012	5.6	1.8	13.8
Playoff Totals	6	–	154	21	56	.375	–	–	–	14	19	.737	–	–	29	9	19	0	–	–	–	56	4.8	1.5	9.3
All-Star Totals	3	–	44	7	15	.467	–	–	–	5	6	.833	–	–	8	2	5	0	–	–	–	19	2.7	0.7	6.3

Diute, Fred Homer b. January 9, 1929 Ht. 6-3 Wt. 210 College: St. Bonaventure

SEASON–TEAM	G	GS	MIN	FGM	FGA	PCT	3FGM	3FGA	PCT	FTM	FTA	PCT	O-RB	D-RB	TOT	AST	PF	DQ	STL	TO	BLK	PTS	RPG	APG	PPG
54-55–Milwaukee	7	–	72	2	21	.095	–	–	–	7	12	.583	–	–	13	4	12	0	–	–	–	11	1.9	0.6	1.6
Reg. Season Totals	7	–	72	2	21	.095	–	–	–	7	12	.583	–	–	13	4	12	0	–	–	–	11	1.9	0.6	1.6

Divac, Vlade b. February 3, 1968 Ht. 7-1 Wt. 260 Country: Serbia

SEASON–TEAM	G	GS	MIN	FGM	FGA	PCT	3FGM	3FGA	PCT	FTM	FTA	PCT	O-RB	D-RB	TOT	AST	PF	DQ	STL	TO	BLK	PTS	RPG	APG	PPG
89-90–L.A. Lakers	82	5	1611	274	549	.499	0	5	.000	153	216	.708	167	345	512	75	240	2	79	110	114	701	6.2	0.9	8.5
90-91–L.A. Lakers	82	81	2310	360	637	.565	5	14	.357	196	279	.703	205	461	666	92	247	3	106	146	127	921	8.1	1.1	11.2
91-92–L.A. Lakers	36	18	979	157	317	.495	5	19	.263	86	112	.768	87	160	247	60	114	3	55	88	35	405	6.9	1.7	11.3
92-93–L.A. Lakers	82	69	2525	397	819	.485	21	75	.280	235	341	.689	220	509	729	232	311	7	128	214	140	1050	8.9	2.8	12.8
93-94–L.A. Lakers	79	73	2685	453	895	.506	9	47	.191	208	303	.686	282	569	851	307	288	5	92	191	112	1123	10.8	3.9	14.2
94-95–L.A. Lakers	80	80	2807	485	957	.507	10	53	.189	297	382	.777	261	568	829	329	305	8	109	205	174	1277	10.4	4.1	16.0
95-96–L.A. Lakers	79	79	2470	414	807	.513	3	18	.167	189	295	.641	198	481	679	261	274	5	76	199	131	1020	8.6	3.3	12.9
96-97–Charlotte	81	80	2840	418	847	.494	11	47	.234	177	259	.683	241	484	725	301	277	6	103	193	180	1024	9.0	3.7	12.6
97-98–Charlotte	64	41	1805	267	536	.498	3	14	.214	130	188	.691	183	335	518	172	179	1	83	114	94	667	8.1	2.7	10.4
98-99–Sacramento	50	50	1761	262	557	.470	11	43	.256	179	255	.702	140	361	501	215	166	2	44	131	51	714	10.0	4.3	14.3
99-00–Sacramento	82	81	2374	384	764	.503	7	26	.269	230	333	.691	174	482	656	244	251	2	103	190	103	1005	8.0	3.0	12.3
Reg. Season Totals	797	657	24167	3871	7685	.504	85	361	.235	2080	2963	.702	2158	4755	6913	2288	2652	44	978	1781	1261	9907	8.7	2.9	12.4
Playoff Totals	73	65	2416	361	735	.491	10	44	.227	218	299	.729	189	380	569	191	269	7	79	175	117	950	7.8	2.6	13.0

Djordjevic, Aleksandar b. August 26, 1967 Ht. 6-2 Wt. 198 Country: Yugoslavia

SEASON–TEAM	G	GS	MIN	FGM	FGA	PCT	3FGM	3FGA	PCT	FTM	FTA	PCT	O-RB	D-RB	TOT	AST	PF	DQ	STL	TO	BLK	PTS	RPG	APG	PPG
96-97–Portland	8	0	61	8	16	.500	5	7	.714	4	5	.800	1	4	5	5	3	0	0	5	0	25	0.6	0.6	3.1
Reg. Season Totals	8	0	61	8	16	.500	5	7	.714	4	5	.800	1	4	5	5	3	0	0	5	0	25	0.6	0.6	3.1

Dodd, Glenn Earl (Earl) b. November 1, 1924 Ht. 6-5 Wt. 175 College: Northeast Missouri State

SEASON–TEAM	G	GS	MIN	FGM	FGA	PCT	3FGM	3FGA	PCT	FTM	FTA	PCT	O-RB	D-RB	TOT	AST	PF	DQ	STL	TO	BLK	PTS	RPG	APG	PPG
49-50–Denver	9	–	–	6	27	.222	–	–	–	3	5	.600	–	–	–	6	13	–	–	–	–	15	–	0.7	1.7
Reg. Season Totals	9	–	–	6	27	.222	–	–	–	3	5	.600	–	–	–	6	13	–	–	–	–	15	–	0.7	1.7

Doleac, Michael Scott b. June 15, 1977 Ht. 6-11 Wt. 262 College: Utah

SEASON–TEAM	G	GS	MIN	FGM	FGA	PCT	3FGM	3FGA	PCT	FTM	FTA	PCT	O-RB	D-RB	TOT	AST	PF	DQ	STL	TO	BLK	PTS	RPG	APG	PPG
98-99–Orlando	49	0	780	125	267	.468	0	0	–	54	80	.675	66	82	148	20	117	1	19	26	17	304	3.0	0.4	6.2
99-00–Orlando	81	29	1335	242	535	.452	1	2	.500	80	95	.842	89	245	334	63	224	3	29	65	34	565	4.1	0.8	7.0
Reg. Season Totals	130	29	2115	367	802	.458	1	2	.500	134	175	.766	155	327	482	83	341	4	48	91	51	869	3.7	0.6	6.7
Playoff Totals	4	0	43	5	18	.278	0	1	.000	7	9	.778	5	7	12	–	6	0	0	3	1	17	3.0	0.0	4.3

Dolhon, Joseph (Joe) b. July 9, 1927 d. January 5, 1981 Ht. 6-0 Wt. 175 College: New York U.

SEASON–TEAM	G	GS	MIN	FGM	FGA	PCT	3FGM	3FGA	PCT	FTM	FTA	PCT	O-RB	D-RB	TOT	AST	PF	DQ	STL	TO	BLK	PTS	RPG	APG	PPG
49-50–Baltimore	64	–	–	143	458	.312	–	–	–	157	214	.734	–	–	–	155	193	–	–	–	–	443	–	2.4	6.9
50-51–Baltimore	13	–	–	17	56	.304	–	–	–	17	23	.739	–	–	18	19	32	1	–	–	–	51	1.4	1.5	3.9
Reg. Season Totals	77	–	–	160	514	.311	–	–	–	174	237	.734	–	–	18	174	225	1	–	–	–	494	1.4	2.3	6.4

Doll, Robert W. (Bob) b. August 10, 1919 d. September 18, 1959 Ht. 6-5 Wt. 195 College: Colorado

SEASON–TEAM	G	GS	MIN	FGM	FGA	PCT	3FGM	3FGA	PCT	FTM	FTA	PCT	O-RB	D-RB	TOT	AST	PF	DQ	STL	TO	BLK	PTS	RPG	APG	PPG
46-47–St. Louis	60	–	–	194	768	.253	–	–	–	134	206	.650	–	–	–	22	167	–	–	–	–	522	–	0.4	8.7
47-48–St. Louis	42	–	–	174	658	.264	–	–	–	98	148	.662	–	–	–	26	107	–	–	–	–	446	–	0.6	10.6
48-49–Boston	47	–	–	145	438	.331	–	–	–	80	117	.684	–	–	–	117	118	–	–	–	–	370	–	2.5	7.9
48-49–Denver (N)	9	–	–	16	–	–	–	–	–	13	28	.464	–	–	–	–	22	–	–	–	–	45	–	–	5.0
49-50–Boston	47	–	–	120	347	.346	–	–	–	75	114	.658	–	–	–	108	117	–	–	–	–	315	–	2.3	6.7
Reg. NBA Totals	196	–	–	633	2211	.286	–	–	–	387	585	.662	–	–	–	273	509	–	–	–	–	1653	–	1.4	8.4
Reg. NBL Totals	9	–	–	16	–	–	–	–	–	13	28	.464	–	–	–	–	22	–	–	–	–	45	–	–	5.0
NBA Playoff Totals	10	–	–	24	169	.178	–	–	–	22	38	.579	–	–	–	5	29	–	–	–	–	70	–	0.4	7.0

Donaldson, James Lee III (J.D.) b. August 16, 1957 Ht. 7-2 Wt. 275 College: Washington State

SEASON–TEAM	G	GS	MIN	FGM	FGA	PCT	3FGM	3FGA	PCT	FTM	FTA	PCT	O-RB	D-RB	TOT	AST	PF	DQ	STL	TO	BLK	PTS	RPG	APG	PPG
80-81–Seattle	68	–	980	129	238	.542	0	0	–	101	170	.594	107	202	309	42	79	0	8	68	74	359	4.5	0.6	5.3
81-82–Seattle	82	1	1710	255	419	.609	0	0	–	151	240	.629	138	352	490	51	186	2	27	115	139	661	6.0	0.6	8.1
82-83–Seattle	82	11	1789	289	496	.583	0	0	–	150	218	.688	131	370	501	97	171	1	19	132	101	728	6.1	1.2	8.9
83-84–San Diego	82	67	2525	360	604	.596	0	0	–	249	327	.761	165	484	649	90	214	1	40	171	139	969	7.9	1.1	11.8
84-85–L.A. Clippers	82	58	2392	351	551	.637	0	0	–	227	303	.749	168	500	668	48	217	1	28	206	130	929	8.1	0.6	11.3
85-86–LAClips-Dallas	83	78	2682	256	459	.558	0	0	–	204	254	.803	171	624	795	96	189	0	28	123	139	716	9.6	1.2	8.6
86-87–Dallas	82	82	3028	311	531	.586	0	0	–	267	329	.812	295	678	973	63	191	0	51	104	136	889	11.9	0.8	10.8
87-88–Dallas	81	81	2523	212	380	.558	0	0	–	147	189	.778	247	508	755	66	175	2	40	113	104	571	9.3	0.8	7.0
88-89–Dallas	53	53	1746	193	337	.573	0	0	–	95	124	.766	158	412	570	38	111	0	24	83	81	481	10.8	0.7	9.1
89-90–Dallas	73	73	2265	258	479	.539	0	0	–	149	213	.700	155	475	630	57	129	0	22	119	47	665	8.6	0.8	9.1
90-91–Dallas	82	82	2800	327	615	.532	0	0	–	165	229	.721	201	526	727	69	181	0	34	146	93	819	8.9	0.8	10.0
91-92–Dallas-N.Y.	58	32	1075	112	245	.457	0	0	–	61	86	.709	99	190	289	33	103	0	8	48	49	285	5.0	0.6	4.9
92-93–Utah	6	1	94	8	14	.571	0	0	–	5	9	.556	6	23	29	1	13	0	1	4	7	21	4.8	0.2	3.5
94-95–Utah	43	40	613	44	74	.595	0	0	–	22	31	.710	19	88	107	14	66	0	6	22	28	110	2.5	0.3	2.6
Reg. Season Totals	957	659	26222	3105	5442	.571	0	0	–	1993	2722	.732	2060	5432	7492	765	2025	7	336	1454	1267	8203	7.8	0.8	8.6
Playoff Totals	51	38	1379	153	244	.627	0	0	–	95	122	.779	118	282	400	35	111	0	18	59	42	401	7.8	0.7	7.9
All-Star Totals	1	0	8	0	0	–	0	0	–	2	2	1.000	1	5	6	1	2	0	0	0	2	2	6.0	1.0	2.0

Donham, Robert E. (Bob) b. October 11, 1926 d. September 21, 1983 Ht. 6-2 Wt. 190 College: Ohio State

SEASON–TEAM	G	GS	MIN	FGM	FGA	PCT	3FGM	3FGA	PCT	FTM	FTA	PCT	O-RB	D-RB	TOT	AST	PF	DQ	STL	TO	BLK	PTS	RPG	APG	PPG
50-51–Boston	68	–	–	151	298	.507	–	–	–	114	229	.498	–	–	235	139	179	3	–	–	–	416	3.5	2.0	6.1
51-52–Boston	66	–	1980	201	413	.487	–	–	–	149	293	.509	–	–	330	228	223	9	–	–	–	551	5.0	3.5	8.3
52-53–Boston	71	–	1435	169	353	.479	–	–	–	113	240	.471	–	–	239	153	213	8	–	–	–	451	3.4	2.2	6.4
53-54–Boston	68	–	1451	141	315	.448	–	–	–	118	213	.554	–	–	267	186	235	11	–	–	–	400	3.9	2.7	5.9
Reg. Season Totals	273	–	4866	662	1379	.480	–	–	–	494	975	.507	–	–	1071	706	850	31	–	–	–	1818	3.9	2.6	6.7
Playoff Totals	17	–	348	31	79	.392	–	–	–	31	76	.408	–	–	66	38	81	9	–	–	–	93	3.0	2.2	5.5

Donovan, Henry Harry (Harry) b. September 10, 1926 Ht. 6-2 Wt. 190 College: Muhlenberg

SEASON–TEAM	G	GS	MIN	FGM	FGA	PCT	3FGM	3FGA	PCT	FTM	FTA	PCT	O-RB	D-RB	TOT	AST	PF	DQ	STL	TO	BLK	PTS	RPG	APG	PPG
49-50–New York	45	–	–	90	275	.327	–	–	–	73	106	.689	–	–	–	38	107	–	–	–	–	253	–	0.8	5.6
Reg. Season Totals	45	–	–	90	275	.327	–	–	–	73	106	.689	–	–	–	38	107	–	–	–	–	253	–	0.8	5.6
Playoff Totals	3	–	–	0	4	.000	–	–	–	2	2	1.000	–	–	–	–	4	–	–	–	–	2	–	0.0	0.7

Donovan, William John (Billy) b. May 30, 1965 Ht. 5-11 Wt. 171 College: Providence

SEASON–TEAM	G	GS	MIN	FGM	FGA	PCT	3FGM	3FGA	PCT	FTM	FTA	PCT	O-RB	D-RB	TOT	AST	PF	DQ	STL	TO	BLK	PTS	RPG	APG	PPG
87-88–New York	44	0	364	44	109	.404	0	7	.000	17	21	.810	5	20	25	87	33	0	16	42	1	105	0.6	2.0	2.4
Reg. Season Totals	44	0	364	44	109	.404	0	7	.000	17	21	.810	5	20	25	87	33	0	16	42	1	105	0.6	2.0	2.4

Dorsey, Jacky b. December 18, 1954 Ht. 6-7 Wt. 230 College: Georgia

SEASON–TEAM	G	GS	MIN	FGM	FGA	PCT	3FGM	3FGA	PCT	FTM	FTA	PCT	O-RB	D-RB	TOT	AST	PF	DQ	STL	TO	BLK	PTS	RPG	APG	PPG
77-78–Denver-Port.	11	–	88	12	31	.387	–	–	–	10	16	.625	11	19	30	5	17	0	2	6	3	34	2.7	0.5	3.1
78-79–Houston	20	–	108	24	43	.558	–	–	–	8	16	.500	12	11	23	2	25	0	1	8	2	56	1.2	0.1	2.8
80-81–Seattle	29	–	253	20	70	.286	0	0	–	13	25	.520	23	65	88	9	47	0	9	14	1	53	3.0	0.3	1.8
Reg. Season Totals	60	–	449	56	144	.389	0	0	–	31	57	.544	46	95	141	16	89	0	12	28	6	143	2.4	0.3	2.4
Playoff Totals	1	–	1	0	0	–	0	0	–	0	0	–	0	0	0	–	0	0	0	0	0	0	0.0	0.0	0.0

Dorsey, Ron b. October 10, 1948 Ht. 6-4 Wt. 200 College: Tennessee State

SEASON–TEAM	G	GS	MIN	FGM	FGA	PCT	3FGM	3FGA	PCT	FTM	FTA	PCT	O-RB	D-RB	TOT	AST	PF	DQ	STL	TO	BLK	PTS	RPG	APG	PPG
71-72–Carolina (A)	1	–	12	2	8	.250	0	1	.000	0	2	.000	–	–	5	0	2	–	–	1	–	4	5.0	0.0	4.0
Reg. ABA Totals	1	–	12	2	8	.250	0	1	.000	0	2	.000	–	–	5	0	2	–	–	1	–	4	5.0	0.0	4.0

Douglas, Bruce b. April 9, 1964 Ht. 6-3 Wt. 195 College: Illinois

SEASON–TEAM	G	GS	MIN	FGM	FGA	PCT	3FGM	3FGA	PCT	FTM	FTA	PCT	O-RB	D-RB	TOT	AST	PF	DQ	STL	TO	BLK	PTS	RPG	APG	PPG
86-87–Sacramento	8	1	98	7	24	.292	0	1	.000	0	4	.000	5	9	14	17	9	0	9	9	0	14	1.8	2.1	1.8
Reg. Season Totals	8	1	98	7	24	.292	0	1	.000	0	4	.000	5	9	14	17	9	0	9	9	0	14	1.8	2.1	1.8

Douglas, John David b. June 12, 1956 Ht. 6-2 Wt. 175 College: John C. Calhoun State (Ala.) C.C.; Kansas

SEASON–TEAM	G	GS	MIN	FGM	FGA	PCT	3FGM	3FGA	PCT	FTM	FTA	PCT	O-RB	D-RB	TOT	AST	PF	DQ	STL	TO	BLK	PTS	RPG	APG	PPG
81-82–San Diego	64	9	1031	181	389	.465	18	59	.305	67	102	.657	27	63	90	146	147	2	48	92	9	447	1.4	2.3	7.0
82-83–San Diego	3	1	12	1	6	.167	1	2	.500	2	2	1.000	0	1	1	1	0	0	0	0	0	5	0.3	0.3	1.7
Reg. Season Totals	67	10	1043	182	395	.461	19	61	.311	69	104	.663	27	64	91	147	147	2	48	92	9	452	1.4	2.2	6.7

D

Douglas, Leon b. August 26, 1954 Ht. 6-10 Wt. 230 College: Alabama

SEASON–TEAM	G	GS	MIN	FGM	FGA	PCT	3FGM	3FGA	PCT	FTM	FTA	PCT	O-RB	D-RB	TOT	AST	PF	DQ	STL	TO	BLK	PTS	RPG	APG	PPG
76-77–Detroit	82	–	1626	245	512	.479	–	–	–	127	229	.555	181	345	526	68	294	10	44	–	81	617	6.4	0.8	7.5
77-78–Detroit	79	–	1993	321	667	.481	–	–	–	221	345	.641	181	401	582	112	295	6	57	197	48	863	7.4	1.4	10.9
78-79–Detroit	78	–	2215	342	698	.490	–	–	–	208	328	.634	248	416	664	74	319	13	39	190	55	892	8.5	0.9	11.4
79-80–Detroit	70	–	1782	221	455	.486	0	1	.000	125	185	.676	171	330	501	121	249	10	30	127	62	567	7.2	1.7	8.1
80-81–Kansas City	79	–	1356	185	323	.573	0	0	–	102	186	.548	150	234	384	69	251	2	25	90	38	472	4.9	0.9	6.0
81-82–Kansas City	63	17	1093	70	140	.500	0	0	–	32	80	.400	111	179	290	35	210	5	15	55	38	172	4.6	0.6	2.7
82-83–Kansas City	5	0	46	2	3	.667	0	0	–	0	2	.000	3	4	7	0	13	0	0	1	3	4	1.4	0.0	0.8
Reg. Season Totals	456	17	10111	1386	2798	.495	0	1	.000	815	1355	.601	1045	1909	2954	479	1631	46	210	660	325	3587	6.5	1.1	7.9
Playoff Totals	18	0	375	19	45	.422	0	0	–	17	42	.405	22	53	75	14	58	1	5	18	8	55	4.2	0.8	3.1

Douglas, Sherman (The General) b. September 15, 1966 Ht. 6-1 Wt. 195 College: Syracuse

SEASON–TEAM	G	GS	MIN	FGM	FGA	PCT	3FGM	3FGA	PCT	FTM	FTA	PCT	O-RB	D-RB	TOT	AST	PF	DQ	STL	TO	BLK	PTS	RPG	APG	PPG
89-90–Miami	81	66	2470	463	938	.494	5	31	.161	224	326	.687	70	136	206	619	187	0	145	246	10	1155	2.5	7.6	14.3
90-91–Miami	73	73	2562	532	1055	.504	4	31	.129	284	414	.686	78	131	209	624	178	2	121	270	5	1352	2.9	8.5	18.5
91-92–Miami-Boston	42	2	752	117	253	.462	1	10	.100	73	107	.682	13	50	63	172	78	0	25	68	9	308	1.5	4.1	7.3
92-93–Boston	79	36	1932	264	530	.498	6	29	.207	84	150	.560	65	97	162	508	166	1	49	161	10	618	2.1	6.4	7.8
93-94–Boston	78	78	2789	425	919	.462	13	56	.232	177	276	.641	70	123	193	683	171	2	89	233	11	1040	2.5	8.8	13.3
94-95–Boston	65	43	2048	365	769	.475	20	82	.244	204	296	.689	48	122	170	446	152	0	80	162	2	954	2.6	6.9	14.7
95-96–Boston-Milw.	79	66	2335	345	685	.504	40	110	.364	160	219	.731	55	125	180	436	163	0	63	194	5	890	2.3	5.5	11.3
96-97–Milwaukee	79	79	2316	306	610	.502	38	114	.333	114	171	.667	57	136	193	427	191	0	78	153	10	764	2.4	5.4	9.7
97-98–New Jersey	80	11	1699	255	515	.495	14	46	.304	115	172	.669	52	83	135	319	156	2	55	110	7	639	1.7	4.0	8.0
98-99–L.A. Clippers	30	19	842	96	219	.438	0	11	.000	55	87	.632	16	42	58	124	54	0	27	61	3	247	1.9	4.1	8.2
99-00–New Jersey	20	2	309	45	90	.500	5	16	.313	25	28	.893	13	16	29	34	26	0	17	24	0	120	1.5	1.7	6.0
Reg. Season Totals	706	475	20054	3213	6583	.488	146	536	.272	1515	2246	.675	537	1061	1598	4392	1522	7	749	1682	72	8087	2.3	6.2	11.5
Playoff Totals	17	10	524	73	182	.401	6	22	.273	26	38	.684	18	40	58	106	35	0	14	46	1	178	3.4	6.2	10.5

Dove, Lloyd (Sonny) b. August 16, 1945 d. February 14, 1983 Ht. 6-8 Wt. 200 College: St. John's (N.Y.)

SEASON–TEAM	G	GS	MIN	FGM	FGA	PCT	3FGM	3FGA	PCT	FTM	FTA	PCT	O-RB	D-RB	TOT	AST	PF	DQ	STL	TO	BLK	PTS	RPG	APG	PPG
67-68–Detroit	28	–	162	22	75	.293	–	–	–	12	26	.462	–	–	52	11	27	0	–	–	–	56	1.9	0.4	2.0
68-69–Detroit	29	–	236	47	100	.470	–	–	–	24	36	.667	–	–	62	12	49	0	–	–	–	118	2.1	0.4	4.1
69-70–New York (A)	80	–	2284	456	987	.462	2	13	.154	240	379	.633	–	–	543	107	295	12	–	–	–	1154	6.8	1.3	14.4
70-71–New York (A)	83	–	2280	467	1006	.464	4	14	.286	186	273	.681	–	–	676	88	304	–	–	–	–	1124	8.1	1.1	13.5
71-72–New York (A)	2	–	9	2	5	.400	0	0	–	2	3	.667	–	–	1	1	4	–	–	2	–	6	0.5	0.5	3.0
Reg. NBA Totals	57	–	398	69	175	.394	–	–	–	36	62	.581	–	–	114	23	76	0	–	–	–	174	2.0	0.4	3.1
Reg. ABA Totals	165	–	4573	925	1998	.463	6	27	.222	428	655	.653	–	–	1220	196	603	12	–	2	–	2284	7.4	1.2	13.8
NBA Playoff Totals	2	–	6	2	4	.500	–	–	–	0	0	–	–	–	2	–	0	0	–	–	–	4	1.0	0.0	2.0
ABA Playoff Totals	12	–	313	53	107	.495	1	4	.250	27	43	.628	27	44	82	10	42	2	–	–	–	134	6.8	0.8	11.2

Dover, Jerry L. b. October 16, 1949 Ht. 5-7 Wt. 155 College: Le Moyne-Owen

SEASON–TEAM	G	GS	MIN	FGM	FGA	PCT	3FGM	3FGA	PCT	FTM	FTA	PCT	O-RB	D-RB	TOT	AST	PF	DQ	STL	TO	BLK	PTS	RPG	APG	PPG
71-72–Memphis (A)	4	–	13	3	9	.333	2	5	.400	0	0	–	–	–	0	1	3	–	–	0	–	8	0.0	0.3	2.0
Reg. ABA Totals	4	–	13	3	9	.333	2	5	.400	0	0	–	–	–	–	1	3	–	–	–	–	8	0.0	0.3	2.0

Downey, William K. (Bill) b. November 11, 1923 Ht. 6-6 Wt. 210 College: Marquette

SEASON–TEAM	G	GS	MIN	FGM	FGA	PCT	3FGM	3FGA	PCT	FTM	FTA	PCT	O-RB	D-RB	TOT	AST	PF	DQ	STL	TO	BLK	PTS	RPG	APG	PPG
47-48–Providence	3	–	–	0	2	.000	–	–	–	0	0	–	–	–	–	0	0	–	–	–	–	0	–	0.0	0.0
Reg. Season Totals	3	–	–	0	2	.000	–	–	–	0	0	–	–	–	–	0	0	–	–	–	–	0	–	0.0	0.0

Downing, Steve b. September 9, 1950 Ht. 6-8 Wt. 225 College: Indiana

SEASON–TEAM	G	GS	MIN	FGM	FGA	PCT	3FGM	3FGA	PCT	FTM	FTA	PCT	O-RB	D-RB	TOT	AST	PF	DQ	STL	TO	BLK	PTS	RPG	APG	PPG
73-74–Boston	24	–	137	21	64	.328	–	–	–	22	38	.579	14	25	39	11	33	0	5	–	0	64	1.6	0.5	2.7
74-75–Boston	3	–	9	0	2	.000	–	–	–	0	2	.000	0	2	2	0	0	0	0	–	0	0	0.7	0.0	0.0
Reg. Season Totals	27	–	146	21	66	.318	–	–	–	22	40	.550	14	27	41	11	33	0	5	–	0	64	1.5	0.4	2.4
Playoff Totals	1	–	4	1	2	.500	–	–	–	0	0	–	2	0	2	–	1	0	0	–	0	2	2.0	0.0	2.0

Doyle, Daniel F. (Danny) b. February 6, 1940 Ht. 6-8 Wt. 200 College: Belmont Abbey

SEASON–TEAM	G	GS	MIN	FGM	FGA	PCT	3FGM	3FGA	PCT	FTM	FTA	PCT	O-RB	D-RB	TOT	AST	PF	DQ	STL	TO	BLK	PTS	RPG	APG	PPG
62-63–Detroit	4	–	25	6	12	.500	–	–	–	4	5	.800	–	–	8	3	4	0	–	–	–	16	2.0	0.8	4.0
Reg. Season Totals	4	–	25	6	12	.500	–	–	–	4	5	.800	–	–	8	3	4	0	–	–	–	16	2.0	0.8	4.0

Dozier, Terry Linnard b. June 29, 1966 Ht. 6-9 Wt. 210 College: South Carolina

SEASON–TEAM	G	GS	MIN	FGM	FGA	PCT	3FGM	3FGA	PCT	FTM	FTA	PCT	O-RB	D-RB	TOT	AST	PF	DQ	STL	TO	BLK	PTS	RPG	APG	PPG
89-90–Charlotte	9	0	92	9	27	.333	0	1	.000	4	8	.500	7	8	15	3	10	0	6	7	2	22	1.7	0.3	2.4
Reg. Season Totals	9	0	92	9	27	.333	0	1	.000	4	8	.500	7	8	15	3	10	0	6	7	2	22	1.7	0.3	2.4

Dreiling, Gregory Alan (Greg) b. November 7, 1963 Ht. 7-1 Wt. 265 College: Kansas

SEASON–TEAM	G	GS	MIN	FGM	FGA	PCT	3FGM	3FGA	PCT	FTM	FTA	PCT	O-RB	D-RB	TOT	AST	PF	DQ	STL	TO	BLK	PTS	RPG	APG	PPG
86-87–Indiana	24	0	128	16	37	.432	0	0	–	10	12	.833	12	31	43	7	42	0	2	7	2	42	1.8	0.3	1.8
87-88–Indiana	20	0	74	8	17	.471	0	0	–	18	26	.692	3	14	17	5	19	0	2	11	4	34	0.9	0.3	1.7
88-89–Indiana	53	4	396	43	77	.558	0	0	–	43	64	.672	39	53	92	18	100	0	5	39	11	129	1.7	0.3	2.4
89-90–Indiana	49	0	307	20	53	.377	0	0	–	25	34	.735	21	66	87	8	69	0	4	19	14	65	1.8	0.2	1.3
90-91–Indiana	73	42	1031	98	194	.505	0	2	.000	63	105	.600	66	189	255	51	178	1	24	57	29	259	3.5	0.7	3.5
91-92–Indiana	60	23	509	43	87	.494	1	1	1.000	30	40	.750	22	74	96	25	123	1	10	31	16	117	1.6	0.4	2.0
92-93–Indiana	43	0	239	19	58	.328	0	4	.000	8	15	.533	26	40	66	8	60	0	5	9	8	46	1.5	0.2	1.1
93-94–Dallas	54	19	685	52	104	.500	1	1	1.000	27	38	.711	47	123	170	31	159	5	16	43	24	132	3.1	0.6	2.4
94-95–Cleveland	58	3	483	42	102	.412	0	0	–	26	41	.634	32	84	116	22	108	1	6	25	22	110	2.0	0.4	1.9
96-97–Dallas	40	3	389	34	74	.459	1	1	1.000	11	27	.407	19	57	76	11	65	1	8	9	7	80	1.9	0.3	2.0
Reg. Season Totals	474	94	4241	375	803	.467	3	9	.333	261	402	.649	287	731	1018	186	923	9	82	250	137	1014	2.1	0.4	2.1
Playoff Totals	9	5	89	6	18	.333	1	1	1.000	4	6	.667	8	12	20	–	22	0	0	3	0	17	2.2	0.0	1.9

Drew, Bryce Homer b. September 21, 1974 Ht. 6-3 Wt. 185 College: Valparaiso

SEASON–TEAM	G	GS	MIN	FGM	FGA	PCT	3FGM	3FGA	PCT	FTM	FTA	PCT	O-RB	D-RB	TOT	AST	PF	DQ	STL	TO	BLK	PTS	RPG	APG	PPG
98-99–Houston	34	0	441	47	129	.364	16	49	.327	8	8	1.000	3	29	32	52	61	2	12	31	4	118	0.9	1.5	3.5
99-00–Houston	72	5	1293	158	413	.383	59	163	.362	45	53	.849	23	80	103	162	79	0	41	66	1	420	1.4	2.3	5.8
Reg. Season Totals	106	5	1734	205	542	.378	75	212	.354	53	61	.869	26	109	135	214	140	2	53	97	5	538	1.3	2.0	5.1
Playoff Totals	1	0	4	1	1	1.000	0	0	–	0	2	.000	1	2	3	2	1	0	0	0	0	2	3.0	2.0	2.0

Drew, John Edward (J.E.) b. September 30, 1954 Ht. 6-6 Wt. 205 College: Gardner-Webb

SEASON–TEAM	G	GS	MIN	FGM	FGA	PCT	3FGM	3FGA	PCT	FTM	FTA	PCT	O-RB	D-RB	TOT	AST	PF	DQ	STL	TO	BLK	PTS	RPG	APG	PPG
74-75–Atlanta	78	–	2289	527	1230	.428	–	–	–	388	544	.713	357	479	836	138	274	4	119	–	39	1442	10.7	1.8	18.5
75-76–Atlanta	77	–	2351	586	1168	.502	–	–	–	488	656	.744	286	374	660	150	261	11	138	–	30	1660	8.6	1.9	21.6
76-77–Atlanta	74	–	2688	689	1416	.487	–	–	–	412	577	.714	280	395	675	133	275	9	102	–	29	1790	9.1	1.8	24.2
77-78–Atlanta	70	–	2203	593	1236	.480	–	–	–	437	575	.760	213	298	511	141	247	8	119	210	27	1623	7.3	2.0	23.2
78-79–Atlanta	79	–	2410	650	1375	.473	–	–	–	495	677	.731	225	297	522	119	332	19	128	211	16	1795	6.6	1.5	22.7
79-80–Atlanta	80	–	2306	535	1182	.453	0	7	.000	489	646	.757	203	268	471	101	313	10	91	240	23	1559	5.9	1.3	19.5
80-81–Atlanta	67	–	2075	500	1096	.456	0	7	.000	454	577	.787	145	238	383	79	264	9	98	194	15	1454	5.7	1.2	21.7
81-82–Atlanta	70	51	2040	465	957	.486	4	12	.333	364	491	.741	169	206	375	96	250	6	64	178	3	1298	5.4	1.4	18.5
82-83–Utah	44	33	1206	318	671	.474	0	5	.000	296	392	.755	98	137	235	97	152	8	35	135	7	932	5.3	2.2	21.2
83-84–Utah	81	4	1797	511	1067	.479	6	22	.273	402	517	.778	146	192	338	135	208	1	88	192	2	1430	4.2	1.7	17.7
84-85–Utah	19	16	463	107	260	.412	0	4	.000	94	122	.770	36	46	82	35	65	0	22	42	2	308	4.3	1.8	16.2
Reg. Season Totals	739	104	21828	5481	11658	.470	10	57	.175	4319	5774	.748	2158	2930	5088	1224	2641	85	1004	1402	193	15291	6.9	1.7	20.7
Playoff Totals	29	2	735	151	350	.431	0	0	–	103	142	.725	55	85	140	24	103	3	21	48	5	405	4.8	0.8	14.0
All-Star Totals	2	1	24	1	7	.143	0	0	–	4	5	.800	2	4	6	0	7	0	2	3	0	6	3.0	0.0	3.0

Drew, Larry Donnell b. April 2, 1958 Ht. 6-1 Wt. 175 College: Missouri

SEASON–TEAM	G	GS	MIN	FGM	FGA	PCT	3FGM	3FGA	PCT	FTM	FTA	PCT	O-RB	D-RB	TOT	AST	PF	DQ	STL	TO	BLK	PTS	RPG	APG	PPG
80-81–Detroit	76	–	1581	197	484	.407	4	17	.235	106	133	.797	24	96	120	249	125	0	88	166	7	504	1.6	3.3	6.6
81-82–Kansas City	81	19	1973	358	757	.473	8	27	.296	150	189	.794	30	119	149	419	150	0	110	174	1	874	1.8	5.2	10.8
82-83–Kansas City	75	74	2690	599	1218	.492	2	16	.125	310	378	.820	44	163	207	610	207	1	126	272	10	1510	2.8	8.1	20.1
83-84–Kansas City	73	73	2363	474	1026	.462	3	10	.300	243	313	.776	33	113	146	558	170	0	121	194	10	1194	2.0	7.6	16.4
84-85–Kansas City	72	66	2373	457	913	.501	7	28	.250	154	194	.794	39	125	164	484	147	0	93	179	8	1075	2.3	6.7	14.9
85-86–Sacramento	75	31	1971	376	776	.485	10	31	.323	128	161	.795	25	100	125	338	134	0	66	133	2	890	1.7	4.5	11.9
86-87–L.A. Clippers	60	22	1566	295	683	.432	12	72	.167	139	166	.837	26	77	103	326	107	0	60	151	2	741	1.7	5.4	12.4
87-88–L.A. Clippers	74	51	2024	328	720	.456	26	90	.289	83	108	.769	21	98	119	383	114	0	65	152	0	765	1.6	5.2	10.3
89-90–L.A. Lakers	80	3	1333	170	383	.444	32	81	.395	46	60	.767	12	86	98	217	92	0	47	95	4	418	1.2	2.7	5.2
90-91–L.A. Lakers	48	2	496	54	125	.432	14	33	.424	17	22	.773	5	29	34	118	40	0	15	49	1	139	0.7	2.5	2.9
Reg. Season Totals	714	341	18370	3308	7085	.467	118	405	.291	1376	1724	.798	259	1006	1265	3702	1286	1	791	1565	45	8110	1.8	5.2	11.4
Playoff Totals	31	3	293	38	85	.447	5	18	.278	14	17	.824	0	15	15	50	33	0	11	18	0	95	0.5	1.6	3.1

Drexler, Clyde Austin (Clyde the Glide) b. June 22, 1962 Ht. 6-7 Wt. 222 College: Houston

SEASON–TEAM	G	GS	MIN	FGM	FGA	PCT	3FGM	3FGA	PCT	FTM	FTA	PCT	O-RB	D-RB	TOT	AST	PF	DQ	STL	TO	BLK	PTS	RPG	APG	PPG
83-84–Portland	82	3	1408	252	559	.451	1	4	.250	123	169	.728	112	123	235	153	209	2	107	123	29	628	2.9	1.9	7.7
84-85–Portland	80	43	2555	573	1161	.494	8	37	.216	223	294	.759	217	259	476	441	265	3	177	223	68	1377	6.0	5.5	17.2
85-86–Portland	75	58	2576	542	1142	.475	12	60	.200	293	381	.769	171	250	421	600	270	8	197	282	46	1389	5.6	8.0	18.5
86-87–Portland	82	82	3114	707	1408	.502	11	47	.234	357	470	.760	227	291	518	566	281	7	204	253	71	1782	6.3	6.9	21.7
87-88–Portland	81	80	3060	849	1679	.506	11	52	.212	476	587	.811	261	272	533	467	250	2	203	236	52	2185	6.6	5.8	27.0
88-89–Portland	78	78	3064	829	1672	.496	27	104	.260	438	548	.799	289	326	615	450	269	2	213	250	54	2123	7.9	5.8	27.2
89-90–Portland	73	73	2683	670	1357	.494	30	106	.283	333	430	.774	208	299	507	432	222	1	145	191	51	1703	6.9	5.9	23.3
90-91–Portland	82	82	2852	645	1338	.482	61	191	.319	416	524	.794	212	334	546	493	226	2	144	232	60	1767	6.7	6.0	21.5
91-92–Portland	76	76	2751	694	1476	.470	114	338	.337	401	505	.794	166	334	500	512	229	2	138	240	70	1903	6.6	6.7	25.0
92-93–Portland	49	49	1671	350	816	.429	31	133	.233	245	292	.839	126	183	309	278	159	1	95	115	37	976	6.3	5.7	19.9
93-94–Portland	68	68	2334	473	1105	.428	71	219	.324	286	368	.777	154	291	445	333	202	2	98	167	34	1303	6.5	4.9	19.2
94-95–Port.-Houston	76	75	2728	571	1238	.461	147	408	.360	364	442	.824	152	328	480	362	206	1	136	186	45	1653	6.3	4.8	21.8
95-96–Houston	52	51	1997	331	764	.433	78	235	.332	265	338	.784	97	276	373	302	153	0	105	134	24	1005	7.2	5.8	19.3
96-97–Houston	62	62	2271	397	899	.442	119	335	.355	201	268	.750	118	255	373	354	151	0	119	156	36	1114	6.0	5.7	18.0
97-98–Houston	70	70	2473	452	1059	.427	106	334	.317	277	346	.801	105	241	346	382	193	0	126	189	42	1287	4.9	5.5	18.4
Reg. Season Totals	1086	950	37537	8335	17673	.472	827	2603	.318	4698	5962	.788	2615	4062	6677	6125	3285	33	2207	2977	719	22195	6.1	5.6	20.4
Playoff Totals	145	140	5572	1076	2408	.447	141	489	.288	670	851	.787	359	643	1002	891	486	7	278	397	108	2963	6.9	6.1	20.4
All-Star Totals	9	4	166	40	79	.506	4	14	.286	12	12	1.000	17	27	44	23	19	0	12	18	6	96	4.9	2.6	10.7

Driggers, Nathan Allen (Nate) b. October 12, 1973 Ht. 6-5 Wt. 215 College: Montevallo

SEASON–TEAM	G	GS	MIN	FGM	FGA	PCT	3FGM	3FGA	PCT	FTM	FTA	PCT	O-RB	D-RB	TOT	AST	PF	DQ	STL	TO	BLK	PTS	RPG	APG	PPG
96-97–Boston	15	0	132	13	43	.302	0	9	.000	10	14	.714	12	10	22	6	10	0	3	6	2	36	1.5	0.4	2.4
Reg. Season Totals	15	0	132	13	43	.302	0	9	.000	10	14	.714	12	10	22	6	10	0	3	6	2	36	1.5	0.4	2.4

Driscoll, Edward Cuthbert Jr. (Terry) b. August 28, 1947 Ht. 6-7 Wt. 215 College: Boston College

SEASON–TEAM	G	GS	MIN	FGM	FGA	PCT	3FGM	3FGA	PCT	FTM	FTA	PCT	O-RB	D-RB	TOT	AST	PF	DQ	STL	TO	BLK	PTS	RPG	APG	PPG
70-71–Detroit	69	–	1255	132	318	.415	–	–	–	108	154	.701	–	–	402	54	212	2	–	–	–	372	5.8	0.8	5.4
71-72–Baltimore	40	–	313	40	104	.385	–	–	–	27	39	.692	–	–	109	23	53	0	–	–	–	107	2.7	0.6	2.7
72-73–Balt.-Milw.	60	–	964	140	327	.428	–	–	–	43	62	.694	–	–	300	55	144	3	–	–	–	323	5.0	0.9	5.4
73-74–Milwaukee	64	–	697	88	187	.471	–	–	–	30	46	.652	73	126	199	54	121	0	21	–	16	206	3.1	0.8	3.2
74-75–Milwaukee	11	–	52	3	13	.231	–	–	–	1	2	.500	7	9	16	3	7	0	1	–	0	7	1.5	0.3	0.6
74-75–St. Louis (A)	30	–	351	46	122	.377	0	0	–	20	27	.741	37	51	88	32	51	–	9	28	6	112	2.9	1.1	3.7
Reg. NBA Totals	244	–	3281	403	949	.425	–	–	–	209	303	.690	80	135	1026	189	537	5	22	–	16	1015	4.2	0.8	4.2
Reg. ABA Totals	30	–	351	46	122	.377	0	0	–	20	27	.741	37	51	88	32	51	–	9	28	6	112	2.9	1.1	3.7
NBA Playoff Totals	16	–	47	6	15	.400	–	–	–	3	3	1.000	9	5	15	4	14	0	2	–	1	15	0.9	0.3	0.9

Drollinger, Ralph Kim b. April 20, 1954 Ht. 7-2 Wt. 250 College: UCLA

SEASON–TEAM	G	GS	MIN	FGM	FGA	PCT	3FGM	3FGA	PCT	FTM	FTA	PCT	O-RB	D-RB	TOT	AST	PF	DQ	STL	TO	BLK	PTS	RPG	APG	PPG
80-81–Dallas	6	–	67	7	14	.500	0	0	–	1	4	.250	5	14	19	14	16	0	1	13	2	15	3.2	2.3	2.5
Reg. Season Totals	6	–	67	7	14	.500	0	0	–	1	4	.250	5	14	19	14	16	0	1	13	2	15	3.2	2.3	2.5

Duckett, Richard J. (Dick) b. March 25, 1933 Ht. 6-1 Wt. 185 College: St. John's (N.Y.)

SEASON–TEAM	G	GS	MIN	FGM	FGA	PCT	3FGM	3FGA	PCT	FTM	FTA	PCT	O-RB	D-RB	TOT	AST	PF	DQ	STL	TO	BLK	PTS	RPG	APG	PPG
57-58–Cincinnati	34	–	424	54	158	.342	–	–	–	24	27	.889	–	–	56	47	60	0	–	–	–	132	1.6	1.4	3.9
Reg. Season Totals	34	–	424	54	158	.342	–	–	–	24	27	.889	–	–	56	47	60	0	–	–	–	132	1.6	1.4	3.9

Duckworth, Kevin Jerome b. April 1, 1964 Ht. 7-0 Wt. 300 College: Eastern Illinois

SEASON–TEAM	G	GS	MIN	FGM	FGA	PCT	3FGM	3FGA	PCT	FTM	FTA	PCT	O-RB	D-RB	TOT	AST	PF	DQ	STL	TO	BLK	PTS	RPG	APG	PPG
86-87–S.A.-Port.	65	1	875	130	273	.476	0	1	.000	92	134	.687	76	147	223	29	192	3	21	78	21	352	3.4	0.4	5.4
87-88–Portland	78	50	2223	450	907	.496	0	0	–	331	430	.770	224	352	576	66	280	5	31	177	32	1231	7.4	0.8	15.8
88-89–Portland	79	79	2662	554	1161	.477	0	2	.000	324	428	.757	246	389	635	60	300	6	56	200	49	1432	8.0	0.8	18.1
89-90–Portland	82	82	2462	548	1146	.478	0	0	–	231	312	.740	184	325	509	91	271	2	36	171	34	1327	6.2	1.1	16.2
90-91–Portland	81	81	2511	521	1084	.481	0	2	.000	240	311	.772	177	354	531	89	251	5	33	186	34	1282	6.6	1.1	15.8
91-92–Portland	82	82	2222	362	786	.461	0	3	.000	156	226	.690	151	346	497	99	264	5	38	143	37	880	6.1	1.2	10.7
92-93–Portland	74	55	1762	301	688	.438	0	2	.000	127	174	.730	118	269	387	70	222	1	45	87	39	729	5.2	0.9	9.9
93-94–Washington	69	52	1485	184	441	.417	0	0	–	88	132	.667	103	222	325	56	223	2	37	101	35	456	4.7	0.8	6.6
94-95–Washington	40	22	818	118	267	.442	2	10	.200	45	70	.643	65	130	195	20	110	3	21	59	24	283	4.9	0.5	7.1
95-96–Milwaukee	8	1	58	3	14	.214	0	0	–	3	6	.500	2	5	7	2	19	0	2	2	0	9	0.9	0.3	1.1
96-97–L.A. Clippers	26	22	384	45	103	.437	3	4	.750	11	16	.688	23	37	60	16	63	1	9	33	11	104	2.3	0.6	4.0
Reg. Season Totals	684	527	17462	3216	6870	.468	5	24	.208	1648	2239	.736	1369	2576	3945	598	2195	33	329	1237	316	8085	5.8	0.9	11.8
Playoff Totals	67	59	1956	323	723	.447	0	1	.000	139	198	.702	143	250	393	84	246	6	30	155	34	785	5.9	1.3	11.7
All-Star Totals	2	0	26	4	8	.500	0	0	–	3	4	.750	3	2	5	0	5	0	1	2	0	11	2.5	0.0	5.5

Dudley, Charles (Grasshopper) b. March 5, 1950 Ht. 6-2 Wt. 180 College: Washington

SEASON–TEAM	G	GS	MIN	FGM	FGA	PCT	3FGM	3FGA	PCT	FTM	FTA	PCT	O-RB	D-RB	TOT	AST	PF	DQ	STL	TO	BLK	PTS	RPG	APG	PPG
72-73–Seattle	12	–	99	10	23	.435	–	–	–	14	16	.875	–	–	6	16	15	0	–	–	–	34	0.5	1.3	2.8
74-75–Golden State	67	–	756	102	217	.470	–	–	–	70	97	.722	61	84	145	103	105	1	40	–	2	274	2.2	1.5	4.1
75-76–Golden State	82	–	1456	182	345	.528	–	–	–	157	245	.641	112	157	269	239	170	0	77	–	2	521	3.3	2.9	6.4
76-77–Golden State	79	–	1682	220	421	.523	–	–	–	129	203	.635	119	177	296	347	169	0	67	–	6	569	3.7	4.4	7.2
77-78–Golden State	78	–	1660	127	249	.510	–	–	–	138	195	.708	86	201	287	409	181	0	68	163	2	392	3.7	5.2	5.0
78-79–Chicago	43	–	684	45	125	.360	–	–	–	28	42	.667	25	61	86	116	82	0	32	64	1	118	2.0	2.7	2.7
Reg. Season Totals	361	–	6337	686	1380	.497	–	–	–	536	798	.672	403	680	1089	1230	722	1	284	227	13	1908	3.0	3.4	5.3
Playoff Totals	36	–	608	56	118	.475	–	–	–	55	84	.655	42	49	91	124	80	0	34	–	3	167	2.5	3.4	4.6

Dudley, Christen Guilford (Chris) b. February 22, 1965 Ht. 6-11 Wt. 260 College: Yale

SEASON–TEAM	G	GS	MIN	FGM	FGA	PCT	3FGM	3FGA	PCT	FTM	FTA	PCT	O-RB	D-RB	TOT	AST	PF	DQ	STL	TO	BLK	PTS	RPG	APG	PPG
87-88–Cleveland	55	1	513	65	137	.474	0	0	–	40	71	.563	74	70	144	23	87	2	13	31	19	170	2.6	0.4	3.1
88-89–Cleveland	61	2	544	73	168	.435	0	1	.000	39	107	.364	72	85	157	21	82	0	9	44	23	185	2.6	0.3	3.0
89-90–Clev.-N.J.	64	30	1356	146	355	.411	0	0	–	58	182	.319	174	249	423	39	164	2	41	84	72	350	6.6	0.6	5.5
90-91–New Jersey	61	25	1560	170	417	.408	0	0	–	94	176	.534	229	282	511	37	217	6	39	80	153	434	8.4	0.6	7.1
91-92–New Jersey	82	21	1902	190	472	.403	0	0	–	80	171	.468	343	396	739	58	275	5	38	79	179	460	9.0	0.7	5.6
92-93–New Jersey	71	16	1398	94	266	.353	0	0	–	57	110	.518	215	298	513	16	195	5	17	54	103	245	7.2	0.2	3.5
93-94–Portland	6	3	86	6	25	.240	0	0	–	2	4	.500	16	8	24	5	18	0	4	2	3	14	4.0	0.8	2.3
94-95–Portland	82	82	2245	181	446	.406	0	1	.000	85	183	.464	325	439	764	34	286	6	43	81	126	447	9.3	0.4	5.5
95-96–Portland	80	61	1924	162	358	.453	0	1	.000	80	157	.510	239	481	720	37	251	4	41	79	100	404	9.0	0.5	5.1
96-97–Portland	81	14	1840	126	293	.430	0	0	–	65	137	.474	204	389	593	41	247	3	39	80	96	317	7.3	0.5	3.9
97-98–New York	51	22	858	58	143	.406	0	0	–	41	92	.446	108	167	275	21	139	4	13	44	51	157	5.4	0.4	3.1
98-99–New York	46	16	685	48	109	.440	0	0	–	19	40	.475	79	114	193	7	116	1	13	24	38	115	4.2	0.2	2.5
99-00–New York	47	3	459	23	67	.343	0	0	–	9	27	.333	63	73	136	5	95	2	7	18	21	55	2.9	0.1	1.2
Reg. Season Totals	787	296	15370	1342	3256	.412	0	3	.000	669	1457	.459	2141	3051	5192	344	2172	40	317	700	984	3353	6.6	0.4	4.3
Playoff Totals	54	16	796	43	105	.410	0	0	–	30	66	.455	85	143	228	17	169	4	24	23	28	116	4.2	0.3	2.1

Duerod, Terry (Sweet Due) b. July 29, 1956 Ht. 6-2 Wt. 180 College: Detroit (Renamed Detroit Mercy)

SEASON–TEAM	G	GS	MIN	FGM	FGA	PCT	3FGM	3FGA	PCT	FTM	FTA	PCT	O-RB	D-RB	TOT	AST	PF	DQ	STL	TO	BLK	PTS	RPG	APG	PPG
79-80–Detroit	67	–	1331	282	598	.472	15	53	.283	45	66	.682	29	69	98	117	102	0	41	79	11	624	1.5	1.7	9.3
80-81–Dallas-Boston	50	–	451	104	234	.444	8	16	.500	31	41	.756	17	27	44	36	27	0	17	35	4	247	0.9	0.7	4.9
81-82–Boston	21	0	146	34	77	.442	0	1	.000	4	12	.333	6	9	15	12	9	0	3	2	1	72	0.7	0.6	3.4
82-83–Golden State	5	0	49	9	19	.474	0	0	–	0	0	–	0	3	3	5	5	0	2	9	1	18	0.6	1.0	3.6
Reg. Season Totals	143	0	1977	429	928	.462	23	70	.329	80	119	.672	52	108	160	170	143	0	63	125	17	961	1.1	1.2	6.7
Playoff Totals	10	0	12	4	10	.400	0	2	.000	0	0	–	0	0	0	–	0	0	1	1	0	8	0.0	0.0	0.8

Duffy, Robert John (Bob John) b. July 5, 1922 Ht. 6-4 Wt. 175 College: Tulane

SEASON–TEAM	G	GS	MIN	FGM	FGA	PCT	3FGM	3FGA	PCT	FTM	FTA	PCT	O-RB	D-RB	TOT	AST	PF	DQ	STL	TO	BLK	PTS	RPG	APG	PPG
46-47–ChStags-Boston	17	–	–	7	32	.219	–	–	–	5	7	.714	–	–	–	0	17	–	–	–	–	19	–	0.0	1.1
Reg. Season Totals	17	–	–	7	32	.219	–	–	–	5	7	.714	–	–	–	0	17	–	–	–	–	19	–	0.0	1.1

Duffy, Robert Joseph (Bob) b. September 26, 1940 Ht. 6-3 Wt. 185 College: Colgate

SEASON–TEAM	G	GS	MIN	FGM	FGA	PCT	3FGM	3FGA	PCT	FTM	FTA	PCT	O-RB	D-RB	TOT	AST	PF	DQ	STL	TO	BLK	PTS	RPG	APG	PPG
62-63–St. Louis	42	–	435	66	174	.379	–	–	–	22	39	.564	–	–	39	83	42	0	–	–	–	154	0.9	2.0	3.7
63-64–St. L.-N.Y.	48	–	662	94	229	.410	–	–	–	44	65	.677	–	–	61	79	48	0	–	–	–	232	1.3	1.6	4.8
64-65–Detroit	4	–	26	4	11	.364	–	–	–	6	7	.857	–	–	4	5	4	0	–	–	–	14	1.0	1.3	3.5
Reg. Season Totals	94	–	1123	164	414	.396	–	–	–	72	111	.649	–	–	104	167	94	0	–	–	–	400	1.1	1.8	4.3
Playoff Totals	5	–	24	6	15	.400	–	–	–	2	2	1.000	–	–	3	3	3	0	–	–	–	14	0.6	0.6	2.8

Dukes, Walter F. b. June 23, 1930 Ht. 7-0 Wt. 220 College: Seton Hall

SEASON–TEAM	G	GS	MIN	FGM	FGA	PCT	3FGM	3FGA	PCT	FTM	FTA	PCT	O-RB	D-RB	TOT	AST	PF	DQ	STL	TO	BLK	PTS	RPG	APG	PPG
55-56–New York	60	–	1290	149	370	.403	–	–	–	167	236	.708	–	–	443	39	211	11	–	–	–	465	7.4	0.7	7.8
56-57–Minneapolis	71	–	1866	228	626	.364	–	–	–	264	383	.689	–	–	794	54	273	10	–	–	–	720	11.2	0.8	10.1
57-58–Detroit	72	–	2184	278	796	.349	–	–	–	247	366	.675	–	–	954	52	311	17	–	–	–	803	13.3	0.7	11.2
58-59–Detroit	72	–	2338	318	904	.352	–	–	–	297	452	.657	–	–	958	64	332	22	–	–	–	933	13.3	0.9	13.0
59-60–Detroit	66	–	2140	314	871	.361	–	–	–	376	508	.740	–	–	883	80	310	20	–	–	–	1004	13.4	1.2	15.2
60-61–Detroit	73	–	2044	286	706	.405	–	–	–	281	400	.703	–	–	1028	139	313	16	–	–	–	853	14.1	1.9	11.7
61-62–Detroit	77	–	1896	256	647	.396	–	–	–	208	291	.715	–	–	803	125	327	20	–	–	–	720	10.4	1.6	9.4
62-63–Detroit	62	–	913	83	255	.325	–	–	–	101	137	.737	–	–	360	55	183	5	–	–	–	267	5.8	0.9	4.3
Reg. Season Totals	553	–	14671	1912	5175	.369	–	–	–	1941	2773	.700	–	–	6223	608	2260	121	–	–	–	5765	11.3	1.1	10.4
Playoff Totals	35	–	1161	151	363	.416	–	–	–	145	204	.711	–	–	432	51	168	14	–	–	–	447	12.3	1.5	12.8
All-Star Totals	2	–	43	5	16	.313	–	–	–	2	3	.667	–	–	19	2	7	0	–	–	–	12	9.5	1.0	6.0

Dumars, Joe III b. May 24, 1963 Ht. 6-3 Wt. 195 College: McNeese State

SEASON–TEAM	G	GS	MIN	FGM	FGA	PCT	3FGM	3FGA	PCT	FTM	FTA	PCT	O-RB	D-RB	TOT	AST	PF	DQ	STL	TO	BLK	PTS	RPG	APG	PPG
85-86–Detroit	82	45	1957	287	597	.481	5	16	.313	190	238	.798	60	59	119	390	200	1	66	158	11	769	1.5	4.8	9.4
86-87–Detroit	79	75	2439	369	749	.493	9	22	.409	184	246	.748	50	117	167	352	194	1	83	171	5	931	2.1	4.5	11.8
87-88–Detroit	82	82	2732	453	960	.472	4	19	.211	251	308	.815	63	137	200	387	155	1	87	172	15	1161	2.4	4.7	14.2
88-89–Detroit	69	67	2408	456	903	.505	14	29	.483	260	306	.850	57	115	172	390	103	1	63	178	5	1186	2.5	5.7	17.2
89-90–Detroit	75	71	2578	508	1058	.480	22	55	.400	297	330	.900	60	152	212	368	129	1	63	145	2	1335	2.8	4.9	17.8
90-91–Detroit	80	80	3046	622	1292	.481	14	45	.311	371	417	.890	62	125	187	443	135	0	89	189	7	1629	2.3	5.5	20.4
91-92–Detroit	82	82	3192	587	1311	.448	49	120	.408	412	475	.867	82	106	188	375	145	0	71	193	12	1635	2.3	4.6	19.9
92-93–Detroit	77	77	3094	677	1454	.466	112	299	.375	343	397	.864	63	85	148	308	141	0	78	138	7	1809	1.9	4.0	23.5
93-94–Detroit	69	69	2591	505	1118	.452	124	320	.388	276	330	.836	35	116	151	261	118	0	63	159	4	1410	2.2	3.8	20.4
94-95–Detroit	67	67	2544	417	970	.430	103	338	.305	277	344	.805	47	111	158	368	153	0	72	219	7	1214	2.4	5.5	18.1
95-96–Detroit	67	40	2193	255	598	.426	121	298	.406	162	197	.822	28	110	138	265	106	0	43	97	3	793	2.1	4.0	11.8
96-97–Detroit	79	79	2923	385	875	.440	166	384	.432	222	256	.867	38	153	191	318	97	0	57	128	1	1158	2.4	4.0	14.7
97-98–Detroit	72	72	2326	329	791	.416	158	426	.371	127	154	.825	14	90	104	253	99	0	44	84	2	943	1.4	3.5	13.1
98-99–Detroit	38	38	1116	144	350	.411	89	221	.403	51	61	.836	12	56	68	134	51	0	23	53	2	428	1.8	3.5	11.3
Reg. Season Totals	1018	944	35139	5994	13026	.460	990	2592	.382	3423	4059	.843	671	1532	2203	4612	1826	5	902	2084	83	16401	2.2	4.5	16.1
Playoff Totals	112	112	4097	646	1398	.462	53	148	.358	407	476	.855	95	162	257	512	227	2	91	205	6	1752	2.3	4.6	15.6
All-Star Totals	6	1	98	14	35	.400	5	15	.333	1	2	.500	1	6	7	20	3	0	1	11	0	34	1.2	3.3	5.7

Dumas, Richard (Rich) b. 1945 Ht. 6-3 Wt. 170 College: Northeastern State (Okla.)

SEASON–TEAM	G	GS	MIN	FGM	FGA	PCT	3FGM	3FGA	PCT	FTM	FTA	PCT	O-RB	D-RB	TOT	AST	PF	DQ	STL	TO	BLK	PTS	RPG	APG	PPG
68-69–Houston (A)	1	–	5	1	5	.200	0	0	–	0	0	–	–	–	1	0	1	0	–	1	–	2	1.0	0.0	2.0
Reg. ABA Totals	1	–	5	1	5	.200	0	0	–	0	0	–	–	–	1	0	1	0	–	1	–	2	1.0	0.0	2.0

Dumas, Richard Wayne b. May 19, 1969 Ht. 6-7 Wt. 225 College: Oklahoma State

SEASON–TEAM	G	GS	MIN	FGM	FGA	PCT	3FGM	3FGA	PCT	FTM	FTA	PCT	O-RB	D-RB	TOT	AST	PF	DQ	STL	TO	BLK	PTS	RPG	APG	PPG
92-93–Phoenix	48	32	1320	302	576	.524	1	3	.333	152	215	.707	100	123	223	60	127	0	85	92	39	757	4.6	1.3	15.8
94-95–Phoenix	15	1	167	37	73	.507	0	1	.000	8	16	.500	18	11	29	7	22	0	10	9	2	82	1.9	0.5	5.5
95-96–Philadelphia	39	14	739	95	203	.468	2	9	.222	49	70	.700	42	57	99	44	79	1	42	49	6	241	2.5	1.1	6.2
Reg. Season Totals	102	47	2226	434	852	.509	3	13	.231	209	301	.694	160	191	351	111	228	1	137	150	47	1080	3.4	1.1	10.6
Playoff Totals	26	20	504	108	208	.519	0	2	.000	37	49	.755	37	29	66	24	52	0	21	28	13	253	2.5	0.9	9.7

Dumas, Tony b. August 25, 1972 Ht. 6-6 Wt. 190 College: Missouri-K.C.

SEASON–TEAM	G	GS	MIN	FGM	FGA	PCT	3FGM	3FGA	PCT	FTM	FTA	PCT	O-RB	D-RB	TOT	AST	PF	DQ	STL	TO	BLK	PTS	RPG	APG	PPG
94-95–Dallas	58	0	613	96	250	.384	22	73	.301	50	77	.649	32	30	62	57	78	0	13	50	4	264	1.1	1.0	4.6
95-96–Dallas	67	12	1284	274	655	.418	74	207	.357	154	257	.599	58	57	115	99	128	0	42	77	13	776	1.7	1.5	11.6
96-97–Dallas-Phoenix	24	1	278	33	96	.344	4	28	.143	16	25	.640	3	13	16	25	45	0	10	16	2	86	0.7	1.0	3.6
97-98–Cleveland	7	0	47	6	12	.500	2	4	.500	0	3	.000	1	4	5	5	5	0	0	5	0	14	0.7	0.7	2.0
Reg. Season Totals	156	13	2222	409	1013	.404	102	312	.327	220	362	.608	94	104	198	186	256	0	65	148	19	1140	1.3	1.2	7.3

Duncan, Andrew (Andy) b. April 17, 1922 Ht. 6-6 Wt. 195 College: Kentucky; William & Mary

SEASON–TEAM	G	GS	MIN	FGM	FGA	PCT	3FGM	3FGA	PCT	FTM	FTA	PCT	O-RB	D-RB	TOT	AST	PF	DQ	STL	TO	BLK	PTS	RPG	APG	PPG
47-48–Rochester (N)	60	–	–	200	–	–	–	–	–	119	199	.598	–	–	–	–	183	–	–	–	–	519	–	–	8.7
48-49–Rochester	55	–	–	162	391	.414	–	–	–	83	135	.615	–	–	–	51	179	–	–	–	–	407	–	0.9	7.4
49-50–Rochester	67	–	–	125	289	.433	–	–	–	60	108	.556	–	–	–	42	160	–	–	–	–	310	–	0.6	4.6
50-51–Boston	14	–	–	7	40	.175	–	–	–	15	22	.682	–	–	30	8	27	0	–	–	–	29	2.1	0.6	2.1
Reg. NBA Totals	136	–	–	294	720	.408	–	–	–	158	265	.596	–	–	30	101	366	0	–	–	–	746	2.1	0.7	5.5
Reg. NBL Totals	60	–	–	200	–	–	–	–	–	119	199	.598	–	–	–	–	183	–	–	–	–	519	–	–	8.7
NBA Playoff Totals	6	–	–	5	28	.321	–	–	–	2	3	.667	–	–	–	6	10	0	–	–	–	12	–	0.5	2.0
NBL Playoff Totals	11	–	–	39	–	–	–	–	–	23	34	.676	–	–	–	–	25	–	–	–	–	101	–	–	9.2

Duncan, Timothy Theodore (Tim) b. April 25, 1976 Ht. 7-0 Wt. 260 College: Wake Forest

SEASON–TEAM	G	GS	MIN	FGM	FGA	PCT	3FGM	3FGA	PCT	FTM	FTA	PCT	O-RB	D-RB	TOT	AST	PF	DQ	STL	TO	BLK	PTS	RPG	APG	PPG
97-98–San Antonio	82	82	3204	706	1287	.549	0	10	.000	319	482	.662	274	703	977	224	254	1	55	279	206	1731	11.9	2.7	21.1
98-99–San Antonio	50	50	1963	418	845	.495	1	7	.143	247	358	.690	159	412	571	121	147	2	45	146	126	1084	11.4	2.4	21.7
99-00–San Antonio	74	74	2875	628	1281	.490	1	11	.091	459	603	.761	262	656	918	234	210	1	66	242	165	1716	12.4	3.2	23.2
Reg. Season Totals	206	206	8042	1752	3413	.513	2	28	.071	1025	1443	.710	695	1771	2466	579	611	4	166	667	497	4531	12.0	2.8	22.0
Playoff Totals	26	26	1107	217	422	.514	0	4	.000	147	203	.724	75	201	276	65	74	2	18	77	68	581	10.6	2.5	22.3
All-Star Totals	2	1	47	13	18	.722	0	1	.000	0	0	–	8	17	25	5	3	0	1	4	1	26	12.5	2.5	13.0

Dunleavy, Michael Joseph (Mike) b. March 21, 1954 Ht. 6-3 Wt. 180 College: South Carolina

SEASON–TEAM	G	GS	MIN	FGM	FGA	PCT	3FGM	3FGA	PCT	FTM	FTA	PCT	O-RB	D-RB	TOT	AST	PF	DQ	STL	TO	BLK	PTS	RPG	APG	PPG
76-77–Philadelphia	32	–	359	60	145	.414	–	–	–	34	45	.756	10	24	34	56	64	1	13	–	2	154	1.1	1.8	4.8
77-78–Phil.-Houston	15	–	119	20	50	.400	–	–	–	13	18	.722	1	9	10	28	12	0	9	12	1	53	0.7	1.9	3.5
78-79–Houston	74	–	1486	215	425	.506	–	–	–	159	184	.864	28	100	128	324	168	2	56	130	5	589	1.7	4.4	8.0
79-80–Houston	51	–	1036	148	319	.464	3	20	.150	111	134	.828	26	74	100	210	120	2	40	110	4	410	2.0	4.1	8.0
80-81–Houston	74	–	1609	310	632	.491	1	16	.063	156	186	.839	28	90	118	268	165	1	64	137	2	777	1.6	3.6	10.5
81-82–Houston	70	15	1315	206	450	.458	33	86	.384	75	106	.708	24	80	104	227	161	0	45	80	3	520	1.5	3.2	7.4
82-83–San Antonio	79	9	1619	213	510	.418	67	194	.345	120	154	.779	18	116	134	437	210	1	74	160	4	613	1.7	5.5	7.8
83-84–Milwaukee	17	12	404	70	127	.551	19	45	.422	32	40	.800	6	22	28	78	51	0	12	36	1	191	1.6	4.6	11.2
84-85–Milwaukee	19	19	433	64	135	.474	16	47	.340	25	29	.862	6	25	31	85	55	1	15	40	3	169	1.6	4.5	8.9
88-89–Milwaukee	2	0	5	1	2	.500	1	2	.500	0	0	–	0	0	0	0	0	0	0	0	0	3	0.0	0.0	1.5
89-90–Milwaukee	5	0	43	4	14	.286	2	9	.222	7	8	.875	0	2	2	10	7	0	1	8	0	17	0.4	2.0	3.4
Reg. Season Totals	438	55	8428	1311	2809	.467	142	419	.339	732	904	.810	147	542	689	1723	1013	8	329	713	25	3496	1.6	3.9	8.0
Playoff Totals	67	15	1228	174	407	.428	32	101	.317	89	104	.856	25	78	103	194	173	3	51	86	2	469	1.5	2.9	7.0

Dunn, Patrick L. (Pat) b. March 17, 1931 d. November 1975 Ht. 6-2 Wt. 170 College: Utah State

SEASON–TEAM	G	GS	MIN	FGM	FGA	PCT	3FGM	3FGA	PCT	FTM	FTA	PCT	O-RB	D-RB	TOT	AST	PF	DQ	STL	TO	BLK	PTS	RPG	APG	PPG
57-58–Philadelphia	28	–	206	28	90	.311	–	–	–	14	17	.824	–	–	31	28	20	0	–	–	–	70	1.1	1.0	2.5
Reg. Season Totals	28	–	206	28	90	.311	–	–	–	14	17	.824	–	–	31	28	20	0	–	–	–	70	1.1	1.0	2.5
Playoff Totals	3	–	8	0	4	.000	–	–	–	0	0	–	–	–	1	1	1	0	–	–	–	0	0.3	0.3	0.0

Dunn, Theodore Roosevelt (T.R.) b. February 1, 1955 Ht. 6-4 Wt. 192 College: Alabama

SEASON–TEAM	G	GS	MIN	FGM	FGA	PCT	3FGM	3FGA	PCT	FTM	FTA	PCT	O-RB	D-RB	TOT	AST	PF	DQ	STL	TO	BLK	PTS	RPG	APG	PPG
77-78–Portland	63	–	768	100	240	.417	–	–	–	37	56	.661	63	84	147	45	74	0	46	35	8	237	2.3	0.7	3.8
78-79–Portland	80	–	1828	246	549	.448	–	–	–	122	158	.772	145	199	344	103	166	1	86	93	23	614	4.3	1.3	7.7
79-80–Portland	82	–	1841	240	551	.436	0	3	.000	84	111	.757	132	192	324	147	145	1	102	91	31	564	4.0	1.8	6.9
80-81–Denver	82	–	1427	146	354	.412	0	2	.000	79	121	.653	133	168	301	81	141	0	66	56	29	371	3.7	1.0	4.5
81-82–Denver	82	80	2519	258	504	.512	0	1	.000	153	215	.712	211	348	559	188	210	1	135	123	36	669	6.8	2.3	8.2
82-83–Denver	82	80	2640	254	527	.482	0	1	.000	119	163	.730	231	384	615	189	218	2	147	113	25	627	7.5	2.3	7.6
83-84–Denver	80	74	2705	174	370	.470	0	1	.000	106	145	.731	195	379	574	228	233	5	173	97	32	454	7.2	2.9	5.7
84-85–Denver	81	81	2290	175	358	.489	0	2	.000	84	116	.724	169	216	385	153	213	3	140	65	14	434	4.8	1.9	5.4
85-86–Denver	82	82	2401	172	379	.454	0	1	.000	68	88	.773	143	234	377	171	228	1	155	51	16	412	4.6	2.1	5.0
86-87–Denver	81	53	1932	118	276	.428	0	2	.000	36	55	.655	91	174	265	147	160	0	100	33	21	272	3.3	1.8	3.4
87-88–Denver	82	1	1534	70	156	.449	0	1	.000	40	52	.769	110	130	240	87	152	0	101	26	11	180	2.9	1.1	2.2
88-89–Phoenix	34	1	321	12	35	.343	0	0	–	9	12	.750	30	30	60	25	35	0	12	6	1	33	1.8	0.7	1.0
89-90–Denver	65	2	657	44	97	.454	0	2	.000	26	39	.667	56	82	138	43	67	1	41	19	4	114	2.1	0.7	1.8
90-91–Denver	17	3	217	21	47	.447	1	4	.250	9	10	.900	20	22	42	24	30	0	12	7	1	52	2.5	1.4	3.1
Reg. Season Totals	993	457	23080	2030	4443	.457	1	20	.050	972	1341	.725	1729	2642	4371	1631	2072	15	1316	815	252	5033	4.4	1.6	5.1
Playoff Totals	76	44	1634	109	244	.447	0	0	–	47	68	.691	130	187	317	104	180	1	95	51	13	265	4.2	1.4	3.5

Duren, John Thomas b. October 30, 1958 Ht. 6-3 Wt. 195 College: Georgetown

SEASON–TEAM	G	GS	MIN	FGM	FGA	PCT	3FGM	3FGA	PCT	FTM	FTA	PCT	O-RB	D-RB	TOT	AST	PF	DQ	STL	TO	BLK	PTS	RPG	APG	PPG
80-81–Utah	40	–	458	33	101	.327	0	1	.000	5	9	.556	8	27	35	54	54	0	18	37	2	71	0.9	1.4	1.8
81-82–Utah	79	9	1056	121	268	.451	3	11	.273	27	37	.730	14	70	84	157	143	0	20	72	4	272	1.1	2.0	3.4
82-83–Indiana	82	24	1433	163	360	.453	0	13	.000	43	54	.796	38	69	107	200	203	2	66	96	5	369	1.3	2.4	4.5
Reg. Season Totals	201	33	2947	317	729	.435	3	25	.120	75	100	.750	60	166	226	411	400	2	104	205	11	712	1.1	2.0	3.5

Durham, Jarrett M. b. August 22, 1949 Ht. 6-5 Wt. 190 College: Duquesne

SEASON–TEAM	G	GS	MIN	FGM	FGA	PCT	3FGM	3FGA	PCT	FTM	FTA	PCT	O-RB	D-RB	TOT	AST	PF	DQ	STL	TO	BLK	PTS	RPG	APG	PPG
71-72–New York (A)	1	–	1	0	0	–	0	0	–	0	0	–	–	–	0	0	0	–	–	1	–	0	0.0	0.0	0.0
Reg. ABA Totals	1	–	1	0	0	–	0	0	–	0	0	–	–	–	–	0	0	–	–	1	–	0	0.0	0.0	0.0

Durham, Patrick Wayne (Pat, Bull) b. March 10, 1967 Ht. 6-7 Wt. 210 College: Colorado State

SEASON–TEAM	G	GS	MIN	FGM	FGA	PCT	3FGM	3FGA	PCT	FTM	FTA	PCT	O-RB	D-RB	TOT	AST	PF	DQ	STL	TO	BLK	PTS	RPG	APG	PPG
92-93–Golden State	5	1	78	6	25	.240	0	0	–	9	12	.750	5	9	14	4	6	0	1	7	1	21	2.8	0.8	4.2
94-95–Minnesota	59	2	852	117	237	.494	5	26	.192	63	96	.656	37	57	94	53	114	0	36	45	32	302	1.6	0.9	5.1
Reg. Season Totals	64	3	930	123	262	.469	5	26	.192	72	108	.667	42	66	108	57	120	0	37	52	33	323	1.7	0.9	5.0

Durrant, Devin George b. October 20, 1960 Ht. 6-7 Wt. 200 College: Brigham Young

SEASON–TEAM	G	GS	MIN	FGM	FGA	PCT	3FGM	3FGA	PCT	FTM	FTA	PCT	O-RB	D-RB	TOT	AST	PF	DQ	STL	TO	BLK	PTS	RPG	APG	PPG
84-85–Indiana	59	8	756	114	274	.416	0	3	.000	72	102	.706	49	75	124	80	106	0	19	77	10	300	2.1	1.4	5.1
85-86–Phoenix	4	0	51	8	21	.381	0	0	–	1	4	.250	2	6	8	5	10	0	3	4	0	17	2.0	1.3	4.3
Reg. Season Totals	63	8	807	122	295	.414	0	3	.000	73	106	.689	51	81	132	85	116	0	22	81	10	317	2.1	1.3	5.0

Durrett, Kenneth L. (Ken) b. December 8, 1948 Ht. 6-7 Wt. 190 College: La Salle

SEASON–TEAM	G	GS	MIN	FGM	FGA	PCT	3FGM	3FGA	PCT	FTM	FTA	PCT	O-RB	D-RB	TOT	AST	PF	DQ	STL	TO	BLK	PTS	RPG	APG	PPG
71-72–Cincinnati	19	–	233	31	79	.392	–	–	–	21	28	.750	–	–	39	14	41	0	–	–	–	83	2.1	0.7	4.4
72-73–K.C.-Omaha	8	–	65	8	21	.381	–	–	–	6	8	.750	–	–	14	3	16	0	–	–	–	22	1.8	0.4	2.8
73-74–K.C.-Omaha	45	–	462	86	176	.489	–	–	–	42	69	.609	28	50	78	19	68	0	13	–	5	214	1.7	0.4	4.8
74-75–K.C.-Omaha-Phil.	48	–	445	67	166	.404	–	–	–	31	52	.596	35	67	102	18	72	0	9	–	8	165	2.1	0.4	3.4
Reg. Season Totals	120	–	1205	192	442	.434	–	–	–	100	157	.637	63	117	233	54	197	0	22	–	13	484	1.9	0.5	4.0

DuVal, Dennis b. March 31, 1952 Ht. 6-3 Wt. 175 College: Syracuse

SEASON–TEAM	G	GS	MIN	FGM	FGA	PCT	3FGM	3FGA	PCT	FTM	FTA	PCT	O-RB	D-RB	TOT	AST	PF	DQ	STL	TO	BLK	PTS	RPG	APG	PPG
74-75–Washington	37	–	137	24	65	.369	–	–	–	12	18	.667	8	15	23	14	34	0	16	–	2	60	0.6	0.4	1.6
75-76–Atlanta	13	–	130	15	43	.349	–	–	–	6	9	.667	1	7	8	20	15	0	6	–	2	36	0.6	1.5	2.8
Reg. Season Totals	50	–	267	39	108	.361	–	–	–	18	27	.667	9	22	31	34	49	0	22	–	4	96	0.6	0.7	1.9
Playoff Totals	5	–	14	3	9	.333	–	–	–	1	2	.500	0	3	3	3	1	0	0	–	0	7	0.6	0.6	1.4

Dwan, John (Jack) b. May 3, 1921 d. August 4, 1993 Ht. 6-4 Wt. 200 College: Loyola (Chicago)

SEASON–TEAM	G	GS	MIN	FGM	FGA	PCT	3FGM	3FGA	PCT	FTM	FTA	PCT	O-RB	D-RB	TOT	AST	PF	DQ	STL	TO	BLK	PTS	RPG	APG	PPG
47-48–Minneapolis (N)	55	–	–	128	–	–	–	–	–	50	73	.685	–	–	–	–	110	–	–	–	–	306	–	–	5.6
48-49–Minneapolis	60	–	–	121	380	.318	–	–	–	34	69	.493	–	–	–	129	157	–	–	–	–	276	–	2.2	4.6
Reg. NBA Totals	60	–	–	121	380	.318	–	–	–	34	69	.493	–	–	–	129	157	–	–	–	–	276	–	2.2	4.6
Reg. NBL Totals	55	–	–	128	–	–	–	–	–	50	73	.685	–	–	–	–	110	–	–	–	–	306	–	–	5.6
NBA Playoff Totals	10	–	–	7	58	.241	–	–	–	4	9	.444	–	–	–	18	23	1	–	–	–	18	–	0.9	1.8
NBL Playoff Totals	10	–	–	27	–	–	–	–	–	5	9	.556	–	–	–	–	28	–	–	–	–	59	–	–	5.9

Dykema, Craig b. June 11, 1959 Ht. 6-8 Wt. 190 College: Long Beach City (Calif.) Coll.(J.C.); Long Beach State

SEASON–TEAM	G	GS	MIN	FGM	FGA	PCT	3FGM	3FGA	PCT	FTM	FTA	PCT	O-RB	D-RB	TOT	AST	PF	DQ	STL	TO	BLK	PTS	RPG	APG	PPG
81-82–Phoenix	32	0	103	17	37	.459	2	4	.500	7	9	.778	3	9	12	15	19	0	2	7	0	43	0.4	0.5	1.3
Reg. Season Totals	32	0	103	17	37	.459	2	4	.500	7	9	.778	3	9	12	15	19	0	2	7	0	43	0.4	0.5	1.3
Playoff Totals	6	0	12	1	6	.167	0	0	–	0	0	–	0	4	4	1	2	0	0	1	0	2	0.7	0.2	0.3

Dyker, Eugene (Gene) b. February 17, 1930 d. January 1966 Ht. 6-6 Wt. 225 College: DePaul

SEASON–TEAM	G	GS	MIN	FGM	FGA	PCT	3FGM	3FGA	PCT	FTM	FTA	PCT	O-RB	D-RB	TOT	AST	PF	DQ	STL	TO	BLK	PTS	RPG	APG	PPG
53-54–Milwaukee	11	–	91	6	26	.231	–	–	–	4	8	.500	–	–	16	5	21	0	–	–	–	16	1.5	0.5	1.5
Reg. Season Totals	11	–	91	6	26	.231	–	–	–	4	8	.500	–	–	16	5	21	0	–	–	–	16	1.5	0.5	1.5

Eackles, Ledell (A-Train) b. November 24, 1966 Ht. 6-5 Wt. 231 College: New Orleans

SEASON–TEAM	G	GS	MIN	FGM	FGA	PCT	3FGM	3FGA	PCT	FTM	FTA	PCT	O-RB	D-RB	TOT	AST	PF	DQ	STL	TO	BLK	PTS	RPG	APG	PPG
88-89–Washington	80	6	1459	318	732	.434	9	40	.225	272	346	.786	100	80	180	123	156	1	41	128	5	917	2.3	1.5	11.5
89-90–Washington	78	8	1696	413	940	.439	19	59	.322	210	280	.750	74	101	175	182	157	0	50	143	4	1055	2.2	2.3	13.5
90-91–Washington	67	17	1616	345	762	.453	14	59	.237	164	222	.739	47	81	128	136	121	0	47	115	10	868	1.9	2.0	13.0
91-92–Washington	65	25	1463	355	759	.468	7	35	.200	139	187	.743	39	139	178	125	145	1	47	75	7	856	2.7	1.9	13.2
94-95–Miami	54	6	898	143	326	.439	18	41	.439	91	126	.722	33	62	95	72	88	0	19	53	2	395	1.8	1.3	7.3
95-96–Washington	55	26	1238	161	377	.427	54	128	.422	98	118	.831	44	104	148	86	84	1	28	57	3	474	2.7	1.6	8.6
97-98–Washington	42	0	547	75	175	.429	16	46	.348	52	59	.881	25	50	75	16	43	0	17	29	0	218	1.8	0.4	5.2
Reg. Season Totals	441	88	8917	1810	4071	.445	137	408	.336	1026	1338	.767	362	617	979	740	794	3	249	600	31	4783	2.2	1.7	10.8

Eakins, James Scott (Jim, Jimbo) b. May 24, 1946 Ht. 6-11 Wt. 215 College: Brigham Young

SEASON–TEAM	G	GS	MIN	FGM	FGA	PCT	3FGM	3FGA	PCT	FTM	FTA	PCT	O-RB	D-RB	TOT	AST	PF	DQ	STL	TO	BLK	PTS	RPG	APG	PPG
68-69–Oakland (A)	78	–	1671	351	646	.543	0	1	.000	309	430	.719	–	–	563	53	234	4	–	141	–	1011	7.2	0.7	13.0
69-70–Washington (A)	82	–	1214	181	364	.497	0	0	–	166	224	.741	–	–	412	71	184	0	–	–	–	528	5.0	0.9	6.4
70-71–Virginia (A)	84	–	2235	332	645	.515	0	0	–	242	319	.759	–	–	778	160	282	–	–	–	–	906	9.3	1.9	10.8
71-72–Virginia (A)	84	–	2718	371	764	.486	0	0	–	288	377	.764	290	517	807	181	298	–	–	189	–	1030	9.6	2.2	12.3
72-73–Virginia (A)	83	–	2559	430	823	.522	0	1	.000	384	479	.802	234	499	733	262	287	5	–	233	131	1244	8.8	3.2	15.0
73-74–Virginia (A)	84	–	2649	445	856	.520	0	1	.000	339	432	.785	296	510	806	236	265	–	65	228	98	1229	9.6	2.8	14.6
74-75–Utah (A)	84	–	2566	380	756	.503	0	0	–	291	348	.836	210	394	604	146	259	–	57	173	85	1051	7.2	1.7	12.5
75-76–Utah-Vir.-N.Y. (A)	73	–	1667	215	477	.451	0	0	–	198	223	.888	167	272	439	88	220	–	34	114	70	628	6.0	1.2	8.6
76-77–Kansas City	82	–	1338	151	336	.449	–	–	–	188	222	.847	112	249	361	119	195	1	29	–	49	490	4.4	1.5	6.0
77-78–S.A.-Milw.	33	–	406	44	86	.512	–	–	–	50	60	.833	29	46	75	29	71	0	7	33	17	138	2.3	0.9	4.2
Reg. NBA Totals	115	–	1744	195	422	.462	–	–	–	238	282	.844	141	295	436	148	266	1	36	33	66	628	3.8	1.3	5.5
Reg. ABA Totals	652	–	17279	2705	5331	.507	0	3	.000	2217	2832	.783	1197	2192	5142	1197	2029	9	156	1078	384	7627	7.9	1.8	11.7
NBA Playoff Totals	3	–	18	1	5	.200	–	–	–	0	0	–	1	0	1	1	2	0	1	1	0	2	0.3	0.3	0.7
ABA Playoff Totals	75	–	1897	317	587	.540	0	1	.000	207	272	.761	153	289	558	117	257	0	22	97	22	841	7.4	1.6	11.2

Earl, Acie Boyd b. June 23, 1970 Ht. 6-11 Wt. 279 College: Iowa

SEASON–TEAM	G	GS	MIN	FGM	FGA	PCT	3FGM	3FGA	PCT	FTM	FTA	PCT	O-RB	D-RB	TOT	AST	PF	DQ	STL	TO	BLK	PTS	RPG	APG	PPG
93-94–Boston	74	8	1149	151	372	.406	0	1	.000	108	160	.675	85	162	247	12	178	5	24	72	53	410	3.3	0.2	5.5
94-95–Boston	30	3	208	26	68	.382	0	0	–	14	29	.483	19	26	45	2	39	0	6	14	8	66	1.5	0.1	2.2
95-96–Toronto	42	7	655	117	276	.424	0	3	.000	82	114	.719	51	78	129	27	73	0	18	49	37	316	3.1	0.6	7.5
96-97–Toronto-Milw.	47	0	500	67	180	.372	0	5	.000	54	84	.643	35	61	96	20	61	0	15	35	28	188	2.0	0.4	4.0
Reg. Season Totals	193	18	2512	361	896	.403	0	9	.000	258	387	.667	190	327	517	61	351	5	63	170	126	980	2.7	0.3	5.1
Playoff Totals	1	0	10	1	3	.333	0	0	–	0	2	.000	1	1	2	–	4	0	0	0	1	2	2.0	0.0	2.0

Earle, Edwin (Ed) b. April 28, 1927 Ht. 6-3 Wt. 190 College: Loyola (Chicago)

SEASON–TEAM	G	GS	MIN	FGM	FGA	PCT	3FGM	3FGA	PCT	FTM	FTA	PCT	O-RB	D-RB	TOT	AST	PF	DQ	STL	TO	BLK	PTS	RPG	APG	PPG
53-54–Syracuse	2	–	12	1	2	.500	–	–	–	2	4	.500	–	–	2	0	0	0	–	–	–	4	1.0	0.0	2.0
Reg. Season Totals	2	–	12	1	2	.500	–	–	–	2	4	.500	–	–	2	0	0	0	–	–	–	4	1.0	0.0	2.0
Playoff Totals	1	–	0	0	0	–	–	–	–	0	0	–	–	–	0	–	0	0	–	–	–	0	0.0	0.0	0.0

Eaton, Mark E. b. January 24, 1957 Ht. 7-4 Wt. 290 College: UCLA

SEASON–TEAM	G	GS	MIN	FGM	FGA	PCT	3FGM	3FGA	PCT	FTM	FTA	PCT	O-RB	D-RB	TOT	AST	PF	DQ	STL	TO	BLK	PTS	RPG	APG	PPG
82-83–Utah	81	32	1528	146	353	.414	0	1	.000	59	90	.656	86	376	462	112	257	6	24	140	275	351	5.7	1.4	4.3
83-84–Utah	82	78	2139	194	416	.466	0	1	.000	73	123	.593	148	447	595	113	303	4	25	98	351	461	7.3	1.4	5.6
84-85–Utah	82	82	2813	302	673	.449	0	0	–	190	267	.712	207	720	927	124	312	5	36	206	456	794	11.3	1.5	9.7
85-86–Utah	80	80	2551	277	589	.470	0	0	–	122	202	.604	172	503	675	101	282	5	33	157	369	676	8.4	1.3	8.5
86-87–Utah	79	79	2505	234	585	.400	0	0	–	140	213	.657	211	486	697	105	273	5	43	142	321	608	8.8	1.3	7.7
87-88–Utah	82	82	2731	226	541	.418	0	0	–	119	191	.623	230	487	717	55	320	8	41	131	304	571	8.7	0.7	7.0
88-89–Utah	82	82	2914	188	407	.462	0	0	–	132	200	.660	227	616	843	83	290	6	40	142	315	508	10.3	1.0	6.2
89-90–Utah	82	82	2281	158	300	.527	0	0	–	79	118	.669	171	430	601	39	238	3	33	75	201	395	7.3	0.5	4.8
90-91–Utah	80	80	2580	169	292	.579	0	0	–	71	112	.634	182	485	667	51	298	6	39	99	188	409	8.3	0.6	5.1
91-92–Utah	81	81	2023	107	240	.446	0	0	–	52	87	.598	150	341	491	40	239	2	36	60	205	266	6.1	0.5	3.3
92-93–Utah	64	57	1104	71	130	.546	0	0	–	35	50	.700	73	191	264	17	143	0	18	43	79	177	4.1	0.3	2.8
Reg. Season Totals	875	815	25169	2072	4526	.458	0	2	.000	1072	1653	.649	1857	5082	6939	840	2955	50	368	1293	3064	5216	7.9	1.0	6.0
Playoff Totals	74	74	2295	180	368	.489	0	0	–	94	147	.639	169	388	557	52	250	5	35	81	210	454	7.5	0.7	6.1
All-Star Totals	1	0	9	0	0	–	0	0	–	0	0	–	0	5	5	0	1	0	0	0	2	0	5.0	0.0	0.0

Eaves, Jerry Lee b. February 8, 1959 Ht. 6-4 Wt. 185 College: Louisville

SEASON–TEAM	G	GS	MIN	FGM	FGA	PCT	3FGM	3FGA	PCT	FTM	FTA	PCT	O-RB	D-RB	TOT	AST	PF	DQ	STL	TO	BLK	PTS	RPG	APG	PPG
82-83–Utah	82	7	1588	280	575	.487	1	8	.125	200	247	.810	34	88	122	210	116	0	51	152	3	761	1.5	2.6	9.3
83-84–Utah	80	1	1034	132	293	.451	0	6	.000	92	132	.697	29	56	85	200	90	0	33	93	5	356	1.1	2.5	4.5
84-85–Atlanta	3	0	37	3	6	.500	0	0	–	5	6	.833	0	0	0	4	6	0	0	4	0	11	0.0	1.3	3.7
86-87–Sacramento	3	0	26	1	8	.125	0	0	–	2	2	1.000	1	0	1	0	6	0	1	2	0	4	0.3	0.0	1.3
Reg. Season Totals	168	8	2685	416	882	.472	1	14	.071	299	387	.773	64	144	208	414	218	0	85	251	8	1132	1.2	2.5	6.7
Playoff Totals	11	0	132	22	46	.478	1	3	.333	10	13	.769	3	7	10	13	10	0	5	7	2	55	0.9	1.2	5.0

Ebben, William Edward (Bill) b. October 7, 1935 Ht. 6-4 Wt. 200 College: Detroit Mercy

SEASON–TEAM	G	GS	MIN	FGM	FGA	PCT	3FGM	3FGA	PCT	FTM	FTA	PCT	O-RB	D-RB	TOT	AST	PF	DQ	STL	TO	BLK	PTS	RPG	APG	PPG
57-58–Detroit	8	–	50	6	28	.214	–	–	–	3	4	.750	–	–	8	4	5	0	–	–	–	15	1.0	0.5	1.9
Reg. Season Totals	8	–	50	6	28	.214	–	–	–	3	4	.750	–	–	8	4	5	0	–	–	–	15	1.0	0.5	1.9

Eberhard, Allen Dean (Al) b. May 10, 1952 Ht. 6-6 Wt. 225 College: Missouri

SEASON–TEAM	G	GS	MIN	FGM	FGA	PCT	3FGM	3FGA	PCT	FTM	FTA	PCT	O-RB	D-RB	TOT	AST	PF	DQ	STL	TO	BLK	PTS	RPG	APG	PPG
74-75–Detroit	34	–	277	31	85	.365	–	–	–	17	21	.810	18	29	47	16	33	0	13	–	1	79	1.4	0.5	2.3
75-76–Detroit	81	–	2066	283	683	.414	–	–	–	191	229	.834	139	251	390	83	250	5	87	–	15	757	4.8	1.0	9.3
76-77–Detroit	68	–	1219	181	380	.476	–	–	–	109	138	.790	76	145	221	50	197	4	45	–	15	471	3.3	0.7	6.9
77-78–Detroit	37	–	576	71	160	.444	–	–	–	41	61	.672	37	65	102	26	64	0	13	23	4	183	2.8	0.7	4.9
Reg. Season Totals	220	–	4138	566	1308	.433	–	–	–	358	449	.797	270	490	760	175	544	9	158	23	35	1490	3.5	0.8	6.8
Playoff Totals	11	–	224	18	48	.375	–	–	–	19	27	.704	13	22	35	9	20	0	9	–	4	55	3.2	0.8	5.0

Ebron, Roy Lester b. August 31, 1951 Ht. 6-9 Wt. 225 College: Louisiana-Lafayette

SEASON–TEAM	G	GS	MIN	FGM	FGA	PCT	3FGM	3FGA	PCT	FTM	FTA	PCT	O-RB	D-RB	TOT	AST	PF	DQ	STL	TO	BLK	PTS	RPG	APG	PPG
73-74–Utah (A)	40	–	529	103	211	.488	0	1	.000	43	84	.512	79	97	176	19	68	–	16	35	32	249	4.4	0.5	6.2
Reg. ABA Totals	40	–	529	103	211	.488	0	1	.000	43	84	.512	79	97	176	19	68	0	16	35	32	249	4.4	0.5	6.2
ABA Playoff Totals	7	–	41	6	19	.316	0	1	.000	5	10	.500	10	5	15	2	6	0	0	2	4	17	2.1	0.3	2.4

Eddie, Patrick b. December 27, 1967 Ht. 6-11 Wt. 240 College: Arkansas State; Mississippi

SEASON–TEAM	G	GS	MIN	FGM	FGA	PCT	3FGM	3FGA	PCT	FTM	FTA	PCT	O-RB	D-RB	TOT	AST	PF	DQ	STL	TO	BLK	PTS	RPG	APG	PPG
91-92–New York	4	0	13	2	9	.222	0	0	–	0	0	–	0	1	1	0	3	0	0	0	0	4	0.3	0.0	1.0
Reg. Season Totals	4	0	13	2	9	.222	0	0	–	0	0	–	0	1	1	0	3	0	0	0	0	4	0.3	0.0	1.0

Eddleman, Thomas Dwight (Dike) b. December 27, 1922 Ht. 6-3 Wt. 190 College: Illinois

SEASON–TEAM	G	GS	MIN	FGM	FGA	PCT	3FGM	3FGA	PCT	FTM	FTA	PCT	O-RB	D-RB	TOT	AST	PF	DQ	STL	TO	BLK	PTS	RPG	APG	PPG
49-50–Tri-Cities	64	–	–	332	906	.366	–	–	–	162	260	.623	–	–	–	142	254	–	–	–	–	826	–	2.2	12.9
50-51–Tri-Cities	68	–	–	398	1120	.355	–	–	–	244	349	.699	–	–	410	170	231	5	–	–	–	1040	6.0	2.5	15.3
51-52–Milw.-FtWayne	65	–	1893	269	809	.333	–	–	–	202	329	.614	–	–	267	134	249	9	–	–	–	740	4.1	2.1	11.4
52-53–Fort Wayne	69	–	1571	241	687	.351	–	–	–	133	237	.561	–	–	236	104	220	5	–	–	–	615	3.4	1.5	8.9
Reg. Season Totals	266	–	3464	1240	3522	.352	–	–	–	741	1175	.631	–	–	913	550	954	19	–	–	–	3221	4.5	2.1	12.1
Playoff Totals	12	–	100	32	129	.380	–	–	–	23	47	.489	–	–	12	20	45	4	–	–	–	87	1.3	1.3	7.3
All-Star Totals	1	–	0	2	9	.222	–	–	–	3	5	.600	–	–	0	3	3	0	–	–	–	7	0.0	3.0	7.0

Edelin, Kenton Scott (Kent) b. May 24, 1962 Ht. 6-8 Wt. 205 College: Virginia

SEASON–TEAM	G	GS	MIN	FGM	FGA	PCT	3FGM	3FGA	PCT	FTM	FTA	PCT	O-RB	D-RB	TOT	AST	PF	DQ	STL	TO	BLK	PTS	RPG	APG	PPG
84-85–Indiana	10	1	143	4	13	.308	0	0	–	3	8	.375	8	18	26	10	39	1	5	3	4	11	2.6	1.0	1.1
Reg. Season Totals	10	1	143	4	13	.308	0	0	–	3	8	.375	8	18	26	10	39	1	5	3	4	11	2.6	1.0	1.1

Edge, Charles (Charlie, Razor) b. February 23, 1950 Ht. 6-6 Wt. 210 College: Le Moyne-Owen

SEASON–TEAM	G	GS	MIN	FGM	FGA	PCT	3FGM	3FGA	PCT	FTM	FTA	PCT	O-RB	D-RB	TOT	AST	PF	DQ	STL	TO	BLK	PTS	RPG	APG	PPG
73-74–Memphis (A)	78	–	1948	312	624	.500	0	1	.000	124	182	.681	250	391	641	70	137	–	64	130	70	748	8.2	0.9	9.6
74-75–Indiana (A)	77	–	1142	195	386	.505	0	3	.000	63	114	.553	164	176	340	39	103	–	53	82	35	453	4.4	0.5	5.9
Reg. ABA Totals	155	–	3090	507	1010	.502	0	4	.000	187	296	.632	414	567	981	109	240	0	117	212	105	1201	6.3	0.7	7.7
ABA Playoff Totals	7	–	42	2	8	.250	0	0	–	0	0	–	4	5	9	2	6	0	0	5	0	4	1.3	0.3	0.6

Edmonds, Bobby Joe b. March 8, 1941 d. November 12, 1991 Ht. 6-6 Wt. 220 College: Tennessee State

SEASON–TEAM	G	GS	MIN	FGM	FGA	PCT	3FGM	3FGA	PCT	FTM	FTA	PCT	O-RB	D-RB	TOT	AST	PF	DQ	STL	TO	BLK	PTS	RPG	APG	PPG
67-68–Indiana (A)	72	–	1338	213	488	.436	1	6	.167	150	229	.655	–	–	374	29	183	4	–	123	–	577	5.2	0.4	8.0
69-70–Indiana (A)	3	–	12	1	5	.200	0	0	–	1	3	.333	–	–	4	0	1	0	–	–	–	3	1.3	0.0	1.0
Reg. ABA Totals	75	–	1350	214	493	.434	1	6	.167	151	232	.651	–	–	378	29	184	4	–	123	–	580	5.0	0.4	7.7
ABA Playoff Totals	3	–	47	6	14	.429	1	2	.500	7	9	.778	–	–	18	2	12	1	–	5	–	20	6.0	0.7	6.7

Edmonson, Keith Andre b. September 28, 1960 Ht. 6-5 Wt. 205 College: Purdue

SEASON–TEAM	G	GS	MIN	FGM	FGA	PCT	3FGM	3FGA	PCT	FTM	FTA	PCT	O-RB	D-RB	TOT	AST	PF	DQ	STL	TO	BLK	PTS	RPG	APG	PPG
82-83–Atlanta	32	2	309	48	139	.345	0	2	.000	16	27	.593	20	19	39	22	41	0	11	20	6	112	1.2	0.7	3.5
83-84–S.A.-Denver	55	0	622	158	321	.492	0	0	–	94	126	.746	46	42	88	34	83	1	26	61	7	410	1.6	0.6	7.5
Reg. Season Totals	87	2	931	206	460	.448	0	2	.000	110	153	.719	66	61	127	56	124	1	37	81	13	522	1.5	0.6	6.0
Playoff Totals	1	0	2	1	1	1.000	0	0	–	0	0	–	1	0	1	1	0	0	0	0	0	2	1.0	1.0	2.0

Edney, Tyus Dwayne b. February 14, 1973 Ht. 5-10 Wt. 152 College: UCLA

SEASON–TEAM	G	GS	MIN	FGM	FGA	PCT	3FGM	3FGA	PCT	FTM	FTA	PCT	O-RB	D-RB	TOT	AST	PF	DQ	STL	TO	BLK	PTS	RPG	APG	PPG
95-96–Sacramento	80	60	2481	305	740	.412	53	144	.368	197	252	.782	63	138	201	491	203	2	89	192	3	860	2.5	6.1	10.8
96-97–Sacramento	70	20	1376	150	391	.384	8	42	.190	177	215	.823	34	79	113	226	98	0	60	112	2	485	1.6	3.2	6.9
97-98–Boston	52	7	623	93	216	.431	3	10	.300	88	111	.793	20	35	55	139	69	0	51	66	1	277	1.1	2.7	5.3
Reg. Season Totals	202	87	4480	548	1347	.407	64	196	.327	462	578	.799	117	252	369	856	370	2	200	370	6	1622	1.8	4.2	8.0
Playoff Totals	4	4	121	18	42	.429	2	8	.250	10	12	.833	2	10	12	11	11	1	8	9	0	48	3.0	2.8	12.0

Edwards, Douglas (Doug) b. January 21, 1971 Ht. 6-7 Wt. 228 College: Florida State

SEASON–TEAM	G	GS	MIN	FGM	FGA	PCT	3FGM	3FGA	PCT	FTM	FTA	PCT	O-RB	D-RB	TOT	AST	PF	DQ	STL	TO	BLK	PTS	RPG	APG	PPG
93-94–Atlanta	16	0	107	17	49	.347	0	1	.000	9	16	.563	7	11	18	8	9	0	2	6	5	43	1.1	0.5	2.7
94-95–Atlanta	38	0	212	22	48	.458	0	1	.000	23	32	.719	19	29	48	13	30	0	5	22	4	67	1.3	0.3	1.8
95-96–Vancouver	31	0	519	32	91	.352	0	4	.000	29	38	.763	35	52	87	39	51	2	10	29	18	93	2.8	1.3	3.0
Reg. Season Totals	85	0	838	71	188	.378	0	6	.000	61	86	.709	61	92	153	60	90	2	17	57	27	203	1.8	0.7	2.4
Playoff Totals	1	0	3	0	0	–	0	0	–	0	0	–	0	0	0	–	0	0	0	0	1	0	0.0	0.0	0.0

Edwards, Franklin Delano b. February 2, 1959 Ht. 6-1 Wt. 190 College: Cleveland State

SEASON–TEAM	G	GS	MIN	FGM	FGA	PCT	3FGM	3FGA	PCT	FTM	FTA	PCT	O-RB	D-RB	TOT	AST	PF	DQ	STL	TO	BLK	PTS	RPG	APG	PPG
81-82–Philadelphia	42	3	291	65	150	.433	0	9	.000	20	27	.741	10	17	27	45	37	0	16	24	5	150	0.6	1.1	3.6
82-83–Philadelphia	81	3	1266	228	483	.472	0	8	.000	86	113	.761	23	62	85	221	119	0	81	110	6	542	1.0	2.7	6.7
83-84–Philadelphia	60	0	654	84	221	.380	0	1	.000	34	48	.708	12	47	59	90	78	1	31	46	5	202	1.0	1.5	3.4
84-85–L.A. Clippers	16	0	198	36	66	.545	0	0	–	19	24	.792	3	11	14	38	10	0	17	17	0	91	0.9	2.4	5.7
85-86–L.A. Clippers	73	19	1491	262	577	.454	1	9	.111	132	151	.874	24	62	86	259	87	0	89	137	4	657	1.2	3.5	9.0
86-87–Sacramento	8	0	122	9	32	.281	0	4	.000	10	14	.714	2	8	10	29	7	0	5	17	1	28	1.3	3.6	3.5
87-88–Sacramento	16	11	414	54	115	.470	0	2	.000	24	32	.750	4	15	19	92	10	0	10	47	1	132	1.2	5.8	8.3
Reg. Season Totals	296	36	4436	738	1644	.449	1	33	.030	325	409	.795	78	222	300	774	348	1	249	398	21	1802	1.0	2.6	6.1
Playoff Totals	21	0	133	25	52	.481	1	1	1.000	22	26	.846	4	10	14	22	7	0	8	8	0	73	0.7	1.0	3.5

E

Edwards, James Franklin b. November 22, 1955 Ht. 7-1 Wt. 252 College: Washington

SEASON–TEAM	G	GS	MIN	FGM	FGA	PCT	3FGM	3FGA	PCT	FTM	FTA	PCT	O-RB	D-RB	TOT	AST	PF	DQ	STL	TO	BLK	PTS	RPG	APG	PPG
77-78–L.A.-Indiana	83	–	2405	495	1093	.453	–	–	–	272	421	.646	197	418	615	85	322	12	53	169	78	1262	7.4	1.0	15.2
78-79–Indiana	82	–	2546	534	1065	.501	–	–	–	298	441	.676	179	514	693	92	363	16	60	162	109	1366	8.5	1.1	16.7
79-80–Indiana	82	–	2314	528	1032	.512	0	1	.000	231	339	.681	179	399	578	127	324	12	55	131	104	1287	7.0	1.5	15.7
80-81–Indiana	81	–	2375	511	1004	.509	0	3	.000	244	347	.703	191	380	571	212	304	7	32	164	128	1266	7.0	2.6	15.6
81-82–Cleveland	77	75	2539	528	1033	.511	0	4	.000	232	339	.684	189	392	581	123	347	17	24	162	117	1288	7.5	1.6	16.7
82-83–Clev.-Phoenix	31	9	667	128	263	.487	0	0	–	69	108	.639	56	99	155	40	110	5	12	49	19	325	5.0	1.3	10.5
83-84–Phoenix	72	67	1897	438	817	.536	0	1	.000	183	254	.720	108	240	348	184	254	3	23	140	30	1059	4.8	2.6	14.7
84-85–Phoenix	70	58	1787	384	766	.501	0	3	.000	276	370	.746	95	292	387	153	237	5	26	162	52	1044	5.5	2.2	14.9
85-86–Phoenix	52	51	1314	318	587	.542	0	0	–	212	302	.702	79	222	301	74	200	5	23	128	29	848	5.8	1.4	16.3
86-87–Phoenix	14	9	304	57	110	.518	0	0	–	54	70	.771	20	40	60	19	42	1	6	15	7	168	4.3	1.4	12.0
87-88–Phoenix-Det.	69	44	1705	302	643	.470	0	1	.000	210	321	.654	119	293	412	78	216	2	16	130	37	814	6.0	1.1	11.8
88-89–Detroit	76	1	1254	211	422	.500	0	2	.000	133	194	.686	68	163	231	49	226	1	11	72	31	555	3.0	0.6	7.3
89-90–Detroit	82	70	2283	462	928	.498	0	3	.000	265	354	.749	112	233	345	63	295	4	23	133	37	1189	4.2	0.8	14.5
90-91–Detroit	72	70	1903	383	792	.484	1	2	.500	215	295	.729	91	186	277	65	249	4	12	126	30	982	3.8	0.9	13.6
91-92–L.A. Clippers	72	11	1437	250	538	.465	0	1	.000	198	271	.731	55	147	202	53	236	1	24	72	33	698	2.8	0.7	9.7
92-93–L.A. Lakers	52	0	617	122	270	.452	0	0	–	84	118	.712	30	70	100	41	122	0	10	51	7	328	1.9	0.8	6.3
93-94–L.A. Lakers	45	2	469	78	168	.464	0	0	–	54	79	.684	11	54	65	22	90	0	4	30	3	210	1.4	0.5	4.7
94-95–Portland	28	0	266	32	83	.386	0	0	–	11	17	.647	10	33	43	8	44	0	5	14	8	75	1.5	0.3	2.7
95-96–Chicago	28	0	274	41	110	.373	0	0	–	16	26	.615	15	25	40	11	61	1	1	21	8	98	1.4	0.4	3.5
Reg. Season Totals	1168	467	28356	5802	11724	.495	1	21	.048	3257	4666	.698	1804	4200	6004	1499	4042	96	420	1931	867	14862	5.1	1.3	12.7
Playoff Totals	111	50	2212	399	853	.468	0	3	.000	232	340	.682	110	244	354	84	325	3	17	126	46	1030	3.2	0.8	9.3

Edwards, Jay Charles b. January 3, 1969 Ht. 6-4 Wt. 185 College: Indiana

SEASON–TEAM	G	GS	MIN	FGM	FGA	PCT	3FGM	3FGA	PCT	FTM	FTA	PCT	O-RB	D-RB	TOT	AST	PF	DQ	STL	TO	BLK	PTS	RPG	APG	PPG
89-90–L.A. Clippers	4	0	26	3	7	.429	0	2	.000	1	3	.333	1	1	2	4	4	0	1	1	0	7	0.5	1.0	1.8
Reg. Season Totals	4	0	26	3	7	.429	0	2	.000	1	3	.333	1	1	2	4	4	0	1	1	0	7	0.5	1.0	1.8

Edwards, Kevin Durell b. October 30, 1965 Ht. 6-3 Wt. 210 College: DePaul

SEASON–TEAM	G	GS	MIN	FGM	FGA	PCT	3FGM	3FGA	PCT	FTM	FTA	PCT	O-RB	D-RB	TOT	AST	PF	DQ	STL	TO	BLK	PTS	RPG	APG	PPG
88-89–Miami	79	62	2349	470	1105	.425	10	37	.270	144	193	.746	85	177	262	349	154	0	139	246	27	1094	3.3	4.4	13.8
89-90–Miami	78	54	2211	395	959	.412	9	30	.300	139	183	.760	77	205	282	252	149	1	125	180	33	938	3.6	3.2	12.0
90-91–Miami	79	16	2000	380	927	.410	24	84	.286	171	213	.803	80	125	205	240	151	2	129	163	46	955	2.6	3.0	12.1
91-92–Miami	81	1	1840	325	716	.454	7	32	.219	162	191	.848	56	155	211	170	138	1	99	120	20	819	2.6	2.1	10.1
92-93–Miami	40	30	1134	216	462	.468	5	17	.294	119	141	.844	48	73	121	120	69	0	68	75	12	556	3.0	3.0	13.9
93-94–New Jersey	82	82	2727	471	1028	.458	35	99	.354	167	217	.770	94	187	281	232	150	0	120	135	34	1144	3.4	2.8	14.0
94-95–New Jersey	14	14	466	69	154	.448	18	45	.400	40	42	.952	10	27	37	27	42	0	19	35	5	196	2.6	1.9	14.0
95-96–New Jersey	34	33	1007	142	390	.364	42	104	.404	68	84	.810	14	61	75	71	67	0	54	68	7	394	2.2	2.1	11.6
96-97–New Jersey	32	0	477	69	183	.377	15	43	.349	37	43	.860	9	34	43	57	34	0	17	49	4	190	1.3	1.8	5.9
97-98–N.J.-Orlando	39	5	487	57	165	.345	6	15	.400	30	35	.857	20	34	54	39	28	0	26	30	1	150	1.4	1.0	3.8
Reg. Season Totals	558	297	14698	2594	6089	.426	171	506	.338	1077	1342	.803	493	1078	1571	1557	982	4	796	1101	189	6436	2.8	2.8	11.5
Playoff Totals	7	4	203	23	63	.365	0	2	.000	18	22	.818	9	14	23	16	12	0	7	14	1	64	3.3	2.3	9.1

Edwards, Theodore (Blue) b. October 31, 1965 Ht. 6-4 Wt. 229 College: East Carolina

SEASON–TEAM	G	GS	MIN	FGM	FGA	PCT	3FGM	3FGA	PCT	FTM	FTA	PCT	O-RB	D-RB	TOT	AST	PF	DQ	STL	TO	BLK	PTS	RPG	APG	PPG
89-90–Utah	82	49	1889	286	564	.507	9	30	.300	146	203	.719	69	182	251	145	280	2	76	152	36	727	3.1	1.8	8.9
90-91–Utah	62	56	1611	244	464	.526	6	24	.250	82	117	.701	51	150	201	108	203	4	57	105	29	576	3.2	1.7	9.3
91-92–Utah	81	81	2283	433	830	.522	39	103	.379	113	146	.774	86	212	298	137	236	1	81	122	46	1018	3.7	1.7	12.6
92-93–Milwaukee	82	81	2729	554	1083	.512	37	106	.349	237	300	.790	123	259	382	214	242	1	129	175	45	1382	4.7	2.6	16.9
93-94–Milwaukee	82	64	2322	382	800	.478	38	106	.358	151	189	.799	104	225	329	171	235	1	83	146	27	953	4.0	2.1	11.6
94-95–Boston-Utah	67	7	1112	181	393	.461	22	75	.293	75	90	.833	50	80	130	77	143	1	43	81	16	459	1.9	1.1	6.9
95-96–Vancouver	82	82	2773	401	956	.419	84	245	.343	157	208	.755	98	248	346	212	243	1	118	170	46	1043	4.2	2.6	12.7
96-97–Vancouver	61	12	1439	182	458	.397	25	89	.281	89	109	.817	49	140	189	114	135	0	38	81	20	478	3.1	1.9	7.8
97-98–Vancouver	81	20	1968	326	742	.439	40	120	.333	180	215	.837	61	156	217	201	183	0	86	134	27	872	2.7	2.5	10.8
98-99–Miami	24	0	283	32	72	.444	4	10	.400	9	13	.692	7	26	33	30	23	0	17	21	5	77	1.4	1.3	3.2
Reg. Season Totals	704	452	18409	3021	6362	.475	304	908	.335	1239	1590	.779	698	1678	2376	1409	1923	11	728	1187	297	7585	3.4	2.0	10.8
Playoff Totals	34	16	722	107	226	.473	5	16	.313	46	60	.767	38	65	103	44	101	0	40	55	6	265	3.0	1.3	7.8

Edwards, William Allen (Bill) b. September 22, 1971 Ht. 6-8 Wt. 215 College: Wright State

SEASON–TEAM	G	GS	MIN	FGM	FGA	PCT	3FGM	3FGA	PCT	FTM	FTA	PCT	O-RB	D-RB	TOT	AST	PF	DQ	STL	TO	BLK	PTS	RPG	APG	PPG
93-94–Philadelphia	3	0	44	2	18	.111	0	5	.000	2	5	.400	5	9	14	4	6	0	3	4	1	6	4.7	1.3	2.0
Reg. Season Totals	3	0	44	2	18	.111	0	5	.000	2	5	.400	5	9	14	4	6	0	3	4	1	6	4.7	1.3	2.0

Egan, John Francis (Johnny) b. January 31, 1939 Ht. 6-0 Wt. 180 College: Providence

SEASON–TEAM	G	GS	MIN	FGM	FGA	PCT	3FGM	3FGA	PCT	FTM	FTA	PCT	O-RB	D-RB	TOT	AST	PF	DQ	STL	TO	BLK	PTS	RPG	APG	PPG
61-62–Detroit	58	–	696	128	301	.425	–	–	–	64	84	.762	–	–	86	102	64	0	–	–	–	320	1.5	1.8	5.5
62-63–Detroit	46	–	752	110	296	.372	–	–	–	53	69	.768	–	–	59	114	70	0	–	–	–	273	1.3	2.5	5.9
63-64–Detroit-N.Y.	66	–	2325	334	758	.441	–	–	–	193	243	.794	–	–	191	358	181	3	–	–	–	861	2.9	5.4	13.0
64-65–New York	74	–	1664	258	529	.488	–	–	–	162	199	.814	–	–	143	252	139	0	–	–	–	678	1.9	3.4	9.2
65-66–N.Y.-Balt.	76	–	1644	259	574	.451	–	–	–	173	227	.762	–	–	183	273	167	1	–	–	–	691	2.4	3.6	9.1
66-67–Baltimore	71	–	1743	267	624	.428	–	–	–	185	219	.845	–	–	180	275	190	3	–	–	–	719	2.5	3.9	10.1
67-68–Baltimore	67	–	930	163	415	.393	–	–	–	142	183	.776	–	–	112	134	127	0	–	–	–	468	1.7	2.0	7.0
68-69–Los Angeles	82	–	1805	246	597	.412	–	–	–	204	240	.850	–	–	147	215	206	1	–	–	–	696	1.8	2.6	8.5
69-70–Los Angeles	72	–	1627	215	491	.438	–	–	–	99	121	.818	–	–	104	216	171	2	–	–	–	529	1.4	3.0	7.3
70-71–Clev.-S.D.	62	–	824	67	178	.376	–	–	–	42	51	.824	–	–	63	112	71	0	–	–	–	176	1.0	1.8	2.8
71-72–Houston	38	–	437	42	104	.404	–	–	–	26	32	.813	–	–	26	51	55	0	–	–	–	110	0.7	1.3	2.9
Reg. Season Totals	712	–	14447	2089	4867	.429	–	–	–	1343	1668	.805	–	–	1294	2102	1441	10	–	–	–	5521	1.8	3.0	7.8
Playoff Totals	42	–	947	165	369	.447	–	–	–	93	117	.795	–	–	67	131	97	1	–	–	–	423	1.6	3.1	10.1

Eggleston, Lonnie J. b. June 8, 1918 Ht. 6-0 Wt. 170 College: Oklahoma State

SEASON–TEAM	G	GS	MIN	FGM	FGA	PCT	3FGM	3FGA	PCT	FTM	FTA	PCT	O-RB	D-RB	TOT	AST	PF	DQ	STL	TO	BLK	PTS	RPG	APG	PPG
48-49–St. Louis	2	–	–	1	4	.250	–	–	–	2	3	.667	–	–	–	1	3	–	–	–	–	4	–	0.5	2.0
Reg. Season Totals	2	–	–	1	4	.250	–	–	–	2	3	.667	–	–	–	1	3	–	–	–	–	4	–	0.5	2.0

Ehlers, Edwin S. (Eddie, Bulbs) b. March 10, 1923 Ht. 6-3 Wt. 200 College: Purdue

SEASON–TEAM	G	GS	MIN	FGM	FGA	PCT	3FGM	3FGA	PCT	FTM	FTA	PCT	O-RB	D-RB	TOT	AST	PF	DQ	STL	TO	BLK	PTS	RPG	APG	PPG
47-48–Boston	40	–	–	104	417	.249	–	–	–	78	144	.542	–	–	–	44	92	–	–	–	–	286	–	1.1	7.2
48-49–Boston	59	–	–	182	583	.312	–	–	–	150	225	.667	–	–	–	133	119	–	–	–	–	514	–	2.3	8.7
Reg. Season Totals	99	–	–	286	1000	.286	–	–	–	228	369	.618	–	–	–	177	211	–	–	–	–	800	–	1.8	8.1

Ehlo, Joel Craig (Craig, Mr. Everything) b. August 11, 1961 Ht. 6-7 Wt. 203 College: Washington State

SEASON–TEAM	G	GS	MIN	FGM	FGA	PCT	3FGM	3FGA	PCT	FTM	FTA	PCT	O-RB	D-RB	TOT	AST	PF	DQ	STL	TO	BLK	PTS	RPG	APG	PPG
83-84–Houston	7	0	63	11	27	.407	0	0	–	1	1	1.000	4	5	9	6	13	0	3	3	0	23	1.3	0.9	3.3
84-85–Houston	45	0	189	34	69	.493	0	3	.000	19	30	.633	8	17	25	26	26	0	11	22	3	87	0.6	0.6	1.9
85-86–Houston	36	0	199	36	84	.429	3	9	.333	23	29	.793	17	29	46	29	22	0	11	15	4	98	1.3	0.8	2.7
86-87–Cleveland	44	15	890	99	239	.414	5	29	.172	70	99	.707	55	106	161	92	80	0	40	61	30	273	3.7	2.1	6.2
87-88–Cleveland	79	27	1709	226	485	.466	22	64	.344	89	132	.674	86	188	274	206	182	0	82	107	30	563	3.5	2.6	7.1
88-89–Cleveland	82	4	1867	249	524	.475	39	100	.390	71	117	.607	100	195	295	266	161	0	110	116	19	608	3.6	3.2	7.4
89-90–Cleveland	81	64	2894	436	940	.464	104	248	.419	126	185	.681	147	292	439	371	226	2	126	161	23	1102	5.4	4.6	13.6
90-91–Cleveland	82	68	2766	344	773	.445	49	149	.329	95	140	.679	142	246	388	376	209	0	121	160	34	832	4.7	4.6	10.1
91-92–Cleveland	63	62	2016	310	684	.453	69	167	.413	87	123	.707	94	213	307	238	150	0	78	104	22	776	4.9	3.8	12.3
92-93–Cleveland	82	73	2559	385	785	.490	93	244	.381	86	120	.717	113	290	403	254	170	0	104	124	22	949	4.9	3.1	11.6
93-94–Atlanta	82	0	2147	316	708	.446	77	221	.348	112	154	.727	71	208	279	273	161	0	136	130	26	821	3.4	3.3	10.0
94-95–Atlanta	49	0	1166	191	422	.453	51	134	.381	44	71	.620	55	92	147	113	86	0	46	73	6	477	3.0	2.3	9.7
95-96–Atlanta	79	8	1758	253	591	.428	82	221	.371	81	103	.786	65	191	256	138	138	0	85	104	9	669	3.2	1.7	8.5
96-97–Seattle	62	0	848	87	248	.351	27	95	.284	13	26	.500	39	71	110	68	71	0	36	45	4	214	1.8	1.1	3.5
Reg. Season Totals	873	321	21071	2977	6579	.453	621	1684	.369	917	1330	.689	996	2143	3139	2456	1695	2	989	1225	232	7492	3.6	2.8	8.6
Playoff Totals	76	30	1843	234	572	.409	57	166	.343	91	124	.734	57	165	222	222	154	0	77	93	13	616	2.9	2.9	8.1

Eichhorst, Richard A. (Dick) b. October 21, 1933 Ht. 6-3 Wt. 200 College: Southeast Missouri State

SEASON–TEAM	G	GS	MIN	FGM	FGA	PCT	3FGM	3FGA	PCT	FTM	FTA	PCT	O-RB	D-RB	TOT	AST	PF	DQ	STL	TO	BLK	PTS	RPG	APG	PPG
61-62–St. Louis	1	–	10	1	2	.500	–	–	–	0	0	–	–	–	1	3	1	0	–	–	–	2	1.0	3.0	2.0
Reg. Season Totals	1	–	10	1	2	.500	–	–	–	0	0	–	–	–	1	3	1	0	–	–	–	2	1.0	3.0	2.0

Eisley, Howard Jonathan b. December 4, 1972 Ht. 6-2 Wt. 180 College: Boston College

SEASON–TEAM	G	GS	MIN	FGM	FGA	PCT	3FGM	3FGA	PCT	FTM	FTA	PCT	O-RB	D-RB	TOT	AST	PF	DQ	STL	TO	BLK	PTS	RPG	APG	PPG
94-95–Minn.-S.A.	49	4	552	40	122	.328	9	37	.243	31	40	.775	12	36	48	95	81	0	18	50	6	120	1.0	1.9	2.4
95-96–Utah	65	0	961	104	242	.430	14	62	.226	65	77	.844	22	56	78	146	130	0	29	77	3	287	1.2	2.2	4.4
96-97–Utah	82	0	1083	139	308	.451	20	72	.278	70	89	.787	20	64	84	198	141	0	44	110	10	368	1.0	2.4	4.5
97-98–Utah	82	18	1726	229	519	.441	48	118	.407	127	149	.852	25	141	166	346	182	3	54	160	13	633	2.0	4.2	7.7
98-99–Utah	50	0	1038	140	314	.446	21	50	.420	67	80	.838	12	82	94	185	122	0	30	109	2	368	1.9	3.7	7.4
99-00–Utah	82	5	2096	282	675	.418	60	163	.368	84	102	.824	23	147	170	347	223	2	59	132	9	708	2.1	4.2	8.6
Reg. Season Totals	410	27	7456	934	2180	.428	172	502	.343	444	537	.827	114	526	640	1317	879	5	234	638	43	2484	1.6	3.2	6.1
Playoff Totals	79	0	1226	143	369	.388	34	98	.347	89	101	.881	16	102	118	216	149	1	31	92	11	409	1.5	2.7	5.2

Ekezie, Obinna Ralph b. August 22, 1975 Ht. 6-9 Wt. 270 College: Maryland

SEASON–TEAM	G	GS	MIN	FGM	FGA	PCT	3FGM	3FGA	PCT	FTM	FTA	PCT	O-RB	D-RB	TOT	AST	PF	DQ	STL	TO	BLK	PTS	RPG	APG	PPG
99-00–Vancouver	39	0	351	41	88	.466	0	0	–	43	64	.672	34	58	92	8	61	0	9	26	4	125	2.4	0.2	3.2
Reg. Season Totals	39	0	351	41	88	.466	0	0	–	43	64	.672	34	58	92	8	61	0	9	26	4	125	2.4	0.2	3.2

Eliason, Donald Carlton (Don) b. July 24, 1918 Ht. 6-2 Wt. 210 College: Hamline

SEASON–TEAM	G	GS	MIN	FGM	FGA	PCT	3FGM	3FGA	PCT	FTM	FTA	PCT	O-RB	D-RB	TOT	AST	PF	DQ	STL	TO	BLK	PTS	RPG	APG	PPG
46-47–Boston	1	–	–	0	1	.000	–	–	–	0	0	–	–	–	–	0	1	–	–	–	–	0	–	0.0	0.0
Reg. Season Totals	1	–	–	0	1	.000	–	–	–	0	0	–	–	–	–	0	1	–	–	–	–	0	–	0.0	0.0

Elie, Mario Antoine b. November 26, 1963 Ht. 6-5 Wt. 225 College: American International

SEASON–TEAM	G	GS	MIN	FGM	FGA	PCT	3FGM	3FGA	PCT	FTM	FTA	PCT	O-RB	D-RB	TOT	AST	PF	DQ	STL	TO	BLK	PTS	RPG	APG	PPG
90-91–Phil.-G.S.	33	0	644	79	159	.497	4	10	.400	75	89	.843	46	64	110	45	85	1	19	30	10	237	3.3	1.4	7.2
91-92–Golden State	79	32	1677	221	424	.521	23	70	.329	155	182	.852	69	158	227	174	159	3	68	83	15	620	2.9	2.2	7.8
92-93–Portland	82	7	1757	240	524	.458	45	129	.349	183	214	.855	59	157	216	177	145	0	74	89	20	708	2.6	2.2	8.6
93-94–Houston	67	8	1606	208	466	.446	56	167	.335	154	179	.860	28	153	181	208	124	0	50	109	8	626	2.7	3.1	9.3
94-95–Houston	81	13	1896	243	487	.499	80	201	.398	144	171	.842	50	146	196	189	158	0	65	104	12	710	2.4	2.3	8.8
95-96–Houston	45	16	1385	180	357	.504	41	127	.323	98	115	.852	47	108	155	138	93	0	45	59	11	499	3.4	3.1	11.1
96-97–Houston	78	77	2687	291	585	.497	120	286	.420	207	231	.896	60	175	235	310	200	2	92	135	12	909	3.0	4.0	11.7
97-98–Houston	73	59	1988	206	456	.452	55	189	.291	145	174	.833	39	117	156	221	115	0	81	100	8	612	2.1	3.0	8.4
98-99–San Antonio	47	37	1291	156	331	.471	40	107	.374	103	119	.866	36	101	137	89	91	0	46	61	12	455	2.9	1.9	9.7
99-00–San Antonio	79	79	2217	195	457	.427	74	186	.398	126	149	.846	48	201	249	193	156	0	73	130	9	590	3.2	2.4	7.5
Reg. Season Totals	664	328	17148	2019	4246	.476	538	1472	.365	1390	1623	.856	482	1380	1862	1744	1326	6	613	900	117	5966	2.8	2.6	9.0
Playoff Totals	112	53	2951	311	688	.452	88	232	.379	239	285	.839	100	229	329	257	254	4	91	140	15	949	2.9	2.3	8.5

Ellefson, E. Ray (Ray) b. November 18, 1922 Ht. 6-8 Wt. 230 College: Oklahoma State; Colorado; West Texas A&M

SEASON–TEAM	G	GS	MIN	FGM	FGA	PCT	3FGM	3FGA	PCT	FTM	FTA	PCT	O-RB	D-RB	TOT	AST	PF	DQ	STL	TO	BLK	PTS	RPG	APG	PPG
48-49–Minneapolis	3	–	–	1	5	.200	–	–	–	0	0	–	–	–	–	0	2	–	–	–	–	2	–	0.0	0.7
48-49–Waterloo (N)	7	–	–	4	–	–	–	–	–	8	11	.727	–	–	–	–	5	–	–	–	–	16	–	–	2.3
50-51–New York	3	–	–	0	4	.000	–	–	–	4	4	1.000	–	–	8	0	6	0	–	–	–	4	2.7	0.0	1.3
Reg. NBA Totals	6	–	–	1	9	.111	–	–	–	4	4	1.000	–	–	8	0	8	0	–	–	–	6	2.7	0.0	1.0
Reg. NBL Totals	7	–	–	4	–	–	–	–	–	8	11	.727	–	–	–	–	5	–	–	–	–	16	–	–	2.3

Elliott, Robert Alan (Bob) b. August 18, 1955 Ht. 6-9 Wt. 225 College: Arizona

SEASON–TEAM	G	GS	MIN	FGM	FGA	PCT	3FGM	3FGA	PCT	FTM	FTA	PCT	O-RB	D-RB	TOT	AST	PF	DQ	STL	TO	BLK	PTS	RPG	APG	PPG
78-79–New Jersey	14	–	282	41	73	.562	–	–	–	41	56	.732	16	40	56	22	34	2	6	26	4	123	4.0	1.6	8.8
79-80–New Jersey	54	–	722	101	228	.443	1	4	.250	104	152	.684	67	118	185	53	97	0	29	88	14	307	3.4	1.0	5.7
80-81–New Jersey	73	–	1320	214	419	.511	1	2	.500	121	202	.599	104	157	261	129	175	3	34	119	16	550	3.6	1.8	7.5
Reg. Season Totals	141	–	2324	356	720	.494	2	6	.333	266	410	.649	187	315	502	204	306	5	69	233	34	980	3.6	1.4	7.0

Elliott, Sean Michael b. February 2, 1968 Ht. 6-8 Wt. 220 College: Arizona

SEASON–TEAM	G	GS	MIN	FGM	FGA	PCT	3FGM	3FGA	PCT	FTM	FTA	PCT	O-RB	D-RB	TOT	AST	PF	DQ	STL	TO	BLK	PTS	RPG	APG	PPG
89-90–San Antonio	81	69	2032	311	647	.481	1	9	.111	187	216	.866	127	170	297	154	172	0	45	112	14	810	3.7	1.9	10.0
90-91–San Antonio	82	82	3044	478	976	.490	20	64	.313	325	402	.808	142	314	456	238	190	2	69	147	33	1301	5.6	2.9	15.9
91-92–San Antonio	82	82	3120	514	1040	.494	25	82	.305	285	331	.861	143	296	439	214	149	0	84	152	29	1338	5.4	2.6	16.3
92-93–San Antonio	70	70	2604	451	918	.491	37	104	.356	268	337	.795	85	237	322	265	132	1	68	152	28	1207	4.6	3.8	17.2
93-94–Detroit	73	73	2409	360	791	.455	26	87	.299	139	173	.803	68	195	263	197	174	3	54	129	27	885	3.6	2.7	12.1
94-95–San Antonio	81	81	2858	502	1072	.468	136	333	.408	326	404	.807	63	224	287	206	216	2	78	151	38	1466	3.5	2.5	18.1
95-96–San Antonio	77	77	2901	525	1127	.466	161	392	.411	326	423	.771	69	327	396	211	178	1	69	198	33	1537	5.1	2.7	20.0
96-97–San Antonio	39	39	1393	196	464	.422	42	126	.333	148	196	.755	48	142	190	124	105	1	24	89	24	582	4.9	3.2	14.9
97-98–San Antonio	36	36	1012	122	303	.403	34	90	.378	56	78	.718	16	108	124	62	92	1	24	57	14	334	3.4	1.7	9.3
98-99–San Antonio	50	50	1509	208	507	.410	39	119	.328	106	140	.757	35	178	213	117	104	1	26	71	17	561	4.3	2.3	11.2
99-00–San Antonio	19	19	391	38	106	.358	13	37	.351	25	32	.781	6	41	47	28	34	0	12	19	2	114	2.5	1.5	6.0
Reg. Season Totals	690	678	23273	3705	7951	.466	534	1443	.370	2191	2732	.802	802	2232	3034	1816	1546	12	553	1277	259	10135	4.4	2.6	14.7
Playoff Totals	73	73	2597	365	811	.450	65	183	.355	266	335	.794	77	238	315	193	199	0	54	134	31	1061	4.3	2.6	14.5
All-Star Totals	2	0	37	6	18	.333	2	6	.333	4	5	.800	3	4	7	2	5	0	0	3	0	18	3.5	1.0	9.0

Ellis, Alexander (Boo) b. February 11, 1936 Ht. 6-5 Wt. 185 College: Niagara

SEASON–TEAM	G	GS	MIN	FGM	FGA	PCT	3FGM	3FGA	PCT	FTM	FTA	PCT	O-RB	D-RB	TOT	AST	PF	DQ	STL	TO	BLK	PTS	RPG	APG	PPG
58-59–Minneapolis	72	–	1202	163	379	.430	–	–	–	102	144	.708	–	–	380	59	137	0	–	–	–	428	5.3	0.8	5.9
59-60–Minneapolis	46	–	671	64	185	.346	–	–	–	51	76	.671	–	–	236	27	64	2	–	–	–	179	5.1	0.6	3.9
Reg. Season Totals	118	–	1873	227	564	.402	–	–	–	153	220	.695	–	–	616	86	201	2	–	–	–	607	5.2	0.7	5.1
Playoff Totals	16	–	291	37	90	.411	–	–	–	22	39	.564	–	–	105	18	37	0	–	–	–	96	6.6	1.1	6.0

Ellis, Dale (Lamar Mundane) b. August 6, 1960 Ht. 6-7 Wt. 215 College: Tennessee

SEASON–TEAM	G	GS	MIN	FGM	FGA	PCT	3FGM	3FGA	PCT	FTM	FTA	PCT	O-RB	D-RB	TOT	AST	PF	DQ	STL	TO	BLK	PTS	RPG	APG	PPG
83-84–Dallas	67	2	1059	225	493	.456	12	29	.414	87	121	.719	106	144	250	56	118	0	41	78	9	549	3.7	0.8	8.2
84-85–Dallas	72	4	1314	274	603	.454	42	109	.385	77	104	.740	100	138	238	56	131	1	46	58	7	667	3.3	0.8	9.3
85-86–Dallas	72	1	1086	193	470	.411	63	173	.364	59	82	.720	86	82	168	37	78	0	40	38	9	508	2.3	0.5	7.1
86-87–Seattle	82	76	3073	785	1520	.516	86	240	.358	385	489	.787	187	260	447	238	267	2	104	238	32	2041	5.5	2.9	24.9
87-88–Seattle	75	73	2790	764	1519	.503	107	259	.413	303	395	.767	167	173	340	197	221	1	74	172	11	1938	4.5	2.6	25.8
88-89–Seattle	82	82	3190	857	1710	.501	162	339	.478	377	462	.816	156	186	342	164	197	0	108	218	22	2253	4.2	2.0	27.5
89-90–Seattle	55	49	2033	502	1011	.497	96	256	.375	193	236	.818	90	148	238	110	124	3	59	119	7	1293	4.3	2.0	23.5
90-91–Seattle-Milw.	51	24	1424	340	718	.474	57	157	.363	120	166	.723	66	107	173	95	112	1	49	81	8	857	3.4	1.9	16.8
91-92–Milwaukee	81	11	2191	485	1034	.469	138	329	.419	164	212	.774	92	161	253	104	151	0	57	119	18	1272	3.1	1.3	15.7
92-93–San Antonio	82	76	2731	545	1092	.499	119	297	.401	157	197	.797	81	231	312	107	179	0	78	111	18	1366	3.8	1.3	16.7
93-94–San Antonio	77	75	2590	478	967	.494	131	332	.395	83	107	.776	70	185	255	80	141	0	66	75	11	1170	3.3	1.0	15.2
94-95–Denver	81	3	1996	351	774	.453	106	263	.403	110	127	.866	56	166	222	57	142	0	37	81	9	918	2.7	0.7	11.3
95-96–Denver	81	52	2626	459	959	.479	150	364	.412	136	179	.760	88	227	315	139	191	1	57	98	7	1204	3.9	1.7	14.9
96-97–Denver	82	51	2940	477	1151	.414	192	528	.364	215	263	.817	99	194	293	165	178	0	60	146	7	1361	3.6	2.0	16.6
97-98–Seattle	79	0	1939	348	700	.497	127	274	.464	111	142	.782	51	133	184	89	128	0	60	74	5	934	2.3	1.1	11.8
98-99–Seattle	48	5	1232	174	395	.441	94	217	.433	53	70	.757	25	90	115	38	77	1	25	45	3	495	2.4	0.8	10.3
99-00–Milw.-Cha.	42	5	564	66	159	.415	37	100	.370	9	13	.692	13	43	56	14	45	0	13	20	0	178	1.3	0.3	4.2
Reg. Season Totals	1209	589	34778	7323	15275	.479	1719	4266	.403	2639	3365	.784	1533	2668	4201	1746	2480	10	974	1771	183	19004	3.5	1.4	15.7
Playoff Totals	73	43	1981	403	909	.443	71	202	.351	134	171	.784	110	163	273	92	163	2	51	97	14	1011	3.7	1.3	13.8
All-Star Totals	1	1	26	12	16	.750	1	1	1.000	2	2	1.000	3	3	6	2	2	0	0	2	0	27	6.0	2.0	27.0

Ellis, Harold b. October 7, 1970 Ht. 6-5 Wt. 220 College: Morehouse

SEASON–TEAM	G	GS	MIN	FGM	FGA	PCT	3FGM	3FGA	PCT	FTM	FTA	PCT	O-RB	D-RB	TOT	AST	PF	DQ	STL	TO	BLK	PTS	RPG	APG	PPG
93-94–L.A. Clippers	49	16	923	159	292	.545	0	4	.000	106	149	.711	94	59	153	31	97	0	73	43	2	424	3.1	0.6	8.7
94-95–L.A. Clippers	69	7	656	91	189	.481	1	13	.077	69	117	.590	56	32	88	40	102	0	67	49	12	252	1.3	0.6	3.7
97-98–Denver	27	3	344	62	111	.559	0	4	.000	40	63	.635	27	23	50	18	53	0	19	19	4	164	1.9	0.7	6.1
Reg. Season Totals	145	26	1923	312	592	.527	1	21	.048	215	329	.653	177	114	291	89	252	0	159	111	18	840	2.0	0.6	5.8

Ellis, Joseph Franklin (Joe) b. May 3, 1944 Ht. 6-6 Wt. 175 College: San Francisco

SEASON–TEAM	G	GS	MIN	FGM	FGA	PCT	3FGM	3FGA	PCT	FTM	FTA	PCT	O-RB	D-RB	TOT	AST	PF	DQ	STL	TO	BLK	PTS	RPG	APG	PPG
66-67–San Francisco	41	–	333	67	164	.409	–	–	–	19	25	.760	–	–	112	27	45	0	–	–	–	153	2.7	0.7	3.7
67-68–San Francisco	51	–	624	111	302	.368	–	–	–	32	50	.640	–	–	195	37	83	2	–	–	–	254	3.8	0.7	5.0
68-69–San Francisco	74	–	1731	371	939	.395	–	–	–	147	201	.731	–	–	481	130	258	13	–	–	–	889	6.5	1.8	12.0
69-70–San Francisco	76	–	2380	501	1223	.410	–	–	–	200	270	.741	–	–	594	139	281	13	–	–	–	1202	7.8	1.8	15.8
70-71–San Francisco	80	–	2275	356	898	.396	–	–	–	151	203	.744	–	–	511	161	287	6	–	–	–	863	6.4	2.0	10.8
71-72–Golden State	78	–	1462	280	681	.411	–	–	–	95	132	.720	–	–	389	97	224	4	–	–	–	655	5.0	1.2	8.4
72-73–Golden State	74	–	1054	199	487	.409	–	–	–	69	93	.742	–	–	282	88	143	2	–	–	–	467	3.8	1.2	6.3
73-74–Golden State	50	–	515	61	190	.321	–	–	–	18	31	.581	37	85	122	37	76	2	33	–	9	140	2.4	0.7	2.8
Reg. Season Totals	524	–	10374	1946	4884	.398	–	–	–	731	1005	.727	37	85	2686	716	1397	42	33	–	9	4623	5.1	1.4	8.8
Playoff Totals	38	–	575	83	270	.307	–	–	–	36	52	.692	0	0	131	23	75	1	0	–	0	202	3.4	0.6	5.3

Ellis, LaPhonso Darnell b. May 5, 1970 Ht. 6-8 Wt. 240 College: Notre Dame

SEASON–TEAM	G	GS	MIN	FGM	FGA	PCT	3FGM	3FGA	PCT	FTM	FTA	PCT	O-RB	D-RB	TOT	AST	PF	DQ	STL	TO	BLK	PTS	RPG	APG	PPG
92-93–Denver	82	82	2749	483	958	.504	2	13	.154	237	317	.748	274	470	744	151	293	8	72	153	111	1205	9.1	1.8	14.7
93-94–Denver	79	79	2699	483	963	.502	7	23	.304	242	359	.674	220	462	682	167	304	6	63	172	80	1215	8.6	2.1	15.4
94-95–Denver	6	0	58	9	25	.360	0	0	–	6	6	1.000	7	10	17	4	12	0	1	5	5	24	2.8	0.7	4.0
95-96–Denver	45	28	1269	189	432	.438	4	22	.182	89	148	.601	93	229	322	74	163	3	36	83	33	471	7.2	1.6	10.5
96-97–Denver	55	49	2002	445	1014	.439	95	259	.367	218	282	.773	107	279	386	131	181	7	44	117	41	1203	7.0	2.4	21.9
97-98–Denver	76	71	2575	410	1007	.407	57	201	.284	206	256	.805	146	398	544	213	226	2	65	173	49	1083	7.2	2.8	14.3
98-99–Atlanta	20	20	539	80	190	.421	1	5	.200	43	61	.705	25	84	109	18	48	1	8	34	7	204	5.5	0.9	10.2
99-00–Atlanta	58	8	1309	209	464	.450	3	21	.143	66	95	.695	98	192	290	59	133	1	32	52	25	487	5.0	1.0	8.4
Reg. Season Totals	421	337	13200	2308	5053	.457	169	544	.311	1107	1524	.726	970	2124	3094	817	1360	28	321	789	351	5892	7.3	1.9	14.0
Playoff Totals	12	12	436	68	142	.479	3	6	.500	38	54	.704	27	70	97	26	46	2	9	19	11	177	8.1	2.2	14.8

Ellis, LeRon Perry b. April 28, 1969 Ht. 6-10 Wt. 240 College: Kentucky; Syracuse

SEASON–TEAM	G	GS	MIN	FGM	FGA	PCT	3FGM	3FGA	PCT	FTM	FTA	PCT	O-RB	D-RB	TOT	AST	PF	DQ	STL	TO	BLK	PTS	RPG	APG	PPG
91-92–L.A. Clippers	29	0	103	17	50	.340	0	0	–	9	19	.474	12	12	24	1	11	0	6	11	9	43	0.8	0.0	1.5
93-94–Charlotte	50	1	680	88	182	.484	0	0	–	45	68	.662	70	118	188	24	83	1	17	21	25	221	3.8	0.5	4.4
95-96–Miami	12	1	74	5	22	.227	0	0	–	3	6	.500	5	3	8	4	11	0	2	3	3	13	0.7	0.3	1.1
Reg. Season Totals	91	2	857	110	254	.433	0	0	–	57	93	.613	87	133	220	29	105	1	25	35	37	277	2.4	0.3	3.0
Playoff Totals	1	0	2	0	0	–	0	0	–	0	0	–	0	0	0	–	0	0	0	0	0	0	0.0	0.0	0.0

Ellis, Leroy b. March 10, 1940 Ht. 6-11 Wt. 210 College: St. John's (N.Y.)

SEASON–TEAM	G	GS	MIN	FGM	FGA	PCT	3FGM	3FGA	PCT	FTM	FTA	PCT	O-RB	D-RB	TOT	AST	PF	DQ	STL	TO	BLK	PTS	RPG	APG	PPG
62-63–Los Angeles	80	–	1628	222	530	.419	–	–	–	133	202	.658	–	–	518	46	194	1	–	–	–	577	6.5	0.6	7.2
63-64–Los Angeles	78	–	1459	200	473	.423	–	–	–	112	170	.659	–	–	498	41	192	3	–	–	–	512	6.4	0.5	6.6
64-65–Los Angeles	80	–	2026	311	700	.444	–	–	–	198	284	.697	–	–	652	49	196	1	–	–	–	820	8.2	0.6	10.3
65-66–Los Angeles	80	–	2219	393	927	.424	–	–	–	186	256	.727	–	–	735	74	232	3	–	–	–	972	9.2	0.9	12.2
66-67–Baltimore	81	–	2938	496	1166	.425	–	–	–	211	286	.738	–	–	970	170	258	3	–	–	–	1203	12.0	2.1	14.9
67-68–Baltimore	78	–	2719	380	800	.475	–	–	–	207	286	.724	–	–	862	158	256	5	–	–	–	967	11.1	2.0	12.4
68-69–Baltimore	80	–	1603	229	527	.435	–	–	–	117	155	.755	–	–	510	73	168	0	–	–	–	575	6.4	0.9	7.2
69-70–Baltimore	72	–	1163	194	414	.469	–	–	–	86	116	.741	–	–	376	47	129	0	–	–	–	474	5.2	0.7	6.6
70-71–Portland	74	–	2581	485	1095	.443	–	–	–	209	261	.801	–	–	907	235	258	5	–	–	–	1179	12.3	3.2	15.9
71-72–Los Angeles	74	–	1081	138	300	.460	–	–	–	66	95	.695	–	–	310	46	115	0	–	–	–	342	4.2	0.6	4.6
72-73–L.A.-Phil.	79	–	2600	421	969	.434	–	–	–	129	161	.801	–	–	777	139	199	2	–	–	–	971	9.8	1.8	12.3
73-74–Philadelphia	81	–	2831	326	722	.452	–	–	–	147	196	.750	292	598	890	189	224	2	86	–	87	799	11.0	2.3	9.9
74-75–Philadelphia	82	–	2183	287	623	.461	–	–	–	72	99	.727	195	387	582	117	178	1	44	–	55	646	7.1	1.4	7.9
75-76–Philadelphia	29	–	489	61	132	.462	–	–	–	17	28	.607	47	75	122	21	62	0	16	–	9	139	4.2	0.7	4.8
Reg. Season Totals	1048	–	27520	4143	9378	.442	–	–	–	1890	2595	.728	534	1060	8709	1405	2661	26	146	–	151	10176	8.3	1.3	9.7
Playoff Totals	64	–	1487	175	424	.413	–	–	–	113	163	.693	0	0	462	44	152	1	0	–	0	463	7.2	0.7	7.2

Ellis, Maurice H. (Bo) b. August 8, 1954 Ht. 6-9 Wt. 200 College: Marquette

SEASON–TEAM	G	GS	MIN	FGM	FGA	PCT	3FGM	3FGA	PCT	FTM	FTA	PCT	O-RB	D-RB	TOT	AST	PF	DQ	STL	TO	BLK	PTS	RPG	APG	PPG
77-78–Denver	78	–	1213	133	320	.416	–	–	–	72	104	.692	114	190	304	73	208	2	49	99	47	338	3.9	0.9	4.3
78-79–Denver	42	–	269	42	92	.457	–	–	–	29	36	.806	17	45	62	10	45	0	10	22	13	113	1.5	0.2	2.7
79-80–Denver	48	–	502	61	136	.449	0	3	.000	40	53	.755	51	65	116	30	67	1	10	24	24	162	2.4	0.6	3.4
Reg. Season Totals	168	–	1984	236	548	.431	0	3	.000	141	193	.731	182	300	482	113	320	3	69	145	84	613	2.9	0.7	3.6
Playoff Totals	15	–	194	19	46	.413	0	0	–	14	17	.824	16	31	47	9	27	0	8	14	9	52	3.1	0.6	3.5

Ellison, Pervis (Never Nervous) b. April 3, 1967 Ht. 6-10 Wt. 242 College: Louisville

SEASON–TEAM	G	GS	MIN	FGM	FGA	PCT	3FGM	3FGA	PCT	FTM	FTA	PCT	O-RB	D-RB	TOT	AST	PF	DQ	STL	TO	BLK	PTS	RPG	APG	PPG
89-90–Sacramento	34	22	866	111	251	.442	0	2	.000	49	78	.628	64	132	196	65	132	4	16	62	57	271	5.8	1.9	8.0
90-91–Washington	76	30	1942	326	636	.513	0	6	.000	139	214	.650	224	361	585	102	268	6	49	146	157	791	7.7	1.3	10.4
91-92–Washington	66	64	2511	547	1014	.539	1	3	.333	227	312	.728	217	523	740	190	222	2	62	196	177	1322	11.2	2.9	20.0
92-93–Washington	49	48	1701	341	655	.521	0	4	.000	170	242	.702	138	295	433	117	154	3	45	110	108	852	8.8	2.4	17.4
93-94–Washington	47	24	1178	137	292	.469	0	3	.000	70	97	.722	77	165	242	70	140	3	25	73	50	344	5.1	1.5	7.3
94-95–Boston	55	11	1083	152	300	.507	0	2	.000	71	99	.717	124	185	309	34	179	5	22	76	54	375	5.6	0.6	6.8
95-96–Boston	69	29	1431	145	295	.492	0	0	–	75	117	.641	151	300	451	62	207	2	39	84	99	365	6.5	0.9	5.3
96-97–Boston	6	4	125	6	16	.375	0	0	–	3	5	.600	9	17	26	4	21	1	5	7	9	15	4.3	0.7	2.5
97-98–Boston	33	8	447	40	70	.571	0	0	–	20	34	.588	52	57	109	31	90	2	20	28	31	100	3.3	0.9	3.0
99-00–Boston	30	5	269	19	43	.442	0	0	–	15	21	.714	29	38	67	13	67	1	10	13	8	53	2.2	0.4	1.8
Reg. Season Totals	465	245	11553	1824	3572	.511	1	20	.050	839	1219	.688	1085	2073	3158	688	1480	29	293	795	750	4488	6.8	1.5	9.7
Playoff Totals	4	0	68	11	19	.579	0	0	–	2	2	1.000	11	6	17	2	17	1	2	4	5	24	4.3	0.5	6.0

Elmore, Leonard J. (Len) b. March 28, 1952 Ht. 6-10 Wt. 225 College: Maryland

SEASON–TEAM	G	GS	MIN	FGM	FGA	PCT	3FGM	3FGA	PCT	FTM	FTA	PCT	O-RB	D-RB	TOT	AST	PF	DQ	STL	TO	BLK	PTS	RPG	APG	PPG
74-75–Indiana (A)	77	–	1414	218	523	.417	1	1	1.000	72	93	.774	148	247	395	35	241	–	67	83	91	509	5.1	0.5	6.6
75-76–Indiana (A)	76	–	2591	480	1193	.402	0	3	.000	152	206	.738	242	577	819	122	310	–	136	175	178	1112	10.8	1.6	14.6
76-77–Indiana	6	–	46	7	17	.412	–	–	–	4	5	.800	7	8	15	2	11	0	0	–	4	18	2.5	0.3	3.0
77-78–Indiana	69	–	1327	142	386	.368	–	–	–	88	132	.667	139	281	420	80	174	4	74	73	71	372	6.1	1.2	5.4
78-79–Indiana	80	–	1264	139	342	.406	–	–	–	56	78	.718	115	287	402	75	183	3	62	73	79	334	5.0	0.9	4.2
79-80–Kansas City	58	–	915	104	242	.430	0	0	–	51	74	.689	74	183	257	64	154	0	41	67	39	259	4.4	1.1	4.5
80-81–Milwaukee	72	–	925	76	212	.358	0	0	–	54	75	.720	68	140	208	69	178	3	37	44	52	206	2.9	1.0	2.9
81-82–New Jersey	81	70	2100	300	652	.460	0	0	–	135	170	.794	167	274	441	100	280	6	92	136	92	735	5.4	1.2	9.1
82-83–New Jersey	74	0	975	97	244	.398	0	1	.000	54	84	.643	81	157	238	39	125	2	44	83	38	248	3.2	0.5	3.4
83-84–New York	65	5	832	64	157	.408	0	0	–	27	38	.711	62	103	165	30	153	3	29	46	30	155	2.5	0.5	2.4
Reg. NBA Totals	505	75	8384	929	2252	.413	0	1	.000	469	656	.715	713	1433	2146	459	1258	21	379	522	405	2327	4.2	0.9	4.6
Reg. ABA Totals	153	–	4005	698	1716	.407	1	4	.250	224	299	.749	390	824	1214	157	551	–	203	258	269	1621	7.9	1.0	10.6
NBA Playoff Totals	11	2	146	15	35	.429	0	0	–	6	8	.750	12	24	36	4	16	0	5	8	3	36	3.3	0.4	3.3
ABA Playoff Totals	21	–	633	92	220	.418	0	0	–	26	38	.684	55	105	160	20	84	–	26	28	41	210	7.6	1.0	10.0

Elston, Darrell Eugene b. August 15, 1952 Ht. 6-4 Wt. 205 College: North Carolina

SEASON–TEAM	G	GS	MIN	FGM	FGA	PCT	3FGM	3FGA	PCT	FTM	FTA	PCT	O-RB	D-RB	TOT	AST	PF	DQ	STL	TO	BLK	PTS	RPG	APG	PPG
74-75–Virginia (A)	72	–	1869	250	613	.408	3	18	.167	93	123	.756	48	115	163	202	166	–	82	126	9	596	2.3	2.8	8.3
76-77–Indiana	5	–	40	2	14	.143	–	–	–	1	2	.500	1	5	6	2	6	0	1	–	0	5	1.2	0.4	1.0
Reg. NBA Totals	5	–	40	2	14	.143	–	–	–	1	2	.500	1	5	6	2	6	0	1	–	0	5	1.2	0.4	1.0
Reg. ABA Totals	72	–	1869	250	613	.408	3	18	.167	93	123	.756	48	115	163	202	166	–	82	126	9	596	2.3	2.8	8.3

Embry, Wayne Richard (Goose) b. March 26, 1937 Ht. 6-8 Wt. 255 College: Miami (Ohio) HOF: 1999

SEASON–TEAM	G	GS	MIN	FGM	FGA	PCT	3FGM	3FGA	PCT	FTM	FTA	PCT	O-RB	D-RB	TOT	AST	PF	DQ	STL	TO	BLK	PTS	RPG	APG	PPG
58-59–Cincinnati	66	–	1590	272	702	.387	–	–	–	206	314	.656	–	–	597	96	232	9	–	–	–	750	9.0	1.5	11.4
59-60–Cincinnati	73	–	1594	303	690	.439	–	–	–	167	325	.514	–	–	692	83	226	1	–	–	–	773	9.5	1.1	10.6
60-61–Cincinnati	79	–	2233	458	1015	.451	–	–	–	221	331	.668	–	–	864	127	286	7	–	–	–	1137	10.9	1.6	14.4
61-62–Cincinnati	75	–	2623	564	1210	.466	–	–	–	356	516	.690	–	–	977	182	286	6	–	–	–	1484	13.0	2.4	19.8
62-63–Cincinnati	76	–	2511	534	1165	.458	–	–	–	343	514	.667	–	–	936	177	286	7	–	–	–	1411	12.3	2.3	18.6
63-64–Cincinnati	80	–	2915	556	1213	.458	–	–	–	271	417	.650	–	–	925	113	325	7	–	–	–	1383	11.6	1.4	17.3
64-65–Cincinnati	74	–	2243	352	772	.456	–	–	–	239	371	.644	–	–	741	92	297	10	–	–	–	943	10.0	1.2	12.7
65-66–Cincinnati	80	–	1882	232	564	.411	–	–	–	141	234	.603	–	–	525	81	287	9	–	–	–	605	6.6	1.0	7.6
66-67–Boston	72	–	729	147	359	.409	–	–	–	82	144	.569	–	–	294	42	137	0	–	–	–	376	4.1	0.6	5.2
67-68–Boston	78	–	1088	193	483	.400	–	–	–	109	185	.589	–	–	321	52	174	1	–	–	–	495	4.1	0.7	6.3
68-69–Milwaukee	78	–	2355	382	894	.427	–	–	–	259	390	.664	–	–	672	149	302	8	–	–	–	1023	8.6	1.9	13.1
Reg. Season Totals	831	–	21763	3993	9067	.440	–	–	–	2394	3741	.640	–	–	7544	1194	2838	65	–	–	–	10380	9.1	1.4	12.5
Playoff Totals	56	–	1347	215	514	.418	–	–	–	136	211	.645	–	–	448	64	206	8	–	–	–	566	8.0	1.1	10.1
All-Star Totals	4	–	64	15	34	.441	–	–	–	2	2	1.000	–	–	18	2	10	0	–	–	–	32	4.5	0.5	8.0

Endress, Ned R. b. March 2, 1918 Ht. 6-2 Wt. 200 College: Akron

SEASON–TEAM	G	GS	MIN	FGM	FGA	PCT	3FGM	3FGA	PCT	FTM	FTA	PCT	O-RB	D-RB	TOT	AST	PF	DQ	STL	TO	BLK	PTS	RPG	APG	PPG
43-44–Cleveland (N)	16	–	–	25	–	–	–	–	–	15	–	–	–	–	–	–	–	–	–	–	–	65	–	–	4.1
44-45–Cleveland (N)	29	–	–	62	–	–	–	–	–	46	–	–	–	–	–	–	–	–	–	–	–	170	–	–	5.9
45-46–Cleveland (N)	22	–	–	58	–	–	–	–	–	36	74	.486	–	–	–	–	41	–	–	–	–	152	–	–	6.9
46-47–Cleveland	16	–	–	3	25	.120	–	–	–	8	15	.533	–	–	–	4	13	–	–	–	–	14	–	0.3	0.9
Reg. NBA Totals	16	–	–	3	25	.120	–	–	–	8	15	.533	–	–	–	4	13	–	–	–	–	14	–	0.3	0.9
Reg. NBL Totals	67	–	–	145	–	–	–	–	–	97	74	.486	–	–	–	–	41	–	–	–	–	387	–	–	5.8
NBL Playoff Totals	4	–	–	5	–	–	–	–	–	3	0	–	–	–	–	–	5	–	–	–	–	13	–	–	3.3

Engler, Christopher Aaron (Chris) b. March 1, 1959 Ht. 6-11 Wt. 250 College: Minnesota; Wyoming

SEASON–TEAM	G	GS	MIN	FGM	FGA	PCT	3FGM	3FGA	PCT	FTM	FTA	PCT	O-RB	D-RB	TOT	AST	PF	DQ	STL	TO	BLK	PTS	RPG	APG	PPG
82-83–Golden State	54	1	369	38	94	.404	0	0	–	5	16	.313	43	61	104	11	95	1	7	24	17	81	1.9	0.2	1.5
83-84–Golden State	46	1	360	33	83	.398	0	0	–	14	23	.609	27	70	97	11	68	0	9	24	3	80	2.1	0.2	1.7
84-85–N.J.-Chicago-Milw.	11	0	82	8	20	.400	0	0	–	5	9	.556	12	18	30	0	5	0	2	2	5	21	2.7	0.0	1.9
86-87–Port.-Milw.-N.J.	30	0	195	23	51	.451	0	0	–	12	16	.750	23	34	57	8	33	0	5	12	11	58	1.9	0.3	1.9
87-88–New Jersey	54	0	399	36	88	.409	0	0	–	31	35	.886	32	66	98	15	73	1	9	29	6	103	1.8	0.3	1.9
Reg. Season Totals	195	2	1405	138	336	.411	0	0	–	67	99	.677	137	249	386	45	274	2	32	91	42	343	2.0	0.2	1.8
Playoff Totals	1	0	6	1	1	1.000	0	0	–	0	0	–	0	2	2	–	2	0	0	0	0	2	2.0	0.0	2.0

Englestad, Wayne Edward b. December 6, 1963 Ht. 6-8 Wt. 245 College: California-Irvine

SEASON–TEAM	G	GS	MIN	FGM	FGA	PCT	3FGM	3FGA	PCT	FTM	FTA	PCT	O-RB	D-RB	TOT	AST	PF	DQ	STL	TO	BLK	PTS	RPG	APG	PPG
88-89–Denver	11	0	50	11	29	.379	0	0	–	6	10	.600	5	11	16	7	12	0	1	3	0	28	1.5	0.6	2.5
Reg. Season Totals	11	0	50	11	29	.379	0	0	–	6	10	.600	5	11	16	7	12	0	1	3	0	28	1.5	0.6	2.5

English, Albert Jay (A.J.) b. July 11, 1967 Ht. 6-5 Wt. 175 College: Virginia Union

SEASON–TEAM	G	GS	MIN	FGM	FGA	PCT	3FGM	3FGA	PCT	FTM	FTA	PCT	O-RB	D-RB	TOT	AST	PF	DQ	STL	TO	BLK	PTS	RPG	APG	PPG
90-91–Washington	70	12	1443	251	572	.439	3	31	.097	111	157	.707	66	81	147	177	127	1	25	114	15	616	2.1	2.5	8.8
91-92–Washington	81	6	1665	366	846	.433	6	34	.176	148	176	.841	74	94	168	143	160	1	32	89	9	886	2.1	1.8	10.9
Reg. Season Totals	151	18	3108	617	1418	.435	9	65	.138	259	333	.778	140	175	315	320	287	2	57	203	24	1502	2.1	2.1	9.9

English, Alexander (Alex) b. January 5, 1954 Ht. 6-8 Wt. 190 College: South Carolina HOF: 1997

SEASON–TEAM	G	GS	MIN	FGM	FGA	PCT	3FGM	3FGA	PCT	FTM	FTA	PCT	O-RB	D-RB	TOT	AST	PF	DQ	STL	TO	BLK	PTS	RPG	APG	PPG
76-77–Milwaukee	60	–	648	132	277	.477	–	–	–	46	60	.767	68	100	168	25	78	0	17	–	18	310	2.8	0.4	5.2
77-78–Milwaukee	82	–	1552	343	633	.542	–	–	–	104	143	.727	144	251	395	129	178	1	41	137	55	790	4.8	1.6	9.6
78-79–Indiana	81	–	2696	563	1102	.511	–	–	–	173	230	.752	253	402	655	271	214	3	70	196	78	1299	8.1	3.3	16.0
79-80–Indiana-Denver	78	–	2401	553	1113	.497	2	6	.333	210	266	.789	269	336	605	224	206	0	73	214	62	1318	7.8	2.9	16.9
80-81–Denver	81	–	3093	768	1555	.494	3	5	.600	390	459	.850	273	373	646	290	255	2	106	241	100	1929	8.0	3.6	23.8
81-82–Denver	82	82	3015	855	1553	.551	0	8	.000	372	443	.840	210	348	558	433	261	2	87	261	120	2082	6.8	5.3	25.4
82-83–Denver	82	82	2988	959	1857	.516	2	12	.167	406	490	.829	263	338	601	397	235	1	116	263	126	2326	7.3	4.8	28.4
83-84–Denver	82	77	2870	907	1714	.529	1	7	.143	352	427	.824	216	248	464	406	252	3	83	222	95	2167	5.7	5.0	26.4
84-85–Denver	81	81	2924	939	1812	.518	1	5	.200	383	462	.829	203	255	458	344	259	1	101	251	46	2262	5.7	4.2	27.9
85-86–Denver	81	81	3024	951	1888	.504	1	5	.200	511	593	.862	192	213	405	320	235	1	73	249	29	2414	5.0	4.0	29.8
86-87–Denver	82	82	3085	965	1920	.503	4	15	.267	411	487	.844	146	198	344	422	216	0	73	214	21	2345	4.2	5.1	28.6
87-88–Denver	80	80	2818	843	1704	.495	0	6	.000	314	379	.828	166	207	373	377	193	1	70	181	23	2000	4.7	4.7	25.0
88-89–Denver	82	82	2990	924	1881	.491	2	8	.250	325	379	.858	148	178	326	383	174	0	66	198	12	2175	4.0	4.7	26.5
89-90–Denver	80	80	2211	635	1293	.491	2	5	.400	161	183	.880	119	167	286	225	130	0	51	93	23	1433	3.6	2.8	17.9
90-91–Dallas	79	26	1748	322	734	.439	0	1	.000	119	140	.850	108	146	254	105	141	0	40	101	25	763	3.2	1.3	9.7
Reg. Season Totals	1193	753	38063	10659	21036	.507	18	83	.217	4277	5141	.832	2778	3760	6538	4351	3027	15	1067	2821	833	25613	5.5	3.6	21.5
Playoff Totals	68	59	2427	668	1328	.503	0	8	.000	325	377	.862	166	205	371	293	188	2	47	142	32	1661	5.5	4.3	24.4
All-Star Totals	8	4	148	36	72	.500	0	0	–	1	2	.500	9	9	18	15	8	0	6	12	4	73	2.3	1.9	9.1

English, Claude W. b. December 26, 1946 Ht. 6-4 Wt. 185 College: Christian Coll. of the Southwest TX (J.C); Rhode Island

SEASON–TEAM	G	GS	MIN	FGM	FGA	PCT	3FGM	3FGA	PCT	FTM	FTA	PCT	O-RB	D-RB	TOT	AST	PF	DQ	STL	TO	BLK	PTS	RPG	APG	PPG
70-71–Portland	18	–	70	11	42	.262	–	–	–	5	7	.714	–	–	20	6	15	0	–	–	–	27	1.1	0.3	1.5
Reg. Season Totals	18	–	70	11	42	.262	–	–	–	5	7	.714	–	–	20	6	15	0	–	–	–	27	1.1	0.3	1.5

English, Scott Garrison b. October 20, 1950 Ht. 6-6 Wt. 205 College: Texas-El Paso; North Carolina

SEASON–TEAM	G	GS	MIN	FGM	FGA	PCT	3FGM	3FGA	PCT	FTM	FTA	PCT	O-RB	D-RB	TOT	AST	PF	DQ	STL	TO	BLK	PTS	RPG	APG	PPG
72-73–Phoenix	29	–	196	36	93	.387	–	–	–	21	29	.724	–	–	44	15	38	0	–	–	–	93	1.5	0.5	3.2
73-74–Virginia (A)	5	–	48	3	15	.200	0	0	–	4	4	1.000	3	13	16	4	9	–	3	9	0	10	3.2	0.8	2.0
74-75–San Diego (A)	71	–	1316	210	494	.425	1	10	.100	69	89	.775	130	233	363	88	115	–	47	88	20	490	5.1	1.2	6.9
Reg. NBA Totals	29	–	196	36	93	.387	–	–	–	21	29	.724	–	–	44	15	38	0	–	–	–	93	1.5	0.5	3.2
Reg. ABA Totals	76	–	1364	213	509	.418	1	10	.100	73	93	.785	133	246	379	92	124	0	50	97	20	500	5.0	1.2	6.6

E

English, Stephen (Jo Jo) b. February 4, 1970 Ht. 6-4 Wt. 195 College: South Carolina

SEASON–TEAM	G	GS	MIN	FGM	FGA	PCT	3FGM	3FGA	PCT	FTM	FTA	PCT	O-RB	D-RB	TOT	AST	PF	DQ	STL	TO	BLK	PTS	RPG	APG	PPG
92-93–Chicago	6	0	31	3	10	.300	0	3	.000	0	2	.000	2	4	6	1	5	0	3	4	2	6	1.0	0.2	1.0
93-94–Chicago	36	0	419	56	129	.434	8	17	.471	10	21	.476	9	36	45	38	61	0	8	36	10	130	1.3	1.1	3.6
94-95–Chicago	8	0	127	15	39	.385	3	12	.250	10	13	.769	1	2	3	7	19	0	7	6	1	43	0.4	0.9	5.4
Reg. Season Totals	50	0	577	74	178	.416	11	32	.344	20	36	.556	12	42	54	46	85	0	18	46	13	179	1.1	0.9	3.6
Playoff Totals	7	0	58	5	12	.417	1	4	.250	3	6	.500	1	2	3	2	4	0	1	1	1	14	0.4	0.3	2.0

Englund, Gene E. b. October 21, 1917 d. November 5, 1995 Ht. 6-5 Wt. 205 College: Wisconsin

SEASON–TEAM	G	GS	MIN	FGM	FGA	PCT	3FGM	3FGA	PCT	FTM	FTA	PCT	O-RB	D-RB	TOT	AST	PF	DQ	STL	TO	BLK	PTS	RPG	APG	PPG
41-42–Oshkosh (N)	22	–	–	61	–	–	–	–	–	42	–	–	–	–	–	–	–	–	–	–	–	164	–	–	7.5
42-43–Oshkosh (N)	17	–	–	41	–	–	–	–	–	48	65	.738	–	–	–	–	64	–	–	–	–	130	–	–	7.6
43-44–Oshkosh (N)	2	–	–	9	–	–	–	–	–	5	–	–	–	–	–	–	–	–	–	–	–	23	–	–	11.5
45-46–Oshkosh (N)	33	–	–	78	–	–	–	–	–	64	102	.627	–	–	–	–	92	–	–	–	–	220	–	–	6.7
46-47–Oshkosh (N)	43	–	–	187	–	–	–	–	–	105	151	.695	–	–	–	–	121	–	–	–	–	479	–	–	11.1
47-48–Oshkosh (N)	58	–	–	246	–	–	–	–	–	242	333	.727	–	–	–	–	204	–	–	–	–	734	–	–	12.7
48-49–Oshkosh (N)	63	–	–	284	–	–	–	–	–	282	393	.718	–	–	–	–	232	–	–	–	–	850	–	–	13.5
49-50–Boston-Tri-Cit	46	–	–	104	274	.380	–	–	–	152	192	.792	–	–	–	41	167	–	–	–	–	360	–	0.9	7.8
Reg. NBA Totals	46	–	–	104	274	.380	–	–	–	152	192	.792	–	–	–	41	167	–	–	–	–	360	–	0.9	7.8
Reg. NBL Totals	238	–	–	906	–	–	–	–	–	788	1044	.710	–	–	–	–	713	–	–	–	–	2600	–	–	10.9
NBA Playoff Totals	2	–	–	1	5	.200	–	–	–	9	11	.818	–	–	–	1	6	–	–	–	–	11	–	0.5	5.5
NBL Playoff Totals	29	–	–	120	–	–	–	–	–	89	93	.677	–	–	–	–	103	–	–	–	–	329	–	–	11.3

Epps, Raymond Edward Jr. (Ray) b. August 20, 1956 Ht. 6-6 Wt. 195 College: Norfolk State

SEASON–TEAM	G	GS	MIN	FGM	FGA	PCT	3FGM	3FGA	PCT	FTM	FTA	PCT	O-RB	D-RB	TOT	AST	PF	DQ	STL	TO	BLK	PTS	RPG	APG	PPG
78-79–Golden State	13	–	72	10	23	.435	–	–	–	6	8	.750	0	5	5	2	7	0	1	2	0	26	0.4	0.2	2.0
Reg. Season Totals	13	–	72	10	23	.435	–	–	–	6	8	.750	0	5	5	2	7	0	1	2	0	26	0.4	0.2	2.0

Erias, Baltico S. (Bo) b. July 30, 1932 Ht. 6-3 Wt. 220 College: Niagara

SEASON–TEAM	G	GS	MIN	FGM	FGA	PCT	3FGM	3FGA	PCT	FTM	FTA	PCT	O-RB	D-RB	TOT	AST	PF	DQ	STL	TO	BLK	PTS	RPG	APG	PPG
57-58–Minneapolis	18	–	401	59	170	.347	–	–	–	30	47	.638	–	–	83	26	52	1	–	–	–	148	4.6	1.4	8.2
Reg. Season Totals	18	–	401	59	170	.347	–	–	–	30	47	.638	–	–	83	26	52	1	–	–	–	148	4.6	1.4	8.2

Erickson, Keith Raymond b. April 19, 1944 Ht. 6-5 Wt. 195 College: UCLA

SEASON–TEAM	G	GS	MIN	FGM	FGA	PCT	3FGM	3FGA	PCT	FTM	FTA	PCT	O-RB	D-RB	TOT	AST	PF	DQ	STL	TO	BLK	PTS	RPG	APG	PPG
65-66–San Francisco	64	–	646	95	267	.356	–	–	–	43	65	.662	–	–	162	38	91	1	–	–	–	233	2.5	0.6	3.6
66-67–Chicago	76	–	1454	235	641	.367	–	–	–	117	159	.736	–	–	338	119	199	2	–	–	–	587	4.4	1.6	7.7
67-68–Chicago	78	–	2257	377	940	.401	–	–	–	194	257	.755	–	–	423	267	276	15	–	–	–	948	5.4	3.4	12.2
68-69–Los Angeles	77	–	1974	264	629	.420	–	–	–	120	175	.686	–	–	308	194	222	6	–	–	–	648	4.0	2.5	8.4
69-70–Los Angeles	68	–	1755	258	563	.458	–	–	–	91	122	.746	–	–	304	209	175	3	–	–	–	607	4.5	3.1	8.9
70-71–Los Angeles	73	–	2272	369	783	.471	–	–	–	85	112	.759	–	–	404	223	241	4	–	–	–	823	5.5	3.1	11.3
71-72–Los Angeles	15	–	262	40	83	.482	–	–	–	6	7	.857	–	–	39	35	26	0	–	–	–	86	2.6	2.3	5.7
72-73–Los Angeles	76	–	1920	299	696	.430	–	–	–	89	110	.809	–	–	337	242	190	3	–	–	–	687	4.4	3.2	9.0
73-74–Phoenix	66	–	2033	393	824	.477	–	–	–	177	221	.801	94	320	414	205	193	3	63	–	20	963	6.3	3.1	14.6
74-75–Phoenix	49	–	1469	237	557	.425	–	–	–	130	156	.833	70	173	243	170	150	3	50	–	12	604	5.0	3.5	12.3
75-76–Phoenix	74	–	1850	305	649	.470	–	–	–	134	157	.854	106	226	332	185	196	4	79	–	6	744	4.5	2.5	10.1
76-77–Phoenix	50	–	949	142	294	.483	–	–	–	37	50	.740	36	108	144	104	122	0	30	–	7	321	2.9	2.1	6.4
Reg. Season Totals	766	–	18841	3014	6926	.435	–	–	–	1223	1591	.769	306	827	3448	1991	2081	44	222	–	45	7251	4.5	2.6	9.5
Playoff Totals	87	–	2393	364	806	.452	–	–	–	144	189	.762	15	52	386	216	286	7	11	–	4	872	4.4	2.5	10.0

Erving, Julius Winfield II (Dr. J) b. February 22, 1950 Ht. 6-7 Wt. 200 College: Massachusetts HOF: 1993

SEASON–TEAM	G	GS	MIN	FGM	FGA	PCT	3FGM	3FGA	PCT	FTM	FTA	PCT	O-RB	D-RB	TOT	AST	PF	DQ	STL	TO	BLK	PTS	RPG	APG	PPG
71-72–Virginia (A)	84	–	3513	910	1826	.498	3	16	.188	467	627	.745	476	843	1319	335	264	–	–	342	–	2290	15.7	4.0	27.3
72-73–Virginia (A)	71	–	2993	894	1804	.496	5	24	.208	475	612	.776	262	605	867	298	197	0	181	326	127	2268	12.2	4.2	31.9
73-74–New York (A)	84	–	3398	914	1785	.512	17	43	.395	454	593	.766	263	636	899	434	270	–	190	341	204	2299	10.7	5.2	27.4
74-75–New York (A)	84	–	3402	914	1806	.506	29	87	.333	486	608	.799	284	630	914	462	256	–	186	301	157	2343	10.9	5.5	27.9
75-76–New York (A)	84	–	3244	949	1873	.507	34	103	.330	530	662	.801	337	588	925	423	221	–	207	307	160	2462	11.0	5.0	29.3
76-77–Philadelphia	82	–	2940	685	1373	.499	–	–	–	400	515	.777	192	503	695	306	251	1	159	–	113	1770	8.5	3.7	21.6
77-78–Philadelphia	74	–	2429	611	1217	.502	–	–	–	306	362	.845	179	302	481	279	207	0	135	238	97	1528	6.5	3.8	20.6
78-79–Philadelphia	78	–	2802	715	1455	.491	–	–	–	373	501	.745	198	366	564	357	207	0	133	315	100	1803	7.2	4.6	23.1
79-80–Philadelphia	78	–	2812	838	1614	.519	4	20	.200	420	534	.787	215	361	576	355	208	0	170	284	140	2100	7.4	4.6	26.9
80-81–Philadelphia	82	–	2874	794	1524	.521	4	18	.222	422	536	.787	244	413	657	364	233	0	173	266	147	2014	8.0	4.4	24.6
81-82–Philadelphia	81	81	2789	780	1428	.546	3	11	.273	411	539	.763	220	337	557	319	229	1	161	214	141	1974	6.9	3.9	24.4
82-83–Philadelphia	72	72	2421	605	1170	.517	2	7	.286	330	435	.759	173	318	491	263	202	1	112	196	131	1542	6.8	3.7	21.4
83-84–Philadelphia	77	77	2683	678	1324	.512	7	21	.333	364	483	.754	190	342	532	309	217	3	141	230	139	1727	6.9	4.0	22.4
84-85–Philadelphia	78	78	2535	610	1236	.494	3	14	.214	338	442	.765	172	242	414	233	199	0	135	208	109	1561	5.3	3.0	20.0
85-86–Philadelphia	74	74	2474	521	1085	.480	9	32	.281	289	368	.785	169	201	370	248	196	3	113	214	82	1340	5.0	3.4	18.1
86-87–Philadelphia	60	60	1918	400	850	.471	14	53	.264	191	235	.813	115	149	264	191	137	0	76	158	94	1005	4.4	3.2	16.8
Reg. NBA Totals	836	442	28677	7237	14276	.507	46	176	.261	3844	4950	.777	2067	3534	5601	3224	2286	9	1508	2323	1293	18364	6.7	3.9	22.0
Reg. ABA Totals	407	–	16550	4581	9094	.504	88	273	.322	2412	3102	.778	1622	3302	4924	1952	1208	0	764	1617	648	11662	12.1	4.8	28.7
NBA Playoff Totals	141	69	5288	1187	2441	.486	7	36	.194	707	908	.779	360	634	994	594	403	1	235	396	239	3088	7.0	4.2	21.9
ABA Playoff Totals	48	–	2064	582	1122	.519	10	40	.250	318	400	.795	199	418	617	247	141	0	52	181	54	1492	12.9	5.1	31.1
NBA All-Star Totals	11	11	316	85	178	.478	1	1	1.000	50	63	.794	34	36	70	35	31	0	18	19	11	221	6.4	3.2	20.1

Eschmeyer, Evan Bruce b. May 30, 1975 Ht. 6-11 Wt. 255 College: Northwestern

SEASON–TEAM	G	GS	MIN	FGM	FGA	PCT	3FGM	3FGA	PCT	FTM	FTA	PCT	O-RB	D-RB	TOT	AST	PF	DQ	STL	TO	BLK	PTS	RPG	APG	PPG
99-00–New Jersey	31	5	373	38	72	.528	0	0	–	15	30	.500	40	68	108	21	84	2	8	21	21	91	3.5	0.7	2.9
Reg. Season Totals	31	5	373	38	72	.528	0	0	–	15	30	.500	40	68	108	21	84	2	8	21	21	91	3.5	0.7	2.9

Eskridge, John I. (Jack) b. January 21, 1924 Ht. 6-5 Wt. 200 College: Kansas

SEASON–TEAM	G	GS	MIN	FGM	FGA	PCT	3FGM	3FGA	PCT	FTM	FTA	PCT	O-RB	D-RB	TOT	AST	PF	DQ	STL	TO	BLK	PTS	RPG	APG	PPG
48-49–Chicago-Ind.	23	–	–	25	69	.362	–	–	–	14	20	.700	–	–	–	14	25	–	–	–	–	64	–	0.6	2.8
Reg. Season Totals	23	–	–	25	69	.362	–	–	–	14	20	.700	–	–	–	14	25	–	–	–	–	64	–	0.6	2.8

Esposito, Vincenzo b. March 1, 1969 Ht. 6-3 Wt. 198 Country: Italy

SEASON–TEAM	G	GS	MIN	FGM	FGA	PCT	3FGM	3FGA	PCT	FTM	FTA	PCT	O-RB	D-RB	TOT	AST	PF	DQ	STL	TO	BLK	PTS	RPG	APG	PPG
95-96–Toronto	30	0	282	36	100	.360	13	56	.232	31	39	.795	4	12	16	23	27	0	7	39	0	116	0.5	0.8	3.9
Reg. Season Totals	30	0	282	36	100	.360	13	56	.232	31	39	.795	4	12	16	23	27	0	7	39	0	116	0.5	0.8	3.9

Evans, Brian Keith b. September 13, 1973 Ht. 6-8 Wt. 220 College: Indiana

SEASON–TEAM	G	GS	MIN	FGM	FGA	PCT	3FGM	3FGA	PCT	FTM	FTA	PCT	O-RB	D-RB	TOT	AST	PF	DQ	STL	TO	BLK	PTS	RPG	APG	PPG
96-97–Orlando	14	0	59	8	22	.364	4	8	.500	0	0	–	1	7	8	7	6	0	1	2	2	20	0.6	0.5	1.4
97-98–Orlando-N.J.	72	1	893	123	312	.394	29	87	.333	46	57	.807	49	88	137	55	101	0	29	38	13	321	1.9	0.8	4.5
98-99–N.J.-Minn.	16	0	145	13	44	.295	4	13	.308	4	4	1.000	6	13	19	15	8	0	5	2	3	34	1.2	0.9	2.1
Reg. Season Totals	102	1	1097	144	378	.381	37	108	.343	50	61	.820	56	108	164	77	115	0	35	42	18	375	1.6	0.8	3.7
Playoff Totals	5	0	11	1	1	1.000	0	0	–	0	0	–	0	1	1	2	0	0	1	0	0	2	0.2	0.4	0.4

Evans, Earl Joseph II b. November 11, 1955 Ht. 6-8 Wt. 205 College: USC; Nevada-Las Vegas

SEASON–TEAM	G	GS	MIN	FGM	FGA	PCT	3FGM	3FGA	PCT	FTM	FTA	PCT	O-RB	D-RB	TOT	AST	PF	DQ	STL	TO	BLK	PTS	RPG	APG	PPG
79-80–Detroit	36	–	381	63	140	.450	7	18	.389	24	42	.571	26	49	75	37	64	0	14	36	1	157	2.1	1.0	4.4
Reg. Season Totals	36	–	381	63	140	.450	7	18	.389	24	42	.571	26	49	75	37	64	0	14	36	1	157	2.1	1.0	4.4

Evans, Michael Leeroyall (Mike) b. April 19, 1955 Ht. 6-1 Wt. 170 College: Kansas State

SEASON–TEAM	G	GS	MIN	FGM	FGA	PCT	3FGM	3FGA	PCT	FTM	FTA	PCT	O-RB	D-RB	TOT	AST	PF	DQ	STL	TO	BLK	PTS	RPG	APG	PPG
79-80–San Antonio	79	–	1246	208	464	.448	12	42	.286	58	85	.682	29	78	107	230	194	2	60	128	9	486	1.4	2.9	6.2
80-81–Milwaukee	71	–	911	134	291	.460	2	14	.143	50	64	.781	22	65	87	167	114	0	34	72	4	320	1.2	2.4	4.5
81-82–Milw.-Clev.	22	0	270	35	86	.407	0	6	.000	13	20	.650	5	17	22	42	36	1	13	26	0	83	1.0	1.9	3.8
82-83–Denver	42	5	695	115	243	.473	0	9	.000	33	41	.805	4	54	58	113	94	3	23	71	3	263	1.4	2.7	6.3
83-84–Denver	78	5	1687	243	564	.431	32	89	.360	111	131	.847	23	115	138	288	175	2	61	117	4	629	1.8	3.7	8.1
84-85–Denver	81	0	1437	323	661	.489	57	157	.363	113	131	.863	26	93	119	231	174	2	65	130	12	816	1.5	2.9	10.1
85-86–Denver	81	1	1389	304	715	.425	39	176	.222	126	149	.846	30	71	101	177	159	1	61	124	1	773	1.2	2.2	9.5
86-87–Denver	81	4	1567	334	729	.458	53	169	.314	96	123	.780	36	92	128	185	149	1	79	107	12	817	1.6	2.3	10.1
87-88–Denver	56	0	656	139	307	.453	36	91	.396	30	37	.811	9	39	48	81	78	0	34	43	6	344	0.9	1.4	6.1
Reg. Season Totals	591	15	9858	1835	4060	.452	231	753	.307	630	781	.807	184	624	808	1514	1173	12	430	818	51	4531	1.4	2.6	7.7
Playoff Totals	58	2	1071	201	485	.414	44	155	.284	80	97	.825	20	86	106	160	127	0	43	97	7	526	1.8	2.8	9.1

Evans, Robert W. (Bob) b. May 31, 1925 Ht. 6-2 Wt. 175 College: Indiana; Butler

SEASON–TEAM	G	GS	MIN	FGM	FGA	PCT	3FGM	3FGA	PCT	FTM	FTA	PCT	O-RB	D-RB	TOT	AST	PF	DQ	STL	TO	BLK	PTS	RPG	APG	PPG
49-50–Indianapolis	47	–	–	56	200	.280	–	–	–	30	44	.682	–	–	–	55	99	–	–	–	–	142	–	1.2	3.0
Reg. Season Totals	47	–	–	56	200	.280	–	–	–	30	44	.682	–	–	–	55	99	–	–	–	–	142	–	1.2	3.0
Playoff Totals	3	–	–	1	8	.250	–	–	–	0	0	–	–	–	–	–	3	–	–	–	–	2	0.0	0.0	0.7

Evans, William D. (Billy) b. March 3, 1947 Ht. 6-0 Wt. 170 College: Boston College

SEASON–TEAM	G	GS	MIN	FGM	FGA	PCT	3FGM	3FGA	PCT	FTM	FTA	PCT	O-RB	D-RB	TOT	AST	PF	DQ	STL	TO	BLK	PTS	RPG	APG	PPG
69-70–New York (A)	53	–	602	32	87	.368	0	2	.000	38	70	.543	–	–	39	100	89	1	–	–	–	102	0.7	1.9	1.9
Reg. ABA Totals	53	–	602	32	87	.368	0	2	.000	38	70	.543	–	–	39	100	89	1	–	–	–	102	0.7	1.9	1.9
ABA Playoff Totals	6	–	27	1	2	.500	0	1	.000	1	3	.333	–	–	3	1	7	0	–	–	–	3	0.5	0.2	0.5

Ewing, Patrick Aloysius b. August 5, 1962 Ht. 7-0 Wt. 255 College: Georgetown

SEASON–TEAM	G	GS	MIN	FGM	FGA	PCT	3FGM	3FGA	PCT	FTM	FTA	PCT	O-RB	D-RB	TOT	AST	PF	DQ	STL	TO	BLK	PTS	RPG	APG	PPG
85-86–New York	50	50	1771	386	814	.474	0	5	.000	226	306	.739	124	327	451	102	191	7	54	172	103	998	9.0	2.0	20.0
86-87–New York	63	63	2206	530	1053	.503	0	7	.000	296	415	.713	157	398	555	104	248	5	89	229	147	1356	8.8	1.7	21.5
87-88–New York	82	82	2546	656	1183	.555	0	3	.000	341	476	.716	245	431	676	125	332	5	104	287	245	1653	8.2	1.5	20.2
88-89–New York	80	80	2896	727	1282	.567	0	6	.000	361	484	.746	213	527	740	188	311	5	117	266	281	1815	9.3	2.4	22.7
89-90–New York	82	82	3165	922	1673	.551	1	4	.250	502	648	.775	235	658	893	182	325	7	78	278	327	2347	10.9	2.2	28.6
90-91–New York	81	81	3104	845	1645	.514	0	6	.000	464	623	.745	194	711	905	244	287	3	80	291	258	2154	11.2	3.0	26.6
91-92–New York	82	82	3150	796	1525	.522	1	6	.167	377	511	.738	228	693	921	156	277	2	88	209	245	1970	11.2	1.9	24.0
92-93–New York	81	81	3003	779	1550	.503	1	7	.143	400	556	.719	191	789	980	151	286	2	74	265	161	1959	12.1	1.9	24.2
93-94–New York	79	79	2972	745	1503	.496	4	14	.286	445	582	.765	219	666	885	179	275	3	90	260	217	1939	11.2	2.3	24.5
94-95–New York	79	79	2920	730	1452	.503	6	21	.286	420	560	.750	157	710	867	212	272	3	68	256	159	1886	11.0	2.7	23.9
95-96–New York	76	76	2783	678	1456	.466	4	28	.143	351	461	.761	157	649	806	160	247	2	68	221	184	1711	10.6	2.1	22.5
96-97–New York	78	78	2887	655	1342	.488	2	9	.222	439	582	.754	175	659	834	156	250	2	69	269	189	1751	10.7	2.0	22.4
97-98–New York	26	26	848	203	403	.504	0	2	.000	134	186	.720	59	206	265	28	74	0	16	77	58	540	10.2	1.1	20.8
98-99–New York	38	38	1300	247	568	.435	0	2	.000	163	231	.706	74	303	377	43	105	1	30	99	100	657	9.9	1.1	17.3
99-00–New York	62	62	2035	361	775	.466	0	2	.000	207	283	.731	140	464	604	58	196	1	36	142	84	929	9.7	0.9	15.0
Reg. Season Totals	1039	1039	37586	9260	18224	.508	19	122	.156	5126	6904	.742	2568	8191	10759	2088	3676	48	1061	3321	2758	23665	10.4	2.0	22.8
Playoff Totals	135	135	5140	1096	2328	.471	8	22	.364	587	814	.721	332	1081	1413	271	510	5	121	343	299	2787	10.5	2.0	20.6
All-Star Totals	9	3	190	44	82	.537	0	0	–	18	26	.692	15	45	60	7	27	0	11	23	16	106	6.7	0.8	11.8

Ezersky, John J. (Johnny) b. 1921 Ht. 6-3 Wt. 175 College: Rhode Island

SEASON–TEAM	G	GS	MIN	FGM	FGA	PCT	3FGM	3FGA	PCT	FTM	FTA	PCT	O-RB	D-RB	TOT	AST	PF	DQ	STL	TO	BLK	PTS	RPG	APG	PPG
47-48–Tri-Cities (N)	5	–	–	9	–	–	–	–	–	5	8	.625	–	–	–	–	–	–	–	–	–	23	–	–	4.6
47-48–Providence	25	–	–	95	376	.253	–	–	–	63	104	.606	–	–	–	16	62	–	–	–	–	253	–	0.6	10.1
48-49–Prov.-Bos.-Balt.	56	–	–	128	407	.314	–	–	–	109	160	.681	–	–	–	67	98	–	–	–	–	365	–	1.2	6.5
49-50–Balt.-Boston	54	–	–	143	487	.294	–	–	–	127	183	.694	–	–	–	86	139	–	–	–	–	413	–	1.6	7.6
Reg. NBA Totals	135	–	–	366	1270	.288	–	–	–	299	447	.669	–	–	–	169	299	–	–	–	–	1031	–	1.3	7.6
Reg. NBL Totals	5	–	–	9	–	–	–	–	–	5	8	.625	–	–	–	–	–	–	–	–	–	23	–	–	4.6

Fabel, Joseph (Joe) b. September 4, 1913 d. 1967 Ht. 6-1 Wt. 190 College: Pittsburgh

SEASON–TEAM	G	GS	MIN	FGM	FGA	PCT	3FGM	3FGA	PCT	FTM	FTA	PCT	O-RB	D-RB	TOT	AST	PF	DQ	STL	TO	BLK	PTS	RPG	APG	PPG
38-39–Pittsburgh (N)	1	–	–	3	–	–	–	–	–	0	–	–	–	–	–	–	–	–	–	–	–	6	–	–	6.0
46-47–Pittsburgh	30	–	–	25	96	.260	–	–	–	13	26	.500	–	–	–	2	64	–	–	–	–	63	–	0.1	2.1
Reg. NBA Totals	30	–	–	25	96	.260	–	–	–	13	26	.500	–	–	–	2	64	–	–	–	–	63	–	0.1	2.1
Reg. NBL Totals	1	–	–	3	–	–	–	–	–	0	–	–	–	–	–	–	–	–	–	–	–	6	–	–	6.0

Fairchild, John Russell b. April 28, 1943 Ht. 6-8 Wt. 205 College: Palomar (Calif.) Coll. (J.C.); Brigham Young

SEASON–TEAM	G	GS	MIN	FGM	FGA	PCT	3FGM	3FGA	PCT	FTM	FTA	PCT	O-RB	D-RB	TOT	AST	PF	DQ	STL	TO	BLK	PTS	RPG	APG	PPG
65-66–Los Angeles	30	–	171	23	89	.258	–	–	–	14	20	.700	–	–	45	11	33	0	–	–	–	60	1.5	0.4	2.0
67-68–Anaheim (A)	62	–	1311	271	620	.437	1	4	.250	135	200	.675	–	–	332	63	155	0	–	103	–	678	5.4	1.0	10.9
68-69–Den.-Indiana (A)	63	–	717	113	294	.384	10	29	.345	89	127	.701	–	–	129	37	98	1	–	74	–	325	2.0	0.6	5.2
69-70–Indiana-Ken. (A)	10	–	78	7	23	.304	3	5	.600	5	10	.500	–	–	17	4	18	0	–	–	–	22	1.7	0.4	2.2
Reg. NBA Totals	30	–	171	23	89	.258	–	–	–	14	20	.700	–	–	45	11	33	0	–	–	–	60	1.5	0.4	2.0
Reg. ABA Totals	135	–	2106	391	937	.417	14	38	.368	229	337	.680	–	–	478	104	271	1	–	177	–	1025	3.5	0.8	7.6
ABA Playoff Totals	9	–	85	19	44	.432	4	10	.400	4	6	.667	–	–	21	3	13	0	–	–	–	46	2.3	0.3	5.1

Farbman, Philip M. (Phil) b. April 3, 1924 Ht. 6-4 Wt. 185 College: C.C.NY; Brooklyn College

SEASON–TEAM	G	GS	MIN	FGM	FGA	PCT	3FGM	3FGA	PCT	FTM	FTA	PCT	O-RB	D-RB	TOT	AST	PF	DQ	STL	TO	BLK	PTS	RPG	APG	PPG
48-49–Phil.-Boston	48	–	–	50	163	.307	–	–	–	55	81	.679	–	–	–	36	86	–	–	–	–	155	–	0.8	3.2
Reg. Season Totals	48	–	–	50	163	.307	–	–	–	55	81	.679	–	–	–	36	86	–	–	–	–	155	–	0.8	3.2

Farley, Richard L. (Dick) b. April 13, 1932 d. October 1, 1969 Ht. 6-4 Wt. 190 College: Indiana

SEASON–TEAM	G	GS	MIN	FGM	FGA	PCT	3FGM	3FGA	PCT	FTM	FTA	PCT	O-RB	D-RB	TOT	AST	PF	DQ	STL	TO	BLK	PTS	RPG	APG	PPG
54-55–Syracuse	69	–	1113	136	353	.385	–	–	–	136	201	.677	–	–	167	111	145	1	–	–	–	408	2.4	1.6	5.9
55-56–Syracuse	72	–	1429	168	451	.373	–	–	–	143	207	.691	–	–	165	151	154	2	–	–	–	479	2.3	2.1	6.7
58-59–Detroit	70	–	1280	177	448	.395	–	–	–	137	186	.737	–	–	195	124	130	2	–	–	–	491	2.8	1.8	7.0
Reg. Season Totals	211	–	3822	481	1252	.384	–	–	–	416	594	.700	–	–	527	386	429	5	–	–	–	1378	2.5	1.8	6.5
Playoff Totals	22	–	370	58	140	.414	–	–	–	34	57	.596	–	–	40	51	66	2	–	–	–	150	1.8	2.3	6.8

Farmer, Don Michael (Mike) b. September 26, 1936 Ht. 6-7 Wt. 210 College: San Francisco

SEASON–TEAM	G	GS	MIN	FGM	FGA	PCT	3FGM	3FGA	PCT	FTM	FTA	PCT	O-RB	D-RB	TOT	AST	PF	DQ	STL	TO	BLK	PTS	RPG	APG	PPG
58-59–New York	72	–	1545	176	498	.353	–	–	–	83	99	.838	–	–	315	66	152	1	–	–	–	435	4.4	0.9	6.0
59-60–New York	67	–	1536	212	568	.373	–	–	–	70	83	.843	–	–	385	57	130	1	–	–	–	494	5.7	0.9	7.4
60-61–N.Y.-Cin.	59	–	1301	180	461	.390	–	–	–	69	94	.734	–	–	380	81	130	1	–	–	–	429	6.4	1.4	7.3
62-63–St. Louis	80	–	1724	239	562	.425	–	–	–	117	139	.842	–	–	369	143	155	0	–	–	–	595	4.6	1.8	7.4
63-64–St. Louis	76	–	1361	178	438	.406	–	–	–	68	83	.819	–	–	225	109	140	0	–	–	–	424	3.0	1.4	5.6
64-65–St. Louis	60	–	1272	167	408	.409	–	–	–	75	94	.798	–	–	258	88	123	0	–	–	–	409	4.3	1.5	6.8
65-66–St. Louis	9	–	79	13	30	.433	–	–	–	4	5	.800	–	–	18	6	10	0	–	–	–	30	2.0	0.7	3.3
Reg. Season Totals	423	–	8818	1165	2965	.393	–	–	–	486	597	.814	–	–	1950	550	840	3	–	–	–	2816	4.6	1.3	6.7
Playoff Totals	25	–	412	53	129	.411	–	–	–	23	32	.719	–	–	79	36	45	0	–	–	–	129	3.2	1.4	5.2

Farmer, James Hubert III (Jim) b. September 23, 1964 Ht. 6-4 Wt. 190 College: Alabama

SEASON–TEAM	G	GS	MIN	FGM	FGA	PCT	3FGM	3FGA	PCT	FTM	FTA	PCT	O-RB	D-RB	TOT	AST	PF	DQ	STL	TO	BLK	PTS	RPG	APG	PPG
87-88–Dallas	30	0	157	26	69	.377	0	6	.000	9	10	.900	9	9	18	16	18	0	3	22	1	61	0.6	0.5	2.0
88-89–Utah	37	0	412	57	142	.401	9	20	.450	29	41	.707	22	33	55	28	41	0	9	26	0	152	1.5	0.8	4.1
89-90–Seattle	38	0	400	89	203	.438	8	27	.296	57	80	.713	17	26	43	25	44	0	17	27	1	243	1.1	0.7	6.4
90-91–Phil.-Denver	27	1	456	101	223	.453	5	23	.217	48	65	.738	29	39	68	38	58	0	13	38	2	255	2.5	1.4	9.4
93-94–Denver	4	0	29	2	6	.333	0	2	.000	0	0	–	0	2	2	4	3	0	0	5	0	4	0.5	1.0	1.0
Reg. Season Totals	136	1	1454	275	643	.428	22	78	.282	143	196	.730	77	109	186	111	164	0	42	118	4	715	1.4	0.8	5.3
Playoff Totals	5	0	14	2	8	.250	0	1	.000	0	0	–	3	1	4	1	2	0	0	2	0	4	0.8	0.2	0.8

Farmer, Tony b. January 3, 1970 Ht. 6-9 Wt. 244 College: Nebraska

SEASON–TEAM	G	GS	MIN	FGM	FGA	PCT	3FGM	3FGA	PCT	FTM	FTA	PCT	O-RB	D-RB	TOT	AST	PF	DQ	STL	TO	BLK	PTS	RPG	APG	PPG
97-98–Charlotte	27	2	169	17	53	.321	2	9	.222	31	39	.795	16	16	32	5	23	0	10	9	4	67	1.2	0.2	2.5
99-00–Golden State	74	9	1199	127	312	.407	8	44	.182	203	265	.766	118	177	295	74	167	1	66	82	16	465	4.0	1.0	6.3
Reg. Season Totals	101	11	1368	144	365	.395	10	53	.189	234	304	.770	134	193	327	79	190	1	76	91	20	532	3.2	0.8	5.3

Faught, Robert Edward (Bob) b. September 2, 1921 Ht. 6-5 Wt. 185 College: Notre Dame

SEASON–TEAM	G	GS	MIN	FGM	FGA	PCT	3FGM	3FGA	PCT	FTM	FTA	PCT	O-RB	D-RB	TOT	AST	PF	DQ	STL	TO	BLK	PTS	RPG	APG	PPG
46-47–Cleveland	51	–	–	141	478	.295	–	–	–	61	106	.575	–	–	–	33	97	–	–	–	–	343	–	0.6	6.7
Reg. Season Totals	51	–	–	141	478	.295	–	–	–	61	106	.575	–	–	–	33	97	–	–	–	–	343	–	0.6	6.7
Playoff Totals	3	–	–	11	32	.344	–	–	–	3	3	1.000	–	–	–	1	10	1	–	–	–	25	–	0.3	8.3

Fedor, Samuel David (Dave) b. December 10, 1940 Ht. 6-6 Wt. 190 College: Florida State

SEASON–TEAM	G	GS	MIN	FGM	FGA	PCT	3FGM	3FGA	PCT	FTM	FTA	PCT	O-RB	D-RB	TOT	AST	PF	DQ	STL	TO	BLK	PTS	RPG	APG	PPG
62-63–San Francisco	7	–	27	3	10	.300	–	–	–	0	1	.000	–	–	6	1	4	0	–	–	–	6	0.9	0.1	0.9
Reg. Season Totals	7	–	27	3	10	.300	–	–	–	0	1	.000	–	–	6	1	4	0	–	–	–	6	0.9	0.1	0.9

Feerick, Robert Joseph (Bob) b. January 2, 1920 d. June 8, 1976 Ht. 6-3 Wt. 190 College: Santa Clara

SEASON–TEAM	G	GS	MIN	FGM	FGA	PCT	3FGM	3FGA	PCT	FTM	FTA	PCT	O-RB	D-RB	TOT	AST	PF	DQ	STL	TO	BLK	PTS	RPG	APG	PPG
45-46–Oshkosh (N)	21	–	–	81	–	–	–	–	–	36	44	.818	–	–	–	–	44	–	–	–	–	198	–	–	9.4
46-47–Washington	55	–	–	364	908	.401	–	–	–	198	260	.762	–	–	–	69	142	–	–	–	–	926	–	1.3	16.8
47-48–Washington	48	–	–	293	861	.340	–	–	–	189	240	.788	–	–	–	56	139	–	–	–	–	775	–	1.2	16.1
48-49–Washington	58	–	–	248	708	.350	–	–	–	256	298	.859	–	–	–	188	171	–	–	–	–	752	–	3.2	13.0
49-50–Washington	60	–	–	172	500	.344	–	–	–	139	174	.799	–	–	–	127	140	–	–	–	–	483	–	2.1	8.1
Reg. NBA Totals	221	–	–	1077	2977	.362	–	–	–	782	972	.805	–	–	–	440	592	–	–	–	–	2936	–	2.0	13.3
Reg. NBL Totals	21	–	–	81	–	–	–	–	–	36	44	.818	–	–	–	–	44	–	–	–	–	198	–	–	9.4
NBA Playoff Totals	9	–	–	38	232	.315	–	–	–	25	33	.758	–	–	–	20	34	2	–	–	–	101	–	1.3	11.2
NBL Playoff Totals	5	–	–	16	–	–	–	–	–	10	0	–	–	–	–	–	6	–	–	–	–	42	–	–	8.4

Feher, Raymond G. (Butch) b. May 19, 1954 Ht. 6-4 Wt. 185 College: Vanderbilt

SEASON–TEAM	G	GS	MIN	FGM	FGA	PCT	3FGM	3FGA	PCT	FTM	FTA	PCT	O-RB	D-RB	TOT	AST	PF	DQ	STL	TO	BLK	PTS	RPG	APG	PPG
76-77–Phoenix	48	–	487	86	162	.531	–	–	–	76	99	.768	18	56	74	36	46	0	11	–	7	248	1.5	0.8	5.2
Reg. Season Totals	48	–	487	86	162	.531	–	–	–	76	99	.768	18	56	74	36	46	0	11	–	7	248	1.5	0.8	5.2

Feick, Jamie b. July 3, 1974 Ht. 6-8 Wt. 255 College: Michigan State

SEASON–TEAM	G	GS	MIN	FGM	FGA	PCT	3FGM	3FGA	PCT	FTM	FTA	PCT	O-RB	D-RB	TOT	AST	PF	DQ	STL	TO	BLK	PTS	RPG	APG	PPG
96-97–Cha.-S.A.	41	0	624	56	157	.357	5	14	.357	34	67	.507	82	132	214	26	78	0	16	31	14	151	5.2	0.6	3.7
97-98–Milwaukee	45	2	450	39	90	.433	4	13	.308	20	41	.488	45	79	124	16	67	0	25	21	17	102	2.8	0.4	2.3
98-99–Milw.-N.J.	28	16	852	67	134	.500	0	0	–	43	60	.717	112	176	288	24	73	0	25	34	18	177	10.3	0.9	6.3
99-00–New Jersey	81	17	2241	181	423	.428	3	3	1.000	94	133	.707	264	491	755	68	206	2	43	59	38	459	9.3	0.8	5.7
Reg. Season Totals	195	35	4167	343	804	.427	12	30	.400	191	301	.635	503	878	1381	134	424	2	109	145	87	889	7.1	0.7	4.6

Feiereisel, Ronald E. (Ron) b. August 6, 1931 Ht. 6-3 Wt. 185 College: DePaul

SEASON–TEAM	G	GS	MIN	FGM	FGA	PCT	3FGM	3FGA	PCT	FTM	FTA	PCT	O-RB	D-RB	TOT	AST	PF	DQ	STL	TO	BLK	PTS	RPG	APG	PPG
55-56–Minneapolis	10	–	59	8	28	.286	–	–	–	14	16	.875	–	–	6	6	9	0	–	–	–	30	0.6	0.6	3.0
Reg. Season Totals	10	–	59	8	28	.286	–	–	–	14	16	.875	–	–	6	6	9	0	–	–	–	30	0.6	0.6	3.0

Feigenbaum, George b. July 2, 1929 Ht. 6-1 Wt. 185 College: Long Island University; Kentucky

SEASON–TEAM	G	GS	MIN	FGM	FGA	PCT	3FGM	3FGA	PCT	FTM	FTA	PCT	O-RB	D-RB	TOT	AST	PF	DQ	STL	TO	BLK	PTS	RPG	APG	PPG
49-50–Baltimore	12	–	–	14	57	.246	–	–	–	8	18	.444	–	–	–	10	15	–	–	–	–	36	–	0.8	3.0
52-53–Milwaukee	5	–	79	4	22	.182	–	–	–	8	15	.533	–	–	7	9	14	1	–	–	–	16	1.4	1.8	3.2
Reg. Season Totals	17	–	79	18	79	.228	–	–	–	16	33	.485	–	–	7	19	29	1	–	–	–	52	1.4	1.1	3.1

Feitl, Dave Scott b. June 8, 1962 Ht. 6-11 Wt. 240 College: Texas-El Paso

SEASON–TEAM	G	GS	MIN	FGM	FGA	PCT	3FGM	3FGA	PCT	FTM	FTA	PCT	O-RB	D-RB	TOT	AST	PF	DQ	STL	TO	BLK	PTS	RPG	APG	PPG
86-87–Houston	62	1	498	88	202	.436	0	1	.000	53	71	.746	39	78	117	22	83	0	9	38	4	229	1.9	0.4	3.7
87-88–Golden State	70	19	1128	182	404	.450	0	4	.000	94	134	.701	83	252	335	53	146	1	15	87	9	458	4.8	0.8	6.5
88-89–Washington	57	36	828	116	266	.436	0	1	.000	54	65	.831	69	133	202	36	136	0	17	65	18	286	3.5	0.6	5.0
90-91–Houston	52	2	372	52	140	.371	0	3	.000	33	44	.750	29	71	100	8	52	0	3	25	12	137	1.9	0.2	2.6
91-92–New Jersey	34	0	175	33	77	.429	0	0	–	16	19	.842	21	40	61	6	22	0	2	19	3	82	1.8	0.2	2.4
Reg. Season Totals	275	58	3001	471	1089	.433	0	9	.000	250	333	.751	241	574	815	125	439	1	46	234	46	1192	3.0	0.5	4.3
Playoff Totals	7	0	11	1	2	.500	0	0	–	2	2	1.000	0	2	2	–	0	0	0	1	0	4	0.3	0.0	0.6

Felix, Raymond Darlington (Ray) b. December 10, 1930 d. July 28, 1991 Ht. 6-11 Wt. 220 College: Long Island University

SEASON–TEAM	G	GS	MIN	FGM	FGA	PCT	3FGM	3FGA	PCT	FTM	FTA	PCT	O-RB	D-RB	TOT	AST	PF	DQ	STL	TO	BLK	PTS	RPG	APG	PPG
53-54–Baltimore	72	–	2672	410	983	.417	–	–	–	449	704	.638	–	–	958	82	253	5	–	–	–	1269	13.3	1.1	17.6
54-55–New York	72	–	2024	364	832	.438	–	–	–	310	498	.622	–	–	818	67	286	11	–	–	–	1038	11.4	0.9	14.4
55-56–New York	72	–	1702	277	668	.415	–	–	–	331	469	.706	–	–	623	47	293	13	–	–	–	885	8.7	0.7	12.3
56-57–New York	72	–	1622	295	709	.416	–	–	–	277	371	.747	–	–	587	36	284	8	–	–	–	867	8.2	0.5	12.0
57-58–New York	72	–	1709	304	688	.442	–	–	–	271	389	.697	–	–	747	52	283	12	–	–	–	879	10.4	0.7	12.2
58-59–New York	72	–	1588	260	700	.371	–	–	–	229	321	.713	–	–	569	49	275	9	–	–	–	749	7.9	0.7	10.4
59-60–N.Y.-Minn.	47	–	883	136	355	.383	–	–	–	70	112	.625	–	–	338	23	177	5	–	–	–	342	7.2	0.5	7.3
60-61–Los Angeles	78	–	1510	189	508	.372	–	–	–	135	193	.699	–	–	539	37	302	12	–	–	–	513	6.9	0.5	6.6
61-62–Los Angeles	80	–	1478	171	398	.430	–	–	–	90	130	.692	–	–	473	55	266	6	–	–	–	432	5.9	0.7	5.4
Reg. Season Totals	637	–	15188	2406	5841	.412	–	–	–	2162	3187	.678	–	–	5652	448	2419	81	–	–	–	6974	8.9	0.7	10.9
Playoff Totals	38	–	836	106	248	.427	–	–	–	89	127	.701	–	–	290	29	143	6	–	–	–	301	7.6	0.8	7.9
All-Star Totals	1	–	32	4	8	.500	–	–	–	5	5	1.000	–	–	11	1	4	0	–	–	–	13	11.0	1.0	13.0

Fendley, John Phillip (Jake) b. June 12, 1929 Ht. 6-1 Wt. 180 College: Northwestern

SEASON–TEAM	G	GS	MIN	FGM	FGA	PCT	3FGM	3FGA	PCT	FTM	FTA	PCT	O-RB	D-RB	TOT	AST	PF	DQ	STL	TO	BLK	PTS	RPG	APG	PPG
51-52–Fort Wayne	58	–	651	54	170	.318	–	–	–	75	95	.789	–	–	80	58	118	3	–	–	–	183	1.4	1.0	3.2
52-53–Fort Wayne	45	–	380	32	80	.400	–	–	–	40	60	.667	–	–	46	36	82	3	–	–	–	104	1.0	0.8	2.3
Reg. Season Totals	103	–	1031	86	250	.344	–	–	–	115	155	.742	–	–	126	94	200	6	–	–	–	287	1.2	0.9	2.8
Playoff Totals	2	–	10	1	8	.250	–	–	–	0	0	–	–	–	3	2	3	0	–	–	–	2	1.0	0.7	1.0

Fenley, William Warren (Bill) b. February 8, 1922 Ht. 6-3 Wt. 190 College: Manhattan

SEASON–TEAM	G	GS	MIN	FGM	FGA	PCT	3FGM	3FGA	PCT	FTM	FTA	PCT	O-RB	D-RB	TOT	AST	PF	DQ	STL	TO	BLK	PTS	RPG	APG	PPG
46-47–Boston	33	–	–	31	138	.225	–	–	–	23	45	.511	–	–	–	16	59	–	–	–	–	85	–	0.5	2.6
Reg. Season Totals	33	–	–	31	138	.225	–	–	–	23	45	.511	–	–	–	16	59	–	–	–	–	85	–	0.5	2.6

Fernsten, Eric Robert b. November 1, 1953 Ht. 6-10 Wt. 205 College: San Francisco

SEASON–TEAM	G	GS	MIN	FGM	FGA	PCT	3FGM	3FGA	PCT	FTM	FTA	PCT	O-RB	D-RB	TOT	AST	PF	DQ	STL	TO	BLK	PTS	RPG	APG	PPG
75-76–Clev.-Chicago	37	–	268	33	86	.384	–	–	–	26	37	.703	25	45	70	19	21	0	7	–	14	92	1.9	0.5	2.5
76-77–Chicago	5	–	61	3	15	.200	–	–	–	8	11	.727	9	7	16	6	9	0	1	–	3	14	3.2	1.2	2.8
79-80–Boston	56	–	431	71	153	.464	0	0	–	33	52	.635	40	56	96	28	43	0	17	20	12	175	1.7	0.5	3.1
80-81–Boston	45	–	279	38	79	.481	0	0	–	20	30	.667	29	33	62	10	29	0	6	20	7	96	1.4	0.2	2.1
81-82–Boston	43	0	202	19	49	.388	0	0	–	19	30	.633	12	30	42	8	23	0	5	13	7	57	1.0	0.2	1.3
83-84–New York	32	0	402	29	52	.558	0	0	–	25	34	.735	29	57	86	11	49	0	16	19	8	83	2.7	0.3	2.6
Reg. Season Totals	218	0	1643	193	434	.445	0	0	–	131	194	.675	144	228	372	82	174	0	52	72	51	517	1.7	0.4	2.4
Playoff Totals	20	0	46	4	13	.308	0	0	–	5	8	.625	6	5	11	1	4	0	1	2	4	13	0.6	0.1	0.7

Ferrari, Albert R. (Al) b. July 6, 1933 Ht. 6-4 Wt. 190 College: Michigan State

SEASON–TEAM	G	GS	MIN	FGM	FGA	PCT	3FGM	3FGA	PCT	FTM	FTA	PCT	O-RB	D-RB	TOT	AST	PF	DQ	STL	TO	BLK	PTS	RPG	APG	PPG
55-56–St. Louis	68	–	1611	191	534	.358	–	–	–	164	236	.695	–	–	186	163	192	3	–	–	–	546	2.7	2.4	8.0
58-59–St. Louis	72	–	1189	134	385	.348	–	–	–	145	199	.729	–	–	142	122	155	1	–	–	–	413	2.0	1.7	5.7
59-60–St. Louis	71	–	1567	216	523	.413	–	–	–	176	225	.782	–	–	162	188	205	7	–	–	–	608	2.3	2.6	8.6
60-61–St. Louis	63	–	1031	117	328	.357	–	–	–	95	116	.819	–	–	115	143	157	4	–	–	–	329	1.8	2.3	5.2
61-62–St. Louis	79	–	2046	208	582	.357	–	–	–	175	219	.799	–	–	213	313	278	9	–	–	–	591	2.7	4.0	7.5
62-63–Chicago	18	–	138	12	37	.324	–	–	–	14	17	.824	–	–	12	14	21	0	–	–	–	38	0.7	0.8	2.1
Reg. Season Totals	371	–	7582	878	2389	.368	–	–	–	769	1012	.760	–	–	830	943	1008	24	–	–	–	2525	2.2	2.5	6.8
Playoff Totals	33	–	736	81	207	.391	–	–	–	94	130	.723	–	–	79	75	97	2	–	–	–	256	2.4	2.3	7.8

Ferreira, Rolando Jr. b. May 24, 1964 Ht. 7-1 Wt. 240 College: Houston

SEASON–TEAM	G	GS	MIN	FGM	FGA	PCT	3FGM	3FGA	PCT	FTM	FTA	PCT	O-RB	D-RB	TOT	AST	PF	DQ	STL	TO	BLK	PTS	RPG	APG	PPG
88-89–Portland	12	0	34	1	18	.056	0	0	–	7	8	.875	4	9	13	1	7	0	0	6	1	9	1.1	0.1	0.8
Reg. Season Totals	12	0	34	1	18	.056	0	0	–	7	8	.875	4	9	13	1	7	0	0	6	1	9	1.1	0.1	0.8

Ferrell, Duane b. February 28, 1965 Ht. 6-7 Wt. 215 College: Georgia Tech

SEASON–TEAM	G	GS	MIN	FGM	FGA	PCT	3FGM	3FGA	PCT	FTM	FTA	PCT	O-RB	D-RB	TOT	AST	PF	DQ	STL	TO	BLK	PTS	RPG	APG	PPG
88-89–Atlanta	41	0	231	35	83	.422	0	0	–	30	44	.682	19	22	41	10	33	0	7	12	6	100	1.0	0.2	2.4
89-90–Atlanta	14	0	29	5	14	.357	0	1	.000	2	6	.333	3	4	7	2	3	0	1	2	0	12	0.5	0.1	0.9
90-91–Atlanta	78	2	1165	174	356	.489	2	3	.667	125	156	.801	97	82	179	55	151	3	33	78	27	475	2.3	0.7	6.1
91-92–Atlanta	66	12	1598	331	632	.524	11	33	.333	166	218	.761	105	105	210	92	134	0	49	99	17	839	3.2	1.4	12.7
92-93–Atlanta	82	15	1736	327	696	.470	9	36	.250	176	226	.779	97	94	191	132	160	1	59	103	17	839	2.3	1.6	10.2
93-94–Atlanta	72	13	1155	184	379	.485	1	9	.111	144	184	.783	62	67	129	65	85	0	44	64	16	513	1.8	0.9	7.1
94-95–Indiana	56	1	607	83	173	.480	1	6	.167	64	85	.753	50	38	88	31	79	0	26	43	6	231	1.6	0.6	4.1
95-96–Indiana	54	6	591	80	166	.482	0	8	.000	42	57	.737	32	61	93	30	83	0	23	34	3	202	1.7	0.6	3.7
96-97–Indiana	62	18	1115	159	337	.472	18	44	.409	58	94	.617	57	84	141	66	120	0	38	55	6	394	2.3	1.1	6.4
97-98–Golden State	50	5	461	41	111	.369	0	6	.000	12	22	.545	25	22	47	26	50	0	21	18	6	94	0.9	0.5	1.9
98-99–Golden State	8	0	46	1	14	.071	0	0	–	3	4	.750	5	1	6	0	4	0	1	1	1	5	0.8	0.0	0.6
Reg. Season Totals	583	72	8734	1420	2961	.480	42	146	.288	822	1096	.750	552	580	1132	509	902	4	302	509	105	3704	1.9	0.9	6.4
Playoff Totals	34	0	468	62	147	.422	3	9	.333	53	77	.688	43	30	73	37	60	0	9	25	5	180	2.1	1.1	5.3

Ferrin, C. Arnold Jr. (Arnie) b. July 29, 1925 Ht. 6-4 Wt. 180 College: Utah

SEASON–TEAM	G	GS	MIN	FGM	FGA	PCT	3FGM	3FGA	PCT	FTM	FTA	PCT	O-RB	D-RB	TOT	AST	PF	DQ	STL	TO	BLK	PTS	RPG	APG	PPG
48-49–Minneapolis	47	–	–	130	378	.344	–	–	–	85	128	.664	–	–	–	76	142	–	–	–	–	345	–	1.6	7.3
49-50–Minneapolis	63	–	–	132	396	.333	–	–	–	76	109	.697	–	–	–	95	147	–	–	–	–	340	–	1.5	5.4
50-51–Minneapolis	68	–	–	119	373	.319	–	–	–	114	164	.695	–	–	271	107	220	8	–	–	–	352	4.0	1.6	5.2
Reg. Season Totals	178	–	–	381	1147	.332	–	–	–	275	401	.686	–	–	271	278	509	8	–	–	–	1037	4.0	1.6	5.8
Playoff Totals	29	–	–	71	384	.339	–	–	–	63	93	.677	–	–	33	118	114	7	–	–	–	205	4.7	2.3	7.1

Ferry, Daniel John Willard (Danny) b. October 17, 1966 Ht. 6-10 Wt. 235 College: Duke

SEASON–TEAM	G	GS	MIN	FGM	FGA	PCT	3FGM	3FGA	PCT	FTM	FTA	PCT	O-RB	D-RB	TOT	AST	PF	DQ	STL	TO	BLK	PTS	RPG	APG	PPG
90-91–Cleveland	81	2	1661	275	643	.428	23	77	.299	124	152	.816	99	187	286	142	230	1	43	120	25	697	3.5	1.8	8.6
91-92–Cleveland	68	1	937	134	328	.409	17	48	.354	61	73	.836	53	160	213	75	135	0	22	46	15	346	3.1	1.1	5.1
92-93–Cleveland	76	1	1461	220	459	.479	34	82	.415	99	113	.876	81	198	279	137	171	1	29	83	49	573	3.7	1.8	7.5
93-94–Cleveland	70	1	965	149	334	.446	14	51	.275	38	43	.884	47	94	141	74	113	0	28	41	22	350	2.0	1.1	5.0
94-95–Cleveland	82	6	1290	223	500	.446	94	233	.403	74	84	.881	30	113	143	96	131	0	27	59	22	614	1.7	1.2	7.5
95-96–Cleveland	82	79	2680	422	919	.459	143	363	.394	103	134	.769	71	238	309	191	233	3	57	122	37	1090	3.8	2.3	13.3
96-97–Cleveland	82	48	2633	341	794	.429	114	284	.401	74	87	.851	82	255	337	151	245	1	56	94	32	870	4.1	1.8	10.6
97-98–Cleveland	69	3	1034	113	286	.395	33	99	.333	32	40	.800	23	91	114	59	118	0	26	53	17	291	1.7	0.9	4.2
98-99–Cleveland	50	10	1058	141	296	.476	38	97	.392	29	33	.879	16	86	102	53	113	0	23	39	10	349	2.0	1.1	7.0
99-00–Cleveland	63	3	1326	189	380	.497	33	75	.440	52	57	.912	55	183	238	67	181	1	22	55	24	463	3.8	1.1	7.3
Reg. Season Totals	723	154	15045	2207	4939	.447	543	1409	.385	686	816	.841	557	1605	2162	1045	1670	7	333	712	253	5643	3.0	1.4	7.8
Playoff Totals	28	3	371	47	117	.402	14	45	.311	17	20	.850	12	48	60	31	45	1	10	14	6	125	2.1	1.1	4.5

Ferry, Robert Dean (Bob) b. May 31, 1937 Ht. 6-8 Wt. 230 College: St. Louis

SEASON–TEAM	G	GS	MIN	FGM	FGA	PCT	3FGM	3FGA	PCT	FTM	FTA	PCT	O-RB	D-RB	TOT	AST	PF	DQ	STL	TO	BLK	PTS	RPG	APG	PPG
59-60–St. Louis	62	–	875	144	338	.426	–	–	–	76	119	.639	–	–	233	40	132	2	–	–	–	364	3.8	0.6	5.9
60-61–Detroit	79	–	1657	350	776	.451	–	–	–	189	255	.741	–	–	500	129	205	1	–	–	–	889	6.3	1.6	11.3
61-62–Detroit	80	–	1918	411	939	.438	–	–	–	286	422	.678	–	–	503	145	199	2	–	–	–	1108	6.3	1.8	13.9
62-63–Detroit	79	–	2479	426	984	.433	–	–	–	220	339	.649	–	–	537	170	246	1	–	–	–	1072	6.8	2.2	13.6
63-64–Detroit	74	–	1522	298	670	.445	–	–	–	186	279	.667	–	–	428	94	174	2	–	–	–	782	5.8	1.3	10.6
64-65–Baltimore	77	–	1280	143	338	.423	–	–	–	122	199	.613	–	–	355	60	156	2	–	–	–	408	4.6	0.8	5.3
65-66–Baltimore	66	–	1229	188	457	.411	–	–	–	105	157	.669	–	–	334	111	134	1	–	–	–	481	5.1	1.7	7.3
66-67–Baltimore	51	–	991	132	315	.419	–	–	–	70	110	.636	–	–	258	92	97	0	–	–	–	334	5.1	1.8	6.5
67-68–Baltimore	59	–	841	128	311	.412	–	–	–	73	117	.624	–	–	186	61	92	0	–	–	–	329	3.2	1.0	5.6
68-69–Baltimore	7	–	36	5	14	.357	–	–	–	3	6	.500	–	–	9	4	3	0	–	–	–	13	1.3	0.6	1.9
Reg. Season Totals	634	–	12828	2225	5142	.433	–	–	–	1330	2003	.664	–	–	3343	906	1438	11	–	–	–	5780	5.3	1.4	9.1
Playoff Totals	42	–	681	115	255	.451	–	–	–	89	145	.614	–	–	198	46	70	0	–	–	–	319	4.7	1.1	7.6

Fields, Kenneth Henry (Kenny) b. February 9, 1962 Ht. 6-5 Wt. 240 College: UCLA

SEASON–TEAM	G	GS	MIN	FGM	FGA	PCT	3FGM	3FGA	PCT	FTM	FTA	PCT	O-RB	D-RB	TOT	AST	PF	DQ	STL	TO	BLK	PTS	RPG	APG	PPG
84-85–Milwaukee	51	1	535	84	191	.440	0	0	–	27	36	.750	41	43	84	38	84	2	9	32	10	195	1.6	0.7	3.8
85-86–Milwaukee	78	3	1120	204	398	.513	0	4	.000	91	132	.689	59	144	203	79	170	3	51	77	15	499	2.6	1.0	6.4
86-87–Milw.-LAClips	48	17	883	159	352	.452	3	12	.250	73	94	.777	63	85	148	61	123	2	32	53	11	394	3.1	1.3	8.2
87-88–L.A. Clippers	7	0	154	16	36	.444	0	0	–	20	26	.769	13	16	29	10	17	0	5	19	2	52	4.1	1.4	7.4
Reg. Season Totals	184	21	2692	463	977	.474	3	16	.188	211	288	.733	176	288	464	188	394	7	97	181	38	1140	2.5	1.0	6.2
Playoff Totals	12	4	158	38	69	.551	1	3	.333	12	23	.522	7	21	28	10	23	0	8	16	0	89	2.3	0.8	7.4

Fields, Robert L. (Bobby) b. October 20, 1949 Ht. 6-3 Wt. 175 College: Brandywine; La Salle

SEASON–TEAM	G	GS	MIN	FGM	FGA	PCT	3FGM	3FGA	PCT	FTM	FTA	PCT	O-RB	D-RB	TOT	AST	PF	DQ	STL	TO	BLK	PTS	RPG	APG	PPG
71-72–Utah (A)	22	–	124	22	48	.458	2	7	.286	8	13	.615	–	–	30	20	33	–	–	21	–	54	1.4	0.9	2.5
Reg. ABA Totals	22	–	124	22	48	.458	2	7	.286	8	13	.615	–	–	30	20	33	–	–	21	–	54	1.4	0.9	2.5

Filipek, Ronald Stanley (Ron) b. February 5, 1944 Ht. 6-5 Wt. 210 College: Tennessee Tech

SEASON–TEAM	G	GS	MIN	FGM	FGA	PCT	3FGM	3FGA	PCT	FTM	FTA	PCT	O-RB	D-RB	TOT	AST	PF	DQ	STL	TO	BLK	PTS	RPG	APG	PPG
67-68–Philadelphia	19	–	73	18	47	.383	–	–	–	7	14	.500	–	–	25	7	12	0	–	–	–	43	1.3	0.4	2.3
Reg. Season Totals	19	–	73	18	47	.383	–	–	–	7	14	.500	–	–	25	7	12	0	–	–	–	43	1.3	0.4	2.3

Fillmore, Gregory Paul (Greg) b. March 7, 1947 Ht. 7-1 Wt. 250 College: Iowa Central C.C.; Cheyney

SEASON–TEAM	G	GS	MIN	FGM	FGA	PCT	3FGM	3FGA	PCT	FTM	FTA	PCT	O-RB	D-RB	TOT	AST	PF	DQ	STL	TO	BLK	PTS	RPG	APG	PPG
70-71–New York	39	–	271	45	102	.441	–	–	–	13	27	.481	–	–	93	17	80	0	–	–	–	103	2.4	0.4	2.6
71-72–New York	10	–	67	7	27	.259	–	–	–	1	3	.333	–	–	15	3	17	0	–	–	–	15	1.5	0.3	1.5
Reg. Season Totals	49	–	338	52	129	.403	–	–	–	14	30	.467	–	–	108	20	97	0	–	–	–	118	2.2	0.4	2.4
Playoff Totals	8	–	24	0	4	.000	–	–	–	0	0	–	–	–	8	1	9	0	–	–	–	0	1.0	0.1	0.0

Finch, Larry O. b. February 16, 1951 Ht. 6-2 Wt. 195 College: Memphis

SEASON–TEAM	G	GS	MIN	FGM	FGA	PCT	3FGM	3FGA	PCT	FTM	FTA	PCT	O-RB	D-RB	TOT	AST	PF	DQ	STL	TO	BLK	PTS	RPG	APG	PPG
73-74–Memphis (A)	65	–	1154	164	399	.411	7	26	.269	108	136	.794	24	50	74	111	162	–	26	95	1	443	1.1	1.7	6.8
74-75–Memphis (A)	63	–	1888	264	593	.445	20	53	.377	115	133	.865	44	99	143	190	164	–	52	90	6	663	2.3	3.0	10.5
Reg. ABA Totals	128	–	3042	428	992	.431	27	79	.342	223	269	.829	68	149	217	301	326	0	78	185	7	1106	1.7	2.4	8.6

Finkel, Henry J. (Hank) b. April 20, 1942 Ht. 7-0 Wt. 240 College: St. Peter's; Dayton

SEASON–TEAM	G	GS	MIN	FGM	FGA	PCT	3FGM	3FGA	PCT	FTM	FTA	PCT	O-RB	D-RB	TOT	AST	PF	DQ	STL	TO	BLK	PTS	RPG	APG	PPG
66-67–Los Angeles	27	–	141	17	47	.362	–	–	–	7	12	.583	–	–	64	5	39	1	–	–	–	41	2.4	0.2	1.5
67-68–San Diego	53	–	1116	242	492	.492	–	–	–	131	191	.686	–	–	375	72	175	5	–	–	–	615	7.1	1.4	11.6
68-69–San Diego	35	–	332	49	111	.441	–	–	–	31	41	.756	–	–	107	21	53	1	–	–	–	129	3.1	0.6	3.7
69-70–Boston	80	–	1866	310	683	.454	–	–	–	156	233	.670	–	–	613	103	292	13	–	–	–	776	7.7	1.3	9.7
70-71–Boston	80	–	1234	214	489	.438	–	–	–	93	127	.732	–	–	343	79	196	5	–	–	–	521	4.3	1.0	6.5
71-72–Boston	78	–	736	103	254	.406	–	–	–	43	74	.581	–	–	251	61	118	4	–	–	–	249	3.2	0.8	3.2
72-73–Boston	76	–	496	78	173	.451	–	–	–	28	52	.538	–	–	151	26	83	0	–	–	–	184	2.0	0.3	2.4
73-74–Boston	60	–	427	60	130	.462	–	–	–	28	43	.651	41	94	135	27	62	1	3	–	7	148	2.3	0.5	2.5
74-75–Boston	62	–	518	52	129	.403	–	–	–	23	43	.535	33	79	112	32	72	0	7	–	3	127	1.8	0.5	2.0
Reg. Season Totals	551	–	6866	1125	2508	.449	–	–	–	540	816	.662	74	173	2151	426	1090	30	10	–	10	2790	3.9	0.8	5.1
Playoff Totals	33	–	175	27	59	.458	–	–	–	4	6	.667	8	8	53	13	29	0	1	–	0	58	1.6	0.4	1.8

Finley, Michael H. b. March 6, 1973 Ht. 6-7 Wt. 215 College: Wisconsin

SEASON–TEAM	G	GS	MIN	FGM	FGA	PCT	3FGM	3FGA	PCT	FTM	FTA	PCT	O-RB	D-RB	TOT	AST	PF	DQ	STL	TO	BLK	PTS	RPG	APG	PPG
95-96–Phoenix	82	72	3212	465	976	.476	61	186	.328	242	323	.749	139	235	374	289	199	1	85	133	31	1233	4.6	3.5	15.0
96-97–Phoenix-Dallas	83	54	2790	475	1071	.444	101	280	.361	198	245	.808	88	284	372	224	138	0	68	164	24	1249	4.5	2.7	15.0
97-98–Dallas	82	82	3394	675	1505	.449	87	244	.357	326	416	.784	150	288	438	405	163	0	132	219	30	1763	5.3	4.9	21.5
98-99–Dallas	50	50	2051	389	876	.444	45	136	.331	186	226	.823	69	194	263	218	96	1	66	107	15	1009	5.3	4.4	20.2
99-00–Dallas	82	82	3464	748	1636	.457	99	247	.401	260	317	.820	122	396	518	438	171	1	109	196	32	1855	6.3	5.3	22.6
Reg. Season Totals	379	340	14911	2752	6064	.454	393	1093	.360	1212	1527	.794	568	1397	1965	1574	767	3	460	819	132	7109	5.2	4.2	18.8
All-Star Totals	1	0	10	5	6	.833	1	2	.500	0	0	–	0	1	1	0	0	0	0	1	0	11	1.0	0.0	11.0

Finn, Daniel Lawrence Jr. (Danny) b. May 27, 1928 Ht. 6-1 Wt. 185 College: St. John's (N.Y.)

SEASON–TEAM	G	GS	MIN	FGM	FGA	PCT	3FGM	3FGA	PCT	FTM	FTA	PCT	O-RB	D-RB	TOT	AST	PF	DQ	STL	TO	BLK	PTS	RPG	APG	PPG
52-53–Philadelphia	31	–	1015	135	409	.330	–	–	–	99	182	.544	–	–	175	146	124	9	–	–	–	369	5.6	4.7	11.9
53-54–Philadelphia	68	–	1562	170	495	.343	–	–	–	126	196	.643	–	–	216	265	215	7	–	–	–	466	3.2	3.9	6.9
54-55–Philadelphia	43	–	820	77	265	.291	–	–	–	53	86	.616	–	–	157	155	114	3	–	–	–	207	3.7	3.6	4.8
Reg. Season Totals	142	–	3397	382	1169	.327	–	–	–	278	464	.599	–	–	548	566	453	19	–	–	–	1042	3.9	4.0	7.3

Fish, Matthew Edward (Matt) b. November 18, 1969 Ht. 6-11 Wt. 235 College: Wilmington

SEASON–TEAM	G	GS	MIN	FGM	FGA	PCT	3FGM	3FGA	PCT	FTM	FTA	PCT	O-RB	D-RB	TOT	AST	PF	DQ	STL	TO	BLK	PTS	RPG	APG	PPG
94-95–L.A. Clippers	26	8	370	49	103	.476	0	1	.000	25	37	.676	32	52	84	17	70	1	16	28	7	123	3.2	0.7	4.7
95-96–N.Y.-Denver	18	1	134	21	36	.583	0	0	–	10	19	.526	10	11	21	8	19	0	3	3	7	52	1.2	0.4	2.9
96-97–Wash.-Miami	6	0	8	1	3	.333	0	0	–	0	0	–	1	4	5	0	2	0	0	2	0	2	0.8	0.0	0.3
Reg. Season Totals	50	9	512	71	142	.500	0	1	.000	35	56	.625	43	67	110	25	91	1	19	33	14	177	2.2	0.5	3.5

Fisher, Derek Lamar b. August 9, 1974 Ht. 6-1 Wt. 200 College: Arkansas-Little Rock

SEASON–TEAM	G	GS	MIN	FGM	FGA	PCT	3FGM	3FGA	PCT	FTM	FTA	PCT	O-RB	D-RB	TOT	AST	PF	DQ	STL	TO	BLK	PTS	RPG	APG	PPG
96-97–L.A. Lakers	80	3	921	104	262	.397	22	73	.301	79	120	.658	25	72	97	119	87	0	41	71	5	309	1.2	1.5	3.9
97-98–L.A. Lakers	82	36	1760	164	378	.434	31	81	.383	115	152	.757	38	155	193	333	126	1	75	119	5	474	2.4	4.1	5.8
98-99–L.A. Lakers	50	21	1131	99	263	.376	38	97	.392	60	79	.759	21	70	91	197	95	0	61	77	1	296	1.8	3.9	5.9
99-00–L.A. Lakers	78	22	1803	167	483	.346	52	166	.313	105	145	.724	22	121	143	216	150	1	80	75	3	491	1.8	2.8	6.3
Reg. Season Totals	290	82	5615	534	1386	.385	143	417	.343	359	496	.724	106	418	524	865	458	2	257	342	14	1570	1.8	3.0	5.4
Playoff Totals	48	21	872	92	225	.409	28	83	.337	51	72	.708	12	67	79	135	87	1	37	41	1	263	1.6	2.8	5.5

Fisher, Richard B. (Rick) b. October 27, 1948 Ht. 6-5 Wt. 220 College: Colorado State

SEASON–TEAM	G	GS	MIN	FGM	FGA	PCT	3FGM	3FGA	PCT	FTM	FTA	PCT	O-RB	D-RB	TOT	AST	PF	DQ	STL	TO	BLK	PTS	RPG	APG	PPG
71-72–Utah-Fla. (A)	12	–	66	18	34	.529	0	0	–	1	1	1.000	–	–	32	5	9	–	–	4	–	37	2.7	0.4	3.1
Reg. ABA Totals	12	–	66	18	34	.529	0	0	–	1	1	1.000	–	–	32	5	9	–	–	4	–	37	2.7	0.4	3.1

Fitzgerald, Richard (Dick) b. November 18, 1920 d. April 13, 1968 Ht. 6-5 Wt. 175 College: Seton Hall

SEASON–TEAM	G	GS	MIN	FGM	FGA	PCT	3FGM	3FGA	PCT	FTM	FTA	PCT	O-RB	D-RB	TOT	AST	PF	DQ	STL	TO	BLK	PTS	RPG	APG	PPG
46-47–Toronto	60	–	–	118	495	.238	–	–	–	41	60	.683	–	–	–	40	89	–	–	–	–	277	–	0.7	4.6
47-48–Providence	1	–	–	0	3	.000	–	–	–	0	0	–	–	–	–	0	1	–	–	–	–	0	–	0.0	0.0
Reg. Season Totals	61	–	–	118	498	.237	–	–	–	41	60	.683	–	–	–	40	90	–	–	–	–	277	–	0.7	4.5

Fitzgerald, Robert (Bob) b. March 14, 1923 d. July 1983 Ht. 6-5 Wt. 190 College: Fordham

SEASON–TEAM	G	GS	MIN	FGM	FGA	PCT	3FGM	3FGA	PCT	FTM	FTA	PCT	O-RB	D-RB	TOT	AST	PF	DQ	STL	TO	BLK	PTS	RPG	APG	PPG
45-46–Rochester (N)	10	–	–	9	–	–	–	–	–	15	–	–	–	–	–	–	–	–	–	–	–	33	–	–	3.3
46-47–Toronto-N.Y.	60	–	–	70	362	.193	–	–	–	81	130	.623	–	–	–	35	153	–	–	–	–	221	–	0.6	3.7
47-48–Syracuse (N)	1	–	–	0	–	–	–	–	–	0	1	.000	–	–	–	–	–	–	–	–	–	0	–	–	0.0
48-49–Rochester	18	–	–	6	29	.207	–	–	–	7	10	.700	–	–	–	12	26	–	–	–	–	19	–	0.7	1.1
Reg. NBA Totals	78	–	–	76	391	.194	–	–	–	88	140	.629	–	–	–	47	179	–	–	–	–	240	–	0.6	3.1
Reg. NBL Totals	11	–	–	9	–	–	–	–	–	15	1	.000	–	–	–	–	–	–	–	–	–	33	–	–	3.0
NBA Playoff Totals	6	–	–	1	11	.091	–	–	–	3	4	.750	–	–	–	1	4	–	–	–	–	5	–	0.1	0.8
NBL Playoff Totals	6	–	–	2	–	–	–	–	–	6	8	.750	–	–	–	–	6	–	–	–	–	10	–	–	1.7

Fleishman, Jerome (Jerry) b. February 14, 1922 Ht. 6-2 Wt. 190 College: New York U.; Long Island University

SEASON–TEAM	G	GS	MIN	FGM	FGA	PCT	3FGM	3FGA	PCT	FTM	FTA	PCT	O-RB	D-RB	TOT	AST	PF	DQ	STL	TO	BLK	PTS	RPG	APG	PPG
46-47–Philadelphia	59	–	–	97	372	.261	–	–	–	69	127	.543	–	–	–	40	101	–	–	–	–	263	–	0.7	4.5
47-48–Philadelphia	46	–	–	119	501	.238	–	–	–	95	138	.688	–	–	–	43	122	–	–	–	–	333	–	0.9	7.2
48-49–Philadelphia	59	–	–	123	424	.290	–	–	–	77	118	.653	–	–	–	120	137	–	–	–	–	323	–	2.0	5.5
49-50–Philadelphia	65	–	–	102	353	.289	–	–	–	93	151	.616	–	–	–	118	129	–	–	–	–	297	–	1.8	4.6
52-53–Phil.-N.Y.	33	–	882	100	303	.330	–	–	–	96	140	.686	–	–	152	108	118	7	–	–	–	296	4.6	3.3	9.0
Reg. Season Totals	262	–	882	541	1953	.277	–	–	–	430	674	.638	–	–	152	429	607	7	–	–	–	1512	4.6	1.6	5.8
Playoff Totals	22	–	26	37	191	.288	–	–	–	31	49	.633	–	–	5	20	45	3	–	–	–	105	2.5	0.7	4.8

Fleming, Albert Jr. (Al) b. April 5, 1954 Ht. 6-7 Wt. 215 College: Arizona

SEASON–TEAM	G	GS	MIN	FGM	FGA	PCT	3FGM	3FGA	PCT	FTM	FTA	PCT	O-RB	D-RB	TOT	AST	PF	DQ	STL	TO	BLK	PTS	RPG	APG	PPG
77-78–Seattle	20	–	97	15	31	.484	–	–	–	10	17	.588	13	17	30	7	16	0	0	16	5	40	1.5	0.4	2.0
Reg. Season Totals	20	–	97	15	31	.484	–	–	–	10	17	.588	13	17	30	7	16	0	0	16	5	40	1.5	0.4	2.0
Playoff Totals	5	–	21	2	6	.333	–	–	–	3	4	.750	1	3	4	2	5	0	1	2	0	7	0.8	0.4	1.4

Fleming, Edward R. (Ed) b. July 25, 1933 Ht. 6-3 Wt. 190 College: Niagara

SEASON–TEAM	G	GS	MIN	FGM	FGA	PCT	3FGM	3FGA	PCT	FTM	FTA	PCT	O-RB	D-RB	TOT	AST	PF	DQ	STL	TO	BLK	PTS	RPG	APG	PPG
55-56–Rochester	71	–	2028	306	824	.371	–	–	–	277	372	.745	–	–	489	197	178	1	–	–	–	889	6.9	2.8	12.5
56-57–Rochester	51	–	927	109	364	.299	–	–	–	139	191	.728	–	–	183	81	94	0	–	–	–	357	3.6	1.6	7.0
57-58–Minneapolis	72	–	1686	226	655	.345	–	–	–	181	255	.710	–	–	492	139	222	5	–	–	–	633	6.8	1.9	8.8
58-59–Minneapolis	71	–	1132	162	419	.387	–	–	–	137	190	.721	–	–	281	89	148	1	–	–	–	461	4.0	1.3	6.5
59-60–Minneapolis	27	–	413	59	141	.418	–	–	–	53	69	.768	–	–	87	38	46	0	–	–	–	171	3.2	1.4	6.3
Reg. Season Totals	292	–	6186	862	2403	.359	–	–	–	787	1077	.731	–	–	1532	544	688	7	–	–	–	2511	5.2	1.9	8.6
Playoff Totals	13	–	178	27	77	.351	–	–	–	22	25	.880	–	–	39	18	32	0	–	–	–	76	3.0	1.4	5.8

Fleming, Vern b. February 4, 1962 Ht. 6-5 Wt. 185 College: Georgia

SEASON–TEAM	G	GS	MIN	FGM	FGA	PCT	3FGM	3FGA	PCT	FTM	FTA	PCT	O-RB	D-RB	TOT	AST	PF	DQ	STL	TO	BLK	PTS	RPG	APG	PPG
84-85–Indiana	80	65	2486	433	922	.470	0	4	.000	260	339	.767	148	175	323	247	232	4	99	197	8	1126	4.0	3.1	14.1
85-86–Indiana	80	77	2870	436	862	.506	1	6	.167	263	353	.745	102	284	386	505	230	3	131	208	5	1136	4.8	6.3	14.2
86-87–Indiana	82	82	2549	370	727	.509	2	10	.200	238	302	.788	109	225	334	473	222	3	109	167	18	980	4.1	5.8	12.0
87-88–Indiana	80	80	2733	442	845	.523	0	13	.000	227	283	.802	106	258	364	568	225	0	115	175	11	1111	4.6	7.1	13.9
88-89–Indiana	76	69	2552	419	814	.515	3	23	.130	243	304	.799	85	225	310	494	212	4	77	192	12	1084	4.1	6.5	14.3
89-90–Indiana	82	82	2876	467	919	.508	12	34	.353	230	294	.782	118	204	322	610	213	1	92	206	10	1176	3.9	7.4	14.3
90-91–Indiana	69	45	1929	356	671	.531	4	18	.222	161	221	.729	83	131	214	369	116	0	76	137	13	877	3.1	5.3	12.7
91-92–Indiana	82	6	1737	294	610	.482	6	27	.222	132	179	.737	69	140	209	266	134	0	56	140	7	726	2.5	3.2	8.9
92-93–Indiana	75	8	1503	280	554	.505	7	36	.194	143	197	.726	63	106	169	224	126	1	63	121	9	710	2.3	3.0	9.5
93-94–Indiana	55	5	1053	147	318	.462	0	4	.000	64	87	.736	27	96	123	173	98	1	40	87	6	358	2.2	3.1	6.5
94-95–Indiana	55	1	686	93	188	.495	0	7	.000	65	90	.722	20	68	88	109	80	0	27	43	1	251	1.6	2.0	4.6
95-96–New Jersey	77	3	1747	227	524	.433	3	28	.107	133	177	.751	49	121	170	255	115	0	41	122	5	590	2.2	3.3	7.7
Reg. Season Totals	893	523	24721	3964	7954	.498	38	210	.181	2159	2826	.764	979	2033	3012	4293	2003	17	926	1795	105	10125	3.4	4.8	11.3
Playoff Totals	37	11	755	109	234	.466	2	14	.143	64	83	.771	37	49	86	114	69	1	22	57	7	284	2.3	3.1	7.7

Flowers, Bruce Douglas b. June 13, 1957 Ht. 6-8 Wt. 225 College: Notre Dame

SEASON–TEAM	G	GS	MIN	FGM	FGA	PCT	3FGM	3FGA	PCT	FTM	FTA	PCT	O-RB	D-RB	TOT	AST	PF	DQ	STL	TO	BLK	PTS	RPG	APG	PPG
82-83–Cleveland	53	5	699	110	206	.534	0	2	.000	41	53	.774	71	109	180	47	99	2	19	43	12	261	3.4	0.9	4.9
Reg. Season Totals	53	5	699	110	206	.534	0	2	.000	41	53	.774	71	109	180	47	99	2	19	43	12	261	3.4	0.9	4.9

Floyd, Eric Augustus (Sleepy) b. March 6, 1960 Ht. 6-3 Wt. 185 College: Georgetown

SEASON–TEAM	G	GS	MIN	FGM	FGA	PCT	3FGM	3FGA	PCT	FTM	FTA	PCT	O-RB	D-RB	TOT	AST	PF	DQ	STL	TO	BLK	PTS	RPG	APG	PPG
82-83–N.J.-G.S.	76	17	1248	226	527	.429	10	25	.400	150	180	.833	56	81	137	138	134	3	58	106	17	612	1.8	1.8	8.1
83-84–Golden State	77	73	2555	484	1045	.463	8	45	.178	315	386	.816	87	184	271	269	216	0	103	196	31	1291	3.5	3.5	16.8
84-85–Golden State	82	82	2873	610	1372	.445	42	143	.294	336	415	.810	62	140	202	406	226	1	134	251	41	1598	2.5	5.0	19.5
85-86–Golden State	82	82	2764	510	1007	.506	39	119	.328	351	441	.796	76	221	297	746	199	2	157	290	16	1410	3.6	9.1	17.2
86-87–Golden State	82	82	3064	503	1030	.488	73	190	.384	462	537	.860	56	212	268	848	199	1	146	280	18	1541	3.3	10.3	18.8
87-88–G.S.-Houston	77	73	2514	420	969	.433	14	72	.194	301	354	.850	77	219	296	544	190	1	95	223	12	1155	3.8	7.1	15.0
88-89–Houston	82	82	2788	396	893	.443	109	292	.373	261	309	.845	48	258	306	709	196	1	124	253	11	1162	3.7	8.6	14.2
89-90–Houston	82	73	2630	362	803	.451	89	234	.380	187	232	.806	46	152	198	600	159	0	94	204	11	1000	2.4	7.3	12.2
90-91–Houston	82	4	1850	386	939	.411	48	176	.273	185	246	.752	52	107	159	317	122	0	95	140	17	1005	1.9	3.9	12.3
91-92–Houston	82	3	1662	286	704	.406	37	123	.301	135	170	.794	34	116	150	239	128	0	57	128	21	744	1.8	2.9	9.1
92-93–Houston	52	10	867	124	305	.407	16	56	.286	81	102	.794	14	72	86	132	59	0	32	68	6	345	1.7	2.5	6.6
93-94–San Antonio	53	2	737	70	209	.335	8	36	.222	52	78	.667	10	60	70	101	71	0	12	61	8	200	1.3	1.9	3.8
94-95–New Jersey	48	1	831	71	212	.335	25	88	.284	30	43	.698	8	46	54	126	73	0	13	51	6	197	1.1	2.6	4.1
Reg. Season Totals	957	584	26383	4448	10015	.444	518	1599	.324	2846	3493	.815	626	1868	2494	5175	1972	9	1120	2251	215	12260	2.6	5.4	12.8
Playoff Totals	36	22	1038	171	374	.457	29	70	.414	96	118	.814	23	54	77	219	58	0	43	92	5	467	2.1	6.1	13.0
All-Star Totals	1	0	19	4	7	.571	1	3	.333	5	7	.714	2	3	5	1	2	0	1	2	0	14	5.0	1.0	14.0

Flynn, Michael David (Mike) b. July 31, 1953 Ht. 6-3 Wt. 190 College: Kentucky

SEASON–TEAM	G	GS	MIN	FGM	FGA	PCT	3FGM	3FGA	PCT	FTM	FTA	PCT	O-RB	D-RB	TOT	AST	PF	DQ	STL	TO	BLK	PTS	RPG	APG	PPG
75-76–Indiana (A)	67	–	1097	166	439	.378	25	99	.253	64	111	.577	63	70	133	133	112	–	44	81	9	421	2.0	2.0	6.3
76-77–Indiana	73	–	1324	250	573	.436	–	–	–	101	142	.711	76	111	187	179	106	0	57	–	6	601	2.6	2.5	8.2
77-78–Indiana	71	–	955	120	267	.449	–	–	–	55	97	.567	47	70	117	142	52	0	41	75	10	295	1.6	2.0	4.2
Reg. NBA Totals	144	–	2279	370	840	.440	–	–	–	156	239	.653	123	181	304	321	158	0	98	75	16	896	2.1	2.2	6.2
Reg. ABA Totals	67	–	1097	166	439	.378	25	99	.253	64	111	.577	63	70	133	133	112	–	44	81	9	421	2.0	2.0	6.3
ABA Playoff Totals	3	–	83	15	30	.500	3	8	.375	8	11	.727	5	5	10	10	6	–	3	5	0	41	3.3	3.3	13.7

Fogle, Larry b. March 19, 1953 Ht. 6-5 Wt. 205 College: Louisiana-Lafayette; Canisius

SEASON–TEAM	G	GS	MIN	FGM	FGA	PCT	3FGM	3FGA	PCT	FTM	FTA	PCT	O-RB	D-RB	TOT	AST	PF	DQ	STL	TO	BLK	PTS	RPG	APG	PPG
75-76–New York	2	–	14	1	5	.200	–	–	–	0	0	–	1	2	3	0	4	0	1	–	0	2	1.5	0.0	1.0
Reg. Season Totals	2	–	14	1	5	.200	–	–	–	0	0	–	1	2	3	0	4	0	1	–	0	2	1.5	0.0	1.0

Foley, John E. (Jack, Jack the Shot) b. April 19, 1939 Ht. 6-5 Wt. 185 College: Holy Cross

SEASON–TEAM	G	GS	MIN	FGM	FGA	PCT	3FGM	3FGA	PCT	FTM	FTA	PCT	O-RB	D-RB	TOT	AST	PF	DQ	STL	TO	BLK	PTS	RPG	APG	PPG
62-63–Boston-N.Y.	11	–	83	20	51	.392	–	–	–	13	15	.867	–	–	16	5	8	0	–	–	–	53	1.5	0.5	4.8
Reg. Season Totals	11	–	83	20	51	.392	–	–	–	13	15	.867	–	–	16	5	8	0	–	–	–	53	1.5	0.5	4.8

Fontaine, Levi b. November 1, 1948 Ht. 6-4 Wt. 190 College: Maryland State

SEASON–TEAM	G	GS	MIN	FGM	FGA	PCT	3FGM	3FGA	PCT	FTM	FTA	PCT	O-RB	D-RB	TOT	AST	PF	DQ	STL	TO	BLK	PTS	RPG	APG	PPG
70-71–San Francisco	35	–	210	53	145	.366	–	–	–	28	37	.757	–	–	15	22	27	0	–	–	–	134	0.4	0.6	3.8
Reg. Season Totals	35	–	210	53	145	.366	–	–	–	28	37	.757	–	–	15	22	27	0	–	–	–	134	0.4	0.6	3.8
Playoff Totals	2	–	9	2	3	.667	–	–	–	1	3	.333	–	–	0	–	2	0	–	–	–	5	0.0	0.0	2.5

Ford, Alphonso Gene b. October 31, 1971 Ht. 6-1 Wt. 190 College: Mississippi Valley State

SEASON–TEAM	G	GS	MIN	FGM	FGA	PCT	3FGM	3FGA	PCT	FTM	FTA	PCT	O-RB	D-RB	TOT	AST	PF	DQ	STL	TO	BLK	PTS	RPG	APG	PPG
93-94–Seattle	6	0	16	7	13	.538	1	1	1.000	1	2	.500	0	0	0	1	2	0	2	1	0	16	0.0	0.2	2.7
94-95–Philadelphia	5	0	98	9	39	.231	0	9	.000	1	2	.500	8	12	20	9	5	0	1	8	0	19	4.0	1.8	3.8
Reg. Season Totals	11	0	114	16	52	.308	1	10	.100	2	4	.500	8	12	20	10	7	0	3	9	0	35	1.8	0.9	3.2

Ford, Christopher Joseph (Chris) b. January 11, 1949 Ht. 6-5 Wt. 190 College: Villanova

SEASON–TEAM	G	GS	MIN	FGM	FGA	PCT	3FGM	3FGA	PCT	FTM	FTA	PCT	O-RB	D-RB	TOT	AST	PF	DQ	STL	TO	BLK	PTS	RPG	APG	PPG
72-73–Detroit	74	–	1537	208	434	.479	–	–	–	60	93	.645	–	–	266	194	133	1	–	–	–	476	3.6	2.6	6.4
73-74–Detroit	82	–	2059	264	595	.444	–	–	–	57	77	.740	109	195	304	279	159	1	148	–	14	585	3.7	3.4	7.1
74-75–Detroit	80	–	1962	206	435	.474	–	–	–	63	95	.663	93	176	269	230	187	0	113	–	26	475	3.4	2.9	5.9
75-76–Detroit	82	–	2198	301	707	.426	–	–	–	83	115	.722	80	211	291	272	222	0	178	–	24	685	3.5	3.3	8.4
76-77–Detroit	82	–	2539	437	918	.476	–	–	–	131	170	.771	96	174	270	337	192	1	179	–	26	1005	3.3	4.1	12.3
77-78–Detroit	82	–	2582	374	777	.481	–	–	–	113	154	.734	117	151	268	381	182	2	166	232	17	861	3.3	4.6	10.5
78-79–Detroit-Boston	81	–	2737	538	1142	.471	–	–	–	172	227	.758	124	150	274	374	209	3	115	210	25	1248	3.4	4.6	15.4
79-80–Boston	73	–	2115	330	709	.465	70	164	.427	86	114	.754	77	104	181	215	178	0	111	105	27	816	2.5	2.9	11.2
80-81–Boston	82	–	2723	314	707	.444	36	109	.330	64	87	.736	72	91	163	295	212	2	100	127	23	728	2.0	3.6	8.9
81-82–Boston	76	53	1591	188	450	.418	20	63	.317	39	56	.696	52	56	108	142	143	0	42	52	10	435	1.4	1.9	5.7
Reg. Season Totals	794	53	22043	3160	6874	.460	126	336	.375	868	1188	.731	820	1308	2394	2719	1817	10	1152	726	192	7314	3.0	3.4	9.2
Playoff Totals	58	0	1477	185	420	.440	11	45	.244	53	77	.688	48	120	168	151	159	2	52	35	15	434	2.9	2.6	7.5

Ford, Donald J. (Don) b. December 31, 1952 Ht. 6-9 Wt. 215 College: New Mexico; Santa Barbara City (Calif.) Coll.(J.C.); California-Santa Barbara

SEASON–TEAM	G	GS	MIN	FGM	FGA	PCT	3FGM	3FGA	PCT	FTM	FTA	PCT	O-RB	D-RB	TOT	AST	PF	DQ	STL	TO	BLK	PTS	RPG	APG	PPG
75-76–Los Angeles	76	–	1838	311	710	.438	–	–	–	104	139	.748	118	215	333	111	186	3	50	–	14	726	4.4	1.5	9.6
76-77–Los Angeles	82	–	1782	262	570	.460	–	–	–	73	102	.716	105	248	353	133	170	0	60	–	21	597	4.3	1.6	7.3
77-78–Los Angeles	79	–	1945	272	576	.472	–	–	–	68	90	.756	106	247	353	142	210	1	68	88	46	612	4.5	1.8	7.7
78-79–Los Angeles	79	–	1540	228	450	.507	–	–	–	72	89	.809	83	185	268	101	177	2	51	93	25	528	3.4	1.3	6.7
79-80–L.A.-Clev.	73	–	999	131	274	.478	1	3	.333	45	53	.849	44	141	185	65	131	0	22	51	21	308	2.5	0.9	4.2
80-81–Cleveland	64	–	996	100	224	.446	0	3	.000	22	24	.917	74	90	164	84	100	1	15	49	12	222	2.6	1.3	3.5
81-82–Cleveland	21	1	201	9	24	.375	0	1	.000	5	6	.833	14	21	35	11	30	0	8	15	0	23	1.7	0.5	1.1
Reg. Season Totals	474	1	9301	1313	2828	.464	1	7	.143	389	503	.773	544	1147	1691	647	1004	7	274	296	139	3016	3.6	1.4	6.4
Playoff Totals	20	0	481	58	131	.443	0	0	–	28	39	.718	26	59	85	44	50	0	21	5	6	144	4.3	2.2	7.2

Ford, Jake b. April 29, 1946 Ht. 6-3 Wt. 180 College: Maryland State

SEASON–TEAM	G	GS	MIN	FGM	FGA	PCT	3FGM	3FGA	PCT	FTM	FTA	PCT	O-RB	D-RB	TOT	AST	PF	DQ	STL	TO	BLK	PTS	RPG	APG	PPG
70-71–Seattle	5	–	68	9	25	.360	–	–	–	16	22	.727	–	–	9	9	11	0	–	–	–	34	1.8	1.8	6.8
71-72–Seattle	26	–	181	33	66	.500	–	–	–	26	33	.788	–	–	11	26	21	0	–	–	–	92	0.4	1.0	3.5
Reg. Season Totals	31	–	249	42	91	.462	–	–	–	42	55	.764	–	–	20	35	32	0	–	–	–	126	0.6	1.1	4.1

Ford, Phil Jackson Jr. b. February 9, 1956 Ht. 6-2 Wt. 175 College: North Carolina

SEASON–TEAM	G	GS	MIN	FGM	FGA	PCT	3FGM	3FGA	PCT	FTM	FTA	PCT	O-RB	D-RB	TOT	AST	PF	DQ	STL	TO	BLK	PTS	RPG	APG	PPG
78-79–Kansas City	79	–	2723	467	1004	.465	–	–	–	326	401	.813	33	149	182	681	245	3	174	323	6	1260	2.3	8.6	15.9
79-80–Kansas City	82	–	2621	489	1058	.462	4	23	.174	346	423	.818	29	143	172	610	208	0	136	282	4	1328	2.1	7.4	16.2
80-81–Kansas City	66	–	2287	424	887	.478	11	36	.306	294	354	.831	26	102	128	580	190	3	99	241	6	1153	1.9	8.8	17.5
81-82–Kansas City	72	65	1952	285	649	.439	7	32	.219	136	166	.819	24	81	105	451	160	0	63	194	1	713	1.5	6.3	9.9
82-83–N.J.-Milw.	77	63	1610	213	445	.479	1	9	.111	97	123	.789	18	85	103	290	190	2	52	134	3	524	1.3	3.8	6.8
83-84–Houston	81	55	2020	236	470	.502	2	15	.133	98	117	.838	28	109	137	410	243	7	59	135	8	572	1.7	5.1	7.1
84-85–Houston	25	1	290	14	47	.298	0	4	.000	16	18	.889	3	24	27	61	33	0	6	17	1	44	1.1	2.4	1.8
Reg. Season Totals	482	184	13503	2128	4560	.467	25	119	.210	1313	1602	.820	161	693	854	3083	1269	15	589	1326	29	5594	1.8	6.4	11.6
Playoff Totals	15	0	416	50	137	.365	3	5	.600	33	46	.717	3	23	26	85	30	0	22	44	0	136	1.7	5.7	9.1

Ford, Robert Alan (Bob) b. January 26, 1950 Ht. 6-7 Wt. 230 College: Purdue

SEASON–TEAM	G	GS	MIN	FGM	FGA	PCT	3FGM	3FGA	PCT	FTM	FTA	PCT	O-RB	D-RB	TOT	AST	PF	DQ	STL	TO	BLK	PTS	RPG	APG	PPG
72-73–Memphis (A)	9	–	74	5	17	.294	0	0	–	4	5	.800	2	10	12	4	8	0	–	4	–	14	1.3	0.4	1.6
Reg. ABA Totals	9	–	74	5	17	.294	0	0	–	4	5	.800	2	10	12	4	8	0	–	4	–	14	1.3	0.4	1.6

Ford, Willard Sherell (Sherell) b. August 26, 1972 Ht. 6-7 Wt. 210 College: Illinois

SEASON–TEAM	G	GS	MIN	FGM	FGA	PCT	3FGM	3FGA	PCT	FTM	FTA	PCT	O-RB	D-RB	TOT	AST	PF	DQ	STL	TO	BLK	PTS	RPG	APG	PPG
95-96–Seattle	28	1	139	30	80	.375	4	25	.160	26	34	.765	12	12	24	5	27	0	8	6	1	90	0.9	0.2	3.2
Reg. Season Totals	28	1	139	30	80	.375	4	25	.160	26	34	.765	12	12	24	5	27	0	8	6	1	90	0.9	0.2	3.2

Forman, Donald J. (Donnie) b. January 17, 1926 Ht. 6-1 Wt. 175 College: New York U.

SEASON–TEAM	G	GS	MIN	FGM	FGA	PCT	3FGM	3FGA	PCT	FTM	FTA	PCT	O-RB	D-RB	TOT	AST	PF	DQ	STL	TO	BLK	PTS	RPG	APG	PPG
48-49–Minneapolis	44	–	–	68	231	.294	–	–	–	43	67	.642	–	–	–	74	94	–	–	–	–	179	–	1.7	4.1
Reg. Season Totals	44	–	–	68	231	.294	–	–	–	43	67	.642	–	–	–	74	94	–	–	–	–	179	–	1.7	4.1
Playoff Totals	9	–	–	3	40	.150	–	–	–	7	11	.636	–	–	–	14	14	–	–	–	–	13	–	0.8	1.4

Forrest, Bayard b. July 8, 1954 Ht. 6-10 Wt. 235 College: Grand Canyon

SEASON–TEAM	G	GS	MIN	FGM	FGA	PCT	3FGM	3FGA	PCT	FTM	FTA	PCT	O-RB	D-RB	TOT	AST	PF	DQ	STL	TO	BLK	PTS	RPG	APG	PPG
77-78–Phoenix	64	–	887	111	238	.466	–	–	–	49	103	.476	84	166	250	129	105	0	23	84	34	271	3.9	2.0	4.2
78-79–Phoenix	75	–	1243	118	272	.434	–	–	–	62	115	.539	110	205	315	167	151	1	29	107	37	298	4.2	2.2	4.0
Reg. Season Totals	139	–	2130	229	510	.449	–	–	–	111	218	.509	194	371	565	296	256	1	52	191	71	569	4.1	2.1	4.1
Playoff Totals	15	–	113	11	19	.579	–	–	–	2	10	.200	9	20	29	11	21	0	4	10	2	24	1.9	0.7	1.6

Fortson, Daniel Anthony (Danny) b. March 27, 1976 Ht. 6-7 Wt. 260 College: Cincinnati

SEASON–TEAM	G	GS	MIN	FGM	FGA	PCT	3FGM	3FGA	PCT	FTM	FTA	PCT	O-RB	D-RB	TOT	AST	PF	DQ	STL	TO	BLK	PTS	RPG	APG	PPG
97-98–Denver	80	23	1811	276	611	.452	1	3	.333	263	339	.776	182	266	448	76	314	7	44	157	30	816	5.6	1.0	10.2
98-99–Denver	50	38	1417	191	386	.495	0	3	.000	168	231	.727	210	371	581	32	212	9	31	77	22	550	11.6	0.6	11.0
99-00–Boston	55	5	856	140	265	.528	0	0	–	139	189	.735	141	225	366	29	180	4	20	67	5	419	6.7	0.5	7.6
Reg. Season Totals	185	66	4084	607	1262	.481	1	6	.167	570	759	.751	533	862	1395	137	706	20	95	301	57	1785	7.5	0.7	9.6

Foster, Fred J. b. March 18, 1946 d. October 4, 1985 Ht. 6-5 Wt. 215 College: Miami (Ohio)

SEASON–TEAM	G	GS	MIN	FGM	FGA	PCT	3FGM	3FGA	PCT	FTM	FTA	PCT	O-RB	D-RB	TOT	AST	PF	DQ	STL	TO	BLK	PTS	RPG	APG	PPG
68-69–Cincinnati	56	–	497	74	193	.383	–	–	–	43	66	.652	–	–	61	36	49	0	–	–	–	191	1.1	0.6	3.4
69-70–Cincinnati	73	–	2077	461	1026	.449	–	–	–	176	243	.724	–	–	310	107	209	2	–	–	–	1098	4.2	1.5	15.0
70-71–Cin.-Phil.	67	–	909	148	368	.402	–	–	–	73	106	.689	–	–	151	61	115	3	–	–	–	369	2.3	0.9	5.5
71-72–Philadelphia	74	–	1699	347	837	.415	–	–	–	185	243	.761	–	–	276	90	184	3	–	–	–	879	3.7	1.2	11.9
72-73–Detroit	63	–	1460	243	627	.388	–	–	–	61	87	.701	–	–	183	94	150	0	–	–	–	547	2.9	1.5	8.7
73-74–Cleveland	58	–	649	112	288	.389	–	–	–	54	64	.844	43	65	108	62	79	0	19	–	6	278	1.9	1.1	4.8
74-75–Cleveland	73	–	1136	217	521	.417	–	–	–	69	97	.711	56	54	110	103	130	1	22	–	2	503	1.5	1.4	6.9
76-77–Buffalo	59	–	689	99	247	.401	–	–	–	30	44	.682	33	43	76	48	92	0	16	–	0	228	1.3	0.8	3.9
Reg. Season Totals	523	–	9116	1701	4107	.414	–	–	–	691	950	.727	132	162	1275	601	1008	9	57	–	8	4093	2.4	1.1	7.8
Playoff Totals	5	–	49	8	19	.421	–	–	–	2	2	1.000	0	0	12	5	6	0	0	–	0	18	2.4	1.0	3.6

Foster, Gregory Clinton (Greg) b. October 3, 1968 Ht. 6-11 Wt. 250 College: UCLA; Texas-El Paso

SEASON–TEAM	G	GS	MIN	FGM	FGA	PCT	3FGM	3FGA	PCT	FTM	FTA	PCT	O-RB	D-RB	TOT	AST	PF	DQ	STL	TO	BLK	PTS	RPG	APG	PPG
90-91–Washington	54	3	606	97	211	.460	0	5	.000	42	61	.689	52	99	151	37	112	1	12	45	22	236	2.8	0.7	4.4
91-92–Washington	49	3	548	89	193	.461	0	1	.000	35	49	.714	43	102	145	35	83	0	6	36	12	213	3.0	0.7	4.3
92-93–Wash.-Atlanta	43	0	298	55	120	.458	0	4	.000	15	21	.714	32	51	83	21	58	0	3	25	14	125	1.9	0.5	2.9
93-94–Milwaukee	3	0	19	4	7	.571	0	0	–	2	2	1.000	0	3	3	0	3	0	0	1	1	10	1.0	0.0	3.3
94-95–Chicago-Minn.	78	3	1144	150	318	.472	7	23	.304	78	111	.703	85	174	259	39	183	0	15	71	28	385	3.3	0.5	4.9
95-96–Utah	73	2	803	107	244	.439	1	8	.125	61	72	.847	53	125	178	25	120	0	7	58	22	276	2.4	0.3	3.8
96-97–Utah	79	12	920	111	245	.453	2	3	.667	54	65	.831	56	131	187	31	145	0	10	54	20	278	2.4	0.4	3.5
97-98–Utah	78	49	1446	186	418	.445	2	9	.222	67	87	.770	85	188	273	51	187	2	15	68	28	441	3.5	0.7	5.7
98-99–Utah	42	1	458	52	138	.377	1	4	.250	13	21	.619	28	55	83	25	63	1	6	24	8	118	2.0	0.6	2.8
99-00–Seattle	60	5	718	91	224	.406	3	15	.200	18	28	.643	16	91	107	41	105	0	10	28	18	203	1.8	0.7	3.4
Reg. Season Totals	559	78	6960	942	2118	.445	16	72	.222	385	517	.745	450	1019	1469	305	1059	4	84	410	173	2285	2.6	0.5	4.1
Playoff Totals	66	16	863	94	221	.425	5	15	.333	40	51	.784	43	112	155	20	149	0	8	40	15	233	2.3	0.3	3.5

Foster, James (Jimmy) b. December 16, 1951 Ht. 6-1 Wt. 175 College: Connecticut

SEASON–TEAM	G	GS	MIN	FGM	FGA	PCT	3FGM	3FGA	PCT	FTM	FTA	PCT	O-RB	D-RB	TOT	AST	PF	DQ	STL	TO	BLK	PTS	RPG	APG	PPG
74-75–St. Louis (A)	41	–	806	78	209	.373	0	6	.000	27	34	.794	19	56	75	143	118	–	39	88	5	183	1.8	3.5	4.5
75-76–Denver (A)	48	–	352	54	145	.372	1	8	.125	39	64	.609	19	23	42	47	78	–	19	63	4	148	0.9	1.0	3.1
Reg. ABA Totals	89	–	1158	132	354	.373	1	14	.071	66	98	.673	38	79	117	190	196	–	58	151	9	331	1.3	2.1	3.7
ABA Playoff Totals	9	–	65	11	24	.458	0	1	.000	7	15	.467	4	4	8	7	13	–	4	8	0	29	0.9	0.8	3.2

Foster, Jeffrey Douglas (Jeff) b. January 16, 1977 Ht. 6-11 Wt. 238 College: Southwest Texas State

SEASON–TEAM	G	GS	MIN	FGM	FGA	PCT	3FGM	3FGA	PCT	FTM	FTA	PCT	O-RB	D-RB	TOT	AST	PF	DQ	STL	TO	BLK	PTS	RPG	APG	PPG
99-00–Indiana	19	0	86	13	23	.565	0	1	.000	17	25	.680	12	20	32	5	18	0	5	2	1	43	1.7	0.3	2.3
Reg. Season Totals	19	0	86	13	23	.565	0	1	.000	17	25	.680	12	20	32	5	18	0	5	2	1	43	1.7	0.3	2.3

Foster, Roderick Allen (Rod) b. October 10, 1960 Ht. 6-1 Wt. 160 College: UCLA

SEASON–TEAM	G	GS	MIN	FGM	FGA	PCT	3FGM	3FGA	PCT	FTM	FTA	PCT	O-RB	D-RB	TOT	AST	PF	DQ	STL	TO	BLK	PTS	RPG	APG	PPG
83-84–Phoenix	80	34	1424	260	580	.448	22	84	.262	122	155	.787	39	81	120	172	193	0	54	108	9	664	1.5	2.2	8.3
84-85–Phoenix	79	1	1318	286	636	.450	41	126	.325	83	110	.755	27	53	80	186	171	1	61	117	0	696	1.0	2.4	8.8
85-86–Phoenix	48	0	704	85	218	.390	9	32	.281	23	32	.719	9	49	58	121	77	0	22	61	1	202	1.2	2.5	4.2
Reg. Season Totals	207	35	3446	631	1434	.440	72	242	.298	228	297	.768	75	183	258	479	441	1	137	286	10	1562	1.2	2.3	7.5
Playoff Totals	19	0	184	17	64	.266	0	9	.000	15	17	.882	6	10	16	25	25	0	10	18	1	49	0.8	1.3	2.6

Foust, Lawrence Michael (Larry) b. June 24, 1928 d. October 27, 1984 Ht. 6-9 Wt. 250 College: La Salle

SEASON–TEAM	G	GS	MIN	FGM	FGA	PCT	3FGM	3FGA	PCT	FTM	FTA	PCT	O-RB	D-RB	TOT	AST	PF	DQ	STL	TO	BLK	PTS	RPG	APG	PPG
50-51–Fort Wayne	68	–	–	327	944	.346	–	–	–	261	396	.659	–	–	681	90	247	6	–	–	–	915	10.0	1.3	13.5
51-52–Fort Wayne	66	–	2615	390	989	.394	–	–	–	267	394	.678	–	–	880	200	245	10	–	–	–	1047	13.3	3.0	15.9
52-53–Fort Wayne	67	–	2303	311	865	.360	–	–	–	336	465	.723	–	–	769	151	267	16	–	–	–	958	11.5	2.3	14.3
53-54–Fort Wayne	72	–	2693	376	919	.409	–	–	–	338	475	.712	–	–	967	161	258	4	–	–	–	1090	13.4	2.2	15.1
54-55–Fort Wayne	70	–	2264	398	818	.487	–	–	–	393	513	.766	–	–	700	118	264	9	–	–	–	1189	10.0	1.7	17.0
55-56–Fort Wayne	72	–	2024	367	821	.447	–	–	–	432	555	.778	–	–	648	127	263	7	–	–	–	1166	9.0	1.8	16.2
56-57–Fort Wayne	61	–	1533	243	617	.394	–	–	–	273	380	.718	–	–	555	71	221	7	–	–	–	759	9.1	1.2	12.4
57-58–Minneapolis	72	–	2200	391	982	.398	–	–	–	428	566	.756	–	–	876	108	299	11	–	–	–	1210	12.2	1.5	16.8
58-59–Minneapolis	72	–	1933	301	771	.390	–	–	–	280	366	.765	–	–	627	91	233	5	–	–	–	882	8.7	1.3	12.3
59-60–Minn.-St. Louis	72	–	1964	312	766	.407	–	–	–	253	320	.791	–	–	621	96	241	7	–	–	–	877	8.6	1.3	12.2
60-61–St. Louis	68	–	1208	194	489	.397	–	–	–	164	208	.788	–	–	389	77	185	0	–	–	–	552	5.7	1.1	8.1
61-62–St. Louis	57	–	1153	204	433	.471	–	–	–	145	178	.815	–	–	328	78	186	3	–	–	–	553	5.8	1.4	9.7
Reg. Season Totals	817	–	21890	3814	9414	.405	–	–	–	3570	4816	.741	–	–	8041	1368	2909	85	–	–	–	11198	9.8	1.7	13.7
Playoff Totals	73	–	2126	301	803	.395	–	–	–	300	384	.781	–	–	775	106	255	9	–	–	–	902	9.8	1.3	12.4
All-Star Totals	7	–	118	17	54	.315	–	–	–	15	16	.938	–	–	49	3	16	0	–	–	–	49	7.0	0.4	7.0

Fowler, Calvin Bernard (Cal) b. February 11, 1940 Ht. 6-0 Wt. 175 College: St. Francis (Pa.)

SEASON–TEAM	G	GS	MIN	FGM	FGA	PCT	3FGM	3FGA	PCT	FTM	FTA	PCT	O-RB	D-RB	TOT	AST	PF	DQ	STL	TO	BLK	PTS	RPG	APG	PPG
69-70–Carolina (A)	78	–	1234	131	288	.455	7	17	.412	74	119	.622	–	–	170	126	156	2	–	–	–	343	2.2	1.6	4.4
Reg. ABA Totals	78	–	1234	131	288	.455	7	17	.412	74	119	.622	–	–	170	126	156	2	–	–	–	343	2.2	1.6	4.4
ABA Playoff Totals	4	–	76	6	14	.429	0	1	.000	7	10	.700	–	–	6	8	11	0	–	–	–	19	1.5	2.0	4.8

Fowler, Jerry A. b. June 20, 1927 Ht. 6-8 Wt. 230 College: Missouri

SEASON–TEAM	G	GS	MIN	FGM	FGA	PCT	3FGM	3FGA	PCT	FTM	FTA	PCT	O-RB	D-RB	TOT	AST	PF	DQ	STL	TO	BLK	PTS	RPG	APG	PPG
51-52–Milwaukee	6	–	41	4	13	.308	–	–	–	1	4	.250	–	–	10	2	9	0	–	–	–	9	1.7	0.3	1.5
Reg. Season Totals	6	–	41	4	13	.308	–	–	–	1	4	.250	–	–	10	2	9	0	–	–	–	9	1.7	0.3	1.5

Fox, Harold b. August 29, 1949 Ht. 6-2 Wt. 175 College: Brevard (Fla.) C.C.; Jacksonville

SEASON–TEAM	G	GS	MIN	FGM	FGA	PCT	3FGM	3FGA	PCT	FTM	FTA	PCT	O-RB	D-RB	TOT	AST	PF	DQ	STL	TO	BLK	PTS	RPG	APG	PPG
72-73–Buffalo	10	–	84	12	32	.375	–	–	–	7	8	.875	–	–	8	10	7	0	–	–	–	31	0.8	1.0	3.1
Reg. Season Totals	10	–	84	12	32	.375	–	–	–	7	8	.875	–	–	8	10	7	0	–	–	–	31	0.8	1.0	3.1

Fox, James L. (Jim) b. April 7, 1943 Ht. 6-10 Wt. 230 College: (Gordon Military); South Carolina

SEASON–TEAM	G	GS	MIN	FGM	FGA	PCT	3FGM	3FGA	PCT	FTM	FTA	PCT	O-RB	D-RB	TOT	AST	PF	DQ	STL	TO	BLK	PTS	RPG	APG	PPG
67-68–Cin.-Detroit	55	–	624	66	161	.410	–	–	–	66	108	.611	–	–	230	29	85	0	–	–	–	198	4.2	0.5	3.6
68-69–Detroit-Phoenix	76	–	2354	318	677	.470	–	–	–	191	267	.715	–	–	818	166	266	6	–	–	–	827	10.8	2.2	10.9
69-70–Phoenix	81	–	2041	413	788	.524	–	–	–	218	283	.770	–	–	570	93	261	7	–	–	–	1044	7.0	1.1	12.9
70-71–Chicago	82	–	1628	280	611	.458	–	–	–	239	321	.745	–	–	598	196	213	0	–	–	–	799	7.3	2.4	9.7
71-72–Chicago-Cin.	81	–	2180	354	788	.449	–	–	–	227	297	.764	–	–	713	86	257	8	–	–	–	935	8.8	1.1	11.5
72-73–Seattle	74	–	2439	316	613	.515	–	–	–	214	265	.808	–	–	827	176	239	6	–	–	–	846	11.2	2.4	11.4
73-74–Seattle	78	–	2179	322	673	.478	–	–	–	241	293	.823	244	470	714	227	247	5	56	–	21	885	9.2	2.9	11.3
74-75–Seattle	75	–	1766	253	540	.469	–	–	–	170	212	.802	128	363	491	137	168	1	48	–	17	676	6.5	1.8	9.0
75-76–Milwaukee	70	–	918	105	203	.517	–	–	–	62	79	.785	82	153	235	42	129	1	27	–	16	272	3.4	0.6	3.9
76-77–New York Nets	71	–	1165	184	398	.462	–	–	–	95	114	.833	100	229	329	49	158	1	20	–	25	463	4.6	0.7	6.5
Reg. Season Totals	743	–	17294	2611	5452	.479	–	–	–	1723	2239	.770	554	1215	5525	1201	2023	35	151	–	79	6945	7.4	1.6	9.3
Playoff Totals	30	–	504	72	183	.393	–	–	–	51	71	.718	6	10	183	33	62	2	0	–	2	195	6.1	1.1	6.5

Fox, Ulrich Alexander (Rick) b. July 24, 1969 Ht. 6-7 Wt. 242 College: North Carolina

SEASON–TEAM	G	GS	MIN	FGM	FGA	PCT	3FGM	3FGA	PCT	FTM	FTA	PCT	O-RB	D-RB	TOT	AST	PF	DQ	STL	TO	BLK	PTS	RPG	APG	PPG
91-92–Boston	81	5	1535	241	525	.459	23	70	.329	139	184	.755	73	147	220	126	230	3	78	123	30	644	2.7	1.6	8.0
92-93–Boston	71	14	1082	184	380	.484	4	23	.174	81	101	.802	55	104	159	113	133	1	61	77	21	453	2.2	1.6	6.4
93-94–Boston	82	53	2096	340	728	.467	33	100	.330	174	230	.757	105	250	355	217	244	4	81	158	52	887	4.3	2.6	10.8
94-95–Boston	53	7	1039	169	351	.481	31	75	.413	95	123	.772	61	94	155	139	154	1	52	78	19	464	2.9	2.6	8.8
95-96–Boston	81	81	2588	421	928	.454	99	272	.364	196	254	.772	158	292	450	369	290	5	113	216	41	1137	5.6	4.6	14.0
96-97–Boston	76	75	2650	433	950	.456	101	278	.363	207	263	.787	114	280	394	286	279	4	167	178	40	1174	5.2	3.8	15.4
97-98–L.A. Lakers	82	82	2709	363	771	.471	86	265	.325	171	230	.743	78	280	358	276	309	4	100	201	48	983	4.4	3.4	12.0
98-99–L.A. Lakers	44	1	944	148	330	.448	32	95	.337	66	89	.742	26	63	89	89	114	1	28	56	10	394	2.0	2.0	9.0
99-00–L.A. Lakers	82	1	1473	206	498	.414	59	181	.326	63	78	.808	63	135	198	138	203	1	52	87	26	534	2.4	1.7	6.5
Reg. Season Totals	652	319	16116	2505	5461	.459	468	1359	.344	1192	1552	.768	733	1645	2378	1753	1956	24	732	1174	287	6670	3.6	2.7	10.2
Playoff Totals	56	14	1078	126	295	.427	47	122	.385	42	51	.824	49	94	143	100	159	4	28	57	11	341	2.6	1.8	6.1

Foyle, Adonal David b. March 19, 1975 Ht. 6-10 Wt. 250 College: Colgate

SEASON–TEAM	G	GS	MIN	FGM	FGA	PCT	3FGM	3FGA	PCT	FTM	FTA	PCT	O-RB	D-RB	TOT	AST	PF	DQ	STL	TO	BLK	PTS	RPG	APG	PPG
97-98–Golden State	55	1	656	69	170	.406	0	1	.000	27	62	.435	73	111	184	14	94	0	13	50	52	165	3.3	0.3	3.0
98-99–Golden State	44	0	614	52	121	.430	0	0	–	25	51	.490	79	115	194	18	90	0	15	31	43	129	4.4	0.4	2.9
99-00–Golden State	76	59	1654	193	380	.508	0	0	–	34	90	.378	174	250	424	42	218	2	26	71	136	420	5.6	0.6	5.5
Reg. Season Totals	175	60	2924	314	671	.468	0	1	.000	86	203	.424	326	476	802	74	402	2	54	152	231	714	4.6	0.4	4.1

Francis, Steve D'Shawn b. February 21, 1978 Ht. 6-3 Wt. 193 College: Maryland

SEASON–TEAM	G	GS	MIN	FGM	FGA	PCT	3FGM	3FGA	PCT	FTM	FTA	PCT	O-RB	D-RB	TOT	AST	PF	DQ	STL	TO	BLK	PTS	RPG	APG	PPG
99-00–Houston	77	77	2776	497	1117	.445	107	310	.345	287	365	.786	152	257	409	507	231	2	118	306	29	1388	5.3	6.6	18.0
Reg. Season Totals	77	77	2776	497	1117	.445	107	310	.345	287	365	.786	152	257	409	507	231	2	118	306	29	1388	5.3	6.6	18.0

Frank, Tellis Joseph Jr. b. April 26, 1965 Ht. 6-10 Wt. 230 College: Western Kentucky

SEASON–TEAM	G	GS	MIN	FGM	FGA	PCT	3FGM	3FGA	PCT	FTM	FTA	PCT	O-RB	D-RB	TOT	AST	PF	DQ	STL	TO	BLK	PTS	RPG	APG	PPG
87-88–Golden State	78	29	1597	242	565	.428	0	1	.000	150	207	.725	95	235	330	111	267	5	53	109	23	634	4.2	1.4	8.1
88-89–Golden State	32	2	245	34	91	.374	0	1	.000	39	51	.765	26	35	61	15	59	1	14	29	6	107	1.9	0.5	3.3
89-90–Miami	77	39	1762	278	607	.458	0	0	–	179	234	.765	151	234	385	85	282	6	51	134	27	735	5.0	1.1	9.5
91-92–Minnesota	10	0	140	18	33	.545	0	0	–	10	15	.667	8	18	26	8	24	0	5	5	4	46	2.6	0.8	4.6
93-94–Minnesota	67	11	959	67	160	.419	0	2	.000	54	76	.711	83	137	220	57	163	1	35	49	35	188	3.3	0.9	2.8
Reg. Season Totals	264	81	4703	639	1456	.439	0	4	.000	432	583	.741	363	659	1022	276	795	13	158	326	95	1710	3.9	1.0	6.5

Frankel, Nathan (Nat) b. November 3, 1913 Ht. 6-2 Wt. 195 College: Brooklyn College

SEASON–TEAM	G	GS	MIN	FGM	FGA	PCT	3FGM	3FGA	PCT	FTM	FTA	PCT	O-RB	D-RB	TOT	AST	PF	DQ	STL	TO	BLK	PTS	RPG	APG	PPG
39-40–Detroit (N)	27	–	–	73	–	–	–	–	–	55	86	.640	–	–	–	–	31	–	–	–	–	201	–	–	7.4
46-47–Pittsburgh	6	–	–	4	27	.148	–	–	–	8	12	.667	–	–	–	3	6	–	–	–	–	16	–	0.5	2.7
Reg. NBA Totals	6	–	–	4	27	.148	–	–	–	8	12	.667	–	–	–	3	6	–	–	–	–	16	–	0.5	2.7
Reg. NBL Totals	27	–	–	73	–	–	–	–	–	55	86	.640	–	–	–	–	31	–	–	–	–	201	–	–	7.4
NBL Playoff Totals	3	–	–	10	–	–	–	–	–	4	2	.000	–	–	–	–	9	–	–	–	–	24	–	–	8.0

Franklin, William Thomas (Will) b. October 19, 1949 Ht. 6-7 Wt. 225 College: Purdue

SEASON–TEAM	G	GS	MIN	FGM	FGA	PCT	3FGM	3FGA	PCT	FTM	FTA	PCT	O-RB	D-RB	TOT	AST	PF	DQ	STL	TO	BLK	PTS	RPG	APG	PPG
72-73–Virginia (A)	73	–	990	218	524	.416	2	7	.286	107	179	.598	123	166	289	50	157	0	–	123	–	545	4.0	0.7	7.5
74-75–San Antonio (A)	24	–	179	32	85	.376	0	1	.000	15	23	.652	39	43	82	10	37	–	3	18	2	79	3.4	0.4	3.3
75-76–San Antonio (A)	10	–	95	12	22	.545	0	0	–	9	16	.563	12	17	29	5	16	–	3	5	3	33	2.9	0.5	3.3
Reg. ABA Totals	107	–	1264	262	631	.415	2	8	.250	131	218	.601	174	226	400	65	210	0	6	146	5	657	3.7	0.6	6.1
ABA Playoff Totals	2	–	10	2	5	.400	0	0	–	0	0	–	3	2	5	0	2	0	0	0	0	4	2.5	0.0	2.0

Franz, Ronald Stephen (Ron) b. October 20, 1945 Ht. 6-7 Wt. 210 College: Kansas

SEASON–TEAM	G	GS	MIN	FGM	FGA	PCT	3FGM	3FGA	PCT	FTM	FTA	PCT	O-RB	D-RB	TOT	AST	PF	DQ	STL	TO	BLK	PTS	RPG	APG	PPG
67-68–Oakland (A)	74	–	2080	354	903	.392	25	97	.258	197	285	.691	–	–	469	129	249	11	–	173	–	930	6.3	1.7	12.6
68-69–New Orleans (A)	73	–	2195	381	850	.448	11	31	.355	286	388	.737	–	–	518	189	233	5	–	174	–	1059	7.1	2.6	14.5
69-70–New Orleans (A)	55	–	1305	231	547	.422	7	25	.280	163	259	.629	–	–	287	91	139	3	–	–	–	632	5.2	1.7	11.5
70-71–Floridians (A)	67	–	1596	309	637	.485	7	22	.318	188	259	.726	–	–	320	97	178	–	–	–	–	813	4.8	1.4	12.1
71-72–Floridians (A)	74	–	1822	342	705	.485	2	11	.182	171	243	.704	–	–	342	94	209	–	–	97	–	857	4.6	1.3	11.6
72-73–Mem.-Dallas (A)	60	–	914	148	303	.488	1	4	.250	145	201	.721	67	125	192	68	112	0	–	78	–	442	3.2	1.1	7.4
Reg. ABA Totals	403	–	9912	1765	3945	.447	53	190	.279	1150	1635	.703	67	125	2128	668	1120	19	–	522	–	4733	5.3	1.7	11.7
ABA Playoff Totals	17	–	389	57	169	.337	1	9	.111	31	53	.585	–	–	82	24	42	0	–	4	–	146	4.8	1.4	8.6

Frazier, Walter Jr. (Walt, Clyde) b. March 29, 1945 Ht. 6-4 Wt. 200 College: Southern Illinois HOF: 1986

SEASON–TEAM	G	GS	MIN	FGM	FGA	PCT	3FGM	3FGA	PCT	FTM	FTA	PCT	O-RB	D-RB	TOT	AST	PF	DQ	STL	TO	BLK	PTS	RPG	APG	PPG
67-68–New York	74	–	1588	256	568	.451	–	–	–	154	235	.655	–	–	313	305	199	2	–	–	–	666	4.2	4.1	9.0
68-69–New York	80	–	2949	531	1052	.505	–	–	–	341	457	.746	–	–	499	635	245	2	–	–	–	1403	6.2	7.9	17.5
69-70–New York	77	–	3040	600	1158	.518	–	–	–	409	547	.748	–	–	465	629	203	1	–	–	–	1609	6.0	8.2	20.9
70-71–New York	80	–	3455	651	1317	.494	–	–	–	434	557	.779	–	–	544	536	240	1	–	–	–	1736	6.8	6.7	21.7
71-72–New York	77	–	3126	669	1307	.512	–	–	–	450	557	.808	–	–	513	446	185	0	–	–	–	1788	6.7	5.8	23.2
72-73–New York	78	–	3181	681	1389	.490	–	–	–	286	350	.817	–	–	570	461	186	0	–	–	–	1648	7.3	5.9	21.1
73-74–New York	80	–	3338	674	1429	.472	–	–	–	295	352	.838	120	416	536	551	212	2	161	–	15	1643	6.7	6.9	20.5
74-75–New York	78	–	3204	672	1391	.483	–	–	–	331	400	.828	90	375	465	474	205	2	190	–	14	1675	6.0	6.1	21.5
75-76–New York	59	–	2427	470	969	.485	–	–	–	186	226	.823	79	321	400	351	163	1	106	–	9	1126	6.8	5.9	19.1
76-77–N.Y. Knicks	76	–	2687	532	1089	.489	–	–	–	259	336	.771	52	241	293	403	194	0	132	–	9	1323	3.9	5.3	17.4
77-78–Cleveland	51	–	1664	336	714	.471	–	–	–	153	180	.850	54	155	209	209	124	1	77	113	13	825	4.1	4.1	16.2
78-79–Cleveland	12	–	279	54	122	.443	–	–	–	21	27	.778	7	13	20	32	22	0	13	22	2	129	1.7	2.7	10.8
79-80–Cleveland	3	–	27	4	11	.364	0	1	.000	2	2	1.000	1	2	3	8	2	0	2	4	1	10	1.0	2.7	3.3
Reg. Season Totals	825	–	30965	6130	12516	.490	0	1	.000	3321	4226	.786	403	1523	4830	5040	2180	12	681	139	63	15581	5.9	6.1	18.9
Playoff Totals	93	–	3953	767	1500	.511	0	0	–	393	523	.751	24	91	666	599	285	2	32	–	4	1927	7.2	6.4	20.7
All-Star Totals	7	–	183	35	78	.449	0	0	–	18	21	.857	1	8	27	26	10	0	9	–	0	88	3.9	3.7	12.6

Frazier, Wilbert B. (Will) b. August 24, 1942 Ht. 6-7 Wt. 210 College: Grambling State

SEASON–TEAM	G	GS	MIN	FGM	FGA	PCT	3FGM	3FGA	PCT	FTM	FTA	PCT	O-RB	D-RB	TOT	AST	PF	DQ	STL	TO	BLK	PTS	RPG	APG	PPG
65-66–San Francisco	2	–	9	0	4	.000	–	–	–	1	2	.500	–	–	5	1	1	0	–	–	–	1	2.5	0.5	0.5
67-68–Houston (A)	76	–	2125	358	870	.411	1	2	.500	228	376	.606	–	–	666	104	219	3	–	146	–	945	8.8	1.4	12.4
68-69–New York (A)	75	–	1370	217	512	.424	0	0	–	120	194	.619	–	–	416	66	200	1	–	75	–	554	5.5	0.9	7.4
Reg. NBA Totals	2	–	9	0	4	.000	–	–	–	1	2	.500	–	–	5	1	1	0	–	–	–	1	2.5	0.5	0.5
Reg. ABA Totals	151	–	3495	575	1382	.416	1	2	.500	348	570	.611	–	–	1082	170	419	4	–	221	–	1499	7.2	1.1	9.9
ABA Playoff Totals	3	–	85	13	29	.448	0	1	.000	3	7	.429	–	–	12	4	11	0	–	5	–	29	4.0	1.3	9.7

Frederick, Anthony b. December 7, 1964 Ht. 6-7 Wt. 205 College: Santa Monica (Calif.) Coll. (J.C.); Pepperdine

SEASON–TEAM	G	GS	MIN	FGM	FGA	PCT	3FGM	3FGA	PCT	FTM	FTA	PCT	O-RB	D-RB	TOT	AST	PF	DQ	STL	TO	BLK	PTS	RPG	APG	PPG
88-89–Indiana	46	0	313	63	125	.504	2	5	.400	24	34	.706	26	26	52	20	59	0	14	34	6	152	1.1	0.4	3.3
90-91–Sacramento	35	3	475	67	168	.399	0	0	–	43	60	.717	36	48	84	44	50	0	22	40	13	177	2.4	1.3	5.1
91-92–Charlotte	66	26	852	161	370	.435	4	17	.235	63	92	.685	75	69	144	71	91	0	40	58	26	389	2.2	1.1	5.9
Reg. Season Totals	147	29	1640	291	663	.439	6	22	.273	130	186	.699	137	143	280	135	200	0	76	132	45	718	1.9	0.9	4.9

Free, World B. (formerly Lloyd B. Free) b. December 9, 1953 Ht. 6-3 Wt. 185 College: Guilford

SEASON–TEAM	G	GS	MIN	FGM	FGA	PCT	3FGM	3FGA	PCT	FTM	FTA	PCT	O-RB	D-RB	TOT	AST	PF	DQ	STL	TO	BLK	PTS	RPG	APG	PPG
75-76–Philadelphia	71	–	1121	239	533	.448	–	–	–	112	186	.602	64	61	125	104	107	0	37	–	6	590	1.8	1.5	8.3
76-77–Philadelphia	78	–	2253	467	1022	.457	–	–	–	334	464	.720	97	140	237	266	207	2	75	–	25	1268	3.0	3.4	16.3
77-78–Philadelphia	76	–	2050	390	857	.455	–	–	–	411	562	.731	92	120	212	306	199	0	68	200	41	1191	2.8	4.0	15.7
78-79–San Diego	78	–	2954	795	1653	.481	–	–	–	654	865	.756	127	174	301	340	253	8	111	297	35	2244	3.9	4.4	28.8
79-80–San Diego	68	–	2585	737	1556	.474	9	25	.360	572	760	.753	129	109	238	283	195	0	81	228	32	2055	3.5	4.2	30.2
80-81–Golden State	65	–	2370	516	1157	.446	5	31	.161	528	649	.814	48	111	159	361	183	1	85	195	11	1565	2.4	5.6	24.1
81-82–Golden State	78	78	2796	650	1452	.448	10	56	.179	479	647	.740	118	130	248	419	222	1	71	208	8	1789	3.2	5.4	22.9
82-83–G.S.-Clev.	73	69	2638	649	1423	.456	15	45	.333	430	583	.738	92	109	201	290	241	4	97	209	15	1743	2.8	4.0	23.9
83-84–Cleveland	75	71	2375	626	1407	.445	22	69	.319	395	504	.784	89	128	217	226	214	2	94	154	8	1669	2.9	3.0	22.3
84-85–Cleveland	71	50	2249	609	1328	.459	71	193	.368	308	411	.749	61	150	211	320	163	0	75	139	16	1597	3.0	4.5	22.5
85-86–Cleveland	75	75	2535	652	1433	.455	71	169	.420	379	486	.780	72	146	218	314	186	1	91	172	19	1754	2.9	4.2	23.4
86-87–Philadelphia	20	2	285	39	123	.317	2	9	.222	36	47	.766	5	14	19	30	26	0	5	18	4	116	1.0	1.5	5.8
87-88–Houston	58	0	682	143	350	.409	8	35	.229	80	100	.800	14	30	44	60	74	2	20	49	3	374	0.8	1.0	6.4
Reg. Season Totals	886	345	26893	6512	14294	.456	213	632	.337	4718	6264	.753	1008	1422	2430	3319	2270	21	910	1869	223	17955	2.7	3.7	20.3
Playoff Totals	34	4	773	166	417	.398	0	5	.000	145	196	.740	26	50	76	103	79	0	25	35	14	477	2.2	3.0	14.0
All-Star Totals	1	1	21	7	13	.538	0	0	–	0	1	.000	1	2	3	5	1	0	0	5	1	14	3.0	5.0	14.0

Freeman, Donald E. (Donnie) b. July 18, 1944 Ht. 6-3 Wt. 185 College: Illinois

SEASON–TEAM	G	GS	MIN	FGM	FGA	PCT	3FGM	3FGA	PCT	FTM	FTA	PCT	O-RB	D-RB	TOT	AST	PF	DQ	STL	TO	BLK	PTS	RPG	APG	PPG
67-68–Minnesota (A)	69	–	2431	414	1013	.409	0	6	.000	296	414	.715	–	–	326	190	185	5	–	187	–	1124	4.7	2.8	16.3
68-69–Miami (A)	78	–	2874	651	1346	.484	2	23	.087	420	534	.787	–	–	285	501	229	7	–	230	–	1724	3.7	6.4	22.1
69-70–Miami (A)	79	–	3164	766	1684	.455	5	19	.263	626	762	.822	–	–	400	291	253	5	–	–	–	2163	5.1	3.7	27.4
70-71–Utah-Texas (A)	66	–	2414	596	1235	.483	0	7	.000	367	459	.800	–	–	324	332	192	–	–	–	–	1559	4.9	5.0	23.6
71-72–Dallas (A)	72	–	2377	628	1336	.470	2	5	.400	475	576	.825	–	–	206	245	177	–	–	176	–	1733	2.9	3.4	24.1
72-73–Indiana (A)	77	–	2170	412	933	.442	2	6	.333	277	343	.808	103	116	219	195	225	0	–	160	–	1103	2.8	2.5	14.3
73-74–Indiana (A)	66	–	1735	383	839	.456	0	2	.000	177	222	.797	91	77	168	165	174	–	48	132	22	943	2.5	2.5	14.3
74-75–San Antonio (A)	77	–	2381	453	1012	.448	0	5	.000	289	352	.821	107	77	184	202	169	–	65	131	15	1195	2.4	2.6	15.5
75-76–Los Angeles	64	–	1480	263	606	.434	–	–	–	163	199	.819	72	108	180	171	160	1	57	–	11	689	2.8	2.7	10.8
Reg. NBA Totals	64	–	1480	263	606	.434	–	–	–	163	199	.819	72	108	180	171	160	1	57	–	11	689	2.8	2.7	10.8
Reg. ABA Totals	584	–	19546	4303	9398	.458	11	73	.151	2927	3662	.799	301	270	2112	2121	1604	17	113	1016	37	11544	3.6	3.6	19.8
ABA Playoff Totals	60	–	1968	405	913	.444	0	10	.000	230	300	.767	13	11	218	198	176	4	6	103	0	1040	3.6	3.3	17.3

Freeman, Gary C. b. July 25, 1948 Ht. 6-9 Wt. 210 College: Oregon State

SEASON–TEAM	G	GS	MIN	FGM	FGA	PCT	3FGM	3FGA	PCT	FTM	FTA	PCT	O-RB	D-RB	TOT	AST	PF	DQ	STL	TO	BLK	PTS	RPG	APG	PPG
70-71–Milw.-Clev.	52	–	382	69	134	.515	–	–	–	29	40	.725	–	–	106	35	67	0	–	–	–	167	2.0	0.7	3.2
Reg. Season Totals	52	–	382	69	134	.515	–	–	–	29	40	.725	–	–	106	35	67	0	–	–	–	167	2.0	0.7	3.2

Freeman, Rodney Lee (Rod) b. November 5, 1950 Ht. 6-7 Wt. 225 College: Vanderbilt

SEASON–TEAM	G	GS	MIN	FGM	FGA	PCT	3FGM	3FGA	PCT	FTM	FTA	PCT	O-RB	D-RB	TOT	AST	PF	DQ	STL	TO	BLK	PTS	RPG	APG	PPG
73-74–Philadelphia	35	–	265	39	103	.379	–	–	–	28	41	.683	22	32	54	14	42	0	12	–	1	106	1.5	0.4	3.0
Reg. Season Totals	35	–	265	39	103	.379	–	–	–	28	41	.683	22	32	54	14	42	0	12	–	1	106	1.5	0.4	3.0

Frey, Frido b. October 26, 1921 Ht. 6-2 Wt. 195 College: St. John's (N.Y.); Long Island University

SEASON–TEAM	G	GS	MIN	FGM	FGA	PCT	3FGM	3FGA	PCT	FTM	FTA	PCT	O-RB	D-RB	TOT	AST	PF	DQ	STL	TO	BLK	PTS	RPG	APG	PPG
46-47–New York	23	–	–	28	97	.289	–	–	–	32	56	.571	–	–	–	14	37	–	–	–	–	88	–	0.6	3.8
Reg. Season Totals	23	–	–	28	97	.289	–	–	–	32	56	.571	–	–	–	14	37	–	–	–	–	88	–	0.6	3.8
Playoff Totals	5	–	–	3	19	.158	–	–	–	4	11	.364	–	–	–	7	11	–	–	–	–	10	–	1.4	2.0

Friend, Lawrence (Larry) b. April 14, 1935 d. February 27, 1998 Ht. 6-4 Wt. 195 College: Los Angeles City (Calif.) Coll. (J.C.); California

SEASON–TEAM	G	GS	MIN	FGM	FGA	PCT	3FGM	3FGA	PCT	FTM	FTA	PCT	O-RB	D-RB	TOT	AST	PF	DQ	STL	TO	BLK	PTS	RPG	APG	PPG
57-58–New York	44	–	569	74	226	.327	–	–	–	27	41	.659	–	–	106	47	54	0	–	–	–	175	2.4	1.1	4.0
Reg. Season Totals	44	–	569	74	226	.327	–	–	–	27	41	.659	–	–	106	47	54	0	–	–	–	175	2.4	1.1	4.0

Frink, Patrick Edward (Pat) b. February 18, 1945 Ht. 6-4 Wt. 195 College: Colorado

SEASON–TEAM	G	GS	MIN	FGM	FGA	PCT	3FGM	3FGA	PCT	FTM	FTA	PCT	O-RB	D-RB	TOT	AST	PF	DQ	STL	TO	BLK	PTS	RPG	APG	PPG
68-69–Cincinnati	48	–	363	50	147	.340	–	–	–	23	29	.793	–	–	41	55	54	1	–	–	–	123	0.9	1.1	2.6
Reg. Season Totals	48	–	363	50	147	.340	–	–	–	23	29	.793	–	–	41	55	54	1	–	–	–	123	0.9	1.1	2.6

Fritsche, James A. (Jim) b. December 10, 1931 Ht. 6-8 Wt. 210 College: Hamline

SEASON–TEAM	G	GS	MIN	FGM	FGA	PCT	3FGM	3FGA	PCT	FTM	FTA	PCT	O-RB	D-RB	TOT	AST	PF	DQ	STL	TO	BLK	PTS	RPG	APG	PPG
53-54–Minn.-Balt.	68	–	1221	116	379	.306	–	–	–	49	68	.721	–	–	217	73	103	0	–	–	–	281	3.2	1.1	4.1
54-55–Fort Wayne	16	–	151	16	48	.333	–	–	–	13	16	.813	–	–	32	4	28	0	–	–	–	45	2.0	0.3	2.8
Reg. Season Totals	84	–	1372	132	427	.309	–	–	–	62	84	.738	–	–	249	77	131	0	–	–	–	326	3.0	0.9	3.9

Fryer, Bernie W. b. December 25, 1949 Ht. 6-3 Wt. 185 College: Brigham Young

SEASON–TEAM	G	GS	MIN	FGM	FGA	PCT	3FGM	3FGA	PCT	FTM	FTA	PCT	O-RB	D-RB	TOT	AST	PF	DQ	STL	TO	BLK	PTS	RPG	APG	PPG
73-74–Portland	80	–	1674	226	491	.460	–	–	–	107	135	.793	60	99	159	279	187	1	92	–	10	559	2.0	3.5	7.0
74-75–New Orleans	31	–	432	47	106	.443	–	–	–	33	43	.767	16	30	46	52	54	0	22	–	0	127	1.5	1.7	4.1
74-75–St. Louis (A)	9	–	264	24	68	.353	0	1	.000	22	28	.786	5	17	22	26	28	–	6	17	0	70	2.4	2.9	7.8
Reg. NBA Totals	111	–	2106	273	597	.457	–	–	–	140	178	.787	76	129	205	331	241	1	114	–	10	686	1.8	3.0	6.2
Reg. ABA Totals	9	–	264	24	68	.353	0	1	.000	22	28	.786	5	17	22	26	28	–	6	17	0	70	2.4	2.9	7.8

Fucarino, Frank A. b. July 24, 1920 Ht. 6-2 Wt. 175 College: Long Island University

SEASON–TEAM	G	GS	MIN	FGM	FGA	PCT	3FGM	3FGA	PCT	FTM	FTA	PCT	O-RB	D-RB	TOT	AST	PF	DQ	STL	TO	BLK	PTS	RPG	APG	PPG
46-47–Toronto	28	–	–	53	198	.268	–	–	–	34	60	.567	–	–	–	8	38	–	–	–	–	140	–	0.3	5.0
Reg. Season Totals	28	–	–	53	198	.268	–	–	–	34	60	.567	–	–	–	8	38	–	–	–	–	140	–	0.3	5.0

Fuetsch, Herman Joseph (Herm, Dutch) b. July 6, 1918 Ht. 6-0 Wt. 170 College: None

SEASON–TEAM	G	GS	MIN	FGM	FGA	PCT	3FGM	3FGA	PCT	FTM	FTA	PCT	O-RB	D-RB	TOT	AST	PF	DQ	STL	TO	BLK	PTS	RPG	APG	PPG
45-46–Cleveland (N)	27	–	–	82	–	–	–	–	–	61	75	.813	–	–	–	–	36	–	–	–	–	225	–	–	8.3
47-48–Baltimore	42	–	–	42	140	.300	–	–	–	25	40	.625	–	–	–	17	39	–	–	–	–	109	–	0.4	2.6
Reg. NBA Totals	42	–	–	42	140	.300	–	–	–	25	40	.625	–	–	–	17	39	–	–	–	–	109	–	0.4	2.6
Reg. NBL Totals	27	–	–	82	–	–	–	–	–	61	75	.813	–	–	–	–	36	–	–	–	–	225	–	–	8.3
NBA Playoff Totals	9	–	–	3	7	.429	–	–	–	6	8	.750	–	–	–	–	13	–	–	–	–	12	–	0.0	1.3

Fulks, Joseph Franklin (Joe, Jumpin' Joe) b. October 26, 1921 d. March 21, 1976 Ht. 6-5 Wt. 190 College: Millsaps; Murray State HOF: 1977

SEASON–TEAM	G	GS	MIN	FGM	FGA	PCT	3FGM	3FGA	PCT	FTM	FTA	PCT	O-RB	D-RB	TOT	AST	PF	DQ	STL	TO	BLK	PTS	RPG	APG	PPG
46-47–Philadelphia	60	–	–	475	1557	.305	–	–	–	439	601	.730	–	–	–	25	199	–	–	–	–	1389	–	0.4	23.2
47-48–Philadelphia	43	–	–	326	1258	.259	–	–	–	297	390	.762	–	–	–	26	162	–	–	–	–	949	–	0.6	22.1
48-49–Philadelphia	60	–	–	529	1689	.313	–	–	–	502	638	.787	–	–	–	74	262	–	–	–	–	1560	–	1.2	26.0
49-50–Philadelphia	68	–	–	336	1209	.278	–	–	–	293	421	.696	–	–	–	56	240	–	–	–	–	965	–	0.8	14.2
50-51–Philadelphia	66	–	–	429	1358	.316	–	–	–	378	442	.855	–	–	523	117	247	8	–	–	–	1236	7.9	1.8	18.7
51-52–Philadelphia	61	–	1904	336	1078	.312	–	–	–	250	303	.825	–	–	368	123	255	13	–	–	–	922	6.0	2.0	15.1
52-53–Philadelphia	70	–	2085	332	960	.346	–	–	–	168	231	.727	–	–	387	138	319	20	–	–	–	832	5.5	2.0	11.9
53-54–Philadelphia	61	–	501	61	229	.266	–	–	–	28	49	.571	–	–	101	28	90	0	–	–	–	150	1.7	0.5	2.5
Reg. Season Totals	489	–	4490	2824	9338	.302	–	–	–	2355	3075	.766	–	–	1379	587	1774	41	–	–	–	8003	5.3	1.2	16.4
Playoff Totals	31	–	140	192	922	.262	–	–	–	204	261	.782	–	–	28	14	121	5	–	–	–	588	5.6	0.4	19.0
All-Star Totals	2	–	9	9	22	.409	–	–	–	7	10	.700	–	–	12	5	7	0	–	–	–	25	6.0	2.5	12.5

Fuller, Anthony Ike (Tony) b. September 4, 1958 Ht. 6-4 Wt. 180 College: Vincennes (Ind.) (J.C.); Pepperdine

SEASON–TEAM	G	GS	MIN	FGM	FGA	PCT	3FGM	3FGA	PCT	FTM	FTA	PCT	O-RB	D-RB	TOT	AST	PF	DQ	STL	TO	BLK	PTS	RPG	APG	PPG
80-81–Detroit	15	–	248	24	66	.364	0	1	.000	12	16	.750	13	29	42	28	25	0	10	23	1	60	2.8	1.9	4.0
Reg. Season Totals	15	–	248	24	66	.364	0	1	.000	12	16	.750	13	29	42	28	25	0	10	23	1	60	2.8	1.9	4.0

Fuller, Carl b. January 10, 1946 Ht. 6-9 Wt. 225 College: Bethune-Cookman

SEASON–TEAM	G	GS	MIN	FGM	FGA	PCT	3FGM	3FGA	PCT	FTM	FTA	PCT	O-RB	D-RB	TOT	AST	PF	DQ	STL	TO	BLK	PTS	RPG	APG	PPG
70-71–Floridians (A)	70	–	1151	170	372	.457	0	1	.000	72	120	.600	–	–	330	54	209	–	–	–	–	412	4.7	0.8	5.9
71-72–Floridians (A)	6	–	63	6	14	.429	0	0	–	9	15	.600	–	–	28	6	11	–	–	7	–	21	4.7	1.0	3.5
Reg. ABA Totals	76	–	1214	176	386	.456	0	1	.000	81	135	.600	–	–	358	60	220	–	–	7	–	433	4.7	0.8	5.7
ABA Playoff Totals	6	–	43	6	22	.273	0	2	.000	4	6	.667	–	–	15	4	11	–	–	–	–	16	2.5	0.7	2.7

Fuller, Todd Douglas b. July 25, 1974 Ht. 6-11 Wt. 255 College: North Carolina State

SEASON–TEAM	G	GS	MIN	FGM	FGA	PCT	3FGM	3FGA	PCT	FTM	FTA	PCT	O-RB	D-RB	TOT	AST	PF	DQ	STL	TO	BLK	PTS	RPG	APG	PPG
96-97–Golden State	75	18	949	114	266	.429	0	0	–	76	110	.691	108	141	249	24	146	0	10	52	20	304	3.3	0.3	4.1
97-98–Golden State	57	1	613	86	205	.420	0	4	.000	55	80	.688	61	135	196	10	89	0	6	37	16	227	3.4	0.2	4.0
98-99–Utah	42	2	462	56	124	.452	0	0	–	30	50	.600	28	73	101	6	60	0	6	27	14	142	2.4	0.1	3.4
99-00–Charlotte	41	2	399	51	122	.418	0	0	–	32	53	.604	36	74	110	5	46	0	9	27	8	134	2.7	0.1	3.3
Reg. Season Totals	215	23	2423	307	717	.428	0	4	.000	193	293	.659	233	423	656	45	341	0	31	143	58	807	3.1	0.2	3.8
Playoff Totals	10	0	105	10	26	.385	0	0	–	6	10	.600	8	20	28	–	21	0	0	5	2	26	2.8	0.0	2.6

Funderburke, Lawrence b. December 15, 1970 Ht. 6-9 Wt. 230 College: Ohio State

SEASON–TEAM	G	GS	MIN	FGM	FGA	PCT	3FGM	3FGA	PCT	FTM	FTA	PCT	O-RB	D-RB	TOT	AST	PF	DQ	STL	TO	BLK	PTS	RPG	APG	PPG
97-98–Sacramento	52	1	1094	191	390	.490	1	7	.143	110	162	.679	80	154	234	63	56	0	19	62	15	493	4.5	1.2	9.5
98-99–Sacramento	47	2	936	167	299	.559	1	5	.200	85	120	.708	101	121	222	30	77	0	22	52	23	420	4.7	0.6	8.9
99-00–Sacramento	75	1	1026	184	352	.523	0	2	.000	115	163	.706	98	136	234	33	91	0	32	40	20	483	3.1	0.4	6.4
Reg. Season Totals	174	4	3056	542	1041	.521	2	14	.143	310	445	.697	279	411	690	126	224	0	73	154	58	1396	4.0	0.7	8.0
Playoff Totals	7	0	65	9	21	.429	0	0	–	2	4	.500	6	9	15	1	3	0	4	3	0	20	2.1	0.1	2.9

Furlow, Terry L. b. October 18, 1954 d. May 23, 1980 Ht. 6-5 Wt. 200 College: Michigan State

SEASON–TEAM	G	GS	MIN	FGM	FGA	PCT	3FGM	3FGA	PCT	FTM	FTA	PCT	O-RB	D-RB	TOT	AST	PF	DQ	STL	TO	BLK	PTS	RPG	APG	PPG
76-77–Philadelphia	32	–	174	34	100	.340	–	–	–	16	18	.889	18	21	39	19	11	0	7	–	2	84	1.2	0.6	2.6
77-78–Cleveland	53	–	827	192	443	.433	–	–	–	88	99	.889	47	60	107	72	67	0	21	77	14	472	2.0	1.4	8.9
78-79–Clev.-Atlanta	78	–	1686	388	804	.483	–	–	–	163	195	.836	76	91	167	184	122	1	58	134	30	939	2.1	2.4	12.0
79-80–Atlanta-Utah	76	–	2122	430	926	.464	24	82	.293	171	196	.872	70	124	194	293	98	0	73	163	23	1055	2.6	3.9	13.9
Reg. Season Totals	239	–	4809	1044	2273	.459	24	82	.293	438	508	.862	211	296	507	568	298	1	159	374	69	2550	2.1	2.4	10.7
Playoff Totals	16	–	310	74	151	.490	0	0	–	36	38	.947	17	25	42	34	18	0	8	15	2	184	2.6	2.1	11.5

Gabor, William A. (Billy, The Human Projectile) b. May 13, 1922 Ht. 5-11 Wt. 180 College: Syracuse

SEASON–TEAM	G	GS	MIN	FGM	FGA	PCT	3FGM	3FGA	PCT	FTM	FTA	PCT	O-RB	D-RB	TOT	AST	PF	DQ	STL	TO	BLK	PTS	RPG	APG	PPG
48-49–Syracuse (N)	58	–	–	115	–	–	–	–	–	125	169	.740	–	–	–	–	163	–	–	–	–	355	–	–	6.1
49-50–Syracuse	56	–	–	226	671	.337	–	–	–	157	228	.689	–	–	–	108	198	–	–	–	–	609	–	1.9	10.9
50-51–Syracuse	61	–	–	255	745	.342	–	–	–	179	242	.740	–	–	150	125	213	7	–	–	–	689	2.5	2.0	11.3
51-52–Syracuse	57	–	1085	173	538	.322	–	–	–	142	183	.776	–	–	93	86	188	5	–	–	–	488	1.6	1.5	8.6
52-53–Syracuse	69	–	1337	215	614	.350	–	–	–	217	284	.764	–	–	104	134	262	11	–	–	–	647	1.5	1.9	9.4
53-54–Syracuse	61	–	1211	204	551	.370	–	–	–	139	194	.716	–	–	96	162	183	4	–	–	–	547	1.6	2.7	9.0
54-55–Syracuse	3	–	47	7	22	.318	–	–	–	3	5	.600	–	–	5	11	6	0	–	–	–	17	1.7	3.7	5.7
Reg. NBA Totals	307	–	3680	1080	3141	.344	–	–	–	837	1136	.737	–	–	448	626	1050	27	–	–	–	2997	1.8	2.0	9.8
Reg. NBL Totals	58	–	–	115	–	–	–	–	–	125	169	.740	–	–	–	–	163	–	–	–	–	355	–	–	6.1
NBA Playoff Totals	36	–	420	92	356	.312	–	–	–	83	114	.728	–	–	81	98	115	6	–	–	–	267	2.4	2.1	7.4
NBL Playoff Totals	6	–	–	12	–	–	–	–	–	12	15	.800	–	–	–	–	25	–	–	–	–	36	–	–	6.0
NBA All-Star Totals	1	–	25	0	3	.000	–	–	–	0	1	.000	–	–	5	2	1	0	–	–	–	0	5.0	2.0	0.0

Gainer, Elmer R. b. 1919 Ht. 6-6 Wt. 205 College: DePaul

SEASON–TEAM	G	GS	MIN	FGM	FGA	PCT	3FGM	3FGA	PCT	FTM	FTA	PCT	O-RB	D-RB	TOT	AST	PF	DQ	STL	TO	BLK	PTS	RPG	APG	PPG
41-42–Fort Wayne (N)	24	–	–	36	–	–	–	–	–	28	–	–	–	–	–	–	–	–	–	–	–	100	–	–	4.2
43-44–Sheboygan (N)	22	–	–	15	–	–	–	–	–	20	–	–	–	–	–	–	–	–	–	–	–	50	–	–	2.3
44-45–Chicago (N)	29	–	–	44	–	–	–	–	–	38	–	–	–	–	–	–	–	–	–	–	–	126	–	–	4.3
45-46–Chicago (N)	5	–	–	2	–	–	–	–	–	2	–	–	–	–	–	–	–	–	–	–	–	6	–	–	1.2
46-47–Anderson (N)	43	–	–	77	–	–	–	–	–	59	79	.747	–	–	–	–	87	–	–	–	–	213	–	–	5.0
47-48–Baltimore	5	–	–	1	9	.111	–	–	–	3	6	.500	–	–	–	3	8	–	–	–	–	5	–	0.6	1.0
48-49–Waterloo (N)	36	–	–	33	–	–	–	–	–	30	39	.769	–	–	–	–	64	–	–	–	–	96	–	–	2.7
49-50–Waterloo	15	–	–	9	35	.257	–	–	–	6	8	.750	–	–	–	7	28	–	–	–	–	24	–	0.5	1.6
Reg. NBA Totals	20	–	–	10	44	.227	–	–	–	9	14	.643	–	–	–	10	36	–	–	–	–	29	–	0.5	1.5
Reg. NBL Totals	159	–	–	207	–	–	–	–	–	177	118	.754	–	–	–	–	151	–	–	–	–	591	–	–	3.7
NBL Playoff Totals	15	–	–	13	–	–	–	–	–	15	7	.286	–	–	–	–	28	–	–	–	–	41	–	–	2.7

Gaines, Corey Yasuto b. June 1, 1965 Ht. 6-4 Wt. 195 College: UCLA; Loyola Marymount

SEASON–TEAM	G	GS	MIN	FGM	FGA	PCT	3FGM	3FGA	PCT	FTM	FTA	PCT	O-RB	D-RB	TOT	AST	PF	DQ	STL	TO	BLK	PTS	RPG	APG	PPG
88-89–New Jersey	32	0	337	27	64	.422	1	5	.200	12	16	.750	3	16	19	67	27	0	15	20	1	67	0.6	2.1	2.1
89-90–Philadelphia	9	0	81	4	12	.333	1	2	.500	1	4	.250	1	4	5	26	11	0	4	10	0	10	0.6	2.9	1.1
90-91–Denver	10	2	226	28	70	.400	5	21	.238	22	26	.846	4	10	14	91	25	0	10	23	2	83	1.4	9.1	8.3
93-94–New York	18	0	78	9	20	.450	2	5	.400	13	15	.867	3	10	13	30	12	0	2	5	0	33	0.7	1.7	1.8
94-95–Philadelphia	11	8	280	24	51	.471	2	15	.133	5	11	.455	1	17	18	33	23	0	8	14	1	55	1.6	3.0	5.0
Reg. Season Totals	80	10	1002	92	217	.424	11	48	.229	53	72	.736	12	57	69	247	98	0	39	72	4	248	0.9	3.1	3.1
Playoff Totals	4	0	28	0	4	.000	0	1	.000	0	0	–	0	2	2	2	4	0	0	0	0	0	0.5	0.5	0.0

Gaines, David (Dave, Smokey) b. February 27, 1942 Ht. 6-1 Wt. 175 College: Le Moyne-Owen

SEASON–TEAM	G	GS	MIN	FGM	FGA	PCT	3FGM	3FGA	PCT	FTM	FTA	PCT	O-RB	D-RB	TOT	AST	PF	DQ	STL	TO	BLK	PTS	RPG	APG	PPG
67-68–Kentucky (A)	3	–	36	4	16	.250	1	1	1.000	1	2	.500	–	–	10	0	4	0	–	0	–	10	3.3	0.0	3.3
Reg. ABA Totals	3	–	36	4	16	.250	1	1	1.000	1	2	.500	–	–	10	0	4	0	–	–	–	10	3.3	0.0	3.3

Gaines, William Roosevelt (Bill) b. March 10, 1946 Ht. 6-4 Wt. 185 College: Texas A&M-Commerce

SEASON–TEAM	G	GS	MIN	FGM	FGA	PCT	3FGM	3FGA	PCT	FTM	FTA	PCT	O-RB	D-RB	TOT	AST	PF	DQ	STL	TO	BLK	PTS	RPG	APG	PPG
68-69–Houston (A)	1	–	5	1	2	.500	0	0	–	0	0	–	–	–	1	0	0	0	–	1	–	2	1.0	0.0	2.0
Reg. ABA Totals	1	–	5	1	2	.500	0	0	–	0	0	–	–	–	1	0	0	0	–	1	–	2	1.0	0.0	2.0

Gale, Michael Eugene (Mike) b. July 18, 1950 Ht. 6-4 Wt. 190 College: Elizabeth City State

SEASON–TEAM	G	GS	MIN	FGM	FGA	PCT	3FGM	3FGA	PCT	FTM	FTA	PCT	O-RB	D-RB	TOT	AST	PF	DQ	STL	TO	BLK	PTS	RPG	APG	PPG
71-72–Kentucky (A)	78	–	1701	201	447	.450	0	3	.000	95	140	.679	–	–	271	200	206	–	–	113	–	497	3.5	2.6	6.4
72-73–Kentucky (A)	81	–	1854	218	463	.471	1	6	.167	100	143	.699	78	163	241	248	207	0	131	108	–	537	3.0	3.1	6.6
73-74–Ken.-N.Y. (A)	80	–	2495	314	720	.436	2	17	.118	105	140	.750	107	261	368	324	242	–	167	178	81	735	4.6	4.1	9.2
74-75–New York (A)	72	–	1624	228	492	.463	7	23	.304	72	91	.791	97	139	236	165	131	–	88	111	47	535	3.3	2.3	7.4
75-76–San Antonio (A)	78	–	1782	230	506	.455	3	17	.176	64	80	.800	48	159	207	244	145	–	123	143	40	527	2.7	3.1	6.8
76-77–San Antonio	82	–	2598	353	754	.468	–	–	–	137	167	.820	54	219	273	473	224	3	191	–	50	843	3.3	5.8	10.3
77-78–San Antonio	70	–	2091	275	581	.473	–	–	–	87	100	.870	57	166	223	376	170	2	159	176	25	637	3.2	5.4	9.1
78-79–San Antonio	82	–	2121	284	612	.464	–	–	–	91	108	.843	40	146	186	374	192	1	152	153	40	659	2.3	4.6	8.0
79-80–San Antonio	67	–	1474	171	377	.454	2	13	.154	97	120	.808	34	118	152	312	134	2	123	115	13	441	2.3	4.7	6.6
80-81–S.A.-Port.	77	–	1112	157	309	.508	2	7	.286	55	68	.809	16	83	99	169	117	0	94	77	7	371	1.3	2.2	4.8
81-82–Golden State	75	70	1793	185	373	.496	0	5	.000	51	65	.785	37	152	189	261	173	1	121	126	28	421	2.5	3.5	5.6
Reg. NBA Totals	453	70	11189	1425	3006	.474	4	25	.160	518	628	.825	238	884	1122	1965	1010	9	840	647	163	3372	2.5	4.3	7.4
Reg. ABA Totals	389	–	9456	1191	2628	.453	13	66	.197	436	594	.734	330	722	1323	1181	931	0	509	653	168	2831	3.4	3.0	7.3
NBA Playoff Totals	28	0	690	84	202	.416	1	4	.250	29	40	.725	25	50	75	122	65	1	37	38	10	198	2.7	4.4	7.1
ABA Playoff Totals	38	–	1048	128	299	.428	3	11	.273	55	66	.833	20	83	137	162	100	0	70	64	34	314	3.6	4.3	8.3

Gallagher, Chad Austin b. May 30, 1969 Ht. 6-10 Wt. 255 College: Creighton

SEASON–TEAM	G	GS	MIN	FGM	FGA	PCT	3FGM	3FGA	PCT	FTM	FTA	PCT	O-RB	D-RB	TOT	AST	PF	DQ	STL	TO	BLK	PTS	RPG	APG	PPG
93-94–Utah	2	0	3	3	3	1.000	0	0	–	0	0	–	0	0	0	0	2	0	0	0	0	6	0.0	0.0	3.0
Reg. Season Totals	2	0	3	3	3	1.000	0	0	–	0	0	–	0	0	0	0	2	0	0	0	0	6	0.0	0.0	3.0

Gallatin, Harry J. (The Horse) b. April 26, 1927 Ht. 6-6 Wt. 215 College: Northeast Missouri State HOF: 1990

SEASON–TEAM	G	GS	MIN	FGM	FGA	PCT	3FGM	3FGA	PCT	FTM	FTA	PCT	O-RB	D-RB	TOT	AST	PF	DQ	STL	TO	BLK	PTS	RPG	APG	PPG
48-49–New York	52	–	–	157	479	.328	–	–	–	120	169	.710	–	–	–	63	127	–	–	–	–	434	–	1.2	8.3
49-50–New York	68	–	–	263	664	.396	–	–	–	277	366	.757	–	–	–	56	215	–	–	–	–	803	–	0.8	11.8
50-51–New York	66	–	–	293	705	.416	–	–	–	259	354	.732	–	–	800	180	244	4	–	–	–	845	12.1	2.7	12.8
51-52–New York	66	–	1931	233	527	.442	–	–	–	275	341	.806	–	–	661	115	223	5	–	–	–	741	10.0	1.7	11.2
52-53–New York	70	–	2333	282	635	.444	–	–	–	301	430	.700	–	–	916	126	224	6	–	–	–	865	13.1	1.8	12.4
53-54–New York	72	–	2690	258	639	.404	–	–	–	433	552	.784	–	–	1098	153	208	2	–	–	–	949	15.3	2.1	13.2
54-55–New York	72	–	2548	330	859	.384	–	–	–	393	483	.814	–	–	995	176	206	5	–	–	–	1053	13.8	2.4	14.6
55-56–New York	72	–	2378	322	834	.386	–	–	–	358	455	.787	–	–	740	168	220	6	–	–	–	1002	10.3	2.3	13.9
56-57–New York	72	–	1943	332	817	.406	–	–	–	415	519	.800	–	–	725	85	202	1	–	–	–	1079	10.1	1.2	15.0
57-58–Detroit	72	–	1990	340	898	.379	–	–	–	392	498	.787	–	–	749	86	217	5	–	–	–	1072	10.4	1.2	14.9
Reg. Season Totals	682	–	15813	2810	7057	.398	–	–	–	3223	4167	.773	–	–	6684	1208	2086	34	–	–	–	8843	11.9	1.8	13.0
Playoff Totals	64	–	1335	242	655	.391	–	–	–	283	383	.762	–	–	610	106	239	9	–	–	–	767	11.3	1.6	12.0
All-Star Totals	7	–	159	19	41	.463	–	–	–	19	27	.704	–	–	65	16	17	0	–	–	–	57	9.3	2.3	8.1

Gambee, David P. (Dave) b. April 16, 1937 Ht. 6-6 Wt. 215 College: Oregon State

SEASON–TEAM	G	GS	MIN	FGM	FGA	PCT	3FGM	3FGA	PCT	FTM	FTA	PCT	O-RB	D-RB	TOT	AST	PF	DQ	STL	TO	BLK	PTS	RPG	APG	PPG
58-59–St. Louis	2	–	7	1	1	1.000	–	–	–	0	0	–	–	–	2	0	2	0	–	–	–	2	1.0	0.0	1.0
59-60–St. Louis-Cin.	61	–	656	117	291	.402	–	–	–	69	106	.651	–	–	229	38	83	1	–	–	–	303	3.8	0.6	5.0
60-61–Syracuse	79	–	2090	397	947	.419	–	–	–	291	352	.827	–	–	581	101	276	6	–	–	–	1085	7.4	1.3	13.7
61-62–Syracuse	80	–	2301	477	1126	.424	–	–	–	384	470	.817	–	–	631	114	275	10	–	–	–	1338	7.9	1.4	16.7
62-63–Syracuse	60	–	1234	235	537	.438	–	–	–	199	238	.836	–	–	289	48	190	2	–	–	–	669	4.8	0.8	11.2
63-64–Philadelphia	41	–	927	149	378	.394	–	–	–	151	185	.816	–	–	256	35	161	6	–	–	–	449	6.2	0.9	11.0
64-65–Philadelphia	80	–	1993	356	864	.412	–	–	–	299	368	.813	–	–	468	113	277	7	–	–	–	1011	5.9	1.4	12.6
65-66–Philadelphia	72	–	1068	168	437	.384	–	–	–	159	187	.850	–	–	273	71	189	3	–	–	–	495	3.8	1.0	6.9
66-67–Philadelphia	63	–	757	150	345	.435	–	–	–	107	125	.856	–	–	197	42	143	5	–	–	–	407	3.1	0.7	6.5
67-68–San Diego	80	–	1755	375	853	.440	–	–	–	321	379	.847	–	–	464	93	253	5	–	–	–	1071	5.8	1.2	13.4
68-69–Milw.-Detroit	59	–	926	210	465	.452	–	–	–	159	195	.815	–	–	257	47	159	4	–	–	–	579	4.4	0.8	9.8
69-70–San Francisco	73	–	951	185	464	.399	–	–	–	156	186	.839	–	–	244	55	172	0	–	–	–	526	3.3	0.8	7.2
Reg. Season Totals	750	–	14665	2820	6708	.420	–	–	–	2295	2791	.822	–	–	3891	757	2180	49	–	–	–	7935	5.2	1.0	10.6
Playoff Totals	43	–	840	118	331	.356	–	–	–	131	157	.834	–	–	188	36	143	3	–	–	–	367	4.4	0.8	8.5

Gamble, Kevin Douglas b. November 13, 1965 Ht. 6-6 Wt. 225 College: Lincoln Trail (Ill.) (J.C.); Iowa

SEASON–TEAM	G	GS	MIN	FGM	FGA	PCT	3FGM	3FGA	PCT	FTM	FTA	PCT	O-RB	D-RB	TOT	AST	PF	DQ	STL	TO	BLK	PTS	RPG	APG	PPG
87-88–Portland	9	0	19	0	3	.000	0	1	.000	0	0	–	2	1	3	1	2	0	2	2	0	0	0.3	0.1	0.0
88-89–Boston	44	6	375	75	136	.551	2	11	.182	35	55	.636	11	31	42	34	40	0	14	19	3	187	1.0	0.8	4.3
89-90–Boston	71	10	990	137	301	.455	3	18	.167	85	107	.794	42	70	112	119	77	1	28	44	8	362	1.6	1.7	5.1
90-91–Boston	82	76	2706	548	933	.587	0	7	.000	185	227	.815	85	182	267	256	237	6	100	148	34	1281	3.3	3.1	15.6
91-92–Boston	82	77	2496	480	908	.529	9	31	.290	139	157	.885	80	206	286	219	200	2	75	97	37	1108	3.5	2.7	13.5
92-93–Boston	82	58	2541	459	906	.507	52	139	.374	123	149	.826	46	200	246	226	185	1	86	81	37	1093	3.0	2.8	13.3
93-94–Boston	75	28	1880	368	804	.458	25	103	.243	103	126	.817	41	118	159	149	134	0	57	77	22	864	2.1	2.0	11.5
94-95–Miami	77	0	1223	220	450	.489	39	98	.398	87	111	.784	29	93	122	119	130	0	52	49	10	566	1.6	1.5	7.4
95-96–Miami-Sac.	65	13	1325	152	379	.401	44	114	.386	38	48	.792	21	92	113	100	147	2	35	43	8	386	1.7	1.5	5.9
96-97–Sacramento	62	2	953	123	286	.430	54	112	.482	7	10	.700	13	94	107	77	76	0	21	27	17	307	1.7	1.2	5.0
Reg. Season Totals	649	270	14508	2562	5106	.502	228	634	.360	802	990	.810	370	1087	1457	1300	1228	12	470	587	176	6154	2.2	2.0	9.5
Playoff Totals	31	26	755	121	249	.486	5	15	.333	24	33	.727	21	45	66	56	63	0	23	23	9	271	2.1	1.8	8.7

Gantt, Robert M. Jr. (Bob) b. June 22, 1922 Ht. 6-4 Wt. 205 College: Duke

SEASON–TEAM	G	GS	MIN	FGM	FGA	PCT	3FGM	3FGA	PCT	FTM	FTA	PCT	O-RB	D-RB	TOT	AST	PF	DQ	STL	TO	BLK	PTS	RPG	APG	PPG
46-47–Washington	23	–	–	29	89	.326	–	–	–	13	28	.464	–	–	–	5	45	–	–	–	–	71	–	0.2	3.1
Reg. Season Totals	23	–	–	29	89	.326	–	–	–	13	28	.464	–	–	–	5	45	–	–	–	–	71	–	0.2	3.1
Playoff Totals	3	–	–	1	6	.333	–	–	–	0	2	.000	–	–	–	–	0	–	–	–	–	2	0.0	0.0	0.7

Gardner, Charles Rutland (Chuck) b. September 30, 1944 Ht. 6-8 Wt. 205 College: Colorado

SEASON–TEAM	G	GS	MIN	FGM	FGA	PCT	3FGM	3FGA	PCT	FTM	FTA	PCT	O-RB	D-RB	TOT	AST	PF	DQ	STL	TO	BLK	PTS	RPG	APG	PPG
67-68–Denver (A)	42	–	487	71	175	.406	0	4	.000	55	79	.696	–	–	136	13	74	1	–	52	–	197	3.2	0.3	4.7
Reg. ABA Totals	42	–	487	71	175	.406	0	4	.000	55	79	.696	–	–	136	13	74	1	–	52	–	197	3.2	0.3	4.7

Gardner, Earl Baker (Red) b. September 18, 1923 Ht. 6-3 Wt. 195 College: Wabash; DePauw

SEASON–TEAM	G	GS	MIN	FGM	FGA	PCT	3FGM	3FGA	PCT	FTM	FTA	PCT	O-RB	D-RB	TOT	AST	PF	DQ	STL	TO	BLK	PTS	RPG	APG	PPG
48-49–Minneapolis	50	–	–	38	101	.376	–	–	–	13	28	.464	–	–	–	19	50	–	–	–	–	89	–	0.4	1.8
Reg. Season Totals	50	–	–	38	101	.376	–	–	–	13	28	.464	–	–	–	19	50	–	–	–	–	89	–	0.4	1.8
Playoff Totals	7	–	–	1	18	.111	–	–	–	2	4	.500	–	–	–	2	3	–	–	–	–	4	–	0.1	0.6

Gardner, Kenneth Kay (Kenny) b. September 27, 1949 Ht. 6-5 Wt. 205 College: Utah

SEASON–TEAM	G	GS	MIN	FGM	FGA	PCT	3FGM	3FGA	PCT	FTM	FTA	PCT	O-RB	D-RB	TOT	AST	PF	DQ	STL	TO	BLK	PTS	RPG	APG	PPG
75-76–Utah (A)	9	–	51	6	18	.333	0	0	–	2	2	1.000	8	5	13	3	9	–	2	1	1	14	1.4	0.3	1.6
Reg. ABA Totals	9	–	51	6	18	.333	0	0	–	2	2	1.000	8	5	13	3	9	–	2	1	1	14	1.4	0.3	1.6

Gardner, Vern B. b. May 14, 1925 d. August 26, 1987 Ht. 6-5 Wt. 200 College: Wyoming; Utah

SEASON–TEAM	G	GS	MIN	FGM	FGA	PCT	3FGM	3FGA	PCT	FTM	FTA	PCT	O-RB	D-RB	TOT	AST	PF	DQ	STL	TO	BLK	PTS	RPG	APG	PPG
49-50–Philadelphia	63	–	–	313	916	.342	–	–	–	227	296	.767	–	–	–	119	236	–	–	–	–	853	–	1.9	13.5
50-51–Philadelphia	61	–	–	129	383	.337	–	–	–	69	97	.711	–	–	237	89	149	6	–	–	–	327	3.9	1.5	5.4
51-52–Philadelphia	27	–	507	72	194	.371	–	–	–	15	23	.652	–	–	112	37	60	2	–	–	–	159	4.1	1.4	5.9
Reg. Season Totals	151	–	507	514	1493	.344	–	–	–	311	416	.748	–	–	349	245	445	8	–	–	–	1339	4.0	1.6	8.9
Playoff Totals	7	–	154	26	71	.366	–	–	–	19	23	.826	–	–	18	5	33	2	–	–	–	71	3.6	0.7	10.1

Garfinkel, Jack (Dutch) b. June 13, 1918 Ht. 6-0 Wt. 190 College: St. John's (N.Y.)

SEASON–TEAM	G	GS	MIN	FGM	FGA	PCT	3FGM	3FGA	PCT	FTM	FTA	PCT	O-RB	D-RB	TOT	AST	PF	DQ	STL	TO	BLK	PTS	RPG	APG	PPG
45-46–Rochester (N)	18	–	–	14	–	–	–	–	–	6	–	–	–	–	–	–	–	–	–	–	–	34	–	–	1.9
46-47–Rochester (N)	10	–	–	5	–	–	–	–	–	3	6	.500	–	–	–	–	–	–	–	–	–	13	–	–	1.3
46-47–Boston	40	–	–	81	304	.266	–	–	–	17	28	.607	–	–	–	58	62	–	–	–	–	179	–	1.5	4.5
47-48–Boston	43	–	–	114	380	.300	–	–	–	35	46	.761	–	–	–	59	78	–	–	–	–	263	–	1.4	6.1
48-49–Boston	9	–	–	12	70	.171	–	–	–	10	14	.714	–	–	–	17	19	–	–	–	–	34	–	1.9	3.8
Reg. NBA Totals	92	–	–	207	754	.275	–	–	–	62	88	.705	–	–	–	134	159	–	–	–	–	476	–	1.5	5.2
Reg. NBL Totals	28	–	–	19	–	–	–	–	–	9	6	.500	–	–	–	–	–	–	–	–	–	47	–	–	1.7
NBA Playoff Totals	3	–	–	7	46	.304	–	–	–	8	10	.800	–	–	–	14	30	–	–	–	–	22	–	2.3	7.3
NBL Playoff Totals	6	–	–	1	–	–	–	–	–	1	3	.333	–	–	–	–	1	–	–	–	–	3	–	–	0.5

Garland, Gary J. b. October 12, 1957 Ht. 6-4 Wt. 180 College: DePaul

SEASON–TEAM	G	GS	MIN	FGM	FGA	PCT	3FGM	3FGA	PCT	FTM	FTA	PCT	O-RB	D-RB	TOT	AST	PF	DQ	STL	TO	BLK	PTS	RPG	APG	PPG
79-80–Denver	78	–	1106	155	356	.435	6	19	.316	18	26	.692	50	88	138	145	80	1	54	73	4	334	1.8	1.9	4.3
Reg. Season Totals	78	–	1106	155	356	.435	6	19	.316	18	26	.692	50	88	138	145	80	1	54	73	4	334	1.8	1.9	4.3

Garland, Winston Kinnard b. December 19, 1964 Ht. 6-2 Wt. 170 College: Southeastern (Iowa) C.C.; Southwest Missouri State

SEASON–TEAM	G	GS	MIN	FGM	FGA	PCT	3FGM	3FGA	PCT	FTM	FTA	PCT	O-RB	D-RB	TOT	AST	PF	DQ	STL	TO	BLK	PTS	RPG	APG	PPG
87-88–Golden State	67	62	2122	340	775	.439	13	39	.333	138	157	.879	68	159	227	429	188	2	116	167	7	831	3.4	6.4	12.4
88-89–Golden State	79	79	2661	466	1074	.434	10	43	.233	203	251	.809	101	227	328	505	216	2	175	187	14	1145	4.2	6.4	14.5
89-90–G.S.-LAClips	79	19	1762	230	573	.401	12	36	.333	102	122	.836	51	163	214	303	152	1	78	158	10	574	2.7	3.8	7.3
90-91–L.A. Clippers	69	26	1702	221	519	.426	4	26	.154	118	157	.752	46	152	198	317	189	3	97	116	10	564	2.9	4.6	8.2
91-92–Denver	78	67	2209	333	750	.444	9	28	.321	171	199	.859	67	123	190	411	206	1	98	175	22	846	2.4	5.3	10.8
92-93–Houston	66	4	1004	152	343	.443	6	13	.462	81	89	.910	32	76	108	138	116	0	39	67	4	391	1.6	2.1	5.9
94-95–Minnesota	73	58	1931	170	410	.415	19	75	.253	89	112	.795	48	120	168	318	184	1	71	105	13	448	2.3	4.4	6.1
Reg. Season Totals	511	315	13391	1912	4444	.430	73	260	.281	902	1087	.830	413	1020	1433	2421	1251	10	674	975	80	4799	2.8	4.7	9.4
Playoff Totals	20	13	516	71	172	.413	1	4	.250	41	45	.911	20	46	66	60	58	2	29	37	2	184	3.3	3.0	9.2

Garmaker, Richard Eugene (Dick) b. October 29, 1932 Ht. 6-3 Wt. 205 College: Hibbing (Minn) C.C.; Minnesota

SEASON–TEAM	G	GS	MIN	FGM	FGA	PCT	3FGM	3FGA	PCT	FTM	FTA	PCT	O-RB	D-RB	TOT	AST	PF	DQ	STL	TO	BLK	PTS	RPG	APG	PPG
55-56–Minneapolis	68	–	870	138	373	.370	–	–	–	112	139	.806	–	–	132	104	127	0	–	–	–	388	1.9	1.5	5.7
56-57–Minneapolis	72	–	2406	406	1015	.400	–	–	–	365	435	.839	–	–	336	190	199	1	–	–	–	1177	4.7	2.6	16.3
57-58–Minneapolis	68	–	2216	390	988	.395	–	–	–	314	411	.764	–	–	365	183	190	2	–	–	–	1094	5.4	2.7	16.1
58-59–Minneapolis	72	–	2493	350	885	.395	–	–	–	284	368	.772	–	–	325	211	226	3	–	–	–	984	4.5	2.9	13.7
59-60–Minn.-N.Y.	70	–	1932	323	815	.396	–	–	–	203	263	.772	–	–	313	206	186	4	–	–	–	849	4.5	2.9	12.1
60-61–New York	71	–	2238	415	943	.440	–	–	–	275	358	.768	–	–	277	220	240	2	–	–	–	1105	3.9	3.1	15.6
Reg. Season Totals	421	–	12155	2022	5019	.403	–	–	–	1553	1974	.787	–	–	1748	1114	1168	12	–	–	–	5597	4.2	2.6	13.3
Playoff Totals	21	–	668	96	253	.379	–	–	–	92	112	.821	–	–	98	67	71	2	–	–	–	284	4.7	3.2	13.5
All-Star Totals	4	–	73	13	36	.361	–	–	–	5	6	.833	–	–	19	6	9	0	–	–	–	31	4.8	1.5	7.8

Garner, Christopher (Chris) b. February 23, 1975 Ht. 5-10 Wt. 156 College: Memphis

SEASON–TEAM	G	GS	MIN	FGM	FGA	PCT	3FGM	3FGA	PCT	FTM	FTA	PCT	O-RB	D-RB	TOT	AST	PF	DQ	STL	TO	BLK	PTS	RPG	APG	PPG
97-98–Toronto	38	0	293	23	70	.329	4	14	.286	3	7	.429	7	17	24	45	50	0	21	25	4	53	0.6	1.2	1.4
Reg. Season Totals	38	0	293	23	70	.329	4	14	.286	3	7	.429	7	17	24	45	50	0	21	25	4	53	0.6	1.2	1.4

Garner, William (Bill) b. June 17, 1940 Ht. 6-11 Wt. 225 College: Portland

SEASON–TEAM	G	GS	MIN	FGM	FGA	PCT	3FGM	3FGA	PCT	FTM	FTA	PCT	O-RB	D-RB	TOT	AST	PF	DQ	STL	TO	BLK	PTS	RPG	APG	PPG
67-68–Anaheim (A)	53	–	514	28	103	.272	0	1	.000	25	50	.500	–	–	119	24	101	4	–	47	–	81	2.2	0.5	1.5
Reg. ABA Totals	53	–	514	28	103	.272	0	1	.000	25	50	.500	–	–	119	24	101	4	–	47	–	81	2.2	0.5	1.5

Garnett, Kevin b. May 19, 1976 Ht. 6-11 Wt. 220 High School: Farragut Academy (Ill.)

SEASON–TEAM	G	GS	MIN	FGM	FGA	PCT	3FGM	3FGA	PCT	FTM	FTA	PCT	O-RB	D-RB	TOT	AST	PF	DQ	STL	TO	BLK	PTS	RPG	APG	PPG
95-96–Minnesota	80	43	2293	361	735	.491	8	28	.286	105	149	.705	175	326	501	145	189	2	86	110	131	835	6.3	1.8	10.4
96-97–Minnesota	77	77	2995	549	1100	.499	6	21	.286	205	272	.754	190	428	618	236	199	2	105	175	163	1309	8.0	3.1	17.0
97-98–Minnesota	82	82	3222	635	1293	.491	3	16	.188	245	332	.738	222	564	786	348	224	1	139	192	150	1518	9.6	4.2	18.5
98-99–Minnesota	47	47	1780	414	900	.460	4	14	.286	145	206	.704	166	323	489	202	152	5	78	135	83	977	10.4	4.3	20.8
99-00–Minnesota	81	81	3243	759	1526	.497	30	81	.370	309	404	.765	223	733	956	401	205	1	120	268	126	1857	11.8	5.0	22.9
Reg. Season Totals	367	330	13533	2718	5554	.489	51	160	.319	1009	1363	.740	976	2374	3350	1332	969	11	528	880	653	6496	9.1	3.6	17.7
Playoff Totals	16	16	660	125	283	.442	3	6	.500	40	51	.784	60	107	167	81	45	0	20	50	26	293	10.4	5.1	18.3
All-Star Totals	3	2	74	17	37	.459	0	2	.000	8	8	1.000	5	18	23	8	3	0	3	3	3	42	7.7	2.7	14.0

Garnett, Marlon b. July 3, 1975 Ht. 6-2 Wt. 186 College: Santa Clara

SEASON–TEAM	G	GS	MIN	FGM	FGA	PCT	3FGM	3FGA	PCT	FTM	FTA	PCT	O-RB	D-RB	TOT	AST	PF	DQ	STL	TO	BLK	PTS	RPG	APG	PPG
98-99–Boston	24	0	205	15	51	.294	6	23	.261	15	20	.750	3	18	21	18	18	0	5	12	1	51	0.9	0.8	2.1
Reg. Season Totals	24	0	205	15	51	.294	6	23	.261	15	20	.750	3	18	21	18	18	0	5	12	1	51	0.9	0.8	2.1

Garnett, William Patrick (Bill) b. April 22, 1960 Ht. 6-9 Wt. 225 College: Wyoming

SEASON–TEAM	G	GS	MIN	FGM	FGA	PCT	3FGM	3FGA	PCT	FTM	FTA	PCT	O-RB	D-RB	TOT	AST	PF	DQ	STL	TO	BLK	PTS	RPG	APG	PPG
82-83–Dallas	75	13	1411	170	319	.533	0	3	.000	129	174	.741	141	265	406	103	245	3	48	81	70	469	5.4	1.4	6.3
83-84–Dallas	80	34	1529	141	299	.472	0	2	.000	129	176	.733	123	208	331	128	217	4	44	68	66	411	4.1	1.6	5.1
84-85–Indiana	65	13	1123	149	310	.481	0	2	.000	120	174	.690	98	188	286	67	196	3	28	92	15	418	4.4	1.0	6.4
85-86–Indiana	80	2	1197	112	239	.469	0	2	.000	116	162	.716	106	169	275	95	174	0	39	91	22	340	3.4	1.2	4.3
Reg. Season Totals	300	62	5260	572	1167	.490	0	9	.000	494	686	.720	468	830	1298	393	832	10	159	332	173	1638	4.3	1.3	5.5
Playoff Totals	8	0	74	15	30	.500	1	1	1.000	7	8	.875	10	12	22	4	10	0	0	1	2	38	2.8	0.5	4.8

Garrett, Calvin Eugene b. July 11, 1956 Ht. 6-7 Wt. 190 College: Austin Peay State; Oral Roberts

SEASON–TEAM	G	GS	MIN	FGM	FGA	PCT	3FGM	3FGA	PCT	FTM	FTA	PCT	O-RB	D-RB	TOT	AST	PF	DQ	STL	TO	BLK	PTS	RPG	APG	PPG
80-81–Houston	70	–	1638	188	415	.453	1	3	.333	50	62	.806	85	179	264	132	167	0	50	90	10	427	3.8	1.9	6.1
81-82–Houston	51	22	858	105	242	.434	3	10	.300	17	26	.654	27	67	94	76	94	0	32	38	6	230	1.8	1.5	4.5
82-83–Houston	4	0	34	4	11	.364	0	1	.000	2	2	1.000	3	4	7	3	4	0	0	3	0	10	1.8	0.8	2.5
83-84–Los Angeles	41	0	478	78	152	.513	2	6	.333	30	39	.769	24	47	71	31	62	2	12	34	2	188	1.7	0.8	4.6
Reg. Season Totals	166	22	3008	375	820	.457	6	20	.300	99	129	.767	139	297	436	242	327	2	94	165	18	855	2.6	1.5	5.2
Playoff Totals	14	0	118	9	22	.409	0	1	.000	7	8	.875	3	12	15	6	10	0	5	6	1	25	1.1	0.4	1.8

Garrett, Dean Heath b. November 27, 1966 Ht. 6-11 Wt. 250 College: Indiana

SEASON–TEAM	G	GS	MIN	FGM	FGA	PCT	3FGM	3FGA	PCT	FTM	FTA	PCT	O-RB	D-RB	TOT	AST	PF	DQ	STL	TO	BLK	PTS	RPG	APG	PPG
96-97–Minnesota	68	47	1665	223	389	.573	0	0	–	96	138	.696	149	346	495	38	158	1	40	34	95	542	7.3	0.6	8.0
97-98–Denver	82	82	2632	242	565	.428	0	0	–	114	176	.648	227	417	644	90	197	0	57	84	133	598	7.9	1.1	7.3
98-99–Minnesota	49	37	1054	116	231	.502	0	0	–	38	51	.745	99	158	257	28	113	0	30	29	45	270	5.2	0.6	5.5
99-00–Minnesota	56	23	604	48	108	.444	0	0	–	18	26	.692	41	99	140	19	94	1	8	21	40	114	2.5	0.3	2.0
Reg. Season Totals	255	189	5955	629	1293	.486	0	0	–	266	391	.680	516	1020	1536	175	562	2	135	168	313	1524	6.0	0.7	6.0
Playoff Totals	10	6	226	26	49	.531	0	0	–	11	17	.647	29	24	53	9	29	1	4	3	7	63	5.3	0.9	6.3

G

Garrett, Eldo **(Dick)** b. January 31, 1947 Ht. 6-3 Wt. 185 College: Southern Illinois

SEASON–TEAM	G	GS	MIN	FGM	FGA	PCT	3FGM	3FGA	PCT	FTM	FTA	PCT	O-RB	D-RB	TOT	AST	PF	DQ	STL	TO	BLK	PTS	RPG	APG	PPG
69-70–Los Angeles	73	–	2318	354	816	.434	–	–	–	138	162	.852	–	–	235	180	236	5	–	–	–	846	3.2	2.5	11.6
70-71–Buffalo	75	–	2375	373	902	.414	–	–	–	218	251	.869	–	–	295	264	290	9	–	–	–	964	3.9	3.5	12.9
71-72–Buffalo	73	–	1905	325	735	.442	–	–	–	136	157	.866	–	–	225	165	225	5	–	–	–	786	3.1	2.3	10.8
72-73–Buffalo	78	–	1805	341	813	.419	–	–	–	96	110	.873	–	–	209	217	217	4	–	–	–	778	2.7	2.8	10.0
73-74–N.Y.-Milw.	40	–	326	43	126	.341	–	–	–	15	19	.789	15	25	40	23	56	0	10	–	1	101	1.0	0.6	2.5
Reg. Season Totals	339	–	8729	1436	3392	.423	–	–	–	603	699	.863	15	25	1004	849	1024	23	10	–	1	3475	3.0	2.5	10.3
Playoff Totals	26	–	641	103	205	.502	–	–	–	30	36	.833	1	2	55	46	75	2	2	–	0	236	2.1	1.8	9.1

Garrett, Rowland G. b. July 16, 1950 Ht. 6-6 Wt. 210 College: Florida State

SEASON–TEAM	G	GS	MIN	FGM	FGA	PCT	3FGM	3FGA	PCT	FTM	FTA	PCT	O-RB	D-RB	TOT	AST	PF	DQ	STL	TO	BLK	PTS	RPG	APG	PPG
72-73–Chicago	35	–	211	52	118	.441	–	–	–	21	31	.677	–	–	61	8	29	0	–	–	–	125	1.7	0.2	3.6
73-74–Chicago	41	–	373	68	184	.370	–	–	–	21	32	.656	31	39	70	11	43	0	5	–	9	157	1.7	0.3	3.8
74-75–Chicago	70	–	1183	228	474	.481	–	–	–	77	97	.794	80	167	247	43	124	0	24	–	13	533	3.5	0.6	7.6
75-76–Chicago-Clev.	55	–	540	108	258	.419	–	–	–	53	65	.815	45	72	117	17	68	0	25	–	7	269	2.1	0.3	4.9
76-77–Clev.-Milw.	62	–	598	106	239	.444	–	–	–	41	51	.804	37	75	112	27	80	0	21	–	10	253	1.8	0.4	4.1
Reg. Season Totals	263	–	2905	562	1273	.441	–	–	–	213	276	.772	193	353	607	106	344	0	75	–	39	1337	2.3	0.4	5.1
Playoff Totals	19	–	155	21	60	.350	–	–	–	4	8	.500	8	22	30	3	28	0	4	–	4	46	1.6	0.2	2.4

Garrick, Thomas S. **(Tom, Chief)** b. July 7, 1966 Ht. 6-2 Wt. 195 College: Rhode Island

SEASON–TEAM	G	GS	MIN	FGM	FGA	PCT	3FGM	3FGA	PCT	FTM	FTA	PCT	O-RB	D-RB	TOT	AST	PF	DQ	STL	TO	BLK	PTS	RPG	APG	PPG
88-89–L.A. Clippers	71	20	1499	176	359	.490	0	13	.000	102	127	.803	37	119	156	243	141	1	78	116	9	454	2.2	3.4	6.4
89-90–L.A. Clippers	73	22	1721	208	421	.494	4	21	.190	88	114	.772	34	128	162	289	151	4	90	117	7	508	2.2	4.0	7.0
90-91–L.A. Clippers	67	0	949	100	236	.424	0	22	.000	60	79	.759	40	87	127	223	101	0	62	66	2	260	1.9	3.3	3.9
91-92–S.A.-Minn.-Dallas	40	5	549	59	143	.413	1	4	.250	18	26	.692	12	44	56	98	54	0	36	44	4	137	1.4	2.5	3.4
Reg. Season Totals	251	47	4718	543	1159	.469	5	60	.083	268	346	.775	123	378	501	853	447	5	266	343	22	1359	2.0	3.4	5.4

Garris, John Brasker b. June 6, 1959 Ht. 6-8 Wt. 205 College: Michigan; Boston College

SEASON–TEAM	G	GS	MIN	FGM	FGA	PCT	3FGM	3FGA	PCT	FTM	FTA	PCT	O-RB	D-RB	TOT	AST	PF	DQ	STL	TO	BLK	PTS	RPG	APG	PPG
83-84–Cleveland	33	1	267	52	102	.510	0	0	–	27	34	.794	35	42	77	10	40	0	8	11	6	131	2.3	0.3	4.0
Reg. Season Totals	33	1	267	52	102	.510	0	0	–	27	34	.794	35	42	77	10	40	0	8	11	6	131	2.3	0.3	4.0

Garris, Kiwane b. September 24, 1974 Ht. 6-2 Wt. 183 College: Illinois

SEASON–TEAM	G	GS	MIN	FGM	FGA	PCT	3FGM	3FGA	PCT	FTM	FTA	PCT	O-RB	D-RB	TOT	AST	PF	DQ	STL	TO	BLK	PTS	RPG	APG	PPG
97-98–Denver	28	0	225	22	65	.338	5	14	.357	19	25	.760	3	16	19	28	22	0	7	15	1	68	0.7	1.0	2.4
99-00–Orlando	3	0	23	2	10	.200	0	1	.000	0	0	–	0	1	1	2	0	0	0	1	0	4	0.3	0.7	1.3
Reg. Season Totals	31	0	248	24	75	.320	5	15	.333	19	25	.760	3	17	20	30	22	0	7	16	1	72	0.6	1.0	2.3

Garrity, Patrick Joseph **(Pat)** b. August 23, 1976 Ht. 6-9 Wt. 238 College: Notre Dame

SEASON–TEAM	G	GS	MIN	FGM	FGA	PCT	3FGM	3FGA	PCT	FTM	FTA	PCT	O-RB	D-RB	TOT	AST	PF	DQ	STL	TO	BLK	PTS	RPG	APG	PPG
98-99–Phoenix	39	9	538	85	170	.500	7	18	.389	40	56	.714	26	49	75	18	62	0	8	20	3	217	1.9	0.5	5.6
99-00–Orlando	82	1	1479	258	585	.441	79	197	.401	80	111	.721	44	166	210	58	197	1	31	85	19	675	2.6	0.7	8.2
Reg. Season Totals	121	10	2017	343	755	.454	86	215	.400	120	167	.719	70	215	285	76	259	1	39	105	22	892	2.4	0.6	7.4
Playoff Totals	3	0	52	9	17	.529	3	3	1.000	6	6	1.000	6	3	9	1	9	0	1	3	1	27	3.0	0.3	9.0

Garvin, James D. **(Jim)** b. February 5, 1950 Ht. 6-7 Wt. 210 College: Boston U.

SEASON–TEAM	G	GS	MIN	FGM	FGA	PCT	3FGM	3FGA	PCT	FTM	FTA	PCT	O-RB	D-RB	TOT	AST	PF	DQ	STL	TO	BLK	PTS	RPG	APG	PPG
73-74–Buffalo	6	–	11	1	4	.250	–	–	–	0	0	–	1	4	5	0	1	0	0	–	0	2	0.8	0.0	0.3
Reg. Season Totals	6	–	11	1	4	.250	–	–	–	0	0	–	1	4	5	0	1	0	0	–	0	2	0.8	0.0	0.3

Gates, Ben Frank **(Frank, Needle)** b. April 12, 1920 d. July 26, 1978 Ht. 6-0 Wt. 165 College: Sam Houston State

SEASON–TEAM	G	GS	MIN	FGM	FGA	PCT	3FGM	3FGA	PCT	FTM	FTA	PCT	O-RB	D-RB	TOT	AST	PF	DQ	STL	TO	BLK	PTS	RPG	APG	PPG
46-47–And.-F.W.(N)	32	–	–	68	–	–	–	–	–	30	52	.577	–	–	–	–	78	–	–	–	–	166	–	–	5.2
48-49–Anderson (N)	64	–	–	150	–	–	–	–	–	78	123	.634	–	–	–	–	166	–	–	–	–	378	–	–	5.9
49-50–Anderson	64	–	–	113	402	.281	–	–	–	61	98	.622	–	–	–	91	147	–	–	–	–	287	–	1.4	4.5
Reg. NBA Totals	64	–	–	113	402	.281	–	–	–	61	98	.622	–	–	–	91	147	–	–	–	–	287	–	1.4	4.5
Reg. NBL Totals	96	–	–	218	–	–	–	–	–	108	175	.617	–	–	–	–	244	–	–	–	–	544	–	–	5.7
NBA Playoff Totals	7	–	–	9	74	.243	–	–	–	7	10	.700	–	–	–	18	16	1	–	–	–	25	–	1.3	3.6
NBL Playoff Totals	14	–	–	22	–	–	–	–	–	14	23	.609	–	–	–	–	33	–	–	–	–	58	–	–	4.1

Gatling, Chris Raymond b. September 3, 1967 Ht. 6-10 Wt. 230 College: Pittsburgh; Old Dominion

SEASON–TEAM	G	GS	MIN	FGM	FGA	PCT	3FGM	3FGA	PCT	FTM	FTA	PCT	O-RB	D-RB	TOT	AST	PF	DQ	STL	TO	BLK	PTS	RPG	APG	PPG
91-92–Golden State	54	1	612	117	206	.568	0	4	.000	72	109	.661	75	107	182	16	101	0	31	44	36	306	3.4	0.3	5.7
92-93–Golden State	70	11	1248	249	462	.539	0	6	.000	150	207	.725	129	191	320	40	197	2	44	102	53	648	4.6	0.6	9.3
93-94–Golden State	82	23	1296	271	461	.588	0	1	.000	129	208	.620	143	254	397	41	223	5	40	84	63	671	4.8	0.5	8.2
94-95–Golden State	58	22	1470	324	512	.633	0	1	.000	148	250	.592	144	299	443	51	184	4	39	117	52	796	7.6	0.9	13.7
95-96–G.S.-Miami	71	2	1427	326	567	.575	0	1	.000	139	207	.671	129	288	417	43	217	0	36	95	40	791	5.9	0.6	11.1
96-97–Dallas-N.J.	47	1	1283	327	623	.525	1	6	.167	236	329	.717	134	236	370	28	138	1	39	120	31	891	7.9	0.6	19.0
97-98–New Jersey	57	16	1359	248	545	.455	1	4	.250	159	265	.600	118	216	334	53	152	2	52	99	29	656	5.9	0.9	11.5
98-99–N.J.-Milw.	48	3	775	117	265	.442	1	8	.125	37	93	.398	52	127	179	32	118	0	32	62	10	272	3.7	0.7	5.7
99-00–Orlando-Denver	85	0	1811	365	802	.455	18	70	.257	266	373	.713	154	348	502	71	246	2	82	169	23	1014	5.9	0.8	11.9
Reg. Season Totals	572	79	11281	2344	4443	.528	21	101	.208	1336	2041	.655	1078	2066	3144	375	1576	16	395	892	337	6045	5.5	0.7	10.6
Playoff Totals	15	2	296	51	104	.490	0	0	–	38	61	.623	33	46	79	7	44	1	9	16	13	140	5.3	0.5	9.3
All-Star Totals	1	0	12	1	8	.125	0	0	–	0	0	–	0	2	2	0	1	0	1	0	0	2	2.0	0.0	2.0

Gattison, Kenneth Clay (Kenny) b. May 23, 1964 Ht. 6-8 Wt. 257 College: Old Dominion

SEASON–TEAM	G	GS	MIN	FGM	FGA	PCT	3FGM	3FGA	PCT	FTM	FTA	PCT	O-RB	D-RB	TOT	AST	PF	DQ	STL	TO	BLK	PTS	RPG	APG	PPG
86-87–Phoenix	77	14	1104	148	311	.476	0	3	.000	108	171	.632	87	183	270	36	178	1	24	88	33	404	3.5	0.5	5.2
88-89–Phoenix	2	0	9	0	1	.000	0	0	–	1	2	.500	0	1	1	0	2	0	0	0	0	1	0.5	0.0	0.5
89-90–Charlotte	63	2	941	148	269	.550	1	1	1.000	75	110	.682	75	122	197	39	150	1	35	67	31	372	3.1	0.6	5.9
90-91–Charlotte	72	6	1552	243	457	.532	0	2	.000	164	248	.661	136	243	379	44	211	3	48	102	67	650	5.3	0.6	9.0
91-92–Charlotte	82	71	2223	423	799	.529	0	2	.000	196	285	.688	177	403	580	131	273	4	59	140	69	1042	7.1	1.6	12.7
92-93–Charlotte	75	5	1475	203	384	.529	0	3	.000	102	169	.604	108	245	353	68	237	3	48	64	55	508	4.7	0.9	6.8
93-94–Charlotte	77	18	1644	233	445	.524	0	0	–	126	195	.646	105	253	358	95	229	3	59	79	46	592	4.6	1.2	7.7
94-95–Charlotte	21	0	409	47	100	.470	0	1	.000	31	51	.608	21	54	75	17	64	1	7	22	15	125	3.6	0.8	6.0
95-96–Vanc.-Orlando	25	14	570	91	190	.479	0	0	–	47	78	.603	35	79	114	14	75	0	10	40	11	229	4.6	0.6	9.2
Reg. Season Totals	494	130	9927	1536	2956	.520	1	12	.083	850	1309	.649	744	1583	2327	444	1419	16	290	602	327	3923	4.7	0.9	7.9
Playoff Totals	13	0	245	27	54	.500	0	0	–	14	29	.483	24	27	51	13	34	0	7	12	1	68	3.9	1.0	5.2

Gayda, Edward C. (Ed) b. May 11, 1927 Ht. 6-4 Wt. 210 College: Washington State

SEASON–TEAM	G	GS	MIN	FGM	FGA	PCT	3FGM	3FGA	PCT	FTM	FTA	PCT	O-RB	D-RB	TOT	AST	PF	DQ	STL	TO	BLK	PTS	RPG	APG	PPG
50-51–Tri-Cities	14	–	–	18	42	.429	–	–	–	18	23	.783	–	–	38	13	32	0	–	–	–	54	2.7	0.9	3.9
Reg. Season Totals	14	–	–	18	42	.429	–	–	–	18	23	.783	–	–	38	13	32	0	–	–	–	54	2.7	0.9	3.9

Gaze, Andrew b. July 24, 1965 Ht. 6-6 Wt. 210 College: Seton Hall

SEASON–TEAM	G	GS	MIN	FGM	FGA	PCT	3FGM	3FGA	PCT	FTM	FTA	PCT	O-RB	D-RB	TOT	AST	PF	DQ	STL	TO	BLK	PTS	RPG	APG	PPG
93-94–Washington	7	0	70	8	17	.471	4	8	.500	2	2	1.000	1	6	7	5	9	0	2	3	1	22	1.0	0.7	3.1
98-99–San Antonio	19	0	58	8	25	.320	5	16	.313	0	0	–	2	3	5	6	7	0	2	4	1	21	0.3	0.3	1.1
Reg. Season Totals	26	0	128	16	42	.381	9	24	.375	2	2	1.000	3	9	12	11	16	0	4	7	2	43	0.5	0.4	1.7

Geary, Reginald Elliot (Reggie) b. August 31, 1973 Ht. 6-2 Wt. 190 College: Arizona

SEASON–TEAM	G	GS	MIN	FGM	FGA	PCT	3FGM	3FGA	PCT	FTM	FTA	PCT	O-RB	D-RB	TOT	AST	PF	DQ	STL	TO	BLK	PTS	RPG	APG	PPG
96-97–Cleveland	39	0	246	22	58	.379	8	21	.381	5	11	.455	4	11	15	36	36	0	13	15	2	57	0.4	0.9	1.5
97-98–San Antonio	62	2	685	56	169	.331	12	40	.300	28	56	.500	19	48	67	74	95	0	37	42	12	152	1.1	1.2	2.5
Reg. Season Totals	101	2	931	78	227	.344	20	61	.328	33	67	.493	23	59	82	110	131	0	50	57	14	209	0.8	1.1	2.1
Playoff Totals	7	0	46	3	7	.429	1	4	.250	2	4	.500	0	2	2	6	10	0	1	2	0	9	0.3	0.9	1.3

Geiger, Matthew Allen (Matt) b. September 10, 1969 Ht. 7-1 Wt. 248 College: Auburn; Georgia Tech

SEASON–TEAM	G	GS	MIN	FGM	FGA	PCT	3FGM	3FGA	PCT	FTM	FTA	PCT	O-RB	D-RB	TOT	AST	PF	DQ	STL	TO	BLK	PTS	RPG	APG	PPG
92-93–Miami	48	2	554	76	145	.524	0	4	.000	62	92	.674	46	74	120	14	123	6	15	36	18	214	2.5	0.3	4.5
93-94–Miami	72	0	1199	202	352	.574	1	5	.200	116	149	.779	119	184	303	32	201	2	36	61	29	521	4.2	0.4	7.2
94-95–Miami	74	43	1712	260	485	.536	4	10	.400	93	143	.650	146	267	413	55	245	5	41	113	51	617	5.6	0.7	8.3
95-96–Charlotte	77	50	2349	357	666	.536	3	8	.375	149	205	.727	201	448	649	60	290	11	46	137	63	866	8.4	0.8	11.2
96-97–Charlotte	49	13	1044	171	350	.489	6	20	.300	89	127	.701	100	158	258	38	153	1	20	67	27	437	5.3	0.8	8.9
97-98–Charlotte	78	42	1839	358	709	.505	1	11	.091	168	236	.712	196	325	521	78	191	1	68	111	87	885	6.7	1.0	11.3
98-99–Philadelphia	50	40	1540	266	555	.479	1	5	.200	141	177	.797	137	225	362	58	157	2	39	101	40	674	7.2	1.2	13.5
99-00–Philadelphia	65	20	1406	260	589	.441	0	4	.000	109	140	.779	154	233	387	39	194	1	29	91	22	629	6.0	0.6	9.7
Reg. Season Totals	513	210	11643	1950	3851	.506	16	67	.239	927	1269	.730	1099	1914	3013	374	1554	29	294	717	337	4843	5.9	0.7	9.4
Playoff Totals	25	8	431	70	157	.446	0	1	.000	47	58	.810	47	71	118	11	60	0	16	21	9	187	4.7	0.4	7.5

George, Devean Jamar b. August 29, 1977 Ht. 6-8 Wt. 220 College: Augsburg

SEASON–TEAM	G	GS	MIN	FGM	FGA	PCT	3FGM	3FGA	PCT	FTM	FTA	PCT	O-RB	D-RB	TOT	AST	PF	DQ	STL	TO	BLK	PTS	RPG	APG	PPG
99-00–L.A. Lakers	49	1	345	56	144	.389	16	47	.340	27	41	.659	29	46	75	12	54	0	10	21	4	155	1.5	0.2	3.2
Reg. Season Totals	49	1	345	56	144	.389	16	47	.340	27	41	.659	29	46	75	12	54	0	10	21	4	155	1.5	0.2	3.2
Playoff Totals	9	0	45	7	19	.368	2	10	.200	6	11	.545	4	6	10	2	5	0	1	3	0	22	1.1	0.2	2.4

George, John Edwin Jr. (Jack) b. November 13, 1928 d. January 30, 1989 Ht. 6-3 Wt. 190 College: Notre Dame; La Salle

SEASON–TEAM	G	GS	MIN	FGM	FGA	PCT	3FGM	3FGA	PCT	FTM	FTA	PCT	O-RB	D-RB	TOT	AST	PF	DQ	STL	TO	BLK	PTS	RPG	APG	PPG
53-54–Philadelphia	71	–	2648	259	736	.352	–	–	–	157	266	.590	–	–	386	312	210	4	–	–	–	675	5.4	4.4	9.5
54-55–Philadelphia	68	–	2480	291	756	.385	–	–	–	192	291	.660	–	–	302	359	191	2	–	–	–	774	4.4	5.3	11.4
55-56–Philadelphia	72	–	2840	352	940	.374	–	–	–	296	391	.757	–	–	313	457	202	1	–	–	–	1000	4.3	6.3	13.9
56-57–Philadelphia	67	–	2229	253	750	.337	–	–	–	200	293	.683	–	–	318	307	165	3	–	–	–	706	4.7	4.6	10.5
57-58–Philadelphia	72	–	1910	232	627	.370	–	–	–	178	242	.736	–	–	288	234	140	1	–	–	–	642	4.0	3.3	8.9
58-59–Phil.-N.Y.	71	–	1881	233	674	.346	–	–	–	153	203	.754	–	–	293	221	149	0	–	–	–	619	4.1	3.1	8.7
59-60–New York	69	–	1604	250	650	.385	–	–	–	155	202	.767	–	–	197	240	148	1	–	–	–	655	2.9	3.5	9.5
60-61–New York	16	–	268	31	93	.333	–	–	–	20	30	.667	–	–	32	39	37	0	–	–	–	82	2.0	2.4	5.1
Reg. Season Totals	506	–	15860	1901	5226	.364	–	–	–	1351	1918	.704	–	–	2129	2169	1242	12	–	–	–	5153	4.2	4.3	10.2
Playoff Totals	22	–	776	87	226	.385	–	–	–	64	85	.753	–	–	96	92	60	2	–	–	–	238	4.4	4.2	10.8
All-Star Totals	2	–	42	5	13	.385	–	–	–	4	4	1.000	–	–	4	7	2	0	–	–	–	14	2.0	3.5	7.0

George, Tate Claude b. May 29, 1968 Ht. 6-5 Wt. 208 College: Connecticut

SEASON–TEAM	G	GS	MIN	FGM	FGA	PCT	3FGM	3FGA	PCT	FTM	FTA	PCT	O-RB	D-RB	TOT	AST	PF	DQ	STL	TO	BLK	PTS	RPG	APG	PPG
90-91–New Jersey	56	11	594	80	193	.415	0	2	.000	32	40	.800	19	28	47	104	58	0	25	42	5	192	0.8	1.9	3.4
91-92–New Jersey	70	2	1037	165	386	.427	1	6	.167	87	106	.821	36	69	105	162	98	0	41	82	3	418	1.5	2.3	6.0
92-93–New Jersey	48	1	380	51	135	.378	0	5	.000	20	24	.833	9	18	27	59	25	0	10	31	3	122	0.6	1.2	2.5
94-95–Phil.-Milw.	3	0	8	1	3	.333	0	1	.000	2	2	1.000	1	0	1	0	1	0	0	2	0	4	0.3	0.0	1.3
Reg. Season Totals	177	14	2019	297	717	.414	1	14	.071	141	172	.820	65	115	180	325	182	0	76	157	11	736	1.0	1.8	4.2
Playoff Totals	6	0	66	9	30	.300	0	0	–	1	3	.333	1	2	3	14	9	0	4	5	1	19	0.5	2.3	3.2

Gerard, Daniel James (Gus) b. July 27, 1953 Ht. 6-8 Wt. 200 College: Virginia

SEASON–TEAM	G	GS	MIN	FGM	FGA	PCT	3FGM	3FGA	PCT	FTM	FTA	PCT	O-RB	D-RB	TOT	AST	PF	DQ	STL	TO	BLK	PTS	RPG	APG	PPG
74-75–St. Louis (A)	84	–	2702	554	1220	.454	1	6	.167	206	279	.738	282	373	655	189	274	–	63	207	111	1315	7.8	2.3	15.7
75-76–St. L.-Denver (A)	82	–	1727	332	795	.418	4	9	.444	175	238	.735	141	296	437	147	238	–	69	186	72	843	5.3	1.8	10.3
76-77–Denver-Buffalo	65	–	1048	201	454	.443	–	–	–	78	117	.667	89	128	217	92	164	1	44	–	62	480	3.3	1.4	7.4
77-78–Buffalo-Detroit	57	–	890	170	395	.430	–	–	–	75	108	.694	55	105	160	53	109	1	36	61	25	415	2.8	0.9	7.3
78-79–Detroit-K.C.	58	–	465	84	194	.433	–	–	–	50	91	.549	40	58	98	21	74	1	20	36	13	218	1.7	0.4	3.8
79-80–Kansas City	73	–	869	159	348	.457	1	3	.333	66	100	.660	77	100	177	43	96	1	41	49	26	385	2.4	0.6	5.3
80-81–K.C.-S.A.	27	–	252	41	111	.369	0	4	.000	27	40	.675	30	37	67	15	41	0	10	15	9	109	2.5	0.6	4.0
Reg. NBA Totals	280	–	3524	655	1502	.436	1	7	.143	296	456	.649	291	428	719	224	484	4	151	161	135	1607	2.6	0.8	5.7
Reg. ABA Totals	166	–	4429	886	2015	.440	5	15	.333	381	517	.737	423	669	1092	336	512	–	132	393	183	2158	6.6	2.0	13.0
NBA Playoff Totals	8	–	50	8	19	.421	0	0	–	4	8	.500	6	10	16	2	8	0	1	5	1	20	2.0	0.3	2.5
ABA Playoff Totals	23	–	410	59	150	.393	0	1	.000	25	38	.658	30	53	83	28	58	–	14	47	14	143	3.6	1.2	6.2

Gervin, Derrick Eugene b. March 28, 1963 Ht. 6-8 Wt. 205 College: Texas-San Antonio

SEASON–TEAM	G	GS	MIN	FGM	FGA	PCT	3FGM	3FGA	PCT	FTM	FTA	PCT	O-RB	D-RB	TOT	AST	PF	DQ	STL	TO	BLK	PTS	RPG	APG	PPG
89-90–New Jersey	21	0	339	93	197	.472	0	3	.000	65	89	.730	29	36	65	8	47	0	20	12	7	251	3.1	0.4	12.0
90-91–New Jersey	56	4	743	164	394	.416	7	28	.250	90	114	.789	40	70	110	30	88	0	19	45	19	425	2.0	0.5	7.6
Reg. Season Totals	77	4	1082	257	591	.435	7	31	.226	155	203	.764	69	106	175	38	135	0	39	57	26	676	2.3	0.5	8.8

Gervin, George (Ice, Iceman) b. April 27, 1952 Ht. 6-7 Wt. 185 College: Long Beach State; Eastern Michigan HOF: 1996

SEASON–TEAM	G	GS	MIN	FGM	FGA	PCT	3FGM	3FGA	PCT	FTM	FTA	PCT	O-RB	D-RB	TOT	AST	PF	DQ	STL	TO	BLK	PTS	RPG	APG	PPG
72-73–Virginia (A)	30	–	689	161	341	.472	6	26	.231	96	118	.814	34	94	128	34	72	0	–	54	–	424	4.3	1.1	14.1
73-74–Vir.-S.A. (A)	74	–	2511	672	1426	.471	8	56	.143	378	464	.815	170	454	624	142	264	–	101	252	120	1730	8.4	1.9	23.4
74-75–San Antonio (A)	84	–	3113	784	1655	.474	17	55	.309	380	458	.830	247	450	697	207	295	–	131	249	138	1965	8.3	2.5	23.4
75-76–San Antonio (A)	81	–	2748	706	1414	.499	14	55	.255	342	399	.857	179	367	546	201	288	–	110	217	119	1768	6.7	2.5	21.8
76-77–San Antonio	82	–	2705	726	1335	.544	–	–	–	443	532	.833	134	320	454	238	286	12	105	–	104	1895	5.5	2.9	23.1
77-78–San Antonio	82	–	2857	864	1611	.536	–	–	–	504	607	.830	118	302	420	302	255	3	136	306	110	2232	5.1	3.7	27.2
78-79–San Antonio	80	–	2888	947	1749	.541	–	–	–	471	570	.826	142	258	400	219	275	5	137	286	91	2365	5.0	2.7	29.6
79-80–San Antonio	78	–	2934	1024	1940	.528	32	102	.314	505	593	.852	154	249	403	202	208	0	110	254	79	2585	5.2	2.6	33.1
80-81–San Antonio	82	–	2765	850	1729	.492	9	35	.257	512	620	.826	126	293	419	260	212	4	94	251	56	2221	5.1	3.2	27.1
81-82–San Antonio	79	79	2817	993	1987	.500	10	36	.278	555	642	.864	138	254	392	187	215	2	77	210	45	2551	5.0	2.4	32.3
82-83–San Antonio	78	78	2830	757	1553	.487	12	33	.364	517	606	.853	111	246	357	264	243	5	88	247	67	2043	4.6	3.4	26.2
83-84–San Antonio	76	76	2584	765	1561	.490	10	24	.417	427	507	.842	106	207	313	220	219	3	79	224	47	1967	4.1	2.9	25.9
84-85–San Antonio	72	69	2091	600	1182	.508	0	10	.000	324	384	.844	79	155	234	178	208	2	66	198	48	1524	3.3	2.5	21.2
85-86–Chicago	82	75	2065	519	1100	.472	4	19	.211	283	322	.879	78	137	215	144	210	4	49	161	23	1325	2.6	1.8	16.2
Reg. NBA Totals	791	377	26536	8045	15747	.511	77	259	.297	4541	5383	.844	1186	2421	3607	2214	2331	40	941	2137	670	20708	4.6	2.8	26.2
Reg. ABA Totals	269	–	9061	2323	4836	.480	45	192	.234	1196	1439	.831	630	1365	1995	584	919	0	342	772	377	5887	7.4	2.2	21.9
NBA Playoff Totals	59	25	2202	622	1225	.508	0	13	.000	348	424	.821	110	231	341	186	207	5	69	187	51	1592	5.8	3.2	27.0
ABA Playoff Totals	25	–	990	237	491	.483	5	21	.238	152	186	.817	78	122	238	54	87	0	15	65	30	631	9.5	2.2	25.2
NBA All-Star Totals	9	7	215	54	108	.500	1	1	1.000	28	36	.778	9	24	33	12	25	0	16	20	9	137	3.7	1.3	15.2

Getchell, Charles Gorham (Gorham) b. August 14, 1920 d. July 1980 Ht. 6-6 Wt. 215 College: Temple

SEASON–TEAM	G	GS	MIN	FGM	FGA	PCT	3FGM	3FGA	PCT	FTM	FTA	PCT	O-RB	D-RB	TOT	AST	PF	DQ	STL	TO	BLK	PTS	RPG	APG	PPG
46-47–Pittsburgh	16	–	–	0	8	.000	–	–	–	5	5	1.000	–	–	–	0	5	–	–	–	–	5	–	0.0	0.3
Reg. Season Totals	16	–	–	0	8	.000	–	–	–	5	5	1.000	–	–	–	0	5	–	–	–	–	5	–	0.0	0.3

Gianelli, John Arec b. June 10, 1950 Ht. 6-10 Wt. 220 College: U. of Pacific

SEASON–TEAM	G	GS	MIN	FGM	FGA	PCT	3FGM	3FGA	PCT	FTM	FTA	PCT	O-RB	D-RB	TOT	AST	PF	DQ	STL	TO	BLK	PTS	RPG	APG	PPG
72-73–New York	52	–	516	79	175	.451	–	–	–	23	33	.697	–	–	150	25	72	0	–	–	–	181	2.9	0.5	3.5
73-74–New York	70	–	1423	208	434	.479	–	–	–	92	121	.760	110	233	343	77	159	1	23	–	42	508	4.9	1.1	7.3
74-75–New York	80	–	2797	343	726	.472	–	–	–	135	195	.692	214	475	689	163	263	3	38	–	118	821	8.6	2.0	10.3
75-76–New York	82	–	2332	325	687	.473	–	–	–	114	160	.713	187	365	552	115	194	1	25	–	62	764	6.7	1.4	9.3
76-77–N.Y.-K-Buffalo	76	–	1913	257	579	.444	–	–	–	90	125	.720	154	321	475	83	171	0	35	–	98	604	6.3	1.1	7.9
77-78–Milwaukee	82	–	2327	307	629	.488	–	–	–	79	123	.642	166	343	509	192	189	4	54	147	92	693	6.2	2.3	8.5
78-79–Milwaukee	82	–	2057	256	527	.486	–	–	–	72	102	.706	122	286	408	160	196	4	44	106	57	584	5.0	2.0	7.1
79-80–Utah	17	–	285	23	66	.348	0	0	–	9	16	.563	14	48	62	17	26	0	6	22	7	55	3.6	1.0	3.2
Reg. Season Totals	541	–	13650	1798	3823	.470	0	0	–	614	875	.702	967	2071	3188	832	1270	13	225	275	476	4210	5.9	1.5	7.8
Playoff Totals	31	–	776	82	189	.434	0	0	–	44	61	.721	60	100	173	40	81	0	12	13	21	208	5.6	1.3	6.7

Gibbs, Dick b. December 20, 1948 Ht. 6-5 Wt. 210 College: Burlington Co. (N.J). Coll. (J.C.); Texas-El Paso

SEASON–TEAM	G	GS	MIN	FGM	FGA	PCT	3FGM	3FGA	PCT	FTM	FTA	PCT	O-RB	D-RB	TOT	AST	PF	DQ	STL	TO	BLK	PTS	RPG	APG	PPG
71-72–Houston	64	–	757	90	265	.340	–	–	–	55	66	.833	–	–	140	51	127	0	–	–	–	235	2.2	0.0	3.7
72-73–Hou.-K.C.-Omaha	67	–	735	80	222	.360	–	–	–	47	63	.746	–	–	94	62	114	1	–	–	–	207	1.4	0.9	3.1
73-74–Seattle	71	–	1528	302	700	.431	–	–	–	162	201	.806	91	132	223	79	195	1	39	–	18	766	3.1	1.1	10.8
74-75–Washington	59	–	424	74	190	.389	–	–	–	48	64	.750	26	35	61	19	60	0	12	–	3	196	1.0	0.3	3.3
75-76–Buffalo	72	–	866	129	301	.429	–	–	–	77	93	.828	42	64	106	49	133	2	16	–	14	335	1.5	0.7	4.7
Reg. Season Totals	333	–	4310	675	1678	.402	–	–	–	389	487	.799	159	231	624	260	629	4	67	–	35	1739	1.9	0.8	5.2
Playoff Totals	11	–	40	7	19	.368	–	–	–	4	4	1.000	0	2	2	4	10	0	3	–	0	18	0.2	0.4	1.6

Gibson, Dee Jr. (Gibby) b. August 25, 1923 Ht. 5-11 Wt. 175 College: Western Kentucky

SEASON–TEAM	G	GS	MIN	FGM	FGA	PCT	3FGM	3FGA	PCT	FTM	FTA	PCT	O-RB	D-RB	TOT	AST	PF	DQ	STL	TO	BLK	PTS	RPG	APG	PPG
48-49–Tri-Cities (N)	64	–	–	94	–	–	–	–	–	113	177	.638	–	–	–	–	137	–	–	–	–	301	–	–	4.7
49-50–Tri-Cities	44	–	–	77	245	.314	–	–	–	127	177	.718	–	–	–	126	113	–	–	–	–	281	–	2.9	6.4
Reg. NBA Totals	44	–	–	77	245	.314	–	–	–	127	177	.718	–	–	–	126	113	–	–	–	–	281	–	2.9	6.4
Reg. NBL Totals	64	–	–	94	–	–	–	–	–	113	177	.638	–	–	–	–	137	–	–	–	–	301	–	–	4.7
NBA Playoff Totals	3	–	–	4	22	.364	–	–	–	3	5	.600	–	–	–	4	11	–	–	–	–	11	–	0.7	3.7
NBL Playoff Totals	6	–	–	19	–	–	–	–	–	19	32	.594	–	–	–	–	19	–	–	–	–	57	–	–	9.5

Gibson, Melvin L. (Mel) b. December 30, 1940 Ht. 6-3 Wt. 180 College: Western Carolina

SEASON–TEAM	G	GS	MIN	FGM	FGA	PCT	3FGM	3FGA	PCT	FTM	FTA	PCT	O-RB	D-RB	TOT	AST	PF	DQ	STL	TO	BLK	PTS	RPG	APG	PPG
63-64–Los Angeles	9	–	53	6	20	.300	–	–	–	1	2	.500	–	–	4	6	10	0	–	–	–	13	0.4	0.7	1.4
Reg. Season Totals	9	–	53	6	20	.300	–	–	–	1	2	.500	–	–	4	6	10	0	–	–	–	13	0.4	0.7	1.4

Gibson, Michael Jerome (Mike) b. October 27, 1960 Ht. 6-11 Wt. 215 College: South Carolina-Spartanburg

SEASON–TEAM	G	GS	MIN	FGM	FGA	PCT	3FGM	3FGA	PCT	FTM	FTA	PCT	O-RB	D-RB	TOT	AST	PF	DQ	STL	TO	BLK	PTS	RPG	APG	PPG
83-84–Washington	32	0	229	21	55	.382	0	0	–	11	17	.647	29	37	66	9	30	1	5	14	7	53	2.1	0.3	1.7
85-86–Detroit	32	0	161	20	51	.392	0	0	–	8	11	.727	15	25	40	5	35	0	8	6	4	48	1.3	0.2	1.5
Reg. Season Totals	64	0	390	41	106	.387	0	0	–	19	28	.679	44	62	106	14	65	1	13	20	11	101	1.7	0.2	1.6

Gibson, Ward B. Jr. (Hoot) b. December 5, 1921 d. February 1, 1958 Ht. 6-5 Wt. 215 College: Creighton

SEASON–TEAM	G	GS	MIN	FGM	FGA	PCT	3FGM	3FGA	PCT	FTM	FTA	PCT	O-RB	D-RB	TOT	AST	PF	DQ	STL	TO	BLK	PTS	RPG	APG	PPG
48-49–Den.-Tri-Cit (N)	62	–	–	291	–	–	–	–	–	223	334	.668	–	–	–	–	180	–	–	–	–	805	–	–	13.0
49-50–Boston-Wat.	32	–	–	67	195	.344	–	–	–	42	64	.656	–	–	–	37	106	–	–	–	–	176	–	1.2	5.5
Reg. NBA Totals	32	–	–	67	195	.344	–	–	–	42	64	.656	–	–	–	37	106	–	–	–	–	176	–	1.2	5.5
Reg. NBL Totals	62	–	–	291	–	–	–	–	–	223	334	.668	–	–	–	–	180	–	–	–	–	805	–	–	13.0
NBL Playoff Totals	6	–	–	9	–	–	–	–	–	6	9	.667	–	–	–	–	16	–	–	–	–	24	–	–	4.0

Gill, Kendall Cedric (K.G.) b. May 25, 1968 Ht. 6-5 Wt. 216 College: Illinois

SEASON–TEAM	G	GS	MIN	FGM	FGA	PCT	3FGM	3FGA	PCT	FTM	FTA	PCT	O-RB	D-RB	TOT	AST	PF	DQ	STL	TO	BLK	PTS	RPG	APG	PPG
90-91–Charlotte	82	36	1944	376	836	.450	2	14	.143	152	182	.835	105	158	263	303	186	0	104	163	39	906	3.2	3.7	11.0
91-92–Charlotte	79	79	2906	666	1427	.467	6	25	.240	284	381	.745	165	237	402	329	237	1	154	180	46	1622	5.1	4.2	20.5
92-93–Charlotte	69	67	2430	463	1032	.449	17	62	.274	224	290	.772	120	220	340	268	191	2	98	174	36	1167	4.9	3.9	16.9
93-94–Seattle	79	77	2435	429	969	.443	38	120	.317	215	275	.782	91	177	268	275	194	1	151	143	32	1111	3.4	3.5	14.1
94-95–Seattle	73	58	2125	392	858	.457	63	171	.368	155	209	.742	99	191	290	192	186	0	117	138	28	1002	4.0	2.6	13.7
95-96–Cha.-N.J.	47	46	1683	246	524	.469	26	79	.329	138	176	.784	72	160	232	260	131	2	64	131	24	656	4.9	5.5	14.0
96-97–New Jersey	82	81	3199	644	1453	.443	74	220	.336	427	536	.797	183	316	499	326	225	2	154	218	46	1789	6.1	4.0	21.8
97-98–New Jersey	81	81	2733	418	974	.429	26	101	.257	225	327	.688	112	279	391	200	268	4	156	124	64	1087	4.8	2.5	13.4
98-99–New Jersey	50	47	1606	236	593	.398	2	17	.118	114	167	.683	61	183	244	123	162	4	134	71	26	588	4.9	2.5	11.8
99-00–New Jersey	76	75	2355	396	956	.414	20	78	.256	181	255	.710	82	201	283	210	211	3	139	89	41	993	3.7	2.8	13.1
Reg. Season Totals	718	647	23416	4266	9622	.443	274	887	.309	2115	2798	.756	1090	2122	3212	2486	1991	19	1271	1431	382	10921	4.5	3.5	15.2
Playoff Totals	21	17	678	118	287	.411	5	23	.217	50	72	.694	37	50	87	49	62	1	35	33	9	291	4.1	2.3	13.9

Gillery, Benjamin (Ben) b. September 19, 1965 Ht. 7-0 Wt. 235 College: Hutchinson (Kan.) C.C.; Georgetown

SEASON–TEAM	G	GS	MIN	FGM	FGA	PCT	3FGM	3FGA	PCT	FTM	FTA	PCT	O-RB	D-RB	TOT	AST	PF	DQ	STL	TO	BLK	PTS	RPG	APG	PPG
88-89–Sacramento	24	0	84	6	19	.316	0	0	–	13	23	.565	7	16	23	2	29	0	2	5	4	25	1.0	0.1	1.0
Reg. Season Totals	24	0	84	6	19	.316	0	0	–	13	23	.565	7	16	23	2	29	0	2	5	4	25	1.0	0.1	1.0

Gillespie, Jack A. b. October 1, 1947 Ht. 6-9 Wt. 220 College: Montana State

SEASON–TEAM	G	GS	MIN	FGM	FGA	PCT	3FGM	3FGA	PCT	FTM	FTA	PCT	O-RB	D-RB	TOT	AST	PF	DQ	STL	TO	BLK	PTS	RPG	APG	PPG
69-70–New York (A)	2	–	27	0	5	.000	0	0	–	2	2	1.000	–	–	7	0	3	0	–	–	–	2	3.5	0.0	1.0
Reg. ABA Totals	2	–	27	0	5	.000	0	0	–	2	2	1.000	–	–	7	0	3	0	–	–	–	2	3.5	0.0	1.0

Gillette, Gene b. 1921 Ht. 6-2 Wt. 205 College: St. Mary's (CA)

SEASON–TEAM	G	GS	MIN	FGM	FGA	PCT	3FGM	3FGA	PCT	FTM	FTA	PCT	O-RB	D-RB	TOT	AST	PF	DQ	STL	TO	BLK	PTS	RPG	APG	PPG
46-47–Washington	14	–	–	1	11	.091	–	–	–	6	9	.667	–	–	–	2	13	–	–	–	–	8	–	0.1	0.6
Reg. Season Totals	14	–	–	1	11	.091	–	–	–	6	9	.667	–	–	–	2	13	–	–	–	–	8	–	0.1	0.6

Gilliam, Armen Louis (The Hammer) b. May 28, 1964 Ht. 6-9 Wt. 260 College: Nevada-Las Vegas

SEASON–TEAM	G	GS	MIN	FGM	FGA	PCT	3FGM	3FGA	PCT	FTM	FTA	PCT	O-RB	D-RB	TOT	AST	PF	DQ	STL	TO	BLK	PTS	RPG	APG	PPG
87-88–Phoenix	55	53	1807	342	720	.475	0	0	–	131	193	.679	134	300	434	72	143	1	58	123	29	815	7.9	1.3	14.8
88-89–Phoenix	74	60	2120	468	930	.503	0	0	–	240	323	.743	165	376	541	52	176	2	54	140	27	1176	7.3	0.7	15.9
89-90–Phoenix-Cha.	76	66	2426	484	940	.515	0	2	.000	303	419	.723	211	388	599	99	212	4	69	183	51	1271	7.9	1.3	16.7
90-91–Cha.-Phil.	75	75	2644	487	1001	.487	0	2	.000	268	329	.815	220	378	598	105	185	2	69	174	53	1242	8.0	1.4	16.6
91-92–Philadelphia	81	81	2771	512	1001	.511	0	2	.000	343	425	.807	234	426	660	118	176	1	51	166	85	1367	8.1	1.5	16.9
92-93–Philadelphia	80	26	1742	359	774	.464	0	1	.000	274	325	.843	136	336	472	116	123	0	37	157	54	992	5.9	1.5	12.4
93-94–New Jersey	82	5	1969	348	682	.510	0	1	.000	274	361	.759	197	303	500	69	129	0	38	106	61	970	6.1	0.8	11.8
94-95–New Jersey	82	30	2472	455	905	.503	0	2	.000	302	392	.770	192	421	613	99	171	0	67	152	89	1212	7.5	1.2	14.8
95-96–New Jersey	78	76	2856	576	1216	.474	0	1	.000	277	350	.791	241	472	713	140	180	1	73	177	53	1429	9.1	1.8	18.3
96-97–Milwaukee	80	25	2050	246	522	.471	0	0	–	199	259	.768	136	361	497	53	206	0	61	105	40	691	6.2	0.7	8.6
97-98–Milwaukee	82	25	2114	327	676	.484	0	4	.000	267	333	.802	146	293	439	104	177	1	65	148	37	921	5.4	1.3	11.2
98-99–Milwaukee	34	5	668	101	223	.453	0	1	.000	79	101	.782	33	93	126	19	48	0	22	36	12	281	3.7	0.6	8.3
99-00–Utah	50	0	782	133	305	.436	0	1	.000	67	86	.779	72	137	209	42	83	0	12	55	16	333	4.2	0.8	6.7
Reg. Season Totals	929	527	26421	4838	9895	.489	0	17	.000	3024	3896	.776	2117	4284	6401	1088	2009	12	676	1722	607	12700	6.9	1.2	13.7
Playoff Totals	34	8	692	111	250	.444	0	1	.000	80	102	.784	39	117	156	18	53	0	14	40	20	302	4.6	0.5	8.9

Gilliam, Herman L. Jr. (Herm) b. May 5, 1946 Ht. 6-3 Wt. 190 College: Purdue

SEASON–TEAM	G	GS	MIN	FGM	FGA	PCT	3FGM	3FGA	PCT	FTM	FTA	PCT	O-RB	D-RB	TOT	AST	PF	DQ	STL	TO	BLK	PTS	RPG	APG	PPG
69-70–Cincinnati	57	–	1161	179	441	.406	–	–	–	68	91	.747	–	–	215	178	163	6	–	–	–	426	3.8	3.1	7.5
70-71–Buffalo	80	–	2082	378	896	.422	–	–	–	142	189	.751	–	–	334	291	246	4	–	–	–	898	4.2	3.6	11.2
71-72–Atlanta	82	–	2337	345	774	.446	–	–	–	145	173	.838	–	–	335	377	232	3	–	–	–	835	4.1	4.6	10.2
72-73–Atlanta	76	–	2741	471	1007	.468	–	–	–	123	150	.820	–	–	399	482	257	8	–	–	–	1065	5.3	6.3	14.0
73-74–Atlanta	62	–	2003	384	846	.454	–	–	–	106	134	.791	61	206	267	355	190	5	134	–	18	874	4.3	5.7	14.1
74-75–Atlanta	60	–	1393	314	736	.427	–	–	–	94	113	.832	76	128	204	170	124	1	77	–	13	722	3.4	2.8	12.0
75-76–Seattle	81	–	1644	299	676	.442	–	–	–	90	116	.776	56	164	220	202	139	0	82	–	12	688	2.7	2.5	8.5
76-77–Portland	80	–	1665	326	744	.438	–	–	–	92	120	.767	64	137	201	170	168	1	76	–	6	744	2.5	2.1	9.3
Reg. Season Totals	578	–	15026	2696	6120	.441	–	–	–	860	1086	.792	257	635	2175	2225	1519	28	369	–	49	6252	3.8	3.8	10.8
Playoff Totals	36	–	751	120	302	.397	–	–	–	29	36	.806	10	21	93	108	73	1	19	–	1	269	2.6	3.0	7.5

Gilmore, Artis (The A. Train) b. September 21, 1948 Ht. 7-2 Wt. 240 College: Gardner-Webb; Jacksonville

SEASON–TEAM	G	GS	MIN	FGM	FGA	PCT	3FGM	3FGA	PCT	FTM	FTA	PCT	O-RB	D-RB	TOT	AST	PF	DQ	STL	TO	BLK	PTS	RPG	APG	PPG
71-72–Kentucky (A)	84	–	3666	806	1348	.598	0	0	–	391	605	.646	421	1070	1491	230	280	–	–	335	422	2003	17.8	2.7	23.8
72-73–Kentucky (A)	84	–	3502	687	1228	.559	1	2	.500	368	572	.643	449	1027	1476	295	302	0	–	286	259	1743	17.6	3.5	20.8
73-74–Kentucky (A)	84	–	3502	621	1260	.493	0	3	.000	326	489	.667	478	1060	1538	329	302	–	57	319	287	1568	18.3	3.9	18.7
74-75–Kentucky (A)	84	–	3493	784	1351	.580	1	2	.500	412	592	.696	427	934	1361	208	318	–	63	344	258	1981	16.2	2.5	23.6
75-76–Kentucky (A)	84	–	3286	773	1401	.552	0	0	–	521	764	.682	402	901	1303	211	341	–	58	295	205	2067	15.5	2.5	24.6
76-77–Chicago	82	–	2877	570	1091	.522	–	–	–	387	586	.660	313	757	1070	199	266	4	44	–	203	1527	13.0	2.4	18.6
77-78–Chicago	82	–	3067	704	1260	.559	–	–	–	471	669	.704	318	753	1071	263	261	4	42	366	181	1879	13.1	3.2	22.9
78-79–Chicago	82	–	3265	753	1310	.575	–	–	–	434	587	.739	293	750	1043	274	280	2	50	310	156	1940	12.7	3.3	23.7
79-80–Chicago	48	–	1568	305	513	.595	0	0	–	245	344	.712	108	324	432	133	167	5	29	133	59	855	9.0	2.8	17.8
80-81–Chicago	82	–	2832	547	816	.670	0	0	–	375	532	.705	220	608	828	172	295	2	47	236	198	1469	10.1	2.1	17.9
81-82–Chicago	82	82	2796	546	837	.652	1	1	1.000	424	552	.768	224	611	835	136	287	4	49	227	220	1517	10.2	1.7	18.5
82-83–San Antonio	82	82	2797	556	888	.626	0	6	.000	367	496	.740	299	685	984	126	273	4	40	254	192	1479	12.0	1.5	18.0
83-84–San Antonio	64	59	2034	351	556	.631	0	3	.000	280	390	.718	213	449	662	70	229	4	36	149	132	982	10.3	1.1	15.3
84-85–San Antonio	81	81	2756	532	854	.623	0	2	.000	484	646	.749	231	615	846	131	306	4	40	241	173	1548	10.4	1.6	19.1
85-86–San Antonio	71	71	2395	423	684	.618	0	1	.000	338	482	.701	166	434	600	102	239	3	39	186	108	1184	8.5	1.4	16.7
86-87–San Antonio	82	74	2405	346	580	.597	0	0	–	242	356	.680	185	394	579	150	235	2	39	178	95	934	7.1	1.8	11.4
87-88–Chicago-Boston	71	27	893	99	181	.547	0	0	–	67	128	.523	69	142	211	21	148	0	15	67	30	265	3.0	0.3	3.7
Reg. NBA Totals	909	476	29685	5732	9570	.599	1	13	.077	4114	5768	.713	2639	6522	9161	1777	2986	38	470	2347	1747	15579	10.1	2.0	17.1
Reg. ABA Totals	420	–	17449	3671	6588	.557	2	7	.286	2018	3022	.668	2177	4992	7169	1273	1543	0	178	1579	1431	9362	17.1	3.0	22.3
NBA Playoff Totals	42	19	1152	179	315	.568	0	0	–	134	197	.680	97	239	336	47	113	1	27	81	71	492	8.0	1.1	11.7
ABA Playoff Totals	58	–	2478	490	877	.559	0	1	.000	296	428	.692	284	647	931	185	213	0	33	224	162	1276	16.1	3.2	22.0
NBA All-Star Totals	6	2	95	18	29	.621	0	0	–	15	19	.789	5	14	19	8	18	0	4	5	4	51	3.2	1.3	8.5

Gilmore, Walt b. February 27, 1947 Ht. 6-6 Wt. 225 College: Fort Valley State

SEASON–TEAM	G	GS	MIN	FGM	FGA	PCT	3FGM	3FGA	PCT	FTM	FTA	PCT	O-RB	D-RB	TOT	AST	PF	DQ	STL	TO	BLK	PTS	RPG	APG	PPG
70-71–Portland	27	–	261	23	54	.426	–	–	–	12	26	.462	–	–	73	12	49	1	–	–	–	58	2.7	0.4	2.1
Reg. Season Totals	27	–	261	23	54	.426	–	–	–	12	26	.462	–	–	73	12	49	1	–	–	–	58	2.7	0.4	2.1

Gilmur, Charles E. Jr. (Chuck) b. August 13, 1922 Ht. 6-4 Wt. 225 College: Washington

SEASON–TEAM	G	GS	MIN	FGM	FGA	PCT	3FGM	3FGA	PCT	FTM	FTA	PCT	O-RB	D-RB	TOT	AST	PF	DQ	STL	TO	BLK	PTS	RPG	APG	PPG
46-47–Chicago	51	–	–	76	253	.300	–	–	–	26	66	.394	–	–	–	21	139	–	–	–	–	178	–	0.4	3.5
47-48–Chicago	48	–	–	181	597	.303	–	–	–	97	148	.655	–	–	–	77	231	–	–	–	–	459	–	1.6	9.6
48-49–Chicago	56	–	–	110	281	.391	–	–	–	66	121	.545	–	–	–	125	194	–	–	–	–	286	–	2.2	5.1
49-50–Washington	68	–	–	127	379	.335	–	–	–	164	241	.680	–	–	–	108	275	–	–	–	–	418	–	1.6	6.1
50-51–Washington	16	–	–	17	61	.279	–	–	–	17	32	.531	–	–	75	17	57	3	–	–	–	51	4.7	1.1	3.2
Reg. Season Totals	239	–	–	511	1571	.325	–	–	–	370	608	.609	–	–	75	348	896	3	–	–	–	1392	4.7	1.5	5.8
Playoff Totals	19	–	–	44	353	.235	–	–	–	25	38	.658	–	–	–	28	107	6	–	–	–	113	–	0.8	5.9

Givens, Jack (Goose) b. September 21, 1956 Ht. 6-5 Wt. 205 College: Kentucky

SEASON–TEAM	G	GS	MIN	FGM	FGA	PCT	3FGM	3FGA	PCT	FTM	FTA	PCT	O-RB	D-RB	TOT	AST	PF	DQ	STL	TO	BLK	PTS	RPG	APG	PPG
78-79–Atlanta	74	–	1347	234	564	.415	–	–	–	102	135	.756	98	116	214	83	121	0	72	75	17	570	2.9	1.1	7.7
79-80–Atlanta	82	–	1254	182	473	.385	0	2	.000	106	128	.828	114	128	242	59	132	1	51	59	19	470	3.0	0.7	5.7
Reg. Season Totals	156	–	2601	416	1037	.401	0	2	.000	208	263	.791	212	244	456	142	253	1	123	134	36	1040	2.9	0.9	6.7
Playoff Totals	13	–	117	13	44	.295	0	0	–	3	3	1.000	8	18	26	6	16	0	3	8	2	29	2.0	0.5	2.2

Glamack, George Gregory (Blind Bomber) b. June 7, 1919 d. March 10, 1987 Ht. 6-9 Wt. 230 College: North Carolina

SEASON–TEAM	G	GS	MIN	FGM	FGA	PCT	3FGM	3FGA	PCT	FTM	FTA	PCT	O-RB	D-RB	TOT	AST	PF	DQ	STL	TO	BLK	PTS	RPG	APG	PPG
41-42–Akron (N)	24	–	–	87	–	–	–	–	–	82	–	–	–	–	–	–	–	–	–	–	–	256	–	–	10.7
45-46–Rochester (N)	34	–	–	151	–	–	–	–	–	115	184	.625	–	–	–	–	108	–	–	–	–	417	–	–	12.3
46-47–Rochester (N)	44	–	–	141	–	–	–	–	–	90	135	.667	–	–	–	–	139	–	–	–	–	372	–	–	8.5
47-48–Indianapolis (N)	57	–	–	215	–	–	–	–	–	162	244	.664	–	–	–	–	151	–	–	–	–	592	–	–	10.4
48-49–Hammond (N)	43	–	–	169	–	–	–	–	–	163	216	.755	–	–	–	–	120	–	–	–	–	501	–	–	11.7
48-49–Indianapolis	11	–	–	30	121	.248	–	–	–	42	55	.764	–	–	–	19	28	–	–	–	–	102	–	1.7	9.3
Reg. NBA Totals	11	–	–	30	121	.248	–	–	–	42	55	.764	–	–	–	19	28	–	–	–	–	102	–	1.7	9.3
Reg. NBL Totals	202	–	–	763	–	–	–	–	–	612	779	.680	–	–	–	–	518	–	–	–	–	2138	–	–	10.6
NBL Playoff Totals	26	–	–	109	–	–	–	–	–	88	97	.753	–	–	–	–	77	–	–	–	–	306	–	–	11.8

Glass, Gerald Damon (World Class) b. November 12, 1967 Ht. 6-6 Wt. 225 College: Delta State; Mississippi

SEASON–TEAM	G	GS	MIN	FGM	FGA	PCT	3FGM	3FGA	PCT	FTM	FTA	PCT	O-RB	D-RB	TOT	AST	PF	DQ	STL	TO	BLK	PTS	RPG	APG	PPG
90-91–Minnesota	51	3	606	149	340	.438	2	17	.118	52	76	.684	54	48	102	42	76	2	28	41	9	352	2.0	0.8	6.9
91-92–Minnesota	75	41	1822	383	871	.440	16	54	.296	77	125	.616	107	153	260	175	171	0	66	103	30	859	3.5	2.3	11.5
92-93–Minn.-Detroit	60	5	848	142	339	.419	7	33	.212	25	39	.641	61	81	142	77	104	1	33	35	18	316	2.4	1.3	5.3
95-96–N.J.-Cha.	15	0	71	12	33	.364	1	6	.167	1	1	1.000	6	2	8	4	10	0	3	0	1	26	0.5	0.3	1.7
Reg. Season Totals	201	49	3347	686	1583	.433	26	110	.236	155	241	.643	228	284	512	298	361	3	130	179	58	1553	2.5	1.5	7.7

Glenn, Mike Theodore (Stinger) b. September 10, 1955 Ht. 6-3 Wt. 175 College: Southern Illinois

SEASON–TEAM	G	GS	MIN	FGM	FGA	PCT	3FGM	3FGA	PCT	FTM	FTA	PCT	O-RB	D-RB	TOT	AST	PF	DQ	STL	TO	BLK	PTS	RPG	APG	PPG
77-78–Buffalo	56	–	947	195	370	.527	–	–	–	51	65	.785	14	65	79	78	98	0	35	50	5	441	1.4	1.4	7.9
78-79–New York	75	–	1171	263	486	.541	–	–	–	57	63	.905	28	54	82	136	113	0	37	64	6	583	1.1	1.8	7.8
79-80–New York	75	–	800	188	364	.516	2	10	.200	63	73	.863	21	45	66	85	79	0	35	38	7	441	0.9	1.1	5.9
80-81–New York	82	–	1506	285	511	.558	4	11	.364	98	110	.891	27	61	88	108	126	0	72	62	5	672	1.1	1.3	8.2
81-82–Atlanta	49	0	833	158	291	.543	1	2	.500	59	67	.881	5	56	61	87	80	0	26	27	3	376	1.2	1.8	7.7
82-83–Atlanta	73	4	1124	230	444	.518	0	1	.000	74	89	.831	16	74	90	125	132	0	30	52	9	534	1.2	1.7	7.3
83-84–Atlanta	81	0	1503	312	554	.563	1	2	.500	56	70	.800	17	87	104	171	146	1	46	63	5	681	1.3	2.1	8.4
84-85–Atlanta	60	5	1126	228	388	.588	0	2	.000	62	76	.816	20	61	81	122	74	0	27	55	0	518	1.4	2.0	8.6
85-86–Milwaukee	38	1	573	94	190	.495	0	0	–	47	49	.959	4	53	57	39	42	0	9	18	3	235	1.5	1.0	6.2
86-87–Milwaukee	4	0	34	5	13	.385	0	0	–	5	7	.714	0	2	2	1	3	0	1	0	0	15	0.5	0.3	3.8
Reg. Season Totals	593	10	9617	1958	3611	.542	8	28	.286	572	669	.855	152	558	710	952	893	1	318	429	43	4496	1.2	1.6	7.6
Playoff Totals	22	0	295	39	86	.453	0	2	.000	19	21	.905	5	21	26	19	28	0	9	16	0	97	1.2	0.9	4.4

Glick, Norman Stanley (Normie) b. November 10, 1927 Ht. 6-7 Wt. 205 College: Loyola Marymount

SEASON–TEAM	G	GS	MIN	FGM	FGA	PCT	3FGM	3FGA	PCT	FTM	FTA	PCT	O-RB	D-RB	TOT	AST	PF	DQ	STL	TO	BLK	PTS	RPG	APG	PPG
49-50–Minneapolis	1	–	–	1	1	1.000	–	–	–	0	0	–	–	–	–	0	1	–	–	–	–	2	–	0.0	2.0
Reg. Season Totals	1	–	–	1	1	1.000	–	–	–	0	0	–	–	–	–	0	1	–	–	–	–	2	–	0.0	2.0

Glouchkov, Georgi Nikolov b. January 10, 1960 Ht. 6-8 Wt. 235 College: Akademik Varna (Bulgaria)

SEASON–TEAM	G	GS	MIN	FGM	FGA	PCT	3FGM	3FGA	PCT	FTM	FTA	PCT	O-RB	D-RB	TOT	AST	PF	DQ	STL	TO	BLK	PTS	RPG	APG	PPG
85-86–Phoenix	49	16	772	84	209	.402	1	1	1.000	70	122	.574	31	132	163	32	124	0	26	76	25	239	3.3	0.7	4.9
Reg. Season Totals	49	16	772	84	209	.402	1	1	1.000	70	122	.574	31	132	163	32	124	0	26	76	25	239	3.3	0.7	4.9

G

Glover, Clarence b. November 1, 1947 Ht. 6-8 Wt. 210 College: Western Kentucky

SEASON–TEAM	G	GS	MIN	FGM	FGA	PCT	3FGM	3FGA	PCT	FTM	FTA	PCT	O-RB	D-RB	TOT	AST	PF	DQ	STL	TO	BLK	PTS	RPG	APG	PPG
71-72–Boston	25	–	119	25	55	.455	–	–	–	15	32	.469	–	–	46	4	26	0	–	–	–	65	1.8	0.2	2.6
Reg. Season Totals	25	–	119	25	55	.455	–	–	–	15	32	.469	–	–	46	4	26	0	–	–	–	65	1.8	0.2	2.6
Playoff Totals	3	–	10	2	6	.333	–	–	–	2	2	1.000	–	–	3	–	1	0	–	–	–	6	1.0	0.0	2.0

Glover, Micaiah Diondae (Dion) b. October 22, 1978 Ht. 6-5 Wt. 228 College: Georgia Tech

SEASON–TEAM	G	GS	MIN	FGM	FGA	PCT	3FGM	3FGA	PCT	FTM	FTA	PCT	O-RB	D-RB	TOT	AST	PF	DQ	STL	TO	BLK	PTS	RPG	APG	PPG
99-00–Atlanta	30	1	446	66	171	.386	12	45	.267	51	70	.729	15	23	38	27	28	0	15	28	4	195	1.3	0.9	6.5
Reg. Season Totals	30	1	446	66	171	.386	12	45	.267	51	70	.729	15	23	38	27	28	0	15	28	4	195	1.3	0.9	6.5

Gminski, Michael Thomas (Mike, G-Man) b. August 3, 1959 Ht. 6-11 Wt. 255 College: Duke

SEASON–TEAM	G	GS	MIN	FGM	FGA	PCT	3FGM	3FGA	PCT	FTM	FTA	PCT	O-RB	D-RB	TOT	AST	PF	DQ	STL	TO	BLK	PTS	RPG	APG	PPG
80-81–New Jersey	56	–	1579	291	688	.423	0	1	.000	155	202	.767	137	282	419	72	127	1	54	128	100	737	7.5	1.3	13.2
81-82–New Jersey	64	6	740	119	270	.441	0	0	–	97	118	.822	70	116	186	41	69	0	17	56	48	335	2.9	0.6	5.2
82-83–New Jersey	80	1	1255	213	426	.500	0	1	.000	175	225	.778	154	228	382	61	118	0	35	126	116	601	4.8	0.8	7.5
83-84–New Jersey	82	2	1655	237	462	.513	0	3	.000	147	184	.799	161	272	433	92	162	0	37	120	70	621	5.3	1.1	7.6
84-85–New Jersey	81	54	2418	380	818	.465	0	1	.000	276	328	.841	229	404	633	158	135	0	38	136	92	1036	7.8	2.0	12.8
85-86–New Jersey	81	78	2525	491	949	.517	0	1	.000	351	393	.893	206	462	668	133	163	0	56	140	71	1333	8.2	1.6	16.5
86-87–New Jersey	72	66	2272	433	947	.457	0	0	–	313	370	.846	192	438	630	99	159	0	52	129	69	1179	8.8	1.4	16.4
87-88–N.J.-Phil.	81	81	2961	505	1126	.448	0	2	.000	355	392	.906	245	569	814	139	176	0	64	177	118	1365	10.0	1.7	16.9
88-89–Philadelphia	82	82	2739	556	1166	.477	0	6	.000	297	341	.871	213	556	769	138	142	0	46	129	106	1409	9.4	1.7	17.2
89-90–Philadelphia	81	81	2659	458	1002	.457	3	17	.176	193	235	.821	196	491	687	128	136	0	43	98	102	1112	8.5	1.6	13.7
90-91–Phil.-Cha.	80	79	2196	357	808	.442	2	14	.143	128	158	.810	186	396	582	93	99	0	40	85	56	844	7.3	1.2	10.6
91-92–Charlotte	35	10	499	90	199	.452	1	3	.333	21	28	.750	37	81	118	31	37	0	11	20	16	202	3.4	0.9	5.8
92-93–Charlotte	34	0	251	42	83	.506	0	0	–	9	10	.900	34	51	85	7	28	0	1	11	9	93	2.5	0.2	2.7
93-94–Cha.-Milw.	29	7	309	36	103	.350	0	0	–	14	18	.778	22	52	74	11	23	0	13	13	16	86	2.6	0.4	3.0
Reg. Season Totals	938	547	24058	4208	9047	.465	6	49	.122	2531	3002	.843	2082	4398	6480	1203	1574	1	507	1368	989	10953	6.9	1.3	11.7
Playoff Totals	35	16	917	148	305	.485	0	5	.000	97	122	.795	55	138	193	29	72	0	22	48	57	393	5.5	0.8	11.2

Godfread, Daniel Joseph (Dan) b. June 14, 1967 Ht. 6-10 Wt. 250 College: Evansville

SEASON–TEAM	G	GS	MIN	FGM	FGA	PCT	3FGM	3FGA	PCT	FTM	FTA	PCT	O-RB	D-RB	TOT	AST	PF	DQ	STL	TO	BLK	PTS	RPG	APG	PPG
90-91–Minnesota	10	0	20	5	12	.417	0	1	.000	3	4	.750	0	2	2	0	5	0	1	0	4	13	0.2	0.0	1.3
91-92–Houston	1	0	2	0	0	–	0	0	–	0	0	–	0	0	0	0	0	0	0	0	0	0	0.0	0.0	0.0
Reg. Season Totals	11	0	22	5	12	.417	0	1	.000	3	4	.750	0	2	2	0	5	0	1	0	4	13	0.2	0.0	1.2

Gola, Thomas Joseph (Tom) b. January 13, 1933 Ht. 6-6 Wt. 205 College: La Salle HOF: 1975

SEASON–TEAM	G	GS	MIN	FGM	FGA	PCT	3FGM	3FGA	PCT	FTM	FTA	PCT	O-RB	D-RB	TOT	AST	PF	DQ	STL	TO	BLK	PTS	RPG	APG	PPG
55-56–Philadelphia	68	–	2346	244	592	.412	–	–	–	244	333	.733	–	–	616	404	272	11	–	–	–	732	9.1	5.9	10.8
57-58–Philadelphia	59	–	2126	295	711	.415	–	–	–	223	299	.746	–	–	639	327	225	11	–	–	–	813	10.8	5.5	13.8
58-59–Philadelphia	64	–	2333	310	773	.401	–	–	–	281	357	.787	–	–	710	269	243	7	–	–	–	901	11.1	4.2	14.1
59-60–Philadelphia	75	–	2870	426	983	.433	–	–	–	270	340	.794	–	–	779	409	311	9	–	–	–	1122	10.4	5.5	15.0
60-61–Philadelphia	74	–	2712	420	940	.447	–	–	–	210	281	.747	–	–	692	292	321	13	–	–	–	1050	9.4	3.9	14.2
61-62–Philadelphia	60	–	2462	322	765	.421	–	–	–	176	230	.765	–	–	587	295	267	16	–	–	–	820	9.8	4.9	13.7
62-63–S.F.-N.Y.	73	–	2670	363	791	.459	–	–	–	170	219	.776	–	–	517	298	295	9	–	–	–	896	7.1	4.1	12.3
63-64–New York	74	–	2156	258	602	.429	–	–	–	154	212	.726	–	–	469	257	278	7	–	–	–	670	6.3	3.5	9.1
64-65–New York	77	–	1727	204	455	.448	–	–	–	133	180	.739	–	–	319	220	269	8	–	–	–	541	4.1	2.9	7.0
65-66–New York	74	–	1127	122	271	.450	–	–	–	82	105	.781	–	–	289	191	207	3	–	–	–	326	3.9	2.6	4.4
Reg. Season Totals	698	–	22529	2964	6883	.431	–	–	–	1943	2556	.760	–	–	5617	2962	2688	94	–	–	–	7871	8.0	4.2	11.3
Playoff Totals	39	–	1470	142	422	.336	–	–	–	148	192	.771	–	–	391	179	164	8	–	–	–	432	10.0	4.6	11.1
All-Star Totals	4	–	70	12	29	.414	–	–	–	5	9	.556	–	–	11	7	10	0	–	–	–	29	2.8	1.8	7.3

Goldfaden, Benjamin Paul (Ben) b. September 6, 1913 Ht. 6-3 Wt. 185 College: George Washington

SEASON–TEAM	G	GS	MIN	FGM	FGA	PCT	3FGM	3FGA	PCT	FTM	FTA	PCT	O-RB	D-RB	TOT	AST	PF	DQ	STL	TO	BLK	PTS	RPG	APG	PPG
46-47–Washington	2	–	–	0	2	.000	–	–	–	2	4	.500	–	–	–	0	3	–	–	–	–	2	–	0.0	1.0
Reg. Season Totals	2	–	–	0	2	.000	–	–	–	2	4	.500	–	–	–	0	3	–	–	–	–	2	–	0.0	1.0

Goldwire, Anthony b. September 6, 1971 Ht. 6-2 Wt. 182 College: Houston

SEASON–TEAM	G	GS	MIN	FGM	FGA	PCT	3FGM	3FGA	PCT	FTM	FTA	PCT	O-RB	D-RB	TOT	AST	PF	DQ	STL	TO	BLK	PTS	RPG	APG	PPG
95-96–Charlotte	42	8	621	76	189	.402	33	83	.398	46	60	.767	8	35	43	112	79	0	16	63	0	231	1.0	2.7	5.5
96-97–Cha.-Denver	60	30	1188	131	330	.397	64	153	.418	61	78	.782	12	72	84	219	104	1	33	76	2	387	1.4	3.7	6.5
97-98–Denver	82	32	2212	269	636	.423	63	164	.384	150	186	.806	40	107	147	277	149	0	86	85	7	751	1.8	3.4	9.2
Reg. Season Totals	184	70	4021	476	1155	.412	160	400	.400	257	324	.793	60	214	274	608	332	1	135	224	9	1369	1.5	3.3	7.4

Gondrezick, Glen Michael (Gondo) b. August 30, 1955 Ht. 6-6 Wt. 220 College: Nevada-Las Vegas

SEASON–TEAM	G	GS	MIN	FGM	FGA	PCT	3FGM	3FGA	PCT	FTM	FTA	PCT	O-RB	D-RB	TOT	AST	PF	DQ	STL	TO	BLK	PTS	RPG	APG	PPG
77-78–New York	72	–	1017	131	339	.386	–	–	–	83	121	.686	92	158	250	83	181	0	56	82	18	345	3.5	1.2	4.8
78-79–New York	75	–	1602	161	326	.494	–	–	–	55	97	.567	147	277	424	106	226	1	98	95	18	377	5.7	1.4	5.0
79-80–Denver	59	–	1020	148	286	.517	2	6	.333	92	121	.760	107	152	259	81	119	0	68	58	16	390	4.4	1.4	6.6
80-81–Denver	73	–	1077	155	329	.471	0	2	.000	112	137	.818	136	171	307	83	185	2	91	69	20	422	4.2	1.1	5.8
81-82–Denver	80	0	1699	250	495	.505	0	3	.000	160	217	.737	140	283	423	152	229	0	92	100	36	660	5.3	1.9	8.3
82-83–Denver	76	2	1130	134	294	.456	0	3	.000	82	114	.719	108	193	301	100	161	0	80	49	9	350	4.0	1.3	4.6
Reg. Season Totals	435	2	7545	979	2069	.473	2	14	.143	584	807	.724	730	1234	1964	605	1101	3	485	453	117	2544	4.5	1.4	5.8
Playoff Totals	15	0	187	25	58	.431	0	1	.000	8	13	.615	22	23	45	19	27	0	7	7	2	58	3.0	1.3	3.9

Gondrezick, Grant b. January 19, 1963 Ht. 6-5 Wt. 205 College: Pepperdine

SEASON–TEAM	G	GS	MIN	FGM	FGA	PCT	3FGM	3FGA	PCT	FTM	FTA	PCT	O-RB	D-RB	TOT	AST	PF	DQ	STL	TO	BLK	PTS	RPG	APG	PPG
86-87–Phoenix	64	1	836	135	300	.450	4	17	.235	75	107	.701	47	63	110	81	91	0	25	56	4	349	1.7	1.3	5.5
88-89–L.A. Clippers	27	0	244	38	95	.400	3	11	.273	26	40	.650	15	21	36	34	36	0	13	17	1	105	1.3	1.3	3.9
Reg. Season Totals	91	1	1080	173	395	.438	7	28	.250	101	147	.687	62	84	146	115	127	0	38	73	5	454	1.6	1.3	5.0

Goodrich, Gail Charles Jr. b. April 23, 1943 Ht. 6-1 Wt. 170 College: UCLA HOF: 1996

SEASON–TEAM	G	GS	MIN	FGM	FGA	PCT	3FGM	3FGA	PCT	FTM	FTA	PCT	O-RB	D-RB	TOT	AST	PF	DQ	STL	TO	BLK	PTS	RPG	APG	PPG
65-66–Los Angeles	65	–	1008	203	503	.404	–	–	–	103	149	.691	–	–	130	103	103	1	–	–	–	509	2.0	1.6	7.8
66-67–Los Angeles	77	–	1780	352	776	.454	–	–	–	253	337	.751	–	–	251	210	194	3	–	–	–	957	3.3	2.7	12.4
67-68–Los Angeles	79	–	2057	395	812	.486	–	–	–	302	392	.770	–	–	199	205	228	2	–	–	–	1092	2.5	2.6	13.8
68-69–Phoenix	81	–	3236	718	1746	.411	–	–	–	495	663	.747	–	–	437	518	253	3	–	–	–	1931	5.4	6.4	23.8
69-70–Phoenix	81	–	3234	568	1251	.454	–	–	–	488	604	.808	–	–	340	605	251	3	–	–	–	1624	4.2	7.5	20.0
70-71–Los Angeles	79	–	2808	558	1174	.475	–	–	–	264	343	.770	–	–	260	380	258	3	–	–	–	1380	3.3	4.8	17.5
71-72–Los Angeles	82	–	3040	826	1695	.487	–	–	–	475	559	.850	–	–	295	365	210	0	–	–	–	2127	3.6	4.5	25.9
72-73–Los Angeles	76	–	2697	750	1615	.464	–	–	–	314	374	.840	–	–	263	332	193	1	–	–	–	1814	3.5	4.4	23.9
73-74–Los Angeles	82	–	3061	784	1773	.442	–	–	–	508	588	.864	95	155	250	427	227	3	126	–	12	2076	3.0	5.2	25.3
74-75–Los Angeles	72	–	2668	656	1429	.459	–	–	–	318	378	.841	96	123	219	420	214	1	102	–	6	1630	3.0	5.8	22.6
75-76–Los Angeles	75	–	2646	583	1321	.441	–	–	–	293	346	.847	94	120	214	421	238	3	123	–	17	1459	2.9	5.6	19.5
76-77–New Orleans	27	–	609	136	305	.446	–	–	–	68	85	.800	25	36	61	74	43	0	22	–	2	340	2.3	2.7	12.6
77-78–New Orleans	81	–	2553	520	1050	.495	–	–	–	264	332	.795	75	102	177	388	186	0	82	205	22	1304	2.2	4.8	16.1
78-79–New Orleans	74	–	2130	382	850	.449	–	–	–	174	204	.853	68	115	183	357	177	1	90	185	13	938	2.5	4.8	12.7
Reg. Season Totals	1031	–	33527	7431	16300	.456	–	–	–	4319	5354	.807	453	651	3279	4805	2775	24	545	390	72	19181	3.2	4.7	18.6
Playoff Totals	80	–	2622	542	1227	.442	–	–	–	366	447	.819	7	9	250	333	219	1	7	–	1	1450	3.1	4.2	18.1
All-Star Totals	5	–	77	16	38	.421	–	–	–	1	2	.500	1	4	9	14	8	0	1	–	0	33	1.8	2.8	6.6

Goodwin, Wilfred R. (Bill, Pop) b. December 22, 1920 Ht. 6-2 Wt. 205 College: None

SEASON–TEAM	G	GS	MIN	FGM	FGA	PCT	3FGM	3FGA	PCT	FTM	FTA	PCT	O-RB	D-RB	TOT	AST	PF	DQ	STL	TO	BLK	PTS	RPG	APG	PPG
45-46–Sheboygan (N)	2	–	–	1	–	–	–	–	–	1	–	–	–	–	–	–	–	–	–	–	–	3	–	–	1.5
46-47–Providence	55	–	–	98	348	.282	–	–	–	60	75	.800	–	–	–	15	94	–	–	–	–	256	–	0.3	4.7
47-48–Providence	24	–	–	36	155	.232	–	–	–	19	27	.704	–	–	–	7	36	–	–	–	–	91	–	0.3	3.8
Reg. NBA Totals	79	–	–	134	503	.266	–	–	–	79	102	.775	–	–	–	22	130	–	–	–	–	347	–	0.3	4.4
Reg. NBL Totals	2	–	–	1	–	–	–	–	–	1	0	–	–	–	–	–	–	–	–	–	–	3	–	–	1.5

Gordon, Lancaster b. June 24, 1962 Ht. 6-3 Wt. 195 College: Louisville

SEASON–TEAM	G	GS	MIN	FGM	FGA	PCT	3FGM	3FGA	PCT	FTM	FTA	PCT	O-RB	D-RB	TOT	AST	PF	DQ	STL	TO	BLK	PTS	RPG	APG	PPG
84-85–L.A. Clippers	63	1	682	110	287	.383	2	9	.222	37	49	.755	26	35	61	88	61	0	33	69	6	259	1.0	1.4	4.1
85-86–L.A. Clippers	60	1	704	130	345	.377	7	28	.250	45	56	.804	24	44	68	60	91	1	33	62	10	312	1.1	1.0	5.2
86-87–L.A. Clippers	70	4	1130	221	545	.406	14	48	.292	70	95	.737	64	62	126	139	106	1	61	102	13	526	1.8	2.0	7.5
87-88–L.A. Clippers	8	0	65	11	31	.355	0	0	–	6	6	1.000	2	2	4	7	8	0	1	4	2	28	0.5	0.9	3.5
Reg. Season Totals	201	6	2581	472	1208	.391	23	85	.271	158	206	.767	116	143	259	294	266	2	128	237	31	1125	1.3	1.5	5.6

Gordon, Paul C. Jr. b. April 8, 1927 Ht. 6-3 Wt. 195 College: Baltimore City (Md.) C.C.; Notre Dame

SEASON–TEAM	G	GS	MIN	FGM	FGA	PCT	3FGM	3FGA	PCT	FTM	FTA	PCT	O-RB	D-RB	TOT	AST	PF	DQ	STL	TO	BLK	PTS	RPG	APG	PPG
49-50–Baltimore	4	–	–	0	6	.000	–	–	–	3	5	.600	–	–	–	3	3	–	–	–	–	3	–	0.8	0.8
Reg. Season Totals	4	–	–	0	6	.000	–	–	–	3	5	.600	–	–	–	3	3	–	–	–	–	3	–	0.8	0.8

Gottlieb, Leo (Ace) b. November 28, 1920 d. August 1972 Ht. 5-11 Wt. 180 College: None

SEASON–TEAM	G	GS	MIN	FGM	FGA	PCT	3FGM	3FGA	PCT	FTM	FTA	PCT	O-RB	D-RB	TOT	AST	PF	DQ	STL	TO	BLK	PTS	RPG	APG	PPG
46-47–New York	57	–	–	149	494	.302	–	–	–	36	55	.655	–	–	–	24	71	–	–	–	–	334	–	0.4	5.9
47-48–New York	27	–	–	59	228	.259	–	–	–	13	21	.619	–	–	–	12	36	–	–	–	–	131	–	0.4	4.9
Reg. Season Totals	84	–	–	208	722	.288	–	–	–	49	76	.645	–	–	–	36	107	–	–	–	–	465	–	0.4	5.5
Playoff Totals	4	–	–	10	39	.256	–	–	–	4	6	.667	–	–	–	1	6	–	–	–	–	24	–	0.3	6.0

Govan, Gerald b. January 2, 1942 Ht. 6-10 Wt. 220 College: St. Mary of the Plains

SEASON–TEAM	G	GS	MIN	FGM	FGA	PCT	3FGM	3FGA	PCT	FTM	FTA	PCT	O-RB	D-RB	TOT	AST	PF	DQ	STL	TO	BLK	PTS	RPG	APG	PPG
67-68–New Orleans (A)	78	–	1587	156	390	.400	1	1	1.000	79	131	.603	–	–	596	95	156	2	–	100	–	392	7.6	1.2	5.0
68-69–New Orleans (A)	77	–	1902	211	537	.393	1	4	.250	134	208	.644	–	–	701	150	238	4	–	162	–	557	9.1	1.9	7.2
69-70–New Orleans (A)	84	–	3701	422	1044	.404	1	11	.091	208	285	.730	285	932	1217	385	273	5	–	–	–	1053	14.5	4.6	12.5
70-71–Memphis (A)	84	–	3698	296	794	.373	1	4	.250	119	191	.623	277	861	1138	407	284	–	–	–	–	712	13.5	4.8	8.5
71-72–Memphis (A)	83	–	3414	277	719	.385	0	0	–	162	230	.704	310	872	1182	348	260	–	–	241	–	716	14.2	4.2	8.6
72-73–Utah (A)	84	–	2408	229	530	.432	0	0	–	81	135	.600	175	620	795	250	279	0	–	168	–	539	9.5	3.0	6.4
73-74–Utah (A)	83	–	2766	255	541	.471	0	2	.000	73	106	.689	142	586	728	245	260	–	60	156	50	583	8.8	3.0	7.0
74-75–Utah (A)	84	–	2791	239	602	.397	1	2	.500	83	105	.790	121	480	601	230	217	–	72	195	36	562	7.2	2.7	6.7
75-76–Virginia (A)	24	–	658	57	131	.435	0	0	–	23	28	.821	44	117	161	54	65	–	7	47	11	137	6.7	2.3	5.7
Reg. ABA Totals	681	–	22925	2142	5288	.405	5	24	.208	962	1419	.678	1354	4468	7119	2164	2032	11	139	1069	97	5251	10.5	3.2	7.7
ABA Playoff Totals	66	–	1930	189	497	.380	1	2	.500	76	109	.697	98	335	657	190	223	2	19	101	26	455	10.0	2.9	6.9

Govedarica, Bato Zdravko b. April 17, 1928 Ht. 5-11 Wt. 185 College: DePaul

SEASON–TEAM	G	GS	MIN	FGM	FGA	PCT	3FGM	3FGA	PCT	FTM	FTA	PCT	O-RB	D-RB	TOT	AST	PF	DQ	STL	TO	BLK	PTS	RPG	APG	PPG
53-54–Syracuse	23	–	258	25	79	.316	–	–	–	25	37	.676	–	–	18	24	44	1	–	–	–	75	0.8	1.0	3.3
Reg. Season Totals	23	–	258	25	79	.316	–	–	–	25	37	.676	–	–	18	24	44	1	–	–	–	75	0.8	1.0	3.3

Graboski, Joseph W. **(Joe, Grabbo)** b. January 15, 1930 d. July 2, 1998 Ht. 6-8 Wt. 230 College: None

SEASON–TEAM	G	GS	MIN	FGM	FGA	PCT	3FGM	3FGA	PCT	FTM	FTA	PCT	O-RB	D-RB	TOT	AST	PF	DQ	STL	TO	BLK	PTS	RPG	APG	PPG
48-49–Chicago	45	–	–	54	157	.344	–	–	–	17	49	.347	–	–	–	18	86	–	–	–	–	125	–	0.4	2.8
49-50–Chicago	57	–	–	75	247	.304	–	–	–	53	89	.596	–	–	–	37	95	–	–	–	–	203	–	0.6	3.6
51-52–Indianapolis	66	–	2439	320	827	.387	–	–	–	264	396	.667	–	–	655	130	254	10	–	–	–	904	9.9	2.0	13.7
52-53–Indianapolis	69	–	2769	272	799	.340	–	–	–	350	513	.682	–	–	687	156	303	18	–	–	–	894	10.0	2.3	13.0
53-54–Philadelphia	71	–	2759	354	1000	.354	–	–	–	236	350	.674	–	–	670	163	223	4	–	–	–	944	9.4	2.3	13.3
54-55–Philadelphia	70	–	2515	373	1096	.340	–	–	–	208	303	.686	–	–	636	182	259	8	–	–	–	954	9.1	2.6	13.6
55-56–Philadelphia	72	–	2375	397	1075	.369	–	–	–	240	340	.706	–	–	642	190	272	5	–	–	–	1034	8.9	2.6	14.4
56-57–Philadelphia	72	–	2501	390	1118	.349	–	–	–	252	322	.783	–	–	614	140	244	5	–	–	–	1032	8.5	1.9	14.3
57-58–Philadelphia	72	–	2077	341	1017	.335	–	–	–	227	303	.749	–	–	570	125	249	3	–	–	–	909	7.9	1.7	12.6
58-59–Philadelphia	72	–	2482	394	1116	.353	–	–	–	270	360	.750	–	–	751	148	249	5	–	–	–	1058	10.4	2.1	14.7
59-60–Philadelphia	73	–	1269	217	583	.372	–	–	–	131	174	.753	–	–	358	111	147	1	–	–	–	565	4.9	1.5	7.7
60-61–Philadelphia	68	–	1011	169	507	.333	–	–	–	127	183	.694	–	–	262	74	148	2	–	–	–	465	3.9	1.1	6.8
61-62–St. L.-Chi.-Syr.	38	–	468	77	221	.348	–	–	–	39	65	.600	–	–	154	28	62	0	–	–	–	193	4.1	0.7	5.1
Reg. Season Totals	845	–	22665	3433	9763	.352	–	–	–	2414	3447	.700	–	–	5999	1502	2591	61	–	–	–	9280	8.1	1.8	11.0
Playoff Totals	40	–	1078	157	471	.333	–	–	–	75	105	.714	–	–	294	81	104	2	–	–	–	389	7.4	2.0	9.7

Grace, Ricky b. August 20, 1967 Ht. 6-1 Wt. 180 College: Midland (Texas) Coll.(J.C.); Oklahoma

SEASON–TEAM	G	GS	MIN	FGM	FGA	PCT	3FGM	3FGA	PCT	FTM	FTA	PCT	O-RB	D-RB	TOT	AST	PF	DQ	STL	TO	BLK	PTS	RPG	APG	PPG
93-94–Atlanta	3	0	8	2	3	.667	0	0	–	0	2	.000	0	1	1	1	3	0	0	0	0	4	0.3	0.3	1.3
Reg. Season Totals	3	0	8	2	3	.667	0	0	–	0	2	.000	0	1	1	1	3	0	0	0	0	4	0.3	0.3	1.3

Graham, Calvin J. **(Cal)** b. June 7, 1944 Ht. 6-2 Wt. 195 College: Gannon

SEASON–TEAM	G	GS	MIN	FGM	FGA	PCT	3FGM	3FGA	PCT	FTM	FTA	PCT	O-RB	D-RB	TOT	AST	PF	DQ	STL	TO	BLK	PTS	RPG	APG	PPG
67-68–Pittsburgh (A)	8	–	52	4	14	.286	0	0	–	5	8	.625	–	–	10	0	12	0	–	1	–	13	1.3	0.0	1.6
Reg. ABA Totals	8	–	52	4	14	.286	0	0	–	5	8	.625	–	–	10	0	12	0	–	1	–	13	1.3	0.0	1.6

Graham, Gregory Lawrence **(Greg)** b. November 26, 1970 Ht. 6-4 Wt. 182 College: Indiana

SEASON–TEAM	G	GS	MIN	FGM	FGA	PCT	3FGM	3FGA	PCT	FTM	FTA	PCT	O-RB	D-RB	TOT	AST	PF	DQ	STL	TO	BLK	PTS	RPG	APG	PPG
93-94–Philadelphia	70	6	889	122	305	.400	2	25	.080	92	110	.836	21	65	86	66	54	0	61	65	4	338	1.2	0.9	4.8
94-95–Philadelphia	50	7	775	95	223	.426	6	28	.214	55	73	.753	19	43	62	66	76	0	29	48	6	251	1.2	1.3	5.0
95-96–Phil.-N.J.	53	5	613	78	193	.404	32	82	.390	52	68	.765	17	40	57	52	64	0	25	46	1	240	1.1	1.0	4.5
96-97–Seattle	28	0	197	29	80	.363	9	31	.290	26	40	.650	2	11	13	11	12	0	12	10	1	93	0.5	0.4	3.3
97-98–Cleveland	6	0	56	7	12	.583	0	3	.000	2	2	1.000	0	1	1	6	7	0	1	10	0	16	0.2	1.0	2.7
Reg. Season Totals	207	18	2530	331	813	.407	49	169	.290	227	293	.775	59	160	219	201	213	0	128	179	12	938	1.1	1.0	4.5
Playoff Totals	6	0	43	4	14	.286	1	4	.250	3	4	.750	0	5	5	6	5	0	2	1	0	12	0.8	1.0	2.0

Graham, Orlando b. May 5, 1965 Ht. 6-8 Wt. 230 College: West Texas A&M; Auburn-Montgomery

SEASON–TEAM	G	GS	MIN	FGM	FGA	PCT	3FGM	3FGA	PCT	FTM	FTA	PCT	O-RB	D-RB	TOT	AST	PF	DQ	STL	TO	BLK	PTS	RPG	APG	PPG
88-89–Golden State	7	0	22	3	10	.300	0	0	–	2	4	.500	8	3	11	0	6	0	0	2	0	8	1.6	0.0	1.1
Reg. Season Totals	7	0	22	3	10	.300	0	0	–	2	4	.500	8	3	11	0	6	0	0	2	0	8	1.6	0.0	1.1
Playoff Totals	2	0	8	1	2	.500	0	0	–	1	2	.500	0	1	1	–	0	0	0	1	0	3	0.5	0.0	1.5

Graham, Paul (Snoop) b. November 28, 1967 Ht. 6-6 Wt. 200 College: Ohio U.

SEASON–TEAM	G	GS	MIN	FGM	FGA	PCT	3FGM	3FGA	PCT	FTM	FTA	PCT	O-RB	D-RB	TOT	AST	PF	DQ	STL	TO	BLK	PTS	RPG	APG	PPG
91-92–Atlanta	78	9	1718	305	682	.447	55	141	.390	126	170	.741	72	159	231	175	193	3	96	91	21	791	3.0	2.2	10.1
92-93–Atlanta	80	11	1508	256	560	.457	42	141	.298	96	131	.733	61	129	190	164	185	0	86	120	6	650	2.4	2.1	8.1
93-94–Atlanta	21	0	128	21	57	.368	3	13	.231	13	17	.765	4	8	12	13	11	0	4	5	5	58	0.6	0.6	2.8
Reg. Season Totals	179	20	3354	582	1299	.448	100	295	.339	235	318	.739	137	296	433	352	389	3	186	216	32	1499	2.4	2.0	8.4
Playoff Totals	3	0	29	3	10	.300	0	3	.000	0	0	–	1	2	3	2	2	0	4	2	0	6	1.0	0.7	2.0

Graham, Robert Malcolm (Mal) b. February 23, 1945 Ht. 6-1 Wt. 185 College: New York U.

SEASON–TEAM	G	GS	MIN	FGM	FGA	PCT	3FGM	3FGA	PCT	FTM	FTA	PCT	O-RB	D-RB	TOT	AST	PF	DQ	STL	TO	BLK	PTS	RPG	APG	PPG
67-68–Boston	78	–	786	117	272	.430	–	–	–	56	88	.636	–	–	94	61	123	0	–	–	–	290	1.2	0.8	3.7
68-69–Boston	22	–	103	13	55	.236	–	–	–	11	14	.786	–	–	24	14	27	0	–	–	–	37	1.1	0.6	1.7
Reg. Season Totals	100	–	889	130	327	.398	–	–	–	67	102	.657	–	–	118	75	150	0	–	–	–	327	1.2	0.8	3.3
Playoff Totals	7	–	25	2	7	.286	–	–	–	1	3	.333	–	–	4	2	3	0	–	–	–	5	0.6	0.3	0.7

Grandholm, James Thomas (Jim) b. October 4, 1960 Ht. 7-0 Wt. 235 College: Florida; South Florida

SEASON–TEAM	G	GS	MIN	FGM	FGA	PCT	3FGM	3FGA	PCT	FTM	FTA	PCT	O-RB	D-RB	TOT	AST	PF	DQ	STL	TO	BLK	PTS	RPG	APG	PPG
90-91–Dallas	26	0	168	30	58	.517	9	17	.529	10	21	.476	20	30	50	8	33	0	2	11	8	79	1.9	0.3	3.0
Reg. Season Totals	26	0	168	30	58	.517	9	17	.529	10	21	.476	20	30	50	8	33	0	2	11	8	79	1.9	0.3	3.0

Grandison, Ronnie Calvin b. July 9, 1964 Ht. 6-6 Wt. 220 College: New Orleans

SEASON–TEAM	G	GS	MIN	FGM	FGA	PCT	3FGM	3FGA	PCT	FTM	FTA	PCT	O-RB	D-RB	TOT	AST	PF	DQ	STL	TO	BLK	PTS	RPG	APG	PPG
88-89–Boston	72	0	528	59	142	.415	0	10	.000	59	80	.738	47	45	92	42	71	0	18	36	3	177	1.3	0.6	2.5
91-92–Charlotte	3	0	25	2	4	.500	0	0	–	6	10	.600	3	8	11	1	4	0	1	3	1	10	3.7	0.3	3.3
94-95–New York	2	0	8	1	4	.250	0	0	–	0	0	–	3	2	5	2	2	0	0	0	0	2	2.5	1.0	1.0
95-96–Mia.-Atl.-N.Y.	28	3	311	22	58	.379	4	14	.286	17	25	.680	20	35	55	13	31	0	12	12	2	65	2.0	0.5	2.3
Reg. Season Totals	105	3	872	84	208	.404	4	24	.167	82	115	.713	73	90	163	58	108	0	31	51	6	254	1.6	0.6	2.4
Playoff Totals	2	0	3	0	1	.000	0	1	.000	0	0	–	0	0	0	–	1	0	0	0	0	0	0.0	0.0	0.0

Granger, Stewart Francis b. October 27, 1961 Ht. 6-3 Wt. 190 College: Villanova

SEASON–TEAM	G	GS	MIN	FGM	FGA	PCT	3FGM	3FGA	PCT	FTM	FTA	PCT	O-RB	D-RB	TOT	AST	PF	DQ	STL	TO	BLK	PTS	RPG	APG	PPG
83-84–Cleveland	56	13	738	97	226	.429	4	13	.308	53	70	.757	8	47	55	134	97	0	24	57	0	251	1.0	2.4	4.5
84-85–Atlanta	9	1	92	6	17	.353	0	1	.000	4	8	.500	1	5	6	12	13	0	2	12	0	16	0.7	1.3	1.8
86-87–New York	15	0	166	20	54	.370	0	3	.000	9	11	.818	6	11	17	27	17	0	7	22	1	49	1.1	1.8	3.3
Reg. Season Totals	80	14	996	123	297	.414	4	17	.235	66	89	.742	15	63	78	173	127	0	33	91	1	316	1.0	2.2	4.0

Grant, Brian Wade b. March 5, 1972 Ht. 6-9 Wt. 254 College: Xavier (Ohio)

SEASON–TEAM	G	GS	MIN	FGM	FGA	PCT	3FGM	3FGA	PCT	FTM	FTA	PCT	O-RB	D-RB	TOT	AST	PF	DQ	STL	TO	BLK	PTS	RPG	APG	PPG
94-95–Sacramento	80	59	2289	413	809	.511	1	4	.250	231	363	.636	207	391	598	99	276	4	49	163	116	1058	7.5	1.2	13.2
95-96–Sacramento	78	75	2398	427	842	.507	4	17	.235	262	358	.732	175	370	545	127	269	9	40	185	103	1120	7.0	1.6	14.4
96-97–Sacramento	24	15	607	91	207	.440	0	0	–	70	90	.778	49	93	142	28	75	0	19	44	25	252	5.9	1.2	10.5
97-98–Portland	61	49	1921	283	557	.508	0	1	.000	171	228	.750	197	358	555	86	184	3	44	110	45	737	9.1	1.4	12.1
98-99–Portland	48	46	1525	183	382	.479	0	0	–	184	226	.814	173	297	470	67	136	1	21	96	34	550	9.8	1.4	11.5
99-00–Portland	63	14	1322	173	352	.491	1	2	.500	112	166	.675	121	223	344	64	166	2	32	84	28	459	5.5	1.0	7.3
Reg. Season Totals	354	258	10062	1570	3149	.499	6	24	.250	1030	1431	.720	922	1732	2654	471	1106	19	205	682	351	4176	7.5	1.3	11.8
Playoff Totals	37	21	1061	127	262	.485	0	0	–	96	143	.671	96	178	274	32	135	3	22	56	32	350	7.4	0.9	9.5

Grant, Gary (The General) b. April 21, 1965 Ht. 6-3 Wt. 185 College: Michigan

SEASON–TEAM	G	GS	MIN	FGM	FGA	PCT	3FGM	3FGA	PCT	FTM	FTA	PCT	O-RB	D-RB	TOT	AST	PF	DQ	STL	TO	BLK	PTS	RPG	APG	PPG
88-89–L.A. Clippers	71	48	1924	361	830	.435	5	22	.227	119	162	.735	80	158	238	506	170	1	144	258	9	846	3.4	7.1	11.9
89-90–L.A. Clippers	44	44	1529	241	517	.466	5	21	.238	88	113	.779	59	136	195	442	120	1	108	206	5	575	4.4	10.0	13.1
90-91–L.A. Clippers	68	65	2105	265	587	.451	9	39	.231	51	74	.689	69	140	209	587	192	4	103	210	12	590	3.1	8.6	8.7
91-92–L.A. Clippers	78	53	2049	275	595	.462	15	51	.294	44	54	.815	34	150	184	538	181	4	138	187	14	609	2.4	6.9	7.8
92-93–L.A. Clippers	74	8	1624	210	476	.441	11	42	.262	55	74	.743	27	112	139	353	168	2	106	129	9	486	1.9	4.8	6.6
93-94–L.A. Clippers	78	8	1533	253	563	.449	17	62	.274	65	76	.855	42	100	142	291	139	1	119	136	12	588	1.8	3.7	7.5
94-95–L.A. Clippers	33	2	470	78	166	.470	4	16	.250	45	55	.818	8	27	35	93	66	0	29	44	3	205	1.1	2.8	6.2
95-96–New York	47	1	596	88	181	.486	8	24	.333	48	58	.828	12	40	52	69	91	0	39	45	3	232	1.1	1.5	4.9
96-97–Miami	28	0	365	39	110	.355	14	46	.304	18	22	.818	8	30	38	45	39	0	16	27	0	110	1.4	1.6	3.9
97-98–Portland	22	2	359	43	93	.462	7	19	.368	12	14	.857	8	40	48	84	30	0	17	24	2	105	2.2	3.8	4.8
98-99–Portland	2	0	7	0	1	.000	0	0	–	0	0	–	0	0	0	3	0	0	1	0	0	0	0.0	1.5	0.0
99-00–Portland	3	0	24	6	14	.429	0	0	–	0	0	–	0	3	3	1	3	0	1	2	0	12	1.0	0.3	4.0
Reg. Season Totals	548	231	12585	1859	4133	.450	95	342	.278	545	702	.776	347	936	1283	3012	1199	13	821	1268	69	4358	2.3	5.5	8.0
Playoff Totals	17	1	221	24	66	.364	3	9	.333	4	6	.667	5	9	14	49	25	0	8	18	3	55	0.8	2.9	3.2

Grant, Gregory Alan **(Greg, Waterbug)** b. August 29, 1966 Ht. 5-7 Wt. 140 College: Morris Brown; Trenton State

SEASON–TEAM	G	GS	MIN	FGM	FGA	PCT	3FGM	3FGA	PCT	FTM	FTA	PCT	O-RB	D-RB	TOT	AST	PF	DQ	STL	TO	BLK	PTS	RPG	APG	PPG
89-90–Phoenix	67	3	678	83	216	.384	3	16	.188	39	59	.661	16	43	59	168	58	0	36	77	1	208	0.9	2.5	3.1
90-91–New York	22	0	107	10	27	.370	1	3	.333	5	6	.833	1	9	10	20	12	0	9	10	0	26	0.5	0.9	1.2
91-92–Cha.-Phil.	68	0	891	99	225	.440	7	18	.389	20	24	.833	14	55	69	217	76	0	45	46	2	225	1.0	3.2	3.3
92-93–Philadelphia	72	0	996	77	220	.350	20	68	.294	20	31	.645	24	43	67	206	73	0	43	54	1	194	0.9	2.9	2.7
94-95–Denver	14	0	151	10	33	.303	2	7	.286	9	12	.750	2	7	9	43	20	1	6	14	2	31	0.6	3.1	2.2
95-96–Phil.-Was.-Den.	31	2	527	35	99	.354	8	34	.235	5	6	.833	7	27	34	97	43	0	22	30	2	83	1.1	3.1	2.7
Reg. Season Totals	274	5	3350	314	820	.383	41	146	.281	98	138	.710	64	184	248	751	282	1	161	231	8	767	0.9	2.7	2.8
Playoff Totals	10	0	67	9	26	.346	1	4	.250	2	2	1.000	5	4	9	15	7	0	3	5	0	21	0.9	1.5	2.1

Grant, Harry Peter Jr. **(Bud)** b. May 20, 1927 Ht. 6-3 Wt. 195 College: Minnesota

SEASON–TEAM	G	GS	MIN	FGM	FGA	PCT	3FGM	3FGA	PCT	FTM	FTA	PCT	O-RB	D-RB	TOT	AST	PF	DQ	STL	TO	BLK	PTS	RPG	APG	PPG
49-50–Minneapolis	35	–	–	42	115	.365	–	–	–	7	17	.412	–	–	–	19	36	–	–	–	–	91	–	0.5	2.6
50-51–Minneapolis	61	–	–	53	184	.288	–	–	–	52	83	.627	–	–	115	71	106	0	–	–	–	158	1.9	1.2	2.6
Reg. Season Totals	96	–	–	95	299	.318	–	–	–	59	100	.590	–	–	115	90	142	0	–	–	–	249	1.9	0.9	2.6
Playoff Totals	18	–	–	22	101	.396	–	–	–	10	17	.588	–	–	5	14	37	0	–	–	–	54	1.0	0.5	3.0

Grant, Harvey **(The General)** b. July 4, 1965 Ht. 6-9 Wt. 225 College: Oklahoma

SEASON–TEAM	G	GS	MIN	FGM	FGA	PCT	3FGM	3FGA	PCT	FTM	FTA	PCT	O-RB	D-RB	TOT	AST	PF	DQ	STL	TO	BLK	PTS	RPG	APG	PPG
88-89–Washington	71	1	1193	181	390	.464	0	1	.000	34	57	.596	75	88	163	79	147	2	35	28	29	396	2.3	1.1	5.6
89-90–Washington	81	25	1846	284	601	.473	0	8	.000	96	137	.701	138	204	342	131	194	1	52	85	43	664	4.2	1.6	8.2
90-91–Washington	77	76	2842	609	1224	.498	2	15	.133	185	249	.743	179	378	557	204	232	2	91	125	61	1405	7.2	2.6	18.2
91-92–Washington	64	60	2388	489	1022	.478	1	8	.125	176	220	.800	157	275	432	170	178	1	74	109	27	1155	6.8	2.7	18.0
92-93–Washington	72	72	2667	560	1149	.487	1	10	.100	218	300	.727	133	279	412	205	168	0	72	90	44	1339	5.7	2.8	18.6
93-94–Portland	77	73	2112	356	774	.460	2	7	.286	84	131	.641	109	242	351	107	179	1	70	56	49	798	4.6	1.4	10.4
94-95–Portland	75	14	1771	286	621	.461	8	26	.308	103	146	.705	103	181	284	82	163	0	56	62	53	683	3.8	1.1	9.1
95-96–Portland	76	75	2394	314	679	.462	21	67	.313	60	110	.545	117	244	361	111	173	1	60	82	43	709	4.8	1.5	9.3
96-97–Washington	78	25	1604	129	314	.411	28	89	.315	30	39	.769	63	193	256	68	167	2	46	30	48	316	3.3	0.9	4.1
97-98–Washington	65	8	895	75	196	.383	1	6	.167	19	30	.633	60	108	168	39	94	1	23	26	15	170	2.6	0.6	2.6
98-99–Philadelphia	47	10	798	62	168	.369	1	6	.167	21	29	.724	36	74	110	23	73	1	20	21	16	146	2.3	0.5	3.1
Reg. Season Totals	783	439	20510	3345	7138	.469	65	243	.267	1026	1448	.709	1170	2266	3436	1219	1768	12	599	714	428	7781	4.4	1.6	9.9
Playoff Totals	19	9	413	45	103	.437	6	17	.353	10	20	.500	14	39	53	13	30	0	4	8	9	106	2.8	0.7	5.6

Grant, Horace Junior b. July 4, 1965 Ht. 6-10 Wt. 245 College: Clemson

SEASON–TEAM	G	GS	MIN	FGM	FGA	PCT	3FGM	3FGA	PCT	FTM	FTA	PCT	O-RB	D-RB	TOT	AST	PF	DQ	STL	TO	BLK	PTS	RPG	APG	PPG
87-88–Chicago	81	6	1827	254	507	.501	0	2	.000	114	182	.626	155	292	447	89	221	3	51	86	53	622	5.5	1.1	7.7
88-89–Chicago	79	79	2809	405	781	.519	0	5	.000	140	199	.704	240	441	681	168	251	1	86	128	62	950	8.6	2.1	12.0
89-90–Chicago	80	80	2753	446	853	.523	0	0	–	179	256	.699	236	393	629	227	230	1	92	110	84	1071	7.9	2.8	13.4
90-91–Chicago	78	76	2641	401	733	.547	1	6	.167	197	277	.711	266	393	659	178	203	2	95	92	69	1000	8.4	2.3	12.8
91-92–Chicago	81	81	2859	457	790	.578	0	2	.000	235	317	.741	344	463	807	217	196	0	100	98	131	1149	10.0	2.7	14.2
92-93–Chicago	77	77	2745	421	829	.508	1	5	.200	174	281	.619	341	388	729	201	218	4	89	110	96	1017	9.5	2.6	13.2
93-94–Chicago	70	69	2570	460	878	.524	0	6	.000	137	230	.596	306	463	769	236	164	0	74	109	84	1057	11.0	3.4	15.1
94-95–Orlando	74	74	2693	401	707	.567	0	8	.000	146	211	.692	223	492	715	173	203	2	76	85	88	948	9.7	2.3	12.8
95-96–Orlando	63	62	2286	347	677	.513	1	6	.167	152	207	.734	178	402	580	170	144	1	62	64	74	847	9.2	2.7	13.4
96-97–Orlando	67	67	2496	358	695	.515	1	6	.167	128	179	.715	206	394	600	163	157	1	101	99	65	845	9.0	2.4	12.6
97-98–Orlando	76	76	2803	393	857	.459	0	7	.000	135	199	.678	228	390	618	172	180	0	81	88	79	921	8.1	2.3	12.1
98-99–Orlando	50	50	1660	198	456	.434	0	2	.000	47	70	.671	117	234	351	90	99	0	46	44	60	443	7.0	1.8	8.9
99-00–Seattle	76	76	2688	266	599	.444	0	4	.000	80	111	.721	167	424	591	188	192	0	55	61	60	612	7.8	2.5	8.1
Reg. Season Totals	952	873	32830	4807	9362	.513	4	59	.068	1864	2719	.686	3007	5169	8176	2272	2458	15	1008	1174	1005	11482	8.6	2.4	12.1
Playoff Totals	150	140	5622	741	1365	.543	1	8	.125	310	436	.711	501	829	1330	332	465	8	153	167	159	1793	8.9	2.2	12.0
All-Star Totals	1	0	17	2	8	.250	0	0	–	0	0	–	6	2	8	2	0	0	1	1	2	4	8.0	2.0	4.0

Grant, Joshua David **(Josh)** b. August 7, 1967 Ht. 6-10 Wt. 225 College: Utah

SEASON–TEAM	G	GS	MIN	FGM	FGA	PCT	3FGM	3FGA	PCT	FTM	FTA	PCT	O-RB	D-RB	TOT	AST	PF	DQ	STL	TO	BLK	PTS	RPG	APG	PPG
93-94–Golden State	53	0	382	59	146	.404	17	61	.279	22	29	.759	27	62	89	24	62	0	18	30	8	157	1.7	0.5	3.0
Reg. Season Totals	53	0	382	59	146	.404	17	61	.279	22	29	.759	27	62	89	24	62	0	18	30	8	157	1.7	0.5	3.0
Playoff Totals	1	0	1	0	0	–	0	0	–	0	0	–	0	0	0	–	0	0	0	0	0	0	0.0	0.0	0.0

Grant, Paul Edward b. January 6, 1974 Ht. 7-0 Wt. 245 College: Boston College; Wisconsin

SEASON–TEAM	G	GS	MIN	FGM	FGA	PCT	3FGM	3FGA	PCT	FTM	FTA	PCT	O-RB	D-RB	TOT	AST	PF	DQ	STL	TO	BLK	PTS	RPG	APG	PPG
98-99–Minn.-Milw.	6	0	13	2	6	.333	0	0	–	0	0	–	1	0	1	0	4	0	1	2	0	4	0.2	0.0	0.7
Reg. Season Totals	6	0	13	2	6	.333	0	0	–	0	0	–	1	0	1	0	4	0	1	2	0	4	0.2	0.0	0.7

Grant, Travis (Machine Gun) b. January 1, 1950 Ht. 6-8 Wt. 215 College: Kentucky State

SEASON–TEAM	G	GS	MIN	FGM	FGA	PCT	3FGM	3FGA	PCT	FTM	FTA	PCT	O-RB	D-RB	TOT	AST	PF	DQ	STL	TO	BLK	PTS	RPG	APG	PPG
72-73–Los Angeles	33	–	153	51	116	.440	–	–	–	23	26	.885	–	–	52	7	19	0	–	–	–	125	1.6	0.2	3.8
73-74–Los Angeles	3	–	6	1	4	.250	–	–	–	1	3	.333	0	1	1	0	1	0	0	–	0	3	0.3	0.0	1.0
73-74–San Diego (A)	56	–	1324	357	681	.524	1	4	.250	141	176	.801	106	192	298	63	118	–	46	88	12	856	5.3	1.1	15.3
74-75–San Diego (A)	53	–	1998	576	1058	.544	1	2	.500	182	218	.835	117	211	328	98	160	–	44	118	21	1335	6.2	1.8	25.2
75-76–Ken.-Indiana (A)	56	–	828	198	398	.497	0	0	–	52	69	.754	61	79	140	43	98	–	16	55	18	448	2.5	0.8	8.0
Reg. NBA Totals	36	–	159	52	120	.433	–	–	–	24	29	.828	0	1	53	7	20	0	0	–	0	128	1.5	0.2	3.6
Reg. ABA Totals	165	–	4150	1131	2137	.529	2	6	.333	375	463	.810	284	482	766	204	376	0	106	261	51	2639	4.6	1.2	16.0
NBA Playoff Totals	2	–	11	4	6	.667	–	–	–	0	0	–	0	0	4	–	1	0	0	–	0	8	2.0	0.0	4.0
ABA Playoff Totals	1	–	1	0	1	.000	0	0	–	0	0	–	0	0	0	0	0	0	0	0	0	0	0.0	0.0	0.0

Grate, Donald (Don) b. August 27, 1923 Ht. 6-2 Wt. 185 College: Ohio State

SEASON–TEAM	G	GS	MIN	FGM	FGA	PCT	3FGM	3FGA	PCT	FTM	FTA	PCT	O-RB	D-RB	TOT	AST	PF	DQ	STL	TO	BLK	PTS	RPG	APG	PPG
47-48–Indianapolis (N)	11	–	–	14	–	–	–	–	–	3	6	.500	–	–	–	–	–	–	–	–	–	31	–	–	2.8
49-50–Sheboygan	2	–	–	1	6	.167	–	–	–	2	2	1.000	–	–	–	3	3	–	–	–	–	4	–	1.5	2.0
Reg. NBA Totals	2	–	–	1	6	.167	–	–	–	2	2	1.000	–	–	–	3	3	–	–	–	–	4	–	1.5	2.0
Reg. NBL Totals	11	–	–	14	–	–	–	–	–	3	6	.500	–	–	–	–	–	–	–	–	–	31	–	–	2.8

G

Graves, Earl G. Jr. (Butch) b. January 5, 1962 Ht. 6-3 Wt. 200 College: Yale

SEASON–TEAM	G	GS	MIN	FGM	FGA	PCT	3FGM	3FGA	PCT	FTM	FTA	PCT	O-RB	D-RB	TOT	AST	PF	DQ	STL	TO	BLK	PTS	RPG	APG	PPG
84-85–Cleveland	4	0	11	2	6	.333	0	1	.000	1	5	.200	0	2	2	1	4	0	1	1	0	5	0.5	0.3	1.3
Reg. Season Totals	4	0	11	2	6	.333	0	1	.000	1	5	.200	0	2	2	1	4	0	1	1	0	5	0.5	0.3	1.3

Gray, Devin Antoine b. March 31, 1972 Ht. 6-6 Wt. 230 College: Clemson

SEASON–TEAM	G	GS	MIN	FGM	FGA	PCT	3FGM	3FGA	PCT	FTM	FTA	PCT	O-RB	D-RB	TOT	AST	PF	DQ	STL	TO	BLK	PTS	RPG	APG	PPG
96-97–Sac.-S.A.	6	0	49	8	26	.308	0	0	–	2	5	.400	6	8	14	2	11	0	4	5	0	18	2.3	0.3	3.0
99-00–Houston	21	2	124	15	37	.405	0	0	–	19	29	.655	11	14	25	5	22	0	5	4	3	49	1.2	0.2	2.3
Reg. Season Totals	27	2	173	23	63	.365	0	0	–	21	34	.618	17	22	39	7	33	0	9	9	3	67	1.4	0.3	2.5

Gray, Edward Jr. (Ed) b. September 27, 1975 Ht. 6-3 Wt. 210 College: Tennessee; Coll. of Southern Idaho (J.C.); California

SEASON–TEAM	G	GS	MIN	FGM	FGA	PCT	3FGM	3FGA	PCT	FTM	FTA	PCT	O-RB	D-RB	TOT	AST	PF	DQ	STL	TO	BLK	PTS	RPG	APG	PPG
97-98–Atlanta	30	3	472	77	202	.381	18	46	.391	55	65	.846	9	36	45	34	73	0	15	30	11	227	1.5	1.1	7.6
98-99–Atlanta	30	3	337	53	182	.291	12	42	.286	28	37	.757	7	21	28	12	30	0	12	29	1	146	0.9	0.4	4.9
Reg. Season Totals	60	6	809	130	384	.339	30	88	.341	83	102	.814	16	57	73	46	103	0	27	59	12	373	1.2	0.8	6.2
Playoff Totals	8	0	71	15	41	.366	4	11	.364	10	11	.909	2	7	9	4	11	1	6	2	1	44	1.1	0.5	5.5

Gray, Evric b. December 13, 1969 Ht. 6-7 Wt. 235 College: Nevada-Las Vegas

SEASON–TEAM	G	GS	MIN	FGM	FGA	PCT	3FGM	3FGA	PCT	FTM	FTA	PCT	O-RB	D-RB	TOT	AST	PF	DQ	STL	TO	BLK	PTS	RPG	APG	PPG
96-97–New Jersey	5	0	42	4	15	.267	1	4	.250	4	4	1.000	1	2	3	2	5	0	1	3	0	13	0.6	0.4	2.6
Reg. Season Totals	5	0	42	4	15	.267	1	4	.250	4	4	1.000	1	2	3	2	5	0	1	3	0	13	0.6	0.4	2.6

Gray, Gary Michael b. February 23, 1945 Ht. 6-1 Wt. 185 College: Oklahoma City

SEASON–TEAM	G	GS	MIN	FGM	FGA	PCT	3FGM	3FGA	PCT	FTM	FTA	PCT	O-RB	D-RB	TOT	AST	PF	DQ	STL	TO	BLK	PTS	RPG	APG	PPG
67-68–Cincinnati	44	–	276	49	134	.366	–	–	–	7	10	.700	–	–	23	26	48	0	–	–	–	105	0.5	0.6	2.4
Reg. Season Totals	44	–	276	49	134	.366	–	–	–	7	10	.700	–	–	23	26	48	0	–	–	–	105	0.5	0.6	2.4

Gray, Leonard Earl b. December 19, 1951 Ht. 6-8 Wt. 240 College: Kansas; Long Beach State

SEASON–TEAM	G	GS	MIN	FGM	FGA	PCT	3FGM	3FGA	PCT	FTM	FTA	PCT	O-RB	D-RB	TOT	AST	PF	DQ	STL	TO	BLK	PTS	RPG	APG	PPG
74-75–Seattle	75	–	2280	378	773	.489	–	–	–	104	144	.722	133	345	478	163	292	9	63	–	24	860	6.4	2.2	11.5
75-76–Seattle	66	–	2139	394	831	.474	–	–	–	126	169	.746	109	289	398	203	260	10	75	–	36	914	6.0	3.1	13.8
76-77–Seattle-Wash.	83	–	1639	258	592	.436	–	–	–	118	158	.747	84	209	293	124	273	9	58	–	31	634	3.5	1.5	7.6
Reg. Season Totals	224	–	6058	1030	2196	.469	–	–	–	348	471	.739	326	843	1169	490	825	28	196	–	91	2408	5.2	2.2	10.8
Playoff Totals	17	–	315	45	101	.446	–	–	–	11	13	.846	13	41	54	21	53	0	14	–	5	101	3.2	1.2	5.9

Gray, Stuart Allan b. May 27, 1963 Ht. 7-0 Wt. 245 College: UCLA

SEASON–TEAM	G	GS	MIN	FGM	FGA	PCT	3FGM	3FGA	PCT	FTM	FTA	PCT	O-RB	D-RB	TOT	AST	PF	DQ	STL	TO	BLK	PTS	RPG	APG	PPG
84-85–Indiana	52	0	391	35	92	.380	0	0	–	32	47	.681	29	94	123	15	82	1	9	51	14	102	2.4	0.3	2.0
85-86–Indiana	67	3	423	54	108	.500	0	0	–	47	74	.635	45	73	118	15	94	0	8	32	11	155	1.8	0.2	2.3
86-87–Indiana	55	1	456	41	101	.406	0	0	–	28	39	.718	39	90	129	26	93	0	10	36	28	110	2.3	0.5	2.0
87-88–Indiana	74	0	807	90	193	.466	0	1	.000	44	73	.603	70	180	250	44	152	1	11	50	32	224	3.4	0.6	3.0
88-89–Indiana	72	0	783	72	153	.471	0	1	.000	44	64	.688	84	161	245	29	128	0	11	48	21	188	3.4	0.4	2.6
89-90–Cha.-N.Y.	58	1	560	42	99	.424	0	5	.000	32	47	.681	40	105	145	19	90	0	15	24	26	116	2.5	0.3	2.0
90-91–New York	8	0	37	4	12	.333	0	0	–	3	3	1.000	2	8	10	0	6	0	0	2	1	11	1.3	0.0	1.4
Reg. Season Totals	386	5	3457	338	758	.446	0	7	.000	230	347	.663	309	711	1020	148	645	2	64	243	133	906	2.6	0.4	2.3
Playoff Totals	7	0	26	2	6	.333	0	0	–	2	4	.500	5	10	15	–	6	0	1	3	0	6	2.1	0.0	0.9

Gray, Sylvester b. July 8, 1967 Ht. 6-6 Wt. 240 College: Memphis

SEASON–TEAM	G	GS	MIN	FGM	FGA	PCT	3FGM	3FGA	PCT	FTM	FTA	PCT	O-RB	D-RB	TOT	AST	PF	DQ	STL	TO	BLK	PTS	RPG	APG	PPG
88-89–Miami	55	15	1220	167	398	.420	1	4	.250	105	156	.673	117	169	286	117	144	1	36	102	25	440	5.2	2.1	8.0
Reg. Season Totals	55	15	1220	167	398	.420	1	4	.250	105	156	.673	117	169	286	117	144	1	36	102	25	440	5.2	2.1	8.0

Gray, Wyndol Woodrow b. March 20, 1922 d. January 29, 1994 Ht. 6-1 Wt. 175 College: Harvard; Bowling Green State

SEASON–TEAM	G	GS	MIN	FGM	FGA	PCT	3FGM	3FGA	PCT	FTM	FTA	PCT	O-RB	D-RB	TOT	AST	PF	DQ	STL	TO	BLK	PTS	RPG	APG	PPG
46-47–Boston	55	–	–	139	476	.292	–	–	–	72	124	.581	–	–	–	47	105	–	–	–	–	350	–	0.9	6.4
47-48–Toledo (N)	2	–	–	2	–	–	–	–	–	2	4	.500	–	–	–	–	4	–	–	–	–	6	–	–	3.0
47-48–Prov.-St. L.	12	–	–	6	37	.162	–	–	–	1	4	.250	–	–	–	3	16	–	–	–	–	13	–	0.3	1.1
Reg. NBA Totals	67	–	–	145	513	.283	–	–	–	73	128	.570	–	–	–	50	121	–	–	–	–	363	–	0.7	5.4
Reg. NBL Totals	2	–	–	2	–	–	–	–	–	2	4	.500	–	–	–	–	4	–	–	–	–	6	–	–	3.0

Grayer, Jeffrey (Jeff) b. December 17, 1965 Ht. 6-5 Wt. 210 College: Iowa State

SEASON–TEAM	G	GS	MIN	FGM	FGA	PCT	3FGM	3FGA	PCT	FTM	FTA	PCT	O-RB	D-RB	TOT	AST	PF	DQ	STL	TO	BLK	PTS	RPG	APG	PPG
88-89–Milwaukee	11	2	200	32	73	.438	0	2	.000	17	20	.850	14	21	35	22	15	0	10	19	1	81	3.2	2.0	7.4
89-90–Milwaukee	71	40	1427	224	487	.460	1	8	.125	99	152	.651	94	123	217	107	125	0	48	82	10	548	3.1	1.5	7.7
90-91–Milwaukee	82	7	1422	210	485	.433	0	3	.000	101	147	.687	111	135	246	123	98	0	48	86	9	521	3.0	1.5	6.4
91-92–Milwaukee	82	11	1659	309	689	.448	19	66	.288	102	153	.667	129	128	257	150	142	0	64	105	13	739	3.1	1.8	9.0
92-93–Golden State	48	12	1025	165	353	.467	2	14	.143	91	136	.669	71	86	157	70	120	1	31	54	8	423	3.3	1.5	8.8
93-94–Golden State	67	4	1096	191	363	.526	2	12	.167	71	118	.602	76	115	191	62	103	0	33	63	13	455	2.9	0.9	6.8
94-95–Philadelphia	47	25	1098	163	381	.428	5	15	.333	58	83	.699	58	91	149	74	80	1	27	56	4	389	3.2	1.6	8.3
96-97–Sacramento	25	0	316	38	83	.458	4	11	.364	11	20	.550	21	17	38	25	42	0	8	15	7	91	1.5	1.0	3.6
97-98–Cha.-G.S.	5	0	34	4	11	.364	2	6	.333	0	0	–	0	4	4	2	7	0	2	4	0	10	0.8	0.4	2.0
Reg. Season Totals	438	101	8277	1336	2925	.457	35	137	.255	550	829	.663	574	720	1294	635	732	2	271	484	65	3257	3.0	1.4	7.4
Playoff Totals	10	0	95	16	33	.485	0	0	–	7	9	.778	4	10	14	8	10	0	2	6	1	39	1.4	0.8	3.9

Greacen, Robert Alexander (Bob) b. September 15, 1947 Ht. 6-7 Wt. 210 College: Rutgers

SEASON–TEAM	G	GS	MIN	FGM	FGA	PCT	3FGM	3FGA	PCT	FTM	FTA	PCT	O-RB	D-RB	TOT	AST	PF	DQ	STL	TO	BLK	PTS	RPG	APG	PPG
69-70–Milwaukee	41	–	292	44	109	.404	–	–	–	18	28	.643	–	–	59	27	49	0	–	–	–	106	1.4	0.7	2.6
70-71–Milwaukee	2	–	43	1	12	.083	–	–	–	3	7	.429	–	–	6	13	7	0	–	–	–	5	3.0	6.5	2.5
71-72–New York (A)	4	–	20	1	2	.500	0	0	–	0	0	–	–	–	2	1	1	–	–	2	–	2	0.5	0.3	0.5
Reg. NBA Totals	43	–	335	45	121	.372	–	–	–	21	35	.600	–	–	65	40	56	0	–	–	–	111	1.5	0.9	2.6
Reg. ABA Totals	4	–	20	1	2	.500	0	0	–	0	0	–	–	–	2	1	1	–	–	2	–	2	0.5	0.3	0.5
NBA Playoff Totals	8	–	24	5	15	.333	–	–	–	4	5	.800	–	–	7	3	4	0	–	–	–	14	0.9	0.4	1.8

Green, A.C. Jr. b. October 4, 1963 Ht. 6-9 Wt. 225 College: Oregon State

SEASON–TEAM	G	GS	MIN	FGM	FGA	PCT	3FGM	3FGA	PCT	FTM	FTA	PCT	O-RB	D-RB	TOT	AST	PF	DQ	STL	TO	BLK	PTS	RPG	APG	PPG
85-86–L.A. Lakers	82	1	1542	209	388	.539	1	6	.167	102	167	.611	160	221	381	54	229	2	49	99	49	521	4.6	0.7	6.4
86-87–L.A. Lakers	79	72	2240	316	587	.538	0	5	.000	220	282	.780	210	405	615	84	171	0	70	102	80	852	7.8	1.1	10.8
87-88–L.A. Lakers	82	64	2636	322	640	.503	0	2	.000	293	379	.773	245	465	710	93	204	0	87	120	45	937	8.7	1.1	11.4
88-89–L.A. Lakers	82	82	2510	401	758	.529	4	17	.235	282	359	.786	258	481	739	103	172	0	94	119	55	1088	9.0	1.3	13.3
89-90–L.A. Lakers	82	82	2709	385	806	.478	13	46	.283	278	370	.751	262	450	712	90	207	0	66	116	50	1061	8.7	1.1	12.9
90-91–L.A. Lakers	82	21	2164	258	542	.476	11	55	.200	223	302	.738	201	315	516	71	117	0	59	99	23	750	6.3	0.9	9.1
91-92–L.A. Lakers	82	53	2902	382	803	.476	12	56	.214	340	457	.744	306	456	762	117	141	0	91	111	36	1116	9.3	1.4	13.6
92-93–L.A. Lakers	82	55	2819	379	706	.537	16	46	.348	277	375	.739	287	424	711	116	149	0	88	116	39	1051	8.7	1.4	12.8
93-94–Phoenix	82	55	2825	465	926	.502	8	35	.229	266	362	.735	275	478	753	137	142	0	70	100	38	1204	9.2	1.7	14.7
94-95–Phoenix	82	52	2687	311	617	.504	43	127	.339	251	343	.732	194	475	669	127	146	0	55	114	31	916	8.2	1.5	11.2
95-96–Phoenix	82	36	2113	215	444	.484	14	52	.269	168	237	.709	166	388	554	72	141	1	45	79	23	612	6.8	0.9	7.5
96-97–Phoenix-Dallas	83	73	2492	234	484	.483	1	20	.050	128	197	.650	222	434	656	69	145	0	70	74	16	597	7.9	0.8	7.2
97-98–Dallas	82	68	2649	242	534	.453	0	4	.000	116	162	.716	219	449	668	123	157	0	78	68	27	600	8.1	1.5	7.3
98-99–Dallas	50	35	924	108	256	.422	0	8	.000	30	52	.577	82	146	228	25	69	0	28	19	8	246	4.6	0.5	4.9
99-00–L.A. Lakers	82	82	1929	173	387	.447	1	4	.250	66	95	.695	160	326	486	80	127	0	53	53	18	413	5.9	1.0	5.0
Reg. Season Totals	1196	831	35141	4400	8878	.496	124	483	.257	3040	4139	.734	3247	5913	9160	1361	2317	3	1003	1389	538	11964	7.7	1.1	10.0
Playoff Totals	150	109	4098	454	955	.475	12	48	.250	392	531	.738	389	691	1080	128	336	2	99	145	46	1312	7.2	0.9	8.7
All-Star Totals	1	1	12	0	3	.000	0	0	–	0	0	–	0	3	3	1	1	0	0	1	1	0	3.0	1.0	0.0

Green, John M. **(Johnny)** b. December 8, 1933 Ht. 6-5 Wt. 200 College: Michigan State

SEASON–TEAM	G	GS	MIN	FGM	FGA	PCT	3FGM	3FGA	PCT	FTM	FTA	PCT	O-RB	D-RB	TOT	AST	PF	DQ	STL	TO	BLK	PTS	RPG	APG	PPG
59-60–New York	69	–	1232	209	468	.447	–	–	–	63	155	.406	–	–	539	52	195	3	–	–	–	481	7.8	0.8	7.0
60-61–New York	78	–	1784	326	758	.430	–	–	–	145	278	.522	–	–	838	97	194	3	–	–	–	797	10.7	1.2	10.2
61-62–New York	80	–	2789	507	1164	.436	–	–	–	261	434	.601	–	–	1066	191	265	4	–	–	–	1275	13.3	2.4	15.9
62-63–New York	80	–	2553	582	1261	.462	–	–	–	280	439	.638	–	–	964	152	243	5	–	–	–	1444	12.1	1.9	18.1
63-64–New York	80	–	2134	482	1026	.470	–	–	–	195	392	.497	–	–	799	157	246	4	–	–	–	1159	10.0	2.0	14.5
64-65–New York	78	–	1720	346	737	.469	–	–	–	165	301	.548	–	–	545	129	194	3	–	–	–	857	7.0	1.7	11.0
65-66–N.Y.-Balt.	79	–	1645	358	668	.536	–	–	–	202	388	.521	–	–	645	107	183	3	–	–	–	918	8.2	1.4	11.6
66-67–Baltimore	61	–	948	203	437	.465	–	–	–	96	207	.464	–	–	394	57	139	7	–	–	–	502	6.5	0.9	8.2
67-68–S.D.-Phil.	77	–	1440	310	676	.459	–	–	–	139	295	.471	–	–	545	80	163	3	–	–	–	759	7.1	1.0	9.9
68-69–Philadelphia	74	–	795	146	282	.518	–	–	–	57	125	.456	–	–	330	47	110	1	–	–	–	349	4.5	0.6	4.7
69-70–Cincinnati	78	–	2278	481	860	.559	–	–	–	254	429	.592	–	–	841	112	268	6	–	–	–	1216	10.8	1.4	15.6
70-71–Cincinnati	75	–	2147	502	855	.587	–	–	–	248	402	.617	–	–	656	89	233	7	–	–	–	1252	8.7	1.2	16.7
71-72–Cincinnati	82	–	1914	331	582	.569	–	–	–	141	250	.564	–	–	560	120	238	5	–	–	–	803	6.8	1.5	9.8
72-73–K.C.-Omaha	66	–	1245	190	317	.599	–	–	–	89	131	.679	–	–	361	59	185	7	–	–	–	469	5.5	0.9	7.1
Reg. Season Totals	1057	–	24624	4973	10091	.493	–	–	–	2335	4226	.553	–	–	9083	1449	2856	61	–	–	–	12281	8.6	1.4	11.6
Playoff Totals	20	–	359	67	115	.583	–	–	–	26	60	.433	–	–	107	13	40	1	–	–	–	160	5.4	0.7	8.0
All-Star Totals	4	–	72	13	19	.684	–	–	–	6	8	.750	–	–	9	0	9	1	–	–	–	32	2.3	0.0	8.0

Green, Kenneth Apple **(Ken)** b. September 19, 1959 Ht. 6-8 Wt. 220 College: Ranger (Texas) Coll. (J.C.); Texas-Pan American

SEASON–TEAM	G	GS	MIN	FGM	FGA	PCT	3FGM	3FGA	PCT	FTM	FTA	PCT	O-RB	D-RB	TOT	AST	PF	DQ	STL	TO	BLK	PTS	RPG	APG	PPG
85-86–New York	7	0	72	13	27	.481	0	0	–	5	9	.556	12	15	27	2	8	0	4	1	0	31	3.9	0.3	4.4
Reg. Season Totals	7	0	72	13	27	.481	0	0	–	5	9	.556	12	15	27	2	8	0	4	1	0	31	3.9	0.3	4.4

Green, Kenneth Leroy **(Kenny)** b. October 11, 1964 Ht. 6-7 Wt. 215 College: Wake Forest

SEASON–TEAM	G	GS	MIN	FGM	FGA	PCT	3FGM	3FGA	PCT	FTM	FTA	PCT	O-RB	D-RB	TOT	AST	PF	DQ	STL	TO	BLK	PTS	RPG	APG	PPG
85-86–Wash.-Phil.	41	0	453	83	192	.432	0	1	.000	35	49	.714	27	46	73	9	53	0	5	35	9	201	1.8	0.2	4.9
86-87–Philadelphia	19	0	172	25	70	.357	0	0	–	14	19	.737	6	22	28	7	8	0	4	15	2	64	1.5	0.4	3.4
Reg. Season Totals	60	0	625	108	262	.412	0	1	.000	49	68	.721	33	68	101	16	61	0	9	50	11	265	1.7	0.3	4.4

Green, Lamar Anthony b. March 22, 1947 Ht. 6-8 Wt. 215 College: Morehead State

SEASON–TEAM	G	GS	MIN	FGM	FGA	PCT	3FGM	3FGA	PCT	FTM	FTA	PCT	O-RB	D-RB	TOT	AST	PF	DQ	STL	TO	BLK	PTS	RPG	APG	PPG
69-70–Phoenix	58	–	700	101	234	.432	–	–	–	41	70	.586	–	–	276	17	115	2	–	–	–	243	4.8	0.3	4.2
70-71–Phoenix	68	–	1326	167	369	.453	–	–	–	64	106	.604	–	–	466	53	202	5	–	–	–	398	6.9	0.8	5.9
71-72–Phoenix	67	–	991	133	298	.446	–	–	–	66	90	.733	–	–	348	45	134	1	–	–	–	332	5.2	0.7	5.0
72-73–Phoenix	80	–	2048	224	520	.431	–	–	–	89	118	.754	–	–	746	89	263	10	–	–	–	537	9.3	1.1	6.7
73-74–Phoenix	72	–	1103	129	317	.407	–	–	–	38	68	.559	85	265	350	43	150	1	32	–	38	296	4.9	0.6	4.1
74-75–New Orleans	15	–	280	24	70	.343	–	–	–	9	20	.450	28	81	109	16	38	0	4	–	5	57	7.3	1.1	3.8
74-75–Virginia (A)	51	–	856	115	270	.426	0	0	–	40	54	.741	86	169	255	47	139	–	13	60	25	270	5.0	0.9	5.3
Reg. NBA Totals	360	–	6448	778	1808	.430	–	–	–	307	472	.650	113	346	2295	263	902	19	36	–	43	1863	6.4	0.7	5.2
Reg. ABA Totals	51	–	856	115	270	.426	0	0	–	40	54	.741	86	169	255	47	139	–	13	60	25	270	5.0	0.9	5.3
NBA Playoff Totals	6	–	69	8	28	.286	–	–	–	2	5	.400	0	0	23	5	8	0	0	–	0	18	3.8	0.8	3.0

Green, Litterial b. March 7, 1970 Ht. 6-1 Wt. 220 College: Georgia

SEASON–TEAM	G	GS	MIN	FGM	FGA	PCT	3FGM	3FGA	PCT	FTM	FTA	PCT	O-RB	D-RB	TOT	AST	PF	DQ	STL	TO	BLK	PTS	RPG	APG	PPG
92-93–Orlando	52	4	626	87	198	.439	1	10	.100	60	96	.625	11	23	34	116	70	0	23	42	4	235	0.7	2.2	4.5
93-94–Orlando	29	0	126	22	57	.386	1	4	.250	28	37	.757	6	6	12	9	16	0	6	13	1	73	0.4	0.3	2.5
96-97–Detroit	45	0	311	30	64	.469	0	10	.000	30	47	.638	6	16	22	41	27	0	16	15	1	90	0.5	0.9	2.0
97-98–Milwaukee	21	0	124	5	23	.217	0	2	.000	15	20	.750	1	6	7	16	11	0	4	8	0	25	0.3	0.8	1.2
98-99–Cleveland	1	0	2	0	1	.000	0	0	–	0	0	–	0	0	0	0	0	0	0	0	0	0	0.0	0.0	0.0
Reg. Season Totals	148	4	1189	144	343	.420	2	26	.077	133	200	.665	24	51	75	182	124	0	49	78	6	423	0.5	1.2	2.9

Green, Luther b. November 13, 1946 Ht. 6-7 Wt. 190 College: Long Island University

SEASON–TEAM	G	GS	MIN	FGM	FGA	PCT	3FGM	3FGA	PCT	FTM	FTA	PCT	O-RB	D-RB	TOT	AST	PF	DQ	STL	TO	BLK	PTS	RPG	APG	PPG
69-70–New York (A)	59	–	739	114	303	.376	0	3	.000	55	97	.567	–	–	263	27	117	2	–	–	–	283	4.5	0.5	4.8
70-71–New York (A)	26	–	164	40	88	.455	0	4	.000	18	44	.409	–	–	55	3	19	–	–	–	–	98	2.1	0.1	3.8
72-73–Philadelphia	5	–	32	0	11	.000	–	–	–	3	9	.333	–	–	3	0	3	0	–	–	–	3	0.6	0.0	0.6
Reg. NBA Totals	5	–	32	0	11	.000	–	–	–	3	9	.333	–	–	3	0	3	0	–	–	–	3	0.6	0.0	0.6
Reg. ABA Totals	85	–	903	154	391	.394	0	7	.000	73	141	.518	–	–	318	30	136	2	–	–	–	381	3.7	0.4	4.5
ABA Playoff Totals	7	–	82	11	29	.379	1	2	.500	10	15	.667	–	–	28	3	22	0	–	–	–	33	4.0	0.4	4.7

Green, Michael Kenneth (Mike) b. August 6, 1951 Ht. 6-10 Wt. 200 College: Louisiana Tech

SEASON–TEAM	G	GS	MIN	FGM	FGA	PCT	3FGM	3FGA	PCT	FTM	FTA	PCT	O-RB	D-RB	TOT	AST	PF	DQ	STL	TO	BLK	PTS	RPG	APG	PPG
73-74–Denver (A)	79	–	1648	367	799	.459	1	2	.500	169	226	.748	225	359	584	64	191	–	47	128	126	904	7.4	0.8	11.4
74-75–Denver (A)	81	–	2557	593	1095	.542	0	4	.000	225	305	.738	282	467	749	101	271	–	85	203	174	1411	9.2	1.2	17.4
75-76–Virginia (A)	54	–	1719	385	832	.463	0	4	.000	154	198	.778	196	323	519	82	187	–	68	136	80	924	9.6	1.5	17.1
76-77–Seattle	76	–	1928	290	658	.441	–	–	–	166	235	.706	191	312	503	120	201	1	45	–	129	746	6.6	1.6	9.8
77-78–Seattle-S.A.	72	–	1382	238	514	.463	–	–	–	107	142	.754	130	229	359	76	193	1	30	105	100	583	5.0	1.1	8.1
78-79–San Antonio	76	–	1641	235	477	.493	–	–	–	101	144	.701	131	223	354	116	230	3	37	89	122	571	4.7	1.5	7.5
79-80–Kansas City	21	–	459	69	159	.434	0	2	.000	24	42	.571	35	78	113	28	55	0	13	36	21	162	5.4	1.3	7.7
Reg. NBA Totals	245	–	5410	832	1808	.460	0	2	.000	398	563	.707	487	842	1329	340	679	5	125	230	372	2062	5.4	1.4	8.4
Reg. ABA Totals	214	–	5924	1345	2726	.493	1	10	.100	548	729	.752	703	1149	1852	247	649	0	200	467	380	3239	8.7	1.2	15.1
NBA Playoff Totals	20	–	524	76	172	.442	0	0	–	23	31	.742	52	65	117	22	80	3	18	26	52	175	5.9	1.1	8.8
ABA Playoff Totals	13	–	487	112	226	.496	0	1	.000	53	60	.883	54	67	121	14	51	0	10	27	21	277	9.3	1.1	21.3

Green, Rickey b. August 18, 1954 Ht. 6-0 Wt. 170 College: Vincennes (Ind.) (J.C.); Michigan

SEASON–TEAM	G	GS	MIN	FGM	FGA	PCT	3FGM	3FGA	PCT	FTM	FTA	PCT	O-RB	D-RB	TOT	AST	PF	DQ	STL	TO	BLK	PTS	RPG	APG	PPG
77-78–Golden State	76	–	1098	143	375	.381	–	–	–	54	90	.600	49	67	116	149	95	0	58	79	1	340	1.5	2.0	4.5
78-79–Detroit	27	–	431	67	177	.379	–	–	–	45	67	.672	15	25	40	63	37	0	25	44	1	179	1.5	2.3	6.6
80-81–Utah	47	–	1307	176	366	.481	0	1	.000	70	97	.722	30	86	116	235	123	2	75	83	1	422	2.5	5.0	9.0
81-82–Utah	81	73	2822	500	1015	.493	0	8	.000	202	264	.765	85	158	243	630	183	0	185	198	9	1202	3.0	7.8	14.8
82-83–Utah	78	78	2783	464	942	.493	2	13	.154	185	232	.797	62	161	223	697	154	0	220	222	4	1115	2.9	8.9	14.3
83-84–Utah	81	81	2768	439	904	.486	2	17	.118	192	234	.821	56	174	230	748	155	1	215	172	13	1072	2.8	9.2	13.2
84-85–Utah	77	77	2431	381	798	.477	6	20	.300	232	267	.869	37	152	189	597	131	0	132	177	3	1000	2.5	7.8	13.0
85-86–Utah	80	44	2012	357	758	.471	5	29	.172	213	250	.852	32	103	135	411	130	0	106	132	6	932	1.7	5.1	11.7
86-87–Utah	81	80	2090	301	644	.467	7	19	.368	172	208	.827	38	125	163	541	108	0	110	133	2	781	2.0	6.7	9.6
87-88–Utah	81	3	1116	157	370	.424	4	19	.211	75	83	.904	14	66	80	300	83	0	57	94	1	393	1.0	3.7	4.9
88-89–Cha.-Milw.	63	2	871	129	264	.489	3	11	.273	30	33	.909	11	58	69	187	35	0	40	61	2	291	1.1	3.0	4.6
89-90–Indiana	69	0	927	100	231	.433	1	11	.091	43	51	.843	9	45	54	182	60	0	51	62	1	244	0.8	2.6	3.5
90-91–Philadelphia	79	75	2248	334	722	.463	8	36	.222	117	141	.830	33	104	137	413	130	0	57	108	6	793	1.7	5.2	10.0
91-92–Boston	26	0	367	46	103	.447	1	4	.250	13	18	.722	3	21	24	68	28	0	17	18	1	106	0.9	2.6	4.1
Reg. Season Totals	946	513	23271	3594	7669	.469	39	188	.207	1643	2035	.807	474	1345	1819	5221	1452	3	1348	1583	51	8870	1.9	5.5	9.4
Playoff Totals	55	36	1275	192	422	.455	7	20	.350	94	111	.847	24	81	105	294	71	0	50	83	4	485	1.9	5.3	8.8
All-Star Totals	1	0	19	3	8	.375	0	0	–	0	0	–	0	0	0	11	1	0	1	4	0	6	0.0	11.0	6.0

Green, Sean Curtis b. February 2, 1970 Ht. 6-5 Wt. 210 College: North Carolina State; Iona

SEASON–TEAM	G	GS	MIN	FGM	FGA	PCT	3FGM	3FGA	PCT	FTM	FTA	PCT	O-RB	D-RB	TOT	AST	PF	DQ	STL	TO	BLK	PTS	RPG	APG	PPG
91-92–Indiana	35	0	256	62	158	.392	2	10	.200	15	28	.536	22	20	42	22	31	0	13	27	6	141	1.2	0.6	4.0
92-93–Indiana	13	0	81	28	55	.509	3	10	.300	3	4	.750	4	5	9	7	11	0	2	9	1	62	0.7	0.5	4.8
93-94–Phil.-Utah	36	0	334	63	183	.344	10	41	.244	13	18	.722	10	24	34	16	21	0	18	27	6	149	0.9	0.4	4.1
Reg. Season Totals	84	0	671	153	396	.386	15	61	.246	31	50	.620	36	49	85	45	63	0	33	63	13	352	1.0	0.5	4.2
Playoff Totals	1	0	3	0	0	–	0	0	–	0	0	–	0	0	0	–	0	0	0	0	0	0	0.0	0.0	0.0

Green, Sidney b. January 4, 1961 Ht. 6-9 Wt. 225 College: Nevada-Las Vegas

SEASON–TEAM	G	GS	MIN	FGM	FGA	PCT	3FGM	3FGA	PCT	FTM	FTA	PCT	O-RB	D-RB	TOT	AST	PF	DQ	STL	TO	BLK	PTS	RPG	APG	PPG
83-84–Chicago	49	0	667	100	228	.439	0	0	–	55	77	.714	58	116	174	25	128	1	18	60	17	255	3.6	0.5	5.2
84-85–Chicago	48	1	740	108	250	.432	0	4	.000	79	98	.806	72	174	246	29	102	0	11	68	11	295	5.1	0.6	6.1
85-86–Chicago	80	68	2307	407	875	.465	0	8	.000	262	335	.782	208	450	658	139	292	5	70	220	37	1076	8.2	1.7	13.5
86-87–Detroit	80	69	1792	256	542	.472	0	2	.000	119	177	.672	196	457	653	62	197	0	41	127	50	631	8.2	0.8	7.9
87-88–New York	82	65	2049	258	585	.441	0	2	.000	126	190	.663	221	421	642	93	318	9	65	148	32	642	7.8	1.1	7.8
88-89–New York	82	0	1277	194	422	.460	0	3	.000	129	170	.759	157	237	394	76	172	0	47	125	18	517	4.8	0.9	6.3
89-90–Orlando	73	31	1860	312	667	.468	1	3	.333	136	209	.651	166	422	588	99	231	4	50	119	26	761	8.1	1.4	10.4
90-91–San Antonio	66	7	1099	177	384	.461	0	3	.000	89	105	.848	98	215	313	52	172	0	32	89	13	443	4.7	0.8	6.7
91-92–San Antonio	80	1	1127	147	344	.427	0	0	–	73	89	.820	92	250	342	36	148	0	29	62	11	367	4.3	0.5	4.6
92-93–S.A.-Cha.	39	0	329	34	89	.382	0	2	.000	25	31	.806	32	86	118	24	37	1	6	20	5	93	3.0	0.6	2.4
Reg. Season Totals	679	242	13247	1993	4386	.454	1	27	.037	1093	1481	.738	1300	2828	4128	635	1797	20	369	1038	220	5080	6.1	0.9	7.5
Playoff Totals	43	4	506	58	135	.430	0	0	–	34	52	.654	56	93	149	18	80	0	5	28	7	150	3.5	0.4	3.5

Green, Sihugo (Si) b. August 20, 1933 d. October 4, 1980 Ht. 6-2 Wt. 185 College: Duquesne

SEASON–TEAM	G	GS	MIN	FGM	FGA	PCT	3FGM	3FGA	PCT	FTM	FTA	PCT	O-RB	D-RB	TOT	AST	PF	DQ	STL	TO	BLK	PTS	RPG	APG	PPG
56-57–Rochester	13	–	423	50	143	.350	–	–	–	49	69	.710			67	47	36	1	–	–	–	149	5.2	3.6	11.5
58-59–Cin.-St. Louis	46	–	1109	146	415	.352	–	–	–	104	160	.650	–	–	252	113	127	1	–	–	–	396	5.5	2.5	8.6
59-60–St. Louis	70	–	1354	159	427	.372	–	–	–	111	175	.634	–	–	257	133	150	3	–	–	–	429	3.7	1.9	6.1
60-61–St. Louis	76	–	1968	263	718	.366	–	–	–	174	247	.704	–	–	380	258	234	2	–	–	–	700	5.0	3.4	9.2
61-62–St. Louis-Chi.	71	–	2388	341	905	.377	–	–	–	218	311	.701	–	–	399	318	226	3	–	–	–	900	5.6	4.5	12.7
62-63–Chicago	73	–	2648	322	783	.411	–	–	–	209	306	.683	–	–	335	422	274	5	–	–	–	853	4.6	5.8	11.7
63-64–Baltimore	75	–	2064	287	691	.415	–	–	–	198	290	.683	–	–	282	215	224	5	–	–	–	772	3.8	2.9	10.3
64-65–Baltimore	70	–	1086	152	368	.413	–	–	–	101	161	.627	–	–	169	140	134	1	–	–	–	405	2.4	2.0	5.8
65-66–Boston	10	–	92	12	31	.387	–	–	–	8	16	.500	–	–	11	9	16	0	–	–	–	32	1.1	0.9	3.2
Reg. Season Totals	504	–	13132	1732	4481	.387	–	–	–	1172	1735	.676	–	–	2152	1655	1421	21	–	–	–	4636	4.3	3.3	9.2
Playoff Totals	41	–	1111	156	360	.433	–	–	–	76	124	.613	–	–	232	165	121	3	–	–	–	388	5.7	4.0	9.5

Green, Steven Michael (Steve) b. October 4, 1953 Ht. 6-7 Wt. 220 College: Indiana

SEASON–TEAM	G	GS	MIN	FGM	FGA	PCT	3FGM	3FGA	PCT	FTM	FTA	PCT	O-RB	D-RB	TOT	AST	PF	DQ	STL	TO	BLK	PTS	RPG	APG	PPG
75-76–Utah-St. L. (A)	52	–	1068	195	438	.445	0	5	.000	84	108	.778	84	110	194	64	150	–	31	72	10	474	3.7	1.2	9.1
76-77–Indiana	70	–	918	183	424	.432	–	–	–	84	113	.743	79	98	177	46	157	2	46	–	12	450	2.5	0.7	6.4
77-78–Indiana	44	–	449	56	128	.438	–	–	–	39	56	.696	31	40	71	30	67	0	14	23	2	151	1.6	0.7	3.4
78-79–Indiana	39	–	265	42	89	.472	–	–	–	20	34	.588	22	30	52	21	39	0	11	17	3	104	1.3	0.5	2.7
Reg. NBA Totals	153	–	1632	281	641	.438	–	–	–	143	203	.704	132	168	300	97	263	2	71	40	17	705	2.0	0.6	4.6
Reg. ABA Totals	52	–	1068	195	438	.445	0	5	.000	84	108	.778	84	110	194	64	150	–	31	72	10	474	3.7	1.2	9.1

Green, Tommie L. (Tommy) b. April 8, 1956 Ht. 6-2 Wt. 185 College: Southern University

SEASON–TEAM	G	GS	MIN	FGM	FGA	PCT	3FGM	3FGA	PCT	FTM	FTA	PCT	O-RB	D-RB	TOT	AST	PF	DQ	STL	TO	BLK	PTS	RPG	APG	PPG
78-79–New Orleans	59	–	809	92	237	.388	–	–	–	48	63	.762	20	48	68	140	111	0	61	89	6	232	1.2	2.4	3.9
Reg. Season Totals	59	–	809	92	237	.388	–	–	–	48	63	.762	20	48	68	140	111	0	61	89	6	232	1.2	2.4	3.9

Greenspan, Gerald (Jerry) b. November 22, 1941 Ht. 6-5 Wt. 195 College: Maryland

SEASON–TEAM	G	GS	MIN	FGM	FGA	PCT	3FGM	3FGA	PCT	FTM	FTA	PCT	O-RB	D-RB	TOT	AST	PF	DQ	STL	TO	BLK	PTS	RPG	APG	PPG
63-64–Philadelphia	20	–	280	32	90	.356	–	–	–	34	50	.680	–	–	72	11	54	0	–	–	–	98	3.6	0.6	4.9
64-65–Philadelphia	5	–	49	8	13	.615	–	–	–	8	8	1.000	–	–	11	0	12	0	–	–	–	24	2.2	0.0	4.8
Reg. Season Totals	25	–	329	40	103	.388	–	–	–	42	58	.724	–	–	83	11	66	0	–	–	–	122	3.3	0.4	4.9

Greenwood, David Kasim b. May 27, 1957 Ht. 6-9 Wt. 230 College: UCLA

SEASON–TEAM	G	GS	MIN	FGM	FGA	PCT	3FGM	3FGA	PCT	FTM	FTA	PCT	O-RB	D-RB	TOT	AST	PF	DQ	STL	TO	BLK	PTS	RPG	APG	PPG
79-80–Chicago	82	–	2791	498	1051	.474	1	7	.143	337	416	.810	223	550	773	182	313	8	60	210	129	1334	9.4	2.2	16.3
80-81–Chicago	82	–	2710	481	989	.486	0	2	.000	217	290	.748	243	481	724	218	282	5	77	192	124	1179	8.8	2.7	14.4
81-82–Chicago	82	82	2914	480	1014	.473	0	3	.000	240	291	.825	192	594	786	262	292	1	70	180	93	1200	9.6	3.2	14.6
82-83–Chicago	79	61	2355	312	686	.455	0	4	.000	165	233	.708	217	548	765	151	261	5	54	154	90	789	9.7	1.9	10.0
83-84–Chicago	78	76	2718	369	753	.490	0	1	.000	213	289	.737	214	572	786	139	265	9	67	149	72	951	10.1	1.8	12.2
84-85–Chicago	61	28	1523	152	332	.458	0	1	.000	67	94	.713	108	280	388	78	190	1	34	63	21	371	6.4	1.3	6.1
85-86–San Antonio	68	24	1910	198	388	.510	0	1	.000	142	184	.772	151	380	531	90	207	3	37	113	52	538	7.8	1.3	7.9
86-87–San Antonio	79	78	2587	336	655	.513	3	6	.500	241	307	.785	256	527	783	237	248	3	71	161	50	916	9.9	3.0	11.6
87-88–San Antonio	45	40	1236	151	328	.460	0	2	.000	83	111	.748	92	208	300	97	134	2	33	74	22	385	6.7	2.2	8.6
88-89–S.A.-Denver	67	18	1403	167	395	.423	0	0	–	132	176	.750	140	262	402	96	201	5	47	91	52	466	6.0	1.4	7.0
89-90–Detroit	37	0	205	22	52	.423	0	0	–	16	29	.552	24	54	78	12	40	0	4	16	9	60	2.1	0.3	1.6
90-91–San Antonio	63	11	1018	85	169	.503	0	2	.000	69	94	.734	61	160	221	52	172	3	29	71	25	239	3.5	0.8	3.8
Reg. Season Totals	823	418	23370	3251	6812	.477	4	29	.138	1922	2514	.765	1921	4616	6537	1614	2605	45	583	1474	739	8428	7.9	2.0	10.2
Playoff Totals	22	7	538	83	149	.557	0	2	.000	21	36	.583	32	83	115	22	70	0	21	26	11	187	5.2	1.0	8.5

Greer, Harold Everett (Hal) b. June 26, 1936 Ht. 6-2 Wt. 175 College: Marshall HOF: 1981

SEASON–TEAM	G	GS	MIN	FGM	FGA	PCT	3FGM	3FGA	PCT	FTM	FTA	PCT	O-RB	D-RB	TOT	AST	PF	DQ	STL	TO	BLK	PTS	RPG	APG	PPG
58-59–Syracuse	68	–	1625	308	679	.454	–	–	–	137	176	.778	–	–	196	101	189	1	–	–	–	753	2.9	1.5	11.1
59-60–Syracuse	70	–	1979	388	815	.476	–	–	–	148	189	.783	–	–	303	188	208	4	–	–	–	924	4.3	2.7	13.2
60-61–Syracuse	79	–	2763	623	1381	.451	–	–	–	305	394	.774	–	–	455	302	242	0	–	–	–	1551	5.8	3.8	19.6
61-62–Syracuse	71	–	2705	644	1442	.447	–	–	–	331	404	.819	–	–	524	313	252	2	–	–	–	1619	7.4	4.4	22.8
62-63–Syracuse	80	–	2631	600	1293	.464	–	–	–	362	434	.834	–	–	457	275	286	4	–	–	–	1562	5.7	3.4	19.5
63-64–Philadelphia	80	–	3157	715	1611	.444	–	–	–	435	525	.829	–	–	484	374	291	6	–	–	–	1865	6.1	4.7	23.3
64-65–Philadelphia	70	–	2600	539	1245	.433	–	–	–	335	413	.811	–	–	355	313	254	7	–	–	–	1413	5.1	4.5	20.2
65-66–Philadelphia	80	–	3326	703	1580	.445	–	–	–	413	514	.804	–	–	473	384	315	6	–	–	–	1819	5.9	4.8	22.7
66-67–Philadelphia	80	–	3086	699	1524	.459	–	–	–	367	466	.788	–	–	422	303	302	5	–	–	–	1765	5.3	3.8	22.1
67-68–Philadelphia	82	–	3263	777	1626	.478	–	–	–	422	549	.769	–	–	444	372	289	6	–	–	–	1976	5.4	4.5	24.1
68-69–Philadelphia	82	–	3311	732	1595	.459	–	–	–	432	543	.796	–	–	435	414	294	8	–	–	–	1896	5.3	5.0	23.1
69-70–Philadelphia	80	–	3024	705	1551	.455	–	–	–	352	432	.815	–	–	376	405	300	8	–	–	–	1762	4.7	5.1	22.0
70-71–Philadelphia	81	–	3060	591	1371	.431	–	–	–	326	405	.805	–	–	364	369	289	4	–	–	–	1508	4.5	4.6	18.6
71-72–Philadelphia	81	52	2410	389	866	.449	–	–	–	181	234	.774	–	–	271	316	268	10	–	–	–	959	3.3	3.9	11.8
72-73–Philadelphia	38	17	848	91	232	.392	–	–	–	32	39	.821	–	–	106	111	76	1	–	–	–	214	2.8	2.9	5.6
Reg. Season Totals	1122	69	39788	8504	18811	.452	–	–	–	4578	5717	.801	–	–	5665	4540	3855	72	–	–	–	21586	5.0	4.0	19.2
Playoff Totals	92	–	3642	705	1657	.425	–	–	–	466	574	.812	–	–	505	393	357	13	–	–	–	1876	5.5	4.3	20.4
All-Star Totals	10	–	207	47	102	.461	–	–	–	26	37	.703	–	–	45	28	29	0	–	–	–	120	4.5	2.8	12.0

Gregor, Gary W. b. August 13, 1945 Ht. 6-7 Wt. 235 College: South Carolina

SEASON–TEAM	G	GS	MIN	FGM	FGA	PCT	3FGM	3FGA	PCT	FTM	FTA	PCT	O-RB	D-RB	TOT	AST	PF	DQ	STL	TO	BLK	PTS	RPG	APG	PPG
68-69–Phoenix	80	–	2182	400	963	.415	–	–	–	85	131	.649	–	–	711	96	249	2	–	–	–	885	8.9	1.2	11.1
69-70–Atlanta	81	–	1603	286	661	.433	–	–	–	88	113	.779	–	–	397	63	159	5	–	–	–	660	4.9	0.8	8.1
70-71–Portland	44	–	1153	181	421	.430	–	–	–	59	89	.663	–	–	334	81	120	2	–	–	–	421	7.6	1.8	9.6
71-72–Portland	82	–	2371	399	884	.451	–	–	–	114	151	.755	–	–	591	187	201	2	–	–	–	912	7.2	2.3	11.1
72-73–Milwaukee	9	–	88	11	33	.333	–	–	–	5	7	.714	–	–	32	9	9	0	–	–	–	27	3.6	1.0	3.0
72-73–New York (A)	40	–	595	99	204	.485	1	1	1.000	32	39	.821	40	110	150	31	84	0	–	41	–	231	3.8	0.8	5.8
73-74–New York (A)	25	–	313	40	85	.471	2	3	.667	9	11	.818	22	49	71	15	48	–	4	10	1	91	2.8	0.6	3.6
Reg. NBA Totals	296	–	7397	1277	2962	.431	–	–	–	351	491	.715	–	–	2065	436	738	11	–	–	–	2905	7.0	1.5	9.8
Reg. ABA Totals	65	–	908	139	289	.481	3	4	.750	41	50	.820	62	159	221	46	132	0	4	51	1	322	3.4	0.7	5.0
NBA Playoff Totals	7	–	67	6	21	.286	–	–	–	4	6	.667	–	–	17	2	14	0	–	–	–	16	2.4	0.3	2.3
ABA Playoff Totals	1	–	12	1	6	.167	0	0	–	2	2	1.000	0	0	4	0	3	0	0	0	0	4	4.0	0.0	4.0

Gregory, Claude Andre b. December 26, 1958 Ht. 6-9 Wt. 235 College: Wisconsin

SEASON–TEAM	G	GS	MIN	FGM	FGA	PCT	3FGM	3FGA	PCT	FTM	FTA	PCT	O-RB	D-RB	TOT	AST	PF	DQ	STL	TO	BLK	PTS	RPG	APG	PPG
85-86–Washington	2	0	2	1	2	.500	0	0	–	0	0	–	2	0	2	0	1	0	1	2	0	2	1.0	0.0	1.0
87-88–L.A. Clippers	23	2	313	61	134	.455	0	1	.000	12	36	.333	37	58	95	16	37	0	9	22	13	134	4.1	0.7	5.8
Reg. Season Totals	25	2	315	62	136	.456	0	1	.000	12	36	.333	39	58	97	16	38	0	10	24	13	136	3.9	0.6	5.4

Greig, John W. b. April 28, 1961 Ht. 6-7 Wt. 215 College: Wenatchee Valley (Wash.) Coll. (J.C.); Oregon

SEASON–TEAM	G	GS	MIN	FGM	FGA	PCT	3FGM	3FGA	PCT	FTM	FTA	PCT	O-RB	D-RB	TOT	AST	PF	DQ	STL	TO	BLK	PTS	RPG	APG	PPG
82-83–Seattle	9	0	26	7	13	.538	0	0	–	5	6	.833	2	4	6	0	4	0	0	2	1	19	0.7	0.0	2.1
Reg. Season Totals	9	0	26	7	13	.538	0	0	–	5	6	.833	2	4	6	0	4	0	0	2	1	19	0.7	0.0	2.1

Grekin, Norman (Norm) b. June 22, 1930 d. September 29, 1981 Ht. 6-5 Wt. 180 College: La Salle

SEASON–TEAM	G	GS	MIN	FGM	FGA	PCT	3FGM	3FGA	PCT	FTM	FTA	PCT	O-RB	D-RB	TOT	AST	PF	DQ	STL	TO	BLK	PTS	RPG	APG	PPG
53-54–Philadelphia	1	–	1	0	0	–	–	–	–	0	0	–	–	–	0	0	1	0	–	–	–	0	0.0	0.0	0.0
Reg. Season Totals	1	–	1	0	0	–	–	–	–	0	0	–	–	–	0	0	1	0	–	–	–	0	0.0	0.0	0.0

Grevey, Kevin Michael b. May 12, 1953 Ht. 6-5 Wt. 210 College: Kentucky

SEASON–TEAM	G	GS	MIN	FGM	FGA	PCT	3FGM	3FGA	PCT	FTM	FTA	PCT	O-RB	D-RB	TOT	AST	PF	DQ	STL	TO	BLK	PTS	RPG	APG	PPG
75-76–Washington	56	–	504	79	213	.371	–	–	–	52	58	.897	24	36	60	27	65	0	13	–	3	210	1.1	0.5	3.8
76-77–Washington	76	–	1306	224	530	.423	–	–	–	79	119	.664	73	105	178	68	148	1	29	–	9	527	2.3	0.9	6.9
77-78–Washington	81	–	2121	505	1128	.448	–	–	–	243	308	.789	124	166	290	155	203	4	61	159	17	1253	3.6	1.9	15.5
78-79–Washington	65	–	1856	418	922	.453	–	–	–	173	224	.772	90	142	232	153	159	1	46	120	14	1009	3.6	2.4	15.5
79-80–Washington	65	–	1818	331	804	.412	34	92	.370	216	249	.867	80	107	187	177	158	0	56	102	16	912	2.9	2.7	14.0
80-81–Washington	75	–	2616	500	1103	.453	45	136	.331	244	290	.841	67	152	219	300	161	1	68	144	17	1289	2.9	4.0	17.2
81-82–Washington	71	62	2164	376	857	.439	28	82	.341	165	193	.855	57	138	195	149	151	1	44	96	23	945	2.7	2.1	13.3
82-83–Washington	41	11	756	114	294	.388	15	38	.395	54	69	.783	18	31	49	49	61	0	18	27	7	297	1.2	1.2	7.2
83-84–Milwaukee	64	3	923	178	395	.451	15	53	.283	75	84	.893	30	51	81	75	95	0	27	45	4	446	1.3	1.2	7.0
84-85–Milwaukee	78	6	1182	190	424	.448	8	33	.242	88	107	.822	27	76	103	94	85	1	30	55	2	476	1.3	1.2	6.1
Reg. Season Totals	672	82	15246	2915	6670	.437	145	434	.334	1389	1701	.817	590	1004	1594	1247	1286	9	392	748	112	7364	2.4	1.9	11.0
Playoff Totals	70	1	1625	310	738	.420	9	18	.500	156	199	.784	65	80	145	102	181	4	38	95	18	785	2.1	1.5	11.2

Grey, Dennis b. August 26, 1947 Ht. 6-8 Wt. 215 College: California Western

SEASON–TEAM	G	GS	MIN	FGM	FGA	PCT	3FGM	3FGA	PCT	FTM	FTA	PCT	O-RB	D-RB	TOT	AST	PF	DQ	STL	TO	BLK	PTS	RPG	APG	PPG
68-69–Los Angeles (A)	58	–	1317	184	439	.419	0	1	.000	157	292	.538	–	–	320	52	196	11	–	129	–	525	5.5	0.9	9.1
69-70–New York (A)	4	–	74	6	24	.250	0	0	–	6	12	.500	–	–	25	0	15	1	–	–	–	18	6.3	0.0	4.5
Reg. ABA Totals	62	–	1391	190	463	.410	0	1	.000	163	304	.536	–	–	345	52	211	12	–	129	–	543	5.6	0.8	8.8

Griffin, Adrian b. July 4, 1974 Ht. 6-5 Wt. 215 College: Seton Hall

SEASON–TEAM	G	GS	MIN	FGM	FGA	PCT	3FGM	3FGA	PCT	FTM	FTA	PCT	O-RB	D-RB	TOT	AST	PF	DQ	STL	TO	BLK	PTS	RPG	APG	PPG
99-00–Boston	72	47	1927	175	413	.424	16	57	.281	119	158	.753	128	244	372	177	222	3	116	93	15	485	5.2	2.5	6.7
Reg. Season Totals	72	47	1927	175	413	.424	16	57	.281	119	158	.753	128	244	372	177	222	3	116	93	15	485	5.2	2.5	6.7

Griffin, Greg b. September 6, 1952 Ht. 6-7 Wt. 190 College: Pasadena City (Calif.) Coll. (J.C.); Idaho State

SEASON–TEAM	G	GS	MIN	FGM	FGA	PCT	3FGM	3FGA	PCT	FTM	FTA	PCT	O-RB	D-RB	TOT	AST	PF	DQ	STL	TO	BLK	PTS	RPG	APG	PPG
77-78–Phoenix	36	–	422	61	169	.361	–	–	–	23	36	.639	44	59	103	24	56	0	16	39	0	145	2.9	0.7	4.0
Reg. Season Totals	36	–	422	61	169	.361	–	–	–	23	36	.639	44	59	103	24	56	0	16	39	0	145	2.9	0.7	4.0
Playoff Totals	2	–	25	3	7	.429	–	–	–	0	0	–	2	2	4	3	5	0	1	2	1	6	2.0	1.5	3.0

Griffin, Paul Arthur b. January 20, 1954 Ht. 6-9 Wt. 205 College: Western Michigan

SEASON–TEAM	G	GS	MIN	FGM	FGA	PCT	3FGM	3FGA	PCT	FTM	FTA	PCT	O-RB	D-RB	TOT	AST	PF	DQ	STL	TO	BLK	PTS	RPG	APG	PPG
76-77–New Orleans	81	–	1645	140	256	.547	–	–	–	145	201	.721	167	328	495	167	241	6	50	–	43	425	6.1	2.1	5.2
77-78–New Orleans	82	–	1853	160	358	.447	–	–	–	112	157	.713	157	353	510	172	228	6	88	150	45	432	6.2	2.1	5.3
78-79–New Orleans	77	–	1398	106	223	.475	–	–	–	91	147	.619	126	265	391	138	198	3	54	117	36	303	5.1	1.8	3.9
79-80–San Antonio	82	–	1812	173	313	.553	0	0	–	174	240	.725	154	284	438	250	306	9	81	131	53	520	5.3	3.0	6.3
80-81–San Antonio	82	–	1930	166	325	.511	0	0	–	170	253	.672	184	321	505	249	207	3	77	132	38	502	6.2	3.0	6.1
81-82–San Antonio	23	0	459	32	66	.485	0	0	–	24	37	.649	29	66	95	54	67	0	20	40	8	88	4.1	2.3	3.8
82-83–San Antonio	53	0	956	60	116	.517	0	0	–	53	76	.697	77	139	216	86	153	0	33	68	25	173	4.1	1.6	3.3
Reg. Season Totals	480	0	10053	837	1657	.505	0	0	–	769	1111	.692	894	1756	2650	1116	1400	27	403	638	248	2443	5.5	2.3	5.1
Playoff Totals	10	0	252	21	38	.553	0	0	–	15	26	.577	19	36	55	35	37	2	6	16	6	57	5.5	3.5	5.7

Griffith, Darrell Steven (Dr. Dunkenstein) b. June 16, 1958 Ht. 6-4 Wt. 190 College: Louisville

SEASON–TEAM	G	GS	MIN	FGM	FGA	PCT	3FGM	3FGA	PCT	FTM	FTA	PCT	O-RB	D-RB	TOT	AST	PF	DQ	STL	TO	BLK	PTS	RPG	APG	PPG
80-81–Utah	81	–	2867	716	1544	.464	10	52	.192	229	320	.716	79	209	288	194	219	0	106	231	40	1671	3.6	2.4	20.6
81-82–Utah	80	79	2597	689	1429	.482	15	52	.288	189	271	.697	128	177	305	187	213	0	95	193	34	1582	3.8	2.3	19.8
82-83–Utah	77	76	2787	752	1554	.484	38	132	.288	167	246	.679	100	204	304	270	184	0	138	252	33	1709	3.9	3.5	22.2
83-84–Utah	82	82	2650	697	1423	.490	91	252	.361	151	217	.696	95	243	338	283	202	1	114	243	23	1636	4.1	3.5	20.0
84-85–Utah	78	78	2776	728	1593	.457	92	257	.358	216	298	.725	124	220	344	243	178	1	133	247	30	1764	4.4	3.1	22.6
86-87–Utah	76	10	1843	463	1038	.446	67	200	.335	149	212	.703	81	146	227	129	167	0	97	135	29	1142	3.0	1.7	15.0
87-88–Utah	52	11	1052	251	585	.429	28	102	.275	59	92	.641	36	91	127	91	102	0	52	67	5	589	2.4	1.8	11.3
88-89–Utah	82	73	2382	466	1045	.446	61	196	.311	142	182	.780	77	253	330	130	175	0	86	141	22	1135	4.0	1.6	13.8
89-90–Utah	82	1	1444	301	649	.464	80	215	.372	51	78	.654	43	123	166	63	149	0	68	75	19	733	2.0	0.8	8.9
90-91–Utah	75	2	1005	174	445	.391	48	138	.348	34	45	.756	17	73	90	37	100	1	42	48	7	430	1.2	0.5	5.7
Reg. Season Totals	765	412	21403	5237	11305	.463	530	1596	.332	1387	1961	.707	780	1739	2519	1627	1689	3	931	1632	242	12391	3.3	2.1	16.2
Playoff Totals	37	21	1038	221	504	.438	46	124	.371	69	97	.711	37	104	141	77	60	0	47	77	11	557	3.8	2.1	15.1

Grigsby, Charles L. (Chuck) b. August 15, 1928 Ht. 6-5 Wt. 190 College: Dayton

SEASON–TEAM	G	GS	MIN	FGM	FGA	PCT	3FGM	3FGA	PCT	FTM	FTA	PCT	O-RB	D-RB	TOT	AST	PF	DQ	STL	TO	BLK	PTS	RPG	APG	PPG
54-55–New York	7	–	45	7	19	.368	–	–	–	2	8	.250	–	–	11	7	9	0	–	–	–	16	1.6	1.0	2.3
Reg. Season Totals	7	–	45	7	19	.368	–	–	–	2	8	.250	–	–	11	7	9	0	–	–	–	16	1.6	1.0	2.3

Grimm, Derek b. August 3, 1974 Ht. 6-10 Wt. 228 College: Missouri

SEASON–TEAM	G	GS	MIN	FGM	FGA	PCT	3FGM	3FGA	PCT	FTM	FTA	PCT	O-RB	D-RB	TOT	AST	PF	DQ	STL	TO	BLK	PTS	RPG	APG	PPG
97-98–Sacramento	9	0	34	4	14	.286	4	12	.333	2	2	1.000	0	4	4	0	6	0	3	3	1	14	0.4	0.0	1.6
Reg. Season Totals	9	0	34	4	14	.286	4	12	.333	2	2	1.000	0	4	4	0	6	0	3	3	1	14	0.4	0.0	1.6

Grimshaw, George W. (Woodie) b. September 24, 1919 d. October 1974 Ht. 6-1 Wt. 185 College: Brown

SEASON–TEAM	G	GS	MIN	FGM	FGA	PCT	3FGM	3FGA	PCT	FTM	FTA	PCT	O-RB	D-RB	TOT	AST	PF	DQ	STL	TO	BLK	PTS	RPG	APG	PPG
46-47–Providence	21	–	–	20	56	.357	–	–	–	21	44	.477	–	–	–	1	25	–	–	–	–	61	–	0.0	2.9
Reg. Season Totals	21	–	–	20	56	.357	–	–	–	21	44	.477	–	–	–	1	25	–	–	–	–	61	–	0.0	2.9

Groat, Richard Morrow (Dick) b. November 4, 1930 Ht. 6-1 Wt. 185 College: Duke

SEASON–TEAM	G	GS	MIN	FGM	FGA	PCT	3FGM	3FGA	PCT	FTM	FTA	PCT	O-RB	D-RB	TOT	AST	PF	DQ	STL	TO	BLK	PTS	RPG	APG	PPG
52-53–Fort Wayne	26	–	663	100	272	.368	–	–	–	109	138	.790	–	–	86	69	90	7	–	–	–	309	3.3	2.7	11.9
Reg. Season Totals	26	–	663	100	272	.368	–	–	–	109	138	.790	–	–	86	69	90	7	–	–	–	309	3.3	2.7	11.9

Gross, Robert Edwin (Bob) b. August 3, 1953 Ht. 6-6 Wt. 200 College: Seattle; Los Angeles Harbor (Calif.) Coll. (J.C.); Long Beach State

SEASON–TEAM	G	GS	MIN	FGM	FGA	PCT	3FGM	3FGA	PCT	FTM	FTA	PCT	O-RB	D-RB	TOT	AST	PF	DQ	STL	TO	BLK	PTS	RPG	APG	PPG
75-76–Portland	76	–	1474	209	400	.523	–	–	–	97	142	.683	138	169	307	163	186	3	91	–	43	515	4.0	2.1	6.8
76-77–Portland	82	–	2232	376	711	.529	–	–	–	183	215	.851	173	221	394	242	255	7	107	–	57	935	4.8	3.0	11.4
77-78–Portland	72	–	2163	381	720	.529	–	–	–	152	190	.800	180	220	400	254	234	5	100	179	52	914	5.6	3.5	12.7
78-79–Portland	53	–	1441	209	443	.472	–	–	–	96	119	.807	106	144	250	184	161	4	70	121	47	514	4.7	3.5	9.7
79-80–Portland	62	–	1581	221	472	.468	1	10	.100	95	114	.833	84	165	249	228	179	3	60	166	47	538	4.0	3.7	8.7
80-81–Portland	82	–	1934	253	479	.528	0	9	.000	135	159	.849	126	202	328	251	238	5	90	151	67	641	4.0	3.1	7.8
81-82–Portland	59	24	1377	173	322	.537	3	6	.500	78	104	.750	101	158	259	125	162	2	75	88	41	427	4.4	2.1	7.2
82-83–San Diego	27	3	373	35	82	.427	1	3	.333	12	19	.632	32	34	66	34	69	1	22	24	7	83	2.4	1.3	3.1
Reg. Season Totals	513	27	12575	1857	3629	.512	5	28	.179	848	1062	.798	940	1313	2253	1481	1484	30	615	729	361	4567	4.4	2.9	8.9
Playoff Totals	25	0	694	122	209	.584	0	0	–	63	74	.851	55	69	124	89	101	5	35	8	17	307	5.0	3.6	12.3

Grosso, Michael James (Mike) b. September 7, 1947 Ht. 6-9 Wt. 230 College: Louisville; South Carolina

SEASON–TEAM	G	GS	MIN	FGM	FGA	PCT	3FGM	3FGA	PCT	FTM	FTA	PCT	O-RB	D-RB	TOT	AST	PF	DQ	STL	TO	BLK	PTS	RPG	APG	PPG
71-72–Pittsburgh (A)	25	–	335	45	102	.441	0	0	–	13	23	.565	–	–	123	11	64	–	–	20	–	103	4.9	0.4	4.1
Reg. ABA Totals	25	–	335	45	102	.441	0	0	–	13	23	.565	–	–	123	11	64	–	–	20	–	103	4.9	0.4	4.1

Grote, Jerry C. b. December 28, 1940 Ht. 6-4 Wt. 215 College: Loyola Marymount

SEASON–TEAM	G	GS	MIN	FGM	FGA	PCT	3FGM	3FGA	PCT	FTM	FTA	PCT	O-RB	D-RB	TOT	AST	PF	DQ	STL	TO	BLK	PTS	RPG	APG	PPG
64-65–Los Angeles	11	–	33	6	11	.545	–	–	–	2	2	1.000	–	–	4	4	5	0	–	–	–	14	0.4	0.4	1.3
Reg. Season Totals	11	–	33	6	11	.545	–	–	–	2	2	1.000	–	–	4	4	5	0	–	–	–	14	0.4	0.4	1.3

Groza, Alex John b. October 7, 1926 d. January 21, 1995 Ht. 6-7 Wt. 220 College: Kentucky

SEASON–TEAM	G	GS	MIN	FGM	FGA	PCT	3FGM	3FGA	PCT	FTM	FTA	PCT	O-RB	D-RB	TOT	AST	PF	DQ	STL	TO	BLK	PTS	RPG	APG	PPG
49-50–Indianapolis	64	–	–	521	1090	.478	–	–	–	454	623	.729	–	–	–	162	221	–	–	–	–	1496	–	2.5	23.4
50-51–Indianapolis	66	–	–	492	1046	.470	–	–	–	445	566	.786	–	–	709	156	237	8	–	–	–	1429	10.7	2.4	21.7
Reg. Season Totals	130	–	–	1013	2136	.474	–	–	–	899	1189	.756	–	–	709	318	458	8	–	–	–	2925	10.7	2.4	22.5
Playoff Totals	9	–	–	80	221	.561	–	–	–	74	91	.813	–	–	42	26	35	1	–	–	–	234	14.0	1.7	26.0
All-Star Totals	1	–	–	8	16	.500	–	–	–	1	1	1.000	–	–	13	1	4	0	–	–	–	17	13.0	1.0	17.0

Grubar, Richard Arthur (Dick) b. July 26, 1947 Ht. 6-4 Wt. 185 College: North Carolina

SEASON–TEAM	G	GS	MIN	FGM	FGA	PCT	3FGM	3FGA	PCT	FTM	FTA	PCT	O-RB	D-RB	TOT	AST	PF	DQ	STL	TO	BLK	PTS	RPG	APG	PPG
69-70–Indiana (A)	2	–	8	2	3	.667	0	0	–	0	0	–	–	–	0	1	1	0	–	–	–	4	0.0	0.5	2.0
Reg. ABA Totals	2	–	8	2	3	.667	0	0	–	0	0	–	–	–	–	1	1	0	–	–	–	4	0.0	0.5	2.0

Grunfeld, Ernest (Ernie) b. April 24, 1955 Ht. 6-6 Wt. 215 College: Tennessee

SEASON–TEAM	G	GS	MIN	FGM	FGA	PCT	3FGM	3FGA	PCT	FTM	FTA	PCT	O-RB	D-RB	TOT	AST	PF	DQ	STL	TO	BLK	PTS	RPG	APG	PPG
77-78–Milwaukee	73	–	1261	204	461	.443	–	–	–	94	143	.657	70	124	194	145	150	1	54	98	19	502	2.7	2.0	6.9
78-79–Milwaukee	82	–	1778	326	661	.493	–	–	–	191	251	.761	124	236	360	216	220	3	58	141	15	843	4.4	2.6	10.3
79-80–Kansas City	80	–	1397	186	420	.443	1	2	.500	101	131	.771	87	145	232	109	151	1	56	81	9	474	2.9	1.4	5.9
80-81–Kansas City	79	–	1584	260	486	.535	0	0	–	75	101	.743	31	175	206	205	155	1	60	88	15	595	2.6	2.6	7.5
81-82–Kansas City	81	11	1892	420	822	.511	2	14	.143	188	229	.821	55	127	182	276	191	0	72	148	39	1030	2.2	3.4	12.7
82-83–New York	77	0	1422	167	377	.443	0	4	.000	81	98	.827	42	121	163	136	172	1	40	84	10	415	2.1	1.8	5.4
83-84–New York	76	6	1119	166	362	.459	2	9	.222	64	83	.771	24	97	121	108	151	0	43	71	7	398	1.6	1.4	5.2
84-85–New York	69	0	1061	188	384	.490	2	8	.250	77	104	.740	41	110	151	105	129	2	50	40	7	455	2.2	1.5	6.6
85-86–New York	76	0	1402	148	355	.417	26	61	.426	90	108	.833	42	164	206	119	192	2	39	50	13	412	2.7	1.6	5.4
Reg. Season Totals	693	17	12916	2065	4328	.477	33	98	.337	961	1248	.770	516	1299	1815	1419	1511	11	472	801	134	5124	2.6	2.0	7.4
Playoff Totals	42	0	944	146	299	.488	2	4	.500	81	98	.827	19	73	92	121	89	1	43	63	12	375	2.2	2.9	8.9

Guarilia, Eugene Michael (Gene) b. September 13, 1937 Ht. 6-5 Wt. 220 College: Potomac State (W.Va.) Coll. (J.C.); George Washington

SEASON–TEAM	G	GS	MIN	FGM	FGA	PCT	3FGM	3FGA	PCT	FTM	FTA	PCT	O-RB	D-RB	TOT	AST	PF	DQ	STL	TO	BLK	PTS	RPG	APG	PPG
59-60–Boston	48	–	423	58	154	.377	–	–	–	29	41	.707	–	–	85	18	57	1	–	–	–	145	1.8	0.4	3.0
60-61–Boston	25	–	209	38	94	.404	–	–	–	3	10	.300	–	–	71	5	28	0	–	–	–	79	2.8	0.2	3.2
61-62–Boston	45	–	367	61	161	.379	–	–	–	41	64	.641	–	–	124	11	56	0	–	–	–	163	2.8	0.2	3.6
62-63–Boston	11	–	83	11	38	.289	–	–	–	4	11	.364	–	–	14	2	5	0	–	–	–	26	1.3	0.2	2.4
Reg. Season Totals	129	–	1082	168	447	.376	–	–	–	77	126	.611	–	–	294	36	146	1	–	–	–	413	2.3	0.3	3.2
Playoff Totals	12	–	67	6	26	.231	–	–	–	8	11	.727	–	–	23	4	10	0	–	–	–	20	1.9	0.3	1.7

Gudmundsson, Karl Petur (Petur) b. October 30, 1958 Ht. 7-2 Wt. 260 College: Washington

SEASON–TEAM	G	GS	MIN	FGM	FGA	PCT	3FGM	3FGA	PCT	FTM	FTA	PCT	O-RB	D-RB	TOT	AST	PF	DQ	STL	TO	BLK	PTS	RPG	APG	PPG
81-82–Portland	68	6	845	83	166	.500	1	1	1.000	52	76	.684	51	135	186	59	163	2	13	73	30	219	2.7	0.9	3.2
85-86–L.A. Lakers	8	2	128	20	37	.541	0	0	–	18	27	.667	17	21	38	3	25	1	3	11	4	58	4.8	0.4	7.3
87-88–San Antonio	69	9	1017	139	280	.496	0	1	.000	117	145	.807	93	230	323	86	197	5	18	103	61	395	4.7	1.2	5.7
88-89–San Antonio	5	3	70	9	25	.360	0	0	–	3	4	.750	5	11	16	5	15	0	1	8	1	21	3.2	1.0	4.2
Reg. Season Totals	150	20	2060	251	508	.494	1	2	.500	190	252	.754	166	397	563	153	400	8	35	195	96	693	3.8	1.0	4.6
Playoff Totals	14	0	117	16	29	.552	0	2	.000	10	15	.667	8	18	26	4	23	1	3	13	4	42	1.9	0.3	3.0

Guerin, Richard V. (Richie) b. May 29, 1932 Ht. 6-4 Wt. 210 College: Iona

SEASON–TEAM	G	GS	MIN	FGM	FGA	PCT	3FGM	3FGA	PCT	FTM	FTA	PCT	O-RB	D-RB	TOT	AST	PF	DQ	STL	TO	BLK	PTS	RPG	APG	PPG
56-57–New York	72	–	1793	257	699	.368	–	–	–	181	292	.620	–	–	334	182	186	3	–	–	–	695	4.6	2.5	9.7
57-58–New York	63	–	2368	344	973	.354	–	–	–	353	511	.691	–	–	489	317	202	3	–	–	–	1041	7.8	5.0	16.5
58-59–New York	71	–	2558	443	1046	.424	–	–	–	405	505	.802	–	–	518	364	255	1	–	–	–	1291	7.3	5.1	18.2
59-60–New York	74	–	2429	579	1379	.420	–	–	–	457	591	.773	–	–	505	468	242	3	–	–	–	1615	6.8	6.3	21.8
60-61–New York	79	–	3023	612	1545	.396	–	–	–	496	626	.792	–	–	628	503	310	3	–	–	–	1720	7.9	6.4	21.8
61-62–New York	78	–	3348	839	1897	.442	–	–	–	625	762	.820	–	–	501	539	299	3	–	–	–	2303	6.4	6.9	29.5
62-63–New York	79	–	2712	596	1380	.432	–	–	–	509	600	.848	–	–	331	348	228	2	–	–	–	1701	4.2	4.4	21.5
63-64–N.Y.-St. Louis	80	–	2366	351	846	.415	–	–	–	347	424	.818	–	–	256	375	276	4	–	–	–	1049	3.2	4.7	13.1
64-65–St. Louis	57	–	1678	295	662	.446	–	–	–	231	301	.767	–	–	149	271	193	1	–	–	–	821	2.6	4.8	14.4
65-66–St. Louis	80	–	2363	414	998	.415	–	–	–	362	446	.812	–	–	314	388	256	4	–	–	–	1190	3.9	4.9	14.9
66-67–St. Louis	80	–	2275	394	904	.436	–	–	–	304	416	.731	–	–	192	345	247	2	–	–	–	1092	2.4	4.3	13.7
68-69–Atlanta	27	–	472	47	111	.423	–	–	–	57	74	.770	–	–	59	99	66	0	–	–	–	151	2.2	3.7	5.6
69-70–Atlanta	8	–	64	3	11	.273	–	–	–	1	1	1.000	–	–	2	12	9	0	–	–	–	7	0.3	1.5	0.9
Reg. Season Totals	848	–	27449	5174	12451	.416	–	–	–	4328	5549	.780	–	–	4278	4211	2769	29	–	–	–	14676	5.0	5.0	17.3
Playoff Totals	42	–	1345	231	539	.429	–	–	–	192	239	.803	–	–	149	214	157	2	–	–	–	654	3.5	5.1	15.6
All-Star Totals	6	–	122	23	56	.411	–	–	–	17	26	.654	–	–	19	18	17	1	–	–	–	63	3.2	3.0	10.5

Gugliotta, Thomas James (Tom, Googs) b. December 19, 1969 Ht. 6-10 Wt. 240 College: North Carolina State

SEASON–TEAM	G	GS	MIN	FGM	FGA	PCT	3FGM	3FGA	PCT	FTM	FTA	PCT	O-RB	D-RB	TOT	AST	PF	DQ	STL	TO	BLK	PTS	RPG	APG	PPG
92-93–Washington	81	81	2795	484	1135	.426	38	135	.281	181	281	.644	219	562	781	306	195	0	134	230	35	1187	9.6	3.8	14.7
93-94–Washington	78	78	2795	540	1159	.466	40	148	.270	213	311	.685	189	539	728	276	174	0	172	247	51	1333	9.3	3.5	17.1
94-95–Wash.-G.S.-Minn.	77	63	2568	371	837	.443	60	186	.323	174	252	.690	165	407	572	279	203	2	132	189	62	976	7.4	3.6	12.7
95-96–Minnesota	78	78	2835	473	1004	.471	26	86	.302	289	374	.773	176	514	690	238	265	1	139	234	96	1261	8.8	3.1	16.2
96-97–Minnesota	81	81	3131	592	1339	.442	24	93	.258	464	566	.820	187	515	702	335	237	3	130	293	89	1672	8.7	4.1	20.6
97-98–Minnesota	41	41	1582	319	635	.502	2	17	.118	183	223	.821	106	250	356	167	102	0	61	109	22	823	8.7	4.1	20.1
98-99–Phoenix	43	43	1563	277	573	.483	2	7	.286	173	218	.794	131	250	381	121	110	0	59	88	21	729	8.9	2.8	17.0
99-00–Phoenix	54	54	1767	310	645	.481	1	8	.125	117	151	.775	141	284	425	124	152	2	80	106	31	738	7.9	2.3	13.7
Reg. Season Totals	533	519	19036	3366	7327	.459	193	680	.284	1794	2376	.755	1314	3321	4635	1846	1438	8	907	1496	407	8719	8.7	3.5	16.4
Playoff Totals	6	6	239	36	87	.414	3	4	.750	12	18	.667	8	33	41	23	23	0	11	14	5	87	6.8	3.8	14.5
All-Star Totals	1	0	19	3	7	.429	0	1	.000	3	4	.750	1	7	8	3	3	0	2	3	0	9	8.0	3.0	9.0

Guibert, Andres b. October 28, 1968 Ht. 6-10 Wt. 242 Country: Cuba

SEASON–TEAM	G	GS	MIN	FGM	FGA	PCT	3FGM	3FGA	PCT	FTM	FTA	PCT	O-RB	D-RB	TOT	AST	PF	DQ	STL	TO	BLK	PTS	RPG	APG	PPG
93-94–Minnesota	5	0	33	6	20	.300	0	0	–	3	6	.500	10	6	16	2	6	0	0	6	1	15	3.2	0.4	3.0
94-95–Minnesota	17	0	167	16	47	.340	0	4	.000	13	19	.684	16	29	45	10	29	0	8	12	1	45	2.6	0.6	2.6
Reg. Season Totals	22	0	200	22	67	.328	0	4	.000	16	25	.640	26	35	61	12	35	0	8	18	2	60	2.8	0.5	2.7

Guidinger, Jay Patrick b. August 18, 1969 Ht. 6-10 Wt. 255 College: Minnesota-Duluth

SEASON–TEAM	G	GS	MIN	FGM	FGA	PCT	3FGM	3FGA	PCT	FTM	FTA	PCT	O-RB	D-RB	TOT	AST	PF	DQ	STL	TO	BLK	PTS	RPG	APG	PPG
92-93–Cleveland	32	5	215	19	55	.345	0	0	–	13	25	.520	26	38	64	17	48	0	9	10	10	51	2.0	0.5	1.6
93-94–Cleveland	32	0	131	16	32	.500	0	0	–	15	21	.714	15	18	33	3	23	0	4	16	5	47	1.0	0.1	1.5
Reg. Season Totals	64	5	346	35	87	.402	0	0	–	28	46	.609	41	56	97	20	71	0	13	26	15	98	1.5	0.3	1.5
Playoff Totals	4	0	15	1	3	.333	0	0	–	0	2	.000	1	0	1	–	1	0	0	2	1	2	0.3	0.0	0.5

Gunther, Coulby b. February 5, 1923 Ht. 6-4 Wt. 190 College: Boston College; St. John's (N.Y.)

SEASON–TEAM	G	GS	MIN	FGM	FGA	PCT	3FGM	3FGA	PCT	FTM	FTA	PCT	O-RB	D-RB	TOT	AST	PF	DQ	STL	TO	BLK	PTS	RPG	APG	PPG
46-47–Pittsburgh	52	–	–	254	756	.336	–	–	–	226	351	.644	–	–	–	32	117	–	–	–	–	734	–	0.6	14.1
48-49–St. Louis	32	–	–	57	181	.315	–	–	–	45	71	.634	–	–	–	33	64	–	–	–	–	159	–	1.0	5.0
Reg. Season Totals	84	–	–	311	937	.332	–	–	–	271	422	.642	–	–	–	65	181	–	–	–	–	893	–	0.8	10.6
Playoff Totals	1	–	–	0	2	.000	–	–	–	0	0	–	–	–	–	–	0	–	–	–	–	0	–	0.0	0.0

Gunther, David C. (Dave) b. July 22, 1937 Ht. 6-7 Wt. 220 College: Iowa

SEASON–TEAM	G	GS	MIN	FGM	FGA	PCT	3FGM	3FGA	PCT	FTM	FTA	PCT	O-RB	D-RB	TOT	AST	PF	DQ	STL	TO	BLK	PTS	RPG	APG	PPG
62-63–San Francisco	1	–	5	1	2	.500	–	–	–	0	0	–	–	–	3	3	1	0	–	–	–	2	3.0	3.0	2.0
Reg. Season Totals	1	–	5	1	2	.500	–	–	–	0	0	–	–	–	3	3	1	0	–	–	–	2	3.0	3.0	2.0

Guokas, Albert G. (Al, Gook) b. August 7, 1925 d. 1990 Ht. 6-5 Wt. 200 College: St. Joseph's (Pa.)

SEASON–TEAM	G	GS	MIN	FGM	FGA	PCT	3FGM	3FGA	PCT	FTM	FTA	PCT	O-RB	D-RB	TOT	AST	PF	DQ	STL	TO	BLK	PTS	RPG	APG	PPG
48-49–Denver (N)	60	–	–	146	–	–	–	–	–	81	129	.628	–	–	–	–	182	–	–	–	–	373	–	–	6.2
49-50–Denver-Phil.	57	–	–	93	299	.311	–	–	–	28	50	.560	–	–	–	95	143	–	–	–	–	214	–	1.7	3.8
Reg. NBA Totals	57	–	–	93	299	.311	–	–	–	28	50	.560	–	–	–	95	143	–	–	–	–	214	–	1.7	3.8
Reg. NBL Totals	60	–	–	146	–	–	–	–	–	81	129	.628	–	–	–	–	182	–	–	–	–	373	–	–	6.2
NBA Playoff Totals	2	–	–	2	4	.500	–	–	–	2	6	.333	–	–	–	5	3	–	–	–	–	6	–	2.5	3.0

Guokas, Matthew George Jr. (Matt) b. February 25, 1944 Ht. 6-6 Wt. 185 College: Miami (Fla.); St. Joseph's (Pa.)

SEASON–TEAM	G	GS	MIN	FGM	FGA	PCT	3FGM	3FGA	PCT	FTM	FTA	PCT	O-RB	D-RB	TOT	AST	PF	DQ	STL	TO	BLK	PTS	RPG	APG	PPG
66-67–Philadelphia	69	–	808	79	203	.389	–	–	–	49	81	.605	–	–	83	105	82	0	–	–	–	207	1.2	1.5	3.0
67-68–Philadelphia	82	–	1612	190	393	.483	–	–	–	118	152	.776	–	–	185	191	172	0	–	–	–	498	2.3	2.3	6.1
68-69–Philadelphia	72	–	838	92	216	.426	–	–	–	54	81	.667	–	–	94	104	121	1	–	–	–	238	1.3	1.4	3.3
69-70–Philadelphia	80	–	1558	189	416	.454	–	–	–	106	149	.711	–	–	216	222	201	0	–	–	–	484	2.7	2.8	6.1
70-71–Phil.-Chicago	79	–	2213	206	418	.493	–	–	–	101	138	.732	–	–	158	342	189	1	–	–	–	513	2.0	4.3	6.5
71-72–Cincinnati	61	–	1975	191	385	.496	–	–	–	64	83	.771	–	–	142	321	150	0	–	–	–	446	2.3	5.3	7.3
72-73–Kansas City-Omaha	79	–	2846	322	565	.570	–	–	–	74	90	.822	–	–	245	403	190	0	–	–	–	718	3.1	5.1	9.1
73-74–K.C.O.-Hou.-Buf.	75	–	1871	195	396	.492	–	–	–	39	60	.650	31	90	121	238	150	3	54	–	21	429	1.6	3.2	5.7
74-75–Chicago	82	–	2089	255	500	.510	–	–	–	78	103	.757	24	115	139	178	154	1	45	–	17	588	1.7	2.2	7.2
75-76–Chicago-K.C.	56	–	793	73	173	.422	–	–	–	18	27	.667	22	41	63	70	76	0	18	–	3	164	1.1	1.3	2.9
Reg. Season Totals	735	–	16603	1792	3665	.489	–	–	–	701	964	.727	77	246	1446	2174	1485	6	117	–	41	4285	2.0	3.0	5.8
Playoff Totals	60	–	1072	101	242	.417	–	–	–	52	67	.776	7	15	118	98	121	0	7	–	2	254	2.0	1.6	4.2

Guokas, Matthew George Sr. (Matt) b. November 11, 1915 d. December 9, 1993 Ht. 6-3 Wt. 195 College: St. Joseph's (Pa.)

SEASON–TEAM	G	GS	MIN	FGM	FGA	PCT	3FGM	3FGA	PCT	FTM	FTA	PCT	O-RB	D-RB	TOT	AST	PF	DQ	STL	TO	BLK	PTS	RPG	APG	PPG
46-47–Philadelphia	47	–	–	28	104	.269	–	–	–	26	47	.553	–	–	–	9	70	–	–	–	–	82	–	0.2	1.7
Reg. Season Totals	47	–	–	28	104	.269	–	–	–	26	47	.553	–	–	–	9	70	–	–	–	–	82	–	0.2	1.7
Playoff Totals	8	–	–	1	15	.067	–	–	–	2	5	.400	–	–	–	–	11	–	–	–	–	4	–	0.0	0.5

Hackett, Rudolph (Rudy) b. May 10, 1953 Ht. 6-9 Wt. 215 College: Syracuse

SEASON–TEAM	G	GS	MIN	FGM	FGA	PCT	3FGM	3FGA	PCT	FTM	FTA	PCT	O-RB	D-RB	TOT	AST	PF	DQ	STL	TO	BLK	PTS	RPG	APG	PPG
75-76–St. Louis (A)	22	–	414	55	131	.420	0	0	–	31	49	.633	20	58	78	28	48	–	15	24	8	141	3.5	1.3	6.4
76-77–N.Y.-Indiana	6	–	46	3	10	.300	–	–	–	8	14	.571	4	9	13	3	8	0	0	–	1	14	2.2	0.5	2.3
Reg. NBA Totals	6	–	46	3	10	.300	–	–	–	8	14	.571	4	9	13	3	8	0	0	–	1	14	2.2	0.5	2.3
Reg. ABA Totals	22	–	414	55	131	.420	0	0	–	31	49	.633	20	58	78	28	48	–	15	24	8	141	3.5	1.3	6.4

Hadnot, James Weldon (Jim) b. January 15, 1940 Ht. 6-10 Wt. 235 College: Providence

SEASON–TEAM	G	GS	MIN	FGM	FGA	PCT	3FGM	3FGA	PCT	FTM	FTA	PCT	O-RB	D-RB	TOT	AST	PF	DQ	STL	TO	BLK	PTS	RPG	APG	PPG
67-68–Oakland (A)	77	–	3004	488	1045	.467	0	2	.000	368	551	.668	303	633	936	135	279	9	–	169	–	1344	12.2	1.8	17.5
Reg. ABA Totals	77	–	3004	488	1045	.467	0	2	.000	368	551	.668	303	633	936	135	279	9	–	169	–	1344	12.2	1.8	17.5

Haffner, Scott Richard b. February 2, 1966 Ht. 6-3 Wt. 180 College: Illinois; Evansville

SEASON–TEAM	G	GS	MIN	FGM	FGA	PCT	3FGM	3FGA	PCT	FTM	FTA	PCT	O-RB	D-RB	TOT	AST	PF	DQ	STL	TO	BLK	PTS	RPG	APG	PPG
89-90–Miami	43	6	559	88	217	.406	3	21	.143	17	25	.680	7	44	51	80	53	0	13	33	2	196	1.2	1.9	4.6
90-91–Charlotte	7	0	50	8	21	.381	0	2	.000	1	2	.500	2	2	4	9	4	0	3	4	1	17	0.6	1.3	2.4
Reg. Season Totals	50	6	609	96	238	.403	3	23	.130	18	27	.667	9	46	55	89	57	0	16	37	3	213	1.1	1.8	4.3

Hagan, Clifford Oldham (Cliff, Li'l Abner) b. December 9, 1931 Ht. 6-4 Wt. 215 College: Kentucky HOF: 1977

SEASON–TEAM	G	GS	MIN	FGM	FGA	PCT	3FGM	3FGA	PCT	FTM	FTA	PCT	O-RB	D-RB	TOT	AST	PF	DQ	STL	TO	BLK	PTS	RPG	APG	PPG
56-57–St. Louis	67	–	971	134	371	.361	–	–	–	100	145	.690	–	–	247	86	165	3	–	–	–	368	3.7	1.3	5.5
57-58–St. Louis	70	–	2190	503	1135	.443	–	–	–	385	501	.768	–	–	707	175	267	9	–	–	–	1391	10.1	2.5	19.9
58-59–St. Louis	72	–	2702	646	1417	.456	–	–	–	415	536	.774	–	–	783	245	275	10	–	–	–	1707	10.9	3.4	23.7
59-60–St. Louis	75	–	2798	719	1549	.464	–	–	–	421	524	.803	–	–	803	299	270	4	–	–	–	1859	10.7	4.0	24.8
60-61–St. Louis	77	–	2701	661	1490	.444	–	–	–	383	467	.820	–	–	715	381	286	9	–	–	–	1705	9.3	4.9	22.1
61-62–St. Louis	77	–	2784	701	1490	.470	–	–	–	362	439	.825	–	–	633	370	282	8	–	–	–	1764	8.2	4.8	22.9
62-63–St. Louis	79	–	1716	491	1055	.465	–	–	–	244	305	.800	–	–	341	193	211	2	–	–	–	1226	4.3	2.4	15.5
63-64–St. Louis	77	–	2279	572	1280	.447	–	–	–	269	331	.813	–	–	377	193	273	4	–	–	–	1413	4.9	2.5	18.4
64-65–St. Louis	77	–	1739	393	901	.436	–	–	–	214	268	.799	–	–	276	136	182	0	–	–	–	1000	3.6	1.8	13.0
65-66–St. Louis	74	–	1851	419	942	.445	–	–	–	176	206	.854	–	–	234	164	177	1	–	–	–	1014	3.2	2.2	13.7
67-68–Dallas (A)	56	–	1737	371	759	.489	0	3	.000	277	351	.789	–	–	334	276	202	6	–	216	–	1019	6.0	4.9	18.2
68-69–Dallas (A)	35	–	579	132	259	.510	0	1	.000	123	144	.854	–	–	102	122	73	2	–	74	–	387	2.9	3.5	11.1
69-70–Dallas (A)	3	–	27	8	13	.615	0	1	.000	1	2	.500	–	–	3	6	2	0	–	–	–	17	1.0	2.0	5.7
Reg. NBA Totals	745	–	21731	5239	11630	.450	–	–	–	2969	3722	.798	–	–	5116	2242	2388	50	–	–	–	13447	6.9	3.0	18.0
Reg. ABA Totals	94	–	2343	511	1031	.496	0	5	.000	401	497	.807	–	–	439	404	277	8	–	290	–	1423	4.7	4.3	15.1
NBA Playoff Totals	90	–	2965	701	1544	.454	–	–	–	432	540	.800	–	–	744	305	320	12	–	–	–	1834	8.3	3.4	20.4
ABA Playoff Totals	5	–	115	19	51	.373	0	0	–	17	23	.739	–	–	19	23	16	1	–	9	–	55	3.8	4.6	11.0
NBA All-Star Totals	4	–	65	8	26	.308	–	–	–	5	5	1.000	–	–	15	6	8	0	–	–	–	21	3.8	1.5	5.3

Hagan, Glenn Kassabin b. June 25, 1955 Ht. 6-0 Wt. 170 College: St. Bonaventure

SEASON–TEAM	G	GS	MIN	FGM	FGA	PCT	3FGM	3FGA	PCT	FTM	FTA	PCT	O-RB	D-RB	TOT	AST	PF	DQ	STL	TO	BLK	PTS	RPG	APG	PPG
81-82–Detroit	4	0	25	3	7	.429	0	0	–	1	1	1.000	2	2	4	8	7	0	3	1	0	7	1.0	2.0	1.8
Reg. Season Totals	4	0	25	3	7	.429	0	0	–	1	1	1.000	2	2	4	8	7	0	3	1	0	7	1.0	2.0	1.8

Hagan, Thomas Medard (Tom) b. January 29, 1947 Ht. 6-4 Wt. 185 College: Vanderbilt

SEASON–TEAM	G	GS	MIN	FGM	FGA	PCT	3FGM	3FGA	PCT	FTM	FTA	PCT	O-RB	D-RB	TOT	AST	PF	DQ	STL	TO	BLK	PTS	RPG	APG	PPG
69-70–Dallas (A)	24	–	226	37	81	.457	7	17	.412	22	29	.759	–	–	30	29	42	0	–	–	–	103	1.3	1.2	4.3
70-71–Texas-Ken. (A)	49	–	690	100	246	.407	12	41	.293	43	63	.683	–	–	83	106	78	–	–	–	–	255	1.7	2.2	5.2
Reg. ABA Totals	73	–	916	137	327	.419	19	58	.328	65	92	.707	–	–	113	135	120	0	–	–	–	358	1.5	1.8	4.9

Hahn, Robert B. (Bob) b. August 25, 1925 Ht. 6-10 Wt. 240 College: North Carolina State

SEASON–TEAM	G	GS	MIN	FGM	FGA	PCT	3FGM	3FGA	PCT	FTM	FTA	PCT	O-RB	D-RB	TOT	AST	PF	DQ	STL	TO	BLK	PTS	RPG	APG	PPG
49-50–Chicago	10	–	–	4	13	.308	–	–	–	2	7	.286	–	–	–	1	17	–	–	–	–	10	–	0.1	1.0
Reg. Season Totals	10	–	–	4	13	.308	–	–	–	2	7	.286	–	–	–	1	17	–	–	–	–	10	–	0.1	1.0

Hairston, Alan Leroy (Al) b. December 11, 1945 Ht. 6-1 Wt. 170 College: St. Clair Co. (Mich.) C.C.; Bowling Green State

SEASON–TEAM	G	GS	MIN	FGM	FGA	PCT	3FGM	3FGA	PCT	FTM	FTA	PCT	O-RB	D-RB	TOT	AST	PF	DQ	STL	TO	BLK	PTS	RPG	APG	PPG
68-69–Seattle	39	–	274	38	114	.333	–	–	–	8	14	.571	–	–	36	38	35	0	–	–	–	84	0.9	1.0	2.2
69-70–Seattle	3	–	20	3	8	.375	–	–	–	1	1	1.000	–	–	5	6	3	0	–	–	–	7	1.7	2.0	2.3
Reg. Season Totals	42	–	294	41	122	.336	–	–	–	9	15	.600	–	–	41	44	38	0	–	–	–	91	1.0	1.0	2.2

Hairston, Harold (Happy) b. May 31, 1942 Ht. 6-7 Wt. 225 College: New York U.

SEASON–TEAM	G	GS	MIN	FGM	FGA	PCT	3FGM	3FGA	PCT	FTM	FTA	PCT	O-RB	D-RB	TOT	AST	PF	DQ	STL	TO	BLK	PTS	RPG	APG	PPG
64-65–Cincinnati	61	–	736	131	351	.373	–	–	–	110	165	.667	–	–	293	27	95	0	–	–	–	372	4.8	0.4	6.1
65-66–Cincinnati	72	–	1794	398	814	.489	–	–	–	220	321	.685	–	–	546	44	216	3	–	–	–	1016	7.6	0.6	14.1
66-67–Cincinnati	79	–	2442	461	962	.479	–	–	–	252	382	.660	–	–	631	62	273	5	–	–	–	1174	8.0	0.8	14.9
67-68–Cin.-Detroit	74	–	2517	481	987	.487	–	–	–	365	522	.699	–	–	617	95	199	1	–	–	–	1327	8.3	1.3	17.9
68-69–Detroit	81	–	2889	530	1131	.469	–	–	–	404	553	.731	–	–	959	109	255	3	–	–	–	1464	11.8	1.3	18.1
69-70–Detroit-L.A.	70	–	2427	483	973	.496	–	–	–	326	413	.789	–	–	775	121	230	9	–	–	–	1292	11.1	1.7	18.5
70-71–Los Angeles	80	–	2921	574	1233	.466	–	–	–	337	431	.782	–	–	797	168	256	2	–	–	–	1485	10.0	2.1	18.6
71-72–Los Angeles	80	–	2748	368	798	.461	–	–	–	311	399	.779	–	–	1045	193	251	2	–	–	–	1047	13.1	2.4	13.1
72-73–Los Angeles	28	–	939	158	328	.482	–	–	–	140	178	.787	–	–	370	68	77	0	–	–	–	456	13.2	2.4	16.3
73-74–Los Angeles	77	–	2634	385	759	.507	–	–	–	343	445	.771	335	705	1040	208	264	2	64	–	17	1113	13.5	2.7	14.5
74-75–Los Angeles	74	–	2283	271	536	.506	–	–	–	217	271	.801	304	642	946	173	218	2	52	–	11	759	12.8	2.3	10.3
Reg. Season Totals	776	–	24330	4240	8872	.478	–	–	–	3025	4080	.741	639	1347	8019	1268	2334	29	116	–	28	11505	10.3	1.6	14.8
Playoff Totals	69	–	2020	307	690	.445	–	–	–	187	255	.733	15	37	559	121	185	4	5	–	1	801	8.1	1.8	11.6

Hairston, Lindsay (Spider) b. December 8, 1951 Ht. 6-7 Wt. 190 College: Michigan State

SEASON–TEAM	G	GS	MIN	FGM	FGA	PCT	3FGM	3FGA	PCT	FTM	FTA	PCT	O-RB	D-RB	TOT	AST	PF	DQ	STL	TO	BLK	PTS	RPG	APG	PPG
75-76–Detroit	47	–	651	104	228	.456	–	–	–	65	112	.580	65	114	179	21	84	2	21	–	32	273	3.8	0.4	5.8
Reg. Season Totals	47	–	651	104	228	.456	–	–	–	65	112	.580	65	114	179	21	84	2	21	–	32	273	3.8	0.4	5.8

H

Halbert, Charles P. (Chuck) b. February 27, 1919 Ht. 6-9 Wt. 225 College: West Texas A&M

SEASON–TEAM	G	GS	MIN	FGM	FGA	PCT	3FGM	3FGA	PCT	FTM	FTA	PCT	O-RB	D-RB	TOT	AST	PF	DQ	STL	TO	BLK	PTS	RPG	APG	PPG
46-47–Chicago	61	–	–	280	915	.306	–	–	–	213	356	.598	–	–	–	46	161	–	–	–	–	773	–	0.8	12.7
47-48–Chicago-Phil.	46	–	–	156	605	.258	–	–	–	140	220	.636	–	–	–	32	126	–	–	–	–	452	–	0.7	9.8
48-49–Boston-Prov.	60	–	–	202	647	.312	–	–	–	214	345	.620	–	–	–	113	175	–	–	–	–	618	–	1.9	10.3
49-50–Washington	68	–	–	108	284	.380	–	–	–	112	175	.640	–	–	–	89	136	–	–	–	–	328	–	1.3	4.8
50-51–Wash.-Balt.	68	–	–	164	449	.365	–	–	–	172	248	.694	–	–	539	158	216	7	–	–	–	500	7.9	2.3	7.4
Reg. Season Totals	303	–	–	910	2900	.314	–	–	–	851	1344	.633	–	–	539	438	814	7	–	–	–	2671	7.9	1.4	8.8
Playoff Totals	26	–	–	106	578	.265	–	–	–	111	185	.600	–	–	–	13	84	2	–	–	–	323	–	0.4	12.4

Halbrook, Harvey Wade (Swede) b. January 30, 1933 d. April 5, 1988 Ht. 7-3 Wt. 235 College: Oregon State

SEASON–TEAM	G	GS	MIN	FGM	FGA	PCT	3FGM	3FGA	PCT	FTM	FTA	PCT	O-RB	D-RB	TOT	AST	PF	DQ	STL	TO	BLK	PTS	RPG	APG	PPG
60-61–Syracuse	79	–	1131	155	463	.335	–	–	–	76	140	.543	–	–	550	31	262	9	–	–	–	386	7.0	0.4	4.9
61-62–Syracuse	64	–	908	152	422	.360	–	–	–	96	151	.636	–	–	399	33	179	7	–	–	–	400	6.2	0.5	6.3
Reg. Season Totals	143	–	2039	307	885	.347	–	–	–	172	291	.591	–	–	949	64	441	16	–	–	–	786	6.6	0.4	5.5
Playoff Totals	8	–	176	24	78	.308	–	–	–	15	22	.682	–	–	85	12	25	1	–	–	–	63	10.6	1.5	7.9

Hale, Hal Ries b. September 21, 1945 Ht. 6-1 Wt. 185 College: Utah State

SEASON–TEAM	G	GS	MIN	FGM	FGA	PCT	3FGM	3FGA	PCT	FTM	FTA	PCT	O-RB	D-RB	TOT	AST	PF	DQ	STL	TO	BLK	PTS	RPG	APG	PPG
67-68–Houston (A)	72	–	1706	133	408	.326	35	112	.313	60	89	.674	–	–	206	144	143	1	–	91	–	361	2.9	2.0	5.0
Reg. ABA Totals	72	–	1706	133	408	.326	35	112	.313	60	89	.674	–	–	206	144	143	1	–	91	–	361	2.9	2.0	5.0
ABA Playoff Totals	3	–	103	6	16	.375	3	3	1.000	7	7	1.000	–	–	8	3	10	0	–	–	–	22	2.7	1.0	7.3

Hale, William Bruce (Bruce) b. August 30, 1918 d. December 30, 1980 Ht. 6-1 Wt. 170 College: Santa Clara

SEASON–TEAM	G	GS	MIN	FGM	FGA	PCT	3FGM	3FGA	PCT	FTM	FTA	PCT	O-RB	D-RB	TOT	AST	PF	DQ	STL	TO	BLK	PTS	RPG	APG	PPG
46-47–Chicago (N)	41	–	–	156	–	–	–	–	–	116	141	.823	–	–	–	–	103	–	–	–	–	428	–	–	10.4
47-48–Indianapolis (N)	48	–	–	196	–	–	–	–	–	155	215	.721	–	–	–	–	136	–	–	–	–	547	–	–	11.4
48-49–Ind.-FtWayne	52	–	–	187	585	.320	–	–	–	172	228	.754	–	–	–	156	112	–	–	–	–	546	–	3.0	10.5
49-50–Indianapolis	64	–	–	217	614	.353	–	–	–	223	285	.782	–	–	–	226	143	–	–	–	–	657	–	3.5	10.3
50-51–Indianapolis	26	–	–	40	135	.296	–	–	–	14	23	.609	–	–	49	42	30	0	–	–	–	94	1.9	1.6	3.6
Reg. NBA Totals	142	–	–	444	1334	.333	–	–	–	409	536	.763	–	–	49	424	285	0	–	–	–	1297	1.9	3.0	9.1
Reg. NBL Totals	89	–	–	352	–	–	–	–	–	271	356	.761	–	–	–	–	239	–	–	–	–	975	–	–	11.0
NBA Playoff Totals	8	–	–	14	80	.350	–	–	–	15	18	.833	–	–	–	34	9	0	–	–	–	43	–	2.8	5.4
NBL Playoff Totals	15	–	–	56	–	–	–	–	–	44	53	.792	–	–	–	–	28	–	–	–	–	156	–	–	10.4

Haley, Jack Kevin b. January 27, 1964 Ht. 6-10 Wt. 242 College: UCLA

SEASON–TEAM	G	GS	MIN	FGM	FGA	PCT	3FGM	3FGA	PCT	FTM	FTA	PCT	O-RB	D-RB	TOT	AST	PF	DQ	STL	TO	BLK	PTS	RPG	APG	PPG
88-89–Chicago	51	1	289	37	78	.474	0	0	–	36	46	.783	21	50	71	10	56	0	11	26	0	110	1.4	0.2	2.2
89-90–Chicago-N.J.	67	26	1084	138	347	.398	0	1	.000	85	125	.680	115	185	300	26	170	1	18	72	12	361	4.5	0.4	5.4
90-91–New Jersey	78	18	1178	161	343	.469	0	0	–	112	181	.619	140	216	356	31	199	0	20	63	21	434	4.6	0.4	5.6
91-92–L.A. Lakers	49	9	394	31	84	.369	0	0	–	14	29	.483	31	64	95	7	75	0	7	25	8	76	1.9	0.1	1.6
93-94–San Antonio	28	0	94	21	48	.438	0	0	–	17	21	.810	6	18	24	1	18	0	0	10	0	59	0.9	0.0	2.1
94-95–San Antonio	31	0	117	26	61	.426	0	1	.000	21	32	.656	8	19	27	2	31	0	3	13	5	73	0.9	0.1	2.4
95-96–Chicago	1	0	7	2	6	.333	0	0	–	1	2	.500	1	1	2	0	2	0	0	1	0	5	2.0	0.0	5.0
96-97–New Jersey	20	0	74	13	37	.351	0	0	–	14	19	.737	13	19	32	5	14	0	1	2	1	40	1.6	0.3	2.0
97-98–New Jersey	16	0	51	5	18	.278	0	1	.000	12	21	.571	5	10	15	0	9	0	0	4	1	22	0.9	0.0	1.4
Reg. Season Totals	341	54	3288	434	1022	.425	0	3	.000	312	476	.655	340	582	922	82	574	1	60	216	48	1180	2.7	0.2	3.5
Playoff Totals	14	0	43	8	22	.364	0	0	–	7	10	.700	6	9	15	4	10	0	0	1	1	23	1.1	0.3	1.6

Halimon, Shaler Jr. b. March 30, 1945 Ht. 6-6 Wt. 200 College: Imperial Valley (Calif.) Coll. (J.C.); Utah State

SEASON–TEAM	G	GS	MIN	FGM	FGA	PCT	3FGM	3FGA	PCT	FTM	FTA	PCT	O-RB	D-RB	TOT	AST	PF	DQ	STL	TO	BLK	PTS	RPG	APG	PPG
68-69–Philadelphia	50	–	350	88	196	.449	–	–	–	10	32	.313	–	–	86	18	34	0	–	–	–	186	1.7	0.4	3.7
69-70–Chicago	38	–	517	96	244	.393	–	–	–	49	73	.671	–	–	68	69	58	0	–	–	–	241	1.8	1.8	6.3
70-71–Chicago-Port.	81	–	1652	301	783	.384	–	–	–	107	162	.660	–	–	417	215	183	1	–	–	–	709	5.1	2.7	8.8
71-72–Atlanta	1	–	4	0	0	–	–	–	–	0	0	–	–	–	0	0	1	0	–	–	–	0	0.0	0.0	0.0
71-72–Dallas (A)	55	–	770	123	294	.418	0	2	.000	62	86	.721	–	–	156	72	89	–	–	46	–	308	2.8	1.3	5.6
72-73–Dallas (A)	29	–	355	59	149	.396	1	7	.143	23	37	.622	16	38	54	49	53	0	–	43	–	142	1.9	1.7	4.9
Reg. NBA Totals	170	–	2523	485	1223	.397	–	–	–	166	267	.622	–	–	571	302	276	1	–	–	–	1136	3.4	1.8	6.7
Reg. ABA Totals	84	–	1125	182	443	.411	1	9	.111	85	123	.691	16	38	210	121	142	0	–	89	–	450	2.5	1.4	5.4
NBA Playoff Totals	6	–	108	22	63	.349	–	–	–	2	3	.667	–	–	20	18	13	0	–	–	–	46	3.3	3.0	7.7
ABA Playoff Totals	4	–	55	9	17	.529	0	0	–	4	7	.571	–	–	13	7	4	0	–	5	–	22	3.3	1.8	5.5

Halliburton, Jeffrey (Jeff) b. July 3, 1949 Ht. 6-5 Wt. 195 College: San Jacinto (Texas) Coll. (J.C.); Drake

SEASON–TEAM	G	GS	MIN	FGM	FGA	PCT	3FGM	3FGA	PCT	FTM	FTA	PCT	O-RB	D-RB	TOT	AST	PF	DQ	STL	TO	BLK	PTS	RPG	APG	PPG
71-72–Atlanta	37	–	288	61	133	.459	–	–	–	25	30	.833	–	–	37	20	50	1	–	–	–	147	1.0	0.5	4.0
72-73–Atlanta-Phil.	55	–	787	172	396	.434	–	–	–	71	88	.807	–	–	108	96	107	1	–	–	–	415	2.0	1.7	7.5
Reg. Season Totals	92	–	1075	233	529	.440	–	–	–	96	118	.814	–	–	145	116	157	2	–	–	–	562	1.6	1.3	6.1
Playoff Totals	1	–	2	0	1	.000	–	–	–	0	0	–	–	–	0	–	0	0	–	–	–	0	0.0	0.0	0.0

Ham, Darvin b. July 23, 1973 Ht. 6-7 Wt. 230 College: Texas Tech

SEASON–TEAM	G	GS	MIN	FGM	FGA	PCT	3FGM	3FGA	PCT	FTM	FTA	PCT	O-RB	D-RB	TOT	AST	PF	DQ	STL	TO	BLK	PTS	RPG	APG	PPG
96-97–Denver-Indiana	36	3	318	33	62	.532	0	0	–	17	35	.486	29	27	56	14	57	3	9	22	8	83	1.6	0.4	2.3
97-98–Washington	71	3	635	55	104	.529	0	0	–	35	74	.473	72	59	131	16	118	1	21	37	25	145	1.8	0.2	2.0
99-00–Milwaukee	35	21	792	71	128	.555	0	1	.000	35	78	.449	85	87	172	42	102	1	29	29	29	177	4.9	1.2	5.1
Reg. Season Totals	142	27	1745	159	294	.541	0	1	.000	87	187	.465	186	173	359	72	277	5	59	88	62	405	2.5	0.5	2.9
Playoff Totals	5	5	144	11	17	.647	0	1	.000	3	9	.333	17	12	29	7	22	0	1	7	8	25	5.8	1.4	5.0

Hamer, Stevie Ray (Steve) b. November 13, 1973 Ht. 7-0 Wt. 245 College: Tennessee

SEASON–TEAM	G	GS	MIN	FGM	FGA	PCT	3FGM	3FGA	PCT	FTM	FTA	PCT	O-RB	D-RB	TOT	AST	PF	DQ	STL	TO	BLK	PTS	RPG	APG	PPG
96-97–Boston	35	3	268	30	57	.526	0	2	.000	16	29	.552	17	43	60	7	39	0	2	13	4	76	1.7	0.2	2.2
Reg. Season Totals	35	3	268	30	57	.526	0	2	.000	16	29	.552	17	43	60	7	39	0	2	13	4	76	1.7	0.2	2.2

Hamilton, Dale B. b. August 16, 1919 Ht. 6-1 Wt. 200 College: Franklin (Ind.)

SEASON–TEAM	G	GS	MIN	FGM	FGA	PCT	3FGM	3FGA	PCT	FTM	FTA	PCT	O-RB	D-RB	TOT	AST	PF	DQ	STL	TO	BLK	PTS	RPG	APG	PPG
39-40–Hammond (N)	7	–	–	5	–	–	–	–	–	1	–	–	–	–	–	–	–	–	–	–	–	11	–	–	1.6
41-42–Fort Wayne (N)	16	–	–	10	–	–	–	–	–	16	–	–	–	–	–	–	–	–	–	–	–	36	–	–	2.3
42-43–Fort Wayne (N)	18	–	–	8	–	–	–	–	–	1	–	–	–	–	–	–	–	–	–	–	–	17	–	–	0.9
43-44–Fort Wayne (N)	11	–	–	2	–	–	–	–	–	0	–	–	–	–	–	–	–	–	–	–	–	4	–	–	0.4
44-45–Fort Wayne (N)	2	–	–	0	–	–	–	–	–	0	–	–	–	–	–	–	–	–	–	–	–	0	–	–	0.0
46-47–Toledo (N)	44	–	–	114	–	–	–	–	–	67	131	.511	–	–	–	–	94	–	–	–	–	295	–	–	6.7
47-48–Toledo (N)	53	–	–	93	–	–	–	–	–	62	133	.466	–	–	–	–	130	–	–	–	–	248	–	–	4.7
48-49–Waterloo (N)	62	–	–	78	–	–	–	–	–	94	179	.525	–	–	–	–	194	–	–	–	–	250	–	–	4.0
49-50–Waterloo	14	–	–	8	33	.242	–	–	–	9	19	.474	–	–	–	17	30	–	–	–	–	25	–	1.2	1.8
Reg. NBA Totals	14	–	–	8	33	.242	–	–	–	9	19	.474	–	–	–	17	30	–	–	–	–	25	–	1.2	1.8
Reg. NBL Totals	213	–	–	310	–	–	–	–	–	241	443	.503	–	–	–	–	418	–	–	–	–	861	–	–	4.0
NBL Playoff Totals	15	–	–	8	–	–	–	–	–	10	20	.350	–	–	–	–	15	–	–	–	–	26	–	–	1.7

Hamilton, Dennis Eugene b. May 8, 1944 Ht. 6-8 Wt. 210 College: Arizona State

SEASON–TEAM	G	GS	MIN	FGM	FGA	PCT	3FGM	3FGA	PCT	FTM	FTA	PCT	O-RB	D-RB	TOT	AST	PF	DQ	STL	TO	BLK	PTS	RPG	APG	PPG
67-68–Los Angeles	44	–	378	54	108	.500	–	–	–	13	13	1.000	–	–	72	30	46	0	–	–	–	121	1.6	0.7	2.8
68-69–Atlanta	25	–	141	37	67	.552	–	–	–	2	5	.400	–	–	29	8	19	0	–	–	–	76	1.2	0.3	3.0
69-70–Pittsburgh (A)	72	–	1331	190	375	.507	0	1	.000	76	100	.760	–	–	340	73	144	0	–	–	–	456	4.7	1.0	6.3
70-71–Kentucky (A)	3	–	11	1	2	.500	0	0	–	1	1	1.000	–	–	1	1	1	–	–	–	–	3	0.3	0.3	1.0
Reg. NBA Totals	69	–	519	91	175	.520	–	–	–	15	18	.833	–	–	101	38	65	0	–	–	–	197	1.5	0.6	2.9
Reg. ABA Totals	75	–	1342	191	377	.507	0	1	.000	77	101	.762	–	–	341	74	145	0	–	–	–	459	4.5	1.0	6.1
NBA Playoff Totals	2	–	11	1	3	.333	–	–	–	0	0	–	–	–	2	1	0	0	–	–	–	2	1.0	0.5	1.0

Hamilton, James Jr. (Joe) b. July 5, 1948 Ht. 5-10 Wt. 180 College: Christian Coll. of the Southwest (Texas) (J.C); North Texas

SEASON–TEAM	G	GS	MIN	FGM	FGA	PCT	3FGM	3FGA	PCT	FTM	FTA	PCT	O-RB	D-RB	TOT	AST	PF	DQ	STL	TO	BLK	PTS	RPG	APG	PPG
70-71–Texas (A)	84	–	2564	500	1184	.422	85	285	.298	233	279	.835	–	–	285	365	279	–	–	–	–	1318	3.4	4.3	15.7
71-72–Dallas (A)	82	–	1959	317	791	.401	46	132	.348	201	256	.785	–	–	194	240	202	–	–	110	–	881	2.4	2.9	10.7
72-73–Dallas (A)	83	–	2359	370	902	.410	66	191	.346	209	262	.798	46	169	215	325	247	0	–	143	–	1015	2.6	3.9	12.2
73-74–S.A.-Ken. (A)	73	–	1961	331	834	.397	37	144	.257	117	143	.818	40	125	165	242	154	–	76	112	5	816	2.3	3.3	11.2
74-75–Kentucky (A)	9	–	124	15	40	.375	3	5	.600	5	6	.833	2	9	11	21	13	–	4	9	0	38	1.2	2.3	4.2
75-76–Utah (A)	13	–	131	31	78	.397	6	21	.286	9	13	.692	5	9	14	15	12	–	8	6	0	77	1.1	1.2	5.9
Reg. ABA Totals	344	–	9098	1564	3829	.408	243	778	.312	774	959	.807	93	312	884	1208	907	0	88	380	5	4145	2.6	3.5	12.0
ABA Playoff Totals	15	–	319	48	145	.331	12	37	.324	27	33	.818	3	20	54	49	38	0	4	19	0	135	3.6	3.3	9.0

Hamilton, Ralph Albert (Ham) b. June 10, 1921 d. June 5, 1993 Ht. 6-1 Wt. 190 College: Indiana

SEASON–TEAM	G	GS	MIN	FGM	FGA	PCT	3FGM	3FGA	PCT	FTM	FTA	PCT	O-RB	D-RB	TOT	AST	PF	DQ	STL	TO	BLK	PTS	RPG	APG	PPG
47-48–Fort Wayne (N)	49	–	–	143	–	–	–	–	–	101	135	.748	–	–	–	–	74	–	–	–	–	387	–	–	7.9
48-49–FtWayne-Ind.	48	–	–	114	447	.255	–	–	–	61	91	.670	–	–	–	83	67	–	–	–	–	289	–	1.7	6.0
Reg. NBA Totals	48	–	–	114	447	.255	–	–	–	61	91	.670	–	–	–	83	67	–	–	–	–	289	–	1.7	6.0
Reg. NBL Totals	49	–	–	143	–	–	–	–	–	101	135	.748	–	–	–	–	74	–	–	–	–	387	–	–	7.9
NBL Playoff Totals	2	–	–	1	–	–	–	–	–	2	4	.500	–	–	–	–	1	–	–	–	–	4	–	–	2.0

Hamilton, Richard Clay b. February 14, 1978 Ht. 6-6 Wt. 185 College: Connecticut

SEASON–TEAM	G	GS	MIN	FGM	FGA	PCT	3FGM	3FGA	PCT	FTM	FTA	PCT	O-RB	D-RB	TOT	AST	PF	DQ	STL	TO	BLK	PTS	RPG	APG	PPG
99-00–Washington	71	12	1373	254	605	.420	28	77	.364	103	133	.774	38	91	129	108	142	2	28	84	6	639	1.8	1.5	9.0
Reg. Season Totals	71	12	1373	254	605	.420	28	77	.364	103	133	.774	38	91	129	108	142	2	28	84	6	639	1.8	1.5	9.0

Hamilton, Roy Lee (Roy Lee) b. July 20, 1957 Ht. 6-2 Wt. 180 College: UCLA

SEASON–TEAM	G	GS	MIN	FGM	FGA	PCT	3FGM	3FGA	PCT	FTM	FTA	PCT	O-RB	D-RB	TOT	AST	PF	DQ	STL	TO	BLK	PTS	RPG	APG	PPG
79-80–Detroit	72	–	1116	115	287	.401	0	2	.000	103	150	.687	45	62	107	192	82	0	48	118	5	333	1.5	2.7	4.6
80-81–Portland	1	–	5	1	3	.333	0	0	–	1	2	.500	2	1	3	0	1	0	0	1	0	3	3.0	0.0	3.0
Reg. Season Totals	73	–	1121	116	290	.400	0	2	.000	104	152	.684	47	63	110	192	83	0	48	119	5	336	1.5	2.6	4.6

Hamilton, Steve Absher b. November 30, 1935 d. December 2, 1997 Ht. 6-7 Wt. 190 College: Purdue; Morehead State

SEASON–TEAM	G	GS	MIN	FGM	FGA	PCT	3FGM	3FGA	PCT	FTM	FTA	PCT	O-RB	D-RB	TOT	AST	PF	DQ	STL	TO	BLK	PTS	RPG	APG	PPG
58-59–Minneapolis	67	–	847	109	294	.371	–	–	–	74	109	.679	–	–	220	36	144	2	–	–	–	292	3.3	0.5	4.4
59-60–Minneapolis	15	–	247	29	77	.377	–	–	–	18	23	.783	–	–	58	7	39	1	–	–	–	76	3.9	0.5	5.1
Reg. Season Totals	82	–	1094	138	371	.372	–	–	–	92	132	.697	–	–	278	43	183	3	–	–	–	368	3.4	0.5	4.5
Playoff Totals	10	–	87	12	43	.279	–	–	–	8	10	.800	–	–	35	5	14	0	–	–	–	32	3.5	0.5	3.2

Hamilton, Thomas b. April 3, 1975 Ht. 7-2 Wt. 330 College: Pittsburgh

SEASON–TEAM	G	GS	MIN	FGM	FGA	PCT	3FGM	3FGA	PCT	FTM	FTA	PCT	O-RB	D-RB	TOT	AST	PF	DQ	STL	TO	BLK	PTS	RPG	APG	PPG
95-96–Boston	11	0	70	9	31	.290	0	0	–	7	18	.389	10	12	22	1	12	0	0	9	9	25	2.0	0.1	2.3
99-00–Houston	22	7	273	35	79	.443	0	0	–	12	23	.522	31	59	90	15	25	0	4	28	14	82	4.1	0.7	3.7
Reg. Season Totals	33	7	343	44	110	.400	0	0	–	19	41	.463	41	71	112	16	37	0	4	37	23	107	3.4	0.5	3.2

Hammink, Geert Hendrik b. April 12, 1969 Ht. 7-0 Wt. 262 College: Louisiana State

SEASON–TEAM	G	GS	MIN	FGM	FGA	PCT	3FGM	3FGA	PCT	FTM	FTA	PCT	O-RB	D-RB	TOT	AST	PF	DQ	STL	TO	BLK	PTS	RPG	APG	PPG
93-94–Orlando	1	0	3	1	3	.333	0	0	–	0	0	–	1	0	1	1	1	0	0	0	0	2	1.0	1.0	2.0
94-95–Orlando	1	0	7	1	3	.333	0	0	–	2	2	1.000	0	2	2	1	1	0	0	0	0	4	2.0	1.0	4.0
95-96–Orlando-G.S.	6	0	17	2	4	.500	0	0	–	4	7	.571	2	2	4	0	2	0	0	2	0	8	0.7	0.0	1.3
Reg. Season Totals	8	0	27	4	10	.400	0	0	–	6	9	.667	3	4	7	2	4	0	0	2	0	14	0.9	0.3	1.8

Hammond, Julian (Julie) b. May 27, 1943 Ht. 6-5 Wt. 210 College: Tulsa

SEASON–TEAM	G	GS	MIN	FGM	FGA	PCT	3FGM	3FGA	PCT	FTM	FTA	PCT	O-RB	D-RB	TOT	AST	PF	DQ	STL	TO	BLK	PTS	RPG	APG	PPG
67-68–Denver (A)	74	–	1364	224	458	.489	0	0	–	143	209	.684	–	–	327	62	112	0	–	98	–	591	4.4	0.8	8.0
68-69–Denver (A)	78	–	2335	329	601	.547	0	0	–	165	253	.652	–	–	600	124	213	3	–	152	–	823	7.7	1.6	10.6
69-70–Denver (A)	69	–	1847	329	660	.498	0	1	.000	169	243	.695	–	–	471	109	183	2	–	–	–	827	6.8	1.6	12.0
70-71–Denver (A)	83	–	2082	435	834	.522	0	0	–	273	375	.728	–	–	523	97	189	–	–	–	–	1143	6.3	1.2	13.8
71-72–Denver (A)	25	–	411	66	140	.471	0	0	–	31	50	.620	–	–	115	29	47	–	–	30	–	163	4.6	1.2	6.5
Reg. ABA Totals	329	–	8039	1383	2693	.514	0	1	.000	781	1130	.691	–	–	2036	421	744	5	–	280	–	3547	6.2	1.3	10.8
ABA Playoff Totals	24	–	739	140	272	.515	0	0	–	63	93	.677	–	–	157	46	92	3	–	11	–	343	6.5	1.9	14.3

Hammonds, Tom Edward (The Terminator) b. March 27, 1967 Ht. 6-9 Wt. 225 College: Georgia Tech

SEASON–TEAM	G	GS	MIN	FGM	FGA	PCT	3FGM	3FGA	PCT	FTM	FTA	PCT	O-RB	D-RB	TOT	AST	PF	DQ	STL	TO	BLK	PTS	RPG	APG	PPG
89-90–Washington	61	8	805	129	295	.437	0	1	.000	63	98	.643	61	107	168	51	98	0	11	46	14	321	2.8	0.8	5.3
90-91–Washington	70	7	1023	155	336	.461	0	4	.000	57	79	.722	58	148	206	43	108	0	15	54	7	367	2.9	0.6	5.2
91-92–Wash.-Cha.	37	19	984	195	400	.488	0	1	.000	50	82	.610	49	136	185	36	118	1	22	58	13	440	5.0	1.0	11.9
92-93–Cha.-Denver	54	5	713	105	221	.475	0	1	.000	38	62	.613	38	89	127	24	77	0	18	34	12	248	2.4	0.4	4.6
93-94–Denver	74	2	877	115	230	.500	0	0	–	71	104	.683	62	137	199	34	91	0	20	41	12	301	2.7	0.5	4.1
94-95–Denver	70	5	956	139	260	.535	0	1	.000	132	177	.746	55	167	222	36	132	1	11	56	14	410	3.2	0.5	5.9
95-96–Denver	71	4	1045	127	268	.474	0	0	–	88	115	.765	85	138	223	23	137	0	23	48	13	342	3.1	0.3	4.8
96-97–Denver	81	8	1758	191	398	.480	0	2	.000	124	172	.721	135	266	401	64	205	0	16	88	24	506	5.0	0.8	6.2
97-98–Minnesota	57	2	1140	127	246	.516	0	1	.000	92	132	.697	100	171	271	36	127	1	15	48	17	346	4.8	0.6	6.1
98-99–Minnesota	49	0	716	82	179	.458	0	0	–	48	75	.640	54	82	136	20	88	1	8	32	7	212	2.8	0.4	4.3
99-00–Minnesota	56	0	372	42	97	.433	0	0	–	33	56	.589	34	67	101	10	55	0	8	21	3	117	1.8	0.2	2.1
Reg. Season Totals	680	60	10389	1407	2930	.480	0	11	.000	796	1152	.691	731	1508	2239	377	1236	4	167	526	136	3610	3.3	0.6	5.3
Playoff Totals	21	1	226	23	51	.451	0	0	–	23	32	.719	18	26	44	5	40	0	0	10	3	69	2.1	0.2	3.3

Hamood, Joseph (Joe) b. September 7, 1943 d. August 19, 1970 Ht. 6-0 Wt. 185 College: Houston

SEASON–TEAM	G	GS	MIN	FGM	FGA	PCT	3FGM	3FGA	PCT	FTM	FTA	PCT	O-RB	D-RB	TOT	AST	PF	DQ	STL	TO	BLK	PTS	RPG	APG	PPG
67-68–Houston (A)	76	–	1839	274	819	.335	16	78	.205	186	252	.738	–	–	217	227	200	2	–	126	–	750	2.9	3.0	9.9
Reg. ABA Totals	76	–	1839	274	819	.335	16	78	.205	186	252	.738	–	–	217	227	200	2	–	126	–	750	2.9	3.0	9.9
ABA Playoff Totals	3	–	42	3	17	.176	0	3	.000	1	2	.500	–	–	5	2	8	0	–	1	–	7	1.7	0.7	2.3

Hancock, Darrin b. November 3, 1971 Ht. 6-7 Wt. 215 College: Garden City (Kan.) C.C.; Kansas

SEASON–TEAM	G	GS	MIN	FGM	FGA	PCT	3FGM	3FGA	PCT	FTM	FTA	PCT	O-RB	D-RB	TOT	AST	PF	DQ	STL	TO	BLK	PTS	RPG	APG	PPG
94-95–Charlotte	46	7	424	68	121	.562	1	3	.333	16	39	.410	14	39	53	30	48	0	19	30	4	153	1.2	0.7	3.3
95-96–Charlotte	63	7	838	112	214	.523	1	3	.333	47	73	.644	40	58	98	47	94	2	28	56	5	272	1.6	0.7	4.3
96-97–Milw.-S.A.-Atlanta	24	0	133	16	35	.457	0	0	–	10	14	.714	4	14	18	12	15	0	9	11	1	42	0.8	0.5	1.8
Reg. Season Totals	133	14	1395	196	370	.530	2	6	.333	73	126	.579	58	111	169	89	157	2	56	97	10	467	1.3	0.7	3.5
Playoff Totals	9	0	51	4	11	.364	0	1	.000	0	3	.000	4	5	9	2	10	0	2	4	1	8	1.0	0.2	0.9

Hankins, Cecil O. b. January 6, 1922 Ht. 6-1 Wt. 175 College: Oklahoma State

SEASON–TEAM	G	GS	MIN	FGM	FGA	PCT	3FGM	3FGA	PCT	FTM	FTA	PCT	O-RB	D-RB	TOT	AST	PF	DQ	STL	TO	BLK	PTS	RPG	APG	PPG
46-47–St. Louis	55	–	–	117	391	.299	–	–	–	90	150	.600	–	–	–	14	49	–	–	–	–	324	–	0.3	5.9
47-48–Boston	25	–	–	23	116	.198	–	–	–	24	35	.686	–	–	–	8	28	–	–	–	–	70	–	0.3	2.8
47-48–Sheboygan (N)	1	–	–	0	–	–	–	–	–	1	1	1.000	–	–	–	–	2	–	–	–	–	1	–	–	1.0
Reg. NBA Totals	80	–	–	140	507	.276	–	–	–	114	185	.616	–	–	–	22	77	–	–	–	–	394	–	0.3	4.9
Reg. NBL Totals	1	–	–	0	–	–	–	–	–	1	1	1.000	–	–	–	–	2	–	–	–	–	1	–	–	1.0
NBA Playoff Totals	2	–	–	2	14	.286	–	–	–	1	2	.500	–	–	–	–	1	–	–	–	–	5	–	0.0	2.5

Hankinson, Phil b. July 26, 1951 d. November 19, 1996 Ht. 6-8 Wt. 195 College: Pennsylvania

SEASON–TEAM	G	GS	MIN	FGM	FGA	PCT	3FGM	3FGA	PCT	FTM	FTA	PCT	O-RB	D-RB	TOT	AST	PF	DQ	STL	TO	BLK	PTS	RPG	APG	PPG
73-74–Boston	28	–	163	50	103	.485	–	–	–	10	13	.769	22	28	50	4	18	0	3	–	1	110	1.8	0.1	3.9
74-75–Boston	3	–	24	6	11	.545	–	–	–	0	0	–	1	6	7	2	3	0	1	–	0	12	2.3	0.7	4.0
Reg. Season Totals	31	–	187	56	114	.491	–	–	–	10	13	.769	23	34	57	6	21	0	4	–	1	122	1.8	0.2	3.9
Playoff Totals	4	–	8	3	7	.429	–	–	–	2	2	1.000	2	1	3	–	0	0	0	–	1	8	0.8	0.0	2.0

Hannum, Alexander Murray (Alex) b. July 19, 1923 Ht. 6-7 Wt. 225 College: USC HOF: 1998

SEASON–TEAM	G	GS	MIN	FGM	FGA	PCT	3FGM	3FGA	PCT	FTM	FTA	PCT	O-RB	D-RB	TOT	AST	PF	DQ	STL	TO	BLK	PTS	RPG	APG	PPG
48-49–Oshkosh (N)	64	–	–	126	–	–	–	–	–	113	191	.592	–	–	–	–	188	–	–	–	–	365	–	–	5.7
49-50–Syracuse	64	–	–	177	488	.363	–	–	–	128	186	.688	–	–	–	129	264	–	–	–	–	482	–	2.0	7.5
50-51–Syracuse	63	–	–	182	494	.368	–	–	–	107	197	.543	–	–	301	119	271	16	–	–	–	471	4.8	1.9	7.5
51-52–Balt.-Roch.	66	–	1508	170	462	.368	–	–	–	98	137	.715	–	–	336	133	271	16	–	–	–	438	5.1	2.0	6.6
52-53–Rochester	68	–	1288	129	360	.358	–	–	–	88	133	.662	–	–	279	81	258	18	–	–	–	346	4.1	1.2	5.1
53-54–Rochester	72	–	1707	175	503	.348	–	–	–	102	164	.622	–	–	350	105	279	11	–	–	–	452	4.9	1.5	6.3
54-55–Milwaukee	53	–	1088	126	358	.352	–	–	–	61	107	.570	–	–	245	105	206	9	–	–	–	313	4.6	2.0	5.9
55-56–St. Louis	71	–	1480	146	453	.322	–	–	–	93	154	.604	–	–	344	157	271	10	–	–	–	385	4.8	2.2	5.4
56-57–FtWayne-St. L.	59	–	642	77	223	.345	–	–	–	37	56	.661	–	–	158	28	135	2	–	–	–	191	2.7	0.5	3.2
Reg. NBA Totals	516	–	7713	1182	3341	.354	–	–	–	714	1134	.630	–	–	2013	857	1955	82	–	–	–	3078	4.5	1.7	6.0
Reg. NBL Totals	64	–	–	126	–	–	–	–	–	113	191	.592	–	–	–	–	188	–	–	–	–	365	–	–	5.7
NBA Playoff Totals	43	–	577	108	342	.415	–	–	–	70	124	.565	–	–	150	63	198	16	–	–	–	286	3.9	1.1	6.7
NBL Playoff Totals	7	–	–	12	–	–	–	–	–	16	26	.615	–	–	–	–	26	–	–	–	–	40	–	–	5.7

Hanrahan, Donald (Don) b. February 6, 1929 Ht. 6-7 Wt. 200 College: Loyola (Chicago)

SEASON–TEAM	G	GS	MIN	FGM	FGA	PCT	3FGM	3FGA	PCT	FTM	FTA	PCT	O-RB	D-RB	TOT	AST	PF	DQ	STL	TO	BLK	PTS	RPG	APG	PPG
52-53–Indianapolis	18	–	121	11	32	.344	–	–	–	11	15	.733	–	–	30	11	24	1	–	–	–	33	1.7	0.6	1.8
Reg. Season Totals	18	–	121	11	32	.344	–	–	–	11	15	.733	–	–	30	11	24	1	–	–	–	33	1.7	0.6	1.8

Hans, Rollen F. (Rolly) b. April 13, 1931 Ht. 6-2 Wt. 210 College: Los Angeles City (Calif.) Coll. (J.C.); Long Island University

SEASON–TEAM	G	GS	MIN	FGM	FGA	PCT	3FGM	3FGA	PCT	FTM	FTA	PCT	O-RB	D-RB	TOT	AST	PF	DQ	STL	TO	BLK	PTS	RPG	APG	PPG
53-54–Baltimore	67	–	1556	191	515	.371	–	–	–	101	180	.561	–	–	160	181	172	1	–	–	–	483	2.4	2.7	7.2
54-55–Baltimore	13	–	178	30	67	.448	–	–	–	13	25	.520	–	–	16	26	20	0	–	–	–	73	1.2	2.0	5.6
Reg. Season Totals	80	–	1734	221	582	.380	–	–	–	114	205	.556	–	–	176	207	192	1	–	–	–	556	2.2	2.6	7.0

Hansen, Glenn R. b. April 21, 1952 Ht. 6-4 Wt. 205 College: Utah State; Louisiana State

SEASON–TEAM	G	GS	MIN	FGM	FGA	PCT	3FGM	3FGA	PCT	FTM	FTA	PCT	O-RB	D-RB	TOT	AST	PF	DQ	STL	TO	BLK	PTS	RPG	APG	PPG
75-76–Kansas City	66	–	1145	173	420	.412	–	–	–	85	117	.726	77	110	187	67	144	1	47	–	13	431	2.8	1.0	6.5
76-77–Kansas City	41	–	289	67	155	.432	–	–	–	23	32	.719	28	31	59	25	44	0	13	–	3	157	1.4	0.6	3.8
77-78–Chicago-K.C.	5	–	13	0	7	.000	–	–	–	0	0	–	1	0	1	1	3	0	1	1	0	0	0.2	0.2	0.0
Reg. Season Totals	112	–	1447	240	582	.412	–	–	–	108	149	.725	106	141	247	93	191	1	61	1	16	588	2.2	0.8	5.3

Hansen, Lars b. September 14, 1954 Ht. 6-10 Wt. 225 College: Washington

SEASON–TEAM	G	GS	MIN	FGM	FGA	PCT	3FGM	3FGA	PCT	FTM	FTA	PCT	O-RB	D-RB	TOT	AST	PF	DQ	STL	TO	BLK	PTS	RPG	APG	PPG
78-79–Seattle	15	–	205	29	57	.509	–	–	–	18	31	.581	22	37	59	14	28	0	1	9	1	76	3.9	0.9	5.1
Reg. Season Totals	15	–	205	29	57	.509	–	–	–	18	31	.581	22	37	59	14	28	0	1	9	1	76	3.9	0.9	5.1

Hansen, Robert Louis II (Bob) b. January 18, 1961 Ht. 6-6 Wt. 195 College: Iowa

SEASON–TEAM	G	GS	MIN	FGM	FGA	PCT	3FGM	3FGA	PCT	FTM	FTA	PCT	O-RB	D-RB	TOT	AST	PF	DQ	STL	TO	BLK	PTS	RPG	APG	PPG
83-84–Utah	55	0	419	65	145	.448	0	8	.000	18	28	.643	13	35	48	44	62	0	15	35	4	148	0.9	0.8	2.7
84-85–Utah	54	4	646	110	225	.489	1	7	.143	40	72	.556	20	50	70	75	88	0	25	49	1	261	1.3	1.4	4.8
85-86–Utah	82	82	2032	299	628	.476	17	50	.340	95	132	.720	82	162	244	193	205	1	74	126	9	710	3.0	2.4	8.7
86-87–Utah	72	72	1453	272	601	.453	16	45	.356	136	179	.760	84	119	203	102	146	0	44	77	6	696	2.8	1.4	9.7
87-88–Utah	81	51	1796	316	611	.517	32	97	.330	113	152	.743	64	123	187	175	193	2	65	91	5	777	2.3	2.2	9.6
88-89–Utah	46	9	964	140	300	.467	19	54	.352	42	75	.560	29	99	128	50	105	0	37	43	6	341	2.8	1.1	7.4
89-90–Utah	81	81	2174	265	568	.467	54	154	.351	33	64	.516	66	163	229	149	194	2	52	79	11	617	2.8	1.8	7.6
90-91–Sacramento	36	24	811	96	256	.375	19	69	.275	18	36	.500	33	63	96	90	72	1	20	34	5	229	2.7	2.5	6.4
91-92–Sac.-Chicago	68	2	809	79	178	.444	7	27	.259	8	22	.364	17	60	77	69	134	0	27	28	3	173	1.1	1.0	2.5
Reg. Season Totals	575	325	11104	1642	3512	.468	165	511	.323	503	760	.662	408	874	1282	947	1199	6	359	562	50	3952	2.2	1.6	6.9
Playoff Totals	49	28	1079	160	336	.476	38	76	.500	57	78	.731	40	83	123	81	121	1	19	58	4	415	2.5	1.7	8.5

Hanson, Reggie b. October 8, 1968 Ht. 6-8 Wt. 195 College: Kentucky

SEASON–TEAM	G	GS	MIN	FGM	FGA	PCT	3FGM	3FGA	PCT	FTM	FTA	PCT	O-RB	D-RB	TOT	AST	PF	DQ	STL	TO	BLK	PTS	RPG	APG	PPG
97-98–Boston	8	0	26	3	6	.500	0	0	–	0	0	–	3	3	6	1	8	0	2	3	1	6	0.8	0.1	0.8
Reg. Season Totals	8	0	26	3	6	.500	0	0	–	0	0	–	3	3	6	1	8	0	2	3	1	6	0.8	0.1	0.8

Hanzlik, William Henry (Bill) b. December 6, 1957 Ht. 6-7 Wt. 200 College: Notre Dame

SEASON–TEAM	G	GS	MIN	FGM	FGA	PCT	3FGM	3FGA	PCT	FTM	FTA	PCT	O-RB	D-RB	TOT	AST	PF	DQ	STL	TO	BLK	PTS	RPG	APG	PPG
80-81–Seattle	74	–	1259	138	289	.478	1	5	.200	119	150	.793	67	86	153	111	168	1	58	84	20	396	2.1	1.5	5.4
81-82–Seattle	81	76	1974	167	357	.468	0	4	.000	138	176	.784	99	167	266	183	250	3	81	106	30	472	3.3	2.3	5.8
82-83–Denver	82	8	1547	187	437	.428	1	7	.143	125	160	.781	80	156	236	268	220	0	75	144	15	500	2.9	3.3	6.1
83-84–Denver	80	14	1469	132	306	.431	3	12	.250	167	207	.807	66	139	205	252	255	6	68	109	19	434	2.6	3.2	5.4
84-85–Denver	80	1	1673	220	522	.421	1	15	.067	180	238	.756	88	119	207	210	291	5	84	115	26	621	2.6	2.6	7.8
85-86–Denver	79	0	1982	331	741	.447	8	41	.195	318	405	.785	88	176	264	316	277	2	107	165	16	988	3.3	4.0	12.5
86-87–Denver	73	10	1990	307	746	.412	22	80	.275	316	402	.786	79	177	256	280	245	3	87	132	28	952	3.5	3.8	13.0
87-88–Denver	77	0	1334	109	287	.380	3	16	.188	129	163	.791	39	132	171	166	185	1	64	95	17	350	2.2	2.2	4.5
88-89–Denver	41	0	701	66	151	.437	1	5	.200	68	87	.782	18	75	93	86	82	1	25	53	5	201	2.3	2.1	4.9
89-90–Denver	81	0	1605	179	396	.452	6	31	.194	136	183	.743	67	140	207	186	249	7	78	87	29	500	2.6	2.3	6.2
Reg. Season Totals	748	109	15534	1836	4232	.434	46	216	.213	1696	2171	.781	691	1367	2058	2058	2222	29	727	1090	205	5414	2.8	2.8	7.2
Playoff Totals	62	15	1327	154	354	.435	5	26	.192	127	165	.770	64	118	182	167	209	5	49	80	29	440	2.9	2.7	7.1

Hardaway, Anfernee Deon (Penny) b. July 18, 1971 Ht. 6-7 Wt. 215 College: Memphis

SEASON–TEAM	G	GS	MIN	FGM	FGA	PCT	3FGM	3FGA	PCT	FTM	FTA	PCT	O-RB	D-RB	TOT	AST	PF	DQ	STL	TO	BLK	PTS	RPG	APG	PPG
93-94–Orlando	82	82	3015	509	1092	.466	50	187	.267	245	330	.742	192	247	439	544	205	2	190	292	51	1313	5.4	6.6	16.0
94-95–Orlando	77	77	2901	585	1142	.512	87	249	.349	356	463	.769	139	197	336	551	158	1	130	258	26	1613	4.4	7.2	20.9
95-96–Orlando	82	82	3015	623	1215	.513	89	283	.314	445	580	.767	129	225	354	582	160	0	166	229	41	1780	4.3	7.1	21.7
96-97–Orlando	59	59	2221	421	941	.447	85	267	.318	283	345	.820	82	181	263	332	123	1	93	145	35	1210	4.5	5.6	20.5
97-98–Orlando	19	15	625	103	273	.377	15	50	.300	90	118	.763	8	68	76	68	45	0	28	46	15	311	4.0	3.6	16.4
98-99–Orlando	50	50	1944	301	717	.420	40	140	.286	149	211	.706	74	210	284	266	111	0	111	150	23	791	5.7	5.3	15.8
99-00–Phoenix	60	60	2253	378	798	.474	33	102	.324	226	286	.790	91	256	347	315	164	1	94	153	38	1015	5.8	5.3	16.9
Reg. Season Totals	429	425	15974	2920	6178	.473	399	1278	.312	1794	2333	.769	715	1384	2099	2658	966	5	812	1273	229	8033	4.9	6.2	18.7
Playoff Totals	54	54	2228	406	885	.459	87	227	.383	263	354	.743	88	161	249	345	163	1	100	165	42	1162	4.6	6.4	21.5
All-Star Totals	4	4	98	20	32	.625	5	12	.417	10	12	.833	8	7	15	24	3	0	4	8	0	55	3.8	6.0	13.8

Hardaway, Timothy Duane (Tim, The Bug) b. September 1, 1966 Ht. 6-0 Wt. 195 College: Texas-El Paso

SEASON–TEAM	G	GS	MIN	FGM	FGA	PCT	3FGM	3FGA	PCT	FTM	FTA	PCT	O-RB	D-RB	TOT	AST	PF	DQ	STL	TO	BLK	PTS	RPG	APG	PPG
89-90–Golden State	79	78	2663	464	985	.471	23	84	.274	211	276	.764	57	253	310	689	232	6	165	260	12	1162	3.9	8.7	14.7
90-91–Golden State	82	82	3215	739	1551	.476	97	252	.385	306	381	.803	87	245	332	793	228	7	214	270	12	1881	4.0	9.7	22.9
91-92–Golden State	81	81	3332	734	1592	.461	127	376	.338	298	389	.766	81	229	310	807	208	1	164	267	13	1893	3.8	10.0	23.4
92-93–Golden State	66	66	2609	522	1168	.447	102	309	.330	273	367	.744	60	203	263	699	152	0	116	220	12	1419	4.0	10.6	21.5
94-95–Golden State	62	62	2321	430	1007	.427	168	444	.378	219	288	.760	46	144	190	578	155	1	88	214	12	1247	3.1	9.3	20.1
95-96–G.S.-Miami	80	46	2534	419	992	.422	138	379	.364	241	305	.790	35	194	229	640	201	3	132	235	17	1217	2.9	8.0	15.2
96-97–Miami	81	81	3136	575	1384	.415	203	590	.344	291	364	.799	49	228	277	695	165	2	151	230	9	1644	3.4	8.6	20.3
97-98–Miami	81	81	3031	558	1296	.431	155	442	.351	257	329	.781	48	251	299	672	200	2	136	224	16	1528	3.7	8.3	18.9
98-99–Miami	48	48	1772	301	752	.400	112	311	.360	121	149	.812	15	137	152	352	102	1	57	131	6	835	3.2	7.3	17.4
99-00–Miami	52	52	1672	246	638	.386	94	256	.367	110	133	.827	25	125	150	385	112	0	49	119	4	696	2.9	7.4	13.4
Reg. Season Totals	712	677	26285	4988	11365	.439	1219	3443	.354	2327	2981	.781	503	2009	2512	6310	1755	23	1272	2170	113	13522	3.5	8.9	19.0
Playoff Totals	50	50	1969	322	813	.396	106	331	.320	175	233	.751	32	136	168	364	116	0	87	154	9	925	3.4	7.3	18.5
All-Star Totals	5	0	84	17	44	.386	8	21	.381	11	14	.786	3	10	13	23	5	0	5	13	0	53	2.6	4.6	10.6

Harding, Reginald **(Reggie)** b. May 4, 1942 d. September 2, 1972 Ht. 7-0 Wt. 255 College: None

SEASON–TEAM	G	GS	MIN	FGM	FGA	PCT	3FGM	3FGA	PCT	FTM	FTA	PCT	O-RB	D-RB	TOT	AST	PF	DQ	STL	TO	BLK	PTS	RPG	APG	PPG
63-64–Detroit	39	–	1158	184	460	.400	–	–	–	61	98	.622	–	–	410	52	119	1	–	–	–	429	10.5	1.3	11.0
64-65–Detroit	78	–	2699	405	987	.410	–	–	–	128	209	.612	–	–	906	179	258	5	–	–	–	938	11.6	2.3	12.0
66-67–Detroit	74	–	1367	172	383	.449	–	–	–	63	103	.612	–	–	455	94	164	2	–	–	–	407	6.1	1.3	5.5
67-68–Chicago	14	–	305	24	71	.338	–	–	–	17	33	.515	–	–	94	18	35	0	–	–	–	65	6.7	1.3	4.6
67-68–Indiana (A)	25	–	840	142	314	.452	0	1	.000	52	90	.578	–	–	334	53	59	0	–	77	–	336	13.4	2.1	13.4
Reg. NBA Totals	205	–	5529	785	1901	.413	–	–	–	269	443	.607	–	–	1865	343	576	8	–	–	–	1839	9.1	1.7	9.0
Reg. ABA Totals	25	–	840	142	314	.452	0	1	.000	52	90	.578	–	–	334	53	59	0	–	77	–	336	13.4	2.1	13.4

Hardnett, Charles **(Charlie)** b. September 13, 1938 Ht. 6-8 Wt. 230 College: Grambling State

SEASON–TEAM	G	GS	MIN	FGM	FGA	PCT	3FGM	3FGA	PCT	FTM	FTA	PCT	O-RB	D-RB	TOT	AST	PF	DQ	STL	TO	BLK	PTS	RPG	APG	PPG
62-63–Chicago	78	–	1657	301	683	.441	–	–	–	225	349	.645	–	–	602	74	225	4	–	–	–	827	7.7	0.9	10.6
63-64–Baltimore	66	–	617	107	260	.412	–	–	–	84	125	.672	–	–	251	27	114	1	–	–	–	298	3.8	0.4	4.5
64-65–Baltimore	20	–	200	25	80	.313	–	–	–	23	39	.590	–	–	77	2	37	0	–	–	–	73	3.9	0.1	3.7
Reg. Season Totals	164	–	2474	433	1023	.423	–	–	–	332	513	.647	–	–	930	103	376	5	–	–	–	1198	5.7	0.6	7.3
Playoff Totals	5	–	22	4	10	.400	–	–	–	2	5	.400	–	–	6	2	2	0	–	–	–	10	1.2	0.4	2.0

Hardy, Alan Timothy b. May 25, 1957 Ht. 6-7 Wt. 195 College: Michigan

SEASON–TEAM	G	GS	MIN	FGM	FGA	PCT	3FGM	3FGA	PCT	FTM	FTA	PCT	O-RB	D-RB	TOT	AST	PF	DQ	STL	TO	BLK	PTS	RPG	APG	PPG
80-81–Los Angeles	22	–	111	22	59	.373	0	0	–	7	10	.700	8	11	19	3	13	0	1	11	9	51	0.9	0.1	2.3
81-82–Detroit	38	0	310	62	136	.456	0	5	.000	18	29	.621	14	20	34	20	32	0	9	20	4	142	0.9	0.5	3.7
Reg. Season Totals	60	0	421	84	195	.431	0	5	.000	25	39	.641	22	31	53	23	45	0	10	31	13	193	0.9	0.4	3.2

Hardy, Darrell Gene b. 1944 Ht. 6-7 Wt. 220 College: Baylor

SEASON–TEAM	G	GS	MIN	FGM	FGA	PCT	3FGM	3FGA	PCT	FTM	FTA	PCT	O-RB	D-RB	TOT	AST	PF	DQ	STL	TO	BLK	PTS	RPG	APG	PPG
67-68–Houston (A)	17	–	172	32	74	.432	0	1	.000	25	35	.714	–	–	56	8	23	0	–	12	–	89	3.3	0.5	5.2
Reg. ABA Totals	17	–	172	32	74	.432	0	1	.000	25	35	.714	–	–	56	8	23	0	–	12	–	89	3.3	0.5	5.2

Hardy, James Percival b. December 1, 1956 Ht. 6-8 Wt. 220 College: San Francisco

SEASON–TEAM	G	GS	MIN	FGM	FGA	PCT	3FGM	3FGA	PCT	FTM	FTA	PCT	O-RB	D-RB	TOT	AST	PF	DQ	STL	TO	BLK	PTS	RPG	APG	PPG
78-79–New Orleans	68	–	1456	196	426	.460	–	–	–	61	88	.693	121	189	310	65	133	1	52	93	61	453	4.6	1.0	6.7
79-80–Utah	76	–	1600	184	363	.507	1	2	.500	51	66	.773	124	275	399	104	207	4	47	105	87	420	5.3	1.4	5.5
80-81–Utah	23	–	509	52	111	.468	0	0	–	11	20	.550	39	94	133	36	58	2	21	23	20	115	5.8	1.6	5.0
81-82–Utah	82	17	1814	179	369	.485	0	1	.000	64	93	.688	153	317	470	110	192	2	58	78	67	422	5.7	1.3	5.1
Reg. Season Totals	249	17	5379	611	1269	.481	1	3	.333	187	267	.700	437	875	1312	315	590	9	178	299	235	1410	5.3	1.3	5.7

Harge, Ira Lee b. March 14, 1941 Ht. 6-9 Wt. 225 College: Burlington Co. (N.J.) Coll. (J.C.); Bowling Green State; New Mexico

SEASON–TEAM	G	GS	MIN	FGM	FGA	PCT	3FGM	3FGA	PCT	FTM	FTA	PCT	O-RB	D-RB	TOT	AST	PF	DQ	STL	TO	BLK	PTS	RPG	APG	PPG
67-68–Pitt.-Oakland (A)	82	–	2699	311	781	.398	0	0	–	202	298	.678	357	681	1038	99	294	7	–	182	–	824	12.7	1.2	10.0
68-69–Oakland (A)	78	–	2095	269	578	.465	0	0	–	123	200	.615	269	547	816	96	245	1	–	222	–	661	10.5	1.2	8.5
69-70–Washington (A)	84	–	2991	415	886	.468	0	0	–	196	289	.678	334	843	1177	200	328	8	–	–	–	1026	14.0	2.4	12.2
70-71–Car.-Fla. (A)	82	–	2934	460	999	.460	2	5	.400	197	306	.644	328	757	1085	202	291	–	–	–	–	1119	13.2	2.5	13.6
71-72–Fla.-Utah (A)	84	–	2264	314	679	.462	0	1	.000	104	150	.693	–	–	780	130	267	–	–	163	–	732	9.3	1.5	8.7
72-73–Utah-Car. (A)	17	–	177	14	40	.350	0	0	–	6	10	.600	15	44	59	9	43	0	–	17	–	34	3.5	0.5	2.0
Reg. ABA Totals	427	–	13160	1783	3963	.450	2	6	.333	828	1253	.661	1303	2872	4955	736	1468	16	–	584	–	4396	11.6	1.7	10.3
ABA Playoff Totals	39	–	1051	132	282	.468	0	3	.000	51	83	.614	112	273	425	61	90	1	–	8	–	315	10.9	1.6	8.1

Hargis, John Arlington **(Shotgun)** b. August 20, 1920 d. January 2, 1986 Ht. 6-2 Wt. 185 College: Texas

SEASON–TEAM	G	GS	MIN	FGM	FGA	PCT	3FGM	3FGA	PCT	FTM	FTA	PCT	O-RB	D-RB	TOT	AST	PF	DQ	STL	TO	BLK	PTS	RPG	APG	PPG
47-48–Anderson (N)	59	–	–	235	–	–	–	–	–	172	329	.523	–	–	–	–	149	–	–	–	–	642	–	–	10.9
48-49–Anderson (N)	57	–	–	169	–	–	–	–	–	106	173	.613	–	–	–	–	129	–	–	–	–	444	–	–	7.8
49-50–Anderson	60	–	–	223	550	.405	–	–	–	197	277	.711	–	–	–	102	170	–	–	–	–	643	–	1.7	10.7
50-51–FtWayne-Tri-Cit	14	–	–	25	66	.379	–	–	–	17	24	.708	–	–	30	9	26	0	–	–	–	67	2.1	0.6	4.8
Reg. NBA Totals	74	–	–	248	616	.403	–	–	–	214	301	.711	–	–	30	111	196	0	–	–	–	710	2.1	1.5	9.6
Reg. NBL Totals	116	–	–	404	–	–	–	–	–	278	502	.554	–	–	–	–	278	–	–	–	–	1086	–	–	9.4
NBA Playoff Totals	8	–	–	32	178	.360	–	–	–	35	47	.745	–	–	–	26	26	1	–	–	–	99	–	1.6	12.4
NBL Playoff Totals	13	–	–	52	–	–	–	–	–	53	81	.654	–	–	–	–	31	–	–	–	–	157	–	–	12.1

Harkness, Jerald B. **(Jerry)** b. May 7, 1940 Ht. 6-2 Wt. 180 College: Loyola (Chicago)

SEASON–TEAM	G	GS	MIN	FGM	FGA	PCT	3FGM	3FGA	PCT	FTM	FTA	PCT	O-RB	D-RB	TOT	AST	PF	DQ	STL	TO	BLK	PTS	RPG	APG	PPG
63-64–New York	5	–	59	13	30	.433	–	–	–	3	8	.375	–	–	6	6	4	0	–	–	–	29	1.2	1.2	5.8
67-68–Indiana (A)	71	–	1241	172	394	.437	1	5	.200	152	223	.682	–	–	193	129	109	1	–	77	–	497	2.7	1.8	7.0
68-69–Indiana (A)	10	–	272	31	67	.463	0	0	–	30	47	.638	–	–	34	21	27	0	–	20	–	92	3.4	2.1	9.2
Reg. NBA Totals	5	–	59	13	30	.433	–	–	–	3	8	.375	–	–	6	6	4	0	–	–	–	29	1.2	1.2	5.8
Reg. ABA Totals	81	–	1513	203	461	.440	1	5	.200	182	270	.674	–	–	227	150	136	1	–	97	–	589	2.8	1.9	7.3
ABA Playoff Totals	3	–	32	4	12	.333	0	0	–	2	2	1.000	–	–	5	5	6	0	–	3	–	10	1.7	1.7	3.3

Harlicka, Jules Peter (Skip) b. October 14, 1946 Ht. 6-1 Wt. 185 College: South Carolina

SEASON–TEAM	G	GS	MIN	FGM	FGA	PCT	3FGM	3FGA	PCT	FTM	FTA	PCT	O-RB	D-RB	TOT	AST	PF	DQ	STL	TO	BLK	PTS	RPG	APG	PPG
68-69–Atlanta	26	–	218	41	90	.456	–	–	–	24	31	.774	–	–	16	37	29	0	–	–	–	106	0.6	1.4	4.1
Reg. Season Totals	26	–	218	41	90	.456	–	–	–	24	31	.774	–	–	16	37	29	0	–	–	–	106	0.6	1.4	4.1
Playoff Totals	1	–	1	0	0	–	–	–	–	0	0	–	–	–	0	–	1	0	–	–	–	0	0.0	0.0	0.0

Harmon, Jerome b. February 6, 1969 Ht. 6-4 Wt. 190 College: Louisville

SEASON–TEAM	G	GS	MIN	FGM	FGA	PCT	3FGM	3FGA	PCT	FTM	FTA	PCT	O-RB	D-RB	TOT	AST	PF	DQ	STL	TO	BLK	PTS	RPG	APG	PPG
94-95–Philadelphia	10	0	158	21	53	.396	1	1	1.000	3	6	.500	9	14	23	12	12	0	9	7	0	46	2.3	1.2	4.6
Reg. Season Totals	10	0	158	21	53	.396	1	1	1.000	3	6	.500	9	14	23	12	12	0	9	7	0	46	2.3	1.2	4.6

Harper, Derek Ricardo b. October 13, 1961 Ht. 6-4 Wt. 206 College: Illinois

SEASON–TEAM	G	GS	MIN	FGM	FGA	PCT	3FGM	3FGA	PCT	FTM	FTA	PCT	O-RB	D-RB	TOT	AST	PF	DQ	STL	TO	BLK	PTS	RPG	APG	PPG
83-84–Dallas	82	1	1712	200	451	.443	3	26	.115	66	98	.673	53	119	172	239	143	0	95	111	21	469	2.1	2.9	5.7
84-85–Dallas	82	1	2218	329	633	.520	21	61	.344	111	154	.721	47	152	199	360	194	1	144	123	37	790	2.4	4.4	9.6
85-86–Dallas	79	39	2150	390	730	.534	12	51	.235	171	229	.747	75	151	226	416	166	1	153	144	23	963	2.9	5.3	12.2
86-87–Dallas	77	76	2556	497	993	.501	76	212	.358	160	234	.684	51	148	199	609	195	0	167	138	25	1230	2.6	7.9	16.0
87-88–Dallas	82	82	3032	536	1167	.459	60	192	.313	261	344	.759	71	175	246	634	164	0	168	190	35	1393	3.0	7.7	17.0
88-89–Dallas	81	81	2968	538	1127	.477	99	278	.356	229	284	.806	46	182	228	570	219	3	172	205	41	1404	2.8	7.0	17.3
89-90–Dallas	82	82	3007	567	1161	.488	89	240	.371	250	315	.794	54	190	244	609	224	1	187	207	26	1473	3.0	7.4	18.0
90-91–Dallas	77	77	2879	572	1226	.467	89	246	.362	286	391	.731	59	174	233	548	222	1	147	177	14	1519	3.0	7.1	19.7
91-92–Dallas	65	64	2252	448	1011	.443	58	186	.312	198	261	.759	49	121	170	373	150	0	101	154	17	1152	2.6	5.7	17.7
92-93–Dallas	62	60	2108	393	939	.419	101	257	.393	239	316	.756	42	81	123	334	145	1	80	136	16	1126	2.0	5.4	18.2
93-94–Dallas-N.Y.	82	55	2204	303	744	.407	73	203	.360	112	163	.687	20	121	141	334	163	0	125	135	8	791	1.7	4.1	9.6
94-95–New York	80	80	2716	337	756	.446	106	292	.363	139	192	.724	31	163	194	458	219	0	79	151	10	919	2.4	5.7	11.5
95-96–New York	82	82	2893	436	939	.464	121	325	.372	156	206	.757	32	170	202	352	201	0	131	178	5	1149	2.5	4.3	14.0
96-97–Dallas	75	29	2210	299	674	.444	60	176	.341	95	128	.742	30	107	137	321	144	0	92	132	12	753	1.8	4.3	10.0
97-98–Orlando	66	45	1761	226	542	.417	59	164	.360	55	79	.696	23	80	103	233	140	0	72	101	10	566	1.6	3.5	8.6
98-99–L.A. Lakers	45	29	1120	120	291	.412	43	117	.368	26	32	.813	13	54	67	187	66	0	44	52	4	309	1.5	4.2	6.9
Reg. Season Totals	1199	883	37786	6191	13384	.463	1070	3026	.354	2554	3426	.745	696	2188	2884	6577	2755	8	1957	2334	304	16006	2.4	5.5	13.3
Playoff Totals	97	75	3094	415	925	.449	96	263	.365	168	236	.712	56	177	233	513	237	1	148	167	11	1094	2.4	5.3	11.3

Harper, Michael Edward (Mike) b. December 9, 1957 Ht. 6-10 Wt. 200 College: North Park

SEASON–TEAM	G	GS	MIN	FGM	FGA	PCT	3FGM	3FGA	PCT	FTM	FTA	PCT	O-RB	D-RB	TOT	AST	PF	DQ	STL	TO	BLK	PTS	RPG	APG	PPG
80-81–Portland	55	–	461	56	136	.412	0	3	.000	37	85	.435	28	65	93	17	73	0	23	32	20	149	1.7	0.3	2.7
81-82–Portland	68	38	1433	184	370	.497	0	1	.000	96	153	.627	127	212	339	54	229	7	55	92	82	464	5.0	0.8	6.8
Reg. Season Totals	123	38	1894	240	506	.474	0	4	.000	133	238	.559	155	277	432	71	302	7	78	124	102	613	3.5	0.6	5.0
Playoff Totals	1	0	6	1	1	1.000	0	0	–	1	1	1.000	0	1	1	–	0	0	0	0	0	3	1.0	0.0	3.0

Harper, Ronald (Ron, Hollywood) b. January 20, 1964 Ht. 6-6 Wt. 215 College: Miami (Ohio)

SEASON–TEAM	G	GS	MIN	FGM	FGA	PCT	3FGM	3FGA	PCT	FTM	FTA	PCT	O-RB	D-RB	TOT	AST	PF	DQ	STL	TO	BLK	PTS	RPG	APG	PPG
86-87–Cleveland	82	82	3064	734	1614	.455	20	94	.213	386	564	.684	169	223	392	394	247	3	209	345	84	1874	4.8	4.8	22.9
87-88–Cleveland	57	52	1830	340	732	.464	3	20	.150	196	278	.705	64	159	223	281	157	3	122	158	52	879	3.9	4.9	15.4
88-89–Cleveland	82	82	2851	587	1149	.511	29	116	.250	323	430	.751	122	287	409	434	224	1	185	230	74	1526	5.0	5.3	18.6
89-90–Clev.-LAClips	35	35	1367	301	637	.473	14	51	.275	182	231	.788	74	132	206	182	105	1	81	100	41	798	5.9	5.2	22.8
90-91–L.A. Clippers	39	34	1383	285	729	.391	48	148	.324	145	217	.668	58	130	188	209	111	0	66	129	35	763	4.8	5.4	19.6
91-92–L.A. Clippers	82	82	3144	569	1292	.440	64	211	.303	293	398	.736	120	327	447	417	199	0	152	252	72	1495	5.5	5.1	18.2
92-93–L.A. Clippers	80	77	2970	542	1203	.451	52	186	.280	307	399	.769	117	308	425	360	212	1	177	222	73	1443	5.3	4.5	18.0
93-94–L.A. Clippers	75	75	2856	569	1335	.426	71	236	.301	299	418	.715	129	331	460	344	167	0	144	242	54	1508	6.1	4.6	20.1
94-95–Chicago	77	53	1536	209	491	.426	31	110	.282	81	131	.618	51	129	180	157	132	1	97	100	27	530	2.3	2.0	6.9
95-96–Chicago	80	80	1886	234	501	.467	28	104	.269	98	139	.705	74	139	213	208	137	0	105	73	32	594	2.7	2.6	7.4
96-97–Chicago	76	74	1740	177	406	.436	68	188	.362	58	82	.707	46	147	193	191	138	0	86	50	38	480	2.5	2.5	6.3
97-98–Chicago	82	82	2284	293	665	.441	16	84	.190	162	216	.750	107	183	290	241	181	0	108	91	48	764	3.5	2.9	9.3
98-99–Chicago	35	35	1107	147	390	.377	27	85	.318	71	101	.703	49	131	180	115	80	0	60	65	35	392	5.1	3.3	11.2
99-00–L.A. Lakers	80	78	2042	212	531	.399	33	106	.311	100	147	.680	96	241	337	270	164	0	85	132	39	557	4.2	3.4	7.0
Reg. Season Totals	962	921	30060	5199	11675	.445	504	1739	.290	2701	3751	.720	1276	2867	4143	3803	2254	10	1677	2189	704	13603	4.3	4.0	14.1
Playoff Totals	106	98	2958	392	873	.449	56	191	.293	160	229	.699	125	284	409	301	241	2	137	120	75	1000	3.9	2.8	9.4

Harpring, Matthew Joseph (Matt) b. May 31, 1976 Ht. 6-7 Wt. 231 College: Georgia Tech

SEASON–TEAM	G	GS	MIN	FGM	FGA	PCT	3FGM	3FGA	PCT	FTM	FTA	PCT	O-RB	D-RB	TOT	AST	PF	DQ	STL	TO	BLK	PTS	RPG	APG	PPG
98-99–Orlando	50	22	1114	148	320	.463	10	25	.400	102	143	.713	88	126	214	45	112	0	30	73	6	408	4.3	0.9	8.2
99-00–Orlando	4	0	63	4	17	.235	2	2	1.000	6	7	.857	5	7	12	8	7	0	5	1	1	16	3.0	2.0	4.0
Reg. Season Totals	54	22	1177	152	337	.451	12	27	.444	108	150	.720	93	133	226	53	119	0	35	74	7	424	4.2	1.0	7.9
Playoff Totals	4	0	82	12	26	.462	1	5	.200	8	11	.727	7	13	20	7	9	0	1	5	0	33	5.0	1.8	8.3

Harrington, Albert (Al) b. February 17, 1980 Ht. 6-9 Wt. 254 High School: St. Patrick's HS (Elizabeth, N.J.)

SEASON–TEAM	G	GS	MIN	FGM	FGA	PCT	3FGM	3FGA	PCT	FTM	FTA	PCT	O-RB	D-RB	TOT	AST	PF	DQ	STL	TO	BLK	PTS	RPG	APG	PPG
98-99–Indiana	21	0	160	18	56	.321	0	5	.000	9	15	.600	20	19	39	5	26	0	4	11	2	45	1.9	0.2	2.1
99-00–Indiana	50	0	854	121	264	.458	8	34	.235	78	111	.703	47	112	159	38	130	0	25	65	9	328	3.2	0.8	6.6
Reg. Season Totals	71	0	1014	139	320	.434	8	39	.205	87	126	.690	67	131	198	43	156	0	29	76	11	373	2.8	0.6	5.3

Harrington, Othella b. January 31, 1974 Ht. 6-9 Wt. 235 College: Georgetown

SEASON–TEAM	G	GS	MIN	FGM	FGA	PCT	3FGM	3FGA	PCT	FTM	FTA	PCT	O-RB	D-RB	TOT	AST	PF	DQ	STL	TO	BLK	PTS	RPG	APG	PPG
96-97–Houston	57	1	860	112	204	.549	0	3	.000	49	81	.605	75	123	198	18	112	2	12	57	22	273	3.5	0.3	4.8
97-98–Houston	58	3	903	129	266	.485	0	1	.000	92	122	.754	73	134	207	24	112	1	10	47	27	350	3.6	0.4	6.0
98-99–Houston	41	10	903	156	304	.513	0	0	–	88	122	.721	72	174	246	15	103	0	6	61	25	400	6.0	0.4	9.8
99-00–Vancouver	82	82	2677	420	830	.506	0	2	.000	236	298	.792	196	367	563	97	287	3	36	217	58	1076	6.9	1.2	13.1
Reg. Season Totals	238	96	5343	817	1604	.509	0	6	.000	465	623	.746	416	798	1214	154	614	6	64	382	132	2099	5.1	0.6	8.8
Playoff Totals	14	0	80	16	28	.571	0	1	.000	15	21	.714	9	16	25	1	4	0	0	5	2	47	1.8	0.1	3.4

Harris, Arthur Carlos Jr. (Art) b. January 13, 1947 Ht. 6-4 Wt. 185 College: Stanford

SEASON–TEAM	G	GS	MIN	FGM	FGA	PCT	3FGM	3FGA	PCT	FTM	FTA	PCT	O-RB	D-RB	TOT	AST	PF	DQ	STL	TO	BLK	PTS	RPG	APG	PPG
68-69–Seattle	80	–	2556	416	1054	.395	–	–	–	161	251	.641	–	–	301	258	326	14	–	–	–	993	3.8	3.2	12.4
69-70–Seattle-Phoenix	81	–	1553	285	723	.394	–	–	–	86	134	.642	–	–	161	231	220	0	–	–	–	656	2.0	2.9	8.1
70-71–Phoenix	56	–	952	199	484	.411	–	–	–	69	113	.611	–	–	100	132	137	0	–	–	–	467	1.8	2.4	8.3
71-72–Phoenix	21	–	145	23	70	.329	–	–	–	9	21	.429	–	–	13	18	26	0	–	–	–	55	0.6	0.9	2.6
Reg. Season Totals	238	–	5206	923	2331	.396	–	–	–	325	519	.626	–	–	575	639	709	14	–	–	–	2171	2.4	2.7	9.1
Playoff Totals	7	–	89	15	42	.357	–	–	–	0	2	.000	–	–	13	12	13	0	–	–	–	30	1.9	1.7	4.3

Harris, Billy b. November 12, 1951 Ht. 6-2 Wt. 190 College: Northern Illinois

SEASON–TEAM	G	GS	MIN	FGM	FGA	PCT	3FGM	3FGA	PCT	FTM	FTA	PCT	O-RB	D-RB	TOT	AST	PF	DQ	STL	TO	BLK	PTS	RPG	APG	PPG
74-75–San Diego (A)	76	–	1221	264	664	.398	16	73	.219	65	96	.677	58	64	122	111	166	–	55	79	6	609	1.6	1.5	8.0
Reg. ABA Totals	76	–	1221	264	664	.398	16	73	.219	65	96	.677	58	64	122	111	166	–	55	79	6	609	1.6	1.5	8.0

Harris, C. Bernard (Bernie) b. November 26, 1950 Ht. 6-10 Wt. 200 College: Virginia Commonwealth

SEASON–TEAM	G	GS	MIN	FGM	FGA	PCT	3FGM	3FGA	PCT	FTM	FTA	PCT	O-RB	D-RB	TOT	AST	PF	DQ	STL	TO	BLK	PTS	RPG	APG	PPG
74-75–Buffalo	11	–	25	2	11	.182	–	–	–	1	2	.500	2	6	8	1	0	0	0	–	1	5	0.7	0.1	0.5
Reg. Season Totals	11	–	25	2	11	.182	–	–	–	1	2	.500	2	6	8	1	0	0	0	–	1	5	0.7	0.1	0.5

Harris, Christopher R. (Chris) b. August 11, 1933 Ht. 6-3 Wt. 190 College: Dayton

SEASON–TEAM	G	GS	MIN	FGM	FGA	PCT	3FGM	3FGA	PCT	FTM	FTA	PCT	O-RB	D-RB	TOT	AST	PF	DQ	STL	TO	BLK	PTS	RPG	APG	PPG
55-56–St. Louis-Roch.	41	–	420	37	149	.248	–	–	–	27	45	.600	–	–	44	44	43	0	–	–	–	101	1.1	1.1	2.5
Reg. Season Totals	41	–	420	37	149	.248	–	–	–	27	45	.600	–	–	44	44	43	0	–	–	–	101	1.1	1.1	2.5

Harris, Lucious H. Jr. b. December 18, 1970 Ht. 6-5 Wt. 205 College: Long Beach State

SEASON–TEAM	G	GS	MIN	FGM	FGA	PCT	3FGM	3FGA	PCT	FTM	FTA	PCT	O-RB	D-RB	TOT	AST	PF	DQ	STL	TO	BLK	PTS	RPG	APG	PPG
93-94–Dallas	77	0	1165	162	385	.421	7	33	.212	87	119	.731	45	112	157	106	117	0	49	78	10	418	2.0	1.4	5.4
94-95–Dallas	79	31	1695	280	610	.459	55	142	.387	136	170	.800	85	135	220	132	105	0	58	77	14	751	2.8	1.7	9.5
95-96–Dallas	61	1	1016	183	397	.461	47	125	.376	68	87	.782	41	81	122	79	56	0	35	46	3	481	2.0	1.3	7.9
96-97–Philadelphia	54	3	813	112	294	.381	36	99	.364	33	47	.702	27	44	71	50	45	0	41	34	3	293	1.3	0.9	5.4
97-98–New Jersey	50	0	671	69	177	.390	12	39	.308	41	55	.745	21	31	52	42	77	0	42	21	5	191	1.0	0.8	3.8
98-99–New Jersey	36	5	602	73	181	.403	11	50	.220	36	48	.750	21	46	67	31	52	1	18	18	7	193	1.9	0.9	5.4
99-00–New Jersey	77	11	1510	198	463	.428	38	115	.330	79	99	.798	53	134	187	100	98	0	65	42	6	513	2.4	1.3	6.7
Reg. Season Totals	434	51	7472	1077	2507	.430	206	603	.342	480	625	.768	293	583	876	540	550	1	308	316	48	2840	2.0	1.2	6.5
Playoff Totals	3	0	52	2	6	.333	0	2	.000	5	6	.833	1	7	8	1	11	0	2	2	0	9	2.7	0.3	3.0

Harris, Robert Azzel (Bob) b. March 16, 1927 Ht. 6-7 Wt. 195 College: Murray State (Okla.) Coll. (J.C.); Oklahoma State

SEASON–TEAM	G	GS	MIN	FGM	FGA	PCT	3FGM	3FGA	PCT	FTM	FTA	PCT	O-RB	D-RB	TOT	AST	PF	DQ	STL	TO	BLK	PTS	RPG	APG	PPG
49-50–Fort Wayne	62	–	–	168	465	.361	–	–	–	140	223	.628	–	–	–	129	190	–	–	–	–	476	–	2.1	7.7
50-51–FtWayne-Bos.	56	–	–	98	295	.332	–	–	–	86	127	.677	–	–	291	64	157	4	–	–	–	282	5.2	1.1	5.0
51-52–Boston	66	–	1899	190	463	.410	–	–	–	134	209	.641	–	–	531	120	194	5	–	–	–	514	8.0	1.8	7.8
52-53–Boston	70	–	1971	192	459	.418	–	–	–	133	226	.588	–	–	485	95	238	6	–	–	–	517	6.9	1.4	7.4
53-54–Boston	71	–	1898	156	409	.381	–	–	–	108	172	.628	–	–	517	94	224	8	–	–	–	420	7.3	1.3	5.9
Reg. Season Totals	325	–	5768	804	2091	.385	–	–	–	601	957	.628	–	–	1824	502	1003	23	–	–	–	2209	6.9	1.5	6.8
Playoff Totals	21	–	430	51	155	.387	–	–	–	56	79	.709	–	–	149	43	88	5	–	–	–	158	6.8	1.7	7.5

Harris, Steven Dwayne (Steve) b. October 15, 1963 Ht. 6-5 Wt. 195 College: Tulsa

SEASON–TEAM	G	GS	MIN	FGM	FGA	PCT	3FGM	3FGA	PCT	FTM	FTA	PCT	O-RB	D-RB	TOT	AST	PF	DQ	STL	TO	BLK	PTS	RPG	APG	PPG
85-86–Houston	57	0	482	103	233	.442	1	5	.200	50	54	.926	25	32	57	50	55	0	21	34	4	257	1.0	0.9	4.5
86-87–Houston	74	3	1174	251	599	.419	0	8	.000	111	130	.854	71	99	170	100	111	1	37	74	16	613	2.3	1.4	8.3
87-88–Houston-G.S.	58	26	1084	223	487	.458	0	7	.000	89	113	.788	53	73	126	87	89	0	50	56	8	535	2.2	1.5	9.2
88-89–Detroit	3	0	7	1	4	.250	0	0	–	2	2	1.000	0	2	2	0	1	0	1	0	0	4	0.7	0.0	1.3
89-90–L.A. Clippers	15	0	93	14	40	.350	0	0	–	3	4	.750	5	5	10	1	9	0	7	5	1	31	0.7	0.1	2.1
Reg. Season Totals	207	29	2840	592	1363	.434	1	20	.050	255	303	.842	154	211	365	238	265	1	116	169	29	1440	1.8	1.1	7.0
Playoff Totals	24	0	174	30	72	.417	0	1	.000	7	11	.636	8	9	17	7	18	0	7	5	3	67	0.7	0.3	2.8

Harris, Tony Dwayne b. May 13, 1967 Ht. 6-3 Wt. 190 College: Johnson Co. (Kan.) C.C.; Delgado (L.A.) C.C.; Southwest Mississippi C.C.; New Orleans

SEASON–TEAM	G	GS	MIN	FGM	FGA	PCT	3FGM	3FGA	PCT	FTM	FTA	PCT	O-RB	D-RB	TOT	AST	PF	DQ	STL	TO	BLK	PTS	RPG	APG	PPG
90-91–Philadelphia	6	0	41	4	16	.250	0	2	.000	2	4	.500	0	1	1	0	5	0	1	3	0	10	0.2	0.0	1.7
93-94–Boston	5	0	88	9	31	.290	3	9	.333	23	25	.920	3	7	10	8	8	0	4	6	0	44	2.0	1.6	8.8
94-95–Boston	3	0	18	3	8	.375	0	1	.000	8	9	.889	0	0	0	0	2	0	0	1	0	14	0.0	0.0	4.7
Reg. Season Totals	14	0	147	16	55	.291	3	12	.250	33	38	.868	3	8	11	8	15	0	5	10	0	68	0.8	0.6	4.9

Harrison, Robert William (Bob, Tiger) b. August 12, 1927 Ht. 6-1 Wt. 190 College: Michigan

SEASON–TEAM	G	GS	MIN	FGM	FGA	PCT	3FGM	3FGA	PCT	FTM	FTA	PCT	O-RB	D-RB	TOT	AST	PF	DQ	STL	TO	BLK	PTS	RPG	APG	PPG
49-50–Minneapolis	66	–	–	125	348	.359	–	–	–	50	74	.676	–	–	–	131	175	–	–	–	–	300	–	2.0	4.5
50-51–Minneapolis	68	–	–	150	432	.347	–	–	–	101	128	.789	–	–	172	195	218	5	–	–	–	401	2.5	2.9	5.9
51-52–Minneapolis	65	–	1712	156	487	.320	–	–	–	89	124	.718	–	–	160	188	203	9	–	–	–	401	2.5	2.9	6.2
52-53–Minneapolis	70	–	1643	195	518	.376	–	–	–	107	165	.648	–	–	153	160	264	16	–	–	–	497	2.2	2.3	7.1
53-54–Minn.-Milw.	64	–	1443	144	449	.321	–	–	–	94	158	.595	–	–	130	139	218	9	–	–	–	382	2.0	2.2	6.0
54-55–Milwaukee	72	–	2300	299	875	.342	–	–	–	126	185	.681	–	–	226	252	291	14	–	–	–	724	3.1	3.5	10.1
55-56–St. Louis	72	–	2219	260	725	.359	–	–	–	97	146	.664	–	–	195	277	246	6	–	–	–	617	2.7	3.8	8.6
56-57–St. Louis-Syr.	66	–	1810	243	629	.386	–	–	–	93	130	.715	–	–	156	161	220	5	–	–	–	579	2.4	2.4	8.8
57-58–Syracuse	72	–	1799	210	604	.348	–	–	–	97	122	.795	–	–	166	169	200	1	–	–	–	517	2.3	2.3	7.2
Reg. Season Totals	615	–	12926	1782	5067	.352	–	–	–	854	1232	.693	–	–	1358	1672	2035	65	–	–	–	4418	2.5	2.7	7.2
Playoff Totals	59	–	1007	138	401	.384	–	–	–	62	90	.689	–	–	121	137	188	10	–	–	–	338	2.3	1.8	5.7
All-Star Totals	1	–	25	2	7	.286	–	–	–	1	2	.500	–	–	0	1	4	0	–	–	–	5	0.0	1.0	5.0

Harvey, Antonio b. July 9, 1970 Ht. 6-11 Wt. 250 College: Southern Illinois; Georgia; Pfeiffer

SEASON–TEAM	G	GS	MIN	FGM	FGA	PCT	3FGM	3FGA	PCT	FTM	FTA	PCT	O-RB	D-RB	TOT	AST	PF	DQ	STL	TO	BLK	PTS	RPG	APG	PPG
93-94–L.A. Lakers	27	6	247	29	79	.367	0	0	–	12	26	.462	26	33	59	5	39	0	8	17	19	70	2.2	0.2	2.6
94-95–L.A. Lakers	59	8	572	77	176	.438	1	1	1.000	24	45	.533	39	63	102	23	87	0	15	25	41	179	1.7	0.4	3.0
95-96–Vanc.-LAClips	55	15	821	83	224	.371	0	2	.000	38	83	.458	69	131	200	15	76	0	27	44	47	204	3.6	0.3	3.7
96-97–Seattle	6	0	26	5	11	.455	0	0	–	5	6	.833	2	8	10	1	8	0	0	1	4	15	1.7	0.2	2.5
99-00–Portland	19	0	137	17	30	.567	0	0	–	7	12	.583	8	25	33	5	20	0	1	12	6	41	1.7	0.3	2.2
Reg. Season Totals	166	29	1803	211	520	.406	1	3	.333	86	172	.500	144	260	404	49	230	0	51	99	117	509	2.4	0.3	3.1
Playoff Totals	3	0	4	0	0	–	0	0	–	0	0	–	0	1	1	–	0	0	0	0	0	0	0.3	0.0	0.0

Haskin, Scott Russell b. September 19, 1970 Ht. 6-11 Wt. 250 College: Oregon State

SEASON–TEAM	G	GS	MIN	FGM	FGA	PCT	3FGM	3FGA	PCT	FTM	FTA	PCT	O-RB	D-RB	TOT	AST	PF	DQ	STL	TO	BLK	PTS	RPG	APG	PPG
93-94–Indiana	27	2	186	21	45	.467	0	0	–	13	19	.684	17	38	55	6	33	0	2	13	15	55	2.0	0.2	2.0
Reg. Season Totals	27	2	186	21	45	.467	0	0	–	13	19	.684	17	38	55	6	33	0	2	13	15	55	2.0	0.2	2.0

Haskins, Clem Smith (The Gem) b. July 11, 1943 Ht. 6-3 Wt. 195 College: Western Kentucky

SEASON–TEAM	G	GS	MIN	FGM	FGA	PCT	3FGM	3FGA	PCT	FTM	FTA	PCT	O-RB	D-RB	TOT	AST	PF	DQ	STL	TO	BLK	PTS	RPG	APG	PPG
67-68–Chicago	76	–	1477	273	650	.420	–	–	–	133	202	.658	–	–	227	165	175	1	–	–	–	679	3.0	2.2	8.9
68-69–Chicago	79	–	2874	537	1275	.421	–	–	–	282	361	.781	–	–	359	306	230	0	–	–	–	1356	4.5	3.9	17.2
69-70–Chicago	82	–	3214	668	1486	.450	–	–	–	332	424	.783	–	–	378	624	237	0	–	–	–	1668	4.6	7.6	20.3
70-71–Phoenix	82	–	2764	562	1277	.440	–	–	–	338	431	.784	–	–	324	383	207	2	–	–	–	1462	4.0	4.7	17.8
71-72–Phoenix	79	–	2453	509	1054	.483	–	–	–	220	258	.853	–	–	270	290	194	1	–	–	–	1238	3.4	3.7	15.7
72-73–Phoenix	77	–	1581	339	731	.464	–	–	–	130	156	.833	–	–	173	203	143	2	–	–	–	808	2.2	2.6	10.5
73-74–Phoenix	81	–	1822	364	792	.460	–	–	–	171	203	.842	78	144	222	259	166	1	81	–	16	899	2.7	3.2	11.1
74-75–Washington	70	–	702	115	290	.397	–	–	–	53	63	.841	29	51	80	79	73	0	23	–	6	283	1.1	1.1	4.0
75-76–Washington	55	–	737	148	269	.550	–	–	–	54	65	.831	12	42	54	73	79	2	23	–	8	350	1.0	1.3	6.4
Reg. Season Totals	681	–	17624	3515	7824	.449	–	–	–	1713	2163	.792	119	237	2087	2382	1504	9	127	–	30	8743	3.1	3.5	12.8
Playoff Totals	28	–	322	68	145	.469	–	–	–	28	38	.737	6	6	37	38	41	0	2	–	1	164	1.3	1.4	5.9

Hassett, Joseph Patrick Jr. **(Joey)** b. September 11, 1955 Ht. 6-5 Wt. 180 College: Providence

SEASON–TEAM	G	GS	MIN	FGM	FGA	PCT	3FGM	3FGA	PCT	FTM	FTA	PCT	O-RB	D-RB	TOT	AST	PF	DQ	STL	TO	BLK	PTS	RPG	APG	PPG
77-78–Seattle	48	–	404	91	205	.444	–	–	–	10	12	.833	14	22	36	41	45	0	21	34	0	192	0.8	0.9	4.0
78-79–Seattle	55	–	463	100	211	.474	–	–	–	23	23	1.000	13	32	45	42	58	0	14	32	4	223	0.8	0.8	4.1
79-80–Indiana	74	–	1135	215	509	.422	69	198	.348	24	29	.828	35	59	94	104	85	0	46	45	8	523	1.3	1.4	7.1
80-81–Dallas-G.S.	41	–	714	143	340	.421	53	156	.340	17	21	.810	24	44	68	74	65	0	13	22	2	356	1.7	1.8	8.7
81-82–Golden State	68	2	787	144	382	.377	71	214	.332	31	37	.838	13	40	53	104	94	1	30	36	3	390	0.8	1.5	5.7
82-83–Golden State	6	2	139	19	44	.432	1	9	.111	0	0	–	3	8	11	21	14	0	2	9	0	39	1.8	3.5	6.5
Reg. Season Totals	292	4	3642	712	1691	.421	194	577	.336	105	122	.861	102	205	307	386	361	1	126	178	17	1723	1.1	1.3	5.9
Playoff Totals	16	0	37	10	20	.500	0	0	–	0	0	–	0	3	3	1	1	0	1	3	0	20	0.2	0.1	1.3

Hassett, William Joseph **(Billy)** b. October 21, 1921 d. November 15, 1992 Ht. 6-1 Wt. 180 College: Georgetown; Notre Dame

SEASON–TEAM	G	GS	MIN	FGM	FGA	PCT	3FGM	3FGA	PCT	FTM	FTA	PCT	O-RB	D-RB	TOT	AST	PF	DQ	STL	TO	BLK	PTS	RPG	APG	PPG
46-47–Tri-Cities (N)	27	–	–	73	–	–	–	–	–	66	101	.653	–	–	–	–	58	–	–	–	–	212	–	–	7.9
47-48–Tri-Cities (N)	56	–	–	199	–	–	–	–	–	203	269	.755	–	–	–	–	145	–	–	–	–	601	–	–	10.7
48-49–Tri-Cities (N)	64	–	–	125	–	–	–	–	–	106	156	.679	–	–	–	–	152	–	–	–	–	356	–	–	5.6
49-50–Tri-Cit-Minn.	60	–	–	84	302	.278	–	–	–	104	161	.646	–	–	–	137	136	–	–	–	–	272	–	2.3	4.5
50-51–Baltimore	31	–	–	45	160	.281	–	–	–	43	63	.683	–	–	35	47	72	1	–	–	–	133	1.1	1.5	4.3
Reg. NBA Totals	91	–	–	129	462	.279	–	–	–	147	224	.656	–	–	35	184	208	1	–	–	–	405	1.1	2.0	4.5
Reg. NBL Totals	147	–	–	397	–	–	–	–	–	375	526	.713	–	–	–	–	355	–	–	–	–	1169	–	–	8.0
NBA Playoff Totals	7	–	–	3	12	.250	–	–	–	3	10	.300	–	–	–	4	8	0	–	–	–	9	–	0.6	1.3
NBL Playoff Totals	11	–	–	29	–	–	–	–	–	34	47	.723	–	–	–	–	27	–	–	–	–	92	–	–	8.4

Hastings, Scott Alan b. June 3, 1960 Ht. 6-10 Wt. 235 College: Arkansas

SEASON–TEAM	G	GS	MIN	FGM	FGA	PCT	3FGM	3FGA	PCT	FTM	FTA	PCT	O-RB	D-RB	TOT	AST	PF	DQ	STL	TO	BLK	PTS	RPG	APG	PPG
82-83–N.Y.-Atlanta	31	0	140	13	38	.342	0	3	.000	11	20	.550	15	26	41	3	34	0	6	9	1	37	1.3	0.1	1.2
83-84–Atlanta	68	8	1135	111	237	.468	1	4	.250	82	104	.788	96	174	270	46	220	7	40	66	36	305	4.0	0.7	4.5
84-85–Atlanta	64	1	825	89	188	.473	0	0	–	63	81	.778	59	100	159	46	135	1	24	50	23	241	2.5	0.7	3.8
85-86–Atlanta	62	0	650	65	159	.409	3	4	.750	60	70	.857	44	80	124	26	118	2	14	40	8	193	2.0	0.4	3.1
86-87–Atlanta	40	0	256	23	68	.338	2	12	.167	23	29	.793	16	54	70	13	35	0	10	13	7	71	1.8	0.3	1.8
87-88–Atlanta	55	0	403	40	82	.488	5	12	.417	25	27	.926	27	70	97	16	67	1	8	14	10	110	1.8	0.3	2.0
88-89–Miami	75	6	1206	143	328	.436	9	28	.321	91	107	.850	72	159	231	59	203	5	32	68	42	386	3.1	0.8	5.1
89-90–Detroit	40	0	166	10	33	.303	3	12	.250	19	22	.864	7	25	32	8	31	0	3	7	3	42	0.8	0.2	1.1
90-91–Detroit	27	0	113	16	28	.571	3	4	.750	13	13	1.000	14	14	28	7	23	0	0	7	0	48	1.0	0.3	1.8
91-92–Denver	40	4	421	17	50	.340	0	9	.000	24	28	.857	30	68	98	26	56	0	10	22	15	58	2.5	0.7	1.5
92-93–Denver	76	0	670	57	112	.509	2	8	.250	40	55	.727	44	93	137	34	115	1	12	29	8	156	1.8	0.4	2.1
Reg. Season Totals	578	19	5985	584	1323	.441	28	96	.292	451	556	.811	424	863	1287	284	1037	17	159	325	153	1647	2.2	0.5	2.8
Playoff Totals	44	0	256	28	50	.560	3	12	.250	18	25	.720	15	32	47	9	51	1	8	13	3	77	1.1	0.2	1.8

Hatton, Walter Vernon **(Vern)** b. January 13, 1936 Ht. 6-3 Wt. 195 College: Kentucky

SEASON–TEAM	G	GS	MIN	FGM	FGA	PCT	3FGM	3FGA	PCT	FTM	FTA	PCT	O-RB	D-RB	TOT	AST	PF	DQ	STL	TO	BLK	PTS	RPG	APG	PPG
58-59–Cin.-Phil.	64	–	1109	149	418	.356	–	–	–	77	105	.733	–	–	178	70	111	0	–	–	–	375	2.8	1.1	5.9
59-60–Philadelphia	67	–	1049	127	356	.357	–	–	–	53	87	.609	–	–	159	82	61	0	–	–	–	307	2.4	1.2	4.6
60-61–Philadelphia	54	–	610	97	304	.319	–	–	–	46	56	.821	–	–	92	59	59	0	–	–	–	240	1.7	1.1	4.4
61-62–Chicago-St. L.	40	–	898	112	331	.338	–	–	–	98	125	.784	–	–	102	99	63	0	–	–	–	322	2.6	2.5	8.1
Reg. Season Totals	225	–	3666	485	1409	.344	–	–	–	274	373	.735	–	–	531	310	294	0	–	–	–	1244	2.4	1.4	5.5
Playoff Totals	6	–	17	4	13	.308	–	–	–	1	3	.333	–	–	3	1	3	0	–	–	–	9	0.5	0.2	1.5

Havlicek, John J. **(Hondo)** b. April 8, 1940 Ht. 6-5 Wt. 205 College: Ohio State HOF: 1983

SEASON–TEAM	G	GS	MIN	FGM	FGA	PCT	3FGM	3FGA	PCT	FTM	FTA	PCT	O-RB	D-RB	TOT	AST	PF	DQ	STL	TO	BLK	PTS	RPG	APG	PPG
62-63–Boston	80	–	2200	483	1085	.445	–	–	–	174	239	.728	–	–	534	179	189	2	–	–	–	1140	6.7	2.2	14.3
63-64–Boston	80	–	2587	640	1535	.417	–	–	–	315	422	.746	–	–	428	238	227	1	–	–	–	1595	5.4	3.0	19.9
64-65–Boston	75	–	2169	570	1420	.401	–	–	–	235	316	.744	–	–	371	199	200	2	–	–	–	1375	4.9	2.7	18.3
65-66–Boston	71	–	2175	530	1328	.399	–	–	–	274	349	.785	–	–	423	210	158	1	–	–	–	1334	6.0	3.0	18.8
66-67–Boston	81	–	2602	684	1540	.444	–	–	–	365	441	.828	–	–	532	278	210	0	–	–	–	1733	6.6	3.4	21.4
67-68–Boston	82	–	2921	666	1551	.429	–	–	–	368	453	.812	–	–	546	384	237	2	–	–	–	1700	6.7	4.7	20.7
68-69–Boston	82	–	3174	692	1709	.405	–	–	–	387	496	.780	–	–	570	441	247	0	–	–	–	1771	7.0	5.4	21.6
69-70–Boston	81	–	3369	736	1585	.464	–	–	–	488	578	.844	–	–	635	550	211	1	–	–	–	1960	7.8	6.8	24.2
70-71–Boston	81	–	3678	892	1982	.450	–	–	–	554	677	.818	–	–	730	607	200	0	–	–	–	2338	9.0	7.5	28.9
71-72–Boston	82	–	3698	897	1957	.458	–	–	–	458	549	.834	–	–	672	614	183	1	–	–	–	2252	8.2	7.5	27.5
72-73–Boston	80	–	3367	766	1704	.450	–	–	–	370	431	.858	–	–	567	529	195	1	–	–	–	1902	7.1	6.6	23.8
73-74–Boston	76	–	3091	685	1502	.456	–	–	–	346	416	.832	138	349	487	447	196	1	95	–	32	1716	6.4	5.9	22.6
74-75–Boston	82	–	3132	642	1411	.455	–	–	–	289	332	.870	154	330	484	432	231	2	110	–	16	1573	5.9	5.3	19.2
75-76–Boston	76	–	2598	504	1121	.450	–	–	–	281	333	.844	116	198	314	278	204	1	97	–	29	1289	4.1	3.7	17.0
76-77–Boston	79	–	2913	580	1283	.452	–	–	–	235	288	.816	109	273	382	400	208	4	84	–	18	1395	4.8	5.1	17.7
77-78–Boston	82	–	2797	546	1217	.449	–	–	–	230	269	.855	93	239	332	328	185	2	90	204	22	1322	4.0	4.0	16.1
Reg. Season Totals	1270	–	46471	10513	23930	.439	–	–	–	5369	6589	.815	610	1389	8007	6114	3281	21	476	204	117	26395	6.3	4.8	20.8
Playoff Totals	172	–	6860	1451	3329	.436	–	–	–	874	1046	.836	79	199	1186	825	527	9	60	–	16	3776	6.9	4.8	22.0
All-Star Totals	13	–	303	74	154	.481	–	–	–	31	41	.756	2	10	46	31	20	0	4	4	0	179	3.5	2.4	13.8

Hawes, Steven Sherburne (Steve) b. May 26, 1950 Ht. 6-9 Wt. 220 College: Washington

SEASON–TEAM	G	GS	MIN	FGM	FGA	PCT	3FGM	3FGA	PCT	FTM	FTA	PCT	O-RB	D-RB	TOT	AST	PF	DQ	STL	TO	BLK	PTS	RPG	APG	PPG
74-75–Houston	55	–	897	140	279	.502	–	–	–	45	55	.818	80	195	275	88	99	1	36	–	36	325	5.0	1.6	5.9
75-76–Houston-Port.	72	–	1411	199	403	.494	–	–	–	87	120	.725	171	326	497	115	169	5	44	–	25	485	6.9	1.6	6.7
76-77–Atlanta	44	–	945	147	305	.482	–	–	–	67	88	.761	78	183	261	63	141	4	36	–	24	361	5.9	1.4	8.2
77-78–Atlanta	75	–	2325	387	854	.453	–	–	–	175	214	.818	180	510	690	190	230	4	78	148	57	949	9.2	2.5	12.7
78-79–Atlanta	81	–	2205	372	756	.492	–	–	–	108	132	.818	190	401	591	184	264	1	79	145	47	852	7.3	2.3	10.5
79-80–Atlanta	82	–	1853	304	605	.502	3	8	.375	150	182	.824	148	348	496	144	205	4	74	121	29	761	6.0	1.8	9.3
80-81–Atlanta	74	–	2309	333	637	.523	1	4	.250	222	278	.799	165	396	561	168	289	13	73	161	32	889	7.6	2.3	12.0
81-82–Atlanta	49	42	1317	178	370	.481	4	10	.400	96	126	.762	89	231	320	142	156	4	36	87	34	456	6.5	2.9	9.3
82-83–Atlanta-Seattle	77	4	1416	163	390	.418	5	21	.238	69	94	.734	81	280	361	95	189	2	38	107	14	400	4.7	1.2	5.2
83-84–Seattle	79	0	1153	114	237	.481	1	4	.250	61	78	.782	50	170	220	99	144	2	24	52	16	290	2.8	1.3	3.7
Reg. Season Totals	688	46	15831	2337	4836	.483	14	47	.298	1080	1367	.790	1232	3040	4272	1288	1886	40	518	821	314	5768	6.2	1.9	8.4
Playoff Totals	32	0	712	96	207	.464	1	2	.500	42	51	.824	58	117	175	71	86	3	23	24	9	235	5.5	2.2	7.3

Hawkins, Cornelius L. (Connie, Hawk) b. July 17, 1942 Ht. 6-8 Wt. 215 College: Iowa HOF: 1992

SEASON–TEAM	G	GS	MIN	FGM	FGA	PCT	3FGM	3FGA	PCT	FTM	FTA	PCT	O-RB	D-RB	TOT	AST	PF	DQ	STL	TO	BLK	PTS	RPG	APG	PPG
67-68–Pittsburgh (A)	70	–	3146	635	1223	.519	2	9	.222	603	789	.764	368	577	945	320	248	2	–	200	–	1875	13.5	4.6	26.8
68-69–Minnesota (A)	47	–	1852	496	971	.511	3	22	.136	425	554	.767	167	367	534	184	166	3	–	155	–	1420	11.4	3.9	30.2
69-70–Phoenix	81	–	3312	709	1447	.490	–	–	–	577	741	.779	–	–	846	391	287	4	–	–	–	1995	10.4	4.8	24.6
70-71–Phoenix	71	–	2662	512	1181	.434	–	–	–	457	560	.816	–	–	643	322	197	2	–	–	–	1481	9.1	4.5	20.9
71-72–Phoenix	76	–	2798	571	1244	.459	–	–	–	456	565	.807	–	–	633	296	235	2	–	–	–	1598	8.3	3.9	21.0
72-73–Phoenix	75	–	2768	441	920	.479	–	–	–	322	404	.797	–	–	641	304	229	5	–	–	–	1204	8.5	4.1	16.1
73-74–Phoenix-L.A.	79	–	2761	404	807	.501	–	–	–	191	251	.761	176	389	565	407	223	1	113	–	81	999	7.2	5.2	12.6
74-75–Los Angeles	43	–	1026	139	324	.429	–	–	–	68	99	.687	54	144	198	120	116	1	51	–	23	346	4.6	2.8	8.0
75-76–Atlanta	74	–	1907	237	530	.447	–	–	–	136	191	.712	102	343	445	212	172	2	80	–	46	610	6.0	2.9	8.2
Reg. NBA Totals	499	–	17234	3013	6453	.467	–	–	–	2207	2811	.785	332	876	3971	2052	1459	17	244	–	150	8233	8.0	4.1	16.5
Reg. ABA Totals	117	–	4998	1131	2194	.515	5	31	.161	1028	1343	.765	535	944	1479	504	414	5	–	355	–	3295	12.6	4.3	28.2
NBA Playoff Totals	12	–	500	83	210	.395	–	–	–	66	81	.815	14	26	137	57	35	0	7	–	1	232	11.4	4.8	19.3
ABA Playoff Totals	21	–	936	210	416	.505	4	8	.500	169	239	.707	39	47	258	91	83	4	–	48	–	593	12.3	4.3	28.2
NBA All-Star Totals	4	–	45	8	16	.500	–	–	–	9	10	.900	0	0	10	5	5	0	0	–	0	25	2.5	1.3	6.3

Hawkins, Hersey R. Jr. b. September 29, 1966 Ht. 6-3 Wt. 200 College: Bradley

SEASON–TEAM	G	GS	MIN	FGM	FGA	PCT	3FGM	3FGA	PCT	FTM	FTA	PCT	O-RB	D-RB	TOT	AST	PF	DQ	STL	TO	BLK	PTS	RPG	APG	PPG
88-89–Philadelphia	79	79	2577	442	971	.455	71	166	.428	241	290	.831	51	174	225	239	184	0	120	158	37	1196	2.8	3.0	15.1
89-90–Philadelphia	82	82	2856	522	1136	.460	84	200	.420	387	436	.888	85	219	304	261	217	2	130	185	28	1515	3.7	3.2	18.5
90-91–Philadelphia	80	80	3110	590	1251	.472	108	270	.400	479	550	.871	48	262	310	299	182	0	178	213	39	1767	3.9	3.7	22.1
91-92–Philadelphia	81	81	3013	521	1127	.462	91	229	.397	403	461	.874	53	218	271	248	174	0	157	189	43	1536	3.3	3.1	19.0
92-93–Philadelphia	81	81	2977	551	1172	.470	122	307	.397	419	487	.860	91	255	346	317	189	0	137	180	30	1643	4.3	3.9	20.3
93-94–Charlotte	82	82	2648	395	859	.460	78	235	.332	312	362	.862	89	288	377	216	167	2	135	158	22	1180	4.6	2.6	14.4
94-95–Charlotte	82	82	2731	390	809	.482	131	298	.440	261	301	.867	60	254	314	262	178	1	122	150	18	1172	3.8	3.2	14.3
95-96–Seattle	82	82	2823	443	936	.473	146	380	.384	249	285	.874	86	211	297	218	172	0	149	164	14	1281	3.6	2.7	15.6
96-97–Seattle	82	82	2755	369	795	.464	143	355	.403	258	295	.875	92	228	320	250	146	1	159	130	12	1139	3.9	3.0	13.9
97-98–Seattle	82	82	2597	280	636	.440	125	301	.415	177	204	.868	71	263	334	221	153	0	148	102	17	862	4.1	2.7	10.5
98-99–Seattle	50	34	1644	171	408	.419	55	180	.306	119	132	.902	51	150	201	123	90	1	80	80	18	516	4.0	2.5	10.3
99-00–Chicago	61	49	1622	159	375	.424	55	141	.390	107	119	.899	31	144	175	134	146	1	74	100	15	480	2.9	2.2	7.9
Reg. Season Totals	924	896	31353	4833	10475	.461	1209	3062	.395	3412	3922	.870	808	2666	3474	2788	1998	8	1589	1809	293	14287	3.8	3.0	15.5
Playoff Totals	68	68	2479	323	708	.456	98	246	.398	287	315	.911	73	204	277	191	184	2	116	122	29	1031	4.1	2.8	15.2
All-Star Totals	1	0	14	3	5	.600	0	1	.000	0	0	–	0	0	0	1	1	0	0	1	0	6	0.0	1.0	6.0

Hawkins, James Marshall (Marshall) b. August 3, 1924 Ht. 6-3 Wt. 210 College: Tennessee

SEASON–TEAM	G	GS	MIN	FGM	FGA	PCT	3FGM	3FGA	PCT	FTM	FTA	PCT	O-RB	D-RB	TOT	AST	PF	DQ	STL	TO	BLK	PTS	RPG	APG	PPG
48-49–Oshkosh (N)	64	–	–	200	–	–	–	–	–	116	160	.725	–	–	–	–	149	–	–	–	–	516	–	–	8.1
49-50–Indianapolis	39	–	–	55	195	.282	–	–	–	42	61	.689	–	–	–	51	87	–	–	–	–	152	–	1.3	3.9
Reg. NBA Totals	39	–	–	55	195	.282	–	–	–	42	61	.689	–	–	–	51	87	–	–	–	–	152	–	1.3	3.9
Reg. NBL Totals	64	–	–	200	–	–	–	–	–	116	160	.725	–	–	–	–	149	–	–	–	–	516	–	–	8.1
NBA Playoff Totals	3	–	–	0	2	.000	–	–	–	0	0	–	–	–	–	–	1	–	–	–	–	0	0.0	0.0	0.0
NBL Playoff Totals	7	–	–	25	–	–	–	–	–	20	27	.741	–	–	–	–	28	–	–	–	–	70	–	–	10.0

Hawkins, Robert (Bubbles) b. June 30, 1954 d. November 28, 1993 Ht. 6-4 Wt. 190 College: Illinois State

SEASON–TEAM	G	GS	MIN	FGM	FGA	PCT	3FGM	3FGA	PCT	FTM	FTA	PCT	O-RB	D-RB	TOT	AST	PF	DQ	STL	TO	BLK	PTS	RPG	APG	PPG
75-76–Golden State	32	–	153	53	104	.510	–	–	–	20	31	.645	16	14	30	16	31	0	10	–	8	126	0.9	0.5	3.9
76-77–New York Nets	52	–	1481	406	909	.447	–	–	–	194	282	.688	67	87	154	93	163	2	77	–	26	1006	3.0	1.8	19.3
77-78–New Jersey	15	–	343	69	150	.460	–	–	–	25	29	.862	21	29	50	37	51	1	22	43	13	163	3.3	2.5	10.9
78-79–Detroit	4	–	28	6	16	.375	–	–	–	6	6	1.000	3	3	6	4	7	0	5	2	0	18	1.5	1.0	4.5
Reg. Season Totals	103	–	2005	534	1179	.453	–	–	–	245	348	.704	107	133	240	150	252	3	114	45	47	1313	2.3	1.5	12.7
Playoff Totals	5	–	12	4	5	.800	–	–	–	2	2	1.000	0	0	0	2	6	0	1	–	0	10	0.0	0.4	2.0

Hawkins, Steven Michael (Michael) b. October 28, 1972 Ht. 6-0 Wt. 180 College: Xavier (Ohio)

SEASON–TEAM	G	GS	MIN	FGM	FGA	PCT	3FGM	3FGA	PCT	FTM	FTA	PCT	O-RB	D-RB	TOT	AST	PF	DQ	STL	TO	BLK	PTS	RPG	APG	PPG
96-97–Boston	29	0	326	29	68	.426	10	31	.323	12	15	.800	9	22	31	64	40	0	16	28	1	80	1.1	2.2	2.8
98-99–Sacramento	24	0	203	14	40	.350	5	19	.263	3	3	1.000	10	15	25	27	14	0	3	13	1	36	1.0	1.1	1.5
99-00–Charlotte	12	0	36	3	13	.231	1	5	.200	1	2	.500	0	7	7	13	2	0	0	3	0	8	0.6	1.1	0.7
Reg. Season Totals	65	0	565	46	121	.380	16	55	.291	16	20	.800	19	44	63	104	56	0	19	44	2	124	1.0	1.6	1.9
Playoff Totals	2	0	10	0	1	.000	0	1	.000	2	2	1.000	0	0	0	–	1	0	0	0	0	2	0.0	0.0	1.0

Hawkins, Thomas Jerome (Tom, Hawk) b. December 22, 1936 Ht. 6-5 Wt. 210 College: Notre Dame

SEASON–TEAM	G	GS	MIN	FGM	FGA	PCT	3FGM	3FGA	PCT	FTM	FTA	PCT	O-RB	D-RB	TOT	AST	PF	DQ	STL	TO	BLK	PTS	RPG	APG	PPG
59-60–Minneapolis	69	–	1467	220	579	.380	–	–	–	106	164	.646	–	–	428	54	188	3	–	–	–	546	6.2	0.8	7.9
60-61–Los Angeles	78	–	1846	310	719	.431	–	–	–	140	235	.596	–	–	479	88	209	2	–	–	–	760	6.1	1.1	9.7
61-62–Los Angeles	79	–	1903	289	704	.411	–	–	–	143	222	.644	–	–	514	95	244	7	–	–	–	721	6.5	1.2	9.1
62-63–Cincinnati	79	–	1721	299	635	.471	–	–	–	147	241	.610	–	–	543	100	197	2	–	–	–	745	6.9	1.3	9.4
63-64–Cincinnati	73	–	1770	256	580	.441	–	–	–	113	188	.601	–	–	435	74	198	4	–	–	–	625	6.0	1.0	8.6
64-65–Cincinnati	79	–	1864	220	538	.409	–	–	–	116	204	.569	–	–	475	80	240	4	–	–	–	556	6.0	1.0	7.0
65-66–Cincinnati	79	–	2126	273	604	.452	–	–	–	116	209	.555	–	–	575	99	274	4	–	–	–	662	7.3	1.3	8.4
66-67–Los Angeles	76	–	1798	275	572	.481	–	–	–	82	173	.474	–	–	434	83	207	1	–	–	–	632	5.7	1.1	8.3
67-68–Los Angeles	78	–	2463	389	779	.499	–	–	–	125	229	.546	–	–	458	117	289	7	–	–	–	903	5.9	1.5	11.6
68-69–Los Angeles	74	–	1507	230	461	.499	–	–	–	62	151	.411	–	–	266	81	168	1	–	–	–	522	3.6	1.1	7.1
Reg. Season Totals	764	–	18465	2761	6171	.447	–	–	–	1150	2016	.570	–	–	4607	871	2214	35	–	–	–	6672	6.0	1.1	8.7
Playoff Totals	96	–	2099	311	677	.459	–	–	–	145	235	.617	–	–	537	106	310	8	–	–	–	767	5.6	1.1	8.0

Hawthorne, Nate b. January 15, 1950 Ht. 6-4 Wt. 190 College: Southern Illinois

SEASON–TEAM	G	GS	MIN	FGM	FGA	PCT	3FGM	3FGA	PCT	FTM	FTA	PCT	O-RB	D-RB	TOT	AST	PF	DQ	STL	TO	BLK	PTS	RPG	APG	PPG
73-74–Los Angeles	33	–	229	38	93	.409	–	–	–	30	48	.625	16	16	32	23	33	1	9	–	6	106	1.0	0.7	3.2
74-75–Phoenix	50	–	618	118	287	.411	–	–	–	61	94	.649	34	58	92	39	94	0	30	–	21	297	1.8	0.8	5.9
75-76–Phoenix	79	–	1144	182	423	.430	–	–	–	115	170	.676	86	123	209	46	147	0	33	–	15	479	2.6	0.6	6.1
Reg. Season Totals	162	–	1991	338	803	.421	–	–	–	206	312	.660	136	197	333	108	274	1	72	–	42	882	2.1	0.7	5.4
Playoff Totals	18	–	95	10	33	.303	–	–	–	12	16	.750	7	11	18	6	20	0	6	–	2	32	1.0	0.3	1.8

Hayes, Elvin Ernest (The Big E) b. November 17, 1945 Ht. 6-9 Wt. 235 College: Houston HOF: 1989

SEASON–TEAM	G	GS	MIN	FGM	FGA	PCT	3FGM	3FGA	PCT	FTM	FTA	PCT	O-RB	D-RB	TOT	AST	PF	DQ	STL	TO	BLK	PTS	RPG	APG	PPG
68-69–San Diego	82	–	3695	930	2082	.447	–	–	–	467	746	.626	–	–	1406	113	266	2	–	–	–	2327	17.1	1.4	28.4
69-70–San Diego	82	–	3665	914	2020	.452	–	–	–	428	622	.688	–	–	1386	162	270	5	–	–	–	2256	16.9	2.0	27.5
70-71–San Diego	82	–	3633	948	2215	.428	–	–	–	454	676	.672	–	–	1362	186	225	1	–	–	–	2350	16.6	2.3	28.7
71-72–Houston	82	–	3461	832	1918	.434	–	–	–	399	615	.649	–	–	1197	270	233	1	–	–	–	2063	14.6	3.3	25.2
72-73–Baltimore	81	–	3347	713	1607	.444	–	–	–	291	434	.671	–	–	1177	127	232	3	–	–	–	1717	14.5	1.6	21.2
73-74–Capital	81	–	3602	689	1627	.423	–	–	–	357	495	.721	354	1109	1463	163	252	1	86	–	240	1735	18.1	2.0	21.4
74-75–Washington	82	–	3465	739	1668	.443	–	–	–	409	534	.766	221	783	1004	206	238	0	158	–	187	1887	12.2	2.5	23.0
75-76–Washington	80	–	2975	649	1381	.470	–	–	–	287	457	.628	210	668	878	121	293	5	104	–	202	1585	11.0	1.5	19.8
76-77–Washington	82	–	3364	760	1516	.501	–	–	–	422	614	.687	289	740	1029	158	312	1	87	–	220	1942	12.5	1.9	23.7
77-78–Washington	81	–	3246	636	1409	.451	–	–	–	326	514	.634	335	740	1075	149	313	7	96	229	159	1598	13.3	1.8	19.7
78-79–Washington	82	–	3105	720	1477	.487	–	–	–	349	534	.654	312	682	994	143	308	5	75	235	190	1789	12.1	1.7	21.8
79-80–Washington	81	–	3183	761	1677	.454	3	13	.231	334	478	.699	269	627	896	129	309	9	62	215	189	1859	11.1	1.6	23.0
80-81–Washington	81	–	2931	584	1296	.451	0	10	.000	271	439	.617	235	554	789	98	300	6	68	189	171	1439	9.7	1.2	17.8
81-82–Houston	82	82	3032	519	1100	.472	0	5	.000	280	422	.664	267	480	747	144	287	4	62	208	104	1318	9.1	1.8	16.1
82-83–Houston	81	43	2302	424	890	.476	2	4	.500	196	287	.683	199	417	616	158	232	2	50	200	81	1046	7.6	2.0	12.9
83-84–Houston	81	4	994	158	389	.406	0	2	.000	86	132	.652	87	173	260	71	123	1	16	82	28	402	3.2	0.9	5.0
Reg. Season Totals	1303	129	50000	10976	24272	.452	5	34	.147	5356	7999	.670	2778	6973	16279	2398	4193	53	864	1358	1771	27313	12.5	1.8	21.0
Playoff Totals	96	3	4160	883	1901	.464	0	0	–	428	656	.652	336	768	1244	185	378	8	97	124	222	2194	13.0	1.9	22.9
All-Star Totals	12	4	264	52	129	.403	0	0	–	22	34	.647	16	38	92	17	37	0	5	5	6	126	7.7	1.4	10.5

Hayes, Jim b. February 18, 1948 Ht. 6-3 Wt. 200 College: Boston U.

SEASON–TEAM	G	GS	MIN	FGM	FGA	PCT	3FGM	3FGA	PCT	FTM	FTA	PCT	O-RB	D-RB	TOT	AST	PF	DQ	STL	TO	BLK	PTS	RPG	APG	PPG
70-71–New York (A)	47	–	494	46	109	.422	0	0	–	52	67	.776	–	–	45	47	73	–	–	–	–	144	1.0	1.0	3.1
Reg. ABA Totals	47	–	494	46	109	.422	0	0	–	52	67	.776	–	–	45	47	73	–	–	–	–	144	1.0	1.0	3.1

Hayes, Steven Leonard (Steve) b. August 2, 1955 Ht. 7-0 Wt. 205 College: Idaho State

SEASON–TEAM	G	GS	MIN	FGM	FGA	PCT	3FGM	3FGA	PCT	FTM	FTA	PCT	O-RB	D-RB	TOT	AST	PF	DQ	STL	TO	BLK	PTS	RPG	APG	PPG
81-82–S.A.-Detroit	35	0	487	54	111	.486	0	0	–	32	53	.604	39	78	117	28	71	0	4	19	20	140	3.3	0.8	4.0
82-83–Cleveland	65	3	1058	104	217	.479	0	1	.000	29	51	.569	102	134	236	36	215	9	17	49	41	237	3.6	0.6	3.6
83-84–Seattle	43	0	253	26	50	.520	0	0	–	5	14	.357	19	43	62	13	52	0	5	13	18	57	1.4	0.3	1.3
84-85–Philadelphia	11	0	101	10	18	.556	0	0	–	2	4	.500	11	23	34	1	19	0	1	2	4	22	3.1	0.1	2.0
85-86–Utah	58	0	397	39	87	.448	0	0	–	11	36	.306	32	45	77	7	81	0	5	16	19	89	1.3	0.1	1.5
Reg. Season Totals	212	3	2296	233	483	.482	0	1	.000	79	158	.500	203	323	526	85	438	9	32	99	102	545	2.5	0.4	2.6
Playoff Totals	1	0	1	1	1	1.000	0	0	–	0	0	–	0	1	1	–	0	0	0	0	0	2	1.0	0.0	2.0

Haywood, Spencer b. April 22, 1949 Ht. 6-8 Wt. 225 College: Trinidad State (Colo.) J.C.; Detroit (Renamed Detroit Mercy)

SEASON–TEAM	G	GS	MIN	FGM	FGA	PCT	3FGM	3FGA	PCT	FTM	FTA	PCT	O-RB	D-RB	TOT	AST	PF	DQ	STL	TO	BLK	PTS	RPG	APG	PPG
69-70–Denver (A)	84	–	3808	986	1998	.493	0	11	.000	547	705	.776	533	1104	1637	190	221	1	–	–	–	2519	19.5	2.3	30.0
70-71–Seattle	33	–	1162	260	579	.449	–	–	–	160	218	.734	–	–	396	48	84	1	–	–	–	680	12.0	1.5	20.6
71-72–Seattle	73	–	3167	717	1557	.461	–	–	–	480	586	.819	–	–	926	148	208	0	–	–	–	1914	12.7	2.0	26.2
72-73–Seattle	77	–	3259	889	1868	.476	–	–	–	473	564	.839	–	–	995	196	213	2	–	–	–	2251	12.9	2.5	29.2
73-74–Seattle	75	–	3039	694	1520	.457	–	–	–	373	458	.814	318	689	1007	240	198	2	65	–	106	1761	13.4	3.2	23.5
74-75–Seattle	68	–	2529	608	1325	.459	–	–	–	309	381	.811	198	432	630	137	173	1	54	–	108	1525	9.3	2.0	22.4
75-76–New York	78	–	2892	605	1360	.445	–	–	–	339	448	.757	234	644	878	92	255	1	53	–	80	1549	11.3	1.2	19.9
76-77–N.Y. Knicks	31	–	1021	202	449	.450	–	–	–	109	131	.832	77	203	280	50	72	0	14	–	29	513	9.0	1.6	16.5
77-78–New York	67	–	1765	412	852	.484	–	–	–	96	135	.711	141	301	442	126	188	1	37	140	72	920	6.6	1.9	13.7
78-79–N.Y.-N.O.	68	–	2361	595	1205	.494	–	–	–	231	292	.791	172	361	533	127	236	8	40	200	82	1421	7.8	1.9	20.9
79-80–Los Angeles	76	–	1544	288	591	.487	1	4	.250	159	206	.772	132	214	346	93	197	2	35	134	57	736	4.6	1.2	9.7
81-82–Washington	76	63	2086	395	829	.476	0	3	.000	219	260	.842	144	278	422	64	249	6	45	175	68	1009	5.6	0.8	13.3
82-83–Washington	38	25	775	125	312	.401	0	1	.000	63	87	.724	77	106	183	30	94	2	12	67	27	313	4.8	0.8	8.2
Reg. NBA Totals	760	88	25600	5790	12447	.465	1	8	.125	3011	3766	.800	1493	3228	7038	1351	2167	26	355	716	629	14592	9.3	1.8	19.2
Reg. ABA Totals	84	–	3808	986	1998	.493	0	11	.000	547	705	.776	533	1104	1637	190	221	1	–	–	–	2519	19.5	2.3	30.0
NBA Playoff Totals	33	7	890	172	384	.448	0	1	.000	97	123	.789	69	119	188	41	98	2	13	45	36	441	5.7	1.2	13.4
ABA Playoff Totals	12	–	568	185	362	.511	1	5	.200	69	83	.831	79	158	237	39	31	0	–	–	–	440	19.8	3.3	36.7
NBA All-Star Totals	4	3	97	20	46	.435	0	0	–	8	9	.889	3	11	31	6	13	0	0	–	3	48	7.8	1.5	12.0

Hazen, John W. b. March 2, 1927 Ht. 6-2 Wt. 175 College: Indiana State

SEASON–TEAM	G	GS	MIN	FGM	FGA	PCT	3FGM	3FGA	PCT	FTM	FTA	PCT	O-RB	D-RB	TOT	AST	PF	DQ	STL	TO	BLK	PTS	RPG	APG	PPG
48-49–Boston	6	–	–	6	17	.353	–	–	–	6	7	.857	–	–	–	3	10	–	–	–	–	18	–	0.5	3.0
Reg. Season Totals	6	–	–	6	17	.353	–	–	–	6	7	.857	–	–	–	3	10	–	–	–	–	18	–	0.5	3.0

Hazzard, Walter Raphael Jr. **(Walt, formerly Mahdi Abdul-Rahman)** b. April 15, 1942 Ht. 6-2 Wt. 190 College: UCLA

SEASON–TEAM	G	GS	MIN	FGM	FGA	PCT	3FGM	3FGA	PCT	FTM	FTA	PCT	O-RB	D-RB	TOT	AST	PF	DQ	STL	TO	BLK	PTS	RPG	APG	PPG
64-65–Los Angeles	66	–	919	117	306	.382	–	–	–	46	71	.648	–	–	111	140	132	0	–	–	–	280	1.7	2.1	4.2
65-66–Los Angeles	80	–	2198	458	1003	.457	–	–	–	182	257	.708	–	–	219	393	224	0	–	–	–	1098	2.7	4.9	13.7
66-67–Los Angeles	79	–	1642	301	706	.426	–	–	–	129	177	.729	–	–	231	323	203	1	–	–	–	731	2.9	4.1	9.3
67-68–Seattle	79	–	2666	733	1662	.441	–	–	–	428	553	.774	–	–	332	493	246	3	–	–	–	1894	4.2	6.2	24.0
68-69–Atlanta	80	–	2420	345	869	.397	–	–	–	208	294	.707	–	–	266	474	264	6	–	–	–	898	3.3	5.9	11.2
69-70–Atlanta	82	–	2757	493	1056	.467	–	–	–	267	330	.809	–	–	329	561	264	3	–	–	–	1253	4.0	6.8	15.3
70-71–Atlanta	82	–	2877	517	1126	.459	–	–	–	315	415	.759	–	–	300	514	276	2	–	–	–	1349	3.7	6.3	16.5
71-72–Buffalo	72	–	2389	450	998	.451	–	–	–	237	303	.782	–	–	213	406	230	2	–	–	–	1137	3.0	5.6	15.8
72-73–Buffalo-G.S.	55	–	763	107	256	.418	–	–	–	47	57	.825	–	–	88	129	110	1	–	–	–	261	1.6	2.3	4.7
73-74–Seattle	49	–	571	76	180	.422	–	–	–	34	45	.756	18	39	57	122	78	0	26	–	6	186	1.2	2.5	3.8
Reg. Season Totals	724	–	19202	3597	8162	.441	–	–	–	1893	2502	.757	18	39	2146	3555	2027	18	26	–	6	9087	3.0	4.9	12.6
Playoff Totals	58	–	1576	268	649	.413	–	–	–	149	202	.738	0	0	169	242	176	1	0	–	0	685	2.9	4.2	11.8
All-Star Totals	1	–	20	4	12	.333	–	–	–	1	1	1.000	0	0	3	3	3	0	0	–	0	9	3.0	3.0	9.0

Heal, Shane b. September 6, 1971 Ht. 6-0 Wt. 180 Country: Australia

SEASON–TEAM	G	GS	MIN	FGM	FGA	PCT	3FGM	3FGA	PCT	FTM	FTA	PCT	O-RB	D-RB	TOT	AST	PF	DQ	STL	TO	BLK	PTS	RPG	APG	PPG
96-97–Minnesota	43	0	236	26	97	.268	20	65	.308	3	5	.600	2	16	18	33	20	0	3	17	3	75	0.4	0.8	1.7
Reg. Season Totals	43	0	236	26	97	.268	20	65	.308	3	5	.600	2	16	18	33	20	0	3	17	3	75	0.4	0.8	1.7
Playoff Totals	2	0	3	2	2	1.000	2	2	1.000	0	0	–	0	0	0	1	0	0	0	0	0	6	0.0	0.5	3.0

Heaney, Brian Patrick b. September 3, 1946 Ht. 6-2 Wt. 180 College: Acadia (Canada)

SEASON–TEAM	G	GS	MIN	FGM	FGA	PCT	3FGM	3FGA	PCT	FTM	FTA	PCT	O-RB	D-RB	TOT	AST	PF	DQ	STL	TO	BLK	PTS	RPG	APG	PPG
69-70–Baltimore	14	–	70	13	24	.542	–	–	–	2	4	.500	–	–	4	6	17	0	–	–	–	28	0.3	0.4	2.0
Reg. Season Totals	14	–	70	13	24	.542	–	–	–	2	4	.500	–	–	4	6	17	0	–	–	–	28	0.3	0.4	2.0
Playoff Totals	6	–	7	0	2	.000	–	–	–	0	0	–	–	–	1	1	0	0	–	–	–	0	0.2	0.2	0.0

Heard, Garfield **(Gar)** b. May 3, 1948 Ht. 6-7 Wt. 220 College: Oklahoma

SEASON–TEAM	G	GS	MIN	FGM	FGA	PCT	3FGM	3FGA	PCT	FTM	FTA	PCT	O-RB	D-RB	TOT	AST	PF	DQ	STL	TO	BLK	PTS	RPG	APG	PPG
70-71–Seattle	65	–	1027	152	399	.381	–	–	–	82	125	.656	–	–	328	45	126	0	–	–	–	386	5.0	0.7	5.9
71-72–Seattle	58	–	1499	190	474	.401	–	–	–	79	128	.617	–	–	442	55	126	2	–	–	–	459	7.6	0.9	7.9
72-73–Seattle-Chi.	81	–	1552	350	824	.425	–	–	–	116	178	.652	–	–	453	60	171	1	–	–	–	816	5.6	0.7	10.1
73-74–Buffalo	81	–	2889	524	1205	.435	–	–	–	191	294	.650	270	677	947	180	300	3	136	–	230	1239	11.7	2.2	15.3
74-75–Buffalo	67	–	2148	318	819	.388	–	–	–	106	188	.564	185	481	666	190	242	2	106	–	120	742	9.9	2.8	11.1
75-76–Buffalo-Phoenix	86	–	2747	392	901	.435	–	–	–	158	248	.637	247	622	869	190	303	2	117	–	96	942	10.1	2.2	11.0
76-77–Phoenix	46	–	1363	173	457	.379	–	–	–	100	138	.725	120	320	440	89	139	2	55	–	55	446	9.6	1.9	9.7
77-78–Phoenix	80	–	2099	265	625	.424	–	–	–	90	147	.612	166	486	652	132	213	0	129	120	101	620	8.2	1.7	7.8
78-79–Phoenix	63	–	1213	162	367	.441	–	–	–	71	103	.689	98	253	351	60	141	1	53	60	57	395	5.6	1.0	6.3
79-80–Phoenix	82	–	1403	171	410	.417	0	2	.000	64	86	.744	118	262	380	97	177	0	84	88	49	406	4.6	1.2	5.0
80-81–San Diego	78	–	1631	149	396	.376	0	7	.000	79	101	.782	120	228	348	122	196	0	104	81	72	377	4.5	1.6	4.8
Reg. Season Totals	787	–	19571	2846	6877	.414	0	9	.000	1136	1736	.654	1324	3329	5876	1220	2134	13	784	349	780	6828	7.5	1.6	8.7
Playoff Totals	59	–	1825	247	589	.419	0	0	–	108	166	.651	146	388	537	96	174	0	80	31	98	602	9.1	1.6	10.2

Hedderick, Herman Arthur (Herm) b. January 1, 1930 Ht. 6-5 Wt. 170 College: Canisius

SEASON–TEAM	G	GS	MIN	FGM	FGA	PCT	3FGM	3FGA	PCT	FTM	FTA	PCT	O-RB	D-RB	TOT	AST	PF	DQ	STL	TO	BLK	PTS	RPG	APG	PPG
54-55–New York	5	–	23	2	9	.222	–	–	–	0	1	.000	–	–	4	2	3	0	–	–	–	4	0.8	0.4	0.8
Reg. Season Totals	5	–	23	2	9	.222	–	–	–	0	1	.000	–	–	4	2	3	0	–	–	–	4	0.8	0.4	0.8

Heggs, Alvin b. December 8, 1967 Ht. 6-8 Wt. 225 College: Texas

SEASON–TEAM	G	GS	MIN	FGM	FGA	PCT	3FGM	3FGA	PCT	FTM	FTA	PCT	O-RB	D-RB	TOT	AST	PF	DQ	STL	TO	BLK	PTS	RPG	APG	PPG
95-96–Houston	4	0	14	3	5	.600	0	0	–	2	3	.667	1	1	2	0	0	0	0	0	0	8	0.5	0.0	2.0
Reg. Season Totals	4	0	14	3	5	.600	0	0	–	2	3	.667	1	1	2	0	0	0	0	0	0	8	0.5	0.0	2.0

Heinsohn, Thomas William (Tom, Tommy, Ack-Ack) b. August 26, 1934 Ht. 6-7 Wt. 220 College: Holy Cross HOF: 1985

SEASON–TEAM	G	GS	MIN	FGM	FGA	PCT	3FGM	3FGA	PCT	FTM	FTA	PCT	O-RB	D-RB	TOT	AST	PF	DQ	STL	TO	BLK	PTS	RPG	APG	PPG
56-57–Boston	72	–	2150	446	1123	.397	–	–	–	271	343	.790	–	–	705	117	304	12	–	–	–	1163	9.8	1.6	16.2
57-58–Boston	69	–	2206	468	1226	.382	–	–	–	294	394	.746	–	–	705	125	274	6	–	–	–	1230	10.2	1.8	17.8
58-59–Boston	66	–	2089	465	1192	.390	–	–	–	312	391	.798	–	–	638	164	271	11	–	–	–	1242	9.7	2.5	18.8
59-60–Boston	75	–	2420	673	1590	.423	–	–	–	283	386	.733	–	–	794	171	275	8	–	–	–	1629	10.6	2.3	21.7
60-61–Boston	74	–	2256	627	1566	.400	–	–	–	325	424	.767	–	–	732	141	260	7	–	–	–	1579	9.9	1.9	21.3
61-62–Boston	79	–	2383	692	1613	.429	–	–	–	358	437	.819	–	–	747	165	280	2	–	–	–	1742	9.5	2.1	22.1
62-63–Boston	76	–	2004	550	1300	.423	–	–	–	340	407	.835	–	–	569	95	270	4	–	–	–	1440	7.5	1.3	18.9
63-64–Boston	76	–	2040	487	1223	.398	–	–	–	283	342	.827	–	–	460	183	268	3	–	–	–	1257	6.1	2.4	16.5
64-65–Boston	67	–	1706	365	954	.383	–	–	–	182	229	.795	–	–	399	157	252	5	–	–	–	912	6.0	2.3	13.6
Reg. Season Totals	654	–	19254	4773	11787	.405	–	–	–	2648	3353	.790	–	–	5749	1318	2454	58	–	–	–	12194	8.8	2.0	18.6
Playoff Totals	104	–	3223	818	2035	.402	–	–	–	422	568	.743	–	–	954	215	417	14	–	–	–	2058	9.2	2.1	19.8
All-Star Totals	5	–	97	22	67	.328	–	–	–	7	8	.875	–	–	20	3	20	0	–	–	–	51	4.0	0.6	10.2

Hemric, Ned Dixon (Dick) b. August 29, 1933 Ht. 6-6 Wt. 220 College: Wake Forest

SEASON–TEAM	G	GS	MIN	FGM	FGA	PCT	3FGM	3FGA	PCT	FTM	FTA	PCT	O-RB	D-RB	TOT	AST	PF	DQ	STL	TO	BLK	PTS	RPG	APG	PPG
55-56–Boston	71	–	1329	161	400	.403	–	–	–	177	273	.648	–	–	399	60	142	2	–	–	–	499	5.6	0.8	7.0
56-57–Boston	67	–	1055	109	317	.344	–	–	–	146	210	.695	–	–	304	42	98	0	–	–	–	364	4.5	0.6	5.4
Reg. Season Totals	138	–	2384	270	717	.377	–	–	–	323	483	.669	–	–	703	102	240	2	–	–	–	863	5.1	0.7	6.3
Playoff Totals	5	–	73	6	31	.194	–	–	–	9	16	.563	–	–	31	2	8	0	–	–	–	21	6.2	0.4	4.2

Henderson, Alan Lybrooks b. December 2, 1972 Ht. 6-9 Wt. 235 College: Indiana

SEASON–TEAM	G	GS	MIN	FGM	FGA	PCT	3FGM	3FGA	PCT	FTM	FTA	PCT	O-RB	D-RB	TOT	AST	PF	DQ	STL	TO	BLK	PTS	RPG	APG	PPG
95-96–Atlanta	79	4	1416	192	434	.442	0	3	.000	119	200	.595	164	192	356	51	217	5	44	87	43	503	4.5	0.6	6.4
96-97–Atlanta	30	0	501	77	162	.475	0	0	–	45	75	.600	47	69	116	23	73	1	21	29	6	199	3.9	0.8	6.6
97-98–Atlanta	69	33	2000	365	753	.485	3	6	.500	253	388	.652	200	242	442	73	175	1	42	110	36	986	6.4	1.1	14.3
98-99–Atlanta	38	37	1142	187	423	.442	0	1	.000	100	149	.671	100	150	250	28	96	1	33	58	19	474	6.6	0.7	12.5
99-00–Atlanta	82	82	2775	429	930	.461	1	10	.100	224	334	.671	265	306	571	77	233	3	81	139	54	1083	7.0	0.9	13.2
Reg. Season Totals	298	156	7834	1250	2702	.463	4	20	.200	741	1146	.647	776	959	1735	252	794	11	221	423	158	3245	5.8	0.8	10.9
Playoff Totals	25	4	411	62	112	.554	0	1	.000	38	54	.704	38	44	82	11	60	0	5	22	8	162	3.3	0.4	6.5

Henderson, Cedric b. October 3, 1965 Ht. 6-8 Wt. 210 College: Georgia

SEASON–TEAM	G	GS	MIN	FGM	FGA	PCT	3FGM	3FGA	PCT	FTM	FTA	PCT	O-RB	D-RB	TOT	AST	PF	DQ	STL	TO	BLK	PTS	RPG	APG	PPG
86-87–Atlanta-Milw.	8	0	16	4	8	.500	0	0	–	3	3	1.000	3	5	8	0	2	0	0	4	0	11	1.0	0.0	1.4
Reg. Season Totals	8	0	16	4	8	.500	0	0	–	3	3	1.000	3	5	8	0	2	0	0	4	0	11	1.0	0.0	1.4

Henderson, Cedric Earl b. March 11, 1975 Ht. 6-7 Wt. 225 College: Memphis

SEASON–TEAM	G	GS	MIN	FGM	FGA	PCT	3FGM	3FGA	PCT	FTM	FTA	PCT	O-RB	D-RB	TOT	AST	PF	DQ	STL	TO	BLK	PTS	RPG	APG	PPG
97-98–Cleveland	82	71	2527	348	725	.480	0	4	.000	136	190	.716	71	254	325	168	238	3	96	165	45	832	4.0	2.0	10.1
98-99–Cleveland	50	48	1517	189	453	.417	2	12	.167	74	91	.813	45	152	197	113	136	2	58	97	24	454	3.9	2.3	9.1
99-00–Cleveland	61	7	1107	129	326	.396	1	15	.067	69	104	.663	34	106	140	55	99	0	39	68	17	328	2.3	0.9	5.4
Reg. Season Totals	193	126	5151	666	1504	.443	3	31	.097	279	385	.725	150	512	662	336	473	5	193	330	86	1614	3.4	1.7	8.4
Playoff Totals	4	4	157	11	28	.393	0	1	.000	8	13	.615	4	13	17	11	14	0	6	13	0	30	4.3	2.8	7.5

Henderson, David McKinley (Dave) b. July 21, 1964 Ht. 6-5 Wt. 195 College: Duke

SEASON–TEAM	G	GS	MIN	FGM	FGA	PCT	3FGM	3FGA	PCT	FTM	FTA	PCT	O-RB	D-RB	TOT	AST	PF	DQ	STL	TO	BLK	PTS	RPG	APG	PPG
87-88–Philadelphia	22	1	351	47	116	.405	0	1	.000	32	47	.681	11	24	35	34	41	0	12	40	5	126	1.6	1.5	5.7
Reg. Season Totals	22	1	351	47	116	.405	0	1	.000	32	47	.681	11	24	35	34	41	0	12	40	5	126	1.6	1.5	5.7

Henderson, Jerome D. b. October 5, 1959 Ht. 6-11 Wt. 230 College: Wabash Valley (Ill.) Coll. (J.C.); New Mexico

SEASON–TEAM	G	GS	MIN	FGM	FGA	PCT	3FGM	3FGA	PCT	FTM	FTA	PCT	O-RB	D-RB	TOT	AST	PF	DQ	STL	TO	BLK	PTS	RPG	APG	PPG
85-86–L.A. Lakers	1	0	3	2	3	.667	0	0	–	0	0	–	0	1	1	0	1	0	0	0	0	4	1.0	0.0	4.0
86-87–Milwaukee	6	0	36	4	13	.308	0	0	–	4	4	1.000	2	5	7	0	12	0	1	6	1	12	1.2	0.0	2.0
Reg. Season Totals	7	0	39	6	16	.375	0	0	–	4	4	1.000	2	6	8	0	13	0	1	6	1	16	1.1	0.0	2.3
Playoff Totals	1	0	1	0	0	–	0	0	–	0	0	–	0	0	0	–	1	0	0	0	0	0	0.0	0.0	0.0

Henderson, Jerome McKinley (Gerald) b. January 16, 1956 Ht. 6-2 Wt. 175 College: Virginia Commonwealth

SEASON–TEAM	G	GS	MIN	FGM	FGA	PCT	3FGM	3FGA	PCT	FTM	FTA	PCT	O-RB	D-RB	TOT	AST	PF	DQ	STL	TO	BLK	PTS	RPG	APG	PPG
79-80–Boston	76	–	1061	191	382	.500	2	6	.333	89	129	.690	37	46	83	147	96	0	45	109	15	473	1.1	1.9	6.2
80-81–Boston	82	–	1608	261	579	.451	1	16	.063	113	157	.720	43	89	132	213	177	0	79	160	12	636	1.6	2.6	7.8
81-82–Boston	82	31	1844	353	705	.501	2	12	.167	125	172	.727	47	105	152	252	199	3	82	150	11	833	1.9	3.1	10.2
82-83–Boston	82	9	1551	286	618	.463	3	16	.188	96	133	.722	57	67	124	195	190	6	95	128	3	671	1.5	2.4	8.2
83-84–Boston	78	78	2088	376	718	.524	20	57	.351	136	177	.768	68	79	147	300	209	1	117	161	14	908	1.9	3.8	11.6
84-85–Seattle	79	78	2648	427	891	.479	9	38	.237	199	255	.780	71	119	190	559	196	1	140	231	9	1062	2.4	7.1	13.4
85-86–Seattle	82	82	2568	434	900	.482	18	52	.346	185	223	.830	89	98	187	487	230	2	138	184	12	1071	2.3	5.9	13.1
86-87–Seattle-N.Y.	74	59	2045	298	674	.442	19	77	.247	190	230	.826	50	125	175	471	208	1	101	172	11	805	2.4	6.4	10.9
87-88–N.Y.-Phil.	75	5	1505	194	453	.428	69	163	.423	138	170	.812	27	80	107	231	187	0	69	133	5	595	1.4	3.1	7.9
88-89–Philadelphia	65	0	986	144	348	.414	33	107	.308	104	127	.819	17	51	68	140	121	1	42	73	3	425	1.0	2.2	6.5
89-90–Milw.-Detroit	57	0	464	53	109	.486	17	38	.447	12	15	.800	11	32	43	74	50	0	16	24	2	135	0.8	1.3	2.4
90-91–Detroit	23	10	392	50	117	.427	7	21	.333	16	21	.762	8	29	37	62	43	0	12	28	2	123	1.6	2.7	5.3
91-92–Hou.-Detroit	16	0	96	12	32	.375	3	8	.375	9	11	.818	1	7	8	10	12	0	3	8	0	36	0.5	0.6	2.3
Reg. Season Totals	871	352	18856	3079	6526	.472	203	611	.332	1412	1820	.776	526	927	1453	3141	1918	15	939	1561	99	7773	1.7	3.6	8.9
Playoff Totals	88	35	1570	259	584	.443	5	32	.156	108	155	.697	63	74	137	229	182	1	78	105	7	631	1.6	2.6	7.2

Henderson, Kevin Dwayne b. March 22, 1964 Ht. 6-4 Wt. 195 College: Cal State-Fullerton

SEASON–TEAM	G	GS	MIN	FGM	FGA	PCT	3FGM	3FGA	PCT	FTM	FTA	PCT	O-RB	D-RB	TOT	AST	PF	DQ	STL	TO	BLK	PTS	RPG	APG	PPG
86-87–Golden State	5	0	45	3	8	.375	0	0	–	2	2	1.000	1	2	3	11	9	0	1	4	0	8	0.6	2.2	1.6
87-88–G.S.-Clev.	17	2	190	21	53	.396	0	1	.000	15	26	.577	9	12	21	23	26	0	8	17	0	57	1.2	1.4	3.4
Reg. Season Totals	22	2	235	24	61	.393	0	1	.000	17	28	.607	10	14	24	34	35	0	9	21	0	65	1.1	1.5	3.0

Henderson, Milton Jr. (J.R.) b. October 30, 1976 Ht. 6-8 Wt. 233 College: UCLA

SEASON–TEAM	G	GS	MIN	FGM	FGA	PCT	3FGM	3FGA	PCT	FTM	FTA	PCT	O-RB	D-RB	TOT	AST	PF	DQ	STL	TO	BLK	PTS	RPG	APG	PPG
98-99–Vancouver	30	0	331	35	96	.365	2	5	.400	25	45	.556	20	27	47	22	29	1	9	18	4	97	1.6	0.7	3.2
Reg. Season Totals	30	0	331	35	96	.365	2	5	.400	25	45	.556	20	27	47	22	29	1	9	18	4	97	1.6	0.7	3.2

Henderson, Thomas Edward (Tom) b. January 26, 1952 Ht. 6-3 Wt. 190 College: San Jacinto (Texas) Coll. (J.C.); Hawaii

SEASON–TEAM	G	GS	MIN	FGM	FGA	PCT	3FGM	3FGA	PCT	FTM	FTA	PCT	O-RB	D-RB	TOT	AST	PF	DQ	STL	TO	BLK	PTS	RPG	APG	PPG
74-75–Atlanta	79	–	2131	367	893	.411	–	–	–	168	241	.697	51	161	212	314	149	0	105	–	7	902	2.7	4.0	11.4
75-76–Atlanta	81	–	2900	469	1136	.413	–	–	–	216	305	.708	58	207	265	374	195	1	137	–	10	1154	3.3	4.6	14.2
76-77–Atlanta-Wash.	87	–	2791	371	826	.449	–	–	–	233	313	.744	43	196	239	598	148	0	138	–	17	975	2.7	6.9	11.2
77-78–Washington	75	–	2315	339	784	.432	–	–	–	179	240	.746	66	127	193	406	131	0	93	195	15	857	2.6	5.4	11.4
78-79–Washington	70	–	2081	299	641	.466	–	–	–	156	195	.800	51	112	163	419	123	0	87	148	10	754	2.3	6.0	10.8
79-80–Houston	66	–	1551	154	323	.477	0	2	.000	56	77	.727	34	77	111	274	107	1	55	102	4	364	1.7	4.2	5.5
80-81–Houston	66	–	1411	137	332	.413	0	3	.000	78	95	.821	30	74	104	307	111	1	53	93	4	352	1.6	4.7	5.3
81-82–Houston	75	23	1721	183	403	.454	0	2	.000	105	150	.700	33	105	138	306	120	0	55	105	7	471	1.8	4.1	6.3
82-83–Houston	51	2	789	107	263	.407	0	2	.000	45	57	.789	18	51	69	138	57	0	37	50	2	259	1.4	2.7	5.1
Reg. Season Totals	650	25	17690	2426	5601	.433	0	9	.000	1236	1673	.739	384	1110	1494	3136	1141	3	760	693	76	6088	2.3	4.8	9.4
Playoff Totals	80	3	2364	270	650	.415	0	2	.000	161	214	.752	64	117	181	431	168	2	79	120	18	701	2.3	5.4	8.8

Hendrickson, Mark Allan b. June 23, 1974 Ht. 6-9 Wt. 220 College: Washington State

SEASON–TEAM	G	GS	MIN	FGM	FGA	PCT	3FGM	3FGA	PCT	FTM	FTA	PCT	O-RB	D-RB	TOT	AST	PF	DQ	STL	TO	BLK	PTS	RPG	APG	PPG
96-97–Philadelphia	29	1	301	32	77	.416	3	12	.250	18	26	.692	35	57	92	3	32	1	10	14	4	85	3.2	0.1	2.9
97-98–Sacramento	48	1	737	58	149	.389	0	5	.000	47	57	.825	33	110	143	41	60	0	26	31	9	163	3.0	0.9	3.4
98-99–New Jersey	22	6	399	39	88	.443	0	1	.000	42	50	.840	27	41	68	13	39	0	12	15	1	120	3.1	0.6	5.5
99-00–Clev.-N.J.	15	0	71	5	8	.625	0	0	–	3	4	.750	3	10	13	6	8	0	2	3	1	13	0.9	0.4	0.9
Reg. Season Totals	114	8	1508	134	322	.416	3	18	.167	110	137	.803	98	218	316	63	139	1	50	63	15	381	2.8	0.6	3.3

Hennessy, Lawrence E. (Larry) b. May 20, 1929 Ht. 6-3 Wt. 185 College: Villanova

SEASON–TEAM	G	GS	MIN	FGM	FGA	PCT	3FGM	3FGA	PCT	FTM	FTA	PCT	O-RB	D-RB	TOT	AST	PF	DQ	STL	TO	BLK	PTS	RPG	APG	PPG
55-56–Philadelphia	53	–	444	85	247	.344	–	–	–	26	32	.813	–	–	49	46	37	0	–	–	–	196	0.9	0.9	3.7
Reg. Season Totals	74	–	817	141	422	.334	–	–	–	49	64	.766	–	–	94	73	65	0	–	–	–	331	1.3	1.4	4.5
Playoff Totals	3	–	11	0	9	.000	–	–	–	0	0	–	–	–	1	2	1	0	–	–	–	0	0.3	0.7	0.0

Henriksen, Donald Anton (Don) b. October 10, 1929 Ht. 6-7 Wt. 225 College: California

SEASON–TEAM	G	GS	MIN	FGM	FGA	PCT	3FGM	3FGA	PCT	FTM	FTA	PCT	O-RB	D-RB	TOT	AST	PF	DQ	STL	TO	BLK	PTS	RPG	APG	PPG
52-53–Baltimore	68	–	2263	199	475	.419	–	–	–	176	281	.626	–	–	506	129	242	12	–	–	–	574	7.4	1.9	8.4
54-55–Balt.-Roch.	70	–	1664	139	406	.342	–	–	–	137	195	.703	–	–	484	111	190	2	–	–	–	415	6.9	1.6	5.9
Reg. Season Totals	138	–	3927	338	881	.384	–	–	–	313	476	.658	–	–	990	240	432	14	–	–	–	989	7.2	1.7	7.2
Playoff Totals	5	–	164	13	27	.481	–	–	–	12	19	.632	–	–	40	11	16	1	–	–	–	38	8.0	2.2	7.6

Henry, Albert J. Jr. (Al, The Tree) b. February 9, 1949 Ht. 6-9 Wt. 190 College: Wisconsin

SEASON–TEAM	G	GS	MIN	FGM	FGA	PCT	3FGM	3FGA	PCT	FTM	FTA	PCT	O-RB	D-RB	TOT	AST	PF	DQ	STL	TO	BLK	PTS	RPG	APG	PPG
70-71–Philadelphia	6	–	26	1	6	.167	–	–	–	5	7	.714	–	–	11	0	1	0	–	–	–	7	1.8	0.0	1.2
71-72–Philadelphia	43	–	421	68	156	.436	–	–	–	51	73	.699	–	–	137	8	42	0	–	–	–	187	3.2	0.2	4.3
Reg. Season Totals	49	–	447	69	162	.426	–	–	–	56	80	.700	–	–	148	8	43	0	–	–	–	194	3.0	0.2	4.0

Henry, Carl J. b. August 16, 1960 Ht. 6-6 Wt. 205 College: Oklahoma City; Kansas

SEASON–TEAM	G	GS	MIN	FGM	FGA	PCT	3FGM	3FGA	PCT	FTM	FTA	PCT	O-RB	D-RB	TOT	AST	PF	DQ	STL	TO	BLK	PTS	RPG	APG	PPG
85-86–Sacramento	28	0	149	31	67	.463	4	10	.400	12	17	.706	8	11	19	4	11	0	5	9	0	78	0.7	0.1	2.8
Reg. Season Totals	28	0	149	31	67	.463	4	10	.400	12	17	.706	8	11	19	4	11	0	5	9	0	78	0.7	0.1	2.8
Playoff Totals	1	0	2	1	1	1.000	1	1	1.000	0	0	–	0	0	0	–	0	0	0	0	0	3	0.0	0.0	3.0

Henry, Conner b. July 21, 1963 Ht. 6-7 Wt. 195 College: California-Santa Barbara

SEASON–TEAM	G	GS	MIN	FGM	FGA	PCT	3FGM	3FGA	PCT	FTM	FTA	PCT	O-RB	D-RB	TOT	AST	PF	DQ	STL	TO	BLK	PTS	RPG	APG	PPG
86-87–Houston-Boston	54	0	323	46	136	.338	13	42	.310	17	27	.630	7	27	34	35	34	0	9	26	1	122	0.6	0.6	2.3
87-88–Bos.-Milw.-Sac.	39	2	433	62	150	.413	20	45	.444	39	47	.830	13	36	49	67	37	0	12	39	5	183	1.3	1.7	4.7
Reg. Season Totals	93	2	756	108	286	.378	33	87	.379	56	74	.757	20	63	83	102	71	0	21	65	6	305	0.9	1.1	3.3
Playoff Totals	11	0	35	8	16	.500	1	5	.200	5	10	.500	3	3	6	–	3	0	0	4	0	22	0.5	0.0	2.0

Henry, Herman (Skeeter) b. December 8, 1967 Ht. 6-7 Wt. 190 College: Oklahoma

SEASON–TEAM	G	GS	MIN	FGM	FGA	PCT	3FGM	3FGA	PCT	FTM	FTA	PCT	O-RB	D-RB	TOT	AST	PF	DQ	STL	TO	BLK	PTS	RPG	APG	PPG
93-94–Phoenix	4	0	15	1	5	.200	0	2	.000	2	4	.500	0	2	2	4	1	0	0	1	0	4	0.5	1.0	1.0
Reg. Season Totals	4	0	15	1	5	.200	0	2	.000	2	4	.500	0	2	2	4	1	0	0	1	0	4	0.5	1.0	1.0
Playoff Totals	3	0	16	1	6	.167	0	2	.000	0	0	–	1	2	3	3	1	0	0	1	0	2	1.0	1.0	0.7

Henry, William Gambrell (Bill, Big Bill) b. December 27, 1924 d. December 1985 Ht. 6-9 Wt. 215 College: Rice

SEASON–TEAM	G	GS	MIN	FGM	FGA	PCT	3FGM	3FGA	PCT	FTM	FTA	PCT	O-RB	D-RB	TOT	AST	PF	DQ	STL	TO	BLK	PTS	RPG	APG	PPG
48-49–Fort Wayne	32	–	–	96	300	.320	–	–	–	125	203	.616	–	–	–	55	110	–	–	–	–	317	–	1.7	9.9
49-50–FtWayne-Tri-Cit	63	–	–	89	278	.320	–	–	–	118	176	.670	–	–	–	48	122	–	–	–	–	296	–	0.8	4.7
Reg. Season Totals	95	–	–	185	578	.320	–	–	–	243	379	.641	–	–	–	103	232	–	–	–	–	613	–	1.1	6.5
Playoff Totals	3	–	–	2	17	.118	–	–	–	5	9	.556	–	–	–	5	14	1	–	–	–	9	–	1.7	3.0

Henson, Steven Michael (Steve) b. February 2, 1968 Ht. 6-1 Wt. 180 College: Kansas State

SEASON–TEAM	G	GS	MIN	FGM	FGA	PCT	3FGM	3FGA	PCT	FTM	FTA	PCT	O-RB	D-RB	TOT	AST	PF	DQ	STL	TO	BLK	PTS	RPG	APG	PPG
90-91–Milwaukee	68	0	690	79	189	.418	18	54	.333	38	42	.905	14	37	51	131	83	0	32	43	0	214	0.8	1.9	3.1
91-92–Milwaukee	50	1	386	52	144	.361	23	48	.479	23	29	.793	17	24	41	82	50	0	15	40	1	150	0.8	1.6	3.0
92-93–Atlanta	53	2	719	71	182	.390	37	80	.463	34	40	.850	12	43	55	155	85	0	30	52	1	213	1.0	2.9	4.0
93-94–Charlotte	3	0	17	1	2	.500	1	1	1.000	0	0	–	0	1	1	5	3	0	0	1	0	3	0.3	1.7	1.0
94-95–Portland	37	0	380	37	86	.430	23	52	.442	22	25	.880	3	23	26	85	52	1	9	30	0	119	0.7	2.3	3.2
97-98–Detroit	23	0	65	13	26	.500	3	8	.375	7	7	1.000	0	2	2	4	9	0	1	6	0	36	0.1	0.2	1.6
98-99–Detroit	4	0	25	1	2	.500	0	0	–	2	2	1.000	0	0	0	3	1	0	1	3	0	4	0.0	0.8	1.0
Reg. Season Totals	238	3	2282	254	631	.403	105	243	.432	126	145	.869	46	130	176	465	283	1	88	175	2	739	0.7	2.0	3.1
Playoff Totals	6	0	87	9	21	.429	4	8	.500	3	4	.750	1	6	7	8	7	0	5	8	0	25	1.2	1.3	4.2

Hentz, Charles (Charlie, Helicopter) b. September 13, 1947 Ht. 6-6 Wt. 235 College: Arkansas-Pine Bluff

SEASON–TEAM	G	GS	MIN	FGM	FGA	PCT	3FGM	3FGA	PCT	FTM	FTA	PCT	O-RB	D-RB	TOT	AST	PF	DQ	STL	TO	BLK	PTS	RPG	APG	PPG
70-71–Pittsburgh (A)	57	–	1075	142	303	.469	0	4	.000	57	98	.582	–	–	386	31	114	–	–	–	–	341	6.8	0.5	6.0
Reg. ABA Totals	57	–	1075	142	303	.469	0	4	.000	57	98	.582	–	–	386	31	114	–	–	–	–	341	6.8	0.5	6.0

Herman, William R. (Bill) b. May 17, 1924 Ht. 6-3 Wt. 170 College: Mount Union

SEASON–TEAM	G	GS	MIN	FGM	FGA	PCT	3FGM	3FGA	PCT	FTM	FTA	PCT	O-RB	D-RB	TOT	AST	PF	DQ	STL	TO	BLK	PTS	RPG	APG	PPG
49-50–Denver	13	–	–	25	65	.385	–	–	–	6	11	.545	–	–	–	15	13	–	–	–	–	56	–	1.2	4.3
Reg. Season Totals	13	–	–	25	65	.385	–	–	–	6	11	.545	–	–	–	15	13	–	–	–	–	56	–	1.2	4.3

Hermsen, Clarence Henry (Kleggie) b. March 12, 1923 d. March 2, 1994 Ht. 6-9 Wt. 235 College: Minnesota

SEASON–TEAM	G	GS	MIN	FGM	FGA	PCT	3FGM	3FGA	PCT	FTM	FTA	PCT	O-RB	D-RB	TOT	AST	PF	DQ	STL	TO	BLK	PTS	RPG	APG	PPG
43-44–Sheboygan (N)	12	–	–	3	–	–	–	–	–	5	–	–	–	–	–	–	–	–	–	–	–	11	–	–	0.9
45-46–Sheboygan (N)	21	–	–	19	–	–	–	–	–	17	–	–	–	–	–	–	–	–	–	–	–	55	–	–	2.6
46-47–Clev.-Toronto	32	–	–	113	394	.287	–	–	–	71	112	.634	–	–	–	25	86	–	–	–	–	297	–	0.8	9.3
47-48–Baltimore	48	–	–	212	765	.277	–	–	–	151	227	.665	–	–	–	48	154	–	–	–	–	575	–	1.0	12.0
48-49–Washington	60	–	–	248	794	.312	–	–	–	212	311	.682	–	–	–	99	257	–	–	–	–	708	–	1.7	11.8
49-50–Chicago	67	–	–	196	615	.319	–	–	–	153	247	.619	–	–	–	98	267	–	–	–	–	545	–	1.5	8.1
50-51–Tri-Cit-Boston	71	–	–	189	644	.293	–	–	–	155	237	.654	–	–	448	92	261	8	–	–	–	533	6.3	1.3	7.5
52-53–Boston-Ind.	10	–	62	4	31	.129	–	–	–	3	5	.600	–	–	19	4	18	0	–	–	–	11	1.9	0.4	1.1
Reg. NBA Totals	288	–	62	962	3243	.297	–	–	–	745	1139	.654	–	–	467	366	1043	8	–	–	–	2669	5.8	1.3	9.3
Reg. NBL Totals	33	–	–	22	–	–	–	–	–	22	0	–	–	–	–	–	–	–	–	–	–	66	–	–	2.0
NBA Playoff Totals	26	–	0	86	481	.264	–	–	–	104	157	.694	–	–	3	42	130	6	–	–	–	276	1.5	1.1	10.6
NBL Playoff Totals	5	–	–	4	–	–	–	–	–	5	8	.000	–	–	–	–	5	–	–	–	–	13	–	–	2.6

Herren, Chris Albert b. September 27, 1975 Ht. 6-2 Wt. 190 College: Fresno State

SEASON–TEAM	G	GS	MIN	FGM	FGA	PCT	3FGM	3FGA	PCT	FTM	FTA	PCT	O-RB	D-RB	TOT	AST	PF	DQ	STL	TO	BLK	PTS	RPG	APG	PPG
99-00–Denver	45	1	597	45	124	.363	24	67	.358	27	40	.675	12	40	52	111	74	0	15	42	2	141	1.2	2.5	3.1
Reg. Season Totals	45	1	597	45	124	.363	24	67	.358	27	40	.675	12	40	52	111	74	0	15	42	2	141	1.2	2.5	3.1

Herrera, Carl Victor b. December 14, 1966 Ht. 6-9 Wt. 225 College: Jacksonville College; Houston

SEASON–TEAM	G	GS	MIN	FGM	FGA	PCT	3FGM	3FGA	PCT	FTM	FTA	PCT	O-RB	D-RB	TOT	AST	PF	DQ	STL	TO	BLK	PTS	RPG	APG	PPG
91-92–Houston	43	7	566	83	161	.516	0	1	.000	25	44	.568	33	66	99	27	60	0	16	37	25	191	2.3	0.6	4.4
92-93–Houston	81	12	1800	240	444	.541	0	2	.000	125	176	.710	148	306	454	61	190	1	47	92	35	605	5.6	0.8	7.5
93-94–Houston	75	0	1292	142	310	.458	0	0	–	69	97	.711	101	184	285	37	159	0	32	69	26	353	3.8	0.5	4.7
94-95–Houston	61	26	1331	171	327	.523	0	2	.000	73	117	.624	98	180	278	44	136	0	40	71	38	415	4.6	0.7	6.8
95-96–San Antonio	44	6	393	40	97	.412	0	1	.000	5	17	.294	30	51	81	16	61	0	9	29	8	85	1.8	0.4	1.9
96-97–San Antonio	75	58	1837	257	593	.433	2	6	.333	81	118	.686	118	222	340	50	217	3	62	95	53	597	4.5	0.7	8.0
97-98–San Antonio	58	1	516	76	175	.434	0	1	.000	18	44	.409	24	67	91	22	71	1	19	38	12	170	1.6	0.4	2.9
98-99–Vanc.-Denver	28	0	307	30	76	.395	0	1	.000	5	11	.455	25	37	62	4	41	0	12	16	7	65	2.2	0.1	2.3
Reg. Season Totals	465	110	8042	1039	2183	.476	2	14	.143	401	624	.643	577	1113	1690	261	935	5	237	447	204	2481	3.6	0.6	5.3
Playoff Totals	41	0	502	55	122	.451	0	2	.000	27	38	.711	32	66	98	13	84	2	10	22	6	137	2.4	0.3	3.3

Herron, Keith Orlando b. June 14, 1956 Ht. 6-6 Wt. 195 College: Villanova

SEASON–TEAM	G	GS	MIN	FGM	FGA	PCT	3FGM	3FGA	PCT	FTM	FTA	PCT	O-RB	D-RB	TOT	AST	PF	DQ	STL	TO	BLK	PTS	RPG	APG	PPG
78-79–Atlanta	14	–	81	14	48	.292	–	–	–	12	13	.923	4	6	10	3	11	0	6	5	2	40	0.7	0.2	2.9
80-81–Detroit	80	–	2270	432	954	.453	2	11	.182	228	267	.854	98	113	211	148	154	1	91	153	26	1094	2.6	1.9	13.7
81-82–Cleveland	30	0	269	39	106	.368	0	1	.000	7	8	.875	10	11	21	23	25	0	8	12	2	85	0.7	0.8	2.8
Reg. Season Totals	124	0	2620	485	1108	.438	2	12	.167	247	288	.858	112	130	242	174	190	1	105	170	30	1219	2.0	1.4	9.8

Hertzberg, Sidney (Sonny) b. July 29, 1922 Ht. 5-10 Wt. 185 College: C.C.NY

SEASON–TEAM	G	GS	MIN	FGM	FGA	PCT	3FGM	3FGA	PCT	FTM	FTA	PCT	O-RB	D-RB	TOT	AST	PF	DQ	STL	TO	BLK	PTS	RPG	APG	PPG
46-47–New York	59	–	–	201	695	.289	–	–	–	113	149	.758	–	–	–	37	109	–	–	–	–	515	–	0.6	8.7
47-48–N.Y.-Wash.	41	–	–	110	414	.266	–	–	–	58	73	.795	–	–	–	23	61	–	–	–	–	278	–	0.6	6.8
48-49–Washington	60	–	–	154	541	.285	–	–	–	134	164	.817	–	–	–	114	140	–	–	–	–	442	–	1.9	7.4
49-50–Boston	68	–	–	275	865	.318	–	–	–	143	191	.749	–	–	–	200	153	–	–	–	–	693	–	2.9	10.2
50-51–Boston	65	–	–	206	651	.316	–	–	–	223	270	.826	–	–	260	244	156	4	–	–	–	635	4.0	3.8	9.8
Reg. Season Totals	293	–	–	946	3166	.299	–	–	–	671	847	.792	–	–	260	618	619	4	–	–	–	2563	4.0	2.1	8.7
Playoff Totals	18	–	–	57	278	.313	–	–	–	50	65	.846	–	–	2	55	62	1	–	–	–	164	1.0	2.1	9.1

Hester, Dan W. b. November 8, 1948 Ht. 6-8 Wt. 220 College: Murray State; Louisiana State

SEASON–TEAM	G	GS	MIN	FGM	FGA	PCT	3FGM	3FGA	PCT	FTM	FTA	PCT	O-RB	D-RB	TOT	AST	PF	DQ	STL	TO	BLK	PTS	RPG	APG	PPG
70-71–Denver-Ken. (A)	42	–	555	97	245	.396	5	12	.417	49	60	.817	–	–	234	35	82	–	–	–	–	248	5.6	0.8	5.9
Reg. ABA Totals	42	–	555	97	245	.396	5	12	.417	49	60	.817	–	–	234	35	82	–	–	–	–	248	5.6	0.8	5.9
ABA Playoff Totals	7	–	42	4	14	.286	0	0	–	8	9	.889	–	–	13	1	9	–	–	–	–	16	1.9	0.1	2.3

Hetzel, Fred W. b. July 21, 1942 Ht. 6-8 Wt. 230 College: Davidson

SEASON–TEAM	G	GS	MIN	FGM	FGA	PCT	3FGM	3FGA	PCT	FTM	FTA	PCT	O-RB	D-RB	TOT	AST	PF	DQ	STL	TO	BLK	PTS	RPG	APG	PPG
65-66–San Francisco	56	–	722	160	401	.399	–	–	–	63	92	.685	–	–	290	27	121	2	–	–	–	383	5.2	0.5	6.8
66-67–San Francisco	77	–	2123	373	932	.400	–	–	–	192	237	.810	–	–	639	111	228	3	–	–	–	938	8.3	1.4	12.2
67-68–San Francisco	77	–	2394	533	1287	.414	–	–	–	395	474	.833	–	–	546	131	262	7	–	–	–	1461	7.1	1.7	19.0
68-69–Milw.-Cin.	84	–	2276	456	1047	.436	–	–	–	299	357	.838	–	–	613	112	287	9	–	–	–	1211	7.3	1.3	14.4
69-70–Philadelphia	63	–	757	156	323	.483	–	–	–	71	85	.835	–	–	207	44	110	3	–	–	–	383	3.3	0.7	6.1
70-71–Los Angeles	59	–	613	111	256	.434	–	–	–	60	77	.779	–	–	149	37	99	3	–	–	–	282	2.5	0.6	4.8
Reg. Season Totals	416	–	8885	1789	4246	.421	–	–	–	1080	1322	.817	–	–	2444	462	1107	27	–	–	–	4658	5.9	1.1	11.2
Playoff Totals	35	–	742	138	323	.427	–	–	–	83	102	.814	–	–	184	44	95	3	–	–	–	359	5.3	1.3	10.3

Hewitt, William Severlyn (Bill) b. August 8, 1944 Ht. 6-7 Wt. 210 College: USC

SEASON–TEAM	G	GS	MIN	FGM	FGA	PCT	3FGM	3FGA	PCT	FTM	FTA	PCT	O-RB	D-RB	TOT	AST	PF	DQ	STL	TO	BLK	PTS	RPG	APG	PPG
68-69–Los Angeles	75	–	1455	239	528	.453	–	–	–	61	106	.575	–	–	332	76	139	1	–	–	–	539	4.4	1.0	7.2
69-70–L.A.-Detroit	65	–	1279	110	298	.369	–	–	–	54	94	.574	–	–	354	64	130	1	–	–	–	274	5.4	1.0	4.2
70-71–Detroit	62	–	1725	203	435	.467	–	–	–	69	120	.575	–	–	454	124	189	5	–	–	–	475	7.3	2.0	7.7
71-72–Detroit	68	–	1203	131	277	.473	–	–	–	41	82	.500	–	–	370	71	134	1	–	–	–	303	5.4	1.0	4.5
72-73–Buffalo	73	–	1332	152	364	.418	–	–	–	41	74	.554	–	–	368	110	154	3	–	–	–	345	5.0	1.5	4.7
74-75–Chicago	18	–	467	56	129	.434	–	–	–	14	23	.609	30	86	116	24	46	1	9	–	10	126	6.4	1.3	7.0
Reg. Season Totals	361	–	7461	891	2031	.439	–	–	–	280	499	.561	30	86	1994	469	792	12	9	–	10	2062	5.5	1.3	5.7
Playoff Totals	15	–	412	61	151	.404	–	–	–	18	29	.621	0	0	78	17	40	0	0	–	0	140	5.2	1.1	9.3

Hewson, John G. (Jack) b. September 7, 1924 Ht. 6-6 Wt. 195 College: Bucknell; Muhlenberg; Temple

SEASON–TEAM	G	GS	MIN	FGM	FGA	PCT	3FGM	3FGA	PCT	FTM	FTA	PCT	O-RB	D-RB	TOT	AST	PF	DQ	STL	TO	BLK	PTS	RPG	APG	PPG
47-48–Boston	24	–	–	22	89	.247	–	–	–	21	30	.700	–	–	–	1	39	–	–	–	–	65	–	0.0	2.7
Reg. Season Totals	24	–	–	22	89	.247	–	–	–	21	30	.700	–	–	–	1	39	–	–	–	–	65	–	0.0	2.7

Heyman, Arthur Bruce (Art) b. June 24, 1941 Ht. 6-5 Wt. 205 College: Duke

SEASON–TEAM	G	GS	MIN	FGM	FGA	PCT	3FGM	3FGA	PCT	FTM	FTA	PCT	O-RB	D-RB	TOT	AST	PF	DQ	STL	TO	BLK	PTS	RPG	APG	PPG
63-64–New York	75	–	2236	432	1003	.431	–	–	–	289	422	.685	–	–	298	256	229	2	–	–	–	1153	4.0	3.4	15.4
64-65–New York	55	–	663	114	267	.427	–	–	–	88	132	.667	–	–	99	79	96	0	–	–	–	316	1.8	1.4	5.7
65-66–Cin.-Phil.	17	–	120	18	52	.346	–	–	–	14	22	.636	–	–	17	11	23	0	–	–	–	50	1.0	0.6	2.9
67-68–N.J.-Pitt. (A)	73	–	2555	457	1058	.432	35	134	.261	400	547	.731	–	–	496	276	188	0	–	239	–	1349	6.8	3.8	18.5
68-69–Minnesota (A)	71	–	2362	350	832	.421	37	118	.314	285	409	.697	–	–	494	217	195	2	–	163	–	1022	7.0	3.1	14.4
69-70–Pitt.-Miami (A)	19	–	310	47	106	.443	0	4	.000	46	65	.708	–	–	57	20	32	1	–	–	–	140	3.0	1.1	7.4
Reg. NBA Totals	147	–	3019	564	1322	.427	–	–	–	391	576	.679	–	–	414	346	348	2	–	–	–	1519	2.8	2.4	10.3
Reg. ABA Totals	163	–	5227	854	1996	.428	72	256	.281	731	1021	.716	–	–	1047	513	415	3	–	402	–	2511	6.4	3.1	15.4
ABA Playoff Totals	22	–	828	135	286	.472	21	55	.382	126	180	.700	–	–	158	78	68	1	–	53	–	417	7.2	3.5	19.0

Hickey, Matthew (Nat) b. January 30, 1902 d. September 1979 Ht. 5-11 Wt. 180 College: None

SEASON–TEAM	G	GS	MIN	FGM	FGA	PCT	3FGM	3FGA	PCT	FTM	FTA	PCT	O-RB	D-RB	TOT	AST	PF	DQ	STL	TO	BLK	PTS	RPG	APG	PPG
44-45–Pittsburgh (N)	2	–	–	3	–	–	–	–	–	2	–	–	–	–	–	–	–	–	–	–	–	8	–	–	4.0
45-46–Indianapolis (N)	13	–	–	30	–	–	–	–	–	13	–	–	–	–	–	–	–	–	–	–	–	73	–	–	5.6
46-47–Tri-Cities (N)	8	–	–	9	–	–	–	–	–	6	12	.500	–	–	–	–	–	–	–	–	–	24	–	–	3.0
47-48–Tri-Cities (N)	3	–	–	1	–	–	–	–	–	1	1	1.000	–	–	–	–	–	–	–	–	–	3	–	–	1.0
47-48–Providence	1	–	–	0	6	.000	–	–	–	2	3	.667	–	–	–	0	5	–	–	–	–	2	–	0.0	2.0
Reg. NBA Totals	1	–	–	0	6	.000	–	–	–	2	3	.667	–	–	–	0	5	–	–	–	–	2	–	0.0	2.0
Reg. NBL Totals	26	–	–	43	–	–	–	–	–	22	13	.538	–	–	–	–	–	–	–	–	–	108	–	–	4.2

Hicks, Phillip James (Phil) b. January 31, 1953 Ht. 6-7 Wt. 205 College: Tulane

SEASON–TEAM	G	GS	MIN	FGM	FGA	PCT	3FGM	3FGA	PCT	FTM	FTA	PCT	O-RB	D-RB	TOT	AST	PF	DQ	STL	TO	BLK	PTS	RPG	APG	PPG
76-77–Hou.-Chi.	37	–	262	41	89	.461	–	–	–	11	13	.846	26	40	66	24	37	0	8	–	0	93	1.8	0.6	2.5
78-79–Denver	20	–	128	18	43	.419	–	–	–	3	5	.600	13	15	28	8	20	0	5	13	0	39	1.4	0.4	2.0
Reg. Season Totals	57	–	390	59	132	.447	–	–	–	14	18	.778	39	55	94	32	57	0	13	13	0	132	1.6	0.6	2.3
Playoff Totals	1	–	4	0	2	.000	–	–	–	0	0	–	1	2	3	–	1	0	0	–	0	0	3.0	0.0	0.0

Higgins, Earle Brent (Sticks) b. December 30, 1946 Ht. 6-8 Wt. 200 College: Casper (Wyo.) Coll. (J.C.); Eastern Michigan

SEASON–TEAM	G	GS	MIN	FGM	FGA	PCT	3FGM	3FGA	PCT	FTM	FTA	PCT	O-RB	D-RB	TOT	AST	PF	DQ	STL	TO	BLK	PTS	RPG	APG	PPG
70-71–Indiana (A)	53	–	467	104	223	.466	3	17	.176	20	30	.667	–	–	128	35	109	–	–	–	–	231	2.4	0.7	4.4
Reg. ABA Totals	53	–	467	104	223	.466	3	17	.176	20	30	.667	–	–	128	35	109	–	–	–	–	231	2.4	0.7	4.4
ABA Playoff Totals	5	–	31	6	20	.300	0	2	.000	6	7	.857	–	–	13	2	5	–	–	–	–	18	2.6	0.4	3.6

Higgins, Michael S. (Mike) b. February 17, 1967 Ht. 6-9 Wt. 220 College: Northern Colorado

SEASON–TEAM	G	GS	MIN	FGM	FGA	PCT	3FGM	3FGA	PCT	FTM	FTA	PCT	O-RB	D-RB	TOT	AST	PF	DQ	STL	TO	BLK	PTS	RPG	APG	PPG
89-90–L.A.L-Den.	11	0	50	3	8	.375	0	0	–	8	10	.800	2	2	4	3	5	0	2	1	2	14	0.4	0.3	1.3
90-91–Sacramento	7	0	61	6	10	.600	0	0	–	4	7	.571	4	1	5	2	16	1	0	4	2	16	0.7	0.3	2.3
Reg. Season Totals	18	0	111	9	18	.500	0	0	–	12	17	.706	6	3	9	5	21	1	2	5	4	30	0.5	0.3	1.7

Higgins, Roderick Dwayne (Rod) b. January 31, 1960 Ht. 6-7 Wt. 217 College: Fresno State

SEASON–TEAM	G	GS	MIN	FGM	FGA	PCT	3FGM	3FGA	PCT	FTM	FTA	PCT	O-RB	D-RB	TOT	AST	PF	DQ	STL	TO	BLK	PTS	RPG	APG	PPG
82-83–Chicago	82	42	2196	313	698	.448	13	41	.317	209	264	.792	159	207	366	175	248	3	66	127	65	848	4.5	2.1	10.3
83-84–Chicago	78	6	1577	193	432	.447	1	22	.045	113	156	.724	87	119	206	116	161	0	49	76	29	500	2.6	1.5	6.4
84-85–Chicago	68	5	942	119	270	.441	10	37	.270	60	90	.667	55	92	147	73	91	0	21	49	13	308	2.2	1.1	4.5
85-86–Sea.-S.A.-N.J.-Chi.	30	0	332	39	106	.368	1	9	.111	19	27	.704	14	37	51	24	49	0	9	13	11	98	1.7	0.8	3.3
86-87–Golden State	73	28	1497	214	412	.519	3	17	.176	200	240	.833	72	165	237	96	145	0	40	76	21	631	3.2	1.3	8.6
87-88–Golden State	68	67	2188	381	725	.526	19	39	.487	273	322	.848	94	199	293	188	188	2	70	111	31	1054	4.3	2.8	15.5
88-89–Golden State	81	1	1887	301	633	.476	66	168	.393	188	229	.821	111	265	376	160	172	2	39	76	42	856	4.6	2.0	10.6
89-90–Golden State	82	22	1993	304	632	.481	67	193	.347	234	285	.821	120	302	422	129	184	0	47	93	53	909	5.1	1.6	11.1
90-91–Golden State	82	9	2024	259	559	.463	73	220	.332	185	226	.819	109	245	354	113	198	2	52	65	37	776	4.3	1.4	9.5
91-92–Golden State	25	6	535	87	211	.412	33	95	.347	48	59	.814	30	55	85	22	75	2	15	15	13	255	3.4	0.9	10.2
92-93–Sacramento	69	4	1425	199	483	.412	43	133	.323	130	151	.861	66	127	193	119	141	0	51	63	29	571	2.8	1.7	8.3
93-94–Cleveland	36	11	547	71	163	.436	22	50	.440	31	42	.738	25	57	82	36	53	1	25	21	14	195	2.3	1.0	5.4
94-95–Golden State	5	2	46	3	12	.250	1	6	.167	3	4	.750	4	3	7	3	7	0	1	1	1	10	1.4	0.6	2.0
Reg. Season Totals	779	203	17189	2483	5336	.465	352	1030	.342	1693	2095	.808	946	1873	2819	1254	1712	12	485	786	359	7011	3.6	1.6	9.0
Playoff Totals	33	22	733	90	205	.439	21	71	.296	61	75	.813	39	74	113	55	78	0	28	23	22	262	3.4	1.7	7.9

Higgins, Sean Marielle (The Dean) b. December 30, 1968 Ht. 6-9 Wt. 215 College: Michigan

SEASON–TEAM	G	GS	MIN	FGM	FGA	PCT	3FGM	3FGA	PCT	FTM	FTA	PCT	O-RB	D-RB	TOT	AST	PF	DQ	STL	TO	BLK	PTS	RPG	APG	PPG
90-91–San Antonio	50	0	464	97	212	.458	3	19	.158	28	33	.848	18	45	63	35	53	0	8	49	1	225	1.3	0.7	4.5
91-92–S.A.-Orlando	38	12	616	127	277	.458	6	25	.240	31	36	.861	29	73	102	41	58	0	16	41	6	291	2.7	1.1	7.7
92-93–Golden State	29	4	591	96	215	.447	13	37	.351	35	47	.745	23	45	68	66	54	0	13	64	5	240	2.3	2.3	8.3
94-95–New Jersey	57	7	735	105	273	.385	23	78	.295	35	40	.875	25	52	77	29	93	1	10	35	9	268	1.4	0.5	4.7
95-96–Philadelphia	44	4	916	134	323	.415	48	129	.372	35	37	.946	20	72	92	55	90	1	24	49	11	351	2.1	1.3	8.0
97-98–Portland	2	0	12	0	5	.000	0	2	.000	0	0	–	0	0	0	0	3	0	2	1	0	0	0.0	0.0	0.0
Reg. Season Totals	220	27	3334	559	1305	.428	93	290	.321	164	193	.850	115	287	402	226	351	2	73	239	32	1375	1.8	1.0	6.3
Playoff Totals	3	0	13	0	2	.000	0	0	–	0	0	–	0	0	0	1	1	0	0	0	0	0	0.0	0.3	0.0

Higgins, William (Bill) b. December 15, 1952 Ht. 6-2 Wt. 185 College: Ashland

SEASON–TEAM	G	GS	MIN	FGM	FGA	PCT	3FGM	3FGA	PCT	FTM	FTA	PCT	O-RB	D-RB	TOT	AST	PF	DQ	STL	TO	BLK	PTS	RPG	APG	PPG
74-75–Virginia (A)	15	–	348	61	139	.439	1	5	.200	15	23	.652	5	16	21	32	41	–	8	40	1	138	1.4	2.1	9.2
Reg. ABA Totals	15	–	348	61	139	.439	1	5	.200	15	23	.652	5	16	21	32	41	–	8	40	1	138	1.4	2.1	9.2

Higgs, Kenneth Lee Jr. (Kenny) b. January 31, 1955 Ht. 6-0 Wt. 180 College: Louisiana State

SEASON–TEAM	G	GS	MIN	FGM	FGA	PCT	3FGM	3FGA	PCT	FTM	FTA	PCT	O-RB	D-RB	TOT	AST	PF	DQ	STL	TO	BLK	PTS	RPG	APG	PPG
78-79–Cleveland	68	–	1050	127	279	.455	–	–	–	85	111	.766	18	84	102	141	176	2	66	47	11	339	1.5	2.1	5.0
80-81–Denver	72	–	1689	209	474	.441	4	34	.118	140	172	.814	24	121	145	408	243	5	101	166	6	562	2.0	5.7	7.8
81-82–Denver	76	49	1696	202	468	.432	4	21	.190	161	197	.817	23	121	144	395	263	8	72	156	6	569	1.9	5.2	7.5
Reg. Season Totals	216	49	4435	538	1221	.441	8	55	.145	386	480	.804	65	326	391	944	682	15	239	369	23	1470	1.8	4.4	6.8
Playoff Totals	3	0	54	8	21	.381	0	2	.000	7	12	.583	1	2	3	6	12	0	3	5	0	23	1.0	2.0	7.7

High, Johnny Harold (Sky) b. April 25, 1957 d. June 13, 1987 Ht. 6-3 Wt. 185 College: Lawson State C.C. AL; Nevada-Reno

SEASON–TEAM	G	GS	MIN	FGM	FGA	PCT	3FGM	3FGA	PCT	FTM	FTA	PCT	O-RB	D-RB	TOT	AST	PF	DQ	STL	TO	BLK	PTS	RPG	APG	PPG
79-80–Phoenix	82	–	1121	144	323	.446	1	7	.143	120	178	.674	69	104	173	119	172	1	71	123	15	409	2.1	1.5	5.0
80-81–Phoenix	81	–	1750	246	576	.427	2	24	.083	183	264	.693	89	139	228	202	251	2	129	188	26	677	2.8	2.5	8.4
82-83–Phoenix	82	2	1155	100	217	.461	1	5	.200	63	136	.463	45	105	150	153	205	0	85	106	34	264	1.8	1.9	3.2
83-84–Phoenix	29	9	512	18	52	.346	0	2	.000	10	29	.345	16	50	66	51	84	1	40	38	11	46	2.3	1.8	1.6
Reg. Season Totals	274	11	4538	508	1168	.435	4	38	.105	376	607	.619	219	398	617	525	712	4	325	455	86	1396	2.3	1.9	5.1
Playoff Totals	18	0	282	31	75	.413	0	3	.000	17	32	.531	26	28	54	32	51	0	15	14	5	79	3.0	1.8	4.4

Hightower, Wayne A. b. January 14, 1940 Ht. 6-8 Wt. 200 College: Kansas

SEASON–TEAM	G	GS	MIN	FGM	FGA	PCT	3FGM	3FGA	PCT	FTM	FTA	PCT	O-RB	D-RB	TOT	AST	PF	DQ	STL	TO	BLK	PTS	RPG	APG	PPG
62-63–San Francisco	66	–	1387	192	543	.354	–	–	–	105	157	.669	–	–	354	51	181	5	–	–	–	489	5.4	0.8	7.4
63-64–San Francisco	79	–	2536	393	1022	.385	–	–	–	260	329	.790	–	–	566	133	269	7	–	–	–	1046	7.2	1.7	13.2
64-65–S.F.-Balt.	75	–	1547	196	570	.344	–	–	–	195	254	.768	–	–	420	54	204	2	–	–	–	587	5.6	0.7	7.8
65-66–Baltimore	24	–	460	63	186	.339	–	–	–	57	78	.731	–	–	131	35	61	2	–	–	–	183	5.5	1.5	7.6
66-67–Balt.-Detroit	72	–	1310	195	567	.344	–	–	–	153	210	.729	–	–	405	64	190	6	–	–	–	543	5.6	0.9	7.5
67-68–Denver (A)	74	–	2459	431	1126	.383	0	6	.000	420	543	.773	–	–	536	143	237	5	–	165	–	1282	7.2	1.9	17.3
68-69–Denver (A)	67	–	2318	311	762	.408	0	2	.000	311	426	.730	–	–	641	203	241	5	–	176	–	933	9.6	3.0	13.9
69-70–Los Angeles (A)	27	–	961	180	403	.447	0	2	.000	129	170	.759	–	–	255	71	101	4	–	–	–	489	9.4	2.6	18.1
70-71–Utah-Texas (A)	68	–	2355	339	848	.400	0	3	.000	268	361	.742	–	–	615	194	204	–	–	–	–	946	9.0	2.9	13.9
71-72–Carolina (A)	13	–	141	20	64	.313	0	2	.000	30	36	.833	–	–	43	11	19	–	–	12	–	70	3.3	0.8	5.4
Reg. NBA Totals	316	–	7240	1039	2888	.360	–	–	–	770	1028	.749	–	–	1876	337	905	22	–	–	–	2848	5.9	1.1	9.0
Reg. ABA Totals	249	–	8234	1281	3203	.400	0	15	.000	1158	1536	.754	–	–	2090	622	802	14	–	353	–	3720	8.4	2.5	14.9
NBA Playoff Totals	22	–	482	56	176	.318	–	–	–	37	55	.673	–	–	107	26	67	1	–	–	–	149	4.9	1.2	6.8
ABA Playoff Totals	16	–	522	71	197	.360	0	1	.000	90	116	.776	–	–	123	34	59	3	–	22	–	232	7.7	2.1	14.5

Hill, Armond G. b. March 31, 1953 Ht. 6-4 Wt. 190 College: Princeton

SEASON–TEAM	G	GS	MIN	FGM	FGA	PCT	3FGM	3FGA	PCT	FTM	FTA	PCT	O-RB	D-RB	TOT	AST	PF	DQ	STL	TO	BLK	PTS	RPG	APG	PPG
76-77–Atlanta	81	–	1825	175	439	.399	–	–	–	139	174	.799	39	104	143	403	245	8	85	–	6	489	1.8	5.0	6.0
77-78–Atlanta	82	–	2530	304	732	.415	–	–	–	189	223	.848	59	172	231	427	302	15	151	240	15	797	2.8	5.2	9.7
78-79–Atlanta	82	–	2527	296	682	.434	–	–	–	246	288	.854	41	123	164	480	292	8	102	202	16	838	2.0	5.9	10.2
79-80–Atlanta	79	–	2092	177	431	.411	1	4	.250	124	146	.849	31	107	138	424	261	7	107	171	8	479	1.7	5.4	6.1
80-81–Atlanta-Seattle	75	–	1738	117	335	.349	0	7	.000	141	172	.820	41	118	159	292	207	3	66	127	11	375	2.1	3.9	5.0
81-82–Seattle-S.D.	40	18	723	53	126	.421	0	2	.000	39	55	.709	12	40	52	106	88	0	21	66	5	145	1.3	2.7	3.6
82-83–Milwaukee	14	3	169	14	26	.538	0	0	–	18	22	.818	5	15	20	27	20	0	9	13	0	46	1.4	1.9	3.3
83-84–Atlanta	15	2	181	14	46	.304	0	0	–	17	21	.810	2	8	10	35	30	1	7	14	0	45	0.7	2.3	3.0
Reg. Season Totals	468	23	11785	1150	2817	.408	1	13	.077	913	1101	.829	230	687	917	2194	1445	42	548	833	61	3214	2.0	4.7	6.9
Playoff Totals	16	0	437	47	116	.405	0	1	.000	23	28	.821	4	22	26	72	54	1	18	39	2	117	1.6	4.5	7.3

Hill, Cleo b. May 24, 1938 Ht. 6-1 Wt. 185 College: Winston-Salem State

SEASON–TEAM	G	GS	MIN	FGM	FGA	PCT	3FGM	3FGA	PCT	FTM	FTA	PCT	O-RB	D-RB	TOT	AST	PF	DQ	STL	TO	BLK	PTS	RPG	APG	PPG
61-62–St. Louis	58	–	1050	107	309	.346	–	–	–	106	137	.774	–	–	178	114	98	1	–	–	–	320	3.1	2.0	5.5
Reg. Season Totals	58	–	1050	107	309	.346	–	–	–	106	137	.774	–	–	178	114	98	1	–	–	–	320	3.1	2.0	5.5

Hill, Gary W. b. October 7, 1941 Ht. 6-4 Wt. 185 College: Oklahoma City

SEASON–TEAM	G	GS	MIN	FGM	FGA	PCT	3FGM	3FGA	PCT	FTM	FTA	PCT	O-RB	D-RB	TOT	AST	PF	DQ	STL	TO	BLK	PTS	RPG	APG	PPG
63-64–San Francisco	67	–	1015	146	384	.380	–	–	–	51	77	.662	–	–	114	103	165	2	–	–	–	343	1.7	1.5	5.1
64-65–S.F.-Balt.	12	–	103	10	36	.278	–	–	–	7	14	.500	–	–	16	7	11	0	–	–	–	27	1.3	0.6	2.3
Reg. Season Totals	79	–	1118	156	420	.371	–	–	–	58	91	.637	–	–	130	110	176	2	–	–	–	370	1.6	1.4	4.7
Playoff Totals	9	–	69	12	24	.500	–	–	–	4	13	.308	–	–	6	8	13	0	–	–	–	28	0.7	0.9	3.1

H

Hill, Grant Henry b. October 5, 1972 Ht. 6-8 Wt. 225 College: Duke

SEASON–TEAM	G	GS	MIN	FGM	FGA	PCT	3FGM	3FGA	PCT	FTM	FTA	PCT	O-RB	D-RB	TOT	AST	PF	DQ	STL	TO	BLK	PTS	RPG	APG	PPG
94-95–Detroit	70	69	2678	508	1064	.477	4	27	.148	374	511	.732	125	320	445	353	203	1	124	202	62	1394	6.4	5.0	19.9
95-96–Detroit	80	80	3260	564	1221	.462	5	26	.192	485	646	.751	127	656	783	548	242	1	100	263	48	1618	9.8	6.9	20.2
96-97–Detroit	80	80	3147	625	1259	.496	10	33	.303	450	633	.711	123	598	721	583	186	0	144	259	48	1710	9.0	7.3	21.4
97-98–Detroit	81	81	3294	615	1361	.452	3	21	.143	479	647	.740	93	530	623	551	196	1	143	285	53	1712	7.7	6.8	21.1
98-99–Detroit	50	50	1852	384	802	.479	0	14	.000	285	379	.752	65	290	355	300	114	0	80	184	27	1053	7.1	6.0	21.1
99-00–Detroit	74	74	2776	696	1422	.489	34	98	.347	480	604	.795	97	393	490	385	190	0	103	240	43	1906	6.6	5.2	25.8
Reg. Season Totals	435	434	17007	3392	7129	.476	56	219	.256	2553	3420	.746	630	2787	3417	2720	1131	3	694	1433	281	9393	7.9	6.3	21.6
Playoff Totals	15	15	549	115	250	.460	2	5	.400	62	79	.785	24	79	103	84	46	0	18	49	7	294	6.9	5.6	19.6
All-Star Totals	5	5	115	25	43	.581	1	2	.500	6	11	.545	3	9	12	17	6	0	6	9	1	57	2.4	3.4	11.4

Hill, Simmie Jr. b. November 14, 1946 Ht. 6-7 Wt. 235 College: Cameron; West Texas A&M; Wichita State; East Texas Baptist

SEASON–TEAM	G	GS	MIN	FGM	FGA	PCT	3FGM	3FGA	PCT	FTM	FTA	PCT	O-RB	D-RB	TOT	AST	PF	DQ	STL	TO	BLK	PTS	RPG	APG	PPG
69-70–L.A.-Miami (A)	53	–	1499	297	709	.419	5	30	.167	126	167	.754	–	–	401	47	201	10	–	–	–	725	7.6	0.9	13.7
71-72–Dallas (A)	70	–	1845	281	629	.447	4	13	.308	129	164	.787	–	–	406	94	234	–	–	125	–	695	5.8	1.3	9.9
72-73–San Diego (A)	69	–	1658	315	743	.424	27	69	.391	103	135	.763	126	225	351	131	221	0	–	150	–	760	5.1	1.9	11.0
73-74–San Antonio (A)	60	–	837	112	244	.459	0	11	.000	45	62	.726	59	113	172	62	145	–	13	63	16	269	2.9	1.0	4.5
Reg. ABA Totals	252	–	5839	1005	2325	.432	36	123	.293	403	528	.763	185	338	1330	334	801	10	13	338	16	2449	5.3	1.3	9.7
ABA Playoff Totals	12	–	226	32	79	.405	0	4	.000	8	12	.667	0	0	39	16	28	0	0	17	0	72	3.3	1.3	6.0

Hill, Tyrone b. March 19, 1968 Ht. 6-9 Wt. 250 College: Xavier (Ohio)

SEASON–TEAM	G	GS	MIN	FGM	FGA	PCT	3FGM	3FGA	PCT	FTM	FTA	PCT	O-RB	D-RB	TOT	AST	PF	DQ	STL	TO	BLK	PTS	RPG	APG	PPG
90-91–Golden State	74	22	1192	147	299	.492	0	0	–	96	152	.632	157	226	383	19	264	8	33	72	30	390	5.2	0.3	5.3
91-92–Golden State	82	75	1886	254	487	.522	0	1	.000	163	235	.694	182	411	593	47	315	7	73	106	43	671	7.2	0.6	8.2
92-93–Golden State	74	66	2070	251	494	.508	0	4	.000	138	221	.624	255	499	754	68	320	8	41	92	40	640	10.2	0.9	8.6
93-94–Cleveland	57	20	1447	216	398	.543	0	2	.000	171	256	.668	184	315	499	46	193	5	53	78	35	603	8.8	0.8	10.6
94-95–Cleveland	70	67	2397	350	694	.504	0	1	.000	263	397	.662	269	496	765	55	245	4	55	151	41	963	10.9	0.8	13.8
95-96–Cleveland	44	2	929	130	254	.512	0	0	–	81	135	.600	94	150	244	33	144	3	31	64	20	341	5.5	0.8	7.8
96-97–Cleveland	74	70	2582	357	595	.600	0	1	.000	241	381	.633	259	477	736	92	268	6	63	147	30	955	9.9	1.2	12.9
97-98–Milwaukee	57	56	2064	208	418	.498	0	1	.000	155	255	.608	212	396	608	88	230	8	67	106	30	571	10.7	1.5	10.0
98-99–Milw.-Phil.	38	23	1104	122	268	.455	0	0	–	81	150	.540	115	172	287	35	145	2	34	59	16	325	7.6	0.9	8.6
99-00–Philadelphia	68	65	2155	318	656	.485	0	1	.000	179	259	.691	220	405	625	52	243	3	64	124	27	815	9.2	0.8	12.0
Reg. Season Totals	638	466	17826	2353	4563	.516	0	11	.000	1568	2441	.642	1947	3547	5494	535	2367	54	514	999	312	6274	8.6	0.8	9.8
Playoff Totals	41	19	990	106	228	.465	0	3	.000	85	142	.599	94	162	256	19	151	6	25	44	9	297	6.2	0.5	7.2
All-Star Totals	1	0	6	1	1	1.000	0	0	–	0	0	–	2	2	4	0	1	0	0	0	0	2	4.0	0.0	2.0

Hillhouse, Arthur Sherwood (Art) b. June 12, 1916 d. October 1980 Ht. 6-7 Wt. 220 College: Rutgers; Long Island University

SEASON–TEAM	G	GS	MIN	FGM	FGA	PCT	3FGM	3FGA	PCT	FTM	FTA	PCT	O-RB	D-RB	TOT	AST	PF	DQ	STL	TO	BLK	PTS	RPG	APG	PPG
46-47–Philadelphia	60	–	–	120	412	.291	–	–	–	120	166	.723	–	–	–	41	139	–	–	–	–	360	–	0.7	6.0
47-48–Philadelphia	11	–	–	14	71	.197	–	–	–	30	37	.811	–	–	–	3	30	–	–	–	–	58	–	0.3	5.3
Reg. Season Totals	71	–	–	134	483	.277	–	–	–	150	203	.739	–	–	–	44	169	–	–	–	–	418	–	0.6	5.9
Playoff Totals	10	–	–	24	144	.264	–	–	–	39	46	.848	–	–	–	10	41	6	–	–	–	87	–	0.6	8.7

Hillman, Darnell (Dr. Dunk) b. August 29, 1949 Ht. 6-9 Wt. 215 College: San Jose State

SEASON–TEAM	G	GS	MIN	FGM	FGA	PCT	3FGM	3FGA	PCT	FTM	FTA	PCT	O-RB	D-RB	TOT	AST	PF	DQ	STL	TO	BLK	PTS	RPG	APG	PPG
71-72–Indiana (A)	73	–	1386	200	410	.488	1	5	.200	114	177	.644	–	–	478	49	210	–	–	84	–	515	6.5	0.7	7.1
72-73–Indiana (A)	84	–	2541	328	735	.446	0	9	.000	148	252	.587	218	517	735	128	291	0	–	154	116	804	8.8	1.5	9.6
73-74–Indiana (A)	83	–	2319	328	658	.498	3	8	.375	99	191	.518	198	478	676	96	295	–	70	177	177	758	8.1	1.2	9.1
74-75–Indiana (A)	81	–	2603	486	923	.527	0	4	.000	152	202	.752	296	451	747	131	330	–	73	209	132	1124	9.2	1.6	13.9
75-76–Indiana (A)	74	–	2166	375	828	.453	1	4	.250	243	336	.723	248	422	670	147	306	–	80	196	80	994	9.1	2.0	13.4
76-77–Indiana	82	–	2302	359	811	.443	–	–	–	161	244	.660	228	465	693	166	353	15	95	–	106	879	8.5	2.0	10.7
77-78–N.J.-Denver	78	–	1966	340	710	.479	–	–	–	167	286	.584	199	378	577	102	290	11	63	175	81	847	7.4	1.3	10.9
78-79–Kansas City	78	–	1618	211	428	.493	–	–	–	125	224	.558	138	293	431	91	288	11	50	134	66	547	5.5	1.2	7.0
79-80–Golden State	49	–	708	82	179	.458	0	0	–	34	68	.500	59	121	180	47	128	2	21	59	24	198	3.7	1.0	4.0
Reg. NBA Totals	287	–	6594	992	2128	.466	0	0	–	487	822	.592	624	1257	1881	406	1059	39	229	368	277	2471	6.6	1.4	8.6
Reg. ABA Totals	395	–	11015	1717	3554	.483	5	30	.167	756	1158	.653	960	1868	3306	551	1432	0	223	820	505	4195	8.4	1.4	10.6
NBA Playoff Totals	18	–	372	41	111	.369	0	0	–	20	32	.625	44	69	113	26	66	1	10	34	10	102	6.3	1.4	5.7
ABA Playoff Totals	72	–	1757	232	466	.498	0	3	.000	107	179	.598	90	174	509	62	222	0	22	103	67	571	7.1	0.9	7.9

Hilton, Fred b. January 15, 1948 Ht. 6-3 Wt. 185 College: Grambling State

SEASON–TEAM	G	GS	MIN	FGM	FGA	PCT	3FGM	3FGA	PCT	FTM	FTA	PCT	O-RB	D-RB	TOT	AST	PF	DQ	STL	TO	BLK	PTS	RPG	APG	PPG
71-72–Buffalo	61	–	1349	309	795	.389	–	–	–	90	122	.738	–	–	156	116	145	0	–	–	–	708	2.6	1.9	11.6
72-73–Buffalo	59	–	731	191	494	.387	–	–	–	41	53	.774	–	–	98	74	100	0	–	–	–	423	1.7	1.3	7.2
Reg. Season Totals	120	–	2080	500	1289	.388	–	–	–	131	175	.749	–	–	254	190	245	0	–	–	–	1131	2.1	1.6	9.4

Hinson, Roy Manus Jr. b. May 2, 1961 Ht. 6-9 Wt. 215 College: Rutgers

SEASON–TEAM	G	GS	MIN	FGM	FGA	PCT	3FGM	3FGA	PCT	FTM	FTA	PCT	O-RB	D-RB	TOT	AST	PF	DQ	STL	TO	BLK	PTS	RPG	APG	PPG
83-84–Cleveland	80	61	1858	184	371	.496	0	0	–	69	117	.590	175	324	499	69	306	11	31	109	145	437	6.2	0.9	5.5
84-85–Cleveland	76	75	2344	465	925	.503	0	3	.000	271	376	.721	186	410	596	68	311	13	51	171	173	1201	7.8	0.9	15.8
85-86–Cleveland	82	82	2834	621	1167	.532	0	4	.000	364	506	.719	167	472	639	102	316	7	62	188	112	1606	7.8	1.2	19.6
86-87–Philadelphia	76	58	2489	393	823	.478	0	1	.000	273	360	.758	150	338	488	60	281	4	45	149	161	1059	6.4	0.8	13.9
87-88–Phil.-N.J.	77	57	2592	453	930	.487	0	2	.000	272	351	.775	159	358	517	99	275	6	69	169	140	1178	6.7	1.3	15.3
88-89–New Jersey	82	39	2542	495	1027	.482	0	2	.000	318	420	.757	152	370	522	71	298	3	34	165	121	1308	6.4	0.9	16.0
89-90–New Jersey	25	19	793	145	286	.507	0	0	–	86	99	.869	61	111	172	22	87	0	14	52	27	376	6.9	0.9	15.0
90-91–New Jersey	9	0	91	20	39	.513	0	0	–	1	3	.333	6	13	19	4	14	0	0	6	3	41	2.1	0.4	4.6
Reg. Season Totals	507	391	15543	2776	5568	.499	0	12	.000	1654	2232	.741	1056	2396	3452	495	1888	44	306	1009	882	7206	6.8	1.0	14.2
Playoff Totals	9	4	279	57	100	.570	0	0	–	39	61	.639	16	37	53	6	36	1	7	10	19	153	5.9	0.7	17.0

Hirsch, Melvin M. (Mel) b. July 31, 1921 d. December 1968 Ht. 5-8 Wt. 165 College: Brooklyn College

SEASON–TEAM	G	GS	MIN	FGM	FGA	PCT	3FGM	3FGA	PCT	FTM	FTA	PCT	O-RB	D-RB	TOT	AST	PF	DQ	STL	TO	BLK	PTS	RPG	APG	PPG
46-47–Boston	13	–	–	9	45	.200	–	–	–	1	2	.500	–	–	–	10	18	–	–	–	–	19	–	0.8	1.5
Reg. Season Totals	13	–	–	9	45	.200	–	–	–	1	2	.500	–	–	–	10	18	–	–	–	–	19	–	0.8	1.5

Hitch, Lewis Rufus (Lew) b. July 16, 1929 Ht. 6-8 Wt. 200 College: Kansas State

SEASON–TEAM	G	GS	MIN	FGM	FGA	PCT	3FGM	3FGA	PCT	FTM	FTA	PCT	O-RB	D-RB	TOT	AST	PF	DQ	STL	TO	BLK	PTS	RPG	APG	PPG
51-52–Minneapolis	61	–	849	77	215	.358	–	–	–	63	94	.670	–	–	243	50	89	3	–	–	–	217	4.0	0.8	3.6
52-53–Minneapolis	70	–	1027	89	255	.349	–	–	–	83	136	.610	–	–	275	66	122	2	–	–	–	261	3.9	0.9	3.7
53-54–Milwaukee	72	–	2452	221	603	.367	–	–	–	133	208	.639	–	–	691	141	176	3	–	–	–	575	9.6	2.0	8.0
54-55–Milw.-Minn.	74	–	1774	167	417	.400	–	–	–	115	169	.680	–	–	438	125	110	0	–	–	–	449	5.9	1.7	6.1
55-56–Minneapolis	69	–	1129	94	235	.400	–	–	–	100	132	.758	–	–	283	77	85	0	–	–	–	288	4.1	1.1	4.2
56-57–Roch.-Phil.	68	–	1133	111	296	.375	–	–	–	63	88	.716	–	–	253	40	103	0	–	–	–	285	3.7	–	4.2
Reg. Season Totals	414	–	8364	759	2021	.376	–	–	–	557	827	.674	–	–	2183	499	685	8	–	–	–	2075	5.3	1.4	5.0
Playoff Totals	38	–	624	45	128	.359	–	–	–	54	94	.574	–	–	177	36	64	1	–	–	–	144	4.1	0.9	3.8

Hodge, Donald Jerome b. February 25, 1969 Ht. 7-0 Wt. 250 College: Temple

SEASON–TEAM	G	GS	MIN	FGM	FGA	PCT	3FGM	3FGA	PCT	FTM	FTA	PCT	O-RB	D-RB	TOT	AST	PF	DQ	STL	TO	BLK	PTS	RPG	APG	PPG
91-92–Dallas	51	27	1058	163	328	.497	0	0	–	100	150	.667	118	157	275	39	128	2	25	75	23	426	5.4	0.8	8.4
92-93–Dallas	79	8	1267	161	400	.403	0	0	–	71	104	.683	93	201	294	75	204	2	33	90	37	393	3.7	0.9	5.0
93-94–Dallas	50	0	428	46	101	.455	0	0	–	44	52	.846	46	49	95	32	66	1	15	30	13	136	1.9	0.6	2.7
94-95–Dallas	54	0	633	83	204	.407	4	14	.286	39	51	.765	40	82	122	41	107	1	10	39	14	209	2.3	0.8	3.9
95-96–Dallas-Cha.	15	0	115	9	24	.375	0	0	–	0	0	–	9	14	23	4	26	0	1	2	8	18	1.5	0.3	1.2
Reg. Season Totals	249	35	3501	462	1057	.437	4	14	.286	254	357	.711	306	503	809	191	531	6	84	236	95	1182	3.2	0.8	4.7

Hodges, Craig Anthony b. June 27, 1960 Ht. 6-3 Wt. 195 College: Long Beach State

SEASON–TEAM	G	GS	MIN	FGM	FGA	PCT	3FGM	3FGA	PCT	FTM	FTA	PCT	O-RB	D-RB	TOT	AST	PF	DQ	STL	TO	BLK	PTS	RPG	APG	PPG
82-83–San Diego	76	48	2022	318	704	.452	20	90	.222	94	130	.723	53	69	122	275	192	3	82	161	4	750	1.6	3.6	9.9
83-84–San Diego	76	28	1571	258	573	.450	10	46	.217	66	88	.750	22	64	86	116	166	2	58	85	1	592	1.1	1.5	7.8
84-85–Milwaukee	82	63	2496	359	733	.490	47	135	.348	106	130	.815	74	112	186	349	262	8	96	135	1	871	2.3	4.3	10.6
85-86–Milwaukee	66	66	1739	284	568	.500	73	162	.451	75	86	.872	39	78	117	229	157	3	74	89	2	716	1.8	3.5	10.8
86-87–Milwaukee	78	43	2147	315	682	.462	85	228	.373	131	147	.891	48	92	140	240	189	3	76	124	7	846	1.8	3.1	10.8
87-88–Milw.-Phoenix	66	0	1445	242	523	.463	86	175	.491	59	71	.831	19	59	78	153	118	1	46	77	2	629	1.2	2.3	9.5
88-89–Phoenix-Chi.	59	6	1204	203	430	.472	75	180	.417	48	57	.842	23	66	89	146	90	0	43	57	4	529	1.5	2.5	9.0
89-90–Chicago	63	0	1055	145	331	.438	87	181	.481	30	33	.909	11	42	53	110	87	1	30	30	2	407	0.8	1.7	6.5
90-91–Chicago	73	0	843	146	344	.424	44	115	.383	26	27	.963	10	32	42	97	74	0	34	35	2	362	0.6	1.3	5.0
91-92–Chicago	56	2	555	93	242	.384	36	96	.375	16	17	.941	7	17	24	54	33	0	14	22	1	238	0.4	1.0	4.3
Reg. Season Totals	695	256	15077	2363	5130	.461	563	1408	.400	651	786	.828	306	631	937	1769	1368	21	553	815	26	5940	1.3	2.5	8.5
Playoff Totals	101	40	2056	292	669	.436	90	248	.363	58	74	.784	39	72	111	203	206	5	95	102	8	732	1.1	2.0	7.2

Hoefer, Adolph Charles (Dutch, Charlie) b. July 12, 1917 Ht. 5-9 Wt. 160 College: Queens College

SEASON–TEAM	G	GS	MIN	FGM	FGA	PCT	3FGM	3FGA	PCT	FTM	FTA	PCT	O-RB	D-RB	TOT	AST	PF	DQ	STL	TO	BLK	PTS	RPG	APG	PPG
46-47–Toronto-Boston	58	–	–	130	514	.253	–	–	–	91	139	.655	–	–	–	33	142	–	–	–	–	351	–	0.6	6.1
47-48–Boston	7	–	–	3	19	.158	–	–	–	4	8	.500	–	–	–	3	17	–	–	–	–	10	–	0.4	1.4
Reg. Season Totals	65	–	–	133	533	.250	–	–	–	95	147	.646	–	–	–	36	159	–	–	–	–	361	–	0.6	5.6

Hoffman, Paul James (Bear, The Body) b. May 5, 1925 d. November 12, 1998 Ht. 6-2 Wt. 205 College: Indiana; Purdue

SEASON–TEAM	G	GS	MIN	FGM	FGA	PCT	3FGM	3FGA	PCT	FTM	FTA	PCT	O-RB	D-RB	TOT	AST	PF	DQ	STL	TO	BLK	PTS	RPG	APG	PPG
47-48–Baltimore	37	–	–	142	408	.348	–	–	–	104	157	.662	–	–	–	23	123	–	–	–	–	388	–	0.6	10.5
49-50–Baltimore	60	–	–	312	914	.341	–	–	–	242	364	.665	–	–	–	161	234	–	–	–	–	866	–	2.7	14.4
50-51–Baltimore	41	–	–	127	399	.318	–	–	–	105	156	.673	–	–	202	111	135	2	–	–	–	359	4.9	2.7	8.8
52-53–Baltimore	69	–	1955	240	656	.366	–	–	–	224	342	.655	–	–	317	237	282	13	–	–	–	704	4.6	3.4	10.2
53-54–Baltimore	72	–	2505	253	761	.332	–	–	–	217	303	.716	–	–	486	285	271	10	–	–	–	723	6.8	4.0	10.0
54-55–Balt.-N.Y.-Phil.	38	–	670	65	216	.301	–	–	–	64	93	.688	–	–	124	94	93	0	–	–	–	194	3.3	2.5	5.1
Reg. Season Totals	317	–	5130	1139	3354	.340	–	–	–	956	1415	.676	–	–	1129	911	1138	25	–	–	–	3234	5.1	2.9	10.2
Playoff Totals	13	–	81	49	191	.304	–	–	–	48	76	.632	–	–	7	21	55	1	–	–	–	146	3.5	1.4	11.2

Hogsett, Robert L. (Bobby) b. January 29, 1941 d. December 5, 1984 Ht. 6-7 Wt. 230 College: Tennessee

SEASON–TEAM	G	GS	MIN	FGM	FGA	PCT	3FGM	3FGA	PCT	FTM	FTA	PCT	O-RB	D-RB	TOT	AST	PF	DQ	STL	TO	BLK	PTS	RPG	APG	PPG
66-67–Detroit	7	–	22	5	16	.313	–	–	–	6	6	1.000	–	–	3	1	5	0	–	–	–	16	0.4	0.1	2.3
67-68–Pittsburgh (A)	13	–	119	7	20	.350	0	0	–	7	17	.412	–	–	23	1	11	0	–	4	–	21	1.8	0.1	1.6
Reg. NBA Totals	7	–	22	5	16	.313	–	–	–	6	6	1.000	–	–	3	1	5	0	–	–	–	16	0.4	0.1	2.3
Reg. ABA Totals	13	–	119	7	20	.350	0	0	–	7	17	.412	–	–	23	1	11	0	–	4	–	21	1.8	0.1	1.6

Hogue, Paul H. (Duke) b. April 28, 1940 Ht. 6-9 Wt. 240 College: Cincinnati

SEASON–TEAM	G	GS	MIN	FGM	FGA	PCT	3FGM	3FGA	PCT	FTM	FTA	PCT	O-RB	D-RB	TOT	AST	PF	DQ	STL	TO	BLK	PTS	RPG	APG	PPG
62-63–New York	50	–	1340	152	419	.363	–	–	–	79	174	.454	–	–	430	42	220	12	–	–	–	383	8.6	0.8	7.7
63-64–N.Y.-Balt.	15	–	147	12	30	.400	–	–	–	2	7	.286	–	–	31	6	35	1	–	–	–	26	2.1	0.4	1.7
Reg. Season Totals	65	–	1487	164	449	.365	–	–	–	81	181	.448	–	–	461	48	255	13	–	–	–	409	7.1	0.7	6.3

Hoiberg, Fredrick Kristian (Fred, The Mayor) b. October 15, 1972 Ht. 6-4 Wt. 203 College: Iowa State

SEASON–TEAM	G	GS	MIN	FGM	FGA	PCT	3FGM	3FGA	PCT	FTM	FTA	PCT	O-RB	D-RB	TOT	AST	PF	DQ	STL	TO	BLK	PTS	RPG	APG	PPG
95-96–Indiana	15	1	85	8	19	.421	1	3	.333	15	18	.833	4	5	9	8	12	0	6	7	1	32	0.6	0.5	2.1
96-97–Indiana	47	0	572	67	156	.429	29	70	.414	61	77	.792	13	68	81	41	51	0	27	22	6	224	1.7	0.9	4.8
97-98–Indiana	65	1	874	85	222	.383	32	85	.376	59	69	.855	14	109	123	45	101	0	40	22	3	261	1.9	0.7	4.0
98-99–Indiana	12	0	87	6	21	.286	1	9	.111	6	6	1.000	2	9	11	4	11	0	0	3	0	19	0.9	0.3	1.6
99-00–Chicago	31	11	845	89	230	.387	32	94	.340	69	76	.908	7	103	110	85	66	0	40	43	2	279	3.5	2.7	9.0
Reg. Season Totals	170	13	2463	255	648	.394	95	261	.364	210	246	.854	40	294	334	183	241	0	113	97	12	815	2.0	1.1	4.8
Playoff Totals	6	0	40	5	12	.417	1	2	.500	2	2	1.000	1	6	7	3	3	0	4	0	0	13	1.2	0.5	2.2

Holcomb, Douglas M. (Doug) b. February 9, 1925 Ht. 6-4 Wt. 200 College: Wisconsin

SEASON–TEAM	G	GS	MIN	FGM	FGA	PCT	3FGM	3FGA	PCT	FTM	FTA	PCT	O-RB	D-RB	TOT	AST	PF	DQ	STL	TO	BLK	PTS	RPG	APG	PPG
48-49–Baltimore	3	–	–	3	12	.250	–	–	–	9	14	.643	–	–	–	5	5	–	–	–	–	15	–	1.7	5.0
Reg. Season Totals	3	–	–	3	12	.250	–	–	–	9	14	.643	–	–	–	5	5	–	–	–	–	15	–	1.7	5.0

Holland, John Bradley (Brad) b. December 6, 1956 Ht. 6-3 Wt. 180 College: UCLA

SEASON–TEAM	G	GS	MIN	FGM	FGA	PCT	3FGM	3FGA	PCT	FTM	FTA	PCT	O-RB	D-RB	TOT	AST	PF	DQ	STL	TO	BLK	PTS	RPG	APG	PPG
79-80–Los Angeles	38	–	197	44	104	.423	3	15	.200	15	16	.938	4	13	17	22	24	0	15	13	1	106	0.4	0.6	2.8
80-81–Los Angeles	41	–	295	47	111	.423	1	3	.333	35	49	.714	9	20	29	23	44	0	21	31	1	130	0.7	0.6	3.2
81-82–Wash.-Milw.	14	3	194	27	78	.346	0	3	.000	3	6	.500	6	7	13	18	13	0	11	8	1	57	0.9	1.3	4.1
Reg. Season Totals	93	3	686	118	293	.403	4	21	.190	53	71	.746	19	40	59	63	81	0	47	52	3	293	0.6	0.7	3.2
Playoff Totals	11	0	36	6	11	.545	0	0	–	4	4	1.000	2	3	5	4	8	0	5	4	0	16	0.5	0.4	1.5

Holland, Joseph Burnett b. September 26, 1925 Ht. 6-4 Wt. 185 College: Berea; Murray State; Iowa; Kentucky

SEASON–TEAM	G	GS	MIN	FGM	FGA	PCT	3FGM	3FGA	PCT	FTM	FTA	PCT	O-RB	D-RB	TOT	AST	PF	DQ	STL	TO	BLK	PTS	RPG	APG	PPG
49-50–Indianapolis	64	–	–	145	453	.320	–	–	–	98	142	.690	–	–	–	130	220	–	–	–	–	388	–	2.0	6.1
50-51–Indianapolis	67	–	–	196	594	.330	–	–	–	78	137	.569	–	–	344	150	228	8	–	–	–	470	5.1	2.2	7.0
51-52–Indianapolis	55	–	737	93	265	.351	–	–	–	40	69	.580	–	–	166	47	90	0	–	–	–	226	3.0	0.9	4.1
Reg. Season Totals	186	–	737	434	1312	.331	–	–	–	216	348	.621	–	–	510	327	538	8	–	–	–	1084	4.2	1.8	5.8
Playoff Totals	9	–	0	38	36	.472	–	–	–	7	19	.368	–	–	12	11	38	3	–	–	–	83	4.0	3.7	9.2

Holland, Wilbur b. November 8, 1951 Ht. 6-0 Wt. 175 College: New Orleans

SEASON–TEAM	G	GS	MIN	FGM	FGA	PCT	3FGM	3FGA	PCT	FTM	FTA	PCT	O-RB	D-RB	TOT	AST	PF	DQ	STL	TO	BLK	PTS	RPG	APG	PPG
75-76–Atlanta	33	–	351	85	213	.399	–	–	–	22	34	.647	15	26	41	26	48	0	20	–	2	192	1.2	0.8	5.8
76-77–Chicago	79	–	2453	509	1120	.454	–	–	–	158	192	.823	78	175	253	253	201	3	169	–	16	1176	3.2	3.2	14.9
77-78–Chicago	82	–	2884	569	1285	.443	–	–	–	223	279	.799	105	189	294	313	258	4	164	223	14	1361	3.6	3.8	16.6
78-79–Chicago	82	–	2483	445	940	.473	–	–	–	141	176	.801	78	176	254	330	240	9	122	185	12	1031	3.1	4.0	12.6
Reg. Season Totals	276	–	8171	1608	3558	.452	–	–	–	544	681	.799	276	566	842	922	747	16	475	408	44	3760	3.1	3.3	13.6
Playoff Totals	3	–	84	17	34	.500	–	–	–	10	10	1.000	5	4	9	3	8	0	1	–	0	44	3.0	1.0	14.7

Hollins, Lionel Eugene b. October 19, 1953 Ht. 6-3 Wt. 185 College: Dodge City (Kan.) C.C.; Arizona State

SEASON–TEAM	G	GS	MIN	FGM	FGA	PCT	3FGM	3FGA	PCT	FTM	FTA	PCT	O-RB	D-RB	TOT	AST	PF	DQ	STL	TO	BLK	PTS	RPG	APG	PPG
75-76–Portland	74	–	1891	311	738	.421	–	–	–	178	247	.721	39	136	175	306	235	5	131	–	28	800	2.4	4.1	10.8
76-77–Portland	76	–	2224	452	1046	.432	–	–	–	215	287	.749	52	158	210	313	265	5	166	–	38	1119	2.8	4.1	14.7
77-78–Portland	81	–	2741	531	1202	.442	–	–	–	223	300	.743	81	196	277	380	268	4	157	241	29	1285	3.4	4.7	15.9
78-79–Portland	64	–	1967	402	886	.454	–	–	–	172	221	.778	32	117	149	325	199	3	114	223	24	976	2.3	5.1	15.3
79-80–Port.-Phil.	47	–	1209	212	526	.403	3	20	.150	101	140	.721	29	60	89	162	103	0	76	128	10	528	1.9	3.4	11.2
80-81–Philadelphia	82	13	2154	327	696	.470	2	15	.133	125	171	.731	47	144	191	352	205	2	104	207	18	781	2.3	4.3	9.5
81-82–Philadelphia	81	81	2257	380	797	.477	2	16	.125	132	188	.702	35	152	187	316	198	1	103	146	20	894	2.3	3.9	11.0
82-83–San Diego	56	54	1844	313	717	.437	3	21	.143	129	179	.721	30	98	128	373	155	2	111	198	14	758	2.3	6.7	13.5
83-84–Detroit	32	0	216	24	63	.381	0	2	.000	11	13	.846	4	18	22	62	26	0	13	24	1	59	0.7	1.9	1.8
84-85–Houston	80	60	1950	249	540	.461	3	13	.231	108	136	.794	33	140	173	417	187	1	78	170	10	609	2.2	5.2	7.6
Reg. Season Totals	673	195	18453	3201	7211	.444	13	87	.149	1394	1882	.741	382	1219	1601	3006	1841	23	1053	1337	192	7809	2.4	4.5	11.6
Playoff Totals	77	3	2293	369	897	.411	0	12	.000	173	236	.733	46	161	207	344	221	4	114	113	11	911	2.7	4.5	11.8
All-Star Totals	1	0	23	3	8	.375	0	0	–	4	5	.800	0	0	0	8	2	0	2	1	0	10	0.0	8.0	10.0

Hollis, Essie B. b. May 16, 1955 Ht. 6-6 Wt. 195 College: St. Bonaventure

SEASON–TEAM	G	GS	MIN	FGM	FGA	PCT	3FGM	3FGA	PCT	FTM	FTA	PCT	O-RB	D-RB	TOT	AST	PF	DQ	STL	TO	BLK	PTS	RPG	APG	PPG
78-79–Detroit	25	–	154	30	75	.400	–	–	–	9	12	.750	21	24	45	6	28	0	11	14	1	69	1.8	0.2	2.8
Reg. Season Totals	25	–	154	30	75	.400	–	–	–	9	12	.750	21	24	45	6	28	0	11	14	1	69	1.8	0.2	2.8

Holman, Dennis R. (Denny) b. October 8, 1945 Ht. 6-3 Wt. 175 College: Southern Methodist

SEASON–TEAM	G	GS	MIN	FGM	FGA	PCT	3FGM	3FGA	PCT	FTM	FTA	PCT	O-RB	D-RB	TOT	AST	PF	DQ	STL	TO	BLK	PTS	RPG	APG	PPG
67-68–Dallas (A)	46	–	554	55	153	.359	4	9	.444	62	103	.602	–	–	78	73	85	1	–	40	–	176	1.7	1.6	3.8
Reg. ABA Totals	46	–	554	55	153	.359	4	9	.444	62	103	.602	–	–	78	73	85	1	–	40	–	176	1.7	1.6	3.8
ABA Playoff Totals	8	–	128	9	31	.290	1	2	.500	12	12	1.000	–	–	16	15	19	0	–	9	–	31	2.0	1.9	3.9

Holstein, James H. (Jim) b. September 24, 1930 Ht. 6-3 Wt. 180 College: Cincinnati

SEASON–TEAM	G	GS	MIN	FGM	FGA	PCT	3FGM	3FGA	PCT	FTM	FTA	PCT	O-RB	D-RB	TOT	AST	PF	DQ	STL	TO	BLK	PTS	RPG	APG	PPG
52-53–Minneapolis	66	–	989	98	274	.358	–	–	–	70	105	.667	–	–	173	74	128	1	–	–	–	266	2.6	1.1	4.0
53-54–Minneapolis	70	–	1155	88	288	.306	–	–	–	64	112	.571	–	–	204	79	140	0	–	–	–	240	2.9	1.1	3.4
54-55–Minneapolis	62	–	980	107	330	.324	–	–	–	67	94	.713	–	–	206	58	107	0	–	–	–	281	3.3	0.9	4.5
55-56–Fort Wayne	27	–	352	24	89	.270	–	–	–	24	37	.649	–	–	76	38	51	1	–	–	–	72	2.8	1.4	2.7
Reg. Season Totals	225	–	3476	317	981	.323	–	–	–	225	348	.647	–	–	659	249	426	2	–	–	–	859	2.9	1.1	3.8
Playoff Totals	32	–	685	51	143	.378	–	–	–	36	56	.643	–	–	130	39	66	0	–	–	–	138	2.9	0.9	4.3

Holt, Alvin William (A.W.) b. August 26, 1946 Ht. 6-7 Wt. 210 College: Jackson State

SEASON–TEAM	G	GS	MIN	FGM	FGA	PCT	3FGM	3FGA	PCT	FTM	FTA	PCT	O-RB	D-RB	TOT	AST	PF	DQ	STL	TO	BLK	PTS	RPG	APG	PPG
70-71–Chicago	6	–	14	1	8	.125	–	–	–	2	3	.667	–	–	4	0	1	0	–	–	–	4	0.7	0.0	0.7
Reg. Season Totals	6	–	14	1	8	.125	–	–	–	2	3	.667	–	–	4	0	1	0	–	–	–	4	0.7	0.0	0.7

Holton, Michael David b. August 4, 1961 Ht. 6-4 Wt. 185 College: UCLA

SEASON–TEAM	G	GS	MIN	FGM	FGA	PCT	3FGM	3FGA	PCT	FTM	FTA	PCT	O-RB	D-RB	TOT	AST	PF	DQ	STL	TO	BLK	PTS	RPG	APG	PPG
84-85–Phoenix	74	59	1761	257	576	.446	14	45	.311	96	118	.814	30	102	132	198	141	0	59	123	6	624	1.8	2.7	8.4
85-86–Phoenix-Chicago	28	0	512	77	175	.440	1	12	.083	28	44	.636	11	22	33	55	47	1	25	27	0	183	1.2	2.0	6.5
86-87–Portland	58	1	479	70	171	.409	7	23	.304	44	55	.800	9	29	38	73	51	0	16	41	2	191	0.7	1.3	3.3
87-88–Portland	82	2	1279	163	353	.462	3	15	.200	107	129	.829	50	99	149	211	154	0	41	86	10	436	1.8	2.6	5.3
88-89–Charlotte	67	60	1696	215	504	.427	3	14	.214	120	143	.839	30	75	105	424	165	0	66	119	12	553	1.6	6.3	8.3
89-90–Charlotte	16	0	109	14	26	.538	0	0	–	1	2	.500	1	1	2	16	19	0	1	13	0	29	0.1	1.0	1.8
Reg. Season Totals	325	122	5836	796	1805	.441	28	109	.257	396	491	.807	131	328	459	977	577	1	208	409	30	2016	1.4	3.0	6.2
Playoff Totals	9	0	98	13	34	.382	0	5	.000	4	4	1.000	1	7	8	15	15	0	2	4	0	30	0.9	1.7	3.3

Holub, Richard W. (Dick) b. October 29, 1921 Ht. 6-6 Wt. 205 College: Long Island University

SEASON–TEAM	G	GS	MIN	FGM	FGA	PCT	3FGM	3FGA	PCT	FTM	FTA	PCT	O-RB	D-RB	TOT	AST	PF	DQ	STL	TO	BLK	PTS	RPG	APG	PPG
47-48–New York	48	–	–	195	662	.295	–	–	–	114	180	.633	–	–	–	37	159	–	–	–	–	504	–	0.8	10.5
Reg. Season Totals	48	–	–	195	662	.295	–	–	–	114	180	.633	–	–	–	37	159	–	–	–	–	504	–	0.8	10.5
Playoff Totals	3	–	–	9	36	.250	–	–	–	8	14	.571	–	–	–	–	12	–	–	–	–	26	–	0.0	8.7

Holup, Joseph J. (Joe) b. February 26, 1934 Ht. 6-6 Wt. 215 College: George Washington

SEASON–TEAM	G	GS	MIN	FGM	FGA	PCT	3FGM	3FGA	PCT	FTM	FTA	PCT	O-RB	D-RB	TOT	AST	PF	DQ	STL	TO	BLK	PTS	RPG	APG	PPG
56-57–Syracuse	71	–	1284	160	487	.329	–	–	–	204	253	.806	–	–	279	84	177	5	–	–	–	524	3.9	1.2	7.4
57-58–Syr.-Detroit	53	–	740	91	278	.327	–	–	–	71	94	.755	–	–	221	36	99	2	–	–	–	253	4.2	0.7	4.8
58-59–Detroit	68	–	1502	209	580	.360	–	–	–	152	200	.760	–	–	352	73	239	12	–	–	–	570	5.2	1.1	8.4
Reg. Season Totals	192	–	3526	460	1345	.342	–	–	–	427	547	.781	–	–	852	193	515	19	–	–	–	1347	4.4	1.0	7.0
Playoff Totals	15	–	258	24	85	.282	–	–	–	26	35	.743	–	–	64	7	30	0	–	–	–	74	4.3	0.5	4.9

Holzman, William (Red) b. August 10, 1920 d. November 13, 1998 Ht. 5-10 Wt. 175 College: Baltimore; C.C.NY HOF: 1985

SEASON–TEAM	G	GS	MIN	FGM	FGA	PCT	3FGM	3FGA	PCT	FTM	FTA	PCT	O-RB	D-RB	TOT	AST	PF	DQ	STL	TO	BLK	PTS	RPG	APG	PPG
45-46–Rochester (N)	34	–	–	143	–	–	–	–	–	77	115	.670	–	–	–	–	54	–	–	–	–	363	–	–	10.7
46-47–Rochester (N)	44	–	–	227	–	–	–	–	–	74	139	.532	–	–	–	–	68	–	–	–	–	528	–	–	12.0
47-48–Rochester (N)	60	–	–	246	–	–	–	–	–	117	182	.643	–	–	–	–	58	–	–	–	–	609	–	–	10.2
48-49–Rochester	60	–	–	225	691	.326	–	–	–	96	157	.611	–	–	–	149	93	–	–	–	–	546	–	2.5	9.1
49-50–Rochester	68	–	–	206	625	.330	–	–	–	144	210	.686	–	–	–	200	67	–	–	–	–	556	–	2.9	8.2
50-51–Rochester	68	–	–	183	561	.326	–	–	–	130	179	.726	–	–	152	147	94	0	–	–	–	496	2.2	2.2	7.3
51-52–Rochester	65	–	1065	104	372	.280	–	–	–	61	85	.718	–	–	106	115	95	1	–	–	–	269	1.6	1.8	4.1
52-53–Rochester	46	–	392	38	149	.255	–	–	–	27	38	.711	–	–	40	35	56	2	–	–	–	103	0.9	0.8	2.2
53-54–Milwaukee	51	–	649	74	224	.330	–	–	–	48	73	.658	–	–	46	75	73	1	–	–	–	196	0.9	1.5	3.8
Reg. NBA Totals	358	–	2106	830	2622	.317	–	–	–	506	742	.682	–	–	344	721	478	4	–	–	–	2166	1.5	2.0	6.1
Reg. NBL Totals	138	–	–	616	–	–	–	–	–	268	436	.615	–	–	–	–	180	–	–	–	–	1500	–	–	10.9
NBA Playoff Totals	28	–	144	55	197	.391	–	–	–	31	52	.596	–	–	32	51	27	0	–	–	–	141	1.1	1.3	5.0
NBL Playoff Totals	28	–	–	107	–	–	–	–	–	53	73	.726	–	–	–	–	39	–	–	–	–	267	–	–	9.5

Honeycutt, Jerald DeWayne b. October 20, 1974 Ht. 6-9 Wt. 254 College: Tulane

SEASON–TEAM	G	GS	MIN	FGM	FGA	PCT	3FGM	3FGA	PCT	FTM	FTA	PCT	O-RB	D-RB	TOT	AST	PF	DQ	STL	TO	BLK	PTS	RPG	APG	PPG
97-98–Milwaukee	38	0	530	90	221	.407	29	77	.377	36	58	.621	27	66	93	33	83	0	20	49	6	245	2.4	0.9	6.4
98-99–Milw.-Phil.	16	0	102	9	32	.281	5	17	.294	7	10	.700	3	9	12	3	16	0	5	9	2	30	0.8	0.2	1.9
Reg. Season Totals	54	0	632	99	253	.391	34	94	.362	43	68	.632	30	75	105	36	99	0	25	58	8	275	1.9	0.7	5.1
Playoff Totals	6	0	12	1	5	.200	0	3	.000	0	0	–	1	0	1	–	3	0	0	1	0	2	0.2	0.0	0.3

Hood, Derek Dwayne b. December 22, 1976 Ht. 6-8 Wt. 222 College: Arkansas

SEASON–TEAM	G	GS	MIN	FGM	FGA	PCT	3FGM	3FGA	PCT	FTM	FTA	PCT	O-RB	D-RB	TOT	AST	PF	DQ	STL	TO	BLK	PTS	RPG	APG	PPG
99-00–Charlotte	2	0	4	0	3	.000	0	0	–	0	0	–	0	1	1	0	0	0	0	0	0	0	0.5	0.0	0.0
Reg. Season Totals	2	0	4	0	3	.000	0	0	–	0	0	–	0	1	1	0	0	0	0	0	0	0	0.5	0.0	0.0

Hooper, Bobby Joe b. December 22, 1946 Ht. 6-0 Wt. 190 College: Dayton

SEASON–TEAM	G	GS	MIN	FGM	FGA	PCT	3FGM	3FGA	PCT	FTM	FTA	PCT	O-RB	D-RB	TOT	AST	PF	DQ	STL	TO	BLK	PTS	RPG	APG	PPG
68-69–Indiana (A)	54	–	955	112	271	.413	4	32	.125	43	59	.729	–	–	109	142	91	0	–	52	–	271	2.0	2.6	5.0
Reg. ABA Totals	54	–	955	112	271	.413	4	32	.125	43	59	.729	–	–	109	142	91	0	–	52	–	271	2.0	2.6	5.0
ABA Playoff Totals	16	–	288	25	74	.338	4	16	.250	22	26	.846	–	–	38	45	41	0	–	–	–	76	2.4	2.8	4.8

Hooser, Carroll L. b. March 5, 1944 Ht. 6-7 Wt. 230 College: Southern Methodist

SEASON–TEAM	G	GS	MIN	FGM	FGA	PCT	3FGM	3FGA	PCT	FTM	FTA	PCT	O-RB	D-RB	TOT	AST	PF	DQ	STL	TO	BLK	PTS	RPG	APG	PPG
67-68–Dallas (A)	56	–	720	128	297	.431	1	1	1.000	59	83	.711	–	–	216	29	139	6	–	49	–	316	3.9	0.5	5.6
Reg. ABA Totals	56	–	720	128	297	.431	1	1	1.000	59	83	.711	–	–	216	29	139	6	–	49	–	316	3.9	0.5	5.6
ABA Playoff Totals	3	–	6	1	2	.500	0	0	–	0	0	–	–	–	2	0	3	0	–	2	–	2	0.7	0.0	0.7

Hoover, Thomas Lee Jr. (Tom) b. January 23, 1941 Ht. 6-10 Wt. 240 College: Villanova

SEASON–TEAM	G	GS	MIN	FGM	FGA	PCT	3FGM	3FGA	PCT	FTM	FTA	PCT	O-RB	D-RB	TOT	AST	PF	DQ	STL	TO	BLK	PTS	RPG	APG	PPG
63-64–New York	59	–	988	102	247	.413	–	–	–	81	132	.614	–	–	331	36	185	4	–	–	–	285	5.6	0.6	4.8
64-65–New York	24	–	153	13	32	.406	–	–	–	8	14	.571	–	–	58	12	37	0	–	–	–	34	2.4	0.5	1.4
66-67–St. Louis	17	–	129	13	31	.419	–	–	–	5	13	.385	–	–	36	8	35	1	–	–	–	31	2.1	0.5	1.8
67-68–Denver (A)	70	–	1588	161	357	.451	4	10	.400	128	206	.621	–	–	491	64	268	8	–	139	–	454	7.0	0.9	6.5
68-69–Hou.-Minn.-N.Y. (A)	53	–	1419	191	408	.468	0	2	.000	125	189	.661	–	–	472	117	223	13	–	172	–	507	8.9	2.2	9.6
Reg. NBA Totals	100	–	1270	128	310	.413	–	–	–	94	159	.591	–	–	425	56	257	5	–	–	–	350	4.3	0.6	3.5
Reg. ABA Totals	123	–	3007	352	765	.460	4	12	.333	253	395	.641	–	–	963	181	491	21	–	311	–	961	7.8	1.5	7.8
NBA Playoff Totals	3	–	11	2	3	.667	–	–	–	0	0	–	–	–	3	1	3	0	–	–	–	4	1.0	0.3	1.3
ABA Playoff Totals	2	–	16	4	7	.571	0	0	–	5	7	.714	–	–	4	1	6	0	–	2	–	13	2.0	0.5	6.5

Hopkins, Robert M. (Bob) b. November 3, 1934 Ht. 6-8 Wt. 205 College: Grambling State

SEASON–TEAM	G	GS	MIN	FGM	FGA	PCT	3FGM	3FGA	PCT	FTM	FTA	PCT	O-RB	D-RB	TOT	AST	PF	DQ	STL	TO	BLK	PTS	RPG	APG	PPG
56-57–Syracuse	62	–	764	130	343	.379	–	–	–	94	126	.746	–	–	233	22	106	0	–	–	–	354	3.8	0.4	5.7
57-58–Syracuse	69	–	1224	221	554	.399	–	–	–	123	161	.764	–	–	392	45	162	5	–	–	–	565	5.7	0.7	8.2
58-59–Syracuse	67	–	1518	246	611	.403	–	–	–	176	234	.752	–	–	436	67	181	5	–	–	–	668	6.5	1.0	10.0
59-60–Syracuse	75	–	1616	257	660	.389	–	–	–	136	174	.782	–	–	465	55	193	4	–	–	–	650	6.2	0.7	8.7
Reg. Season Totals	273	–	5122	854	2168	.394	–	–	–	529	695	.761	–	–	1526	189	642	14	–	–	–	2237	5.6	0.7	8.2
Playoff Totals	18	–	334	38	117	.325	–	–	–	45	58	.776	–	–	99	11	57	2	–	–	–	121	5.5	0.6	6.7

Hoppen, David Dirk (Dave) b. March 13, 1964 Ht. 6-11 Wt. 235 College: Nebraska

SEASON–TEAM	G	GS	MIN	FGM	FGA	PCT	3FGM	3FGA	PCT	FTM	FTA	PCT	O-RB	D-RB	TOT	AST	PF	DQ	STL	TO	BLK	PTS	RPG	APG	PPG
87-88–Milw.-G.S.	39	8	642	84	183	.459	0	1	.000	54	62	.871	58	116	174	32	87	1	13	37	6	222	4.5	0.8	5.7
88-89–Charlotte	77	36	1419	199	353	.564	1	2	.500	101	139	.727	123	261	384	57	239	4	25	77	21	500	5.0	0.7	6.5
89-90–Charlotte	10	2	135	16	41	.390	0	0	–	8	10	.800	19	17	36	6	26	0	2	8	1	40	3.6	0.6	4.0
90-91–Cha.-Phil.	30	0	155	24	44	.545	0	2	.000	16	22	.727	18	21	39	3	29	0	3	13	1	64	1.3	0.1	2.1
91-92–Philadelphia	11	0	40	2	7	.286	0	0	–	5	10	.500	1	9	10	2	6	0	0	3	0	9	0.9	0.2	0.8
92-93–New Jersey	2	0	10	1	1	1.000	0	0	–	0	2	.000	1	3	4	0	2	0	0	0	0	2	2.0	0.0	1.0
Reg. Season Totals	169	46	2401	326	629	.518	1	5	.200	184	245	.751	220	427	647	100	389	5	43	138	29	837	3.8	0.6	5.0
Playoff Totals	3	0	9	3	3	1.000	0	0	–	0	2	.000	0	3	3	–	1	0	0	0	0	6	1.0	0.0	2.0

Hopson, Dennis b. April 22, 1965 Ht. 6-5 Wt. 200 College: Ohio State

SEASON–TEAM	G	GS	MIN	FGM	FGA	PCT	3FGM	3FGA	PCT	FTM	FTA	PCT	O-RB	D-RB	TOT	AST	PF	DQ	STL	TO	BLK	PTS	RPG	APG	PPG
87-88–New Jersey	61	19	1365	222	549	.404	12	45	.267	131	177	.740	63	80	143	118	145	0	57	119	25	587	2.3	1.9	9.6
88-89–New Jersey	62	36	1551	299	714	.419	4	27	.148	186	219	.849	91	111	202	103	150	0	70	102	30	788	3.3	1.7	12.7
89-90–New Jersey	79	64	2551	474	1093	.434	32	101	.317	271	342	.792	113	166	279	151	183	1	100	168	51	1251	3.5	1.9	15.8
90-91–Chicago	61	0	728	104	244	.426	1	5	.200	55	83	.663	49	60	109	65	79	0	25	59	14	264	1.8	1.1	4.3
91-92–Chicago-Sac.	71	0	1314	276	593	.465	12	47	.255	179	253	.708	105	101	206	102	115	0	67	100	39	743	2.9	1.4	10.5
Reg. Season Totals	334	119	7509	1375	3193	.431	61	225	.271	822	1074	.765	421	518	939	539	672	1	319	548	159	3633	2.8	1.6	10.9
Playoff Totals	5	0	18	2	6	.333	0	0	–	4	9	.444	2	2	4	1	2	0	0	1	1	8	0.8	0.2	1.6

Horan, John F. (Johnny, The Vertical Hyphen) b. November 24, 1932 d. November 14, 1980 Ht. 6-8 Wt. 190 College: Dayton

SEASON–TEAM	G	GS	MIN	FGM	FGA	PCT	3FGM	3FGA	PCT	FTM	FTA	PCT	O-RB	D-RB	TOT	AST	PF	DQ	STL	TO	BLK	PTS	RPG	APG	PPG
55-56–FtWayne-Minn.	19	–	93	12	42	.286	–	–	–	10	11	.909	–	–	10	2	21	0	–	–	–	34	0.5	0.1	1.8
Reg. Season Totals	19	–	93	12	42	.286	–	–	–	10	11	.909	–	–	10	2	21	0	–	–	–	34	0.5	0.1	1.8

Hordges, Cedrick Tyrone b. January 8, 1957 Ht. 6-8 Wt. 220 College: Auburn; South Carolina

SEASON–TEAM	G	GS	MIN	FGM	FGA	PCT	3FGM	3FGA	PCT	FTM	FTA	PCT	O-RB	D-RB	TOT	AST	PF	DQ	STL	TO	BLK	PTS	RPG	APG	PPG
80-81–Denver	68	–	1599	221	480	.460	0	3	.000	130	186	.699	120	338	458	104	226	4	33	120	19	572	6.7	1.5	8.4
81-82–Denver	77	1	1372	204	414	.493	3	13	.231	116	199	.583	119	276	395	65	230	1	26	111	19	527	5.1	0.8	6.8
Reg. Season Totals	145	1	2971	425	894	.475	3	16	.188	246	385	.639	239	614	853	169	456	5	59	231	38	1099	5.9	1.2	7.6
Playoff Totals	3	0	45	8	19	.421	0	1	.000	3	4	.750	2	11	13	2	4	0	1	4	0	19	4.3	0.7	6.3

Horford, Alfredo William (Tito) b. January 19, 1966 Ht. 7-1 Wt. 245 College: Louisiana State; Miami (Fla.)

SEASON–TEAM	G	GS	MIN	FGM	FGA	PCT	3FGM	3FGA	PCT	FTM	FTA	PCT	O-RB	D-RB	TOT	AST	PF	DQ	STL	TO	BLK	PTS	RPG	APG	PPG
88-89–Milwaukee	25	0	112	15	46	.326	0	0	–	12	19	.632	9	13	22	3	14	0	1	15	7	42	0.9	0.1	1.7
89-90–Milwaukee	35	0	236	18	62	.290	0	0	–	15	24	.625	19	40	59	2	33	0	5	14	16	51	1.7	0.1	1.5
93-94–Washington	3	0	28	0	2	.000	0	0	–	0	0	–	1	2	3	0	3	0	1	1	3	0	1.0	0.0	0.0
Reg. Season Totals	63	0	376	33	110	.300	0	0	–	27	43	.628	29	55	84	5	50	0	7	30	26	93	1.3	0.1	1.5
Playoff Totals	2	0	2	1	1	1.000	0	0	–	0	0	–	0	0	0	–	0	0	0	0	0	2	0.0	0.0	1.0

Horn, Ronald Leroy (Ron) b. May 24, 1938 Ht. 6-7 Wt. 225 College: Indiana

SEASON–TEAM	G	GS	MIN	FGM	FGA	PCT	3FGM	3FGA	PCT	FTM	FTA	PCT	O-RB	D-RB	TOT	AST	PF	DQ	STL	TO	BLK	PTS	RPG	APG	PPG
61-62–St. Louis	3	–	25	1	12	.083	–	–	–	1	2	.500	–	–	6	1	4	0	–	–	–	3	2.0	0.3	1.0
62-63–Los Angeles	28	–	289	27	82	.329	–	–	–	20	29	.690	–	–	71	10	46	0	–	–	–	74	2.5	0.4	2.6
67-68–Denver (A)	1	–	6	0	2	.000	0	0	–	2	2	1.000	–	–	1	0	0	0	–	1	–	2	1.0	0.0	2.0
Reg. NBA Totals	31	–	314	28	94	.298	–	–	–	21	31	.677	–	–	77	11	50	0	–	–	–	77	2.5	0.4	2.5
Reg. ABA Totals	1	–	6	0	2	.000	0	0	–	2	2	1.000	–	–	1	0	0	0	–	1	–	2	1.0	0.0	2.0
NBA Playoff Totals	7	–	55	4	12	.333	–	–	–	4	5	.800	–	–	11	2	13	0	–	–	–	12	1.6	0.3	1.7

Hornacek, Jeffrey John (Jeff) b. May 3, 1963 Ht. 6-4 Wt. 190 College: Iowa State

SEASON–TEAM	G	GS	MIN	FGM	FGA	PCT	3FGM	3FGA	PCT	FTM	FTA	PCT	O-RB	D-RB	TOT	AST	PF	DQ	STL	TO	BLK	PTS	RPG	APG	PPG
86-87–Phoenix	80	3	1561	159	350	.454	12	43	.279	94	121	.777	41	143	184	361	130	0	70	153	5	424	2.3	4.5	5.3
87-88–Phoenix	82	49	2243	306	605	.506	17	58	.293	152	185	.822	71	191	262	540	151	0	107	156	10	781	3.2	6.6	9.5
88-89–Phoenix	78	73	2487	440	889	.495	27	81	.333	147	178	.826	75	191	266	465	188	0	129	111	8	1054	3.4	6.0	13.5
89-90–Phoenix	67	60	2278	483	901	.536	40	98	.408	173	202	.856	86	227	313	337	144	2	117	125	14	1179	4.7	5.0	17.6
90-91–Phoenix	80	77	2733	544	1051	.518	61	146	.418	201	224	.897	74	247	321	409	185	1	111	130	16	1350	4.0	5.1	16.9
91-92–Phoenix	81	81	3078	635	1240	.512	83	189	.439	279	315	.886	106	301	407	411	218	1	158	170	31	1632	5.0	5.1	20.1
92-93–Philadelphia	79	78	2860	582	1239	.470	97	249	.390	250	289	.865	84	258	342	548	203	2	131	222	21	1511	4.3	6.9	19.1
93-94–Phil.-Utah	80	62	2820	472	1004	.470	70	208	.337	260	296	.878	60	219	279	419	186	0	127	171	13	1274	3.5	5.2	15.9
94-95–Utah	81	81	2696	482	937	.514	89	219	.406	284	322	.882	53	157	210	347	181	1	129	145	17	1337	2.6	4.3	16.5
95-96–Utah	82	59	2588	442	880	.502	104	223	.466	259	290	.893	62	147	209	340	171	1	106	127	20	1247	2.5	4.1	15.2
96-97–Utah	82	82	2592	413	856	.482	72	195	.369	293	326	.899	60	181	241	361	188	1	124	134	26	1191	2.9	4.4	14.5
97-98–Utah	80	80	2460	399	828	.482	56	127	.441	285	322	.885	65	205	270	349	175	1	109	132	15	1139	3.4	4.4	14.2
98-99–Utah	48	48	1435	214	449	.477	34	81	.420	125	140	.893	33	127	160	192	95	0	52	82	14	587	3.3	4.0	12.2
99-00–Utah	77	77	2133	358	728	.492	66	138	.478	171	180	.950	49	133	182	202	149	1	66	113	16	953	2.4	2.6	12.4
Reg. Season Totals	1077	910	33964	5929	11957	.496	828	2055	.403	2973	3390	.877	919	2727	3646	5281	2364	11	1536	1971	226	15659	3.4	4.9	14.5
Playoff Totals	140	140	4766	741	1578	.470	122	282	.433	488	551	.886	136	391	527	525	384	6	170	231	25	2092	3.8	3.8	14.9
All-Star Totals	1	0	24	5	7	.714	1	2	.500	0	0	–	1	1	2	3	0	0	1	0	0	11	2.0	3.0	11.0

Horry, Robert Keith b. August 25, 1970 Ht. 6-10 Wt. 235 College: Alabama

SEASON–TEAM	G	GS	MIN	FGM	FGA	PCT	3FGM	3FGA	PCT	FTM	FTA	PCT	O-RB	D-RB	TOT	AST	PF	DQ	STL	TO	BLK	PTS	RPG	APG	PPG
92-93–Houston	79	79	2330	323	682	.474	12	47	.255	143	200	.715	113	279	392	191	210	1	80	156	83	801	5.0	2.4	10.1
93-94–Houston	81	81	2370	322	702	.459	44	136	.324	115	157	.732	128	312	440	231	186	0	119	137	75	803	5.4	2.9	9.9
94-95–Houston	64	61	2074	240	537	.447	86	227	.379	86	113	.761	81	243	324	216	161	0	94	122	76	652	5.1	3.4	10.2
95-96–Houston	71	71	2634	300	732	.410	142	388	.366	111	143	.776	97	315	412	281	197	3	116	160	109	853	5.8	4.0	12.0
96-97–Phoenix-Lakers	54	29	1395	157	360	.436	49	154	.318	60	90	.667	68	169	237	110	153	2	66	72	55	423	4.4	2.0	7.8
97-98–L.A. Lakers	72	71	2192	200	420	.476	19	93	.204	117	169	.692	186	356	542	163	238	5	112	99	94	536	7.5	2.3	7.4
98-99–L.A. Lakers	38	5	744	67	146	.459	20	45	.444	34	46	.739	56	96	152	56	103	2	36	49	39	188	4.0	1.5	4.9
99-00–L.A. Lakers	76	0	1685	159	363	.438	29	94	.309	89	113	.788	133	228	361	118	189	0	84	73	80	436	4.8	1.6	5.7
Reg. Season Totals	535	397	15424	1768	3942	.449	401	1184	.339	755	1031	.732	862	1998	2860	1366	1437	13	707	868	611	4692	5.3	2.6	8.8
Playoff Totals	118	87	3797	402	906	.444	148	398	.372	220	309	.712	203	503	706	342	385	8	156	161	121	1172	6.0	2.9	9.9

Horton, Edward C. (Ed) b. December 17, 1967 Ht. 6-8 Wt. 230 College: Iowa

SEASON–TEAM	G	GS	MIN	FGM	FGA	PCT	3FGM	3FGA	PCT	FTM	FTA	PCT	O-RB	D-RB	TOT	AST	PF	DQ	STL	TO	BLK	PTS	RPG	APG	PPG
89-90–Washington	45	10	374	80	162	.494	0	4	.000	42	69	.609	59	49	108	19	63	1	9	39	5	202	2.4	0.4	4.5
Reg. Season Totals	45	10	374	80	162	.494	0	4	.000	42	69	.609	59	49	108	19	63	1	9	39	5	202	2.4	0.4	4.5

Hosket, Wilmer Frederick (Bill) b. December 20, 1946 Ht. 6-8 Wt. 225 College: Ohio State

SEASON–TEAM	G	GS	MIN	FGM	FGA	PCT	3FGM	3FGA	PCT	FTM	FTA	PCT	O-RB	D-RB	TOT	AST	PF	DQ	STL	TO	BLK	PTS	RPG	APG	PPG
68-69–New York	50	–	351	53	123	.431	–	–	–	24	42	.571	–	–	94	19	77	0	–	–	–	130	1.9	0.4	2.6
69-70–New York	36	–	235	46	91	.505	–	–	–	26	33	.788	–	–	63	17	36	0	–	–	–	118	1.8	0.5	3.3
70-71–Buffalo	13	–	217	47	90	.522	–	–	–	11	17	.647	–	–	75	20	27	1	–	–	–	105	5.8	1.5	8.1
71-72–Buffalo	44	–	592	89	181	.492	–	–	–	42	52	.808	–	–	123	38	79	0	–	–	–	220	2.8	0.9	5.0
Reg. Season Totals	143	–	1395	235	485	.485	–	–	–	103	144	.715	–	–	355	94	219	1	–	–	–	573	2.5	0.7	4.0
Playoff Totals	9	–	51	7	16	.438	–	–	–	3	5	.600	–	–	12	4	9	0	–	–	–	17	1.3	0.4	1.9

Houbregs, Robert J. (Bob, Houby) b. March 12, 1932 Ht. 6-8 Wt. 225 College: Washington HOF: 1986

SEASON–TEAM	G	GS	MIN	FGM	FGA	PCT	3FGM	3FGA	PCT	FTM	FTA	PCT	O-RB	D-RB	TOT	AST	PF	DQ	STL	TO	BLK	PTS	RPG	APG	PPG
53-54–Milw.-Balt.	70	–	1970	209	562	.372	–	–	–	190	266	.714	–	–	375	123	209	2	–	–	–	608	5.4	1.8	8.7
54-55–Balt.-Bos.-FtWayne	64	–	1326	148	386	.383	–	–	–	129	182	.709	–	–	297	86	180	5	–	–	–	425	4.6	1.3	6.6
55-56–Fort Wayne	70	–	1535	247	575	.430	–	–	–	283	383	.739	–	–	414	159	147	0	–	–	–	777	5.9	2.3	11.1
56-57–Fort Wayne	60	–	1592	253	585	.432	–	–	–	167	234	.714	–	–	401	113	118	2	–	–	–	673	6.7	1.9	11.2
57-58–Detroit	17	–	302	49	137	.358	–	–	–	30	43	.698	–	–	65	19	36	0	–	–	–	128	3.8	1.1	7.5
Reg. Season Totals	281	–	6725	906	2245	.404	–	–	–	799	1108	.721	–	–	1552	500	690	9	–	–	–	2611	5.5	1.8	9.3
Playoff Totals	23	–	468	67	158	.424	–	–	–	68	92	.739	–	–	135	36	55	1	–	–	–	202	5.9	1.6	8.8

Houston, Allan Wade b. April 20, 1971 Ht. 6-6 Wt. 200 College: Tennessee

SEASON–TEAM	G	GS	MIN	FGM	FGA	PCT	3FGM	3FGA	PCT	FTM	FTA	PCT	O-RB	D-RB	TOT	AST	PF	DQ	STL	TO	BLK	PTS	RPG	APG	PPG
93-94–Detroit	79	20	1519	272	671	.405	35	117	.299	89	108	.824	19	101	120	100	165	2	34	99	13	668	1.5	1.3	8.5
94-95–Detroit	76	39	1996	398	859	.463	158	373	.424	147	171	.860	29	138	167	164	182	0	61	113	14	1101	2.2	2.2	14.5
95-96–Detroit	82	75	3072	564	1244	.453	191	447	.427	298	362	.823	54	246	300	250	233	1	61	233	16	1617	3.7	3.0	19.7
96-97–New York	81	81	2681	437	1032	.423	148	384	.385	175	218	.803	43	197	240	179	233	6	41	167	18	1197	3.0	2.2	14.8
97-98–New York	82	82	2848	571	1277	.447	82	213	.385	285	335	.851	43	231	274	212	207	2	63	200	24	1509	3.3	2.6	18.4
98-99–New York	50	50	1815	294	703	.418	57	140	.407	168	195	.862	20	132	152	137	115	1	35	130	9	813	3.0	2.7	16.3
99-00–New York	82	82	3169	614	1271	.483	106	243	.436	280	334	.838	38	233	271	224	219	1	65	186	14	1614	3.3	2.7	19.7
Reg. Season Totals	532	429	17100	3150	7057	.446	777	1917	.405	1442	1723	.837	246	1278	1524	1266	1354	13	360	1128	108	8519	2.9	2.4	16.0
Playoff Totals	58	58	2336	397	906	.438	70	170	.412	246	281	.875	19	156	175	132	134	0	38	153	9	1110	3.0	2.3	19.1
All-Star Totals	1	0	18	3	10	.300	1	3	.333	4	4	1.000	0	0	0	2	1	0	1	1	0	11	0.0	2.0	11.0

Houston, Byron Dwight b. November 22, 1969 Ht. 6-5 Wt. 250 College: Oklahoma State

SEASON–TEAM	G	GS	MIN	FGM	FGA	PCT	3FGM	3FGA	PCT	FTM	FTA	PCT	O-RB	D-RB	TOT	AST	PF	DQ	STL	TO	BLK	PTS	RPG	APG	PPG
92-93–Golden State	79	8	1274	145	325	.446	2	7	.286	129	194	.665	119	196	315	69	253	12	44	87	43	421	4.0	0.9	5.3
93-94–Golden State	71	2	866	81	177	.458	1	7	.143	33	54	.611	67	127	194	32	181	4	33	49	31	196	2.7	0.5	2.8
94-95–Seattle	39	0	258	49	107	.458	6	22	.273	28	38	.737	20	35	55	6	50	0	13	20	5	132	1.4	0.2	3.4
95-96–Sacramento	25	0	276	32	64	.500	1	3	.333	21	26	.808	31	53	84	7	59	2	13	17	7	86	3.4	0.3	3.4
Reg. Season Totals	214	10	2674	307	673	.456	10	39	.256	211	312	.676	237	411	648	114	543	18	103	173	86	835	3.0	0.5	3.9
Playoff Totals	4	2	47	6	9	.667	0	0	–	3	5	.600	2	3	5	3	9	0	1	0	2	15	1.3	0.8	3.8

Hovasse, Tom b. January 31, 1967 Ht. 6-8 Wt. 205 College: Penn State

SEASON–TEAM	G	GS	MIN	FGM	FGA	PCT	3FGM	3FGA	PCT	FTM	FTA	PCT	O-RB	D-RB	TOT	AST	PF	DQ	STL	TO	BLK	PTS	RPG	APG	PPG
94-95–Atlanta	2	0	4	0	1	.000	0	1	.000	0	0	–	0	0	0	0	1	0	1	0	0	0	0.0	0.0	0.0
Reg. Season Totals	2	0	4	0	1	.000	0	1	.000	0	0	–	0	0	0	0	1	0	1	0	0	0	0.0	0.0	0.0

Howard, Brian Eugene b. October 19, 1967 Ht. 6-6 Wt. 210 College: North Carolina State

SEASON–TEAM	G	GS	MIN	FGM	FGA	PCT	3FGM	3FGA	PCT	FTM	FTA	PCT	O-RB	D-RB	TOT	AST	PF	DQ	STL	TO	BLK	PTS	RPG	APG	PPG
91-92–Dallas	27	0	318	54	104	.519	1	2	.500	22	31	.710	17	34	51	14	55	2	11	15	8	131	1.9	0.5	4.9
92-93–Dallas	68	22	1295	183	414	.442	1	7	.143	72	94	.766	66	146	212	67	217	8	55	68	34	439	3.1	1.0	6.5
Reg. Season Totals	95	22	1613	237	518	.458	2	9	.222	94	125	.752	83	180	263	81	272	10	66	83	42	570	2.8	0.9	6.0

Howard, Gregory Darryle (Greg, Stretch) b. January 8, 1948 Ht. 6-9 Wt. 215 College: Hartnell (Calif.) Coll. (J.C.); New Mexico

SEASON–TEAM	G	GS	MIN	FGM	FGA	PCT	3FGM	3FGA	PCT	FTM	FTA	PCT	O-RB	D-RB	TOT	AST	PF	DQ	STL	TO	BLK	PTS	RPG	APG	PPG
70-71–Phoenix	44	–	426	68	173	.393	–	–	–	37	58	.638	–	–	119	26	67	0	–	–	–	173	2.7	0.6	3.9
71-72–Cleveland	48	–	426	50	131	.382	–	–	–	39	51	.765	–	–	108	27	50	0	–	–	–	139	2.3	0.6	2.9
Reg. Season Totals	92	–	852	118	304	.388	–	–	–	76	109	.697	–	–	227	53	117	0	–	–	–	312	2.5	0.6	3.4

Howard, Juwan Antonio
b. February 7, 1973 Ht. 6-9 Wt. 250 College: Michigan

SEASON–TEAM	G	GS	MIN	FGM	FGA	PCT	3FGM	3FGA	PCT	FTM	FTA	PCT	O-RB	D-RB	TOT	AST	PF	DQ	STL	TO	BLK	PTS	RPG	APG	PPG
94-95–Washington	65	52	2348	455	931	.489	0	7	.000	194	292	.664	184	361	545	165	236	2	52	166	15	1104	8.4	2.5	17.0
95-96–Washington	81	81	3294	733	1500	.489	4	13	.308	319	426	.749	188	472	660	360	269	3	67	303	39	1789	8.1	4.4	22.1
96-97–Washington	82	82	3324	638	1313	.486	0	2	.000	294	389	.756	202	450	652	311	259	3	93	246	23	1570	8.0	3.8	19.1
97-98–Washington	64	64	2559	463	991	.467	0	2	.000	258	358	.721	161	288	449	208	225	3	82	185	23	1184	7.0	3.3	18.5
98-99–Washington	36	36	1430	286	604	.474	0	3	.000	110	146	.753	90	203	293	107	130	1	42	95	14	682	8.1	3.0	18.9
99-00–Washington	82	82	2909	509	1108	.459	0	7	.000	202	275	.735	132	338	470	247	299	2	67	225	21	1220	5.7	3.0	14.9
Reg. Season Totals	410	397	15864	3084	6447	.478	4	34	.118	1377	1886	.730	957	2112	3069	1398	1418	14	403	1220	135	7549	7.5	3.4	18.4
Playoff Totals	3	3	129	20	43	.465	0	0	–	16	18	.889	10	8	18	5	9	0	2	3	2	56	6.0	1.7	18.7
All-Star Totals	1	0	16	1	5	.200	0	0	–	0	0	–	4	2	6	2	3	0	1	0	0	2	6.0	2.0	2.0

Howard, Maurice (Mo)
b. August 24, 1954 Ht. 6-2 Wt. 175 College: Maryland

SEASON–TEAM	G	GS	MIN	FGM	FGA	PCT	3FGM	3FGA	PCT	FTM	FTA	PCT	O-RB	D-RB	TOT	AST	PF	DQ	STL	TO	BLK	PTS	RPG	APG	PPG
76-77–Clev.-N.O.	32	–	345	64	132	.485	–	–	–	24	35	.686	17	22	39	42	51	0	17	–	8	152	1.2	1.3	4.8
Reg. Season Totals	32	–	345	64	132	.485	–	–	–	24	35	.686	17	22	39	42	51	0	17	–	8	152	1.2	1.3	4.8

Howard, Stephen Christopher
b. July 15, 1970 Ht. 6-9 Wt. 250 College: DePaul

SEASON–TEAM	G	GS	MIN	FGM	FGA	PCT	3FGM	3FGA	PCT	FTM	FTA	PCT	O-RB	D-RB	TOT	AST	PF	DQ	STL	TO	BLK	PTS	RPG	APG	PPG
92-93–Utah	49	0	260	35	93	.376	0	0	–	34	53	.642	26	34	60	10	58	0	15	23	12	104	1.2	0.2	2.1
93-94–Utah	9	0	53	10	17	.588	0	0	–	11	16	.688	10	6	16	1	13	0	1	6	3	31	1.8	0.1	3.4
96-97–S.A.-Utah	49	0	418	62	108	.574	0	0	–	52	81	.642	29	56	85	11	62	0	19	25	12	176	1.7	0.2	3.6
97-98–Seattle	13	0	53	8	21	.381	0	0	–	9	18	.500	6	6	12	3	13	0	3	6	1	25	0.9	0.2	1.9
Reg. Season Totals	120	0	784	115	239	.481	0	0	–	106	168	.631	71	102	173	25	146	0	38	60	28	336	1.4	0.2	2.8
Playoff Totals	15	0	40	6	17	.353	0	0	–	11	15	.733	3	8	11	–	13	0	1	2	0	23	0.7	0.0	1.5

Howard, Wilbur Otis (Otis)
b. November 5, 1956 Ht. 6-7 Wt. 220 College: Austin Peay State

SEASON–TEAM	G	GS	MIN	FGM	FGA	PCT	3FGM	3FGA	PCT	FTM	FTA	PCT	O-RB	D-RB	TOT	AST	PF	DQ	STL	TO	BLK	PTS	RPG	APG	PPG
78-79–Milw.-Detroit	14	–	113	24	56	.429	–	–	–	11	23	.478	18	23	41	5	24	0	2	7	2	59	2.9	0.4	4.2
Reg. Season Totals	14	–	113	24	56	.429	–	–	–	11	23	.478	18	23	41	5	24	0	2	7	2	59	2.9	0.4	4.2

Howell, Bailey E.
b. January 20, 1937 Ht. 6-7 Wt. 220 College: Mississippi State HOF: 1997

SEASON–TEAM	G	GS	MIN	FGM	FGA	PCT	3FGM	3FGA	PCT	FTM	FTA	PCT	O-RB	D-RB	TOT	AST	PF	DQ	STL	TO	BLK	PTS	RPG	APG	PPG
59-60–Detroit	75	–	2346	510	1119	.456	–	–	–	312	422	.739	–	–	790	63	282	13	–	–	–	1332	10.5	0.8	17.8
60-61–Detroit	77	–	2952	607	1293	.469	–	–	–	601	798	.753	–	–	1111	196	297	10	–	–	–	1815	14.4	2.5	23.6
61-62–Detroit	79	–	2857	553	1193	.464	–	–	–	470	612	.768	–	–	996	186	317	10	–	–	–	1576	12.6	2.4	19.9
62-63–Detroit	79	–	2971	637	1235	.516	–	–	–	519	650	.798	–	–	910	232	300	9	–	–	–	1793	11.5	2.9	22.7
63-64–Detroit	77	–	2700	598	1267	.472	–	–	–	470	581	.809	–	–	776	205	290	9	–	–	–	1666	10.1	2.7	21.6
64-65–Baltimore	80	–	2975	515	1040	.495	–	–	–	504	629	.801	–	–	869	208	345	10	–	–	–	1534	10.9	2.6	19.2
65-66–Baltimore	78	–	2328	481	986	.488	–	–	–	402	551	.730	–	–	773	155	306	12	–	–	–	1364	9.9	2.0	17.5
66-67–Boston	81	–	2503	636	1242	.512	–	–	–	349	471	.741	–	–	677	103	296	4	–	–	–	1621	8.4	1.3	20.0
67-68–Boston	82	–	2801	643	1336	.481	–	–	–	335	461	.727	–	–	805	133	285	4	–	–	–	1621	9.8	1.6	19.8
68-69–Boston	78	–	2527	612	1257	.487	–	–	–	313	426	.735	–	–	685	137	285	3	–	–	–	1537	8.8	1.8	19.7
69-70–Boston	82	–	2078	399	931	.429	–	–	–	235	308	.763	–	–	550	120	261	4	–	–	–	1033	6.7	1.5	12.6
70-71–Philadelphia	82	–	1589	324	686	.472	–	–	–	230	315	.730	–	–	441	115	234	2	–	–	–	878	5.4	1.4	10.7
Reg. Season Totals	950	–	30627	6515	13585	.480	–	–	–	4740	6224	.762	–	–	9383	1853	3498	90	–	–	–	17770	9.9	2.0	18.7
Playoff Totals	86	–	2712	542	1165	.465	–	–	–	317	433	.732	–	–	687	130	376	21	–	–	–	1401	8.0	1.5	16.3
All-Star Totals	6	–	81	13	33	.394	–	–	–	6	8	.750	–	–	10	8	12	0	–	–	–	32	1.7	1.3	5.3

Hubbard, Phillip Gregory (Phil)
b. December 13, 1956 Ht. 6-8 Wt. 215 College: Michigan

SEASON–TEAM	G	GS	MIN	FGM	FGA	PCT	3FGM	3FGA	PCT	FTM	FTA	PCT	O-RB	D-RB	TOT	AST	PF	DQ	STL	TO	BLK	PTS	RPG	APG	PPG
79-80–Detroit	64	–	1189	210	451	.466	0	2	.000	165	220	.750	114	206	320	70	202	9	48	120	10	585	5.0	1.1	9.1
80-81–Detroit	80	–	2289	433	880	.492	1	3	.333	294	426	.690	236	350	586	150	317	14	80	229	20	1161	7.3	1.9	14.5
81-82–Detroit-Clev.	83	40	1839	326	665	.490	0	4	.000	191	280	.682	187	286	473	91	292	3	65	161	19	843	5.7	1.1	10.2
82-83–Cleveland	82	38	1953	288	597	.482	0	2	.000	204	296	.689	222	249	471	89	271	11	87	158	8	780	5.7	1.1	9.5
83-84–Cleveland	80	6	1799	321	628	.511	0	1	.000	221	299	.739	172	208	380	86	244	3	71	115	6	863	4.8	1.1	10.8
84-85–Cleveland	76	55	2249	415	822	.505	0	4	.000	371	494	.751	214	265	479	114	258	8	81	178	9	1201	6.3	1.5	15.8
85-86–Cleveland	23	21	640	93	198	.470	0	1	.000	76	112	.679	48	72	120	29	78	2	20	66	3	262	5.2	1.3	11.4
86-87–Cleveland	68	68	2083	321	605	.531	0	4	.000	162	272	.596	178	210	388	136	224	6	66	156	7	804	5.7	2.0	11.8
87-88–Cleveland	78	59	1631	237	485	.489	0	5	.000	182	243	.749	117	164	281	81	167	1	50	118	7	656	3.6	1.0	8.4
88-89–Cleveland	31	0	191	28	63	.444	0	0	–	17	25	.680	14	26	40	11	20	0	6	9	0	73	1.3	0.4	2.4
Reg. Season Totals	665	287	15863	2672	5394	.495	1	26	.038	1883	2667	.706	1502	2036	3538	857	2073	57	574	1310	89	7228	5.3	1.3	10.9
Playoff Totals	8	4	123	25	51	.490	1	1	1.000	13	18	.722	12	11	23	3	17	0	3	8	0	64	2.9	0.4	8.0

Hubbard, Robert Cecil (Bob) b. December 27, 1922 Ht. 6-6 Wt. 215 College: Springfield

SEASON–TEAM	G	GS	MIN	FGM	FGA	PCT	3FGM	3FGA	PCT	FTM	FTA	PCT	O-RB	D-RB	TOT	AST	PF	DQ	STL	TO	BLK	PTS	RPG	APG	PPG
47-48–Tri-Cities (N)	20	–	–	27	–	–	–	–	–	22	26	.846	–	–	–	–	–	–	–	–	–	76	–	–	3.8
47-48–Providence	28	–	–	58	199	.291	–	–	–	36	52	.692	–	–	–	11	34	–	–	–	–	152	–	0.4	5.4
48-49–Providence	34	–	–	25	135	.185	–	–	–	22	34	.647	–	–	–	18	39	–	–	–	–	72	–	0.5	2.1
Reg. NBA Totals	62	–	–	83	334	.249	–	–	–	58	86	.674	–	–	–	29	73	–	–	–	–	224	–	0.5	3.6
Reg. NBL Totals	20	–	–	27	–	–	–	–	–	22	26	.846	–	–	–	–	–	–	–	–	–	76	–	–	3.8

Hudson, Louis Clyde (Lou, Super Lou) b. July 11, 1944 Ht. 6-5 Wt. 215 College: Minnesota

SEASON–TEAM	G	GS	MIN	FGM	FGA	PCT	3FGM	3FGA	PCT	FTM	FTA	PCT	O-RB	D-RB	TOT	AST	PF	DQ	STL	TO	BLK	PTS	RPG	APG	PPG
66-67–St. Louis	80	–	2446	620	1328	.467	–	–	–	231	327	.706	–	–	435	95	277	3	–	–	–	1471	5.4	1.2	18.4
67-68–St. Louis	46	–	966	227	500	.454	–	–	–	120	164	.732	–	–	193	65	113	2	–	–	–	574	4.2	1.4	12.5
68-69–Atlanta	81	–	2869	716	1455	.492	–	–	–	338	435	.777	–	–	533	216	248	0	–	–	–	1770	6.6	2.7	21.9
69-70–Atlanta	80	–	3091	830	1564	.531	–	–	–	371	450	.824	–	–	373	276	225	1	–	–	–	2031	4.7	3.5	25.4
70-71–Atlanta	76	–	3113	829	1713	.484	–	–	–	381	502	.759	–	–	386	257	186	0	–	–	–	2039	5.1	3.4	26.8
71-72–Atlanta	77	–	3042	775	1540	.503	–	–	–	349	430	.812	–	–	385	309	225	0	–	–	–	1899	5.0	4.0	24.7
72-73–Atlanta	75	–	3027	816	1710	.477	–	–	–	397	481	.825	–	–	467	258	197	1	–	–	–	2029	6.2	3.4	27.1
73-74–Atlanta	65	–	2588	678	1356	.500	–	–	–	295	353	.836	126	224	350	213	205	3	160	–	29	1651	5.4	3.3	25.4
74-75–Atlanta	11	–	380	97	225	.431	–	–	–	48	57	.842	14	33	47	40	33	1	13	–	2	242	4.3	3.6	22.0
75-76–Atlanta	81	–	2558	569	1205	.472	–	–	–	237	291	.814	104	196	300	214	241	3	124	–	17	1375	3.7	2.6	17.0
76-77–Atlanta	58	–	1745	413	905	.456	–	–	–	142	169	.840	48	81	129	155	160	2	67	–	19	968	2.2	2.7	16.7
77-78–Los Angeles	82	–	2283	493	992	.497	–	–	–	137	177	.774	80	108	188	193	196	0	94	150	14	1123	2.3	2.4	13.7
78-79–Los Angeles	78	–	1686	329	636	.517	–	–	–	110	124	.887	64	76	140	141	133	1	58	99	17	768	1.8	1.8	9.8
Reg. Season Totals	890	–	29794	7392	15129	.489	–	–	–	3156	3960	.797	436	718	3926	2432	2439	17	516	249	98	17940	4.4	2.7	20.2
Playoff Totals	61	–	2199	519	1164	.446	–	–	–	262	326	.804	8	5	318	164	196	4	6	10	0	1300	5.2	2.7	21.3
All-Star Totals	6	–	99	26	61	.426	–	–	–	14	15	.933	1	2	13	6	11	0	0	–	1	66	2.2	1.0	11.0

Hudson, Troy b. March 13, 1976 Ht. 6-1 Wt. 170 College: Southern Illinois

SEASON–TEAM	G	GS	MIN	FGM	FGA	PCT	3FGM	3FGA	PCT	FTM	FTA	PCT	O-RB	D-RB	TOT	AST	PF	DQ	STL	TO	BLK	PTS	RPG	APG	PPG
97-98–Utah	8	0	23	6	14	.429	0	3	.000	0	0	–	1	1	2	4	1	0	2	1	0	12	0.3	0.5	1.5
98-99–L.A. Clippers	25	6	524	60	150	.400	15	47	.319	34	38	.895	15	40	55	92	28	1	11	38	2	169	2.2	3.7	6.8
99-00–L.A. Clippers	62	38	1592	204	541	.377	60	193	.311	77	95	.811	28	120	148	242	65	0	43	108	0	545	2.4	3.9	8.8
Reg. Season Totals	95	44	2139	270	705	.383	75	243	.309	111	133	.835	44	161	205	338	94	1	56	147	2	726	2.2	3.6	7.6

Hughes, Alfredrick b. July 19, 1962 Ht. 6-5 Wt. 215 College: Loyola (Chicago)

SEASON–TEAM	G	GS	MIN	FGM	FGA	PCT	3FGM	3FGA	PCT	FTM	FTA	PCT	O-RB	D-RB	TOT	AST	PF	DQ	STL	TO	BLK	PTS	RPG	APG	PPG
85-86–San Antonio	68	0	866	152	372	.409	3	17	.176	49	84	.583	49	64	113	61	79	0	26	63	5	356	1.7	0.9	5.2
Reg. Season Totals	68	0	866	152	372	.409	3	17	.176	49	84	.583	49	64	113	61	79	0	26	63	5	356	1.7	0.9	5.2
Playoff Totals	3	0	18	4	9	.444	0	0	–	0	0	–	0	0	0	1	3	0	1	1	0	8	0.0	0.3	2.7

Hughes, Eddie b. May 26, 1960 Ht. 5-10 Wt. 165 College: Colorado State

SEASON–TEAM	G	GS	MIN	FGM	FGA	PCT	3FGM	3FGA	PCT	FTM	FTA	PCT	O-RB	D-RB	TOT	AST	PF	DQ	STL	TO	BLK	PTS	RPG	APG	PPG
87-88–Utah	11	0	42	5	13	.385	1	6	.167	6	6	1.000	3	1	4	8	5	0	0	6	0	17	0.4	0.7	1.5
88-89–Denver	26	1	224	28	64	.438	7	22	.318	7	12	.583	6	13	19	35	30	0	17	11	2	70	0.7	1.3	2.7
89-90–Denver	60	7	892	83	202	.411	20	49	.408	23	34	.676	15	55	70	116	87	0	48	39	1	209	1.2	1.9	3.5
Reg. Season Totals	97	8	1158	116	279	.416	28	77	.364	36	52	.692	24	69	93	159	122	0	65	56	3	296	1.0	1.6	3.1
Playoff Totals	7	0	16	2	7	.286	1	3	.333	0	0	–	0	0	0	1	1	0	1	1	0	5	0.0	0.1	0.7

Hughes, Kim Galen b. June 4, 1952 Ht. 6-11 Wt. 220 College: Wisconsin

SEASON–TEAM	G	GS	MIN	FGM	FGA	PCT	3FGM	3FGA	PCT	FTM	FTA	PCT	O-RB	D-RB	TOT	AST	PF	DQ	STL	TO	BLK	PTS	RPG	APG	PPG
75-76–New York (A)	84	–	2162	300	566	.530	0	0	–	92	202	.455	341	434	775	55	292	–	98	102	120	692	9.2	0.7	8.2
76-77–New York Nets	81	–	2081	151	354	.427	–	–	–	19	69	.275	189	375	564	98	308	9	122	–	119	321	7.0	1.2	4.0
77-78–New Jersey	56	–	854	57	160	.356	–	–	–	9	29	.310	95	145	240	38	163	9	49	57	49	123	4.3	0.7	2.2
78-79–Denver	81	–	1086	98	182	.538	–	–	–	18	45	.400	112	223	335	74	215	2	56	78	102	214	4.1	0.9	2.6
79-80–Denver	70	–	1208	102	202	.505	0	0	–	15	41	.366	125	201	326	74	184	3	66	50	77	219	4.7	1.1	3.1
80-81–Denver-Clev.	53	–	490	27	70	.386	0	0	–	1	2	.500	48	79	127	35	106	2	28	44	35	55	2.4	0.7	1.0
Reg. NBA Totals	341	–	5719	435	968	.449	0	0	–	62	186	.333	569	1023	1592	319	976	25	321	229	382	932	4.7	0.9	2.7
Reg. ABA Totals	84	–	2162	300	566	.530	0	0	–	92	202	.455	341	434	775	55	292	–	98	102	120	692	9.2	0.7	8.2
NBA Playoff Totals	3	–	35	1	2	.500	0	0	–	1	2	.500	3	8	11	–	8	0	2	3	0	3	3.7	0.0	1.0
ABA Playoff Totals	12	–	266	29	57	.509	0	0	–	2	5	.400	34	38	72	9	53	–	10	9	13	60	6.0	0.8	5.0

Hughes, Larry Darnell b. January 23, 1979 Ht. 6-5 Wt. 185 College: St. Louis

SEASON–TEAM	G	GS	MIN	FGM	FGA	PCT	3FGM	3FGA	PCT	FTM	FTA	PCT	O-RB	D-RB	TOT	AST	PF	DQ	STL	TO	BLK	PTS	RPG	APG	PPG
98-99–Philadelphia	50	1	988	170	414	.411	8	52	.154	107	151	.709	83	106	189	77	97	0	44	68	14	455	3.8	1.5	9.1
99-00–Phil.-G.S.	82	37	2324	459	1147	.400	29	125	.232	279	377	.740	113	236	349	205	191	2	115	195	28	1226	4.3	2.5	15.0
Reg. Season Totals	132	38	3312	629	1561	.403	37	177	.209	386	528	.731	196	342	538	282	288	2	159	263	42	1681	4.1	2.1	12.7
Playoff Totals	8	2	198	31	77	.403	0	7	.000	20	24	.833	17	20	37	16	21	0	15	12	9	82	4.6	2.0	10.3

Hughes, Rick b. August 22, 1973 Ht. 6-9 Wt. 235 College: Thomas More

SEASON–TEAM	G	GS	MIN	FGM	FGA	PCT	3FGM	3FGA	PCT	FTM	FTA	PCT	O-RB	D-RB	TOT	AST	PF	DQ	STL	TO	BLK	PTS	RPG	APG	PPG
99-00–Dallas	21	0	224	35	72	.486	0	1	.000	12	26	.462	24	25	49	9	30	0	3	14	1	82	2.3	0.4	3.9
Reg. Season Totals	21	0	224	35	72	.486	0	1	.000	12	26	.462	24	25	49	9	30	0	3	14	1	82	2.3	0.4	3.9

Hummer, John R. b. May 4, 1948 Ht. 6-9 Wt. 230 College: Princeton

SEASON–TEAM	G	GS	MIN	FGM	FGA	PCT	3FGM	3FGA	PCT	FTM	FTA	PCT	O-RB	D-RB	TOT	AST	PF	DQ	STL	TO	BLK	PTS	RPG	APG	PPG
70-71–Buffalo	81	–	2637	339	764	.444	–	–	–	235	405	.580	–	–	717	163	284	10	–	–	–	913	8.9	2.0	11.3
71-72–Buffalo	55	–	1186	113	290	.390	–	–	–	58	124	.468	–	–	229	72	178	4	–	–	–	284	4.2	1.3	5.2
72-73–Buffalo	66	–	1546	206	464	.444	–	–	–	115	205	.561	–	–	323	138	185	5	–	–	–	527	4.9	2.1	8.0
73-74–Chi.-Seattle	53	–	1119	144	305	.472	–	–	–	59	124	.476	84	199	283	107	119	0	28	–	22	347	5.3	2.0	6.5
74-75–Seattle	43	–	568	41	108	.380	–	–	–	14	51	.275	28	76	104	38	63	0	8	–	7	96	2.4	0.9	2.2
75-76–Seattle	29	–	364	32	67	.478	–	–	–	17	41	.415	21	56	77	25	71	5	6	–	9	81	2.7	0.9	2.8
Reg. Season Totals	327	–	7420	875	1998	.438	–	–	–	498	950	.524	133	331	1733	543	900	24	42	–	38	2248	5.3	1.7	6.9
Playoff Totals	9	–	84	2	10	.200	–	–	–	0	0	–	2	8	10	4	10	0	2	–	0	4	1.1	0.4	0.4

Humphries, John Jay (Jay) b. October 17, 1962 Ht. 6-3 Wt. 185 College: Colorado

SEASON–TEAM	G	GS	MIN	FGM	FGA	PCT	3FGM	3FGA	PCT	FTM	FTA	PCT	O-RB	D-RB	TOT	AST	PF	DQ	STL	TO	BLK	PTS	RPG	APG	PPG
84-85–Phoenix	80	39	2062	279	626	.446	4	20	.200	141	170	.829	32	132	164	350	209	2	107	167	8	703	2.1	4.4	8.8
85-86–Phoenix	82	82	2733	352	735	.479	4	29	.138	197	257	.767	56	204	260	526	222	1	132	190	9	905	3.2	6.4	11.0
86-87–Phoenix	82	82	2579	359	753	.477	5	27	.185	200	260	.769	62	198	260	632	239	1	112	195	9	923	3.2	7.7	11.3
87-88–Phoenix-Milw.	68	33	1809	284	538	.528	3	18	.167	112	153	.732	49	125	174	395	177	1	81	127	5	683	2.6	5.8	10.0
88-89–Milwaukee	73	50	2220	345	714	.483	25	94	.266	129	158	.816	70	119	189	405	187	1	142	160	5	844	2.6	5.5	11.6
89-90–Milwaukee	81	81	2818	496	1005	.494	21	70	.300	224	285	.786	80	189	269	472	253	2	156	151	11	1237	3.3	5.8	15.3
90-91–Milwaukee	80	80	2726	482	960	.502	60	161	.373	191	239	.799	57	163	220	538	237	2	129	151	7	1215	2.8	6.7	15.2
91-92–Milwaukee	71	71	2261	377	803	.469	42	144	.292	195	249	.783	44	140	184	466	210	2	119	148	13	991	2.6	6.6	14.0
92-93–Utah	78	20	2034	287	659	.436	15	75	.200	101	130	.777	40	103	143	317	236	3	101	132	11	690	1.8	4.1	8.8
93-94–Utah	75	19	1619	233	535	.436	38	96	.396	57	76	.750	35	92	127	219	168	0	65	95	11	561	1.7	2.9	7.5
94-95–Utah-Boston	18	0	201	8	34	.235	2	4	.500	2	4	.500	4	9	13	19	35	0	9	17	0	20	0.7	1.1	1.1
Reg. Season Totals	788	557	23062	3502	7362	.476	219	738	.297	1549	1981	.782	529	1474	2003	4339	2173	15	1153	1533	89	8772	2.5	5.5	11.1
Playoff Totals	41	17	1104	151	323	.467	15	56	.268	79	101	.782	26	67	93	187	123	2	32	57	5	396	2.3	4.6	9.7

Hundley, Rodney Clark (Rod, Hot Rod) b. October 26, 1934 Ht. 6-4 Wt. 185 College: West Virginia

SEASON–TEAM	G	GS	MIN	FGM	FGA	PCT	3FGM	3FGA	PCT	FTM	FTA	PCT	O-RB	D-RB	TOT	AST	PF	DQ	STL	TO	BLK	PTS	RPG	APG	PPG
57-58–Minneapolis	65	–	1154	174	548	.318	–	–	–	104	162	.642	–	–	186	121	99	0	–	–	–	452	2.9	1.9	7.0
58-59–Minneapolis	71	–	1664	259	719	.360	–	–	–	164	218	.752	–	–	250	205	139	0	–	–	–	682	3.5	2.9	9.6
59-60–Minneapolis	73	–	2279	365	1019	.358	–	–	–	203	273	.744	–	–	390	338	194	0	–	–	–	933	5.3	4.6	12.8
60-61–Los Angeles	79	–	2179	323	921	.351	–	–	–	223	296	.753	–	–	289	350	144	0	–	–	–	869	3.7	4.4	11.0
61-62–Los Angeles	78	–	1492	173	509	.340	–	–	–	83	127	.654	–	–	199	290	129	1	–	–	–	429	2.6	3.7	5.5
62-63–Los Angeles	65	–	785	88	262	.336	–	–	–	84	119	.706	–	–	106	151	81	0	–	–	–	260	1.6	2.3	4.0
Reg. Season Totals	431	–	9553	1382	3978	.347	–	–	–	861	1195	.721	–	–	1420	1455	786	1	–	–	–	3625	3.3	3.4	8.4
Playoff Totals	53	–	1020	101	316	.320	–	–	–	68	95	.716	–	–	149	157	80	0	–	–	–	270	2.8	3.0	5.1
All-Star Totals	2	–	37	11	22	.500	–	–	–	2	2	1.000	–	–	3	4	3	0	–	–	–	24	1.5	2.0	12.0

Hunter, Cedric R. b. January 16, 1965 Ht. 6-0 Wt. 180 College: Kansas

SEASON–TEAM	G	GS	MIN	FGM	FGA	PCT	3FGM	3FGA	PCT	FTM	FTA	PCT	O-RB	D-RB	TOT	AST	PF	DQ	STL	TO	BLK	PTS	RPG	APG	PPG
91-92–Charlotte	1	0	1	0	0	–	0	0	–	0	0	–	0	0	0	0	0	0	0	0	0	0	0.0	0.0	0.0
Reg. Season Totals	1	0	1	0	0	–	0	0	–	0	0	–	0	0	0	0	0	0	0	0	0	0	0.0	0.0	0.0

Hunter, Leslie (Les, Big Game) b. August 16, 1942 Ht. 6-7 Wt. 210 College: Loyola (Chicago)

SEASON–TEAM	G	GS	MIN	FGM	FGA	PCT	3FGM	3FGA	PCT	FTM	FTA	PCT	O-RB	D-RB	TOT	AST	PF	DQ	STL	TO	BLK	PTS	RPG	APG	PPG
64-65–Baltimore	24	–	114	18	64	.281	–	–	–	6	14	.429	–	–	50	11	16	0	–	–	–	42	2.1	0.5	1.8
67-68–Minnesota (A)	75	–	2552	513	1207	.425	2	17	.118	290	468	.620	332	406	738	116	297	7	–	204	–	1318	9.8	1.5	17.6
68-69–Miami (A)	77	–	2537	476	1073	.444	0	5	.000	335	448	.748	–	–	743	127	311	14	–	220	–	1287	9.6	1.6	16.7
69-70–New York (A)	79	–	2859	486	1122	.433	6	41	.146	317	432	.734	–	–	673	215	335	15	–	–	–	1295	8.5	2.7	16.4
70-71–N.Y.-Ken. (A)	80	–	1525	288	645	.447	10	49	.204	159	223	.713	–	–	493	95	253	–	–	–	–	745	6.2	1.2	9.3
71-72–Kentucky (A)	70	–	967	183	383	.478	5	16	.313	101	144	.701	–	–	225	93	154	–	–	93	–	472	3.2	1.3	6.7
72-73–Memphis (A)	63	–	1333	236	474	.498	9	33	.273	95	135	.704	94	208	302	95	183	0	–	95	–	576	4.8	1.5	9.1
Reg. NBA Totals	24	–	114	18	64	.281	–	–	–	6	14	.429	–	–	50	11	16	0	–	–	–	42	2.1	0.5	1.8
Reg. ABA Totals	444	–	11773	2182	4904	.445	32	161	.199	1297	1850	.701	426	614	3174	741	1533	36	–	612	–	5693	7.1	1.7	12.8
ABA Playoff Totals	52	–	1302	250	613	.408	8	28	.286	167	253	.660	–	–	349	89	177	5	–	37	–	675	6.7	1.7	13.0

H

Hunter, Lindsey Benson Jr. b. December 3, 1970 Ht. 6-2 Wt. 195 College: Alcorn State; Jackson State

SEASON–TEAM	G	GS	MIN	FGM	FGA	PCT	3FGM	3FGA	PCT	FTM	FTA	PCT	O-RB	D-RB	TOT	AST	PF	DQ	STL	TO	BLK	PTS	RPG	APG	PPG
93-94–Detroit	82	26	2172	335	893	.375	69	207	.333	104	142	.732	47	142	189	390	174	1	121	184	10	843	2.3	4.8	10.3
94-95–Detroit	42	26	944	119	318	.374	36	108	.333	40	55	.727	24	51	75	159	94	1	51	79	7	314	1.8	3.8	7.5
95-96–Detroit	80	48	2138	239	628	.381	117	289	.405	84	120	.700	44	150	194	188	185	0	84	80	18	679	2.4	2.4	8.5
96-97–Detroit	82	76	3023	421	1042	.404	166	468	.355	158	203	.778	59	174	233	154	206	1	129	96	24	1166	2.8	1.9	14.2
97-98–Detroit	71	67	2505	316	826	.383	85	265	.321	145	196	.740	61	186	247	224	174	3	123	110	10	862	3.5	3.2	12.1
98-99–Detroit	49	49	1755	228	524	.435	59	153	.386	67	89	.753	26	142	168	193	126	2	86	92	8	582	3.4	3.9	11.9
99-00–Detroit	82	82	2919	379	892	.425	168	389	.432	117	154	.760	35	215	250	327	216	2	129	145	22	1043	3.0	4.0	12.7
Reg. Season Totals	488	374	15456	2037	5123	.398	700	1879	.373	715	959	.746	296	1060	1356	1635	1175	10	723	786	99	5489	2.8	3.4	11.2
Playoff Totals	15	13	510	55	159	.346	17	53	.321	15	20	.750	10	32	42	24	26	0	19	13	2	142	2.8	1.6	9.5

Hurley, Robert Matthew (Bobby) b. June 28, 1971 Ht. 6-0 Wt. 165 College: Duke

SEASON–TEAM	G	GS	MIN	FGM	FGA	PCT	3FGM	3FGA	PCT	FTM	FTA	PCT	O-RB	D-RB	TOT	AST	PF	DQ	STL	TO	BLK	PTS	RPG	APG	PPG
93-94–Sacramento	19	19	499	54	146	.370	2	16	.125	24	30	.800	6	28	34	115	28	0	13	48	1	134	1.8	6.1	7.1
94-95–Sacramento	68	6	1105	103	284	.363	21	76	.276	58	76	.763	14	56	70	226	79	0	29	110	0	285	1.0	3.3	4.2
95-96–Sacramento	72	22	1059	65	230	.283	22	76	.289	68	85	.800	12	63	75	216	121	0	28	86	3	220	1.0	3.0	3.1
96-97–Sacramento	49	12	632	46	125	.368	14	45	.311	37	53	.698	9	29	38	146	53	0	27	55	3	143	0.8	3.0	2.9
97-98–Sac.-Vanc.	61	3	875	93	238	.391	5	22	.227	59	76	.776	12	54	66	177	79	0	23	86	0	250	1.1	2.9	4.1
Reg. Season Totals	269	62	4170	361	1023	.353	64	235	.272	246	320	.769	53	230	283	880	360	0	120	385	7	1032	1.1	3.3	3.8
Playoff Totals	1	0	2	0	0	–	0	0	–	0	0	–	0	0	0	–	0	0	0	0	0	0	0.0	0.0	0.0

Hurley, Roy Leonard b. August 12, 1922 d. October 14, 1993 Ht. 6-2 Wt. 170 College: Indiana; Murray State

SEASON–TEAM	G	GS	MIN	FGM	FGA	PCT	3FGM	3FGA	PCT	FTM	FTA	PCT	O-RB	D-RB	TOT	AST	PF	DQ	STL	TO	BLK	PTS	RPG	APG	PPG
45-46–Indianapolis (N)	30	–	–	76	–	–	–	–	–	24	38	.632	–	–	–	–	68	–	–	–	–	176	–	–	5.9
46-47–Toronto	46	–	–	100	447	.224	–	–	–	39	64	.609	–	–	–	34	85	–	–	–	–	239	–	0.7	5.2
47-48–Tri-Cit-Syr. (N)	16	–	–	19	–	–	–	–	–	13	21	.619	–	–	–	–	–	–	–	–	–	51	–	–	3.2
Reg. NBA Totals	46	–	–	100	447	.224	–	–	–	39	64	.609	–	–	–	34	85	–	–	–	–	239	–	0.7	5.2
Reg. NBL Totals	46	–	–	95	–	–	–	–	–	37	59	.627	–	–	–	–	68	–	–	–	–	227	–	–	4.9

Huston, Geoffrey Angier (Geoff) b. November 8, 1957 Ht. 6-2 Wt. 175 College: Texas Tech

SEASON–TEAM	G	GS	MIN	FGM	FGA	PCT	3FGM	3FGA	PCT	FTM	FTA	PCT	O-RB	D-RB	TOT	AST	PF	DQ	STL	TO	BLK	PTS	RPG	APG	PPG
79-80–New York	71	–	923	94	241	.390	3	17	.176	28	38	.737	14	44	58	159	83	0	39	73	5	219	0.8	2.2	3.1
80-81–Dallas-Clev.	81	–	2434	461	942	.489	1	5	.200	150	212	.708	45	93	138	394	148	1	58	179	7	1073	1.7	4.9	13.2
81-82–Cleveland	78	43	2409	325	672	.484	3	10	.300	153	200	.765	53	97	150	590	169	1	70	171	11	806	1.9	7.6	10.3
82-83–Cleveland	80	79	2716	401	832	.482	4	12	.333	168	245	.686	41	118	159	487	215	1	74	195	4	974	2.0	6.1	12.2
83-84–Cleveland	77	56	2041	348	699	.498	2	11	.182	110	154	.714	32	64	96	413	126	0	38	145	1	808	1.2	5.4	10.5
84-85–Cleveland	8	0	93	12	25	.480	0	0	–	2	3	.667	0	1	1	23	8	0	0	8	0	26	0.1	2.9	3.3
85-86–Golden State	82	0	1208	140	273	.513	2	6	.333	63	92	.685	10	55	65	342	67	0	38	83	4	345	0.8	4.2	4.2
86-87–L.A. Clippers	19	8	428	55	121	.455	1	2	.500	18	34	.529	6	11	17	101	28	0	14	45	0	129	0.9	5.3	6.8
Reg. Season Totals	496	186	12252	1836	3805	.483	16	63	.254	692	978	.708	201	483	684	2509	844	3	331	899	32	4380	1.4	5.1	8.8

Huston, Paul F. (Shad) b. June 2, 1925 Ht. 6-3 Wt. 175 College: Ohio State

SEASON–TEAM	G	GS	MIN	FGM	FGA	PCT	3FGM	3FGA	PCT	FTM	FTA	PCT	O-RB	D-RB	TOT	AST	PF	DQ	STL	TO	BLK	PTS	RPG	APG	PPG
47-48–Chicago	46	–	–	51	215	.237	–	–	–	62	89	.697	–	–	–	27	82	–	–	–	–	164	–	0.6	3.6
Reg. Season Totals	46	–	–	51	215	.237	–	–	–	62	89	.697	–	–	–	27	82	–	–	–	–	164	–	0.6	3.6
Playoff Totals	5	–	–	3	38	.158	–	–	–	7	13	.538	–	–	–	4	28	–	–	–	–	13	–	0.4	2.6

Hutchins, Melvin R. (Mel, Hutch) b. November 22, 1928 Ht. 6-6 Wt. 200 College: Brigham Young

SEASON–TEAM	G	GS	MIN	FGM	FGA	PCT	3FGM	3FGA	PCT	FTM	FTA	PCT	O-RB	D-RB	TOT	AST	PF	DQ	STL	TO	BLK	PTS	RPG	APG	PPG
51-52–Milwaukee	66	–	2618	231	633	.365	–	–	–	145	225	.644	–	–	880	190	192	5	–	–	–	607	13.3	2.9	9.2
52-53–Milwaukee	71	–	2891	319	842	.379	–	–	–	193	295	.654	–	–	793	227	214	5	–	–	–	831	11.2	3.2	11.7
53-54–Fort Wayne	72	–	2934	295	736	.401	–	–	–	151	223	.677	–	–	695	210	229	4	–	–	–	741	9.7	2.9	10.3
54-55–Fort Wayne	72	–	2860	341	903	.378	–	–	–	182	257	.708	–	–	665	247	232	0	–	–	–	864	9.2	3.4	12.0
55-56–Fort Wayne	66	–	2240	325	764	.425	–	–	–	142	221	.643	–	–	496	180	166	1	–	–	–	792	7.5	2.7	12.0
56-57–Fort Wayne	72	–	2647	369	953	.387	–	–	–	152	206	.738	–	–	571	210	182	0	–	–	–	890	7.9	2.9	12.4
57-58–New York	18	–	384	51	131	.389	–	–	–	24	43	.558	–	–	86	34	31	0	–	–	–	126	4.8	1.9	7.0
Reg. Season Totals	437	–	16574	1931	4962	.389	–	–	–	989	1470	.673	–	–	4186	1298	1246	15	–	–	–	4851	9.6	3.0	11.1
Playoff Totals	27	–	1186	118	363	.353	–	–	–	80	121	.661	–	–	274	76	100	5	–	–	–	316	8.8	2.5	11.7
All-Star Totals	4	–	114	11	39	.282	–	–	–	4	8	.500	–	–	21	7	7	0	–	–	–	26	5.3	1.8	6.5

Hutton, Joseph W. Jr. (Joe) b. October 6, 1928 Ht. 6-1 Wt. 170 College: Hamline

SEASON–TEAM	G	GS	MIN	FGM	FGA	PCT	3FGM	3FGA	PCT	FTM	FTA	PCT	O-RB	D-RB	TOT	AST	PF	DQ	STL	TO	BLK	PTS	RPG	APG	PPG
50-51–Minneapolis	60	–	–	59	180	.328	–	–	–	29	43	.674	–	–	102	53	89	1	–	–	–	147	1.7	0.9	2.5
51-52–Minneapolis	60	–	723	53	158	.335	–	–	–	49	70	.700	–	–	85	62	110	1	–	–	–	155	1.4	1.0	2.6
Reg. Season Totals	120	–	723	112	338	.331	–	–	–	78	113	.690	–	–	187	115	199	2	–	–	–	302	1.6	1.0	2.5
Playoff Totals	22	–	235	12	40	.425	–	–	–	11	18	.611	–	–	23	18	22	0	–	–	–	35	1.1	0.9	1.6

Hyder, Gregory Peck (Greg) b. June 21, 1948 Ht. 6-6 Wt. 215 College: Eastern New Mexico

SEASON–TEAM	G	GS	MIN	FGM	FGA	PCT	3FGM	3FGA	PCT	FTM	FTA	PCT	O-RB	D-RB	TOT	AST	PF	DQ	STL	TO	BLK	PTS	RPG	APG	PPG
70-71–Cincinnati	77	–	1359	183	409	.447	–	–	–	51	71	.718	–	–	332	48	187	2	–	–	–	417	4.3	0.6	5.4
Reg. Season Totals	77	–	1359	183	409	.447	–	–	–	51	71	.718	–	–	332	48	187	2	–	–	–	417	4.3	0.6	5.4

Iavaroni, Marcus John (Marc) b. September 15, 1956 Ht. 6-10 Wt. 225 College: Virginia

SEASON–TEAM	G	GS	MIN	FGM	FGA	PCT	3FGM	3FGA	PCT	FTM	FTA	PCT	O-RB	D-RB	TOT	AST	PF	DQ	STL	TO	BLK	PTS	RPG	APG	PPG
82-83–Philadelphia	80	77	1612	163	353	.462	0	2	.000	78	113	.690	117	212	329	83	238	0	32	133	44	404	4.1	1.0	5.1
83-84–Philadelphia	78	71	1532	149	322	.463	0	2	.000	97	131	.740	91	219	310	95	222	1	36	124	55	395	4.0	1.2	5.1
84-85–Phil.-S.A.	69	43	1334	162	354	.458	0	4	.000	87	128	.680	95	209	304	119	217	5	35	119	35	411	4.4	1.7	6.0
85-86–S.A.-Utah	68	9	1014	110	244	.451	0	2	.000	76	115	.661	63	146	209	82	163	0	32	72	17	296	3.1	1.2	4.4
86-87–Utah	78	0	845	100	215	.465	0	4	.000	78	116	.672	64	109	173	36	154	0	16	56	11	278	2.2	0.5	3.6
87-88–Utah	81	71	1238	143	308	.464	0	2	.000	78	99	.788	94	174	268	67	162	1	23	83	25	364	3.3	0.8	4.5
88-89–Utah	77	50	796	72	163	.442	0	1	.000	36	44	.818	41	91	132	32	99	0	11	52	13	180	1.7	0.4	2.3
Reg. Season Totals	531	321	8371	899	1959	.459	0	17	.000	530	746	.710	565	1160	1725	514	1255	7	185	639	200	2328	3.2	1.0	4.4
Playoff Totals	43	31	721	76	151	.503	1	4	.250	48	67	.716	50	82	132	59	126	3	17	49	15	201	3.1	1.4	4.7

Ilgauskas, Zydrunas b. June 5, 1975 Ht. 7-3 Wt. 260 Country: Lithuania

SEASON–TEAM	G	GS	MIN	FGM	FGA	PCT	3FGM	3FGA	PCT	FTM	FTA	PCT	O-RB	D-RB	TOT	AST	PF	DQ	STL	TO	BLK	PTS	RPG	APG	PPG
97-98–Cleveland	82	81	2379	454	876	.518	1	4	.250	230	302	.762	279	444	723	71	288	4	52	146	135	1139	8.8	0.9	13.9
98-99–Cleveland	5	5	171	29	57	.509	0	0	–	18	30	.600	17	27	44	4	24	1	4	9	7	76	8.8	0.8	15.2
Reg. Season Totals	87	86	2550	483	933	.518	1	4	.250	248	332	.747	296	471	767	75	312	5	56	155	142	1215	8.8	0.9	14.0
Playoff Totals	4	4	147	28	49	.571	0	0	–	13	25	.520	14	16	30	2	22	2	2	10	5	69	7.5	0.5	17.3

Imhoff, Darrall Tucker (Big D) b. October 11, 1938 Ht. 6-10 Wt. 220 College: California

SEASON–TEAM	G	GS	MIN	FGM	FGA	PCT	3FGM	3FGA	PCT	FTM	FTA	PCT	O-RB	D-RB	TOT	AST	PF	DQ	STL	TO	BLK	PTS	RPG	APG	PPG
60-61–New York	62	–	994	122	310	.394	–	–	–	49	96	.510	–	–	296	51	143	2	–	–	–	293	4.8	0.8	4.7
61-62–New York	76	–	1481	186	482	.386	–	–	–	80	139	.576	–	–	470	82	230	10	–	–	–	452	6.2	1.1	5.9
62-63–Detroit	45	–	458	48	153	.314	–	–	–	24	50	.480	–	–	155	28	66	1	–	–	–	120	3.4	0.6	2.7
63-64–Detroit	58	–	871	104	251	.414	–	–	–	69	114	.605	–	–	283	56	167	5	–	–	–	277	4.9	1.0	4.8
64-65–Los Angeles	76	–	1521	145	311	.466	–	–	–	88	154	.571	–	–	500	87	238	7	–	–	–	378	6.6	1.1	5.0
65-66–Los Angeles	77	–	1413	151	337	.448	–	–	–	77	136	.566	–	–	509	113	234	7	–	–	–	379	6.6	1.5	4.9
66-67–Los Angeles	81	–	2725	370	780	.474	–	–	–	127	207	.614	–	–	1080	222	281	7	–	–	–	867	13.3	2.7	10.7
67-68–Los Angeles	82	–	2271	293	613	.478	–	–	–	177	286	.619	–	–	893	206	264	3	–	–	–	763	10.9	2.5	9.3
68-69–Philadelphia	82	–	2360	279	593	.470	–	–	–	194	325	.597	–	–	792	218	310	12	–	–	–	752	9.7	2.7	9.2
69-70–Philadelphia	79	–	2474	430	796	.540	–	–	–	215	331	.650	–	–	754	211	294	7	–	–	–	1075	9.5	2.7	13.6
70-71–Cincinnati	34	–	826	119	258	.461	–	–	–	37	73	.507	–	–	233	79	120	5	–	–	–	275	6.9	2.3	8.1
71-72–Cin.-Port.	49	–	480	52	132	.394	–	–	–	24	43	.558	–	–	134	52	98	2	–	–	–	128	2.7	1.1	2.6
Reg. Season Totals	801	–	17874	2299	5016	.458	–	–	–	1161	1954	.594	–	–	6099	1405	2445	68	–	–	–	5759	7.6	1.8	7.2
Playoff Totals	54	–	1251	139	291	.478	–	–	–	76	131	.580	–	–	442	101	179	2	–	–	–	354	8.2	1.9	6.6
All-Star Totals	1	–	6	0	7	.000	–	–	–	0	0	–	–	–	7	1	1	0	–	–	–	0	7.0	1.0	0.0

Ingelsby, Tom b. February 12, 1951 Ht. 6-3 Wt. 185 College: Villanova

SEASON–TEAM	G	GS	MIN	FGM	FGA	PCT	3FGM	3FGA	PCT	FTM	FTA	PCT	O-RB	D-RB	TOT	AST	PF	DQ	STL	TO	BLK	PTS	RPG	APG	PPG
73-74–Atlanta	48	–	398	50	131	.382	–	–	–	29	37	.784	10	34	44	37	43	0	19	–	4	129	0.9	0.8	2.7
74-75–St. Louis (A)	22	–	344	44	90	.489	1	5	.200	20	27	.741	22	28	50	38	19	–	14	17	1	109	2.3	1.7	5.0
75-76–San Diego (A)	5	–	14	1	3	.333	0	0	–	2	2	1.000	1	2	3	0	1	–	0	0	0	4	0.6	0.0	0.8
Reg. NBA Totals	48	–	398	50	131	.382	–	–	–	29	37	.784	10	34	44	37	43	0	19	–	4	129	0.9	0.8	2.7
Reg. ABA Totals	27	–	358	45	93	.484	1	5	.200	22	29	.759	23	30	53	38	20	–	14	17	1	113	2.0	1.4	4.2

Ingram, Joel McCoy (McCoy) b. August 31, 1931 Ht. 6-0 Wt. 210 College: Jackson State

SEASON–TEAM	G	GS	MIN	FGM	FGA	PCT	3FGM	3FGA	PCT	FTM	FTA	PCT	O-RB	D-RB	TOT	AST	PF	DQ	STL	TO	BLK	PTS	RPG	APG	PPG
57-58–Minneapolis	24	–	267	27	103	.262	–	–	–	13	28	.464	–	–	116	20	44	1	–	–	–	67	4.8	0.8	2.8
Reg. Season Totals	24	–	267	27	103	.262	–	–	–	13	28	.464	–	–	116	20	44	1	–	–	–	67	4.8	0.8	2.8

Inniger, Ervin Lee Jr. (Irv) b. January 16, 1945 Ht. 6-4 Wt. 190 College: Indiana

SEASON–TEAM	G	GS	MIN	FGM	FGA	PCT	3FGM	3FGA	PCT	FTM	FTA	PCT	O-RB	D-RB	TOT	AST	PF	DQ	STL	TO	BLK	PTS	RPG	APG	PPG
67-68–Minnesota (A)	75	–	1993	345	790	.437	5	35	.143	99	137	.723	–	–	325	115	201	2	–	94	–	794	4.3	1.5	10.6
68-69–Miami (A)	34	–	484	73	182	.401	3	13	.231	21	25	.840	–	–	60	41	59	0	–	30	–	170	1.8	1.2	5.0
Reg. ABA Totals	109	–	2477	418	972	.430	8	48	.167	120	162	.741	–	–	385	156	260	2	–	124	–	964	3.5	1.4	8.8
ABA Playoff Totals	10	–	364	55	140	.393	2	11	.182	26	32	.813	–	–	57	35	36	0	–	15	–	138	5.7	3.5	13.8

Irvin, Byron Edward b. December 2, 1966 Ht. 6-6 Wt. 195 College: Arkansas; Missouri

SEASON–TEAM	G	GS	MIN	FGM	FGA	PCT	3FGM	3FGA	PCT	FTM	FTA	PCT	O-RB	D-RB	TOT	AST	PF	DQ	STL	TO	BLK	PTS	RPG	APG	PPG
89-90–Portland	50	2	488	96	203	.473	5	14	.357	61	91	.670	30	44	74	47	40	0	28	39	1	258	1.5	0.9	5.2
90-91–Washington	33	4	316	60	129	.465	1	5	.200	50	61	.820	24	21	45	24	32	0	15	16	2	171	1.4	0.7	5.2
92-93–Washington	4	2	45	9	18	.500	1	1	1.000	3	6	.500	2	2	4	2	5	0	1	4	0	22	1.0	0.5	5.5
Reg. Season Totals	87	8	849	165	350	.471	7	20	.350	114	158	.722	56	67	123	73	77	0	44	59	3	451	1.4	0.8	5.2
Playoff Totals	4	0	47	5	22	.227	0	0	–	5	6	.833	4	4	8	5	7	0	2	3	0	15	2.0	1.3	3.8

Irvine, George R. (Hawkeye) b. February 1, 1948 Ht. 6-6 Wt. 200 College: Washington

SEASON–TEAM	G	GS	MIN	FGM	FGA	PCT	3FGM	3FGA	PCT	FTM	FTA	PCT	O-RB	D-RB	TOT	AST	PF	DQ	STL	TO	BLK	PTS	RPG	APG	PPG
70-71–Virginia (A)	34	–	338	83	149	.557	2	8	.250	26	35	.743	–	–	65	25	67	–	–	–	–	194	1.9	0.7	5.7
71-72–Virginia (A)	75	–	1362	200	397	.504	3	10	.300	54	75	.720	–	–	217	70	202	–	–	74	–	457	2.9	0.9	6.1
72-73–Virginia (A)	79	–	2075	424	805	.527	7	33	.212	169	203	.833	108	188	296	149	267	0	–	138	–	1024	3.7	1.9	13.0
73-74–Virginia (A)	75	–	1140	254	516	.492	12	46	.261	120	138	.870	56	121	177	76	134	–	28	67	16	640	2.4	1.0	8.5
74-75–Virginia (A)	59	–	1522	311	589	.528	13	37	.351	139	164	.848	73	130	203	108	171	–	32	94	12	774	3.4	1.8	13.1
75-76–Denver (A)	3	–	14	2	6	.333	0	1	.000	0	0	–	1	0	1	0	1	–	0	1	0	4	0.3	0.0	1.3
Reg. ABA Totals	325	–	6451	1274	2462	.517	37	135	.274	508	615	.826	238	439	959	428	842	0	60	374	28	3093	3.0	1.3	9.5
ABA Playoff Totals	28	–	472	89	162	.549	1	10	.100	41	47	.872	3	8	48	27	73	0	3	29	1	220	1.7	1.0	7.9

Issel, Daniel Paul (Dan) b. October 25, 1948 Ht. 6-9 Wt. 240 College: Kentucky HOF: 1992

SEASON–TEAM	G	GS	MIN	FGM	FGA	PCT	3FGM	3FGA	PCT	FTM	FTA	PCT	O-RB	D-RB	TOT	AST	PF	DQ	STL	TO	BLK	PTS	RPG	APG	PPG
70-71–Kentucky (A)	83	–	3274	938	1924	.488	0	5	.000	604	748	.807	421	672	1093	162	323	–	–	–	–	2480	13.2	2.0	29.9
71-72–Kentucky (A)	83	–	3570	972	2001	.486	3	11	.273	591	753	.785	353	578	931	195	242	–	–	244	–	2538	11.2	2.3	30.6
72-73–Kentucky (A)	84	–	3531	902	1757	.513	3	15	.200	485	635	.764	329	593	922	220	255	0	–	216	–	2292	11.0	2.6	27.3
73-74–Kentucky (A)	83	–	3347	829	1726	.480	3	17	.176	457	581	.787	346	501	847	137	199	–	69	171	32	2118	10.2	1.7	25.5
74-75–Kentucky (A)	83	–	2864	614	1303	.471	0	5	.000	237	321	.738	258	452	710	188	197	–	76	157	48	1465	8.6	2.3	17.7
75-76–Denver (A)	84	–	2856	752	1472	.511	1	4	.250	425	521	.816	303	620	923	201	266	–	100	200	56	1930	11.0	2.4	23.0
76-77–Denver	79	–	2507	660	1282	.515	–	–	–	445	558	.797	211	485	696	177	246	7	91	–	29	1765	8.8	2.2	22.3
77-78–Denver	82	–	2851	659	1287	.512	–	–	–	428	547	.782	253	577	830	304	279	5	100	259	41	1746	10.1	3.7	21.3
78-79–Denver	81	–	2742	532	1030	.517	–	–	–	316	419	.754	240	498	738	255	233	6	61	171	46	1380	9.1	3.1	17.0
79-80–Denver	82	–	2938	715	1416	.505	4	12	.333	517	667	.775	236	483	719	198	190	1	88	163	54	1951	8.8	2.4	23.8
80-81–Denver	80	–	2641	614	1220	.503	2	12	.167	519	684	.759	229	447	676	158	249	6	83	130	53	1749	8.5	2.0	21.9
81-82–Denver	81	81	2472	651	1236	.527	4	6	.667	546	655	.834	174	434	608	179	245	4	67	169	55	1852	7.5	2.2	22.9
82-83–Denver	80	80	2431	661	1296	.510	4	19	.211	400	479	.835	151	445	596	223	227	0	83	174	43	1726	7.5	2.8	21.6
83-84–Denver	76	66	2076	569	1153	.493	4	19	.211	364	428	.850	112	401	513	173	182	2	60	122	44	1506	6.8	2.3	19.8
84-85–Denver	77	9	1684	363	791	.459	1	7	.143	257	319	.806	80	251	331	137	171	1	65	93	31	984	4.3	1.8	12.8
Reg. NBA Totals	718	236	22342	5424	10711	.506	19	75	.253	3792	4756	.797	1686	4021	5707	1804	2022	32	698	1281	396	14659	7.9	2.5	20.4
Reg. ABA Totals	500	–	19442	5007	10183	.492	10	57	.175	2799	3559	.786	2010	3416	5426	1103	1482	0	245	988	136	12823	10.9	2.2	25.6
NBA Playoff Totals	53	20	1599	402	810	.496	2	4	.500	223	269	.829	111	282	393	145	157	1	42	93	24	1029	7.4	2.7	19.4
ABA Playoff Totals	80	–	3119	744	1543	.482	1	8	.125	416	508	.819	278	584	862	136	308	0	51	148	37	1905	10.8	1.7	23.8
NBA All-Star Totals	1	1	10	0	3	.000	0	0	–	0	0	–	1	0	1	0	0	0	0	–	0	0	1.0	0.0	0.0

Iuzzolino, Michael Alan (Mike) b. January 22, 1968 Ht. 5-11 Wt. 175 College: Penn State; St. Francis (Pa.)

SEASON–TEAM	G	GS	MIN	FGM	FGA	PCT	3FGM	3FGA	PCT	FTM	FTA	PCT	O-RB	D-RB	TOT	AST	PF	DQ	STL	TO	BLK	PTS	RPG	APG	PPG
91-92–Dallas	52	21	1280	160	355	.451	59	136	.434	107	128	.836	27	71	98	194	79	0	33	92	1	486	1.9	3.7	9.3
92-93–Dallas	70	23	1769	221	478	.462	54	144	.375	114	149	.765	31	109	140	328	101	0	49	129	6	610	2.0	4.7	8.7
Reg. Season Totals	122	44	3049	381	833	.457	113	280	.404	221	277	.798	58	180	238	522	180	0	82	221	7	1096	2.0	4.3	9.0

Iverson, Allen b. June 7, 1975 Ht. 6-0 Wt. 165 College: Georgetown

SEASON–TEAM	G	GS	MIN	FGM	FGA	PCT	3FGM	3FGA	PCT	FTM	FTA	PCT	O-RB	D-RB	TOT	AST	PF	DQ	STL	TO	BLK	PTS	RPG	APG	PPG
96-97–Philadelphia	76	74	3045	625	1504	.416	155	455	.341	382	544	.702	115	197	312	567	233	5	157	337	24	1787	4.1	7.5	23.5
97-98–Philadelphia	80	80	3150	649	1407	.461	70	235	.298	390	535	.729	86	210	296	494	200	2	176	244	25	1758	3.7	6.2	22.0
98-99–Philadelphia	48	48	1990	435	1056	.412	58	199	.291	356	474	.751	66	170	236	223	98	0	110	167	7	1284	4.9	4.6	26.8
99-00–Philadelphia	70	70	2853	729	1733	.421	89	261	.341	442	620	.713	71	196	267	328	162	1	144	230	5	1989	3.8	4.7	28.4
Reg. Season Totals	274	272	11038	2438	5700	.428	372	1150	.323	1570	2173	.723	338	773	1111	1612	693	8	587	978	61	6818	4.1	5.9	24.9
Playoff Totals	18	18	802	179	451	.397	27	92	.293	105	144	.729	28	45	73	84	43	0	32	56	3	490	4.1	4.7	27.2
All-Star Totals	1	1	28	10	18	.556	2	2	1.000	4	5	.800	2	0	2	9	0	0	2	5	0	26	2.0	9.0	26.0

Iverson, Willie b. October 8, 1945 Ht. 6-0 Wt. 180 College: Central Michigan

SEASON–TEAM	G	GS	MIN	FGM	FGA	PCT	3FGM	3FGA	PCT	FTM	FTA	PCT	O-RB	D-RB	TOT	AST	PF	DQ	STL	TO	BLK	PTS	RPG	APG	PPG
68-69–Miami (A)	28	–	531	50	146	.342	0	2	.000	36	60	.600	–	–	46	80	47	0	–	55	–	136	1.6	2.9	4.9
Reg. ABA Totals	28	–	531	50	146	.342	0	2	.000	36	60	.600	–	–	46	80	47	0	–	55	–	136	1.6	2.9	4.9

Ivory, Elvin Dennis (Little E.) b. July 2, 1948 Ht. 6-8 Wt. 215 College: Southeastern Louisiana

SEASON–TEAM	G	GS	MIN	FGM	FGA	PCT	3FGM	3FGA	PCT	FTM	FTA	PCT	O-RB	D-RB	TOT	AST	PF	DQ	STL	TO	BLK	PTS	RPG	APG	PPG
68-69–Los Angeles (A)	20	–	188	38	87	.437	1	4	.250	11	17	.647	–	–	166	9	38	0	–	14	–	88	8.3	0.5	4.4
Reg. ABA Totals	20	–	188	38	87	.437	1	4	.250	11	17	.647	–	–	166	9	38	0	–	14	–	88	8.3	0.5	4.4

Jabali, Warren (formerly Warren Edward Armstrong) b. August 29, 1946 Ht. 6-2 Wt. 200 College: Wichita State

SEASON–TEAM	G	GS	MIN	FGM	FGA	PCT	3FGM	3FGA	PCT	FTM	FTA	PCT	O-RB	D-RB	TOT	AST	PF	DQ	STL	TO	BLK	PTS	RPG	APG	PPG
68-69–Oakland (A)	71	–	2545	573	1276	.449	11	44	.250	373	545	.684	–	–	688	252	263	4	–	307	–	1530	9.7	3.5	21.5
69-70–Washington (A)	40	–	1510	342	768	.445	19	62	.306	210	293	.717	–	–	416	173	143	5	–	–	–	913	10.4	4.3	22.8
70-71–Indiana (A)	62	–	1586	227	554	.410	47	163	.288	181	238	.761	–	–	298	214	205	–	–	–	–	682	4.8	3.5	11.0
71-72–Floridians (A)	81	–	3313	569	1304	.436	102	285	.358	375	496	.756	–	–	656	495	298	–	–	332	–	1615	8.1	6.1	19.9
72-73–Denver (A)	82	–	2738	441	974	.453	36	140	.257	480	596	.805	129	295	424	539	280	0	–	302	–	1398	5.2	6.6	17.0
73-74–Denver (A)	49	–	1711	257	657	.391	45	123	.366	220	274	.803	82	164	246	358	167	–	97	195	10	779	5.0	7.3	15.9
74-75–San Diego (A)	62	–	1861	254	648	.392	62	193	.321	179	227	.789	72	185	257	358	188	–	112	184	19	749	4.1	5.8	12.1
Reg. ABA Totals	447	–	15264	2663	6181	.431	322	1010	.319	2018	2669	.756	283	644	2985	2389	1544	9	209	1320	29	7666	6.7	5.3	17.1
ABA Playoff Totals	36	–	1209	221	532	.415	11	66	.167	198	282	.702	81	178	306	115	111	1	0	30	0	651	8.5	3.2	18.1

Jackson, Alvin (Al) b. July 29, 1943 Ht. 6-1 Wt. 185 College: Wilberforce

SEASON–TEAM	G	GS	MIN	FGM	FGA	PCT	3FGM	3FGA	PCT	FTM	FTA	PCT	O-RB	D-RB	TOT	AST	PF	DQ	STL	TO	BLK	PTS	RPG	APG	PPG
67-68–Cincinnati	2	–	17	0	3	.000	–	–	–	0	0	–	–	–	0	1	6	0	–	–	–	0	0.0	0.5	0.0
Reg. Season Totals	2	–	17	0	3	.000	–	–	–	0	0	–	–	–	0	1	6	0	–	–	–	0	0.0	0.5	0.0

Jackson, Anthony Eugene (Tony) b. January 17, 1958 Ht. 6-0 Wt. 170 College: Florida State

SEASON–TEAM	G	GS	MIN	FGM	FGA	PCT	3FGM	3FGA	PCT	FTM	FTA	PCT	O-RB	D-RB	TOT	AST	PF	DQ	STL	TO	BLK	PTS	RPG	APG	PPG
80-81–Los Angeles	2	–	14	1	3	.333	0	0	–	0	0	–	0	2	2	2	1	0	2	0	0	2	1.0	1.0	1.0
Reg. Season Totals	2	–	14	1	3	.333	0	0	–	0	0	–	0	2	2	2	1	0	2	0	0	2	1.0	1.0	1.0

Jackson, Bobby b. March 13, 1973 Ht. 6-1 Wt. 185 College: Western Nebraska C.C.; Minnesota

SEASON–TEAM	G	GS	MIN	FGM	FGA	PCT	3FGM	3FGA	PCT	FTM	FTA	PCT	O-RB	D-RB	TOT	AST	PF	DQ	STL	TO	BLK	PTS	RPG	APG	PPG
97-98–Denver	68	53	2042	310	791	.392	21	81	.259	149	183	.814	78	224	302	317	160	0	105	184	11	790	4.4	4.7	11.6
98-99–Minnesota	50	12	941	141	348	.405	10	27	.370	61	79	.772	43	92	135	167	75	1	39	75	3	353	2.7	3.3	7.1
99-00–Minnesota	73	10	1034	140	346	.405	13	46	.283	76	98	.776	50	103	153	172	114	0	48	58	7	369	2.1	2.4	5.1
Reg. Season Totals	191	75	4017	591	1485	.398	44	154	.286	286	360	.794	171	419	590	656	349	1	192	317	21	1512	3.1	3.4	7.9
Playoff Totals	7	0	57	6	18	.333	1	6	.167	6	6	1.000	1	8	9	6	7	0	2	3	1	19	1.3	0.9	2.7

Jackson, Chris Wayne (see Mahmoud Abdul-Rauf)

Jackson, Gregory (Greg) b. August 2, 1952 Ht. 6-0 Wt. 185 College: Guilford

SEASON–TEAM	G	GS	MIN	FGM	FGA	PCT	3FGM	3FGA	PCT	FTM	FTA	PCT	O-RB	D-RB	TOT	AST	PF	DQ	STL	TO	BLK	PTS	RPG	APG	PPG
74-75–N.Y.-Phoenix	49	–	802	73	176	.415	–	–	–	36	62	.581	19	50	69	96	130	5	23	–	9	182	1.4	2.0	3.7
Reg. Season Totals	49	–	802	73	176	.415	–	–	–	36	62	.581	19	50	69	96	130	5	23	–	9	182	1.4	2.0	3.7

Jackson, James Arthur (Jim) b. October 14, 1970 Ht. 6-6 Wt. 220 College: Ohio State

SEASON–TEAM	G	GS	MIN	FGM	FGA	PCT	3FGM	3FGA	PCT	FTM	FTA	PCT	O-RB	D-RB	TOT	AST	PF	DQ	STL	TO	BLK	PTS	RPG	APG	PPG
92-93–Dallas	28	28	938	184	466	.395	21	73	.288	68	92	.739	42	80	122	131	80	0	40	115	11	457	4.4	4.7	16.3
93-94–Dallas	82	82	3066	637	1432	.445	17	60	.283	285	347	.821	169	219	388	374	161	0	87	334	25	1576	4.7	4.6	19.2
94-95–Dallas	51	51	1982	484	1026	.472	35	110	.318	306	380	.805	120	140	260	191	92	0	28	160	12	1309	5.1	3.7	25.7
95-96–Dallas	82	82	2820	569	1308	.435	121	333	.363	345	418	.825	173	237	410	235	165	0	47	191	22	1604	5.0	2.9	19.6
96-97–Dallas-N.J.	77	77	2831	444	1029	.431	86	247	.348	252	310	.813	132	279	411	316	194	0	86	208	32	1226	5.3	4.1	15.9
97-98–Phil.-G.S.	79	78	3046	476	1107	.430	61	191	.319	229	282	.812	130	270	400	381	186	0	79	263	8	1242	5.1	4.8	15.7
98-99–Portland	49	9	1175	152	370	.411	25	90	.278	85	101	.842	36	123	159	128	80	0	43	82	6	414	3.2	2.6	8.4
99-00–Atlanta	79	76	2767	507	1235	.411	117	303	.386	186	212	.877	101	293	394	230	167	0	57	185	10	1317	5.0	2.9	16.7
Reg. Season Totals	527	483	18625	3453	7973	.433	483	1407	.343	1756	2142	.820	903	1641	2544	1986	1125	0	467	1538	126	9145	4.8	3.8	17.4
Playoff Totals	13	0	265	26	72	.361	5	18	.278	38	42	.905	8	22	30	19	26	0	7	18	1	95	2.3	1.5	7.3

Jackson, Jaren b. October 27, 1967 Ht. 6-6 Wt. 225 College: Georgetown

SEASON–TEAM	G	GS	MIN	FGM	FGA	PCT	3FGM	3FGA	PCT	FTM	FTA	PCT	O-RB	D-RB	TOT	AST	PF	DQ	STL	TO	BLK	PTS	RPG	APG	PPG
89-90–New Jersey	28	0	160	25	69	.362	0	3	.000	17	21	.810	16	8	24	13	16	0	13	18	1	67	0.9	0.5	2.4
91-92–Golden State	5	0	54	11	23	.478	0	0	–	4	6	.667	5	5	10	3	7	1	2	4	0	26	2.0	0.6	5.2
92-93–L.A. Clippers	34	0	350	53	128	.414	2	5	.400	23	27	.852	19	20	39	35	45	1	19	17	5	131	1.1	1.0	3.9
93-94–Portland	29	0	187	34	87	.391	0	6	.000	12	14	.857	6	11	17	27	20	0	4	14	2	80	0.6	0.9	2.8
94-95–Philadelphia	21	1	257	25	68	.368	4	15	.267	16	24	.667	18	24	42	19	33	0	9	17	5	70	2.0	0.9	3.3
95-96–Houston	4	0	33	0	8	.000	0	5	.000	8	10	.800	0	3	3	0	5	0	1	0	0	8	0.8	0.0	2.0
96-97–Washington	75	0	1133	134	329	.407	53	158	.335	53	69	.768	31	101	132	65	131	0	45	60	16	374	1.8	0.9	5.0
97-98–San Antonio	82	45	2226	258	654	.394	112	297	.377	94	118	.797	55	155	210	156	222	3	60	104	8	722	2.6	1.9	8.8
98-99–San Antonio	47	13	861	108	284	.380	53	147	.361	32	39	.821	21	78	99	49	63	0	41	37	9	301	2.1	1.0	6.4
99-00–San Antonio	81	12	1691	186	488	.381	108	306	.353	33	51	.647	34	147	181	118	157	1	54	66	7	513	2.2	1.5	6.3
Reg. Season Totals	406	71	6952	834	2138	.390	332	942	.352	292	379	.770	205	552	757	485	699	6	248	337	53	2292	1.9	1.2	5.6
Playoff Totals	36	8	723	85	235	.362	49	147	.333	25	38	.658	15	73	88	37	78	1	21	37	1	244	2.4	1.0	6.8

Jackson, Jermaine b. June 6, 1976 Ht. 6-5 Wt. 204 College: Detroit Mercy

SEASON–TEAM	G	GS	MIN	FGM	FGA	PCT	3FGM	3FGA	PCT	FTM	FTA	PCT	O-RB	D-RB	TOT	AST	PF	DQ	STL	TO	BLK	PTS	RPG	APG	PPG
99-00–Detroit	7	0	73	1	11	.091	0	1	.000	5	8	.625	1	10	11	4	7	0	3	7	0	7	1.6	0.6	1.0
Reg. Season Totals	7	0	73	1	11	.091	0	1	.000	5	8	.625	1	10	11	4	7	0	3	7	0	7	1.6	0.6	1.0

Jackson, Lucious B. **(Luke)** b. October 31, 1941 Ht. 6-9 Wt. 250 College: Quincy; Texas Southern; Texas-Pan American

SEASON–TEAM	G	GS	MIN	FGM	FGA	PCT	3FGM	3FGA	PCT	FTM	FTA	PCT	O-RB	D-RB	TOT	AST	PF	DQ	STL	TO	BLK	PTS	RPG	APG	PPG
64-65–Philadelphia	76	–	2590	419	1013	.414	–	–	–	288	404	.713	–	–	980	93	251	4	–	–	–	1126	12.9	1.2	14.8
65-66–Philadelphia	79	–	1966	246	614	.401	–	–	–	158	214	.738	–	–	676	132	216	2	–	–	–	650	8.6	1.7	8.2
66-67–Philadelphia	81	–	2377	386	882	.438	–	–	–	198	261	.759	–	–	724	114	276	6	–	–	–	970	8.9	1.4	12.0
67-68–Philadelphia	82	–	2570	401	927	.433	–	–	–	166	231	.719	–	–	872	139	287	6	–	–	–	968	10.6	1.7	11.8
68-69–Philadelphia	25	–	840	145	332	.437	–	–	–	69	97	.711	–	–	286	54	102	3	–	–	–	359	11.4	2.2	14.4
69-70–Philadelphia	37	–	583	71	181	.392	–	–	–	60	81	.741	–	–	198	50	80	0	–	–	–	202	5.4	1.4	5.5
70-71–Philadelphia	79	–	1774	199	529	.376	–	–	–	131	189	.693	–	–	568	148	211	3	–	–	–	529	7.2	1.9	6.7
71-72–Philadelphia	63	–	1083	137	346	.396	–	–	–	92	133	.692	–	–	309	88	141	1	–	–	–	366	4.9	1.4	5.8
Reg. Season Totals	522	–	13783	2004	4824	.415	–	–	–	1162	1610	.722	–	–	4613	818	1564	25	–	–	–	5170	8.8	1.6	9.9
Playoff Totals	56	–	1692	216	555	.389	–	–	–	113	152	.743	–	–	508	92	186	7	–	–	–	545	9.1	1.6	9.7
All-Star Totals	1	–	15	2	5	.400	–	–	–	1	2	.500	–	–	1	1	4	0	–	–	–	5	1.0	1.0	5.0

Jackson, Mark A. b. April 1, 1965 Ht. 6-3 Wt. 185 College: St. John's (N.Y.)

SEASON–TEAM	G	GS	MIN	FGM	FGA	PCT	3FGM	3FGA	PCT	FTM	FTA	PCT	O-RB	D-RB	TOT	AST	PF	DQ	STL	TO	BLK	PTS	RPG	APG	PPG
87-88–New York	82	80	3249	438	1013	.432	32	126	.254	206	266	.774	120	276	396	868	244	2	205	258	6	1114	4.8	10.6	13.6
88-89–New York	72	72	2477	479	1025	.467	81	240	.338	180	258	.698	106	235	341	619	163	1	139	226	7	1219	4.7	8.6	16.9
89-90–New York	82	69	2428	327	749	.437	35	131	.267	120	165	.727	106	212	318	604	121	0	109	211	4	809	3.9	7.4	9.9
90-91–New York	72	21	1595	250	508	.492	13	51	.255	117	160	.731	62	135	197	452	81	0	60	135	9	630	2.7	6.3	8.8
91-92–New York	81	81	2461	367	747	.491	11	43	.256	171	222	.770	95	210	305	694	153	0	112	211	13	916	3.8	8.6	11.3
92-93–L.A. Clippers	82	81	3117	459	945	.486	22	82	.268	241	300	.803	129	259	388	724	158	0	136	220	12	1181	4.7	8.8	14.4
93-94–L.A. Clippers	79	79	2711	331	732	.452	36	127	.283	167	211	.791	107	241	348	678	115	0	120	232	6	865	4.4	8.6	10.9
94-95–Indiana	82	67	2402	239	566	.422	27	87	.310	119	153	.778	73	233	306	616	148	0	105	210	16	624	3.7	7.5	7.6
95-96–Indiana	81	81	2643	296	626	.473	64	149	.430	150	191	.785	66	241	307	635	153	0	100	201	5	806	3.8	7.8	10.0
96-97–Denver-Indiana	82	82	3054	289	679	.426	66	178	.371	168	213	.789	91	304	395	935	161	0	97	274	12	812	4.8	11.4	9.9
97-98–Indiana	82	82	2413	249	598	.416	43	137	.314	137	180	.761	67	255	322	713	132	0	84	174	2	678	3.9	8.7	8.3
98-99–Indiana	49	49	1382	138	329	.419	32	103	.311	65	79	.823	33	151	184	386	58	0	42	99	3	373	3.8	7.9	7.6
99-00–Indiana	81	81	2190	246	570	.432	89	221	.403	79	98	.806	63	233	296	650	111	0	76	174	10	660	3.7	8.0	8.1
Reg. Season Totals	1007	925	32122	4108	9087	.452	551	1675	.329	1920	2496	.769	1118	2985	4103	8574	1798	3	1385	2625	105	10687	4.1	8.5	10.6
Playoff Totals	116	104	3498	402	937	.429	90	261	.345	208	269	.773	108	335	443	857	207	0	118	276	8	1102	3.8	7.4	9.5
All-Star Totals	1	0	16	3	5	.600	1	1	1.000	2	4	.500	1	1	2	4	1	0	1	2	1	9	2.0	4.0	9.0

Jackson, Mervin P. Jr. **(Merv, The Magician)** b. August 15, 1946 Ht. 6-3 Wt. 175 College: Utah

SEASON–TEAM	G	GS	MIN	FGM	FGA	PCT	3FGM	3FGA	PCT	FTM	FTA	PCT	O-RB	D-RB	TOT	AST	PF	DQ	STL	TO	BLK	PTS	RPG	APG	PPG
68-69–Los Angeles (A)	71	–	2314	423	1000	.423	19	62	.306	249	302	.825	–	–	299	237	262	9	–	191	–	1114	4.2	3.3	15.7
69-70–Los Angeles (A)	52	–	1118	169	475	.356	16	44	.364	92	114	.807	–	–	138	114	145	4	–	–	–	446	2.7	2.2	8.6
70-71–Utah (A)	65	–	1902	351	836	.420	7	20	.350	196	244	.803	–	–	262	225	207	–	–	–	–	905	4.0	3.5	13.9
71-72–Utah (A)	52	–	1136	185	412	.449	5	15	.333	92	109	.844	–	–	123	155	150	–	–	88	–	467	2.4	3.0	9.0
72-73–Memphis (A)	22	–	420	34	103	.330	4	11	.364	28	35	.800	9	29	38	82	61	1	–	35	–	100	1.7	3.7	4.5
Reg. ABA Totals	262	–	6890	1162	2826	.411	51	152	.336	657	804	.817	9	29	860	813	825	14	–	314	–	3032	3.3	3.1	11.6
ABA Playoff Totals	46	–	1391	250	543	.460	12	30	.400	97	120	.808	–	–	179	188	144	0	–	16	–	609	3.9	4.1	13.2

Jackson, Michael b. July 13, 1964 Ht. 6-2 Wt. 185 College: Georgetown

SEASON–TEAM	G	GS	MIN	FGM	FGA	PCT	3FGM	3FGA	PCT	FTM	FTA	PCT	O-RB	D-RB	TOT	AST	PF	DQ	STL	TO	BLK	PTS	RPG	APG	PPG
87-88–Sacramento	58	0	760	64	171	.374	6	25	.240	23	32	.719	17	42	59	179	81	0	20	58	5	157	1.0	3.1	2.7
88-89–Sacramento	14	0	70	9	24	.375	2	6	.333	1	2	.500	1	3	4	11	12	0	3	4	0	21	0.3	0.8	1.5
89-90–Sacramento	17	0	58	3	11	.273	1	2	.500	3	6	.500	2	5	7	8	3	0	5	4	0	10	0.4	0.5	0.6
Reg. Season Totals	89	0	888	76	206	.369	9	33	.273	27	40	.675	20	50	70	198	96	0	28	66	5	188	0.8	2.2	2.1

Jackson, Michael **(Mike)** b. July 31, 1949 Ht. 6-7 Wt. 230 College: Allan Hancock (Calif.) Coll. (J.C.); Los Angeles State

SEASON–TEAM	G	GS	MIN	FGM	FGA	PCT	3FGM	3FGA	PCT	FTM	FTA	PCT	O-RB	D-RB	TOT	AST	PF	DQ	STL	TO	BLK	PTS	RPG	APG	PPG
72-73–Utah (A)	30	–	191	36	83	.434	0	0	–	28	46	.609	24	38	62	2	46	0	–	27	–	100	2.1	0.1	3.3
73-74–Utah-Mem. (A)	72	–	1474	247	489	.505	3	7	.429	110	152	.724	140	240	380	57	222	–	25	109	15	607	5.3	0.8	8.4
74-75–Virginia (A)	82	–	2023	382	724	.528	1	3	.333	232	295	.786	183	274	457	82	308	–	47	212	19	997	5.6	1.0	12.2
75-76–Virginia (A)	80	–	2230	390	781	.499	0	5	.000	199	250	.796	209	398	607	113	306	–	45	190	29	979	7.6	1.4	12.2
Reg. ABA Totals	264	–	5918	1055	2077	.508	4	15	.267	569	743	.766	556	950	1506	254	882	0	117	538	63	2683	5.7	1.0	10.2
ABA Playoff Totals	1	–	2	0	0	–	0	0	–	0	0	–	0	0	–	0	2	0	0	0	0	0	0.0	0.0	0.0

Jackson, Myron b. May 6, 1964 Ht. 6-3 Wt. 185 College: Arkansas-Little Rock

SEASON–TEAM	G	GS	MIN	FGM	FGA	PCT	3FGM	3FGA	PCT	FTM	FTA	PCT	O-RB	D-RB	TOT	AST	PF	DQ	STL	TO	BLK	PTS	RPG	APG	PPG
86-87–Dallas	8	0	22	2	9	.222	0	0	–	7	8	.875	1	2	3	6	1	0	1	5	0	11	0.4	0.8	1.4
Reg. Season Totals	8	0	22	2	9	.222	0	0	–	7	8	.875	1	2	3	6	1	0	1	5	0	11	0.4	0.8	1.4

Jackson, Philip D. (Phil, Action) b. September 17, 1945 Ht. 6-8 Wt. 220 College: North Dakota

SEASON–TEAM	G	GS	MIN	FGM	FGA	PCT	3FGM	3FGA	PCT	FTM	FTA	PCT	O-RB	D-RB	TOT	AST	PF	DQ	STL	TO	BLK	PTS	RPG	APG	PPG
67-68–New York	75	–	1093	182	455	.400	–	–	–	99	168	.589	–	–	338	55	212	3	–	–	–	463	4.5	0.7	6.2
68-69–New York	47	–	924	126	294	.429	–	–	–	80	119	.672	–	–	246	43	168	6	–	–	–	332	5.2	0.9	7.1
70-71–New York	71	–	771	118	263	.449	–	–	–	95	133	.714	–	–	238	31	169	4	–	–	–	331	3.4	0.4	4.7
71-72–New York	80	–	1273	205	466	.440	–	–	–	167	228	.732	–	–	326	72	224	4	–	–	–	577	4.1	0.9	7.2
72-73–New York	80	–	1393	245	553	.443	–	–	–	154	195	.790	–	–	344	94	218	2	–	–	–	644	4.3	1.2	8.1
73-74–New York	82	–	2050	361	757	.477	–	–	–	191	246	.776	123	355	478	134	277	7	42	–	67	913	5.8	1.6	11.1
74-75–New York	78	–	2285	324	712	.455	–	–	–	193	253	.763	137	463	600	136	330	10	84	–	53	841	7.7	1.7	10.8
75-76–New York	80	–	1461	185	387	.478	–	–	–	110	150	.733	80	263	343	105	275	3	41	–	20	480	4.3	1.3	6.0
76-77–N.Y. Knicks	76	–	1033	102	232	.440	–	–	–	51	71	.718	75	154	229	85	184	4	33	–	18	255	3.0	1.1	3.4
77-78–New York	63	–	654	55	115	.478	–	–	–	43	56	.768	29	81	110	46	106	0	31	47	15	153	1.7	0.7	2.4
78-79–New Jersey	59	–	1070	144	303	.475	–	–	–	86	105	.819	59	119	178	85	168	7	45	78	22	374	3.0	1.4	6.3
79-80–New Jersey	16	–	194	29	46	.630	0	2	.000	7	10	.700	12	12	24	12	35	1	5	9	4	65	1.5	0.8	4.1
Reg. Season Totals	807	–	14201	2076	4583	.453	0	2	.000	1276	1734	.736	515	1447	3454	898	2366	51	281	134	199	5428	4.3	1.1	6.7
Playoff Totals	67	–	1223	200	437	.458	0	0	–	115	147	.782	26	69	284	63	208	4	18	4	8	515	4.2	0.9	7.7

Jackson, Ralph A. III b. October 26, 1962 Ht. 6-2 Wt. 190 College: UCLA

SEASON–TEAM	G	GS	MIN	FGM	FGA	PCT	3FGM	3FGA	PCT	FTM	FTA	PCT	O-RB	D-RB	TOT	AST	PF	DQ	STL	TO	BLK	PTS	RPG	APG	PPG
84-85–Indiana	1	0	12	1	3	.333	0	0	–	0	0	–	1	0	1	4	1	0	2	1	0	2	1.0	4.0	2.0
Reg. Season Totals	1	0	12	1	3	.333	0	0	–	0	0	–	1	0	1	4	1	0	2	1	0	2	1.0	4.0	2.0

Jackson, Randell b. January 16, 1976 Ht. 6-11 Wt. 215 College: Florida State

SEASON–TEAM	G	GS	MIN	FGM	FGA	PCT	3FGM	3FGA	PCT	FTM	FTA	PCT	O-RB	D-RB	TOT	AST	PF	DQ	STL	TO	BLK	PTS	RPG	APG	PPG
98-99–Washington	27	8	271	46	108	.426	1	7	.143	21	32	.656	30	24	54	8	29	0	3	26	11	114	2.0	0.3	4.2
99-00–Dallas	1	0	1	0	0	–	0	0	–	0	0	–	0	0	0	0	0	0	0	0	0	0	0.0	0.0	0.0
Reg. Season Totals	28	8	272	46	108	.426	1	7	.143	21	32	.656	30	24	54	8	29	0	3	26	11	114	1.9	0.3	4.1

Jackson, Stanley Leon b. October 10, 1970 Ht. 6-3 Wt. 185 College: Alabama-Birmingham

SEASON–TEAM	G	GS	MIN	FGM	FGA	PCT	3FGM	3FGA	PCT	FTM	FTA	PCT	O-RB	D-RB	TOT	AST	PF	DQ	STL	TO	BLK	PTS	RPG	APG	PPG
93-94–Minnesota	17	0	92	17	33	.515	1	5	.200	3	3	1.000	12	15	27	16	13	0	5	10	0	38	1.6	0.9	2.2
Reg. Season Totals	17	0	92	17	33	.515	1	5	.200	3	3	1.000	12	15	27	16	13	0	5	10	0	38	1.6	0.9	2.2

Jackson, Tony B. b. November 7, 1942 Ht. 6-4 Wt. 200 College: St. John's (N.Y.)

SEASON–TEAM	G	GS	MIN	FGM	FGA	PCT	3FGM	3FGA	PCT	FTM	FTA	PCT	O-RB	D-RB	TOT	AST	PF	DQ	STL	TO	BLK	PTS	RPG	APG	PPG
67-68–New Jersey (A)	74	–	2638	449	1171	.383	91	302	.301	450	543	.829	–	–	500	140	184	1	–	144	–	1439	6.8	1.9	19.4
68-69–N.Y.-Minn.-Hou. (A)	64	–	1453	210	588	.357	32	145	.221	299	337	.887	–	–	241	139	147	2	–	153	–	751	3.8	2.2	11.7
Reg. ABA Totals	138	–	4091	659	1759	.375	123	447	.275	749	880	.851	–	–	741	279	331	3	–	297	–	2190	5.4	2.0	15.9

Jackson, Tracy Cordell b. April 21, 1959 Ht. 6-6 Wt. 215 College: Notre Dame

SEASON–TEAM	G	GS	MIN	FGM	FGA	PCT	3FGM	3FGA	PCT	FTM	FTA	PCT	O-RB	D-RB	TOT	AST	PF	DQ	STL	TO	BLK	PTS	RPG	APG	PPG
81-82–Boston-Chi.	49	0	478	79	172	.459	0	0	–	38	49	.776	35	28	63	27	48	0	14	24	3	196	1.3	0.6	4.0
82-83–Chicago	78	3	1309	199	426	.467	2	13	.154	92	126	.730	87	92	179	105	132	0	64	83	11	492	2.3	1.3	6.3
83-84–Indiana	2	0	10	1	4	.250	0	0	–	4	4	1.000	1	0	1	0	3	0	0	1	0	6	0.5	0.0	3.0
Reg. Season Totals	129	3	1797	279	602	.463	2	13	.154	134	179	.749	123	120	243	132	183	0	78	108	14	694	1.9	1.0	5.4

Jackson, Wardell b. July 18, 1951 Ht. 6-7 Wt. 200 College: Ohio State

SEASON–TEAM	G	GS	MIN	FGM	FGA	PCT	3FGM	3FGA	PCT	FTM	FTA	PCT	O-RB	D-RB	TOT	AST	PF	DQ	STL	TO	BLK	PTS	RPG	APG	PPG
74-75–Seattle	56	–	939	96	242	.397	–	–	–	51	71	.718	53	80	133	30	126	2	26	–	5	243	2.4	0.5	4.3
Reg. Season Totals	56	–	939	96	242	.397	–	–	–	51	71	.718	53	80	133	30	126	2	26	–	5	243	2.4	0.5	4.3

Jacobs, Winfred O. (Fred) b. December 2, 1922 Ht. 6-3 Wt. 175 College: Denver

SEASON–TEAM	G	GS	MIN	FGM	FGA	PCT	3FGM	3FGA	PCT	FTM	FTA	PCT	O-RB	D-RB	TOT	AST	PF	DQ	STL	TO	BLK	PTS	RPG	APG	PPG
46-47–St. Louis	18	–	–	19	69	.275	–	–	–	12	25	.480	–	–	–	5	25	–	–	–	–	50	–	0.3	2.8
Reg. Season Totals	18	–	–	19	69	.275	–	–	–	12	25	.480	–	–	–	5	25	–	–	–	–	50	–	0.3	2.8

Jacobson, Samuel Ryan (Sam) b. July 22, 1975 Ht. 6-4 Wt. 219 College: Minnesota

SEASON–TEAM	G	GS	MIN	FGM	FGA	PCT	3FGM	3FGA	PCT	FTM	FTA	PCT	O-RB	D-RB	TOT	AST	PF	DQ	STL	TO	BLK	PTS	RPG	APG	PPG
98-99–L.A. Lakers	2	0	12	3	5	.600	0	1	.000	2	2	1.000	0	3	3	0	2	0	0	1	0	8	1.5	0.0	4.0
99-00–Lakers-G.S.	52	5	681	108	212	.509	9	24	.375	30	41	.732	25	46	71	32	113	3	30	33	3	255	1.4	0.6	4.9
Reg. Season Totals	54	5	693	111	217	.512	9	25	.360	32	43	.744	25	49	74	32	115	3	30	34	3	263	1.4	0.6	4.9

Jamerson, John David (Dave) b. August 13, 1967 Ht. 6-5 Wt. 190 College: Ohio U.

SEASON–TEAM	G	GS	MIN	FGM	FGA	PCT	3FGM	3FGA	PCT	FTM	FTA	PCT	O-RB	D-RB	TOT	AST	PF	DQ	STL	TO	BLK	PTS	RPG	APG	PPG
90-91–Houston	37	0	202	43	113	.381	5	19	.263	22	27	.815	9	21	30	27	24	0	6	20	1	113	0.8	0.7	3.1
91-92–Houston	48	0	378	79	191	.414	8	28	.286	25	27	.926	22	21	43	33	39	0	17	24	0	191	0.9	0.7	4.0
93-94–Utah-N.J.	5	0	14	0	7	.000	0	0	–	2	3	.667	0	4	4	1	0	0	0	1	0	2	0.8	0.2	0.4
Reg. Season Totals	90	0	594	122	311	.392	13	47	.277	49	57	.860	31	46	77	61	63	0	23	45	1	306	0.9	0.7	3.4
Playoff Totals	2	0	21	5	13	.385	0	1	.000	6	6	1.000	1	2	3	4	4	0	1	1	0	16	1.5	2.0	8.0

James, Aaron (A.J.) b. October 5, 1952 Ht. 6-8 Wt. 210 College: Grambling State

SEASON–TEAM	G	GS	MIN	FGM	FGA	PCT	3FGM	3FGA	PCT	FTM	FTA	PCT	O-RB	D-RB	TOT	AST	PF	DQ	STL	TO	BLK	PTS	RPG	APG	PPG
74-75–New Orleans	76	–	1731	370	776	.477	–	–	–	147	189	.778	140	226	366	66	217	4	41	–	15	887	4.8	0.9	11.7
75-76–New Orleans	75	–	1346	262	594	.441	–	–	–	153	204	.750	93	156	249	59	172	1	33	–	6	677	3.3	0.8	9.0
76-77–New Orleans	52	–	1059	238	486	.490	–	–	–	89	114	.781	56	130	186	55	127	1	20	–	5	565	3.6	1.1	10.9
77-78–New Orleans	80	–	2118	428	861	.497	–	–	–	117	157	.745	163	258	421	112	254	5	36	130	22	973	5.3	1.4	12.2
78-79–New Orleans	73	–	1417	311	630	.494	–	–	–	105	140	.750	97	151	248	78	202	1	28	111	21	727	3.4	1.1	10.0
Reg. Season Totals	356	–	7671	1609	3347	.481	–	–	–	611	804	.760	549	921	1470	370	972	12	158	241	69	3829	4.1	1.0	10.8

James, Harold Gene (Gene, Goose) b. February 15, 1925 Ht. 6-4 Wt. 180 College: Marshall

SEASON–TEAM	G	GS	MIN	FGM	FGA	PCT	3FGM	3FGA	PCT	FTM	FTA	PCT	O-RB	D-RB	TOT	AST	PF	DQ	STL	TO	BLK	PTS	RPG	APG	PPG
48-49–New York	11	–	–	18	48	.375	–	–	–	6	12	.500	–	–	–	5	20	–	–	–	–	42	–	0.5	3.8
49-50–New York	29	–	–	19	64	.297	–	–	–	14	31	.452	–	–	–	20	53	–	–	–	–	52	–	0.7	1.8
50-51–N.Y.-Balt.	48	–	–	79	235	.336	–	–	–	44	71	.620	–	–	141	70	118	2	–	–	–	202	2.9	1.5	4.2
Reg. Season Totals	88	–	–	116	347	.334	–	–	–	64	114	.561	–	–	141	95	191	2	–	–	–	296	2.9	1.1	3.4
Playoff Totals	4	–	–	1	14	.071	–	–	–	2	4	.500	–	–	–	4	8	0	–	–	–	4	–	0.7	1.0

James, Henry Charles b. July 29, 1965 Ht. 6-8 Wt. 220 College: South Plains (Texas) Coll. (J.C.); St. Mary's (Texas)

SEASON–TEAM	G	GS	MIN	FGM	FGA	PCT	3FGM	3FGA	PCT	FTM	FTA	PCT	O-RB	D-RB	TOT	AST	PF	DQ	STL	TO	BLK	PTS	RPG	APG	PPG
90-91–Cleveland	37	4	505	112	254	.441	24	60	.400	52	72	.722	26	53	79	32	59	1	15	37	5	300	2.1	0.9	8.1
91-92–Cleveland	65	5	866	164	403	.407	29	90	.322	61	76	.803	35	77	112	25	94	1	16	43	11	418	1.7	0.4	6.4
92-93–Sac.-Utah	10	0	88	21	51	.412	3	13	.231	22	26	.846	7	4	11	1	9	0	3	7	0	67	1.1	0.1	6.7
93-94–L.A. Clippers	12	0	75	16	42	.381	4	18	.222	5	5	1.000	6	8	14	1	9	0	2	2	0	41	1.2	0.1	3.4
95-96–Houston	7	0	58	10	24	.417	5	15	.333	5	5	1.000	3	3	6	2	13	0	0	4	0	30	0.9	0.3	4.3
96-97–Atlanta	53	15	945	125	306	.408	76	181	.420	30	36	.833	27	54	81	21	98	1	11	29	1	356	1.5	0.4	6.7
97-98–Cleveland	28	0	166	24	59	.407	11	25	.440	21	22	.955	2	13	15	5	24	0	1	12	1	80	0.5	0.2	2.9
Reg. Season Totals	212	24	2703	472	1139	.414	152	402	.378	196	242	.810	106	212	318	87	306	3	48	134	18	1292	1.5	0.4	6.1
Playoff Totals	16	0	67	4	23	.174	2	9	.222	2	4	.500	2	1	3	4	14	0	2	5	0	12	0.2	0.3	0.8

James, Jerome Keith b. November 17, 1975 Ht. 7-1 Wt. 300 College: Florida A&M

SEASON–TEAM	G	GS	MIN	FGM	FGA	PCT	3FGM	3FGA	PCT	FTM	FTA	PCT	O-RB	D-RB	TOT	AST	PF	DQ	STL	TO	BLK	PTS	RPG	APG	PPG
98-99–Sacramento	16	0	42	9	24	.375	0	0	–	6	12	.500	6	11	17	1	11	0	2	9	6	24	1.1	0.1	1.5
Reg. Season Totals	16	0	42	9	24	.375	0	0	–	6	12	.500	6	11	17	1	11	0	2	9	6	24	1.1	0.1	1.5
Playoff Totals	1	0	4	1	2	.500	0	0	–	3	4	.750	1	1	2	–	1	0	0	1	0	5	2.0	0.0	5.0

James, Mack William (Billy) b. February 11, 1950 Ht. 6-3 Wt. 185 College: Marshall

SEASON–TEAM	G	GS	MIN	FGM	FGA	PCT	3FGM	3FGA	PCT	FTM	FTA	PCT	O-RB	D-RB	TOT	AST	PF	DQ	STL	TO	BLK	PTS	RPG	APG	PPG
73-74–Kentucky (A)	1	–	10	1	3	.333	0	0	–	0	0	–	0	0	0	1	3	–	0	1	0	2	0.0	1.0	2.0
Reg. ABA Totals	1	–	10	1	3	.333	0	0	–	0	0	–	0	0	–	1	3	0	0	1	0	2	0.0	1.0	2.0

James, Tim O'Connor b. December 25, 1976 Ht. 6-7 Wt. 212 College: Miami (Fla.)

SEASON–TEAM	G	GS	MIN	FGM	FGA	PCT	3FGM	3FGA	PCT	FTM	FTA	PCT	O-RB	D-RB	TOT	AST	PF	DQ	STL	TO	BLK	PTS	RPG	APG	PPG
99-00–Miami	4	0	23	5	14	.357	0	0	–	1	3	.333	3	1	4	2	1	0	0	2	3	11	1.0	0.5	2.8
Reg. Season Totals	4	0	23	5	14	.357	0	0	–	1	3	.333	3	1	4	2	1	0	0	2	3	11	1.0	0.5	2.8

Jamison, Antawn Cortez b. June 12, 1976 Ht. 6-9 Wt. 223 College: North Carolina

SEASON–TEAM	G	GS	MIN	FGM	FGA	PCT	3FGM	3FGA	PCT	FTM	FTA	PCT	O-RB	D-RB	TOT	AST	PF	DQ	STL	TO	BLK	PTS	RPG	APG	PPG
98-99–Golden State	47	24	1058	178	394	.452	3	10	.300	90	153	.588	131	170	301	34	102	1	38	68	16	449	6.4	0.7	9.6
99-00–Golden State	43	41	1556	356	756	.471	2	7	.286	127	208	.611	172	187	359	90	115	0	30	113	15	841	8.3	2.1	19.6
Reg. Season Totals	90	65	2614	534	1150	.464	5	17	.294	217	361	.601	303	357	660	124	217	1	68	181	31	1290	7.3	1.4	14.3

Jamison, Harold Sherill (Big O) b. November 20, 1976 Ht. 6-8 Wt. 260 College: Clemson

SEASON–TEAM	G	GS	MIN	FGM	FGA	PCT	3FGM	3FGA	PCT	FTM	FTA	PCT	O-RB	D-RB	TOT	AST	PF	DQ	STL	TO	BLK	PTS	RPG	APG	PPG
99-00–Miami	12	0	74	7	20	.350	0	0	–	4	18	.222	16	5	21	4	17	0	2	4	1	18	1.8	0.3	1.5
Reg. Season Totals	12	0	74	7	20	.350	0	0	–	4	18	.222	16	5	21	4	17	0	2	4	1	18	1.8	0.3	1.5

Janisch, John Albert b. March 15, 1920 d. August 25, 1992 Ht. 6-3 Wt. 200 College: Valparaiso

SEASON–TEAM	G	GS	MIN	FGM	FGA	PCT	3FGM	3FGA	PCT	FTM	FTA	PCT	O-RB	D-RB	TOT	AST	PF	DQ	STL	TO	BLK	PTS	RPG	APG	PPG
46-47–Detroit	60	–	–	283	983	.288	–	–	–	131	198	.662	–	–	–	49	132	–	–	–	–	697	–	0.8	11.6
47-48–Boston-Prov.	10	–	–	14	50	.280	–	–	–	9	16	.563	–	–	–	2	5	–	–	–	–	37	–	0.2	3.7
47-48–Flint (N)	36	–	–	36	–	–	–	–	–	21	28	.750	–	–	–	–	38	–	–	–	–	93	–	–	2.6
Reg. NBA Totals	70	–	–	297	1033	.288	–	–	–	140	214	.654	–	–	–	51	137	–	–	–	–	734	–	0.7	10.5
Reg. NBL Totals	36	–	–	36	–	–	–	–	–	21	28	.750	–	–	–	–	38	–	–	–	–	93	–	–	2.6

Janotta, Howard (Howie) b. October 19, 1924 Ht. 6-3 Wt. 185 College: Seton Hall

SEASON–TEAM	G	GS	MIN	FGM	FGA	PCT	3FGM	3FGA	PCT	FTM	FTA	PCT	O-RB	D-RB	TOT	AST	PF	DQ	STL	TO	BLK	PTS	RPG	APG	PPG
49-50–Baltimore	9	–	–	9	30	.300	–	–	–	13	16	.813	–	–	–	4	10	–	–	–	–	31	–	0.4	3.4
Reg. Season Totals	9	–	–	9	30	.300	–	–	–	13	16	.813	–	–	–	4	10	–	–	–	–	31	–	0.4	3.4

Jaros, Anthony Joseph (Tony) b. February 22, 1920 d. April 22, 1995 Ht. 6-3 Wt. 185 College: Minnesota

SEASON–TEAM	G	GS	MIN	FGM	FGA	PCT	3FGM	3FGA	PCT	FTM	FTA	PCT	O-RB	D-RB	TOT	AST	PF	DQ	STL	TO	BLK	PTS	RPG	APG	PPG
46-47–Chicago	59	–	–	177	613	.289	–	–	–	128	181	.707	–	–	–	28	156	–	–	–	–	482	–	0.5	8.2
47-48–Minneapolis (N)	58	–	–	95	–	–	–	–	–	83	114	.728	–	–	–	–	90	–	–	–	–	273	–	–	4.7
48-49–Minneapolis	59	–	–	132	385	.343	–	–	–	79	110	.718	–	–	–	58	114	–	–	–	–	343	–	1.0	5.8
49-50–Minneapolis	61	–	–	84	289	.291	–	–	–	72	96	.750	–	–	–	60	106	–	–	–	–	240	–	1.0	3.9
50-51–Minneapolis	63	–	–	88	287	.307	–	–	–	65	103	.631	–	–	131	72	131	0	–	–	–	241	2.1	1.1	3.8
Reg. NBA Totals	242	–	–	481	1574	.306	–	–	–	344	490	.702	–	–	131	218	507	0	–	–	–	1306	2.1	0.9	5.4
Reg. NBL Totals	58	–	–	95	–	–	–	–	–	83	114	.728	–	–	–	–	90	–	–	–	–	273	–	–	4.7
NBA Playoff Totals	30	–	–	66	418	.287	–	–	–	49	67	.731	–	–	7	33	73	2	–	–	–	181	1.0	0.6	6.0
NBL Playoff Totals	10	–	–	29	–	–	–	–	–	22	33	.667	–	–	–	–	29	–	–	–	–	80	–	–	8.0

J

Jarvis, James C. (Jim) b. March 3, 1943 Ht. 6-1 Wt. 175 College: Oregon State

SEASON–TEAM	G	GS	MIN	FGM	FGA	PCT	3FGM	3FGA	PCT	FTM	FTA	PCT	O-RB	D-RB	TOT	AST	PF	DQ	STL	TO	BLK	PTS	RPG	APG	PPG
67-68–Pittsburgh (A)	63	–	818	132	343	.385	12	48	.250	53	64	.828	–	–	106	72	103	0	–	48	–	329	1.7	1.1	5.2
68-69–Minn.-L.A. (A)	62	–	911	147	402	.366	19	47	.404	86	109	.789	–	–	129	80	137	1	–	71	–	399	2.1	1.3	6.4
Reg. ABA Totals	125	–	1729	279	745	.374	31	95	.326	139	173	.803	–	–	235	152	240	1	–	119	–	728	1.9	1.2	5.8
ABA Playoff Totals	15	–	211	39	89	.438	0	2	.000	16	20	.800	–	–	21	15	29	0	–	11	–	94	1.4	1.0	6.3

Jeannette, Harry Edward (Buddy) b. September 15, 1917 d. March 11, 1998 Ht. 5-11 Wt. 175 College: Washington & Jefferson HOF: 1994

SEASON–TEAM	G	GS	MIN	FGM	FGA	PCT	3FGM	3FGA	PCT	FTM	FTA	PCT	O-RB	D-RB	TOT	AST	PF	DQ	STL	TO	BLK	PTS	RPG	APG	PPG
38-39–Cleveland (N)	26	–	–	54	–	–	–	–	–	65	–	–	–	–	–	–	57	–	–	–	–	173	–	–	6.7
39-40–Detroit (N)	25	–	–	45	–	–	–	–	–	52	80	.650	–	–	–	–	62	–	–	–	–	142	–	–	5.7
40-41–Detroit (N)	23	–	–	75	–	–	–	–	–	54	86	.628	–	–	–	–	56	–	–	–	–	204	–	–	8.9
42-43–Sheboygan (N)	4	–	–	24	–	–	–	–	–	14	17	.824	–	–	–	–	8	–	–	–	–	62	–	–	15.5
43-44–Fort Wayne (N)	22	–	–	68	–	–	–	–	–	48	65	.738	–	–	–	–	46	–	–	–	–	184	–	–	8.4
44-45–Fort Wayne (N)	27	–	–	85	–	–	–	–	–	82	111	.739	–	–	–	–	67	–	–	–	–	252	–	–	9.3
45-46–Fort Wayne (N)	34	–	–	99	–	–	–	–	–	105	136	.772	–	–	–	–	184	–	–	–	–	303	–	–	8.9
47-48–Baltimore	46	–	–	150	430	.349	–	–	–	191	252	.758	–	–	–	70	147	–	–	–	–	491	–	1.5	10.7
48-49–Baltimore	56	–	–	73	199	.367	–	–	–	167	213	.784	–	–	–	124	157	–	–	–	–	313	–	2.2	5.6
49-50–Baltimore	37	–	–	42	148	.284	–	–	–	109	133	.820	–	–	–	93	82	–	–	–	–	193	–	2.5	5.2
Reg. NBA Totals	139	–	–	265	777	.341	–	–	–	467	598	.781	–	–	–	287	386	–	–	–	–	997	–	2.1	7.2
Reg. NBL Totals	161	–	–	450	–	–	–	–	–	420	495	.717	–	–	–	–	480	–	–	–	–	1320	–	–	8.2
NBA Playoff Totals	14	–	–	32	90	.433	–	–	–	41	46	.891	–	–	–	20	67	1	–	–	–	105	–	1.3	7.5
NBL Playoff Totals	27	–	–	71	–	–	–	–	–	68	32	.781	–	–	–	–	69	–	–	–	–	210	–	–	7.8

Jeelani, Abdul Qadir (formerly Gary Cole) b. February 10, 1954 Ht. 6-8 Wt. 210 College: Wisconsin-Parkside

SEASON–TEAM	G	GS	MIN	FGM	FGA	PCT	3FGM	3FGA	PCT	FTM	FTA	PCT	O-RB	D-RB	TOT	AST	PF	DQ	STL	TO	BLK	PTS	RPG	APG	PPG
79-80–Portland	77	–	1286	288	565	.510	0	6	.000	161	204	.789	114	156	270	95	155	0	40	117	40	737	3.5	1.2	9.6
80-81–Dallas	66	–	1108	187	440	.425	0	1	.000	179	220	.814	83	147	230	65	123	2	44	87	31	553	3.5	1.0	8.4
Reg. Season Totals	143	–	2394	475	1005	.473	0	7	.000	340	424	.802	197	303	500	160	278	2	84	204	71	1290	3.5	1.1	9.0

Jennings, Keith Russell (Mister) b. November 2, 1968 Ht. 5-7 Wt. 160 College: East Tennessee State

SEASON–TEAM	G	GS	MIN	FGM	FGA	PCT	3FGM	3FGA	PCT	FTM	FTA	PCT	O-RB	D-RB	TOT	AST	PF	DQ	STL	TO	BLK	PTS	RPG	APG	PPG
92-93–Golden State	8	0	136	25	42	.595	5	9	.556	14	18	.778	2	9	11	23	18	0	4	7	0	69	1.4	2.9	8.6
93-94–Golden State	76	2	1097	138	342	.404	56	151	.371	100	120	.833	16	73	89	218	62	0	65	74	0	432	1.2	2.9	5.7
94-95–Golden State	80	24	1722	190	425	.447	75	204	.368	134	153	.876	26	122	148	373	133	0	95	120	2	589	1.9	4.7	7.4
Reg. Season Totals	164	26	2955	353	809	.436	136	364	.374	248	291	.852	44	204	248	614	213	0	164	201	2	1090	1.5	3.7	6.6
Playoff Totals	3	0	39	4	13	.308	1	5	.200	6	7	.857	1	4	5	4	11	0	1	4	0	15	1.7	1.3	5.0

Jent, Chris b. January 11, 1970 Ht. 6-7 Wt. 220 College: Ohio State

SEASON–TEAM	G	GS	MIN	FGM	FGA	PCT	3FGM	3FGA	PCT	FTM	FTA	PCT	O-RB	D-RB	TOT	AST	PF	DQ	STL	TO	BLK	PTS	RPG	APG	PPG
93-94–Houston	3	0	78	13	26	.500	4	11	.364	1	2	.500	4	11	15	7	13	1	0	5	0	31	5.0	2.3	10.3
96-97–New York	3	0	10	2	6	.333	2	3	.667	0	0	–	1	0	1	1	2	0	0	0	0	6	0.3	0.3	2.0
Reg. Season Totals	6	0	88	15	32	.469	6	14	.429	1	2	.500	5	11	16	8	15	1	0	5	0	37	2.7	1.3	6.2
Playoff Totals	11	0	62	5	20	.250	3	13	.231	0	0	–	1	8	9	7	7	0	2	3	0	13	0.8	0.6	1.2

Jepsen, Leslie Burnell (Les, Big Boy) b. June 24, 1967 Ht. 7-0 Wt. 240 College: Iowa

SEASON–TEAM	G	GS	MIN	FGM	FGA	PCT	3FGM	3FGA	PCT	FTM	FTA	PCT	O-RB	D-RB	TOT	AST	PF	DQ	STL	TO	BLK	PTS	RPG	APG	PPG
90-91–Golden State	21	0	105	11	36	.306	0	1	.000	6	9	.667	17	20	37	1	16	0	1	3	3	28	1.8	0.0	1.3
91-92–Sacramento	31	0	87	9	24	.375	0	1	.000	7	11	.636	12	18	30	1	17	0	1	3	5	25	1.0	0.0	0.8
Reg. Season Totals	52	0	192	20	60	.333	0	2	.000	13	20	.650	29	38	67	2	33	0	2	6	8	53	1.3	0.0	1.0

Jeter, Harold (Hal) b. May 17, 1945 Ht. 6-3 Wt. 195 College: Drake

SEASON–TEAM	G	GS	MIN	FGM	FGA	PCT	3FGM	3FGA	PCT	FTM	FTA	PCT	O-RB	D-RB	TOT	AST	PF	DQ	STL	TO	BLK	PTS	RPG	APG	PPG
69-70–Washington (A)	5	–	19	1	4	.250	0	0	–	0	0	–	–	–	1	0	8	0	–	–	–	2	0.2	0.0	0.4
Reg. ABA Totals	5	–	19	1	4	.250	0	0	–	0	0	–	–	–	1	0	8	0	–	–	–	2	0.2	0.0	0.4

Johnson, Alfonso Jr. (Buck) b. January 3, 1964 Ht. 6-7 Wt. 200 College: Alabama

SEASON–TEAM	G	GS	MIN	FGM	FGA	PCT	3FGM	3FGA	PCT	FTM	FTA	PCT	O-RB	D-RB	TOT	AST	PF	DQ	STL	TO	BLK	PTS	RPG	APG	PPG
86-87–Houston	60	3	520	94	201	.468	0	1	.000	40	58	.690	38	50	88	40	81	0	17	37	15	228	1.5	0.7	3.8
87-88–Houston	70	2	879	155	298	.520	1	8	.125	67	91	.736	77	91	168	49	127	0	30	54	26	378	2.4	0.7	5.4
88-89–Houston	67	51	1850	270	515	.524	1	9	.111	101	134	.754	114	172	286	126	213	4	64	110	35	642	4.3	1.9	9.6
89-90–Houston	82	82	2832	504	1019	.495	2	17	.118	205	270	.759	113	268	381	252	321	8	104	167	62	1215	4.6	3.1	14.8
90-91–Houston	73	70	2279	416	873	.477	2	15	.133	157	216	.727	108	222	330	142	240	5	81	122	47	991	4.5	1.9	13.6
91-92–Houston	80	69	2202	290	633	.458	1	9	.111	104	143	.727	95	217	312	158	234	2	72	104	49	685	3.9	2.0	8.6
92-93–Washington	73	19	1287	193	403	.479	0	3	.000	92	126	.730	78	117	195	89	187	2	36	70	18	478	2.7	1.2	6.5
Reg. Season Totals	505	296	11849	1922	3942	.488	7	62	.113	766	1038	.738	623	1137	1760	856	1403	21	404	664	252	4617	3.5	1.7	9.1
Playoff Totals	20	11	382	53	125	.424	0	2	.000	24	33	.727	20	28	48	29	46	0	12	21	5	130	2.4	1.5	6.5

Johnson, Andrew Jr. (Andy) b. April 21, 1931 Ht. 6-5 Wt. 215 College: Portland

SEASON–TEAM	G	GS	MIN	FGM	FGA	PCT	3FGM	3FGA	PCT	FTM	FTA	PCT	O-RB	D-RB	TOT	AST	PF	DQ	STL	TO	BLK	PTS	RPG	APG	PPG
58-59–Philadelphia	67	–	1158	174	466	.373	–	–	–	115	191	.602	–	–	212	90	176	4	–	–	–	463	3.2	1.3	6.9
59-60–Philadelphia	75	–	1421	245	648	.378	–	–	–	125	208	.601	–	–	282	152	196	5	–	–	–	615	3.8	2.0	8.2
60-61–Philadelphia	79	–	2000	299	834	.359	–	–	–	157	275	.571	–	–	345	205	249	3	–	–	–	755	4.4	2.6	9.6
61-62–Chicago	71	–	2193	365	814	.448	–	–	–	284	452	.628	–	–	351	228	247	5	–	–	–	1014	4.9	3.2	14.3
Reg. Season Totals	292	–	6772	1083	2762	.392	–	–	–	681	1126	.605	–	–	1190	675	868	17	–	–	–	2847	4.1	2.3	9.8
Playoff Totals	12	–	233	35	89	.393	–	–	–	30	56	.536	–	–	55	22	37	2	–	–	–	100	4.6	1.8	8.3

Johnson, Anthony Mark b. October 2, 1974 Ht. 6-3 Wt. 190 College: Charleston (S.C.)

SEASON–TEAM	G	GS	MIN	FGM	FGA	PCT	3FGM	3FGA	PCT	FTM	FTA	PCT	O-RB	D-RB	TOT	AST	PF	DQ	STL	TO	BLK	PTS	RPG	APG	PPG
97-98–Sacramento	77	62	2266	226	609	.371	42	128	.328	80	110	.727	51	120	171	329	188	1	64	120	6	574	2.2	4.3	7.5
98-99–Atlanta	49	2	885	91	225	.404	5	19	.263	57	82	.695	16	59	75	107	67	0	35	65	7	244	1.5	2.2	5.0
99-00–Atlanta-Orlando	56	6	637	62	164	.378	2	11	.182	28	39	.718	21	30	51	72	58	0	33	32	4	154	0.9	1.3	2.8
Reg. Season Totals	182	70	3788	379	998	.380	49	158	.310	165	231	.714	88	209	297	508	313	1	132	217	17	972	1.6	2.8	5.3
Playoff Totals	9	0	111	8	29	.276	1	2	.500	7	10	.700	3	6	9	10	9	0	1	5	1	24	1.0	1.1	2.7

Johnson, Arnitz L. (Arnie) b. May 17, 1920 Ht. 6-5 Wt. 240 College: Bemidji State

SEASON–TEAM	G	GS	MIN	FGM	FGA	PCT	3FGM	3FGA	PCT	FTM	FTA	PCT	O-RB	D-RB	TOT	AST	PF	DQ	STL	TO	BLK	PTS	RPG	APG	PPG
46-47–Rochester (N)	32	–	–	68	–	–	–	–	–	68	98	.694	–	–	–	–	74	–	–	–	–	204	–	–	6.4
47-48–Rochester (N)	57	–	–	101	–	–	–	–	–	97	147	.660	–	–	–	–	153	–	–	–	–	299	–	–	5.2
48-49–Rochester	60	–	–	156	375	.416	–	–	–	199	284	.701	–	–	–	80	247	–	–	–	–	511	–	1.3	8.5
49-50–Rochester	68	–	–	149	376	.396	–	–	–	200	294	.680	–	–	–	141	260		–	–	–	498	–	2.1	7.3
50-51–Rochester	68	–	–	185	403	.459	–	–	–	269	371	.725	–	–	449	175	290	11	–	–	–	639	6.6	2.6	9.4
51-52–Rochester	66	–	2158	178	411	.433	–	–	–	301	387	.778	–	–	404	182	259	9	–	–	–	657	6.1	2.8	10.0
52-53–Rochester	70	–	1984	140	369	.379	–	–	–	303	405	.748	–	–	419	153	282	14	–	–	–	583	6.0	2.2	8.3
Reg. NBA Totals	332	–	4142	808	1934	.418	–	–	–	1272	1741	.731	–	–	1272	731	1338	34	–	–	–	2888	6.2	2.2	8.7
Reg. NBL Totals	89	–	–	169	–	–	–	–	–	165	245	.673	–	–	–	–	227	–	–	–	–	503	–	–	5.7
NBA Playoff Totals	29	–	419	77	260	.369	–	–	–	124	165	.752	–	–	206	118	137	5	–	–	–	278	7.1	2.9	9.6
NBL Playoff Totals	11	–	–	23	–	–	–	–	–	20	24	.833	–	–	–	–	21	–	–	–	–	66	–	–	6.0

Johnson, Avery (Taz) b. March 25, 1965 Ht. 5-11 Wt. 180 College: Southern University

SEASON–TEAM	G	GS	MIN	FGM	FGA	PCT	3FGM	3FGA	PCT	FTM	FTA	PCT	O-RB	D-RB	TOT	AST	PF	DQ	STL	TO	BLK	PTS	RPG	APG	PPG
88-89–Seattle	43	0	291	29	83	.349	1	9	.111	9	16	.563	11	13	24	73	34	0	21	18	3	68	0.6	1.7	1.6
89-90–Seattle	53	10	575	55	142	.387	1	4	.250	29	40	.725	21	22	43	162	55	0	26	48	1	140	0.8	3.1	2.6
90-91–Denver-S.A.	68	14	959	130	277	.469	1	9	.111	59	87	.678	22	55	77	230	62	0	47	74	4	320	1.1	3.4	4.7
91-92–S.A.-Houston	69	15	1235	158	330	.479	4	15	.267	66	101	.653	13	67	80	266	89	1	61	110	9	386	1.2	3.9	5.6
92-93–San Antonio	75	49	2030	256	510	.502	0	8	.000	144	182	.791	20	126	146	561	141	0	85	145	16	656	1.9	7.5	8.7
93-94–Golden State	82	70	2332	356	724	.492	0	12	.000	178	253	.704	41	135	176	433	160	0	113	172	8	890	2.1	5.3	10.9
94-95–San Antonio	82	82	3011	448	863	.519	3	22	.136	202	295	.685	49	159	208	670	154	0	114	207	13	1101	2.5	8.2	13.4
95-96–San Antonio	82	82	3084	438	887	.494	6	31	.194	189	262	.721	37	169	206	789	179	1	119	195	21	1071	2.5	9.6	13.1
96-97–San Antonio	76	76	2472	327	685	.477	6	26	.231	140	203	.690	32	115	147	513	158	1	96	146	15	800	1.9	6.8	10.5
97-98–San Antonio	75	73	2674	321	671	.478	2	13	.154	122	168	.726	30	120	150	591	140	0	84	165	18	766	2.0	7.9	10.2
98-99–San Antonio	50	50	1672	218	461	.473	1	12	.083	50	88	.568	22	96	118	369	101	0	51	112	11	487	2.4	7.4	9.7
99-00–San Antonio	82	82	2571	402	850	.473	1	9	.111	114	155	.735	33	125	158	491	150	0	76	140	18	919	1.9	6.0	11.2
Reg. Season Totals	837	603	22906	3138	6483	.484	26	170	.153	1302	1850	.704	331	1202	1533	5148	1423	3	893	1532	137	7604	1.8	6.2	9.1
Playoff Totals	77	65	2526	364	731	.498	1	15	.067	144	215	.670	39	131	170	521	150	0	92	161	10	873	2.2	6.8	11.3

Johnson, Charles (Charlie, C.J.) b. March 31, 1949 Ht. 6-0 Wt. 170 College: California

SEASON–TEAM	G	GS	MIN	FGM	FGA	PCT	3FGM	3FGA	PCT	FTM	FTA	PCT	O-RB	D-RB	TOT	AST	PF	DQ	STL	TO	BLK	PTS	RPG	APG	PPG
72-73–Golden State	70	–	887	171	400	.428	–	–	–	33	46	.717	–	–	132	118	105	0	–	–	–	375	1.9	1.7	5.4
73-74–Golden State	59	–	1051	194	468	.415	–	–	–	38	55	.691	49	126	175	102	111	1	62	–	7	426	3.0	1.7	7.2
74-75–Golden State	79	–	2171	394	957	.412	–	–	–	75	102	.735	134	177	311	233	204	2	138	–	8	863	3.9	2.9	10.9
75-76–Golden State	81	–	1549	342	732	.467	–	–	–	60	79	.759	77	125	202	122	178	1	100	–	7	744	2.5	1.5	9.2
76-77–Golden State	79	–	1196	255	583	.437	–	–	–	49	69	.710	50	91	141	91	134	1	77	–	7	559	1.8	1.2	7.1
77-78–G.S.-Wash.	71	–	1299	237	581	.408	–	–	–	49	61	.803	43	112	155	130	129	0	62	73	5	523	2.2	1.8	7.4
78-79–Washington	82	–	1819	342	786	.435	–	–	–	67	79	.848	70	132	202	177	161	0	95	87	6	751	2.5	2.2	9.2
Reg. Season Totals	521	–	9972	1935	4507	.429	–	–	–	371	491	.756	423	763	1318	973	1022	5	534	160	40	4241	2.5	1.9	8.1
Playoff Totals	85	–	1723	321	806	.398	–	–	–	80	107	.748	71	126	207	142	201	1	88	37	10	722	2.4	1.7	8.5

J

Johnson, Clarence Stephen (Steve) b. November 3, 1957 Ht. 6-10 Wt. 235 College: Oregon State

SEASON–TEAM	G	GS	MIN	FGM	FGA	PCT	3FGM	3FGA	PCT	FTM	FTA	PCT	O-RB	D-RB	TOT	AST	PF	DQ	STL	TO	BLK	PTS	RPG	APG	PPG
81-82–Kansas City	78	50	1741	395	644	.613	0	0	–	212	330	.642	152	307	459	91	372	25	39	197	89	1002	5.9	1.2	12.8
82-83–Kansas City	79	21	1544	371	595	.624	0	0	–	186	324	.574	140	258	398	95	323	9	40	180	83	928	5.0	1.2	11.7
83-84–K.C.-Chicago	81	21	1487	302	540	.559	0	0	–	165	287	.575	162	256	418	81	307	15	37	164	69	769	5.2	1.0	9.5
84-85–Chicago	74	54	1659	281	516	.545	0	3	.000	181	252	.718	146	291	437	64	265	7	37	151	62	743	5.9	0.9	10.0
85-86–San Antonio	71	55	1828	362	573	.632	0	0	–	259	373	.694	143	319	462	95	291	13	44	191	66	983	6.5	1.3	13.8
86-87–Portland	79	74	2345	494	889	.556	0	0	–	342	490	.698	194	372	566	155	340	16	49	276	76	1330	7.2	2.0	16.8
87-88–Portland	43	33	1050	258	488	.529	0	1	.000	146	249	.586	84	158	242	57	151	4	17	122	32	662	5.6	1.3	15.4
88-89–Portland	72	11	1477	296	565	.524	0	0	–	129	245	.527	135	223	358	105	254	3	20	140	44	721	5.0	1.5	10.0
89-90–Minn.-Seattle	25	0	259	48	92	.522	0	0	–	21	35	.600	19	34	53	17	56	0	3	31	5	117	2.1	0.7	4.7
90-91–Golden State	24	8	228	34	63	.540	0	0	–	22	37	.595	18	39	57	17	50	1	4	25	4	90	2.4	0.7	3.8
Reg. Season Totals	626	327	13618	2841	4965	.572	0	4	.000	1663	2622	.634	1193	2257	3450	777	2409	93	290	1477	530	7345	5.5	1.2	11.7
Playoff Totals	13	4	246	37	91	.407	0	0	–	37	59	.627	23	34	57	6	40	1	4	20	2	111	4.4	0.5	8.5

Johnson, Clayton H. b. July 18, 1956 Ht. 6-4 Wt. 175 College: Penn Valley (Mo.) C.C.; Missouri

SEASON–TEAM	G	GS	MIN	FGM	FGA	PCT	3FGM	3FGA	PCT	FTM	FTA	PCT	O-RB	D-RB	TOT	AST	PF	DQ	STL	TO	BLK	PTS	RPG	APG	PPG
81-82–Los Angeles	7	0	65	11	20	.550	0	0	–	3	6	.500	8	4	12	7	13	0	3	7	3	25	1.7	1.0	3.6
82-83–Los Angeles	48	0	447	53	135	.393	0	2	.000	38	48	.792	40	29	69	24	62	0	22	25	4	144	1.4	0.5	3.0
83-84–Seattle	25	0	176	20	50	.400	1	1	1.000	14	22	.636	6	6	12	14	24	0	8	12	2	55	0.5	0.6	2.2
Reg. Season Totals	80	0	688	84	205	.410	1	3	.333	55	76	.724	54	39	93	45	99	0	33	44	9	224	1.2	0.6	2.8
Playoff Totals	17	0	67	11	20	.550	0	2	.000	2	2	1.000	4	4	8	3	12	0	3	2	0	24	0.5	0.2	1.4

Johnson, Clemon b. September 12, 1956 Ht. 6-10 Wt. 240 College: Florida A&M

SEASON–TEAM	G	GS	MIN	FGM	FGA	PCT	3FGM	3FGA	PCT	FTM	FTA	PCT	O-RB	D-RB	TOT	AST	PF	DQ	STL	TO	BLK	PTS	RPG	APG	PPG
78-79–Portland	74	–	794	102	217	.470	–	–	–	36	74	.486	83	143	226	78	121	1	23	65	36	240	3.1	1.1	3.2
79-80–Indiana	79	–	1541	199	396	.503	0	0	–	74	117	.632	145	249	394	115	211	2	48	78	121	472	5.0	1.5	6.0
80-81–Indiana	81	–	1643	235	466	.504	0	1	.000	112	189	.593	173	295	468	144	185	1	44	121	119	582	5.8	1.8	7.2
81-82–Indiana	79	42	1979	312	641	.487	0	0	–	123	189	.651	184	387	571	127	241	3	60	138	110	747	7.2	1.6	9.5
82-83–Indiana-Phil.	83	11	1914	299	581	.515	0	1	.000	111	180	.617	190	334	524	139	221	3	67	124	92	709	6.3	1.7	8.5
83-84–Philadelphia	80	10	1721	193	412	.468	0	0	–	69	113	.611	131	267	398	55	205	1	35	95	65	455	5.0	0.7	5.7
84-85–Philadelphia	58	0	875	117	235	.498	0	1	.000	36	49	.735	92	129	221	33	112	0	15	43	44	270	3.8	0.6	4.7
85-86–Philadelphia	75	2	1069	105	223	.471	0	0	–	51	81	.630	106	149	255	15	129	0	23	38	62	261	3.4	0.2	3.5
86-87–Seattle	78	7	1051	88	178	.494	0	2	.000	70	110	.636	106	171	277	21	137	0	21	36	42	246	3.6	0.3	3.2
87-88–Seattle	74	26	723	49	105	.467	0	0	–	22	32	.688	66	108	174	17	104	0	13	29	24	120	2.4	0.2	1.6
Reg. Season Totals	761	98	13310	1699	3454	.492	0	5	.000	704	1134	.621	1276	2232	3508	744	1666	11	349	767	715	4102	4.6	1.0	5.4
Playoff Totals	66	9	1118	107	230	.465	0	1	.000	56	92	.609	104	134	238	26	139	0	33	52	52	270	3.6	0.4	4.1

Johnson, Darryl b. October 26, 1965 Ht. 6-1 Wt. 185 College: Michigan State

SEASON–TEAM	G	GS	MIN	FGM	FGA	PCT	3FGM	3FGA	PCT	FTM	FTA	PCT	O-RB	D-RB	TOT	AST	PF	DQ	STL	TO	BLK	PTS	RPG	APG	PPG
95-96–Cleveland	11	0	28	5	12	.417	0	1	.000	2	2	1.000	2	0	2	1	3	0	0	1	0	12	0.2	0.1	1.1
Reg. Season Totals	11	0	28	5	12	.417	0	1	.000	2	2	1.000	2	0	2	1	3	0	0	1	0	12	0.2	0.1	1.1

Johnson, Dave M. b. November 16, 1970 Ht. 6-7 Wt. 210 College: Syracuse

SEASON–TEAM	G	GS	MIN	FGM	FGA	PCT	3FGM	3FGA	PCT	FTM	FTA	PCT	O-RB	D-RB	TOT	AST	PF	DQ	STL	TO	BLK	PTS	RPG	APG	PPG
92-93–Portland	42	0	356	57	149	.383	3	14	.214	40	59	.678	18	30	48	13	23	0	8	28	1	157	1.1	0.3	3.7
93-94–Chicago	17	0	119	17	54	.315	0	1	.000	13	21	.619	9	7	16	4	7	0	4	9	0	47	0.9	0.2	2.8
Reg. Season Totals	59	0	475	74	203	.365	3	15	.200	53	80	.663	27	37	64	17	30	0	12	37	1	204	1.1	0.3	3.5

Johnson, David Ralph (Boag, Ralph) b. December 6, 1921 Ht. 5-11 Wt. 170 College: Huntington College

SEASON–TEAM	G	GS	MIN	FGM	FGA	PCT	3FGM	3FGA	PCT	FTM	FTA	PCT	O-RB	D-RB	TOT	AST	PF	DQ	STL	TO	BLK	PTS	RPG	APG	PPG
47-48–Anderson (N)	57	–	–	84	–	–	–	–	–	31	53	.585	–	–	–	–	99	–	–	–	–	199	–	–	3.5
48-49–Anderson (N)	64	–	–	218	–	–	–	–	–	85	129	.659	–	–	–	–	178	–	–	–	–	521	–	–	8.1
49-50–And.-FtWayne	67	–	–	243	779	.312	–	–	–	104	129	.806	–	–	–	171	207	–	–	–	–	590	–	2.6	8.8
50-51–Fort Wayne	68	–	–	235	737	.319	–	–	–	114	162	.704	–	–	275	183	247	11	–	–	–	584	4.0	2.7	8.6
51-52–Fort Wayne	66	–	2265	211	592	.356	–	–	–	101	140	.721	–	–	222	210	243	6	–	–	–	523	3.4	3.2	7.9
52-53–Fort Wayne	3	–	30	3	9	.333	–	–	–	2	3	.667	–	–	1	5	6	0	–	–	–	8	0.3	1.7	2.7
Reg. NBA Totals	204	–	2295	692	2117	.327	–	–	–	321	434	.740	–	–	498	569	703	17	–	–	–	1705	3.6	2.8	8.4
Reg. NBL Totals	121	–	–	302	–	–	–	–	–	116	182	.637	–	–	–	–	277	–	–	–	–	720	–	–	6.0
NBA Playoff Totals	9	–	140	28	96	.323	–	–	–	14	19	.737	–	–	19	29	41	3	–	–	–	70	2.7	2.6	7.8
NBL Playoff Totals	13	–	–	49	–	–	–	–	–	21	27	.778	–	–	–	–	33	–	–	–	–	119	–	–	9.2

Johnson, DeMarco Antonio b. October 6, 1975 Ht. 6-9 Wt. 245 College: North Carolina-Charlotte

SEASON–TEAM	G	GS	MIN	FGM	FGA	PCT	3FGM	3FGA	PCT	FTM	FTA	PCT	O-RB	D-RB	TOT	AST	PF	DQ	STL	TO	BLK	PTS	RPG	APG	PPG
99-00–New York	5	0	37	3	9	.333	0	0	–	0	0	–	3	4	7	0	5	0	1	3	0	6	1.4	0.0	1.2
Reg. Season Totals	5	0	37	3	9	.333	0	0	–	0	0	–	3	4	7	0	5	0	1	3	0	6	1.4	0.0	1.2

Johnson, Dennis Wayne (D.J.) b. September 18, 1954 Ht. 6-4 Wt. 200 College: Los Angeles Harbor (Calif.) Coll. (J.C.); Pepperdine

SEASON–TEAM	G	GS	MIN	FGM	FGA	PCT	3FGM	3FGA	PCT	FTM	FTA	PCT	O-RB	D-RB	TOT	AST	PF	DQ	STL	TO	BLK	PTS	RPG	APG	PPG
76-77–Seattle	81	–	1667	285	566	.504	–	–	–	179	287	.624	161	141	302	123	221	3	123	–	57	749	3.7	1.5	9.2
77-78–Seattle	81	–	2209	367	881	.417	–	–	–	297	406	.732	152	142	294	230	213	2	118	164	51	1031	3.6	2.8	12.7
78-79–Seattle	80	–	2717	482	1110	.434	–	–	–	306	392	.781	146	228	374	280	209	2	100	191	97	1270	4.7	3.5	15.9
79-80–Seattle	81	–	2937	574	1361	.422	12	58	.207	380	487	.780	173	241	414	332	267	6	144	227	82	1540	5.1	4.1	19.0
80-81–Phoenix	79	–	2615	532	1220	.436	11	51	.216	411	501	.820	160	203	363	291	244	2	136	208	61	1486	4.6	3.7	18.8
81-82–Phoenix	80	77	2937	577	1228	.470	8	42	.190	399	495	.806	142	268	410	369	253	6	105	233	55	1561	5.1	4.6	19.5
82-83–Phoenix	77	74	2551	398	861	.462	5	31	.161	292	369	.791	92	243	335	388	204	1	97	204	39	1093	4.4	5.0	14.2
83-84–Boston	80	78	2665	384	878	.437	4	32	.125	281	330	.852	87	193	280	338	251	6	93	172	57	1053	3.5	4.2	13.2
84-85–Boston	80	77	2976	493	1066	.462	7	26	.269	261	306	.853	91	226	317	543	224	2	96	212	39	1254	4.0	6.8	15.7
85-86–Boston	78	78	2732	482	1060	.455	6	42	.143	243	297	.818	69	199	268	456	206	3	110	173	35	1213	3.4	5.8	15.6
86-87–Boston	79	78	2933	423	953	.444	7	62	.113	209	251	.833	45	216	261	594	201	0	87	177	38	1062	3.3	7.5	13.4
87-88–Boston	77	74	2670	352	803	.438	12	46	.261	255	298	.856	62	178	240	598	204	0	93	195	29	971	3.1	7.8	12.6
88-89–Boston	72	72	2309	277	638	.434	7	50	.140	160	195	.821	31	159	190	472	211	3	94	175	21	721	2.6	6.6	10.0
89-90–Boston	75	65	2036	206	475	.434	1	24	.042	118	140	.843	48	153	201	485	179	2	81	117	14	531	2.7	6.5	7.1
Reg. Season Totals	1100	673	35954	5832	13100	.445	80	464	.172	3791	4754	.797	1459	2790	4249	5499	3087	38	1477	2448	675	15535	3.9	5.0	14.1
Playoff Totals	180	117	6994	1167	2661	.439	26	110	.236	756	943	.802	262	519	781	1006	575	8	247	480	113	3116	4.3	5.6	17.3
All-Star Totals	5	0	98	20	37	.541	0	0	–	19	22	.864	7	11	18	9	10	0	5	9	4	59	3.6	1.8	11.8

Johnson, Earvin Jr. (Magic) b. August 14, 1959 Ht. 6-9 Wt. 220 College: Michigan State

SEASON–TEAM	G	GS	MIN	FGM	FGA	PCT	3FGM	3FGA	PCT	FTM	FTA	PCT	O-RB	D-RB	TOT	AST	PF	DQ	STL	TO	BLK	PTS	RPG	APG	PPG
79-80–Los Angeles	77	–	2795	503	949	.530	7	31	.226	374	462	.810	166	430	596	563	218	1	187	305	41	1387	7.7	7.3	18.0
80-81–Los Angeles	37	–	1371	312	587	.532	3	17	.176	171	225	.760	101	219	320	317	100	0	127	143	27	798	8.6	8.6	21.6
81-82–Los Angeles	78	77	2991	556	1036	.537	6	29	.207	329	433	.760	252	499	751	743	223	1	208	286	34	1447	9.6	9.5	18.6
82-83–Los Angeles	79	79	2907	511	933	.548	0	21	.000	304	380	.800	214	469	683	829	200	1	176	301	47	1326	8.6	10.5	16.8
83-84–Los Angeles	67	66	2567	441	780	.565	6	29	.207	290	358	.810	99	392	491	875	169	1	150	306	49	1178	7.3	13.1	17.6
84-85–L.A. Lakers	77	77	2781	504	899	.561	7	37	.189	391	464	.843	90	386	476	968	155	0	113	305	25	1406	6.2	12.6	18.3
85-86–L.A. Lakers	72	70	2578	483	918	.526	10	43	.233	378	434	.871	85	341	426	907	133	0	113	273	16	1354	5.9	12.6	18.8
86-87–L.A. Lakers	80	80	2904	683	1308	.522	8	39	.205	535	631	.848	122	382	504	977	168	0	138	300	36	1909	6.3	12.2	23.9
87-88–L.A. Lakers	72	70	2637	490	996	.492	11	56	.196	417	489	.853	88	361	449	858	147	0	114	269	13	1408	6.2	11.9	19.6
88-89–L.A. Lakers	77	77	2886	579	1137	.509	59	188	.314	513	563	.911	111	496	607	988	172	0	138	312	22	1730	7.9	12.8	22.5
89-90–L.A. Lakers	79	79	2937	546	1138	.480	106	276	.384	567	637	.890	128	394	522	907	167	1	132	289	34	1765	6.6	11.5	22.3
90-91–L.A. Lakers	79	79	2933	466	976	.477	80	250	.320	519	573	.906	105	446	551	989	150	0	102	314	17	1531	7.0	12.5	19.4
95-96–L.A. Lakers	32	9	958	137	294	.466	22	58	.379	172	201	.856	40	143	183	220	48	0	26	103	13	468	5.7	6.9	14.6
Reg. Season Totals	906	763	33245	6211	11951	.520	325	1074	.303	4960	5850	.848	1601	4958	6559	10141	2050	5	1724	3506	374	17707	7.2	11.2	19.5
Playoff Totals	190	167	7538	1291	2552	.506	51	212	.241	1068	1274	.838	349	1116	1465	2346	524	3	358	696	64	3701	7.7	12.3	19.5
All-Star Totals	11	10	331	64	131	.489	10	21	.476	38	42	.905	21	36	57	127	25	0	21	48	7	176	5.2	11.5	16.0

Johnson, Ed L. b. June 17, 1944 Ht. 6-9 Wt. 205 College: Tennessee State

SEASON–TEAM	G	GS	MIN	FGM	FGA	PCT	3FGM	3FGA	PCT	FTM	FTA	PCT	O-RB	D-RB	TOT	AST	PF	DQ	STL	TO	BLK	PTS	RPG	APG	PPG
68-69–Los Angeles (A)	58	–	1662	263	548	.480	0	1	.000	156	303	.515	–	–	539	58	281	18	–	127	–	682	9.3	1.0	11.8
69-70–New York (A)	74	–	2486	405	848	.478	1	2	.500	226	404	.559	328	551	879	88	305	18	–	–	–	1037	11.9	1.2	14.0
70-71–N.Y.-Texas (A)	34	–	751	119	265	.449	0	0	–	82	130	.631	–	–	270	34	101	–	–	–	–	320	7.9	1.0	9.4
Reg. ABA Totals	166	–	4899	787	1661	.474	1	3	.333	464	837	.554	328	551	1688	180	687	36	–	127	–	2039	10.2	1.1	12.3
ABA Playoff Totals	7	–	216	32	69	.464	0	0	–	30	52	.577	–	–	67	5	31	4	–	–	–	94	9.6	0.7	13.4

Johnson, Edward Arnet (Eddie) b. May 1, 1959 Ht. 6-7 Wt. 215 College: Illinois

SEASON–TEAM	G	GS	MIN	FGM	FGA	PCT	3FGM	3FGA	PCT	FTM	FTA	PCT	O-RB	D-RB	TOT	AST	PF	DQ	STL	TO	BLK	PTS	RPG	APG	PPG
81-82–Kansas City	74	27	1517	295	643	.459	1	11	.091	99	149	.664	128	194	322	109	210	6	50	97	14	690	4.4	1.5	9.3
82-83–Kansas City	82	82	2933	677	1370	.494	20	71	.282	247	317	.779	191	310	501	216	259	3	70	181	20	1621	6.1	2.6	19.8
83-84–Kansas City	82	82	2920	753	1552	.485	20	64	.313	268	331	.810	165	290	455	296	266	4	76	213	21	1794	5.5	3.6	21.9
84-85–Kansas City	82	81	3029	769	1565	.491	13	54	.241	325	373	.871	151	256	407	273	237	2	83	225	22	1876	5.0	3.3	22.9
85-86–Sacramento	82	30	2514	623	1311	.475	4	20	.200	280	343	.816	173	246	419	214	237	0	54	191	17	1530	5.1	2.6	18.7
86-87–Sacramento	81	30	2457	606	1309	.463	37	118	.314	267	322	.829	146	207	353	251	218	4	42	163	19	1516	4.4	3.1	18.7
87-88–Phoenix	73	59	2177	533	1110	.480	24	94	.255	204	240	.850	121	197	318	180	190	0	33	139	9	1294	4.4	2.5	17.7
88-89–Phoenix	70	7	2043	608	1224	.497	71	172	.413	217	250	.868	91	215	306	162	198	0	47	122	7	1504	4.4	2.3	21.5
89-90–Phoenix	64	4	1811	411	907	.453	70	184	.380	188	205	.917	69	177	246	107	174	4	32	108	10	1080	3.8	1.7	16.9
90-91–Phoenix-Seattle	81	27	2085	543	1122	.484	39	120	.325	229	257	.891	107	164	271	111	181	0	58	122	9	1354	3.3	1.4	16.7
91-92–Seattle	81	19	2366	534	1164	.459	27	107	.252	291	338	.861	118	174	292	161	199	0	55	130	11	1386	3.6	2.0	17.1
92-93–Seattle	82	0	1869	463	991	.467	17	56	.304	234	257	.911	124	148	272	135	173	0	36	134	4	1177	3.3	1.6	14.4
93-94–Charlotte	73	27	1460	339	738	.459	59	150	.393	99	127	.780	80	144	224	125	143	2	36	84	8	836	3.1	1.7	11.5
95-96–Indiana	62	1	1002	180	436	.413	45	128	.352	70	79	.886	45	108	153	69	104	1	20	56	4	475	2.5	1.1	7.7
96-97–Ind.-Den.-Hou.	52	2	913	160	362	.442	49	131	.374	55	68	.809	27	111	138	52	81	0	15	47	2	424	2.7	1.0	8.2
97-98–Houston	75	1	1490	227	544	.417	66	198	.333	113	136	.831	50	103	153	88	89	0	32	62	3	633	2.0	1.2	8.4
98-99–Houston	3	0	18	6	13	.462	0	1	.000	0	0	–	0	2	2	1	3	0	0	2	0	12	0.7	0.3	4.0
Reg. Season Totals	1199	479	32604	7727	16361	.472	562	1679	.335	3186	3792	.840	1786	3046	4832	2550	2962	26	739	2076	180	19202	4.0	2.1	16.0
Playoff Totals	89	9	2114	452	1054	.429	67	216	.310	197	228	.864	113	199	312	102	199	3	46	98	13	1168	3.5	1.1	13.1

Johnson, Edward Jr. (Eddie, Fast Eddie) b. February 24, 1955 Ht. 6-2 Wt. 180 College: Auburn

SEASON–TEAM	G	GS	MIN	FGM	FGA	PCT	3FGM	3FGA	PCT	FTM	FTA	PCT	O-RB	D-RB	TOT	AST	PF	DQ	STL	TO	BLK	PTS	RPG	APG	PPG
77-78–Atlanta	79	–	1875	332	686	.484	–	–	–	164	201	.816	51	102	153	235	232	4	100	168	4	828	1.9	3.0	10.5
78-79–Atlanta	78	–	2413	501	982	.510	–	–	–	243	292	.832	65	105	170	360	241	6	121	213	11	1245	2.2	4.6	16.0
79-80–Atlanta	79	–	2622	590	1212	.487	5	13	.385	280	338	.828	95	105	200	370	216	2	120	189	24	1465	2.5	4.7	18.5
80-81–Atlanta	75	–	2693	573	1136	.504	6	20	.300	279	356	.784	60	119	179	407	188	2	126	197	11	1431	2.4	5.4	19.1
81-82–Atlanta	68	57	2314	455	1011	.450	7	30	.233	294	385	.764	63	128	191	358	188	1	102	186	16	1211	2.8	5.3	17.8
82-83–Atlanta	61	57	1813	389	858	.453	14	41	.341	186	237	.785	26	98	124	318	138	2	61	156	6	978	2.0	5.2	16.0
83-84–Atlanta	67	43	1893	353	798	.442	16	43	.372	164	213	.770	31	115	146	374	155	2	58	173	7	886	2.2	5.6	13.2
84-85–Atlanta	73	66	2367	453	946	.479	22	72	.306	265	332	.798	38	154	192	566	184	1	43	244	7	1193	2.6	7.8	16.3
85-86–Atlanta-Clev.	71	9	1477	284	621	.457	29	85	.341	112	155	.723	30	91	121	333	128	1	18	150	2	709	1.7	4.7	10.0
86-87–Seattle	24	0	508	85	186	.457	5	15	.333	42	55	.764	11	35	46	115	36	0	12	41	1	217	1.9	4.8	9.0
Reg. Season Totals	675	232	19975	4015	8436	.476	104	319	.326	2029	2564	.791	470	1052	1522	3436	1706	21	761	1717	89	10163	2.3	5.1	15.1
Playoff Totals	37	3	885	174	359	.485	3	11	.273	91	117	.778	20	56	76	150	79	1	31	58	6	442	2.1	4.1	11.9
All-Star Totals	2	2	60	18	28	.643	0	0	–	2	3	.667	2	1	3	9	3	0	7	5	0	38	1.5	4.5	19.0

Johnson, Eric b. February 7, 1966 Ht. 6-2 Wt. 205 College: Baylor; Nebraska

SEASON–TEAM	G	GS	MIN	FGM	FGA	PCT	3FGM	3FGA	PCT	FTM	FTA	PCT	O-RB	D-RB	TOT	AST	PF	DQ	STL	TO	BLK	PTS	RPG	APG	PPG
89-90–Utah	48	2	272	20	84	.238	1	6	.167	13	17	.765	8	20	28	64	49	1	17	26	2	54	0.6	1.3	1.1
Reg. Season Totals	48	2	272	20	84	.238	1	6	.167	13	17	.765	8	20	28	64	49	1	17	26	2	54	0.6	1.3	1.1
Playoff Totals	1	0	3	0	0	–	0	0	–	0	0	–	0	0	0	–	0	0	0	0	0	0	0.0	0.0	0.0

Johnson, Ervin Jr. b. December 21, 1967 Ht. 6-11 Wt. 245 College: New Orleans

SEASON–TEAM	G	GS	MIN	FGM	FGA	PCT	3FGM	3FGA	PCT	FTM	FTA	PCT	O-RB	D-RB	TOT	AST	PF	DQ	STL	TO	BLK	PTS	RPG	APG	PPG
93-94–Seattle	45	3	280	44	106	.415	0	0	–	29	46	.630	48	70	118	7	45	0	10	24	22	117	2.6	0.2	2.6
94-95–Seattle	64	30	907	85	192	.443	0	1	.000	29	46	.630	101	188	289	16	163	1	17	54	67	199	4.5	0.3	3.1
95-96–Seattle	81	60	1519	180	352	.511	1	3	.333	85	127	.669	129	304	433	48	245	3	40	98	129	446	5.3	0.6	5.5
96-97–Denver	82	82	2599	243	467	.520	0	2	.000	96	156	.615	231	682	913	71	288	5	65	118	227	582	11.1	0.9	7.1
97-98–Milwaukee	81	81	2261	253	471	.537	0	0	–	143	238	.601	242	443	685	59	321	7	79	117	158	649	8.5	0.7	8.0
98-99–Milwaukee	50	7	1027	96	189	.508	0	0	–	64	105	.610	120	200	320	19	151	1	29	47	57	256	6.4	0.4	5.1
99-00–Milwaukee	80	74	2129	144	279	.516	0	1	.000	95	157	.605	233	415	648	44	298	6	81	80	127	383	8.1	0.6	4.8
Reg. Season Totals	483	337	10722	1045	2056	.508	1	7	.143	541	875	.618	1104	2302	3406	264	1511	23	321	538	787	2632	7.1	0.5	5.4
Playoff Totals	32	27	562	43	110	.391	0	0	–	27	37	.730	58	104	162	10	90	0	15	19	30	113	5.1	0.3	3.5

J

Johnson, Franklin Lenard (Frank) b. November 23, 1958 Ht. 6-3 Wt. 185 College: Wake Forest

SEASON–TEAM	G	GS	MIN	FGM	FGA	PCT	3FGM	3FGA	PCT	FTM	FTA	PCT	O-RB	D-RB	TOT	AST	PF	DQ	STL	TO	BLK	PTS	RPG	APG	PPG
81-82–Washington	79	29	2027	336	812	.414	17	79	.215	153	204	.750	34	113	147	380	196	1	76	160	7	842	1.9	4.8	10.7
82-83–Washington	68	65	2324	321	786	.408	14	61	.230	196	261	.751	46	132	178	549	170	1	110	238	6	852	2.6	8.1	12.5
83-84–Washington	82	81	2686	392	840	.467	11	43	.256	187	252	.742	58	126	184	567	174	1	96	191	6	982	2.2	6.9	12.0
84-85–Washington	46	1	925	175	358	.489	6	17	.353	72	96	.750	23	40	63	143	72	0	43	59	3	428	1.4	3.1	9.3
85-86–Washington	14	9	402	69	154	.448	0	3	.000	38	54	.704	7	21	28	76	30	0	11	29	1	176	2.0	5.4	12.6
86-87–Washington	18	10	399	59	128	.461	0	1	.000	35	49	.714	10	20	30	58	31	0	21	31	0	153	1.7	3.2	8.5
87-88–Washington	75	17	1258	216	498	.434	1	9	.111	121	149	.812	39	82	121	188	120	0	70	99	4	554	1.6	2.5	7.4
88-89–Houston	67	0	879	109	246	.443	1	6	.167	75	93	.806	22	57	79	181	91	0	42	102	0	294	1.2	2.7	4.4
92-93–Phoenix	77	0	1122	136	312	.436	1	12	.083	59	76	.776	41	72	113	186	112	0	60	80	8	332	1.5	2.4	4.3
93-94–Phoenix	70	5	875	134	299	.448	2	12	.167	54	69	.783	29	53	82	148	120	0	41	65	1	324	1.2	2.1	4.6
Reg. Season Totals	596	217	12897	1947	4433	.439	53	243	.218	990	1303	.760	309	716	1025	2476	1116	3	570	1054	36	4937	1.7	4.2	8.3
Playoff Totals	54	11	801	102	257	.397	8	29	.276	78	91	.857	20	43	63	126	87	0	31	60	0	290	1.2	2.3	5.4

Johnson, George E. b. June 19, 1947 Ht. 6-11 Wt. 245 College: Stephen F. Austin State

SEASON–TEAM	G	GS	MIN	FGM	FGA	PCT	3FGM	3FGA	PCT	FTM	FTA	PCT	O-RB	D-RB	TOT	AST	PF	DQ	STL	TO	BLK	PTS	RPG	APG	PPG
70-71–Baltimore	24	–	337	41	100	.410	–	–	–	11	30	.367	–	–	114	10	63	1	–	–	–	93	4.8	0.4	3.9
71-72–Dallas (A)	67	–	1477	128	282	.454	0	0	–	61	103	.592	–	–	464	59	209	–	–	84	–	317	6.9	0.9	4.7
72-73–Houston	19	–	169	20	39	.513	–	–	–	3	4	.750	–	–	45	3	33	0	–	–	–	43	2.4	0.2	2.3
73-74–Houston	26	–	238	23	51	.451	–	–	–	8	17	.471	20	41	61	9	46	1	8	–	8	54	2.3	0.3	2.1
Reg. NBA Totals	69	–	744	84	190	.442	–	–	–	22	51	.431	20	41	220	22	142	2	8	–	8	190	3.2	0.3	2.8
Reg. ABA Totals	67	–	1477	128	282	.454	0	0	–	61	103	.592	–	–	464	59	209	–	–	84	–	317	6.9	0.9	4.7
NBA Playoff Totals	11	–	35	7	13	.538	–	–	–	1	2	.500	0	0	11	2	9	0	0	–	0	15	1.0	0.2	1.4
ABA Playoff Totals	4	–	96	3	9	.333	0	0	–	0	0	–	–	–	24	9	16	–	–	6	–	6	6.0	2.3	1.5

Johnson, George L. b. December 8, 1956 Ht. 6-7 Wt. 210 College: St. John's (N.Y.)

SEASON–TEAM	G	GS	MIN	FGM	FGA	PCT	3FGM	3FGA	PCT	FTM	FTA	PCT	O-RB	D-RB	TOT	AST	PF	DQ	STL	TO	BLK	PTS	RPG	APG	PPG
78-79–Milwaukee	67	–	1157	165	342	.482	–	–	–	84	117	.718	106	254	360	81	187	5	75	100	49	414	5.4	1.2	6.2
79-80–Denver	75	–	1938	309	649	.476	2	9	.222	148	189	.783	190	394	584	157	260	4	84	148	67	768	7.8	2.1	10.2
80-81–Indiana	43	–	930	182	394	.462	0	5	.000	93	122	.762	99	179	278	86	120	1	47	85	23	457	6.5	2.0	10.6
81-82–Indiana	59	4	720	120	291	.412	0	2	.000	60	80	.750	72	145	217	40	147	2	36	68	27	300	3.7	0.7	5.1
82-83–Indiana	82	64	2297	409	858	.477	7	38	.184	126	172	.733	176	369	545	220	279	6	77	242	53	951	6.6	2.7	11.6
83-84–Indiana	81	20	2073	411	884	.465	11	47	.234	223	270	.826	139	321	460	195	256	3	82	186	49	1056	5.7	2.4	13.0
84-85–Philadelphia	55	3	756	107	263	.407	1	10	.100	49	56	.875	48	116	164	38	99	0	31	49	16	264	3.0	0.7	4.8
85-86–Washington	2	0	7	1	3	.333	0	0	–	2	2	1.000	1	1	2	0	1	0	0	1	0	4	1.0	0.0	2.0
Reg. Season Totals	464	91	9878	1704	3684	.463	21	111	.189	785	1008	.779	831	1779	2610	817	1349	21	432	879	284	4214	5.6	1.8	9.1
Playoff Totals	7	0	47	10	16	.625	1	1	1.000	0	0	–	4	7	11	1	3	0	0	3	0	21	1.6	0.1	3.0

Johnson, George Thomas b. December 18, 1948 Ht. 6-11 Wt. 205 College: Dillard

SEASON–TEAM	G	GS	MIN	FGM	FGA	PCT	3FGM	3FGA	PCT	FTM	FTA	PCT	O-RB	D-RB	TOT	AST	PF	DQ	STL	TO	BLK	PTS	RPG	APG	PPG
72-73–Golden State	56	–	349	41	100	.410	–	–	–	7	17	.412	–	–	138	8	40	0	–	–	–	89	2.5	0.1	1.6
73-74–Golden State	66	–	1291	173	358	.483	–	–	–	59	107	.551	190	332	522	73	176	3	35	–	124	405	7.9	1.1	6.1
74-75–Golden State	82	–	1439	152	319	.476	–	–	–	60	91	.659	217	357	574	67	206	1	32	–	136	364	7.0	0.8	4.4
75-76–Golden State	82	–	1745	165	341	.484	–	–	–	70	104	.673	200	427	627	82	275	6	51	–	174	400	7.6	1.0	4.9
76-77–G.S.-Buffalo	78	–	1652	198	429	.462	–	–	–	71	98	.724	204	407	611	104	246	8	37	–	177	467	7.8	1.3	6.0
77-78–New Jersey	81	–	2411	285	721	.395	–	–	–	133	185	.719	245	534	779	111	339	20	78	221	274	703	9.6	1.4	8.7
78-79–New Jersey	78	–	2058	206	483	.427	–	–	–	105	138	.761	201	415	616	88	315	8	68	178	253	517	7.9	1.1	6.6
79-80–New Jersey	81		2119	248	543	.457	0	1	.000	89	126	.706	192	410	602	173	312	7	53	199	258	585	7.4	2.1	7.2
80-81–San Antonio	82	–	1935	164	347	.473	0	0	–	80	109	.734	215	387	602	92	273	3	47	110	278	408	7.3	1.1	5.0
81-82–San Antonio	75	62	1578	91	195	.467	0	0	–	43	64	.672	152	302	454	79	259	6	20	92	234	225	6.1	1.1	3.0
82-83–Atlanta	37	0	461	25	57	.439	0	0	–	14	19	.737	44	73	117	17	69	0	10	19	59	64	3.2	0.5	1.7
84-85–New Jersey	65	0	800	42	79	.532	1	1	1.000	22	27	.815	74	111	185	22	151	2	19	39	78	107	2.8	0.3	1.6
85-86–Seattle	41	0	264	12	23	.522	0	0	–	11	16	.688	26	34	60	13	46	0	6	14	37	35	1.5	0.3	0.9
Reg. Season Totals	904	62	18102	1802	3995	.451	1	2	.500	764	1101	.694	1960	3789	5887	929	2707	64	456	872	2082	4369	6.5	1.0	4.8
Playoff Totals	59	9	1043	103	187	.551	0	0	–	42	68	.618	136	211	361	55	165	2	34	15	101	248	6.1	0.9	4.2

Johnson, Gus Jr. (Honeycomb) b. December 13, 1935 d. April 29, 1987 Ht. 6-6 Wt. 230 College: ; Akron; Idaho

SEASON–TEAM	G	GS	MIN	FGM	FGA	PCT	3FGM	3FGA	PCT	FTM	FTA	PCT	O-RB	D-RB	TOT	AST	PF	DQ	STL	TO	BLK	PTS	RPG	APG	PPG
63-64–Baltimore	78	–	2847	571	1329	.430	–	–	–	210	319	.658	–	–	1064	169	321	11	–	–	–	1352	13.6	2.2	17.3
64-65–Baltimore	76	–	2899	577	1379	.418	–	–	–	261	386	.676	–	–	988	270	258	4	–	–	–	1415	13.0	3.6	18.6
65-66–Baltimore	41	–	1284	273	661	.413	–	–	–	131	178	.736	–	–	546	114	136	3	–	–	–	677	13.3	2.8	16.5
66-67–Baltimore	73	–	2626	620	1377	.450	–	–	–	271	383	.708	–	–	855	194	281	7	–	–	–	1511	11.7	2.7	20.7
67-68–Baltimore	60	–	2271	482	1033	.467	–	–	–	180	270	.667	–	–	782	159	223	7	–	–	–	1144	13.0	2.7	19.1
68-69–Baltimore	49	–	1671	359	782	.459	–	–	–	160	223	.717	–	–	568	97	176	1	–	–	–	878	11.6	2.0	17.9
69-70–Baltimore	78	–	2919	578	1282	.451	–	–	–	197	272	.724	–	–	1086	264	269	6	–	–	–	1353	13.9	3.4	17.3
70-71–Baltimore	66	–	2538	494	1090	.453	–	–	–	214	290	.738	–	–	1128	192	227	4	–	–	–	1202	17.1	2.9	18.2
71-72–Baltimore	39	–	668	103	269	.383	–	–	–	43	63	.683	–	–	226	51	91	0	–	–	–	249	5.8	1.3	6.4
72-73–Phoenix	21	–	417	69	181	.381	–	–	–	25	36	.694	–	–	136	31	55	0	–	–	–	163	6.5	1.5	7.8
72-73–Indiana (A)	50	–	753	132	299	.441	4	21	.190	31	42	.738	85	160	245	62	113	1	–	70	–	299	4.9	1.2	6.0
Reg. NBA Totals	581	–	20140	4126	9383	.440	–	–	–	1692	2420	.699	–	–	7379	1541	2037	43	–	–	–	9944	12.7	2.7	17.1
Reg. ABA Totals	50	–	753	132	299	.441	4	21	.190	31	42	.738	85	160	245	62	113	1	–	70	–	299	4.9	1.2	6.0
NBA Playoff Totals	34	–	1125	177	446	.397	–	–	–	98	129	.760	–	–	330	76	110	1	–	–	–	452	9.7	2.2	13.3
ABA Playoff Totals	17	–	184	15	59	.254	0	3	.000	12	16	.750	–	–	69	15	27	0	–	18	–	42	4.1	0.9	2.5
NBA All-Star Totals	5	–	99	24	56	.429	–	–	–	19	25	.760	–	–	35	6	12	0	–	–	–	67	7.0	1.2	13.4

Johnson, Harold H. b. January 20, 1920 Ht. 6-6 Wt. 240 College: Indiana State

SEASON–TEAM	G	GS	MIN	FGM	FGA	PCT	3FGM	3FGA	PCT	FTM	FTA	PCT	O-RB	D-RB	TOT	AST	PF	DQ	STL	TO	BLK	PTS	RPG	APG	PPG
46-47–Detroit	27	–	–	4	20	.200	–	–	–	7	14	.500	–	–	–	11	13	–	–	–	–	15	–	0.4	0.6
Reg. Season Totals	27	–	–	4	20	.200	–	–	–	7	14	.500	–	–	–	11	13	–	–	–	–	15	–	0.4	0.6

Johnson, John Howard Getty (J.J.) b. October 18, 1947 Ht. 6-7 Wt. 200 College: Northwest (Wyo.) Coll. (J.C.); Iowa

SEASON–TEAM	G	GS	MIN	FGM	FGA	PCT	3FGM	3FGA	PCT	FTM	FTA	PCT	O-RB	D-RB	TOT	AST	PF	DQ	STL	TO	BLK	PTS	RPG	APG	PPG
70-71–Cleveland	67	–	2310	435	1032	.422	–	–	–	240	298	.805	–	–	453	323	251	3	–	–	–	1110	6.8	4.8	16.6
71-72–Cleveland	82	–	3041	557	1286	.433	–	–	–	277	353	.785	–	–	631	415	268	2	–	–	–	1391	7.7	5.1	17.0
72-73–Cleveland	82	–	2815	492	1143	.430	–	–	–	199	271	.734	–	–	552	309	246	3	–	–	–	1183	6.7	3.8	14.4
73-74–Portland	69	–	2287	459	990	.464	–	–	–	212	261	.812	160	355	515	284	221	1	69	–	29	1130	7.5	4.1	16.4
74-75–Portland	80	–	2540	527	1082	.487	–	–	–	236	301	.784	162	339	501	240	249	3	75	–	39	1290	6.3	3.0	16.1
75-76–Port.-Houston	76	–	1697	316	697	.453	–	–	–	120	155	.774	94	238	332	217	194	1	57	–	36	752	4.4	2.9	9.9
76-77–Houston	79	–	1738	319	696	.458	–	–	–	94	132	.712	75	191	266	163	199	1	47	–	24	732	3.4	2.1	9.3
77-78–Hou.-Seattle	77	–	1823	342	824	.415	–	–	–	133	177	.751	102	208	310	211	197	0	43	169	19	817	4.0	2.7	10.6
78-79–Seattle	82	–	2386	356	821	.434	–	–	–	190	250	.760	127	285	412	358	245	2	59	254	25	902	5.0	4.4	11.0
79-80–Seattle	81	–	2533	377	772	.488	0	0	–	161	201	.801	163	263	426	424	213	1	76	247	35	915	5.3	5.2	11.3
80-81–Seattle	80	–	2324	373	866	.431	0	1	.000	173	214	.808	135	227	362	312	202	2	57	230	25	919	4.5	3.9	11.5
81-82–Seattle	14	1	187	22	45	.489	0	0	–	15	20	.750	3	15	18	29	20	0	4	17	3	59	1.3	2.1	4.2
Reg. Season Totals	869	1	25681	4575	10254	.446	0	1	.000	2050	2633	.779	1021	2121	4778	3285	2505	19	487	917	235	11200	5.5	3.8	12.9
Playoff Totals	73	0	2002	295	656	.450	0	1	.000	121	173	.699	133	226	359	275	195	1	43	184	12	711	4.9	3.8	9.7
All-Star Totals	2	0	5	0	2	.000	0	0	–	0	0	–	0	0	1	1	1	0	0	–	0	0	0.5	0.5	0.0

Johnson, Kannard b. June 24, 1965 Ht. 6-9 Wt. 220 College: Western Kentucky

SEASON–TEAM	G	GS	MIN	FGM	FGA	PCT	3FGM	3FGA	PCT	FTM	FTA	PCT	O-RB	D-RB	TOT	AST	PF	DQ	STL	TO	BLK	PTS	RPG	APG	PPG
87-88–Cleveland	4	0	12	1	3	.333	0	0	–	0	0	–	0	0	0	0	1	0	1	2	0	2	0.0	0.0	0.5
Reg. Season Totals	4	0	12	1	3	.333	0	0	–	0	0	–	0	0	0	0	1	0	1	2	0	2	0.0	0.0	0.5

Johnson, Kenneth H. (Ken) b. November 7, 1962 Ht. 6-8 Wt. 240 College: USC; Michigan State

SEASON–TEAM	G	GS	MIN	FGM	FGA	PCT	3FGM	3FGA	PCT	FTM	FTA	PCT	O-RB	D-RB	TOT	AST	PF	DQ	STL	TO	BLK	PTS	RPG	APG	PPG
85-86–Portland	64	0	815	113	214	.528	0	0	–	37	85	.435	90	153	243	19	147	1	13	59	22	263	3.8	0.3	4.1
Reg. Season Totals	64	0	815	113	214	.528	0	0	–	37	85	.435	90	153	243	19	147	1	13	59	22	263	3.8	0.3	4.1
Playoff Totals	2	0	11	0	0	–	0	0	–	0	0	–	0	2	2	–	1	0	2	1	0	0	1.0	0.0	0.0

Johnson, Kevin Maurice (K.J.) b. March 4, 1966 Ht. 6-1 Wt. 190 College: California

SEASON–TEAM	G	GS	MIN	FGM	FGA	PCT	3FGM	3FGA	PCT	FTM	FTA	PCT	O-RB	D-RB	TOT	AST	PF	DQ	STL	TO	BLK	PTS	RPG	APG	PPG
87-88–Clev.-Phoenix	80	28	1917	275	596	.461	5	24	.208	177	211	.839	36	155	191	437	155	1	103	146	24	732	2.4	5.5	9.2
88-89–Phoenix	81	81	3179	570	1128	.505	2	22	.091	508	576	.882	46	294	340	991	226	1	135	322	24	1650	4.2	12.2	20.4
89-90–Phoenix	74	74	2782	578	1159	.499	8	41	.195	501	598	.838	42	228	270	846	143	0	95	263	14	1665	3.6	11.4	22.5
90-91–Phoenix	77	76	2772	591	1145	.516	9	44	.205	519	616	.843	54	217	271	781	174	0	163	269	11	1710	3.5	10.1	22.2
91-92–Phoenix	78	78	2899	539	1125	.479	10	46	.217	448	555	.807	61	231	292	836	180	0	116	272	23	1536	3.7	10.7	19.7
92-93–Phoenix	49	47	1643	282	565	.499	1	8	.125	226	276	.819	30	74	104	384	100	0	85	151	19	791	2.1	7.8	16.1
93-94–Phoenix	67	67	2449	477	980	.487	6	27	.222	380	464	.819	55	112	167	637	127	1	125	235	10	1340	2.5	9.5	20.0
94-95–Phoenix	47	35	1352	246	523	.470	4	26	.154	234	289	.810	32	83	115	360	88	0	47	105	18	730	2.4	7.7	15.5
95-96–Phoenix	56	55	2007	342	674	.507	21	57	.368	342	398	.859	42	179	221	517	144	0	82	170	13	1047	3.9	9.2	18.7
96-97–Phoenix	70	70	2658	441	890	.496	89	202	.441	439	515	.852	54	199	253	653	141	0	102	217	12	1410	3.6	9.3	20.1
97-98–Phoenix	50	12	1290	155	347	.447	4	26	.154	162	186	.871	35	129	164	245	57	0	27	101	8	476	3.3	4.9	9.5
99-00–Phoenix	6	0	113	16	28	.571	1	1	1.000	7	7	1.000	0	16	16	24	6	0	2	7	0	40	2.7	4.0	6.7
Reg. Season Totals	735	623	25061	4512	9160	.493	160	524	.305	3943	4691	.841	487	1917	2404	6711	1541	3	1082	2258	176	13127	3.3	9.1	17.9
Playoff Totals	105	93	3879	705	1504	.469	22	90	.244	594	713	.833	70	279	349	935	233	3	132	354	30	2026	3.3	8.9	19.3
All-Star Totals	3	1	51	6	12	.500	0	0	–	1	3	.333	1	2	3	13	5	0	4	8	1	13	1.0	4.3	4.3

Johnson, Larry b. November 28, 1954 Ht. 6-3 Wt. 205 College: Kentucky

SEASON–TEAM	G	GS	MIN	FGM	FGA	PCT	3FGM	3FGA	PCT	FTM	FTA	PCT	O-RB	D-RB	TOT	AST	PF	DQ	STL	TO	BLK	PTS	RPG	APG	PPG
77-78–Buffalo	4	–	38	3	13	.231	–	–	–	0	2	.000	1	4	5	7	3	0	5	3	2	6	1.3	1.8	1.5
Reg. Season Totals	4	–	38	3	13	.231	–	–	–	0	2	.000	1	4	5	7	3	0	5	3	2	6	1.3	1.8	1.5

Johnson, Larry Demetric (Grandmama) b. March 14, 1969 Ht. 6-7 Wt. 235 College: Odessa (Texas) Coll. (J.C.); Nevada-Las Vegas

SEASON–TEAM	G	GS	MIN	FGM	FGA	PCT	3FGM	3FGA	PCT	FTM	FTA	PCT	O-RB	D-RB	TOT	AST	PF	DQ	STL	TO	BLK	PTS	RPG	APG	PPG
91-92–Charlotte	82	77	3047	616	1258	.490	5	22	.227	339	409	.829	323	576	899	292	225	3	81	160	51	1576	11.0	3.6	19.2
92-93–Charlotte	82	82	3323	728	1385	.526	18	71	.254	336	438	.767	281	583	864	353	187	0	53	227	27	1810	10.5	4.3	22.1
93-94–Charlotte	51	51	1757	346	672	.515	5	21	.238	137	197	.695	143	305	448	184	131	0	29	116	14	834	8.8	3.6	16.4
94-95–Charlotte	81	81	3234	585	1219	.480	81	210	.386	274	354	.774	190	395	585	369	174	2	78	207	28	1525	7.2	4.6	18.8
95-96–Charlotte	81	81	3274	583	1225	.476	67	183	.366	427	564	.757	249	434	683	355	173	0	55	182	43	1660	8.4	4.4	20.5
96-97–New York	76	76	2613	376	735	.512	34	105	.324	190	274	.693	165	228	393	174	249	3	64	136	36	976	5.2	2.3	12.8
97-98–New York	70	70	2412	429	884	.485	15	63	.238	214	283	.756	175	226	401	150	193	2	40	127	13	1087	5.7	2.1	15.5
98-99–New York	49	48	1639	210	458	.459	33	92	.359	134	164	.817	91	193	284	119	147	1	34	89	10	587	5.8	2.4	12.0
99-00–New York	70	68	2281	282	652	.433	58	174	.333	128	167	.766	87	293	380	175	205	1	42	94	7	750	5.4	2.5	10.7
Reg. Season Totals	642	634	23580	4155	8488	.490	316	941	.336	2179	2850	.765	1704	3233	4937	2171	1684	12	476	1338	229	10805	7.7	3.4	16.8
Playoff Totals	66	66	2397	351	727	.483	47	155	.303	188	245	.767	102	249	351	134	202	3	55	121	11	937	5.3	2.0	14.2
All-Star Totals	2	1	36	4	9	.444	1	1	1.000	2	2	1.000	4	4	8	2	1	0	0	1	0	11	4.0	1.0	5.5

Johnson, Lee b. June 16, 1957 Ht. 6-11 Wt. 205 College: McCook (Neb.) C.C.; Montana; Texas A&M-Commerce

SEASON–TEAM	G	GS	MIN	FGM	FGA	PCT	3FGM	3FGA	PCT	FTM	FTA	PCT	O-RB	D-RB	TOT	AST	PF	DQ	STL	TO	BLK	PTS	RPG	APG	PPG
80-81–Houston-Detroit	12	–	90	7	25	.280	0	0	–	3	5	.600	6	16	22	1	18	0	0	7	5	17	1.8	0.1	1.4
Reg. Season Totals	12	–	90	7	25	.280	0	0	–	3	5	.600	6	16	22	1	18	0	0	7	5	17	1.8	0.1	1.4

Johnson, Lynbert R. (Cheese) b. September 7, 1957 Ht. 6-6 Wt. 195 College: Wichita State

SEASON–TEAM	G	GS	MIN	FGM	FGA	PCT	3FGM	3FGA	PCT	FTM	FTA	PCT	O-RB	D-RB	TOT	AST	PF	DQ	STL	TO	BLK	PTS	RPG	APG	PPG
79-80–Golden State	9	–	53	12	30	.400	0	0	–	3	5	.600	6	8	14	2	11	0	1	4	0	27	1.6	0.2	3.0
Reg. Season Totals	9	–	53	12	30	.400	0	0	–	3	5	.600	6	8	14	2	11	0	1	4	0	27	1.6	0.2	3.0

Johnson, Marques Kevin b. February 8, 1956 Ht. 6-7 Wt. 220 College: UCLA

SEASON–TEAM	G	GS	MIN	FGM	FGA	PCT	3FGM	3FGA	PCT	FTM	FTA	PCT	O-RB	D-RB	TOT	AST	PF	DQ	STL	TO	BLK	PTS	RPG	APG	PPG
77-78–Milwaukee	80	–	2765	628	1204	.522	–	–	–	301	409	.736	292	555	847	190	221	3	92	175	103	1557	10.6	2.4	19.5
78-79–Milwaukee	77	–	2779	820	1491	.550	–	–	–	332	437	.760	212	374	586	234	186	1	116	170	89	1972	7.6	3.0	25.6
79-80–Milwaukee	77	–	2686	689	1267	.544	2	9	.222	291	368	.791	217	349	566	273	173	0	100	185	70	1671	7.4	3.5	21.7
80-81–Milwaukee	76	–	2542	636	1153	.552	0	9	.000	269	381	.706	225	293	518	346	196	1	115	190	41	1541	6.8	4.6	20.3
81-82–Milwaukee	60	52	1900	404	760	.532	0	4	.000	182	260	.700	153	211	364	213	142	1	59	145	35	990	6.1	3.6	16.5
82-83–Milwaukee	80	80	2853	723	1420	.509	4	20	.200	264	359	.735	196	366	562	363	211	0	100	196	56	1714	7.0	4.5	21.4
83-84–Milwaukee	74	74	2715	646	1288	.502	2	13	.154	241	340	.709	173	307	480	315	194	1	115	180	45	1535	6.5	4.3	20.7
84-85–L.A. Clippers	72	68	2448	494	1094	.452	3	13	.231	190	260	.731	184	244	428	248	193	2	72	176	30	1181	5.9	3.4	16.4
85-86–L.A. Clippers	75	75	2605	613	1201	.510	1	15	.067	298	392	.760	156	260	416	283	214	2	107	183	50	1525	5.5	3.8	20.3
86-87–L.A. Clippers	10	10	302	68	155	.439	0	6	.000	30	42	.714	9	24	33	28	24	0	12	17	5	166	3.3	2.8	16.6
89-90–Golden State	10	0	99	12	32	.375	2	3	.667	14	17	.824	8	9	17	9	12	0	0	10	1	40	1.7	0.9	4.0
Reg. Season Totals	691	359	23694	5733	11065	.518	14	92	.152	2412	3265	.739	1825	2992	4817	2502	1766	11	888	1627	525	13892	7.0	3.6	20.1
Playoff Totals	54	31	2112	471	964	.489	3	13	.231	218	311	.701	173	254	427	198	156	0	56	111	45	1163	7.9	3.7	21.5
All-Star Totals	5	2	106	11	35	.314	0	0	–	12	16	.750	9	10	19	9	9	0	1	1	2	34	3.8	1.8	6.8

Johnson, Neil A. b. April 17, 1943 Ht. 6-7 Wt. 220 College: Tulsa; Creighton

SEASON–TEAM	G	GS	MIN	FGM	FGA	PCT	3FGM	3FGA	PCT	FTM	FTA	PCT	O-RB	D-RB	TOT	AST	PF	DQ	STL	TO	BLK	PTS	RPG	APG	PPG
66-67–New York	51	–	522	59	171	.345	–	–	–	57	86	.663	–	–	167	38	102	0	–	–	–	175	3.3	0.7	3.4
67-68–New York	43	–	286	44	106	.415	–	–	–	23	48	.479	–	–	75	33	63	0	–	–	–	111	1.7	0.8	2.6
68-69–Phoenix	80	–	1319	177	368	.481	–	–	–	110	177	.621	–	–	396	134	214	3	–	–	–	464	5.0	1.7	5.8
69-70–Phoenix	28	–	136	20	60	.333	–	–	–	8	12	.667	–	–	47	12	38	0	–	–	–	48	1.7	0.4	1.7
70-71–Virginia (A)	78	–	1838	398	758	.525	0	2	.000	194	259	.749	–	–	668	179	295	–	–	–	–	990	8.6	2.3	12.7
71-72–Virginia (A)	31	–	874	128	273	.469	1	3	.333	65	94	.691	–	–	286	78	123	–	–	67	–	322	9.2	2.5	10.4
72-73–Virginia (A)	69	–	1442	210	429	.490	0	1	.000	103	156	.660	156	208	364	158	232	5	–	131	–	523	5.3	2.3	7.6
Reg. NBA Totals	202	–	2263	300	705	.426	–	–	–	198	323	.613	–	–	685	217	417	3	–	–	–	798	3.4	1.1	4.0
Reg. ABA Totals	178	–	4154	736	1460	.504	1	6	.167	362	509	.711	156	208	1318	415	650	5	–	198	–	1835	7.4	2.3	10.3
NBA Playoff Totals	8	–	77	11	34	.324	–	–	–	7	8	.875	–	–	30	5	13	0	–	–	–	29	3.8	0.6	3.6
ABA Playoff Totals	17	–	351	54	118	.458	1	1	1.000	35	52	.673	–	–	121	37	70	0	–	7	–	144	7.1	2.2	8.5

Johnson, Ollie b. May 11, 1949 Ht. 6-6 Wt. 200 College: Philadelphia (Pa.) C.C.; Temple

SEASON–TEAM	G	GS	MIN	FGM	FGA	PCT	3FGM	3FGA	PCT	FTM	FTA	PCT	O-RB	D-RB	TOT	AST	PF	DQ	STL	TO	BLK	PTS	RPG	APG	PPG
72-73–Portland	78	–	2138	308	620	.497	–	–	–	156	206	.757	–	–	417	200	166	0	–	–	–	772	5.3	2.6	9.9
73-74–Portland	79	–	1718	209	434	.482	–	–	–	77	94	.819	116	208	324	167	179	2	60	–	30	495	4.1	2.1	6.3
74-75–N.O.-K.C.-Omaha	73	–	1667	203	429	.473	–	–	–	95	114	.833	87	156	243	110	172	1	59	–	33	501	3.3	1.5	6.9
75-76–Kansas City	81	–	2150	348	678	.513	–	–	–	125	149	.839	116	241	357	146	217	4	67	–	42	821	4.4	1.8	10.1
76-77–Kansas City	81	–	1386	218	446	.489	–	–	–	101	115	.878	68	144	212	105	169	1	43	–	21	537	2.6	1.3	6.6
77-78–Atlanta	82	–	1704	292	619	.472	–	–	–	111	130	.854	89	171	260	120	180	2	80	107	36	695	3.2	1.5	8.5
78-79–Chicago	71	–	1734	281	540	.520	–	–	–	88	110	.800	58	169	227	163	182	2	54	114	33	650	3.2	2.3	9.2
79-80–Chicago	79	–	1535	262	527	.497	1	11	.091	82	93	.882	50	113	163	161	165	0	59	96	24	607	2.1	2.0	7.7
80-81–Philadelphia	40	–	372	87	158	.551	1	6	.167	27	31	.871	8	47	55	30	45	0	20	25	2	202	1.4	0.8	5.1
81-82–Philadelphia	26	0	150	27	54	.500	1	3	.333	6	7	.857	7	15	22	10	28	0	13	13	3	61	0.8	0.4	2.3
Reg. Season Totals	690	0	14554	2235	4505	.496	3	20	.150	868	1049	.827	599	1264	2280	1212	1503	12	455	355	224	5341	3.3	1.8	7.7
Playoff Totals	16	0	209	33	77	.429	0	1	.000	12	12	1.000	13	18	31	10	21	0	10	2	6	78	1.9	0.6	4.9

Johnson, Reginald (Reggie) b. June 25, 1957 Ht. 6-9 Wt. 210 College: Tennessee

SEASON–TEAM	G	GS	MIN	FGM	FGA	PCT	3FGM	3FGA	PCT	FTM	FTA	PCT	O-RB	D-RB	TOT	AST	PF	DQ	STL	TO	BLK	PTS	RPG	APG	PPG
80-81–San Antonio	79	–	1716	340	682	.499	0	1	.000	128	193	.663	132	226	358	78	283	8	45	130	48	808	4.5	1.0	10.2
81-82–S.A.-Clev.-K.C.	75	48	1904	351	662	.530	0	1	.000	118	156	.756	140	311	451	73	257	5	33	100	60	820	6.0	1.0	10.9
82-83–K.C.-Phil.	79	8	1541	247	509	.485	1	4	.250	95	130	.731	107	184	291	71	232	3	26	104	43	590	3.7	0.9	7.5
83-84–New Jersey	72	4	818	127	256	.496	0	1	.000	92	126	.730	53	85	138	40	141	1	24	59	18	346	1.9	0.6	4.8
Reg. Season Totals	305	60	5979	1065	2109	.505	1	7	.143	433	605	.716	432	806	1238	262	913	17	128	393	169	2564	4.1	0.9	8.4
Playoff Totals	19	0	273	37	81	.457	0	0	–	26	33	.788	16	23	39	19	34	2	5	17	6	100	2.1	1.0	5.3

Johnson, Richard Lewis (Rich) b. December 18, 1946 Ht. 6-9 Wt. 210 College: Grambling State

SEASON–TEAM	G	GS	MIN	FGM	FGA	PCT	3FGM	3FGA	PCT	FTM	FTA	PCT	O-RB	D-RB	TOT	AST	PF	DQ	STL	TO	BLK	PTS	RPG	APG	PPG
68-69–Boston	31	–	163	29	76	.382	–	–	–	11	23	.478	–	–	52	7	40	0	–	–	–	69	1.7	0.2	2.2
69-70–Boston	65	–	898	167	361	.463	–	–	–	46	70	.657	–	–	208	32	155	3	–	–	–	380	3.2	0.5	5.8
70-71–Boston	1	–	13	4	5	.800	–	–	–	0	0	–	–	–	5	0	3	0	–	–	–	8	5.0	0.0	8.0
70-71–Fla.-Car.-Pitt. (A)	38	–	542	92	191	.482	0	0	–	36	54	.667	–	–	152	19	83	–	–	–	–	220	4.0	0.5	5.8
Reg. NBA Totals	97	–	1074	200	442	.452	–	–	–	57	93	.613	–	–	265	39	198	3	–	–	–	457	2.7	0.4	4.7
Reg. ABA Totals	38	–	542	92	191	.482	0	0	–	36	54	.667	–	–	152	19	83	–	–	–	–	220	4.0	0.5	5.8
NBA Playoff Totals	2	–	4	1	1	1.000	–	–	–	0	0	–	–	–	2	–	0	0	–	–	–	2	1.0	0.0	1.0

Johnson, Ronald F. (Ron) b. July 20, 1938 Ht. 6-8 Wt. 215 College: Minnesota

SEASON–TEAM	G	GS	MIN	FGM	FGA	PCT	3FGM	3FGA	PCT	FTM	FTA	PCT	O-RB	D-RB	TOT	AST	PF	DQ	STL	TO	BLK	PTS	RPG	APG	PPG
60-61–Detroit-L.A.	14	–	92	13	43	.302	–	–	–	11	17	.647	–	–	29	2	10	0	–	–	–	37	2.1	0.1	2.6
Reg. Season Totals	14	–	92	13	43	.302	–	–	–	11	17	.647	–	–	29	2	10	0	–	–	–	37	2.1	0.1	2.6

Johnson, Steffond O'Shea b. November 4, 1962 Ht. 6-8 Wt. 240 College: Louisiana State; San Diego State

SEASON–TEAM	G	GS	MIN	FGM	FGA	PCT	3FGM	3FGA	PCT	FTM	FTA	PCT	O-RB	D-RB	TOT	AST	PF	DQ	STL	TO	BLK	PTS	RPG	APG	PPG
86-87–L.A. Clippers	29	0	234	27	64	.422	0	3	.000	20	38	.526	15	28	43	5	55	2	9	18	2	74	1.5	0.2	2.6
Reg. Season Totals	29	0	234	27	64	.422	0	3	.000	20	38	.526	15	28	43	5	55	2	9	18	2	74	1.5	0.2	2.6

Johnson, Stewart (Stew) b. August 19, 1944 Ht. 6-9 Wt. 225 College: Murray State

SEASON–TEAM	G	GS	MIN	FGM	FGA	PCT	3FGM	3FGA	PCT	FTM	FTA	PCT	O-RB	D-RB	TOT	AST	PF	DQ	STL	TO	BLK	PTS	RPG	APG	PPG
67-68–Ken.-N.J. (A)	72	–	1475	255	743	.343	25	79	.316	69	113	.611	–	–	415	49	147	2	–	89	–	604	5.8	0.7	8.4
68-69–N.Y.-Hou. (A)	78	–	2484	616	1444	.427	64	183	.350	199	253	.787	–	–	604	142	178	1	–	172	–	1495	7.7	1.8	19.2
69-70–Pittsburgh (A)	81	–	2347	544	1337	.407	15	55	.273	137	176	.778	–	–	547	120	210	2	–	–	–	1240	6.8	1.5	15.3
70-71–Pittsburgh (A)	84	–	2595	593	1350	.439	12	40	.300	144	171	.842	–	–	646	123	221	–	–	–	–	1342	7.7	1.5	16.0
71-72–Pitt.-Car. (A)	67	–	1534	368	874	.421	16	47	.340	73	99	.737	–	–	382	88	159	–	–	91	–	825	5.7	1.3	12.3
72-73–San Diego (A)	80	–	2952	769	1748	.440	37	133	.278	195	238	.819	178	419	597	174	258	6	–	161	–	1770	7.5	2.2	22.1
73-74–San Diego (A)	84	–	2652	716	1668	.429	59	190	.311	199	235	.847	181	350	531	127	162	–	72	136	13	1690	6.3	1.5	20.1
74-75–S.D.-Mem. (A)	81	–	2812	664	1493	.445	40	132	.303	63	86	.733	138	355	493	138	228	–	97	118	28	1431	6.1	1.7	17.7
75-76–S.D.-S.A. (A)	20	–	350	61	197	.310	1	13	.077	18	22	.818	22	26	48	23	35	–	8	13	1	141	2.4	1.2	7.1
Reg. ABA Totals	647	–	19201	4586	10854	.423	269	872	.308	1097	1393	.788	519	1150	4263	984	1598	11	177	780	42	10538	6.6	1.5	16.3
ABA Playoff Totals	15	–	569	103	264	.390	12	30	.400	20	25	.800	20	48	93	33	32	0	16	23	7	238	6.2	2.2	15.9

Johnson, Vincent **(Vinnie, Microwave)** b. September 1, 1956 Ht. 6-2 Wt. 200 College: McLennan (Texas) C.C.; Baylor

SEASON–TEAM	G	GS	MIN	FGM	FGA	PCT	3FGM	3FGA	PCT	FTM	FTA	PCT	O-RB	D-RB	TOT	AST	PF	DQ	STL	TO	BLK	PTS	RPG	APG	PPG
79-80–Seattle	38	–	325	45	115	.391	0	1	.000	31	39	.795	19	36	55	54	40	0	19	42	4	121	1.4	1.4	3.2
80-81–Seattle	81	–	2311	419	785	.534	1	5	.200	214	270	.793	193	173	366	341	198	0	78	216	20	1053	4.5	4.2	13.0
81-82–Seattle-Detroit	74	15	1295	217	444	.489	3	12	.250	107	142	.754	82	77	159	171	101	0	56	96	25	544	2.1	2.3	7.4
82-83–Detroit	82	51	2511	520	1013	.513	11	40	.275	245	315	.778	167	186	353	301	263	2	93	152	49	1296	4.3	3.7	15.8
83-84–Detroit	82	0	1909	426	901	.473	4	19	.211	207	275	.753	130	107	237	271	196	1	44	135	19	1063	2.9	3.3	13.0
84-85–Detroit	82	16	2093	428	942	.454	5	27	.185	190	247	.769	134	118	252	325	205	2	71	135	20	1051	3.1	4.0	12.8
85-86–Detroit	79	12	1978	465	996	.467	2	13	.154	165	214	.771	119	107	226	269	180	2	80	88	23	1097	2.9	3.4	13.9
86-87–Detroit	78	8	2166	533	1154	.462	4	14	.286	158	201	.786	123	134	257	300	159	0	92	133	16	1228	3.3	3.8	15.7
87-88–Detroit	82	1	1935	425	959	.443	5	24	.208	147	217	.677	90	141	231	267	164	0	58	152	18	1002	2.8	3.3	12.2
88-89–Detroit	82	21	2073	462	996	.464	13	44	.295	193	263	.734	109	146	255	242	155	0	74	105	17	1130	3.1	3.0	13.8
89-90–Detroit	82	12	1972	334	775	.431	5	34	.147	131	196	.668	108	148	256	255	143	0	71	123	13	804	3.1	3.1	9.8
90-91–Detroit	82	28	2390	406	936	.434	11	34	.324	135	209	.646	110	170	280	271	166	0	75	118	15	958	3.4	3.3	11.7
91-92–San Antonio	60	23	1350	202	499	.405	19	60	.317	55	85	.647	67	115	182	145	93	0	41	74	14	478	3.0	2.4	8.0
Reg. Season Totals	984	187	24308	4882	10515	.464	83	327	.254	1978	2673	.740	1451	1658	3109	3212	2063	7	852	1569	253	11825	3.2	3.3	12.0
Playoff Totals	116	3	2671	578	1275	.453	17	62	.274	214	284	.754	167	197	364	306	234	0	65	142	22	1387	3.1	2.6	12.0

Johnson, Wallace Edgar **(Mickey)** b. August 31, 1952 Ht. 6-10 Wt. 190 College: Aurora

SEASON–TEAM	G	GS	MIN	FGM	FGA	PCT	3FGM	3FGA	PCT	FTM	FTA	PCT	O-RB	D-RB	TOT	AST	PF	DQ	STL	TO	BLK	PTS	RPG	APG	PPG
74-75–Chicago	38	–	291	53	118	.449	–	–	–	37	58	.638	32	62	94	20	57	1	10	–	11	143	2.5	0.5	3.8
75-76–Chicago	81	–	2390	478	1033	.463	–	–	–	283	360	.786	279	479	758	130	292	8	93	–	66	1239	9.4	1.6	15.3
76-77–Chicago	81	–	2847	538	1205	.446	–	–	–	324	407	.796	297	531	828	195	315	10	103	–	64	1400	10.2	2.4	17.3
77-78–Chicago	81	–	2870	561	1215	.462	–	–	–	362	446	.812	218	520	738	267	317	8	92	270	68	1484	9.1	3.3	18.3
78-79–Chicago	82	–	2594	496	1105	.449	–	–	–	273	329	.830	193	434	627	380	286	9	88	312	59	1265	7.6	4.6	15.4
79-80–Indiana	82	–	2647	588	1271	.463	5	32	.156	385	482	.799	258	423	681	344	291	11	153	286	112	1566	8.3	4.2	19.1
80-81–Milwaukee	82	–	2118	379	846	.448	3	18	.167	262	332	.789	183	362	545	286	256	4	94	230	71	1023	6.6	3.5	12.5
81-82–Milwaukee	76	71	1934	372	757	.491	1	7	.143	233	291	.801	133	321	454	215	240	4	72	191	45	978	6.0	2.8	12.9
82-83–Milw.-N.J.-G.S.	78	16	2053	391	921	.425	3	36	.083	312	380	.821	163	331	494	255	288	10	82	238	46	1097	6.3	3.3	14.1
83-84–Golden State	78	25	2122	359	852	.421	5	29	.172	339	432	.785	198	320	518	219	290	3	101	216	30	1062	6.6	2.8	13.6
84-85–Golden State	66	9	1565	304	714	.426	7	30	.233	260	316	.823	149	247	396	149	221	5	70	142	35	875	6.0	2.3	13.3
85-86–New Jersey	79	4	1574	214	507	.422	5	24	.208	183	233	.785	98	234	332	217	248	1	67	165	25	616	4.2	2.7	7.8
Reg. Season Totals	904	125	25005	4733	10544	.449	29	176	.165	3253	4066	.800	2201	4264	6465	2677	3101	74	1025	2050	632	12748	7.2	3.0	14.1
Playoff Totals	22	1	559	109	234	.466	0	4	.000	84	101	.832	55	74	129	40	74	1	24	37	13	302	5.9	1.8	13.7

Johnston, Donald Neil **(Neil, Gabby)** b. February 4, 1929 d. September 27, 1978 Ht. 6-8 Wt. 215 College: Ohio State HOF: 1989

SEASON–TEAM	G	GS	MIN	FGM	FGA	PCT	3FGM	3FGA	PCT	FTM	FTA	PCT	O-RB	D-RB	TOT	AST	PF	DQ	STL	TO	BLK	PTS	RPG	APG	PPG
51-52–Philadelphia	64	–	993	141	299	.472	–	–	–	100	151	.662	–	–	342	39	154	5	–	–	–	382	5.3	0.6	6.0
52-53–Philadelphia	70	–	3166	504	1114	.452	–	–	–	556	794	.700	–	–	976	197	248	6	–	–	–	1564	13.9	2.8	22.3
53-54–Philadelphia	72	–	3296	591	1317	.449	–	–	–	577	772	.747	–	–	797	203	259	7	–	–	–	1759	11.1	2.8	24.4
54-55–Philadelphia	72	–	2917	521	1184	.440	–	–	–	589	769	.766	–	–	1085	215	255	4	–	–	–	1631	15.1	3.0	22.7
55-56–Philadelphia	70	–	2594	499	1092	.457	–	–	–	549	685	.801	–	–	872	225	251	8	–	–	–	1547	12.5	3.2	22.1
56-57–Philadelphia	69	–	2531	520	1163	.447	–	–	–	535	648	.826	–	–	855	203	231	2	–	–	–	1575	12.4	2.9	22.8
57-58–Philadelphia	71	–	2408	473	1102	.429	–	–	–	442	540	.819	–	–	790	166	233	4	–	–	–	1388	11.1	2.3	19.5
58-59–Philadelphia	28	–	393	54	164	.329	–	–	–	69	88	.784	–	–	139	21	50	0	–	–	–	177	5.0	0.8	6.3
Reg. Season Totals	516	–	18298	3303	7435	.444	–	–	–	3417	4447	.768	–	–	5856	1269	1681	36	–	–	–	10023	11.3	2.5	19.4
Playoff Totals	23	–	734	121	310	.390	–	–	–	102	139	.734	–	–	257	75	76	0	–	–	–	344	11.2	3.3	15.0
All-Star Totals	6	–	132	27	63	.429	–	–	–	16	23	.696	–	–	52	6	13	0	–	–	–	70	8.7	1.0	11.7

Johnston, Nate b. December 18, 1966 Ht. 6-8 Wt. 210 College: Tampa

SEASON–TEAM	G	GS	MIN	FGM	FGA	PCT	3FGM	3FGA	PCT	FTM	FTA	PCT	O-RB	D-RB	TOT	AST	PF	DQ	STL	TO	BLK	PTS	RPG	APG	PPG
89-90–Utah-Port.	21	0	87	18	48	.375	1	4	.250	9	13	.692	13	10	23	1	11	1	3	6	8	46	1.1	0.0	2.2
Reg. Season Totals	21	0	87	18	48	.375	1	4	.250	9	13	.692	13	10	23	1	11	1	3	6	8	46	1.1	0.0	2.2
Playoff Totals	3	0	19	6	11	.545	0	0	–	1	1	1.000	2	4	6	1	5	0	1	0	1	13	2.0	0.3	4.3

Johnstone, James Robert **(Jim)** b. September 20, 1960 Ht. 6-11 Wt. 245 College: Wake Forest

SEASON–TEAM	G	GS	MIN	FGM	FGA	PCT	3FGM	3FGA	PCT	FTM	FTA	PCT	O-RB	D-RB	TOT	AST	PF	DQ	STL	TO	BLK	PTS	RPG	APG	PPG
82-83–S.A.-Detroit	23	0	191	11	30	.367	0	0	–	9	20	.450	15	31	46	11	33	0	3	15	7	31	2.0	0.5	1.3
Reg. Season Totals	23	0	191	11	30	.367	0	0	–	9	20	.450	15	31	46	11	33	0	3	15	7	31	2.0	0.5	1.3

Jolliff, Howard **(Howie)** b. July 20, 1938 Ht. 6-7 Wt. 220 College: Ohio U.

SEASON–TEAM	G	GS	MIN	FGM	FGA	PCT	3FGM	3FGA	PCT	FTM	FTA	PCT	O-RB	D-RB	TOT	AST	PF	DQ	STL	TO	BLK	PTS	RPG	APG	PPG
60-61–Los Angeles	46	–	352	46	141	.326	–	–	–	11	23	.478	–	–	141	16	53	0	–	–	–	103	3.1	0.3	2.2
61-62–Los Angeles	64	–	1094	104	253	.411	–	–	–	41	78	.526	–	–	383	76	175	4	–	–	–	249	6.0	1.2	3.9
62-63–Los Angeles	28	–	293	15	55	.273	–	–	–	6	9	.667	–	–	62	20	49	1	–	–	–	36	2.2	0.7	1.3
Reg. Season Totals	138	–	1739	165	449	.367	–	–	–	58	110	.527	–	–	586	112	277	5	–	–	–	388	4.2	0.8	2.8
Playoff Totals	13	–	112	8	22	.364	–	–	–	8	8	1.000	–	–	53	15	21	1	–	–	–	24	4.1	1.2	1.8

Jones, Anthony Hamilton b. September 13, 1962 Ht. 6-6 Wt. 195 College: Georgetown; Nevada-Las Vegas

SEASON–TEAM	G	GS	MIN	FGM	FGA	PCT	3FGM	3FGA	PCT	FTM	FTA	PCT	O-RB	D-RB	TOT	AST	PF	DQ	STL	TO	BLK	PTS	RPG	APG	PPG
86-87–Wash.-S.A.	65	4	858	133	322	.413	7	20	.350	50	65	.769	40	64	104	73	79	0	42	49	19	323	1.6	1.1	5.0
88-89–Chicago-Dallas	33	0	196	29	79	.367	4	16	.250	14	16	.875	14	14	28	17	20	0	11	5	3	76	0.8	0.5	2.3
89-90–Dallas	66	0	650	72	194	.371	4	13	.308	47	69	.681	33	49	82	29	77	0	32	42	16	195	1.2	0.4	3.0
Reg. Season Totals	164	4	1704	234	595	.393	15	49	.306	111	150	.740	87	127	214	119	176	0	85	96	38	594	1.3	0.7	3.6
Playoff Totals	1	0	3	0	0	–	0	0	–	0	0	–	0	0	0	–	0	0	0	0	0	0	0.0	0.0	0.0

Jones, Askia b. December 3, 1971 Ht. 6-5 Wt. 205 College: Kansas State

SEASON–TEAM	G	GS	MIN	FGM	FGA	PCT	3FGM	3FGA	PCT	FTM	FTA	PCT	O-RB	D-RB	TOT	AST	PF	DQ	STL	TO	BLK	PTS	RPG	APG	PPG
94-95–Minnesota	11	0	139	15	44	.341	2	12	.167	13	16	.813	6	5	11	16	19	0	6	9	0	45	1.0	1.5	4.1
Reg. Season Totals	11	0	139	15	44	.341	2	12	.167	13	16	.813	6	5	11	16	19	0	6	9	0	45	1.0	1.5	4.1

Jones, Caldwell b. August 4, 1950 Ht. 6-11 Wt. 230 College: Albany State (GA)

SEASON–TEAM	G	GS	MIN	FGM	FGA	PCT	3FGM	3FGA	PCT	FTM	FTA	PCT	O-RB	D-RB	TOT	AST	PF	DQ	STL	TO	BLK	PTS	RPG	APG	PPG
73-74–San Diego (A)	79	–	2929	507	1091	.465	2	8	.250	171	230	.743	322	773	1095	144	319	–	64	155	316	1187	13.9	1.8	15.0
74-75–San Diego (A)	76	–	3004	606	1240	.489	3	11	.273	264	335	.788	311	763	1074	162	269	–	60	192	246	1479	14.1	2.1	19.5
75-76–S.D.-Ken.-St. L. (A)	76	–	2674	423	900	.470	0	7	.000	140	186	.753	246	607	853	147	321	–	81	166	218	986	11.2	1.9	13.0
76-77–Philadelphia	82	57	2023	215	424	.507	–	–	–	64	116	.552	190	476	666	92	301	3	43	–	200	494	8.1	1.1	6.0
77-78–Philadelphia	80	69	1636	169	359	.471	–	–	–	96	153	.627	165	405	570	92	281	4	26	128	127	434	7.1	1.2	5.4
78-79–Philadelphia	78	75	2171	302	637	.474	–	–	–	121	162	.747	177	570	747	151	303	10	39	156	157	725	9.6	1.9	9.3
79-80–Philadelphia	80	80	2771	232	532	.436	0	2	.000	124	178	.697	219	731	950	164	298	5	43	218	162	588	11.9	2.1	7.4
80-81–Philadelphia	81	81	2639	218	485	.449	0	0	–	148	193	.767	200	613	813	122	271	2	53	168	134	584	10.0	1.5	7.2
81-82–Philadelphia	81	47	2446	231	465	.497	0	3	.000	179	219	.817	164	544	708	100	301	3	38	155	146	641	8.7	1.2	7.9
82-83–Houston	82	82	2440	307	677	.453	0	2	.000	162	206	.786	222	446	668	138	278	2	46	171	131	776	8.1	1.7	9.5
83-84–Houston	81	73	2506	318	633	.502	1	3	.333	164	196	.837	168	414	582	156	335	7	46	158	80	801	7.2	1.9	9.9
84-85–Chicago	42	32	885	53	115	.461	0	2	.000	36	47	.766	49	162	211	34	125	3	12	40	31	142	5.0	0.8	3.4
85-86–Portland	80	19	1437	126	254	.496	0	7	.000	124	150	.827	105	250	355	74	244	2	38	102	61	376	4.4	0.9	4.7
86-87–Portland	78	37	1578	111	224	.496	0	2	.000	97	124	.782	114	341	455	64	227	5	23	87	77	319	5.8	0.8	4.1
87-88–Portland	79	77	1778	128	263	.487	0	4	.000	78	106	.736	105	303	408	81	251	0	29	82	99	334	5.2	1.0	4.2
88-89–Portland	72	40	1279	77	183	.421	0	1	.000	48	61	.787	88	212	300	59	166	0	24	83	85	202	4.2	0.8	2.8
89-90–San Antonio	72	2	885	67	144	.465	1	5	.200	38	54	.704	76	154	230	20	146	2	20	48	27	173	3.2	0.3	2.4
Reg. NBA Totals	1068	771	26474	2554	5395	.473	2	31	.065	1479	1965	.753	2042	5621	7663	1347	3527	48	480	1596	1517	6589	7.2	1.3	6.2
Reg. ABA Totals	231	–	8607	1536	3231	.475	5	26	.192	575	751	.766	879	2143	3022	453	909	0	205	513	780	3652	13.1	2.0	15.8
NBA Playoff Totals	119	30	3466	322	665	.484	0	4	.000	170	224	.759	267	732	999	147	426	9	51	157	223	814	8.4	1.2	6.8
ABA Playoff Totals	6	–	277	36	88	.409	0	0	–	11	16	.688	21	73	94	15	19	0	6	9	14	83	15.7	2.5	13.8

Jones, Charles b. July 17, 1975 Ht. 6-3 Wt. 180 College: Long Island University

SEASON–TEAM	G	GS	MIN	FGM	FGA	PCT	3FGM	3FGA	PCT	FTM	FTA	PCT	O-RB	D-RB	TOT	AST	PF	DQ	STL	TO	BLK	PTS	RPG	APG	PPG
98-99–Chicago	29	5	476	39	123	.317	19	61	.311	11	22	.500	9	33	42	41	30	0	18	29	5	108	1.4	1.4	3.7
99-00–L.A. Clippers	56	0	662	66	201	.328	39	118	.331	17	23	.739	17	45	62	94	46	0	30	28	5	188	1.1	1.7	3.4
Reg. Season Totals	85	5	1138	105	324	.324	58	179	.324	28	45	.622	26	78	104	135	76	0	48	57	10	296	1.2	1.6	3.5

Jones, Charles (C.J., Gadget) b. April 3, 1957 Ht. 6-9 Wt. 215 College: Albany State (GA)

SEASON–TEAM	G	GS	MIN	FGM	FGA	PCT	3FGM	3FGA	PCT	FTM	FTA	PCT	O-RB	D-RB	TOT	AST	PF	DQ	STL	TO	BLK	PTS	RPG	APG	PPG
83-84–Philadelphia	1	0	3	0	1	.000	0	0	–	1	4	.250	0	0	0	0	1	0	0	0	0	1	0.0	0.0	1.0
84-85–Chicago-Wash.	31	4	667	67	127	.528	0	0	–	40	58	.690	71	113	184	26	107	3	22	25	79	174	5.9	0.8	5.6
85-86–Washington	81	58	1609	129	254	.508	0	2	.000	54	86	.628	122	199	321	76	235	2	57	71	133	312	4.0	0.9	3.9
86-87–Washington	79	64	1609	118	249	.474	0	1	.000	48	76	.632	144	212	356	80	252	2	67	77	165	284	4.5	1.0	3.6
87-88–Washington	69	49	1313	72	177	.407	0	1	.000	53	75	.707	106	219	325	59	226	5	53	57	113	197	4.7	0.9	2.9
88-89–Washington	53	45	1154	60	125	.480	0	1	.000	16	25	.640	77	180	257	42	187	4	39	39	76	136	4.8	0.8	2.6
89-90–Washington	81	81	2240	94	185	.508	0	0	–	68	105	.648	145	359	504	139	296	10	50	76	197	256	6.2	1.7	3.2
90-91–Washington	62	54	1499	67	124	.540	0	0	–	29	50	.580	119	240	359	48	199	2	51	46	124	163	5.8	0.8	2.6
91-92–Washington	75	32	1365	33	90	.367	0	0	–	20	40	.500	105	212	317	62	214	0	43	39	92	86	4.2	0.8	1.1
92-93–Washington	67	21	1206	33	63	.524	0	1	.000	22	38	.579	87	190	277	42	144	1	38	38	77	88	4.1	0.6	1.3
93-94–Detroit	42	0	877	36	78	.462	0	1	.000	19	34	.559	89	146	235	29	136	3	14	12	43	91	5.6	0.7	2.2
94-95–Houston	3	0	36	1	3	.333	0	0	–	1	2	.500	2	5	7	0	8	0	0	0	1	3	2.3	0.0	1.0
95-96–Houston	46	0	297	6	19	.316	0	0	–	4	13	.308	28	46	74	12	44	0	5	3	24	16	1.6	0.3	0.3
96-97–Houston	12	0	93	2	5	.400	0	0	–	0	0	–	5	8	13	3	8	0	2	0	4	4	1.1	0.3	0.3
97-98–Houston	24	0	127	7	10	.700	0	0	–	1	2	.500	12	12	24	5	22	0	1	4	6	15	1.0	0.2	0.6
Reg. Season Totals	726	408	14095	725	1510	.480	0	7	.000	376	608	.618	1112	2141	3253	623	2079	32	442	487	1134	1826	4.5	0.9	2.5
Playoff Totals	44	9	591	23	54	.426	0	1	.000	20	36	.556	36	72	108	13	115	0	13	17	31	66	2.5	0.3	1.5

J

Jones, Charles Alexander b. January 12, 1962 Ht. 6-8 Wt. 215 College: Louisville

SEASON–TEAM	G	GS	MIN	FGM	FGA	PCT	3FGM	3FGA	PCT	FTM	FTA	PCT	O-RB	D-RB	TOT	AST	PF	DQ	STL	TO	BLK	PTS	RPG	APG	PPG
84-85–Phoenix	78	14	1565	236	454	.520	0	4	.000	182	281	.648	139	255	394	128	149	0	45	143	61	654	5.1	1.6	8.4
85-86–Phoenix	43	18	742	75	164	.457	0	1	.000	50	98	.510	65	128	193	52	87	0	32	57	25	200	4.5	1.2	4.7
87-88–Portland	37	0	186	16	40	.400	0	1	.000	19	33	.576	11	20	31	8	28	0	3	12	6	51	0.8	0.2	1.4
88-89–Washington	43	0	516	38	82	.463	1	3	.333	33	53	.623	54	86	140	18	49	0	18	22	16	110	3.3	0.4	2.6
Reg. Season Totals	201	32	3009	365	740	.493	1	9	.111	284	465	.611	269	489	758	206	313	0	98	234	108	1015	3.8	1.0	5.0
Playoff Totals	4	0	36	3	6	.500	0	0	–	6	6	1.000	1	3	4	3	4	0	0	3	3	12	1.0	0.8	3.0

Jones, Clarence William (Bill) b. March 18, 1966 Ht. 6-7 Wt. 185 College: Iowa

SEASON–TEAM	G	GS	MIN	FGM	FGA	PCT	3FGM	3FGA	PCT	FTM	FTA	PCT	O-RB	D-RB	TOT	AST	PF	DQ	STL	TO	BLK	PTS	RPG	APG	PPG
88-89–New Jersey	37	0	307	50	102	.490	0	1	.000	29	43	.674	20	27	47	20	38	0	17	18	6	129	1.3	0.5	3.5
Reg. Season Totals	37	0	307	50	102	.490	0	1	.000	29	43	.674	20	27	47	20	38	0	17	18	6	129	1.3	0.5	3.5

Jones, Damon b. August 25, 1976 Ht. 6-3 Wt. 185 College: Houston

SEASON–TEAM	G	GS	MIN	FGM	FGA	PCT	3FGM	3FGA	PCT	FTM	FTA	PCT	O-RB	D-RB	TOT	AST	PF	DQ	STL	TO	BLK	PTS	RPG	APG	PPG
98-99–N.J.-Boston	24	0	344	43	119	.361	25	62	.403	14	17	.824	6	38	44	42	23	0	13	17	0	125	1.8	1.8	5.2
99-00–G.S.-Dallas	55	1	612	80	208	.385	41	114	.360	32	48	.667	12	43	55	96	34	0	18	40	1	233	1.0	1.7	4.2
Reg. Season Totals	79	1	956	123	327	.376	66	176	.375	46	65	.708	18	81	99	138	57	0	31	57	1	358	1.3	1.7	4.5

Jones, Dontae' Antijuaine b. June 2, 1975 Ht. 6-8 Wt. 220 College: Mississippi State

SEASON–TEAM	G	GS	MIN	FGM	FGA	PCT	3FGM	3FGA	PCT	FTM	FTA	PCT	O-RB	D-RB	TOT	AST	PF	DQ	STL	TO	BLK	PTS	RPG	APG	PPG
97-98–Boston	15	0	91	19	57	.333	6	23	.261	0	0	–	3	6	9	5	12	0	2	11	3	44	0.6	0.3	2.9
Reg. Season Totals	15	0	91	19	57	.333	6	23	.261	0	0	–	3	6	9	5	12	0	2	11	3	44	0.6	0.3	2.9

Jones, Dwight E. b. February 27, 1952 Ht. 6-10 Wt. 210 College: Houston

SEASON–TEAM	G	GS	MIN	FGM	FGA	PCT	3FGM	3FGA	PCT	FTM	FTA	PCT	O-RB	D-RB	TOT	AST	PF	DQ	STL	TO	BLK	PTS	RPG	APG	PPG
73-74–Atlanta	74	–	1448	238	502	.474	–	–	–	116	156	.744	145	309	454	86	197	3	29	–	64	592	6.1	1.2	8.0
74-75–Atlanta	75	–	2086	323	752	.430	–	–	–	132	183	.721	236	461	697	152	226	1	51	–	51	778	9.3	2.0	10.4
75-76–Atlanta	66	–	1762	251	542	.463	–	–	–	163	219	.744	171	353	524	83	214	8	52	–	61	665	7.9	1.3	10.1
76-77–Houston	74	–	1239	167	338	.494	–	–	–	101	126	.802	98	186	284	48	175	1	38	–	19	435	3.8	0.6	5.9
77-78–Houston	82	–	2476	346	777	.445	–	–	–	181	233	.777	215	426	641	109	265	2	77	165	39	873	7.8	1.3	10.6
78-79–Houston	81	–	1215	181	395	.458	–	–	–	96	132	.727	110	218	328	57	204	1	34	102	26	458	4.0	0.7	5.7
79-80–Houston-Chicago	74	–	1448	257	506	.508	0	0	–	146	201	.726	114	254	368	101	207	0	28	122	42	660	5.0	1.4	8.9
80-81–Chicago	81	–	1574	245	507	.483	0	0	–	125	161	.776	127	274	401	99	200	1	40	126	36	615	5.0	1.2	7.6
81-82–Chicago	78	18	2040	303	572	.530	1	1	1.000	172	238	.723	156	351	507	114	217	0	49	155	36	779	6.5	1.5	10.0
82-83–Chicago-L.A.	81	2	1164	148	325	.455	0	1	.000	79	123	.642	84	225	309	62	172	0	31	101	23	375	3.8	0.8	4.6
Reg. Season Totals	766	20	16452	2459	5216	.471	1	2	.500	1311	1772	.740	1456	3057	4513	911	2077	17	429	771	397	6230	5.9	1.2	8.1
Playoff Totals	27	0	555	69	153	.451	0	0	–	43	51	.843	39	95	134	29	67	2	15	27	10	181	5.0	1.1	6.7

Jones, Earl b. January 13, 1961 Ht. 7-0 Wt. 230 College: District of Columbia

SEASON–TEAM	G	GS	MIN	FGM	FGA	PCT	3FGM	3FGA	PCT	FTM	FTA	PCT	O-RB	D-RB	TOT	AST	PF	DQ	STL	TO	BLK	PTS	RPG	APG	PPG
84-85–L.A. Lakers	2	0	7	0	1	.000	0	0	–	0	0	–	0	0	0	0	0	0	0	1	0	0	0.0	0.0	0.0
85-86–Milwaukee	12	0	43	5	12	.417	0	0	–	3	4	.750	4	6	10	4	13	0	0	7	1	13	0.8	0.3	1.1
Reg. Season Totals	14	0	50	5	13	.385	0	0	–	3	4	.750	4	6	10	4	13	0	0	8	1	13	0.7	0.3	0.9

Jones, Eddie Charles b. October 20, 1971 Ht. 6-6 Wt. 200 College: Temple

SEASON–TEAM	G	GS	MIN	FGM	FGA	PCT	3FGM	3FGA	PCT	FTM	FTA	PCT	O-RB	D-RB	TOT	AST	PF	DQ	STL	TO	BLK	PTS	RPG	APG	PPG
94-95–L.A. Lakers	64	58	1981	342	744	.460	91	246	.370	122	169	.722	79	170	249	128	175	1	131	75	41	897	3.9	2.0	14.0
95-96–L.A. Lakers	70	66	2184	337	685	.492	83	227	.366	136	184	.739	45	188	233	246	162	0	129	99	45	893	3.3	3.5	12.8
96-97–L.A. Lakers	80	80	2998	473	1081	.438	152	389	.391	276	337	.819	90	236	326	270	226	3	189	169	49	1374	4.1	3.4	17.2
97-98–L.A. Lakers	80	80	2910	486	1005	.484	143	368	.389	234	306	.765	85	217	302	246	164	0	160	146	55	1349	3.8	3.1	16.9
98-99–Lakers-Cha.	50	50	1881	260	595	.437	48	142	.338	212	271	.782	50	144	194	186	128	1	125	93	58	780	3.9	3.7	15.6
99-00–Charlotte	72	72	2807	478	1119	.427	128	341	.375	362	419	.864	81	262	343	305	176	1	192	160	49	1446	4.8	4.2	20.1
Reg. Season Totals	416	406	14761	2376	5229	.454	645	1713	.377	1342	1686	.796	430	1217	1647	1381	1031	6	926	742	297	6739	4.0	3.3	16.2
Playoff Totals	40	30	1371	181	407	.445	60	144	.417	124	156	.795	38	117	155	106	116	0	61	56	38	546	3.9	2.7	13.7
All-Star Totals	3	1	63	14	30	.467	2	11	.182	5	9	.556	9	7	16	5	3	0	4	4	2	35	5.3	1.7	11.7

Jones, Edgar Jr. (E.J.) b. June 17, 1956 Ht. 6-10 Wt. 225 College: Nevada-Reno

SEASON–TEAM	G	GS	MIN	FGM	FGA	PCT	3FGM	3FGA	PCT	FTM	FTA	PCT	O-RB	D-RB	TOT	AST	PF	DQ	STL	TO	BLK	PTS	RPG	APG	PPG
80-81–New Jersey	60	–	950	189	357	.529	0	4	.000	146	218	.670	92	171	263	43	185	4	36	101	81	524	4.4	0.7	8.7
81-82–Detroit	48	19	802	142	259	.548	1	2	.500	90	129	.698	70	137	207	40	149	3	28	66	92	375	4.3	0.8	7.8
82-83–Detroit-S.A.	77	28	1658	237	479	.495	2	9	.222	201	286	.703	136	312	448	89	267	10	42	146	108	677	5.8	1.2	8.8
83-84–San Antonio	81	33	1770	322	644	.500	6	19	.316	176	242	.727	143	306	449	85	298	7	64	125	107	826	5.5	1.0	10.2
84-85–S.A.-Clev.	44	5	769	130	275	.473	0	4	.000	82	111	.739	50	121	171	29	123	2	20	61	29	342	3.9	0.7	7.8
85-86–Cleveland	53	6	1011	187	370	.505	7	23	.304	132	178	.742	71	136	207	45	142	0	30	64	38	513	3.9	0.8	9.7
Reg. Season Totals	363	91	6960	1207	2384	.506	16	61	.262	827	1164	.710	562	1183	1745	331	1164	26	220	563	455	3257	4.8	0.9	9.0
Playoff Totals	15	0	238	37	80	.463	0	3	.000	26	41	.634	25	36	61	20	50	1	8	20	14	100	4.1	1.3	6.7

Jones, J. Collis (Collis) b. July 3, 1949 Ht. 6-7 Wt. 205 College: Notre Dame

SEASON–TEAM	G	GS	MIN	FGM	FGA	PCT	3FGM	3FGA	PCT	FTM	FTA	PCT	O-RB	D-RB	TOT	AST	PF	DQ	STL	TO	BLK	PTS	RPG	APG	PPG
71-72–Dallas (A)	78	–	1428	163	372	.438	1	4	.250	98	154	.636	–	–	334	78	200	–	–	83	–	425	4.3	1.0	5.4
72-73–Dallas (A)	81	–	2204	357	768	.465	0	6	.000	227	318	.714	262	260	522	143	230	3	–	145	–	941	6.4	1.8	11.6
73-74–Kentucky (A)	58	–	719	102	263	.388	0	3	.000	51	78	.654	94	90	184	36	91	–	21	38	13	255	3.2	0.6	4.4
74-75–Memphis (A)	81	–	1880	333	702	.474	5	15	.333	134	177	.757	150	219	369	81	186	–	105	69	33	805	4.6	1.0	9.9
Reg. ABA Totals	298	–	6231	955	2105	.454	6	28	.214	510	727	.702	506	569	1409	338	707	3	126	335	46	2426	4.7	1.1	8.1
ABA Playoff Totals	12	–	256	28	73	.384	0	1	.000	15	26	.577	15	20	49	4	28	0	9	11	1	71	4.1	0.3	5.9

Jones, Jacob (Jake) b. May 9, 1949 Ht. 6-3 Wt. 180 College: Assumption

SEASON–TEAM	G	GS	MIN	FGM	FGA	PCT	3FGM	3FGA	PCT	FTM	FTA	PCT	O-RB	D-RB	TOT	AST	PF	DQ	STL	TO	BLK	PTS	RPG	APG	PPG
71-72–Phil.-Cin.	17	–	202	28	72	.389	–	–	–	20	31	.645	–	–	26	12	22	0	–	–	–	76	1.5	0.7	4.5
Reg. Season Totals	17	–	202	28	72	.389	–	–	–	20	31	.645	–	–	26	12	22	0	–	–	–	76	1.5	0.7	4.5

Jones, James (Jimmy) b. January 1, 1945 Ht. 6-4 Wt. 190 College: Grambling State

SEASON–TEAM	G	GS	MIN	FGM	FGA	PCT	3FGM	3FGA	PCT	FTM	FTA	PCT	O-RB	D-RB	TOT	AST	PF	DQ	STL	TO	BLK	PTS	RPG	APG	PPG
67-68–New Orleans (A)	78	–	3255	551	1181	.467	2	9	.222	360	508	.709	–	–	443	179	243	6	–	241	–	1464	5.7	2.3	18.8
68-69–New Orleans (A)	77	–	3188	764	1429	.535	1	7	.143	521	647	.805	–	–	441	437	225	4	–	198	–	2050	5.7	5.7	26.6
69-70–New Orleans (A)	70	–	2513	533	1072	.497	2	9	.222	380	469	.810	–	–	315	340	238	5	–	–	–	1448	4.5	4.9	20.7
70-71–Memphis (A)	80	–	3004	593	1220	.486	4	7	.571	374	481	.778	–	–	386	468	240	–	–	–	–	1564	4.8	5.9	19.6
71-72–Utah (A)	78	–	2903	462	903	.512	1	6	.167	282	362	.779	–	–	377	485	252	–	–	270	–	1207	4.8	6.2	15.5
72-73–Utah (A)	80	–	2848	496	948	.523	0	1	.000	345	432	.799	72	263	335	448	271	5	–	267	–	1337	4.2	5.6	16.7
73-74–Utah (A)	83	–	3162	583	1060	.550	0	1	.000	229	259	.884	103	258	361	429	205	–	154	238	32	1395	4.3	5.2	16.8
74-75–Washington	73	–	1424	207	400	.518	–	–	–	103	142	.725	36	101	137	162	190	0	76	–	10	517	1.9	2.2	7.1
75-76–Washington	64	–	1133	153	308	.497	–	–	–	72	94	.766	32	99	131	120	127	1	33	–	5	378	2.0	1.9	5.9
76-77–Washington	3	–	33	2	9	.222	–	–	–	2	4	.500	1	3	4	1	4	0	2	–	0	6	1.3	0.3	2.0
Reg. NBA Totals	140	–	2590	362	717	.505	–	–	–	177	240	.738	69	203	272	283	321	1	111	–	15	901	1.9	2.0	6.4
Reg. ABA Totals	546	–	20873	3982	7813	.510	10	40	.250	2491	3158	.789	175	521	2658	2786	1674	20	154	1214	32	10465	4.9	5.1	19.2
NBA Playoff Totals	18	–	371	51	109	.468	–	–	–	28	32	.875	7	32	39	31	36	0	26	–	1	130	2.2	1.7	7.2
ABA Playoff Totals	71	–	2853	602	1155	.521	0	7	.000	336	448	.750	30	57	371	340	244	2	27	153	5	1540	5.2	4.8	21.7

Jones, John (Johnny) b. March 12, 1943 Ht. 6-7 Wt. 205 College: Los Angeles State

SEASON–TEAM	G	GS	MIN	FGM	FGA	PCT	3FGM	3FGA	PCT	FTM	FTA	PCT	O-RB	D-RB	TOT	AST	PF	DQ	STL	TO	BLK	PTS	RPG	APG	PPG
67-68–Boston	51	–	475	86	253	.340	–	–	–	42	68	.618	–	–	114	26	60	0	–	–	–	214	2.2	0.5	4.2
68-69–Kentucky (A)	29	–	449	81	213	.380	0	3	.000	41	71	.577	–	–	117	34	53	0	–	39	–	203	4.0	1.2	7.0
Reg. NBA Totals	51	–	475	86	253	.340	–	–	–	42	68	.618	–	–	114	26	60	0	–	–	–	214	2.2	0.5	4.2
Reg. ABA Totals	29	–	449	81	213	.380	0	3	.000	41	71	.577	–	–	117	34	53	0	–	39	–	203	4.0	1.2	7.0
NBA Playoff Totals	5	–	10	3	6	.500	–	–	–	0	0	–	–	–	4	–	2	0	–	–	–	6	0.8	0.0	1.2

Jones, Jumaine Lanard b. February 10, 1979 Ht. 6-8 Wt. 218 College: Georgia

SEASON–TEAM	G	GS	MIN	FGM	FGA	PCT	3FGM	3FGA	PCT	FTM	FTA	PCT	O-RB	D-RB	TOT	AST	PF	DQ	STL	TO	BLK	PTS	RPG	APG	PPG
99-00–Philadelphia	33	0	138	22	58	.379	2	4	.500	11	18	.611	16	22	38	5	10	0	6	14	5	57	1.2	0.2	1.7
Reg. Season Totals	33	0	138	22	58	.379	2	4	.500	11	18	.611	16	22	38	5	10	0	6	14	5	57	1.2	0.2	1.7
Playoff Totals	4	0	8	1	3	.333	0	2	.000	0	0	–	0	0	0	–	0	0	0	0	0	2	0.0	0.0	0.5

Jones, K.C. b. May 25, 1932 Ht. 6-1 Wt. 200 College: San Francisco HOF: 1988

SEASON–TEAM	G	GS	MIN	FGM	FGA	PCT	3FGM	3FGA	PCT	FTM	FTA	PCT	O-RB	D-RB	TOT	AST	PF	DQ	STL	TO	BLK	PTS	RPG	APG	PPG
58-59–Boston	49	–	609	65	192	.339	–	–	–	41	68	.603	–	–	127	70	58	0	–	–	–	171	2.6	1.4	3.5
59-60–Boston	74	–	1274	169	414	.408	–	–	–	128	170	.753	–	–	199	189	109	1	–	–	–	466	2.7	2.6	6.3
60-61–Boston	78	–	1605	203	601	.338	–	–	–	186	280	.664	–	–	279	253	190	3	–	–	–	592	3.6	3.2	7.6
61-62–Boston	80	–	2054	294	724	.406	–	–	–	147	232	.634	–	–	298	343	206	1	–	–	–	735	3.7	4.3	9.2
62-63–Boston	79	–	1945	230	591	.389	–	–	–	112	177	.633	–	–	263	317	221	3	–	–	–	572	3.3	4.0	7.2
63-64–Boston	80	–	2424	283	722	.392	–	–	–	88	168	.524	–	–	372	407	253	0	–	–	–	654	4.7	5.1	8.2
64-65–Boston	78	–	2434	253	639	.396	–	–	–	143	227	.630	–	–	318	437	263	5	–	–	–	649	4.1	5.6	8.3
65-66–Boston	80	–	2710	240	619	.388	–	–	–	209	303	.690	–	–	304	503	243	4	–	–	–	689	3.8	6.3	8.6
66-67–Boston	78	–	2446	182	459	.397	–	–	–	119	189	.630	–	–	239	389	273	7	–	–	–	483	3.1	5.0	6.2
Reg. Season Totals	676	–	17501	1919	4961	.387	–	–	–	1173	1814	.647	–	–	2399	2908	1816	24	–	–	–	5011	3.5	4.3	7.4
Playoff Totals	105	–	2499	241	656	.367	–	–	–	186	269	.691	–	–	320	396	335	4	–	–	–	668	3.0	3.8	6.4

Jones, Major James Brooks b. July 9, 1953 Ht. 6-9 Wt. 225 College: Albany State (GA)

SEASON–TEAM	G	GS	MIN	FGM	FGA	PCT	3FGM	3FGA	PCT	FTM	FTA	PCT	O-RB	D-RB	TOT	AST	PF	DQ	STL	TO	BLK	PTS	RPG	APG	PPG
79-80–Houston	82	–	1545	188	392	.480	1	3	.333	61	108	.565	147	234	381	67	186	0	50	112	67	438	4.6	0.8	5.3
80-81–Houston	68	–	1003	117	252	.464	0	1	.000	64	101	.634	96	138	234	41	112	0	18	57	23	298	3.4	0.6	4.4
81-82–Houston	60	6	746	113	213	.531	0	3	.000	42	77	.545	80	122	202	25	100	0	20	50	29	268	3.4	0.4	4.5
82-83–Houston	60	4	878	142	311	.457	0	2	.000	56	102	.549	114	149	263	39	104	0	22	83	22	340	4.4	0.7	5.7
83-84–Houston	57	5	473	70	130	.538	0	0	–	30	49	.612	33	82	115	28	63	0	14	30	14	170	2.0	0.5	3.0
84-85–Detroit	47	0	418	48	87	.552	0	0	–	33	51	.647	48	80	128	15	58	0	9	35	14	129	2.7	0.3	2.7
Reg. Season Totals	374	15	5063	678	1385	.490	1	9	.111	286	488	.586	518	805	1323	215	623	0	133	367	169	1643	3.5	0.6	4.4
Playoff Totals	19	0	162	22	40	.550	0	0	–	8	14	.571	15	25	40	9	23	0	3	6	4	52	2.1	0.5	2.7

Jones, Mark Anthony b. April 10, 1961 Ht. 6-1 Wt. 175 College: St. Bonaventure

SEASON–TEAM	G	GS	MIN	FGM	FGA	PCT	3FGM	3FGA	PCT	FTM	FTA	PCT	O-RB	D-RB	TOT	AST	PF	DQ	STL	TO	BLK	PTS	RPG	APG	PPG
83-84–New Jersey	6	0	16	3	6	.500	0	1	.000	1	2	.500	2	0	2	5	2	0	0	2	0	7	0.3	0.8	1.2
Reg. Season Totals	6	0	16	3	6	.500	0	1	.000	1	2	.500	2	0	2	5	2	0	0	2	0	7	0.3	0.8	1.2

Jones, Ozell b. November 20, 1960 Ht. 6-11 Wt. 235 College: Wichita State; Cal State-Fullerton

SEASON–TEAM	G	GS	MIN	FGM	FGA	PCT	3FGM	3FGA	PCT	FTM	FTA	PCT	O-RB	D-RB	TOT	AST	PF	DQ	STL	TO	BLK	PTS	RPG	APG	PPG
84-85–San Antonio	67	6	888	106	180	.589	0	1	.000	33	83	.398	65	173	238	56	139	1	30	61	57	245	3.6	0.8	3.7
85-86–L.A. Clippers	3	0	18	0	2	.000	0	0	–	0	0	–	0	2	2	0	5	0	2	3	1	0	0.7	0.0	0.0
Reg. Season Totals	70	6	906	106	182	.582	0	1	.000	33	83	.398	65	175	240	56	144	1	32	64	58	245	3.4	0.8	3.5
Playoff Totals	5	0	73	8	11	.727	0	0	–	1	6	.167	5	12	17	4	18	1	1	7	4	17	3.4	0.8	3.4

Jones, Richard Wesley (Rich, House) b. December 27, 1946 Ht. 6-8 Wt. 230 College: Illinois; Memphis

SEASON–TEAM	G	GS	MIN	FGM	FGA	PCT	3FGM	3FGA	PCT	FTM	FTA	PCT	O-RB	D-RB	TOT	AST	PF	DQ	STL	TO	BLK	PTS	RPG	APG	PPG
69-70–Dallas (A)	2	–	50	9	20	.450	0	0	–	10	11	.909	–	–	23	1	11	1	–	–	–	28	11.5	0.5	14.0
70-71–Texas (A)	79	–	2074	371	910	.408	33	95	.347	175	230	.761	–	–	525	182	246	–	–	–	–	950	6.6	2.3	12.0
71-72–Dallas (A)	82	–	2932	475	1053	.451	14	47	.298	212	279	.760	–	–	696	222	298	–	–	152	–	1176	8.5	2.7	14.3
72-73–Dallas (A)	67	–	2691	564	1364	.413	43	127	.339	324	414	.783	174	493	667	274	240	5	–	225	–	1495	10.0	4.1	22.3
73-74–San Antonio (A)	78	–	2843	510	1175	.434	13	46	.283	186	241	.772	170	411	581	268	273	–	70	145	13	1219	7.4	3.4	15.6
74-75–San Antonio (A)	83	–	3097	649	1480	.439	13	50	.260	287	374	.767	247	398	645	270	297	–	88	210	32	1598	7.8	3.3	19.3
75-76–New York (A)	83	–	2427	441	1153	.382	15	67	.224	199	261	.762	103	325	428	131	294	–	81	159	21	1096	5.2	1.6	13.2
76-77–New York Nets	34	–	877	134	348	.385	–	–	–	92	121	.760	48	146	194	46	109	2	38	–	11	360	5.7	1.4	10.6
Reg. NBA Totals	34	–	877	134	348	.385	–	–	–	92	121	.760	48	146	194	46	109	2	38	–	11	360	5.7	1.4	10.6
Reg. ABA Totals	474	–	16114	3019	7155	.422	131	432	.303	1393	1810	.770	694	1627	3565	1348	1659	6	239	891	66	7562	7.5	2.8	16.0
ABA Playoff Totals	39	–	1177	195	502	.388	7	38	.184	62	92	.674	48	130	255	90	145	0	33	62	14	459	6.5	2.3	11.8

Jones, Robert Clyde (Bobby) b. December 18, 1951 Ht. 6-9 Wt. 210 College: North Carolina

SEASON–TEAM	G	GS	MIN	FGM	FGA	PCT	3FGM	3FGA	PCT	FTM	FTA	PCT	O-RB	D-RB	TOT	AST	PF	DQ	STL	TO	BLK	PTS	RPG	APG	PPG
74-75–Denver (A)	84	–	2706	529	876	.604	0	1	.000	187	269	.695	230	462	692	303	263	–	167	234	153	1245	8.2	3.6	14.8
75-76–Denver (A)	83	–	2845	510	878	.581	0	0	–	215	308	.698	241	550	791	331	253	–	170	232	184	1235	9.5	4.0	14.9
76-77–Denver	82	–	2419	501	879	.570	–	–	–	236	329	.717	174	504	678	264	238	3	186	–	162	1238	8.3	3.2	15.1
77-78–Denver	75	–	2440	440	761	.578	–	–	–	208	277	.751	164	472	636	252	221	2	137	194	126	1088	8.5	3.4	14.5
78-79–Philadelphia	80	9	2304	378	704	.537	–	–	–	209	277	.755	199	332	531	201	245	2	107	165	96	965	6.6	2.5	12.1
79-80–Philadelphia	81	18	2125	398	748	.532	0	3	.000	257	329	.781	152	298	450	146	223	3	102	146	118	1053	5.6	1.8	13.0
80-81–Philadelphia	81	16	2046	407	755	.539	0	3	.000	282	347	.813	142	293	435	226	226	2	95	149	74	1096	5.4	2.8	13.5
81-82–Philadelphia	76	21	2181	416	737	.564	0	3	.000	263	333	.790	109	284	393	189	211	3	99	145	112	1095	5.2	2.5	14.4
82-83–Philadelphia	74	12	1749	250	460	.543	0	1	.000	165	208	.793	102	242	344	142	199	4	85	109	91	665	4.6	1.9	9.0
83-84–Philadelphia	75	5	1761	226	432	.523	0	1	.000	167	213	.784	92	231	323	187	199	1	107	101	103	619	4.3	2.5	8.3
84-85–Philadelphia	80	13	1633	207	385	.538	0	4	.000	186	216	.861	105	192	297	155	183	2	84	118	50	600	3.7	1.9	7.5
85-86–Philadelphia	70	12	1519	189	338	.559	0	1	.000	114	145	.786	49	120	169	126	159	0	48	90	50	492	2.4	1.8	7.0
Reg. NBA Totals	774	106	20177	3412	6199	.550	0	16	.000	2087	2674	.780	1288	2968	4256	1888	2104	22	1050	1217	982	8911	5.5	2.4	11.5
Reg. ABA Totals	167	–	5551	1039	1754	.592	0	1	.000	402	577	.697	471	1012	1483	634	516	–	337	466	337	2480	8.9	3.8	14.9
NBA Playoff Totals	125	31	3431	553	1034	.535	0	3	.000	347	429	.809	219	395	614	284	400	4	132	187	156	1453	4.9	2.3	11.6
ABA Playoff Totals	26	–	859	143	256	.559	0	1	.000	61	81	.753	76	147	223	97	102	–	28	65	32	347	8.6	3.7	13.3
NBA All-Star Totals	4	1	62	9	23	.391	0	0	–	2	3	.667	3	11	14	6	8	0	2	1	3	20	3.5	1.5	5.0

Jones, Robin Dale b. February 2, 1954 Ht. 6-9 Wt. 225 College: St. Louis

SEASON–TEAM	G	GS	MIN	FGM	FGA	PCT	3FGM	3FGA	PCT	FTM	FTA	PCT	O-RB	D-RB	TOT	AST	PF	DQ	STL	TO	BLK	PTS	RPG	APG	PPG
76-77–Portland	63	–	1065	139	299	.465	–	–	–	66	109	.606	103	193	296	80	124	3	37	–	38	344	4.7	1.3	5.5
77-78–Houston	12	–	66	11	20	.550	–	–	–	4	10	.400	5	9	14	2	16	0	1	7	1	26	1.2	0.2	2.2
Reg. Season Totals	75	–	1131	150	319	.470	–	–	–	70	119	.588	108	202	310	82	140	3	38	7	39	370	4.1	1.1	4.9
Playoff Totals	19	–	105	15	32	.469	–	–	–	6	9	.667	8	15	23	9	24	0	4	–	4	36	1.2	0.5	1.9

Jones, Ronald Jerome (Popeye) b. June 17, 1970 Ht. 6-8 Wt. 250 College: Murray State

SEASON–TEAM	G	GS	MIN	FGM	FGA	PCT	3FGM	3FGA	PCT	FTM	FTA	PCT	O-RB	D-RB	TOT	AST	PF	DQ	STL	TO	BLK	PTS	RPG	APG	PPG
93-94–Dallas	81	47	1773	195	407	.479	0	1	.000	78	107	.729	299	306	605	99	246	2	61	94	31	468	7.5	1.2	5.8
94-95–Dallas	80	80	2385	372	839	.443	1	12	.083	80	124	.645	329	515	844	163	267	5	35	124	27	825	10.6	2.0	10.3
95-96–Dallas	68	68	2322	327	733	.446	14	39	.359	102	133	.767	260	477	737	132	262	8	54	109	27	770	10.8	1.9	11.3
96-97–Toronto	79	61	2421	258	537	.480	1	13	.077	99	121	.818	270	410	680	84	269	3	58	116	39	616	8.6	1.1	7.8
97-98–Toronto-Boston	14	4	352	52	127	.409	2	3	.667	14	19	.737	50	52	102	18	39	0	10	16	3	120	7.3	1.3	8.6
98-99–Boston	18	2	206	20	51	.392	0	1	.000	14	17	.824	28	24	52	15	31	0	5	7	0	54	2.9	0.8	3.0
99-00–Denver	40	1	330	44	104	.423	2	3	.667	14	19	.737	41	62	103	19	50	1	3	13	6	104	2.6	0.5	2.6
Reg. Season Totals	380	263	9789	1268	2798	.453	20	72	.278	401	540	.743	1277	1846	3123	530	1164	19	226	479	133	2957	8.2	1.4	7.8

Jones, Ryan Nicholas (Nick) b. March 28, 1945 Ht. 6-2 Wt. 190 College: Oregon

SEASON–TEAM	G	GS	MIN	FGM	FGA	PCT	3FGM	3FGA	PCT	FTM	FTA	PCT	O-RB	D-RB	TOT	AST	PF	DQ	STL	TO	BLK	PTS	RPG	APG	PPG
67-68–San Diego	42	–	603	86	232	.371	–	–	–	55	69	.797	–	–	67	89	84	0	–	–	–	227	1.6	2.1	5.4
68-69–Dallas-Miami (A)	7	–	81	9	28	.321	0	2	.000	2	6	.333	–	–	8	6	14	0	–	6	–	20	1.1	0.9	2.9
70-71–San Francisco	81	–	1183	225	523	.430	–	–	–	111	151	.735	–	–	110	113	192	2	–	–	–	561	1.4	1.4	6.9
71-72–Golden State	65	–	478	82	196	.418	–	–	–	51	61	.836	–	–	39	45	109	0	–	–	–	215	0.6	0.7	3.3
72-73–Dallas (A)	3	–	16	3	8	.375	0	0	–	2	3	.667	1	–	1	1	4	0	–	2	–	8	0.3	0.3	2.7
Reg. NBA Totals	188	–	2264	393	951	.413	–	–	–	217	281	.772	–	–	216	247	385	2	–	–	–	1003	1.1	1.3	5.3
Reg. ABA Totals	10	–	97	12	36	.333	0	2	.000	4	9	.444	1	–	9	7	18	0	–	8	–	28	0.9	0.7	2.8
NBA Playoff Totals	7	–	84	8	28	.286	–	–	–	17	20	.850	–	–	5	7	9	0	–	–	–	33	0.7	1.0	4.7

Jones, Samuel (Sam, Mr. Clutch) b. June 24, 1933 Ht. 6-4 Wt. 205 College: North Carolina Central HOF: 1983

SEASON–TEAM	G	GS	MIN	FGM	FGA	PCT	3FGM	3FGA	PCT	FTM	FTA	PCT	O-RB	D-RB	TOT	AST	PF	DQ	STL	TO	BLK	PTS	RPG	APG	PPG
57-58–Boston	56	–	594	100	233	.429	–	–	–	60	84	.714	–	–	160	37	42	0	–	–	–	260	2.9	0.7	4.6
58-59–Boston	71	–	1466	305	703	.434	–	–	–	151	196	.770	–	–	428	101	102	0	–	–	–	761	6.0	1.4	10.7
59-60–Boston	74	–	1512	355	782	.454	–	–	–	168	220	.764	–	–	375	125	101	1	–	–	–	878	5.1	1.7	11.9
60-61–Boston	78	–	2028	480	1069	.449	–	–	–	211	268	.787	–	–	421	217	148	1	–	–	–	1171	5.4	2.8	15.0
61-62–Boston	78	–	2388	596	1284	.464	–	–	–	243	297	.818	–	–	458	232	149	0	–	–	–	1435	5.9	3.0	18.4
62-63–Boston	76	–	2323	621	1305	.476	–	–	–	257	324	.793	–	–	396	241	162	1	–	–	–	1499	5.2	3.2	19.7
63-64–Boston	76	–	2381	612	1359	.450	–	–	–	249	318	.783	–	–	349	202	192	1	–	–	–	1473	4.6	2.7	19.4
64-65–Boston	80	–	2885	821	1818	.452	–	–	–	428	522	.820	–	–	411	223	176	0	–	–	–	2070	5.1	2.8	25.9
65-66–Boston	67	–	2155	626	1335	.469	–	–	–	325	407	.799	–	–	347	216	170	0	–	–	–	1577	5.2	3.2	23.5
66-67–Boston	72	–	2325	638	1406	.454	–	–	–	318	371	.857	–	–	338	217	191	1	–	–	–	1594	4.7	3.0	22.1
67-68–Boston	73	–	2408	621	1348	.461	–	–	–	311	376	.827	–	–	357	216	181	0	–	–	–	1553	4.9	3.0	21.3
68-69–Boston	70	–	1820	496	1103	.450	–	–	–	148	189	.783	–	–	265	182	121	0	–	–	–	1140	3.8	2.6	16.3
Reg. Season Totals	871	–	24285	6271	13745	.456	–	–	–	2869	3572	.803	–	–	4305	2209	1735	5	–	–	–	15411	4.9	2.5	17.7
Playoff Totals	154	–	4654	1149	2571	.447	–	–	–	611	753	.811	–	–	718	358	391	5	–	–	–	2909	4.7	2.3	18.9
All-Star Totals	5	–	102	18	56	.321	–	–	–	5	6	.833	–	–	14	15	6	0	–	–	–	41	2.8	3.0	8.2

J

Jones, Shelton b. April 6, 1966 Ht. 6-9 Wt. 210 College: St. John's (N.Y.)

SEASON–TEAM	G	GS	MIN	FGM	FGA	PCT	3FGM	3FGA	PCT	FTM	FTA	PCT	O-RB	D-RB	TOT	AST	PF	DQ	STL	TO	BLK	PTS	RPG	APG	PPG
88-89–S.A.-G.S.-Phil.	51	34	682	93	209	.445	0	1	.000	58	80	.725	32	81	113	42	58	0	21	47	15	244	2.2	0.8	4.8
Reg. Season Totals	51	34	682	93	209	.445	0	1	.000	58	80	.725	32	81	113	42	58	0	21	47	15	244	2.2	0.8	4.8

Jones, Stephen Howard (Steve, Snapper) b. October 17, 1942 Ht. 6-5 Wt. 205 College: Oregon

SEASON–TEAM	G	GS	MIN	FGM	FGA	PCT	3FGM	3FGA	PCT	FTM	FTA	PCT	O-RB	D-RB	TOT	AST	PF	DQ	STL	TO	BLK	PTS	RPG	APG	PPG
67-68–Oakland (A)	76	–	1950	278	665	.418	23	54	.426	186	233	.798	–	–	343	111	239	7	–	135	–	765	4.5	1.5	10.1
68-69–New Orleans (A)	78	–	3024	576	1372	.420	52	151	.344	348	437	.796	–	–	393	226	280	4	–	192	–	1552	5.0	2.9	19.9
69-70–New Orleans (A)	84	–	3116	689	1558	.442	15	66	.227	412	495	.832	–	–	388	195	290	3	–	–	–	1805	4.6	2.3	21.5
70-71–Memphis (A)	83	–	2923	732	1556	.470	40	108	.370	332	400	.830	–	–	299	182	234		–	–	–	1836	3.6	2.2	22.1
71-72–Dallas (A)	84	–	3091	572	1343	.426	26	78	.333	367	422	.870	–	–	317	237	268	–	–	205	–	1537	3.8	2.8	18.3
72-73–Dallas-Car. (A)	80	–	2129	430	883	.487	13	31	.419	200	247	.810	56	168	224	119	220	3	–	150	–	1073	2.8	1.5	13.4
73-74–Car.-Denver (A)	86	–	2092	400	899	.445	13	43	.302	128	168	.762	62	172	234	185	223	–	26	175	15	941	2.7	2.2	10.9
74-75–St. Louis (A)	69	–	1884	287	654	.439	4	19	.211	171	206	.830	43	151	194	197	131	–	53	147	7	749	2.8	2.9	10.9
75-76–Portland	64	–	819	168	380	.442	–	–	–	78	94	.830	13	62	75	63	96	0	17	–	6	414	1.2	1.0	6.5
Reg. NBA Totals	64	–	819	168	380	.442	–	–	–	78	94	.830	13	62	75	63	96	0	17	–	6	414	1.2	1.0	6.5
Reg. ABA Totals	640	–	20209	3964	8930	.444	186	550	.338	2144	2608	.822	161	491	2392	1452	1885	17	79	1004	22	10258	3.7	2.3	16.0
ABA Playoff Totals	37	–	1224	224	505	.444	8	30	.267	111	141	.787	1	13	144	61	132	0	2	42	3	567	3.9	1.6	15.3

Jones, Wali (formerly Walter Jones) b. February 14, 1942 Ht. 6-2 Wt. 180 College: Villanova

SEASON–TEAM	G	GS	MIN	FGM	FGA	PCT	3FGM	3FGA	PCT	FTM	FTA	PCT	O-RB	D-RB	TOT	AST	PF	DQ	STL	TO	BLK	PTS	RPG	APG	PPG
64-65–Baltimore	77	–	1250	154	411	.375	–	–	–	99	136	.728	–	–	140	200	196	1	–	–	–	407	1.8	2.6	5.3
65-66–Philadelphia	80	–	2196	296	799	.370	–	–	–	128	172	.744	–	–	169	273	250	6	–	–	–	720	2.1	3.4	9.0
66-67–Philadelphia	81	–	2249	423	982	.431	–	–	–	223	266	.838	–	–	265	303	246	6	–	–	–	1069	3.3	3.7	13.2
67-68–Philadelphia	77	–	2058	413	1040	.397	–	–	–	159	202	.787	–	–	219	245	225	5	–	–	–	985	2.8	3.2	12.8
68-69–Philadelphia	81	–	2340	432	1005	.430	–	–	–	207	256	.809	–	–	251	292	280	5	–	–	–	1071	3.1	3.6	13.2
69-70–Philadelphia	78	–	1740	366	851	.430	–	–	–	190	226	.841	–	–	173	276	210	2	–	–	–	922	2.2	3.5	11.8
70-71–Philadelphia	41	1	962	168	418	.402	–	–	–	79	101	.782	–	–	64	128	110	1	–	–	–	415	1.6	3.1	10.1
71-72–Milwaukee	48	–	1030	144	354	.407	–	–	–	74	90	.822	–	–	75	141	112	0	–	–	–	362	1.6	2.9	7.5
72-73–Milwaukee	27	–	419	59	145	.407	–	–	–	16	18	.889	–	–	29	56	39	0	–	–	–	134	1.1	2.1	5.0
74-75–Utah (A)	71	–	1339	212	524	.405	6	25	.240	102	124	.823	15	62	77	152	147	–	42	76	3	532	1.1	2.1	7.5
75-76–Detroit-Phil.	17	1	176	23	49	.469	–	–	–	9	13	.692	0	9	9	33	27	0	6	–	0	55	0.5	1.9	3.2
Reg. NBA Totals	607	2	14420	2478	6054	.409	–	–	–	1184	1480	.800	0	9	1394	1947	1695	26	6	–	0	6140	2.3	3.2	10.1
Reg. ABA Totals	71	–	1339	212	524	.405	6	25	.240	102	124	.823	15	62	77	152	147	–	42	76	3	532	1.1	2.1	7.5
NBA Playoff Totals	70	–	1761	333	821	.406	–	–	–	167	215	.777	0	1	166	202	234	5	0	–	0	833	2.4	2.9	11.9
ABA Playoff Totals	5	–	46	8	21	.381	0	0	–	6	6	1.000	1	1	2	4	6	–	4	7	0	22	0.4	0.8	4.4

Jones, Wallace C. (Wah Wah) b. July 14, 1926 Ht. 6-4 Wt. 225 College: Kentucky

SEASON–TEAM	G	GS	MIN	FGM	FGA	PCT	3FGM	3FGA	PCT	FTM	FTA	PCT	O-RB	D-RB	TOT	AST	PF	DQ	STL	TO	BLK	PTS	RPG	APG	PPG
49-50–Indianapolis	60	–	–	264	706	.374	–	–	–	223	297	.751	–	–	–	194	241	–	–	–	–	751	–	3.2	12.5
50-51–Indianapolis	22	–	–	93	237	.392	–	–	–	61	77	.792	–	–	125	85	74	4	–	–	–	247	5.7	3.9	11.2
51-52–Indianapolis	58	–	1320	164	524	.313	–	–	–	102	136	.750	–	–	283	150	137	3	–	–	–	430	4.9	2.6	7.4
Reg. Season Totals	140	–	1320	521	1467	.355	–	–	–	386	510	.757	–	–	408	429	452	7	–	–	–	1428	5.1	3.1	10.2
Playoff Totals	6	–	16	23	148	.304	–	–	–	29	34	.853	–	–	0	44	28	3	–	–	–	75	0.0	3.7	12.5

Jones, Walter (Larry) b. September 22, 1942 Ht. 6-3 Wt. 180 College: Toledo

SEASON–TEAM	G	GS	MIN	FGM	FGA	PCT	3FGM	3FGA	PCT	FTM	FTA	PCT	O-RB	D-RB	TOT	AST	PF	DQ	STL	TO	BLK	PTS	RPG	APG	PPG
64-65–Philadelphia	23	–	359	47	153	.307	–	–	–	37	52	.712	–	–	57	40	46	2	–	–	–	131	2.5	1.7	5.7
67-68–Denver (A)	76	–	3085	602	1409	.427	8	42	.190	530	683	.776	–	–	599	270	268	4	–	232	–	1742	7.9	3.6	22.9
68-69–Denver (A)	75	–	3042	759	1631	.465	24	100	.240	591	760	.778	–	–	493	258	273	3	–	218	–	2133	6.6	3.4	28.4
69-70–Denver (A)	75	–	3027	625	1441	.434	41	165	.248	579	732	.791	–	–	391	426	228	1	–	–	–	1870	5.2	5.7	24.9
70-71–Floridians (A)	84	–	3611	764	1636	.467	45	124	.363	471	587	.802	–	–	453	390	269	–	–	–	–	2044	5.4	4.6	24.3
71-72–Floridians (A)	66	–	2255	423	797	.531	18	60	.300	300	373	.804	–	–	309	210	203	–	–	135	–	1164	4.7	3.2	17.6
72-73–Utah-Dallas (A)	80	–	1701	240	521	.461	16	57	.281	202	244	.828	88	151	239	206	184	2	–	104	–	698	3.0	2.6	8.7
73-74–Philadelphia	72	60	1876	263	622	.423	–	–	–	197	235	.838	71	113	184	230	116	0	85	–	18	723	2.6	3.2	10.0
Reg. NBA Totals	95	60	2235	310	775	.400	–	–	–	234	287	.815	71	113	241	270	162	2	85	–	18	854	2.5	2.8	9.0
Reg. ABA Totals	456	–	16721	3413	7435	.459	152	548	.277	2673	3379	.791	88	151	2484	1760	1425	10	–	689	–	9651	5.4	3.9	21.2
NBA Playoff Totals	5	–	25	5	12	.417	–	–	–	7	11	.636	0	0	4	2	5	0	0	–	0	17	0.8	0.4	3.4
ABA Playoff Totals	30	–	1189	220	485	.454	10	37	.270	195	238	.819	–	–	160	158	99	0	–	9	–	645	5.3	5.3	21.5

Jones, Wilbert (Wil) b. February 27, 1947 Ht. 6-8 Wt. 205 College: Albany State (GA)

SEASON–TEAM	G	GS	MIN	FGM	FGA	PCT	3FGM	3FGA	PCT	FTM	FTA	PCT	O-RB	D-RB	TOT	AST	PF	DQ	STL	TO	BLK	PTS	RPG	APG	PPG
69-70–Miami (A)	74	–	1697	243	616	.394	2	11	.182	118	162	.728	–	–	565	48	207	5	–	–	–	606	7.6	0.6	8.2
70-71–Memphis (A)	84	–	2234	391	812	.482	1	13	.077	174	258	.674	–	–	680	152	249	–	–	–	–	957	8.1	1.8	11.4
71-72–Memphis (A)	84	–	3098	506	1078	.469	2	16	.125	240	320	.750	371	505	876	154	322	–	–	160	–	1254	10.4	1.8	14.9
72-73–Memphis (A)	76	–	2316	344	722	.476	1	7	.143	146	198	.737	245	359	604	117	281	9	–	130	–	835	7.9	1.5	11.0
73-74–Memphis (A)	81	–	2842	453	997	.454	3	26	.115	163	220	.741	205	460	665	205	276	–	105	184	82	1072	8.2	2.5	13.2
74-75–Kentucky (A)	84	–	2689	458	948	.483	0	5	.000	139	189	.735	198	409	607	256	353	–	108	199	70	1055	7.2	3.0	12.6
75-76–Kentucky (A)	83	–	2635	483	1015	.476	3	6	.500	158	204	.775	243	382	625	209	326	–	84	200	54	1127	7.5	2.5	13.6
76-77–Indiana	80	–	2709	438	1019	.430	–	–	–	166	223	.744	218	386	604	189	305	10	102	–	80	1042	7.6	2.4	13.0
77-78–Buffalo	79	–	1711	226	514	.440	–	–	–	84	119	.706	106	228	334	116	255	7	70	137	43	536	4.2	1.5	6.8
Reg. NBA Totals	159	–	4420	664	1533	.433	–	–	–	250	342	.731	324	614	938	305	560	17	172	137	123	1578	5.9	1.9	9.9
Reg. ABA Totals	566	–	17511	2878	6188	.465	12	84	.143	1138	1551	.734	1262	2115	4622	1141	2014	14	297	873	206	6906	8.2	2.0	12.2
ABA Playoff Totals	29	–	936	142	306	.464	0	2	.000	39	47	.830	95	121	216	81	118	0	28	51	12	323	7.4	2.8	11.1

Jones, William A. (Willie) b. June 29, 1936 Ht. 6-3 Wt. 185 College: Northwestern

SEASON–TEAM	G	GS	MIN	FGM	FGA	PCT	3FGM	3FGA	PCT	FTM	FTA	PCT	O-RB	D-RB	TOT	AST	PF	DQ	STL	TO	BLK	PTS	RPG	APG	PPG
60-61–Detroit	35	–	452	78	216	.361	–	–	–	40	63	.635	–	–	94	63	90	2	–	–	–	196	2.7	1.8	5.6
61-62–Detroit	69	–	1006	177	475	.373	–	–	–	64	101	.634	–	–	177	115	137	1	–	–	–	418	2.6	1.7	6.1
62-63–Detroit	79	–	1470	305	730	.418	–	–	–	118	164	.720	–	–	233	188	207	4	–	–	–	728	2.9	2.4	9.2
63-64–Detroit	77	–	1539	265	680	.390	–	–	–	100	141	.709	–	–	253	172	211	5	–	–	–	630	3.3	2.2	8.2
64-65–Detroit	12	–	101	21	52	.404	–	–	–	2	6	.333	–	–	10	7	13	0	–	–	–	44	0.8	0.6	3.7
Reg. Season Totals	272	–	4568	846	2153	.393	–	–	–	324	475	.682	–	–	767	545	658	12	–	–	–	2016	2.8	2.0	7.4
Playoff Totals	16	–	287	66	158	.418	–	–	–	25	29	.862	–	–	37	43	43	2	–	–	–	157	2.3	2.7	9.8

Jones, Willie D. (Hutch) b. September 1, 1959 Ht. 6-8 Wt. 195 College: Buffalo State; Vanderbilt

SEASON–TEAM	G	GS	MIN	FGM	FGA	PCT	3FGM	3FGA	PCT	FTM	FTA	PCT	O-RB	D-RB	TOT	AST	PF	DQ	STL	TO	BLK	PTS	RPG	APG	PPG
82-83–San Diego	9	0	85	17	37	.459	0	0	–	6	6	1.000	10	7	17	4	14	0	3	6	0	40	1.9	0.4	4.4
83-84–San Diego	4	0	18	0	3	.000	0	0	–	1	4	.250	0	0	0	0	0	0	1	2	0	1	0.0	0.0	0.3
Reg. Season Totals	13	0	103	17	40	.425	0	0	–	7	10	.700	10	7	17	4	14	0	4	8	0	41	1.3	0.3	3.2

Jordan, Adonis Adelecino b. August 21, 1970 Ht. 5-11 Wt. 170 College: Kansas

SEASON–TEAM	G	GS	MIN	FGM	FGA	PCT	3FGM	3FGA	PCT	FTM	FTA	PCT	O-RB	D-RB	TOT	AST	PF	DQ	STL	TO	BLK	PTS	RPG	APG	PPG
93-94–Denver	6	0	79	6	23	.261	3	10	.300	0	0	–	3	3	6	19	6	0	0	6	1	15	1.0	3.2	2.5
98-99–Milwaukee	4	0	18	2	4	.500	0	2	.000	2	4	.500	0	0	0	3	0	0	3	2	0	6	0.0	0.8	1.5
Reg. Season Totals	10	0	97	8	27	.296	3	12	.250	2	4	.500	3	3	6	22	6	0	3	8	1	21	0.6	2.2	2.1

Jordan, Charles C. b. January 31, 1954 Ht. 6-8 Wt. 220 College: Canisius

SEASON–TEAM	G	GS	MIN	FGM	FGA	PCT	3FGM	3FGA	PCT	FTM	FTA	PCT	O-RB	D-RB	TOT	AST	PF	DQ	STL	TO	BLK	PTS	RPG	APG	PPG
75-76–Indiana (A)	71	–	855	162	373	.434	2	10	.200	43	72	.597	94	122	216	53	184	–	33	84	13	369	3.0	0.7	5.2
Reg. ABA Totals	71	–	855	162	373	.434	2	10	.200	43	72	.597	94	122	216	53	184	–	33	84	13	369	3.0	0.7	5.2
ABA Playoff Totals	2	–	18	1	6	.167	0	0	–	0	0	–	0	5	5	2	9	–	2	1	0	2	2.5	1.0	1.0

Jordan, Edward Montgomery (Eddie, Fast Eddie) b. January 29, 1955 Ht. 6-1 Wt. 170 College: Rutgers

SEASON–TEAM	G	GS	MIN	FGM	FGA	PCT	3FGM	3FGA	PCT	FTM	FTA	PCT	O-RB	D-RB	TOT	AST	PF	DQ	STL	TO	BLK	PTS	RPG	APG	PPG
77-78–Clev.-N.J.	73	–	1213	215	538	.400	–	–	–	131	167	.784	35	84	119	177	94	0	126	106	19	561	1.6	2.4	7.7
78-79–New Jersey	82	–	2260	401	960	.418	–	–	–	213	274	.777	74	141	215	365	209	0	201	244	40	1015	2.6	4.5	12.4
79-80–New Jersey	82	–	2657	437	1017	.430	12	48	.250	201	258	.779	62	208	270	557	238	7	223	258	27	1087	3.3	6.8	13.3
80-81–N.J.-L.A.	74	–	1226	150	352	.426	6	22	.273	87	127	.685	30	68	98	241	165	0	98	143	8	393	1.3	3.3	5.3
81-82–Los Angeles	58	0	608	89	208	.428	1	9	.111	43	54	.796	4	39	43	131	98	0	62	66	1	222	0.7	2.3	3.8
82-83–Los Angeles	35	0	333	40	132	.303	3	16	.188	11	17	.647	8	18	26	80	52	0	31	54	1	94	0.7	2.3	2.7
83-84–Port.-L.A.	16	0	210	17	49	.347	0	3	.000	8	12	.667	3	14	17	44	37	0	25	26	0	42	1.1	2.8	2.6
Reg. Season Totals	420	0	8507	1349	3256	.414	22	98	.224	694	909	.763	216	572	788	1595	893	7	766	897	96	3414	1.9	3.8	8.1
Playoff Totals	7	0	93	15	40	.375	0	1	.000	8	9	.889	6	9	15	23	6	0	10	7	3	38	2.1	3.3	5.4

Jordan, Michael Jeffrey (Air Jordan, Air, M.J.) b. February 17, 1963 Ht. 6-6 Wt. 216 College: North Carolina

SEASON–TEAM	G	GS	MIN	FGM	FGA	PCT	3FGM	3FGA	PCT	FTM	FTA	PCT	O-RB	D-RB	TOT	AST	PF	DQ	STL	TO	BLK	PTS	RPG	APG	PPG
84-85–Chicago	82	82	3144	837	1625	.515	9	52	.173	630	746	.845	167	367	534	481	285	4	196	291	69	2313	6.5	5.9	28.2
85-86–Chicago	18	7	451	150	328	.457	3	18	.167	105	125	.840	23	41	64	53	46	0	37	45	21	408	3.6	2.9	22.7
86-87–Chicago	82	82	3281	1098	2279	.482	12	66	.182	833	972	.857	166	264	430	377	237	0	236	272	125	3041	5.2	4.6	37.1
87-88–Chicago	82	82	3311	1069	1998	.535	7	53	.132	723	860	.841	139	310	449	485	270	2	259	252	131	2868	5.5	5.9	35.0
88-89–Chicago	81	81	3255	966	1795	.538	27	98	.276	674	793	.850	149	503	652	650	247	2	234	290	65	2633	8.0	8.0	32.5
89-90–Chicago	82	82	3197	1034	1964	.526	92	245	.376	593	699	.848	143	422	565	519	241	0	227	247	54	2753	6.9	6.3	33.6
90-91–Chicago	82	82	3034	990	1837	.539	29	93	.312	571	671	.851	118	374	492	453	229	1	223	202	83	2580	6.0	5.5	31.5
91-92–Chicago	80	80	3102	943	1818	.519	27	100	.270	491	590	.832	91	420	511	489	201	1	182	200	75	2404	6.4	6.1	30.1
92-93–Chicago	78	78	3067	992	2003	.495	81	230	.352	476	569	.837	135	387	522	428	188	0	221	207	61	2541	6.7	5.5	32.6
94-95–Chicago	17	17	668	166	404	.411	16	32	.500	109	136	.801	25	92	117	90	47	0	30	35	13	457	6.9	5.3	26.9
95-96–Chicago	82	82	3090	916	1850	.495	111	260	.427	548	657	.834	148	395	543	352	195	0	180	197	42	2491	6.6	4.3	30.4
96-97–Chicago	82	82	3106	920	1892	.486	111	297	.374	480	576	.833	113	369	482	352	156	0	140	166	44	2431	5.9	4.3	29.6
97-98–Chicago	82	82	3181	881	1893	.465	30	126	.238	565	721	.784	130	345	475	283	151	0	141	185	45	2357	5.8	3.5	28.7
Reg. Season Totals	930	919	35887	10962	21686	.505	555	1670	.332	6798	8115	.838	1547	4289	5836	5012	2493	10	2306	2589	828	29277	6.3	5.4	31.5
Playoff Totals	179	179	7474	2188	4497	.487	148	446	.332	1463	1766	.828	305	847	1152	1022	541	3	376	546	158	5987	6.4	5.7	33.4
All-Star Totals	11	11	324	97	193	.503	3	9	.333	37	50	.740	20	32	52	49	27	0	33	39	6	234	4.7	4.5	21.3

Jordan, Reginald (Reggie) b. January 26, 1968 Ht. 6-4 Wt. 195 College: New Mexico State

SEASON–TEAM	G	GS	MIN	FGM	FGA	PCT	3FGM	3FGA	PCT	FTM	FTA	PCT	O-RB	D-RB	TOT	AST	PF	DQ	STL	TO	BLK	PTS	RPG	APG	PPG
93-94–L.A. Lakers	23	0	259	44	103	.427	2	4	.500	35	51	.686	46	21	67	26	26	0	14	14	5	125	2.9	1.1	5.4
95-96–Atlanta	24	0	247	36	71	.507	0	0	–	22	38	.579	23	29	52	29	30	0	12	19	7	94	2.2	1.2	3.9
96-97–Port.-Det.-Minn.	19	0	130	16	26	.615	0	0	–	8	17	.471	11	16	27	12	15	0	7	8	3	40	1.4	0.6	2.1
97-98–Minnesota	57	1	487	54	113	.478	0	1	.000	41	72	.569	57	40	97	50	63	0	35	30	9	149	1.7	0.9	2.6
98-99–Minnesota	27	1	296	15	54	.278	0	0	–	21	38	.553	27	32	59	41	38	0	12	14	5	51	2.2	1.5	1.9
99-00–Washington	36	0	243	17	53	.321	0	1	.000	7	13	.538	16	25	41	32	29	0	12	19	2	41	1.1	0.9	1.1
Reg. Season Totals	186	2	1662	182	420	.433	2	6	.333	134	229	.585	180	163	343	190	201	0	92	104	31	500	1.8	1.0	2.7
Playoff Totals	12	0	88	12	21	.571	1	1	1.000	4	9	.444	4	11	15	12	12	0	6	3	1	29	1.3	1.0	2.4

Jordan, Thomas b. May 23, 1968 Ht. 6-10 Wt. 220 College: Oklahoma State

SEASON–TEAM	G	GS	MIN	FGM	FGA	PCT	3FGM	3FGA	PCT	FTM	FTA	PCT	O-RB	D-RB	TOT	AST	PF	DQ	STL	TO	BLK	PTS	RPG	APG	PPG
92-93–Philadelphia	4	0	106	18	41	.439	0	0	–	8	17	.471	5	14	19	3	14	0	3	12	5	44	4.8	0.8	11.0
Reg. Season Totals	4	0	106	18	41	.439	0	0	–	8	17	.471	5	14	19	3	14	0	3	12	5	44	4.8	0.8	11.0

Jordan, Walter Lee b. February 19, 1956 Ht. 6-7 Wt. 205 College: Purdue

SEASON–TEAM	G	GS	MIN	FGM	FGA	PCT	3FGM	3FGA	PCT	FTM	FTA	PCT	O-RB	D-RB	TOT	AST	PF	DQ	STL	TO	BLK	PTS	RPG	APG	PPG
80-81–Cleveland	30	–	207	29	75	.387	0	0	–	10	17	.588	23	19	42	11	35	0	11	17	5	68	1.4	0.4	2.3
Reg. Season Totals	30	–	207	29	75	.387	0	0	–	10	17	.588	23	19	42	11	35	0	11	17	5	68	1.4	0.4	2.3

Jordon, Phil b. September 12, 1933 d. June 7, 1965 Ht. 6-10 Wt. 205 College: Whitworth

SEASON–TEAM	G	GS	MIN	FGM	FGA	PCT	3FGM	3FGA	PCT	FTM	FTA	PCT	O-RB	D-RB	TOT	AST	PF	DQ	STL	TO	BLK	PTS	RPG	APG	PPG
56-57–New York	9	–	91	18	49	.367	–	–	–	8	12	.667	–	–	34	2	15	0	–	–	–	44	3.8	0.2	4.9
57-58–N.Y.-Detroit	58	–	898	193	467	.413	–	–	–	64	93	.688	–	–	301	37	108	1	–	–	–	450	5.2	0.6	7.8
58-59–Detroit	72	–	2058	399	967	.413	–	–	–	231	303	.762	–	–	594	83	193	1	–	–	–	1029	8.3	1.2	14.3
59-60–Cincinnati	75	–	2066	381	970	.393	–	–	–	242	338	.716	–	–	624	207	227	7	–	–	–	1004	8.3	2.8	13.4
60-61–Cin.-N.Y.	79	–	2064	360	932	.386	–	–	–	208	297	.700	–	–	674	181	273	5	–	–	–	928	8.5	2.3	11.7
61-62–New York	76	–	2195	403	1028	.392	–	–	–	96	168	.571	–	–	482	156	258	7	–	–	–	902	6.3	2.1	11.9
62-63–St. Louis	73	–	1420	211	527	.400	–	–	–	56	101	.554	–	–	319	103	172	3	–	–	–	478	4.4	1.4	6.5
Reg. Season Totals	442	–	10792	1965	4940	.398	–	–	–	905	1312	.690	–	–	3028	769	1246	24	–	–	–	4835	6.9	1.7	10.9
Playoff Totals	16	–	243	36	99	.364	–	–	–	33	42	.786	–	–	51	14	34	0	–	–	–	105	3.2	0.9	6.6

Jorgensen, John J. (Johnny) b. December 28, 1921 d. January 19, 1973 Ht. 6-2 Wt. 185 College: William & Mary; DePaul

SEASON–TEAM	G	GS	MIN	FGM	FGA	PCT	3FGM	3FGA	PCT	FTM	FTA	PCT	O-RB	D-RB	TOT	AST	PF	DQ	STL	TO	BLK	PTS	RPG	APG	PPG
47-48–Chicago-Balt.	3	–	–	4	9	.444	–	–	–	1	1	1.000	–	–	–	0	2	–	–	–	–	9	–	0.0	3.0
47-48–Minneapolis (N)	38	–	–	37	–	–	–	–	–	27	49	.551	–	–	–	–	52	–	–	–	–	101	–	–	2.7
48-49–Minneapolis	48	–	–	41	114	.360	–	–	–	24	33	.727	–	–	–	33	68	–	–	–	–	106	–	0.7	2.2
Reg. NBA Totals	51	–	–	45	123	.366	–	–	–	25	34	.735	–	–	–	33	70	–	–	–	–	115	–	0.6	2.3
Reg. NBL Totals	38	–	–	37	–	–	–	–	–	27	49	.551	–	–	–	–	52	–	–	–	–	101	–	–	2.7
NBA Playoff Totals	5	–	–	3	14	.429	–	–	–	1	1	1.000	–	–	–	–	4	–	–	–	–	7	–	0.0	1.4
NBL Playoff Totals	10	–	–	11	–	–	–	–	–	4	8	.500	–	–	–	–	20	–	–	–	–	26	–	–	2.6

Jorgensen, Noble Gordon (Jorgy) b. May 18, 1925 d. November 1982 Ht. 6-9 Wt. 230 College: Iowa; Westminster

SEASON–TEAM	G	GS	MIN	FGM	FGA	PCT	3FGM	3FGA	PCT	FTM	FTA	PCT	O-RB	D-RB	TOT	AST	PF	DQ	STL	TO	BLK	PTS	RPG	APG	PPG
46-47–Pittsburgh	15	–	–	25	112	.223	–	–	–	16	25	.640	–	–	–	4	40	–	–	–	–	66	–	0.3	4.4
48-49–Sheboygan (N)	63	–	–	218	–	–	–	–	–	194	255	.761	–	–	–	–	189	–	–	–	–	630	–	–	10.0
49-50–Sheboygan	54	–	–	218	618	.353	–	–	–	268	350	.766	–	–	–	90	201	–	–	–	–	704	–	1.7	13.0
50-51–Tri-Cit-Syr.	63	–	–	223	600	.372	–	–	–	182	265	.687	–	–	338	91	237	8	–	–	–	628	5.4	1.4	10.0
51-52–Syracuse	66	–	1318	190	460	.413	–	–	–	149	187	.797	–	–	288	63	190	2	–	–	–	529	4.4	1.0	8.0
52-53–Syracuse	70	–	1355	145	436	.333	–	–	–	146	199	.734	–	–	236	76	247	7	–	–	–	436	3.4	1.1	6.2
Reg. NBA Totals	268	–	2673	801	2226	.360	–	–	–	761	1026	.742	–	–	862	324	915	17	–	–	–	2363	4.3	1.2	8.8
Reg. NBL Totals	63	–	–	218	–	–	–	–	–	194	255	.761	–	–	–	–	189	–	–	–	–	630	–	–	10.0
NBA Playoff Totals	19	–	306	59	192	.396	–	–	–	58	88	.659	–	–	58	31	75	4	–	–	–	176	3.6	1.4	9.3
NBL Playoff Totals	2	–	–	11	–	–	–	–	–	7	8	.875	–	–	–	–	7	–	–	–	–	29	–	–	14.5

Jorgensen, Roger Kennedy b. September 2, 1920 Ht. 6-5 Wt. 200 College: Pittsburgh; Ohio State

SEASON–TEAM	G	GS	MIN	FGM	FGA	PCT	3FGM	3FGA	PCT	FTM	FTA	PCT	O-RB	D-RB	TOT	AST	PF	DQ	STL	TO	BLK	PTS	RPG	APG	PPG
46-47–Pittsburgh	28	–	–	14	54	.259	–	–	–	13	19	.684	–	–	–	1	36	–	–	–	–	41	–	0.0	1.5
Reg. Season Totals	28	–	–	14	54	.259	–	–	–	13	19	.684	–	–	–	1	36	–	–	–	–	41	–	0.0	1.5

Joseph, Yvon b. October 31, 1957 Ht. 6-11 Wt. 245 College: Miami-Dade (Fla.) C.C. North; Georgia Tech

SEASON–TEAM	G	GS	MIN	FGM	FGA	PCT	3FGM	3FGA	PCT	FTM	FTA	PCT	O-RB	D-RB	TOT	AST	PF	DQ	STL	TO	BLK	PTS	RPG	APG	PPG
85-86–New Jersey	1	0	5	0	0	–	0	0	–	2	2	1.000	0	0	0	0	1	0	0	0	0	2	0.0	0.0	2.0
Reg. Season Totals	1	0	5	0	0	–	0	0	–	2	2	1.000	0	0	0	0	1	0	0	0	0	2	0.0	0.0	2.0

Joyce, Kevin F. b. June 27, 1951 Ht. 6-3 Wt. 190 College: South Carolina

SEASON–TEAM	G	GS	MIN	FGM	FGA	PCT	3FGM	3FGA	PCT	FTM	FTA	PCT	O-RB	D-RB	TOT	AST	PF	DQ	STL	TO	BLK	PTS	RPG	APG	PPG
73-74–Indiana (A)	56	–	987	171	432	.396	5	27	.185	64	78	.821	33	59	92	128	86	–	32	80	8	411	1.6	2.3	7.3
74-75–Indiana (A)	81	–	2828	530	1245	.426	8	42	.190	142	180	.789	60	103	163	322	259	–	107	151	23	1210	2.0	4.0	14.9
75-76–S.D.-Ken. (A)	43	–	916	114	311	.367	2	12	.167	55	74	.743	7	42	49	130	96	–	31	91	3	285	1.1	3.0	6.6
Reg. ABA Totals	180	–	4731	815	1988	.410	15	81	.185	261	332	.786	100	204	304	580	441	0	170	322	34	1906	1.7	3.2	10.6
ABA Playoff Totals	37	–	846	115	300	.383	7	20	.350	50	63	.794	7	36	43	87	89	0	24	58	11	287	1.2	2.4	7.8

Joyner, Harry C. (Butch) b. April 26, 1945 Ht. 6-5 Wt. 200 College: Indiana

SEASON–TEAM	G	GS	MIN	FGM	FGA	PCT	3FGM	3FGA	PCT	FTM	FTA	PCT	O-RB	D-RB	TOT	AST	PF	DQ	STL	TO	BLK	PTS	RPG	APG	PPG
68-69–Indiana (A)	2	–	5	0	0	–	0	0	–	0	0	–	–	–	1	0	1	0	–	0	–	0	0.5	0.0	0.0
Reg. ABA Totals	2	–	5	0	0	–	0	0	–	0	0	–	–	–	1	0	1	0	–	–	–	0	0.5	0.0	0.0

Judkins, Jeffrey Reed (Jeff) b. March 23, 1956 Ht. 6-6 Wt. 185 College: Utah

SEASON–TEAM	G	GS	MIN	FGM	FGA	PCT	3FGM	3FGA	PCT	FTM	FTA	PCT	O-RB	D-RB	TOT	AST	PF	DQ	STL	TO	BLK	PTS	RPG	APG	PPG
78-79–Boston	81	–	1521	295	587	.503	–	–	–	119	146	.815	70	121	191	145	184	1	81	109	12	709	2.4	1.8	8.8
79-80–Boston	65	–	674	139	276	.504	11	27	.407	62	76	.816	32	34	66	47	91	0	29	49	5	351	1.0	0.7	5.4
80-81–Utah	62	–	666	92	216	.426	9	28	.321	45	51	.882	29	64	93	59	84	0	16	30	2	238	1.5	1.0	3.8
81-82–Detroit	30	0	251	31	81	.383	1	10	.100	16	26	.615	14	20	34	14	33	0	6	9	5	79	1.1	0.5	2.6
82-83–Portland	34	0	309	39	88	.443	2	8	.250	25	30	.833	18	25	43	17	39	0	15	17	2	105	1.3	0.5	3.1
Reg. Season Totals	272	0	3421	596	1248	.478	23	73	.315	267	329	.812	163	264	427	282	431	1	147	214	26	1482	1.6	1.0	5.4
Playoff Totals	7	0	10	4	8	.500	1	3	.333	0	0	–	3	1	4	–	0	0	1	0	0	9	0.6	0.0	1.3

Kachan, Edwin John (Whitey) b. September 15, 1925 Ht. 6-2 Wt. 175 College: DePaul

SEASON–TEAM	G	GS	MIN	FGM	FGA	PCT	3FGM	3FGA	PCT	FTM	FTA	PCT	O-RB	D-RB	TOT	AST	PF	DQ	STL	TO	BLK	PTS	RPG	APG	PPG
48-49–Chicago-Minn.	52	–	–	38	142	.268	–	–	–	36	56	.643	–	–	–	37	81	–	–	–	–	112	–	0.7	2.2
Reg. Season Totals	52	–	–	38	142	.268	–	–	–	36	56	.643	–	–	–	37	81	–	–	–	–	112	–	0.7	2.2
Playoff Totals	8	–	–	2	5	.400	–	–	–	0	0	–	–	–	–	2	3	–	–	–	–	4	–	0.3	0.5

Kaftan, George A. (The Golden Greek) b. February 22, 1928 Ht. 6-3 Wt. 190 College: Holy Cross

SEASON–TEAM	G	GS	MIN	FGM	FGA	PCT	3FGM	3FGA	PCT	FTM	FTA	PCT	O-RB	D-RB	TOT	AST	PF	DQ	STL	TO	BLK	PTS	RPG	APG	PPG
48-49–Boston	21	–	–	116	315	.368	–	–	–	72	115	.626	–	–	–	61	28	–	–	–	–	304	–	2.9	14.5
49-50–Boston	55	–	–	199	535	.372	–	–	–	136	208	.654	–	–	–	145	92	–	–	–	–	534	–	2.6	9.7
50-51–New York	61	–	–	111	286	.388	–	–	–	78	125	.624	–	–	153	74	102	1	–	–	–	300	2.5	1.2	4.9
51-52–New York	52	–	955	115	307	.375	–	–	–	92	134	.687	–	–	196	88	107	0	–	–	–	322	3.8	1.7	6.2
52-53–Baltimore	23	–	380	45	142	.317	–	–	–	44	67	.657	–	–	75	31	59	2	–	–	–	134	3.3	1.3	5.8
Reg. Season Totals	212	–	1335	586	1585	.370	–	–	–	422	649	.650	–	–	424	399	388	3	–	–	–	1594	3.1	1.9	7.5
Playoff Totals	22	–	287	32	84	.381	–	–	–	29	45	.644	–	–	36	24	48	3	–	–	–	93	1.8	1.2	4.2

Kalafat, Edward L. (Ed) b. October 13, 1932 Ht. 6-6 Wt. 245 College: Minnesota

SEASON–TEAM	G	GS	MIN	FGM	FGA	PCT	3FGM	3FGA	PCT	FTM	FTA	PCT	O-RB	D-RB	TOT	AST	PF	DQ	STL	TO	BLK	PTS	RPG	APG	PPG
54-55–Minneapolis	72	–	1102	118	375	.315	–	–	–	111	168	.661	–	–	317	75	205	9	–	–	–	347	4.4	1.0	4.8
55-56–Minneapolis	72	–	1639	194	540	.359	–	–	–	186	252	.738	–	–	440	130	236	2	–	–	–	574	6.1	1.8	8.0
56-57–Minneapolis	65	–	1617	178	507	.351	–	–	–	197	298	.661	–	–	425	105	243	9	–	–	–	553	6.5	1.6	8.5
Reg. Season Totals	209	–	4358	490	1422	.345	–	–	–	494	718	.688	–	–	1182	310	684	20	–	–	–	1474	5.7	1.5	7.1
Playoff Totals	15	–	235	32	79	.405	–	–	–	39	60	.650	–	–	63	11	49	3	–	–	–	103	4.2	0.7	6.9

Kaplowitz, Ralph (Kappy) b. May 18, 1919 Ht. 6-2 Wt. 170 College: New York U.

SEASON–TEAM	G	GS	MIN	FGM	FGA	PCT	3FGM	3FGA	PCT	FTM	FTA	PCT	O-RB	D-RB	TOT	AST	PF	DQ	STL	TO	BLK	PTS	RPG	APG	PPG
46-47–N.Y.-Phil.	57	–	–	146	532	.274	–	–	–	111	151	.735	–	–	–	38	122	–	–	–	–	403	–	0.7	7.1
47-48–Philadelphia	48	–	–	71	292	.243	–	–	–	47	60	.783	–	–	–	19	100	–	–	–	–	189	–	0.4	3.9
Reg. Season Totals	105	–	–	217	824	.263	–	–	–	158	211	.749	–	–	–	57	222	–	–	–	–	592	–	0.5	5.6
Playoff Totals	23	–	–	54	191	.283	–	–	–	44	56	.786	–	–	–	13	47	–	–	–	–	152	–	0.6	6.6

Kappen, Anthony George (Tony) b. April 13, 1919 d. December 18, 1993 Ht. 5-10 Wt. 165 College: None

SEASON–TEAM	G	GS	MIN	FGM	FGA	PCT	3FGM	3FGA	PCT	FTM	FTA	PCT	O-RB	D-RB	TOT	AST	PF	DQ	STL	TO	BLK	PTS	RPG	APG	PPG
46-47–Pitt.-Boston	59	–	–	128	537	.238	–	–	–	128	161	.795	–	–	–	28	78	–	–	–	–	384	–	0.5	6.5
Reg. Season Totals	59	–	–	128	537	.238	–	–	–	128	161	.795	–	–	–	28	78	–	–	–	–	384	–	0.5	6.5

Karl, George Matthew b. May 12, 1951 Ht. 6-2 Wt. 185 College: North Carolina

SEASON–TEAM	G	GS	MIN	FGM	FGA	PCT	3FGM	3FGA	PCT	FTM	FTA	PCT	O-RB	D-RB	TOT	AST	PF	DQ	STL	TO	BLK	PTS	RPG	APG	PPG
73-74–San Antonio (A)	74	–	1339	236	502	.470	8	22	.364	94	113	.832	41	85	126	160	161	–	65	92	10	574	1.7	2.2	7.8
74-75–San Antonio (A)	82	–	1629	261	534	.489	4	23	.174	137	177	.774	47	108	155	334	207	–	96	158	7	663	1.9	4.1	8.1
75-76–San Antonio (A)	75	–	1200	150	334	.449	0	9	.000	81	106	.764	13	53	66	250	149	–	60	108	3	381	0.9	3.3	5.1
76-77–San Antonio	29	–	251	25	73	.342	–	–	–	29	42	.690	4	13	17	46	36	0	10	–	0	79	0.6	1.6	2.7
77-78–San Antonio	4	–	30	2	6	.333	–	–	–	2	2	1.000	0	5	5	5	6	0	1	4	0	6	1.3	1.3	1.5
Reg. NBA Totals	33	–	281	27	79	.342	–	–	–	31	44	.705	4	18	22	51	42	0	11	4	0	85	0.7	1.5	2.6
Reg. ABA Totals	231	–	4168	647	1370	.472	12	54	.222	312	396	.788	101	246	347	744	517	0	221	358	20	1618	1.5	3.2	7.0
NBA Playoff Totals	1	–	1	0	0	–	–	–	–	0	0	–	0	0	0	–	0	0	0	–	0	0	0.0	0.0	0.0
ABA Playoff Totals	17	–	245	24	58	.414	0	3	.000	11	18	.611	4	18	22	45	36	0	16	19	0	59	1.3	2.6	3.5

Kasid, Edward (Ed) b. August 13, 1923 Ht. 5-11 Wt. 185 College: None

SEASON–TEAM	G	GS	MIN	FGM	FGA	PCT	3FGM	3FGA	PCT	FTM	FTA	PCT	O-RB	D-RB	TOT	AST	PF	DQ	STL	TO	BLK	PTS	RPG	APG	PPG
46-47–Toronto	8	–	–	6	21	.286	–	–	–	0	6	.000	–	–	–	6	8	–	–	–	–	12	–	0.8	1.5
Reg. Season Totals	8	–	–	6	21	.286	–	–	–	0	6	.000	–	–	–	6	8	–	–	–	–	12	–	0.8	1.5

Katkaveck, Leo Frank b. April 17, 1923 Ht. 6-0 Wt. 185 College: North Carolina State

SEASON–TEAM	G	GS	MIN	FGM	FGA	PCT	3FGM	3FGA	PCT	FTM	FTA	PCT	O-RB	D-RB	TOT	AST	PF	DQ	STL	TO	BLK	PTS	RPG	APG	PPG
48-49–Washington	53	–	–	84	253	.332	–	–	–	53	71	.746	–	–	–	68	110	–	–	–	–	221	–	1.3	4.2
49-50–Washington	54	–	–	101	330	.306	–	–	–	34	56	.607	–	–	–	68	102	–	–	–	–	236	–	1.3	4.4
Reg. Season Totals	107	–	–	185	583	.317	–	–	–	87	127	.685	–	–	–	136	212	–	–	–	–	457	–	1.3	4.3
Playoff Totals	11	–	–	9	63	.222	–	–	–	8	14	.714	–	–	–	20	21	–	–	–	–	26	–	1.2	2.4

Kauffman, Robert (Bob, Horse) b. July 13, 1946 Ht. 6-8 Wt. 240 College: Guilford

SEASON–TEAM	G	GS	MIN	FGM	FGA	PCT	3FGM	3FGA	PCT	FTM	FTA	PCT	O-RB	D-RB	TOT	AST	PF	DQ	STL	TO	BLK	PTS	RPG	APG	PPG
68-69–Seattle	82	–	1660	219	496	.442	–	–	–	203	289	.702	–	–	484	83	252	8	–	–	–	641	5.9	1.0	7.8
69-70–Chicago	64	–	775	94	221	.425	–	–	–	88	123	.715	–	–	211	76	117	1	–	–	–	276	3.3	1.2	4.3
70-71–Buffalo	78	–	2778	616	1309	.471	–	–	–	359	485	.740	–	–	837	354	263	8	–	–	–	1591	10.7	4.5	20.4
71-72–Buffalo	77	–	3205	558	1123	.497	–	–	–	341	429	.795	–	–	787	297	273	7	–	–	–	1457	10.2	3.9	18.9
72-73–Buffalo	77	–	3049	535	1059	.505	–	–	–	280	359	.780	–	–	855	396	211	1	–	–	–	1350	11.1	5.1	17.5
73-74–Buffalo	74	–	1304	171	366	.467	–	–	–	107	150	.713	97	229	326	142	155	0	37	–	18	449	4.4	1.9	6.1
74-75–Atlanta	73	–	797	113	261	.433	–	–	–	59	84	.702	67	115	182	81	103	1	19	–	4	285	2.5	1.1	3.9
Reg. Season Totals	525	–	13568	2306	4835	.477	–	–	–	1437	1919	.749	164	344	3682	1429	1374	26	56	–	22	6049	7.0	2.7	11.5
Playoff Totals	5	–	24	2	6	.333	–	–	–	2	5	.400	1	0	7	6	5	0	0	–	0	6	1.4	1.2	1.2
All-Star Totals	3	–	20	2	5	.400	–	–	–	1	2	.500	0	0	2	2	4	0	0	–	0	5	0.7	0.7	1.7

Kautz, Wilbert (Wibs) b. September 7, 1915 d. May 1979 Ht. 6-0 Wt. 180 College: Loyola (Chicago)

SEASON–TEAM	G	GS	MIN	FGM	FGA	PCT	3FGM	3FGA	PCT	FTM	FTA	PCT	O-RB	D-RB	TOT	AST	PF	DQ	STL	TO	BLK	PTS	RPG	APG	PPG
39-40–Chicago (N)	28	–	–	105	–	–	–	–	–	63	116	.543	–	–	–	–	55	–	–	–	–	273	–	–	9.8
40-41–Chicago (N)	21	–	–	94	–	–	–	–	–	39	63	.619	–	–	–	–	31	–	–	–	–	227	–	–	10.8
41-42–Chicago (N)	20	–	–	85	–	–	–	–	–	40	–	–	–	–	–	–	–	–	–	–	–	210	–	–	10.5
46-47–Chicago	50	–	–	107	420	.255	–	–	–	39	73	.534	–	–	–	37	114	–	–	–	–	253	–	0.7	5.1
Reg. NBA Totals	50	–	–	107	420	.255	–	–	–	39	73	.534	–	–	–	37	114	–	–	–	–	253	–	0.7	5.1
Reg. NBL Totals	69	–	–	284	–	–	–	–	–	142	179	.570	–	–	–	–	86	–	–	–	–	710	–	–	10.3
NBA Playoff Totals	10	–	–	10	71	.211	–	–	–	2	5	.400	–	–	–	–	17	–	–	–	–	22	0.0	0.0	2.2

Kea, Clarence Leroy b. February 2, 1959 Ht. 6-7 Wt. 220 College: Lamar

SEASON–TEAM	G	GS	MIN	FGM	FGA	PCT	3FGM	3FGA	PCT	FTM	FTA	PCT	O-RB	D-RB	TOT	AST	PF	DQ	STL	TO	BLK	PTS	RPG	APG	PPG
80-81–Dallas	16	–	199	37	81	.457	0	1	.000	43	62	.694	28	39	67	5	44	2	6	16	1	117	4.2	0.3	7.3
81-82–Dallas	35	0	248	26	49	.531	0	0	–	29	42	.690	26	35	61	14	55	0	4	16	3	81	1.7	0.4	2.3
Reg. Season Totals	51	0	447	63	130	.485	0	1	.000	72	104	.692	54	74	128	19	99	2	10	32	4	198	2.5	0.4	3.9

Kearns, Michael Joseph b. June 18, 1929 Ht. 6-2 Wt. 180 College: Princeton

SEASON–TEAM	G	GS	MIN	FGM	FGA	PCT	3FGM	3FGA	PCT	FTM	FTA	PCT	O-RB	D-RB	TOT	AST	PF	DQ	STL	TO	BLK	PTS	RPG	APG	PPG
54-55–Philadelphia	6	–	25	0	5	.000	–	–	–	1	4	.250	–	–	3	5	1	0	–	–	–	1	0.5	0.8	0.2
Reg. Season Totals	6	–	25	0	5	.000	–	–	–	1	4	.250	–	–	3	5	1	0	–	–	–	1	0.5	0.8	0.2

Kearns, Thomas Francis Jr. (Tommy) b. October 6, 1936 Ht. 5-11 Wt. 185 College: North Carolina

SEASON–TEAM	G	GS	MIN	FGM	FGA	PCT	3FGM	3FGA	PCT	FTM	FTA	PCT	O-RB	D-RB	TOT	AST	PF	DQ	STL	TO	BLK	PTS	RPG	APG	PPG
58-59–Syracuse	1	–	7	1	1	1.000	–	–	–	0	0	–	–	–	0	0	1	0	–	–	–	2	0.0	0.0	2.0
Reg. Season Totals	1	–	7	1	1	1.000	–	–	–	0	0	–	–	–	0	0	1	0	–	–	–	2	0.0	0.0	2.0

Keefe, Adam Thomas b. February 22, 1970 Ht. 6-9 Wt. 230 College: Stanford

SEASON–TEAM	G	GS	MIN	FGM	FGA	PCT	3FGM	3FGA	PCT	FTM	FTA	PCT	O-RB	D-RB	TOT	AST	PF	DQ	STL	TO	BLK	PTS	RPG	APG	PPG
92-93–Atlanta	82	6	1549	188	376	.500	0	1	.000	166	237	.700	171	261	432	80	195	1	57	100	16	542	5.3	1.0	6.6
93-94–Atlanta	63	1	763	96	213	.451	0	0	–	81	111	.730	77	124	201	34	80	0	20	60	9	273	3.2	0.5	4.3
94-95–Utah	75	0	1270	172	298	.577	0	0	–	117	173	.676	135	192	327	30	141	0	36	62	25	461	4.4	0.4	6.1
95-96–Utah	82	0	1708	180	346	.520	0	4	.000	139	201	.692	176	279	455	64	174	0	51	88	41	499	5.5	0.8	6.1
96-97–Utah	62	0	915	82	160	.513	0	1	.000	71	103	.689	75	141	216	32	97	0	30	45	13	235	3.5	0.5	3.8
97-98–Utah	80	75	2047	229	424	.540	0	0	–	162	200	.810	179	259	438	89	172	0	52	71	24	620	5.5	1.1	7.8
98-99–Utah	44	0	642	56	124	.452	0	4	.000	62	89	.697	51	91	142	28	63	0	16	33	12	174	3.2	0.6	4.0
99-00–Utah	62	3	604	53	130	.408	0	1	.000	29	36	.806	45	91	136	34	90	0	17	46	13	135	2.2	0.5	2.2
Reg. Season Totals	550	85	9498	1056	2071	.510	0	11	.000	827	1150	.719	909	1438	2347	391	1012	1	279	505	153	2939	4.3	0.7	5.3
Playoff Totals	64	10	676	73	134	.545	1	2	.500	43	66	.652	47	103	150	19	83	0	20	28	9	190	2.3	0.3	3.0

Keeling, Harold A. b. September 18, 1963 Ht. 6-4 Wt. 185 College: Santa Clara

SEASON–TEAM	G	GS	MIN	FGM	FGA	PCT	3FGM	3FGA	PCT	FTM	FTA	PCT	O-RB	D-RB	TOT	AST	PF	DQ	STL	TO	BLK	PTS	RPG	APG	PPG
85-86–Dallas	20	0	75	17	39	.436	0	0	–	10	14	.714	3	3	6	10	9	0	7	7	0	44	0.3	0.5	2.2
Reg. Season Totals	20	0	75	17	39	.436	0	0	–	10	14	.714	3	3	6	10	9	0	7	7	0	44	0.3	0.5	2.2
Playoff Totals	1	0	1	0	0	–	0	0	–	0	0	–	0	0	0	–	0	0	0	0	0	0	0.0	0.0	0.0

Keller, Gary J. b. June 13, 1944 Ht. 6-9 Wt. 220 College: Florida

SEASON–TEAM	G	GS	MIN	FGM	FGA	PCT	3FGM	3FGA	PCT	FTM	FTA	PCT	O-RB	D-RB	TOT	AST	PF	DQ	STL	TO	BLK	PTS	RPG	APG	PPG
67-68–Minnesota (A)	69	–	1211	184	483	.381	0	2	.000	139	214	.650	–	–	383	39	168	7	–	87	–	507	5.6	0.6	7.3
68-69–Miami (A)	53	–	503	78	192	.406	0	3	.000	72	120	.600	–	–	167	8	102	2	–	41	–	228	3.2	0.2	4.3
Reg. ABA Totals	122	–	1714	262	675	.388	0	5	.000	211	334	.632	–	–	550	47	270	9	–	128	–	735	4.5	0.4	6.0
ABA Playoff Totals	16	–	199	37	88	.420	0	0	–	19	33	.576	–	–	73	11	39	0	–	15	–	93	4.6	0.7	5.8

Keller, Kenneth W. (Ken) b. 1922 d. February 24, 1983 Ht. 6-1 Wt. 180 College: Vermont; St. John's (N.Y.)

SEASON–TEAM	G	GS	MIN	FGM	FGA	PCT	3FGM	3FGA	PCT	FTM	FTA	PCT	O-RB	D-RB	TOT	AST	PF	DQ	STL	TO	BLK	PTS	RPG	APG	PPG
46-47–Wash.-Prov.	28	–	–	10	30	.333	–	–	–	2	5	.400	–	–	–	1	15	–	–	–	–	22	–	0.0	0.8
Reg. Season Totals	28	–	–	10	30	.333	–	–	–	2	5	.400	–	–	–	1	15	–	–	–	–	22	–	0.0	0.8

Keller, William Curry (Billy) b. August 30, 1947 Ht. 5-10 Wt. 180 College: Purdue

SEASON–TEAM	G	GS	MIN	FGM	FGA	PCT	3FGM	3FGA	PCT	FTM	FTA	PCT	O-RB	D-RB	TOT	AST	PF	DQ	STL	TO	BLK	PTS	RPG	APG	PPG
69-70–Indiana (A)	82	–	1482	252	634	.397	42	154	.273	164	193	.850	–	–	174	235	153	0	–	–	–	710	2.1	2.9	8.7
70-71–Indiana (A)	83	–	2490	417	980	.426	84	230	.365	267	308	.867	–	–	240	437	170	–	–	–	–	1185	2.9	5.3	14.3
71-72–Indiana (A)	76	–	1729	264	619	.426	56	169	.331	153	174	.879	–	–	164	264	118	–	–	131	–	737	2.2	3.5	9.7
72-73–Indiana (A)	83	–	2251	421	973	.433	71	222	.320	234	269	.870	82	122	204	361	162	1	–	171	–	1147	2.5	4.3	13.8
73-74–Indiana (A)	75	–	1428	279	615	.454	50	131	.382	107	123	.870	44	84	128	172	83	–	37	100	3	715	1.7	2.3	9.5
74-75–Indiana (A)	79	–	1918	397	908	.437	80	240	.333	113	128	.883	90	121	211	204	101	–	59	109	3	987	2.7	2.6	12.5
75-76–Indiana (A)	78	–	2311	410	1011	.406	123	349	.352	164	183	.896	81	147	228	307	116	–	59	148	5	1107	2.9	3.9	14.2
Reg. ABA Totals	556	–	13609	2440	5740	.425	506	1495	.338	1202	1378	.872	297	474	1349	1980	903	1	155	659	11	6588	2.4	3.6	11.8
ABA Playoff Totals	95	–	2504	415	975	.426	87	255	.341	222	255	.871	17	28	225	334	184	0	13	82	0	1139	2.4	3.5	12.0

Kelley, Richard Ryland (Rich) b. March 23, 1953 Ht. 7-0 Wt. 235 College: Stanford

SEASON–TEAM	G	GS	MIN	FGM	FGA	PCT	3FGM	3FGA	PCT	FTM	FTA	PCT	O-RB	D-RB	TOT	AST	PF	DQ	STL	TO	BLK	PTS	RPG	APG	PPG
75-76–New Orleans	75	–	1346	184	379	.485	–	–	–	159	205	.776	193	335	528	155	209	5	52	–	60	527	7.0	2.1	7.0
76-77–New Orleans	76	–	1505	184	386	.477	–	–	–	156	197	.792	210	377	587	208	244	7	45	–	63	524	7.7	2.7	6.9
77-78–New Orleans	82	–	2119	304	602	.505	–	–	–	225	289	.779	249	510	759	233	293	6	89	225	129	833	9.3	2.8	10.2
78-79–New Orleans	80	–	2705	440	870	.506	–	–	–	373	458	.814	303	723	1026	285	309	8	126	288	166	1253	12.8	3.6	15.7
79-80–N.J.-Phoenix	80	–	1839	229	484	.473	0	3	.000	244	310	.787	200	315	515	178	273	5	78	198	96	702	6.4	2.2	8.8
80-81–Phoenix	81	–	1686	196	387	.506	0	2	.000	175	231	.758	131	310	441	282	210	0	79	209	63	567	5.4	3.5	7.0
81-82–Phoenix	81	39	1892	236	505	.467	0	1	.000	167	223	.749	168	329	497	293	292	14	64	244	71	639	6.1	3.6	7.9
82-83–Denver-Utah	70	23	1345	130	293	.444	0	0	–	142	175	.811	131	273	404	138	221	4	54	118	39	402	5.8	2.0	5.7
83-84–Utah	75	30	1674	132	264	.500	0	0	–	124	162	.765	140	350	490	157	273	6	55	148	29	388	6.5	2.1	5.2
84-85–Utah	77	34	1276	103	216	.477	0	2	.000	84	112	.750	118	232	350	120	227	5	42	124	30	290	4.5	1.6	3.8
85-86–Sacramento	37	0	324	28	49	.571	0	2	.000	18	22	.818	29	52	81	43	62	0	10	22	3	74	2.2	1.2	2.0
Reg. Season Totals	814	126	17711	2166	4435	.488	0	10	.000	1867	2384	.783	1872	3806	5678	2092	2613	60	694	1576	749	6199	7.0	2.6	7.6
Playoff Totals	45	12	860	92	197	.467	0	2	.000	75	94	.798	95	151	246	105	133	2	39	69	24	259	5.5	2.3	5.8

Kellogg, Clark Clifton Jr. (Special K) b. July 2, 1961 Ht. 6-7 Wt. 225 College: Ohio State

SEASON–TEAM	G	GS	MIN	FGM	FGA	PCT	3FGM	3FGA	PCT	FTM	FTA	PCT	O-RB	D-RB	TOT	AST	PF	DQ	STL	TO	BLK	PTS	RPG	APG	PPG
82-83–Indiana	81	81	2761	680	1420	.479	4	18	.222	261	352	.741	340	520	860	223	298	6	141	217	43	1625	10.6	2.8	20.1
83-84–Indiana	79	79	2676	619	1193	.519	7	21	.333	261	340	.768	230	489	719	234	242	2	121	218	28	1506	9.1	3.0	19.1
84-85–Indiana	77	65	2449	562	1112	.505	7	14	.500	301	396	.760	224	500	724	244	247	2	86	231	26	1432	9.4	3.2	18.6
85-86–Indiana	19	12	568	139	294	.473	4	13	.308	53	69	.768	51	117	168	57	59	2	28	61	8	335	8.8	3.0	17.6
86-87–Indiana	4	4	60	8	22	.364	1	2	.500	3	4	.750	7	4	11	6	12	0	5	4	0	20	2.8	1.5	5.0
Reg. Season Totals	260	241	8514	2008	4041	.497	23	68	.338	879	1161	.757	852	1630	2482	764	858	12	381	731	105	4918	9.5	2.9	18.9

Kelly, Arvesta b. November 20, 1945 Ht. 6-3 Wt. 195 College: Lincoln (MO)

SEASON–TEAM	G	GS	MIN	FGM	FGA	PCT	3FGM	3FGA	PCT	FTM	FTA	PCT	O-RB	D-RB	TOT	AST	PF	DQ	STL	TO	BLK	PTS	RPG	APG	PPG
67-68–Pittsburgh (A)	16	–	146	26	76	.342	3	13	.231	8	13	.615	–	–	33	13	34	0	–	10	–	63	2.1	0.8	3.9
68-69–Minnesota (A)	68	–	1066	155	425	.365	25	105	.238	63	103	.612	–	–	157	61	141	0	–	89	–	398	2.3	0.9	5.9
69-70–Pittsburgh (A)	70	–	2391	384	778	.494	21	74	.284	168	257	.654	–	–	267	226	195	4	–	–	–	957	3.8	3.2	13.7
70-71–Car.-Pitt. (A)	22	–	180	20	35	.571	0	3	.000	18	31	.581	–	–	25	17	34	–	–	–	–	58	1.1	0.8	2.6
71-72–Pitt.-Indiana (A)	12	–	112	13	29	.448	1	3	.333	3	4	.750	–	–	15	14	20	–	–	8	–	30	1.3	1.2	2.5
Reg. ABA Totals	188	–	3895	598	1343	.445	50	198	.253	260	408	.637	–	–	497	331	424	4	–	107	–	1506	2.6	1.8	8.0
ABA Playoff Totals	13	–	77	13	36	.361	7	18	.389	7	8	.875	–	–	16	5	22	0	–	2	–	40	1.2	0.4	3.1

Kelly, Gerard Allan (Jerry) b. June 14, 1918 Ht. 6-3 Wt. 185 College: Marshall

SEASON–TEAM	G	GS	MIN	FGM	FGA	PCT	3FGM	3FGA	PCT	FTM	FTA	PCT	O-RB	D-RB	TOT	AST	PF	DQ	STL	TO	BLK	PTS	RPG	APG	PPG
46-47–Boston	43	–	–	91	313	.291	–	–	–	74	111	.667	–	–	–	21	128	–	–	–	–	256	–	0.5	6.0
47-48–Providence	3	–	–	3	10	.300	–	–	–	0	1	.000	–	–	–	0	3	–	–	–	–	6	–	0.0	2.0
Reg. Season Totals	46	–	–	94	323	.291	–	–	–	74	112	.661	–	–	–	21	131	–	–	–	–	262	–	0.5	5.7

Kelly, Thomas Edward (Tom) b. March 5, 1924 Ht. 6-2 Wt. 170 College: New York U.

SEASON–TEAM	G	GS	MIN	FGM	FGA	PCT	3FGM	3FGA	PCT	FTM	FTA	PCT	O-RB	D-RB	TOT	AST	PF	DQ	STL	TO	BLK	PTS	RPG	APG	PPG
48-49–Boston	27	–	–	73	218	.335	–	–	–	45	73	.616	–	–	–	38	73	–	–	–	–	191	–	1.4	7.1
Reg. Season Totals	27	–	–	73	218	.335	–	–	–	45	73	.616	–	–	–	38	73	–	–	–	–	191	–	1.4	7.1

Kelser, Gregory (Greg, Special K) b. September 17, 1957 Ht. 6-7 Wt. 195 College: Michigan State

SEASON–TEAM	G	GS	MIN	FGM	FGA	PCT	3FGM	3FGA	PCT	FTM	FTA	PCT	O-RB	D-RB	TOT	AST	PF	DQ	STL	TO	BLK	PTS	RPG	APG	PPG
79-80–Detroit	50	–	1231	280	593	.472	3	15	.200	146	203	.719	124	152	276	108	176	5	60	140	34	709	5.5	2.2	14.2
80-81–Detroit	25	–	654	120	285	.421	0	2	.000	68	106	.642	53	67	120	45	89	0	34	78	29	308	4.8	1.8	12.3
81-82–Detroit-Seattle	60	10	741	116	271	.428	0	3	.000	105	160	.656	80	113	193	57	131	0	18	84	21	337	3.2	1.0	5.6
82-83–Seattle	80	9	1507	247	450	.549	0	3	.000	173	257	.673	158	245	403	97	243	5	52	149	35	667	5.0	1.2	8.3
83-84–San Diego	80	21	1783	313	603	.519	2	6	.333	250	356	.702	188	203	391	91	249	3	68	195	31	878	4.9	1.1	11.0
84-85–Indiana	10	0	114	21	53	.396	0	1	.000	20	28	.714	6	13	19	13	16	0	7	12	0	62	1.9	1.3	6.2
Reg. Season Totals	305	40	6030	1097	2255	.486	5	30	.167	762	1110	.686	609	793	1402	411	904	13	239	658	150	2961	4.6	1.3	9.7
Playoff Totals	5	0	25	2	7	.286	0	0	–	4	4	1.000	4	5	9	2	6	0	1	2	0	8	1.8	0.4	1.6

Kelso, Ben b. April 11, 1949 Ht. 6-3 Wt. 195 College: Central Michigan

SEASON–TEAM	G	GS	MIN	FGM	FGA	PCT	3FGM	3FGA	PCT	FTM	FTA	PCT	O-RB	D-RB	TOT	AST	PF	DQ	STL	TO	BLK	PTS	RPG	APG	PPG
73-74–Detroit	46	–	298	35	96	.365	–	–	–	15	22	.682	15	16	31	18	45	0	12	–	1	85	0.7	0.4	1.8
Reg. Season Totals	46	–	298	35	96	.365	–	–	–	15	22	.682	15	16	31	18	45	0	12	–	1	85	0.7	0.4	1.8
Playoff Totals	1	–	1	0	2	.000	–	–	–	0	0	–	0	1	1	1	0	0	0	–	0	0	1.0	1.0	0.0

Kemp, Shawn T. (The ReignMan) b. November 26, 1969 Ht. 6-10 Wt. 280 College: Kentucky; Trinity Valley (Texas) C.C.

SEASON–TEAM	G	GS	MIN	FGM	FGA	PCT	3FGM	3FGA	PCT	FTM	FTA	PCT	O-RB	D-RB	TOT	AST	PF	DQ	STL	TO	BLK	PTS	RPG	APG	PPG
89-90–Seattle	81	1	1120	203	424	.479	2	12	.167	117	159	.736	146	200	346	26	204	5	47	107	70	525	4.3	0.3	6.5
90-91–Seattle	81	66	2442	462	909	.508	2	12	.167	288	436	.661	267	412	679	144	319	11	77	202	123	1214	8.4	1.8	15.0
91-92–Seattle	64	23	1808	362	718	.504	0	3	.000	270	361	.748	264	401	665	86	261	13	70	156	124	994	10.4	1.3	15.5
92-93–Seattle	78	68	2582	515	1047	.492	0	4	.000	358	503	.712	287	546	833	155	327	13	119	217	146	1388	10.7	2.0	17.8
93-94–Seattle	79	73	2597	533	990	.538	1	4	.250	364	491	.741	312	539	851	207	312	11	142	259	166	1431	10.8	2.6	18.1
94-95–Seattle	82	79	2679	545	997	.547	2	7	.286	438	585	.749	318	575	893	149	337	9	102	259	122	1530	10.9	1.8	18.7
95-96–Seattle	79	76	2631	526	937	.561	5	12	.417	493	664	.742	276	628	904	173	299	6	93	315	127	1550	11.4	2.2	19.6
96-97–Seattle	81	75	2750	526	1032	.510	12	33	.364	452	609	.742	275	532	807	156	320	11	125	280	81	1516	10.0	1.9	18.7
97-98–Cleveland	80	80	2769	518	1164	.445	2	8	.250	404	556	.727	219	526	745	197	310	15	108	271	90	1442	9.3	2.5	18.0
98-99–Cleveland	42	42	1475	277	575	.482	1	2	.500	307	389	.789	131	257	388	101	159	2	48	127	45	862	9.2	2.4	20.5
99-00–Cleveland	82	82	2492	484	1160	.417	2	6	.333	493	635	.776	231	494	725	138	371	13	100	291	96	1463	8.8	1.7	17.8
Reg. Season Totals	829	665	25345	4951	9953	.497	29	103	.282	3984	5388	.739	2726	5110	7836	1532	3219	109	1031	2484	1190	13915	9.5	1.8	16.8
Playoff Totals	78	78	2830	504	1004	.502	3	15	.200	479	600	.798	311	519	830	161	325	8	98	269	137	1490	10.6	2.1	19.1
All-Star Totals	6	5	120	22	48	.458	1	5	.200	9	12	.750	13	22	35	10	19	0	6	18	4	54	5.8	1.7	9.0

Kempton, Timothy Joseph (Tim) b. January 25, 1964 Ht. 6-10 Wt. 255 College: Notre Dame

SEASON–TEAM	G	GS	MIN	FGM	FGA	PCT	3FGM	3FGA	PCT	FTM	FTA	PCT	O-RB	D-RB	TOT	AST	PF	DQ	STL	TO	BLK	PTS	RPG	APG	PPG
86-87–L.A. Clippers	66	6	936	97	206	.471	0	1	.000	95	137	.693	70	124	194	53	162	6	38	49	12	289	2.9	0.8	4.4
88-89–Charlotte	79	0	1341	171	335	.510	0	1	.000	142	207	.686	91	213	304	102	215	3	41	121	14	484	3.8	1.3	6.1
89-90–Denver	71	14	1061	153	312	.490	0	1	.000	77	114	.675	51	167	218	118	144	2	30	80	9	383	3.1	1.7	5.4
92-93–Phoenix	30	0	167	19	48	.396	0	0	–	18	31	.581	12	27	39	19	30	0	4	16	4	56	1.3	0.6	1.9
93-94–Phoenix-Cha.-Clev.	13	0	136	15	38	.395	0	0	–	9	16	.563	10	14	24	9	33	0	6	11	2	39	1.8	0.7	3.0
95-96–Atlanta	3	0	11	0	0	–	0	0	–	0	0	–	0	2	2	1	5	0	0	1	0	0	0.7	0.3	0.0
96-97–San Antonio	10	0	59	1	5	.200	0	0	–	2	2	1.000	3	5	8	2	4	0	1	7	1	4	0.8	0.2	0.4
97-98–Orlando-Toronto	8	0	47	2	9	.222	0	0	–	0	0	–	4	2	6	3	10	0	1	4	2	4	0.8	0.4	0.5
Reg. Season Totals	280	20	3758	458	953	.481	0	3	.000	343	507	.677	241	554	795	307	603	11	121	289	44	1259	2.8	1.1	4.5
Playoff Totals	6	2	121	17	34	.500	0	0	–	10	10	1.000	11	10	21	12	17	0	3	6	0	44	3.5	2.0	7.3

Kendrick, Frank Edward b. September 11, 1950 Ht. 6-6 Wt. 200 College: Purdue

SEASON–TEAM	G	GS	MIN	FGM	FGA	PCT	3FGM	3FGA	PCT	FTM	FTA	PCT	O-RB	D-RB	TOT	AST	PF	DQ	STL	TO	BLK	PTS	RPG	APG	PPG
74-75–Golden State	24	–	121	31	77	.403	–	–	–	18	22	.818	19	17	36	6	22	0	11	–	3	80	1.5	0.3	3.3
Reg. Season Totals	24	–	121	31	77	.403	–	–	–	18	22	.818	19	17	36	6	22	0	11	–	3	80	1.5	0.3	3.3

Kennedy, Eugene (Goo) b. August 23, 1949 Ht. 6-6 Wt. 205 College: Texas Christian

SEASON–TEAM	G	GS	MIN	FGM	FGA	PCT	3FGM	3FGA	PCT	FTM	FTA	PCT	O-RB	D-RB	TOT	AST	PF	DQ	STL	TO	BLK	PTS	RPG	APG	PPG
71-72–Dallas (A)	65	–	1453	234	406	.576	0	0	–	88	133	.662	–	–	485	65	262	–	–	75	–	556	7.5	1.0	8.6
72-73–Dallas (A)	70	–	1809	365	664	.550	0	0	–	148	232	.638	167	323	490	75	275	8	–	113	–	878	7.0	1.1	12.5
73-74–San Antonio (A)	76	–	1440	194	352	.551	0	0	–	60	87	.690	121	266	387	83	240	–	59	79	15	448	5.1	1.1	5.9
74-75–St. Louis (A)	74	–	1532	281	536	.524	1	1	1.000	129	178	.725	171	202	373	59	190	–	64	92	10	692	5.0	0.8	9.4
75-76–Utah (A)	16	–	271	38	69	.551	0	0	–	24	37	.649	30	50	80	11	43	–	10	12	2	100	5.0	0.7	6.3
76-77–Houston	32	–	277	31	58	.534	–	–	–	3	8	.375	14	37	51	6	45	1	7	–	5	65	1.6	0.2	2.0
Reg. NBA Totals	32	–	277	31	58	.534	–	–	–	3	8	.375	14	37	51	6	45	1	7	–	5	65	1.6	0.2	2.0
Reg. ABA Totals	301	–	6505	1112	2027	.549	1	1	1.000	449	667	.673	489	841	1815	293	1010	8	133	371	27	2674	6.0	1.0	8.9
NBA Playoff Totals	6	–	35	5	10	.500	–	–	–	2	2	1.000	4	8	12	–	6	0	0	–	0	12	2.0	0.0	2.0
ABA Playoff Totals	16	–	165	29	62	.468	0	1	.000	15	20	.750	15	21	42	6	31	0	1	9	1	73	2.6	0.4	4.6

Kennedy, Joseph A. (Joe) b. January 12, 1947 Ht. 6-6 Wt. 210 College: Duke

SEASON–TEAM	G	GS	MIN	FGM	FGA	PCT	3FGM	3FGA	PCT	FTM	FTA	PCT	O-RB	D-RB	TOT	AST	PF	DQ	STL	TO	BLK	PTS	RPG	APG	PPG
68-69–Seattle	72	–	1241	174	441	.395	–	–	–	98	124	.790	–	–	241	60	158	2	–	–	–	446	3.3	0.8	6.2
69-70–Seattle	14	–	82	3	34	.088	–	–	–	2	2	1.000	–	–	20	7	7	0	–	–	–	8	1.4	0.5	0.6
70-71–Pittsburgh (A)	82	–	1382	189	498	.380	0	2	.000	130	160	.813	–	–	341	73	156	–	–	–	–	508	4.2	0.9	6.2
Reg. NBA Totals	86	–	1323	177	475	.373	–	–	–	100	126	.794	–	–	261	67	165	2	–	–	–	454	3.0	0.8	5.3
Reg. ABA Totals	82	–	1382	189	498	.380	0	2	.000	130	160	.813	–	–	341	73	156	–	–	–	–	508	4.2	0.9	6.2

Kennedy, William F. (Pickles) b. May 17, 1938 Ht. 5-11 Wt. 180 College: Temple

SEASON–TEAM	G	GS	MIN	FGM	FGA	PCT	3FGM	3FGA	PCT	FTM	FTA	PCT	O-RB	D-RB	TOT	AST	PF	DQ	STL	TO	BLK	PTS	RPG	APG	PPG
60-61–Philadelphia	7	–	52	4	21	.190	–	–	–	4	6	.667	–	–	8	9	6	0	–	–	–	12	1.1	1.3	1.7
Reg. Season Totals	7	–	52	4	21	.190	–	–	–	4	6	.667	–	–	8	9	6	0	–	–	–	12	1.1	1.3	1.7

Kenon, Larry Joe **(Special K)** b. December 13, 1952 Ht. 6-9 Wt. 210 College: Amarillo (Texas) Coll. (J.C.); Memphis

SEASON–TEAM	G	GS	MIN	FGM	FGA	PCT	3FGM	3FGA	PCT	FTM	FTA	PCT	O-RB	D-RB	TOT	AST	PF	DQ	STL	TO	BLK	PTS	RPG	APG	PPG
73-74–New York (A)	84	–	2908	589	1274	.462	0	1	.000	156	222	.703	375	587	962	112	251	–	79	250	19	1334	11.5	1.3	15.9
74-75–New York (A)	84	–	3165	676	1327	.509	1	2	.500	217	282	.770	279	621	900	122	229	–	107	206	30	1570	10.7	1.5	18.7
75-76–San Antonio (A)	81	–	2920	647	1344	.481	0	1	.000	221	283	.781	287	610	897	151	165	–	91	243	43	1515	11.1	1.9	18.7
76-77–San Antonio	78	–	2936	706	1435	.492	–	–	–	293	356	.823	282	597	879	229	190	0	167	–	60	1705	11.3	2.9	21.9
77-78–San Antonio	81	–	2869	698	1426	.489	–	–	–	276	323	.854	245	528	773	268	209	2	115	279	24	1672	9.5	3.3	20.6
78-79–San Antonio	81	–	2947	748	1484	.504	–	–	–	295	349	.845	260	530	790	335	192	1	154	300	19	1791	9.8	4.1	22.1
79-80–San Antonio	78	–	2798	647	1333	.485	1	9	.111	270	345	.783	258	517	775	231	192	0	111	232	18	1565	9.9	3.0	20.1
80-81–Chicago	77	–	2161	454	946	.480	0	0	–	180	245	.735	179	219	398	120	160	2	75	161	18	1088	5.2	1.6	14.1
81-82–Chicago	60	30	1036	192	412	.466	0	0	–	50	88	.568	72	108	180	65	71	0	30	82	7	434	3.0	1.1	7.2
82-83–Chicago-G.S.-Clev.	48	7	770	119	257	.463	0	1	.000	42	57	.737	66	81	147	39	64	0	23	47	9	280	3.1	0.8	5.8
Reg. NBA Totals	503	37	15517	3564	7293	.489	1	10	.100	1406	1763	.798	1362	2580	3942	1287	1078	5	675	1101	155	8535	7.8	2.6	17.0
Reg. ABA Totals	249	–	8993	1912	3945	.485	1	4	.250	594	787	.755	941	1818	2759	385	645	0	277	699	92	4419	11.1	1.5	17.7
NBA Playoff Totals	31	0	1031	218	508	.429	0	1	.000	65	93	.699	99	171	270	82	84	1	34	58	5	501	8.7	2.6	16.2
ABA Playoff Totals	26	–	946	209	423	.494	1	3	.333	59	78	.756	118	189	307	46	66	0	30	90	6	478	11.8	1.8	18.4
NBA All-Star Totals	2	1	27	9	18	.500	0	0	–	1	2	.500	3	3	6	1	0	0	0	2	0	19	3.0	0.5	9.5

Kenville, William McGill **(Billy, The Kid)** b. December 1, 1930 Ht. 6-2 Wt. 190 College: St. Bonaventure

SEASON–TEAM	G	GS	MIN	FGM	FGA	PCT	3FGM	3FGA	PCT	FTM	FTA	PCT	O-RB	D-RB	TOT	AST	PF	DQ	STL	TO	BLK	PTS	RPG	APG	PPG
53-54–Syracuse	72	–	1405	149	388	.384	–	–	–	136	182	.747	–	–	247	122	138	0	–	–	–	434	3.4	1.7	6.0
54-55–Syracuse	70	–	1380	172	482	.357	–	–	–	154	201	.766	–	–	247	150	132	1	–	–	–	498	3.5	2.1	7.1
55-56–Syracuse	72	–	1278	170	448	.379	–	–	–	195	257	.759	–	–	215	159	132	0	–	–	–	535	3.0	2.2	7.4
56-57–Fort Wayne	71	–	1701	204	608	.336	–	–	–	174	218	.798	–	–	324	172	169	3	–	–	–	582	4.6	2.4	8.2
57-58–Detroit	35	–	649	106	280	.379	–	–	–	46	75	.613	–	–	102	66	68	0	–	–	–	258	2.9	1.9	7.4
59-60–Detroit	25	–	365	47	131	.359	–	–	–	33	41	.805	–	–	71	46	31	0	–	–	–	127	2.8	1.8	5.1
Reg. Season Totals	345	–	6778	848	2337	.363	–	–	–	738	974	.758	–	–	1206	715	670	4	–	–	–	2434	3.5	2.1	7.1
Playoff Totals	41	–	990	89	223	.399	–	–	–	106	153	.693	–	–	155	74	103	2	–	–	–	284	3.0	1.5	6.9

Kerner, Jonathan b. June 6, 1974 Ht. 6-11 Wt. 245 College: East Carolina

SEASON–TEAM	G	GS	MIN	FGM	FGA	PCT	3FGM	3FGA	PCT	FTM	FTA	PCT	O-RB	D-RB	TOT	AST	PF	DQ	STL	TO	BLK	PTS	RPG	APG	PPG
98-99–Orlando	1	0	5	0	1	.000	0	0	–	0	0	–	0	0	0	0	2	0	0	0	0	0	0.0	0.0	0.0
Reg. Season Totals	1	0	5	0	1	.000	0	0	–	0	0	–	0	0	0	0	2	0	0	0	0	0	0.0	0.0	0.0

Kerr, John G. **(Johnny, Red)** b. July 17, 1932 Ht. 6-9 Wt. 230 College: Illinois

SEASON–TEAM	G	GS	MIN	FGM	FGA	PCT	3FGM	3FGA	PCT	FTM	FTA	PCT	O-RB	D-RB	TOT	AST	PF	DQ	STL	TO	BLK	PTS	RPG	APG	PPG
54-55–Syracuse	72	–	1529	301	718	.419	–	–	–	152	223	.682	–	–	474	80	165	2	–	–	–	754	6.6	1.1	10.5
55-56–Syracuse	72	–	2114	377	935	.403	–	–	–	207	316	.655	–	–	607	84	168	3	–	–	–	961	8.4	1.2	13.3
56-57–Syracuse	72	–	2191	333	827	.403	–	–	–	225	313	.719	–	–	807	90	190	3	–	–	–	891	11.2	1.3	12.4
57-58–Syracuse	72	–	2384	407	1020	.399	–	–	–	280	422	.664	–	–	963	88	197	4	–	–	–	1094	13.4	1.2	15.2
58-59–Syracuse	72	–	2671	502	1139	.441	–	–	–	281	367	.766	–	–	1008	142	183	1	–	–	–	1285	14.0	2.0	17.8
59-60–Syracuse	75	–	2372	436	1111	.392	–	–	–	233	310	.752	–	–	913	167	207	4	–	–	–	1105	12.2	2.2	14.7
60-61–Syracuse	79	–	2676	419	1056	.397	–	–	–	218	299	.729	–	–	951	199	230	4	–	–	–	1056	12.0	2.5	13.4
61-62–Syracuse	80	–	2768	541	1220	.443	–	–	–	222	302	.735	–	–	1176	243	272	7	–	–	–	1304	14.7	3.0	16.3
62-63–Syracuse	80	–	2561	507	1069	.474	–	–	–	241	320	.753	–	–	1039	214	208	3	–	–	–	1255	13.0	2.7	15.7
63-64–Philadelphia	80	–	2938	536	1250	.429	–	–	–	268	357	.751	–	–	1017	275	187	2	–	–	–	1340	12.7	3.4	16.8
64-65–Philadelphia	80	–	1810	264	714	.370	–	–	–	126	181	.696	–	–	551	197	132	1	–	–	–	654	6.9	2.5	8.2
65-66–Baltimore	71	–	1770	286	692	.413	–	–	–	209	272	.768	–	–	586	225	148	0	–	–	–	781	8.3	3.2	11.0
Reg. Season Totals	905	–	27784	4909	11751	.418	–	–	–	2662	3682	.723	–	–	10092	2004	2287	34	–	–	–	12480	11.2	2.2	13.8
Playoff Totals	76	–	2275	370	959	.386	–	–	–	193	281	.687	–	–	827	152	173	0	–	–	–	933	10.9	2.0	12.3
All-Star Totals	3	–	48	5	22	.227	–	–	–	3	5	.600	–	–	19	3	5	0	–	–	–	13	6.3	1.0	4.3

Kerr, Stephen Douglas **(Steve)** b. September 27, 1965 Ht. 6-3 Wt. 180 College: Arizona

SEASON–TEAM	G	GS	MIN	FGM	FGA	PCT	3FGM	3FGA	PCT	FTM	FTA	PCT	O-RB	D-RB	TOT	AST	PF	DQ	STL	TO	BLK	PTS	RPG	APG	PPG
88-89–Phoenix	26	0	157	20	46	.435	8	17	.471	6	9	.667	3	14	17	24	12	0	7	6	0	54	0.7	0.9	2.1
89-90–Cleveland	78	5	1664	192	432	.444	73	144	.507	63	73	.863	12	86	98	248	59	0	45	74	7	520	1.3	3.2	6.7
90-91–Cleveland	57	4	905	99	223	.444	28	62	.452	45	53	.849	5	32	37	131	52	0	29	40	4	271	0.6	2.3	4.8
91-92–Cleveland	48	20	847	121	237	.511	32	74	.432	45	54	.833	14	64	78	110	29	0	27	31	10	319	1.6	2.3	6.6
92-93–Clev.-Orlando	52	0	481	53	122	.434	6	26	.231	22	24	.917	5	40	45	70	36	0	10	27	1	134	0.9	1.3	2.6
93-94–Chicago	82	0	2036	287	577	.497	52	124	.419	83	97	.856	26	105	131	210	97	0	75	57	3	709	1.6	2.6	8.6
94-95–Chicago	82	0	1839	261	495	.527	89	170	.524	63	81	.778	20	99	119	151	114	0	44	48	3	674	1.5	1.8	8.2
95-96–Chicago	82	0	1919	244	482	.506	122	237	.515	78	84	.929	25	85	110	192	109	0	63	42	2	688	1.3	2.3	8.4
96-97–Chicago	82	0	1861	249	467	.533	110	237	.464	54	67	.806	29	101	130	175	98	0	67	43	3	662	1.6	2.1	8.1
97-98–Chicago	50	0	1119	137	302	.454	57	130	.438	45	49	.918	14	63	77	96	71	0	26	27	5	376	1.5	1.9	7.5
98-99–San Antonio	44	0	734	68	174	.391	25	80	.313	31	35	.886	6	38	44	49	28	0	23	22	3	192	1.0	1.1	4.4
99-00–San Antonio	32	0	268	32	74	.432	16	31	.516	9	11	.818	3	16	19	12	14	0	4	7	0	89	0.6	0.4	2.8
Reg. Season Totals	715	29	13830	1763	3631	.486	618	1332	.464	544	637	.854	162	743	905	1468	719	0	420	424	41	4688	1.3	2.1	6.6
Playoff Totals	106	3	1811	167	401	.416	72	198	.364	76	86	.884	23	71	94	139	122	0	57	37	2	482	0.9	1.3	4.5

Kerris, John E. **(Jack)** b. January 30, 1925 Ht. 6-6 Wt. 215 College: Loyola (Chicago)

SEASON–TEAM	G	GS	MIN	FGM	FGA	PCT	3FGM	3FGA	PCT	FTM	FTA	PCT	O-RB	D-RB	TOT	AST	PF	DQ	STL	TO	BLK	PTS	RPG	APG	PPG
49-50–Tri-Cit-FtWayne	68	–	–	157	481	.326	–	–	–	169	260	.650	–	–	–	118	175	–	–	–	–	483	–	1.7	7.1
50-51–Fort Wayne	68	–	–	255	689	.370	–	–	–	201	295	.681	–	–	477	181	253	12	–	–	–	711	7.0	2.7	10.5
51-52–Fort Wayne	66	–	2148	186	480	.388	–	–	–	217	325	.668	–	–	514	212	265	16	–	–	–	589	7.8	3.2	8.9
52-53–FtWayne-Balt.	69	–	1424	93	256	.363	–	–	–	88	140	.629	–	–	295	156	165	7	–	–	–	274	4.3	2.3	4.0
Reg. Season Totals	271	–	3572	691	1906	.363	–	–	–	675	1020	.662	–	–	1286	667	858	35	–	–	–	2057	6.3	2.5	7.6
Playoff Totals	11	–	157	30	92	.337	–	–	–	32	58	.552	–	–	58	33	47	3	–	–	–	92	6.4	2.5	8.4

Kersey, Jerome b. June 26, 1962 Ht. 6-7 Wt. 245 College: Longwood

SEASON–TEAM	G	GS	MIN	FGM	FGA	PCT	3FGM	3FGA	PCT	FTM	FTA	PCT	O-RB	D-RB	TOT	AST	PF	DQ	STL	TO	BLK	PTS	RPG	APG	PPG
84-85–Portland	77	0	958	178	372	.478	0	3	.000	117	181	.646	95	111	206	63	147	1	49	66	29	473	2.7	0.8	6.1
85-86–Portland	79	2	1217	258	470	.549	0	6	.000	156	229	.681	137	156	293	83	208	2	85	113	32	672	3.7	1.1	8.5
86-87–Portland	82	8	2088	373	733	.509	1	23	.043	262	364	.720	201	295	496	194	328	5	122	149	77	1009	6.0	2.4	12.3
87-88–Portland	79	75	2888	611	1225	.499	3	15	.200	291	396	.735	211	446	657	243	302	8	127	161	65	1516	8.3	3.1	19.2
88-89–Portland	76	76	2716	533	1137	.469	6	21	.286	258	372	.694	246	383	629	243	277	6	137	167	84	1330	8.3	3.2	17.5
89-90–Portland	82	82	2843	519	1085	.478	3	20	.150	269	390	.690	251	439	690	188	304	7	121	144	63	1310	8.4	2.3	16.0
90-91–Portland	73	72	2359	424	887	.478	4	13	.308	232	327	.709	169	312	481	227	251	4	101	149	76	1084	6.6	3.1	14.8
91-92–Portland	77	76	2553	398	852	.467	1	8	.125	174	262	.664	241	392	633	243	254	1	114	151	71	971	8.2	3.2	12.6
92-93–Portland	65	50	1719	281	642	.438	8	28	.286	116	183	.634	126	280	406	121	181	2	80	84	41	686	6.2	1.9	10.6
93-94–Portland	78	6	1276	203	469	.433	1	8	.125	101	135	.748	130	201	331	75	213	1	71	63	49	508	4.2	1.0	6.5
94-95–Portland	63	0	1143	203	489	.415	7	27	.259	95	124	.766	93	163	256	82	173	1	52	64	35	508	4.1	1.3	8.1
95-96–Golden State	76	58	1620	205	500	.410	3	17	.176	97	147	.660	154	209	363	114	205	2	91	75	45	510	4.8	1.5	6.7
96-97–L.A. Lakers	70	44	1766	194	449	.432	17	65	.262	71	118	.602	112	251	363	89	219	0	119	74	49	476	5.2	1.3	6.8
97-98–Seattle	37	2	717	97	233	.416	1	10	.100	39	65	.600	56	79	135	44	104	1	52	36	14	234	3.6	1.2	6.3
98-99–San Antonio	45	0	699	68	200	.340	3	14	.214	6	14	.429	42	88	130	41	92	1	37	30	14	145	2.9	0.9	3.2
99-00–San Antonio	72	18	1310	146	354	.412	0	9	.000	29	41	.707	58	167	225	69	161	0	67	51	47	321	3.1	1.0	4.5
Reg. Season Totals	1131	569	27872	4691	10097	.465	58	287	.202	2313	3348	.691	2322	3972	6294	2119	3419	42	1425	1577	791	11753	5.6	1.9	10.4
Playoff Totals	126	71	3394	599	1277	.469	2	21	.095	357	491	.727	283	434	717	233	427	10	168	163	80	1557	5.7	1.8	12.4

Kerwin, Thomas Vincent **(Tom)** b. July 7, 1944 Ht. 6-7 Wt. 210 College: Centenary

SEASON–TEAM	G	GS	MIN	FGM	FGA	PCT	3FGM	3FGA	PCT	FTM	FTA	PCT	O-RB	D-RB	TOT	AST	PF	DQ	STL	TO	BLK	PTS	RPG	APG	PPG
67-68–Pittsburgh (A)	13	–	68	7	22	.318	0	0	–	0	2	.000	–	–	20	1	5	0	–	2	–	14	1.5	0.1	1.1
Reg. ABA Totals	13	–	68	7	22	.318	0	0	–	0	2	.000	–	–	20	1	5	0	–	2	–	14	1.5	0.1	1.1

Kessler, Alec Christopher b. January 13, 1967 Ht. 6-11 Wt. 250 College: Georgia

SEASON–TEAM	G	GS	MIN	FGM	FGA	PCT	3FGM	3FGA	PCT	FTM	FTA	PCT	O-RB	D-RB	TOT	AST	PF	DQ	STL	TO	BLK	PTS	RPG	APG	PPG
90-91–Miami	78	18	1259	199	468	.425	0	4	.000	88	131	.672	115	221	336	31	189	1	17	108	26	486	4.3	0.4	6.2
91-92–Miami	77	4	1197	158	383	.413	0	0	–	94	115	.817	114	200	314	34	185	3	17	58	32	410	4.1	0.4	5.3
92-93–Miami	40	2	415	57	122	.467	5	11	.455	36	47	.766	25	66	91	14	63	0	4	21	12	155	2.3	0.4	3.9
93-94–Miami	15	0	66	11	25	.440	5	9	.556	6	8	.750	4	6	10	2	14	0	1	5	1	33	0.7	0.1	2.2
Reg. Season Totals	210	24	2937	425	998	.426	10	24	.417	224	301	.744	258	493	751	81	451	4	39	192	71	1084	3.6	0.4	5.2
Playoff Totals	2	0	12	0	2	.000	0	0	–	2	2	1.000	0	1	1	–	1	0	0	1	0	2	0.5	0.0	1.0

Ketner, Lari Arthur b. February 1, 1977 Ht. 6-10 Wt. 285 College: Massachusetts

SEASON–TEAM	G	GS	MIN	FGM	FGA	PCT	3FGM	3FGA	PCT	FTM	FTA	PCT	O-RB	D-RB	TOT	AST	PF	DQ	STL	TO	BLK	PTS	RPG	APG	PPG
99-00–Chicago-Clev.	22	0	132	13	32	.406	0	0	–	8	12	.667	12	22	34	1	20	1	4	10	3	34	1.5	0.0	1.5
Reg. Season Totals	22	0	132	13	32	.406	0	0	–	8	12	.667	12	22	34	1	20	1	4	10	3	34	1.5	0.0	1.5

Keye, Julius b. September 5, 1946 d. September 13, 1984 Ht. 6-10 Wt. 225 College: Alcorn State; South Carolina State

SEASON–TEAM	G	GS	MIN	FGM	FGA	PCT	3FGM	3FGA	PCT	FTM	FTA	PCT	O-RB	D-RB	TOT	AST	PF	DQ	STL	TO	BLK	PTS	RPG	APG	PPG
69-70–Denver (A)	77	–	1641	245	618	.396	0	7	.000	116	193	.601	–	–	530	47	209	2	–	–	–	606	6.9	0.6	7.9
70-71–Denver (A)	83	–	3634	505	1182	.427	0	5	.000	212	317	.669	370	1084	1454	140	317	–	–	–	–	1222	17.5	1.7	14.7
71-72–Denver (A)	84	–	2557	192	476	.403	0	2	.000	108	174	.621	315	667	982	153	346	–	–	139	–	492	11.7	1.8	5.9
72-73–Denver (A)	83	–	3016	163	375	.435	3	8	.375	130	233	.558	275	617	892	180	269	3	–	134	–	459	10.7	2.2	5.5
73-74–Denver (A)	79	–	2595	147	329	.447	1	5	.200	57	84	.679	225	464	689	135	240	–	40	87	149	352	8.7	1.7	4.5
74-75–Memphis (A)	12	–	233	12	47	.255	0	0	–	6	8	.750	16	39	55	2	26	–	4	8	5	30	4.6	0.2	2.5
Reg. ABA Totals	418	–	13676	1264	3027	.418	4	27	.148	629	1009	.623	1201	2871	4602	657	1407	5	44	368	154	3161	11.0	1.6	7.6
ABA Playoff Totals	19	–	643	57	135	.422	0	2	.000	15	31	.484	73	108	210	42	62	0	0	21	17	129	11.1	2.2	6.8

Keys, Randolph **(Rudy)** b. April 19, 1966 Ht. 6-7 Wt. 210 College: Southern Mississippi

SEASON–TEAM	G	GS	MIN	FGM	FGA	PCT	3FGM	3FGA	PCT	FTM	FTA	PCT	O-RB	D-RB	TOT	AST	PF	DQ	STL	TO	BLK	PTS	RPG	APG	PPG
88-89–Cleveland	42	0	331	74	172	.430	1	10	.100	20	29	.690	23	33	56	19	51	0	12	21	6	169	1.3	0.5	4.0
89-90–Clev.-Cha.	80	18	1615	293	678	.432	14	43	.326	101	140	.721	100	153	253	88	224	1	68	84	8	701	3.2	1.1	8.8
90-91–Charlotte	44	0	473	59	145	.407	3	14	.214	19	33	.576	40	60	100	18	93	0	22	35	15	140	2.3	0.4	3.2
94-95–L.A. Lakers	6	0	83	9	26	.346	0	9	.000	2	2	1.000	6	11	17	2	16	0	1	2	2	20	2.8	0.3	3.3
95-96–Milwaukee	69	1	816	87	208	.418	22	71	.310	36	43	.837	41	84	125	65	139	2	32	33	14	232	1.8	0.9	3.4
Reg. Season Totals	241	19	3318	522	1229	.425	40	147	.272	178	247	.721	210	341	551	192	523	3	135	175	45	1262	2.3	0.8	5.2
Playoff Totals	1	0	12	0	3	.000	0	1	.000	0	0	–	0	3	3	1	1	0	0	2	0	0	3.0	1.0	0.0

Kidd, Jason Fredrick b. March 23, 1973 Ht. 6-4 Wt. 212 College: California

SEASON–TEAM	G	GS	MIN	FGM	FGA	PCT	3FGM	3FGA	PCT	FTM	FTA	PCT	O-RB	D-RB	TOT	AST	PF	DQ	STL	TO	BLK	PTS	RPG	APG	PPG
94-95–Dallas	79	79	2668	330	857	.385	70	257	.272	192	275	.698	152	278	430	607	146	0	151	250	24	922	5.4	7.7	11.7
95-96–Dallas	81	81	3034	493	1293	.381	133	396	.336	229	331	.692	203	350	553	783	155	0	175	328	26	1348	6.8	9.7	16.6
96-97–Dallas-Phoenix	55	45	1964	213	529	.403	61	165	.370	112	165	.679	64	185	249	496	114	0	124	142	20	599	4.5	9.0	10.9
97-98–Phoenix	82	82	3118	357	859	.416	73	233	.313	167	209	.799	108	402	510	745	142	0	162	261	26	954	6.2	9.1	11.6
98-99–Phoenix	50	50	2060	310	698	.444	45	123	.366	181	239	.757	87	252	339	539	108	1	114	150	19	846	6.8	10.8	16.9
99-00–Phoenix	67	67	2616	350	855	.409	56	166	.337	203	245	.829	96	387	483	678	148	2	134	226	28	959	7.2	10.1	14.3
Reg. Season Totals	414	404	15460	2053	5091	.403	438	1340	.327	1084	1464	.740	710	1854	2564	3848	813	3	860	1357	143	5628	6.2	9.3	13.6
Playoff Totals	18	18	733	83	209	.397	20	67	.299	35	51	.686	18	82	100	164	50	0	43	57	6	221	5.6	9.1	12.3
All-Star Totals	3	2	75	7	14	.500	4	8	.500	0	0	–	2	10	12	33	3	0	6	10	0	18	4.0	11.0	6.0

Kidd, Warren Lynn b. September 9, 1970 Ht. 6-9 Wt. 235 College: Middle Tennessee State

SEASON–TEAM	G	GS	MIN	FGM	FGA	PCT	3FGM	3FGA	PCT	FTM	FTA	PCT	O-RB	D-RB	TOT	AST	PF	DQ	STL	TO	BLK	PTS	RPG	APG	PPG
93-94–Philadelphia	68	14	884	100	169	.592	0	0	–	47	86	.547	76	157	233	19	129	0	19	44	23	247	3.4	0.3	3.6
Reg. Season Totals	68	14	884	100	169	.592	0	0	–	47	86	.547	76	157	233	19	129	0	19	44	23	247	3.4	0.3	3.6

Kiffin, Irvin A. Jr. b. August 8, 1951 Ht. 6-9 Wt. 225 College: Virginia Union; Oklahoma Baptist

SEASON–TEAM	G	GS	MIN	FGM	FGA	PCT	3FGM	3FGA	PCT	FTM	FTA	PCT	O-RB	D-RB	TOT	AST	PF	DQ	STL	TO	BLK	PTS	RPG	APG	PPG
79-80–San Antonio	26	–	212	32	96	.333	0	0	–	18	25	.720	12	28	40	19	43	0	10	30	2	82	1.5	0.7	3.2
Reg. Season Totals	26	–	212	32	96	.333	0	0	–	18	25	.720	12	28	40	19	43	0	10	30	2	82	1.5	0.7	3.2

Kiley, John F. (Jack) b. January 5, 1929 d. February 16, 1982 Ht. 6-1 Wt. 170 College: Syracuse

SEASON–TEAM	G	GS	MIN	FGM	FGA	PCT	3FGM	3FGA	PCT	FTM	FTA	PCT	O-RB	D-RB	TOT	AST	PF	DQ	STL	TO	BLK	PTS	RPG	APG	PPG
51-52–Fort Wayne	47	–	477	44	193	.228	–	–	–	30	54	.556	–	–	49	62	54	2	–	–	–	118	1.0	1.3	2.5
52-53–Fort Wayne	6	–	27	2	10	.200	–	–	–	2	2	1.000	–	–	2	3	7	0	–	–	–	6	0.3	0.5	1.0
Reg. Season Totals	53	–	504	46	203	.227	–	–	–	32	56	.571	–	–	51	65	61	2	–	–	–	124	1.0	1.2	2.3
Playoff Totals	1	–	4	1	6	.333	–	–	–	0	0	–	–	–	0	2	0	0	–	–	–	2	0.0	1.0	2.0

Killum, Earnest (Ernie) b. June 11, 1948 Ht. 6-3 Wt. 185 College: Stetson

SEASON–TEAM	G	GS	MIN	FGM	FGA	PCT	3FGM	3FGA	PCT	FTM	FTA	PCT	O-RB	D-RB	TOT	AST	PF	DQ	STL	TO	BLK	PTS	RPG	APG	PPG
70-71–Los Angeles	4	–	12	0	4	.000	–	–	–	1	1	1.000	–	–	2	0	1	0	–	–	–	1	0.5	0.0	0.3
Reg. Season Totals	4	–	12	0	4	.000	–	–	–	1	1	1.000	–	–	2	0	1	0	–	–	–	1	0.5	0.0	0.3
Playoff Totals	2	–	4	1	1	1.000	–	–	–	2	3	.667	–	–	0	–	1	0	–	–	–	4	0.0	0.0	2.0

Kilpatrick, Carl b. May 16, 1956 Ht. 6-10 Wt. 230 College: Kilgore (Texas) Coll. (J.C.); Louisiana-Monroe

SEASON–TEAM	G	GS	MIN	FGM	FGA	PCT	3FGM	3FGA	PCT	FTM	FTA	PCT	O-RB	D-RB	TOT	AST	PF	DQ	STL	TO	BLK	PTS	RPG	APG	PPG
79-80–Utah	2	–	6	1	2	.500	0	0	–	1	2	.500	1	3	4	0	1	0	0	0	0	3	2.0	0.0	1.5
Reg. Season Totals	2	–	6	1	2	.500	0	0	–	1	2	.500	1	3	4	0	1	0	0	0	0	3	2.0	0.0	1.5

Kimball, Thomas (Toby) b. September 7, 1942 Ht. 6-8 Wt. 220 College: Connecticut

SEASON–TEAM	G	GS	MIN	FGM	FGA	PCT	3FGM	3FGA	PCT	FTM	FTA	PCT	O-RB	D-RB	TOT	AST	PF	DQ	STL	TO	BLK	PTS	RPG	APG	PPG
66-67–Boston	38	–	222	35	97	.361	–	–	–	27	40	.675	–	–	146	13	42	0	–	–	–	97	3.8	0.3	2.6
67-68–San Diego	81	–	2519	354	894	.396	–	–	–	181	306	.592	–	–	947	147	273	3	–	–	–	889	11.7	1.8	11.0
68-69–San Diego	76	–	1680	239	537	.445	–	–	–	117	250	.468	–	–	669	90	216	6	–	–	–	595	8.8	1.2	7.8
69-70–San Diego	77	–	1622	218	508	.429	–	–	–	107	185	.578	–	–	621	95	187	1	–	–	–	543	8.1	1.2	7.1
70-71–San Diego	80	–	1100	111	287	.387	–	–	–	51	108	.472	–	–	406	62	128	1	–	–	–	273	5.1	0.8	3.4
71-72–Milwaukee	74	–	971	107	229	.467	–	–	–	44	81	.543	–	–	312	60	137	0	–	–	–	258	4.2	0.8	3.5
72-73–K.C.-Omaha	67	–	643	96	220	.436	–	–	–	44	67	.657	–	–	191	27	86	2	–	–	–	236	2.9	0.4	3.5
73-74–Philadelphia	75	1	1592	216	456	.474	–	–	–	127	185	.686	185	367	552	73	199	1	49	–	23	559	7.4	1.0	7.5
74-75–New Orleans	3	–	90	7	23	.304	–	–	–	6	7	.857	8	18	26	4	12	0	2	–	0	20	8.7	1.3	6.7
Reg. Season Totals	571	1	10439	1383	3251	.425	–	–	–	704	1229	.573	193	385	3870	571	1280	14	51	–	23	3470	6.8	1.0	6.1
Playoff Totals	14	–	237	28	67	.418	–	–	–	15	27	.556	0	0	83	6	21	0	0	–	0	71	5.9	0.4	5.1

Kimble, Gregory Kevin (Bo) b. April 9, 1966 Ht. 6-4 Wt. 190 College: USC; Loyola Marymount

SEASON–TEAM	G	GS	MIN	FGM	FGA	PCT	3FGM	3FGA	PCT	FTM	FTA	PCT	O-RB	D-RB	TOT	AST	PF	DQ	STL	TO	BLK	PTS	RPG	APG	PPG
90-91–L.A. Clippers	62	22	1004	159	418	.380	19	65	.292	92	119	.773	42	77	119	76	158	2	30	77	8	429	1.9	1.2	6.9
91-92–L.A. Clippers	34	0	277	44	111	.396	4	13	.308	20	31	.645	13	19	32	17	37	0	10	15	6	112	0.9	0.5	3.3
92-93–New York	9	0	55	14	33	.424	2	8	.250	3	8	.375	3	8	11	5	10	0	1	6	0	33	1.2	0.6	3.7
Reg. Season Totals	105	22	1336	217	562	.386	25	86	.291	115	158	.728	58	104	162	98	205	2	41	98	14	574	1.5	0.9	5.5
Playoff Totals	3	0	5	0	1	.000	0	0	–	0	0	–	0	0	0	1	2	0	0	1	0	0	0.0	0.3	0.0

Kimbrough, Stan b. April 24, 1966 Ht. 5-11 Wt. 155 College: Central Florida; Xavier (Ohio)

SEASON–TEAM	G	GS	MIN	FGM	FGA	PCT	3FGM	3FGA	PCT	FTM	FTA	PCT	O-RB	D-RB	TOT	AST	PF	DQ	STL	TO	BLK	PTS	RPG	APG	PPG
89-90–Detroit	10	0	50	7	16	.438	0	0	–	2	2	1.000	4	3	7	5	4	0	4	4	0	16	0.7	0.5	1.6
92-93–Sacramento	3	0	15	2	6	.333	1	2	.500	0	0	–	0	0	0	1	1	0	1	0	0	5	0.0	0.3	1.7
Reg. Season Totals	13	0	65	9	22	.409	1	2	.500	2	2	1.000	4	3	7	6	5	0	5	4	0	21	0.5	0.5	1.6

K

Kinch, Chadwick Oliver (Chad) b. May 22, 1958 d. April 3, 1994 Ht. 6-4 Wt. 190 College: North Carolina-Charlotte

SEASON–TEAM	G	GS	MIN	FGM	FGA	PCT	3FGM	3FGA	PCT	FTM	FTA	PCT	O-RB	D-RB	TOT	AST	PF	DQ	STL	TO	BLK	PTS	RPG	APG	PPG
80-81–Clev.-Dallas	41	–	353	52	141	.369	0	0	–	14	18	.778	7	26	33	45	33	0	11	30	6	118	0.8	1.1	2.9
Reg. Season Totals	41	–	353	52	141	.369	0	0	–	14	18	.778	7	26	33	45	33	0	11	30	6	118	0.8	1.1	2.9

King, Albert b. December 17, 1959 Ht. 6-6 Wt. 215 College: Maryland

SEASON–TEAM	G	GS	MIN	FGM	FGA	PCT	3FGM	3FGA	PCT	FTM	FTA	PCT	O-RB	D-RB	TOT	AST	PF	DQ	STL	TO	BLK	PTS	RPG	APG	PPG
81-82–New Jersey	76	52	1694	391	812	.482	3	13	.231	133	171	.778	105	207	312	142	261	4	64	180	36	918	4.1	1.9	12.1
82-83–New Jersey	79	75	2447	582	1226	.475	6	23	.261	176	227	.775	157	299	456	291	278	5	95	245	41	1346	5.8	3.7	17.0
83-84–New Jersey	79	53	2103	465	946	.492	3	22	.136	232	295	.786	125	263	388	203	258	6	91	208	33	1165	4.9	2.6	14.7
84-85–New Jersey	42	7	860	226	460	.491	0	8	.000	85	104	.817	70	89	159	58	110	0	41	65	9	537	3.8	1.4	12.8
85-86–New Jersey	73	69	1998	438	961	.456	4	23	.174	167	203	.823	116	250	366	181	205	4	58	181	24	1047	5.0	2.5	14.3
86-87–New Jersey	61	15	1291	244	573	.426	13	32	.406	81	100	.810	82	132	214	103	177	5	34	103	28	582	3.5	1.7	9.5
87-88–Philadelphia	72	44	1593	211	540	.391	17	49	.347	78	103	.757	71	145	216	109	219	4	39	93	18	517	3.0	1.5	7.2
88-89–San Antonio	46	11	791	141	327	.431	8	32	.250	37	48	.771	33	107	140	79	97	2	27	74	7	327	3.0	1.7	7.1
91-92–Washington	6	0	59	11	30	.367	2	7	.286	7	8	.875	1	10	11	5	7	0	3	2	0	31	1.8	0.8	5.2
Reg. Season Totals	534	326	12836	2709	5875	.461	56	209	.268	996	1259	.791	760	1502	2262	1171	1612	30	452	1151	196	6470	4.2	2.2	12.1
Playoff Totals	21	10	624	135	298	.453	3	9	.333	54	74	.730	44	66	110	49	81	3	26	47	8	327	5.2	2.3	15.6

King, Bernard b. December 4, 1956 Ht. 6-7 Wt. 205 College: Tennessee

SEASON–TEAM	G	GS	MIN	FGM	FGA	PCT	3FGM	3FGA	PCT	FTM	FTA	PCT	O-RB	D-RB	TOT	AST	PF	DQ	STL	TO	BLK	PTS	RPG	APG	PPG
77-78–New Jersey	79	–	3092	798	1665	.479	–	–	–	313	462	.677	265	486	751	193	302	5	122	311	36	1909	9.5	2.4	24.2
78-79–New Jersey	82	–	2859	710	1359	.522	–	–	–	349	619	.564	251	418	669	295	326	10	118	323	39	1769	8.2	3.6	21.6
79-80–Utah	19	–	419	71	137	.518	0	0	–	34	63	.540	24	64	88	52	66	3	7	50	4	176	4.6	2.7	9.3
80-81–Golden State	81	–	2914	731	1244	.588	2	6	.333	307	437	.703	178	373	551	287	304	5	72	265	34	1771	6.8	3.5	21.9
81-82–Golden State	79	77	2861	740	1307	.566	1	5	.200	352	499	.705	140	329	469	282	285	6	78	267	23	1833	5.9	3.6	23.2
82-83–New York	68	68	2207	603	1142	.528	0	6	.000	280	388	.722	99	227	326	195	233	5	90	197	13	1486	4.8	2.9	21.9
83-84–New York	77	76	2667	795	1391	.572	0	4	.000	437	561	.779	123	271	394	164	273	2	75	197	17	2027	5.1	2.1	26.3
84-85–New York	55	55	2063	691	1303	.530	1	10	.100	426	552	.772	114	203	317	204	191	3	71	204	15	1809	5.8	3.7	32.9
86-87–New York	6	4	214	52	105	.495	0	0	–	32	43	.744	13	19	32	19	14	0	2	15	0	136	5.3	3.2	22.7
87-88–Washington	69	38	2044	470	938	.501	1	6	.167	247	324	.762	86	194	280	192	202	3	49	211	10	1188	4.1	2.8	17.2
88-89–Washington	81	81	2559	654	1371	.477	5	30	.167	361	441	.819	133	251	384	294	219	1	64	227	13	1674	4.7	3.6	20.7
89-90–Washington	82	82	2687	711	1459	.487	3	23	.130	412	513	.803	129	275	404	376	230	1	51	248	7	1837	4.9	4.6	22.4
90-91–Washington	64	64	2401	713	1511	.472	8	37	.216	383	485	.790	114	205	319	292	187	1	56	255	16	1817	5.0	4.6	28.4
92-93–New Jersey	32	2	430	91	177	.514	2	7	.286	39	57	.684	35	41	76	18	53	0	11	21	3	223	2.4	0.6	7.0
Reg. Season Totals	874	547	29417	7830	15109	.518	23	134	.172	3972	5444	.730	1704	3356	5060	2863	2885	45	866	2791	230	19655	5.8	3.3	22.5
Playoff Totals	28	23	934	269	481	.559	1	4	.250	148	203	.729	45	76	121	65	94	0	24	62	6	687	4.3	2.3	24.5
All-Star Totals	4	1	84	18	38	.474	0	0	–	9	13	.692	8	9	17	9	10	0	3	4	2	45	4.3	2.3	11.3

King, Christopher Donnell (Chris) b. July 24, 1969 Ht. 6-8 Wt. 215 College: Wake Forest

SEASON–TEAM	G	GS	MIN	FGM	FGA	PCT	3FGM	3FGA	PCT	FTM	FTA	PCT	O-RB	D-RB	TOT	AST	PF	DQ	STL	TO	BLK	PTS	RPG	APG	PPG
93-94–Seattle	15	0	86	19	48	.396	2	7	.286	15	26	.577	5	10	15	11	12	0	4	12	0	55	1.0	0.7	3.7
95-96–Vancouver	80	66	1930	250	585	.427	44	113	.389	90	136	.662	102	183	285	104	163	0	68	103	33	634	3.6	1.3	7.9
98-99–Utah	8	0	42	2	7	.286	0	0	–	0	4	.000	1	10	11	1	8	0	2	4	1	4	1.4	0.1	0.5
Reg. Season Totals	103	66	2058	271	640	.423	46	120	.383	105	166	.633	108	203	311	116	183	0	74	119	34	693	3.0	1.1	6.7
Playoff Totals	2	0	7	0	1	.000	0	0	–	0	2	.000	0	0	0	–	1	0	1	0	0	0	0.0	0.0	0.0

King, Daniel (Dan) b. January 7, 1931 Ht. 6-6 Wt. 220 College: Western Kentucky

SEASON–TEAM	G	GS	MIN	FGM	FGA	PCT	3FGM	3FGA	PCT	FTM	FTA	PCT	O-RB	D-RB	TOT	AST	PF	DQ	STL	TO	BLK	PTS	RPG	APG	PPG
54-55–Baltimore	12	–	103	7	22	.318	–	–	–	5	10	.500	–	–	25	3	5	0	–	–	–	19	2.1	0.3	1.6
Reg. Season Totals	12	–	103	7	22	.318	–	–	–	5	10	.500	–	–	25	3	5	0	–	–	–	19	2.1	0.3	1.6

King, Frankie Alexander b. June 6, 1972 Ht. 6-1 Wt. 185 College: Western Carolina

SEASON–TEAM	G	GS	MIN	FGM	FGA	PCT	3FGM	3FGA	PCT	FTM	FTA	PCT	O-RB	D-RB	TOT	AST	PF	DQ	STL	TO	BLK	PTS	RPG	APG	PPG
95-96–L.A. Lakers	6	0	20	3	11	.273	0	1	.000	1	3	.333	1	1	2	2	4	0	2	2	0	7	0.3	0.3	1.2
96-97–Philadelphia	7	0	59	7	17	.412	1	2	.500	5	5	1.000	4	10	14	5	7	0	4	3	0	20	2.0	0.7	2.9
Reg. Season Totals	13	0	79	10	28	.357	1	3	.333	6	8	.750	5	11	16	7	11	0	6	5	0	27	1.2	0.5	2.1

King, George Smith Jr. b. August 16, 1928 Ht. 6-0 Wt. 185 College: Charleston (W.Va)

SEASON–TEAM	G	GS	MIN	FGM	FGA	PCT	3FGM	3FGA	PCT	FTM	FTA	PCT	O-RB	D-RB	TOT	AST	PF	DQ	STL	TO	BLK	PTS	RPG	APG	PPG
51-52–Syracuse	66	–	1889	235	579	.406	–	–	–	188	264	.712	–	–	274	244	199	6	–	–	–	658	4.2	3.7	10.0
52-53–Syracuse	71	–	2519	255	635	.402	–	–	–	284	442	.643	–	–	281	364	244	2	–	–	–	794	4.0	5.1	11.2
53-54–Syracuse	72	–	2370	280	744	.376	–	–	–	257	410	.627	–	–	268	272	179	2	–	–	–	817	3.7	3.8	11.3
54-55–Syracuse	67	–	2015	228	605	.377	–	–	–	140	229	.611	–	–	227	331	148	0	–	–	–	596	3.4	4.9	8.9
55-56–Syracuse	72	–	2343	284	763	.372	–	–	–	176	275	.640	–	–	250	410	150	2	–	–	–	744	3.5	5.7	10.3
57-58–Cincinnati	63	–	2272	235	645	.364	–	–	–	140	227	.617	–	–	306	337	124	0	–	–	–	610	4.9	5.3	9.7
Reg. Season Totals	411	–	13408	1517	3971	.382	–	–	–	1185	1847	.642	–	–	1606	1958	1044	12	–	–	–	4219	3.9	4.8	10.3
Playoff Totals	39	–	1599	142	382	.372	–	–	–	145	212	.684	–	–	169	186	113	3	–	–	–	429	3.5	4.2	11.0

King, Gerard b. November 25, 1972 Ht. 6-9 Wt. 250 College: Nicholls State

SEASON–TEAM	G	GS	MIN	FGM	FGA	PCT	3FGM	3FGA	PCT	FTM	FTA	PCT	O-RB	D-RB	TOT	AST	PF	DQ	STL	TO	BLK	PTS	RPG	APG	PPG
98-99–San Antonio	19	0	63	6	14	.429	0	0	–	11	18	.611	6	8	14	4	12	0	2	4	1	23	0.7	0.2	1.2
99-00–Washington	62	28	1060	139	277	.502	0	0	–	49	66	.742	84	166	250	49	132	1	34	41	15	327	4.0	0.8	5.3
Reg. Season Totals	81	28	1123	145	291	.498	0	0	–	60	84	.714	90	174	264	53	144	1	36	45	16	350	3.3	0.7	4.3
Playoff Totals	8	0	14	2	4	.500	0	0	–	0	0	–	0	4	4	1	2	0	0	1	1	4	0.5	0.1	0.5

King, James Leonard (Jim, Country) b. February 7, 1941 Ht. 6-2 Wt. 175 College: Tulsa

SEASON–TEAM	G	GS	MIN	FGM	FGA	PCT	3FGM	3FGA	PCT	FTM	FTA	PCT	O-RB	D-RB	TOT	AST	PF	DQ	STL	TO	BLK	PTS	RPG	APG	PPG
63-64–Los Angeles	60	–	762	84	198	.424	–	–	–	66	101	.653	–	–	113	110	99	0	–	–	–	234	1.9	1.8	3.9
64-65–Los Angeles	77	–	1671	184	469	.392	–	–	–	118	151	.781	–	–	214	178	193	2	–	–	–	486	2.8	2.3	6.3
65-66–Los Angeles	76	–	1499	238	545	.437	–	–	–	94	115	.817	–	–	204	223	181	1	–	–	–	570	2.7	2.9	7.5
66-67–San Francisco	67	–	1667	286	685	.418	–	–	–	174	221	.787	–	–	319	240	193	5	–	–	–	746	4.8	3.6	11.1
67-68–San Francisco	54	–	1743	340	800	.425	–	–	–	217	268	.810	–	–	243	226	172	1	–	–	–	897	4.5	4.2	16.6
68-69–San Francisco	46	–	1010	137	394	.348	–	–	–	78	108	.722	–	–	120	123	99	1	–	–	–	352	2.6	2.7	7.7
69-70–S.F.-Cin.	34	–	391	53	129	.411	–	–	–	33	41	.805	–	–	62	52	47	0	–	–	–	139	1.8	1.5	4.1
70-71–Chicago	55	–	645	100	228	.439	–	–	–	64	79	.810	–	–	68	78	55	0	–	–	–	264	1.2	1.4	4.8
71-72–Chicago	73	–	1014	162	356	.455	–	–	–	89	113	.788	–	–	81	101	103	0	–	–	–	413	1.1	1.4	5.7
72-73–Chicago	65	–	785	116	263	.441	–	–	–	44	52	.846	–	–	76	81	76	0	–	–	–	276	1.2	1.2	4.2
Reg. Season Totals	607	–	11187	1700	4067	.418	–	–	–	977	1249	.782	–	–	1500	1412	1218	10	–	–	–	4377	2.5	2.3	7.2
Playoff Totals	73	–	1452	246	564	.436	–	–	–	110	151	.728	–	–	246	182	196	4	–	–	–	602	3.4	2.5	8.2
All-Star Totals	1	–	7	1	4	.250	–	–	–	2	3	.667	–	–	1	2	3	0	–	–	–	4	1.0	2.0	4.0

King, Jimmy Hal b. August 9, 1973 Ht. 6-5 Wt. 210 College: Michigan

SEASON–TEAM	G	GS	MIN	FGM	FGA	PCT	3FGM	3FGA	PCT	FTM	FTA	PCT	O-RB	D-RB	TOT	AST	PF	DQ	STL	TO	BLK	PTS	RPG	APG	PPG
95-96–Toronto	62	1	868	110	255	.431	5	34	.147	54	77	.701	43	67	110	88	76	0	21	60	13	279	1.8	1.4	4.5
96-97–Denver	2	0	22	2	6	.333	0	0	–	2	4	.500	2	0	2	2	2	0	3	1	0	6	1.0	1.0	3.0
Reg. Season Totals	64	1	890	112	261	.429	5	34	.147	56	81	.691	45	67	112	90	78	0	24	61	13	285	1.8	1.4	4.5

King, Loyd Harold b. May 29, 1949 Ht. 6-2 Wt. 180 College: Virginia Tech

SEASON–TEAM	G	GS	MIN	FGM	FGA	PCT	3FGM	3FGA	PCT	FTM	FTA	PCT	O-RB	D-RB	TOT	AST	PF	DQ	STL	TO	BLK	PTS	RPG	APG	PPG
71-72–Memphis (A)	74	–	1153	185	494	.374	21	87	.241	96	119	.807	–	–	113	103	168	–	–	76	–	487	1.5	1.4	6.6
72-73–Memphis (A)	10	–	102	6	29	.207	0	3	.000	7	8	.875	2	10	12	14	20	0	–	4	–	19	1.2	1.4	1.9
Reg. ABA Totals	84	–	1255	191	523	.365	21	90	.233	103	127	.811	2	10	125	117	188	0	–	80	–	506	1.5	1.4	6.0

King, Maurice E. (Maury) b. March 12, 1935 Ht. 6-2 Wt. 195 College: Kansas

SEASON–TEAM	G	GS	MIN	FGM	FGA	PCT	3FGM	3FGA	PCT	FTM	FTA	PCT	O-RB	D-RB	TOT	AST	PF	DQ	STL	TO	BLK	PTS	RPG	APG	PPG
59-60–Boston	1	–	19	5	8	.625	–	–	–	0	1	.000	–	–	4	2	3	0	–	–	–	10	4.0	2.0	10.0
62-63–Chicago	37	–	954	94	241	.390	–	–	–	28	34	.824	–	–	102	142	87	0	–	–	–	216	2.8	3.8	5.8
Reg. Season Totals	38	–	973	99	249	.398	–	–	–	28	35	.800	–	–	106	144	90	0	–	–	–	226	2.8	3.8	5.9

King, Reginald Biddings (Reggie) b. February 14, 1957 Ht. 6-6 Wt. 240 College: Alabama

SEASON–TEAM	G	GS	MIN	FGM	FGA	PCT	3FGM	3FGA	PCT	FTM	FTA	PCT	O-RB	D-RB	TOT	AST	PF	DQ	STL	TO	BLK	PTS	RPG	APG	PPG
79-80–Kansas City	82	–	2052	257	499	.515	0	1	.000	159	219	.726	184	382	566	106	230	2	69	100	31	673	6.9	1.3	8.2
80-81–Kansas City	81	–	2743	472	867	.544	0	0	–	264	386	.684	235	551	786	122	227	2	102	164	41	1208	9.7	1.5	14.9
81-82–Kansas City	80	76	2609	383	752	.509	0	0	–	201	285	.705	162	361	523	173	221	6	84	155	29	967	6.5	2.2	12.1
82-83–Kansas City	58	5	995	104	225	.462	0	0	–	73	96	.760	91	149	240	58	94	1	28	65	11	281	4.1	1.0	4.8
83-84–Seattle	77	42	2086	233	448	.520	0	2	.000	136	206	.660	134	336	470	179	159	2	54	127	24	602	6.1	2.3	7.8
84-85–Seattle	60	5	860	63	149	.423	0	0	–	41	59	.695	44	78	122	53	74	1	28	42	11	167	2.0	0.9	2.8
Reg. Season Totals	438	128	11345	1512	2940	.514	0	3	.000	874	1251	.699	850	1857	2707	691	1005	14	365	653	147	3898	6.2	1.6	8.9
Playoff Totals	23	0	788	137	281	.488	0	1	.000	80	111	.721	69	122	191	35	73	0	21	44	13	354	8.3	1.5	15.4

King, Richard Thomas (Rich) b. April 4, 1969 Ht. 7-2 Wt. 265 College: Nebraska

SEASON–TEAM	G	GS	MIN	FGM	FGA	PCT	3FGM	3FGA	PCT	FTM	FTA	PCT	O-RB	D-RB	TOT	AST	PF	DQ	STL	TO	BLK	PTS	RPG	APG	PPG
91-92–Seattle	40	2	213	27	71	.380	0	1	.000	34	45	.756	20	29	49	12	42	0	4	18	5	88	1.2	0.3	2.2
92-93–Seattle	3	0	12	2	5	.400	0	0	–	2	2	1.000	1	4	5	1	1	0	0	3	0	6	1.7	0.3	2.0
93-94–Seattle	27	0	78	15	34	.441	0	1	.000	11	22	.500	9	11	20	8	18	0	1	7	2	41	0.7	0.3	1.5
94-95–Seattle	2	0	6	0	2	.000	0	0	–	0	2	.000	0	0	0	0	1	0	0	0	0	0	0.0	0.0	0.0
Reg. Season Totals	72	2	309	44	112	.393	0	2	.000	47	71	.662	30	44	74	21	62	0	5	28	7	135	1.0	0.3	1.9

King, Ron b. 1951 Ht. 6-4 Wt. 195 College: Florida State

SEASON–TEAM	G	GS	MIN	FGM	FGA	PCT	3FGM	3FGA	PCT	FTM	FTA	PCT	O-RB	D-RB	TOT	AST	PF	DQ	STL	TO	BLK	PTS	RPG	APG	PPG
73-74–Kentucky (A)	9	–	126	24	70	.343	2	6	.333	14	17	.824	8	11	19	14	14	–	5	7	2	64	2.1	1.6	7.1
Reg. ABA Totals	9	–	126	24	70	.343	2	6	.333	14	17	.824	8	11	19	14	14	0	5	7	2	64	2.1	1.6	7.1

King, Ronald Stacey (Stacey) b. January 29, 1967 Ht. 6-11 Wt. 250 College: Oklahoma

SEASON–TEAM	G	GS	MIN	FGM	FGA	PCT	3FGM	3FGA	PCT	FTM	FTA	PCT	O-RB	D-RB	TOT	AST	PF	DQ	STL	TO	BLK	PTS	RPG	APG	PPG
89-90–Chicago	82	2	1777	267	530	.504	0	1	.000	194	267	.727	169	215	384	87	215	0	38	119	58	728	4.7	1.1	8.9
90-91–Chicago	76	6	1198	156	334	.467	0	2	.000	107	152	.704	72	136	208	65	134	0	24	91	42	419	2.7	0.9	5.5
91-92–Chicago	79	12	1268	215	425	.506	2	5	.400	119	158	.753	87	118	205	77	129	0	21	76	25	551	2.6	1.0	7.0
92-93–Chicago	76	3	1059	160	340	.471	2	6	.333	86	122	.705	105	102	207	71	128	0	26	70	20	408	2.7	0.9	5.4
93-94–Chicago-Minn.	49	30	1053	146	341	.428	0	2	.000	93	136	.684	90	151	241	58	121	1	31	83	42	385	4.9	1.2	7.9
94-95–Minnesota	50	10	792	99	212	.467	0	1	.000	68	102	.667	54	111	165	26	126	1	24	64	20	266	3.3	0.5	5.3
95-96–Miami	15	0	156	17	36	.472	0	0	–	4	8	.500	9	14	23	2	39	2	7	18	2	38	1.5	0.1	2.5
96-97–Boston-Dallas	11	0	103	11	22	.500	0	0	–	2	7	.286	11	16	27	1	14	0	2	6	1	24	2.5	0.1	2.2
Reg. Season Totals	438	63	7406	1071	2240	.478	4	17	.235	673	952	.707	597	863	1460	387	906	4	173	527	210	2819	3.3	0.9	6.4
Playoff Totals	61	2	719	89	227	.392	2	4	.500	84	114	.737	53	83	136	31	98	0	21	50	15	264	2.2	0.5	4.3

King, Thomas Van Dyke (Tom) b. March 9, 1924 Ht. 6-1 Wt. 165 College: Michigan

SEASON–TEAM	G	GS	MIN	FGM	FGA	PCT	3FGM	3FGA	PCT	FTM	FTA	PCT	O-RB	D-RB	TOT	AST	PF	DQ	STL	TO	BLK	PTS	RPG	APG	PPG
46-47–Detroit	58	–	–	97	410	.237	–	–	–	101	160	.631	–	–	–	32	102	–	–	–	–	295	–	0.6	5.1
Reg. Season Totals	58	–	–	97	410	.237	–	–	–	101	160	.631	–	–	–	32	102	–	–	–	–	295	–	0.6	5.1

Kinney, Robert Paul (Bob, Hi-Pocket) b. September 16, 1920 d. September 2, 1985 Ht. 6-6 Wt. 215 College: Rice

SEASON–TEAM	G	GS	MIN	FGM	FGA	PCT	3FGM	3FGA	PCT	FTM	FTA	PCT	O-RB	D-RB	TOT	AST	PF	DQ	STL	TO	BLK	PTS	RPG	APG	PPG
45-46–Fort Wayne (N)	13	–	–	16	–	–	–	–	–	2	–	–	–	–	–	–	–	–	–	–	–	34	–	–	2.6
46-47–Fort Wayne (N)	44	–	–	102	–	–	–	–	–	42	84	.500	–	–	–	–	129	–	–	–	–	246	–	–	5.6
47-48–Fort Wayne (N)	58	–	–	149	–	–	–	–	–	92	147	.626	–	–	–	–	192	–	–	–	–	390	–	–	6.7
48-49–FtWayne-Boston	58	–	–	161	495	.325	–	–	–	136	234	.581	–	–	–	77	224	–	–	–	–	458	–	1.3	7.9
49-50–Boston	60	–	–	233	621	.375	–	–	–	201	320	.628	–	–	–	100	251	–	–	–	–	667	–	1.7	11.1
Reg. NBA Totals	118	–	–	394	1116	.353	–	–	–	337	554	.608	–	–	–	177	475	–	–	–	–	1125	–	1.5	9.5
Reg. NBL Totals	115	–	–	267	–	–	–	–	–	136	231	.580	–	–	–	–	321	–	–	–	–	670	–	–	5.8
NBL Playoff Totals	15	–	–	43	–	–	–	–	–	21	32	.656	–	–	–	–	44	–	–	–	–	107	–	–	7.1

Kirk, Walton Jr. (Walt, Junior) b. September 3, 1924 Ht. 6-3 Wt. 175 College: Illinois

SEASON–TEAM	G	GS	MIN	FGM	FGA	PCT	3FGM	3FGA	PCT	FTM	FTA	PCT	O-RB	D-RB	TOT	AST	PF	DQ	STL	TO	BLK	PTS	RPG	APG	PPG
47-48–Fort Wayne (N)	45	–	–	62	–	–	–	–	–	44	90	.489	–	–	–	–	–	–	–	–	–	168	–	–	3.7
48-49–FtWayne-Ind.	49	–	–	140	406	.345	–	–	–	167	231	.723	–	–	–	118	127	–	–	–	–	447	–	2.4	9.1
49-50–And.-Tri-Cit	58	–	–	97	361	.269	–	–	–	155	216	.718	–	–	–	103	155	–	–	–	–	349	–	1.8	6.0
51-52–Milwaukee	11	–	396	28	101	.277	–	–	–	55	78	.705	–	–	44	28	47	3	–	–	–	111	4.0	2.5	10.1
Reg. NBA Totals	118	–	396	265	868	.305	–	–	–	377	525	.718	–	–	44	249	329	3	–	–	–	907	4.0	2.1	7.7
Reg. NBL Totals	45	–	–	62	–	–	–	–	–	44	90	.489	–	–	–	–	–	–	–	–	–	168	–	–	3.7
NBA Playoff Totals	3	–	0	2	7	.286	–	–	–	1	6	.167	–	–	–	1	8	0	–	–	–	5	–	0.3	1.7
NBL Playoff Totals	3	–	–	3	–	–	–	–	–	1	6	.167	–	–	–	–	8	–	–	–	–	7	–	–	2.3

Kirkland, Wilber b. 1947 Ht. 6-7 Wt. 195 College: Cheyney

SEASON–TEAM	G	GS	MIN	FGM	FGA	PCT	3FGM	3FGA	PCT	FTM	FTA	PCT	O-RB	D-RB	TOT	AST	PF	DQ	STL	TO	BLK	PTS	RPG	APG	PPG
69-70–Pittsburgh (A)	2	–	27	3	7	.429	0	0	–	0	0	–	–	–	11	1	5	0	–	–	–	6	5.5	0.5	3.0
Reg. ABA Totals	2	–	27	3	7	.429	0	0	–	0	0	–	–	–	11	1	5	0	–	–	–	6	5.5	0.5	3.0

Kissane, James J. Jr. (Jim) b. August 17, 1946 Ht. 6-7 Wt. 210 College: Boston College

SEASON–TEAM	G	GS	MIN	FGM	FGA	PCT	3FGM	3FGA	PCT	FTM	FTA	PCT	O-RB	D-RB	TOT	AST	PF	DQ	STL	TO	BLK	PTS	RPG	APG	PPG
68-69–Minnesota (A)	2	–	15	2	6	.333	0	0	–	2	2	1.000	–	–	3	0	3	0	–	1	–	6	1.5	0.0	3.0
Reg. ABA Totals	2	–	15	2	6	.333	0	0	–	2	2	1.000	–	–	3	0	3	0	–	1	–	6	1.5	0.0	3.0

Kistler, Douglas C. (Doug) b. March 21, 1938 d. February 29, 1980 Ht. 6-9 Wt. 210 College: Duke

SEASON–TEAM	G	GS	MIN	FGM	FGA	PCT	3FGM	3FGA	PCT	FTM	FTA	PCT	O-RB	D-RB	TOT	AST	PF	DQ	STL	TO	BLK	PTS	RPG	APG	PPG
61-62–New York	5	–	13	3	6	.500	–	–	–	2	4	.500	–	–	1	0	2	0	–	–	–	8	0.2	0.0	1.6
Reg. Season Totals	5	–	13	3	6	.500	–	–	–	2	4	.500	–	–	1	0	2	0	–	–	–	8	0.2	0.0	1.6

Kitchen, Curtis b. January 30, 1964 Ht. 6-9 Wt. 235 College: South Florida

SEASON–TEAM	G	GS	MIN	FGM	FGA	PCT	3FGM	3FGA	PCT	FTM	FTA	PCT	O-RB	D-RB	TOT	AST	PF	DQ	STL	TO	BLK	PTS	RPG	APG	PPG
86-87–Seattle	6	0	31	3	6	.500	0	1	.000	3	4	.750	4	5	9	1	4	0	2	0	3	9	1.5	0.2	1.5
Reg. Season Totals	6	0	31	3	6	.500	0	1	.000	3	4	.750	4	5	9	1	4	0	2	0	3	9	1.5	0.2	1.5
Playoff Totals	8	0	23	1	2	.500	0	0	–	0	4	.000	2	4	6	–	7	0	0	0	2	2	0.8	0.0	0.3

Kite, Gregory Fuller (Greg) b. August 5, 1961 Ht. 6-11 Wt. 263 College: Brigham Young

SEASON–TEAM	G	GS	MIN	FGM	FGA	PCT	3FGM	3FGA	PCT	FTM	FTA	PCT	O-RB	D-RB	TOT	AST	PF	DQ	STL	TO	BLK	PTS	RPG	APG	PPG
83-84–Boston	35	1	197	30	66	.455	0	0	–	5	16	.313	27	35	62	7	42	0	1	20	5	65	1.8	0.2	1.9
84-85–Boston	55	4	424	33	88	.375	0	0	–	22	32	.688	38	51	89	17	84	3	3	29	10	88	1.6	0.3	1.6
85-86–Boston	64	2	464	34	91	.374	0	1	.000	15	39	.385	35	93	128	17	81	1	3	32	28	83	2.0	0.3	1.3
86-87–Boston	74	1	745	47	110	.427	0	1	.000	29	76	.382	61	108	169	27	148	2	17	34	46	123	2.3	0.4	1.7
87-88–Boston-LAClips	53	19	1063	92	205	.449	0	1	.000	40	79	.506	85	179	264	47	153	1	19	73	58	224	5.0	0.9	4.2
88-89–LAClips-Cha.	70	24	942	65	151	.430	0	0	–	20	41	.488	81	162	243	36	161	1	27	58	54	150	3.5	0.5	2.1
89-90–Sacramento	71	47	1515	101	234	.432	1	1	1.000	27	54	.500	131	246	377	76	201	2	31	76	51	230	5.3	1.1	3.2
90-91–Orlando	82	82	2225	166	338	.491	0	0	–	63	123	.512	189	399	588	59	298	4	25	102	81	395	7.2	0.7	4.8
91-92–Orlando	72	44	1479	94	215	.437	0	1	.000	40	68	.588	156	246	402	44	212	2	30	61	57	228	5.6	0.6	3.2
92-93–Orlando	64	1	640	38	84	.452	0	1	.000	13	24	.542	66	127	193	10	133	1	13	35	12	89	3.0	0.2	1.4
93-94–Orlando	29	0	309	13	35	.371	0	0	–	8	22	.364	22	48	70	4	61	0	2	17	12	34	2.4	0.1	1.2
94-95–N.Y.-Indiana	11	0	77	3	17	.176	0	0	–	2	10	.200	12	10	22	1	15	0	0	6	0	8	2.0	0.1	0.7
Reg. Season Totals	680	225	10080	716	1634	.438	1	6	.167	284	584	.486	903	1704	2607	345	1589	17	171	543	414	1717	3.8	0.5	2.5
Playoff Totals	61	1	378	21	53	.396	0	0	–	15	24	.625	33	64	97	17	94	1	6	17	13	57	1.6	0.3	0.9

Kittles, Kerry b. June 12, 1974 Ht. 6-5 Wt. 180 College: Villanova

SEASON–TEAM	G	GS	MIN	FGM	FGA	PCT	3FGM	3FGA	PCT	FTM	FTA	PCT	O-RB	D-RB	TOT	AST	PF	DQ	STL	TO	BLK	PTS	RPG	APG	PPG
96-97–New Jersey	82	57	3012	507	1189	.426	158	419	.377	175	227	.771	106	213	319	249	165	1	157	127	35	1347	3.9	3.0	16.4
97-98–New Jersey	77	76	2814	508	1154	.440	110	263	.418	202	250	.808	132	230	362	176	152	0	132	106	37	1328	4.7	2.3	17.2
98-99–New Jersey	46	40	1570	227	613	.370	50	158	.316	88	114	.772	52	139	191	116	82	0	79	66	26	592	4.2	2.5	12.9
99-00–New Jersey	62	61	1896	305	698	.437	96	240	.400	101	127	.795	46	179	225	142	120	0	79	56	19	807	3.6	2.3	13.0
Reg. Season Totals	267	234	9292	1547	3654	.423	414	1080	.383	566	718	.788	336	761	1097	683	519	1	447	355	117	4074	4.1	2.6	15.3
Playoff Totals	3	3	126	17	40	.425	5	13	.385	10	11	.909	0	15	15	8	12	1	4	7	2	49	5.0	2.7	16.3

Kleine, Joseph William (Joe) b. January 4, 1962 Ht. 7-0 Wt. 271 College: Notre Dame; Arkansas

SEASON–TEAM	G	GS	MIN	FGM	FGA	PCT	3FGM	3FGA	PCT	FTM	FTA	PCT	O-RB	D-RB	TOT	AST	PF	DQ	STL	TO	BLK	PTS	RPG	APG	PPG
85-86–Sacramento	80	18	1180	160	344	.465	0	0	–	94	130	.723	113	260	373	46	224	1	24	107	34	414	4.7	0.6	5.2
86-87–Sacramento	79	31	1658	256	543	.471	0	1	.000	110	140	.786	173	310	483	71	213	2	35	90	30	622	6.1	0.9	7.9
87-88–Sacramento	82	60	1999	324	686	.472	0	0	–	153	188	.814	179	400	579	93	228	1	28	107	59	801	7.1	1.1	9.8
88-89–Sac.-Boston	75	13	1411	175	432	.405	0	2	.000	134	152	.882	124	254	378	67	192	2	33	104	23	484	5.0	0.9	6.5
89-90–Boston	81	4	1365	176	367	.480	0	4	.000	83	100	.830	117	238	355	46	170	0	15	64	27	435	4.4	0.6	5.4
90-91–Boston	72	1	850	102	218	.468	0	2	.000	54	69	.783	71	173	244	21	108	0	15	53	14	258	3.4	0.3	3.6
91-92–Boston	70	3	991	144	293	.491	4	8	.500	34	48	.708	94	202	296	32	99	0	23	27	14	326	4.2	0.5	4.7
92-93–Boston	78	3	1129	108	267	.404	0	6	.000	41	58	.707	113	233	346	39	123	0	17	37	17	257	4.4	0.5	3.3
93-94–Phoenix	74	4	848	125	256	.488	5	11	.455	30	39	.769	50	143	193	45	118	1	14	35	19	285	2.6	0.6	3.9
94-95–Phoenix	75	42	968	119	265	.449	0	2	.000	42	49	.857	82	177	259	39	174	2	14	35	18	280	3.5	0.5	3.7
95-96–Phoenix	56	9	663	71	169	.420	2	7	.286	20	25	.800	36	96	132	44	113	0	13	37	6	164	2.4	0.8	2.9
96-97–Phoenix-L.A.L.-N.J.	59	10	848	69	170	.406	2	3	.667	28	38	.737	62	141	203	35	110	0	17	41	18	168	3.4	0.6	2.8
97-98–Chicago	46	1	397	39	106	.368	0	0	–	15	18	.833	27	50	77	30	63	0	4	28	5	93	1.7	0.7	2.0
98-99–Phoenix	31	5	374	30	74	.405	0	2	.000	8	12	.667	27	40	67	12	46	0	8	10	1	68	2.2	0.4	2.2
99-00–Portland	7	0	31	4	11	.364	0	0	–	3	3	1.000	0	6	6	2	7	0	1	2	0	11	0.9	0.3	1.6
Reg. Season Totals	965	204	14712	1902	4201	.453	13	48	.271	849	1069	.794	1268	2723	3991	622	1988	9	261	777	285	4666	4.1	0.6	4.8
Playoff Totals	50	11	592	84	163	.515	1	5	.200	23	29	.793	40	93	133	18	103	0	11	26	15	192	2.7	0.4	3.8

Klier, Leo Anthony (Crystal) b. May 21, 1923 Ht. 6-2 Wt. 170 College: Notre Dame

SEASON–TEAM	G	GS	MIN	FGM	FGA	PCT	3FGM	3FGA	PCT	FTM	FTA	PCT	O-RB	D-RB	TOT	AST	PF	DQ	STL	TO	BLK	PTS	RPG	APG	PPG
46-47–Indianapolis (N)	44	–	–	162	–	–	–	–	–	93	128	.727	–	–	–	–	97	–	–	–	–	417	–	–	9.5
47-48–Indianapolis (N)	56	–	–	227	–	–	–	–	–	152	223	.682	–	–	–	–	159	–	–	–	–	606	–	–	10.8
48-49–Fort Wayne	47	–	–	125	492	.254	–	–	–	97	137	.708	–	–	–	56	124	–	–	–	–	347	–	1.2	7.4
49-50–Fort Wayne	66	–	–	157	516	.304	–	–	–	141	190	.742	–	–	–	121	177	–	–	–	–	455	–	1.8	6.9
Reg. NBA Totals	113	–	–	282	1008	.280	–	–	–	238	327	.728	–	–	–	177	301	–	–	–	–	802	–	1.6	7.1
Reg. NBL Totals	100	–	–	389	–	–	–	–	–	245	351	.698	–	–	–	–	256	–	–	–	–	1023	–	–	10.2
NBA Playoff Totals	2	–	–	0	6	.000	–	–	–	1	1	1.000	–	–	–	6	1	–	–	–	–	1	–	1.5	0.5
NBL Playoff Totals	9	–	–	32	–	–	–	–	–	26	34	.735	–	–	–	–	22	–	–	–	–	90	–	–	10.0

Klotz, Louis Herman (Herm, Red) b. October 21, 1921 Ht. 5-7 Wt. 150 College: Villanova

SEASON–TEAM	G	GS	MIN	FGM	FGA	PCT	3FGM	3FGA	PCT	FTM	FTA	PCT	O-RB	D-RB	TOT	AST	PF	DQ	STL	TO	BLK	PTS	RPG	APG	PPG
47-48–Baltimore	11	–	–	7	31	.226	–	–	–	1	3	.333	–	–	–	7	3	–	–	–	–	15	–	0.6	1.4
Reg. Season Totals	11	–	–	7	31	.226	–	–	–	1	3	.333	–	–	–	7	3	–	–	–	–	15	–	0.6	1.4
Playoff Totals	6	–	–	2	10	.200	–	–	–	2	3	.667	–	–	–	1	3	–	–	–	–	6	–	0.1	1.0

Klueh, Duane M. b. January 6, 1926 Ht. 6-3 Wt. 175 College: Indiana State

SEASON–TEAM	G	GS	MIN	FGM	FGA	PCT	3FGM	3FGA	PCT	FTM	FTA	PCT	O-RB	D-RB	TOT	AST	PF	DQ	STL	TO	BLK	PTS	RPG	APG	PPG
49-50–Denver-FtWayne	52	–	–	159	414	.384	–	–	–	157	222	.707	–	–	–	91	111	–	–	–	–	475	–	1.8	9.1
50-51–Fort Wayne	61	–	–	157	458	.343	–	–	–	135	184	.734	–	–	183	82	143	5	–	–	–	449	3.0	1.3	7.4
Reg. Season Totals	113	–	–	316	872	.362	–	–	–	292	406	.719	–	–	183	173	254	5	–	–	–	924	3.0	1.5	8.2
Playoff Totals	4	–	–	3	16	.188	–	–	–	5	5	1.000	–	–	3	6	10	1	–	–	–	11	1.5	1.5	2.8

Kluttz, Lonnie Gene (Gene) b. September 17, 1945 Ht. 6-7 Wt. 220 College: North Carolina A&T

SEASON–TEAM	G	GS	MIN	FGM	FGA	PCT	3FGM	3FGA	PCT	FTM	FTA	PCT	O-RB	D-RB	TOT	AST	PF	DQ	STL	TO	BLK	PTS	RPG	APG	PPG
70-71–Carolina (A)	3	–	8	0	4	.000	0	0	–	0	0	–	–	–	5	0	3	–	–	–	–	0	1.7	0.0	0.0
Reg. ABA Totals	3	–	8	0	4	.000	0	0	–	0	0	–	–	–	5	0	3	–	–	–	–	0	1.7	0.0	0.0

Knight, Brevin b. November 8, 1975 Ht. 5-10 Wt. 170 College: Stanford

SEASON–TEAM	G	GS	MIN	FGM	FGA	PCT	3FGM	3FGA	PCT	FTM	FTA	PCT	O-RB	D-RB	TOT	AST	PF	DQ	STL	TO	BLK	PTS	RPG	APG	PPG
97-98–Cleveland	80	76	2483	261	592	.441	0	7	.000	201	251	.801	67	186	253	656	271	5	196	194	18	723	3.2	8.2	9.0
98-99–Cleveland	39	38	1186	134	315	.425	0	5	.000	105	141	.745	16	115	131	302	115	1	70	105	7	373	3.4	7.7	9.6
99-00–Cleveland	65	46	1754	230	558	.412	2	10	.200	140	184	.761	38	155	193	458	185	2	107	157	21	602	3.0	7.0	9.3
Reg. Season Totals	184	160	5423	625	1465	.427	2	22	.091	446	576	.774	121	456	577	1416	571	8	373	456	46	1698	3.1	7.7	9.2
Playoff Totals	4	4	132	6	21	.286	0	0	–	6	10	.600	0	16	16	23	16	1	10	8	1	18	4.0	5.8	4.5

Knight, Negele Oscar b. March 6, 1967 Ht. 6-1 Wt. 182 College: Dayton

SEASON–TEAM	G	GS	MIN	FGM	FGA	PCT	3FGM	3FGA	PCT	FTM	FTA	PCT	O-RB	D-RB	TOT	AST	PF	DQ	STL	TO	BLK	PTS	RPG	APG	PPG
90-91–Phoenix	64	6	792	131	308	.425	6	25	.240	71	118	.602	20	51	71	191	83	0	20	76	7	339	1.1	3.0	5.3
91-92–Phoenix	42	1	631	103	217	.475	4	13	.308	33	48	.688	16	30	46	112	58	0	24	58	3	243	1.1	2.7	5.8
92-93–Phoenix	52	35	888	124	317	.391	0	7	.000	67	86	.779	28	36	64	145	66	1	23	73	4	315	1.2	2.8	6.1
93-94–Phoenix-S.A.	65	18	1438	225	475	.474	4	21	.190	141	174	.810	28	75	103	197	121	0	34	94	11	595	1.6	3.0	9.2
94-95–Port.-Detroit	47	17	708	85	214	.397	11	28	.393	18	25	.720	21	40	61	127	70	0	21	49	5	199	1.3	2.7	4.2
98-99–Toronto	6	0	56	3	8	.375	0	1	.000	2	4	.500	1	5	6	8	5	0	1	7	0	8	1.0	1.3	1.3
Reg. Season Totals	276	77	4513	671	1539	.436	25	95	.263	332	455	.730	114	237	351	780	403	1	123	357	30	1699	1.3	2.8	6.2
Playoff Totals	17	1	198	35	83	.422	1	6	.167	16	19	.842	5	8	13	28	17	0	4	14	1	87	0.8	1.6	5.1

Knight, Robert (Bob) b. 1931 Ht. 6-2 Wt. 185 College: None

SEASON–TEAM	G	GS	MIN	FGM	FGA	PCT	3FGM	3FGA	PCT	FTM	FTA	PCT	O-RB	D-RB	TOT	AST	PF	DQ	STL	TO	BLK	PTS	RPG	APG	PPG
54-55–New York	2	–	29	3	7	.429	–	–	–	1	1	1.000	–	–	1	8	6	0	–	–	–	7	0.5	4.0	3.5
Reg. Season Totals	2	–	29	3	7	.429	–	–	–	1	1	1.000	–	–	1	8	6	0	–	–	–	7	0.5	4.0	3.5

Knight, Ronald Eugene (Ron) b. August 4, 1947 Ht. 6-7 Wt. 215 College: Los Angeles State

SEASON–TEAM	G	GS	MIN	FGM	FGA	PCT	3FGM	3FGA	PCT	FTM	FTA	PCT	O-RB	D-RB	TOT	AST	PF	DQ	STL	TO	BLK	PTS	RPG	APG	PPG
70-71–Portland	52	–	662	99	230	.430	–	–	–	19	38	.500	–	–	167	50	99	1	–	–	–	217	3.2	1.0	4.2
71-72–Portland	49	–	483	112	257	.436	–	–	–	31	62	.500	–	–	116	33	52	0	–	–	–	255	2.4	0.7	5.2
Reg. Season Totals	101	–	1145	211	487	.433	–	–	–	50	100	.500	–	–	283	83	151	1	–	–	–	472	2.8	0.8	4.7

Knight, Toby Thomas b. May 3, 1955 Ht. 6-9 Wt. 210 College: Notre Dame

SEASON–TEAM	G	GS	MIN	FGM	FGA	PCT	3FGM	3FGA	PCT	FTM	FTA	PCT	O-RB	D-RB	TOT	AST	PF	DQ	STL	TO	BLK	PTS	RPG	APG	PPG
77-78–New York	80	–	1169	222	465	.477	–	–	–	63	97	.649	121	200	321	38	211	1	50	97	28	507	4.0	0.5	6.3
78-79–New York	82	–	2667	609	1174	.519	–	–	–	145	206	.704	201	347	548	124	309	7	61	163	60	1363	6.7	1.5	16.6
79-80–New York	81	–	2945	669	1265	.529	0	2	.000	211	261	.808	201	292	493	150	302	4	117	163	86	1549	6.1	1.9	19.1
81-82–New York	40	0	550	102	183	.557	0	0	–	17	25	.680	33	49	82	23	74	0	14	21	11	221	2.1	0.6	5.5
Reg. Season Totals	283	0	7331	1602	3087	.519	0	2	.000	436	589	.740	556	888	1444	335	896	12	242	444	185	3640	5.1	1.2	12.9
Playoff Totals	6	0	48	6	20	.300	0	0	–	4	8	.500	9	10	19	1	9	0	1	3	4	16	3.2	0.2	2.7

Knight, Travis James b. September 13, 1974 Ht. 7-0 Wt. 235 College: Connecticut

SEASON–TEAM	G	GS	MIN	FGM	FGA	PCT	3FGM	3FGA	PCT	FTM	FTA	PCT	O-RB	D-RB	TOT	AST	PF	DQ	STL	TO	BLK	PTS	RPG	APG	PPG
96-97–L.A. Lakers	71	14	1156	140	275	.509	0	0	–	62	100	.620	130	189	319	39	170	2	31	49	58	342	4.5	0.5	4.8
97-98–Boston	74	21	1503	193	438	.441	15	55	.273	81	103	.786	146	219	365	104	253	3	54	87	82	482	4.9	1.4	6.5
98-99–L.A. Lakers	37	23	525	67	130	.515	0	1	.000	22	29	.759	34	94	128	31	108	2	21	35	27	156	3.5	0.8	4.2
99-00–L.A. Lakers	63	0	410	46	118	.390	0	0	–	17	28	.607	46	83	129	23	88	1	6	26	23	109	2.0	0.4	1.7
Reg. Season Totals	245	58	3594	446	961	.464	15	56	.268	182	260	.700	356	585	941	197	619	8	112	197	190	1089	3.8	0.8	4.4
Playoff Totals	26	0	151	17	28	.607	0	0	–	6	12	.500	6	22	28	4	39	1	4	11	6	40	1.1	0.2	1.5

Knight, William R. (Billy) b. June 9, 1952 Ht. 6-6 Wt. 200 College: Pittsburgh

SEASON–TEAM	G	GS	MIN	FGM	FGA	PCT	3FGM	3FGA	PCT	FTM	FTA	PCT	O-RB	D-RB	TOT	AST	PF	DQ	STL	TO	BLK	PTS	RPG	APG	PPG
74-75–Indiana (A)	80	–	2559	580	1087	.534	4	16	.250	207	259	.799	284	348	632	168	194	–	115	236	29	1371	7.9	2.1	17.1
75-76–Indiana (A)	70	–	2775	774	1567	.494	6	15	.400	415	501	.828	294	414	708	259	206	–	92	299	23	1969	10.1	3.7	28.1
76-77–Indiana	78	–	3117	831	1687	.493	–	–	–	413	506	.816	223	359	582	260	197	0	117	–	19	2075	7.5	3.3	26.6
77-78–Buffalo	53	–	2155	457	926	.494	–	–	–	301	372	.809	126	257	383	161	137	0	82	167	13	1215	7.2	3.0	22.9
78-79–Boston-Ind.	79	–	2095	441	835	.528	–	–	–	249	296	.841	94	253	347	152	160	1	63	225	8	1131	4.4	1.9	14.3
79-80–Indiana	75	–	1910	385	722	.533	4	15	.267	212	262	.809	136	225	361	155	96	0	82	132	9	986	4.8	2.1	13.1
80-81–Indiana	82	–	2385	546	1025	.533	3	19	.158	341	410	.832	191	219	410	157	155	1	84	177	12	1436	5.0	1.9	17.5
81-82–Indiana	81	19	1803	378	764	.495	9	32	.281	233	282	.826	97	160	257	118	132	0	63	137	14	998	3.2	1.5	12.3
82-83–Indiana	80	54	2262	512	984	.520	3	19	.158	343	408	.841	152	172	324	192	143	0	66	193	8	1370	4.1	2.4	17.1
83-84–Kansas City	75	39	1885	358	729	.491	4	14	.286	243	283	.859	89	166	255	160	122	0	54	155	6	963	3.4	2.1	12.8
84-85–K.C.-S.A.	68	1	800	156	354	.441	11	25	.440	64	73	.877	50	68	118	80	62	0	16	70	2	387	1.7	1.2	5.7
Reg. NBA Totals	671	113	18412	4064	8026	.506	34	124	.274	2399	2892	.830	1158	1879	3037	1435	1204	2	627	1256	91	10561	4.5	2.1	15.7
Reg. ABA Totals	150	–	5334	1354	2654	.510	10	31	.323	622	760	.818	578	762	1340	427	400	–	207	535	52	3340	8.9	2.8	22.3
NBA Playoff Totals	10	0	153	32	69	.464	0	4	.000	7	10	.700	11	10	21	10	9	0	3	9	0	71	2.1	1.0	7.1
ABA Playoff Totals	21	–	906	217	384	.565	0	3	.000	101	119	.849	74	118	192	55	54	–	19	75	1	535	9.1	2.6	25.5
NBA All-Star Totals	1	0	12	1	5	.200	0	0	–	2	2	1.000	1	4	5	0	0	0	2	–	0	4	5.0	0.0	4.0

Knorek, Lee J. b. July 15, 1921 Ht. 6-7 Wt. 215 College: DeSales; Denison; Detroit Mercy

SEASON–TEAM	G	GS	MIN	FGM	FGA	PCT	3FGM	3FGA	PCT	FTM	FTA	PCT	O-RB	D-RB	TOT	AST	PF	DQ	STL	TO	BLK	PTS	RPG	APG	PPG
46-47–New York	22	–	–	62	219	.283	–	–	–	47	72	.653	–	–	–	21	64	–	–	–	–	171	–	1.0	7.8
47-48–New York	48	–	–	99	369	.268	–	–	–	61	120	.508	–	–	–	50	171	–	–	–	–	259	–	1.0	5.4
48-49–New York	60	–	–	156	457	.341	–	–	–	131	183	.716	–	–	–	135	258	–	–	–	–	443	–	2.3	7.4
49-50–Baltimore	1	–	–	0	2	.000	–	–	–	0	0	–	–	–	–	0	4	–	–	–	–	0	–	0.0	0.0
Reg. Season Totals	131	–	–	317	1047	.303	–	–	–	239	375	.637	–	–	–	206	497	–	–	–	–	873	–	1.6	6.7
Playoff Totals	14	–	–	50	131	.382	–	–	–	30	49	.633	–	–	–	23	59	6	–	–	–	130	–	1.4	9.3

Knostman, Richard W. (Dick) b. August 9, 1931 Ht. 6-6 Wt. 215 College: Kansas State

SEASON–TEAM	G	GS	MIN	FGM	FGA	PCT	3FGM	3FGA	PCT	FTM	FTA	PCT	O-RB	D-RB	TOT	AST	PF	DQ	STL	TO	BLK	PTS	RPG	APG	PPG
53-54–Syracuse	5	–	47	3	10	.300	–	–	–	7	11	.636	–	–	17	6	9	0	–	–	–	13	3.4	1.2	2.6
Reg. Season Totals	5	–	47	3	10	.300	–	–	–	7	11	.636	–	–	17	6	9	0	–	–	–	13	3.4	1.2	2.6

Knowles, W. Rodney (Rod) b. February 27, 1946 Ht. 6-9 Wt. 215 College: Davidson

SEASON–TEAM	G	GS	MIN	FGM	FGA	PCT	3FGM	3FGA	PCT	FTM	FTA	PCT	O-RB	D-RB	TOT	AST	PF	DQ	STL	TO	BLK	PTS	RPG	APG	PPG
68-69–Phoenix	8	–	40	4	14	.286	–	–	–	1	3	.333	–	–	9	0	10	0	–	–	–	9	1.1	0.0	1.1
68-69–New York (A)	1	–	3	0	0	–	0	0	–	0	0	–	–	–	0	0	1	0	–	0	–	0	0.0	0.0	0.0
Reg. NBA Totals	8	–	40	4	14	.286	–	–	–	1	3	.333	–	–	9	0	10	0	–	–	–	9	1.1	0.0	1.1
Reg. ABA Totals	1	–	3	0	0	–	0	0	–	0	0	–	–	–	0	0	1	0	–	–	–	0	0.0	0.0	0.0

Kofoed, Bart b. March 24, 1964 Ht. 6-4 Wt. 210 College: Hastings; Nebraska-Kearney

SEASON–TEAM	G	GS	MIN	FGM	FGA	PCT	3FGM	3FGA	PCT	FTM	FTA	PCT	O-RB	D-RB	TOT	AST	PF	DQ	STL	TO	BLK	PTS	RPG	APG	PPG
87-88–Utah	36	0	225	18	48	.375	2	7	.286	8	13	.615	4	11	15	23	42	0	6	18	1	46	0.4	0.6	1.3
88-89–Utah	19	0	176	12	33	.364	0	1	.000	6	11	.545	4	7	11	20	22	0	9	13	0	30	0.6	1.1	1.6
90-91–Golden State	5	0	21	0	3	.000	0	0	–	3	6	.500	2	1	3	4	4	0	0	2	0	3	0.6	0.8	0.6
91-92–Seattle	44	0	239	25	53	.472	1	7	.143	15	26	.577	6	20	26	51	26	0	2	20	2	66	0.6	1.2	1.5
92-93–Boston	7	0	41	3	13	.231	0	1	.000	11	14	.786	0	1	1	10	1	0	2	3	1	17	0.1	1.4	2.4
Reg. Season Totals	111	0	702	58	150	.387	3	16	.188	43	70	.614	16	40	56	108	95	0	19	56	4	162	0.5	1.0	1.5
Playoff Totals	10	0	109	9	23	.391	1	5	.200	2	2	1.000	3	11	14	11	18	0	1	9	0	21	1.4	1.1	2.1

Kojis, Donald R. (Don) b. July 15, 1939 Ht. 6-3 Wt. 215 College: Marquette

SEASON–TEAM	G	GS	MIN	FGM	FGA	PCT	3FGM	3FGA	PCT	FTM	FTA	PCT	O-RB	D-RB	TOT	AST	PF	DQ	STL	TO	BLK	PTS	RPG	APG	PPG
63-64–Baltimore	78	–	1148	203	484	.419	–	–	–	82	146	.562	–	–	309	57	123	0	–	–	–	488	4.0	0.7	6.3
64-65–Detroit	65	–	836	180	416	.433	–	–	–	62	98	.633	–	–	243	63	115	1	–	–	–	422	3.7	1.0	6.5
65-66–Detroit	60	–	783	182	439	.415	–	–	–	76	141	.539	–	–	260	42	94	0	–	–	–	440	4.3	0.7	7.3
66-67–Chicago	78	–	1655	329	773	.426	–	–	–	134	222	.604	–	–	479	70	204	3	–	–	–	792	6.1	0.9	10.2
67-68–San Diego	69	–	2548	530	1189	.446	–	–	–	300	413	.726	–	–	710	176	259	5	–	–	–	1360	10.3	2.6	19.7
68-69–San Diego	81	–	3130	687	1582	.434	–	–	–	446	596	.748	–	–	776	214	303	6	–	–	–	1820	9.6	2.6	22.5
69-70–San Diego	56	–	1578	338	756	.447	–	–	–	181	241	.751	–	–	388	78	135	1	–	–	–	857	6.9	1.4	15.3
70-71–Seattle	79	–	2143	454	1018	.446	–	–	–	249	320	.778	–	–	435	130	220	3	–	–	–	1157	5.5	1.6	14.6
71-72–Seattle	73	–	1857	322	687	.469	–	–	–	188	237	.793	–	–	335	82	168	1	–	–	–	832	4.6	1.1	11.4
72-73–K.C.-Omaha	77	–	1240	276	575	.480	–	–	–	106	137	.774	–	–	198	80	128	0	–	–	–	658	2.6	1.0	8.5
73-74–K.C.-Omaha	77	–	2091	400	836	.478	–	–	–	210	272	.772	126	257	383	110	157	2	77	–	15	1010	5.0	1.4	13.1
74-75–K.C.-Omaha	21	–	232	46	98	.469	–	–	–	20	30	.667	14	25	39	10	31	0	12	–	1	112	1.9	0.5	5.3
Reg. Season Totals	814	–	19241	3947	8853	.446	–	–	–	2054	2853	.720	140	282	4555	1112	1937	22	89	–	16	9948	5.6	1.4	12.2
Playoff Totals	13	–	358	72	163	.442	–	–	–	35	45	.778	1	3	85	26	35	1	1	–	0	179	6.5	2.0	13.8
All-Star Totals	2	–	26	4	12	.333	–	–	–	4	5	.800	0	0	7	4	1	0	0	–	0	12	3.5	2.0	6.0

Komenich, Milan (Milo) b. June 22, 1920 d. May 25, 1977 Ht. 6-7 Wt. 220 College: Wyoming

SEASON–TEAM	G	GS	MIN	FGM	FGA	PCT	3FGM	3FGA	PCT	FTM	FTA	PCT	O-RB	D-RB	TOT	AST	PF	DQ	STL	TO	BLK	PTS	RPG	APG	PPG
46-47–Fort Wayne (N)	36	–	–	50	–	–	–	–	–	23	50	.460	–	–	–	–	59	–	–	–	–	123	–	–	3.4
47-48–FtWayne-And. (N)	50	–	–	127	–	–	–	–	–	44	95	.463	–	–	–	–	119	–	–	–	–	298	–	–	6.0
48-49–Anderson (N)	64	–	–	243	–	–	–	–	–	124	217	.571	–	–	–	–	209	–	–	–	–	610	–	–	9.5
49-50–Anderson	64	–	–	244	861	.283	–	–	–	146	250	.584	–	–	–	124	246	–	–	–	–	634	–	1.9	9.9
Reg. NBA Totals	64	–	–	244	861	.283	–	–	–	146	250	.584	–	–	–	124	246	–	–	–	–	634	–	1.9	9.9
Reg. NBL Totals	150	–	–	420	–	–	–	–	–	191	362	.528	–	–	–	–	387	–	–	–	–	1031	–	–	6.9
NBA Playoff Totals	8	–	–	26	214	.243	–	–	–	16	28	.571	–	–	–	28	37	1	–	–	–	68	–	1.8	8.5
NBL Playoff Totals	21	–	–	50	–	–	–	–	–	39	69	.565	–	–	–	–	49	–	–	–	–	139	–	–	6.6

Komives, Howard K. (Howie, Butch) b. May 9, 1941 Ht. 6-1 Wt. 185 College: Bowling Green State

SEASON–TEAM	G	GS	MIN	FGM	FGA	PCT	3FGM	3FGA	PCT	FTM	FTA	PCT	O-RB	D-RB	TOT	AST	PF	DQ	STL	TO	BLK	PTS	RPG	APG	PPG
64-65–New York	80	–	2378	381	1020	.374	–	–	–	212	254	.835	–	–	195	265	246	2	–	–	–	974	2.4	3.3	12.2
65-66–New York	80	–	2612	436	1116	.391	–	–	–	241	280	.861	–	–	281	425	278	5	–	–	–	1113	3.5	5.3	13.9
66-67–New York	65	–	2282	402	995	.404	–	–	–	217	253	.858	–	–	183	401	213	1	–	–	–	1021	2.8	6.2	15.7
67-68–New York	78	–	1660	233	631	.369	–	–	–	132	161	.820	–	–	168	246	170	1	–	–	–	598	2.2	3.2	7.7
68-69–N.Y.-Detroit	85	–	2562	379	974	.389	–	–	–	211	264	.799	–	–	299	403	274	1	–	–	–	969	3.5	4.7	11.4
69-70–Detroit	82	–	2418	363	878	.413	–	–	–	190	234	.812	–	–	193	312	247	2	–	–	–	916	2.4	3.8	11.2
70-71–Detroit	82	–	1932	275	715	.385	–	–	–	121	151	.801	–	–	152	262	184	0	–	–	–	671	1.9	3.2	8.2
71-72–Detroit	79	–	2071	262	702	.373	–	–	–	164	203	.808	–	–	172	291	196	0	–	–	–	688	2.2	3.7	8.7
72-73–Buffalo	67	–	1468	163	429	.380	–	–	–	85	98	.867	–	–	118	239	155	1	–	–	–	411	1.8	3.6	6.1
73-74–K.C.-Omaha	44	–	830	78	192	.406	–	–	–	33	38	.868	10	33	43	97	83	0	32	–	3	189	1.0	2.2	4.3
Reg. Season Totals	742	–	20213	2972	7652	.388	–	–	–	1606	1936	.830	10	33	1804	2941	2046	13	32	–	3	7550	2.4	4.0	10.2
Playoff Totals	10	–	263	31	103	.301	–	–	–	14	19	.737	0	0	25	38	35	1	0	–	0	76	2.5	3.8	7.6

Koncak, Jon Francis (Kak) b. May 17, 1963 Ht. 7-0 Wt. 255 College: Southern Methodist

SEASON–TEAM	G	GS	MIN	FGM	FGA	PCT	3FGM	3FGA	PCT	FTM	FTA	PCT	O-RB	D-RB	TOT	AST	PF	DQ	STL	TO	BLK	PTS	RPG	APG	PPG
85-86–Atlanta	82	15	1695	263	519	.507	0	1	.000	156	257	.607	171	296	467	55	296	10	37	111	69	682	5.7	0.7	8.3
86-87–Atlanta	82	19	1684	169	352	.480	0	1	.000	125	191	.654	153	340	493	31	262	2	52	92	76	463	6.0	0.4	5.6
87-88–Atlanta	49	22	1073	98	203	.483	0	2	.000	83	136	.610	103	230	333	19	161	1	36	53	56	279	6.8	0.4	5.7
88-89–Atlanta	74	22	1531	141	269	.524	0	3	.000	63	114	.553	147	306	453	56	238	4	54	60	98	345	6.1	0.8	4.7
89-90–Atlanta	54	28	977	78	127	.614	0	1	.000	42	79	.532	58	168	226	23	182	4	38	47	34	198	4.2	0.4	3.7
90-91–Atlanta	77	61	1931	140	321	.436	1	8	.125	32	54	.593	101	274	375	124	265	6	74	50	76	313	4.9	1.6	4.1
91-92–Atlanta	77	14	1489	111	284	.391	0	12	.000	19	29	.655	62	199	261	132	207	2	50	54	67	241	3.4	1.7	3.1
92-93–Atlanta	78	65	1975	124	267	.464	3	8	.375	24	50	.480	100	327	427	140	264	6	75	52	100	275	5.5	1.8	3.5
93-94–Atlanta	82	78	1823	159	369	.431	0	3	.000	24	36	.667	83	282	365	102	236	1	63	44	125	342	4.5	1.2	4.2
94-95–Atlanta	62	20	943	77	187	.412	12	36	.333	13	24	.542	23	161	184	52	137	1	36	20	46	179	3.0	0.8	2.9
95-96–Orlando	67	35	1288	84	175	.480	3	9	.333	32	57	.561	63	209	272	51	226	7	27	41	44	203	4.1	0.8	3.0
Reg. Season Totals	784	379	16409	1444	3073	.470	19	84	.226	613	1027	.597	1064	2792	3856	785	2474	44	542	624	791	3520	4.9	1.0	4.5
Playoff Totals	53	27	1028	75	168	.446	0	0	–	70	108	.648	57	150	207	39	171	4	27	29	47	220	3.9	0.7	4.2

Kondla, Thomas A. (Tom) b. November 30, 1946 Ht. 6-8 Wt. 225 College: Minnesota

SEASON–TEAM	G	GS	MIN	FGM	FGA	PCT	3FGM	3FGA	PCT	FTM	FTA	PCT	O-RB	D-RB	TOT	AST	PF	DQ	STL	TO	BLK	PTS	RPG	APG	PPG
68-69–Minn.-Hou. (A)	42	–	353	58	145	.400	0	1	.000	22	46	.478	–	–	125	13	56	0	–	23	–	138	3.0	0.3	3.3
Reg. ABA Totals	42	–	353	58	145	.400	0	1	.000	22	46	.478	–	–	125	13	56	0	–	23	–	138	3.0	0.3	3.3

Koper, Herbert L. (Bud) b. August 9, 1942 Ht. 6-6 Wt. 210 College: Oklahoma City

SEASON–TEAM	G	GS	MIN	FGM	FGA	PCT	3FGM	3FGA	PCT	FTM	FTA	PCT	O-RB	D-RB	TOT	AST	PF	DQ	STL	TO	BLK	PTS	RPG	APG	PPG
64-65–San Francisco	56	–	631	106	241	.440	–	–	–	35	42	.833	–	–	61	43	59	1	–	–	–	247	1.1	0.8	4.4
Reg. Season Totals	56	–	631	106	241	.440	–	–	–	35	42	.833	–	–	61	43	59	1	–	–	–	247	1.1	0.8	4.4

Kopicki, Joseph Gerard (Joe) b. June 12, 1960 Ht. 6-9 Wt. 240 College: Detroit Mercy

SEASON–TEAM	G	GS	MIN	FGM	FGA	PCT	3FGM	3FGA	PCT	FTM	FTA	PCT	O-RB	D-RB	TOT	AST	PF	DQ	STL	TO	BLK	PTS	RPG	APG	PPG
82-83–Washington	17	1	201	23	51	.451	0	1	.000	21	25	.840	18	44	62	9	21	0	9	8	2	67	3.6	0.5	3.9
83-84–Washington	59	2	678	64	132	.485	1	7	.143	91	112	.813	64	102	166	46	71	0	15	39	5	220	2.8	0.8	3.7
84-85–Denver	42	0	308	50	95	.526	2	3	.667	43	54	.796	29	57	86	29	58	0	13	28	1	145	2.0	0.7	3.5
Reg. Season Totals	118	3	1187	137	278	.493	3	11	.273	155	191	.812	111	203	314	84	150	0	37	75	8	432	2.7	0.7	3.7
Playoff Totals	10	0	57	9	22	.409	0	0	–	9	17	.529	2	16	18	4	11	0	1	3	1	27	1.8	0.4	2.7

Kornet, Francis Milton (Frank) b. January 27, 1967 Ht. 6-9 Wt. 225 College: Vanderbilt

SEASON–TEAM	G	GS	MIN	FGM	FGA	PCT	3FGM	3FGA	PCT	FTM	FTA	PCT	O-RB	D-RB	TOT	AST	PF	DQ	STL	TO	BLK	PTS	RPG	APG	PPG
89-90–Milwaukee	57	0	438	42	114	.368	5	20	.250	24	39	.615	25	46	71	21	54	0	14	23	3	113	1.2	0.4	2.0
90-91–Milwaukee	32	0	157	23	62	.371	5	18	.278	7	13	.538	10	14	24	9	28	0	5	11	1	58	0.8	0.3	1.8
Reg. Season Totals	89	0	595	65	176	.369	10	38	.263	31	52	.596	35	60	95	30	82	0	19	34	4	171	1.1	0.3	1.9
Playoff Totals	2	0	4	0	1	.000	0	1	.000	0	0	–	0	1	1	–	1	0	0	1	0	0	0.5	0.0	0.0

Koski, Anthony P. **(Tony)** b. June 26, 1946 Ht. 6-8 Wt. 215 College: Providence

SEASON–TEAM	G	GS	MIN	FGM	FGA	PCT	3FGM	3FGA	PCT	FTM	FTA	PCT	O-RB	D-RB	TOT	AST	PF	DQ	STL	TO	BLK	PTS	RPG	APG	PPG
68-69–New York (A)	5	–	30	2	7	.286	0	0	–	2	2	1.000	–	–	7	4	9	0	–	2	–	6	1.4	0.8	1.2
Reg. ABA Totals	5	–	30	2	7	.286	0	0	–	2	2	1.000	–	–	7	4	9	0	–	2	–	6	1.4	0.8	1.2

Kosmalski, Leonard J. **(Len)** b. November 29, 1951 Ht. 7-0 Wt. 245 College: Tennessee

SEASON–TEAM	G	GS	MIN	FGM	FGA	PCT	3FGM	3FGA	PCT	FTM	FTA	PCT	O-RB	D-RB	TOT	AST	PF	DQ	STL	TO	BLK	PTS	RPG	APG	PPG
74-75–K.C.-Omaha	67	–	413	33	83	.398	–	–	–	24	29	.828	31	88	119	41	64	0	6	–	6	90	1.8	0.6	1.3
75-76–Kansas City	9	–	93	8	20	.400	–	–	–	4	7	.571	9	16	25	12	11	0	3	–	4	20	2.8	1.3	2.2
Reg. Season Totals	76	–	506	41	103	.398	–	–	–	28	36	.778	40	104	144	53	75	0	9	–	10	110	1.9	0.7	1.4
Playoff Totals	6	–	29	2	3	.667	–	–	–	2	3	.667	1	9	10	5	4	0	1	–	0	6	1.7	0.8	1.0

Kostecka, Andrew **(Andy)** b. February 10, 1921 Ht. 6-3 Wt. 205 College: Georgetown

SEASON–TEAM	G	GS	MIN	FGM	FGA	PCT	3FGM	3FGA	PCT	FTM	FTA	PCT	O-RB	D-RB	TOT	AST	PF	DQ	STL	TO	BLK	PTS	RPG	APG	PPG
48-49–Indianapolis	21	–	–	46	110	.418	–	–	–	43	70	.614	–	–	–	14	48	–	–	–	–	135	–	0.7	6.4
Reg. Season Totals	21	–	–	46	110	.418	–	–	–	43	70	.614	–	–	–	14	48	–	–	–	–	135	–	0.7	6.4

Kottman, Harold M. b. August 22, 1922 Ht. 6-8 Wt. 220 College: Culver-Stockton

SEASON–TEAM	G	GS	MIN	FGM	FGA	PCT	3FGM	3FGA	PCT	FTM	FTA	PCT	O-RB	D-RB	TOT	AST	PF	DQ	STL	TO	BLK	PTS	RPG	APG	PPG
46-47–Boston	53	–	–	59	188	.314	–	–	–	47	101	.465	–	–	–	17	58	–	–	–	–	165	–	0.3	3.1
Reg. Season Totals	53	–	–	59	188	.314	–	–	–	47	101	.465	–	–	–	17	58	–	–	–	–	165	–	0.3	3.1

Kozelko, Thomas William b. July 1, 1951 Ht. 6-8 Wt. 220 College: Toledo

SEASON–TEAM	G	GS	MIN	FGM	FGA	PCT	3FGM	3FGA	PCT	FTM	FTA	PCT	O-RB	D-RB	TOT	AST	PF	DQ	STL	TO	BLK	PTS	RPG	APG	PPG
73-74–Capital	49	–	573	59	133	.444	–	–	–	23	32	.719	52	72	124	25	82	3	21	–	7	141	2.5	0.5	2.9
74-75–Washington	73	–	754	60	167	.359	–	–	–	31	36	.861	50	90	140	41	125	4	28	–	5	151	1.9	0.6	2.1
75-76–Washington	67	–	584	48	99	.485	–	–	–	19	30	.633	19	63	82	33	74	0	19	–	4	115	1.2	0.5	1.7
Reg. Season Totals	189	–	1911	167	399	.419	–	–	–	73	98	.745	121	225	346	99	281	7	68	–	16	407	1.8	0.5	2.2
Playoff Totals	25	–	126	15	25	.600	–	–	–	9	11	.818	9	8	17	2	18	1	0	–	1	39	0.7	0.1	1.6

Kozlicki, Ronald F. **(Ron, Koz)** b. December 12, 1944 Ht. 6-7 Wt. 215 College: Northwestern

SEASON–TEAM	G	GS	MIN	FGM	FGA	PCT	3FGM	3FGA	PCT	FTM	FTA	PCT	O-RB	D-RB	TOT	AST	PF	DQ	STL	TO	BLK	PTS	RPG	APG	PPG
67-68–Indiana (A)	37	–	354	41	121	.339	6	29	.207	21	34	.618	–	–	69	14	31	0	–	19	–	109	1.9	0.4	2.9
Reg. ABA Totals	37	–	354	41	121	.339	6	29	.207	21	34	.618	–	–	69	14	31	0	–	19	–	109	1.9	0.4	2.9
ABA Playoff Totals	2	–	5	0	2	.000	0	1	.000	0	0	–	–	–	1	0	1	0	–	1	–	0	0.5	0.0	0.0

Kramer, Arvid b. October 2, 1956 Ht. 6-9 Wt. 220 College: Augustana (S.D.)

SEASON–TEAM	G	GS	MIN	FGM	FGA	PCT	3FGM	3FGA	PCT	FTM	FTA	PCT	O-RB	D-RB	TOT	AST	PF	DQ	STL	TO	BLK	PTS	RPG	APG	PPG
79-80–Denver	8	–	45	7	22	.318	0	0	–	2	2	1.000	6	6	12	3	8	0	0	5	5	16	1.5	0.4	2.0
Reg. Season Totals	8	–	45	7	22	.318	0	0	–	2	2	1.000	6	6	12	3	8	0	0	5	5	16	1.5	0.4	2.0

Kramer, Barry D. b. November 10, 1942 Ht. 6-4 Wt. 200 College: New York U.

SEASON–TEAM	G	GS	MIN	FGM	FGA	PCT	3FGM	3FGA	PCT	FTM	FTA	PCT	O-RB	D-RB	TOT	AST	PF	DQ	STL	TO	BLK	PTS	RPG	APG	PPG
64-65–S.F.-N.Y.	52	–	507	63	186	.339	–	–	–	60	84	.714	–	–	100	41	67	1	–	–	–	186	1.9	0.8	3.6
69-70–New York (A)	7	–	56	10	31	.323	0	1	.000	7	8	.875	–	–	13	3	10	0	–	–	–	27	1.9	0.4	3.9
Reg. NBA Totals	52	–	507	63	186	.339	–	–	–	60	84	.714	–	–	100	41	67	1	–	–	–	186	1.9	0.8	3.6
Reg. ABA Totals	7	–	56	10	31	.323	0	1	.000	7	8	.875	–	–	13	3	10	0	–	–	–	27	1.9	0.4	3.9

Kramer, Joel Bruce b. November 30, 1955 Ht. 6-7 Wt. 205 College: San Diego State

SEASON–TEAM	G	GS	MIN	FGM	FGA	PCT	3FGM	3FGA	PCT	FTM	FTA	PCT	O-RB	D-RB	TOT	AST	PF	DQ	STL	TO	BLK	PTS	RPG	APG	PPG
78-79–Phoenix	82	–	1401	181	370	.489	–	–	–	125	176	.710	134	203	337	92	224	2	45	98	23	487	4.1	1.1	5.9
79-80–Phoenix	54	–	711	67	143	.469	0	1	.000	56	70	.800	49	102	151	75	104	0	26	51	5	190	2.8	1.4	3.5
80-81–Phoenix	82	–	1065	136	258	.527	0	1	.000	63	91	.692	77	155	232	88	132	0	35	67	17	335	2.8	1.1	4.1
81-82–Phoenix	56	0	549	55	133	.414	0	0	–	33	42	.786	36	72	108	51	62	0	19	26	11	143	1.9	0.9	2.6
82-83–Phoenix	54	4	458	44	104	.423	0	1	.000	14	16	.875	41	47	88	37	63	0	15	22	6	102	1.6	0.7	1.9
Reg. Season Totals	328	4	4184	483	1008	.479	0	3	.000	291	395	.737	337	579	916	343	585	2	140	264	62	1257	2.8	1.0	3.8
Playoff Totals	28	0	384	50	93	.538	0	0	–	29	41	.707	25	53	78	24	64	2	12	18	9	129	2.8	0.9	4.6

Kramer, Steven P. **(Steve)** b. January 1, 1945 Ht. 6-5 Wt. 205 College: Brigham Young

SEASON–TEAM	G	GS	MIN	FGM	FGA	PCT	3FGM	3FGA	PCT	FTM	FTA	PCT	O-RB	D-RB	TOT	AST	PF	DQ	STL	TO	BLK	PTS	RPG	APG	PPG
67-68–Anaheim (A)	50	–	1140	218	497	.439	1	5	.200	129	165	.782	–	–	173	85	149	3	–	96	–	566	3.5	1.7	11.3
68-69–Houston (A)	23	–	701	113	281	.402	0	1	.000	95	117	.812	–	–	85	112	96	4	–	69	–	321	3.7	4.9	14.0
69-70–Carolina (A)	51	–	447	49	107	.458	0	2	.000	63	86	.733	–	–	52	39	70	0	–	–	–	161	1.0	0.8	3.2
Reg. ABA Totals	124	–	2288	380	885	.429	1	8	.125	287	368	.780	–	–	310	236	315	7	–	165	–	1048	2.5	1.9	8.5
ABA Playoff Totals	2	–	20	2	5	.400	0	0	–	3	3	1.000	–	–	4	2	3	0	–	–	–	7	2.0	1.0	3.5

Kraus, Daniel Joseph (Dan) b. February 13, 1923 Ht. 6-0 Wt. 195 College: Georgetown

SEASON–TEAM	G	GS	MIN	FGM	FGA	PCT	3FGM	3FGA	PCT	FTM	FTA	PCT	O-RB	D-RB	TOT	AST	PF	DQ	STL	TO	BLK	PTS	RPG	APG	PPG
48-49–Baltimore	13	–	–	5	35	.143	–	–	–	11	24	.458	–	–	–	7	24	–	–	–	–	21	–	0.5	1.6
Reg. Season Totals	13	–	–	5	35	.143	–	–	–	11	24	.458	–	–	–	7	24	–	–	–	–	21	–	0.5	1.6

Krautblatt, Herbert (Herb) b. November 19, 1926 Ht. 6-1 Wt. 190 College: Rider

SEASON–TEAM	G	GS	MIN	FGM	FGA	PCT	3FGM	3FGA	PCT	FTM	FTA	PCT	O-RB	D-RB	TOT	AST	PF	DQ	STL	TO	BLK	PTS	RPG	APG	PPG
48-49–Baltimore	10	–	–	4	18	.222	–	–	–	5	11	.455	–	–	–	4	14	–	–	–	–	13	–	0.4	1.3
Reg. Season Totals	10	–	–	4	18	.222	–	–	–	5	11	.455	–	–	–	4	14	–	–	–	–	13	–	0.4	1.3

Krebs, James (Jim, Red) b. September 8, 1935 d. May 6, 1965 Ht. 6-8 Wt. 230 College: Southern Methodist

SEASON–TEAM	G	GS	MIN	FGM	FGA	PCT	3FGM	3FGA	PCT	FTM	FTA	PCT	O-RB	D-RB	TOT	AST	PF	DQ	STL	TO	BLK	PTS	RPG	APG	PPG
57-58–Minneapolis	68	–	1259	199	527	.378	–	–	–	135	176	.767	–	–	502	27	182	4	–	–	–	533	7.4	0.4	7.8
58-59–Minneapolis	72	–	1578	271	679	.399	–	–	–	92	123	.748	–	–	491	50	212	4	–	–	–	634	6.8	0.7	8.8
59-60–Minneapolis	75	–	1269	237	605	.392	–	–	–	98	136	.721	–	–	327	38	210	2	–	–	–	572	4.4	0.5	7.6
60-61–Los Angeles	75	–	1655	271	692	.392	–	–	–	75	93	.806	–	–	456	68	223	2	–	–	–	617	6.1	0.9	8.2
61-62–Los Angeles	78	–	2012	312	701	.445	–	–	–	156	208	.750	–	–	616	110	290	9	–	–	–	780	7.9	1.4	10.0
62-63–Los Angeles	79	–	1913	272	627	.434	–	–	–	115	154	.747	–	–	502	87	256	2	–	–	–	659	6.4	1.1	8.3
63-64–Los Angeles	68	–	975	134	357	.375	–	–	–	65	85	.765	–	–	283	49	166	6	–	–	–	333	4.2	0.7	4.9
Reg. Season Totals	515	–	10661	1696	4188	.405	–	–	–	736	975	.755	–	–	3177	429	1539	29	–	–	–	4128	6.2	0.8	8.0
Playoff Totals	62	–	1129	127	341	.372	–	–	–	75	96	.781	–	–	348	53	211	12	–	–	–	329	5.6	0.9	5.3

Kreklow, Wayne R. b. January 4, 1957 Ht. 6-4 Wt. 180 College: Drake

SEASON–TEAM	G	GS	MIN	FGM	FGA	PCT	3FGM	3FGA	PCT	FTM	FTA	PCT	O-RB	D-RB	TOT	AST	PF	DQ	STL	TO	BLK	PTS	RPG	APG	PPG
80-81–Boston	25	–	100	11	47	.234	1	4	.250	7	10	.700	2	10	12	9	20	0	2	10	1	30	0.5	0.4	1.2
Reg. Season Totals	25	–	100	11	47	.234	1	4	.250	7	10	.700	2	10	12	9	20	0	2	10	1	30	0.5	0.4	1.2

Kron, Thomas M. (Tommy) b. February 28, 1943 Ht. 6-5 Wt. 200 College: Kentucky

SEASON–TEAM	G	GS	MIN	FGM	FGA	PCT	3FGM	3FGA	PCT	FTM	FTA	PCT	O-RB	D-RB	TOT	AST	PF	DQ	STL	TO	BLK	PTS	RPG	APG	PPG
66-67–St. Louis	32	–	221	27	87	.310	–	–	–	13	19	.684	–	–	36	46	35	0	–	–	–	67	1.1	1.4	2.1
67-68–Seattle	76	–	1794	277	699	.396	–	–	–	184	233	.790	–	–	355	281	231	4	–	–	–	738	4.7	3.7	9.7
68-69–Seattle	76	–	1124	146	372	.392	–	–	–	96	137	.701	–	–	212	191	179	2	–	–	–	388	2.8	2.5	5.1
69-70–Kentucky (A)	40	–	493	55	147	.374	7	19	.368	41	46	.891	–	–	69	87	80	1	–	–	–	158	1.7	2.2	4.0
Reg. NBA Totals	184	–	3139	450	1158	.389	–	–	–	293	389	.753	–	–	603	518	445	6	–	–	–	1193	3.3	2.8	6.5
Reg. ABA Totals	40	–	493	55	147	.374	7	19	.368	41	46	.891	–	–	69	87	80	1	–	–	–	158	1.7	2.2	4.0
NBA Playoff Totals	1	–	1	0	1	.000	–	–	–	0	0	–	–	–	0	–	1	0	–	–	–	0	0.0	0.0	0.0

Kropp, Thomas Carl (Tom) b. February 12, 1953 Ht. 6-3 Wt. 205 College: Nebraska-Kearney

SEASON–TEAM	G	GS	MIN	FGM	FGA	PCT	3FGM	3FGA	PCT	FTM	FTA	PCT	O-RB	D-RB	TOT	AST	PF	DQ	STL	TO	BLK	PTS	RPG	APG	PPG
75-76–Washington	25	–	72	7	30	.233	–	–	–	5	6	.833	5	10	15	8	20	0	2	–	0	19	0.6	0.3	0.8
76-77–Chicago	53	–	480	73	152	.480	–	–	–	28	41	.683	21	26	47	39	77	1	18	–	1	174	0.9	0.7	3.3
Reg. Season Totals	78	–	552	80	182	.440	–	–	–	33	47	.702	26	36	62	47	97	1	20	–	1	193	0.8	0.6	2.5
Playoff Totals	2	–	4	1	1	1.000	–	–	–	0	0	–	0	0	0	–	3	0	0	–	0	2	0.0	0.0	1.0

Krystkowiak, Larry Brett (Special K) b. September 23, 1964 Ht. 6-9 Wt. 240 College: Montana

SEASON–TEAM	G	GS	MIN	FGM	FGA	PCT	3FGM	3FGA	PCT	FTM	FTA	PCT	O-RB	D-RB	TOT	AST	PF	DQ	STL	TO	BLK	PTS	RPG	APG	PPG
86-87–San Antonio	68	2	1004	170	373	.456	1	12	.083	110	148	.743	77	162	239	85	141	1	22	67	12	451	3.5	1.3	6.6
87-88–Milwaukee	50	7	1050	128	266	.481	0	3	.000	103	127	.811	88	143	231	50	137	0	18	57	8	359	4.6	1.0	7.2
88-89–Milwaukee	80	77	2472	362	766	.473	4	12	.333	289	351	.823	198	412	610	107	219	0	93	147	9	1017	7.6	1.3	12.7
89-90–Milwaukee	16	7	381	43	118	.364	0	2	.000	26	33	.788	16	60	76	25	41	0	10	19	2	112	4.8	1.6	7.0
91-92–Milwaukee	79	16	1848	293	660	.444	0	5	.000	128	169	.757	131	298	429	114	218	2	54	115	12	714	5.4	1.4	9.0
92-93–Utah	71	0	1362	198	425	.466	0	1	.000	117	147	.796	74	205	279	68	181	1	42	62	13	513	3.9	1.0	7.2
93-94–Orlando	34	11	682	71	148	.480	0	1	.000	31	39	.795	38	85	123	35	74	0	14	29	4	173	3.6	1.0	5.1
94-95–Chicago	19	14	287	28	72	.389	0	0	–	27	30	.900	19	40	59	26	34	0	9	25	2	83	3.1	1.4	4.4
96-97–L.A. Lakers	3	0	11	1	2	.500	0	0	–	1	2	.500	2	3	5	3	3	0	2	1	0	3	1.7	1.0	1.0
Reg. Season Totals	420	134	9097	1294	2830	.457	5	36	.139	832	1046	.795	643	1408	2051	513	1048	4	264	522	62	3425	4.9	1.2	8.2
Playoff Totals	20	16	527	50	122	.410	0	2	.000	47	53	.887	35	74	109	30	53	0	10	24	3	147	5.5	1.5	7.4

Kuberski, Stephen Paul (Steve) b. November 6, 1947 Ht. 6-8 Wt. 215 College: Illinois; Bradley

SEASON–TEAM	G	GS	MIN	FGM	FGA	PCT	3FGM	3FGA	PCT	FTM	FTA	PCT	O-RB	D-RB	TOT	AST	PF	DQ	STL	TO	BLK	PTS	RPG	APG	PPG
69-70–Boston	51	–	797	130	335	.388	–	–	–	64	92	.696	–	–	257	29	87	0	–	–	–	324	5.0	0.6	6.4
70-71–Boston	82	–	1867	313	745	.420	–	–	–	133	183	.727	–	–	538	78	198	1	–	–	–	759	6.6	1.0	9.3
71-72–Boston	71	–	1128	185	444	.417	–	–	–	80	102	.784	–	–	320	46	130	1	–	–	–	450	4.5	0.6	6.3
72-73–Boston	78	–	762	140	347	.403	–	–	–	65	84	.774	–	–	197	26	92	0	–	–	–	345	2.5	0.3	4.4
73-74–Boston	78	–	985	157	368	.427	–	–	–	86	111	.775	96	141	237	38	125	0	7	–	7	400	3.0	0.5	5.1
74-75–Milwaukee	59	–	517	62	159	.390	–	–	–	44	56	.786	52	71	123	35	59	0	11	–	3	168	2.1	0.6	2.8
75-76–Buffalo-Boston	70	–	967	135	291	.464	–	–	–	71	79	.899	90	169	259	47	133	1	12	–	13	341	3.7	0.7	4.9
76-77–Boston	76	–	860	131	312	.420	–	–	–	63	83	.759	76	133	209	39	89	0	7	–	5	325	2.8	0.5	4.3
77-78–Boston	3	–	14	1	4	.250	–	–	–	0	0	–	1	5	6	0	2	0	1	2	0	2	2.0	0.0	0.7
Reg. Season Totals	568	–	7897	1254	3005	.417	–	–	–	606	790	.767	315	519	2146	338	915	3	38	2	28	3114	3.8	0.6	5.5
Playoff Totals	50	–	614	110	239	.460	–	–	–	65	84	.774	24	47	148	24	85	0	1	–	4	285	3.0	0.5	5.7

Kubiak, Leo R. b. December 25, 1927 Ht. 5-11 Wt. 175 College: Bowling Green State

SEASON–TEAM	G	GS	MIN	FGM	FGA	PCT	3FGM	3FGA	PCT	FTM	FTA	PCT	O-RB	D-RB	TOT	AST	PF	DQ	STL	TO	BLK	PTS	RPG	APG	PPG
48-49–Waterloo (N)	62	–	–	177	–	–	–	–	–	108	142	.761	–	–	–	–	177	–	–	–	–	462	–	–	7.5
49-50–Waterloo	62	–	–	259	794	.326	–	–	–	192	236	.814	–	–	–	201	250	–	–	–	–	710	–	3.2	11.5
Reg. NBA Totals	62	–	–	259	794	.326	–	–	–	192	236	.814	–	–	–	201	250	–	–	–	–	710	–	3.2	11.5
Reg. NBL Totals	62	–	–	177	–	–	–	–	–	108	142	.761	–	–	–	–	177	–	–	–	–	462	–	–	7.5

Kuczenski, Bruce John b. February 3, 1961 Ht. 6-10 Wt. 230 College: Connecticut

SEASON–TEAM	G	GS	MIN	FGM	FGA	PCT	3FGM	3FGA	PCT	FTM	FTA	PCT	O-RB	D-RB	TOT	AST	PF	DQ	STL	TO	BLK	PTS	RPG	APG	PPG
83-84–N.J.-Phil.-Indiana	15	2	119	10	37	.270	0	0	–	8	12	.667	7	16	23	8	18	0	1	15	1	28	1.5	0.5	1.9
Reg. Season Totals	15	2	119	10	37	.270	0	0	–	8	12	.667	7	16	23	8	18	0	1	15	1	28	1.5	0.5	1.9

Kudelka, Frank Carl (Apples) b. June 25, 1925 d. May 4, 1993 Ht. 6-2 Wt. 195 College: St. Mary's (Calif.)

SEASON–TEAM	G	GS	MIN	FGM	FGA	PCT	3FGM	3FGA	PCT	FTM	FTA	PCT	O-RB	D-RB	TOT	AST	PF	DQ	STL	TO	BLK	PTS	RPG	APG	PPG
49-50–Chicago	65	–	–	172	528	.326	–	–	–	89	140	.636	–	–	–	132	198	–	–	–	–	433	–	2.0	6.7
50-51–Wash.-Boston	62	–	–	179	518	.346	–	–	–	83	119	.697	–	–	158	105	211	8	–	–	–	441	2.5	1.7	7.1
51-52–Baltimore	65	–	1583	204	614	.332	–	–	–	198	258	.767	–	–	275	183	220	11	–	–	–	606	4.2	2.8	9.3
52-53–Balt.-Phil.	36	–	567	59	193	.306	–	–	–	44	68	.647	–	–	88	70	109	2	–	–	–	162	2.4	1.9	4.5
Reg. Season Totals	228	–	2150	614	1853	.331	–	–	–	414	585	.708	–	–	521	490	738	21	–	–	–	1642	3.2	2.1	7.2
Playoff Totals	3	–	0	4	24	.250	–	–	–	1	5	.200	–	–	5	10	7	0	–	–	–	9	5.0	2.0	3.0

Kuester, John DeWitt Jr. b. February 6, 1955 Ht. 6-2 Wt. 180 College: North Carolina

SEASON–TEAM	G	GS	MIN	FGM	FGA	PCT	3FGM	3FGA	PCT	FTM	FTA	PCT	O-RB	D-RB	TOT	AST	PF	DQ	STL	TO	BLK	PTS	RPG	APG	PPG
77-78–Kansas City	78	–	1215	145	319	.455	–	–	–	87	105	.829	19	95	114	252	143	1	58	97	1	377	1.5	3.2	4.8
78-79–Denver	33	–	212	16	52	.308	–	–	–	13	14	.929	5	8	13	37	29	0	18	20	1	45	0.4	1.1	1.4
79-80–Indiana	24	–	100	12	34	.353	0	1	.000	5	7	.714	3	11	14	16	8	0	7	5	1	29	0.6	0.7	1.2
Reg. Season Totals	135	–	1527	173	405	.427	0	1	.000	105	126	.833	27	114	141	305	180	1	83	122	3	451	1.0	2.3	3.3

Kuka, Raphael Eugene (Ray) b. February 17, 1922 d. March 27, 1990 Ht. 6-3 Wt. 200 College: Montana State; Notre Dame

SEASON–TEAM	G	GS	MIN	FGM	FGA	PCT	3FGM	3FGA	PCT	FTM	FTA	PCT	O-RB	D-RB	TOT	AST	PF	DQ	STL	TO	BLK	PTS	RPG	APG	PPG
47-48–New York	44	–	–	89	273	.326	–	–	–	50	84	.595	–	–	–	27	117	–	–	–	–	228	–	0.6	5.2
48-49–New York	8	–	–	10	36	.278	–	–	–	5	9	.556	–	–	–	11	16	–	–	–	–	25	–	1.4	3.1
Reg. Season Totals	52	–	–	99	309	.320	–	–	–	55	93	.591	–	–	–	38	133	–	–	–	–	253	–	0.7	4.9
Playoff Totals	3	–	–	3	10	.300	–	–	–	2	2	1.000	–	–	–	–	12	–	–	–	–	8	–	0.0	2.7

Kukoc, Toni (Euro-Magic) b. September 18, 1968 Ht. 6-11 Wt. 235 Country: Croatia

SEASON–TEAM	G	GS	MIN	FGM	FGA	PCT	3FGM	3FGA	PCT	FTM	FTA	PCT	O-RB	D-RB	TOT	AST	PF	DQ	STL	TO	BLK	PTS	RPG	APG	PPG
93-94–Chicago	75	8	1808	313	726	.431	32	118	.271	156	210	.743	98	199	297	252	122	0	81	167	33	814	4.0	3.4	10.9
94-95–Chicago	81	55	2584	487	967	.504	62	198	.313	235	314	.748	155	285	440	372	163	1	102	165	16	1271	5.4	4.6	15.7
95-96–Chicago	81	20	2103	386	787	.490	87	216	.403	206	267	.772	115	208	323	287	150	0	64	114	28	1065	4.0	3.5	13.1
96-97–Chicago	57	15	1610	285	605	.471	50	151	.331	134	174	.770	94	167	261	256	97	1	60	91	29	754	4.6	4.5	13.2
97-98–Chicago	74	52	2235	383	841	.455	63	174	.362	155	219	.708	121	206	327	314	149	0	76	154	37	984	4.4	4.2	13.3
98-99–Chicago	44	44	1654	315	750	.420	39	137	.285	159	215	.740	65	245	310	235	82	0	49	121	11	828	7.0	5.3	18.8
99-00–Chicago-Phil.	56	31	1784	297	728	.408	44	168	.262	192	265	.725	75	198	273	265	112	0	77	146	28	830	4.9	4.7	14.8
Reg. Season Totals	468	225	13778	2466	5404	.456	377	1162	.324	1237	1664	.743	723	1508	2231	1981	875	2	509	958	182	6546	4.8	4.2	14.0
Playoff Totals	85	32	2322	329	765	.430	88	267	.330	165	234	.705	94	249	343	282	184	1	78	121	26	911	4.0	3.3	10.7

Kunnert, Kevin Robert b. November 11, 1951 Ht. 7-0 Wt. 230 College: Iowa

SEASON–TEAM	G	GS	MIN	FGM	FGA	PCT	3FGM	3FGA	PCT	FTM	FTA	PCT	O-RB	D-RB	TOT	AST	PF	DQ	STL	TO	BLK	PTS	RPG	APG	PPG
73-74–Buffalo-Hou.	64	–	701	105	215	.488	–	–	–	21	33	.636	83	134	217	43	151	1	10	–	54	231	3.4	0.7	3.6
74-75–Houston	75	–	1801	346	676	.512	–	–	–	116	169	.686	214	417	631	108	223	2	34	–	84	808	8.4	1.4	10.8
75-76–Houston	80	–	2335	465	954	.487	–	–	–	102	156	.654	267	520	787	155	315	14	57	–	105	1032	9.8	1.9	12.9
76-77–Houston	81	–	2050	333	685	.486	–	–	–	93	126	.738	210	459	669	154	361	17	35	–	105	759	8.3	1.9	9.4
77-78–Houston	80	–	2152	368	842	.437	–	–	–	93	135	.689	262	431	693	97	315	13	44	141	90	829	8.7	1.2	10.4
78-79–San Diego	81	–	1684	234	501	.467	–	–	–	56	85	.659	202	367	569	113	309	7	45	141	118	524	7.0	1.4	6.5
79-80–Portland	18	–	302	50	114	.439	0	0	–	26	43	.605	37	75	112	29	59	1	7	41	22	126	6.2	1.6	7.0
80-81–Portland	55	–	842	101	216	.468	0	0	–	42	54	.778	98	189	287	67	143	1	17	50	32	244	5.2	1.2	4.4
81-82–Portland	21	0	237	20	48	.417	0	0	–	9	17	.529	20	46	66	18	51	1	3	18	6	49	3.1	0.9	2.3
Reg. Season Totals	555	0	12104	2022	4251	.476	0	0	–	558	818	.682	1393	2638	4031	784	1927	57	252	391	616	4602	7.3	1.4	8.3
Playoff Totals	23	0	615	91	195	.467	0	1	.000	30	53	.566	61	115	176	27	95	3	7	3	21	212	7.7	1.2	9.2

Kunze, Terry D. b. March 11, 1943 Ht. 6-4 Wt. 210 College: Minnesota

SEASON–TEAM	G	GS	MIN	FGM	FGA	PCT	3FGM	3FGA	PCT	FTM	FTA	PCT	O-RB	D-RB	TOT	AST	PF	DQ	STL	TO	BLK	PTS	RPG	APG	PPG
67-68–Minnesota (A)	46	–	662	83	245	.339	5	11	.455	59	102	.578	–	–	75	47	77	0	–	58	–	230	1.6	1.0	5.0
Reg. ABA Totals	46	–	662	83	245	.339	5	11	.455	59	102	.578	–	–	75	47	77	0	–	58	–	230	1.6	1.0	5.0

Kupchak, Mitchell (Mitch) b. May 24, 1954 Ht. 6-9 Wt. 230 College: North Carolina

SEASON–TEAM	G	GS	MIN	FGM	FGA	PCT	3FGM	3FGA	PCT	FTM	FTA	PCT	O-RB	D-RB	TOT	AST	PF	DQ	STL	TO	BLK	PTS	RPG	APG	PPG
76-77–Washington	82	–	1513	341	596	.572	–	–	–	170	246	.691	183	311	494	62	204	3	22	–	34	852	6.0	0.8	10.4
77-78–Washington	67	–	1759	393	768	.512	–	–	–	280	402	.697	162	298	460	71	196	1	28	184	42	1066	6.9	1.1	15.9
78-79–Washington	66	–	1604	369	685	.539	–	–	–	223	300	.743	152	278	430	88	141	0	23	120	23	961	6.5	1.3	14.6
79-80–Washington	40	–	451	67	160	.419	0	2	.000	52	75	.693	32	73	105	16	49	1	8	40	8	186	2.6	0.4	4.7
80-81–Washington	82	–	1934	392	747	.525	0	1	.000	240	340	.706	198	371	569	62	195	1	36	161	26	1024	6.9	0.8	12.5
81-82–Los Angeles	26	26	821	153	267	.573	0	0	–	65	98	.663	64	146	210	33	80	1	12	43	10	371	8.1	1.3	14.3
83-84–Los Angeles	34	3	324	41	108	.380	0	0	–	22	34	.647	35	52	87	7	46	0	4	22	6	104	2.6	0.2	3.1
84-85–L.A. Lakers	58	3	716	123	244	.504	0	0	–	60	91	.659	68	116	184	21	104	0	19	48	20	306	3.2	0.4	5.3
85-86–L.A. Lakers	55	0	783	124	257	.482	0	1	.000	84	112	.750	69	122	191	17	102	0	12	64	7	332	3.5	0.3	6.0
Reg. Season Totals	510	32	9905	2003	3832	.523	0	4	.000	1196	1698	.704	963	1767	2730	377	1117	7	164	682	176	5202	5.4	0.7	10.2
Playoff Totals	68	0	1215	202	426	.474	0	1	.000	120	185	.649	121	200	321	44	164	1	13	66	15	524	4.7	0.6	7.7

Kupec, Charles J. (C.J.) b. January 16, 1953 Ht. 6-6 Wt. 220 College: Michigan

SEASON–TEAM	G	GS	MIN	FGM	FGA	PCT	3FGM	3FGA	PCT	FTM	FTA	PCT	O-RB	D-RB	TOT	AST	PF	DQ	STL	TO	BLK	PTS	RPG	APG	PPG
75-76–Los Angeles	16	–	55	10	40	.250	–	–	–	7	11	.636	4	19	23	5	7	0	3	–	0	27	1.4	0.3	1.7
76-77–Los Angeles	82	–	908	153	342	.447	–	–	–	78	101	.772	76	123	199	53	113	0	18	–	4	384	2.4	0.6	4.7
77-78–Houston	49	–	626	84	197	.426	–	–	–	27	33	.818	27	64	91	50	54	0	10	24	3	195	1.9	1.0	4.0
Reg. Season Totals	147	–	1589	247	579	.427	–	–	–	112	145	.772	107	206	313	108	174	0	31	24	7	606	2.1	0.7	4.1
Playoff Totals	11	–	57	8	18	.444	–	–	–	5	7	.714	3	13	16	4	7	0	3	–	0	21	1.5	0.4	1.9

Lacefield, Reggie b. April 10, 1945 Ht. 6-6 Wt. 230 College: Western Michigan

SEASON–TEAM	G	GS	MIN	FGM	FGA	PCT	3FGM	3FGA	PCT	FTM	FTA	PCT	O-RB	D-RB	TOT	AST	PF	DQ	STL	TO	BLK	PTS	RPG	APG	PPG
68-69–Kentucky (A)	8	–	48	11	22	.500	0	1	.000	2	4	.500	–	–	11	0	9	0	–	3	–	24	1.4	0.0	3.0
Reg. ABA Totals	8	–	48	11	22	.500	0	1	.000	2	4	.500	–	–	11	0	9	0	–	3	–	24	1.4	0.0	3.0

Lacey, Samuel (Sam) b. March 28, 1948 Ht. 6-10 Wt. 235 College: New Mexico State

SEASON–TEAM	G	GS	MIN	FGM	FGA	PCT	3FGM	3FGA	PCT	FTM	FTA	PCT	O-RB	D-RB	TOT	AST	PF	DQ	STL	TO	BLK	PTS	RPG	APG	PPG
70-71–Cincinnati	81	–	2648	467	1117	.418	–	–	–	156	227	.687	–	–	913	117	270	8	–	–	–	1090	11.3	1.4	13.5
71-72–Cincinnati	81	–	2832	410	972	.422	–	–	–	119	169	.704	–	–	968	173	284	6	–	–	–	939	12.0	2.1	11.6
72-73–K.C.-Omaha	79	–	2930	471	994	.474	–	–	–	126	178	.708	–	–	933	189	283	6	–	–	–	1068	11.8	2.4	13.5
73-74–K.C.-Omaha	79	–	3107	467	982	.476	–	–	–	185	247	.749	293	762	1055	299	254	3	126	–	184	1119	13.4	3.8	14.2
74-75–K.C.-Omaha	81	–	3378	392	917	.427	–	–	–	144	191	.754	228	921	1149	428	274	4	139	–	168	928	14.2	5.3	11.5
75-76–Kansas City	81	–	3083	409	1019	.401	–	–	–	217	286	.759	218	806	1024	378	286	7	132	–	134	1035	12.6	4.7	12.8
76-77–Kansas City	82	–	2595	327	774	.422	–	–	–	215	282	.762	189	545	734	386	292	9	119	–	133	869	9.0	4.7	10.6
77-78–Kansas City	77	–	2131	265	590	.449	–	–	–	134	187	.717	155	487	642	300	264	7	120	186	108	664	8.3	3.9	8.6
78-79–Kansas City	82	–	2627	350	697	.502	–	–	–	167	226	.739	179	523	702	430	309	11	106	245	141	867	8.6	5.2	10.6
79-80–Kansas City	81	–	2412	303	677	.448	0	1	.000	137	185	.741	172	473	645	460	307	8	111	211	109	743	8.0	5.7	9.2
80-81–Kansas City	82	–	2228	237	536	.442	1	5	.200	92	117	.786	131	453	584	399	302	5	95	182	120	567	7.1	4.9	6.9
81-82–K.C.-N.J.	56	7	670	67	154	.435	0	1	.000	27	37	.730	20	87	107	77	139	1	22	56	38	161	1.9	1.4	2.9
82-83–Cleveland	60	33	1232	111	264	.420	2	9	.222	29	37	.784	62	169	231	118	209	3	29	98	25	253	3.9	2.0	4.2
Reg. Season Totals	1002	40	31873	4276	9693	.441	3	16	.188	1748	2369	.738	1647	5226	9687	3754	3473	78	999	978	1160	10303	9.7	3.7	10.3
Playoff Totals	29	0	1074	107	267	.401	1	4	.250	59	76	.776	68	219	287	144	113	5	56	66	44	274	9.9	5.0	9.4
All-Star Totals	1	0	17	2	6	.333	0	0	–	2	2	1.000	3	4	7	1	2	0	2	–	1	6	7.0	1.0	6.0

Lackey, Robert (Bob) b. April 4, 1949 Ht. 6-6 Wt. 210 College: Casper (Wyo.) Coll. (J.C.); Marquette

SEASON–TEAM	G	GS	MIN	FGM	FGA	PCT	3FGM	3FGA	PCT	FTM	FTA	PCT	O-RB	D-RB	TOT	AST	PF	DQ	STL	TO	BLK	PTS	RPG	APG	PPG
72-73–New York (A)	68	–	1185	153	355	.431	2	5	.400	99	167	.593	60	100	160	136	170	0	–	120	–	407	2.4	2.0	6.0
73-74–New York (A)	3	–	15	3	7	.429	0	0	–	0	0	–	3	1	4	1	2	–	1	1	0	6	1.3	0.3	2.0
Reg. ABA Totals	71	–	1200	156	362	.431	2	5	.400	99	167	.593	63	101	164	137	172	0	1	121	0	413	2.3	1.9	5.8
ABA Playoff Totals	5	–	60	4	8	.500	0	2	.000	4	11	.364	0	0	8	5	10	0	0	7	0	12	1.6	1.0	2.4

LaCour, Fred b. February 7, 1938 d. August 1972 Ht. 6-5 Wt. 210 College: San Francisco

SEASON–TEAM	G	GS	MIN	FGM	FGA	PCT	3FGM	3FGA	PCT	FTM	FTA	PCT	O-RB	D-RB	TOT	AST	PF	DQ	STL	TO	BLK	PTS	RPG	APG	PPG
60-61–St. Louis	55	–	722	123	295	.417	–	–	–	63	84	.750	–	–	178	84	73	0	–	–	–	309	3.2	1.5	5.6
61-62–St. Louis	73	–	1507	230	536	.429	–	–	–	106	130	.815	–	–	272	166	168	3	–	–	–	566	3.7	2.3	7.8
62-63–San Francisco	16	–	171	28	73	.384	–	–	–	9	16	.563	–	–	24	19	27	0	–	–	–	65	1.5	1.2	4.1
Reg. Season Totals	144	–	2400	381	904	.421	–	–	–	178	230	.774	–	–	474	269	268	3	–	–	–	940	3.3	1.9	6.5
Playoff Totals	5	–	47	7	21	.333	–	–	–	6	7	.857	–	–	6	4	6	0	–	–	–	20	1.2	0.8	4.0

Lacy, Edgar Eddie b. August 2, 1944 Ht. 6-6 Wt. 190 College: UCLA

SEASON–TEAM	G	GS	MIN	FGM	FGA	PCT	3FGM	3FGA	PCT	FTM	FTA	PCT	O-RB	D-RB	TOT	AST	PF	DQ	STL	TO	BLK	PTS	RPG	APG	PPG
68-69–Los Angeles (A)	46	–	609	98	219	.447	0	2	.000	38	67	.567	–	–	180	30	92	1	–	63	–	234	3.9	0.7	5.1
Reg. ABA Totals	46	–	609	98	219	.447	0	2	.000	38	67	.567	–	–	180	30	92	1	–	63	–	234	3.9	0.7	5.1

Ladner, Wendall b. October 6, 1948 d. June 24, 1975 Ht. 6-5 Wt. 220 College: Southern Mississippi

SEASON–TEAM	G	GS	MIN	FGM	FGA	PCT	3FGM	3FGA	PCT	FTM	FTA	PCT	O-RB	D-RB	TOT	AST	PF	DQ	STL	TO	BLK	PTS	RPG	APG	PPG
70-71–Memphis (A)	77	–	2504	572	1308	.437	8	29	.276	154	219	.703	337	538	875	160	334	–	–	–	–	1306	11.4	2.1	17.0
71-72–Mem.-Car. (A)	82	–	2446	491	1287	.382	61	236	.258	122	159	.767	244	589	833	166	347	–	–	215	–	1165	10.2	2.0	14.2
72-73–Mem.-Ken. (A)	52	–	932	146	446	.327	12	53	.226	55	73	.753	94	183	277	107	186	4	–	78	–	359	5.3	2.1	6.9
73-74–Ken.-N.Y. (A)	64	–	1565	244	670	.364	24	90	.267	29	53	.547	110	318	428	149	233	–	108	128	6	541	6.7	2.3	8.5
74-75–New York (A)	25	–	436	45	173	.260	7	36	.194	6	10	.600	21	47	68	39	68	–	32	23	1	103	2.7	1.6	4.1
Reg. ABA Totals	300	–	7883	1498	3884	.386	112	444	.252	366	514	.712	806	1675	2481	621	1168	4	140	444	7	3474	8.3	2.1	11.6
ABA Playoff Totals	40	–	718	131	359	.365	23	86	.267	20	33	.606	19	56	171	69	145	0	56	45	0	305	4.3	1.7	7.6

Laettner, Christian Donald b. August 17, 1969 Ht. 6-11 Wt. 245 College: Duke

SEASON–TEAM	G	GS	MIN	FGM	FGA	PCT	3FGM	3FGA	PCT	FTM	FTA	PCT	O-RB	D-RB	TOT	AST	PF	DQ	STL	TO	BLK	PTS	RPG	APG	PPG
92-93–Minnesota	81	81	2823	503	1061	.474	4	40	.100	462	553	.835	171	537	708	223	290	4	105	275	83	1472	8.7	2.8	18.2
93-94–Minnesota	70	67	2428	396	883	.448	6	25	.240	375	479	.783	160	442	602	307	264	6	87	259	86	1173	8.6	4.4	16.8
94-95–Minnesota	81	80	2770	450	920	.489	13	40	.325	409	500	.818	164	449	613	234	302	4	101	225	87	1322	7.6	2.9	16.3
95-96–Minn.-Atlanta	74	71	2495	442	907	.487	9	39	.231	324	396	.818	184	354	538	197	276	7	71	187	71	1217	7.3	2.7	16.4
96-97–Atlanta	82	82	3140	548	1128	.486	31	88	.352	359	440	.816	212	508	720	223	277	8	102	218	64	1486	8.8	2.7	18.1
97-98–Atlanta	74	49	2282	354	730	.485	6	27	.222	306	354	.864	142	345	487	190	246	6	71	183	73	1020	6.6	2.6	13.8
98-99–Detroit	16	0	337	38	106	.358	1	3	.333	44	57	.772	21	33	54	24	30	0	15	19	12	121	3.4	1.5	7.6
99-00–Detroit	82	82	2443	379	801	.473	7	24	.292	237	292	.812	175	378	553	186	326	10	83	186	45	1002	6.7	2.3	12.2
Reg. Season Totals	560	512	18718	3110	6536	.476	77	286	.269	2516	3071	.819	1229	3046	4275	1584	2011	45	635	1552	521	8813	7.6	2.8	15.7
Playoff Totals	32	23	1022	160	374	.428	5	27	.185	118	149	.792	57	130	187	62	117	2	32	66	21	443	5.8	1.9	13.8
All-Star Totals	1	0	24	3	5	.600	0	0	–	1	1	1.000	4	7	11	2	4	0	1	2	1	7	11.0	2.0	7.0

LaFrentz, Raef Andrew b. May 29, 1976 Ht. 6-11 Wt. 240 College: Kansas

SEASON–TEAM	G	GS	MIN	FGM	FGA	PCT	3FGM	3FGA	PCT	FTM	FTA	PCT	O-RB	D-RB	TOT	AST	PF	DQ	STL	TO	BLK	PTS	RPG	APG	PPG
98-99–Denver	12	12	387	59	129	.457	12	31	.387	36	48	.750	33	58	91	8	38	2	9	9	17	166	7.6	0.7	13.8
99-00–Denver	81	80	2435	392	879	.446	60	183	.328	162	236	.686	170	471	641	97	292	6	42	96	180	1006	7.9	1.2	12.4
Reg. Season Totals	93	92	2822	451	1008	.447	72	214	.336	198	284	.697	203	529	732	105	330	8	51	105	197	1172	7.9	1.1	12.6

LaGarde, Thomas Joseph (Tom) b. February 10, 1955 Ht. 6-10 Wt. 220 College: North Carolina

SEASON–TEAM	G	GS	MIN	FGM	FGA	PCT	3FGM	3FGA	PCT	FTM	FTA	PCT	O-RB	D-RB	TOT	AST	PF	DQ	STL	TO	BLK	PTS	RPG	APG	PPG
77-78–Denver	77	–	868	96	237	.405	–	–	–	114	150	.760	75	139	214	47	146	1	17	101	17	306	2.8	0.6	4.0
78-79–Seattle	23	–	575	98	181	.541	–	–	–	57	95	.600	61	129	190	32	75	2	6	47	18	253	8.3	1.4	11.0
79-80–Seattle	82	–	1164	146	306	.477	0	0	–	90	137	.657	127	185	312	91	206	2	19	97	34	382	3.8	1.1	4.7
80-81–Dallas	82	–	2670	417	888	.470	0	0	–	288	444	.649	177	488	665	237	293	6	35	206	45	1122	8.1	2.9	13.7
81-82–Dallas	47	28	909	113	269	.420	0	2	.000	86	166	.518	63	147	210	49	138	3	17	82	17	312	4.5	1.0	6.6
84-85–New Jersey	1	0	8	0	1	.000	0	0	–	1	2	.500	1	1	2	0	2	0	0	1	0	1	2.0	0.0	1.0
Reg. Season Totals	312	28	6194	870	1882	.462	0	2	.000	636	994	.640	504	1089	1593	456	860	14	94	534	131	2376	5.1	1.5	7.6
Playoff Totals	23	0	240	27	65	.415	0	0	–	14	18	.778	22	36	58	19	37	0	2	16	2	68	2.5	0.8	3.0

Laimbeer, William Jr. **(Bill, Lambs)** b. May 19, 1957 Ht. 6-11 Wt. 255 College: Owens (Ohio) C.C.; Notre Dame

SEASON–TEAM	G	GS	MIN	FGM	FGA	PCT	3FGM	3FGA	PCT	FTM	FTA	PCT	O-RB	D-RB	TOT	AST	PF	DQ	STL	TO	BLK	PTS	RPG	APG	PPG
80-81–Cleveland	81	–	2460	337	670	.503	0	0	–	117	153	.765	266	427	693	216	332	14	56	132	78	791	8.6	2.7	9.8
81-82–Clev.-Detroit	80	34	1829	265	536	.494	4	13	.308	184	232	.793	234	383	617	100	296	5	39	121	64	718	7.7	1.3	9.0
82-83–Detroit	82	82	2871	436	877	.497	2	13	.154	245	310	.790	282	711	993	263	320	9	51	176	118	1119	12.1	3.2	13.6
83-84–Detroit	82	82	2864	553	1044	.530	0	11	.000	316	365	.866	329	674	1003	149	273	4	49	151	84	1422	12.2	1.8	17.3
84-85–Detroit	82	82	2892	595	1177	.506	4	18	.222	244	306	.797	295	718	1013	154	308	4	69	129	71	1438	12.4	1.9	17.5
85-86–Detroit	82	82	2891	545	1107	.492	4	14	.286	266	319	.834	305	770	1075	146	291	4	59	133	65	1360	13.1	1.8	16.6
86-87–Detroit	82	82	2854	506	1010	.501	6	21	.286	245	274	.894	243	712	955	151	283	4	72	120	69	1263	11.6	1.8	15.4
87-88–Detroit	82	82	2897	455	923	.493	13	39	.333	187	214	.874	165	667	832	199	284	6	66	136	78	1110	10.1	2.4	13.5
88-89–Detroit	81	81	2640	449	900	.499	30	86	.349	178	212	.840	138	638	776	177	259	2	51	129	100	1106	9.6	2.2	13.7
89-90–Detroit	81	81	2675	380	785	.484	57	158	.361	164	192	.854	166	614	780	171	278	4	57	98	84	981	9.6	2.1	12.1
90-91–Detroit	82	81	2668	372	778	.478	37	125	.296	123	147	.837	173	564	737	157	242	3	38	98	56	904	9.0	1.9	11.0
91-92–Detroit	81	46	2234	342	727	.470	32	85	.376	67	75	.893	104	347	451	160	225	0	51	102	54	783	5.6	2.0	9.7
92-93–Detroit	79	41	1933	292	574	.509	10	27	.370	93	104	.894	110	309	419	127	212	4	46	59	40	687	5.3	1.6	8.7
93-94–Detroit	11	5	248	47	90	.522	3	9	.333	11	13	.846	9	47	56	14	30	0	6	10	4	108	5.1	1.3	9.8
Reg. Season Totals	1068	861	33956	5574	11198	.498	202	619	.326	2440	2916	.837	2819	7581	10400	2184	3633	63	710	1594	965	13790	9.7	2.0	12.9
Playoff Totals	113	112	3735	549	1174	.468	44	137	.321	212	259	.819	257	840	1097	195	408	13	84	143	83	1354	9.7	1.7	12.0
All-Star Totals	4	0	45	13	20	.650	0	0	–	2	3	.667	3	8	11	2	7	0	2	1	2	28	2.8	0.5	7.0

Lalich, Peter T. **(Pete)** b. June 23, 1920 Ht. 6-2 Wt. 190 College: Ohio U.

SEASON–TEAM	G	GS	MIN	FGM	FGA	PCT	3FGM	3FGA	PCT	FTM	FTA	PCT	O-RB	D-RB	TOT	AST	PF	DQ	STL	TO	BLK	PTS	RPG	APG	PPG
42-43–Sheboygan (N)	1	–	–	0	–	–	–	–	–	0	–	–	–	–	–	–	–	–	–	–	–	0	–	–	0.0
43-44–Cleveland (N)	17	–	–	44	–	–	–	–	–	21	–	–	–	–	–	–	–	–	–	–	–	109	–	–	6.4
44-45–Pittsburgh (N)	9	–	–	8	–	–	–	–	–	4	–	–	–	–	–	–	–	–	–	–	–	20	–	–	2.2
45-46–Youngstown (N)	11	–	–	2	–	–	–	–	–	3	–	–	–	–	–	–	–	–	–	–	–	7	–	–	0.6
46-47–Cleveland	1	–	–	0	1	.000	–	–	–	0	0	–	–	–	–	0	1	–	–	–	–	0	–	0.0	0.0
Reg. NBA Totals	1	–	–	0	1	.000	–	–	–	0	0	–	–	–	–	0	1	–	–	–	–	0	–	0.0	0.0
Reg. NBL Totals	38	–	–	54	–	–	–	–	–	28	0	–	–	–	–	–	–	–	–	–	–	136	–	–	3.6
NBL Playoff Totals	2	–	–	1	–	–	–	–	–	2	0	–	–	–	–	–	5	–	–	–	–	4	–	–	2.0

Lamar, Dwight **(Bo)** b. April 7, 1951 Ht. 6-1 Wt. 180 College: Louisiana-Lafayette

SEASON–TEAM	G	GS	MIN	FGM	FGA	PCT	3FGM	3FGA	PCT	FTM	FTA	PCT	O-RB	D-RB	TOT	AST	PF	DQ	STL	TO	BLK	PTS	RPG	APG	PPG
73-74–San Diego (A)	84	–	2824	686	1726	.397	69	247	.279	272	350	.777	105	187	292	288	155	–	129	183	13	1713	3.5	3.4	20.4
74-75–San Diego (A)	77	–	2917	667	1571	.425	25	109	.229	247	315	.784	88	151	239	427	150	–	129	238	12	1606	3.1	5.5	20.9
75-76–S.D.-Indiana (A)	41	–	1130	277	668	.415	24	86	.279	79	106	.745	46	70	116	171	58	–	42	95	2	657	2.8	4.2	16.0
76-77–Los Angeles	71	–	1165	228	561	.406	–	–	–	46	68	.676	30	62	92	177	73	0	59	–	3	502	1.3	2.5	7.1
Reg. NBA Totals	71	–	1165	228	561	.406	–	–	–	46	68	.676	30	62	92	177	73	0	59	–	3	502	1.3	2.5	7.1
Reg. ABA Totals	202	–	6871	1630	3965	.411	118	442	.267	598	771	.776	239	408	647	886	363	0	300	516	27	3976	3.2	4.4	19.7
NBA Playoff Totals	10	–	109	12	41	.293	–	–	–	9	10	.900	0	9	9	14	12	0	3	–	0	33	0.9	1.4	3.3
ABA Playoff Totals	6	–	241	71	161	.441	7	17	.412	16	19	.842	7	17	24	21	19	0	11	22	2	165	4.0	3.5	27.5

Lambert, John Edward b. January 14, 1953 Ht. 6-10 Wt. 225 College: USC

SEASON–TEAM	G	GS	MIN	FGM	FGA	PCT	3FGM	3FGA	PCT	FTM	FTA	PCT	O-RB	D-RB	TOT	AST	PF	DQ	STL	TO	BLK	PTS	RPG	APG	PPG
75-76–Cleveland	54	–	333	49	110	.445	–	–	–	25	37	.676	37	65	102	16	54	0	8	–	12	123	1.9	0.3	2.3
76-77–Cleveland	63	–	555	67	157	.427	–	–	–	25	36	.694	62	92	154	31	75	0	16	–	18	159	2.4	0.5	2.5
77-78–Cleveland	76	–	1075	142	336	.423	–	–	–	27	48	.563	125	199	324	38	169	0	27	62	50	311	4.3	0.5	4.1
78-79–Cleveland	70	–	1030	148	329	.450	–	–	–	35	55	.636	116	174	290	43	163	0	25	65	29	331	4.1	0.6	4.7
79-80–Cleveland	74	–	1324	165	400	.413	0	3	.000	73	101	.723	138	214	352	56	203	4	47	64	42	403	4.8	0.8	5.4
80-81–Clev.-K.C.	46	–	483	68	165	.412	0	2	.000	18	23	.783	28	65	93	27	76	0	12	19	5	154	2.0	0.6	3.3
81-82–K.C.-S.A.	63	7	764	86	197	.437	1	7	.143	34	42	.810	55	123	178	37	123	0	18	48	16	207	2.8	0.6	3.3
Reg. Season Totals	446	7	5564	725	1694	.428	1	12	.083	237	342	.693	561	932	1493	248	863	4	153	258	172	1688	3.3	0.6	3.8
Playoff Totals	28	0	250	30	75	.400	0	4	.000	8	10	.800	25	35	60	11	35	0	8	6	6	68	2.1	0.4	2.4

Lamp, Jeffrey Alan **(Jeff)** b. March 9, 1959 Ht. 6-6 Wt. 195 College: Virginia

SEASON–TEAM	G	GS	MIN	FGM	FGA	PCT	3FGM	3FGA	PCT	FTM	FTA	PCT	O-RB	D-RB	TOT	AST	PF	DQ	STL	TO	BLK	PTS	RPG	APG	PPG
81-82–Portland	54	0	617	100	196	.510	0	1	.000	50	61	.820	24	40	64	28	83	0	16	45	1	250	1.2	0.5	4.6
82-83–Portland	59	1	690	107	252	.425	1	6	.167	42	52	.808	25	51	76	58	67	0	20	38	3	257	1.3	1.0	4.4
83-84–Portland	64	0	660	128	261	.490	2	13	.154	60	67	.896	23	40	63	51	67	0	22	52	4	318	1.0	0.8	5.0
85-86–Milw.-S.A.	74	2	1321	245	514	.477	7	30	.233	111	133	.835	53	147	200	117	155	1	39	68	4	608	2.7	1.6	8.2
87-88–L.A. Lakers	3	0	7	0	0	–	0	0	–	2	2	1.000	0	0	0	0	1	0	0	0	0	2	0.0	0.0	0.7
88-89–L.A. Lakers	37	0	176	27	69	.391	2	4	.500	4	5	.800	6	28	34	15	27	0	8	16	2	60	0.9	0.4	1.6
Reg. Season Totals	291	3	3471	607	1292	.470	12	54	.222	269	320	.841	131	306	437	269	400	1	105	219	14	1495	1.5	0.9	5.1
Playoff Totals	12	0	79	13	32	.406	1	3	.333	1	2	.500	3	1	4	8	10	0	1	6	0	28	0.3	0.7	2.3

Lampley, Jimmy D. b. July 2, 1960 Ht. 6-11 Wt. 230 College: Vanderbilt; Arkansas-Little Rock

SEASON–TEAM	G	GS	MIN	FGM	FGA	PCT	3FGM	3FGA	PCT	FTM	FTA	PCT	O-RB	D-RB	TOT	AST	PF	DQ	STL	TO	BLK	PTS	RPG	APG	PPG
86-87–Philadelphia	1	0	16	1	3	.333	0	0	–	1	2	.500	1	4	5	0	0	0	1	1	0	3	5.0	0.0	3.0
Reg. Season Totals	1	0	16	1	3	.333	0	0	–	1	2	.500	1	4	5	0	0	0	1	1	0	3	5.0	0.0	3.0

Landsberger, Mark Walter b. May 21, 1955 Ht. 6-8 Wt. 225 College: Allan Hancock (Calif.) Coll. (J.C.); Minnesota; Arizona State

SEASON–TEAM	G	GS	MIN	FGM	FGA	PCT	3FGM	3FGA	PCT	FTM	FTA	PCT	O-RB	D-RB	TOT	AST	PF	DQ	STL	TO	BLK	PTS	RPG	APG	PPG
77-78–Chicago	62	–	926	127	251	.506	–	–	–	91	157	.580	110	191	301	41	78	0	21	69	6	345	4.9	0.7	5.6
78-79–Chicago	80	–	1959	278	585	.475	–	–	–	91	194	.469	292	450	742	68	125	0	27	149	22	647	9.3	0.9	8.1
79-80–Chicago-L.A.	77	–	1510	249	483	.516	0	0	–	116	222	.523	226	387	613	46	140	1	33	100	22	614	8.0	0.6	8.0
80-81–Los Angeles	69	–	1086	164	327	.502	0	1	.000	62	116	.534	152	225	377	27	135	0	19	65	6	390	5.5	0.4	5.7
81-82–Los Angeles	75	1	1134	144	329	.438	0	2	.000	33	65	.508	164	237	401	32	134	0	10	49	7	321	5.3	0.4	4.3
82-83–Los Angeles	39	4	356	43	102	.422	0	0	–	12	25	.480	55	73	128	12	48	0	8	20	4	98	3.3	0.3	2.5
83-84–Atlanta	35	0	335	19	51	.373	0	0	–	15	26	.577	42	77	119	10	32	0	6	21	3	53	3.4	0.3	1.5
Reg. Season Totals	437	5	7306	1024	2128	.481	0	3	.000	420	805	.522	1041	1640	2681	236	692	1	124	473	70	2468	6.1	0.5	5.6
Playoff Totals	41	0	433	42	114	.368	0	2	.000	12	20	.600	65	86	151	7	77	0	4	21	4	96	3.7	0.2	2.3

Lane, Jerome b. December 4, 1966 Ht. 6-6 Wt. 230 College: Pittsburgh

SEASON–TEAM	G	GS	MIN	FGM	FGA	PCT	3FGM	3FGA	PCT	FTM	FTA	PCT	O-RB	D-RB	TOT	AST	PF	DQ	STL	TO	BLK	PTS	RPG	APG	PPG
88-89–Denver	54	1	550	109	256	.426	0	7	.000	43	112	.384	87	113	200	60	105	1	20	50	4	261	3.7	1.1	4.8
89-90–Denver	67	46	956	145	309	.469	0	5	.000	44	120	.367	144	217	361	105	189	1	53	85	17	334	5.4	1.6	5.0
90-91–Denver	62	25	1383	202	461	.438	1	4	.250	58	141	.411	280	298	578	123	192	1	51	105	14	463	9.3	2.0	7.5
91-92–Den.-Ind.-Milw.	14	5	177	14	46	.304	0	0	–	9	27	.333	32	34	66	17	28	0	2	14	1	37	4.7	1.2	2.6
92-93–Cleveland	21	2	149	27	54	.500	0	0	–	5	20	.250	24	29	53	17	32	0	12	7	3	59	2.5	0.8	2.8
Reg. Season Totals	218	79	3215	497	1126	.441	1	16	.063	159	420	.379	567	691	1258	322	546	3	138	261	39	1154	5.8	1.5	5.3
Playoff Totals	4	2	35	2	10	.200	0	1	.000	3	4	.750	1	6	7	4	8	0	0	2	0	7	1.8	1.0	1.8

Lang, Andrew Charles Jr. b. June 28, 1966 Ht. 6-11 Wt. 275 College: Arkansas

SEASON–TEAM	G	GS	MIN	FGM	FGA	PCT	3FGM	3FGA	PCT	FTM	FTA	PCT	O-RB	D-RB	TOT	AST	PF	DQ	STL	TO	BLK	PTS	RPG	APG	PPG
88-89–Phoenix	62	25	526	60	117	.513	0	0	–	39	60	.650	54	93	147	9	112	1	17	28	48	159	2.4	0.1	2.6
89-90–Phoenix	74	0	1011	97	174	.557	0	0	–	64	98	.653	83	188	271	21	171	1	22	41	133	258	3.7	0.3	3.5
90-91–Phoenix	63	18	1152	109	189	.577	0	1	.000	93	130	.715	113	190	303	27	168	2	17	45	127	311	4.8	0.4	4.9
91-92–Phoenix	81	71	1965	248	475	.522	0	1	.000	126	164	.768	170	376	546	43	306	8	48	87	201	622	6.7	0.5	7.7
92-93–Philadelphia	73	59	1861	149	351	.425	1	5	.200	87	114	.763	136	300	436	79	261	4	46	89	141	386	6.0	1.1	5.3
93-94–Atlanta	82	0	1608	215	458	.469	1	4	.250	73	106	.689	126	187	313	51	192	2	38	81	87	504	3.8	0.6	6.1
94-95–Atlanta	82	63	2340	320	677	.473	2	3	.667	152	188	.809	154	302	456	72	271	4	45	108	144	794	5.6	0.9	9.7
95-96–Atlanta-Minn.	71	69	2365	353	790	.447	1	5	.200	125	156	.801	153	302	455	65	241	4	42	124	126	832	6.4	0.9	11.7
96-97–Milwaukee	52	52	1194	115	248	.464	0	0	–	44	61	.721	94	184	278	25	140	4	26	39	47	274	5.3	0.5	5.3
97-98–Milwaukee	57	0	692	54	143	.378	0	1	.000	44	57	.772	56	97	153	16	101	0	18	33	27	152	2.7	0.3	2.7
98-99–Chicago	21	13	386	32	99	.323	0	0	–	16	23	.696	33	60	93	13	43	0	5	17	12	80	4.4	0.6	3.8
99-00–New York	19	10	244	28	64	.438	0	0	–	3	7	.429	16	44	60	3	31	0	8	5	6	59	3.2	0.2	3.1
Reg. Season Totals	737	380	15344	1780	3785	.470	5	20	.250	866	1164	.744	1188	2323	3511	424	2037	30	332	697	1099	4431	4.8	0.6	6.0
Playoff Totals	42	11	683	68	153	.444	0	1	.000	57	74	.770	44	91	135	12	112	3	15	39	50	193	3.2	0.3	4.6

Lang, Antonio Maurice b. May 15, 1972 Ht. 6-8 Wt. 230 College: Duke

SEASON–TEAM	G	GS	MIN	FGM	FGA	PCT	3FGM	3FGA	PCT	FTM	FTA	PCT	O-RB	D-RB	TOT	AST	PF	DQ	STL	TO	BLK	PTS	RPG	APG	PPG
94-95–Phoenix	12	0	53	4	10	.400	0	0	–	3	4	.750	3	1	4	1	11	0	0	5	2	11	0.3	0.1	0.9
95-96–Cleveland	41	0	367	41	77	.532	0	2	.000	34	47	.723	17	36	53	12	61	0	14	24	12	116	1.3	0.3	2.8
96-97–Cleveland	64	1	843	68	162	.420	0	6	.000	35	48	.729	52	75	127	33	111	0	33	50	30	171	2.0	0.5	2.7
97-98–Miami	6	0	29	3	5	.600	0	0	–	6	8	.750	2	3	5	1	3	0	2	4	0	12	0.8	0.2	2.0
98-99–Cleveland	10	0	65	4	6	.667	0	0	–	5	9	.556	6	10	16	1	13	0	2	4	1	13	1.6	0.1	1.3
99-00–Toronto-Phil.	10	0	38	1	6	.167	0	0	–	4	5	.800	0	5	5	2	8	0	4	2	1	6	0.5	0.2	0.6
Reg. Season Totals	143	1	1395	121	266	.455	0	8	.000	87	121	.719	80	130	210	50	207	0	55	89	46	329	1.5	0.3	2.3
Playoff Totals	1	0	2	0	0	–	0	0	–	0	0	–	0	0	0	–	0	0	0	0	0	0	0.0	0.0	0.0

Langdon, Trajan Shaka b. May 13, 1976 Ht. 6-3 Wt. 195 College: Duke

SEASON–TEAM	G	GS	MIN	FGM	FGA	PCT	3FGM	3FGA	PCT	FTM	FTA	PCT	O-RB	D-RB	TOT	AST	PF	DQ	STL	TO	BLK	PTS	RPG	APG	PPG
99-00–Cleveland	10	0	145	15	40	.375	8	19	.421	11	11	1.000	4	11	15	11	16	0	5	6	0	49	1.5	1.1	4.9
Reg. Season Totals	10	0	145	15	40	.375	8	19	.421	11	11	1.000	4	11	15	11	16	0	5	6	0	49	1.5	1.1	4.9

Lanier, Robert Jerry Jr. (Bob) b. September 10, 1948 Ht. 6-11 Wt. 260 College: St. Bonaventure HOF: 1991

SEASON–TEAM	G	GS	MIN	FGM	FGA	PCT	3FGM	3FGA	PCT	FTM	FTA	PCT	O-RB	D-RB	TOT	AST	PF	DQ	STL	TO	BLK	PTS	RPG	APG	PPG
70-71–Detroit	82	–	2017	504	1108	.455	–	–	–	273	376	.726	–	–	665	146	272	4	–	–	–	1281	8.1	1.8	15.6
71-72–Detroit	80	–	3092	834	1690	.493	–	–	–	388	505	.768	–	–	1132	248	297	6	–	–	–	2056	14.2	3.1	25.7
72-73–Detroit	81	–	3150	810	1654	.490	–	–	–	307	397	.773	–	–	1205	260	278	4	–	–	–	1927	14.9	3.2	23.8
73-74–Detroit	81	–	3047	748	1483	.504	–	–	–	326	409	.797	269	805	1074	343	273	7	110	–	247	1822	13.3	4.2	22.5
74-75–Detroit	76	–	2987	731	1433	.510	–	–	–	361	450	.802	225	689	914	350	237	1	75	–	172	1823	12.0	4.6	24.0
75-76–Detroit	64	–	2363	541	1017	.532	–	–	–	284	370	.768	217	529	746	217	203	2	79	–	86	1366	11.7	3.4	21.3
76-77–Detroit	64	–	2446	678	1269	.534	–	–	–	260	318	.818	200	545	745	214	174	0	70	–	126	1616	11.6	3.3	25.3
77-78–Detroit	63	–	2311	622	1159	.537	–	–	–	298	386	.772	197	518	715	216	185	2	82	225	93	1542	11.3	3.4	24.5
78-79–Detroit	53	–	1835	489	950	.515	–	–	–	275	367	.749	164	330	494	140	181	5	50	175	75	1253	9.3	2.6	23.6
79-80–Detroit-Milw.	63	–	2131	466	867	.537	1	6	.167	277	354	.782	152	400	552	184	200	3	74	162	89	1210	8.8	2.9	19.2
80-81–Milwaukee	67	–	1753	376	716	.525	1	1	1.000	208	277	.751	128	285	413	179	184	0	73	139	81	961	6.2	2.7	14.3
81-82–Milwaukee	74	72	1986	407	729	.558	0	2	.000	182	242	.752	92	296	388	219	211	3	72	166	56	996	5.2	3.0	13.5
82-83–Milwaukee	39	35	978	163	332	.491	0	1	.000	91	133	.684	58	142	200	105	125	2	34	82	24	417	5.1	2.7	10.7
83-84–Milwaukee	72	72	2007	392	685	.572	0	3	.000	194	274	.708	141	314	455	186	228	8	58	163	51	978	6.3	2.6	13.6
Reg. Season Totals	959	179	32103	7761	15092	.514	2	13	.154	3724	4858	.767	1843	4853	9698	3007	3048	47	777	1112	1100	19248	10.1	3.1	20.1
Playoff Totals	67	31	2361	508	955	.532	0	1	.000	228	297	.768	179	466	645	235	233	7	62	105	99	1244	9.6	3.5	18.6
All-Star Totals	8	0	121	32	55	.582	0	0	–	10	12	.833	14	22	45	12	15	0	4	2	5	74	5.6	1.5	9.3

Lantz, Stuart Burrell (Stu) b. July 13, 1946 Ht. 6-3 Wt. 180 College: Nebraska

SEASON–TEAM	G	GS	MIN	FGM	FGA	PCT	3FGM	3FGA	PCT	FTM	FTA	PCT	O-RB	D-RB	TOT	AST	PF	DQ	STL	TO	BLK	PTS	RPG	APG	PPG
68-69–San Diego	73	–	1378	220	482	.456	–	–	–	129	167	.772	–	–	236	99	178	0	–	–	–	569	3.2	1.4	7.8
69-70–San Diego	82	–	2471	455	1027	.443	–	–	–	278	361	.770	–	–	255	287	238	2	–	–	–	1188	3.1	3.5	14.5
70-71–San Diego	82	–	3102	585	1305	.448	–	–	–	519	644	.806	–	–	406	344	230	3	–	–	–	1689	5.0	4.2	20.6
71-72–Houston	81	–	3097	557	1279	.435	–	–	–	387	462	.838	–	–	345	337	211	2	–	–	–	1501	4.3	4.2	18.5
72-73–Detroit	51	–	1603	185	455	.407	–	–	–	120	150	.800	–	–	172	138	117	0	–	–	–	490	3.4	2.7	9.6
73-74–Detroit	50	–	980	154	361	.427	–	–	–	139	164	.848	34	79	113	97	79	0	38	–	3	447	2.3	1.9	8.9
74-75–N.O.-L.A.	75	–	1783	228	561	.406	–	–	–	192	229	.838	88	106	194	188	162	1	56	–	12	648	2.6	2.5	8.6
75-76–Los Angeles	53	–	853	85	204	.417	–	–	–	80	89	.899	28	71	99	76	105	1	27	–	3	250	1.9	1.4	4.7
Reg. Season Totals	547	–	15267	2469	5674	.435	–	–	–	1844	2266	.814	150	256	1820	1566	1320	9	121	–	18	6782	3.3	2.9	12.4
Playoff Totals	13	–	435	58	128	.453	–	–	–	49	59	.831	10	19	50	24	41	0	2	–	0	165	3.8	1.8	12.7

Larese, York Bruno b. July 18, 1938 Ht. 6-4 Wt. 185 College: North Carolina

SEASON–TEAM	G	GS	MIN	FGM	FGA	PCT	3FGM	3FGA	PCT	FTM	FTA	PCT	O-RB	D-RB	TOT	AST	PF	DQ	STL	TO	BLK	PTS	RPG	APG	PPG
61-62–Chicago-Phil.	59	–	703	122	327	.373	–	–	–	58	72	.806	–	–	77	94	104	0	–	–	–	302	1.3	1.6	5.1
Reg. Season Totals	59	–	703	122	327	.373	–	–	–	58	72	.806	–	–	77	94	104	0	–	–	–	302	1.3	1.6	5.1
Playoff Totals	9	–	78	11	35	.314	–	–	–	8	12	.667	–	–	15	5	14	0	–	–	–	30	1.7	0.6	3.3

LaRue, Rusty b. December 10, 1973 Ht. 6-3 Wt. 185 College: Wake Forest

SEASON–TEAM	G	GS	MIN	FGM	FGA	PCT	3FGM	3FGA	PCT	FTM	FTA	PCT	O-RB	D-RB	TOT	AST	PF	DQ	STL	TO	BLK	PTS	RPG	APG	PPG
97-98–Chicago	14	0	140	20	49	.408	4	16	.250	5	8	.625	1	7	8	5	12	0	3	6	1	49	0.6	0.4	3.5
98-99–Chicago	43	6	732	78	217	.359	30	89	.337	17	17	1.000	9	47	56	63	66	0	33	34	3	203	1.3	1.5	4.7
99-00–Chicago	4	1	129	15	43	.349	2	14	.143	5	7	.714	1	9	10	11	9	0	7	7	0	37	2.5	2.8	9.3
Reg. Season Totals	61	7	1001	113	309	.366	36	119	.303	27	32	.844	11	63	74	79	87	0	43	47	4	289	1.2	1.3	4.7

LaRusso, Rudolph A. (Rudy) b. November 11, 1937 Ht. 6-8 Wt. 220 College: Dartmouth

SEASON–TEAM	G	GS	MIN	FGM	FGA	PCT	3FGM	3FGA	PCT	FTM	FTA	PCT	O-RB	D-RB	TOT	AST	PF	DQ	STL	TO	BLK	PTS	RPG	APG	PPG
59-60–Minneapolis	71	–	2092	355	913	.389	–	–	–	265	357	.742	–	–	679	83	222	8	–	–	–	975	9.6	1.2	13.7
60-61–Los Angeles	79	–	2593	416	992	.419	–	–	–	323	409	.790	–	–	781	135	280	8	–	–	–	1155	9.9	1.7	14.6
61-62–Los Angeles	80	–	2754	516	1108	.466	–	–	–	342	448	.763	–	–	828	179	255	5	–	–	–	1374	10.4	2.2	17.2
62-63–Los Angeles	75	–	2505	321	761	.422	–	–	–	282	393	.718	–	–	747	187	255	5	–	–	–	924	10.0	2.5	12.3
63-64–Los Angeles	79	–	2746	337	776	.434	–	–	–	298	397	.751	–	–	800	190	268	5	–	–	–	972	10.1	2.4	12.3
64-65–Los Angeles	77	–	2588	381	827	.461	–	–	–	321	415	.773	–	–	725	198	258	3	–	–	–	1083	9.4	2.6	14.1
65-66–Los Angeles	76	–	2316	410	897	.457	–	–	–	350	445	.787	–	–	660	165	261	9	–	–	–	1170	8.7	2.2	15.4
66-67–Los Angeles	45	–	1292	211	509	.415	–	–	–	156	224	.696	–	–	351	78	149	6	–	–	–	578	7.8	1.7	12.8
67-68–San Francisco	79	–	2819	602	1389	.433	–	–	–	522	661	.790	–	–	741	182	337	14	–	–	–	1726	9.4	2.3	21.8
68-69–San Francisco	75	–	2782	553	1349	.410	–	–	–	444	559	.794	–	–	624	159	268	9	–	–	–	1550	8.3	2.1	20.7
Reg. Season Totals	736	–	24487	4102	9521	.431	–	–	–	3303	4308	.767	–	–	6936	1556	2553	72	–	–	–	11507	9.4	2.1	15.6
Playoff Totals	93	–	3188	467	1152	.405	–	–	–	410	546	.751	–	–	779	194	366	13	–	–	–	1344	8.4	2.1	14.5
All-Star Totals	4	–	70	13	27	.481	–	–	–	3	9	.333	–	–	17	6	6	0	–	–	–	29	4.3	1.5	7.3

Laskowski, John b. June 7, 1953 Ht. 6-6 Wt. 190 College: Indiana

SEASON–TEAM	G	GS	MIN	FGM	FGA	PCT	3FGM	3FGA	PCT	FTM	FTA	PCT	O-RB	D-RB	TOT	AST	PF	DQ	STL	TO	BLK	PTS	RPG	APG	PPG
75-76–Chicago	71	–	1570	284	690	.412	–	–	–	87	120	.725	52	167	219	55	90	0	56	–	10	655	3.1	0.8	9.2
76-77–Chicago	47	–	562	75	212	.354	–	–	–	27	30	.900	16	47	63	44	22	0	32	–	2	177	1.3	0.9	3.8
Reg. Season Totals	118	–	2132	359	902	.398	–	–	–	114	150	.760	68	214	282	99	112	0	88	–	12	832	2.4	0.8	7.1

Lattin, David (Dave, Big Daddy) b. December 23, 1943 Ht. 6-7 Wt. 230 College: Texas-El Paso

SEASON–TEAM	G	GS	MIN	FGM	FGA	PCT	3FGM	3FGA	PCT	FTM	FTA	PCT	O-RB	D-RB	TOT	AST	PF	DQ	STL	TO	BLK	PTS	RPG	APG	PPG
67-68–San Francisco	44	–	257	37	102	.363	–	–	–	23	33	.697	–	–	104	14	94	4	–	–	–	97	2.4	0.3	2.2
68-69–Phoenix	68	–	987	150	366	.410	–	–	–	109	172	.634	–	–	323	48	163	5	–	–	–	409	4.8	0.7	6.0
70-71–Pittsburgh (A)	71	–	1135	177	377	.469	0	1	.000	108	177	.610	–	–	467	64	215	–	–	–	–	462	6.6	0.9	6.5
71-72–Pittsburgh (A)	64	–	1482	329	605	.544	0	1	.000	148	242	.612	–	–	375	51	178	–	–	108	–	806	5.9	0.8	12.6
72-73–Memphis (A)	16	–	296	48	104	.462	0	1	.000	34	45	.756	21	42	63	7	45	0	–	32	–	130	3.9	0.4	8.1
Reg. NBA Totals	112	–	1244	187	468	.400	–	–	–	132	205	.644	–	–	427	62	257	9	–	–	–	506	3.8	0.6	4.5
Reg. ABA Totals	151	–	2913	554	1086	.510	0	3	.000	290	464	.625	21	42	905	122	438	0	–	140	–	1398	6.0	0.8	9.3
NBA Playoff Totals	5	–	27	1	5	.200	–	–	–	5	6	.833	–	–	5	1	9	0	–	–	–	7	1.0	0.2	1.4

Lauderdale, Priest b. August 31, 1973 Ht. 7-4 Wt. 325 College: Central State (Ohio)

SEASON–TEAM	G	GS	MIN	FGM	FGA	PCT	3FGM	3FGA	PCT	FTM	FTA	PCT	O-RB	D-RB	TOT	AST	PF	DQ	STL	TO	BLK	PTS	RPG	APG	PPG
96-97–Atlanta	35	0	180	49	89	.551	0	1	.000	13	23	.565	16	27	43	12	39	0	1	37	9	111	1.2	0.3	3.2
97-98–Denver	39	0	345	53	127	.417	0	0	–	38	69	.551	27	73	100	21	63	0	7	46	17	144	2.6	0.5	3.7
Reg. Season Totals	74	0	525	102	216	.472	0	1	.000	51	92	.554	43	100	143	33	102	0	8	83	26	255	1.9	0.4	3.4
Playoff Totals	3	0	7	0	3	.000	0	0	–	0	0	–	1	1	2	–	1	0	0	3	0	0	0.7	0.0	0.0

Laurel, Richard b. July 11, 1954 Ht. 6-7 Wt. 195 College: Hofstra

SEASON–TEAM	G	GS	MIN	FGM	FGA	PCT	3FGM	3FGA	PCT	FTM	FTA	PCT	O-RB	D-RB	TOT	AST	PF	DQ	STL	TO	BLK	PTS	RPG	APG	PPG
77-78–Milwaukee	10	–	57	10	31	.323	–	–	–	4	4	1.000	6	4	10	3	10	0	3	4	1	24	1.0	0.3	2.4
Reg. Season Totals	10	–	57	10	31	.323	–	–	–	4	4	1.000	6	4	10	3	10	0	3	4	1	24	1.0	0.3	2.4

Laurie, Harry b. November 2, 1944 Ht. 6-1 Wt. 180 College: Loyola (Chicago); St. Peter's

SEASON–TEAM	G	GS	MIN	FGM	FGA	PCT	3FGM	3FGA	PCT	FTM	FTA	PCT	O-RB	D-RB	TOT	AST	PF	DQ	STL	TO	BLK	PTS	RPG	APG	PPG
70-71–Pittsburgh (A)	9	–	57	3	12	.250	0	0	–	7	11	.636	–	–	15	8	16	–	–	–	–	13	1.7	0.9	1.4
Reg. ABA Totals	9	–	57	3	12	.250	0	0	–	7	11	.636	–	–	15	8	16	–	–	–	–	13	1.7	0.9	1.4

Lautenbach, Walter Henry (Walt) b. November 17, 1922 Ht. 6-2 Wt. 190 College: Wisconsin

SEASON–TEAM	G	GS	MIN	FGM	FGA	PCT	3FGM	3FGA	PCT	FTM	FTA	PCT	O-RB	D-RB	TOT	AST	PF	DQ	STL	TO	BLK	PTS	RPG	APG	PPG
47-48–Oshkosh (N)	60	–	–	159	–	–	–	–	–	36	60	.600	–	–	–	–	130	–	–	–	–	354	–	–	5.9
48-49–Oshkosh (N)	61	–	–	104	–	–	–	–	–	26	45	.578	–	–	–	–	84	–	–	–	–	234	–	–	3.8
49-50–Sheboygan	55	–	–	100	332	.301	–	–	–	38	55	.691	–	–	–	73	122	–	–	–	–	238	–	1.3	4.3
Reg. NBA Totals	55	–	–	100	332	.301	–	–	–	38	55	.691	–	–	–	73	122	–	–	–	–	238	–	1.3	4.3
Reg. NBL Totals	121	–	–	263	–	–	–	–	–	62	105	.590	–	–	–	–	214	–	–	–	–	588	–	–	4.9
NBL Playoff Totals	11	–	–	26	–	–	–	–	–	11	18	.611	–	–	–	–	28	–	–	–	–	63	–	–	5.7

Lavelli, Anthony (Tony) b. July 11, 1926 Ht. 6-3 Wt. 185 College: Yale

SEASON–TEAM	G	GS	MIN	FGM	FGA	PCT	3FGM	3FGA	PCT	FTM	FTA	PCT	O-RB	D-RB	TOT	AST	PF	DQ	STL	TO	BLK	PTS	RPG	APG	PPG
49-50–Boston	56	–	–	162	436	.372	–	–	–	168	197	.853	–	–	–	40	107	–	–	–	–	492	–	0.7	8.8
50-51–New York	30	–	–	32	93	.344	–	–	–	35	41	.854	–	–	59	23	56	1	–	–	–	99	2.0	0.8	3.3
Reg. Season Totals	86	–	–	194	529	.367	–	–	–	203	238	.853	–	–	59	63	163	1	–	–	–	591	2.0	0.7	6.9
Playoff Totals	2	–	–	1	5	.200	–	–	–	2	2	1.000	–	–	1	1	2	0	–	–	–	4	0.5	0.5	2.0

Lavoy, Robert William (Bob) b. June 29, 1926 Ht. 6-7 Wt. 185 College: Illinois; Western Kentucky

SEASON–TEAM	G	GS	MIN	FGM	FGA	PCT	3FGM	3FGA	PCT	FTM	FTA	PCT	O-RB	D-RB	TOT	AST	PF	DQ	STL	TO	BLK	PTS	RPG	APG	PPG
50-51–Indianapolis	63	–	–	221	619	.357	–	–	–	84	133	.632	–	–	310	76	190	2	–	–	–	526	4.9	1.2	8.3
51-52–Indianapolis	63	–	1829	240	604	.397	–	–	–	168	223	.753	–	–	479	107	210	5	–	–	–	648	7.6	1.7	10.3
52-53–Indianapolis	70	–	2327	225	560	.402	–	–	–	168	242	.694	–	–	528	130	274	18	–	–	–	618	7.5	1.9	8.8
53-54–Milw.-Syr.	68	–	1277	135	356	.379	–	–	–	94	129	.729	–	–	317	78	215	2	–	–	–	364	4.7	1.1	5.4
Reg. Season Totals	264	–	5433	821	2139	.384	–	–	–	514	727	.707	–	–	1634	391	889	27	–	–	–	2156	6.2	1.5	8.2
Playoff Totals	20	–	561	50	148	.338	–	–	–	55	73	.753	–	–	141	34	74	2	–	–	–	155	6.4	1.5	7.8

Lawrence, Edmund (Ed) b. December 8, 1952 Ht. 7-0 Wt. 240 College: McNeese State

SEASON–TEAM	G	GS	MIN	FGM	FGA	PCT	3FGM	3FGA	PCT	FTM	FTA	PCT	O-RB	D-RB	TOT	AST	PF	DQ	STL	TO	BLK	PTS	RPG	APG	PPG
80-81–Detroit	3	–	19	5	8	.625	0	0	–	2	4	.500	2	2	4	1	6	0	1	1	0	12	1.3	0.3	4.0
Reg. Season Totals	3	–	19	5	8	.625	0	0	–	2	4	.500	2	2	4	1	6	0	1	1	0	12	1.3	0.3	4.0

Lawson, Jason L. b. September 2, 1974 Ht. 6-11 Wt. 240 College: Villanova

SEASON–TEAM	G	GS	MIN	FGM	FGA	PCT	3FGM	3FGA	PCT	FTM	FTA	PCT	O-RB	D-RB	TOT	AST	PF	DQ	STL	TO	BLK	PTS	RPG	APG	PPG
97-98–Orlando	17	0	80	9	15	.600	0	0	–	8	10	.800	8	19	27	5	14	1	4	2	4	26	1.6	0.3	1.5
Reg. Season Totals	17	0	80	9	15	.600	0	0	–	8	10	.800	8	19	27	5	14	1	4	2	4	26	1.6	0.3	1.5

Layton, Dennis (Mo) b. December 24, 1948 Ht. 6-1 Wt. 180 College: Phoenix Coll. AZ (J.C.); USC

SEASON–TEAM	G	GS	MIN	FGM	FGA	PCT	3FGM	3FGA	PCT	FTM	FTA	PCT	O-RB	D-RB	TOT	AST	PF	DQ	STL	TO	BLK	PTS	RPG	APG	PPG
71-72–Phoenix	80	–	1849	304	717	.424	–	–	–	122	165	.739	–	–	164	247	219	0	–	–	–	730	2.1	3.1	9.1
72-73–Phoenix	65	–	990	187	434	.431	–	–	–	90	119	.756	–	–	77	139	127	2	–	–	–	464	1.2	2.1	7.1
73-74–Portland	22	–	327	55	112	.491	–	–	–	14	26	.538	7	26	33	51	45	0	9	–	1	124	1.5	2.3	5.6
73-74–Memphis (A)	3	–	65	8	17	.471	0	0	–	3	3	1.000	1	3	4	7	4	–	0	7	1	19	1.3	2.3	6.3
76-77–N.Y. Knicks	56	–	765	134	277	.484	–	–	–	58	73	.795	11	36	47	154	87	0	21	–	6	326	0.8	2.8	5.8
77-78–San Antonio	41	–	498	85	168	.506	–	–	–	12	13	.923	4	28	32	108	51	0	21	59	4	182	0.8	2.6	4.4
Reg. NBA Totals	264	–	4429	765	1708	.448	–	–	–	296	396	.747	22	90	353	699	529	2	51	59	11	1826	1.3	2.6	6.9
Reg. ABA Totals	3	–	65	8	17	.471	0	0	–	3	3	1.000	1	3	4	7	4	0	0	7	1	19	1.3	2.3	6.3

Leaks, Emanuel (Manny) b. November 27, 1945 Ht. 6-8 Wt. 230 College: Niagara

SEASON–TEAM	G	GS	MIN	FGM	FGA	PCT	3FGM	3FGA	PCT	FTM	FTA	PCT	O-RB	D-RB	TOT	AST	PF	DQ	STL	TO	BLK	PTS	RPG	APG	PPG
68-69–Ken.-N.Y.-Dallas (A)	78	–	2089	299	756	.396	0	1	.000	160	229	.699	–	–	763	92	253	4	–	97	–	758	9.8	1.2	9.7
69-70–Dallas (A)	84	–	3086	636	1287	.494	0	2	.000	305	428	.713	427	620	1047	100	283	11	–	–	–	1577	12.5	1.2	18.8
70-71–Texas-N.Y. (A)	80	–	2614	510	1080	.472	0	1	.000	279	381	.732	317	538	855	104	211	–	–	–	–	1299	10.7	1.3	16.2
71-72–N.Y.-Utah-Fla. (A)	69	–	1443	240	580	.414	0	1	.000	74	121	.612	–	–	412	55	136	–	–	73	–	554	6.0	0.8	8.0
72-73–Philadelphia	82	–	2530	377	933	.404	–	–	–	144	200	.720	–	–	677	95	191	5	–	–	–	898	8.3	1.2	11.0
73-74–Capital	53	–	845	79	232	.341	–	–	–	58	83	.699	94	150	244	25	95	1	10	–	39	216	4.6	0.5	4.1
Reg. NBA Totals	135	–	3375	456	1165	.391	–	–	–	202	283	.714	94	150	921	120	286	6	10	–	39	1114	6.8	0.9	8.3
Reg. ABA Totals	311	–	9232	1685	3703	.455	0	5	.000	818	1159	.706	744	1158	3077	351	883	15	–	170	–	4188	9.9	1.1	13.5
NBA Playoff Totals	2	–	5	1	2	.500	–	–	–	0	0	–	1	1	2	–	1	0	0	–	0	2	1.0	0.0	1.0
ABA Playoff Totals	19	–	640	111	236	.470	0	0	–	46	65	.708	23	63	196	20	58	0	–	–	–	268	10.3	1.1	14.1

Lear, Harold C. Jr. (Hal, King) b. January 31, 1935 Ht. 6-0 Wt. 165 College: Temple

SEASON–TEAM	G	GS	MIN	FGM	FGA	PCT	3FGM	3FGA	PCT	FTM	FTA	PCT	O-RB	D-RB	TOT	AST	PF	DQ	STL	TO	BLK	PTS	RPG	APG	PPG
56-57–Philadelphia	3	–	14	2	6	.333	–	–	–	0	0	–	–	–	1	1	3	0	–	–	–	4	0.3	0.3	1.3
Reg. Season Totals	3	–	14	2	6	.333	–	–	–	0	0	–	–	–	1	1	3	0	–	–	–	4	0.3	0.3	1.3

Leavell, Allen Frazier b. May 27, 1957 Ht. 6-1 Wt. 170 College: Oklahoma City

SEASON–TEAM	G	GS	MIN	FGM	FGA	PCT	3FGM	3FGA	PCT	FTM	FTA	PCT	O-RB	D-RB	TOT	AST	PF	DQ	STL	TO	BLK	PTS	RPG	APG	PPG
79-80–Houston	77	–	2123	330	656	.503	3	19	.158	180	221	.814	57	127	184	417	197	1	127	205	28	843	2.4	5.4	10.9
80-81–Houston	79	–	1686	258	548	.471	2	17	.118	124	149	.832	30	104	134	384	160	1	97	189	15	642	1.7	4.9	8.1
81-82–Houston	79	61	2150	370	793	.467	9	31	.290	115	135	.852	49	119	168	457	182	2	150	153	15	864	2.1	5.8	10.9
82-83–Houston	79	76	2602	439	1059	.415	42	175	.240	247	297	.832	64	131	195	530	215	0	165	198	14	1167	2.5	6.7	14.8
83-84–Houston	82	27	2009	349	731	.477	11	71	.155	238	286	.832	31	86	117	459	199	2	107	184	12	947	1.4	5.6	11.5
84-85–Houston	42	0	536	88	209	.421	8	37	.216	44	57	.772	8	29	37	102	61	0	23	51	4	228	0.9	2.4	5.4
85-86–Houston	74	12	1190	212	458	.463	24	67	.358	135	158	.854	6	61	67	234	126	1	58	88	8	583	0.9	3.2	7.9
86-87–Houston	53	11	1175	147	358	.411	18	57	.316	100	119	.840	14	47	61	224	126	1	53	64	10	412	1.2	4.2	7.8
87-88–Houston	80	54	2150	291	666	.437	19	88	.216	218	251	.869	22	126	148	405	162	1	124	130	9	819	1.9	5.1	10.2
88-89–Houston	55	3	627	65	188	.346	5	41	.122	44	60	.733	13	40	53	127	61	0	25	62	5	179	1.0	2.3	3.3
Reg. Season Totals	700	244	16248	2549	5666	.450	141	603	.234	1445	1733	.834	294	870	1164	3339	1489	9	929	1324	120	6684	1.7	4.8	9.5
Playoff Totals	63	13	1072	138	377	.366	13	44	.295	113	131	.863	18	62	80	203	109	2	58	74	8	402	1.3	3.2	6.4

Lebo, Jeffrey Brian (Jeff) b. October 5, 1966 Ht. 6-2 Wt. 180 College: North Carolina

SEASON–TEAM	G	GS	MIN	FGM	FGA	PCT	3FGM	3FGA	PCT	FTM	FTA	PCT	O-RB	D-RB	TOT	AST	PF	DQ	STL	TO	BLK	PTS	RPG	APG	PPG
89-90–San Antonio	4	0	32	2	7	.286	0	0	–	2	2	1.000	2	2	4	3	7	0	2	1	0	6	1.0	0.8	1.5
Reg. Season Totals	4	0	32	2	7	.286	0	0	–	2	2	1.000	2	2	4	3	7	0	2	1	0	6	1.0	0.8	1.5

Leckner, Eric Charles b. May 27, 1966 Ht. 6-11 Wt. 265 College: Wyoming

SEASON–TEAM	G	GS	MIN	FGM	FGA	PCT	3FGM	3FGA	PCT	FTM	FTA	PCT	O-RB	D-RB	TOT	AST	PF	DQ	STL	TO	BLK	PTS	RPG	APG	PPG
88-89–Utah	75	0	779	120	220	.545	0	0	–	79	113	.699	48	151	199	16	174	1	8	69	22	319	2.7	0.2	4.3
89-90–Utah	77	0	764	125	222	.563	0	0	–	81	109	.743	48	144	192	19	157	0	15	63	23	331	2.5	0.2	4.3
90-91–Sac.-Cha.	72	2	1122	131	294	.446	0	0	–	62	111	.559	82	213	295	39	192	4	14	69	22	324	4.1	0.5	4.5
91-92–Charlotte	59	2	716	79	154	.513	0	1	.000	38	51	.745	49	157	206	31	114	1	9	39	18	196	3.5	0.5	3.3
93-94–Philadelphia	71	36	1163	139	286	.486	0	2	.000	84	130	.646	75	207	282	86	190	2	18	86	34	362	4.0	1.2	5.1
94-95–Detroit	57	11	623	87	165	.527	0	2	.000	51	72	.708	47	127	174	14	122	1	15	39	15	225	3.1	0.2	3.9
95-96–Detroit	18	8	155	18	29	.621	0	0	–	8	13	.615	8	26	34	1	30	0	2	11	4	44	1.9	0.1	2.4
96-97–N.Y.-Cha.-Vanc.	20	1	126	14	33	.424	0	0	–	6	12	.500	5	31	36	5	35	0	3	10	2	34	1.8	0.3	1.7
Reg. Season Totals	449	60	5448	713	1403	.508	0	5	.000	409	611	.669	362	1056	1418	211	1014	9	84	386	140	1835	3.2	0.5	4.1
Playoff Totals	7	0	41	7	14	.500	1	1	1.000	5	9	.556	3	7	10	2	12	0	0	4	0	20	1.4	0.3	2.9

Lee, Alfred (Butch) b. December 5, 1956 Ht. 6-0 Wt. 185 College: Marquette

SEASON–TEAM	G	GS	MIN	FGM	FGA	PCT	3FGM	3FGA	PCT	FTM	FTA	PCT	O-RB	D-RB	TOT	AST	PF	DQ	STL	TO	BLK	PTS	RPG	APG	PPG
78-79–Atlanta-Clev.	82	–	1779	290	634	.457	–	–	–	175	230	.761	33	93	126	295	146	0	86	154	1	755	1.5	3.6	9.2
79-80–Clev.-L.A.	14	–	55	6	24	.250	0	0	–	6	8	.750	7	4	11	12	2	0	1	10	0	18	0.8	0.9	1.3
Reg. Season Totals	96	–	1834	296	658	.450	0	0	–	181	238	.761	40	97	137	307	148	0	87	164	1	773	1.4	3.2	8.1
Playoff Totals	3	–	6	0	0	–	0	0	–	2	2	1.000	0	1	1	–	2	0	0	3	0	2	0.3	0.0	0.7

Lee, Clyde Wayne b. March 14, 1944 Ht. 6-10 Wt. 215 College: Vanderbilt

SEASON–TEAM	G	GS	MIN	FGM	FGA	PCT	3FGM	3FGA	PCT	FTM	FTA	PCT	O-RB	D-RB	TOT	AST	PF	DQ	STL	TO	BLK	PTS	RPG	APG	PPG
66-67–San Francisco	74	–	1247	205	503	.408	–	–	–	105	166	.633	–	–	551	77	168	5	–	–	–	515	7.4	1.0	7.0
67-68–San Francisco	82	–	2699	373	894	.417	–	–	–	229	335	.684	–	–	1141	135	331	10	–	–	–	975	13.9	1.6	11.9
68-69–San Francisco	65	–	2237	268	674	.398	–	–	–	160	256	.625	–	–	897	82	225	1	–	–	–	696	13.8	1.3	10.7
69-70–San Francisco	82	–	2641	362	822	.440	–	–	–	178	300	.593	–	–	929	80	263	5	–	–	–	902	11.3	1.0	11.0
70-71–San Francisco	82	–	1392	194	428	.453	–	–	–	111	199	.558	–	–	570	63	137	0	–	–	–	499	7.0	0.8	6.1
71-72–Golden State	78	–	2674	256	544	.471	–	–	–	120	222	.541	–	–	1132	85	244	4	–	–	–	632	14.5	1.1	8.1
72-73–Golden State	66	–	1476	170	365	.466	–	–	–	74	131	.565	–	–	598	34	183	5	–	–	–	414	9.1	0.5	6.3
73-74–Golden State	54	–	1642	129	284	.454	–	–	–	62	107	.579	188	410	598	68	179	3	27	–	17	320	11.1	1.3	5.9
74-75–Atlanta-Phil.	80	–	2456	176	427	.412	–	–	–	119	177	.672	288	469	757	105	285	9	30	–	20	471	9.5	1.3	5.9
75-76–Philadelphia	79	–	1421	123	282	.436	–	–	–	63	95	.663	164	289	453	59	188	0	23	–	27	309	5.7	0.7	3.9
Reg. Season Totals	742	–	19885	2256	5223	.432	–	–	–	1221	1988	.614	640	1168	7626	788	2203	42	80	–	64	5733	10.3	1.1	7.7
Playoff Totals	51	–	1398	146	368	.397	–	–	–	68	116	.586	4	12	519	61	157	3	0	–	1	360	10.2	1.2	7.1
All-Star Totals	1	–	18	2	8	.250	–	–	–	2	4	.500	0	0	11	2	3	0	0	–	0	6	11.0	2.0	6.0

Lee, David G. (Dave) b. March 31, 1942 Ht. 6-7 Wt. 225 College: San Francisco

SEASON–TEAM	G	GS	MIN	FGM	FGA	PCT	3FGM	3FGA	PCT	FTM	FTA	PCT	O-RB	D-RB	TOT	AST	PF	DQ	STL	TO	BLK	PTS	RPG	APG	PPG
67-68–Oakland (A)	54	–	753	125	276	.453	2	6	.333	120	140	.857	–	–	184	20	83	2	–	42	–	372	3.4	0.4	6.9
68-69–New Orleans (A)	4	–	16	1	9	.111	0	0	–	0	0	–	–	–	3	0	0	0	–	2	–	2	0.8	0.0	0.5
Reg. ABA Totals	58	–	769	126	285	.442	2	6	.333	120	140	.857	–	–	187	20	83	2	–	44	–	374	3.2	0.3	6.4

Lee, Douglas Edward (Doug) b. October 24, 1964 Ht. 6-6 Wt. 210 College: Texas A&M; Purdue

SEASON–TEAM	G	GS	MIN	FGM	FGA	PCT	3FGM	3FGA	PCT	FTM	FTA	PCT	O-RB	D-RB	TOT	AST	PF	DQ	STL	TO	BLK	PTS	RPG	APG	PPG
91-92–New Jersey	46	0	307	50	116	.431	10	37	.270	10	19	.526	17	18	35	22	39	0	11	12	1	120	0.8	0.5	2.6
92-93–New Jersey	5	0	33	2	7	.286	1	3	.333	0	0	–	0	2	2	5	7	0	0	3	1	5	0.4	1.0	1.0
94-95–Sacramento	22	0	75	9	25	.360	7	18	.389	18	21	.857	0	5	5	5	18	0	6	5	3	43	0.2	0.2	2.0
Reg. Season Totals	73	0	415	61	148	.412	18	58	.310	28	40	.700	17	25	42	32	64	0	17	20	5	168	0.6	0.4	2.3
Playoff Totals	2	0	6	0	3	.000	0	2	.000	0	0	–	0	0	0	1	1	0	0	0	1	0	0.0	0.5	0.0

Lee, George C. b. November 23, 1936 Ht. 6-4 Wt. 200 College: Michigan

SEASON–TEAM	G	GS	MIN	FGM	FGA	PCT	3FGM	3FGA	PCT	FTM	FTA	PCT	O-RB	D-RB	TOT	AST	PF	DQ	STL	TO	BLK	PTS	RPG	APG	PPG
60-61–Detroit	74	–	1735	310	776	.399	–	–	–	276	394	.701	–	–	490	89	158	1	–	–	–	896	6.6	1.2	12.1
61-62–Detroit	75	–	1351	179	500	.358	–	–	–	213	280	.761	–	–	349	64	128	1	–	–	–	571	4.7	0.9	7.6
62-63–San Francisco	64	–	1192	149	394	.378	–	–	–	152	193	.788	–	–	217	64	113	0	–	–	–	450	3.4	1.0	7.0
63-64–San Francisco	54	–	522	64	169	.379	–	–	–	47	71	.662	–	–	97	25	67	0	–	–	–	175	1.8	0.5	3.2
64-65–San Francisco	19	–	247	27	77	.351	–	–	–	38	52	.731	–	–	55	12	22	0	–	–	–	92	2.9	0.6	4.8
66-67–San Francisco	1	–	5	3	4	.750	–	–	–	6	7	.857	–	–	0	0	0	0	–	–	–	12	0.0	0.0	12.0
67-68–San Francisco	10	–	106	8	35	.229	–	–	–	17	24	.708	–	–	27	4	16	0	–	–	–	33	2.7	0.4	3.3
Reg. Season Totals	297	–	5158	740	1955	.379	–	–	–	749	1021	.734	–	–	1235	258	504	2	–	–	–	2229	4.2	0.9	7.5
Playoff Totals	21	–	262	48	110	.436	–	–	–	38	54	.704	–	–	58	19	32	0	–	–	–	134	2.8	0.9	6.4

Lee, Gregory Scott (Greg) b. December 12, 1951 Ht. 6-3 Wt. 195 College: UCLA

SEASON–TEAM	G	GS	MIN	FGM	FGA	PCT	3FGM	3FGA	PCT	FTM	FTA	PCT	O-RB	D-RB	TOT	AST	PF	DQ	STL	TO	BLK	PTS	RPG	APG	PPG
74-75–San Diego (A)	5	–	63	8	15	.533	0	0	–	2	2	1.000	1	2	3	13	6	–	4	6	0	18	0.6	2.6	3.6
75-76–Portland	5	–	35	2	4	.500	–	–	–	2	2	1.000	0	2	2	11	6	0	2	–	0	6	0.4	2.2	1.2
Reg. NBA Totals	5	–	35	2	4	.500	–	–	–	2	2	1.000	0	2	2	11	6	0	2	–	0	6	0.4	2.2	1.2
Reg. ABA Totals	5	–	63	8	15	.533	0	0	–	2	2	1.000	1	2	3	13	6	–	4	6	0	18	0.6	2.6	3.6

Lee, Keith DeWayne b. December 28, 1962 Ht. 6-10 Wt. 220 College: Memphis

SEASON–TEAM	G	GS	MIN	FGM	FGA	PCT	3FGM	3FGA	PCT	FTM	FTA	PCT	O-RB	D-RB	TOT	AST	PF	DQ	STL	TO	BLK	PTS	RPG	APG	PPG
85-86–Cleveland	58	38	1197	177	380	.466	2	9	.222	75	96	.781	116	235	351	67	204	9	29	78	37	431	6.1	1.2	7.4
86-87–Cleveland	67	1	870	170	374	.455	0	1	.000	72	101	.713	93	158	251	69	147	0	25	85	40	412	3.7	1.0	6.1
88-89–New Jersey	57	4	840	109	258	.422	0	2	.000	53	71	.746	73	186	259	42	138	1	20	53	33	271	4.5	0.7	4.8
Reg. Season Totals	182	43	2907	456	1012	.451	2	12	.167	200	268	.746	282	579	861	178	489	10	74	216	110	1114	4.7	1.0	6.1

Lee, Kurk b. June 3, 1967 Ht. 6-3 Wt. 190 College: Western Kentucky; Towson State

SEASON–TEAM	G	GS	MIN	FGM	FGA	PCT	3FGM	3FGA	PCT	FTM	FTA	PCT	O-RB	D-RB	TOT	AST	PF	DQ	STL	TO	BLK	PTS	RPG	APG	PPG
90-91–New Jersey	48	0	265	19	71	.268	3	15	.200	25	28	.893	7	23	30	34	39	0	11	20	2	66	0.6	0.7	1.4
Reg. Season Totals	48	0	265	19	71	.268	3	15	.200	25	28	.893	7	23	30	34	39	0	11	20	2	66	0.6	0.7	1.4

Lee, Richard (Dick) College: None

SEASON–TEAM	G	GS	MIN	FGM	FGA	PCT	3FGM	3FGA	PCT	FTM	FTA	PCT	O-RB	D-RB	TOT	AST	PF	DQ	STL	TO	BLK	PTS	RPG	APG	PPG
67-68–Anaheim (A)	2	–	2	0	0	–	0	0	–	0	0	–	–	–	1	1	0	0	–	0	–	0	0.5	0.5	0.0
Reg. ABA Totals	2	–	2	0	0	–	0	0	–	0	0	–	–	–	1	1	0	0	–	–	–	0	0.5	0.5	0.0

Lee, Rock Alan b. May 1, 1955 Ht. 6-10 Wt. 220 College: California; San Diego State

SEASON–TEAM	G	GS	MIN	FGM	FGA	PCT	3FGM	3FGA	PCT	FTM	FTA	PCT	O-RB	D-RB	TOT	AST	PF	DQ	STL	TO	BLK	PTS	RPG	APG	PPG
81-82–San Diego	2	0	10	1	2	.500	0	0	–	0	4	.000	0	1	1	2	3	0	0	0	0	2	0.5	1.0	1.0
Reg. Season Totals	2	0	10	1	2	.500	0	0	–	0	4	.000	0	1	1	2	3	0	0	0	0	2	0.5	1.0	1.0

Lee, Ronald Henry (Ron) b. November 2, 1952 Ht. 6-4 Wt. 195 College: Oregon

SEASON–TEAM	G	GS	MIN	FGM	FGA	PCT	3FGM	3FGA	PCT	FTM	FTA	PCT	O-RB	D-RB	TOT	AST	PF	DQ	STL	TO	BLK	PTS	RPG	APG	PPG
76-77–Phoenix	82	–	1849	347	786	.441	–	–	–	142	210	.676	99	200	299	263	276	10	156	–	33	836	3.6	3.2	10.2
77-78–Phoenix	82	–	1928	417	950	.439	–	–	–	170	228	.746	95	159	254	305	257	3	225	221	17	1004	3.1	3.7	12.2
78-79–Phoenix-N.O.	60	–	1346	218	507	.430	–	–	–	98	141	.695	63	105	168	205	182	3	107	165	6	534	2.8	3.4	8.9
79-80–Atlanta-Detroit	61	–	1167	113	305	.370	22	59	.373	44	70	.629	40	83	123	241	172	5	99	101	17	292	2.0	4.0	4.8
80-81–Detroit	82	–	1829	113	323	.350	2	13	.154	113	156	.724	65	155	220	362	260	4	166	173	29	341	2.7	4.4	4.2
81-82–Detroit	81	7	1467	88	246	.358	18	59	.305	84	119	.706	35	120	155	312	221	3	116	123	20	278	1.9	3.9	3.4
Reg. Season Totals	448	7	9586	1296	3117	.416	42	131	.321	651	924	.705	397	822	1219	1688	1368	28	869	783	122	3285	2.7	3.8	7.3
Playoff Totals	2	0	41	5	16	.313	0	0	–	2	2	1.000	2	4	6	3	7	0	4	4	0	12	3.0	1.5	6.0

Lee, Russell E. b. January 27, 1950 Ht. 6-5 Wt. 185 College: Marshall

SEASON–TEAM	G	GS	MIN	FGM	FGA	PCT	3FGM	3FGA	PCT	FTM	FTA	PCT	O-RB	D-RB	TOT	AST	PF	DQ	STL	TO	BLK	PTS	RPG	APG	PPG
72-73–Milwaukee	46	–	277	49	127	.386	–	–	–	32	43	.744	–	–	43	38	36	0	–	–	–	130	0.9	0.8	2.8
73-74–Milwaukee	36	–	166	38	94	.404	–	–	–	11	16	.688	16	24	40	20	29	0	11	–	0	87	1.1	0.6	2.4
74-75–New Orleans	15	–	139	29	76	.382	–	–	–	7	14	.500	15	16	31	7	17	1	11	–	3	65	2.1	0.5	4.3
Reg. Season Totals	97	–	582	116	297	.391	–	–	–	50	73	.685	31	40	114	65	82	1	22	–	3	282	1.2	0.7	2.9
Playoff Totals	11	–	25	13	22	.591	–	–	–	1	4	.250	1	2	7	3	1	0	3	–	1	27	0.6	0.3	2.5

Leede, Edward Horst (Ed) b. July 17, 1927 Ht. 6-3 Wt. 185 College: Dartmouth

SEASON–TEAM	G	GS	MIN	FGM	FGA	PCT	3FGM	3FGA	PCT	FTM	FTA	PCT	O-RB	D-RB	TOT	AST	PF	DQ	STL	TO	BLK	PTS	RPG	APG	PPG
49-50–Boston	64	–	–	174	507	.343	–	–	–	223	316	.706	–	–	–	130	167	–	–	–	–	571	–	2.0	8.9
50-51–Boston	57	–	–	119	370	.322	–	–	–	140	189	.741	–	–	118	95	144	3	–	–	–	378	2.1	1.7	6.6
Reg. Season Totals	121	–	–	293	877	.334	–	–	–	363	505	.719	–	–	118	225	311	3	–	–	–	949	2.1	1.9	7.8
Playoff Totals	2	–	–	1	7	.143	–	–	–	1	1	1.000	–	–	0	2	3	0	–	–	–	3	0.0	1.0	1.5

Lefkowitz, Henry A. (Hank) b. August 31, 1923 Ht. 6-2 Wt. 190 College: Case Western Reserve

SEASON–TEAM	G	GS	MIN	FGM	FGA	PCT	3FGM	3FGA	PCT	FTM	FTA	PCT	O-RB	D-RB	TOT	AST	PF	DQ	STL	TO	BLK	PTS	RPG	APG	PPG
46-47–Cleveland	24	–	–	22	114	.193	–	–	–	7	13	.538	–	–	–	4	35	–	–	–	–	51	–	0.2	2.1
Reg. Season Totals	24	–	–	22	114	.193	–	–	–	7	13	.538	–	–	–	4	35	–	–	–	–	51	–	0.2	2.1
Playoff Totals	3	–	–	4	18	.222	–	–	–	1	1	1.000	–	–	–	–	4	–	–	–	–	9	–	0.0	3.0

Legler, Timothy Eugene (Tim) b. December 26, 1966 Ht. 6-4 Wt. 220 College: La Salle

SEASON–TEAM	G	GS	MIN	FGM	FGA	PCT	3FGM	3FGA	PCT	FTM	FTA	PCT	O-RB	D-RB	TOT	AST	PF	DQ	STL	TO	BLK	PTS	RPG	APG	PPG
89-90–Phoenix	11	0	83	11	29	.379	0	1	.000	6	6	1.000	4	4	8	6	12	0	2	4	0	28	0.7	0.5	2.5
90-91–Denver	10	0	148	25	72	.347	3	12	.250	5	6	.833	8	10	18	12	20	0	2	4	0	58	1.8	1.2	5.8
92-93–Utah-Dallas	33	0	635	105	241	.436	22	65	.338	57	71	.803	25	34	59	46	63	0	24	28	6	289	1.8	1.4	8.8
93-94–Dallas	79	0	1322	231	528	.438	52	139	.374	142	169	.840	36	92	128	120	133	0	52	60	13	656	1.6	1.5	8.3
94-95–Golden State	24	0	371	60	115	.522	26	50	.520	30	34	.882	12	28	40	27	33	0	12	20	1	176	1.7	1.1	7.3
95-96–Washington	77	0	1775	233	460	.507	128	245	.522	132	153	.863	29	111	140	136	141	0	45	45	12	726	1.8	1.8	9.4
96-97–Washington	15	0	182	15	48	.313	8	29	.276	6	7	.857	0	21	21	7	21	0	3	9	5	44	1.4	0.5	2.9
97-98–Washington	8	0	76	3	19	.158	0	6	.000	3	4	.750	2	2	4	3	11	0	1	4	0	9	0.5	0.4	1.1
98-99–Washington	30	0	377	51	115	.443	14	35	.400	3	6	.500	8	32	40	21	42	0	4	14	3	119	1.3	0.7	4.0
99-00–Golden State	23	4	284	28	78	.359	7	21	.333	14	18	.778	4	19	23	24	33	0	4	6	1	77	1.0	1.0	3.3
Reg. Season Totals	310	4	5253	762	1705	.447	260	603	.431	398	474	.840	128	353	481	402	509	0	149	194	41	2182	1.6	1.3	7.0
Playoff Totals	3	0	19	0	2	.000	0	1	.000	1	2	.500	0	1	1	2	2	0	0	0	0	1	0.3	0.7	0.3

Lehmann, George b. May 1, 1942 Ht. 6-2 Wt. 185 College: Campbell

SEASON–TEAM	G	GS	MIN	FGM	FGA	PCT	3FGM	3FGA	PCT	FTM	FTA	PCT	O-RB	D-RB	TOT	AST	PF	DQ	STL	TO	BLK	PTS	RPG	APG	PPG
67-68–St. Louis	55	–	497	59	172	.343	–	–	–	35	43	.814	–	–	44	93	54	0	–	–	–	153	0.8	1.7	2.8
68-69–Atlanta	11	–	138	26	67	.388	–	–	–	8	12	.667	–	–	9	27	18	0	–	–	–	60	0.8	2.5	5.5
68-69–Los Angeles (A)	32	–	937	212	511	.415	48	137	.350	132	164	.805	–	–	73	159	96	1	–	122	–	604	2.3	5.0	18.9
69-70–L.A.-N.Y.-Miami (A)	81	–	1994	318	847	.375	92	286	.322	180	211	.853	–	–	121	256	189	0	–	–	–	908	1.5	3.2	11.2
70-71–Carolina (A)	83	–	2918	535	1186	.451	154	382	.403	214	256	.836	–	–	203	464	221	–	–	–	–	1438	2.4	5.6	17.3
71-72–Car.-Memphis (A)	53	–	1921	303	663	.457	71	199	.357	169	192	.880	–	–	98	411	155	–	–	210	–	846	1.8	7.8	16.0
72-73–Memphis (A)	28	–	753	95	240	.396	26	67	.388	61	74	.824	7	27	34	150	74	1	–	65	–	277	1.2	5.4	9.9
73-74–Memphis (A)	33	–	554	68	177	.384	18	50	.360	18	19	.947	8	29	37	117	52	–	13	53	4	172	1.1	3.5	5.2
Reg. NBA Totals	66	–	635	85	239	.356	–	–	–	43	55	.782	–	–	53	120	72	0	–	–	–	213	0.8	1.8	3.2
Reg. ABA Totals	310	–	9077	1531	3624	.422	409	1121	.365	774	916	.845	15	56	566	1557	787	2	13	450	4	4245	1.8	5.0	13.7
NBA Playoff Totals	1	–	2	0	1	.000	–	–	–	0	0	–	–	–	0	2	1	0	–	–	–	0	0.0	2.0	0.0

Lenard, Voshon Kelan b. May 14, 1973 Ht. 6-4 Wt. 205 College: Minnesota

SEASON–TEAM	G	GS	MIN	FGM	FGA	PCT	3FGM	3FGA	PCT	FTM	FTA	PCT	O-RB	D-RB	TOT	AST	PF	DQ	STL	TO	BLK	PTS	RPG	APG	PPG
95-96–Miami	30	0	323	53	141	.376	36	101	.356	34	43	.791	12	40	52	31	31	0	6	23	1	176	1.7	1.0	5.9
96-97–Miami	73	47	2111	314	684	.459	183	442	.414	86	105	.819	38	179	217	161	168	1	50	109	18	897	3.0	2.2	12.3
97-98–Miami	81	81	2621	363	854	.425	153	378	.405	141	179	.788	72	220	292	180	219	0	58	99	16	1020	3.6	2.2	12.6
98-99–Miami	12	2	190	31	79	.392	12	35	.343	8	11	.727	4	12	16	10	18	0	3	7	1	82	1.3	0.8	6.8
99-00–Miami	53	13	1434	228	560	.407	89	228	.390	84	106	.792	37	116	153	136	127	2	41	80	15	629	2.9	2.6	11.9
Reg. Season Totals	249	143	6679	989	2318	.427	473	1184	.399	353	444	.795	163	567	730	518	563	3	158	318	51	2804	2.9	2.1	11.3
Playoff Totals	26	22	791	99	229	.432	54	131	.412	51	61	.836	13	57	70	46	73	0	12	42	6	303	2.7	1.8	11.7

Lentz, Leary Lee b. February 23, 1945 Ht. 6-6 Wt. 200 College: Houston

SEASON–TEAM	G	GS	MIN	FGM	FGA	PCT	3FGM	3FGA	PCT	FTM	FTA	PCT	O-RB	D-RB	TOT	AST	PF	DQ	STL	TO	BLK	PTS	RPG	APG	PPG
67-68–Houston (A)	78	–	2504	343	845	.406	0	3	.000	147	221	.665	–	–	648	89	175	0	–	97	–	833	8.3	1.1	10.7
68-69–Hou.-N.Y. (A)	70	–	1129	135	334	.404	0	1	.000	76	117	.650	–	–	271	31	103	1	–	52	–	346	3.9	0.4	4.9
Reg. ABA Totals	148	–	3633	478	1179	.405	0	4	.000	223	338	.660	–	–	919	120	278	1	–	149	–	1179	6.2	0.8	8.0
ABA Playoff Totals	3	–	73	12	26	.462	0	0	–	1	3	.333	–	–	19	3	6	0	–	2	–	25	6.3	1.0	8.3

Leonard, Gary Francis b. February 16, 1967 Ht. 7-1 Wt. 265 College: Missouri

SEASON–TEAM	G	GS	MIN	FGM	FGA	PCT	3FGM	3FGA	PCT	FTM	FTA	PCT	O-RB	D-RB	TOT	AST	PF	DQ	STL	TO	BLK	PTS	RPG	APG	PPG
89-90–Minnesota	22	0	127	13	31	.419	0	1	.000	6	14	.429	10	17	27	1	26	0	3	8	9	32	1.2	0.0	1.5
90-91–Atlanta	4	0	9	0	0	–	0	0	–	2	4	.500	0	2	2	0	2	0	0	0	1	2	0.5	0.0	0.5
91-92–Atlanta	5	0	13	4	6	.667	0	0	–	2	2	1.000	3	2	5	1	3	0	1	1	0	10	1.0	0.2	2.0
Reg. Season Totals	31	0	149	17	37	.459	0	1	.000	10	20	.500	13	21	34	2	31	0	4	9	10	44	1.1	0.1	1.4
Playoff Totals	2	0	5	2	2	1.000	0	0	–	0	0	–	0	2	2	–	0	0	0	0	0	4	1.0	0.0	2.0

Leonard, William Robert (Bob, Slick) b. July 17, 1932 Ht. 6-3 Wt. 185 College: Indiana

SEASON–TEAM	G	GS	MIN	FGM	FGA	PCT	3FGM	3FGA	PCT	FTM	FTA	PCT	O-RB	D-RB	TOT	AST	PF	DQ	STL	TO	BLK	PTS	RPG	APG	PPG
56-57–Minneapolis	72	–	1943	303	867	.349	–	–	–	186	241	.772	–	–	220	169	140	0	–	–	–	792	3.1	2.3	11.0
57-58–Minneapolis	66	–	2074	266	794	.335	–	–	–	205	268	.765	–	–	237	218	145	0	–	–	–	737	3.6	3.3	11.2
58-59–Minneapolis	58	–	1598	206	552	.373	–	–	–	120	160	.750	–	–	178	186	119	0	–	–	–	532	3.1	3.2	9.2
59-60–Minneapolis	73	–	2074	231	717	.322	–	–	–	136	193	.705	–	–	245	252	171	3	–	–	–	598	3.4	3.5	8.2
60-61–Los Angeles	55	–	600	61	207	.295	–	–	–	71	100	.710	–	–	70	81	70	0	–	–	–	193	1.3	1.5	3.5
61-62–Chicago	70	–	2464	423	1128	.375	–	–	–	279	371	.752	–	–	199	378	186	0	–	–	–	1125	2.8	5.4	16.1
62-63–Chicago	32	–	879	84	245	.343	–	–	–	59	85	.694	–	–	68	143	84	1	–	–	–	227	2.1	4.5	7.1
Reg. Season Totals	426	–	11632	1574	4510	.349	–	–	–	1056	1418	.745	–	–	1217	1427	915	4	–	–	–	4204	2.9	3.3	9.9
Playoff Totals	34	–	924	130	364	.357	–	–	–	74	98	.755	–	–	93	165	77	0	–	–	–	334	2.7	4.9	9.8

Les, James Allen (Jim) b. August 18, 1963 Ht. 5-11 Wt. 175 College: Bradley

SEASON–TEAM	G	GS	MIN	FGM	FGA	PCT	3FGM	3FGA	PCT	FTM	FTA	PCT	O-RB	D-RB	TOT	AST	PF	DQ	STL	TO	BLK	PTS	RPG	APG	PPG
88-89–Utah	82	0	781	40	133	.301	1	14	.071	57	73	.781	23	64	87	215	88	0	27	88	5	138	1.1	2.6	1.7
89-90–Utah-LAClips	7	0	92	5	14	.357	0	1	.000	13	17	.765	3	4	7	21	9	0	3	10	0	23	1.0	3.0	3.3
90-91–Sacramento	55	8	1399	119	268	.444	71	154	.461	86	103	.835	18	93	111	299	141	0	57	75	4	395	2.0	5.4	7.2
91-92–Sacramento	62	5	712	74	192	.385	45	131	.344	38	47	.809	11	52	63	143	58	0	31	42	3	231	1.0	2.3	3.7
92-93–Sacramento	73	0	881	110	259	.425	66	154	.429	42	50	.840	20	69	89	169	81	0	40	48	7	328	1.2	2.3	4.5
93-94–Sacramento	18	0	169	13	34	.382	8	18	.444	11	13	.846	5	8	13	39	16	0	7	11	1	45	0.7	2.2	2.5
94-95–Atlanta	24	0	188	11	38	.289	5	23	.217	23	27	.852	6	20	26	44	28	0	4	21	0	50	1.1	1.8	2.1
Reg. Season Totals	321	13	4222	372	938	.397	196	495	.396	270	330	.818	86	310	396	930	421	0	169	295	20	1210	1.2	2.9	3.8
Playoff Totals	3	0	5	0	0	–	0	0	–	0	0	–	0	0	0	1	2	0	0	1	0	0	0.0	0.3	0.0

Lester, Ronnie b. January 1, 1959 Ht. 6-2 Wt. 175 College: Iowa

SEASON–TEAM	G	GS	MIN	FGM	FGA	PCT	3FGM	3FGA	PCT	FTM	FTA	PCT	O-RB	D-RB	TOT	AST	PF	DQ	STL	TO	BLK	PTS	RPG	APG	PPG
80-81–Chicago	8	–	83	10	24	.417	0	0	–	10	11	.909	3	3	6	7	5	0	2	9	0	30	0.8	0.9	3.8
81-82–Chicago	75	74	2252	329	657	.501	4	8	.500	208	256	.813	75	138	213	362	158	2	80	185	14	870	2.8	4.8	11.6
82-83–Chicago	65	38	1437	202	446	.453	0	5	.000	124	171	.725	46	126	172	332	121	2	51	134	6	528	2.6	5.1	8.1
83-84–Chicago	43	3	687	78	188	.415	1	5	.200	75	87	.862	20	26	46	168	59	1	30	72	6	232	1.1	3.9	5.4
84-85–L.A. Lakers	32	1	278	34	82	.415	0	1	.000	21	31	.677	4	22	26	80	25	0	15	32	3	89	0.8	2.5	2.8
85-86–L.A. Lakers	27	0	222	26	52	.500	0	3	.000	15	19	.789	0	10	10	54	27	0	9	42	3	67	0.4	2.0	2.5
Reg. Season Totals	250	116	4959	679	1449	.469	5	22	.227	453	575	.788	148	325	473	1003	395	5	187	474	32	1816	1.9	4.0	7.3
Playoff Totals	14	0	96	13	33	.394	0	1	.000	12	16	.750	7	7	14	13	11	0	2	9	0	38	1.0	0.9	2.7

Lett, Clifford Earl b. December 23, 1965 Ht. 6-3 Wt. 170 College: Florida

SEASON–TEAM	G	GS	MIN	FGM	FGA	PCT	3FGM	3FGA	PCT	FTM	FTA	PCT	O-RB	D-RB	TOT	AST	PF	DQ	STL	TO	BLK	PTS	RPG	APG	PPG
89-90–Chicago	4	0	28	2	8	.250	0	0	–	0	0	–	0	0	0	1	8	0	0	2	0	4	0.0	0.3	1.0
90-91–San Antonio	7	0	99	14	29	.483	0	1	.000	6	9	.667	1	6	7	7	9	0	2	8	1	34	1.0	1.0	4.9
Reg. Season Totals	11	0	127	16	37	.432	0	1	.000	6	9	.667	1	6	7	8	17	0	2	10	1	38	0.6	0.7	3.5

Levane, Andrew Joseph (Fuzzy) b. April 11, 1920 Ht. 6-2 Wt. 190 College: St. John's (N.Y.)

SEASON–TEAM	G	GS	MIN	FGM	FGA	PCT	3FGM	3FGA	PCT	FTM	FTA	PCT	O-RB	D-RB	TOT	AST	PF	DQ	STL	TO	BLK	PTS	RPG	APG	PPG
45-46–Rochester (N)	22	–	–	52	–	–	–	–	–	8	19	.421	–	–	–	–	23	–	–	–	–	112	–	–	5.1
46-47–Rochester (N)	39	–	–	133	–	–	–	–	–	49	87	.563	–	–	–	–	83	–	–	–	–	315	–	–	8.1
47-48–Rochester (N)	54	–	–	147	–	–	–	–	–	45	62	.726	–	–	–	–	100	–	–	–	–	339	–	–	6.3
48-49–Rochester	36	–	–	55	193	.285	–	–	–	13	21	.619	–	–	–	39	37	–	–	–	–	123	–	1.1	3.4
49-50–Syracuse	60	–	–	139	418	.333	–	–	–	54	85	.635	–	–	–	156	106	–	–	–	–	332	–	2.6	5.5
52-53–Milwaukee	7	–	68	3	24	.125	–	–	–	2	3	.667	–	–	9	9	15	0	–	–	–	8	1.3	1.3	1.1
Reg. NBA Totals	103	–	68	197	635	.310	–	–	–	69	109	.633	–	–	9	204	158	0	–	–	–	463	1.3	2.0	4.5
Reg. NBL Totals	115	–	–	332	–	–	–	–	–	102	168	.607	–	–	–	–	206	–	–	–	–	766	–	–	6.7
NBA Playoff Totals	9	–	0	13	57	.368	–	–	–	5	5	1.000	–	–	–	22	12	0	–	–	–	31	–	1.4	3.4
NBL Playoff Totals	23	–	–	57	–	–	–	–	–	22	32	.688	–	–	–	–	43	–	–	–	–	136	–	–	5.9

Lever, Lafayette (Fat) b. August 18, 1960 Ht. 6-3 Wt. 180 College: Arizona State

SEASON–TEAM	G	GS	MIN	FGM	FGA	PCT	3FGM	3FGA	PCT	FTM	FTA	PCT	O-RB	D-RB	TOT	AST	PF	DQ	STL	TO	BLK	PTS	RPG	APG	PPG
82-83–Portland	81	45	2020	256	594	.431	5	15	.333	116	159	.730	85	140	225	426	179	2	153	137	15	633	2.8	5.3	7.8
83-84–Portland	81	22	2010	313	701	.447	3	15	.200	159	214	.743	96	122	218	372	178	1	135	125	31	788	2.7	4.6	9.7
84-85–Denver	82	82	2559	424	985	.430	6	24	.250	197	256	.770	147	264	411	613	226	1	202	203	30	1051	5.0	7.5	12.8
85-86–Denver	78	77	2616	468	1061	.441	12	38	.316	132	182	.725	136	284	420	584	204	3	178	210	15	1080	5.4	7.5	13.8
86-87–Denver	82	82	3054	643	1370	.469	22	92	.239	244	312	.782	216	513	729	654	219	1	201	167	34	1552	8.9	8.0	18.9
87-88–Denver	82	82	3061	643	1360	.473	12	57	.211	248	316	.785	203	462	665	639	214	0	223	182	21	1546	8.1	7.8	18.9
88-89–Denver	71	71	2745	558	1221	.457	23	66	.348	270	344	.785	187	475	662	559	178	1	195	157	20	1409	9.3	7.9	19.8
89-90–Denver	79	79	2832	568	1283	.443	36	87	.414	271	337	.804	230	504	734	517	172	1	168	156	13	1443	9.3	6.5	18.3
90-91–Dallas	4	0	86	9	23	.391	0	3	.000	11	14	.786	3	12	15	12	5	0	6	10	3	29	3.8	3.0	7.3
91-92–Dallas	31	5	884	135	349	.387	17	52	.327	60	80	.750	56	105	161	107	73	0	46	36	12	347	5.2	3.5	11.2
93-94–Dallas	81	54	1947	227	557	.408	26	74	.351	75	98	.765	83	200	283	213	155	1	159	88	15	555	3.5	2.6	6.9
Reg. Season Totals	752	599	23814	4244	9504	.447	162	523	.310	1783	2312	.771	1442	3081	4523	4696	1803	11	1666	1471	209	10433	6.0	6.2	13.9
Playoff Totals	48	33	1441	227	548	.414	18	44	.409	124	160	.775	85	191	276	297	118	0	89	81	9	596	5.8	6.2	12.4
All-Star Totals	2	1	53	14	27	.519	0	2	.000	5	6	.833	0	7	7	5	4	0	2	0	0	33	3.5	2.5	16.5

Levingston, Clifford Eugene (Cliff) b. January 4, 1961 Ht. 6-8 Wt. 225 College: Wichita State

SEASON–TEAM	G	GS	MIN	FGM	FGA	PCT	3FGM	3FGA	PCT	FTM	FTA	PCT	O-RB	D-RB	TOT	AST	PF	DQ	STL	TO	BLK	PTS	RPG	APG	PPG
82-83–Detroit	62	5	879	131	270	.485	0	1	.000	84	147	.571	104	128	232	52	125	2	23	73	36	346	3.7	0.8	5.6
83-84–Detroit	80	24	1746	229	436	.525	0	3	.000	125	186	.672	234	311	545	109	281	7	44	77	78	583	6.8	1.4	7.3
84-85–Atlanta	74	53	2017	291	552	.527	0	2	.000	145	222	.653	230	336	566	104	231	3	70	133	69	727	7.6	1.4	9.8
85-86–Atlanta	81	35	1945	294	551	.534	0	1	.000	164	242	.678	193	341	534	72	260	5	76	113	39	752	6.6	0.9	9.3
86-87–Atlanta	82	10	1848	251	496	.506	0	3	.000	155	212	.731	219	314	533	40	261	4	48	72	68	657	6.5	0.5	8.0
87-88–Atlanta	82	32	2135	314	564	.557	1	2	.500	190	246	.772	228	276	504	71	287	5	52	94	84	819	6.1	0.9	10.0
88-89–Atlanta	80	52	2184	300	568	.528	1	5	.200	133	191	.696	194	304	498	75	270	4	97	105	70	734	6.2	0.9	9.2
89-90–Atlanta	75	5	1706	216	424	.509	1	5	.200	83	122	.680	113	206	319	80	216	2	55	49	41	516	4.3	1.1	6.9
90-91–Chicago	78	0	1013	127	282	.450	1	4	.250	59	91	.648	99	126	225	56	143	0	29	50	43	314	2.9	0.7	4.0
91-92–Chicago	79	0	1020	125	251	.498	1	6	.167	60	96	.625	109	118	227	66	134	0	27	42	45	311	2.9	0.8	3.9
94-95–Denver	57	0	469	55	130	.423	0	1	.000	19	45	.422	49	75	124	27	91	0	13	21	20	129	2.2	0.5	2.3
Reg. Season Totals	830	216	16962	2333	4524	.516	5	33	.152	1217	1800	.676	1772	2535	4307	752	2299	32	534	829	593	5888	5.2	0.9	7.1
Playoff Totals	82	0	1047	120	239	.502	2	4	.500	70	105	.667	103	130	233	33	162	0	27	42	37	312	2.8	0.4	3.8

Lewis, Cedric b. September 24, 1969 Ht. 6-10 Wt. 235 College: Maryland

SEASON–TEAM	G	GS	MIN	FGM	FGA	PCT	3FGM	3FGA	PCT	FTM	FTA	PCT	O-RB	D-RB	TOT	AST	PF	DQ	STL	TO	BLK	PTS	RPG	APG	PPG
95-96–Washington	3	0	4	2	3	.667	0	0	–	0	0	–	2	0	2	0	0	0	1	0	0	4	0.7	0.0	1.3
Reg. Season Totals	3	0	4	2	3	.667	0	0	–	0	0	–	2	0	2	0	0	0	1	0	0	4	0.7	0.0	1.3

Lewis, Frederick B. Jr. (Fred) b. January 6, 1921 d. December 27, 1994 Ht. 6-2 Wt. 195 College: Long Island University; Eastern Kentucky

SEASON–TEAM	G	GS	MIN	FGM	FGA	PCT	3FGM	3FGA	PCT	FTM	FTA	PCT	O-RB	D-RB	TOT	AST	PF	DQ	STL	TO	BLK	PTS	RPG	APG	PPG
46-47–Sheboygan (N)	44	–	–	230	–	–	–	–	–	125	170	.735	–	–	–	–	106	–	–	–	–	585	–	–	13.3
47-48–She.-Ind. (N)	44	–	–	169	–	–	–	–	–	101	137	.737	–	–	–	–	100	–	–	–	–	439	–	–	10.0
48-49–Ind.-Balt.	61	–	–	272	834	.326	–	–	–	138	181	.762	–	–	–	107	167	–	–	–	–	682	–	1.8	11.2
49-50–Balt.-Phil.	34	–	–	46	184	.250	–	–	–	25	32	.781	–	–	–	25	40	–	–	–	–	117	–	0.7	3.4
Reg. NBA Totals	95	–	–	318	1018	.312	–	–	–	163	213	.765	–	–	–	132	207	–	–	–	–	799	–	1.4	8.4
Reg. NBL Totals	88	–	–	399	–	–	–	–	–	226	307	.736	–	–	–	–	206	–	–	–	–	1024	–	–	11.6
NBA Playoff Totals	3	–	–	15	35	.429	–	–	–	7	10	.700	–	–	–	3	13	–	–	–	–	37	–	1.0	12.3
NBL Playoff Totals	9	–	–	41	–	–	–	–	–	14	18	.611	–	–	–	–	14	–	–	–	–	96	–	–	10.7

Lewis, Frederick L. (Freddie) b. July 1, 1943 Ht. 6-0 Wt. 180 College: Eastern Arizona Coll. (J.C.); Arizona State

SEASON–TEAM	G	GS	MIN	FGM	FGA	PCT	3FGM	3FGA	PCT	FTM	FTA	PCT	O-RB	D-RB	TOT	AST	PF	DQ	STL	TO	BLK	PTS	RPG	APG	PPG
66-67–Cincinnati	32	–	334	60	153	.392	–	–	–	29	41	.707	–	–	44	40	49	1	–	–	–	149	1.4	1.3	4.7
67-68–Indiana (A)	76	–	2921	542	1287	.421	16	74	.216	465	583	.798	–	–	440	183	217	2	–	209	–	1565	5.8	2.4	20.6
68-69–Indiana (A)	78	–	3055	572	1300	.440	22	83	.265	419	510	.822	–	–	374	346	289	5	–	224	–	1585	4.8	4.4	20.3
69-70–Indiana (A)	81	–	2877	448	1065	.421	47	177	.266	383	485	.790	–	–	277	289	294	5	–	–	–	1326	3.4	3.6	16.4
70-71–Indiana (A)	81	–	3034	547	1241	.441	59	194	.304	372	461	.807	–	–	336	433	249	–	–	–	–	1525	4.1	5.3	18.8
71-72–Indiana (A)	77	–	2714	405	947	.428	31	100	.310	341	396	.861	–	–	327	362	230	–	–	194	–	1182	4.2	4.7	15.4
72-73–Indiana (A)	72	–	2217	375	860	.436	38	110	.345	287	349	.822	97	131	228	288	204	4	–	173	–	1075	3.2	4.0	14.9
73-74–Indiana (A)	78	–	2164	290	728	.398	13	72	.181	182	219	.831	84	117	201	322	189	–	99	169	11	775	2.6	4.1	9.9
74-75–Mem.-St. L. (A)	69	–	2790	579	1232	.470	18	67	.269	355	421	.843	111	154	265	367	161	–	147	206	3	1531	3.8	5.3	22.2
75-76–St. Louis (A)	74	–	2266	403	953	.423	31	106	.292	259	317	.817	67	146	213	293	183	–	109	193	7	1096	2.9	4.0	14.8
76-77–Indiana	32	–	552	81	199	.407	–	–	–	62	77	.805	17	30	47	56	58	0	18	–	2	224	1.5	1.8	7.0
Reg. NBA Totals	64	–	886	141	352	.401	–	–	–	91	118	.771	17	30	91	96	107	1	18	–	2	373	1.4	1.5	5.8
Reg. ABA Totals	686	–	24038	4161	9613	.433	275	983	.280	3063	3741	.819	359	548	2661	2883	2016	16	355	1368	21	11660	3.9	4.2	17.0
NBA Playoff Totals	3	–	9	4	9	.444	–	–	–	0	0	–	0	0	4	–	1	0	0	–	0	8	1.3	0.0	2.7
ABA Playoff Totals	106	–	4151	712	1679	.424	43	175	.246	548	643	.852	41	55	437	458	348	2	56	160	2	2015	4.1	4.3	19.0

Lewis, Grady W. b. March 25, 1917 Ht. 6-7 Wt. 215 College: Southwestern Oklahoma State; Oklahoma

SEASON–TEAM	G	GS	MIN	FGM	FGA	PCT	3FGM	3FGA	PCT	FTM	FTA	PCT	O-RB	D-RB	TOT	AST	PF	DQ	STL	TO	BLK	PTS	RPG	APG	PPG
46-47–Detroit	60	–	–	106	520	.204	–	–	–	75	138	.543	–	–	–	54	166	–	–	–	–	287	–	0.9	4.8
47-48–St. Louis-Balt.	45	–	–	114	425	.268	–	–	–	87	135	.644	–	–	–	41	151	–	–	–	–	315	–	0.9	7.0
48-49–St. Louis	34	–	–	53	137	.387	–	–	–	42	70	.600	–	–	–	37	104	–	–	–	–	148	–	1.1	4.4
Reg. Season Totals	139	–	–	273	1082	.252	–	–	–	204	343	.595	–	–	–	132	421	–	–	–	–	750	–	0.9	5.4
Playoff Totals	11	–	–	23	109	.211	–	–	–	22	29	.759	–	–	–	9	49	4	–	–	–	68	–	0.8	6.2

Lewis, Martin b. April 28, 1975 Ht. 6-6 Wt. 225 College: Seward Co. (Kan.) C.C.

SEASON–TEAM	G	GS	MIN	FGM	FGA	PCT	3FGM	3FGA	PCT	FTM	FTA	PCT	O-RB	D-RB	TOT	AST	PF	DQ	STL	TO	BLK	PTS	RPG	APG	PPG
95-96–Toronto	16	0	189	29	60	.483	2	7	.286	15	25	.600	15	14	29	3	21	0	8	14	3	75	1.8	0.2	4.7
96-97–Toronto	9	0	50	6	14	.429	1	3	.333	1	2	.500	4	2	6	4	8	0	1	1	2	14	0.7	0.4	1.6
Reg. Season Totals	25	0	239	35	74	.473	3	10	.300	16	27	.593	19	16	35	7	29	0	9	15	5	89	1.4	0.3	3.6

Lewis, Michael J. (Mike) b. March 18, 1946 Ht. 6-8 Wt. 225 College: Duke

SEASON–TEAM	G	GS	MIN	FGM	FGA	PCT	3FGM	3FGA	PCT	FTM	FTA	PCT	O-RB	D-RB	TOT	AST	PF	DQ	STL	TO	BLK	PTS	RPG	APG	PPG
68-69–Ind.-Minn. (A)	76	–	1617	247	566	.436	0	2	.000	153	235	.651	–	–	632	107	246	8	–	138	–	647	8.3	1.4	8.5
69-70–Pittsburgh (A)	78	–	2698	499	1006	.496	0	0	–	269	356	.756	370	684	1054	268	306	7	–	–	–	1267	13.5	3.4	16.2
70-71–Pittsburgh (A)	83	–	2741	420	825	.509	0	0	–	235	306	.768	435	778	1213	268	332	–	–	–	–	1075	14.6	3.2	13.0
71-72–Pittsburgh (A)	82	–	2618	385	713	.540	0	0	–	165	226	.730	357	639	996	316	315	–	–	237	–	935	12.1	3.9	11.4
72-73–Carolina (A)	15	–	430	59	119	.496	0	0	–	33	41	.805	44	78	122	41	48	1	–	27	–	151	8.1	2.7	10.1
73-74–Carolina (A)	3	–	14	3	8	.375	0	0	–	0	0	–	3	2	5	0	2	–	0	1	0	6	1.7	0.0	2.0
Reg. ABA Totals	337	–	10118	1613	3237	.498	0	2	.000	855	1164	.735	1209	2181	4022	1000	1249	16	0	403	0	4081	11.9	3.0	12.1
ABA Playoff Totals	7	–	131	20	52	.385	0	0	–	10	19	.526	0	0	47	11	28	2	0	0	0	50	6.7	1.6	7.1

Lewis, Quincy Lavell b. June 26, 1977 Ht. 6-7 Wt. 215 College: Minnesota

SEASON–TEAM	G	GS	MIN	FGM	FGA	PCT	3FGM	3FGA	PCT	FTM	FTA	PCT	O-RB	D-RB	TOT	AST	PF	DQ	STL	TO	BLK	PTS	RPG	APG	PPG
99-00–Utah	74	0	896	111	298	.372	23	63	.365	38	52	.731	46	67	113	40	158	0	24	46	15	283	1.5	0.5	3.8
Reg. Season Totals	74	0	896	111	298	.372	23	63	.365	38	52	.731	46	67	113	40	158	0	24	46	15	283	1.5	0.5	3.8
Playoff Totals	8	0	106	10	27	.370	2	6	.333	4	5	.800	2	13	15	2	24	0	3	3	7	26	1.9	0.3	3.3

Lewis, Ralph Adolphus b. March 28, 1963 Ht. 6-6 Wt. 200 College: La Salle

SEASON–TEAM	G	GS	MIN	FGM	FGA	PCT	3FGM	3FGA	PCT	FTM	FTA	PCT	O-RB	D-RB	TOT	AST	PF	DQ	STL	TO	BLK	PTS	RPG	APG	PPG
87-88–Detroit	50	0	310	27	87	.310	0	1	.000	29	48	.604	17	34	51	14	36	0	13	19	4	83	1.0	0.3	1.7
88-89–Charlotte	42	0	336	58	121	.479	1	3	.333	19	39	.487	35	26	61	15	28	0	11	24	3	136	1.5	0.4	3.2
89-90–Detroit-Cha.	7	0	26	4	7	.571	0	0	–	2	2	1.000	4	2	6	0	3	0	1	2	0	10	0.9	0.0	1.4
Reg. Season Totals	99	0	672	89	215	.414	1	4	.250	50	89	.562	56	62	118	29	67	0	25	45	7	229	1.2	0.3	2.3
Playoff Totals	10	0	17	2	6	.333	0	1	.000	0	0	–	3	5	8	1	2	0	0	0	0	4	0.8	0.1	0.4

Lewis, Rashard Quovon b. August 8, 1979 Ht. 6-10 Wt. 215 High School: Alief Elsik HS (Texas)

SEASON–TEAM	G	GS	MIN	FGM	FGA	PCT	3FGM	3FGA	PCT	FTM	FTA	PCT	O-RB	D-RB	TOT	AST	PF	DQ	STL	TO	BLK	PTS	RPG	APG	PPG
98-99–Seattle	20	7	145	19	52	.365	1	6	.167	8	14	.571	13	12	25	4	19	0	8	20	1	47	1.3	0.2	2.4
99-00–Seattle	82	8	1575	275	566	.486	40	120	.333	84	123	.683	127	209	336	70	163	0	62	78	36	674	4.1	0.9	8.2
Reg. Season Totals	102	15	1720	294	618	.476	41	126	.325	92	137	.672	140	221	361	74	182	0	70	98	37	721	3.5	0.7	7.1
Playoff Totals	5	5	157	26	59	.441	9	19	.474	16	20	.800	12	19	31	3	11	0	5	10	3	77	6.2	0.6	15.4

Lewis, Reginald C. (Reggie) b. November 21, 1965 d. July 27, 1993 Ht. 6-7 Wt. 195 College: Northeastern

SEASON–TEAM	G	GS	MIN	FGM	FGA	PCT	3FGM	3FGA	PCT	FTM	FTA	PCT	O-RB	D-RB	TOT	AST	PF	DQ	STL	TO	BLK	PTS	RPG	APG	PPG
87-88–Boston	49	0	405	90	193	.466	0	4	.000	40	57	.702	28	35	63	26	54	0	16	30	15	220	1.3	0.5	4.5
88-89–Boston	81	57	2657	604	1242	.486	3	22	.136	284	361	.787	116	261	377	218	258	5	124	142	72	1495	4.7	2.7	18.5
89-90–Boston	79	54	2522	540	1089	.496	4	15	.267	256	317	.808	109	238	347	225	216	2	88	120	63	1340	4.4	2.8	17.0
90-91–Boston	79	79	2878	598	1219	.491	1	13	.077	281	340	.826	119	291	410	201	234	1	98	147	85	1478	5.2	2.5	18.7
91-92–Boston	82	82	3070	703	1397	.503	5	21	.238	292	343	.851	117	277	394	185	258	4	125	136	105	1703	4.8	2.3	20.8
92-93–Boston	80	80	3144	663	1410	.470	14	60	.233	326	376	.867	88	259	347	298	248	1	118	133	77	1666	4.3	3.7	20.8
Reg. Season Totals	450	352	14676	3198	6550	.488	27	135	.200	1479	1794	.824	577	1361	1938	1153	1268	13	569	708	417	7902	4.3	2.6	17.6
Playoff Totals	42	30	1278	293	575	.510	2	15	.133	146	188	.777	54	121	175	109	110	3	51	57	19	734	4.2	2.6	17.5
All-Star Totals	1	0	15	3	7	.429	0	0	–	1	2	.500	4	0	4	2	3	0	0	1	1	7	4.0	2.0	7.0

Lewis, Robert Franklin (Bobby) b. March 20, 1945 Ht. 6-3 Wt. 185 College: North Carolina

SEASON–TEAM	G	GS	MIN	FGM	FGA	PCT	3FGM	3FGA	PCT	FTM	FTA	PCT	O-RB	D-RB	TOT	AST	PF	DQ	STL	TO	BLK	PTS	RPG	APG	PPG
67-68–San Francisco	41	–	342	59	151	.391	–	–	–	61	79	.772	–	–	56	41	40	0	–	–	–	179	1.4	1.0	4.4
68-69–San Francisco	62	–	756	113	290	.390	–	–	–	83	113	.735	–	–	114	76	117	0	–	–	–	309	1.8	1.2	5.0
69-70–San Francisco	73	–	1353	213	557	.382	–	–	–	100	152	.658	–	–	157	194	170	0	–	–	–	526	2.2	2.7	7.2
70-71–Cleveland	79	–	1852	179	484	.370	–	–	–	109	152	.717	–	–	206	244	176	1	–	–	–	467	2.6	3.1	5.9
Reg. Season Totals	255	–	4303	564	1482	.381	–	–	–	353	496	.712	–	–	533	555	503	1	–	–	–	1481	2.1	2.2	5.8
Playoff Totals	6	–	63	13	31	.419	–	–	–	1	3	.333	–	–	5	6	12	0	–	–	–	27	0.8	1.0	4.5

Liberty, Marcus (Doc) b. October 27, 1968 Ht. 6-8 Wt. 205 College: Illinois

SEASON–TEAM	G	GS	MIN	FGM	FGA	PCT	3FGM	3FGA	PCT	FTM	FTA	PCT	O-RB	D-RB	TOT	AST	PF	DQ	STL	TO	BLK	PTS	RPG	APG	PPG
90-91–Denver	76	18	1171	216	513	.421	17	57	.298	58	92	.630	117	104	221	64	153	2	48	71	19	507	2.9	0.8	6.7
91-92–Denver	75	13	1527	275	621	.443	17	50	.340	131	180	.728	144	164	308	58	165	3	66	90	29	698	4.1	0.8	9.3
92-93–Denver	78	32	1585	252	620	.406	22	59	.373	102	156	.654	131	204	335	105	143	0	64	79	21	628	4.3	1.3	8.1
93-94–Den.-Detroit	38	0	285	40	123	.325	10	28	.357	19	39	.487	26	35	61	17	34	0	11	24	4	109	1.6	0.4	2.9
Reg. Season Totals	267	63	4568	783	1877	.417	66	194	.340	310	467	.664	418	507	925	244	495	5	189	264	73	1942	3.5	0.9	7.3

Lichti, Todd Samuel b. January 8, 1967 Ht. 6-4 Wt. 205 College: Stanford

SEASON–TEAM	G	GS	MIN	FGM	FGA	PCT	3FGM	3FGA	PCT	FTM	FTA	PCT	O-RB	D-RB	TOT	AST	PF	DQ	STL	TO	BLK	PTS	RPG	APG	PPG
89-90–Denver	79	4	1326	250	514	.486	0	14	.000	130	174	.747	49	102	151	116	145	1	55	95	13	630	1.9	1.5	8.0
90-91–Denver	29	25	860	166	378	.439	14	47	.298	59	69	.855	49	63	112	72	65	1	46	33	8	405	3.9	2.5	14.0
91-92–Denver	68	10	1176	173	376	.460	1	9	.111	99	118	.839	36	82	118	74	131	0	43	72	12	446	1.7	1.1	6.6
92-93–Denver	48	12	752	124	276	.449	2	6	.333	81	102	.794	35	67	102	52	60	0	28	49	11	331	2.1	1.1	6.9
93-94–Orlando-G.S.-Bos.	13	0	126	20	51	.392	2	2	1.000	16	25	.640	8	14	22	11	16	0	7	5	1	58	1.7	0.8	4.5
Reg. Season Totals	237	51	4240	733	1595	.460	19	78	.244	385	488	.789	177	328	505	325	417	2	179	254	45	1870	2.1	1.4	7.9
Playoff Totals	3	0	70	15	29	.517	0	1	.000	14	19	.737	5	13	18	9	6	0	1	8	0	44	6.0	3.0	14.7

Liebowitz, Barry b. 1943 Ht. 6-2 Wt. 180 College: Long Island University

SEASON–TEAM	G	GS	MIN	FGM	FGA	PCT	3FGM	3FGA	PCT	FTM	FTA	PCT	O-RB	D-RB	TOT	AST	PF	DQ	STL	TO	BLK	PTS	RPG	APG	PPG
67-68–Pitt.-N.J.-Oakland (A)	82	–	2168	320	873	.367	6	39	.154	248	308	.805	–	–	170	301	208	1	–	224	–	894	2.1	3.7	10.9
Reg. ABA Totals	82	–	2168	320	873	.367	6	39	.154	248	308	.805	–	–	170	301	208	1	–	224	–	894	2.1	3.7	10.9

Ligon, Jim (Goose) b. February 22, 1944 Ht. 6-7 Wt. 215 College: None

SEASON–TEAM	G	GS	MIN	FGM	FGA	PCT	3FGM	3FGA	PCT	FTM	FTA	PCT	O-RB	D-RB	TOT	AST	PF	DQ	STL	TO	BLK	PTS	RPG	APG	PPG
67-68–Kentucky (A)	78	–	2801	428	942	.454	1	4	.250	405	595	.681	370	559	929	143	307	6	–	188	–	1262	11.9	1.8	16.2
68-69–Kentucky (A)	75	–	2815	391	879	.445	1	5	.200	337	510	.661	328	491	819	172	312	6	–	193	–	1120	10.9	2.3	14.9
69-70–Kentucky (A)	84	–	3130	507	1000	.507	0	2	.000	287	445	.645	399	695	1094	190	360	13	–	–	–	1301	13.0	2.3	15.5
70-71–Kentucky (A)	84	–	2753	429	795	.540	0	6	.000	214	391	.547	312	677	989	211	331	–	–	–	–	1072	11.8	2.5	12.8
71-72–Ken.-Pitt. (A)	82	–	2341	213	428	.498	1	6	.167	141	217	.650	–	–	700	163	265	–	–	126	–	568	8.5	2.0	6.9
72-73–Virginia (A)	12	–	360	58	103	.563	0	0	–	28	43	.651	36	58	94	20	40	0	–	21	–	144	7.8	1.7	12.0
73-74–Virginia (A)	19	–	360	37	85	.435	0	1	.000	19	25	.760	45	50	95	11	43	–	9	24	9	93	5.0	0.6	4.9
Reg. ABA Totals	434	–	14560	2063	4232	.487	3	24	.125	1431	2226	.643	1490	2530	4720	910	1658	25	9	552	9	5560	10.9	2.1	12.8
ABA Playoff Totals	46	–	1521	211	439	.481	0	3	.000	166	249	.667	163	295	516	76	129	1	0	20	1	588	11.2	1.7	12.8

Ligon, William N. (Bill) b. May 19, 1952 Ht. 6-4 Wt. 180 College: Vanderbilt

SEASON–TEAM	G	GS	MIN	FGM	FGA	PCT	3FGM	3FGA	PCT	FTM	FTA	PCT	O-RB	D-RB	TOT	AST	PF	DQ	STL	TO	BLK	PTS	RPG	APG	PPG
74-75–Detroit	38	–	272	55	143	.385	–	–	–	16	25	.640	14	12	26	25	31	0	8	–	9	126	0.7	0.7	3.3
Reg. Season Totals	38	–	272	55	143	.385	–	–	–	16	25	.640	14	12	26	25	31	0	8	–	9	126	0.7	0.7	3.3
Playoff Totals	2	–	7	1	1	1.000	–	–	–	0	0	–	0	0	0	–	1	0	0	–	0	2	0.0	0.0	1.0

Lingenfelter, Steven Rodney (Steve) b. June 10, 1958 Ht. 6-9 Wt. 225 College: Minnesota; South Dakota State

SEASON–TEAM	G	GS	MIN	FGM	FGA	PCT	3FGM	3FGA	PCT	FTM	FTA	PCT	O-RB	D-RB	TOT	AST	PF	DQ	STL	TO	BLK	PTS	RPG	APG	PPG
82-83–Washington	7	0	53	4	6	.667	0	0	–	0	4	.000	1	11	12	4	16	1	1	5	3	8	1.7	0.6	1.1
83-84–San Antonio	3	0	14	1	1	1.000	0	0	–	0	2	.000	3	1	4	1	6	0	0	1	0	2	1.3	0.3	0.7
Reg. Season Totals	10	0	67	5	7	.714	0	0	–	0	6	.000	4	12	16	5	22	1	1	6	3	10	1.6	0.5	1.0

Lister, Alton Lavelle b. October 1, 1958 Ht. 7-0 Wt. 245 College: San Jacinto (Texas) Coll. (J.C.); Arizona State

SEASON–TEAM	G	GS	MIN	FGM	FGA	PCT	3FGM	3FGA	PCT	FTM	FTA	PCT	O-RB	D-RB	TOT	AST	PF	DQ	STL	TO	BLK	PTS	RPG	APG	PPG
81-82–Milwaukee	80	23	1186	149	287	.519	0	0	–	64	123	.520	108	279	387	84	239	4	18	129	118	362	4.8	1.1	4.5
82-83–Milwaukee	80	37	1885	272	514	.529	0	0	–	130	242	.537	168	400	568	111	328	18	50	186	177	674	7.1	1.4	8.4
83-84–Milwaukee	82	72	1955	256	512	.500	0	0	–	114	182	.626	156	447	603	110	327	11	41	153	140	626	7.4	1.3	7.6
84-85–Milwaukee	81	80	2091	322	598	.538	0	1	.000	154	262	.588	219	428	647	127	287	5	49	183	167	798	8.0	1.6	9.9
85-86–Milwaukee	81	19	1812	318	577	.551	0	2	.000	160	266	.602	199	393	592	101	300	8	49	161	142	796	7.3	1.2	9.8
86-87–Seattle	75	75	2288	346	687	.504	0	1	.000	179	265	.675	223	482	705	110	289	11	32	169	180	871	9.4	1.5	11.6
87-88–Seattle	82	55	1812	173	343	.504	1	2	.500	114	188	.606	200	427	627	58	319	8	27	90	140	461	7.6	0.7	5.6
88-89–Seattle	82	82	1806	271	543	.499	0	0	–	115	178	.646	207	338	545	54	310	3	28	117	180	657	6.6	0.7	8.0
89-90–Golden State	3	0	40	4	8	.500	0	1	.000	4	7	.571	5	3	8	2	8	0	1	0	0	12	2.7	0.7	4.0
90-91–Golden State	77	65	1552	188	393	.478	0	1	.000	115	202	.569	121	362	483	93	282	4	20	106	90	491	6.3	1.2	6.4
91-92–Golden State	26	12	293	44	79	.557	0	0	–	14	33	.424	21	71	92	14	61	0	5	20	16	102	3.5	0.5	3.9
92-93–Golden State	20	9	174	19	42	.452	0	0	–	7	13	.538	15	29	44	5	40	0	0	18	9	45	2.2	0.3	2.3
94-95–Milwaukee	60	32	776	66	134	.493	0	1	.000	35	70	.500	67	169	236	12	146	3	16	38	57	167	3.9	0.2	2.8
95-96–Milw.-Boston	64	19	735	51	105	.486	0	0	–	41	64	.641	67	213	280	19	136	1	6	48	42	143	4.4	0.3	2.2
96-97–Boston	53	2	516	32	77	.416	0	0	–	23	31	.742	66	102	168	13	95	1	8	30	14	87	3.2	0.2	1.6
97-98–Portland	7	0	44	3	8	.375	0	0	–	0	0	–	2	9	11	1	12	0	1	2	1	6	1.6	0.1	0.9
Reg. Season Totals	953	582	18965	2514	4907	.512	1	9	.111	1269	2126	.597	1844	4152	5996	914	3179	77	351	1450	1473	6298	6.3	1.0	6.6
Playoff Totals	87	59	1797	241	477	.505	0	2	.000	135	211	.640	179	327	506	70	319	10	39	126	142	617	5.8	0.8	7.1

Little, Samuel Ray (Sammy) b. March 29, 1946 Ht. 6-0 Wt. 180 College: Delta State

SEASON–TEAM	G	GS	MIN	FGM	FGA	PCT	3FGM	3FGA	PCT	FTM	FTA	PCT	O-RB	D-RB	TOT	AST	PF	DQ	STL	TO	BLK	PTS	RPG	APG	PPG
69-70–Kentucky (A)	3	–	11	2	4	.500	0	1	.000	1	1	1.000	–	–	1	2	4	0	–	–	–	5	0.3	0.7	1.7
Reg. ABA Totals	3	–	11	2	4	.500	0	1	.000	1	1	1.000	–	–	1	2	4	0	–	–	–	5	0.3	0.7	1.7

Littles, Eugene Scape (Gene) b. June 29, 1943 Ht. 6-1 Wt. 180 College: High Point

SEASON–TEAM	G	GS	MIN	FGM	FGA	PCT	3FGM	3FGA	PCT	FTM	FTA	PCT	O-RB	D-RB	TOT	AST	PF	DQ	STL	TO	BLK	PTS	RPG	APG	PPG
69-70–Carolina (A)	82	–	2832	414	817	.507	0	3	.000	197	254	.776	–	–	415	282	255	0	–	–	–	1025	5.1	3.4	12.5
70-71–Carolina (A)	70	–	1495	223	501	.445	4	14	.286	117	168	.696	–	–	205	173	175	–	–	–	–	567	2.9	2.5	8.1
71-72–Carolina (A)	69	–	2006	280	605	.463	7	26	.269	178	237	.751	–	–	276	237	180	–	–	104	–	745	4.0	3.4	10.8
72-73–Carolina (A)	84	–	2060	310	622	.498	8	30	.267	179	246	.728	104	158	262	245	198	0	–	125	–	807	3.1	2.9	9.6
73-74–Carolina (A)	84	–	2017	294	626	.470	4	23	.174	115	161	.714	87	144	231	280	159	–	105	122	17	707	2.8	3.3	8.4
74-75–Kentucky (A)	61	–	900	85	202	.421	2	8	.250	43	58	.741	30	56	86	119	81	–	52	62	4	215	1.4	2.0	3.5
Reg. ABA Totals	450	–	11310	1606	3373	.476	25	104	.240	829	1124	.738	221	358	1475	1336	1048	0	157	413	21	4066	3.3	3.0	9.0
ABA Playoff Totals	28	–	492	65	143	.455	4	9	.444	29	49	.592	8	8	70	52	43	1	26	16	0	163	2.5	1.9	5.8

Livingston, Randy Anthony b. April 2, 1975 Ht. 6-4 Wt. 209 College: Louisiana State

SEASON–TEAM	G	GS	MIN	FGM	FGA	PCT	3FGM	3FGA	PCT	FTM	FTA	PCT	O-RB	D-RB	TOT	AST	PF	DQ	STL	TO	BLK	PTS	RPG	APG	PPG
96-97–Houston	64	0	981	100	229	.437	9	22	.409	42	65	.646	32	62	94	155	107	0	39	102	12	251	1.5	2.4	3.9
97-98–Atlanta	12	0	82	3	12	.250	0	0	–	4	5	.800	1	5	6	5	6	0	7	6	2	10	0.5	0.4	0.8
98-99–Phoenix	1	0	22	5	8	.625	0	0	–	2	2	1.000	0	2	2	3	1	0	2	1	0	12	2.0	3.0	12.0
99-00–Phoenix	79	15	1081	155	373	.416	19	55	.345	52	62	.839	25	105	130	170	129	1	49	92	13	381	1.6	2.2	4.8
Reg. Season Totals	156	15	2166	263	622	.423	28	77	.364	100	134	.746	58	174	232	333	243	1	97	201	27	654	1.5	2.1	4.2
Playoff Totals	12	3	102	13	46	.283	3	8	.375	4	4	1.000	7	7	14	10	13	0	6	7	1	33	1.2	0.8	2.8

Livingstone, George Ronald (Ron) b. October 9, 1925 Ht. 6-10 Wt. 220 College: Modesto (Calif.) J.C.; Wyoming; St. Mary's (Calif.)

SEASON–TEAM	G	GS	MIN	FGM	FGA	PCT	3FGM	3FGA	PCT	FTM	FTA	PCT	O-RB	D-RB	TOT	AST	PF	DQ	STL	TO	BLK	PTS	RPG	APG	PPG
49-50–Balt.-Phil.	54	–	–	163	579	.282	–	–	–	122	177	.689	–	–	–	141	260	–	–	–	–	448	–	2.6	8.3
50-51–Philadelphia	63	–	–	104	353	.295	–	–	–	76	109	.697	–	–	297	76	220	10	–	–	–	284	4.7	1.2	4.5
Reg. Season Totals	117	–	–	267	932	.286	–	–	–	198	286	.692	–	–	297	217	480	10	–	–	–	732	4.7	1.9	6.3
Playoff Totals	4	–	–	8	19	.421	–	–	–	4	7	.571	–	–	2	5	13	2	–	–	–	20	1.0	1.3	5.0

Llamas, Horacio Grey b. July 17, 1973 Ht. 6-11 Wt. 285 College: Grand Canyon

SEASON–TEAM	G	GS	MIN	FGM	FGA	PCT	3FGM	3FGA	PCT	FTM	FTA	PCT	O-RB	D-RB	TOT	AST	PF	DQ	STL	TO	BLK	PTS	RPG	APG	PPG
96-97–Phoenix	20	2	101	15	28	.536	0	0	–	4	8	.500	4	14	18	4	25	0	10	11	5	34	0.9	0.2	1.7
97-98–Phoenix	8	0	42	8	21	.381	1	3	.333	7	10	.700	4	14	18	1	14	0	1	9	3	24	2.3	0.1	3.0
Reg. Season Totals	28	2	143	23	49	.469	1	3	.333	11	18	.611	8	28	36	5	39	0	11	20	8	58	1.3	0.2	2.1

Lloyd, Charles P. Jr. (Chuck) b. May 22, 1947 Ht. 6-8 Wt. 220 College: Yankton

SEASON–TEAM	G	GS	MIN	FGM	FGA	PCT	3FGM	3FGA	PCT	FTM	FTA	PCT	O-RB	D-RB	TOT	AST	PF	DQ	STL	TO	BLK	PTS	RPG	APG	PPG
70-71–Carolina (A)	14	–	118	23	51	.451	0	0	–	20	30	.667	–	–	25	6	25	–	–	–	–	66	1.8	0.4	4.7
Reg. ABA Totals	14	–	118	23	51	.451	0	0	–	20	30	.667	–	–	25	6	25	–	–	–	–	66	1.8	0.4	4.7

Lloyd, Earl Francis (Big Cat) b. April 3, 1928 Ht. 6-6 Wt. 220 College: West Virginia State

SEASON-TEAM	G	GS	MIN	FGM	FGA	PCT	3FGM	3FGA	PCT	FTM	FTA	PCT	O-RB	D-RB	TOT	AST	PF	DQ	STL	TO	BLK	PTS	RPG	APG	PPG
50-51–Washington	7	–	–	16	35	.457	–	–	–	11	13	.846	–	–	47	11	26	0	–	–	–	43	6.7	1.6	6.1
52-53–Syracuse	64	–	1806	156	453	.344	–	–	–	160	231	.693	–	–	444	64	241	6	–	–	–	472	6.9	1.0	7.4
53-54–Syracuse	72	–	2206	249	666	.374	–	–	–	156	209	.746	–	–	529	115	303	12	–	–	–	654	7.3	1.6	9.1
54-55–Syracuse	72	–	2212	286	784	.365	–	–	–	159	212	.750	–	–	553	151	283	4	–	–	–	731	7.7	2.1	10.2
55-56–Syracuse	72	–	1837	213	636	.335	–	–	–	186	241	.772	–	–	492	116	267	6	–	–	–	612	6.8	1.6	8.5
56-57–Syracuse	72	–	1965	256	687	.373	–	–	–	134	179	.749	–	–	435	114	282	10	–	–	–	646	6.0	1.6	9.0
57-58–Syracuse	61	–	1045	119	359	.331	–	–	–	79	106	.745	–	–	287	60	179	3	–	–	–	317	4.7	1.0	5.2
58-59–Detroit	72	–	1796	234	670	.349	–	–	–	137	182	.753	–	–	500	90	291	15	–	–	–	605	6.9	1.3	8.4
59-60–Detroit	68	–	1610	237	665	.356	–	–	–	128	160	.800	–	–	322	89	226	1	–	–	–	602	4.7	1.3	8.9
Reg. Season Totals	560	–	14477	1766	4955	.356	–	–	–	1150	1533	.750	–	–	3609	810	2098	57	–	–	–	4682	6.4	1.4	8.4
Playoff Totals	44	–	1290	131	388	.338	–	–	–	96	129	.744	–	–	304	93	171	2	–	–	–	358	5.8	1.8	8.1

Lloyd, Lewis Kevin b. February 22, 1959 Ht. 6-6 Wt. 205 College: New Mexico Mil. Inst. (J.C.); Drake

SEASON-TEAM	G	GS	MIN	FGM	FGA	PCT	3FGM	3FGA	PCT	FTM	FTA	PCT	O-RB	D-RB	TOT	AST	PF	DQ	STL	TO	BLK	PTS	RPG	APG	PPG
81-82–Golden State	16	0	95	25	45	.556	0	0	–	7	11	.636	9	7	16	6	20	0	5	14	1	57	1.0	0.4	3.6
82-83–Golden State	73	24	1350	293	566	.518	1	4	.250	100	139	.719	77	183	260	130	109	0	61	118	31	687	3.6	1.8	9.4
83-84–Houston	82	82	2578	610	1182	.516	3	13	.231	235	298	.789	128	167	295	321	211	4	102	245	44	1458	3.6	3.9	17.8
84-85–Houston	82	58	2128	457	869	.526	2	8	.250	161	220	.732	98	133	231	280	196	1	73	177	28	1077	2.8	3.4	13.1
85-86–Houston	82	82	2444	592	1119	.529	3	14	.214	199	236	.843	155	169	324	300	216	0	102	194	24	1386	4.0	3.7	16.9
86-87–Houston	32	14	688	165	310	.532	1	7	.143	65	86	.756	13	35	48	90	69	0	19	52	5	396	1.5	2.8	12.4
89-90–Phil.-Houston	21	0	123	30	53	.566	0	0	–	9	16	.563	8	10	18	11	12	0	3	20	0	69	0.9	0.5	3.3
Reg. Season Totals	388	260	9406	2172	4144	.524	10	46	.217	776	1006	.771	488	704	1192	1138	833	5	365	820	133	5130	3.1	2.9	13.2
Playoff Totals	25	25	763	154	318	.484	2	5	.400	57	72	.792	49	46	95	111	59	0	23	57	14	367	3.8	4.4	14.7

Lloyd, Robert E. (Bobby) b. January 3, 1946 Ht. 6-2 Wt. 185 College: Rutgers

SEASON-TEAM	G	GS	MIN	FGM	FGA	PCT	3FGM	3FGA	PCT	FTM	FTA	PCT	O-RB	D-RB	TOT	AST	PF	DQ	STL	TO	BLK	PTS	RPG	APG	PPG
67-68–New Jersey (A)	58	–	995	147	349	.421	3	8	.375	170	199	.854	–	–	108	93	114	1	–	74	–	467	1.9	1.6	8.1
68-69–New York (A)	67	–	1358	215	541	.397	12	31	.387	218	246	.886	–	–	112	136	176	1	–	95	–	660	1.7	2.0	9.9
Reg. ABA Totals	125	–	2353	362	890	.407	15	39	.385	388	445	.872	–	–	220	229	290	2	–	169	–	1127	1.8	1.8	9.0

Lloyd, Scott G. b. December 19, 1952 Ht. 6-10 Wt. 230 College: Arizona State

SEASON-TEAM	G	GS	MIN	FGM	FGA	PCT	3FGM	3FGA	PCT	FTM	FTA	PCT	O-RB	D-RB	TOT	AST	PF	DQ	STL	TO	BLK	PTS	RPG	APG	PPG
76-77–Milwaukee	69	–	1025	153	324	.472	–	–	–	95	126	.754	81	129	210	33	158	5	21	–	13	401	3.0	0.5	5.8
77-78–Milw.-Buffalo	70	–	678	80	193	.415	–	–	–	49	68	.721	52	93	145	44	105	1	14	43	14	209	2.1	0.6	3.0
78-79–S.D.-Chicago	72	–	496	42	122	.344	–	–	–	27	47	.574	49	47	96	32	92	0	10	51	8	111	1.3	0.4	1.5
80-81–Dallas	72	–	2186	245	547	.448	0	2	.000	147	205	.717	161	293	454	159	269	8	34	145	25	637	6.3	2.2	8.8
81-82–Dallas	74	17	1047	108	285	.379	2	4	.500	69	91	.758	60	103	163	67	175	6	15	59	7	287	2.2	0.9	3.9
82-83–Dallas	15	0	206	19	50	.380	0	1	.000	11	17	.647	19	27	46	21	24	0	6	6	6	49	3.1	1.4	3.3
Reg. Season Totals	372	17	5638	647	1521	.425	2	7	.286	398	554	.718	422	692	1114	356	823	20	100	304	73	1694	3.0	1.0	4.6

Lochmann, Reinhold D. (Riney) b. May 26, 1944 Ht. 6-6 Wt. 215 College: Kansas

SEASON-TEAM	G	GS	MIN	FGM	FGA	PCT	3FGM	3FGA	PCT	FTM	FTA	PCT	O-RB	D-RB	TOT	AST	PF	DQ	STL	TO	BLK	PTS	RPG	APG	PPG
67-68–Dallas (A)	63	–	808	108	285	.379	1	4	.250	49	79	.620	–	–	166	44	113	2	–	40	–	266	2.6	0.7	4.2
68-69–Dallas (A)	60	–	950	115	279	.412	1	4	.250	60	97	.619	–	–	204	59	138	4	–	50	–	291	3.4	1.0	4.9
69-70–Dallas (A)	47	–	447	73	166	.440	3	8	.375	25	45	.556	–	–	96	40	61	0	–	–	–	174	2.0	0.9	3.7
Reg. ABA Totals	170	–	2205	296	730	.405	5	16	.313	134	221	.606	–	–	466	143	312	6	–	90	–	731	2.7	0.8	4.3
ABA Playoff Totals	8	–	51	5	14	.357	0	0	–	3	3	1.000	–	–	7	1	7	0	–	–	–	13	0.9	0.1	1.6

Lochmueller, Robert L. (Bob) b. June 5, 1927 Ht. 6-5 Wt. 185 College: Louisville

SEASON-TEAM	G	GS	MIN	FGM	FGA	PCT	3FGM	3FGA	PCT	FTM	FTA	PCT	O-RB	D-RB	TOT	AST	PF	DQ	STL	TO	BLK	PTS	RPG	APG	PPG
52-53–Syracuse	62	–	802	79	245	.322	–	–	–	74	122	.607	–	–	162	47	143	1	–	–	–	232	2.6	0.8	3.7
Reg. Season Totals	62	–	802	79	245	.322	–	–	–	74	122	.607	–	–	162	47	143	1	–	–	–	232	2.6	0.8	3.7
Playoff Totals	2	–	21	2	10	.200	–	–	–	1	4	.250	–	–	5	2	12	2	–	–	–	5	2.5	1.0	2.5

Lock, Robert Alan (Rob) b. May 22, 1966 Ht. 6-9 Wt. 235 College: Kentucky

SEASON-TEAM	G	GS	MIN	FGM	FGA	PCT	3FGM	3FGA	PCT	FTM	FTA	PCT	O-RB	D-RB	TOT	AST	PF	DQ	STL	TO	BLK	PTS	RPG	APG	PPG
88-89–L.A. Clippers	20	0	110	9	32	.281	0	0	–	12	15	.800	14	18	32	4	15	0	3	13	4	30	1.6	0.2	1.5
Reg. Season Totals	20	0	110	9	32	.281	0	0	–	12	15	.800	14	18	32	4	15	0	3	13	4	30	1.6	0.2	1.5

Lockhart, Darrell b. September 14, 1960 Ht. 6-9 Wt. 245 College: Auburn

SEASON-TEAM	G	GS	MIN	FGM	FGA	PCT	3FGM	3FGA	PCT	FTM	FTA	PCT	O-RB	D-RB	TOT	AST	PF	DQ	STL	TO	BLK	PTS	RPG	APG	PPG
83-84–San Antonio	2	0	14	2	2	1.000	0	0	–	0	0	–	0	3	3	0	5	0	0	2	0	4	1.5	0.0	2.0
Reg. Season Totals	2	0	14	2	2	1.000	0	0	–	0	0	–	0	3	3	0	5	0	0	2	0	4	1.5	0.0	2.0

Lockhart, Ian DeWitt b. June 25, 1967 Ht. 6-8 Wt. 240 College: Tennessee

SEASON–TEAM	G	GS	MIN	FGM	FGA	PCT	3FGM	3FGA	PCT	FTM	FTA	PCT	O-RB	D-RB	TOT	AST	PF	DQ	STL	TO	BLK	PTS	RPG	APG	PPG
90-91–Phoenix	1	0	2	1	1	1.000	0	0	–	2	2	1.000	0	0	0	0	0	0	0	0	0	4	0.0	0.0	4.0
Reg. Season Totals	1	0	2	1	1	1.000	0	0	–	2	2	1.000	0	0	0	0	0	0	0	0	0	4	0.0	0.0	4.0

Loder, Kevin Allen b. March 15, 1959 Ht. 6-6 Wt. 205 College: Kentucky State; Alabama State

SEASON–TEAM	G	GS	MIN	FGM	FGA	PCT	3FGM	3FGA	PCT	FTM	FTA	PCT	O-RB	D-RB	TOT	AST	PF	DQ	STL	TO	BLK	PTS	RPG	APG	PPG
81-82–Kansas City	71	13	1139	208	448	.464	0	11	.000	77	107	.720	69	126	195	88	147	0	35	68	30	493	2.7	1.2	6.9
82-83–Kansas City	66	13	818	138	300	.460	5	9	.556	53	80	.663	37	88	125	72	98	0	29	64	8	334	1.9	1.1	5.1
83-84–K.C.-S.D.	11	0	137	19	43	.442	1	3	.333	9	13	.692	7	11	18	14	16	0	3	11	5	48	1.6	1.3	4.4
Reg. Season Totals	148	26	2094	365	791	.461	6	23	.261	139	200	.695	113	225	338	174	261	0	67	143	43	875	2.3	1.2	5.9

Lofgran, Donald b. November 18, 1928 d. June 1976 Ht. 6-5 Wt. 200 College: Grant Tech; San Francisco

SEASON–TEAM	G	GS	MIN	FGM	FGA	PCT	3FGM	3FGA	PCT	FTM	FTA	PCT	O-RB	D-RB	TOT	AST	PF	DQ	STL	TO	BLK	PTS	RPG	APG	PPG
50-51–Syr.-Ind.	61	–	–	79	270	.293	–	–	–	79	127	.622	–	–	157	36	132	4	–	–	–	237	2.6	0.6	3.9
51-52–Indianapolis	63	–	1254	149	417	.357	–	–	–	156	219	.712	–	–	257	48	147	3	–	–	–	454	4.1	0.8	7.2
52-53–Philadelphia	64	–	1788	173	525	.330	–	–	–	126	173	.728	–	–	339	106	178	6	–	–	–	472	5.3	1.7	7.4
53-54–Milwaukee	21	–	380	35	112	.313	–	–	–	32	49	.653	–	–	64	26	34	0	–	–	–	102	3.0	1.2	4.9
Reg. Season Totals	209	–	3422	436	1324	.329	–	–	–	393	568	.692	–	–	817	216	491	13	–	–	–	1265	3.9	1.0	6.1
Playoff Totals	3	–	20	2	8	.250	–	–	–	1	1	1.000	–	–	1	–	6	0	–	–	–	5	0.2	0.0	1.7

Logan, Henry Lee b. March 14, 1946 Ht. 6-0 Wt. 185 College: Western Carolina

SEASON–TEAM	G	GS	MIN	FGM	FGA	PCT	3FGM	3FGA	PCT	FTM	FTA	PCT	O-RB	D-RB	TOT	AST	PF	DQ	STL	TO	BLK	PTS	RPG	APG	PPG
68-69–Oakland (A)	76	–	1751	339	694	.488	1	4	.250	268	382	.702	–	–	287	185	226	4	–	188	–	947	3.8	2.4	12.5
69-70–Washington (A)	32	–	659	110	269	.409	0	3	.000	91	127	.717	–	–	89	59	93	3	–	–	–	311	2.8	1.8	9.7
Reg. ABA Totals	108	–	2410	449	963	.466	1	7	.143	359	509	.705	–	–	376	244	319	7	–	188	–	1258	3.5	2.3	11.6
ABA Playoff Totals	17	–	381	75	176	.426	0	0	–	68	101	.673	–	–	40	34	50	3	–	–	–	218	2.4	2.0	12.8

Logan, John Arnold (Johnny) b. January 1, 1921 d. September 16, 1977 Ht. 6-2 Wt. 175 College: Indiana

SEASON–TEAM	G	GS	MIN	FGM	FGA	PCT	3FGM	3FGA	PCT	FTM	FTA	PCT	O-RB	D-RB	TOT	AST	PF	DQ	STL	TO	BLK	PTS	RPG	APG	PPG
46-47–St. Louis	61	–	–	290	1043	.278	–	–	–	190	254	.748	–	–	–	78	136	–	–	–	–	770	–	1.3	12.6
47-48–St. Louis	48	–	–	221	734	.301	–	–	–	202	272	.743	–	–	–	62	141	–	–	–	–	644	–	1.3	13.4
48-49–St. Louis	57	–	–	282	816	.346	–	–	–	239	302	.791	–	–	–	276	191	–	–	–	–	803	–	4.8	14.1
49-50–St. Louis	62	–	–	251	759	.331	–	–	–	253	323	.783	–	–	–	240	206	–	–	–	–	755	–	3.9	12.2
50-51–Tri-Cities	29	–	–	81	257	.315	–	–	–	62	83	.747	–	–	134	127	66	2	–	–	–	224	4.6	4.4	7.7
Reg. Season Totals	257	–	–	1125	3609	.312	–	–	–	946	1234	.767	–	–	134	783	740	2	–	–	–	3196	4.6	3.0	12.4
Playoff Totals	10	–	–	34	177	.266	–	–	–	39	55	.709	–	–	–	30	36	0	–	–	–	107	–	2.0	10.7

Lohaus, Brad Allen b. September 29, 1964 Ht. 6-11 Wt. 230 College: Iowa

SEASON–TEAM	G	GS	MIN	FGM	FGA	PCT	3FGM	3FGA	PCT	FTM	FTA	PCT	O-RB	D-RB	TOT	AST	PF	DQ	STL	TO	BLK	PTS	RPG	APG	PPG
87-88–Boston	70	4	718	122	246	.496	3	13	.231	50	62	.806	46	92	138	49	123	1	20	59	41	297	2.0	0.7	4.2
88-89–Boston-Sac.	77	25	1214	210	486	.432	1	11	.091	81	103	.786	84	172	256	66	161	1	30	77	56	502	3.3	0.9	6.5
89-90–Minn.-Milw.	80	41	1943	305	663	.460	47	137	.343	75	103	.728	98	300	398	168	211	3	58	109	88	732	5.0	2.1	9.2
90-91–Milwaukee	81	3	1219	179	415	.431	33	119	.277	37	54	.685	59	158	217	75	170	3	50	60	74	428	2.7	0.9	5.3
91-92–Milwaukee	70	8	1081	162	360	.450	57	144	.396	27	41	.659	65	184	249	74	144	5	40	46	71	408	3.6	1.1	5.8
92-93–Milwaukee	80	24	1766	283	614	.461	85	230	.370	73	101	.723	59	217	276	127	178	1	47	93	74	724	3.5	1.6	9.1
93-94–Milwaukee	67	2	962	102	281	.363	46	134	.343	20	29	.690	33	117	150	62	142	3	30	58	55	270	2.2	0.9	4.0
94-95–Miami	61	1	730	97	231	.420	63	155	.406	10	15	.667	28	74	102	43	85	2	20	29	25	267	1.7	0.7	4.4
95-96–S.A.-N.Y.	55	8	598	71	175	.406	51	122	.418	4	5	.800	7	57	64	44	70	0	10	20	17	197	1.2	0.8	3.6
96-97–Toronto	6	0	45	4	15	.267	2	7	.286	0	0	–	1	6	7	1	6	0	1	1	0	10	1.2	0.2	1.7
97-98–San Antonio	9	0	102	7	21	.333	4	14	.286	1	3	.333	3	9	12	5	10	0	1	3	2	19	1.3	0.6	2.1
Reg. Season Totals	656	116	10378	1542	3507	.440	392	1086	.361	378	516	.733	483	1386	1869	714	1300	19	307	555	503	3854	2.8	1.1	5.9
Playoff Totals	20	4	224	29	68	.426	9	26	.346	1	2	.500	9	33	42	7	27	1	9	13	10	68	2.1	0.4	3.4

Long, Grant Andrew b. March 12, 1966 Ht. 6-9 Wt. 248 College: Eastern Michigan

SEASON–TEAM	G	GS	MIN	FGM	FGA	PCT	3FGM	3FGA	PCT	FTM	FTA	PCT	O-RB	D-RB	TOT	AST	PF	DQ	STL	TO	BLK	PTS	RPG	APG	PPG
88-89–Miami	82	73	2435	336	692	.486	0	5	.000	304	406	.749	240	306	546	149	337	13	122	201	48	976	6.7	1.8	11.9
89-90–Miami	81	31	1856	257	532	.483	0	3	.000	172	241	.714	156	246	402	96	300	11	91	139	38	686	5.0	1.2	8.5
90-91–Miami	80	66	2514	276	561	.492	1	6	.167	181	230	.787	225	343	568	176	295	10	119	156	43	734	7.1	2.2	9.2
91-92–Miami	82	82	3063	440	890	.494	6	22	.273	326	404	.807	259	432	691	225	248	2	139	185	40	1212	8.4	2.7	14.8
92-93–Miami	76	62	2728	397	847	.469	6	26	.231	261	341	.765	197	371	568	182	264	8	104	133	31	1061	7.5	2.4	14.0
93-94–Miami	69	59	2201	300	672	.446	1	6	.167	187	238	.786	190	305	495	170	244	5	89	125	26	788	7.2	2.5	11.4
94-95–Miami-Atlanta	81	79	2641	342	716	.478	11	31	.355	244	325	.751	191	415	606	131	243	3	109	155	34	939	7.5	1.6	11.6
95-96–Atlanta	82	82	3008	395	838	.471	31	86	.360	257	337	.763	248	540	788	183	233	3	108	157	34	1078	9.6	2.2	13.1
96-97–Detroit	65	24	1166	123	275	.447	17	47	.362	63	84	.750	88	134	222	39	106	0	43	48	6	326	3.4	0.6	5.0
97-98–Detroit	40	17	739	50	117	.427	0	4	.000	41	57	.719	57	93	150	25	91	2	29	22	12	141	3.8	0.6	3.5
98-99–Atlanta	50	13	1380	151	359	.421	3	18	.167	184	235	.783	100	196	296	53	143	0	57	74	16	489	5.9	1.1	9.8
99-00–Vancouver	42	1	920	74	167	.443	0	4	.000	55	71	.775	86	148	234	43	108	1	45	49	10	203	5.6	1.0	4.8
Reg. Season Totals	830	589	24651	3141	6666	.471	76	258	.295	2275	2969	.766	2037	3529	5566	1472	2612	58	1055	1444	338	8633	6.7	1.8	10.4
Playoff Totals	34	27	1146	131	317	.413	7	35	.200	102	135	.756	92	146	238	58	103	2	41	65	10	371	7.0	1.7	10.9

Long, John Eddie b. August 28, 1956 Ht. 6-5 Wt. 200 College: Detroit Mercy

SEASON–TEAM	G	GS	MIN	FGM	FGA	PCT	3FGM	3FGA	PCT	FTM	FTA	PCT	O-RB	D-RB	TOT	AST	PF	DQ	STL	TO	BLK	PTS	RPG	APG	PPG
78-79–Detroit	82	–	2498	581	1240	.469	–	–	–	157	190	.826	127	139	266	121	224	1	102	137	19	1319	3.2	1.5	16.1
79-80–Detroit	69	–	2364	588	1164	.505	1	12	.083	160	194	.825	152	185	337	206	221	4	129	206	26	1337	4.9	3.0	19.4
80-81–Detroit	59	–	1750	441	957	.461	2	11	.182	160	184	.870	95	102	197	106	164	3	95	151	22	1044	3.3	1.8	17.7
81-82–Detroit	69	66	2211	637	1294	.492	2	15	.133	238	275	.865	95	162	257	148	173	0	65	167	25	1514	3.7	2.1	21.9
82-83–Detroit	70	30	1485	312	692	.451	2	7	.286	111	146	.760	56	124	180	105	130	1	44	144	12	737	2.6	1.5	10.5
83-84–Detroit	82	82	2514	545	1155	.472	1	5	.200	243	275	.884	139	150	289	205	199	1	93	143	18	1334	3.5	2.5	16.3
84-85–Detroit	66	55	1820	431	885	.487	5	15	.333	106	123	.862	81	109	190	130	139	0	71	98	14	973	2.9	2.0	14.7
85-86–Detroit	62	30	1176	264	548	.482	3	16	.188	89	104	.856	47	51	98	82	92	0	41	59	13	620	1.6	1.3	10.0
86-87–Indiana	80	68	2265	490	1170	.419	19	67	.284	219	246	.890	75	142	217	258	167	1	96	153	8	1218	2.7	3.2	15.2
87-88–Indiana	81	81	2022	417	879	.474	34	77	.442	166	183	.907	72	157	229	173	164	1	84	127	11	1034	2.8	2.1	12.8
88-89–Ind.-Detroit	68	1	919	147	359	.409	8	20	.400	70	76	.921	18	59	77	80	84	1	29	57	3	372	1.1	1.2	5.5
89-90–Atlanta	48	19	1030	174	384	.453	10	29	.345	46	55	.836	26	57	83	85	66	0	45	75	5	404	1.7	1.8	8.4
90-91–Detroit	25	0	256	35	85	.412	2	6	.333	24	25	.960	9	23	32	18	17	0	9	14	2	96	1.3	0.7	3.8
96-97–Toronto	32	0	370	46	117	.393	12	34	.353	25	28	.893	6	34	40	21	28	0	9	24	2	129	1.3	0.7	4.0
Reg. Season Totals	893	432	22680	5108	10929	.467	101	314	.322	1814	2104	.862	998	1494	2492	1738	1868	13	912	1555	180	12131	2.8	1.9	13.6
Playoff Totals	23	18	534	87	218	.399	2	11	.182	47	49	.959	19	16	35	24	54	0	28	28	2	223	1.5	1.0	9.7

Long, Paul Richard b. February 8, 1944 Ht. 6-2 Wt. 180 College: Wake Forest; Virginia Tech

SEASON–TEAM	G	GS	MIN	FGM	FGA	PCT	3FGM	3FGA	PCT	FTM	FTA	PCT	O-RB	D-RB	TOT	AST	PF	DQ	STL	TO	BLK	PTS	RPG	APG	PPG
67-68–Detroit	16	–	93	23	51	.451	–	–	–	11	15	.733	–	–	15	12	13	0	–	–	–	57	0.9	0.8	3.6
68-69–Kentucky (A)	9	–	82	9	40	.225	0	0	–	17	21	.810	–	–	9	12	21	0	–	15	–	35	1.0	1.3	3.9
69-70–Detroit	25	–	130	28	62	.452	–	–	–	27	38	.711	–	–	11	17	22	0	–	–	–	83	0.4	0.7	3.3
70-71–Buffalo	30	–	213	57	120	.475	–	–	–	20	24	.833	–	–	31	25	23	0	–	–	–	134	1.0	0.8	4.5
Reg. NBA Totals	71	–	436	108	233	.464	–	–	–	58	77	.753	–	–	57	54	58	0	–	–	–	274	0.8	0.8	3.9
Reg. ABA Totals	9	–	82	9	40	.225	0	0	–	17	21	.810	–	–	9	12	21	0	–	15	–	35	1.0	1.3	3.9
NBA Playoff Totals	1	–	4	3	3	1.000	–	–	–	0	0	–	–	–	0	1	1	0	–	–	–	6	0.0	1.0	6.0

Long, Willie b. March 1, 1950 Ht. 6-8 Wt. 230 College: New Mexico

SEASON–TEAM	G	GS	MIN	FGM	FGA	PCT	3FGM	3FGA	PCT	FTM	FTA	PCT	O-RB	D-RB	TOT	AST	PF	DQ	STL	TO	BLK	PTS	RPG	APG	PPG
71-72–Floridians (A)	75	–	1925	336	761	.442	0	1	.000	206	291	.708	–	–	513	66	215	–	–	137	–	878	6.8	0.9	11.7
72-73–Denver (A)	56	–	1050	183	458	.400	0	2	.000	138	177	.780	99	191	290	43	147	3	–	95	–	504	5.2	0.8	9.0
73-74–Denver (A)	82	–	2058	383	925	.414	0	2	.000	270	325	.831	197	269	466	100	244	–	54	157	13	1036	5.7	1.2	12.6
Reg. ABA Totals	213	–	5033	902	2144	.421	0	5	.000	614	793	.774	296	460	1269	209	606	3	54	389	13	2418	6.0	1.0	11.4
ABA Playoff Totals	8	–	209	29	77	.377	0	0	–	23	31	.742	14	26	49	5	29	0	0	20	0	81	6.1	0.6	10.1

Longley, Lucien James (Luc) b. January 19, 1969 Ht. 7-2 Wt. 260 College: New Mexico

SEASON–TEAM	G	GS	MIN	FGM	FGA	PCT	3FGM	3FGA	PCT	FTM	FTA	PCT	O-RB	D-RB	TOT	AST	PF	DQ	STL	TO	BLK	PTS	RPG	APG	PPG
91-92–Minnesota	66	3	991	114	249	.458	0	0	–	53	80	.663	67	190	257	53	157	0	35	83	64	281	3.9	0.8	4.3
92-93–Minnesota	55	25	1045	133	292	.455	0	0	–	53	74	.716	71	169	240	51	169	4	47	88	77	319	4.4	0.9	5.8
93-94–Minn.-Chi.	76	46	1502	219	465	.471	0	1	.000	90	125	.720	129	304	433	109	216	3	45	119	79	528	5.7	1.4	6.9
94-95–Chicago	55	0	1001	135	302	.447	0	2	.000	88	107	.822	82	181	263	73	177	5	24	86	45	358	4.8	1.3	6.5
95-96–Chicago	62	62	1641	242	502	.482	0	0	–	80	103	.777	104	214	318	119	223	4	22	114	84	564	5.1	1.9	9.1
96-97–Chicago	59	59	1472	221	485	.456	0	2	.000	95	120	.792	121	211	332	141	191	5	23	111	66	537	5.6	2.4	9.1
97-98–Chicago	58	58	1703	277	609	.455	0	0	–	109	148	.736	113	228	341	161	206	7	34	130	62	663	5.9	2.8	11.4
98-99–Phoenix	39	39	933	140	290	.483	0	0	–	59	76	.776	59	162	221	45	119	0	23	53	21	339	5.7	1.2	8.7
99-00–Phoenix	72	68	1417	186	399	.466	0	0	–	80	97	.825	100	223	323	77	221	1	22	136	42	452	4.5	1.1	6.3
Reg. Season Totals	542	360	11705	1667	3593	.464	0	5	.000	707	930	.760	846	1882	2728	829	1679	29	275	920	540	4041	5.0	1.5	7.5
Playoff Totals	87	74	1914	241	517	.466	0	0	–	95	133	.714	140	232	372	136	338	8	46	145	73	577	4.3	1.6	6.6

Lopez, Luis Felipe (Felipe) b. December 19, 1974 Ht. 6-6 Wt. 195 College: St. John's (N.Y.)

SEASON–TEAM	G	GS	MIN	FGM	FGA	PCT	3FGM	3FGA	PCT	FTM	FTA	PCT	O-RB	D-RB	TOT	AST	PF	DQ	STL	TO	BLK	PTS	RPG	APG	PPG
98-99–Vancouver	47	32	1218	169	379	.446	12	44	.273	87	135	.644	69	97	166	62	128	0	49	82	14	437	3.5	1.3	9.3
99-00–Vancouver	65	0	781	111	261	.425	3	18	.167	67	109	.615	59	65	124	44	94	0	32	53	17	292	1.9	0.7	4.5
Reg. Season Totals	112	32	1999	280	640	.438	15	62	.242	154	244	.631	128	162	290	106	222	0	81	135	31	729	2.6	0.9	6.5

Lorthridge, Ryan b. July 27, 1972 Ht. 6-4 Wt. 190 College: Jackson State

SEASON–TEAM	G	GS	MIN	FGM	FGA	PCT	3FGM	3FGA	PCT	FTM	FTA	PCT	O-RB	D-RB	TOT	AST	PF	DQ	STL	TO	BLK	PTS	RPG	APG	PPG
94-95–Golden State	37	2	672	106	223	.475	3	14	.214	57	88	.648	24	47	71	101	42	0	28	57	1	272	1.9	2.7	7.4
Reg. Season Totals	37	2	672	106	223	.475	3	14	.214	57	88	.648	24	47	71	101	42	0	28	57	1	272	1.9	2.7	7.4

Loscutoff, James Jr. (Jim, Jungle Jim) b. February 4, 1930 Ht. 6-5 Wt. 230 College: Sacramento City (Calif.) Coll. (J.C.); Grant Tech; Oregon

SEASON–TEAM	G	GS	MIN	FGM	FGA	PCT	3FGM	3FGA	PCT	FTM	FTA	PCT	O-RB	D-RB	TOT	AST	PF	DQ	STL	TO	BLK	PTS	RPG	APG	PPG
55-56–Boston	71	–	1582	226	628	.360	–	–	–	139	207	.671	–	–	622	65	213	4	–	–	–	591	8.8	0.9	8.3
56-57–Boston	70	–	2220	306	888	.345	–	–	–	132	187	.706	–	–	730	89	244	5	–	–	–	744	10.4	1.3	10.6
57-58–Boston	5	–	56	11	31	.355	–	–	–	1	3	.333	–	–	20	1	8	0	–	–	–	23	4.0	0.2	4.6
58-59–Boston	66	–	1680	242	686	.353	–	–	–	62	84	.738	–	–	460	60	285	15	–	–	–	546	7.0	0.9	8.3
59-60–Boston	28	–	536	66	205	.322	–	–	–	22	36	.611	–	–	108	12	108	6	–	–	–	154	3.9	0.4	5.5
60-61–Boston	76	–	1153	144	478	.301	–	–	–	49	76	.645	–	–	291	25	238	5	–	–	–	337	3.8	0.3	4.4
61-62–Boston	79	–	1146	188	519	.362	–	–	–	45	84	.536	–	–	329	51	185	3	–	–	–	421	4.2	0.6	5.3
62-63–Boston	63	–	607	94	251	.375	–	–	–	22	42	.524	–	–	157	25	126	1	–	–	–	210	2.5	0.4	3.3
63-64–Boston	53	–	451	56	182	.308	–	–	–	18	31	.581	–	–	131	25	90	1	–	–	–	130	2.5	0.5	2.5
Reg. Season Totals	511	–	9431	1333	3868	.345	–	–	–	490	750	.653	–	–	2848	353	1497	40	–	–	–	3156	5.6	0.7	6.2
Playoff Totals	57	–	997	136	420	.324	–	–	–	48	79	.608	–	–	299	32	219	8	–	–	–	320	5.2	0.6	5.6

Lott, Plummer E. b. December 11, 1945 Ht. 6-5 Wt. 210 College: Seattle

SEASON–TEAM	G	GS	MIN	FGM	FGA	PCT	3FGM	3FGA	PCT	FTM	FTA	PCT	O-RB	D-RB	TOT	AST	PF	DQ	STL	TO	BLK	PTS	RPG	APG	PPG
67-68–Seattle	44	–	478	46	148	.311	–	–	–	19	31	.613	–	–	93	36	65	1	–	–	–	111	2.1	0.8	2.5
68-69–Seattle	23	–	160	17	66	.258	–	–	–	2	5	.400	–	–	30	7	9	0	–	–	–	36	1.3	0.3	1.6
Reg. Season Totals	67	–	638	63	214	.294	–	–	–	21	36	.583	–	–	123	43	74	1	–	–	–	147	1.8	0.6	2.2

Loughery, Kevin Michael (Murph) b. March 28, 1940 Ht. 6-3 Wt. 190 College: St. John's (N.Y.); Boston College

SEASON–TEAM	G	GS	MIN	FGM	FGA	PCT	3FGM	3FGA	PCT	FTM	FTA	PCT	O-RB	D-RB	TOT	AST	PF	DQ	STL	TO	BLK	PTS	RPG	APG	PPG
62-63–Detroit	57	–	845	146	397	.368	–	–	–	71	100	.710	–	–	109	104	135	1	–	–	–	363	1.9	1.8	6.4
63-64–Detroit-Balt.	66	–	1459	236	631	.374	–	–	–	126	177	.712	–	–	138	182	175	2	–	–	–	598	2.1	2.8	9.1
64-65–Baltimore	80	–	2417	406	957	.424	–	–	–	212	281	.754	–	–	235	296	320	13	–	–	–	1024	2.9	3.7	12.8
65-66–Baltimore	74	–	2455	526	1264	.416	–	–	–	297	358	.830	–	–	227	356	273	8	–	–	–	1349	3.1	4.8	18.2
66-67–Baltimore	76	–	2577	520	1306	.398	–	–	–	340	412	.825	–	–	349	288	294	10	–	–	–	1380	4.6	3.8	18.2
67-68–Baltimore	77	–	2297	458	1127	.406	–	–	–	305	392	.778	–	–	247	256	301	13	–	–	–	1221	3.2	3.3	15.9
68-69–Baltimore	80	–	3135	717	1636	.438	–	–	–	372	463	.803	–	–	266	384	299	3	–	–	–	1806	3.3	4.8	22.6
69-70–Baltimore	55	–	2037	477	1082	.441	–	–	–	253	298	.849	–	–	168	292	183	3	–	–	–	1207	3.1	5.3	21.9
70-71–Baltimore	82	–	2260	481	1193	.403	–	–	–	275	331	.831	–	–	219	301	246	2	–	–	–	1237	2.7	3.7	15.1
71-72–Balt.-Phil.	76	–	1771	341	809	.422	–	–	–	263	320	.822	–	–	183	196	213	3	–	–	–	945	2.4	2.6	12.4
72-73–Philadelphia	32	–	955	169	427	.396	–	–	–	107	130	.823	–	–	113	148	104	0	–	–	–	445	3.5	4.6	13.9
Reg. Season Totals	755	–	22208	4477	10829	.413	–	–	–	2621	3262	.803	–	–	2254	2803	2543	58	–	–	–	11575	3.0	3.7	15.3
Playoff Totals	43	–	1176	196	522	.375	–	–	–	140	186	.753	–	–	107	116	140	2	–	–	–	532	2.5	2.7	12.4

Love, Robert (Bob, Butterbean) b. December 8, 1942 Ht. 6-8 Wt. 215 College: Southern University

SEASON–TEAM	G	GS	MIN	FGM	FGA	PCT	3FGM	3FGA	PCT	FTM	FTA	PCT	O-RB	D-RB	TOT	AST	PF	DQ	STL	TO	BLK	PTS	RPG	APG	PPG
66-67–Cincinnati	66	–	1074	173	403	.429	–	–	–	93	147	.633	–	–	257	49	153	3	–	–	–	439	3.9	0.7	6.7
67-68–Cincinnati	72	–	1068	193	455	.424	–	–	–	78	114	.684	–	–	209	55	141	1	–	–	–	464	2.9	0.8	6.4
68-69–Milw.-Chicago	49	–	542	108	272	.397	–	–	–	71	96	.740	–	–	150	17	59	0	–	–	–	287	3.1	0.3	5.9
69-70–Chicago	82	–	3123	640	1373	.466	–	–	–	442	525	.842	–	–	712	148	260	2	–	–	–	1722	8.7	1.8	21.0
70-71–Chicago	81	–	3482	765	1710	.447	–	–	–	513	619	.829	–	–	690	185	259	0	–	–	–	2043	8.5	2.3	25.2
71-72–Chicago	79	–	3108	819	1854	.442	–	–	–	399	509	.784	–	–	518	125	235	2	–	–	–	2037	6.6	1.6	25.8
72-73–Chicago	82	–	3033	774	1794	.431	–	–	–	347	421	.824	–	–	532	119	240	1	–	–	–	1895	6.5	1.5	23.1
73-74–Chicago	82	–	3292	731	1752	.417	–	–	–	323	395	.818	183	309	492	130	221	1	84	–	28	1785	6.0	1.6	21.8
74-75–Chicago	61	–	2401	539	1256	.429	–	–	–	264	318	.830	99	286	385	102	209	3	63	–	12	1342	6.3	1.7	22.0
75-76–Chicago	76	–	2823	543	1391	.390	–	–	–	362	452	.801	191	319	510	145	233	3	63	–	10	1448	6.7	1.9	19.1
76-77–Chi.-N.Y.-Seattle	59	–	1174	162	428	.379	–	–	–	109	132	.826	79	119	198	48	120	1	22	–	6	433	3.4	0.8	7.3
Reg. Season Totals	789	–	25120	5447	12688	.429	–	–	–	3001	3728	.805	552	1033	4653	1123	2130	17	232	–	56	13895	5.9	1.4	17.6
Playoff Totals	47	–	2061	441	1023	.431	–	–	–	194	250	.776	58	103	352	87	144	1	24	–	10	1076	7.5	1.9	22.9
All-Star Totals	3	–	49	12	27	.444	–	–	–	6	9	.667	0	0	13	0	4	0	0	–	0	30	4.3	0.0	10.0

Love, Stanley S. (Stan) b. April 9, 1949 Ht. 6-9 Wt. 215 College: Oregon

SEASON–TEAM	G	GS	MIN	FGM	FGA	PCT	3FGM	3FGA	PCT	FTM	FTA	PCT	O-RB	D-RB	TOT	AST	PF	DQ	STL	TO	BLK	PTS	RPG	APG	PPG
71-72–Baltimore	74	–	1327	242	536	.451	–	–	–	103	140	.736	–	–	338	52	202	0	–	–	–	587	4.6	0.7	7.9
72-73–Baltimore	72	–	995	190	436	.436	–	–	–	79	100	.790	–	–	300	46	175	0	–	–	–	459	4.2	0.6	6.4
73-74–Los Angeles	51	–	698	119	278	.428	–	–	–	49	64	.766	54	116	170	48	132	3	28	–	20	287	3.3	0.9	5.6
74-75–Los Angeles	30	–	431	85	194	.438	–	–	–	47	66	.712	31	66	97	26	69	1	16	–	13	217	3.2	0.9	7.2
74-75–San Antonio (A)	12	–	64	13	30	.433	0	0	–	3	4	.750	6	18	24	9	16	–	0	6	4	29	2.0	0.8	2.4
Reg. NBA Totals	227	–	3451	636	1444	.440	–	–	–	278	370	.751	85	182	905	172	578	4	44	–	33	1550	4.0	0.8	6.8
Reg. ABA Totals	12	–	64	13	30	.433	0	0	–	3	4	.750	6	18	24	9	16	–	0	6	4	29	2.0	0.8	2.4
NBA Playoff Totals	7	–	30	3	10	.300	–	–	–	2	3	.667	1	2	10	2	4	0	1	–	0	8	1.4	0.3	1.1

Lovellette, Clyde Edward b. September 7, 1929 Ht. 6-9 Wt. 235 College: Kansas HOF: 1988

SEASON–TEAM	G	GS	MIN	FGM	FGA	PCT	3FGM	3FGA	PCT	FTM	FTA	PCT	O-RB	D-RB	TOT	AST	PF	DQ	STL	TO	BLK	PTS	RPG	APG	PPG
53-54–Minneapolis	72	–	1255	237	560	.423	–	–	–	114	164	.695	–	–	419	51	210	2	–	–	–	588	5.8	0.7	8.2
54-55–Minneapolis	70	–	2361	519	1192	.435	–	–	–	273	398	.686	–	–	802	100	262	6	–	–	–	1311	11.5	1.4	18.7
55-56–Minneapolis	71	–	2518	594	1370	.434	–	–	–	338	469	.721	–	–	992	164	245	5	–	–	–	1526	14.0	2.3	21.5
56-57–Minneapolis	69	–	2492	574	1348	.426	–	–	–	286	399	.717	–	–	932	139	251	4	–	–	–	1434	13.5	2.0	20.8
57-58–Cincinnati	71	–	2589	679	1540	.441	–	–	–	301	405	.743	–	–	862	134	236	3	–	–	–	1659	12.1	1.9	23.4
58-59–St. Louis	70	–	1599	402	885	.454	–	–	–	205	250	.820	–	–	605	91	216	1	–	–	–	1009	8.6	1.3	14.4
59-60–St. Louis	68	–	1953	550	1174	.468	–	–	–	316	385	.821	–	–	721	127	248	6	–	–	–	1416	10.6	1.9	20.8
60-61–St. Louis	67	–	2111	599	1321	.453	–	–	–	273	329	.830	–	–	677	172	248	4	–	–	–	1471	10.1	2.6	22.0
61-62–St. Louis	40	–	1192	341	724	.471	–	–	–	155	187	.829	–	–	350	68	136	4	–	–	–	837	8.8	1.7	20.9
62-63–Boston	61	–	568	161	376	.428	–	–	–	73	98	.745	–	–	177	27	137	0	–	–	–	395	2.9	0.4	6.5
63-64–Boston	45	–	437	128	305	.420	–	–	–	45	57	.789	–	–	126	24	100	0	–	–	–	301	2.8	0.5	6.7
Reg. Season Totals	704	–	19075	4784	10795	.443	–	–	–	2379	3141	.757	–	–	6663	1097	2289	35	–	–	–	11947	9.5	1.6	17.0
Playoff Totals	69	–	1907	372	898	.419	–	–	–	221	328	.674	–	–	683	96	232	4	–	–	–	965	8.3	1.2	14.0
All-Star Totals	3	–	71	19	40	.475	–	–	–	2	4	.500	–	–	28	4	9	0	–	–	–	40	9.3	1.3	13.3

Lowe, Sidney Rochell b. January 21, 1960 Ht. 6-0 Wt. 195 College: North Carolina State

SEASON–TEAM	G	GS	MIN	FGM	FGA	PCT	3FGM	3FGA	PCT	FTM	FTA	PCT	O-RB	D-RB	TOT	AST	PF	DQ	STL	TO	BLK	PTS	RPG	APG	PPG
83-84–Indiana	78	2	1238	107	259	.413	2	18	.111	108	139	.777	30	92	122	269	112	0	93	106	5	324	1.6	3.4	4.2
84-85–Detroit-Atlanta	21	0	190	10	27	.370	0	1	.000	8	8	1.000	4	12	16	50	28	0	11	13	0	28	0.8	2.4	1.3
88-89–Charlotte	14	0	250	8	25	.320	0	2	.000	7	11	.636	6	28	34	93	28	0	14	9	0	23	2.4	6.6	1.6
89-90–Minnesota	80	38	1744	73	229	.319	2	9	.222	39	54	.722	41	122	163	337	114	0	73	63	4	187	2.0	4.2	2.3
Reg. Season Totals	193	40	3422	198	540	.367	4	30	.133	162	212	.764	81	254	335	749	282	0	191	191	9	562	1.7	3.9	2.9

Lowery, Charles P. **(Chuck)** b. November 12, 1949 Ht. 6-3 Wt. 185 College: Puget Sound

SEASON–TEAM	G	GS	MIN	FGM	FGA	PCT	3FGM	3FGA	PCT	FTM	FTA	PCT	O-RB	D-RB	TOT	AST	PF	DQ	STL	TO	BLK	PTS	RPG	APG	PPG
71-72–Milwaukee	20	–	134	17	38	.447	–	–	–	11	18	.611	–	–	19	14	16	1	–	–	–	45	1.0	0.7	2.3
Reg. Season Totals	20	–	134	17	38	.447	–	–	–	11	18	.611	–	–	19	14	16	1	–	–	–	45	1.0	0.7	2.3
Playoff Totals	7	–	26	2	8	.250	–	–	–	2	3	.667	–	–	3	1	4	0	–	–	–	6	0.4	0.1	0.9

Lucas, Albert Thomas **(Al, Lukey)** b. July 4, 1922 d. April 26, 1995 Ht. 6-3 Wt. 195 College: Fordham

SEASON–TEAM	G	GS	MIN	FGM	FGA	PCT	3FGM	3FGA	PCT	FTM	FTA	PCT	O-RB	D-RB	TOT	AST	PF	DQ	STL	TO	BLK	PTS	RPG	APG	PPG
44-45–Sheboygan (N)	26	–	–	57	–	–	–	–	–	36	–	–	–	–	–	–	–	–	–	–	–	150	–	–	5.8
45-46–Sheboygan (N)	32	–	–	75	–	–	–	–	–	24	38	.632	–	–	–	–	66	–	–	–	–	174	–	–	5.4
46-47–Sheboygan (N)	42	–	–	87	–	–	–	–	–	32	60	.533	–	–	–	–	74	–	–	–	–	206	–	–	4.9
47-48–Sheboygan (N)	58	–	–	98	–	–	–	–	–	39	56	.696	–	–	–	–	135	–	–	–	–	235	–	–	4.1
48-49–Boston	2	–	–	1	3	.333	–	–	–	0	0	–	–	–	–	2	0	–	–	–	–	2	–	1.0	1.0
Reg. NBA Totals	2	–	–	1	3	.333	–	–	–	0	0	–	–	–	–	2	0	–	–	–	–	2	–	1.0	1.0
Reg. NBL Totals	158	–	–	317	–	–	–	–	–	131	154	.617	–	–	–	–	275	–	–	–	–	765	–	–	4.8
NBL Playoff Totals	17	–	–	31	–	–	–	–	–	15	22	.636	–	–	–	–	29	–	–	–	–	77	–	–	4.5

Lucas, Jerry Ray **(Luke)** b. March 30, 1940 Ht. 6-8 Wt. 230 College: Ohio State HOF: 1979

SEASON–TEAM	G	GS	MIN	FGM	FGA	PCT	3FGM	3FGA	PCT	FTM	FTA	PCT	O-RB	D-RB	TOT	AST	PF	DQ	STL	TO	BLK	PTS	RPG	APG	PPG
63-64–Cincinnati	79	–	3273	545	1035	.527	–	–	–	310	398	.779	–	–	1375	204	300	6	–	–	–	1400	17.4	2.6	17.7
64-65–Cincinnati	66	–	2864	558	1121	.498	–	–	–	298	366	.814	–	–	1321	157	214	1	–	–	–	1414	20.0	2.4	21.4
65-66–Cincinnati	79	–	3517	690	1523	.453	–	–	–	317	403	.787	–	–	1668	213	274	5	–	–	–	1697	21.1	2.7	21.5
66-67–Cincinnati	81	–	3558	577	1257	.459	–	–	–	284	359	.791	–	–	1547	268	280	2	–	–	–	1438	19.1	3.3	17.8
67-68–Cincinnati	82	–	3619	707	1361	.519	–	–	–	346	445	.778	–	–	1560	251	243	3	–	–	–	1760	19.0	3.1	21.5
68-69–Cincinnati	74	–	3075	555	1007	.551	–	–	–	247	327	.755	–	–	1360	306	206	0	–	–	–	1357	18.4	4.1	18.3
69-70–Cin.-S.F.	67	–	2420	405	799	.507	–	–	–	200	255	.784	–	–	951	173	166	2	–	–	–	1010	14.2	2.6	15.1
70-71–San Francisco	80	–	3251	623	1250	.498	–	–	–	289	367	.787	–	–	1265	293	197	0	–	–	–	1535	15.8	3.7	19.2
71-72–New York	77	–	2926	543	1060	.512	–	–	–	197	249	.791	–	–	1011	318	218	1	–	–	–	1283	13.1	4.1	16.7
72-73–New York	71	–	2001	312	608	.513	–	–	–	80	100	.800	–	–	510	317	157	0	–	–	–	704	7.2	4.5	9.9
73-74–New York	73	–	1627	194	420	.462	–	–	–	67	96	.698	62	312	374	230	134	0	28	–	24	455	5.1	3.2	6.2
Reg. Season Totals	829	–	32131	5709	11441	.499	–	–	–	2635	3365	.783	62	312	12942	2730	2389	20	28	–	24	14053	15.6	3.3	17.0
Playoff Totals	72	–	2370	367	786	.467	–	–	–	162	206	.786	6	16	717	214	197	2	4	–	0	896	10.0	3.0	12.4
All-Star Totals	7	–	183	35	64	.547	–	–	–	19	21	.905	0	0	64	12	20	0	0	–	0	89	9.1	1.7	12.7

Lucas, John Harding Jr. b. October 31, 1953 Ht. 6-3 Wt. 180 College: Maryland

SEASON–TEAM	G	GS	MIN	FGM	FGA	PCT	3FGM	3FGA	PCT	FTM	FTA	PCT	O-RB	D-RB	TOT	AST	PF	DQ	STL	TO	BLK	PTS	RPG	APG	PPG
76-77–Houston	82	–	2531	388	814	.477	–	–	–	135	171	.789	55	164	219	463	174	0	125	–	19	911	2.7	5.6	11.1
77-78–Houston	82	–	2933	412	947	.435	–	–	–	193	250	.772	51	204	255	768	208	1	160	213	9	1017	3.1	9.4	12.4
78-79–Golden State	82	–	3095	530	1146	.462	–	–	–	264	321	.822	65	182	247	762	229	1	152	255	9	1324	3.0	9.3	16.1
79-80–Golden State	80	–	2763	388	830	.467	12	42	.286	222	289	.768	61	159	220	602	196	2	138	184	3	1010	2.8	7.5	12.6
80-81–Golden State	66	–	1919	222	506	.439	4	24	.167	107	145	.738	34	120	154	464	140	1	83	185	2	555	2.3	7.0	8.4
81-82–Washington	79	53	1940	263	618	.426	2	22	.091	138	176	.784	40	126	166	551	105	0	95	156	6	666	2.1	7.0	8.4
82-83–Washington	35	0	386	62	131	.473	0	5	.000	21	42	.500	8	21	29	102	18	0	25	47	1	145	0.8	2.9	4.1
83-84–San Antonio	63	39	1807	275	595	.462	19	69	.275	120	157	.764	23	157	180	673	123	1	92	147	5	689	2.9	10.7	10.9
84-85–Houston	47	21	1158	206	446	.462	21	66	.318	103	129	.798	21	64	85	318	78	0	62	102	2	536	1.8	6.8	11.4
85-86–Houston	65	65	2120	365	818	.446	45	146	.308	231	298	.775	33	110	143	571	124	0	77	149	5	1006	2.2	8.8	15.5
86-87–Milwaukee	43	40	1358	285	624	.457	46	126	.365	137	174	.787	29	96	125	290	82	0	71	89	6	753	2.9	6.7	17.5
87-88–Milwaukee	81	22	1766	281	631	.445	51	151	.338	130	162	.802	29	130	159	392	102	1	88	125	3	743	2.0	4.8	9.2
88-89–Seattle	74	8	842	119	299	.398	18	68	.265	54	77	.701	22	57	79	260	53	0	60	66	1	310	1.1	3.5	4.2
89-90–Houston	49	18	938	109	291	.375	26	87	.299	42	55	.764	19	71	90	238	59	0	45	85	2	286	1.8	4.9	5.8
Reg. Season Totals	928	266	25556	3905	8696	.449	244	806	.303	1897	2446	.776	490	1661	2151	6454	1691	7	1273	1803	73	9951	2.3	7.0	10.7
Playoff Totals	45	16	1135	198	439	.451	18	69	.261	88	118	.746	20	76	96	219	80	1	52	39	6	502	2.1	4.9	11.2

Lucas, Maurice D. (Luke) b. February 18, 1952 Ht. 6-9 Wt. 215 College: Marquette

SEASON–TEAM	G	GS	MIN	FGM	FGA	PCT	3FGM	3FGA	PCT	FTM	FTA	PCT	O-RB	D-RB	TOT	AST	PF	DQ	STL	TO	BLK	PTS	RPG	APG	PPG
74-75–St. Louis (A)	80	–	2464	438	937	.467	2	9	.222	180	229	.786	282	534	816	287	301	–	89	208	64	1058	10.2	3.6	13.2
75-76–St. L.-Ken. (A)	86	–	2861	620	1346	.461	3	18	.167	217	283	.767	297	673	970	224	332	–	75	298	57	1460	11.3	2.6	17.0
76-77–Portland	79	–	2863	632	1357	.466	–	–	–	335	438	.765	271	628	899	229	294	6	83	–	56	1599	11.4	2.9	20.2
77-78–Portland	68	–	2119	453	989	.458	–	–	–	207	270	.767	186	435	621	173	221	3	61	192	56	1113	9.1	2.5	16.4
78-79–Portland	69	–	2462	568	1208	.470	–	–	–	270	345	.783	192	524	716	215	254	3	66	233	81	1406	10.4	3.1	20.4
79-80–Port.-N.J.	63	–	1884	371	813	.456	2	9	.222	179	239	.749	143	394	537	208	223	2	42	218	62	923	8.5	3.3	14.7
80-81–New Jersey	68	–	2162	404	835	.484	0	2	.000	191	254	.752	153	422	575	173	260	3	57	176	59	999	8.5	2.5	14.7
81-82–New York	80	74	2671	505	1001	.504	0	3	.000	253	349	.725	274	629	903	179	309	4	68	173	70	1263	11.3	2.2	15.8
82-83–Phoenix	77	71	2586	495	1045	.474	1	3	.333	278	356	.781	201	598	799	219	274	5	56	221	43	1269	10.4	2.8	16.5
83-84–Phoenix	75	69	2309	451	908	.497	0	5	.000	293	383	.765	208	517	725	203	235	2	55	177	39	1195	9.7	2.7	15.9
84-85–Phoenix	63	22	1670	346	727	.476	0	4	.000	150	200	.750	138	419	557	145	183	0	39	151	17	842	8.8	2.3	13.4
85-86–L.A. Lakers	77	8	1750	302	653	.462	1	2	.500	180	230	.783	164	402	566	84	253	1	45	121	24	785	7.4	1.1	10.2
86-87–Seattle	63	0	1120	175	388	.451	0	5	.000	150	187	.802	88	219	307	65	171	1	34	75	21	500	4.9	1.0	7.9
87-88–Portland	73	0	1191	168	373	.450	0	3	.000	109	148	.736	101	214	315	94	188	0	33	73	10	445	4.3	1.3	6.1
Reg. NBA Totals	855	244	24787	4870	10297	.473	4	36	.111	2595	3399	.763	2119	5401	7520	1987	2865	30	639	1810	538	12339	8.8	2.3	14.4
Reg. ABA Totals	166	–	5325	1058	2283	.463	5	27	.185	397	512	.775	579	1207	1786	511	633	–	164	506	121	2518	10.8	3.1	15.2
NBA Playoff Totals	82	18	2426	472	975	.484	0	1	.000	215	289	.744	180	510	690	225	310	6	71	107	46	1159	8.4	2.7	14.1
ABA Playoff Totals	20	–	705	143	305	.469	0	1	.000	42	60	.700	89	166	255	72	92	–	20	49	20	328	12.8	3.6	16.4
NBA All-Star Totals	4	2	90	16	40	.400	0	0	–	2	3	.667	10	21	31	8	10	0	2	4	1	34	7.8	2.0	8.5

Luckenbill, Theodore (Ted) b. July 27, 1939 Ht. 6-6 Wt. 205 College: Houston

SEASON–TEAM	G	GS	MIN	FGM	FGA	PCT	3FGM	3FGA	PCT	FTM	FTA	PCT	O-RB	D-RB	TOT	AST	PF	DQ	STL	TO	BLK	PTS	RPG	APG	PPG
61-62–Philadelphia	67	–	396	43	120	.358	–	–	–	49	76	.645	–	–	110	27	67	0	–	–	–	135	1.6	0.4	2.0
62-63–San Francisco	20	–	201	26	68	.382	–	–	–	9	20	.450	–	–	56	8	34	0	–	–	–	61	2.8	0.4	3.1
Reg. Season Totals	87	–	597	69	188	.367	–	–	–	58	96	.604	–	–	166	35	101	0	–	–	–	196	1.9	0.4	2.3
Playoff Totals	4	–	17	0	5	.000	–	–	–	2	5	.400	–	–	3	1	3	0	–	–	–	2	0.8	0.3	0.5

Lue, Tyronn Jamar b. May 3, 1977 Ht. 6-0 Wt. 175 College: Nebraska

SEASON–TEAM	G	GS	MIN	FGM	FGA	PCT	3FGM	3FGA	PCT	FTM	FTA	PCT	O-RB	D-RB	TOT	AST	PF	DQ	STL	TO	BLK	PTS	RPG	APG	PPG
98-99–L.A. Lakers	15	0	188	28	65	.431	7	16	.438	12	21	.571	2	4	6	25	28	0	5	11	0	75	0.4	1.7	5.0
99-00–L.A. Lakers	8	0	146	19	39	.487	4	8	.500	6	8	.750	2	10	12	17	17	0	3	9	0	48	1.5	2.1	6.0
Reg. Season Totals	23	0	334	47	104	.452	11	24	.458	18	29	.621	4	14	18	42	45	0	8	20	0	123	0.8	1.8	5.3
Playoff Totals	3	0	33	7	17	.412	0	2	.000	0	0	–	0	2	2	6	4	0	2	4	0	14	0.7	2.0	4.7

Luisi, James A. (Jim) b. November 2, 1928 Ht. 6-2 Wt. 180 College: St. Francis (N.Y.)

SEASON–TEAM	G	GS	MIN	FGM	FGA	PCT	3FGM	3FGA	PCT	FTM	FTA	PCT	O-RB	D-RB	TOT	AST	PF	DQ	STL	TO	BLK	PTS	RPG	APG	PPG
53-54–Baltimore	31	–	367	31	95	.326	–	–	–	27	41	.659	–	–	25	35	45	0	–	–	–	89	0.8	1.1	2.9
Reg. Season Totals	31	–	367	31	95	.326	–	–	–	27	41	.659	–	–	25	35	45	0	–	–	–	89	0.8	1.1	2.9

Lujack, Aloysius R. (Al) b. October 5, 1921 Ht. 6-3 Wt. 220 College: Georgetown

SEASON–TEAM	G	GS	MIN	FGM	FGA	PCT	3FGM	3FGA	PCT	FTM	FTA	PCT	O-RB	D-RB	TOT	AST	PF	DQ	STL	TO	BLK	PTS	RPG	APG	PPG
46-47–Washington	5	–	–	1	8	.125	–	–	–	2	5	.400	–	–	–	0	6	–	–	–	–	4	–	0.0	0.8
Reg. Season Totals	5	–	–	1	8	.125	–	–	–	2	5	.400	–	–	–	0	6	–	–	–	–	4	–	0.0	0.8

L

Lumpkin, Phil b. December 20, 1951 Ht. 6-0 Wt. 165 College: Miami (Ohio)

SEASON–TEAM	G	GS	MIN	FGM	FGA	PCT	3FGM	3FGA	PCT	FTM	FTA	PCT	O-RB	D-RB	TOT	AST	PF	DQ	STL	TO	BLK	PTS	RPG	APG	PPG
74-75–Portland	48	–	792	86	190	.453	–	–	–	30	39	.769	10	49	59	177	80	1	20	–	3	202	1.2	3.7	4.2
75-76–Phoenix	34	–	370	22	65	.338	–	–	–	26	30	.867	7	16	23	48	26	0	15	–	0	70	0.7	1.4	2.1
Reg. Season Totals	82	–	1162	108	255	.424	–	–	–	56	69	.812	17	65	82	225	106	1	35	–	3	272	1.0	2.7	3.3
Playoff Totals	17	–	136	10	30	.333	–	–	–	11	14	.786	5	8	13	21	8	0	2	–	0	31	0.8	1.2	1.8

Lumpp, Raymond G. (Ray) b. July 11, 1923 Ht. 6-1 Wt. 180 College: New York U.

SEASON–TEAM	G	GS	MIN	FGM	FGA	PCT	3FGM	3FGA	PCT	FTM	FTA	PCT	O-RB	D-RB	TOT	AST	PF	DQ	STL	TO	BLK	PTS	RPG	APG	PPG
48-49–Ind.-N.Y.	61	–	–	279	800	.349	–	–	–	219	283	.774	–	–	–	158	173	–	–	–	–	777	–	2.6	12.7
49-50–New York	58	–	–	91	283	.322	–	–	–	86	108	.796	–	–	–	90	117	–	–	–	–	268	–	1.6	4.6
50-51–New York	64	–	–	153	379	.404	–	–	–	124	160	.775	–	–	125	115	160	2	–	–	–	430	2.0	1.8	6.7
51-52–New York	62	–	1317	184	476	.387	–	–	–	90	119	.756	–	–	125	123	165	4	–	–	–	458	2.0	2.0	7.4
52-53–N.Y.-Balt.	55	–	1422	188	506	.372	–	–	–	153	206	.743	–	–	141	168	178	5	–	–	–	529	2.6	3.1	9.6
Reg. Season Totals	300	–	2739	895	2444	.366	–	–	–	672	876	.767	–	–	391	654	793	11	–	–	–	2462	2.2	2.2	8.2
Playoff Totals	37	–	296	75	247	.308	–	–	–	79	96	.823	–	–	47	57	119	5	–	–	–	229	1.7	1.4	6.2

Lynam, Robert Bracey (R.B.) b. 1944 Ht. 6-1 Wt. 190 College: Oklahoma Baptist

SEASON–TEAM	G	GS	MIN	FGM	FGA	PCT	3FGM	3FGA	PCT	FTM	FTA	PCT	O-RB	D-RB	TOT	AST	PF	DQ	STL	TO	BLK	PTS	RPG	APG	PPG
67-68–Denver (A)	7	–	39	5	17	.294	0	1	.000	7	8	.875	–	–	5	0	10	0	–	5	–	17	0.7	0.0	2.4
Reg. ABA Totals	7	–	39	5	17	.294	0	1	.000	7	8	.875	–	–	5	0	10	0	–	5	–	17	0.7	0.0	2.4

Lynch, George DeWitt III b. September 3, 1970 Ht. 6-8 Wt. 228 College: North Carolina

SEASON–TEAM	G	GS	MIN	FGM	FGA	PCT	3FGM	3FGA	PCT	FTM	FTA	PCT	O-RB	D-RB	TOT	AST	PF	DQ	STL	TO	BLK	PTS	RPG	APG	PPG
93-94–L.A. Lakers	71	46	1762	291	573	.508	0	5	.000	99	166	.596	220	190	410	96	177	1	102	87	27	681	5.8	1.4	9.6
94-95–L.A. Lakers	56	15	953	138	295	.468	3	21	.143	62	86	.721	75	109	184	62	86	0	51	73	10	341	3.3	1.1	6.1
95-96–L.A. Lakers	76	6	1012	117	272	.430	4	13	.308	53	80	.663	82	127	209	51	106	0	47	40	10	291	2.8	0.7	3.8
96-97–Vancouver	41	27	1059	137	291	.471	8	31	.258	60	97	.619	98	163	261	76	97	1	63	64	17	342	6.4	1.9	8.3
97-98–Vancouver	82	0	1493	248	516	.481	9	30	.300	111	158	.703	147	215	362	122	161	0	65	104	41	616	4.4	1.5	7.5
98-99–Philadelphia	43	43	1315	147	349	.421	9	23	.391	53	84	.631	110	169	279	76	142	2	85	79	22	356	6.5	1.8	8.3
99-00–Philadelphia	75	75	2416	297	644	.461	15	36	.417	113	183	.617	216	366	582	136	231	2	119	120	38	722	7.8	1.8	9.6
Reg. Season Totals	444	212	10010	1375	2940	.468	48	159	.302	551	854	.645	948	1339	2287	619	1000	6	532	567	165	3349	5.2	1.4	7.5
Playoff Totals	30	16	693	68	166	.410	4	19	.211	39	55	.709	67	90	157	38	89	2	35	32	7	179	5.2	1.3	6.0

Lynch, Kevin Joseph b. December 24, 1968 Ht. 6-5 Wt. 195 College: Minnesota

SEASON–TEAM	G	GS	MIN	FGM	FGA	PCT	3FGM	3FGA	PCT	FTM	FTA	PCT	O-RB	D-RB	TOT	AST	PF	DQ	STL	TO	BLK	PTS	RPG	APG	PPG
91-92–Charlotte	55	3	819	93	223	.417	3	8	.375	35	46	.761	30	55	85	83	107	0	37	44	9	224	1.5	1.5	4.1
92-93–Charlotte	40	8	324	30	59	.508	0	1	.000	26	38	.684	12	23	35	25	44	0	11	24	6	86	0.9	0.6	2.2
Reg. Season Totals	95	11	1143	123	282	.436	3	9	.333	61	84	.726	42	78	120	108	151	0	48	68	15	310	1.3	1.1	3.3
Playoff Totals	1	0	3	0	0	–	0	0	–	0	0	–	0	0	0	1	0	0	0	0	0	0	0.0	1.0	0.0

Lynn, Lonnie b. May 24, 1943 Ht. 6-7 Wt. 215 College: Upper Iowa; Wilberforce

SEASON–TEAM	G	GS	MIN	FGM	FGA	PCT	3FGM	3FGA	PCT	FTM	FTA	PCT	O-RB	D-RB	TOT	AST	PF	DQ	STL	TO	BLK	PTS	RPG	APG	PPG
69-70–Denver-Pitt. (A)	52	–	779	112	275	.407	0	3	.000	36	74	.486	–	–	258	43	120	1	–	–	–	260	5.0	0.8	5.0
Reg. ABA Totals	52	–	779	112	275	.407	0	3	.000	36	74	.486	–	–	258	43	120	1	–	–	–	260	5.0	0.8	5.0

Lynn, Michael Edward (Mike) b. November 25, 1945 Ht. 6-7 Wt. 215 College: UCLA

SEASON–TEAM	G	GS	MIN	FGM	FGA	PCT	3FGM	3FGA	PCT	FTM	FTA	PCT	O-RB	D-RB	TOT	AST	PF	DQ	STL	TO	BLK	PTS	RPG	APG	PPG
69-70–Los Angeles	44	–	403	44	133	.331	–	–	–	31	48	.646	–	–	64	30	87	4	–	–	–	119	1.5	0.7	2.7
70-71–Buffalo	5	–	25	2	7	.286	–	–	–	3	3	1.000	–	–	4	1	9	0	–	–	–	7	0.8	0.2	1.4
Reg. Season Totals	49	–	428	46	140	.329	–	–	–	34	51	.667	–	–	68	31	96	4	–	–	–	126	1.4	0.6	2.6
Playoff Totals	3	–	6	2	3	.667	–	–	–	0	0	–	–	–	2	1	1	0	–	–	–	4	0.7	0.3	1.3

Macaluso, Michael Emelius (Mike) b. July 20, 1951 Ht. 6-5 Wt. 210 College: Canisius

SEASON–TEAM	G	GS	MIN	FGM	FGA	PCT	3FGM	3FGA	PCT	FTM	FTA	PCT	O-RB	D-RB	TOT	AST	PF	DQ	STL	TO	BLK	PTS	RPG	APG	PPG
73-74–Buffalo	30	–	112	19	44	.432	–	–	–	10	17	.588	10	15	25	3	31	0	7	–	1	48	0.8	0.1	1.6
Reg. Season Totals	30	–	112	19	44	.432	–	–	–	10	17	.588	10	15	25	3	31	0	7	–	1	48	0.8	0.1	1.6

Macauley, Charles Edward Jr. (Ed, Easy Ed) b. March 22, 1928 Ht. 6-8 Wt. 190 College: St. Louis HOF: 1960

SEASON–TEAM	G	GS	MIN	FGM	FGA	PCT	3FGM	3FGA	PCT	FTM	FTA	PCT	O-RB	D-RB	TOT	AST	PF	DQ	STL	TO	BLK	PTS	RPG	APG	PPG
49-50–St. Louis	67	–	–	351	882	.398	–	–	–	379	528	.718	–	–	–	200	221	–	–	–	–	1081	–	3.0	16.1
50-51–Boston	68	–	–	459	985	.466	–	–	–	466	614	.759	–	–	616	252	205	4	–	–	–	1384	9.1	3.7	20.4
51-52–Boston	66	–	2631	384	888	.432	–	–	–	496	621	.799	–	–	529	232	174	0	–	–	–	1264	8.0	3.5	19.2
52-53–Boston	69	–	2902	451	997	.452	–	–	–	500	667	.750	–	–	629	280	188	0	–	–	–	1402	9.1	4.1	20.3
53-54–Boston	71	–	2792	462	950	.486	–	–	–	420	554	.758	–	–	571	271	168	1	–	–	–	1344	8.0	3.8	18.9
54-55–Boston	71	–	2706	403	951	.424	–	–	–	442	558	.792	–	–	600	275	171	0	–	–	–	1248	8.5	3.9	17.6
55-56–Boston	71	–	2354	420	995	.422	–	–	–	400	504	.794	–	–	422	211	158	2	–	–	–	1240	5.9	3.0	17.5
56-57–St. Louis	72	–	2582	414	987	.419	–	–	–	359	479	.749	–	–	440	202	206	2	–	–	–	1187	6.1	2.8	16.5
57-58–St. Louis	72	–	1908	376	879	.428	–	–	–	267	369	.724	–	–	478	143	156	2	–	–	–	1019	6.6	2.0	14.2
58-59–St. Louis	14	–	196	22	75	.293	–	–	–	21	35	.600	–	–	40	13	20	1	–	–	–	65	2.9	0.9	4.6
Reg. Season Totals	641	–	18071	3742	8589	.436	–	–	–	3750	4929	.761	–	–	4325	2079	1667	12	–	–	–	11234	7.5	3.2	17.5
Playoff Totals	47	–	1414	218	499	.437	–	–	–	212	291	.729	–	–	337	138	141	6	–	–	–	648	6.6	2.9	13.8
All-Star Totals	7	–	154	24	62	.387	–	–	–	35	41	.854	–	–	32	18	13	0	–	–	–	83	4.6	2.6	11.9

MacCulloch, Todd Carlyle b. January 27, 1976 Ht. 7-0 Wt. 280 College: Washington

SEASON–TEAM	G	GS	MIN	FGM	FGA	PCT	3FGM	3FGA	PCT	FTM	FTA	PCT	O-RB	D-RB	TOT	AST	PF	DQ	STL	TO	BLK	PTS	RPG	APG	PPG
99-00–Philadelphia	56	6	528	89	161	.553	0	0	–	28	54	.519	48	98	146	13	94	0	11	26	37	206	2.6	0.2	3.7
Reg. Season Totals	56	6	528	89	161	.553	0	0	–	28	54	.519	48	98	146	13	94	0	11	26	37	206	2.6	0.2	3.7
Playoff Totals	5	0	24	2	3	.667	0	0	–	4	6	.667	3	6	9	–	2	0	0	0	0	8	1.8	0.0	1.6

MacGilvray, Ronald (Ronnie) b. July 20, 1930 Ht. 6-2 Wt. 185 College: St. John's (N.Y.)

SEASON–TEAM	G	GS	MIN	FGM	FGA	PCT	3FGM	3FGA	PCT	FTM	FTA	PCT	O-RB	D-RB	TOT	AST	PF	DQ	STL	TO	BLK	PTS	RPG	APG	PPG
54-55–Milwaukee	6	–	57	2	12	.167	–	–	–	4	7	.571	–	–	9	11	5	0	–	–	–	8	1.5	1.8	1.3
Reg. Season Totals	6	–	57	2	12	.167	–	–	–	4	7	.571	–	–	9	11	5	0	–	–	–	8	1.5	1.8	1.3

Mack, Oliver (Ollie) b. June 6, 1957 Ht. 6-3 Wt. 195 College: San Jacinto (Texas) Coll. (J.C.); East Carolina

SEASON–TEAM	G	GS	MIN	FGM	FGA	PCT	3FGM	3FGA	PCT	FTM	FTA	PCT	O-RB	D-RB	TOT	AST	PF	DQ	STL	TO	BLK	PTS	RPG	APG	PPG
79-80–L.A.-Chicago	50	–	681	98	199	.492	0	5	.000	38	51	.745	32	39	71	53	50	0	24	35	3	234	1.4	1.1	4.7
80-81–Chicago-Dallas	65	–	1682	279	606	.460	0	9	.000	80	125	.640	92	138	230	163	117	0	56	70	7	638	3.5	2.5	9.8
81-82–Dallas	13	3	150	19	59	.322	0	2	.000	6	8	.750	8	10	18	14	6	0	5	4	1	44	1.4	1.1	3.4
Reg. Season Totals	128	3	2513	396	864	.458	0	16	.000	124	184	.674	132	187	319	230	173	0	85	109	11	916	2.5	1.8	7.2

Mack, Sam b. May 26, 1970 Ht. 6-7 Wt. 220 College: Iowa State; Arizona State; Tyler (Texas) J.C.; Houston

SEASON–TEAM	G	GS	MIN	FGM	FGA	PCT	3FGM	3FGA	PCT	FTM	FTA	PCT	O-RB	D-RB	TOT	AST	PF	DQ	STL	TO	BLK	PTS	RPG	APG	PPG
92-93–San Antonio	40	0	267	47	118	.398	3	22	.136	45	58	.776	18	30	48	15	44	0	14	22	5	142	1.2	0.4	3.6
95-96–Houston	31	20	868	121	287	.422	54	135	.400	39	46	.848	18	80	98	79	75	0	22	28	9	335	3.2	2.5	10.8
96-97–Houston	52	10	904	105	262	.401	47	142	.331	35	42	.833	20	86	106	58	67	0	29	42	6	292	2.0	1.1	5.6
97-98–Vancouver	57	54	1414	222	559	.397	110	269	.409	62	77	.805	30	103	133	101	117	0	41	69	11	616	2.3	1.8	10.8
98-99–Vanc.-Houston	44	15	1083	167	384	.435	87	219	.397	51	58	.879	14	81	95	55	94	1	35	33	4	472	2.2	1.3	10.7
99-00–Golden State	23	5	333	37	122	.303	21	64	.328	19	20	.950	7	32	39	24	45	0	18	19	1	114	1.7	1.0	5.0
Reg. Season Totals	247	104	4869	699	1732	.404	322	851	.378	251	301	.834	107	412	519	332	442	1	159	213	36	1971	2.1	1.3	8.0
Playoff Totals	10	0	170	18	53	.340	12	35	.343	14	20	.700	1	17	18	8	12	0	5	7	0	62	1.8	0.8	6.2

Mackey, Malcolm Malik b. July 11, 1970 Ht. 6-9 Wt. 248 College: Georgia Tech

SEASON–TEAM	G	GS	MIN	FGM	FGA	PCT	3FGM	3FGA	PCT	FTM	FTA	PCT	O-RB	D-RB	TOT	AST	PF	DQ	STL	TO	BLK	PTS	RPG	APG	PPG
93-94–Phoenix	22	0	69	14	37	.378	0	2	.000	4	8	.500	12	12	24	1	9	0	0	2	3	32	1.1	0.0	1.5
Reg. Season Totals	22	0	69	14	37	.378	0	2	.000	4	8	.500	12	12	24	1	9	0	0	2	3	32	1.1	0.0	1.5

Macklin, Durand (Rudy) b. February 19, 1958 Ht. 6-7 Wt. 215 College: Louisiana State

SEASON–TEAM	G	GS	MIN	FGM	FGA	PCT	3FGM	3FGA	PCT	FTM	FTA	PCT	O-RB	D-RB	TOT	AST	PF	DQ	STL	TO	BLK	PTS	RPG	APG	PPG
81-82–Atlanta	79	32	1516	210	484	.434	0	3	.000	134	173	.775	113	150	263	47	225	5	40	112	20	554	3.3	0.6	7.0
82-83–Atlanta	73	20	1171	170	360	.472	0	4	.000	101	131	.771	85	105	190	71	189	4	41	89	10	441	2.6	1.0	6.0
83-84–New York	8	0	65	12	30	.400	0	0	–	11	13	.846	5	6	11	3	17	0	1	6	0	35	1.4	0.4	4.4
Reg. Season Totals	160	52	2752	392	874	.449	0	7	.000	246	317	.776	203	261	464	121	431	9	82	207	30	1030	2.9	0.8	6.4
Playoff Totals	5	3	108	15	32	.469	0	1	.000	14	16	.875	7	11	18	3	18	1	2	7	2	44	3.6	0.6	8.8

Macknowski, John Andrew (Johnny, Whitey) b. January 7, 1923 Ht. 6-1 Wt. 185 College: Seton Hall

SEASON–TEAM	G	GS	MIN	FGM	FGA	PCT	3FGM	3FGA	PCT	FTM	FTA	PCT	O-RB	D-RB	TOT	AST	PF	DQ	STL	TO	BLK	PTS	RPG	APG	PPG
48-49–Syracuse (N)	62	–	–	146	–	–	–	–	–	128	178	.719	–	–	–	–	128	–	–	–	–	420	–	–	6.8
49-50–Syracuse	59	–	–	154	463	.333	–	–	–	131	178	.736	–	–	–	65	128	–	–	–	–	439	–	1.1	7.4
50-51–Syracuse	58	–	–	131	435	.301	–	–	–	122	170	.718	–	–	110	69	134	3	–	–	–	384	1.9	1.2	6.6
Reg. NBA Totals	117	–	–	285	898	.317	–	–	–	253	348	.727	–	–	110	134	262	3	–	–	–	823	1.9	1.1	7.0
Reg. NBL Totals	62	–	–	146	–	–	–	–	–	128	178	.719	–	–	–	–	128	–	–	–	–	420	–	–	6.8
NBA Playoff Totals	13	–	–	45	189	.397	–	–	–	41	55	.745	–	–	7	42	22	0	–	–	–	131	3.5	2.1	10.1
NBL Playoff Totals	6	–	–	3	–	–	–	–	–	7	9	.778	–	–	–	–	7	–	–	–	–	13	–	–	2.2

MacLean, Donald James (Don) b. January 16, 1970 Ht. 6-10 Wt. 235 College: UCLA

SEASON–TEAM	G	GS	MIN	FGM	FGA	PCT	3FGM	3FGA	PCT	FTM	FTA	PCT	O-RB	D-RB	TOT	AST	PF	DQ	STL	TO	BLK	PTS	RPG	APG	PPG
92-93–Washington	62	4	674	157	361	.435	3	6	.500	90	111	.811	33	89	122	39	82	0	11	42	4	407	2.0	0.6	6.6
93-94–Washington	75	69	2487	517	1030	.502	3	21	.143	328	398	.824	140	327	467	160	169	0	47	152	22	1365	6.2	2.1	18.2
94-95–Washington	39	20	1052	158	361	.438	10	40	.250	104	136	.765	46	119	165	51	97	0	15	44	3	430	4.2	1.3	11.0
95-96–Denver	56	5	1107	233	547	.426	14	49	.286	145	198	.732	62	143	205	89	105	1	21	68	5	625	3.7	1.6	11.2
96-97–Philadelphia	37	2	733	163	365	.447	12	38	.316	64	97	.660	41	99	140	37	71	0	12	47	10	402	3.8	1.0	10.9
97-98–New Jersey	9	0	42	1	10	.100	1	2	.500	0	0	–	3	2	5	0	7	0	0	2	0	3	0.6	0.0	0.3
98-99–Seattle	17	10	365	63	159	.396	9	33	.273	50	80	.625	18	47	65	16	34	0	5	25	5	185	3.8	0.9	10.9
99-00–Phoenix	16	0	143	18	49	.367	2	6	.333	4	6	.667	6	17	23	8	24	0	2	8	1	42	1.4	0.5	2.6
Reg. Season Totals	311	110	6603	1310	2882	.455	54	195	.277	785	1026	.765	349	843	1192	400	589	1	113	388	50	3459	3.8	1.3	11.1

Macon, Mark L. b. April 14, 1969 Ht. 6-5 Wt. 200 College: Temple

SEASON–TEAM	G	GS	MIN	FGM	FGA	PCT	3FGM	3FGA	PCT	FTM	FTA	PCT	O-RB	D-RB	TOT	AST	PF	DQ	STL	TO	BLK	PTS	RPG	APG	PPG
91-92–Denver	76	67	2304	333	889	.375	4	30	.133	135	185	.730	80	140	220	168	242	4	154	155	14	805	2.9	2.2	10.6
92-93–Denver	48	27	1141	158	381	.415	0	6	.000	42	60	.700	33	70	103	126	135	2	69	72	3	358	2.1	2.6	7.5
93-94–Den.-Detroit	42	1	496	69	184	.375	2	10	.200	23	34	.676	18	23	41	51	73	0	39	40	1	163	1.0	1.2	3.9
94-95–Detroit	55	6	721	101	265	.381	20	62	.323	54	68	.794	29	47	76	63	97	1	67	41	1	276	1.4	1.1	5.0
95-96–Detroit	23	0	287	29	67	.433	7	15	.467	9	11	.818	10	12	22	16	34	0	15	9	0	74	1.0	0.7	3.2
98-99–Detroit	7	3	69	4	20	.200	1	3	.333	0	0	–	3	2	5	4	6	0	5	6	1	9	0.7	0.6	1.3
Reg. Season Totals	251	104	5018	694	1806	.384	34	126	.270	263	358	.735	173	294	467	428	587	7	349	323	20	1685	1.9	1.7	6.7

Macy, Kyle Robert b. April 9, 1957 Ht. 6-3 Wt. 175 College: Purdue; Kentucky

SEASON–TEAM	G	GS	MIN	FGM	FGA	PCT	3FGM	3FGA	PCT	FTM	FTA	PCT	O-RB	D-RB	TOT	AST	PF	DQ	STL	TO	BLK	PTS	RPG	APG	PPG
80-81–Phoenix	82	–	1469	272	532	.511	12	51	.235	107	119	.899	44	88	132	160	120	0	76	95	5	663	1.6	2.0	8.1
81-82–Phoenix	82	72	2845	486	945	.514	39	100	.390	152	169	.899	78	183	261	384	185	1	143	125	9	1163	3.2	4.7	14.2
82-83–Phoenix	82	9	1836	328	634	.517	23	76	.303	129	148	.872	41	124	165	278	130	0	64	90	8	808	2.0	3.4	9.9
83-84–Phoenix	82	45	2402	357	713	.501	23	70	.329	95	114	.833	49	137	186	353	181	0	123	116	6	832	2.3	4.3	10.1
84-85–Phoenix	65	52	2018	282	582	.485	23	85	.271	127	140	.907	33	146	179	380	128	0	85	111	3	714	2.8	5.8	11.0
85-86–Chicago	82	79	2426	286	592	.483	58	140	.414	73	90	.811	41	137	178	446	201	1	81	117	11	703	2.2	5.4	8.6
86-87–Indiana	76	0	1250	164	341	.481	14	46	.304	34	41	.829	25	88	113	197	136	0	59	58	7	376	1.5	2.6	4.9
Reg. Season Totals	551	257	14246	2175	4339	.501	192	568	.338	717	821	.873	311	903	1214	2198	1081	2	631	712	49	5259	2.2	4.0	9.5
Playoff Totals	44	28	1258	169	363	.466	20	53	.377	44	53	.830	34	78	112	170	99	0	44	56	3	402	2.5	3.9	9.1

Maddox, Jack C. b. December 10, 1921 Ht. 6-3 Wt. 190 College: West Texas A&M

SEASON–TEAM	G	GS	MIN	FGM	FGA	PCT	3FGM	3FGA	PCT	FTM	FTA	PCT	O-RB	D-RB	TOT	AST	PF	DQ	STL	TO	BLK	PTS	RPG	APG	PPG
46-47–Oshkosh (N)	43	–	–	102	–	–	–	–	–	33	39	.846	–	–	–	–	53	–	–	–	–	237	–	–	5.5
47-48–Oshkosh (N)	60	–	–	146	–	–	–	–	–	59	90	.656	–	–	–	–	112	–	–	–	–	351	–	–	5.9
48-49–Hammond (N)	17	–	–	39	–	–	–	–	–	18	29	.621	–	–	–	–	28	–	–	–	–	96	–	–	5.6
48-49–Indianapolis	1	–	–	0	0	–	–	–	–	0	0	–	–	–	–	1	0	–	–	–	–	0	–	1.0	0.0
Reg. NBA Totals	1	–	–	0	0	–	–	–	–	0	0	–	–	–	–	1	0	–	–	–	–	0	–	1.0	0.0
Reg. NBL Totals	120	–	–	287	–	–	–	–	–	110	158	.696	–	–	–	–	193	–	–	–	–	684	–	–	5.7
NBL Playoff Totals	10	–	–	7	–	–	–	–	–	2	4	.500	–	–	–	–	5	–	–	–	–	16	–	–	1.6

Madkins, Gerald Jr. b. April 18, 1969 Ht. 6-4 Wt. 200 College: UCLA

SEASON–TEAM	G	GS	MIN	FGM	FGA	PCT	3FGM	3FGA	PCT	FTM	FTA	PCT	O-RB	D-RB	TOT	AST	PF	DQ	STL	TO	BLK	PTS	RPG	APG	PPG
93-94–Cleveland	22	0	149	11	31	.355	5	15	.333	8	10	.800	1	10	11	19	16	0	9	13	0	35	0.5	0.9	1.6
94-95–Cleveland	7	0	28	2	6	.333	1	2	.500	3	4	.750	0	0	0	1	2	0	2	3	0	8	0.0	0.1	1.1
97-98–Miami-G.S.	19	0	243	13	34	.382	6	15	.400	5	7	.714	2	13	15	45	18	0	13	13	1	37	0.8	2.4	1.9
Reg. Season Totals	48	0	420	26	71	.366	12	32	.375	16	21	.762	3	23	26	65	36	0	24	29	1	80	0.5	1.4	1.7

Mager, Norman Clifford (Norm) b. March 23, 1926 Ht. 6-5 Wt. 185 College: St. John's (N.Y.); C.C.NY

SEASON–TEAM	G	GS	MIN	FGM	FGA	PCT	3FGM	3FGA	PCT	FTM	FTA	PCT	O-RB	D-RB	TOT	AST	PF	DQ	STL	TO	BLK	PTS	RPG	APG	PPG
50-51–Baltimore	24	–	–	40	142	.282	–	–	–	44	56	.786	–	–	47	22	68	3	–	–	–	124	2.0	0.9	5.2
Reg. Season Totals	24	–	–	40	142	.282	–	–	–	44	56	.786	–	–	47	22	68	3	–	–	–	124	2.0	0.9	5.2

Maggette, Corey Antoine b. November 12, 1979 Ht. 6-6 Wt. 218 College: Duke

SEASON–TEAM	G	GS	MIN	FGM	FGA	PCT	3FGM	3FGA	PCT	FTM	FTA	PCT	O-RB	D-RB	TOT	AST	PF	DQ	STL	TO	BLK	PTS	RPG	APG	PPG
99-00–Orlando	77	5	1370	224	469	.478	2	11	.182	196	261	.751	123	180	303	61	169	1	24	138	26	646	3.9	0.8	8.4
Reg. Season Totals	77	5	1370	224	469	.478	2	11	.182	196	261	.751	123	180	303	61	169	1	24	138	26	646	3.9	0.8	8.4

Magley, David John (Dave) b. November 24, 1959 Ht. 6-8 Wt. 210 College: Kansas

SEASON–TEAM	G	GS	MIN	FGM	FGA	PCT	3FGM	3FGA	PCT	FTM	FTA	PCT	O-RB	D-RB	TOT	AST	PF	DQ	STL	TO	BLK	PTS	RPG	APG	PPG
82-83–Cleveland	14	0	56	4	16	.250	0	1	.000	4	8	.500	2	8	10	2	5	0	2	2	0	12	0.7	0.1	0.9
Reg. Season Totals	14	0	56	4	16	.250	0	1	.000	4	8	.500	2	8	10	2	5	0	2	2	0	12	0.7	0.1	0.9

Mahaffey, Randolph (Randy) b. September 28, 1945 Ht. 6-7 Wt. 210 College: Clemson

SEASON–TEAM	G	GS	MIN	FGM	FGA	PCT	3FGM	3FGA	PCT	FTM	FTA	PCT	O-RB	D-RB	TOT	AST	PF	DQ	STL	TO	BLK	PTS	RPG	APG	PPG
67-68–Kentucky (A)	75	–	2325	373	875	.426	0	2	.000	281	411	.684	259	425	684	129	278	15	–	224	–	1027	9.1	1.7	13.7
68-69–Ken.-N.Y. (A)	79	–	2353	351	828	.424	0	2	.000	232	329	.705	–	–	571	99	261	8	–	243	–	934	7.2	1.3	11.8
69-70–Carolina (A)	84	–	2558	367	821	.447	0	4	.000	194	283	.686	–	–	681	164	275	7	–	–	–	928	8.1	2.0	11.0
70-71–Carolina (A)	83	–	2353	385	791	.487	0	8	.000	156	239	.653	–	–	618	115	304	–	–	–	–	926	7.4	1.4	11.2
Reg. ABA Totals	321	–	9589	1476	3315	.445	0	16	.000	863	1262	.684	259	425	2554	507	1118	30	–	467	–	3815	8.0	1.6	11.9
ABA Playoff Totals	9	–	238	43	91	.473	0	0	–	27	38	.711	–	–	50	11	16	1	–	16	–	113	5.6	1.2	12.6

Mahnken, John E. (Long John) b. June 16, 1922 Ht. 6-8 Wt. 220 College: Georgetown

SEASON–TEAM	G	GS	MIN	FGM	FGA	PCT	3FGM	3FGA	PCT	FTM	FTA	PCT	O-RB	D-RB	TOT	AST	PF	DQ	STL	TO	BLK	PTS	RPG	APG	PPG
45-46–Rochester (N)	16	–	–	50	–	–	–	–	–	23	39	.590	–	–	–	–	56	–	–	–	–	123	–	–	7.7
46-47–Washington	60	–	–	223	876	.255	–	–	–	111	163	.681	–	–	–	60	181	–	–	–	–	557	–	1.0	9.3
47-48–Washington	48	–	–	131	526	.249	–	–	–	54	88	.614	–	–	–	31	151	–	–	–	–	316	–	0.6	6.6
48-49–Balt.-Ind.-Ft.Wayne	57	–	–	215	830	.259	–	–	–	104	167	.623	–	–	–	125	215	–	–	–	–	534	–	2.2	9.4
49-50–Ft.Wayne-Tri-Cit-Bos.	62	–	–	132	495	.267	–	–	–	77	115	.670	–	–	–	108	231	–	–	–	–	341	–	1.7	5.5
50-51–Boston-Ind.	58	–	–	111	351	.316	–	–	–	45	70	.643	–	–	219	77	164	6	–	–	–	267	3.8	1.3	4.6
51-52–Boston	60	–	581	78	227	.344	–	–	–	26	43	.605	–	–	132	63	91	2	–	–	–	182	2.2	1.1	3.0
52-53–Boston	69	–	771	76	252	.302	–	–	–	39	56	.696	–	–	182	75	110	1	–	–	–	191	2.6	1.1	2.8
Reg. NBA Totals	414	–	1352	966	3557	.272	–	–	–	456	702	.650	–	–	533	539	1143	9	–	–	–	2388	2.9	1.3	5.8
Reg. NBL Totals	16	–	–	50	–	–	–	–	–	23	39	.590	–	–	–	–	56	–	–	–	–	123	–	–	7.7
NBA Playoff Totals	18	–	122	27	224	.223	–	–	–	24	31	.774	–	–	40	20	62	7	–	–	–	78	3.3	0.8	4.3
NBL Playoff Totals	7	–	–	19	–	–	–	–	–	8	11	.727	–	–	–	–	24	–	–	–	–	46	–	–	6.6

Mahoney, Brian C. b. December 17, 1948 Ht. 6-3 Wt. 175 College: Manhattan

SEASON–TEAM	G	GS	MIN	FGM	FGA	PCT	3FGM	3FGA	PCT	FTM	FTA	PCT	O-RB	D-RB	TOT	AST	PF	DQ	STL	TO	BLK	PTS	RPG	APG	PPG
72-73–New York (A)	19	–	181	17	57	.298	0	2	.000	24	40	.600	4	10	14	12	35	1	–	17	–	58	0.7	0.6	3.1
Reg. ABA Totals	19	–	181	17	57	.298	0	2	.000	24	40	.600	4	10	14	12	35	1	–	17	–	58	0.7	0.6	3.1

Mahoney, Francis H. (Mo) b. November 20, 1927 Ht. 6-3 Wt. 205 College: Brown

SEASON–TEAM	G	GS	MIN	FGM	FGA	PCT	3FGM	3FGA	PCT	FTM	FTA	PCT	O-RB	D-RB	TOT	AST	PF	DQ	STL	TO	BLK	PTS	RPG	APG	PPG
52-53–Boston	6	–	34	4	10	.400	–	–	–	4	5	.800	–	–	7	1	7	0	–	–	–	12	1.2	0.2	2.0
53-54–Baltimore	2	–	11	0	2	.000	–	–	–	0	0	–	–	–	2	1	0	0	–	–	–	0	1.0	0.5	0.0
Reg. Season Totals	8	–	45	4	12	.333	–	–	–	4	5	.800	–	–	9	2	7	0	–	–	–	12	1.1	0.3	1.5
Playoff Totals	4	–	45	3	14	.214	–	–	–	3	5	.600	–	–	7	2	14	0	–	–	–	9	1.8	0.5	2.3

Mahorn, Derrick Allen (Rick) b. September 21, 1958 Ht. 6-10 Wt. 260 College: Hampton

SEASON–TEAM	G	GS	MIN	FGM	FGA	PCT	3FGM	3FGA	PCT	FTM	FTA	PCT	O-RB	D-RB	TOT	AST	PF	DQ	STL	TO	BLK	PTS	RPG	APG	PPG
80-81–Washington	52	–	696	111	219	.507	0	0	–	27	40	.675	67	148	215	25	134	3	21	38	44	249	4.1	0.5	4.8
81-82–Washington	80	80	2664	414	816	.507	0	3	.000	148	234	.632	149	555	704	150	349	12	57	162	138	976	8.8	1.9	12.2
82-83–Washington	82	82	3023	376	768	.490	0	3	.000	146	254	.575	171	608	779	115	335	13	86	170	148	898	9.5	1.4	11.0
83-84–Washington	82	82	2701	307	605	.507	0	0	–	125	192	.651	169	569	738	131	358	14	62	142	123	739	9.0	1.6	9.0
84-85–Washington	77	63	2072	206	413	.499	0	0	–	71	104	.683	150	458	608	121	308	11	59	133	104	483	7.9	1.6	6.3
85-86–Detroit	80	12	1442	157	345	.455	0	1	.000	81	119	.681	121	291	412	64	261	4	40	109	61	395	5.2	0.8	4.9
86-87–Detroit	63	6	1278	144	322	.447	0	0	–	96	117	.821	93	282	375	38	221	4	32	73	50	384	6.0	0.6	6.1
87-88–Detroit	67	64	1963	276	481	.574	1	2	.500	164	217	.756	159	406	565	60	262	4	43	119	42	717	8.4	0.9	10.7
88-89–Detroit	72	61	1795	203	393	.517	0	2	.000	116	155	.748	141	355	496	59	206	1	40	97	66	522	6.9	0.8	7.3
89-90–Philadelphia	75	66	2271	313	630	.497	2	9	.222	183	256	.715	167	401	568	98	251	2	44	104	103	811	7.6	1.3	10.8
90-91–Philadelphia	80	74	2439	261	559	.467	0	9	.000	189	240	.788	151	470	621	118	276	6	79	127	56	711	7.8	1.5	8.9
92-93–New Jersey	74	9	1077	101	214	.472	1	3	.333	88	110	.800	93	186	279	33	156	0	19	58	31	291	3.8	0.4	3.9
93-94–New Jersey	28	0	226	23	47	.489	0	1	.000	13	20	.650	16	38	54	5	38	0	3	7	5	59	1.9	0.2	2.1
94-95–New Jersey	58	7	630	79	151	.523	1	3	.333	39	49	.796	45	117	162	26	93	0	11	34	12	198	2.8	0.4	3.4
95-96–New Jersey	50	0	450	43	122	.352	0	1	.000	34	47	.723	31	79	110	16	72	0	14	30	13	120	2.2	0.3	2.4
96-97–Detroit	22	7	218	20	54	.370	0	1	.000	16	22	.727	19	34	53	6	34	0	4	10	3	56	2.4	0.3	2.5
97-98–Detroit	59	0	707	59	129	.457	0	0	–	23	34	.676	65	130	195	15	123	0	14	37	7	141	3.3	0.3	2.4
98-99–Philadelphia	16	0	127	5	18	.278	0	0	–	3	8	.375	7	16	23	2	22	0	5	6	1	13	1.4	0.1	0.8
Reg. Season Totals	1117	613	25779	3098	6286	.493	5	38	.132	1562	2218	.704	1814	5143	6957	1082	3499	74	633	1456	1007	7763	6.2	1.0	6.9
Playoff Totals	106	86	2429	249	528	.472	0	3	.000	114	152	.750	150	429	579	72	348	6	42	93	63	612	5.5	0.7	5.8

Majerle, Daniel Lewis (Dan, Thunder Dan) b. September 9, 1965 Ht. 6-6 Wt. 222 College: Central Michigan

SEASON–TEAM	G	GS	MIN	FGM	FGA	PCT	3FGM	3FGA	PCT	FTM	FTA	PCT	O-RB	D-RB	TOT	AST	PF	DQ	STL	TO	BLK	PTS	RPG	APG	PPG
88-89–Phoenix	54	5	1354	181	432	.419	27	82	.329	78	127	.614	62	147	209	130	139	1	63	48	14	467	3.9	2.4	8.6
89-90–Phoenix	73	23	2244	296	698	.424	19	80	.238	198	260	.762	144	286	430	188	177	5	100	82	32	809	5.9	2.6	11.1
90-91–Phoenix	77	7	2281	397	821	.484	30	86	.349	227	298	.762	168	250	418	216	162	0	106	114	40	1051	5.4	2.8	13.6
91-92–Phoenix	82	15	2853	551	1153	.478	87	228	.382	229	303	.756	148	335	483	274	158	0	131	102	43	1418	5.9	3.3	17.3
92-93–Phoenix	82	82	3199	509	1096	.464	167	438	.381	203	261	.778	120	263	383	311	180	0	138	133	33	1388	4.7	3.8	16.9
93-94–Phoenix	80	76	3207	476	1138	.418	192	503	.382	176	238	.739	120	229	349	275	153	0	129	137	43	1320	4.4	3.4	16.5
94-95–Phoenix	82	46	3091	438	1031	.425	199	548	.363	206	282	.730	104	271	375	340	155	0	96	105	38	1281	4.6	4.1	15.6
95-96–Cleveland	82	15	2367	303	748	.405	146	414	.353	120	169	.710	70	235	305	214	131	0	81	93	34	872	3.7	2.6	10.6
96-97–Miami	36	26	1264	141	347	.406	68	201	.338	40	59	.678	45	117	162	116	75	0	54	50	14	390	4.5	3.2	10.8
97-98–Miami	72	22	1928	184	439	.419	111	295	.376	40	51	.784	48	220	268	157	139	2	68	65	15	519	3.7	2.2	7.2
98-99–Miami	48	48	1624	118	298	.396	68	203	.335	33	46	.717	21	187	208	150	100	0	38	55	7	337	4.3	3.1	7.0
99-00–Miami	69	69	2308	170	422	.403	110	304	.362	56	69	.812	27	306	333	206	156	1	89	62	17	506	4.8	3.0	7.3
Reg. Season Totals	837	434	27720	3764	8623	.437	1224	3382	.362	1606	2163	.742	1077	2846	3923	2577	1725	9	1093	1046	330	10358	4.7	3.1	12.4
Playoff Totals	120	53	4168	503	1206	.417	177	499	.355	242	320	.756	150	449	599	299	278	0	161	126	52	1425	5.0	2.5	11.9
All-Star Totals	3	1	58	12	28	.429	5	15	.333	3	4	.750	3	12	15	8	3	0	1	1	2	32	5.0	2.7	10.7

Malamed, Lionel b. November 15, 1924 d. September 17, 1989 Ht. 5-9 Wt. 150 College: C.C.NY

SEASON–TEAM	G	GS	MIN	FGM	FGA	PCT	3FGM	3FGA	PCT	FTM	FTA	PCT	O-RB	D-RB	TOT	AST	PF	DQ	STL	TO	BLK	PTS	RPG	APG	PPG
48-49–Ind.-Roch.	44	–	–	97	290	.334	–	–	–	64	77	.831	–	–	–	61	53	–	–	–	–	258	–	1.4	5.9
Reg. Season Totals	44	–	–	97	290	.334	–	–	–	64	77	.831	–	–	–	61	53	–	–	–	–	258	–	1.4	5.9

Malone, Jeffrey Nigel (Jeff) b. June 28, 1961 Ht. 6-4 Wt. 205 College: Mississippi State

SEASON–TEAM	G	GS	MIN	FGM	FGA	PCT	3FGM	3FGA	PCT	FTM	FTA	PCT	O-RB	D-RB	TOT	AST	PF	DQ	STL	TO	BLK	PTS	RPG	APG	PPG
83-84–Washington	81	2	1976	408	918	.444	24	74	.324	142	172	.826	57	98	155	151	162	1	23	110	13	982	1.9	1.9	12.1
84-85–Washington	76	61	2613	605	1213	.499	15	72	.208	211	250	.844	60	146	206	184	176	1	52	107	9	1436	2.7	2.4	18.9
85-86–Washington	80	80	2992	735	1522	.483	3	17	.176	322	371	.868	66	222	288	191	180	2	70	168	12	1795	3.6	2.4	22.4
86-87–Washington	80	79	2763	689	1509	.457	4	26	.154	376	425	.885	50	168	218	298	154	0	75	182	13	1758	2.7	3.7	22.0
87-88–Washington	80	80	2655	648	1360	.476	10	24	.417	335	380	.882	44	162	206	237	198	1	51	172	13	1641	2.6	3.0	20.5
88-89–Washington	76	75	2418	677	1410	.480	1	19	.053	296	340	.871	55	124	179	219	155	0	39	165	14	1651	2.4	2.9	21.7
89-90–Washington	75	74	2567	781	1592	.491	1	6	.167	257	293	.877	54	152	206	243	116	1	48	125	6	1820	2.7	3.2	24.3
90-91–Utah	69	69	2466	525	1034	.508	1	6	.167	231	252	.917	36	170	206	143	128	0	50	108	6	1282	3.0	2.1	18.6
91-92–Utah	81	81	2922	691	1353	.511	1	12	.083	256	285	.898	49	184	233	180	126	1	56	140	5	1639	2.9	2.2	20.2
92-93–Utah	79	59	2558	595	1205	.494	3	9	.333	236	277	.852	31	142	173	128	117	0	42	125	4	1429	2.2	1.6	18.1
93-94–Utah-Phil.	77	73	2560	525	1081	.486	7	12	.583	205	247	.830	51	148	199	125	123	0	40	85	5	1262	2.6	1.6	16.4
94-95–Philadelphia	19	19	660	144	284	.507	11	28	.393	51	59	.864	11	44	55	29	35	0	15	29	0	350	2.9	1.5	18.4
95-96–Phil.-Miami	32	3	510	76	193	.394	5	16	.313	29	32	.906	8	32	40	26	25	0	16	22	0	186	1.3	0.8	5.8
Reg. Season Totals	905	755	29660	7099	14674	.484	86	321	.268	2947	3383	.871	572	1792	2364	2154	1695	7	577	1538	100	17231	2.6	2.4	19.0
Playoff Totals	51	47	1809	382	812	.470	2	12	.167	190	223	.852	35	106	141	110	123	1	39	90	12	956	2.8	2.2	18.7
All-Star Totals	2	0	25	6	10	.600	0	1	.000	0	0	–	1	2	3	6	1	0	1	1	0	12	1.5	3.0	6.0

Malone, Karl (The Mailman) b. July 24, 1963 Ht. 6-9 Wt. 256 College: Louisiana Tech

SEASON–TEAM	G	GS	MIN	FGM	FGA	PCT	3FGM	3FGA	PCT	FTM	FTA	PCT	O-RB	D-RB	TOT	AST	PF	DQ	STL	TO	BLK	PTS	RPG	APG	PPG
85-86–Utah	81	76	2475	504	1016	.496	0	2	.000	195	405	.481	174	544	718	236	295	2	105	279	44	1203	8.9	2.9	14.9
86-87–Utah	82	82	2857	728	1422	.512	0	7	.000	323	540	.598	278	577	855	158	323	6	104	237	60	1779	10.4	1.9	21.7
87-88–Utah	82	82	3198	858	1650	.520	0	5	.000	552	789	.700	277	709	986	199	296	2	117	325	50	2268	12.0	2.4	27.7
88-89–Utah	80	80	3126	809	1559	.519	5	16	.313	703	918	.766	259	594	853	219	286	3	144	285	70	2326	10.7	2.7	29.1
89-90–Utah	82	82	3122	914	1627	.562	16	43	.372	696	913	.762	232	679	911	226	259	1	121	304	50	2540	11.1	2.8	31.0
90-91–Utah	82	82	3302	847	1608	.527	4	14	.286	684	888	.770	236	731	967	270	268	2	89	244	79	2382	11.8	3.3	29.0
91-92–Utah	81	81	3054	798	1516	.526	3	17	.176	673	865	.778	225	684	909	241	226	2	108	248	51	2272	11.2	3.0	28.0
92-93–Utah	82	82	3099	797	1443	.552	4	20	.200	619	836	.740	227	692	919	308	261	2	124	240	85	2217	11.2	3.8	27.0
93-94–Utah	82	82	3329	772	1552	.497	8	32	.250	511	736	.694	235	705	940	328	268	2	125	234	126	2063	11.5	4.0	25.2
94-95–Utah	82	82	3126	830	1548	.536	11	41	.268	516	695	.742	156	715	871	285	269	2	129	236	85	2187	10.6	3.5	26.7
95-96–Utah	82	82	3113	789	1520	.519	16	40	.400	512	708	.723	175	629	804	345	245	1	138	199	56	2106	9.8	4.2	25.7
96-97–Utah	82	82	2998	864	1571	.550	0	13	.000	521	690	.755	193	616	809	368	217	0	113	233	48	2249	9.9	4.5	27.4
97-98–Utah	81	81	3030	780	1472	.530	2	6	.333	628	825	.761	189	645	834	316	237	0	96	247	70	2190	10.3	3.9	27.0
98-99–Utah	49	49	1832	393	797	.493	0	1	.000	378	480	.788	107	356	463	201	134	0	62	162	28	1164	9.4	4.1	23.8
99-00–Utah	82	82	2947	752	1476	.509	2	8	.250	589	739	.797	169	610	779	304	229	1	79	231	71	2095	9.5	3.7	25.5
Reg. Season Totals	1192	1187	44608	11435	21777	.525	71	265	.268	8100	11027	.735	3132	9486	12618	4004	3813	26	1654	3704	973	31041	10.6	3.4	26.0
Playoff Totals	158	158	6556	1532	3272	.468	5	32	.156	1134	1534	.739	446	1323	1769	483	558	6	216	453	124	4203	11.2	3.1	26.6
All-Star Totals	11	8	240	58	105	.552	0	0	–	29	40	.725	19	54	73	19	16	0	12	15	5	145	6.6	1.7	13.2

Malone, Moses Eugene b. March 23, 1955 Ht. 6-10 Wt. 255 College: None

SEASON–TEAM	G	GS	MIN	FGM	FGA	PCT	3FGM	3FGA	PCT	FTM	FTA	PCT	O-RB	D-RB	TOT	AST	PF	DQ	STL	TO	BLK	PTS	RPG	APG	PPG
74-75–Utah (A)	83	–	3205	591	1035	.571	0	1	.000	375	591	.635	455	754	1209	82	288	–	85	320	128	1557	14.6	1.0	18.8
75-76–St. Louis (A)	43	–	1168	251	490	.512	0	2	.000	112	183	.612	196	217	413	58	113	–	25	140	28	614	9.6	1.3	14.3
76-77–Buffalo-Hou.	82	–	2506	389	810	.480	–	–	–	305	440	.693	437	635	1072	89	275	3	67	–	181	1083	13.1	1.1	13.2
77-78–Houston	59	–	2107	413	828	.499	–	–	–	318	443	.718	380	506	886	31	179	2	48	220	76	1144	15.0	0.5	19.4
78-79–Houston	82	–	3390	716	1325	.540	–	–	–	599	811	.739	587	857	1444	147	223	0	79	326	119	2031	17.6	1.8	24.8
79-80–Houston	82	–	3140	778	1549	.502	0	6	.000	563	783	.719	573	617	1190	147	210	0	80	300	107	2119	14.5	1.8	25.8
80-81–Houston	80	–	3245	806	1545	.522	1	3	.333	609	804	.757	474	706	1180	141	223	0	83	308	150	2222	14.8	1.8	27.8
81-82–Houston	81	81	3398	945	1822	.519	0	6	.000	630	827	.762	558	630	1188	142	208	0	76	294	125	2520	14.7	1.8	31.1
82-83–Philadelphia	78	78	2922	654	1305	.501	0	1	.000	600	788	.761	445	749	1194	101	206	0	89	264	157	1908	15.3	1.3	24.5
83-84–Philadelphia	71	71	2613	532	1101	.483	0	4	.000	545	727	.750	352	598	950	96	188	0	71	250	110	1609	13.4	1.4	22.7
84-85–Philadelphia	79	79	2957	602	1284	.469	0	2	.000	737	904	.815	385	646	1031	130	216	0	67	286	123	1941	13.1	1.6	24.6
85-86–Philadelphia	74	74	2706	571	1246	.458	0	1	.000	617	784	.787	339	533	872	90	194	0	67	261	71	1759	11.8	1.2	23.8
86-87–Washington	73	70	2488	595	1311	.454	0	11	.000	570	692	.824	340	484	824	120	139	0	59	202	92	1760	11.3	1.6	24.1
87-88–Washington	79	78	2692	531	1090	.487	2	7	.286	543	689	.788	372	512	884	112	160	0	59	249	72	1607	11.2	1.4	20.3
88-89–Atlanta	81	80	2878	538	1096	.491	0	12	.000	561	711	.789	386	570	956	112	154	0	79	245	100	1637	11.8	1.4	20.2
89-90–Atlanta	81	81	2735	517	1077	.480	1	9	.111	493	631	.781	364	448	812	130	158	0	47	232	84	1528	10.0	1.6	18.9
90-91–Atlanta	82	15	1912	280	598	.468	0	7	.000	309	372	.831	271	396	667	68	134	0	30	137	74	869	8.1	0.8	10.6
91-92–Milwaukee	82	77	2511	440	929	.474	3	8	.375	396	504	.786	320	424	744	93	136	0	74	150	64	1279	9.1	1.1	15.6
92-93–Milwaukee	11	0	104	13	42	.310	0	0	–	24	31	.774	22	24	46	7	6	0	1	10	8	50	4.2	0.6	4.5
93-94–Philadelphia	55	0	618	102	232	.440	0	1	.000	90	117	.769	106	120	226	34	52	0	11	59	17	294	4.1	0.6	5.3
94-95–San Antonio	17	0	149	13	35	.371	1	2	.500	22	32	.688	20	26	46	6	15	0	2	11	3	49	2.7	0.4	2.9
Reg. NBA Totals	1329	784	45071	9435	19225	.491	8	80	.100	8531	11090	.769	6731	9481	16212	1796	3076	5	1089	3804	1733	27409	12.2	1.4	20.6
Reg. ABA Totals	126	–	4373	842	1525	.552	0	3	.000	487	774	.629	651	971	1622	140	401	–	110	460	156	2171	12.9	1.1	17.2
NBA Playoff Totals	94	47	3796	750	1566	.479	1	7	.143	576	756	.762	510	785	1295	136	244	0	84	215	151	2077	13.8	1.4	22.1
ABA Playoff Totals	6	–	235	51	80	.638	0	0	–	34	51	.667	47	58	105	9	21	–	0	13	9	136	17.5	1.5	22.7
NBA All-Star Totals	11	8	271	44	98	.449	0	0	–	40	67	.597	44	64	108	15	26	0	9	19	6	128	9.8	1.4	11.6

Maloney, Matthew Patrick (Matt) b. December 6, 1971 Ht. 6-3 Wt. 200 College: Pennsylvania

SEASON–TEAM	G	GS	MIN	FGM	FGA	PCT	3FGM	3FGA	PCT	FTM	FTA	PCT	O-RB	D-RB	TOT	AST	PF	DQ	STL	TO	BLK	PTS	RPG	APG	PPG
96-97–Houston	82	82	2386	271	615	.441	154	381	.404	71	93	.763	19	141	160	303	125	0	82	122	1	767	2.0	3.7	9.4
97-98–Houston	78	78	2217	239	586	.408	126	346	.364	65	78	.833	16	126	142	219	99	0	62	107	5	669	1.8	2.8	8.6
98-99–Houston	15	7	186	5	28	.179	1	15	.067	10	11	.909	2	8	10	21	7	0	4	14	0	21	0.7	1.4	1.4
99-00–Chicago	51	12	1175	114	318	.358	62	174	.356	37	45	.822	10	54	64	138	42	0	32	63	3	327	1.3	2.7	6.4
Reg. Season Totals	226	179	5964	629	1547	.407	343	916	.374	183	227	.806	47	329	376	681	273	0	180	306	9	1784	1.7	3.0	7.9
Playoff Totals	21	21	691	71	183	.388	48	128	.375	22	30	.733	1	26	27	68	42	0	12	42	5	212	1.3	3.2	10.1

Malovic, Stephen L. b. July 21, 1956 Ht. 6-10 Wt. 230 College: USC; San Diego State

SEASON–TEAM	G	GS	MIN	FGM	FGA	PCT	3FGM	3FGA	PCT	FTM	FTA	PCT	O-RB	D-RB	TOT	AST	PF	DQ	STL	TO	BLK	PTS	RPG	APG	PPG
79-80–Was.-S.D.-Det.	39	–	445	31	67	.463	0	0	–	18	27	.667	36	50	86	26	51	0	8	23	6	80	2.2	0.7	2.1
Reg. Season Totals	39	–	445	31	67	.463	0	0	–	18	27	.667	36	50	86	26	51	0	8	23	6	80	2.2	0.7	2.1

Maloy, Michael Alvin (Mike) b. May 10, 1949 Ht. 6-7 Wt. 230 College: Davidson

SEASON–TEAM	G	GS	MIN	FGM	FGA	PCT	3FGM	3FGA	PCT	FTM	FTA	PCT	O-RB	D-RB	TOT	AST	PF	DQ	STL	TO	BLK	PTS	RPG	APG	PPG
70-71–Virginia (A)	55	–	725	149	334	.446	0	1	.000	98	139	.705	–	–	236	43	125	–	–	–	–	396	4.3	0.8	7.2
71-72–Virginia (A)	7	–	73	12	35	.343	0	0	–	2	2	1.000	–	–	17	2	14	–	–	9	–	26	2.4	0.3	3.7
72-73–Dallas (A)	9	–	63	7	27	.259	0	0	–	6	10	.600	6	9	15	3	14	0	–	4	–	20	1.7	0.3	2.2
Reg. ABA Totals	71	–	861	168	396	.424	0	1	.000	106	151	.702	6	9	268	48	153	0	–	13	–	442	3.8	0.7	6.2
ABA Playoff Totals	1	–	2	1	3	.333	0	0	–	0	0	–	–	–	1	0	0	0	–	–	–	2	1.0	0.0	2.0

Manakas, Theodore (Ted) b. February 22, 1951 Ht. 6-2 Wt. 180 College: Princeton

SEASON–TEAM	G	GS	MIN	FGM	FGA	PCT	3FGM	3FGA	PCT	FTM	FTA	PCT	O-RB	D-RB	TOT	AST	PF	DQ	STL	TO	BLK	PTS	RPG	APG	PPG
73-74–K.C.-Omaha	5	–	45	4	10	.400	–	–	–	4	4	1.000	0	3	3	2	4	0	1	–	0	12	0.6	0.4	2.4
Reg. Season Totals	5	–	45	4	10	.400	–	–	–	4	4	1.000	0	3	3	2	4	0	1	–	0	12	0.6	0.4	2.4

Mandic, John J. b. October 3, 1919 Ht. 6-4 Wt. 205 College: Oregon State

SEASON–TEAM	G	GS	MIN	FGM	FGA	PCT	3FGM	3FGA	PCT	FTM	FTA	PCT	O-RB	D-RB	TOT	AST	PF	DQ	STL	TO	BLK	PTS	RPG	APG	PPG
47-48–Rochester (N)	33	–	–	32	–	–	–	–	–	13	23	.565	–	–	–	–	57	–	–	–	–	77	–	–	2.3
48-49–Indianapolis	56	–	–	97	302	.321	–	–	–	75	115	.652	–	–	–	80	151	–	–	–	–	269	–	1.4	4.8
49-50–Wash.-Balt.	25	–	–	22	75	.293	–	–	–	22	32	.688	–	–	–	8	54	–	–	–	–	66	–	0.3	2.6
Reg. NBA Totals	81	–	–	119	377	.316	–	–	–	97	147	.660	–	–	–	88	205	–	–	–	–	335	–	1.1	4.1
Reg. NBL Totals	33	–	–	32	–	–	–	–	–	13	23	.565	–	–	–	–	57	–	–	–	–	77	–	–	2.3
NBL Playoff Totals	5	–	–	2	–	–	–	–	–	2	4	.500	–	–	–	–	9	–	–	–	–	6	–	–	1.2

Mangiapane, Francis E. (Frank) b. August 25, 1925 Ht. 5-10 Wt. 195 College: New York U.

SEASON–TEAM	G	GS	MIN	FGM	FGA	PCT	3FGM	3FGA	PCT	FTM	FTA	PCT	O-RB	D-RB	TOT	AST	PF	DQ	STL	TO	BLK	PTS	RPG	APG	PPG
46-47–New York	6	–	–	2	13	.154	–	–	–	1	3	.333	–	–	–	0	6	–	–	–	–	5	–	0.0	0.8
Reg. Season Totals	6	–	–	2	13	.154	–	–	–	1	3	.333	–	–	–	0	6	–	–	–	–	5	–	0.0	0.8

Manning, Daniel Ricardo (Danny, D.) b. May 17, 1966 Ht. 6-10 Wt. 244 College: Kansas

SEASON–TEAM	G	GS	MIN	FGM	FGA	PCT	3FGM	3FGA	PCT	FTM	FTA	PCT	O-RB	D-RB	TOT	AST	PF	DQ	STL	TO	BLK	PTS	RPG	APG	PPG
88-89–L.A. Clippers	26	18	950	177	358	.494	1	5	.200	79	103	.767	70	101	171	81	89	1	44	93	25	434	6.6	3.1	16.7
89-90–L.A. Clippers	71	42	2269	440	826	.533	0	5	.000	274	370	.741	142	280	422	187	261	4	91	188	39	1154	5.9	2.6	16.3
90-91–L.A. Clippers	73	47	2197	470	905	.519	0	3	.000	219	306	.716	169	257	426	196	281	5	117	188	62	1159	5.8	2.7	15.9
91-92–L.A. Clippers	82	82	2904	650	1199	.542	0	5	.000	279	385	.725	229	335	564	285	293	5	135	210	122	1579	6.9	3.5	19.3
92-93–L.A. Clippers	79	77	2761	702	1379	.509	8	30	.267	388	484	.802	198	322	520	207	323	8	108	230	101	1800	6.6	2.6	22.8
93-94–LAClips-Atlanta	68	66	2520	586	1201	.488	3	17	.176	228	341	.669	131	334	465	261	260	2	99	233	82	1403	6.8	3.8	20.6
94-95–Phoenix	46	19	1510	340	622	.547	6	21	.286	136	202	.673	97	179	276	154	176	1	41	121	57	822	6.0	3.3	17.9
95-96–Phoenix	33	4	816	178	388	.459	3	14	.214	82	109	.752	30	113	143	65	121	2	38	77	24	441	4.3	2.0	13.4
96-97–Phoenix	77	17	2134	426	795	.536	7	36	.194	181	251	.721	137	332	469	173	268	7	81	161	74	1040	6.1	2.2	13.5
97-98–Phoenix	70	11	1794	390	756	.516	0	7	.000	167	226	.739	110	282	392	139	201	2	71	100	46	947	5.6	2.0	13.5
98-99–Phoenix	50	5	1184	187	386	.484	1	9	.111	78	112	.696	62	157	219	113	129	1	36	69	38	453	4.4	2.3	9.1
99-00–Milwaukee	72	0	1217	149	339	.440	1	4	.250	34	52	.654	50	158	208	73	183	2	62	55	29	333	2.9	1.0	4.6
Reg. Season Totals	747	388	22256	4695	9154	.513	30	156	.192	2145	2941	.729	1425	2850	4275	1934	2585	40	923	1725	699	11565	5.7	2.6	15.5
Playoff Totals	34	22	1081	227	456	.498	1	9	.111	122	159	.767	63	125	188	77	127	3	39	69	26	577	5.5	2.3	17.0
All-Star Totals	2	0	35	9	12	.750	0	0	–	0	0	–	1	7	8	3	5	0	0	0	1	18	4.0	1.5	9.0

Manning, Edward R. (Ed) b. January 2, 1944 Ht. 6-7 Wt. 215 College: Jackson State

SEASON–TEAM	G	GS	MIN	FGM	FGA	PCT	3FGM	3FGA	PCT	FTM	FTA	PCT	O-RB	D-RB	TOT	AST	PF	DQ	STL	TO	BLK	PTS	RPG	APG	PPG
67-68–Baltimore	71	–	951	112	259	.432	–	–	–	60	99	.606	–	–	375	32	153	3	–	–	–	284	5.3	0.5	4.0
68-69–Baltimore	63	–	727	129	288	.448	–	–	–	35	54	.648	–	–	246	21	120	0	–	–	–	293	3.9	0.3	4.7
69-70–Balt.-Chicago	67	–	777	119	321	.371	–	–	–	42	56	.750	–	–	232	36	122	1	–	–	–	280	3.5	0.5	4.2
70-71–Portland	79	–	1558	243	559	.435	–	–	–	75	93	.806	–	–	411	111	198	3	–	–	–	561	5.2	1.4	7.1
71-72–Carolina (A)	77	–	1648	228	499	.457	0	3	.000	95	114	.833	–	–	441	58	227	–	–	83	–	551	5.7	0.8	7.2
72-73–Carolina (A)	83	–	1631	263	554	.475	0	1	.000	64	84	.762	110	283	393	64	247	4	–	84	–	590	4.7	0.8	7.1
73-74–Carolina (A)	82	–	1816	297	609	.488	1	2	.500	86	101	.851	105	265	370	100	210	–	93	95	16	681	4.5	1.2	8.3
74-75–New York (A)	70	–	992	103	243	.424	0	2	.000	35	42	.833	59	153	212	58	144	–	40	57	9	241	3.0	0.8	3.4
75-76–Indiana (A)	12	–	134	24	60	.400	0	0	–	12	17	.706	15	22	37	14	18	–	4	7	2	60	3.1	1.2	5.0
Reg. NBA Totals	280	–	4013	603	1427	.423	–	–	–	212	302	.702	–	–	1264	200	593	7	–	–	–	1418	4.5	0.7	5.1
Reg. ABA Totals	324	–	6221	915	1965	.466	1	8	.125	292	358	.816	289	723	1453	294	846	4	137	326	27	2123	4.5	0.9	6.6
NBA Playoff Totals	6	–	92	12	28	.429	–	–	–	1	2	.500	–	–	32	4	13	0	–	–	–	25	5.3	0.7	4.2
ABA Playoff Totals	19	–	361	64	126	.508	1	2	.500	24	29	.828	4	10	71	8	53	0	0	18	1	153	3.7	0.4	8.1

Manning, Guy R. b. February 4, 1944 Ht. 6-6 Wt. 205 College: Prairie View A&M

SEASON–TEAM	G	GS	MIN	FGM	FGA	PCT	3FGM	3FGA	PCT	FTM	FTA	PCT	O-RB	D-RB	TOT	AST	PF	DQ	STL	TO	BLK	PTS	RPG	APG	PPG
67-68–Houston (A)	59	–	1107	206	502	.410	2	6	.333	115	199	.578	–	–	311	37	151	4	–	53	–	529	5.3	0.6	9.0
68-69–Houston (A)	14	–	167	27	95	.284	0	2	.000	21	37	.568	–	–	42	2	20	0	–	12	–	75	3.0	0.1	5.4
Reg. ABA Totals	73	–	1274	233	597	.390	2	8	.250	136	236	.576	–	–	353	39	171	4	–	65	–	604	4.8	0.5	8.3
ABA Playoff Totals	3	–	66	15	34	.441	0	0	–	11	19	.579	–	–	19	2	11	0	–	5	–	41	6.3	0.7	13.7

Manning, Richard Alan (Rich) b. June 23, 1970 Ht. 6-11 Wt. 260 College: Washington

SEASON–TEAM	G	GS	MIN	FGM	FGA	PCT	3FGM	3FGA	PCT	FTM	FTA	PCT	O-RB	D-RB	TOT	AST	PF	DQ	STL	TO	BLK	PTS	RPG	APG	PPG
95-96–Vancouver	29	0	311	49	113	.434	0	1	.000	9	14	.643	16	39	55	7	37	0	3	17	6	107	1.9	0.2	3.7
96-97–Vanc.-LAClips	26	2	201	32	82	.390	2	4	.500	9	14	.643	16	23	39	3	29	0	4	7	2	75	1.5	0.1	2.9
Reg. Season Totals	55	2	512	81	195	.415	2	5	.400	18	28	.643	32	62	94	10	66	0	7	24	8	182	1.7	0.2	3.3
Playoff Totals	3	0	21	2	9	.222	0	0	–	5	6	.833	3	1	4	1	5	0	0	0	1	9	1.3	0.3	3.0

Mannion, Pace Shewan b. September 22, 1960 Ht. 6-7 Wt. 190 College: Utah

SEASON–TEAM	G	GS	MIN	FGM	FGA	PCT	3FGM	3FGA	PCT	FTM	FTA	PCT	O-RB	D-RB	TOT	AST	PF	DQ	STL	TO	BLK	PTS	RPG	APG	PPG
83-84–Golden State	57	0	469	50	126	.397	3	13	.231	18	23	.783	23	36	59	47	63	0	25	23	2	121	1.0	0.8	2.1
84-85–Utah	34	0	190	27	63	.429	0	1	.000	16	23	.696	12	11	23	27	17	0	16	18	3	70	0.7	0.8	2.1
85-86–Utah	57	0	673	97	214	.453	8	42	.190	53	82	.646	26	56	82	55	68	0	32	41	5	255	1.4	1.0	4.5
86-87–New Jersey	23	3	284	31	94	.330	3	9	.333	18	31	.581	10	29	39	45	32	0	18	23	4	83	1.7	2.0	3.6
87-88–Milwaukee	35	1	477	48	118	.407	2	12	.167	25	37	.676	17	34	51	55	53	0	13	24	7	123	1.5	1.6	3.5
88-89–Detroit-Atlanta	10	0	32	4	8	.500	0	2	.000	0	0	–	0	5	5	2	5	0	3	3	0	8	0.5	0.2	0.8
Reg. Season Totals	216	4	2125	257	623	.413	16	79	.203	130	196	.663	88	171	259	231	238	0	107	132	21	660	1.2	1.1	3.1
Playoff Totals	8	0	41	4	12	.333	0	1	.000	10	12	.833	3	4	7	4	5	0	1	7	2	18	0.9	0.5	2.3

Mantis, Nicholas (Nick) b. December 7, 1935 Ht. 6-3 Wt. 190 College: Northwestern

SEASON–TEAM	G	GS	MIN	FGM	FGA	PCT	3FGM	3FGA	PCT	FTM	FTA	PCT	O-RB	D-RB	TOT	AST	PF	DQ	STL	TO	BLK	PTS	RPG	APG	PPG
59-60–Minneapolis	10	–	71	10	39	.256	–	–	–	1	2	.500	–	–	6	9	8	0	–	–	–	21	0.6	0.9	2.1
62-63–St. L.-Chicago	32	–	684	94	244	.385	–	–	–	27	49	.551	–	–	85	83	94	0	–	–	–	215	2.7	2.6	6.7
Reg. Season Totals	42	–	755	104	283	.367	–	–	–	28	51	.549	–	–	91	92	102	0	–	–	–	236	2.2	2.2	5.6

Maravich, Peter (Press) b. August 20, 1920 d. April 15, 1987 Ht. 6-0 Wt. 185 College: Davis & Elkins

SEASON–TEAM	G	GS	MIN	FGM	FGA	PCT	3FGM	3FGA	PCT	FTM	FTA	PCT	O-RB	D-RB	TOT	AST	PF	DQ	STL	TO	BLK	PTS	RPG	APG	PPG
45-46–Youngstown (N)	32	–	–	72	–	–	–	–	–	34	51	.667	–	–	–	–	76	–	–	–	–	178	–	–	5.6
46-47–Pittsburgh	51	–	–	102	375	.272	–	–	–	30	58	.517	–	–	–	6	102	–	–	–	–	234	–	0.1	4.6
Reg. NBA Totals	51	–	–	102	375	.272	–	–	–	30	58	.517	–	–	–	6	102	–	–	–	–	234	–	0.1	4.6
Reg. NBL Totals	32	–	–	72	–	–	–	–	–	34	51	.667	–	–	–	–	76	–	–	–	–	178	–	–	5.6

Maravich, Peter Press (Pete, Pistol Pete) b. June 22, 1947 d. January 5, 1988 Ht. 6-5 Wt. 200 College: Louisiana State HOF: 1986

SEASON–TEAM	G	GS	MIN	FGM	FGA	PCT	3FGM	3FGA	PCT	FTM	FTA	PCT	O-RB	D-RB	TOT	AST	PF	DQ	STL	TO	BLK	PTS	RPG	APG	PPG
70-71–Atlanta	81	–	2926	738	1613	.458	–	–	–	404	505	.800	–	–	298	355	238	1	–	–	–	1880	3.7	4.4	23.2
71-72–Atlanta	66	–	2302	460	1077	.427	–	–	–	355	438	.811	–	–	256	393	207	0	–	–	–	1275	3.9	6.0	19.3
72-73–Atlanta	79	–	3089	789	1788	.441	–	–	–	485	606	.800	–	–	346	546	245	1	–	–	–	2063	4.4	6.9	26.1
73-74–Atlanta	76	–	2903	819	1791	.457	–	–	–	469	568	.826	98	276	374	396	261	4	111	–	13	2107	4.9	5.2	27.7
74-75–New Orleans	79	–	2853	655	1562	.419	–	–	–	390	481	.811	93	329	422	488	227	4	120	–	18	1700	5.3	6.2	21.5
75-76–New Orleans	62	–	2373	604	1316	.459	–	–	–	396	488	.811	46	254	300	332	197	3	87	–	23	1604	4.8	5.4	25.9
76-77–New Orleans	73	–	3041	886	2047	.433	–	–	–	501	600	.835	90	284	374	392	191	1	84	–	22	2273	5.1	5.4	31.1
77-78–New Orleans	50	–	2041	556	1253	.444	–	–	–	240	276	.870	49	129	178	335	116	1	101	248	8	1352	3.6	6.7	27.0
78-79–New Orleans	49	–	1824	436	1035	.421	–	–	–	233	277	.841	33	88	121	243	104	2	60	200	18	1105	2.5	5.0	22.6
79-80–Utah-Boston	43	–	964	244	543	.449	10	15	.667	91	105	.867	17	61	78	83	79	1	24	82	6	589	1.8	1.9	13.7
Reg. Season Totals	658	–	24316	6187	14025	.441	10	15	.667	3564	4344	.820	426	1421	2747	3563	1865	18	587	530	108	15948	4.2	5.4	24.2
Playoff Totals	26	–	756	190	449	.423	2	6	.333	105	134	.784	0	8	95	98	74	1	3	9	0	487	3.7	3.8	18.7
All-Star Totals	4	–	79	18	44	.409	0	0	–	7	9	.778	1	4	8	15	8	0	4	4	0	43	2.0	3.8	10.8

Marble, Roy Lane Jr. b. December 13, 1966 Ht. 6-6 Wt. 190 College: Iowa

SEASON–TEAM	G	GS	MIN	FGM	FGA	PCT	3FGM	3FGA	PCT	FTM	FTA	PCT	O-RB	D-RB	TOT	AST	PF	DQ	STL	TO	BLK	PTS	RPG	APG	PPG
89-90–Atlanta	24	0	162	16	58	.276	0	2	.000	19	29	.655	15	9	24	11	16	0	7	14	1	51	1.0	0.5	2.1
93-94–Denver	5	0	32	2	12	.167	0	0	–	0	3	.000	3	5	8	1	1	0	0	3	2	4	1.6	0.2	0.8
Reg. Season Totals	29	0	194	18	70	.257	0	2	.000	19	32	.594	18	14	32	12	17	0	7	17	3	55	1.1	0.4	1.9

Marbury, Stephon Xzavior b. February 20, 1977 Ht. 6-2 Wt. 180 College: Georgia Tech

SEASON–TEAM	G	GS	MIN	FGM	FGA	PCT	3FGM	3FGA	PCT	FTM	FTA	PCT	O-RB	D-RB	TOT	AST	PF	DQ	STL	TO	BLK	PTS	RPG	APG	PPG
96-97–Minnesota	67	64	2324	355	871	.408	102	288	.354	245	337	.727	54	130	184	522	159	2	67	210	19	1057	2.7	7.8	15.8
97-98–Minnesota	82	81	3112	513	1237	.415	95	304	.313	329	450	.731	58	172	230	704	222	0	104	256	7	1450	2.8	8.6	17.7
98-99–Minn.-N.J.	49	49	1895	378	883	.428	66	197	.335	222	278	.799	37	105	142	437	125	0	59	164	8	1044	2.9	8.9	21.3
99-00–New Jersey	74	74	2881	569	1317	.432	66	233	.283	436	536	.813	61	179	240	622	195	4	112	270	15	1640	3.2	8.4	22.2
Reg. Season Totals	272	268	10212	1815	4308	.421	329	1022	.322	1232	1601	.770	210	586	796	2285	701	6	342	900	49	5191	2.9	8.4	19.1
Playoff Totals	8	8	326	48	137	.350	13	45	.289	24	33	.727	7	21	28	61	25	0	14	27	0	133	3.5	7.6	16.6

Marciulionis, Raimondas Sarunas (Sarunas, Rooney) b. June 13, 1964 Ht. 6-5 Wt. 215 Country: Lithuania

SEASON–TEAM	G	GS	MIN	FGM	FGA	PCT	3FGM	3FGA	PCT	FTM	FTA	PCT	O-RB	D-RB	TOT	AST	PF	DQ	STL	TO	BLK	PTS	RPG	APG	PPG
89-90–Golden State	75	3	1695	289	557	.519	10	39	.256	317	403	.787	84	137	221	121	230	5	94	137	7	905	2.9	1.6	12.1
90-91–Golden State	50	10	987	183	365	.501	1	6	.167	178	246	.724	51	67	118	85	136	4	62	75	4	545	2.4	1.7	10.9
91-92–Golden State	72	5	2117	491	912	.538	3	10	.300	376	477	.788	68	140	208	243	237	4	116	193	10	1361	2.9	3.4	18.9
92-93–Golden State	30	8	836	178	328	.543	3	15	.200	162	213	.761	40	57	97	105	92	1	51	76	2	521	3.2	3.5	17.4
94-95–Seattle	66	4	1194	216	457	.473	35	87	.402	145	198	.732	17	51	68	110	126	1	72	98	3	612	1.0	1.7	9.3
95-96–Sacramento	53	0	1039	176	389	.452	64	157	.408	155	200	.775	20	57	77	118	112	1	52	96	4	571	1.5	2.2	10.8
96-97–Denver	17	0	255	38	101	.376	11	30	.367	29	36	.806	12	18	30	25	38	0	12	40	1	116	1.8	1.5	6.8
Reg. Season Totals	363	30	8123	1571	3109	.505	127	344	.369	1362	1773	.768	292	527	819	807	971	16	459	715	31	4631	2.3	2.2	12.8
Playoff Totals	17	0	440	75	160	.469	5	21	.238	78	95	.821	15	24	39	61	40	1	24	28	2	233	2.3	3.6	13.7

Mariaschin, Saul George b. September 1, 1924 Ht. 5-11 Wt. 165 College: Bloomsburg; Syracuse; Harvard

SEASON–TEAM	G	GS	MIN	FGM	FGA	PCT	3FGM	3FGA	PCT	FTM	FTA	PCT	O-RB	D-RB	TOT	AST	PF	DQ	STL	TO	BLK	PTS	RPG	APG	PPG
47-48–Boston	43	–	–	125	463	.270	–	–	–	83	117	.709	–	–	–	60	121	–	–	–	–	333	–	1.4	7.7
Reg. Season Totals	43	–	–	125	463	.270	–	–	–	83	117	.709	–	–	–	60	121	–	–	–	–	333	–	1.4	7.7
Playoff Totals	3	–	–	10	84	.238	–	–	–	9	14	.643	–	–	–	2	24	–	–	–	–	29	–	0.3	9.7

Marin, John Warren (Jack) b. October 12, 1944 Ht. 6-6 Wt. 200 College: Duke

SEASON–TEAM	G	GS	MIN	FGM	FGA	PCT	3FGM	3FGA	PCT	FTM	FTA	PCT	O-RB	D-RB	TOT	AST	PF	DQ	STL	TO	BLK	PTS	RPG	APG	PPG
66-67–Baltimore	74	–	1323	283	632	.448	–	–	–	145	187	.775	–	–	313	75	199	6	–	–	–	711	4.2	1.0	9.6
67-68–Baltimore	82	–	2037	429	932	.460	–	–	–	250	314	.796	–	–	473	110	246	4	–	–	–	1108	5.8	1.3	13.5
68-69–Baltimore	82	–	2710	505	1109	.455	–	–	–	292	352	.830	–	–	608	231	275	4	–	–	–	1302	7.4	2.8	15.9
69-70–Baltimore	82	–	2947	666	1363	.489	–	–	–	286	339	.844	–	–	537	217	248	6	–	–	–	1618	6.5	2.6	19.7
70-71–Baltimore	82	–	2920	626	1360	.460	–	–	–	290	342	.848	–	–	513	217	261	3	–	–	–	1542	6.3	2.6	18.8
71-72–Baltimore	78	–	2927	690	1444	.478	–	–	–	356	398	.894	–	–	528	169	240	2	–	–	–	1736	6.8	2.2	22.3
72-73–Houston	81	–	3019	624	1334	.468	–	–	–	248	292	.849	–	–	499	291	247	4	–	–	–	1496	6.2	3.6	18.5
73-74–Hou.-Buffalo	74	–	1782	355	709	.501	–	–	–	153	179	.855	59	169	228	167	213	5	46	–	26	863	3.1	2.3	11.7
74-75–Buffalo	81	–	2147	380	836	.455	–	–	–	193	222	.869	104	259	363	133	238	7	51	–	16	953	4.5	1.6	11.8
75-76–Buffalo-Chi.	79	–	1909	343	812	.422	–	–	–	161	188	.856	69	183	252	141	164	0	45	–	11	847	3.2	1.8	10.7
76-77–Chicago	54	–	869	167	359	.465	–	–	–	31	39	.795	27	64	91	62	85	0	13	–	6	365	1.7	1.1	6.8
Reg. Season Totals	849	–	24590	5068	10890	.465	–	–	–	2405	2852	.843	259	675	4405	1813	2416	41	155	–	59	12541	5.2	2.1	14.8
Playoff Totals	51	–	1679	292	649	.450	–	–	–	173	210	.824	10	27	283	120	151	2	9	–	1	757	5.5	2.4	14.8
All-Star Totals	2	–	26	7	14	.500	–	–	–	1	1	1.000	0	0	4	2	2	0	0	–	0	15	2.0	1.0	7.5

Marion, Shawn Dwayne b. May 7, 1978 Ht. 6-7 Wt. 215 College: Nevada-Las Vegas

SEASON–TEAM	G	GS	MIN	FGM	FGA	PCT	3FGM	3FGA	PCT	FTM	FTA	PCT	O-RB	D-RB	TOT	AST	PF	DQ	STL	TO	BLK	PTS	RPG	APG	PPG
99-00–Phoenix	51	38	1260	222	471	.471	4	22	.182	72	85	.847	105	227	332	69	113	0	38	51	53	520	6.5	1.4	10.2
Reg. Season Totals	51	38	1260	222	471	.471	4	22	.182	72	85	.847	105	227	332	69	113	0	38	51	53	520	6.5	1.4	10.2
Playoff Totals	9	9	281	36	86	.419	1	6	.167	9	11	.818	21	58	79	7	17	0	6	7	14	82	8.8	0.8	9.1

Marks, Sean Andrew b. August 23, 1975 Ht. 6-10 Wt. 250 College: California

SEASON–TEAM	G	GS	MIN	FGM	FGA	PCT	3FGM	3FGA	PCT	FTM	FTA	PCT	O-RB	D-RB	TOT	AST	PF	DQ	STL	TO	BLK	PTS	RPG	APG	PPG
98-99–Toronto	8	0	28	5	8	.625	0	0	–	1	2	.500	0	1	1	0	3	0	1	3	0	11	0.1	0.0	1.4
99-00–Toronto	5	0	12	2	6	.333	0	1	.000	4	4	1.000	0	2	2	0	3	0	1	3	1	8	0.4	0.0	1.6
Reg. Season Totals	13	0	40	7	14	.500	0	1	.000	5	6	.833	0	3	3	0	6	0	2	6	1	19	0.2	0.0	1.5

Marlatt, Harvey W. b. August 26, 1948 Ht. 6-3 Wt. 185 College: Eastern Michigan

SEASON–TEAM	G	GS	MIN	FGM	FGA	PCT	3FGM	3FGA	PCT	FTM	FTA	PCT	O-RB	D-RB	TOT	AST	PF	DQ	STL	TO	BLK	PTS	RPG	APG	PPG
70-71–Detroit	23	–	214	25	80	.313	–	–	–	15	18	.833	–	–	23	30	27	0	–	–	–	65	1.0	1.3	2.8
71-72–Detroit	31	–	506	60	149	.403	–	–	–	36	42	.857	–	–	62	60	64	1	–	–	–	156	2.0	1.9	5.0
72-73–Detroit	7	–	26	2	4	.500	–	–	–	0	0	–	–	–	1	4	1	0	–	–	–	4	0.1	0.6	0.6
Reg. Season Totals	61	–	746	87	233	.373	–	–	–	51	60	.850	–	–	86	94	92	1	–	–	–	225	1.4	1.5	3.7

Marsh, Eric Clifton (Ricky) b. March 10, 1954 Ht. 6-3 Wt. 200 College: Nebraska; Manhattan

SEASON–TEAM	G	GS	MIN	FGM	FGA	PCT	3FGM	3FGA	PCT	FTM	FTA	PCT	O-RB	D-RB	TOT	AST	PF	DQ	STL	TO	BLK	PTS	RPG	APG	PPG
77-78–Golden State	60	–	851	123	289	.426	–	–	–	23	33	.697	16	59	75	90	111	0	29	50	19	269	1.3	1.5	4.5
Reg. Season Totals	60	–	851	123	289	.426	–	–	–	23	33	.697	16	59	75	90	111	0	29	50	19	269	1.3	1.5	4.5

Marsh, James (Jim) b. April 26, 1946 Ht. 6-7 Wt. 215 College: USC

SEASON–TEAM	G	GS	MIN	FGM	FGA	PCT	3FGM	3FGA	PCT	FTM	FTA	PCT	O-RB	D-RB	TOT	AST	PF	DQ	STL	TO	BLK	PTS	RPG	APG	PPG
71-72–Portland	39	–	375	39	117	.333	–	–	–	41	59	.695	–	–	84	30	50	0	–	–	–	119	2.2	0.8	3.1
Reg. Season Totals	39	–	375	39	117	.333	–	–	–	41	59	.695	–	–	84	30	50	0	–	–	–	119	2.2	0.8	3.1

Marshall, Donny E. b. July 17, 1972 Ht. 6-7 Wt. 230 College: Connecticut

SEASON–TEAM	G	GS	MIN	FGM	FGA	PCT	3FGM	3FGA	PCT	FTM	FTA	PCT	O-RB	D-RB	TOT	AST	PF	DQ	STL	TO	BLK	PTS	RPG	APG	PPG
95-96–Cleveland	34	0	208	24	68	.353	7	30	.233	22	35	.629	9	17	26	7	26	0	8	7	2	77	0.8	0.2	2.3
96-97–Cleveland	56	0	548	52	160	.325	33	87	.379	38	54	.704	22	48	70	24	60	0	24	32	3	175	1.3	0.4	3.1
99-00–Cleveland	6	0	39	3	11	.273	0	3	.000	5	6	.833	0	1	1	0	7	0	2	3	0	11	0.2	0.0	1.8
Reg. Season Totals	96	0	795	79	239	.331	40	120	.333	65	95	.684	31	66	97	31	93	0	34	42	5	263	1.0	0.3	2.7
Playoff Totals	1	0	1	0	0	–	0	0	–	0	0	–	0	0	0	–	0	0	0	0	0	0	0.0	0.0	0.0

Marshall, Donyell Lamar b. May 18, 1973 Ht. 6-9 Wt. 230 College: Connecticut

SEASON–TEAM	G	GS	MIN	FGM	FGA	PCT	3FGM	3FGA	PCT	FTM	FTA	PCT	O-RB	D-RB	TOT	AST	PF	DQ	STL	TO	BLK	PTS	RPG	APG	PPG
94-95–Minn.-G.S.	72	31	2086	345	876	.394	69	243	.284	147	222	.662	137	268	405	105	157	1	45	115	88	906	5.6	1.5	12.6
95-96–Golden State	62	6	934	125	314	.398	28	94	.298	64	83	.771	65	148	213	49	83	0	22	48	31	342	3.4	0.8	5.5
96-97–Golden State	61	20	1022	174	421	.413	35	111	.315	61	98	.622	92	184	276	54	96	0	25	55	46	444	4.5	0.9	7.3
97-98–Golden State	73	73	2611	451	1090	.414	63	201	.313	158	216	.731	210	418	628	159	226	1	95	147	73	1123	8.6	2.2	15.4
98-99–Golden State	48	20	1250	208	494	.421	26	72	.361	88	121	.727	115	227	342	66	123	1	47	80	37	530	7.1	1.4	11.0
99-00–Golden State	64	51	2071	331	840	.394	49	138	.355	199	255	.780	189	448	637	167	180	1	68	123	68	910	10.0	2.6	14.2
Reg. Season Totals	380	201	9974	1634	4035	.405	270	859	.314	717	995	.721	808	1693	2501	600	865	4	302	568	343	4255	6.6	1.6	11.2

Marshall, John Thomas (Tom) b. January 6, 1931 Ht. 6-4 Wt. 215 College: Western Kentucky

SEASON–TEAM	G	GS	MIN	FGM	FGA	PCT	3FGM	3FGA	PCT	FTM	FTA	PCT	O-RB	D-RB	TOT	AST	PF	DQ	STL	TO	BLK	PTS	RPG	APG	PPG
54-55–Rochester	72	–	1337	223	505	.442	–	–	–	131	194	.675	–	–	256	111	99	0	–	–	–	577	3.6	1.5	8.0
56-57–Rochester	40	–	460	56	163	.344	–	–	–	47	58	.810	–	–	83	31	33	0	–	–	–	159	2.1	0.8	4.0
57-58–Detroit-Cin.	38	–	518	52	166	.313	–	–	–	48	63	.762	–	–	101	19	43	0	–	–	–	152	2.7	0.5	4.0
58-59–Cincinnati	18	–	272	23	79	.291	–	–	–	18	29	.621	–	–	52	27	22	0	–	–	–	64	2.9	1.5	3.6
Reg. Season Totals	168	–	2587	354	913	.388	–	–	–	244	344	.709	–	–	492	188	197	0	–	–	–	952	2.9	1.1	5.7
Playoff Totals	5	–	83	10	37	.270	–	–	–	7	10	.700	–	–	33	4	2	0	–	–	–	27	6.6	0.8	5.4

Marshall, Vester b. December 22, 1948 Ht. 6-7 Wt. 200 College: Oklahoma

SEASON–TEAM	G	GS	MIN	FGM	FGA	PCT	3FGM	3FGA	PCT	FTM	FTA	PCT	O-RB	D-RB	TOT	AST	PF	DQ	STL	TO	BLK	PTS	RPG	APG	PPG
73-74–Seattle	13	–	174	7	29	.241	–	–	–	3	7	.429	14	23	37	4	20	0	4	–	3	17	2.8	0.3	1.3
Reg. Season Totals	13	–	174	7	29	.241	–	–	–	3	7	.429	14	23	37	4	20	0	4	–	3	17	2.8	0.3	1.3

Martin, Brian b. August 18, 1962 Ht. 6-9 Wt. 215 College: Hutchinson (Kan.) C.C.; Kansas

SEASON–TEAM	G	GS	MIN	FGM	FGA	PCT	3FGM	3FGA	PCT	FTM	FTA	PCT	O-RB	D-RB	TOT	AST	PF	DQ	STL	TO	BLK	PTS	RPG	APG	PPG
85-86–Seattle-Port.	8	0	21	3	7	.429	0	0	–	0	2	.000	1	3	4	0	7	0	0	2	1	6	0.5	0.0	0.8
Reg. Season Totals	8	0	21	3	7	.429	0	0	–	0	2	.000	1	3	4	0	7	0	0	2	1	6	0.5	0.0	0.8

Martin, Cuonzo LaMar b. September 23, 1971 Ht. 6-6 Wt. 215 College: Purdue

SEASON–TEAM	G	GS	MIN	FGM	FGA	PCT	3FGM	3FGA	PCT	FTM	FTA	PCT	O-RB	D-RB	TOT	AST	PF	DQ	STL	TO	BLK	PTS	RPG	APG	PPG
95-96–Vancouver	4	0	19	3	5	.600	3	3	1.000	0	2	.000	1	1	2	2	1	0	1	1	0	9	0.5	0.5	2.3
96-97–Milwaukee	3	0	13	0	7	.000	0	2	.000	0	0	–	1	0	1	1	1	0	0	1	0	0	0.3	0.3	0.0
Reg. Season Totals	7	0	32	3	12	.250	3	5	.600	0	2	.000	2	1	3	3	2	0	1	2	0	9	0.4	0.4	1.3

Martin, Darrick David b. March 6, 1971 Ht. 5-11 Wt. 170 College: UCLA

SEASON–TEAM	G	GS	MIN	FGM	FGA	PCT	3FGM	3FGA	PCT	FTM	FTA	PCT	O-RB	D-RB	TOT	AST	PF	DQ	STL	TO	BLK	PTS	RPG	APG	PPG
94-95–Minnesota	34	9	803	95	233	.408	7	38	.184	57	65	.877	14	50	64	133	88	0	34	62	0	254	1.9	3.9	7.5
95-96–Vanc.-Minn.	59	16	1149	147	362	.406	20	69	.290	101	120	.842	16	66	82	217	123	0	53	107	3	415	1.4	3.7	7.0
96-97–L.A. Clippers	82	64	1820	292	718	.407	91	234	.389	218	250	.872	26	87	113	339	165	1	57	127	2	893	1.4	4.1	10.9
97-98–L.A. Clippers	82	63	2299	275	730	.377	107	293	.365	184	217	.848	19	145	164	331	198	2	82	154	10	841	2.0	4.0	10.3
98-99–L.A. Clippers	37	25	941	102	278	.367	31	106	.292	61	76	.803	5	43	48	144	82	1	43	67	4	296	1.3	3.9	8.0
99-00–Sacramento	71	1	893	133	350	.380	38	124	.306	98	119	.824	7	37	44	122	89	0	28	62	2	402	0.6	1.7	5.7
Reg. Season Totals	365	178	7905	1044	2671	.391	294	864	.340	719	847	.849	87	428	515	1286	745	4	297	579	21	3101	1.4	3.5	8.5
Playoff Totals	5	3	98	14	34	.412	6	12	.500	9	13	.692	2	3	5	15	13	0	1	5	0	43	1.0	3.0	8.6

Martin, Donald E. (Dino) b. May 25, 1920 d. July 24, 1999 Ht. 5-9 Wt. 160 College: Georgetown

SEASON–TEAM	G	GS	MIN	FGM	FGA	PCT	3FGM	3FGA	PCT	FTM	FTA	PCT	O-RB	D-RB	TOT	AST	PF	DQ	STL	TO	BLK	PTS	RPG	APG	PPG
46-47–Providence	60	–	–	311	1022	.304	–	–	–	111	168	.661	–	–	–	59	98	–	–	–	–	733	–	1.0	12.2
47-48–Providence	32	–	–	46	193	.238	–	–	–	9	20	.450	–	–	–	14	17	–	–	–	–	101	–	0.4	3.2
Reg. Season Totals	92	–	–	357	1215	.294	–	–	–	120	188	.638	–	–	–	73	115	–	–	–	–	834	–	0.8	9.1

Martin, Fernando b. March 25, 1962 d. December 3, 1989 Ht. 6-10 Wt. 240 Country: Spain

SEASON–TEAM	G	GS	MIN	FGM	FGA	PCT	3FGM	3FGA	PCT	FTM	FTA	PCT	O-RB	D-RB	TOT	AST	PF	DQ	STL	TO	BLK	PTS	RPG	APG	PPG
86-87–Portland	24	0	146	9	31	.290	0	1	.000	4	11	.364	8	20	28	9	24	0	7	20	1	22	1.2	0.4	0.9
Reg. Season Totals	24	0	146	9	31	.290	0	1	.000	4	11	.364	8	20	28	9	24	0	7	20	1	22	1.2	0.4	0.9
Playoff Totals	1	0	1	0	1	.000	0	0	–	0	0	–	0	0	0	–	0	0	0	0	0	0	0.0	0.0	0.0

Martin, James Donald (Don) b. February 7, 1920 d. July 24, 1999 Ht. 6-7 Wt. 210 College: Central Missouri State

SEASON–TEAM	G	GS	MIN	FGM	FGA	PCT	3FGM	3FGA	PCT	FTM	FTA	PCT	O-RB	D-RB	TOT	AST	PF	DQ	STL	TO	BLK	PTS	RPG	APG	PPG
46-47–St. Louis	54	–	–	89	304	.293	–	–	–	13	31	.419	–	–	–	9	75	–	–	–	–	191	–	0.2	3.5
47-48–St. Louis	39	–	–	35	150	.233	–	–	–	15	33	.455	–	–	–	2	61	–	–	–	–	85	–	0.1	2.2
48-49–St. L.-Balt.	44	–	–	52	170	.306	–	–	–	30	47	.638	–	–	–	25	115	–	–	–	–	134	–	0.6	3.0
Reg. Season Totals	137	–	–	176	624	.282	–	–	–	58	111	.523	–	–	–	36	251	–	–	–	–	410	–	0.3	3.0
Playoff Totals	9	–	–	9	92	.141	–	–	–	3	1	–	–	–	–	3	19	1	–	–	–	21	0.0	0.3	2.3

Martin, Jeffery Allen (Jeff) b. January 14, 1967 Ht. 6-5 Wt. 195 College: Murray State

SEASON–TEAM	G	GS	MIN	FGM	FGA	PCT	3FGM	3FGA	PCT	FTM	FTA	PCT	O-RB	D-RB	TOT	AST	PF	DQ	STL	TO	BLK	PTS	RPG	APG	PPG
89-90–L.A. Clippers	69	23	1351	170	414	.411	2	15	.133	91	129	.705	78	81	159	44	97	0	41	47	16	433	2.3	0.6	6.3
90-91–L.A. Clippers	74	26	1334	214	507	.422	27	88	.307	68	100	.680	53	78	131	65	104	0	37	49	31	523	1.8	0.9	7.1
Reg. Season Totals	143	49	2685	384	921	.417	29	103	.282	159	229	.694	131	159	290	109	201	0	78	96	47	956	2.0	0.8	6.7

Martin, LaRue b. March 30, 1950 Ht. 6-11 Wt. 210 College: Loyola (Chicago)

SEASON–TEAM	G	GS	MIN	FGM	FGA	PCT	3FGM	3FGA	PCT	FTM	FTA	PCT	O-RB	D-RB	TOT	AST	PF	DQ	STL	TO	BLK	PTS	RPG	APG	PPG
72-73–Portland	77	–	996	145	366	.396	–	–	–	50	77	.649	–	–	358	42	162	0	–	–	–	340	4.6	0.5	4.4
73-74–Portland	50	–	538	101	232	.435	–	–	–	42	66	.636	74	107	181	20	90	0	7	–	26	244	3.6	0.4	4.9
74-75–Portland	81	–	1372	236	522	.452	–	–	–	99	142	.697	136	272	408	69	239	5	33	–	49	571	5.0	0.9	7.0
75-76–Portland	63	–	889	109	302	.361	–	–	–	57	77	.740	68	243	311	72	126	1	6	–	23	275	4.9	1.1	4.4
Reg. Season Totals	271	–	3795	591	1422	.416	–	–	–	248	362	.685	278	622	1258	203	617	6	46	–	98	1430	4.6	0.7	5.3

Martin, Maurice (Mo) b. July 2, 1964 Ht. 6-6 Wt. 200 College: St. Joseph's (Pa.)

SEASON–TEAM	G	GS	MIN	FGM	FGA	PCT	3FGM	3FGA	PCT	FTM	FTA	PCT	O-RB	D-RB	TOT	AST	PF	DQ	STL	TO	BLK	PTS	RPG	APG	PPG
86-87–Denver	43	0	286	51	135	.378	3	15	.200	42	66	.636	12	29	41	35	48	0	13	33	6	147	1.0	0.8	3.4
87-88–Denver	26	0	136	23	61	.377	1	4	.250	10	21	.476	13	11	24	14	21	0	6	10	3	57	0.9	0.5	2.2
Reg. Season Totals	69	0	422	74	196	.378	4	19	.211	52	87	.598	25	40	65	49	69	0	19	43	9	204	0.9	0.7	3.0
Playoff Totals	6	0	63	13	34	.382	0	2	.000	12	18	.667	4	6	10	10	13	0	0	6	2	38	1.7	1.7	6.3

Martin, Phillip Roger (Phil) b. April 2, 1928 Ht. 6-3 Wt. 190 College: Toledo

SEASON–TEAM	G	GS	MIN	FGM	FGA	PCT	3FGM	3FGA	PCT	FTM	FTA	PCT	O-RB	D-RB	TOT	AST	PF	DQ	STL	TO	BLK	PTS	RPG	APG	PPG
54-55–Milwaukee	7	–	47	5	19	.263	–	–	–	2	2	1.000	–	–	10	6	7	0	–	–	–	12	1.4	0.9	1.7
Reg. Season Totals	7	–	47	5	19	.263	–	–	–	2	2	1.000	–	–	10	6	7	0	–	–	–	12	1.4	0.9	1.7

Martin, Robert W. (Bob) b. October 7, 1969 Ht. 7-0 Wt. 255 College: Minnesota

SEASON–TEAM	G	GS	MIN	FGM	FGA	PCT	3FGM	3FGA	PCT	FTM	FTA	PCT	O-RB	D-RB	TOT	AST	PF	DQ	STL	TO	BLK	PTS	RPG	APG	PPG
93-94–L.A. Clippers	53	1	535	40	88	.455	0	0	–	31	51	.608	36	81	117	17	106	1	8	29	33	111	2.2	0.3	2.1
94-95–L.A. Clippers	1	0	14	1	5	.200	0	0	–	0	0	–	2	0	2	1	2	0	0	0	1	2	2.0	1.0	2.0
Reg. Season Totals	54	1	549	41	93	.441	0	0	–	31	51	.608	38	81	119	18	108	1	8	29	34	113	2.2	0.3	2.1

Martin, Ronald Barry (Whitey) b. April 11, 1939 Ht. 6-2 Wt. 185 College: St. Bonaventure

SEASON–TEAM	G	GS	MIN	FGM	FGA	PCT	3FGM	3FGA	PCT	FTM	FTA	PCT	O-RB	D-RB	TOT	AST	PF	DQ	STL	TO	BLK	PTS	RPG	APG	PPG
61-62–New York	66	–	1018	95	292	.325	–	–	–	37	55	.673	–	–	158	115	158	4	–	–	–	227	2.4	1.7	3.4
Reg. Season Totals	66	–	1018	95	292	.325	–	–	–	37	55	.673	–	–	158	115	158	4	–	–	–	227	2.4	1.7	3.4

Martin, Slater Nelson Jr. (Dugie) b. October 22, 1925 Ht. 5-10 Wt. 170 College: Texas HOF: 1981

SEASON–TEAM	G	GS	MIN	FGM	FGA	PCT	3FGM	3FGA	PCT	FTM	FTA	PCT	O-RB	D-RB	TOT	AST	PF	DQ	STL	TO	BLK	PTS	RPG	APG	PPG
49-50–Minneapolis	67	–	–	106	302	.351	–	–	–	59	93	.634	–	–	–	148	162	–	–	–	–	271	–	2.2	4.0
50-51–Minneapolis	68	–	–	227	627	.362	–	–	–	121	177	.684	–	–	246	235	199	3	–	–	–	575	3.6	3.5	8.5
51-52–Minneapolis	66	–	2480	237	632	.375	–	–	–	142	190	.747	–	–	228	249	226	9	–	–	–	616	3.5	3.8	9.3
52-53–Minneapolis	70	–	2556	260	634	.410	–	–	–	224	287	.780	–	–	186	250	246	4	–	–	–	744	2.7	3.6	10.6
53-54–Minneapolis	69	–	2472	254	654	.388	–	–	–	176	243	.724	–	–	166	253	198	3	–	–	–	684	2.4	3.7	9.9
54-55–Minneapolis	72	–	2784	350	919	.381	–	–	–	276	359	.769	–	–	260	427	221	7	–	–	–	976	3.6	5.9	13.6
55-56–Minneapolis	72	–	2838	309	863	.358	–	–	–	329	395	.833	–	–	260	445	202	2	–	–	–	947	3.6	6.2	13.2
56-57–N.Y.-St. Louis	66	–	2401	244	736	.332	–	–	–	230	291	.790	–	–	288	269	193	1	–	–	–	718	4.4	4.1	10.9
57-58–St. Louis	60	–	2098	258	768	.336	–	–	–	206	276	.746	–	–	228	218	187	0	–	–	–	722	3.8	3.6	12.0
58-59–St. Louis	71	–	2504	245	706	.347	–	–	–	197	254	.776	–	–	253	336	230	8	–	–	–	687	3.6	4.7	9.7
59-60–St. Louis	64	–	1756	142	383	.371	–	–	–	113	155	.729	–	–	187	330	174	2	–	–	–	397	2.9	5.2	6.2
Reg. Season Totals	745	–	21889	2632	7224	.364	–	–	–	2073	2720	.762	–	–	2302	3160	2238	39	–	–	–	7337	3.4	4.2	9.8
Playoff Totals	92	–	3711	304	947	.351	–	–	–	317	443	.716	–	–	314	466	343	10	–	–	–	925	3.2	3.8	10.1
All-Star Totals	7	–	180	16	53	.302	–	–	–	8	12	.667	–	–	15	28	19	0	–	–	–	40	2.1	4.0	5.7

Martin, William (Bill) b. August 16, 1962 Ht. 6-7 Wt. 205 College: Georgetown

SEASON–TEAM	G	GS	MIN	FGM	FGA	PCT	3FGM	3FGA	PCT	FTM	FTA	PCT	O-RB	D-RB	TOT	AST	PF	DQ	STL	TO	BLK	PTS	RPG	APG	PPG
85-86–Indiana	66	0	691	143	298	.480	0	8	.000	46	54	.852	42	60	102	52	108	1	21	58	7	332	1.5	0.8	5.0
86-87–New York	8	0	68	9	25	.360	0	0	–	7	8	.875	2	5	7	0	5	0	4	7	2	25	0.9	0.0	3.1
87-88–Phoenix	10	0	101	16	51	.314	0	1	.000	8	13	.615	9	18	27	6	16	0	5	9	0	40	2.7	0.6	4.0
Reg. Season Totals	84	0	860	168	374	.449	0	9	.000	61	75	.813	53	83	136	58	129	1	30	74	9	397	1.6	0.7	4.7

Mashburn, Jamal b. November 29, 1972 Ht. 6-8 Wt. 241 College: Kentucky

SEASON–TEAM	G	GS	MIN	FGM	FGA	PCT	3FGM	3FGA	PCT	FTM	FTA	PCT	O-RB	D-RB	TOT	AST	PF	DQ	STL	TO	BLK	PTS	RPG	APG	PPG
93-94–Dallas	79	73	2896	561	1382	.406	85	299	.284	306	438	.699	107	246	353	266	205	0	89	245	14	1513	4.5	3.4	19.2
94-95–Dallas	80	80	2980	683	1566	.436	113	344	.328	447	605	.739	116	215	331	298	190	0	82	235	8	1926	4.1	3.7	24.1
95-96–Dallas	18	18	669	145	383	.379	35	102	.343	97	133	.729	37	60	97	50	39	0	14	55	3	422	5.4	2.8	23.4
96-97–Dallas-Miami	69	51	2164	286	743	.385	90	277	.325	160	228	.702	69	225	294	204	186	4	78	114	12	822	4.3	3.0	11.9
97-98–Miami	48	48	1729	251	577	.435	37	122	.303	184	231	.797	72	164	236	132	137	1	43	108	14	723	4.9	2.8	15.1
98-99–Miami	24	23	855	134	297	.451	13	30	.433	75	104	.721	24	122	146	75	58	0	20	60	3	356	6.1	3.1	14.8
99-00–Miami	76	76	2828	515	1158	.445	112	278	.403	186	239	.778	64	317	381	298	215	3	79	180	14	1328	5.0	3.9	17.5
Reg. Season Totals	394	369	14121	2575	6106	.422	485	1452	.334	1455	1978	.736	489	1349	1838	1323	1030	8	405	997	68	7090	4.7	3.4	18.0
Playoff Totals	37	35	1258	159	419	.379	45	120	.375	71	95	.747	39	126	165	86	120	4	33	73	5	434	4.5	2.3	11.7

Masino, Alfred Albert (Al) b. February 5, 1928 Ht. 5-11 Wt. 175 College: Canisius

SEASON–TEAM	G	GS	MIN	FGM	FGA	PCT	3FGM	3FGA	PCT	FTM	FTA	PCT	O-RB	D-RB	TOT	AST	PF	DQ	STL	TO	BLK	PTS	RPG	APG	PPG
52-53–Milwaukee	72	–	1773	134	400	.335	–	–	–	128	204	.627	–	–	177	160	252	12	–	–	–	396	2.5	2.2	5.5
53-54–Roch.-Syr.	27	–	181	26	62	.419	–	–	–	30	49	.612	–	–	28	22	44	0	–	–	–	82	1.0	0.8	3.0
Reg. Season Totals	99	–	1954	160	462	.346	–	–	–	158	253	.625	–	–	205	182	296	12	–	–	–	478	2.1	1.8	4.8
Playoff Totals	13	–	96	7	20	.350	–	–	–	7	15	.467	–	–	6	7	23	0	–	–	–	21	0.5	0.5	1.6

Mason, Anthony George Douglas b. December 14, 1966 Ht. 6-8 Wt. 270 College: Tennessee State

SEASON–TEAM	G	GS	MIN	FGM	FGA	PCT	3FGM	3FGA	PCT	FTM	FTA	PCT	O-RB	D-RB	TOT	AST	PF	DQ	STL	TO	BLK	PTS	RPG	APG	PPG
89-90–New Jersey	21	0	108	14	40	.350	0	0	–	9	15	.600	11	23	34	7	20	0	2	11	2	37	1.6	0.3	1.8
90-91–Denver	3	0	21	2	4	.500	0	0	–	6	8	.750	3	2	5	0	6	0	1	0	0	10	1.7	0.0	3.3
91-92–New York	82	0	2198	203	399	.509	0	0	–	167	260	.642	216	357	573	106	229	0	46	101	20	573	7.0	1.3	7.0
92-93–New York	81	0	2482	316	629	.502	0	0	–	199	292	.682	231	409	640	170	240	2	43	137	19	831	7.9	2.1	10.3
93-94–New York	73	12	1903	206	433	.476	0	1	.000	116	161	.720	158	269	427	151	190	2	31	107	9	528	5.8	2.1	7.2
94-95–New York	77	11	2496	287	507	.566	0	1	.000	191	298	.641	182	468	650	240	253	3	69	123	21	765	8.4	3.1	9.9
95-96–New York	82	82	3457	449	798	.563	0	0	–	298	414	.720	220	544	764	363	246	3	69	211	34	1196	9.3	4.4	14.6
96-97–Charlotte	73	73	3143	433	825	.525	1	3	.333	319	428	.745	186	643	829	414	202	3	76	165	33	1186	11.4	5.7	16.2
97-98–Charlotte	81	80	3148	389	764	.509	0	4	.000	261	402	.649	177	649	826	342	182	1	68	146	18	1039	10.2	4.2	12.8
99-00–Charlotte	82	81	3133	317	661	.480	0	1	.000	314	421	.746	145	554	699	367	220	0	74	160	29	948	8.5	4.5	11.6
Reg. Season Totals	655	339	22089	2616	5060	.517	1	10	.100	1880	2699	.697	1529	3918	5447	2160	1788	14	479	1161	185	7113	8.3	3.3	10.9
Playoff Totals	87	24	2837	321	606	.530	0	3	.000	228	345	.661	217	390	607	209	234	2	50	160	27	870	7.0	2.4	10.0

Massenburg, Tony Arnel b. July 13, 1967 Ht. 6-9 Wt. 250 College: Maryland

SEASON–TEAM	G	GS	MIN	FGM	FGA	PCT	3FGM	3FGA	PCT	FTM	FTA	PCT	O-RB	D-RB	TOT	AST	PF	DQ	STL	TO	BLK	PTS	RPG	APG	PPG
90-91–San Antonio	35	0	161	27	60	.450	0	0	–	28	45	.622	23	35	58	4	26	0	4	13	9	82	1.7	0.1	2.3
91-92–S.A.-Cha.-Bos.-G.S.	18	0	90	10	25	.400	0	0	–	9	15	.600	7	18	25	0	21	0	1	9	1	29	1.4	0.0	1.6
94-95–L.A. Clippers	80	50	2127	282	601	.469	0	3	.000	177	235	.753	160	295	455	67	253	2	48	118	58	741	5.7	0.8	9.3
95-96–Toronto-Phil.	54	28	1463	214	432	.495	0	3	.000	111	157	.707	127	225	352	30	140	0	28	73	20	539	6.5	0.6	10.0
96-97–New Jersey	79	49	1954	219	452	.485	0	1	.000	130	206	.631	222	295	517	23	217	2	38	91	50	568	6.5	0.3	7.2
97-98–Vancouver	61	13	894	148	309	.479	0	0	–	100	137	.730	80	152	232	21	123	0	25	60	24	396	3.8	0.3	6.5
98-99–Vancouver	43	35	1143	189	388	.487	0	2	.000	103	155	.665	83	174	257	23	108	0	26	64	39	481	6.0	0.5	11.2
99-00–Houston	10	0	109	16	36	.444	0	0	–	14	16	.875	7	20	27	3	13	0	2	9	5	46	2.7	0.3	4.6
Reg. Season Totals	380	175	7941	1105	2303	.480	0	9	.000	672	966	.696	709	1214	1923	171	901	4	172	437	206	2882	5.1	0.5	7.6
Playoff Totals	1	0	1	0	0	–	0	0	–	0	0	–	0	0	0	–	0	0	0	0	0	0	0.0	0.0	0.0

Mast, Edward (Eddie) b. October 3, 1948 d. October 18, 1994 Ht. 6-9 Wt. 220 College: Temple

SEASON–TEAM	G	GS	MIN	FGM	FGA	PCT	3FGM	3FGA	PCT	FTM	FTA	PCT	O-RB	D-RB	TOT	AST	PF	DQ	STL	TO	BLK	PTS	RPG	APG	PPG
70-71–New York	30	–	164	25	66	.379	–	–	–	11	20	.550	–	–	56	4	25	0	–	–	–	61	1.9	0.1	2.0
71-72–New York	40	–	270	39	112	.348	–	–	–	25	41	.610	–	–	73	10	39	0	–	–	–	103	1.8	0.3	2.6
72-73–Atlanta	42	–	447	50	118	.424	–	–	–	19	30	.633	–	–	136	37	50	0	–	–	–	119	3.2	0.9	2.8
Reg. Season Totals	112	–	881	114	296	.385	–	–	–	55	91	.604	–	–	265	51	114	0	–	–	–	283	2.4	0.5	2.5
Playoff Totals	16	–	49	11	17	.647	–	–	–	1	5	.200	–	–	15	2	7	0	–	–	–	23	0.9	0.1	1.4

Mathis, Johnny C. b. July 14, 1943 Ht. 6-6 Wt. 220 College: Savannah State

SEASON–TEAM	G	GS	MIN	FGM	FGA	PCT	3FGM	3FGA	PCT	FTM	FTA	PCT	O-RB	D-RB	TOT	AST	PF	DQ	STL	TO	BLK	PTS	RPG	APG	PPG
67-68–New Jersey (A)	51	–	656	69	186	.371	0	2	.000	35	55	.636	–	–	194	28	102	3	–	42	–	173	3.8	0.5	3.4
Reg. ABA Totals	51	–	656	69	186	.371	0	2	.000	35	55	.636	–	–	194	28	102	3	–	42	–	173	3.8	0.5	3.4

Matthews, Wesley Joel b. August 24, 1959 Ht. 6-1 Wt. 170 College: Wisconsin

SEASON–TEAM	G	GS	MIN	FGM	FGA	PCT	3FGM	3FGA	PCT	FTM	FTA	PCT	O-RB	D-RB	TOT	AST	PF	DQ	STL	TO	BLK	PTS	RPG	APG	PPG
80-81–Wash.-Atlanta	79	–	2266	385	779	.494	5	21	.238	202	252	.802	46	93	139	411	242	2	107	261	17	977	1.8	5.2	12.4
81-82–Atlanta	47	5	837	131	298	.440	2	8	.250	60	79	.759	19	39	58	139	129	3	53	63	2	324	1.2	3.0	6.9
82-83–Atlanta	64	0	1187	171	424	.403	14	48	.292	86	112	.768	25	66	91	249	129	0	60	123	8	442	1.4	3.9	6.9
83-84–Atlanta-Phil.	20	5	388	61	131	.466	1	8	.125	27	36	.750	7	20	27	83	45	0	16	40	3	150	1.4	4.2	7.5
84-85–Chicago	78	38	1523	191	386	.495	2	16	.125	59	85	.694	16	51	67	354	133	0	73	124	12	443	0.9	4.5	5.7
85-86–San Antonio	75	46	1853	320	603	.531	4	25	.160	173	211	.820	30	101	131	476	168	1	87	232	32	817	1.7	6.3	10.9
86-87–L.A. Lakers	50	0	532	89	187	.476	1	3	.333	29	36	.806	13	34	47	100	53	0	23	51	4	208	0.9	2.0	4.2
87-88–L.A. Lakers	51	8	706	114	248	.460	7	30	.233	54	65	.831	16	50	66	138	65	0	25	69	3	289	1.3	2.7	5.7
89-90–Atlanta	1	0	13	1	3	.333	0	1	.000	2	2	1.000	0	0	0	5	0	0	0	0	0	4	0.0	5.0	4.0
Reg. Season Totals	465	102	9305	1463	3059	.478	36	160	.225	692	878	.788	172	454	626	1955	964	6	444	963	81	3654	1.3	4.2	7.9
Playoff Totals	38	7	384	68	141	.482	1	9	.111	36	45	.800	3	15	18	66	43	0	14	43	2	173	0.5	1.7	4.6

Maughan, Ariel Leishman (Ace) b. February 23, 1923 d. August 4, 1997 Ht. 6-4 Wt. 190 College: Utah State

SEASON–TEAM	G	GS	MIN	FGM	FGA	PCT	3FGM	3FGA	PCT	FTM	FTA	PCT	O-RB	D-RB	TOT	AST	PF	DQ	STL	TO	BLK	PTS	RPG	APG	PPG
46-47–Detroit	59	–	–	224	929	.241	–	–	–	84	114	.737	–	–	–	57	180	–	–	–	–	532	–	1.0	9.0
47-48–Prov.-St. L.	42	–	–	76	256	.297	–	–	–	32	53	.604	–	–	–	6	89	–	–	–	–	184	–	0.1	4.4
48-49–St. Louis	55	–	–	206	650	.317	–	–	–	184	285	.646	–	–	–	99	134	–	–	–	–	596	–	1.8	10.8
49-50–St. Louis	68	–	–	160	574	.279	–	–	–	157	205	.766	–	–	–	101	174	–	–	–	–	477	–	1.5	7.0
50-51–Washington	35	–	–	78	250	.312	–	–	–	101	120	.842	–	–	141	48	91	2	–	–	–	257	4.0	1.4	7.3
Reg. Season Totals	259	–	–	744	2659	.280	–	–	–	558	777	.718	–	–	141	311	668	2	–	–	–	2046	4.0	1.2	7.9
Playoff Totals	9	–	–	32	134	.239	–	–	–	18	26	.692	–	–	–	7	25	1	–	–	–	82	–	0.6	9.1

Maxey, Marlon Lee b. February 19, 1969 Ht. 6-8 Wt. 250 College: Minnesota; Texas-El Paso

SEASON–TEAM	G	GS	MIN	FGM	FGA	PCT	3FGM	3FGA	PCT	FTM	FTA	PCT	O-RB	D-RB	TOT	AST	PF	DQ	STL	TO	BLK	PTS	RPG	APG	PPG
92-93–Minnesota	43	3	520	93	169	.550	0	1	.000	45	70	.643	66	98	164	12	75	0	11	38	18	231	3.8	0.3	5.4
93-94–Minnesota	55	2	626	89	167	.533	0	2	.000	70	98	.714	75	124	199	10	113	1	16	40	33	248	3.6	0.2	4.5
Reg. Season Totals	98	5	1146	182	336	.542	0	3	.000	115	168	.685	141	222	363	22	188	1	27	78	51	479	3.7	0.2	4.9

Maxwell, Cedric Bryan (Cornbread) b. November 21, 1955 Ht. 6-8 Wt. 205 College: North Carolina-Charlotte

SEASON–TEAM	G	GS	MIN	FGM	FGA	PCT	3FGM	3FGA	PCT	FTM	FTA	PCT	O-RB	D-RB	TOT	AST	PF	DQ	STL	TO	BLK	PTS	RPG	APG	PPG
77-78–Boston	72	–	1213	170	316	.538	–	–	–	188	250	.752	138	241	379	68	151	2	53	122	48	528	5.3	0.9	7.3
78-79–Boston	80	–	2969	472	808	.584	–	–	–	574	716	.802	272	519	791	228	266	4	98	273	74	1518	9.9	2.9	19.0
79-80–Boston	80	–	2744	457	750	.609	0	0	–	436	554	.787	284	420	704	199	266	6	76	230	61	1350	8.8	2.5	16.9
80-81–Boston	81	–	2730	441	750	.588	0	1	.000	352	450	.782	222	303	525	219	256	5	79	180	68	1234	6.5	2.7	15.2
81-82–Boston	78	73	2590	397	724	.548	0	3	.000	357	478	.747	218	281	499	183	263	6	79	174	49	1151	6.4	2.3	14.8
82-83–Boston	79	72	2252	331	663	.499	0	1	.000	280	345	.812	185	237	422	186	202	3	65	165	39	942	5.3	2.4	11.9
83-84–Boston	80	78	2502	317	596	.532	1	6	.167	320	425	.753	201	260	461	205	224	4	63	203	24	955	5.8	2.6	11.9
84-85–Boston	57	51	1495	201	377	.533	0	2	.000	231	278	.831	98	144	242	102	140	2	36	98	15	633	4.2	1.8	11.1
85-86–L.A. Clippers	76	72	2458	314	661	.475	0	3	.000	447	562	.795	241	383	624	215	252	2	61	206	29	1075	8.2	2.8	14.1
86-87–LAClips-Hou.	81	31	1968	253	477	.530	0	1	.000	303	391	.775	175	260	435	197	178	1	39	136	14	809	5.4	2.4	10.0
87-88–Houston	71	0	848	80	171	.468	0	2	.000	110	143	.769	74	105	179	60	75	0	22	54	12	270	2.5	0.8	3.8
Reg. Season Totals	835	622	23769	3433	6293	.546	1	19	.053	3598	4592	.784	2108	3153	5261	1862	2273	35	671	1841	433	10465	6.3	2.2	12.5
Playoff Totals	102	42	2731	375	688	.545	0	2	.000	366	471	.777	233	320	553	194	260	2	74	172	50	1116	5.4	1.9	10.9

Maxwell, Vernon (Mad Max) b. September 12, 1965 Ht. 6-4 Wt. 190 College: Florida

SEASON–TEAM	G	GS	MIN	FGM	FGA	PCT	3FGM	3FGA	PCT	FTM	FTA	PCT	O-RB	D-RB	TOT	AST	PF	DQ	STL	TO	BLK	PTS	RPG	APG	PPG
88-89–San Antonio	79	36	2065	357	827	.432	32	129	.248	181	243	.745	49	153	202	301	136	0	86	178	8	927	2.6	3.8	11.7
89-90–S.A.-Houston	79	12	1987	275	627	.439	28	105	.267	136	211	.645	50	178	228	296	148	0	84	143	10	714	2.9	3.7	9.0
90-91–Houston	82	79	2870	504	1247	.404	172	510	.337	217	296	.733	41	197	238	303	179	2	127	171	15	1397	2.9	3.7	17.0
91-92–Houston	80	80	2700	502	1216	.413	162	473	.342	206	267	.772	37	206	243	326	200	3	104	178	28	1372	3.0	4.1	17.2
92-93–Houston	71	68	2251	349	858	.407	120	361	.332	164	228	.719	29	192	221	297	124	1	86	140	8	982	3.1	4.2	13.8
93-94–Houston	75	73	2571	380	976	.389	120	403	.298	143	191	.749	42	187	229	380	143	0	125	185	20	1023	3.1	5.1	13.6
94-95–Houston	64	54	2038	306	777	.394	143	441	.324	99	144	.688	18	146	164	274	157	1	75	137	13	854	2.6	4.3	13.3
95-96–Philadelphia	75	57	2467	410	1052	.390	146	460	.317	251	332	.756	39	190	229	330	182	1	96	215	12	1217	3.1	4.4	16.2
96-97–San Antonio	72	31	2068	340	906	.375	115	372	.309	134	180	.744	27	132	159	153	168	1	87	121	19	929	2.2	2.1	12.9
97-98–Orlando-Cha.	42	0	636	103	258	.399	37	112	.330	48	60	.800	14	43	57	52	71	1	16	40	4	291	1.4	1.2	6.9
98-99–Sacramento	46	1	1007	164	421	.390	80	231	.346	84	114	.737	13	72	85	76	111	1	30	67	3	492	1.8	1.7	10.7
99-00–Seattle	47	0	989	169	490	.345	67	223	.300	108	148	.730	15	64	79	75	83	0	38	53	9	513	1.7	1.6	10.9
Reg. Season Totals	812	377	23649	3859	9655	.400	1222	3820	.320	1771	2414	.734	374	1760	2134	2863	1702	11	954	1628	149	10711	2.6	3.5	13.2
Playoff Totals	45	37	1605	238	635	.375	84	274	.307	78	112	.696	25	112	137	160	105	1	44	86	5	638	3.0	3.6	14.2

May, Donald John (Don) b. January 3, 1946 Ht. 6-4 Wt. 220 College: Dayton

SEASON–TEAM	G	GS	MIN	FGM	FGA	PCT	3FGM	3FGA	PCT	FTM	FTA	PCT	O-RB	D-RB	TOT	AST	PF	DQ	STL	TO	BLK	PTS	RPG	APG	PPG
68-69–New York	48	–	560	81	223	.363	–	–	–	42	58	.724	–	–	114	35	64	0	–	–	–	204	2.4	0.7	4.3
69-70–New York	37	–	238	39	101	.386	–	–	–	18	19	.947	–	–	52	17	42	0	–	–	–	96	1.4	0.5	2.6
70-71–Buffalo	76	–	2666	629	1336	.471	–	–	–	277	350	.791	–	–	567	150	219	4	–	–	–	1535	7.5	2.0	20.2
71-72–Atlanta	75	–	1285	234	476	.492	–	–	–	126	164	.768	–	–	217	55	133	0	–	–	–	594	2.9	0.7	7.9
72-73–Atlanta-Phil.	58	–	919	189	424	.446	–	–	–	75	93	.806	–	–	210	64	135	1	–	–	–	453	3.6	1.1	7.8
73-74–Philadelphia	56	–	812	152	367	.414	–	–	–	89	102	.873	25	111	136	63	137	0	25	–	8	393	2.4	1.1	7.0
74-75–K.C.-Omaha	29	–	139	27	54	.500	–	–	–	10	12	.833	4	9	13	5	21	0	4	–	2	64	0.4	0.2	2.2
Reg. Season Totals	379	–	6619	1351	2981	.453	–	–	–	637	798	.798	29	120	1309	389	751	5	29	–	10	3339	3.5	1.0	8.8
Playoff Totals	14	–	126	14	42	.333	–	–	–	13	17	.765	0	0	31	9	12	0	0	–	0	41	2.2	0.6	2.9

May, Scott Glenn
b. March 19, 1954 Ht. 6-7 Wt. 215 College: Indiana

SEASON–TEAM	G	GS	MIN	FGM	FGA	PCT	3FGM	3FGA	PCT	FTM	FTA	PCT	O-RB	D-RB	TOT	AST	PF	DQ	STL	TO	BLK	PTS	RPG	APG	PPG
76-77–Chicago	72	–	2369	431	955	.451	–	–	–	188	227	.828	141	296	437	145	185	2	78	–	17	1050	6.1	2.0	14.6
77-78–Chicago	55	–	1802	280	617	.454	–	–	–	175	216	.810	118	214	332	114	170	4	50	125	6	735	6.0	2.1	13.4
78-79–Chicago	37	–	403	59	136	.434	–	–	–	30	40	.750	14	50	64	39	51	0	22	51	1	148	1.7	1.1	4.0
79-80–Chicago	54	–	1298	264	587	.450	0	4	.000	144	172	.837	78	140	218	104	126	2	45	77	5	672	4.0	1.9	12.4
80-81–Chicago	63	–	815	165	338	.488	0	0	–	113	149	.758	62	93	155	63	83	0	35	71	7	443	2.5	1.0	7.0
81-82–Milwaukee	65	7	1187	212	417	.508	0	4	.000	159	193	.824	85	133	218	133	151	2	50	92	6	583	3.4	2.0	9.0
82-83–Detroit	9	1	155	21	50	.420	0	0	–	17	21	.810	10	16	26	12	24	1	5	13	2	59	2.9	1.3	6.6
Reg. Season Totals	355	8	8029	1432	3100	.462	0	8	.000	826	1018	.811	508	942	1450	610	790	11	285	429	44	3690	4.1	1.7	10.4
Playoff Totals	7	0	147	14	46	.304	0	0	–	21	29	.724	13	12	25	13	16	0	10	6	2	49	3.6	1.9	7.0

Mayberry, Orva Lee Jr. (Lee)
b. June 12, 1970 Ht. 6-1 Wt. 180 College: Arkansas

SEASON–TEAM	G	GS	MIN	FGM	FGA	PCT	3FGM	3FGA	PCT	FTM	FTA	PCT	O-RB	D-RB	TOT	AST	PF	DQ	STL	TO	BLK	PTS	RPG	APG	PPG
92-93–Milwaukee	82	4	1503	171	375	.456	43	110	.391	39	68	.574	26	92	118	273	148	1	59	85	7	424	1.4	3.3	5.2
93-94–Milwaukee	82	6	1472	167	402	.415	41	119	.345	58	84	.690	26	75	101	215	114	0	46	97	4	433	1.2	2.6	5.3
94-95–Milwaukee	82	50	1744	172	408	.422	72	177	.407	58	83	.699	21	61	82	276	123	0	51	106	4	474	1.0	3.4	5.8
95-96–Milwaukee	82	20	1705	153	364	.420	75	189	.397	41	68	.603	21	69	90	302	144	1	64	89	10	422	1.1	3.7	5.1
96-97–Vancouver	80	38	1952	149	370	.403	83	221	.376	29	46	.630	29	105	134	329	159	0	60	90	8	410	1.7	4.1	5.1
97-98–Vancouver	79	32	1835	131	349	.375	63	180	.350	38	51	.745	19	95	114	349	164	1	65	113	10	363	1.4	4.4	4.6
98-99–Vancouver	9	0	126	7	19	.368	2	10	.200	4	5	.800	0	3	3	23	13	0	7	11	0	20	0.3	2.6	2.2
Reg. Season Totals	496	150	10337	950	2287	.415	379	1006	.377	267	405	.659	142	500	642	1767	865	3	352	591	43	2546	1.3	3.6	5.1

Mayes, Clyde C. Jr.
b. March 17, 1953 Ht. 6-8 Wt. 230 College: Furman

SEASON–TEAM	G	GS	MIN	FGM	FGA	PCT	3FGM	3FGA	PCT	FTM	FTA	PCT	O-RB	D-RB	TOT	AST	PF	DQ	STL	TO	BLK	PTS	RPG	APG	PPG
75-76–Milwaukee	65	–	948	114	248	.460	–	–	–	56	97	.577	97	166	263	37	154	7	9	–	42	284	4.0	0.6	4.4
76-77–Ind.-Buffalo-Port.	9	–	52	5	19	.263	–	–	–	3	7	.429	10	6	16	3	12	0	0	–	4	13	1.8	0.3	1.4
Reg. Season Totals	74	–	1000	119	267	.446	–	–	–	59	104	.567	107	172	279	40	166	7	9	–	46	297	3.8	0.5	4.0
Playoff Totals	3	–	41	1	5	.200	–	–	–	3	4	.750	0	6	6	1	6	1	1	–	1	5	2.0	0.3	1.7

Mayes, Tharon R.
b. September 9, 1968 Ht. 6-3 Wt. 175 College: Florida State

SEASON–TEAM	G	GS	MIN	FGM	FGA	PCT	3FGM	3FGA	PCT	FTM	FTA	PCT	O-RB	D-RB	TOT	AST	PF	DQ	STL	TO	BLK	PTS	RPG	APG	PPG
91-92–Phil.-LAClips	24	0	255	30	99	.303	15	41	.366	24	36	.667	3	13	16	35	41	0	16	31	2	99	0.7	1.5	4.1
Reg. Season Totals	24	0	255	30	99	.303	15	41	.366	24	36	.667	3	13	16	35	41	0	16	31	2	99	0.7	1.5	4.1

Mayfield, Kendall (Ken)
b. May 11, 1948 Ht. 6-2 Wt. 185 College: Coffeyville (Kan.) C.C.; Tuskegee

SEASON–TEAM	G	GS	MIN	FGM	FGA	PCT	3FGM	3FGA	PCT	FTM	FTA	PCT	O-RB	D-RB	TOT	AST	PF	DQ	STL	TO	BLK	PTS	RPG	APG	PPG
75-76–New York	13	–	64	17	46	.370	–	–	–	3	3	1.000	1	7	8	4	18	0	0	–	0	37	0.6	0.3	2.8
Reg. Season Totals	13	–	64	17	46	.370	–	–	–	3	3	1.000	1	7	8	4	18	0	0	–	0	37	0.6	0.3	2.8

Mayfield, William Henry (Bill)
b. October 17, 1957 Ht. 6-7 Wt. 210 College: Iowa

SEASON–TEAM	G	GS	MIN	FGM	FGA	PCT	3FGM	3FGA	PCT	FTM	FTA	PCT	O-RB	D-RB	TOT	AST	PF	DQ	STL	TO	BLK	PTS	RPG	APG	PPG
80-81–Golden State	7	–	54	8	18	.444	0	0	–	1	2	.500	7	2	9	1	8	0	0	3	1	17	1.3	0.1	2.4
Reg. Season Totals	7	–	54	8	18	.444	0	0	–	1	2	.500	7	2	9	1	8	0	0	3	1	17	1.3	0.1	2.4

Mays, Travis Cortez
b. June 19, 1968 Ht. 6-2 Wt. 190 College: Texas

SEASON–TEAM	G	GS	MIN	FGM	FGA	PCT	3FGM	3FGA	PCT	FTM	FTA	PCT	O-RB	D-RB	TOT	AST	PF	DQ	STL	TO	BLK	PTS	RPG	APG	PPG
90-91–Sacramento	64	55	2145	294	724	.406	72	197	.365	255	331	.770	54	124	178	253	169	1	81	159	11	915	2.8	4.0	14.3
91-92–Atlanta	2	0	32	6	14	.429	3	6	.500	2	2	1.000	1	1	2	1	4	0	0	3	0	17	1.0	0.5	8.5
92-93–Atlanta	49	9	787	129	309	.417	29	84	.345	54	82	.659	20	33	53	72	59	0	21	51	3	341	1.1	1.5	7.0
Reg. Season Totals	115	64	2964	429	1047	.410	104	287	.362	311	415	.749	75	158	233	326	232	1	102	213	14	1273	2.0	2.8	11.1
Playoff Totals	1	0	20	2	4	.500	0	1	.000	0	0	–	0	1	1	–	3	0	0	1	0	4	1.0	0.0	4.0

Mazza, Matthew Anthony (Matt)
b. September 23, 1923 Ht. 6-3 Wt. 210 College: Canisius; Michigan State

SEASON–TEAM	G	GS	MIN	FGM	FGA	PCT	3FGM	3FGA	PCT	FTM	FTA	PCT	O-RB	D-RB	TOT	AST	PF	DQ	STL	TO	BLK	PTS	RPG	APG	PPG
49-50–Sheboygan	26	–	–	33	110	.300	–	–	–	32	45	.711	–	–	–	29	34	–	–	–	–	98	–	1.1	3.8
Reg. Season Totals	26	–	–	33	110	.300	–	–	–	32	45	.711	–	–	–	29	34	–	–	–	–	98	–	1.1	3.8

McAdoo, Robert Allen Jr. (Bob) b. September 25, 1951 Ht. 6-9 Wt. 210 College: Vincennes (Ind.) (J.C.); North Carolina HOF: 2000

SEASON–TEAM	G	GS	MIN	FGM	FGA	PCT	3FGM	3FGA	PCT	FTM	FTA	PCT	O-RB	D-RB	TOT	AST	PF	DQ	STL	TO	BLK	PTS	RPG	APG	PPG
72-73–Buffalo	80	–	2562	585	1293	.452	–	–	–	271	350	.774	–	–	728	139	256	6	–	–	–	1441	9.1	1.7	18.0
73-74–Buffalo	74	–	3185	901	1647	.547	–	–	–	459	579	.793	281	836	1117	170	252	3	88	–	246	2261	15.1	2.3	30.6
74-75–Buffalo	82	–	3539	1095	2138	.512	–	–	–	641	796	.805	307	848	1155	179	278	3	92	–	174	2831	14.1	2.2	34.5
75-76–Buffalo	78	–	3328	934	1918	.487	–	–	–	559	734	.762	241	724	965	315	298	5	93	–	160	2427	12.4	4.0	31.1
76-77–Buffalo-N.Y.-K	72	–	2798	740	1445	.512	–	–	–	381	516	.738	199	727	926	205	262	3	77	–	99	1861	12.9	2.8	25.8
77-78–New York	79	–	3182	814	1564	.520	–	–	–	469	645	.727	236	774	1010	298	297	6	105	346	126	2097	12.8	3.8	26.5
78-79–N.Y.-Boston	60	–	2231	596	1127	.529	–	–	–	295	450	.656	130	390	520	168	189	3	74	217	67	1487	8.7	2.8	24.8
79-80–Detroit	58	–	2097	492	1025	.480	3	24	.125	235	322	.730	100	367	467	200	178	3	73	238	65	1222	8.1	3.4	21.1
80-81–Detroit-N.J.	16	–	321	68	157	.433	0	1	.000	29	41	.707	17	50	67	30	38	0	17	32	13	165	4.2	1.9	10.3
81-82–Los Angeles	41	0	746	151	330	.458	0	5	.000	90	126	.714	45	114	159	32	109	1	22	51	36	392	3.9	0.8	9.6
82-83–Los Angeles	47	1	1019	292	562	.520	0	1	.000	119	163	.730	76	171	247	39	153	2	40	68	40	703	5.3	0.8	15.0
83-84–Los Angeles	70	0	1456	352	748	.471	0	5	.000	212	264	.803	82	207	289	74	182	0	42	127	50	916	4.1	1.1	13.1
84-85–L.A. Lakers	66	0	1254	284	546	.520	0	1	.000	122	162	.753	79	216	295	67	170	0	18	95	53	690	4.5	1.0	10.5
85-86–Philadelphia	29	0	609	116	251	.462	0	0	–	62	81	.765	25	78	103	35	64	0	10	49	18	294	3.6	1.2	10.1
Reg. Season Totals	852	1	28327	7420	14751	.503	3	37	.081	3944	5229	.754	1818	5502	8048	1951	2726	35	751	1223	1147	18787	9.4	2.3	22.1
Playoff Totals	94	0	2714	698	1423	.491	2	8	.250	320	442	.724	180	531	711	127	318	9	72	145	151	1718	7.6	1.4	18.3
All-Star Totals	4	2	88	24	41	.585	0	0	–	10	15	.667	10	10	20	4	15	0	1	3	1	58	5.0	1.0	14.5

McBride, Kenneth S. (Ken) b. 1931 Ht. 6-3 Wt. 195 College: Maryland Eastern Shore

SEASON–TEAM	G	GS	MIN	FGM	FGA	PCT	3FGM	3FGA	PCT	FTM	FTA	PCT	O-RB	D-RB	TOT	AST	PF	DQ	STL	TO	BLK	PTS	RPG	APG	PPG
54-55–Milwaukee	12	–	249	48	147	.327	–	–	–	21	29	.724	–	–	31	14	31	0	–	–	–	117	2.6	1.2	9.8
Reg. Season Totals	12	–	249	48	147	.327	–	–	–	21	29	.724	–	–	31	14	31	0	–	–	–	117	2.6	1.2	9.8

McCann, Brendan Michael b. July 5, 1935 Ht. 6-2 Wt. 180 College: St. Bonaventure

SEASON–TEAM	G	GS	MIN	FGM	FGA	PCT	3FGM	3FGA	PCT	FTM	FTA	PCT	O-RB	D-RB	TOT	AST	PF	DQ	STL	TO	BLK	PTS	RPG	APG	PPG
57-58–New York	36	–	295	22	100	.220	–	–	–	25	37	.676	–	–	45	54	34	0	–	–	–	69	1.3	1.5	1.9
58-59–New York	1	–	7	0	3	.000	–	–	–	0	0	–	–	–	1	1	1	0	–	–	–	0	1.0	1.0	0.0
59-60–New York	4	–	29	1	10	.100	–	–	–	3	3	1.000	–	–	4	10	2	0	–	–	–	5	1.0	2.5	1.3
Reg. Season Totals	41	–	331	23	113	.204	–	–	–	28	40	.700	–	–	50	65	37	0	–	–	–	74	1.2	1.6	1.8

McCann, Robert Glen (Bob) b. April 22, 1964 Ht. 6-7 Wt. 245 College: Upsala; Morehead State

SEASON–TEAM	G	GS	MIN	FGM	FGA	PCT	3FGM	3FGA	PCT	FTM	FTA	PCT	O-RB	D-RB	TOT	AST	PF	DQ	STL	TO	BLK	PTS	RPG	APG	PPG
89-90–Dallas	10	0	62	7	21	.333	0	0	–	12	14	.857	4	8	12	6	7	0	2	6	2	26	1.2	0.6	2.6
91-92–Detroit	26	0	129	13	33	.394	0	1	.000	4	13	.308	12	18	30	6	23	0	6	7	4	30	1.2	0.2	1.2
92-93–Minnesota	79	7	1536	200	410	.488	0	2	.000	95	152	.625	92	190	282	68	202	2	51	79	58	495	3.6	0.9	6.3
95-96–Washington	62	0	653	76	153	.497	1	2	.500	35	74	.473	46	97	143	24	116	0	21	42	15	188	2.3	0.4	3.0
97-98–Toronto	1	0	5	0	1	.000	0	0	–	0	0	–	0	1	1	0	1	0	0	0	0	0	1.0	0.0	0.0
Reg. Season Totals	178	7	2385	296	618	.479	1	5	.200	146	253	.577	154	314	468	104	349	2	80	134	79	739	2.6	0.6	4.2
Playoff Totals	1	0	13	3	6	.500	0	0	–	0	0	–	1	1	2	–	2	0	0	2	1	6	2.0	0.0	6.0

McCants, Melvin Lamont (Mel) b. August 19, 1967 Ht. 6-8 Wt. 240 College: Purdue

SEASON–TEAM	G	GS	MIN	FGM	FGA	PCT	3FGM	3FGA	PCT	FTM	FTA	PCT	O-RB	D-RB	TOT	AST	PF	DQ	STL	TO	BLK	PTS	RPG	APG	PPG
89-90–L.A. Lakers	13	0	65	8	26	.308	0	0	–	6	8	.750	1	5	6	2	11	0	3	1	1	22	0.5	0.2	1.7
Reg. Season Totals	13	0	65	8	26	.308	0	0	–	6	8	.750	1	5	6	2	11	0	3	1	1	22	0.5	0.2	1.7
Playoff Totals	2	0	5	0	0	–	0	0	–	0	0	–	0	0	0	–	1	0	0	0	0	0	0.0	0.0	0.0

McCarron, Michael (Mike) b. March 2, 1922 d. October 2, 1991 Ht. 5-11 Wt. 180 College: Seton Hall

SEASON–TEAM	G	GS	MIN	FGM	FGA	PCT	3FGM	3FGA	PCT	FTM	FTA	PCT	O-RB	D-RB	TOT	AST	PF	DQ	STL	TO	BLK	PTS	RPG	APG	PPG
46-47–Toronto	60	–	–	236	838	.282	–	–	–	177	288	.615	–	–	–	59	184	–	–	–	–	649	–	1.0	10.8
49-50–Balt.-St. Louis	8	–	–	3	15	.200	–	–	–	3	5	.600	–	–	–	3	5	–	–	–	–	9	–	0.4	1.1
Reg. Season Totals	68	–	–	239	853	.280	–	–	–	180	293	.614	–	–	–	62	189	–	–	–	–	658	–	0.9	9.7

McCarter, Andre Eugene b. August 25, 1953 Ht. 6-3 Wt. 190 College: UCLA

SEASON–TEAM	G	GS	MIN	FGM	FGA	PCT	3FGM	3FGA	PCT	FTM	FTA	PCT	O-RB	D-RB	TOT	AST	PF	DQ	STL	TO	BLK	PTS	RPG	APG	PPG
76-77–Kansas City	59	–	725	119	257	.463	–	–	–	32	45	.711	16	39	55	99	63	0	23	–	0	270	0.9	1.7	4.6
77-78–Kansas City	1	–	9	0	2	.000	–	–	–	0	0	–	0	1	1	0	1	0	0	0	0	0	1.0	0.0	0.0
80-81–Washington	43	–	448	51	135	.378	2	8	.250	18	24	.750	16	23	39	73	36	0	14	24	0	122	0.9	1.7	2.8
Reg. Season Totals	103	–	1182	170	394	.431	2	8	.250	50	69	.725	32	63	95	172	100	0	37	24	0	392	0.9	1.7	3.8

McCarter, Willie J. b. July 26, 1946 Ht. 6-3 Wt. 175 College: Drake

SEASON–TEAM	G	GS	MIN	FGM	FGA	PCT	3FGM	3FGA	PCT	FTM	FTA	PCT	O-RB	D-RB	TOT	AST	PF	DQ	STL	TO	BLK	PTS	RPG	APG	PPG
69-70–Los Angeles	40	–	861	132	349	.378	–	–	–	43	60	.717	–	–	83	93	71	0	–	–	–	307	2.1	2.3	7.7
70-71–Los Angeles	76	–	1369	247	592	.417	–	–	–	46	77	.597	–	–	122	126	152	0	–	–	–	540	1.6	1.7	7.1
71-72–Portland	39	–	612	103	257	.401	–	–	–	37	55	.673	–	–	43	85	58	0	–	–	–	243	1.1	2.2	6.2
Reg. Season Totals	155	–	2842	482	1198	.402	–	–	–	126	192	.656	–	–	248	304	281	0	–	–	–	1090	1.6	2.0	7.0
Playoff Totals	17	–	246	30	83	.361	–	–	–	2	7	.286	–	–	29	20	32	0	–	–	–	62	1.7	1.2	3.6

McCarthy, John Joseph (Johnny) b. April 25, 1934 Ht. 6-1 Wt. 185 College: Canisius

SEASON–TEAM	G	GS	MIN	FGM	FGA	PCT	3FGM	3FGA	PCT	FTM	FTA	PCT	O-RB	D-RB	TOT	AST	PF	DQ	STL	TO	BLK	PTS	RPG	APG	PPG
56-57–Rochester	72	–	1560	173	460	.376	–	–	–	130	193	.674	–	–	201	107	130	0	–	–	–	476	2.8	1.5	6.6
58-59–Cincinnati	47	–	1827	245	657	.373	–	–	–	116	174	.667	–	–	227	225	158	4	–	–	–	606	4.8	4.8	12.9
59-60–St. Louis	75	–	2383	240	730	.329	–	–	–	149	226	.659	–	–	301	328	233	3	–	–	–	629	4.0	4.4	8.4
60-61–St. Louis	79	–	2519	266	746	.357	–	–	–	122	226	.540	–	–	325	430	272	8	–	–	–	654	4.1	5.4	8.3
61-62–St. Louis	15	–	333	18	73	.247	–	–	–	12	27	.444	–	–	56	70	50	1	–	–	–	48	3.7	4.7	3.2
63-64–Boston	28	–	206	16	48	.333	–	–	–	5	13	.385	–	–	35	24	42	0	–	–	–	37	1.3	0.9	1.3
Reg. Season Totals	316	–	8828	958	2714	.353	–	–	–	534	859	.622	–	–	1145	1184	885	16	–	–	–	2450	3.6	3.7	7.8
Playoff Totals	27	–	808	63	162	.389	–	–	–	33	45	.733	–	–	96	132	78	0	–	–	–	159	3.6	4.9	5.9

McCarty, Howard T. (Howie) b. 1919 d. 1973 Ht. 6-2 Wt. 190 College: Wayne State (Mich.)

SEASON–TEAM	G	GS	MIN	FGM	FGA	PCT	3FGM	3FGA	PCT	FTM	FTA	PCT	O-RB	D-RB	TOT	AST	PF	DQ	STL	TO	BLK	PTS	RPG	APG	PPG
45-46–Cleveland (N)	13	–	–	40	–	–	–	–	–	13	–	–	–	–	–	–	–	–	–	–	–	93	–	–	7.2
46-47–Detroit (N)	16	–	–	46	–	–	–	–	–	29	75	.387	–	–	–	–	–	–	–	–	–	121	–	–	7.6
46-47–Detroit	19	–	–	10	82	.122	–	–	–	1	10	.100	–	–	–	2	22	–	–	–	–	21	–	0.1	1.1
Reg. NBA Totals	19	–	–	10	82	.122	–	–	–	1	10	.100	–	–	–	2	22	–	–	–	–	21	–	0.1	1.1
Reg. NBL Totals	29	–	–	86	–	–	–	–	–	42	75	.387	–	–	–	–	–	–	–	–	–	214	–	–	7.4

McCarty, Kelly Deshawn b. August 24, 1975 Ht. 6-7 Wt. 200 College: Southern Mississippi

SEASON–TEAM	G	GS	MIN	FGM	FGA	PCT	3FGM	3FGA	PCT	FTM	FTA	PCT	O-RB	D-RB	TOT	AST	PF	DQ	STL	TO	BLK	PTS	RPG	APG	PPG
98-99–Denver	2	0	4	2	3	.667	0	0	–	0	0	–	2	1	3	0	0	0	0	2	0	4	1.5	0.0	2.0
Reg. Season Totals	2	0	4	2	3	.667	0	0	–	0	0	–	2	1	3	0	0	0	0	2	0	4	1.5	0.0	2.0

McCarty, Walter Lee b. February 1, 1974 Ht. 6-10 Wt. 230 College: Kentucky

SEASON–TEAM	G	GS	MIN	FGM	FGA	PCT	3FGM	3FGA	PCT	FTM	FTA	PCT	O-RB	D-RB	TOT	AST	PF	DQ	STL	TO	BLK	PTS	RPG	APG	PPG
96-97–New York	35	0	192	26	68	.382	4	14	.286	8	14	.571	8	15	23	13	38	0	7	17	9	64	0.7	0.4	1.8
97-98–Boston	82	64	2340	295	730	.404	54	175	.309	144	194	.742	141	223	364	177	274	6	110	141	44	788	4.4	2.2	9.6
98-99–Boston	32	4	659	64	177	.362	13	50	.260	40	57	.702	36	79	115	40	88	0	24	40	13	181	3.6	1.3	5.7
99-00–Boston	61	5	879	78	230	.339	34	110	.309	39	54	.722	33	77	110	70	83	1	24	67	23	229	1.8	1.1	3.8
Reg. Season Totals	210	73	4070	463	1205	.384	105	349	.301	231	319	.724	218	394	612	300	483	7	165	265	89	1262	2.9	1.4	6.0
Playoff Totals	2	0	4	2	2	1.000	0	0	–	0	0	–	0	0	0	–	0	0	1	0	0	4	0.0	0.0	2.0

McCaskill, Amal Omari b. October 28, 1973 Ht. 6-11 Wt. 245 College: Marquette

SEASON–TEAM	G	GS	MIN	FGM	FGA	PCT	3FGM	3FGA	PCT	FTM	FTA	PCT	O-RB	D-RB	TOT	AST	PF	DQ	STL	TO	BLK	PTS	RPG	APG	PPG
96-97–Orlando	17	1	109	10	32	.313	0	2	.000	8	12	.667	4	18	22	7	7	0	3	11	5	28	1.3	0.4	1.6
Reg. Season Totals	17	1	109	10	32	.313	0	2	.000	8	12	.667	4	18	22	7	7	0	3	11	5	28	1.3	0.4	1.6
Playoff Totals	2	0	7	2	3	.667	0	0	–	1	3	.333	0	3	3	1	1	0	0	0	0	5	1.5	0.5	2.5

McClain, Dwayne Edward b. February 7, 1963 Ht. 6-6 Wt. 185 College: Villanova

SEASON–TEAM	G	GS	MIN	FGM	FGA	PCT	3FGM	3FGA	PCT	FTM	FTA	PCT	O-RB	D-RB	TOT	AST	PF	DQ	STL	TO	BLK	PTS	RPG	APG	PPG
85-86–Indiana	45	4	461	69	180	.383	1	9	.111	18	35	.514	14	16	30	67	61	0	38	40	4	157	0.7	1.5	3.5
Reg. Season Totals	45	4	461	69	180	.383	1	9	.111	18	35	.514	14	16	30	67	61	0	38	40	4	157	0.7	1.5	3.5

McClain, Theodore (Ted, Hound Dog) b. August 30, 1946 Ht. 6-2 Wt. 190 College: Tennessee State

SEASON–TEAM	G	GS	MIN	FGM	FGA	PCT	3FGM	3FGA	PCT	FTM	FTA	PCT	O-RB	D-RB	TOT	AST	PF	DQ	STL	TO	BLK	PTS	RPG	APG	PPG
71-72–Carolina (A)	64	–	900	148	415	.357	13	53	.245	110	142	.775	–	–	120	120	144	–	–	116	–	419	1.9	1.9	6.5
72-73–Carolina (A)	84	–	1816	325	652	.498	8	24	.333	145	204	.711	108	155	263	225	256	1	120	185	–	803	3.1	2.7	9.6
73-74–Carolina (A)	84	–	2582	423	872	.485	2	27	.074	251	325	.772	121	237	358	348	326	–	250	239	25	1099	4.3	4.1	13.1
74-75–Kentucky (A)	72	–	1971	256	582	.440	1	8	.125	104	138	.754	65	203	268	365	231	–	130	167	15	617	3.7	5.1	8.6
75-76–Ken.-N.Y. (A)	73	–	1927	267	631	.423	3	12	.250	136	170	.800	52	156	208	310	277	–	138	194	23	673	2.8	4.2	9.2
76-77–Denver	72	–	2002	245	551	.445	–	–	–	99	133	.744	52	177	229	324	255	9	106	–	13	589	3.2	4.5	8.2
77-78–Buffalo-Phil.	70	–	1020	123	280	.439	–	–	–	57	73	.781	20	92	112	157	124	2	58	90	6	303	1.6	2.2	4.3
78-79–Phoenix	36	–	465	62	132	.470	–	–	–	42	46	.913	25	44	69	60	51	0	19	54	0	166	1.9	1.7	4.6
Reg. NBA Totals	178	–	3487	430	963	.447	–	–	–	198	252	.786	97	313	410	541	430	11	183	144	19	1058	2.3	3.0	5.9
Reg. ABA Totals	377	–	9196	1419	3152	.450	27	124	.218	746	979	.762	346	751	1217	1368	1234	1	638	901	63	3611	3.2	3.6	9.6
NBA Playoff Totals	25	–	304	37	90	.411	–	–	–	19	24	.792	12	24	36	50	36	0	21	21	2	93	1.4	2.0	3.7
ABA Playoff Totals	39	–	1007	128	341	.375	1	13	.077	56	78	.718	29	84	156	127	130	0	41	78	6	313	4.0	3.3	8.0

McCloskey, John William (Jack) b. September 19, 1925 Ht. 6-2 Wt. 190 College: Pennsylvania

SEASON–TEAM	G	GS	MIN	FGM	FGA	PCT	3FGM	3FGA	PCT	FTM	FTA	PCT	O-RB	D-RB	TOT	AST	PF	DQ	STL	TO	BLK	PTS	RPG	APG	PPG
52-53–Philadelphia	1	–	16	3	9	.333	–	–	–	0	0	–	–	–	3	1	2	0	–	–	–	6	3.0	1.0	6.0
Reg. Season Totals	1	–	16	3	9	.333	–	–	–	0	0	–	–	–	3	1	2	0	–	–	–	6	3.0	1.0	6.0

McCloud, George Aaron b. May 27, 1967 Ht. 6-8 Wt. 225 College: Florida State

SEASON–TEAM	G	GS	MIN	FGM	FGA	PCT	3FGM	3FGA	PCT	FTM	FTA	PCT	O-RB	D-RB	TOT	AST	PF	DQ	STL	TO	BLK	PTS	RPG	APG	PPG
89-90–Indiana	44	0	413	45	144	.313	13	40	.325	15	19	.789	12	30	42	45	56	0	19	36	3	118	1.0	1.0	2.7
90-91–Indiana	74	0	1070	131	351	.373	43	124	.347	38	49	.776	35	83	118	150	141	1	40	91	11	343	1.6	2.0	4.6
91-92–Indiana	51	5	892	128	313	.409	32	94	.340	50	64	.781	45	87	132	116	95	1	26	62	11	338	2.6	2.3	6.6
92-93–Indiana	78	21	1500	216	525	.411	58	181	.320	75	102	.735	60	145	205	192	165	0	53	107	11	565	2.6	2.5	7.2
94-95–Dallas	42	3	802	144	328	.439	34	89	.382	80	96	.833	82	65	147	53	71	0	23	40	9	402	3.5	1.3	9.6
95-96–Dallas	79	63	2846	530	1281	.414	257	678	.379	180	224	.804	116	263	379	212	212	1	113	166	38	1497	4.8	2.7	18.9
96-97–Dallas-Lakers	64	28	1493	238	578	.412	99	254	.390	83	101	.822	36	143	179	109	126	1	61	61	8	658	2.8	1.7	10.3
97-98–Phoenix	63	13	1213	173	427	.405	71	208	.341	39	51	.765	45	173	218	84	132	1	54	63	13	456	3.5	1.3	7.2
98-99–Phoenix	48	16	1245	142	324	.438	69	166	.416	75	87	.862	34	128	162	79	128	0	45	49	14	428	3.4	1.6	8.9
99-00–Denver	78	11	2118	266	638	.417	107	283	.378	148	181	.818	72	213	285	246	180	2	48	134	26	787	3.7	3.2	10.1
Reg. Season Totals	621	160	13592	2013	4909	.410	783	2117	.370	783	974	.804	537	1330	1867	1286	1306	7	482	809	144	5592	3.0	2.1	9.0
Playoff Totals	14	5	342	49	108	.454	26	59	.441	19	29	.655	8	38	46	30	49	0	12	18	3	143	3.3	2.1	10.2

McConathy, John R. b. April 9, 1930 Ht. 6-5 Wt. 195 College: Northwestern State-Louisiana

SEASON–TEAM	G	GS	MIN	FGM	FGA	PCT	3FGM	3FGA	PCT	FTM	FTA	PCT	O-RB	D-RB	TOT	AST	PF	DQ	STL	TO	BLK	PTS	RPG	APG	PPG
51-52–Milwaukee	11	–	106	4	29	.138	–	–	–	6	14	.429	–	–	20	8	7	0	–	–	–	14	1.8	0.7	1.3
Reg. Season Totals	11	–	106	4	29	.138	–	–	–	6	14	.429	–	–	20	8	7	0	–	–	–	14	1.8	0.7	1.3

McConnell, Paul Joseph (Bucky) b. July 1, 1928 Ht. 5-10 Wt. 170 College: Marshall

SEASON–TEAM	G	GS	MIN	FGM	FGA	PCT	3FGM	3FGA	PCT	FTM	FTA	PCT	O-RB	D-RB	TOT	AST	PF	DQ	STL	TO	BLK	PTS	RPG	APG	PPG
52-53–Milwaukee	14	–	297	27	71	.380	–	–	–	14	29	.483	–	–	34	41	39	0	–	–	–	68	2.4	2.9	4.9
Reg. Season Totals	14	–	297	27	71	.380	–	–	–	14	29	.483	–	–	34	41	39	0	–	–	–	68	2.4	2.9	4.9

McCord, Keith Rennae b. June 22, 1957 Ht. 6-7 Wt. 210 College: Alabama-Birmingham; Alabama

SEASON–TEAM	G	GS	MIN	FGM	FGA	PCT	3FGM	3FGA	PCT	FTM	FTA	PCT	O-RB	D-RB	TOT	AST	PF	DQ	STL	TO	BLK	PTS	RPG	APG	PPG
80-81–Washington	2	–	9	2	4	.500	0	0	–	0	0	–	1	1	2	1	0	0	0	2	0	4	1.0	0.5	2.0
Reg. Season Totals	2	–	9	2	4	.500	0	0	–	0	0	–	1	1	2	1	0	0	0	2	0	4	1.0	0.5	2.0

McCormick, Timothy Daniel (Tim) b. March 10, 1962 Ht. 6-11 Wt. 240 College: Michigan

SEASON–TEAM	G	GS	MIN	FGM	FGA	PCT	3FGM	3FGA	PCT	FTM	FTA	PCT	O-RB	D-RB	TOT	AST	PF	DQ	STL	TO	BLK	PTS	RPG	APG	PPG
84-85–Seattle	78	27	1584	269	483	.557	0	1	.000	188	263	.715	146	252	398	78	207	2	18	114	33	726	5.1	1.0	9.3
85-86–Seattle	77	42	1705	253	444	.570	1	2	.500	174	244	.713	140	263	403	83	219	4	19	110	28	681	5.2	1.1	8.8
86-87–Philadelphia	81	79	2817	391	718	.545	0	4	.000	251	349	.719	180	431	611	114	270	4	36	153	64	1033	7.5	1.4	12.8
87-88–Phil.-N.J.	70	55	2114	348	648	.537	0	2	.000	145	215	.674	146	321	467	118	234	3	32	111	23	841	6.7	1.7	12.0
88-89–Houston	81	0	1257	169	351	.481	0	4	.000	87	129	.674	87	174	261	54	193	0	18	68	24	425	3.2	0.7	5.2
89-90–Houston	18	0	116	10	29	.345	0	0	–	10	19	.526	8	19	27	3	24	0	3	10	1	30	1.5	0.2	1.7
90-91–Atlanta	56	7	689	93	187	.497	0	3	.000	66	90	.733	56	109	165	32	91	1	11	45	14	252	2.9	0.6	4.5
91-92–New York	22	0	108	14	33	.424	0	0	–	14	21	.667	14	20	34	9	18	0	2	8	0	42	1.5	0.4	1.9
Reg. Season Totals	483	210	10390	1547	2893	.535	1	16	.063	935	1330	.703	777	1589	2366	491	1256	14	139	619	187	4030	4.9	1.0	8.3
Playoff Totals	15	5	214	22	49	.449	0	1	.000	15	18	.833	11	46	57	6	35	0	4	7	4	59	3.8	0.4	3.9

McCoy, Jelani Marwan b. December 6, 1977 Ht. 6-10 Wt. 245 College: UCLA

SEASON–TEAM	G	GS	MIN	FGM	FGA	PCT	3FGM	3FGA	PCT	FTM	FTA	PCT	O-RB	D-RB	TOT	AST	PF	DQ	STL	TO	BLK	PTS	RPG	APG	PPG
98-99–Seattle	26	0	331	56	76	.737	0	0	–	21	42	.500	27	52	79	4	42	0	11	10	20	133	3.0	0.2	5.1
99-00–Seattle	58	2	746	102	177	.576	0	0	–	45	91	.495	54	125	179	24	127	0	15	45	46	249	3.1	0.4	4.3
Reg. Season Totals	84	2	1077	158	253	.625	0	0	–	66	133	.496	81	177	258	28	169	0	26	55	66	382	3.1	0.3	4.5
Playoff Totals	3	0	26	2	5	.400	0	0	–	0	3	.000	0	6	6	2	6	0	0	2	0	4	2.0	0.7	1.3

McCracken, Paul George b. September 11, 1950 Ht. 6-4 Wt. 180 College: Cal State-Northridge

SEASON–TEAM	G	GS	MIN	FGM	FGA	PCT	3FGM	3FGA	PCT	FTM	FTA	PCT	O-RB	D-RB	TOT	AST	PF	DQ	STL	TO	BLK	PTS	RPG	APG	PPG
72-73–Houston	24	–	305	44	89	.494	–	–	–	23	39	.590	–	–	51	17	32	0	–	–	–	111	2.1	0.7	4.6
73-74–Houston	4	–	13	1	4	.250	–	–	–	0	0	–	1	5	6	2	3	0	0	–	0	2	1.5	0.5	0.5
76-77–Chicago	9	–	119	18	47	.383	–	–	–	11	18	.611	6	10	16	14	17	0	6	–	0	47	1.8	1.6	5.2
Reg. Season Totals	37	–	437	63	140	.450	–	–	–	34	57	.596	7	15	73	33	52	0	6	–	0	160	2.0	0.9	4.3

McCray, Carlton Lamont (Scooter) b. February 8, 1960 Ht. 6-9 Wt. 215 College: Louisville

SEASON–TEAM	G	GS	MIN	FGM	FGA	PCT	3FGM	3FGA	PCT	FTM	FTA	PCT	O-RB	D-RB	TOT	AST	PF	DQ	STL	TO	BLK	PTS	RPG	APG	PPG
83-84–Seattle	47	6	520	47	121	.388	0	0	–	35	50	.700	45	70	115	44	73	1	11	34	19	129	2.4	0.9	2.7
84-85–Seattle	6	0	93	6	10	.600	0	0	–	3	4	.750	6	11	17	7	13	0	1	10	3	15	2.8	1.2	2.5
86-87–Cleveland	24	2	279	30	65	.462	0	0	–	20	41	.488	19	39	58	23	28	0	9	24	4	80	2.4	1.0	3.3
Reg. Season Totals	77	8	892	83	196	.423	0	0	–	58	95	.611	70	120	190	74	114	1	21	68	26	224	2.5	1.0	2.9
Playoff Totals	4	0	38	4	6	.667	0	1	.000	0	1	.000	3	3	6	3	8	0	1	0	0	8	1.5	0.8	2.0

McCray, Rodney Earl b. August 29, 1961 Ht. 6-8 Wt. 235 College: Louisville

SEASON–TEAM	G	GS	MIN	FGM	FGA	PCT	3FGM	3FGA	PCT	FTM	FTA	PCT	O-RB	D-RB	TOT	AST	PF	DQ	STL	TO	BLK	PTS	RPG	APG	PPG
83-84–Houston	79	36	2081	335	672	.499	1	4	.250	182	249	.731	173	277	450	176	205	1	53	120	54	853	5.7	2.2	10.8
84-85–Houston	82	82	3001	476	890	.535	0	6	.000	231	313	.738	201	338	539	355	215	2	90	178	75	1183	6.6	4.3	14.4
85-86–Houston	82	82	2610	338	629	.537	0	3	.000	171	222	.770	159	361	520	292	197	2	50	130	58	847	6.3	3.6	10.3
86-87–Houston	81	81	3136	432	783	.552	0	9	.000	306	393	.779	190	388	578	434	172	2	88	208	53	1170	7.1	5.4	14.4
87-88–Houston	81	80	2689	359	746	.481	0	4	.000	288	367	.785	232	399	631	264	166	2	57	144	51	1006	7.8	3.3	12.4
88-89–Sacramento	68	65	2435	340	729	.466	5	22	.227	169	234	.722	143	371	514	293	121	0	57	168	36	854	7.6	4.3	12.6
89-90–Sacramento	82	82	3238	537	1043	.515	11	42	.262	273	348	.784	192	477	669	377	176	0	60	174	70	1358	8.2	4.6	16.6
90-91–Dallas	74	68	2561	336	679	.495	13	39	.333	159	198	.803	153	407	560	259	203	3	70	129	51	844	7.6	3.5	11.4
91-92–Dallas	75	48	2106	271	622	.436	25	85	.294	110	153	.719	149	319	468	219	180	2	48	115	30	677	6.2	2.9	9.0
92-93–Chicago	64	5	1019	92	204	.451	2	5	.400	36	52	.692	53	105	158	81	99	0	12	53	15	222	2.5	1.3	3.5
Reg. Season Totals	768	629	24876	3516	6997	.503	57	219	.260	1925	2529	.761	1645	3442	5087	2750	1734	14	585	1419	493	9014	6.6	3.6	11.7
Playoff Totals	46	39	1650	197	374	.527	0	6	.000	109	147	.741	81	190	271	206	99	0	33	87	33	503	5.9	4.5	10.9

McCullough, John P. b. October 5, 1956 Ht. 6-4 Wt. 190 College: Oklahoma

SEASON–TEAM	G	GS	MIN	FGM	FGA	PCT	3FGM	3FGA	PCT	FTM	FTA	PCT	O-RB	D-RB	TOT	AST	PF	DQ	STL	TO	BLK	PTS	RPG	APG	PPG
81-82–Phoenix	8	0	23	9	13	.692	0	0	–	3	5	.600	1	3	4	3	3	0	2	3	0	21	0.5	0.4	2.6
Reg. Season Totals	8	0	23	9	13	.692	0	0	–	3	5	.600	1	3	4	3	3	0	2	3	0	21	0.5	0.4	2.6

McDaniel, Clint b. February 26, 1972 Ht. 6-4 Wt. 180 College: Arkansas

SEASON–TEAM	G	GS	MIN	FGM	FGA	PCT	3FGM	3FGA	PCT	FTM	FTA	PCT	O-RB	D-RB	TOT	AST	PF	DQ	STL	TO	BLK	PTS	RPG	APG	PPG
95-96–Sacramento	12	0	71	8	23	.348	2	6	.333	12	16	.750	3	7	10	7	10	0	5	2	0	30	0.8	0.6	2.5
Reg. Season Totals	12	0	71	8	23	.348	2	6	.333	12	16	.750	3	7	10	7	10	0	5	2	0	30	0.8	0.6	2.5

McDaniel, Xavier Maurice (X-Man) b. June 4, 1963 Ht. 6-7 Wt. 218 College: Wichita State

SEASON–TEAM	G	GS	MIN	FGM	FGA	PCT	3FGM	3FGA	PCT	FTM	FTA	PCT	O-RB	D-RB	TOT	AST	PF	DQ	STL	TO	BLK	PTS	RPG	APG	PPG
85-86–Seattle	82	80	2706	576	1176	.490	2	10	.200	250	364	.687	307	348	655	193	305	8	101	248	37	1404	8.0	2.4	17.1
86-87–Seattle	82	82	3031	806	1583	.509	3	14	.214	275	395	.696	338	367	705	207	300	4	115	234	52	1890	8.6	2.5	23.0
87-88–Seattle	78	77	2703	687	1407	.488	14	50	.280	281	393	.715	206	312	518	263	230	2	96	223	52	1669	6.6	3.4	21.4
88-89–Seattle	82	10	2385	677	1385	.489	11	36	.306	312	426	.732	177	256	433	134	231	0	84	210	40	1677	5.3	1.6	20.5
89-90–Seattle	69	67	2432	611	1233	.496	5	17	.294	244	333	.733	165	282	447	171	231	2	73	187	36	1471	6.5	2.5	21.3
90-91–Seattle-Phoenix	81	79	2634	590	1186	.497	0	8	.000	193	267	.723	173	384	557	187	264	2	76	184	46	1373	6.9	2.3	17.0
91-92–New York	82	82	2344	488	1021	.478	12	39	.308	137	192	.714	176	284	460	149	241	3	57	147	24	1125	5.6	1.8	13.7
92-93–Boston	82	27	2215	457	924	.495	6	22	.273	191	241	.793	168	321	489	163	249	4	72	171	51	1111	6.0	2.0	13.5
93-94–Boston	82	5	1971	387	839	.461	10	41	.244	144	213	.676	142	258	400	126	193	0	48	116	39	928	4.9	1.5	11.3
94-95–Boston	68	15	1430	246	546	.451	6	21	.286	89	125	.712	94	206	300	108	146	0	30	89	20	587	4.4	1.6	8.6
96-97–New Jersey	62	5	1170	138	355	.389	5	25	.200	65	89	.730	124	194	318	65	144	0	36	70	17	346	5.1	1.0	5.6
97-98–New Jersey	20	0	180	10	30	.333	0	0	–	5	8	.625	12	19	31	9	23	0	3	8	2	25	1.6	0.5	1.3
Reg. Season Totals	870	529	25201	5673	11685	.485	74	283	.261	2186	3046	.718	2082	3231	5313	1775	2557	25	791	1887	416	13606	6.1	2.0	15.6
Playoff Totals	51	43	1733	365	787	.464	11	39	.282	126	189	.667	145	212	357	131	173	3	36	125	22	867	7.0	2.6	17.0
All-Star Totals	1	0	13	1	9	.111	0	0	–	0	0	–	1	1	2	0	1	0	0	1	0	2	2.0	0.0	2.0

McDaniels, James Ronald (Jim) b. April 2, 1948 Ht. 7-0 Wt. 230 College: Western Kentucky

SEASON–TEAM	G	GS	MIN	FGM	FGA	PCT	3FGM	3FGA	PCT	FTM	FTA	PCT	O-RB	D-RB	TOT	AST	PF	DQ	STL	TO	BLK	PTS	RPG	APG	PPG
71-72–Carolina (A)	58	–	2172	659	1276	.516	0	0	–	234	324	.722	249	565	814	97	251	–	–	167	–	1552	14.0	1.7	26.8
71-72–Seattle	12	–	235	51	123	.415	–	–	–	11	18	.611	–	–	82	9	26	0	–	–	–	113	6.8	0.8	9.4
72-73–Seattle	68	–	1095	154	386	.399	–	–	–	70	100	.700	–	–	345	78	140	4	–	–	–	378	5.1	1.1	5.6
73-74–Seattle	27	–	439	63	173	.364	–	–	–	23	43	.535	51	77	128	24	48	0	7	–	15	149	4.7	0.9	5.5
75-76–Kentucky (A)	29	–	365	78	165	.473	0	0	–	23	28	.821	40	84	124	21	64	–	8	37	17	179	4.3	0.7	6.2
75-76–Los Angeles	35	–	242	41	102	.402	–	–	–	9	9	1.000	26	48	74	15	40	1	4	–	10	91	2.1	0.4	2.6
77-78–Buffalo	42	–	694	100	234	.427	–	–	–	36	42	.857	46	135	181	44	112	3	4	50	37	236	4.3	1.0	5.6
Reg. NBA Totals	184	–	2705	409	1018	.402	–	–	–	149	212	.703	123	260	810	170	366	8	15	50	62	967	4.4	0.9	5.3
Reg. ABA Totals	87	–	2537	737	1441	.511	0	0	–	257	352	.730	289	649	938	118	315	0	8	204	17	1731	10.8	1.4	19.9
ABA Playoff Totals	10	–	98	19	41	.463	0	0	–	4	7	.571	9	26	35	5	16	0	3	4	5	42	3.5	0.5	4.2

McDonald, Benjamin (Ben) b. July 20, 1962 Ht. 6-8 Wt. 225 College: California-Irvine

SEASON–TEAM	G	GS	MIN	FGM	FGA	PCT	3FGM	3FGA	PCT	FTM	FTA	PCT	O-RB	D-RB	TOT	AST	PF	DQ	STL	TO	BLK	PTS	RPG	APG	PPG
85-86–Cleveland	21	0	266	28	58	.483	0	1	.000	5	8	.625	15	23	38	9	30	0	7	10	1	61	1.8	0.4	2.9
86-87–Golden State	63	34	1284	164	360	.456	1	8	.125	24	38	.632	63	120	183	84	200	5	27	43	8	353	2.9	1.3	5.6
87-88–Golden State	81	41	2039	258	552	.467	9	35	.257	87	111	.784	133	202	335	138	246	4	39	93	8	612	4.1	1.7	7.6
88-89–Golden State	11	0	103	13	19	.684	0	0	–	9	15	.600	4	8	12	5	11	0	4	3	0	35	1.1	0.5	3.2
Reg. Season Totals	176	75	3692	463	989	.468	10	44	.227	125	172	.727	215	353	568	236	487	9	77	149	17	1061	3.2	1.3	6.0
Playoff Totals	10	0	85	3	21	.143	0	5	.000	2	4	.500	6	8	14	10	15	0	5	4	1	8	1.4	1.0	0.8

M

McDonald, Glenn Stuart b. March 18, 1952 Ht. 6-6 Wt. 190 College: Long Beach State

SEASON–TEAM	G	GS	MIN	FGM	FGA	PCT	3FGM	3FGA	PCT	FTM	FTA	PCT	O-RB	D-RB	TOT	AST	PF	DQ	STL	TO	BLK	PTS	RPG	APG	PPG
74-75–Boston	62	–	395	70	182	.385	–	–	–	28	37	.757	20	48	68	24	58	0	8	–	5	168	1.1	0.4	2.7
75-76–Boston	75	–	1019	191	456	.419	–	–	–	40	56	.714	56	79	135	68	123	0	39	–	20	422	1.8	0.9	5.6
76-77–Milwaukee	9	–	79	8	34	.235	–	–	–	3	4	.750	8	4	12	7	11	0	4	–	0	19	1.3	0.8	2.1
Reg. Season Totals	146	–	1493	269	672	.400	–	–	–	71	97	.732	84	131	215	99	192	0	51	–	25	609	1.5	0.7	4.2
Playoff Totals	19	–	98	10	38	.263	–	–	–	6	9	.667	2	12	14	6	16	0	2	–	0	26	0.7	0.3	1.4

McDonald, Michael DeWayne (Mike) b. February 13, 1969 Ht. 6-10 Wt. 232 College: New Orleans

SEASON–TEAM	G	GS	MIN	FGM	FGA	PCT	3FGM	3FGA	PCT	FTM	FTA	PCT	O-RB	D-RB	TOT	AST	PF	DQ	STL	TO	BLK	PTS	RPG	APG	PPG
97-98–Charlotte	1	0	4	0	0	–	0	0	–	0	0	–	1	0	1	0	1	0	0	2	0	0	1.0	0.0	0.0
Reg. Season Totals	1	0	4	0	0	–	0	0	–	0	0	–	1	0	1	0	1	0	0	2	0	0	1.0	0.0	0.0

McDonald, Roderick William (Rod) b. April 9, 1945 d. February 7, 1994 Ht. 6-6 Wt. 205 College: Whitworth

SEASON–TEAM	G	GS	MIN	FGM	FGA	PCT	3FGM	3FGA	PCT	FTM	FTA	PCT	O-RB	D-RB	TOT	AST	PF	DQ	STL	TO	BLK	PTS	RPG	APG	PPG
70-71–Utah (A)	29	–	206	50	109	.459	2	2	1.000	15	25	.600	–	–	93	7	41	–	–	–	–	117	3.2	0.2	4.0
71-72–Utah (A)	33	–	231	34	76	.447	0	2	.000	27	37	.730	–	–	74	18	40	–	–	23	–	95	2.2	0.5	2.9
72-73–Utah (A)	25	–	142	27	63	.429	1	4	.250	15	19	.789	13	17	30	15	19	0	–	14	–	70	1.2	0.6	2.8
Reg. ABA Totals	87	–	579	111	248	.448	3	8	.375	57	81	.704	13	17	197	40	100	0	–	37	–	282	2.3	0.5	3.2
ABA Playoff Totals	9	–	36	12	18	.667	1	2	.500	1	3	.333	–	–	14	2	6	0	–	–	–	26	1.6	0.2	2.9

McDowell, Hank Leigh b. November 13, 1959 Ht. 6-9 Wt. 215 College: Memphis

SEASON–TEAM	G	GS	MIN	FGM	FGA	PCT	3FGM	3FGA	PCT	FTM	FTA	PCT	O-RB	D-RB	TOT	AST	PF	DQ	STL	TO	BLK	PTS	RPG	APG	PPG
81-82–Golden State	30	1	335	34	84	.405	0	0	–	27	41	.659	41	59	100	20	52	1	6	21	8	95	3.3	0.7	3.2
82-83–G.S.-Port.	56	0	505	58	126	.460	0	2	.000	47	61	.770	54	65	119	24	84	0	8	40	11	163	2.1	0.4	2.9
83-84–San Diego	57	0	611	85	197	.431	0	3	.000	38	56	.679	63	92	155	37	77	0	14	49	2	208	2.7	0.6	3.6
84-85–Houston	34	0	132	20	42	.476	0	1	.000	7	10	.700	7	15	22	9	22	0	3	8	5	47	0.6	0.3	1.4
85-86–Houston	22	0	204	24	42	.571	0	2	.000	17	25	.680	12	37	49	6	25	0	1	10	3	65	2.2	0.3	3.0
86-87–Milwaukee	7	0	70	8	17	.471	0	0	–	6	7	.857	9	10	19	2	14	0	2	3	0	22	2.7	0.3	3.1
Reg. Season Totals	206	1	1857	229	508	.451	0	8	.000	142	200	.710	186	278	464	98	274	1	34	131	29	600	2.3	0.5	2.9
Playoff Totals	15	0	37	2	8	.250	0	0	–	5	8	.625	4	6	10	4	8	0	0	2	0	9	0.7	0.3	0.6

McDyess, Antonio Keithflen b. September 7, 1974 Ht. 6-9 Wt. 220 College: Alabama

SEASON–TEAM	G	GS	MIN	FGM	FGA	PCT	3FGM	3FGA	PCT	FTM	FTA	PCT	O-RB	D-RB	TOT	AST	PF	DQ	STL	TO	BLK	PTS	RPG	APG	PPG
95-96–Denver	76	75	2280	427	881	.485	0	4	.000	166	243	.683	229	343	572	75	250	4	54	154	114	1020	7.5	1.0	13.4
96-97–Denver	74	73	2565	536	1157	.463	6	35	.171	274	387	.708	155	382	537	106	276	9	62	199	126	1352	7.3	1.4	18.3
97-98–Phoenix	81	81	2441	497	927	.536	0	2	.000	231	329	.702	206	407	613	106	292	6	100	142	135	1225	7.6	1.3	15.1
98-99–Denver	50	50	1937	415	882	.471	1	9	.111	230	338	.680	168	369	537	82	175	5	73	138	115	1061	10.7	1.6	21.2
99-00–Denver	81	81	2698	614	1211	.507	0	2	.000	323	516	.626	234	451	685	159	316	12	69	230	139	1551	8.5	2.0	19.1
Reg. Season Totals	362	360	11921	2489	5058	.492	7	52	.135	1224	1813	.675	992	1952	2944	528	1309	36	358	863	629	6209	8.1	1.5	17.2
Playoff Totals	4	4	147	31	65	.477	0	0	–	9	14	.643	18	35	53	4	12	0	2	5	6	71	13.3	1.0	17.8

McElroy, James Charles Jr. (Jim) b. October 4, 1953 Ht. 6-3 Wt. 190 College: Monroe (N.Y.) C.C.; Central Michigan

SEASON–TEAM	G	GS	MIN	FGM	FGA	PCT	3FGM	3FGA	PCT	FTM	FTA	PCT	O-RB	D-RB	TOT	AST	PF	DQ	STL	TO	BLK	PTS	RPG	APG	PPG
75-76–New Orleans	51	–	1134	151	296	.510	–	–	–	81	110	.736	34	76	110	107	70	0	44	–	4	383	2.2	2.1	7.5
76-77–New Orleans	73	–	2029	301	640	.470	–	–	–	169	217	.779	55	128	183	260	119	3	60	–	8	771	2.5	3.6	10.6
77-78–New Orleans	74	–	1760	287	607	.473	–	–	–	123	167	.737	44	104	148	292	110	0	58	141	34	697	2.0	3.9	9.4
78-79–New Orleans	79	–	2698	539	1097	.491	–	–	–	259	340	.762	61	154	215	453	183	1	148	237	49	1337	2.7	5.7	16.9
79-80–Detroit-Atlanta	67	–	1528	228	527	.433	5	21	.238	132	172	.767	32	67	99	227	123	2	46	131	19	593	1.5	3.4	8.9
80-81–Atlanta	54	–	680	78	202	.386	1	8	.125	48	59	.814	10	38	48	84	62	0	20	79	9	205	0.9	1.6	3.8
81-82–Atlanta	20	17	349	52	125	.416	1	5	.200	29	36	.806	6	11	17	39	44	0	8	22	4	134	0.9	2.0	6.7
Reg. Season Totals	418	17	10178	1636	3494	.468	7	34	.206	841	1101	.764	242	578	820	1462	711	6	384	610	127	4120	2.0	3.5	9.9
Playoff Totals	5	0	32	4	9	.444	0	1	.000	4	5	.800	1	1	2	4	1	0	0	2	0	12	0.4	0.8	2.4

McFarland, Patrick Aloysius (Pat) b. December 7, 1951 Ht. 6-5 Wt. 185 College: St. Joseph's (Pa.)

SEASON–TEAM	G	GS	MIN	FGM	FGA	PCT	3FGM	3FGA	PCT	FTM	FTA	PCT	O-RB	D-RB	TOT	AST	PF	DQ	STL	TO	BLK	PTS	RPG	APG	PPG
73-74–Denver (A)	67	–	757	159	359	.443	8	24	.333	35	52	.673	60	74	134	64	69	–	23	41	6	361	2.0	1.0	5.4
74-75–Denver (A)	70	–	945	200	424	.472	2	16	.125	52	66	.788	37	83	120	116	60	–	47	108	5	454	1.7	1.7	6.5
75-76–San Diego (A)	11	–	275	55	120	.458	1	2	.500	21	22	.955	17	27	44	39	20	–	6	29	1	132	4.0	3.5	12.0
Reg. ABA Totals	148	–	1977	414	903	.458	11	42	.262	108	140	.771	114	184	298	219	149	0	76	178	12	947	2.0	1.5	6.4
ABA Playoff Totals	5	–	30	2	8	.250	0	2	.000	2	2	1.000	1	2	3	2	3	0	0	6	0	6	0.6	0.4	1.2

McGaha, Fred Melvin (Mel) b. September 26, 1926 Ht. 6-1 Wt. 190 College: Arkansas

SEASON–TEAM	G	GS	MIN	FGM	FGA	PCT	3FGM	3FGA	PCT	FTM	FTA	PCT	O-RB	D-RB	TOT	AST	PF	DQ	STL	TO	BLK	PTS	RPG	APG	PPG
48-49–New York	51	–	–	62	195	.318	–	–	–	52	88	.591	–	–	–	51	104	–	–	–	–	176	–	1.0	3.5
Reg. Season Totals	51	–	–	62	195	.318	–	–	–	52	88	.591	–	–	–	51	104	–	–	–	–	176	–	1.0	3.5
Playoff Totals	2	–	–	0	3	.000	–	–	–	1	2	.500	–	–	–	2	6	–	–	–	–	1	–	1.0	0.5

McGee, Michael Ray (Mike) b. July 29, 1959 Ht. 6-5 Wt. 205 College: Michigan

SEASON–TEAM	G	GS	MIN	FGM	FGA	PCT	3FGM	3FGA	PCT	FTM	FTA	PCT	O-RB	D-RB	TOT	AST	PF	DQ	STL	TO	BLK	PTS	RPG	APG	PPG
81-82–Los Angeles	39	0	352	80	172	.465	0	4	.000	31	53	.585	34	15	49	16	59	0	18	34	3	191	1.3	0.4	4.9
82-83–Los Angeles	39	7	381	69	163	.423	1	7	.143	17	23	.739	33	20	53	26	50	1	11	27	5	156	1.4	0.7	4.0
83-84–Los Angeles	77	45	1425	347	584	.594	2	13	.154	61	113	.540	117	76	193	81	176	0	49	111	6	757	2.5	1.1	9.8
84-85–L.A. Lakers	76	3	1170	329	612	.538	22	61	.361	94	160	.588	97	68	165	71	147	1	39	81	7	774	2.2	0.9	10.2
85-86–L.A. Lakers	71	19	1213	252	544	.463	41	114	.360	42	64	.656	51	89	140	83	131	0	53	70	7	587	2.0	1.2	8.3
86-87–Atlanta	76	6	1420	311	677	.459	86	229	.376	80	137	.584	71	88	159	149	156	1	61	104	2	788	2.1	2.0	10.4
87-88–Atlanta-Sac.	48	0	1003	223	530	.421	53	160	.331	76	102	.745	55	73	128	71	81	0	52	65	6	575	2.7	1.5	12.0
88-89–New Jersey	80	49	2027	434	917	.473	93	255	.365	77	144	.535	73	116	189	116	184	1	80	124	12	1038	2.4	1.5	13.0
89-90–Phoenix	14	7	280	42	87	.483	8	23	.348	10	21	.476	11	25	36	16	28	0	8	14	1	102	2.6	1.1	7.3
Reg. Season Totals	520	136	9271	2087	4286	.487	306	866	.353	488	817	.597	542	570	1112	629	1012	4	371	630	49	4968	2.1	1.2	9.6
Playoff Totals	68	13	838	201	400	.503	21	61	.344	63	103	.612	63	46	109	55	100	0	23	54	3	486	1.6	0.8	7.1

McGill, Bill (The Hill) b. September 16, 1939 Ht. 6-9 Wt. 225 College: Utah

SEASON–TEAM	G	GS	MIN	FGM	FGA	PCT	3FGM	3FGA	PCT	FTM	FTA	PCT	O-RB	D-RB	TOT	AST	PF	DQ	STL	TO	BLK	PTS	RPG	APG	PPG
62-63–Chicago	60	–	590	181	353	.513	–	–	–	80	119	.672	–	–	161	38	118	1	–	–	–	442	2.7	0.6	7.4
63-64–Balt.-N.Y.	74	–	1784	456	937	.487	–	–	–	204	282	.723	–	–	414	121	217	7	–	–	–	1116	5.6	1.6	15.1
64-65–St. Louis-L.A.	24	–	133	21	65	.323	–	–	–	13	17	.765	–	–	36	9	32	1	–	–	–	55	1.5	0.4	2.3
68-69–Denver (A)	78	–	1760	411	745	.552	0	0	–	180	264	.682	–	–	460	102	289	13	–	149	–	1002	5.9	1.3	12.8
69-70–Pitt.-L.A.-Dal. (A)	59	–	830	201	369	.545	0	0	–	77	108	.713	–	–	215	60	140	1	–	–	–	479	3.6	1.0	8.1
Reg. NBA Totals	158	–	2507	658	1355	.486	–	–	–	297	418	.711	–	–	611	168	367	9	–	–	–	1613	3.9	1.1	10.2
Reg. ABA Totals	137	–	2590	612	1114	.549	0	0	–	257	372	.691	–	–	675	162	429	14	–	149	–	1481	4.9	1.2	10.8
NBA Playoff Totals	5	–	34	5	9	.556	–	–	–	1	1	1.000	–	–	9	2	9	1	–	–	–	11	1.8	0.4	2.2
ABA Playoff Totals	7	–	96	19	39	.487	0	0	–	9	10	.900	–	–	23	6	26	2	–	–	–	47	3.3	0.9	6.7

McGinnis, George F. b. August 12, 1950 Ht. 6-8 Wt. 235 College: Indiana

SEASON–TEAM	G	GS	MIN	FGM	FGA	PCT	3FGM	3FGA	PCT	FTM	FTA	PCT	O-RB	D-RB	TOT	AST	PF	DQ	STL	TO	BLK	PTS	RPG	APG	PPG
71-72–Indiana (A)	73	–	2179	465	999	.465	6	38	.158	298	462	.645	290	421	711	137	260	–	–	256	–	1234	9.7	1.9	16.9
72-73–Indiana (A)	82	–	3347	868	1755	.495	8	32	.250	517	778	.665	434	588	1022	205	348	0	160	401	–	2261	12.5	2.5	27.6
73-74–Indiana (A)	80	–	3266	789	1686	.468	5	34	.147	488	715	.683	422	775	1197	267	325	–	159	393	40	2071	15.0	3.3	25.9
74-75–Indiana (A)	79	–	3193	873	1934	.451	62	175	.354	545	753	.724	396	730	1126	495	303	–	206	422	56	2353	14.3	6.3	29.8
75-76–Philadelphia	77	–	2946	647	1552	.417	–	–	–	475	642	.740	260	707	967	359	334	13	198	–	41	1769	12.6	4.7	23.0
76-77–Philadelphia	79	–	2769	659	1439	.458	–	–	–	372	546	.681	324	587	911	302	299	4	163	–	37	1690	11.5	3.8	21.4
77-78–Philadelphia	78	–	2533	588	1270	.463	–	–	–	411	574	.716	282	528	810	294	287	6	137	312	27	1587	10.4	3.8	20.3
78-79–Denver	76	–	2552	603	1273	.474	–	–	–	509	765	.665	256	608	864	283	321	16	129	346	52	1715	11.4	3.7	22.6
79-80–Denver-Indiana	73	–	2208	400	886	.451	2	15	.133	270	488	.553	222	477	699	333	303	12	101	281	23	1072	9.6	4.6	14.7
80-81–Indiana	69	–	1845	348	768	.453	0	7	.000	207	385	.538	164	364	528	210	242	3	99	221	28	903	7.7	3.0	13.1
81-82–Indiana	76	4	1341	141	378	.373	0	3	.000	72	159	.453	93	305	398	204	198	4	96	131	28	354	5.2	2.7	4.7
Reg. NBA Totals	528	4	16194	3386	7566	.448	2	25	.080	2316	3559	.651	1601	3576	5177	1985	1984	58	923	1291	236	9090	9.8	3.8	17.2
Reg. ABA Totals	314	–	11985	2995	6374	.470	81	279	.290	1848	2708	.682	1542	2514	4056	1104	1236	0	525	1472	96	7919	12.9	3.5	25.2
NBA Playoff Totals	34	0	1035	187	474	.395	0	0	–	121	189	.640	97	230	327	118	143	4	41	43	11	495	9.6	3.5	14.6
ABA Playoff Totals	70	–	2680	599	1334	.449	29	100	.290	431	620	.695	345	556	901	286	301	0	74	281	27	1658	12.9	4.1	23.7
NBA All-Star Totals	3	2	70	11	30	.367	0	0	–	8	17	.471	8	12	20	7	9	0	9	0	0	30	6.7	2.3	10.0

McGlocklin, Jon P. b. June 10, 1943 Ht. 6-5 Wt. 205 College: Indiana

SEASON–TEAM	G	GS	MIN	FGM	FGA	PCT	3FGM	3FGA	PCT	FTM	FTA	PCT	O-RB	D-RB	TOT	AST	PF	DQ	STL	TO	BLK	PTS	RPG	APG	PPG
65-66–Cincinnati	72	–	852	153	363	.421	–	–	–	62	79	.785	–	–	133	88	77	0	–	–	–	368	1.8	1.2	5.1
66-67–Cincinnati	60	–	1194	217	493	.440	–	–	–	74	104	.712	–	–	164	93	84	0	–	–	–	508	2.7	1.6	8.5
67-68–San Diego	65	–	1876	316	757	.417	–	–	–	156	180	.867	–	–	199	178	117	0	–	–	–	788	3.1	2.7	12.1
68-69–Milwaukee	80	–	2888	662	1358	.487	–	–	–	246	292	.842	–	–	343	312	186	1	–	–	–	1570	4.3	3.9	19.6
69-70–Milwaukee	82	–	2966	639	1206	.530	–	–	–	169	198	.854	–	–	252	303	164	0	–	–	–	1447	3.1	3.7	17.6
70-71–Milwaukee	82	–	2891	574	1073	.535	–	–	–	144	167	.862	–	–	223	305	189	0	–	–	–	1292	2.7	3.7	15.8
71-72–Milwaukee	80	–	2213	374	733	.510	–	–	–	109	126	.865	–	–	181	231	146	0	–	–	–	857	2.3	2.9	10.7
72-73–Milwaukee	80	–	1951	351	699	.502	–	–	–	63	73	.863	–	–	158	236	119	0	–	–	–	765	2.0	3.0	9.6
73-74–Milwaukee	79	–	1910	329	693	.475	–	–	–	72	80	.900	33	106	139	241	128	1	43	–	7	730	1.8	3.1	9.2
74-75–Milwaukee	79	–	1853	323	651	.496	–	–	–	63	72	.875	25	94	119	255	142	2	51	–	6	709	1.5	3.2	9.0
75-76–Milwaukee	33	–	336	63	148	.426	–	–	–	9	10	.900	3	14	17	38	18	0	8	–	0	135	0.5	1.2	4.1
Reg. Season Totals	792	–	20930	4001	8174	.489	–	–	–	1167	1381	.845	61	214	1928	2280	1370	4	102	–	13	9169	2.4	2.9	11.6
Playoff Totals	55	–	1528	266	544	.489	–	–	–	75	91	.824	2	15	102	123	121	0	7	–	1	607	1.9	2.2	11.0
All-Star Totals	1	–	7	1	2	.500	–	–	–	0	0	–	0	0	1	0	0	0	0	–	0	2	1.0	0.0	2.0

McGrady, Tracy Lamar (T-Mac) b. May 24, 1979 Ht. 6-8 Wt. 210 High School: Mount Zion Christian Academy

SEASON–TEAM	G	GS	MIN	FGM	FGA	PCT	3FGM	3FGA	PCT	FTM	FTA	PCT	O-RB	D-RB	TOT	AST	PF	DQ	STL	TO	BLK	PTS	RPG	APG	PPG
97-98–Toronto	64	17	1179	179	398	.450	14	41	.341	79	111	.712	105	164	269	98	86	0	49	66	61	451	4.2	1.5	7.0
98-99–Toronto	49	2	1106	168	385	.436	8	35	.229	114	157	.726	120	158	278	113	94	1	52	80	66	458	5.7	2.3	9.3
99-00–Toronto	79	34	2462	459	1018	.451	18	65	.277	277	392	.707	188	313	501	263	201	2	90	160	151	1213	6.3	3.3	15.4
Reg. Season Totals	192	53	4747	806	1801	.448	40	141	.284	470	660	.712	413	635	1048	474	381	3	191	306	278	2122	5.5	2.5	11.1
Playoff Totals	3	3	111	17	44	.386	2	7	.286	14	16	.875	10	11	21	9	10	0	3	10	3	50	7.0	3.0	16.7

M

McGregor, Gilbert Ray (Gil) b. June 14, 1949 Ht. 6-8 Wt. 240 College: Wake Forest

SEASON–TEAM	G	GS	MIN	FGM	FGA	PCT	3FGM	3FGA	PCT	FTM	FTA	PCT	O-RB	D-RB	TOT	AST	PF	DQ	STL	TO	BLK	PTS	RPG	APG	PPG
71-72–Cincinnati	42	–	532	66	182	.363	–	–	–	39	56	.696	–	–	148	18	120	4	–	–	–	171	3.5	0.4	4.1
Reg. Season Totals	42	–	532	66	182	.363	–	–	–	39	56	.696	–	–	148	18	120	4	–	–	–	171	3.5	0.4	4.1

McGriff, Elton Wayne (Mac) b. August 21, 1942 Ht. 6-9 Wt. 225 College: Creighton

SEASON–TEAM	G	GS	MIN	FGM	FGA	PCT	3FGM	3FGA	PCT	FTM	FTA	PCT	O-RB	D-RB	TOT	AST	PF	DQ	STL	TO	BLK	PTS	RPG	APG	PPG
67-68–Dallas (A)	20	–	369	49	89	.551	0	0	–	33	62	.532	–	–	114	2	65	3	–	21	–	131	5.7	0.1	6.6
68-69–Dal.-N.O.-Ken. (A)	36	–	495	75	171	.439	0	1	.000	57	90	.633	–	–	144	8	85	1	–	32	–	207	4.0	0.2	5.8
Reg. ABA Totals	56	–	864	124	260	.477	0	1	.000	90	152	.592	–	–	258	10	150	4	–	53	–	338	4.6	0.2	6.0
ABA Playoff Totals	13	–	267	38	91	.418	0	0	–	27	48	.563	–	–	99	8	49	3	–	22	–	103	7.6	0.6	7.9

McGuire, Alfred (Allie) b. July 10, 1951 Ht. 6-3 Wt. 175 College: Marquette

SEASON–TEAM	G	GS	MIN	FGM	FGA	PCT	3FGM	3FGA	PCT	FTM	FTA	PCT	O-RB	D-RB	TOT	AST	PF	DQ	STL	TO	BLK	PTS	RPG	APG	PPG
73-74–New York	2	–	10	2	4	.500	–	–	–	0	0	–	0	2	2	1	2	0	0	–	0	4	1.0	0.5	2.0
Reg. Season Totals	2	–	10	2	4	.500	–	–	–	0	0	–	0	2	2	1	2	0	0	–	0	4	1.0	0.5	2.0

McGuire, Alfred James (Al) b. September 7, 1928 Ht. 6-2 Wt. 180 College: St. John's (N.Y.) HOF: 1992

SEASON–TEAM	G	GS	MIN	FGM	FGA	PCT	3FGM	3FGA	PCT	FTM	FTA	PCT	O-RB	D-RB	TOT	AST	PF	DQ	STL	TO	BLK	PTS	RPG	APG	PPG
51-52–New York	59	–	788	72	167	.431	–	–	–	64	122	.525	–	–	121	107	136	8	–	–	–	208	2.1	1.8	3.5
52-53–New York	58	–	1231	112	287	.390	–	–	–	128	201	.637	–	–	167	145	206	8	–	–	–	352	2.9	2.5	6.1
53-54–New York	64	–	849	58	177	.328	–	–	–	58	133	.436	–	–	121	103	144	2	–	–	–	174	1.9	1.6	2.7
54-55–Baltimore	10	–	98	9	32	.281	–	–	–	5	7	.714	–	–	9	8	15	0	–	–	–	23	0.9	0.8	2.3
Reg. Season Totals	191	–	2966	251	663	.379	–	–	–	255	463	.551	–	–	418	363	501	18	–	–	–	757	2.2	1.9	4.0
Playoff Totals	24	–	372	31	82	.378	–	–	–	22	43	.512	–	–	28	30	60	3	–	–	–	84	1.2	1.3	3.5

McGuire, Richard Joseph (Dick, Tricky Dick) b. January 25, 1926 Ht. 6-0 Wt. 180 College: St. John's (N.Y.); Dartmouth HOF: 1993

SEASON–TEAM	G	GS	MIN	FGM	FGA	PCT	3FGM	3FGA	PCT	FTM	FTA	PCT	O-RB	D-RB	TOT	AST	PF	DQ	STL	TO	BLK	PTS	RPG	APG	PPG
49-50–New York	68	–	–	190	563	.337	–	–	–	204	313	.652	–	–	–	386	160	–	–	–	–	584	–	5.7	8.6
50-51–New York	64	–	–	179	482	.371	–	–	–	179	276	.649	–	–	334	400	154	2	–	–	–	537	5.2	6.3	8.4
51-52–New York	64	–	2018	204	474	.430	–	–	–	183	290	.631	–	–	332	388	181	4	–	–	–	591	5.2	6.1	9.2
52-53–New York	61	–	1783	142	373	.381	–	–	–	153	269	.569	–	–	280	296	172	3	–	–	–	437	4.6	4.9	7.2
53-54–New York	68	–	2343	201	493	.408	–	–	–	220	345	.638	–	–	310	354	199	3	–	–	–	622	4.6	5.2	9.1
54-55–New York	71	–	2310	226	581	.389	–	–	–	195	303	.644	–	–	322	542	143	0	–	–	–	647	4.5	7.6	9.1
55-56–New York	62	–	1685	152	438	.347	–	–	–	121	193	.627	–	–	220	362	146	0	–	–	–	425	3.5	5.8	6.9
56-57–New York	72	–	1191	140	366	.383	–	–	–	105	163	.644	–	–	146	222	103	0	–	–	–	385	2.0	3.1	5.3
57-58–Detroit	69	–	2311	203	544	.373	–	–	–	150	225	.667	–	–	291	454	178	0	–	–	–	556	4.2	6.6	8.1
58-59–Detroit	71	–	2063	232	543	.427	–	–	–	191	258	.740	–	–	285	443	147	1	–	–	–	655	4.0	6.2	9.2
59-60–Detroit	68	–	1466	179	402	.445	–	–	–	124	201	.617	–	–	264	358	112	0	–	–	–	482	3.9	5.3	7.1
Reg. Season Totals	738	–	17170	2048	5259	.389	–	–	–	1825	2836	.644	–	–	2784	4205	1695	13	–	–	–	5921	4.2	5.7	8.0
Playoff Totals	63	–	1628	179	452	.407	–	–	–	163	274	.595	–	–	284	357	187	3	–	–	–	521	4.8	5.6	8.3
All-Star Totals	7	–	151	12	31	.387	–	–	–	5	12	.417	–	–	23	38	11	0	–	–	–	29	3.3	5.4	4.1

McHale, Kevin Edward b. December 19, 1957 Ht. 6-10 Wt. 210 College: Minnesota HOF: 1999

SEASON–TEAM	G	GS	MIN	FGM	FGA	PCT	3FGM	3FGA	PCT	FTM	FTA	PCT	O-RB	D-RB	TOT	AST	PF	DQ	STL	TO	BLK	PTS	RPG	APG	PPG
80-81–Boston	82	–	1645	355	666	.533	0	2	.000	108	159	.679	155	204	359	55	260	3	27	110	151	818	4.4	0.7	10.0
81-82–Boston	82	33	2332	465	875	.531	0	0	–	187	248	.754	191	365	556	91	264	1	30	137	185	1117	6.8	1.1	13.6
82-83–Boston	82	13	2345	483	893	.541	0	1	.000	193	269	.717	215	338	553	104	241	3	34	159	192	1159	6.7	1.3	14.1
83-84–Boston	82	10	2577	587	1055	.556	1	3	.333	336	439	.765	208	402	610	104	243	5	23	150	126	1511	7.4	1.3	18.4
84-85–Boston	79	31	2653	605	1062	.570	0	6	.000	355	467	.760	229	483	712	141	234	3	28	157	120	1565	9.0	1.8	19.8
85-86–Boston	68	62	2397	561	978	.574	0	0	–	326	420	.776	171	380	551	181	192	2	29	149	134	1448	8.1	2.7	21.3
86-87–Boston	77	77	3060	790	1307	.604	0	4	.000	428	512	.836	247	516	763	198	240	1	38	197	172	2008	9.9	2.6	26.1
87-88–Boston	64	63	2390	550	911	.604	0	0	–	346	434	.797	159	377	536	171	179	1	27	141	92	1446	8.4	2.7	22.6
88-89–Boston	78	74	2876	661	1211	.546	0	4	.000	436	533	.818	223	414	637	172	223	2	26	196	97	1758	8.2	2.2	22.5
89-90–Boston	82	25	2722	648	1181	.549	23	69	.333	393	440	.893	201	476	677	172	250	3	30	183	157	1712	8.3	2.1	20.9
90-91–Boston	68	10	2067	504	912	.553	15	37	.405	228	275	.829	145	335	480	126	194	2	25	140	146	1251	7.1	1.9	18.4
91-92–Boston	56	1	1398	323	634	.509	0	13	.000	134	163	.822	119	211	330	82	112	1	11	82	59	780	5.9	1.5	13.9
92-93–Boston	71	0	1656	298	649	.459	2	18	.111	164	195	.841	95	263	358	73	126	0	16	92	59	762	5.0	1.0	10.7
Reg. Season Totals	971	399	30118	6830	12334	.554	41	157	.261	3634	4554	.798	2358	4764	7122	1670	2758	27	344	1893	1690	17335	7.3	1.7	17.9
Playoff Totals	169	85	5716	1204	2145	.561	8	21	.381	766	972	.788	456	797	1253	274	571	8	65	326	281	3182	7.4	1.6	18.8
All-Star Totals	7	0	125	24	48	.500	1	2	.500	12	14	.857	13	24	37	8	21	0	1	5	12	61	5.3	1.1	8.7

McHartley, Maurice Franklin (Mo) b. August 1, 1942 Ht. 6-3 Wt. 200 College: North Carolina A&T

SEASON–TEAM	G	GS	MIN	FGM	FGA	PCT	3FGM	3FGA	PCT	FTM	FTA	PCT	O-RB	D-RB	TOT	AST	PF	DQ	STL	TO	BLK	PTS	RPG	APG	PPG
67-68–Dallas (A)	58	–	2175	330	825	.400	3	17	.176	225	324	.694	–	–	273	230	216	5	–	241	–	888	4.7	4.0	15.3
68-69–N.Y.-Miami (A)	76	–	2148	390	962	.405	6	27	.222	263	331	.795	–	–	211	269	251	5	–	269	–	1049	2.8	3.5	13.8
69-70–Mia.-Pitt.-Dal. (A)	55	–	992	155	388	.399	6	36	.167	98	130	.754	–	–	115	142	158	3	–	–	–	414	2.1	2.6	7.5
Reg. ABA Totals	189	–	5315	875	2175	.402	15	80	.188	586	785	.746	–	–	599	641	625	13	–	510	–	2351	3.2	3.4	12.4
ABA Playoff Totals	25	–	699	127	337	.377	2	9	.222	90	114	.789	–	–	98	92	88	3	–	35	–	346	3.9	3.7	13.8

McIlvaine, James Michael (Jim) b. July 30, 1972 Ht. 7-1 Wt. 264 College: Marquette

SEASON–TEAM	G	GS	MIN	FGM	FGA	PCT	3FGM	3FGA	PCT	FTM	FTA	PCT	O-RB	D-RB	TOT	AST	PF	DQ	STL	TO	BLK	PTS	RPG	APG	PPG
94-95–Washington	55	0	534	34	71	.479	0	0	–	28	41	.683	40	65	105	10	95	0	10	19	60	96	1.9	0.2	1.7
95-96–Washington	80	6	1195	62	145	.428	0	0	–	58	105	.552	66	164	230	11	171	0	21	36	166	182	2.9	0.1	2.3
96-97–Seattle	82	79	1477	130	276	.471	1	7	.143	53	107	.495	132	198	330	23	247	4	39	62	164	314	4.0	0.3	3.8
97-98–Seattle	78	72	1211	101	223	.453	0	3	.000	45	81	.556	96	163	259	19	240	3	24	54	137	247	3.3	0.2	3.2
98-99–New Jersey	22	1	269	22	51	.431	0	0	–	4	6	.667	31	23	54	2	59	1	9	13	32	48	2.5	0.1	2.2
99-00–New Jersey	66	53	1048	64	154	.416	0	0	–	29	56	.518	106	124	230	36	205	2	26	38	117	157	3.5	0.5	2.4
Reg. Season Totals	383	211	5734	413	920	.449	1	10	.100	217	396	.548	471	737	1208	101	1017	10	129	222	676	1044	3.2	0.3	2.7
Playoff Totals	11	4	87	10	27	.370	0	1	.000	2	4	.500	8	4	12	1	29	1	3	2	8	22	1.1	0.1	2.0

McInnis, Jeffrey Lemans (Jeff) b. October 22, 1974 Ht. 6-4 Wt. 190 College: North Carolina

SEASON–TEAM	G	GS	MIN	FGM	FGA	PCT	3FGM	3FGA	PCT	FTM	FTA	PCT	O-RB	D-RB	TOT	AST	PF	DQ	STL	TO	BLK	PTS	RPG	APG	PPG
96-97–Denver	13	0	117	23	49	.469	12	26	.462	7	10	.700	2	4	6	18	16	0	2	13	1	65	0.5	1.4	5.0
98-99–Washington	35	6	427	50	134	.373	9	35	.257	21	28	.750	9	12	21	73	36	0	19	30	1	130	0.6	2.1	3.7
99-00–L.A. Clippers	25	10	597	80	186	.430	7	21	.333	13	17	.765	18	54	72	89	55	0	15	27	2	180	2.9	3.6	7.2
Reg. Season Totals	73	16	1141	153	369	.415	28	82	.341	41	55	.745	29	70	99	180	107	0	36	70	4	375	1.4	2.5	5.1

McIntosh, Kennedy (Kenny) b. January 21, 1949 Ht. 6-7 Wt. 225 College: Eastern Michigan

SEASON–TEAM	G	GS	MIN	FGM	FGA	PCT	3FGM	3FGA	PCT	FTM	FTA	PCT	O-RB	D-RB	TOT	AST	PF	DQ	STL	TO	BLK	PTS	RPG	APG	PPG
71-72–Chicago	43	–	405	57	168	.339	–	–	–	21	44	.477	–	–	89	18	41	0	–	–	–	135	2.1	0.4	3.1
72-73–Chicago-Seattle	59	–	1138	115	341	.337	–	–	–	40	67	.597	–	–	231	54	102	1	–	–	–	270	3.9	0.9	4.6
73-74–Seattle	69	–	2056	223	573	.389	–	–	–	65	107	.607	111	250	361	94	178	4	52	–	29	511	5.2	1.4	7.4
74-75–Seattle	6	–	101	6	29	.207	–	–	–	6	9	.667	6	9	15	7	12	0	4	–	3	18	2.5	1.2	3.0
Reg. Season Totals	177	–	3700	401	1111	.361	–	–	–	132	227	.581	117	259	696	173	333	5	56	–	32	934	3.9	1.0	5.3

McIntyre, Robert (Bob) b. January 23, 1944 Ht. 6-7 Wt. 215 College: St. John's (N.Y.)

SEASON–TEAM	G	GS	MIN	FGM	FGA	PCT	3FGM	3FGA	PCT	FTM	FTA	PCT	O-RB	D-RB	TOT	AST	PF	DQ	STL	TO	BLK	PTS	RPG	APG	PPG
67-68–New Jersey (A)	21	–	451	70	187	.374	0	1	.000	34	58	.586	–	–	101	11	27	0	–	27	–	174	4.8	0.5	8.3
69-70–New York (A)	7	–	94	12	32	.375	1	3	.333	0	1	.000	–	–	20	5	8	0	–	–	–	25	2.9	0.7	3.6
Reg. ABA Totals	28	–	545	82	219	.374	1	4	.250	34	59	.576	–	–	121	16	35	0	–	27	–	199	4.3	0.6	7.1

McKee, Gerald (Jerry) b. August 4, 1946 Ht. 6-3 Wt. 190 College: Ohio U.

SEASON–TEAM	G	GS	MIN	FGM	FGA	PCT	3FGM	3FGA	PCT	FTM	FTA	PCT	O-RB	D-RB	TOT	AST	PF	DQ	STL	TO	BLK	PTS	RPG	APG	PPG
69-70–Indiana (A)	1	–	3	0	1	.000	0	0	–	0	0	–	–	–	0	0	0	0	–	–	–	0	0.0	0.0	0.0
Reg. ABA Totals	1	–	3	0	1	.000	0	0	–	0	0	–	–	–	–	0	0	0	–	–	–	0	0.0	0.0	0.0

McKenna, Kevin Robert b. January 8, 1959 Ht. 6-5 Wt. 195 College: Creighton

SEASON–TEAM	G	GS	MIN	FGM	FGA	PCT	3FGM	3FGA	PCT	FTM	FTA	PCT	O-RB	D-RB	TOT	AST	PF	DQ	STL	TO	BLK	PTS	RPG	APG	PPG
81-82–Los Angeles	36	0	237	28	87	.322	0	2	.000	11	17	.647	18	11	29	14	45	0	10	20	2	67	0.8	0.4	1.9
83-84–Indiana	61	13	923	152	371	.410	3	17	.176	80	98	.816	30	65	95	114	133	3	46	62	5	387	1.6	1.9	6.3
84-85–New Jersey	29	7	535	61	134	.455	5	13	.385	38	43	.884	20	29	49	58	63	0	30	32	7	165	1.7	2.0	5.7
85-86–Washington	30	1	430	61	166	.367	27	77	.351	25	30	.833	9	27	36	23	54	1	29	18	2	174	1.2	0.8	5.8
86-87–New Jersey	56	3	942	153	337	.454	52	124	.419	43	57	.754	21	56	77	93	141	0	54	53	7	401	1.4	1.7	7.2
87-88–New Jersey	31	2	393	43	109	.394	16	50	.320	24	25	.960	4	27	31	40	55	1	15	19	2	126	1.0	1.3	4.1
Reg. Season Totals	243	26	3460	498	1204	.414	103	283	.364	221	270	.819	102	215	317	342	491	5	184	204	25	1320	1.3	1.4	5.4
Playoff Totals	1	0	2	0	0	–	0	0	–	0	0	–	0	0	0	–	0	0	0	0	0	0	0.0	0.0	0.0

McKenzie, Forrest Walton b. February 16, 1963 Ht. 6-7 Wt. 200 College: Loyola Marymount

SEASON–TEAM	G	GS	MIN	FGM	FGA	PCT	3FGM	3FGA	PCT	FTM	FTA	PCT	O-RB	D-RB	TOT	AST	PF	DQ	STL	TO	BLK	PTS	RPG	APG	PPG
86-87–San Antonio	6	0	42	7	28	.250	1	2	.500	2	2	1.000	2	5	7	1	9	0	1	3	0	17	1.2	0.2	2.8
Reg. Season Totals	6	0	42	7	28	.250	1	2	.500	2	2	1.000	2	5	7	1	9	0	1	3	0	17	1.2	0.2	2.8

McKenzie, Stanley (Stan) b. October 6, 1944 Ht. 6-5 Wt. 210 College: New York U.

SEASON–TEAM	G	GS	MIN	FGM	FGA	PCT	3FGM	3FGA	PCT	FTM	FTA	PCT	O-RB	D-RB	TOT	AST	PF	DQ	STL	TO	BLK	PTS	RPG	APG	PPG
67-68–Baltimore	50	–	653	73	182	.401	–	–	–	58	88	.659	–	–	121	24	98	1	–	–	–	204	2.4	0.5	4.1
68-69–Phoenix	80	–	1569	264	618	.427	–	–	–	219	287	.763	–	–	251	123	191	3	–	–	–	747	3.1	1.5	9.3
69-70–Phoenix	58	–	525	81	206	.393	–	–	–	58	73	.795	–	–	93	52	67	1	–	–	–	220	1.6	0.9	3.8
70-71–Portland	82	–	2290	398	902	.441	–	–	–	331	396	.836	–	–	309	235	238	2	–	–	–	1127	3.8	2.9	13.7
71-72–Portland	82	–	2036	410	834	.492	–	–	–	315	379	.831	–	–	272	148	240	2	–	–	–	1135	3.3	1.8	13.8
72-73–Port.-Houston	33	–	294	48	119	.403	–	–	–	30	37	.811	–	–	55	23	43	1	–	–	–	126	1.7	0.7	3.8
73-74–Houston	11	–	112	7	24	.292	–	–	–	6	8	.750	3	13	16	6	17	0	3	–	0	20	1.5	0.5	1.8
Reg. Season Totals	396	–	7479	1281	2885	.444	–	–	–	1017	1268	.802	3	13	1117	611	894	10	3	–	0	3579	2.8	1.5	9.0
Playoff Totals	7	–	71	8	29	.276	–	–	–	4	5	.800	0	0	9	3	14	0	0	–	0	20	1.3	0.4	2.9

McKey, Derrick Wayne (Heavy D) b. October 10, 1966 Ht. 6-10 Wt. 241 College: Alabama

SEASON–TEAM	G	GS	MIN	FGM	FGA	PCT	3FGM	3FGA	PCT	FTM	FTA	PCT	O-RB	D-RB	TOT	AST	PF	DQ	STL	TO	BLK	PTS	RPG	APG	PPG
87-88–Seattle	82	4	1706	255	519	.491	11	30	.367	173	224	.772	115	213	328	107	237	3	70	108	63	694	4.0	1.3	8.5
88-89–Seattle	82	82	2804	487	970	.502	30	89	.337	301	375	.803	167	297	464	219	264	4	105	188	70	1305	5.7	2.7	15.9
89-90–Seattle	80	80	2748	468	949	.493	3	23	.130	315	403	.782	170	319	489	187	247	2	87	192	81	1254	6.1	2.3	15.7
90-91–Seattle	73	55	2503	438	847	.517	4	19	.211	235	278	.845	172	251	423	169	220	2	91	158	56	1115	5.8	2.3	15.3
91-92–Seattle	52	44	1757	285	604	.472	19	50	.380	188	222	.847	95	173	268	120	142	2	61	114	47	777	5.2	2.3	14.9
92-93–Seattle	77	68	2439	387	780	.496	40	112	.357	220	297	.741	121	206	327	197	208	5	105	152	58	1034	4.2	2.6	13.4
93-94–Indiana	76	76	2613	355	710	.500	9	31	.290	192	254	.756	129	273	402	327	248	1	111	228	49	911	5.3	4.3	12.0
94-95–Indiana	81	81	2805	411	833	.493	32	89	.360	221	297	.744	125	269	394	276	260	5	125	168	49	1075	4.9	3.4	13.3
95-96–Indiana	75	75	2440	346	712	.486	17	68	.250	170	221	.769	123	238	361	262	246	4	83	143	44	879	4.8	3.5	11.7
96-97–Indiana	50	49	1449	148	379	.391	15	58	.259	89	123	.724	80	161	241	135	141	1	47	83	30	400	4.8	2.7	8.0
97-98–Indiana	57	4	1316	150	327	.459	4	17	.235	55	77	.714	74	137	211	88	156	1	57	79	30	359	3.7	1.5	6.3
98-99–Indiana	13	0	244	23	52	.442	0	1	.000	14	17	.824	18	23	41	13	24	0	12	12	4	60	3.2	1.0	4.6
99-00–Indiana	32	0	634	43	108	.398	10	23	.435	43	56	.768	29	106	135	35	81	0	29	19	13	139	4.2	1.1	4.3
Reg. Season Totals	830	618	25458	3796	7790	.487	194	610	.318	2216	2844	.779	1418	2666	4084	2135	2474	30	983	1644	594	10002	4.9	2.6	12.1
Playoff Totals	134	72	3711	430	926	.464	38	128	.297	264	354	.746	222	389	611	314	424	5	109	223	86	1162	4.6	2.3	8.7

McKie, Aaron Fitzgerald b. October 2, 1972 Ht. 6-5 Wt. 209 College: Temple

SEASON–TEAM	G	GS	MIN	FGM	FGA	PCT	3FGM	3FGA	PCT	FTM	FTA	PCT	O-RB	D-RB	TOT	AST	PF	DQ	STL	TO	BLK	PTS	RPG	APG	PPG
94-95–Portland	45	20	827	116	261	.444	11	28	.393	50	73	.685	35	94	129	89	97	1	36	39	16	293	2.9	2.0	6.5
95-96–Portland	81	73	2259	337	722	.467	38	117	.325	152	199	.764	86	218	304	205	205	5	92	135	21	864	3.8	2.5	10.7
96-97–Port.-Detroit	83	11	1625	150	365	.411	41	103	.398	92	110	.836	40	181	221	161	130	1	77	90	22	433	2.7	1.9	5.2
97-98–Detroit-Phil.	81	32	1813	139	381	.365	12	63	.190	42	55	.764	58	173	231	175	164	0	101	76	13	332	2.9	2.2	4.1
98-99–Philadelphia	50	4	959	95	237	.401	6	31	.194	44	62	.710	27	113	140	100	90	1	63	57	3	240	2.8	2.0	4.8
99-00–Philadelphia	82	14	1952	244	593	.411	44	121	.364	121	146	.829	47	199	246	240	194	3	108	113	18	653	3.0	2.9	8.0
Reg. Season Totals	422	154	9435	1081	2559	.422	152	463	.328	501	645	.777	293	978	1271	970	880	11	477	510	93	2815	3.0	2.3	6.7
Playoff Totals	29	10	693	83	190	.437	16	51	.314	39	47	.830	13	68	81	77	72	0	23	29	6	221	2.8	2.7	7.6

McKinney, Carlton B. b. October 21, 1964 Ht. 6-5 Wt. 210 College: Tulsa; Southern Methodist

SEASON–TEAM	G	GS	MIN	FGM	FGA	PCT	3FGM	3FGA	PCT	FTM	FTA	PCT	O-RB	D-RB	TOT	AST	PF	DQ	STL	TO	BLK	PTS	RPG	APG	PPG
89-90–L.A. Clippers	7	0	104	8	32	.250	0	1	.000	2	4	.500	4	8	12	7	15	1	6	7	1	18	1.7	1.0	2.6
91-92–New York	2	0	9	2	9	.222	0	0	–	0	0	–	0	1	1	0	1	0	0	0	0	4	0.5	0.0	2.0
Reg. Season Totals	9	0	113	10	41	.244	0	1	.000	2	4	.500	4	9	13	7	16	1	6	7	1	22	1.4	0.8	2.4

McKinney, Horace Albert (Bones) b. January 1, 1919 d. May 16, 1997 Ht. 6-6 Wt. 185 College: North Carolina; North Carolina State

SEASON–TEAM	G	GS	MIN	FGM	FGA	PCT	3FGM	3FGA	PCT	FTM	FTA	PCT	O-RB	D-RB	TOT	AST	PF	DQ	STL	TO	BLK	PTS	RPG	APG	PPG
46-47–Washington	58	–	–	275	987	.279	–	–	–	145	210	.690	–	–	–	69	162	–	–	–	–	695	–	1.2	12.0
47-48–Washington	43	–	–	182	680	.268	–	–	–	121	188	.644	–	–	–	36	176	–	–	–	–	485	–	0.8	11.3
48-49–Washington	57	–	–	263	801	.328	–	–	–	197	279	.706	–	–	–	114	216	–	–	–	–	723	–	2.0	12.7
49-50–Washington	53	–	–	187	631	.296	–	–	–	118	152	.776	–	–	–	88	185	–	–	–	–	492	–	1.7	9.3
50-51–Wash.-Boston	44	–	–	102	327	.312	–	–	–	58	81	.716	–	–	198	85	136	6	–	–	–	262	4.5	1.9	6.0
51-52–Boston	63	–	1083	136	418	.325	–	–	–	65	80	.813	–	–	175	111	148	4	–	–	–	337	2.8	1.8	5.3
Reg. Season Totals	318	–	1083	1145	3844	.298	–	–	–	704	990	.711	–	–	373	503	1023	10	–	–	–	2994	3.5	1.6	9.4
Playoff Totals	23	–	20	82	426	.291	–	–	–	68	102	.696	–	–	16	33	84	4	–	–	–	232	3.2	0.9	10.1

McKinney, William Mervin (Billy) b. June 5, 1955 Ht. 6-0 Wt. 160 College: Northwestern

SEASON–TEAM	G	GS	MIN	FGM	FGA	PCT	3FGM	3FGA	PCT	FTM	FTA	PCT	O-RB	D-RB	TOT	AST	PF	DQ	STL	TO	BLK	PTS	RPG	APG	PPG
78-79–Kansas City	78	–	1242	240	477	.503	–	–	–	129	162	.796	20	65	85	253	121	0	58	124	3	609	1.1	3.2	7.8
79-80–Kansas City	76	–	1333	206	459	.449	1	10	.100	107	133	.805	20	66	86	248	87	0	58	89	5	520	1.1	3.3	6.8
80-81–Utah-Denver	84	–	2166	327	645	.507	2	12	.167	162	188	.862	36	148	184	360	231	3	99	158	11	818	2.2	4.3	9.7
81-82–Denver	81	27	1963	369	699	.528	0	17	.000	137	170	.806	29	113	142	338	186	0	69	115	16	875	1.8	4.2	10.8
82-83–Denver	68	38	1559	266	546	.487	0	7	.000	136	167	.814	21	100	121	288	142	0	39	101	5	668	1.8	4.2	9.8
83-84–San Diego	80	0	843	136	305	.446	0	2	.000	39	46	.848	7	47	54	161	84	0	27	48	0	311	0.7	2.0	3.9
85-86–Chicago	9	0	83	10	23	.435	0	0	–	2	2	1.000	1	4	5	13	9	0	3	2	0	22	0.6	1.4	2.4
Reg. Season Totals	476	65	9189	1554	3154	.493	3	48	.063	712	868	.820	134	543	677	1661	860	3	353	637	40	3823	1.4	3.5	8.0
Playoff Totals	19	3	334	59	118	.500	0	2	.000	26	37	.703	13	16	29	60	31	0	10	27	0	144	1.5	3.2	7.6

McLemore, McCoy Jr. b. April 3, 1942 Ht. 6-7 Wt. 230 College: Moberly Area (Kan.) C.C.; Drake

SEASON–TEAM	G	GS	MIN	FGM	FGA	PCT	3FGM	3FGA	PCT	FTM	FTA	PCT	O-RB	D-RB	TOT	AST	PF	DQ	STL	TO	BLK	PTS	RPG	APG	PPG
64-65–San Francisco	78	–	1731	244	725	.337	–	–	–	157	220	.714	–	–	488	81	224	6	–	–	–	645	6.3	1.0	8.3
65-66–San Francisco	80	–	1467	225	528	.426	–	–	–	142	191	.743	–	–	488	55	197	4	–	–	–	592	6.1	0.7	7.4
66-67–Chicago	79	–	1382	258	670	.385	–	–	–	210	272	.772	–	–	374	62	189	2	–	–	–	726	4.7	0.8	9.2
67-68–Chicago	76	–	2100	374	940	.398	–	–	–	215	276	.779	–	–	430	130	219	4	–	–	–	963	5.7	1.7	12.7
68-69–Phoenix-Detroit	81	–	1620	282	722	.391	–	–	–	169	214	.790	–	–	404	94	186	4	–	–	–	733	5.0	1.2	9.0
69-70–Detroit	73	–	1421	233	500	.466	–	–	–	119	145	.821	–	–	336	83	159	3	–	–	–	585	4.6	1.1	8.0
70-71–Clev.-Milw.	86	–	2254	303	787	.385	–	–	–	204	261	.782	–	–	568	206	235	2	–	–	–	810	6.6	2.4	9.4
71-72–Milw.-Houston	27	–	246	28	71	.394	–	–	–	20	24	.833	–	–	73	22	33	1	–	–	–	76	2.7	0.8	2.8
Reg. Season Totals	580	–	12221	1947	4943	.394	–	–	–	1236	1603	.771	–	–	3161	733	1442	26	–	–	–	5130	5.5	1.3	8.8
Playoff Totals	18	–	239	34	91	.374	–	–	–	30	38	.789	–	–	49	17	31	1	–	–	–	98	2.7	0.9	5.4

McLeod, George L. b. January 3, 1931 Ht. 6-5 Wt. 200 College: Texas Christian

SEASON–TEAM	G	GS	MIN	FGM	FGA	PCT	3FGM	3FGA	PCT	FTM	FTA	PCT	O-RB	D-RB	TOT	AST	PF	DQ	STL	TO	BLK	PTS	RPG	APG	PPG
52-53–Baltimore	10	–	85	2	16	.125	–	–	–	8	15	.533	–	–	21	4	16	0	–	–	–	12	2.1	0.4	1.2
Reg. Season Totals	10	–	85	2	16	.125	–	–	–	8	15	.533	–	–	21	4	16	0	–	–	–	12	2.1	0.4	1.2

McLeod, Roshown b. November 17, 1975 Ht. 6-8 Wt. 221 College: St. John's (N.Y.); Duke

SEASON–TEAM	G	GS	MIN	FGM	FGA	PCT	3FGM	3FGA	PCT	FTM	FTA	PCT	O-RB	D-RB	TOT	AST	PF	DQ	STL	TO	BLK	PTS	RPG	APG	PPG
98-99–Atlanta	34	0	348	62	163	.380	1	10	.100	37	45	.822	12	38	50	14	24	0	2	23	1	162	1.5	0.4	4.8
99-00–Atlanta	44	20	860	131	332	.395	2	13	.154	54	70	.771	41	97	138	52	84	0	16	59	5	318	3.1	1.2	7.2
Reg. Season Totals	78	20	1208	193	495	.390	3	23	.130	91	115	.791	53	135	188	66	108	0	18	82	6	480	2.4	0.8	6.2
Playoff Totals	6	0	49	11	21	.524	0	0	–	4	4	1.000	1	2	3	1	3	0	1	1	1	26	0.5	0.2	4.3

McMahon, John Joseph (Jack) b. December 3, 1928 d. June 11, 1969 Ht. 6-1 Wt. 185 College: St. John's (N.Y.)

SEASON–TEAM	G	GS	MIN	FGM	FGA	PCT	3FGM	3FGA	PCT	FTM	FTA	PCT	O-RB	D-RB	TOT	AST	PF	DQ	STL	TO	BLK	PTS	RPG	APG	PPG
52-53–Rochester	70	–	1665	176	534	.330	–	–	–	155	236	.657	–	–	183	186	253	16	–	–	–	507	2.6	2.7	7.2
53-54–Rochester	71	–	1891	250	691	.362	–	–	–	211	303	.696	–	–	211	238	221	6	–	–	–	711	3.0	3.4	10.0
54-55–Rochester	72	–	1807	251	721	.348	–	–	–	143	225	.636	–	–	211	246	179	1	–	–	–	645	2.9	3.4	9.0
55-56–Roch.-St. Louis	70	–	1713	202	615	.328	–	–	–	110	185	.595	–	–	180	222	170	1	–	–	–	514	2.6	3.2	7.3
56-57–St. Louis	72	–	2344	239	725	.330	–	–	–	142	225	.631	–	–	222	367	213	2	–	–	–	620	3.1	5.1	8.6
57-58–St. Louis	72	–	2239	216	719	.300	–	–	–	134	221	.606	–	–	195	333	184	2	–	–	–	566	2.7	4.6	7.9
58-59–St. Louis	72	–	2235	248	692	.358	–	–	–	96	156	.615	–	–	164	298	221	2	–	–	–	592	2.3	4.1	8.2
59-60–St. Louis	25	–	334	33	93	.355	–	–	–	16	29	.552	–	–	24	49	42	1	–	–	–	82	1.0	2.0	3.3
Reg. Season Totals	524	–	14228	1615	4790	.337	–	–	–	1007	1580	.637	–	–	1390	1939	1483	31	–	–	–	4237	2.7	3.7	8.1
Playoff Totals	49	–	1715	191	539	.378	–	–	–	91	164	.555	–	–	173	227	163	7	–	–	–	473	3.1	4.1	9.7

McMillan, Nathaniel (Nate, Mac) b. August 3, 1964 Ht. 6-5 Wt. 210 College: Chowan (N.C.) Coll.; North Carolina State

SEASON–TEAM	G	GS	MIN	FGM	FGA	PCT	3FGM	3FGA	PCT	FTM	FTA	PCT	O-RB	D-RB	TOT	AST	PF	DQ	STL	TO	BLK	PTS	RPG	APG	PPG
86-87–Seattle	71	50	1972	143	301	.475	0	7	.000	87	141	.617	101	230	331	583	238	4	125	155	45	373	4.7	8.2	5.3
87-88–Seattle	82	82	2453	235	496	.474	9	24	.375	145	205	.707	117	221	338	702	238	1	169	189	47	624	4.1	8.6	7.6
88-89–Seattle	75	74	2341	199	485	.410	15	70	.214	119	189	.630	143	245	388	696	236	3	156	211	42	532	5.2	9.3	7.1
89-90–Seattle	82	69	2338	207	438	.473	11	31	.355	98	153	.641	127	276	403	598	289	7	140	187	37	523	4.9	7.3	6.4
90-91–Seattle	78	0	1434	132	305	.433	17	48	.354	57	93	.613	71	180	251	371	211	6	104	122	20	338	3.2	4.8	4.3
91-92–Seattle	72	30	1652	177	405	.437	27	98	.276	54	84	.643	92	160	252	359	218	4	129	112	29	435	3.5	5.0	6.0
92-93–Seattle	73	25	1977	213	459	.464	25	65	.385	95	134	.709	84	222	306	384	240	6	173	139	33	546	4.2	5.3	7.5
93-94–Seattle	73	8	1887	177	396	.447	52	133	.391	31	55	.564	50	233	283	387	201	1	216	126	22	437	3.9	5.3	6.0
94-95–Seattle	80	18	2070	166	397	.418	53	155	.342	34	58	.586	65	237	302	421	275	8	165	126	53	419	3.8	5.3	5.2
95-96–Seattle	55	14	1261	100	238	.420	46	121	.380	29	41	.707	41	169	210	197	143	3	95	75	18	275	3.8	3.6	5.0
96-97–Seattle	37	2	798	61	149	.409	28	84	.333	19	29	.655	15	103	118	140	78	0	58	32	6	169	3.2	3.8	4.6
97-98–Seattle	18	1	279	23	67	.343	15	34	.441	1	1	1.000	13	27	40	55	41	0	14	12	4	62	2.2	3.1	3.4
Reg. Season Totals	796	373	20462	1833	4136	.443	298	870	.343	769	1183	.650	919	2303	3222	4893	2408	43	1544	1486	356	4733	4.0	6.1	5.9
Playoff Totals	98	34	2186	184	483	.381	37	128	.289	84	133	.632	98	245	343	505	271	5	131	139	43	489	3.5	5.2	5.0

McMillen, Charles Thomas (Tom) b. May 26, 1952 Ht. 6-11 Wt. 220 College: Maryland

SEASON–TEAM	G	GS	MIN	FGM	FGA	PCT	3FGM	3FGA	PCT	FTM	FTA	PCT	O-RB	D-RB	TOT	AST	PF	DQ	STL	TO	BLK	PTS	RPG	APG	PPG
75-76–Buffalo	50	–	708	96	222	.432	–	–	–	41	54	.759	64	122	186	69	87	1	7	–	6	233	3.7	1.4	4.7
76-77–Buffalo-N.Y.-K	76	–	1492	274	563	.487	–	–	–	96	123	.780	114	275	389	67	163	0	11	–	6	644	5.1	0.9	8.5
77-78–N.Y.-Atlanta	68	–	1683	280	568	.493	–	–	–	116	145	.800	151	265	416	84	233	8	33	109	16	676	6.1	1.2	9.9
78-79–Atlanta	82	–	1392	232	498	.466	–	–	–	106	119	.891	131	201	332	69	211	2	15	87	32	570	4.0	0.8	7.0
79-80–Atlanta	53	–	1071	191	382	.500	0	1	.000	81	107	.757	70	150	220	62	126	2	36	64	14	463	4.2	1.2	8.7
80-81–Atlanta	79	–	1564	253	519	.487	1	6	.167	80	108	.741	96	199	295	72	165	0	23	81	25	587	3.7	0.9	7.4
81-82–Atlanta	73	23	1792	291	572	.509	1	3	.333	140	170	.824	102	234	336	129	202	1	25	124	23	723	4.6	1.8	9.9
82-83–Atlanta	61	4	1364	198	424	.467	0	1	.000	108	133	.812	57	160	217	76	143	2	17	80	24	504	3.6	1.2	8.3
83-84–Washington	62	5	1294	222	447	.497	1	6	.167	127	156	.814	64	135	199	73	162	0	14	70	17	572	3.2	1.2	9.2
84-85–Washington	69	21	1547	252	534	.472	0	5	.000	112	135	.830	64	146	210	52	163	3	8	44	17	616	3.0	0.8	8.9
85-86–Washington	56	1	863	131	285	.460	0	1	.000	64	79	.810	44	69	113	35	85	0	9	34	10	326	2.0	0.6	5.8
Reg. Season Totals	729	54	14770	2420	5014	.483	3	23	.130	1071	1329	.806	957	1956	2913	788	1740	19	198	693	190	5914	4.0	1.1	8.1
Playoff Totals	26	0	430	58	132	.439	0	1	.000	23	29	.793	30	53	83	22	50	1	10	20	3	139	3.2	0.8	5.3

McMillian, James M. (Jim) b. March 11, 1948 Ht. 6-5 Wt. 225 College: Columbia

SEASON–TEAM	G	GS	MIN	FGM	FGA	PCT	3FGM	3FGA	PCT	FTM	FTA	PCT	O-RB	D-RB	TOT	AST	PF	DQ	STL	TO	BLK	PTS	RPG	APG	PPG
70-71–Los Angeles	81	–	1747	289	629	.459	–	–	–	100	130	.769	–	–	330	133	122	1	–	–	–	678	4.1	1.6	8.4
71-72–Los Angeles	80	–	3050	642	1331	.482	–	–	–	219	277	.791	–	–	522	209	209	0	–	–	–	1503	6.5	2.6	18.8
72-73–Los Angeles	81	–	2953	655	1431	.458	–	–	–	223	264	.845	–	–	447	221	176	0	–	–	–	1533	5.5	2.7	18.9
73-74–Buffalo	82	–	3322	600	1214	.494	–	–	–	325	379	.858	216	394	610	256	186	0	129	–	26	1525	7.4	3.1	18.6
74-75–Buffalo	62	–	2132	347	695	.499	–	–	–	194	231	.840	127	258	385	156	129	0	69	–	15	888	6.2	2.5	14.3
75-76–Buffalo	74	–	2610	492	918	.536	–	–	–	188	219	.858	134	256	390	205	141	0	88	–	14	1172	5.3	2.8	15.8
76-77–N.Y. Knicks	67	–	2158	298	642	.464	–	–	–	67	86	.779	66	241	307	139	103	0	63	–	5	663	4.6	2.1	9.9
77-78–New York	81	–	1977	288	623	.462	–	–	–	115	134	.858	80	209	289	205	116	0	76	104	17	691	3.6	2.5	8.5
78-79–Portland	23	–	278	33	74	.446	–	–	–	17	21	.810	16	23	39	33	18	0	10	16	3	83	1.7	1.4	3.6
Reg. Season Totals	631	–	20227	3644	7557	.482	–	–	–	1448	1741	.832	639	1381	3319	1557	1200	1	435	120	80	8736	5.3	2.5	13.8
Playoff Totals	72	–	2722	497	1101	.451	–	–	–	200	253	.791	54	91	377	137	169	1	36	7	7	1194	5.2	1.9	16.6

McMillon, Shellie Jr. b. March 11, 1936 d. July 11, 1980 Ht. 6-5 Wt. 205 College: Bradley

SEASON–TEAM	G	GS	MIN	FGM	FGA	PCT	3FGM	3FGA	PCT	FTM	FTA	PCT	O-RB	D-RB	TOT	AST	PF	DQ	STL	TO	BLK	PTS	RPG	APG	PPG
58-59–Detroit	48	–	700	127	289	.439	–	–	–	55	104	.529	–	–	285	26	110	2	–	–	–	309	5.9	0.5	6.4
59-60–Detroit	75	–	1416	267	627	.426	–	–	–	132	199	.663	–	–	431	49	198	3	–	–	–	666	5.7	0.7	8.9
60-61–Detroit	78	–	1636	322	752	.428	–	–	–	140	201	.697	–	–	487	98	238	6	–	–	–	784	6.2	1.3	10.1
61-62–Detroit-St. L.	62	–	1225	265	591	.448	–	–	–	108	182	.593	–	–	368	59	202	10	–	–	–	638	5.9	1.0	10.3
Reg. Season Totals	263	–	4977	981	2259	.434	–	–	–	435	686	.634	–	–	1571	232	748	21	–	–	–	2397	6.0	0.9	9.1
Playoff Totals	9	–	168	28	71	.394	–	–	–	22	29	.759	–	–	39	9	37	3	–	–	–	78	4.3	1.0	8.7

McMullan, Malcolm H. (Mal) b. August 23, 1927 d. April 13, 1995 Ht. 6-5 Wt. 210 College: Xavier (Ohio); Kentucky

SEASON–TEAM	G	GS	MIN	FGM	FGA	PCT	3FGM	3FGA	PCT	FTM	FTA	PCT	O-RB	D-RB	TOT	AST	PF	DQ	STL	TO	BLK	PTS	RPG	APG	PPG
49-50–Indianapolis	58	–	–	123	380	.324	–	–	–	77	141	.546	–	–	–	87	212	–	–	–	–	323	–	1.5	5.6
50-51–Indianapolis	51	–	–	78	277	.282	–	–	–	48	82	.585	–	–	128	33	109	2	–	–	–	204	2.5	0.6	4.0
Reg. Season Totals	109	–	–	201	657	.306	–	–	–	125	223	.561	–	–	128	120	321	2	–	–	–	527	2.5	1.1	4.8
Playoff Totals	6	–	–	4	42	.190	–	–	–	6	7	.857	–	–	–	18	19	1	–	–	–	14	–	1.5	2.3

McNabb, Chester (Chet) b. 1921 Ht. 6-2 Wt. 200 College: Arizona State; West Texas A&M

SEASON–TEAM	G	GS	MIN	FGM	FGA	PCT	3FGM	3FGA	PCT	FTM	FTA	PCT	O-RB	D-RB	TOT	AST	PF	DQ	STL	TO	BLK	PTS	RPG	APG	PPG
47-48–Baltimore	2	–	–	0	1	.000	–	–	–	0	0	–	–	–	–	0	1	–	–	–	–	0	–	0.0	0.0
Reg. Season Totals	2	–	–	0	1	.000	–	–	–	0	0	–	–	–	–	0	1	–	–	–	–	0	–	0.0	0.0

McNamara, Mark Robert b. June 8, 1959 Ht. 6-11 Wt. 235 College: Santa Clara; California

SEASON–TEAM	G	GS	MIN	FGM	FGA	PCT	3FGM	3FGA	PCT	FTM	FTA	PCT	O-RB	D-RB	TOT	AST	PF	DQ	STL	TO	BLK	PTS	RPG	APG	PPG
82-83–Philadelphia	36	2	182	29	64	.453	0	0	–	20	45	.444	34	42	76	7	42	1	3	36	3	78	2.1	0.2	2.2
83-84–San Antonio	70	3	1037	157	253	.621	0	0	–	74	157	.471	137	180	317	31	138	2	14	89	12	388	4.5	0.4	5.5
84-85–S.A.-K.C.	45	0	273	40	76	.526	0	0	–	32	62	.516	31	43	74	6	27	0	7	19	8	112	1.6	0.1	2.5
86-87–Philadelphia	11	1	113	14	30	.467	0	0	–	7	19	.368	17	19	36	2	17	0	1	8	0	35	3.3	0.2	3.2
87-88–Philadelphia	42	18	581	52	133	.391	0	0	–	48	66	.727	66	91	157	18	67	0	4	26	12	152	3.7	0.4	3.6
88-89–L.A. Lakers	39	0	318	32	64	.500	0	0	–	49	78	.628	38	62	100	10	51	0	4	24	3	113	2.6	0.3	2.9
89-90–L.A. Lakers	33	1	190	38	86	.442	0	0	–	26	40	.650	22	41	63	3	31	1	2	21	1	102	1.9	0.1	3.1
90-91–Orlando	2	0	13	0	1	.000	0	0	–	0	0	–	0	4	4	0	1	0	0	0	0	0	2.0	0.0	0.0
Reg. Season Totals	278	25	2707	362	707	.512	0	0	–	256	467	.548	345	482	827	77	374	4	35	223	39	980	3.0	0.3	3.5
Playoff Totals	8	0	16	5	9	.556	0	0	–	1	2	.500	0	4	4	–	1	0	0	0	0	11	0.5	0.0	1.4

McNamee, John Joseph (Joe) b. September 24, 1926 Ht. 6-6 Wt. 210 College: San Francisco

SEASON–TEAM	G	GS	MIN	FGM	FGA	PCT	3FGM	3FGA	PCT	FTM	FTA	PCT	O-RB	D-RB	TOT	AST	PF	DQ	STL	TO	BLK	PTS	RPG	APG	PPG
50-51–Rochester	60	–	–	48	167	.287	–	–	–	27	42	.643	–	–	101	18	88	2	–	–	–	123	1.7	0.3	2.1
51-52–Roch.-Balt.	58	–	695	68	222	.306	–	–	–	30	50	.600	–	–	137	40	108	4	–	–	–	166	2.4	0.7	2.9
Reg. Season Totals	118	–	695	116	389	.298	–	–	–	57	92	.620	–	–	238	58	196	6	–	–	–	289	2.0	0.5	2.4
Playoff Totals	13	–	0	12	41	.293	–	–	–	9	12	.750	–	–	35	9	26	0	–	–	–	33	2.7	0.7	2.5

McNealy, Christopher (Chris) b. July 15, 1961 Ht. 6-7 Wt. 215 College: Santa Barbara City (Calif.) Coll. (J.C.); San Jose State

SEASON–TEAM	G	GS	MIN	FGM	FGA	PCT	3FGM	3FGA	PCT	FTM	FTA	PCT	O-RB	D-RB	TOT	AST	PF	DQ	STL	TO	BLK	PTS	RPG	APG	PPG
85-86–New York	30	6	627	70	144	.486	0	0	–	31	47	.660	62	141	203	41	88	2	38	35	12	171	6.8	1.4	5.7
86-87–New York	59	16	972	88	179	.492	0	0	–	52	80	.650	74	153	227	46	136	1	36	64	16	228	3.8	0.8	3.9
87-88–New York	19	0	265	23	74	.311	0	0	–	21	31	.677	24	40	64	23	50	1	16	17	2	67	3.4	1.2	3.5
Reg. Season Totals	108	22	1864	181	397	.456	0	0	–	104	158	.658	160	334	494	110	274	4	90	116	30	466	4.6	1.0	4.3

McNeill, Larry (The Hawk) b. January 31, 1951 Ht. 6-9 Wt. 195 College: Marquette

SEASON–TEAM	G	GS	MIN	FGM	FGA	PCT	3FGM	3FGA	PCT	FTM	FTA	PCT	O-RB	D-RB	TOT	AST	PF	DQ	STL	TO	BLK	PTS	RPG	APG	PPG
73-74–K.C.-Omaha	54	–	516	106	220	.482	–	–	–	99	140	.707	60	86	146	24	76	0	35	–	6	311	2.7	0.4	5.8
74-75–K.C.-Omaha	80	–	1749	296	645	.459	–	–	–	189	241	.784	149	348	497	73	229	1	69	–	27	781	6.2	0.9	9.8
75-76–Kansas City	82	–	1613	295	610	.484	–	–	–	207	273	.758	157	353	510	72	244	2	51	–	32	797	6.2	0.9	9.7
76-77–N.Y.-G.S.	24	–	230	47	112	.420	–	–	–	52	61	.852	28	47	75	6	32	1	10	–	2	146	3.1	0.3	6.1
77-78–G.S.-Buffalo	46	–	940	162	356	.455	–	–	–	145	175	.829	80	122	202	47	114	1	18	67	11	469	4.4	1.0	10.2
78-79–Detroit	11	–	46	9	20	.450	–	–	–	11	12	.917	3	7	10	3	7	0	0	4	0	29	0.9	0.3	2.6
Reg. Season Totals	297	–	5094	915	1963	.466	–	–	–	703	902	.779	477	963	1440	225	702	5	183	71	78	2533	4.8	0.8	8.5
Playoff Totals	12	–	124	29	44	.659	–	–	–	19	24	.792	9	19	28	2	23	2	3	–	2	77	2.3	0.2	6.4

McNeill, Robert J. (Bob) b. October 22, 1938 Ht. 6-1 Wt. 180 College: St. Joseph's (Pa.)

SEASON–TEAM	G	GS	MIN	FGM	FGA	PCT	3FGM	3FGA	PCT	FTM	FTA	PCT	O-RB	D-RB	TOT	AST	PF	DQ	STL	TO	BLK	PTS	RPG	APG	PPG
60-61–New York	75	–	1387	166	427	.389	–	–	–	105	126	.833	–	–	123	238	148	2	–	–	–	437	1.6	3.2	5.8
61-62–Phil.-L.A.	50	–	441	56	136	.412	–	–	–	26	34	.765	–	–	56	89	56	0	–	–	–	138	1.1	1.8	2.8
Reg. Season Totals	125	–	1828	222	563	.394	–	–	–	131	160	.819	–	–	179	327	204	2	–	–	–	575	1.4	2.6	4.6
Playoff Totals	5	–	30	4	7	.571	–	–	–	1	2	.500	–	–	6	5	6	0	–	–	–	9	1.2	1.0	1.8

McNulty, Carl Edwin b. February 14, 1930 Ht. 6-3 Wt. 185 College: Purdue

SEASON–TEAM	G	GS	MIN	FGM	FGA	PCT	3FGM	3FGA	PCT	FTM	FTA	PCT	O-RB	D-RB	TOT	AST	PF	DQ	STL	TO	BLK	PTS	RPG	APG	PPG
54-55–Milwaukee	1	–	14	1	6	.167	–	–	–	0	0	–	–	–	0	0	1	0	–	–	–	2	0.0	0.0	2.0
Reg. Season Totals	1	–	14	1	6	.167	–	–	–	0	0	–	–	–	0	0	1	0	–	–	–	2	0.0	0.0	2.0

McPipe, Roy b. May 5, 1950 Ht. 6-3 Wt. 205 College: Eastern Montana

SEASON–TEAM	G	GS	MIN	FGM	FGA	PCT	3FGM	3FGA	PCT	FTM	FTA	PCT	O-RB	D-RB	TOT	AST	PF	DQ	STL	TO	BLK	PTS	RPG	APG	PPG
74-75–Utah (A)	5	–	44	8	24	.333	2	4	.500	3	4	.750	2	3	5	1	5	–	1	10	0	21	1.0	0.2	4.2
Reg. ABA Totals	5	–	44	8	24	.333	2	4	.500	3	4	.750	2	3	5	1	5	–	1	10	0	21	1.0	0.2	4.2

McQueen, Cozell b. January 18, 1962 Ht. 6-11 Wt. 235 College: North Carolina State

SEASON–TEAM	G	GS	MIN	FGM	FGA	PCT	3FGM	3FGA	PCT	FTM	FTA	PCT	O-RB	D-RB	TOT	AST	PF	DQ	STL	TO	BLK	PTS	RPG	APG	PPG
86-87–Detroit	3	0	7	3	3	1.000	0	0	–	0	0	–	3	5	8	0	1	0	0	0	1	6	2.7	0.0	2.0
Reg. Season Totals	3	0	7	3	3	1.000	0	0	–	0	0	–	3	5	8	0	1	0	0	0	1	6	2.7	0.0	2.0

McReynolds, Thales b. June 8, 1943 d. July 3, 1988 Ht. 6-3 Wt. 185 College: Miles (Mont.) C.C.

SEASON–TEAM	G	GS	MIN	FGM	FGA	PCT	3FGM	3FGA	PCT	FTM	FTA	PCT	O-RB	D-RB	TOT	AST	PF	DQ	STL	TO	BLK	PTS	RPG	APG	PPG
65-66–Baltimore	5	–	28	1	12	.083	–	–	–	1	2	.500	–	–	6	1	0	0	–	–	–	3	1.2	0.2	0.6
Reg. Season Totals	5	–	28	1	12	.083	–	–	–	1	2	.500	–	–	6	1	0	0	–	–	–	3	1.2	0.2	0.6

McWilliams, Eric Lee b. April 18, 1950 Ht. 6-8 Wt. 200 College: Pasadena City (Calif.) Coll. (J.C.); Long Beach State

SEASON–TEAM	G	GS	MIN	FGM	FGA	PCT	3FGM	3FGA	PCT	FTM	FTA	PCT	O-RB	D-RB	TOT	AST	PF	DQ	STL	TO	BLK	PTS	RPG	APG	PPG
72-73–Houston	44	–	245	34	98	.347	–	–	–	18	37	.486	–	–	60	5	46	0	–	–	–	86	1.4	0.1	2.0
Reg. Season Totals	44	–	245	34	98	.347	–	–	–	18	37	.486	–	–	60	5	46	0	–	–	–	86	1.4	0.1	2.0

Mearns, George b. April 18, 1922 d. December 27, 1997 Ht. 6-3 Wt. 175 College: Rhode Island

SEASON–TEAM	G	GS	MIN	FGM	FGA	PCT	3FGM	3FGA	PCT	FTM	FTA	PCT	O-RB	D-RB	TOT	AST	PF	DQ	STL	TO	BLK	PTS	RPG	APG	PPG
46-47–Providence	57	–	–	128	478	.268	–	–	–	126	175	.720	–	–	–	35	137	–	–	–	–	382	–	0.6	6.7
47-48–Providence	24	–	–	23	115	.200	–	–	–	15	31	.484	–	–	–	10	65	–	–	–	–	61	–	0.4	2.5
Reg. Season Totals	81	–	–	151	593	.255	–	–	–	141	206	.684	–	–	–	45	202	–	–	–	–	443	–	0.6	5.5

Mee, LaFarrell Darnell (Darnell) b. February 11, 1971 Ht. 6-5 Wt. 175 College: Western Kentucky

SEASON–TEAM	G	GS	MIN	FGM	FGA	PCT	3FGM	3FGA	PCT	FTM	FTA	PCT	O-RB	D-RB	TOT	AST	PF	DQ	STL	TO	BLK	PTS	RPG	APG	PPG
93-94–Denver	38	0	285	28	88	.318	5	24	.208	12	27	.444	17	18	35	16	34	0	15	18	13	73	0.9	0.4	1.9
94-95–Denver	2	0	8	1	5	.200	1	3	.333	0	0	–	0	1	1	2	0	0	1	0	0	3	0.5	1.0	1.5
Reg. Season Totals	40	0	293	29	93	.312	6	27	.222	12	27	.444	17	19	36	18	34	0	16	18	13	76	0.9	0.5	1.9
Playoff Totals	3	0	30	3	6	.500	1	4	.250	0	0	–	0	2	2	2	4	0	3	3	0	7	0.7	0.7	2.3

Meely, Cliff b. July 10, 1947 Ht. 6-8 Wt. 215 College: Northeastern Christian J.C. (Pa.); Colorado

SEASON–TEAM	G	GS	MIN	FGM	FGA	PCT	3FGM	3FGA	PCT	FTM	FTA	PCT	O-RB	D-RB	TOT	AST	PF	DQ	STL	TO	BLK	PTS	RPG	APG	PPG
71-72–Houston	77	–	1815	315	776	.406	–	–	–	133	197	.675	–	–	507	119	254	9	–	–	–	763	6.6	1.5	9.9
72-73–Houston	82	–	1694	268	657	.408	–	–	–	92	137	.672	–	–	496	91	263	6	–	–	–	628	6.0	1.1	7.7
73-74–Houston	77	–	1754	330	773	.427	–	–	–	90	140	.643	103	336	439	124	234	5	53	–	77	750	5.7	1.6	9.7
74-75–Houston	48	–	753	156	349	.447	–	–	–	68	94	.723	55	109	164	45	117	4	21	–	21	380	3.4	0.9	7.9
75-76–Houston-L.A.	34	–	313	52	132	.394	–	–	–	33	48	.688	22	75	97	19	61	1	14	–	8	137	2.9	0.6	4.0
Reg. Season Totals	318	–	6329	1121	2687	.417	–	–	–	416	616	.675	180	520	1703	398	929	25	88	–	106	2658	5.4	1.3	8.4

Meents, Scott E. b. January 4, 1964 Ht. 6-10 Wt. 225 College: Illinois

SEASON–TEAM	G	GS	MIN	FGM	FGA	PCT	3FGM	3FGA	PCT	FTM	FTA	PCT	O-RB	D-RB	TOT	AST	PF	DQ	STL	TO	BLK	PTS	RPG	APG	PPG
89-90–Seattle	26	0	148	19	44	.432	0	0	–	17	23	.739	7	23	30	7	12	0	4	9	3	55	1.2	0.3	2.1
90-91–Seattle	13	0	53	7	28	.250	1	1	1.000	2	4	.500	3	7	10	8	5	0	7	6	4	17	0.8	0.6	1.3
Reg. Season Totals	39	0	201	26	72	.361	1	1	1.000	19	27	.704	10	30	40	15	17	0	11	15	7	72	1.0	0.4	1.8
Playoff Totals	2	0	8	2	4	.500	0	0	–	0	1	.000	0	1	1	–	1	0	1	0	0	4	0.5	0.0	2.0

Mehen, Richard P. (Dick) b. May 20, 1922 d. December 14, 1986 Ht. 6-6 Wt. 195 College: Tennessee

SEASON–TEAM	G	GS	MIN	FGM	FGA	PCT	3FGM	3FGA	PCT	FTM	FTA	PCT	O-RB	D-RB	TOT	AST	PF	DQ	STL	TO	BLK	PTS	RPG	APG	PPG
47-48–Toledo (N)	57	–	–	151	–	–	–	–	–	85	125	.680	–	–	–	–	95	–	–	–	–	387	–	–	6.8
48-49–Waterloo (N)	62	–	–	315	–	–	–	–	–	211	304	.694	–	–	–	–	195	–	–	–	–	841	–	–	13.6
49-50–Waterloo	62	–	–	347	826	.420	–	–	–	198	281	.705	–	–	–	191	203	–	–	–	–	892	–	3.1	14.4
50-51–Balt.-Bos.-Ft.W.	66	–	–	192	532	.361	–	–	–	90	123	.732	–	–	223	188	149	4	–	–	–	474	3.4	2.8	7.2
51-52–Milwaukee	65	–	2294	293	824	.356	–	–	–	117	167	.701	–	–	282	171	209	10	–	–	–	703	4.3	2.6	10.8
Reg. NBA Totals	193	–	2294	832	2182	.381	–	–	–	405	571	.709	–	–	505	550	561	14	–	–	–	2069	3.9	2.8	10.7
Reg. NBL Totals	119	–	–	466	–	–	–	–	–	296	429	.690	–	–	–	–	290	–	–	–	–	1228	–	–	10.3
NBA Playoff Totals	3	–	0	12	29	.414	–	–	–	2	4	.500	–	–	14	3	9	0	–	–	–	26	4.7	1.0	8.7

Meineke, Donald E. (Don, Monk) b. October 30, 1930 Ht. 6-7 Wt. 210 College: Dayton

SEASON–TEAM	G	GS	MIN	FGM	FGA	PCT	3FGM	3FGA	PCT	FTM	FTA	PCT	O-RB	D-RB	TOT	AST	PF	DQ	STL	TO	BLK	PTS	RPG	APG	PPG
52-53–Fort Wayne	68	–	2250	240	630	.381	–	–	–	245	313	.783	–	–	466	148	334	26	–	–	–	725	6.9	2.2	10.7
53-54–Fort Wayne	71	–	1466	135	393	.344	–	–	–	136	169	.805	–	–	372	81	214	6	–	–	–	406	5.2	1.1	5.7
54-55–Fort Wayne	68	–	1026	136	366	.372	–	–	–	119	170	.700	–	–	246	64	153	1	–	–	–	391	3.6	0.9	5.8
55-56–Rochester	69	–	1248	154	414	.372	–	–	–	181	232	.780	–	–	316	102	191	4	–	–	–	489	4.6	1.5	7.1
57-58–Cincinnati	67	–	792	125	351	.356	–	–	–	77	119	.647	–	–	226	38	155	3	–	–	–	327	3.4	0.6	4.9
Reg. Season Totals	343	–	6782	790	2154	.367	–	–	–	758	1003	.756	–	–	1626	433	1047	40	–	–	–	2338	4.7	1.3	6.8
Playoff Totals	25	–	595	40	127	.331	–	–	–	66	89	.742	–	–	115	32	72	5	–	–	–	146	4.0	1.1	5.8

Meinhold, Carl Marvin (Red) b. March 29, 1926 Ht. 6-2 Wt. 185 College: Long Island University

SEASON–TEAM	G	GS	MIN	FGM	FGA	PCT	3FGM	3FGA	PCT	FTM	FTA	PCT	O-RB	D-RB	TOT	AST	PF	DQ	STL	TO	BLK	PTS	RPG	APG	PPG
47-48–Baltimore	48	–	–	108	356	.303	–	–	–	37	60	.617	–	–	–	16	64	–	–	–	–	253	–	0.3	5.3
48-49–Chicago-Prov.	50	–	–	101	306	.330	–	–	–	61	96	.635	–	–	–	47	60	–	–	–	–	263	–	0.9	5.3
Reg. Season Totals	98	–	–	209	662	.316	–	–	–	98	156	.628	–	–	–	63	124	–	–	–	–	516	–	0.6	5.3
Playoff Totals	11	–	–	17	74	.270	–	–	–	6	13	.462	–	–	–	–	7	–	–	–	–	40	–	0.0	3.6

Melchionni, Gary Dennis b. January 19, 1951 Ht. 6-2 Wt. 185 College: Duke

SEASON–TEAM	G	GS	MIN	FGM	FGA	PCT	3FGM	3FGA	PCT	FTM	FTA	PCT	O-RB	D-RB	TOT	AST	PF	DQ	STL	TO	BLK	PTS	RPG	APG	PPG
73-74–Phoenix	69	–	1251	202	439	.460	–	–	–	92	107	.860	46	96	142	142	85	1	41	–	9	496	2.1	2.1	7.2
74-75–Phoenix	68	–	1529	232	539	.430	–	–	–	114	141	.809	45	142	187	156	116	1	48	–	12	578	2.8	2.3	8.5
Reg. Season Totals	137	–	2780	434	978	.444	–	–	–	206	248	.831	91	238	329	298	201	2	89	–	21	1074	2.4	2.2	7.8

Melchionni, William P. (Bill) b. October 19, 1944 Ht. 6-1 Wt. 165 College: Villanova

SEASON–TEAM	G	GS	MIN	FGM	FGA	PCT	3FGM	3FGA	PCT	FTM	FTA	PCT	O-RB	D-RB	TOT	AST	PF	DQ	STL	TO	BLK	PTS	RPG	APG	PPG
66-67–Philadelphia	73	–	692	138	353	.391	–	–	–	39	60	.650	–	–	98	98	73	0	–	–	–	315	1.3	1.3	4.3
67-68–Philadelphia	71	–	758	146	336	.435	–	–	–	33	47	.702	–	–	104	105	75	0	–	–	–	325	1.5	1.5	4.6
69-70–New York (A)	80	–	3157	479	1030	.465	5	28	.179	255	311	.820	–	–	230	457	282	7	–	–	–	1218	2.9	5.7	15.2
70-71–New York (A)	81	–	3284	561	1244	.451	2	22	.091	301	370	.814	–	–	237	672	273	–	–	–	–	1425	2.9	8.3	17.6
71-72–New York (A)	80	–	3326	672	1346	.499	2	19	.105	336	416	.808	–	–	248	669	275	–	–	314	–	1682	3.1	8.4	21.0
72-73–New York (A)	61	–	1849	291	646	.450	6	15	.400	163	194	.840	19	108	127	453	155	0	–	184	–	751	2.1	7.4	12.3
73-74–New York (A)	56	–	1146	116	276	.420	5	23	.217	59	71	.831	13	64	77	207	94	–	51	86	5	296	1.4	3.7	5.3
74-75–New York (A)	77	–	1384	201	413	.487	8	27	.296	62	78	.795	12	63	75	320	105	–	69	106	7	472	1.0	4.2	6.1
75-76–New York (A)	67	–	1191	149	358	.416	9	23	.391	79	93	.849	13	75	88	266	66	–	52	95	8	386	1.3	4.0	5.8
Reg. NBA Totals	144	–	1450	284	689	.412	–	–	–	72	107	.673	–	–	202	203	148	0	–	–	–	640	1.4	1.4	4.4
Reg. ABA Totals	502	–	15337	2469	5313	.465	37	157	.236	1255	1533	.819	57	310	1082	3044	1250	7	172	785	20	6230	2.2	6.1	12.4
NBA Playoff Totals	10	–	55	8	26	.308	–	–	–	2	6	.333	–	–	7	11	4	0	–	–	–	18	0.7	1.1	1.8
ABA Playoff Totals	45	–	1275	203	450	.451	3	18	.167	118	142	.831	6	20	91	227	139	5	4	65	1	527	2.0	5.0	11.7

Melvin, Edward H. (Ed) b. February 13, 1916 Ht. 5-9 Wt. 170 College: Duquesne

SEASON–TEAM	G	GS	MIN	FGM	FGA	PCT	3FGM	3FGA	PCT	FTM	FTA	PCT	O-RB	D-RB	TOT	AST	PF	DQ	STL	TO	BLK	PTS	RPG	APG	PPG
46-47–Pittsburgh	57	–	–	99	376	.263	–	–	–	83	127	.654	–	–	–	37	150	–	–	–	–	281	–	0.6	4.9
Reg. Season Totals	57	–	–	99	376	.263	–	–	–	83	127	.654	–	–	–	37	150	–	–	–	–	281	–	0.6	4.9

Meminger, Dean P. (The Dream) b. May 13, 1948 Ht. 6-1 Wt. 175 College: Marquette

SEASON–TEAM	G	GS	MIN	FGM	FGA	PCT	3FGM	3FGA	PCT	FTM	FTA	PCT	O-RB	D-RB	TOT	AST	PF	DQ	STL	TO	BLK	PTS	RPG	APG	PPG
71-72–New York	78	–	1173	139	293	.474	–	–	–	79	140	.564	–	–	185	103	137	0	–	–	–	357	2.4	1.3	4.6
72-73–New York	80	–	1453	188	365	.515	–	–	–	81	129	.628	–	–	229	133	109	1	–	–	–	457	2.9	1.7	5.7
73-74–New York	78	–	2079	274	539	.508	–	–	–	103	160	.644	125	156	281	162	161	0	62	–	8	651	3.6	2.1	8.3
74-75–Atlanta	80	–	2177	233	500	.466	–	–	–	168	263	.639	84	130	214	397	160	0	118	–	11	634	2.7	5.0	7.9
75-76–Atlanta	68	–	1418	155	379	.409	–	–	–	100	152	.658	65	86	151	222	116	0	54	–	8	410	2.2	3.3	6.0
76-77–N.Y. Knicks	32	–	254	15	36	.417	–	–	–	13	23	.565	12	14	26	29	17	0	8	–	1	43	0.8	0.9	1.3
Reg. Season Totals	416	–	8554	1004	2112	.475	–	–	–	544	867	.627	286	386	1086	1046	700	1	242	–	28	2552	2.6	2.5	6.1
Playoff Totals	45	–	779	66	145	.455	–	–	–	37	66	.561	9	15	104	82	85	1	4	–	0	169	2.3	1.8	3.8

Mencel, Charles J. (Chuck) b. April 21, 1933 Ht. 6-0 Wt. 170 College: Minnesota

SEASON–TEAM	G	GS	MIN	FGM	FGA	PCT	3FGM	3FGA	PCT	FTM	FTA	PCT	O-RB	D-RB	TOT	AST	PF	DQ	STL	TO	BLK	PTS	RPG	APG	PPG
55-56–Minneapolis	69	–	973	120	375	.320	–	–	–	78	96	.813	–	–	110	132	74	1	–	–	–	318	1.6	1.9	4.6
56-57–Minneapolis	72	–	1848	243	688	.353	–	–	–	179	240	.746	–	–	237	201	95	0	–	–	–	665	3.3	2.8	9.2
Reg. Season Totals	141	–	2821	363	1063	.341	–	–	–	257	336	.765	–	–	347	333	169	1	–	–	–	983	2.5	2.4	7.0
Playoff Totals	8	–	150	19	55	.345	–	–	–	13	16	.813	–	–	18	14	11	0	–	–	–	51	2.3	1.8	6.4

Mengelt, John P. (Crash) b. October 16, 1949 Ht. 6-2 Wt. 195 College: Auburn

SEASON–TEAM	G	GS	MIN	FGM	FGA	PCT	3FGM	3FGA	PCT	FTM	FTA	PCT	O-RB	D-RB	TOT	AST	PF	DQ	STL	TO	BLK	PTS	RPG	APG	PPG
71-72–Cincinnati	78	–	1438	287	605	.474	–	–	–	208	252	.825	–	–	148	146	163	0	–	–	–	782	1.9	1.9	10.0
72-73–K.C.-Omaha.Det.	79	–	1647	320	651	.492	–	–	–	127	160	.794	–	–	181	153	148	0	–	–	–	767	2.3	1.9	9.7
73-74–Detroit	77	–	1555	249	558	.446	–	–	–	182	229	.795	40	166	206	148	164	2	68	–	7	680	2.7	1.9	8.8
74-75–Detroit	80	–	1995	336	701	.479	–	–	–	211	248	.851	38	153	191	201	198	2	72	–	4	883	2.4	2.5	11.0
75-76–Detroit	67	–	1105	264	540	.489	–	–	–	192	237	.810	27	88	115	108	138	1	40	–	5	720	1.7	1.6	10.7
76-77–Chicago	61	–	1178	209	458	.456	–	–	–	89	113	.788	29	81	110	114	102	2	37	–	4	507	1.8	1.9	8.3
77-78–Chicago	81	–	1767	325	675	.481	–	–	–	184	238	.773	41	88	129	232	169	0	51	124	4	834	1.6	2.9	10.3
78-79–Chicago	75	–	1705	338	689	.491	–	–	–	150	182	.824	25	93	118	187	148	1	46	120	4	826	1.6	2.5	11.0
79-80–Chicago	36	–	387	90	166	.542	0	6	.000	39	49	.796	3	20	23	38	54	0	10	36	0	219	0.6	1.1	6.1
80-81–Golden State	2	–	11	0	4	.000	0	0	–	0	0	–	0	0	0	2	0	0	0	0	0	0	0.0	1.0	0.0
Reg. Season Totals	636	–	12788	2418	5047	.479	0	6	.000	1382	1708	.809	203	689	1221	1329	1284	8	324	280	28	6218	1.9	2.1	9.8
Playoff Totals	19	–	290	62	119	.521	0	0	–	43	55	.782	6	27	33	33	40	0	11	–	2	167	1.7	1.7	8.8

Menke, Kenneth H. (Ken, Angles) b. October 2, 1922 Ht. 6-0 Wt. 170 College: Illinois

SEASON–TEAM	G	GS	MIN	FGM	FGA	PCT	3FGM	3FGA	PCT	FTM	FTA	PCT	O-RB	D-RB	TOT	AST	PF	DQ	STL	TO	BLK	PTS	RPG	APG	PPG
47-48–Fort Wayne (N)	44	–	–	39	–	–	–	–	–	45	57	.789	–	–	–	–	49	–	–	–	–	123	–	–	2.8
49-50–Waterloo	6	–	–	6	17	.353	–	–	–	3	8	.375	–	–	–	7	7	–	–	–	–	15	–	1.2	2.5
Reg. NBA Totals	6	–	–	6	17	.353	–	–	–	3	8	.375	–	–	–	7	7	–	–	–	–	15	–	1.2	2.5
Reg. NBL Totals	44	–	–	39	–	–	–	–	–	45	57	.789	–	–	–	–	49	–	–	–	–	123	–	–	2.8
NBL Playoff Totals	1	–	–	1	–	–	–	–	–	0	0	–	–	–	–	–	1	–	–	–	–	2	–	–	2.0

Menyard, DeWitt b. 1944 Ht. 6-10 Wt. 210 College: Allan Hancock (Calif.) Coll. (J.C.); Utah

SEASON–TEAM	G	GS	MIN	FGM	FGA	PCT	3FGM	3FGA	PCT	FTM	FTA	PCT	O-RB	D-RB	TOT	AST	PF	DQ	STL	TO	BLK	PTS	RPG	APG	PPG
67-68–Houston (A)	71	–	1756	256	692	.370	0	0	–	131	197	.665	–	–	551	84	218	5	–	99	–	643	7.8	1.2	9.1
Reg. ABA Totals	71	–	1756	256	692	.370	0	0	–	131	197	.665	–	–	551	84	218	5	–	99	–	643	7.8	1.2	9.1
ABA Playoff Totals	3	–	64	7	18	.389	0	1	.000	1	3	.333	–	–	11	0	8	0	–	3	–	15	3.7	0.0	5.0

Mercer, Ronald Eugene (Ron) b. May 18, 1976 Ht. 6-7 Wt. 210 College: Kentucky

SEASON–TEAM	G	GS	MIN	FGM	FGA	PCT	3FGM	3FGA	PCT	FTM	FTA	PCT	O-RB	D-RB	TOT	AST	PF	DQ	STL	TO	BLK	PTS	RPG	APG	PPG
97-98–Boston	80	62	2662	515	1145	.450	3	28	.107	188	224	.839	109	171	280	176	213	2	125	132	17	1221	3.5	2.2	15.3
98-99–Boston	41	40	1551	305	707	.431	5	30	.167	83	105	.790	37	118	155	104	81	1	67	89	12	698	3.8	2.5	17.0
99-00–Den.-Orlando	68	68	2377	460	1080	.426	15	48	.313	213	270	.789	64	186	250	158	151	2	75	151	23	1148	3.7	2.3	16.9
Reg. Season Totals	189	170	6590	1280	2932	.437	23	106	.217	484	599	.808	210	475	685	438	445	5	267	372	52	3067	3.6	2.3	16.2

Meriweather, Joe C. b. October 26, 1953 Ht. 6-10 Wt. 215 College: Southern Illinois

SEASON–TEAM	G	GS	MIN	FGM	FGA	PCT	3FGM	3FGA	PCT	FTM	FTA	PCT	O-RB	D-RB	TOT	AST	PF	DQ	STL	TO	BLK	PTS	RPG	APG	PPG
75-76–Houston	81	–	2042	338	684	.494	–	–	–	154	239	.644	163	353	516	82	219	4	36	–	120	830	6.4	1.0	10.2
76-77–Atlanta	73	–	2068	319	607	.526	–	–	–	182	255	.714	216	380	596	82	324	21	41	–	82	820	8.2	1.1	11.2
77-78–New Orleans	54	–	1277	194	411	.472	–	–	–	87	133	.654	135	237	372	58	188	8	18	94	118	475	6.9	1.1	8.8
78-79–N.O.-N.Y.	77	–	1693	242	500	.484	–	–	–	126	187	.674	143	266	409	79	283	10	40	130	94	610	5.3	1.0	7.9
79-80–New York	65	–	1565	252	477	.528	0	1	.000	78	121	.645	122	228	350	66	239	8	37	112	120	582	5.4	1.0	9.0
80-81–Kansas City	74	–	1514	206	415	.496	0	0	–	148	213	.695	126	267	393	77	219	4	27	125	80	560	5.3	1.0	7.6
81-82–Kansas City	18	10	380	47	91	.516	0	0	–	31	40	.775	25	63	88	17	68	1	13	25	21	125	4.9	0.9	6.9
82-83–Kansas City	78	74	1706	258	453	.570	0	0	–	102	163	.626	150	274	424	64	285	4	47	118	86	618	5.4	0.8	7.9
83-84–Kansas City	73	31	1501	193	363	.532	0	0	–	94	123	.764	111	242	353	51	247	8	35	83	61	480	4.8	0.7	6.6
84-85–Kansas City	76	4	1061	121	243	.498	1	2	.500	96	124	.774	94	169	263	27	181	1	17	50	28	339	3.5	0.4	4.5
Reg. Season Totals	669	119	14807	2170	4244	.511	1	3	.333	1098	1598	.687	1285	2479	3764	603	2253	69	311	737	810	5439	5.6	0.9	8.1
Playoff Totals	10	0	199	24	49	.490	0	0	–	8	14	.571	12	19	31	5	31	1	5	9	7	56	3.1	0.5	5.6

Meriwether, Porter L. b. March 16, 1940 Ht. 6-2 Wt. 180 College: Tennessee State

SEASON–TEAM	G	GS	MIN	FGM	FGA	PCT	3FGM	3FGA	PCT	FTM	FTA	PCT	O-RB	D-RB	TOT	AST	PF	DQ	STL	TO	BLK	PTS	RPG	APG	PPG
62-63–Syracuse	31	–	268	48	122	.393	–	–	–	23	33	.697	–	–	29	43	19	0	–	–	–	119	0.9	1.4	3.8
Reg. Season Totals	31	–	268	48	122	.393	–	–	–	23	33	.697	–	–	29	43	19	0	–	–	–	119	0.9	1.4	3.8

Meschery, Thomas N. (Tom) b. October 26, 1938 Ht. 6-6 Wt. 215 College: St. Mary's (Calif.)

SEASON–TEAM	G	GS	MIN	FGM	FGA	PCT	3FGM	3FGA	PCT	FTM	FTA	PCT	O-RB	D-RB	TOT	AST	PF	DQ	STL	TO	BLK	PTS	RPG	APG	PPG
61-62–Philadelphia	80	–	2509	375	929	.404	–	–	–	216	262	.824	–	–	729	145	330	15	–	–	–	966	9.1	1.8	12.1
62-63–San Francisco	64	–	2245	397	935	.425	–	–	–	228	313	.728	–	–	624	104	249	11	–	–	–	1022	9.8	1.6	16.0
63-64–San Francisco	80	–	2422	436	951	.458	–	–	–	207	295	.702	–	–	612	149	288	6	–	–	–	1079	7.7	1.9	13.5
64-65–San Francisco	79	–	2408	361	917	.394	–	–	–	278	370	.751	–	–	655	106	279	6	–	–	–	1000	8.3	1.3	12.7
65-66–San Francisco	80	–	2383	401	895	.448	–	–	–	224	293	.765	–	–	716	81	285	7	–	–	–	1026	9.0	1.0	12.8
66-67–San Francisco	72	–	1846	293	706	.415	–	–	–	175	244	.717	–	–	549	94	264	8	–	–	–	761	7.6	1.3	10.6
67-68–Seattle	82	–	2857	473	1008	.469	–	–	–	244	345	.707	–	–	840	193	323	14	–	–	–	1190	10.2	2.4	14.5
68-69–Seattle	82	–	2673	462	1019	.453	–	–	–	220	299	.736	–	–	822	194	304	7	–	–	–	1144	10.0	2.4	14.0
69-70–Seattle	80	–	2294	394	818	.482	–	–	–	196	248	.790	–	–	666	157	317	13	–	–	–	984	8.3	2.0	12.3
70-71–Seattle	79	–	1822	285	615	.463	–	–	–	162	216	.750	–	–	485	108	202	2	–	–	–	732	6.1	1.4	9.3
Reg. Season Totals	778	–	23459	3877	8793	.441	–	–	–	2150	2885	.745	–	–	6698	1331	2841	89	–	–	–	9904	8.6	1.7	12.7
Playoff Totals	39	–	1321	248	570	.435	–	–	–	140	173	.809	–	–	344	78	153	7	–	–	–	636	8.8	2.0	16.3
All-Star Totals	1	–	8	1	3	.333	–	–	–	1	2	.500	–	–	1	1	1	0	–	–	–	3	1.0	1.0	3.0

Meyer, Loren Henry b. December 30, 1972 Ht. 6-10 Wt. 260 College: Iowa State

SEASON–TEAM	G	GS	MIN	FGM	FGA	PCT	3FGM	3FGA	PCT	FTM	FTA	PCT	O-RB	D-RB	TOT	AST	PF	DQ	STL	TO	BLK	PTS	RPG	APG	PPG
95-96–Dallas	72	21	1266	145	330	.439	3	11	.273	70	102	.686	114	205	319	57	224	6	20	67	32	363	4.4	0.8	5.0
96-97–Dallas-Phoenix	54	33	708	108	244	.443	4	7	.571	46	64	.719	53	92	145	19	125	3	11	62	15	266	2.7	0.4	4.9
98-99–Denver	14	0	70	7	28	.250	1	5	.200	1	2	.500	4	12	16	1	22	0	0	4	3	16	1.1	0.1	1.1
Reg. Season Totals	140	54	2044	260	602	.432	8	23	.348	117	168	.696	171	309	480	77	371	9	31	133	50	645	3.4	0.6	4.6
Playoff Totals	3	0	14	0	4	.000	0	1	.000	0	0	–	2	4	6	1	0	0	0	3	2	0	2.0	0.3	0.0

Meyer, William J. (Bill) b. August 30, 1943 Ht. 6-3 Wt. 195 College: Hiram

SEASON–TEAM	G	GS	MIN	FGM	FGA	PCT	3FGM	3FGA	PCT	FTM	FTA	PCT	O-RB	D-RB	TOT	AST	PF	DQ	STL	TO	BLK	PTS	RPG	APG	PPG
67-68–Pittsburgh (A)	7	–	45	10	22	.455	0	0	–	2	2	1.000	–	–	5	1	7	0	–	2	–	22	0.7	0.1	3.1
Reg. ABA Totals	7	–	45	10	22	.455	0	0	–	2	2	1.000	–	–	5	1	7	0	–	2	–	22	0.7	0.1	3.1

Meyers, David William (Dave) b. April 21, 1953 Ht. 6-9 Wt. 215 College: UCLA

SEASON–TEAM	G	GS	MIN	FGM	FGA	PCT	3FGM	3FGA	PCT	FTM	FTA	PCT	O-RB	D-RB	TOT	AST	PF	DQ	STL	TO	BLK	PTS	RPG	APG	PPG
75-76–Milwaukee	72	–	1589	198	472	.419	–	–	–	135	210	.643	121	324	445	100	145	0	72	–	25	531	6.2	1.4	7.4
76-77–Milwaukee	50	–	1262	179	383	.467	–	–	–	127	192	.661	122	219	341	86	152	4	42	–	32	485	6.8	1.7	9.7
77-78–Milwaukee	80	–	2416	432	938	.461	–	–	–	314	435	.722	144	393	537	241	240	2	86	213	46	1178	6.7	3.0	14.7
79-80–Milwaukee	79	–	2204	399	830	.481	1	5	.200	156	246	.634	140	308	448	225	218	3	72	182	40	955	5.7	2.8	12.1
Reg. Season Totals	281	–	7471	1208	2623	.461	1	5	.200	732	1083	.676	527	1244	1771	652	755	9	272	395	143	3149	6.3	2.3	11.2
Playoff Totals	19	–	528	75	172	.436	0	3	.000	56	89	.629	45	78	123	51	65	1	17	40	17	206	6.5	2.7	10.8

Miasek, Stanley (Stan) b. August 8, 1924 d. October 18, 1989 Ht. 6-5 Wt. 210 College: None

SEASON–TEAM	G	GS	MIN	FGM	FGA	PCT	3FGM	3FGA	PCT	FTM	FTA	PCT	O-RB	D-RB	TOT	AST	PF	DQ	STL	TO	BLK	PTS	RPG	APG	PPG
46-47–Detroit	60	–	–	331	1154	.287	–	–	–	233	385	.605	–	–	–	93	208	–	–	–	–	895	–	1.6	14.9
47-48–Chicago	48	–	–	263	867	.303	–	–	–	190	310	.613	–	–	–	31	192	–	–	–	–	716	–	0.6	14.9
48-49–Chicago	58	–	–	169	488	.346	–	–	–	113	216	.523	–	–	–	57	208	–	–	–	–	451	–	1.0	7.8
49-50–Chicago	68	–	–	176	462	.381	–	–	–	146	221	.661	–	–	–	75	264	–	–	–	–	498	–	1.1	7.3
51-52–Baltimore	66	–	2174	258	707	.365	–	–	–	263	372	.707	–	–	639	140	257	12	–	–	–	779	9.7	2.1	11.8
52-53–Balt.-Milw.	65	–	1584	178	488	.365	–	–	–	156	248	.629	–	–	360	122	229	13	–	–	–	512	5.5	1.9	7.9
Reg. Season Totals	365	–	3758	1375	4166	.330	–	–	–	1101	1752	.628	–	–	999	518	1358	25	–	–	–	3851	7.6	1.4	10.6
Playoff Totals	8	–	0	36	192	.375	–	–	–	24	43	.558	–	–	–	8	65	1	–	–	–	96	–	0.5	12.0

Micheaux, Larry Wayne b. March 24, 1960 Ht. 6-9 Wt. 220 College: Houston

SEASON–TEAM	G	GS	MIN	FGM	FGA	PCT	3FGM	3FGA	PCT	FTM	FTA	PCT	O-RB	D-RB	TOT	AST	PF	DQ	STL	TO	BLK	PTS	RPG	APG	PPG
83-84–Kansas City	39	0	332	49	90	.544	0	0	–	21	39	.538	40	73	113	19	46	0	21	21	11	119	2.9	0.5	3.1
84-85–Milw.-Houston	57	0	565	91	157	.580	0	3	.000	29	43	.674	62	81	143	30	75	0	20	36	21	211	2.5	0.5	3.7
Reg. Season Totals	96	0	897	140	247	.567	0	3	.000	50	82	.610	102	154	256	49	121	0	41	57	32	330	2.7	0.5	3.4
Playoff Totals	8	0	122	18	37	.486	0	1	.000	10	20	.500	24	18	42	3	18	0	0	5	7	46	5.3	0.4	5.8

Mihalik, Zigmund John (Red) b. September 22, 1916 Ht. 6-0 Wt. 180 College: None HOF: 1986

SEASON–TEAM	G	GS	MIN	FGM	FGA	PCT	3FGM	3FGA	PCT	FTM	FTA	PCT	O-RB	D-RB	TOT	AST	PF	DQ	STL	TO	BLK	PTS	RPG	APG	PPG
46-47–Pittsburgh	7	–	–	3	9	.333	–	–	–	0	0	–	–	–	–	0	10	–	–	–	–	6	–	0.0	0.9
46-47–Youngstown (N)	31	–	–	41	–	–	–	–	–	12	29	.414	–	–	–	–	–	–	–	–	–	94	–	–	3.0
Reg. NBA Totals	7	–	–	3	9	.333	–	–	–	0	0	–	–	–	–	0	10	–	–	–	–	6	–	0.0	0.9
Reg. NBL Totals	31	–	–	41	–	–	–	–	–	12	29	.414	–	–	–	–	–	–	–	–	–	94	–	–	3.0

Mikan, Edward Anton (Ed) b. October 20, 1925 d. October 22, 1999 Ht. 6-8 Wt. 230 College: DePaul

SEASON–TEAM	G	GS	MIN	FGM	FGA	PCT	3FGM	3FGA	PCT	FTM	FTA	PCT	O-RB	D-RB	TOT	AST	PF	DQ	STL	TO	BLK	PTS	RPG	APG	PPG
48-49–Chicago	60	–	–	229	729	.314	–	–	–	136	183	.743	–	–	–	62	191	–	–	–	–	594	–	1.0	9.9
49-50–Chicago-Roch.	65	–	–	89	321	.277	–	–	–	92	120	.767	–	–	–	42	143	–	–	–	–	270	–	0.6	4.2
50-51–Roch.-Wash.-Phil.	61	–	–	193	556	.347	–	–	–	137	189	.725	–	–	344	63	194	6	–	–	–	523	5.6	1.0	8.6
51-52–Philadelphia	66	–	1781	202	571	.354	–	–	–	116	148	.784	–	–	492	87	252	7	–	–	–	520	7.5	1.3	7.9
52-53–Phil.-Ind.	62	–	927	78	292	.267	–	–	–	79	98	.806	–	–	237	39	124	0	–	–	–	235	3.8	0.6	3.8
53-54–Boston	9	–	71	8	24	.333	–	–	–	5	9	.556	–	–	20	3	15	0	–	–	–	21	2.2	0.3	2.3
Reg. Season Totals	323	–	2779	799	2493	.320	–	–	–	565	747	.756	–	–	1093	296	919	13	–	–	–	2163	5.5	0.9	6.7
Playoff Totals	11	–	180	31	158	.247	–	–	–	29	35	.829	–	–	48	9	36	0	–	–	–	91	6.9	0.7	8.3

Mikan, George Lawrence III (Larry) b. April 8, 1948 Ht. 6-7 Wt. 210 College: Minnesota

SEASON–TEAM	G	GS	MIN	FGM	FGA	PCT	3FGM	3FGA	PCT	FTM	FTA	PCT	O-RB	D-RB	TOT	AST	PF	DQ	STL	TO	BLK	PTS	RPG	APG	PPG
70-71–Cleveland	53	–	536	62	186	.333	–	–	–	34	55	.618	–	–	139	41	56	1	–	–	–	158	2.6	0.8	3.0
Reg. Season Totals	53	–	536	62	186	.333	–	–	–	34	55	.618	–	–	139	41	56	1	–	–	–	158	2.6	0.8	3.0

Mikan, George Lawrence Jr. b. June 18, 1924 Ht. 6-10 Wt. 245 College: DePaul HOF: 1959

SEASON–TEAM	G	GS	MIN	FGM	FGA	PCT	3FGM	3FGA	PCT	FTM	FTA	PCT	O-RB	D-RB	TOT	AST	PF	DQ	STL	TO	BLK	PTS	RPG	APG	PPG
46-47–Chicago (N)	25	–	–	147	–	–	–	–	–	119	164	.726	–	–	–	–	96	–	–	–	–	413	–	–	16.5
47-48–Minneapolis (N)	56	–	–	406	–	–	–	–	–	383	509	.752	–	–	–	–	210	–	–	–	–	1195	–	–	21.3
48-49–Minneapolis	60	–	–	583	1403	.416	–	–	–	532	689	.772	–	–	–	218	260	–	–	–	–	1698	–	3.6	28.3
49-50–Minneapolis	68	–	–	649	1595	.407	–	–	–	567	728	.779	–	–	–	197	297	–	–	–	–	1865	–	2.9	27.4
50-51–Minneapolis	68	–	–	678	1584	.428	–	–	–	576	717	.803	–	–	958	208	308	14	–	–	–	1932	14.1	3.1	28.4
51-52–Minneapolis	64	–	2572	545	1414	.385	–	–	–	433	555	.780	–	–	866	194	286	14	–	–	–	1523	13.5	3.0	23.8
52-53–Minneapolis	70	–	2651	500	1252	.399	–	–	–	442	567	.780	–	–	1007	201	290	12	–	–	–	1442	14.4	2.9	20.6
53-54–Minneapolis	72	–	2362	441	1160	.380	–	–	–	424	546	.777	–	–	1028	174	268	4	–	–	–	1306	14.3	2.4	18.1
55-56–Minneapolis	37	–	765	148	375	.395	–	–	–	94	122	.770	–	–	308	53	153	6	–	–	–	390	8.3	1.4	10.5
Reg. NBA Totals	439	–	8350	3544	8783	.404	–	–	–	3068	3924	.782	–	–	4167	1245	1862	50	–	–	–	10156	13.4	2.8	23.1
Reg. NBL Totals	81	–	–	553	–	–	–	–	–	502	673	.746	–	–	–	–	306	–	–	–	–	1608	–	–	19.9
NBA Playoff Totals	70	–	1500	563	1394	.404	–	–	–	554	705	.786	–	–	665	155	305	12	–	–	–	1680	13.9	2.2	24.0
NBL Playoff Totals	21	–	–	160	–	–	–	–	–	141	196	.699	–	–	–	–	85	–	–	–	–	461	–	–	22.0
NBA All-Star Totals	4	–	100	28	80	.350	–	–	–	22	27	.815	–	–	51	7	14	0	–	–	–	78	12.8	1.8	19.5

Mikkelsen, Arild Verner (Vern) b. October 21, 1928 Ht. 6-7 Wt. 230 College: Hamline HOF: 1995

SEASON–TEAM	G	GS	MIN	FGM	FGA	PCT	3FGM	3FGA	PCT	FTM	FTA	PCT	O-RB	D-RB	TOT	AST	PF	DQ	STL	TO	BLK	PTS	RPG	APG	PPG
49-50–Minneapolis	68	–	–	288	722	.399	–	–	–	215	286	.752	–	–	–	123	222	–	–	–	–	791	–	1.8	11.6
50-51–Minneapolis	64	–	–	359	893	.402	–	–	–	186	275	.676	–	–	655	181	260	13	–	–	–	904	10.2	2.8	14.1
51-52–Minneapolis	66	–	2345	363	866	.419	–	–	–	283	372	.761	–	–	681	180	282	16	–	–	–	1009	10.3	2.7	15.3
52-53–Minneapolis	70	–	2465	378	868	.435	–	–	–	291	387	.752	–	–	654	148	289	14	–	–	–	1047	9.3	2.1	15.0
53-54–Minneapolis	72	–	2247	288	771	.374	–	–	–	221	298	.742	–	–	615	119	264	7	–	–	–	797	8.5	1.7	11.1
54-55–Minneapolis	71	–	2559	440	1043	.422	–	–	–	447	598	.747	–	–	722	145	319	14	–	–	–	1327	10.2	2.0	18.7
55-56–Minneapolis	72	–	2100	317	821	.386	–	–	–	328	408	.804	–	–	608	173	319	17	–	–	–	962	8.4	2.4	13.4
56-57–Minneapolis	72	–	2198	322	854	.377	–	–	–	342	424	.807	–	–	630	121	312	18	–	–	–	986	8.8	1.7	13.7
57-58–Minneapolis	72	–	2390	439	1070	.410	–	–	–	370	471	.786	–	–	805	166	299	20	–	–	–	1248	11.2	2.3	17.3
58-59–Minneapolis	72	–	2139	353	904	.390	–	–	–	286	355	.806	–	–	570	159	246	8	–	–	–	992	7.9	2.2	13.8
Reg. Season Totals	699	–	18443	3547	8812	.403	–	–	–	2969	3874	.766	–	–	5940	1515	2812	127	–	–	–	10063	9.4	2.2	14.4
Playoff Totals	85	–	2785	396	1172	.397	–	–	–	350	442	.792	–	–	710	200	397	27	–	–	–	1142	7.7	1.7	13.4
All-Star Totals	6	–	110	27	70	.386	–	–	–	13	20	.650	–	–	52	8	20	0	–	–	–	67	8.7	1.3	11.2

Miksis, Alfonse K. b. February 2, 1928 Ht. 6-7 Wt. 210 College: Western Illinois

SEASON–TEAM	G	GS	MIN	FGM	FGA	PCT	3FGM	3FGA	PCT	FTM	FTA	PCT	O-RB	D-RB	TOT	AST	PF	DQ	STL	TO	BLK	PTS	RPG	APG	PPG
49-50–Waterloo	8	–	–	5	21	.238	–	–	–	17	21	.810	–	–	–	4	22	–	–	–	–	27	–	0.5	3.4
Reg. Season Totals	8	–	–	5	21	.238	–	–	–	17	21	.810	–	–	–	4	22	–	–	–	–	27	–	0.5	3.4

Miles, Edward Jr. (Eddie) b. July 5, 1940 Ht. 6-4 Wt. 195 College: Seattle

SEASON–TEAM	G	GS	MIN	FGM	FGA	PCT	3FGM	3FGA	PCT	FTM	FTA	PCT	O-RB	D-RB	TOT	AST	PF	DQ	STL	TO	BLK	PTS	RPG	APG	PPG
63-64–Detroit	60	–	811	131	371	.353	–	–	–	62	87	.713	–	–	95	58	92	0	–	–	–	324	1.6	1.0	5.4
64-65–Detroit	76	–	2074	439	994	.442	–	–	–	166	223	.744	–	–	258	157	201	1	–	–	–	1044	3.4	2.1	13.7
65-66–Detroit	80	–	2788	634	1418	.447	–	–	–	298	402	.741	–	–	302	221	203	2	–	–	–	1566	3.8	2.8	19.6
66-67–Detroit	81	–	2419	582	1363	.427	–	–	–	261	338	.772	–	–	298	181	216	2	–	–	–	1425	3.7	2.2	17.6
67-68–Detroit	76	–	2303	561	1180	.475	–	–	–	282	369	.764	–	–	264	215	200	3	–	–	–	1404	3.5	2.8	18.5
68-69–Detroit	80	–	2252	441	983	.449	–	–	–	182	273	.667	–	–	283	180	201	0	–	–	–	1064	3.5	2.3	13.3
69-70–Detroit-Balt.	47	–	1295	238	541	.440	–	–	–	133	175	.760	–	–	177	86	107	0	–	–	–	609	3.8	1.8	13.0
70-71–Baltimore	63	–	1541	252	591	.426	–	–	–	118	147	.803	–	–	167	110	119	0	–	–	–	622	2.7	1.7	9.9
71-72–New York	42	–	198	23	64	.359	–	–	–	16	18	.889	–	–	16	17	46	0	–	–	–	62	0.4	0.4	1.5
Reg. Season Totals	605	–	15681	3301	7505	.440	–	–	–	1518	2032	.747	–	–	1860	1225	1385	8	–	–	–	8120	3.1	2.0	13.4
Playoff Totals	20	–	277	43	111	.387	–	–	–	13	17	.765	–	–	35	16	23	0	–	–	–	99	1.8	0.8	5.0
All-Star Totals	1	–	28	8	16	.500	–	–	–	1	5	.200	–	–	1	0	1	0	–	–	–	17	1.0	0.0	17.0

Milic, Marko b. May 7, 1977 Ht. 6-6 Wt. 235 Country: Slovenia

SEASON–TEAM	G	GS	MIN	FGM	FGA	PCT	3FGM	3FGA	PCT	FTM	FTA	PCT	O-RB	D-RB	TOT	AST	PF	DQ	STL	TO	BLK	PTS	RPG	APG	PPG
97-98–Phoenix	33	0	163	39	64	.609	3	6	.500	11	17	.647	10	15	25	12	17	0	10	21	0	92	0.8	0.4	2.8
98-99–Phoenix	11	0	53	8	20	.400	0	1	.000	0	0	–	3	2	5	2	7	0	3	6	1	16	0.5	0.2	1.5
Reg. Season Totals	44	0	216	47	84	.560	3	7	.429	11	17	.647	13	17	30	14	24	0	13	27	1	108	0.7	0.3	2.5
Playoff Totals	2	0	4	2	3	.667	0	0	–	0	0	–	0	1	1	–	1	0	1	0	0	4	0.5	0.0	2.0

Militzok, Nathan (Nat) b. May 3, 1923 Ht. 6-3 Wt. 195 College: C.C.NY; Hofstra; Cornell

SEASON–TEAM	G	GS	MIN	FGM	FGA	PCT	3FGM	3FGA	PCT	FTM	FTA	PCT	O-RB	D-RB	TOT	AST	PF	DQ	STL	TO	BLK	PTS	RPG	APG	PPG
46-47–N.Y.-Toronto	56	–	–	90	343	.262	–	–	–	64	112	.571	–	–	–	42	120	–	–	–	–	244	–	0.8	4.4
Reg. Season Totals	56	–	–	90	343	.262	–	–	–	64	112	.571	–	–	–	42	120	–	–	–	–	244	–	0.8	4.4

Milkovich, Ed b. 1916 Ht. 5-9 Wt. 170 College: Duquesne

SEASON–TEAM	G	GS	MIN	FGM	FGA	PCT	3FGM	3FGA	PCT	FTM	FTA	PCT	O-RB	D-RB	TOT	AST	PF	DQ	STL	TO	BLK	PTS	RPG	APG	PPG
46-47–Pittsburgh	57	–	–	99	376	.000	–	–	–	83	127	.000	–	–	–	37	150	–	–	–	–	281	–	–	4.9
Reg. Season Totals	57	–	–	99	376	.000	–	–	–	83	127	.000	–	–	–	37	150	–	–	–	–	281	–	–	4.9

Miller, Andre Lloyd b. March 19, 1976 Ht. 6-2 Wt. 203 College: Utah

SEASON–TEAM	G	GS	MIN	FGM	FGA	PCT	3FGM	3FGA	PCT	FTM	FTA	PCT	O-RB	D-RB	TOT	AST	PF	DQ	STL	TO	BLK	PTS	RPG	APG	PPG
99-00–Cleveland	82	36	2093	339	755	.449	10	49	.204	226	292	.774	85	195	280	476	194	1	84	166	17	914	3.4	5.8	11.1
Reg. Season Totals	82	36	2093	339	755	.449	10	49	.204	226	292	.774	85	195	280	476	194	1	84	166	17	914	3.4	5.8	11.1

Miller, Anthony (Pig) b. October 27, 1971 Ht. 6-9 Wt. 255 College: Michigan State

SEASON–TEAM	G	GS	MIN	FGM	FGA	PCT	3FGM	3FGA	PCT	FTM	FTA	PCT	O-RB	D-RB	TOT	AST	PF	DQ	STL	TO	BLK	PTS	RPG	APG	PPG
94-95–L.A. Lakers	46	1	527	70	132	.530	2	5	.400	47	76	.618	67	85	152	35	77	2	20	38	7	189	3.3	0.8	4.1
95-96–L.A. Lakers	27	0	123	15	35	.429	0	2	.000	6	10	.600	11	14	25	4	19	0	4	8	1	36	0.9	0.1	1.3
96-97–Atlanta	1	0	14	0	5	.000	0	0	–	0	0	–	2	5	7	0	2	0	0	0	0	0	7.0	0.0	0.0
97-98–Atlanta	37	0	228	29	52	.558	0	0	–	21	39	.538	30	40	70	3	41	0	15	14	3	79	1.9	0.1	2.1
98-99–Houston	29	0	249	28	60	.467	0	1	.000	14	22	.636	26	41	67	7	34	0	7	9	5	70	2.3	0.2	2.4
99-00–Houston	35	14	476	52	97	.536	0	0	–	26	51	.510	49	115	164	16	68	1	11	19	10	130	4.7	0.5	3.7
Reg. Season Totals	175	15	1617	194	381	.509	2	8	.250	114	198	.576	185	300	485	65	241	3	57	88	26	504	2.8	0.4	2.9
Playoff Totals	8	0	48	3	10	.300	0	0	–	2	2	1.000	7	8	15	2	7	0	3	4	1	8	1.9	0.3	1.0

Miller, Brad b. April 12, 1976 Ht. 7-0 Wt. 261 College: Purdue

SEASON–TEAM	G	GS	MIN	FGM	FGA	PCT	3FGM	3FGA	PCT	FTM	FTA	PCT	O-RB	D-RB	TOT	AST	PF	DQ	STL	TO	BLK	PTS	RPG	APG	PPG
98-99–Charlotte	38	0	469	78	138	.565	1	2	.500	81	102	.794	35	82	117	22	65	0	9	32	18	238	3.1	0.6	6.3
99-00–Charlotte	55	4	961	135	293	.461	0	2	.000	153	195	.785	113	180	293	45	111	1	23	48	35	423	5.3	0.8	7.7
Reg. Season Totals	93	4	1430	213	431	.494	1	4	.250	234	297	.788	148	262	410	67	176	1	32	80	53	661	4.4	0.7	7.1
Playoff Totals	4	0	62	9	17	.529	0	0	–	12	15	.800	8	5	13	3	11	0	0	9	3	30	3.3	0.8	7.5

Miller, Edwin B. (Eddie) b. June 18, 1931 Ht. 6-8 Wt. 225 College: Syracuse

SEASON–TEAM	G	GS	MIN	FGM	FGA	PCT	3FGM	3FGA	PCT	FTM	FTA	PCT	O-RB	D-RB	TOT	AST	PF	DQ	STL	TO	BLK	PTS	RPG	APG	PPG
52-53–Milw.-Balt.	70	–	2018	273	781	.350	–	–	–	187	287	.652	–	–	669	115	250	12	–	–	–	733	9.6	1.6	10.5
53-54–Baltimore	72	–	1657	244	600	.407	–	–	–	231	317	.729	–	–	537	95	194	0	–	–	–	719	7.5	1.3	10.0
Reg. Season Totals	142	–	3675	517	1381	.374	–	–	–	418	604	.692	–	–	1206	210	444	12	–	–	–	1452	8.5	1.5	10.2
Playoff Totals	2	–	93	13	34	.382	–	–	–	7	16	.438	–	–	36	5	9	0	–	–	–	33	18.0	2.5	16.5

Miller, Harry David (Moose) b. July 28, 1923 Ht. 6-4 Wt. 230 College: Seton Hall; North Carolina

SEASON–TEAM	G	GS	MIN	FGM	FGA	PCT	3FGM	3FGA	PCT	FTM	FTA	PCT	O-RB	D-RB	TOT	AST	PF	DQ	STL	TO	BLK	PTS	RPG	APG	PPG
46-47–Toronto	53	–	–	58	260	.223	–	–	–	36	82	.439	–	–	–	42	119	–	–	–	–	152	–	0.8	2.9
Reg. Season Totals	53	–	–	58	260	.223	–	–	–	36	82	.439	–	–	–	42	119	–	–	–	–	152	–	0.8	2.9

Miller, Jay Julian (Jay Jay) b. July 19, 1943 Ht. 6-5 Wt. 210 College: Notre Dame

SEASON–TEAM	G	GS	MIN	FGM	FGA	PCT	3FGM	3FGA	PCT	FTM	FTA	PCT	O-RB	D-RB	TOT	AST	PF	DQ	STL	TO	BLK	PTS	RPG	APG	PPG
67-68–St. Louis	8	–	52	8	31	.258	–	–	–	4	7	.571	–	–	7	1	11	0	–	–	–	20	0.9	0.1	2.5
68-69–Milwaukee	3	–	27	2	10	.200	–	–	–	5	7	.714	–	–	2	0	4	0	–	–	–	9	0.7	0.0	3.0
68-69–L.A.-Indiana (A)	52	–	742	147	356	.413	0	0	–	127	176	.722	–	–	113	29	103	2	–	71	–	421	2.2	0.6	8.1
69-70–Indiana (A)	52	–	415	75	167	.449	0	1	.000	41	57	.719	–	–	80	16	72	2	–	–	–	191	1.5	0.3	3.7
70-71–Indiana (A)	2	–	9	4	5	.800	0	0	–	0	0	–	–	–	3	1	1	–	–	–	–	8	1.5	0.5	4.0
Reg. NBA Totals	11	–	79	10	41	.244	–	–	–	9	14	.643	–	–	9	1	15	0	–	–	–	29	0.8	0.1	2.6
Reg. ABA Totals	106	–	1166	226	528	.428	0	1	.000	168	233	.721	–	–	196	46	176	4	–	71	–	620	1.8	0.4	5.8
ABA Playoff Totals	14	–	72	16	38	.421	0	0	–	4	10	.400	–	–	25	2	18	0	–	–	–	36	1.8	0.1	2.6

Miller, Lawrence James (Larry, Mills) b. April 4, 1946 Ht. 6-4 Wt. 210 College: North Carolina

SEASON–TEAM	G	GS	MIN	FGM	FGA	PCT	3FGM	3FGA	PCT	FTM	FTA	PCT	O-RB	D-RB	TOT	AST	PF	DQ	STL	TO	BLK	PTS	RPG	APG	PPG
68-69–Los Angeles (A)	78	–	2871	473	1162	.407	42	139	.302	340	475	.716	–	–	599	177	193	0	–	182	–	1328	7.7	2.3	17.0
69-70–L.A.-Car. (A)	80	–	2037	317	758	.418	15	74	.203	223	331	.674	–	–	414	147	173	0	–	–	–	872	5.2	1.8	10.9
70-71–Carolina (A)	77	–	2140	364	795	.458	13	61	.213	197	272	.724	–	–	457	167	181	–	–	–	–	938	5.9	2.2	12.2
71-72–Carolina (A)	83	–	3199	562	1228	.458	12	47	.255	393	497	.791	–	–	399	235	232	–	–	191	–	1529	4.8	2.8	18.4
72-73–San Diego (A)	83	–	2700	450	1080	.417	0	7	.000	306	422	.725	171	184	355	281	174	0	–	168	–	1206	4.3	3.4	14.5
73-74–S.D.-Vir. (A)	80	–	1968	281	638	.440	0	3	.000	151	228	.662	87	122	209	144	138	–	56	120	6	713	2.6	1.8	8.9
74-75–Utah (A)	5	–	26	3	9	.333	0	0	–	3	3	1.000	1	0	1	4	0	–	1	2	0	9	0.2	0.8	1.8
Reg. ABA Totals	486	–	14941	2450	5670	.432	82	331	.248	1613	2228	.724	259	306	2434	1155	1091	0	57	663	6	6595	5.0	2.4	13.6
ABA Playoff Totals	9	–	153	20	61	.328	2	5	.400	19	23	.826	0	0	20	20	3	0	0	7	0	61	2.2	2.2	6.8

Miller, Oliver J. (Big O) b. April 6, 1970 Ht. 6-9 Wt. 315 College: Arkansas

SEASON–TEAM	G	GS	MIN	FGM	FGA	PCT	3FGM	3FGA	PCT	FTM	FTA	PCT	O-RB	D-RB	TOT	AST	PF	DQ	STL	TO	BLK	PTS	RPG	APG	PPG
92-93–Phoenix	56	1	1069	121	255	.475	0	3	.000	71	100	.710	70	205	275	118	145	0	38	108	100	313	4.9	2.1	5.6
93-94–Phoenix	69	30	1786	277	455	.609	2	9	.222	80	137	.584	140	336	476	244	230	1	83	164	156	636	6.9	3.5	9.2
94-95–Detroit	64	22	1558	232	418	.555	3	13	.231	78	124	.629	162	313	475	93	217	1	60	115	116	545	7.4	1.5	8.5
95-96–Toronto	76	72	2516	418	795	.526	0	11	.000	146	221	.661	177	385	562	219	277	4	108	202	143	982	7.4	2.9	12.9
96-97–Dallas-Toronto	61	8	1152	123	238	.517	0	2	.000	48	79	.608	105	201	306	87	181	1	47	90	63	294	5.0	1.4	4.8
97-98–Toronto	64	53	1628	170	369	.461	0	4	.000	61	101	.604	146	254	400	196	184	1	58	131	72	401	6.3	3.1	6.3
98-99–Sacramento	4	0	35	5	11	.455	0	0	–	0	0	–	7	1	8	0	3	0	0	4	2	10	2.0	0.0	2.5
99-00–Phoenix	51	9	1088	137	233	.588	0	0	–	49	73	.671	87	174	261	68	132	1	42	74	80	323	5.1	1.3	6.3
Reg. Season Totals	445	195	10832	1483	2774	.535	5	42	.119	533	835	.638	894	1869	2763	1025	1369	9	436	888	732	3504	6.2	2.3	7.9
Playoff Totals	41	4	696	89	157	.567	0	5	.000	36	66	.545	49	127	176	65	106	0	27	57	73	214	4.3	1.6	5.2

Miller, Reginald Wayne (Reggie) b. August 24, 1965 Ht. 6-7 Wt. 185 College: UCLA

SEASON–TEAM	G	GS	MIN	FGM	FGA	PCT	3FGM	3FGA	PCT	FTM	FTA	PCT	O-RB	D-RB	TOT	AST	PF	DQ	STL	TO	BLK	PTS	RPG	APG	PPG
87-88–Indiana	82	1	1840	306	627	.488	61	172	.355	149	186	.801	95	95	190	132	157	0	53	101	19	822	2.3	1.6	10.0
88-89–Indiana	74	70	2536	398	831	.479	98	244	.402	287	340	.844	73	219	292	227	170	2	93	143	29	1181	3.9	3.1	16.0
89-90–Indiana	82	82	3192	661	1287	.514	150	362	.414	544	627	.868	95	200	295	311	175	1	110	222	18	2016	3.6	3.8	24.6
90-91–Indiana	82	82	2972	596	1164	.512	112	322	.348	551	600	.918	81	200	281	331	165	1	109	163	13	1855	3.4	4.0	22.6
91-92–Indiana	82	82	3120	562	1121	.501	129	341	.378	442	515	.858	82	236	318	314	210	1	105	157	26	1695	3.9	3.8	20.7
92-93–Indiana	82	82	2954	571	1193	.479	167	419	.399	427	485	.880	67	191	258	262	182	0	120	145	26	1736	3.1	3.2	21.2
93-94–Indiana	79	79	2638	524	1042	.503	123	292	.421	403	444	.908	30	182	212	248	193	2	119	175	24	1574	2.7	3.1	19.9
94-95–Indiana	81	81	2665	505	1092	.462	195	470	.415	383	427	.897	30	180	210	242	157	0	98	151	16	1588	2.6	3.0	19.6
95-96–Indiana	76	76	2621	504	1066	.473	168	410	.410	430	498	.863	38	176	214	253	175	0	77	189	13	1606	2.8	3.3	21.1
96-97–Indiana	81	81	2966	552	1244	.444	229	536	.427	418	475	.880	53	233	286	273	172	1	75	166	25	1751	3.5	3.4	21.6
97-98–Indiana	81	81	2795	516	1081	.477	164	382	.429	382	440	.868	46	186	232	171	148	2	78	128	11	1578	2.9	2.1	19.5
98-99–Indiana	50	50	1787	294	671	.438	106	275	.385	226	247	.915	25	110	135	112	101	1	37	76	9	920	2.7	2.2	18.4
99-00–Indiana	81	81	2987	466	1041	.448	165	404	.408	373	406	.919	50	189	239	187	126	0	85	129	25	1470	3.0	2.3	18.1
Reg. Season Totals	1013	928	35073	6455	13460	.480	1867	4629	.403	5015	5690	.881	765	2397	3162	3063	2131	11	1159	1945	254	19792	3.1	3.0	19.5
Playoff Totals	100	100	3872	736	1614	.456	243	599	.406	605	683	.886	62	227	289	254	202	1	106	176	26	2320	2.9	2.5	23.2
All-Star Totals	5	1	96	16	35	.457	5	19	.263	3	4	.750	0	5	5	10	6	0	5	3	1	40	1.0	2.0	8.0

Miller, Richard Mathias (Dick) b. April 26, 1958 Ht. 6-6 Wt. 220 College: Toledo

SEASON–TEAM	G	GS	MIN	FGM	FGA	PCT	3FGM	3FGA	PCT	FTM	FTA	PCT	O-RB	D-RB	TOT	AST	PF	DQ	STL	TO	BLK	PTS	RPG	APG	PPG
80-81–Indiana-Utah	8	–	53	4	9	.444	0	1	.000	0	0	–	2	5	7	5	5	0	4	8	0	8	0.9	0.6	1.0
Reg. Season Totals	8	–	53	4	9	.444	0	1	.000	0	0	–	2	5	7	5	5	0	4	8	0	8	0.9	0.6	1.0

Miller, Robert E. (Bob) b. July 9, 1956 Ht. 6-10 Wt. 230 College: Cincinnati

SEASON–TEAM	G	GS	MIN	FGM	FGA	PCT	3FGM	3FGA	PCT	FTM	FTA	PCT	O-RB	D-RB	TOT	AST	PF	DQ	STL	TO	BLK	PTS	RPG	APG	PPG
83-84–San Antonio	2	0	8	2	3	.667	0	0	–	0	0	–	2	3	5	1	5	0	0	0	1	4	2.5	0.5	2.0
Reg. Season Totals	2	0	8	2	3	.667	0	0	–	0	0	–	2	3	5	1	5	0	0	0	1	4	2.5	0.5	2.0

Miller, Walter P. (Walt) b. July 30, 1915 Ht. 6-2 Wt. 190 College: Duquesne

SEASON–TEAM	G	GS	MIN	FGM	FGA	PCT	3FGM	3FGA	PCT	FTM	FTA	PCT	O-RB	D-RB	TOT	AST	PF	DQ	STL	TO	BLK	PTS	RPG	APG	PPG
37-38–Pittsburgh (N)	9	–	–	18	–	–	–	–	–	10	–	–	–	–	–	–	–	–	–	–	–	46	–	–	5.1
38-39–Pittsburgh (N)	19	–	–	52	–	–	–	–	–	44	–	–	–	–	–	–	–	–	–	–	–	148	–	–	7.8
45-46–Youngstown (N)	10	–	–	4	–	–	–	–	–	5	–	–	–	–	–	–	–	–	–	–	–	13	–	–	1.3
46-47–Pittsburgh	12	–	–	7	21	.333	–	–	–	9	18	.500	–	–	–	6	16	–	–	–	–	23	–	0.5	1.9
Reg. NBA Totals	12	–	–	7	21	.333	–	–	–	9	18	.500	–	–	–	6	16	–	–	–	–	23	–	0.5	1.9
Reg. NBL Totals	38	–	–	74	–	–	–	–	–	59	0	–	–	–	–	–	–	–	–	–	–	207	–	–	5.4

Miller, William Ralph (Bill) b. November 24, 1924 Ht. 6-3 Wt. 190 College: North Carolina

SEASON–TEAM	G	GS	MIN	FGM	FGA	PCT	3FGM	3FGA	PCT	FTM	FTA	PCT	O-RB	D-RB	TOT	AST	PF	DQ	STL	TO	BLK	PTS	RPG	APG	PPG
48-49–Chicago-St. L.	28	–	–	21	72	.292	–	–	–	11	20	.550	–	–	–	20	32	–	–	–	–	53	–	0.7	1.9
Reg. Season Totals	28	–	–	21	72	.292	–	–	–	11	20	.550	–	–	–	20	32	–	–	–	–	53	–	0.7	1.9
Playoff Totals	1	–	–	0	0	–	–	–	–	0	2	.000	–	–	–	–	0	–	–	–	–	0	–	–	0.0

Mills, Christopher Lemonte (Chris) b. January 25, 1970 Ht. 6-7 Wt. 216 College: Kentucky; Arizona

SEASON–TEAM	G	GS	MIN	FGM	FGA	PCT	3FGM	3FGA	PCT	FTM	FTA	PCT	O-RB	D-RB	TOT	AST	PF	DQ	STL	TO	BLK	PTS	RPG	APG	PPG
93-94–Cleveland	79	18	2022	284	677	.419	38	122	.311	137	176	.778	134	267	401	128	232	3	54	89	50	743	5.1	1.6	9.4
94-95–Cleveland	80	79	2814	359	855	.420	94	240	.392	174	213	.817	99	267	366	154	242	2	59	120	35	986	4.6	1.9	12.3
95-96–Cleveland	80	80	3060	454	971	.468	79	210	.376	218	263	.829	112	331	443	188	241	1	73	121	52	1205	5.5	2.4	15.1
96-97–Cleveland	80	79	3167	405	894	.453	86	220	.391	176	209	.842	118	379	497	198	222	1	86	120	41	1072	6.2	2.5	13.4
97-98–New York	80	29	2183	292	675	.433	40	137	.292	152	189	.804	120	288	408	133	218	3	45	107	30	776	5.1	1.7	9.7
98-99–Golden State	47	24	1395	186	453	.411	32	115	.278	79	96	.823	49	188	237	103	125	1	39	58	14	483	5.0	2.2	10.3
99-00–Golden State	20	11	649	123	292	.421	8	30	.267	68	84	.810	46	77	123	47	60	0	18	25	4	322	6.2	2.4	16.1
Reg. Season Totals	466	320	15290	2103	4817	.437	377	1074	.351	1004	1230	.816	678	1797	2475	951	1340	11	374	640	226	5587	5.3	2.0	12.0
Playoff Totals	19	10	524	65	143	.455	16	34	.471	25	29	.862	25	57	82	29	58	1	20	20	7	171	4.3	1.5	9.0

Mills, John (Long John) b. September 7, 1919 Ht. 6-8 Wt. 210 College: Western Kentucky

SEASON–TEAM	G	GS	MIN	FGM	FGA	PCT	3FGM	3FGA	PCT	FTM	FTA	PCT	O-RB	D-RB	TOT	AST	PF	DQ	STL	TO	BLK	PTS	RPG	APG	PPG
44-45–Cleveland (N)	29	–	–	29	–	–	–	–	–	42	–	–	–	–	–	–	–	–	–	–	–	100	–	–	3.4
45-46–Cleveland (N)	19	–	–	13	–	–	–	–	–	25	–	–	–	–	–	–	–	–	–	–	–	51	–	–	2.7
46-47–Pittsburgh	47	–	–	55	187	.294	–	–	–	71	129	.550	–	–	–	9	94	–	–	–	–	181	–	0.2	3.9
Reg. NBA Totals	47	–	–	55	187	.294	–	–	–	71	129	.550	–	–	–	9	94	–	–	–	–	181	–	0.2	3.9
Reg. NBL Totals	48	–	–	42	–	–	–	–	–	67	0	–	–	–	–	–	–	–	–	–	–	151	–	–	3.1
NBL Playoff Totals	2	–	–	3	–	–	–	–	–	6	0	–	–	–	–	–	3	–	–	–	–	12	–	–	6.0

Mills, Terry Richard (T) b. December 21, 1967 Ht. 6-10 Wt. 250 College: Michigan

SEASON–TEAM	G	GS	MIN	FGM	FGA	PCT	3FGM	3FGA	PCT	FTM	FTA	PCT	O-RB	D-RB	TOT	AST	PF	DQ	STL	TO	BLK	PTS	RPG	APG	PPG
90-91–Denver-N.J.	55	2	819	134	288	.465	0	4	.000	47	66	.712	82	147	229	33	100	0	35	43	29	315	4.2	0.6	5.7
91-92–New Jersey	82	24	1714	310	670	.463	8	23	.348	114	152	.750	187	266	453	84	200	3	48	82	41	742	5.5	1.0	9.0
92-93–Detroit	81	46	2183	494	1072	.461	10	36	.278	201	254	.791	176	296	472	111	282	6	44	142	50	1199	5.8	1.4	14.8
93-94–Detroit	80	74	2773	588	1151	.511	24	73	.329	181	227	.797	193	479	672	177	309	6	64	153	62	1381	8.4	2.2	17.3
94-95–Detroit	72	69	2514	417	933	.447	109	285	.382	175	219	.799	124	434	558	160	253	5	68	144	33	1118	7.8	2.2	15.5
95-96–Detroit	82	5	1656	283	675	.419	82	207	.396	121	157	.771	108	244	352	98	197	0	42	98	20	769	4.3	1.2	9.4
96-97–Detroit	79	5	1997	312	702	.444	175	415	.422	58	70	.829	68	309	377	99	161	1	35	85	27	857	4.8	1.3	10.8
97-98–Miami	50	0	782	81	206	.393	25	81	.309	25	33	.758	34	118	152	39	129	1	19	45	9	212	3.0	0.8	4.2
98-99–Miami	1	0	29	3	8	.375	2	4	.500	1	2	.500	3	1	4	0	3	0	1	3	0	9	4.0	0.0	9.0
99-00–Detroit	82	78	1842	214	488	.439	95	242	.393	25	34	.735	50	340	390	85	242	4	38	46	24	548	4.8	1.0	6.7
Reg. Season Totals	664	303	16309	2836	6193	.458	530	1370	.387	948	1214	.781	1025	2634	3659	886	1876	26	394	841	295	7150	5.5	1.3	10.8
Playoff Totals	17	7	409	49	122	.402	17	48	.354	16	25	.640	16	57	73	20	53	1	10	14	2	131	4.3	1.2	7.7

Miner, Harold David (Baby Jordan) b. May 5, 1971 Ht. 6-5 Wt. 214 College: USC

SEASON–TEAM	G	GS	MIN	FGM	FGA	PCT	3FGM	3FGA	PCT	FTM	FTA	PCT	O-RB	D-RB	TOT	AST	PF	DQ	STL	TO	BLK	PTS	RPG	APG	PPG
92-93–Miami	73	0	1383	292	615	.475	3	9	.333	163	214	.762	74	73	147	73	130	2	34	92	8	750	2.0	1.0	10.3
93-94–Miami	63	31	1358	254	532	.477	4	6	.667	149	180	.828	75	81	156	95	132	0	31	95	13	661	2.5	1.5	10.5
94-95–Miami	45	16	871	123	305	.403	14	49	.286	69	95	.726	38	79	117	69	85	0	15	77	6	329	2.6	1.5	7.3
95-96–Cleveland	19	0	136	23	52	.442	2	10	.200	13	13	1.000	4	8	12	8	23	1	0	14	0	61	0.6	0.4	3.2
Reg. Season Totals	200	47	3748	692	1504	.460	23	74	.311	394	502	.785	191	241	432	245	370	3	80	278	27	1801	2.2	1.2	9.0
Playoff Totals	4	0	57	12	26	.462	0	0	–	8	11	.727	3	5	8	2	4	0	1	2	0	32	2.0	0.5	8.0

Minniefield, Dirk DeWayne b. January 17, 1961 Ht. 6-3 Wt. 180 College: Kentucky

SEASON–TEAM	G	GS	MIN	FGM	FGA	PCT	3FGM	3FGA	PCT	FTM	FTA	PCT	O-RB	D-RB	TOT	AST	PF	DQ	STL	TO	BLK	PTS	RPG	APG	PPG
85-86–Cleveland	76	2	1131	167	347	.481	10	37	.270	73	93	.785	43	88	131	269	165	1	65	108	1	417	1.7	3.5	5.5
86-87–Clev.-Houston	74	52	1600	218	482	.452	11	39	.282	62	90	.689	29	111	140	348	174	2	72	157	7	509	1.9	4.7	6.9
87-88–G.S.-Boston	72	6	1070	108	221	.489	4	16	.250	41	55	.745	30	66	96	228	133	0	59	93	3	261	1.3	3.2	3.6
Reg. Season Totals	222	60	3801	493	1050	.470	25	92	.272	176	238	.739	102	265	367	845	472	3	196	358	11	1187	1.7	3.8	5.3
Playoff Totals	19	0	77	10	22	.455	2	5	.400	8	8	1.000	3	1	4	13	21	0	3	14	0	30	0.2	0.7	1.6

Minor, Davage (Dave) b. February 23, 1922 Ht. 6-2 Wt. 185 College: Toledo; UCLA

SEASON–TEAM	G	GS	MIN	FGM	FGA	PCT	3FGM	3FGA	PCT	FTM	FTA	PCT	O-RB	D-RB	TOT	AST	PF	DQ	STL	TO	BLK	PTS	RPG	APG	PPG
51-52–Baltimore	57	–	1558	185	522	.354	–	–	–	101	132	.765	–	–	275	160	161	2	–	–	–	471	4.8	2.8	8.3
52-53–Balt.-Milw.	59	–	1610	154	420	.367	–	–	–	98	132	.742	–	–	252	128	211	11	–	–	–	406	4.3	2.2	6.9
Reg. Season Totals	116	–	3168	339	942	.360	–	–	–	199	264	.754	–	–	527	288	372	13	–	–	–	877	4.5	2.5	7.6

Minor, Greg Magado b. September 8, 1971 Ht. 6-6 Wt. 230 College: Louisville

SEASON–TEAM	G	GS	MIN	FGM	FGA	PCT	3FGM	3FGA	PCT	FTM	FTA	PCT	O-RB	D-RB	TOT	AST	PF	DQ	STL	TO	BLK	PTS	RPG	APG	PPG
94-95–Boston	63	8	945	155	301	.515	2	12	.167	65	78	.833	49	88	137	66	89	0	32	44	16	377	2.2	1.0	6.0
95-96–Boston	78	47	1761	320	640	.500	7	27	.259	99	130	.762	93	164	257	146	161	0	36	78	11	746	3.3	1.9	9.6
96-97–Boston	23	15	547	94	196	.480	1	8	.125	31	36	.861	30	50	80	34	45	0	15	22	2	220	3.5	1.5	9.6
97-98–Boston	69	16	1126	140	321	.436	6	31	.194	59	86	.686	55	95	150	88	100	0	53	43	11	345	2.2	1.3	5.0
98-99–Boston	44	7	765	85	204	.417	8	28	.286	36	48	.750	31	86	117	50	69	1	20	38	6	214	2.7	1.1	4.9
Reg. Season Totals	277	93	5144	794	1662	.478	24	106	.226	290	378	.767	258	483	741	384	464	1	156	225	46	1902	2.7	1.4	6.9
Playoff Totals	4	0	37	5	13	.385	0	0	–	1	1	1.000	1	0	1	2	3	0	1	1	1	11	0.3	0.5	2.8

Minor, Mark William b. May 14, 1950 Ht. 6-6 Wt. 215 College: Ohio State

SEASON–TEAM	G	GS	MIN	FGM	FGA	PCT	3FGM	3FGA	PCT	FTM	FTA	PCT	O-RB	D-RB	TOT	AST	PF	DQ	STL	TO	BLK	PTS	RPG	APG	PPG
72-73–Boston	4	–	20	1	4	.250	–	–	–	3	4	.750	–	–	4	2	5	0	–	–	–	5	1.0	0.5	1.3
Reg. Season Totals	4	–	20	1	4	.250	–	–	–	3	4	.750	–	–	4	2	5	0	–	–	–	5	1.0	0.5	1.3

Misaka, Wataru (Wat) b. December 21, 1923 Ht. 5-7 Wt. 150 College: Utah

SEASON–TEAM	G	GS	MIN	FGM	FGA	PCT	3FGM	3FGA	PCT	FTM	FTA	PCT	O-RB	D-RB	TOT	AST	PF	DQ	STL	TO	BLK	PTS	RPG	APG	PPG
47-48–New York	3	–	–	3	13	.231	–	–	–	1	3	.333	–	–	–	0	7	–	–	–	–	7	–	0.0	2.3
Reg. Season Totals	3	–	–	3	13	.231	–	–	–	1	3	.333	–	–	–	0	7	–	–	–	–	7	–	0.0	2.3

Miskiri, Jason Oliver b. August 19, 1975 Ht. 6-2 Wt. 175 College: George Mason

SEASON–TEAM	G	GS	MIN	FGM	FGA	PCT	3FGM	3FGA	PCT	FTM	FTA	PCT	O-RB	D-RB	TOT	AST	PF	DQ	STL	TO	BLK	PTS	RPG	APG	PPG
99-00–Charlotte	1	0	3	0	1	.000	0	1	.000	0	0	–	0	0	0	1	2	0	0	0	0	0	0.0	1.0	0.0
Reg. Season Totals	1	0	3	0	1	.000	0	1	.000	0	0	–	0	0	0	1	2	0	0	0	0	0	0.0	1.0	0.0

Mitchell, Ernest Todd (Todd) b. July 26, 1966 Ht. 6-7 Wt. 205 College: Purdue

SEASON–TEAM	G	GS	MIN	FGM	FGA	PCT	3FGM	3FGA	PCT	FTM	FTA	PCT	O-RB	D-RB	TOT	AST	PF	DQ	STL	TO	BLK	PTS	RPG	APG	PPG
88-89–Miami-S.A.	24	0	353	43	97	.443	0	0	–	37	64	.578	18	32	50	21	51	0	16	33	2	123	2.1	0.9	5.1
Reg. Season Totals	24	0	353	43	97	.443	0	0	–	37	64	.578	18	32	50	21	51	0	16	33	2	123	2.1	0.9	5.1

Mitchell, Leland b. February 22, 1941 Ht. 6-4 Wt. 210 College: Pearl River (Miss.) C.C.; Mississippi State

SEASON–TEAM	G	GS	MIN	FGM	FGA	PCT	3FGM	3FGA	PCT	FTM	FTA	PCT	O-RB	D-RB	TOT	AST	PF	DQ	STL	TO	BLK	PTS	RPG	APG	PPG
67-68–New Orleans (A)	78	–	1091	122	350	.349	21	76	.276	56	85	.659	–	–	182	73	159	1	–	108	–	321	2.3	0.9	4.1
Reg. ABA Totals	78	–	1091	122	350	.349	21	76	.276	56	85	.659	–	–	182	73	159	1	–	108	–	321	2.3	0.9	4.1
ABA Playoff Totals	7	–	57	1	9	.111	0	4	.000	1	2	.500	–	–	3	3	8	0	–	5	–	3	0.4	0.4	0.4

Mitchell, Michael Anthony (Mike) b. January 1, 1956 Ht. 6-7 Wt. 215 College: Auburn

SEASON–TEAM	G	GS	MIN	FGM	FGA	PCT	3FGM	3FGA	PCT	FTM	FTA	PCT	O-RB	D-RB	TOT	AST	PF	DQ	STL	TO	BLK	PTS	RPG	APG	PPG
78-79–Cleveland	80	–	1576	362	706	.513	–	–	–	131	178	.736	127	202	329	60	215	6	51	102	29	855	4.1	0.8	10.7
79-80–Cleveland	82	–	2802	775	1482	.523	0	6	.000	270	343	.787	206	385	591	93	259	4	70	172	77	1820	7.2	1.1	22.2
80-81–Cleveland	82	–	3194	853	1791	.476	4	9	.444	302	385	.784	215	287	502	139	199	0	63	175	52	2012	6.1	1.7	24.5
81-82–Clev.-S.A.	84	83	3063	753	1477	.510	0	7	.000	220	302	.728	244	346	590	82	277	4	60	153	43	1726	7.0	1.0	20.5
82-83–San Antonio	80	79	2803	686	1342	.511	0	3	.000	219	289	.758	188	349	537	98	248	6	57	126	52	1591	6.7	1.2	19.9
83-84–San Antonio	79	79	2853	779	1597	.488	6	14	.429	275	353	.779	188	382	570	93	251	6	62	141	73	1839	7.2	1.2	23.3
84-85–San Antonio	82	82	2853	775	1558	.497	5	23	.217	269	346	.777	145	272	417	151	219	1	61	144	27	1824	5.1	1.8	22.2
85-86–San Antonio	82	82	2970	802	1697	.473	0	12	.000	317	392	.809	134	275	409	188	175	0	56	184	25	1921	5.0	2.3	23.4
86-87–San Antonio	40	18	922	208	478	.435	1	2	.500	92	112	.821	38	65	103	38	68	0	19	51	9	509	2.6	1.0	12.7
87-88–San Antonio	68	20	1501	378	784	.482	3	12	.250	160	194	.825	54	144	198	68	101	0	31	52	13	919	2.9	1.0	13.5
Reg. Season Totals	759	443	24537	6371	12912	.493	19	88	.216	2255	2894	.779	1539	2707	4246	1010	2012	27	530	1300	400	15016	5.6	1.3	19.8
Playoff Totals	35	31	1163	273	544	.502	1	3	.333	99	130	.762	76	148	224	47	90	2	19	75	28	646	6.4	1.3	18.5
All-Star Totals	1	0	15	6	12	.500	0	0	–	2	2	1.000	4	0	4	2	2	0	1	1	0	14	4.0	2.0	14.0

Mitchell, Murray C. b. March 19, 1923 Ht. 6-6 College: Sam Houston State

SEASON–TEAM	G	GS	MIN	FGM	FGA	PCT	3FGM	3FGA	PCT	FTM	FTA	PCT	O-RB	D-RB	TOT	AST	PF	DQ	STL	TO	BLK	PTS	RPG	APG	PPG
49-50–Anderson	2	–	–	1	3	.333	–	–	–	0	0	–	–	–	–	2	1	–	–	–	–	2	–	1.0	1.0
Reg. Season Totals	2	–	–	1	3	.333	–	–	–	0	0	–	–	–	–	2	1	–	–	–	–	2	–	1.0	1.0

Mitchell, Samuel E. Jr. (Sam) b. September 2, 1963 Ht. 6-7 Wt. 215 College: Mercer

SEASON–TEAM	G	GS	MIN	FGM	FGA	PCT	3FGM	3FGA	PCT	FTM	FTA	PCT	O-RB	D-RB	TOT	AST	PF	DQ	STL	TO	BLK	PTS	RPG	APG	PPG
89-90–Minnesota	80	30	2414	372	834	.446	0	9	.000	268	349	.768	180	282	462	89	301	7	66	96	54	1012	5.8	1.1	12.7
90-91–Minnesota	82	60	3121	445	1010	.441	0	9	.000	307	396	.775	188	332	520	133	338	13	66	104	57	1197	6.3	1.6	14.6
91-92–Minnesota	82	63	2151	307	725	.423	2	11	.182	209	266	.786	158	315	473	94	230	3	53	97	39	825	5.8	1.1	10.1
92-93–Indiana	81	1	1402	215	483	.445	4	23	.174	150	185	.811	93	155	248	76	207	1	23	51	10	584	3.1	0.9	7.2
93-94–Indiana	75	18	1084	140	306	.458	0	5	.000	82	110	.745	71	119	190	65	152	1	33	50	9	362	2.5	0.9	4.8
94-95–Indiana	81	12	1377	201	413	.487	1	10	.100	126	174	.724	95	148	243	61	206	0	43	54	20	529	3.0	0.8	6.5
95-96–Minnesota	78	42	2145	303	618	.490	1	18	.056	237	291	.814	107	232	339	74	220	3	49	87	26	844	4.3	0.9	10.8
96-97–Minnesota	82	5	2044	269	603	.446	4	25	.160	224	295	.759	112	214	326	79	232	1	51	93	20	766	4.0	1.0	9.3
97-98–Minnesota	81	33	2239	371	800	.464	15	43	.349	243	292	.832	118	267	385	107	200	0	64	66	22	1000	4.8	1.3	12.3
98-99–Minnesota	50	20	1344	213	522	.408	9	38	.237	126	165	.764	55	127	182	98	111	1	35	34	16	561	3.6	2.0	11.2
99-00–Minnesota	66	24	1227	168	376	.447	10	23	.435	81	92	.880	28	110	138	111	116	0	27	44	14	427	2.1	1.7	6.5
Reg. Season Totals	838	308	20548	3004	6690	.449	46	214	.215	2053	2615	.785	1205	2301	3506	987	2313	30	510	776	287	8107	4.2	1.2	9.7
Playoff Totals	52	6	770	93	227	.410	6	28	.214	61	76	.803	38	83	121	28	112	0	8	38	8	253	2.3	0.5	4.9

Mix, Steven Charles (Steve) b. December 30, 1947 Ht. 6-7 Wt. 215 College: Toledo

SEASON–TEAM	G	GS	MIN	FGM	FGA	PCT	3FGM	3FGA	PCT	FTM	FTA	PCT	O-RB	D-RB	TOT	AST	PF	DQ	STL	TO	BLK	PTS	RPG	APG	PPG
69-70–Detroit	18	–	276	48	100	.480	–	–	–	23	39	.590	–	–	64	15	31	0	–	–	–	119	3.6	0.8	6.6
70-71–Detroit	35	–	731	111	249	.446	–	–	–	68	89	.764	–	–	164	34	72	0	–	–	–	290	4.7	1.0	8.3
71-72–Detroit	8	–	104	15	47	.319	–	–	–	7	12	.583	–	–	23	4	7	0	–	–	–	37	2.9	0.5	4.6
71-72–Denver (A)	1	–	4	1	1	1.000	0	0	–	0	0	–	–	–	1	0	1	–	–	0	–	2	1.0	0.0	2.0
73-74–Philadelphia	82	–	2969	495	1042	.475	–	–	–	228	288	.792	305	559	864	152	305	9	212	–	37	1218	10.5	1.9	14.9
74-75–Philadelphia	46	–	1748	280	582	.481	–	–	–	159	205	.776	155	345	500	99	175	6	79	–	21	719	10.9	2.2	15.6
75-76–Philadelphia	81	–	3039	421	844	.499	–	–	–	287	351	.818	215	447	662	216	288	6	158	–	29	1129	8.2	2.7	13.9
76-77–Philadelphia	75	–	1958	288	551	.523	–	–	–	215	263	.817	127	249	376	152	167	0	90	–	20	791	5.0	2.0	10.5
77-78–Philadelphia	82	–	1819	291	560	.520	–	–	–	175	220	.795	96	201	297	174	158	1	87	131	3	757	3.6	2.1	9.2
78-79–Philadelphia	74	–	1269	265	493	.538	–	–	–	161	201	.801	109	184	293	121	112	0	57	100	16	691	4.0	1.6	9.3
79-80–Philadelphia	81	–	1543	363	703	.516	4	10	.400	207	249	.831	114	176	290	149	114	0	67	132	9	937	3.6	1.8	11.6
80-81–Philadelphia	72	–	1327	288	575	.501	0	3	.000	200	240	.833	105	159	264	114	107	0	59	88	18	776	3.7	1.6	10.8
81-82–Philadelphia	75	0	1235	202	399	.506	1	4	.250	136	172	.791	92	133	225	93	86	0	42	67	17	541	3.0	1.2	7.2
82-83–Milw.-L.A.	58	20	809	137	283	.484	1	4	.250	75	88	.852	38	99	137	70	71	0	33	45	3	350	2.4	1.2	6.0
Reg. NBA Totals	787	20	18827	3204	6428	.498	6	21	.286	1941	2417	.803	1356	2552	4159	1393	1693	22	884	563	173	8355	5.3	1.8	10.6
Reg. ABA Totals	1	–	4	1	1	1.000	0	0	–	0	0	–	–	–	1	0	1	–	–	–	–	2	1.0	0.0	2.0
NBA Playoff Totals	89	0	1442	244	494	.494	1	2	.500	153	177	.864	90	158	248	137	143	1	65	53	13	642	2.8	1.5	7.2
NBA All-Star Totals	1	0	11	2	5	.400	0	0	–	0	0	–	0	2	2	0	2	0	0	–	0	4	2.0	0.0	4.0

Mikvy, William P. (Bill, Owl Without A Vowel) b. January 19, 1931 Ht. 6-4 Wt. 190 College: Temple

SEASON–TEAM	G	GS	MIN	FGM	FGA	PCT	3FGM	3FGA	PCT	FTM	FTA	PCT	O-RB	D-RB	TOT	AST	PF	DQ	STL	TO	BLK	PTS	RPG	APG	PPG
52-53–Philadelphia	31	–	608	75	246	.305	–	–	–	31	48	.646	–	–	101	62	54	1	–	–	–	181	3.3	2.0	5.8
Reg. Season Totals	31	–	608	75	246	.305	–	–	–	31	48	.646	–	–	101	62	54	1	–	–	–	181	3.3	2.0	5.8

Mobley, Cuttino Rashawn b. September 1, 1974 Ht. 6-4 Wt. 190 College: Rhode Island

SEASON–TEAM	G	GS	MIN	FGM	FGA	PCT	3FGM	3FGA	PCT	FTM	FTA	PCT	O-RB	D-RB	TOT	AST	PF	DQ	STL	TO	BLK	PTS	RPG	APG	PPG
98-99–Houston	49	37	1456	172	405	.425	53	148	.358	90	110	.818	22	89	111	121	98	0	44	79	23	487	2.3	2.5	9.9
99-00–Houston	81	8	2496	437	1016	.430	104	292	.356	299	353	.847	59	229	288	208	171	0	87	186	32	1277	3.6	2.6	15.8
Reg. Season Totals	130	45	3952	609	1421	.429	157	440	.357	389	463	.840	81	318	399	329	269	0	131	265	55	1764	3.1	2.5	13.6
Playoff Totals	4	4	94	7	15	.467	4	7	.571	10	11	.909	0	4	4	11	11	0	2	5	0	28	1.0	2.8	7.0

Mobley, Eric b. February 1, 1970 Ht. 6-11 Wt. 235 College: Pittsburgh

SEASON–TEAM	G	GS	MIN	FGM	FGA	PCT	3FGM	3FGA	PCT	FTM	FTA	PCT	O-RB	D-RB	TOT	AST	PF	DQ	STL	TO	BLK	PTS	RPG	APG	PPG
94-95–Milwaukee	46	26	587	78	132	.591	2	2	1.000	22	45	.489	55	98	153	21	63	0	8	24	27	180	3.3	0.5	3.9
95-96–Milw.-Vanc.	39	4	676	74	138	.536	1	2	.500	39	87	.448	54	86	140	22	87	1	14	50	24	188	3.6	0.6	4.8
96-97–Vancouver	28	8	307	28	63	.444	0	0	–	16	30	.533	30	28	58	14	44	0	5	29	10	72	2.1	0.5	2.6
Reg. Season Totals	113	38	1570	180	333	.541	3	4	.750	77	162	.475	139	212	351	57	194	1	27	103	61	440	3.1	0.5	3.9

Modzelewski, Stan (see Stanley J. Stutz)

Moe, Douglas Edwin (Doug) b. September 21, 1938 Ht. 6-5 Wt. 220 College: Elon; North Carolina

SEASON–TEAM	G	GS	MIN	FGM	FGA	PCT	3FGM	3FGA	PCT	FTM	FTA	PCT	O-RB	D-RB	TOT	AST	PF	DQ	STL	TO	BLK	PTS	RPG	APG	PPG
67-68–New Orleans (A)	78	–	3113	665	1610	.413	3	22	.136	551	693	.795	249	546	795	202	282	4	–	199	–	1884	10.2	2.6	24.2
68-69–Oakland (A)	75	–	2528	529	1227	.431	5	14	.357	360	444	.811	–	–	614	151	266	9	–	181	–	1423	8.2	2.0	19.0
69-70–Carolina (A)	80	–	2671	535	1254	.427	8	34	.235	304	399	.762	–	–	437	425	282	8	–	–	–	1382	5.5	5.3	17.3
70-71–Virginia (A)	78	–	2297	397	871	.456	2	10	.200	221	259	.853	–	–	473	270	284	–	–	–	–	1017	6.1	3.5	13.0
71-72–Virginia (A)	67	–	1472	175	415	.422	1	9	.111	104	129	.806	–	–	241	149	172	–	–	112	–	455	3.6	2.2	6.8
Reg. ABA Totals	378	–	12081	2301	5377	.428	19	89	.213	1540	1924	.800	249	546	2560	1197	1286	21	–	492	–	6161	6.8	3.2	16.3
ABA Playoff Totals	60	–	2142	411	968	.425	5	23	.217	259	342	.757	–	–	419	160	240	4	–	79	–	1086	7.0	2.7	18.1

Moffett, Larry b. November 5, 1954 Ht. 6-9 Wt. 210 College: Compton (Calif.) C.C.; Murray State; Nevada-Las Vegas

SEASON–TEAM	G	GS	MIN	FGM	FGA	PCT	3FGM	3FGA	PCT	FTM	FTA	PCT	O-RB	D-RB	TOT	AST	PF	DQ	STL	TO	BLK	PTS	RPG	APG	PPG
77-78–Houston	20	–	110	5	17	.294	–	–	–	6	10	.600	10	11	21	7	16	0	2	8	2	16	1.1	0.4	0.8
Reg. Season Totals	20	–	110	5	17	.294	–	–	–	6	10	.600	10	11	21	7	16	0	2	8	2	16	1.1	0.4	0.8

Mogus, Leo b. April 13, 1921 d. 1975 Ht. 6-4 Wt. 205 College: Youngstown State

SEASON–TEAM	G	GS	MIN	FGM	FGA	PCT	3FGM	3FGA	PCT	FTM	FTA	PCT	O-RB	D-RB	TOT	AST	PF	DQ	STL	TO	BLK	PTS	RPG	APG	PPG
45-46–Youngstown (N)	16	–	–	61	–	–	–	–	–	66	98	.673	–	–	–	–	40	–	–	–	–	188	–	–	11.8
46-47–Clev.-Toronto	58	–	–	259	879	.295	–	–	–	235	325	.723	–	–	–	84	176	–	–	–	–	753	–	1.4	13.0
48-49–Balt.-FtWayne-Ind.	52	–	–	172	509	.338	–	–	–	177	243	.728	–	–	–	104	170	–	–	–	–	521	–	2.0	10.0
49-50–Philadelphia	64	–	–	172	434	.396	–	–	–	218	300	.727	–	–	–	99	169	–	–	–	–	562	–	1.5	8.8
50-51–Philadelphia	57	–	–	43	122	.352	–	–	–	53	86	.616	–	–	102	32	60	0	–	–	–	139	1.8	0.6	2.4
Reg. NBA Totals	231	–	–	646	1944	.332	–	–	–	683	954	.716	–	–	102	319	575	0	–	–	–	1975	1.8	1.4	8.5
Reg. NBL Totals	16	–	–	61	–	–	–	–	–	66	98	.673	–	–	–	–	40	–	–	–	–	188	–	–	11.8
NBA Playoff Totals	4	–	–	3	18	.167	–	–	–	4	7	.571	–	–	–	7	10	0	–	–	–	10	–	3.5	2.5

Mohammed, Nazr Tahiru b. September 5, 1977 Ht. 6-10 Wt. 221 College: Kentucky

SEASON–TEAM	G	GS	MIN	FGM	FGA	PCT	3FGM	3FGA	PCT	FTM	FTA	PCT	O-RB	D-RB	TOT	AST	PF	DQ	STL	TO	BLK	PTS	RPG	APG	PPG
98-99–Philadelphia	26	0	121	15	42	.357	0	0	–	12	21	.571	18	19	37	2	22	0	5	12	4	42	1.4	0.1	1.6
99-00–Philadelphia	28	3	190	21	54	.389	0	0	–	12	22	.545	16	34	50	2	29	0	4	18	12	54	1.8	0.1	1.9
Reg. Season Totals	54	3	311	36	96	.375	0	0	–	24	43	.558	34	53	87	4	51	0	9	30	16	96	1.6	0.1	1.8
Playoff Totals	3	0	3	0	0	–	0	0	–	0	0	–	0	0	0	–	0	0	0	0	0	0	0.0	0.0	0.0

Mokeski, Paul Keen (Mo) b. January 3, 1957 Ht. 7-0 Wt. 250 College: Kansas

SEASON–TEAM	G	GS	MIN	FGM	FGA	PCT	3FGM	3FGA	PCT	FTM	FTA	PCT	O-RB	D-RB	TOT	AST	PF	DQ	STL	TO	BLK	PTS	RPG	APG	PPG
79-80–Houston	12	–	113	11	33	.333	0	0	–	7	9	.778	14	15	29	2	24	0	1	10	6	29	2.4	0.2	2.4
80-81–Detroit	80	–	1815	224	458	.489	0	1	.000	120	200	.600	141	277	418	135	267	7	38	160	73	568	5.2	1.7	7.1
81-82–Clev.-Detroit	67	4	868	84	193	.435	0	3	.000	48	63	.762	59	149	208	35	171	2	33	55	40	216	3.1	0.5	3.2
82-83–Clev.-Milw.	73	19	1128	119	260	.458	0	1	.000	50	68	.735	76	184	260	49	223	9	21	67	44	288	3.6	0.7	3.9
83-84–Milwaukee	68	4	838	102	213	.479	1	3	.333	50	72	.694	51	115	166	44	168	1	11	44	29	255	2.4	0.6	3.8
84-85–Milwaukee	79	6	1586	205	429	.478	0	2	.000	81	116	.698	107	303	410	99	266	6	28	85	35	491	5.2	1.3	6.2
85-86–Milwaukee	45	0	521	59	139	.424	0	0	–	25	34	.735	36	103	139	30	92	1	6	25	6	143	3.1	0.7	3.2
86-87–Milwaukee	62	3	626	52	129	.403	0	1	.000	46	64	.719	45	93	138	22	126	0	18	22	13	150	2.2	0.4	2.4
87-88–Milwaukee	60	0	848	100	210	.476	0	4	.000	51	72	.708	70	151	221	22	194	5	27	49	29	251	3.7	0.4	4.2
88-89–Milwaukee	74	0	690	59	164	.360	7	26	.269	40	51	.784	63	124	187	36	153	0	29	35	21	165	2.5	0.5	2.2
89-90–Cleveland	38	1	449	63	150	.420	0	1	.000	25	36	.694	27	72	99	17	76	0	8	26	10	151	2.6	0.4	4.0
90-91–Golden State	36	1	257	21	59	.356	3	9	.333	12	15	.800	20	47	67	9	58	0	8	7	3	57	1.9	0.3	1.6
Reg. Season Totals	694	38	9739	1099	2437	.451	11	51	.216	555	800	.694	709	1633	2342	500	1818	31	228	585	309	2764	3.4	0.7	4.0
Playoff Totals	69	0	815	89	183	.486	1	4	.250	72	97	.742	59	148	207	33	166	3	26	39	23	251	3.0	0.5	3.6

Molinas, Jacob L. (Jack) b. October 1931 d. August 3, 1975 Ht. 6-6 Wt. 200 College: Columbia

SEASON–TEAM	G	GS	MIN	FGM	FGA	PCT	3FGM	3FGA	PCT	FTM	FTA	PCT	O-RB	D-RB	TOT	AST	PF	DQ	STL	TO	BLK	PTS	RPG	APG	PPG
53-54–Fort Wayne	29	–	993	108	278	.388	–	–	–	134	176	.761	–	–	209	47	74	2	–	–	–	350	7.2	1.6	12.1
Reg. Season Totals	29	–	993	108	278	.388	–	–	–	134	176	.761	–	–	209	47	74	2	–	–	–	350	7.2	1.6	12.1

Molis, Wayne J. b. April 17, 1943 Ht. 6-8 Wt. 230 College: Chicago State; Illinois Tech

SEASON–TEAM	G	GS	MIN	FGM	FGA	PCT	3FGM	3FGA	PCT	FTM	FTA	PCT	O-RB	D-RB	TOT	AST	PF	DQ	STL	TO	BLK	PTS	RPG	APG	PPG
66-67–New York	13	–	75	19	51	.373	–	–	–	7	13	.538	–	–	22	2	9	0	–	–	–	45	1.7	0.2	3.5
67-68–Oak.-Hou. (A)	46	–	535	96	225	.427	2	3	.667	41	61	.672	–	–	170	39	49	1	–	26	–	235	3.7	0.8	5.1
Reg. NBA Totals	13	–	75	19	51	.373	–	–	–	7	13	.538	–	–	22	2	9	0	–	–	–	45	1.7	0.2	3.5
Reg. ABA Totals	46	–	535	96	225	.427	2	3	.667	41	61	.672	–	–	170	39	49	1	–	26	–	235	3.7	0.8	5.1
NBA Playoff Totals	1	–	10	0	2	.000	–	–	–	0	0	–	–	–	1	1	1	0	–	–	–	0	1.0	1.0	0.0

Moncrief, Sidney A. b. September 21, 1957 Ht. 6-4 Wt. 190 College: Arkansas

SEASON–TEAM	G	GS	MIN	FGM	FGA	PCT	3FGM	3FGA	PCT	FTM	FTA	PCT	O-RB	D-RB	TOT	AST	PF	DQ	STL	TO	BLK	PTS	RPG	APG	PPG
79-80–Milwaukee	77	–	1557	211	451	.468	0	1	.000	232	292	.795	154	184	338	133	106	0	72	117	16	654	4.4	1.7	8.5
80-81–Milwaukee	80	–	2417	400	739	.541	2	9	.222	320	398	.804	186	220	406	264	156	1	90	145	37	1122	5.1	3.3	14.0
81-82–Milwaukee	80	80	2980	556	1063	.523	1	14	.071	468	573	.817	221	313	534	382	206	3	138	208	22	1581	6.7	4.8	19.8
82-83–Milwaukee	76	76	2710	606	1156	.524	1	10	.100	499	604	.826	192	245	437	300	180	1	113	197	23	1712	5.8	3.9	22.5
83-84–Milwaukee	79	79	3075	560	1125	.498	5	18	.278	529	624	.848	215	313	528	358	204	2	108	217	27	1654	6.7	4.5	20.9
84-85–Milwaukee	73	72	2734	561	1162	.483	9	33	.273	454	548	.828	149	242	391	382	197	1	117	184	39	1585	5.4	5.2	21.7
85-86–Milwaukee	73	72	2567	470	962	.489	33	103	.320	498	580	.859	115	219	334	357	178	1	103	174	18	1471	4.6	4.9	20.2
86-87–Milwaukee	39	30	992	158	324	.488	8	31	.258	136	162	.840	57	70	127	121	73	0	27	63	10	460	3.3	3.1	11.8
87-88–Milwaukee	56	51	1428	217	444	.489	5	31	.161	164	196	.837	58	122	180	204	109	0	41	86	12	603	3.2	3.6	10.8
88-89–Milwaukee	62	50	1594	261	532	.491	25	73	.342	205	237	.865	46	126	172	188	114	1	65	94	13	752	2.8	3.0	12.1
90-91–Atlanta	72	3	1096	117	240	.488	21	64	.328	82	105	.781	31	97	128	104	112	0	50	66	9	337	1.8	1.4	4.7
Reg. Season Totals	767	513	23150	4117	8198	.502	110	387	.284	3587	4319	.831	1424	2151	3575	2793	1635	10	924	1551	226	11931	4.7	3.6	15.6
Playoff Totals	93	71	3226	491	1033	.475	17	58	.293	488	602	.811	189	280	469	317	285	3	106	224	36	1487	5.0	3.4	16.0
All-Star Totals	5	2	119	19	47	.404	1	1	1.000	19	22	.864	12	10	22	12	7	0	12	8	2	58	4.4	2.4	11.6

Money, Eric V. b. February 6, 1955 Ht. 6-0 Wt. 170 College: Arizona

SEASON–TEAM	G	GS	MIN	FGM	FGA	PCT	3FGM	3FGA	PCT	FTM	FTA	PCT	O-RB	D-RB	TOT	AST	PF	DQ	STL	TO	BLK	PTS	RPG	APG	PPG
74-75–Detroit	66	–	889	144	319	.451	–	–	–	31	45	.689	27	61	88	101	121	3	33	–	2	319	1.3	1.5	4.8
75-76–Detroit	80	–	2267	449	947	.474	–	–	–	145	180	.806	77	130	207	338	243	4	137	–	11	1043	2.6	4.2	13.0
76-77–Detroit	73	–	1586	329	631	.521	–	–	–	90	114	.789	43	81	124	243	199	3	91	–	14	748	1.7	3.3	10.2
77-78–Detroit	76	–	2557	600	1200	.500	–	–	–	214	298	.718	90	119	209	356	237	5	123	322	12	1414	2.8	4.7	18.6
78-79–N.J.-Phil.	69	–	1979	444	893	.497	–	–	–	170	237	.717	70	92	162	331	202	2	87	235	12	1058	2.3	4.7	15.3
79-80–Phil.-Detroit	61	–	1549	273	546	.500	0	0	–	83	106	.783	31	73	104	254	146	3	53	155	11	629	1.7	4.2	10.3
Reg. Season Totals	425	–	10827	2239	4536	.494	0	0	–	733	980	.748	338	556	894	1623	1148	20	524	712	62	5211	2.1	3.8	12.3
Playoff Totals	20	–	505	96	210	.457	0	0	–	30	38	.789	18	24	42	93	62	1	23	22	1	222	2.1	4.7	11.1

Monroe, Rodney Eugene (Ice) b. April 16, 1968 Ht. 6-3 Wt. 185 College: North Carolina State

SEASON–TEAM	G	GS	MIN	FGM	FGA	PCT	3FGM	3FGA	PCT	FTM	FTA	PCT	O-RB	D-RB	TOT	AST	PF	DQ	STL	TO	BLK	PTS	RPG	APG	PPG
91-92–Atlanta	38	0	313	53	144	.368	6	27	.222	19	23	.826	12	21	33	27	19	0	12	23	2	131	0.9	0.7	3.4
Reg. Season Totals	38	0	313	53	144	.368	6	27	.222	19	23	.826	12	21	33	27	19	0	12	23	2	131	0.9	0.7	3.4

Monroe, Vernon Earl (Earl, Earl the Pearl) b. November 21, 1944 Ht. 6-3 Wt. 185 College: Winston-Salem State HOF: 1989

SEASON–TEAM	G	GS	MIN	FGM	FGA	PCT	3FGM	3FGA	PCT	FTM	FTA	PCT	O-RB	D-RB	TOT	AST	PF	DQ	STL	TO	BLK	PTS	RPG	APG	PPG
67-68–Baltimore	82	–	3012	742	1637	.453	–	–	–	507	649	.781	–	–	465	349	282	3	–	–	–	1991	5.7	4.3	24.3
68-69–Baltimore	80	–	3075	809	1837	.440	–	–	–	447	582	.768	–	–	280	392	261	1	–	–	–	2065	3.5	4.9	25.8
69-70–Baltimore	82	–	3051	695	1557	.446	–	–	–	532	641	.830	–	–	257	402	258	3	–	–	–	1922	3.1	4.9	23.4
70-71–Baltimore	81	–	2843	663	1501	.442	–	–	–	406	506	.802	–	–	213	354	220	3	–	–	–	1732	2.6	4.4	21.4
71-72–Balt.-N.Y.	63	–	1337	287	662	.434	–	–	–	175	224	.781	–	–	100	142	139	1	–	–	–	749	1.6	2.3	11.9
72-73–New York	75	–	2370	496	1016	.488	–	–	–	171	208	.822	–	–	245	288	195	1	–	–	–	1163	3.3	3.8	15.5
73-74–New York	41	–	1194	240	513	.468	–	–	–	93	113	.823	22	99	121	110	97	0	34	–	19	573	3.0	2.7	14.0
74-75–New York	78	–	2814	668	1462	.457	–	–	–	297	359	.827	56	271	327	270	200	0	108	–	29	1633	4.2	3.5	20.9
75-76–New York	76	–	2889	647	1354	.478	–	–	–	280	356	.787	48	225	273	304	209	1	111	–	22	1574	3.6	4.0	20.7
76-77–N.Y. Knicks	77	–	2656	613	1185	.517	–	–	–	307	366	.839	45	178	223	366	197	0	91	–	23	1533	2.9	4.8	19.9
77-78–New York	76	–	2369	556	1123	.495	–	–	–	242	291	.832	47	135	182	361	189	0	60	179	19	1354	2.4	4.8	17.8
78-79–New York	64	–	1393	329	699	.471	–	–	–	129	154	.838	26	48	74	189	123	0	48	98	6	787	1.2	3.0	12.3
79-80–New York	51	–	633	161	352	.457	0	0	–	56	64	.875	16	20	36	67	46	0	21	28	3	378	0.7	1.3	7.4
Reg. Season Totals	926	–	29636	6906	14898	.464	0	0	–	3642	4513	.807	260	976	2796	3594	2416	13	473	305	121	17454	3.0	3.9	18.8
Playoff Totals	82	–	2715	567	1292	.439	0	0	–	337	426	.791	10	52	266	264	216	0	18	6	11	1471	3.2	3.2	17.9
All-Star Totals	4	–	85	14	39	.359	0	0	–	12	17	.706	0	3	12	11	10	0	1	–	0	40	3.0	2.8	10.0

Montgomery, Howard (Howie) b. August 22, 1940 Ht. 6-6 Wt. 220 College: Texas-Pan American

SEASON–TEAM	G	GS	MIN	FGM	FGA	PCT	3FGM	3FGA	PCT	FTM	FTA	PCT	O-RB	D-RB	TOT	AST	PF	DQ	STL	TO	BLK	PTS	RPG	APG	PPG
62-63–San Francisco	20	–	364	65	153	.425	–	–	–	14	23	.609	–	–	69	21	35	1	–	–	–	144	3.5	1.1	7.2
Reg. Season Totals	20	–	364	65	153	.425	–	–	–	14	23	.609	–	–	69	21	35	1	–	–	–	144	3.5	1.1	7.2

Montross, Eric Scott b. September 23, 1971 Ht. 7-0 Wt. 270 College: North Carolina

SEASON–TEAM	G	GS	MIN	FGM	FGA	PCT	3FGM	3FGA	PCT	FTM	FTA	PCT	O-RB	D-RB	TOT	AST	PF	DQ	STL	TO	BLK	PTS	RPG	APG	PPG
94-95–Boston	78	75	2315	307	575	.534	0	1	.000	167	263	.635	196	370	566	36	299	10	29	112	61	781	7.3	0.5	10.0
95-96–Boston	61	59	1432	196	346	.566	0	0	–	50	133	.376	119	233	352	43	181	1	19	83	29	442	5.8	0.7	7.2
96-97–Dallas-N.J.	78	77	1828	159	349	.456	0	0	–	21	62	.339	181	337	518	61	268	5	20	77	73	339	6.6	0.8	4.3
97-98–Phil.-Detroit	48	30	691	61	144	.424	0	0	–	16	40	.400	69	130	199	11	127	1	13	29	27	138	4.1	0.2	2.9
98-99–Detroit	46	2	577	42	80	.525	0	1	.000	11	32	.344	45	94	139	14	107	1	12	16	27	95	3.0	0.3	2.1
99-00–Detroit	51	0	332	17	55	.309	0	0	–	6	12	.500	18	54	72	7	81	0	6	22	9	40	1.4	0.1	0.8
Reg. Season Totals	362	243	7175	782	1549	.505	0	2	.000	271	542	.500	628	1218	1846	172	1063	18	99	339	226	1835	5.1	0.5	5.1
Playoff Totals	11	4	137	8	17	.471	0	0	–	4	8	.500	10	14	24	–	30	0	0	8	2	20	2.2	0.0	1.8

Mooney, James J. (Jim) b. July 8, 1930 Ht. 6-5 Wt. 215 College: Villanova

SEASON–TEAM	G	GS	MIN	FGM	FGA	PCT	3FGM	3FGA	PCT	FTM	FTA	PCT	O-RB	D-RB	TOT	AST	PF	DQ	STL	TO	BLK	PTS	RPG	APG	PPG
52-53–Philadelphia	18	–	529	54	148	.365	–	–	–	27	40	.675	–	–	70	35	50	1	–	–	–	135	3.9	1.9	7.5
Reg. Season Totals	18	–	529	54	148	.365	–	–	–	27	40	.675	–	–	70	35	50	1	–	–	–	135	3.9	1.9	7.5

Moore, Andre M. b. July 2, 1964 Ht. 6-9 Wt. 215 College: Illinois; Loyola (Chicago)

SEASON–TEAM	G	GS	MIN	FGM	FGA	PCT	3FGM	3FGA	PCT	FTM	FTA	PCT	O-RB	D-RB	TOT	AST	PF	DQ	STL	TO	BLK	PTS	RPG	APG	PPG
87-88–Denver-Milw.	10	0	50	9	27	.333	0	0	–	6	8	.750	6	8	14	6	6	0	2	4	1	24	1.4	0.6	2.4
Reg. Season Totals	10	0	50	9	27	.333	0	0	–	6	8	.750	6	8	14	6	6	0	2	4	1	24	1.4	0.6	2.4

Moore, Eugene Wilbert (Gene) b. July 29, 1945 Ht. 6-9 Wt. 235 College: St. Louis

SEASON–TEAM	G	GS	MIN	FGM	FGA	PCT	3FGM	3FGA	PCT	FTM	FTA	PCT	O-RB	D-RB	TOT	AST	PF	DQ	STL	TO	BLK	PTS	RPG	APG	PPG
68-69–Kentucky (A)	76	–	2026	417	920	.453	0	2	.000	204	290	.703	318	499	817	90	311	18	–	160	–	1038	10.8	1.2	13.7
69-70–Kentucky (A)	83	–	2613	630	1390	.453	2	4	.500	209	311	.672	345	657	1002	188	382	25	–	–	–	1471	12.1	2.3	17.7
70-71–Texas (A)	84	–	2243	467	972	.480	2	6	.333	189	280	.675	285	565	850	101	303	–	–	–	–	1125	10.1	1.2	13.4
71-72–Dallas-N.Y. (A)	77	–	1412	253	545	.464	1	3	.333	89	120	.742	–	–	483	53	221	–	–	150	–	596	6.3	0.7	7.7
72-73–San Diego (A)	83	–	2481	400	804	.498	4	11	.364	180	260	.692	324	550	874	152	369	0	–	227	–	984	10.5	1.8	11.9
73-74–San Diego (A)	49	–	897	154	340	.453	1	7	.143	41	85	.482	96	196	292	59	133	–	26	74	51	350	6.0	1.2	7.1
74-75–St. Louis (A)	13	–	108	13	32	.406	0	0	–	4	4	1.000	15	27	42	5	11	–	4	12	7	30	3.2	0.4	2.3
Reg. ABA Totals	465	–	11780	2334	5003	.467	10	33	.303	916	1350	.679	1383	2494	4360	648	1730	43	30	623	58	5594	9.4	1.4	12.0
ABA Playoff Totals	47	–	933	196	440	.445	0	1	.000	87	120	.725	99	200	366	52	153	9	0	18	0	479	7.8	1.1	10.2

Moore, John Brian (Johnny) b. March 3, 1958 Ht. 6-1 Wt. 175 College: Texas

SEASON–TEAM	G	GS	MIN	FGM	FGA	PCT	3FGM	3FGA	PCT	FTM	FTA	PCT	O-RB	D-RB	TOT	AST	PF	DQ	STL	TO	BLK	PTS	RPG	APG	PPG
80-81–San Antonio	82	–	1578	249	520	.479	1	19	.053	105	172	.610	58	138	196	373	178	0	120	154	22	604	2.4	4.5	7.4
81-82–San Antonio	79	78	2294	309	667	.463	1	21	.048	122	182	.670	62	213	275	762	254	6	163	175	12	741	3.5	9.6	9.4
82-83–San Antonio	77	73	2552	394	841	.468	5	22	.227	148	199	.744	65	212	277	753	247	2	194	226	32	941	3.6	9.8	12.2
83-84–San Antonio	59	42	1650	231	518	.446	28	87	.322	105	139	.755	37	141	178	566	168	2	123	143	20	595	3.0	9.6	10.1
84-85–San Antonio	82	82	2689	416	910	.457	25	89	.281	189	248	.762	94	284	378	816	247	3	229	236	18	1046	4.6	10.0	12.8
85-86–San Antonio	28	23	856	150	303	.495	4	22	.182	59	86	.686	25	61	86	252	78	0	70	81	6	363	3.1	9.0	13.0
86-87–San Antonio	55	27	1234	198	448	.442	22	79	.278	56	70	.800	32	68	100	250	97	0	83	102	3	474	1.8	4.5	8.6
87-88–S.A.-N.J.	5	0	61	4	10	.400	0	1	.000	0	0	–	2	4	6	12	1	0	3	7	0	8	1.2	2.4	1.6
89-90–San Antonio	53	8	516	47	126	.373	8	34	.235	16	27	.593	16	36	52	82	55	0	32	39	3	118	1.0	1.5	2.2
Reg. Season Totals	520	333	13430	1998	4343	.460	94	374	.251	800	1123	.712	391	1157	1548	3866	1325	13	1017	1163	116	4890	3.0	7.4	9.4
Playoff Totals	41	25	1084	193	394	.490	10	32	.313	69	101	.683	41	91	132	344	121	0	70	74	13	465	3.2	8.4	11.3

Moore, John T. (Jackie) b. September 24, 1932 Ht. 6-5 Wt. 180 College: La Salle

SEASON–TEAM	G	GS	MIN	FGM	FGA	PCT	3FGM	3FGA	PCT	FTM	FTA	PCT	O-RB	D-RB	TOT	AST	PF	DQ	STL	TO	BLK	PTS	RPG	APG	PPG
54-55–Syr.-Milw.-Phil.	23	–	376	44	115	.383	–	–	–	22	47	.468	–	–	105	20	62	2	–	–	–	110	4.6	0.9	4.8
55-56–Philadelphia	54	–	402	50	129	.388	–	–	–	32	53	.604	–	–	117	26	80	1	–	–	–	132	2.2	0.5	2.4
56-57–Philadelphia	57	–	400	43	106	.406	–	–	–	37	46	.804	–	–	116	21	75	1	–	–	–	123	2.0	0.4	2.2
Reg. Season Totals	134	–	1178	137	350	.391	–	–	–	91	146	.623	–	–	338	67	217	4	–	–	–	365	2.5	0.5	2.7
Playoff Totals	9	–	53	8	20	.400	–	–	–	2	6	.333	–	–	17	2	14	0	–	–	–	18	1.9	0.2	2.0

Moore, Lawrence b. 1944 Ht. 6-7 Wt. 215 College: None

SEASON–TEAM	G	GS	MIN	FGM	FGA	PCT	3FGM	3FGA	PCT	FTM	FTA	PCT	O-RB	D-RB	TOT	AST	PF	DQ	STL	TO	BLK	PTS	RPG	APG	PPG
67-68–Anaheim (A)	12	–	78	8	33	.242	0	5	.000	11	13	.846	–	–	16	1	17	0	–	7	–	27	1.3	0.1	2.3
Reg. ABA Totals	12	–	78	8	33	.242	0	5	.000	11	13	.846	–	–	16	1	17	0	–	7	–	27	1.3	0.1	2.3

Moore, Lowes Lee b. May 5, 1957 Ht. 6-1 Wt. 170 College: West Virginia

SEASON–TEAM	G	GS	MIN	FGM	FGA	PCT	3FGM	3FGA	PCT	FTM	FTA	PCT	O-RB	D-RB	TOT	AST	PF	DQ	STL	TO	BLK	PTS	RPG	APG	PPG
80-81–New Jersey	71	–	1406	212	478	.444	4	27	.148	69	92	.750	43	125	168	228	179	1	61	108	17	497	2.4	3.2	7.0
81-82–Cleveland	4	0	70	19	38	.500	1	5	.200	6	8	.750	1	3	4	15	15	1	6	5	1	45	1.0	3.8	11.3
82-83–San Diego	37	3	642	81	190	.426	6	23	.261	42	56	.750	15	40	55	73	72	1	22	46	1	210	1.5	2.0	5.7
Reg. Season Totals	112	3	2118	312	706	.442	11	55	.200	117	156	.750	59	168	227	316	266	3	89	159	19	752	2.0	2.8	6.7

Moore, Mikki b. November 4, 1975 Ht. 7-0 Wt. 225 College: Nebraska

SEASON–TEAM	G	GS	MIN	FGM	FGA	PCT	3FGM	3FGA	PCT	FTM	FTA	PCT	O-RB	D-RB	TOT	AST	PF	DQ	STL	TO	BLK	PTS	RPG	APG	PPG
98-99–Detroit	2	0	6	1	1	1.000	0	0	–	2	2	1.000	0	1	1	0	0	0	0	0	0	4	0.5	0.0	2.0
99-00–Detroit	29	0	488	87	140	.621	0	0	–	54	68	.794	44	68	112	17	104	5	9	23	31	228	3.9	0.6	7.9
Reg. Season Totals	31	0	494	88	141	.624	0	0	–	56	70	.800	44	69	113	17	104	5	9	23	31	232	3.6	0.5	7.5
Playoff Totals	3	0	42	5	12	.417	0	0	–	8	8	1.000	7	5	12	3	9	0	1	4	0	18	4.0	1.0	6.0

Moore, Otto George (Say No Moore) b. August 27, 1946 Ht. 6-11 Wt. 205 College: Texas-Pan American

SEASON–TEAM	G	GS	MIN	FGM	FGA	PCT	3FGM	3FGA	PCT	FTM	FTA	PCT	O-RB	D-RB	TOT	AST	PF	DQ	STL	TO	BLK	PTS	RPG	APG	PPG
68-69–Detroit	74	–	1605	241	544	.443	–	–	–	88	168	.524	–	–	524	68	182	2	–	–	–	570	7.1	0.9	7.7
69-70–Detroit	81	–	2523	383	805	.476	–	–	–	194	305	.636	–	–	900	104	232	3	–	–	–	960	11.1	1.3	11.9
70-71–Detroit	82	–	1926	310	696	.445	–	–	–	121	219	.553	–	–	700	88	182	0	–	–	–	741	8.5	1.1	9.0
71-72–Phoenix	81	–	1624	260	597	.436	–	–	–	94	156	.603	–	–	540	88	212	2	–	–	–	614	6.7	1.1	7.6
72-73–Houston	82	–	2712	418	859	.487	–	–	–	127	211	.602	–	–	868	167	239	4	–	–	–	963	10.6	2.0	11.7
73-74–Hou.-K.C.-Omaha	78	–	946	120	240	.500	–	–	–	39	62	.629	80	204	284	65	99	2	26	–	49	279	3.6	0.8	3.6
74-75–Detroit-N.O.	42	–	1066	118	262	.450	–	–	–	46	69	.667	92	238	330	83	148	3	21	–	40	282	7.9	2.0	6.7
75-76–New Orleans	81	–	2407	293	672	.436	–	–	–	144	226	.637	162	631	793	216	250	3	85	–	136	730	9.8	2.7	9.0
76-77–New Orleans	81	–	2084	193	477	.405	–	–	–	91	134	.679	170	466	636	181	231	3	54	–	117	477	7.9	2.2	5.9
Reg. Season Totals	682	–	16893	2336	5152	.453	–	–	–	944	1550	.609	504	1539	5575	1060	1775	22	186	–	342	5616	8.2	1.6	8.2

Moore, Richard b. 1945 Ht. 6-2 Wt. 190 College: Villanova; Hiram

SEASON–TEAM	G	GS	MIN	FGM	FGA	PCT	3FGM	3FGA	PCT	FTM	FTA	PCT	O-RB	D-RB	TOT	AST	PF	DQ	STL	TO	BLK	PTS	RPG	APG	PPG
67-68–Denver (A)	18	–	211	24	71	.338	0	2	.000	21	28	.750	–	–	19	8	16	0	–	24	–	69	1.1	0.4	3.8
Reg. ABA Totals	18	–	211	24	71	.338	0	2	.000	21	28	.750	–	–	19	8	16	0	–	24	–	69	1.1	0.4	3.8

Moore, Ronald Keith (Ron) b. January 16, 1962 Ht. 7-0 Wt. 260 College: Salem (N.C.); West Virginia State

SEASON–TEAM	G	GS	MIN	FGM	FGA	PCT	3FGM	3FGA	PCT	FTM	FTA	PCT	O-RB	D-RB	TOT	AST	PF	DQ	STL	TO	BLK	PTS	RPG	APG	PPG
87-88–Detroit-Phoenix	14	0	59	9	29	.310	0	0	–	6	8	.750	2	6	8	1	21	0	5	4	0	24	0.6	0.1	1.7
Reg. Season Totals	14	0	59	9	29	.310	0	0	–	6	8	.750	2	6	8	1	21	0	5	4	0	24	0.6	0.1	1.7

Moore, Tracy Lamont b. December 28, 1965 Ht. 6-4 Wt. 200 College: Tulsa

SEASON–TEAM	G	GS	MIN	FGM	FGA	PCT	3FGM	3FGA	PCT	FTM	FTA	PCT	O-RB	D-RB	TOT	AST	PF	DQ	STL	TO	BLK	PTS	RPG	APG	PPG
91-92–Dallas	42	2	782	130	325	.400	30	84	.357	65	78	.833	31	51	82	48	97	0	32	44	4	355	2.0	1.1	8.5
92-93–Dallas	39	1	510	103	249	.414	23	67	.343	53	61	.869	23	29	52	47	54	0	21	32	4	282	1.3	1.2	7.2
93-94–Detroit	3	0	10	2	3	.667	0	0	–	2	2	1.000	0	1	1	0	0	0	2	0	0	6	0.3	0.0	2.0
95-96–Houston	8	2	190	30	76	.395	13	30	.433	18	19	.947	10	12	22	6	16	0	2	8	0	91	2.8	0.8	11.4
96-97–Houston	27	1	237	33	85	.388	11	43	.256	22	31	.710	11	15	26	20	19	0	5	14	0	99	1.0	0.7	3.7
Reg. Season Totals	119	6	1729	298	738	.404	77	224	.344	160	191	.838	75	108	183	121	186	0	62	98	8	833	1.5	1.0	7.0

Moreland, Jack (Jackie) b. March 11, 1938 d. December 19, 1971 Ht. 6-7 Wt. 215 College: North Carolina State; Louisiana Tech

SEASON–TEAM	G	GS	MIN	FGM	FGA	PCT	3FGM	3FGA	PCT	FTM	FTA	PCT	O-RB	D-RB	TOT	AST	PF	DQ	STL	TO	BLK	PTS	RPG	APG	PPG
60-61–Detroit	64	–	1003	191	477	.400	–	–	–	86	132	.652	–	–	315	52	174	3	–	–	–	468	4.9	0.8	7.3
61-62–Detroit	74	–	1219	205	487	.421	–	–	–	139	186	.747	–	–	427	76	179	2	–	–	–	549	5.8	1.0	7.4
62-63–Detroit	78	–	1516	271	622	.436	–	–	–	145	214	.678	–	–	449	114	226	5	–	–	–	687	5.8	1.5	8.8
63-64–Detroit	78	–	1780	272	639	.426	–	–	–	164	210	.781	–	–	405	121	268	9	–	–	–	708	5.2	1.6	9.1
64-65–Detroit	54	–	732	103	296	.348	–	–	–	66	104	.635	–	–	183	69	151	4	–	–	–	272	3.4	1.3	5.0
67-68–New Orleans (A)	76	–	2332	459	1051	.437	2	4	.500	192	263	.730	–	–	619	138	289	13	–	124	–	1112	8.1	1.8	14.6
68-69–New Orleans (A)	78	–	2714	468	1109	.422	2	8	.250	221	313	.706	–	–	633	207	310	11	–	171	–	1159	8.1	2.7	14.9
69-70–New Orleans (A)	80	–	2321	317	765	.414	2	8	.250	139	176	.790	–	–	386	160	250	8	–	–	–	775	4.8	2.0	9.7
Reg. NBA Totals	348	–	6250	1042	2521	.413	–	–	–	600	846	.709	–	–	1779	432	998	23	–	–	–	2684	5.1	1.2	7.7
Reg. ABA Totals	234	–	7367	1244	2925	.425	6	20	.300	552	752	.734	–	–	1638	505	849	32	–	295	–	3046	7.0	2.2	13.0
NBA Playoff Totals	14	–	223	44	90	.489	–	–	–	15	22	.682	–	–	62	16	50	1	–	–	–	103	4.4	1.1	7.4
ABA Playoff Totals	28	–	829	143	342	.418	0	2	.000	61	92	.663	–	–	193	70	123	4	–	27	–	347	6.9	2.5	12.4

Morgan, Munden Guy (Guy) b. August 23, 1960 Ht. 6-8 Wt. 215 College: Wake Forest

SEASON–TEAM	G	GS	MIN	FGM	FGA	PCT	3FGM	3FGA	PCT	FTM	FTA	PCT	O-RB	D-RB	TOT	AST	PF	DQ	STL	TO	BLK	PTS	RPG	APG	PPG
82-83–Indiana	8	0	46	7	24	.292	0	0	–	1	4	.250	6	11	17	7	7	0	2	2	0	15	2.1	0.9	1.9
Reg. Season Totals	8	0	46	7	24	.292	0	0	–	1	4	.250	6	11	17	7	7	0	2	2	0	15	2.1	0.9	1.9

Morgan, Rex b. October 27, 1948 Ht. 6-5 Wt. 190 College: Lakeland (Ohio) C.C.; Jacksonville

SEASON–TEAM	G	GS	MIN	FGM	FGA	PCT	3FGM	3FGA	PCT	FTM	FTA	PCT	O-RB	D-RB	TOT	AST	PF	DQ	STL	TO	BLK	PTS	RPG	APG	PPG
70-71–Boston	34	–	266	41	102	.402	–	–	–	35	54	.648	–	–	61	22	58	2	–	–	–	117	1.8	0.6	3.4
71-72–Boston	28	–	150	16	50	.320	–	–	–	23	31	.742	–	–	30	17	34	0	–	–	–	55	1.1	0.6	2.0
Reg. Season Totals	62	–	416	57	152	.375	–	–	–	58	85	.682	–	–	91	39	92	2	–	–	–	172	1.5	0.6	2.8
Playoff Totals	4	–	10	1	7	.143	–	–	–	1	3	.333	–	–	5	–	6	0	–	–	–	3	1.3	0.0	0.8

Morgenthaler, Elmore Robert (Elmo) b. August 3, 1922 Ht. 7-1 Wt. 230 College: Boston College; New Mexico Mines & Tech

SEASON–TEAM	G	GS	MIN	FGM	FGA	PCT	3FGM	3FGA	PCT	FTM	FTA	PCT	O-RB	D-RB	TOT	AST	PF	DQ	STL	TO	BLK	PTS	RPG	APG	PPG
46-47–Providence	11	–	–	4	13	.308	–	–	–	7	12	.583	–	–	–	3	3	–	–	–	–	15	–	0.3	1.4
48-49–Philadelphia	20	–	–	15	39	.385	–	–	–	12	18	.667	–	–	–	7	18	–	–	–	–	42	–	0.4	2.1
Reg. Season Totals	31	–	–	19	52	.365	–	–	–	19	30	.633	–	–	–	10	21	–	–	–	–	57	–	0.3	1.8

Morningstar, Darren b. April 22, 1969 Ht. 6-10 Wt. 235 College: Pittsburgh

SEASON–TEAM	G	GS	MIN	FGM	FGA	PCT	3FGM	3FGA	PCT	FTM	FTA	PCT	O-RB	D-RB	TOT	AST	PF	DQ	STL	TO	BLK	PTS	RPG	APG	PPG
93-94–Dallas-Utah	23	15	367	39	82	.476	0	0	–	18	30	.600	31	50	81	15	70	1	14	19	2	96	3.5	0.7	4.2
Reg. Season Totals	23	15	367	39	82	.476	0	0	–	18	30	.600	31	50	81	15	70	1	14	19	2	96	3.5	0.7	4.2

Morris, Christopher Vernard (Chris) b. January 20, 1966 Ht. 6-8 Wt. 228 College: Auburn

SEASON–TEAM	G	GS	MIN	FGM	FGA	PCT	3FGM	3FGA	PCT	FTM	FTA	PCT	O-RB	D-RB	TOT	AST	PF	DQ	STL	TO	BLK	PTS	RPG	APG	PPG
88-89–New Jersey	76	48	2096	414	905	.457	64	175	.366	182	254	.717	188	209	397	119	250	4	102	190	60	1074	5.2	1.6	14.1
89-90–New Jersey	80	76	2449	449	1065	.422	61	193	.316	228	316	.722	194	228	422	143	219	1	130	185	79	1187	5.3	1.8	14.8
90-91–New Jersey	79	68	2553	409	962	.425	45	179	.251	179	244	.734	210	311	521	220	248	5	138	167	96	1042	6.6	2.8	13.2
91-92–New Jersey	77	74	2394	346	726	.477	22	110	.200	165	231	.714	199	295	494	197	211	2	129	171	81	879	6.4	2.6	11.4
92-93–New Jersey	77	57	2302	436	907	.481	17	76	.224	197	248	.794	227	227	454	106	171	2	144	119	52	1086	5.9	1.4	14.1
93-94–New Jersey	50	27	1349	203	454	.447	53	147	.361	85	118	.720	91	137	228	83	120	2	55	52	49	544	4.6	1.7	10.9
94-95–New Jersey	71	49	2131	351	856	.410	106	317	.334	142	195	.728	181	221	402	147	155	0	86	117	51	950	5.7	2.1	13.4
95-96–Utah	66	33	1424	265	606	.437	63	197	.320	98	127	.772	100	129	229	77	140	1	63	71	20	691	3.5	1.2	10.5
96-97–Utah	73	1	977	122	299	.408	31	113	.274	39	54	.722	37	125	162	43	121	3	29	45	24	314	2.2	0.6	4.3
97-98–Utah	54	1	538	85	207	.411	19	62	.306	44	61	.721	35	79	114	24	61	0	25	33	17	233	2.1	0.4	4.3
98-99–Phoenix	44	2	535	64	149	.430	16	56	.286	40	46	.870	54	67	121	23	54	0	16	21	11	184	2.8	0.5	4.2
Reg. Season Totals	747	436	18748	3144	7136	.441	497	1625	.306	1399	1894	.739	1516	2028	3544	1182	1750	20	917	1171	540	8184	4.7	1.6	11.0
Playoff Totals	69	24	1142	173	389	.445	39	132	.295	63	84	.750	72	152	224	53	115	0	46	45	32	448	3.2	0.8	6.5

Morris, Glen Max (Max) b. March 14, 1925 d. January 8, 1998 Ht. 6-2 Wt. 195 College: Illinois; Northwestern

SEASON–TEAM	G	GS	MIN	FGM	FGA	PCT	3FGM	3FGA	PCT	FTM	FTA	PCT	O-RB	D-RB	TOT	AST	PF	DQ	STL	TO	BLK	PTS	RPG	APG	PPG
46-47–Chicago (N)	33	–	–	44	–	–	–	–	–	33	63	.524	–	–	–	–	59	–	–	–	–	121	–	–	3.7
47-48–Sheboygan (N)	39	–	–	132	–	–	–	–	–	132	215	.614	–	–	–	–	107	–	–	–	–	396	–	–	10.2
48-49–Sheboygan (N)	41	–	–	70	–	–	–	–	–	68	104	.654	–	–	–	–	83	–	–	–	–	208	–	–	5.1
49-50–Sheboygan	62	–	–	252	694	.363	–	–	–	277	415	.667	–	–	–	194	172	–	–	–	–	781	–	3.1	12.6
Reg. NBA Totals	62	–	–	252	694	.363	–	–	–	277	415	.667	–	–	–	194	172	–	–	–	–	781	–	3.1	12.6
Reg. NBL Totals	113	–	–	246	–	–	–	–	–	233	382	.610	–	–	–	–	249	–	–	–	–	725	–	–	6.4
NBA Playoff Totals	3	–	–	14	80	.350	–	–	–	15	26	.577	–	–	–	28	9	–	–	–	–	43	–	4.7	14.3
NBL Playoff Totals	12	–	–	12	–	–	–	–	–	4	10	.400	–	–	–	–	27	–	–	–	–	28	–	–	2.3

Morris, Isaiah Butch b. April 2, 1969 Ht. 6-8 Wt. 230 College: San Jacinto (Texas) Coll. (J.C.); Arkansas

SEASON–TEAM	G	GS	MIN	FGM	FGA	PCT	3FGM	3FGA	PCT	FTM	FTA	PCT	O-RB	D-RB	TOT	AST	PF	DQ	STL	TO	BLK	PTS	RPG	APG	PPG
92-93–Detroit	25	0	102	26	57	.456	0	0	–	3	4	.750	6	6	12	4	14	0	3	8	1	55	0.5	0.2	2.2
Reg. Season Totals	25	0	102	26	57	.456	0	0	–	3	4	.750	6	6	12	4	14	0	3	8	1	55	0.5	0.2	2.2

Morrison, Dwight W. (Red) b. April 26, 1932 Ht. 6-8 Wt. 225 College: Idaho

SEASON–TEAM	G	GS	MIN	FGM	FGA	PCT	3FGM	3FGA	PCT	FTM	FTA	PCT	O-RB	D-RB	TOT	AST	PF	DQ	STL	TO	BLK	PTS	RPG	APG	PPG
54-55–Boston	71	–	1227	120	284	.423	–	–	–	72	115	.626	–	–	451	82	222	10	–	–	–	312	6.4	1.2	4.4
55-56–Boston	71	–	910	89	240	.371	–	–	–	44	89	.494	–	–	345	53	159	5	–	–	–	222	4.9	0.7	3.1
57-58–St. Louis	13	–	79	9	26	.346	–	–	–	3	4	.750	–	–	26	0	12	0	–	–	–	21	2.0	0.0	1.6
Reg. Season Totals	155	–	2216	218	550	.396	–	–	–	119	208	.572	–	–	822	135	393	15	–	–	–	555	5.3	0.9	3.6
Playoff Totals	10	–	57	5	15	.333	–	–	–	1	7	.143	–	–	25	1	27	1	–	–	–	11	2.5	0.1	1.1

Morrison, John Russell b. May 2, 1945 Ht. 6-2 Wt. 190 College: Canisius

SEASON–TEAM	G	GS	MIN	FGM	FGA	PCT	3FGM	3FGA	PCT	FTM	FTA	PCT	O-RB	D-RB	TOT	AST	PF	DQ	STL	TO	BLK	PTS	RPG	APG	PPG
67-68–Denver (A)	9	–	76	10	34	.294	1	6	.167	6	9	.667	–	–	9	7	15	0	–	9	–	27	1.0	0.8	3.0
Reg. ABA Totals	9	–	76	10	34	.294	1	6	.167	6	9	.667	–	–	9	7	15	0	–	9	–	27	1.0	0.8	3.0

Morrison, Michael Fitzgerald (Mike) b. August 16, 1967 Ht. 6-4 Wt. 195 College: Loyola (Balt.)

SEASON–TEAM	G	GS	MIN	FGM	FGA	PCT	3FGM	3FGA	PCT	FTM	FTA	PCT	O-RB	D-RB	TOT	AST	PF	DQ	STL	TO	BLK	PTS	RPG	APG	PPG
89-90–Phoenix	36	1	153	23	68	.338	2	7	.286	24	30	.800	7	13	20	11	20	0	2	23	0	72	0.6	0.3	2.0
Reg. Season Totals	36	1	153	23	68	.338	2	7	.286	24	30	.800	7	13	20	11	20	0	2	23	0	72	0.6	0.3	2.0

Morton, Dwayne Lamont b. August 10, 1971 Ht. 6-7 Wt. 195 College: Louisville

SEASON–TEAM	G	GS	MIN	FGM	FGA	PCT	3FGM	3FGA	PCT	FTM	FTA	PCT	O-RB	D-RB	TOT	AST	PF	DQ	STL	TO	BLK	PTS	RPG	APG	PPG
94-95–Golden State	41	6	395	50	129	.388	9	25	.360	58	85	.682	21	37	58	18	45	1	11	27	15	167	1.4	0.4	4.1
Reg. Season Totals	41	6	395	50	129	.388	9	25	.360	58	85	.682	21	37	58	18	45	1	11	27	15	167	1.4	0.4	4.1

Morton, John Jr. (Salt) b. May 18, 1967 Ht. 6-3 Wt. 195 College: Seton Hall

SEASON–TEAM	G	GS	MIN	FGM	FGA	PCT	3FGM	3FGA	PCT	FTM	FTA	PCT	O-RB	D-RB	TOT	AST	PF	DQ	STL	TO	BLK	PTS	RPG	APG	PPG
89-90–Cleveland	37	3	402	48	161	.298	7	30	.233	43	62	.694	7	25	32	67	30	0	18	51	4	146	0.9	1.8	3.9
90-91–Cleveland	66	2	1207	120	274	.438	4	12	.333	113	139	.813	41	62	103	243	112	1	61	107	18	357	1.6	3.7	5.4
91-92–Clev.-Miami	25	0	270	36	93	.387	2	16	.125	32	38	.842	6	20	26	32	23	0	13	28	1	106	1.0	1.3	4.2
Reg. Season Totals	128	5	1879	204	528	.386	13	58	.224	188	239	.787	54	107	161	342	165	1	92	186	23	609	1.3	2.7	4.8
Playoff Totals	3	0	11	2	5	.400	0	0	–	4	4	1.000	0	0	0	–	1	0	0	2	0	8	0.0	0.0	2.7

Morton, Richard b. February 2, 1966 Ht. 6-3 Wt. 190 College: Cal State-Fullerton

SEASON–TEAM	G	GS	MIN	FGM	FGA	PCT	3FGM	3FGA	PCT	FTM	FTA	PCT	O-RB	D-RB	TOT	AST	PF	DQ	STL	TO	BLK	PTS	RPG	APG	PPG
88-89–Indiana	2	0	11	3	4	.750	0	0	–	0	0	–	0	0	0	1	2	0	0	1	0	6	0.0	0.5	3.0
Reg. Season Totals	2	0	11	3	4	.750	0	0	–	0	0	–	0	0	0	1	2	0	0	1	0	6	0.0	0.5	3.0

Mosley, Glenn E. b. December 26, 1955 Ht. 6-8 Wt. 195 College: Seton Hall

SEASON–TEAM	G	GS	MIN	FGM	FGA	PCT	3FGM	3FGA	PCT	FTM	FTA	PCT	O-RB	D-RB	TOT	AST	PF	DQ	STL	TO	BLK	PTS	RPG	APG	PPG
77-78–Philadelphia	6	–	21	5	13	.385	–	–	–	3	7	.429	0	5	5	2	5	0	0	5	0	13	0.8	0.3	2.2
78-79–San Antonio	26	–	221	31	75	.413	–	–	–	23	38	.605	27	37	64	19	35	0	8	20	10	85	2.5	0.7	3.3
Reg. Season Totals	32	–	242	36	88	.409	–	–	–	26	45	.578	27	42	69	21	40	0	8	25	10	98	2.2	0.7	3.1
Playoff Totals	3	–	6	2	3	.667	–	–	–	1	3	.333	0	1	1	1	0	0	0	0	1	5	0.3	0.3	1.7

Moss, Perry Victor b. November 11, 1958 Ht. 6-2 Wt. 185 College: Northeastern

SEASON–TEAM	G	GS	MIN	FGM	FGA	PCT	3FGM	3FGA	PCT	FTM	FTA	PCT	O-RB	D-RB	TOT	AST	PF	DQ	STL	TO	BLK	PTS	RPG	APG	PPG
85-86–Wash.-Phil.	72	0	1012	116	292	.397	7	32	.219	65	89	.730	34	81	115	108	132	1	56	79	15	304	1.6	1.5	4.2
86-87–Golden State	64	0	698	91	207	.440	1	14	.071	49	69	.710	29	66	95	90	96	0	42	57	3	232	1.5	1.4	3.6
Reg. Season Totals	136	0	1710	207	499	.415	8	46	.174	114	158	.722	63	147	210	198	228	1	98	136	18	536	1.5	1.5	3.9
Playoff Totals	15	0	73	10	22	.455	1	2	.500	9	10	.900	2	6	8	7	11	0	6	7	1	30	0.5	0.5	2.0

Moten, Lawrence Edward III b. March 25, 1972 Ht. 6-5 Wt. 190 College: Syracuse

SEASON–TEAM	G	GS	MIN	FGM	FGA	PCT	3FGM	3FGA	PCT	FTM	FTA	PCT	O-RB	D-RB	TOT	AST	PF	DQ	STL	TO	BLK	PTS	RPG	APG	PPG
95-96–Vancouver	44	3	573	112	247	.453	18	55	.327	49	75	.653	36	25	61	50	54	0	29	44	8	291	1.4	1.1	6.6
96-97–Vancouver	67	18	1214	171	441	.388	41	141	.291	64	99	.646	43	76	119	129	83	0	48	81	24	447	1.8	1.9	6.7
97-98–Washington	8	0	27	3	13	.231	0	1	.000	3	4	.750	1	0	1	3	6	0	0	1	0	9	0.1	0.4	1.1
Reg. Season Totals	119	21	1814	286	701	.408	59	197	.299	116	178	.652	80	101	181	182	143	0	77	126	32	747	1.5	1.5	6.3

Mount, Richard Carl (Rick) b. January 5, 1947 Ht. 6-4 Wt. 185 College: Purdue

SEASON–TEAM	G	GS	MIN	FGM	FGA	PCT	3FGM	3FGA	PCT	FTM	FTA	PCT	O-RB	D-RB	TOT	AST	PF	DQ	STL	TO	BLK	PTS	RPG	APG	PPG
70-71–Indiana (A)	66	–	832	149	402	.371	23	79	.291	116	145	.800	–	–	71	107	127	–	–	–	–	437	1.1	1.6	6.6
71-72–Indiana (A)	78	–	2126	420	949	.443	57	180	.317	216	261	.828	–	–	155	230	233	–	–	142	–	1113	2.0	2.9	14.3
72-73–Kentucky (A)	61	–	1780	369	804	.459	9	30	.300	159	198	.803	50	88	138	194	172	0	–	119	–	906	2.3	3.2	14.9
73-74–Ken.-Utah (A)	52	–	753	179	410	.437	12	46	.261	59	71	.831	27	33	60	66	77	–	27	48	1	429	1.2	1.3	8.3
74-75–Memphis (A)	26	–	895	181	431	.420	20	47	.426	63	73	.863	14	37	51	79	44	–	28	41	7	445	2.0	3.0	17.1
Reg. ABA Totals	283	–	6386	1298	2996	.433	121	382	.317	613	748	.820	91	158	475	676	653	0	55	350	8	3330	1.7	2.4	11.8
ABA Playoff Totals	65	–	1498	290	714	.406	28	85	.329	120	143	.839	7	17	104	106	128	0	9	75	6	728	1.6	1.6	11.2

Mourning, Alonzo (Zo) b. February 8, 1970 Ht. 6-10 Wt. 261 College: Georgetown

SEASON–TEAM	G	GS	MIN	FGM	FGA	PCT	3FGM	3FGA	PCT	FTM	FTA	PCT	O-RB	D-RB	TOT	AST	PF	DQ	STL	TO	BLK	PTS	RPG	APG	PPG
92-93–Charlotte	78	78	2644	572	1119	.511	0	3	.000	495	634	.781	263	542	805	76	286	6	27	236	271	1639	10.3	1.0	21.0
93-94–Charlotte	60	59	2018	427	845	.505	0	2	.000	433	568	.762	177	433	610	86	207	3	27	199	188	1287	10.2	1.4	21.5
94-95–Charlotte	77	77	2941	571	1101	.519	11	34	.324	490	644	.761	200	561	761	111	275	5	49	241	225	1643	9.9	1.4	21.3
95-96–Miami	70	70	2671	563	1076	.523	9	30	.300	488	712	.685	218	509	727	159	245	5	70	262	189	1623	10.4	2.3	23.2
96-97–Miami	66	65	2320	473	885	.534	1	9	.111	363	565	.642	189	467	656	104	272	9	56	226	189	1310	9.9	1.6	19.8
97-98–Miami	58	56	1939	403	732	.551	0	0	–	309	465	.665	193	365	558	52	208	4	40	179	130	1115	9.6	0.9	19.2
98-99–Miami	46	46	1753	324	634	.511	0	2	.000	276	423	.652	166	341	507	74	161	1	34	139	180	924	11.0	1.6	20.1
99-00–Miami	79	78	2748	652	1184	.551	0	4	.000	414	582	.711	215	538	753	123	308	8	40	217	294	1718	9.5	1.6	21.7
Reg. Season Totals	534	529	19034	3985	7576	.526	21	84	.250	3268	4593	.712	1621	3756	5377	785	1962	41	343	1699	1666	11259	10.1	1.5	21.1
Playoff Totals	52	52	1971	362	744	.487	7	19	.368	329	493	.667	137	371	508	69	217	5	35	181	150	1060	9.8	1.3	20.4
All-Star Totals	3	1	59	12	26	.462	0	1	.000	3	5	.600	2	14	16	2	11	0	3	4	6	27	5.3	0.7	9.0

Mrazovich, Charles (Chuck) b. February 26, 1924 Ht. 6-5 Wt. 185 College: Eastern Kentucky

SEASON–TEAM	G	GS	MIN	FGM	FGA	PCT	3FGM	3FGA	PCT	FTM	FTA	PCT	O-RB	D-RB	TOT	AST	PF	DQ	STL	TO	BLK	PTS	RPG	APG	PPG
50-51–Indianapolis	23	–	–	24	73	.329	–	–	–	28	46	.609	–	–	33	12	48	1	–	–	–	76	1.4	0.5	3.3
Reg. Season Totals	23	–	–	24	73	.329	–	–	–	28	46	.609	–	–	33	12	48	1	–	–	–	76	1.4	0.5	3.3

Mueller, Erwin L. b. March 12, 1944 Ht. 6-8 Wt. 230 College: San Francisco

SEASON–TEAM	G	GS	MIN	FGM	FGA	PCT	3FGM	3FGA	PCT	FTM	FTA	PCT	O-RB	D-RB	TOT	AST	PF	DQ	STL	TO	BLK	PTS	RPG	APG	PPG
66-67–Chicago	80	–	2136	422	957	.441	–	–	–	171	260	.658	–	–	497	131	223	2	–	–	–	1015	6.2	1.6	12.7
67-68–Chicago-L.A.	74	–	1788	223	489	.456	–	–	–	107	185	.578	–	–	389	154	164	3	–	–	–	553	5.3	2.1	7.5
68-69–Chi.-Seattle	78	–	1355	144	384	.375	–	–	–	89	162	.549	–	–	297	186	143	1	–	–	–	377	3.8	2.4	4.8
69-70–Seattle-Detroit	78	–	2353	300	646	.464	–	–	–	189	263	.719	–	–	483	205	192	1	–	–	–	789	6.2	2.6	10.1
70-71–Detroit	52	–	1224	126	309	.408	–	–	–	60	108	.556	–	–	223	113	99	0	–	–	–	312	4.3	2.2	6.0
71-72–Detroit	42	–	605	68	197	.345	–	–	–	43	74	.581	–	–	147	57	64	0	–	–	–	179	3.5	1.4	4.3
72-73–Detroit	21	–	80	9	31	.290	–	–	–	5	7	.714	–	–	14	7	13	0	–	–	–	23	0.7	0.3	1.1
72-73–Virginia (A)	17	–	205	17	53	.321	0	0	–	3	10	.300	17	30	47	26	24	0	–	22	–	37	2.8	1.5	2.2
73-74–Memphis (A)	3	–	20	0	4	.000	0	0	–	2	5	.400	0	3	3	2	5	–	0	3	0	2	1.0	0.7	0.7
Reg. NBA Totals	425	–	9541	1292	3013	.429	–	–	–	664	1059	.627	–	–	2050	853	898	7	–	–	–	3248	4.8	2.0	7.6
Reg. ABA Totals	20	–	225	17	57	.298	0	0	–	5	15	.333	17	33	50	28	29	0	0	25	0	39	2.5	1.4	2.0
NBA Playoff Totals	17	–	334	28	85	.329	–	–	–	15	28	.536	–	–	68	27	39	0	–	–	–	71	4.0	1.6	4.2
ABA Playoff Totals	5	–	112	5	18	.278	1	1	1.000	6	7	.857	0	0	19	15	10	0	0	11	0	17	3.8	3.0	3.4

Mullaney, Joseph A. (Joe) b. November 17, 1925 d. March 8, 2000 Ht. 6-0 Wt. 165 College: Holy Cross

SEASON–TEAM	G	GS	MIN	FGM	FGA	PCT	3FGM	3FGA	PCT	FTM	FTA	PCT	O-RB	D-RB	TOT	AST	PF	DQ	STL	TO	BLK	PTS	RPG	APG	PPG
49-50–Boston	37	–	–	9	70	.129	–	–	–	12	15	.800	–	–	–	52	30	–	–	–	–	30	–	1.4	0.8
Reg. Season Totals	37	–	–	9	70	.129	–	–	–	12	15	.800	–	–	–	52	30	–	–	–	–	30	–	1.4	0.8

Mullens, Robert J. (Bob) b. November 1, 1922 Ht. 6-1 Wt. 175 College: Fordham

SEASON–TEAM	G	GS	MIN	FGM	FGA	PCT	3FGM	3FGA	PCT	FTM	FTA	PCT	O-RB	D-RB	TOT	AST	PF	DQ	STL	TO	BLK	PTS	RPG	APG	PPG
46-47–N.Y.-Toronto	54	–	–	125	445	.281	–	–	–	64	102	.627	–	–	–	54	94	–	–	–	–	314	–	1.0	5.8
Reg. Season Totals	54	–	–	125	445	.281	–	–	–	64	102	.627	–	–	–	54	94	–	–	–	–	314	–	1.0	5.8

Mullin, Christopher Paul (Chris) b. July 30, 1963 Ht. 6-7 Wt. 215 College: St. John's (N.Y.)

SEASON–TEAM	G	GS	MIN	FGM	FGA	PCT	3FGM	3FGA	PCT	FTM	FTA	PCT	O-RB	D-RB	TOT	AST	PF	DQ	STL	TO	BLK	PTS	RPG	APG	PPG
85-86–Golden State	55	30	1391	287	620	.463	5	27	.185	189	211	.896	42	73	115	105	130	1	70	75	23	768	2.1	1.9	14.0
86-87–Golden State	82	82	2377	477	928	.514	19	63	.302	269	326	.825	39	142	181	261	217	1	98	154	36	1242	2.2	3.2	15.1
87-88–Golden State	60	55	2033	470	926	.508	34	97	.351	239	270	.885	58	147	205	290	136	3	113	156	32	1213	3.4	4.8	20.2
88-89–Golden State	82	82	3093	830	1630	.509	23	100	.230	493	553	.892	152	331	483	415	178	1	176	296	39	2176	5.9	5.1	26.5
89-90–Golden State	78	78	2830	682	1272	.536	87	234	.372	505	568	.889	130	333	463	319	142	1	123	239	45	1956	5.9	4.1	25.1
90-91–Golden State	82	82	3315	777	1449	.536	40	133	.301	513	580	.884	141	302	443	329	176	2	173	245	63	2107	5.4	4.0	25.7
91-92–Golden State	81	81	3346	830	1584	.524	64	175	.366	350	420	.833	127	323	450	286	171	1	173	202	62	2074	5.6	3.5	25.6
92-93–Golden State	46	46	1902	474	930	.510	60	133	.451	183	226	.810	42	190	232	166	76	0	68	139	41	1191	5.0	3.6	25.9
93-94–Golden State	62	39	2324	410	869	.472	55	151	.364	165	219	.753	64	281	345	315	114	0	107	178	53	1040	5.6	5.1	16.8
94-95–Golden State	25	23	890	170	348	.489	42	93	.452	94	107	.879	25	90	115	125	53	0	38	93	19	476	4.6	5.0	19.0
95-96–Golden State	55	19	1617	269	539	.499	59	150	.393	137	160	.856	44	115	159	194	127	0	75	122	32	734	2.9	3.5	13.3
96-97–Golden State	79	63	2733	438	792	.553	83	202	.411	184	213	.864	75	242	317	322	155	0	130	192	33	1143	4.0	4.1	14.5
97-98–Indiana	82	82	2177	333	692	.481	107	243	.440	154	164	.939	38	211	249	186	186	0	95	117	39	927	3.0	2.3	11.3
98-99–Indiana	50	50	1179	177	371	.477	73	157	.465	80	92	.870	25	135	160	81	101	0	47	60	13	507	3.2	1.6	10.1
99-00–Indiana	47	2	582	80	187	.428	45	110	.409	37	41	.902	14	62	76	37	60	0	28	28	9	242	1.6	0.8	5.1
Reg. Season Totals	966	814	31789	6704	13137	.510	796	2068	.385	3592	4150	.866	1016	2977	3993	3431	2022	10	1514	2296	539	17796	4.1	3.6	18.4
Playoff Totals	71	63	2057	366	740	.495	67	164	.409	183	213	.859	46	191	237	148	145	0	74	136	45	982	3.3	2.1	13.8
All-Star Totals	4	2	78	12	24	.500	2	2	1.000	7	8	.875	3	5	8	8	2	0	4	5	1	33	2.0	2.0	8.3

Mullins, Jeffrey Vincent Jr. (Jeff, Pork Chop) b. March 18, 1942 Ht. 6-4 Wt. 190 College: Duke

SEASON–TEAM	G	GS	MIN	FGM	FGA	PCT	3FGM	3FGA	PCT	FTM	FTA	PCT	O-RB	D-RB	TOT	AST	PF	DQ	STL	TO	BLK	PTS	RPG	APG	PPG
64-65–St. Louis	44	–	492	87	209	.416	–	–	–	41	61	.672	–	–	102	44	60	0	–	–	–	215	2.3	1.0	4.9
65-66–St. Louis	44	–	587	113	296	.382	–	–	–	29	36	.806	–	–	69	66	68	1	–	–	–	255	1.6	1.5	5.8
66-67–San Francisco	75	–	1835	421	919	.458	–	–	–	150	214	.701	–	–	388	226	195	5	–	–	–	992	5.2	3.0	13.2
67-68–San Francisco	79	–	2805	610	1391	.439	–	–	–	273	344	.794	–	–	447	351	271	2	–	–	–	1493	5.7	4.4	18.9
68-69–San Francisco	78	–	2916	697	1517	.459	–	–	–	381	452	.843	–	–	460	339	251	4	–	–	–	1775	5.9	4.3	22.8
69-70–San Francisco	74	–	2861	656	1426	.460	–	–	–	320	378	.847	–	–	382	360	240	4	–	–	–	1632	5.2	4.9	22.1
70-71–San Francisco	75	–	2909	630	1308	.482	–	–	–	302	358	.844	–	–	341	332	246	5	–	–	–	1562	4.5	4.4	20.8
71-72–Golden State	80	–	3214	685	1466	.467	–	–	–	350	441	.794	–	–	444	471	260	5	–	–	–	1720	5.6	5.9	21.5
72-73–Golden State	81	–	3005	651	1321	.493	–	–	–	143	172	.831	–	–	363	337	201	2	–	–	–	1445	4.5	4.2	17.8
73-74–Golden State	77	–	2498	541	1144	.473	–	–	–	168	192	.875	86	190	276	305	214	2	69	–	22	1250	3.6	4.0	16.2
74-75–Golden State	66	–	1141	234	514	.455	–	–	–	71	87	.816	46	77	123	153	123	0	57	–	14	539	1.9	2.3	8.2
75-76–Golden State	29	–	311	58	120	.483	–	–	–	23	29	.793	12	20	32	39	36	0	14	–	1	139	1.1	1.3	4.8
Reg. Season Totals	802	–	24574	5383	11631	.463	–	–	–	2251	2764	.814	144	287	3427	3023	2165	30	140	–	37	13017	4.3	3.8	16.2
Playoff Totals	83	–	2255	462	1030	.449	–	–	–	160	213	.751	19	20	304	259	217	5	12	–	2	1084	3.7	3.1	13.1
All-Star Totals	3	–	42	11	20	.550	–	–	–	0	0	–	0	0	5	6	6	0	0	–	0	22	1.7	2.0	7.3
95-96–Atlanta-Boston	33	0	151	16	41	.390	0	0	–	5	8	.625	11	17	28	3	29	0	2	3	5	37	0.8	0.1	1.1

Munk, Christian (Chris) b. August 5, 1967 Ht. 6-9 Wt. 225 College: USC

SEASON–TEAM	G	GS	MIN	FGM	FGA	PCT	3FGM	3FGA	PCT	FTM	FTA	PCT	O-RB	D-RB	TOT	AST	PF	DQ	STL	TO	BLK	PTS	RPG	APG	PPG
90-91–Utah	11	0	29	3	7	.429	0	0	–	7	12	.583	5	9	14	1	5	0	1	5	2	13	1.3	0.1	1.2
Reg. Season Totals	11	0	29	3	7	.429	0	0	–	7	12	.583	5	9	14	1	5	0	1	5	2	13	1.3	0.1	1.2

Munroe, George B. b. January 5, 1922 Ht. 5-11 Wt. 170 College: Columbia; Dartmouth

SEASON–TEAM	G	GS	MIN	FGM	FGA	PCT	3FGM	3FGA	PCT	FTM	FTA	PCT	O-RB	D-RB	TOT	AST	PF	DQ	STL	TO	BLK	PTS	RPG	APG	PPG
46-47–St. Louis	59	–	–	164	623	.263	–	–	–	86	133	.647	–	–	–	17	91	–	–	–	–	414	–	0.3	7.0
47-48–Boston	21	–	–	27	91	.297	–	–	–	17	26	.654	–	–	–	3	20	–	–	–	–	71	–	0.1	3.4
Reg. Season Totals	80	–	–	191	714	.268	–	–	–	103	159	.648	–	–	–	20	111	–	–	–	–	485	–	0.3	6.1
Playoff Totals	6	–	–	16	72	.444	–	–	–	6	9	.667	–	–	–	2	12	–	–	–	–	38	–	0.2	6.3

Murdock, Eric Lloyd b. June 14, 1968 Ht. 6-1 Wt. 200 College: Providence

SEASON–TEAM	G	GS	MIN	FGM	FGA	PCT	3FGM	3FGA	PCT	FTM	FTA	PCT	O-RB	D-RB	TOT	AST	PF	DQ	STL	TO	BLK	PTS	RPG	APG	PPG
91-92–Utah	50	0	478	76	183	.415	5	26	.192	46	61	.754	21	33	54	92	52	0	30	50	7	203	1.1	1.8	4.1
92-93–Milwaukee	79	78	2437	438	936	.468	31	119	.261	231	296	.780	95	189	284	603	177	2	174	207	7	1138	3.6	7.6	14.4
93-94–Milwaukee	82	76	2533	477	1019	.468	69	168	.411	234	288	.813	91	170	261	546	189	2	197	206	12	1257	3.2	6.7	15.3
94-95–Milwaukee	75	32	2158	338	814	.415	90	240	.375	211	267	.790	48	166	214	482	139	0	113	194	12	977	2.9	6.4	13.0
95-96–Milw.-Vanc.	73	14	1673	244	587	.416	45	145	.310	114	143	.797	26	143	169	327	140	0	135	132	9	647	2.3	4.5	8.9
96-97–Denver	12	0	114	15	33	.455	4	10	.400	11	12	.917	1	10	11	24	9	0	9	11	2	45	0.9	2.0	3.8
97-98–Miami	82	1	1395	177	419	.422	28	91	.308	125	156	.801	39	117	156	219	173	1	103	104	13	507	1.9	2.7	6.2
98-99–New Jersey	15	8	401	45	114	.395	8	22	.364	21	26	.808	3	32	35	66	35	1	22	29	2	119	2.3	4.4	7.9
99-00–L.A. Clippers	40	15	693	79	205	.385	16	42	.381	51	80	.638	15	62	77	108	67	0	47	58	5	225	1.9	2.7	5.6
Reg. Season Totals	508	224	11882	1889	4310	.438	296	863	.343	1044	1329	.786	339	922	1261	2467	981	6	830	991	69	5118	2.5	4.9	10.1
Playoff Totals	8	0	136	14	37	.378	2	10	.200	25	30	.833	3	20	23	16	12	0	8	7	1	55	2.9	2.0	6.9

M

Muresan, Gheorghe (My Giant) b. February 14, 1971 Ht. 7-7 Wt. 303 College: Cluj (Romania)

SEASON–TEAM	G	GS	MIN	FGM	FGA	PCT	3FGM	3FGA	PCT	FTM	FTA	PCT	O-RB	D-RB	TOT	AST	PF	DQ	STL	TO	BLK	PTS	RPG	APG	PPG
93-94–Washington	54	2	650	128	235	.545	0	0	–	48	71	.676	66	126	192	18	120	1	28	54	48	304	3.6	0.3	5.6
94-95–Washington	73	58	1720	303	541	.560	0	0	–	124	175	.709	179	309	488	38	259	6	48	115	127	730	6.7	0.5	10.0
95-96–Washington	76	76	2242	466	798	.584	0	1	.000	172	278	.619	248	480	728	56	297	8	52	143	172	1104	9.6	0.7	14.5
96-97–Washington	73	69	1849	327	541	.604	0	0	–	123	199	.618	141	340	481	29	230	3	43	117	96	777	6.6	0.4	10.6
98-99–New Jersey	1	0	1	0	1	.000	0	0	–	0	0	–	0	0	0	0	0	0	0	1	0	0	0.0	0.0	0.0
99-00–New Jersey	30	2	267	41	90	.456	0	0	–	23	38	.605	24	44	68	9	52	0	0	16	12	105	2.3	0.3	3.5
Reg. Season Totals	307	207	6729	1265	2206	.573	0	1	.000	490	761	.644	658	1299	1957	150	958	18	171	446	455	3020	6.4	0.5	9.8
Playoff Totals	3	3	70	4	9	.444	0	0	–	7	8	.875	2	16	18	–	6	0	0	11	4	15	6.0	0.0	5.0

Murphy, Allen b. July 15, 1952 Ht. 6-5 Wt. 190 College: Louisville

SEASON–TEAM	G	GS	MIN	FGM	FGA	PCT	3FGM	3FGA	PCT	FTM	FTA	PCT	O-RB	D-RB	TOT	AST	PF	DQ	STL	TO	BLK	PTS	RPG	APG	PPG
75-76–Kentucky (A)	29	–	248	43	114	.377	0	1	.000	27	37	.730	24	23	47	13	52	–	10	27	8	113	1.6	0.4	3.9
76-77–Los Angeles	2	–	18	1	5	.200	–	–	–	3	7	.429	3	1	4	0	5	0	0	–	0	5	2.0	0.0	2.5
Reg. NBA Totals	2	–	18	1	5	.200	–	–	–	3	7	.429	3	1	4	0	5	0	0	–	0	5	2.0	0.0	2.5
Reg. ABA Totals	29	–	248	43	114	.377	0	1	.000	27	37	.730	24	23	47	13	52	–	10	27	8	113	1.6	0.4	3.9

Murphy, Calvin Jerome (Cal) b. May 9, 1948 Ht. 5-9 Wt. 165 College: Niagara HOF: 1992

SEASON–TEAM	G	GS	MIN	FGM	FGA	PCT	3FGM	3FGA	PCT	FTM	FTA	PCT	O-RB	D-RB	TOT	AST	PF	DQ	STL	TO	BLK	PTS	RPG	APG	PPG
70-71–San Diego	82	–	2020	471	1029	.458	–	–	–	356	434	.820	–	–	245	329	263	4	–	–	–	1298	3.0	4.0	15.8
71-72–Houston	82	–	2538	571	1255	.455	–	–	–	349	392	.890	–	–	258	393	298	6	–	–	–	1491	3.1	4.8	18.2
72-73–Houston	77	–	1697	381	820	.465	–	–	–	239	269	.888	–	–	149	262	211	3	–	–	–	1001	1.9	3.4	13.0
73-74–Houston	81	–	2922	671	1285	.522	–	–	–	310	357	.868	51	137	188	603	310	8	157	–	4	1652	2.3	7.4	20.4
74-75–Houston	78	–	2513	557	1152	.484	–	–	–	341	386	.883	52	121	173	381	281	8	128	–	4	1455	2.2	4.9	18.7
75-76–Houston	82	–	2995	675	1369	.493	–	–	–	372	410	.907	52	157	209	596	294	3	151	–	6	1722	2.5	7.3	21.0
76-77–Houston	82	–	2764	596	1216	.490	–	–	–	272	307	.886	54	118	172	386	281	6	144	–	8	1464	2.1	4.7	17.9
77-78–Houston	76	–	2900	852	1737	.491	–	–	–	245	267	.918	57	107	164	259	241	4	112	173	3	1949	2.2	3.4	25.6
78-79–Houston	82	–	2941	707	1424	.496	–	–	–	246	265	.928	78	95	173	351	288	5	117	187	6	1660	2.1	4.3	20.2
79-80–Houston	76	–	2676	624	1267	.493	1	25	.040	271	302	.897	68	82	150	299	269	3	143	162	9	1520	2.0	3.9	20.0
80-81–Houston	76	–	2014	528	1074	.492	4	17	.235	206	215	.958	33	54	87	222	209	0	111	129	6	1266	1.1	2.9	16.7
81-82–Houston	64	0	1204	277	648	.427	1	16	.063	100	110	.909	20	41	61	163	142	0	43	82	1	655	1.0	2.5	10.2
82-83–Houston	64	0	1423	337	754	.447	4	14	.286	138	150	.920	34	40	74	158	163	3	59	89	4	816	1.2	2.5	12.8
Reg. Season Totals	1002	0	30607	7247	15030	.482	10	72	.139	3445	3864	.892	499	952	2103	4402	3250	53	1165	822	51	17949	2.1	4.4	17.9
Playoff Totals	51	0	1660	388	817	.475	4	14	.286	165	177	.932	31	47	78	213	197	4	79	64	4	945	1.5	4.2	18.5
All-Star Totals	1	0	15	3	5	.600	0	0	–	0	0	–	0	1	1	5	4	0	2	4	0	6	1.0	5.0	6.0

Murphy, Jay Dennis b. June 26, 1962 Ht. 6-9 Wt. 220 College: Boston College

SEASON–TEAM	G	GS	MIN	FGM	FGA	PCT	3FGM	3FGA	PCT	FTM	FTA	PCT	O-RB	D-RB	TOT	AST	PF	DQ	STL	TO	BLK	PTS	RPG	APG	PPG
84-85–L.A. Clippers	23	0	149	8	50	.160	0	1	.000	12	21	.571	6	35	41	4	21	0	1	8	2	28	1.8	0.2	1.2
85-86–L.A. Clippers	14	0	100	16	45	.356	0	2	.000	9	14	.643	7	8	15	3	12	0	4	5	3	41	1.1	0.2	2.9
86-87–Washington	21	0	141	31	72	.431	0	0	–	9	16	.563	17	22	39	5	21	0	3	6	2	71	1.9	0.2	3.4
87-88–Washington	9	0	46	8	23	.348	0	0	–	4	5	.800	4	12	16	1	5	0	0	5	0	20	1.8	0.1	2.2
Reg. Season Totals	67	0	436	63	190	.332	0	3	.000	34	56	.607	34	77	111	13	59	0	8	24	7	160	1.7	0.2	2.4

Murphy, John Francis (Moe) b. September 13, 1924 Ht. 6-2 Wt. 175 College: None

SEASON–TEAM	G	GS	MIN	FGM	FGA	PCT	3FGM	3FGA	PCT	FTM	FTA	PCT	O-RB	D-RB	TOT	AST	PF	DQ	STL	TO	BLK	PTS	RPG	APG	PPG
46-47–N.Y.-Phil.	20	–	–	11	40	.275	–	–	–	10	15	.667	–	–	–	0	8	–	–	–	–	32	–	0.0	1.6
Reg. Season Totals	20	–	–	11	40	.275	–	–	–	10	15	.667	–	–	–	0	8	–	–	–	–	32	–	0.0	1.6

Murphy, Richard D. (Dick) b. March 10, 1921 d. October 22, 1973 Ht. 6-1 Wt. 180 College: Manhattan; Marshall

SEASON–TEAM	G	GS	MIN	FGM	FGA	PCT	3FGM	3FGA	PCT	FTM	FTA	PCT	O-RB	D-RB	TOT	AST	PF	DQ	STL	TO	BLK	PTS	RPG	APG	PPG
46-47–N.Y.-Boston	31	–	–	15	75	.200	–	–	–	4	9	.444	–	–	–	8	15	–	–	–	–	34	–	0.3	1.1
Reg. Season Totals	31	–	–	15	75	.200	–	–	–	4	9	.444	–	–	–	8	15	–	–	–	–	34	–	0.3	1.1

Murphy, Ronald T. (Ronnie) b. July 29, 1964 Ht. 6-5 Wt. 225 College: Jacksonville

SEASON–TEAM	G	GS	MIN	FGM	FGA	PCT	3FGM	3FGA	PCT	FTM	FTA	PCT	O-RB	D-RB	TOT	AST	PF	DQ	STL	TO	BLK	PTS	RPG	APG	PPG
87-88–Portland	18	0	89	14	49	.286	1	4	.250	7	11	.636	5	6	11	6	14	0	5	8	1	36	0.6	0.3	2.0
Reg. Season Totals	18	0	89	14	49	.286	1	4	.250	7	11	.636	5	6	11	6	14	0	5	8	1	36	0.6	0.3	2.0

Murphy, Tod James b. December 24, 1963 Ht. 6-9 Wt. 220 College: California-Irvine

SEASON–TEAM	G	GS	MIN	FGM	FGA	PCT	3FGM	3FGA	PCT	FTM	FTA	PCT	O-RB	D-RB	TOT	AST	PF	DQ	STL	TO	BLK	PTS	RPG	APG	PPG
87-88–L.A. Clippers	1	0	19	1	1	1.000	0	0	–	3	4	.750	1	1	2	2	2	0	1	0	0	5	2.0	2.0	5.0
89-90–Minnesota	82	59	2493	260	552	.471	16	43	.372	144	203	.709	207	357	564	106	229	2	76	61	60	680	6.9	1.3	8.3
90-91–Minnesota	52	19	1063	90	227	.396	1	17	.059	70	105	.667	92	163	255	60	101	1	25	32	20	251	4.9	1.2	4.8
91-92–Minnesota	47	3	429	39	80	.488	1	2	.500	19	34	.559	36	74	110	11	40	0	9	18	8	98	2.3	0.2	2.1
93-94–Detroit-G.S.	9	0	67	6	12	.500	0	0	–	3	6	.500	4	6	10	4	10	0	2	1	0	15	1.1	0.4	1.7
Reg. Season Totals	191	81	4071	396	872	.454	18	62	.290	239	352	.679	340	601	941	183	382	3	113	112	88	1049	4.9	1.0	5.5

Murray, Kenneth Stanley Jr. (Ken) b. April 20, 1928 Ht. 6-2 Wt. 195 College: St. Bonaventure

SEASON–TEAM	G	GS	MIN	FGM	FGA	PCT	3FGM	3FGA	PCT	FTM	FTA	PCT	O-RB	D-RB	TOT	AST	PF	DQ	STL	TO	BLK	PTS	RPG	APG	PPG
50-51–Balt.-FtWayne	66	–	–	301	887	.339	–	–	–	248	332	.747	–	–	355	202	164	7	–	–	–	850	5.4	3.1	12.9
53-54–Fort Wayne	49	–	528	53	195	.272	–	–	–	43	60	.717	–	–	65	56	60	0	–	–	–	149	1.3	1.1	3.0
54-55–Balt.-Phil.	66	–	1590	187	535	.350	–	–	–	98	129	.760	–	–	179	224	126	1	–	–	–	472	2.7	3.4	7.2
Reg. Season Totals	181	–	2118	541	1617	.335	–	–	–	389	521	.747	–	–	599	482	350	8	–	–	–	1471	3.3	2.7	8.1
Playoff Totals	6	–	30	17	68	.338	–	–	–	6	7	.857	–	–	14	10	13	0	–	–	–	40	1.6	1.1	6.7

Murray, Lamond Maurice b. April 20, 1973 Ht. 6-7 Wt. 236 College: California

SEASON–TEAM	G	GS	MIN	FGM	FGA	PCT	3FGM	3FGA	PCT	FTM	FTA	PCT	O-RB	D-RB	TOT	AST	PF	DQ	STL	TO	BLK	PTS	RPG	APG	PPG
94-95–L.A. Clippers	81	61	2556	439	1093	.402	65	218	.298	199	264	.754	132	222	354	133	180	3	72	163	55	1142	4.4	1.6	14.1
95-96–L.A. Clippers	77	32	1816	257	575	.447	37	116	.319	99	132	.750	89	157	246	84	151	0	61	108	25	650	3.2	1.1	8.4
96-97–L.A. Clippers	74	1	1295	181	435	.416	31	91	.341	156	211	.739	85	148	233	57	113	3	53	86	29	549	3.1	0.8	7.4
97-98–L.A. Clippers	79	65	2579	473	984	.481	54	153	.353	220	294	.748	172	312	484	142	193	3	118	171	54	1220	6.1	1.8	15.4
98-99–L.A. Clippers	50	13	1317	226	578	.391	34	103	.330	126	157	.803	59	136	195	61	107	1	58	99	20	612	3.9	1.2	12.2
99-00–Cleveland	74	72	2365	460	1019	.451	51	139	.367	204	268	.761	127	296	423	132	208	2	105	184	36	1175	5.7	1.8	15.9
Reg. Season Totals	435	244	11928	2036	4684	.435	272	820	.332	1004	1326	.757	664	1271	1935	609	952	12	467	811	219	5348	4.4	1.4	12.3
Playoff Totals	3	0	65	6	20	.300	2	8	.250	7	7	1.000	2	9	11	3	7	0	2	4	3	21	3.7	1.0	7.0

Murray, Tracy Lamonte b. July 25, 1971 Ht. 6-7 Wt. 228 College: UCLA

SEASON–TEAM	G	GS	MIN	FGM	FGA	PCT	3FGM	3FGA	PCT	FTM	FTA	PCT	O-RB	D-RB	TOT	AST	PF	DQ	STL	TO	BLK	PTS	RPG	APG	PPG
92-93–Portland	48	14	495	108	260	.415	21	70	.300	35	40	.875	40	43	83	11	59	0	8	31	5	272	1.7	0.2	5.7
93-94–Portland	66	1	820	167	355	.470	50	109	.459	50	72	.694	43	68	111	31	76	0	21	37	20	434	1.7	0.5	6.6
94-95–Port.-Houston	54	3	516	95	233	.408	35	86	.407	33	42	.786	20	39	59	19	73	0	14	35	4	258	1.1	0.4	4.8
95-96–Toronto	82	37	2458	496	1092	.454	151	358	.422	182	219	.831	114	238	352	131	208	2	87	132	40	1325	4.3	1.6	16.2
96-97–Washington	82	1	1814	288	678	.425	106	300	.353	135	161	.839	84	169	253	78	150	1	69	86	19	817	3.1	1.0	10.0
97-98–Washington	82	12	2227	449	1007	.446	158	403	.392	182	209	.871	75	202	277	84	167	0	67	102	25	1238	3.4	1.0	15.1
98-99–Washington	36	0	653	83	237	.350	33	103	.320	34	42	.810	18	63	81	27	65	0	21	29	6	233	2.3	0.8	6.5
99-00–Washington	80	8	1831	290	670	.433	113	263	.430	120	141	.851	63	208	271	72	185	2	45	84	24	813	3.4	0.9	10.2
Reg. Season Totals	530	76	10814	1976	4532	.436	667	1692	.394	771	926	.833	457	1030	1487	453	983	5	332	536	143	5390	2.8	0.9	10.2
Playoff Totals	5	0	98	20	36	.556	5	11	.455	16	17	.941	6	6	12	3	13	0	5	0	2	61	2.4	0.6	12.2

Murrell, Willie Vernon b. September 13, 1941 Ht. 6-6 Wt. 225 College: Eastern Oklahoma St. (J.C.); Kansas State

SEASON–TEAM	G	GS	MIN	FGM	FGA	PCT	3FGM	3FGA	PCT	FTM	FTA	PCT	O-RB	D-RB	TOT	AST	PF	DQ	STL	TO	BLK	PTS	RPG	APG	PPG
67-68–Denver (A)	71	–	2495	498	1069	.466	3	11	.273	166	236	.703	–	–	637	64	200	1	–	116	–	1165	9.0	0.9	16.4
68-69–Miami (A)	75	–	2493	476	1019	.467	4	18	.222	191	269	.710	–	–	566	103	239	5	–	159	–	1147	7.5	1.4	15.3
69-70–Miami-Ken. (A)	82	–	1759	276	596	.463	7	17	.412	117	154	.760	–	–	452	66	201	2	–	–	–	676	5.5	0.8	8.2
Reg. ABA Totals	228	–	6747	1250	2684	.466	14	46	.304	474	659	.719	–	–	1655	233	640	8	–	275	–	2988	7.3	1.0	13.1
ABA Playoff Totals	24	–	689	130	278	.468	1	6	.167	56	69	.812	–	–	159	29	73	1	–	8	–	317	6.6	1.2	13.2

Murrey, Dorie S. b. September 7, 1943 Ht. 6-8 Wt. 215 College: Detroit Mercy

SEASON–TEAM	G	GS	MIN	FGM	FGA	PCT	3FGM	3FGA	PCT	FTM	FTA	PCT	O-RB	D-RB	TOT	AST	PF	DQ	STL	TO	BLK	PTS	RPG	APG	PPG
66-67–Detroit	35	–	311	33	82	.402	–	–	–	32	54	.593	–	–	102	12	57	2	–	–	–	98	2.9	0.3	2.8
67-68–Seattle	81	–	1494	211	484	.436	–	–	–	168	244	.689	–	–	600	68	273	7	–	–	–	590	7.4	0.8	7.3
68-69–Seattle	38	–	465	75	194	.387	–	–	–	62	97	.639	–	–	149	21	81	1	–	–	–	212	3.9	0.6	5.6
69-70–Seattle	81	–	1079	153	343	.446	–	–	–	136	186	.731	–	–	357	76	191	4	–	–	–	442	4.4	0.9	5.5
70-71–Port.-Balt.	71	–	716	78	178	.438	–	–	–	75	112	.670	–	–	221	32	149	4	–	–	–	231	3.1	0.5	3.3
71-72–Baltimore	51	–	421	43	113	.381	–	–	–	24	39	.615	–	–	126	17	76	2	–	–	–	110	2.5	0.3	2.2
Reg. Season Totals	357	–	4486	593	1394	.425	–	–	–	497	732	.679	–	–	1555	226	827	20	–	–	–	1683	4.4	0.6	4.7
Playoff Totals	17	–	93	13	27	.481	–	–	–	7	11	.636	–	–	33	1	6	0	–	–	–	33	1.9	0.1	1.9

Musi, Angelo Jr. b. July 25, 1918 Ht. 5-9 Wt. 145 College: Temple

SEASON–TEAM	G	GS	MIN	FGM	FGA	PCT	3FGM	3FGA	PCT	FTM	FTA	PCT	O-RB	D-RB	TOT	AST	PF	DQ	STL	TO	BLK	PTS	RPG	APG	PPG
46-47–Philadelphia	60	–	–	230	818	.281	–	–	–	102	123	.829	–	–	–	26	120	–	–	–	–	562	–	0.4	9.4
47-48–Philadelphia	43	–	–	134	485	.276	–	–	–	51	73	.699	–	–	–	10	56	–	–	–	–	319	–	0.2	7.4
48-49–Philadelphia	58	–	–	194	618	.314	–	–	–	90	119	.756	–	–	–	81	108	–	–	–	–	478	–	1.4	8.2
Reg. Season Totals	161	–	–	558	1921	.290	–	–	–	243	315	.771	–	–	–	117	284	–	–	–	–	1359	–	0.7	8.4
Playoff Totals	25	–	–	77	417	.259	–	–	–	44	59	.746	–	–	–	17	58	–	–	–	–	198	–	0.5	7.9

Mustaf, Terrah Jerrod (Jerrod) b. October 28, 1969 Ht. 6-10 Wt. 245 College: Maryland

SEASON–TEAM	G	GS	MIN	FGM	FGA	PCT	3FGM	3FGA	PCT	FTM	FTA	PCT	O-RB	D-RB	TOT	AST	PF	DQ	STL	TO	BLK	PTS	RPG	APG	PPG
90-91–New York	62	5	825	106	228	.465	0	1	.000	56	87	.644	51	118	169	36	109	0	15	61	14	268	2.7	0.6	4.3
91-92–Phoenix	52	3	545	92	193	.477	0	0	–	49	71	.690	45	100	145	45	59	0	21	51	16	233	2.8	0.9	4.5
92-93–Phoenix	32	9	336	57	130	.438	0	1	.000	33	53	.623	29	54	83	10	40	0	14	22	11	147	2.6	0.3	4.6
93-94–Phoenix	33	2	196	30	84	.357	0	0	–	13	22	.591	20	35	55	8	29	0	4	10	5	73	1.7	0.2	2.2
Reg. Season Totals	179	19	1902	285	635	.449	0	2	.000	151	233	.648	145	307	452	99	237	0	54	144	46	721	2.5	0.6	4.0
Playoff Totals	10	0	32	7	10	.700	0	0	–	4	5	.800	3	4	7	–	2	0	0	1	2	18	0.7	0.0	1.8

M

Mutombo, Dikembe Mpolondo Jean-Jacque b. June 25, 1966 Ht. 7-2 Wt. 261 College: Georgetown

SEASON–TEAM	G	GS	MIN	FGM	FGA	PCT	3FGM	3FGA	PCT	FTM	FTA	PCT	O-RB	D-RB	TOT	AST	PF	DQ	STL	TO	BLK	PTS	RPG	APG	PPG
91-92–Denver	71	71	2716	428	869	.493	0	0	–	321	500	.642	316	554	870	156	273	1	43	252	210	1177	12.3	2.2	16.6
92-93–Denver	82	82	3029	398	781	.510	0	0	–	335	492	.681	344	726	1070	147	284	5	43	216	287	1131	13.0	1.8	13.8
93-94–Denver	82	82	2853	365	642	.569	0	1	.000	256	439	.583	286	685	971	127	262	2	59	206	336	986	11.8	1.5	12.0
94-95–Denver	82	82	3100	349	628	.556	0	0	–	248	379	.654	319	710	1029	113	284	2	40	192	321	946	12.5	1.4	11.5
95-96–Denver	74	74	2713	284	569	.499	0	1	.000	246	354	.695	249	622	871	108	258	4	38	150	332	814	11.8	1.5	11.0
96-97–Atlanta	80	80	2973	380	721	.527	0	0	–	306	434	.705	268	661	929	110	249	3	49	186	264	1066	11.6	1.4	13.3
97-98–Atlanta	82	82	2917	399	743	.537	0	0	–	303	452	.670	276	656	932	82	254	1	34	168	277	1101	11.4	1.0	13.4
98-99–Atlanta	50	50	1829	173	338	.512	0	0	–	195	285	.684	192	418	610	57	145	2	16	94	147	541	12.2	1.1	10.8
99-00–Atlanta	82	82	2984	322	573	.562	0	0	–	298	421	.708	304	853	1157	105	248	3	27	174	269	942	14.1	1.3	11.5
Reg. Season Totals	685	685	25114	3098	5864	.528	0	2	.000	2508	3756	.668	2554	5885	8439	1005	2257	23	349	1638	2443	8704	12.3	1.5	12.7
Playoff Totals	38	38	1526	161	299	.538	0	0	–	154	234	.658	130	332	462	47	125	1	15	83	134	476	12.2	1.2	12.5
All-Star Totals	6	2	91	17	30	.567	0	0	–	2	4	.500	15	27	42	2	9	0	1	8	6	36	7.0	0.3	6.0

Muursepp, Martin b. September 26, 1974 Ht. 6-9 Wt. 235 College: BC Kalev Tallinn (Estonia)

SEASON–TEAM	G	GS	MIN	FGM	FGA	PCT	3FGM	3FGA	PCT	FTM	FTA	PCT	O-RB	D-RB	TOT	AST	PF	DQ	STL	TO	BLK	PTS	RPG	APG	PPG
96-97–Miami-Dallas	42	0	348	54	131	.412	4	24	.167	44	70	.629	35	32	67	20	58	1	12	18	11	156	1.6	0.5	3.7
97-98–Dallas	41	7	603	83	191	.435	16	38	.421	51	67	.761	46	68	114	30	96	1	29	29	14	233	2.8	0.7	5.7
Reg. Season Totals	83	7	951	137	322	.425	20	62	.323	95	137	.693	81	100	181	50	154	2	41	47	25	389	2.2	0.6	4.7

Myers, Peter E. (Pete, Skeeter Hawk) b. September 15, 1963 Ht. 6-6 Wt. 190 College: Arkansas-Little Rock

SEASON–TEAM	G	GS	MIN	FGM	FGA	PCT	3FGM	3FGA	PCT	FTM	FTA	PCT	O-RB	D-RB	TOT	AST	PF	DQ	STL	TO	BLK	PTS	RPG	APG	PPG
86-87–Chicago	29	0	155	19	52	.365	0	6	.000	28	43	.651	8	9	17	21	25	0	14	10	2	66	0.6	0.7	2.3
87-88–San Antonio	22	0	328	43	95	.453	0	4	.000	26	39	.667	11	26	37	48	30	0	17	33	6	112	1.7	2.2	5.1
88-89–Phil.-N.Y.	33	0	270	31	73	.425	0	2	.000	33	48	.688	15	18	33	48	44	0	20	23	2	95	1.0	1.5	2.9
89-90–N.Y.-N.J.	52	2	751	89	225	.396	0	7	.000	66	100	.660	33	63	96	135	109	0	35	76	11	244	1.8	2.6	4.7
90-91–San Antonio	8	1	103	10	23	.435	0	1	.000	9	11	.818	2	16	18	14	14	0	3	14	3	29	2.3	1.8	3.6
93-94–Chicago	82	81	2030	253	556	.455	8	29	.276	136	194	.701	54	127	181	245	195	1	78	136	20	650	2.2	3.0	7.9
94-95–Chicago	71	14	1270	119	287	.415	10	39	.256	70	114	.614	57	82	139	148	125	1	58	88	15	318	2.0	2.1	4.5
95-96–Miami-Cha.	71	2	1092	91	247	.368	14	58	.241	80	122	.656	35	105	140	145	132	1	34	81	17	276	2.0	2.0	3.9
97-98–New York	9	0	40	5	10	.500	0	0	–	4	6	.667	5	5	10	3	7	0	4	4	0	14	1.1	0.3	1.6
Reg. Season Totals	377	100	6039	660	1568	.421	32	146	.219	452	677	.668	220	451	671	807	681	3	263	465	76	1804	1.8	2.1	4.8
Playoff Totals	24	10	329	34	71	.479	1	6	.167	18	33	.545	17	15	32	37	33	0	12	21	6	87	1.3	1.5	3.6

Naber, Robert E. (Bob) b. September 3, 1929 Ht. 6-3 Wt. 185 College: Louisville

SEASON–TEAM	G	GS	MIN	FGM	FGA	PCT	3FGM	3FGA	PCT	FTM	FTA	PCT	O-RB	D-RB	TOT	AST	PF	DQ	STL	TO	BLK	PTS	RPG	APG	PPG
52-53–Indianapolis	4	–	11	0	4	.000	–	–	–	1	2	.500	–	–	5	1	6	0	–	–	–	1	1.3	0.3	0.3
Reg. Season Totals	4	–	11	0	4	.000	–	–	–	1	2	.500	–	–	5	1	6	0	–	–	–	1	1.3	0.3	0.3

Nachamkin, Boris Alexander b. December 6, 1933 Ht. 6-6 Wt. 210 College: New York U.

SEASON–TEAM	G	GS	MIN	FGM	FGA	PCT	3FGM	3FGA	PCT	FTM	FTA	PCT	O-RB	D-RB	TOT	AST	PF	DQ	STL	TO	BLK	PTS	RPG	APG	PPG
54-55–Rochester	6	–	59	6	20	.300	–	–	–	8	13	.615	–	–	19	3	6	0	–	–	–	20	3.2	0.5	3.3
Reg. Season Totals	6	–	59	6	20	.300	–	–	–	8	13	.615	–	–	19	3	6	0	–	–	–	20	3.2	0.5	3.3

Nagel, Gerald R. (Jerry) b. May 18, 1928 Ht. 6-0 Wt. 190 College: Loyola (Chicago)

SEASON–TEAM	G	GS	MIN	FGM	FGA	PCT	3FGM	3FGA	PCT	FTM	FTA	PCT	O-RB	D-RB	TOT	AST	PF	DQ	STL	TO	BLK	PTS	RPG	APG	PPG
49-50–Fort Wayne	14	–	–	6	28	.214	–	–	–	1	4	.250	–	–	–	18	11	–	–	–	–	13	–	1.3	0.9
Reg. Season Totals	14	–	–	6	28	.214	–	–	–	1	4	.250	–	–	–	18	11	–	–	–	–	13	–	1.3	0.9

Nagy, Frederick Karl (Fritz) b. January 3, 1924 d. June 5, 1989 Ht. 6-2 Wt. 185 College: North Carolina; Akron

SEASON–TEAM	G	GS	MIN	FGM	FGA	PCT	3FGM	3FGA	PCT	FTM	FTA	PCT	O-RB	D-RB	TOT	AST	PF	DQ	STL	TO	BLK	PTS	RPG	APG	PPG
47-48–Indianapolis (N)	39	–	–	42	–	–	–	–	–	42	63	.667	–	–	–	–	53	–	–	–	–	126	–	–	3.2
48-49–Indianapolis	50	–	–	94	271	.347	–	–	–	65	97	.670	–	–	–	68	84	–	–	–	–	253	–	1.4	5.1
Reg. NBA Totals	50	–	–	94	271	.347	–	–	–	65	97	.670	–	–	–	68	84	–	–	–	–	253	–	1.4	5.1
Reg. NBL Totals	39	–	–	42	–	–	–	–	–	42	63	.667	–	–	–	–	53	–	–	–	–	126	–	–	3.2
NBL Playoff Totals	4	–	–	1	–	–	–	–	–	6	8	.750	–	–	–	–	2	–	–	–	–	8	–	–	2.0

Nance, Larry Donell b. February 12, 1959 Ht. 6-10 Wt. 235 College: Clemson

SEASON–TEAM	G	GS	MIN	FGM	FGA	PCT	3FGM	3FGA	PCT	FTM	FTA	PCT	O-RB	D-RB	TOT	AST	PF	DQ	STL	TO	BLK	PTS	RPG	APG	PPG
81-82–Phoenix	80	0	1186	227	436	.521	0	1	.000	75	117	.641	95	161	256	82	169	2	42	104	71	529	3.2	1.0	6.6
82-83–Phoenix	82	82	2914	588	1069	.550	1	3	.333	193	287	.672	239	471	710	197	254	4	99	190	217	1370	8.7	2.4	16.7
83-84–Phoenix	82	82	2899	601	1044	.576	0	7	.000	249	352	.707	227	451	678	214	274	5	86	177	174	1451	8.3	2.6	17.7
84-85–Phoenix	61	55	2202	515	877	.587	1	2	.500	180	254	.709	195	341	536	159	185	2	88	136	104	1211	8.8	2.6	19.9
85-86–Phoenix	73	69	2484	582	1001	.581	0	8	.000	310	444	.698	169	449	618	240	247	6	70	210	130	1474	8.5	3.3	20.2
86-87–Phoenix	69	67	2569	585	1062	.551	1	5	.200	381	493	.773	188	411	599	233	223	4	86	149	148	1552	8.7	3.4	22.5
87-88–Phoenix-Clev.	67	60	2383	487	920	.529	2	6	.333	304	390	.779	193	414	607	207	242	10	63	155	159	1280	9.1	3.1	19.1
88-89–Cleveland	73	72	2526	496	920	.539	0	4	.000	267	334	.799	156	425	581	159	186	0	57	117	206	1259	8.0	2.2	17.2
89-90–Cleveland	62	53	2065	412	807	.511	1	1	1.000	186	239	.778	162	354	516	161	185	3	54	110	122	1011	8.3	2.6	16.3
90-91–Cleveland	80	78	2927	635	1211	.524	2	8	.250	265	330	.803	201	485	686	237	219	3	66	131	200	1537	8.6	3.0	19.2
91-92–Cleveland	81	81	2880	556	1032	.539	0	6	.000	263	320	.822	213	457	670	232	200	2	80	87	243	1375	8.3	2.9	17.0
92-93–Cleveland	77	77	2753	533	971	.549	0	4	.000	202	247	.818	184	484	668	223	223	3	54	107	198	1268	8.7	2.9	16.5
93-94–Cleveland	33	19	909	153	314	.487	0	0	–	64	85	.753	77	150	227	49	96	1	27	38	55	370	6.9	1.5	11.2
Reg. Season Totals	920	795	30697	6370	11664	.546	8	55	.145	2939	3892	.755	2299	5053	7352	2393	2703	45	872	1711	2027	15687	8.0	2.6	17.1
Playoff Totals	68	61	2428	440	813	.541	0	1	.000	190	256	.742	184	351	535	160	220	5	59	108	144	1070	7.9	2.4	15.7
All-Star Totals	3	0	44	15	21	.714	0	0	–	3	4	.750	5	9	14	2	9	0	2	2	4	33	4.7	0.7	11.0

Napolitano, Paul Wally b. February 3, 1923 Ht. 6-2 Wt. 185 College: San Francisco

SEASON–TEAM	G	GS	MIN	FGM	FGA	PCT	3FGM	3FGA	PCT	FTM	FTA	PCT	O-RB	D-RB	TOT	AST	PF	DQ	STL	TO	BLK	PTS	RPG	APG	PPG
47-48–Minneapolis (N)	52	–	–	72	–	–	–	–	–	11	21	.524	–	–	–	–	48	–	–	–	–	155	–	–	3.0
48-49–Indianapolis	1	–	–	0	0	–	–	–	–	0	0	–	–	–	–	0	0	–	–	–	–	0	–	0.0	0.0
Reg. NBA Totals	1	–	–	0	0	–	–	–	–	0	0	–	–	–	–	0	0	–	–	–	–	0	–	0.0	0.0
Reg. NBL Totals	52	–	–	72	–	–	–	–	–	11	21	.524	–	–	–	–	48	–	–	–	–	155	–	–	3.0
NBL Playoff Totals	9	–	–	8	–	–	–	–	–	4	5	.800	–	–	–	–	3	–	–	–	–	20	–	–	2.2

Nash, Charles Francis (Cotton) b. July 24, 1942 Ht. 6-6 Wt. 220 College: Kentucky

SEASON–TEAM	G	GS	MIN	FGM	FGA	PCT	3FGM	3FGA	PCT	FTM	FTA	PCT	O-RB	D-RB	TOT	AST	PF	DQ	STL	TO	BLK	PTS	RPG	APG	PPG
64-65–L.A.-S.F.	45	–	357	47	145	.324	–	–	–	43	52	.827	–	–	83	19	57	0	–	–	–	137	1.8	0.4	3.0
67-68–Kentucky (A)	39	–	786	106	305	.348	0	1	.000	121	162	.747	–	–	190	46	63	0	–	49	–	333	4.9	1.2	8.5
Reg. NBA Totals	45	–	357	47	145	.324	–	–	–	43	52	.827	–	–	83	19	57	0	–	–	–	137	1.8	0.4	3.0
Reg. ABA Totals	39	–	786	106	305	.348	0	1	.000	121	162	.747	–	–	190	46	63	0	–	49	–	333	4.9	1.2	8.5

Nash, Robert Lee Jr. (Bob) b. August 24, 1950 Ht. 6-8 Wt. 195 College: San Jacinto (Texas) Coll. (J.C.); Hawaii

SEASON–TEAM	G	GS	MIN	FGM	FGA	PCT	3FGM	3FGA	PCT	FTM	FTA	PCT	O-RB	D-RB	TOT	AST	PF	DQ	STL	TO	BLK	PTS	RPG	APG	PPG
72-73–Detroit	36	–	169	16	72	.222	–	–	–	11	17	.647	–	–	34	16	30	0	–	–	–	43	0.9	0.4	1.2
73-74–Detroit	35	–	281	41	115	.357	–	–	–	24	39	.615	31	43	74	14	35	0	3	–	10	106	2.1	0.4	3.0
74-75–San Diego (A)	17	–	175	27	78	.346	0	2	.000	13	18	.722	20	35	55	12	30	–	4	16	2	67	3.2	0.7	3.9
77-78–Kansas City	66	–	800	157	304	.516	–	–	–	50	69	.725	75	94	169	46	75	0	27	47	18	364	2.6	0.7	5.5
78-79–Kansas City	82	–	1307	227	522	.435	–	–	–	69	86	.802	76	130	206	71	135	0	29	82	15	523	2.5	0.9	6.4
Reg. NBA Totals	219	–	2557	441	1013	.435	–	–	–	154	211	.730	182	267	483	147	275	0	59	129	43	1036	2.2	0.7	4.7
Reg. ABA Totals	17	–	175	27	78	.346	0	2	.000	13	18	.722	20	35	55	12	30	–	4	16	2	67	3.2	0.7	3.9
NBA Playoff Totals	5	–	64	8	27	.296	–	–	–	8	10	.800	6	5	11	–	10	0	0	7	4	24	2.2	0.0	4.8

Nash, Stephen John (Steve) b. February 7, 1974 Ht. 6-3 Wt. 195 College: Santa Clara

SEASON–TEAM	G	GS	MIN	FGM	FGA	PCT	3FGM	3FGA	PCT	FTM	FTA	PCT	O-RB	D-RB	TOT	AST	PF	DQ	STL	TO	BLK	PTS	RPG	APG	PPG
96-97–Phoenix	65	2	684	74	175	.423	23	55	.418	42	51	.824	16	47	63	138	92	1	20	63	0	213	1.0	2.1	3.3
97-98–Phoenix	76	9	1664	268	584	.459	81	195	.415	74	86	.860	32	128	160	262	145	1	63	98	4	691	2.1	3.4	9.1
98-99–Dallas	40	40	1269	114	314	.363	49	131	.374	38	46	.826	32	82	114	219	98	2	37	83	2	315	2.9	5.5	7.9
99-00–Dallas	56	27	1532	173	363	.477	60	149	.403	75	85	.882	34	87	121	272	122	1	37	102	3	481	2.2	4.9	8.6
Reg. Season Totals	237	78	5149	629	1436	.438	213	530	.402	229	268	.854	114	344	458	891	457	5	157	346	9	1700	1.9	3.8	7.2
Playoff Totals	8	1	66	10	27	.370	2	9	.222	5	8	.625	3	8	11	8	12	0	3	5	1	27	1.4	1.0	3.4

Nater, Swen Eric b. January 14, 1950 Ht. 6-11 Wt. 250 College: Cypress (Calif.) Coll. (J.C.); UCLA

SEASON–TEAM	G	GS	MIN	FGM	FGA	PCT	3FGM	3FGA	PCT	FTM	FTA	PCT	O-RB	D-RB	TOT	AST	PF	DQ	STL	TO	BLK	PTS	RPG	APG	PPG
73-74–Vir.-S.A. (A)	79	–	2375	467	846	.552	0	1	.000	180	254	.709	286	712	998	129	214	–	32	200	63	1114	12.6	1.6	14.1
74-75–San Antonio (A)	78	–	2713	495	914	.542	0	1	.000	185	246	.752	369	910	1279	97	240	–	43	185	87	1175	16.4	1.2	15.1
75-76–N.Y.-Vir. (A)	76	–	1790	320	651	.492	0	4	.000	108	155	.697	229	537	766	55	238	–	31	170	51	748	10.1	0.7	9.8
76-77–Milwaukee	72	–	1960	383	725	.528	–	–	–	172	228	.754	266	599	865	108	214	7	54	–	51	938	12.0	1.5	13.0
77-78–Buffalo	78	–	2778	501	994	.504	–	–	–	208	272	.765	278	751	1029	216	274	3	40	225	47	1210	13.2	2.8	15.5
78-79–San Diego	79	–	2006	357	627	.569	–	–	–	132	165	.800	218	483	701	140	244	6	38	170	29	846	8.9	1.8	10.7
79-80–San Diego	81	–	2860	443	799	.554	0	2	.000	196	273	.718	352	864	1216	233	259	3	45	257	37	1082	15.0	2.9	13.4
80-81–San Diego	82	–	2809	517	935	.553	0	0	–	244	307	.795	295	722	1017	199	295	8	49	211	46	1278	12.4	2.4	15.6
81-82–San Diego	21	7	575	101	175	.577	1	1	1.000	59	79	.747	46	146	192	30	64	1	6	48	9	262	9.1	1.4	12.5
82-83–San Diego	7	0	51	6	20	.300	0	0	–	4	4	1.000	2	11	13	1	1	0	1	3	0	16	1.9	0.1	2.3
83-84–Los Angeles	69	0	829	124	253	.490	0	1	.000	63	91	.692	81	183	264	27	150	0	25	68	7	311	3.8	0.4	4.5
Reg. NBA Totals	489	7	13868	2432	4528	.537	1	4	.250	1078	1419	.760	1538	3759	5297	954	1501	28	258	982	226	5943	10.8	2.0	12.2
Reg. ABA Totals	233	–	6878	1282	2411	.532	0	6	.000	473	655	.722	884	2159	3043	281	692	0	106	555	201	3037	13.1	1.2	13.0
NBA Playoff Totals	17	0	146	19	38	.500	0	0	–	20	26	.769	16	24	40	1	27	0	1	8	2	58	2.4	0.1	3.4
ABA Playoff Totals	13	–	445	87	169	.515	0	0	–	19	35	.543	51	130	181	21	39	0	4	24	11	193	13.9	1.6	14.8

Nathan, Howard b. January 21, 1972 Ht. 5-10 Wt. 185 College: N.E. Louisiana (Renamed Louisiana-Monroe)

SEASON–TEAM	G	GS	MIN	FGM	FGA	PCT	3FGM	3FGA	PCT	FTM	FTA	PCT	O-RB	D-RB	TOT	AST	PF	DQ	STL	TO	BLK	PTS	RPG	APG	PPG
95-96–Atlanta	5	0	15	5	9	.556	0	1	.000	3	4	.750	0	0	0	2	2	0	3	8	0	13	0.0	0.4	2.6
Reg. Season Totals	5	0	15	5	9	.556	0	1	.000	3	4	.750	0	0	0	2	2	0	3	8	0	13	0.0	0.4	2.6

Natt, Calvin Leon b. January 8, 1957 Ht. 6-6 Wt. 220 College: N.E. Louisiana (Renamed Louisiana-Monroe)

SEASON–TEAM	G	GS	MIN	FGM	FGA	PCT	3FGM	3FGA	PCT	FTM	FTA	PCT	O-RB	D-RB	TOT	AST	PF	DQ	STL	TO	BLK	PTS	RPG	APG	PPG
79-80–N.J.-Port.	78	–	2857	622	1298	.479	3	9	.333	306	419	.730	239	452	691	169	205	1	102	198	34	1553	8.9	2.2	19.9
80-81–Portland	74	–	2111	395	794	.497	4	8	.500	200	283	.707	149	282	431	159	188	2	73	163	18	994	5.8	2.1	13.4
81-82–Portland	75	71	2599	515	894	.576	2	8	.250	294	392	.750	193	420	613	150	175	1	62	140	36	1326	8.2	2.0	17.7
82-83–Portland	80	80	2879	644	1187	.543	3	20	.150	339	428	.792	214	385	599	171	184	2	63	203	29	1630	7.5	2.1	20.4
83-84–Portland	79	74	2638	500	857	.583	2	17	.118	275	345	.797	166	310	476	179	218	3	69	166	22	1277	6.0	2.3	16.2
84-85–Denver	78	76	2657	685	1255	.546	0	3	.000	447	564	.793	209	401	610	238	182	1	75	190	33	1817	7.8	3.1	23.3
85-86–Denver	69	62	2007	469	930	.504	2	6	.333	278	347	.801	125	311	436	164	143	0	58	130	13	1218	6.3	2.4	17.7
86-87–Denver	1	1	20	4	10	.400	0	0	–	2	2	1.000	2	3	5	2	2	0	1	1	0	10	5.0	2.0	10.0
87-88–Denver	27	7	533	102	208	.490	0	1	.000	54	73	.740	35	61	96	47	43	0	13	30	3	258	3.6	1.7	9.6
88-89–Denver-S.A.	24	0	353	47	116	.405	0	1	.000	57	79	.722	28	50	78	18	32	0	8	30	3	151	3.3	0.8	6.3
89-90–Indiana	14	0	164	20	31	.645	0	0	–	17	22	.773	10	25	35	9	14	0	1	5	0	57	2.5	0.6	4.1
Reg. Season Totals	599	371	18818	4003	7580	.528	16	73	.219	2269	2954	.768	1370	2700	4070	1306	1386	10	525	1256	191	10291	6.8	2.2	17.2
Playoff Totals	45	33	1504	320	636	.503	2	9	.222	184	250	.736	97	229	326	109	100	0	27	91	12	826	7.2	2.4	18.4
All-Star Totals	1	0	11	1	3	.333	0	0	–	1	2	.500	0	3	3	1	1	0	0	1	0	3	3.0	1.0	3.0

Natt, Kenneth Wayne (Kenny) b. October 5, 1958 Ht. 6-3 Wt. 185 N.E. Louisiana (Renamed Louisiana-Monroe)

SEASON–TEAM	G	GS	MIN	FGM	FGA	PCT	3FGM	3FGA	PCT	FTM	FTA	PCT	O-RB	D-RB	TOT	AST	PF	DQ	STL	TO	BLK	PTS	RPG	APG	PPG
80-81–Indiana	19	–	149	25	77	.325	2	8	.250	7	11	.636	9	6	15	10	18	0	5	10	1	59	0.8	0.5	3.1
82-83–Utah	22	0	210	38	73	.521	0	2	.000	9	14	.643	6	16	22	28	36	0	5	22	0	85	1.0	1.3	3.9
84-85–Utah-K.C.	8	0	29	2	6	.333	0	0	–	2	4	.500	2	1	3	3	3	0	2	3	0	6	0.4	0.4	0.8
Reg. Season Totals	49	0	388	65	156	.417	2	10	.200	18	29	.621	17	23	40	41	57	0	12	35	1	150	0.8	0.8	3.1

Naulls, William Dean (Willie) b. October 7, 1934 Ht. 6-6 Wt. 225 College: UCLA

SEASON–TEAM	G	GS	MIN	FGM	FGA	PCT	3FGM	3FGA	PCT	FTM	FTA	PCT	O-RB	D-RB	TOT	AST	PF	DQ	STL	TO	BLK	PTS	RPG	APG	PPG
56-57–St. Louis-N.Y.	71	–	1778	293	820	.357	–	–	–	132	195	.677	–	–	617	84	186	1	–	–	–	718	8.7	1.2	10.1
57-58–New York	68	–	2369	472	1189	.397	–	–	–	284	344	.826	–	–	799	97	220	4	–	–	–	1228	11.8	1.4	18.1
58-59–New York	68	–	2061	405	1072	.378	–	–	–	258	311	.830	–	–	723	102	233	8	–	–	–	1068	10.6	1.5	15.7
59-60–New York	65	–	2250	551	1286	.428	–	–	–	286	342	.836	–	–	921	138	214	4	–	–	–	1388	14.2	2.1	21.4
60-61–New York	79	–	2976	737	1723	.428	–	–	–	372	456	.816	–	–	1055	191	268	5	–	–	–	1846	13.4	2.4	23.4
61-62–New York	75	–	2978	747	1798	.415	–	–	–	383	455	.842	–	–	867	192	260	6	–	–	–	1877	11.6	2.6	25.0
62-63–N.Y.-S.F.	70	–	1901	370	887	.417	–	–	–	166	207	.802	–	–	515	102	205	3	–	–	–	906	7.4	1.5	12.9
63-64–Boston	78	–	1409	321	769	.417	–	–	–	125	157	.796	–	–	356	64	208	0	–	–	–	767	4.6	0.8	9.8
64-65–Boston	71	–	1465	302	786	.384	–	–	–	143	176	.813	–	–	336	72	225	5	–	–	–	747	4.7	1.0	10.5
65-66–Boston	71	–	1433	328	815	.402	–	–	–	104	131	.794	–	–	319	72	197	4	–	–	–	760	4.5	1.0	10.7
Reg. Season Totals	716	–	20620	4526	11145	.406	–	–	–	2253	2774	.812	–	–	6508	1114	2216	40	–	–	–	11305	9.1	1.6	15.8
Playoff Totals	35	–	495	99	267	.371	–	–	–	50	67	.746	–	–	134	21	92	2	–	–	–	248	3.8	0.6	7.1
All-Star Totals	4	–	77	17	50	.340	–	–	–	6	8	.750	–	–	26	2	8	0	–	–	–	40	6.5	0.5	10.0

Ndiaye, Makhtar Vincent b. December 12, 1973 Ht. 6-10 Wt. 231 College: North Carolina

SEASON–TEAM	G	GS	MIN	FGM	FGA	PCT	3FGM	3FGA	PCT	FTM	FTA	PCT	O-RB	D-RB	TOT	AST	PF	DQ	STL	TO	BLK	PTS	RPG	APG	PPG
98-99–Vancouver	4	0	27	1	4	.250	0	0	–	3	4	.750	3	2	5	1	9	0	0	1	1	5	1.3	0.3	1.3
Reg. Season Totals	4	0	27	1	4	.250	0	0	–	3	4	.750	3	2	5	1	9	0	0	1	1	5	1.3	0.3	1.3

Neal, Craig Duane b. February 16, 1964 Ht. 6-6 Wt. 170 College: Georgia Tech

SEASON–TEAM	G	GS	MIN	FGM	FGA	PCT	3FGM	3FGA	PCT	FTM	FTA	PCT	O-RB	D-RB	TOT	AST	PF	DQ	STL	TO	BLK	PTS	RPG	APG	PPG
88-89–Port.-Miami	53	0	500	45	123	.366	10	34	.294	14	23	.609	7	22	29	118	70	0	24	54	4	114	0.5	2.2	2.2
90-91–Denver	10	0	125	14	35	.400	3	9	.333	13	22	.591	2	14	16	37	26	1	4	19	0	44	1.6	3.7	4.4
Reg. Season Totals	63	0	625	59	158	.373	13	43	.302	27	45	.600	9	36	45	155	96	1	28	73	4	158	0.7	2.5	2.5

Neal, James Ellerbe (Jim) b. May 21, 1930 Ht. 6-11 Wt. 235 College: Wofford

SEASON–TEAM	G	GS	MIN	FGM	FGA	PCT	3FGM	3FGA	PCT	FTM	FTA	PCT	O-RB	D-RB	TOT	AST	PF	DQ	STL	TO	BLK	PTS	RPG	APG	PPG
53-54–Syracuse	67	–	899	117	369	.317	–	–	–	78	132	.591	–	–	257	24	139	0	–	–	–	312	3.8	0.4	4.7
54-55–Baltimore	13	–	194	12	59	.203	–	–	–	15	22	.682	–	–	47	9	27	0	–	–	–	39	3.6	0.7	3.0
Reg. Season Totals	80	–	1093	129	428	.301	–	–	–	93	154	.604	–	–	304	33	166	0	–	–	–	351	3.8	0.4	4.4
Playoff Totals	11	–	151	13	34	.382	–	–	–	5	13	.385	–	–	54	3	14	0	–	–	–	31	2.6	0.2	2.8

Neal, Lloyd b. December 10, 1950 Ht. 6-7 Wt. 225 College: Tennessee State

SEASON–TEAM	G	GS	MIN	FGM	FGA	PCT	3FGM	3FGA	PCT	FTM	FTA	PCT	O-RB	D-RB	TOT	AST	PF	DQ	STL	TO	BLK	PTS	RPG	APG	PPG
72-73–Portland	82	–	2723	455	921	.494	–	–	–	187	293	.638	–	–	967	146	305	6	–	–	–	1097	11.8	1.8	13.4
73-74–Portland	80	–	1517	246	502	.490	–	–	–	117	168	.696	150	344	494	89	190	0	45	–	73	609	6.2	1.1	7.6
74-75–Portland	82	–	2278	409	869	.471	–	–	–	189	295	.641	186	501	687	139	239	2	43	–	87	1007	8.4	1.7	12.3
75-76–Portland	68	–	2320	435	904	.481	–	–	–	186	268	.694	145	440	585	118	254	4	53	–	107	1056	8.6	1.7	15.5
76-77–Portland	58	–	955	160	340	.471	–	–	–	77	114	.675	87	168	255	58	148	0	8	–	35	397	4.4	1.0	6.8
77-78–Portland	61	–	1174	272	540	.504	–	–	–	127	177	.718	116	257	373	81	128	0	29	96	21	671	6.1	1.3	11.0
78-79–Portland	4	–	48	4	11	.364	–	–	–	1	1	1.000	2	7	9	1	7	0	0	6	1	9	2.3	0.3	2.3
Reg. Season Totals	435	–	11015	1981	4087	.485	–	–	–	884	1316	.672	686	1717	3370	632	1271	12	178	102	324	4846	7.7	1.5	11.1
Playoff Totals	22	–	253	37	84	.440	–	–	–	18	27	.667	23	58	81	19	39	0	2	6	12	92	3.7	0.9	4.2

Nealy, Eddie Carl (Ed) b. February 19, 1960 Ht. 6-7 Wt. 240 College: Kansas State

SEASON–TEAM	G	GS	MIN	FGM	FGA	PCT	3FGM	3FGA	PCT	FTM	FTA	PCT	O-RB	D-RB	TOT	AST	PF	DQ	STL	TO	BLK	PTS	RPG	APG	PPG
82-83–Kansas City	82	61	1643	147	247	.595	0	0	–	70	114	.614	170	315	485	62	247	4	68	51	12	364	5.9	0.8	4.4
83-84–Kansas City	71	1	960	63	126	.500	0	0	–	48	60	.800	73	149	222	50	138	1	41	33	9	174	3.1	0.7	2.5
84-85–Kansas City	22	0	225	26	44	.591	0	0	–	10	19	.526	15	29	44	18	26	0	3	12	1	62	2.0	0.8	2.8
86-87–San Antonio	60	7	980	84	192	.438	4	31	.129	51	69	.739	96	188	284	83	144	1	40	36	11	223	4.7	1.4	3.7
87-88–San Antonio	68	1	837	50	109	.459	1	2	.500	41	63	.651	82	140	222	49	94	0	29	27	5	142	3.3	0.7	2.1
88-89–Chi.-Phoenix	43	0	258	13	36	.361	0	2	.000	4	9	.444	22	56	78	14	45	0	7	7	1	30	1.8	0.3	0.7
89-90–Chicago	46	0	503	37	70	.529	0	2	.000	30	41	.732	46	92	138	28	67	0	16	17	4	104	3.0	0.6	2.3
90-91–Phoenix	55	0	573	45	97	.464	5	16	.313	28	38	.737	44	107	151	36	46	0	24	19	4	123	2.7	0.7	2.2
91-92–Phoenix	52	4	505	62	121	.512	20	50	.400	16	24	.667	25	86	111	37	45	0	16	17	2	160	2.1	0.7	3.1
92-93–G.S.-Chicago	41	4	308	26	69	.377	8	27	.296	9	12	.750	12	52	64	15	41	0	12	7	2	69	1.6	0.4	1.7
Reg. Season Totals	540	78	6792	553	1111	.498	38	130	.292	307	449	.684	585	1214	1799	392	893	6	256	226	51	1451	3.3	0.7	2.7
Playoff Totals	33	0	376	30	68	.441	5	15	.333	19	27	.704	28	63	91	15	66	1	14	10	1	84	2.8	0.5	2.5

Negratti, Albert Edward (Al) b. June 12, 1921 d. January 19, 1998 Ht. 6-4 Wt. 200 College: Seton Hall

SEASON–TEAM	G	GS	MIN	FGM	FGA	PCT	3FGM	3FGA	PCT	FTM	FTA	PCT	O-RB	D-RB	TOT	AST	PF	DQ	STL	TO	BLK	PTS	RPG	APG	PPG
45-46–Rochester (N)	16	–	–	19	–	–	–	–	–	10	–	–	–	–	–	–	–	–	–	–	–	48	–	–	3.0
46-47–Rochester (N)	33	–	–	15	–	–	–	–	–	14	24	.583	–	–	–	–	–	–	–	–	–	44	–	–	1.3
46-47–Washington	11	–	–	13	69	.188	–	–	–	5	8	.625	–	–	–	5	20	–	–	–	–	31	–	0.5	2.8
Reg. NBA Totals	11	–	–	13	69	.188	–	–	–	5	8	.625	–	–	–	5	20	–	–	–	–	31	–	0.5	2.8
Reg. NBL Totals	49	–	–	34	–	–	–	–	–	24	24	.583	–	–	–	–	–	–	–	–	–	92	–	–	1.9
NBL Playoff Totals	18	–	–	12	–	–	–	–	–	11	17	.647	–	–	–	–	32	–	–	–	–	35	–	–	1.9

Nelson, Barry G. b. September 19, 1949 Ht. 6-10 Wt. 230 College: Duquesne

SEASON–TEAM	G	GS	MIN	FGM	FGA	PCT	3FGM	3FGA	PCT	FTM	FTA	PCT	O-RB	D-RB	TOT	AST	PF	DQ	STL	TO	BLK	PTS	RPG	APG	PPG
71-72–Milwaukee	28	–	102	15	36	.417	–	–	–	5	10	.500	–	–	20	7	21	0	–	–	–	35	0.7	0.3	1.3
Reg. Season Totals	28	–	102	15	36	.417	–	–	–	5	10	.500	–	–	20	7	21	0	–	–	–	35	0.7	0.3	1.3
Playoff Totals	2	–	5	0	0	–	–	–	–	0	0	–	–	–	1	1	1	0	–	–	–	0	0.5	0.5	0.0

Nelson, Donald Arvid (Don, Nellie) b. May 15, 1940 Ht. 6-6 Wt. 210 College: Iowa

SEASON–TEAM	G	GS	MIN	FGM	FGA	PCT	3FGM	3FGA	PCT	FTM	FTA	PCT	O-RB	D-RB	TOT	AST	PF	DQ	STL	TO	BLK	PTS	RPG	APG	PPG
62-63–Chicago	62	–	1071	129	293	.440	–	–	–	161	221	.729	–	–	279	72	136	3	–	–	–	419	4.5	1.2	6.8
63-64–Los Angeles	80	–	1406	135	323	.418	–	–	–	149	201	.741	–	–	323	76	181	1	–	–	–	419	4.0	1.0	5.2
64-65–Los Angeles	39	–	238	36	85	.424	–	–	–	20	26	.769	–	–	73	24	40	1	–	–	–	92	1.9	0.6	2.4
65-66–Boston	75	–	1765	271	618	.439	–	–	–	223	326	.684	–	–	403	79	187	1	–	–	–	765	5.4	1.1	10.2
66-67–Boston	79	–	1202	227	509	.446	–	–	–	141	190	.742	–	–	295	65	143	0	–	–	–	595	3.7	0.8	7.5
67-68–Boston	82	–	1498	312	632	.494	–	–	–	195	268	.728	–	–	431	103	178	1	–	–	–	819	5.3	1.3	10.0
68-69–Boston	82	–	1773	374	771	.485	–	–	–	201	259	.776	–	–	458	92	198	2	–	–	–	949	5.6	1.1	11.6
69-70–Boston	82	–	2224	461	920	.501	–	–	–	337	435	.775	–	–	601	148	238	3	–	–	–	1259	7.3	1.8	15.4
70-71–Boston	82	–	2254	412	881	.468	–	–	–	317	426	.744	–	–	565	153	232	2	–	–	–	1141	6.9	1.9	13.9
71-72–Boston	82	–	2086	389	811	.480	–	–	–	356	452	.788	–	–	453	192	220	3	–	–	–	1134	5.5	2.3	13.8
72-73–Boston	72	–	1425	309	649	.476	–	–	–	159	188	.846	–	–	315	102	155	1	–	–	–	777	4.4	1.4	10.8
73-74–Boston	82	–	1748	364	717	.508	–	–	–	215	273	.788	90	255	345	162	189	1	19	–	13	943	4.2	2.0	11.5
74-75–Boston	79	–	2052	423	785	.539	–	–	–	263	318	.827	127	342	469	181	239	2	32	–	15	1109	5.9	2.3	14.0
75-76–Boston	75	–	943	175	379	.462	–	–	–	127	161	.789	56	126	182	77	115	0	14	–	7	477	2.4	1.0	6.4
Reg. Season Totals	1053	–	21685	4017	8373	.480	–	–	–	2864	3744	.765	273	723	5192	1526	2451	21	65	–	35	10898	4.9	1.4	10.3
Playoff Totals	150	–	3209	585	1175	.498	–	–	–	407	498	.817	60	135	719	210	399	5	13	–	7	1577	4.8	1.4	10.5

Nelson, Louis (Louie, Sweets) b. May 28, 1951 Ht. 6-3 Wt. 190 College: Washington

SEASON–TEAM	G	GS	MIN	FGM	FGA	PCT	3FGM	3FGA	PCT	FTM	FTA	PCT	O-RB	D-RB	TOT	AST	PF	DQ	STL	TO	BLK	PTS	RPG	APG	PPG
73-74–Capital	49	–	556	93	215	.433	–	–	–	53	73	.726	26	44	70	52	62	0	31	–	2	239	1.4	1.1	4.9
74-75–New Orleans	72	–	1898	307	679	.452	–	–	–	192	250	.768	75	121	196	178	186	1	65	–	6	806	2.7	2.5	11.2
75-76–New Orleans	66	–	2030	327	755	.433	–	–	–	169	230	.735	81	121	202	169	147	1	82	–	6	823	3.1	2.6	12.5
76-77–San Antonio	4	–	57	7	14	.500	–	–	–	4	7	.571	2	5	7	3	9	0	2	–	0	18	1.8	0.8	4.5
77-78–K.C.-N.J.	33	–	406	85	211	.403	–	–	–	57	84	.679	13	39	52	34	33	0	22	48	7	227	1.6	1.0	6.9
Reg. Season Totals	224	–	4947	819	1874	.437	–	–	–	475	644	.738	197	330	527	436	437	2	202	48	21	2113	2.4	1.9	9.4

Nelson, Ron b. October 7, 1946 Ht. 6-2 Wt. 175 College: New Mexico

SEASON–TEAM	G	GS	MIN	FGM	FGA	PCT	3FGM	3FGA	PCT	FTM	FTA	PCT	O-RB	D-RB	TOT	AST	PF	DQ	STL	TO	BLK	PTS	RPG	APG	PPG
70-71–Floridians (A)	59	–	490	72	172	.419	1	3	.333	41	54	.759	–	–	53	47	95	–	–	–	–	186	0.9	0.8	3.2
Reg. ABA Totals	59	–	490	72	172	.419	1	3	.333	41	54	.759	–	–	53	47	95	–	–	–	–	186	0.9	0.8	3.2
ABA Playoff Totals	1	–	2	0	1	.000	0	0	–	0	0	–	–	–	1	0	0	–	–	–	–	0	1.0	0.0	0.0

Nembhard, Ruben b. February 20, 1972 Ht. 6-3 Wt. 215 College: Weber State

SEASON–TEAM	G	GS	MIN	FGM	FGA	PCT	3FGM	3FGA	PCT	FTM	FTA	PCT	O-RB	D-RB	TOT	AST	PF	DQ	STL	TO	BLK	PTS	RPG	APG	PPG
96-97–Utah-Port.	10	0	113	16	37	.432	0	6	.000	8	10	.800	3	5	8	17	12	0	9	8	0	40	0.8	1.7	4.0
Reg. Season Totals	10	0	113	16	37	.432	0	6	.000	8	10	.800	3	5	8	17	12	0	9	8	0	40	0.8	1.7	4.0

Nemelka, Richard S. (Dick) b. October 1, 1943 Ht. 6-0 Wt. 175 College: Brigham Young

SEASON–TEAM	G	GS	MIN	FGM	FGA	PCT	3FGM	3FGA	PCT	FTM	FTA	PCT	O-RB	D-RB	TOT	AST	PF	DQ	STL	TO	BLK	PTS	RPG	APG	PPG
70-71–Utah (A)	39	–	504	82	213	.385	20	62	.323	32	49	.653	–	–	59	57	60	–	–	–	–	216	1.5	1.5	5.5
Reg. ABA Totals	39	–	504	82	213	.385	20	62	.323	32	49	.653	–	–	59	57	60	–	–	–	–	216	1.5	1.5	5.5
ABA Playoff Totals	9	–	51	7	21	.333	1	9	.111	4	5	.800	–	–	9	9	12	–	–	–	–	19	1.0	1.0	2.1

Nesby, Tyrone b. January 31, 1976 Ht. 6-6 Wt. 225 College: Nevada-Las Vegas

SEASON–TEAM	G	GS	MIN	FGM	FGA	PCT	3FGM	3FGA	PCT	FTM	FTA	PCT	O-RB	D-RB	TOT	AST	PF	DQ	STL	TO	BLK	PTS	RPG	APG	PPG
98-99–L.A. Clippers	50	36	1288	182	405	.449	35	96	.365	104	133	.782	57	118	175	82	143	2	77	53	20	503	3.5	1.6	10.1
99-00–L.A. Clippers	73	39	2317	364	915	.398	94	281	.335	151	191	.791	82	193	275	121	205	5	75	102	31	973	3.8	1.7	13.3
Reg. Season Totals	123	75	3605	546	1320	.414	129	377	.342	255	324	.787	139	311	450	203	348	7	152	155	51	1476	3.7	1.7	12.0

Nessley, Martin Scott b. February 16, 1965 Ht. 7-2 Wt. 260 College: Duke

SEASON–TEAM	G	GS	MIN	FGM	FGA	PCT	3FGM	3FGA	PCT	FTM	FTA	PCT	O-RB	D-RB	TOT	AST	PF	DQ	STL	TO	BLK	PTS	RPG	APG	PPG
87-88–LAClips-Sac.	44	0	336	20	52	.385	0	0	–	8	18	.444	23	59	82	16	89	1	8	23	12	48	1.9	0.4	1.1
Reg. Season Totals	44	0	336	20	52	.385	0	0	–	8	18	.444	23	59	82	16	89	1	8	23	12	48	1.9	0.4	1.1

Nesterovic, Radoslav b. May 30, 1976 Ht. 7-0 Wt. 248 Country: Slovenia

SEASON–TEAM	G	GS	MIN	FGM	FGA	PCT	3FGM	3FGA	PCT	FTM	FTA	PCT	O-RB	D-RB	TOT	AST	PF	DQ	STL	TO	BLK	PTS	RPG	APG	PPG
98-99–Minnesota	2	0	30	3	12	.250	0	0	–	2	2	1.000	3	5	8	1	5	0	0	1	0	8	4.0	0.5	4.0
99-00–Minnesota	82	55	1723	206	433	.476	0	2	.000	59	103	.573	135	244	379	93	262	9	21	71	85	471	4.6	1.1	5.7
Reg. Season Totals	84	55	1753	209	445	.470	0	2	.000	61	105	.581	138	249	387	94	267	9	21	72	85	479	4.6	1.1	5.7
Playoff Totals	7	4	155	15	33	.455	0	0	–	3	6	.500	9	11	20	9	24	1	3	5	7	33	2.9	1.3	4.7

Netolicky, Robert (Bob, Neto) b. August 2, 1942 Ht. 6-9 Wt. 225 College: Drake

SEASON–TEAM	G	GS	MIN	FGM	FGA	PCT	3FGM	3FGA	PCT	FTM	FTA	PCT	O-RB	D-RB	TOT	AST	PF	DQ	STL	TO	BLK	PTS	RPG	APG	PPG
67-68–Indiana (A)	71	–	2385	468	928	.504	0	1	.000	220	369	.596	313	506	819	69	162	0	–	143	–	1156	11.5	1.0	16.3
68-69–Indiana (A)	78	–	2721	583	1145	.509	0	5	.000	306	491	.623	313	485	798	87	231	4	–	178	–	1472	10.2	1.1	18.9
69-70–Indiana (A)	82	–	3222	673	1393	.483	2	7	.286	343	502	.683	337	539	876	123	206	2	–	–	–	1691	10.7	1.5	20.6
70-71–Indiana (A)	82	–	3137	651	1305	.499	2	8	.250	237	333	.712	–	–	774	104	192	–	–	–	–	1541	9.4	1.3	18.8
71-72–Indiana (A)	83	–	2905	522	1090	.479	4	19	.211	202	279	.724	–	–	764	83	185	–	–	166	–	1250	9.2	1.0	15.1
72-73–Dallas (A)	84	–	3409	650	1347	.483	0	4	.000	269	404	.666	338	513	851	239	166	0	–	214	–	1569	10.1	2.8	18.7
73-74–S.A.-Ind. (A)	75	–	1645	314	644	.488	2	6	.333	106	165	.642	173	220	393	94	113	–	28	98	33	736	5.2	1.3	9.8
74-75–Indiana (A)	59	–	1077	189	375	.504	2	12	.167	62	98	.633	98	133	231	49	108	–	9	55	18	442	3.9	0.8	7.5
75-76–Indiana (A)	4	–	53	8	21	.381	0	0	–	3	3	1.000	7	5	12	0	2	–	0	5	1	19	3.0	0.0	4.8
Reg. ABA Totals	618	–	20554	4058	8248	.492	12	62	.194	1748	2644	.661	1579	2401	5518	848	1365	6	37	859	52	9876	8.9	1.4	16.0
ABA Playoff Totals	73	–	2385	475	945	.503	0	4	.000	193	297	.650	158	255	645	61	177	2	0	25	1	1143	8.8	0.8	15.7

Neumann, Johnny b. September 11, 1951 Ht. 6-6 Wt. 200 College: Mississippi

SEASON–TEAM	G	GS	MIN	FGM	FGA	PCT	3FGM	3FGA	PCT	FTM	FTA	PCT	O-RB	D-RB	TOT	AST	PF	DQ	STL	TO	BLK	PTS	RPG	APG	PPG
71-72–Memphis (A)	77	–	1969	545	1328	.410	26	128	.203	293	385	.761	–	–	322	147	285	–	–	239	–	1409	4.2	1.9	18.3
72-73–Memphis (A)	79	–	2787	605	1283	.472	9	51	.176	329	423	.778	146	164	310	470	304	5	–	345	–	1548	3.9	5.9	19.6
73-74–Mem.-Utah (A)	87	–	2056	482	1070	.450	18	74	.243	166	215	.772	108	118	226	254	283	–	95	248	26	1148	2.6	2.9	13.2
74-75–Vir.-Indiana (A)	52	–	931	186	445	.418	21	78	.269	52	75	.693	42	47	89	135	131	–	26	82	11	445	1.7	2.6	8.6
75-76–Vir.-Ken. (A)	77	–	1589	393	949	.414	71	208	.341	151	189	.799	80	121	201	171	222	–	68	174	26	1008	2.6	2.2	13.1
76-77–Buffalo-L.A.	63	–	937	161	397	.406	–	–	–	59	87	.678	24	48	72	141	134	2	31	–	10	381	1.1	2.2	6.0
77-78–Indiana	20	–	216	35	86	.407	–	–	–	13	18	.722	5	9	14	27	24	0	6	22	1	83	0.7	1.4	4.2
Reg. NBA Totals	83	–	1153	196	483	.406	–	–	–	72	105	.686	29	57	86	168	158	2	37	22	11	464	1.0	2.0	5.6
Reg. ABA Totals	372	–	9332	2211	5075	.436	145	539	.269	991	1287	.770	376	450	1148	1177	1225	5	189	1088	63	5558	3.1	3.2	14.9
NBA Playoff Totals	6	–	68	11	29	.379	–	–	–	2	4	.500	0	2	2	9	14	0	3	–	2	24	0.3	1.5	4.0
ABA Playoff Totals	23	–	285	67	168	.399	6	22	.273	24	27	.889	18	18	36	22	41	0	10	26	3	164	1.6	1.0	7.1

Neumann, Paul R. b. January 30, 1938 Ht. 6-1 Wt. 175 College: Stanford

SEASON–TEAM	G	GS	MIN	FGM	FGA	PCT	3FGM	3FGA	PCT	FTM	FTA	PCT	O-RB	D-RB	TOT	AST	PF	DQ	STL	TO	BLK	PTS	RPG	APG	PPG
61-62–Syracuse	77	–	1265	172	401	.429	–	–	–	133	172	.773	–	–	194	176	203	3	–	–	–	477	2.5	2.3	6.2
62-63–Syracuse	80	–	1581	237	503	.471	–	–	–	181	222	.815	–	–	200	227	221	5	–	–	–	655	2.5	2.8	8.2
63-64–Philadelphia	74	–	1973	324	732	.443	–	–	–	210	266	.789	–	–	246	291	211	1	–	–	–	858	3.3	3.9	11.6
64-65–Phil.-S.F.	76	–	2034	365	772	.473	–	–	–	234	303	.772	–	–	198	233	218	3	–	–	–	964	2.6	3.1	12.7
65-66–San Francisco	66	–	1729	343	817	.420	–	–	–	265	317	.836	–	–	208	184	174	0	–	–	–	951	3.2	2.8	14.4
66-67–San Francisco	78	–	2421	386	911	.424	–	–	–	312	390	.800	–	–	272	342	266	4	–	–	–	1084	3.5	4.4	13.9
Reg. Season Totals	451	–	11003	1827	4136	.442	–	–	–	1335	1670	.799	–	–	1318	1453	1293	16	–	–	–	4989	2.9	3.2	11.1
Playoff Totals	29	–	608	76	194	.392	–	–	–	65	85	.765	–	–	61	82	87	0	–	–	–	217	2.1	2.8	7.5

Nevitt, Charles Goodrich (Chuck) b. June 13, 1959 Ht. 7-5 Wt. 250 College: North Carolina State

SEASON–TEAM	G	GS	MIN	FGM	FGA	PCT	3FGM	3FGA	PCT	FTM	FTA	PCT	O-RB	D-RB	TOT	AST	PF	DQ	STL	TO	BLK	PTS	RPG	APG	PPG
82-83–Houston	6	0	64	11	15	.733	0	0	–	1	4	.250	6	11	17	0	14	0	1	7	12	23	2.8	0.0	3.8
84-85–L.A. Lakers	11	0	59	5	17	.294	0	0	–	2	8	.250	5	15	20	3	20	0	0	10	15	12	1.8	0.3	1.1
85-86–Lakers-Detroit	29	0	126	15	43	.349	0	0	–	19	26	.731	13	19	32	7	35	0	4	12	19	49	1.1	0.2	1.7
86-87–Detroit	41	0	267	31	63	.492	0	0	–	14	24	.583	36	47	83	4	73	0	7	21	30	76	2.0	0.1	1.9
87-88–Detroit	17	0	63	7	21	.333	0	0	–	3	6	.500	4	14	18	0	12	0	1	2	5	17	1.1	0.0	1.0
88-89–Houston	43	0	228	27	62	.435	0	0	–	11	16	.688	17	47	64	3	51	1	5	22	29	65	1.5	0.1	1.5
89-90–Houston	3	0	9	2	2	1.000	0	0	–	0	0	–	0	3	3	1	3	0	0	2	1	4	1.0	0.3	1.3
91-92–Chicago	4	0	9	1	3	.333	0	0	–	0	0	–	0	1	1	1	2	0	0	3	0	2	0.3	0.3	0.5
93-94–San Antonio	1	0	1	0	0	–	0	0	–	3	6	.500	1	0	1	0	1	0	0	1	0	3	1.0	0.0	3.0
Reg. Season Totals	155	0	826	99	226	.438	0	0	–	53	90	.589	82	157	239	19	211	1	18	80	111	251	1.5	0.1	1.6
Playoff Totals	16	0	55	5	16	.313	0	0	–	6	10	.600	6	10	16	1	13	0	4	6	9	16	1.0	0.1	1.0

Newbern, Melvin b. June 11, 1967 Ht. 6-4 Wt. 200 College: Minnesota

SEASON–TEAM	G	GS	MIN	FGM	FGA	PCT	3FGM	3FGA	PCT	FTM	FTA	PCT	O-RB	D-RB	TOT	AST	PF	DQ	STL	TO	BLK	PTS	RPG	APG	PPG
92-93–Detroit	33	1	311	42	113	.372	1	8	.125	34	60	.567	19	18	37	57	42	0	23	32	1	119	1.1	1.7	3.6
Reg. Season Totals	33	1	311	42	113	.372	1	8	.125	34	60	.567	19	18	37	57	42	0	23	32	1	119	1.1	1.7	3.6

Newbill, Ivano Miguel b. December 12, 1970 Ht. 6-11 Wt. 245 College: Georgia Tech

SEASON–TEAM	G	GS	MIN	FGM	FGA	PCT	3FGM	3FGA	PCT	FTM	FTA	PCT	O-RB	D-RB	TOT	AST	PF	DQ	STL	TO	BLK	PTS	RPG	APG	PPG
94-95–Detroit	34	0	331	16	45	.356	0	0	–	8	22	.364	40	41	81	17	60	0	12	12	11	40	2.4	0.5	1.2
96-97–Atlanta	72	2	850	40	91	.440	0	0	–	20	52	.385	76	128	204	24	115	1	28	42	15	100	2.8	0.3	1.4
97-98–Vancouver	28	2	249	20	57	.351	1	1	1.000	17	30	.567	24	45	69	9	38	0	10	17	3	58	2.5	0.3	2.1
Reg. Season Totals	134	4	1430	76	193	.394	1	1	1.000	45	104	.433	140	214	354	50	213	1	50	71	29	198	2.6	0.4	1.5
Playoff Totals	3	0	5	0	0	–	0	0	–	0	0	–	0	1	1	1	2	0	0	1	0	0	0.3	0.3	0.0

Newlin, Michael F. (Mike) b. January 2, 1949 Ht. 6-4 Wt. 200 College: Utah

SEASON–TEAM	G	GS	MIN	FGM	FGA	PCT	3FGM	3FGA	PCT	FTM	FTA	PCT	O-RB	D-RB	TOT	AST	PF	DQ	STL	TO	BLK	PTS	RPG	APG	PPG
71-72–Houston	82	–	1495	256	618	.414	–	–	–	108	144	.750	–	–	228	135	233	6	–	–	–	620	2.8	1.6	7.6
72-73–Houston	82	–	2658	534	1206	.443	–	–	–	327	369	.886	–	–	340	409	301	5	–	–	–	1395	4.1	5.0	17.0
73-74–Houston	76	–	2591	510	1139	.448	–	–	–	380	444	.856	77	185	262	363	259	5	87	–	9	1400	3.4	4.8	18.4
74-75–Houston	79	–	2709	436	905	.482	–	–	–	265	305	.869	55	205	260	403	288	4	111	–	7	1137	3.3	5.1	14.4
75-76–Houston	82	–	3065	569	1123	.507	–	–	–	385	445	.865	72	264	336	457	263	5	106	–	5	1523	4.1	5.6	18.6
76-77–Houston	82	–	2119	387	850	.455	–	–	–	269	304	.885	53	151	204	320	226	2	60	–	3	1043	2.5	3.9	12.7
77-78–Houston	45	–	1181	216	495	.436	–	–	–	152	174	.874	36	84	120	203	128	1	52	120	9	584	2.7	4.5	13.0
78-79–Houston	76	–	1828	283	581	.487	–	–	–	212	243	.872	51	119	170	291	218	3	51	175	9	778	2.2	3.8	10.2
79-80–New Jersey	78	–	2510	611	1329	.460	45	152	.296	367	415	.884	101	163	264	314	195	1	115	231	4	1634	3.4	4.0	20.9
80-81–New Jersey	79	–	2911	632	1272	.497	10	30	.333	414	466	.888	78	141	219	299	237	2	87	248	9	1688	2.8	3.8	21.4
81-82–New York	76	32	1507	286	615	.465	7	23	.304	126	147	.857	36	55	91	170	194	2	33	104	3	705	1.2	2.2	9.3
Reg. Season Totals	837	32	24574	4720	10133	.466	62	205	.302	3005	3456	.870	559	1367	2494	3364	2542	36	702	878	58	12507	3.0	4.0	14.9
Playoff Totals	22	0	682	135	270	.500	0	0	–	55	65	.846	21	52	73	103	72	1	28	6	1	325	3.3	4.7	14.8

Newman, John Sylvester Jr. (Johnny) b. November 28, 1963 Ht. 6-7 Wt. 210 College: Richmond

SEASON–TEAM	G	GS	MIN	FGM	FGA	PCT	3FGM	3FGA	PCT	FTM	FTA	PCT	O-RB	D-RB	TOT	AST	PF	DQ	STL	TO	BLK	PTS	RPG	APG	PPG
86-87–Cleveland	59	0	630	113	275	.411	1	22	.045	66	76	.868	36	34	70	27	67	0	20	46	7	293	1.2	0.5	5.0
87-88–New York	77	25	1589	270	620	.435	26	93	.280	207	246	.841	87	72	159	62	204	5	72	103	11	773	2.1	0.8	10.0
88-89–New York	81	80	2336	455	957	.475	97	287	.338	286	351	.815	93	113	206	162	259	4	111	153	23	1293	2.5	2.0	16.0
89-90–New York	80	69	2277	374	786	.476	45	142	.317	239	299	.799	60	131	191	180	254	3	95	143	22	1032	2.4	2.3	12.9
90-91–Charlotte	81	81	2477	478	1017	.470	30	84	.357	385	476	.809	94	160	254	188	278	7	100	189	17	1371	3.1	2.3	16.9
91-92–Charlotte	55	55	1651	295	618	.477	13	46	.283	236	308	.766	71	108	179	146	181	4	70	129	14	839	3.3	2.7	15.3
92-93–Charlotte	64	27	1471	279	534	.522	12	45	.267	194	240	.808	72	71	143	117	154	1	45	90	19	764	2.2	1.8	11.9
93-94–Cha.-N.J.	81	18	1697	313	664	.471	24	90	.267	182	225	.809	86	94	180	72	196	3	69	90	27	832	2.2	0.9	10.3
94-95–Milwaukee	82	11	1896	226	488	.463	45	128	.352	137	171	.801	72	101	173	91	234	3	69	86	13	634	2.1	1.1	7.7
95-96–Milwaukee	82	82	2690	321	649	.495	61	162	.377	186	232	.802	66	134	200	154	257	4	90	108	15	889	2.4	1.9	10.8
96-97–Milwaukee	82	4	2060	246	547	.450	34	98	.347	189	247	.765	66	120	186	116	257	4	73	115	17	715	2.3	1.4	8.7
97-98–Denver	74	15	2176	344	799	.431	36	105	.343	365	445	.820	50	91	141	138	208	2	77	147	24	1089	1.9	1.9	14.7
98-99–Cleveland	50	2	949	106	251	.422	23	61	.377	68	84	.810	15	60	75	41	126	2	28	41	12	303	1.5	0.8	6.1
99-00–New Jersey	82	9	1763	278	623	.446	72	190	.379	192	229	.838	39	115	154	65	207	0	53	89	11	820	1.9	0.8	10.0
Reg. Season Totals	1030	478	25662	4098	8828	.464	519	1553	.334	2932	3629	.808	907	1404	2311	1559	2882	42	972	1529	232	11647	2.2	1.5	11.3
Playoff Totals	36	20	829	150	328	.457	13	56	.232	105	137	.766	41	40	81	54	114	2	35	59	8	418	2.3	1.5	11.6

Newmark, David L. (Dave) b. September 11, 1946 Ht. 7-0 Wt. 250 College: Columbia

SEASON–TEAM	G	GS	MIN	FGM	FGA	PCT	3FGM	3FGA	PCT	FTM	FTA	PCT	O-RB	D-RB	TOT	AST	PF	DQ	STL	TO	BLK	PTS	RPG	APG	PPG
68-69–Chicago	81	–	1159	185	475	.389	–	–	–	86	139	.619	–	–	347	58	205	7	–	–	–	456	4.3	0.7	5.6
69-70–Atlanta	64	–	612	127	296	.429	–	–	–	59	77	.766	–	–	174	42	128	3	–	–	–	313	2.7	0.7	4.9
70-71–Carolina (A)	31	–	457	100	209	.478	0	0	–	34	60	.567	–	–	157	28	84	–	–	–	–	234	5.1	0.9	7.5
Reg. NBA Totals	145	–	1771	312	771	.405	–	–	–	145	216	.671	–	–	521	100	333	10	–	–	–	769	3.6	0.7	5.3
Reg. ABA Totals	31	–	457	100	209	.478	0	0	–	34	60	.567	–	–	157	28	84	–	–	–	–	234	5.1	0.9	7.5
NBA Playoff Totals	6	–	42	15	33	.455	–	–	–	4	4	1.000	–	–	12	2	8	0	–	–	–	34	2.0	0.3	5.7

Newton, Bill R. b. December 22, 1950 Ht. 6-9 Wt. 225 College: Louisiana State

SEASON–TEAM	G	GS	MIN	FGM	FGA	PCT	3FGM	3FGA	PCT	FTM	FTA	PCT	O-RB	D-RB	TOT	AST	PF	DQ	STL	TO	BLK	PTS	RPG	APG	PPG
72-73–Indiana (A)	24	–	117	24	56	.429	1	2	.500	9	18	.500	21	26	47	9	40	1	–	10	–	58	2.0	0.4	2.4
73-74–Indiana (A)	11	–	73	7	15	.467	0	0	–	1	2	.500	1	17	18	5	12	–	2	7	0	15	1.6	0.5	1.4
Reg. ABA Totals	35	–	190	31	71	.437	1	2	.500	10	20	.500	22	43	65	14	52	1	2	17	0	73	1.9	0.4	2.1
ABA Playoff Totals	4	–	7	2	5	.400	0	1	.000	0	0	–	0	0	5	0	3	0	0	1	0	4	1.3	0.0	1.0

Nichols, Jack Edward b. April 9, 1926 d. December 24, 1992 Ht. 6-7 Wt. 230 College: Washington; USC

SEASON–TEAM	G	GS	MIN	FGM	FGA	PCT	3FGM	3FGA	PCT	FTM	FTA	PCT	O-RB	D-RB	TOT	AST	PF	DQ	STL	TO	BLK	PTS	RPG	APG	PPG
48-49–Washington	34	–	–	153	392	.390	–	–	–	92	126	.730	–	–	–	56	118	–	–	–	–	398	–	1.6	11.7
49-50–Wash.-Tri-Cit	67	–	–	310	848	.366	–	–	–	259	344	.753	–	–	–	142	179	–	–	–	–	879	–	2.1	13.1
50-51–Tri-Cities	5	–	–	18	48	.375	–	–	–	10	13	.769	–	–	52	14	18	0	–	–	–	46	10.4	2.8	9.2
52-53–Milwaukee	69	–	2626	425	1170	.363	–	–	–	240	339	.708	–	–	533	196	237	9	–	–	–	1090	7.7	2.8	15.8
53-54–Milw.-Boston	75	–	1607	163	528	.309	–	–	–	113	152	.743	–	–	363	104	187	2	–	–	–	439	4.8	1.4	5.9
54-55–Boston	64	–	1910	249	656	.380	–	–	–	138	177	.780	–	–	533	144	238	10	–	–	–	636	8.3	2.3	9.9
55-56–Boston	60	–	1964	330	799	.413	–	–	–	200	253	.791	–	–	625	160	228	7	–	–	–	860	10.4	2.7	14.3
56-57–Boston	61	–	1372	195	537	.363	–	–	–	108	136	.794	–	–	374	85	185	4	–	–	–	498	6.1	1.4	8.2
57-58–Boston	69	–	1224	170	484	.351	–	–	–	59	80	.738	–	–	302	63	123	1	–	–	–	399	4.4	0.9	5.8
Reg. Season Totals	504	–	10703	2013	5462	.369	–	–	–	1219	1620	.752	–	–	2782	964	1513	33	–	–	–	5245	6.9	1.9	10.4
Playoff Totals	51	–	807	201	621	.393	–	–	–	117	161	.739	–	–	209	135	171	2	–	–	–	519	5.6	2.3	10.2

Nickerson, Gaylon b. February 5, 1969 Ht. 6-3 Wt. 190 College: Northwestern Okla. State

SEASON–TEAM	G	GS	MIN	FGM	FGA	PCT	3FGM	3FGA	PCT	FTM	FTA	PCT	O-RB	D-RB	TOT	AST	PF	DQ	STL	TO	BLK	PTS	RPG	APG	PPG
96-97–S.A.-Wash.	4	0	42	4	12	.333	0	2	.000	7	7	1.000	1	4	5	1	1	0	1	1	1	15	1.3	0.3	3.8
Reg. Season Totals	4	0	42	4	12	.333	0	2	.000	7	7	1.000	1	4	5	1	1	0	1	1	1	15	1.3	0.3	3.8

Nicks, Orlando Carl (Carl) b. October 6, 1958 Ht. 6-2 Wt. 180 College: Gulf Coast (Fla.) C.C.; Indiana State

SEASON–TEAM	G	GS	MIN	FGM	FGA	PCT	3FGM	3FGA	PCT	FTM	FTA	PCT	O-RB	D-RB	TOT	AST	PF	DQ	STL	TO	BLK	PTS	RPG	APG	PPG
80-81–Denver-Utah	67	–	1109	172	359	.479	0	4	.000	71	126	.563	37	73	110	149	141	0	60	116	3	415	1.6	2.2	6.2
81-82–Utah	80	1	1322	252	555	.454	0	5	.000	85	150	.567	67	94	161	89	184	0	66	101	4	589	2.0	1.1	7.4
82-83–Cleveland	9	2	148	26	59	.441	0	1	.000	11	17	.647	8	18	26	11	17	0	6	11	0	63	2.9	1.2	7.0
Reg. Season Totals	156	3	2579	450	973	.462	0	10	.000	167	293	.570	112	185	297	249	342	0	132	228	7	1067	1.9	1.6	6.8

Niemann, Richard W. (Rich) b. July 2, 1946 Ht. 7-0 Wt. 245 College: St. Louis

SEASON–TEAM	G	GS	MIN	FGM	FGA	PCT	3FGM	3FGA	PCT	FTM	FTA	PCT	O-RB	D-RB	TOT	AST	PF	DQ	STL	TO	BLK	PTS	RPG	APG	PPG
68-69–Detroit-Milw.	34	–	272	44	106	.415	–	–	–	19	25	.760	–	–	100	16	61	1	–	–	–	107	2.9	0.5	3.1
69-70–Boston	6	–	18	2	5	.400	–	–	–	2	2	1.000	–	–	6	2	10	0	–	–	–	6	1.0	0.3	1.0
69-70–Carolina (A)	63	–	1466	285	601	.474	0	0	–	141	192	.734	–	–	563	87	219	7	–	–	–	711	8.9	1.4	11.3
70-71–Floridians (A)	51	–	642	121	241	.502	0	0	–	43	60	.717	–	–	255	29	137	–	–	–	–	285	5.0	0.6	5.6
71-72–Dallas (A)	33	–	524	48	98	.490	0	0	–	25	34	.735	–	–	155	24	87	–	–	27	–	121	4.7	0.7	3.7
Reg. NBA Totals	40	–	290	46	111	.414	–	–	–	21	27	.778	–	–	106	18	71	1	–	–	–	113	2.7	0.5	2.8
Reg. ABA Totals	147	–	2632	454	940	.483	0	0	–	209	286	.731	–	–	973	140	443	7	–	27	–	1117	6.6	1.0	7.6
ABA Playoff Totals	5	–	53	7	18	.389	0	0	–	3	3	1.000	–	–	12	2	11	0	–	–	–	17	2.4	0.4	3.4

Niemiera, John Richard (Richie) b. May 26, 1921 Ht. 6-1 Wt. 165 College: Notre Dame

SEASON–TEAM	G	GS	MIN	FGM	FGA	PCT	3FGM	3FGA	PCT	FTM	FTA	PCT	O-RB	D-RB	TOT	AST	PF	DQ	STL	TO	BLK	PTS	RPG	APG	PPG
46-47–Fort Wayne (N)	13	–	–	28	–	–	–	–	–	17	23	.739	–	–	–	–	–	–	–	–	–	73	–	–	5.6
47-48–Fort Wayne (N)	59	–	–	118	–	–	–	–	–	97	135	.719	–	–	–	–	113	–	–	–	–	333	–	–	5.6
48-49–Fort Wayne	55	–	–	115	331	.347	–	–	–	132	165	.800	–	–	–	96	115	–	–	–	–	362	–	1.7	6.6
49-50–FtWayne-And.	60	–	–	110	350	.314	–	–	–	104	139	.748	–	–	–	116	77	–	–	–	–	324	–	1.9	5.4
Reg. NBA Totals	115	–	–	225	681	.330	–	–	–	236	304	.776	–	–	–	212	192	–	–	–	–	686	–	1.8	6.0
Reg. NBL Totals	72	–	–	146	–	–	–	–	–	114	158	.722	–	–	–	–	113	–	–	–	–	406	–	–	5.6
NBA Playoff Totals	8	–	–	11	27	.407	–	–	–	6	8	.750	–	–	–	8	10	–	–	–	–	28	–	1.0	3.5
NBL Playoff Totals	10	–	–	21	–	–	–	–	–	12	16	.750	–	–	–	–	12	–	–	–	–	54	–	–	5.4

Niles, Michael Donnell (Mike) b. March 31, 1955 Ht. 6-6 Wt. 225 College: Cal State-Fullerton

SEASON–TEAM	G	GS	MIN	FGM	FGA	PCT	3FGM	3FGA	PCT	FTM	FTA	PCT	O-RB	D-RB	TOT	AST	PF	DQ	STL	TO	BLK	PTS	RPG	APG	PPG
80-81–Phoenix	44	–	231	48	138	.348	2	4	.500	17	37	.459	26	32	58	15	41	0	8	25	1	115	1.3	0.3	2.6
Reg. Season Totals	44	–	231	48	138	.348	2	4	.500	17	37	.459	26	32	58	15	41	0	8	25	1	115	1.3	0.3	2.6
Playoff Totals	2	–	4	0	5	.000	0	0	–	0	0	–	0	0	0	–	0	0	1	0	0	0	0.0	0.0	0.0

Nimphius, Kurt Allen b. March 13, 1958 Ht. 6-11 Wt. 225 College: Arizona State

SEASON–TEAM	G	GS	MIN	FGM	FGA	PCT	3FGM	3FGA	PCT	FTM	FTA	PCT	O-RB	D-RB	TOT	AST	PF	DQ	STL	TO	BLK	PTS	RPG	APG	PPG
81-82–Dallas	63	27	1085	137	297	.461	0	0	–	63	108	.583	92	203	295	61	190	5	17	56	82	337	4.7	1.0	5.3
82-83–Dallas	81	12	1515	174	355	.490	1	1	1.000	77	140	.550	157	247	404	115	287	11	24	66	111	426	5.0	1.4	5.3
83-84–Dallas	82	46	2284	272	523	.520	1	4	.250	101	162	.623	182	331	513	176	283	5	41	98	144	646	6.3	2.1	7.9
84-85–Dallas	82	40	2010	196	434	.452	0	6	.000	108	140	.771	136	272	408	183	262	4	30	95	126	500	5.0	2.2	6.1
85-86–Dallas-LAClips	80	66	2226	351	694	.506	0	3	.000	194	262	.740	152	301	453	62	267	8	33	120	105	896	5.7	0.8	11.2
86-87–LAClips-Detroit	66	11	1088	155	330	.470	0	4	.000	81	120	.675	80	107	187	25	156	1	20	63	54	391	2.8	0.4	5.9
87-88–San Antonio	72	7	919	128	257	.498	0	1	.000	60	83	.723	62	91	153	53	141	2	22	49	56	316	2.1	0.7	4.4
89-90–Philadelphia	38	1	314	38	91	.418	0	1	.000	14	30	.467	22	39	61	6	45	0	4	12	18	90	1.6	0.2	2.4
Reg. Season Totals	564	210	11441	1451	2981	.487	2	20	.100	698	1045	.668	883	1591	2474	681	1631	36	191	559	696	3602	4.4	1.2	6.4
Playoff Totals	25	0	306	26	65	.400	0	0	–	18	23	.783	34	47	81	18	52	0	2	14	19	70	3.2	0.7	2.8

Nix, Dyron Patrick b. February 11, 1967 Ht. 6-7 Wt. 210 College: Tennessee

SEASON–TEAM	G	GS	MIN	FGM	FGA	PCT	3FGM	3FGA	PCT	FTM	FTA	PCT	O-RB	D-RB	TOT	AST	PF	DQ	STL	TO	BLK	PTS	RPG	APG	PPG
89-90–Indiana	20	0	109	14	39	.359	0	0	–	11	16	.688	8	18	26	5	15	0	3	7	1	39	1.3	0.3	2.0
Reg. Season Totals	20	0	109	14	39	.359	0	0	–	11	16	.688	8	18	26	5	15	0	3	7	1	39	1.3	0.3	2.0

Nixon, Norman Ellard (Norm) b. October 11, 1955 Ht. 6-2 Wt. 175 College: Duquesne

SEASON–TEAM	G	GS	MIN	FGM	FGA	PCT	3FGM	3FGA	PCT	FTM	FTA	PCT	O-RB	D-RB	TOT	AST	PF	DQ	STL	TO	BLK	PTS	RPG	APG	PPG
77-78–Los Angeles	81	–	2779	496	998	.497	–	–	–	115	161	.714	41	198	239	553	259	3	138	251	7	1107	3.0	6.8	13.7
78-79–Los Angeles	82	–	3145	623	1149	.542	–	–	–	158	204	.775	48	183	231	737	250	6	201	231	17	1404	2.8	9.0	17.1
79-80–Los Angeles	82	–	3226	624	1209	.516	1	8	.125	197	253	.779	52	177	229	642	241	1	147	288	14	1446	2.8	7.8	17.6
80-81–Los Angeles	79	–	2962	576	1210	.476	2	12	.167	196	252	.778	64	168	232	696	226	2	146	285	11	1350	2.9	8.8	17.1
81-82–Los Angeles	82	82	3024	628	1274	.493	3	12	.250	181	224	.808	38	138	176	652	264	3	132	238	7	1440	2.1	8.0	17.6
82-83–Los Angeles	79	79	2711	533	1123	.475	0	13	.000	125	168	.744	61	144	205	566	176	1	104	237	4	1191	2.6	7.2	15.1
83-84–San Diego	82	82	3053	587	1270	.462	11	46	.239	206	271	.760	56	147	203	914	180	1	94	257	4	1391	2.5	11.1	17.0
84-85–L.A. Clippers	81	81	2894	596	1281	.465	33	99	.333	170	218	.780	55	163	218	711	175	2	95	273	4	1395	2.7	8.8	17.2
85-86–L.A. Clippers	67	62	2138	403	921	.438	42	121	.347	131	162	.809	45	135	180	576	143	0	84	190	3	979	2.7	8.6	14.6
88-89–L.A. Clippers	53	30	1318	153	370	.414	8	29	.276	48	65	.738	13	65	78	339	69	0	46	118	0	362	1.5	6.4	6.8
Reg. Season Totals	768	416	27250	5219	10805	.483	100	340	.294	1527	1978	.772	473	1518	1991	6386	1983	19	1187	2368	71	12065	2.6	8.3	15.7
Playoff Totals	58	28	2287	440	921	.478	5	15	.333	142	186	.763	50	145	195	465	201	1	89	151	8	1027	3.4	8.0	17.7
All-Star Totals	2	0	38	12	21	.571	0	0	–	1	2	.500	0	2	2	10	0	0	2	1	0	25	1.0	5.0	12.5

Noble, Charles E. **(Chuck)** b. July 24, 1931 Ht. 6-4 Wt. 195 College: Louisville

SEASON–TEAM	G	GS	MIN	FGM	FGA	PCT	3FGM	3FGA	PCT	FTM	FTA	PCT	O-RB	D-RB	TOT	AST	PF	DQ	STL	TO	BLK	PTS	RPG	APG	PPG
55-56–Fort Wayne	72	–	2013	270	767	.352	–	–	–	146	195	.749	–	–	261	282	253	3	–	–	–	686	3.6	3.9	9.5
56-57–Fort Wayne	54	–	1260	200	556	.360	–	–	–	76	102	.745	–	–	135	180	161	2	–	–	–	476	2.5	3.3	8.8
57-58–Detroit	61	–	1363	199	601	.331	–	–	–	56	77	.727	–	–	140	153	166	0	–	–	–	454	2.3	2.5	7.4
58-59–Detroit	65	–	939	189	560	.338	–	–	–	83	113	.735	–	–	115	114	126	0	–	–	–	461	1.8	1.8	7.1
59-60–Detroit	58	–	1621	276	774	.357	–	–	–	101	138	.732	–	–	201	265	172	2	–	–	–	653	3.5	4.6	11.3
60-61–Detroit	75	–	1655	196	566	.346	–	–	–	82	115	.713	–	–	180	287	195	4	–	–	–	474	2.4	3.8	6.3
61-62–Detroit	26	–	361	32	113	.283	–	–	–	8	15	.533	–	–	43	63	55	1	–	–	–	72	1.7	2.4	2.8
Reg. Season Totals	411	–	9212	1362	3937	.346	–	–	–	552	755	.731	–	–	1075	1344	1128	12	–	–	–	3276	2.6	3.3	8.0
Playoff Totals	29	–	591	79	244	.324	–	–	–	28	36	.778	–	–	63	86	71	2	–	–	–	186	2.2	3.0	6.4
All-Star Totals	1	–	11	0	5	.000	–	–	–	0	0	–	–	–	1	3	1	0	–	–	–	0	1.0	3.0	0.0

Noel, Paul Wendel b. August 4, 1924 Ht. 6-4 Wt. 185 College: Kentucky

SEASON–TEAM	G	GS	MIN	FGM	FGA	PCT	3FGM	3FGA	PCT	FTM	FTA	PCT	O-RB	D-RB	TOT	AST	PF	DQ	STL	TO	BLK	PTS	RPG	APG	PPG
47-48–New York	29	–	–	40	138	.290	–	–	–	19	30	.633	–	–	–	3	41	–	–	–	–	99	–	0.1	3.4
48-49–New York	47	–	–	70	277	.253	–	–	–	37	60	.617	–	–	–	33	84	–	–	–	–	177	–	0.7	3.8
49-50–New York	65	–	–	98	291	.337	–	–	–	53	87	.609	–	–	–	67	132	–	–	–	–	249	–	1.0	3.8
50-51–Rochester	52	–	–	49	174	.282	–	–	–	32	45	.711	–	–	81	34	61	1	–	–	–	130	1.6	0.7	2.5
51-52–Rochester	8	–	32	2	9	.222	–	–	–	2	3	.667	–	–	4	3	6	0	–	–	–	6	0.5	0.4	0.8
Reg. Season Totals	201	–	32	259	889	.291	–	–	–	143	225	.636	–	–	85	140	324	1	–	–	–	661	1.4	0.7	3.3
Playoff Totals	21	–	0	13	48	.313	–	–	–	10	15	.667	–	–	9	6	35	1	–	–	–	36	1.8	0.3	1.7

Nolan, James S. **(Jim)** b. June 9, 1927 d. April 19, 1983 Ht. 6-8 Wt. 210 College: Georgia Tech

SEASON–TEAM	G	GS	MIN	FGM	FGA	PCT	3FGM	3FGA	PCT	FTM	FTA	PCT	O-RB	D-RB	TOT	AST	PF	DQ	STL	TO	BLK	PTS	RPG	APG	PPG
49-50–Philadelphia	5	–	–	4	21	.190	–	–	–	0	0	–	–	–	–	4	14	–	–	–	–	8	–	0.8	1.6
Reg. Season Totals	5	–	–	4	21	.190	–	–	–	0	0	–	–	–	–	4	14	–	–	–	–	8	–	0.8	1.6

Nolen, Paul E. b. September 3, 1929 Ht. 6-10 Wt. 215 College: Texas Tech

SEASON–TEAM	G	GS	MIN	FGM	FGA	PCT	3FGM	3FGA	PCT	FTM	FTA	PCT	O-RB	D-RB	TOT	AST	PF	DQ	STL	TO	BLK	PTS	RPG	APG	PPG
53-54–Baltimore	1	–	2	0	1	.000	–	–	–	0	0	–	–	–	1	0	1	0	–	–	–	0	1.0	0.0	0.0
Reg. Season Totals	1	–	2	0	1	.000	–	–	–	0	0	–	–	–	1	0	1	0	–	–	–	0	1.0	0.0	0.0

Nordgaard, Jeffrey Wallace **(Jeff)** b. February 23, 1973 Ht. 6-7 Wt. 225 College: Wisconsin-Green Bay

SEASON–TEAM	G	GS	MIN	FGM	FGA	PCT	3FGM	3FGA	PCT	FTM	FTA	PCT	O-RB	D-RB	TOT	AST	PF	DQ	STL	TO	BLK	PTS	RPG	APG	PPG
97-98–Milwaukee	13	0	48	5	18	.278	0	0	–	8	9	.889	4	10	14	3	7	0	2	3	0	18	1.1	0.2	1.4
Reg. Season Totals	13	0	48	5	18	.278	0	0	–	8	9	.889	4	10	14	3	7	0	2	3	0	18	1.1	0.2	1.4

Nordmann, Robert **(Bevo)** b. December 11, 1939 Ht. 6-10 Wt. 225 College: St. Louis

SEASON–TEAM	G	GS	MIN	FGM	FGA	PCT	3FGM	3FGA	PCT	FTM	FTA	PCT	O-RB	D-RB	TOT	AST	PF	DQ	STL	TO	BLK	PTS	RPG	APG	PPG
61-62–Cincinnati	58	–	344	51	126	.405	–	–	–	29	57	.509	–	–	128	18	81	1	–	–	–	131	2.2	0.3	2.3
62-63–St. Louis-N.Y.	53	–	1000	156	319	.489	–	–	–	59	122	.484	–	–	316	47	156	6	–	–	–	371	6.0	0.9	7.0
63-64–N.Y.-St. Louis	19	–	259	27	66	.409	–	–	–	9	19	.474	–	–	65	5	51	1	–	–	–	63	3.4	0.3	3.3
64-65–Boston	3	–	25	3	5	.600	–	–	–	0	0	–	–	–	8	3	5	0	–	–	–	6	2.7	1.0	2.0
Reg. Season Totals	133	–	1628	237	516	.459	–	–	–	97	198	.490	–	–	517	73	293	8	–	–	–	571	3.9	0.5	4.3
Playoff Totals	2	–	5	0	1	.000	–	–	–	0	0	–	–	–	2	–	1	0	–	–	–	0	1.0	0.0	0.0

Norlander, John A. **(Johnny)** b. March 5, 1921 Ht. 6-3 Wt. 180 College: Hamline

SEASON–TEAM	G	GS	MIN	FGM	FGA	PCT	3FGM	3FGA	PCT	FTM	FTA	PCT	O-RB	D-RB	TOT	AST	PF	DQ	STL	TO	BLK	PTS	RPG	APG	PPG
46-47–Washington	60	–	–	223	698	.319	–	–	–	180	276	.652	–	–	–	50	122	–	–	–	–	626	–	0.8	10.4
47-48–Washington	48	–	–	167	543	.308	–	–	–	135	182	.742	–	–	–	44	102	–	–	–	–	469	–	0.9	9.8
48-49–Washington	60	–	–	164	454	.361	–	–	–	116	171	.678	–	–	–	86	124	–	–	–	–	444	–	1.4	7.4
49-50–Washington	40	–	–	99	293	.338	–	–	–	53	85	.624	–	–	–	33	71	–	–	–	–	251	–	0.8	6.3
50-51–Washington	9	–	–	6	19	.316	–	–	–	9	14	.643	–	–	9	5	14	0	–	–	–	21	1.0	0.6	2.3
Reg. Season Totals	217	–	–	659	2007	.328	–	–	–	493	728	.677	–	–	9	218	433	0	–	–	–	1811	1.0	1.0	8.3
Playoff Totals	17	–	–	39	226	.305	–	–	–	33	49	.796	–	–	–	17	40	0	–	–	–	111	–	0.5	6.5

Norman, Coniel **(Connie, Popcorn)** b. September 24, 1953 Ht. 6-3 Wt. 175 College: Arizona

SEASON–TEAM	G	GS	MIN	FGM	FGA	PCT	3FGM	3FGA	PCT	FTM	FTA	PCT	O-RB	D-RB	TOT	AST	PF	DQ	STL	TO	BLK	PTS	RPG	APG	PPG
74-75–Philadelphia	12	–	72	23	44	.523	–	–	–	2	3	.667	3	9	12	4	9	0	3	–	1	48	1.0	0.3	4.0
75-76–Philadelphia	65	–	818	183	422	.434	–	–	–	20	24	.833	51	50	101	66	87	1	28	–	7	386	1.6	1.0	5.9
78-79–San Diego	22	–	323	71	165	.430	–	–	–	19	23	.826	13	19	32	24	35	0	10	22	3	161	1.5	1.1	7.3
Reg. Season Totals	99	–	1213	277	631	.439	–	–	–	41	50	.820	67	78	145	94	131	1	41	22	11	595	1.5	0.9	6.0
Playoff Totals	1	–	1	1	1	1.000	–	–	–	0	0	–	0	1	1	–	0	0	0	–	0	2	1.0	0.0	2.0

Norman, Kenneth Darnel (Ken, Snake) b. September 5, 1964 Ht. 6-8 Wt. 228 College: Illinois

SEASON–TEAM	G	GS	MIN	FGM	FGA	PCT	3FGM	3FGA	PCT	FTM	FTA	PCT	O-RB	D-RB	TOT	AST	PF	DQ	STL	TO	BLK	PTS	RPG	APG	PPG
87-88–L.A. Clippers	66	28	1435	241	500	.482	0	10	.000	87	170	.512	100	163	263	78	123	0	44	103	34	569	4.0	1.2	8.6
88-89–L.A. Clippers	80	79	3020	638	1271	.502	4	21	.190	170	270	.630	245	422	667	277	223	2	106	206	66	1450	8.3	3.5	18.1
89-90–L.A. Clippers	70	64	2334	484	949	.510	7	16	.438	153	242	.632	143	327	470	160	196	0	78	190	59	1128	6.7	2.3	16.1
90-91–L.A. Clippers	70	45	2309	520	1037	.501	6	32	.188	173	275	.629	177	320	497	159	192	0	63	139	63	1219	7.1	2.3	17.4
91-92–L.A. Clippers	77	24	2009	402	821	.490	4	28	.143	121	226	.535	158	290	448	125	145	0	53	100	66	929	5.8	1.6	12.1
92-93–L.A. Clippers	76	71	2477	498	975	.511	10	38	.263	131	220	.595	209	362	571	165	156	0	59	125	58	1137	7.5	2.2	15.0
93-94–Milwaukee	82	75	2539	412	919	.448	63	189	.333	92	183	.503	169	331	500	222	209	2	58	150	46	979	6.1	2.7	11.9
94-95–Atlanta	74	27	1879	388	856	.453	98	285	.344	64	140	.457	103	259	362	94	154	0	34	96	20	938	4.9	1.3	12.7
95-96–Atlanta	34	28	770	127	273	.465	33	84	.393	17	48	.354	40	92	132	63	68	0	15	46	16	304	3.9	1.9	8.9
96-97–Atlanta	17	0	220	27	94	.287	6	38	.158	4	12	.333	8	31	39	12	17	0	7	18	3	64	2.3	0.7	3.8
Reg. Season Totals	646	441	18992	3737	7695	.486	231	741	.312	1012	1786	.567	1352	2597	3949	1355	1483	4	517	1173	431	8717	6.1	2.1	13.5
Playoff Totals	13	10	390	59	138	.428	4	18	.222	21	46	.457	35	64	99	30	39	1	8	10	4	143	7.6	2.3	11.0

Norris, Audie James b. December 18, 1960 Ht. 6-9 Wt. 250 College: Jackson State

SEASON–TEAM	G	GS	MIN	FGM	FGA	PCT	3FGM	3FGA	PCT	FTM	FTA	PCT	O-RB	D-RB	TOT	AST	PF	DQ	STL	TO	BLK	PTS	RPG	APG	PPG
82-83–Portland	30	0	311	26	63	.413	0	0	–	14	30	.467	25	44	69	24	61	0	13	33	2	66	2.3	0.8	2.2
83-84–Portland	79	1	1157	124	246	.504	0	0	–	104	149	.698	82	175	257	76	231	2	30	114	34	352	3.3	1.0	4.5
84-85–Portland	78	13	1117	133	245	.543	0	3	.000	135	203	.665	90	160	250	47	221	7	42	100	33	401	3.2	0.6	5.1
Reg. Season Totals	187	14	2585	283	554	.511	0	3	.000	253	382	.662	197	379	576	147	513	9	85	247	69	819	3.1	0.8	4.4
Playoff Totals	20	0	214	32	55	.582	0	0	–	15	32	.469	31	40	71	12	43	1	7	18	8	79	3.6	0.6	4.0

Norris, Martyn (Moochie) b. July 27, 1973 Ht. 6-1 Wt. 175 College: West Florida

SEASON–TEAM	G	GS	MIN	FGM	FGA	PCT	3FGM	3FGA	PCT	FTM	FTA	PCT	O-RB	D-RB	TOT	AST	PF	DQ	STL	TO	BLK	PTS	RPG	APG	PPG
96-97–Vancouver	8	0	89	4	22	.182	2	10	.200	2	5	.400	3	9	12	23	5	0	4	5	0	12	1.5	2.9	1.5
98-99–Seattle	12	0	140	13	40	.325	6	15	.400	6	16	.375	4	16	20	24	17	0	7	16	0	38	1.7	2.0	3.2
99-00–Houston	30	0	502	69	159	.434	12	29	.414	57	73	.781	16	52	68	94	32	0	23	30	1	207	2.3	3.1	6.9
Reg. Season Totals	50	0	731	86	221	.389	20	54	.370	65	94	.691	23	77	100	141	54	0	34	51	1	257	2.0	2.8	5.1

Norris, Sylvester b. February 18, 1957 Ht. 6-11 Wt. 225 College: Jackson State

SEASON–TEAM	G	GS	MIN	FGM	FGA	PCT	3FGM	3FGA	PCT	FTM	FTA	PCT	O-RB	D-RB	TOT	AST	PF	DQ	STL	TO	BLK	PTS	RPG	APG	PPG
79-80–San Antonio	17	–	189	18	43	.419	0	0	–	4	6	.667	10	33	43	6	41	1	3	19	12	40	2.5	0.4	2.4
Reg. Season Totals	17	–	189	18	43	.419	0	0	–	4	6	.667	10	33	43	6	41	1	3	19	12	40	2.5	0.4	2.4

Norwood, Willie B. b. August 8, 1947 Ht. 6-7 Wt. 220 College: Alcorn State

SEASON–TEAM	G	GS	MIN	FGM	FGA	PCT	3FGM	3FGA	PCT	FTM	FTA	PCT	O-RB	D-RB	TOT	AST	PF	DQ	STL	TO	BLK	PTS	RPG	APG	PPG
71-72–Detroit	78	–	1272	222	440	.505	–	–	–	140	215	.651	–	–	316	43	229	4	–	–	–	584	4.1	0.6	7.5
72-73–Detroit	79	–	1282	249	504	.494	–	–	–	154	225	.684	–	–	324	56	182	0	–	–	–	652	4.1	0.7	8.3
73-74–Detroit	74	–	1178	247	484	.510	–	–	–	95	143	.664	95	134	229	58	156	2	60	–	9	589	3.1	0.8	8.0
74-75–Detroit	24	–	347	64	123	.520	–	–	–	31	42	.738	31	57	88	16	51	0	23	–	0	159	3.7	0.7	6.6
75-76–Seattle	64	–	1004	146	301	.485	–	–	–	152	203	.749	91	138	229	59	139	3	42	–	4	444	3.6	0.9	6.9
76-77–Seattle	76	–	1647	216	461	.469	–	–	–	151	206	.733	127	165	292	99	191	1	62	–	6	583	3.8	1.3	7.7
77-78–Detroit-Port.	35	–	611	74	181	.409	–	–	–	50	75	.667	49	70	119	33	101	1	31	56	3	198	3.4	0.9	5.7
Reg. Season Totals	430	–	7341	1218	2494	.488	–	–	–	773	1109	.697	393	564	1597	364	1049	11	218	56	22	3209	3.7	0.8	7.5
Playoff Totals	14	–	290	38	81	.469	–	–	–	16	23	.696	22	23	45	13	43	4	8	2	3	92	3.2	0.9	6.6

Nostrand, George Thomas b. January 25, 1924 d. November 8, 1981 Ht. 6-8 Wt. 195 College: High Point; Wyoming

SEASON–TEAM	G	GS	MIN	FGM	FGA	PCT	3FGM	3FGA	PCT	FTM	FTA	PCT	O-RB	D-RB	TOT	AST	PF	DQ	STL	TO	BLK	PTS	RPG	APG	PPG
46-47–Toronto-Clev.	61	–	–	192	656	.293	–	–	–	98	210	.467	–	–	–	31	145	–	–	–	–	482	–	0.5	7.9
47-48–Providence	45	–	–	196	660	.297	–	–	–	129	239	.540	–	–	–	30	148	–	–	–	–	521	–	0.7	11.6
48-49–Prov.-Boston	60	–	–	212	651	.326	–	–	–	165	284	.581	–	–	–	94	164	–	–	–	–	589	–	1.6	9.8
49-50–Bos.-Tri-Cit-Chi.	55	–	–	78	255	.306	–	–	–	56	99	.566	–	–	–	29	118	–	–	–	–	212	–	0.5	3.9
Reg. Season Totals	221	–	–	678	2222	.305	–	–	–	448	832	.538	–	–	–	184	575	–	–	–	–	1804	–	0.8	8.2
Playoff Totals	3	–	–	14	40	.350	–	–	–	5	7	.714	–	–	–	3	10	1	–	–	–	33	–	1.0	11.0

Noszka, Stanley M. (Stan) b. September 19, 1920 Ht. 6-1 Wt. 185 College: Duquesne

SEASON–TEAM	G	GS	MIN	FGM	FGA	PCT	3FGM	3FGA	PCT	FTM	FTA	PCT	O-RB	D-RB	TOT	AST	PF	DQ	STL	TO	BLK	PTS	RPG	APG	PPG
45-46–Youngstown (N)	2	–	–	0	–	–	–	–	–	1	–	–	–	–	–	–	–	–	–	–	–	1	–	–	0.5
46-47–Pittsburgh	58	–	–	199	693	.287	–	–	–	109	157	.694	–	–	–	39	163	–	–	–	–	507	–	0.7	8.7
47-48–Boston	22	–	–	27	97	.278	–	–	–	24	35	.686	–	–	–	4	52	–	–	–	–	78	–	0.2	3.5
48-49–Boston	30	–	–	30	123	.244	–	–	–	15	30	.500	–	–	–	25	56	–	–	–	–	75	–	0.8	2.5
Reg. NBA Totals	110	–	–	256	913	.280	–	–	–	148	222	.667	–	–	–	68	271	–	–	–	–	660	–	0.6	6.0
Reg. NBL Totals	2	–	–	0	–	–	–	–	–	–	1	–	–	–	–	–	–	–	–	–	–	1	–	–	0.5
NBA Playoff Totals	3	–	–	10	60	.333	–	–	–	5	8	.625	–	–	–	4	22	–	–	–	–	25	–	0.7	8.3

N

Novak, Michael D. **(Mike)** b. April 23, 1915 d. August 15, 1978 Ht. 6-9 Wt. 220 College: Loyola (Chicago)

SEASON–TEAM	G	GS	MIN	FGM	FGA	PCT	3FGM	3FGA	PCT	FTM	FTA	PCT	O-RB	D-RB	TOT	AST	PF	DQ	STL	TO	BLK	PTS	RPG	APG	PPG
39-40–Chicago (N)	28	–	–	114	–	–	–	–	–	65	114	.570	–	–	–	–	62	–	–	–	–	293	–	–	10.5
40-41–Chicago (N)	23	–	–	56	–	–	–	–	–	34	74	.459	–	–	–	–	66	–	–	–	–	146	–	–	6.3
41-42–Chicago (N)	19	–	–	58	–	–	–	–	–	31	–	–	–	–	–	–	–	–	–	–	–	147	–	–	7.7
42-43–Chicago (N)	18	–	–	50	–	–	–	–	–	35	50	.700	–	–	–	–	51	–	–	–	–	135	–	–	7.5
43-44–Sheboygan (N)	22	–	–	39	–	–	–	–	–	14	–	–	–	–	–	–	–	–	–	–	–	92	–	–	4.2
44-45–Sheboygan (N)	27	–	–	88	–	–	–	–	–	57	–	–	–	–	–	–	–	–	–	–	–	233	–	–	8.6
45-46–Sheboygan (N)	34	–	–	111	–	–	–	–	–	88	144	.611	–	–	–	–	63	–	–	–	–	310	–	–	9.1
46-47–She.-Syr. (N)	36	–	–	153	–	–	–	–	–	73	136	.537	–	–	–	–	129	–	–	–	–	379	–	–	10.5
47-48–Syracuse (N)	60	–	–	211	–	–	–	–	–	124	201	.617	–	–	–	–	201	–	–	–	–	546	–	–	9.1
48-49–Rochester	60	–	–	124	363	.342	–	–	–	72	124	.581	–	–	–	112	188	–	–	–	–	320	–	1.9	5.3
49-50–Roch.-Phil.	60	–	–	37	149	.248	–	–	–	25	47	.532	–	–	–	61	139	–	–	–	–	99	–	1.0	1.7
53-54–Syracuse	5	–	24	0	7	.000	–	–	–	1	2	.500	–	–	2	2	9	0	–	–	–	1	0.4	0.4	0.2
Reg. NBA Totals	125	–	24	161	519	.310	–	–	–	98	173	.566	–	–	2	175	336	0	–	–	–	420	0.4	1.4	3.4
Reg. NBL Totals	267	–	–	880	–	–	–	–	–	521	719	.583	–	–	–	–	572	–	–	–	–	2281	–	–	8.5
NBA Playoff Totals	4	–	0	6	41	.268	–	–	–	1	1	1.000	–	–	–	20	13	0	–	–	–	13	–	2.5	3.3
NBL Playoff Totals	32	–	–	90	–	–	–	–	–	65	69	.565	–	–	–	–	77	–	–	–	–	245	–	–	7.7

Nowell, Melvyn P. **(Mel)** b. December 27, 1939 Ht. 6-2 Wt. 170 College: Ohio State

SEASON–TEAM	G	GS	MIN	FGM	FGA	PCT	3FGM	3FGA	PCT	FTM	FTA	PCT	O-RB	D-RB	TOT	AST	PF	DQ	STL	TO	BLK	PTS	RPG	APG	PPG
62-63–Chicago	39	–	589	92	237	.388	–	–	–	48	66	.727	–	–	67	84	86	0	–	–	–	232	1.7	2.2	5.9
67-68–New Jersey (A)	76	–	1555	273	679	.402	9	32	.281	176	213	.826	–	–	193	155	188	1	–	142	–	731	2.5	2.0	9.6
Reg. NBA Totals	39	–	589	92	237	.388	–	–	–	48	66	.727	–	–	67	84	86	0	–	–	–	232	1.7	2.2	5.9
Reg. ABA Totals	76	–	1555	273	679	.402	9	32	.281	176	213	.826	–	–	193	155	188	1	–	142	–	731	2.5	2.0	9.6

Nowitzki, Dirk b. June 19, 1978 Ht. 7-0 Wt. 237 Country: Germany

SEASON–TEAM	G	GS	MIN	FGM	FGA	PCT	3FGM	3FGA	PCT	FTM	FTA	PCT	O-RB	D-RB	TOT	AST	PF	DQ	STL	TO	BLK	PTS	RPG	APG	PPG
98-99–Dallas	47	24	958	136	336	.405	14	68	.206	99	128	.773	41	121	162	47	105	5	29	73	27	385	3.4	1.0	8.2
99-00–Dallas	82	81	2938	515	1118	.461	116	306	.379	289	348	.830	102	430	532	203	256	4	63	141	68	1435	6.5	2.5	17.5
Reg. Season Totals	129	105	3896	651	1454	.448	130	374	.348	388	476	.815	143	551	694	250	361	9	92	214	95	1820	5.4	1.9	14.1

Nutt, Dennis Clay b. March 25, 1963 Ht. 6-2 Wt. 170 College: Texas Christian

SEASON–TEAM	G	GS	MIN	FGM	FGA	PCT	3FGM	3FGA	PCT	FTM	FTA	PCT	O-RB	D-RB	TOT	AST	PF	DQ	STL	TO	BLK	PTS	RPG	APG	PPG
86-87–Dallas	25	0	91	16	40	.400	5	17	.294	20	22	.909	1	7	8	16	6	0	7	10	0	57	0.3	0.6	2.3
Reg. Season Totals	25	0	91	16	40	.400	5	17	.294	20	22	.909	1	7	8	16	6	0	7	10	0	57	0.3	0.6	2.3
Playoff Totals	1	0	10	1	5	.200	0	2	.000	0	0	–	1	1	2	1	0	0	0	1	0	2	2.0	1.0	2.0

Nwosu, Obinna Julius **(Julius)** b. May 1, 1971 Ht. 6-10 Wt. 255 College: Liberty

SEASON–TEAM	G	GS	MIN	FGM	FGA	PCT	3FGM	3FGA	PCT	FTM	FTA	PCT	O-RB	D-RB	TOT	AST	PF	DQ	STL	TO	BLK	PTS	RPG	APG	PPG
94-95–San Antonio	23	0	84	9	28	.321	0	0	–	13	17	.765	11	13	24	3	20	0	0	9	3	31	1.0	0.1	1.3
Reg. Season Totals	23	0	84	9	28	.321	0	0	–	13	17	.765	11	13	24	3	20	0	0	9	3	31	1.0	0.1	1.3
Playoff Totals	2	0	7	0	2	.000	0	0	–	0	0	–	1	1	2	–	1	0	0	1	0	0	1.0	0.0	0.0

Oakley, Charles b. December 18, 1963 Ht. 6-9 Wt. 245 College: Virginia Union

SEASON–TEAM	G	GS	MIN	FGM	FGA	PCT	3FGM	3FGA	PCT	FTM	FTA	PCT	O-RB	D-RB	TOT	AST	PF	DQ	STL	TO	BLK	PTS	RPG	APG	PPG
85-86–Chicago	77	30	1772	281	541	.519	0	3	.000	178	269	.662	255	409	664	133	250	9	68	175	30	740	8.6	1.7	9.6
86-87–Chicago	82	81	2980	468	1052	.445	11	30	.367	245	357	.686	299	775	1074	296	315	4	85	299	36	1192	13.1	3.6	14.5
87-88–Chicago	82	82	2816	375	776	.483	3	12	.250	261	359	.727	326	740	1066	248	272	2	68	241	28	1014	13.0	3.0	12.4
88-89–New York	82	82	2604	426	835	.510	12	48	.250	197	255	.773	343	518	861	187	270	1	104	248	14	1061	10.5	2.3	12.9
89-90–New York	61	61	2196	336	641	.524	0	3	.000	217	285	.761	258	469	727	146	220	3	64	165	16	889	11.9	2.4	14.6
90-91–New York	76	74	2739	307	595	.516	0	2	.000	239	305	.784	305	615	920	204	288	4	62	215	17	853	12.1	2.7	11.2
91-92–New York	82	82	2309	210	402	.522	0	3	.000	86	117	.735	256	444	700	133	258	2	67	123	15	506	8.5	1.6	6.2
92-93–New York	82	82	2230	219	431	.508	0	1	.000	127	176	.722	288	420	708	126	289	5	85	124	15	565	8.6	1.5	6.9
93-94–New York	82	82	2932	363	760	.478	0	3	.000	243	313	.776	349	616	965	218	293	4	110	193	18	969	11.8	2.7	11.8
94-95–New York	50	49	1567	192	393	.489	3	12	.250	119	150	.793	155	290	445	126	179	3	60	103	7	506	8.9	2.5	10.1
95-96–New York	53	51	1775	211	448	.471	7	26	.269	175	210	.833	162	298	460	137	195	6	58	104	14	604	8.7	2.6	11.4
96-97–New York	80	80	2873	339	694	.488	5	19	.263	181	224	.808	246	535	781	221	305	4	111	171	21	864	9.8	2.8	10.8
97-98–New York	79	79	2734	307	698	.440	0	6	.000	97	114	.851	218	506	724	201	280	4	123	126	22	711	9.2	2.5	9.0
98-99–Toronto	50	50	1633	140	327	.428	1	5	.200	67	83	.807	96	278	374	168	182	4	46	96	21	348	7.5	3.4	7.0
99-00–Toronto	80	80	2431	234	560	.418	14	41	.341	66	85	.776	117	423	540	253	294	6	102	154	45	548	6.8	3.2	6.9
Reg. Season Totals	1098	1045	35591	4408	9153	.482	56	214	.262	2498	3302	.757	3673	7336	11009	2797	3890	61	1213	2537	319	11370	10.0	2.5	10.4
Playoff Totals	132	130	4717	537	1164	.461	12	33	.364	353	469	.753	499	870	1369	262	474	6	166	286	35	1439	10.4	2.0	10.9
All-Star Totals	1	0	11	1	3	.333	0	0	–	0	0	–	1	2	3	3	3	0	0	0	0	2	3.0	3.0	2.0

O'Bannon, Charles Edward
b. February 22, 1975 Ht. 6-5 Wt. 209 College: UCLA

SEASON–TEAM	G	GS	MIN	FGM	FGA	PCT	3FGM	3FGA	PCT	FTM	FTA	PCT	O-RB	D-RB	TOT	AST	PF	DQ	STL	TO	BLK	PTS	RPG	APG	PPG
97-98–Detroit	30	0	234	26	69	.377	0	3	.000	12	15	.800	14	19	33	17	15	0	9	9	1	64	1.1	0.6	2.1
98-99–Detroit	18	1	165	24	56	.429	0	1	.000	8	8	1.000	18	16	34	12	22	0	2	8	3	56	1.9	0.7	3.1
Reg. Season Totals	48	1	399	50	125	.400	0	4	.000	20	23	.870	32	35	67	29	37	0	11	17	4	120	1.4	0.6	2.5
Playoff Totals	4	0	9	2	3	.667	0	0	–	0	0	–	1	0	1	1	0	0	0	3	0	4	0.3	0.3	1.0

O'Bannon, Edward Charles Jr. (Ed)
b. August 14, 1972 Ht. 6-8 Wt. 222 College: UCLA

SEASON–TEAM	G	GS	MIN	FGM	FGA	PCT	3FGM	3FGA	PCT	FTM	FTA	PCT	O-RB	D-RB	TOT	AST	PF	DQ	STL	TO	BLK	PTS	RPG	APG	PPG
95-96–New Jersey	64	29	1253	156	400	.390	10	56	.179	77	108	.713	65	103	168	63	95	0	44	62	11	399	2.6	1.0	6.2
96-97–N.J.-Dallas	64	5	809	93	279	.333	18	70	.257	31	35	.886	50	98	148	39	97	0	29	20	12	235	2.3	0.6	3.7
Reg. Season Totals	128	34	2062	249	679	.367	28	126	.222	108	143	.755	115	201	316	102	192	0	73	82	23	634	2.5	0.8	5.0

O'Boyle, John W.
b. March 7, 1928 Ht. 6-2 Wt. 185 College: Modesto (Calif.) J.C.; Colorado State

SEASON–TEAM	G	GS	MIN	FGM	FGA	PCT	3FGM	3FGA	PCT	FTM	FTA	PCT	O-RB	D-RB	TOT	AST	PF	DQ	STL	TO	BLK	PTS	RPG	APG	PPG
52-53–Milwaukee	5	–	97	8	26	.308	–	–	–	5	7	.714	–	–	10	5	20	1	–	–	–	21	2.0	1.0	4.2
Reg. Season Totals	5	–	97	8	26	.308	–	–	–	5	7	.714	–	–	10	5	20	1	–	–	–	21	2.0	1.0	4.2

O'Brien, James J. (Jimmy)
b. April 9, 1949 Ht. 6-2 Wt. 170 College: Boston College

SEASON–TEAM	G	GS	MIN	FGM	FGA	PCT	3FGM	3FGA	PCT	FTM	FTA	PCT	O-RB	D-RB	TOT	AST	PF	DQ	STL	TO	BLK	PTS	RPG	APG	PPG
71-72–Pitt.-Ken. (A)	84	–	1778	173	436	.397	7	32	.219	65	80	.813	–	–	206	373	189	–	–	152	–	418	2.5	4.4	5.0
72-73–Kentucky (A)	68	–	1014	126	317	.397	0	9	.000	68	89	.764	27	65	92	174	103	0	–	77	–	320	1.4	2.6	4.7
73-74–Ken.-S.D. (A)	72	–	1320	211	513	.411	7	27	.259	79	95	.832	49	85	134	254	79	–	63	113	1	508	1.9	3.5	7.1
74-75–San Diego (A)	79	–	2036	210	525	.400	4	34	.118	125	142	.880	50	136	186	443	147	–	89	192	2	549	2.4	5.6	6.9
Reg. ABA Totals	303	–	6148	720	1791	.402	18	102	.176	337	406	.830	126	286	618	1244	518	0	152	534	3	1795	2.0	4.1	5.9
ABA Playoff Totals	30	–	610	57	148	.385	2	7	.286	46	55	.836	1	8	46	111	41	0	25	40	1	162	1.5	3.7	5.4

O'Brien, James M. (Jim)
b. November 7, 1951 Ht. 6-7 Wt. 200 College: Maryland

SEASON–TEAM	G	GS	MIN	FGM	FGA	PCT	3FGM	3FGA	PCT	FTM	FTA	PCT	O-RB	D-RB	TOT	AST	PF	DQ	STL	TO	BLK	PTS	RPG	APG	PPG
73-74–New York (A)	11	–	54	15	37	.405	0	4	.000	9	15	.600	13	4	17	6	5	–	3	8	3	39	1.5	0.5	3.5
74-75–Memphis (A)	47	–	611	88	203	.433	6	26	.231	47	60	.783	45	76	121	81	56	–	38	73	23	229	2.6	1.7	4.9
Reg. ABA Totals	58	–	665	103	240	.429	6	30	.200	56	75	.747	58	80	138	87	61	0	41	81	26	268	2.4	1.5	4.6
ABA Playoff Totals	7	–	42	6	19	.316	0	1	.000	2	2	1.000	2	6	8	8	3	0	3	1	0	14	1.1	1.1	2.0

O'Brien, Ralph E. (Buckshot)
b. April 28, 1928 Ht. 5-9 Wt. 160 College: Butler

SEASON–TEAM	G	GS	MIN	FGM	FGA	PCT	3FGM	3FGA	PCT	FTM	FTA	PCT	O-RB	D-RB	TOT	AST	PF	DQ	STL	TO	BLK	PTS	RPG	APG	PPG
51-52–Indianapolis	64	–	1577	228	613	.372	–	–	–	122	149	.819	–	–	122	124	115	0	–	–	–	578	1.9	1.9	9.0
52-53–Ind.-Ft.W-Balt.	55	–	758	96	286	.336	–	–	–	78	92	.848	–	–	70	56	74	0	–	–	–	270	1.3	1.0	4.9
Reg. Season Totals	119	–	2335	324	899	.360	–	–	–	200	241	.830	–	–	192	180	189	0	–	–	–	848	1.6	1.5	7.1
Playoff Totals	3	–	116	5	13	.385	–	–	–	7	7	1.000	–	–	7	6	3	0	–	–	–	17	1.4	1.2	5.7

O'Brien, Robert (Bob)
b. January 26, 1927 Ht. 6-4 Wt. 190 College: Kansas; Pepperdine

SEASON–TEAM	G	GS	MIN	FGM	FGA	PCT	3FGM	3FGA	PCT	FTM	FTA	PCT	O-RB	D-RB	TOT	AST	PF	DQ	STL	TO	BLK	PTS	RPG	APG	PPG
47-48–Philadelphia	22	–	–	17	81	.210	–	–	–	15	26	.577	–	–	–	1	40	–	–	–	–	49	–	0.0	2.2
48-49–Phil.-St. Louis	24	–	–	10	50	.200	–	–	–	12	32	.375	–	–	–	9	32	–	–	–	–	32	–	0.4	1.3
Reg. Season Totals	46	–	–	27	131	.206	–	–	–	27	58	.466	–	–	–	10	72	–	–	–	–	81	–	0.2	1.8
Playoff Totals	9	–	–	9	38	.237	–	–	–	10	15	.667	–	–	–	3	13	–	–	–	–	28	–	0.3	3.1

O'Connell, Dermott F. (Dermie)
b. April 13, 1928 d. October 5, 1988 Ht. 6-0 Wt. 175 College: Holy Cross

SEASON–TEAM	G	GS	MIN	FGM	FGA	PCT	3FGM	3FGA	PCT	FTM	FTA	PCT	O-RB	D-RB	TOT	AST	PF	DQ	STL	TO	BLK	PTS	RPG	APG	PPG
48-49–Boston	21	–	–	87	315	.276	–	–	–	30	56	.536	–	–	–	65	40	–	–	–	–	204	–	3.1	9.7
49-50–Boston-St. Louis	61	–	–	111	425	.261	–	–	–	47	89	.528	–	–	–	91	91	–	–	–	–	269	–	1.5	4.4
Reg. Season Totals	82	–	–	198	740	.268	–	–	–	77	145	.531	–	–	–	156	131	–	–	–	–	473	–	1.9	5.8

Odom, Lamar Joseph
b. November 6, 1979 Ht. 6-10 Wt. 220 College: Nevada-Las Vegas; Rhode Island

SEASON–TEAM	G	GS	MIN	FGM	FGA	PCT	3FGM	3FGA	PCT	FTM	FTA	PCT	O-RB	D-RB	TOT	AST	PF	DQ	STL	TO	BLK	PTS	RPG	APG	PPG
99-00–L.A. Clippers	76	70	2767	449	1024	.438	59	164	.360	302	420	.719	159	436	595	317	291	13	91	258	95	1259	7.8	4.2	16.6
Reg. Season Totals	76	70	2767	449	1024	.438	59	164	.360	302	420	.719	159	436	595	317	291	13	91	258	95	1259	7.8	4.2	16.6

O'Donnell, Andrew J. (Andy)
b. March 10, 1925 Ht. 6-1 Wt. 180 College: Loyola (Balt.)

SEASON–TEAM	G	GS	MIN	FGM	FGA	PCT	3FGM	3FGA	PCT	FTM	FTA	PCT	O-RB	D-RB	TOT	AST	PF	DQ	STL	TO	BLK	PTS	RPG	APG	PPG
49-50–Baltimore	25	–	–	38	108	.352	–	–	–	14	18	.778	–	–	–	17	32	–	–	–	–	90	–	0.7	3.6
Reg. Season Totals	25	–	–	38	108	.352	–	–	–	14	18	.778	–	–	–	17	32	–	–	–	–	90	–	0.7	3.6

Ogden, Carlos (Bud) b. December 29, 1946 Ht. 6-6 Wt. 215 College: Santa Clara

SEASON–TEAM	G	GS	MIN	FGM	FGA	PCT	3FGM	3FGA	PCT	FTM	FTA	PCT	O-RB	D-RB	TOT	AST	PF	DQ	STL	TO	BLK	PTS	RPG	APG	PPG
69-70–Philadelphia	47	–	357	82	172	.477	–	–	–	27	39	.692	–	–	86	31	62	2	–	–	–	191	1.8	0.7	4.1
70-71–Philadelphia	27	–	133	24	66	.364	–	–	–	18	26	.692	–	–	20	17	21	0	–	–	–	66	0.7	0.6	2.4
Reg. Season Totals	74	–	490	106	238	.445	–	–	–	45	65	.692	–	–	106	48	83	2	–	–	–	257	1.4	0.6	3.5
Playoff Totals	2	–	16	5	11	.455	–	–	–	2	4	.500	–	–	3	6	1	0	–	–	–	12	1.5	3.0	6.0

Ogden, Ralph b. January 25, 1948 Ht. 6-5 Wt. 205 College: Santa Clara

SEASON–TEAM	G	GS	MIN	FGM	FGA	PCT	3FGM	3FGA	PCT	FTM	FTA	PCT	O-RB	D-RB	TOT	AST	PF	DQ	STL	TO	BLK	PTS	RPG	APG	PPG
70-71–San Francisco	32	–	162	17	71	.239	–	–	–	8	12	.667	–	–	32	9	17	0	–	–	–	42	1.0	0.3	1.3
Reg. Season Totals	32	–	162	17	71	.239	–	–	–	8	12	.667	–	–	32	9	17	0	–	–	–	42	1.0	0.3	1.3
Playoff Totals	2	–	15	1	5	.200	–	–	–	4	4	1.000	–	–	4	1	0	0	–	–	–	6	2.0	0.5	3.0

Ogg, Raymond Alan (Alan) b. July 5, 1967 Ht. 7-2 Wt. 245 College: Alabama-Birmingham

SEASON–TEAM	G	GS	MIN	FGM	FGA	PCT	3FGM	3FGA	PCT	FTM	FTA	PCT	O-RB	D-RB	TOT	AST	PF	DQ	STL	TO	BLK	PTS	RPG	APG	PPG
90-91–Miami	31	1	261	24	55	.436	0	2	.000	6	10	.600	15	34	49	2	53	1	6	8	27	54	1.6	0.1	1.7
91-92–Miami	43	0	367	46	84	.548	0	0	–	16	30	.533	30	44	74	7	73	0	5	19	28	108	1.7	0.2	2.5
92-93–Milw.-Wash.	6	0	29	5	13	.385	0	0	–	3	4	.750	3	7	10	4	6	0	1	3	3	13	1.7	0.7	2.2
Reg. Season Totals	80	1	657	75	152	.493	0	2	.000	25	44	.568	48	85	133	13	132	1	12	30	58	175	1.7	0.2	2.2
Playoff Totals	3	0	15	1	3	.333	0	0	–	1	2	.500	0	1	1	–	3	0	1	0	3	3	0.3	0.0	1.0

O'Grady, Francis David (Buddy) b. January 19, 1920 d. February 19, 1992 Ht. 5-11 Wt. 160 College: Georgetown

SEASON–TEAM	G	GS	MIN	FGM	FGA	PCT	3FGM	3FGA	PCT	FTM	FTA	PCT	O-RB	D-RB	TOT	AST	PF	DQ	STL	TO	BLK	PTS	RPG	APG	PPG
45-46–Rochester (N)	1	–	–	0	–	–	–	–	–	0	–	–	–	–	–	–	–	–	–	–	–	0	–	–	0.0
46-47–Washington	55	–	–	55	231	.238	–	–	–	38	53	.717	–	–	–	20	60	–	–	–	–	148	–	0.4	2.7
47-48–St. Louis	44	–	–	67	257	.261	–	–	–	36	54	.667	–	–	–	9	61	–	–	–	–	170	–	0.2	3.9
48-49–St. Louis-Prov.	47	–	–	85	293	.290	–	–	–	49	71	.690	–	–	–	68	57	–	–	–	–	219	–	1.4	4.7
Reg. NBA Totals	146	–	–	207	781	.265	–	–	–	123	178	.691	–	–	–	97	178	–	–	–	–	537	–	0.7	3.7
Reg. NBL Totals	1	–	–	0	–	–	–	–	–	0	0	–	–	–	–	–	–	–	–	–	–	0	–	–	0.0
NBA Playoff Totals	14	–	–	13	73	.205	–	–	–	8	8	1.000	–	–	–	–	10	–	–	–	–	34	0.0	0.0	2.4

O'Hanlon, Francis Brian (Fran) b. August 24, 1948 Ht. 6-1 Wt. 175 College: Villanova

SEASON–TEAM	G	GS	MIN	FGM	FGA	PCT	3FGM	3FGA	PCT	FTM	FTA	PCT	O-RB	D-RB	TOT	AST	PF	DQ	STL	TO	BLK	PTS	RPG	APG	PPG
70-71–Floridians (A)	14	–	101	8	22	.364	0	1	.000	6	9	.667	–	–	4	13	18	–	–	–	–	22	0.3	0.9	1.6
Reg. ABA Totals	14	–	101	8	22	.364	0	1	.000	6	9	.667	–	–	4	13	18	–	–	–	–	22	0.3	0.9	1.6

Ohl, Donald Jay (Don) b. April 18, 1936 Ht. 6-3 Wt. 190 College: Illinois

SEASON–TEAM	G	GS	MIN	FGM	FGA	PCT	3FGM	3FGA	PCT	FTM	FTA	PCT	O-RB	D-RB	TOT	AST	PF	DQ	STL	TO	BLK	PTS	RPG	APG	PPG
60-61–Detroit	79	–	2172	427	1085	.394	–	–	–	200	278	.719	–	–	256	265	224	3	–	–	–	1054	3.2	3.4	13.3
61-62–Detroit	77	–	2526	555	1250	.444	–	–	–	201	280	.718	–	–	267	244	173	2	–	–	–	1311	3.5	3.2	17.0
62-63–Detroit	80	–	2961	636	1450	.439	–	–	–	275	380	.724	–	–	239	325	234	3	–	–	–	1547	3.0	4.1	19.3
63-64–Detroit	71	–	2366	500	1224	.408	–	–	–	225	331	.680	–	–	180	225	219	3	–	–	–	1225	2.5	3.2	17.3
64-65–Baltimore	77	–	2821	568	1297	.438	–	–	–	284	388	.732	–	–	336	250	274	7	–	–	–	1420	4.4	3.2	18.4
65-66–Baltimore	73	–	2645	593	1334	.445	–	–	–	316	430	.735	–	–	280	290	208	1	–	–	–	1502	3.8	4.0	20.6
66-67–Baltimore	58	–	2024	452	1002	.451	–	–	–	276	354	.780	–	–	189	168	153	1	–	–	–	1180	3.3	2.9	20.3
67-68–Balt.-St. Louis	70	–	1919	393	891	.441	–	–	–	197	254	.776	–	–	175	157	184	1	–	–	–	983	2.5	2.2	14.0
68-69–Atlanta	76	–	1995	385	901	.427	–	–	–	147	208	.707	–	–	170	221	232	5	–	–	–	917	2.2	2.9	12.1
69-70–Atlanta	66	–	984	176	372	.473	–	–	–	58	72	.806	–	–	71	98	113	1	–	–	–	410	1.1	1.5	6.2
Reg. Season Totals	727	–	22413	4685	10806	.434	–	–	–	2179	2975	.732	–	–	2163	2243	2014	27	–	–	–	11549	3.0	3.1	15.9
Playoff Totals	47	–	1482	320	749	.427	–	–	–	155	206	.752	–	–	161	130	154	3	–	–	–	795	3.4	2.8	16.9
All-Star Totals	5	–	87	16	43	.372	–	–	–	14	15	.933	–	–	9	7	10	0	–	–	–	46	1.8	1.4	9.2

O'Keefe, Richard T. (Dick) b. September 29, 1923 Ht. 6-2 Wt. 185 College: Santa Clara

SEASON–TEAM	G	GS	MIN	FGM	FGA	PCT	3FGM	3FGA	PCT	FTM	FTA	PCT	O-RB	D-RB	TOT	AST	PF	DQ	STL	TO	BLK	PTS	RPG	APG	PPG
47-48–Washington	37	–	–	63	257	.245	–	–	–	30	59	.508	–	–	–	18	85	–	–	–	–	156	–	0.5	4.2
48-49–Washington	50	–	–	70	274	.255	–	–	–	51	99	.515	–	–	–	43	119	–	–	–	–	191	–	0.9	3.8
49-50–Washington	68	–	–	162	529	.306	–	–	–	150	203	.739	–	–	–	74	247	–	–	–	–	474	–	1.1	7.0
50-51–Washington	17	–	–	21	102	.206	–	–	–	25	39	.641	–	–	37	25	48	0	–	–	–	67	2.2	1.5	3.9
Reg. Season Totals	172	–	–	316	1162	.272	–	–	–	256	400	.640	–	–	37	160	499	0	–	–	–	888	2.2	0.9	5.2
Playoff Totals	13	–	–	26	118	.364	–	–	–	20	31	.710	–	–	–	22	55	0	–	–	–	72	–	1.0	5.5

O'Keefe, Thomas V. (Tommy) b. July 16, 1926 Ht. 6-2 Wt. 185 College: Notre Dame; Georgetown

SEASON–TEAM	G	GS	MIN	FGM	FGA	PCT	3FGM	3FGA	PCT	FTM	FTA	PCT	O-RB	D-RB	TOT	AST	PF	DQ	STL	TO	BLK	PTS	RPG	APG	PPG
50-51–Balt.-Wash.	6	–	–	10	28	.357	–	–	–	3	4	.750	–	–	7	10	5	0	–	–	–	23	1.2	1.7	3.8
Reg. Season Totals	6	–	–	10	28	.357	–	–	–	3	4	.750	–	–	7	10	5	0	–	–	–	23	1.2	1.7	3.8

O'Koren, Michael F. **(Mike)** b. February 7, 1958 Ht. 6-7 Wt. 205 College: North Carolina

SEASON–TEAM	G	GS	MIN	FGM	FGA	PCT	3FGM	3FGA	PCT	FTM	FTA	PCT	O-RB	D-RB	TOT	AST	PF	DQ	STL	TO	BLK	PTS	RPG	APG	PPG
80-81–New Jersey	79	–	2473	365	751	.486	5	18	.278	135	212	.637	179	299	478	252	243	8	86	146	27	870	6.1	3.2	11.0
81-82–New Jersey	80	32	2018	383	778	.492	8	23	.348	135	189	.714	111	194	305	192	175	0	83	147	13	909	3.8	2.4	11.4
82-83–New Jersey	46	14	803	136	259	.525	2	9	.222	34	48	.708	42	72	114	82	67	0	42	62	11	308	2.5	1.8	6.7
83-84–New Jersey	73	25	1191	186	385	.483	5	28	.179	53	87	.609	71	104	175	95	148	3	34	75	11	430	2.4	1.3	5.9
84-85–New Jersey	43	29	1119	194	393	.494	8	21	.381	42	67	.627	46	120	166	102	115	1	32	51	16	438	3.9	2.4	10.2
85-86–New Jersey	67	11	1031	160	336	.476	7	27	.259	23	39	.590	33	102	135	118	134	3	29	54	9	350	2.0	1.8	5.2
86-87–Washington	15	0	123	16	42	.381	0	2	.000	0	2	.000	6	8	14	13	10	0	2	6	0	32	0.9	0.9	2.1
87-88–New Jersey	4	0	52	9	16	.563	0	1	.000	0	4	.000	1	3	4	2	2	0	3	0	2	18	1.0	0.5	4.5
Reg. Season Totals	407	111	8810	1449	2960	.490	35	129	.271	422	648	.651	489	902	1391	856	894	15	311	541	89	3355	3.4	2.1	8.2
Playoff Totals	20	11	333	34	91	.374	0	3	.000	6	10	.600	21	40	61	33	59	2	6	20	5	74	3.1	1.7	3.7

Olajuwon, Hakeem Abdul **(Hakeem the Dream)** b. January 21, 1963 Ht. 7-0 Wt. 255 College: Houston

SEASON–TEAM	G	GS	MIN	FGM	FGA	PCT	3FGM	3FGA	PCT	FTM	FTA	PCT	O-RB	D-RB	TOT	AST	PF	DQ	STL	TO	BLK	PTS	RPG	APG	PPG
84-85–Houston	82	82	2914	677	1258	.538	0	0	–	338	551	.613	440	534	974	111	344	10	99	234	220	1692	11.9	1.4	20.6
85-86–Houston	68	68	2467	625	1188	.526	0	0	–	347	538	.645	333	448	781	137	271	9	134	195	231	1597	11.5	2.0	23.5
86-87–Houston	75	75	2760	677	1332	.508	1	5	.200	400	570	.702	315	543	858	220	294	8	140	228	254	1755	11.4	2.9	23.4
87-88–Houston	79	79	2825	712	1385	.514	0	4	.000	381	548	.695	302	657	959	163	324	7	162	243	214	1805	12.1	2.1	22.8
88-89–Houston	82	82	3024	790	1556	.508	0	10	.000	454	652	.696	338	767	1105	149	329	10	213	275	282	2034	13.5	1.8	24.8
89-90–Houston	82	82	3124	806	1609	.501	1	6	.167	382	536	.713	299	850	1149	234	314	6	174	316	376	1995	14.0	2.9	24.3
90-91–Houston	56	50	2062	487	959	.508	0	4	.000	213	277	.769	219	551	770	131	221	5	121	174	221	1187	13.8	2.3	21.2
91-92–Houston	70	69	2636	591	1177	.502	0	1	.000	328	428	.766	246	599	845	157	263	7	127	187	304	1510	12.1	2.2	21.6
92-93–Houston	82	82	3242	848	1603	.529	0	8	.000	444	570	.779	283	785	1068	291	305	5	150	262	342	2140	13.0	3.5	26.1
93-94–Houston	80	80	3277	894	1694	.528	8	19	.421	388	542	.716	229	726	955	287	289	4	128	271	297	2184	11.9	3.6	27.3
94-95–Houston	72	72	2853	798	1545	.517	3	16	.188	406	537	.756	172	603	775	255	250	3	133	237	242	2005	10.8	3.5	27.8
95-96–Houston	72	72	2797	768	1494	.514	3	14	.214	397	548	.724	176	608	784	257	242	0	113	247	207	1936	10.9	3.6	26.9
96-97–Houston	78	78	2852	727	1426	.510	5	16	.313	351	446	.787	173	543	716	236	249	3	117	281	173	1810	9.2	3.0	23.2
97-98–Houston	47	45	1633	306	633	.483	0	3	.000	160	212	.755	116	344	460	143	152	0	84	126	96	772	9.8	3.0	16.4
98-99–Houston	50	50	1784	373	725	.514	4	13	.308	195	272	.717	106	372	478	88	160	3	82	139	123	945	9.6	1.8	18.9
99-00–Houston	44	28	1049	193	421	.458	0	2	.000	69	112	.616	65	209	274	61	88	0	41	73	70	455	6.2	1.4	10.3
Reg. Season Totals	1119	1094	41299	10272	20005	.513	25	121	.207	5253	7339	.716	3812	9139	12951	2920	4095	80	2018	3488	3652	25822	11.6	2.6	23.1
Playoff Totals	140	140	5663	1492	2825	.528	4	18	.222	739	1028	.719	462	1140	1602	456	553	5	238	418	468	3727	11.4	3.3	26.6
All-Star Totals	12	8	270	45	110	.409	1	1	1.000	26	50	.520	38	56	94	17	31	1	15	26	23	117	7.8	1.4	9.8

Olberding, Mark Allen b. April 21, 1956 Ht. 6-8 Wt. 230 College: Minnesota

SEASON–TEAM	G	GS	MIN	FGM	FGA	PCT	3FGM	3FGA	PCT	FTM	FTA	PCT	O-RB	D-RB	TOT	AST	PF	DQ	STL	TO	BLK	PTS	RPG	APG	PPG
75-76–S.D.-S.A. (A)	81	–	2055	302	607	.498	0	0	–	191	247	.773	184	346	530	142	249	–	50	141	37	795	6.5	1.8	9.8
76-77–San Antonio	82	–	1949	301	598	.503	–	–	–	251	316	.794	162	287	449	119	277	6	59	–	29	853	5.5	1.5	10.4
77-78–San Antonio	79	–	1773	231	480	.481	–	–	–	184	227	.811	104	269	373	131	235	1	45	118	26	646	4.7	1.7	8.2
78-79–San Antonio	80	–	1885	261	551	.474	–	–	–	233	290	.803	96	333	429	211	282	2	53	163	18	755	5.4	2.6	9.4
79-80–San Antonio	75	–	2111	291	609	.478	0	3	.000	210	264	.795	83	335	418	327	274	7	67	180	22	792	5.6	4.4	10.6
80-81–San Antonio	82	–	2408	348	685	.508	1	7	.143	315	380	.829	146	325	471	277	307	6	75	202	31	1012	5.7	3.4	12.3
81-82–San Antonio	68	63	2098	333	705	.472	2	12	.167	273	338	.808	118	321	439	202	253	5	57	139	29	941	6.5	3.0	13.8
82-83–Chicago	80	31	1817	251	522	.481	2	12	.167	194	248	.782	108	250	358	131	246	3	50	152	9	698	4.5	1.6	8.7
83-84–Kansas City	81	81	2160	249	504	.494	0	1	.000	261	318	.821	119	326	445	192	291	2	50	166	28	759	5.5	2.4	9.4
84-85–Kansas City	81	62	2277	265	528	.502	0	3	.000	293	352	.832	139	374	513	243	298	8	56	185	11	823	6.3	3.0	10.2
85-86–Sacramento	81	64	2157	225	403	.558	0	2	.000	162	210	.771	113	310	423	266	276	3	43	148	23	612	5.2	3.3	7.6
86-87–Sacramento	76	0	1002	69	165	.418	0	1	.000	116	131	.885	50	135	185	91	144	0	18	56	9	254	2.4	1.2	3.3
Reg. NBA Totals	865	301	21637	2824	5750	.491	5	41	.122	2492	3074	.811	1238	3265	4503	2190	2883	43	573	1509	235	8145	5.2	2.5	9.4
Reg. ABA Totals	81	–	2055	302	607	.498	0	0	–	191	247	.773	184	346	530	142	249	–	50	141	37	795	6.5	1.8	9.8
NBA Playoff Totals	47	15	1366	204	435	.469	1	4	.250	112	144	.778	67	188	255	131	183	5	35	95	20	521	5.4	2.8	11.1
ABA Playoff Totals	7	–	73	5	15	.333	0	0	–	3	6	.500	7	15	22	3	15	–	3	4	2	13	3.1	0.4	1.9

Oldham, Jawann b. July 4, 1957 Ht. 7-0 Wt. 220 College: Seattle

SEASON–TEAM	G	GS	MIN	FGM	FGA	PCT	3FGM	3FGA	PCT	FTM	FTA	PCT	O-RB	D-RB	TOT	AST	PF	DQ	STL	TO	BLK	PTS	RPG	APG	PPG
80-81–Denver	4	–	21	2	6	.333	0	0	–	0	0	–	3	2	5	0	3	0	0	2	2	4	1.3	0.0	1.0
81-82–Houston	22	0	124	13	36	.361	0	0	–	8	14	.571	7	17	24	3	28	0	2	6	10	34	1.1	0.1	1.5
82-83–Chicago	16	0	171	31	58	.534	0	0	–	12	22	.545	18	29	47	5	30	1	5	13	13	74	2.9	0.3	4.6
83-84–Chicago	64	0	870	110	218	.505	0	0	–	39	66	.591	75	158	233	33	139	2	15	83	76	259	3.6	0.5	4.0
84-85–Chicago	63	0	993	89	192	.464	0	1	.000	34	50	.680	79	157	236	31	166	3	11	58	127	212	3.7	0.5	3.4
85-86–Chicago	52	47	1276	167	323	.517	0	1	.000	53	91	.582	112	194	306	37	206	6	28	86	134	387	5.9	0.7	7.4
86-87–New York	44	9	776	71	174	.408	0	1	.000	31	57	.544	51	128	179	19	95	1	22	48	71	173	4.1	0.4	3.9
87-88–Sacramento	54	13	946	119	250	.476	0	0	–	59	87	.678	82	222	304	33	143	2	12	62	110	297	5.6	0.6	5.5
89-90–Orlando-Lakers	6	0	45	3	6	.500	0	0	–	3	7	.429	4	12	16	1	9	0	2	4	3	9	2.7	0.2	1.5
90-91–Indiana	4	0	19	3	6	.500	0	0	–	0	0	–	0	3	3	0	1	0	0	0	0	6	0.8	0.0	1.5
Reg. Season Totals	329	69	5241	608	1269	.479	0	3	.000	239	394	.607	431	922	1353	162	820	15	97	362	546	1455	4.1	0.5	4.4
Playoff Totals	5	0	95	7	16	.438	0	0	–	0	0	–	9	15	24	3	19	1	6	12	7	14	4.8	0.6	2.8

Oldham, John O. **(Johnny)** b. June 22, 1923 Ht. 6-3 Wt. 185 College: Western Kentucky

SEASON–TEAM	G	GS	MIN	FGM	FGA	PCT	3FGM	3FGA	PCT	FTM	FTA	PCT	O-RB	D-RB	TOT	AST	PF	DQ	STL	TO	BLK	PTS	RPG	APG	PPG
49-50–Fort Wayne	59	–	–	127	426	.298	–	–	–	103	145	.710	–	–	–	99	192	–	–	–	–	357	–	1.7	6.1
50-51–Fort Wayne	68	–	–	199	597	.333	–	–	–	171	292	.586	–	–	242	127	242	15	–	–	–	569	3.6	1.9	8.4
Reg. Season Totals	127	–	–	326	1023	.319	–	–	–	274	437	.627	–	–	242	226	434	15	–	–	–	926	3.6	1.8	7.3
Playoff Totals	7	–	–	18	70	.429	–	–	–	18	27	.667	–	–	5	13	28	1	–	–	–	54	1.7	1.2	7.7

Oleynick, Frank b. February 20, 1955 Ht. 6-2 Wt. 190 College: Seattle

SEASON–TEAM	G	GS	MIN	FGM	FGA	PCT	3FGM	3FGA	PCT	FTM	FTA	PCT	O-RB	D-RB	TOT	AST	PF	DQ	STL	TO	BLK	PTS	RPG	APG	PPG
75-76–Seattle	52	–	650	127	316	.402	–	–	–	53	77	.688	10	35	45	53	62	0	21	–	6	307	0.9	1.0	5.9
76-77–Seattle	50	–	516	81	223	.363	–	–	–	39	53	.736	13	32	45	60	48	0	13	–	4	201	0.9	1.2	4.0
Reg. Season Totals	102	–	1166	208	539	.386	–	–	–	92	130	.708	23	67	90	113	110	0	34	–	10	508	0.9	1.1	5.0

Olive, John b. March 1, 1955 Ht. 6-7 Wt. 215 College: Villanova

SEASON–TEAM	G	GS	MIN	FGM	FGA	PCT	3FGM	3FGA	PCT	FTM	FTA	PCT	O-RB	D-RB	TOT	AST	PF	DQ	STL	TO	BLK	PTS	RPG	APG	PPG
78-79–San Diego	34	–	189	13	40	.325	–	–	–	18	23	.783	3	16	19	3	32	0	4	13	0	44	0.6	0.1	1.3
79-80–San Diego	1	–	15	0	2	.000	0	0	–	0	0	–	0	1	1	0	2	0	0	2	0	0	1.0	0.0	0.0
Reg. Season Totals	35	–	204	13	42	.310	0	0	–	18	23	.783	3	17	20	3	34	0	4	15	0	44	0.6	0.1	1.3

Oliver, Brian Darnell b. June 1, 1968 Ht. 6-4 Wt. 210 College: Georgia Tech

SEASON–TEAM	G	GS	MIN	FGM	FGA	PCT	3FGM	3FGA	PCT	FTM	FTA	PCT	O-RB	D-RB	TOT	AST	PF	DQ	STL	TO	BLK	PTS	RPG	APG	PPG
90-91–Philadelphia	73	4	800	111	272	.408	5	18	.278	52	71	.732	18	62	80	88	76	0	34	50	4	279	1.1	1.2	3.8
91-92–Philadelphia	34	0	279	33	100	.330	0	4	.000	15	22	.682	10	20	30	20	33	0	10	24	2	81	0.9	0.6	2.4
94-95–Washington	6	0	42	4	9	.444	0	0	–	6	8	.750	0	4	4	4	8	0	0	3	0	14	0.7	0.7	2.3
97-98–Atlanta	5	0	61	7	19	.368	0	0	–	1	4	.250	3	6	9	2	4	0	1	1	0	15	1.8	0.4	3.0
Reg. Season Totals	118	4	1182	155	400	.388	5	22	.227	74	105	.705	31	92	123	114	121	0	45	78	6	389	1.0	1.0	3.3
Playoff Totals	4	0	15	2	6	.333	0	0	–	2	2	1.000	0	0	0	1	4	0	1	0	0	6	0.0	0.3	1.5

Oliver, Jimmy Allen b. July 12, 1969 Ht. 6-5 Wt. 210 College: Purdue

SEASON–TEAM	G	GS	MIN	FGM	FGA	PCT	3FGM	3FGA	PCT	FTM	FTA	PCT	O-RB	D-RB	TOT	AST	PF	DQ	STL	TO	BLK	PTS	RPG	APG	PPG
91-92–Cleveland	27	8	252	39	98	.398	1	9	.111	17	22	.773	9	18	27	20	22	0	9	9	2	96	1.0	0.7	3.6
93-94–Boston	44	6	540	89	214	.416	13	32	.406	25	33	.758	8	38	46	33	39	0	16	21	1	216	1.0	0.8	4.9
96-97–Toronto	4	0	43	4	13	.308	1	6	.167	2	2	1.000	1	4	5	1	2	0	2	3	0	11	1.3	0.3	2.8
97-98–Washington	1	0	10	2	4	.500	1	2	.500	0	0	–	0	2	2	1	1	0	0	0	0	5	2.0	1.0	5.0
98-99–Phoenix	2	0	11	1	3	.333	1	1	1.000	0	0	–	0	0	0	0	2	0	0	0	0	3	0.0	0.0	1.5
Reg. Season Totals	78	14	856	135	332	.407	17	50	.340	44	57	.772	18	62	80	55	66	0	27	33	3	331	1.0	0.7	4.2

Ollie, Kevin Jermaine b. December 27, 1972 Ht. 6-4 Wt. 195 College: Connecticut

SEASON–TEAM	G	GS	MIN	FGM	FGA	PCT	3FGM	3FGA	PCT	FTM	FTA	PCT	O-RB	D-RB	TOT	AST	PF	DQ	STL	TO	BLK	PTS	RPG	APG	PPG
97-98–Dallas-Orlando	35	0	430	37	98	.378	0	1	.000	49	70	.700	9	30	39	65	31	0	13	44	0	123	1.1	1.9	3.5
98-99–Sac.-Orlando	8	0	72	4	14	.286	0	0	–	5	7	.714	0	7	7	3	9	0	3	3	1	13	0.9	0.4	1.6
99-00–Philadelphia	40	0	290	22	49	.449	0	0	–	28	37	.757	4	27	31	46	27	0	10	10	0	72	0.8	1.2	1.8
Reg. Season Totals	83	0	792	63	161	.391	0	1	.000	82	114	.719	13	64	77	114	67	0	26	57	1	208	0.9	1.4	2.5
Playoff Totals	10	0	65	6	12	.500	0	0	–	8	9	.889	0	5	5	12	5	0	2	3	0	20	0.5	1.2	2.0

Ollrich, Gene W. **(Moe)** b. June 30, 1922 Ht. 5-11 Wt. 160 College: Drake

SEASON–TEAM	G	GS	MIN	FGM	FGA	PCT	3FGM	3FGA	PCT	FTM	FTA	PCT	O-RB	D-RB	TOT	AST	PF	DQ	STL	TO	BLK	PTS	RPG	APG	PPG
49-50–Waterloo	14	–	–	17	72	.236	–	–	–	10	14	.714	–	–	–	24	34	–	–	–	–	44	–	1.7	3.1
Reg. Season Totals	14	–	–	17	72	.236	–	–	–	10	14	.714	–	–	–	24	34	–	–	–	–	44	–	1.7	3.1

Olowokandi, Michael **(Kandi)** b. April 3, 1975 Ht. 7-0 Wt. 269 College: U. of Pacific

SEASON–TEAM	G	GS	MIN	FGM	FGA	PCT	3FGM	3FGA	PCT	FTM	FTA	PCT	O-RB	D-RB	TOT	AST	PF	DQ	STL	TO	BLK	PTS	RPG	APG	PPG
98-99–L.A. Clippers	45	36	1279	172	399	.431	0	0	–	57	118	.483	120	237	357	25	137	2	27	85	55	401	7.9	0.6	8.9
99-00–L.A. Clippers	80	77	2493	330	756	.437	0	0	–	123	189	.651	194	462	656	38	304	10	35	177	140	783	8.2	0.5	9.8
Reg. Season Totals	125	113	3772	502	1155	.435	0	0	–	180	307	.586	314	699	1013	63	441	12	62	262	195	1184	8.1	0.5	9.5

Olsen, Enoch Eli III (Bud) b. July 25, 1940 Ht. 6-8 Wt. 225 College: Louisville

SEASON–TEAM	G	GS	MIN	FGM	FGA	PCT	3FGM	3FGA	PCT	FTM	FTA	PCT	O-RB	D-RB	TOT	AST	PF	DQ	STL	TO	BLK	PTS	RPG	APG	PPG
62-63–Cincinnati	52	–	373	43	133	.323	–	–	–	27	39	.692	–	–	105	42	78	0	–	–	–	113	2.0	0.8	2.2
63-64–Cincinnati	49	–	513	85	210	.405	–	–	–	32	57	.561	–	–	149	29	78	0	–	–	–	202	3.0	0.6	4.1
64-65–Cincinnati	79	–	1372	224	512	.438	–	–	–	144	195	.738	–	–	333	84	203	5	–	–	–	592	4.2	1.1	7.5
65-66–Cin.-S.F.	59	–	602	81	193	.420	–	–	–	39	88	.443	–	–	192	20	81	1	–	–	–	201	3.3	0.3	3.4
66-67–San Francisco	40	–	348	75	167	.449	–	–	–	23	58	.397	–	–	103	32	51	1	–	–	–	173	2.6	0.8	4.3
67-68–Seattle	73	–	897	130	285	.456	–	–	–	17	62	.274	–	–	204	75	136	1	–	–	–	277	2.8	1.0	3.8
68-69–Boston-Detroit	17	–	113	15	42	.357	–	–	–	4	18	.222	–	–	25	11	14	0	–	–	–	34	1.5	0.6	2.0
69-70–Kentucky (A)	84	–	1375	158	330	.479	1	4	.250	26	73	.356	–	–	374	249	234	5	–	–	–	343	4.5	3.0	4.1
Reg. NBA Totals	369	–	4218	653	1542	.423	–	–	–	286	517	.553	–	–	1111	293	641	8	–	–	–	1592	3.0	0.8	4.3
Reg. ABA Totals	84	–	1375	158	330	.479	1	4	.250	26	73	.356	–	–	374	249	234	5	–	–	–	343	4.5	3.0	4.1
NBA Playoff Totals	15	–	84	21	45	.467	–	–	–	4	12	.333	–	–	32	6	16	0	–	–	–	46	2.1	0.4	3.1
ABA Playoff Totals	12	–	211	18	43	.419	0	1	.000	1	7	.143	–	–	61	39	45	2	–	–	–	37	5.1	3.3	3.1

O'Malley, V. Grady (Grady) b. April 25, 1948 Ht. 6-5 Wt. 205 College: Manhattan

SEASON–TEAM	G	GS	MIN	FGM	FGA	PCT	3FGM	3FGA	PCT	FTM	FTA	PCT	O-RB	D-RB	TOT	AST	PF	DQ	STL	TO	BLK	PTS	RPG	APG	PPG
69-70–Atlanta	24	–	113	21	60	.350	–	–	–	8	19	.421	–	–	26	10	12	0	–	–	–	50	1.1	0.4	2.1
Reg. Season Totals	24	–	113	21	60	.350	–	–	–	8	19	.421	–	–	26	10	12	0	–	–	–	50	1.1	0.4	2.1

O'Neal, Jermaine b. October 13, 1978 Ht. 6-11 Wt. 226 High School: Eau Claire HS (S.C.)

SEASON–TEAM	G	GS	MIN	FGM	FGA	PCT	3FGM	3FGA	PCT	FTM	FTA	PCT	O-RB	D-RB	TOT	AST	PF	DQ	STL	TO	BLK	PTS	RPG	APG	PPG
96-97–Portland	45	0	458	69	153	.451	0	1	.000	47	78	.603	39	85	124	8	46	0	2	27	26	185	2.8	0.2	4.1
97-98–Portland	60	9	808	112	231	.485	0	2	.000	45	89	.506	80	121	201	17	101	0	15	55	58	269	3.4	0.3	4.5
98-99–Portland	36	1	311	36	83	.434	0	1	.000	18	35	.514	42	55	97	13	41	0	4	14	14	90	2.7	0.4	2.5
99-00–Portland	70	8	859	108	222	.486	0	1	.000	57	98	.582	97	132	229	18	127	1	11	47	55	273	3.3	0.3	3.9
Reg. Season Totals	211	18	2436	325	689	.472	0	5	.000	167	300	.557	258	393	651	56	315	1	32	143	153	817	3.1	0.3	3.9
Playoff Totals	20	0	100	7	26	.269	0	2	.000	12	23	.522	11	15	26	2	21	0	0	2	9	26	1.3	0.1	1.3

O'Neal, Shaquille Rashaun (Shaq) b. March 6, 1972 Ht. 7-1 Wt. 315 College: Louisiana State

SEASON–TEAM	G	GS	MIN	FGM	FGA	PCT	3FGM	3FGA	PCT	FTM	FTA	PCT	O-RB	D-RB	TOT	AST	PF	DQ	STL	TO	BLK	PTS	RPG	APG	PPG
92-93–Orlando	81	81	3071	733	1304	.562	0	2	.000	427	721	.592	342	780	1122	152	321	8	60	307	286	1893	13.9	1.9	23.4
93-94–Orlando	81	81	3224	953	1591	.599	0	2	.000	471	850	.554	384	688	1072	195	281	3	76	222	231	2377	13.2	2.4	29.3
94-95–Orlando	79	79	2923	930	1594	.583	0	5	.000	455	854	.533	328	573	901	214	258	1	73	204	192	2315	11.4	2.7	29.3
95-96–Orlando	54	52	1946	592	1033	.573	1	2	.500	249	511	.487	182	414	596	155	193	1	34	155	115	1434	11.0	2.9	26.6
96-97–L.A. Lakers	51	51	1941	552	991	.557	0	4	.000	232	479	.484	195	445	640	159	180	2	46	146	147	1336	12.5	3.1	26.2
97-98–L.A. Lakers	60	57	2175	670	1147	.584	0	0	–	359	681	.527	208	473	681	142	193	1	39	175	144	1699	11.4	2.4	28.3
98-99–L.A. Lakers	49	49	1705	510	885	.576	0	1	.000	269	498	.540	187	338	525	114	155	4	36	122	82	1289	10.7	2.3	26.3
99-00–L.A. Lakers	79	79	3163	956	1665	.574	0	1	.000	432	824	.524	336	742	1078	299	255	2	36	223	239	2344	13.6	3.8	29.7
Reg. Season Totals	534	529	20148	5896	10210	.577	1	17	.059	2894	5418	.534	2162	4453	6615	1430	1836	22	400	1554	1436	14687	12.4	2.7	27.5
Playoff Totals	89	89	3532	961	1690	.569	0	0	–	547	1095	.500	410	675	1085	288	311	4	61	266	193	2469	12.2	3.2	27.7
All-Star Totals	6	6	148	41	83	.494	0	1	.000	21	44	.477	20	27	47	6	14	0	5	10	11	103	7.8	1.0	17.2

O'Neill, Mike b. 1927 Ht. 6-3 Wt. 210 College: California

SEASON–TEAM	G	GS	MIN	FGM	FGA	PCT	3FGM	3FGA	PCT	FTM	FTA	PCT	O-RB	D-RB	TOT	AST	PF	DQ	STL	TO	BLK	PTS	RPG	APG	PPG
52-53–Milwaukee	4	–	50	4	17	.235	–	–	–	4	4	1.000	–	–	9	3	10	1	–	–	–	12	2.3	0.8	3.0
Reg. Season Totals	4	–	50	4	17	.235	–	–	–	4	4	1.000	–	–	9	3	10	1	–	–	–	12	2.3	0.8	3.0

Orms, Barry D. b. May 1, 1946 Ht. 6-3 Wt. 190 College: St. Louis

SEASON–TEAM	G	GS	MIN	FGM	FGA	PCT	3FGM	3FGA	PCT	FTM	FTA	PCT	O-RB	D-RB	TOT	AST	PF	DQ	STL	TO	BLK	PTS	RPG	APG	PPG
68-69–Baltimore	64	–	916	76	246	.309	–	–	–	29	60	.483	–	–	158	49	155	3	–	–	–	181	2.5	0.8	2.8
69-70–Indiana-Pitt. (A)	77	–	2091	272	695	.391	5	26	.192	152	276	.551	–	–	347	132	215	3	–	–	–	701	4.5	1.7	9.1
Reg. NBA Totals	64	–	916	76	246	.309	–	–	–	29	60	.483	–	–	158	49	155	3	–	–	–	181	2.5	0.8	2.8
Reg. ABA Totals	77	–	2091	272	695	.391	5	26	.192	152	276	.551	–	–	347	132	215	3	–	–	–	701	4.5	1.7	9.1
NBA Playoff Totals	3	–	10	0	0	–	–	–	–	0	0	–	–	–	1	–	2	0	–	–	–	0	0.3	0.0	0.0

Orr, John M. (Johnny) b. June 10, 1927 Ht. 6-3 Wt. 205 College: Beloit; Illinois

SEASON–TEAM	G	GS	MIN	FGM	FGA	PCT	3FGM	3FGA	PCT	FTM	FTA	PCT	O-RB	D-RB	TOT	AST	PF	DQ	STL	TO	BLK	PTS	RPG	APG	PPG
49-50–St. Louis-Wat.	34	–	–	40	118	.339	–	–	–	12	14	.857	–	–	–	20	34	–	–	–	–	92	–	0.6	2.7
Reg. Season Totals	34	–	–	40	118	.339	–	–	–	12	14	.857	–	–	–	20	34	–	–	–	–	92	–	0.6	2.7

Orr, Louis M. b. May 7, 1958 Ht. 6-8 Wt. 175 College: Syracuse

SEASON–TEAM	G	GS	MIN	FGM	FGA	PCT	3FGM	3FGA	PCT	FTM	FTA	PCT	O-RB	D-RB	TOT	AST	PF	DQ	STL	TO	BLK	PTS	RPG	APG	PPG
80-81–Indiana	82	–	1787	348	709	.491	0	6	.000	163	202	.807	172	189	361	132	153	0	55	123	25	859	4.4	1.6	10.5
81-82–Indiana	80	41	1951	357	719	.497	1	8	.125	203	254	.799	127	204	331	134	182	1	56	137	26	918	4.1	1.7	11.5
82-83–New York	82	14	1666	274	593	.462	0	2	.000	140	175	.800	94	134	228	94	134	0	64	93	24	688	2.8	1.1	8.4
83-84–New York	78	20	1640	262	572	.458	0	0	–	173	211	.820	101	127	228	61	142	0	66	95	17	697	2.9	0.8	8.9
84-85–New York	79	31	2452	372	766	.486	1	10	.100	262	334	.784	171	220	391	134	195	1	100	138	27	1007	4.9	1.7	12.7
85-86–New York	74	64	2237	330	741	.445	0	4	.000	218	278	.784	123	189	312	179	177	4	61	118	26	878	4.2	2.4	11.9
86-87–New York	65	8	1440	166	389	.427	1	5	.200	125	172	.727	102	130	232	110	123	0	47	70	18	458	3.6	1.7	7.0
87-88–New York	29	0	180	16	50	.320	0	1	.000	8	16	.500	13	21	34	9	27	0	6	14	0	40	1.2	0.3	1.4
Reg. Season Totals	569	178	13353	2125	4539	.468	3	36	.083	1292	1642	.787	903	1214	2117	853	1133	6	455	788	163	5545	3.7	1.5	9.7
Playoff Totals	22	0	393	56	143	.392	0	0	–	32	38	.842	37	46	83	13	46	1	14	24	6	144	3.8	0.6	6.5

Ortiz, Jose Rafael (Piculin) b. October 25, 1963 Ht. 6-10 Wt. 225 College: Oregon State

SEASON–TEAM	G	GS	MIN	FGM	FGA	PCT	3FGM	3FGA	PCT	FTM	FTA	PCT	O-RB	D-RB	TOT	AST	PF	DQ	STL	TO	BLK	PTS	RPG	APG	PPG
88-89–Utah	51	15	327	55	125	.440	0	1	.000	31	52	.596	30	28	58	11	40	0	8	36	7	141	1.1	0.2	2.8
89-90–Utah	13	0	64	19	42	.452	1	2	.500	3	5	.600	8	7	15	7	15	0	2	5	1	42	1.2	0.5	3.2
Reg. Season Totals	64	15	391	74	167	.443	1	3	.333	34	57	.596	38	35	73	18	55	0	10	41	8	183	1.1	0.3	2.9

Osborne, Charles H. (Chuck) b. January 21, 1939 d. April 1979 Ht. 6-6 Wt. 210 College: Western Kentucky

SEASON–TEAM	G	GS	MIN	FGM	FGA	PCT	3FGM	3FGA	PCT	FTM	FTA	PCT	O-RB	D-RB	TOT	AST	PF	DQ	STL	TO	BLK	PTS	RPG	APG	PPG
61-62–Syracuse	4	–	21	1	8	.125	–	–	–	3	4	.750	–	–	9	1	3	0	–	–	–	5	2.3	0.3	1.3
Reg. Season Totals	4	–	21	1	8	.125	–	–	–	3	4	.750	–	–	9	1	3	0	–	–	–	5	2.3	0.3	1.3

O'Shea, Kevin Christopher b. July 10, 1925 Ht. 6-2 Wt. 175 College: Notre Dame

SEASON–TEAM	G	GS	MIN	FGM	FGA	PCT	3FGM	3FGA	PCT	FTM	FTA	PCT	O-RB	D-RB	TOT	AST	PF	DQ	STL	TO	BLK	PTS	RPG	APG	PPG
50-51–Minneapolis	63	–	–	87	267	.326	–	–	–	97	134	.724	–	–	125	100	99	1	–	–	–	271	2.0	1.6	4.3
51-52–Milw.-Balt.	65	–	1725	153	466	.328	–	–	–	144	210	.686	–	–	201	171	175	7	–	–	–	450	3.1	2.6	6.9
52-53–Baltimore	46	–	643	71	189	.376	–	–	–	48	81	.593	–	–	76	87	82	1	–	–	–	190	1.7	1.9	4.1
Reg. Season Totals	174	–	2368	311	922	.337	–	–	–	289	425	.680	–	–	402	358	356	9	–	–	–	911	2.3	2.1	5.2
Playoff Totals	6	–	0	1	7	.143	–	–	–	3	4	.750	–	–	5	1	8	0	–	–	–	5	1.3	0.3	0.8

O'Shields, Garland L. (Mule) b. May 23, 1921 Ht. 6-1 Wt. 195 College: Spartanburg (S.C.) Tech J.C.; Tennessee

SEASON–TEAM	G	GS	MIN	FGM	FGA	PCT	3FGM	3FGA	PCT	FTM	FTA	PCT	O-RB	D-RB	TOT	AST	PF	DQ	STL	TO	BLK	PTS	RPG	APG	PPG
46-47–Chicago	9	–	–	2	11	.182	–	–	–	0	2	.000	–	–	–	1	8	–	–	–	–	4	–	0.1	0.4
47-48–Syracuse (N)	5	–	–	3	–	–	–	–	–	3	4	.750	–	–	–	–	–	–	–	–	–	9	–	–	1.8
Reg. NBA Totals	9	–	–	2	11	.182	–	–	–	0	2	.000	–	–	–	1	8	–	–	–	–	4	–	0.1	0.4
Reg. NBL Totals	5	–	–	3	–	–	–	–	–	3	4	.750	–	–	–	–	–	–	–	–	–	9	–	–	1.8

Osterkorn, Walter Raymond (Wally) b. July 6, 1928 Ht. 6-5 Wt. 215 College: Illinois

SEASON–TEAM	G	GS	MIN	FGM	FGA	PCT	3FGM	3FGA	PCT	FTM	FTA	PCT	O-RB	D-RB	TOT	AST	PF	DQ	STL	TO	BLK	PTS	RPG	APG	PPG
51-52–Syracuse	66	–	1721	145	413	.351	–	–	–	199	335	.594	–	–	444	117	226	8	–	–	–	489	6.7	1.8	7.4
52-53–Syracuse	49	–	1016	85	262	.324	–	–	–	106	168	.631	–	–	217	61	129	2	–	–	–	276	4.4	1.2	5.6
53-54–Syracuse	70	–	2164	203	586	.346	–	–	–	209	361	.579	–	–	487	151	209	1	–	–	–	615	7.0	2.2	8.8
54-55–Syracuse	19	–	286	20	97	.206	–	–	–	16	32	.500	–	–	70	17	32	0	–	–	–	56	3.7	0.9	2.9
Reg. Season Totals	204	–	5187	453	1358	.334	–	–	–	530	896	.592	–	–	1218	346	596	11	–	–	–	1436	6.0	1.7	7.0
Playoff Totals	33	–	1378	83	232	.358	–	–	–	93	158	.589	–	–	318	92	97	2	–	–	–	259	7.2	2.3	7.8

Ostertag, Gregory Donovan (Greg) b. March 6, 1973 Ht. 7-2 Wt. 280 College: Kansas

SEASON–TEAM	G	GS	MIN	FGM	FGA	PCT	3FGM	3FGA	PCT	FTM	FTA	PCT	O-RB	D-RB	TOT	AST	PF	DQ	STL	TO	BLK	PTS	RPG	APG	PPG
95-96–Utah	57	10	661	86	182	.473	0	0	–	36	54	.667	57	118	175	5	91	1	5	25	63	208	3.1	0.1	3.6
96-97–Utah	77	70	1818	210	408	.515	0	4	.000	139	205	.678	180	385	565	27	233	2	24	74	152	559	7.3	0.4	7.3
97-98–Utah	63	23	1288	115	239	.481	0	0	–	67	140	.479	134	240	374	25	166	1	28	74	132	297	5.9	0.4	4.7
98-99–Utah	48	48	1340	99	208	.476	0	0	–	75	121	.620	105	243	348	23	140	2	12	45	131	273	7.3	0.5	5.7
99-00–Utah	81	3	1606	124	267	.464	0	1	.000	119	187	.636	172	310	482	18	196	2	20	79	172	367	6.0	0.2	4.5
Reg. Season Totals	326	154	6713	634	1304	.486	0	5	.000	436	707	.617	648	1296	1944	98	826	8	89	297	650	1704	6.0	0.3	5.2
Playoff Totals	73	32	1440	103	228	.452	0	0	–	79	131	.603	132	246	378	20	202	3	23	50	146	285	5.2	0.3	3.9

O'Sullivan, Daniel James (Dan) b. March 3, 1968 Ht. 6-10 Wt. 250 College: Fordham

SEASON–TEAM	G	GS	MIN	FGM	FGA	PCT	3FGM	3FGA	PCT	FTM	FTA	PCT	O-RB	D-RB	TOT	AST	PF	DQ	STL	TO	BLK	PTS	RPG	APG	PPG
90-91–Utah	21	0	85	7	16	.438	0	0	–	7	11	.636	5	12	17	4	18	0	1	4	1	21	0.8	0.2	1.0
92-93–N.J.-Milw.	6	0	17	3	5	.600	0	0	–	3	4	.750	2	4	6	1	4	0	1	0	0	9	1.0	0.2	1.5
93-94–Detroit	13	0	56	4	12	.333	0	0	–	9	12	.750	2	8	10	3	10	0	0	3	0	17	0.8	0.2	1.3
95-96–Toronto	5	2	139	13	35	.371	0	1	.000	7	8	.875	13	19	32	2	13	0	2	5	4	33	6.4	0.4	6.6
Reg. Season Totals	45	2	297	27	68	.397	0	1	.000	26	35	.743	22	43	65	10	45	0	4	12	5	80	1.4	0.2	1.8

Othick, Matthew Brian (Matt) b. March 16, 1969 Ht. 6-2 Wt. 165 College: Arizona

SEASON–TEAM	G	GS	MIN	FGM	FGA	PCT	3FGM	3FGA	PCT	FTM	FTA	PCT	O-RB	D-RB	TOT	AST	PF	DQ	STL	TO	BLK	PTS	RPG	APG	PPG
92-93–San Antonio	4	0	39	3	5	.600	2	4	.500	0	2	.000	1	1	2	7	7	0	1	4	0	8	0.5	1.8	2.0
Reg. Season Totals	4	0	39	3	5	.600	2	4	.500	0	2	.000	1	1	2	7	7	0	1	4	0	8	0.5	1.8	2.0

Otten, Donald F. (Don) b. April 18, 1921 d. September 18, 1985 Ht. 7-0 Wt. 250 College: Bowling Green State

SEASON–TEAM	G	GS	MIN	FGM	FGA	PCT	3FGM	3FGA	PCT	FTM	FTA	PCT	O-RB	D-RB	TOT	AST	PF	DQ	STL	TO	BLK	PTS	RPG	APG	PPG
46-47–Tri-Cities (N)	44	–	–	200	–	–	–	–	–	169	261	.648	–	–	–	–	98	–	–	–	–	569	–	–	12.9
47-48–Tri-Cities (N)	60	–	–	282	–	–	–	–	–	260	392	.663	–	–	–	–	184	–	–	–	–	824	–	–	13.7
48-49–Tri-Cities (N)	64	–	–	301	–	–	–	–	–	297	424	.700	–	–	–	–	205	–	–	–	–	899	–	–	14.0
49-50–Tri-Cit-Wash.	64	–	–	242	648	.373	–	–	–	341	463	.737	–	–	–	91	246	–	–	–	–	825	–	1.4	12.9
50-51–Wash.-Balt.-Ft.W	67	–	–	162	479	.338	–	–	–	246	308	.799	–	–	404	62	255	15	–	–	–	570	6.0	0.9	8.5
51-52–FtWayne-Milw.	64	–	1789	222	636	.349	–	–	–	323	418	.773	–	–	435	123	218	11	–	–	–	767	6.8	1.9	12.0
52-53–Milwaukee	24	–	384	34	87	.391	–	–	–	64	91	.703	–	–	89	21	68	4	–	–	–	132	3.7	0.9	5.5
Reg. NBA Totals	219	–	2173	660	1850	.357	–	–	–	974	1280	.761	–	–	928	297	787	30	–	–	–	2294	6.0	1.4	10.5
Reg. NBL Totals	168	–	–	783	–	–	–	–	–	726	1077	.674	–	–	–	–	487	–	–	–	–	2292	–	–	13.6
NBA Playoff Totals	5	–	0	18	51	.353	–	–	–	34	42	.810	–	–	19	14	22	1	–	–	–	70	6.3	2.8	14.0
NBL Playoff Totals	12	–	–	58	–	–	–	–	–	73	93	.785	–	–	–	–	41	–	–	–	–	189	–	–	15.8

Otten, Mac William b. December 16, 1925 Ht. 6-7 Wt. 220 College: Bowling Green State

SEASON–TEAM	G	GS	MIN	FGM	FGA	PCT	3FGM	3FGA	PCT	FTM	FTA	PCT	O-RB	D-RB	TOT	AST	PF	DQ	STL	TO	BLK	PTS	RPG	APG	PPG
49-50–Tri-Cit-St. L.	59	–	–	51	155	.329	–	–	–	40	81	.494	–	–	–	36	119	–	–	–	–	142	–	0.6	2.4
Reg. Season Totals	59	–	–	51	155	.329	–	–	–	40	81	.494	–	–	–	36	119	–	–	–	–	142	–	0.6	2.4

Outlaw, Charles (Bo) b. April 13, 1971 Ht. 6-8 Wt. 210 College: Houston

SEASON–TEAM	G	GS	MIN	FGM	FGA	PCT	3FGM	3FGA	PCT	FTM	FTA	PCT	O-RB	D-RB	TOT	AST	PF	DQ	STL	TO	BLK	PTS	RPG	APG	PPG
93-94–L.A. Clippers	37	14	871	98	167	.587	0	2	.000	61	103	.592	81	131	212	36	94	1	36	31	37	257	5.7	1.0	6.9
94-95–L.A. Clippers	81	31	1655	170	325	.523	0	5	.000	82	186	.441	121	192	313	84	227	4	90	78	151	422	3.9	1.0	5.2
95-96–L.A. Clippers	80	3	985	107	186	.575	0	3	.000	72	162	.444	87	113	200	50	127	0	44	45	91	286	2.5	0.6	3.6
96-97–L.A. Clippers	82	25	2195	254	417	.609	0	8	.000	117	232	.504	174	280	454	157	227	5	94	107	142	625	5.5	1.9	7.6
97-98–Orlando	82	76	2953	301	543	.554	1	4	.250	180	313	.575	255	382	637	216	260	1	107	175	181	783	7.8	2.6	9.5
98-99–Orlando	31	22	851	84	154	.545	0	3	.000	35	81	.432	54	113	167	56	79	1	40	58	43	203	5.4	1.8	6.5
99-00–Orlando	82	55	2326	204	339	.602	0	3	.000	82	162	.506	202	323	525	245	203	0	113	133	148	490	6.4	3.0	6.0
Reg. Season Totals	475	226	11836	1218	2131	.572	1	28	.036	629	1239	.508	974	1534	2508	844	1217	12	524	627	793	3066	5.3	1.8	6.5
Playoff Totals	7	0	149	12	21	.571	0	1	.000	9	23	.391	9	20	29	6	14	0	2	9	10	33	4.1	0.9	4.7

Overton, Claudell (Claude) b. December 16, 1927 Ht. 6-2 Wt. 195 College: East Central (Okla.)

SEASON–TEAM	G	GS	MIN	FGM	FGA	PCT	3FGM	3FGA	PCT	FTM	FTA	PCT	O-RB	D-RB	TOT	AST	PF	DQ	STL	TO	BLK	PTS	RPG	APG	PPG
52-53–Philadelphia	15	–	182	19	75	.253	–	–	–	20	30	.667	–	–	25	15	25	0	–	–	–	58	1.7	1.0	3.9
Reg. Season Totals	15	–	182	19	75	.253	–	–	–	20	30	.667	–	–	25	15	25	0	–	–	–	58	1.7	1.0	3.9

Overton, Douglas M. (Doug) b. August 3, 1969 Ht. 6-3 Wt. 190 College: La Salle

SEASON–TEAM	G	GS	MIN	FGM	FGA	PCT	3FGM	3FGA	PCT	FTM	FTA	PCT	O-RB	D-RB	TOT	AST	PF	DQ	STL	TO	BLK	PTS	RPG	APG	PPG
92-93–Washington	45	13	990	152	323	.471	3	13	.231	59	81	.728	25	81	106	157	81	0	31	72	6	366	2.4	3.5	8.1
93-94–Washington	61	1	749	87	216	.403	1	11	.091	43	52	.827	19	50	69	92	48	0	21	54	1	218	1.1	1.5	3.6
94-95–Washington	82	20	1704	207	498	.416	53	125	.424	109	125	.872	26	117	143	246	126	1	53	104	2	576	1.7	3.0	7.0
95-96–Denver	55	0	607	67	178	.376	8	26	.308	40	55	.727	8	55	63	106	49	0	13	40	5	182	1.1	1.9	3.3
96-97–Philadelphia	61	4	634	81	190	.426	10	40	.250	45	48	.938	18	50	68	101	44	0	24	39	0	217	1.1	1.7	3.6
97-98–Philadelphia	23	2	277	24	63	.381	0	3	.000	14	16	.875	2	12	14	37	34	0	8	23	1	62	0.6	1.6	2.7
98-99–Orlando-N.J.-Phil.	24	1	244	36	84	.429	2	7	.286	18	20	.900	7	14	21	23	18	0	5	20	1	92	0.9	1.0	3.8
99-00–Boston	48	0	432	61	154	.396	10	28	.357	20	21	.952	14	19	33	53	46	0	10	20	0	152	0.7	1.1	3.2
Reg. Season Totals	399	41	5637	715	1706	.419	87	253	.344	348	418	.833	119	398	517	815	446	1	165	372	16	1865	1.3	2.0	4.7

Owens, Billy Eugene b. May 1, 1969 Ht. 6-9 Wt. 225 College: Syracuse

SEASON–TEAM	G	GS	MIN	FGM	FGA	PCT	3FGM	3FGA	PCT	FTM	FTA	PCT	O-RB	D-RB	TOT	AST	PF	DQ	STL	TO	BLK	PTS	RPG	APG	PPG
91-92–Golden State	80	77	2510	468	891	.525	1	9	.111	204	312	.654	243	396	639	188	276	4	90	179	65	1141	8.0	2.4	14.3
92-93–Golden State	37	37	1201	247	493	.501	1	11	.091	117	183	.639	108	156	264	144	105	1	35	106	28	612	7.1	3.9	16.5
93-94–Golden State	79	72	2738	492	971	.507	3	15	.200	199	326	.610	230	410	640	326	269	5	83	214	60	1186	8.1	4.1	15.0
94-95–Miami	70	60	2296	403	820	.491	2	22	.091	194	313	.620	203	299	502	246	205	6	80	204	30	1002	7.2	3.5	14.3
95-96–Miami-Sac.	62	51	1982	323	673	.480	5	18	.278	157	247	.636	143	268	411	204	192	2	49	164	38	808	6.6	3.3	13.0
96-97–Sacramento	66	56	1995	299	640	.467	25	72	.347	101	145	.697	134	258	392	187	187	4	62	133	25	724	5.9	2.8	11.0
97-98–Sacramento	78	78	2348	338	728	.464	26	70	.371	116	197	.589	170	412	582	219	231	5	93	153	38	818	7.5	2.8	10.5
98-99–Seattle	21	19	451	65	165	.394	5	11	.455	28	35	.800	35	45	80	38	37	0	12	33	4	163	3.8	1.8	7.8
99-00–Phil.-G.S.	62	11	1305	150	358	.419	11	34	.324	63	106	.594	99	202	301	97	166	1	33	85	21	374	4.9	1.6	6.0
Reg. Season Totals	555	461	16826	2785	5739	.485	79	262	.302	1179	1864	.633	1365	2446	3811	1649	1668	28	537	1271	309	6828	6.9	3.0	12.3
Playoff Totals	11	11	415	70	141	.496	0	5	.000	29	45	.644	30	59	89	40	42	1	16	24	5	169	8.1	3.6	15.4

Owens, Eddie b. December 26, 1953 Ht. 6-7 Wt. 210 College: Nevada-Las Vegas

SEASON–TEAM	G	GS	MIN	FGM	FGA	PCT	3FGM	3FGA	PCT	FTM	FTA	PCT	O-RB	D-RB	TOT	AST	PF	DQ	STL	TO	BLK	PTS	RPG	APG	PPG
77-78–Buffalo	8	–	63	9	21	.429	–	–	–	3	6	.500	5	5	10	5	9	0	1	3	0	21	1.3	0.6	2.6
Reg. Season Totals	8	–	63	9	21	.429	–	–	–	3	6	.500	5	5	10	5	9	0	1	3	0	21	1.3	0.6	2.6

Owens, James L. (Red) b. September 2, 1925 d. October 11, 1988 Ht. 6-3 Wt. 185 College: Baylor

SEASON–TEAM	G	GS	MIN	FGM	FGA	PCT	3FGM	3FGA	PCT	FTM	FTA	PCT	O-RB	D-RB	TOT	AST	PF	DQ	STL	TO	BLK	PTS	RPG	APG	PPG
49-50–Tri-Cit-And.	61	–	–	86	288	.299	–	–	–	68	101	.673	–	–	–	73	152	–	–	–	–	240	–	1.2	3.9
51-52–Balt.-Milw.	29	–	626	83	252	.329	–	–	–	64	114	.561	–	–	102	64	92	5	–	–	–	230	3.5	2.2	7.9
Reg. Season Totals	90	–	626	169	540	.313	–	–	–	132	215	.614	–	–	102	137	244	5	–	–	–	470	3.5	1.5	5.2
Playoff Totals	8	–	0	26	89	.292	–	–	–	28	41	.683	–	–	–	19	37	2	–	–	–	80	–	2.4	10.0

Owens, Jim b. May 1, 1950 Ht. 6-5 Wt. 200 College: Arizona State

SEASON–TEAM	G	GS	MIN	FGM	FGA	PCT	3FGM	3FGA	PCT	FTM	FTA	PCT	O-RB	D-RB	TOT	AST	PF	DQ	STL	TO	BLK	PTS	RPG	APG	PPG
73-74–Phoenix	17	–	101	21	39	.538	–	–	–	11	14	.786	1	8	9	15	6	0	5	–	0	53	0.5	0.9	3.1
74-75–Phoenix	41	–	432	56	145	.386	–	–	–	12	16	.750	7	36	43	49	27	0	16	–	2	124	1.0	1.2	3.0
Reg. Season Totals	58	–	533	77	184	.418	–	–	–	23	30	.767	8	44	52	64	33	0	21	–	2	177	0.9	1.1	3.1

Owens, Keith Kensel b. May 31, 1969 Ht. 6-7 Wt. 225 College: UCLA

SEASON–TEAM	G	GS	MIN	FGM	FGA	PCT	3FGM	3FGA	PCT	FTM	FTA	PCT	O-RB	D-RB	TOT	AST	PF	DQ	STL	TO	BLK	PTS	RPG	APG	PPG
91-92–L.A. Lakers	20	0	80	9	32	.281	0	0	–	8	10	.800	8	7	15	3	11	0	5	2	4	26	0.8	0.2	1.3
Reg. Season Totals	20	0	80	9	32	.281	0	0	–	8	10	.800	8	7	15	3	11	0	5	2	4	26	0.8	0.2	1.3

Owens, Thomas William (Tom) b. June 28, 1949 Ht. 6-10 Wt. 225 College: South Carolina

SEASON–TEAM	G	GS	MIN	FGM	FGA	PCT	3FGM	3FGA	PCT	FTM	FTA	PCT	O-RB	D-RB	TOT	AST	PF	DQ	STL	TO	BLK	PTS	RPG	APG	PPG
71-72–Mem.-Car. (A)	69	–	1118	197	402	.490	1	5	.200	109	175	.623	–	–	390	51	170	–	–	83	–	504	5.7	0.7	7.3
72-73–Carolina (A)	83	–	2209	393	727	.541	0	2	.000	193	284	.680	229	417	646	94	318	10	–	173	–	979	7.8	1.1	11.8
73-74–Carolina (A)	81	–	2284	444	843	.527	2	6	.333	226	294	.769	301	416	717	127	308	–	54	171	41	1116	8.9	1.6	13.8
74-75–St. L.-Mem. (A)	82	–	2647	511	969	.527	0	2	.000	217	289	.751	296	609	905	208	261	–	36	153	82	1239	11.0	2.5	15.1
75-76–Ken.-Ind.-S.A. (A)	74	–	1107	178	369	.482	0	0	–	92	129	.713	115	202	317	69	200	–	11	74	41	448	4.3	0.9	6.1
76-77–Houston	46	–	462	68	135	.504	–	–	–	52	76	.684	47	95	142	18	96	2	4	–	13	188	3.1	0.4	4.1
77-78–Portland	82	–	1714	313	639	.490	–	–	–	206	278	.741	195	346	541	160	263	7	33	152	37	832	6.6	2.0	10.1
78-79–Portland	82	–	2791	600	1095	.548	–	–	–	320	403	.794	263	477	740	301	329	15	59	247	58	1520	9.0	3.7	18.5
79-80–Portland	76	–	2337	518	1008	.514	1	2	.500	213	283	.753	189	384	573	194	270	5	45	174	53	1250	7.5	2.6	16.4
80-81–Portland	79	–	1843	322	630	.511	0	4	.000	191	250	.764	165	291	456	140	273	10	36	130	47	835	5.8	1.8	10.6
81-82–Indiana	74	40	1599	299	636	.470	1	2	.500	181	226	.801	142	230	372	127	259	7	41	137	37	780	5.0	1.7	10.5
82-83–Detroit	49	4	725	81	192	.422	0	0	–	45	66	.682	66	120	186	44	115	0	12	48	14	207	3.8	0.9	4.2
Reg. NBA Totals	488	44	11471	2201	4335	.508	2	8	.250	1208	1582	.764	1067	1943	3010	984	1605	46	230	888	259	5612	6.2	2.0	11.5
Reg. ABA Totals	389	–	9365	1723	3310	.521	3	15	.200	837	1171	.715	941	1644	2975	549	1257	10	101	654	164	4286	7.6	1.4	11.0
NBA Playoff Totals	16	0	375	67	127	.528	0	0	–	25	37	.676	35	47	82	33	62	3	11	19	10	159	5.1	2.1	9.9
ABA Playoff Totals	28	–	751	136	274	.496	0	1	.000	66	96	.688	90	148	238	36	102	0	6	33	15	338	8.5	1.3	12.1

Owes, Ray b. December 12, 1972 Ht. 6-9 Wt. 224 College: Arizona

SEASON–TEAM	G	GS	MIN	FGM	FGA	PCT	3FGM	3FGA	PCT	FTM	FTA	PCT	O-RB	D-RB	TOT	AST	PF	DQ	STL	TO	BLK	PTS	RPG	APG	PPG
96-97–Golden State	57	1	592	75	180	.417	1	5	.200	26	46	.565	64	99	163	15	86	1	15	23	20	177	2.9	0.3	3.1
Reg. Season Totals	57	1	592	75	180	.417	1	5	.200	26	46	.565	64	99	163	15	86	1	15	23	20	177	2.9	0.3	3.1

Pace, Joseph (Joe) b. December 18, 1953 Ht. 6-10 Wt. 220 College: Coppin State; Maryland Eastern Shore

SEASON–TEAM	G	GS	MIN	FGM	FGA	PCT	3FGM	3FGA	PCT	FTM	FTA	PCT	O-RB	D-RB	TOT	AST	PF	DQ	STL	TO	BLK	PTS	RPG	APG	PPG
76-77–Washington	30	–	119	24	55	.436	–	–	–	16	29	.552	16	18	34	4	29	0	2	–	17	64	1.1	0.1	2.1
77-78–Washington	49	–	438	67	140	.479	–	–	–	57	93	.613	50	84	134	23	86	1	12	44	21	191	2.7	0.5	3.9
Reg. Season Totals	79	–	557	91	195	.467	–	–	–	73	122	.598	66	102	168	27	115	1	14	44	38	255	2.1	0.3	3.2
Playoff Totals	9	–	52	7	10	.700	–	–	–	11	15	.733	5	15	20	1	17	1	1	5	6	25	2.2	0.1	2.8

Pack, Robert John Jr. b. February 3, 1969 Ht. 6-2 Wt. 190 College: Tyler (Texas) J.C.; USC

SEASON–TEAM	G	GS	MIN	FGM	FGA	PCT	3FGM	3FGA	PCT	FTM	FTA	PCT	O-RB	D-RB	TOT	AST	PF	DQ	STL	TO	BLK	PTS	RPG	APG	PPG
91-92–Portland	72	0	894	115	272	.423	0	10	.000	102	127	.803	32	65	97	140	101	0	40	92	4	332	1.3	1.9	4.6
92-93–Denver	77	1	1579	285	606	.470	1	8	.125	239	311	.768	52	108	160	335	182	1	81	185	10	810	2.1	4.4	10.5
93-94–Denver	66	4	1382	223	503	.443	6	29	.207	179	236	.758	25	98	123	356	147	1	81	204	9	631	1.9	5.4	9.6
94-95–Denver	42	32	1144	170	395	.430	30	72	.417	137	175	.783	19	94	113	290	101	1	61	134	6	507	2.7	6.9	12.1
95-96–Washington	31	31	1084	190	444	.428	26	98	.265	154	182	.846	29	103	132	242	68	0	62	114	1	560	4.3	7.8	18.1
96-97–N.J.-Dallas	54	42	1782	272	693	.392	31	112	.277	196	243	.807	28	118	146	452	139	0	94	217	6	771	2.7	8.4	14.3
97-98–Dallas	12	10	292	33	98	.337	3	6	.500	25	36	.694	8	26	34	42	17	0	20	38	1	94	2.8	3.5	7.8
98-99–Dallas	25	0	468	75	174	.431	0	4	.000	72	88	.818	9	27	36	81	41	0	20	49	1	222	1.4	3.2	8.9
99-00–Dallas	29	22	665	96	230	.417	4	11	.364	63	78	.808	7	35	42	168	44	0	31	76	3	259	1.4	5.8	8.9
Reg. Season Totals	408	142	9290	1459	3415	.427	101	350	.289	1167	1476	.791	209	674	883	2106	840	3	490	1109	41	4186	2.2	5.2	10.3
Playoff Totals	26	0	384	52	136	.382	6	20	.300	42	59	.712	7	27	34	58	51	0	23	49	7	152	1.3	2.2	5.8

Pack, Wayne (Six-Pack) b. July 5, 1950 Ht. 6-0 Wt. 165 College: Tennessee Tech

SEASON–TEAM	G	GS	MIN	FGM	FGA	PCT	3FGM	3FGA	PCT	FTM	FTA	PCT	O-RB	D-RB	TOT	AST	PF	DQ	STL	TO	BLK	PTS	RPG	APG	PPG
74-75–Indiana (A)	21	–	189	23	60	.383	5	17	.294	10	12	.833	7	13	20	13	21	–	6	13	0	61	1.0	0.6	2.9
Reg. ABA Totals	21	–	189	23	60	.383	5	17	.294	10	12	.833	7	13	20	13	21	–	6	13	0	61	1.0	0.6	2.9

Paddio, Gerald James b. April 21, 1965 Ht. 6-7 Wt. 205 College: Seminole (Okla.) J.C.; Kilgore (Texas) Coll. (J.C.); Nevada-Las Vegas

SEASON–TEAM	G	GS	MIN	FGM	FGA	PCT	3FGM	3FGA	PCT	FTM	FTA	PCT	O-RB	D-RB	TOT	AST	PF	DQ	STL	TO	BLK	PTS	RPG	APG	PPG
90-91–Cleveland	70	22	1181	212	506	.419	6	24	.250	74	93	.796	38	80	118	90	71	0	20	71	6	504	1.7	1.3	7.2
92-93–Seattle	41	3	307	71	159	.447	2	8	.250	14	21	.667	17	33	50	33	24	0	14	16	6	158	1.2	0.8	3.9
93-94–Ind.-N.Y.-Wash.	18	1	137	22	60	.367	0	1	.000	9	16	.563	5	11	16	11	9	0	4	6	0	53	0.9	0.6	2.9
Reg. Season Totals	129	26	1625	305	725	.421	8	33	.242	97	130	.746	60	124	184	134	104	0	38	93	12	715	1.4	1.0	5.5
Playoff Totals	9	0	30	7	14	.500	0	1	.000	0	0	–	1	2	3	4	1	0	2	2	1	14	0.3	0.4	1.6

Padgett, Scott Anthony b. April 19, 1976 Ht. 6-9 Wt. 240 College: Kentucky

SEASON–TEAM	G	GS	MIN	FGM	FGA	PCT	3FGM	3FGA	PCT	FTM	FTA	PCT	O-RB	D-RB	TOT	AST	PF	DQ	STL	TO	BLK	PTS	RPG	APG	PPG
99-00–Utah	47	9	432	44	140	.314	13	44	.295	19	27	.704	24	64	88	25	55	1	14	22	8	120	1.9	0.5	2.6
Reg. Season Totals	47	9	432	44	140	.314	13	44	.295	19	27	.704	24	64	88	25	55	1	14	22	8	120	1.9	0.5	2.6
Playoff Totals	8	0	59	6	16	.375	3	9	.333	0	0	–	3	14	17	5	10	0	1	4	2	15	2.1	0.6	1.9

Pagett, Dana P. b. March 29, 1949 Ht. 6-2 Wt. 180 College: USC

SEASON–TEAM	G	GS	MIN	FGM	FGA	PCT	3FGM	3FGA	PCT	FTM	FTA	PCT	O-RB	D-RB	TOT	AST	PF	DQ	STL	TO	BLK	PTS	RPG	APG	PPG
71-72–Virginia (A)	5	–	34	1	9	.111	1	3	.333	2	3	.667	–	–	3	6	8	–	–	3	–	5	0.6	1.2	1.0
Reg. ABA Totals	5	–	34	1	9	.111	1	3	.333	2	3	.667	–	–	3	6	8	–	–	3	–	5	0.6	1.2	1.0

Paine, Frederick Vincent Jr. (Fred) b. December 7, 1925 Ht. 6-5 Wt. 210 College: Westminster (Pa.)

SEASON–TEAM	G	GS	MIN	FGM	FGA	PCT	3FGM	3FGA	PCT	FTM	FTA	PCT	O-RB	D-RB	TOT	AST	PF	DQ	STL	TO	BLK	PTS	RPG	APG	PPG
48-49–Providence	3	–	–	3	19	.158	–	–	–	1	5	.200	–	–	–	1	3	–	–	–	–	7	–	0.3	2.3
Reg. Season Totals	3	–	–	3	19	.158	–	–	–	1	5	.200	–	–	–	1	3	–	–	–	–	7	–	0.3	2.3

Palacio, Milt b. February 7, 1978 Ht. 6-3 Wt. 195 College: Colorado State

SEASON–TEAM	G	GS	MIN	FGM	FGA	PCT	3FGM	3FGA	PCT	FTM	FTA	PCT	O-RB	D-RB	TOT	AST	PF	DQ	STL	TO	BLK	PTS	RPG	APG	PPG
99-00–Vancouver	53	0	394	43	98	.439	0	2	.000	22	37	.595	17	34	51	48	32	0	20	44	0	108	1.0	0.9	2.0
Reg. Season Totals	53	0	394	43	98	.439	0	2	.000	22	37	.595	17	34	51	48	32	0	20	44	0	108	1.0	0.9	2.0

Palazzi, Togo Anthony b. August 8, 1932 Ht. 6-4 Wt. 205 College: Holy Cross

SEASON–TEAM	G	GS	MIN	FGM	FGA	PCT	3FGM	3FGA	PCT	FTM	FTA	PCT	O-RB	D-RB	TOT	AST	PF	DQ	STL	TO	BLK	PTS	RPG	APG	PPG
54-55–Boston	53	–	504	101	253	.399	–	–	–	45	60	.750	–	–	146	30	60	1	–	–	–	247	2.8	0.6	4.7
55-56–Boston	63	–	703	145	373	.389	–	–	–	85	124	.685	–	–	182	42	87	0	–	–	–	375	2.9	0.7	6.0
56-57–Boston-Syr.	63	–	1013	210	571	.368	–	–	–	136	175	.777	–	–	262	49	117	1	–	–	–	556	4.2	0.8	8.8
57-58–Syracuse	67	–	1001	228	579	.394	–	–	–	123	171	.719	–	–	243	42	125	0	–	–	–	579	3.6	0.6	8.6
58-59–Syracuse	71	–	1053	240	612	.392	–	–	–	115	158	.728	–	–	266	67	174	5	–	–	–	595	3.7	0.9	8.4
59-60–Syracuse	7	–	70	13	41	.317	–	–	–	4	8	.500	–	–	14	3	7	0	–	–	–	30	2.0	0.4	4.3
Reg. Season Totals	324	–	4344	937	2429	.386	–	–	–	508	696	.730	–	–	1113	233	570	7	–	–	–	2382	3.4	0.7	7.4
Playoff Totals	23	–	216	48	136	.353	–	–	–	25	39	.641	–	–	59	12	33	0	–	–	–	121	2.6	0.5	5.3

Palmer, Errol b. 1945 Ht. 6-5 Wt. 195 College: DePaul

SEASON–TEAM	G	GS	MIN	FGM	FGA	PCT	3FGM	3FGA	PCT	FTM	FTA	PCT	O-RB	D-RB	TOT	AST	PF	DQ	STL	TO	BLK	PTS	RPG	APG	PPG
67-68–Minnesota (A)	63	–	1191	165	453	.364	0	0	–	170	253	.672	–	–	471	91	169	2	–	78	–	500	7.5	1.4	7.9
Reg. ABA Totals	63	–	1191	165	453	.364	0	0	–	170	253	.672	–	–	471	91	169	2	–	78	–	500	7.5	1.4	7.9
ABA Playoff Totals	6	–	75	10	25	.400	0	0	–	8	10	.800	–	–	27	7	17	0	–	7	–	28	4.5	1.2	4.7

Palmer, James G. (Jim) b. June 8, 1933 Ht. 6-8 Wt. 225 College: Dayton

SEASON–TEAM	G	GS	MIN	FGM	FGA	PCT	3FGM	3FGA	PCT	FTM	FTA	PCT	O-RB	D-RB	TOT	AST	PF	DQ	STL	TO	BLK	PTS	RPG	APG	PPG
58-59–Cincinnati	67	–	1624	256	633	.404	–	–	–	178	246	.724	–	–	472	65	211	7	–	–	–	690	7.0	1.0	10.3
59-60–Cin.-N.Y.	74	–	1482	246	574	.429	–	–	–	119	174	.684	–	–	389	70	224	6	–	–	–	611	5.3	0.9	8.3
60-61–New York	55	–	688	125	310	.403	–	–	–	44	65	.677	–	–	179	30	128	0	–	–	–	294	3.3	0.5	5.3
Reg. Season Totals	196	–	3794	627	1517	.413	–	–	–	341	485	.703	–	–	1040	165	563	13	–	–	–	1595	5.3	0.8	8.1

Palmer, John S. (Bud) b. September 14, 1921 Ht. 6-4 Wt. 185 College: Princeton

SEASON–TEAM	G	GS	MIN	FGM	FGA	PCT	3FGM	3FGA	PCT	FTM	FTA	PCT	O-RB	D-RB	TOT	AST	PF	DQ	STL	TO	BLK	PTS	RPG	APG	PPG
46-47–New York	42	–	–	160	521	.307	–	–	–	81	121	.669	–	–	–	34	110	–	–	–	–	401	–	0.8	9.5
47-48–New York	48	–	–	224	710	.315	–	–	–	174	234	.744	–	–	–	45	149	–	–	–	–	622	–	0.9	13.0
48-49–New York	58	–	–	240	685	.350	–	–	–	234	307	.762	–	–	–	108	206	–	–	–	–	714	–	1.9	12.3
Reg. Season Totals	148	–	–	624	1916	.326	–	–	–	489	662	.739	–	–	–	187	465	–	–	–	–	1737	–	1.3	11.7
Playoff Totals	14	–	–	76	213	.380	–	–	–	49	70	.729	–	–	–	17	61	5	–	–	–	201	–	1.1	14.4

Palmer, Walter Scott b. October 23, 1968 Ht. 7-2 Wt. 215 College: Dartmouth

SEASON–TEAM	G	GS	MIN	FGM	FGA	PCT	3FGM	3FGA	PCT	FTM	FTA	PCT	O-RB	D-RB	TOT	AST	PF	DQ	STL	TO	BLK	PTS	RPG	APG	PPG
90-91–Utah	28	0	85	15	45	.333	0	1	.000	10	15	.667	6	15	21	6	20	0	3	6	4	40	0.8	0.2	1.4
92-93–Dallas	20	0	124	27	57	.474	0	0	–	6	9	.667	12	32	44	5	29	0	1	10	5	60	2.2	0.3	3.0
Reg. Season Totals	48	0	209	42	102	.412	0	1	.000	16	24	.667	18	47	65	11	49	0	4	16	9	100	1.4	0.2	2.1
Playoff Totals	2	0	6	1	4	.250	0	0	–	0	0	–	0	1	1	–	3	0	0	1	0	2	0.5	0.0	1.0

Parham, Estes Foster (Easy) b. December 27, 1921 d. October 1982 Ht. 6-3 Wt. 200 College: Texas Wesleyan

SEASON–TEAM	G	GS	MIN	FGM	FGA	PCT	3FGM	3FGA	PCT	FTM	FTA	PCT	O-RB	D-RB	TOT	AST	PF	DQ	STL	TO	BLK	PTS	RPG	APG	PPG
48-49–St. Louis	60	–	–	124	404	.307	–	–	–	96	172	.558	–	–	–	151	134	–	–	–	–	344	–	2.5	5.7
49-50–St. Louis	66	–	–	137	421	.325	–	–	–	88	178	.494	–	–	–	132	158	–	–	–	–	362	–	2.0	5.5
50-51–Philadelphia	7	–	–	3	7	.429	–	–	–	4	9	.444	–	–	12	3	5	0	–	–	–	10	1.7	0.4	1.4
Reg. Season Totals	133	–	–	264	832	.317	–	–	–	188	359	.524	–	–	12	286	297	0	–	–	–	716	1.7	2.2	5.4
Playoff Totals	2	–	–	5	17	.412	–	–	–	0	0	–	–	–	–	12	6	1	–	–	–	10	–	3.0	5.0

Parish, Robert Lee (The Chief) b. August 30, 1953 Ht. 7-1 Wt. 244 College: Centenary

SEASON–TEAM	G	GS	MIN	FGM	FGA	PCT	3FGM	3FGA	PCT	FTM	FTA	PCT	O-RB	D-RB	TOT	AST	PF	DQ	STL	TO	BLK	PTS	RPG	APG	PPG
76-77–Golden State	77	–	1384	288	573	.503	–	–	–	121	171	.708	201	342	543	74	224	7	55	–	94	697	7.1	1.0	9.1
77-78–Golden State	82	–	1969	430	911	.472	–	–	–	165	264	.625	211	469	680	95	291	10	79	201	123	1025	8.3	1.2	12.5
78-79–Golden State	76	–	2411	554	1110	.499	–	–	–	196	281	.698	265	651	916	115	303	10	100	233	217	1304	12.1	1.5	17.2
79-80–Golden State	72	–	2119	510	1006	.507	0	1	.000	203	284	.715	247	536	783	122	248	6	58	225	115	1223	10.9	1.7	17.0
80-81–Boston	82	–	2298	635	1166	.545	0	1	.000	282	397	.710	245	532	777	144	310	9	81	191	214	1552	9.5	1.8	18.9
81-82–Boston	80	78	2534	669	1235	.542	0	0	–	252	355	.710	288	578	866	140	267	5	68	221	192	1590	10.8	1.8	19.9
82-83–Boston	78	76	2459	619	1125	.550	0	1	.000	271	388	.698	260	567	827	141	222	4	79	185	148	1509	10.6	1.8	19.3
83-84–Boston	80	79	2867	623	1140	.546	0	0	–	274	368	.745	243	614	857	139	266	7	55	184	116	1520	10.7	1.7	19.0
84-85–Boston	79	78	2850	551	1016	.542	0	0	–	292	393	.743	263	577	840	125	223	2	56	186	101	1394	10.6	1.6	17.6
85-86–Boston	81	80	2567	530	966	.549	0	0	–	245	335	.731	246	524	770	145	215	3	65	187	116	1305	9.5	1.8	16.1
86-87–Boston	80	80	2995	588	1057	.556	0	1	.000	227	309	.735	254	597	851	173	266	5	64	191	144	1403	10.6	2.2	17.5
87-88–Boston	74	73	2312	442	750	.589	0	1	.000	177	241	.734	173	455	628	115	198	5	55	154	84	1061	8.5	1.6	14.3
88-89–Boston	80	80	2840	596	1045	.570	0	0	–	294	409	.719	342	654	996	175	209	2	79	200	116	1486	12.5	2.2	18.6
89-90–Boston	79	78	2396	505	871	.580	0	0	–	233	312	.747	259	537	796	103	189	2	38	169	69	1243	10.1	1.3	15.7
90-91–Boston	81	81	2441	485	811	.598	0	1	.000	237	309	.767	271	585	856	66	197	1	66	153	103	1207	10.6	0.8	14.9
91-92–Boston	79	79	2285	468	874	.535	0	0	–	179	232	.772	219	486	705	70	172	2	68	131	97	1115	8.9	0.9	14.1
92-93–Boston	79	79	2146	416	777	.535	0	0	–	162	235	.689	246	494	740	61	201	3	57	120	107	994	9.4	0.8	12.6
93-94–Boston	74	74	1987	356	725	.491	0	0	–	154	208	.740	141	401	542	82	190	3	42	108	96	866	7.3	1.1	11.7
94-95–Charlotte	81	4	1352	159	372	.427	0	0	–	71	101	.703	93	257	350	44	132	0	27	66	36	389	4.3	0.5	4.8
95-96–Charlotte	74	34	1086	120	241	.498	0	0	–	50	71	.704	89	214	303	29	80	0	21	50	54	290	4.1	0.4	3.9
96-97–Chicago	43	3	406	70	143	.490	0	0	–	21	31	.677	42	47	89	22	40	0	6	28	19	161	2.1	0.5	3.7
Reg. Season Totals	1611	1056	45704	9614	17914	.537	0	6	.000	4106	5694	.721	4598	10117	14715	2180	4443	86	1219	3183	2361	23334	9.1	1.4	14.5
Playoff Totals	184	151	6177	1132	2239	.506	0	1	.000	556	770	.722	571	1194	1765	234	617	16	145	365	309	2820	9.6	1.3	15.3
All-Star Totals	9	1	142	36	68	.529	0	0	–	14	21	.667	16	37	53	8	15	0	4	10	8	86	5.9	0.9	9.6

Park, Medford R. (Med) b. April 11, 1933 d. July 23, 1998 Ht. 6-2 Wt. 205 College: Missouri

SEASON–TEAM	G	GS	MIN	FGM	FGA	PCT	3FGM	3FGA	PCT	FTM	FTA	PCT	O-RB	D-RB	TOT	AST	PF	DQ	STL	TO	BLK	PTS	RPG	APG	PPG
55-56–St. Louis	40	–	424	53	152	.349	–	–	–	44	70	.629	–	–	94	40	64	0	–	–	–	150	2.4	1.0	3.8
56-57–St. Louis	66	–	1130	118	324	.364	–	–	–	108	146	.740	–	–	200	94	137	2	–	–	–	344	3.0	1.4	5.2
57-58–St. Louis	71	–	1103	133	363	.366	–	–	–	118	162	.728	–	–	184	76	106	0	–	–	–	384	2.6	1.1	5.4
58-59–St. Louis-Cin.	62	–	1126	145	361	.402	–	–	–	115	150	.767	–	–	188	108	93	0	–	–	–	405	3.0	1.7	6.5
59-60–Cincinnati	74	–	1849	226	582	.388	–	–	–	189	260	.727	–	–	301	214	180	2	–	–	–	641	4.1	2.9	8.7
Reg. Season Totals	313	–	5632	675	1782	.379	–	–	–	574	788	.728	–	–	967	532	580	4	–	–	–	1924	3.1	1.7	6.1
Playoff Totals	26	–	418	38	121	.314	–	–	–	53	77	.688	–	–	74	35	61	1	–	–	–	129	2.8	1.3	5.0

Parker, Anthony Michael b. June 19, 1975 Ht. 6-6 Wt. 215 College: Bradley

SEASON–TEAM	G	GS	MIN	FGM	FGA	PCT	3FGM	3FGA	PCT	FTM	FTA	PCT	O-RB	D-RB	TOT	AST	PF	DQ	STL	TO	BLK	PTS	RPG	APG	PPG
97-98–Philadelphia	37	0	196	25	63	.397	9	28	.321	13	20	.650	8	18	26	19	17	0	11	11	3	72	0.7	0.5	1.9
98-99–Philadelphia	2	0	3	1	1	1.000	0	0	–	0	0	–	0	0	0	0	0	0	0	0	0	2	0.0	0.0	1.0
99-00–Orlando	16	0	185	24	57	.421	1	14	.071	8	11	.727	5	22	27	10	13	0	8	11	4	57	1.7	0.6	3.6
Reg. Season Totals	55	0	384	50	121	.413	10	42	.238	21	31	.677	13	40	53	29	30	0	19	22	7	131	1.0	0.5	2.4

Parker, Robert S. Jr. (Sonny) b. March 22, 1955 Ht. 6-6 Wt. 210 College: Mineral Area (Mo.) Coll. (J.C.); Texas A&M

SEASON–TEAM	G	GS	MIN	FGM	FGA	PCT	3FGM	3FGA	PCT	FTM	FTA	PCT	O-RB	D-RB	TOT	AST	PF	DQ	STL	TO	BLK	PTS	RPG	APG	PPG
76-77–Golden State	65	–	889	154	292	.527	–	–	–	71	92	.772	85	88	173	59	77	0	53	–	26	379	2.7	0.9	5.8
77-78–Golden State	82	–	2069	406	783	.519	–	–	–	122	173	.705	167	222	389	155	186	0	135	128	36	934	4.7	1.9	11.4
78-79–Golden State	79	–	2893	512	1019	.502	–	–	–	175	222	.788	164	280	444	291	187	0	144	193	33	1199	5.6	3.7	15.2
79-80–Golden State	82	–	2849	483	988	.489	0	2	.000	237	302	.785	166	298	464	254	195	2	173	163	32	1203	5.7	3.1	14.7
80-81–Golden State	73	–	1317	191	388	.492	0	0	–	94	128	.734	101	93	194	106	112	0	67	84	13	476	2.7	1.5	6.5
81-82–Golden State	71	0	899	116	245	.473	0	0	–	48	72	.667	73	104	177	89	101	0	39	51	10	280	2.5	1.3	3.9
Reg. Season Totals	452	0	10916	1862	3715	.501	0	2	.000	747	989	.755	756	1085	1841	954	858	2	611	619	150	4471	4.1	2.1	9.9
Playoff Totals	10	0	120	19	36	.528	0	0	–	4	4	1.000	9	19	28	9	9	0	5	–	2	42	2.8	0.9	4.2

Parkhill, Barry b. May 10, 1951 Ht. 6-4 Wt. 185 College: Virginia

SEASON–TEAM	G	GS	MIN	FGM	FGA	PCT	3FGM	3FGA	PCT	FTM	FTA	PCT	O-RB	D-RB	TOT	AST	PF	DQ	STL	TO	BLK	PTS	RPG	APG	PPG
73-74–Virginia (A)	60	–	869	115	310	.371	3	16	.188	50	61	.820	13	52	65	96	151	–	28	80	12	283	1.1	1.6	4.7
74-75–Virginia (A)	78	–	1870	266	638	.417	0	8	.000	75	100	.750	27	106	133	226	228	–	50	170	11	607	1.7	2.9	7.8
75-76–St. Louis (A)	35	–	377	37	100	.370	1	11	.091	5	8	.625	2	24	26	64	46	–	9	29	7	80	0.7	1.8	2.3
Reg. ABA Totals	173	–	3116	418	1048	.399	4	35	.114	130	169	.769	42	182	224	386	425	0	87	279	30	970	1.3	2.2	5.6
ABA Playoff Totals	3	–	9	3	7	.429	0	0	–	0	0	–	0	1	1	2	0	0	1	0	0	6	0.3	0.7	2.0

Parkinson, Jack Gordon b. March 4, 1924 Ht. 6-0 Wt. 175 College: Kentucky

SEASON–TEAM	G	GS	MIN	FGM	FGA	PCT	3FGM	3FGA	PCT	FTM	FTA	PCT	O-RB	D-RB	TOT	AST	PF	DQ	STL	TO	BLK	PTS	RPG	APG	PPG
49-50–Indianapolis	4	–	–	1	12	.083	–	–	–	1	1	1.000	–	–	–	2	3	–	–	–	–	3	–	0.5	0.8
Reg. Season Totals	4	–	–	1	12	.083	–	–	–	1	1	1.000	–	–	–	2	3	–	–	–	–	3	–	0.5	0.8

Parks, Charles (Charley) b. 1946 Ht. 6-5 Wt. 210 College: Idaho State

SEASON–TEAM	G	GS	MIN	FGM	FGA	PCT	3FGM	3FGA	PCT	FTM	FTA	PCT	O-RB	D-RB	TOT	AST	PF	DQ	STL	TO	BLK	PTS	RPG	APG	PPG
68-69–Denver (A)	2	–	5	0	1	.000	0	0	–	0	0	–	–	–	0	0	1	0	–	0	–	0	0.0	0.0	0.0
Reg. ABA Totals	2	–	5	0	1	.000	0	0	–	0	0	–	–	–	–	0	1	0	–	–	–	0	0.0	0.0	0.0

Parks, Cherokee Bryan b. October 11, 1972 Ht. 6-11 Wt. 240 College: Duke

SEASON–TEAM	G	GS	MIN	FGM	FGA	PCT	3FGM	3FGA	PCT	FTM	FTA	PCT	O-RB	D-RB	TOT	AST	PF	DQ	STL	TO	BLK	PTS	RPG	APG	PPG
95-96–Dallas	64	3	869	101	247	.409	7	26	.269	41	62	.661	66	150	216	29	100	0	25	31	32	250	3.4	0.5	3.9
96-97–Minnesota	76	0	961	103	202	.510	0	1	.000	46	76	.605	83	112	195	34	150	2	41	32	48	252	2.6	0.4	3.3
97-98–Minnesota	79	43	1703	224	449	.499	0	1	.000	110	169	.651	140	297	437	53	237	4	36	66	86	558	5.5	0.7	7.1
98-99–Vancouver	48	41	1118	118	275	.429	0	1	.000	30	55	.545	75	168	243	36	114	0	28	49	28	266	5.1	0.8	5.5
99-00–Vancouver	56	14	808	72	145	.497	0	1	.000	24	37	.649	55	128	183	35	115	2	29	28	45	168	3.3	0.6	3.0
Reg. Season Totals	323	101	5459	618	1318	.469	7	30	.233	251	399	.629	419	855	1274	187	716	8	159	206	239	1494	3.9	0.6	4.6
Playoff Totals	2	0	12	2	3	.667	0	0	–	0	0	–	0	5	5	–	5	0	1	0	0	4	2.5	0.0	2.0

Parks, Richard E. (Rich) b. October 28, 1943 d. August 1978 Ht. 6-7 Wt. 235 College: Tulsa; St. Louis

SEASON–TEAM	G	GS	MIN	FGM	FGA	PCT	3FGM	3FGA	PCT	FTM	FTA	PCT	O-RB	D-RB	TOT	AST	PF	DQ	STL	TO	BLK	PTS	RPG	APG	PPG
67-68–Pittsburgh (A)	40	–	374	59	133	.444	1	3	.333	12	21	.571	–	–	116	14	68	3	–	19	–	131	2.9	0.4	3.3
Reg. ABA Totals	40	–	374	59	133	.444	1	3	.333	12	21	.571	–	–	116	14	68	3	–	19	–	131	2.9	0.4	3.3
ABA Playoff Totals	5	–	7	0	2	.000	0	1	.000	1	4	.250	–	–	2	0	3	0	–	–	–	1	0.4	0.0	0.2

Parr, Jack b. March 13, 1936 Ht. 6-9 Wt. 220 College: Kansas State

SEASON–TEAM	G	GS	MIN	FGM	FGA	PCT	3FGM	3FGA	PCT	FTM	FTA	PCT	O-RB	D-RB	TOT	AST	PF	DQ	STL	TO	BLK	PTS	RPG	APG	PPG
58-59–Cincinnati	66	–	1037	109	307	.355	–	–	–	44	73	.603	–	–	278	51	138	1	–	–	–	262	4.2	0.8	4.0
Reg. Season Totals	66	–	1037	109	307	.355	–	–	–	44	73	.603	–	–	278	51	138	1	–	–	–	262	4.2	0.8	4.0

Parrack, Doyle Kenneth b. December 6, 1921 Ht. 6-0 Wt. 165 College: Oklahoma State

SEASON–TEAM	G	GS	MIN	FGM	FGA	PCT	3FGM	3FGA	PCT	FTM	FTA	PCT	O-RB	D-RB	TOT	AST	PF	DQ	STL	TO	BLK	PTS	RPG	APG	PPG
46-47–Chicago	58	–	–	110	413	.266	–	–	–	52	80	.650	–	–	–	20	77	–	–	–	–	272	–	0.3	4.7
Reg. Season Totals	58	–	–	110	413	.266	–	–	–	52	80	.650	–	–	–	20	77	–	–	–	–	272	–	0.3	4.7
Playoff Totals	10	–	–	0	18	.000	–	–	–	3	3	1.000	–	–	–	2	4	–	–	–	–	3	0.0	0.1	0.3

Parsley, Charles H. (Charlie) b. October 13, 1925 Ht. 6-2 Wt. 175 College: Western Kentucky

SEASON–TEAM	G	GS	MIN	FGM	FGA	PCT	3FGM	3FGA	PCT	FTM	FTA	PCT	O-RB	D-RB	TOT	AST	PF	DQ	STL	TO	BLK	PTS	RPG	APG	PPG
49-50–Philadelphia	9	–	–	8	31	.258	–	–	–	6	7	.857	–	–	–	8	7	–	–	–	–	22	–	0.9	2.4
Reg. Season Totals	9	–	–	8	31	.258	–	–	–	6	7	.857	–	–	–	8	7	–	–	–	–	22	–	0.9	2.4

Paspalj, Zarko b. March 27, 1966 Ht. 6-9 Wt. 215 College: None

SEASON–TEAM	G	GS	MIN	FGM	FGA	PCT	3FGM	3FGA	PCT	FTM	FTA	PCT	O-RB	D-RB	TOT	AST	PF	DQ	STL	TO	BLK	PTS	RPG	APG	PPG
89-90–San Antonio	28	1	181	27	79	.342	0	1	.000	18	22	.818	15	15	30	10	37	0	3	21	7	72	1.1	0.4	2.6
Reg. Season Totals	28	1	181	27	79	.342	0	1	.000	18	22	.818	15	15	30	10	37	0	3	21	7	72	1.1	0.4	2.6

Passaglia, Martin Harold (Marty) b. April 22, 1919 Ht. 6-1 Wt. 170 College: Santa Clara

SEASON–TEAM	G	GS	MIN	FGM	FGA	PCT	3FGM	3FGA	PCT	FTM	FTA	PCT	O-RB	D-RB	TOT	AST	PF	DQ	STL	TO	BLK	PTS	RPG	APG	PPG
46-47–Washington	43	–	–	51	221	.231	–	–	–	18	32	.563	–	–	–	9	44	–	–	–	–	120	–	0.2	2.8
48-49–Indianapolis	19	–	–	14	57	.246	–	–	–	3	4	.750	–	–	–	17	17	–	–	–	–	31	–	0.9	1.6
Reg. Season Totals	62	–	–	65	278	.234	–	–	–	21	36	.583	–	–	–	26	61	–	–	–	–	151	–	0.4	2.4
Playoff Totals	7	–	–	2	28	.143	–	–	–	1	4	.250	–	–	–	–	11	–	–	–	–	5	0.0	0.0	0.7

Pastushok, George A. b. 1923 Ht. 6-1 Wt. 195 College: Manhattan; St. John's (N.Y.)

SEASON–TEAM	G	GS	MIN	FGM	FGA	PCT	3FGM	3FGA	PCT	FTM	FTA	PCT	O-RB	D-RB	TOT	AST	PF	DQ	STL	TO	BLK	PTS	RPG	APG	PPG
46-47–Providence	39	–	–	48	183	.262	–	–	–	25	46	.543	–	–	–	15	42	–	–	–	–	121	–	0.4	3.1
Reg. Season Totals	39	–	–	48	183	.262	–	–	–	25	46	.543	–	–	–	15	42	–	–	–	–	121	–	0.4	3.1

Patrick, Myles b. November 16, 1954 Ht. 6-8 Wt. 220 College: Auburn

SEASON–TEAM	G	GS	MIN	FGM	FGA	PCT	3FGM	3FGA	PCT	FTM	FTA	PCT	O-RB	D-RB	TOT	AST	PF	DQ	STL	TO	BLK	PTS	RPG	APG	PPG
80-81–Los Angeles	3	–	9	2	5	.400	0	0	–	1	2	.500	1	1	2	1	3	0	0	1	0	5	0.7	0.3	1.7
Reg. Season Totals	3	–	9	2	5	.400	0	0	–	1	2	.500	1	1	2	1	3	0	0	1	0	5	0.7	0.3	1.7

Patrick, Stanley A. (Stan) b. May 5, 1922 d. January 1, 2000 Ht. 6-3 Wt. 215 College: Santa Clara; Illinois

SEASON–TEAM	G	GS	MIN	FGM	FGA	PCT	3FGM	3FGA	PCT	FTM	FTA	PCT	O-RB	D-RB	TOT	AST	PF	DQ	STL	TO	BLK	PTS	RPG	APG	PPG
44-45–Chicago (N)	28	–	–	187	–	–	–	–	–	84	–	–	–	–	–	–	–	–	–	–	–	458	–	–	16.4
45-46–Chicago (N)	33	–	–	123	–	–	–	–	–	66	100	.660	–	–	–	–	42	–	–	–	–	312	–	–	9.5
46-47–Chicago (N)	42	–	–	72	–	–	–	–	–	36	67	.537	–	–	–	–	61	–	–	–	–	180	–	–	4.3
47-48–Flint (N)	48	–	–	149	–	–	–	–	–	90	144	.625	–	–	–	–	104	–	–	–	–	388	–	–	8.1
48-49–Hammond (N)	61	–	–	150	–	–	–	–	–	127	192	.661	–	–	–	–	97	–	–	–	–	427	–	–	7.0
49-50–Wat.-She.	53	–	–	116	294	.395	–	–	–	89	147	.605	–	–	–	74	76	–	–	–	–	321	–	1.4	6.1
Reg. NBA Totals	53	–	–	116	294	.395	–	–	–	89	147	.605	–	–	–	74	76	–	–	–	–	321	–	1.4	6.1
Reg. NBL Totals	212	–	–	681	–	–	–	–	–	403	503	.634	–	–	–	–	304	–	–	–	–	1765	–	–	8.3
NBA Playoff Totals	3	–	–	4	7	.571	–	–	–	2	3	.667	–	–	–	1	2	–	–	–	–	10	0.0	0.3	3.3
NBL Playoff Totals	16	–	–	39	–	–	–	–	–	16	26	.538	–	–	–	–	35	–	–	–	–	94	–	–	5.9

Patterson, Andrae Malone b. November 12, 1975 Ht. 6-9 Wt. 238 College: Indiana

SEASON–TEAM	G	GS	MIN	FGM	FGA	PCT	3FGM	3FGA	PCT	FTM	FTA	PCT	O-RB	D-RB	TOT	AST	PF	DQ	STL	TO	BLK	PTS	RPG	APG	PPG
98-99–Minnesota	35	0	284	43	97	.443	0	5	.000	28	36	.778	30	35	65	15	62	1	19	22	7	114	1.9	0.4	3.3
99-00–Minnesota	5	0	20	3	4	.750	0	0	–	0	0	–	1	1	2	1	4	0	1	1	0	6	0.4	0.2	1.2
Reg. Season Totals	40	0	304	46	101	.455	0	5	.000	28	36	.778	31	36	67	16	66	1	20	23	7	120	1.7	0.4	3.0
Playoff Totals	2	0	7	0	0	–	0	0	–	0	0	–	1	3	4	2	1	0	0	1	0	0	2.0	1.0	0.0

Patterson, George b. November 26, 1939 Ht. 6-8 Wt. 230 College: Toledo

SEASON–TEAM	G	GS	MIN	FGM	FGA	PCT	3FGM	3FGA	PCT	FTM	FTA	PCT	O-RB	D-RB	TOT	AST	PF	DQ	STL	TO	BLK	PTS	RPG	APG	PPG
67-68–Detroit	59	–	559	44	133	.331	–	–	–	32	38	.842	–	–	159	51	85	0	–	–	–	120	2.7	0.9	2.0
Reg. Season Totals	59	–	559	44	133	.331	–	–	–	32	38	.842	–	–	159	51	85	0	–	–	–	120	2.7	0.9	2.0
Playoff Totals	1	–	4	0	0	–	–	–	–	0	0	–	–	–	1	1	0	0	–	–	–	0	1.0	1.0	0.0

Patterson, Ruben Nathaniel b. July 31, 1975 Ht. 6-6 Wt. 227 College: Cincinnati

SEASON–TEAM	G	GS	MIN	FGM	FGA	PCT	3FGM	3FGA	PCT	FTM	FTA	PCT	O-RB	D-RB	TOT	AST	PF	DQ	STL	TO	BLK	PTS	RPG	APG	PPG
98-99–L.A. Lakers	24	2	144	21	51	.412	1	6	.167	22	31	.710	17	13	30	2	16	0	5	12	3	65	1.3	0.1	2.7
99-00–Seattle	81	74	2097	354	661	.536	12	27	.444	222	321	.692	218	216	434	126	190	0	94	144	40	942	5.4	1.6	11.6
Reg. Season Totals	105	76	2241	375	712	.527	13	33	.394	244	352	.693	235	229	464	128	206	0	99	156	43	1007	4.4	1.2	9.6
Playoff Totals	8	0	89	14	27	.519	0	2	.000	13	15	.867	9	6	15	2	6	0	3	9	2	41	1.9	0.3	5.1

Patterson, Steven J. (Steve) b. June 24, 1948 Ht. 6-9 Wt. 225 College: UCLA

SEASON–TEAM	G	GS	MIN	FGM	FGA	PCT	3FGM	3FGA	PCT	FTM	FTA	PCT	O-RB	D-RB	TOT	AST	PF	DQ	STL	TO	BLK	PTS	RPG	APG	PPG
71-72–Cleveland	65	–	775	94	263	.357	–	–	–	23	46	.500	–	–	228	54	80	0	–	–	–	211	3.5	0.8	3.2
72-73–Cleveland	62	–	710	71	198	.359	–	–	–	34	65	.523	–	–	228	51	79	1	–	–	–	176	3.7	0.8	2.8
73-74–Cleveland	76	–	1910	262	599	.437	–	–	–	69	112	.616	223	396	619	165	193	3	48	–	58	593	8.1	2.2	7.8
74-75–Cleveland	81	–	1269	161	387	.416	–	–	–	48	73	.658	112	217	329	93	128	1	21	–	20	370	4.1	1.1	4.6
75-76–Clev.-Chicago	66	–	918	84	220	.382	–	–	–	34	54	.630	80	148	228	80	93	1	16	–	16	202	3.5	1.2	3.1
Reg. Season Totals	350	–	5582	672	1667	.403	–	–	–	208	350	.594	415	761	1632	443	573	6	85	–	94	1552	4.7	1.3	4.4

Patterson, Tommie J. (Tommy) b. October 15, 1948 Ht. 6-6 Wt. 220 College: Ouachita Baptist

SEASON–TEAM	G	GS	MIN	FGM	FGA	PCT	3FGM	3FGA	PCT	FTM	FTA	PCT	O-RB	D-RB	TOT	AST	PF	DQ	STL	TO	BLK	PTS	RPG	APG	PPG
72-73–Baltimore	23	–	92	21	49	.429	–	–	–	13	16	.813	–	–	22	3	18	0	–	–	–	55	1.0	0.1	2.4
73-74–Capital	2	–	8	0	1	.000	–	–	–	1	2	.500	1	1	2	2	0	0	0	–	0	1	1.0	1.0	0.5
Reg. Season Totals	25	–	100	21	50	.420	–	–	–	14	18	.778	1	1	24	5	18	0	0	–	0	56	1.0	0.2	2.2
Playoff Totals	1	–	1	0	0	–	–	–	–	0	0	–	0	0	0	–	0	0	0	–	0	0	0.0	0.0	0.0

Patterson, Worthington R. (Worthy) b. June 17, 1931 Ht. 6-2 Wt. 175 College: Connecticut

SEASON–TEAM	G	GS	MIN	FGM	FGA	PCT	3FGM	3FGA	PCT	FTM	FTA	PCT	O-RB	D-RB	TOT	AST	PF	DQ	STL	TO	BLK	PTS	RPG	APG	PPG
57-58–St. Louis	4	–	3	3	8	.375	–	–	–	1	2	.500	–	–	2	2	3	0	–	–	–	7	0.5	0.5	1.8
Reg. Season Totals	4	–	3	3	8	.375	–	–	–	1	2	.500	–	–	2	2	3	0	–	–	–	7	0.5	0.5	1.8

Paulk, Charles (Charlie) b. June 14, 1946 Ht. 6-9 Wt. 220 College: Tulsa; Northeastern State (Okla.)

SEASON–TEAM	G	GS	MIN	FGM	FGA	PCT	3FGM	3FGA	PCT	FTM	FTA	PCT	O-RB	D-RB	TOT	AST	PF	DQ	STL	TO	BLK	PTS	RPG	APG	PPG
68-69–Milwaukee	17	–	217	19	84	.226	–	–	–	13	23	.565	–	–	78	3	26	0	–	–	–	51	4.6	0.2	3.0
70-71–Cincinnati	68	–	1213	274	637	.430	–	–	–	79	131	.603	–	–	320	27	186	6	–	–	–	627	4.7	0.4	9.2
71-72–Chicago-N.Y.	35	–	211	24	88	.273	–	–	–	15	21	.714	–	–	64	11	31	0	–	–	–	63	1.8	0.3	1.8
Reg. Season Totals	120	–	1641	317	809	.392	–	–	–	107	175	.611	–	–	462	41	243	6	–	–	–	741	3.9	0.3	6.2
Playoff Totals	7	–	13	3	10	.300	–	–	–	0	0	–	–	–	5	–	5	0	–	–	–	6	0.7	0.0	0.9

Paulson, Gerald Arthur (Jerry) b. July 21, 1935 d. March 6, 1986 Ht. 6-2 Wt. 185 College: Manhattan

SEASON–TEAM	G	GS	MIN	FGM	FGA	PCT	3FGM	3FGA	PCT	FTM	FTA	PCT	O-RB	D-RB	TOT	AST	PF	DQ	STL	TO	BLK	PTS	RPG	APG	PPG
57-58–Cincinnati	6	–	68	8	23	.348	–	–	–	4	6	.667	–	–	10	4	5	0	–	–	–	20	1.7	0.7	3.3
Reg. Season Totals	6	–	68	8	23	.348	–	–	–	4	6	.667	–	–	10	4	5	0	–	–	–	20	1.7	0.7	3.3

Paultz, William Edward (Billy, The Whopper) b. July 30, 1948 Ht. 6-11 Wt. 245 College: Cameron; St. John's (N.Y.)

SEASON–TEAM	G	GS	MIN	FGM	FGA	PCT	3FGM	3FGA	PCT	FTM	FTA	PCT	O-RB	D-RB	TOT	AST	PF	DQ	STL	TO	BLK	PTS	RPG	APG	PPG
70-71–New York (A)	83	–	2758	510	973	.524	0	2	.000	201	269	.747	239	701	940	160	274	–	–	–	–	1221	11.3	1.9	14.7
71-72–New York (A)	83	–	2824	498	1021	.488	0	3	.000	207	299	.692	263	772	1035	128	298	–	–	214	–	1203	12.5	1.5	14.5
72-73–New York (A)	81	–	2800	532	1027	.518	0	2	.000	287	405	.709	279	736	1015	189	259	5	–	213	214	1351	12.5	2.3	16.7
73-74–New York (A)	77	–	2596	519	1051	.494	0	1	.000	222	308	.721	211	571	782	167	238	–	60	175	147	1260	10.2	2.2	16.4
74-75–New York (A)	80	–	2826	524	1080	.485	0	3	.000	214	286	.748	174	598	772	179	273	–	59	149	137	1262	9.7	2.2	15.8
75-76–San Antonio (A)	83	–	2958	566	1124	.504	0	2	.000	238	324	.735	210	652	862	340	232	–	61	231	253	1370	10.4	4.1	16.5
76-77–San Antonio	82	–	2694	521	1102	.473	–	–	–	238	320	.744	192	495	687	223	262	5	55	–	173	1280	8.4	2.7	15.6
77-78–San Antonio	80	–	2479	518	979	.529	–	–	–	230	306	.752	172	503	675	213	222	3	42	167	194	1266	8.4	2.7	15.8
78-79–San Antonio	79	–	2122	399	758	.526	–	–	–	114	194	.588	169	456	625	178	204	4	35	157	125	912	7.9	2.3	11.5
79-80–S.A.-Houston	84	–	2193	327	673	.486	0	1	.000	109	182	.599	187	399	586	188	213	3	69	115	84	763	7.0	2.2	9.1
80-81–Houston	81	–	1659	262	517	.507	0	0	–	75	153	.490	111	280	391	105	182	1	28	89	72	599	4.8	1.3	7.4
81-82–Houston	65	3	807	89	226	.394	0	0	–	34	65	.523	54	126	180	41	99	0	15	45	22	212	2.8	0.6	3.3
82-83–Houston-S.A.	64	0	820	101	227	.445	0	0	–	27	59	.458	64	136	200	61	109	0	17	47	18	229	3.1	1.0	3.6
83-84–Atlanta	40	4	486	36	88	.409	0	0	–	17	33	.515	35	78	113	18	57	0	8	22	7	89	2.8	0.5	2.2
84-85–Utah	62	0	370	32	87	.368	0	0	–	18	28	.643	24	72	96	16	51	0	6	30	11	82	1.5	0.3	1.3
Reg. NBA Totals	637	7	13630	2285	4657	.491	0	1	.000	862	1340	.643	1008	2545	3553	1043	1399	16	275	672	706	5432	5.6	1.6	8.5
Reg. ABA Totals	487	–	16762	3149	6276	.502	0	13	.000	1369	1891	.724	1376	4030	5406	1163	1574	5	180	982	751	7667	11.1	2.4	15.7
NBA Playoff Totals	70	0	1616	215	505	.426	0	1	.000	85	129	.659	113	267	380	106	157	1	30	67	54	515	5.4	1.5	7.4
ABA Playoff Totals	56	–	2172	372	733	.508	1	3	.333	206	285	.723	159	523	682	115	216	0	13	115	65	951	12.2	2.1	17.0

Paxson, James Edward Sr. (Jim) b. December 19, 1932 Ht. 6-6 Wt. 200 College: Dayton

SEASON–TEAM	G	GS	MIN	FGM	FGA	PCT	3FGM	3FGA	PCT	FTM	FTA	PCT	O-RB	D-RB	TOT	AST	PF	DQ	STL	TO	BLK	PTS	RPG	APG	PPG
56-57–Minneapolis	71	–	1274	138	485	.285	–	–	–	170	236	.720	–	–	266	86	163	3	–	–	–	446	3.7	1.2	6.3
57-58–Cincinnati	67	–	1795	225	639	.352	–	–	–	209	285	.733	–	–	350	139	183	2	–	–	–	659	5.2	2.1	9.8
Reg. Season Totals	138	–	3069	363	1124	.323	–	–	–	379	521	.727	–	–	616	225	346	5	–	–	–	1105	4.5	1.6	8.0
Playoff Totals	7	–	84	12	47	.255	–	–	–	13	22	.591	–	–	22	8	11	0	–	–	–	37	3.1	1.1	5.3

Paxson, James Joseph (Jim) b. July 9, 1957 Ht. 6-6 Wt. 200 College: Dayton

SEASON–TEAM	G	GS	MIN	FGM	FGA	PCT	3FGM	3FGA	PCT	FTM	FTA	PCT	O-RB	D-RB	TOT	AST	PF	DQ	STL	TO	BLK	PTS	RPG	APG	PPG
79-80–Portland	72	–	1270	189	460	.411	1	22	.045	64	90	.711	25	84	109	144	97	0	48	93	5	443	1.5	2.0	6.2
80-81–Portland	79	–	2701	585	1092	.536	2	30	.067	182	248	.734	74	137	211	299	172	1	140	131	9	1354	2.7	3.8	17.1
81-82–Portland	82	82	2756	662	1259	.526	8	35	.229	220	287	.767	75	146	221	276	159	0	129	144	12	1552	2.7	3.4	18.9
82-83–Portland	81	81	2740	682	1323	.515	4	25	.160	388	478	.812	68	106	174	231	160	0	140	156	17	1756	2.1	2.9	21.7
83-84–Portland	81	81	2686	680	1322	.514	17	59	.288	345	410	.841	68	105	173	251	165	0	122	142	10	1722	2.1	3.1	21.3
84-85–Portland	68	57	2253	508	988	.514	6	39	.154	196	248	.790	69	153	222	264	115	0	101	108	5	1218	3.3	3.9	17.9
85-86–Portland	75	31	1931	372	792	.470	20	62	.323	217	244	.889	42	106	148	278	156	3	94	112	5	981	2.0	3.7	13.1
86-87–Portland	72	1	1798	337	733	.460	26	98	.265	174	216	.806	41	98	139	237	134	0	76	108	12	874	1.9	3.3	12.1
87-88–Port.-Boston	45	3	801	137	298	.460	5	21	.238	68	79	.861	15	30	45	76	73	0	30	39	5	347	1.0	1.7	7.7
88-89–Boston	57	7	1138	202	445	.454	4	24	.167	84	103	.816	18	56	74	107	96	0	38	57	8	492	1.3	1.9	8.6
89-90–Boston	72	25	1283	191	422	.453	5	20	.250	73	90	.811	24	53	77	137	115	0	33	54	5	460	1.1	1.9	6.4
Reg. Season Totals	784	368	21357	4545	9134	.498	98	435	.225	2011	2493	.807	519	1074	1593	2300	1442	4	951	1144	93	11199	2.0	2.9	14.3
Playoff Totals	53	12	1107	212	458	.463	8	30	.267	122	151	.808	27	53	80	100	81	1	38	56	4	554	1.5	1.9	10.5
All-Star Totals	2	0	31	10	16	.625	0	0	–	1	2	.500	1	2	3	3	0	0	2	4	0	21	1.5	1.5	10.5

Paxson, John MacBeth b. September 29, 1960 Ht. 6-2 Wt. 185 College: Notre Dame

SEASON–TEAM	G	GS	MIN	FGM	FGA	PCT	3FGM	3FGA	PCT	FTM	FTA	PCT	O-RB	D-RB	TOT	AST	PF	DQ	STL	TO	BLK	PTS	RPG	APG	PPG
83-84–San Antonio	49	0	458	61	137	.445	4	22	.182	16	26	.615	4	29	33	149	47	0	10	32	2	142	0.7	3.0	2.9
84-85–San Antonio	78	1	1259	196	385	.509	10	34	.294	84	100	.840	19	49	68	215	117	0	45	81	3	486	0.9	2.8	6.2
85-86–Chicago	75	3	1570	153	328	.466	15	51	.294	74	92	.804	18	76	94	274	172	2	55	63	2	395	1.3	3.7	5.3
86-87–Chicago	82	64	2689	386	793	.487	52	140	.371	106	131	.809	22	117	139	467	207	1	66	105	8	930	1.7	5.7	11.3
87-88–Chicago	81	30	1888	287	582	.493	33	95	.347	33	45	.733	16	88	104	303	154	2	49	64	1	640	1.3	3.7	7.9
88-89–Chicago	78	20	1738	246	513	.480	44	133	.331	31	36	.861	13	81	94	308	162	1	53	71	6	567	1.2	3.9	7.3
89-90–Chicago	82	82	2365	365	708	.516	33	92	.359	56	68	.824	27	92	119	335	176	1	83	85	6	819	1.5	4.1	10.0
90-91–Chicago	82	82	1971	317	578	.548	42	96	.438	34	41	.829	15	76	91	297	136	0	62	69	3	710	1.1	3.6	8.7
91-92–Chicago	79	79	1946	257	487	.528	12	44	.273	29	37	.784	21	75	96	241	142	0	49	44	9	555	1.2	3.1	7.0
92-93–Chicago	59	8	1030	105	233	.451	19	41	.463	17	20	.850	9	39	48	136	99	0	38	31	2	246	0.8	2.3	4.2
93-94–Chicago	27	0	343	30	68	.441	9	22	.409	1	2	.500	3	17	20	33	18	0	7	6	2	70	0.7	1.2	2.6
Reg. Season Totals	772	369	17257	2403	4812	.499	273	770	.355	481	598	.804	167	739	906	2758	1430	7	517	651	44	5560	1.2	3.6	7.2
Playoff Totals	119	57	2617	306	620	.494	45	122	.369	91	105	.867	11	98	109	306	249	6	65	71	3	748	0.9	2.6	6.3

Payak, John Jr. (Johnny) b. November 20, 1926 Ht. 6-4 Wt. 180 College: Bowling Green State

SEASON–TEAM	G	GS	MIN	FGM	FGA	PCT	3FGM	3FGA	PCT	FTM	FTA	PCT	O-RB	D-RB	TOT	AST	PF	DQ	STL	TO	BLK	PTS	RPG	APG	PPG
49-50–Phil.-Wat.	52	–	–	98	331	.296	–	–	–	121	173	.699	–	–	–	86	113	–	–	–	–	317	–	1.7	6.1
52-53–Milwaukee	68	–	1470	128	373	.343	–	–	–	180	248	.726	–	–	114	140	194	7	–	–	–	436	1.7	2.1	6.4
Reg. Season Totals	120	–	1470	226	704	.321	–	–	–	301	421	.715	–	–	114	226	307	7	–	–	–	753	1.7	1.9	6.3

Payne, Kenneth Victor (Kenny) b. November 25, 1966 Ht. 6-8 Wt. 220 College: Louisville

SEASON–TEAM	G	GS	MIN	FGM	FGA	PCT	3FGM	3FGA	PCT	FTM	FTA	PCT	O-RB	D-RB	TOT	AST	PF	DQ	STL	TO	BLK	PTS	RPG	APG	PPG
89-90–Philadelphia	35	4	216	47	108	.435	4	10	.400	16	18	.889	11	15	26	10	37	0	7	20	6	114	0.7	0.3	3.3
90-91–Philadelphia	47	6	444	68	189	.360	4	18	.222	26	29	.897	17	49	66	16	43	0	10	21	6	166	1.4	0.3	3.5
91-92–Philadelphia	49	3	353	65	145	.448	5	12	.417	9	13	.692	13	41	54	17	34	0	16	19	8	144	1.1	0.3	2.9
92-93–Philadelphia	13	0	154	38	90	.422	4	18	.222	4	4	1.000	4	20	24	18	15	0	5	7	2	84	1.8	1.4	6.5
Reg. Season Totals	144	13	1167	218	532	.410	17	58	.293	55	64	.859	45	125	170	61	129	0	38	67	22	508	1.2	0.4	3.5
Playoff Totals	3	0	10	2	5	.400	0	2	.000	2	2	1.000	1	1	2	–	3	0	0	1	0	6	0.7	0.0	2.0

Payne, Tom b. November 19, 1950 Ht. 7-2 Wt. 240 College: Kentucky

SEASON–TEAM	G	GS	MIN	FGM	FGA	PCT	3FGM	3FGA	PCT	FTM	FTA	PCT	O-RB	D-RB	TOT	AST	PF	DQ	STL	TO	BLK	PTS	RPG	APG	PPG
71-72–Atlanta	29	–	227	45	103	.437	–	–	–	29	46	.630	–	–	69	15	40	0	–	–	–	119	2.4	0.5	4.1
Reg. Season Totals	29	–	227	45	103	.437	–	–	–	29	46	.630	–	–	69	15	40	0	–	–	–	119	2.4	0.5	4.1
Playoff Totals	1	–	5	1	1	1.000	–	–	–	2	5	.400	–	–	4	–	1	0	–	–	–	4	4.0	0.0	4.0

Payton, Gary Dwayne (The Glove) b. July 23, 1968 Ht. 6-4 Wt. 180 College: Oregon State

SEASON–TEAM	G	GS	MIN	FGM	FGA	PCT	3FGM	3FGA	PCT	FTM	FTA	PCT	O-RB	D-RB	TOT	AST	PF	DQ	STL	TO	BLK	PTS	RPG	APG	PPG
90-91–Seattle	82	82	2244	259	575	.450	1	13	.077	69	97	.711	108	135	243	528	249	3	165	180	15	588	3.0	6.4	7.2
91-92–Seattle	81	79	2549	331	734	.451	3	23	.130	99	148	.669	123	172	295	506	248	0	147	174	21	764	3.6	6.2	9.4
92-93–Seattle	82	78	2548	476	963	.494	7	34	.206	151	196	.770	95	186	281	399	250	1	177	148	21	1110	3.4	4.9	13.5
93-94–Seattle	82	82	2881	584	1159	.504	15	54	.278	166	279	.595	105	164	269	494	227	0	188	173	19	1349	3.3	6.0	16.5
94-95–Seattle	82	82	3015	685	1345	.509	70	232	.302	249	348	.716	108	173	281	583	206	1	204	201	13	1689	3.4	7.1	20.6
95-96–Seattle	81	81	3162	618	1276	.484	98	299	.328	229	306	.748	104	235	339	608	221	1	231	260	19	1563	4.2	7.5	19.3
96-97–Seattle	82	82	3213	706	1482	.476	119	380	.313	254	355	.715	106	272	378	583	208	1	197	215	13	1785	4.6	7.1	21.8
97-98–Seattle	82	82	3145	579	1278	.453	134	397	.338	279	375	.744	77	299	376	679	195	0	185	229	18	1571	4.6	8.3	19.2
98-99–Seattle	50	50	2008	401	923	.434	83	281	.295	199	276	.721	62	182	244	436	115	0	109	154	12	1084	4.9	8.7	21.7
99-00–Seattle	82	82	3425	747	1666	.448	177	520	.340	311	423	.735	100	429	529	732	178	0	153	224	18	1982	6.5	8.9	24.2
Reg. Season Totals	786	780	28190	5386	11401	.472	707	2233	.317	2006	2803	.716	988	2247	3235	5548	2097	7	1756	1958	169	13485	4.1	7.1	17.2
Playoff Totals	89	89	3420	612	1341	.456	100	276	.362	233	328	.710	101	268	369	543	276	3	153	210	21	1557	4.1	6.1	17.5
All-Star Totals	6	2	140	23	54	.426	2	16	.125	11	11	1.000	10	14	24	60	7	0	14	19	0	59	4.0	10.0	9.8

Payton, Melvin E. (Mel) b. July 16, 1926 Ht. 6-4 Wt. 185 College: Tulane

SEASON–TEAM	G	GS	MIN	FGM	FGA	PCT	3FGM	3FGA	PCT	FTM	FTA	PCT	O-RB	D-RB	TOT	AST	PF	DQ	STL	TO	BLK	PTS	RPG	APG	PPG
51-52–Philadelphia	45	–	471	54	140	.386	–	–	–	21	28	.750	–	–	83	45	68	2	–	–	–	129	1.8	1.0	2.9
52-53–Indianapolis	66	–	1424	173	485	.357	–	–	–	120	161	.745	–	–	313	81	118	0	–	–	–	466	4.7	1.2	7.1
Reg. Season Totals	111	–	1895	227	625	.363	–	–	–	141	189	.746	–	–	396	126	186	2	–	–	–	595	3.6	1.1	5.4
Playoff Totals	5	–	72	8	19	.421	–	–	–	9	10	.900	–	–	9	1	13	0	–	–	–	25	1.8	0.2	5.0

Pearcy, George W. (Wig) b. July 2, 1919 Ht. 6-1 Wt. 165 College: Indiana State

SEASON–TEAM	G	GS	MIN	FGM	FGA	PCT	3FGM	3FGA	PCT	FTM	FTA	PCT	O-RB	D-RB	TOT	AST	PF	DQ	STL	TO	BLK	PTS	RPG	APG	PPG
46-47–Detroit	37	–	–	31	130	.238	–	–	–	32	44	.727	–	–	–	13	68	–	–	–	–	94	–	0.4	2.5
Reg. Season Totals	37	–	–	31	130	.238	–	–	–	32	44	.727	–	–	–	13	68	–	–	–	–	94	–	0.4	2.5

Pearcy, Henry Earl b. July 21, 1922 Ht. 6-1 Wt. 170 College: Indiana State

SEASON–TEAM	G	GS	MIN	FGM	FGA	PCT	3FGM	3FGA	PCT	FTM	FTA	PCT	O-RB	D-RB	TOT	AST	PF	DQ	STL	TO	BLK	PTS	RPG	APG	PPG
46-47–Detroit	29	–	–	24	108	.222	–	–	–	25	34	.735	–	–	–	7	20	–	–	–	–	73	–	0.2	2.5
Reg. Season Totals	29	–	–	24	108	.222	–	–	–	25	34	.735	–	–	–	7	20	–	–	–	–	73	–	0.2	2.5

Peck, Wiley J. b. September 15, 1957 Ht. 6-7 Wt. 220 College: Mississippi State

SEASON–TEAM	G	GS	MIN	FGM	FGA	PCT	3FGM	3FGA	PCT	FTM	FTA	PCT	O-RB	D-RB	TOT	AST	PF	DQ	STL	TO	BLK	PTS	RPG	APG	PPG
79-80–San Antonio	52	–	628	73	169	.432	0	2	.000	34	55	.618	66	117	183	33	100	2	17	48	23	180	3.5	0.6	3.5
Reg. Season Totals	52	–	628	73	169	.432	0	2	.000	34	55	.618	66	117	183	33	100	2	17	48	23	180	3.5	0.6	3.5
Playoff Totals	2	–	9	0	3	.000	0	0	–	0	0	–	0	3	3	–	1	0	0	0	1	0	1.5	0.0	0.0

Peek, Richard Shelby (Rich) b. October 28, 1943 Ht. 6-11 Wt. 230 College: Louisiana Tech; Florida

SEASON–TEAM	G	GS	MIN	FGM	FGA	PCT	3FGM	3FGA	PCT	FTM	FTA	PCT	O-RB	D-RB	TOT	AST	PF	DQ	STL	TO	BLK	PTS	RPG	APG	PPG
67-68–Dallas (A)	51	–	759	101	209	.483	0	0	–	35	65	.538	–	–	197	22	94	1	–	49	–	237	3.9	0.4	4.6
Reg. ABA Totals	51	–	759	101	209	.483	0	0	–	35	65	.538	–	–	197	22	94	1	–	49	–	237	3.9	0.4	4.6
ABA Playoff Totals	8	–	137	18	37	.486	0	0	–	7	15	.467	–	–	42	3	17	1	–	10	–	43	5.3	0.4	5.4

Peeler, Anthony Eugene b. November 25, 1969 Ht. 6-4 Wt. 208 College: Missouri

SEASON–TEAM	G	GS	MIN	FGM	FGA	PCT	3FGM	3FGA	PCT	FTM	FTA	PCT	O-RB	D-RB	TOT	AST	PF	DQ	STL	TO	BLK	PTS	RPG	APG	PPG
92-93–L.A. Lakers	77	11	1656	297	634	.468	46	118	.390	162	206	.786	64	115	179	166	193	0	60	123	14	802	2.3	2.2	10.4
93-94–L.A. Lakers	30	30	923	176	409	.430	14	63	.222	57	71	.803	48	61	109	94	93	0	43	59	8	423	3.6	3.1	14.1
94-95–L.A. Lakers	73	24	1559	285	659	.432	84	216	.389	102	128	.797	62	106	168	122	143	1	52	82	13	756	2.3	1.7	10.4
95-96–L.A. Lakers	73	12	1608	272	602	.452	105	254	.413	61	86	.709	45	92	137	118	139	0	59	56	10	710	1.9	1.6	9.7
96-97–Vancouver	72	57	2291	402	1011	.398	128	343	.373	109	133	.820	54	193	247	256	168	0	105	157	17	1041	3.4	3.6	14.5
97-98–Vanc.-Minn.	38	32	1193	190	420	.452	53	125	.424	36	47	.766	37	86	123	137	97	0	61	51	6	469	3.2	3.6	12.3
98-99–Minnesota	28	28	810	103	272	.379	34	114	.298	30	41	.732	30	54	84	78	60	0	35	38	6	270	3.0	2.8	9.6
99-00–Minnesota	82	22	2073	316	725	.436	85	255	.333	87	109	.798	58	174	232	195	171	1	62	85	10	804	2.8	2.4	9.8
Reg. Season Totals	473	216	12113	2041	4732	.431	549	1488	.369	644	821	.784	398	881	1279	1166	1064	2	477	651	84	5275	2.7	2.5	11.2
Playoff Totals	26	19	768	94	242	.388	36	99	.364	31	38	.816	35	64	99	57	65	1	33	28	6	255	3.8	2.2	9.8

Peeples, George Albert b. October 30, 1943 Ht. 6-8 Wt. 205 College: Iowa

SEASON–TEAM	G	GS	MIN	FGM	FGA	PCT	3FGM	3FGA	PCT	FTM	FTA	PCT	O-RB	D-RB	TOT	AST	PF	DQ	STL	TO	BLK	PTS	RPG	APG	PPG
67-68–Indiana (A)	65	–	1203	138	339	.407	0	3	.000	115	188	.612	–	–	378	29	136	1	–	71	–	391	5.8	0.4	6.0
68-69–Indiana (A)	64	–	1111	122	278	.439	0	0	–	101	142	.711	–	–	358	33	137	2	–	73	–	345	5.6	0.5	5.4
69-70–Carolina (A)	83	–	2220	279	682	.409	0	7	.000	209	315	.663	–	–	685	123	232	0	–	–	–	767	8.3	1.5	9.2
70-71–Carolina (A)	82	–	2220	377	773	.488	0	1	.000	202	335	.603	–	–	771	110	279	–	–	–	–	956	9.4	1.3	11.7
71-72–Dallas (A)	6	–	125	11	25	.440	0	0	–	7	11	.636	–	–	35	5	10	–	–	9	–	29	5.8	0.8	4.8
72-73–Indiana (A)	9	–	56	4	14	.286	0	0	–	6	11	.545	3	12	15	4	14	0	–	6	–	14	1.7	0.4	1.6
Reg. ABA Totals	309	–	6935	931	2111	.441	0	11	.000	640	1002	.639	3	12	2242	304	808	3	–	159	–	2502	7.3	1.0	8.1
ABA Playoff Totals	24	–	607	59	144	.410	0	1	.000	49	73	.671	15	39	201	19	64	1	–	4	–	167	8.4	0.8	7.0

Pelkington, John Francis Robert Jr. (Jake, Pelky) b. January 3, 1916 d. May 1, 1982 Ht. 6-6 Wt. 225 College: Manhattan

SEASON–TEAM	G	GS	MIN	FGM	FGA	PCT	3FGM	3FGA	PCT	FTM	FTA	PCT	O-RB	D-RB	TOT	AST	PF	DQ	STL	TO	BLK	PTS	RPG	APG	PPG
40-41–Akron Goodyear (N)	24	–	–	57	–	–	–	–	–	70	102	.686	–	–	–	–	87	–	–	–	–	184	–	–	7.7
42-43–Fort Wayne (N)	23	–	–	83	–	–	–	–	–	70	100	.700	–	–	–	–	65	–	–	–	–	236	–	–	10.3
43-44–Fort Wayne (N)	20	–	–	46	–	–	–	–	–	40	–	–	–	–	–	–	–	–	–	–	–	132	–	–	6.6
44-45–Fort Wayne (N)	30	–	–	85	–	–	–	–	–	76	–	–	–	–	–	–	–	–	–	–	–	246	–	–	8.2
45-46–Fort Wayne (N)	33	–	–	94	–	–	–	–	–	76	104	.731	–	–	–	–	89	–	–	–	–	264	–	–	8.0
46-47–Fort Wayne (N)	42	–	–	129	–	–	–	–	–	125	166	.753	–	–	–	–	117	–	–	–	–	383	–	–	9.1
47-48–Fort Wayne (N)	54	–	–	174	–	–	–	–	–	156	214	.729	–	–	–	–	156	–	–	–	–	504	–	–	9.3
48-49–FtWayne-Balt.	54	–	–	193	469	.412	–	–	–	211	267	.790	–	–	–	131	216	–	–	–	–	597	–	2.4	11.1
Reg. NBA Totals	54	–	–	193	469	.412	–	–	–	211	267	.790	–	–	–	131	216	–	–	–	–	597	–	2.4	11.1
Reg. NBL Totals	226	–	–	668	–	–	–	–	–	613	686	.724	–	–	–	–	514	–	–	–	–	1949	–	–	8.6
NBA Playoff Totals	3	–	–	13	33	.394	–	–	–	27	35	.771	–	–	–	3	13	1	–	–	–	53	–	1.0	17.7
NBL Playoff Totals	34	–	–	82	–	–	–	–	–	73	66	.667	–	–	–	–	93	–	–	–	–	237	–	–	7.0

Pellom, Samuel Troy (Sam) b. October 2, 1951 Ht. 6-9 Wt. 225 College: Buffalo State

SEASON–TEAM	G	GS	MIN	FGM	FGA	PCT	3FGM	3FGA	PCT	FTM	FTA	PCT	O-RB	D-RB	TOT	AST	PF	DQ	STL	TO	BLK	PTS	RPG	APG	PPG
79-80–Atlanta	44	–	373	44	108	.407	0	0	–	21	30	.700	28	64	92	18	70	0	12	18	12	109	2.1	0.4	2.5
80-81–Atlanta	77	–	1472	186	380	.489	0	1	.000	81	116	.698	122	234	356	48	228	6	50	99	92	453	4.6	0.6	5.9
81-82–Atlanta	69	4	1037	114	251	.454	0	1	.000	61	79	.772	90	139	229	28	164	0	29	57	47	289	3.3	0.4	4.2
82-83–Atlanta-Milw.	6	0	29	6	16	.375	0	0	–	0	0	–	2	6	8	1	3	0	0	2	0	12	1.3	0.2	2.0
Reg. Season Totals	196	4	2911	350	755	.464	0	2	.000	163	225	.724	242	443	685	95	465	6	91	176	151	863	3.5	0.5	4.4
Playoff Totals	5	0	22	1	6	.167	0	0	–	1	3	.333	1	0	1	1	3	0	0	0	1	3	0.2	0.2	0.6

Pender, Jerry Lee b. February 12, 1950 Ht. 6-2 Wt. 195 College: Merced (Calif.) Coll. (J.C.); Fresno State

SEASON–TEAM	G	GS	MIN	FGM	FGA	PCT	3FGM	3FGA	PCT	FTM	FTA	PCT	O-RB	D-RB	TOT	AST	PF	DQ	STL	TO	BLK	PTS	RPG	APG	PPG
73-74–San Diego (A)	11	–	68	8	30	.267	1	3	.333	10	13	.769	3	2	5	4	11	–	6	9	0	27	0.5	0.4	2.5
Reg. ABA Totals	11	–	68	8	30	.267	1	3	.333	10	13	.769	3	2	5	4	11	0	6	9	0	27	0.5	0.4	2.5

Peplowski, Michael Walter (Mike) b. October 15, 1970 Ht. 6-10 Wt. 270 College: Michigan State

SEASON–TEAM	G	GS	MIN	FGM	FGA	PCT	3FGM	3FGA	PCT	FTM	FTA	PCT	O-RB	D-RB	TOT	AST	PF	DQ	STL	TO	BLK	PTS	RPG	APG	PPG
93-94–Sacramento	55	19	667	76	141	.539	0	1	.000	24	44	.545	49	120	169	24	131	2	17	34	25	176	3.1	0.4	3.2
94-95–Detroit	6	0	21	5	5	1.000	0	0	–	1	2	.500	1	2	3	1	10	0	1	2	0	11	0.5	0.2	1.8
95-96–Wash.-Milw.	7	0	17	3	5	.600	0	0	–	1	3	.333	1	3	4	1	10	0	1	2	2	7	0.6	0.1	1.0
Reg. Season Totals	68	19	705	84	151	.556	0	1	.000	26	49	.531	51	125	176	26	151	2	19	38	27	194	2.6	0.4	2.9

Perdue, William Edward III (Will) b. August 29, 1965 Ht. 7-0 Wt. 240 College: Vanderbilt

SEASON–TEAM	G	GS	MIN	FGM	FGA	PCT	3FGM	3FGA	PCT	FTM	FTA	PCT	O-RB	D-RB	TOT	AST	PF	DQ	STL	TO	BLK	PTS	RPG	APG	PPG
88-89–Chicago	30	0	190	29	72	.403	0	0	–	8	14	.571	18	27	45	11	38	0	4	15	6	66	1.5	0.4	2.2
89-90–Chicago	77	11	884	111	268	.414	0	5	.000	72	104	.692	88	126	214	46	150	0	19	65	26	294	2.8	0.6	3.8
90-91–Chicago	74	3	972	116	235	.494	0	3	.000	75	112	.670	122	214	336	47	147	1	23	75	57	307	4.5	0.6	4.1
91-92–Chicago	77	7	1007	152	278	.547	1	2	.500	45	91	.495	108	204	312	80	133	1	16	72	43	350	4.1	1.0	4.5
92-93–Chicago	72	16	998	137	246	.557	0	1	.000	67	111	.604	103	184	287	74	139	2	22	74	47	341	4.0	1.0	4.7
93-94–Chicago	43	6	397	47	112	.420	0	1	.000	23	32	.719	40	86	126	34	61	0	8	42	11	117	2.9	0.8	2.7
94-95–Chicago	78	78	1592	254	459	.553	0	1	.000	113	194	.582	211	311	522	90	220	3	26	116	56	621	6.7	1.2	8.0
95-96–San Antonio	80	22	1396	173	331	.523	0	1	.000	67	125	.536	175	310	485	33	183	0	28	86	75	413	6.1	0.4	5.2
96-97–San Antonio	65	34	1918	233	410	.568	0	0	–	99	171	.579	251	387	638	38	184	2	32	87	102	565	9.8	0.6	8.7
97-98–San Antonio	79	30	1491	162	295	.549	0	1	.000	70	133	.526	177	358	535	57	137	0	22	81	50	394	6.8	0.7	5.0
98-99–San Antonio	37	1	445	38	60	.633	0	0	–	14	26	.538	33	105	138	18	63	0	9	22	10	90	3.7	0.5	2.4
99-00–Chicago	67	15	1012	59	168	.351	0	0	–	50	105	.476	88	174	262	65	126	1	14	78	42	168	3.9	1.0	2.5
Reg. Season Totals	779	223	12302	1511	2934	.515	1	15	.067	703	1218	.577	1414	2486	3900	593	1581	10	223	813	525	3726	5.0	0.8	4.8
Playoff Totals	105	11	1251	139	264	.527	1	4	.250	88	137	.642	152	223	375	34	206	2	15	73	42	367	3.6	0.3	3.5

Perkins, Samuel Bruce (Sam, Big Smooth; Sleepy) b. June 14, 1961 Ht. 6-9 Wt. 260 College: North Carolina

SEASON–TEAM	G	GS	MIN	FGM	FGA	PCT	3FGM	3FGA	PCT	FTM	FTA	PCT	O-RB	D-RB	TOT	AST	PF	DQ	STL	TO	BLK	PTS	RPG	APG	PPG
84-85–Dallas	82	42	2317	347	736	.471	9	36	.250	200	244	.820	189	416	605	135	236	1	63	102	63	903	7.4	1.6	11.0
85-86–Dallas	80	79	2626	458	910	.503	11	33	.333	307	377	.814	195	490	685	153	212	2	75	145	94	1234	8.6	1.9	15.4
86-87–Dallas	80	80	2687	461	957	.482	19	54	.352	245	296	.828	197	419	616	146	269	6	109	132	77	1186	7.7	1.8	14.8
87-88–Dallas	75	75	2499	394	876	.450	5	30	.167	273	332	.822	201	400	601	118	227	2	74	119	54	1066	8.0	1.6	14.2
88-89–Dallas	78	77	2860	445	959	.464	7	38	.184	274	329	.833	235	453	688	127	224	1	76	141	92	1171	8.8	1.6	15.0
89-90–Dallas	76	70	2668	435	883	.493	6	28	.214	330	424	.778	209	363	572	175	225	4	88	148	64	1206	7.5	2.3	15.9
90-91–L.A. Lakers	73	66	2504	368	744	.495	18	64	.281	229	279	.821	167	371	538	108	247	2	64	103	78	983	7.4	1.5	13.5
91-92–L.A. Lakers	63	63	2332	361	803	.450	15	69	.217	304	372	.817	192	364	556	141	192	1	64	83	62	1041	8.8	2.2	16.5
92-93–Lakers-Seattle	79	62	2351	381	799	.477	24	71	.338	250	305	.820	163	361	524	156	225	0	60	108	82	1036	6.6	2.0	13.1
93-94–Seattle	81	41	2170	341	779	.438	99	270	.367	218	272	.801	120	246	366	111	197	0	67	103	31	999	4.5	1.4	12.3
94-95–Seattle	82	37	2356	346	742	.466	136	343	.397	215	269	.799	96	302	398	135	186	0	72	77	45	1043	4.9	1.6	12.7
95-96–Seattle	82	20	2169	325	797	.408	129	363	.355	191	241	.793	101	266	367	120	174	1	83	82	48	970	4.5	1.5	11.8
96-97–Seattle	81	4	1976	290	661	.439	122	309	.395	187	229	.817	74	226	300	103	134	0	69	77	49	889	3.7	1.3	11.0
97-98–Seattle	81	0	1675	196	471	.416	87	222	.392	101	128	.789	53	202	255	113	158	0	62	62	29	580	3.1	1.4	7.2
98-99–Indiana	48	0	789	80	200	.400	35	90	.389	43	60	.717	36	102	138	25	74	0	15	22	14	238	2.9	0.5	5.0
99-00–Indiana	81	0	1620	184	441	.417	89	218	.408	80	97	.825	64	225	289	68	136	0	31	63	33	537	3.6	0.8	6.6
Reg. Season Totals	1222	716	35599	5412	11758	.460	811	2238	.362	3447	4254	.810	2292	5206	7498	1934	3116	20	1072	1567	915	15082	6.1	1.6	12.3
Playoff Totals	164	84	4766	654	1471	.445	151	415	.364	397	506	.785	254	678	932	246	438	6	118	207	126	1856	5.7	1.5	11.3

Perkins, Warren C. (Red) b. February 2, 1924 Ht. 6-3 Wt. 190 College: Tulane

SEASON–TEAM	G	GS	MIN	FGM	FGA	PCT	3FGM	3FGA	PCT	FTM	FTA	PCT	O-RB	D-RB	TOT	AST	PF	DQ	STL	TO	BLK	PTS	RPG	APG	PPG
49-50–Tri-Cities	60	–	–	128	422	.303	–	–	–	115	195	.590	–	–	–	114	260	–	–	–	–	371	–	1.9	6.2
50-51–Tri-Cities	66	–	–	135	428	.315	–	–	–	126	195	.646	–	–	319	143	232	13	–	–	–	396	4.8	2.2	6.0
Reg. Season Totals	126	–	–	263	850	.309	–	–	–	241	390	.618	–	–	319	257	492	13	–	–	–	767	4.8	2.0	6.1
Playoff Totals	2	–	–	1	2	.500	–	–	–	0	0	–	–	–	–	2	4	0	–	–	–	2	–	0.5	1.0

Perry, Aulcie b. July 3, 1950 Ht. 6-10 Wt. 210 College: Bethune-Cookman

SEASON–TEAM	G	GS	MIN	FGM	FGA	PCT	3FGM	3FGA	PCT	FTM	FTA	PCT	O-RB	D-RB	TOT	AST	PF	DQ	STL	TO	BLK	PTS	RPG	APG	PPG
74-75–Virginia (A)	21	–	415	81	186	.435	0	1	.000	19	30	.633	40	65	105	20	58	–	12	34	16	181	5.0	1.0	8.6
Reg. ABA Totals	21	–	415	81	186	.435	0	1	.000	19	30	.633	40	65	105	20	58	–	12	34	16	181	5.0	1.0	8.6

Perry, Curtis R. b. September 13, 1948 Ht. 6-7 Wt. 220 College: Southwest Missouri State

SEASON–TEAM	G	GS	MIN	FGM	FGA	PCT	3FGM	3FGA	PCT	FTM	FTA	PCT	O-RB	D-RB	TOT	AST	PF	DQ	STL	TO	BLK	PTS	RPG	APG	PPG
70-71–San Diego	18	–	100	21	48	.438	–	–	–	11	20	.550	–	–	30	5	22	0	–	–	–	53	1.7	0.3	2.9
71-72–Houston-Milw.	75	–	1826	181	486	.372	–	–	–	76	119	.639	–	–	593	100	261	14	–	–	–	438	7.9	1.3	5.8
72-73–Milwaukee	67	–	2094	265	575	.461	–	–	–	83	126	.659	–	–	644	123	246	6	–	–	–	613	9.6	1.8	9.1
73-74–Milwaukee	81	–	2386	325	729	.446	–	–	–	78	134	.582	242	461	703	183	301	8	104	–	97	728	8.7	2.3	9.0
74-75–Phoenix	79	–	2688	437	917	.477	–	–	–	184	256	.719	347	593	940	186	288	10	108	–	78	1058	11.9	2.4	13.4
75-76–Phoenix	71	–	2353	386	776	.497	–	–	–	175	239	.732	197	487	684	182	269	5	84	–	66	947	9.6	2.6	13.3
76-77–Phoenix	44	–	1391	179	414	.432	–	–	–	112	142	.789	149	246	395	79	163	3	49	–	28	470	9.0	1.8	10.7
77-78–Phoenix	45	–	818	110	243	.453	–	–	–	51	65	.785	87	163	250	48	120	2	34	63	22	271	5.6	1.1	6.0
Reg. Season Totals	480	–	13656	1904	4188	.455	–	–	–	770	1101	.699	1022	1950	4239	906	1670	48	379	63	291	4578	8.8	1.9	9.5
Playoff Totals	52	–	1546	213	453	.470	–	–	–	72	109	.661	97	130	437	75	189	7	22	–	19	498	8.4	1.4	9.6

Perry, Elliot Lamonte (Socks) b. March 28, 1969 Ht. 6-0 Wt. 152 College: Memphis

SEASON–TEAM	G	GS	MIN	FGM	FGA	PCT	3FGM	3FGA	PCT	FTM	FTA	PCT	O-RB	D-RB	TOT	AST	PF	DQ	STL	TO	BLK	PTS	RPG	APG	PPG
91-92–LAClips-Cha.	50	0	437	49	129	.380	1	7	.143	27	41	.659	14	25	39	78	36	0	34	50	3	126	0.8	1.6	2.5
93-94–Phoenix	27	9	432	42	113	.372	0	3	.000	21	28	.750	12	27	39	125	36	0	25	43	1	105	1.4	4.6	3.9
94-95–Phoenix	82	51	1977	306	588	.520	25	60	.417	158	195	.810	51	100	151	394	142	0	156	163	4	795	1.8	4.8	9.7
95-96–Phoenix	81	26	1668	261	549	.475	24	59	.407	151	194	.778	34	102	136	353	140	1	87	146	5	697	1.7	4.4	8.6
96-97–Milwaukee	82	3	1595	217	458	.474	49	137	.358	79	106	.745	24	100	124	247	117	0	98	111	3	562	1.5	3.0	6.9
97-98–Milwaukee	81	33	1752	241	561	.430	17	50	.340	92	109	.844	21	87	108	230	129	1	90	128	2	591	1.3	2.8	7.3
98-99–Milw.-N.J.	35	0	290	39	103	.379	10	24	.417	10	14	.714	7	27	34	47	25	0	20	34	0	98	1.0	1.3	2.8
99-00–New Jersey	60	5	803	128	294	.435	11	39	.282	50	62	.806	13	48	61	139	47	0	39	60	1	317	1.0	2.3	5.3
Reg. Season Totals	498	127	8954	1283	2795	.459	137	379	.361	588	749	.785	176	516	692	1613	672	2	549	735	19	3291	1.4	3.2	6.6
Playoff Totals	17	0	170	28	63	.444	2	5	.400	20	26	.769	3	9	12	25	13	0	8	10	0	78	0.7	1.5	4.6

Perry, Ron b. December 29, 1943 Ht. 6-3 Wt. 190 College: Virginia Tech

SEASON–TEAM	G	GS	MIN	FGM	FGA	PCT	3FGM	3FGA	PCT	FTM	FTA	PCT	O-RB	D-RB	TOT	AST	PF	DQ	STL	TO	BLK	PTS	RPG	APG	PPG
67-68–Minnesota (A)	67	–	2125	339	878	.386	62	178	.348	118	179	.659	–	–	223	139	151	2	–	169	–	858	3.3	2.1	12.8
68-69–Mi.-N.Y.-Ind. (A)	74	–	2385	402	1060	.379	67	192	.349	212	292	.726	–	–	241	244	255	8	–	201	–	1083	3.3	3.3	14.6
69-70–Car.-N.O. (A)	46	–	522	104	272	.382	10	35	.286	69	97	.711	–	–	53	37	78	1	–	–	–	287	1.2	0.8	6.2
Reg. ABA Totals	187	–	5032	845	2210	.382	139	405	.343	399	568	.702	–	–	517	420	484	11	–	370	–	2228	2.8	2.2	11.9
ABA Playoff Totals	17	–	202	34	114	.298	11	38	.289	18	27	.667	–	–	21	18	33	0	–	–	–	97	1.2	1.1	5.7

Perry, Timothy D. (Tim) b. June 4, 1965 Ht. 6-9 Wt. 220 College: Temple

SEASON–TEAM	G	GS	MIN	FGM	FGA	PCT	3FGM	3FGA	PCT	FTM	FTA	PCT	O-RB	D-RB	TOT	AST	PF	DQ	STL	TO	BLK	PTS	RPG	APG	PPG
88-89–Phoenix	62	15	614	108	201	.537	1	4	.250	40	65	.615	61	71	132	18	47	0	19	37	32	257	2.1	0.3	4.1
89-90–Phoenix	60	18	612	100	195	.513	1	1	1.000	53	90	.589	79	73	152	17	76	0	21	47	22	254	2.5	0.3	4.2
90-91–Phoenix	46	2	587	75	144	.521	0	5	.000	43	70	.614	53	73	126	27	60	1	23	32	43	193	2.7	0.6	4.2
91-92–Phoenix	80	69	2483	413	789	.523	3	8	.375	153	215	.712	204	347	551	134	237	2	44	141	116	982	6.9	1.7	12.3
92-93–Philadelphia	81	51	2104	287	613	.468	10	49	.204	147	207	.710	154	255	409	126	159	0	40	123	91	731	5.0	1.6	9.0
93-94–Philadelphia	80	68	2336	272	625	.435	73	200	.365	102	176	.580	117	287	404	94	154	1	60	80	82	719	5.1	1.2	9.0
94-95–Philadelphia	42	1	446	27	78	.346	0	14	.000	22	40	.550	38	51	89	12	51	0	10	21	15	76	2.1	0.3	1.8
95-96–Phil.-N.J.	30	1	254	31	65	.477	4	8	.500	5	9	.556	21	27	48	8	16	0	4	10	13	71	1.6	0.3	2.4
Reg. Season Totals	481	225	9436	1313	2710	.485	92	289	.318	565	872	.648	727	1184	1911	436	800	4	221	491	414	3283	4.0	0.9	6.8
Playoff Totals	23	8	302	53	92	.576	0	0	–	31	52	.596	23	39	62	13	44	1	8	20	13	137	2.7	0.6	6.0

Person, Chuck Connors (Rifleman) b. June 27, 1964 Ht. 6-8 Wt. 241 College: Auburn

SEASON–TEAM	G	GS	MIN	FGM	FGA	PCT	3FGM	3FGA	PCT	FTM	FTA	PCT	O-RB	D-RB	TOT	AST	PF	DQ	STL	TO	BLK	PTS	RPG	APG	PPG
86-87–Indiana	82	78	2956	635	1358	.468	49	138	.355	222	297	.747	168	509	677	295	310	4	90	211	16	1541	8.3	3.6	18.8
87-88–Indiana	79	71	2807	575	1252	.459	59	177	.333	132	197	.670	171	365	536	309	266	4	73	210	8	1341	6.8	3.9	17.0
88-89–Indiana	80	79	3012	711	1453	.489	63	205	.307	243	307	.792	144	372	516	289	280	12	83	308	18	1728	6.5	3.6	21.6
89-90–Indiana	77	73	2714	605	1242	.487	94	253	.372	211	270	.781	126	319	445	230	217	1	53	170	20	1515	5.8	3.0	19.7
90-91–Indiana	80	79	2566	620	1231	.504	69	203	.340	165	229	.721	121	296	417	238	221	1	56	184	17	1474	5.2	3.0	18.4
91-92–Indiana	81	81	2923	616	1284	.480	132	354	.373	133	197	.675	114	312	426	382	247	5	68	216	18	1497	5.3	4.7	18.5
92-93–Minnesota	78	75	2985	541	1248	.433	118	332	.355	109	168	.649	98	335	433	343	198	2	67	219	30	1309	5.6	4.4	16.8
93-94–Minnesota	77	37	2029	356	843	.422	100	272	.368	82	108	.759	55	198	253	185	164	0	45	121	12	894	3.3	2.4	11.6
94-95–San Antonio	81	1	2033	317	750	.423	172	445	.387	66	102	.647	49	209	258	106	198	0	45	102	12	872	3.2	1.3	10.8
95-96–San Antonio	80	16	2131	308	705	.437	190	463	.410	67	104	.644	76	337	413	100	197	2	49	91	26	873	5.2	1.3	10.9
97-98–San Antonio	61	11	1455	143	398	.359	95	276	.344	28	37	.757	17	187	204	86	121	1	29	67	10	409	3.3	1.4	6.7
98-99–Charlotte	50	21	990	112	289	.388	55	157	.350	24	32	.750	17	115	132	60	90	0	20	41	8	303	2.6	1.2	6.1
99-00–Seattle	37	0	340	37	123	.301	24	95	.253	4	8	.500	6	47	53	22	56	1	5	12	2	102	1.4	0.6	2.8
Reg. Season Totals	943	622	28941	5576	12176	.458	1220	3370	.362	1486	2056	.723	1162	3601	4763	2645	2565	33	683	1952	197	13858	5.1	2.8	14.7
Playoff Totals	51	15	1332	208	464	.448	77	197	.391	84	114	.737	23	161	184	86	120	2	23	60	12	577	3.6	1.7	11.3

P

Person, Wesley Lavon b. March 28, 1971 Ht. 6-6 Wt. 195 College: Auburn

SEASON–TEAM	G	GS	MIN	FGM	FGA	PCT	3FGM	3FGA	PCT	FTM	FTA	PCT	O-RB	D-RB	TOT	AST	PF	DQ	STL	TO	BLK	PTS	RPG	APG	PPG
94-95–Phoenix	78	56	1800	309	638	.484	116	266	.436	80	101	.792	67	134	201	105	149	0	48	79	24	814	2.6	1.3	10.4
95-96–Phoenix	82	47	2609	390	877	.445	117	313	.374	148	192	.771	56	265	321	138	148	0	55	89	22	1045	3.9	1.7	12.7
96-97–Phoenix	80	42	2326	409	903	.453	171	414	.413	91	114	.798	68	224	292	123	102	0	86	76	20	1080	3.7	1.5	13.5
97-98–Cleveland	82	82	3198	440	957	.460	192	447	.430	132	170	.776	65	298	363	188	108	0	129	110	49	1204	4.4	2.3	14.7
98-99–Cleveland	45	42	1342	198	437	.453	75	200	.375	32	53	.604	19	123	142	80	52	0	37	41	16	503	3.2	1.8	11.2
99-00–Cleveland	79	38	2056	280	654	.428	106	250	.424	61	77	.792	44	223	267	146	119	1	40	60	19	727	3.4	1.8	9.2
Reg. Season Totals	446	307	13331	2026	4466	.454	777	1890	.411	544	707	.769	319	1267	1586	780	678	1	395	455	150	5373	3.6	1.7	12.0
Playoff Totals	23	19	729	92	221	.416	47	126	.373	32	39	.821	24	62	86	30	36	0	13	19	6	263	3.7	1.3	11.4

Petersen, James Richard (Jim, Pete) b. February 22, 1962 Ht. 6-10 Wt. 235 College: Minnesota

SEASON–TEAM	G	GS	MIN	FGM	FGA	PCT	3FGM	3FGA	PCT	FTM	FTA	PCT	O-RB	D-RB	TOT	AST	PF	DQ	STL	TO	BLK	PTS	RPG	APG	PPG
84-85–Houston	60	0	714	70	144	.486	0	0	–	50	66	.758	44	103	147	29	125	1	14	71	32	190	2.5	0.5	3.2
85-86–Houston	82	20	1664	196	411	.477	0	3	.000	113	160	.706	149	247	396	85	231	2	38	84	54	505	4.8	1.0	6.2
86-87–Houston	82	56	2403	386	755	.511	0	4	.000	152	209	.727	177	380	557	127	268	5	43	152	102	924	6.8	1.5	11.3
87-88–Houston	69	50	1793	249	488	.510	1	6	.167	114	153	.745	145	291	436	106	203	3	36	119	40	613	6.3	1.5	8.9
88-89–Sacramento	66	40	1633	278	606	.459	0	8	.000	115	154	.747	121	292	413	81	236	8	47	147	68	671	6.3	1.2	10.2
89-90–Golden State	43	19	592	60	141	.426	0	1	.000	52	73	.712	49	111	160	23	103	0	17	36	20	172	3.7	0.5	4.0
90-91–Golden State	62	21	834	114	236	.483	1	4	.250	50	76	.658	69	131	200	27	153	2	13	48	41	279	3.2	0.4	4.5
91-92–Golden State	27	2	169	18	40	.450	0	2	.000	7	10	.700	12	33	45	9	35	0	5	5	6	43	1.7	0.3	1.6
Reg. Season Totals	491	208	9802	1371	2821	.486	2	28	.071	653	901	.725	766	1588	2354	487	1354	21	213	662	363	3397	4.8	1.0	6.9
Playoff Totals	46	4	788	97	200	.485	0	0	–	47	71	.662	73	134	207	37	132	4	17	33	17	241	4.5	0.8	5.2

Petersen, Loy M. b. July 26, 1945 Ht. 6-5 Wt. 205 College: Oregon State

SEASON–TEAM	G	GS	MIN	FGM	FGA	PCT	3FGM	3FGA	PCT	FTM	FTA	PCT	O-RB	D-RB	TOT	AST	PF	DQ	STL	TO	BLK	PTS	RPG	APG	PPG
68-69–Chicago	38	–	299	44	109	.404	–	–	–	19	27	.704	–	–	41	25	39	0	–	–	–	107	1.1	0.7	2.8
69-70–Chicago	31	–	231	33	90	.367	–	–	–	26	39	.667	–	–	26	23	22	0	–	–	–	92	0.8	0.7	3.0
Reg. Season Totals	69	–	530	77	199	.387	–	–	–	45	66	.682	–	–	67	48	61	0	–	–	–	199	1.0	0.7	2.9

Peterson, Edward T. (Ed) b. June 27, 1924 d. March 20, 1984 Ht. 6-9 Wt. 230 College: Cornell College

SEASON–TEAM	G	GS	MIN	FGM	FGA	PCT	3FGM	3FGA	PCT	FTM	FTA	PCT	O-RB	D-RB	TOT	AST	PF	DQ	STL	TO	BLK	PTS	RPG	APG	PPG
48-49–Syracuse (N)	63	–	–	165	–	–	–	–	–	104	177	.588	–	–	–	–	203	–	–	–	–	434	–	–	6.9
49-50–Syracuse	62	–	–	167	390	.428	–	–	–	111	185	.600	–	–	–	33	198	–	–	–	–	445	–	0.5	7.2
50-51–Syr.-Tri-Cit	53	–	–	130	384	.339	–	–	–	99	150	.660	–	–	288	66	188	9	–	–	–	359	5.4	1.2	6.8
Reg. NBA Totals	115	–	–	297	774	.384	–	–	–	210	335	.627	–	–	288	99	386	9	–	–	–	804	5.4	0.9	7.0
Reg. NBL Totals	63	–	–	165	–	–	–	–	–	104	177	.588	–	–	–	–	203	–	–	–	–	434	–	–	6.9
NBA Playoff Totals	11	–	–	18	75	.400	–	–	–	8	14	.571	–	–	–	2	33	2	–	–	–	44	–	0.1	4.0
NBL Playoff Totals	6	–	–	14	–	–	–	–	–	16	28	.571	–	–	–	–	21	–	–	–	–	44	–	–	7.3

Peterson, Melvin Lowell (Mel) b. March 23, 1938 Ht. 6-4 Wt. 185 College: Wheaton

SEASON–TEAM	G	GS	MIN	FGM	FGA	PCT	3FGM	3FGA	PCT	FTM	FTA	PCT	O-RB	D-RB	TOT	AST	PF	DQ	STL	TO	BLK	PTS	RPG	APG	PPG
63-64–Baltimore	2	–	3	1	1	1.000	–	–	–	0	0	–	–	–	1	0	2	0	–	–	–	2	0.5	0.0	1.0
67-68–Oakland (A)	77	–	1589	323	756	.427	9	34	.265	76	93	.817	–	–	451	104	161	1	–	114	–	731	5.9	1.4	9.5
68-69–Oakland (A)	51	–	709	132	263	.502	0	2	.000	12	15	.800	–	–	170	55	61	0	–	43	–	276	3.3	1.1	5.4
69-70–Los Angeles (A)	4	–	53	10	35	.286	0	4	.000	3	3	1.000	–	–	13	1	4	0	–	–	–	23	3.3	0.3	5.8
Reg. NBA Totals	2	–	3	1	1	1.000	–	–	–	0	0	–	–	–	1	0	2	0	–	–	–	2	0.5	0.0	1.0
Reg. ABA Totals	132	–	2351	465	1054	.441	9	40	.225	91	111	.820	–	–	634	160	226	1	–	157	–	1030	4.8	1.2	7.8
ABA Playoff Totals	18	–	120	21	36	.583	1	2	.500	8	14	.571	–	–	34	6	13	0	–	–	–	51	1.9	0.3	2.8

Peterson, Robert (Bob) b. January 25, 1932 Ht. 6-5 Wt. 210 College: Oregon

SEASON–TEAM	G	GS	MIN	FGM	FGA	PCT	3FGM	3FGA	PCT	FTM	FTA	PCT	O-RB	D-RB	TOT	AST	PF	DQ	STL	TO	BLK	PTS	RPG	APG	PPG
53-54–Balt.-Milw.	8	–	60	3	10	.300	–	–	–	9	11	.818	–	–	12	3	15	1	–	–	–	15	1.5	0.4	1.9
54-55–New York	37	–	503	62	169	.367	–	–	–	30	45	.667	–	–	154	31	80	2	–	–	–	154	4.2	0.8	4.2
55-56–New York	58	–	779	121	303	.399	–	–	–	68	104	.654	–	–	223	44	123	0	–	–	–	310	3.8	0.8	5.3
Reg. Season Totals	103	–	1342	186	482	.386	–	–	–	107	160	.669	–	–	389	78	218	3	–	–	–	479	3.8	0.8	4.7
Playoff Totals	3	–	81	7	15	.467	–	–	–	10	11	.909	–	–	16	5	3	0	–	–	–	24	5.3	1.7	8.0

Petrie, Geoffrey Michael (Geoff) b. April 17, 1948 Ht. 6-4 Wt. 190 College: Princeton

SEASON–TEAM	G	GS	MIN	FGM	FGA	PCT	3FGM	3FGA	PCT	FTM	FTA	PCT	O-RB	D-RB	TOT	AST	PF	DQ	STL	TO	BLK	PTS	RPG	APG	PPG
70-71–Portland	82	–	3032	784	1770	.443	–	–	–	463	600	.772	–	–	280	390	196	1	–	–	–	2031	3.4	4.8	24.8
71-72–Portland	60	–	2155	465	1115	.417	–	–	–	202	256	.789	–	–	133	248	108	0	–	–	–	1132	2.2	4.1	18.9
72-73–Portland	79	–	3134	836	1801	.464	–	–	–	298	383	.778	–	–	273	350	163	2	–	–	–	1970	3.5	4.4	24.9
73-74–Portland	73	–	2800	740	1537	.481	–	–	–	291	341	.853	64	144	208	315	199	2	84	–	15	1771	2.8	4.3	24.3
74-75–Portland	80	–	3109	602	1319	.456	–	–	–	261	311	.839	38	171	209	424	215	1	81	–	13	1465	2.6	5.3	18.3
75-76–Portland	72	–	2557	543	1177	.461	–	–	–	277	334	.829	38	130	168	330	194	0	82	–	5	1363	2.3	4.6	18.9
Reg. Season Totals	446	–	16787	3970	8719	.455	–	–	–	1792	2225	.805	140	445	1271	2057	1075	6	247	–	33	9732	2.8	4.6	21.8
All-Star Totals	2	–	31	3	14	.214	–	–	–	2	2	1.000	1	1	2	5	1	0	1	–	0	8	1.0	2.5	4.0

Petrovic, Drazen b. October 22, 1964 d. June 7, 1993 Ht. 6-5 Wt. 200 College: University of Zagreb (Yugoslavia)

SEASON–TEAM	G	GS	MIN	FGM	FGA	PCT	3FGM	3FGA	PCT	FTM	FTA	PCT	O-RB	D-RB	TOT	AST	PF	DQ	STL	TO	BLK	PTS	RPG	APG	PPG
89-90–Portland	77	0	967	207	427	.485	34	74	.459	135	160	.844	50	61	111	116	134	0	23	96	2	583	1.4	1.5	7.6
90-91–Port.-N.J.	61	0	1015	243	493	.493	23	65	.354	114	137	.832	51	59	110	86	132	0	43	81	1	623	1.8	1.4	10.2
91-92–New Jersey	82	82	3027	668	1315	.508	123	277	.444	232	287	.808	97	161	258	252	248	3	105	215	11	1691	3.1	3.1	20.6
92-93–New Jersey	70	67	2660	587	1134	.518	75	167	.449	315	362	.870	42	148	190	247	237	5	94	204	13	1564	2.7	3.5	22.3
Reg. Season Totals	290	149	7669	1705	3369	.506	255	583	.437	796	946	.841	240	429	669	701	751	8	265	596	27	4461	2.3	2.4	15.4
Playoff Totals	29	9	609	119	251	.474	11	34	.324	48	69	.696	16	35	51	42	68	0	12	50	1	297	1.8	1.4	10.2

Petruska, Richard b. January 25, 1969 Ht. 6-10 Wt. 260 College: Loyola Marymount; UCLA

SEASON–TEAM	G	GS	MIN	FGM	FGA	PCT	3FGM	3FGA	PCT	FTM	FTA	PCT	O-RB	D-RB	TOT	AST	PF	DQ	STL	TO	BLK	PTS	RPG	APG	PPG
93-94–Houston	22	0	92	20	46	.435	7	15	.467	6	8	.750	9	22	31	1	15	0	2	15	3	53	1.4	0.0	2.4
Reg. Season Totals	22	0	92	20	46	.435	7	15	.467	6	8	.750	9	22	31	1	15	0	2	15	3	53	1.4	0.0	2.4

Pettit, Robert E. Lee Jr. (Bob) b. December 12, 1932 Ht. 6-9 Wt. 215 College: Louisiana State HOF: 1970

SEASON–TEAM	G	GS	MIN	FGM	FGA	PCT	3FGM	3FGA	PCT	FTM	FTA	PCT	O-RB	D-RB	TOT	AST	PF	DQ	STL	TO	BLK	PTS	RPG	APG	PPG
54-55–Milwaukee	72	–	2659	520	1279	.407	–	–	–	426	567	.751	–	–	994	229	258	5	–	–	–	1466	13.8	3.2	20.4
55-56–St. Louis	72	–	2794	646	1507	.429	–	–	–	557	757	.736	–	–	1164	189	202	1	–	–	–	1849	16.2	2.6	25.7
56-57–St. Louis	71	–	2491	613	1477	.415	–	–	–	529	684	.773	–	–	1037	133	181	1	–	–	–	1755	14.6	1.9	24.7
57-58–St. Louis	70	–	2528	581	1418	.410	–	–	–	557	744	.749	–	–	1216	157	222	6	–	–	–	1719	17.4	2.2	24.6
58-59–St. Louis	72	–	2873	719	1640	.438	–	–	–	667	879	.759	–	–	1182	221	200	3	–	–	–	2105	16.4	3.1	29.2
59-60–St. Louis	72	–	2896	669	1526	.438	–	–	–	544	722	.753	–	–	1221	257	204	0	–	–	–	1882	17.0	3.6	26.1
60-61–St. Louis	76	–	3027	769	1720	.447	–	–	–	582	804	.724	–	–	1540	262	217	1	–	–	–	2120	20.3	3.4	27.9
61-62–St. Louis	78	–	3282	867	1928	.450	–	–	–	695	901	.771	–	–	1459	289	296	4	–	–	–	2429	18.7	3.7	31.1
62-63–St. Louis	79	–	3090	778	1746	.446	–	–	–	685	885	.774	–	–	1191	245	282	8	–	–	–	2241	15.1	3.1	28.4
63-64–St. Louis	80	–	3296	791	1708	.463	–	–	–	608	771	.789	–	–	1224	259	300	3	–	–	–	2190	15.3	3.2	27.4
64-65–St. Louis	50	–	1754	396	923	.429	–	–	–	332	405	.820	–	–	621	128	167	0	–	–	–	1124	12.4	2.6	22.5
Reg. Season Totals	792	–	30690	7349	16872	.436	–	–	–	6182	8119	.761	–	–	12849	2369	2529	32	–	–	–	20880	16.2	3.0	26.4
Playoff Totals	88	–	3545	766	1834	.418	–	–	–	708	915	.774	–	–	1304	241	277	1	–	–	–	2240	14.8	2.7	25.5
All-Star Totals	11	–	360	81	193	.420	–	–	–	62	80	.775	–	–	178	23	25	0	–	–	–	224	16.2	2.1	20.4

Pettway, Jerry b. February 13, 1944 Ht. 6-3 Wt. 185 College: Northwood

SEASON–TEAM	G	GS	MIN	FGM	FGA	PCT	3FGM	3FGA	PCT	FTM	FTA	PCT	O-RB	D-RB	TOT	AST	PF	DQ	STL	TO	BLK	PTS	RPG	APG	PPG
67-68–Houston (A)	76	–	1572	289	838	.345	16	57	.281	119	183	.650	–	–	274	103	132	2	–	82	–	713	3.6	1.4	9.4
68-69–Houston (A)	11	–	264	37	123	.301	0	5	.000	5	7	.714	–	–	29	17	19	0	–	16	–	79	2.6	1.5	7.2
Reg. ABA Totals	87	–	1836	326	961	.339	16	62	.258	124	190	.653	–	–	303	120	151	2	–	98	–	792	3.5	1.4	9.1
ABA Playoff Totals	3	–	62	12	29	.414	1	2	.500	4	5	.800	–	–	14	5	5	0	–	2	–	29	4.7	1.7	9.7

Phegley, Roger Dale b. October 16, 1956 Ht. 6-7 Wt. 205 College: Bradley

SEASON–TEAM	G	GS	MIN	FGM	FGA	PCT	3FGM	3FGA	PCT	FTM	FTA	PCT	O-RB	D-RB	TOT	AST	PF	DQ	STL	TO	BLK	PTS	RPG	APG	PPG
78-79–Washington	29	–	153	28	78	.359	–	–	–	24	29	.828	5	17	22	15	21	0	5	17	2	80	0.8	0.5	2.8
79-80–Wash.-N.J.	78	–	1512	350	733	.477	4	9	.444	177	203	.872	75	110	185	102	158	1	34	119	7	881	2.4	1.3	11.3
80-81–Cleveland	82	–	2269	474	965	.491	8	28	.286	224	267	.839	90	156	246	184	262	7	65	165	15	1180	3.0	2.2	14.4
81-82–Clev.-S.A.	81	9	1183	233	507	.460	5	31	.161	85	109	.780	61	93	154	114	152	0	36	66	8	556	1.9	1.4	6.9
82-83–San Antonio	62	4	599	120	267	.449	3	14	.214	43	56	.768	39	45	84	60	92	0	30	49	8	286	1.4	1.0	4.6
83-84–S.A.-Dallas	13	0	87	11	35	.314	2	5	.400	4	4	1.000	2	9	11	11	11	0	1	6	0	28	0.8	0.8	2.2
Reg. Season Totals	345	13	5803	1216	2585	.470	22	87	.253	557	668	.834	272	430	702	486	696	8	171	422	40	3011	2.0	1.4	8.7
Playoff Totals	14	0	49	9	23	.391	3	6	.500	5	6	.833	1	7	8	2	7	0	2	4	0	26	0.6	0.1	1.9

Phelan, James J. (Jim) b. March 19, 1929 Ht. 6-1 Wt. 175 College: La Salle

SEASON–TEAM	G	GS	MIN	FGM	FGA	PCT	3FGM	3FGA	PCT	FTM	FTA	PCT	O-RB	D-RB	TOT	AST	PF	DQ	STL	TO	BLK	PTS	RPG	APG	PPG
53-54–Philadelphia	4	–	33	0	6	.000	–	–	–	3	6	.500	–	–	5	2	9	0	–	–	–	3	1.3	0.5	0.8
Reg. Season Totals	4	–	33	0	6	.000	–	–	–	3	6	.500	–	–	5	2	9	0	–	–	–	3	1.3	0.5	0.8

Phelan, John Edward (Jack) b. November 6, 1925 Ht. 6-5 Wt. 195 College: DePaul

SEASON–TEAM	G	GS	MIN	FGM	FGA	PCT	3FGM	3FGA	PCT	FTM	FTA	PCT	O-RB	D-RB	TOT	AST	PF	DQ	STL	TO	BLK	PTS	RPG	APG	PPG
49-50–Wat.-She.	55	–	–	87	268	.325	–	–	–	52	90	.578	–	–	–	57	151	–	–	–	–	226	–	1.0	4.1
Reg. Season Totals	55	–	–	87	268	.325	–	–	–	52	90	.578	–	–	–	57	151	–	–	–	–	226	–	1.0	4.1
Playoff Totals	3	–	–	4	10	.400	–	–	–	2	3	.667	–	–	–	3	10	–	–	–	–	10	–	1.0	3.3

Phelps, Derrick Michael b. July 31, 1972 Ht. 6-4 Wt. 181 College: North Carolina

SEASON–TEAM	G	GS	MIN	FGM	FGA	PCT	3FGM	3FGA	PCT	FTM	FTA	PCT	O-RB	D-RB	TOT	AST	PF	DQ	STL	TO	BLK	PTS	RPG	APG	PPG
94-95–Sacramento	3	0	5	0	1	.000	0	0	–	0	2	.000	0	0	0	1	3	0	0	0	0	0	0.0	0.3	0.0
Reg. Season Totals	3	0	5	0	1	.000	0	0	–	0	2	.000	0	0	0	1	3	0	0	0	0	0	0.0	0.3	0.0

Phelps, Michael (Mike) b. October 3, 1961 Ht. 6-4 Wt. 185 College: Alcorn State

SEASON–TEAM	G	GS	MIN	FGM	FGA	PCT	3FGM	3FGA	PCT	FTM	FTA	PCT	O-RB	D-RB	TOT	AST	PF	DQ	STL	TO	BLK	PTS	RPG	APG	PPG
85-86–Seattle	70	18	880	117	286	.409	1	12	.083	44	74	.595	29	60	89	71	86	0	45	62	1	279	1.3	1.0	4.0
86-87–Seattle	60	6	469	75	176	.426	1	10	.100	31	44	.705	16	34	50	64	60	0	21	32	2	182	0.8	1.1	3.0
87-88–L.A. Clippers	2	0	23	3	7	.429	0	0	–	3	4	.750	0	2	2	3	1	0	5	2	0	9	1.0	1.5	4.5
Reg. Season Totals	132	24	1372	195	469	.416	2	22	.091	78	122	.639	45	96	141	138	147	0	71	96	3	470	1.1	1.0	3.6

Phillip, Andrew Michael (Andy) b. March 7, 1922 Ht. 6-3 Wt. 195 College: Illinois HOF: 1961

SEASON–TEAM	G	GS	MIN	FGM	FGA	PCT	3FGM	3FGA	PCT	FTM	FTA	PCT	O-RB	D-RB	TOT	AST	PF	DQ	STL	TO	BLK	PTS	RPG	APG	PPG
47-48–Chicago	32	–	–	143	425	.336	–	–	–	60	103	.583	–	–	–	74	75	–	–	–	–	346	–	2.3	10.8
48-49–Chicago	60	–	–	285	818	.348	–	–	–	148	219	.676	–	–	–	319	205	–	–	–	–	718	–	5.3	12.0
49-50–Chicago	65	–	–	284	814	.349	–	–	–	190	270	.704	–	–	–	377	210	–	–	–	–	758	–	5.8	11.7
50-51–Philadelphia	66	–	–	275	690	.399	–	–	–	190	253	.751	–	–	446	414	221	8	–	–	–	740	6.8	6.3	11.2
51-52–Philadelphia	66	–	2933	279	762	.366	–	–	–	232	308	.753	–	–	434	539	218	6	–	–	–	790	6.6	8.2	12.0
52-53–Phil.-FtWayne	70	–	2690	250	629	.397	–	–	–	222	301	.738	–	–	364	397	229	9	–	–	–	722	5.2	5.7	10.3
53-54–Fort Wayne	71	–	2705	255	680	.375	–	–	–	241	330	.730	–	–	265	449	204	4	–	–	–	751	3.7	6.3	10.6
54-55–Fort Wayne	64	–	2332	202	545	.371	–	–	–	213	308	.692	–	–	290	491	166	1	–	–	–	617	4.5	7.7	9.6
55-56–Fort Wayne	70	–	2078	148	405	.365	–	–	–	112	199	.563	–	–	257	410	155	2	–	–	–	408	3.7	5.9	5.8
56-57–Boston	67	–	1476	105	277	.379	–	–	–	88	137	.642	–	–	181	168	121	1	–	–	–	298	2.7	2.5	4.4
57-58–Boston	70	–	1164	97	273	.355	–	–	–	42	71	.592	–	–	158	121	121	0	–	–	–	236	2.3	1.7	3.4
Reg. Season Totals	701	–	15378	2323	6318	.368	–	–	–	1738	2499	.695	–	–	2395	3759	1925	31	–	–	–	6384	4.4	5.4	9.1
Playoff Totals	67	–	1682	137	553	.327	–	–	–	154	221	.697	–	–	205	293	187	2	–	–	–	428	3.3	3.7	6.4
All-Star Totals	5	–	113	15	31	.484	–	–	–	4	5	.800	–	–	25	31	8	0	–	–	–	34	5.0	6.2	6.8

Phillips, Donald Eugene (Gene) b. October 25, 1948 Ht. 6-4 Wt. 175 College: Southern Methodist

SEASON–TEAM	G	GS	MIN	FGM	FGA	PCT	3FGM	3FGA	PCT	FTM	FTA	PCT	O-RB	D-RB	TOT	AST	PF	DQ	STL	TO	BLK	PTS	RPG	APG	PPG
71-72–Dallas (A)	28	–	174	30	76	.395	7	17	.412	11	14	.786	–	–	21	13	23	–	–	8	–	78	0.8	0.5	2.8
72-73–Dallas (A)	3	–	10	0	5	.000	0	3	.000	0	0	–	–	–	0	1	3	0	–	0	–	0	0.0	0.3	0.0
Reg. ABA Totals	31	–	184	30	81	.370	7	20	.350	11	14	.786	–	–	21	14	26	0	–	8	–	78	0.7	0.5	2.5
ABA Playoff Totals	1	–	2	0	0	–	0	0	–	0	0	–	–	–	–	0	0	0	–	–	–	0	0.0	0.0	0.0

Phillips, Eddie Lee b. September 29, 1961 Ht. 6-7 Wt. 225 College: Alabama

SEASON–TEAM	G	GS	MIN	FGM	FGA	PCT	3FGM	3FGA	PCT	FTM	FTA	PCT	O-RB	D-RB	TOT	AST	PF	DQ	STL	TO	BLK	PTS	RPG	APG	PPG
82-83–New Jersey	48	0	416	56	138	.406	0	2	.000	40	59	.678	27	50	77	29	58	0	14	50	8	152	1.6	0.6	3.2
Reg. Season Totals	48	0	416	56	138	.406	0	2	.000	40	59	.678	27	50	77	29	58	0	14	50	8	152	1.6	0.6	3.2
Playoff Totals	2	0	12	3	6	.500	0	2	.000	1	4	.250	3	2	5	3	2	0	0	1	0	7	2.5	1.5	3.5

Phillips, Gary A. b. December 7, 1939 Ht. 6-3 Wt. 190 College: Houston

SEASON–TEAM	G	GS	MIN	FGM	FGA	PCT	3FGM	3FGA	PCT	FTM	FTA	PCT	O-RB	D-RB	TOT	AST	PF	DQ	STL	TO	BLK	PTS	RPG	APG	PPG
61-62–Boston	67	–	713	110	310	.355	–	–	–	50	86	.581	–	–	107	64	109	0	–	–	–	270	1.6	1.0	4.0
62-63–San Francisco	75	–	1801	256	643	.398	–	–	–	97	152	.638	–	–	225	137	185	7	–	–	–	609	3.0	1.8	8.1
63-64–San Francisco	66	–	2010	256	691	.370	–	–	–	146	218	.670	–	–	248	203	245	8	–	–	–	658	3.8	3.1	10.0
64-65–San Francisco	73	–	1541	198	553	.358	–	–	–	120	199	.603	–	–	189	148	184	3	–	–	–	516	2.6	2.0	7.1
65-66–San Francisco	67	–	867	106	303	.350	–	–	–	54	87	.621	–	–	134	113	97	0	–	–	–	266	2.0	1.7	4.0
Reg. Season Totals	348	–	6932	926	2500	.370	–	–	–	467	742	.629	–	–	903	665	820	18	–	–	–	2319	2.6	1.9	6.7
Playoff Totals	17	–	288	36	113	.319	–	–	–	34	51	.667	–	–	27	21	42	2	–	–	–	106	1.6	1.2	6.2

Phills, Bobby Ray II b. December 20, 1969 d. January 12, 2000 Ht. 6-5 Wt. 226 College: Southern University

SEASON–TEAM	G	GS	MIN	FGM	FGA	PCT	3FGM	3FGA	PCT	FTM	FTA	PCT	O-RB	D-RB	TOT	AST	PF	DQ	STL	TO	BLK	PTS	RPG	APG	PPG
91-92–Cleveland	10	0	65	12	28	.429	0	2	.000	7	11	.636	4	4	8	4	3	0	3	8	1	31	0.8	0.4	3.1
92-93–Cleveland	31	0	139	38	82	.463	2	5	.400	15	25	.600	6	11	17	10	19	0	10	18	2	93	0.5	0.3	3.0
93-94–Cleveland	72	53	1531	242	514	.471	1	12	.083	113	157	.720	71	141	212	133	135	1	67	63	12	598	2.9	1.8	8.3
94-95–Cleveland	80	79	2500	338	816	.414	19	55	.345	183	235	.779	90	175	265	180	206	0	115	113	25	878	3.3	2.3	11.0
95-96–Cleveland	72	69	2530	386	826	.467	93	211	.441	186	240	.775	62	199	261	271	192	3	102	126	27	1051	3.6	3.8	14.6
96-97–Cleveland	69	65	2375	328	766	.428	85	216	.394	125	174	.718	63	182	245	233	174	1	113	135	21	866	3.6	3.4	12.6
97-98–Charlotte	62	61	1887	246	552	.446	44	114	.386	106	140	.757	59	157	216	187	181	2	81	108	18	642	3.5	3.0	10.4
98-99–Charlotte	43	43	1574	215	497	.433	68	172	.395	115	168	.685	39	135	174	149	124	1	60	92	25	613	4.0	3.5	14.3
99-00–Charlotte	28	9	825	152	335	.454	30	91	.330	47	65	.723	17	54	71	79	72	2	41	48	8	381	2.5	2.8	13.6
Reg. Season Totals	467	379	13426	1957	4416	.443	342	878	.390	897	1215	.738	411	1058	1469	1246	1106	10	592	711	139	5153	3.1	2.7	11.0
Playoff Totals	26	18	600	71	178	.399	12	36	.333	24	40	.600	19	50	69	48	48	0	24	35	3	178	2.7	1.8	6.8

Piatkowski, Eric Todd b. September 30, 1970 Ht. 6-7 Wt. 215 College: Nebraska

SEASON–TEAM	G	GS	MIN	FGM	FGA	PCT	3FGM	3FGA	PCT	FTM	FTA	PCT	O-RB	D-RB	TOT	AST	PF	DQ	STL	TO	BLK	PTS	RPG	APG	PPG
94-95–L.A. Clippers	81	11	1208	201	456	.441	74	198	.374	90	115	.783	63	70	133	77	150	1	37	63	15	566	1.6	1.0	7.0
95-96–L.A. Clippers	65	1	784	98	242	.405	38	114	.333	67	82	.817	40	63	103	48	83	0	24	45	10	301	1.6	0.7	4.6
96-97–L.A. Clippers	65	0	747	134	298	.450	51	120	.425	69	84	.821	49	56	105	52	85	0	33	46	10	388	1.6	0.8	6.0
97-98–L.A. Clippers	67	35	1740	257	568	.452	106	259	.409	140	170	.824	70	166	236	85	137	0	51	80	12	760	3.5	1.3	11.3
98-99–L.A. Clippers	49	38	1242	180	417	.432	65	165	.394	88	102	.863	39	101	140	53	86	0	44	53	6	513	2.9	1.1	10.5
99-00–L.A. Clippers	75	23	1712	238	573	.415	93	243	.383	85	100	.850	74	148	222	81	140	0	44	57	13	654	3.0	1.1	8.7
Reg. Season Totals	402	108	7433	1108	2554	.434	427	1099	.389	539	653	.825	335	604	939	396	681	1	233	344	66	3182	2.3	1.0	7.9
Playoff Totals	3	0	38	4	11	.364	2	5	.400	6	7	.857	1	1	2	–	5	0	1	0	0	16	0.7	0.0	5.3

Piatkowski, Walter Jr. (Walt) b. June 11, 1945 Ht. 6-8 Wt. 225 College: Bowling Green State

SEASON–TEAM	G	GS	MIN	FGM	FGA	PCT	3FGM	3FGA	PCT	FTM	FTA	PCT	O-RB	D-RB	TOT	AST	PF	DQ	STL	TO	BLK	PTS	RPG	APG	PPG
68-69–Denver (A)	77	–	1819	399	956	.417	27	82	.329	117	151	.775	–	–	363	46	226	2	–	100	–	942	4.7	0.6	12.2
69-70–Denver (A)	74	–	1302	215	535	.402	11	50	.220	76	99	.768	–	–	252	41	180	1	–	–	–	517	3.4	0.6	7.0
71-72–Floridians (A)	6	–	28	3	16	.188	0	0	–	0	0	–	–	–	2	2	2	–	–	3	–	6	0.3	0.3	1.0
Reg. ABA Totals	157	–	3149	617	1507	.409	38	132	.288	193	250	.772	–	–	617	89	408	3	–	103	–	1465	3.9	0.6	9.3
ABA Playoff Totals	13	–	251	60	135	.444	2	13	.154	12	15	.800	–	–	40	10	41	1	–	–	–	134	3.1	0.8	10.3

Pierce, Paul Anthony b. October 13, 1977 Ht. 6-7 Wt. 220 College: Kansas

SEASON–TEAM	G	GS	MIN	FGM	FGA	PCT	3FGM	3FGA	PCT	FTM	FTA	PCT	O-RB	D-RB	TOT	AST	PF	DQ	STL	TO	BLK	PTS	RPG	APG	PPG
98-99–Boston	48	47	1632	284	647	.439	84	204	.412	139	195	.713	117	192	309	115	139	1	82	113	50	791	6.4	2.4	16.5
99-00–Boston	73	72	2583	486	1099	.442	96	280	.343	359	450	.798	83	313	396	221	237	5	152	178	62	1427	5.4	3.0	19.5
Reg. Season Totals	121	119	4215	770	1746	.441	180	484	.372	498	645	.772	200	505	705	336	376	6	234	291	112	2218	5.8	2.8	18.3

Pierce, Ricky Charles b. August 19, 1959 Ht. 6-4 Wt. 215 College: Walla Walla (Wash.) C.C; Rice

SEASON–TEAM	G	GS	MIN	FGM	FGA	PCT	3FGM	3FGA	PCT	FTM	FTA	PCT	O-RB	D-RB	TOT	AST	PF	DQ	STL	TO	BLK	PTS	RPG	APG	PPG
82-83–Detroit	39	1	265	33	88	.375	1	7	.143	18	32	.563	15	20	35	14	42	0	8	18	4	85	0.9	0.4	2.2
83-84–San Diego	69	35	1280	268	570	.470	0	9	.000	149	173	.861	59	76	135	60	143	1	27	81	13	685	2.0	0.9	9.9
84-85–Milwaukee	44	3	882	165	307	.537	1	4	.250	102	124	.823	49	68	117	94	117	0	34	63	5	433	2.7	2.1	9.8
85-86–Milwaukee	81	8	2147	429	798	.538	3	23	.130	266	310	.858	94	137	231	177	252	6	83	107	6	1127	2.9	2.2	13.9
86-87–Milwaukee	79	31	2505	575	1077	.534	3	28	.107	387	440	.880	117	149	266	144	222	0	64	120	24	1540	3.4	1.8	19.5
87-88–Milwaukee	37	0	965	248	486	.510	3	14	.214	107	122	.877	30	53	83	73	94	0	21	57	7	606	2.2	2.0	16.4
88-89–Milwaukee	75	4	2078	527	1018	.518	8	36	.222	255	297	.859	82	115	197	156	193	1	77	112	19	1317	2.6	2.1	17.6
89-90–Milwaukee	59	0	1709	503	987	.510	46	133	.346	307	366	.839	64	103	167	133	158	2	50	129	7	1359	2.8	2.3	23.0
90-91–Milw.-Seattle	78	2	2167	561	1156	.485	46	116	.397	430	471	.913	67	124	191	168	170	1	60	147	13	1598	2.4	2.2	20.5
91-92–Seattle	78	78	2658	620	1306	.475	33	123	.268	417	455	.916	93	140	233	241	213	2	86	189	20	1690	3.0	3.1	21.7
92-93–Seattle	77	72	2218	524	1071	.489	42	113	.372	313	352	.889	58	134	192	220	167	0	100	160	7	1403	2.5	2.9	18.2
93-94–Seattle	51	0	1022	272	577	.471	6	32	.188	189	211	.896	29	54	83	91	84	0	42	64	5	739	1.6	1.8	14.5
94-95–Golden State	27	6	673	111	254	.437	23	70	.329	93	106	.877	12	52	64	40	38	0	22	24	2	338	2.4	1.5	12.5
95-96–Indiana	76	2	1404	264	590	.447	35	104	.337	174	205	.849	40	96	136	101	188	1	57	93	6	737	1.8	1.3	9.7
96-97–Denver-Cha.	60	27	1250	239	497	.481	42	95	.442	139	155	.897	36	85	121	80	97	0	28	68	9	659	2.0	1.3	11.0
97-98–Milwaukee	39	0	442	52	143	.364	4	13	.308	43	52	.827	19	26	45	34	35	0	9	21	0	151	1.2	0.9	3.9
Reg. Season Totals	969	269	23665	5391	10925	.493	296	920	.322	3389	3871	.875	864	1432	2296	1826	2213	14	768	1453	147	14467	2.4	1.9	14.9
Playoff Totals	97	37	2656	532	1142	.466	33	93	.355	350	404	.866	97	132	229	187	266	2	70	154	20	1447	2.4	1.9	14.9
All-Star Totals	1	0	19	4	8	.500	0	0	–	1	1	1.000	0	2	2	2	2	0	0	2	0	9	2.0	2.0	9.0

Pietkiewicz, Stanley Thomas (Stan) b. July 14, 1956 Ht. 6-5 Wt. 200 College: Auburn

SEASON–TEAM	G	GS	MIN	FGM	FGA	PCT	3FGM	3FGA	PCT	FTM	FTA	PCT	O-RB	D-RB	TOT	AST	PF	DQ	STL	TO	BLK	PTS	RPG	APG	PPG
78-79–San Diego	4	–	32	1	8	.125	–	–	–	2	2	1.000	0	6	6	3	5	0	1	1	0	4	1.5	0.8	1.0
79-80–San Diego	50	–	577	91	179	.508	9	36	.250	37	46	.804	26	19	45	94	52	1	25	51	4	228	0.9	1.9	4.6
80-81–S.D.-Dallas	42	–	461	57	138	.413	19	48	.396	11	14	.786	13	29	42	77	28	0	15	22	2	144	1.0	1.8	3.4
Reg. Season Totals	96	–	1070	149	325	.458	28	84	.333	50	62	.806	39	54	93	174	85	1	41	74	6	376	1.0	1.8	3.9

Pilch, John A. b. July 11, 1925 Ht. 6-3 Wt. 185 College: Wyoming

SEASON–TEAM	G	GS	MIN	FGM	FGA	PCT	3FGM	3FGA	PCT	FTM	FTA	PCT	O-RB	D-RB	TOT	AST	PF	DQ	STL	TO	BLK	PTS	RPG	APG	PPG
51-52–Minneapolis	9	–	41	1	10	.100	–	–	–	3	6	.500	–	–	9	2	10	0	–	–	–	5	1.0	0.2	0.6
Reg. Season Totals	9	–	41	1	10	.100	–	–	–	3	6	.500	–	–	9	2	10	0	–	–	–	5	1.0	0.2	0.6

Pinckney, Edward Lewis (Ed, E-Z Ed) b. March 27, 1963 Ht. 6-9 Wt. 240 College: Villanova

SEASON–TEAM	G	GS	MIN	FGM	FGA	PCT	3FGM	3FGA	PCT	FTM	FTA	PCT	O-RB	D-RB	TOT	AST	PF	DQ	STL	TO	BLK	PTS	RPG	APG	PPG
85-86–Phoenix	80	24	1602	255	457	.558	0	2	.000	171	254	.673	95	213	308	90	190	3	71	148	37	681	3.9	1.1	8.5
86-87–Phoenix	80	65	2250	290	497	.584	0	2	.000	257	348	.739	179	401	580	116	196	1	86	135	54	837	7.3	1.5	10.5
87-88–Sacramento	79	7	1177	179	343	.522	0	2	.000	133	178	.747	94	136	230	66	118	0	39	77	32	491	2.9	0.8	6.2
88-89–Sac.-Boston	80	33	2012	319	622	.513	0	6	.000	280	350	.800	166	283	449	118	202	2	83	119	66	918	5.6	1.5	11.5
89-90–Boston	77	50	1082	135	249	.542	0	1	.000	92	119	.773	93	132	225	68	126	1	34	56	42	362	2.9	0.9	4.7
90-91–Boston	70	16	1165	131	243	.539	0	1	.000	104	116	.897	155	186	341	45	147	0	61	45	43	366	4.9	0.6	5.2
91-92–Boston	81	36	1917	203	378	.537	0	1	.000	207	255	.812	252	312	564	62	158	1	70	73	56	613	7.0	0.8	7.6
92-93–Boston	7	5	151	10	24	.417	0	0	–	12	13	.923	14	29	43	1	13	0	4	8	7	32	6.1	0.1	4.6
93-94–Boston	76	35	1524	151	289	.522	0	0	–	92	125	.736	160	318	478	62	131	0	58	62	44	394	6.3	0.8	5.2
94-95–Milwaukee	62	17	835	48	97	.495	0	0	–	44	62	.710	65	146	211	21	64	0	34	26	17	140	3.4	0.3	2.3
95-96–Toronto-Phil.	74	47	1710	171	335	.510	0	3	.000	136	179	.760	189	269	458	72	156	1	64	77	28	478	6.2	1.0	6.5
96-97–Miami	27	0	273	23	43	.535	0	0	–	20	25	.800	25	40	65	6	30	0	8	19	9	66	2.4	0.2	2.4
Reg. Season Totals	793	335	15698	1915	3577	.535	0	18	.000	1548	2024	.765	1487	2465	3952	727	1531	9	612	845	435	5378	5.0	0.9	6.8
Playoff Totals	30	8	560	62	101	.614	0	1	.000	52	63	.825	63	72	135	11	57	0	19	21	12	176	4.5	0.4	5.9

Pinone, John Gabriel Jr. b. February 19, 1961 Ht. 6-8 Wt. 230 College: Villanova

SEASON–TEAM	G	GS	MIN	FGM	FGA	PCT	3FGM	3FGA	PCT	FTM	FTA	PCT	O-RB	D-RB	TOT	AST	PF	DQ	STL	TO	BLK	PTS	RPG	APG	PPG
83-84–Atlanta	7	0	65	7	13	.538	0	0	–	6	10	.600	0	10	10	3	11	0	2	5	1	20	1.4	0.4	2.9
Reg. Season Totals	7	0	65	7	13	.538	0	0	–	6	10	.600	0	10	10	3	11	0	2	5	1	20	1.4	0.4	2.9

Piontek, David Vincent (Dave) b. August 27, 1934 Ht. 6-6 Wt. 230 College: Xavier (Ohio)

SEASON–TEAM	G	GS	MIN	FGM	FGA	PCT	3FGM	3FGA	PCT	FTM	FTA	PCT	O-RB	D-RB	TOT	AST	PF	DQ	STL	TO	BLK	PTS	RPG	APG	PPG
56-57–Rochester	71	–	1759	257	637	.403	–	–	–	122	183	.667	–	–	351	108	141	1	–	–	–	636	4.9	1.5	9.0
57-58–Cincinnati	71	–	1032	150	397	.378	–	–	–	95	151	.629	–	–	254	52	134	2	–	–	–	395	3.6	0.7	5.6
58-59–Cincinnati	72	–	1674	305	813	.375	–	–	–	156	227	.687	–	–	385	124	162	3	–	–	–	766	5.3	1.7	10.6
59-60–Cin.-St. Louis	77	–	1833	292	728	.401	–	–	–	129	202	.639	–	–	461	118	211	5	–	–	–	713	6.0	1.5	9.3
60-61–St. Louis	29	–	254	47	96	.490	–	–	–	16	31	.516	–	–	68	19	31	0	–	–	–	110	2.3	0.7	3.8
61-62–Chicago	45	–	614	83	225	.369	–	–	–	39	59	.661	–	–	155	31	89	1	–	–	–	205	3.4	0.7	4.6
62-63–Cincinnati	48	–	457	60	158	.380	–	–	–	10	16	.625	–	–	96	26	67	0	–	–	–	130	2.0	0.5	2.7
Reg. Season Totals	413	–	7623	1194	3054	.391	–	–	–	567	869	.652	–	–	1770	478	835	12	–	–	–	2955	4.3	1.2	7.2
Playoff Totals	25	–	327	40	113	.354	–	–	–	24	37	.649	–	–	70	20	44	1	–	–	–	104	2.8	0.8	4.2

Piotrowski, Thomas Tracy (Tom) b. October 17, 1960 Ht. 7-1 Wt. 240 College: La Salle

SEASON–TEAM	G	GS	MIN	FGM	FGA	PCT	3FGM	3FGA	PCT	FTM	FTA	PCT	O-RB	D-RB	TOT	AST	PF	DQ	STL	TO	BLK	PTS	RPG	APG	PPG
83-84–Portland	18	0	78	12	26	.462	0	0	–	6	6	1.000	6	10	16	5	22	0	1	6	3	30	0.9	0.3	1.7
Reg. Season Totals	18	0	78	12	26	.462	0	0	–	6	6	1.000	6	10	16	5	22	0	1	6	3	30	0.9	0.3	1.7

Pippen, Scottie b. September 25, 1965 Ht. 6-7 Wt. 228 College: Central Arkansas

SEASON–TEAM	G	GS	MIN	FGM	FGA	PCT	3FGM	3FGA	PCT	FTM	FTA	PCT	O-RB	D-RB	TOT	AST	PF	DQ	STL	TO	BLK	PTS	RPG	APG	PPG
87-88–Chicago	79	0	1650	261	564	.463	4	23	.174	99	172	.576	115	183	298	169	214	3	91	131	52	625	3.8	2.1	7.9
88-89–Chicago	73	56	2413	413	867	.476	21	77	.273	201	301	.668	138	307	445	256	261	8	139	199	61	1048	6.1	3.5	14.4
89-90–Chicago	82	82	3148	562	1150	.489	28	112	.250	199	295	.675	150	397	547	444	298	6	211	278	101	1351	6.7	5.4	16.5
90-91–Chicago	82	82	3014	600	1153	.520	21	68	.309	240	340	.706	163	432	595	511	270	3	193	232	93	1461	7.3	6.2	17.8
91-92–Chicago	82	82	3164	687	1359	.506	16	80	.200	330	434	.760	185	445	630	572	242	2	155	253	93	1720	7.7	7.0	21.0
92-93–Chicago	81	81	3123	628	1327	.473	22	93	.237	232	350	.663	203	418	621	507	219	3	173	246	73	1510	7.7	6.3	18.6
93-94–Chicago	72	72	2759	627	1278	.491	63	197	.320	270	409	.660	173	456	629	403	227	1	211	232	58	1587	8.7	5.6	22.0
94-95–Chicago	79	79	3014	634	1320	.480	109	316	.345	315	440	.716	175	464	639	409	238	4	232	271	89	1692	8.1	5.2	21.4
95-96–Chicago	77	77	2825	563	1216	.463	150	401	.374	220	324	.679	152	344	496	452	198	0	133	207	57	1496	6.4	5.9	19.4
96-97–Chicago	82	82	3095	648	1366	.474	156	424	.368	204	291	.701	160	371	531	467	213	2	154	214	45	1656	6.5	5.7	20.2
97-98–Chicago	44	44	1652	315	704	.447	61	192	.318	150	193	.777	53	174	227	254	116	0	79	109	43	841	5.2	5.8	19.1
98-99–Houston	50	50	2011	261	604	.432	72	212	.340	132	183	.721	63	260	323	293	118	0	98	159	37	726	6.5	5.9	14.5
99-00–Portland	82	82	2749	388	860	.451	86	263	.327	160	223	.717	114	399	513	406	208	0	117	208	41	1022	6.3	5.0	12.5
Reg. Season Totals	965	869	34617	6587	13768	.478	809	2458	.329	2752	3955	.696	1844	4650	6494	5143	2822	32	1986	2739	843	16735	6.7	5.3	17.3
Playoff Totals	198	193	7814	1292	2910	.444	188	623	.302	757	1048	.722	454	1073	1527	1011	650	9	383	573	181	3529	7.7	5.1	17.8
All-Star Totals	7	6	173	34	77	.442	7	22	.318	10	16	.625	8	31	39	17	8	0	17	16	6	85	5.6	2.4	12.1

Pittman, Charles E. (Charlie) b. March 23, 1958 Ht. 6-8 Wt. 220 College: Merced (Calif.) Coll. (J.C.); Maryland

SEASON–TEAM	G	GS	MIN	FGM	FGA	PCT	3FGM	3FGA	PCT	FTM	FTA	PCT	O-RB	D-RB	TOT	AST	PF	DQ	STL	TO	BLK	PTS	RPG	APG	PPG
82-83–Phoenix	28	0	170	19	40	.475	0	1	.000	25	37	.676	13	18	31	7	41	0	2	22	7	63	1.1	0.3	2.3
83-84–Phoenix	69	8	989	126	209	.603	0	2	.000	69	101	.683	76	138	214	70	129	1	16	81	22	321	3.1	1.0	4.7
84-85–Phoenix	68	3	1001	107	227	.471	0	2	.000	109	146	.747	90	137	227	69	144	1	20	100	21	323	3.3	1.0	4.8
85-86–Phoenix	69	17	1132	127	218	.583	0	0	–	99	141	.702	99	147	246	58	140	2	37	107	23	353	3.6	0.8	5.1
Reg. Season Totals	234	28	3292	379	694	.546	0	5	.000	302	425	.711	278	440	718	204	454	4	75	310	73	1060	3.1	0.9	4.5
Playoff Totals	21	4	336	42	74	.568	0	1	.000	30	46	.652	31	52	83	21	41	0	5	25	8	114	4.0	1.0	5.4

Plummer, Gary b. February 21, 1962 Ht. 6-9 Wt. 215 College: Boston U.

SEASON–TEAM	G	GS	MIN	FGM	FGA	PCT	3FGM	3FGA	PCT	FTM	FTA	PCT	O-RB	D-RB	TOT	AST	PF	DQ	STL	TO	BLK	PTS	RPG	APG	PPG
84-85–Golden State	66	0	702	92	232	.397	1	4	.250	65	92	.707	54	80	134	26	127	1	15	50	14	250	2.0	0.4	3.8
92-93–Denver	60	0	737	106	228	.465	0	3	.000	69	95	.726	53	120	173	40	141	1	14	78	11	281	2.9	0.7	4.7
Reg. Season Totals	126	0	1439	198	460	.430	1	7	.143	134	187	.717	107	200	307	66	268	2	29	128	25	531	2.4	0.5	4.2

Polee, Dwayne L. b. March 2, 1963 Ht. 6-5 Wt. 180 College: Nevada-Las Vegas; Pepperdine

SEASON–TEAM	G	GS	MIN	FGM	FGA	PCT	3FGM	3FGA	PCT	FTM	FTA	PCT	O-RB	D-RB	TOT	AST	PF	DQ	STL	TO	BLK	PTS	RPG	APG	PPG
86-87–L.A. Clippers	1	0	6	1	4	.250	0	3	.000	0	0	–	0	0	0	0	3	0	1	1	0	2	0.0	0.0	2.0
Reg. Season Totals	1	0	6	1	4	.250	0	3	.000	0	0	–	0	0	0	0	3	0	1	1	0	2	0.0	0.0	2.0

Pollard, James Clifford (Jim, The Kangaroo Kid) b. July 9, 1922 d. January 22, 1993 Ht. 6-4 Wt. 190 College: Stanford HOF: 1977

SEASON–TEAM	G	GS	MIN	FGM	FGA	PCT	3FGM	3FGA	PCT	FTM	FTA	PCT	O-RB	D-RB	TOT	AST	PF	DQ	STL	TO	BLK	PTS	RPG	APG	PPG
47-48–Minneapolis (N)	59	–	–	310	–	–	–	–	–	140	207	.676	–	–	–	–	147	–	–	–	–	760	–	–	12.9
48-49–Minneapolis	53	–	–	314	792	.396	–	–	–	156	227	.687	–	–	–	142	144	–	–	–	–	784	–	2.7	14.8
49-50–Minneapolis	66	–	–	394	1140	.346	–	–	–	185	242	.764	–	–	–	252	143	–	–	–	–	973	–	3.8	14.7
50-51–Minneapolis	54	–	–	256	728	.352	–	–	–	117	156	.750	–	–	484	184	157	4	–	–	–	629	9.0	3.4	11.6
51-52–Minneapolis	65	–	2545	411	1155	.356	–	–	–	183	260	.704	–	–	593	234	199	4	–	–	–	1005	9.1	3.6	15.5
52-53–Minneapolis	66	–	2403	333	933	.357	–	–	–	193	251	.769	–	–	452	231	194	3	–	–	–	859	6.8	3.5	13.0
53-54–Minneapolis	71	–	2483	326	882	.370	–	–	–	179	230	.778	–	–	500	214	161	0	–	–	–	831	7.0	3.0	11.7
54-55–Minneapolis	63	–	1960	265	749	.354	–	–	–	151	186	.812	–	–	458	160	147	3	–	–	–	681	7.3	2.5	10.8
Reg. NBA Totals	438	–	9391	2299	6379	.360	–	–	–	1164	1552	.750	–	–	2487	1417	1145	14	–	–	–	5762	7.8	3.2	13.2
Reg. NBL Totals	59	–	–	310	–	–	–	–	–	140	207	.676	–	–	–	–	147	–	–	–	–	760	–	–	12.9
NBA Playoff Totals	72	–	2583	349	1405	.325	–	–	–	278	370	.751	–	–	556	413	205	6	–	–	–	976	8.1	3.7	13.6
NBL Playoff Totals	10	–	–	48	–	–	–	–	–	27	41	.659	–	–	–	–	29	–	–	–	–	123	–	–	12.3
NBA All-Star Totals	4	–	97	21	69	.304	–	–	–	6	8	.750	–	–	22	13	8	0	–	–	–	48	5.5	3.3	12.0

Pollard, Scot b. February 12, 1975 Ht. 6-11 Wt. 265 College: Kansas

SEASON–TEAM	G	GS	MIN	FGM	FGA	PCT	3FGM	3FGA	PCT	FTM	FTA	PCT	O-RB	D-RB	TOT	AST	PF	DQ	STL	TO	BLK	PTS	RPG	APG	PPG
97-98–Detroit	33	0	317	35	70	.500	0	0	–	19	23	.826	34	40	74	9	48	0	8	12	10	89	2.2	0.3	2.7
98-99–Atlanta-Sac.	16	5	259	33	61	.541	0	0	–	16	23	.696	38	44	82	4	41	0	8	5	18	82	5.1	0.3	5.1
99-00–Sacramento	76	5	1336	149	283	.527	0	0	–	114	159	.717	168	236	404	43	213	3	55	50	59	412	5.3	0.6	5.4
Reg. Season Totals	125	10	1912	217	414	.524	0	0	–	149	205	.727	240	320	560	56	302	3	71	67	87	583	4.5	0.4	4.7
Playoff Totals	10	0	144	15	25	.600	0	0	–	5	11	.455	11	16	27	2	31	1	6	5	7	35	2.7	0.2	3.5

Polson, Ralph M. b. October 26, 1929 Ht. 6-7 Wt. 205 College: Whitworth

SEASON–TEAM	G	GS	MIN	FGM	FGA	PCT	3FGM	3FGA	PCT	FTM	FTA	PCT	O-RB	D-RB	TOT	AST	PF	DQ	STL	TO	BLK	PTS	RPG	APG	PPG
52-53–N.Y.-Phil.	49	–	810	65	179	.363	–	–	–	61	96	.635	–	–	211	24	102	5	–	–	–	191	4.3	0.5	3.9
Reg. Season Totals	49	–	810	65	179	.363	–	–	–	61	96	.635	–	–	211	24	102	5	–	–	–	191	4.3	0.5	3.9

P

Polynice, Olden (O.P.) b. November 21, 1964 Ht. 7-0 Wt. 250 College: Virginia

SEASON–TEAM	G	GS	MIN	FGM	FGA	PCT	3FGM	3FGA	PCT	FTM	FTA	PCT	O-RB	D-RB	TOT	AST	PF	DQ	STL	TO	BLK	PTS	RPG	APG	PPG
87-88–Seattle	82	0	1080	118	254	.465	0	2	.000	101	158	.639	122	208	330	33	215	1	32	81	26	337	4.0	0.4	4.1
88-89–Seattle	80	0	835	91	180	.506	0	2	.000	51	86	.593	98	108	206	21	164	0	37	46	30	233	2.6	0.3	2.9
89-90–Seattle	79	7	1085	156	289	.540	1	2	.500	47	99	.475	128	172	300	15	187	0	25	35	21	360	3.8	0.2	4.6
90-91–Seattle-L.A.C	79	30	2092	316	564	.560	0	1	.000	146	252	.579	220	333	553	42	192	1	43	88	32	778	7.0	0.5	9.8
91-92–L.A. Clippers	76	65	1834	244	470	.519	0	1	.000	125	201	.622	195	341	536	46	165	0	45	83	20	613	7.1	0.6	8.1
92-93–Detroit	67	18	1299	210	429	.490	0	1	.000	66	142	.465	181	237	418	29	126	0	31	54	21	486	6.2	0.4	7.3
93-94–Detroit-Sac.	68	65	2402	346	662	.523	0	2	.000	97	191	.508	299	510	809	41	189	2	42	78	67	789	11.9	0.6	11.6
94-95–Sacramento	81	81	2534	376	691	.544	1	1	1.000	124	194	.639	277	448	725	62	238	0	48	113	52	877	9.0	0.8	10.8
95-96–Sacramento	81	80	2441	431	818	.527	1	3	.333	122	203	.601	257	507	764	58	250	3	52	127	66	985	9.4	0.7	12.2
96-97–Sacramento	82	82	2893	442	967	.457	0	6	.000	141	251	.562	272	500	772	178	298	4	46	166	80	1025	9.4	2.2	12.5
97-98–Sacramento	70	25	1458	249	542	.459	0	1	.000	52	115	.452	173	266	439	107	158	0	37	98	45	550	6.3	1.5	7.9
98-99–Seattle	48	47	1481	169	358	.472	1	1	1.000	29	94	.309	184	241	425	43	150	0	20	49	30	368	8.9	0.9	7.7
99-00–Utah	82	79	1819	203	398	.510	1	2	.500	28	90	.311	166	287	453	37	260	1	30	70	84	435	5.5	0.5	5.3
Reg. Season Totals	975	579	23253	3351	6622	.506	5	25	.200	1129	2076	.544	2572	4158	6730	712	2592	12	488	1088	574	7836	6.9	0.7	8.0
Playoff Totals	32	14	670	89	162	.549	1	1	1.000	18	36	.500	71	131	202	11	100	2	14	23	20	197	6.3	0.3	6.2

Pondexter, Clifton (Cliff) b. September 15, 1954 Ht. 6-9 Wt. 235 College: Long Beach State

SEASON–TEAM	G	GS	MIN	FGM	FGA	PCT	3FGM	3FGA	PCT	FTM	FTA	PCT	O-RB	D-RB	TOT	AST	PF	DQ	STL	TO	BLK	PTS	RPG	APG	PPG
75-76–Chicago	75	–	1326	156	380	.411	–	–	–	122	182	.670	113	268	381	90	134	4	28	–	26	434	5.1	1.2	5.8
76-77–Chicago	78	–	996	107	257	.416	–	–	–	42	65	.646	77	159	236	41	82	0	34	–	11	256	3.0	0.5	3.3
77-78–Chicago	44	–	534	37	85	.435	–	–	–	14	20	.700	36	94	130	87	66	0	19	30	15	88	3.0	2.0	2.0
Reg. Season Totals	197	–	2856	300	722	.416	–	–	–	178	267	.667	226	521	747	218	282	4	81	30	52	778	3.8	1.1	3.9
Playoff Totals	3	–	12	0	1	.000	–	–	–	2	2	1.000	0	3	3	1	0	0	0	–	0	2	1.0	0.3	0.7

Pope, David b. April 15, 1962 Ht. 6-7 Wt. 220 College: Norfolk State

SEASON–TEAM	G	GS	MIN	FGM	FGA	PCT	3FGM	3FGA	PCT	FTM	FTA	PCT	O-RB	D-RB	TOT	AST	PF	DQ	STL	TO	BLK	PTS	RPG	APG	PPG
84-85–Kansas City	22	0	129	17	53	.321	0	1	.000	7	13	.538	9	9	18	5	30	0	3	7	3	41	0.8	0.2	1.9
85-86–Seattle	11	0	74	9	20	.450	1	1	1.000	2	4	.500	6	5	11	4	11	0	2	2	1	21	1.0	0.4	1.9
Reg. Season Totals	33	0	203	26	73	.356	1	2	.500	9	17	.529	15	14	29	9	41	0	5	9	4	62	0.9	0.3	1.9

Pope, Mark Edward b. September 11, 1972 Ht. 6-10 Wt. 235 College: Kentucky

SEASON–TEAM	G	GS	MIN	FGM	FGA	PCT	3FGM	3FGA	PCT	FTM	FTA	PCT	O-RB	D-RB	TOT	AST	PF	DQ	STL	TO	BLK	PTS	RPG	APG	PPG
97-98–Indiana	28	0	193	14	41	.341	1	3	.333	10	17	.588	9	17	26	7	36	0	3	10	6	39	0.9	0.3	1.4
98-99–Indiana	4	0	26	1	7	.143	0	4	.000	0	1	.000	2	2	4	0	6	0	0	1	0	2	1.0	0.0	0.5
Reg. Season Totals	32	0	219	15	48	.313	1	7	.143	10	18	.556	11	19	30	7	42	0	3	11	6	41	0.9	0.2	1.3
Playoff Totals	7	0	42	4	6	.667	0	1	.000	1	1	1.000	2	3	5	1	8	0	1	1	0	9	0.7	0.1	1.3

Popson, David G. (Dave) b. May 17, 1964 Ht. 6-10 Wt. 220 College: North Carolina

SEASON–TEAM	G	GS	MIN	FGM	FGA	PCT	3FGM	3FGA	PCT	FTM	FTA	PCT	O-RB	D-RB	TOT	AST	PF	DQ	STL	TO	BLK	PTS	RPG	APG	PPG
88-89–LAClips-Miami	17	0	106	16	40	.400	0	0	–	2	4	.500	12	15	27	8	17	0	1	10	3	34	1.6	0.5	2.0
90-91–Boston	19	0	64	13	32	.406	0	0	–	9	10	.900	7	7	14	2	12	0	1	6	2	35	0.7	0.1	1.8
91-92–Milwaukee	5	0	26	3	7	.429	0	1	.000	1	2	.500	2	3	5	3	5	0	2	4	1	7	1.0	0.6	1.4
Reg. Season Totals	41	0	196	32	79	.405	0	1	.000	12	16	.750	21	25	46	13	34	0	4	20	6	76	1.1	0.3	1.9

Poquette, Benedict Jay (Ben, Gentle Ben) b. May 7, 1955 Ht. 6-9 Wt. 235 College: Central Michigan

SEASON–TEAM	G	GS	MIN	FGM	FGA	PCT	3FGM	3FGA	PCT	FTM	FTA	PCT	O-RB	D-RB	TOT	AST	PF	DQ	STL	TO	BLK	PTS	RPG	APG	PPG
77-78–Detroit	52	–	626	95	225	.422	–	–	–	42	60	.700	50	95	145	20	69	1	10	40	22	232	2.8	0.4	4.5
78-79–Detroit	76	–	1337	198	464	.427	–	–	–	111	142	.782	99	237	336	57	198	4	38	65	98	507	4.4	0.8	6.7
79-80–Utah	82	–	2349	296	566	.523	0	2	.000	139	167	.832	124	436	560	131	283	8	45	103	162	731	6.8	1.6	8.9
80-81–Utah	82	–	2808	324	614	.528	3	6	.500	126	162	.778	160	469	629	161	342	18	67	122	174	777	7.7	2.0	9.5
81-82–Utah	82	56	1698	220	428	.514	3	10	.300	97	120	.808	117	294	411	94	235	4	51	69	65	540	5.0	1.1	6.6
82-83–Utah	75	50	2331	329	697	.472	1	5	.200	166	221	.751	155	366	521	168	264	5	64	100	116	825	6.9	2.2	11.0
83-84–Cleveland	51	4	858	75	171	.439	1	5	.200	34	43	.791	57	125	182	49	114	1	20	28	33	185	3.6	1.0	3.6
84-85–Cleveland	79	6	1656	210	457	.460	3	17	.176	109	137	.796	148	325	473	79	220	3	47	70	58	532	6.0	1.0	6.7
85-86–Cleveland	81	3	1496	166	348	.477	2	10	.200	72	100	.720	121	252	373	78	187	2	33	68	32	406	4.6	1.0	5.0
86-87–Clev.-Chicago	58	2	604	62	122	.508	0	4	.000	40	50	.800	30	71	101	35	77	1	9	21	34	164	1.7	0.6	2.8
Reg. Season Totals	718	121	15763	1975	4092	.483	13	59	.220	936	1202	.779	1061	2670	3731	872	1989	47	384	686	794	4899	5.2	1.2	6.8
Playoff Totals	4	0	91	13	21	.619	0	0	–	4	5	.800	4	10	14	1	16	2	2	4	6	30	3.5	0.3	7.5

Porter, Howard (Geezer) b. August 31, 1948 Ht. 6-8 Wt. 220 College: Villanova

SEASON–TEAM	G	GS	MIN	FGM	FGA	PCT	3FGM	3FGA	PCT	FTM	FTA	PCT	O-RB	D-RB	TOT	AST	PF	DQ	STL	TO	BLK	PTS	RPG	APG	PPG
71-72–Chicago	67	–	730	171	403	.424	–	–	–	59	77	.766	–	–	183	24	88	0	–	–	–	401	2.7	0.4	6.0
72-73–Chicago	43	–	407	98	217	.452	–	–	–	22	29	.759	–	–	118	16	52	1	–	–	–	218	2.7	0.4	5.1
73-74–Chicago	73	–	1229	296	658	.450	–	–	–	92	115	.800	86	199	285	32	116	0	23	–	39	684	3.9	0.4	9.4
74-75–N.Y.-Detroit	58	–	1163	201	412	.488	–	–	–	66	79	.835	79	175	254	19	93	0	23	–	26	468	4.4	0.3	8.1
75-76–Detroit	75	–	1482	298	635	.469	–	–	–	73	97	.753	81	214	295	25	133	0	31	–	36	669	3.9	0.3	8.9
76-77–Detroit	78	–	2200	465	962	.483	–	–	–	103	120	.858	155	303	458	53	202	0	50	–	73	1033	5.9	0.7	13.2
77-78–Detroit-N.J.	63	–	1323	309	635	.487	–	–	–	124	155	.800	100	179	279	42	134	0	29	55	38	742	4.4	0.7	11.8
Reg. Season Totals	457	–	8534	1838	3922	.469	–	–	–	539	672	.802	501	1070	1872	211	818	1	156	55	212	4215	4.1	0.5	9.2
Playoff Totals	36	–	663	151	329	.459	–	–	–	33	39	.846	51	72	152	18	59	0	18	–	15	335	4.2	0.5	9.3

Porter, Kevin b. April 17, 1950 Ht. 6-0 Wt. 175 College: St. Francis (Pa.)

SEASON–TEAM	G	GS	MIN	FGM	FGA	PCT	3FGM	3FGA	PCT	FTM	FTA	PCT	O-RB	D-RB	TOT	AST	PF	DQ	STL	TO	BLK	PTS	RPG	APG	PPG
72-73–Baltimore	71	–	1217	205	451	.455	–	–	–	62	101	.614	–	–	72	237	206	5	–	–	–	472	1.0	3.3	6.6
73-74–Capital	81	–	2339	477	997	.478	–	–	–	180	249	.723	79	100	179	469	319	14	95	–	9	1134	2.2	5.8	14.0
74-75–Washington	81	–	2589	406	827	.491	–	–	–	131	186	.704	55	97	152	650	320	12	152	–	11	943	1.9	8.0	11.6
75-76–Detroit	19	–	687	99	235	.421	–	–	–	42	56	.750	14	30	44	193	83	3	35	–	3	240	2.3	10.2	12.6
76-77–Detroit	81	–	2117	310	605	.512	–	–	–	97	133	.729	28	70	98	592	271	8	88	–	8	717	1.2	7.3	8.9
77-78–Detroit-N.J.	82	–	2813	495	1055	.469	–	–	–	244	320	.763	53	161	214	837	283	6	123	360	15	1234	2.6	10.2	15.0
78-79–Detroit	82	–	3064	534	1110	.481	–	–	–	192	266	.722	62	147	209	1099	302	5	158	337	5	1260	2.5	13.4	15.4
79-80–Washington	70	–	1494	201	438	.459	0	4	.000	110	137	.803	25	57	82	457	180	1	59	164	11	512	1.2	6.5	7.3
80-81–Washington	81	–	2577	446	859	.519	3	12	.250	191	247	.773	35	89	124	734	257	4	110	251	10	1086	1.5	9.1	13.4
82-83–Washington	11	0	210	21	40	.525	0	0	–	5	6	.833	2	3	5	46	30	0	10	21	0	47	0.5	4.2	4.3
Reg. Season Totals	659	0	19107	3194	6617	.483	3	16	.188	1254	1701	.737	353	754	1179	5314	2251	58	830	1133	72	7645	1.8	8.1	11.6
Playoff Totals	33	0	971	150	324	.463	0	1	.000	63	97	.649	26	40	68	191	128	5	33	4	0	363	2.1	5.8	11.0

Porter, Terry b. April 8, 1963 Ht. 6-3 Wt. 205 College: Wisconsin-Stevens Point

SEASON–TEAM	G	GS	MIN	FGM	FGA	PCT	3FGM	3FGA	PCT	FTM	FTA	PCT	O-RB	D-RB	TOT	AST	PF	DQ	STL	TO	BLK	PTS	RPG	APG	PPG
85-86–Portland	79	3	1214	212	447	.474	13	42	.310	125	155	.806	35	82	117	198	136	0	81	106	1	562	1.5	2.5	7.1
86-87–Portland	80	80	2714	376	770	.488	13	60	.217	280	334	.838	70	267	337	715	192	0	159	255	9	1045	4.2	8.9	13.1
87-88–Portland	82	82	2991	462	890	.519	24	69	.348	274	324	.846	65	313	378	831	204	1	150	244	16	1222	4.6	10.1	14.9
88-89–Portland	81	81	3102	540	1146	.471	79	219	.361	272	324	.840	85	282	367	770	187	1	146	248	8	1431	4.5	9.5	17.7
89-90–Portland	80	80	2781	448	969	.462	89	238	.374	421	472	.892	59	213	272	726	150	0	151	245	4	1406	3.4	9.1	17.6
90-91–Portland	81	81	2665	486	944	.515	130	313	.415	279	339	.823	52	230	282	649	151	2	158	189	12	1381	3.5	8.0	17.0
91-92–Portland	82	82	2784	521	1129	.461	128	324	.395	315	368	.856	51	204	255	477	155	1	127	188	12	1485	3.1	5.8	18.1
92-93–Portland	81	81	2883	503	1108	.454	143	345	.414	327	388	.843	58	258	316	419	122	0	101	199	10	1476	3.9	5.2	18.2
93-94–Portland	77	34	2074	348	836	.416	110	282	.390	204	234	.872	45	170	215	401	132	0	79	166	18	1010	2.8	5.2	13.1
94-95–Portland	35	9	770	105	267	.393	44	114	.386	58	82	.707	18	63	81	133	60	0	30	58	2	312	2.3	3.8	8.9
95-96–Minnesota	82	40	2072	269	608	.442	71	226	.314	164	209	.785	36	176	212	452	154	0	89	173	15	773	2.6	5.5	9.4
96-97–Minnesota	82	20	1568	187	449	.416	67	200	.335	127	166	.765	31	145	176	295	104	0	54	128	11	568	2.1	3.6	6.9
97-98–Minnesota	82	8	1786	259	577	.449	92	233	.395	167	195	.856	37	131	168	271	103	0	63	104	16	777	2.0	3.3	9.5
98-99–Miami	50	1	1365	172	370	.465	58	141	.411	123	148	.831	13	127	140	146	97	0	48	74	11	525	2.8	2.9	10.5
99-00–San Antonio	68	8	1613	207	463	.447	90	207	.435	137	170	.806	24	167	191	221	79	0	50	100	9	641	2.8	3.3	9.4
Reg. Season Totals	1122	690	32382	5095	10973	.464	1151	3013	.382	3273	3908	.838	679	2828	3507	6704	2026	5	1486	2477	154	14614	3.1	6.0	13.0
Playoff Totals	101	77	3482	568	1199	.474	133	350	.380	418	503	.831	71	267	338	572	220	1	122	209	14	1687	3.3	5.7	16.7
All-Star Totals	2	0	34	5	14	.357	1	7	.143	0	0	–	1	2	3	7	3	0	3	4	1	11	1.5	3.5	5.5

Porter, Willie William b. July 3, 1942 Ht. 6-7 Wt. 205 College: Tennessee State

SEASON–TEAM	G	GS	MIN	FGM	FGA	PCT	3FGM	3FGA	PCT	FTM	FTA	PCT	O-RB	D-RB	TOT	AST	PF	DQ	STL	TO	BLK	PTS	RPG	APG	PPG
67-68–Oakland-Pitt. (A)	56	–	1294	225	546	.412	0	0	–	199	294	.677	–	–	449	59	190	11	–	155	–	649	8.0	1.1	11.6
68-69–Minn.-Hou. (A)	13	–	148	28	52	.538	0	0	–	17	31	.548	–	–	55	6	23	0	–	11	–	73	4.2	0.5	5.6
Reg. ABA Totals	69	–	1442	253	598	.423	0	0	–	216	325	.665	–	–	504	65	213	11	–	166	–	722	7.3	0.9	10.5
ABA Playoff Totals	14	–	167	19	43	.442	0	0	–	20	29	.690	–	–	69	6	43	0	–	18	–	58	4.9	0.4	4.1

Portman, Robert M. (Bob) b. March 22, 1947 Ht. 6-5 Wt. 200 College: Creighton

SEASON–TEAM	G	GS	MIN	FGM	FGA	PCT	3FGM	3FGA	PCT	FTM	FTA	PCT	O-RB	D-RB	TOT	AST	PF	DQ	STL	TO	BLK	PTS	RPG	APG	PPG
69-70–San Francisco	60	–	813	177	398	.445	–	–	–	66	85	.776	–	–	224	28	77	0	–	–	–	420	3.7	0.5	7.0
70-71–San Francisco	68	–	1395	221	483	.458	–	–	–	77	106	.726	–	–	321	67	130	0	–	–	–	519	4.7	1.0	7.6
71-72–Golden State	61	–	553	89	221	.403	–	–	–	53	60	.883	–	–	133	26	69	0	–	–	–	231	2.2	0.4	3.8
72-73–Golden State	32	–	176	32	70	.457	–	–	–	20	26	.769	–	–	51	7	16	0	–	–	–	84	1.6	0.2	2.6
Reg. Season Totals	221	–	2937	519	1172	.443	–	–	–	216	277	.780	–	–	729	128	292	0	–	–	–	1254	3.3	0.6	5.7
Playoff Totals	11	–	149	24	61	.393	–	–	–	11	14	.786	–	–	30	3	14	0	–	–	–	59	2.7	0.3	5.4

Posey, James Mikley Mantell b. January 13, 1977 Ht. 6-8 Wt. 215 College: Xavier (Ohio)

SEASON–TEAM	G	GS	MIN	FGM	FGA	PCT	3FGM	3FGA	PCT	FTM	FTA	PCT	O-RB	D-RB	TOT	AST	PF	DQ	STL	TO	BLK	PTS	RPG	APG	PPG
99-00–Denver	81	77	2052	230	536	.429	82	220	.373	120	150	.800	85	232	317	146	207	1	98	95	33	662	3.9	1.8	8.2
Reg. Season Totals	81	77	2052	230	536	.429	82	220	.373	120	150	.800	85	232	317	146	207	1	98	95	33	662	3.9	1.8	8.2

Postley, John b. May 30, 1940 d. July 1970 Ht. 6-5 Wt. 220 College: Bethune-Cookman

SEASON–TEAM	G	GS	MIN	FGM	FGA	PCT	3FGM	3FGA	PCT	FTM	FTA	PCT	O-RB	D-RB	TOT	AST	PF	DQ	STL	TO	BLK	PTS	RPG	APG	PPG
67-68–Pittsburgh (A)	1	–	6	1	3	.333	0	0	–	0	0	–	–	–	6	1	1	0	–	1	–	2	6.0	1.0	2.0
Reg. ABA Totals	1	–	6	1	3	.333	0	0	–	0	0	–	–	–	6	1	1	0	–	1	–	2	6.0	1.0	2.0

Potapenko, Vitaly Nikolaevich (The Ukraine Train) b. March 21, 1975 Ht. 6-10 Wt. 280 College: Wright State

SEASON–TEAM	G	GS	MIN	FGM	FGA	PCT	3FGM	3FGA	PCT	FTM	FTA	PCT	O-RB	D-RB	TOT	AST	PF	DQ	STL	TO	BLK	PTS	RPG	APG	PPG
96-97–Cleveland	80	3	1238	186	423	.440	1	2	.500	92	125	.736	105	112	217	40	216	3	26	109	34	465	2.7	0.5	5.8
97-98–Cleveland	80	0	1412	234	488	.480	0	1	.000	102	144	.708	110	203	313	57	198	2	27	132	28	570	3.9	0.7	7.1
98-99–Clev.-Boston	50	44	1394	204	412	.495	0	1	.000	91	155	.587	114	218	332	75	169	4	35	100	36	499	6.6	1.5	10.0
99-00–Boston	79	72	1797	307	615	.499	0	1	.000	109	160	.681	182	317	499	77	239	4	41	145	29	723	6.3	1.0	9.2
Reg. Season Totals	289	119	5841	931	1938	.480	1	5	.200	394	584	.675	511	850	1361	249	822	13	129	486	127	2257	4.7	0.9	7.8
Playoff Totals	4	0	70	6	15	.400	0	0	–	5	10	.500	3	8	11	3	8	0	2	6	0	17	2.8	0.8	4.3

Powell, Cincinnatus (Cincy) b. February 25, 1942 Ht. 6-7 Wt. 225 College: Portland; Xavier (New Orleans)

SEASON–TEAM	G	GS	MIN	FGM	FGA	PCT	3FGM	3FGA	PCT	FTM	FTA	PCT	O-RB	D-RB	TOT	AST	PF	DQ	STL	TO	BLK	PTS	RPG	APG	PPG
67-68–Dallas (A)	77	–	2524	533	1089	.489	1	4	.250	343	496	.692	–	–	694	106	254	7	–	190	–	1410	9.0	1.4	18.3
68-69–Dallas (A)	75	–	2573	555	1179	.471	2	7	.286	342	470	.728	–	–	671	173	275	5	–	212	–	1454	8.9	2.3	19.4
69-70–Dallas (A)	76	–	2624	562	1200	.468	2	12	.167	402	519	.775	–	–	682	192	250	6	–	–	–	1528	9.0	2.5	20.1
70-71–Kentucky (A)	81	–	2933	578	1173	.493	4	16	.250	302	398	.759	311	579	890	255	323	–	–	–	–	1462	11.0	3.1	18.0
71-72–Kentucky (A)	65	–	2288	430	907	.474	4	13	.308	185	256	.723	–	–	500	237	219	–	–	178	–	1049	7.7	3.6	16.1
72-73–Utah (A)	83	–	1985	423	853	.496	3	13	.231	167	240	.696	135	285	420	137	249	7	–	137	–	1016	5.1	1.7	12.2
73-74–Virginia (A)	82	–	2485	528	1167	.452	10	31	.323	209	296	.706	171	348	519	136	270	–	46	186	32	1275	6.3	1.7	15.5
74-75–Virginia (A)	60	–	1224	214	530	.404	5	17	.294	119	180	.661	74	132	206	94	138	–	27	91	8	552	3.4	1.6	9.2
Reg. ABA Totals	599	–	18636	3823	8098	.472	31	113	.274	2069	2855	.725	691	1344	4582	1330	1978	25	73	994	40	9746	7.6	2.2	16.3
ABA Playoff Totals	61	–	2020	412	989	.417	5	18	.278	242	321	.754	119	258	593	123	224	0	3	75	1	1071	9.7	2.0	17.6

Pradd, Marlbert (Marl) b. November 17, 1944 Ht. 6-3 Wt. 170 College: Dillard

SEASON–TEAM	G	GS	MIN	FGM	FGA	PCT	3FGM	3FGA	PCT	FTM	FTA	PCT	O-RB	D-RB	TOT	AST	PF	DQ	STL	TO	BLK	PTS	RPG	APG	PPG
67-68–New Orleans (A)	29	–	125	27	60	.450	0	0	–	20	27	.741	–	–	26	3	22	0	–	18	–	74	0.9	0.1	2.6
68-69–New Orleans (A)	50	–	323	81	186	.435	3	13	.231	93	119	.782	–	–	50	23	60	0	–	34	–	258	1.0	0.5	5.2
Reg. ABA Totals	79	–	448	108	246	.439	3	13	.231	113	146	.774	–	–	76	26	82	0	–	52	–	332	1.0	0.3	4.2
ABA Playoff Totals	13	–	57	13	31	.419	4	6	.667	10	18	.556	–	–	9	1	10	0	–	3	–	40	0.7	0.1	3.1

Pratt, Michael P. (Mike) b. August 4, 1948 Ht. 6-4 Wt. 205 College: Kentucky

SEASON–TEAM	G	GS	MIN	FGM	FGA	PCT	3FGM	3FGA	PCT	FTM	FTA	PCT	O-RB	D-RB	TOT	AST	PF	DQ	STL	TO	BLK	PTS	RPG	APG	PPG
70-71–Kentucky (A)	78	–	1213	173	416	.416	3	11	.273	91	121	.752	–	–	225	188	135	–	–	–	–	440	2.9	2.4	5.6
71-72–Kentucky (A)	65	–	889	133	301	.442	16	40	.400	84	98	.857	–	–	158	98	151	–	–	81	–	366	2.4	1.5	5.6
Reg. ABA Totals	143	–	2102	306	717	.427	19	51	.373	175	219	.799	–	–	383	286	286	–	–	81	–	806	2.7	2.0	5.6
ABA Playoff Totals	25	–	488	80	187	.428	1	6	.167	42	52	.808	–	–	83	68	53	–	–	11	–	203	3.3	2.7	8.1

Pressey, Paul Matthew b. December 24, 1958 Ht. 6-5 Wt. 205 College: Western Texas Coll. (J.C.); Tulsa

SEASON–TEAM	G	GS	MIN	FGM	FGA	PCT	3FGM	3FGA	PCT	FTM	FTA	PCT	O-RB	D-RB	TOT	AST	PF	DQ	STL	TO	BLK	PTS	RPG	APG	PPG
82-83–Milwaukee	79	18	1528	213	466	.457	1	9	.111	105	176	.597	83	198	281	207	174	2	99	162	47	532	3.6	2.6	6.7
83-84–Milwaukee	81	18	1730	276	528	.523	2	9	.222	120	200	.600	102	180	282	252	241	6	86	157	50	674	3.5	3.1	8.3
84-85–Milwaukee	80	80	2876	480	928	.517	7	20	.350	317	418	.758	149	280	429	543	258	4	129	247	56	1284	5.4	6.8	16.1
85-86–Milwaukee	80	80	2704	411	843	.488	8	44	.182	316	392	.806	127	272	399	623	247	4	168	240	71	1146	5.0	7.8	14.3
86-87–Milwaukee	61	60	2057	294	616	.477	16	55	.291	242	328	.738	98	198	296	441	213	4	110	186	47	846	4.9	7.2	13.9
87-88–Milwaukee	75	75	2484	345	702	.491	8	39	.205	285	357	.798	130	245	375	523	233	6	112	198	34	983	5.0	7.0	13.1
88-89–Milwaukee	67	62	2170	307	648	.474	12	55	.218	187	241	.776	73	189	262	439	221	2	119	184	44	813	3.9	6.6	12.1
89-90–Milwaukee	57	2	1400	239	506	.472	6	43	.140	144	190	.758	59	113	172	244	149	3	71	109	23	628	3.0	4.3	11.0
90-91–San Antonio	70	18	1683	201	426	.472	16	57	.281	110	133	.827	50	126	176	271	174	1	63	130	32	528	2.5	3.9	7.5
91-92–San Antonio	56	7	759	60	161	.373	3	21	.143	28	41	.683	22	73	95	142	86	0	29	64	19	151	1.7	2.5	2.7
92-93–Golden State	18	0	268	29	66	.439	0	4	.000	21	27	.778	8	23	31	30	36	0	11	23	5	79	1.7	1.7	4.4
Reg. Season Totals	724	420	19659	2855	5890	.485	79	356	.222	1875	2503	.749	901	1897	2798	3715	2032	32	997	1700	428	7664	3.9	5.1	10.6
Playoff Totals	75	50	2269	321	682	.471	11	45	.244	228	313	.728	113	203	316	420	261	6	116	207	49	881	4.2	5.6	11.7

Pressley, Dominic Ivan b. May 30, 1964 Ht. 6-2 Wt. 175 College: Boston College

SEASON–TEAM	G	GS	MIN	FGM	FGA	PCT	3FGM	3FGA	PCT	FTM	FTA	PCT	O-RB	D-RB	TOT	AST	PF	DQ	STL	TO	BLK	PTS	RPG	APG	PPG
88-89–Wash.-Chicago	13	0	124	9	31	.290	0	2	.000	5	9	.556	3	12	15	26	11	0	4	11	0	23	1.2	2.0	1.8
Reg. Season Totals	13	0	124	9	31	.290	0	2	.000	5	9	.556	3	12	15	26	11	0	4	11	0	23	1.2	2.0	1.8

Pressley, Harold b. July 14, 1963 Ht. 6-8 Wt. 210 College: Villanova

SEASON–TEAM	G	GS	MIN	FGM	FGA	PCT	3FGM	3FGA	PCT	FTM	FTA	PCT	O-RB	D-RB	TOT	AST	PF	DQ	STL	TO	BLK	PTS	RPG	APG	PPG
86-87–Sacramento	67	23	913	134	317	.423	7	28	.250	35	48	.729	68	108	176	120	96	1	40	63	21	310	2.6	1.8	4.6
87-88–Sacramento	80	49	2029	318	702	.453	36	110	.327	103	130	.792	139	230	369	185	211	4	84	135	55	775	4.6	2.3	9.7
88-89–Sacramento	80	36	2257	383	873	.439	119	295	.403	96	123	.780	216	269	485	174	215	1	93	124	76	981	6.1	2.2	12.3
89-90–Sacramento	72	10	1603	240	566	.424	46	148	.311	110	141	.780	94	215	309	149	148	0	58	88	36	636	4.3	2.1	8.8
Reg. Season Totals	299	118	6802	1075	2458	.437	208	581	.358	344	442	.778	517	822	1339	628	670	6	275	410	188	2702	4.5	2.1	9.0

Previs, Stephen Richard (Steve) b. February 9, 1950 Ht. 6-3 Wt. 185 College: North Carolina

SEASON–TEAM	G	GS	MIN	FGM	FGA	PCT	3FGM	3FGA	PCT	FTM	FTA	PCT	O-RB	D-RB	TOT	AST	PF	DQ	STL	TO	BLK	PTS	RPG	APG	PPG
72-73–Carolina (A)	30	–	147	23	60	.383	1	8	.125	8	15	.533	6	8	14	24	26	0	–	13	–	55	0.5	0.8	1.8
Reg. ABA Totals	30	–	147	23	60	.383	1	8	.125	8	15	.533	6	8	14	24	26	0	–	13	–	55	0.5	0.8	1.8
ABA Playoff Totals	2	–	11	1	7	.143	1	2	.500	0	0	–	–	–	3	3	2	0	–	4	–	3	1.5	1.5	1.5

Price, Anthony (Tony) b. January 5, 1957 Ht. 6-6 Wt. 200 College: Pennsylvania

SEASON–TEAM	G	GS	MIN	FGM	FGA	PCT	3FGM	3FGA	PCT	FTM	FTA	PCT	O-RB	D-RB	TOT	AST	PF	DQ	STL	TO	BLK	PTS	RPG	APG	PPG
80-81–San Diego	5	–	29	2	7	.286	0	0	–	0	0	–	0	0	0	3	3	0	2	2	1	4	0.0	0.6	0.8
Reg. Season Totals	5	–	29	2	7	.286	0	0	–	0	0	–	0	0	0	3	3	0	2	2	1	4	0.0	0.6	0.8

Price, Hartley Brent (Brent) b. December 9, 1968 Ht. 6-1 Wt. 185 College: South Carolina; Oklahoma

SEASON–TEAM	G	GS	MIN	FGM	FGA	PCT	3FGM	3FGA	PCT	FTM	FTA	PCT	O-RB	D-RB	TOT	AST	PF	DQ	STL	TO	BLK	PTS	RPG	APG	PPG
92-93–Washington	68	9	859	100	279	.358	8	48	.167	54	68	.794	28	75	103	154	90	0	56	85	3	262	1.5	2.3	3.9
93-94–Washington	65	13	1035	141	326	.433	50	150	.333	68	87	.782	31	59	90	213	114	1	55	119	2	400	1.4	3.3	6.2
95-96–Washington	81	50	2042	252	534	.472	139	301	.462	167	191	.874	38	190	228	416	184	3	78	153	4	810	2.8	5.1	10.0
96-97–Houston	25	0	390	44	105	.419	17	53	.321	21	21	1.000	10	19	29	65	34	0	17	32	0	126	1.2	2.6	5.0
97-98–Houston	72	2	1332	128	310	.413	73	187	.390	77	98	.786	37	70	107	192	163	3	52	111	4	406	1.5	2.7	5.6
98-99–Houston	40	6	806	100	207	.483	46	112	.411	46	61	.754	18	60	78	113	90	0	33	65	1	292	2.0	2.8	7.3
99-00–Vancouver	41	0	424	41	119	.345	25	68	.368	34	39	.872	8	29	37	69	63	0	17	47	1	141	0.9	1.7	3.4
Reg. Season Totals	392	80	6888	806	1880	.429	358	919	.390	467	565	.827	170	502	672	1222	738	7	308	612	15	2437	1.7	3.1	6.2
Playoff Totals	9	0	173	17	39	.436	10	27	.370	8	9	.889	4	13	17	20	17	1	8	12	1	52	1.9	2.2	5.8

Price, James E. (Jim) b. November 27, 1949 Ht. 6-3 Wt. 195 College: Louisville

SEASON–TEAM	G	GS	MIN	FGM	FGA	PCT	3FGM	3FGA	PCT	FTM	FTA	PCT	O-RB	D-RB	TOT	AST	PF	DQ	STL	TO	BLK	PTS	RPG	APG	PPG
72-73–Los Angeles	59	–	828	158	359	.440	–	–	–	60	73	.822	–	–	115	97	119	1	–	–	–	376	1.9	1.6	6.4
73-74–Los Angeles	82	–	2628	538	1197	.449	–	–	–	187	234	.799	120	258	378	369	229	2	157	–	29	1263	4.6	4.5	15.4
74-75–L.A.-Milw.	50	–	1870	317	717	.442	–	–	–	169	194	.871	62	136	198	286	182	1	111	–	24	803	4.0	5.7	16.1
75-76–Milwaukee	80	–	2525	398	958	.415	–	–	–	141	166	.849	74	187	261	395	264	3	148	–	32	937	3.3	4.9	11.7
76-77–Milw.-Buf.-Den.	81	–	1828	253	567	.446	–	–	–	83	103	.806	50	181	231	261	247	3	128	–	20	589	2.9	3.2	7.3
77-78–Denver-Detroit	83	–	1929	294	656	.448	–	–	–	135	169	.799	57	203	260	260	200	0	114	175	9	723	3.1	3.1	8.7
78-79–Los Angeles	75	–	1207	171	344	.497	–	–	–	55	79	.696	26	97	123	218	128	0	66	100	12	397	1.6	2.9	5.3
Reg. Season Totals	510	–	12815	2129	4798	.444	–	–	–	830	1018	.815	389	1062	1566	1886	1369	10	724	275	126	5088	3.1	3.7	10.0
Playoff Totals	23	–	482	59	168	.351	–	–	–	20	32	.625	15	36	55	62	61	1	25	8	1	138	2.4	2.7	6.0
All-Star Totals	1	–	17	3	9	.333	–	–	–	2	2	1.000	0	2	2	0	4	0	2	–	0	8	2.0	0.0	8.0

Price, Michael (Mike) b. September 11, 1948 Ht. 6-3 Wt. 200 College: Illinois

SEASON–TEAM	G	GS	MIN	FGM	FGA	PCT	3FGM	3FGA	PCT	FTM	FTA	PCT	O-RB	D-RB	TOT	AST	PF	DQ	STL	TO	BLK	PTS	RPG	APG	PPG
70-71–New York	56	–	251	30	81	.370	–	–	–	24	34	.706	–	–	29	12	57	0	–	–	–	84	0.5	0.2	1.5
71-72–New York	6	–	40	5	14	.357	–	–	–	9	11	.818	–	–	6	6	10	0	–	–	–	19	1.0	1.0	3.2
71-72–Indiana (A)	4	–	25	3	9	.333	0	0	–	0	0	–	–	–	5	1	4	–	–	4	–	6	1.3	0.3	1.5
72-73–Philadelphia	57	–	751	125	301	.415	–	–	–	38	47	.809	–	–	117	71	106	0	–	–	–	288	2.1	1.2	5.1
Reg. NBA Totals	119	–	1042	160	396	.404	–	–	–	71	92	.772	–	–	152	89	173	0	–	–	–	391	1.3	0.7	3.3
Reg. ABA Totals	4	–	25	3	9	.333	0	0	–	0	0	–	–	–	5	1	4	–	–	4	–	6	1.3	0.3	1.5
NBA Playoff Totals	8	–	26	4	11	.364	–	–	–	4	6	.667	–	–	5	5	11	0	–	–	–	12	0.6	0.6	1.5

Price, William Mark (Mark) b. February 15, 1964 Ht. 6-0 Wt. 180 College: Georgia Tech

SEASON–TEAM	G	GS	MIN	FGM	FGA	PCT	3FGM	3FGA	PCT	FTM	FTA	PCT	O-RB	D-RB	TOT	AST	PF	DQ	STL	TO	BLK	PTS	RPG	APG	PPG
86-87–Cleveland	67	0	1217	173	424	.408	23	70	.329	95	114	.833	33	84	117	202	75	1	43	105	4	464	1.7	3.0	6.9
87-88–Cleveland	80	79	2626	493	974	.506	72	148	.486	221	252	.877	54	126	180	480	119	1	99	184	12	1279	2.3	6.0	16.0
88-89–Cleveland	75	74	2728	529	1006	.526	93	211	.441	263	292	.901	48	178	226	631	98	0	115	212	7	1414	3.0	8.4	18.9
89-90–Cleveland	73	73	2706	489	1066	.459	152	374	.406	300	338	.888	66	185	251	666	89	0	114	214	5	1430	3.4	9.1	19.6
90-91–Cleveland	16	16	571	97	195	.497	18	53	.340	59	62	.952	8	37	45	166	23	0	42	56	2	271	2.8	10.4	16.9
91-92–Cleveland	72	72	2138	438	897	.488	101	261	.387	270	285	.947	38	135	173	535	113	0	94	159	12	1247	2.4	7.4	17.3
92-93–Cleveland	75	74	2380	477	986	.484	122	293	.416	289	305	.948	37	164	201	602	105	0	89	196	11	1365	2.7	8.0	18.2
93-94–Cleveland	76	73	2386	480	1005	.478	118	297	.397	238	268	.888	39	189	228	589	93	0	103	189	11	1316	3.0	7.8	17.3
94-95–Cleveland	48	34	1375	253	612	.413	103	253	.407	148	162	.914	25	87	112	335	50	0	35	142	4	757	2.3	7.0	15.8
95-96–Washington	7	1	127	18	60	.300	10	30	.333	10	10	1.000	1	6	7	18	7	0	6	10	0	56	1.0	2.6	8.0
96-97–Golden State	70	49	1876	263	589	.447	112	283	.396	155	171	.906	36	143	179	342	100	0	67	161	3	793	2.6	4.9	11.3
97-98–Orlando	63	33	1430	229	531	.431	52	155	.335	87	103	.845	24	105	129	297	92	0	53	162	5	597	2.0	4.7	9.5
Reg. Season Totals	722	578	21560	3939	8345	.472	976	2428	.402	2135	2362	.904	409	1439	1848	4863	964	2	860	1790	76	10989	2.6	6.7	15.2
Playoff Totals	47	47	1691	280	603	.464	56	166	.337	202	214	.944	21	103	124	327	81	1	64	158	5	818	2.6	7.0	17.4
All-Star Totals	4	0	80	18	35	.514	9	19	.474	9	10	.900	1	5	6	13	9	0	5	8	1	54	1.5	3.3	13.5

P

Priddy, Robert B. (Bob) b. March 24, 1930 Ht. 6-3 Wt. 190 College: New Mexico State

SEASON–TEAM	G	GS	MIN	FGM	FGA	PCT	3FGM	3FGA	PCT	FTM	FTA	PCT	O-RB	D-RB	TOT	AST	PF	DQ	STL	TO	BLK	PTS	RPG	APG	PPG
52-53–Baltimore	16	–	149	14	38	.368	–	–	–	8	14	.571	–	–	36	7	36	3	–	–	–	36	2.3	0.4	2.3
Reg. Season Totals	16	–	149	14	38	.368	–	–	–	8	14	.571	–	–	36	7	36	3	–	–	–	36	2.3	0.4	2.3
Playoff Totals	1	–	1	0	0	–	–	–	–	0	0	–	–	–	0	–	1	0	–	–	–	0	0.0	0.0	0.0

Pritchard, John D. b. January 23, 1927 Ht. 6-9 Wt. 220 College: Drake

SEASON–TEAM	G	GS	MIN	FGM	FGA	PCT	3FGM	3FGA	PCT	FTM	FTA	PCT	O-RB	D-RB	TOT	AST	PF	DQ	STL	TO	BLK	PTS	RPG	APG	PPG
49-50–Waterloo	7	–	–	9	29	.310	–	–	–	4	11	.364	–	–	–	8	14	–	–	–	–	22	–	1.1	3.1
Reg. Season Totals	7	–	–	9	29	.310	–	–	–	4	11	.364	–	–	–	8	14	–	–	–	–	22	–	1.1	3.1

Pritchard, Kevin Lee b. July 17, 1967 Ht. 6-3 Wt. 180 College: Kansas

SEASON–TEAM	G	GS	MIN	FGM	FGA	PCT	3FGM	3FGA	PCT	FTM	FTA	PCT	O-RB	D-RB	TOT	AST	PF	DQ	STL	TO	BLK	PTS	RPG	APG	PPG
90-91–Golden State	62	1	773	88	229	.384	5	31	.161	62	77	.805	16	49	65	81	104	1	30	59	8	243	1.0	1.3	3.9
91-92–Boston	11	0	136	16	34	.471	0	3	.000	14	18	.778	1	10	11	30	17	0	3	11	4	46	1.0	2.7	4.2
94-95–Phil.-Miami	19	0	194	13	32	.406	2	8	.250	16	21	.762	0	12	12	34	22	0	2	12	1	44	0.6	1.8	2.3
95-96–Washington	2	0	22	2	3	.667	1	1	1.000	2	3	.667	0	2	2	7	3	0	2	0	0	7	1.0	3.5	3.5
Reg. Season Totals	94	1	1125	119	298	.399	8	43	.186	94	119	.790	17	73	90	152	146	1	37	82	13	340	1.0	1.6	3.6

Profit, Bronta Laron (Laron) b. August 5, 1977 Ht. 6-5 Wt. 204 College: Maryland

SEASON–TEAM	G	GS	MIN	FGM	FGA	PCT	3FGM	3FGA	PCT	FTM	FTA	PCT	O-RB	D-RB	TOT	AST	PF	DQ	STL	TO	BLK	PTS	RPG	APG	PPG
99-00–Washington	33	1	225	21	59	.356	3	17	.176	4	10	.400	2	24	26	25	26	0	7	19	4	49	0.8	0.8	1.5
Reg. Season Totals	33	1	225	21	59	.356	3	17	.176	4	10	.400	2	24	26	25	26	0	7	19	4	49	0.8	0.8	1.5

Pugh, Leslie (Les) b. September 18, 1923 Ht. 6-7 Wt. 195 College: Ohio State

SEASON–TEAM	G	GS	MIN	FGM	FGA	PCT	3FGM	3FGA	PCT	FTM	FTA	PCT	O-RB	D-RB	TOT	AST	PF	DQ	STL	TO	BLK	PTS	RPG	APG	PPG
48-49–Providence	60	–	–	168	556	.302	–	–	–	125	167	.749	–	–	–	59	168	–	–	–	–	461	–	1.0	7.7
49-50–Baltimore	56	–	–	68	273	.249	–	–	–	115	136	.846	–	–	–	16	118	–	–	–	–	251	–	0.3	4.5
Reg. Season Totals	116	–	–	236	829	.285	–	–	–	240	303	.792	–	–	–	75	286	–	–	–	–	712	–	0.6	6.1

Pugh, Roy b. 1923 Ht. 6-6 Wt. 210 College: Southern Methodist

SEASON–TEAM	G	GS	MIN	FGM	FGA	PCT	3FGM	3FGA	PCT	FTM	FTA	PCT	O-RB	D-RB	TOT	AST	PF	DQ	STL	TO	BLK	PTS	RPG	APG	PPG
47-48–Indianapolis (N)	4	–	–	1	–	–	–	–	–	2	4	.500	–	–	–	–	–	–	–	–	–	4	–	–	1.0
48-49–Ft.W-Ind.-Phil.	23	–	–	13	51	.255	–	–	–	6	19	.316	–	–	–	9	17	–	–	–	–	32	–	0.4	1.4
Reg. NBA Totals	23	–	–	13	51	.255	–	–	–	6	19	.316	–	–	–	9	17	–	–	–	–	32	–	0.4	1.4
Reg. NBL Totals	4	–	–	1	–	–	–	–	–	2	4	.500	–	–	–	–	–	–	–	–	–	4	–	–	1.0

Pullard, Anthony Quinn b. June 23, 1966 Ht. 6-10 Wt. 245 College: McNeese State

SEASON–TEAM	G	GS	MIN	FGM	FGA	PCT	3FGM	3FGA	PCT	FTM	FTA	PCT	O-RB	D-RB	TOT	AST	PF	DQ	STL	TO	BLK	PTS	RPG	APG	PPG
92-93–Milwaukee	8	0	37	8	18	.444	0	0	–	1	3	.333	2	6	8	2	5	0	2	5	2	17	1.0	0.3	2.1
Reg. Season Totals	8	0	37	8	18	.444	0	0	–	1	3	.333	2	6	8	2	5	0	2	5	2	17	1.0	0.3	2.1

Putman, James Donald (Don) b. November 13, 1922 Ht. 6-1 Wt. 170 College: Colorado; Denver

SEASON–TEAM	G	GS	MIN	FGM	FGA	PCT	3FGM	3FGA	PCT	FTM	FTA	PCT	O-RB	D-RB	TOT	AST	PF	DQ	STL	TO	BLK	PTS	RPG	APG	PPG
46-47–St. Louis	58	–	–	156	635	.246	–	–	–	68	105	.648	–	–	–	30	106	–	–	–	–	380	–	0.5	6.6
47-48–St. Louis	42	–	–	105	399	.263	–	–	–	57	84	.679	–	–	–	25	95	–	–	–	–	267	–	0.6	6.4
48-49–St. Louis	59	–	–	98	330	.297	–	–	–	52	97	.536	–	–	–	140	132	–	–	–	–	248	–	2.4	4.2
49-50–St. Louis	57	–	–	51	200	.255	–	–	–	33	52	.635	–	–	–	90	116	–	–	–	–	135	–	1.6	2.4
Reg. Season Totals	216	–	–	410	1564	.262	–	–	–	210	338	.621	–	–	–	285	449	–	–	–	–	1030	–	1.3	4.8
Playoff Totals	12	–	–	17	107	.234	–	–	–	8	19	.421	–	–	–	15	28	1	–	–	–	42	–	0.9	3.5

Quick, Robert L. (Bob) b. March 5, 1946 Ht. 6-5 Wt. 215 College: Xavier (Ohio)

SEASON–TEAM	G	GS	MIN	FGM	FGA	PCT	3FGM	3FGA	PCT	FTM	FTA	PCT	O-RB	D-RB	TOT	AST	PF	DQ	STL	TO	BLK	PTS	RPG	APG	PPG
68-69–Baltimore	28	–	154	30	73	.411	–	–	–	27	44	.614	–	–	25	12	14	0	–	–	–	87	0.9	0.4	3.1
69-70–Balt.-Detroit	34	–	364	63	139	.453	–	–	–	49	71	.690	–	–	75	14	50	0	–	–	–	175	2.2	0.4	5.1
70-71–Detroit	56	–	1146	155	341	.455	–	–	–	138	176	.784	–	–	230	56	142	1	–	–	–	448	4.1	1.0	8.0
71-72–Detroit	18	–	204	39	82	.476	–	–	–	34	45	.756	–	–	51	11	29	0	–	–	–	112	2.8	0.6	6.2
71-72–Dallas (A)	6	–	57	8	15	.533	0	0	–	10	10	1.000	–	–	14	1	9	–	–	4	–	26	2.3	0.2	4.3
Reg. NBA Totals	136	–	1868	287	635	.452	–	–	–	248	336	.738	–	–	381	93	235	1	–	–	–	822	2.8	0.7	6.0
Reg. ABA Totals	6	–	57	8	15	.533	0	0	–	10	10	1.000	–	–	14	1	9	–	–	4	–	26	2.3	0.2	4.3
NBA Playoff Totals	2	–	9	2	3	.667	–	–	–	0	2	.000	–	–	1	–	1	0	–	–	–	4	0.5	0.0	2.0

Quinnett, Brian Ralph b. May 30, 1966 Ht. 6-8 Wt. 235 College: Washington State

SEASON–TEAM	G	GS	MIN	FGM	FGA	PCT	3FGM	3FGA	PCT	FTM	FTA	PCT	O-RB	D-RB	TOT	AST	PF	DQ	STL	TO	BLK	PTS	RPG	APG	PPG
89-90–New York	31	0	193	19	58	.328	0	2	.000	2	3	.667	9	19	28	11	27	0	3	4	4	40	0.9	0.4	1.3
90-91–New York	68	5	1011	139	303	.459	15	43	.349	26	36	.722	65	80	145	53	100	0	22	52	13	319	2.1	0.8	4.7
91-92–N.Y.-Dallas	39	0	326	43	124	.347	13	41	.317	16	26	.615	16	35	51	12	32	0	16	16	8	115	1.3	0.3	2.9
Reg. Season Totals	138	5	1530	201	485	.414	28	86	.326	44	65	.677	90	134	224	76	159	0	41	72	25	474	1.6	0.6	3.4
Playoff Totals	6	0	52	6	12	.500	2	4	.500	0	0	–	5	4	9	5	4	0	1	3	0	14	1.5	0.8	2.3

Rackley, Luther Jr. (Luke) b. June 11, 1946 Ht. 6-10 Wt. 220 College: Xavier (Ohio)

SEASON–TEAM	G	GS	MIN	FGM	FGA	PCT	3FGM	3FGA	PCT	FTM	FTA	PCT	O-RB	D-RB	TOT	AST	PF	DQ	STL	TO	BLK	PTS	RPG	APG	PPG
69-70–Cincinnati	66	–	1256	190	423	.449	–	–	–	124	195	.636	–	–	378	56	204	5	–	–	–	504	5.7	0.8	7.6
70-71–Cleveland	74	–	1434	219	470	.466	–	–	–	121	190	.637	–	–	394	66	186	3	–	–	–	559	5.3	0.9	7.6
71-72–Clev.-N.Y.	71	–	683	103	240	.429	–	–	–	50	88	.568	–	–	208	21	107	0	–	–	–	256	2.9	0.3	3.6
72-73–New York	1	–	2	0	0	–	–	–	–	0	0	–	–	–	1	0	2	0	–	–	–	0	1.0	0.0	0.0
72-73–Memphis (A)	57	–	893	170	344	.494	0	1	.000	78	120	.650	90	197	287	36	130	2	–	50	–	418	5.0	0.6	7.3
73-74–Philadelphia	9	–	68	5	13	.385	–	–	–	8	11	.727	5	17	22	0	11	0	3	–	4	18	2.4	0.0	2.0
Reg. NBA Totals	221	–	3443	517	1146	.451	–	–	–	303	484	.626	5	17	1003	143	510	8	3	–	4	1337	4.5	0.6	6.0
Reg. ABA Totals	57	–	893	170	344	.494	0	1	.000	78	120	.650	90	197	287	36	130	2	–	50	–	418	5.0	0.6	7.3
NBA Playoff Totals	11	–	29	2	14	.143	–	–	–	4	4	1.000	0	0	7	1	7	0	0	–	0	8	0.6	0.1	0.7

Rader, Howard (Howie) b. March 29, 1921 d. February 2, 1991 Ht. 6-1 Wt. 190 College: Long Island University

SEASON–TEAM	G	GS	MIN	FGM	FGA	PCT	3FGM	3FGA	PCT	FTM	FTA	PCT	O-RB	D-RB	TOT	AST	PF	DQ	STL	TO	BLK	PTS	RPG	APG	PPG
46-47–Tri-Cities (N)	41	–	–	76	–	–	–	–	–	43	64	.672	–	–	–	–	93	–	–	–	–	195	–	–	4.8
47-48–Tri-Cities (N)	45	–	–	44	–	–	–	–	–	29	54	.537	–	–	–	–	90	–	–	–	–	117	–	–	2.6
48-49–Baltimore	13	–	–	7	45	.156	–	–	–	3	10	.300	–	–	–	14	25	–	–	–	–	17	–	1.1	1.3
Reg. NBA Totals	13	–	–	7	45	.156	–	–	–	3	10	.300	–	–	–	14	25	–	–	–	–	17	–	1.1	1.3
Reg. NBL Totals	86	–	–	120	–	–	–	–	–	72	118	.610	–	–	–	–	183	–	–	–	–	312	–	–	3.6
NBL Playoff Totals	6	–	–	8	–	–	–	–	–	6	12	.500	–	–	–	–	11	–	–	–	–	22	–	–	3.7

Radford, Mark Jeffrey b. July 5, 1959 Ht. 6-4 Wt. 190 College: Oregon State

SEASON–TEAM	G	GS	MIN	FGM	FGA	PCT	3FGM	3FGA	PCT	FTM	FTA	PCT	O-RB	D-RB	TOT	AST	PF	DQ	STL	TO	BLK	PTS	RPG	APG	PPG
81-82–Seattle	43	0	369	54	100	.540	2	3	.667	35	69	.507	13	16	29	57	65	0	16	42	2	145	0.7	1.3	3.4
82-83–Seattle	54	2	439	84	172	.488	4	18	.222	30	73	.411	12	35	47	104	78	0	34	74	4	202	0.9	1.9	3.7
Reg. Season Totals	97	2	808	138	272	.507	6	21	.286	65	142	.458	25	51	76	161	143	0	50	116	6	347	0.8	1.7	3.6

Radford, Wayne b. May 29, 1956 Ht. 6-3 Wt. 205 College: Indiana

SEASON–TEAM	G	GS	MIN	FGM	FGA	PCT	3FGM	3FGA	PCT	FTM	FTA	PCT	O-RB	D-RB	TOT	AST	PF	DQ	STL	TO	BLK	PTS	RPG	APG	PPG
78-79–Indiana	52	–	649	83	175	.474	–	–	–	36	45	.800	25	43	68	57	61	0	30	45	1	202	1.3	1.1	3.9
Reg. Season Totals	52	–	649	83	175	.474	–	–	–	36	45	.800	25	43	68	57	61	0	30	45	1	202	1.3	1.1	3.9

Radja, Dino b. April 24, 1967 Ht. 6-11 Wt. 255 Country: Croatia

SEASON–TEAM	G	GS	MIN	FGM	FGA	PCT	3FGM	3FGA	PCT	FTM	FTA	PCT	O-RB	D-RB	TOT	AST	PF	DQ	STL	TO	BLK	PTS	RPG	APG	PPG
93-94–Boston	80	47	2303	491	942	.521	0	1	.000	226	301	.751	191	386	577	114	276	2	70	149	67	1208	7.2	1.4	15.1
94-95–Boston	66	48	2147	450	919	.490	0	1	.000	233	307	.759	149	424	573	111	232	5	60	159	86	1133	8.7	1.7	17.2
95-96–Boston	53	52	1984	426	852	.500	0	0	–	191	275	.695	113	409	522	83	161	2	48	117	81	1043	9.8	1.6	19.7
96-97–Boston	25	25	874	149	339	.440	0	1	.000	51	71	.718	44	167	211	48	76	2	23	70	48	349	8.4	1.9	14.0
Reg. Season Totals	224	172	7308	1516	3052	.497	0	3	.000	701	954	.735	497	1386	1883	356	745	11	201	495	282	3733	8.4	1.6	16.7
Playoff Totals	4	3	153	20	50	.400	0	0	–	20	28	.714	4	24	28	9	19	0	4	9	5	60	7.0	2.3	15.0

Radojevic, Aleksandar (Alek) b. August 8, 1976 Ht. 7-3 Wt. 245 College: Barton County (Kan.) C.C.

SEASON–TEAM	G	GS	MIN	FGM	FGA	PCT	3FGM	3FGA	PCT	FTM	FTA	PCT	O-RB	D-RB	TOT	AST	PF	DQ	STL	TO	BLK	PTS	RPG	APG	PPG
99-00–Toronto	3	0	24	2	7	.286	0	0	–	3	6	.500	2	6	8	1	5	0	2	5	1	7	2.7	0.3	2.3
Reg. Season Totals	3	0	24	2	7	.286	0	0	–	3	6	.500	2	6	8	1	5	0	2	5	1	7	2.7	0.3	2.3

Radovich, Frank Raymond b. March 3, 1938 Ht. 6-8 Wt. 235 College: Indiana

SEASON–TEAM	G	GS	MIN	FGM	FGA	PCT	3FGM	3FGA	PCT	FTM	FTA	PCT	O-RB	D-RB	TOT	AST	PF	DQ	STL	TO	BLK	PTS	RPG	APG	PPG
61-62–Philadelphia	37	–	175	37	93	.398	–	–	–	13	26	.500	–	–	51	4	27	0	–	–	–	87	1.4	0.1	2.4
Reg. Season Totals	37	–	175	37	93	.398	–	–	–	13	26	.500	–	–	51	4	27	0	–	–	–	87	1.4	0.1	2.4
Playoff Totals	2	–	12	1	6	.167	–	–	–	2	4	.500	–	–	3	–	2	0	–	–	–	4	1.5	0.0	2.0

Radovich, George Lewis (Moe) b. May 5, 1929 Ht. 6-0 Wt. 160 College: Wyoming

SEASON–TEAM	G	GS	MIN	FGM	FGA	PCT	3FGM	3FGA	PCT	FTM	FTA	PCT	O-RB	D-RB	TOT	AST	PF	DQ	STL	TO	BLK	PTS	RPG	APG	PPG
52-53–Philadelphia	4	–	33	5	13	.385	–	–	–	4	4	1.000	–	–	1	8	5	0	–	–	–	14	0.3	2.0	3.5
Reg. Season Totals	4	–	33	5	13	.385	–	–	–	4	4	1.000	–	–	1	8	5	0	–	–	–	14	0.3	2.0	3.5

Radziszewski, Raymond A. (Ray) b. March 1, 1935 Ht. 6-5 Wt. 210 College: St. Joseph's (Pa.)

SEASON–TEAM	G	GS	MIN	FGM	FGA	PCT	3FGM	3FGA	PCT	FTM	FTA	PCT	O-RB	D-RB	TOT	AST	PF	DQ	STL	TO	BLK	PTS	RPG	APG	PPG
57-58–Philadelphia	1	–	6	0	3	.000	–	–	–	0	0	–	–	–	2	1	1	0	–	–	–	0	2.0	1.0	0.0
Reg. Season Totals	1	–	6	0	3	.000	–	–	–	0	0	–	–	–	2	1	1	0	–	–	–	0	2.0	1.0	0.0

Ragelis, Raymond Ernest (Ray) b. December 10, 1928 d. September 19, 1983 Ht. 6-4 Wt. 205 College: Northwestern

SEASON–TEAM	G	GS	MIN	FGM	FGA	PCT	3FGM	3FGA	PCT	FTM	FTA	PCT	O-RB	D-RB	TOT	AST	PF	DQ	STL	TO	BLK	PTS	RPG	APG	PPG
51-52–Rochester	51	–	337	25	96	.260	–	–	–	18	29	.621	–	–	76	31	62	1	–	–	–	68	1.5	0.6	1.3
Reg. Season Totals	51	–	337	25	96	.260	–	–	–	18	29	.621	–	–	76	31	62	1	–	–	–	68	1.5	0.6	1.3
Playoff Totals	5	–	14	0	2	.000	–	–	–	0	0	–	–	–	2	2	0	0	–	–	–	0	0.3	0.3	0.0

Raiken, Sherwin H. b. October 29, 1928 Ht. 6-2 Wt. 185 College: Villanova

SEASON–TEAM	G	GS	MIN	FGM	FGA	PCT	3FGM	3FGA	PCT	FTM	FTA	PCT	O-RB	D-RB	TOT	AST	PF	DQ	STL	TO	BLK	PTS	RPG	APG	PPG
52-53–New York	6	–	63	3	21	.143	–	–	–	3	8	.375	–	–	8	6	10	0	–	–	–	9	1.3	1.0	1.5
Reg. Season Totals	6	–	63	3	21	.143	–	–	–	3	8	.375	–	–	8	6	10	0	–	–	–	9	1.3	1.0	1.5
Playoff Totals	4	–	19	4	5	.800	–	–	–	0	1	.000	–	–	1	2	3	0	–	–	–	8	0.3	0.5	2.0

Rains, Edward Eugene (Ed) b. December 24, 1956 Ht. 6-7 Wt. 195 College: South Alabama

SEASON–TEAM	G	GS	MIN	FGM	FGA	PCT	3FGM	3FGA	PCT	FTM	FTA	PCT	O-RB	D-RB	TOT	AST	PF	DQ	STL	TO	BLK	PTS	RPG	APG	PPG
81-82–San Antonio	49	15	637	77	177	.435	0	2	.000	38	64	.594	37	43	80	40	74	0	18	25	2	192	1.6	0.8	3.9
82-83–San Antonio	34	1	292	33	83	.398	0	1	.000	29	43	.674	25	19	44	22	35	0	10	25	1	95	1.3	0.6	2.8
Reg. Season Totals	83	16	929	110	260	.423	0	3	.000	67	107	.626	62	62	124	62	109	0	28	50	3	287	1.5	0.7	3.5
Playoff Totals	8	0	41	5	11	.455	0	1	.000	4	9	.444	4	5	9	2	5	0	1	2	0	14	1.1	0.3	1.8

Rambis, Darrell Kurt (Kurt, Rambo) b. February 25, 1958 Ht. 6-8 Wt. 215 College: Santa Clara

SEASON–TEAM	G	GS	MIN	FGM	FGA	PCT	3FGM	3FGA	PCT	FTM	FTA	PCT	O-RB	D-RB	TOT	AST	PF	DQ	STL	TO	BLK	PTS	RPG	APG	PPG
81-82–Los Angeles	64	43	1131	118	228	.518	0	1	.000	59	117	.504	116	232	348	56	167	2	60	77	76	295	5.4	0.9	4.6
82-83–Los Angeles	78	77	1806	235	413	.569	0	2	.000	114	166	.687	164	367	531	90	233	2	105	145	63	584	6.8	1.2	7.5
83-84–Los Angeles	47	31	743	63	113	.558	0	0	–	42	66	.636	82	184	266	34	108	0	30	56	14	168	5.7	0.7	3.6
84-85–L.A. Lakers	82	46	1617	181	327	.554	0	0	–	68	103	.660	164	364	528	69	211	0	82	97	47	430	6.4	0.8	5.2
85-86–L.A. Lakers	74	74	1573	160	269	.595	0	0	–	88	122	.721	156	361	517	69	198	0	66	97	33	408	7.0	0.9	5.5
86-87–L.A. Lakers	78	10	1514	163	313	.521	0	0	–	120	157	.764	159	294	453	63	201	1	74	104	41	446	5.8	0.8	5.7
87-88–L.A. Lakers	70	20	845	102	186	.548	0	0	–	73	93	.785	103	165	268	54	103	0	39	59	13	277	3.8	0.8	4.0
88-89–Charlotte	75	75	2233	325	627	.518	0	3	.000	182	248	.734	269	434	703	159	208	4	100	148	57	832	9.4	2.1	11.1
89-90–Cha.-Phoenix	74	61	1904	190	373	.509	0	3	.000	82	127	.646	156	369	525	135	208	0	100	104	37	462	7.1	1.8	6.2
90-91–Phoenix	62	17	900	83	167	.497	0	2	.000	60	85	.706	77	189	266	64	107	1	25	45	11	226	4.3	1.0	3.6
91-92–Phoenix	28	5	381	38	82	.463	0	0	–	14	18	.778	23	83	106	37	46	0	12	25	14	90	3.8	1.3	3.2
92-93–Phoenix-Sac.	72	1	822	67	129	.519	0	2	.000	43	65	.662	77	150	227	53	122	0	43	42	18	177	3.2	0.7	2.5
93-94–L.A. Lakers	50	1	635	59	114	.518	0	1	.000	46	71	.648	84	105	189	32	89	0	22	26	23	164	3.8	0.6	3.3
94-95–L.A. Lakers	26	1	195	18	35	.514	0	0	–	8	12	.667	10	24	34	16	35	0	3	8	9	44	1.3	0.6	1.7
Reg. Season Totals	880	462	16299	1802	3376	.534	0	14	.000	999	1450	.689	1640	3321	4961	931	2036	10	761	1033	456	4603	5.6	1.1	5.2
Playoff Totals	139	105	2565	284	495	.574	0	1	.000	151	215	.702	236	528	764	119	373	0	85	141	68	719	5.5	0.9	5.2

Ramsey, Calvin (Cal) b. July 13, 1937 Ht. 6-4 Wt. 200 College: New York U.

SEASON–TEAM	G	GS	MIN	FGM	FGA	PCT	3FGM	3FGA	PCT	FTM	FTA	PCT	O-RB	D-RB	TOT	AST	PF	DQ	STL	TO	BLK	PTS	RPG	APG	PPG
59-60–St. Louis-N.Y.	11	–	195	39	96	.406	–	–	–	19	33	.576	–	–	66	9	25	1	–	–	–	97	6.0	0.8	8.8
60-61–Syracuse	2	–	27	2	11	.182	–	–	–	2	4	.500	–	–	7	3	7	0	–	–	–	6	3.5	1.5	3.0
Reg. Season Totals	13	–	222	41	107	.383	–	–	–	21	37	.568	–	–	73	12	32	1	–	–	–	103	5.6	0.9	7.9

Ramsey, Frank Vernon Jr. b. July 13, 1931 Ht. 6-3 Wt. 190 College: Kentucky HOF: 1981

SEASON–TEAM	G	GS	MIN	FGM	FGA	PCT	3FGM	3FGA	PCT	FTM	FTA	PCT	O-RB	D-RB	TOT	AST	PF	DQ	STL	TO	BLK	PTS	RPG	APG	PPG
54-55–Boston	64	–	1754	236	592	.399	–	–	–	243	322	.755	–	–	402	185	250	11	–	–	–	715	6.3	2.9	11.2
56-57–Boston	35	–	807	137	349	.393	–	–	–	144	182	.791	–	–	178	67	113	3	–	–	–	418	5.1	1.9	11.9
57-58–Boston	69	–	2047	377	900	.419	–	–	–	383	472	.811	–	–	504	167	245	8	–	–	–	1137	7.3	2.4	16.5
58-59–Boston	72	–	2013	383	1013	.378	–	–	–	341	436	.782	–	–	491	147	266	11	–	–	–	1107	6.8	2.0	15.4
59-60–Boston	73	–	2009	422	1062	.397	–	–	–	273	347	.787	–	–	506	137	251	10	–	–	–	1117	6.9	1.9	15.3
60-61–Boston	79	–	2019	448	1100	.407	–	–	–	295	354	.833	–	–	431	146	284	14	–	–	–	1191	5.5	1.8	15.1
61-62–Boston	79	–	1913	436	1019	.428	–	–	–	334	405	.825	–	–	387	109	245	10	–	–	–	1206	4.9	1.4	15.3
62-63–Boston	77	–	1541	284	743	.382	–	–	–	271	332	.816	–	–	288	95	259	13	–	–	–	839	3.7	1.2	10.9
63-64–Boston	75	–	1227	226	604	.374	–	–	–	196	233	.841	–	–	223	81	245	7	–	–	–	648	3.0	1.1	8.6
Reg. Season Totals	623	–	15330	2949	7382	.399	–	–	–	2480	3083	.804	–	–	3410	1134	2158	87	–	–	–	8378	5.5	1.8	13.4
Playoff Totals	98	–	2396	469	1105	.424	–	–	–	393	476	.826	–	–	492	151	362	14	–	–	–	1331	5.0	1.5	13.6

Ramsey, Raymond L. (Ray) b. July 18, 1921 Ht. 6-2 Wt. 165 College: Bradley

SEASON–TEAM	G	GS	MIN	FGM	FGA	PCT	3FGM	3FGA	PCT	FTM	FTA	PCT	O-RB	D-RB	TOT	AST	PF	DQ	STL	TO	BLK	PTS	RPG	APG	PPG
47-48–Tri-Cities (N)	2	–	–	0	–	–	–	–	–	0	0	–	–	–	–	–	–	–	–	–	–	0	–	–	0.0
48-49–Baltimore	2	–	–	0	1	.000	–	–	–	2	2	1.000	–	–	–	0	0	–	–	–	–	2	–	0.0	1.0
Reg. NBA Totals	2	–	–	0	1	.000	–	–	–	2	2	1.000	–	–	–	0	0	–	–	–	–	2	–	0.0	1.0
Reg. NBL Totals	2	–	–	0	–	–	–	–	–	0	0	–	–	–	–	–	–	–	–	–	–	0	–	–	0.0

Randall, Mark Christopher b. September 30, 1967 Ht. 6-9 Wt. 235 College: Kansas

SEASON–TEAM	G	GS	MIN	FGM	FGA	PCT	3FGM	3FGA	PCT	FTM	FTA	PCT	O-RB	D-RB	TOT	AST	PF	DQ	STL	TO	BLK	PTS	RPG	APG	PPG
91-92–Chicago-Minn.	54	0	441	68	149	.456	3	16	.188	32	43	.744	39	32	71	33	39	0	12	25	3	171	1.3	0.6	3.2
92-93–Minn.-Detroit	37	0	248	40	80	.500	1	8	.125	16	26	.615	27	28	55	11	33	0	4	17	2	97	1.5	0.3	2.6
93-94–Denver	28	0	155	17	50	.340	2	14	.143	22	28	.786	9	13	22	11	18	0	8	10	3	58	0.8	0.4	2.1
94-95–Denver	8	0	39	3	10	.300	0	1	.000	0	0	–	4	8	12	1	5	0	0	1	0	6	1.5	0.1	0.8
Reg. Season Totals	127	0	883	128	289	.443	6	39	.154	70	97	.722	79	81	160	56	95	0	24	53	8	332	1.3	0.4	2.6
Playoff Totals	2	0	6	0	1	.000	0	0	–	0	0	–	1	4	5	–	1	0	0	1	1	0	2.5	0.0	0.0

Rank, Wallace Aliifua (Wally) b. March 1, 1958 Ht. 6-6 Wt. 220 College: San Jose State

SEASON–TEAM	G	GS	MIN	FGM	FGA	PCT	3FGM	3FGA	PCT	FTM	FTA	PCT	O-RB	D-RB	TOT	AST	PF	DQ	STL	TO	BLK	PTS	RPG	APG	PPG
80-81–San Diego	25	–	153	21	57	.368	0	0	–	13	28	.464	17	13	30	17	33	1	7	26	1	55	1.2	0.7	2.2
Reg. Season Totals	25	–	153	21	57	.368	0	0	–	13	28	.464	17	13	30	17	33	1	7	26	1	55	1.2	0.7	2.2

Ransey, Kelvin b. May 3, 1958 Ht. 6-2 Wt. 170 College: Ohio State

SEASON–TEAM	G	GS	MIN	FGM	FGA	PCT	3FGM	3FGA	PCT	FTM	FTA	PCT	O-RB	D-RB	TOT	AST	PF	DQ	STL	TO	BLK	PTS	RPG	APG	PPG
80-81–Portland	80	–	2431	525	1162	.452	3	31	.097	164	219	.749	42	153	195	555	201	1	88	232	9	1217	2.4	6.9	15.2
81-82–Portland	78	68	2418	504	1094	.461	3	38	.079	242	318	.761	39	147	186	555	169	1	97	229	4	1253	2.4	7.1	16.1
82-83–Dallas	76	4	1607	343	746	.460	2	16	.125	152	199	.764	44	103	147	280	109	1	58	129	4	840	1.9	3.7	11.1
83-84–New Jersey	80	50	1937	304	700	.434	7	32	.219	145	183	.792	28	99	127	483	182	2	91	141	6	760	1.6	6.0	9.5
84-85–New Jersey	81	29	1689	300	654	.459	2	11	.182	122	142	.859	40	90	130	355	134	0	87	113	7	724	1.6	4.4	8.9
85-86–New Jersey	79	15	1504	231	505	.457	3	24	.125	121	148	.818	34	82	116	252	128	0	51	114	4	586	1.5	3.2	7.4
Reg. Season Totals	474	166	11586	2207	4861	.454	20	152	.132	946	1209	.782	227	674	901	2480	923	5	472	958	34	5380	1.9	5.2	11.4
Playoff Totals	14	6	306	45	117	.385	2	5	.400	14	19	.737	8	17	25	64	33	0	9	22	3	106	1.8	4.6	7.6

Ranzino, Samuel Salvadore (Sam) b. June 21, 1927 Ht. 6-1 Wt. 185 College: North Carolina State

SEASON–TEAM	G	GS	MIN	FGM	FGA	PCT	3FGM	3FGA	PCT	FTM	FTA	PCT	O-RB	D-RB	TOT	AST	PF	DQ	STL	TO	BLK	PTS	RPG	APG	PPG
51-52–Rochester	39	–	234	30	90	.333	–	–	–	26	37	.703	–	–	39	25	63	2	–	–	–	86	1.0	0.6	2.2
Reg. Season Totals	39	–	234	30	90	.333	–	–	–	26	37	.703	–	–	39	25	63	2	–	–	–	86	1.0	0.6	2.2

Rascoe, Robert B. (Bobby) b. July 22, 1940 Ht. 6-4 Wt. 205 College: Western Kentucky

SEASON–TEAM	G	GS	MIN	FGM	FGA	PCT	3FGM	3FGA	PCT	FTM	FTA	PCT	O-RB	D-RB	TOT	AST	PF	DQ	STL	TO	BLK	PTS	RPG	APG	PPG
67-68–Kentucky (A)	77	–	1606	245	563	.435	0	5	.000	190	249	.763	–	–	284	102	158	2	–	86	–	680	3.7	1.3	8.8
68-69–Kentucky (A)	78	–	1247	201	477	.421	3	15	.200	129	167	.772	–	–	150	105	131	1	–	93	–	534	1.9	1.3	6.8
69-70–Kentucky (A)	4	–	34	4	21	.190	0	1	.000	6	7	.857	–	–	4	1	3	0	–	–	–	14	1.0	0.3	3.5
Reg. ABA Totals	159	–	2887	450	1061	.424	3	21	.143	325	423	.768	–	–	438	208	292	3	–	179	–	1228	2.8	1.3	7.7
ABA Playoff Totals	12	–	251	42	90	.467	0	1	.000	34	36	.944	–	–	25	13	32	0	–	5	–	118	2.1	1.1	9.8

Rasmussen, Blair Allen b. November 13, 1962 Ht. 7-0 Wt. 250 College: Oregon

SEASON–TEAM	G	GS	MIN	FGM	FGA	PCT	3FGM	3FGA	PCT	FTM	FTA	PCT	O-RB	D-RB	TOT	AST	PF	DQ	STL	TO	BLK	PTS	RPG	APG	PPG
85-86–Denver	48	1	330	61	150	.407	0	0	–	31	39	.795	37	60	97	16	63	0	3	40	10	153	2.0	0.3	3.2
86-87–Denver	74	23	1421	268	570	.470	0	0	–	169	231	.732	183	282	465	60	224	6	24	79	58	705	6.3	0.8	9.5
87-88–Denver	79	45	1779	435	884	.492	0	0	–	132	170	.776	130	307	437	78	241	2	22	73	81	1002	5.5	1.0	12.7
88-89–Denver	77	22	1308	257	577	.445	0	0	–	69	81	.852	105	182	287	49	194	2	29	49	41	583	3.7	0.6	7.6
89-90–Denver	81	55	1995	445	895	.497	0	1	.000	111	134	.828	174	420	594	82	300	10	40	75	104	1001	7.3	1.0	12.4
90-91–Denver	70	69	2325	405	885	.458	2	5	.400	63	93	.677	170	508	678	70	307	15	52	81	132	875	9.7	1.0	12.5
91-92–Atlanta	81	61	1968	347	726	.478	5	23	.217	30	40	.750	94	299	393	107	233	1	35	51	48	729	4.9	1.3	9.0
92-93–Atlanta	22	6	283	30	80	.375	2	6	.333	9	13	.692	20	35	55	5	61	2	5	12	10	71	2.5	0.2	3.2
Reg. Season Totals	532	282	11409	2248	4767	.472	9	35	.257	614	801	.767	913	2093	3006	467	1623	38	210	460	484	5119	5.7	0.9	9.6
Playoff Totals	29	18	632	140	316	.443	0	0	–	65	81	.802	68	112	180	25	84	1	10	21	27	345	6.2	0.9	11.9

Ratkovicz, George b. November 13, 1922 Ht. 6-7 Wt. 225 College: None

SEASON–TEAM	G	GS	MIN	FGM	FGA	PCT	3FGM	3FGA	PCT	FTM	FTA	PCT	O-RB	D-RB	TOT	AST	PF	DQ	STL	TO	BLK	PTS	RPG	APG	PPG
41-42–Chicago (N)	13	–	–	9	–	–	–	–	–	14	–	–	–	–	–	–	–	–	–	–	–	32	–	–	2.5
45-46–Chicago (N)	33	–	–	80	–	–	–	–	–	66	113	.584	–	–	–	–	91	–	–	–	–	226	–	–	6.8
46-47–Chicago (N)	37	–	–	43	–	–	–	–	–	26	58	.448	–	–	–	–	68	–	–	–	–	112	–	–	3.0
47-48–Rochester (N)	53	–	–	79	–	–	–	–	–	76	119	.639	–	–	–	–	135	–	–	–	–	234	–	–	4.4
48-49–Tri-Cities (N)	64	–	–	109	–	–	–	–	–	106	175	.606	–	–	–	–	207	–	–	–	–	324	–	–	5.1
49-50–Syracuse	62	–	–	162	439	.369	–	–	–	211	348	.606	–	–	–	124	201	–	–	–	–	535	–	2.0	8.6
50-51–Syracuse	66	–	–	264	636	.415	–	–	–	321	439	.731	–	–	547	193	256	11	–	–	–	849	8.3	2.9	12.9
51-52–Syracuse	66	–	1356	165	473	.349	–	–	–	163	242	.674	–	–	328	90	235	8	–	–	–	493	5.0	1.4	7.5
52-53–Balt.-Milw.	71	–	2235	208	619	.336	–	–	–	262	373	.702	–	–	522	217	287	16	–	–	–	678	7.4	3.1	9.5
53-54–Milwaukee	69	–	2170	197	501	.393	–	–	–	176	273	.645	–	–	523	154	255	11	–	–	–	570	7.6	2.2	8.3
54-55–Milwaukee	9	–	102	3	19	.158	–	–	–	10	23	.435	–	–	17	13	15	0	–	–	–	16	1.9	1.4	1.8
Reg. NBA Totals	343	–	5863	999	2687	.372	–	–	–	1143	1698	.673	–	–	1937	791	1249	46	–	–	–	3141	6.9	2.3	9.2
Reg. NBL Totals	200	–	–	320	–	–	–	–	–	288	465	.589	–	–	–	–	501	–	–	–	–	928	–	–	4.6
NBA Playoff Totals	24	–	106	80	272	.397	–	–	–	99	148	.669	–	–	85	48	94	2	–	–	–	259	6.5	1.5	10.8
NBL Playoff Totals	27	–	–	39	–	–	–	–	–	40	58	.672	–	–	–	–	74	–	–	–	–	118	–	–	4.4

Ratleff, William Edward (Ed) b. March 29, 1950 Ht. 6-6 Wt. 195 College: Long Beach State

SEASON–TEAM	G	GS	MIN	FGM	FGA	PCT	3FGM	3FGA	PCT	FTM	FTA	PCT	O-RB	D-RB	TOT	AST	PF	DQ	STL	TO	BLK	PTS	RPG	APG	PPG
73-74–Houston	81	–	1773	254	585	.434	–	–	–	103	129	.798	93	193	286	181	182	2	90	–	27	611	3.5	2.2	7.5
74-75–Houston	80	–	2563	392	851	.461	–	–	–	157	190	.826	185	274	459	259	231	5	146	–	51	941	5.7	3.2	11.8
75-76–Houston	72	–	2401	314	647	.485	–	–	–	168	206	.816	107	272	379	260	234	4	114	–	37	796	5.3	3.6	11.1
76-77–Houston	37	–	533	70	161	.435	–	–	–	26	42	.619	24	53	77	43	45	0	20	–	6	166	2.1	1.2	4.5
77-78–Houston	68	–	1163	130	310	.419	–	–	–	39	47	.830	56	106	162	153	109	0	60	67	22	299	2.4	2.3	4.4
Reg. Season Totals	338	–	8433	1160	2554	.454	–	–	–	493	614	.803	465	898	1363	896	801	11	430	67	143	2813	4.0	2.7	8.3
Playoff Totals	8	–	291	36	87	.414	–	–	–	17	20	.850	24	29	53	35	31	0	14	–	1	89	6.6	4.4	11.1

Ratliff, Michael D. (Mike) b. June 7, 1951 Ht. 6-10 Wt. 230 College: Wisconsin-Eau Claire

SEASON–TEAM	G	GS	MIN	FGM	FGA	PCT	3FGM	3FGA	PCT	FTM	FTA	PCT	O-RB	D-RB	TOT	AST	PF	DQ	STL	TO	BLK	PTS	RPG	APG	PPG
72-73–K.C.-Omaha	58	–	681	98	235	.417	–	–	–	45	84	.536	–	–	194	38	111	1	–	–	–	241	3.3	0.7	4.2
73-74–K.C.-Omaha	2	–	4	0	0	–	–	–	–	0	0	–	0	0	0	0	0	0	0	–	0	0	0.0	0.0	0.0
Reg. Season Totals	60	–	685	98	235	.417	–	–	–	45	84	.536	0	0	194	38	111	1	0	–	0	241	3.2	0.6	4.0

Ratliff, Theo Curtis b. April 17, 1973 Ht. 6-10 Wt. 225 College: Wyoming

SEASON–TEAM	G	GS	MIN	FGM	FGA	PCT	3FGM	3FGA	PCT	FTM	FTA	PCT	O-RB	D-RB	TOT	AST	PF	DQ	STL	TO	BLK	PTS	RPG	APG	PPG
95-96–Detroit	75	2	1305	128	230	.557	0	1	.000	85	120	.708	110	187	297	13	144	1	16	56	116	341	4.0	0.2	4.5
96-97–Detroit	76	38	1292	179	337	.531	0	0	–	81	116	.698	109	147	256	13	181	2	29	56	111	439	3.4	0.2	5.8
97-98–Detroit-Phil.	82	67	2447	306	597	.513	0	0	–	197	281	.701	221	326	547	57	292	8	50	116	258	809	6.7	0.7	9.9
98-99–Philadelphia	50	50	1627	197	419	.470	0	0	–	166	229	.725	139	268	407	30	180	8	45	92	149	560	8.1	0.6	11.2
99-00–Philadelphia	57	56	1795	247	491	.503	0	0	–	182	236	.771	140	295	435	36	185	4	32	108	171	676	7.6	0.6	11.9
Reg. Season Totals	340	213	8466	1057	2074	.510	0	1	.000	711	982	.724	719	1223	1942	149	982	23	172	428	805	2825	5.7	0.4	8.3
Playoff Totals	21	17	600	71	148	.480	0	0	–	47	70	.671	53	81	134	16	59	1	16	27	52	189	6.4	0.8	9.0

Rautins, Leo R. b. March 20, 1960 Ht. 6-8 Wt. 215 College: Minnesota; Syracuse

SEASON–TEAM	G	GS	MIN	FGM	FGA	PCT	3FGM	3FGA	PCT	FTM	FTA	PCT	O-RB	D-RB	TOT	AST	PF	DQ	STL	TO	BLK	PTS	RPG	APG	PPG
83-84–Philadelphia	28	3	196	21	58	.362	0	0	–	6	10	.600	9	24	33	29	31	0	9	19	2	48	1.2	1.0	1.7
84-85–Atlanta	4	0	12	0	2	.000	0	0	–	0	0	–	1	1	2	3	3	0	0	1	0	0	0.5	0.8	0.0
Reg. Season Totals	32	3	208	21	60	.350	0	0	–	6	10	.600	10	25	35	32	34	0	9	20	2	48	1.1	1.0	1.5
Playoff Totals	3	0	5	1	3	.333	1	2	.500	0	0	–	2	0	2	1	2	0	1	0	0	3	0.7	0.3	1.0

Ray, Clifford b. January 21, 1949 Ht. 6-9 Wt. 235 College: Oklahoma

SEASON–TEAM	G	GS	MIN	FGM	FGA	PCT	3FGM	3FGA	PCT	FTM	FTA	PCT	O-RB	D-RB	TOT	AST	PF	DQ	STL	TO	BLK	PTS	RPG	APG	PPG
71-72–Chicago	82	–	1872	222	445	.499	–	–	–	134	218	.615	–	–	869	254	296	5	–	–	–	578	10.6	3.1	7.0
72-73–Chicago	73	–	2009	254	516	.492	–	–	–	117	189	.619	–	–	797	271	232	5	–	–	–	625	10.9	3.7	8.6
73-74–Chicago	80	–	2632	313	612	.511	–	–	–	121	199	.608	285	692	977	246	281	5	58	–	173	747	12.2	3.1	9.3
74-75–Golden State	82	–	2519	299	573	.522	–	–	–	171	284	.602	259	611	870	178	305	9	95	–	116	769	10.6	2.2	9.4
75-76–Golden State	82	–	2184	212	404	.525	–	–	–	140	230	.609	270	506	776	149	247	2	78	–	83	564	9.5	1.8	6.9
76-77–Golden State	77	–	2018	263	450	.584	–	–	–	105	199	.528	199	416	615	112	242	5	74	–	81	631	8.0	1.5	8.2
77-78–Golden State	79	–	2268	272	476	.571	–	–	–	148	243	.609	236	522	758	147	291	9	74	150	90	692	9.6	1.9	8.8
78-79–Golden State	82	–	1917	231	439	.526	–	–	–	106	190	.558	213	395	608	136	264	4	47	153	50	568	7.4	1.7	6.9
79-80–Golden State	81	–	1683	203	383	.530	0	2	.000	84	149	.564	122	344	466	183	266	6	51	155	32	490	5.8	2.3	6.0
80-81–Golden State	66	–	838	64	152	.421	0	0	–	29	62	.468	73	144	217	52	194	2	24	74	13	157	3.3	0.8	2.4
Reg. Season Totals	784	–	19940	2333	4450	.524	0	2	.000	1155	1963	.588	1657	3630	6953	1728	2618	52	501	532	638	5821	8.9	2.2	7.4
Playoff Totals	60	–	1735	207	385	.538	0	0	–	82	139	.590	196	337	608	125	206	2	51	–	70	496	10.1	2.1	8.3

Ray, Donald L. (Don, Duck) b. July 8, 1921 Ht. 6-6 Wt. 190 College: Western Kentucky

SEASON–TEAM	G	GS	MIN	FGM	FGA	PCT	3FGM	3FGA	PCT	FTM	FTA	PCT	O-RB	D-RB	TOT	AST	PF	DQ	STL	TO	BLK	PTS	RPG	APG	PPG
48-49–Tri-Cities (N)	46	–	–	123	–	–	–	–	–	80	117	.684	–	–	–	–	103	–	–	–	–	326	–	–	7.1
49-50–Tri-Cities	61	–	–	130	403	.323	–	–	–	104	149	.698	–	–	–	60	147	–	–	–	–	364	–	1.0	6.0
Reg. NBA Totals	61	–	–	130	403	.323	–	–	–	104	149	.698	–	–	–	60	147	–	–	–	–	364	–	1.0	6.0
Reg. NBL Totals	46	–	–	123	–	–	–	–	–	80	117	.684	–	–	–	–	103	–	–	–	–	326	–	–	7.1
NBA Playoff Totals	3	–	–	4	26	.308	–	–	–	10	11	.909	–	–	–	–	7	1	–	–	–	18	–	0.0	6.0
NBL Playoff Totals	6	–	–	16	–	–	–	–	–	17	21	.810	–	–	–	–	18	–	–	–	–	49	–	–	8.2

Ray, James E. (Jim) b. January 12, 1934 Ht. 6-1 Wt. 180 College: Toledo

SEASON–TEAM	G	GS	MIN	FGM	FGA	PCT	3FGM	3FGA	PCT	FTM	FTA	PCT	O-RB	D-RB	TOT	AST	PF	DQ	STL	TO	BLK	PTS	RPG	APG	PPG
56-57–Syracuse	4	–	43	2	11	.182	–	–	–	3	5	.600	–	–	5	3	4	0	–	–	–	7	1.3	0.8	1.8
59-60–Syracuse	4	–	21	1	6	.167	–	–	–	0	0	–	–	–	0	2	3	0	–	–	–	2	0.0	0.5	0.5
Reg. Season Totals	8	–	64	3	17	.176	–	–	–	3	5	.600	–	–	5	5	7	0	–	–	–	9	0.6	0.6	1.1

Ray, James Earl b. July 27, 1957 Ht. 6-8 Wt. 215 College: Jacksonville

SEASON–TEAM	G	GS	MIN	FGM	FGA	PCT	3FGM	3FGA	PCT	FTM	FTA	PCT	O-RB	D-RB	TOT	AST	PF	DQ	STL	TO	BLK	PTS	RPG	APG	PPG
80-81–Denver	18	–	148	15	49	.306	0	1	.000	7	10	.700	13	24	37	11	31	0	4	13	4	37	2.1	0.6	2.1
81-82–Denver	40	4	262	51	116	.440	1	1	1.000	21	36	.583	18	47	65	26	59	0	10	37	16	124	1.6	0.7	3.1
82-83–Denver	45	3	433	70	153	.458	0	1	.000	33	51	.647	37	89	126	39	83	2	24	50	19	173	2.8	0.9	3.8
Reg. Season Totals	103	7	843	136	318	.428	1	3	.333	61	97	.629	68	160	228	76	173	2	38	100	39	334	2.2	0.7	3.2
Playoff Totals	4	0	20	1	6	.167	0	0	–	1	4	.250	1	2	3	–	4	0	0	0	2	3	0.8	0.0	0.8

Rayl, James R. (Jimmy, Splendid Splinter) b. June 21, 1941 Ht. 6-2 Wt. 175 College: Indiana

SEASON–TEAM	G	GS	MIN	FGM	FGA	PCT	3FGM	3FGA	PCT	FTM	FTA	PCT	O-RB	D-RB	TOT	AST	PF	DQ	STL	TO	BLK	PTS	RPG	APG	PPG
67-68–Indiana (A)	74	–	2193	317	819	.387	57	175	.326	195	243	.802	–	–	238	210	197	1	–	193	–	886	3.2	2.8	12.0
68-69–Indiana (A)	27	–	567	72	202	.356	34	92	.370	61	68	.897	–	–	67	63	80	2	–	50	–	239	2.5	2.3	8.9
Reg. ABA Totals	101	–	2760	389	1021	.381	91	267	.341	256	311	.823	–	–	305	273	277	3	–	243	–	1125	3.0	2.7	11.1
ABA Playoff Totals	3	–	118	15	42	.357	4	14	.286	5	7	.714	–	–	10	14	14	0	–	9	–	39	3.3	4.7	13.0

Raymond, Craig Milford b. April 5, 1945 Ht. 6-11 Wt. 240 College: Brigham Young

SEASON–TEAM	G	GS	MIN	FGM	FGA	PCT	3FGM	3FGA	PCT	FTM	FTA	PCT	O-RB	D-RB	TOT	AST	PF	DQ	STL	TO	BLK	PTS	RPG	APG	PPG
68-69–Philadelphia	27	–	177	22	64	.344	–	–	–	11	17	.647	–	–	68	8	46	2	–	–	–	55	2.5	0.3	2.0
69-70–Pitt.-L.A. (A)	80	–	2356	386	812	.475	0	1	.000	190	304	.625	–	–	796	154	274	8	–	–	–	962	10.0	1.9	12.0
70-71–Memphis (A)	56	–	1102	142	330	.430	0	1	.000	67	106	.632	–	–	289	91	124	–	–	–	–	351	5.2	1.6	6.3
71-72–Floridians (A)	64	–	889	104	227	.458	0	3	.000	48	76	.632	–	–	284	67	108	–	–	91	–	256	4.4	1.0	4.0
72-73–S.D.-Ind. (A)	14	–	168	12	39	.308	0	0	–	10	14	.714	23	50	73	7	24	0	–	15	–	34	5.2	0.5	2.4
Reg. NBA Totals	27	–	177	22	64	.344	–	–	–	11	17	.647	–	–	68	8	46	2	–	–	–	55	2.5	0.3	2.0
Reg. ABA Totals	214	–	4515	644	1408	.457	0	5	.000	315	500	.630	23	50	1442	319	530	8	–	106	–	1603	6.7	1.5	7.5
ABA Playoff Totals	23	–	743	131	270	.485	0	0	–	74	96	.771	45	209	280	44	7	0	–	1	–	336	12.2	1.9	14.6

Rea, Connie Mack b. January 27, 1935 Ht. 6-3 Wt. 175 College: Centenary; Vanderbilt

SEASON–TEAM	G	GS	MIN	FGM	FGA	PCT	3FGM	3FGA	PCT	FTM	FTA	PCT	O-RB	D-RB	TOT	AST	PF	DQ	STL	TO	BLK	PTS	RPG	APG	PPG
53-54–Baltimore	20	–	154	9	43	.209	–	–	–	5	16	.313	–	–	31	16	13	0	–	–	–	23	1.6	0.8	1.2
Reg. Season Totals	20	–	154	9	43	.209	–	–	–	5	16	.313	–	–	31	16	13	0	–	–	–	23	1.6	0.8	1.2

Reaves, Joe L. b. May 27, 1950 Ht. 6-6 Wt. 220 College: Bethel College (Tenn.)

SEASON–TEAM	G	GS	MIN	FGM	FGA	PCT	3FGM	3FGA	PCT	FTM	FTA	PCT	O-RB	D-RB	TOT	AST	PF	DQ	STL	TO	BLK	PTS	RPG	APG	PPG
73-74–Phoenix	7	–	38	6	11	.545	–	–	–	4	11	.364	2	6	8	1	6	0	0	–	2	16	1.1	0.1	2.3
73-74–Memphis (A)	12	–	172	30	70	.429	0	0	–	4	6	.667	17	29	46	6	23	–	2	17	7	64	3.8	0.5	5.3
Reg. NBA Totals	7	–	38	6	11	.545	–	–	–	4	11	.364	2	6	8	1	6	0	0	–	2	16	1.1	0.1	2.3
Reg. ABA Totals	12	–	172	30	70	.429	0	0	–	4	6	.667	17	29	46	6	23	0	2	17	7	64	3.8	0.5	5.3

Recasner, Eldridge David b. December 14, 1967 Ht. 6-4 Wt. 190 College: Washington

SEASON–TEAM	G	GS	MIN	FGM	FGA	PCT	3FGM	3FGA	PCT	FTM	FTA	PCT	O-RB	D-RB	TOT	AST	PF	DQ	STL	TO	BLK	PTS	RPG	APG	PPG
94-95–Denver	3	0	13	1	6	.167	0	1	.000	4	4	1.000	0	2	2	1	0	0	3	2	0	6	0.7	0.3	2.0
95-96–Houston	63	27	1275	149	359	.415	81	191	.424	57	66	.864	31	113	144	170	111	1	23	61	5	436	2.3	2.7	6.9
96-97–Atlanta	71	4	1207	148	350	.423	58	140	.414	51	58	.879	35	80	115	94	97	0	38	65	4	405	1.6	1.3	5.7
97-98–Atlanta	59	14	1454	206	452	.456	62	148	.419	74	79	.937	32	110	142	117	94	0	41	91	1	548	2.4	2.0	9.3
98-99–Charlotte	44	2	708	82	184	.446	24	60	.400	34	39	.872	20	57	77	91	66	0	17	58	1	222	1.8	2.1	5.0
99-00–Charlotte	7	0	28	3	7	.429	1	4	.250	0	0	–	0	4	4	5	1	0	0	0	0	7	0.6	0.7	1.0
Reg. Season Totals	247	47	4685	589	1358	.434	226	544	.415	220	246	.894	118	366	484	478	369	1	122	277	11	1624	2.0	1.9	6.6
Playoff Totals	15	0	218	21	54	.389	11	24	.458	7	10	.700	3	13	16	19	16	0	4	10	0	60	1.1	1.3	4.0

Reddout, Franklin P. (Frank) b. 1931 Ht. 6-5 Wt. 195 College: Syracuse

SEASON–TEAM	G	GS	MIN	FGM	FGA	PCT	3FGM	3FGA	PCT	FTM	FTA	PCT	O-RB	D-RB	TOT	AST	PF	DQ	STL	TO	BLK	PTS	RPG	APG	PPG
53-54–Rochester	7	–	18	5	6	.833	–	–	–	3	4	.750	–	–	9	0	6	0	–	–	–	13	1.3	0.0	1.9
Reg. Season Totals	7	–	18	5	6	.833	–	–	–	3	4	.750	–	–	9	0	6	0	–	–	–	13	1.3	0.0	1.9

Redmond, Marlon Bernard b. April 15, 1955 Ht. 6-6 Wt. 200 College: San Francisco

SEASON–TEAM	G	GS	MIN	FGM	FGA	PCT	3FGM	3FGA	PCT	FTM	FTA	PCT	O-RB	D-RB	TOT	AST	PF	DQ	STL	TO	BLK	PTS	RPG	APG	PPG
78-79–K.C.-Phil.	53	–	759	163	387	.421	–	–	–	31	50	.620	57	52	109	58	96	2	28	57	16	357	2.1	1.1	6.7
79-80–Kansas City	24	–	298	59	138	.428	0	9	.000	24	34	.706	18	34	52	19	27	0	4	19	9	142	2.2	0.8	5.9
Reg. Season Totals	77	–	1057	222	525	.423	0	9	.000	55	84	.655	75	86	161	77	123	2	32	76	25	499	2.1	1.0	6.5
Playoff Totals	1	–	2	0	2	.000	0	0	–	0	0	–	0	0	0	–	0	0	0	0	0	0	0.0	0.0	0.0

Reed, Hubert F. (Hub) b. October 4, 1936 Ht. 6-9 Wt. 220 College: Oklahoma City

SEASON–TEAM	G	GS	MIN	FGM	FGA	PCT	3FGM	3FGA	PCT	FTM	FTA	PCT	O-RB	D-RB	TOT	AST	PF	DQ	STL	TO	BLK	PTS	RPG	APG	PPG
58-59–St. Louis	65	–	950	136	317	.429	–	–	–	53	71	.746	–	–	317	32	171	2	–	–	–	325	4.9	0.5	5.0
59-60–St. Louis-Cin.	71	–	1820	270	601	.449	–	–	–	134	184	.728	–	–	614	69	230	6	–	–	–	674	8.6	1.0	9.5
60-61–Cincinnati	75	–	1216	156	364	.429	–	–	–	85	122	.697	–	–	367	69	199	7	–	–	–	397	4.9	0.9	5.3
61-62–Cincinnati	80	–	1446	203	460	.441	–	–	–	60	82	.732	–	–	440	53	267	9	–	–	–	466	5.5	0.7	5.8
62-63–Cincinnati	80	–	1299	199	427	.466	–	–	–	74	98	.755	–	–	398	83	261	7	–	–	–	472	5.0	1.0	5.9
63-64–Los Angeles	46	–	386	33	91	.363	–	–	–	10	15	.667	–	–	107	23	73	0	–	–	–	76	2.3	0.5	1.7
64-65–Detroit	62	–	753	84	221	.380	–	–	–	40	58	.690	–	–	206	38	136	2	–	–	–	208	3.3	0.6	3.4
Reg. Season Totals	479	–	7870	1081	2481	.436	–	–	–	456	630	.724	–	–	2449	367	1337	33	–	–	–	2618	5.1	0.8	5.5
Playoff Totals	21	–	319	43	106	.406	–	–	–	21	30	.700	–	–	103	16	56	0	–	–	–	107	4.9	0.8	5.1

Reed, Ronald Lee (Ron) b. November 2, 1942 Ht. 6-5 Wt. 205 College: Notre Dame

SEASON–TEAM	G	GS	MIN	FGM	FGA	PCT	3FGM	3FGA	PCT	FTM	FTA	PCT	O-RB	D-RB	TOT	AST	PF	DQ	STL	TO	BLK	PTS	RPG	APG	PPG
65-66–Detroit	57	–	997	186	524	.355	–	–	–	54	100	.540	–	–	339	92	133	1	–	–	–	426	5.9	1.6	7.5
66-67–Detroit	61	–	1248	223	600	.372	–	–	–	79	133	.594	–	–	423	81	145	2	–	–	–	525	6.9	1.3	8.6
Reg. Season Totals	118	–	2245	409	1124	.364	–	–	–	133	233	.571	–	–	762	173	278	3	–	–	–	951	6.5	1.5	8.1

Reed, Willis Jr. b. June 25, 1942 Ht. 6-10 Wt. 235 College: Grambling State HOF: 1981

SEASON–TEAM	G	GS	MIN	FGM	FGA	PCT	3FGM	3FGA	PCT	FTM	FTA	PCT	O-RB	D-RB	TOT	AST	PF	DQ	STL	TO	BLK	PTS	RPG	APG	PPG
64-65–New York	80	–	3042	629	1457	.432	–	–	–	302	407	.742	–	–	1175	133	339	14	–	–	–	1560	14.7	1.7	19.5
65-66–New York	76	–	2537	438	1009	.434	–	–	–	302	399	.757	–	–	883	91	323	13	–	–	–	1178	11.6	1.2	15.5
66-67–New York	78	–	2824	635	1298	.489	–	–	–	358	487	.735	–	–	1136	126	293	9	–	–	–	1628	14.6	1.6	20.9
67-68–New York	81	–	2879	659	1346	.490	–	–	–	367	509	.721	–	–	1073	159	343	12	–	–	–	1685	13.2	2.0	20.8
68-69–New York	82	–	3108	704	1351	.521	–	–	–	325	435	.747	–	–	1191	190	314	7	–	–	–	1733	14.5	2.3	21.1
69-70–New York	81	–	3089	702	1385	.507	–	–	–	351	464	.756	–	–	1126	161	287	2	–	–	–	1755	13.9	2.0	21.7
70-71–New York	73	–	2855	614	1330	.462	–	–	–	299	381	.785	–	–	1003	148	228	1	–	–	–	1527	13.7	2.0	20.9
71-72–New York	11	–	363	60	137	.438	–	–	–	27	39	.692	–	–	96	22	30	0	–	–	–	147	8.7	2.0	13.4
72-73–New York	69	–	1876	334	705	.474	–	–	–	92	124	.742	–	–	590	126	205	0	–	–	–	760	8.6	1.8	11.0
73-74–New York	19	–	500	84	184	.457	–	–	–	42	53	.792	47	94	141	30	49	0	12	–	21	210	7.4	1.6	11.1
Reg. Season Totals	650	–	23073	4859	10202	.476	–	–	–	2465	3298	.747	47	94	8414	1186	2411	58	12	–	21	12183	12.9	1.8	18.7
Playoff Totals	78	–	2641	570	1203	.474	–	–	–	218	285	.765	4	18	801	149	275	4	2	–	0	1358	10.3	1.9	17.4
All-Star Totals	7	–	161	38	84	.452	–	–	–	12	16	.750	0	0	58	7	20	1	0	–	0	88	8.3	1.0	12.6

Reeves, Bryant (Big Country) b. June 8, 1973 Ht. 7-0 Wt. 275 College: Oklahoma State

SEASON–TEAM	G	GS	MIN	FGM	FGA	PCT	3FGM	3FGA	PCT	FTM	FTA	PCT	O-RB	D-RB	TOT	AST	PF	DQ	STL	TO	BLK	PTS	RPG	APG	PPG
95-96–Vancouver	77	63	2460	401	877	.457	0	3	.000	219	299	.732	178	392	570	109	226	2	43	157	55	1021	7.4	1.4	13.3
96-97–Vancouver	75	75	2777	498	1025	.486	1	11	.091	216	307	.704	174	436	610	160	270	3	29	175	67	1213	8.1	2.1	16.2
97-98–Vancouver	74	74	2527	492	941	.523	0	4	.000	223	316	.706	196	389	585	155	278	6	39	156	80	1207	7.9	2.1	16.3
98-99–Vancouver	25	14	702	102	251	.406	0	1	.000	67	116	.578	50	88	138	37	103	3	13	47	8	271	5.5	1.5	10.8
99-00–Vancouver	69	67	1773	252	562	.448	0	4	.000	107	165	.648	126	264	390	82	245	8	33	119	38	611	5.7	1.2	8.9
Reg. Season Totals	320	293	10239	1745	3656	.477	1	23	.043	832	1203	.692	724	1569	2293	543	1122	22	157	654	248	4323	7.2	1.7	13.5

Reeves, Khalid b. July 15, 1972 Ht. 6-3 Wt. 201 College: Arizona

SEASON–TEAM	G	GS	MIN	FGM	FGA	PCT	3FGM	3FGA	PCT	FTM	FTA	PCT	O-RB	D-RB	TOT	AST	PF	DQ	STL	TO	BLK	PTS	RPG	APG	PPG
94-95–Miami	67	17	1462	206	465	.443	67	171	.392	140	196	.714	52	134	186	288	139	1	77	132	10	619	2.8	4.3	9.2
95-96–Cha.-N.J.	51	12	833	95	227	.419	28	91	.308	61	82	.744	18	61	79	118	115	2	37	63	3	279	1.5	2.3	5.5
96-97–N.J.-Dallas	63	30	1432	184	470	.391	83	227	.366	65	87	.747	34	85	119	226	159	3	34	108	9	516	1.9	3.6	8.2
97-98–Dallas	82	54	1950	248	593	.418	56	152	.368	165	213	.775	54	131	185	230	195	3	80	130	10	717	2.3	2.8	8.7
98-99–Dallas-Detroit	11	0	112	8	21	.381	1	3	.333	8	14	.571	3	4	7	11	13	0	4	7	0	25	0.6	1.0	2.3
99-00–Chicago	3	0	48	3	12	.250	0	3	.000	5	5	1.000	2	2	4	13	8	0	2	6	0	11	1.3	4.3	3.7
Reg. Season Totals	277	113	5837	744	1788	.416	235	647	.363	444	597	.744	163	417	580	886	629	9	234	446	32	2167	2.1	3.2	7.8

Regan, Richard Joseph (Richie) b. November 30, 1930 Ht. 6-2 Wt. 180 College: Seton Hall

SEASON–TEAM	G	GS	MIN	FGM	FGA	PCT	3FGM	3FGA	PCT	FTM	FTA	PCT	O-RB	D-RB	TOT	AST	PF	DQ	STL	TO	BLK	PTS	RPG	APG	PPG
55-56–Rochester	72	–	1746	240	681	.352	–	–	–	85	133	.639	–	–	174	222	179	4	–	–	–	565	2.4	3.1	7.8
56-57–Rochester	71	–	2100	257	780	.329	–	–	–	182	235	.774	–	–	205	222	179	1	–	–	–	696	2.9	3.1	9.8
57-58–Cincinnati	72	–	1648	202	569	.355	–	–	–	120	172	.698	–	–	175	185	174	0	–	–	–	524	2.4	2.6	7.3
Reg. Season Totals	215	–	5494	699	2030	.344	–	–	–	387	540	.717	–	–	554	629	532	5	–	–	–	1785	2.6	2.9	8.3
Playoff Totals	2	–	63	12	26	.462	–	–	–	0	1	.000	–	–	9	3	5	0	–	–	–	24	4.5	1.5	12.0
All-Star Totals	1	–	21	2	7	.286	–	–	–	0	0	–	–	–	4	1	0	0	–	–	–	4	4.0	1.0	4.0

Rehfeldt, Donald (Don) b. January 7, 1927 d. October 17, 1980 Ht. 6-6 Wt. 210 College: Wisconsin

SEASON–TEAM	G	GS	MIN	FGM	FGA	PCT	3FGM	3FGA	PCT	FTM	FTA	PCT	O-RB	D-RB	TOT	AST	PF	DQ	STL	TO	BLK	PTS	RPG	APG	PPG
50-51–Baltimore	59	–	–	164	426	.385	–	–	–	103	139	.741	–	–	251	68	146	4	–	–	–	431	4.3	1.2	7.3
51-52–Balt.-Milw.	39	–	788	99	285	.347	–	–	–	63	80	.788	–	–	243	50	102	2	–	–	–	261	6.2	1.3	6.7
Reg. Season Totals	98	–	788	263	711	.370	–	–	–	166	219	.758	–	–	494	118	248	6	–	–	–	692	5.0	1.2	7.1

Reid, Don Corey b. December 30, 1973 Ht. 6-8 Wt. 250 College: Georgetown

SEASON–TEAM	G	GS	MIN	FGM	FGA	PCT	3FGM	3FGA	PCT	FTM	FTA	PCT	O-RB	D-RB	TOT	AST	PF	DQ	STL	TO	BLK	PTS	RPG	APG	PPG
95-96–Detroit	69	46	997	106	187	.567	0	0	–	51	77	.662	78	125	203	11	199	2	47	41	40	263	2.9	0.2	3.8
96-97–Detroit	47	14	462	54	112	.482	0	1	.000	24	32	.750	36	65	101	14	105	1	16	23	15	132	2.1	0.3	2.8
97-98–Detroit	68	44	994	94	176	.534	0	0	–	50	71	.704	77	98	175	26	183	2	25	28	55	238	2.6	0.4	3.5
98-99–Detroit	47	30	935	97	174	.557	0	0	–	48	79	.608	66	104	170	33	156	2	27	36	43	242	3.6	0.7	5.1
99-00–Detroit-Wash.	38	3	498	60	112	.536	0	0	–	24	34	.706	31	71	102	11	118	5	24	23	31	144	2.7	0.3	3.8
Reg. Season Totals	269	137	3886	411	761	.540	0	1	.000	197	293	.672	288	463	751	95	761	12	139	151	184	1019	2.8	0.4	3.8
Playoff Totals	8	0	50	3	6	.500	0	0	–	5	7	.714	2	4	6	2	10	0	0	1	2	11	0.8	0.3	1.4

Reid, Herman Jr. (J.R.) b. March 31, 1968 Ht. 6-10 Wt. 250 College: North Carolina

SEASON–TEAM	G	GS	MIN	FGM	FGA	PCT	3FGM	3FGA	PCT	FTM	FTA	PCT	O-RB	D-RB	TOT	AST	PF	DQ	STL	TO	BLK	PTS	RPG	APG	PPG
89-90–Charlotte	82	82	2757	358	814	.440	0	5	.000	192	289	.664	199	492	691	101	292	7	92	172	54	908	8.4	1.2	11.1
90-91–Charlotte	80	80	2467	360	773	.466	0	2	.000	182	259	.703	154	348	502	89	286	6	87	153	47	902	6.3	1.1	11.3
91-92–Charlotte	51	7	1257	213	435	.490	0	3	.000	134	190	.705	96	221	317	81	159	0	49	84	23	560	6.2	1.6	11.0
92-93–Cha.-S.A.	83	25	1887	283	595	.476	0	5	.000	214	280	.764	120	336	456	80	266	3	47	125	31	780	5.5	1.0	9.4
93-94–San Antonio	70	11	1344	260	530	.491	0	3	.000	107	153	.699	91	129	220	73	165	0	43	84	25	627	3.1	1.0	9.0
94-95–San Antonio	81	37	1566	201	396	.508	1	2	.500	160	233	.687	120	273	393	55	230	2	60	113	32	563	4.9	0.7	7.0
95-96–S.A.-N.Y.	65	21	1313	160	324	.494	0	1	.000	107	142	.754	73	182	255	42	187	0	43	79	17	427	3.9	0.6	6.6
97-98–Charlotte	79	1	1109	146	318	.459	3	8	.375	89	122	.730	72	138	210	51	172	1	35	65	19	384	2.7	0.6	4.9
98-99–Cha.-Lakers	41	26	1029	132	277	.477	0	1	.000	105	137	.766	45	167	212	48	135	3	37	51	10	369	5.2	1.2	9.0
99-00–Milwaukee	34	7	602	53	127	.417	1	7	.143	43	56	.768	29	88	117	18	81	2	19	20	5	150	3.4	0.5	4.4
Reg. Season Totals	666	297	15331	2166	4589	.472	5	37	.135	1333	1861	.716	999	2374	3373	638	1973	24	512	946	263	5670	5.1	1.0	8.5
Playoff Totals	47	11	784	86	197	.437	0	3	.000	77	97	.794	49	118	167	33	135	1	23	43	21	249	3.6	0.7	5.3

Reid, James (Jim) b. August 3, 1945 Ht. 6-6 Wt. 210 College: Winston-Salem State

SEASON–TEAM	G	GS	MIN	FGM	FGA	PCT	3FGM	3FGA	PCT	FTM	FTA	PCT	O-RB	D-RB	TOT	AST	PF	DQ	STL	TO	BLK	PTS	RPG	APG	PPG
67-68–Philadelphia	6	–	52	10	20	.500	–	–	–	1	5	.200	–	–	11	3	6	0	–	–	–	21	1.8	0.5	3.5
Reg. Season Totals	6	–	52	10	20	.500	–	–	–	1	5	.200	–	–	11	3	6	0	–	–	–	21	1.8	0.5	3.5

Reid, Robert Keith b. August 30, 1955 Ht. 6-8 Wt. 210 College: St. Mary's (Texas)

SEASON–TEAM	G	GS	MIN	FGM	FGA	PCT	3FGM	3FGA	PCT	FTM	FTA	PCT	O-RB	D-RB	TOT	AST	PF	DQ	STL	TO	BLK	PTS	RPG	APG	PPG
77-78–Houston	80	–	1849	261	574	.455	–	–	–	63	96	.656	111	248	359	121	277	8	67	81	51	585	4.5	1.5	7.3
78-79–Houston	82	–	2259	382	777	.492	–	–	–	131	186	.704	129	354	483	230	302	7	75	131	48	895	5.9	2.8	10.9
79-80–Houston	76	–	2304	419	861	.487	0	3	.000	153	208	.736	140	301	441	244	281	2	132	164	57	991	5.8	3.2	13.0
80-81–Houston	82	–	2963	536	1113	.482	0	4	.000	229	303	.756	164	419	583	344	325	4	163	198	66	1301	7.1	4.2	15.9
81-82–Houston	77	75	2913	437	958	.456	1	10	.100	160	214	.748	175	336	511	314	297	2	115	157	48	1035	6.6	4.1	13.4
83-84–Houston	64	28	1936	406	857	.474	2	8	.250	81	123	.659	97	244	341	217	243	5	88	92	30	895	5.3	3.4	14.0
84-85–Houston	82	0	1763	312	648	.481	1	16	.063	88	126	.698	81	192	273	171	196	1	48	101	22	713	3.3	2.1	8.7
85-86–Houston	82	5	2157	409	881	.464	6	33	.182	162	214	.757	67	234	301	222	231	3	91	96	16	986	3.7	2.7	12.0
86-87–Houston	75	63	2594	420	1006	.417	53	162	.327	136	177	.768	47	242	289	323	232	2	75	104	21	1029	3.9	4.3	13.7
87-88–Houston	62	31	980	165	356	.463	13	34	.382	50	63	.794	38	87	125	67	118	0	27	41	5	393	2.0	1.1	6.3
88-89–Charlotte	82	54	2152	519	1214	.428	17	52	.327	152	196	.776	82	220	302	153	235	2	53	106	20	1207	3.7	1.9	14.7
89-90–Port.-Cha.	72	28	1202	175	447	.391	10	32	.313	54	86	.628	34	117	151	90	153	0	38	45	16	414	2.1	1.3	5.8
90-91–Philadelphia	3	0	37	2	14	.143	0	0	–	0	0	–	2	7	9	4	3	0	1	3	3	4	3.0	1.3	1.3
Reg. Season Totals	919	284	25109	4443	9706	.458	103	354	.291	1459	1992	.732	1167	3001	4168	2500	2893	36	973	1319	403	10448	4.5	2.7	11.4
Playoff Totals	79	37	2740	430	983	.437	8	53	.151	157	217	.724	110	281	391	335	277	3	106	148	41	1025	4.9	4.2	13.0

Reid, William Jennings Jr. (Billy) b. September 10, 1957 Ht. 6-5 Wt. 190 College: Anderson (S.C.) (J.C.); New Mexico; San Francisco

SEASON–TEAM	G	GS	MIN	FGM	FGA	PCT	3FGM	3FGA	PCT	FTM	FTA	PCT	O-RB	D-RB	TOT	AST	PF	DQ	STL	TO	BLK	PTS	RPG	APG	PPG
80-81–Golden State	59	–	597	84	185	.454	0	5	.000	22	39	.564	27	33	60	71	111	0	33	78	5	190	1.0	1.2	3.2
Reg. Season Totals	59	–	597	84	185	.454	0	5	.000	22	39	.564	27	33	60	71	111	0	33	78	5	190	1.0	1.2	3.2

Reiser, Joseph Francis (Chick) b. December 17, 1914 d. July 30, 1996 Ht. 5-11 Wt. 165 College: Pratt Institute; New York U.

SEASON–TEAM	G	GS	MIN	FGM	FGA	PCT	3FGM	3FGA	PCT	FTM	FTA	PCT	O-RB	D-RB	TOT	AST	PF	DQ	STL	TO	BLK	PTS	RPG	APG	PPG
43-44–Fort Wayne (N)	22	–	–	28	–	–	–	–	–	25	–	–	–	–	–	–	–	–	–	–	–	81	–	–	3.7
44-45–Fort Wayne (N)	30	–	–	82	–	–	–	–	–	53	–	–	–	–	–	–	–	–	–	–	–	217	–	–	7.2
45-46–Fort Wayne (N)	34	–	–	90	–	–	–	–	–	53	80	.663	–	–	–	–	93	–	–	–	–	233	–	–	6.9
46-47–Fort Wayne (N)	44	–	–	153	–	–	–	–	–	104	139	.748	–	–	–	–	153	–	–	–	–	410	–	–	9.3
47-48–Baltimore	47	–	–	202	628	.322	–	–	–	137	185	.741	–	–	–	40	175	–	–	–	–	541	–	0.9	11.5
48-49–Baltimore	57	–	–	219	653	.335	–	–	–	188	257	.732	–	–	–	132	202	–	–	–	–	626	–	2.3	11.0
49-50–Washington	67	–	–	197	646	.305	–	–	–	212	254	.835	–	–	–	174	223	–	–	–	–	606	–	2.6	9.0
Reg. NBA Totals	171	–	–	618	1927	.321	–	–	–	537	696	.772	–	–	–	346	600	–	–	–	–	1773	–	2.0	10.4
Reg. NBL Totals	130	–	–	353	–	–	–	–	–	235	219	.717	–	–	–	–	246	–	–	–	–	941	–	–	7.2
NBA Playoff Totals	16	–	–	49	216	.273	–	–	–	58	73	.795	–	–	–	20	84	3	–	–	–	156	–	1.1	9.8
NBL Playoff Totals	24	–	–	77	–	–	–	–	–	45	47	.660	–	–	–	–	77	–	–	–	–	199	–	–	8.3

Rellford, Richard Allen b. February 16, 1964 Ht. 6-6 Wt. 230 College: Michigan

SEASON–TEAM	G	GS	MIN	FGM	FGA	PCT	3FGM	3FGA	PCT	FTM	FTA	PCT	O-RB	D-RB	TOT	AST	PF	DQ	STL	TO	BLK	PTS	RPG	APG	PPG
87-88–San Antonio	4	0	42	5	8	.625	0	0	–	6	8	.750	2	5	7	1	3	0	0	4	3	16	1.8	0.3	4.0
Reg. Season Totals	4	0	42	5	8	.625	0	0	–	6	8	.750	2	5	7	1	3	0	0	4	3	16	1.8	0.3	4.0

Rencher, Terrence Lamont b. February 19, 1973 Ht. 6-3 Wt. 185 College: Texas

SEASON–TEAM	G	GS	MIN	FGM	FGA	PCT	3FGM	3FGA	PCT	FTM	FTA	PCT	O-RB	D-RB	TOT	AST	PF	DQ	STL	TO	BLK	PTS	RPG	APG	PPG
95-96–Miami-Phoenix	36	1	405	33	100	.330	9	29	.310	31	46	.674	9	35	44	54	37	0	16	43	2	106	1.2	1.5	2.9
Reg. Season Totals	36	1	405	33	100	.330	9	29	.310	31	46	.674	9	35	44	54	37	0	16	43	2	106	1.2	1.5	2.9

Rennicke, John W. b. August 11, 1929 Ht. 6-2 Wt. 205 College: Drake

SEASON–TEAM	G	GS	MIN	FGM	FGA	PCT	3FGM	3FGA	PCT	FTM	FTA	PCT	O-RB	D-RB	TOT	AST	PF	DQ	STL	TO	BLK	PTS	RPG	APG	PPG
51-52–Milwaukee	6	–	54	4	18	.222	–	–	–	3	9	.333	–	–	9	1	7	0	–	–	–	11	1.5	0.2	1.8
Reg. Season Totals	6	–	54	4	18	.222	–	–	–	3	9	.333	–	–	9	1	7	0	–	–	–	11	1.5	0.2	1.8

Rensberger, Robert Lamar (Rob) b. March 7, 1921 Ht. 6-2 Wt. 170 College: Notre Dame

SEASON–TEAM	G	GS	MIN	FGM	FGA	PCT	3FGM	3FGA	PCT	FTM	FTA	PCT	O-RB	D-RB	TOT	AST	PF	DQ	STL	TO	BLK	PTS	RPG	APG	PPG
45-46–Chicago (N)	16	–	–	6	–	–	–	–	–	3	–	–	–	–	–	–	–	–	–	–	–	15	–	–	0.9
46-47–Chicago	3	–	–	0	7	.000	–	–	–	0	0	–	–	–	–	0	4	–	–	–	–	0	–	0.0	0.0
Reg. NBA Totals	3	–	–	0	7	.000	–	–	–	0	0	–	–	–	–	0	4	–	–	–	–	0	–	0.0	0.0
Reg. NBL Totals	16	–	–	6	–	–	–	–	–	3	0	–	–	–	–	–	–	–	–	–	–	15	–	–	0.9

Respert, Shawn Christopher b. February 6, 1972 Ht. 6-2 Wt. 195 College: Michigan State

SEASON–TEAM	G	GS	MIN	FGM	FGA	PCT	3FGM	3FGA	PCT	FTM	FTA	PCT	O-RB	D-RB	TOT	AST	PF	DQ	STL	TO	BLK	PTS	RPG	APG	PPG
95-96–Milwaukee	62	0	845	113	292	.387	42	122	.344	35	42	.833	28	46	74	68	67	0	32	42	4	303	1.2	1.1	4.9
96-97–Milw.-Toronto	41	0	495	59	139	.424	20	57	.351	34	39	.872	14	25	39	40	40	0	20	30	2	172	1.0	1.0	4.2
97-98–Toronto-Dallas	57	4	911	130	293	.444	31	93	.333	48	61	.787	37	63	100	61	75	0	34	48	1	339	1.8	1.1	5.9
98-99–Phoenix	12	1	99	13	36	.361	4	13	.308	7	10	.700	2	11	13	8	10	0	5	5	0	37	1.1	0.7	3.1
Reg. Season Totals	172	5	2350	315	760	.414	97	285	.340	124	152	.816	81	145	226	177	192	0	91	125	7	851	1.3	1.0	4.9

Restani, Kevin Gilbert (Big Bird) b. December 23, 1951 Ht. 6-9 Wt. 225 College: San Francisco

SEASON–TEAM	G	GS	MIN	FGM	FGA	PCT	3FGM	3FGA	PCT	FTM	FTA	PCT	O-RB	D-RB	TOT	AST	PF	DQ	STL	TO	BLK	PTS	RPG	APG	PPG
74-75–Milwaukee	76	–	1755	188	427	.440	–	–	–	35	49	.714	131	272	403	119	172	1	36	–	19	411	5.3	1.6	5.4
75-76–Milwaukee	82	–	1650	234	493	.475	–	–	–	24	42	.571	115	261	376	96	151	3	36	–	12	492	4.6	1.2	6.0
76-77–Milwaukee	64	–	1116	173	334	.518	–	–	–	12	24	.500	81	181	262	88	102	0	33	–	11	358	4.1	1.4	5.6
77-78–Milw.-K.C.	54	–	547	72	167	.431	–	–	–	9	13	.692	36	72	108	30	41	0	5	17	5	153	2.0	0.6	2.8
78-79–Milwaukee	81	–	1598	262	529	.495	–	–	–	51	73	.699	141	244	385	122	155	0	30	96	27	575	4.8	1.5	7.1
79-80–San Antonio	82	–	1966	369	727	.508	5	29	.172	131	161	.814	142	244	386	189	186	0	54	129	12	874	4.7	2.3	10.7
80-81–San Antonio	64	–	999	192	369	.520	3	8	.375	62	88	.705	71	103	174	81	103	0	16	68	14	449	2.7	1.3	7.0
81-82–S.A.-Clev.	47	0	483	32	88	.364	0	2	.000	10	16	.625	39	73	112	22	56	0	11	20	11	74	2.4	0.5	1.6
Reg. Season Totals	550	0	10114	1522	3134	.486	8	39	.205	334	466	.717	756	1450	2206	747	966	4	221	330	111	3386	4.0	1.4	6.2
Playoff Totals	9	0	118	19	36	.528	0	1	.000	4	9	.444	8	15	23	4	10	0	1	3	2	42	2.6	0.4	4.7

Reynolds, George b. November 23, 1947 Ht. 6-4 Wt. 195 College: Houston

SEASON–TEAM	G	GS	MIN	FGM	FGA	PCT	3FGM	3FGA	PCT	FTM	FTA	PCT	O-RB	D-RB	TOT	AST	PF	DQ	STL	TO	BLK	PTS	RPG	APG	PPG
69-70–Detroit	10	–	44	8	19	.421	–	–	–	5	7	.714	–	–	14	12	10	0	–	–	–	21	1.4	1.2	2.1
Reg. Season Totals	10	–	44	8	19	.421	–	–	–	5	7	.714	–	–	14	12	10	0	–	–	–	21	1.4	1.2	2.1

Reynolds, Jerry (Ice) b. December 23, 1962 Ht. 6-8 Wt. 205 College: Louisiana State

SEASON–TEAM	G	GS	MIN	FGM	FGA	PCT	3FGM	3FGA	PCT	FTM	FTA	PCT	O-RB	D-RB	TOT	AST	PF	DQ	STL	TO	BLK	PTS	RPG	APG	PPG
85-86–Milwaukee	55	8	508	72	162	.444	1	2	.500	58	104	.558	37	43	80	86	57	0	43	52	19	203	1.5	1.6	3.7
86-87–Milwaukee	58	24	963	140	356	.393	6	18	.333	118	184	.641	72	101	173	106	91	0	50	82	30	404	3.0	1.8	7.0
87-88–Milwaukee	62	21	1161	188	419	.449	3	7	.429	119	154	.773	70	90	160	104	97	0	74	104	32	498	2.6	1.7	8.0
88-89–Seattle	56	0	737	149	357	.417	3	15	.200	127	167	.760	49	51	100	62	58	0	53	57	26	428	1.8	1.1	7.6
89-90–Orlando	67	40	1817	309	741	.417	1	14	.071	239	322	.742	91	232	323	180	162	1	93	139	64	858	4.8	2.7	12.8
90-91–Orlando	80	9	1843	344	793	.434	10	34	.294	336	419	.802	88	211	299	203	123	0	95	172	56	1034	3.7	2.5	12.9
91-92–Orlando	46	16	1159	197	518	.380	3	24	.125	158	189	.836	47	102	149	151	69	0	63	96	17	555	3.2	3.3	12.1
95-96–Milwaukee	19	0	191	21	53	.396	1	10	.100	13	21	.619	13	20	33	12	20	0	15	16	6	56	1.7	0.6	2.9
Reg. Season Totals	443	118	8379	1420	3399	.418	28	124	.226	1168	1560	.749	467	850	1317	904	677	1	486	718	250	4036	3.0	2.0	9.1
Playoff Totals	18	0	97	19	48	.396	1	6	.167	14	23	.609	5	11	16	8	12	0	9	9	9	53	0.9	0.4	2.9

Rhine, Kendall Lee b. February 13, 1943 Ht. 6-10 Wt. 240 College: Rice

SEASON–TEAM	G	GS	MIN	FGM	FGA	PCT	3FGM	3FGA	PCT	FTM	FTA	PCT	O-RB	D-RB	TOT	AST	PF	DQ	STL	TO	BLK	PTS	RPG	APG	PPG
67-68–Kentucky (A)	52	–	552	50	158	.316	0	1	.000	27	56	.482	–	–	235	31	120	2	–	36	–	127	4.5	0.6	2.4
68-69–Houston (A)	73	–	2116	255	629	.405	0	1	.000	149	265	.562	307	497	804	150	321	16	–	119	–	659	11.0	2.1	9.0
Reg. ABA Totals	125	–	2668	305	787	.388	0	2	.000	176	321	.548	307	497	1039	181	441	18	–	155	–	786	8.3	1.4	6.3
ABA Playoff Totals	5	–	62	5	17	.294	0	0	–	0	7	.000	–	–	15	4	16	0	–	4	–	10	3.0	0.8	2.0

Rhodes, Eugene Stephen (Gene) b. September 2, 1927 Ht. 6-1 Wt. 170 College: Western Kentucky

SEASON–TEAM	G	GS	MIN	FGM	FGA	PCT	3FGM	3FGA	PCT	FTM	FTA	PCT	O-RB	D-RB	TOT	AST	PF	DQ	STL	TO	BLK	PTS	RPG	APG	PPG
52-53–Indianapolis	65	–	1162	109	342	.319	–	–	–	119	169	.704	–	–	98	91	78	2	–	–	–	337	1.5	1.4	5.2
Reg. Season Totals	65	–	1162	109	342	.319	–	–	–	119	169	.704	–	–	98	91	78	2	–	–	–	337	1.5	1.4	5.2
Playoff Totals	2	–	51	4	14	.286	–	–	–	1	4	.250	–	–	7	5	5	0	–	–	–	9	3.5	2.5	4.5

Rhodes, Rodrick b. September 24, 1973 Ht. 6-6 Wt. 225 College: Kentucky; USC

SEASON–TEAM	G	GS	MIN	FGM	FGA	PCT	3FGM	3FGA	PCT	FTM	FTA	PCT	O-RB	D-RB	TOT	AST	PF	DQ	STL	TO	BLK	PTS	RPG	APG	PPG
97-98–Houston	58	13	1070	112	305	.367	2	8	.250	111	180	.617	28	42	70	110	125	0	62	97	10	337	1.2	1.9	5.8
98-99–Houston-Vanc.	13	1	156	13	52	.250	1	7	.143	16	25	.640	9	8	17	11	21	0	5	20	2	43	1.3	0.8	3.3
99-00–Phil.-Dallas	1	0	8	0	3	.000	0	0	–	0	0	–	1	0	1	0	0	0	2	2	0	0	1.0	0.0	0.0
Reg. Season Totals	72	14	1234	125	360	.347	3	15	.200	127	205	.620	38	50	88	121	146	0	69	119	12	380	1.2	1.7	5.3
Playoff Totals	3	0	7	2	3	.667	0	0	–	2	4	.500	0	1	1	–	0	0	1	1	0	6	0.3	0.0	2.0

Rice, Glen Anthony b. May 28, 1967 Ht. 6-8 Wt. 220 College: Michigan

SEASON–TEAM	G	GS	MIN	FGM	FGA	PCT	3FGM	3FGA	PCT	FTM	FTA	PCT	O-RB	D-RB	TOT	AST	PF	DQ	STL	TO	BLK	PTS	RPG	APG	PPG
89-90–Miami	77	60	2311	470	1071	.439	17	69	.246	91	124	.734	100	252	352	138	198	1	67	113	27	1048	4.6	1.8	13.6
90-91–Miami	77	77	2646	550	1193	.461	71	184	.386	171	209	.818	85	296	381	189	216	0	101	166	26	1342	4.9	2.5	17.4
91-92–Miami	79	79	3007	672	1432	.469	155	396	.391	266	318	.836	84	310	394	184	170	0	90	145	35	1765	5.0	2.3	22.3
92-93–Miami	82	82	3082	582	1324	.440	148	386	.383	242	295	.820	92	332	424	180	201	0	92	157	25	1554	5.2	2.2	19.0
93-94–Miami	81	81	2999	663	1421	.467	132	346	.382	250	284	.880	76	358	434	184	186	0	110	130	32	1708	5.4	2.3	21.1
94-95–Miami	82	82	3014	667	1403	.475	185	451	.410	312	365	.855	99	279	378	192	203	1	112	153	14	1831	4.6	2.3	22.3
95-96–Charlotte	79	79	3142	610	1296	.471	171	403	.424	319	381	.837	86	292	378	232	217	1	91	163	19	1710	4.8	2.9	21.6
96-97–Charlotte	79	78	3362	722	1513	.477	207	440	.470	464	535	.867	67	251	318	160	190	0	72	177	26	2115	4.0	2.0	26.8
97-98–Charlotte	82	82	3295	634	1386	.457	130	300	.433	428	504	.849	89	264	353	182	200	0	77	182	22	1826	4.3	2.2	22.3
98-99–Char.-L.A.L.	27	25	985	171	396	.432	53	135	.393	77	90	.856	9	90	99	71	67	1	17	45	6	472	3.7	2.6	17.5
99-00–L.A. Lakers	80	80	2530	421	980	.430	84	229	.367	346	396	.874	56	271	327	176	179	0	47	114	12	1272	4.1	2.2	15.9
Reg. Season Totals	825	805	30373	6162	13415	.459	1353	3339	.405	2966	3501	.847	843	2995	3838	1888	2027	4	876	1545	244	16643	4.7	2.3	20.2
Playoff Totals	50	50	1893	298	691	.431	65	182	.357	162	192	.844	35	192	227	98	123	0	42	82	11	823	4.5	2.0	16.5
All-Star Totals	3	0	56	17	43	.395	9	15	.600	6	6	1.000	2	1	3	3	4	0	2	4	0	49	1.0	1.0	16.3

Richardson, Clint Dewitt b. August 7, 1956 Ht. 6-3 Wt. 195 College: Seattle

SEASON–TEAM	G	GS	MIN	FGM	FGA	PCT	3FGM	3FGA	PCT	FTM	FTA	PCT	O-RB	D-RB	TOT	AST	PF	DQ	STL	TO	BLK	PTS	RPG	APG	PPG
79-80–Philadelphia	52	–	988	159	348	.457	1	3	.333	28	45	.622	55	68	123	107	97	0	24	64	15	347	2.4	2.1	6.7
80-81–Philadelphia	77	–	1313	227	464	.489	0	1	.000	84	108	.778	83	93	176	152	102	0	36	110	10	538	2.3	2.0	7.0
81-82–Philadelphia	77	0	1040	140	310	.452	2	2	1.000	69	88	.784	55	63	118	109	109	0	36	79	9	351	1.5	1.4	4.6
82-83–Philadelphia	77	1	1755	259	559	.463	0	6	.000	71	111	.640	98	149	247	168	164	0	71	99	18	589	3.2	2.2	7.6
83-84–Philadelphia	69	12	1571	221	473	.467	0	4	.000	79	103	.767	62	103	165	155	145	0	49	100	23	521	2.4	2.2	7.6
84-85–Philadelphia	74	20	1531	183	404	.453	1	3	.333	76	89	.854	60	95	155	157	143	0	37	78	15	443	2.1	2.1	6.0
85-86–Indiana	82	61	2224	335	736	.455	1	9	.111	123	147	.837	69	182	251	372	153	1	58	136	8	794	3.1	4.5	9.7
86-87–Indiana	78	14	1396	218	467	.467	6	17	.353	59	74	.797	51	92	143	241	106	0	49	85	7	501	1.8	3.1	6.4
Reg. Season Totals	586	108	11818	1742	3761	.463	11	45	.244	589	765	.770	533	845	1378	1461	1019	1	360	751	105	4084	2.4	2.5	7.0
Playoff Totals	72	1	1387	178	357	.499	0	3	.000	62	90	.689	73	120	193	120	152	0	48	70	14	418	2.7	1.7	5.8

Richardson, Jerome Jr. (Pooh) b. May 14, 1966 Ht. 6-1 Wt. 200 College: UCLA

SEASON–TEAM	G	GS	MIN	FGM	FGA	PCT	3FGM	3FGA	PCT	FTM	FTA	PCT	O-RB	D-RB	TOT	AST	PF	DQ	STL	TO	BLK	PTS	RPG	APG	PPG
89-90–Minnesota	82	48	2581	426	925	.461	23	83	.277	63	107	.589	55	162	217	554	143	0	133	141	25	938	2.6	6.8	11.4
90-91–Minnesota	82	82	3154	635	1350	.470	42	128	.328	89	165	.539	82	204	286	734	114	0	131	174	13	1401	3.5	9.0	17.1
91-92–Minnesota	82	82	2922	587	1261	.466	53	155	.342	123	178	.691	91	210	301	685	152	0	119	204	25	1350	3.7	8.4	16.5
92-93–Indiana	74	73	2396	337	703	.479	3	29	.103	92	124	.742	63	204	267	573	132	1	94	167	12	769	3.6	7.7	10.4
93-94–Indiana	37	25	1022	160	354	.452	3	12	.250	47	77	.610	28	82	110	237	78	0	32	88	3	370	3.0	6.4	10.0
94-95–L.A. Clippers	80	77	2864	353	897	.394	87	244	.357	81	125	.648	38	223	261	632	218	1	129	171	12	874	3.3	7.9	10.9
95-96–L.A. Clippers	63	61	2013	281	664	.423	94	245	.384	78	105	.743	35	123	158	340	134	0	77	95	13	734	2.5	5.4	11.7
96-97–L.A. Clippers	59	18	1065	131	344	.381	42	128	.328	26	43	.605	25	73	98	169	82	0	54	62	5	330	1.7	2.9	5.6
97-98–L.A. Clippers	69	17	1252	124	333	.372	11	57	.193	30	43	.698	17	79	96	226	71	0	44	54	3	289	1.4	3.3	4.2
98-99–L.A. Clippers	11	0	130	12	36	.333	0	6	.000	4	4	1.000	1	12	13	30	5	0	4	9	0	28	1.2	2.7	2.5
Reg. Season Totals	639	483	19399	3046	6867	.444	358	1087	.329	633	971	.652	435	1372	1807	4180	1129	2	817	1165	111	7083	2.8	6.5	11.1
Playoff Totals	6	1	113	8	19	.421	1	2	.500	4	7	.571	1	10	11	26	11	1	3	7	0	21	1.8	4.3	3.5

Richardson, Micheal Ray (Micheal Ray, Sugar Ray) b. April 11, 1955 Ht. 6-5 Wt. 190 College: Montana

SEASON–TEAM	G	GS	MIN	FGM	FGA	PCT	3FGM	3FGA	PCT	FTM	FTA	PCT	O-RB	D-RB	TOT	AST	PF	DQ	STL	TO	BLK	PTS	RPG	APG	PPG
78-79–New York	72	–	1218	200	483	.414	–	–	–	69	128	.539	78	155	233	213	188	2	100	141	18	469	3.2	3.0	6.5
79-80–New York	82	–	3060	502	1063	.472	27	110	.245	223	338	.660	151	388	539	832	260	3	265	359	35	1254	6.6	10.1	15.3
80-81–New York	79	–	3175	523	1116	.469	23	102	.225	224	338	.663	173	372	545	627	258	2	232	302	35	1293	6.9	7.9	16.4
81-82–New York	82	79	3044	619	1343	.461	19	101	.188	212	303	.700	177	388	565	572	317	3	213	291	41	1469	6.9	7.0	17.9
82-83–G.S.-N.J.	64	51	2076	346	815	.425	8	51	.157	106	163	.650	113	182	295	432	240	4	182	244	24	806	4.6	6.8	12.6
83-84–New Jersey	48	25	1285	243	528	.460	14	58	.241	76	108	.704	56	116	172	214	156	4	103	118	20	576	3.6	4.5	12.0
84-85–New Jersey	82	82	3127	690	1470	.469	29	115	.252	240	313	.767	156	301	457	669	277	3	243	249	22	1649	5.6	8.2	20.1
85-86–New Jersey	47	39	1604	296	661	.448	4	27	.148	141	179	.788	77	173	250	340	163	2	125	150	11	737	5.3	7.2	15.7
Reg. Season Totals	556	276	18589	3419	7479	.457	124	564	.220	1291	1870	.690	981	2075	3056	3899	1859	23	1463	1854	206	8253	5.5	7.0	14.8
Playoff Totals	18	16	712	108	280	.386	6	29	.207	60	87	.690	32	67	99	129	63	1	50	50	4	282	5.5	7.2	15.7
All-Star Totals	4	0	70	15	32	.469	0	3	.000	2	4	.500	5	5	10	10	9	0	9	7	0	32	2.5	2.5	8.0

Richmond, Mitchell James (Mitch, Rock) b. June 30, 1965 Ht. 6-5 Wt. 220 College: Moberly Area (Kan.) C.C.; Kansas State

SEASON–TEAM	G	GS	MIN	FGM	FGA	PCT	3FGM	3FGA	PCT	FTM	FTA	PCT	O-RB	D-RB	TOT	AST	PF	DQ	STL	TO	BLK	PTS	RPG	APG	PPG
88-89–Golden State	79	79	2717	649	1386	.468	33	90	.367	410	506	.810	158	310	468	334	223	5	82	269	13	1741	5.9	4.2	22.0
89-90–Golden State	78	78	2799	640	1287	.497	34	95	.358	406	469	.866	98	262	360	223	210	3	98	201	24	1720	4.6	2.9	22.1
90-91–Golden State	77	77	3027	703	1424	.494	40	115	.348	394	465	.847	147	305	452	238	207	0	126	230	34	1840	5.9	3.1	23.9
91-92–Sacramento	80	80	3095	685	1465	.468	103	268	.384	330	406	.813	62	257	319	411	231	1	92	247	34	1803	4.0	5.1	22.5
92-93–Sacramento	45	45	1728	371	782	.474	48	130	.369	197	233	.845	18	136	154	221	137	3	53	130	9	987	3.4	4.9	21.9
93-94–Sacramento	78	78	2897	635	1428	.445	127	312	.407	426	511	.834	70	216	286	313	211	3	103	216	17	1823	3.7	4.0	23.4
94-95–Sacramento	82	82	3172	668	1497	.446	156	424	.368	375	445	.843	69	288	357	311	227	2	91	234	29	1867	4.4	3.8	22.8
95-96–Sacramento	81	81	2946	611	1368	.447	225	515	.437	425	491	.866	54	215	269	255	233	6	125	220	19	1872	3.3	3.1	23.1
96-97–Sacramento	81	81	3125	717	1578	.454	204	477	.428	457	531	.861	59	260	319	338	211	1	118	237	24	2095	3.9	4.2	25.9
97-98–Sacramento	70	70	2569	543	1220	.445	130	334	.389	407	471	.864	50	179	229	279	154	0	88	181	15	1623	3.3	4.0	23.2
98-99–Washington	50	50	1912	331	803	.412	70	221	.317	251	293	.857	30	142	172	122	121	1	64	136	10	983	3.4	2.4	19.7
99-00–Washington	74	69	2397	447	1049	.426	93	241	.386	298	340	.876	37	176	213	185	191	2	110	154	13	1285	2.9	2.5	17.4
Reg. Season Totals	875	870	32384	7000	15287	.458	1263	3222	.392	4376	5161	.848	852	2746	3598	3230	2356	27	1150	2455	241	19639	4.1	3.7	22.4
Playoff Totals	21	21	832	171	358	.478	19	63	.302	85	97	.876	23	99	122	69	64	1	22	56	7	446	5.8	3.3	21.2
All-Star Totals	5	1	110	25	57	.439	6	12	.500	1	2	.500	4	8	12	13	1	0	1	5	0	57	2.4	2.6	11.4

Richter, John Fritz b. March 12, 1937 Ht. 6-9 Wt. 225 College: Paul Smith's (N.Y.) (J.C.); North Carolina State

SEASON–TEAM	G	GS	MIN	FGM	FGA	PCT	3FGM	3FGA	PCT	FTM	FTA	PCT	O-RB	D-RB	TOT	AST	PF	DQ	STL	TO	BLK	PTS	RPG	APG	PPG
59-60–Boston	66	–	808	113	332	.340	–	–	–	59	117	.504	–	–	312	27	158	1	–	–	–	285	4.7	0.4	4.3
Reg. Season Totals	66	–	808	113	332	.340	–	–	–	59	117	.504	–	–	312	27	158	1	–	–	–	285	4.7	0.4	4.3
Playoff Totals	8	–	95	15	38	.395	–	–	–	5	14	.357	–	–	29	2	17	1	–	–	–	35	3.6	0.3	4.4

Ricketts, Richard James Jr. (Dick) b. December 4, 1933 d. March 6, 1988 Ht. 6-7 Wt. 220 College: Duquesne

SEASON–TEAM	G	GS	MIN	FGM	FGA	PCT	3FGM	3FGA	PCT	FTM	FTA	PCT	O-RB	D-RB	TOT	AST	PF	DQ	STL	TO	BLK	PTS	RPG	APG	PPG
55-56–St. Louis-Roch.	68	–	1943	235	752	.313	–	–	–	138	195	.708	–	–	490	206	287	14	–	–	–	608	7.2	3.0	8.9
56-57–Rochester	72	–	2114	299	869	.344	–	–	–	206	297	.694	–	–	437	127	307	12	–	–	–	804	6.1	1.8	11.2
57-58–Cincinnati	72	–	1620	215	664	.324	–	–	–	132	196	.673	–	–	410	114	277	8	–	–	–	562	5.7	1.6	7.8
Reg. Season Totals	212	–	5677	749	2285	.328	–	–	–	476	688	.692	–	–	1337	447	871	34	–	–	–	1974	6.3	2.1	9.3
Playoff Totals	2	–	31	5	15	.333	–	–	–	5	5	1.000	–	–	10	2	9	0	–	–	–	15	5.0	1.0	7.5

Rider, Isaiah Jr. (J.R.) b. March 12, 1971 Ht. 6-5 Wt. 215 College: Allen County (Kan.) C.C.; Antelope Valley (Calif.) Coll. (J.C.); Nevada-Las Vegas

SEASON–TEAM	G	GS	MIN	FGM	FGA	PCT	3FGM	3FGA	PCT	FTM	FTA	PCT	O-RB	D-RB	TOT	AST	PF	DQ	STL	TO	BLK	PTS	RPG	APG	PPG
93-94–Minnesota	79	60	2415	522	1115	.468	54	150	.360	215	265	.811	118	197	315	202	194	0	54	218	28	1313	4.0	2.6	16.6
94-95–Minnesota	75	67	2645	558	1249	.447	139	396	.351	277	339	.817	90	159	249	245	194	3	69	232	23	1532	3.3	3.3	20.4
95-96–Minnesota	75	68	2594	560	1206	.464	102	275	.371	248	296	.838	99	210	309	213	204	2	48	201	23	1470	4.1	2.8	19.6
96-97–Portland	76	68	2563	456	983	.464	99	257	.385	212	261	.812	94	210	304	198	199	2	45	212	19	1223	4.0	2.6	16.1
97-98–Portland	74	66	2786	551	1302	.423	135	420	.321	221	267	.828	99	247	346	231	188	1	55	187	19	1458	4.7	3.1	19.7
98-99–Portland	47	41	1385	249	605	.412	42	111	.378	111	147	.755	59	137	196	104	100	0	25	95	9	651	4.2	2.2	13.9
99-00–Atlanta	60	47	2084	449	1072	.419	56	180	.311	204	260	.785	63	195	258	219	132	3	41	168	6	1158	4.3	3.7	19.3
Reg. Season Totals	486	417	16472	3345	7532	.444	627	1789	.350	1488	1835	.811	622	1355	1977	1412	1211	11	337	1313	127	8805	4.1	2.9	18.1
Playoff Totals	21	21	753	114	273	.418	18	53	.340	98	114	.860	25	53	78	65	52	0	19	61	0	344	3.7	3.1	16.4

Ridgle, Jackie Lendell b. February 13, 1948 d. August 26, 1998 Ht. 6-4 Wt. 195 College: California

SEASON–TEAM	G	GS	MIN	FGM	FGA	PCT	3FGM	3FGA	PCT	FTM	FTA	PCT	O-RB	D-RB	TOT	AST	PF	DQ	STL	TO	BLK	PTS	RPG	APG	PPG
71-72–Cleveland	32	–	107	19	44	.432	–	–	–	19	26	.731	–	–	15	7	15	0	–	–	–	57	0.5	0.2	1.8
Reg. Season Totals	32	–	107	19	44	.432	–	–	–	19	26	.731	–	–	15	7	15	0	–	–	–	57	0.5	0.2	1.8

Riebe, Melvin Russell (Mel, Mouse) b. July 12, 1916 d. July 25, 1977 Ht. 5-11 Wt. 180 College: Wooster

SEASON–TEAM	G	GS	MIN	FGM	FGA	PCT	3FGM	3FGA	PCT	FTM	FTA	PCT	O-RB	D-RB	TOT	AST	PF	DQ	STL	TO	BLK	PTS	RPG	APG	PPG
43-44–Cleveland (N)	18	–	–	113	–	–	–	–	–	97	134	.724	–	–	–	–	48	–	–	–	–	323	–	–	17.9
44-45–Cleveland (N)	30	–	–	223	–	–	–	–	–	161	–	–	–	–	–	–	86	–	–	–	–	607	–	–	20.2
45-46–Cleveland (N)	5	–	–	23	–	–	–	–	–	26	–	–	–	–	–	–	–	–	–	–	–	72	–	–	14.4
46-47–Cleveland	55	–	–	276	898	.307	–	–	–	111	173	.642	–	–	–	67	169	–	–	–	–	663	–	1.2	12.1
47-48–Boston	48	–	–	202	653	.309	–	–	–	85	137	.620	–	–	–	41	137	–	–	–	–	489	–	0.9	10.2
48-49–Boston-Prov.	43	–	–	172	589	.292	–	–	–	79	133	.594	–	–	–	104	110	–	–	–	–	423	–	2.4	9.8
Reg. NBA Totals	146	–	–	650	2140	.304	–	–	–	275	443	.621	–	–	–	212	416	–	–	–	–	1575	–	1.5	10.8
Reg. NBL Totals	53	–	–	359	–	–	–	–	–	284	134	.724	–	–	–	–	134	–	–	–	–	1002	–	–	18.9
NBA Playoff Totals	6	–	–	23	123	.301	–	–	–	17	26	.654	–	–	–	8	23	–	–	–	–	63	–	0.9	10.5
NBL Playoff Totals	4	–	–	23	–	–	–	–	–	20	0	–	–	–	–	–	8	–	–	–	–	66	–	–	16.5

Riedy, Robert F. (Bob) b. August 26, 1945 Ht. 6-6 Wt. 215 College: Duke

SEASON–TEAM	G	GS	MIN	FGM	FGA	PCT	3FGM	3FGA	PCT	FTM	FTA	PCT	O-RB	D-RB	TOT	AST	PF	DQ	STL	TO	BLK	PTS	RPG	APG	PPG
67-68–Houston (A)	23	–	331	45	129	.349	0	0	–	41	67	.612	–	–	68	5	27	0	–	21	–	131	3.0	0.2	5.7
Reg. ABA Totals	23	–	331	45	129	.349	0	0	–	41	67	.612	–	–	68	5	27	0	–	21	–	131	3.0	0.2	5.7

Riffey, James R. (Jim) b. December 14, 1923 Ht. 6-4 Wt. 200 College: Tulane

SEASON–TEAM	G	GS	MIN	FGM	FGA	PCT	3FGM	3FGA	PCT	FTM	FTA	PCT	O-RB	D-RB	TOT	AST	PF	DQ	STL	TO	BLK	PTS	RPG	APG	PPG
50-51–Fort Wayne	35	–	–	65	185	.351	–	–	–	20	26	.769	–	–	61	16	54	0	–	–	–	150	1.7	0.5	4.3
Reg. Season Totals	35	–	–	65	185	.351	–	–	–	20	26	.769	–	–	61	16	54	0	–	–	–	150	1.7	0.5	4.3

Riker, Thomas E. (Tom) b. February 28, 1950 Ht. 6-10 Wt. 225 College: South Carolina

SEASON–TEAM	G	GS	MIN	FGM	FGA	PCT	3FGM	3FGA	PCT	FTM	FTA	PCT	O-RB	D-RB	TOT	AST	PF	DQ	STL	TO	BLK	PTS	RPG	APG	PPG
72-73–New York	14	–	65	10	24	.417	–	–	–	15	24	.625	–	–	16	2	15	0	–	–	–	35	1.1	0.1	2.5
73-74–New York	17	–	57	13	29	.448	–	–	–	12	17	.706	9	6	15	3	6	0	0	–	0	38	0.9	0.2	2.2
74-75–New York	51	–	483	53	147	.361	–	–	–	46	82	.561	40	67	107	19	64	0	15	–	5	152	2.1	0.4	3.0
Reg. Season Totals	82	–	605	76	200	.380	–	–	–	73	123	.593	49	73	138	24	85	0	15	–	5	225	1.7	0.3	2.7
Playoff Totals	1	–	8	1	2	.500	–	–	–	0	0	–	1	1	2	1	1	0	0	–	0	2	2.0	1.0	2.0

Riley, Eric Kendall b. June 2, 1970 Ht. 7-0 Wt. 245 College: Michigan

SEASON–TEAM	G	GS	MIN	FGM	FGA	PCT	3FGM	3FGA	PCT	FTM	FTA	PCT	O-RB	D-RB	TOT	AST	PF	DQ	STL	TO	BLK	PTS	RPG	APG	PPG
93-94–Houston	47	2	219	34	70	.486	0	1	.000	20	37	.541	24	35	59	9	30	0	5	15	9	88	1.3	0.2	1.9
94-95–L.A. Clippers	40	4	434	65	145	.448	0	1	.000	47	64	.734	45	67	112	11	78	1	17	31	35	177	2.8	0.3	4.4
95-96–Minnesota	25	10	310	35	74	.473	0	1	.000	22	28	.786	32	44	76	5	42	0	8	17	16	92	3.0	0.2	3.7
97-98–Dallas	39	14	544	56	135	.415	0	1	.000	27	36	.750	43	90	133	22	80	0	15	37	46	139	3.4	0.6	3.6
98-99–Boston	35	11	337	28	54	.519	0	0	–	22	31	.710	36	63	99	13	73	2	9	26	26	78	2.8	0.4	2.2
Reg. Season Totals	186	41	1844	218	478	.456	0	4	.000	138	196	.704	180	299	479	60	303	3	54	126	132	574	2.6	0.3	3.1

Riley, Patrick James (Pat) b. March 20, 1945 Ht. 6-4 Wt. 205 College: Kentucky

SEASON–TEAM	G	GS	MIN	FGM	FGA	PCT	3FGM	3FGA	PCT	FTM	FTA	PCT	O-RB	D-RB	TOT	AST	PF	DQ	STL	TO	BLK	PTS	RPG	APG	PPG
67-68–San Diego	80	–	1263	250	660	.379	–	–	–	128	202	.634	–	–	177	138	205	1	–	–	–	628	2.2	1.7	7.9
68-69–San Diego	56	–	1027	202	498	.406	–	–	–	90	134	.672	–	–	112	136	146	1	–	–	–	494	2.0	2.4	8.8
69-70–San Diego	36	–	474	75	180	.417	–	–	–	40	55	.727	–	–	57	85	68	0	–	–	–	190	1.6	2.4	5.3
70-71–Los Angeles	54	–	506	105	254	.413	–	–	–	56	87	.644	–	–	54	72	84	0	–	–	–	266	1.0	1.3	4.9
71-72–Los Angeles	67	–	926	197	441	.447	–	–	–	55	74	.743	–	–	127	75	110	0	–	–	–	449	1.9	1.1	6.7
72-73–Los Angeles	55	–	801	167	390	.428	–	–	–	65	82	.793	–	–	65	81	126	0	–	–	–	399	1.2	1.5	7.3
73-74–Los Angeles	72	–	1361	287	667	.430	–	–	–	110	144	.764	38	90	128	148	173	1	54	–	3	684	1.8	2.1	9.5
74-75–Los Angeles	46	–	1016	219	523	.419	–	–	–	69	93	.742	25	60	85	121	128	0	36	–	4	507	1.8	2.6	11.0
75-76–L.A.-Phoenix	62	–	813	117	301	.389	–	–	–	55	77	.714	16	34	50	57	112	0	22	–	6	289	0.8	0.9	4.7
Reg. Season Totals	528	–	8187	1619	3914	.414	–	–	–	668	948	.705	79	184	855	913	1152	3	112	–	13	3906	1.6	1.7	7.4
Playoff Totals	44	–	641	111	297	.374	–	–	–	29	38	.763	3	3	66	52	86	0	4	–	0	251	1.5	1.2	5.7

Riley, Robert J. (Bob) b. July 6, 1948 Ht. 6-9 Wt. 235 College: Mount St. Mary's

SEASON–TEAM	G	GS	MIN	FGM	FGA	PCT	3FGM	3FGA	PCT	FTM	FTA	PCT	O-RB	D-RB	TOT	AST	PF	DQ	STL	TO	BLK	PTS	RPG	APG	PPG
70-71–Atlanta	7	–	39	4	9	.444	–	–	–	5	9	.556	–	–	12	1	5	0	–	–	–	13	1.7	0.1	1.9
Reg. Season Totals	7	–	39	4	9	.444	–	–	–	5	9	.556	–	–	12	1	5	0	–	–	–	13	1.7	0.1	1.9

Riley, Ronald Jay (Ron) b. November 11, 1950 Ht. 6-8 Wt. 200 College: USC

SEASON–TEAM	G	GS	MIN	FGM	FGA	PCT	3FGM	3FGA	PCT	FTM	FTA	PCT	O-RB	D-RB	TOT	AST	PF	DQ	STL	TO	BLK	PTS	RPG	APG	PPG
72-73–K.C.-Omaha	74	–	1634	273	634	.431	–	–	–	79	116	.681	–	–	507	76	226	3	–	–	–	625	6.9	1.0	8.4
73-74–K.C.-O.-Hou.	48	–	591	81	202	.401	–	–	–	24	38	.632	48	129	177	37	95	0	18	–	24	186	3.7	0.8	3.9
74-75–Houston	77	–	1578	196	470	.417	–	–	–	71	97	.732	137	243	380	130	197	3	56	–	22	463	4.9	1.7	6.0
75-76–Houston	65	–	1049	115	280	.411	–	–	–	38	56	.679	91	213	304	75	137	1	32	–	21	268	4.7	1.2	4.1
Reg. Season Totals	264	–	4852	665	1586	.419	–	–	–	212	307	.691	276	585	1368	318	655	7	106	–	67	1542	5.2	1.2	5.8
Playoff Totals	8	–	152	25	42	.595	–	–	–	6	16	.375	12	24	36	15	18	0	9	–	2	56	4.5	1.9	7.0

Rinaldi, Richard P. (Rich) b. August 3, 1949 Ht. 6-3 Wt. 195 College: St. Peter's

SEASON–TEAM	G	GS	MIN	FGM	FGA	PCT	3FGM	3FGA	PCT	FTM	FTA	PCT	O-RB	D-RB	TOT	AST	PF	DQ	STL	TO	BLK	PTS	RPG	APG	PPG
71-72–Baltimore	39	–	159	42	104	.404	–	–	–	20	30	.667	–	–	18	15	25	0	–	–	–	104	0.5	0.4	2.7
72-73–Baltimore	33	–	646	116	284	.408	–	–	–	48	64	.750	–	–	68	48	40	0	–	–	–	280	2.1	1.5	8.5
73-74–Capital	7	–	48	3	22	.136	–	–	–	3	4	.750	2	5	7	10	7	0	3	–	1	9	1.0	1.4	1.3
73-74–New York (A)	5	–	28	4	14	.286	0	1	.000	4	4	1.000	5	0	5	1	3	–	2	1	0	12	1.0	0.2	2.4
Reg. NBA Totals	79	–	853	161	410	.393	–	–	–	71	98	.724	2	5	93	73	72	0	3	–	1	393	1.2	0.9	5.0
Reg. ABA Totals	5	–	28	4	14	.286	0	1	.000	4	4	1.000	5	0	5	1	3	0	2	1	0	12	1.0	0.2	2.4
NBA Playoff Totals	3	–	6	1	2	.500	–	–	–	0	0	–	0	0	0	1	3	0	0	–	0	2	0.0	0.3	0.7

R

Riordan, Michael W. (Mike) b. July 9, 1945 Ht. 6-4 Wt. 200 College: Providence

SEASON–TEAM	G	GS	MIN	FGM	FGA	PCT	3FGM	3FGA	PCT	FTM	FTA	PCT	O-RB	D-RB	TOT	AST	PF	DQ	STL	TO	BLK	PTS	RPG	APG	PPG
68-69–New York	54	–	397	49	144	.340	–	–	–	28	42	.667	–	–	57	46	93	1	–	–	–	126	1.1	0.9	2.3
69-70–New York	81	–	1677	255	549	.464	–	–	–	114	165	.691	–	–	194	201	192	1	–	–	–	624	2.4	2.5	7.7
70-71–New York	82	–	1320	162	388	.418	–	–	–	67	108	.620	–	–	169	121	151	0	–	–	–	391	2.1	1.5	4.8
71-72–N.Y.-Balt.	58	–	1377	233	499	.467	–	–	–	84	124	.677	–	–	128	126	129	0	–	–	–	550	2.2	2.2	9.5
72-73–Baltimore	82	–	3466	652	1278	.510	–	–	–	179	218	.821	–	–	404	426	216	0	–	–	–	1483	4.9	5.2	18.1
73-74–Capital	81	–	3230	577	1223	.472	–	–	–	136	174	.782	120	260	380	264	237	2	102	–	14	1290	4.7	3.3	15.9
74-75–Washington	74	–	2191	520	1057	.492	–	–	–	98	117	.838	90	194	284	198	238	4	72	–	6	1138	3.8	2.7	15.4
75-76–Washington	78	–	1943	291	662	.440	–	–	–	71	96	.740	44	143	187	122	201	2	54	–	13	653	2.4	1.6	8.4
76-77–Washington	49	–	289	34	94	.362	–	–	–	11	15	.733	7	20	27	20	33	0	3	–	2	79	0.6	0.4	1.6
Reg. Season Totals	639	–	15890	2773	5894	.470	–	–	–	788	1059	.744	261	617	1830	1524	1490	10	231	–	35	6334	2.9	2.4	9.9
Playoff Totals	84	–	1648	253	567	.446	–	–	–	107	138	.775	20	53	199	111	203	1	20	–	4	613	2.4	1.3	7.3

Risen, Arnold D. **(Arnie, Stilts)** b. October 9, 1924 Ht. 6-9 Wt. 200 College: Ohio State HOF: 1998

SEASON–TEAM	G	GS	MIN	FGM	FGA	PCT	3FGM	3FGA	PCT	FTM	FTA	PCT	O-RB	D-RB	TOT	AST	PF	DQ	STL	TO	BLK	PTS	RPG	APG	PPG
45-46–Indianapolis (N)	18	–	–	77	–	–	–	–	–	65	110	.591	–	–	–	–	75	–	–	–	–	219	–	–	12.2
46-47–Indianapolis (N)	44	–	–	204	–	–	–	–	–	174	276	.630	–	–	–	–	150	–	–	–	–	582	–	–	13.2
47-48–Ind.-Roch. (N)	61	–	–	282	–	–	–	–	–	241	352	.685	–	–	–	–	198	–	–	–	–	805	–	–	13.2
48-49–Rochester	60	–	–	345	816	.423	–	–	–	305	462	.660	–	–	–	100	216	–	–	–	–	995	–	1.7	16.6
49-50–Rochester	62	–	–	206	598	.344	–	–	–	213	321	.664	–	–	–	92	228	–	–	–	–	625	–	1.5	10.1
50-51–Rochester	66	–	–	377	940	.401	–	–	–	323	440	.734	–	–	795	158	278	9	–	–	–	1077	12.0	2.4	16.3
51-52–Rochester	66	–	2396	365	926	.394	–	–	–	302	431	.701	–	–	841	150	258	3	–	–	–	1032	12.7	2.3	15.6
52-53–Rochester	68	–	2288	295	802	.368	–	–	–	294	429	.685	–	–	745	135	274	10	–	–	–	884	11.0	2.0	13.0
53-54–Rochester	72	–	2385	321	872	.368	–	–	–	307	430	.714	–	–	728	120	284	9	–	–	–	949	10.1	1.7	13.2
54-55–Rochester	69	–	1970	259	699	.371	–	–	–	279	375	.744	–	–	703	112	253	10	–	–	–	797	10.2	1.6	11.6
55-56–Boston	68	–	1597	189	493	.383	–	–	–	170	240	.708	–	–	553	88	300	17	–	–	–	548	8.1	1.3	8.1
56-57–Boston	43	–	935	119	307	.388	–	–	–	106	156	.679	–	–	286	53	163	4	–	–	–	344	6.7	1.2	8.0
57-58–Boston	63	–	1119	134	397	.338	–	–	–	114	167	.683	–	–	360	50	195	5	–	–	–	382	5.7	0.8	6.1
Reg. NBA Totals	637	–	12690	2610	6850	.381	–	–	–	2413	3451	.699	–	–	5011	1058	2449	67	–	–	–	7633	9.7	1.7	12.0
Reg. NBL Totals	123	–	–	563	–	–	–	–	–	480	738	.650	–	–	–	–	423	–	–	–	–	1606	–	–	13.1
NBA Playoff Totals	61	–	1452	263	820	.385	–	–	–	264	392	.673	–	–	690	113	255	11	–	–	–	790	10.3	1.4	13.0
NBL Playoff Totals	12	–	–	67	–	–	–	–	–	61	74	.730	–	–	–	–	44	–	–	–	–	195	–	–	16.3
NBA All-Star Totals	3	–	58	9	24	.375	–	–	–	1	5	.200	–	–	21	3	11	0	–	–	–	19	7.0	1.0	6.3

Ritter, Goebel Franklin **(Tex)** b. February 26, 1924 Ht. 6-2 Wt. 185 College: Eastern Kentucky

SEASON–TEAM	G	GS	MIN	FGM	FGA	PCT	3FGM	3FGA	PCT	FTM	FTA	PCT	O-RB	D-RB	TOT	AST	PF	DQ	STL	TO	BLK	PTS	RPG	APG	PPG
48-49–New York	55	–	–	123	353	.348	–	–	–	91	146	.623	–	–	–	57	71	–	–	–	–	337	–	1.0	6.1
49-50–New York	62	–	–	100	297	.337	–	–	–	125	176	.710	–	–	–	51	101	–	–	–	–	325	–	0.8	5.2
50-51–New York	34	–	–	39	103	.379	–	–	–	49	71	.690	–	–	65	37	52	1	–	–	–	127	1.9	1.1	3.7
Reg. Season Totals	151	–	–	262	753	.348	–	–	–	265	393	.674	–	–	65	145	224	1	–	–	–	789	1.9	1.0	5.2
Playoff Totals	13	–	–	21	84	.286	–	–	–	37	50	.760	–	–	2	11	44	2	–	–	–	79	0.7	0.7	6.1

Rivas, Ramon b. June 3, 1966 Ht. 6-10 Wt. 260 College: Temple

SEASON–TEAM	G	GS	MIN	FGM	FGA	PCT	3FGM	3FGA	PCT	FTM	FTA	PCT	O-RB	D-RB	TOT	AST	PF	DQ	STL	TO	BLK	PTS	RPG	APG	PPG
88-89–Boston	28	0	91	12	31	.387	0	1	.000	16	25	.640	9	15	24	3	21	0	4	9	1	40	0.9	0.1	1.4
Reg. Season Totals	28	0	91	12	31	.387	0	1	.000	16	25	.640	9	15	24	3	21	0	4	9	1	40	0.9	0.1	1.4

Rivers, David Lee b. January 20, 1965 Ht. 6-0 Wt. 175 College: Notre Dame

SEASON–TEAM	G	GS	MIN	FGM	FGA	PCT	3FGM	3FGA	PCT	FTM	FTA	PCT	O-RB	D-RB	TOT	AST	PF	DQ	STL	TO	BLK	PTS	RPG	APG	PPG
88-89–L.A. Lakers	47	0	440	49	122	.402	1	6	.167	35	42	.833	13	30	43	106	50	0	23	61	9	134	0.9	2.3	2.9
89-90–L.A. Clippers	52	11	724	80	197	.406	0	5	.000	59	78	.756	30	55	85	155	53	0	31	88	0	219	1.6	3.0	4.2
91-92–L.A. Clippers	15	0	122	10	30	.333	0	1	.000	10	11	.909	10	9	19	21	14	0	7	17	1	30	1.3	1.4	2.0
Reg. Season Totals	114	11	1286	139	349	.398	1	12	.083	104	131	.794	53	94	147	282	117	0	61	166	10	383	1.3	2.5	3.4
Playoff Totals	6	0	33	4	12	.333	0	2	.000	7	8	.875	1	3	4	6	6	0	0	4	0	15	0.7	1.0	2.5

Rivers, Glenn Anton **(Doc)** b. October 13, 1961 Ht. 6-4 Wt. 210 College: Marquette

SEASON–TEAM	G	GS	MIN	FGM	FGA	PCT	3FGM	3FGA	PCT	FTM	FTA	PCT	O-RB	D-RB	TOT	AST	PF	DQ	STL	TO	BLK	PTS	RPG	APG	PPG
83-84–Atlanta	81	47	1938	250	541	.462	2	12	.167	255	325	.785	72	148	220	314	286	8	127	174	30	757	2.7	3.9	9.3
84-85–Atlanta	69	58	2126	334	701	.476	15	36	.417	291	378	.770	66	148	214	410	250	7	163	176	53	974	3.1	5.9	14.1
85-86–Atlanta	53	50	1571	220	464	.474	0	16	.000	172	283	.608	49	113	162	443	185	2	120	141	13	612	3.1	8.4	11.5
86-87–Atlanta	82	82	2590	342	758	.451	4	21	.190	365	441	.828	83	216	299	823	287	5	171	217	30	1053	3.6	10.0	12.8
87-88–Atlanta	80	80	2502	403	890	.453	9	33	.273	319	421	.758	83	283	366	747	272	3	140	210	41	1134	4.6	9.3	14.2
88-89–Atlanta	76	76	2462	371	816	.455	43	124	.347	247	287	.861	89	197	286	525	263	6	181	158	40	1032	3.8	6.9	13.6
89-90–Atlanta	48	44	1526	218	480	.454	24	66	.364	138	170	.812	47	153	200	264	151	2	116	98	22	598	4.2	5.5	12.5
90-91–Atlanta	79	79	2586	444	1020	.435	88	262	.336	221	262	.844	47	206	253	340	216	2	148	125	47	1197	3.2	4.3	15.2
91-92–L.A. Clippers	59	25	1658	226	533	.424	26	92	.283	163	196	.832	23	124	147	233	166	2	111	92	19	641	2.5	3.9	10.9
92-93–New York	77	45	1886	216	494	.437	39	123	.317	133	162	.821	26	166	192	405	215	2	123	114	9	604	2.5	5.3	7.8
93-94–New York	19	19	499	55	127	.433	19	52	.365	14	22	.636	4	35	39	100	44	0	25	29	5	143	2.1	5.3	7.5
94-95–N.Y.-S.A.	63	0	989	108	302	.358	45	127	.354	60	82	.732	15	94	109	162	150	2	65	60	21	321	1.7	2.6	5.1
95-96–San Antonio	78	0	1235	108	290	.372	47	137	.343	48	64	.750	30	108	138	123	175	0	73	57	21	311	1.8	1.6	4.0
Reg. Season Totals	864	605	23568	3295	7416	.444	361	1101	.328	2426	3093	.784	634	1991	2625	4889	2660	41	1563	1651	351	9377	3.0	5.7	10.9
Playoff Totals	81	62	2393	308	691	.446	50	148	.338	260	339	.767	54	216	270	479	265	5	125	153	23	926	3.3	5.9	11.4
All-Star Totals	1	0	16	2	4	.500	0	0	–	5	11	.455	0	3	3	6	3	0	0	3	0	9	3.0	6.0	9.0

Robbins, Austin (Red) b. September 30, 1944 Ht. 6-8 Wt. 200 College: Chipola (Fla.) J.C.; Tennessee

SEASON–TEAM	G	GS	MIN	FGM	FGA	PCT	3FGM	3FGA	PCT	FTM	FTA	PCT	O-RB	D-RB	TOT	AST	PF	DQ	STL	TO	BLK	PTS	RPG	APG	PPG
67-68–New Orleans (A)	73	–	2159	448	918	.488	2	6	.333	245	308	.795	366	528	894	73	157	0	–	115	–	1143	12.2	1.0	15.7
68-69–New Orleans (A)	76	–	2736	456	1035	.441	7	29	.241	291	361	.806	368	656	1024	142	200	1	–	121	–	1210	13.5	1.9	15.9
69-70–New Orleans (A)	82	–	3266	525	1091	.481	7	23	.304	285	366	.779	427	905	1332	182	251	1	–	–	–	1342	16.2	2.2	16.4
70-71–Utah (A)	82	–	2995	396	908	.436	11	44	.250	227	272	.835	303	673	976	178	203	–	–	–	–	1030	11.9	2.2	12.6
71-72–Utah (A)	78	–	2567	379	752	.504	29	71	.408	167	201	.831	–	–	711	124	171	–	–	86	–	954	9.1	1.6	12.2
72-73–San Diego (A)	58	–	1618	218	525	.415	9	30	.300	131	155	.845	159	258	417	99	134	2	–	85	–	576	7.2	1.7	9.9
73-74–S.D.-Ken. (A)	80	–	1627	276	577	.478	1	13	.077	116	136	.853	144	242	386	89	112	–	40	89	34	669	4.8	1.1	8.4
74-75–Ken.-Vir. (A)	57	–	1777	307	648	.474	3	10	.300	162	187	.866	153	262	415	114	106	–	31	97	31	779	7.3	2.0	13.7
Reg. ABA Totals	586	–	18745	3005	6454	.466	69	226	.305	1624	1986	.818	1920	3524	6155	1001	1334	4	71	593	65	7703	10.5	1.7	13.1
ABA Playoff Totals	67	–	2079	335	706	.475	9	32	.281	186	244	.762	138	296	729	109	155	0	4	64	5	865	10.9	1.6	12.9

Robbins, Lee Roy b. February 11, 1922 d. April 8, 1968 Ht. 6-3 Wt. 175 College: Colorado

SEASON–TEAM	G	GS	MIN	FGM	FGA	PCT	3FGM	3FGA	PCT	FTM	FTA	PCT	O-RB	D-RB	TOT	AST	PF	DQ	STL	TO	BLK	PTS	RPG	APG	PPG
47-48–Providence	31	–	–	72	260	.277	–	–	–	51	93	.548	–	–	–	7	93	–	–	–	–	195	–	0.2	6.3
48-49–Providence	16	–	–	9	25	.360	–	–	–	11	17	.647	–	–	–	12	24	–	–	–	–	29	–	0.8	1.8
Reg. Season Totals	47	–	–	81	285	.284	–	–	–	62	110	.564	–	–	–	19	117	–	–	–	–	224	–	0.4	4.8

Roberson, Rick b. July 7, 1947 Ht. 6-9 Wt. 235 College: Cincinnati

SEASON–TEAM	G	GS	MIN	FGM	FGA	PCT	3FGM	3FGA	PCT	FTM	FTA	PCT	O-RB	D-RB	TOT	AST	PF	DQ	STL	TO	BLK	PTS	RPG	APG	PPG
69-70–Los Angeles	74	–	2005	262	586	.447	–	–	–	120	212	.566	–	–	672	92	256	7	–	–	–	644	9.1	1.2	8.7
70-71–Los Angeles	65	–	909	125	301	.415	–	–	–	88	143	.615	–	–	304	47	125	1	–	–	–	338	4.7	0.7	5.2
71-72–Cleveland	63	–	2207	304	688	.442	–	–	–	215	366	.587	–	–	801	109	251	7	–	–	–	823	12.7	1.7	13.1
72-73–Cleveland	62	–	2127	307	709	.433	–	–	–	167	290	.576	–	–	693	134	249	5	–	–	–	781	11.2	2.2	12.6
73-74–Portland	69	–	2060	364	797	.457	–	–	–	205	316	.649	251	450	701	133	252	4	65	–	55	933	10.2	1.9	13.5
74-75–New Orleans	16	–	339	48	108	.444	–	–	–	23	40	.575	39	79	118	23	49	0	7	–	8	119	7.4	1.4	7.4
75-76–Kansas City	74	–	709	73	180	.406	–	–	–	42	103	.408	74	159	233	53	126	1	18	–	17	188	3.1	0.7	2.5
Reg. Season Totals	423	–	10356	1483	3369	.440	–	–	–	860	1470	.585	364	688	3522	591	1308	25	90	–	80	3826	8.3	1.4	9.0
Playoff Totals	18	–	154	18	47	.383	–	–	–	10	17	.588	0	0	42	4	27	0	0	–	0	46	2.3	0.2	2.6

Roberts, Anthony Jerome b. April 15, 1955 d. March 29, 1997 Ht. 6-5 Wt. 195 College: Oral Roberts

SEASON–TEAM	G	GS	MIN	FGM	FGA	PCT	3FGM	3FGA	PCT	FTM	FTA	PCT	O-RB	D-RB	TOT	AST	PF	DQ	STL	TO	BLK	PTS	RPG	APG	PPG
77-78–Denver	82	–	1598	311	736	.423	–	–	–	153	212	.722	135	216	351	105	212	1	40	118	7	775	4.3	1.3	9.5
78-79–Denver	63	–	1236	211	498	.424	–	–	–	76	110	.691	106	152	258	107	142	2	20	65	2	498	4.1	1.7	7.9
79-80–Denver	23	–	486	69	181	.381	0	1	.000	39	60	.650	54	55	109	20	52	1	13	28	3	177	4.7	0.9	7.7
80-81–Washington	26	–	350	54	144	.375	0	0	–	19	29	.655	18	50	68	20	52	0	11	28	0	127	2.6	0.8	4.9
83-84–Denver	19	0	197	34	91	.374	0	0	–	13	18	.722	20	31	51	13	43	1	5	17	1	81	2.7	0.7	4.3
Reg. Season Totals	213	0	3867	679	1650	.412	0	1	.000	300	429	.699	333	504	837	265	501	5	89	256	13	1658	3.9	1.2	7.8
Playoff Totals	16	0	480	99	232	.427	0	0	–	47	61	.770	50	71	121	36	66	3	13	30	7	245	7.6	2.3	15.3

Roberts, Frederick Clark (Fred) b. August 14, 1960 Ht. 6-10 Wt. 210 College: Brigham Young

SEASON–TEAM	G	GS	MIN	FGM	FGA	PCT	3FGM	3FGA	PCT	FTM	FTA	PCT	O-RB	D-RB	TOT	AST	PF	DQ	STL	TO	BLK	PTS	RPG	APG	PPG
83-84–San Antonio	79	8	1531	214	399	.536	1	4	.250	144	172	.837	102	202	304	98	219	4	52	100	38	573	3.8	1.2	7.3
84-85–S.A.-Utah	74	0	1178	208	418	.498	1	1	1.000	150	182	.824	78	108	186	87	141	0	28	89	22	567	2.5	1.2	7.7
85-86–Utah	58	0	469	74	167	.443	1	2	.500	67	87	.770	31	49	80	27	72	0	8	53	6	216	1.4	0.5	3.7
86-87–Boston	73	11	1079	139	270	.515	0	3	.000	124	153	.810	54	136	190	62	129	1	22	89	20	402	2.6	0.8	5.5
87-88–Boston	74	14	1032	161	330	.488	0	6	.000	128	165	.776	60	102	162	81	118	0	16	68	15	450	2.2	1.1	6.1
88-89–Milwaukee	71	3	1251	155	319	.486	3	14	.214	104	129	.806	68	141	209	66	126	0	36	80	23	417	2.9	0.9	5.9
89-90–Milwaukee	82	66	2235	330	666	.495	2	11	.182	195	249	.783	107	204	311	147	210	5	56	130	25	857	3.8	1.8	10.5
90-91–Milwaukee	82	82	2114	357	670	.533	4	25	.160	170	209	.813	107	174	281	135	190	2	63	135	29	888	3.4	1.6	10.8
91-92–Milwaukee	80	63	1746	311	645	.482	19	37	.514	128	171	.749	103	154	257	122	177	0	52	122	40	769	3.2	1.5	9.6
92-93–Milwaukee	79	5	1488	226	428	.528	12	29	.414	135	169	.799	91	146	237	118	138	0	57	67	27	599	3.0	1.5	7.6
94-95–Cleveland	21	0	223	28	72	.389	4	11	.364	20	26	.769	13	21	34	8	26	1	6	7	3	80	1.6	0.4	3.8
95-96–L.A. Lakers	33	1	317	48	97	.495	4	14	.286	22	28	.786	18	29	47	26	24	0	16	24	4	122	1.4	0.8	3.7
96-97–Dallas	12	0	40	6	15	.400	0	0	–	10	14	.714	2	8	10	0	2	0	0	5	1	22	0.8	0.0	1.8
Reg. Season Totals	818	253	14703	2257	4496	.502	51	157	.325	1397	1754	.796	834	1474	2308	977	1572	13	412	969	253	5962	2.8	1.2	7.3
Playoff Totals	67	16	1063	148	299	.495	0	5	.000	111	144	.771	56	84	140	57	131	2	23	63	12	407	2.1	0.9	6.1

Roberts, Joseph (Joe) b. May 18, 1936 Ht. 6-6 Wt. 215 College: Ohio State

SEASON–TEAM	G	GS	MIN	FGM	FGA	PCT	3FGM	3FGA	PCT	FTM	FTA	PCT	O-RB	D-RB	TOT	AST	PF	DQ	STL	TO	BLK	PTS	RPG	APG	PPG
60-61–Syracuse	68	–	800	130	351	.370	–	–	–	62	104	.596	–	–	243	43	125	0	–	–	–	322	3.6	0.6	4.7
61-62–Syracuse	80	–	1642	243	619	.393	–	–	–	129	194	.665	–	–	538	50	230	4	–	–	–	615	6.7	0.6	7.7
62-63–Syracuse	33	–	466	73	196	.372	–	–	–	35	51	.686	–	–	155	16	66	1	–	–	–	181	4.7	0.5	5.5
67-68–Kentucky (A)	37	–	564	54	146	.370	1	3	.333	28	50	.560	–	–	139	14	64	1	–	30	–	137	3.8	0.4	3.7
Reg. NBA Totals	181	–	2908	446	1166	.383	–	–	–	226	349	.648	–	–	936	109	421	5	–	–	–	1118	5.2	0.6	6.2
Reg. ABA Totals	37	–	564	54	146	.370	1	3	.333	28	50	.560	–	–	139	14	64	1	–	30	–	137	3.8	0.4	3.7
NBA Playoff Totals	9	–	84	11	32	.344	–	–	–	10	14	.714	–	–	32	–	12	0	–	–	–	32	3.6	0.0	3.6
ABA Playoff Totals	5	–	63	5	15	.333	0	0	–	2	6	.333	–	–	15	1	13	0	–	3	–	12	3.0	0.2	2.4

Roberts, Marvin James **(Marv)** b. January 29, 1950 Ht. 6-8 Wt. 220 College: Utah State

SEASON–TEAM	G	GS	MIN	FGM	FGA	PCT	3FGM	3FGA	PCT	FTM	FTA	PCT	O-RB	D-RB	TOT	AST	PF	DQ	STL	TO	BLK	PTS	RPG	APG	PPG
71-72–Denver (A)	68	–	1047	217	533	.407	1	4	.250	86	120	.717	–	–	294	61	150	–	–	77	–	521	4.3	0.9	7.7
72-73–Denver (A)	77	–	1959	374	807	.463	1	3	.333	201	255	.788	180	218	398	95	194	3	–	110	–	950	5.2	1.2	12.3
73-74–Denver-Car. (A)	74	–	1599	266	598	.445	1	1	1.000	129	164	.787	161	210	371	119	153	–	47	100	7	662	5.0	1.6	8.9
74-75–Kentucky (A)	83	–	1370	201	467	.430	0	1	.000	127	164	.774	91	155	246	103	200	–	27	100	4	529	3.0	1.2	6.4
75-76–Ken.-Vir. (A)	72	–	1559	259	621	.417	0	0	–	107	137	.781	104	132	236	120	151	–	36	100	8	625	3.3	1.7	8.7
76-77–Los Angeles	28	–	209	27	76	.355	–	–	–	4	6	.667	9	16	25	19	34	0	4	–	2	58	0.9	0.7	2.1
Reg. NBA Totals	28	–	209	27	76	.355	–	–	–	4	6	.667	9	16	25	19	34	0	4	–	2	58	0.9	0.7	2.1
Reg. ABA Totals	374	–	7534	1317	3026	.435	3	9	.333	650	840	.774	536	715	1545	498	848	3	110	487	19	3287	4.1	1.3	8.8
ABA Playoff Totals	24	–	422	86	178	.483	0	1	.000	45	57	.789	38	41	84	31	45	0	5	22	1	217	3.5	1.3	9.0

Roberts, Stanley Corvet b. February 7, 1970 Ht. 7-0 Wt. 290 College: Louisiana State

SEASON–TEAM	G	GS	MIN	FGM	FGA	PCT	3FGM	3FGA	PCT	FTM	FTA	PCT	O-RB	D-RB	TOT	AST	PF	DQ	STL	TO	BLK	PTS	RPG	APG	PPG
91-92–Orlando	55	34	1118	236	446	.529	0	1	.000	101	196	.515	113	223	336	39	221	7	22	78	83	573	6.1	0.7	10.4
92-93–L.A. Clippers	77	76	1816	375	711	.527	0	0	–	120	246	.488	181	297	478	59	332	15	34	121	141	870	6.2	0.8	11.3
93-94–L.A. Clippers	14	14	350	43	100	.430	0	0	–	18	44	.409	27	66	93	11	54	2	6	24	25	104	6.6	0.8	7.4
95-96–L.A. Clippers	51	7	795	141	304	.464	0	0	–	74	133	.556	42	120	162	41	153	3	15	48	39	356	3.2	0.8	7.0
96-97–L.A. Clippers	18	2	378	63	148	.426	0	0	–	45	64	.703	24	67	91	9	57	2	8	23	23	171	5.1	0.5	9.5
97-98–Minnesota	74	44	1328	191	386	.495	0	0	–	75	156	.481	109	254	363	27	226	5	24	70	72	457	4.9	0.4	6.2
98-99–Houston	6	0	33	5	13	.385	0	0	–	4	8	.500	4	7	11	0	2	0	0	4	1	14	1.8	0.0	2.3
99-00–Philadelphia	5	1	51	5	16	.313	0	1	.000	0	3	.000	6	9	15	3	15	0	1	2	1	10	3.0	0.6	2.0
Reg. Season Totals	300	178	5869	1059	2124	.499	0	2	.000	437	850	.514	506	1043	1549	189	1060	34	110	370	385	2555	5.2	0.6	8.5
Playoff Totals	9	5	177	26	57	.456	0	1	.000	7	22	.318	18	28	46	1	29	2	3	11	7	59	5.1	0.1	6.6

Roberts, William **(Bill)** b. 1925 Ht. 6-9 Wt. 210 College: Wyoming

SEASON–TEAM	G	GS	MIN	FGM	FGA	PCT	3FGM	3FGA	PCT	FTM	FTA	PCT	O-RB	D-RB	TOT	AST	PF	DQ	STL	TO	BLK	PTS	RPG	APG	PPG
48-49–Chi.-Bos.-St. L.	50	–	–	89	267	.333	–	–	–	44	63	.698	–	–	–	41	113	–	–	–	–	222	–	0.8	4.4
49-50–St. Louis	67	–	–	77	222	.347	–	–	–	28	39	.718	–	–	–	24	90	–	–	–	–	182	–	0.4	2.7
Reg. Season Totals	117	–	–	166	489	.339	–	–	–	72	102	.706	–	–	–	65	203	–	–	–	–	404	–	0.6	3.5
Playoff Totals	2	–	–	10	29	.345	–	–	–	2	5	.400	–	–	–	2	10	–	–	–	–	22	–	1.0	11.0

Robertson, Alvin Cyrrale b. July 22, 1962 Ht. 6-4 Wt. 208 College: Arkansas

SEASON–TEAM	G	GS	MIN	FGM	FGA	PCT	3FGM	3FGA	PCT	FTM	FTA	PCT	O-RB	D-RB	TOT	AST	PF	DQ	STL	TO	BLK	PTS	RPG	APG	PPG
84-85–San Antonio	79	9	1685	299	600	.498	4	11	.364	124	169	.734	116	149	265	275	217	1	127	167	24	726	3.4	3.5	9.2
85-86–San Antonio	82	82	2878	562	1093	.514	8	29	.276	260	327	.795	184	332	516	448	296	4	301	256	40	1392	6.3	5.5	17.0
86-87–San Antonio	81	78	2697	589	1264	.466	13	48	.271	244	324	.753	186	238	424	421	264	2	260	243	35	1435	5.2	5.2	17.7
87-88–San Antonio	82	82	2978	655	1408	.465	27	95	.284	273	365	.748	165	333	498	557	300	4	243	251	69	1610	6.1	6.8	19.6
88-89–San Antonio	65	65	2287	465	962	.483	9	45	.200	183	253	.723	157	227	384	393	259	6	197	231	36	1122	5.9	6.0	17.3
89-90–Milwaukee	81	81	2599	476	946	.503	4	26	.154	197	266	.741	230	329	559	445	280	2	207	217	17	1153	6.9	5.5	14.2
90-91–Milwaukee	81	81	2598	438	904	.485	23	63	.365	199	263	.757	191	268	459	444	273	5	246	212	16	1098	5.7	5.5	13.6
91-92–Milwaukee	82	79	2463	396	922	.430	67	210	.319	151	198	.763	175	175	350	360	263	5	210	223	32	1010	4.3	4.4	12.3
92-93–Milw.-Detroit	69	54	2006	247	539	.458	40	122	.328	84	128	.656	107	162	269	263	218	1	155	133	18	618	3.9	3.8	9.0
95-96–Toronto	77	69	2478	285	607	.470	41	151	.272	107	158	.677	110	232	342	323	268	5	166	183	36	718	4.4	4.2	9.3
Reg. Season Totals	779	680	24669	4412	9245	.477	236	800	.295	1822	2451	.743	1621	2445	4066	3929	2638	35	2112	2116	323	10882	5.2	5.0	14.0
Playoff Totals	13	13	490	102	198	.515	6	17	.353	52	69	.754	27	42	69	81	53	1	36	39	2	262	5.3	6.2	20.2
All-Star Totals	4	2	60	7	18	.389	0	0	–	4	4	1.000	3	10	13	7	3	0	2	10	0	18	3.3	1.8	4.5

Robertson, Oscar Palmer **(The Big O)** b. November 24, 1938 Ht. 6-5 Wt. 210 College: Cincinnati HOF: 1979

SEASON–TEAM	G	GS	MIN	FGM	FGA	PCT	3FGM	3FGA	PCT	FTM	FTA	PCT	O-RB	D-RB	TOT	AST	PF	DQ	STL	TO	BLK	PTS	RPG	APG	PPG
60-61–Cincinnati	71	–	3032	756	1600	.473	–	–	–	653	794	.822	–	–	716	690	219	3	–	–	–	2165	10.1	9.7	30.5
61-62–Cincinnati	79	–	3503	866	1810	.478	–	–	–	700	872	.803	–	–	985	899	258	1	–	–	–	2432	12.5	11.4	30.8
62-63–Cincinnati	80	–	3521	825	1593	.518	–	–	–	614	758	.810	–	–	835	758	293	1	–	–	–	2264	10.4	9.5	28.3
63-64–Cincinnati	79	–	3559	840	1740	.483	–	–	–	800	938	.853	–	–	783	868	280	3	–	–	–	2480	9.9	11.0	31.4
64-65–Cincinnati	75	–	3421	807	1681	.480	–	–	–	665	793	.839	–	–	674	861	205	2	–	–	–	2279	9.0	11.5	30.4
65-66–Cincinnati	76	–	3493	818	1723	.475	–	–	–	742	881	.842	–	–	586	847	227	1	–	–	–	2378	7.7	11.1	31.3
66-67–Cincinnati	79	–	3468	838	1699	.493	–	–	–	736	843	.873	–	–	486	845	226	2	–	–	–	2412	6.2	10.7	30.5
67-68–Cincinnati	65	–	2765	660	1321	.500	–	–	–	576	660	.873	–	–	391	633	199	2	–	–	–	1896	6.0	9.7	29.2
68-69–Cincinnati	79	–	3461	656	1351	.486	–	–	–	643	767	.838	–	–	502	772	231	2	–	–	–	1955	6.4	9.8	24.7
69-70–Cincinnati	69	–	2865	647	1267	.511	–	–	–	454	561	.809	–	–	422	558	175	1	–	–	–	1748	6.1	8.1	25.3
70-71–Milwaukee	81	–	3194	592	1193	.496	–	–	–	385	453	.850	–	–	462	668	203	0	–	–	–	1569	5.7	8.2	19.4
71-72–Milwaukee	64	–	2390	419	887	.472	–	–	–	276	330	.836	–	–	323	491	116	0	–	–	–	1114	5.0	7.7	17.4
72-73–Milwaukee	73	–	2737	446	983	.454	–	–	–	238	281	.847	–	–	360	551	167	0	–	–	–	1130	4.9	7.5	15.5
73-74–Milwaukee	70	–	2477	338	772	.438	–	–	–	212	254	.835	71	208	279	446	132	0	77	–	4	888	4.0	6.4	12.7
Reg. Season Totals	1040	–	43886	9508	19620	.485	–	–	–	7694	9185	.838	71	208	7804	9887	2931	18	77	–	4	26710	7.5	9.5	25.7
Playoff Totals	86	–	3673	675	1466	.460	–	–	–	560	655	.855	15	39	578	769	267	3	15	–	4	1910	6.7	8.9	22.2
All-Star Totals	12	–	380	88	172	.512	–	–	–	70	98	.714	0	0	69	81	41	0	0	–	0	246	5.8	6.8	20.5

Robertson, Ryan Ashley b. October 2, 1976 Ht. 6-5 Wt. 190 College: Kansas

SEASON–TEAM	G	GS	MIN	FGM	FGA	PCT	3FGM	3FGA	PCT	FTM	FTA	PCT	O-RB	D-RB	TOT	AST	PF	DQ	STL	TO	BLK	PTS	RPG	APG	PPG
99-00–Sacramento	1	0	25	2	6	.333	0	2	.000	1	1	1.000	0	0	0	0	0	0	0	0	0	5	0.0	0.0	5.0
Reg. Season Totals	1	0	25	2	6	.333	0	2	.000	1	1	1.000	0	0	0	0	0	0	0	0	0	5	0.0	0.0	5.0

Robertson, Tony b. January 1, 1956 Ht. 6-4 Wt. 195 College: West Virginia

SEASON–TEAM	G	GS	MIN	FGM	FGA	PCT	3FGM	3FGA	PCT	FTM	FTA	PCT	O-RB	D-RB	TOT	AST	PF	DQ	STL	TO	BLK	PTS	RPG	APG	PPG
77-78–Atlanta	63	–	929	168	381	.441	–	–	–	37	53	.698	15	55	70	103	133	2	74	88	5	373	1.1	1.6	5.9
78-79–Golden State	12	–	74	15	40	.375	–	–	–	6	9	.667	6	4	10	4	10	0	8	8	0	36	0.8	0.3	3.0
Reg. Season Totals	75	–	1003	183	421	.435	–	–	–	43	62	.694	21	59	80	107	143	2	82	96	5	409	1.1	1.4	5.5
Playoff Totals	2	–	12	2	6	.333	–	–	–	1	2	.500	0	0	0	–	3	0	0	0	0	5	0.0	0.0	2.5

Robey, Frederick Robert (Rick) b. January 30, 1956 Ht. 6-11 Wt. 230 College: Kentucky

SEASON–TEAM	G	GS	MIN	FGM	FGA	PCT	3FGM	3FGA	PCT	FTM	FTA	PCT	O-RB	D-RB	TOT	AST	PF	DQ	STL	TO	BLK	PTS	RPG	APG	PPG
78-79–Indiana-Bos.	79	–	1763	322	673	.478	–	–	–	174	224	.777	168	345	513	132	232	4	48	164	15	818	6.5	1.7	10.4
79-80–Boston	82	–	1918	379	727	.521	0	1	.000	184	269	.684	209	321	530	92	244	2	53	151	15	942	6.5	1.1	11.5
80-81–Boston	82	–	1569	298	547	.545	0	1	.000	144	251	.574	132	258	390	126	204	0	38	141	19	740	4.8	1.5	9.0
81-82–Boston	80	4	1186	185	375	.493	0	2	.000	84	157	.535	114	181	295	68	183	2	27	92	14	454	3.7	0.9	5.7
82-83–Boston	59	6	855	100	214	.467	0	0	–	45	78	.577	79	140	219	65	131	1	13	72	8	245	3.7	1.1	4.2
83-84–Phoenix	61	4	856	140	257	.545	1	1	1.000	61	88	.693	80	118	198	65	120	0	20	77	14	342	3.2	1.1	5.6
84-85–Phoenix	4	0	48	2	9	.222	0	0	–	1	2	.500	3	5	8	5	7	0	2	8	0	5	2.0	1.3	1.3
85-86–Phoenix	46	1	629	72	191	.377	0	3	.000	33	48	.688	40	108	148	58	92	1	19	66	5	177	3.2	1.3	3.8
Reg. Season Totals	493	15	8824	1498	2993	.501	1	8	.125	726	1117	.650	825	1476	2301	611	1213	10	220	771	90	3723	4.7	1.2	7.6
Playoff Totals	53	0	610	87	194	.448	0	3	.000	42	78	.538	55	84	139	29	107	0	13	44	11	216	2.6	0.5	4.1

Robinson, Christopher Sean (Chris) b. February 17, 1973 Ht. 6-5 Wt. 200 College: Western Kentucky

SEASON–TEAM	G	GS	MIN	FGM	FGA	PCT	3FGM	3FGA	PCT	FTM	FTA	PCT	O-RB	D-RB	TOT	AST	PF	DQ	STL	TO	BLK	PTS	RPG	APG	PPG
96-97–Vancouver	41	6	681	69	182	.379	34	89	.382	16	26	.615	23	48	71	65	85	2	28	34	9	188	1.7	1.6	4.6
97-98–Vanc.-Sac.	35	0	414	65	174	.374	24	66	.364	8	16	.500	9	37	46	39	50	0	19	33	4	162	1.3	1.1	4.6
Reg. Season Totals	76	6	1095	134	356	.376	58	155	.374	24	42	.571	32	85	117	104	135	2	47	67	13	350	1.5	1.4	4.6

Robinson, Clifford Ralph (Cliff) b. December 16, 1966 Ht. 6-10 Wt. 225 College: Connecticut

SEASON–TEAM	G	GS	MIN	FGM	FGA	PCT	3FGM	3FGA	PCT	FTM	FTA	PCT	O-RB	D-RB	TOT	AST	PF	DQ	STL	TO	BLK	PTS	RPG	APG	PPG
89-90–Portland	82	0	1565	298	751	.397	12	44	.273	138	251	.550	110	198	308	72	226	4	53	129	53	746	3.8	0.9	9.1
90-91–Portland	82	11	1940	373	806	.463	6	19	.316	205	314	.653	123	226	349	151	263	2	78	133	76	957	4.3	1.8	11.7
91-92–Portland	82	7	2124	398	854	.466	1	11	.091	219	330	.664	140	276	416	137	274	11	85	154	107	1016	5.1	1.7	12.4
92-93–Portland	82	12	2575	632	1336	.473	19	77	.247	287	416	.690	165	377	542	182	287	8	98	173	163	1570	6.6	2.2	19.1
93-94–Portland	82	64	2853	641	1404	.457	13	53	.245	352	460	.765	164	386	550	159	263	0	118	169	111	1647	6.7	1.9	20.1
94-95–Portland	75	73	2725	597	1320	.452	142	383	.371	265	382	.694	152	271	423	198	240	3	79	158	82	1601	5.6	2.6	21.3
95-96–Portland	78	76	2980	553	1306	.423	178	471	.378	360	542	.664	123	320	443	190	248	3	86	194	68	1644	5.7	2.4	21.1
96-97–Portland	81	79	3077	444	1043	.426	121	350	.346	215	309	.696	90	231	321	261	251	6	99	172	66	1224	4.0	3.2	15.1
97-98–Phoenix	80	64	2359	429	895	.479	27	84	.321	248	360	.689	152	258	410	170	249	5	92	140	90	1133	5.1	2.1	14.2
98-99–Phoenix	50	35	1740	299	629	.475	58	139	.417	163	234	.697	69	158	227	128	153	2	75	88	59	819	4.5	2.6	16.4
99-00–Phoenix	80	67	2839	530	1142	.464	120	324	.370	298	381	.782	105	254	359	224	239	3	90	166	61	1478	4.5	2.8	18.5
Reg. Season Totals	854	488	26777	5194	11486	.452	697	1955	.357	2750	3979	.691	1393	2955	4348	1872	2693	47	953	1676	936	13835	5.1	2.2	16.2
Playoff Totals	94	38	2550	391	967	.404	32	129	.248	222	362	.613	156	270	426	158	343	8	88	161	94	1036	4.5	1.7	11.0
All-Star Totals	1	0	18	5	8	.625	0	1	.000	0	0	–	1	1	2	5	0	0	1	0	0	10	2.0	5.0	10.0

Robinson, Clifford Trent (Cliff) b. March 13, 1960 Ht. 6-9 Wt. 220 College: USC

SEASON–TEAM	G	GS	MIN	FGM	FGA	PCT	3FGM	3FGA	PCT	FTM	FTA	PCT	O-RB	D-RB	TOT	AST	PF	DQ	STL	TO	BLK	PTS	RPG	APG	PPG
79-80–New Jersey	70	–	1661	391	833	.469	1	4	.250	168	242	.694	174	332	506	98	178	1	61	137	34	951	7.2	1.4	13.6
80-81–New Jersey	63	–	1822	525	1070	.491	1	1	1.000	178	248	.718	120	361	481	105	216	6	58	182	52	1229	7.6	1.7	19.5
81-82–K.C.-Clev.	68	59	2175	518	1143	.453	0	4	.000	222	313	.709	174	435	609	120	222	4	88	149	103	1258	9.0	1.8	18.5
82-83–Cleveland	77	75	2601	587	1230	.477	0	5	.000	213	301	.708	190	666	856	145	272	7	61	224	58	1387	11.1	1.9	18.0
83-84–Cleveland	73	70	2402	533	1185	.450	1	2	.500	234	334	.701	156	597	753	185	195	2	51	187	32	1301	10.3	2.5	17.8
84-85–Washington	60	37	1870	422	896	.471	1	2	.500	158	213	.742	141	405	546	149	187	4	51	161	47	1003	9.1	2.5	16.7
85-86–Washington	78	78	2563	595	1255	.474	1	3	.333	269	353	.762	180	500	680	186	217	2	98	206	44	1460	8.7	2.4	18.7
86-87–Philadelphia	55	30	1586	338	729	.464	0	4	.000	139	184	.755	86	221	307	89	150	1	86	123	30	815	5.6	1.6	14.8
87-88–Philadelphia	62	51	2110	483	1041	.464	2	9	.222	210	293	.717	116	289	405	131	192	4	79	161	39	1178	6.5	2.1	19.0
88-89–Philadelphia	14	13	416	90	187	.481	0	1	.000	32	44	.727	19	56	75	32	37	0	17	34	2	212	5.4	2.3	15.1
91-92–L.A. Lakers	9	0	78	11	27	.407	0	1	.000	7	8	.875	7	12	19	9	4	0	5	7	0	29	2.1	1.0	3.2
Reg. Season Totals	629	413	19284	4493	9596	.468	7	36	.194	1830	2533	.722	1363	3874	5237	1249	1870	31	655	1571	441	10823	8.3	2.0	17.2
Playoff Totals	17	14	462	104	220	.473	0	0	–	42	66	.636	41	81	122	28	54	1	20	28	13	250	7.2	1.6	14.7

Robinson, David Maurice **(The Admiral)** b. August 6, 1965 Ht. 7-1 Wt. 250 College: Navy

SEASON–TEAM	G	GS	MIN	FGM	FGA	PCT	3FGM	3FGA	PCT	FTM	FTA	PCT	O-RB	D-RB	TOT	AST	PF	DQ	STL	TO	BLK	PTS	RPG	APG	PPG
89-90–San Antonio	82	81	3002	690	1300	.531	0	2	.000	613	837	.732	303	680	983	164	259	3	138	257	319	1993	12.0	2.0	24.3
90-91–San Antonio	82	81	3095	754	1366	.552	1	7	.143	592	777	.762	335	728	1063	208	264	5	127	270	320	2101	13.0	2.5	25.6
91-92–San Antonio	68	68	2564	592	1074	.551	1	8	.125	393	561	.701	261	568	829	181	219	2	158	182	305	1578	12.2	2.7	23.2
92-93–San Antonio	82	82	3211	676	1348	.501	3	17	.176	561	766	.732	229	727	956	301	239	5	127	241	264	1916	11.7	3.7	23.4
93-94–San Antonio	80	80	3241	840	1658	.507	10	29	.345	693	925	.749	241	614	855	381	228	3	139	253	265	2383	10.7	4.8	29.8
94-95–San Antonio	81	81	3074	788	1487	.530	6	20	.300	656	847	.774	234	643	877	236	230	2	134	233	262	2238	10.8	2.9	27.6
95-96–San Antonio	82	82	3019	711	1378	.516	3	9	.333	626	823	.761	319	681	1000	247	262	1	111	190	271	2051	12.2	3.0	25.0
96-97–San Antonio	6	6	147	36	72	.500	0	0	–	34	52	.654	19	32	51	8	9	0	6	8	6	106	8.5	1.3	17.7
97-98–San Antonio	73	73	2457	544	1065	.511	1	4	.250	485	660	.735	239	536	775	199	204	2	64	202	192	1574	10.6	2.7	21.6
98-99–San Antonio	49	49	1554	268	527	.509	0	1	.000	239	363	.658	148	344	492	103	143	0	69	108	119	775	10.0	2.1	15.8
99-00–San Antonio	80	80	2557	528	1031	.512	0	2	.000	371	511	.726	193	577	770	142	247	1	97	164	183	1427	9.6	1.8	17.8
Reg. Season Totals	765	763	27921	6427	12306	.522	25	99	.253	5263	7122	.739	2521	6130	8651	2170	2304	24	1170	2108	2506	18142	11.3	2.8	23.7
Playoff Totals	83	83	3192	620	1308	.474	1	9	.111	566	789	.717	277	696	973	232	304	6	113	226	247	1807	11.7	2.8	21.8
All-Star Totals	9	3	174	47	80	.588	0	0	–	39	55	.709	20	38	58	8	23	0	13	10	13	133	6.4	0.9	14.8

Robinson, Eddie b. April 19, 1976 Ht. 6-9 Wt. 210 College: Central Oklahoma

SEASON–TEAM	G	GS	MIN	FGM	FGA	PCT	3FGM	3FGA	PCT	FTM	FTA	PCT	O-RB	D-RB	TOT	AST	PF	DQ	STL	TO	BLK	PTS	RPG	APG	PPG
99-00–Charlotte	67	8	1112	212	386	.549	0	4	.000	47	64	.734	54	130	184	32	67	0	48	39	25	471	2.7	0.5	7.0
Reg. Season Totals	67	8	1112	212	386	.549	0	4	.000	47	64	.734	54	130	184	32	67	0	48	39	25	471	2.7	0.5	7.0
Playoff Totals	4	0	45	5	12	.417	0	0	–	2	2	1.000	1	2	3	4	2	0	2	1	1	12	0.8	1.0	3.0

Robinson, Flynn James b. April 28, 1941 Ht. 6-1 Wt. 190 College: Wyoming

SEASON–TEAM	G	GS	MIN	FGM	FGA	PCT	3FGM	3FGA	PCT	FTM	FTA	PCT	O-RB	D-RB	TOT	AST	PF	DQ	STL	TO	BLK	PTS	RPG	APG	PPG
66-67–Cincinnati	76	–	1140	274	599	.457	–	–	–	120	154	.779	–	–	133	110	197	3	–	–	–	668	1.8	1.4	8.8
67-68–Cin.-Chicago	75	–	2046	444	1010	.440	–	–	–	288	351	.821	–	–	272	219	184	1	–	–	–	1176	3.6	2.9	15.7
68-69–Chicago-Milw.	83	–	2616	625	1442	.433	–	–	–	412	491	.839	–	–	306	377	261	7	–	–	–	1662	3.7	4.5	20.0
69-70–Milwaukee	81	–	2762	663	1391	.477	–	–	–	439	489	.898	–	–	263	449	254	5	–	–	–	1765	3.2	5.5	21.8
70-71–Cincinnati	71	–	1368	374	817	.458	–	–	–	195	228	.855	–	–	143	138	161	0	–	–	–	943	2.0	1.9	13.3
71-72–Los Angeles	64	–	1007	262	535	.490	–	–	–	111	129	.860	–	–	115	138	139	2	–	–	–	635	1.8	2.2	9.9
72-73–L.A.-Balt.	44	–	630	133	288	.462	–	–	–	32	39	.821	–	–	62	85	71	0	–	–	–	298	1.4	1.9	6.8
73-74–San Diego (A)	49	–	779	185	405	.457	8	30	.267	52	68	.765	28	50	78	112	72	–	23	50	2	430	1.6	2.3	8.8
Reg. NBA Totals	494	–	11569	2775	6082	.456	–	–	–	1597	1881	.849	–	–	1294	1516	1267	18	–	–	–	7147	2.6	3.1	14.5
Reg. ABA Totals	49	–	779	185	405	.457	8	30	.267	52	68	.765	28	50	78	112	72	0	23	50	2	430	1.6	2.3	8.8
NBA Playoff Totals	27	–	626	129	318	.406	–	–	–	70	88	.795	–	–	54	76	57	0	–	–	–	328	2.0	2.8	12.1
NBA All-Star Totals	1	–	8	3	4	.750	–	–	–	0	0	–	–	–	1	2	2	0	–	–	–	6	1.0	2.0	6.0

Robinson, Glenn A. **(Big Dog)** b. January 10, 1973 Ht. 6-7 Wt. 230 College: Purdue

SEASON–TEAM	G	GS	MIN	FGM	FGA	PCT	3FGM	3FGA	PCT	FTM	FTA	PCT	O-RB	D-RB	TOT	AST	PF	DQ	STL	TO	BLK	PTS	RPG	APG	PPG
94-95–Milwaukee	80	76	2958	636	1410	.451	86	268	.321	397	499	.796	169	344	513	197	234	2	115	313	22	1755	6.4	2.5	21.9
95-96–Milwaukee	82	82	3249	627	1382	.454	90	263	.342	316	389	.812	136	368	504	293	236	2	95	282	42	1660	6.1	3.6	20.2
96-97–Milwaukee	80	79	3114	669	1438	.465	63	180	.350	288	364	.791	130	372	502	248	225	5	103	269	68	1689	6.3	3.1	21.1
97-98–Milwaukee	56	56	2294	534	1136	.470	25	65	.385	215	266	.808	82	225	307	158	164	2	69	200	34	1308	5.5	2.8	23.4
98-99–Milwaukee	47	47	1579	347	756	.459	31	79	.392	140	161	.870	73	203	276	100	114	1	46	106	41	865	5.9	2.1	18.4
99-00–Milwaukee	81	81	2909	690	1461	.472	86	237	.363	227	283	.802	107	378	485	193	212	3	78	223	41	1693	6.0	2.4	20.9
Reg. Season Totals	426	421	16103	3503	7583	.462	381	1092	.349	1583	1962	.807	697	1890	2587	1189	1185	15	506	1393	248	8970	6.1	2.8	21.1
Playoff Totals	8	8	292	53	130	.408	6	15	.400	27	31	.871	4	42	46	18	23	0	11	25	6	139	5.8	2.3	17.4
All-Star Totals	1	0	17	5	10	.500	0	0	–	0	0	–	2	4	6	0	0	0	0	0	0	10	6.0	0.0	10.0

Robinson, Jackie b. May 20, 1955 Ht. 6-6 Wt. 210 College: Nevada-Las Vegas

SEASON–TEAM	G	GS	MIN	FGM	FGA	PCT	3FGM	3FGA	PCT	FTM	FTA	PCT	O-RB	D-RB	TOT	AST	PF	DQ	STL	TO	BLK	PTS	RPG	APG	PPG
78-79–Seattle	12	–	105	19	41	.463	–	–	–	8	15	.533	9	10	19	13	9	0	5	11	1	46	1.6	1.1	3.8
79-80–Detroit	7	–	51	9	17	.529	0	1	.000	9	11	.818	3	2	5	0	8	0	3	2	3	27	0.7	0.0	3.9
81-82–Chicago	3	0	29	3	9	.333	0	0	–	4	4	1.000	3	0	3	0	1	0	0	1	0	10	1.0	0.0	3.3
Reg. Season Totals	22	0	185	31	67	.463	0	1	.000	21	30	.700	15	12	27	13	18	0	8	14	4	83	1.2	0.6	3.8

Robinson, James **(Hollywood)** b. August 31, 1970 Ht. 6-2 Wt. 180 College: Alabama

SEASON–TEAM	G	GS	MIN	FGM	FGA	PCT	3FGM	3FGA	PCT	FTM	FTA	PCT	O-RB	D-RB	TOT	AST	PF	DQ	STL	TO	BLK	PTS	RPG	APG	PPG
93-94–Portland	58	3	673	104	285	.365	23	73	.315	45	67	.672	34	44	78	68	69	0	30	52	15	276	1.3	1.2	4.8
94-95–Portland	71	25	1539	255	624	.409	76	223	.341	65	110	.591	42	90	132	180	142	0	48	127	13	651	1.9	2.5	9.2
95-96–Portland	76	5	1627	229	574	.399	102	284	.359	89	135	.659	44	113	157	150	146	0	34	111	16	649	2.1	2.0	8.5
96-97–Minnesota	69	5	1309	196	482	.407	102	267	.382	78	114	.684	24	88	112	126	125	1	30	69	8	572	1.6	1.8	8.3
97-98–L.A. Clippers	70	13	1231	195	501	.389	74	225	.329	77	107	.720	37	74	111	135	101	0	37	97	10	541	1.6	1.9	7.7
98-99–LAClips-Minn.	31	0	506	67	185	.362	21	74	.284	28	41	.683	18	44	62	56	60	0	22	44	8	183	2.0	1.8	5.9
Reg. Season Totals	375	51	6885	1046	2651	.395	398	1146	.347	382	574	.666	199	453	652	715	643	1	201	500	70	2872	1.7	1.9	7.7
Playoff Totals	14	0	99	15	39	.385	10	24	.417	1	2	.500	3	5	8	13	13	0	4	7	2	41	0.6	0.9	2.9

Robinson, Larry b. January 11, 1968 Ht. 6-3 Wt. 180 College: Eastern Oklahoma St. (J.C.); Centenary

SEASON–TEAM	G	GS	MIN	FGM	FGA	PCT	3FGM	3FGA	PCT	FTM	FTA	PCT	O-RB	D-RB	TOT	AST	PF	DQ	STL	TO	BLK	PTS	RPG	APG	PPG
90-91–G.S.-Wash.	36	10	425	62	150	.413	0	1	.000	15	27	.556	29	22	51	35	49	0	16	27	1	139	1.4	1.0	3.9
91-92–Boston	1	0	6	1	5	.200	0	0	–	0	0	–	2	0	2	1	3	0	0	1	0	2	2.0	1.0	2.0
92-93–Washington	4	0	33	6	16	.375	0	1	.000	3	5	.600	1	2	3	3	0	0	1	1	1	15	0.8	0.8	3.8
93-94–Houston	6	0	55	10	20	.500	2	8	.250	3	8	.375	4	6	10	6	8	0	7	10	0	25	1.7	1.0	4.2
97-98–Vancouver	6	0	41	6	19	.316	3	6	.500	2	2	1.000	2	10	12	1	0	0	4	2	0	17	2.0	0.2	2.8
Reg. Season Totals	53	10	560	85	210	.405	5	16	.313	23	42	.548	38	40	78	46	60	0	28	41	2	198	1.5	0.9	3.7

Robinson, Leonard Eugene (Truck) b. October 4, 1951 Ht. 6-7 Wt. 225 College: Tennessee State

SEASON–TEAM	G	GS	MIN	FGM	FGA	PCT	3FGM	3FGA	PCT	FTM	FTA	PCT	O-RB	D-RB	TOT	AST	PF	DQ	STL	TO	BLK	PTS	RPG	APG	PPG
74-75–Washington	76	–	995	191	393	.486	–	–	–	60	115	.522	94	207	301	40	132	0	36	–	32	442	4.0	0.5	5.8
75-76–Washington	82	–	2055	354	779	.454	–	–	–	211	314	.672	139	418	557	113	239	3	42	–	107	919	6.8	1.4	11.2
76-77–Wash.-Atlanta	77	–	2777	574	1200	.478	–	–	–	314	430	.730	252	576	828	142	253	3	66	–	38	1462	10.8	1.8	19.0
77-78–New Orleans	82	–	3638	748	1683	.444	–	–	–	366	572	.640	298	990	1288	171	265	5	73	301	79	1862	15.7	2.1	22.7
78-79–N.O.-Phoenix	69	–	2537	566	1152	.491	–	–	–	324	462	.701	195	607	802	113	206	2	46	233	75	1456	11.6	1.6	21.1
79-80–Phoenix	82	–	2710	545	1064	.512	0	0	–	325	487	.667	213	557	770	142	262	2	58	251	59	1415	9.4	1.7	17.3
80-81–Phoenix	82	–	3088	647	1280	.505	0	0	–	249	396	.629	216	573	789	206	220	1	68	250	38	1543	9.6	2.5	18.8
81-82–Phoenix	74	72	2745	579	1128	.513	1	1	1.000	255	371	.687	202	519	721	179	215	2	42	202	28	1414	9.7	2.4	19.1
82-83–New York	81	76	2426	326	706	.462	0	0	–	118	201	.587	199	458	657	145	241	4	57	190	24	770	8.1	1.8	9.5
83-84–New York	65	63	2135	284	581	.489	0	0	–	133	206	.646	171	374	545	94	217	6	43	160	27	701	8.4	1.4	10.8
84-85–New York	2	1	35	2	5	.400	0	0	–	0	2	.000	6	3	9	3	3	0	2	5	3	4	4.5	1.5	2.0
Reg. Season Totals	772	212	25141	4816	9971	.483	1	1	1.000	2355	3556	.662	1985	5282	7267	1348	2253	28	533	1592	510	11988	9.4	1.7	15.5
Playoff Totals	74	25	1736	241	538	.448	0	0	–	122	198	.616	151	354	505	77	204	3	47	103	46	604	6.8	1.0	8.2
All-Star Totals	2	0	45	6	13	.462	0	0	–	1	2	.500	4	7	11	3	6	0	0	7	0	13	5.5	1.5	6.5

Robinson, Oliver Leon Jr. b. March 13, 1960 Ht. 6-4 Wt. 185 College: Alabama-Birmingham

SEASON–TEAM	G	GS	MIN	FGM	FGA	PCT	3FGM	3FGA	PCT	FTM	FTA	PCT	O-RB	D-RB	TOT	AST	PF	DQ	STL	TO	BLK	PTS	RPG	APG	PPG
82-83–San Antonio	35	0	147	35	97	.361	1	11	.091	30	45	.667	6	11	17	21	18	0	4	13	2	101	0.5	0.6	2.9
Reg. Season Totals	35	0	147	35	97	.361	1	11	.091	30	45	.667	6	11	17	21	18	0	4	13	2	101	0.5	0.6	2.9

Robinson, Ronnie b. March 9, 1951 Ht. 6-8 Wt. 220 College: Memphis

SEASON–TEAM	G	GS	MIN	FGM	FGA	PCT	3FGM	3FGA	PCT	FTM	FTA	PCT	O-RB	D-RB	TOT	AST	PF	DQ	STL	TO	BLK	PTS	RPG	APG	PPG
73-74–Utah-Mem. (A)	62	–	1170	174	394	.442	0	1	.000	49	73	.671	103	178	281	49	123	–	20	68	9	397	4.5	0.8	6.4
74-75–Memphis (A)	10	–	102	18	38	.474	0	0	–	4	6	.667	10	17	27	4	14	–	5	7	0	40	2.7	0.4	4.0
Reg. ABA Totals	72	–	1272	192	432	.444	0	1	.000	53	79	.671	113	195	308	53	137	0	25	75	9	437	4.3	0.7	6.1

Robinson, Rumeal James (Meal Time) b. November 13, 1966 Ht. 6-2 Wt. 195 College: Michigan

SEASON–TEAM	G	GS	MIN	FGM	FGA	PCT	3FGM	3FGA	PCT	FTM	FTA	PCT	O-RB	D-RB	TOT	AST	PF	DQ	STL	TO	BLK	PTS	RPG	APG	PPG
90-91–Atlanta	47	16	674	108	242	.446	2	11	.182	47	80	.588	20	51	71	132	65	0	32	76	8	265	1.5	2.8	5.6
91-92–Atlanta	81	64	2220	423	928	.456	34	104	.327	175	275	.636	64	155	219	446	178	0	105	206	24	1055	2.7	5.5	13.0
92-93–New Jersey	80	28	1585	270	638	.423	20	56	.357	112	195	.574	49	110	159	323	169	2	96	140	12	672	2.0	4.0	8.4
93-94–N.J.-Cha.	31	0	396	55	152	.362	8	20	.400	13	29	.448	6	26	32	63	48	0	18	43	3	131	1.0	2.0	4.2
95-96–Portland	43	14	715	92	221	.416	30	79	.380	33	51	.647	19	59	78	142	79	1	26	72	5	247	1.8	3.3	5.7
96-97–L.A.L.-Phoe.-Port.	54	3	508	66	164	.402	18	56	.321	26	35	.743	6	41	47	73	60	0	24	43	2	176	0.9	1.4	3.3
Reg. Season Totals	336	125	6098	1014	2345	.432	112	326	.344	406	665	.611	164	442	606	1179	599	3	301	580	54	2546	1.8	3.5	7.6
Playoff Totals	16	5	216	32	78	.410	6	18	.333	7	12	.583	4	12	16	44	33	0	10	28	0	77	1.0	2.8	4.8

Robinson, Samuel Lee (Sam) b. January 1, 1948 Ht. 6-7 Wt. 200 College: Long Beach State

SEASON–TEAM	G	GS	MIN	FGM	FGA	PCT	3FGM	3FGA	PCT	FTM	FTA	PCT	O-RB	D-RB	TOT	AST	PF	DQ	STL	TO	BLK	PTS	RPG	APG	PPG
70-71–Floridians (A)	83	–	2172	405	896	.452	4	19	.211	103	134	.769	–	–	410	112	182	–	–	–	–	917	4.9	1.3	11.0
71-72–Floridians (A)	51	–	686	126	300	.420	0	2	.000	54	68	.794	–	–	136	48	70	–	–	24	–	306	2.7	0.9	6.0
Reg. ABA Totals	134	–	2858	531	1196	.444	4	21	.190	157	202	.777	–	–	546	160	252	–	–	24	–	1223	4.1	1.2	9.1
ABA Playoff Totals	10	–	192	42	90	.467	0	0	–	21	23	.913	–	–	41	8	28	–	–	3	–	105	4.1	0.8	10.5

Robinson, Wayne Howard b. April 19, 1958 Ht. 6-8 Wt. 217 College: Virginia Tech

SEASON–TEAM	G	GS	MIN	FGM	FGA	PCT	3FGM	3FGA	PCT	FTM	FTA	PCT	O-RB	D-RB	TOT	AST	PF	DQ	STL	TO	BLK	PTS	RPG	APG	PPG
80-81–Detroit	81	–	1592	234	509	.460	0	6	.000	175	240	.729	117	177	294	112	186	2	46	149	24	643	3.6	1.4	7.9
Reg. Season Totals	81	–	1592	234	509	.460	0	6	.000	175	240	.729	117	177	294	112	186	2	46	149	24	643	3.6	1.4	7.9

Robinson, Wilbert Jr. (Wil) b. December 25, 1949 Ht. 6-2 Wt. 175 College: West Virginia

SEASON–TEAM	G	GS	MIN	FGM	FGA	PCT	3FGM	3FGA	PCT	FTM	FTA	PCT	O-RB	D-RB	TOT	AST	PF	DQ	STL	TO	BLK	PTS	RPG	APG	PPG
73-74–Memphis (A)	45	–	956	166	402	.413	0	6	.000	57	67	.851	28	51	79	132	124	–	51	92	9	389	1.8	2.9	8.6
Reg. ABA Totals	45	–	956	166	402	.413	0	6	.000	57	67	.851	28	51	79	132	124	0	51	92	9	389	1.8	2.9	8.6

Robinzine, William Clintard (Bill) b. January 20, 1953 d. September 16, 1982 Ht. 6-7 Wt. 230 College: DePaul

SEASON–TEAM	G	GS	MIN	FGM	FGA	PCT	3FGM	3FGA	PCT	FTM	FTA	PCT	O-RB	D-RB	TOT	AST	PF	DQ	STL	TO	BLK	PTS	RPG	APG	PPG
75-76–Kansas City	75	–	1327	229	499	.459	–	–	–	145	198	.732	128	227	355	60	290	19	80	–	8	603	4.7	0.8	8.0
76-77–Kansas City	75	–	1594	307	677	.453	–	–	–	159	216	.736	164	310	474	95	283	7	86	–	13	773	6.3	1.3	10.3
77-78–Kansas City	82	–	1748	305	677	.451	–	–	–	206	271	.760	173	366	539	72	281	5	74	172	11	816	6.6	0.9	10.0
78-79–Kansas City	82	–	2179	459	837	.548	–	–	–	180	246	.732	218	420	638	104	367	16	105	179	15	1098	7.8	1.3	13.4
79-80–Kansas City	81	–	1917	362	723	.501	1	2	.500	200	274	.730	184	342	526	62	311	5	106	148	23	925	6.5	0.8	11.4
80-81–Clev.-Dallas	78	–	2016	392	826	.475	1	6	.167	218	281	.776	168	365	533	118	275	6	75	187	9	1003	6.8	1.5	12.9
81-82–Utah	56	9	651	131	294	.446	0	0	–	61	75	.813	56	88	144	49	156	5	37	83	5	323	2.6	0.9	5.8
Reg. Season Totals	529	9	11432	2185	4533	.482	2	8	.250	1169	1561	.749	1091	2118	3209	560	1963	63	563	769	84	5541	6.1	1.1	10.5
Playoff Totals	8	0	187	35	75	.467	0	0	–	13	18	.722	22	32	54	3	26	1	16	14	0	83	6.8	0.4	10.4

Robisch, David George (Dave, Robo) b. December 22, 1949 Ht. 6-10 Wt. 235 College: Kansas

SEASON–TEAM	G	GS	MIN	FGM	FGA	PCT	3FGM	3FGA	PCT	FTM	FTA	PCT	O-RB	D-RB	TOT	AST	PF	DQ	STL	TO	BLK	PTS	RPG	APG	PPG
71-72–Denver (A)	84	–	2420	505	1138	.444	0	5	.000	294	419	.702	–	–	804	201	251	–	–	113	–	1304	9.6	2.4	15.5
72-73–Denver (A)	83	–	2647	521	1010	.516	0	1	.000	309	409	.756	248	496	744	170	271	8	–	134	–	1351	9.0	2.0	16.3
73-74–Denver (A)	84	–	2469	449	950	.473	0	0	–	318	411	.774	217	491	708	152	225	–	45	103	66	1216	8.4	1.8	14.5
74-75–Denver (A)	84	–	1899	392	779	.503	0	1	.000	304	346	.879	161	342	503	153	205	–	46	108	48	1088	6.0	1.8	13.0
75-76–S.D.-Ind. (A)	87	–	2789	436	1033	.422	0	3	.000	324	381	.850	281	513	794	166	200	–	71	113	59	1196	9.1	1.9	13.7
76-77–Indiana	80	–	1966	369	811	.455	–	–	–	213	256	.832	171	383	554	158	169	1	55	–	37	951	6.9	2.0	11.9
77-78–Indiana-L.A.	78	–	1277	177	430	.412	–	–	–	100	129	.775	100	252	352	88	130	1	39	71	29	454	4.5	1.1	5.8
78-79–Los Angeles	80	–	1219	150	336	.446	–	–	–	86	115	.748	82	203	285	97	108	0	20	53	25	386	3.6	1.2	4.8
79-80–Cleveland	82	–	2670	489	940	.520	0	3	.000	277	329	.842	225	433	658	192	211	2	53	138	53	1255	8.0	2.3	15.3
80-81–Clev.-Denver	84	–	2116	330	740	.446	0	0	–	200	247	.810	157	342	499	173	173	0	37	83	34	860	5.9	2.1	10.2
81-82–Denver	12	0	257	48	106	.453	0	0	–	48	55	.873	14	49	63	32	29	0	3	13	4	144	5.3	2.7	12.0
82-83–Denver	61	0	711	96	251	.382	0	1	.000	92	118	.780	34	117	151	53	61	0	10	45	9	284	2.5	0.9	4.7
83-84–Denver-S.A.-K.C.	31	0	340	35	96	.365	0	0	–	22	26	.846	15	43	58	20	36	1	3	12	2	92	1.9	0.6	3.0
Reg. NBA Totals	508	0	10556	1694	3710	.457	0	4	.000	1038	1275	.814	798	1822	2620	813	917	5	220	415	193	4426	5.2	1.6	8.7
Reg. ABA Totals	422	–	12224	2303	4910	.469	0	10	.000	1549	1966	.788	907	1842	3553	842	1152	8	162	571	173	6155	8.4	2.0	14.6
NBA Playoff Totals	14	0	152	21	48	.438	0	0	–	7	11	.636	17	29	46	6	18	0	2	8	2	49	3.3	0.4	3.5
ABA Playoff Totals	28	–	909	174	401	.434	0	0	–	116	152	.763	97	165	262	53	85	0	14	30	8	464	9.4	1.9	16.6

Rocha, Ephraim J. (Red) b. September 18, 1923 Ht. 6-9 Wt. 185 College: Hawaii; Oregon State

SEASON–TEAM	G	GS	MIN	FGM	FGA	PCT	3FGM	3FGA	PCT	FTM	FTA	PCT	O-RB	D-RB	TOT	AST	PF	DQ	STL	TO	BLK	PTS	RPG	APG	PPG
47-48–St. Louis	48	–	–	232	740	.314	–	–	–	147	213	.690	–	–	–	39	209	–	–	–	–	611	–	0.8	12.7
48-49–St. Louis	58	–	–	223	574	.389	–	–	–	162	211	.768	–	–	–	157	251	–	–	–	–	608	–	2.7	10.5
49-50–St. Louis	65	–	–	275	679	.405	–	–	–	220	313	.703	–	–	–	155	257	–	–	–	–	770	–	2.4	11.8
50-51–Baltimore	64	–	–	297	843	.352	–	–	–	242	299	.809	–	–	511	147	242	9	–	–	–	836	8.0	2.3	13.1
51-52–Syracuse	66	–	2543	300	749	.401	–	–	–	254	330	.770	–	–	549	128	249	4	–	–	–	854	8.3	1.9	12.9
52-53–Syracuse	69	–	2454	268	690	.388	–	–	–	234	310	.755	–	–	510	137	257	5	–	–	–	770	7.4	2.0	11.2
54-55–Syracuse	72	–	2473	295	801	.368	–	–	–	222	284	.782	–	–	489	178	242	5	–	–	–	812	6.8	2.5	11.3
55-56–Syracuse	72	–	1883	250	692	.361	–	–	–	220	281	.783	–	–	416	131	244	6	–	–	–	720	5.8	1.8	10.0
56-57–Fort Wayne	72	–	1154	136	390	.349	–	–	–	109	144	.757	–	–	272	81	162	1	–	–	–	381	3.8	1.1	5.3
Reg. Season Totals	586	–	10507	2276	6158	.370	–	–	–	1810	2385	.759	–	–	2747	1153	2113	30	–	–	–	6362	6.6	2.0	10.9
Playoff Totals	39	–	1153	165	473	.357	–	–	–	141	190	.742	–	–	197	64	172	10	–	–	–	471	6.6	1.6	12.1
All-Star Totals	2	–	28	7	21	.333	–	–	–	6	6	1.000	–	–	7	5	6	0	–	–	–	20	3.5	2.5	10.0

Roche, John Michael (Johnny) b. September 26, 1949 Ht. 6-3 Wt. 170 College: South Carolina

SEASON–TEAM	G	GS	MIN	FGM	FGA	PCT	3FGM	3FGA	PCT	FTM	FTA	PCT	O-RB	D-RB	TOT	AST	PF	DQ	STL	TO	BLK	PTS	RPG	APG	PPG
71-72–New York (A)	82	–	2593	403	859	.469	12	35	.343	240	311	.772	–	–	172	259	211	–	–	188	–	1058	2.1	3.2	12.9
72-73–New York (A)	77	–	2615	404	909	.444	34	103	.330	265	347	.764	33	113	146	348	170	0	–	207	–	1107	1.9	4.5	14.4
73-74–N.Y.-Ken. (A)	84	–	2180	397	829	.479	36	105	.343	148	177	.836	34	88	122	363	157	–	57	184	15	978	1.5	4.3	11.6
74-75–Ken.-Utah (A)	58	–	1387	241	509	.473	13	44	.295	85	106	.802	21	72	93	191	103	–	49	105	7	580	1.6	3.3	10.0
75-76–Utah (A)	16	–	484	112	212	.528	9	26	.346	31	41	.756	5	20	25	79	47	–	14	51	1	264	1.6	4.9	16.5
75-76–Los Angeles	15	–	52	3	14	.214	–	–	–	2	4	.500	0	3	3	6	7	0	0	–	0	8	0.2	0.4	0.5
79-80–Denver	82	–	2286	354	741	.478	49	129	.380	175	202	.866	24	91	115	405	139	0	82	159	12	932	1.4	4.9	11.4
80-81–Denver	26	–	611	82	179	.458	9	27	.333	58	77	.753	5	32	37	140	44	0	17	52	8	231	1.4	5.4	8.9
81-82–Denver	39	2	501	68	150	.453	23	52	.442	28	38	.737	4	19	23	89	40	0	15	29	2	187	0.6	2.3	4.8
Reg. NBA Totals	162	2	3450	507	1084	.468	81	208	.389	263	321	.819	33	145	178	640	230	0	114	240	22	1358	1.1	4.0	8.4
Reg. ABA Totals	317	–	9259	1557	3318	.469	104	313	.332	769	982	.783	93	293	558	1240	688	0	120	735	23	3987	1.8	3.9	12.6
ABA Playoff Totals	36	–	1239	259	543	.477	27	65	.415	115	156	.737	11	13	56	164	71	0	12	95	4	660	1.6	4.6	18.3

Rock, Eugene (Gene) b. November 4, 1921 Ht. 5-9 Wt. 155 College: USC

SEASON–TEAM	G	GS	MIN	FGM	FGA	PCT	3FGM	3FGA	PCT	FTM	FTA	PCT	O-RB	D-RB	TOT	AST	PF	DQ	STL	TO	BLK	PTS	RPG	APG	PPG
47-48–Chicago	11	–	–	4	18	.222	–	–	–	2	4	.500	–	–	–	0	8	–	–	–	–	10	–	0.0	0.9
Reg. Season Totals	11	–	–	4	18	.222	–	–	–	2	4	.500	–	–	–	0	8	–	–	–	–	10	–	0.0	0.9
Playoff Totals	2	–	–	0	0	–	–	–	–	0	1	.000	–	–	–	–	0	–	–	–	–	0	–	–	0.0

Rocker, Jack L. b. August 12, 1922 Ht. 6-5 Wt. 185 College: California

SEASON–TEAM	G	GS	MIN	FGM	FGA	PCT	3FGM	3FGA	PCT	FTM	FTA	PCT	O-RB	D-RB	TOT	AST	PF	DQ	STL	TO	BLK	PTS	RPG	APG	PPG
47-48–Minneapolis (N)	5	–	–	2	–	–	–	–	–	0	0	–	–	–	–	–	–	–	–	–	–	4	–	–	0.8
47-48–Philadelphia	9	–	–	8	22	.364	–	–	–	1	1	1.000	–	–	–	3	2	–	–	–	–	17	–	0.3	1.9
Reg. NBA Totals	9	–	–	8	22	.364	–	–	–	1	1	1.000	–	–	–	3	2	–	–	–	–	17	–	0.3	1.9
Reg. NBL Totals	5	–	–	2	–	–	–	–	–	0	0	–	–	–	–	–	–	–	–	–	–	4	–	–	0.8

Rodgers, Guy William Jr. b. September 1, 1935 Ht. 6-0 Wt. 185 College: Temple

SEASON–TEAM	G	GS	MIN	FGM	FGA	PCT	3FGM	3FGA	PCT	FTM	FTA	PCT	O-RB	D-RB	TOT	AST	PF	DQ	STL	TO	BLK	PTS	RPG	APG	PPG
58-59–Philadelphia	45	–	1565	211	535	.394	–	–	–	61	112	.545	–	–	281	261	132	1	–	–	–	483	6.2	5.8	10.7
59-60–Philadelphia	68	–	2483	338	870	.389	–	–	–	111	181	.613	–	–	391	482	196	3	–	–	–	787	5.8	7.1	11.6
60-61–Philadelphia	78	–	2905	397	1029	.386	–	–	–	206	300	.687	–	–	509	677	262	3	–	–	–	1000	6.5	8.7	12.8
61-62–Philadelphia	80	–	2650	267	749	.356	–	–	–	121	182	.665	–	–	348	643	312	12	–	–	–	655	4.4	8.0	8.2
62-63–San Francisco	79	–	3249	445	1150	.387	–	–	–	208	286	.727	–	–	394	825	296	7	–	–	–	1098	5.0	10.4	13.9
63-64–San Francisco	79	–	2695	337	923	.365	–	–	–	198	280	.707	–	–	328	556	245	4	–	–	–	872	4.2	7.0	11.0
64-65–San Francisco	79	–	2699	465	1225	.380	–	–	–	223	325	.686	–	–	323	565	256	4	–	–	–	1153	4.1	7.2	14.6
65-66–San Francisco	79	–	2902	586	1571	.373	–	–	–	296	407	.727	–	–	421	846	241	6	–	–	–	1468	5.3	10.7	18.6
66-67–Chicago	81	–	3063	538	1377	.391	–	–	–	383	475	.806	–	–	346	908	243	1	–	–	–	1459	4.3	11.2	18.0
67-68–Chicago-Cin.	79	–	1546	148	426	.347	–	–	–	107	133	.805	–	–	150	380	167	1	–	–	–	403	1.9	4.8	5.1
68-69–Milwaukee	81	–	2157	325	862	.377	–	–	–	184	232	.793	–	–	226	561	207	2	–	–	–	834	2.8	6.9	10.3
69-70–Milwaukee	64	–	749	68	191	.356	–	–	–	67	90	.744	–	–	74	213	73	1	–	–	–	203	1.2	3.3	3.2
Reg. Season Totals	892	–	28663	4125	10908	.378	–	–	–	2165	3003	.721	–	–	3791	6917	2630	45	–	–	–	10415	4.3	7.8	11.7
Playoff Totals	46	–	1557	198	565	.350	–	–	–	112	175	.640	–	–	257	286	176	9	–	–	–	508	5.6	6.2	11.0
All-Star Totals	4	–	101	10	27	.370	–	–	–	2	3	.667	–	–	13	25	13	0	–	–	–	22	3.3	6.3	5.5

Rodgers, Willie Daniel b. September 11, 1945 Ht. 6-3 Wt. 195 College: Oklahoma

SEASON–TEAM	G	GS	MIN	FGM	FGA	PCT	3FGM	3FGA	PCT	FTM	FTA	PCT	O-RB	D-RB	TOT	AST	PF	DQ	STL	TO	BLK	PTS	RPG	APG	PPG
68-69–Denver (A)	40	–	294	27	80	.338	0	3	.000	31	52	.596	–	–	47	16	51	1	–	30	–	85	1.2	0.4	2.1
Reg. ABA Totals	40	–	294	27	80	.338	0	3	.000	31	52	.596	–	–	47	16	51	1	–	30	–	85	1.2	0.4	2.1

Rodman, Dennis Keith (The Worm) b. May 13, 1961 Ht. 6-8 Wt. 220 College: Southeastern Oklahoma State

SEASON–TEAM	G	GS	MIN	FGM	FGA	PCT	3FGM	3FGA	PCT	FTM	FTA	PCT	O-RB	D-RB	TOT	AST	PF	DQ	STL	TO	BLK	PTS	RPG	APG	PPG
86-87–Detroit	77	1	1155	213	391	.545	0	1	.000	74	126	.587	163	169	332	56	166	1	38	93	48	500	4.3	0.7	6.5
87-88–Detroit	82	32	2147	398	709	.561	5	17	.294	152	284	.535	318	397	715	110	273	5	75	156	45	953	8.7	1.3	11.6
88-89–Detroit	82	8	2208	316	531	.595	6	26	.231	97	155	.626	327	445	772	99	292	4	55	126	76	735	9.4	1.2	9.0
89-90–Detroit	82	43	2377	288	496	.581	1	9	.111	142	217	.654	336	456	792	72	276	2	52	90	60	719	9.7	0.9	8.8
90-91–Detroit	82	77	2747	276	560	.493	6	30	.200	111	176	.631	361	665	1026	85	281	7	65	94	55	669	12.5	1.0	8.2
91-92–Detroit	82	80	3301	342	635	.539	32	101	.317	84	140	.600	523	1007	1530	191	248	0	68	140	70	800	18.7	2.3	9.8
92-93–Detroit	62	55	2410	183	429	.427	15	73	.205	87	163	.534	367	765	1132	102	201	0	48	103	45	468	18.3	1.6	7.5
93-94–San Antonio	79	51	2989	156	292	.534	5	24	.208	53	102	.520	453	914	1367	184	229	0	52	138	32	370	17.3	2.3	4.7
94-95–San Antonio	49	26	1568	137	240	.571	0	2	.000	75	111	.676	274	549	823	97	159	1	31	98	23	349	16.8	2.0	7.1
95-96–Chicago	64	57	2088	146	304	.480	3	27	.111	56	106	.528	356	596	952	160	196	1	36	138	27	351	14.9	2.5	5.5
96-97–Chicago	55	54	1947	128	286	.448	5	19	.263	50	88	.568	320	563	883	170	172	1	32	111	19	311	16.1	3.1	5.7
97-98–Chicago	80	66	2856	155	360	.431	4	23	.174	61	111	.550	421	780	1201	230	238	2	47	147	18	375	15.0	2.9	4.7
98-99–L.A. Lakers	23	11	657	16	46	.348	0	2	.000	17	39	.436	62	196	258	30	71	0	10	31	12	49	11.2	1.3	2.1
99-00–Dallas	12	12	389	12	31	.387	0	1	.000	10	14	.714	48	123	171	14	41	2	2	19	1	34	14.3	1.2	2.8
Reg. Season Totals	911	573	28839	2766	5310	.521	82	355	.231	1069	1832	.584	4329	7625	11954	1600	2843	26	611	1484	531	6683	13.1	1.8	7.3
Playoff Totals	169	89	4789	442	902	.490	7	47	.149	190	352	.540	626	1050	1676	205	630	12	106	258	97	1081	9.9	1.2	6.4
All-Star Totals	2	0	36	4	11	.364	0	0	–	0	0	–	10	7	17	1	2	0	1	4	1	8	8.5	0.5	4.0

Roe, Louis Marquel (Lou) b. July 14, 1972 Ht. 6-7 Wt. 220 College: Massachusetts

SEASON–TEAM	G	GS	MIN	FGM	FGA	PCT	3FGM	3FGA	PCT	FTM	FTA	PCT	O-RB	D-RB	TOT	AST	PF	DQ	STL	TO	BLK	PTS	RPG	APG	PPG
95-96–Detroit	49	2	372	32	90	.356	2	9	.222	24	32	.750	30	48	78	15	42	0	10	17	8	90	1.6	0.3	1.8
96-97–Golden State	17	0	107	14	48	.292	3	11	.273	9	19	.474	7	7	14	6	10	0	3	11	1	40	0.8	0.4	2.4
Reg. Season Totals	66	2	479	46	138	.333	5	20	.250	33	51	.647	37	55	92	21	52	0	13	28	9	130	1.4	0.3	2.0
Playoff Totals	2	0	7	0	1	.000	0	0	–	0	0	–	1	1	2	–	1	0	1	0	0	0	1.0	0.0	0.0

Rogers, Carlos Deon b. February 6, 1971 Ht. 6-11 Wt. 232 College: Tennessee State

SEASON–TEAM	G	GS	MIN	FGM	FGA	PCT	3FGM	3FGA	PCT	FTM	FTA	PCT	O-RB	D-RB	TOT	AST	PF	DQ	STL	TO	BLK	PTS	RPG	APG	PPG
94-95–Golden State	49	18	1017	180	340	.529	2	14	.143	76	146	.521	108	170	278	37	124	2	22	84	52	438	5.7	0.8	8.9
95-96–Toronto	56	18	1043	178	344	.517	3	21	.143	71	130	.546	80	90	170	35	87	0	25	61	48	430	3.0	0.6	7.7
96-97–Toronto	56	3	1397	212	404	.525	25	66	.379	102	170	.600	120	184	304	37	140	1	42	53	69	551	5.4	0.7	9.8
97-98–Toronto-Port.	21	0	376	47	91	.516	0	2	.000	18	32	.563	35	32	67	18	35	0	10	14	8	112	3.2	0.9	5.3
98-99–Portland	2	0	8	2	2	1.000	0	0	–	1	4	.250	0	1	1	1	2	0	0	0	0	5	0.5	0.5	2.5
99-00–Houston	53	15	1101	170	324	.525	1	14	.071	81	137	.591	98	177	275	42	77	0	14	63	34	422	5.2	0.8	8.0
Reg. Season Totals	237	54	4942	789	1505	.524	31	117	.265	349	619	.564	441	654	1095	170	465	3	113	275	211	1958	4.6	0.7	8.3

Rogers, Harry J. (Tree) b. December 31, 1950 Ht. 6-7 Wt. 195 College: St. Louis

SEASON–TEAM	G	GS	MIN	FGM	FGA	PCT	3FGM	3FGA	PCT	FTM	FTA	PCT	O-RB	D-RB	TOT	AST	PF	DQ	STL	TO	BLK	PTS	RPG	APG	PPG
75-76–St. Louis (A)	18	–	298	60	124	.484	0	2	.000	17	24	.708	38	58	96	15	34	–	12	21	6	137	5.3	0.8	7.6
Reg. ABA Totals	18	–	298	60	124	.484	0	2	.000	17	24	.708	38	58	96	15	34	–	12	21	6	137	5.3	0.8	7.6

Rogers, John Bernard (Johnny) b. December 30, 1963 Ht. 6-10 Wt. 230 College: Stanford; California-Irvine

SEASON–TEAM	G	GS	MIN	FGM	FGA	PCT	3FGM	3FGA	PCT	FTM	FTA	PCT	O-RB	D-RB	TOT	AST	PF	DQ	STL	TO	BLK	PTS	RPG	APG	PPG
86-87–Sacramento	45	15	468	90	185	.486	0	5	.000	9	15	.600	30	47	77	26	66	0	9	20	8	189	1.7	0.6	4.2
87-88–Cleveland	24	0	168	26	61	.426	0	2	.000	10	13	.769	8	19	27	3	23	0	4	10	3	62	1.1	0.1	2.6
Reg. Season Totals	69	15	636	116	246	.472	0	7	.000	19	28	.679	38	66	104	29	89	0	13	30	11	251	1.5	0.4	3.6

Rogers, Marshall Lee b. August 27, 1953 Ht. 6-1 Wt. 190 College: Texas-Pan American

SEASON–TEAM	G	GS	MIN	FGM	FGA	PCT	3FGM	3FGA	PCT	FTM	FTA	PCT	O-RB	D-RB	TOT	AST	PF	DQ	STL	TO	BLK	PTS	RPG	APG	PPG
76-77–Golden State	26	–	176	43	116	.371	–	–	–	14	15	.933	6	5	11	10	33	0	8	–	3	100	0.4	0.4	3.8
Reg. Season Totals	26	–	176	43	116	.371	–	–	–	14	15	.933	6	5	11	10	33	0	8	–	3	100	0.4	0.4	3.8
Playoff Totals	1	–	3	0	2	.000	–	–	–	2	2	1.000	0	1	1	–	0	0	0	–	0	2	1.0	0.0	2.0

Rogers, Rodney Ray Jr. b. June 20, 1971 Ht. 6-7 Wt. 255 College: Wake Forest

SEASON–TEAM	G	GS	MIN	FGM	FGA	PCT	3FGM	3FGA	PCT	FTM	FTA	PCT	O-RB	D-RB	TOT	AST	PF	DQ	STL	TO	BLK	PTS	RPG	APG	PPG
93-94–Denver	79	14	1406	239	545	.439	35	92	.380	127	189	.672	90	136	226	101	195	3	63	131	48	640	2.9	1.3	8.1
94-95–Denver	80	77	2142	375	769	.488	50	148	.338	179	275	.651	132	253	385	161	281	7	95	173	46	979	4.8	2.0	12.2
95-96–L.A. Clippers	67	51	1950	306	641	.477	49	153	.320	113	180	.628	113	173	286	167	216	2	75	144	35	774	4.3	2.5	11.6
96-97–L.A. Clippers	81	62	2480	408	884	.462	65	180	.361	191	288	.663	137	274	411	222	272	5	88	221	61	1072	5.1	2.7	13.2
97-98–L.A. Clippers	76	70	2499	426	935	.456	72	212	.340	225	328	.686	155	269	424	202	242	5	93	193	38	1149	5.6	2.7	15.1
98-99–L.A. Clippers	47	7	968	131	297	.441	18	63	.286	68	101	.673	65	114	179	77	140	2	47	66	22	348	3.8	1.6	7.4
99-00–Phoenix	82	7	2286	428	881	.486	115	262	.439	159	249	.639	138	309	447	170	290	5	94	163	47	1130	5.5	2.1	13.8
Reg. Season Totals	512	288	13731	2313	4952	.467	404	1110	.364	1062	1610	.660	830	1528	2358	1100	1636	29	555	1091	297	6092	4.6	2.1	11.9
Playoff Totals	27	6	614	91	215	.423	17	69	.246	47	70	.671	28	73	101	41	82	2	24	35	23	246	3.7	1.5	9.1

Rogers, Roy Jr. b. August 19, 1973 Ht. 6-10 Wt. 235 College: Alabama

SEASON–TEAM	G	GS	MIN	FGM	FGA	PCT	3FGM	3FGA	PCT	FTM	FTA	PCT	O-RB	D-RB	TOT	AST	PF	DQ	STL	TO	BLK	PTS	RPG	APG	PPG
96-97–Vancouver	82	50	1848	244	483	.505	1	1	1.000	54	94	.574	139	247	386	46	214	1	21	86	163	543	4.7	0.6	6.6
97-98–Boston-Toronto	15	0	106	9	25	.360	0	0	–	2	6	.333	8	9	17	2	18	0	3	5	8	20	1.1	0.1	1.3
99-00–Denver	40	0	355	35	88	.398	0	1	.000	19	41	.463	33	47	80	9	36	0	2	10	38	89	2.0	0.2	2.2
Reg. Season Totals	137	50	2309	288	596	.483	1	2	.500	75	141	.532	180	303	483	57	268	1	26	101	209	652	3.5	0.4	4.8

Roges, Albert A. (Al) b. October 25, 1930 Ht. 6-4 Wt. 195 College: Los Angeles City (Calif.) Coll. (J.C.); Long Island University

SEASON–TEAM	G	GS	MIN	FGM	FGA	PCT	3FGM	3FGA	PCT	FTM	FTA	PCT	O-RB	D-RB	TOT	AST	PF	DQ	STL	TO	BLK	PTS	RPG	APG	PPG
53-54–Baltimore	67	–	1937	220	614	.358	–	–	–	130	179	.726	–	–	213	160	177	1	–	–	–	570	3.2	2.4	8.5
54-55–Balt.-FtWayne	17	–	201	23	61	.377	–	–	–	15	24	.625	–	–	24	19	20	0	–	–	–	61	1.4	1.1	3.6
Reg. Season Totals	84	–	2138	243	675	.360	–	–	–	145	203	.714	–	–	237	179	197	1	–	–	–	631	2.8	2.1	7.5

Rohloff, Kenneth Lawrance (Ken) b. April 18, 1939 Ht. 6-0 Wt. 195 College: North Carolina State

SEASON–TEAM	G	GS	MIN	FGM	FGA	PCT	3FGM	3FGA	PCT	FTM	FTA	PCT	O-RB	D-RB	TOT	AST	PF	DQ	STL	TO	BLK	PTS	RPG	APG	PPG
63-64–St. Louis	2	–	7	0	1	.000	–	–	–	0	0	–	–	–	0	1	4	0	–	–	–	0	0.0	0.5	0.0
Reg. Season Totals	2	–	7	0	1	.000	–	–	–	0	0	–	–	–	0	1	4	0	–	–	–	0	0.0	0.5	0.0

Rollins, Kenneth H. (Kenny) b. September 14, 1923 Ht. 6-0 Wt. 170 College: Kentucky

SEASON–TEAM	G	GS	MIN	FGM	FGA	PCT	3FGM	3FGA	PCT	FTM	FTA	PCT	O-RB	D-RB	TOT	AST	PF	DQ	STL	TO	BLK	PTS	RPG	APG	PPG
48-49–Chicago	59	–	–	144	520	.277	–	–	–	77	104	.740	–	–	–	167	150	–	–	–	–	365	–	2.8	6.2
49-50–Chicago	66	–	–	144	421	.342	–	–	–	66	89	.742	–	–	–	131	129	–	–	–	–	354	–	2.0	5.4
52-53–Boston	43	–	426	38	115	.330	–	–	–	22	27	.815	–	–	45	46	63	1	–	–	–	98	1.0	1.1	2.3
Reg. Season Totals	168	–	426	326	1056	.309	–	–	–	165	220	.750	–	–	45	344	342	1	–	–	–	817	1.0	2.0	4.9
Playoff Totals	10	–	65	6	33	.182	–	–	–	8	8	1.000	–	–	8	11	20	0	–	–	–	20	1.3	0.8	2.0

Rollins, Philip Lee (Phil) b. January 19, 1934 Ht. 6-2 Wt. 190 College: Louisville

SEASON–TEAM	G	GS	MIN	FGM	FGA	PCT	3FGM	3FGA	PCT	FTM	FTA	PCT	O-RB	D-RB	TOT	AST	PF	DQ	STL	TO	BLK	PTS	RPG	APG	PPG
58-59–Phil.-Cin.	44	–	691	83	231	.359	–	–	–	63	90	.700	–	–	118	102	49	0	–	–	–	229	2.7	2.3	5.2
59-60–Cincinnati	72	–	1235	158	386	.409	–	–	–	77	127	.606	–	–	180	233	150	1	–	–	–	393	2.5	3.2	5.5
60-61–Cin.-St. L.-N.Y.	60	–	816	109	293	.372	–	–	–	58	88	.659	–	–	97	123	121	1	–	–	–	276	1.6	2.1	4.6
Reg. Season Totals	176	–	2742	350	910	.385	–	–	–	198	305	.649	–	–	395	458	320	2	–	–	–	898	2.2	2.6	5.1

Rollins, Wayne Monte (Tree) b. June 16, 1955 Ht. 7-1 Wt. 255 College: Clemson

SEASON–TEAM	G	GS	MIN	FGM	FGA	PCT	3FGM	3FGA	PCT	FTM	FTA	PCT	O-RB	D-RB	TOT	AST	PF	DQ	STL	TO	BLK	PTS	RPG	APG	PPG
77-78–Atlanta	80	–	1795	253	520	.487	–	–	–	104	148	.703	179	373	552	79	326	16	57	121	218	610	6.9	1.0	7.6
78-79–Atlanta	81	–	1900	297	555	.535	–	–	–	89	141	.631	219	369	588	49	328	19	46	87	254	683	7.3	0.6	8.4
79-80–Atlanta	82	–	2123	287	514	.558	0	0	–	157	220	.714	283	491	774	76	322	12	54	99	244	731	9.4	0.9	8.9
80-81–Atlanta	40	–	1044	116	210	.552	0	1	.000	46	57	.807	102	184	286	35	151	7	29	57	117	278	7.2	0.9	7.0
81-82–Atlanta	79	39	2018	202	346	.584	0	0	–	79	129	.612	168	443	611	59	285	4	35	79	224	483	7.7	0.7	6.1
82-83–Atlanta	80	80	2472	261	512	.510	0	1	.000	98	135	.726	210	533	743	75	294	7	49	95	343	620	9.3	0.9	7.8
83-84–Atlanta	77	76	2351	274	529	.518	0	0	–	118	190	.621	200	393	593	62	297	9	35	101	277	666	7.7	0.8	8.6
84-85–Atlanta	70	60	1750	186	339	.549	0	0	–	67	93	.720	113	329	442	52	213	6	35	80	167	439	6.3	0.7	6.3
85-86–Atlanta	74	61	1781	173	347	.499	0	1	.000	69	90	.767	131	327	458	41	239	5	38	91	167	415	6.2	0.6	5.6
86-87–Atlanta	75	58	1764	171	313	.546	0	0	–	63	87	.724	155	333	488	22	240	1	43	61	140	405	6.5	0.3	5.4
87-88–Atlanta	76	59	1765	133	260	.512	0	0	–	70	80	.875	142	317	459	20	229	2	31	51	132	336	6.0	0.3	4.4
88-89–Cleveland	60	2	583	62	138	.449	0	1	.000	12	19	.632	38	101	139	19	89	0	11	22	38	136	2.3	0.3	2.3
89-90–Cleveland	48	19	674	57	125	.456	0	1	.000	11	16	.688	58	95	153	24	83	3	13	35	53	125	3.2	0.5	2.6
90-91–Detroit	37	0	202	14	33	.424	0	0	–	8	14	.571	13	29	42	4	35	0	2	15	20	36	1.1	0.1	1.0
91-92–Houston	59	5	697	46	86	.535	0	0	–	26	30	.867	61	110	171	15	85	0	14	18	62	118	2.9	0.3	2.0
92-93–Houston	42	0	247	11	41	.268	0	2	.000	9	12	.750	12	48	60	10	43	0	6	9	15	31	1.4	0.2	0.7
93-94–Orlando	45	1	384	29	53	.547	0	0	–	18	30	.600	33	63	96	9	55	1	7	13	35	76	2.1	0.2	1.7
94-95–Orlando	51	3	478	20	42	.476	0	0	–	21	31	.677	31	64	95	9	63	0	7	23	36	61	1.9	0.2	1.2
Reg. Season Totals	1156	460	24028	2592	4963	.522	0	7	.000	1065	1522	.700	2148	4602	6750	660	3377	92	512	1057	2542	6249	5.8	0.6	5.4
Playoff Totals	93	40	1804	146	289	.505	0	1	.000	68	109	.624	139	293	432	29	269	10	33	79	134	360	4.6	0.3	3.9

Romar, Lorenzo b. November 13, 1958 Ht. 6-1 Wt. 175 College: Cerritos (Calif.) Coll. (J.C.); Washington

SEASON–TEAM	G	GS	MIN	FGM	FGA	PCT	3FGM	3FGA	PCT	FTM	FTA	PCT	O-RB	D-RB	TOT	AST	PF	DQ	STL	TO	BLK	PTS	RPG	APG	PPG
80-81–Golden State	53	–	726	87	211	.412	2	6	.333	43	63	.683	10	46	56	136	64	0	27	52	3	219	1.1	2.6	4.1
81-82–Golden State	79	11	1259	203	403	.504	3	15	.200	79	96	.823	12	86	98	226	103	0	60	89	13	488	1.2	2.9	6.2
82-83–Golden State	82	64	2130	266	572	.465	10	33	.303	78	105	.743	23	115	138	455	142	0	98	141	5	620	1.7	5.5	7.6
83-84–G.S.-Milw.	68	9	1022	161	351	.459	4	33	.121	67	94	.713	21	72	93	193	77	0	55	63	8	393	1.4	2.8	5.8
84-85–Milw.-Detroit	9	0	51	3	16	.188	0	3	.000	5	5	1.000	0	0	0	12	7	0	4	5	0	11	0.0	1.3	1.2
Reg. Season Totals	291	84	5188	720	1553	.464	19	90	.211	272	363	.749	66	319	385	1022	393	0	244	350	29	1731	1.3	3.5	5.9
Playoff Totals	13	0	67	9	20	.450	0	3	.000	7	11	.636	0	3	3	15	9	0	0	5	0	25	0.2	1.2	1.9

Rook, Jerry G. b. October 27, 1943 Ht. 6-5 Wt. 220 College: Arkansas State

SEASON–TEAM	G	GS	MIN	FGM	FGA	PCT	3FGM	3FGA	PCT	FTM	FTA	PCT	O-RB	D-RB	TOT	AST	PF	DQ	STL	TO	BLK	PTS	RPG	APG	PPG
69-70–New Orleans (A)	28	–	155	37	82	.451	0	2	.000	11	13	.846	–	–	31	10	21	0	–	–	–	85	1.1	0.4	3.0
Reg. ABA Totals	28	–	155	37	82	.451	0	2	.000	11	13	.846	–	–	31	10	21	0	–	–	–	85	1.1	0.4	3.0

Rooks, Sean Lester b. September 9, 1969 Ht. 6-10 Wt. 270 College: Arizona

SEASON–TEAM	G	GS	MIN	FGM	FGA	PCT	3FGM	3FGA	PCT	FTM	FTA	PCT	O-RB	D-RB	TOT	AST	PF	DQ	STL	TO	BLK	PTS	RPG	APG	PPG
92-93–Dallas	72	68	2087	368	747	.493	0	2	.000	234	389	.602	196	340	536	95	204	2	38	160	81	970	7.4	1.3	13.5
93-94–Dallas	47	28	1255	193	393	.491	0	1	.000	150	210	.714	84	175	259	49	109	0	21	80	44	536	5.5	1.0	11.4
94-95–Minnesota	80	70	2405	289	615	.470	0	5	.000	290	381	.761	165	321	486	97	208	1	29	142	71	868	6.1	1.2	10.9
95-96–Minn.-Atlanta	65	7	1117	144	285	.505	1	7	.143	135	202	.668	81	174	255	47	141	0	23	80	42	424	3.9	0.7	6.5
96-97–L.A. Lakers	69	3	735	87	185	.470	0	1	.000	91	130	.700	56	107	163	42	123	1	17	51	38	265	2.4	0.6	3.8
97-98–L.A. Lakers	41	1	425	46	101	.455	0	0	–	47	79	.595	46	72	118	24	68	0	2	19	23	139	2.9	0.6	3.4
98-99–L.A. Lakers	36	0	315	32	79	.405	0	2	.000	34	48	.708	33	39	72	9	61	0	2	21	9	98	2.0	0.3	2.7
99-00–Dallas	71	13	1001	122	283	.431	0	0	–	65	89	.730	82	166	248	68	169	0	29	70	52	309	3.5	1.0	4.4
Reg. Season Totals	481	190	9340	1281	2688	.477	1	18	.056	1046	1528	.685	743	1394	2137	431	1083	4	161	623	360	3609	4.4	0.9	7.5
Playoff Totals	29	0	253	24	49	.490	0	0	–	24	35	.686	20	22	42	11	60	0	7	13	11	72	1.4	0.4	2.5

Rose, Jalen b. January 30, 1973 Ht. 6-8 Wt. 210 College: Michigan

SEASON–TEAM	G	GS	MIN	FGM	FGA	PCT	3FGM	3FGA	PCT	FTM	FTA	PCT	O-RB	D-RB	TOT	AST	PF	DQ	STL	TO	BLK	PTS	RPG	APG	PPG
94-95–Denver	81	37	1798	227	500	.454	36	114	.316	173	234	.739	57	160	217	389	206	0	65	160	22	663	2.7	4.8	8.2
95-96–Denver	80	37	2134	290	604	.480	32	108	.296	191	277	.690	46	214	260	495	229	3	53	234	39	803	3.3	6.2	10.0
96-97–Indiana	66	6	1188	172	377	.456	21	72	.292	117	156	.750	27	94	121	155	136	1	57	107	18	482	1.8	2.3	7.3
97-98–Indiana	82	0	1706	290	607	.478	25	73	.342	166	228	.728	28	167	195	155	171	0	56	132	14	771	2.4	1.9	9.4
98-99–Indiana	49	1	1238	200	496	.403	17	65	.262	125	158	.791	34	120	154	93	128	0	50	72	15	542	3.1	1.9	11.1
99-00–Indiana	80	80	2978	563	1196	.471	77	196	.393	254	307	.827	42	345	387	320	234	1	84	188	49	1457	4.8	4.0	18.2
Reg. Season Totals	438	161	11042	1742	3780	.461	208	628	.331	1026	1360	.754	234	1100	1334	1607	1104	5	365	893	157	4718	3.0	3.7	10.8
Playoff Totals	54	26	1711	293	657	.446	45	113	.398	158	199	.794	26	144	170	156	156	0	43	109	24	789	3.1	2.9	14.6

Rose, Malik Jabari b. November 23, 1974 Ht. 6-7 Wt. 255 College: Drexel

SEASON–TEAM	G	GS	MIN	FGM	FGA	PCT	3FGM	3FGA	PCT	FTM	FTA	PCT	O-RB	D-RB	TOT	AST	PF	DQ	STL	TO	BLK	PTS	RPG	APG	PPG
96-97–Charlotte	54	1	525	61	128	.477	0	2	.000	38	62	.613	70	94	164	32	114	3	28	41	17	160	3.0	0.6	3.0
97-98–San Antonio	53	0	429	59	136	.434	1	3	.333	39	61	.639	40	50	90	19	79	1	21	44	7	158	1.7	0.4	3.0
98-99–San Antonio	47	0	608	93	201	.463	0	1	.000	98	146	.671	90	92	182	29	120	0	40	56	22	284	3.9	0.6	6.0
99-00–San Antonio	74	3	1341	176	385	.457	1	3	.333	143	198	.722	133	202	335	47	232	2	35	99	52	496	4.5	0.6	6.7
Reg. Season Totals	228	4	2903	389	850	.458	2	9	.222	318	467	.681	333	438	771	127	545	6	124	240	98	1098	3.4	0.6	4.8
Playoff Totals	28	0	307	28	66	.424	0	0	–	25	39	.641	29	41	70	6	68	0	10	23	7	81	2.5	0.2	2.9

Rose, Robert Paul (Bob) b. December 27, 1964 Ht. 6-5 Wt. 185 College: George Mason

SEASON–TEAM	G	GS	MIN	FGM	FGA	PCT	3FGM	3FGA	PCT	FTM	FTA	PCT	O-RB	D-RB	TOT	AST	PF	DQ	STL	TO	BLK	PTS	RPG	APG	PPG
88-89–L.A. Clippers	2	0	3	0	1	.000	0	0	–	0	0	–	1	1	2	0	0	0	0	0	0	0	1.0	0.0	0.0
Reg. Season Totals	2	0	3	0	1	.000	0	0	–	0	0	–	1	1	2	0	0	0	0	0	0	0	1.0	0.0	0.0

Rosenberg, Alexander (Petey) b. April 7, 1918 d. June 29, 1997 Ht. 5-10 Wt. 165 College: St. Joseph's (Pa.)

SEASON–TEAM	G	GS	MIN	FGM	FGA	PCT	3FGM	3FGA	PCT	FTM	FTA	PCT	O-RB	D-RB	TOT	AST	PF	DQ	STL	TO	BLK	PTS	RPG	APG	PPG
46-47–Philadelphia	51	–	–	60	287	.209	–	–	–	30	49	.612	–	–	–	27	64	–	–	–	–	150	–	0.5	2.9
Reg. Season Totals	51	–	–	60	287	.209	–	–	–	30	49	.612	–	–	–	27	64	–	–	–	–	150	–	0.5	2.9
Playoff Totals	11	–	–	1	22	.045	–	–	–	0	3	.000	–	–	–	4	4	–	–	–	–	2	0.0	0.3	0.2

Rosenbluth, Leonard Robert (Lennie) b. January 22, 1933 Ht. 6-5 Wt. 200 College: North Carolina

SEASON–TEAM	G	GS	MIN	FGM	FGA	PCT	3FGM	3FGA	PCT	FTM	FTA	PCT	O-RB	D-RB	TOT	AST	PF	DQ	STL	TO	BLK	PTS	RPG	APG	PPG
57-58–Philadelphia	53	–	373	91	265	.343	–	–	–	53	84	.631	–	–	91	23	39	0	–	–	–	235	1.7	0.4	4.4
58-59–Philadelphia	29	–	205	43	145	.297	–	–	–	21	29	.724	–	–	54	6	20	0	–	–	–	107	1.9	0.2	3.7
Reg. Season Totals	82	–	578	134	410	.327	–	–	–	74	113	.655	–	–	145	29	59	0	–	–	–	342	1.8	0.4	4.2
Playoff Totals	4	–	11	3	9	.333	–	–	–	2	3	.667	–	–	3	–	0	0	–	–	–	8	0.8	0.0	2.0

Rosenstein, Henry (Hank) b. June 16, 1920 Ht. 6-4 Wt. 185 College: C.C.NY

SEASON–TEAM	G	GS	MIN	FGM	FGA	PCT	3FGM	3FGA	PCT	FTM	FTA	PCT	O-RB	D-RB	TOT	AST	PF	DQ	STL	TO	BLK	PTS	RPG	APG	PPG
46-47–N.Y.-Prov.	60	–	–	119	390	.305	–	–	–	144	225	.640	–	–	–	36	172	–	–	–	–	382	–	0.6	6.4
Reg. Season Totals	60	–	–	119	390	.305	–	–	–	144	225	.640	–	–	–	36	172	–	–	–	–	382	–	0.6	6.4

Rosenthal, Richard Anthony (Dick) b. January 20, 1933 Ht. 6-5 Wt. 205 College: Notre Dame

SEASON–TEAM	G	GS	MIN	FGM	FGA	PCT	3FGM	3FGA	PCT	FTM	FTA	PCT	O-RB	D-RB	TOT	AST	PF	DQ	STL	TO	BLK	PTS	RPG	APG	PPG
54-55–Fort Wayne	67	–	1406	197	523	.377	–	–	–	130	181	.718	–	–	300	153	179	2	–	–	–	524	4.5	2.3	7.8
56-57–Fort Wayne	18	–	188	21	79	.266	–	–	–	9	17	.529	–	–	52	17	22	0	–	–	–	51	2.9	0.9	2.8
Reg. Season Totals	85	–	1594	218	602	.362	–	–	–	139	198	.702	–	–	352	170	201	2	–	–	–	575	4.1	2.0	6.8
Playoff Totals	11	–	209	27	84	.321	–	–	–	28	39	.718	–	–	48	26	39	1	–	–	–	82	4.4	2.4	7.5

Roth, Douglas Keith (Doug) b. August 24, 1967 Ht. 6-11 Wt. 255 College: Tennessee

SEASON–TEAM	G	GS	MIN	FGM	FGA	PCT	3FGM	3FGA	PCT	FTM	FTA	PCT	O-RB	D-RB	TOT	AST	PF	DQ	STL	TO	BLK	PTS	RPG	APG	PPG
89-90–Washington	42	0	412	37	86	.430	0	1	.000	7	14	.500	44	76	120	20	70	1	8	16	13	81	2.9	0.5	1.9
Reg. Season Totals	42	0	412	37	86	.430	0	1	.000	7	14	.500	44	76	120	20	70	1	8	16	13	81	2.9	0.5	1.9

Roth, Scott Edward b. June 3, 1963 Ht. 6-8 Wt. 215 College: Wisconsin

SEASON–TEAM	G	GS	MIN	FGM	FGA	PCT	3FGM	3FGA	PCT	FTM	FTA	PCT	O-RB	D-RB	TOT	AST	PF	DQ	STL	TO	BLK	PTS	RPG	APG	PPG
87-88–Utah	26	0	201	30	74	.405	2	11	.182	22	30	.733	7	21	28	16	37	0	12	11	0	84	1.1	0.6	3.2
88-89–Utah-S.A.	63	3	536	59	167	.353	3	16	.188	60	87	.690	20	44	64	55	69	0	24	40	5	181	1.0	0.9	2.9
89-90–Minnesota	71	3	1061	159	420	.379	18	52	.346	150	201	.746	34	78	112	115	144	1	51	85	6	486	1.6	1.6	6.8
Reg. Season Totals	160	6	1798	248	661	.375	23	79	.291	232	318	.730	61	143	204	186	250	1	87	136	11	751	1.3	1.2	4.7
Playoff Totals	6	0	10	1	3	.333	0	0	–	0	0	–	0	0	0	–	0	0	2	0	0	2	0.0	0.0	0.3

Rothenberg, Irwin P. (Irv) b. December 31, 1921 Ht. 6-8 Wt. 215 College: Long Island University

SEASON–TEAM	G	GS	MIN	FGM	FGA	PCT	3FGM	3FGA	PCT	FTM	FTA	PCT	O-RB	D-RB	TOT	AST	PF	DQ	STL	TO	BLK	PTS	RPG	APG	PPG
46-47–Cleveland	29	–	–	36	167	.216	–	–	–	30	54	.556	–	–	–	15	62	–	–	–	–	102	–	0.5	3.5
47-48–Was.-Bal.-St.L.	49	–	–	103	364	.283	–	–	–	87	150	.580	–	–	–	7	115	–	–	–	–	293	–	0.1	6.0
48-49–New York	53	–	–	101	367	.275	–	–	–	112	174	.644	–	–	–	68	174	–	–	–	–	314	–	1.3	5.9
Reg. Season Totals	131	–	–	240	898	.267	–	–	–	229	378	.606	–	–	–	90	351	–	–	–	–	709	–	0.7	5.4
Playoff Totals	11	–	–	9	62	.177	–	–	–	6	19	.368	–	–	–	3	22	–	–	–	–	24	–	0.2	2.2

Rottner, Marvin (Mickey) b. March 23, 1919 Ht. 5-10 Wt. 180 College: Loyola (Chicago)

SEASON–TEAM	G	GS	MIN	FGM	FGA	PCT	3FGM	3FGA	PCT	FTM	FTA	PCT	O-RB	D-RB	TOT	AST	PF	DQ	STL	TO	BLK	PTS	RPG	APG	PPG
45-46–Sheboygan (N)	5	–	–	10	–	–	–	–	–	0	–	–	–	–	–	–	–	–	–	–	–	20	–	–	4.0
46-47–Chicago	56	–	–	190	655	.290	–	–	–	43	79	.544	–	–	–	93	109	–	–	–	–	423	–	1.7	7.6
47-48–Chicago	44	–	–	53	184	.288	–	–	–	11	34	.324	–	–	–	46	49	–	–	–	–	117	–	1.0	2.7
Reg. NBA Totals	100	–	–	243	839	.290	–	–	–	54	113	.478	–	–	–	139	158	–	–	–	–	540	–	1.4	5.4
Reg. NBL Totals	5	–	–	10	–	–	–	–	–	0	0	–	–	–	–	–	–	–	–	–	–	20	–	–	4.0
NBA Playoff Totals	16	–	–	8	110	.136	–	–	–	2	7	.286	–	–	–	10	35	1	–	–	–	18	0.0	0.4	1.1
NBL Playoff Totals	8	–	–	10	–	–	–	–	–	4	1	.000	–	–	–	–	5	–	–	–	–	24	–	–	3.0

Roundfield, Danny Thomas (Dan, Rounds) b. May 26, 1953 Ht. 6-8 Wt. 205 College: Central Michigan

SEASON–TEAM	G	GS	MIN	FGM	FGA	PCT	3FGM	3FGA	PCT	FTM	FTA	PCT	O-RB	D-RB	TOT	AST	PF	DQ	STL	TO	BLK	PTS	RPG	APG	PPG
75-76–Indiana (A)	67	–	767	131	309	.424	0	2	.000	77	122	.631	131	128	259	35	161	–	31	64	43	339	3.9	0.5	5.1
76-77–Indiana	61	–	1645	342	734	.466	–	–	–	164	239	.686	179	339	518	69	243	8	61	–	131	848	8.5	1.1	13.9
77-78–Indiana	79	–	2423	421	861	.489	–	–	–	218	300	.727	275	527	802	196	297	4	81	194	149	1060	10.2	2.5	13.4
78-79–Atlanta	80	–	2539	462	916	.504	–	–	–	300	420	.714	326	539	865	131	358	16	87	209	176	1224	10.8	1.6	15.3
79-80–Atlanta	81	–	2588	502	1007	.499	0	4	.000	330	465	.710	293	544	837	184	317	6	101	233	139	1334	10.3	2.3	16.5
80-81–Atlanta	63	–	2128	426	808	.527	0	1	.000	256	355	.721	231	403	634	161	258	8	76	178	119	1108	10.1	2.6	17.6
81-82–Atlanta	61	58	2217	424	910	.466	1	5	.200	285	375	.760	227	494	721	162	210	3	64	183	93	1134	11.8	2.7	18.6
82-83–Atlanta	77	76	2811	561	1193	.470	5	27	.185	337	450	.749	259	621	880	225	239	1	60	245	115	1464	11.4	2.9	19.0
83-84–Atlanta	73	72	2610	503	1038	.485	0	11	.000	374	486	.770	206	515	721	184	221	2	61	205	74	1380	9.9	2.5	18.9
84-85–Detroit	56	43	1492	236	505	.467	0	2	.000	139	178	.781	175	278	453	102	147	0	26	123	54	611	8.1	1.8	10.9
85-86–Washington	79	21	2321	322	660	.488	0	6	.000	273	362	.754	210	432	642	167	194	1	36	187	51	917	8.1	2.1	11.6
86-87–Washington	36	0	669	90	220	.409	1	5	.200	57	72	.792	64	106	170	39	77	0	11	49	16	238	4.7	1.1	6.6
Reg. NBA Totals	746	270	23443	4289	8852	.485	7	61	.115	2733	3702	.738	2445	4798	7243	1620	2561	49	664	1806	1117	11318	9.7	2.2	15.2
Reg. ABA Totals	67	–	767	131	309	.424	0	2	.000	77	122	.631	131	128	259	35	161	–	31	64	43	339	3.9	0.5	5.1
NBA Playoff Totals	38	18	1304	225	478	.471	1	4	.250	126	174	.724	126	252	378	81	133	5	26	98	56	577	9.9	2.1	15.2
ABA Playoff Totals	2	–	25	7	12	.583	0	0	–	8	9	.889	4	6	10	0	6	–	2	0	4	22	5.0	0.0	11.0
NBA All-Star Totals	1	0	27	7	15	.467	0	0	–	4	9	.444	9	4	13	0	2	0	1	3	2	18	13.0	0.0	18.0

Roux, Gifford H. (Giff) b. June 28, 1923 Ht. 6-5 Wt. 195 College: Kansas

SEASON–TEAM	G	GS	MIN	FGM	FGA	PCT	3FGM	3FGA	PCT	FTM	FTA	PCT	O-RB	D-RB	TOT	AST	PF	DQ	STL	TO	BLK	PTS	RPG	APG	PPG
46-47–St. Louis	60	–	–	142	478	.297	–	–	–	70	160	.438	–	–	–	17	95	–	–	–	–	354	–	0.3	5.9
47-48–St. Louis	46	–	–	68	258	.264	–	–	–	40	68	.588	–	–	–	12	60	–	–	–	–	176	–	0.3	3.8
48-49–St. Louis-Prov.	45	–	–	29	118	.246	–	–	–	29	44	.659	–	–	–	20	30	–	–	–	–	87	–	0.4	1.9
Reg. Season Totals	151	–	–	239	854	.280	–	–	–	139	272	.511	–	–	–	49	185	–	–	–	–	617	–	0.3	4.1
Playoff Totals	8	–	–	13	82	.293	–	–	–	3	9	.333	–	–	–	–	9	–	–	–	–	29	–	0.0	3.6

Rowan, Ronald Lewis (Ron) b. April 23, 1962 Ht. 6-5 Wt. 200 College: Notre Dame; St. John's (N.Y.)

SEASON–TEAM	G	GS	MIN	FGM	FGA	PCT	3FGM	3FGA	PCT	FTM	FTA	PCT	O-RB	D-RB	TOT	AST	PF	DQ	STL	TO	BLK	PTS	RPG	APG	PPG
86-87–Portland	7	0	16	4	9	.444	1	1	1.000	3	4	.750	1	0	1	1	1	0	4	3	0	12	0.1	0.1	1.7
Reg. Season Totals	7	0	16	4	9	.444	1	1	1.000	3	4	.750	1	0	1	1	1	0	4	3	0	12	0.1	0.1	1.7

Rowe, Curtis Jr. b. July 2, 1949 Ht. 6-7 Wt. 225 College: UCLA

SEASON–TEAM	G	GS	MIN	FGM	FGA	PCT	3FGM	3FGA	PCT	FTM	FTA	PCT	O-RB	D-RB	TOT	AST	PF	DQ	STL	TO	BLK	PTS	RPG	APG	PPG
71-72–Detroit	82	–	2661	369	802	.460	–	–	–	192	287	.669	–	–	699	99	171	1	–	–	–	930	8.5	1.2	11.3
72-73–Detroit	81	–	3009	547	1053	.519	–	–	–	210	327	.642	–	–	760	172	191	0	–	–	–	1304	9.4	2.1	16.1
73-74–Detroit	82	–	2499	380	769	.494	–	–	–	118	169	.698	167	348	515	136	177	1	49	–	36	878	6.3	1.7	10.7
74-75–Detroit	82	–	2787	422	874	.483	–	–	–	171	227	.753	174	411	585	121	190	0	50	–	44	1015	7.1	1.5	12.4
75-76–Detroit	80	–	2998	514	1098	.468	–	–	–	252	342	.737	231	466	697	183	209	3	47	–	45	1280	8.7	2.3	16.0
76-77–Boston	79	–	2190	315	632	.498	–	–	–	170	240	.708	188	375	563	107	215	3	24	–	47	800	7.1	1.4	10.1
77-78–Boston	51	–	911	123	273	.451	–	–	–	66	89	.742	74	129	203	45	94	1	14	76	8	312	4.0	0.9	6.1
78-79–Boston	53	–	1222	151	346	.436	–	–	–	52	75	.693	79	163	242	69	105	2	15	88	13	354	4.6	1.3	6.7
Reg. Season Totals	590	–	18277	2821	5847	.482	–	–	–	1231	1756	.701	913	1892	4264	932	1352	11	199	164	193	6873	7.2	1.6	11.6
Playoff Totals	28	–	927	127	264	.481	–	–	–	69	95	.726	78	142	220	62	85	2	11	–	23	323	7.9	2.2	11.5
All-Star Totals	1	–	8	0	2	.000	–	–	–	1	2	.500	0	2	2	0	2	0	0	–	0	1	2.0	0.0	1.0

Rowinski, James (Jim) b. January 4, 1961 Ht. 6-8 Wt. 260 College: Purdue

SEASON–TEAM	G	GS	MIN	FGM	FGA	PCT	3FGM	3FGA	PCT	FTM	FTA	PCT	O-RB	D-RB	TOT	AST	PF	DQ	STL	TO	BLK	PTS	RPG	APG	PPG
88-89–Detroit-Phil.	9	0	15	1	4	.250	0	0	–	5	6	.833	1	4	5	0	0	0	0	0	0	7	0.6	0.0	0.8
89-90–Miami	14	0	112	14	32	.438	0	0	–	22	26	.846	17	12	29	5	19	0	1	10	2	50	2.1	0.4	3.6
Reg. Season Totals	23	0	127	15	36	.417	0	0	–	27	32	.844	18	16	34	5	19	0	1	10	2	57	1.5	0.2	2.5

Rowland, Derrick b. June 21, 1959 Ht. 6-5 Wt. 195 College: Potsdam State

SEASON–TEAM	G	GS	MIN	FGM	FGA	PCT	3FGM	3FGA	PCT	FTM	FTA	PCT	O-RB	D-RB	TOT	AST	PF	DQ	STL	TO	BLK	PTS	RPG	APG	PPG
85-86–Milwaukee	2	0	9	1	3	.333	0	0	–	1	2	.500	0	1	1	1	1	0	0	0	0	3	0.5	0.5	1.5
Reg. Season Totals	2	0	9	1	3	.333	0	0	–	1	2	.500	0	1	1	1	1	0	0	0	0	3	0.5	0.5	1.5

Rowsom, Brian Maurice b. October 23, 1965 Ht. 6-9 Wt. 220 College: North Carolina-Wilmington

SEASON–TEAM	G	GS	MIN	FGM	FGA	PCT	3FGM	3FGA	PCT	FTM	FTA	PCT	O-RB	D-RB	TOT	AST	PF	DQ	STL	TO	BLK	PTS	RPG	APG	PPG
87-88–Indiana	4	0	16	0	6	.000	0	0	–	6	6	1.000	1	4	5	1	3	0	1	1	0	6	1.3	0.3	1.5
88-89–Charlotte	34	0	517	80	162	.494	1	1	1.000	65	81	.802	56	81	137	24	69	1	10	18	12	226	4.0	0.7	6.6
89-90–Charlotte	44	2	559	78	179	.436	1	2	.500	68	83	.819	44	87	131	22	58	0	18	25	11	225	3.0	0.5	5.1
Reg. Season Totals	82	2	1092	158	347	.455	2	3	.667	139	170	.818	101	172	273	47	130	1	29	44	23	457	3.3	0.6	5.6

Royal, Donald Adam b. May 22, 1966 Ht. 6-8 Wt. 218 College: Notre Dame

SEASON–TEAM	G	GS	MIN	FGM	FGA	PCT	3FGM	3FGA	PCT	FTM	FTA	PCT	O-RB	D-RB	TOT	AST	PF	DQ	STL	TO	BLK	PTS	RPG	APG	PPG
89-90–Minnesota	66	0	746	117	255	.459	0	1	.000	153	197	.777	69	68	137	43	107	0	32	81	8	387	2.1	0.7	5.9
91-92–San Antonio	60	4	718	80	178	.449	0	0	–	92	133	.692	65	59	124	34	73	0	25	39	7	252	2.1	0.6	4.2
92-93–Orlando	77	0	1636	194	391	.496	0	3	.000	318	390	.815	116	179	295	80	179	4	36	113	25	706	3.8	1.0	9.2
93-94–Orlando	74	0	1357	174	347	.501	0	2	.000	199	269	.740	94	154	248	61	121	1	50	76	16	547	3.4	0.8	7.4
94-95–Orlando	70	68	1841	206	434	.475	0	4	.000	223	299	.746	83	196	279	198	156	0	45	125	16	635	4.0	2.8	9.1
95-96–Orlando	64	7	963	106	216	.491	0	2	.000	125	164	.762	57	96	153	42	97	0	29	52	15	337	2.4	0.7	5.3
96-97–Orl.-G.S.-Cha.	62	4	858	62	146	.425	0	2	.000	94	117	.803	52	102	154	25	100	0	23	47	11	218	2.5	0.4	3.5
97-98–Orlando-Cha.	31	5	323	25	69	.362	0	0	–	29	33	.879	18	23	41	17	35	0	7	10	1	79	1.3	0.5	2.5
Reg. Season Totals	504	88	8442	964	2036	.473	0	14	.000	1233	1602	.770	554	877	1431	500	868	5	247	543	99	3161	2.8	1.0	6.3
Playoff Totals	36	8	424	32	76	.421	0	0	–	43	61	.705	16	36	52	16	44	0	6	24	3	107	1.4	0.4	3.0

Royals, Reggie b. September 18, 1954 Ht. 6-10 Wt. 200 College: Florida State

SEASON–TEAM	G	GS	MIN	FGM	FGA	PCT	3FGM	3FGA	PCT	FTM	FTA	PCT	O-RB	D-RB	TOT	AST	PF	DQ	STL	TO	BLK	PTS	RPG	APG	PPG
74-75–San Diego (A)	2	–	11	2	4	.500	0	0	–	0	0	–	0	0	0	0	1	–	0	0	0	4	0.0	0.0	2.0
Reg. ABA Totals	2	–	11	2	4	.500	0	0	–	0	0	–	0	0	–	0	1	–	0	0	0	4	0.0	0.0	2.0

Royer, Robert D. (Bob) b. October 15, 1927 d. May 30, 1973 Ht. 5-10 Wt. 155 College: Kansas City (Mo.) C.C.; Indiana State

SEASON–TEAM	G	GS	MIN	FGM	FGA	PCT	3FGM	3FGA	PCT	FTM	FTA	PCT	O-RB	D-RB	TOT	AST	PF	DQ	STL	TO	BLK	PTS	RPG	APG	PPG
49-50–Denver	42	–	–	78	231	.338	–	–	–	41	58	.707	–	–	–	85	72	–	–	–	–	197	–	2.0	4.7
Reg. Season Totals	42	–	–	78	231	.338	–	–	–	41	58	.707	–	–	–	85	72	–	–	–	–	197	–	2.0	4.7

Rozier, Clifford Glen II b. October 31, 1972 Ht. 6-11 Wt. 255 College: Louisville

SEASON–TEAM	G	GS	MIN	FGM	FGA	PCT	3FGM	3FGA	PCT	FTM	FTA	PCT	O-RB	D-RB	TOT	AST	PF	DQ	STL	TO	BLK	PTS	RPG	APG	PPG
94-95–Golden State	66	34	1494	189	390	.485	2	7	.286	68	152	.447	200	286	486	45	196	2	35	89	39	448	7.4	0.7	6.8
95-96–Golden State	59	1	723	79	135	.585	0	2	.000	26	55	.473	71	100	171	22	135	0	19	40	30	184	2.9	0.4	3.1
96-97–G.S.-Orl.-Tor.	42	29	737	79	174	.454	0	2	.000	31	61	.508	102	132	234	31	97	2	24	29	44	189	5.6	0.7	4.5
97-98–Minnesota	6	0	30	3	6	.500	0	0	–	0	1	.000	3	3	6	0	7	0	0	4	0	6	1.0	0.0	1.0
Reg. Season Totals	173	64	2984	350	705	.496	2	11	.182	125	269	.465	376	521	897	98	435	4	78	162	113	827	5.2	0.6	4.8

Rudd, Edward Delane (Delaney) b. November 8, 1962 Ht. 6-2 Wt. 195 College: Wake Forest

SEASON–TEAM	G	GS	MIN	FGM	FGA	PCT	3FGM	3FGA	PCT	FTM	FTA	PCT	O-RB	D-RB	TOT	AST	PF	DQ	STL	TO	BLK	PTS	RPG	APG	PPG
89-90–Utah	77	2	850	111	259	.429	16	56	.286	35	53	.660	12	43	55	177	81	0	22	88	1	273	0.7	2.3	3.5
90-91–Utah	82	0	874	124	285	.435	17	61	.279	59	71	.831	14	52	66	216	92	0	36	102	2	324	0.8	2.6	4.0
91-92–Utah	65	0	538	75	188	.399	11	47	.234	32	42	.762	15	39	54	109	64	0	15	49	1	193	0.8	1.7	3.0
92-93–Portland	15	1	95	7	36	.194	1	11	.091	11	14	.786	4	5	9	17	7	0	1	11	0	26	0.6	1.1	1.7
Reg. Season Totals	239	3	2357	317	768	.413	45	175	.257	137	180	.761	45	139	184	519	244	0	74	250	4	816	0.8	2.2	3.4
Playoff Totals	24	0	187	27	65	.415	7	26	.269	6	10	.600	3	6	9	49	27	0	7	10	0	67	0.4	2.0	2.8

Rudd, John William b. August 7, 1955 Ht. 6-7 Wt. 230 College: McNeese State

SEASON–TEAM	G	GS	MIN	FGM	FGA	PCT	3FGM	3FGA	PCT	FTM	FTA	PCT	O-RB	D-RB	TOT	AST	PF	DQ	STL	TO	BLK	PTS	RPG	APG	PPG
78-79–New York	58	–	723	59	133	.444	–	–	–	66	93	.710	69	98	167	35	95	1	17	59	8	184	2.9	0.6	3.2
Reg. Season Totals	58	–	723	59	133	.444	–	–	–	66	93	.710	69	98	167	35	95	1	17	59	8	184	2.9	0.6	3.2

Rudometkin, John (Rudo) b. June 6, 1940 Ht. 6-6 Wt. 205 College: Allan Hancock (Calif.) Coll. (J.C.); USC

SEASON–TEAM	G	GS	MIN	FGM	FGA	PCT	3FGM	3FGA	PCT	FTM	FTA	PCT	O-RB	D-RB	TOT	AST	PF	DQ	STL	TO	BLK	PTS	RPG	APG	PPG
62-63–New York	56	–	572	108	307	.352	–	–	–	73	95	.768	–	–	149	30	58	0	–	–	–	289	2.7	0.5	5.2
63-64–New York	52	–	696	154	326	.472	–	–	–	87	116	.750	–	–	164	26	86	0	–	–	–	395	3.2	0.5	7.6
64-65–N.Y.-S.F.	23	–	376	52	154	.338	–	–	–	34	50	.680	–	–	99	16	54	0	–	–	–	138	4.3	0.7	6.0
Reg. Season Totals	131	–	1644	314	787	.399	–	–	–	194	261	.743	–	–	412	72	198	0	–	–	–	822	3.1	0.5	6.3

Ruffin, Michael David b. January 21, 1977 Ht. 6-9 Wt. 246 College: Tulsa

SEASON–TEAM	G	GS	MIN	FGM	FGA	PCT	3FGM	3FGA	PCT	FTM	FTA	PCT	O-RB	D-RB	TOT	AST	PF	DQ	STL	TO	BLK	PTS	RPG	APG	PPG
99-00–Chicago	71	6	975	58	138	.420	0	0	–	43	88	.489	117	133	250	44	170	1	26	59	26	159	3.5	0.6	2.2
Reg. Season Totals	71	6	975	58	138	.420	0	0	–	43	88	.489	117	133	250	44	170	1	26	59	26	159	3.5	0.6	2.2

Ruffin, Trevor b. September 26, 1970 Ht. 6-1 Wt. 199 College: Hawaii

SEASON–TEAM	G	GS	MIN	FGM	FGA	PCT	3FGM	3FGA	PCT	FTM	FTA	PCT	O-RB	D-RB	TOT	AST	PF	DQ	STL	TO	BLK	PTS	RPG	APG	PPG
94-95–Phoenix	49	1	319	84	197	.426	38	99	.384	27	38	.711	8	15	23	48	52	0	14	47	2	233	0.5	1.0	4.8
95-96–Philadelphia	61	23	1551	263	648	.406	104	284	.366	148	182	.813	21	111	132	269	132	0	43	149	2	778	2.2	4.4	12.8
Reg. Season Totals	110	24	1870	347	845	.411	142	383	.371	175	220	.795	29	126	155	317	184	0	57	196	4	1011	1.4	2.9	9.2
Playoff Totals	5	0	11	4	8	.500	1	4	.250	1	5	.200	0	3	3	2	0	0	1	0	0	10	0.6	0.4	2.0

Ruffner, Paul b. October 15, 1948 Ht. 6-10 Wt. 225 College: Cerritos (Calif.) Coll. (J.C.); Brigham Young

SEASON–TEAM	G	GS	MIN	FGM	FGA	PCT	3FGM	3FGA	PCT	FTM	FTA	PCT	O-RB	D-RB	TOT	AST	PF	DQ	STL	TO	BLK	PTS	RPG	APG	PPG
70-71–Chicago	10	–	60	15	35	.429	–	–	–	4	8	.500	–	–	16	2	10	0	–	–	–	34	1.6	0.2	3.4
71-72–Pittsburgh (A)	79	–	1059	182	381	.478	0	0	–	84	115	.730	–	–	341	52	178	–	–	69	–	448	4.3	0.7	5.7
73-74–Buffalo	20	–	51	11	27	.407	–	–	–	8	13	.615	4	7	11	0	10	0	1	–	1	30	0.6	0.0	1.5
74-75–Buffalo	22	–	103	22	47	.468	–	–	–	1	5	.200	12	10	22	7	22	0	3	–	3	45	1.0	0.3	2.0
75-76–St. Louis (A)	2	–	5	2	3	.667	0	0	–	0	0	–	1	2	3	0	0	–	0	0	0	4	1.5	0.0	2.0
Reg. NBA Totals	52	–	214	48	109	.440	–	–	–	13	26	.500	16	17	49	9	42	0	4	–	4	109	0.9	0.2	2.1
Reg. ABA Totals	81	–	1064	184	384	.479	0	0	–	84	115	.730	1	2	344	52	178	0	0	69	0	452	4.2	0.6	5.6
NBA Playoff Totals	2	–	7	0	6	.000	–	–	–	0	0	–	0	2	4	–	0	0	0	–	0	0	2.0	0.0	0.0

Ruklick, Joseph (Joe) b. August 3, 1938 Ht. 6-9 Wt. 220 College: Northwestern

SEASON–TEAM	G	GS	MIN	FGM	FGA	PCT	3FGM	3FGA	PCT	FTM	FTA	PCT	O-RB	D-RB	TOT	AST	PF	DQ	STL	TO	BLK	PTS	RPG	APG	PPG
59-60–Philadelphia	39	–	384	85	214	.397	–	–	–	26	36	.722	–	–	137	24	70	0	–	–	–	196	3.5	0.6	5.0
60-61–Philadelphia	29	–	223	43	120	.358	–	–	–	8	13	.615	–	–	62	10	38	0	–	–	–	94	2.1	0.3	3.2
61-62–Philadelphia	46	–	302	48	147	.327	–	–	–	12	26	.462	–	–	87	14	56	1	–	–	–	108	1.9	0.3	2.3
Reg. Season Totals	114	–	909	176	481	.366	–	–	–	46	75	.613	–	–	286	48	164	1	–	–	–	398	2.5	0.4	3.5
Playoff Totals	6	–	23	3	13	.231	–	–	–	1	2	.500	–	–	9	–	5	0	–	–	–	7	1.5	0.0	1.2

Ruland, Jeffrey Alan (Jeff) b. December 16, 1958 Ht. 6-10 Wt. 275 College: Iona

SEASON–TEAM	G	GS	MIN	FGM	FGA	PCT	3FGM	3FGA	PCT	FTM	FTA	PCT	O-RB	D-RB	TOT	AST	PF	DQ	STL	TO	BLK	PTS	RPG	APG	PPG
81-82–Washington	82	0	2214	420	749	.561	1	3	.333	342	455	.752	253	509	762	134	319	7	44	237	58	1183	9.3	1.6	14.4
82-83–Washington	79	47	2862	580	1051	.552	1	3	.333	375	544	.689	293	578	871	234	312	12	74	297	77	1536	11.0	3.0	19.4
83-84–Washington	75	75	3082	599	1035	.579	1	7	.143	466	636	.733	265	657	922	296	285	8	68	342	72	1665	12.3	3.9	22.2
84-85–Washington	37	36	1436	250	439	.569	0	2	.000	200	292	.685	127	283	410	162	128	2	31	179	27	700	11.1	4.4	18.9
85-86–Washington	30	24	1114	212	383	.554	0	4	.000	145	200	.725	107	213	320	159	100	1	23	121	25	569	10.7	5.3	19.0
86-87–Philadelphia	5	2	116	19	28	.679	0	0	–	9	12	.750	12	16	28	10	13	0	0	10	4	47	5.6	2.0	9.4
91-92–Philadelphia	13	5	209	20	38	.526	0	0	–	11	16	.688	16	31	47	5	45	0	7	20	4	51	3.6	0.4	3.9
92-93–Detroit	11	0	55	5	11	.455	0	0	–	2	4	.500	9	9	18	2	16	0	2	6	0	12	1.6	0.2	1.1
Reg. Season Totals	332	189	11088	2105	3734	.564	3	19	.158	1550	2159	.718	1082	2296	3378	1002	1218	30	249	1212	267	5763	10.2	3.0	17.4
Playoff Totals	17	7	640	110	211	.521	0	4	.000	93	120	.775	62	101	163	67	60	1	14	71	13	313	9.6	3.9	18.4
All-Star Totals	1	0	13	2	3	.667	0	0	–	2	2	1.000	1	3	4	2	2	0	1	2	0	6	4.0	2.0	6.0

Rule, Bobby Frank (Bob, Golden) b. June 29, 1944 Ht. 6-9 Wt. 220 College: Riverside (Calif.) C.C.; Colorado State

SEASON–TEAM	G	GS	MIN	FGM	FGA	PCT	3FGM	3FGA	PCT	FTM	FTA	PCT	O-RB	D-RB	TOT	AST	PF	DQ	STL	TO	BLK	PTS	RPG	APG	PPG
67-68–Seattle	82	–	2424	568	1162	.489	–	–	–	348	529	.658	–	–	776	99	316	10	–	–	–	1484	9.5	1.2	18.1
68-69–Seattle	82	–	3104	776	1655	.469	–	–	–	413	606	.682	–	–	941	141	322	8	–	–	–	1965	11.5	1.7	24.0
69-70–Seattle	80	–	2959	789	1705	.463	–	–	–	387	542	.714	–	–	825	144	278	6	–	–	–	1965	10.3	1.8	24.6
70-71–Seattle	4	–	142	47	98	.480	–	–	–	25	30	.833	–	–	46	7	14	0	–	–	–	119	11.5	1.8	29.8
71-72–Seattle-Phil.	76	53	2230	461	1058	.436	–	–	–	226	335	.675	–	–	534	116	189	4	–	–	–	1148	7.0	1.5	15.1
72-73–Phil.-Clev.	52	–	452	60	158	.380	–	–	–	20	31	.645	–	–	108	38	68	0	–	–	–	140	2.1	0.7	2.7
73-74–Cleveland	26	–	540	76	192	.396	–	–	–	34	46	.739	43	60	103	47	71	0	12	–	10	186	4.0	1.8	7.2
74-75–Milwaukee	1	–	11	0	1	.000	–	–	–	0	0	–	0	0	0	2	2	0	0	–	0	0	0.0	2.0	0.0
Reg. Season Totals	403	–	11862	2777	6029	.461	–	–	–	1453	2119	.686	43	60	3333	594	1260	28	12	–	10	7007	8.3	1.5	17.4
All-Star Totals	1	–	13	2	6	.333	–	–	–	1	1	1.000	0	0	4	0	2	0	0	–	0	5	4.0	0.0	5.0

Rullo, Generoso Charles (Jerry) b. June 23, 1922 Ht. 5-10 Wt. 165 College: Temple

SEASON–TEAM	G	GS	MIN	FGM	FGA	PCT	3FGM	3FGA	PCT	FTM	FTA	PCT	O-RB	D-RB	TOT	AST	PF	DQ	STL	TO	BLK	PTS	RPG	APG	PPG
46-47–Philadelphia	50	–	–	52	174	.299	–	–	–	23	47	.489	–	–	–	20	61	–	–	–	–	127	–	0.4	2.5
47-48–Baltimore	2	–	–	0	4	.000	–	–	–	0	0	–	–	–	–	0	1	–	–	–	–	0	–	0.0	0.0
48-49–Philadelphia	39	–	–	53	183	.290	–	–	–	31	45	.689	–	–	–	48	71	–	–	–	–	137	–	1.2	3.5
49-50–Philadelphia	4	–	–	3	9	.333	–	–	–	1	1	1.000	–	–	–	2	2	–	–	–	–	7	–	0.5	1.8
Reg. Season Totals	95	–	–	108	370	.292	–	–	–	55	93	.591	–	–	–	70	135	–	–	–	–	271	–	0.7	2.9
Playoff Totals	10	–	–	5	27	.185	–	–	–	3	3	1.000	–	–	–	1	10	1	–	–	–	13	0.0	0.1	1.3

Rusconi, Stefano b. February 10, 1968 Ht. 6-10 Wt. 240 Country: Italy

SEASON–TEAM	G	GS	MIN	FGM	FGA	PCT	3FGM	3FGA	PCT	FTM	FTA	PCT	O-RB	D-RB	TOT	AST	PF	DQ	STL	TO	BLK	PTS	RPG	APG	PPG
95-96–Phoenix	7	0	30	3	9	.333	0	0	–	2	5	.400	3	3	6	3	10	0	0	3	2	8	0.9	0.4	1.1
Reg. Season Totals	7	0	30	3	9	.333	0	0	–	2	5	.400	3	3	6	3	10	0	0	3	2	8	0.9	0.4	1.1

Russell, Bryon Demetrise b. December 31, 1970 Ht. 6-7 Wt. 225 College: Long Beach State

SEASON–TEAM	G	GS	MIN	FGM	FGA	PCT	3FGM	3FGA	PCT	FTM	FTA	PCT	O-RB	D-RB	TOT	AST	PF	DQ	STL	TO	BLK	PTS	RPG	APG	PPG
93-94–Utah	67	48	1121	135	279	.484	2	22	.091	62	101	.614	61	120	181	54	138	0	68	55	19	334	2.7	0.8	5.0
94-95–Utah	63	15	860	104	238	.437	13	44	.295	62	93	.667	44	97	141	34	101	0	48	42	11	283	2.2	0.5	4.5
95-96–Utah	59	9	577	56	142	.394	14	40	.350	48	67	.716	28	62	90	29	66	0	29	36	8	174	1.5	0.5	2.9
96-97–Utah	81	81	2525	297	620	.479	108	264	.409	171	244	.701	79	252	331	123	237	2	129	94	27	873	4.1	1.5	10.8
97-98–Utah	82	7	2219	226	525	.430	73	214	.341	213	278	.766	78	248	326	101	229	2	90	81	31	738	4.0	1.2	9.0
98-99–Utah	50	50	1770	217	468	.464	52	147	.354	136	171	.795	65	201	266	74	154	3	76	76	15	622	5.3	1.5	12.4
99-00–Utah	82	70	2900	408	914	.446	106	268	.396	237	316	.750	99	328	427	158	255	3	128	101	23	1159	5.2	1.9	14.1
Reg. Season Totals	484	280	11972	1443	3186	.453	368	999	.368	929	1270	.731	454	1308	1762	573	1180	10	568	485	134	4183	3.6	1.2	8.6
Playoff Totals	87	54	2722	321	710	.452	110	305	.361	184	247	.745	78	312	390	111	219	1	102	74	27	936	4.5	1.3	10.8

Russell, Cazzie Lee Jr. b. June 7, 1944 Ht. 6-5 Wt. 220 College: Michigan

SEASON–TEAM	G	GS	MIN	FGM	FGA	PCT	3FGM	3FGA	PCT	FTM	FTA	PCT	O-RB	D-RB	TOT	AST	PF	DQ	STL	TO	BLK	PTS	RPG	APG	PPG
66-67–New York	77	–	1696	344	789	.436	–	–	–	179	228	.785	–	–	251	187	174	1	–	–	–	867	3.3	2.4	11.3
67-68–New York	82	–	2296	551	1192	.462	–	–	–	282	349	.808	–	–	374	195	223	2	–	–	–	1384	4.6	2.4	16.9
68-69–New York	50	–	1645	362	804	.450	–	–	–	191	240	.796	–	–	209	115	140	1	–	–	–	915	4.2	2.3	18.3
69-70–New York	78	–	1563	385	773	.498	–	–	–	124	160	.775	–	–	236	135	137	0	–	–	–	894	3.0	1.7	11.5
70-71–New York	57	–	1056	216	504	.429	–	–	–	92	119	.773	–	–	192	77	74	0	–	–	–	524	3.4	1.4	9.2
71-72–Golden State	79	–	2902	689	1514	.455	–	–	–	315	378	.833	–	–	428	248	176	0	–	–	–	1693	5.4	3.1	21.4
72-73–Golden State	80	–	2429	541	1182	.458	–	–	–	172	199	.864	–	–	350	187	171	0	–	–	–	1254	4.4	2.3	15.7
73-74–Golden State	82	–	2574	738	1531	.482	–	–	–	208	249	.835	142	211	353	192	194	1	54	–	17	1684	4.3	2.3	20.5
74-75–Los Angeles	40	–	1055	264	580	.455	–	–	–	101	113	.894	34	81	115	109	56	0	27	–	2	629	2.9	2.7	15.7
75-76–Los Angeles	74	–	1625	371	802	.463	–	–	–	132	148	.892	50	133	183	122	122	0	53	–	3	874	2.5	1.6	11.8
76-77–Los Angeles	82	–	2583	578	1179	.490	–	–	–	188	219	.858	86	208	294	210	163	1	86	–	7	1344	3.6	2.6	16.4
77-78–Chicago	36	–	789	133	304	.438	–	–	–	49	57	.860	31	52	83	61	63	1	19	35	4	315	2.3	1.7	8.8
Reg. Season Totals	817	–	22213	5172	11154	.464	–	–	–	2033	2459	.827	343	685	3068	1838	1693	7	239	35	33	12377	3.8	2.2	15.1
Playoff Totals	72	–	1566	359	781	.460	–	–	–	134	154	.870	22	26	222	97	151	1	16	–	1	852	3.1	1.3	11.8
All-Star Totals	1	–	20	4	13	.308	–	–	–	2	2	1.000	0	0	1	0	1	0	0	–	0	10	1.0	0.0	10.0

Russell, Frank b. April 17, 1949 Ht. 6-3 Wt. 180 College: Detroit Mercy

SEASON–TEAM	G	GS	MIN	FGM	FGA	PCT	3FGM	3FGA	PCT	FTM	FTA	PCT	O-RB	D-RB	TOT	AST	PF	DQ	STL	TO	BLK	PTS	RPG	APG	PPG
72-73–Chicago	23	–	131	29	77	.377	–	–	–	16	18	.889	–	–	17	15	12	0	–	–	–	74	0.7	0.7	3.2
Reg. Season Totals	23	–	131	29	77	.377	–	–	–	16	18	.889	–	–	17	15	12	0	–	–	–	74	0.7	0.7	3.2

Russell, Michael Campanella (Campy) b. January 12, 1952 Ht. 6-8 Wt. 215 College: Michigan

SEASON–TEAM	G	GS	MIN	FGM	FGA	PCT	3FGM	3FGA	PCT	FTM	FTA	PCT	O-RB	D-RB	TOT	AST	PF	DQ	STL	TO	BLK	PTS	RPG	APG	PPG
74-75–Cleveland	68	–	754	150	365	.411	–	–	–	124	165	.752	43	109	152	45	100	0	21	–	3	424	2.2	0.7	6.2
75-76–Cleveland	82	–	1961	483	1003	.482	–	–	–	266	344	.773	134	211	345	107	231	5	69	–	10	1232	4.2	1.3	15.0
76-77–Cleveland	70	–	2109	435	1003	.434	–	–	–	288	370	.778	144	275	419	189	196	3	70	–	24	1158	6.0	2.7	16.5
77-78–Cleveland	72	–	2520	523	1168	.448	–	–	–	352	469	.751	154	304	458	278	193	3	88	206	12	1398	6.4	3.9	19.4
78-79–Cleveland	74	–	2859	603	1268	.476	–	–	–	417	523	.797	147	356	503	348	222	2	98	259	25	1623	6.8	4.7	21.9
79-80–Cleveland	41	–	1331	284	630	.451	1	9	.111	178	239	.745	76	149	225	173	113	1	72	148	20	747	5.5	4.2	18.2
80-81–New York	79	–	2865	508	1095	.464	8	26	.308	268	343	.781	109	244	353	257	248	2	99	212	8	1292	4.5	3.3	16.4
81-82–New York	77	63	2358	410	858	.478	25	57	.439	228	294	.776	86	150	236	284	221	1	77	195	12	1073	3.1	3.7	13.9
84-85–Cleveland	3	0	24	2	7	.286	0	1	.000	2	3	.667	0	5	5	3	3	0	0	5	0	6	1.7	1.0	2.0
Reg. Season Totals	566	63	16781	3398	7397	.459	34	93	.366	2123	2750	.772	893	1803	2696	1684	1527	17	594	1025	114	8953	4.8	3.0	15.8
Playoff Totals	20	0	605	120	288	.417	0	2	.000	91	108	.843	43	78	121	44	79	0	18	18	10	331	6.1	2.2	16.6
All-Star Totals	1	0	13	2	8	.250	0	0	–	0	0	–	1	0	1	0	0	0	0	1	0	4	1.0	0.0	4.0

Russell, Pierre Angelo b. December 13, 1949 Ht. 6-4 Wt. 190 College: Kansas

SEASON–TEAM	G	GS	MIN	FGM	FGA	PCT	3FGM	3FGA	PCT	FTM	FTA	PCT	O-RB	D-RB	TOT	AST	PF	DQ	STL	TO	BLK	PTS	RPG	APG	PPG
71-72–Kentucky (A)	51	–	397	65	153	.425	0	3	.000	16	21	.762	–	–	93	51	56	–	–	33	–	146	1.8	1.0	2.9
72-73–Kentucky (A)	59	–	618	119	266	.447	2	17	.118	49	78	.628	54	75	129	61	80	0	–	33	–	289	2.2	1.0	4.9
Reg. ABA Totals	110	–	1015	184	419	.439	2	20	.100	65	99	.657	54	75	222	112	136	0	–	66	–	435	2.0	1.0	4.0
ABA Playoff Totals	12	–	37	7	12	.583	0	0	–	3	6	.500	–	–	12	2	5	0	–	1	–	17	1.0	0.2	1.4

Russell, Rubin B. Jr. b. November 7, 1944 Ht. 6-3 Wt. 180 College: Parsons; North Texas

SEASON–TEAM	G	GS	MIN	FGM	FGA	PCT	3FGM	3FGA	PCT	FTM	FTA	PCT	O-RB	D-RB	TOT	AST	PF	DQ	STL	TO	BLK	PTS	RPG	APG	PPG
67-68–Dallas-Ken. (A)	26	–	269	56	158	.354	4	22	.182	25	41	.610	–	–	52	7	40	0	–	32	–	141	2.0	0.3	5.4
Reg. ABA Totals	26	–	269	56	158	.354	4	22	.182	25	41	.610	–	–	52	7	40	0	–	32	–	141	2.0	0.3	5.4

Russell, Walker D. b. October 26, 1960 Ht. 6-5 Wt. 195 College: Merritt (Calif.) Coll. (J.C.); Houston; Western Michigan

SEASON–TEAM	G	GS	MIN	FGM	FGA	PCT	3FGM	3FGA	PCT	FTM	FTA	PCT	O-RB	D-RB	TOT	AST	PF	DQ	STL	TO	BLK	PTS	RPG	APG	PPG
82-83–Detroit	68	1	757	67	184	.364	2	18	.111	47	58	.810	19	54	73	131	71	0	16	92	1	183	1.1	1.9	2.7
83-84–Detroit	16	0	119	14	42	.333	1	2	.500	12	13	.923	6	13	19	22	25	0	4	9	0	41	1.2	1.4	2.6
84-85–Atlanta	21	2	377	34	63	.540	1	1	1.000	14	17	.824	8	32	40	66	37	1	17	40	4	83	1.9	3.1	4.0
85-86–Detroit	1	0	2	0	1	.000	0	0	–	0	0	–	0	0	0	1	0	0	0	0	0	0	0.0	1.0	0.0
86-87–Indiana	48	0	511	64	165	.388	2	16	.125	27	37	.730	18	37	55	129	62	0	20	60	5	157	1.1	2.7	3.3
87-88–Detroit	1	0	1	0	1	.000	0	1	.000	0	0	–	0	0	0	1	0	0	0	0	0	0	0.0	1.0	0.0
Reg. Season Totals	155	3	1767	179	456	.393	6	38	.158	100	125	.800	51	136	187	350	195	1	57	201	10	464	1.2	2.3	3.0
Playoff Totals	7	0	10	2	5	.400	0	0	–	2	2	1.000	0	0	0	1	1	0	1	1	0	6	0.0	0.1	0.9

Russell, William Felton (Bill) b. February 12, 1934 Ht. 6-10 Wt. 220 College: San Francisco HOF: 1974

SEASON–TEAM	G	GS	MIN	FGM	FGA	PCT	3FGM	3FGA	PCT	FTM	FTA	PCT	O-RB	D-RB	TOT	AST	PF	DQ	STL	TO	BLK	PTS	RPG	APG	PPG
56-57–Boston	48	–	1695	277	649	.427	–	–	–	152	309	.492	–	–	943	88	143	2	–	–	–	706	19.6	1.8	14.7
57-58–Boston	69	–	2640	456	1032	.442	–	–	–	230	443	.519	–	–	1564	202	181	2	–	–	–	1142	22.7	2.9	16.6
58-59–Boston	70	–	2979	456	997	.457	–	–	–	256	428	.598	–	–	1612	222	161	3	–	–	–	1168	23.0	3.2	16.7
59-60–Boston	74	–	3146	555	1189	.467	–	–	–	240	392	.612	–	–	1778	277	210	0	–	–	–	1350	24.0	3.7	18.2
60-61–Boston	78	–	3458	532	1250	.426	–	–	–	258	469	.550	–	–	1868	268	155	0	–	–	–	1322	23.9	3.4	16.9
61-62–Boston	76	–	3433	575	1258	.457	–	–	–	286	481	.595	–	–	1790	341	207	3	–	–	–	1436	23.6	4.5	18.9
62-63–Boston	78	–	3500	511	1182	.432	–	–	–	287	517	.555	–	–	1843	348	189	1	–	–	–	1309	23.6	4.5	16.8
63-64–Boston	78	–	3482	466	1077	.433	–	–	–	236	429	.550	–	–	1930	370	190	0	–	–	–	1168	24.7	4.7	15.0
64-65–Boston	78	–	3466	429	980	.438	–	–	–	244	426	.573	–	–	1878	410	204	1	–	–	–	1102	24.1	5.3	14.1
65-66–Boston	78	–	3386	391	943	.415	–	–	–	223	405	.551	–	–	1779	371	221	4	–	–	–	1005	22.8	4.8	12.9
66-67–Boston	81	–	3297	395	870	.454	–	–	–	285	467	.610	–	–	1700	472	258	4	–	–	–	1075	21.0	5.8	13.3
67-68–Boston	78	–	2953	365	858	.425	–	–	–	247	460	.537	–	–	1451	357	242	2	–	–	–	977	18.6	4.6	12.5
68-69–Boston	77	–	3291	279	645	.433	–	–	–	204	388	.526	–	–	1484	374	231	2	–	–	–	762	19.3	4.9	9.9
Reg. Season Totals	963	–	40726	5687	12930	.440	–	–	–	3148	5614	.561	–	–	21620	4100	2592	24	–	–	–	14522	22.5	4.3	15.1
Playoff Totals	165	–	7497	1003	2335	.430	–	–	–	667	1106	.603	–	–	4104	770	546	8	–	–	–	2673	24.9	4.7	16.2
All-Star Totals	12	–	343	51	111	.459	–	–	–	18	34	.529	–	–	139	39	37	1	–	–	–	120	11.6	3.3	10.0

Sabonis, Arvydas b. December 19, 1964 Ht. 7-3 Wt. 292 Country: Lithuania

SEASON–TEAM	G	GS	MIN	FGM	FGA	PCT	3FGM	3FGA	PCT	FTM	FTA	PCT	O-RB	D-RB	TOT	AST	PF	DQ	STL	TO	BLK	PTS	RPG	APG	PPG
95-96–Portland	73	21	1735	394	723	.545	39	104	.375	231	305	.757	147	441	588	130	211	2	64	154	78	1058	8.1	1.8	14.5
96-97–Portland	69	68	1762	328	658	.498	49	132	.371	223	287	.777	114	433	547	146	203	4	63	151	84	928	7.9	2.1	13.4
97-98–Portland	73	73	2333	407	826	.493	30	115	.261	323	405	.798	149	580	729	218	267	7	65	190	80	1167	10.0	3.0	16.0
98-99–Portland	50	48	1349	232	478	.485	7	24	.292	135	175	.771	88	305	393	119	147	2	34	85	63	606	7.9	2.4	12.1
99-00–Portland	66	61	1688	302	598	.505	7	19	.368	167	198	.843	97	416	513	118	184	3	43	97	78	778	7.8	1.8	11.8
Reg. Season Totals	331	271	8867	1663	3283	.507	132	394	.335	1079	1370	.788	595	2175	2770	731	1012	18	269	677	383	4537	8.4	2.2	13.7
Playoff Totals	42	42	1277	184	426	.432	15	45	.333	140	174	.805	58	271	329	84	149	4	43	74	37	523	7.8	2.0	12.5

Sadowski, Edward Frank (Ed, Big Ed) b. July 11, 1917 d. September 18, 1990 Ht. 6-5 Wt. 240 College: Seton Hall

SEASON–TEAM	G	GS	MIN	FGM	FGA	PCT	3FGM	3FGA	PCT	FTM	FTA	PCT	O-RB	D-RB	TOT	AST	PF	DQ	STL	TO	BLK	PTS	RPG	APG	PPG
40-41–Detroit (N)	24	–	–	95	–	–	–	–	–	66	101	.653	–	–	–	–	63	–	–	–	–	256	–	–	10.7
44-45–Fort Wayne (N)	1	–	–	4	–	–	–	–	–	2	–	–	–	–	–	–	–	–	–	–	–	10	–	–	10.0
45-46–Fort Wayne (N)	34	–	–	122	–	–	–	–	–	82	120	.683	–	–	–	–	94	–	–	–	–	326	–	–	9.6
46-47–Toronto-Clev.	53	–	–	329	891	.369	–	–	–	219	328	.668	–	–	–	46	194	–	–	–	–	877	–	0.9	16.5
47-48–Boston	47	–	–	308	953	.323	–	–	–	294	422	.697	–	–	–	74	182	–	–	–	–	910	–	1.6	19.4
48-49–Philadelphia	60	–	–	340	839	.405	–	–	–	240	350	.686	–	–	–	160	273	–	–	–	–	920	–	2.7	15.3
49-50–Phil.-Balt.	69	–	–	299	922	.324	–	–	–	274	373	.735	–	–	–	136	244	–	–	–	–	872	–	2.0	12.6
Reg. NBA Totals	229	–	–	1276	3605	.354	–	–	–	1027	1473	.697	–	–	–	416	893	–	–	–	–	3579	–	1.8	15.6
Reg. NBL Totals	59	–	–	221	–	–	–	–	–	150	221	.670	–	–	–	–	157	–	–	–	–	592	–	–	10.0
NBA Playoff Totals	8	–	–	47	194	.340	–	–	–	58	85	.682	–	–	–	20	50	–	–	–	–	152	–	1.8	19.0
NBL Playoff Totals	14	–	–	44	–	–	–	–	–	37	31	.710	–	–	–	–	38	–	–	–	–	125	–	–	8.9

Sailors, Kenneth L. (Kenny) b. January 14, 1922 Ht. 5-10 Wt. 195 College: Wyoming

SEASON–TEAM	G	GS	MIN	FGM	FGA	PCT	3FGM	3FGA	PCT	FTM	FTA	PCT	O-RB	D-RB	TOT	AST	PF	DQ	STL	TO	BLK	PTS	RPG	APG	PPG
46-47–Cleveland	58	–	–	229	741	.309	–	–	–	119	200	.595	–	–	–	134	177	–	–	–	–	577	–	2.3	9.9
47-48–Chi.-Phil.-Prov.	44	–	–	207	689	.300	–	–	–	110	159	.692	–	–	–	59	162	–	–	–	–	524	–	1.3	11.9
48-49–Providence	57	–	–	309	906	.341	–	–	–	281	367	.766	–	–	–	209	239	–	–	–	–	899	–	3.7	15.8
49-50–Denver	57	–	–	329	944	.349	–	–	–	329	456	.721	–	–	–	229	242	–	–	–	–	987	–	4.0	17.3
50-51–Boston-Balt.	60	–	–	181	533	.340	–	–	–	131	180	.728	–	–	120	150	196	8	–	–	–	493	2.0	2.5	8.2
Reg. Season Totals	276	–	–	1255	3813	.329	–	–	–	970	1362	.712	–	–	120	781	1016	8	–	–	–	3480	2.0	2.8	12.6
Playoff Totals	2	–	–	6	16	.375	–	–	–	3	4	.750	–	–	–	4	8	1	–	–	–	15	–	2.0	7.5

Salley, John Thomas (Spider) b. May 16, 1964 Ht. 6-11 Wt. 255 College: Georgia Tech

SEASON–TEAM	G	GS	MIN	FGM	FGA	PCT	3FGM	3FGA	PCT	FTM	FTA	PCT	O-RB	D-RB	TOT	AST	PF	DQ	STL	TO	BLK	PTS	RPG	APG	PPG
86-87–Detroit	82	2	1463	163	290	.562	0	1	.000	105	171	.614	108	188	296	54	256	5	44	74	125	431	3.6	0.7	5.3
87-88–Detroit	82	16	2003	258	456	.566	0	0	–	185	261	.709	166	236	402	113	294	4	53	120	137	701	4.9	1.4	8.5
88-89–Detroit	67	21	1458	166	333	.498	0	2	.000	135	195	.692	134	201	335	75	197	3	40	100	72	467	5.0	1.1	7.0
89-90–Detroit	82	12	1914	209	408	.512	1	4	.250	174	244	.713	154	285	439	67	282	7	51	97	153	593	5.4	0.8	7.2
90-91–Detroit	74	1	1649	179	377	.475	0	1	.000	186	256	.727	137	190	327	70	240	7	52	91	112	544	4.4	0.9	7.4
91-92–Detroit	72	38	1774	249	486	.512	0	3	.000	186	260	.715	106	190	296	116	222	1	49	102	110	684	4.1	1.6	9.5
92-93–Miami	51	34	1422	154	307	.502	0	0	–	115	144	.799	113	200	313	83	192	7	32	101	70	423	6.1	1.6	8.3
93-94–Miami	76	45	1910	208	436	.477	2	3	.667	164	225	.729	132	275	407	135	260	4	56	94	78	582	5.4	1.8	7.7
94-95–Miami	75	50	1955	197	395	.499	0	0	–	153	207	.739	110	226	336	123	279	5	47	97	85	547	4.5	1.6	7.3
95-96–Toronto-Chicago	42	6	673	63	140	.450	0	0	–	59	85	.694	46	94	140	54	110	3	19	55	27	185	3.3	1.3	4.4
99-00–L.A. Lakers	45	3	303	25	69	.362	0	0	–	21	28	.750	20	45	65	26	67	1	8	18	14	71	1.4	0.6	1.6
Reg. Season Totals	748	228	16524	1871	3697	.506	3	14	.214	1483	2076	.714	1226	2130	3356	916	2399	47	451	949	983	5228	4.5	1.2	7.0
Playoff Totals	134	6	2694	296	586	.505	0	2	.000	265	384	.690	244	344	588	104	420	7	49	107	159	857	4.4	0.8	6.4

Salvadori, Albert Julian (Al) b. May 6, 1945 Ht. 6-9 Wt. 220 College: South Carolina

SEASON–TEAM	G	GS	MIN	FGM	FGA	PCT	3FGM	3FGA	PCT	FTM	FTA	PCT	O-RB	D-RB	TOT	AST	PF	DQ	STL	TO	BLK	PTS	RPG	APG	PPG
67-68–Oakland (A)	17	–	186	21	58	.362	1	1	1.000	11	16	.688	–	–	46	4	28	0	–	12	–	54	2.7	0.2	3.2
Reg. ABA Totals	17	–	186	21	58	.362	1	1	1.000	11	16	.688	–	–	46	4	28	0	–	12	–	54	2.7	0.2	3.2

Salvadori, Kevin Michael b. December 30, 1970 Ht. 7-0 Wt. 231 College: North Carolina

SEASON–TEAM	G	GS	MIN	FGM	FGA	PCT	3FGM	3FGA	PCT	FTM	FTA	PCT	O-RB	D-RB	TOT	AST	PF	DQ	STL	TO	BLK	PTS	RPG	APG	PPG
96-97–Sacramento	23	0	154	12	33	.364	0	0	–	13	18	.722	6	19	25	10	17	0	2	12	13	37	1.1	0.4	1.6
97-98–Sacramento	16	0	87	1	13	.077	0	0	–	3	6	.500	5	15	20	3	12	0	0	5	11	5	1.3	0.2	0.3
Reg. Season Totals	39	0	241	13	46	.283	0	0	–	16	24	.667	11	34	45	13	29	0	2	17	24	42	1.2	0.3	1.1

Sampson, Ralph Lee Jr. b. July 7, 1960 Ht. 7-4 Wt. 235 College: Virginia

SEASON–TEAM	G	GS	MIN	FGM	FGA	PCT	3FGM	3FGA	PCT	FTM	FTA	PCT	O-RB	D-RB	TOT	AST	PF	DQ	STL	TO	BLK	PTS	RPG	APG	PPG
83-84–Houston	82	82	2693	716	1369	.523	1	4	.250	287	434	.661	293	620	913	163	339	16	70	294	197	1720	11.1	2.0	21.0
84-85–Houston	82	82	3086	753	1499	.502	0	6	.000	303	448	.676	227	626	853	224	306	10	81	326	168	1809	10.4	2.7	22.1
85-86–Houston	79	76	2864	624	1280	.488	2	15	.133	241	376	.641	258	621	879	283	308	12	99	285	129	1491	11.1	3.6	18.9
86-87–Houston	43	32	1326	277	566	.489	0	3	.000	118	189	.624	88	284	372	120	169	6	40	126	58	672	8.7	2.8	15.6
87-88–Houston-G.S.	48	44	1663	299	682	.438	2	11	.182	149	196	.760	140	322	462	122	164	3	41	171	88	749	9.6	2.5	15.6
88-89–Golden State	61	36	1086	164	365	.449	3	8	.375	62	95	.653	105	202	307	77	170	3	31	90	65	393	5.0	1.3	6.4
89-90–Sacramento	26	7	417	48	129	.372	1	4	.250	12	23	.522	11	73	84	28	66	1	14	34	22	109	3.2	1.1	4.2
90-91–Sacramento	25	4	348	34	93	.366	1	5	.200	5	19	.263	41	70	111	17	54	0	11	27	17	74	4.4	0.7	3.0
91-92–Washington	10	0	108	9	29	.310	0	2	.000	4	6	.667	11	19	30	4	14	1	3	10	8	22	3.0	0.4	2.2
Reg. Season Totals	456	363	13591	2924	6012	.486	10	58	.172	1181	1786	.661	1174	2837	4011	1038	1590	52	390	1363	752	7039	8.8	2.3	15.4
Playoff Totals	38	36	1307	283	569	.497	3	8	.375	142	202	.703	124	276	400	109	157	4	35	123	57	711	10.5	2.9	18.7
All-Star Totals	3	2	66	21	33	.636	0	0	–	7	10	.700	5	14	19	2	13	0	0	6	1	49	6.3	0.7	16.3

Sanders, Albert T. III (Al, Apple) b. January 1, 1950 d. May 4, 1994 Ht. 6-7 Wt. 240 College: Louisiana State

SEASON–TEAM	G	GS	MIN	FGM	FGA	PCT	3FGM	3FGA	PCT	FTM	FTA	PCT	O-RB	D-RB	TOT	AST	PF	DQ	STL	TO	BLK	PTS	RPG	APG	PPG
72-73–Virginia (A)	4	–	25	2	2	1.000	0	0	–	4	6	.667	–	5	5	0	4	0	–	3	–	8	1.3	0.0	2.0
Reg. ABA Totals	4	–	25	2	2	1.000	0	0	–	4	6	.667	–	5	5	0	4	0	–	3	–	8	1.3	0.0	2.0

Sanders, Frankie J. b. January 23, 1957 Ht. 6-6 Wt. 200 College: Southern University

SEASON–TEAM	G	GS	MIN	FGM	FGA	PCT	3FGM	3FGA	PCT	FTM	FTA	PCT	O-RB	D-RB	TOT	AST	PF	DQ	STL	TO	BLK	PTS	RPG	APG	PPG
78-79–S.A.-Boston	46	–	479	105	246	.427	–	–	–	54	68	.794	35	75	110	52	69	1	21	55	6	264	2.4	1.1	5.7
80-81–Kansas City	23	–	186	34	77	.442	0	3	.000	20	22	.909	6	15	21	17	20	0	16	21	1	88	0.9	0.7	3.8
Reg. Season Totals	69	–	665	139	323	.430	0	3	.000	74	90	.822	41	90	131	69	89	1	37	76	7	352	1.9	1.0	5.1
Playoff Totals	9	–	50	9	18	.500	1	2	.500	4	4	1.000	4	1	5	2	8	0	3	8	0	23	0.6	0.2	2.6

Sanders, Jeffery Raynard (Jeff) b. January 14, 1966 Ht. 6-8 Wt. 240 College: Georgia Southern

SEASON–TEAM	G	GS	MIN	FGM	FGA	PCT	3FGM	3FGA	PCT	FTM	FTA	PCT	O-RB	D-RB	TOT	AST	PF	DQ	STL	TO	BLK	PTS	RPG	APG	PPG
89-90–Chicago	31	0	182	13	40	.325	0	0	–	2	4	.500	17	22	39	9	27	0	4	15	4	28	1.3	0.3	0.9
90-91–Charlotte	3	0	43	6	14	.429	0	0	–	1	2	.500	3	6	9	1	6	0	1	1	1	13	3.0	0.3	4.3
91-92–Atlanta	12	0	117	20	45	.444	0	0	–	7	9	.778	9	17	26	9	15	0	5	5	3	47	2.2	0.8	3.9
92-93–Atlanta	9	0	120	10	25	.400	0	0	–	4	8	.500	12	17	29	6	16	0	8	11	1	24	3.2	0.7	2.7
Reg. Season Totals	55	0	462	49	124	.395	0	0	–	14	23	.609	41	62	103	25	64	0	18	32	9	112	1.9	0.5	2.0
Playoff Totals	3	0	3	1	1	1.000	0	0	–	0	0	–	0	0	0	–	0	0	0	0	0	2	0.0	0.0	0.7

Sanders, Michael Anthony (Mike) b. May 7, 1960 Ht. 6-6 Wt. 210 College: UCLA

SEASON–TEAM	G	GS	MIN	FGM	FGA	PCT	3FGM	3FGA	PCT	FTM	FTA	PCT	O-RB	D-RB	TOT	AST	PF	DQ	STL	TO	BLK	PTS	RPG	APG	PPG
82-83–San Antonio	26	0	393	76	157	.484	0	2	.000	31	43	.721	31	63	94	19	57	0	18	28	6	183	3.6	0.7	7.0
83-84–Phoenix	50	0	586	97	203	.478	0	0	–	29	42	.690	40	63	103	44	101	0	23	44	12	223	2.1	0.9	4.5
84-85–Phoenix	21	11	418	85	175	.486	0	0	–	45	59	.763	38	51	89	29	59	0	23	34	4	215	4.2	1.4	10.2
85-86–Phoenix	82	5	1644	347	676	.513	3	15	.200	208	257	.809	104	169	273	150	236	3	76	143	31	905	3.3	1.8	11.0
86-87–Phoenix	82	4	1655	357	722	.494	2	17	.118	143	183	.781	101	170	271	126	210	1	61	105	23	859	3.3	1.5	10.5
87-88–Phoenix-Clev.	59	16	883	153	303	.505	0	1	.000	59	76	.776	38	71	109	56	131	1	31	50	9	365	1.8	0.9	6.2
88-89–Cleveland	82	82	2102	332	733	.453	3	10	.300	97	135	.719	98	209	307	133	230	2	89	104	32	764	3.7	1.6	9.3
89-90–Indiana	82	13	1531	225	479	.470	5	14	.357	55	75	.733	78	152	230	89	220	1	43	79	23	510	2.8	1.1	6.2
90-91–Indiana	80	7	1357	206	494	.417	4	20	.200	47	57	.825	73	112	185	106	198	1	37	65	26	463	2.3	1.3	5.8
91-92–Indiana-Clev.	31	20	633	92	161	.571	1	3	.333	36	47	.766	27	69	96	53	83	1	24	22	10	221	3.1	1.7	7.1
92-93–Cleveland	53	51	1189	197	396	.497	1	4	.250	59	78	.756	52	118	170	75	150	2	39	57	30	454	3.2	1.4	8.6
Reg. Season Totals	648	209	12391	2167	4499	.482	19	86	.221	809	1052	.769	680	1247	1927	880	1675	12	464	731	206	5162	3.0	1.4	8.0
Playoff Totals	67	35	1117	181	362	.500	3	9	.333	60	77	.779	70	98	168	85	166	0	43	73	22	425	2.5	1.3	6.3

Sanders, Thomas Ernest (Satch) b. November 8, 1938 Ht. 6-6 Wt. 210 College: New York U.

SEASON–TEAM	G	GS	MIN	FGM	FGA	PCT	3FGM	3FGA	PCT	FTM	FTA	PCT	O-RB	D-RB	TOT	AST	PF	DQ	STL	TO	BLK	PTS	RPG	APG	PPG
60-61–Boston	68	–	1084	148	352	.420	–	–	–	67	100	.670	–	–	385	44	131	1	–	–	–	363	5.7	0.6	5.3
61-62–Boston	80	–	2325	350	804	.435	–	–	–	197	263	.749	–	–	762	74	279	9	–	–	–	897	9.5	0.9	11.2
62-63–Boston	80	–	2148	339	744	.456	–	–	–	186	252	.738	–	–	576	95	262	5	–	–	–	864	7.2	1.2	10.8
63-64–Boston	80	–	2370	349	836	.417	–	–	–	213	280	.761	–	–	667	102	277	6	–	–	–	911	8.3	1.3	11.4
64-65–Boston	80	–	2459	374	871	.429	–	–	–	193	259	.745	–	–	661	92	318	15	–	–	–	941	8.3	1.2	11.8
65-66–Boston	72	–	1896	349	816	.428	–	–	–	211	276	.764	–	–	508	90	317	19	–	–	–	909	7.1	1.3	12.6
66-67–Boston	81	–	1926	323	755	.428	–	–	–	178	218	.817	–	–	439	91	304	6	–	–	–	824	5.4	1.1	10.2
67-68–Boston	78	–	1981	296	691	.428	–	–	–	200	255	.784	–	–	454	100	300	12	–	–	–	792	5.8	1.3	10.2
68-69–Boston	82	–	2184	364	847	.430	–	–	–	187	255	.733	–	–	574	110	293	9	–	–	–	915	7.0	1.3	11.2
69-70–Boston	57	–	1616	246	555	.443	–	–	–	161	183	.880	–	–	314	92	199	5	–	–	–	653	5.5	1.6	11.5
70-71–Boston	17	–	121	16	44	.364	–	–	–	7	8	.875	–	–	17	11	25	0	–	–	–	39	1.0	0.6	2.3
71-72–Boston	82	–	1631	215	524	.410	–	–	–	111	136	.816	–	–	353	98	257	7	–	–	–	541	4.3	1.2	6.6
72-73–Boston	59	–	423	47	149	.315	–	–	–	23	35	.657	–	–	88	27	82	0	–	–	–	117	1.5	0.5	2.0
Reg. Season Totals	916	–	22164	3416	7988	.428	–	–	–	1934	2520	.767	–	–	5798	1026	3044	94	–	–	–	8766	6.3	1.1	9.6
Playoff Totals	130	–	3039	465	1066	.436	–	–	–	212	296	.716	–	–	760	127	508	26	–	–	–	1142	5.8	1.0	8.8

Sanford, Ron b. June 11, 1946 Ht. 6-9 Wt. 215 College: New Mexico

SEASON–TEAM	G	GS	MIN	FGM	FGA	PCT	3FGM	3FGA	PCT	FTM	FTA	PCT	O-RB	D-RB	TOT	AST	PF	DQ	STL	TO	BLK	PTS	RPG	APG	PPG
71-72–Dallas (A)	1	–	2	0	0	–	0	0	–	0	0	–	–	–	0	0	1	–	–	0	–	0	0.0	0.0	0.0
Reg. ABA Totals	1	–	2	0	0	–	0	0	–	0	0	–	–	–	–	0	1	–	–	–	–	0	0.0	0.0	0.0

Santini, Robert (Bob) b. February 17, 1935 Ht. 6-5 Wt. 190 College: Iona

SEASON–TEAM	G	GS	MIN	FGM	FGA	PCT	3FGM	3FGA	PCT	FTM	FTA	PCT	O-RB	D-RB	TOT	AST	PF	DQ	STL	TO	BLK	PTS	RPG	APG	PPG
55-56–New York	4	–	23	5	10	.500	–	–	–	1	2	.500	–	–	3	1	4	0	–	–	–	11	0.8	0.3	2.8
Reg. Season Totals	4	–	23	5	10	.500	–	–	–	1	2	.500	–	–	3	1	4	0	–	–	–	11	0.8	0.3	2.8

Sappleton, Wayne B. b. November 17, 1960 Ht. 6-9 Wt. 230 College: Loyola (Chicago)

SEASON–TEAM	G	GS	MIN	FGM	FGA	PCT	3FGM	3FGA	PCT	FTM	FTA	PCT	O-RB	D-RB	TOT	AST	PF	DQ	STL	TO	BLK	PTS	RPG	APG	PPG
84-85–New Jersey	33	0	298	41	87	.471	0	0	–	14	34	.412	28	47	75	7	50	0	7	21	4	96	2.3	0.2	2.9
Reg. Season Totals	33	0	298	41	87	.471	0	0	–	14	34	.412	28	47	75	7	50	0	7	21	4	96	2.3	0.2	2.9

Sasser, Jason Jermane b. January 13, 1974 Ht. 6-7 Wt. 225 College: Texas Tech

SEASON–TEAM	G	GS	MIN	FGM	FGA	PCT	3FGM	3FGA	PCT	FTM	FTA	PCT	O-RB	D-RB	TOT	AST	PF	DQ	STL	TO	BLK	PTS	RPG	APG	PPG
96-97–S.A.-Dallas	8	0	69	9	23	.391	1	3	.333	0	0	–	1	7	8	2	11	0	3	2	0	19	1.0	0.3	2.4
98-99–Vancouver	6	0	39	5	11	.455	0	0	–	1	2	.500	2	5	7	2	4	0	2	2	0	11	1.2	0.3	1.8
Reg. Season Totals	14	0	108	14	34	.412	1	3	.333	1	2	.500	3	12	15	4	15	0	5	4	0	30	1.1	0.3	2.1

Saul, Frank Benjamin Jr. (Pep) b. February 16, 1924 Ht. 6-2 Wt. 185 College: Seton Hall

SEASON–TEAM	G	GS	MIN	FGM	FGA	PCT	3FGM	3FGA	PCT	FTM	FTA	PCT	O-RB	D-RB	TOT	AST	PF	DQ	STL	TO	BLK	PTS	RPG	APG	PPG
49-50–Rochester	49	–	–	74	183	.404	–	–	–	34	47	.723	–	–	–	28	33	–	–	–	–	182	–	0.6	3.7
50-51–Rochester	65	–	–	105	310	.339	–	–	–	72	105	.686	–	–	84	68	85	0	–	–	–	282	1.3	1.0	4.3
51-52–Balt.-Minn.	64	–	1479	157	436	.360	–	–	–	119	153	.778	–	–	165	147	120	3	–	–	–	433	2.6	2.3	6.8
52-53–Minneapolis	70	–	1796	187	471	.397	–	–	–	142	200	.710	–	–	141	110	174	3	–	–	–	516	2.0	1.6	7.4
53-54–Minneapolis	71	–	1805	162	467	.347	–	–	–	128	170	.753	–	–	159	139	149	3	–	–	–	452	2.2	2.0	6.4
54-55–Milwaukee	65	–	1139	96	303	.317	–	–	–	95	123	.772	–	–	134	104	126	0	–	–	–	287	2.1	1.6	4.4
Reg. Season Totals	384	–	6219	781	2170	.360	–	–	–	590	798	.739	–	–	683	596	687	9	–	–	–	2152	2.0	1.6	5.6
Playoff Totals	49	–	1281	116	295	.431	–	–	–	89	121	.736	–	–	121	105	119	2	–	–	–	321	2.0	1.6	6.6

S

Sauldsberry, Woodrow Jr. **(Woody)** b. July 11, 1934 Ht. 6-7 Wt. 220 College: Texas Southern

SEASON–TEAM	G	GS	MIN	FGM	FGA	PCT	3FGM	3FGA	PCT	FTM	FTA	PCT	O-RB	D-RB	TOT	AST	PF	DQ	STL	TO	BLK	PTS	RPG	APG	PPG
57-58–Philadelphia	71	–	2377	389	1082	.360	–	–	–	134	218	.615	–	–	729	58	245	3	–	–	–	912	10.3	0.8	12.8
58-59–Philadelphia	72	–	2743	501	1380	.363	–	–	–	110	176	.625	–	–	826	71	276	12	–	–	–	1112	11.5	1.0	15.4
59-60–Philadelphia	71	–	1848	325	974	.334	–	–	–	55	103	.534	–	–	447	112	203	2	–	–	–	705	6.3	1.6	9.9
60-61–St. Louis	69	–	1491	230	768	.299	–	–	–	56	100	.560	–	–	491	74	197	3	–	–	–	516	7.1	1.1	7.5
61-62–St. L.-Chicago	63	–	1765	298	869	.343	–	–	–	79	123	.642	–	–	536	90	179	5	–	–	–	675	8.5	1.4	10.7
62-63–Chicago-St. L.	77	–	2034	366	966	.379	–	–	–	107	163	.656	–	–	447	78	241	4	–	–	–	839	5.8	1.0	10.9
65-66–Boston	39	–	530	80	249	.321	–	–	–	11	22	.500	–	–	142	15	94	0	–	–	–	171	3.6	0.4	4.4
Reg. Season Totals	462	–	12788	2189	6288	.348	–	–	–	552	905	.610	–	–	3618	498	1435	29	–	–	–	4930	7.8	1.1	10.7
Playoff Totals	29	–	995	174	496	.351	–	–	–	35	62	.565	–	–	259	52	118	4	–	–	–	383	8.9	1.8	13.2
All-Star Totals	1	–	18	5	11	.455	–	–	–	4	4	1.000	–	–	2	3	2	0	–	–	–	14	2.0	3.0	14.0

Saulters, Glynn b. February 10, 1945 Ht. 6-2 Wt. 175 College: N.E. Louisiana (Renamed Louisiana-Monroe)

SEASON–TEAM	G	GS	MIN	FGM	FGA	PCT	3FGM	3FGA	PCT	FTM	FTA	PCT	O-RB	D-RB	TOT	AST	PF	DQ	STL	TO	BLK	PTS	RPG	APG	PPG
68-69–New Orleans (A)	22	–	120	22	70	.314	0	1	.000	15	22	.682	–	–	19	11	25	0	–	11	–	59	0.9	0.5	2.7
Reg. ABA Totals	22	–	120	22	70	.314	0	1	.000	15	22	.682	–	–	19	11	25	0	–	11	–	59	0.9	0.5	2.7

Saunders, James Frederick **(Fred)** b. June 13, 1951 Ht. 6-7 Wt. 210 College: Syracuse

SEASON–TEAM	G	GS	MIN	FGM	FGA	PCT	3FGM	3FGA	PCT	FTM	FTA	PCT	O-RB	D-RB	TOT	AST	PF	DQ	STL	TO	BLK	PTS	RPG	APG	PPG
74-75–Phoenix	69	–	1059	176	406	.433	–	–	–	66	95	.695	82	171	253	80	151	3	41	–	15	418	3.7	1.2	6.1
75-76–Phoenix	17	–	146	28	64	.438	–	–	–	6	11	.545	11	26	37	13	23	0	5	–	1	62	2.2	0.8	3.6
76-77–Boston	68	–	1051	184	395	.466	–	–	–	35	53	.660	73	150	223	85	191	3	26	–	7	403	3.3	1.3	5.9
77-78–Boston-N.O.	56	–	643	99	234	.423	–	–	–	26	36	.722	38	73	111	46	106	3	21	42	14	224	2.0	0.8	4.0
Reg. Season Totals	210	–	2899	487	1099	.443	–	–	–	133	195	.682	204	420	624	224	471	9	93	42	37	1107	3.0	1.1	5.3
Playoff Totals	9	–	66	12	33	.364	–	–	–	5	6	.833	1	8	9	5	21	0	1	–	0	29	1.0	0.6	3.2

Savage, Donald Joseph **(Don)** b. April 9, 1928 Ht. 6-3 Wt. 205 College: Le Moyne

SEASON–TEAM	G	GS	MIN	FGM	FGA	PCT	3FGM	3FGA	PCT	FTM	FTA	PCT	O-RB	D-RB	TOT	AST	PF	DQ	STL	TO	BLK	PTS	RPG	APG	PPG
51-52–Syracuse	12	–	118	9	43	.209	–	–	–	18	28	.643	–	–	24	12	22	0	–	–	–	36	2.0	1.0	3.0
56-57–Syracuse	5	–	55	6	19	.316	–	–	–	6	7	.857	–	–	7	2	7	0	–	–	–	18	1.4	0.4	3.6
Reg. Season Totals	17	–	173	15	62	.242	–	–	–	24	35	.686	–	–	31	14	29	0	–	–	–	54	1.8	0.8	3.2

Sawyer, Alan Leigh b. January 1, 1928 Ht. 6-5 Wt. 195 College: UCLA

SEASON–TEAM	G	GS	MIN	FGM	FGA	PCT	3FGM	3FGA	PCT	FTM	FTA	PCT	O-RB	D-RB	TOT	AST	PF	DQ	STL	TO	BLK	PTS	RPG	APG	PPG
50-51–Washington	33	–	–	87	215	.405	–	–	–	43	54	.796	–	–	125	25	75	1	–	–	–	217	3.8	0.8	6.6
Reg. Season Totals	33	–	–	87	215	.405	–	–	–	43	54	.796	–	–	125	25	75	1	–	–	–	217	3.8	0.8	6.6

Scales, DeWayne Jay **(Hot Man)** b. December 28, 1958 Ht. 6-8 Wt. 215 College: Louisiana State

SEASON–TEAM	G	GS	MIN	FGM	FGA	PCT	3FGM	3FGA	PCT	FTM	FTA	PCT	O-RB	D-RB	TOT	AST	PF	DQ	STL	TO	BLK	PTS	RPG	APG	PPG
80-81–New York	44	–	484	94	225	.418	1	6	.167	26	39	.667	47	85	132	10	54	0	12	30	4	215	3.0	0.2	4.9
81-82–New York	3	0	24	1	5	.200	0	0	–	1	2	.500	2	3	5	0	3	0	1	2	1	3	1.7	0.0	1.0
83-84–Washington	2	0	13	3	5	.600	0	0	–	0	2	.000	0	3	3	0	1	0	1	2	0	6	1.5	0.0	3.0
Reg. Season Totals	49	0	521	98	235	.417	1	6	.167	27	43	.628	49	91	140	10	58	0	14	34	5	224	2.9	0.2	4.6

Schade, Frank b. January 22, 1950 Ht. 6-1 Wt. 170 College: Wisconsin-Eau Claire; Texas-El Paso

SEASON–TEAM	G	GS	MIN	FGM	FGA	PCT	3FGM	3FGA	PCT	FTM	FTA	PCT	O-RB	D-RB	TOT	AST	PF	DQ	STL	TO	BLK	PTS	RPG	APG	PPG
72-73–K.C.-Omaha	9	–	76	2	7	.286	–	–	–	6	6	1.000	–	–	6	10	12	0	–	–	–	10	0.7	1.1	1.1
Reg. Season Totals	9	–	76	2	7	.286	–	–	–	6	6	1.000	–	–	6	10	12	0	–	–	–	10	0.7	1.1	1.1

Schadler, Bernard R. **(Ben)** b. March 9, 1924 Ht. 6-2 Wt. 185 College: Northwestern

SEASON–TEAM	G	GS	MIN	FGM	FGA	PCT	3FGM	3FGA	PCT	FTM	FTA	PCT	O-RB	D-RB	TOT	AST	PF	DQ	STL	TO	BLK	PTS	RPG	APG	PPG
47-48–Chicago	37	–	–	23	116	.198	–	–	–	10	13	.769	–	–	–	6	40	–	–	–	–	56	–	0.2	1.5
48-49–Det.-Wat. (N)	53	–	–	150	–	–	–	–	–	58	89	.652	–	–	–	–	104	–	–	–	–	358	–	–	6.8
Reg. NBA Totals	37	–	–	23	116	.198	–	–	–	10	13	.769	–	–	–	6	40	–	–	–	–	56	–	0.2	1.5
Reg. NBL Totals	53	–	–	150	–	–	–	–	–	58	89	.652	–	–	–	–	104	–	–	–	–	358	–	–	6.8
NBA Playoff Totals	4	–	–	5	46	.217	–	–	–	0	2	.000	–	–	–	2	8	–	–	–	–	10	–	0.3	2.5

Schaefer, Herman H. (Herm) b. December 20, 1919 d. March 21, 1980 Ht. 6-0 Wt. 175 College: Indiana

SEASON–TEAM	G	GS	MIN	FGM	FGA	PCT	3FGM	3FGA	PCT	FTM	FTA	PCT	O-RB	D-RB	TOT	AST	PF	DQ	STL	TO	BLK	PTS	RPG	APG	PPG
41-42–Fort Wayne (N)	24	–	–	85	–	–	–	–	–	37	–	–	–	–	–	–	–	–	–	–	–	207	–	–	8.6
42-43–Fort Wayne (N)	21	–	–	36	–	–	–	–	–	12	–	–	–	–	–	–	–	–	–	–	–	84	–	–	4.0
45-46–Fort Wayne (N)	15	–	–	10	–	–	–	–	–	3	–	–	–	–	–	–	–	–	–	–	–	23	–	–	1.5
46-47–Indianapolis (N)	44	–	–	147	–	–	–	–	–	65	90	.722	–	–	–	–	45	–	–	–	–	359	–	–	8.2
47-48–Ind.-Minn. (N)	57	–	–	110	–	–	–	–	–	78	96	.813	–	–	–	–	74	–	–	–	–	298	–	–	5.2
48-49–Minneapolis	58	–	–	214	572	.374	–	–	–	174	213	.817	–	–	–	185	121	–	–	–	–	602	–	3.2	10.4
49-50–Minneapolis	65	–	–	122	314	.389	–	–	–	86	101	.851	–	–	–	203	104	–	–	–	–	330	–	3.1	5.1
Reg. NBA Totals	123	–	–	336	886	.379	–	–	–	260	314	.828	–	–	–	388	225	–	–	–	–	932	–	3.2	7.6
Reg. NBL Totals	161	–	–	388	–	–	–	–	–	195	186	.769	–	–	–	–	119	–	–	–	–	971	–	–	6.0
NBA Playoff Totals	22	–	–	64	292	.438	–	–	–	47	53	.887	–	–	–	94	33	–	–	–	–	175	–	2.1	8.0
NBL Playoff Totals	26	–	–	92	–	–	–	–	–	53	52	.808	–	–	–	–	31	–	–	–	–	237	–	–	9.1

Schaeffer, William G. (Billy) b. December 11, 1951 Ht. 6-5 Wt. 200 College: St. John's (N.Y.)

SEASON–TEAM	G	GS	MIN	FGM	FGA	PCT	3FGM	3FGA	PCT	FTM	FTA	PCT	O-RB	D-RB	TOT	AST	PF	DQ	STL	TO	BLK	PTS	RPG	APG	PPG
73-74–New York (A)	59	–	871	171	344	.497	2	9	.222	41	54	.759	49	92	141	37	140	–	24	53	9	385	2.4	0.6	6.5
74-75–New York (A)	27	–	280	61	131	.466	2	7	.286	15	25	.600	15	22	37	20	36	–	9	18	2	139	1.4	0.7	5.1
75-76–N.Y.-Vir. (A)	51	–	637	114	258	.442	2	10	.200	48	63	.762	39	72	111	37	72	–	19	35	9	278	2.2	0.7	5.5
Reg. ABA Totals	137	–	1788	346	733	.472	6	26	.231	104	142	.732	103	186	289	94	248	0	52	106	20	802	2.1	0.7	5.9
ABA Playoff Totals	5	–	23	8	16	.500	0	0	–	3	4	.750	6	3	9	3	3	0	0	1	0	19	1.8	0.6	3.8

Schafer, Robert Thomas (Bob) b. 1933 Ht. 6-3 Wt. 195 College: Villanova

SEASON–TEAM	G	GS	MIN	FGM	FGA	PCT	3FGM	3FGA	PCT	FTM	FTA	PCT	O-RB	D-RB	TOT	AST	PF	DQ	STL	TO	BLK	PTS	RPG	APG	PPG
55-56–Phil.-St. Louis	54	–	578	81	270	.300	–	–	–	62	81	.765	–	–	71	53	75	0	–	–	–	224	1.3	1.0	4.1
Reg. Season Totals	65	–	745	100	336	.298	–	–	–	73	94	.777	–	–	82	68	91	0	–	–	–	273	1.3	1.3	4.2
Playoff Totals	4	–	39	3	20	.150	–	–	–	5	6	.833	–	–	9	1	8	1	–	–	–	11	2.3	0.3	2.8

Scharnus, Benedict Michael (Ben, Whitey) b. December 11, 1917 d. March 19, 1982 Ht. 6-2 Wt. 175 College: Seton Hall

SEASON–TEAM	G	GS	MIN	FGM	FGA	PCT	3FGM	3FGA	PCT	FTM	FTA	PCT	O-RB	D-RB	TOT	AST	PF	DQ	STL	TO	BLK	PTS	RPG	APG	PPG
46-47–Cleveland	51	–	–	33	165	.200	–	–	–	37	59	.627	–	–	–	19	83	–	–	–	–	103	–	0.4	2.0
48-49–Providence	1	–	–	0	1	.000	–	–	–	0	1	.000	–	–	–	0	0	–	–	–	–	0	–	0.0	0.0
Reg. Season Totals	52	–	–	33	166	.199	–	–	–	37	60	.617	–	–	–	19	83	–	–	–	–	103	–	0.4	2.0
Playoff Totals	3	–	–	6	21	.286	–	–	–	5	9	.556	–	–	–	2	10	1	–	–	–	17	–	0.7	5.7

Schatzman, Marvin J. (Marv) b. February 18, 1927 Ht. 6-5 Wt. 200 College: St. Louis

SEASON–TEAM	G	GS	MIN	FGM	FGA	PCT	3FGM	3FGA	PCT	FTM	FTA	PCT	O-RB	D-RB	TOT	AST	PF	DQ	STL	TO	BLK	PTS	RPG	APG	PPG
49-50–Baltimore	34	–	–	43	174	.247	–	–	–	29	50	.580	–	–	–	38	49	–	–	–	–	115	–	1.1	3.4
Reg. Season Totals	34	–	–	43	174	.247	–	–	–	29	50	.580	–	–	–	38	49	–	–	–	–	115	–	1.1	3.4

Schaus, Frederick Appleton (Fred) b. June 30, 1925 Ht. 6-5 Wt. 210 College: West Virginia

SEASON–TEAM	G	GS	MIN	FGM	FGA	PCT	3FGM	3FGA	PCT	FTM	FTA	PCT	O-RB	D-RB	TOT	AST	PF	DQ	STL	TO	BLK	PTS	RPG	APG	PPG
49-50–Fort Wayne	68	–	–	351	996	.352	–	–	–	270	330	.818	–	–	–	176	232	–	–	–	–	972	–	2.6	14.3
50-51–Fort Wayne	68	–	–	312	918	.340	–	–	–	404	484	.835	–	–	495	184	240	11	–	–	–	1028	7.3	2.7	15.1
51-52–Fort Wayne	62	–	2581	281	778	.361	–	–	–	310	372	.833	–	–	434	247	221	7	–	–	–	872	7.0	4.0	14.1
52-53–Fort Wayne	69	–	2541	240	719	.334	–	–	–	243	296	.821	–	–	413	245	261	11	–	–	–	723	6.0	3.6	10.5
53-54–FtWayne-N.Y.	67	–	1515	161	415	.388	–	–	–	153	195	.785	–	–	267	109	176	3	–	–	–	475	4.0	1.6	7.1
Reg. Season Totals	334	–	6637	1345	3826	.352	–	–	–	1380	1677	.823	–	–	1609	961	1130	32	–	–	–	4070	6.0	2.9	12.2
Playoff Totals	21	–	543	78	315	.349	–	–	–	91	112	.813	–	–	100	80	86	4	–	–	–	247	5.3	3.0	11.8
All-Star Totals	1	–	0	2	9	.222	–	–	–	4	4	1.000	–	–	4	2	3	0	–	–	–	8	4.0	2.0	8.0

S

Schayes, Adolph (Dolph) b. May 19, 1928 Ht. 6-8 Wt. 220 College: New York U. HOF: 1972

SEASON–TEAM	G	GS	MIN	FGM	FGA	PCT	3FGM	3FGA	PCT	FTM	FTA	PCT	O-RB	D-RB	TOT	AST	PF	DQ	STL	TO	BLK	PTS	RPG	APG	PPG
48-49–Syracuse (N)	63	–	–	271	–	–	–	–	–	267	370	.722	–	–	–	–	232	–	–	–	–	809	–	–	12.8
49-50–Syracuse	64	–	–	348	903	.385	–	–	–	376	486	.774	–	–	–	259	225	–	–	–	–	1072	–	4.0	16.8
50-51–Syracuse	66	–	–	332	930	.357	–	–	–	457	608	.752	–	–	1080	251	271	9	–	–	–	1121	16.4	3.8	17.0
51-52–Syracuse	63	–	2004	263	740	.355	–	–	–	342	424	.807	–	–	773	182	213	5	–	–	–	868	12.3	2.9	13.8
52-53–Syracuse	71	–	2668	375	1002	.374	–	–	–	512	619	.827	–	–	920	227	271	9	–	–	–	1262	13.0	3.2	17.8
53-54–Syracuse	72	–	2655	370	973	.380	–	–	–	488	590	.827	–	–	870	214	232	4	–	–	–	1228	12.1	3.0	17.1
54-55–Syracuse	72	–	2526	422	1103	.383	–	–	–	489	587	.833	–	–	887	213	247	6	–	–	–	1333	12.3	3.0	18.5
55-56–Syracuse	72	–	2517	465	1202	.387	–	–	–	542	632	.858	–	–	891	200	251	9	–	–	–	1472	12.4	2.8	20.4
56-57–Syracuse	72	–	2851	496	1308	.379	–	–	–	625	691	.904	–	–	1008	229	219	5	–	–	–	1617	14.0	3.2	22.5
57-58–Syracuse	72	–	2918	581	1458	.398	–	–	–	629	696	.904	–	–	1022	224	244	6	–	–	–	1791	14.2	3.1	24.9
58-59–Syracuse	72	–	2645	504	1304	.387	–	–	–	526	609	.864	–	–	962	178	280	9	–	–	–	1534	13.4	2.5	21.3
59-60–Syracuse	75	–	2741	578	1440	.401	–	–	–	533	597	.893	–	–	959	256	263	10	–	–	–	1689	12.8	3.4	22.5
60-61–Syracuse	79	–	3007	594	1595	.372	–	–	–	680	783	.868	–	–	960	296	296	9	–	–	–	1868	12.2	3.7	23.6
61-62–Syracuse	56	–	1480	268	751	.357	–	–	–	286	319	.897	–	–	439	120	167	4	–	–	–	822	7.8	2.1	14.7
62-63–Syracuse	66	–	1438	223	575	.388	–	–	–	181	206	.879	–	–	375	175	177	2	–	–	–	627	5.7	2.7	9.5
63-64–Philadelphia	24	–	350	44	143	.308	–	–	–	46	57	.807	–	–	110	48	76	3	–	–	–	134	4.6	2.0	5.6
Reg. NBA Totals	996	–	29800	5863	15427	.380	–	–	–	6712	7904	.849	–	–	11256	3072	3432	90	–	–	–	18438	12.1	3.1	18.5
Reg. NBL Totals	63	–	–	271	–	–	–	–	–	267	370	.722	–	–	–	–	232	–	–	–	–	809	–	–	12.8
NBA Playoff Totals	97	–	3016	582	1587	.393	–	–	–	722	875	.825	–	–	1150	281	371	12	–	–	–	1886	11.9	2.5	19.4
NBL Playoff Totals	6	–	–	27	–	–	–	–	–	32	42	.762	–	–	–	–	26	–	–	–	–	86	–	–	14.3
NBA All-Star Totals	11	–	248	48	109	.440	–	–	–	42	50	.840	–	–	105	17	32	1	–	–	–	138	9.5	1.5	12.5

Schayes, Daniel Leslie (Danny) b. May 10, 1959 Ht. 6-11 Wt. 260 College: Syracuse

SEASON–TEAM	G	GS	MIN	FGM	FGA	PCT	3FGM	3FGA	PCT	FTM	FTA	PCT	O-RB	D-RB	TOT	AST	PF	DQ	STL	TO	BLK	PTS	RPG	APG	PPG
81-82–Utah	82	20	1623	252	524	.481	0	1	.000	140	185	.757	131	296	427	146	292	4	46	151	72	644	5.2	1.8	7.9
82-83–Utah-Denver	82	50	2284	342	749	.457	0	1	.000	228	295	.773	200	435	635	205	325	8	54	253	98	912	7.7	2.5	11.1
83-84–Denver	82	15	1420	183	371	.493	0	2	.000	215	272	.790	145	288	433	91	308	5	32	119	60	581	5.3	1.1	7.1
84-85–Denver	56	0	542	60	129	.465	0	0	–	79	97	.814	48	96	144	38	98	2	20	44	25	199	2.6	0.7	3.6
85-86–Denver	80	13	1654	221	440	.502	0	1	.000	216	278	.777	154	285	439	79	298	7	42	105	63	658	5.5	1.0	8.2
86-87–Denver	76	41	1556	210	405	.519	0	0	–	229	294	.779	120	260	380	85	266	5	20	95	74	649	5.0	1.1	8.5
87-88–Denver	81	74	2166	361	668	.540	0	2	.000	407	487	.836	200	462	662	106	323	9	62	155	92	1129	8.2	1.3	13.9
88-89–Denver	76	64	1918	317	607	.522	3	9	.333	332	402	.826	142	358	500	105	320	8	42	160	81	969	6.6	1.4	12.8
89-90–Denver	53	22	1194	163	330	.494	0	4	.000	225	264	.852	117	225	342	61	200	7	41	72	45	551	6.5	1.2	10.4
90-91–Milwaukee	82	38	2228	298	597	.499	0	5	.000	274	328	.835	174	361	535	98	264	4	55	106	61	870	6.5	1.2	10.6
91-92–Milwaukee	43	4	726	83	199	.417	0	0	–	74	96	.771	58	110	168	34	98	0	19	41	19	240	3.9	0.8	5.6
92-93–Milwaukee	70	7	1124	105	263	.399	0	3	.000	112	137	.818	72	177	249	78	148	1	36	65	36	322	3.6	1.1	4.6
93-94–Milw.-Lakers	36	6	363	28	84	.333	0	0	–	29	32	.906	31	48	79	13	45	0	10	23	10	85	2.2	0.4	2.4
94-95–Phoenix	69	27	823	126	248	.508	1	1	1.000	50	69	.725	57	151	208	89	170	0	20	64	37	303	3.0	1.3	4.4
95-96–Miami	32	6	399	32	94	.340	0	0	–	37	46	.804	29	60	89	9	60	0	11	23	16	101	2.8	0.3	3.2
96-97–Orlando	45	6	540	47	120	.392	0	1	.000	39	52	.750	41	84	125	14	74	0	15	27	16	133	2.8	0.3	3.0
97-98–Orlando	74	33	1272	155	371	.418	0	0	–	96	119	.807	97	145	242	44	182	0	34	61	33	406	3.3	0.6	5.5
98-99–Orlando	19	1	143	11	29	.379	0	0	–	6	8	.750	3	11	14	4	23	0	1	8	2	28	0.7	0.2	1.5
Reg. Season Totals	1138	427	21975	2994	6228	.481	4	30	.133	2788	3461	.806	1819	3852	5671	1299	3494	60	560	1572	840	8780	5.0	1.1	7.7
Playoff Totals	69	22	1416	189	365	.518	0	2	.000	163	198	.823	108	223	331	76	227	2	26	98	47	541	4.8	1.1	7.8

Schectman, Oscar B. (Ossie) b. March 30, 1919 Ht. 6-0 Wt. 175 College: Long Island University

SEASON–TEAM	G	GS	MIN	FGM	FGA	PCT	3FGM	3FGA	PCT	FTM	FTA	PCT	O-RB	D-RB	TOT	AST	PF	DQ	STL	TO	BLK	PTS	RPG	APG	PPG
46-47–New York	54	–	–	162	588	.276	–	–	–	111	179	.620	–	–	–	109	115	–	–	–	–	435	–	2.0	8.1
Reg. Season Totals	54	–	–	162	588	.276	–	–	–	111	179	.620	–	–	–	109	115	–	–	–	–	435	–	2.0	8.1

Scheffler, Stephen Robert (Steve) b. September 3, 1967 Ht. 6-9 Wt. 250 College: Purdue

SEASON–TEAM	G	GS	MIN	FGM	FGA	PCT	3FGM	3FGA	PCT	FTM	FTA	PCT	O-RB	D-RB	TOT	AST	PF	DQ	STL	TO	BLK	PTS	RPG	APG	PPG
90-91–Charlotte	39	0	227	20	39	.513	0	0	–	19	21	.905	21	24	45	9	20	0	6	4	2	59	1.2	0.2	1.5
91-92–Sac.-Denver	11	0	61	6	9	.667	0	0	–	9	12	.750	10	4	14	0	10	0	3	1	1	21	1.3	0.0	1.9
92-93–Seattle	29	5	166	25	48	.521	0	0	–	16	24	.667	15	21	36	5	37	0	6	5	1	66	1.2	0.2	2.3
93-94–Seattle	35	1	152	28	46	.609	0	0	–	19	20	.950	11	15	26	6	25	0	7	8	0	75	0.7	0.2	2.1
94-95–Seattle	18	0	102	12	23	.522	0	0	–	15	18	.833	8	15	23	4	9	0	2	3	2	39	1.3	0.2	2.2
95-96–Seattle	35	2	181	24	45	.533	1	5	.200	9	19	.474	15	18	33	2	25	0	6	8	2	58	0.9	0.1	1.7
96-97–Seattle	7	0	29	6	7	.857	0	0	–	1	2	.500	1	2	3	0	5	0	0	5	0	13	0.4	0.0	1.9
Reg. Season Totals	174	8	918	121	217	.558	1	5	.200	88	116	.759	81	99	180	26	131	0	30	34	8	331	1.0	0.1	1.9
Playoff Totals	19	0	54	7	16	.438	0	0	–	4	8	.500	8	12	20	3	4	0	4	1	0	18	1.1	0.2	0.9

Scheffler, Thomas Mark (Tom) b. October 27, 1954 Ht. 6-11 Wt. 240 College: Purdue

SEASON–TEAM	G	GS	MIN	FGM	FGA	PCT	3FGM	3FGA	PCT	FTM	FTA	PCT	O-RB	D-RB	TOT	AST	PF	DQ	STL	TO	BLK	PTS	RPG	APG	PPG
84-85–Portland	39	0	268	21	51	.412	0	0	–	10	20	.500	18	58	76	11	48	0	8	15	11	52	1.9	0.3	1.3
Reg. Season Totals	39	0	268	21	51	.412	0	0	–	10	20	.500	18	58	76	11	48	0	8	15	11	52	1.9	0.3	1.3
Playoff Totals	3	0	10	2	3	.667	0	0	–	3	4	.750	3	2	5	–	0	0	1	1	0	7	1.7	0.0	2.3

Schellhase, David Gene Jr. (Dave) b. October 14, 1944 Ht. 6-3 Wt. 205 College: Purdue

SEASON–TEAM	G	GS	MIN	FGM	FGA	PCT	3FGM	3FGA	PCT	FTM	FTA	PCT	O-RB	D-RB	TOT	AST	PF	DQ	STL	TO	BLK	PTS	RPG	APG	PPG
66-67–Chicago	31	–	212	40	111	.360	–	–	–	14	22	.636	–	–	29	23	27	0	–	–	–	94	0.9	0.7	3.0
67-68–Chicago	42	–	301	47	138	.341	–	–	–	20	38	.526	–	–	47	37	43	0	–	–	–	114	1.1	0.9	2.7
Reg. Season Totals	73	–	513	87	249	.349	–	–	–	34	60	.567	–	–	76	60	70	0	–	–	–	208	1.0	0.8	2.8
Playoff Totals	3	–	8	1	5	.200	–	–	–	1	2	.500	–	–	1	–	0	0	–	–	–	3	0.3	0.0	1.0

Scherer, Herbert Frederick (Herb) b. December 21, 1929 Ht. 6-9 Wt. 215 College: Long Island University

SEASON–TEAM	G	GS	MIN	FGM	FGA	PCT	3FGM	3FGA	PCT	FTM	FTA	PCT	O-RB	D-RB	TOT	AST	PF	DQ	STL	TO	BLK	PTS	RPG	APG	PPG
50-51–Tri-Cities	20	–	–	24	84	.286	–	–	–	20	35	.571	–	–	50	17	56	1	–	–	–	68	2.5	0.9	3.4
51-52–New York	12	–	167	19	65	.292	–	–	–	9	14	.643	–	–	26	6	25	0	–	–	–	47	2.2	0.5	3.9
Reg. Season Totals	32	–	167	43	149	.289	–	–	–	29	49	.592	–	–	76	23	81	1	–	–	–	115	2.4	0.7	3.6

Schintzius, Dwayne Kenneth b. October 14, 1968 Ht. 7-2 Wt. 285 College: Florida

SEASON–TEAM	G	GS	MIN	FGM	FGA	PCT	3FGM	3FGA	PCT	FTM	FTA	PCT	O-RB	D-RB	TOT	AST	PF	DQ	STL	TO	BLK	PTS	RPG	APG	PPG
90-91–San Antonio	42	7	398	68	155	.439	0	2	.000	22	40	.550	28	93	121	17	64	0	2	34	29	158	2.9	0.4	3.8
91-92–Sacramento	33	0	400	50	117	.427	0	4	.000	10	12	.833	43	75	118	20	67	1	6	19	28	110	3.6	0.6	3.3
92-93–New Jersey	5	0	35	2	7	.286	0	0	–	3	3	1.000	2	6	8	2	4	0	2	0	2	7	1.6	0.4	1.4
93-94–New Jersey	30	7	319	29	84	.345	0	0	–	10	17	.588	26	63	89	13	49	1	7	13	17	68	3.0	0.4	2.3
94-95–New Jersey	43	11	318	41	108	.380	0	0	–	6	11	.545	29	52	81	15	45	0	3	17	17	88	1.9	0.3	2.0
95-96–Indiana	33	8	297	49	110	.445	0	0	–	13	21	.619	23	55	78	14	53	0	9	19	12	111	2.4	0.4	3.4
96-97–L.A. Clippers	15	0	116	13	36	.361	1	2	.500	7	8	.875	9	13	22	4	22	0	1	7	9	34	1.5	0.3	2.3
98-99–Boston	16	0	67	4	16	.250	0	0	–	3	4	.750	7	12	19	8	17	0	0	10	3	11	1.2	0.5	0.7
Reg. Season Totals	217	33	1950	256	633	.404	1	8	.125	74	116	.638	167	369	536	93	321	2	30	119	117	587	2.5	0.4	2.7
Playoff Totals	5	0	106	13	29	.448	0	0	–	3	6	.500	6	19	25	4	12	0	1	3	6	29	5.0	0.8	5.8

Schlueter, Dale Wayne b. November 12, 1945 Ht. 6-10 Wt. 225 College: Colorado State

SEASON–TEAM	G	GS	MIN	FGM	FGA	PCT	3FGM	3FGA	PCT	FTM	FTA	PCT	O-RB	D-RB	TOT	AST	PF	DQ	STL	TO	BLK	PTS	RPG	APG	PPG
68-69–San Francisco	31	–	559	68	157	.433	–	–	–	45	82	.549	–	–	216	30	81	3	–	–	–	181	7.0	1.0	5.8
69-70–San Francisco	63	–	685	82	167	.491	–	–	–	60	97	.619	–	–	231	25	108	0	–	–	–	224	3.7	0.4	3.6
70-71–Portland	80	–	1823	257	527	.488	–	–	–	143	218	.656	–	–	629	192	265	4	–	–	–	657	7.9	2.4	8.2
71-72–Portland	81	–	2693	353	672	.525	–	–	–	241	326	.739	–	–	860	285	277	3	–	–	–	947	10.6	3.5	11.7
72-73–Philadelphia	78	–	1136	166	317	.524	–	–	–	86	123	.699	–	–	354	103	166	0	–	–	–	418	4.5	1.3	5.4
73-74–Atlanta	57	–	547	63	135	.467	–	–	–	38	50	.760	54	101	155	45	84	0	25	–	22	164	2.7	0.8	2.9
74-75–Buffalo	76	–	962	92	178	.517	–	–	–	84	121	.694	78	186	264	104	163	0	18	–	42	268	3.5	1.4	3.5
75-76–Buffalo	71	–	773	61	122	.500	–	–	–	54	81	.667	58	166	224	80	141	1	13	–	17	176	3.2	1.1	2.5
76-77–Phoenix	39	–	337	26	72	.361	–	–	–	18	31	.581	30	50	80	38	62	0	8	–	8	70	2.1	1.0	1.8
77-78–Portland	10	–	109	8	19	.421	–	–	–	9	18	.500	5	16	21	18	20	0	3	15	2	25	2.1	1.8	2.5
Reg. Season Totals	586	–	9624	1176	2366	.497	–	–	–	778	1147	.678	225	519	3034	920	1367	11	67	15	91	3130	5.2	1.6	5.3
Playoff Totals	17	–	109	14	26	.538	–	–	–	13	24	.542	7	14	43	4	21	0	2	–	3	41	2.5	0.2	2.4

Schnellbacher, Otto O. (The Claw) b. April 15, 1923 Ht. 6-5 Wt. 185 College: Kansas

SEASON–TEAM	G	GS	MIN	FGM	FGA	PCT	3FGM	3FGA	PCT	FTM	FTA	PCT	O-RB	D-RB	TOT	AST	PF	DQ	STL	TO	BLK	PTS	RPG	APG	PPG
48-49–Prov.-St. Louis	43	–	–	93	280	.332	–	–	–	89	133	.669	–	–	–	64	109	–	–	–	–	275	–	1.5	6.4
Reg. Season Totals	43	–	–	93	280	.332	–	–	–	89	133	.669	–	–	–	64	109	–	–	–	–	275	–	1.5	6.4
Playoff Totals	2	–	–	6	20	.300	–	–	–	6	12	.500	–	–	–	6	9	1	–	–	–	18	–	3.0	9.0

Schnittker, Richard D. (Dick) b. May 27, 1928 Ht. 6-5 Wt. 205 College: Ohio State

SEASON–TEAM	G	GS	MIN	FGM	FGA	PCT	3FGM	3FGA	PCT	FTM	FTA	PCT	O-RB	D-RB	TOT	AST	PF	DQ	STL	TO	BLK	PTS	RPG	APG	PPG
50-51–Washington	29	–	–	85	219	.388	–	–	–	123	139	.885	–	–	153	42	76	0	–	–	–	293	5.3	1.4	10.1
53-54–Minneapolis	71	–	1040	122	307	.397	–	–	–	86	132	.652	–	–	178	59	178	3	–	–	–	330	2.5	0.8	4.6
54-55–Minneapolis	72	–	1798	226	583	.388	–	–	–	298	362	.823	–	–	349	114	231	7	–	–	–	750	4.8	1.6	10.4
55-56–Minneapolis	72	–	1930	254	647	.393	–	–	–	304	355	.856	–	–	296	142	253	4	–	–	–	812	4.1	2.0	11.3
56-57–Minneapolis	70	–	997	113	351	.322	–	–	–	160	193	.829	–	–	185	52	144	3	–	–	–	386	2.6	0.7	5.5
57-58–Minneapolis	50	–	979	128	357	.359	–	–	–	201	237	.848	–	–	211	71	126	5	–	–	–	457	4.2	1.4	9.1
Reg. Season Totals	364	–	6744	928	2464	.377	–	–	–	1172	1418	.827	–	–	1372	480	1008	22	–	–	–	3028	3.8	1.3	8.3
Playoff Totals	35	–	665	44	140	.321	–	–	–	76	106	.717	–	–	104	30	83	3	–	–	–	164	2.2	0.6	4.7

Schoene, Russell (Russ) b. April 16, 1960 Ht. 6-10 Wt. 210 College: Mineral Area (Mo.) Coll. (J.C.); Tennessee-Chattanooga

SEASON–TEAM	G	GS	MIN	FGM	FGA	PCT	3FGM	3FGA	PCT	FTM	FTA	PCT	O-RB	D-RB	TOT	AST	PF	DQ	STL	TO	BLK	PTS	RPG	APG	PPG
82-83–Phil.-Indiana	77	7	1222	207	435	.476	1	4	.250	61	83	.735	96	159	255	59	192	3	25	81	23	476	3.3	0.8	6.2
86-87–Seattle	63	0	579	71	190	.374	2	13	.154	29	46	.630	52	65	117	27	94	1	20	42	11	173	1.9	0.4	2.7
87-88–Seattle	81	2	973	208	454	.458	17	58	.293	51	63	.810	78	120	198	53	151	0	39	57	13	484	2.4	0.7	6.0
88-89–Seattle	69	1	774	135	349	.387	42	110	.382	46	57	.807	58	107	165	36	136	1	37	48	24	358	2.4	0.5	5.2
Reg. Season Totals	290	10	3548	621	1428	.435	62	185	.335	187	249	.751	284	451	735	175	573	5	121	228	71	1491	2.5	0.6	5.1
Playoff Totals	22	0	205	21	57	.368	4	17	.235	14	18	.778	10	28	38	7	31	1	4	4	4	60	1.7	0.3	2.7

Scholz, David A. (Dave) b. April 12, 1948 Ht. 6-8 Wt. 220 College: Illinois

SEASON–TEAM	G	GS	MIN	FGM	FGA	PCT	3FGM	3FGA	PCT	FTM	FTA	PCT	O-RB	D-RB	TOT	AST	PF	DQ	STL	TO	BLK	PTS	RPG	APG	PPG
69-70–Philadelphia	1	0	1	1	1	1.000	–	–	–	0	0	–	–	–	0	0	0	0	–	–	–	2	0.0	0.0	2.0
Reg. Season Totals	1	0	1	1	1	1.000	–	–	–	0	0	–	–	–	0	0	0	0	–	–	–	2	0.0	0.0	2.0

Schoon, Milton W. (Milt) b. February 25, 1922 Ht. 6-9 Wt. 230 College: Valparaiso

SEASON–TEAM	G	GS	MIN	FGM	FGA	PCT	3FGM	3FGA	PCT	FTM	FTA	PCT	O-RB	D-RB	TOT	AST	PF	DQ	STL	TO	BLK	PTS	RPG	APG	PPG
46-47–Detroit	41	–	–	43	199	.216	–	–	–	34	80	.425	–	–	–	12	75	–	–	–	–	120	–	0.3	2.9
47-48–Flint (N)	55	–	–	114	–	–	–	–	–	120	214	.561	–	–	–	–	194	–	–	–	–	348	–	–	6.3
48-49–Sheboygan (N)	57	–	–	81	–	–	–	–	–	109	184	.592	–	–	–	–	143	–	–	–	–	271	–	–	4.8
49-50–Sheboygan	62	–	–	150	366	.410	–	–	–	196	300	.653	–	–	–	84	190	–	–	–	–	496	–	1.4	8.0
Reg. NBA Totals	103	–	–	193	565	.342	–	–	–	230	380	.605	–	–	–	96	265	–	–	–	–	616	–	0.9	6.0
Reg. NBL Totals	112	–	–	195	–	–	–	–	–	229	398	.575	–	–	–	–	337	–	–	–	–	619	–	–	5.5
NBA Playoff Totals	3	–	–	5	34	.294	–	–	–	7	10	.700	–	–	–	6	6	–	–	–	–	17	–	1.0	5.7
NBL Playoff Totals	2	–	–	2	–	–	–	–	–	2	5	.400	–	–	–	–	10	–	–	–	–	6	–	–	3.0

Schrempf, Detlef b. January 21, 1963 Ht. 6-10 Wt. 235 College: Washington

SEASON–TEAM	G	GS	MIN	FGM	FGA	PCT	3FGM	3FGA	PCT	FTM	FTA	PCT	O-RB	D-RB	TOT	AST	PF	DQ	STL	TO	BLK	PTS	RPG	APG	PPG
85-86–Dallas	64	12	969	142	315	.451	3	7	.429	110	152	.724	70	128	198	88	166	1	23	84	10	397	3.1	1.4	6.2
86-87–Dallas	81	5	1711	265	561	.472	33	69	.478	193	260	.742	87	216	303	161	224	2	50	110	16	756	3.7	2.0	9.3
87-88–Dallas	82	4	1587	246	539	.456	5	32	.156	201	266	.756	102	177	279	159	189	0	42	108	32	698	3.4	1.9	8.5
88-89–Dallas-Ind.	69	13	1850	274	578	.474	7	35	.200	273	350	.780	126	269	395	179	220	3	53	133	19	828	5.7	2.6	12.0
89-90–Indiana	78	18	2573	424	822	.516	17	48	.354	402	490	.820	149	471	620	247	271	6	59	180	16	1267	7.9	3.2	16.2
90-91–Indiana	82	3	2632	432	831	.520	15	40	.375	441	539	.818	178	482	660	301	262	3	58	175	22	1320	8.0	3.7	16.1
91-92–Indiana	80	4	2605	496	925	.536	23	71	.324	365	441	.828	202	568	770	312	286	4	62	191	37	1380	9.6	3.9	17.3
92-93–Indiana	82	60	3098	517	1085	.476	8	52	.154	525	653	.804	210	570	780	493	305	3	79	243	27	1567	9.5	6.0	19.1
93-94–Seattle	81	80	2728	445	903	.493	22	68	.324	300	390	.769	144	310	454	275	273	3	73	173	9	1212	5.6	3.4	15.0
94-95–Seattle	82	82	2886	521	997	.523	93	181	.514	437	521	.839	135	373	508	310	252	0	93	176	35	1572	6.2	3.8	19.2
95-96–Seattle	63	60	2200	360	740	.486	73	179	.408	287	370	.776	73	255	328	276	179	0	56	146	8	1080	5.2	4.4	17.1
96-97–Seattle	61	60	2192	356	724	.492	57	161	.354	253	316	.801	87	307	394	266	151	0	63	150	16	1022	6.5	4.4	16.8
97-98–Seattle	78	78	2742	437	898	.487	61	147	.415	297	352	.844	135	419	554	341	205	0	60	168	19	1232	7.1	4.4	15.8
98-99–Seattle	50	39	1765	259	549	.472	34	86	.395	200	243	.823	77	293	370	184	152	0	41	103	26	752	7.4	3.7	15.0
99-00–Portland	77	6	1662	187	433	.432	21	52	.404	179	215	.833	79	253	332	197	182	0	37	100	17	574	4.3	2.6	7.5
Reg. Season Totals	1110	524	33200	5361	10900	.492	472	1228	.384	4463	5558	.803	1854	5091	6945	3789	3317	25	849	2240	309	15657	6.3	3.4	14.1
Playoff Totals	111	59	3306	484	1043	.464	55	150	.367	395	500	.790	143	417	560	295	306	2	62	223	26	1418	5.0	2.7	12.8
All-Star Totals	3	0	51	10	22	.455	2	8	.250	1	3	.333	1	10	11	7	9	0	0	2	1	23	3.7	2.3	7.7

Schultz, Howard Henry (Howie, Stretch) b. July 3, 1922 Ht. 6-6 Wt. 220 College: Hamline

SEASON–TEAM	G	GS	MIN	FGM	FGA	PCT	3FGM	3FGA	PCT	FTM	FTA	PCT	O-RB	D-RB	TOT	AST	PF	DQ	STL	TO	BLK	PTS	RPG	APG	PPG
46-47–Anderson (N)	41	–	–	155	–	–	–	–	–	147	213	.690	–	–	–	–	124	–	–	–	–	457	–	–	11.1
47-48–Anderson (N)	60	–	–	213	–	–	–	–	–	179	258	.694	–	–	–	–	194	–	–	–	–	605	–	–	10.1
48-49–Anderson (N)	64	–	–	176	–	–	–	–	–	186	256	.727	–	–	–	–	204	–	–	–	–	538	–	–	8.4
49-50–And.-FtWayne	67	–	–	179	671	.267	–	–	–	196	282	.695	–	–	–	169	244	–	–	–	–	554	–	2.5	8.3
51-52–Minneapolis	66	–	1301	89	315	.283	–	–	–	90	119	.756	–	–	246	102	197	13	–	–	–	268	3.7	1.5	4.1
52-53–Minneapolis	40	–	474	24	90	.267	–	–	–	43	62	.694	–	–	80	29	73	1	–	–	–	91	2.0	0.7	2.3
Reg. NBA Totals	173	–	1775	292	1076	.271	–	–	–	329	463	.711	–	–	326	300	514	14	–	–	–	913	3.1	1.7	5.3
Reg. NBL Totals	165	–	–	544	–	–	–	–	–	512	727	.704	–	–	–	–	522	–	–	–	–	1600	–	–	9.7
NBA Playoff Totals	16	–	151	21	81	.272	–	–	–	20	28	.714	–	–	26	13	36	3	–	–	–	62	1.5	0.6	3.9
NBL Playoff Totals	13	–	–	36	–	–	–	–	–	47	70	.671	–	–	–	–	46	–	–	–	–	119	–	–	9.2

Schulz, Richard A. (Dick) b. January 3, 1917 d. June 26, 1998 Ht. 6-2 Wt. 205 College: Wisconsin

SEASON–TEAM	G	GS	MIN	FGM	FGA	PCT	3FGM	3FGA	PCT	FTM	FTA	PCT	O-RB	D-RB	TOT	AST	PF	DQ	STL	TO	BLK	PTS	RPG	APG	PPG
42-43–Sheboygan (N)	1	–	–	0	–	–	–	–	–	0	–	–	–	–	–	–	–	–	–	–	–	0	–	–	0.0
43-44–Sheboygan (N)	20	–	–	18	–	–	–	–	–	10	–	–	–	–	–	–	–	–	–	–	–	46	–	–	2.3
44-45–Sheboygan (N)	29	–	–	86	–	–	–	–	–	71	–	–	–	–	–	–	–	–	–	–	–	243	–	–	8.4
45-46–Sheboygan (N)	29	–	–	56	–	–	–	–	–	66	94	.702	–	–	–	–	39	–	–	–	–	178	–	–	6.1
46-47–Clev.-Toronto	57	–	–	130	548	.237	–	–	–	94	138	.681	–	–	–	56	123	–	–	–	–	354	–	1.0	6.2
47-48–Baltimore	48	–	–	133	469	.284	–	–	–	117	160	.731	–	–	–	28	116	–	–	–	–	383	–	0.6	8.0
48-49–Washington	50	–	–	65	278	.234	–	–	–	65	91	.714	–	–	–	53	107	–	–	–	–	195	–	1.1	3.9
49-50–Wash.-Tri-Cit-She.	50	–	–	63	212	.297	–	–	–	83	110	.755	–	–	–	66	106	–	–	–	–	209	–	1.3	4.2
Reg. NBA Totals	205	–	–	391	1507	.259	–	–	–	359	499	.719	–	–	–	203	452	–	–	–	–	1141	–	1.0	5.6
Reg. NBL Totals	79	–	–	160	–	–	–	–	–	147	94	.702	–	–	–	–	39	–	–	–	–	467	–	–	5.9
NBA Playoff Totals	25	–	–	40	256	.211	–	–	–	68	99	.687	–	–	–	59	85	–	–	–	–	148	–	1.7	5.9
NBL Playoff Totals	21	–	–	52	–	–	–	–	–	67	61	.656	–	–	–	–	45	–	–	–	–	171	–	–	8.1

Schurig, Roger Paul b. April 3, 1942 Ht. 6-3 Wt. 185 College: Vanderbilt

SEASON–TEAM	G	GS	MIN	FGM	FGA	PCT	3FGM	3FGA	PCT	FTM	FTA	PCT	O-RB	D-RB	TOT	AST	PF	DQ	STL	TO	BLK	PTS	RPG	APG	PPG
67-68–Houston (A)	21	–	252	35	94	.372	3	8	.375	27	36	.750	–	–	29	18	38	0	–	23	–	100	1.4	0.9	4.8
Reg. ABA Totals	21	–	252	35	94	.372	3	8	.375	27	36	.750	–	–	29	18	38	0	–	23	–	100	1.4	0.9	4.8

Schweitz, John Elwood b. April 19, 1960 Ht. 6-6 Wt. 210 College: Richmond

SEASON–TEAM	G	GS	MIN	FGM	FGA	PCT	3FGM	3FGA	PCT	FTM	FTA	PCT	O-RB	D-RB	TOT	AST	PF	DQ	STL	TO	BLK	PTS	RPG	APG	PPG
84-85–Seattle	19	0	110	25	74	.338	0	4	.000	7	10	.700	6	15	21	18	12	0	0	14	1	57	1.1	0.9	3.0
86-87–Detroit	3	0	7	0	1	.000	0	0	–	0	0	–	0	1	1	0	2	0	0	2	0	0	0.3	0.0	0.0
Reg. Season Totals	22	0	117	25	75	.333	0	4	.000	7	10	.700	6	16	22	18	14	0	0	16	1	57	1.0	0.8	2.6

Scolari, Fred J. (Freddie, Fat Freddie) b. March 1, 1922 Ht. 5-11 Wt. 180 College: San Francisco

SEASON–TEAM	G	GS	MIN	FGM	FGA	PCT	3FGM	3FGA	PCT	FTM	FTA	PCT	O-RB	D-RB	TOT	AST	PF	DQ	STL	TO	BLK	PTS	RPG	APG	PPG
46-47–Washington	58	–	–	291	989	.294	–	–	–	146	180	.811	–	–	–	58	159	–	–	–	–	728	–	1.0	12.6
47-48–Washington	47	–	–	229	780	.294	–	–	–	131	179	.732	–	–	–	58	153	–	–	–	–	589	–	1.2	12.5
48-49–Washington	48	–	–	196	633	.310	–	–	–	146	183	.798	–	–	–	100	150	–	–	–	–	538	–	2.1	11.2
49-50–Washington	66	–	–	312	910	.343	–	–	–	236	287	.822	–	–	–	175	181	–	–	–	–	860	–	2.7	13.0
50-51–Wash.-Syr.	66	–	–	302	923	.327	–	–	–	279	331	.843	–	–	218	255	183	1	–	–	–	883	3.3	3.9	13.4
51-52–Baltimore	64	–	2242	290	867	.334	–	–	–	353	423	.835	–	–	214	303	213	6	–	–	–	933	3.3	4.7	14.6
52-53–Balt.-FtWayne	62	–	2123	277	809	.342	–	–	–	276	327	.844	–	–	209	233	212	4	–	–	–	830	3.4	3.8	13.4
53-54–Fort Wayne	64	–	1589	159	491	.324	–	–	–	144	180	.800	–	–	139	131	155	1	–	–	–	462	2.2	2.0	7.2
54-55–Boston	59	–	619	76	249	.305	–	–	–	39	49	.796	–	–	77	93	76	0	–	–	–	191	1.3	1.6	3.2
Reg. Season Totals	534	–	6573	2132	6651	.321	–	–	–	1750	2139	.818	–	–	857	1406	1482	12	–	–	–	6014	2.7	2.6	11.3
Playoff Totals	41	–	417	134	645	.285	–	–	–	141	179	.788	–	–	85	96	117	3	–	–	–	409	3.0	1.6	10.0
All-Star Totals	1	–	15	5	9	.556	–	–	–	0	0	–	–	–	0	2	0	0	–	–	–	10	0.0	2.0	10.0

Scott, Alvin Leroy b. September 14, 1955 Ht. 6-7 Wt. 185 College: Oral Roberts

SEASON–TEAM	G	GS	MIN	FGM	FGA	PCT	3FGM	3FGA	PCT	FTM	FTA	PCT	O-RB	D-RB	TOT	AST	PF	DQ	STL	TO	BLK	PTS	RPG	APG	PPG
77-78–Phoenix	81	–	1538	180	369	.488	–	–	–	132	191	.691	135	222	357	88	158	0	52	85	40	492	4.4	1.1	6.1
78-79–Phoenix	81	–	1737	212	396	.535	–	–	–	120	168	.714	104	256	360	126	139	2	80	99	62	544	4.4	1.6	6.7
79-80–Phoenix	79	–	1303	127	301	.422	1	3	.333	95	122	.779	89	139	228	98	101	0	47	92	53	350	2.9	1.2	4.4
80-81–Phoenix	82	–	1423	173	348	.497	1	6	.167	97	127	.764	101	167	268	114	124	0	60	77	70	444	3.3	1.4	5.4
81-82–Phoenix	81	38	1740	189	380	.497	0	2	.000	108	148	.730	97	197	294	149	169	0	59	98	70	486	3.6	1.8	6.0
82-83–Phoenix	81	9	1139	124	259	.479	0	2	.000	81	110	.736	60	164	224	97	133	0	48	64	31	329	2.8	1.2	4.1
83-84–Phoenix	65	5	735	55	124	.444	1	2	.500	56	72	.778	29	71	100	48	85	0	19	42	20	167	1.5	0.7	2.6
84-85–Phoenix	77	18	1238	111	259	.429	1	5	.200	53	74	.716	46	115	161	127	125	0	39	60	25	276	2.1	1.6	3.6
Reg. Season Totals	627	70	10853	1171	2436	.481	4	20	.200	742	1012	.733	661	1331	1992	847	1034	2	404	617	371	3088	3.2	1.4	4.9
Playoff Totals	61	1	878	88	206	.427	1	7	.143	47	72	.653	57	92	149	78	77	0	29	52	51	224	2.4	1.3	3.7

Scott, Brent b. June 15, 1971 Ht. 6-10 Wt. 250 College: Rice

SEASON–TEAM	G	GS	MIN	FGM	FGA	PCT	3FGM	3FGA	PCT	FTM	FTA	PCT	O-RB	D-RB	TOT	AST	PF	DQ	STL	TO	BLK	PTS	RPG	APG	PPG
96-97–Indiana	16	0	55	8	17	.471	0	0	–	3	6	.500	3	6	9	3	14	0	1	4	1	19	0.6	0.2	1.2
Reg. Season Totals	16	0	55	8	17	.471	0	0	–	3	6	.500	3	6	9	3	14	0	1	4	1	19	0.6	0.2	1.2

Scott, Byron Antom b. March 28, 1961 Ht. 6-4 Wt. 205 College: Arizona State

SEASON–TEAM	G	GS	MIN	FGM	FGA	PCT	3FGM	3FGA	PCT	FTM	FTA	PCT	O-RB	D-RB	TOT	AST	PF	DQ	STL	TO	BLK	PTS	RPG	APG	PPG
83-84–Los Angeles	74	49	1637	334	690	.484	8	34	.235	112	139	.806	50	114	164	177	174	0	81	116	19	788	2.2	2.4	10.6
84-85–L.A. Lakers	81	65	2305	541	1003	.539	26	60	.433	187	228	.820	57	153	210	244	197	1	100	138	17	1295	2.6	3.0	16.0
85-86–L.A. Lakers	76	62	2190	507	989	.513	22	61	.361	138	176	.784	55	134	189	164	167	0	85	110	15	1174	2.5	2.2	15.4
86-87–L.A. Lakers	82	82	2729	554	1134	.489	65	149	.436	224	251	.892	63	223	286	281	163	0	125	144	18	1397	3.5	3.4	17.0
87-88–L.A. Lakers	81	81	3048	710	1348	.527	62	179	.346	272	317	.858	76	257	333	335	204	2	155	161	27	1754	4.1	4.1	21.7
88-89–L.A. Lakers	74	73	2605	588	1198	.491	77	193	.399	195	226	.863	72	230	302	231	181	1	114	157	27	1448	4.1	3.1	19.6
89-90–L.A. Lakers	77	77	2593	472	1005	.470	93	220	.423	160	209	.766	51	191	242	274	180	2	77	122	31	1197	3.1	3.6	15.5
90-91–L.A. Lakers	82	82	2630	501	1051	.477	71	219	.324	118	148	.797	54	192	246	177	146	0	95	85	21	1191	3.0	2.2	14.5
91-92–L.A. Lakers	82	82	2679	460	1005	.458	54	157	.344	244	291	.838	74	236	310	226	140	0	105	119	28	1218	3.8	2.8	14.9
92-93–L.A. Lakers	58	53	1677	296	659	.449	44	135	.326	156	184	.848	27	107	134	157	98	0	55	70	13	792	2.3	2.7	13.7
93-94–Indiana	67	2	1197	256	548	.467	27	74	.365	157	195	.805	19	91	110	133	80	0	62	103	9	696	1.6	2.0	10.4
94-95–Indiana	80	1	1528	265	583	.455	79	203	.389	193	227	.850	18	133	151	108	123	1	61	119	13	802	1.9	1.4	10.0
95-96–Vancouver	80	0	1894	271	676	.401	74	221	.335	203	243	.835	40	152	192	123	126	0	63	100	22	819	2.4	1.5	10.2
96-97–L.A. Lakers	79	8	1440	163	379	.430	73	188	.388	127	151	.841	21	97	118	99	72	0	46	53	16	526	1.5	1.3	6.7
Reg. Season Totals	1073	717	30152	5918	12268	.482	775	2093	.370	2486	2985	.833	677	2310	2987	2729	2051	7	1224	1597	276	15097	2.8	2.5	14.1
Playoff Totals	183	122	5365	934	1937	.482	134	339	.395	449	548	.819	136	400	536	390	445	2	226	266	30	2451	2.9	2.1	13.4

Scott, Charles Thomas (Charlie) b. December 15, 1946 Ht. 6-6 Wt. 175 College: North Carolina

SEASON–TEAM	G	GS	MIN	FGM	FGA	PCT	3FGM	3FGA	PCT	FTM	FTA	PCT	O-RB	D-RB	TOT	AST	PF	DQ	STL	TO	BLK	PTS	RPG	APG	PPG
70-71–Virginia (A)	84	–	3185	902	1947	.463	16	65	.246	456	611	.746	–	–	438	472	298	–	–	–	–	2276	5.2	5.6	27.1
71-72–Virginia (A)	73	–	3061	985	2192	.449	29	110	.264	525	654	.803	–	–	374	347	261	–	–	340	–	2524	5.1	4.8	34.6
71-72–Phoenix	6	–	177	48	113	.425	–	–	–	17	21	.810	–	–	23	26	19	0	–	–	–	113	3.8	4.3	18.8
72-73–Phoenix	81	–	3062	806	1809	.446	–	–	–	436	556	.784	–	–	342	495	306	5	–	–	–	2048	4.2	6.1	25.3
73-74–Phoenix	52	–	2003	538	1171	.459	–	–	–	246	315	.781	64	158	222	271	194	6	99	–	22	1322	4.3	5.2	25.4
74-75–Phoenix	69	–	2592	703	1594	.441	–	–	–	274	351	.781	72	201	273	311	296	11	111	–	24	1680	4.0	4.5	24.3
75-76–Boston	82	–	2913	588	1309	.449	–	–	–	267	335	.797	106	252	358	341	356	17	103	–	24	1443	4.4	4.2	17.6
76-77–Boston	43	–	1581	326	734	.444	–	–	–	129	173	.746	52	139	191	196	155	3	60	–	12	781	4.4	4.6	18.2
77-78–Boston-L.A.	79	–	2473	435	994	.438	–	–	–	194	260	.746	62	187	249	378	252	6	110	238	17	1064	3.2	4.8	13.5
78-79–Denver	79	–	2617	393	854	.460	–	–	–	161	215	.749	54	156	210	428	284	12	78	255	30	947	2.7	5.4	12.0
79-80–Denver	69	–	1860	276	688	.401	2	11	.182	85	118	.720	51	115	166	250	197	3	47	163	23	639	2.4	3.6	9.3
Reg. NBA Totals	560	–	19278	4113	9266	.444	2	11	.182	1809	2344	.772	461	1208	2034	2696	2059	63	608	656	152	10037	3.6	4.8	17.9
Reg. ABA Totals	157	–	6246	1887	4139	.456	45	175	.257	981	1265	.775	–	–	812	819	559	–	–	340	–	4800	5.2	5.2	30.6
NBA Playoff Totals	33	–	1177	195	494	.395	0	0	–	113	146	.774	46	95	141	133	158	14	40	21	12	503	4.3	4.0	15.2
ABA Playoff Totals	12	–	504	115	281	.409	8	31	.258	83	110	.755	–	–	79	82	45	–	–	–	–	321	6.6	6.8	26.8
NBA All-Star Totals	3	–	49	1	15	.067	0	0	–	2	2	1.000	1	2	5	7	6	0	0	–	1	4	1.7	2.3	1.3

Scott, Dennis Eugene (3-D) b. September 5, 1968 Ht. 6-8 Wt. 229 College: Georgia Tech

SEASON–TEAM	G	GS	MIN	FGM	FGA	PCT	3FGM	3FGA	PCT	FTM	FTA	PCT	O-RB	D-RB	TOT	AST	PF	DQ	STL	TO	BLK	PTS	RPG	APG	PPG
90-91–Orlando	82	73	2336	503	1183	.425	125	334	.374	153	204	.750	62	173	235	134	203	1	62	127	25	1284	2.9	1.6	15.7
91-92–Orlando	18	15	608	133	331	.402	29	89	.326	64	71	.901	14	52	66	35	49	1	20	31	9	359	3.7	1.9	19.9
92-93–Orlando	54	43	1759	329	763	.431	108	268	.403	92	117	.786	38	148	186	136	131	3	57	104	18	858	3.4	2.5	15.9
93-94–Orlando	82	37	2283	384	949	.405	155	388	.399	123	159	.774	54	164	218	216	161	0	81	93	32	1046	2.7	2.6	12.8
94-95–Orlando	62	10	1499	283	645	.439	150	352	.426	86	114	.754	25	121	146	131	119	1	45	57	14	802	2.4	2.1	12.9
95-96–Orlando	82	82	3041	491	1117	.440	267	628	.425	182	222	.820	63	246	309	243	169	1	90	122	29	1431	3.8	3.0	17.5
96-97–Orlando	66	62	2166	298	749	.398	147	373	.394	80	101	.792	40	163	203	139	138	2	74	81	19	823	3.1	2.1	12.5
97-98–Dallas-Phoenix	81	45	2290	329	828	.397	125	342	.365	105	130	.808	47	200	247	153	152	1	53	104	39	888	3.0	1.9	11.0
98-99–N.Y.-Minn.	36	9	738	87	213	.408	37	97	.381	23	31	.742	8	50	58	40	49	0	15	19	3	234	1.6	1.1	6.5
99-00–Vancouver	66	0	1263	125	333	.375	71	189	.376	48	57	.842	16	90	106	69	104	0	28	30	9	369	1.6	1.0	5.6
Reg. Season Totals	629	376	17983	2962	7111	.417	1214	3060	.397	956	1206	.793	367	1407	1774	1296	1275	10	525	768	197	8094	2.8	2.1	12.9
Playoff Totals	45	31	1447	184	461	.399	95	261	.364	56	72	.778	23	106	129	77	116	0	36	60	9	519	2.9	1.7	11.5

Scott, James b. June 30, 1972 Ht. 6-6 Wt. 195 College: St. John's (N.Y.)

SEASON–TEAM	G	GS	MIN	FGM	FGA	PCT	3FGM	3FGA	PCT	FTM	FTA	PCT	O-RB	D-RB	TOT	AST	PF	DQ	STL	TO	BLK	PTS	RPG	APG	PPG
96-97–Miami	8	0	32	0	8	.000	0	4	.000	1	2	.500	1	5	6	3	5	0	2	2	0	1	0.8	0.4	0.1
Reg. Season Totals	8	0	32	0	8	.000	0	4	.000	1	2	.500	1	5	6	3	5	0	2	2	0	1	0.8	0.4	0.1

Scott, John Raymond (Ray) b. July 12, 1938 Ht. 6-9 Wt. 215 College: Portland

SEASON–TEAM	G	GS	MIN	FGM	FGA	PCT	3FGM	3FGA	PCT	FTM	FTA	PCT	O-RB	D-RB	TOT	AST	PF	DQ	STL	TO	BLK	PTS	RPG	APG	PPG
61-62–Detroit	75	–	2087	370	956	.387	–	–	–	255	388	.657	–	–	865	132	232	6	–	–	–	995	11.5	1.8	13.3
62-63–Detroit	76	–	2538	460	1110	.414	–	–	–	308	457	.674	–	–	772	191	263	9	–	–	–	1228	10.2	2.5	16.2
63-64–Detroit	80	–	2964	539	1307	.412	–	–	–	328	456	.719	–	–	1078	244	296	7	–	–	–	1406	13.5	3.1	17.6
64-65–Detroit	66	–	2167	402	1092	.368	–	–	–	220	314	.701	–	–	634	239	209	5	–	–	–	1024	9.6	3.6	15.5
65-66–Detroit	79	–	2652	544	1309	.416	–	–	–	323	435	.743	–	–	755	238	209	1	–	–	–	1411	9.6	3.0	17.9
66-67–Detroit-Balt.	72	–	2446	458	1144	.400	–	–	–	256	366	.699	–	–	760	160	215	2	–	–	–	1172	10.6	2.2	16.3
67-68–Baltimore	81	–	2924	490	1189	.412	–	–	–	348	447	.779	–	–	1111	167	252	2	–	–	–	1328	13.7	2.1	16.4
68-69–Baltimore	82	–	2168	386	929	.416	–	–	–	195	257	.759	–	–	722	133	212	1	–	–	–	967	8.8	1.6	11.8
69-70–Baltimore	73	–	1393	257	605	.425	–	–	–	139	173	.803	–	–	457	114	147	0	–	–	–	653	6.3	1.6	8.9
70-71–Virginia (A)	72	–	1552	420	933	.450	1	1	1.000	187	236	.792	–	–	573	123	180	–	–	–	–	1028	8.0	1.7	14.3
71-72–Virginia (A)	55	–	818	163	393	.415	2	4	.500	89	114	.781	–	–	252	40	90	–	–	55	–	417	4.6	0.7	7.6
Reg. NBA Totals	684	–	21339	3906	9641	.405	–	–	–	2372	3293	.720	–	–	7154	1618	2035	33	–	–	–	10184	10.5	2.4	14.9
Reg. ABA Totals	127	–	2370	583	1326	.440	3	5	.600	276	350	.789	–	–	825	163	270	–	–	55	–	1445	6.5	1.3	11.4
NBA Playoff Totals	25	–	782	130	333	.390	–	–	–	61	102	.598	–	–	246	60	82	2	–	–	–	321	9.8	2.4	12.8
ABA Playoff Totals	23	–	476	132	262	.504	0	0	–	75	94	.798	–	–	136	38	68	–	–	16	–	339	5.9	1.7	14.7

Scott, Shawnelle b. June 16, 1972 Ht. 6-11 Wt. 250 College: St. John's (N.Y.)

SEASON–TEAM	G	GS	MIN	FGM	FGA	PCT	3FGM	3FGA	PCT	FTM	FTA	PCT	O-RB	D-RB	TOT	AST	PF	DQ	STL	TO	BLK	PTS	RPG	APG	PPG
96-97–Cleveland	16	0	50	8	16	.500	0	0	–	4	11	.364	8	8	16	0	6	0	0	0	3	20	1.0	0.0	1.3
97-98–Cleveland	41	0	188	16	36	.444	0	0	–	12	18	.667	20	39	59	8	45	0	6	10	8	44	1.4	0.2	1.1
Reg. Season Totals	57	0	238	24	52	.462	0	0	–	16	29	.552	28	47	75	8	51	0	6	10	11	64	1.3	0.1	1.1
Playoff Totals	1	0	3	1	2	.500	0	0	–	0	0	–	0	0	0	–	0	0	0	1	1	2	0.0	0.0	2.0

Scott, Willie b. 1947 Ht. 6-5 Wt. 210 College: Alabama State

SEASON–TEAM	G	GS	MIN	FGM	FGA	PCT	3FGM	3FGA	PCT	FTM	FTA	PCT	O-RB	D-RB	TOT	AST	PF	DQ	STL	TO	BLK	PTS	RPG	APG	PPG
69-70–Dallas (A)	8	–	51	6	15	.400	0	0	–	1	6	.167	–	–	4	2	16	0	–	–	–	13	0.5	0.3	1.6
Reg. ABA Totals	8	–	51	6	15	.400	0	0	–	1	6	.167	–	–	4	2	16	0	–	–	–	13	0.5	0.3	1.6

Scranton, Paul Earl Jr. b. April 30, 1944 Ht. 6-5 Wt. 230 College: Cal Poly-Pomona

SEASON–TEAM	G	GS	MIN	FGM	FGA	PCT	3FGM	3FGA	PCT	FTM	FTA	PCT	O-RB	D-RB	TOT	AST	PF	DQ	STL	TO	BLK	PTS	RPG	APG	PPG
67-68–Anaheim (A)	5	–	41	4	9	.444	0	0	–	1	4	.250	–	–	16	1	5	0	–	1	–	9	3.2	0.2	1.8
Reg. ABA Totals	5	–	41	4	9	.444	0	0	–	1	4	.250	–	–	16	1	5	0	–	1	–	9	3.2	0.2	1.8

Scurry, Carey b. December 4, 1962 Ht. 6-7 Wt. 190 College: Northeastern Oklahoma A&M (J.C.); Long Island University

SEASON–TEAM	G	GS	MIN	FGM	FGA	PCT	3FGM	3FGA	PCT	FTM	FTA	PCT	O-RB	D-RB	TOT	AST	PF	DQ	STL	TO	BLK	PTS	RPG	APG	PPG
85-86–Utah	78	0	1168	142	301	.472	1	11	.091	78	126	.619	97	145	242	85	171	2	78	96	66	363	3.1	1.1	4.7
86-87–Utah	69	5	753	123	247	.498	4	14	.286	94	134	.701	97	101	198	57	124	1	55	56	54	344	2.9	0.8	5.0
87-88–Utah-N.Y.	33	0	455	55	118	.466	3	8	.375	27	39	.692	30	54	84	50	81	0	49	43	23	140	2.5	1.5	4.2
Reg. Season Totals	180	5	2376	320	666	.480	8	33	.242	199	299	.666	224	300	524	192	376	3	182	195	143	847	2.9	1.1	4.7
Playoff Totals	8	0	111	18	42	.429	1	4	.250	4	9	.444	17	13	30	3	22	0	5	4	9	41	3.8	0.4	5.1

Seals, Bruce A. b. June 18, 1953 Ht. 6-8 Wt. 210 College: Xavier (La.)

SEASON–TEAM	G	GS	MIN	FGM	FGA	PCT	3FGM	3FGA	PCT	FTM	FTA	PCT	O-RB	D-RB	TOT	AST	PF	DQ	STL	TO	BLK	PTS	RPG	APG	PPG
73-74–Utah (A)	78	–	1358	229	605	.379	19	90	.211	68	108	.630	100	179	279	54	199	–	57	81	57	545	3.6	0.7	7.0
74-75–Utah (A)	35	–	371	60	142	.423	0	3	.000	20	26	.769	43	54	97	13	67	–	15	24	16	140	2.8	0.4	4.0
75-76–Seattle	81	–	2435	388	889	.436	–	–	–	181	267	.678	157	350	507	119	314	11	64	–	44	957	6.3	1.5	11.8
76-77–Seattle	81	–	1977	378	851	.444	–	–	–	138	195	.708	118	236	354	93	262	6	49	–	58	894	4.4	1.1	11.0
77-78–Seattle	73	–	1322	230	551	.417	–	–	–	111	175	.634	62	164	226	81	210	4	41	103	33	571	3.1	1.1	7.8
Reg. NBA Totals	235	–	5734	996	2291	.435	–	–	–	430	637	.675	337	750	1087	293	786	21	154	103	135	2422	4.6	1.2	10.3
Reg. ABA Totals	113	–	1729	289	747	.387	19	93	.204	88	134	.657	143	233	376	67	266	0	72	105	73	685	3.3	0.6	6.1
NBA Playoff Totals	15	–	273	42	105	.400	–	–	–	21	33	.636	22	34	56	11	36	0	7	6	8	105	3.7	0.7	7.0
ABA Playoff Totals	18	–	301	50	112	.446	2	10	.200	13	23	.565	28	35	63	14	48	0	7	17	4	115	3.5	0.8	6.4

Seals, Shea b. August 26, 1975 Ht. 6-5 Wt. 210 College: Tulsa

SEASON–TEAM	G	GS	MIN	FGM	FGA	PCT	3FGM	3FGA	PCT	FTM	FTA	PCT	O-RB	D-RB	TOT	AST	PF	DQ	STL	TO	BLK	PTS	RPG	APG	PPG
97-98–L.A. Lakers	4	0	9	1	8	.125	0	3	.000	2	4	.500	3	1	4	0	1	0	1	0	0	4	1.0	0.0	1.0
Reg. Season Totals	4	0	9	1	8	.125	0	3	.000	2	4	.500	3	1	4	0	1	0	1	0	0	4	1.0	0.0	1.0

Sealy, Malik b. February 1, 1970 d. May 20, 2000 Ht. 6-8 Wt. 200 College: St. John's (N.Y.)

SEASON–TEAM	G	GS	MIN	FGM	FGA	PCT	3FGM	3FGA	PCT	FTM	FTA	PCT	O-RB	D-RB	TOT	AST	PF	DQ	STL	TO	BLK	PTS	RPG	APG	PPG
92-93–Indiana	58	2	672	136	319	.426	7	31	.226	51	74	.689	60	52	112	47	74	0	36	58	7	330	1.9	0.8	5.7
93-94–Indiana	43	5	623	111	274	.405	4	16	.250	59	87	.678	43	75	118	48	84	0	31	51	8	285	2.7	1.1	6.6
94-95–L.A. Clippers	60	41	1604	291	669	.435	22	73	.301	174	223	.780	77	137	214	107	173	2	72	83	25	778	3.6	1.8	13.0
95-96–L.A. Clippers	62	48	1601	272	655	.415	21	100	.210	147	184	.799	76	164	240	116	150	2	84	113	28	712	3.9	1.9	11.5
96-97–L.A. Clippers	80	79	2456	373	942	.396	79	222	.356	254	290	.876	59	179	238	165	185	4	124	154	45	1079	3.0	2.1	13.5
97-98–Detroit	77	10	1641	216	505	.428	9	41	.220	150	182	.824	48	171	219	100	156	2	65	79	20	591	2.8	1.3	7.7
98-99–Minnesota	31	7	731	95	231	.411	6	23	.261	55	61	.902	23	69	92	36	68	0	30	33	5	251	3.0	1.2	8.1
99-00–Minnesota	82	61	2392	371	780	.476	10	35	.286	177	218	.812	119	233	352	197	197	1	76	110	19	929	4.3	2.4	11.3
Reg. Season Totals	493	253	11720	1865	4375	.426	158	541	.292	1067	1319	.809	505	1080	1585	816	1087	11	518	681	157	4955	3.2	1.7	10.1
Playoff Totals	14	7	289	39	94	.415	2	9	.222	28	38	.737	10	19	29	13	25	1	3	16	1	108	2.1	0.9	7.7

Searcy, Edwin (Ed) b. April 17, 1952 Ht. 6-6 Wt. 210 College: St. John's (N.Y.)

SEASON–TEAM	G	GS	MIN	FGM	FGA	PCT	3FGM	3FGA	PCT	FTM	FTA	PCT	O-RB	D-RB	TOT	AST	PF	DQ	STL	TO	BLK	PTS	RPG	APG	PPG
75-76–Boston	4	–	12	2	6	.333	–	–	–	2	2	1.000	0	0	0	1	4	0	0	–	0	6	0.0	0.3	1.5
Reg. Season Totals	4	–	12	2	6	.333	–	–	–	2	2	1.000	0	0	0	1	4	0	0	–	0	6	0.0	0.3	1.5

Sears, Kenneth Robert (Ken, Big Cat) b. August 17, 1933 Ht. 6-9 Wt. 200 College: Santa Clara

SEASON–TEAM	G	GS	MIN	FGM	FGA	PCT	3FGM	3FGA	PCT	FTM	FTA	PCT	O-RB	D-RB	TOT	AST	PF	DQ	STL	TO	BLK	PTS	RPG	APG	PPG
55-56–New York	70	–	2069	319	728	.438	–	–	–	258	324	.796	–	–	616	114	201	4	–	–	–	896	8.8	1.6	12.8
56-57–New York	72	–	2516	343	821	.418	–	–	–	383	485	.790	–	–	614	101	226	2	–	–	–	1069	8.5	1.4	14.8
57-58–New York	72	–	2685	445	1014	.439	–	–	–	452	550	.822	–	–	785	126	251	7	–	–	–	1342	10.9	1.8	18.6
58-59–New York	71	–	2498	491	1002	.490	–	–	–	506	588	.861	–	–	658	136	237	6	–	–	–	1488	9.3	1.9	21.0
59-60–New York	64	–	2099	412	863	.477	–	–	–	363	418	.868	–	–	876	127	191	2	–	–	–	1187	13.7	2.0	18.5
60-61–New York	52	–	1396	241	568	.424	–	–	–	268	325	.825	–	–	293	102	165	6	–	–	–	750	5.6	2.0	14.4
62-63–N.Y.-S.F.	77	–	1141	161	304	.530	–	–	–	131	168	.780	–	–	206	95	128	0	–	–	–	453	2.7	1.2	5.9
63-64–San Francisco	51	–	519	53	120	.442	–	–	–	64	79	.810	–	–	94	42	71	0	–	–	–	170	1.8	0.8	3.3
Reg. Season Totals	529	–	14923	2465	5420	.455	–	–	–	2425	2937	.826	–	–	4142	843	1470	27	–	–	–	7355	7.8	1.6	13.9
Playoff Totals	9	–	88	16	37	.432	–	–	–	13	15	.867	–	–	29	9	10	0	–	–	–	45	3.2	1.0	5.0
All-Star Totals	2	–	40	9	17	.529	–	–	–	9	10	.900	–	–	9	1	5	0	–	–	–	27	4.5	0.5	13.5

See, Marshall Wayne (Wayne) b. November 3, 1923 Ht. 6-3 Wt. 190 College: Northern Arizona

SEASON–TEAM	G	GS	MIN	FGM	FGA	PCT	3FGM	3FGA	PCT	FTM	FTA	PCT	O-RB	D-RB	TOT	AST	PF	DQ	STL	TO	BLK	PTS	RPG	APG	PPG
49-50–Waterloo	61	–	–	113	303	.373	–	–	–	94	135	.696	–	–	–	143	147	–	–	–	–	320	–	2.3	5.2
Reg. Season Totals	61	–	–	113	303	.373	–	–	–	94	135	.696	–	–	–	143	147	–	–	–	–	320	–	2.3	5.2

Seikaly, Ronald F. (Rony) b. May 10, 1965 Ht. 6-11 Wt. 253 College: Syracuse

SEASON–TEAM	G	GS	MIN	FGM	FGA	PCT	3FGM	3FGA	PCT	FTM	FTA	PCT	O-RB	D-RB	TOT	AST	PF	DQ	STL	TO	BLK	PTS	RPG	APG	PPG
88-89–Miami	78	62	1962	333	744	.448	1	4	.250	181	354	.511	204	345	549	55	258	8	46	200	96	848	7.0	0.7	10.9
89-90–Miami	74	72	2409	486	968	.502	0	1	.000	256	431	.594	253	513	766	78	258	8	78	236	124	1228	10.4	1.1	16.6
90-91–Miami	64	59	2171	395	822	.481	2	6	.333	258	417	.619	207	502	709	95	213	2	51	205	86	1050	11.1	1.5	16.4
91-92–Miami	79	78	2800	463	947	.489	0	3	.000	370	505	.733	307	627	934	109	278	2	40	216	121	1296	11.8	1.4	16.4
92-93–Miami	72	64	2456	417	868	.480	1	8	.125	397	540	.735	259	587	846	100	260	3	38	203	83	1232	11.8	1.4	17.1
93-94–Miami	72	60	2410	392	803	.488	0	2	.000	304	422	.720	244	496	740	136	279	8	59	195	100	1088	10.3	1.9	15.1
94-95–Golden State	36	35	1035	162	314	.516	0	0	–	111	160	.694	77	189	266	45	122	1	20	104	37	435	7.4	1.3	12.1
95-96–Golden State	64	60	1813	285	568	.502	2	3	.667	204	282	.723	166	333	499	71	219	5	40	180	69	776	7.8	1.1	12.1
96-97–Orlando	74	68	2615	460	907	.507	0	3	.000	357	500	.714	274	427	701	92	275	4	49	218	107	1277	9.5	1.2	17.3
97-98–Orlando-N.J.	56	49	1636	250	579	.432	0	2	.000	246	332	.741	146	247	393	77	164	2	28	146	43	746	7.0	1.4	13.3
98-99–New Jersey	9	0	88	4	20	.200	0	0	–	7	18	.389	5	16	21	2	15	0	4	10	6	15	2.3	0.2	1.7
Reg. Season Totals	678	607	21395	3647	7540	.484	6	32	.188	2691	3961	.679	2142	4282	6424	860	2341	43	453	1913	872	9991	9.5	1.3	14.7
Playoff Totals	14	9	405	47	98	.480	0	0	–	46	68	.676	38	64	102	12	51	1	7	28	15	140	7.3	0.9	10.0

Selbo, Glen L. b. March 29, 1926 Ht. 6-3 Wt. 195 College: Western Michigan; Michigan; Wisconsin

SEASON–TEAM	G	GS	MIN	FGM	FGA	PCT	3FGM	3FGA	PCT	FTM	FTA	PCT	O-RB	D-RB	TOT	AST	PF	DQ	STL	TO	BLK	PTS	RPG	APG	PPG
47-48–Oshkosh (N)	59	–	–	157	–	–	–	–	–	62	100	.620	–	–	–	–	85	–	–	–	–	376	–	–	6.4
48-49–Oshkosh (N)	60	–	–	119	–	–	–	–	–	77	114	.675	–	–	–	–	94	–	–	–	–	315	–	–	5.3
49-50–Sheboygan	13	–	–	10	51	.196	–	–	–	22	29	.759	–	–	–	23	15	–	–	–	–	42	–	1.8	3.2
Reg. NBA Totals	13	–	–	10	51	.196	–	–	–	22	29	.759	–	–	–	23	15	–	–	–	–	42	–	1.8	3.2
Reg. NBL Totals	119	–	–	276	–	–	–	–	–	139	214	.650	–	–	–	–	179	–	–	–	–	691	–	–	5.8
NBL Playoff Totals	4	–	–	5	–	–	–	–	–	5	6	.833	–	–	–	–	12	–	–	–	–	15	–	–	3.8

Sellers, Bradley Donn (Brad) b. December 17, 1962 Ht. 7-0 Wt. 220 College: Wisconsin; Ohio State

SEASON–TEAM	G	GS	MIN	FGM	FGA	PCT	3FGM	3FGA	PCT	FTM	FTA	PCT	O-RB	D-RB	TOT	AST	PF	DQ	STL	TO	BLK	PTS	RPG	APG	PPG
86-87–Chicago	80	17	1751	276	606	.455	2	10	.200	126	173	.728	155	218	373	102	194	1	44	84	68	680	4.7	1.3	8.5
87-88–Chicago	82	76	2212	326	714	.457	1	7	.143	124	157	.790	107	143	250	141	174	0	34	91	66	777	3.0	1.7	9.5
88-89–Chicago	80	25	1732	231	476	.485	3	6	.500	86	101	.851	85	142	227	99	176	2	35	72	69	551	2.8	1.2	6.9
89-90–Seattle-Minn.	59	0	700	103	254	.406	0	5	.000	58	73	.795	39	50	89	33	74	1	17	46	22	264	1.5	0.6	4.5
91-92–Detroit	43	1	226	41	88	.466	0	1	.000	20	26	.769	15	27	42	14	20	0	1	15	10	102	1.0	0.3	2.4
92-93–Detroit-Minn.	54	4	533	49	130	.377	0	1	.000	37	39	.949	27	56	83	46	40	0	6	27	11	135	1.5	0.9	2.5
Reg. Season Totals	398	123	7154	1026	2268	.452	6	30	.200	451	569	.793	428	636	1064	435	678	4	137	335	246	2509	2.7	1.1	6.3
Playoff Totals	28	4	402	45	124	.363	0	0	–	30	34	.882	27	32	59	28	47	0	5	12	12	120	2.1	1.0	4.3

Sellers, Phillip Jr. (Phil) b. November 20, 1953 Ht. 6-4 Wt. 195 College: Rutgers

SEASON–TEAM	G	GS	MIN	FGM	FGA	PCT	3FGM	3FGA	PCT	FTM	FTA	PCT	O-RB	D-RB	TOT	AST	PF	DQ	STL	TO	BLK	PTS	RPG	APG	PPG
76-77–Detroit	44	–	329	73	190	.384	–	–	–	52	72	.722	19	22	41	25	56	0	22	–	0	198	0.9	0.6	4.5
Reg. Season Totals	44	–	329	73	190	.384	–	–	–	52	72	.722	19	22	41	25	56	0	22	–	0	198	0.9	0.6	4.5
Playoff Totals	1	–	6	1	4	.250	–	–	–	1	4	.250	1	1	2	–	2	0	0	–	0	3	2.0	0.0	3.0

Seltz, Rolland A. (Rollie) b. January 25, 1924 Ht. 5-10 Wt. 170 College: Hamline

SEASON–TEAM	G	GS	MIN	FGM	FGA	PCT	3FGM	3FGA	PCT	FTM	FTA	PCT	O-RB	D-RB	TOT	AST	PF	DQ	STL	TO	BLK	PTS	RPG	APG	PPG
46-47–Anderson (N)	41	–	–	123	–	–	–	–	–	104	143	.727	–	–	–	–	97	–	–	–	–	350	–	–	8.5
47-48–Anderson (N)	59	–	–	118	–	–	–	–	–	90	119	.756	–	–	–	–	110	–	–	–	–	326	–	–	5.5
48-49–Waterloo (N)	62	–	–	188	–	–	–	–	–	127	174	.730	–	–	–	–	139	–	–	–	–	503	–	–	8.1
49-50–Anderson	34	–	–	93	309	.301	–	–	–	80	104	.769	–	–	–	64	72	–	–	–	–	266	–	1.9	7.8
Reg. NBA Totals	34	–	–	93	309	.301	–	–	–	80	104	.769	–	–	–	64	72	–	–	–	–	266	–	1.9	7.8
Reg. NBL Totals	162	–	–	429	–	–	–	–	–	321	436	.736	–	–	–	–	346	–	–	–	–	1179	–	–	7.3
NBL Playoff Totals	6	–	–	11	–	–	–	–	–	4	4	1.000	–	–	–	–	6	–	–	–	–	26	–	–	4.3

Selvage, Lester Revell (Les) b. March 7, 1943 Ht. 6-1 Wt. 175 College: Northeast Missouri State

SEASON–TEAM	G	GS	MIN	FGM	FGA	PCT	3FGM	3FGA	PCT	FTM	FTA	PCT	O-RB	D-RB	TOT	AST	PF	DQ	STL	TO	BLK	PTS	RPG	APG	PPG
67-68–Anaheim (A)	78	–	2432	371	1044	.355	147	461	.319	206	278	.741	–	–	217	247	239	3	–	195	–	1095	2.8	3.2	14.0
69-70–Los Angeles (A)	4	–	17	4	14	.286	0	4	.000	0	0	–	–	–	2	5	2	0	–	–	–	8	0.5	1.3	2.0
Reg. ABA Totals	82	–	2449	375	1058	.354	147	465	.316	206	278	.741	–	–	219	252	241	3	–	195	–	1103	2.7	3.1	13.5
ABA Playoff Totals	1	–	1	0	0	–	0	0	–	0	0	–	–	–	–	0	0	0	–	–	–	0	0.0	0.0	0.0

Selvy, Franklin Delano (Frank) b. November 9, 1932 Ht. 6-3 Wt. 180 College: Furman

SEASON–TEAM	G	GS	MIN	FGM	FGA	PCT	3FGM	3FGA	PCT	FTM	FTA	PCT	O-RB	D-RB	TOT	AST	PF	DQ	STL	TO	BLK	PTS	RPG	APG	PPG
54-55–Balt.-Milw.	71	–	2668	452	1195	.378	–	–	–	444	610	.728	–	–	394	245	230	3	–	–	–	1348	5.5	3.5	19.0
55-56–St. Louis	17	–	444	67	183	.366	–	–	–	53	71	.746	–	–	54	35	38	1	–	–	–	187	3.2	2.1	11.0
57-58–St. Louis-Minn.	38	–	426	44	167	.263	–	–	–	47	77	.610	–	–	88	35	44	0	–	–	–	135	2.3	0.9	3.6
58-59–New York	68	–	1448	233	605	.385	–	–	–	201	262	.767	–	–	248	96	113	1	–	–	–	667	3.6	1.4	9.8
59-60–Syr.-Minn.	62	–	1308	205	521	.393	–	–	–	153	208	.736	–	–	175	111	101	1	–	–	–	563	2.8	1.8	9.1
60-61–Los Angeles	77	–	2153	311	767	.405	–	–	–	210	279	.753	–	–	299	246	219	3	–	–	–	832	3.9	3.2	10.8
61-62–Los Angeles	79	–	2806	433	1032	.420	–	–	–	298	404	.738	–	–	412	381	232	0	–	–	–	1164	5.2	4.8	14.7
62-63–Los Angeles	80	–	2369	317	747	.424	–	–	–	192	269	.714	–	–	289	281	149	0	–	–	–	826	3.6	3.5	10.3
63-64–Los Angeles	73	–	1286	160	423	.378	–	–	–	78	122	.639	–	–	139	149	115	1	–	–	–	398	1.9	2.0	5.5
Reg. Season Totals	565	–	14908	2222	5640	.394	–	–	–	1676	2302	.728	–	–	2098	1579	1241	10	–	–	–	6120	3.7	2.8	10.8
Playoff Totals	52	–	1608	219	554	.395	–	–	–	151	192	.786	–	–	226	189	147	1	–	–	–	589	4.3	3.6	11.3
All-Star Totals	2	–	30	2	10	.200	–	–	–	3	4	.750	–	–	7	2	5	0	–	–	–	7	3.5	1.0	3.5

Seminoff, James (Jim) b. September 1, 1922 Ht. 6-2 Wt. 190 College: USC

SEASON–TEAM	G	GS	MIN	FGM	FGA	PCT	3FGM	3FGA	PCT	FTM	FTA	PCT	O-RB	D-RB	TOT	AST	PF	DQ	STL	TO	BLK	PTS	RPG	APG	PPG
46-47–Chicago	60	–	–	184	586	.314	–	–	–	71	130	.546	–	–	–	63	155	–	–	–	–	439	–	1.1	7.3
47-48–Chicago	48	–	–	113	381	.297	–	–	–	73	105	.695	–	–	–	89	105	–	–	–	–	299	–	1.9	6.2
48-49–Boston	58	–	–	153	487	.314	–	–	–	151	219	.689	–	–	–	229	195	–	–	–	–	457	–	3.9	7.9
49-50–Boston	65	–	–	85	283	.300	–	–	–	142	188	.755	–	–	–	249	154	–	–	–	–	312	–	3.8	4.8
Reg. Season Totals	231	–	–	535	1737	.308	–	–	–	437	642	.681	–	–	–	630	609	–	–	–	–	1507	–	2.7	6.5
Playoff Totals	17	–	–	47	373	.239	–	–	–	30	46	.652	–	–	–	30	69	1	–	–	–	124	0.0	1.0	7.3

Senesky, George Lawrence b. April 4, 1922 Ht. 6-2 Wt. 180 College: St. Joseph's (Pa.)

SEASON–TEAM	G	GS	MIN	FGM	FGA	PCT	3FGM	3FGA	PCT	FTM	FTA	PCT	O-RB	D-RB	TOT	AST	PF	DQ	STL	TO	BLK	PTS	RPG	APG	PPG
46-47–Philadelphia	58	–	–	142	531	.267	–	–	–	82	124	.661	–	–	–	34	83	–	–	–	–	366	–	0.6	6.3
47-48–Philadelphia	47	–	–	158	570	.277	–	–	–	98	147	.667	–	–	–	52	90	–	–	–	–	414	–	1.1	8.8
48-49–Philadelphia	60	–	–	138	516	.267	–	–	–	111	152	.730	–	–	–	233	133	–	–	–	–	387	–	3.9	6.5
49-50–Philadelphia	68	–	–	227	709	.320	–	–	–	157	223	.704	–	–	–	264	164	–	–	–	–	611	–	3.9	9.0
50-51–Philadelphia	65	–	–	249	703	.354	–	–	–	181	238	.761	–	–	326	342	144	1	–	–	–	679	5.0	5.3	10.4
51-52–Philadelphia	57	–	1925	164	454	.361	–	–	–	146	194	.753	–	–	232	280	123	0	–	–	–	474	4.1	4.9	8.3
52-53–Philadelphia	69	–	2336	160	485	.330	–	–	–	93	146	.637	–	–	254	264	166	1	–	–	–	413	3.7	3.8	6.0
53-54–Philadelphia	58	–	771	41	119	.345	–	–	–	29	53	.547	–	–	66	84	79	0	–	–	–	111	1.1	1.4	1.9
Reg. Season Totals	482	–	5032	1279	4087	.313	–	–	–	897	1277	.702	–	–	878	1553	982	2	–	–	–	3455	3.5	3.2	7.2
Playoff Totals	32	–	240	125	491	.318	–	–	–	72	103	.699	–	–	19	54	72	0	–	–	–	322	3.8	1.4	10.1

Sewell, Tom b. March 11, 1962 Ht. 6-5 Wt. 185 College: Amarillo (Texas) Coll. (J.C.); Lamar

SEASON–TEAM	G	GS	MIN	FGM	FGA	PCT	3FGM	3FGA	PCT	FTM	FTA	PCT	O-RB	D-RB	TOT	AST	PF	DQ	STL	TO	BLK	PTS	RPG	APG	PPG
84-85–Washington	21	0	87	9	36	.250	0	2	.000	2	4	.500	2	2	4	6	13	0	3	7	1	20	0.2	0.3	1.0
Reg. Season Totals	21	0	87	9	36	.250	0	2	.000	2	4	.500	2	2	4	6	13	0	3	7	1	20	0.2	0.3	1.0

Seymour, Paul Norman b. January 30, 1928 d. May 6, 1998 Ht. 6-2 Wt. 180 College: Toledo

SEASON–TEAM	G	GS	MIN	FGM	FGA	PCT	3FGM	3FGA	PCT	FTM	FTA	PCT	O-RB	D-RB	TOT	AST	PF	DQ	STL	TO	BLK	PTS	RPG	APG	PPG
46-47–Toledo (N)	33	–	–	41	–	–	–	–	–	17	30	.567	–	–	–	–	–	–	–	–	–	99	–	–	3.0
47-48–Syracuse (N)	30	–	–	79	–	–	–	–	–	47	64	.734	–	–	–	–	54	–	–	–	–	205	–	–	6.8
47-48–Baltimore	22	–	–	27	101	.267	–	–	–	22	37	.595	–	–	–	6	34	–	–	–	–	76	–	0.3	3.5
48-49–Syracuse (N)	63	–	–	120	–	–	–	–	–	70	106	.660	–	–	–	–	150	–	–	–	–	310	–	–	4.9
49-50–Syracuse	62	–	–	175	524	.334	–	–	–	126	176	.716	–	–	–	189	157	–	–	–	–	476	–	3.0	7.7
50-51–Syracuse	51	–	–	125	385	.325	–	–	–	117	159	.736	–	–	194	187	138	0	–	–	–	367	3.8	3.7	7.2
51-52–Syracuse	66	–	2209	206	615	.335	–	–	–	186	245	.759	–	–	225	220	165	4	–	–	–	598	3.4	3.3	9.1
52-53–Syracuse	67	–	2684	306	798	.383	–	–	–	340	416	.817	–	–	246	294	210	3	–	–	–	952	3.7	4.4	14.2
53-54–Syracuse	71	–	2727	316	838	.377	–	–	–	299	368	.813	–	–	291	364	187	2	–	–	–	931	4.1	5.1	13.1
54-55–Syracuse	72	–	2950	375	1036	.362	–	–	–	300	370	.811	–	–	309	483	137	0	–	–	–	1050	4.3	6.7	14.6
55-56–Syracuse	57	–	1826	227	670	.339	–	–	–	188	233	.807	–	–	152	276	130	1	–	–	–	642	2.7	4.8	11.3
56-57–Syracuse	65	–	1235	143	442	.324	–	–	–	101	123	.821	–	–	130	193	91	0	–	–	–	387	2.0	3.0	6.0
57-58–Syracuse	64	–	763	107	315	.340	–	–	–	53	63	.841	–	–	107	93	88	0	–	–	–	267	1.7	1.5	4.2
58-59–Syracuse	21	–	266	32	98	.327	–	–	–	26	29	.897	–	–	39	36	25	0	–	–	–	90	1.9	1.7	4.3
59-60–Syracuse	4	–	7	0	4	.000	–	–	–	0	0	–	–	–	1	0	1	0	–	–	–	0	0.3	0.0	0.0
Reg. NBA Totals	622	–	14667	2039	5826	.350	–	–	–	1758	2219	.792	–	–	1694	2341	1363	10	–	–	–	5836	3.1	3.8	9.4
Reg. NBL Totals	126	–	–	240	–	–	–	–	–	134	200	.670	–	–	–	–	204	–	–	–	–	614	–	–	4.9
NBA Playoff Totals	66	–	2156	208	693	.326	–	–	–	234	284	.824	–	–	191	318	185	4	–	–	–	650	2.9	4.0	9.8
NBL Playoff Totals	14	–	–	36	–	–	–	–	–	19	26	.731	–	–	–	–	35	–	–	–	–	91	–	–	6.5
NBA All-Star Totals	3	–	49	7	17	.412	–	–	–	7	8	.875	–	–	7	6	4	0	–	–	–	21	2.3	2.0	7.0

Shaback, Nicholas (Nick) b. September 10, 1918 Ht. 5-11 Wt. 180 College: None

SEASON–TEAM	G	GS	MIN	FGM	FGA	PCT	3FGM	3FGA	PCT	FTM	FTA	PCT	O-RB	D-RB	TOT	AST	PF	DQ	STL	TO	BLK	PTS	RPG	APG	PPG
46-47–Cleveland	53	–	–	102	385	.265	–	–	–	38	53	.717	–	–	–	29	75	–	–	–	–	242	–	0.5	4.6
Reg. Season Totals	53	–	–	102	385	.265	–	–	–	38	53	.717	–	–	–	29	75	–	–	–	–	242	–	0.5	4.6
Playoff Totals	3	–	–	6	22	.273	–	–	–	3	5	.600	–	–	–	–	6	–	–	–	–	15	–	0.0	5.0

Shackelford, Ray Lynn (Lynn) b. August 27, 1947 Ht. 6-5 Wt. 195 College: UCLA

SEASON–TEAM	G	GS	MIN	FGM	FGA	PCT	3FGM	3FGA	PCT	FTM	FTA	PCT	O-RB	D-RB	TOT	AST	PF	DQ	STL	TO	BLK	PTS	RPG	APG	PPG
69-70–Miami (A)	22	–	183	22	72	.306	4	13	.308	10	13	.769	–	–	27	11	34	0	–	–	–	58	1.2	0.5	2.6
Reg. ABA Totals	22	–	183	22	72	.306	4	13	.308	10	13	.769	–	–	27	11	34	0	–	–	–	58	1.2	0.5	2.6

Shackleford, Charles Edward b. April 22, 1966 Ht. 6-11 Wt. 245 College: North Carolina State

SEASON–TEAM	G	GS	MIN	FGM	FGA	PCT	3FGM	3FGA	PCT	FTM	FTA	PCT	O-RB	D-RB	TOT	AST	PF	DQ	STL	TO	BLK	PTS	RPG	APG	PPG
88-89–New Jersey	60	0	484	83	168	.494	0	1	.000	21	42	.500	50	103	153	21	71	0	15	27	18	187	2.6	0.4	3.1
89-90–New Jersey	70	37	1557	247	535	.462	0	1	.000	79	115	.687	180	299	479	56	183	1	40	116	35	573	6.8	0.8	8.2
91-92–Philadelphia	72	62	1399	205	422	.486	0	1	.000	63	95	.663	145	270	415	46	205	3	38	62	51	473	5.8	0.6	6.6
92-93–Philadelphia	48	0	568	80	164	.488	0	2	.000	31	49	.633	65	140	205	26	92	1	13	36	25	191	4.3	0.5	4.0
94-95–Minnesota	21	2	239	39	65	.600	0	0	–	16	20	.800	16	51	67	8	47	0	8	8	6	94	3.2	0.4	4.5
98-99–Charlotte	32	4	367	44	90	.489	0	0	–	19	29	.655	41	88	129	13	66	1	5	27	13	107	4.0	0.4	3.3
Reg. Season Totals	303	105	4614	698	1444	.483	0	5	.000	229	350	.654	497	951	1448	170	664	6	119	276	148	1625	4.8	0.6	5.4

Shaeffer, Carl Edgel b. October 25, 1924 d. October 25, 1974 Ht. 6-3 Wt. 185 College: Alabama

SEASON–TEAM	G	GS	MIN	FGM	FGA	PCT	3FGM	3FGA	PCT	FTM	FTA	PCT	O-RB	D-RB	TOT	AST	PF	DQ	STL	TO	BLK	PTS	RPG	APG	PPG
49-50–Indianapolis	43	–	–	59	160	.369	–	–	–	32	57	.561	–	–	–	40	103	–	–	–	–	150	–	0.9	3.5
50-51–Indianapolis	10	–	–	6	22	.273	–	–	–	3	3	1.000	–	–	10	6	15	0	–	–	–	15	1.0	0.6	1.5
Reg. Season Totals	53	–	–	65	182	.357	–	–	–	35	60	.583	–	–	10	46	118	0	–	–	–	165	1.0	0.9	3.1
Playoff Totals	6	–	–	7	42	.333	–	–	–	7	13	.538	–	–	–	14	19	1	–	–	–	21	–	1.2	3.5

Shaffer, Lee Philip II b. February 23, 1939 Ht. 6-7 Wt. 220 College: North Carolina

SEASON–TEAM	G	GS	MIN	FGM	FGA	PCT	3FGM	3FGA	PCT	FTM	FTA	PCT	O-RB	D-RB	TOT	AST	PF	DQ	STL	TO	BLK	PTS	RPG	APG	PPG
61-62–Syracuse	75	–	2083	514	1180	.436	–	–	–	239	310	.771	–	–	511	99	266	6	–	–	–	1267	6.8	1.3	16.9
62-63–Syracuse	80	–	2392	597	1393	.429	–	–	–	294	375	.784	–	–	524	97	249	5	–	–	–	1488	6.6	1.2	18.6
63-64–Philadelphia	41	–	1013	217	587	.370	–	–	–	102	133	.767	–	–	205	36	116	1	–	–	–	536	5.0	0.9	13.1
Reg. Season Totals	196	–	5488	1328	3160	.420	–	–	–	635	818	.776	–	–	1240	232	631	12	–	–	–	3291	6.3	1.2	16.8
Playoff Totals	13	–	387	99	238	.416	–	–	–	49	63	.778	–	–	82	15	41	0	–	–	–	247	6.3	1.2	19.0
All-Star Totals	1	–	19	6	13	.462	–	–	–	0	0	–	–	–	1	1	3	0	–	–	–	12	1.0	1.0	12.0

Shammgod, God b. April 29, 1976 Ht. 6-0 Wt. 182 College: Providence

SEASON–TEAM	G	GS	MIN	FGM	FGA	PCT	3FGM	3FGA	PCT	FTM	FTA	PCT	O-RB	D-RB	TOT	AST	PF	DQ	STL	TO	BLK	PTS	RPG	APG	PPG
97-98–Washington	20	0	146	19	58	.328	0	2	.000	23	30	.767	2	5	7	36	27	0	7	21	1	61	0.4	1.8	3.1
Reg. Season Totals	20	0	146	19	58	.328	0	2	.000	23	30	.767	2	5	7	36	27	0	7	21	1	61	0.4	1.8	3.1

Shannon, Earl F. b. November 23, 1921 Ht. 5-11 Wt. 170 College: Rhode Island

SEASON–TEAM	G	GS	MIN	FGM	FGA	PCT	3FGM	3FGA	PCT	FTM	FTA	PCT	O-RB	D-RB	TOT	AST	PF	DQ	STL	TO	BLK	PTS	RPG	APG	PPG
46-47–Providence	57	–	–	245	722	.339	–	–	–	197	348	.566	–	–	–	84	169	–	–	–	–	687	–	1.5	12.1
47-48–Providence	45	–	–	123	469	.262	–	–	–	116	183	.634	–	–	–	49	106	–	–	–	–	362	–	1.1	8.0
48-49–Prov.-Boston	32	–	–	34	127	.268	–	–	–	39	58	.672	–	–	–	44	33	–	–	–	–	107	–	1.4	3.3
Reg. Season Totals	134	–	–	402	1318	.305	–	–	–	352	589	.598	–	–	–	177	308	–	–	–	–	1156	–	1.3	8.6

Shannon, Howard Payne (Howie) b. June 10, 1923 Ht. 6-2 Wt. 175 College: Kansas State; North Texas

SEASON–TEAM	G	GS	MIN	FGM	FGA	PCT	3FGM	3FGA	PCT	FTM	FTA	PCT	O-RB	D-RB	TOT	AST	PF	DQ	STL	TO	BLK	PTS	RPG	APG	PPG
48-49–Providence	55	–	–	292	802	.364	–	–	–	152	189	.804	–	–	–	125	154	–	–	–	–	736	–	2.3	13.4
49-50–Boston	67	–	–	222	646	.344	–	–	–	143	182	.786	–	–	–	174	148	–	–	–	–	587	–	2.6	8.8
Reg. Season Totals	122	–	–	514	1448	.355	–	–	–	295	371	.795	–	–	–	299	302	–	–	–	–	1323	–	2.5	10.8

Share, Charles Edward (Charlie, Chuck) b. March 14, 1927 Ht. 6-11 Wt. 245 College: Bowling Green State

SEASON–TEAM	G	GS	MIN	FGM	FGA	PCT	3FGM	3FGA	PCT	FTM	FTA	PCT	O-RB	D-RB	TOT	AST	PF	DQ	STL	TO	BLK	PTS	RPG	APG	PPG
51-52–Fort Wayne	63	–	882	76	236	.322	–	–	–	96	155	.619	–	–	331	66	141	9	–	–	–	248	5.3	1.0	3.9
52-53–Fort Wayne	67	–	1044	91	254	.358	–	–	–	172	234	.735	–	–	373	74	213	13	–	–	–	354	5.6	1.1	5.3
53-54–FtWayne-Milw.	68	–	1576	188	493	.381	–	–	–	188	275	.684	–	–	555	80	210	8	–	–	–	564	8.2	1.2	8.3
54-55–Milwaukee	69	–	1685	235	577	.407	–	–	–	351	492	.713	–	–	684	84	273	17	–	–	–	821	9.9	1.2	11.9
55-56–St. Louis	72	–	1975	315	733	.430	–	–	–	346	498	.695	–	–	774	131	318	13	–	–	–	976	10.8	1.8	13.6
56-57–St. Louis	72	–	1673	235	535	.439	–	–	–	269	393	.684	–	–	642	79	269	15	–	–	–	739	8.9	1.1	10.3
57-58–St. Louis	72	–	1824	216	545	.396	–	–	–	190	293	.648	–	–	749	130	279	15	–	–	–	622	10.4	1.8	8.6
58-59–St. Louis	72	–	1713	147	381	.386	–	–	–	139	184	.755	–	–	657	103	261	6	–	–	–	433	9.1	1.4	6.0
59-60–St. Louis-Minn.	41	–	651	59	151	.391	–	–	–	53	80	.663	–	–	221	62	142	9	–	–	–	171	5.4	1.5	4.2
Reg. Season Totals	596	–	13023	1562	3905	.400	–	–	–	1804	2604	.693	–	–	4986	809	2106	105	–	–	–	4928	8.4	1.4	8.3
Playoff Totals	54	–	1111	124	290	.438	–	–	–	135	205	.659	–	–	362	62	224	17	–	–	–	383	6.5	1.1	7.1

Sharman, William Walton (Bill) b. May 25, 1926 Ht. 6-1 Wt. 190 College: USC HOF: 1975

SEASON–TEAM	G	GS	MIN	FGM	FGA	PCT	3FGM	3FGA	PCT	FTM	FTA	PCT	O-RB	D-RB	TOT	AST	PF	DQ	STL	TO	BLK	PTS	RPG	APG	PPG
50-51–Washington	31	–	–	141	361	.391	–	–	–	96	108	.889	–	–	96	39	86	3	–	–	–	378	3.1	1.3	12.2
51-52–Boston	63	–	1389	244	628	.389	–	–	–	183	213	.859	–	–	221	151	181	3	–	–	–	671	3.5	2.4	10.7
52-53–Boston	71	–	2333	403	925	.436	–	–	–	341	401	.850	–	–	288	191	240	7	–	–	–	1147	4.1	2.7	16.2
53-54–Boston	72	–	2467	412	915	.450	–	–	–	331	392	.844	–	–	255	229	211	4	–	–	–	1155	3.5	3.2	16.0
54-55–Boston	68	–	2453	453	1062	.427	–	–	–	347	387	.897	–	–	302	280	212	2	–	–	–	1253	4.4	4.1	18.4
55-56–Boston	72	–	2698	538	1229	.438	–	–	–	358	413	.867	–	–	259	339	197	1	–	–	–	1434	3.6	4.7	19.9
56-57–Boston	67	–	2403	516	1241	.416	–	–	–	381	421	.905	–	–	286	236	188	1	–	–	–	1413	4.3	3.5	21.1
57-58–Boston	63	–	2214	550	1297	.424	–	–	–	302	338	.893	–	–	295	167	156	3	–	–	–	1402	4.7	2.7	22.3
58-59–Boston	72	–	2382	562	1377	.408	–	–	–	342	367	.932	–	–	292	179	173	1	–	–	–	1466	4.1	2.5	20.4
59-60–Boston	71	–	1916	559	1225	.456	–	–	–	252	291	.866	–	–	262	144	154	2	–	–	–	1370	3.7	2.0	19.3
60-61–Boston	61	–	1538	383	908	.422	–	–	–	210	228	.921	–	–	223	146	127	0	–	–	–	976	3.7	2.4	16.0
Reg. Season Totals	711	–	21793	4761	11168	.426	–	–	–	3143	3559	.883	–	–	2779	2101	1925	27	–	–	–	12665	3.9	3.0	17.8
Playoff Totals	78	–	2573	538	1262	.426	–	–	–	370	404	.916	–	–	306	201	220	6	–	–	–	1446	3.7	2.6	18.5
All-Star Totals	8	–	194	40	104	.385	–	–	–	22	27	.815	–	–	31	16	16	0	–	–	–	102	3.9	2.0	12.8

Shasky, John Paul b. July 31, 1964 Ht. 6-11 Wt. 240 College: Minnesota

SEASON–TEAM	G	GS	MIN	FGM	FGA	PCT	3FGM	3FGA	PCT	FTM	FTA	PCT	O-RB	D-RB	TOT	AST	PF	DQ	STL	TO	BLK	PTS	RPG	APG	PPG
88-89–Miami	65	4	944	121	248	.488	0	2	.000	115	167	.689	96	136	232	22	94	0	14	46	13	357	3.6	0.3	5.5
89-90–Golden State	14	0	51	4	14	.286	0	0	–	2	6	.333	4	9	13	1	10	0	1	2	2	10	0.9	0.1	0.7
90-91–Dallas	57	0	510	51	116	.440	0	0	–	48	79	.608	58	76	134	11	75	0	14	27	20	150	2.4	0.2	2.6
Reg. Season Totals	136	4	1505	176	378	.466	0	2	.000	165	252	.655	158	221	379	34	179	0	29	75	35	517	2.8	0.3	3.8

Shavlik, Ronald Dean (Ron) b. December 4, 1933 d. June 27, 1983 Ht. 6-8 Wt. 200 College: North Carolina State

SEASON–TEAM	G	GS	MIN	FGM	FGA	PCT	3FGM	3FGA	PCT	FTM	FTA	PCT	O-RB	D-RB	TOT	AST	PF	DQ	STL	TO	BLK	PTS	RPG	APG	PPG
56-57–New York	7	–	72	4	22	.182	–	–	–	2	5	.400	–	–	22	0	12	0	–	–	–	10	3.1	0.0	1.4
57-58–New York	1	–	2	0	1	.000	–	–	–	0	0	–	–	–	1	0	0	0	–	–	–	0	1.0	0.0	0.0
Reg. Season Totals	8	–	74	4	23	.174	–	–	–	2	5	.400	–	–	23	0	12	0	–	–	–	10	2.9	0.0	1.3

Shaw, Brian K. b. March 22, 1966 Ht. 6-6 Wt. 200 College: St. Mary's (Calif.); California-Santa Barbara

SEASON–TEAM	G	GS	MIN	FGM	FGA	PCT	3FGM	3FGA	PCT	FTM	FTA	PCT	O-RB	D-RB	TOT	AST	PF	DQ	STL	TO	BLK	PTS	RPG	APG	PPG
88-89–Boston	82	54	2301	297	686	.433	0	13	.000	109	132	.826	119	257	376	472	211	1	78	188	27	703	4.6	5.8	8.6
90-91–Boston	79	79	2772	442	942	.469	3	27	.111	204	249	.819	104	266	370	602	206	1	105	223	34	1091	4.7	7.6	13.8
91-92–Boston-Miami	63	26	1423	209	513	.407	5	23	.217	72	91	.791	50	154	204	250	115	0	57	99	22	495	3.2	4.0	7.9
92-93–Miami	68	45	1603	197	501	.393	43	130	.331	61	78	.782	70	187	257	235	163	2	48	96	19	498	3.8	3.5	7.3
93-94–Miami	77	52	2037	278	667	.417	73	216	.338	64	89	.719	104	246	350	385	195	1	71	173	21	693	4.5	5.0	9.0
94-95–Orlando	78	9	1836	192	494	.389	48	184	.261	70	95	.737	52	189	241	406	184	1	73	184	18	502	3.1	5.2	6.4
95-96–Orlando	75	1	1679	182	486	.374	41	144	.285	91	114	.798	58	166	224	336	160	1	58	173	11	496	3.0	4.5	6.6
96-97–Orlando	77	31	1867	189	516	.366	63	194	.325	111	140	.793	47	147	194	319	197	3	67	170	26	552	2.5	4.1	7.2
97-98–G.S.-Phil.	59	34	1530	154	446	.345	28	95	.295	36	52	.692	37	178	215	261	148	4	49	99	17	372	3.6	4.4	6.3
98-99–Portland	1	0	5	0	1	.000	0	0	–	0	0	–	0	1	1	1	1	0	0	1	0	0	1.0	1.0	0.0
99-00–L.A. Lakers	74	2	1249	123	322	.382	18	58	.310	41	54	.759	45	171	216	201	105	0	35	75	14	305	2.9	2.7	4.1
Reg. Season Totals	733	333	18302	2263	5574	.406	322	1084	.297	859	1094	.785	686	1962	2648	3468	1685	14	641	1481	209	5707	3.6	4.7	7.8
Playoff Totals	80	27	1699	213	515	.414	52	155	.335	83	115	.722	46	185	231	278	193	1	47	121	11	561	2.9	3.5	7.0

Shaw, Joseph Casey (Casey) b. July 20, 1975 Ht. 6-11 Wt. 260 College: Toledo

SEASON–TEAM	G	GS	MIN	FGM	FGA	PCT	3FGM	3FGA	PCT	FTM	FTA	PCT	O-RB	D-RB	TOT	AST	PF	DQ	STL	TO	BLK	PTS	RPG	APG	PPG
98-99–Philadelphia	9	0	14	1	8	.125	0	0	–	0	0	–	3	0	3	0	2	0	0	2	0	2	0.3	0.0	0.2
Reg. Season Totals	9	0	14	1	8	.125	0	0	–	0	0	–	3	0	3	0	2	0	0	2	0	2	0.3	0.0	0.2

Shea, Robert F. (Bob) b. September 11, 1924 Ht. 6-2 Wt. 195 College: Rhode Island

SEASON–TEAM	G	GS	MIN	FGM	FGA	PCT	3FGM	3FGA	PCT	FTM	FTA	PCT	O-RB	D-RB	TOT	AST	PF	DQ	STL	TO	BLK	PTS	RPG	APG	PPG
46-47–Providence	43	–	–	37	153	.242	–	–	–	19	33	.576	–	–	–	6	42	–	–	–	–	93	–	0.1	2.2
Reg. Season Totals	43	–	–	37	153	.242	–	–	–	19	33	.576	–	–	–	6	42	–	–	–	–	93	–	0.1	2.2

Sheffield, Frederick J. (Fred) b. November 5, 1923 Ht. 6-2 Wt. 165 College: Utah

SEASON–TEAM	G	GS	MIN	FGM	FGA	PCT	3FGM	3FGA	PCT	FTM	FTA	PCT	O-RB	D-RB	TOT	AST	PF	DQ	STL	TO	BLK	PTS	RPG	APG	PPG
46-47–Philadelphia	22	–	–	29	146	.199	–	–	–	16	26	.615	–	–	–	4	34	–	–	–	–	74	–	0.2	3.4
Reg. Season Totals	22	–	–	29	146	.199	–	–	–	16	26	.615	–	–	–	4	34	–	–	–	–	74	–	0.2	3.4

Shelton, Craig Anthony b. May 1, 1957 Ht. 6-7 Wt. 210 College: Georgetown

SEASON–TEAM	G	GS	MIN	FGM	FGA	PCT	3FGM	3FGA	PCT	FTM	FTA	PCT	O-RB	D-RB	TOT	AST	PF	DQ	STL	TO	BLK	PTS	RPG	APG	PPG
80-81–Atlanta	55	–	586	100	219	.457	0	1	.000	35	58	.603	59	79	138	27	128	1	18	61	5	235	2.5	0.5	4.3
81-82–Atlanta	4	0	21	2	6	.333	0	0	–	1	2	.500	1	2	3	0	3	0	1	0	0	5	0.8	0.0	1.3
Reg. Season Totals	59	0	607	102	225	.453	0	1	.000	36	60	.600	60	81	141	27	131	1	19	61	5	240	2.4	0.5	4.1

Shelton, Lonnie Jewel b. October 19, 1955 Ht. 6-8 Wt. 240 College: Oregon State

SEASON–TEAM	G	GS	MIN	FGM	FGA	PCT	3FGM	3FGA	PCT	FTM	FTA	PCT	O-RB	D-RB	TOT	AST	PF	DQ	STL	TO	BLK	PTS	RPG	APG	PPG
76-77–N.Y. Knicks	82	–	2104	398	836	.476	–	–	–	159	225	.707	220	413	633	149	363	10	125	–	98	955	7.7	1.8	11.6
77-78–New York	82	–	2319	508	988	.514	–	–	–	203	276	.736	204	376	580	195	350	11	109	228	112	1219	7.1	2.4	14.9
78-79–Seattle	76	–	2158	446	859	.519	–	–	–	131	189	.693	182	286	468	110	266	7	76	188	75	1023	6.2	1.4	13.5
79-80–Seattle	76	–	2243	425	802	.530	1	5	.200	184	241	.763	199	383	582	145	292	11	92	169	79	1035	7.7	1.9	13.6
80-81–Seattle	14	–	440	73	174	.420	0	0	–	36	55	.655	31	47	78	35	48	0	22	41	3	182	5.6	2.5	13.0
81-82–Seattle	81	81	2667	508	1046	.486	0	8	.000	188	240	.783	161	348	509	252	317	12	99	199	43	1204	6.3	3.1	14.9
82-83–Seattle	82	79	2572	437	915	.478	1	6	.167	141	187	.754	158	337	495	237	310	8	75	172	72	1016	6.0	2.9	12.4
83-84–Cleveland	79	78	2101	371	779	.476	1	5	.200	107	140	.764	140	241	381	179	279	9	76	165	55	850	4.8	2.3	10.8
84-85–Cleveland	57	14	1244	158	363	.435	0	5	.000	51	77	.662	82	185	267	96	187	3	44	74	18	367	4.7	1.7	6.4
85-86–Cleveland	44	1	682	92	188	.489	0	2	.000	14	16	.875	38	105	143	61	128	2	21	48	4	198	3.3	1.4	4.5
Reg. Season Totals	673	253	18530	3416	6950	.492	3	31	.097	1214	1646	.738	1415	2721	4136	1459	2540	73	739	1284	559	8049	6.1	2.2	12.0
Playoff Totals	52	10	1611	268	553	.485	0	4	.000	88	132	.667	157	256	413	101	228	10	52	110	43	624	7.9	1.9	12.0
All-Star Totals	1	1	20	3	3	1.000	0	0	–	1	2	.500	4	5	9	1	4	0	1	2	0	7	9.0	1.0	7.0

Shepherd, Billy L. b. November 18, 1949 Ht. 5-10 Wt. 165 College: Butler

SEASON–TEAM	G	GS	MIN	FGM	FGA	PCT	3FGM	3FGA	PCT	FTM	FTA	PCT	O-RB	D-RB	TOT	AST	PF	DQ	STL	TO	BLK	PTS	RPG	APG	PPG
72-73–Virginia (A)	16	–	68	7	35	.200	4	16	.250	9	10	.900	2	3	5	8	12	0	–	8	–	27	0.3	0.5	1.7
73-74–San Diego (A)	84	–	1738	200	530	.377	65	202	.322	42	66	.636	22	85	107	371	102	–	97	120	10	507	1.3	4.4	6.0
74-75–Memphis (A)	69	–	1315	161	386	.417	60	143	.420	52	72	.722	14	65	79	278	68	–	66	91	9	434	1.1	4.0	6.3
Reg. ABA Totals	169	–	3121	368	951	.387	129	361	.357	103	148	.696	38	153	191	657	182	0	163	219	19	968	1.1	3.9	5.7
ABA Playoff Totals	11	–	227	27	86	.314	11	39	.282	9	9	1.000	3	13	16	33	14	0	11	19	2	74	1.5	3.0	6.7

Sheppard, Jeff b. December 29, 1974 Ht. 6-3 Wt. 190 College: Kentucky

SEASON–TEAM	G	GS	MIN	FGM	FGA	PCT	3FGM	3FGA	PCT	FTM	FTA	PCT	O-RB	D-RB	TOT	AST	PF	DQ	STL	TO	BLK	PTS	RPG	APG	PPG
98-99–Atlanta	18	5	185	15	39	.385	2	7	.286	8	13	.615	6	16	22	16	12	0	3	7	0	40	1.2	0.9	2.2
Reg. Season Totals	18	5	185	15	39	.385	2	7	.286	8	13	.615	6	16	22	16	12	0	3	7	0	40	1.2	0.9	2.2
Playoff Totals	4	0	12	0	3	.000	0	0	–	0	0	–	2	0	2	2	0	0	1	0	0	0	0.5	0.5	0.0

Sheppard, Steve (Bear) b. March 21, 1954 Ht. 6-6 Wt. 215 College: Maryland

SEASON–TEAM	G	GS	MIN	FGM	FGA	PCT	3FGM	3FGA	PCT	FTM	FTA	PCT	O-RB	D-RB	TOT	AST	PF	DQ	STL	TO	BLK	PTS	RPG	APG	PPG
77-78–Chicago	64	–	698	119	262	.454	–	–	–	37	56	.661	67	64	131	43	72	0	14	46	3	275	2.0	0.7	4.3
78-79–Chi.-Detroit	42	–	279	36	76	.474	–	–	–	20	34	.588	25	22	47	19	26	0	8	25	1	92	1.1	0.5	2.2
Reg. Season Totals	106	–	977	155	338	.459	–	–	–	57	90	.633	92	86	178	62	98	0	22	71	4	367	1.7	0.6	3.5

Sherod, Edmund b. September 13, 1959 Ht. 6-2 Wt. 170 College: Virginia Commonwealth

SEASON–TEAM	G	GS	MIN	FGM	FGA	PCT	3FGM	3FGA	PCT	FTM	FTA	PCT	O-RB	D-RB	TOT	AST	PF	DQ	STL	TO	BLK	PTS	RPG	APG	PPG
82-83–New York	64	37	1624	171	421	.406	1	13	.077	52	80	.650	43	106	149	311	112	2	96	104	14	395	2.3	4.9	6.2
Reg. Season Totals	64	37	1624	171	421	.406	1	13	.077	52	80	.650	43	106	149	311	112	2	96	104	14	395	2.3	4.9	6.2
Playoff Totals	6	0	23	1	5	.200	0	0	–	0	0	–	1	1	2	4	3	0	4	1	0	2	0.3	0.7	0.3

Shipp, Charles William (Charley, Jo-Jo) b. December 3, 1913 d. March 21, 1988 Ht. 6-1 Wt. 200 College: Catholic U.

SEASON–TEAM	G	GS	MIN	FGM	FGA	PCT	3FGM	3FGA	PCT	FTM	FTA	PCT	O-RB	D-RB	TOT	AST	PF	DQ	STL	TO	BLK	PTS	RPG	APG	PPG
37-38–Akron Goodyear (N)	16	–	–	38	–	–	–	–	–	14	–	–	–	–	–	–	37	–	–	–	–	90	–	–	5.6
38-39–Akron Goodyear (N)	24	–	–	59	–	–	–	–	–	24	–	–	–	–	–	–	56	–	–	–	–	142	–	–	5.9
39-40–Oshkosh (N)	28	–	–	74	–	–	–	–	–	26	59	.441	–	–	–	–	64	–	–	–	–	174	–	–	6.2
40-41–Oshkosh (N)	22	–	–	46	–	–	–	–	–	21	38	.553	–	–	–	–	50	–	–	–	–	113	–	–	5.1
41-42–Oshkosh (N)	24	–	–	70	–	–	–	–	–	38	53	.717	–	–	–	–	54	–	–	–	–	178	–	–	7.4
42-43–Oshkosh (N)	23	–	–	52	–	–	–	–	–	36	67	.537	–	–	–	–	62	–	–	–	–	140	–	–	6.1
43-44–Oshkosh (N)	20	–	–	57	–	–	–	–	–	36	–	–	–	–	–	–	47	–	–	–	–	150	–	–	7.5
44-45–Fort Wayne (N)	30	–	–	31	–	–	–	–	–	16	–	–	–	–	–	–	57	–	–	–	–	78	–	–	2.6
45-46–Fort Wayne (N)	34	–	–	42	–	–	–	–	–	14	24	.583	–	–	–	–	49	–	–	–	–	98	–	–	2.9
46-47–FtWayne-And. (N)	44	–	–	89	–	–	–	–	–	58	83	.699	–	–	–	–	98	–	–	–	–	236	–	–	5.4
47-48–Anderson (N)	55	–	–	103	–	–	–	–	–	63	95	.663	–	–	–	–	136	–	–	–	–	269	–	–	4.9
48-49–Waterloo (N)	56	–	–	104	–	–	–	–	–	59	90	.656	–	–	–	–	105	–	–	–	–	267	–	–	4.8
49-50–Waterloo	23	–	–	35	137	.255	–	–	–	37	51	.725	–	–	–	46	46	–	–	–	–	107	–	2.0	4.7
Reg. NBA Totals	23	–	–	35	137	.255	–	–	–	37	51	.725	–	–	–	46	46	–	–	–	–	107	–	2.0	4.7
Reg. NBL Totals	376	–	–	765	–	–	–	–	–	405	509	.619	–	–	–	–	815	–	–	–	–	1935	–	–	5.1
NBL Playoff Totals	40	–	–	44	–	–	–	–	–	48	18	.611	–	–	–	–	65	–	–	–	–	136	–	–	3.4

Short, Eugene (Gene) b. August 7, 1953 Ht. 6-7 Wt. 200 College: Jackson State

SEASON–TEAM	G	GS	MIN	FGM	FGA	PCT	3FGM	3FGA	PCT	FTM	FTA	PCT	O-RB	D-RB	TOT	AST	PF	DQ	STL	TO	BLK	PTS	RPG	APG	PPG
75-76–Seattle-N.Y.	34	–	222	32	91	.352	–	–	–	20	32	.625	19	29	48	10	36	0	8	–	3	84	1.4	0.3	2.5
Reg. Season Totals	34	–	222	32	91	.352	–	–	–	20	32	.625	19	29	48	10	36	0	8	–	3	84	1.4	0.3	2.5

Short, Purvis b. July 2, 1957 Ht. 6-7 Wt. 220 College: Jackson State

SEASON–TEAM	G	GS	MIN	FGM	FGA	PCT	3FGM	3FGA	PCT	FTM	FTA	PCT	O-RB	D-RB	TOT	AST	PF	DQ	STL	TO	BLK	PTS	RPG	APG	PPG
78-79–Golden State	75	–	1703	369	771	.479	–	–	–	57	85	.671	127	220	347	97	233	6	54	111	12	795	4.6	1.3	10.6
79-80–Golden State	62	–	1636	461	916	.503	0	6	.000	134	165	.812	119	197	316	123	186	4	63	122	9	1056	5.1	2.0	17.0
80-81–Golden State	79	–	2309	549	1157	.475	3	17	.176	168	205	.820	151	240	391	249	244	3	78	143	19	1269	4.9	3.2	16.1
81-82–Golden State	76	8	1782	456	935	.488	6	28	.214	177	221	.801	123	143	266	209	220	3	65	122	10	1095	3.5	2.8	14.4
82-83–Golden State	67	57	2397	589	1209	.487	4	15	.267	255	308	.828	145	209	354	228	242	3	94	194	14	1437	5.3	3.4	21.4
83-84–Golden State	79	76	2945	714	1509	.473	22	72	.306	353	445	.793	184	254	438	246	252	2	103	228	11	1803	5.5	3.1	22.8
84-85–Golden State	78	77	3081	819	1780	.460	47	150	.313	501	613	.817	157	241	398	234	255	4	116	241	27	2186	5.1	3.0	28.0
85-86–Golden State	64	63	2427	633	1313	.482	15	49	.306	351	406	.865	126	203	329	237	229	5	92	184	22	1632	5.1	3.7	25.5
86-87–Golden State	34	15	950	240	501	.479	4	17	.235	137	160	.856	55	82	137	86	103	1	45	68	7	621	4.0	2.5	18.3
87-88–Houston	81	11	1949	474	986	.481	5	21	.238	206	240	.858	71	151	222	162	197	0	58	118	14	1159	2.7	2.0	14.3
88-89–Houston	65	16	1157	198	480	.413	9	33	.273	77	89	.865	65	114	179	107	116	1	44	70	13	482	2.8	1.6	7.4
89-90–New Jersey	82	24	2213	432	950	.455	10	35	.286	198	237	.835	101	147	248	145	202	2	66	119	20	1072	3.0	1.8	13.1
Reg. Season Totals	842	347	24549	5934	12507	.474	125	443	.282	2614	3174	.824	1424	2201	3625	2123	2479	34	878	1720	178	14607	4.3	2.5	17.3
Playoff Totals	18	2	361	72	170	.424	0	5	.000	43	49	.878	23	29	52	30	49	0	13	26	2	187	2.9	1.7	10.4

Shouse, Dexter Wayne b. March 24, 1963 Ht. 6-2 Wt. 200 College: Panola (Texas) Coll. (J.C.); South Alabama

SEASON–TEAM	G	GS	MIN	FGM	FGA	PCT	3FGM	3FGA	PCT	FTM	FTA	PCT	O-RB	D-RB	TOT	AST	PF	DQ	STL	TO	BLK	PTS	RPG	APG	PPG
89-90–Philadelphia	3	0	18	0	4	.000	0	1	.000	0	0	–	0	0	0	2	2	0	1	2	1	0	0.0	0.7	0.0
Reg. Season Totals	3	0	18	0	4	.000	0	1	.000	0	0	–	0	0	0	2	2	0	1	2	1	0	0.0	0.7	0.0

Shrider, Richard G. **(Dick)** b. February 7, 1923 Ht. 6-2 Wt. 190 College: Ohio U.

SEASON–TEAM	G	GS	MIN	FGM	FGA	PCT	3FGM	3FGA	PCT	FTM	FTA	PCT	O-RB	D-RB	TOT	AST	PF	DQ	STL	TO	BLK	PTS	RPG	APG	PPG
48-49–Detroit (N)	3	–	–	3	–	–	–	–	–	3	6	.500	–	–	–	–	–	–	–	–	–	9	–	–	3.0
48-49–New York	4	–	–	0	0	–	–	–	–	1	3	.333	–	–	–	2	2	–	–	–	–	1	–	0.5	0.3
Reg. NBA Totals	4	–	–	0	0	–	–	–	–	1	3	.333	–	–	–	2	2	–	–	–	–	1	–	0.5	0.3
Reg. NBL Totals	3	–	–	3	–	–	–	–	–	3	6	.500	–	–	–	–	–	–	–	–	–	9	–	–	3.0

Shue, Eugene William **(Gene)** b. December 18, 1931 Ht. 6-2 Wt. 175 College: Maryland

SEASON–TEAM	G	GS	MIN	FGM	FGA	PCT	3FGM	3FGA	PCT	FTM	FTA	PCT	O-RB	D-RB	TOT	AST	PF	DQ	STL	TO	BLK	PTS	RPG	APG	PPG
54-55–Phil.-N.Y.	62	–	947	100	289	.346	–	–	–	59	78	.756	–	–	154	89	64	0	–	–	–	259	2.5	1.4	4.2
55-56–New York	72	–	1750	240	625	.384	–	–	–	181	237	.764	–	–	212	179	111	0	–	–	–	661	2.9	2.5	9.2
56-57–Fort Wayne	72	–	2470	273	710	.385	–	–	–	241	316	.763	–	–	421	238	137	0	–	–	–	787	5.8	3.3	10.9
57-58–Detroit	63	–	2333	353	919	.384	–	–	–	276	327	.844	–	–	333	172	150	1	–	–	–	982	5.3	2.7	15.6
58-59–Detroit	72	–	2745	464	1197	.388	–	–	–	338	421	.803	–	–	335	231	129	1	–	–	–	1266	4.7	3.2	17.6
59-60–Detroit	75	–	3338	620	1501	.413	–	–	–	472	541	.872	–	–	409	295	146	2	–	–	–	1712	5.5	3.9	22.8
60-61–Detroit	78	–	3361	650	1545	.421	–	–	–	465	543	.856	–	–	334	530	207	1	–	–	–	1765	4.3	6.8	22.6
61-62–Detroit	80	–	3143	580	1422	.408	–	–	–	362	447	.810	–	–	372	465	192	1	–	–	–	1522	4.7	5.8	19.0
62-63–New York	78	–	2288	354	894	.396	–	–	–	208	302	.689	–	–	191	259	171	0	–	–	–	916	2.4	3.3	11.7
63-64–Baltimore	47	–	963	81	276	.293	–	–	–	36	61	.590	–	–	94	150	98	2	–	–	–	198	2.0	3.2	4.2
Reg. Season Totals	699	–	23338	3715	9378	.396	–	–	–	2638	3273	.806	–	–	2855	2608	1405	8	–	–	–	10068	4.1	3.7	14.4
Playoff Totals	32	–	1171	207	488	.424	–	–	–	155	184	.842	–	–	133	132	75	0	–	–	–	569	4.2	4.1	17.8
All-Star Totals	5	–	130	29	51	.569	–	–	–	8	12	.667	–	–	20	19	11	0	–	–	–	66	4.0	3.8	13.2

Shumate, John H. b. April 6, 1952 Ht. 6-9 Wt. 235 College: Notre Dame

SEASON–TEAM	G	GS	MIN	FGM	FGA	PCT	3FGM	3FGA	PCT	FTM	FTA	PCT	O-RB	D-RB	TOT	AST	PF	DQ	STL	TO	BLK	PTS	RPG	APG	PPG
75-76–Phoenix-Buffalo	75	–	1976	332	592	.561	–	–	–	212	326	.650	143	411	554	127	159	2	82	–	34	876	7.4	1.7	11.7
76-77–Buffalo	74	–	2601	407	810	.502	–	–	–	302	450	.671	163	538	701	159	197	1	90	–	84	1116	9.5	2.1	15.1
77-78–Buffalo-Detroit	80	–	2760	391	773	.506	–	–	–	400	508	.787	157	525	682	180	200	2	90	232	52	1182	8.5	2.3	14.8
79-80–Det.-Hou.-S.A.	65	–	1337	207	392	.528	0	1	.000	165	216	.764	108	255	363	84	126	1	40	91	45	579	5.6	1.3	8.9
80-81–S.A.-Seattle	24	–	527	56	131	.427	0	0	–	55	76	.724	34	54	88	24	49	0	21	42	9	167	3.7	1.0	7.0
Reg. Season Totals	318	–	9201	1393	2698	.516	0	1	.000	1134	1576	.720	605	1783	2388	574	731	6	323	365	224	3920	7.5	1.8	12.3
Playoff Totals	12	–	440	63	112	.563	0	0	–	22	41	.537	32	58	90	30	38	0	13	5	17	148	7.5	2.5	12.3

Sibert, Sam Lewis b. February 11, 1949 Ht. 6-7 Wt. 215 College: Eastern Oklahoma St. (J.C.); Texas Tech; Kentucky State

SEASON–TEAM	G	GS	MIN	FGM	FGA	PCT	3FGM	3FGA	PCT	FTM	FTA	PCT	O-RB	D-RB	TOT	AST	PF	DQ	STL	TO	BLK	PTS	RPG	APG	PPG
72-73–K.C.-Omaha	5	–	26	4	13	.308	–	–	–	4	5	.800	–	–	4	0	4	0	–	–	–	12	0.8	0.0	2.4
Reg. Season Totals	5	–	26	4	13	.308	–	–	–	4	5	.800	–	–	4	0	4	0	–	–	–	12	0.8	0.0	2.4

Sibley, Donald **(Mark)** b. November 13, 1950 Ht. 6-2 Wt. 175 College: Northwestern

SEASON–TEAM	G	GS	MIN	FGM	FGA	PCT	3FGM	3FGA	PCT	FTM	FTA	PCT	O-RB	D-RB	TOT	AST	PF	DQ	STL	TO	BLK	PTS	RPG	APG	PPG
73-74–Portland	28	–	124	20	56	.357	–	–	–	6	7	.857	9	16	25	13	23	0	4	–	1	46	0.9	0.5	1.6
Reg. Season Totals	28	–	124	20	56	.357	–	–	–	6	7	.857	9	16	25	13	23	0	4	–	1	46	0.9	0.5	1.6

Sichting, Jerry Lee b. November 29, 1956 Ht. 6-1 Wt. 180 College: Purdue

SEASON–TEAM	G	GS	MIN	FGM	FGA	PCT	3FGM	3FGA	PCT	FTM	FTA	PCT	O-RB	D-RB	TOT	AST	PF	DQ	STL	TO	BLK	PTS	RPG	APG	PPG
80-81–Indiana	47	–	450	34	95	.358	0	5	.000	25	32	.781	11	32	43	70	38	0	23	28	1	93	0.9	1.5	2.0
81-82–Indiana	51	0	800	91	194	.469	1	9	.111	29	38	.763	14	41	55	117	63	0	33	42	1	212	1.1	2.3	4.2
82-83–Indiana	78	58	2435	316	661	.478	3	18	.167	92	107	.860	33	122	155	433	185	0	104	138	2	727	2.0	5.6	9.3
83-84–Indiana	80	80	2497	397	746	.532	6	20	.300	117	135	.867	44	127	171	457	179	0	90	144	8	917	2.1	5.7	11.5
84-85–Indiana	70	25	1808	325	624	.521	9	37	.243	112	128	.875	24	90	114	264	116	0	47	102	4	771	1.6	3.8	11.0
85-86–Boston	82	7	1596	235	412	.570	6	16	.375	61	66	.924	27	77	104	188	118	0	50	73	0	537	1.3	2.3	6.5
86-87–Boston	78	15	1566	202	398	.508	7	26	.269	37	42	.881	22	69	91	187	124	0	40	61	1	448	1.2	2.4	5.7
87-88–Boston-Port.	52	1	694	93	172	.541	10	22	.455	17	23	.739	9	27	36	93	60	0	21	22	0	213	0.7	1.8	4.1
88-89–Portland	25	1	390	46	104	.442	3	12	.250	7	8	.875	9	20	29	59	17	0	15	25	0	102	1.2	2.4	4.1
89-90–Cha.-Milw.	35	8	496	50	125	.400	3	12	.250	18	22	.818	3	16	19	94	40	0	16	22	2	121	0.5	2.7	3.5
Reg. Season Totals	598	195	12732	1789	3531	.507	48	177	.271	515	601	.857	196	621	817	1962	940	0	439	657	19	4141	1.4	3.3	6.9
Playoff Totals	47	4	655	64	153	.418	1	7	.143	11	17	.647	11	28	39	79	59	0	16	18	0	140	0.8	1.7	3.0

Sidle, Donald Roy (Don) b. June 21, 1946 d. May 1987 Ht. 6-9 Wt. 215 College: Oklahoma

SEASON–TEAM	G	GS	MIN	FGM	FGA	PCT	3FGM	3FGA	PCT	FTM	FTA	PCT	O-RB	D-RB	TOT	AST	PF	DQ	STL	TO	BLK	PTS	RPG	APG	PPG
68-69–Miami (A)	77	–	1984	305	656	.465	0	4	.000	321	450	.713	–	–	551	73	212	3	–	142	–	931	7.2	0.9	12.1
69-70–Miami (A)	84	–	3493	639	1320	.484	1	6	.167	469	634	.740	432	650	1082	129	272	3	–	–	–	1748	12.9	1.5	20.8
70-71–Denver-Ind. (A)	84	–	2151	425	851	.499	2	9	.222	241	331	.728	–	–	635	97	233	–	–	–	–	1093	7.6	1.2	13.0
71-72–Ind.-Mem. (A)	69	–	960	175	384	.456	1	10	.100	124	195	.636	–	–	234	26	96	–	–	56	–	475	3.4	0.4	6.9
Reg. ABA Totals	314	–	8588	1544	3211	.481	4	29	.138	1155	1610	.717	432	650	2502	325	813	6	–	198	–	4247	8.0	1.0	13.5
ABA Playoff Totals	20	–	428	68	141	.482	0	1	.000	53	76	.697	–	–	122	21	43	1	–	–	–	189	6.1	1.1	9.5

Siegfried, Larry E. b. May 22, 1939 Ht. 6-4 Wt. 190 College: Ohio State

SEASON–TEAM	G	GS	MIN	FGM	FGA	PCT	3FGM	3FGA	PCT	FTM	FTA	PCT	O-RB	D-RB	TOT	AST	PF	DQ	STL	TO	BLK	PTS	RPG	APG	PPG
63-64–Boston	31	–	261	35	110	.318	–	–	–	31	39	.795	–	–	51	40	33	0	–	–	–	101	1.6	1.3	3.3
64-65–Boston	72	–	996	173	417	.415	–	–	–	109	140	.779	–	–	134	119	108	1	–	–	–	455	1.9	1.7	6.3
65-66–Boston	71	–	1675	349	825	.423	–	–	–	274	311	.881	–	–	196	165	157	1	–	–	–	972	2.8	2.3	13.7
66-67–Boston	73	–	1891	368	833	.442	–	–	–	294	347	.847	–	–	228	250	207	1	–	–	–	1030	3.1	3.4	14.1
67-68–Boston	62	–	1937	261	629	.415	–	–	–	236	272	.868	–	–	215	289	194	2	–	–	–	758	3.5	4.7	12.2
68-69–Boston	79	–	2560	392	1031	.380	–	–	–	336	389	.864	–	–	282	370	222	0	–	–	–	1120	3.6	4.7	14.2
69-70–Boston	78	–	2081	382	902	.424	–	–	–	220	257	.856	–	–	212	299	187	2	–	–	–	984	2.7	3.8	12.6
70-71–San Diego	53	–	1673	146	378	.386	–	–	–	130	153	.850	–	–	207	346	146	0	–	–	–	422	3.9	6.5	8.0
71-72–Hou.-Atlanta	31	–	558	43	123	.350	–	–	–	32	37	.865	–	–	42	72	53	0	–	–	–	118	1.4	2.3	3.8
Reg. Season Totals	550	–	13632	2149	5248	.409	–	–	–	1662	1945	.854	–	–	1567	1950	1307	7	–	–	–	5960	2.8	3.5	10.8
Playoff Totals	79	–	1826	301	753	.400	–	–	–	256	307	.834	–	–	199	209	249	5	–	–	–	858	2.5	2.6	10.9

Siewert, Ralph Paul (Sky) b. December 31, 1923 d. June 1991 Ht. 7-1 Wt. 235 College: Dakota Wesleyan

SEASON–TEAM	G	GS	MIN	FGM	FGA	PCT	3FGM	3FGA	PCT	FTM	FTA	PCT	O-RB	D-RB	TOT	AST	PF	DQ	STL	TO	BLK	PTS	RPG	APG	PPG
46-47–St. L.-Toronto	21	–	–	6	44	.136	–	–	–	8	15	.533	–	–	–	4	18	–	–	–	–	20	–	0.2	1.0
Reg. Season Totals	21	–	–	6	44	.136	–	–	–	8	15	.533	–	–	–	4	18	–	–	–	–	20	–	0.2	1.0

Sikma, Jack Wayne b. November 14, 1955 Ht. 6-11 Wt. 250 College: Illinois Wesleyan

SEASON–TEAM	G	GS	MIN	FGM	FGA	PCT	3FGM	3FGA	PCT	FTM	FTA	PCT	O-RB	D-RB	TOT	AST	PF	DQ	STL	TO	BLK	PTS	RPG	APG	PPG
77-78–Seattle	82	–	2238	342	752	.455	–	–	–	192	247	.777	196	482	678	134	300	6	68	186	40	876	8.3	1.6	10.7
78-79–Seattle	82	–	2958	476	1034	.460	–	–	–	329	404	.814	232	781	1013	261	295	4	82	253	67	1281	12.4	3.2	15.6
79-80–Seattle	82	–	2793	470	989	.475	0	1	.000	235	292	.805	198	710	908	279	232	5	68	202	77	1175	11.1	3.4	14.3
80-81–Seattle	82	–	2920	595	1311	.454	0	5	.000	340	413	.823	184	668	852	248	282	5	78	201	93	1530	10.4	3.0	18.7
81-82–Seattle	82	82	3049	581	1212	.479	2	13	.154	447	523	.855	223	815	1038	277	268	5	102	213	107	1611	12.7	3.4	19.6
82-83–Seattle	75	71	2564	484	1043	.464	0	8	.000	400	478	.837	213	645	858	233	263	4	87	190	65	1368	11.4	3.1	18.2
83-84–Seattle	82	82	2993	576	1155	.499	0	2	.000	411	480	.856	225	686	911	327	301	6	95	236	92	1563	11.1	4.0	19.1
84-85–Seattle	68	68	2402	461	943	.489	2	10	.200	335	393	.852	164	559	723	285	239	1	83	160	91	1259	10.6	4.2	18.5
85-86–Seattle	80	78	2790	508	1100	.462	0	13	.000	355	411	.864	146	602	748	301	293	4	92	214	73	1371	9.4	3.8	17.1
86-87–Milwaukee	82	82	2536	390	842	.463	0	2	.000	265	313	.847	208	614	822	203	328	14	88	160	90	1045	10.0	2.5	12.7
87-88–Milwaukee	82	82	2923	514	1058	.486	3	14	.214	321	348	.922	195	514	709	279	316	11	93	157	80	1352	8.6	3.4	16.5
88-89–Milwaukee	80	80	2587	360	835	.431	82	216	.380	266	294	.905	141	482	623	289	300	6	85	145	61	1068	7.8	3.6	13.4
89-90–Milwaukee	71	70	2250	344	827	.416	68	199	.342	230	260	.885	109	383	492	229	244	5	76	139	48	986	6.9	3.2	13.9
90-91–Milwaukee	77	44	1940	295	691	.427	46	135	.341	166	197	.843	108	333	441	143	218	4	65	130	64	802	5.7	1.9	10.4
Reg. Season Totals	1107	739	36943	6396	13792	.464	203	618	.328	4292	5053	.849	2542	8274	10816	3488	3879	80	1162	2586	1048	17287	9.8	3.2	15.6
Playoff Totals	102	45	3558	556	1249	.445	11	45	.244	338	407	.830	226	719	945	244	432	17	97	209	80	1461	9.3	2.4	14.3
All-Star Totals	7	0	147	24	51	.471	0	2	.000	7	8	.875	12	30	42	11	20	0	9	6	7	55	6.0	1.6	7.9

Silas, James Edward (Snake, Captain Late) b. February 11, 1949 Ht. 6-2 Wt. 190 College: Stephen F. Austin St.

SEASON–TEAM	G	GS	MIN	FGM	FGA	PCT	3FGM	3FGA	PCT	FTM	FTA	PCT	O-RB	D-RB	TOT	AST	PF	DQ	STL	TO	BLK	PTS	RPG	APG	PPG
72-73–Dallas (A)	78	–	2417	341	679	.502	0	0	–	389	467	.833	109	227	336	244	262	2	–	192	–	1071	4.3	3.1	13.7
73-74–San Antonio (A)	84	–	3096	486	1017	.478	0	1	.000	349	420	.831	83	260	343	319	256	–	90	220	8	1321	4.1	3.8	15.7
74-75–San Antonio (A)	82	–	3105	578	1136	.509	0	2	.000	430	486	.885	73	237	310	398	232	–	111	230	17	1586	3.8	4.9	19.3
75-76–San Antonio (A)	84	–	3112	718	1384	.519	0	2	.000	564	647	.872	111	224	335	452	263	–	155	254	24	2000	4.0	5.4	23.8
76-77–San Antonio	22	–	356	61	142	.430	–	–	–	87	107	.813	7	25	32	50	36	0	13	–	3	209	1.5	2.3	9.5
77-78–San Antonio	37	–	311	43	97	.443	–	–	–	60	73	.822	4	19	23	38	29	0	11	30	1	146	0.6	1.0	3.9
78-79–San Antonio	79	–	2171	466	922	.505	–	–	–	334	402	.831	35	148	183	273	215	1	76	199	20	1266	2.3	3.5	16.0
79-80–San Antonio	77	–	2293	513	999	.514	0	4	.000	339	382	.887	45	122	167	347	206	2	61	192	14	1365	2.2	4.5	17.7
80-81–San Antonio	75	–	2055	476	997	.477	0	2	.000	374	440	.850	44	187	231	285	129	0	51	159	12	1326	3.1	3.8	17.7
81-82–Cleveland	67	34	1447	251	573	.438	0	5	.000	246	286	.860	26	83	109	222	109	0	40	107	6	748	1.6	3.3	11.2
Reg. NBA Totals	357	34	8633	1810	3730	.485	0	11	.000	1440	1690	.852	161	584	745	1215	724	3	252	687	56	5060	2.1	3.4	14.2
Reg. ABA Totals	328	–	11730	2123	4216	.504	0	5	.000	1732	2020	.857	376	948	1324	1413	1013	2	356	896	49	5978	4.0	4.3	18.2
NBA Playoff Totals	27	0	745	148	330	.448	0	0	–	101	125	.808	18	46	64	95	57	1	32	60	2	397	2.4	3.5	14.7
ABA Playoff Totals	14	–	591	93	202	.460	0	1	.000	61	82	.744	16	44	60	92	45	0	24	39	2	247	4.3	6.6	17.6

Silas, Paul Theron b. July 12, 1943 Ht. 6-7 Wt. 230 College: Creighton

SEASON–TEAM	G	GS	MIN	FGM	FGA	PCT	3FGM	3FGA	PCT	FTM	FTA	PCT	O-RB	D-RB	TOT	AST	PF	DQ	STL	TO	BLK	PTS	RPG	APG	PPG
64-65–St. Louis	79	–	1243	140	375	.373	–	–	–	83	164	.506	–	–	576	48	161	1	–	–	–	363	7.3	0.6	4.6
65-66–St. Louis	46	–	586	70	173	.405	–	–	–	35	61	.574	–	–	236	22	72	0	–	–	–	175	5.1	0.5	3.8
66-67–St. Louis	77	–	1570	207	482	.429	–	–	–	113	213	.531	–	–	669	74	208	4	–	–	–	527	8.7	1.0	6.8
67-68–St. Louis	82	–	2652	399	871	.458	–	–	–	299	424	.705	–	–	958	162	243	4	–	–	–	1097	11.7	2.0	13.4
68-69–Atlanta	79	–	1853	241	575	.419	–	–	–	204	333	.613	–	–	745	140	166	0	–	–	–	686	9.4	1.8	8.7
69-70–Phoenix	78	–	2836	373	804	.464	–	–	–	250	412	.607	–	–	916	214	266	5	–	–	–	996	11.7	2.7	12.8
70-71–Phoenix	81	–	2944	338	789	.428	–	–	–	285	416	.685	–	–	1015	247	227	4	–	–	–	961	12.5	3.0	11.9
71-72–Phoenix	80	–	3082	485	1031	.470	–	–	–	433	560	.773	–	–	955	343	201	2	–	–	–	1403	11.9	4.3	17.5
72-73–Boston	80	–	2618	400	851	.470	–	–	–	266	380	.700	–	–	1039	251	197	1	–	–	–	1066	13.0	3.1	13.3
73-74–Boston	82	–	2599	340	772	.440	–	–	–	264	337	.783	334	581	915	186	246	3	63	–	20	944	11.2	2.3	11.5
74-75–Boston	82	–	2661	312	749	.417	–	–	–	244	344	.709	348	677	1025	224	229	3	60	–	22	868	12.5	2.7	10.6
75-76–Boston	81	–	2662	315	740	.426	–	–	–	236	333	.709	365	660	1025	203	227	3	56	–	33	866	12.7	2.5	10.7
76-77–Denver	81	–	1959	206	572	.360	–	–	–	170	255	.667	236	370	606	132	183	0	58	–	23	582	7.5	1.6	7.2
77-78–Seattle	82	–	2172	184	464	.397	–	–	–	109	186	.586	289	377	666	145	182	0	65	152	16	477	8.1	1.8	5.8
78-79–Seattle	82	–	1957	170	402	.423	–	–	–	116	194	.598	259	316	575	115	177	3	31	98	19	456	7.0	1.4	5.6
79-80–Seattle	82	–	1595	113	299	.378	0	0	–	89	136	.654	204	232	436	66	120	0	25	83	5	315	5.3	0.8	3.8
Reg. Season Totals	1254	–	34989	4293	9949	.432	0	0	–	3196	4748	.673	2035	3213	12357	2572	3105	33	358	333	138	11782	9.9	2.1	9.4
Playoff Totals	163	–	4619	396	998	.397	0	0	–	332	480	.692	339	628	1527	335	469	7	81	73	34	1124	9.4	2.1	6.9
All-Star Totals	2	–	30	2	10	.200	0	0	–	4	5	.800	0	2	11	3	3	0	4	–	0	8	5.5	1.5	4.0

Silliman, Michael Barnwell (Mike) b. May 4, 1944 Ht. 6-6 Wt. 225 College: Army

SEASON–TEAM	G	GS	MIN	FGM	FGA	PCT	3FGM	3FGA	PCT	FTM	FTA	PCT	O-RB	D-RB	TOT	AST	PF	DQ	STL	TO	BLK	PTS	RPG	APG	PPG
70-71–Buffalo	36	–	366	36	79	.456	–	–	–	19	39	.487	–	–	62	23	37	0	–	–	–	91	1.7	0.6	2.5
Reg. Season Totals	36	–	366	36	79	.456	–	–	–	19	39	.487	–	–	62	23	37	0	–	–	–	91	1.7	0.6	2.5

Simmons, Cornelius Leo (Connie) b. March 15, 1925 d. April 15, 1989 Ht. 6-8 Wt. 225 College: None

SEASON–TEAM	G	GS	MIN	FGM	FGA	PCT	3FGM	3FGA	PCT	FTM	FTA	PCT	O-RB	D-RB	TOT	AST	PF	DQ	STL	TO	BLK	PTS	RPG	APG	PPG
46-47–Boston	60	–	–	246	768	.320	–	–	–	128	189	.677	–	–	–	62	130	–	–	–	–	620	–	1.0	10.3
47-48–Boston-Balt.	45	–	–	162	545	.297	–	–	–	62	108	.574	–	–	–	24	122	–	–	–	–	386	–	0.5	8.6
48-49–Baltimore	60	–	–	299	794	.377	–	–	–	181	265	.683	–	–	–	116	215	–	–	–	–	779	–	1.9	13.0
49-50–New York	60	–	–	241	729	.331	–	–	–	198	299	.662	–	–	–	102	203	–	–	–	–	680	–	1.7	11.3
50-51–New York	66	–	–	229	613	.374	–	–	–	146	208	.702	–	–	426	117	222	8	–	–	–	604	6.5	1.8	9.2
51-52–New York	66	–	1558	227	600	.378	–	–	–	175	254	.689	–	–	471	121	214	8	–	–	–	629	7.1	1.8	9.5
52-53–New York	65	–	1707	240	637	.377	–	–	–	249	340	.732	–	–	458	127	252	9	–	–	–	729	7.0	2.0	11.2
53-54–New York	72	–	2006	255	713	.358	–	–	–	210	305	.689	–	–	484	128	234	1	–	–	–	720	6.7	1.8	10.0
54-55–Balt.-Syr.	36	–	862	137	384	.357	–	–	–	72	114	.632	–	–	220	61	109	2	–	–	–	346	6.1	1.7	9.6
55-56–Rochester	68	–	903	144	428	.336	–	–	–	78	129	.605	–	–	235	82	142	2	–	–	–	366	3.5	1.2	5.4
Reg. Season Totals	598	–	7036	2180	6211	.351	–	–	–	1499	2211	.678	–	–	2294	940	1843	30	–	–	–	5859	6.2	1.6	9.8
Playoff Totals	62	–	1003	278	742	.380	–	–	–	286	390	.733	–	–	327	99	256	8	–	–	–	842	7.4	1.6	13.6

Simmons, Grant M. b. March 7, 1943 Ht. 6-3 Wt. 190 College: Nebraska

SEASON–TEAM	G	GS	MIN	FGM	FGA	PCT	3FGM	3FGA	PCT	FTM	FTA	PCT	O-RB	D-RB	TOT	AST	PF	DQ	STL	TO	BLK	PTS	RPG	APG	PPG
67-68–Denver (A)	78	–	2264	292	688	.424	1	22	.045	208	295	.705	–	–	240	182	236	3	–	153	–	793	3.1	2.3	10.2
68-69–Denver (A)	17	–	252	22	59	.373	1	2	.500	20	29	.690	–	–	26	15	42	2	–	17	–	65	1.5	0.9	3.8
Reg. ABA Totals	95	–	2516	314	747	.420	2	24	.083	228	324	.704	–	–	266	197	278	5	–	170	–	858	2.8	2.1	9.0
ABA Playoff Totals	7	–	154	13	37	.351	0	1	.000	12	16	.750	–	–	22	15	21	1	–	10	–	38	3.1	2.1	5.4

Simmons, John Earl **(Johnny)** b. July 7, 1924 Ht. 6-1 Wt. 185 College: New York U.

SEASON–TEAM	G	GS	MIN	FGM	FGA	PCT	3FGM	3FGA	PCT	FTM	FTA	PCT	O-RB	D-RB	TOT	AST	PF	DQ	STL	TO	BLK	PTS	RPG	APG	PPG
46-47–Boston	60	–	–	120	429	.280	–	–	–	78	127	.614	–	–	–	29	78	–	–	–	–	318	–	0.5	5.3
Reg. Season Totals	60	–	–	120	429	.280	–	–	–	78	127	.614	–	–	–	29	78	–	–	–	–	318	–	0.5	5.3

Simmons, Lionel James **(L-Train)** b. November 14, 1968 Ht. 6-7 Wt. 210 College: La Salle

SEASON–TEAM	G	GS	MIN	FGM	FGA	PCT	3FGM	3FGA	PCT	FTM	FTA	PCT	O-RB	D-RB	TOT	AST	PF	DQ	STL	TO	BLK	PTS	RPG	APG	PPG
90-91–Sacramento	79	79	2978	549	1301	.422	3	11	.273	320	435	.736	193	504	697	315	249	0	113	230	85	1421	8.8	4.0	18.0
91-92–Sacramento	78	78	2895	527	1162	.454	1	5	.200	281	365	.770	149	485	634	337	205	0	135	218	132	1336	8.1	4.3	17.1
92-93–Sacramento	69	68	2502	468	1055	.444	1	11	.091	298	364	.819	156	339	495	312	197	4	95	196	38	1235	7.2	4.5	17.9
93-94–Sacramento	75	74	2702	436	996	.438	6	17	.353	251	323	.777	168	394	562	305	189	2	104	183	50	1129	7.5	4.1	15.1
94-95–Sacramento	58	3	1064	131	312	.420	6	16	.375	59	84	.702	61	135	196	89	118	0	28	70	23	327	3.4	1.5	5.6
95-96–Sacramento	54	5	810	86	217	.396	19	51	.373	55	75	.733	41	104	145	83	85	0	31	51	20	246	2.7	1.5	4.6
96-97–Sacramento	41	0	521	45	136	.331	7	30	.233	42	48	.875	30	74	104	57	63	0	8	34	13	139	2.5	1.4	3.4
Reg. Season Totals	454	307	13472	2242	5179	.433	43	141	.305	1306	1694	.771	798	2035	2833	1498	1106	6	514	982	361	5833	6.2	3.3	12.8
Playoff Totals	4	0	77	15	33	.455	3	9	.333	5	7	.714	4	8	12	8	12	0	6	6	2	38	3.0	2.0	9.5

Simon, Miles Julian b. November 21, 1975 Ht. 6-3 Wt. 202 College: Arizona

SEASON–TEAM	G	GS	MIN	FGM	FGA	PCT	3FGM	3FGA	PCT	FTM	FTA	PCT	O-RB	D-RB	TOT	AST	PF	DQ	STL	TO	BLK	PTS	RPG	APG	PPG
98-99–Orlando	5	0	19	1	5	.200	0	2	.000	0	0	–	1	1	2	0	1	0	1	3	0	2	0.4	0.0	0.4
Reg. Season Totals	5	0	19	1	5	.200	0	2	.000	0	0	–	1	1	2	0	1	0	1	3	0	2	0.4	0.0	0.4

Simon, Walter J. **(Walt)** b. December 1, 1939 Ht. 6-6 Wt. 200 College: Benedict

SEASON–TEAM	G	GS	MIN	FGM	FGA	PCT	3FGM	3FGA	PCT	FTM	FTA	PCT	O-RB	D-RB	TOT	AST	PF	DQ	STL	TO	BLK	PTS	RPG	APG	PPG
67-68–New Jersey (A)	78	–	2518	433	955	.453	1	15	.067	169	266	.635	–	–	524	212	272	8	–	173	–	1036	6.7	2.7	13.3
68-69–New York (A)	68	–	2750	570	1296	.440	6	27	.222	290	417	.695	–	–	554	234	289	5	–	183	–	1436	8.1	3.4	21.1
69-70–New York (A)	81	–	2696	454	1030	.441	1	20	.050	253	338	.749	–	–	474	294	296	5	–	–	–	1162	5.9	3.6	14.3
70-71–Kentucky (A)	84	–	1411	274	578	.474	1	11	.091	100	156	.641	–	–	315	156	253	–	–	–	–	649	3.8	1.9	7.7
71-72–Kentucky (A)	67	–	1111	243	464	.524	1	10	.100	109	156	.699	–	–	233	137	157	–	–	72	–	596	3.5	2.0	8.9
72-73–Kentucky (A)	83	–	2403	432	897	.482	3	17	.176	143	191	.749	122	273	395	336	271	6	–	156	–	1010	4.8	4.0	12.2
73-74–Kentucky (A)	80	–	1164	233	492	.474	2	13	.154	57	68	.838	62	147	209	117	133	–	38	77	10	525	2.6	1.5	6.6
Reg. ABA Totals	541	–	14053	2639	5712	.462	15	113	.133	1121	1592	.704	184	420	2704	1486	1671	24	38	661	10	6414	5.0	2.7	11.9
ABA Playoff Totals	59	–	1435	231	514	.449	0	18	.000	93	118	.788	3	6	264	162	204	1	24	45	14	555	4.5	2.7	9.4

Simpkins, LuBara Dixon **(Dickey)** b. April 6, 1972 Ht. 6-9 Wt. 255 College: Providence

SEASON–TEAM	G	GS	MIN	FGM	FGA	PCT	3FGM	3FGA	PCT	FTM	FTA	PCT	O-RB	D-RB	TOT	AST	PF	DQ	STL	TO	BLK	PTS	RPG	APG	PPG
94-95–Chicago	59	5	586	78	184	.424	0	0	–	50	72	.694	60	91	151	37	72	0	10	45	7	206	2.6	0.6	3.5
95-96–Chicago	60	12	685	77	160	.481	1	1	1.000	61	97	.629	66	90	156	38	78	0	9	56	8	216	2.6	0.6	3.6
96-97–Chicago	48	0	395	31	93	.333	1	4	.250	28	40	.700	36	56	92	31	44	0	5	35	5	91	1.9	0.6	1.9
97-98–G.S.-Chicago	40	0	433	48	89	.539	0	2	.000	36	70	.514	27	50	77	33	54	0	9	32	5	132	1.9	0.8	3.3
98-99–Chicago	50	35	1448	150	324	.463	0	1	.000	156	242	.645	110	229	339	65	128	1	36	72	13	456	6.8	1.3	9.1
99-00–Chicago	69	48	1651	111	274	.405	0	1	.000	65	120	.542	124	248	372	100	217	4	22	128	22	287	5.4	1.4	4.2
Reg. Season Totals	326	100	5198	495	1124	.440	2	9	.222	396	641	.618	423	764	1187	304	593	5	91	368	60	1388	3.6	0.9	4.3
Playoff Totals	13	0	74	6	16	.375	0	0	–	4	9	.444	4	9	13	3	10	0	2	3	1	16	1.0	0.2	1.2

Simpson, Ralph Derek b. August 10, 1949 Ht. 6-5 Wt. 200 College: Michigan State

SEASON–TEAM	G	GS	MIN	FGM	FGA	PCT	3FGM	3FGA	PCT	FTM	FTA	PCT	O-RB	D-RB	TOT	AST	PF	DQ	STL	TO	BLK	PTS	RPG	APG	PPG
70-71–Denver (A)	81	–	1820	460	1108	.415	17	60	.283	215	285	.754	–	–	231	168	152	–	–	–	–	1152	2.9	2.1	14.2
71-72–Denver (A)	84	–	3006	920	2000	.460	3	22	.136	457	568	.805	–	–	398	258	244	–	–	266	–	2300	4.7	3.1	27.4
72-73–Denver (A)	81	–	2589	732	1670	.438	5	24	.208	421	556	.757	140	231	371	222	241	2	127	283	–	1890	4.6	2.7	23.3
73-74–Denver (A)	75	–	2244	597	1395	.428	2	24	.083	208	276	.754	113	213	326	191	190	–	103	196	12	1404	4.3	2.5	18.7
74-75–Denver (A)	82	–	2863	694	1374	.505	1	12	.083	303	402	.754	108	283	391	442	214	–	166	314	19	1692	4.8	5.4	20.6
75-76–Denver (A)	84	–	3121	619	1211	.511	4	24	.167	273	350	.780	121	333	454	597	183	–	153	360	23	1515	5.4	7.1	18.0
76-77–Detroit	77	–	1597	356	834	.427	–	–	–	138	195	.708	48	133	181	180	100	0	68	–	5	850	2.4	2.3	11.0
77-78–Detroit-Denver	64	–	1323	216	576	.375	–	–	–	85	104	.817	53	104	157	159	90	1	75	126	7	517	2.5	2.5	8.1
78-79–Phil.-N.J.	68	–	979	174	433	.402	–	–	–	76	111	.685	35	61	96	126	57	0	37	100	5	424	1.4	1.8	6.2
79-80–New Jersey	8	–	81	18	47	.383	0	2	.000	5	10	.500	6	5	11	14	3	0	9	12	0	41	1.4	1.8	5.1
Reg. NBA Totals	217	–	3980	764	1890	.404	0	2	.000	304	420	.724	142	303	445	479	250	1	189	238	17	1832	2.1	2.2	8.4
Reg. ABA Totals	487	–	15643	4022	8758	.459	32	166	.193	1877	2437	.770	482	1060	2171	1878	1224	2	549	1419	54	9953	4.5	3.9	20.4
NBA Playoff Totals	17	–	252	45	109	.413	0	0	–	16	23	.696	6	18	24	41	21	0	4	22	2	106	1.4	2.4	6.2
ABA Playoff Totals	38	–	1501	322	731	.440	4	16	.250	186	226	.823	35	91	181	185	104	0	43	146	7	834	4.8	4.9	21.9

Sims, Alvin b. October 18, 1974 Ht. 6-4 Wt. 235 College: Louisville

SEASON–TEAM	G	GS	MIN	FGM	FGA	PCT	3FGM	3FGA	PCT	FTM	FTA	PCT	O-RB	D-RB	TOT	AST	PF	DQ	STL	TO	BLK	PTS	RPG	APG	PPG
98-99–Phoenix	4	0	25	4	10	.400	1	1	1.000	2	5	.400	3	1	4	5	2	0	2	6	0	11	1.0	1.3	2.8
Reg. Season Totals	4	0	25	4	10	.400	1	1	1.000	2	5	.400	3	1	4	5	2	0	2	6	0	11	1.0	1.3	2.8

Sims, H. Douglas (Doug) b. June 29, 1943 Ht. 6-7 Wt. 195 College: Kent State

SEASON–TEAM	G	GS	MIN	FGM	FGA	PCT	3FGM	3FGA	PCT	FTM	FTA	PCT	O-RB	D-RB	TOT	AST	PF	DQ	STL	TO	BLK	PTS	RPG	APG	PPG
68-69–Cincinnati	4	–	12	2	5	.400	–	–	–	0	0	–	–	–	4	0	4	0	–	–	–	4	1.0	0.0	1.0
Reg. Season Totals	4	–	12	2	5	.400	–	–	–	0	0	–	–	–	4	0	4	0	–	–	–	4	1.0	0.0	1.0

Sims, Robert Antell Jr. (Bob) b. October 9, 1938 Ht. 6-5 Wt. 220 College: Pepperdine

SEASON–TEAM	G	GS	MIN	FGM	FGA	PCT	3FGM	3FGA	PCT	FTM	FTA	PCT	O-RB	D-RB	TOT	AST	PF	DQ	STL	TO	BLK	PTS	RPG	APG	PPG
61-62–L.A.-St. Louis	65	–	1345	193	491	.393	–	–	–	123	216	.569	–	–	183	154	187	4	–	–	–	509	2.8	2.4	7.8
67-68–Anaheim (A)	2	–	19	2	7	.286	0	0	–	4	6	.667	–	–	1	2	6	1	–	0	–	8	0.5	1.0	4.0
Reg. NBA Totals	65	–	1345	193	491	.393	–	–	–	123	216	.569	–	–	183	154	187	4	–	–	–	509	2.8	2.4	7.8
Reg. ABA Totals	2	–	19	2	7	.286	0	0	–	4	6	.667	–	–	1	2	6	1	–	–	–	8	0.5	1.0	4.0

Sims, Scott Alan b. April 18, 1955 Ht. 6-1 Wt. 170 College: Missouri

SEASON–TEAM	G	GS	MIN	FGM	FGA	PCT	3FGM	3FGA	PCT	FTM	FTA	PCT	O-RB	D-RB	TOT	AST	PF	DQ	STL	TO	BLK	PTS	RPG	APG	PPG
77-78–San Antonio	12	–	95	10	26	.385	–	–	–	10	15	.667	5	8	13	20	16	0	3	19	0	30	1.1	1.7	2.5
Reg. Season Totals	12	–	95	10	26	.385	–	–	–	10	15	.667	5	8	13	20	16	0	3	19	0	30	1.1	1.7	2.5

Singleton, McKinley b. October 29, 1961 Ht. 6-5 Wt. 175 College: Shelby State (Tenn.) C.C.; Alabama-Birmingham

SEASON–TEAM	G	GS	MIN	FGM	FGA	PCT	3FGM	3FGA	PCT	FTM	FTA	PCT	O-RB	D-RB	TOT	AST	PF	DQ	STL	TO	BLK	PTS	RPG	APG	PPG
86-87–New York	2	0	10	2	3	.667	0	1	.000	0	0	–	0	0	0	1	1	0	0	0	0	4	0.0	0.5	2.0
Reg. Season Totals	2	0	10	2	3	.667	0	1	.000	0	0	–	0	0	0	1	1	0	0	0	0	4	0.0	0.5	2.0

Sinicola, Emilio J. (Zeke) b. January 25, 1929 Ht. 5-10 Wt. 165 College: Niagara

SEASON–TEAM	G	GS	MIN	FGM	FGA	PCT	3FGM	3FGA	PCT	FTM	FTA	PCT	O-RB	D-RB	TOT	AST	PF	DQ	STL	TO	BLK	PTS	RPG	APG	PPG
51-52–Fort Wayne	3	–	15	1	4	.250	–	–	–	0	2	.000	–	–	1	0	2	0	–	–	–	2	0.3	0.0	0.7
53-54–Fort Wayne	9	–	53	4	16	.250	–	–	–	3	6	.500	–	–	1	3	8	0	–	–	–	11	0.1	0.3	1.2
Reg. Season Totals	12	–	68	5	20	.250	–	–	–	3	8	.375	–	–	2	3	10	0	–	–	–	13	0.2	0.3	1.1

Sitton, Charles E. (Charlie) b. July 3, 1962 Ht. 6-8 Wt. 210 College: Oregon State

SEASON–TEAM	G	GS	MIN	FGM	FGA	PCT	3FGM	3FGA	PCT	FTM	FTA	PCT	O-RB	D-RB	TOT	AST	PF	DQ	STL	TO	BLK	PTS	RPG	APG	PPG
84-85–Dallas	43	0	304	39	94	.415	0	2	.000	13	25	.520	24	36	60	26	50	0	7	19	6	91	1.4	0.6	2.1
Reg. Season Totals	43	0	304	39	94	.415	0	2	.000	13	25	.520	24	36	60	26	50	0	7	19	6	91	1.4	0.6	2.1

Skiles, Scott Allen b. March 5, 1964 Ht. 6-1 Wt. 185 College: Michigan State

SEASON–TEAM	G	GS	MIN	FGM	FGA	PCT	3FGM	3FGA	PCT	FTM	FTA	PCT	O-RB	D-RB	TOT	AST	PF	DQ	STL	TO	BLK	PTS	RPG	APG	PPG
86-87–Milwaukee	13	0	205	18	62	.290	3	14	.214	10	12	.833	6	20	26	45	18	0	5	21	1	49	2.0	3.5	3.8
87-88–Indiana	51	2	760	86	209	.411	6	20	.300	45	54	.833	11	55	66	180	97	0	22	76	3	223	1.3	3.5	4.4
88-89–Indiana	80	13	1571	198	442	.448	20	75	.267	130	144	.903	21	128	149	390	151	1	64	177	2	546	1.9	4.9	6.8
89-90–Orlando	70	32	1460	190	464	.409	52	132	.394	104	119	.874	23	136	159	334	126	0	36	90	4	536	2.3	4.8	7.7
90-91–Orlando	79	66	2714	462	1039	.445	93	228	.408	340	377	.902	57	213	270	660	192	2	89	252	4	1357	3.4	8.4	17.2
91-92–Orlando	75	63	2377	359	868	.414	91	250	.364	248	277	.895	36	166	202	544	188	0	74	233	5	1057	2.7	7.3	14.1
92-93–Orlando	78	78	3086	416	891	.467	80	235	.340	289	324	.892	52	238	290	735	244	4	86	267	2	1201	3.7	9.4	15.4
93-94–Orlando	82	46	2303	276	644	.429	68	165	.412	195	222	.878	42	147	189	503	171	1	47	193	2	815	2.3	6.1	9.9
94-95–Washington	62	62	2077	265	583	.455	96	228	.421	179	202	.886	26	133	159	452	135	2	70	172	6	805	2.6	7.3	13.0
95-96–Philadelphia	10	9	236	20	57	.351	15	34	.441	8	10	.800	1	15	16	38	21	0	7	16	0	63	1.6	3.8	6.3
Reg. Season Totals	600	371	16789	2290	5259	.435	524	1381	.379	1548	1741	.889	275	1251	1526	3881	1343	10	500	1497	29	6652	2.5	6.5	11.1
Playoff Totals	2	0	23	4	8	.500	0	2	.000	1	1	1.000	1	0	1	3	2	0	0	5	0	9	0.5	1.5	4.5

Skinner, Albert L. Jr. (Al) b. June 16, 1952 Ht. 6-3 Wt. 195 College: Massachusetts

SEASON–TEAM	G	GS	MIN	FGM	FGA	PCT	3FGM	3FGA	PCT	FTM	FTA	PCT	O-RB	D-RB	TOT	AST	PF	DQ	STL	TO	BLK	PTS	RPG	APG	PPG
74-75–New York (A)	51	–	773	130	266	.489	1	3	.333	72	94	.766	42	78	120	121	111	–	29	68	13	333	2.4	2.4	6.5
75-76–New York (A)	83	–	2082	330	702	.470	2	8	.250	203	241	.842	96	211	307	280	252	–	91	169	50	865	3.7	3.4	10.4
76-77–New York Nets	79	–	2256	382	887	.431	–	–	–	231	292	.791	112	251	363	289	279	7	103	–	53	995	4.6	3.7	12.6
77-78–N.J.-Detroit	77	–	1551	222	488	.455	–	–	–	162	203	.798	67	157	224	146	242	6	65	161	20	606	2.9	1.9	7.9
78-79–N.J.-Phil.	45	–	643	91	214	.425	–	–	–	99	114	.868	27	59	86	89	114	2	40	72	3	281	1.9	2.0	6.2
79-80–Philadelphia	2	0	10	1	2	.500	0	0	–	0	0	–	0	0	0	2	1	0	0	2	0	2	0.0	1.0	1.0
Reg. NBA Totals	203	–	4460	696	1591	.437	0	0	–	492	609	.808	206	467	673	526	636	15	208	235	76	1884	3.3	2.6	9.3
Reg. ABA Totals	134	–	2855	460	968	.475	3	11	.273	275	335	.821	138	289	427	401	363	–	120	237	63	1198	3.2	3.0	8.9
NBA Playoff Totals	5	–	47	6	17	.353	0	0	–	6	8	.750	5	5	10	11	6	0	3	6	1	18	2.0	2.2	3.6
ABA Playoff Totals	14	–	296	45	103	.437	1	1	1.000	42	54	.778	25	25	50	28	46	–	21	26	2	133	3.6	2.0	9.5

Skinner, Brian b. May 19, 1976 Ht. 6-9 Wt. 255 College: Baylor

SEASON–TEAM	G	GS	MIN	FGM	FGA	PCT	3FGM	3FGA	PCT	FTM	FTA	PCT	O-RB	D-RB	TOT	AST	PF	DQ	STL	TO	BLK	PTS	RPG	APG	PPG
98-99–L.A. Clippers	21	0	258	33	71	.465	0	0	–	20	33	.606	20	33	53	1	20	0	10	19	13	86	2.5	0.0	4.1
99-00–L.A. Clippers	33	9	775	68	134	.507	0	0	–	43	65	.662	63	138	201	11	75	0	16	37	44	179	6.1	0.3	5.4
Reg. Season Totals	54	9	1033	101	205	.493	0	0	–	63	98	.643	83	171	254	12	95	0	26	56	57	265	4.7	0.2	4.9

Skinner, Talvin (Tab) b. September 10, 1952 Ht. 6-5 Wt. 210 College: Maryland Eastern. Shore

SEASON–TEAM	G	GS	MIN	FGM	FGA	PCT	3FGM	3FGA	PCT	FTM	FTA	PCT	O-RB	D-RB	TOT	AST	PF	DQ	STL	TO	BLK	PTS	RPG	APG	PPG
74-75–Seattle	73	–	1574	142	347	.409	–	–	–	63	97	.649	135	209	344	85	161	0	49	–	17	347	4.7	1.2	4.8
75-76–Seattle	72	–	1224	132	285	.463	–	–	–	49	80	.613	89	175	264	67	116	1	50	–	7	313	3.7	0.9	4.3
Reg. Season Totals	145	–	2798	274	632	.434	–	–	–	112	177	.633	224	384	608	152	277	1	99	–	24	660	4.2	1.0	4.6
Playoff Totals	15	–	297	25	59	.424	–	–	–	25	34	.735	17	36	53	19	35	0	14	–	4	75	3.5	1.3	5.0

Skoog, Myer Upton (Whitey) b. November 2, 1926 Ht. 5-11 Wt. 180 College: Minnesota

SEASON–TEAM	G	GS	MIN	FGM	FGA	PCT	3FGM	3FGA	PCT	FTM	FTA	PCT	O-RB	D-RB	TOT	AST	PF	DQ	STL	TO	BLK	PTS	RPG	APG	PPG
51-52–Minneapolis	35	–	988	102	296	.345	–	–	–	30	38	.789	–	–	122	60	94	4	–	–	–	234	3.5	1.7	6.7
52-53–Minneapolis	68	–	996	102	264	.386	–	–	–	46	61	.754	–	–	121	82	137	2	–	–	–	250	1.8	1.2	3.7
53-54–Minneapolis	71	–	1877	212	530	.400	–	–	–	72	97	.742	–	–	224	179	234	5	–	–	–	496	3.2	2.5	7.0
54-55–Minneapolis	72	–	2365	330	836	.395	–	–	–	125	155	.806	–	–	303	251	265	10	–	–	–	785	4.2	3.5	10.9
55-56–Minneapolis	72	–	2311	340	854	.398	–	–	–	155	193	.803	–	–	291	255	232	5	–	–	–	835	4.0	3.5	11.6
56-57–Minneapolis	23	–	656	78	220	.355	–	–	–	44	47	.936	–	–	72	76	65	1	–	–	–	200	3.1	3.3	8.7
Reg. Season Totals	341	–	9193	1164	3000	.388	–	–	–	472	591	.799	–	–	1133	903	1027	27	–	–	–	2800	3.3	2.6	8.2
Playoff Totals	34	–	1329	115	299	.405	–	–	–	49	72	.681	–	–	172	93	130	5	–	–	–	279	3.7	2.0	8.2

Slade, Jeffrey Alan (Jeff) b. March 1, 1941 Ht. 6-6 Wt. 220 College: Kenyon

SEASON–TEAM	G	GS	MIN	FGM	FGA	PCT	3FGM	3FGA	PCT	FTM	FTA	PCT	O-RB	D-RB	TOT	AST	PF	DQ	STL	TO	BLK	PTS	RPG	APG	PPG
62-63–Chicago	3	–	20	2	5	.400	–	–	–	0	1	.000	–	–	7	0	3	0	–	–	–	4	2.3	0.0	1.3
Reg. Season Totals	3	–	20	2	5	.400	–	–	–	0	1	.000	–	–	7	0	3	0	–	–	–	4	2.3	0.0	1.3

Slater, Reginald Dwayne (Reggie) b. August 27, 1970 Ht. 6-7 Wt. 255 College: Wyoming

SEASON–TEAM	G	GS	MIN	FGM	FGA	PCT	3FGM	3FGA	PCT	FTM	FTA	PCT	O-RB	D-RB	TOT	AST	PF	DQ	STL	TO	BLK	PTS	RPG	APG	PPG
94-95–Denver	25	0	236	40	81	.494	0	0	–	40	55	.727	21	36	57	12	47	0	7	26	3	120	2.3	0.5	4.8
95-96–Port.-Den.-Dallas	11	0	72	14	27	.519	0	0	–	3	7	.429	4	11	15	2	11	0	2	9	3	31	1.4	0.2	2.8
96-97–Toronto	26	0	406	82	149	.550	0	2	.000	39	75	.520	40	55	95	21	34	0	9	29	6	203	3.7	0.8	7.8
97-98–Toronto	78	28	1662	211	459	.460	0	0	–	203	322	.630	134	171	305	74	201	4	45	102	30	625	3.9	0.9	8.0
98-99–Toronto	30	0	263	31	81	.383	0	0	–	53	85	.624	36	34	70	5	50	0	3	25	3	115	2.3	0.2	3.8
Reg. Season Totals	170	28	2639	378	797	.474	0	2	.000	338	544	.621	235	307	542	114	343	4	66	191	45	1094	3.2	0.7	6.4

Slaughter, James W. (Jim) b. May 13, 1928 Ht. 6-11 Wt. 215 College: South Carolina

SEASON–TEAM	G	GS	MIN	FGM	FGA	PCT	3FGM	3FGA	PCT	FTM	FTA	PCT	O-RB	D-RB	TOT	AST	PF	DQ	STL	TO	BLK	PTS	RPG	APG	PPG
51-52–Baltimore	28	–	525	53	165	.321	–	–	–	41	68	.603	–	–	148	25	81	0	–	–	–	147	5.3	0.9	5.3
Reg. Season Totals	28	–	525	53	165	.321	–	–	–	41	68	.603	–	–	148	25	81	0	–	–	–	147	5.3	0.9	5.3

Slaughter, Jose Dan b. September 9, 1960 Ht. 6-5 Wt. 215 College: Portland

SEASON–TEAM	G	GS	MIN	FGM	FGA	PCT	3FGM	3FGA	PCT	FTM	FTA	PCT	O-RB	D-RB	TOT	AST	PF	DQ	STL	TO	BLK	PTS	RPG	APG	PPG
82-83–Indiana	63	1	515	89	238	.374	9	41	.220	38	59	.644	34	34	68	52	93	0	36	42	7	225	1.1	0.8	3.6
Reg. Season Totals	63	1	515	89	238	.374	9	41	.220	38	59	.644	34	34	68	52	93	0	36	42	7	225	1.1	0.8	3.6

Sloan, Gerald Eugene (Jerry, Spider) b. March 28, 1942 Ht. 6-5 Wt. 195 College: Illinois; Evansville

SEASON–TEAM	G	GS	MIN	FGM	FGA	PCT	3FGM	3FGA	PCT	FTM	FTA	PCT	O-RB	D-RB	TOT	AST	PF	DQ	STL	TO	BLK	PTS	RPG	APG	PPG
65-66–Baltimore	59	–	952	120	289	.415	–	–	–	98	139	.705	–	–	230	110	176	7	–	–	–	338	3.9	1.9	5.7
66-67–Chicago	80	–	2942	525	1214	.432	–	–	–	340	427	.796	–	–	726	170	293	7	–	–	–	1390	9.1	2.1	17.4
67-68–Chicago	77	–	2454	369	959	.385	–	–	–	289	386	.749	–	–	591	229	291	11	–	–	–	1027	7.7	3.0	13.3
68-69–Chicago	78	–	2939	488	1170	.417	–	–	–	333	447	.745	–	–	619	276	313	6	–	–	–	1309	7.9	3.5	16.8
69-70–Chicago	53	–	1822	310	737	.421	–	–	–	207	318	.651	–	–	372	165	179	3	–	–	–	827	7.0	3.1	15.6
70-71–Chicago	80	–	3140	592	1342	.441	–	–	–	278	389	.715	–	–	701	281	289	5	–	–	–	1462	8.8	3.5	18.3
71-72–Chicago	82	–	3035	535	1206	.444	–	–	–	258	391	.660	–	–	691	211	309	8	–	–	–	1328	8.4	2.6	16.2
72-73–Chicago	69	–	2412	301	733	.411	–	–	–	94	133	.707	–	–	475	151	235	5	–	–	–	696	6.9	2.2	10.1
73-74–Chicago	77	–	2860	412	921	.447	–	–	–	194	273	.711	150	406	556	149	273	3	183	–	10	1018	7.2	1.9	13.2
74-75–Chicago	78	–	2577	380	865	.439	–	–	–	193	258	.748	177	361	538	161	265	5	171	–	17	953	6.9	2.1	12.2
75-76–Chicago	22	–	617	84	210	.400	–	–	–	55	78	.705	40	76	116	22	77	1	27	–	5	223	5.3	1.0	10.1
Reg. Season Totals	755	–	25750	4116	9646	.427	–	–	–	2339	3239	.722	367	843	5615	1925	2700	61	381	–	32	10571	7.4	2.5	14.0
Playoff Totals	51	–	1888	294	689	.427	–	–	–	128	189	.677	42	116	412	109	187	4	27	–	1	716	8.1	2.1	14.0
All-Star Totals	2	–	40	6	17	.353	–	–	–	0	1	.000	0	0	7	4	10	0	0	–	0	12	3.5	2.0	6.0

Sluby, Tom Griffin b. February 18, 1962 Ht. 6-4 Wt. 200 College: Notre Dame

SEASON–TEAM	G	GS	MIN	FGM	FGA	PCT	3FGM	3FGA	PCT	FTM	FTA	PCT	O-RB	D-RB	TOT	AST	PF	DQ	STL	TO	BLK	PTS	RPG	APG	PPG
84-85–Dallas	31	0	151	30	58	.517	0	2	.000	13	21	.619	5	7	12	16	18	0	3	11	0	73	0.4	0.5	2.4
Reg. Season Totals	31	0	151	30	58	.517	0	2	.000	13	21	.619	5	7	12	16	18	0	3	11	0	73	0.4	0.5	2.4

Smart, Jonathan Keith (Keith) b. September 21, 1964 Ht. 6-1 Wt. 175 College: Garden City (Kan.) C.C.; Indiana

SEASON–TEAM	G	GS	MIN	FGM	FGA	PCT	3FGM	3FGA	PCT	FTM	FTA	PCT	O-RB	D-RB	TOT	AST	PF	DQ	STL	TO	BLK	PTS	RPG	APG	PPG
88-89–San Antonio	2	0	12	0	2	.000	0	1	.000	2	2	1.000	0	1	1	2	0	0	0	2	0	2	0.5	1.0	1.0
Reg. Season Totals	2	0	12	0	2	.000	0	1	.000	2	2	1.000	0	1	1	2	0	0	0	2	0	2	0.5	1.0	1.0

Smawley, Belus Van b. March 20, 1918 Ht. 6-1 Wt. 195 College: Appalachian State

SEASON–TEAM	G	GS	MIN	FGM	FGA	PCT	3FGM	3FGA	PCT	FTM	FTA	PCT	O-RB	D-RB	TOT	AST	PF	DQ	STL	TO	BLK	PTS	RPG	APG	PPG
46-47–St. Louis	22	–	–	113	352	.321	–	–	–	36	47	.766	–	–	–	10	37	–	–	–	–	262	–	0.5	11.9
47-48–St. Louis	48	–	–	212	688	.308	–	–	–	111	150	.740	–	–	–	18	88	–	–	–	–	535	–	0.4	11.1
48-49–St. Louis	59	–	–	352	946	.372	–	–	–	210	281	.747	–	–	–	183	145	–	–	–	–	914	–	3.1	15.5
49-50–St. Louis	61	–	–	287	832	.345	–	–	–	260	314	.828	–	–	–	215	160	–	–	–	–	834	–	3.5	13.7
50-51–Syr.-Balt.	60	–	–	252	663	.380	–	–	–	227	267	.850	–	–	178	161	145	4	–	–	–	731	3.0	2.7	12.2
51-52–Baltimore	11	–	0	13	63	.206	–	–	–	14	17	.824	–	–	18	8	9	0	–	–	–	40	1.6	0.7	3.6
Reg. Season Totals	261	–	0	1229	3544	.347	–	–	–	858	1076	.797	–	–	196	595	584	4	–	–	–	3316	2.8	2.3	12.7
Playoff Totals	11	–	0	54	246	.321	–	–	–	20	29	.690	–	–	–	4	31	1	–	–	–	128	–	0.3	11.6

Smiley, A. John (Jack, Smiles) b. December 22, 1922 Ht. 6-3 Wt. 190 College: Illinois

SEASON–TEAM	G	GS	MIN	FGM	FGA	PCT	3FGM	3FGA	PCT	FTM	FTA	PCT	O-RB	D-RB	TOT	AST	PF	DQ	STL	TO	BLK	PTS	RPG	APG	PPG
47-48–Fort Wayne (N)	60	–	–	105	–	–	–	–	–	90	135	.667	–	–	–	–	168	–	–	–	–	300	–	–	5.0
48-49–Fort Wayne	59	–	–	141	571	.247	–	–	–	112	164	.683	–	–	–	138	202	–	–	–	–	394	–	2.3	6.7
49-50–And.-Wat.	59	–	–	98	364	.269	–	–	–	136	201	.677	–	–	–	161	193	–	–	–	–	332	–	2.7	5.6
Reg. NBA Totals	118	–	–	239	935	.256	–	–	–	248	365	.679	–	–	–	299	395	–	–	–	–	726	–	2.5	6.2
Reg. NBL Totals	60	–	–	105	–	–	–	–	–	90	135	.667	–	–	–	–	168	–	–	–	–	300	–	–	5.0
NBL Playoff Totals	4	–	–	7	–	–	–	–	–	6	8	.750	–	–	–	–	11	–	–	–	–	20	–	–	5.0

Smith, Adrian Howard (Odie) b. October 5, 1936 Ht. 6-1 Wt. 180 College: Northeast (Miss.) C.C.; Kentucky

SEASON–TEAM	G	GS	MIN	FGM	FGA	PCT	3FGM	3FGA	PCT	FTM	FTA	PCT	O-RB	D-RB	TOT	AST	PF	DQ	STL	TO	BLK	PTS	RPG	APG	PPG
61-62–Cincinnati	80	–	1462	202	499	.405	–	–	–	172	222	.775	–	–	151	167	101	0	–	–	–	576	1.9	2.1	7.2
62-63–Cincinnati	79	–	1522	241	544	.443	–	–	–	223	275	.811	–	–	174	141	157	1	–	–	–	705	2.2	1.8	8.9
63-64–Cincinnati	66	–	1524	234	576	.406	–	–	–	154	197	.782	–	–	147	145	164	1	–	–	–	622	2.2	2.2	9.4
64-65–Cincinnati	80	–	2745	463	1016	.456	–	–	–	284	342	.830	–	–	220	240	199	2	–	–	–	1210	2.8	3.0	15.1
65-66–Cincinnati	80	–	2982	531	1310	.405	–	–	–	408	480	.850	–	–	287	256	276	1	–	–	–	1470	3.6	3.2	18.4
66-67–Cincinnati	81	–	2636	502	1147	.438	–	–	–	343	380	.903	–	–	205	187	272	0	–	–	–	1347	2.5	2.3	16.6
67-68–Cincinnati	82	–	2783	480	1035	.464	–	–	–	320	386	.829	–	–	185	272	259	6	–	–	–	1280	2.3	3.3	15.6
68-69–Cincinnati	73	–	1336	243	562	.432	–	–	–	217	269	.807	–	–	105	127	166	1	–	–	–	703	1.4	1.7	9.6
69-70–Cin.-S.F.	77	–	1087	153	416	.368	–	–	–	152	170	.894	–	–	82	133	122	0	–	–	–	458	1.1	1.7	5.9
70-71–San Francisco	21	–	247	38	89	.427	–	–	–	35	41	.854	–	–	24	30	24	0	–	–	–	111	1.1	1.4	5.3
71-72–Virginia (A)	53	–	686	87	195	.446	2	11	.182	92	103	.893	–	–	46	42	89	–	–	34	–	268	0.9	0.8	5.1
Reg. NBA Totals	719	–	18324	3087	7194	.429	–	–	–	2308	2762	.836	–	–	1580	1698	1740	12	–	–	–	8482	2.2	2.4	11.8
Reg. ABA Totals	53	–	686	87	195	.446	2	11	.182	92	103	.893	–	–	46	42	89	–	–	34	–	268	0.9	0.8	5.1
NBA Playoff Totals	36	–	746	107	282	.379	–	–	–	92	112	.821	–	–	61	80	60	0	–	–	–	306	1.7	2.2	8.5
ABA Playoff Totals	11	–	297	46	99	.465	1	5	.200	32	37	.865	–	–	19	17	28	–	–	11	–	125	1.7	1.5	11.4
NBA All-Star Totals	1	–	26	9	18	.500	–	–	–	6	6	1.000	–	–	8	3	5	0	–	–	–	24	8.0	3.0	24.0

Smith, Alan Richard (Al) b. January 15, 1947 Ht. 6-1 Wt. 185 College: Bradley

SEASON–TEAM	G	GS	MIN	FGM	FGA	PCT	3FGM	3FGA	PCT	FTM	FTA	PCT	O-RB	D-RB	TOT	AST	PF	DQ	STL	TO	BLK	PTS	RPG	APG	PPG
71-72–Denver (A)	83	–	1764	292	675	.433	32	107	.299	153	211	.725	–	–	226	249	244	–	–	163	–	769	2.7	3.0	9.3
72-73–Denver (A)	83	–	2343	315	767	.411	17	90	.189	272	352	.773	68	146	214	477	295	7	–	261	–	919	2.6	5.7	11.1
73-74–Denver (A)	76	–	2435	311	779	.399	22	72	.306	187	242	.773	56	185	241	619	257	–	100	273	7	831	3.2	8.1	10.9
74-75–Utah (A)	80	–	2037	225	582	.387	34	94	.362	157	193	.813	39	108	147	375	230	–	59	201	3	641	1.8	4.7	8.0
75-76–Utah (A)	15	–	392	42	105	.400	6	17	.353	48	59	.814	13	24	37	73	45	–	10	29	2	138	2.5	4.9	9.2
Reg. ABA Totals	337	–	8971	1185	2908	.407	111	380	.292	817	1057	.773	176	463	865	1793	1071	7	169	927	12	3298	2.6	5.3	9.8
ABA Playoff Totals	18	–	449	59	154	.383	5	16	.313	39	45	.867	2	10	55	68	55	0	2	47	0	162	3.1	3.8	9.0

Smith, Charles Anton (Tony) b. June 14, 1968 Ht. 6-4 Wt. 205 College: Marquette

SEASON–TEAM	G	GS	MIN	FGM	FGA	PCT	3FGM	3FGA	PCT	FTM	FTA	PCT	O-RB	D-RB	TOT	AST	PF	DQ	STL	TO	BLK	PTS	RPG	APG	PPG
90-91–L.A. Lakers	64	1	695	97	220	.441	0	7	.000	40	57	.702	24	47	71	135	80	0	28	69	12	234	1.1	2.1	3.7
91-92–L.A. Lakers	63	0	820	113	283	.399	0	11	.000	49	75	.653	31	45	76	109	91	0	39	50	8	275	1.2	1.7	4.4
92-93–L.A. Lakers	55	9	752	133	275	.484	2	11	.182	62	82	.756	46	41	87	63	72	1	50	40	7	330	1.6	1.1	6.0
93-94–L.A. Lakers	73	31	1617	272	617	.441	16	50	.320	85	119	.714	106	89	195	148	128	1	59	76	14	645	2.7	2.0	8.8
94-95–L.A. Lakers	61	4	1024	132	309	.427	32	91	.352	44	63	.698	43	64	107	102	111	0	46	50	7	340	1.8	1.7	5.6
95-96–Phoenix-Miami	59	3	938	116	274	.423	38	116	.328	28	46	.609	30	65	95	154	106	2	37	66	10	298	1.6	2.6	5.1
96-97–Charlotte	69	39	1291	138	337	.409	32	99	.323	38	59	.644	38	56	94	150	110	2	48	73	19	346	1.4	2.2	5.0
97-98–Milwaukee	7	0	80	8	24	.333	0	4	.000	3	4	.750	4	3	7	10	7	0	5	9	2	19	1.0	1.4	2.7
Reg. Season Totals	451	87	7217	1009	2339	.431	120	389	.308	349	505	.691	322	410	732	871	705	6	312	433	79	2487	1.6	1.9	5.5
Playoff Totals	27	0	250	34	81	.420	9	27	.333	10	18	.556	13	8	21	22	34	1	11	22	1	87	0.8	0.8	3.2

Smith, Charles Cornelius b. August 22, 1975 Ht. 6-4 Wt. 194 College: New Mexico

SEASON–TEAM	G	GS	MIN	FGM	FGA	PCT	3FGM	3FGA	PCT	FTM	FTA	PCT	O-RB	D-RB	TOT	AST	PF	DQ	STL	TO	BLK	PTS	RPG	APG	PPG
97-98–Miami-LAClips	34	0	292	49	125	.392	15	47	.319	6	11	.545	13	14	27	21	24	0	12	27	6	119	0.8	0.6	3.5
98-99–L.A. Clippers	23	10	317	35	97	.361	7	33	.212	7	16	.438	7	17	24	13	35	0	17	20	14	84	1.0	0.6	3.7
Reg. Season Totals	57	10	609	84	222	.378	22	80	.275	13	27	.481	20	31	51	34	59	0	29	47	20	203	0.9	0.6	3.6

Smith, Charles Daniel (Mr. Fluid) b. July 16, 1965 Ht. 6-10 Wt. 245 College: Pittsburgh

SEASON–TEAM	G	GS	MIN	FGM	FGA	PCT	3FGM	3FGA	PCT	FTM	FTA	PCT	O-RB	D-RB	TOT	AST	PF	DQ	STL	TO	BLK	PTS	RPG	APG	PPG
88-89–L.A. Clippers	71	56	2161	435	878	.495	0	3	.000	285	393	.725	173	292	465	103	273	6	68	146	89	1155	6.5	1.5	16.3
89-90–L.A. Clippers	78	76	2732	595	1145	.520	1	12	.083	454	572	.794	177	347	524	114	294	6	86	162	119	1645	6.7	1.5	21.1
90-91–L.A. Clippers	74	74	2703	548	1168	.469	0	7	.000	384	484	.793	216	392	608	134	267	4	81	165	145	1480	8.2	1.8	20.0
91-92–L.A. Clippers	49	25	1310	251	539	.466	0	6	.000	212	270	.785	95	206	301	56	159	2	41	69	98	714	6.1	1.1	14.6
92-93–New York	81	68	2172	358	764	.469	0	2	.000	287	367	.782	170	262	432	142	254	4	48	155	96	1003	5.3	1.8	12.4
93-94–New York	43	21	1105	176	397	.443	8	16	.500	87	121	.719	66	99	165	50	144	4	26	64	45	447	3.8	1.2	10.4
94-95–New York	76	58	2150	352	747	.471	7	31	.226	255	322	.792	144	180	324	120	286	6	49	147	95	966	4.3	1.6	12.7
95-96–N.Y.-S.A.	73	34	1716	244	578	.422	2	15	.133	119	163	.730	133	229	362	65	224	3	50	106	80	609	5.0	0.9	8.3
96-97–San Antonio	19	7	329	34	84	.405	0	1	.000	20	26	.769	18	47	65	14	44	0	13	22	22	88	3.4	0.7	4.6
Reg. Season Totals	564	419	16378	2993	6300	.475	18	93	.194	2103	2718	.774	1192	2054	3246	798	1945	35	462	1036	789	8107	5.8	1.4	14.4
Playoff Totals	66	57	1616	247	514	.481	0	5	.000	122	173	.705	102	160	262	77	240	4	45	103	77	616	4.0	1.2	9.3

Smith, Charles Edward IV b. November 29, 1967 Ht. 6-2 Wt. 170 College: Georgetown

SEASON–TEAM	G	GS	MIN	FGM	FGA	PCT	3FGM	3FGA	PCT	FTM	FTA	PCT	O-RB	D-RB	TOT	AST	PF	DQ	STL	TO	BLK	PTS	RPG	APG	PPG
89-90–Boston	60	0	519	59	133	.444	0	7	.000	53	76	.697	14	55	69	103	75	0	35	36	3	171	1.2	1.7	2.9
90-91–Boston	5	0	30	3	7	.429	0	0	–	3	5	.600	0	2	2	6	7	0	1	3	0	9	0.4	1.2	1.8
95-96–Minnesota	8	0	39	3	10	.300	0	3	.000	0	2	.000	0	5	5	6	7	0	1	5	0	6	0.6	0.8	0.8
Reg. Season Totals	73	0	588	65	150	.433	0	10	.000	56	83	.675	14	62	76	115	89	0	37	44	3	186	1.0	1.6	2.5
Playoff Totals	3	0	9	1	2	.500	0	0	–	0	0	–	1	0	1	3	0	0	1	0	0	2	0.3	1.0	0.7

Smith, Chris G. b. May 17, 1970 Ht. 6-3 Wt. 191 College: Connecticut

SEASON–TEAM	G	GS	MIN	FGM	FGA	PCT	3FGM	3FGA	PCT	FTM	FTA	PCT	O-RB	D-RB	TOT	AST	PF	DQ	STL	TO	BLK	PTS	RPG	APG	PPG
92-93–Minnesota	80	6	1266	125	289	.433	2	14	.143	95	120	.792	32	64	96	196	96	1	48	68	16	347	1.2	2.5	4.3
93-94–Minnesota	80	16	1617	184	423	.435	10	39	.256	95	141	.674	15	107	122	285	131	1	38	101	18	473	1.5	3.6	5.9
94-95–Minnesota	64	17	1073	116	264	.439	47	108	.435	41	63	.651	14	59	73	146	119	0	32	50	22	320	1.1	2.3	5.0
Reg. Season Totals	224	39	3956	425	976	.435	59	161	.366	231	324	.713	61	230	291	627	346	2	118	219	56	1140	1.3	2.8	5.1

Smith, Clinton b. January 19, 1964 Ht. 6-6 Wt. 210 College: Central Arizona Coll. (J.C.); Ohio State; Cleveland State

SEASON–TEAM	G	GS	MIN	FGM	FGA	PCT	3FGM	3FGA	PCT	FTM	FTA	PCT	O-RB	D-RB	TOT	AST	PF	DQ	STL	TO	BLK	PTS	RPG	APG	PPG
86-87–Golden State	41	0	341	50	117	.427	0	2	.000	27	36	.750	26	30	56	45	36	0	13	26	1	127	1.4	1.1	3.1
90-91–Washington	5	0	45	2	4	.500	0	0	–	3	6	.500	2	2	4	4	3	0	1	1	0	7	0.8	0.8	1.4
Reg. Season Totals	46	0	386	52	121	.430	0	2	.000	30	42	.714	28	32	60	49	39	0	14	27	1	134	1.3	1.1	2.9

Smith, Delbert Bower (Deb) b. January 7, 1920 Ht. 6-3 Wt. 180 College: Utah

SEASON–TEAM	G	GS	MIN	FGM	FGA	PCT	3FGM	3FGA	PCT	FTM	FTA	PCT	O-RB	D-RB	TOT	AST	PF	DQ	STL	TO	BLK	PTS	RPG	APG	PPG
46-47–St. Louis	48	–	–	32	119	.269	–	–	–	9	21	.429	–	–	–	6	47	–	–	–	–	73	–	0.1	1.5
Reg. Season Totals	48	–	–	32	119	.269	–	–	–	9	21	.429	–	–	–	6	47	–	–	–	–	73	–	0.1	1.5
Playoff Totals	1	–	–	0	0	–	–	–	–	0	1	.000	–	–	–	–	1	–	–	–	–	0	–	–	0.0

Smith, Derek Ervin b. November 1, 1961 d. August 9, 1996 Ht. 6-7 Wt. 220 College: Louisville

SEASON–TEAM	G	GS	MIN	FGM	FGA	PCT	3FGM	3FGA	PCT	FTM	FTA	PCT	O-RB	D-RB	TOT	AST	PF	DQ	STL	TO	BLK	PTS	RPG	APG	PPG
82-83–Golden State	27	0	154	21	51	.412	0	2	.000	17	25	.680	10	28	38	2	40	0	0	11	4	59	1.4	0.1	2.2
83-84–San Diego	61	20	1297	238	436	.546	1	6	.167	123	163	.755	54	116	170	82	165	2	33	78	22	600	2.8	1.3	9.8
84-85–L.A. Clippers	80	80	2762	682	1271	.537	3	19	.158	400	504	.794	174	253	427	216	317	8	77	230	52	1767	5.3	2.7	22.1
85-86–L.A. Clippers	11	9	339	100	181	.552	1	2	.500	58	84	.690	20	21	41	31	35	2	9	33	13	259	3.7	2.8	23.5
86-87–Sacramento	52	42	1658	338	757	.446	9	33	.273	178	228	.781	60	122	182	204	184	3	46	126	23	863	3.5	3.9	16.6
87-88–Sacramento	35	18	899	174	364	.478	8	23	.348	87	113	.770	35	68	103	89	108	2	21	48	17	443	2.9	2.5	12.7
88-89–Sac.-Phil.	65	38	1295	216	496	.435	7	31	.226	129	188	.686	61	106	167	128	164	4	43	88	23	568	2.6	2.0	8.7
89-90–Philadelphia	75	7	1405	261	514	.508	16	36	.444	130	186	.699	62	110	172	109	198	2	35	85	20	668	2.3	1.5	8.9
90-91–Boston	2	0	16	1	4	.250	0	1	.000	3	4	.750	0	0	0	5	3	0	1	1	1	5	0.0	2.5	2.5
Reg. Season Totals	408	214	9825	2031	4074	.499	45	153	.294	1125	1495	.753	476	824	1300	866	1214	23	265	700	175	5232	3.2	2.1	12.8
Playoff Totals	14	3	149	23	43	.535	0	2	.000	13	18	.722	4	12	16	9	32	0	5	15	1	59	1.1	0.6	4.2

Smith, Donald (Don) b. October 10, 1951 Ht. 6-0 Wt. 165 College: Dayton

SEASON–TEAM	G	GS	MIN	FGM	FGA	PCT	3FGM	3FGA	PCT	FTM	FTA	PCT	O-RB	D-RB	TOT	AST	PF	DQ	STL	TO	BLK	PTS	RPG	APG	PPG
74-75–Philadelphia	54	0	538	131	321	.408	–	–	–	21	21	1.000	14	16	30	47	45	0	20	–	3	283	0.6	0.9	5.2
Reg. Season Totals	54	0	538	131	321	.408	–	–	–	21	21	1.000	14	16	30	47	45	0	20	–	3	283	0.6	0.9	5.2

Smith, Donald E. (Des) b. July 27, 1920 d. March 1, 1996 Ht. 6-2 Wt. 190 College: Minnesota

SEASON–TEAM	G	GS	MIN	FGM	FGA	PCT	3FGM	3FGA	PCT	FTM	FTA	PCT	O-RB	D-RB	TOT	AST	PF	DQ	STL	TO	BLK	PTS	RPG	APG	PPG
42-43–Oshkosh (N)	13	–	–	22	–	–	–	–	–	15	–	–	–	–	–	–	–	–	–	–	–	59	–	–	4.5
45-46–Oshkosh (N)	9	–	–	1	–	–	–	–	–	6	–	–	–	–	–	–	–	–	–	–	–	8	–	–	0.9
46-47–Oshkosh-Ind. (N)	12	–	–	5	–	–	–	–	–	5	8	.625	–	–	–	–	–	–	–	–	–	15	–	–	1.3
47-48–Minneapolis (N)	57	–	–	69	–	–	–	–	–	62	94	.660	–	–	–	–	98	–	–	–	–	200	–	–	3.5
48-49–Minneapolis	8	–	–	2	13	.154	–	–	–	2	3	.667	–	–	–	2	6	–	–	–	–	6	–	0.3	0.8
Reg. NBA Totals	8	–	–	2	13	.154	–	–	–	2	3	.667	–	–	–	2	6	–	–	–	–	6	–	0.3	0.8
Reg. NBL Totals	91	–	–	97	–	–	–	–	–	88	102	.657	–	–	–	–	98	–	–	–	–	282	–	–	3.1
NBL Playoff Totals	12	–	–	14	–	–	–	–	–	11	12	.750	–	–	–	–	23	–	–	–	–	39	–	–	3.3

Smith, Douglas (Doug) b. September 17, 1969 Ht. 6-10 Wt. 220 College: Missouri

SEASON–TEAM	G	GS	MIN	FGM	FGA	PCT	3FGM	3FGA	PCT	FTM	FTA	PCT	O-RB	D-RB	TOT	AST	PF	DQ	STL	TO	BLK	PTS	RPG	APG	PPG
91-92–Dallas	76	32	1707	291	702	.415	0	11	.000	89	121	.736	129	262	391	129	259	5	62	97	34	671	5.1	1.7	8.8
92-93–Dallas	61	42	1524	289	666	.434	0	4	.000	56	74	.757	96	232	328	104	280	12	48	115	52	634	5.4	1.7	10.4
93-94–Dallas	79	42	1684	295	678	.435	2	9	.222	106	127	.835	114	235	349	119	287	3	82	93	38	698	4.4	1.5	8.8
94-95–Dallas	63	0	826	131	314	.417	1	12	.083	57	75	.760	43	101	144	44	132	1	29	37	26	320	2.3	0.7	5.1
95-96–Boston	17	2	92	14	39	.359	0	0	–	5	8	.625	12	10	22	4	21	0	3	11	0	33	1.3	0.2	1.9
Reg. Season Totals	296	118	5833	1020	2399	.425	3	36	.083	313	405	.773	394	840	1234	400	979	21	224	353	150	2356	4.2	1.4	8.0

Smith, Edward Bernard (Ed) b. July 5, 1929 Ht. 6-6 Wt. 195 College: Harvard

SEASON–TEAM	G	GS	MIN	FGM	FGA	PCT	3FGM	3FGA	PCT	FTM	FTA	PCT	O-RB	D-RB	TOT	AST	PF	DQ	STL	TO	BLK	PTS	RPG	APG	PPG
53-54–New York	11	–	104	11	45	.244	–	–	–	6	10	.600	–	–	26	9	15	0	–	–	–	28	2.4	0.8	2.5
Reg. Season Totals	11	–	104	11	45	.244	–	–	–	6	10	.600	–	–	26	9	15	0	–	–	–	28	2.4	0.8	2.5

Smith, Elmore b. May 9, 1949 Ht. 7-1 Wt. 250 College: Wiley; Kentucky State

SEASON–TEAM	G	GS	MIN	FGM	FGA	PCT	3FGM	3FGA	PCT	FTM	FTA	PCT	O-RB	D-RB	TOT	AST	PF	DQ	STL	TO	BLK	PTS	RPG	APG	PPG
71-72–Buffalo	78	–	3186	579	1275	.454	–	–	–	194	363	.534	–	–	1184	111	306	10	–	–	–	1352	15.2	1.4	17.3
72-73–Buffalo	76	–	2829	600	1244	.482	–	–	–	188	337	.558	–	–	946	192	295	16	–	–	–	1388	12.4	2.5	18.3
73-74–Los Angeles	81	–	2922	434	949	.457	–	–	–	147	249	.590	204	702	906	150	309	8	71	–	393	1015	11.2	1.9	12.5
74-75–Los Angeles	74	–	2341	346	702	.493	–	–	–	112	231	.485	210	600	810	145	255	6	84	–	216	804	10.9	2.0	10.9
75-76–Milwaukee	78	–	2809	498	962	.518	–	–	–	222	351	.632	201	692	893	97	268	7	78	–	238	1218	11.4	1.2	15.6
76-77–Milw.-Clev.	70	–	1464	241	507	.475	–	–	–	117	213	.549	114	325	439	43	207	4	35	–	144	599	6.3	0.6	8.6
77-78–Cleveland	81	–	1996	402	809	.497	–	–	–	205	309	.663	178	500	678	57	241	4	50	141	176	1009	8.4	0.7	12.5
78-79–Cleveland	24	–	332	69	130	.531	–	–	–	18	26	.692	45	61	106	13	60	0	7	42	16	156	4.4	0.5	6.5
Reg. Season Totals	562	–	17879	3169	6578	.482	–	–	–	1203	2079	.579	952	2880	5962	808	1941	55	325	183	1183	7541	10.6	1.4	13.4
Playoff Totals	13	–	387	86	172	.500	–	–	–	34	52	.654	36	82	118	8	53	0	17	5	25	206	9.1	0.6	15.8

Smith, Garfield b. November 18, 1945 Ht. 6-9 Wt. 235 College: Eastern Kentucky

SEASON–TEAM	G	GS	MIN	FGM	FGA	PCT	3FGM	3FGA	PCT	FTM	FTA	PCT	O-RB	D-RB	TOT	AST	PF	DQ	STL	TO	BLK	PTS	RPG	APG	PPG
70-71–Boston	37	–	281	42	116	.362	–	–	–	22	56	.393	–	–	95	9	53	0	–	–	–	106	2.6	0.2	2.9
71-72–Boston	26	–	134	28	66	.424	–	–	–	6	31	.194	–	–	37	8	22	0	–	–	–	62	1.4	0.3	2.4
72-73–San Diego (A)	71	–	1055	116	244	.475	0	0	–	28	93	.301	140	166	306	39	197	4	–	33	–	260	4.3	0.5	3.7
Reg. NBA Totals	63	–	415	70	182	.385	–	–	–	28	87	.322	–	–	132	17	75	0	–	–	–	168	2.1	0.3	2.7
Reg. ABA Totals	71	–	1055	116	244	.475	0	0	–	28	93	.301	140	166	306	39	197	4	–	33	–	260	4.3	0.5	3.7
NBA Playoff Totals	4	–	6	1	5	.200	–	–	–	0	3	.000	–	–	1	–	1	0	–	–	–	2	0.3	0.0	0.5
ABA Playoff Totals	4	–	63	5	17	.294	0	0	–	2	7	.286	–	–	21	1	9	0	–	1	–	12	5.3	0.3	3.0

Smith, Gregory Darnell (Greg) b. January 28, 1947 Ht. 6-5 Wt. 195 College: Western Kentucky

SEASON–TEAM	G	GS	MIN	FGM	FGA	PCT	3FGM	3FGA	PCT	FTM	FTA	PCT	O-RB	D-RB	TOT	AST	PF	DQ	STL	TO	BLK	PTS	RPG	APG	PPG
68-69–Milwaukee	79	–	2207	276	613	.450	–	–	–	91	155	.587	–	–	804	137	264	12	–	–	–	643	10.2	1.7	8.1
69-70–Milwaukee	82	–	2368	339	664	.511	–	–	–	125	174	.718	–	–	712	156	304	8	–	–	–	803	8.7	1.9	9.8
70-71–Milwaukee	82	–	2428	409	799	.512	–	–	–	141	213	.662	–	–	589	227	284	5	–	–	–	959	7.2	2.8	11.7
71-72–Milw.-Houston	82	–	2256	309	671	.461	–	–	–	111	168	.661	–	–	483	222	259	4	–	–	–	729	5.9	2.7	8.9
72-73–Houston-Port.	76	–	1610	234	485	.482	–	–	–	75	128	.586	–	–	383	122	218	8	–	–	–	543	5.0	1.6	7.1
73-74–Portland	67	–	878	99	228	.434	–	–	–	48	79	.608	65	124	189	78	126	1	41	–	6	246	2.8	1.2	3.7
74-75–Portland	55	–	519	71	146	.486	–	–	–	32	48	.667	29	60	89	27	96	1	22	–	6	174	1.6	0.5	3.2
75-76–Portland	1	–	3	0	1	.000	–	–	–	0	0	–	0	0	0	0	2	0	0	–	0	0	0.0	0.0	0.0
Reg. Season Totals	524	–	12269	1737	3607	.482	–	–	–	623	965	.646	94	184	3249	969	1553	39	63	–	12	4097	6.2	1.8	7.8
Playoff Totals	24	–	783	117	222	.527	–	–	–	35	62	.565	0	0	205	58	79	1	0	–	0	269	8.5	2.4	11.2

Smith, James Oliver (Jim) b. April 12, 1958 Ht. 6-9 Wt. 225 College: Ohio State

SEASON–TEAM	G	GS	MIN	FGM	FGA	PCT	3FGM	3FGA	PCT	FTM	FTA	PCT	O-RB	D-RB	TOT	AST	PF	DQ	STL	TO	BLK	PTS	RPG	APG	PPG
81-82–San Diego	72	3	858	86	169	.509	0	0	–	39	85	.459	72	110	182	46	185	5	22	47	51	211	2.5	0.6	2.9
82-83–Detroit	4	0	18	3	4	.750	0	0	–	2	4	.500	0	5	5	0	4	0	0	0	0	8	1.3	0.0	2.0
Reg. Season Totals	76	3	876	89	173	.514	0	0	–	41	89	.461	72	115	187	46	189	5	22	47	51	219	2.5	0.6	2.9

Smith, John Jr. b. May 24, 1944 Ht. 7-0 Wt. 235 College: Southern Colorado

SEASON–TEAM	G	GS	MIN	FGM	FGA	PCT	3FGM	3FGA	PCT	FTM	FTA	PCT	O-RB	D-RB	TOT	AST	PF	DQ	STL	TO	BLK	PTS	RPG	APG	PPG
68-69–Dallas (A)	77	–	2172	246	623	.395	0	0	–	116	214	.542	271	538	809	58	328	19	–	117	–	608	10.5	0.8	7.9
69-70–Dallas-Pitt.-N.Y. (A)	70	–	1190	105	284	.370	0	2	.000	56	94	.596	–	–	404	58	185	5	–	–	–	266	5.8	0.8	3.8
Reg. ABA Totals	147	–	3362	351	907	.387	0	2	.000	172	308	.558	271	538	1213	116	513	24	–	117	–	874	8.3	0.8	5.9
ABA Playoff Totals	9	–	141	16	34	.471	0	1	.000	7	13	.538	–	–	44	8	21	0	–	–	–	39	4.9	0.9	4.3

Smith, Joseph Leynard (Joe) b. July 26, 1975 Ht. 6-10 Wt. 225 College: Maryland

SEASON–TEAM	G	GS	MIN	FGM	FGA	PCT	3FGM	3FGA	PCT	FTM	FTA	PCT	O-RB	D-RB	TOT	AST	PF	DQ	STL	TO	BLK	PTS	RPG	APG	PPG
95-96–Golden State	82	82	2821	469	1024	.458	10	28	.357	303	392	.773	300	417	717	79	224	5	85	138	134	1251	8.7	1.0	15.3
96-97–Golden State	80	80	3086	587	1293	.454	12	46	.261	307	377	.814	261	418	679	125	244	3	74	192	86	1493	8.5	1.6	18.7
97-98–G.S.-Phil.	79	55	2344	464	1070	.434	0	8	.000	227	293	.775	199	272	471	94	263	2	62	158	51	1155	6.0	1.2	14.6
98-99–Minnesota	43	42	1418	223	522	.427	0	3	.000	142	188	.755	154	200	354	68	147	3	32	66	66	588	8.2	1.6	13.7
99-00–Minnesota	78	9	1975	289	623	.464	1	1	1.000	195	258	.756	186	298	484	88	302	8	45	119	85	774	6.2	1.1	9.9
Reg. Season Totals	362	268	11644	2032	4532	.448	23	86	.267	1174	1508	.779	1100	1605	2705	454	1180	21	298	673	422	5261	7.5	1.3	14.5
Playoff Totals	8	4	199	19	54	.352	0	1	.000	10	13	.769	17	21	38	6	30	0	5	9	9	48	4.8	0.8	6.0

Smith, Keith LeWayne b. March 9, 1964 Ht. 6-3 Wt. 195 College: Loyola Marymount

SEASON–TEAM	G	GS	MIN	FGM	FGA	PCT	3FGM	3FGA	PCT	FTM	FTA	PCT	O-RB	D-RB	TOT	AST	PF	DQ	STL	TO	BLK	PTS	RPG	APG	PPG
86-87–Milwaukee	42	4	461	57	150	.380	3	9	.333	21	28	.750	13	19	32	43	74	0	25	30	3	138	0.8	1.0	3.3
Reg. Season Totals	42	4	461	57	150	.380	3	9	.333	21	28	.750	13	19	32	43	74	0	25	30	3	138	0.8	1.0	3.3

Smith, Kenneth Wayne (Ken) b. July 12, 1953 Ht. 6-7 Wt. 185 College: Lon Morris (Texas) Coll. (J.C.); Tulsa

SEASON–TEAM	G	GS	MIN	FGM	FGA	PCT	3FGM	3FGA	PCT	FTM	FTA	PCT	O-RB	D-RB	TOT	AST	PF	DQ	STL	TO	BLK	PTS	RPG	APG	PPG
75-76–San Antonio (A)	19	–	164	34	83	.410	1	5	.200	13	16	.813	9	15	24	7	22	–	4	8	0	82	1.3	0.4	4.3
Reg. ABA Totals	19	–	164	34	83	.410	1	5	.200	13	16	.813	9	15	24	7	22	–	4	8	0	82	1.3	0.4	4.3

Smith, Kenny b. March 8, 1965 Ht. 6-3 Wt. 170 College: North Carolina

SEASON–TEAM	G	GS	MIN	FGM	FGA	PCT	3FGM	3FGA	PCT	FTM	FTA	PCT	O-RB	D-RB	TOT	AST	PF	DQ	STL	TO	BLK	PTS	RPG	APG	PPG
87-88–Sacramento	61	60	2170	331	694	.477	12	39	.308	167	204	.819	40	98	138	434	140	1	92	184	8	841	2.3	7.1	13.8
88-89–Sacramento	81	81	3145	547	1183	.462	46	128	.359	263	357	.737	49	177	226	621	173	0	102	249	7	1403	2.8	7.7	17.3
89-90–Sac.-Atlanta	79	51	2421	378	811	.466	26	83	.313	161	196	.821	18	139	157	445	143	0	79	169	8	943	2.0	5.6	11.9
90-91–Houston	78	78	2699	522	1003	.520	49	135	.363	287	340	.844	36	127	163	554	131	0	106	237	11	1380	2.1	7.1	17.7
91-92–Houston	81	80	2735	432	910	.475	54	137	.394	219	253	.866	34	143	177	562	112	0	104	227	7	1137	2.2	6.9	14.0
92-93–Houston	82	82	2422	387	744	.520	96	219	.438	195	222	.878	28	132	160	446	110	0	80	163	7	1065	2.0	5.4	13.0
93-94–Houston	78	78	2209	341	711	.480	89	220	.405	135	155	.871	24	114	138	327	121	0	59	126	4	906	1.8	4.2	11.6
94-95–Houston	81	81	2030	287	593	.484	142	331	.429	126	148	.851	27	128	155	323	109	1	71	123	10	842	1.9	4.0	10.4
95-96–Houston	68	56	1617	201	464	.433	91	238	.382	87	106	.821	21	75	96	245	116	1	47	100	3	580	1.4	3.6	8.5
96-97–Det.-Orl.-Den.	48	3	765	101	239	.423	59	135	.437	39	45	.867	4	40	44	116	30	0	19	71	0	300	0.9	2.4	6.3
Reg. Season Totals	737	650	22213	3527	7352	.480	664	1665	.399	1679	2026	.829	281	1173	1454	4073	1185	3	759	1649	65	9397	2.0	5.5	12.8
Playoff Totals	68	68	2043	268	586	.457	117	261	.448	127	150	.847	22	125	147	305	123	0	54	104	9	780	2.2	4.5	11.5

Smith, LaBradford Corvey b. April 3, 1969 Ht. 6-3 Wt. 205 College: Louisville

SEASON–TEAM	G	GS	MIN	FGM	FGA	PCT	3FGM	3FGA	PCT	FTM	FTA	PCT	O-RB	D-RB	TOT	AST	PF	DQ	STL	TO	BLK	PTS	RPG	APG	PPG
91-92–Washington	48	5	708	100	246	.407	2	21	.095	45	56	.804	30	51	81	99	98	0	44	63	1	247	1.7	2.1	5.1
92-93–Washington	69	33	1546	261	570	.458	8	23	.348	109	127	.858	26	80	106	186	178	2	58	103	9	639	1.5	2.7	9.3
93-94–Wash.-Sac.	66	2	877	124	306	.405	21	60	.350	63	84	.750	34	50	84	109	96	2	40	50	5	332	1.3	1.7	5.0
Reg. Season Totals	183	40	3131	485	1122	.432	31	104	.298	217	267	.813	90	181	271	394	372	4	142	216	15	1218	1.5	2.2	6.7

Smith, Larry (Mr. Mean) b. January 18, 1958 Ht. 6-8 Wt. 225 College: Alcorn State

SEASON–TEAM	G	GS	MIN	FGM	FGA	PCT	3FGM	3FGA	PCT	FTM	FTA	PCT	O-RB	D-RB	TOT	AST	PF	DQ	STL	TO	BLK	PTS	RPG	APG	PPG
80-81–Golden State	82	–	2578	304	594	.512	0	0	–	177	301	.588	433	561	994	93	316	10	70	146	63	785	12.1	1.1	9.6
81-82–Golden State	74	55	2213	220	412	.534	0	1	.000	88	159	.553	279	534	813	83	291	7	65	105	54	528	11.0	1.1	7.1
82-83–Golden State	49	41	1433	180	306	.588	0	0	–	53	99	.535	209	276	485	46	186	5	36	83	20	413	9.9	0.9	8.4
83-84–Golden State	75	63	2091	244	436	.560	0	0	–	94	168	.560	282	390	672	72	274	6	61	124	22	582	9.0	1.0	7.8
84-85–Golden State	80	78	2497	366	690	.530	0	0	–	155	256	.605	405	464	869	96	285	5	78	160	54	887	10.9	1.2	11.1
85-86–Golden State	77	74	2441	314	586	.536	0	1	.000	112	227	.493	384	472	856	95	286	7	62	135	50	740	11.1	1.2	9.6
86-87–Golden State	80	78	2374	297	544	.546	0	1	.000	113	197	.574	366	551	917	95	295	7	71	135	56	707	11.5	1.2	8.8
87-88–Golden State	20	10	499	58	123	.472	0	1	.000	11	27	.407	79	103	182	25	63	1	12	36	11	127	9.1	1.3	6.4
88-89–Golden State	80	78	1897	219	397	.552	0	0	–	18	58	.310	272	380	652	118	248	2	61	110	54	456	8.2	1.5	5.7
89-90–Houston	74	0	1300	101	213	.474	0	2	.000	20	55	.364	180	272	452	69	203	3	56	70	28	222	6.1	0.9	3.0
90-91–Houston	81	28	1923	128	263	.487	0	0	–	12	50	.240	302	407	709	88	265	6	83	93	22	268	8.8	1.1	3.3
91-92–Houston	45	7	800	50	92	.543	0	1	.000	4	11	.364	107	149	256	33	121	3	21	44	7	104	5.7	0.7	2.3
92-93–San Antonio	66	13	833	38	87	.437	0	0	–	9	22	.409	103	165	268	28	133	2	23	39	16	85	4.1	0.4	1.3
Reg. Season Totals	883	525	22879	2519	4743	.531	0	7	.000	866	1630	.531	3401	4724	8125	941	2966	64	699	1280	457	5904	9.2	1.1	6.7
Playoff Totals	31	18	657	56	112	.500	0	1	.000	20	29	.690	99	120	219	43	101	0	27	28	20	132	7.1	1.4	4.3

Smith, Michael b. March 28, 1972 Ht. 6-8 Wt. 240 College: Providence

SEASON–TEAM	G	GS	MIN	FGM	FGA	PCT	3FGM	3FGA	PCT	FTM	FTA	PCT	O-RB	D-RB	TOT	AST	PF	DQ	STL	TO	BLK	PTS	RPG	APG	PPG
94-95–Sacramento	82	0	1736	220	406	.542	0	2	.000	127	262	.485	174	312	486	67	235	1	61	106	49	567	5.9	0.8	6.9
95-96–Sacramento	65	0	1384	144	238	.605	1	1	1.000	68	177	.384	143	246	389	110	166	0	47	72	46	357	6.0	1.7	5.5
96-97–Sacramento	81	52	2526	202	375	.539	0	0	–	128	258	.496	257	512	769	191	251	3	82	130	60	532	9.5	2.4	6.6
97-98–Sac.-Vanc.	48	33	1053	93	194	.479	0	1	.000	65	103	.631	120	186	306	88	95	0	41	51	15	251	6.4	1.8	5.2
98-99–Vancouver	48	10	1098	77	144	.535	0	1	.000	76	128	.594	135	215	350	48	107	0	46	60	18	230	7.3	1.0	4.8
99-00–Washington	46	46	1145	108	192	.563	0	1	.000	73	101	.723	121	210	331	56	127	0	27	45	23	289	7.2	1.2	6.3
Reg. Season Totals	370	141	8942	844	1549	.545	1	6	.167	537	1029	.522	950	1681	2631	560	981	4	304	464	211	2226	7.1	1.5	6.0
Playoff Totals	4	0	87	7	12	.583	0	0	–	5	11	.455	7	15	22	8	14	0	1	2	2	19	5.5	2.0	4.8

Smith, Michael John b. May 19, 1965 Ht. 6-10 Wt. 225 College: Brigham Young

SEASON–TEAM	G	GS	MIN	FGM	FGA	PCT	3FGM	3FGA	PCT	FTM	FTA	PCT	O-RB	D-RB	TOT	AST	PF	DQ	STL	TO	BLK	PTS	RPG	APG	PPG
89-90–Boston	65	7	620	136	286	.476	2	28	.071	53	64	.828	40	60	100	79	51	0	9	54	1	327	1.5	1.2	5.0
90-91–Boston	47	3	389	95	200	.475	6	24	.250	22	27	.815	21	35	56	43	27	0	6	37	2	218	1.2	0.9	4.6
94-95–L.A. Clippers	29	0	319	63	134	.470	1	8	.125	26	30	.867	13	43	56	20	41	0	6	18	2	153	1.9	0.7	5.3
Reg. Season Totals	141	10	1328	294	620	.474	9	60	.150	101	121	.835	74	138	212	142	119	0	21	109	5	698	1.5	1.0	5.0
Playoff Totals	6	0	22	6	10	.600	0	3	.000	7	7	1.000	0	0	0	1	3	0	1	1	0	19	0.0	0.2	3.2

Smith, Otis Fitzgerald b. January 30, 1964 Ht. 6-5 Wt. 210 College: Jacksonville

SEASON–TEAM	G	GS	MIN	FGM	FGA	PCT	3FGM	3FGA	PCT	FTM	FTA	PCT	O-RB	D-RB	TOT	AST	PF	DQ	STL	TO	BLK	PTS	RPG	APG	PPG
86-87–Denver	28	0	168	33	79	.418	0	2	.000	12	21	.571	17	17	34	22	30	0	1	19	1	78	1.2	0.8	2.8
87-88–Denver-G.S.	72	18	1549	325	662	.491	13	41	.317	178	229	.777	126	121	247	155	160	0	91	107	42	841	3.4	2.2	11.7
88-89–Golden State	80	5	1597	311	715	.435	7	37	.189	174	218	.798	128	202	330	140	165	1	88	129	40	803	4.1	1.8	10.0
89-90–Orlando	65	35	1644	348	708	.492	10	40	.250	169	222	.761	117	183	300	147	174	0	76	102	57	875	4.6	2.3	13.5
90-91–Orlando	75	39	1885	407	902	.451	9	46	.196	221	301	.734	176	213	389	169	190	1	85	140	35	1044	5.2	2.3	13.9
91-92–Orlando	55	5	877	116	318	.365	8	21	.381	70	91	.769	40	76	116	57	85	1	36	62	13	310	2.1	1.0	5.6
Reg. Season Totals	375	102	7720	1540	3384	.455	47	187	.251	824	1082	.762	604	812	1416	690	804	3	377	559	188	3951	3.8	1.8	10.5
Playoff Totals	7	0	68	11	30	.367	0	0	–	7	11	.636	7	11	18	10	6	0	2	6	3	29	2.6	1.4	4.1

Smith, Pete b. 1947 Ht. 6-6 Wt. 205 College: Cincinnati; Valdosta State; Pepperdine

SEASON–TEAM	G	GS	MIN	FGM	FGA	PCT	3FGM	3FGA	PCT	FTM	FTA	PCT	O-RB	D-RB	TOT	AST	PF	DQ	STL	TO	BLK	PTS	RPG	APG	PPG
72-73–San Diego (A)	5	–	32	2	12	.167	0	2	.000	0	0	–	3	5	8	1	5	0	–	5	–	4	1.6	0.2	0.8
Reg. ABA Totals	5	–	32	2	12	.167	0	2	.000	0	0	–	3	5	8	1	5	0	–	5	–	4	1.6	0.2	0.8

Smith, Philip Arnold (Phil) b. April 22, 1952 Ht. 6-4 Wt. 185 College: San Francisco

SEASON–TEAM	G	GS	MIN	FGM	FGA	PCT	3FGM	3FGA	PCT	FTM	FTA	PCT	O-RB	D-RB	TOT	AST	PF	DQ	STL	TO	BLK	PTS	RPG	APG	PPG
74-75–Golden State	74	–	1055	221	464	.476	–	–	–	127	158	.804	51	89	140	135	141	0	62	–	0	569	1.9	1.8	7.7
75-76–Golden State	82	–	2793	659	1383	.477	–	–	–	323	410	.788	133	243	376	362	223	0	108	–	18	1641	4.6	4.4	20.0
76-77–Golden State	82	–	2880	631	1318	.479	–	–	–	295	376	.785	101	231	332	328	227	0	98	–	29	1557	4.0	4.0	19.0
77-78–Golden State	82	–	2940	648	1373	.472	–	–	–	316	389	.812	100	200	300	393	219	2	108	266	27	1612	3.7	4.8	19.7
78-79–Golden State	59	–	2288	489	977	.501	–	–	–	194	255	.761	48	164	212	261	159	3	101	170	23	1172	3.6	4.4	19.9
79-80–Golden State	51	–	1552	325	685	.474	7	22	.318	135	171	.789	28	118	146	187	154	1	62	121	15	792	2.9	3.7	15.5
80-81–San Diego	76	–	2378	519	1057	.491	4	18	.222	237	313	.757	49	107	156	372	231	1	84	176	18	1279	2.1	4.9	16.8
81-82–S.D.-Seattle	74	41	2042	340	761	.447	5	27	.185	163	223	.731	51	135	186	307	213	0	67	155	27	848	2.5	4.1	11.5
82-83–Seattle	79	17	1238	175	400	.438	3	8	.375	101	133	.759	27	103	130	216	113	0	44	102	8	454	1.6	2.7	5.7
Reg. Season Totals	659	58	19166	4007	8418	.476	19	75	.253	1891	2428	.779	588	1390	1978	2561	1680	7	734	990	165	9924	3.0	3.9	15.1
Playoff Totals	49	0	1210	234	517	.453	0	1	.000	120	167	.719	43	107	150	143	99	1	49	6	18	588	3.1	2.9	12.0
All-Star Totals	2	0	40	9	20	.450	0	0	–	2	6	.333	1	6	7	8	4	0	1	–	0	20	3.5	4.0	10.0

Smith, Randolph (Randy) b. December 12, 1948 Ht. 6-3 Wt. 180 College: Buffalo State

SEASON–TEAM	G	GS	MIN	FGM	FGA	PCT	3FGM	3FGA	PCT	FTM	FTA	PCT	O-RB	D-RB	TOT	AST	PF	DQ	STL	TO	BLK	PTS	RPG	APG	PPG
71-72–Buffalo	76	–	2094	432	896	.482	–	–	–	158	254	.622	–	–	368	189	202	2	–	–	–	1022	4.8	2.5	13.4
72-73–Buffalo	82	–	2603	511	1154	.443	–	–	–	192	264	.727	–	–	391	422	247	1	–	–	–	1214	4.8	5.1	14.8
73-74–Buffalo	82	–	2745	531	1079	.492	–	–	–	205	288	.712	87	228	315	383	261	4	203	–	4	1267	3.8	4.7	15.5
74-75–Buffalo	82	–	3001	610	1261	.484	–	–	–	236	295	.800	95	249	344	534	247	2	137	–	3	1456	4.2	6.5	17.8
75-76–Buffalo	82	–	3167	702	1422	.494	–	–	–	383	469	.817	104	313	417	484	274	5	153	–	4	1787	5.1	5.9	21.8
76-77–Buffalo	82	–	3094	702	1504	.467	–	–	–	294	386	.762	134	323	457	441	264	2	176	–	8	1698	5.6	5.4	20.7
77-78–Buffalo	82	–	3314	789	1697	.465	–	–	–	443	554	.800	110	200	310	458	224	2	172	286	11	2021	3.8	5.6	24.6
78-79–San Diego	82	–	3111	693	1523	.455	–	–	–	292	359	.813	102	193	295	395	177	1	177	255	5	1678	3.6	4.8	20.5
79-80–Cleveland	82	–	2677	599	1326	.452	10	53	.189	233	283	.823	93	163	256	363	190	1	125	200	7	1441	3.1	4.4	17.6
80-81–Cleveland	82	–	2199	486	1043	.466	1	28	.036	221	271	.815	46	147	193	357	132	0	113	195	14	1194	2.4	4.4	14.6
81-82–New York	82	40	2033	348	748	.465	3	11	.273	122	151	.808	53	102	155	255	199	1	91	124	1	821	1.9	3.1	10.0
82-83–S.D.-Atlanta	80	16	1406	273	565	.483	3	18	.167	114	131	.870	37	59	96	206	139	1	56	98	0	663	1.2	2.6	8.3
Reg. Season Totals	976	56	31444	6676	14218	.470	17	110	.155	2893	3705	.781	861	1977	3597	4487	2556	22	1403	1158	57	16262	3.7	4.6	16.7
Playoff Totals	24	0	914	168	361	.465	0	0	–	84	103	.816	18	91	109	157	80	1	43	0	2	420	4.5	6.5	17.5
All-Star Totals	2	0	44	15	21	.714	0	0	–	5	6	.833	4	4	8	9	5	0	3	3	1	35	4.0	4.5	17.5

Smith, Reginald D. (Reggie) b. August 21, 1970 Ht. 6-10 Wt. 250 College: Texas Christian

SEASON–TEAM	G	GS	MIN	FGM	FGA	PCT	3FGM	3FGA	PCT	FTM	FTA	PCT	O-RB	D-RB	TOT	AST	PF	DQ	STL	TO	BLK	PTS	RPG	APG	PPG
92-93–Portland	23	0	68	10	27	.370	0	1	.000	3	14	.214	15	6	21	1	16	0	4	4	1	23	0.9	0.0	1.0
93-94–Portland	43	9	316	29	72	.403	0	0	–	18	38	.474	40	59	99	4	47	0	12	12	6	76	2.3	0.1	1.8
Reg. Season Totals	66	9	384	39	99	.394	0	1	.000	21	52	.404	55	65	120	5	63	0	16	16	7	99	1.8	0.1	1.5

Smith, Robert (Bingo) b. February 26, 1946 Ht. 6-5 Wt. 210 College: Tulsa

SEASON–TEAM	G	GS	MIN	FGM	FGA	PCT	3FGM	3FGA	PCT	FTM	FTA	PCT	O-RB	D-RB	TOT	AST	PF	DQ	STL	TO	BLK	PTS	RPG	APG	PPG
69-70–San Diego	75	–	1198	242	567	.427	–	–	–	66	96	.688	–	–	328	75	119	0	–	–	–	550	4.4	1.0	7.3
70-71–Cleveland	77	–	2332	495	1106	.448	–	–	–	178	234	.761	–	–	429	258	175	4	–	–	–	1168	5.6	3.4	15.2
71-72–Cleveland	82	–	2734	527	1190	.443	–	–	–	178	224	.795	–	–	502	247	222	3	–	–	–	1232	6.1	3.0	15.0
72-73–Cleveland	73	–	1068	268	603	.444	–	–	–	64	81	.790	–	–	199	108	80	0	–	–	–	600	2.7	1.5	8.2
73-74–Cleveland	82	–	2612	536	1179	.455	–	–	–	139	169	.822	134	301	435	198	242	4	89	–	30	1211	5.3	2.4	14.8
74-75–Cleveland	82	–	2636	585	1212	.483	–	–	–	132	160	.825	108	299	407	229	227	1	80	–	26	1302	5.0	2.8	15.9
75-76–Cleveland	81	–	2338	495	1121	.442	–	–	–	111	136	.816	83	258	341	155	231	0	58	–	36	1101	4.2	1.9	13.6
76-77–Cleveland	81	–	2135	513	1149	.446	–	–	–	148	181	.818	92	225	317	152	211	3	61	–	30	1174	3.9	1.9	14.5
77-78–Cleveland	82	–	1581	369	840	.439	–	–	–	108	135	.800	65	142	207	91	155	1	38	81	21	846	2.5	1.1	10.3
78-79–Cleveland	72	–	1650	361	784	.460	–	–	–	83	106	.783	77	129	206	121	188	2	43	75	7	805	2.9	1.7	11.2
79-80–Clev.-S.D.	78	–	2123	385	891	.432	23	81	.284	100	115	.870	94	165	259	100	209	4	62	81	17	893	3.3	1.3	11.4
Reg. Season Totals	865	–	22407	4776	10642	.449	23	81	.284	1307	1637	.798	653	1519	3630	1734	2059	22	431	237	167	10882	4.2	2.0	12.6
Playoff Totals	18	–	470	88	216	.407	0	0	–	25	28	.893	16	38	54	35	48	1	14	1	4	201	3.0	1.9	11.2

Smith, Robert Joseph (Bobby) b. August 20, 1937 Ht. 6-4 Wt. 190 College: West Virginia

SEASON–TEAM	G	GS	MIN	FGM	FGA	PCT	3FGM	3FGA	PCT	FTM	FTA	PCT	O-RB	D-RB	TOT	AST	PF	DQ	STL	TO	BLK	PTS	RPG	APG	PPG
59-60–Minneapolis	10	–	130	13	54	.241	–	–	–	11	16	.688	–	–	33	14	10	0	–	–	–	37	3.3	1.4	3.7
61-62–Los Angeles	3	–	7	0	1	.000	–	–	–	0	0	–	–	–	0	0	1	0	–	–	–	0	0.0	0.0	0.0
Reg. Season Totals	13	–	137	13	55	.236	–	–	–	11	16	.688	–	–	33	14	11	0	–	–	–	37	2.5	1.1	2.8

Smith, Robert Leroy b. March 10, 1955 Ht. 5-11 Wt. 165 College: Arizona Western Coll. (J.C.); Nevada-Las Vegas

SEASON–TEAM	G	GS	MIN	FGM	FGA	PCT	3FGM	3FGA	PCT	FTM	FTA	PCT	O-RB	D-RB	TOT	AST	PF	DQ	STL	TO	BLK	PTS	RPG	APG	PPG
77-78–Denver	45	–	378	50	97	.515	–	–	–	21	24	.875	6	30	36	39	52	0	18	20	3	121	0.8	0.9	2.7
78-79–Denver	82	–	1479	184	436	.422	–	–	–	159	180	.883	41	105	146	208	165	1	58	95	13	527	1.8	2.5	6.4
79-80–Utah-N.J.	65	–	809	118	269	.439	8	26	.308	80	92	.870	20	59	79	92	105	1	26	53	4	324	1.2	1.4	5.0
80-81–Cleveland	1	–	20	2	5	.400	0	0	–	4	4	1.000	1	2	3	3	6	1	0	3	0	8	3.0	3.0	8.0
81-82–Milwaukee	17	1	316	52	110	.473	2	10	.200	10	12	.833	1	13	14	44	35	0	10	14	1	116	0.8	2.6	6.8
82-83–S.D.-S.A.	12	0	68	7	24	.292	0	2	.000	9	10	.900	1	5	6	8	13	0	5	6	0	23	0.5	0.7	1.9
84-85–Cleveland	7	0	48	4	17	.235	0	4	.000	8	10	.800	0	4	4	7	6	0	2	3	0	16	0.6	1.0	2.3
Reg. Season Totals	229	1	3118	417	958	.435	10	42	.238	291	332	.877	70	218	288	401	382	3	119	194	21	1135	1.3	1.8	5.0
Playoff Totals	26	0	208	31	68	.456	2	8	.250	16	19	.842	10	13	23	39	25	0	10	12	0	80	0.9	1.5	3.1

Smith, Sam b. January 27, 1944 Ht. 6-7 Wt. 230 College: Louisville; Kentucky Wesleyan

SEASON–TEAM	G	GS	MIN	FGM	FGA	PCT	3FGM	3FGA	PCT	FTM	FTA	PCT	O-RB	D-RB	TOT	AST	PF	DQ	STL	TO	BLK	PTS	RPG	APG	PPG
67-68–Minnesota (A)	77	–	2175	284	750	.379	2	6	.333	185	280	.661	–	–	586	81	171	1	–	94	–	755	7.6	1.1	9.8
68-69–Kentucky (A)	62	–	1421	173	437	.396	1	10	.100	114	172	.663	–	–	390	64	143	0	–	70	–	461	6.3	1.0	7.4
69-70–Kentucky (A)	81	–	2405	307	724	.424	1	4	.250	163	249	.655	–	–	719	109	202	4	–	–	–	778	8.9	1.3	9.6
70-71–Ken.-Utah (A)	35	–	302	39	93	.419	1	5	.200	24	39	.615	–	–	81	20	42	–	–	–	–	103	2.3	0.6	2.9
Reg. ABA Totals	255	–	6303	803	2004	.401	5	25	.200	486	740	.657	–	–	1776	274	558	5	–	164	–	2097	7.0	1.1	8.2
ABA Playoff Totals	32	–	895	131	304	.431	0	4	.000	70	105	.667	–	–	222	34	64	0	–	15	–	332	6.9	1.1	10.4

Smith, Sam b. January 8, 1955 Ht. 6-4 Wt. 200 College: Seminole Coll. (Fla.) (J.C.); Nevada-Las Vegas

SEASON–TEAM	G	GS	MIN	FGM	FGA	PCT	3FGM	3FGA	PCT	FTM	FTA	PCT	O-RB	D-RB	TOT	AST	PF	DQ	STL	TO	BLK	PTS	RPG	APG	PPG
78-79–Milwaukee	16	–	125	19	47	.404	–	–	–	18	24	.750	0	9	9	16	12	0	8	8	7	56	0.6	1.0	3.5
79-80–Chicago	30	–	496	97	230	.422	8	35	.229	57	63	.905	22	32	54	42	54	0	25	33	7	259	1.8	1.4	8.6
Reg. Season Totals	46	–	621	116	277	.419	8	35	.229	75	87	.862	22	41	63	58	66	0	33	41	14	315	1.4	1.3	6.8

Smith, Steven Delano (Steve) b. March 31, 1969 Ht. 6-8 Wt. 215 College: Michigan State

SEASON–TEAM	G	GS	MIN	FGM	FGA	PCT	3FGM	3FGA	PCT	FTM	FTA	PCT	O-RB	D-RB	TOT	AST	PF	DQ	STL	TO	BLK	PTS	RPG	APG	PPG
91-92–Miami	61	59	1806	297	654	.454	40	125	.320	95	127	.748	81	107	188	278	162	1	59	152	19	729	3.1	4.6	12.0
92-93–Miami	48	43	1610	279	619	.451	53	132	.402	155	197	.787	56	141	197	267	148	3	50	129	16	766	4.1	5.6	16.0
93-94–Miami	78	77	2776	491	1076	.456	91	262	.347	273	327	.835	156	196	352	394	217	6	84	202	35	1346	4.5	5.1	17.3
94-95–Miami-Atlanta	80	61	2665	428	1005	.426	137	416	.329	312	371	.841	104	172	276	274	225	2	62	155	33	1305	3.5	3.4	16.3
95-96–Atlanta	80	80	2856	494	1143	.432	140	423	.331	318	385	.826	124	202	326	224	207	1	68	151	17	1446	4.1	2.8	18.1
96-97–Atlanta	72	72	2818	491	1145	.429	130	388	.335	333	393	.847	90	148	238	305	173	2	62	176	23	1445	3.3	4.2	20.1
97-98–Atlanta	73	73	2857	489	1101	.444	97	276	.351	389	455	.855	133	176	309	292	219	4	75	176	29	1464	4.2	4.0	20.1
98-99–Atlanta	36	36	1314	217	540	.402	47	139	.338	191	225	.849	50	101	151	118	100	2	36	99	11	672	4.2	3.3	18.7
99-00–Portland	82	81	2689	420	900	.467	96	241	.398	289	340	.850	123	190	313	209	214	0	71	117	31	1225	3.8	2.5	14.9
Reg. Season Totals	610	582	21391	3606	8183	.441	831	2402	.346	2355	2820	.835	917	1433	2350	2361	1665	21	567	1357	214	10398	3.9	3.9	17.0
Playoff Totals	60	60	2362	379	869	.436	114	273	.418	264	313	.843	77	129	206	164	190	1	66	113	27	1136	3.4	2.7	18.9
All-Star Totals	1	0	16	6	12	.500	2	5	.400	0	0	–	2	1	3	0	0	0	0	0	0	14	3.0	0.0	14.0

Smith, Stevin b. January 23, 1972 Ht. 6-2 Wt. 208 College: Arizona State

SEASON–TEAM	G	GS	MIN	FGM	FGA	PCT	3FGM	3FGA	PCT	FTM	FTA	PCT	O-RB	D-RB	TOT	AST	PF	DQ	STL	TO	BLK	PTS	RPG	APG	PPG
96-97–Dallas	8	0	60	6	18	.333	1	6	.167	1	1	1.000	2	8	10	4	9	0	1	4	0	14	1.3	0.5	1.8
Reg. Season Totals	8	0	60	6	18	.333	1	6	.167	1	1	1.000	2	8	10	4	9	0	1	4	0	14	1.3	0.5	1.8

Smith, William A. (Bill) b. February 14, 1949 Ht. 7-0 Wt. 220 College: Syracuse

SEASON–TEAM	G	GS	MIN	FGM	FGA	PCT	3FGM	3FGA	PCT	FTM	FTA	PCT	O-RB	D-RB	TOT	AST	PF	DQ	STL	TO	BLK	PTS	RPG	APG	PPG
71-72–Portland	22	–	448	72	173	.416	–	–	–	38	64	.594	–	–	135	19	73	3	–	–	–	182	6.1	0.9	8.3
72-73–Portland	8	–	43	9	15	.600	–	–	–	5	8	.625	–	–	8	1	8	0	–	–	–	23	1.0	0.1	2.9
Reg. Season Totals	30	–	491	81	188	.431	–	–	–	43	72	.597	–	–	143	20	81	3	–	–	–	205	4.8	0.7	6.8

Smith, William C. (Willie) b. October 26, 1953 Ht. 6-2 Wt. 180 College: Seminole (Fla.) Coll. (J.C.); Missouri

SEASON–TEAM	G	GS	MIN	FGM	FGA	PCT	3FGM	3FGA	PCT	FTM	FTA	PCT	O-RB	D-RB	TOT	AST	PF	DQ	STL	TO	BLK	PTS	RPG	APG	PPG
76-77–Chicago	2	–	11	0	1	.000	–	–	–	0	0	–	0	0	0	0	1	0	0	–	0	0	0.0	0.0	0.0
77-78–Indiana	1	–	7	0	0	–	–	–	–	0	0	–	0	0	0	1	1	0	0	0	0	0	0.0	1.0	0.0
78-79–Portland	13	–	131	23	44	.523	–	–	–	12	17	.706	7	6	13	17	19	0	10	14	1	58	1.0	1.3	4.5
79-80–Cleveland	62	–	1051	121	315	.384	17	71	.239	40	52	.769	56	65	121	259	110	1	75	95	1	299	2.0	4.2	4.8
Reg. Season Totals	78	–	1200	144	360	.400	17	71	.239	52	69	.754	63	71	134	277	131	1	85	109	2	357	1.7	3.6	4.6

Smith, William F. (Bill) b. April 26, 1939 Ht. 6-5 Wt. 190 College: St. Peter's

SEASON–TEAM	G	GS	MIN	FGM	FGA	PCT	3FGM	3FGA	PCT	FTM	FTA	PCT	O-RB	D-RB	TOT	AST	PF	DQ	STL	TO	BLK	PTS	RPG	APG	PPG
61-62–New York	9	–	83	8	33	.242	–	–	–	7	8	.875	–	–	16	7	6	0	–	–	–	23	1.8	0.8	2.6
Reg. Season Totals	9	–	83	8	33	.242	–	–	–	7	8	.875	–	–	16	7	6	0	–	–	–	23	1.8	0.8	2.6

Smits, Rik (Dutch Boy in Paint) b. August 23, 1966 Ht. 7-4 Wt. 265 College: Marist

SEASON–TEAM	G	GS	MIN	FGM	FGA	PCT	3FGM	3FGA	PCT	FTM	FTA	PCT	O-RB	D-RB	TOT	AST	PF	DQ	STL	TO	BLK	PTS	RPG	APG	PPG
88-89–Indiana	82	71	2041	386	746	.517	0	1	.000	184	255	.722	185	315	500	70	310	14	37	130	151	956	6.1	0.9	11.7
89-90–Indiana	82	82	2404	515	967	.533	0	1	.000	241	297	.811	135	377	512	142	328	11	45	143	169	1271	6.2	1.7	15.5
90-91–Indiana	76	38	1690	342	705	.485	0	0	–	144	189	.762	116	241	357	84	246	3	24	86	111	828	4.7	1.1	10.9
91-92–Indiana	74	55	1772	436	855	.510	0	2	.000	152	193	.788	124	293	417	116	231	4	29	130	100	1024	5.6	1.6	13.8
92-93–Indiana	81	81	2072	494	1017	.486	0	0	–	167	228	.732	126	306	432	121	285	5	27	147	75	1155	5.3	1.5	14.3
93-94–Indiana	78	75	2113	493	923	.534	0	1	.000	238	300	.793	135	348	483	156	281	11	49	151	82	1224	6.2	2.0	15.7
94-95–Indiana	78	78	2381	558	1060	.526	0	2	.000	284	377	.753	192	409	601	111	278	6	40	189	79	1400	7.7	1.4	17.9
95-96–Indiana	63	63	1901	466	894	.521	1	5	.200	231	293	.788	119	314	433	110	226	5	21	160	45	1164	6.9	1.7	18.5
96-97–Indiana	52	52	1518	356	733	.486	2	8	.250	173	217	.797	105	256	361	67	175	3	22	126	59	887	6.9	1.3	17.1
97-98–Indiana	73	69	2085	514	1038	.495	0	3	.000	188	240	.783	127	378	505	101	243	9	40	134	88	1216	6.9	1.4	16.7
98-99–Indiana	49	49	1271	310	633	.490	0	2	.000	108	132	.818	73	202	275	52	159	1	18	75	52	728	5.6	1.1	14.9
99-00–Indiana	79	79	1852	431	890	.484	0	1	.000	156	211	.739	94	307	401	85	249	1	20	108	100	1018	5.1	1.1	12.9
Reg. Season Totals	867	792	23100	5301	10461	.507	3	26	.115	2266	2932	.773	1531	3746	5277	1215	3011	73	372	1579	1111	12871	6.1	1.4	14.8
Playoff Totals	104	96	2747	623	1230	.507	1	4	.250	290	350	.829	149	391	540	135	419	13	51	185	90	1537	5.2	1.3	14.8
All-Star Totals	1	0	21	3	7	.429	0	0	–	4	4	1.000	2	5	7	4	3	0	0	0	2	10	7.0	4.0	10.0

Smrek, Michael Frank (Mike) b. August 31, 1962 Ht. 7-0 Wt. 250 College: Canisius

SEASON–TEAM	G	GS	MIN	FGM	FGA	PCT	3FGM	3FGA	PCT	FTM	FTA	PCT	O-RB	D-RB	TOT	AST	PF	DQ	STL	TO	BLK	PTS	RPG	APG	PPG
85-86–Chicago	38	5	408	46	122	.377	0	2	.000	16	29	.552	46	64	110	19	95	0	6	29	23	108	2.9	0.5	2.8
86-87–L.A. Lakers	35	3	233	30	60	.500	0	0	–	16	25	.640	13	24	37	5	70	1	4	19	13	76	1.1	0.1	2.2
87-88–L.A. Lakers	48	2	421	44	103	.427	0	0	–	44	66	.667	27	58	85	8	105	3	7	30	42	132	1.8	0.2	2.8
88-89–San Antonio	43	18	623	72	153	.471	0	0	–	49	76	.645	42	87	129	12	102	2	13	48	58	193	3.0	0.3	4.5
89-90–Golden State	13	3	107	10	24	.417	0	0	–	1	6	.167	11	23	34	1	18	0	4	9	11	21	2.6	0.1	1.6
90-91–G.S.-LAClips	15	0	95	9	27	.333	0	0	–	6	12	.500	7	19	26	4	27	1	3	3	3	24	1.7	0.3	1.6
91-92–Golden State	2	0	3	0	0	–	0	0	–	0	0	–	0	1	1	0	0	0	0	0	0	0	0.5	0.0	0.0
Reg. Season Totals	194	31	1890	211	489	.431	0	2	.000	132	214	.617	146	276	422	49	417	7	37	138	150	554	2.2	0.3	2.9
Playoff Totals	21	0	72	3	16	.188	0	0	–	5	9	.556	4	9	13	–	21	0	1	3	10	11	0.6	0.0	0.5

Smyth, Joseph George (Joe) b. May 22, 1929 Ht. 6-3 Wt. 215 College: Niagara

SEASON–TEAM	G	GS	MIN	FGM	FGA	PCT	3FGM	3FGA	PCT	FTM	FTA	PCT	O-RB	D-RB	TOT	AST	PF	DQ	STL	TO	BLK	PTS	RPG	APG	PPG
53-54–N.Y.-Balt.	40	–	495	48	138	.348	–	–	–	35	65	.538	–	–	98	49	53	0	–	–	–	131	2.5	1.2	3.3
Reg. Season Totals	40	–	495	48	138	.348	–	–	–	35	65	.538	–	–	98	49	53	0	–	–	–	131	2.5	1.2	3.3

Snow, Eric b. April 24, 1973 Ht. 6-3 Wt. 204 College: Michigan State

SEASON–TEAM	G	GS	MIN	FGM	FGA	PCT	3FGM	3FGA	PCT	FTM	FTA	PCT	O-RB	D-RB	TOT	AST	PF	DQ	STL	TO	BLK	PTS	RPG	APG	PPG
95-96–Seattle	43	1	389	42	100	.420	2	10	.200	29	49	.592	9	34	43	73	53	0	28	38	0	115	1.0	1.7	2.7
96-97–Seattle	67	0	775	74	164	.451	4	15	.267	47	66	.712	17	53	70	159	94	0	37	48	3	199	1.0	2.4	3.0
97-98–Seattle-Phil.	64	0	918	79	184	.429	2	17	.118	49	71	.690	19	62	81	177	114	0	60	63	5	209	1.3	2.8	3.3
98-99–Philadelphia	48	48	1716	149	348	.428	5	21	.238	110	150	.733	25	137	162	301	149	2	100	111	1	413	3.4	6.3	8.6
99-00–Philadelphia	82	80	2866	257	597	.430	11	45	.244	126	177	.712	42	219	261	624	243	2	140	162	8	651	3.2	7.6	7.9
Reg. Season Totals	304	129	6664	601	1393	.431	24	108	.222	361	513	.704	112	505	617	1334	653	4	365	422	17	1587	2.0	4.4	5.2
Playoff Totals	31	12	516	58	137	.423	8	23	.348	27	33	.818	3	46	49	110	50	0	18	36	2	151	1.6	3.5	4.9

Snyder, Richard J. Jr. (Dick) b. February 1, 1944 Ht. 6-5 Wt. 210 College: Davidson

SEASON–TEAM	G	GS	MIN	FGM	FGA	PCT	3FGM	3FGA	PCT	FTM	FTA	PCT	O-RB	D-RB	TOT	AST	PF	DQ	STL	TO	BLK	PTS	RPG	APG	PPG
66-67–St. Louis	55	–	676	144	333	.432	–	–	–	46	61	.754	–	–	91	59	82	1	–	–	–	334	1.7	1.1	6.1
67-68–St. Louis	75	–	1622	257	613	.419	–	–	–	129	167	.772	–	–	194	164	215	5	–	–	–	643	2.6	2.2	8.6
68-69–Phoenix	81	–	2108	399	846	.472	–	–	–	185	255	.725	–	–	328	211	213	2	–	–	–	983	4.0	2.6	12.1
69-70–Phoenix-Seattle	82	–	2437	456	863	.528	–	–	–	169	208	.813	–	–	323	342	277	8	–	–	–	1081	3.9	4.2	13.2
70-71–Seattle	82	–	2824	645	1215	.531	–	–	–	302	361	.837	–	–	257	352	249	6	–	–	–	1592	3.1	4.3	19.4
71-72–Seattle	73	–	2534	496	937	.529	–	–	–	218	259	.842	–	–	228	283	200	3	–	–	–	1210	3.1	3.9	16.6
72-73–Seattle	82	–	3060	473	1022	.463	–	–	–	186	216	.861	–	–	323	311	216	2	–	–	–	1132	3.9	3.8	13.8
73-74–Seattle	74	–	2670	572	1189	.481	–	–	–	194	224	.866	90	216	306	265	257	4	90	–	26	1338	4.1	3.6	18.1
74-75–Cleveland	82	–	2590	498	988	.504	–	–	–	165	195	.846	37	201	238	281	226	3	69	–	43	1161	2.9	3.4	14.2
75-76–Cleveland	82	–	2274	441	881	.501	–	–	–	155	188	.824	50	148	198	220	215	0	59	–	33	1037	2.4	2.7	12.6
76-77–Cleveland	82	–	1685	316	693	.456	–	–	–	127	149	.852	47	102	149	160	177	2	45	–	30	759	1.8	2.0	9.3
77-78–Cleveland	58	–	660	112	252	.444	–	–	–	56	64	.875	9	40	49	56	74	0	23	48	19	280	0.8	1.0	4.8
78-79–Seattle	56	–	536	81	187	.433	–	–	–	43	51	.843	15	33	48	63	52	0	14	36	6	205	0.9	1.1	3.7
Reg. Season Totals	964	–	25676	4890	10019	.488	–	–	–	1975	2398	.824	248	740	2732	2767	2453	36	300	84	157	11755	2.8	2.9	12.2
Playoff Totals	31	–	572	97	233	.416	–	–	–	30	41	.732	14	31	50	49	55	1	16	8	11	224	1.6	1.6	7.2

Sobek, George Edward (Chips) b. February 10, 1920 d. April 9, 1990 Ht. 6-2 Wt. 180 College: Notre Dame

SEASON–TEAM	G	GS	MIN	FGM	FGA	PCT	3FGM	3FGA	PCT	FTM	FTA	PCT	O-RB	D-RB	TOT	AST	PF	DQ	STL	TO	BLK	PTS	RPG	APG	PPG
45-46–Indianapolis (N)	1	–	–	2	–	–	–	–	–	1	–	–	–	–	–	–	–	–	–	–	–	5	–	–	5.0
46-47–Toledo (N)	42	–	–	186	–	–	–	–	–	179	248	.722	–	–	–	–	106	–	–	–	–	551	–	–	13.1
47-48–Toledo (N)	48	–	–	118	–	–	–	–	–	124	170	.729	–	–	–	–	110	–	–	–	–	360	–	–	7.5
48-49–Hammond (N)	57	–	–	143	–	–	–	–	–	232	322	.720	–	–	–	–	167	–	–	–	–	518	–	–	9.1
49-50–Sheboygan	60	–	–	95	251	.378	–	–	–	156	205	.761	–	–	–	95	158	–	–	–	–	346	–	1.6	5.8
Reg. NBA Totals	60	–	–	95	251	.378	–	–	–	156	205	.761	–	–	–	95	158	–	–	–	–	346	–	1.6	5.8
Reg. NBL Totals	148	–	–	449	–	–	–	–	–	536	740	.723	–	–	–	–	383	–	–	–	–	1434	–	–	9.7
NBA Playoff Totals	3	–	–	10	40	.500	–	–	–	12	15	.800	–	–	–	6	15	2	–	–	–	32	–	1.0	10.7
NBL Playoff Totals	7	–	–	18	–	–	–	–	–	20	27	.741	–	–	–	–	25	–	–	–	–	56	–	–	8.0

Sobers, Ricky Brad b. January 15, 1953 Ht. 6-3 Wt. 200 College: Coll. of Southern Idaho (J.C.); Nevada-Las Vegas

SEASON–TEAM	G	GS	MIN	FGM	FGA	PCT	3FGM	3FGA	PCT	FTM	FTA	PCT	O-RB	D-RB	TOT	AST	PF	DQ	STL	TO	BLK	PTS	RPG	APG	PPG
75-76–Phoenix	78	–	1898	280	623	.449	–	–	–	158	192	.823	80	179	259	215	253	6	106	–	7	718	3.3	2.8	9.2
76-77–Phoenix	79	–	2005	414	834	.496	–	–	–	243	289	.841	82	152	234	238	258	3	93	–	14	1071	3.0	3.0	13.6
77-78–Indiana	79	–	3019	553	1221	.453	–	–	–	330	400	.825	92	235	327	584	308	10	170	352	23	1436	4.1	7.4	18.2
78-79–Indiana	81	–	2825	553	1194	.463	–	–	–	298	338	.882	118	183	301	450	315	8	138	304	23	1404	3.7	5.6	17.3
79-80–Chicago	82	–	2673	470	1002	.469	21	68	.309	200	239	.837	75	167	242	426	294	4	136	282	17	1161	3.0	5.2	14.2
80-81–Chicago	71	–	1803	355	769	.462	17	66	.258	231	247	.935	46	98	144	284	225	3	98	206	17	958	2.0	4.0	13.5
81-82–Chicago	80	6	1938	363	801	.453	19	76	.250	195	254	.768	37	105	142	301	238	6	73	217	18	940	1.8	3.8	11.8
82-83–Washington	41	39	1438	234	534	.438	23	55	.418	154	185	.832	35	67	102	218	158	3	61	147	14	645	2.5	5.3	15.7
83-84–Washington	81	81	2624	508	1115	.456	29	111	.261	221	264	.837	51	128	179	377	278	10	117	222	17	1266	2.2	4.7	15.6
84-85–Seattle	71	12	1490	280	628	.446	8	28	.286	132	162	.815	27	76	103	252	156	0	49	158	9	700	1.5	3.5	9.9
85-86–Seattle	78	0	1279	240	541	.444	13	43	.302	110	125	.880	29	70	99	180	139	1	44	85	2	603	1.3	2.3	7.7
Reg. Season Totals	821	138	22992	4250	9262	.459	130	447	.291	2272	2695	.843	672	1460	2132	3525	2622	54	1085	1973	161	10902	2.6	4.3	13.3
Playoff Totals	29	4	875	156	343	.455	4	16	.250	71	85	.835	25	54	79	117	122	5	27	24	8	387	2.7	4.0	13.3

Sobie, Ronald Charles (Ron, formerly Ronald Charles Sobieszczyk) b. September 21, 1934 Ht. 6-3 Wt. 195 College: DePaul

SEASON–TEAM	G	GS	MIN	FGM	FGA	PCT	3FGM	3FGA	PCT	FTM	FTA	PCT	O-RB	D-RB	TOT	AST	PF	DQ	STL	TO	BLK	PTS	RPG	APG	PPG
56-57–New York	71	–	1378	166	442	.376	–	–	–	152	199	.764	–	–	326	129	158	0	–	–	–	484	4.6	1.8	6.8
57-58–New York	55	–	1399	217	539	.403	–	–	–	196	239	.820	–	–	263	125	147	3	–	–	–	630	4.8	2.3	11.5
58-59–New York	50	–	857	144	400	.360	–	–	–	112	133	.842	–	–	154	78	84	0	–	–	–	400	3.1	1.6	8.0
59-60–N.Y.-Minn.	16	–	234	37	108	.343	–	–	–	31	37	.838	–	–	48	21	32	0	–	–	–	105	3.0	1.3	6.6
Reg. Season Totals	192	–	3868	564	1489	.379	–	–	–	491	608	.808	–	–	791	353	421	3	–	–	–	1619	4.1	1.8	8.4

Sojourner, Mike b. October 16, 1953 Ht. 6-9 Wt. 225 College: Utah

SEASON–TEAM	G	GS	MIN	FGM	FGA	PCT	3FGM	3FGA	PCT	FTM	FTA	PCT	O-RB	D-RB	TOT	AST	PF	DQ	STL	TO	BLK	PTS	RPG	APG	PPG
74-75–Atlanta	73	–	2129	378	775	.488	–	–	–	95	146	.651	196	446	642	93	217	10	35	–	57	851	8.8	1.3	11.7
75-76–Atlanta	67	–	1602	248	524	.473	–	–	–	80	119	.672	126	323	449	58	174	2	38	–	40	576	6.7	0.9	8.6
76-77–Atlanta	51	–	551	95	203	.468	–	–	–	41	57	.719	49	97	146	21	66	0	15	–	9	231	2.9	0.4	4.5
Reg. Season Totals	191	–	4282	721	1502	.480	–	–	–	216	322	.671	371	866	1237	172	457	12	88	–	106	1658	6.5	0.9	8.7

Sojourner, Willard (Willie, Rainbow) b. September 10, 1948 Ht. 6-8 Wt. 225 College: Weber State

SEASON–TEAM	G	GS	MIN	FGM	FGA	PCT	3FGM	3FGA	PCT	FTM	FTA	PCT	O-RB	D-RB	TOT	AST	PF	DQ	STL	TO	BLK	PTS	RPG	APG	PPG
71-72–Virginia (A)	84	–	1313	222	448	.496	0	0	–	124	193	.642	–	–	514	56	222	–	–	86	–	568	6.1	0.7	6.8
72-73–Virginia (A)	64	–	1065	199	410	.485	0	0	–	84	128	.656	121	243	364	75	187	4	–	80	–	482	5.7	1.2	7.5
73-74–New York (A)	82	–	1316	202	419	.482	0	3	.000	54	64	.844	110	225	335	54	205	–	24	85	88	458	4.1	0.7	5.6
74-75–New York (A)	79	–	1020	155	324	.478	1	3	.333	49	70	.700	94	181	275	42	190	–	16	63	64	360	3.5	0.5	4.6
Reg. ABA Totals	309	–	4714	778	1601	.486	1	6	.167	311	455	.684	325	649	1488	227	804	4	40	314	152	1868	4.8	0.7	6.0
ABA Playoff Totals	32	–	297	44	91	.484	0	0	–	14	20	.700	24	23	76	18	52	0	2	30	21	102	2.4	0.6	3.2

Somerset, Willard F. (Willie) b. March 17, 1942 Ht. 5-10 Wt. 170 College: Duquesne

SEASON–TEAM	G	GS	MIN	FGM	FGA	PCT	3FGM	3FGA	PCT	FTM	FTA	PCT	O-RB	D-RB	TOT	AST	PF	DQ	STL	TO	BLK	PTS	RPG	APG	PPG
65-66–Baltimore	8	–	98	18	43	.419	–	–	–	9	11	.818	–	–	15	9	21	0	–	–	–	45	1.9	1.1	5.6
67-68–Houston (A)	61	–	2334	467	1042	.448	33	107	.308	359	460	.780	–	–	305	225	211	5	–	164	–	1326	5.0	3.7	21.7
68-69–Houston-N.Y. (A)	74	–	3118	619	1510	.410	36	139	.259	484	583	.830	–	–	332	280	261	4	–	215	–	1758	4.5	3.8	23.8
Reg. NBA Totals	8	–	98	18	43	.419	–	–	–	9	11	.818	–	–	15	9	21	0	–	–	–	45	1.9	1.1	5.6
Reg. ABA Totals	135	–	5452	1086	2552	.426	69	246	.280	843	1043	.808	–	–	637	505	472	9	–	379	–	3084	4.7	3.7	22.8
ABA Playoff Totals	3	–	131	30	73	.411	4	14	.286	27	34	.794	–	–	25	9	11	0	–	16	–	91	8.3	3.0	30.3

Sorenson, David Lowell (Dave) b. July 8, 1948 Ht. 6-8 Wt. 225 College: Ohio State

SEASON–TEAM	G	GS	MIN	FGM	FGA	PCT	3FGM	3FGA	PCT	FTM	FTA	PCT	O-RB	D-RB	TOT	AST	PF	DQ	STL	TO	BLK	PTS	RPG	APG	PPG
70-71–Cleveland	79	–	1940	353	794	.445	–	–	–	184	229	.803	–	–	486	163	181	3	–	–	–	890	6.2	2.1	11.3
71-72–Cleveland	76	–	1162	213	475	.448	–	–	–	106	136	.779	–	–	301	81	120	1	–	–	–	532	4.0	1.1	7.0
72-73–Clev.-Phil.	58	–	755	124	293	.423	–	–	–	64	90	.711	–	–	210	36	107	0	–	–	–	312	3.6	0.6	5.4
Reg. Season Totals	213	–	3857	690	1562	.442	–	–	–	354	455	.778	–	–	997	280	408	4	–	–	–	1734	4.7	1.3	8.1

Sovran, Gino b. December 17, 1924 Ht. 6-2 Wt. 175 College: Assumption; Detroit Mercy

SEASON–TEAM	G	GS	MIN	FGM	FGA	PCT	3FGM	3FGA	PCT	FTM	FTA	PCT	O-RB	D-RB	TOT	AST	PF	DQ	STL	TO	BLK	PTS	RPG	APG	PPG
46-47–Toronto	6	–	–	5	15	.333	–	–	–	1	2	.500	–	–	–	1	5	–	–	–	–	11	–	0.2	1.8
Reg. Season Totals	6	–	–	5	15	.333	–	–	–	1	2	.500	–	–	–	1	5	–	–	–	–	11	–	0.2	1.8

Spain, John Kenneth (Ken) b. October 6, 1946 Ht. 6-9 Wt. 235 College: Houston

SEASON–TEAM	G	GS	MIN	FGM	FGA	PCT	3FGM	3FGA	PCT	FTM	FTA	PCT	O-RB	D-RB	TOT	AST	PF	DQ	STL	TO	BLK	PTS	RPG	APG	PPG
70-71–Pittsburgh (A)	11	–	112	8	22	.364	0	0	–	8	17	.471	–	–	40	2	17	–	–	–	–	24	3.6	0.2	2.2
Reg. ABA Totals	11	–	112	8	22	.364	0	0	–	8	17	.471	–	–	40	2	17	–	–	–	–	24	3.6	0.2	2.2

Spanarkel, James Gerard (Jim) b. June 28, 1957 Ht. 6-5 Wt. 190 College: Duke

SEASON–TEAM	G	GS	MIN	FGM	FGA	PCT	3FGM	3FGA	PCT	FTM	FTA	PCT	O-RB	D-RB	TOT	AST	PF	DQ	STL	TO	BLK	PTS	RPG	APG	PPG
79-80–Philadelphia	40	0	442	72	153	.471	0	2	.000	54	65	.831	27	27	54	51	58	0	12	57	6	198	1.4	1.3	5.0
80-81–Dallas	82	–	2317	404	866	.467	1	10	.100	375	423	.887	142	155	297	232	230	3	117	172	20	1184	3.6	2.8	14.4
81-82–Dallas	82	1	1755	270	564	.479	8	24	.333	279	327	.853	99	111	210	206	140	0	86	111	9	827	2.6	2.5	10.1
82-83–Dallas	48	4	722	91	197	.462	2	10	.200	88	113	.779	27	57	84	78	59	0	27	55	3	272	1.8	1.6	5.7
83-84–Dallas	7	0	54	7	16	.438	1	2	.500	9	13	.692	5	2	7	5	8	0	6	4	0	24	1.0	0.7	3.4
Reg. Season Totals	259	5	5290	844	1796	.470	12	48	.250	805	941	.855	300	352	652	572	495	3	248	399	38	2505	2.5	2.2	9.7
Playoff Totals	5	0	8	0	2	.000	0	0	–	2	2	1.000	0	1	1	1	1	0	0	0	0	2	0.2	0.2	0.4

Sparks, Daniel E. (Dan) b. April 17, 1945 Ht. 6-8 Wt. 200 College: Vincennes (Ind.) (J.C.); Weber State

SEASON–TEAM	G	GS	MIN	FGM	FGA	PCT	3FGM	3FGA	PCT	FTM	FTA	PCT	O-RB	D-RB	TOT	AST	PF	DQ	STL	TO	BLK	PTS	RPG	APG	PPG
68-69–Miami (A)	64	–	1138	153	396	.386	0	0	–	113	165	.685	–	–	287	43	171	5	–	70	–	419	4.5	0.7	6.5
69-70–Miami (A)	3	–	52	7	18	.389	0	0	–	5	6	.833	–	–	16	2	7	0	–	–	–	19	5.3	0.7	6.3
Reg. ABA Totals	67	–	1190	160	414	.386	0	0	–	118	171	.690	–	–	303	45	178	5	–	70	–	438	4.5	0.7	6.5
ABA Playoff Totals	12	–	251	29	65	.446	0	0	–	19	30	.633	–	–	57	8	35	0	–	–	–	77	4.8	0.7	6.4

Sparrow, Guy P. b. November 2, 1932 Ht. 6-6 Wt. 220 College: Detroit Mercy

SEASON–TEAM	G	GS	MIN	FGM	FGA	PCT	3FGM	3FGA	PCT	FTM	FTA	PCT	O-RB	D-RB	TOT	AST	PF	DQ	STL	TO	BLK	PTS	RPG	APG	PPG
57-58–New York	72	–	1661	318	838	.379	–	–	–	165	257	.642	–	–	461	69	232	6	–	–	–	801	6.4	1.0	11.1
58-59–N.Y.-Phil.	67	–	842	129	406	.318	–	–	–	78	138	.565	–	–	244	67	158	3	–	–	–	336	3.6	1.0	5.0
59-60–Philadelphia	11	–	80	14	45	.311	–	–	–	2	8	.250	–	–	23	6	20	0	–	–	–	30	2.1	0.5	2.7
Reg. Season Totals	150	–	2583	461	1289	.358	–	–	–	245	403	.608	–	–	728	142	410	9	–	–	–	1167	4.9	0.9	7.8

Sparrow, Rory Darnell b. June 12, 1958 Ht. 6-2 Wt. 175 College: Villanova

SEASON–TEAM	G	GS	MIN	FGM	FGA	PCT	3FGM	3FGA	PCT	FTM	FTA	PCT	O-RB	D-RB	TOT	AST	PF	DQ	STL	TO	BLK	PTS	RPG	APG	PPG
80-81–New Jersey	15	0	212	22	63	.349	0	0	–	12	16	.750	7	11	18	32	15	0	13	18	3	56	1.2	2.1	3.7
81-82–Atlanta	82	82	2610	366	730	.501	1	15	.067	124	148	.838	53	171	224	424	240	2	87	145	13	857	2.7	5.2	10.5
82-83–Atlanta-N.Y.	81	58	2428	392	810	.484	5	22	.227	147	199	.739	61	169	230	397	255	4	107	197	5	936	2.8	4.9	11.6
83-84–New York	79	74	2436	350	738	.474	10	39	.256	108	131	.824	48	141	189	539	230	4	100	210	8	818	2.4	6.8	10.4
84-85–New York	79	41	2292	326	662	.492	7	31	.226	122	141	.865	38	131	169	557	200	2	81	150	9	781	2.1	7.1	9.9
85-86–New York	74	74	2344	345	723	.477	5	20	.250	101	127	.795	50	120	170	472	182	1	85	154	14	796	2.3	6.4	10.8
86-87–New York	80	30	1951	263	590	.446	11	42	.262	71	89	.798	29	86	115	432	160	0	67	140	6	608	1.4	5.4	7.6
87-88–N.Y.-Chicago	58	25	1044	117	293	.399	2	13	.154	24	33	.727	15	57	72	167	79	1	41	58	3	260	1.2	2.9	4.5
88-89–Miami	80	79	2613	444	982	.452	18	74	.243	94	107	.879	55	161	216	429	168	0	103	204	17	1000	2.7	5.4	12.5
89-90–Miami	82	25	1756	210	510	.412	8	40	.200	59	77	.766	37	101	138	298	140	0	49	99	4	487	1.7	3.6	5.9
90-91–Sacramento	80	74	2375	371	756	.491	31	78	.397	58	83	.699	45	141	186	362	189	1	83	126	16	831	2.3	4.5	10.4
91-92–Chi.-Lakers	46	0	489	58	151	.384	3	15	.200	8	13	.615	3	25	28	83	57	0	12	33	5	127	0.6	1.8	2.8
Reg. Season Totals	836	562	22550	3264	7008	.466	101	389	.260	928	1164	.797	441	1314	1755	4192	1915	15	828	1534	103	7557	2.1	5.0	9.0
Playoff Totals	30	20	782	100	240	.417	5	16	.313	52	65	.800	16	35	51	161	82	3	26	54	1	257	1.7	5.4	8.6

Spears, Marion Odicca (Odie) b. June 26, 1925 d. March 28, 1985 Ht. 6-5 Wt. 205 College: Western Kentucky

SEASON–TEAM	G	GS	MIN	FGM	FGA	PCT	3FGM	3FGA	PCT	FTM	FTA	PCT	O-RB	D-RB	TOT	AST	PF	DQ	STL	TO	BLK	PTS	RPG	APG	PPG
48-49–Chicago	57	–	–	200	631	.317	–	–	–	131	197	.665	–	–	–	97	200	–	–	–	–	531	–	1.7	9.3
49-50–Chicago	68	–	–	277	775	.357	–	–	–	158	230	.687	–	–	–	159	250	–	–	–	–	712	–	2.3	10.5
51-52–Rochester	66	–	1673	225	570	.395	–	–	–	116	152	.763	–	–	303	163	225	8	–	–	–	566	4.6	2.5	8.6
52-53–Rochester	62	–	1414	198	494	.401	–	–	–	199	243	.819	–	–	251	113	227	15	–	–	–	595	4.0	1.8	9.6
53-54–Rochester	72	–	1633	184	505	.364	–	–	–	183	238	.769	–	–	310	109	211	5	–	–	–	551	4.3	1.5	7.7
54-55–Rochester	71	–	1888	226	585	.386	–	–	–	220	271	.812	–	–	299	148	252	6	–	–	–	672	4.2	2.1	9.5
55-56–Fort Wayne	72	–	1378	166	468	.355	–	–	–	159	201	.791	–	–	231	121	191	2	–	–	–	491	3.2	1.7	6.8
56-57–FtWayne-St. L.	11	–	118	12	38	.316	–	–	–	19	22	.864	–	–	15	7	24	0	–	–	–	43	1.4	0.6	3.9
Reg. Season Totals	479	–	8104	1488	4066	.366	–	–	–	1185	1554	.763	–	–	1409	917	1580	36	–	–	–	4161	4.0	1.9	8.7
Playoff Totals	32	–	817	74	286	.339	–	–	–	58	91	.637	–	–	123	64	116	5	–	–	–	206	3.1	1.3	6.4

Spector, Arthur Edward (Art, Speed) b. October 17, 1920 d. June 18, 1987 Ht. 6-4 Wt. 200 College: Villanova

SEASON–TEAM	G	GS	MIN	FGM	FGA	PCT	3FGM	3FGA	PCT	FTM	FTA	PCT	O-RB	D-RB	TOT	AST	PF	DQ	STL	TO	BLK	PTS	RPG	APG	PPG
46-47–Boston	55	–	–	123	460	.267	–	–	–	83	150	.553	–	–	–	46	130	–	–	–	–	329	–	0.8	6.0
47-48–Boston	48	–	–	67	243	.276	–	–	–	60	92	.652	–	–	–	17	106	–	–	–	–	194	–	0.4	4.0
48-49–Boston	59	–	–	130	434	.300	–	–	–	64	116	.552	–	–	–	77	111	–	–	–	–	324	–	1.3	5.5
49-50–Boston	7	–	–	2	12	.167	–	–	–	1	4	.250	–	–	–	3	4	–	–	–	–	5	–	0.4	0.7
Reg. Season Totals	169	–	–	322	1149	.280	–	–	–	208	362	.575	–	–	–	143	351	–	–	–	–	852	–	0.8	5.0
Playoff Totals	3	–	–	2	18	.222	–	–	–	2	3	.667	–	–	–	–	18	–	–	–	–	6	–	0.0	2.0

Spencer, Andre b. July 20, 1964 Ht. 6-6 Wt. 210 College: Bakersfield (Calif.) Coll. (J.C.); Northern Arizona

SEASON–TEAM	G	GS	MIN	FGM	FGA	PCT	3FGM	3FGA	PCT	FTM	FTA	PCT	O-RB	D-RB	TOT	AST	PF	DQ	STL	TO	BLK	PTS	RPG	APG	PPG
92-93–Atlanta-G.S.	20	1	422	73	163	.448	0	2	.000	41	54	.759	38	43	81	24	64	0	17	26	7	187	4.1	1.2	9.4
93-94–G.S.-Sac.	28	1	349	52	118	.441	0	0	–	55	77	.714	30	43	73	22	43	0	19	21	7	159	2.6	0.8	5.7
Reg. Season Totals	48	2	771	125	281	.445	0	2	.000	96	131	.733	68	86	154	46	107	0	36	47	14	346	3.2	1.0	7.2

Spencer, Elmore b. December 6, 1969 Ht. 7-0 Wt. 270 College: Georgia, Connors State (Okla.) Coll. (J.C.); Clark County (Nev.) C.C.; UNLV

SEASON–TEAM	G	GS	MIN	FGM	FGA	PCT	3FGM	3FGA	PCT	FTM	FTA	PCT	O-RB	D-RB	TOT	AST	PF	DQ	STL	TO	BLK	PTS	RPG	APG	PPG
92-93–L.A. Clippers	44	4	280	44	82	.537	0	0	–	16	32	.500	17	45	62	8	54	0	8	26	18	104	1.4	0.2	2.4
93-94–L.A. Clippers	76	63	1930	288	540	.533	0	2	.000	97	162	.599	96	319	415	75	208	3	30	168	127	673	5.5	1.0	8.9
94-95–L.A. Clippers	19	8	368	52	118	.441	0	1	.000	28	50	.560	11	54	65	25	62	0	14	48	23	132	3.4	1.3	6.9
95-96–Denver-Port.	17	0	58	5	13	.385	0	0	–	4	6	.667	3	10	13	1	12	1	0	6	2	14	0.8	0.1	0.8
96-97–Seattle	1	0	5	0	1	.000	0	0	–	0	0	–	0	0	0	0	0	0	1	1	0	0	0.0	0.0	0.0
Reg. Season Totals	157	75	2641	389	754	.516	0	3	.000	145	250	.580	127	428	555	109	336	4	53	249	170	923	3.5	0.7	5.9
Playoff Totals	3	0	5	0	2	.000	0	0	–	0	2	.000	1	0	1	–	1	0	0	0	0	0	0.3	0.0	0.0

Spencer, Felton LaFrance b. January 5, 1968 Ht. 7-0 Wt. 265 College: Louisville

SEASON–TEAM	G	GS	MIN	FGM	FGA	PCT	3FGM	3FGA	PCT	FTM	FTA	PCT	O-RB	D-RB	TOT	AST	PF	DQ	STL	TO	BLK	PTS	RPG	APG	PPG
90-91–Minnesota	81	46	2099	195	381	.512	0	1	.000	182	252	.722	272	369	641	25	337	14	48	77	121	572	7.9	0.3	7.1
91-92–Minnesota	61	54	1481	141	331	.426	0	0	–	123	178	.691	167	268	435	53	241	7	27	70	79	405	7.1	0.9	6.6
92-93–Minnesota	71	48	1296	105	226	.465	0	0	–	83	127	.654	134	190	324	17	243	10	23	70	66	293	4.6	0.2	4.1
93-94–Utah	79	79	2210	256	507	.505	0	0	–	165	272	.607	235	423	658	43	304	5	41	127	67	677	8.3	0.5	8.6
94-95–Utah	34	34	905	105	215	.488	0	0	–	107	135	.793	90	170	260	17	131	3	12	68	32	317	7.6	0.5	9.3
95-96–Utah	71	70	1267	146	281	.520	0	0	–	104	151	.689	100	206	306	11	240	1	20	77	54	396	4.3	0.2	5.6
96-97–Orlando-G.S.	73	65	1558	139	284	.489	0	0	–	94	161	.584	157	259	416	22	275	7	34	88	50	372	5.7	0.3	5.1
97-98–Golden State	68	0	813	59	129	.457	0	0	–	44	79	.557	93	133	226	17	175	3	23	49	37	162	3.3	0.3	2.4
98-99–Golden State	26	0	159	15	33	.455	0	0	–	12	26	.462	18	28	46	0	41	0	5	9	10	42	1.8	0.0	1.6
99-00–San Antonio	26	0	149	15	33	.455	0	0	–	20	30	.667	15	24	39	3	32	0	6	9	8	50	1.5	0.1	1.9
Reg. Season Totals	590	396	11937	1176	2420	.486	0	1	.000	934	1411	.662	1281	2070	3351	208	2019	50	239	644	524	3286	5.7	0.4	5.6
Playoff Totals	34	34	768	70	158	.443	0	1	.000	38	59	.644	87	102	189	9	131	3	8	43	42	178	5.6	0.3	5.2

Spicer, Lewis G. (Lou) b. November 12, 1922 d. June 23, 1981 Ht. 6-2 Wt. 195 College: Syracuse

SEASON–TEAM	G	GS	MIN	FGM	FGA	PCT	3FGM	3FGA	PCT	FTM	FTA	PCT	O-RB	D-RB	TOT	AST	PF	DQ	STL	TO	BLK	PTS	RPG	APG	PPG
46-47–Providence	4	–	–	0	7	.000	–	–	–	1	2	.500	–	–	–	0	3	–	–	–	–	1	–	0.0	0.3
Reg. Season Totals	4	–	–	0	7	.000	–	–	–	1	2	.500	–	–	–	0	3	–	–	–	–	1	–	0.0	0.3

Spitzer, Craig W. b. December 18, 1945 Ht. 7-0 Wt. 225 College: Tulane

SEASON–TEAM	G	GS	MIN	FGM	FGA	PCT	3FGM	3FGA	PCT	FTM	FTA	PCT	O-RB	D-RB	TOT	AST	PF	DQ	STL	TO	BLK	PTS	RPG	APG	PPG
67-68–Chicago	10	–	44	8	21	.381	–	–	–	2	3	.667	–	–	24	0	4	0	–	–	–	18	2.4	0.0	1.8
Reg. Season Totals	10	–	44	8	21	.381	–	–	–	2	3	.667	–	–	24	0	4	0	–	–	–	18	2.4	0.0	1.8
Playoff Totals	1	–	3	0	3	.000	–	–	–	0	0	–	–	–	3	1	0	0	–	–	–	0	3.0	1.0	0.0

Spoelstra, Arthur Cornelius (Art) b. September 11, 1932 Ht. 6-9 Wt. 220 College: Western Kentucky

SEASON–TEAM	G	GS	MIN	FGM	FGA	PCT	3FGM	3FGA	PCT	FTM	FTA	PCT	O-RB	D-RB	TOT	AST	PF	DQ	STL	TO	BLK	PTS	RPG	APG	PPG
54-55–Rochester	70	–	1127	159	399	.398	–	–	–	108	156	.692	–	–	285	58	170	2	–	–	–	426	4.1	0.8	6.1
55-56–Rochester	72	–	1640	226	576	.392	–	–	–	163	238	.685	–	–	436	95	248	11	–	–	–	615	6.1	1.3	8.5
56-57–Rochester	69	–	1176	217	559	.388	–	–	–	88	120	.733	–	–	220	56	168	5	–	–	–	522	3.2	0.8	7.6
57-58–Minn.-N.Y.	67	–	1305	161	419	.384	–	–	–	127	187	.679	–	–	332	57	225	11	–	–	–	449	5.0	0.9	6.7
Reg. Season Totals	278	–	5248	763	1953	.391	–	–	–	486	701	.693	–	–	1273	266	811	29	–	–	–	2012	4.6	1.0	7.2
Playoff Totals	3	–	28	7	14	.500	–	–	–	1	1	1.000	–	–	9	–	11	0	–	–	–	15	3.0	0.0	5.0

Spraggins, Warren Bruce (Bruce) b. 1940 Ht. 6-5 Wt. 190 College: Virginia Union

SEASON–TEAM	G	GS	MIN	FGM	FGA	PCT	3FGM	3FGA	PCT	FTM	FTA	PCT	O-RB	D-RB	TOT	AST	PF	DQ	STL	TO	BLK	PTS	RPG	APG	PPG
67-68–New Jersey (A)	70	–	1590	306	686	.446	2	5	.400	238	336	.708	–	–	329	66	173	2	–	81	–	852	4.7	0.9	12.2
Reg. ABA Totals	70	–	1590	306	686	.446	2	5	.400	238	336	.708	–	–	329	66	173	2	–	81	–	852	4.7	0.9	12.2

Sprewell, Latrell Fontaine b. September 8, 1970 Ht. 6-5 Wt. 190 College: Three Rivers (Mo.) C.C.; Alabama

SEASON–TEAM	G	GS	MIN	FGM	FGA	PCT	3FGM	3FGA	PCT	FTM	FTA	PCT	O-RB	D-RB	TOT	AST	PF	DQ	STL	TO	BLK	PTS	RPG	APG	PPG
92-93–Golden State	77	69	2741	449	968	.464	73	198	.369	211	283	.746	79	192	271	295	166	2	126	203	52	1182	3.5	3.8	15.4
93-94–Golden State	82	82	3533	613	1417	.433	141	391	.361	353	456	.774	80	321	401	385	158	0	180	226	76	1720	4.9	4.7	21.0
94-95–Golden State	69	69	2771	490	1171	.418	90	326	.276	350	448	.781	58	198	256	279	108	0	112	230	46	1420	3.7	4.0	20.6
95-96–Golden State	78	78	3064	515	1202	.428	91	282	.323	352	446	.789	124	256	380	328	150	1	127	222	45	1473	4.9	4.2	18.9
96-97–Golden State	80	79	3353	649	1444	.449	147	415	.354	493	585	.843	58	308	366	507	153	0	132	322	45	1938	4.6	6.3	24.2
97-98–Golden State	14	13	547	110	277	.397	9	48	.188	70	94	.745	7	44	51	68	26	0	19	44	5	299	3.6	4.9	21.4
98-99–New York	37	4	1233	215	518	.415	21	77	.273	155	191	.812	41	115	156	91	65	0	46	79	2	606	4.2	2.5	16.4
99-00–New York	82	82	3276	568	1305	.435	44	127	.346	344	397	.866	49	300	349	332	184	0	109	226	22	1524	4.3	4.0	18.6
Reg. Season Totals	519	476	20518	3609	8302	.435	616	1864	.330	2328	2900	.803	496	1734	2230	2285	1010	3	851	1552	293	10162	4.3	4.4	19.6
Playoff Totals	39	27	1565	281	672	.418	22	78	.282	190	233	.815	37	138	175	122	83	1	39	104	14	774	4.5	3.1	19.8
All-Star Totals	3	1	62	14	29	.483	1	7	.143	8	14	.571	7	7	14	6	3	0	5	4	0	37	4.7	2.0	12.3

Spriggs, Larry Michael b. September 8, 1959 Ht. 6-7 Wt. 230 College: San Jacinto (Texas) Coll. (J.C.); Howard

SEASON–TEAM	G	GS	MIN	FGM	FGA	PCT	3FGM	3FGA	PCT	FTM	FTA	PCT	O-RB	D-RB	TOT	AST	PF	DQ	STL	TO	BLK	PTS	RPG	APG	PPG
81-82–Houston	4	0	37	7	11	.636	0	0	–	0	2	.000	2	4	6	4	7	0	2	4	0	14	1.5	1.0	3.5
82-83–Chicago	9	0	39	8	20	.400	0	0	–	5	7	.714	2	7	9	3	3	0	1	2	2	21	1.0	0.3	2.3
83-84–Los Angeles	38	0	363	44	82	.537	0	2	.000	36	50	.720	16	45	61	30	55	0	12	34	4	124	1.6	0.8	3.3
84-85–L.A. Lakers	75	32	1292	194	354	.548	0	3	.000	112	146	.767	77	150	227	132	195	2	47	115	13	500	3.0	1.8	6.7
85-86–L.A. Lakers	43	7	471	88	192	.458	0	1	.000	38	49	.776	28	53	81	49	78	0	18	54	9	214	1.9	1.1	5.0
Reg. Season Totals	169	39	2202	341	659	.517	0	6	.000	191	254	.752	125	259	384	218	338	2	80	209	28	873	2.3	1.3	5.2
Playoff Totals	30	0	297	55	106	.519	0	2	.000	39	51	.765	21	47	68	40	50	0	5	33	6	149	2.3	1.3	5.0

Springer, James E. (Jim) b. June 17, 1926 Ht. 6-9 Wt. 235 Country: Germany

SEASON–TEAM	G	GS	MIN	FGM	FGA	PCT	3FGM	3FGA	PCT	FTM	FTA	PCT	O-RB	D-RB	TOT	AST	PF	DQ	STL	TO	BLK	PTS	RPG	APG	PPG
47-48–And.-Ind. (N)	25	–	–	12	–	–	–	–	–	25	40	.625	–	–	–	–	29	–	–	–	–	49	–	–	2.0
48-49–Indianapolis	2	–	–	0	0	–	–	–	–	1	1	1.000	–	–	–	0	0	–	–	–	–	1	–	0.0	0.5
Reg. NBA Totals	2	–	–	0	0	–	–	–	–	1	1	1.000	–	–	–	0	0	–	–	–	–	1	–	0.0	0.5
Reg. NBL Totals	25	–	–	12	–	–	–	–	–	25	40	.625	–	–	–	–	29	–	–	–	–	49	–	–	2.0
NBL Playoff Totals	3	–	–	0	–	–	–	–	–	0	2	.000	–	–	–	–	3	–	–	–	–	0	–	–	0.0

Spruill, James Winfred (Jim) b. February 26, 1923 Ht. 6-2 Wt. 225 College: Rice

SEASON–TEAM	G	GS	MIN	FGM	FGA	PCT	3FGM	3FGA	PCT	FTM	FTA	PCT	O-RB	D-RB	TOT	AST	PF	DQ	STL	TO	BLK	PTS	RPG	APG	PPG
48-49–Indianapolis	1	–	–	1	3	.333	–	–	–	0	0	–	–	–	–	0	3	–	–	–	–	2	–	0.0	2.0
Reg. Season Totals	1	–	–	1	3	.333	–	–	–	0	0	–	–	–	–	0	3	–	–	–	–	2	–	0.0	2.0

Stacey, Robert L. (see Stacey Arceneaux)

Stack, Ryan Eugene b. July 24, 1975 Ht. 6-11 Wt. 221 College: South Carolina

SEASON–TEAM	G	GS	MIN	FGM	FGA	PCT	3FGM	3FGA	PCT	FTM	FTA	PCT	O-RB	D-RB	TOT	AST	PF	DQ	STL	TO	BLK	PTS	RPG	APG	PPG
98-99–Cleveland	18	0	199	14	37	.378	0	0	–	19	20	.950	19	15	34	5	31	0	2	9	11	47	1.9	0.3	2.6
99-00–Cleveland	25	0	198	17	51	.333	0	1	.000	18	27	.667	15	30	45	5	47	3	4	17	11	52	1.8	0.2	2.1
Reg. Season Totals	43	0	397	31	88	.352	0	1	.000	37	47	.787	34	45	79	10	78	3	6	26	22	99	1.8	0.2	2.3

Stackhouse, Jerry Darnell b. November 5, 1974 Ht. 6-6 Wt. 218 College: North Carolina

SEASON–TEAM	G	GS	MIN	FGM	FGA	PCT	3FGM	3FGA	PCT	FTM	FTA	PCT	O-RB	D-RB	TOT	AST	PF	DQ	STL	TO	BLK	PTS	RPG	APG	PPG
95-96–Philadelphia	72	71	2701	452	1091	.414	93	292	.318	387	518	.747	90	175	265	278	179	0	76	252	79	1384	3.7	3.9	19.2
96-97–Philadelphia	81	81	3166	533	1308	.407	102	342	.298	511	667	.766	156	182	338	253	219	2	93	316	63	1679	4.2	3.1	20.7
97-98–Phil.-Detroit	79	37	2545	424	975	.435	47	195	.241	354	450	.787	105	161	266	241	175	2	89	224	59	1249	3.4	3.1	15.8
98-99–Detroit	42	9	1188	181	488	.371	35	126	.278	210	247	.850	26	81	107	118	79	0	34	121	19	607	2.5	2.8	14.5
99-00–Detroit	82	82	3148	619	1447	.428	83	288	.288	618	758	.815	118	197	315	365	188	1	103	311	36	1939	3.8	4.5	23.6
Reg. Season Totals	356	280	12748	2209	5309	.416	360	1243	.290	2080	2640	.788	495	796	1291	1255	840	5	395	1224	256	6858	3.6	3.5	19.3
Playoff Totals	8	3	244	42	105	.400	5	15	.333	35	45	.778	4	16	20	16	15	0	4	24	1	124	2.5	2.0	15.5
All-Star Totals	1	0	14	4	7	.571	0	0	–	0	0	–	0	1	1	2	2	0	0	1	0	8	1.0	2.0	8.0

Stacom, Kevin M. b. September 4, 1951 Ht. 6-3 Wt. 185 College: Holy Cross; Providence

SEASON–TEAM	G	GS	MIN	FGM	FGA	PCT	3FGM	3FGA	PCT	FTM	FTA	PCT	O-RB	D-RB	TOT	AST	PF	DQ	STL	TO	BLK	PTS	RPG	APG	PPG
74-75–Boston	61	–	447	72	159	.453	–	–	–	29	33	.879	30	25	55	49	65	0	11	–	3	173	0.9	0.8	2.8
75-76–Boston	77	–	1114	170	387	.439	–	–	–	68	91	.747	62	99	161	128	117	0	23	–	5	408	2.1	1.7	5.3
76-77–Boston	79	–	1051	179	438	.409	–	–	–	46	58	.793	40	57	97	117	65	0	19	–	3	404	1.2	1.5	5.1
77-78–Boston	55	–	1006	206	484	.426	–	–	–	54	71	.761	26	80	106	111	60	0	28	69	3	466	1.9	2.0	8.5
78-79–Indiana-Bos.	68	–	831	128	342	.374	–	–	–	44	60	.733	30	55	85	112	47	0	29	80	1	300	1.3	1.6	4.4
81-82–Milwaukee	7	0	90	14	34	.412	1	2	.500	1	2	.500	2	5	7	7	6	0	1	9	0	30	1.0	1.0	4.3
Reg. Season Totals	347	0	4539	769	1844	.417	1	2	.500	242	315	.768	190	321	511	524	360	0	111	158	15	1781	1.5	1.5	5.1
Playoff Totals	26	0	227	16	53	.302	0	0	–	9	12	.750	9	10	19	21	24	0	5	–	0	41	0.7	0.8	1.6

Staggs, James Ervin (Erv) b. 1948 Ht. 6-6 Wt. 195 College: Cheyney

SEASON–TEAM	G	GS	MIN	FGM	FGA	PCT	3FGM	3FGA	PCT	FTM	FTA	PCT	O-RB	D-RB	TOT	AST	PF	DQ	STL	TO	BLK	PTS	RPG	APG	PPG
69-70–Miami (A)	53	–	1058	189	474	.399	2	7	.286	73	114	.640	–	–	122	76	155	7	–	–	–	453	2.3	1.4	8.5
Reg. ABA Totals	53	–	1058	189	474	.399	2	7	.286	73	114	.640	–	–	122	76	155	7	–	–	–	453	2.3	1.4	8.5

Stallworth, David A. (Dave, The Rave) b. December 20, 1941 Ht. 6-7 Wt. 200 College: Wichita State

SEASON–TEAM	G	GS	MIN	FGM	FGA	PCT	3FGM	3FGA	PCT	FTM	FTA	PCT	O-RB	D-RB	TOT	AST	PF	DQ	STL	TO	BLK	PTS	RPG	APG	PPG
65-66–New York	80	–	1893	373	820	.455	–	–	–	258	376	.686	–	–	492	186	237	4	–	–	–	1004	6.2	2.3	12.6
66-67–New York	76	–	1889	380	816	.466	–	–	–	229	320	.716	–	–	472	144	226	4	–	–	–	989	6.2	1.9	13.0
69-70–New York	82	–	1375	239	557	.429	–	–	–	161	225	.716	–	–	323	139	194	2	–	–	–	639	3.9	1.7	7.8
70-71–New York	81	–	1565	295	685	.431	–	–	–	169	230	.735	–	–	352	106	175	1	–	–	–	759	4.3	1.3	9.4
71-72–N.Y.-Balt.	78	–	2040	336	778	.432	–	–	–	152	188	.809	–	–	433	158	217	3	–	–	–	824	5.6	2.0	10.6
72-73–Baltimore	73	–	1217	180	435	.414	–	–	–	78	101	.772	–	–	236	112	139	1	–	–	–	438	3.2	1.5	6.0
73-74–Capital	45	–	458	75	187	.401	–	–	–	47	55	.855	52	73	125	25	61	0	28	–	4	197	2.8	0.6	4.4
74-75–New York	7	–	57	5	18	.278	–	–	–	0	0	–	6	14	20	2	10	0	3	–	3	10	2.9	0.3	1.4
Reg. Season Totals	522	–	10494	1883	4296	.438	–	–	–	1094	1495	.732	58	87	2453	872	1259	15	31	–	7	4860	4.7	1.7	9.3
Playoff Totals	40	–	579	92	230	.400	–	–	–	52	68	.765	0	0	137	36	79	0	0	–	0	236	3.4	0.9	5.9

Stallworth, Isaac (Bud) b. January 18, 1950 Ht. 6-5 Wt. 190 College: Kansas

SEASON–TEAM	G	GS	MIN	FGM	FGA	PCT	3FGM	3FGA	PCT	FTM	FTA	PCT	O-RB	D-RB	TOT	AST	PF	DQ	STL	TO	BLK	PTS	RPG	APG	PPG
72-73–Seattle	77	–	1225	198	522	.379	–	–	–	86	114	.754	–	–	225	58	138	0	–	–	–	482	2.9	0.8	6.3
73-74–Seattle	67	–	1019	188	479	.392	–	–	–	48	77	.623	51	123	174	33	129	0	21	–	12	424	2.6	0.5	6.3
74-75–New Orleans	73	–	1668	298	710	.420	–	–	–	125	182	.687	78	168	246	46	208	4	59	–	11	721	3.4	0.6	9.9
75-76–New Orleans	56	–	1051	211	483	.437	–	–	–	85	124	.685	42	103	145	53	135	1	30	–	17	507	2.6	0.9	9.1
76-77–New Orleans	40	–	526	126	272	.463	–	–	–	17	29	.586	19	52	71	23	76	1	19	–	11	269	1.8	0.6	6.7
Reg. Season Totals	313	–	5489	1021	2466	.414	–	–	–	361	526	.686	190	446	861	213	686	6	129	–	51	2403	2.8	0.7	7.7

Stanczak, Edmund A. (Ed, Moose) b. August 15, 1921 Ht. 6-3 Wt. 205 College: None

SEASON–TEAM	G	GS	MIN	FGM	FGA	PCT	3FGM	3FGA	PCT	FTM	FTA	PCT	O-RB	D-RB	TOT	AST	PF	DQ	STL	TO	BLK	PTS	RPG	APG	PPG
46-47–Anderson (N)	44	–	–	142	–	–	–	–	–	118	201	.587	–	–	–	–	109	–	–	–	–	402	–	–	9.1
47-48–Anderson (N)	55	–	–	73	–	–	–	–	–	61	102	.598	–	–	–	–	95	–	–	–	–	207	–	–	3.8
48-49–Anderson (N)	64	–	–	191	–	–	–	–	–	202	275	.735	–	–	–	–	209	–	–	–	–	584	–	–	9.1
49-50–Anderson	57	–	–	159	456	.349	–	–	–	203	270	.752	–	–	–	67	166	–	–	–	–	521	–	1.2	9.1
50-51–Boston	17	–	–	11	48	.229	–	–	–	35	43	.814	–	–	34	6	6	0	–	–	–	57	2.0	0.4	3.4
Reg. NBA Totals	74	–	–	170	504	.337	–	–	–	238	313	.760	–	–	34	73	172	0	–	–	–	578	2.0	1.0	7.8
Reg. NBL Totals	163	–	–	406	–	–	–	–	–	381	578	.659	–	–	–	–	413	–	–	–	–	1193	–	–	7.3
NBA Playoff Totals	8	–	–	14	96	.292	–	–	–	23	30	.767	–	–	–	20	26	1	–	–	–	51	–	1.3	6.4
NBL Playoff Totals	13	–	–	17	–	–	–	–	–	27	46	.587	–	–	–	–	41	–	–	–	–	61	–	–	4.7

Stansbury, Terence R. b. February 27, 1961 Ht. 6-5 Wt. 175 College: Temple

SEASON–TEAM	G	GS	MIN	FGM	FGA	PCT	3FGM	3FGA	PCT	FTM	FTA	PCT	O-RB	D-RB	TOT	AST	PF	DQ	STL	TO	BLK	PTS	RPG	APG	PPG
84-85–Indiana	74	14	1278	210	458	.459	4	25	.160	102	126	.810	39	75	114	127	205	2	47	80	12	526	1.5	1.7	7.1
85-86–Indiana	74	17	1331	191	441	.433	9	53	.170	107	132	.811	29	110	139	206	200	2	59	139	8	498	1.9	2.8	6.7
86-87–Seattle	44	0	375	67	156	.429	11	29	.379	31	50	.620	8	16	24	57	78	0	13	29	0	176	0.5	1.3	4.0
Reg. Season Totals	192	31	2984	468	1055	.444	24	107	.224	240	308	.779	76	201	277	390	483	4	119	248	20	1200	1.4	2.0	6.3

Starks, John Levell b. August 10, 1965 Ht. 6-5 Wt. 185 College: Northern Oklahoma Coll. (J.C.); Rogers State (Okla.) Coll. (J.C.); Oklahoma Junior College; Oklahoma State

SEASON–TEAM	G	GS	MIN	FGM	FGA	PCT	3FGM	3FGA	PCT	FTM	FTA	PCT	O-RB	D-RB	TOT	AST	PF	DQ	STL	TO	BLK	PTS	RPG	APG	PPG
88-89–Golden State	36	0	316	51	125	.408	10	26	.385	34	52	.654	15	26	41	27	36	0	23	39	3	146	1.1	0.8	4.1
90-91–New York	61	10	1173	180	410	.439	27	93	.290	79	105	.752	30	101	131	204	137	1	59	74	17	466	2.1	3.3	7.6
91-92–New York	82	0	2118	405	902	.449	94	270	.348	235	302	.778	45	146	191	276	231	4	103	150	18	1139	2.3	3.4	13.9
92-93–New York	80	51	2477	513	1199	.428	108	336	.321	263	331	.795	54	150	204	404	234	3	91	173	12	1397	2.6	5.1	17.5
93-94–New York	59	54	2057	410	977	.420	113	337	.335	187	248	.754	37	148	185	348	191	4	95	184	6	1120	3.1	5.9	19.0
94-95–New York	80	78	2725	419	1062	.395	217	611	.355	168	228	.737	34	185	219	411	257	3	92	160	4	1223	2.7	5.1	15.3
95-96–New York	81	71	2491	375	846	.443	143	396	.361	131	174	.753	31	206	237	315	226	2	103	156	11	1024	2.9	3.9	12.6
96-97–New York	77	1	2042	369	856	.431	150	407	.369	173	225	.769	36	169	205	217	196	2	90	158	11	1061	2.7	2.8	13.8
97-98–New York	82	10	2188	372	947	.393	130	398	.327	185	235	.787	48	182	230	219	205	2	78	143	5	1059	2.8	2.7	12.9
98-99–Golden State	50	50	1686	269	728	.370	78	269	.290	74	100	.740	33	130	163	235	135	3	69	83	5	690	3.3	4.7	13.8
99-00–G.S.-Chicago	37	30	1190	203	542	.375	59	171	.345	50	59	.847	10	91	101	181	102	1	42	67	4	515	2.7	4.9	13.9
Reg. Season Totals	725	355	20463	3566	8594	.415	1129	3314	.341	1579	2059	.767	373	1534	1907	2837	1950	25	845	1387	96	9840	2.6	3.9	13.6
Playoff Totals	93	55	2999	446	1057	.422	175	471	.372	285	376	.758	37	231	268	392	318	4	119	222	8	1352	2.9	4.2	14.5
All-Star Totals	1	0	20	4	9	.444	1	3	.333	0	0	–	1	2	3	3	1	0	1	2	0	9	3.0	3.0	9.0

Starr, Keith Edward b. March 14, 1954 Ht. 6-7 Wt. 195 College: Pittsburgh

SEASON–TEAM	G	GS	MIN	FGM	FGA	PCT	3FGM	3FGA	PCT	FTM	FTA	PCT	O-RB	D-RB	TOT	AST	PF	DQ	STL	TO	BLK	PTS	RPG	APG	PPG
76-77–Chicago	17	–	65	6	24	.250	–	–	–	2	2	1.000	6	4	10	6	11	0	1	–	0	14	0.6	0.4	0.8
Reg. Season Totals	17	–	65	6	24	.250	–	–	–	2	2	1.000	6	4	10	6	11	0	1	–	0	14	0.6	0.4	0.8

Staverman, Larry Joseph b. October 11, 1936 Ht. 6-7 Wt. 205 College: Thomas More

SEASON–TEAM	G	GS	MIN	FGM	FGA	PCT	3FGM	3FGA	PCT	FTM	FTA	PCT	O-RB	D-RB	TOT	AST	PF	DQ	STL	TO	BLK	PTS	RPG	APG	PPG
58-59–Cincinnati	57	–	681	101	215	.470	–	–	–	45	59	.763	–	–	218	54	103	0	–	–	–	247	3.8	0.9	4.3
59-60–Cincinnati	49	–	479	70	149	.470	–	–	–	47	64	.734	–	–	180	36	98	0	–	–	–	187	3.7	0.7	3.8
60-61–Cincinnati	66	–	944	111	249	.446	–	–	–	79	93	.849	–	–	287	86	164	4	–	–	–	301	4.3	1.3	4.6
62-63–Chicago	33	–	602	94	194	.485	–	–	–	49	62	.790	–	–	158	43	94	3	–	–	–	237	4.8	1.3	7.2
63-64–Balt.-Det.-Cin.	60	–	674	98	212	.462	–	–	–	69	90	.767	–	–	176	32	118	3	–	–	–	265	2.9	0.5	4.4
Reg. Season Totals	265	–	3380	474	1019	.465	–	–	–	289	368	.785	–	–	1019	251	577	10	–	–	–	1237	3.8	0.9	4.7
Playoff Totals	7	–	70	11	23	.478	–	–	–	15	19	.789	–	–	26	5	16	0	–	–	–	37	3.7	0.7	5.3

Steele, Larry Nelson b. May 5, 1949 Ht. 6-5 Wt. 180 College: Kentucky

SEASON–TEAM	G	GS	MIN	FGM	FGA	PCT	3FGM	3FGA	PCT	FTM	FTA	PCT	O-RB	D-RB	TOT	AST	PF	DQ	STL	TO	BLK	PTS	RPG	APG	PPG
71-72–Portland	72	–	1311	148	308	.481	–	–	–	70	97	.722	–	–	282	161	198	8	–	–	–	366	3.9	2.2	5.1
72-73–Portland	66	–	1301	159	329	.483	–	–	–	71	89	.798	–	–	154	156	181	4	–	–	–	389	2.3	2.4	5.9
73-74–Portland	81	–	2648	325	680	.478	–	–	–	135	171	.789	89	221	310	323	295	10	217	–	32	785	3.8	4.0	9.7
74-75–Portland	76	–	2389	265	484	.548	–	–	–	122	146	.836	86	140	226	287	254	6	183	–	16	652	3.0	3.8	8.6
75-76–Portland	81	–	2382	322	651	.495	–	–	–	154	203	.759	77	215	292	324	289	8	170	–	19	798	3.6	4.0	9.9
76-77–Portland	81	–	1680	326	652	.500	–	–	–	183	227	.806	71	117	188	172	216	3	118	–	13	835	2.3	2.1	10.3
77-78–Portland	65	–	1132	210	447	.470	–	–	–	100	122	.820	34	79	113	87	138	2	59	66	5	520	1.7	1.3	8.0
78-79–Portland	72	–	1488	203	483	.420	–	–	–	112	136	.824	58	113	171	142	208	4	74	96	10	518	2.4	2.0	7.2
79-80–Portland	16	–	446	62	146	.425	0	4	.000	22	27	.815	13	32	45	67	53	0	25	33	1	146	2.8	4.2	9.1
Reg. Season Totals	610	–	14777	2020	4180	.483	0	4	.000	969	1218	.796	428	917	1781	1719	1832	45	846	195	96	5009	2.9	2.8	8.2
Playoff Totals	27	–	525	67	158	.424	0	0	–	51	62	.823	26	38	64	39	60	0	26	15	2	185	2.4	1.4	6.9

Steigenga, Matthew Todd (Matt) b. March 27, 1970 Ht. 6-7 Wt. 200 College: Michigan State

SEASON–TEAM	G	GS	MIN	FGM	FGA	PCT	3FGM	3FGA	PCT	FTM	FTA	PCT	O-RB	D-RB	TOT	AST	PF	DQ	STL	TO	BLK	PTS	RPG	APG	PPG
96-97–Chicago	2	0	12	1	4	.250	0	2	.000	1	2	.500	0	3	3	2	1	0	1	2	1	3	1.5	1.0	1.5
Reg. Season Totals	2	0	12	1	4	.250	0	2	.000	1	2	.500	0	3	3	2	1	0	1	2	1	3	1.5	1.0	1.5

Stepania, Vladimir b. August 5, 1976 Ht. 7-0 Wt. 236 Country: Slovenia

SEASON–TEAM	G	GS	MIN	FGM	FGA	PCT	3FGM	3FGA	PCT	FTM	FTA	PCT	O-RB	D-RB	TOT	AST	PF	DQ	STL	TO	BLK	PTS	RPG	APG	PPG
98-99–Seattle	23	6	313	53	125	.424	0	3	.000	21	40	.525	27	48	75	12	58	0	10	32	23	127	3.3	0.5	5.5
99-00–Seattle	30	1	202	29	79	.367	0	6	.000	17	36	.472	21	26	47	3	44	0	10	22	11	75	1.6	0.1	2.5
Reg. Season Totals	53	7	515	82	204	.402	0	9	.000	38	76	.500	48	74	122	15	102	0	20	54	34	202	2.3	0.3	3.8

Stephens, Everette Louis b. October 21, 1966 Ht. 6-2 Wt. 175 College: Purdue

SEASON–TEAM	G	GS	MIN	FGM	FGA	PCT	3FGM	3FGA	PCT	FTM	FTA	PCT	O-RB	D-RB	TOT	AST	PF	DQ	STL	TO	BLK	PTS	RPG	APG	PPG
88-89–Indiana	35	0	209	23	72	.319	2	10	.200	17	22	.773	11	12	23	37	22	0	9	29	4	65	0.7	1.1	1.9
90-91–Milwaukee	3	0	6	2	3	.667	0	0	–	2	2	1.000	0	0	0	2	0	0	0	0	0	6	0.0	0.7	2.0
Reg. Season Totals	38	0	215	25	75	.333	2	10	.200	19	24	.792	11	12	23	39	22	0	9	29	4	71	0.6	1.0	1.9

Stephens, Joe b. January 28, 1973 Ht. 6-7 Wt. 210 College: Arkansas-Little Rock

SEASON–TEAM	G	GS	MIN	FGM	FGA	PCT	3FGM	3FGA	PCT	FTM	FTA	PCT	O-RB	D-RB	TOT	AST	PF	DQ	STL	TO	BLK	PTS	RPG	APG	PPG
96-97–Houston	2	0	9	1	5	.200	1	3	.333	0	0	–	2	1	3	0	3	0	3	3	0	3	1.5	0.0	1.5
97-98–Houston	7	0	37	10	28	.357	3	10	.300	4	6	.667	3	3	6	1	2	0	2	2	0	27	0.9	0.1	3.9
99-00–Vancouver	13	0	181	19	51	.373	0	8	.000	3	4	.750	13	23	36	11	9	0	7	6	3	41	2.8	0.8	3.2
Reg. Season Totals	22	0	227	30	84	.357	4	21	.190	7	10	.700	18	27	45	12	14	0	12	11	3	71	2.0	0.5	3.2

Stephens, John Francis (Jack) b. May 18, 1933 Ht. 6-3 Wt. 185 College: Notre Dame

SEASON–TEAM	G	GS	MIN	FGM	FGA	PCT	3FGM	3FGA	PCT	FTM	FTA	PCT	O-RB	D-RB	TOT	AST	PF	DQ	STL	TO	BLK	PTS	RPG	APG	PPG
55-56–St. Louis	72	–	2219	248	643	.386	–	–	–	247	357	.692	–	–	377	207	144	6	–	–	–	743	5.2	2.9	10.3
Reg. Season Totals	72	–	2219	248	643	.386	–	–	–	247	357	.692	–	–	377	207	144	6	–	–	–	743	5.2	2.9	10.3
Playoff Totals	7	–	116	12	41	.293	–	–	–	15	25	.600	–	–	23	9	9	0	–	–	–	39	3.3	1.3	5.6

Steppe, Michael Holbrook (Brook) b. November 7, 1959 Ht. 6-5 Wt. 195 College: Northern Illinois; Georgia Tech

SEASON–TEAM	G	GS	MIN	FGM	FGA	PCT	3FGM	3FGA	PCT	FTM	FTA	PCT	O-RB	D-RB	TOT	AST	PF	DQ	STL	TO	BLK	PTS	RPG	APG	PPG
82-83–Kansas City	62	6	606	84	176	.477	1	7	.143	76	100	.760	25	48	73	68	92	0	26	55	3	245	1.2	1.1	4.0
83-84–Indiana	61	13	857	148	314	.471	0	3	.000	134	161	.832	43	79	122	79	93	0	34	83	6	430	2.0	1.3	7.0
84-85–Detroit	54	0	486	83	178	.466	0	1	.000	87	104	.837	25	32	57	36	61	0	16	43	4	253	1.1	0.7	4.7
86-87–Sacramento	34	7	665	95	199	.477	3	9	.333	73	88	.830	21	40	61	81	56	0	18	54	3	266	1.8	2.4	7.8
88-89–Portland	27	2	244	33	78	.423	5	9	.556	32	37	.865	13	19	32	16	32	0	11	13	1	103	1.2	0.6	3.8
Reg. Season Totals	238	28	2858	443	945	.469	9	29	.310	402	490	.820	127	218	345	280	334	0	105	248	17	1297	1.4	1.2	5.4
Playoff Totals	4	0	20	2	7	.286	0	1	.000	4	6	.667	1	2	3	2	3	0	0	2	0	8	0.8	0.5	2.0

Stevens, Barry Wayne b. January 17, 1963 Ht. 6-5 Wt. 195 College: Iowa State

SEASON–TEAM	G	GS	MIN	FGM	FGA	PCT	3FGM	3FGA	PCT	FTM	FTA	PCT	O-RB	D-RB	TOT	AST	PF	DQ	STL	TO	BLK	PTS	RPG	APG	PPG
92-93–Golden State	2	0	6	1	2	.500	0	0	–	0	0	–	2	0	2	0	1	0	0	0	0	2	1.0	0.0	1.0
Reg. Season Totals	2	0	6	1	2	.500	0	0	–	0	0	–	2	0	2	0	1	0	0	0	0	2	1.0	0.0	1.0

Stevens, Wayne b. June 19, 1936 Ht. 6-3 Wt. 185 College: Cincinnati

SEASON–TEAM	G	GS	MIN	FGM	FGA	PCT	3FGM	3FGA	PCT	FTM	FTA	PCT	O-RB	D-RB	TOT	AST	PF	DQ	STL	TO	BLK	PTS	RPG	APG	PPG
59-60–Cincinnati	8	–	49	3	19	.158	–	–	–	7	10	.700	–	–	16	4	4	0	–	–	–	13	2.0	0.5	1.6
Reg. Season Totals	8	–	49	3	19	.158	–	–	–	7	10	.700	–	–	16	4	4	0	–	–	–	13	2.0	0.5	1.6

Stewart, Dennis Edward b. April 11, 1947 Ht. 6-6 Wt. 220 College: Michigan

SEASON–TEAM	G	GS	MIN	FGM	FGA	PCT	3FGM	3FGA	PCT	FTM	FTA	PCT	O-RB	D-RB	TOT	AST	PF	DQ	STL	TO	BLK	PTS	RPG	APG	PPG
70-71–Baltimore	2	–	6	1	4	.250	–	–	–	2	2	1.000	–	–	3	1	0	0	–	–	–	4	1.5	0.5	2.0
70-71–Floridians (A)	10	–	66	15	44	.341	1	3	.333	5	7	.714	–	–	14	1	12	–	–	–	–	36	1.4	0.1	3.6
Reg. NBA Totals	2	–	6	1	4	.250	–	–	–	2	2	1.000	–	–	3	1	0	0	–	–	–	4	1.5	0.5	2.0
Reg. ABA Totals	10	–	66	15	44	.341	1	3	.333	5	7	.714	–	–	14	1	12	–	–	–	–	36	1.4	0.1	3.6

Stewart, Kebu b. December 19, 1973 Ht. 6-8 Wt. 239 College: Nevada-Las Vegas; Cal State-Bakersfield

SEASON–TEAM	G	GS	MIN	FGM	FGA	PCT	3FGM	3FGA	PCT	FTM	FTA	PCT	O-RB	D-RB	TOT	AST	PF	DQ	STL	TO	BLK	PTS	RPG	APG	PPG
97-98–Philadelphia	15	0	110	12	26	.462	0	0	–	16	25	.640	9	22	31	2	13	0	5	8	2	40	2.1	0.1	2.7
Reg. Season Totals	15	0	110	12	26	.462	0	0	–	16	25	.640	9	22	31	2	13	0	5	8	2	40	2.1	0.1	2.7

Stewart, Larry b. September 21, 1968 Ht. 6-8 Wt. 230 College: Coppin State

SEASON–TEAM	G	GS	MIN	FGM	FGA	PCT	3FGM	3FGA	PCT	FTM	FTA	PCT	O-RB	D-RB	TOT	AST	PF	DQ	STL	TO	BLK	PTS	RPG	APG	PPG
91-92–Washington	76	43	2229	303	590	.514	0	3	.000	188	233	.807	186	263	449	120	225	3	51	112	44	794	5.9	1.6	10.4
92-93–Washington	81	8	1823	306	564	.543	0	2	.000	184	253	.727	154	229	383	146	191	1	47	153	29	796	4.7	1.8	9.8
93-94–Washington	3	0	35	3	8	.375	0	0	–	7	10	.700	1	6	7	2	4	0	2	2	1	13	2.3	0.7	4.3
94-95–Washington	40	0	346	41	89	.461	0	2	.000	20	30	.667	28	39	67	18	52	0	16	16	9	102	1.7	0.5	2.6
96-97–Seattle	70	21	982	112	252	.444	9	37	.243	67	93	.720	75	96	171	52	108	0	31	63	23	300	2.4	0.7	4.3
Reg. Season Totals	270	72	5415	765	1503	.509	9	44	.205	466	619	.753	444	633	1077	338	580	4	147	346	106	2005	4.0	1.3	7.4
Playoff Totals	4	0	16	5	6	.833	1	2	.500	2	2	1.000	0	1	1	2	4	0	2	2	1	13	0.3	0.5	3.3

Stewart, Michael b. April 24, 1975 Ht. 6-10 Wt. 230 College: California

SEASON–TEAM	G	GS	MIN	FGM	FGA	PCT	3FGM	3FGA	PCT	FTM	FTA	PCT	O-RB	D-RB	TOT	AST	PF	DQ	STL	TO	BLK	PTS	RPG	APG	PPG
97-98–Sacramento	81	37	1761	155	323	.480	0	0	–	65	142	.458	197	339	536	61	251	6	29	85	195	375	6.6	0.8	4.6
98-99–Toronto	42	2	394	22	53	.415	0	0	–	17	25	.680	43	56	99	5	76	0	4	12	28	61	2.4	0.1	1.5
99-00–Toronto	42	1	389	20	53	.377	0	0	–	18	32	.563	33	61	94	6	81	3	5	17	19	58	2.2	0.1	1.4
Reg. Season Totals	165	40	2544	197	429	.459	0	0	–	100	199	.503	273	456	729	72	408	9	38	114	242	494	4.4	0.4	3.0

Stewart, Norman E. (Norm) b. January 20, 1935 Ht. 6-5 Wt. 205 College: Missouri

SEASON–TEAM	G	GS	MIN	FGM	FGA	PCT	3FGM	3FGA	PCT	FTM	FTA	PCT	O-RB	D-RB	TOT	AST	PF	DQ	STL	TO	BLK	PTS	RPG	APG	PPG
56-57–St. Louis	5	–	37	4	15	.267	–	–	–	2	6	.333	–	–	5	2	9	0	–	–	–	10	1.0	0.4	2.0
Reg. Season Totals	5	–	37	4	15	.267	–	–	–	2	6	.333	–	–	5	2	9	0	–	–	–	10	1.0	0.4	2.0

Stipanovich, Stephen Samuel (Steve) b. November 17, 1960 Ht. 7-0 Wt. 250 College: Missouri

SEASON–TEAM	G	GS	MIN	FGM	FGA	PCT	3FGM	3FGA	PCT	FTM	FTA	PCT	O-RB	D-RB	TOT	AST	PF	DQ	STL	TO	BLK	PTS	RPG	APG	PPG
83-84–Indiana	81	73	2426	392	816	.480	3	16	.188	183	243	.753	116	446	562	170	303	4	73	161	67	970	6.9	2.1	12.0
84-85–Indiana	82	66	2315	414	871	.475	1	11	.091	297	372	.798	141	473	614	199	265	4	71	184	78	1126	7.5	2.4	13.7
85-86–Indiana	79	65	2397	416	885	.470	2	10	.200	242	315	.768	173	450	623	206	261	1	75	146	69	1076	7.9	2.6	13.6
86-87–Indiana	81	81	2761	382	760	.503	1	4	.250	307	367	.837	184	486	670	180	304	9	106	130	97	1072	8.3	2.2	13.2
87-88–Indiana	80	80	2692	411	828	.496	3	15	.200	254	314	.809	157	505	662	183	302	8	90	156	69	1079	8.3	2.3	13.5
Reg. Season Totals	403	365	12591	2015	4160	.484	10	56	.179	1283	1611	.796	771	2360	3131	938	1435	26	415	777	380	5323	7.8	2.3	13.2
Playoff Totals	4	4	149	21	38	.553	0	1	.000	13	19	.684	7	23	30	3	14	0	3	4	2	55	7.5	0.8	13.8

Stith, Bryant Lamonica b. December 10, 1970 Ht. 6-5 Wt. 210 College: Virginia

SEASON–TEAM	G	GS	MIN	FGM	FGA	PCT	3FGM	3FGA	PCT	FTM	FTA	PCT	O-RB	D-RB	TOT	AST	PF	DQ	STL	TO	BLK	PTS	RPG	APG	PPG
92-93–Denver	39	12	865	124	278	.446	0	4	.000	99	119	.832	39	85	124	49	82	0	24	44	5	347	3.2	1.3	8.9
93-94–Denver	82	82	2853	365	811	.450	2	9	.222	291	351	.829	119	230	349	199	165	0	116	131	16	1023	4.3	2.4	12.5
94-95–Denver	81	51	2329	312	661	.472	20	68	.294	267	324	.824	95	173	268	153	142	0	91	110	18	911	3.3	1.9	11.2
95-96–Denver	82	77	2810	379	911	.416	41	148	.277	320	379	.844	125	275	400	241	187	3	114	157	16	1119	4.9	2.9	13.6
96-97–Denver	52	52	1788	251	603	.416	70	182	.385	202	234	.863	74	143	217	133	119	1	60	101	20	774	4.2	2.6	14.9
97-98–Denver	31	15	718	75	225	.333	10	48	.208	75	86	.872	15	50	65	50	52	0	21	35	8	235	2.1	1.6	7.6
98-99–Denver	46	32	1194	114	290	.393	31	106	.292	61	71	.859	30	77	107	82	65	0	28	45	15	320	2.3	1.8	7.0
99-00–Denver	45	6	691	86	189	.455	17	56	.304	64	77	.831	23	61	84	61	56	0	18	33	12	253	1.9	1.4	5.6
Reg. Season Totals	458	327	13248	1706	3968	.430	191	621	.308	1379	1641	.840	520	1094	1614	968	868	4	472	656	110	4982	3.5	2.1	10.9
Playoff Totals	15	13	498	60	134	.448	1	7	.143	65	79	.823	26	39	65	33	30	0	12	14	3	186	4.3	2.2	12.4

Stith, Samuel Elwood (Sam) b. July 22, 1937 Ht. 6-2 Wt. 185 College: St. Bonaventure

SEASON–TEAM	G	GS	MIN	FGM	FGA	PCT	3FGM	3FGA	PCT	FTM	FTA	PCT	O-RB	D-RB	TOT	AST	PF	DQ	STL	TO	BLK	PTS	RPG	APG	PPG
61-62–New York	32	–	440	59	162	.364	–	–	–	23	38	.605	–	–	51	60	55	0	–	–	–	141	1.6	1.9	4.4
Reg. Season Totals	32	–	440	59	162	.364	–	–	–	23	38	.605	–	–	51	60	55	0	–	–	–	141	1.6	1.9	4.4

Stith, Thomas Alvin (Tom) b. January 21, 1939 Ht. 6-5 Wt. 210 College: St. Bonaventure

SEASON–TEAM	G	GS	MIN	FGM	FGA	PCT	3FGM	3FGA	PCT	FTM	FTA	PCT	O-RB	D-RB	TOT	AST	PF	DQ	STL	TO	BLK	PTS	RPG	APG	PPG
62-63–New York	25	–	209	37	110	.336	–	–	–	3	10	.300	–	–	39	18	23	0	–	–	–	77	1.6	0.7	3.1
Reg. Season Totals	25	–	209	37	110	.336	–	–	–	3	10	.300	–	–	39	18	23	0	–	–	–	77	1.6	0.7	3.1

Stivrins, Alex Frank b. November 29, 1962 Ht. 6-8 Wt. 220 College: Creighton; Colorado

SEASON–TEAM	G	GS	MIN	FGM	FGA	PCT	3FGM	3FGA	PCT	FTM	FTA	PCT	O-RB	D-RB	TOT	AST	PF	DQ	STL	TO	BLK	PTS	RPG	APG	PPG
85-86–Seattle	3	0	14	1	4	.250	0	0	–	1	4	.250	3	0	3	1	2	0	0	3	0	3	1.0	0.3	1.0
92-93–Atl.-LAClips-Milw.-Pho.	19	0	76	19	39	.487	0	2	.000	3	4	.750	7	12	19	3	11	0	2	7	2	41	1.0	0.2	2.2
Reg. Season Totals	22	0	90	20	43	.465	0	2	.000	4	8	.500	10	12	22	4	13	0	2	10	2	44	1.0	0.2	2.0

Stockton, John Houston (Stock) b. March 26, 1962 Ht. 6-1 Wt. 175 College: Gonzaga

SEASON–TEAM	G	GS	MIN	FGM	FGA	PCT	3FGM	3FGA	PCT	FTM	FTA	PCT	O-RB	D-RB	TOT	AST	PF	DQ	STL	TO	BLK	PTS	RPG	APG	PPG
84-85–Utah	82	5	1490	157	333	.471	2	11	.182	142	193	.736	26	79	105	415	203	3	109	150	11	458	1.3	5.1	5.6
85-86–Utah	82	38	1935	228	466	.489	2	15	.133	172	205	.839	33	146	179	610	227	2	157	168	10	630	2.2	7.4	7.7
86-87–Utah	82	2	1858	231	463	.499	7	38	.184	179	229	.782	32	119	151	670	224	1	177	164	14	648	1.8	8.2	7.9
87-88–Utah	82	79	2842	454	791	.574	24	67	.358	272	324	.840	54	183	237	1128	247	5	242	262	16	1204	2.9	13.8	14.7
88-89–Utah	82	82	3171	497	923	.538	16	66	.242	390	452	.863	83	165	248	1118	241	3	263	308	14	1400	3.0	13.6	17.1
89-90–Utah	78	78	2915	472	918	.514	47	113	.416	354	432	.819	57	149	206	1134	233	3	207	272	18	1345	2.6	14.5	17.2
90-91–Utah	82	82	3103	496	978	.507	58	168	.345	363	434	.836	46	191	237	1164	233	1	234	298	16	1413	2.9	14.2	17.2
91-92–Utah	82	82	3002	453	939	.482	83	204	.407	308	366	.842	68	202	270	1126	234	3	244	286	22	1297	3.3	13.7	15.8
92-93–Utah	82	82	2863	437	899	.486	72	187	.385	293	367	.798	64	173	237	987	224	2	199	266	21	1239	2.9	12.0	15.1
93-94–Utah	82	82	2969	458	868	.528	48	149	.322	272	338	.805	72	186	258	1031	236	3	199	266	22	1236	3.1	12.6	15.1
94-95–Utah	82	82	2867	429	791	.542	102	227	.449	246	306	.804	57	194	251	1011	215	3	194	267	22	1206	3.1	12.3	14.7
95-96–Utah	82	82	2915	440	818	.538	95	225	.422	234	282	.830	54	172	226	916	207	1	140	246	15	1209	2.8	11.2	14.7
96-97–Utah	82	82	2896	416	759	.548	76	180	.422	275	325	.846	45	183	228	860	194	2	166	248	15	1183	2.8	10.5	14.4
97-98–Utah	64	64	1858	270	511	.528	39	91	.429	191	231	.827	35	131	166	543	138	0	89	161	10	770	2.6	8.5	12.0
98-99–Utah	50	50	1410	200	410	.488	16	50	.320	137	169	.811	31	115	146	374	107	0	81	110	13	553	2.9	7.5	11.1
99-00–Utah	82	82	2432	363	725	.501	43	121	.355	221	257	.860	45	170	215	703	192	0	143	179	15	990	2.6	8.6	12.1
Reg. Season Totals	1258	1054	40526	6001	11592	.518	730	1912	.382	4049	4910	.825	802	2558	3360	13790	3355	32	2844	3651	254	16781	2.7	11.0	13.3
Playoff Totals	168	151	5922	802	1693	.474	109	325	.335	568	705	.806	143	405	548	1716	491	0	309	488	45	2281	3.3	10.2	13.6
All-Star Totals	10	4	197	35	66	.530	7	21	.333	4	6	.667	2	15	17	71	20	0	16	29	1	81	1.7	7.1	8.1

Stojakovic, Predrag b. September 6, 1977 Ht. 6-9 Wt. 229 Country: Yugoslavia

SEASON–TEAM	G	GS	MIN	FGM	FGA	PCT	3FGM	3FGA	PCT	FTM	FTA	PCT	O-RB	D-RB	TOT	AST	PF	DQ	STL	TO	BLK	PTS	RPG	APG	PPG
98-99–Sacramento	48	1	1025	141	373	.378	57	178	.320	63	74	.851	43	100	143	72	43	0	41	53	7	402	3.0	1.5	8.4
99-00–Sacramento	74	11	1749	321	717	.448	100	267	.375	135	153	.882	74	202	276	106	97	0	52	88	7	877	3.7	1.4	11.9
Reg. Season Totals	122	12	2774	462	1090	.424	157	445	.353	198	227	.872	117	302	419	178	140	0	93	141	14	1279	3.4	1.5	10.5
Playoff Totals	10	0	237	25	66	.379	9	27	.333	9	12	.750	14	22	36	5	14	0	7	11	0	68	3.6	0.5	6.8

Stokes, Edward Kobie (Ed) b. September 3, 1971 Ht. 7-0 Wt. 264 College: Arizona

SEASON–TEAM	G	GS	MIN	FGM	FGA	PCT	3FGM	3FGA	PCT	FTM	FTA	PCT	O-RB	D-RB	TOT	AST	PF	DQ	STL	TO	BLK	PTS	RPG	APG	PPG
97-98–Toronto	4	0	17	1	3	.333	0	0	–	1	2	.500	1	3	4	1	4	0	1	2	2	3	1.0	0.3	0.8
Reg. Season Totals	4	0	17	1	3	.333	0	0	–	1	2	.500	1	3	4	1	4	0	1	2	2	3	1.0	0.3	0.8

Stokes, Gregory Lewis (Greg) b. August 5, 1963 Ht. 6-10 Wt. 220 College: Iowa

SEASON–TEAM	G	GS	MIN	FGM	FGA	PCT	3FGM	3FGA	PCT	FTM	FTA	PCT	O-RB	D-RB	TOT	AST	PF	DQ	STL	TO	BLK	PTS	RPG	APG	PPG
85-86–Philadelphia	31	13	350	56	119	.471	0	1	.000	14	21	.667	27	30	57	17	56	0	14	19	11	126	1.8	0.5	4.1
89-90–Sacramento	11	0	34	1	9	.111	0	0	–	2	2	1.000	2	3	5	0	8	0	0	3	0	4	0.5	0.0	0.4
Reg. Season Totals	42	13	384	57	128	.445	0	1	.000	16	23	.696	29	33	62	17	64	0	14	22	11	130	1.5	0.4	3.1
Playoff Totals	7	7	90	8	28	.286	0	0	–	11	13	.846	6	7	13	4	12	0	2	4	6	27	1.9	0.6	3.9

Stokes, Maurice (Mo) b. June 17, 1933 d. April 6, 1970 Ht. 6-7 Wt. 240 College: St. Francis (Pa.)

SEASON–TEAM	G	GS	MIN	FGM	FGA	PCT	3FGM	3FGA	PCT	FTM	FTA	PCT	O-RB	D-RB	TOT	AST	PF	DQ	STL	TO	BLK	PTS	RPG	APG	PPG
55-56–Rochester	67	–	2323	403	1137	.354	–	–	–	319	447	.714	–	–	1094	328	276	11	–	–	–	1125	16.3	4.9	16.8
56-57–Rochester	72	–	2761	434	1249	.347	–	–	–	256	385	.665	–	–	1256	331	287	12	–	–	–	1124	17.4	4.6	15.6
57-58–Cincinnati	63	–	2460	414	1181	.351	–	–	–	238	333	.715	–	–	1142	403	226	9	–	–	–	1066	18.1	6.4	16.9
Reg. Season Totals	202	–	7544	1251	3567	.351	–	–	–	813	1165	.698	–	–	3492	1062	789	32	–	–	–	3315	17.3	5.3	16.4
Playoff Totals	1	–	39	3	12	.250	–	–	–	6	7	.857	–	–	15	2	3	0	–	–	–	12	15.0	2.0	12.0
All-Star Totals	3	–	87	15	43	.349	–	–	–	9	15	.600	–	–	42	12	8	0	–	–	–	39	14.0	4.0	13.0

Stolkey, Arthur F. (Art) b. October 23, 1920 Ht. 6-1 Wt. 180 College: Detroit Mercy

SEASON–TEAM	G	GS	MIN	FGM	FGA	PCT	3FGM	3FGA	PCT	FTM	FTA	PCT	O-RB	D-RB	TOT	AST	PF	DQ	STL	TO	BLK	PTS	RPG	APG	PPG
46-47–Detroit	23	–	–	36	164	.220	–	–	–	30	44	.682	–	–	–	38	72	–	–	–	–	102	–	1.7	4.4
Reg. Season Totals	23	–	–	36	164	.220	–	–	–	30	44	.682	–	–	–	38	72	–	–	–	–	102	–	1.7	4.4

Stoll, Randy C. b. 1945 Ht. 6-7 Wt. 235 College: Washington State

SEASON–TEAM	G	GS	MIN	FGM	FGA	PCT	3FGM	3FGA	PCT	FTM	FTA	PCT	O-RB	D-RB	TOT	AST	PF	DQ	STL	TO	BLK	PTS	RPG	APG	PPG
67-68–Anaheim (A)	25	–	403	66	138	.478	0	0	–	10	25	.400	–	–	91	12	42	0	–	28	–	142	3.6	0.5	5.7
Reg. ABA Totals	25	–	403	66	138	.478	0	0	–	10	25	.400	–	–	91	12	42	0	–	28	–	142	3.6	0.5	5.7

Stone, George (Radar) b. February 9, 1946 Ht. 6-7 Wt. 215 College: Marshall

SEASON–TEAM	G	GS	MIN	FGM	FGA	PCT	3FGM	3FGA	PCT	FTM	FTA	PCT	O-RB	D-RB	TOT	AST	PF	DQ	STL	TO	BLK	PTS	RPG	APG	PPG
68-69–Los Angeles (A)	74	–	2199	437	964	.453	28	74	.378	261	337	.774	–	–	504	57	254	8	–	124	–	1163	6.8	0.8	15.7
69-70–Los Angeles (A)	83	–	2639	512	1194	.429	65	206	.316	239	306	.781	–	–	551	145	280	4	–	–	–	1328	6.6	1.7	16.0
70-71–Utah (A)	78	–	1734	372	808	.460	50	157	.318	121	156	.776	–	–	363	106	173	–	–	–	–	915	4.7	1.4	11.7
71-72–Utah-Car. (A)	24	–	381	49	123	.398	1	9	.111	25	28	.893	–	–	62	25	40	–	–	22	–	124	2.6	1.0	5.2
Reg. ABA Totals	259	–	6953	1370	3089	.444	144	446	.323	646	827	.781	–	–	1480	333	747	12	–	146	–	3530	5.7	1.3	13.6
ABA Playoff Totals	35	–	1148	249	597	.417	18	83	.217	93	118	.788	–	–	262	71	97	0	–	–	–	609	7.5	2.0	17.4

Stoudamire, Damon Lamon b. September 3, 1973 Ht. 5-10 Wt. 171 College: Arizona

SEASON–TEAM	G	GS	MIN	FGM	FGA	PCT	3FGM	3FGA	PCT	FTM	FTA	PCT	O-RB	D-RB	TOT	AST	PF	DQ	STL	TO	BLK	PTS	RPG	APG	PPG
95-96–Toronto	70	70	2865	481	1129	.426	133	337	.395	236	296	.797	59	222	281	653	166	0	98	267	19	1331	4.0	9.3	19.0
96-97–Toronto	81	81	3311	564	1407	.401	176	496	.355	330	401	.823	86	244	330	709	162	1	123	288	13	1634	4.1	8.8	20.2
97-98–Toronto-Port.	71	71	2839	448	1091	.411	91	304	.299	238	287	.829	87	211	298	580	150	0	113	223	7	1225	4.2	8.2	17.3
98-99–Portland	50	50	1673	249	629	.396	44	142	.310	89	122	.730	41	126	167	312	81	0	49	110	4	631	3.3	6.2	12.6
99-00–Portland	78	78	2372	386	894	.432	80	212	.377	122	145	.841	61	182	243	405	173	0	77	149	1	974	3.1	5.2	12.5
Reg. Season Totals	350	350	13060	2128	5150	.413	524	1491	.351	1015	1251	.811	334	985	1319	2659	732	1	460	1037	44	5795	3.8	7.6	16.6
Playoff Totals	33	33	1016	130	327	.398	28	74	.378	57	71	.803	21	79	100	169	87	1	21	73	6	345	3.0	5.1	10.5

Stovall, Paul L. b. August 16, 1948 d. January 9, 1978 Ht. 6-5 Wt. 225 College: Pratt (Kan.) C.C.; Arizona State

SEASON–TEAM	G	GS	MIN	FGM	FGA	PCT	3FGM	3FGA	PCT	FTM	FTA	PCT	O-RB	D-RB	TOT	AST	PF	DQ	STL	TO	BLK	PTS	RPG	APG	PPG
72-73–Phoenix	25	–	211	26	76	.342	–	–	–	24	38	.632	–	–	61	13	37	0	–	–	–	76	2.4	0.5	3.0
73-74–San Diego (A)	13	–	194	36	73	.493	0	0	–	28	44	.636	21	37	58	12	32	–	4	21	6	100	4.5	0.9	7.7
Reg. NBA Totals	25	–	211	26	76	.342	–	–	–	24	38	.632	–	–	61	13	37	0	–	–	–	76	2.4	0.5	3.0
Reg. ABA Totals	13	–	194	36	73	.493	0	0	–	28	44	.636	21	37	58	12	32	0	4	21	6	100	4.5	0.9	7.7

Strawder, Joe Tom b. September 21, 1940 Ht. 6-10 Wt. 235 College: Bradley

SEASON–TEAM	G	GS	MIN	FGM	FGA	PCT	3FGM	3FGA	PCT	FTM	FTA	PCT	O-RB	D-RB	TOT	AST	PF	DQ	STL	TO	BLK	PTS	RPG	APG	PPG
65-66–Detroit	79	–	2180	250	613	.408	–	–	–	176	256	.688	–	–	820	78	305	10	–	–	–	676	10.4	1.0	8.6
66-67–Detroit	79	–	2156	281	660	.426	–	–	–	188	262	.718	–	–	791	82	344	19	–	–	–	750	10.0	1.0	9.5
67-68–Detroit	73	–	2029	206	456	.452	–	–	–	139	215	.647	–	–	685	85	312	18	–	–	–	551	9.4	1.2	7.5
Reg. Season Totals	231	–	6365	737	1729	.426	–	–	–	503	733	.686	–	–	2296	245	961	47	–	–	–	1977	9.9	1.1	8.6
Playoff Totals	6	–	177	14	42	.333	–	–	–	14	22	.636	–	–	65	9	27	1	–	–	–	42	10.8	1.5	7.0

Stricker, William Louis (Bill) b. January 22, 1948 Ht. 6-9 Wt. 220 College: U. of Pacific

SEASON–TEAM	G	GS	MIN	FGM	FGA	PCT	3FGM	3FGA	PCT	FTM	FTA	PCT	O-RB	D-RB	TOT	AST	PF	DQ	STL	TO	BLK	PTS	RPG	APG	PPG
70-71–Portland	1	–	2	2	3	.667	–	–	–	0	0	–	–	–	0	0	1	0	–	–	–	4	0.0	0.0	4.0
Reg. Season Totals	1	–	2	2	3	.667	–	–	–	0	0	–	–	–	0	0	1	0	–	–	–	4	0.0	0.0	4.0

Strickland, Demerick Montae (Erick) b. November 25, 1973 Ht. 6-3 Wt. 210 College: Nebraska

SEASON–TEAM	G	GS	MIN	FGM	FGA	PCT	3FGM	3FGA	PCT	FTM	FTA	PCT	O-RB	D-RB	TOT	AST	PF	DQ	STL	TO	BLK	PTS	RPG	APG	PPG
96-97–Dallas	28	15	759	102	256	.398	28	92	.304	65	80	.813	21	69	90	68	75	3	27	66	5	297	3.2	2.4	10.6
97-98–Dallas	67	19	1505	199	558	.357	48	163	.294	65	84	.774	35	126	161	167	140	1	56	106	8	511	2.4	2.5	7.6
98-99–Dallas	33	2	567	89	221	.403	18	59	.305	53	65	.815	12	71	83	64	44	0	40	36	2	249	2.5	1.9	7.5
99-00–Dallas	68	67	2025	316	730	.433	73	186	.392	162	195	.831	69	254	323	211	190	3	105	102	13	867	4.8	3.1	12.8
Reg. Season Totals	196	103	4856	706	1765	.400	167	500	.334	345	424	.814	137	520	657	510	449	7	228	310	28	1924	3.4	2.6	9.8

Strickland, Mark b. July 14, 1970 Ht. 6-10 Wt. 220 College: Temple

SEASON–TEAM	G	GS	MIN	FGM	FGA	PCT	3FGM	3FGA	PCT	FTM	FTA	PCT	O-RB	D-RB	TOT	AST	PF	DQ	STL	TO	BLK	PTS	RPG	APG	PPG
94-95–Indiana	4	0	9	1	3	.333	0	0	–	1	2	.500	2	2	4	0	0	0	0	1	1	3	1.0	0.0	0.8
96-97–Miami	31	0	153	25	60	.417	0	1	.000	12	21	.571	16	21	37	1	17	0	4	15	10	62	1.2	0.0	2.0
97-98–Miami	51	8	847	145	269	.539	0	1	.000	59	82	.720	80	133	213	26	87	0	18	47	34	349	4.2	0.5	6.8
98-99–Miami	32	1	357	50	101	.495	0	1	.000	19	26	.731	26	52	78	9	28	0	7	13	8	119	2.4	0.3	3.7
99-00–Miami	58	5	663	122	224	.545	0	0	–	40	56	.714	44	96	140	22	68	0	15	24	18	284	2.4	0.4	4.9
Reg. Season Totals	176	14	2029	343	657	.522	0	3	.000	131	187	.701	168	304	472	58	200	0	44	100	71	817	2.7	0.3	4.6
Playoff Totals	10	0	62	10	18	.556	0	0	–	3	8	.375	3	10	13	1	4	0	4	4	1	23	1.3	0.1	2.3

Strickland, Rodney (Rod) b. July 11, 1966 Ht. 6-3 Wt. 185 College: DePaul

SEASON–TEAM	G	GS	MIN	FGM	FGA	PCT	3FGM	3FGA	PCT	FTM	FTA	PCT	O-RB	D-RB	TOT	AST	PF	DQ	STL	TO	BLK	PTS	RPG	APG	PPG
88-89–New York	81	10	1358	265	567	.467	19	59	.322	172	231	.745	51	109	160	319	142	2	98	148	3	721	2.0	3.9	8.9
89-90–N.Y.-S.A.	82	24	2140	343	756	.454	8	30	.267	174	278	.626	90	169	259	468	160	3	127	170	14	868	3.2	5.7	10.6
90-91–San Antonio	58	56	2076	314	651	.482	11	33	.333	161	211	.763	57	162	219	463	125	0	117	156	11	800	3.8	8.0	13.8
91-92–San Antonio	57	54	2053	300	659	.455	5	15	.333	182	265	.687	92	173	265	491	122	0	118	160	17	787	4.6	8.6	13.8
92-93–Portland	78	35	2474	396	816	.485	4	30	.133	273	381	.717	120	217	337	559	153	1	131	199	24	1069	4.3	7.2	13.7
93-94–Portland	82	58	2889	528	1093	.483	2	10	.200	353	471	.749	122	248	370	740	171	0	147	257	24	1411	4.5	9.0	17.2
94-95–Portland	64	61	2267	441	946	.466	46	123	.374	283	380	.745	73	244	317	562	118	0	123	209	9	1211	5.0	8.8	18.9
95-96–Portland	67	63	2526	471	1023	.460	38	111	.342	276	423	.652	89	208	297	640	135	2	97	255	16	1256	4.4	9.6	18.7
96-97–Washington	82	81	2997	515	1105	.466	13	77	.169	367	497	.738	95	240	335	727	166	2	143	270	14	1410	4.1	8.9	17.2
97-98–Washington	76	76	3020	490	1130	.434	12	48	.250	357	492	.726	112	293	405	801	182	2	126	266	25	1349	5.3	10.5	17.8
98-99–Washington	44	43	1632	251	603	.416	12	42	.286	176	236	.746	56	156	212	434	91	0	76	142	5	690	4.8	9.9	15.7
99-00–Washington	69	67	2188	327	762	.429	1	21	.048	214	305	.702	73	186	259	519	147	1	94	187	18	869	3.8	7.5	12.6
Reg. Season Totals	840	628	27620	4641	10111	.459	171	599	.285	2988	4170	.717	1030	2405	3435	6723	1712	13	1397	2419	180	12441	4.1	8.0	14.8
Playoff Totals	44	35	1505	262	590	.444	10	35	.286	129	185	.697	63	134	197	371	129	2	50	116	9	663	4.5	8.4	15.1

Strickland, Roger (The Rifle) b. September 4, 1940 Ht. 6-5 Wt. 200 College: Jacksonville

SEASON–TEAM	G	GS	MIN	FGM	FGA	PCT	3FGM	3FGA	PCT	FTM	FTA	PCT	O-RB	D-RB	TOT	AST	PF	DQ	STL	TO	BLK	PTS	RPG	APG	PPG
63-64–Baltimore	1	–	4	1	3	.333	–	–	–	0	0	–	–	–	0	0	1	0	–	–	–	2	0.0	0.0	2.0
Reg. Season Totals	1	–	4	1	3	.333	–	–	–	0	0	–	–	–	0	0	1	0	–	–	–	2	0.0	0.0	2.0

Stroeder, John b. July 24, 1958 Ht. 6-10 Wt. 260 College: Montana

SEASON–TEAM	G	GS	MIN	FGM	FGA	PCT	3FGM	3FGA	PCT	FTM	FTA	PCT	O-RB	D-RB	TOT	AST	PF	DQ	STL	TO	BLK	PTS	RPG	APG	PPG
87-88–Milwaukee	41	0	271	29	79	.367	0	2	.000	20	30	.667	24	47	71	20	48	0	3	24	12	78	1.7	0.5	1.9
88-89–S.A.-G.S.	5	0	22	2	5	.400	0	0	–	0	0	–	5	9	14	3	3	0	0	3	2	4	2.8	0.6	0.8
Reg. Season Totals	46	0	293	31	84	.369	0	2	.000	20	30	.667	29	56	85	23	51	0	3	27	14	82	1.8	0.5	1.8
Playoff Totals	1	0	1	1	1	1.000	1	1	1.000	0	0	–	0	0	0	–	0	0	0	0	0	3	0.0	0.0	3.0

Strong, Derek Lamar b. February 9, 1968 Ht. 6-9 Wt. 240 College: Xavier (Ohio)

SEASON–TEAM	G	GS	MIN	FGM	FGA	PCT	3FGM	3FGA	PCT	FTM	FTA	PCT	O-RB	D-RB	TOT	AST	PF	DQ	STL	TO	BLK	PTS	RPG	APG	PPG
91-92–Washington	1	0	12	0	4	.000	0	0	–	3	4	.750	1	4	5	1	1	0	0	1	0	3	5.0	1.0	3.0
92-93–Milwaukee	23	0	339	42	92	.457	4	8	.500	68	85	.800	40	75	115	14	20	0	11	13	1	156	5.0	0.6	6.8
93-94–Milwaukee	67	11	1131	141	341	.413	3	13	.231	159	206	.772	109	172	281	48	69	1	38	61	14	444	4.2	0.7	6.6
94-95–Boston	70	24	1344	149	329	.453	2	7	.286	141	172	.820	136	239	375	44	143	0	24	79	13	441	5.4	0.6	6.3
95-96–L.A. Lakers	63	0	746	72	169	.426	1	9	.111	69	85	.812	60	118	178	32	80	1	18	20	12	214	2.8	0.5	3.4
96-97–Orlando	82	21	2004	262	586	.447	0	13	.000	175	218	.803	174	345	519	73	196	2	47	102	20	699	6.3	0.9	8.5
97-98–Orlando	58	8	1638	259	617	.420	0	4	.000	218	279	.781	152	275	427	51	122	0	31	74	24	736	7.4	0.9	12.7
98-99–Orlando	44	0	695	76	180	.422	0	2	.000	71	99	.717	66	95	161	17	64	0	15	37	7	223	3.7	0.4	5.1
99-00–Orlando	20	0	148	21	48	.438	1	4	.250	11	14	.786	11	33	44	4	15	0	5	12	2	54	2.2	0.2	2.7
Reg. Season Totals	428	64	8057	1022	2366	.432	11	60	.183	915	1162	.787	749	1356	2105	284	710	4	189	399	93	2970	4.9	0.7	6.9
Playoff Totals	10	6	292	26	54	.481	0	1	.000	24	33	.727	33	41	74	7	29	1	6	20	3	76	7.4	0.7	7.6

Strothers, William Lamont (Lamont) b. May 10, 1968 Ht. 6-4 Wt. 190 College: Christopher Newport

SEASON–TEAM	G	GS	MIN	FGM	FGA	PCT	3FGM	3FGA	PCT	FTM	FTA	PCT	O-RB	D-RB	TOT	AST	PF	DQ	STL	TO	BLK	PTS	RPG	APG	PPG
91-92–Portland	4	0	17	4	12	.333	0	2	.000	2	4	.500	1	0	1	1	2	0	1	2	1	10	0.3	0.3	2.5
92-93–Dallas	9	0	138	20	61	.328	2	13	.154	8	10	.800	8	6	14	13	13	0	8	15	0	50	1.6	1.4	5.6
Reg. Season Totals	13	0	155	24	73	.329	2	15	.133	10	14	.714	9	6	15	14	15	0	9	17	1	60	1.2	1.1	4.6

Stroud, John Busby b. October 29, 1957 Ht. 6-7 Wt. 215 College: Mississippi

SEASON–TEAM	G	GS	MIN	FGM	FGA	PCT	3FGM	3FGA	PCT	FTM	FTA	PCT	O-RB	D-RB	TOT	AST	PF	DQ	STL	TO	BLK	PTS	RPG	APG	PPG
80-81–Houston	9	–	88	11	34	.324	0	0	–	3	4	.750	7	6	13	9	7	0	1	4	0	25	1.4	1.0	2.8
Reg. Season Totals	9	–	88	11	34	.324	0	0	–	3	4	.750	7	6	13	9	7	0	1	4	0	25	1.4	1.0	2.8

Stroud, William D. (Red) b. May 2, 1941 Ht. 6-0 Wt. 160 College: Mississippi State

SEASON–TEAM	G	GS	MIN	FGM	FGA	PCT	3FGM	3FGA	PCT	FTM	FTA	PCT	O-RB	D-RB	TOT	AST	PF	DQ	STL	TO	BLK	PTS	RPG	APG	PPG
67-68–New Orleans (A)	7	–	33	5	11	.455	1	1	1.000	9	10	.900	–	–	2	1	7	0	–	9	–	20	0.3	0.1	2.9
Reg. ABA Totals	7	–	33	5	11	.455	1	1	1.000	9	10	.900	–	–	2	1	7	0	–	9	–	20	0.3	0.1	2.9

Stump, Eugene Andrew (Gene) b. November 13, 1923 Ht. 6-2 Wt. 185 College: DePaul

SEASON–TEAM	G	GS	MIN	FGM	FGA	PCT	3FGM	3FGA	PCT	FTM	FTA	PCT	O-RB	D-RB	TOT	AST	PF	DQ	STL	TO	BLK	PTS	RPG	APG	PPG
47-48–Boston	43	–	–	59	247	.239	–	–	–	24	38	.632	–	–	–	18	66	–	–	–	–	142	–	0.4	3.3
48-49–Boston	56	–	–	193	580	.333	–	–	–	92	129	.713	–	–	–	56	102	–	–	–	–	478	–	1.0	8.5
49-50–Minn.-Wat.	49	–	–	63	213	.296	–	–	–	37	54	.685	–	–	–	44	59	–	–	–	–	163	–	0.9	3.3
Reg. Season Totals	148	–	–	315	1040	.303	–	–	–	153	221	.692	–	–	–	118	227	–	–	–	–	783	–	0.8	5.3
Playoff Totals	4	–	–	1	6	.333	–	–	–	0	0	–	–	–	–	–	4	–	–	–	–	2	0.0	0.0	0.5

Stutz, Stanley J. (Stan, formerly Stan Modzelewski) b. April 14, 1920 d. October 28, 1975 Ht. 5-10 Wt. 170 College: Rhode Island

SEASON–TEAM	G	GS	MIN	FGM	FGA	PCT	3FGM	3FGA	PCT	FTM	FTA	PCT	O-RB	D-RB	TOT	AST	PF	DQ	STL	TO	BLK	PTS	RPG	APG	PPG
46-47–New York	60	–	–	172	641	.268	–	–	–	133	170	.782	–	–	–	49	127	–	–	–	–	477	–	0.8	8.0
47-48–New York	47	–	–	109	501	.218	–	–	–	113	135	.837	–	–	–	57	121	–	–	–	–	331	–	1.2	7.0
48-49–Baltimore	59	–	–	121	431	.281	–	–	–	131	159	.824	–	–	–	82	149	–	–	–	–	373	–	1.4	6.3
Reg. Season Totals	166	–	–	402	1573	.256	–	–	–	377	464	.813	–	–	–	188	397	–	–	–	–	1181	–	1.1	7.1
Playoff Totals	11	–	–	32	117	.274	–	–	–	40	49	.816	–	–	–	8	31	–	–	–	–	104	–	0.7	9.5

Suiter, Gary G. b. January 18, 1945 Ht. 6-9 Wt. 235 College: Midwestern State

SEASON–TEAM	G	GS	MIN	FGM	FGA	PCT	3FGM	3FGA	PCT	FTM	FTA	PCT	O-RB	D-RB	TOT	AST	PF	DQ	STL	TO	BLK	PTS	RPG	APG	PPG
70-71–Cleveland	30	–	140	19	54	.352	–	–	–	4	9	.444	–	–	41	2	20	0	–	–	–	42	1.4	0.1	1.4
Reg. Season Totals	30	–	140	19	54	.352	–	–	–	4	9	.444	–	–	41	2	20	0	–	–	–	42	1.4	0.1	1.4

Sumpter, Barry b. November 11, 1965 Ht. 6-11 Wt. 245 College: Louisville; Austin Peay State

SEASON–TEAM	G	GS	MIN	FGM	FGA	PCT	3FGM	3FGA	PCT	FTM	FTA	PCT	O-RB	D-RB	TOT	AST	PF	DQ	STL	TO	BLK	PTS	RPG	APG	PPG
88-89–L.A. Clippers	1	0	1	0	1	.000	0	0	–	0	0	–	0	0	0	0	0	0	0	0	0	0	0.0	0.0	0.0
Reg. Season Totals	1	0	1	0	1	.000	0	0	–	0	0	–	0	0	0	0	0	0	0	0	0	0	0.0	0.0	0.0

Sunderlage, Don J. b. December 20, 1929 d. July 15, 1961 Ht. 6-1 Wt. 180 College: Illinois

SEASON–TEAM	G	GS	MIN	FGM	FGA	PCT	3FGM	3FGA	PCT	FTM	FTA	PCT	O-RB	D-RB	TOT	AST	PF	DQ	STL	TO	BLK	PTS	RPG	APG	PPG
53-54–Milwaukee	68	–	2232	254	748	.340	–	–	–	252	337	.748	–	–	225	187	263	8	–	–	–	760	3.3	2.8	11.2
54-55–Minneapolis	45	–	404	33	133	.248	–	–	–	48	73	.658	–	–	56	37	57	0	–	–	–	114	1.2	0.8	2.5
Reg. Season Totals	113	–	2636	287	881	.326	–	–	–	300	410	.732	–	–	281	224	320	8	–	–	–	874	2.5	2.0	7.7
All-Star Totals	1	–	6	1	2	.500	–	–	–	2	2	1.000	–	–	0	1	1	0	–	–	–	4	0.0	1.0	4.0

Sundov, Bruno b. February 10, 1980 Ht. 7-2 Wt. 220 Country: Croatia

SEASON–TEAM	G	GS	MIN	FGM	FGA	PCT	3FGM	3FGA	PCT	FTM	FTA	PCT	O-RB	D-RB	TOT	AST	PF	DQ	STL	TO	BLK	PTS	RPG	APG	PPG
98-99–Dallas	3	0	11	2	7	.286	0	0	–	0	0	–	0	0	0	1	4	0	0	1	0	4	0.0	0.3	1.3
99-00–Dallas	14	0	61	12	31	.387	0	0	–	2	2	1.000	5	7	12	2	16	0	2	4	2	26	0.9	0.1	1.9
Reg. Season Totals	17	0	72	14	38	.368	0	0	–	2	2	1.000	5	7	12	3	20	0	2	5	2	30	0.7	0.2	1.8

Sundvold, Jon Thomas (Sunny) b. July 2, 1961 Ht. 6-2 Wt. 170 College: Missouri

SEASON–TEAM	G	GS	MIN	FGM	FGA	PCT	3FGM	3FGA	PCT	FTM	FTA	PCT	O-RB	D-RB	TOT	AST	PF	DQ	STL	TO	BLK	PTS	RPG	APG	PPG
83-84–Seattle	73	2	1284	217	488	.445	9	37	.243	64	72	.889	23	68	91	239	81	0	29	81	1	507	1.2	3.3	6.9
84-85–Seattle	73	1	1150	170	400	.425	12	38	.316	48	59	.814	17	53	70	206	87	0	36	85	1	400	1.0	2.8	5.5
85-86–San Antonio	70	4	1150	220	476	.462	21	60	.350	39	48	.813	22	58	80	261	110	0	34	85	0	500	1.1	3.7	7.1
86-87–San Antonio	76	42	1765	365	751	.486	50	149	.336	70	84	.833	20	78	98	315	109	1	35	97	0	850	1.3	4.1	11.2
87-88–San Antonio	52	12	1024	176	379	.464	26	64	.406	43	48	.896	14	34	48	183	54	0	27	57	2	421	0.9	3.5	8.1
88-89–Miami	68	8	1338	307	675	.455	48	92	.522	47	57	.825	18	69	87	137	78	0	27	87	1	709	1.3	2.0	10.4
89-90–Miami	63	2	867	148	363	.408	44	100	.440	44	52	.846	15	56	71	102	69	0	25	52	0	384	1.1	1.6	6.1
90-91–Miami	24	0	225	43	107	.402	15	35	.429	11	11	1.000	3	6	9	24	11	0	7	16	0	112	0.4	1.0	4.7
91-92–Miami	3	0	8	1	3	.333	1	1	1.000	0	0	–	0	0	0	2	2	0	0	0	0	3	0.0	0.7	1.0
Reg. Season Totals	502	71	8811	1647	3642	.452	226	576	.392	366	431	.849	132	422	554	1469	601	1	220	560	5	3886	1.1	2.9	7.7
Playoff Totals	10	3	157	25	57	.439	4	18	.222	5	6	.833	2	5	7	25	6	0	4	9	0	59	0.7	2.5	5.9

Sura, Robert Jr. (Bob) b. March 25, 1973 Ht. 6-5 Wt. 200 College: Florida State

SEASON–TEAM	G	GS	MIN	FGM	FGA	PCT	3FGM	3FGA	PCT	FTM	FTA	PCT	O-RB	D-RB	TOT	AST	PF	DQ	STL	TO	BLK	PTS	RPG	APG	PPG
95-96–Cleveland	79	3	1150	148	360	.411	27	78	.346	99	141	.702	34	101	135	233	126	1	56	115	21	422	1.7	2.9	5.3
96-97–Cleveland	82	23	2269	253	587	.431	53	164	.323	196	319	.614	76	232	308	390	218	3	90	181	33	755	3.8	4.8	9.2
97-98–Cleveland	46	4	942	87	231	.377	19	60	.317	74	131	.565	25	69	94	171	113	0	44	93	7	267	2.0	3.7	5.8
98-99–Cleveland	50	6	841	70	210	.333	9	45	.200	65	103	.631	21	81	102	152	98	1	46	67	14	214	2.0	3.0	4.3
99-00–Cleveland	73	45	2216	356	815	.437	122	332	.367	175	251	.697	50	238	288	284	201	0	91	148	19	1009	3.9	3.9	13.8
Reg. Season Totals	330	81	7418	914	2203	.415	230	679	.339	609	945	.644	206	721	927	1230	756	5	327	604	94	2667	2.8	3.7	8.1
Playoff Totals	6	0	49	3	8	.375	0	2	.000	2	3	.667	0	4	4	7	8	0	2	6	0	8	0.7	1.2	1.3

Surhoff, Richard C. Jr. (Dick) b. November 16, 1929 d. May 1, 1987 Ht. 6-4 Wt. 210 College: Long Island University; Marshall

SEASON–TEAM	G	GS	MIN	FGM	FGA	PCT	3FGM	3FGA	PCT	FTM	FTA	PCT	O-RB	D-RB	TOT	AST	PF	DQ	STL	TO	BLK	PTS	RPG	APG	PPG
52-53–New York	26	–	187	13	61	.213	–	–	–	19	30	.633	–	–	25	9	36	1	–	–	–	45	1.0	0.3	1.7
53-54–Milwaukee	32	–	358	43	129	.333	–	–	–	47	62	.758	–	–	69	23	53	0	–	–	–	133	2.2	0.7	4.2
Reg. Season Totals	58	–	545	56	190	.295	–	–	–	66	92	.717	–	–	94	32	89	1	–	–	–	178	1.6	0.6	3.1
Playoff Totals	4	–	13	2	4	.500	–	–	–	0	0	–	–	–	2	2	2	0	–	–	–	4	0.5	0.5	1.0

Sutor, George J. b. September 14, 1943 Ht. 6-8 Wt. 240 College: La Salle

SEASON–TEAM	G	GS	MIN	FGM	FGA	PCT	3FGM	3FGA	PCT	FTM	FTA	PCT	O-RB	D-RB	TOT	AST	PF	DQ	STL	TO	BLK	PTS	RPG	APG	PPG
67-68–Kentucky (A)	1	–	5	0	0	–	0	0	–	0	0	–	–	–	1	0	2	0	–	0	–	0	1.0	0.0	0.0
68-69–Minnesota (A)	64	–	886	139	397	.350	0	2	.000	71	114	.623	–	–	348	27	170	8	–	60	–	349	5.4	0.4	5.5
69-70–Car.-Miami (A)	14	–	147	12	46	.261	0	1	.000	7	17	.412	–	–	55	3	31	0	–	–	–	31	3.9	0.2	2.2
Reg. ABA Totals	79	–	1038	151	443	.341	0	3	.000	78	131	.595	–	–	404	30	203	8	–	60	–	380	5.1	0.4	4.8
ABA Playoff Totals	1	–	3	0	1	.000	0	0	–	0	1	.000	–	–	–	0	2	0	–	–	–	0	0.0	0.0	0.0

Suttle, Dane Lee b. August 9, 1961 Ht. 6-3 Wt. 190 College: Pepperdine

SEASON–TEAM	G	GS	MIN	FGM	FGA	PCT	3FGM	3FGA	PCT	FTM	FTA	PCT	O-RB	D-RB	TOT	AST	PF	DQ	STL	TO	BLK	PTS	RPG	APG	PPG
83-84–Kansas City	40	1	469	109	214	.509	0	3	.000	40	47	.851	21	25	46	46	46	0	20	32	0	258	1.2	1.2	6.5
84-85–Kansas City	6	0	24	6	13	.462	0	1	.000	2	2	1.000	0	3	3	2	3	0	1	1	0	14	0.5	0.3	2.3
Reg. Season Totals	46	1	493	115	227	.507	0	4	.000	42	49	.857	21	28	49	48	49	0	21	33	0	272	1.1	1.0	5.9

Sutton, Gregory Ray (Greg) b. December 3, 1967 Ht. 6-2 Wt. 185 College: Langston; Oral Roberts

SEASON–TEAM	G	GS	MIN	FGM	FGA	PCT	3FGM	3FGA	PCT	FTM	FTA	PCT	O-RB	D-RB	TOT	AST	PF	DQ	STL	TO	BLK	PTS	RPG	APG	PPG
91-92–San Antonio	67	2	601	93	240	.388	26	89	.292	34	45	.756	6	41	47	91	111	0	26	70	9	246	0.7	1.4	3.7
94-95–Charlotte	53	4	690	94	230	.409	43	115	.374	32	45	.711	8	48	56	91	114	0	33	51	2	263	1.1	1.7	5.0
95-96–Cha.-Phil.	48	2	655	85	217	.392	47	117	.402	35	46	.761	8	42	50	102	92	0	25	62	2	252	1.0	2.1	5.3
Reg. Season Totals	168	8	1946	272	687	.396	116	321	.361	101	136	.743	22	131	153	284	317	0	84	183	13	761	0.9	1.7	4.5
Playoff Totals	5	0	38	2	13	.154	0	7	.000	3	3	1.000	3	2	5	5	4	0	1	1	1	7	1.0	1.0	1.4

Swagerty, Keith M. b. October 30, 1945 Ht. 6-7 Wt. 235 College: U. of Pacific

SEASON–TEAM	G	GS	MIN	FGM	FGA	PCT	3FGM	3FGA	PCT	FTM	FTA	PCT	O-RB	D-RB	TOT	AST	PF	DQ	STL	TO	BLK	PTS	RPG	APG	PPG
68-69–Houston (A)	77	–	2447	362	883	.410	0	5	.000	256	421	.608	326	496	822	92	238	5	–	112	–	980	10.7	1.2	12.7
69-70–Kentucky (A)	3	–	30	2	9	.222	0	1	.000	3	3	1.000	–	–	6	3	4	0	–	–	–	7	2.0	1.0	2.3
Reg. ABA Totals	80	–	2477	364	892	.408	0	6	.000	259	424	.611	326	496	828	95	242	5	–	112	–	987	10.4	1.2	12.3

Swain, Bennie S. b. December 16, 1933 Ht. 6-8 Wt. 220 College: Texas Southern

SEASON–TEAM	G	GS	MIN	FGM	FGA	PCT	3FGM	3FGA	PCT	FTM	FTA	PCT	O-RB	D-RB	TOT	AST	PF	DQ	STL	TO	BLK	PTS	RPG	APG	PPG
58-59–Boston	58	–	708	99	244	.406	–	–	–	67	110	.609	–	–	262	29	127	3	–	–	–	265	4.5	0.5	4.6
Reg. Season Totals	58	–	708	99	244	.406	–	–	–	67	110	.609	–	–	262	29	127	3	–	–	–	265	4.5	0.5	4.6
Playoff Totals	5	–	27	2	6	.333	–	–	–	1	2	.500	–	–	14	1	4	0	–	–	–	5	2.8	0.2	1.0

S

Swanson, Norman P. (Norm) b. October 4, 1930 Ht. 6-6 Wt. 210 College: Detroit Mercy

SEASON–TEAM	G	GS	MIN	FGM	FGA	PCT	3FGM	3FGA	PCT	FTM	FTA	PCT	O-RB	D-RB	TOT	AST	PF	DQ	STL	TO	BLK	PTS	RPG	APG	PPG
53-54–Rochester	63	–	611	31	137	.226	–	–	–	38	64	.594	–	–	110	33	91	3	–	–	–	100	1.7	0.5	1.6
Reg. Season Totals	63	–	611	31	137	.226	–	–	–	38	64	.594	–	–	110	33	91	3	–	–	–	100	1.7	0.5	1.6
Playoff Totals	8	–	46	3	14	.429	–	–	–	2	3	.667	–	–	10	–	5	0	–	–	–	8	0.8	0.0	1.0

Swartz, Daniel S. (Dan, Dogpatch) b. December 23, 1934 Ht. 6-4 Wt. 215 College: Kentucky; Morehead State

SEASON–TEAM	G	GS	MIN	FGM	FGA	PCT	3FGM	3FGA	PCT	FTM	FTA	PCT	O-RB	D-RB	TOT	AST	PF	DQ	STL	TO	BLK	PTS	RPG	APG	PPG
62-63–Boston	39	–	335	57	150	.380	–	–	–	61	72	.847	–	–	88	21	92	0	–	–	–	175	2.3	0.5	4.5
Reg. Season Totals	39	–	335	57	150	.380	–	–	–	61	72	.847	–	–	88	21	92	0	–	–	–	175	2.3	0.5	4.5
Playoff Totals	1	–	4	0	0	–	–	–	–	0	0	–	–	–	0	–	0	0	–	–	–	0	0.0	0.0	0.0

Swift, Harley E. Jr. (Skeeter) b. June 19, 1946 Ht. 6-3 Wt. 210 College: East Tennessee State

SEASON–TEAM	G	GS	MIN	FGM	FGA	PCT	3FGM	3FGA	PCT	FTM	FTA	PCT	O-RB	D-RB	TOT	AST	PF	DQ	STL	TO	BLK	PTS	RPG	APG	PPG
69-70–New Orleans (A)	66	–	1089	215	546	.394	38	125	.304	139	168	.827	–	–	100	77	208	4	–	–	–	607	1.5	1.2	9.2
70-71–Mem.-Pitt. (A)	80	–	2134	402	895	.449	39	150	.260	206	246	.837	–	–	233	269	264	–	–	–	–	1049	2.9	3.4	13.1
71-72–Pittsburgh (A)	79	–	2340	401	856	.468	33	100	.330	224	265	.845	–	–	200	309	277	–	–	252	–	1059	2.5	3.9	13.4
72-73–Dallas (A)	42	–	1123	177	374	.473	19	49	.388	128	149	.859	20	62	82	150	140	1	–	136	–	501	2.0	3.6	11.9
73-74–San Antonio (A)	16	–	153	23	67	.343	1	12	.083	16	20	.800	5	11	16	15	26	–	3	13	0	63	1.0	0.9	3.9
Reg. ABA Totals	283	–	6839	1218	2738	.445	130	436	.298	713	848	.841	25	73	631	820	915	5	3	401	0	3279	2.2	2.9	11.6

Swinson, Aaron Anthony b. December 21, 1970 Ht. 6-5 Wt. 230 College: Auburn

SEASON–TEAM	G	GS	MIN	FGM	FGA	PCT	3FGM	3FGA	PCT	FTM	FTA	PCT	O-RB	D-RB	TOT	AST	PF	DQ	STL	TO	BLK	PTS	RPG	APG	PPG
94-95–Phoenix	9	0	51	10	18	.556	0	0	–	4	5	.800	3	5	8	3	8	0	1	5	0	24	0.9	0.3	2.7
Reg. Season Totals	9	0	51	10	18	.556	0	0	–	4	5	.800	3	5	8	3	8	0	1	5	0	24	0.9	0.3	2.7

Sydnor, Wallace B. (Buck) b. September 19, 1921 Ht. 5-10 Wt. 175 College: Western Kentucky

SEASON–TEAM	G	GS	MIN	FGM	FGA	PCT	3FGM	3FGA	PCT	FTM	FTA	PCT	O-RB	D-RB	TOT	AST	PF	DQ	STL	TO	BLK	PTS	RPG	APG	PPG
46-47–Chicago	15	–	–	5	26	.192	–	–	–	5	10	.500	–	–	–	0	6	–	–	–	–	15	–	0.0	1.0
Reg. Season Totals	15	–	–	5	26	.192	–	–	–	5	10	.500	–	–	–	0	6	–	–	–	–	15	–	0.0	1.0

Sykes, Larry b. April 11, 1973 Ht. 6-9 Wt. 255 College: Xavier (Ohio)

SEASON–TEAM	G	GS	MIN	FGM	FGA	PCT	3FGM	3FGA	PCT	FTM	FTA	PCT	O-RB	D-RB	TOT	AST	PF	DQ	STL	TO	BLK	PTS	RPG	APG	PPG
95-96–Boston	1	0	2	0	0	–	0	0	–	0	0	–	1	1	2	0	0	0	0	1	0	0	2.0	0.0	0.0
Reg. Season Totals	1	0	2	0	0	–	0	0	–	0	0	–	1	1	2	0	0	0	0	1	0	0	2.0	0.0	0.0

Szabo, Brett b. February 1, 1968 Ht. 6-11 Wt. 230 College: Augustana (S.D.)

SEASON–TEAM	G	GS	MIN	FGM	FGA	PCT	3FGM	3FGA	PCT	FTM	FTA	PCT	O-RB	D-RB	TOT	AST	PF	DQ	STL	TO	BLK	PTS	RPG	APG	PPG
96-97–Boston	70	24	662	54	121	.446	0	1	.000	45	61	.738	56	109	165	17	119	0	16	41	32	153	2.4	0.2	2.2
Reg. Season Totals	70	24	662	54	121	.446	0	1	.000	45	61	.738	56	109	165	17	119	0	16	41	32	153	2.4	0.2	2.2

Szczerbiak, Walter (Walt) b. August 21, 1949 Ht. 6-6 Wt. 210 College: George Washington

SEASON–TEAM	G	GS	MIN	FGM	FGA	PCT	3FGM	3FGA	PCT	FTM	FTA	PCT	O-RB	D-RB	TOT	AST	PF	DQ	STL	TO	BLK	PTS	RPG	APG	PPG
71-72–Pittsburgh (A)	53	–	598	149	237	.629	0	2	.000	35	53	.660	–	–	150	41	100	–	–	50	–	333	2.8	0.8	6.3
Reg. ABA Totals	53	–	598	149	237	.629	0	2	.000	35	53	.660	–	–	150	41	100	–	–	50	–	333	2.8	0.8	6.3

Szczerbiak, Walter Robert (Wally) b. March 5, 1977 Ht. 6-7 Wt. 243 College: Miami (Ohio)

SEASON–TEAM	G	GS	MIN	FGM	FGA	PCT	3FGM	3FGA	PCT	FTM	FTA	PCT	O-RB	D-RB	TOT	AST	PF	DQ	STL	TO	BLK	PTS	RPG	APG	PPG
99-00–Minnesota	73	53	2171	342	669	.511	28	78	.359	133	161	.826	89	183	272	201	175	3	58	83	23	845	3.7	2.8	11.6
Reg. Season Totals	73	53	2171	342	669	.511	28	78	.359	133	161	.826	89	183	272	201	175	3	58	83	23	845	3.7	2.8	11.6
Playoff Totals	4	4	94	12	30	.400	0	3	.000	0	0	–	2	6	8	2	7	0	3	1	1	24	2.0	0.5	6.0

Tabak, Zan b. June 15, 1970 Ht. 7-0 Wt. 245 Country: Croatia

SEASON–TEAM	G	GS	MIN	FGM	FGA	PCT	3FGM	3FGA	PCT	FTM	FTA	PCT	O-RB	D-RB	TOT	AST	PF	DQ	STL	TO	BLK	PTS	RPG	APG	PPG
94-95–Houston	37	0	182	24	53	.453	0	1	.000	27	44	.614	23	34	57	4	37	0	2	18	7	75	1.5	0.1	2.0
95-96–Toronto	67	18	1332	225	414	.543	0	1	.000	64	114	.561	117	203	320	62	204	2	24	101	31	514	4.8	0.9	7.7
96-97–Toronto	13	4	218	32	71	.451	0	0	–	20	29	.690	20	29	49	14	35	0	6	21	11	84	3.8	1.1	6.5
97-98–Toronto-Boston	57	34	984	142	304	.467	0	1	.000	23	61	.377	84	128	212	48	163	2	20	61	38	307	3.7	0.8	5.4
99-00–Indiana	18	0	114	16	34	.471	0	0	–	5	8	.625	16	16	32	4	13	0	3	11	9	37	1.8	0.2	2.1
Reg. Season Totals	192	56	2830	439	876	.501	0	3	.000	139	256	.543	260	410	670	132	452	4	55	212	96	1017	3.5	0.7	5.3
Playoff Totals	18	0	78	6	13	.462	0	0	–	6	6	1.000	5	12	17	1	15	0	1	3	5	18	0.9	0.1	1.0

Tannenbaum, Sidney (Sid) b. October 8, 1925 d. September 4, 1986 Ht. 6-0 Wt. 160 College: New York U.

SEASON–TEAM	G	GS	MIN	FGM	FGA	PCT	3FGM	3FGA	PCT	FTM	FTA	PCT	O-RB	D-RB	TOT	AST	PF	DQ	STL	TO	BLK	PTS	RPG	APG	PPG
47-48–New York	24	–	–	90	360	.250	–	–	–	62	74	.838	–	–	–	37	33	–	–	–	–	242	–	1.5	10.1
48-49–N.Y.-Balt.	46	–	–	146	501	.291	–	–	–	99	120	.825	–	–	–	125	74	–	–	–	–	391	–	2.7	8.5
Reg. Season Totals	70	–	–	236	861	.274	–	–	–	161	194	.830	–	–	–	162	107	–	–	–	–	633	–	2.3	9.0
Playoff Totals	6	–	–	17	62	.274	–	–	–	13	16	.813	–	–	–	14	13	–	–	–	–	47	–	2.3	7.8

Tarpley, Roy James Jr. b. November 28, 1964 Ht. 7-0 Wt. 245 College: Michigan

SEASON–TEAM	G	GS	MIN	FGM	FGA	PCT	3FGM	3FGA	PCT	FTM	FTA	PCT	O-RB	D-RB	TOT	AST	PF	DQ	STL	TO	BLK	PTS	RPG	APG	PPG
86-87–Dallas	75	1	1405	233	499	.467	1	3	.333	94	139	.676	180	353	533	52	232	3	56	101	79	561	7.1	0.7	7.5
87-88–Dallas	81	9	2307	444	888	.500	0	5	.000	205	277	.740	360	599	959	86	313	8	103	172	86	1093	11.8	1.1	13.5
88-89–Dallas	19	6	591	131	242	.541	0	1	.000	66	96	.688	77	141	218	17	70	2	28	45	30	328	11.5	0.9	17.3
89-90–Dallas	45	35	1648	314	696	.451	0	6	.000	130	172	.756	189	400	589	67	160	0	79	117	70	758	13.1	1.5	16.8
90-91–Dallas	5	5	171	43	79	.544	0	1	.000	16	18	.889	16	39	55	12	20	0	6	13	9	102	11.0	2.4	20.4
94-95–Dallas	55	1	1354	292	610	.479	5	18	.278	102	122	.836	142	307	449	58	155	2	45	109	55	691	8.2	1.1	12.6
Reg. Season Totals	280	57	7476	1457	3014	.483	6	34	.176	613	824	.744	964	1839	2803	292	950	15	317	557	329	3533	10.0	1.0	12.6
Playoff Totals	24	4	806	171	335	.510	0	4	.000	65	92	.707	115	192	307	32	99	4	29	48	43	407	12.8	1.3	17.0

Tart, Levern Donihue (Doc) b. June 1, 1942 Ht. 6-3 Wt. 195 College: Bradley

SEASON–TEAM	G	GS	MIN	FGM	FGA	PCT	3FGM	3FGA	PCT	FTM	FTA	PCT	O-RB	D-RB	TOT	AST	PF	DQ	STL	TO	BLK	PTS	RPG	APG	PPG
67-68–Oak.-N.J. (A)	73	–	2853	633	1500	.422	1	15	.067	451	566	.797	–	–	394	249	212	0	–	277	–	1718	5.4	3.4	23.5
68-69–N.Y.-Hou.-Den. (A)	61	–	1403	274	649	.422	0	3	.000	193	255	.757	–	–	195	143	141	2	–	149	–	741	3.2	2.3	12.1
69-70–New York (A)	80	–	3210	756	1528	.495	11	35	.314	412	526	.783	–	–	546	264	268	4	–	–	–	1935	6.8	3.3	24.2
70-71–N.Y.-Texas (A)	60	–	1806	357	862	.414	10	34	.294	198	253	.783	–	–	239	174	171	–	–	–	–	922	4.0	2.9	15.4
Reg. ABA Totals	274	–	9272	2020	4539	.445	22	87	.253	1254	1600	.784	–	–	1374	830	792	6	–	426	–	5316	5.0	3.0	19.4
ABA Playoff Totals	11	–	414	102	230	.443	4	18	.222	59	72	.819	–	–	53	69	35	0	–	–	–	267	4.8	6.3	24.3

Tatum, William Earl (Earl) b. July 26, 1953 Ht. 6-4 Wt. 185 College: Marquette

SEASON–TEAM	G	GS	MIN	FGM	FGA	PCT	3FGM	3FGA	PCT	FTM	FTA	PCT	O-RB	D-RB	TOT	AST	PF	DQ	STL	TO	BLK	PTS	RPG	APG	PPG
76-77–Los Angeles	68	–	1249	283	607	.466	–	–	–	72	100	.720	83	153	236	118	168	1	85	–	22	638	3.5	1.7	9.4
77-78–L.A.-Indiana	82	–	2522	510	1087	.469	–	–	–	153	196	.781	79	216	295	296	257	5	140	184	40	1173	3.6	3.6	14.3
78-79–Boston-Detroit	79	–	1233	280	627	.447	–	–	–	52	71	.732	41	84	125	73	165	3	78	88	34	612	1.6	0.9	7.7
79-80–Cleveland	33	–	225	36	94	.383	2	6	.333	11	19	.579	11	15	26	20	29	0	16	17	5	85	0.8	0.6	2.6
Reg. Season Totals	262	–	5229	1109	2415	.459	2	6	.333	288	386	.746	214	468	682	507	619	9	319	289	101	2508	2.6	1.9	9.6
Playoff Totals	11	–	356	67	134	.500	0	0	–	16	24	.667	16	38	54	27	34	2	15	–	9	150	4.9	2.5	13.6

Taylor, Anthony Paul b. November 30, 1965 Ht. 6-4 Wt. 175 College: Oregon

SEASON–TEAM	G	GS	MIN	FGM	FGA	PCT	3FGM	3FGA	PCT	FTM	FTA	PCT	O-RB	D-RB	TOT	AST	PF	DQ	STL	TO	BLK	PTS	RPG	APG	PPG
88-89–Miami	21	7	368	60	151	.397	0	2	.000	24	32	.750	11	23	34	43	37	0	22	20	5	144	1.6	2.0	6.9
Reg. Season Totals	21	7	368	60	151	.397	0	2	.000	24	32	.750	11	23	34	43	37	0	22	20	5	144	1.6	2.0	6.9

Taylor, Brian Dwight b. June 9, 1951 Ht. 6-2 Wt. 185 College: Princeton

SEASON–TEAM	G	GS	MIN	FGM	FGA	PCT	3FGM	3FGA	PCT	FTM	FTA	PCT	O-RB	D-RB	TOT	AST	PF	DQ	STL	TO	BLK	PTS	RPG	APG	PPG
72-73–New York (A)	63	–	2038	395	767	.515	4	25	.160	168	226	.743	77	126	203	175	219	5	–	137	–	962	3.2	2.8	15.3
73-74–New York (A)	75	–	2505	363	762	.476	8	29	.276	100	143	.699	92	122	214	341	192	–	154	164	22	834	2.9	4.5	11.1
74-75–New York (A)	79	–	2611	472	920	.513	10	46	.217	150	196	.765	86	146	232	282	216	–	221	152	26	1104	2.9	3.6	14.0
75-76–New York (A)	54	–	1733	354	724	.489	32	76	.421	164	207	.792	70	92	162	204	138	–	125	153	22	904	3.0	3.8	16.7
76-77–Kansas City	72	–	2488	501	995	.504	–	–	–	225	275	.818	88	150	238	320	206	1	199	–	16	1227	3.3	4.4	17.0
77-78–Denver	39	–	1222	182	403	.452	–	–	–	88	115	.765	30	68	98	132	120	1	71	77	9	452	2.5	3.4	11.6
78-79–San Diego	20	–	212	30	83	.361	–	–	–	16	18	.889	13	13	26	20	34	0	24	17	0	76	1.3	1.0	3.8
79-80–San Diego	78	–	2754	418	895	.467	90	239	.377	130	162	.802	76	112	188	335	246	6	147	141	25	1056	2.4	4.3	13.5
80-81–San Diego	80	–	2312	310	591	.525	44	115	.383	146	185	.789	58	93	151	440	212	0	118	111	23	810	1.9	5.5	10.1
81-82–San Diego	41	40	1274	165	328	.503	23	63	.365	90	110	.818	26	70	96	229	113	1	47	82	9	443	2.3	5.6	10.8
Reg. NBA Totals	330	40	10262	1606	3295	.487	157	417	.376	695	865	.803	291	506	797	1476	931	9	606	428	82	4064	2.4	4.5	12.3
Reg. ABA Totals	271	–	8887	1584	3173	.499	54	176	.307	582	772	.754	325	486	811	1002	765	5	500	606	70	3804	3.0	3.7	14.0
ABA Playoff Totals	37	–	1334	208	473	.440	12	37	.324	73	95	.768	51	56	123	133	117	0	66	81	8	501	3.3	3.6	13.5

Taylor, Cornelius F. (Jay) b. October 3, 1967 Ht. 6-3 Wt. 190 College: Eastern Illinois

SEASON–TEAM	G	GS	MIN	FGM	FGA	PCT	3FGM	3FGA	PCT	FTM	FTA	PCT	O-RB	D-RB	TOT	AST	PF	DQ	STL	TO	BLK	PTS	RPG	APG	PPG
89-90–New Jersey	17	0	114	21	52	.404	3	13	.231	6	9	.667	5	6	11	5	9	0	5	10	3	51	0.6	0.3	3.0
Reg. Season Totals	17	0	114	21	52	.404	3	13	.231	6	9	.667	5	6	11	5	9	0	5	10	3	51	0.6	0.3	3.0

Taylor, Fredrick Ollie (Fred) b. February 5, 1948 Ht. 6-5 Wt. 180 College: Texas-Pan American

SEASON–TEAM	G	GS	MIN	FGM	FGA	PCT	3FGM	3FGA	PCT	FTM	FTA	PCT	O-RB	D-RB	TOT	AST	PF	DQ	STL	TO	BLK	PTS	RPG	APG	PPG
70-71–Phoenix	54	–	552	110	284	.387	–	–	–	78	125	.624	–	–	86	51	113	0	–	–	–	298	1.6	0.9	5.5
71-72–Phoenix-Cin.	34	–	283	36	117	.308	–	–	–	15	32	.469	–	–	54	18	40	0	–	–	–	87	1.6	0.5	2.6
Reg. Season Totals	88	–	835	146	401	.364	–	–	–	93	157	.592	–	–	140	69	153	0	–	–	–	385	1.6	0.8	4.4

T

Taylor, Jeffrey (Jeff) b. January 1, 1960 Ht. 6-4 Wt. 175 College: Texas Tech

SEASON–TEAM	G	GS	MIN	FGM	FGA	PCT	3FGM	3FGA	PCT	FTM	FTA	PCT	O-RB	D-RB	TOT	AST	PF	DQ	STL	TO	BLK	PTS	RPG	APG	PPG
82-83–Houston	44	5	774	64	160	.400	0	1	.000	30	46	.652	25	53	78	110	82	1	40	60	15	158	1.8	2.5	3.6
86-87–Detroit	12	0	44	6	10	.600	0	0	–	9	10	.900	1	3	4	3	4	0	2	8	1	21	0.3	0.3	1.8
Reg. Season Totals	56	5	818	70	170	.412	0	1	.000	39	56	.696	26	56	82	113	86	1	42	68	16	179	1.5	2.0	3.2

Taylor, Johnny Antonio b. June 4, 1974 Ht. 6-9 Wt. 220 College: Knoxville; Indian Hills (Iowa) C.C.; Knoxville College; Tenn.-Chattanooga

SEASON–TEAM	G	GS	MIN	FGM	FGA	PCT	3FGM	3FGA	PCT	FTM	FTA	PCT	O-RB	D-RB	TOT	AST	PF	DQ	STL	TO	BLK	PTS	RPG	APG	PPG
97-98–Orlando	12	0	108	13	37	.351	1	2	.500	11	16	.688	4	9	13	1	22	0	3	8	2	38	1.1	0.1	3.2
98-99–Denver	36	9	724	82	198	.414	26	68	.382	17	23	.739	30	71	101	24	97	1	28	34	17	207	2.8	0.7	5.8
99-00–Denver-Orlando	6	0	34	5	14	.357	1	1	1.000	0	0	–	2	4	6	1	5	0	1	2	1	11	1.0	0.2	1.8
Reg. Season Totals	54	9	866	100	249	.402	28	71	.394	28	39	.718	36	84	120	26	124	1	32	44	20	256	2.2	0.5	4.7

Taylor, Leonard Chester Jr. b. May 2, 1966 Ht. 6-8 Wt. 220 College: California

SEASON–TEAM	G	GS	MIN	FGM	FGA	PCT	3FGM	3FGA	PCT	FTM	FTA	PCT	O-RB	D-RB	TOT	AST	PF	DQ	STL	TO	BLK	PTS	RPG	APG	PPG
89-90–Golden State	10	0	37	0	6	.000	0	1	.000	11	16	.688	4	8	12	1	4	0	0	5	0	11	1.2	0.1	1.1
Reg. Season Totals	10	0	37	0	6	.000	0	1	.000	11	16	.688	4	8	12	1	4	0	0	5	0	11	1.2	0.1	1.1

Taylor, Maurice De Shawn b. October 30, 1976 Ht. 6-9 Wt. 260 College: Michigan

SEASON–TEAM	G	GS	MIN	FGM	FGA	PCT	3FGM	3FGA	PCT	FTM	FTA	PCT	O-RB	D-RB	TOT	AST	PF	DQ	STL	TO	BLK	PTS	RPG	APG	PPG
97-98–L.A. Clippers	71	3	1513	321	675	.476	0	1	.000	173	244	.709	118	178	296	53	222	7	34	107	40	815	4.2	0.7	11.5
98-99–L.A. Clippers	46	45	1505	311	675	.461	1	6	.167	150	206	.728	100	142	242	67	179	5	16	120	29	773	5.3	1.5	16.8
99-00–L.A. Clippers	62	60	2227	458	988	.464	1	8	.125	143	201	.711	96	304	400	101	217	4	51	169	48	1060	6.5	1.6	17.1
Reg. Season Totals	179	108	5245	1090	2338	.466	2	15	.133	466	651	.716	314	624	938	221	618	16	101	396	117	2648	5.2	1.2	14.8

Taylor, Oliver Harold (Ollie) b. March 7, 1947 Ht. 6-2 Wt. 195 College: Houston

SEASON–TEAM	G	GS	MIN	FGM	FGA	PCT	3FGM	3FGA	PCT	FTM	FTA	PCT	O-RB	D-RB	TOT	AST	PF	DQ	STL	TO	BLK	PTS	RPG	APG	PPG
70-71–New York (A)	80	–	1617	251	496	.506	5	12	.417	187	277	.675	–	–	307	146	231	–	–	–	–	694	3.8	1.8	8.7
71-72–New York (A)	82	–	1891	245	542	.452	0	6	.000	218	308	.708	–	–	330	153	213	–	–	153	–	708	4.0	1.9	8.6
72-73–San Diego (A)	69	–	2121	325	757	.429	11	55	.200	286	425	.673	156	209	365	275	191	1	–	207	–	947	5.3	4.0	13.7
73-74–N.Y.-Car. (A)	31	–	519	65	150	.433	2	4	.500	58	86	.674	34	54	88	54	63	–	20	58	6	190	2.8	1.7	6.1
Reg. ABA Totals	262	–	6148	886	1945	.456	18	77	.234	749	1096	.683	190	263	1090	628	698	1	20	418	6	2539	4.2	2.4	9.7
ABA Playoff Totals	31	–	994	118	270	.437	3	9	.333	83	116	.716	3	0	148	73	92	0	2	87	0	322	4.8	2.4	10.4

Taylor, Roland Morris (Fatty) b. March 13, 1946 Ht. 6-0 Wt. 180 College: Edison (Fla.) C.C.; La Salle

SEASON–TEAM	G	GS	MIN	FGM	FGA	PCT	3FGM	3FGA	PCT	FTM	FTA	PCT	O-RB	D-RB	TOT	AST	PF	DQ	STL	TO	BLK	PTS	RPG	APG	PPG
69-70–Washington (A)	83	–	1994	243	520	.467	1	6	.167	178	264	.674	–	–	377	201	285	4	–	–	–	665	4.5	2.4	8.0
70-71–Virginia (A)	84	–	1629	180	393	.458	4	22	.182	175	256	.684	–	–	263	225	228	–	–	–	–	539	3.1	2.7	6.4
71-72–Virginia (A)	84	–	2669	306	680	.450	1	15	.067	164	258	.636	–	–	416	321	302	–	–	206	–	777	5.0	3.8	9.3
72-73–Virginia (A)	78	–	2553	316	679	.465	3	7	.429	150	248	.605	137	181	318	374	266	3	210	237	–	785	4.1	4.8	10.1
73-74–Virginia (A)	80	–	2812	292	709	.412	3	19	.158	185	256	.723	124	253	377	416	270	–	215	279	15	772	4.7	5.2	9.7
74-75–Denver (A)	76	–	2018	251	586	.428	6	21	.286	129	172	.750	85	136	221	337	238	–	172	248	16	637	2.9	4.4	8.4
75-76–Virginia (A)	76	–	2483	243	600	.405	11	51	.216	125	173	.723	117	224	341	401	212	–	206	247	16	622	4.5	5.3	8.2
76-77–Denver	79	–	1548	132	314	.420	–	–	–	37	65	.569	90	121	211	288	202	0	132	–	9	301	2.7	3.6	3.8
Reg. NBA Totals	79	–	1548	132	314	.420	–	–	–	37	65	.569	90	121	211	288	202	0	132	–	9	301	2.7	3.6	3.8
Reg. ABA Totals	561	–	16158	1831	4167	.439	29	141	.206	1106	1627	.680	463	794	2313	2275	1801	7	803	1217	47	4797	4.1	4.1	8.6
NBA Playoff Totals	1	–	1	0	0	–	–	–	–	0	0	–	0	0	0	–	0	0	0	–	0	0	0.0	0.0	0.0
ABA Playoff Totals	53	–	1336	127	313	.406	3	14	.214	74	104	.712	28	35	200	167	163	0	35	89	5	331	3.8	3.2	6.2

Taylor, Ronald (Ron) b. November 21, 1947 Ht. 7-1 Wt. 265 College: USC

SEASON–TEAM	G	GS	MIN	FGM	FGA	PCT	3FGM	3FGA	PCT	FTM	FTA	PCT	O-RB	D-RB	TOT	AST	PF	DQ	STL	TO	BLK	PTS	RPG	APG	PPG
69-70–Wash.-N.Y. (A)	75	–	910	156	327	.477	0	0	–	57	102	.559	–	–	293	64	218	11	–	–	–	369	3.9	0.9	4.9
70-71–Virginia (A)	1	–	25	1	9	.111	0	0	–	0	1	.000	–	–	0	4	2	–	–	–	–	2	0.0	4.0	2.0
71-72–Pittsburgh (A)	1	–	4	0	1	.000	0	0	–	0	0	–	–	–	1	0	5	–	–	1	–	0	1.0	0.0	0.0
Reg. ABA Totals	77	–	939	157	337	.466	0	0	–	57	103	.553	–	–	294	68	225	11	–	1	–	371	3.8	0.9	4.8
ABA Playoff Totals	2	–	5	0	4	.000	0	0	–	0	1	.000	–	–	2	0	0	0	–	–	–	0	1.0	0.0	0.0

Taylor, Vincent Caldwell (Vince) b. September 11, 1960 Ht. 6-5 Wt. 180 College: Duke

SEASON–TEAM	G	GS	MIN	FGM	FGA	PCT	3FGM	3FGA	PCT	FTM	FTA	PCT	O-RB	D-RB	TOT	AST	PF	DQ	STL	TO	BLK	PTS	RPG	APG	PPG
82-83–New York	31	0	321	37	102	.363	0	0	–	21	32	.656	19	17	36	41	54	1	20	30	2	95	1.2	1.3	3.1
Reg. Season Totals	31	0	321	37	102	.363	0	0	–	21	32	.656	19	17	36	41	54	1	20	30	2	95	1.2	1.3	3.1

Teagle, Terry Michael b. April 10, 1960 Ht. 6-5 Wt. 195 College: Baylor

SEASON–TEAM	G	GS	MIN	FGM	FGA	PCT	3FGM	3FGA	PCT	FTM	FTA	PCT	O-RB	D-RB	TOT	AST	PF	DQ	STL	TO	BLK	PTS	RPG	APG	PPG
82-83–Houston	73	44	1708	332	776	.428	10	29	.345	87	125	.696	74	120	194	150	171	0	53	137	18	761	2.7	2.1	10.4
83-84–Houston	68	0	616	148	315	.470	7	27	.259	37	44	.841	28	50	78	63	81	1	13	62	4	340	1.1	0.9	5.0
84-85–Detroit-G.S.	21	3	349	74	137	.540	2	4	.500	25	35	.714	22	21	43	14	36	0	13	15	5	175	2.0	0.7	8.3
85-86–Golden State	82	52	2158	475	958	.496	4	25	.160	211	265	.796	96	139	235	115	241	2	71	136	34	1165	2.9	1.4	14.2
86-87–Golden State	82	0	1650	370	808	.458	0	10	.000	182	234	.778	68	107	175	105	190	0	68	117	13	922	2.1	1.3	11.2
87-88–Golden State	47	4	958	248	546	.454	1	9	.111	97	121	.802	41	40	81	61	95	0	32	80	4	594	1.7	1.3	12.6
88-89–Golden State	66	41	1569	409	859	.476	2	12	.167	182	225	.809	110	153	263	96	173	2	79	116	17	1002	4.0	1.5	15.2
89-90–Golden State	82	49	2376	538	1122	.480	3	14	.214	244	294	.830	114	253	367	155	231	3	91	144	15	1323	4.5	1.9	16.1
90-91–L.A. Lakers	82	0	1498	335	757	.443	0	9	.000	145	177	.819	82	99	181	82	165	1	31	83	8	815	2.2	1.0	9.9
91-92–L.A. Lakers	82	0	1602	364	805	.452	1	4	.250	151	197	.766	91	92	183	113	148	0	66	114	9	880	2.2	1.4	10.7
92-93–Houston	2	0	25	2	7	.286	0	0	–	1	2	.500	0	3	3	2	1	0	0	1	0	5	1.5	1.0	2.5
Reg. Season Totals	687	193	14509	3295	7090	.465	30	143	.210	1362	1719	.792	726	1077	1803	956	1532	9	517	1005	127	7982	2.6	1.4	11.6
Playoff Totals	45	3	885	203	450	.451	0	4	.000	89	114	.781	39	59	98	42	104	1	29	54	10	495	2.2	0.9	11.0

Temple, Collis Jr. b. November 8, 1952 Ht. 6-8 Wt. 220 College: Louisiana State

SEASON–TEAM	G	GS	MIN	FGM	FGA	PCT	3FGM	3FGA	PCT	FTM	FTA	PCT	O-RB	D-RB	TOT	AST	PF	DQ	STL	TO	BLK	PTS	RPG	APG	PPG
74-75–San Antonio (A)	24	–	102	17	41	.415	0	1	.000	8	10	.800	14	17	31	15	29	–	4	12	4	42	1.3	0.6	1.8
Reg. ABA Totals	24	–	102	17	41	.415	0	1	.000	8	10	.800	14	17	31	15	29	–	4	12	4	42	1.3	0.6	1.8

Terrell, Ira Edmondson b. June 19, 1954 Ht. 6-8 Wt. 205 College: Southern Methodist

SEASON–TEAM	G	GS	MIN	FGM	FGA	PCT	3FGM	3FGA	PCT	FTM	FTA	PCT	O-RB	D-RB	TOT	AST	PF	DQ	STL	TO	BLK	PTS	RPG	APG	PPG
76-77–Phoenix	78	–	1751	277	545	.508	–	–	–	111	176	.631	99	288	387	103	165	0	41	–	47	665	5.0	1.3	8.5
78-79–N.O.-Port.	49	–	732	93	198	.470	–	–	–	35	53	.660	44	102	146	41	100	0	22	53	28	221	3.0	0.8	4.5
Reg. Season Totals	127	–	2483	370	743	.498	–	–	–	146	229	.638	143	390	533	144	265	0	63	53	75	886	4.2	1.1	7.0
Playoff Totals	1	–	6	0	4	.000	–	–	–	0	0	–	0	2	2	–	0	0	0	0	0	0	2.0	0.0	0.0

Terry, Allen Charles (Chuck) b. September 27, 1950 Ht. 6-6 Wt. 215 College: Long Beach State

SEASON–TEAM	G	GS	MIN	FGM	FGA	PCT	3FGM	3FGA	PCT	FTM	FTA	PCT	O-RB	D-RB	TOT	AST	PF	DQ	STL	TO	BLK	PTS	RPG	APG	PPG
72-73–Milwaukee	67	–	693	55	162	.340	–	–	–	17	24	.708	–	–	145	40	116	1	–	–	–	127	2.2	0.6	1.9
73-74–Milwaukee	7	–	32	4	12	.333	–	–	–	0	0	–	1	2	3	4	4	0	2	–	0	8	0.4	0.6	1.1
73-74–San Antonio (A)	61	–	1093	132	294	.449	1	2	.500	36	41	.878	67	99	166	72	139	–	18	33	5	301	2.7	1.2	4.9
74-75–San Antonio (A)	79	–	1186	148	313	.473	3	8	.375	39	53	.736	77	140	217	69	146	–	37	37	3	338	2.7	0.9	4.3
75-76–New York (A)	66	–	970	96	246	.390	6	21	.286	22	29	.759	45	99	144	38	116	–	36	21	6	220	2.2	0.6	3.3
76-77–New York Nets	61	–	1075	128	318	.403	–	–	–	48	62	.774	43	100	143	39	120	0	58	–	10	304	2.3	0.6	5.0
Reg. NBA Totals	135	–	1800	187	492	.380	–	–	–	65	86	.756	44	102	291	83	240	1	60	–	10	439	2.2	0.6	3.3
Reg. ABA Totals	206	–	3249	376	853	.441	10	31	.323	97	123	.789	189	338	527	179	401	0	91	91	14	859	2.6	0.9	4.2
NBA Playoff Totals	5	–	18	4	5	.800	–	–	–	0	0	–	0	0	3	1	2	0	0	–	0	8	0.6	0.2	1.6
ABA Playoff Totals	16	–	261	23	56	.411	0	2	.000	7	10	.700	13	32	45	10	30	0	3	9	1	53	2.8	0.6	3.3

Terry, Carlos Fernando b. June 22, 1956 d. March 12, 1989 Ht. 6-5 Wt. 215 College: Winston-Salem State

SEASON–TEAM	G	GS	MIN	FGM	FGA	PCT	3FGM	3FGA	PCT	FTM	FTA	PCT	O-RB	D-RB	TOT	AST	PF	DQ	STL	TO	BLK	PTS	RPG	APG	PPG
80-81–Washington	26	–	504	80	160	.500	0	6	.000	28	42	.667	43	73	116	70	68	1	27	57	13	188	4.5	2.7	7.2
81-82–Washington	13	0	60	3	15	.200	0	3	.000	3	4	.750	5	7	12	8	15	0	3	5	1	9	0.9	0.6	0.7
82-83–Washington	55	3	514	39	106	.368	0	2	.000	10	15	.667	27	72	99	46	79	1	24	20	13	88	1.8	0.8	1.6
Reg. Season Totals	94	3	1078	122	281	.434	0	11	.000	41	61	.672	75	152	227	124	162	2	54	82	27	285	2.4	1.3	3.0
Playoff Totals	3	0	5	0	0	–	0	0	–	0	0	–	0	1	1	–	0	0	0	0	0	0	0.3	0.0	0.0

Terry, Claude Lewis b. January 12, 1950 Ht. 6-5 Wt. 195 College: Stanford

SEASON–TEAM	G	GS	MIN	FGM	FGA	PCT	3FGM	3FGA	PCT	FTM	FTA	PCT	O-RB	D-RB	TOT	AST	PF	DQ	STL	TO	BLK	PTS	RPG	APG	PPG
72-73–Denver (A)	68	–	667	120	285	.421	10	24	.417	74	114	.649	–	–	75	62	111	0	–	69	–	324	1.1	0.9	4.8
73-74–Denver (A)	60	–	587	113	255	.443	14	35	.400	60	69	.870	26	45	71	73	64	–	12	57	3	300	1.2	1.2	5.0
74-75–Denver (A)	70	–	989	193	364	.530	10	25	.400	70	92	.761	57	83	140	111	82	–	33	80	2	466	2.0	1.6	6.7
75-76–Denver (A)	79	–	1349	232	500	.464	13	55	.236	80	89	.899	42	110	152	146	116	–	40	96	5	557	1.9	1.8	7.1
76-77–Buffalo-Atlanta	45	–	545	96	191	.503	–	–	–	36	44	.818	12	34	46	58	48	0	20	–	1	228	1.0	1.3	5.1
77-78–Atlanta	27	–	166	25	68	.368	–	–	–	9	11	.818	3	12	15	7	14	0	6	8	0	59	0.6	0.3	2.2
Reg. NBA Totals	72	–	711	121	259	.467	–	–	–	45	55	.818	15	46	61	65	62	0	26	8	1	287	0.8	0.9	4.0
Reg. ABA Totals	277	–	3592	658	1404	.469	47	139	.338	284	364	.780	125	238	438	392	373	0	85	302	10	1647	1.6	1.4	5.9
ABA Playoff Totals	28	–	330	43	117	.368	1	19	.053	17	23	.739	9	25	37	32	38	0	8	23	2	104	1.3	1.1	3.7

Terry, Jason b. September 15, 1977 Ht. 6-2 Wt. 172 College: Arizona

SEASON–TEAM	G	GS	MIN	FGM	FGA	PCT	3FGM	3FGA	PCT	FTM	FTA	PCT	O-RB	D-RB	TOT	AST	PF	DQ	STL	TO	BLK	PTS	RPG	APG	PPG
99-00–Atlanta	81	27	1888	249	600	.415	46	157	.293	113	140	.807	24	142	166	346	133	0	90	156	10	657	2.0	4.3	8.1
Reg. Season Totals	81	27	1888	249	600	.415	46	157	.293	113	140	.807	24	142	166	346	133	0	90	156	10	657	2.0	4.3	8.1

Thacker, Thomas Porter **(Tom, Tack)** b. November 2, 1939 Ht. 6-2 Wt. 170 College: Cincinnati

SEASON–TEAM	G	GS	MIN	FGM	FGA	PCT	3FGM	3FGA	PCT	FTM	FTA	PCT	O-RB	D-RB	TOT	AST	PF	DQ	STL	TO	BLK	PTS	RPG	APG	PPG
63-64–Cincinnati	48	–	457	53	181	.293	–	–	–	26	53	.491	–	–	115	51	51	0	–	–	–	132	2.4	1.1	2.8
64-65–Cincinnati	55	–	470	56	168	.333	–	–	–	23	47	.489	–	–	127	41	64	0	–	–	–	135	2.3	0.7	2.5
65-66–Cincinnati	50	–	478	84	207	.406	–	–	–	15	38	.395	–	–	119	61	85	0	–	–	–	183	2.4	1.2	3.7
67-68–Boston	65	–	782	114	272	.419	–	–	–	43	84	.512	–	–	161	69	165	2	–	–	–	271	2.5	1.1	4.2
68-69–Indiana (A)	18	–	346	40	117	.342	0	2	.000	18	31	.581	–	–	67	52	51	0	–	26	–	98	3.7	2.9	5.4
69-70–Indiana (A)	70	–	1016	70	212	.330	10	39	.256	38	69	.551	–	–	211	185	177	2	–	–	–	188	3.0	2.6	2.7
70-71–Indiana (A)	8	–	92	6	17	.353	0	3	.000	1	1	1.000	–	–	22	7	18	–	–	–	–	13	2.8	0.9	1.6
Reg. NBA Totals	218	–	2187	307	828	.371	–	–	–	107	222	.482	–	–	522	222	365	2	–	–	–	721	2.4	1.0	3.3
Reg. ABA Totals	96	–	1454	116	346	.335	10	44	.227	57	101	.564	–	–	300	244	246	2	–	26	–	299	3.1	2.5	3.1
NBA Playoff Totals	31	–	217	25	82	.305	–	–	–	9	19	.474	–	–	51	19	46	0	–	–	–	59	1.6	0.6	1.9
ABA Playoff Totals	30	–	578	48	155	.310	3	16	.188	34	58	.586	–	–	125	105	90	1	–	–	–	133	4.2	3.5	4.4

Theard, Floyd b. September 5, 1944 d. April 11, 1985 Ht. 6-1 Wt. 170 College: Kentucky State

SEASON–TEAM	G	GS	MIN	FGM	FGA	PCT	3FGM	3FGA	PCT	FTM	FTA	PCT	O-RB	D-RB	TOT	AST	PF	DQ	STL	TO	BLK	PTS	RPG	APG	PPG
69-70–Denver (A)	25	–	406	39	113	.345	0	1	.000	18	28	.643	–	–	51	44	49	1	–	–	–	96	2.0	1.8	3.8
Reg. ABA Totals	25	–	406	39	113	.345	0	1	.000	18	28	.643	–	–	51	44	49	1	–	–	–	96	2.0	1.8	3.8

Theus, Reggie Wayne b. October 13, 1957 Ht. 6-6 Wt. 205 College: Nevada-Las Vegas

SEASON–TEAM	G	GS	MIN	FGM	FGA	PCT	3FGM	3FGA	PCT	FTM	FTA	PCT	O-RB	D-RB	TOT	AST	PF	DQ	STL	TO	BLK	PTS	RPG	APG	PPG
78-79–Chicago	82	–	2753	537	1119	.480	–	–	–	264	347	.761	92	136	228	429	270	2	93	303	18	1338	2.8	5.2	16.3
79-80–Chicago	82	–	3029	566	1172	.483	28	105	.267	500	597	.838	143	186	329	515	262	4	114	348	20	1660	4.0	6.3	20.2
80-81–Chicago	82	–	2820	543	1097	.495	18	90	.200	445	550	.809	124	163	287	426	258	1	122	259	20	1549	3.5	5.2	18.9
81-82–Chicago	82	82	2838	560	1194	.469	25	100	.250	363	449	.808	115	197	312	476	243	1	87	277	16	1508	3.8	5.8	18.4
82-83–Chicago	82	81	2856	749	1567	.478	21	91	.231	434	542	.801	91	209	300	484	281	6	143	321	17	1953	3.7	5.9	23.8
83-84–Chicago-K.C.	61	35	1498	262	625	.419	7	42	.167	214	281	.762	50	79	129	352	171	3	50	156	12	745	2.1	5.8	12.2
84-85–Kansas City	82	80	2543	501	1029	.487	5	38	.132	334	387	.863	106	164	270	656	250	0	95	307	18	1341	3.3	8.0	16.4
85-86–Sacramento	82	82	2919	546	1137	.480	6	35	.171	405	490	.827	73	231	304	788	231	3	112	327	20	1503	3.7	9.6	18.3
86-87–Sacramento	79	76	2872	577	1223	.472	17	78	.218	429	495	.867	86	180	266	692	208	3	78	289	16	1600	3.4	8.8	20.3
87-88–Sacramento	73	73	2653	619	1318	.470	16	59	.271	320	385	.831	72	160	232	463	173	0	59	234	16	1574	3.2	6.3	21.6
88-89–Atlanta	82	82	2517	497	1067	.466	17	58	.293	285	335	.851	86	156	242	387	236	0	108	194	16	1296	3.0	4.7	15.8
89-90–Orlando	76	71	2350	517	1178	.439	26	105	.248	378	443	.853	75	146	221	407	194	1	60	226	12	1438	2.9	5.4	18.9
90-91–New Jersey	81	81	2955	583	1247	.468	52	144	.361	292	343	.851	69	160	229	378	231	0	85	252	35	1510	2.8	4.7	18.6
Reg. Season Totals	1026	743	34603	7057	14973	.471	238	945	.252	4663	5644	.826	1182	2167	3349	6453	3008	24	1206	3493	236	19015	3.3	6.3	18.5
Playoff Totals	17	11	542	89	218	.408	2	15	.133	64	77	.831	17	30	47	97	58	1	18	48	2	244	2.8	5.7	14.4
All-Star Totals	2	1	27	4	12	.333	0	0	–	0	0	–	1	1	2	4	1	0	2	6	0	8	1.0	2.0	4.0

Thibeaux, Peter C. b. October 3, 1961 Ht. 6-7 Wt. 210 College: St. Mary's (Calif.)

SEASON–TEAM	G	GS	MIN	FGM	FGA	PCT	3FGM	3FGA	PCT	FTM	FTA	PCT	O-RB	D-RB	TOT	AST	PF	DQ	STL	TO	BLK	PTS	RPG	APG	PPG
84-85–Golden State	51	1	461	94	195	.482	0	2	.000	43	67	.642	29	40	69	17	85	1	11	34	17	231	1.4	0.3	4.5
85-86–Golden State	42	8	531	100	233	.429	2	5	.400	29	48	.604	28	47	75	28	82	1	23	39	15	231	1.8	0.7	5.5
Reg. Season Totals	93	9	992	194	428	.453	2	7	.286	72	115	.626	57	87	144	45	167	2	34	73	32	462	1.5	0.5	5.0

Thieben, William Bernard **(Bill)** b. March 28, 1935 Ht. 6-7 Wt. 215 College: Hofstra

SEASON–TEAM	G	GS	MIN	FGM	FGA	PCT	3FGM	3FGA	PCT	FTM	FTA	PCT	O-RB	D-RB	TOT	AST	PF	DQ	STL	TO	BLK	PTS	RPG	APG	PPG
56-57–Fort Wayne	58	–	633	90	256	.352	–	–	–	57	87	.655	–	–	207	17	78	0	–	–	–	237	3.6	0.3	4.1
57-58–Detroit	27	–	243	42	143	.294	–	–	–	16	27	.593	–	–	65	7	44	0	–	–	–	100	2.4	0.3	3.7
Reg. Season Totals	85	–	876	132	399	.331	–	–	–	73	114	.640	–	–	272	24	122	0	–	–	–	337	3.2	0.3	4.0
Playoff Totals	2	–	28	6	7	.857	–	–	–	2	6	.333	–	–	6	3	5	0	–	–	–	14	3.0	1.5	7.0

Thigpen, Justus b. August 13, 1947 Ht. 6-1 Wt. 170 College: Charles Stewart Mott (Mich.) C.C.; Weber State

SEASON–TEAM	G	GS	MIN	FGM	FGA	PCT	3FGM	3FGA	PCT	FTM	FTA	PCT	O-RB	D-RB	TOT	AST	PF	DQ	STL	TO	BLK	PTS	RPG	APG	PPG
69-70–Pittsburgh (A)	3	–	58	5	19	.263	0	0	–	1	3	.333	–	–	8	4	14	1	–	–	–	11	2.7	1.3	3.7
72-73–Detroit	18	–	99	23	57	.404	–	–	–	0	0	–	–	–	9	8	18	0	–	–	–	46	0.5	0.4	2.6
73-74–K.C.-Omaha	1	–	2	1	3	.333	–	–	–	0	0	–	1	0	1	0	0	0	0	–	0	2	1.0	0.0	2.0
Reg. NBA Totals	19	–	101	24	60	.400	–	–	–	0	0	–	1	0	10	8	18	0	0	–	0	48	0.5	0.4	2.5
Reg. ABA Totals	3	–	58	5	19	.263	0	0	–	1	3	.333	–	–	8	4	14	1	–	–	–	11	2.7	1.3	3.7

Thirdkill, David b. April 12, 1960 Ht. 6-7 Wt. 215 College: Coll. of Southern Idaho (J.C.); Bradley

SEASON–TEAM	G	GS	MIN	FGM	FGA	PCT	3FGM	3FGA	PCT	FTM	FTA	PCT	O-RB	D-RB	TOT	AST	PF	DQ	STL	TO	BLK	PTS	RPG	APG	PPG
82-83–Phoenix	49	2	521	74	170	.435	1	7	.143	45	78	.577	28	44	72	36	93	1	19	48	4	194	1.5	0.7	4.0
83-84–Detroit	46	0	291	31	72	.431	0	1	.000	15	31	.484	9	22	31	27	44	0	10	19	3	77	0.7	0.6	1.7
84-85–Det.-Milw.-S.A.	18	3	183	20	38	.526	0	1	.000	11	19	.579	10	7	17	4	22	0	5	14	3	51	0.9	0.2	2.8
85-86–Boston	49	0	385	54	110	.491	0	1	.000	55	88	.625	27	43	70	15	55	0	11	19	3	163	1.4	0.3	3.3
86-87–Boston	17	0	89	10	24	.417	0	1	.000	5	16	.313	5	14	19	2	12	0	2	5	0	25	1.1	0.1	1.5
Reg. Season Totals	179	5	1469	189	414	.457	1	11	.091	131	232	.565	79	130	209	84	226	1	47	105	13	510	1.2	0.5	2.8
Playoff Totals	18	0	69	7	22	.318	0	3	.000	7	15	.467	1	9	10	5	9	0	2	7	0	21	0.6	0.3	1.2

Thomas, Carl b. October 3, 1969 Ht. 6-4 Wt. 195 College: Eastern Michigan

SEASON–TEAM	G	GS	MIN	FGM	FGA	PCT	3FGM	3FGA	PCT	FTM	FTA	PCT	O-RB	D-RB	TOT	AST	PF	DQ	STL	TO	BLK	PTS	RPG	APG	PPG
91-92–Sacramento	1	0	31	5	12	.417	1	2	.500	1	2	.500	0	0	0	1	3	0	1	1	0	12	0.0	1.0	12.0
96-97–Cleveland	19	0	77	9	24	.375	2	12	.167	1	1	1.000	3	10	13	8	7	0	2	6	1	21	0.7	0.4	1.1
97-98–Orl.-G.S.-Clev.	43	0	426	56	140	.400	20	59	.339	16	25	.640	10	37	47	19	39	0	21	18	7	148	1.1	0.4	3.4
Reg. Season Totals	63	0	534	70	176	.398	23	73	.315	18	28	.643	13	47	60	28	49	0	24	25	8	181	1.0	0.4	2.9
Playoff Totals	1	0	11	0	1	.000	0	0	–	2	3	.667	1	0	1	–	2	0	0	0	0	2	1.0	0.0	2.0

Thomas, Charles b. October 3, 1969 Ht. 6-3 Wt. 175 College: Eastern Michigan

SEASON–TEAM	G	GS	MIN	FGM	FGA	PCT	3FGM	3FGA	PCT	FTM	FTA	PCT	O-RB	D-RB	TOT	AST	PF	DQ	STL	TO	BLK	PTS	RPG	APG	PPG
91-92–Detroit	36	0	156	18	51	.353	2	17	.118	10	15	.667	6	16	22	22	20	0	4	17	1	48	0.6	0.6	1.3
Reg. Season Totals	36	0	156	18	51	.353	2	17	.118	10	15	.667	6	16	22	22	20	0	4	17	1	48	0.6	0.6	1.3

Thomas, Irving b. January 2, 1966 Ht. 6-9 Wt. 230 College: Kentucky; Florida State

SEASON–TEAM	G	GS	MIN	FGM	FGA	PCT	3FGM	3FGA	PCT	FTM	FTA	PCT	O-RB	D-RB	TOT	AST	PF	DQ	STL	TO	BLK	PTS	RPG	APG	PPG
90-91–L.A. Lakers	26	0	108	17	50	.340	0	0	–	12	21	.571	14	17	31	10	24	0	4	13	1	46	1.2	0.4	1.8
Reg. Season Totals	26	0	108	17	50	.340	0	0	–	12	21	.571	14	17	31	10	24	0	4	13	1	46	1.2	0.4	1.8
Playoff Totals	3	0	5	1	1	1.000	0	0	–	0	0	–	0	0	0	–	0	0	0	0	0	2	0.0	0.0	0.7

Thomas, Isiah Lord III (Zeke) b. April 30, 1961 Ht. 6-1 Wt. 185 College: Indiana HOF: 2000

SEASON–TEAM	G	GS	MIN	FGM	FGA	PCT	3FGM	3FGA	PCT	FTM	FTA	PCT	O-RB	D-RB	TOT	AST	PF	DQ	STL	TO	BLK	PTS	RPG	APG	PPG
81-82–Detroit	72	72	2433	453	1068	.424	17	59	.288	302	429	.704	57	152	209	565	253	2	150	299	17	1225	2.9	7.8	17.0
82-83–Detroit	81	81	3093	725	1537	.472	36	125	.288	368	518	.710	105	223	328	634	318	8	199	326	29	1854	4.0	7.8	22.9
83-84–Detroit	82	82	3007	669	1448	.462	22	65	.338	388	529	.733	103	224	327	914	324	8	204	307	33	1748	4.0	11.1	21.3
84-85–Detroit	81	81	3089	646	1410	.458	29	113	.257	399	493	.809	114	247	361	1123	288	8	187	302	25	1720	4.5	13.9	21.2
85-86–Detroit	77	77	2790	609	1248	.488	26	84	.310	365	462	.790	83	194	277	830	245	9	171	289	20	1609	3.6	10.8	20.9
86-87–Detroit	81	81	3013	626	1353	.463	19	98	.194	400	521	.768	82	237	319	813	251	5	153	343	20	1671	3.9	10.0	20.6
87-88–Detroit	81	81	2927	621	1341	.463	30	97	.309	305	394	.774	64	214	278	678	217	0	141	273	17	1577	3.4	8.4	19.5
88-89–Detroit	80	76	2924	569	1227	.464	33	121	.273	287	351	.818	49	224	273	663	209	0	133	298	20	1458	3.4	8.3	18.2
89-90–Detroit	81	81	2993	579	1322	.438	42	136	.309	292	377	.775	74	234	308	765	206	0	139	322	19	1492	3.8	9.4	18.4
90-91–Detroit	48	46	1657	289	665	.435	19	65	.292	179	229	.782	35	125	160	446	118	4	75	185	10	776	3.3	9.3	16.2
91-92–Detroit	78	78	2918	564	1264	.446	25	86	.291	292	378	.772	68	179	247	560	194	2	118	252	15	1445	3.2	7.2	18.5
92-93–Detroit	79	79	2922	526	1258	.418	61	198	.308	278	377	.737	71	161	232	671	222	2	123	284	18	1391	2.9	8.5	17.6
93-94–Detroit	58	56	1750	318	763	.417	39	126	.310	181	258	.702	46	113	159	399	126	0	68	202	6	856	2.7	6.9	14.8
Reg. Season Totals	979	971	35516	7194	15904	.452	398	1373	.290	4036	5316	.759	951	2527	3478	9061	2971	48	1861	3682	249	18822	3.6	9.3	19.2
Playoff Totals	111	109	4216	825	1869	.441	81	234	.346	530	689	.769	134	390	524	987	363	8	234	369	38	2261	4.7	8.9	20.4
All-Star Totals	11	10	318	76	133	.571	6	15	.400	27	35	.771	12	15	27	97	17	0	31	41	0	185	2.5	8.8	16.8

Thomas, Jamel b. July 19, 1976 Ht. 6-6 Wt. 219 College: Providence

SEASON–TEAM	G	GS	MIN	FGM	FGA	PCT	3FGM	3FGA	PCT	FTM	FTA	PCT	O-RB	D-RB	TOT	AST	PF	DQ	STL	TO	BLK	PTS	RPG	APG	PPG
99-00–Boston-G.S.-Port.	7	0	46	8	18	.444	0	3	.000	1	1	1.000	1	4	5	6	2	0	1	5	0	17	0.7	0.9	2.4
Reg. Season Totals	7	0	46	8	18	.444	0	3	.000	1	1	1.000	1	4	5	6	2	0	1	5	0	17	0.7	0.9	2.4

Thomas, James Edward (Jim) b. October 19, 1960 Ht. 6-3 Wt. 190 College: Indiana

SEASON–TEAM	G	GS	MIN	FGM	FGA	PCT	3FGM	3FGA	PCT	FTM	FTA	PCT	O-RB	D-RB	TOT	AST	PF	DQ	STL	TO	BLK	PTS	RPG	APG	PPG
83-84–Indiana	72	15	1219	187	403	.464	1	11	.091	80	110	.727	59	90	149	130	115	1	60	69	6	455	2.1	1.8	6.3
84-85–Indiana	80	52	2059	347	726	.478	8	42	.190	183	234	.782	74	187	261	234	195	2	76	131	5	885	3.3	2.9	11.1
85-86–L.A. Clippers	6	0	69	6	15	.400	0	0	–	1	2	.500	3	5	8	12	12	0	5	9	1	13	1.3	2.0	2.2
90-91–Minnesota	3	0	14	1	4	.250	0	0	–	0	0	–	0	0	0	1	0	0	1	1	0	2	0.0	0.3	0.7
Reg. Season Totals	161	67	3361	541	1148	.471	9	53	.170	264	346	.763	136	282	418	377	322	3	142	210	12	1355	2.6	2.3	8.4

Thomas, John G. b. September 8, 1975 Ht. 6-9 Wt. 265 College: Minnesota

SEASON–TEAM	G	GS	MIN	FGM	FGA	PCT	3FGM	3FGA	PCT	FTM	FTA	PCT	O-RB	D-RB	TOT	AST	PF	DQ	STL	TO	BLK	PTS	RPG	APG	PPG
97-98–Boston-Toronto	54	2	535	55	113	.487	0	0	–	41	54	.759	48	58	106	17	97	0	22	46	12	151	2.0	0.3	2.8
98-99–Toronto	39	11	593	71	123	.577	0	1	.000	27	48	.563	65	69	134	15	82	0	17	21	9	169	3.4	0.4	4.3
99-00–Toronto	55	6	477	49	107	.458	0	1	.000	16	41	.390	37	38	75	9	106	1	12	14	14	114	1.4	0.2	2.1
Reg. Season Totals	148	19	1605	175	343	.510	0	2	.000	84	143	.587	150	165	315	41	285	1	51	81	35	434	2.1	0.3	2.9
Playoff Totals	1	0	1	0	0	–	0	0	–	0	0	–	0	0	0	–	0	0	0	0	0	0	0.0	0.0	0.0

Thomas, Joseph Randle (Joe) b. March 9, 1948 Ht. 6-6 Wt. 205 College: Marquette

SEASON–TEAM	G	GS	MIN	FGM	FGA	PCT	3FGM	3FGA	PCT	FTM	FTA	PCT	O-RB	D-RB	TOT	AST	PF	DQ	STL	TO	BLK	PTS	RPG	APG	PPG
70-71–Phoenix	39	–	204	23	86	.267	–	–	–	9	20	.450	–	–	43	17	19	0	–	–	–	55	1.1	0.4	1.4
Reg. Season Totals	39	–	204	23	86	.267	–	–	–	9	20	.450	–	–	43	17	19	0	–	–	–	55	1.1	0.4	1.4

T

Thomas, Kenneth Cornelius (Kenny) b. July 25, 1977 Ht. 6-8 Wt. 260 College: New Mexico

SEASON–TEAM	G	GS	MIN	FGM	FGA	PCT	3FGM	3FGA	PCT	FTM	FTA	PCT	O-RB	D-RB	TOT	AST	PF	DQ	STL	TO	BLK	PTS	RPG	APG	PPG
99-00–Houston	72	29	1797	212	531	.399	32	122	.262	138	209	.660	147	290	437	113	167	0	54	112	22	594	6.1	1.6	8.3
Reg. Season Totals	72	29	1797	212	531	.399	32	122	.262	138	209	.660	147	290	437	113	167	0	54	112	22	594	6.1	1.6	8.3

Thomas, Kurt Vincent b. October 4, 1972 Ht. 6-9 Wt. 230 College: Texas Christian

SEASON–TEAM	G	GS	MIN	FGM	FGA	PCT	3FGM	3FGA	PCT	FTM	FTA	PCT	O-RB	D-RB	TOT	AST	PF	DQ	STL	TO	BLK	PTS	RPG	APG	PPG
95-96–Miami	74	42	1655	274	547	.501	0	2	.000	118	178	.663	122	317	439	46	271	7	47	98	36	666	5.9	0.6	9.0
96-97–Miami-Dallas	18	9	374	39	105	.371	0	1	.000	35	46	.761	31	76	107	9	67	3	12	25	9	113	5.9	0.5	6.3
97-98–Dallas	5	0	73	17	45	.378	0	0	–	3	3	1.000	8	16	24	3	19	1	1	10	0	37	4.8	0.6	7.4
98-99–New York	50	44	1182	170	368	.462	0	1	.000	66	108	.611	82	204	286	55	159	3	45	73	17	406	5.7	1.1	8.1
99-00–New York	80	21	1971	270	535	.505	1	3	.333	100	128	.781	144	361	505	82	278	6	51	105	42	641	6.3	1.0	8.0
Reg. Season Totals	227	116	5255	770	1600	.481	1	7	.143	322	463	.695	387	974	1361	195	794	20	156	311	104	1863	6.0	0.9	8.2
Playoff Totals	39	15	730	80	189	.423	0	0	–	27	37	.730	60	116	176	15	133	2	20	38	19	187	4.5	0.4	4.8

Thomas, Ronald Morton (Ron) b. November 19, 1950 Ht. 6-6 Wt. 215 College: Trinity Valley (Tex.) C.C.; Louisville

SEASON–TEAM	G	GS	MIN	FGM	FGA	PCT	3FGM	3FGA	PCT	FTM	FTA	PCT	O-RB	D-RB	TOT	AST	PF	DQ	STL	TO	BLK	PTS	RPG	APG	PPG
72-73–Kentucky (A)	31	–	369	62	132	.470	0	2	.000	21	41	.512	53	62	115	23	73	2	–	21	–	145	3.7	0.7	4.7
73-74–Kentucky (A)	71	–	976	128	273	.469	1	7	.143	37	63	.587	112	177	289	62	156	–	48	71	7	294	4.1	0.9	4.1
74-75–Kentucky (A)	79	–	830	115	256	.449	1	3	.333	57	119	.479	124	176	300	46	133	–	51	71	14	288	3.8	0.6	3.6
75-76–Kentucky (A)	83	–	1117	134	277	.484	1	2	.500	55	94	.585	148	223	371	67	168	–	61	71	18	324	4.5	0.8	3.9
Reg. ABA Totals	264	–	3292	439	938	.468	3	14	.214	170	317	.536	437	638	1075	198	530	2	160	234	39	1051	4.1	0.8	4.0
ABA Playoff Totals	50	–	665	98	188	.521	0	1	.000	32	62	.516	57	90	222	37	106	0	18	45	6	228	4.4	0.7	4.6

Thomas, Terry C. b. August 20, 1953 Ht. 6-8 Wt. 220 College: Detroit Mercy

SEASON–TEAM	G	GS	MIN	FGM	FGA	PCT	3FGM	3FGA	PCT	FTM	FTA	PCT	O-RB	D-RB	TOT	AST	PF	DQ	STL	TO	BLK	PTS	RPG	APG	PPG
75-76–Detroit	28	–	136	28	65	.431	–	–	–	21	29	.724	15	21	36	3	21	1	4	–	2	77	1.3	0.1	2.8
Reg. Season Totals	28	–	136	28	65	.431	–	–	–	21	29	.724	15	21	36	3	21	1	4	–	2	77	1.3	0.1	2.8
Playoff Totals	4	–	6	0	5	.000	–	–	–	0	0	–	1	0	1	–	1	0	0	–	0	0	0.3	0.0	0.0

Thomas, Timothy Mark (Tim) b. February 26, 1977 Ht. 6-10 Wt. 230 College: Villanova

SEASON–TEAM	G	GS	MIN	FGM	FGA	PCT	3FGM	3FGA	PCT	FTM	FTA	PCT	O-RB	D-RB	TOT	AST	PF	DQ	STL	TO	BLK	PTS	RPG	APG	PPG
97-98–Philadelphia	77	48	1779	306	684	.447	62	171	.363	171	231	.740	107	181	288	90	185	2	54	118	17	845	3.7	1.2	11.0
98-99–Phil.-Milw.	50	26	812	132	279	.473	21	68	.309	73	112	.652	49	77	126	46	107	2	26	46	12	358	2.5	0.9	7.2
99-00–Milwaukee	80	1	2093	347	753	.461	63	182	.346	188	243	.774	100	232	332	113	227	3	59	129	31	945	4.2	1.4	11.8
Reg. Season Totals	207	75	4684	785	1716	.457	146	421	.347	432	586	.737	256	490	746	249	519	7	139	293	60	2148	3.6	1.2	10.4
Playoff Totals	8	3	202	37	77	.481	5	17	.294	21	29	.724	10	26	36	11	25	0	2	6	5	100	4.5	1.4	12.5

Thomas, Willis (Lefty) b. 1937 Ht. 6-2 Wt. 185 College: Los Angeles Harbor (Calif.) Coll. (J.C.); Tennessee State

SEASON–TEAM	G	GS	MIN	FGM	FGA	PCT	3FGM	3FGA	PCT	FTM	FTA	PCT	O-RB	D-RB	TOT	AST	PF	DQ	STL	TO	BLK	PTS	RPG	APG	PPG
67-68–Den.-Anaheim (A)	62	–	1068	243	550	.442	0	3	.000	69	93	.742	–	–	114	55	107	1	–	94	–	555	1.8	0.9	9.0
Reg. ABA Totals	62	–	1068	243	550	.442	0	3	.000	69	93	.742	–	–	114	55	107	1	–	94	–	555	1.8	0.9	9.0

Thompson, Bernard b. August 30, 1962 Ht. 6-6 Wt. 210 College: Fresno State

SEASON–TEAM	G	GS	MIN	FGM	FGA	PCT	3FGM	3FGA	PCT	FTM	FTA	PCT	O-RB	D-RB	TOT	AST	PF	DQ	STL	TO	BLK	PTS	RPG	APG	PPG
84-85–Portland	59	0	535	79	212	.373	0	8	.000	39	51	.765	37	39	76	52	79	0	31	35	10	197	1.3	0.9	3.3
85-86–Phoenix	61	20	1281	195	399	.489	0	2	.000	127	157	.809	58	83	141	132	151	0	51	90	10	517	2.3	2.2	8.5
86-87–Phoenix	24	2	331	42	105	.400	0	3	.000	27	33	.818	20	11	31	18	53	0	11	16	5	111	1.3	0.8	4.6
87-88–Phoenix	37	7	566	74	159	.465	0	2	.000	43	60	.717	40	36	76	51	75	1	21	21	1	191	2.1	1.4	5.2
88-89–Houston	23	0	222	20	59	.339	0	2	.000	22	26	.846	9	19	28	13	33	0	13	19	1	62	1.2	0.6	2.7
Reg. Season Totals	204	29	2935	410	934	.439	0	17	.000	258	327	.789	164	188	352	266	391	1	127	181	27	1078	1.7	1.3	5.3
Playoff Totals	2	0	10	0	5	.000	0	0	–	2	2	1.000	1	2	3	2	1	0	0	0	1	2	1.5	1.0	1.0

Thompson, Brooks James b. July 19, 1970 Ht. 6-4 Wt. 193 College: Oklahoma State

SEASON–TEAM	G	GS	MIN	FGM	FGA	PCT	3FGM	3FGA	PCT	FTM	FTA	PCT	O-RB	D-RB	TOT	AST	PF	DQ	STL	TO	BLK	PTS	RPG	APG	PPG
94-95–Orlando	38	2	246	45	114	.395	18	58	.310	8	12	.667	7	16	23	43	46	1	10	27	2	116	0.6	1.1	3.1
95-96–Orlando	33	0	246	48	103	.466	25	64	.391	19	27	.704	4	20	24	31	35	0	12	24	0	140	0.7	0.9	4.2
96-97–Utah-Denver	67	6	1055	162	406	.399	97	244	.398	24	38	.632	18	78	96	180	126	0	55	87	2	445	1.4	2.7	6.6
97-98–Phoenix-N.Y.	30	0	167	23	56	.411	9	30	.300	4	8	.500	1	14	15	27	22	0	10	16	1	59	0.5	0.9	2.0
Reg. Season Totals	168	8	1714	278	679	.409	149	396	.376	55	85	.647	30	128	158	281	229	1	87	154	5	760	0.9	1.7	4.5
Playoff Totals	8	0	59	13	25	.520	4	10	.400	8	11	.727	4	3	7	10	8	0	0	11	2	38	0.9	1.3	4.8

Thompson, Cornelius Allen (Corny) b. February 5, 1960 Ht. 6-8 Wt. 225 College: Connecticut

SEASON–TEAM	G	GS	MIN	FGM	FGA	PCT	3FGM	3FGA	PCT	FTM	FTA	PCT	O-RB	D-RB	TOT	AST	PF	DQ	STL	TO	BLK	PTS	RPG	APG	PPG
82-83–Dallas	44	2	520	43	137	.314	0	0	–	36	46	.783	41	79	120	34	92	0	12	31	7	122	2.7	0.8	2.8
Reg. Season Totals	44	2	520	43	137	.314	0	0	–	36	46	.783	41	79	120	34	92	0	12	31	7	122	2.7	0.8	2.8

Thompson, David O'Neil b. July 13, 1954 Ht. 6-4 Wt. 195 College: North Carolina State HOF: 1996

SEASON–TEAM	G	GS	MIN	FGM	FGA	PCT	3FGM	3FGA	PCT	FTM	FTA	PCT	O-RB	D-RB	TOT	AST	PF	DQ	STL	TO	BLK	PTS	RPG	APG	PPG
75-76–Denver (A)	83	–	3101	807	1567	.515	3	19	.158	541	681	.794	228	297	525	308	282	–	136	250	102	2158	6.3	3.7	26.0
76-77–Denver	82	–	3001	824	1626	.507	–	–	–	477	623	.766	138	196	334	337	236	1	114	–	53	2125	4.1	4.1	25.9
77-78–Denver	80	–	3025	826	1584	.521	–	–	–	520	668	.778	156	234	390	362	213	1	92	245	99	2172	4.9	4.5	27.2
78-79–Denver	76	–	2670	693	1353	.512	–	–	–	439	583	.753	109	165	274	225	180	2	70	186	82	1825	3.6	3.0	24.0
79-80–Denver	39	–	1239	289	617	.468	7	19	.368	254	335	.758	56	118	174	124	106	0	39	116	38	839	4.5	3.2	21.5
80-81–Denver	77	–	2620	734	1451	.506	10	39	.256	489	615	.795	107	180	287	231	231	3	53	250	60	1967	3.7	3.0	25.5
81-82–Denver	61	5	1246	313	644	.486	4	14	.286	276	339	.814	57	91	148	117	149	1	34	142	29	906	2.4	1.9	14.9
82-83–Seattle	75	64	2155	445	925	.481	2	10	.200	298	380	.784	96	174	270	222	142	0	47	163	33	1190	3.6	3.0	15.9
83-84–Seattle	19	0	349	89	165	.539	0	1	.000	62	73	.849	18	26	44	13	30	0	10	27	13	240	2.3	0.7	12.6
Reg. NBA Totals	509	69	16305	4213	8365	.504	23	83	.277	2815	3616	.778	737	1184	1921	1631	1287	8	459	1129	407	11264	3.8	3.2	22.1
Reg. ABA Totals	83	–	3101	807	1567	.515	3	19	.158	541	681	.794	228	297	525	308	282	–	136	250	102	2158	6.3	3.7	26.0
NBA Playoff Totals	27	2	971	249	539	.462	1	3	.333	120	161	.745	42	73	115	101	83	1	24	63	27	619	4.3	3.7	22.9
ABA Playoff Totals	13	–	508	127	237	.536	1	4	.250	88	105	.838	32	51	83	39	54	–	16	50	5	343	6.4	3.0	26.4
NBA All-Star Totals	4	4	115	33	49	.673	0	0	–	9	17	.529	3	13	16	10	13	0	6	8	1	75	4.0	2.5	18.8

Thompson, George b. November 29, 1947 Ht. 6-2 Wt. 215 College: Marquette

SEASON–TEAM	G	GS	MIN	FGM	FGA	PCT	3FGM	3FGA	PCT	FTM	FTA	PCT	O-RB	D-RB	TOT	AST	PF	DQ	STL	TO	BLK	PTS	RPG	APG	PPG
69-70–Pittsburgh (A)	54	–	1017	259	587	.441	7	32	.219	176	260	.677	–	–	94	73	109	0	–	–	–	701	1.7	1.4	13.0
70-71–Pittsburgh (A)	82	–	2470	575	1220	.471	23	90	.256	347	485	.715	–	–	291	207	217	–	–	–	–	1520	3.5	2.5	18.5
71-72–Pittsburgh (A)	70	–	2904	696	1448	.481	41	132	.311	455	584	.779	–	–	353	257	201	–	–	217	–	1888	5.0	3.7	27.0
72-73–Memphis (A)	80	–	2925	579	1269	.456	20	73	.274	549	700	.784	95	170	265	403	246	1	–	245	–	1727	3.3	5.0	21.6
73-74–Memphis (A)	78	–	2732	539	1134	.475	10	54	.185	410	519	.790	93	180	273	396	234	–	117	210	24	1498	3.5	5.1	19.2
74-75–Milwaukee	73	–	1983	306	691	.443	–	–	–	168	214	.785	50	131	181	225	203	5	66	–	6	780	2.5	3.1	10.7
Reg. NBA Totals	73	–	1983	306	691	.443	–	–	–	168	214	.785	50	131	181	225	203	5	66	–	6	780	2.5	3.1	10.7
Reg. ABA Totals	364	–	12048	2648	5658	.468	101	381	.265	1937	2548	.760	188	350	1276	1336	1007	1	117	672	24	7334	3.5	3.7	20.1

Thompson, John R. Jr. b. September 2, 1941 Ht. 6-10 Wt. 230 College: Providence

SEASON–TEAM	G	GS	MIN	FGM	FGA	PCT	3FGM	3FGA	PCT	FTM	FTA	PCT	O-RB	D-RB	TOT	AST	PF	DQ	STL	TO	BLK	PTS	RPG	APG	PPG
64-65–Boston	64	–	699	84	209	.402	–	–	–	62	105	.590	–	–	230	16	141	1	–	–	–	230	3.6	0.3	3.6
65-66–Boston	10	–	72	14	30	.467	–	–	–	4	6	.667	–	–	30	3	15	0	–	–	–	32	3.0	0.3	3.2
Reg. Season Totals	74	–	771	98	239	.410	–	–	–	66	111	.595	–	–	260	19	156	1	–	–	–	262	3.5	0.3	3.5
Playoff Totals	6	–	32	3	14	.214	–	–	–	7	7	1.000	–	–	16	1	4	0	–	–	–	13	2.7	0.2	2.2

Thompson, John Sigred (Jack) b. March 26, 1946 Ht. 6-1 Wt. 185 College: South Carolina

SEASON–TEAM	G	GS	MIN	FGM	FGA	PCT	3FGM	3FGA	PCT	FTM	FTA	PCT	O-RB	D-RB	TOT	AST	PF	DQ	STL	TO	BLK	PTS	RPG	APG	PPG
68-69–Indiana (A)	2	–	4	1	3	.333	0	1	.000	0	0	–	–	–	1	2	0	0	–	2	–	2	0.5	1.0	1.0
Reg. ABA Totals	2	–	4	1	3	.333	0	1	.000	0	0	–	–	–	1	2	0	0	–	2	–	2	0.5	1.0	1.0

Thompson, Kevin Lamont b. February 7, 1971 Ht. 6-11 Wt. 260 College: North Carolina State

SEASON–TEAM	G	GS	MIN	FGM	FGA	PCT	3FGM	3FGA	PCT	FTM	FTA	PCT	O-RB	D-RB	TOT	AST	PF	DQ	STL	TO	BLK	PTS	RPG	APG	PPG
93-94–Portland	14	0	58	6	14	.429	0	1	.000	1	2	.500	7	6	13	3	11	0	0	5	2	13	0.9	0.2	0.9
Reg. Season Totals	14	0	58	6	14	.429	0	1	.000	1	2	.500	7	6	13	3	11	0	0	5	2	13	0.9	0.2	0.9

Thompson, LaSalle III (Tank) b. June 23, 1961 Ht. 6-10 Wt. 260 College: Texas

SEASON–TEAM	G	GS	MIN	FGM	FGA	PCT	3FGM	3FGA	PCT	FTM	FTA	PCT	O-RB	D-RB	TOT	AST	PF	DQ	STL	TO	BLK	PTS	RPG	APG	PPG
82-83–Kansas City	71	3	987	147	287	.512	0	1	.000	89	137	.650	133	242	375	33	186	1	40	96	61	383	5.3	0.5	5.4
83-84–Kansas City	80	38	1915	333	637	.523	0	0	–	160	223	.717	260	449	709	86	327	8	71	168	145	826	8.9	1.1	10.3
84-85–Kansas City	82	77	2458	369	695	.531	0	0	–	227	315	.721	274	580	854	130	328	4	98	202	128	965	10.4	1.6	11.8
85-86–Sacramento	80	64	2377	411	794	.518	0	1	.000	202	276	.732	252	518	770	168	295	8	71	184	109	1024	9.6	2.1	12.8
86-87–Sacramento	82	53	2166	362	752	.481	0	5	.000	188	255	.737	237	450	687	122	290	6	69	143	126	912	8.4	1.5	11.1
87-88–Sacramento	69	9	1257	215	456	.471	2	5	.400	118	164	.720	138	289	427	68	217	1	54	109	73	550	6.2	1.0	8.0
88-89–Sac.-Indiana	76	71	2329	416	850	.489	0	1	.000	227	281	.808	224	494	718	81	285	12	79	179	94	1059	9.4	1.1	13.9
89-90–Indiana	82	60	2126	223	471	.473	1	5	.200	107	134	.799	175	455	630	106	313	11	65	150	71	554	7.7	1.3	6.8
90-91–Indiana	82	77	1946	276	565	.488	1	5	.200	72	104	.692	154	409	563	147	265	4	63	168	63	625	6.9	1.8	7.6
91-92–Indiana	80	49	1299	168	359	.468	0	2	.000	58	71	.817	98	283	381	102	207	0	52	98	34	394	4.8	1.3	4.9
92-93–Indiana	63	0	730	104	213	.488	0	1	.000	29	39	.744	55	123	178	34	137	0	29	47	24	237	2.8	0.5	3.8
93-94–Indiana	30	1	282	27	77	.351	0	0	–	16	30	.533	26	49	75	16	59	1	10	23	8	70	2.5	0.5	2.3
94-95–Indiana	38	3	453	49	118	.415	0	0	–	14	16	.875	28	61	89	18	76	0	18	33	10	112	2.3	0.5	2.9
95-96–Philadelphia	44	11	773	33	83	.398	0	0	–	19	24	.792	62	137	199	26	125	5	19	37	20	85	4.5	0.6	1.9
96-97–Denver-Indiana	26	0	140	3	19	.158	0	0	–	4	6	.667	7	27	34	2	33	0	3	9	6	10	1.3	0.1	0.4
Reg. Season Totals	985	516	21238	3136	6376	.492	4	26	.154	1530	2075	.737	2123	4566	6689	1139	3143	61	741	1646	972	7806	6.8	1.2	7.9
Playoff Totals	28	14	547	71	163	.436	0	0	–	36	45	.800	49	99	148	28	79	0	16	37	25	178	5.3	1.0	6.4

T

Thompson, Mychal George b. January 30, 1955 Ht. 6-10 Wt. 235 College: Minnesota

SEASON–TEAM	G	GS	MIN	FGM	FGA	PCT	3FGM	3FGA	PCT	FTM	FTA	PCT	O-RB	D-RB	TOT	AST	PF	DQ	STL	TO	BLK	PTS	RPG	APG	PPG
78-79–Portland	73	–	2144	460	938	.490	–	–	–	154	269	.572	198	406	604	176	270	10	67	205	134	1074	8.3	2.4	14.7
80-81–Portland	79	–	2790	569	1151	.494	0	1	.000	207	323	.641	223	463	686	284	260	5	62	241	170	1345	8.7	3.6	17.0
81-82–Portland	79	78	3129	681	1303	.523	0	0	–	280	446	.628	258	663	921	319	233	2	69	245	107	1642	11.7	4.0	20.8
82-83–Portland	80	80	3017	505	1033	.489	0	1	.000	249	401	.621	183	570	753	380	213	1	68	281	110	1259	9.4	4.8	15.7
83-84–Portland	79	74	2648	487	929	.524	0	2	.000	266	399	.667	235	453	688	308	237	2	84	235	108	1240	8.7	3.9	15.7
84-85–Portland	79	55	2616	572	1111	.515	0	0	–	307	449	.684	211	407	618	205	216	0	78	231	104	1451	7.8	2.6	18.4
85-86–Portland	82	78	2569	503	1011	.498	0	0	–	198	309	.641	181	427	608	176	267	5	76	196	35	1204	7.4	2.1	14.7
86-87–S.A.-Lakers	82	7	1890	359	797	.450	1	2	.500	219	297	.737	138	274	412	115	202	1	45	134	71	938	5.0	1.4	11.4
87-88–L.A. Lakers	80	0	2007	370	722	.512	0	3	.000	185	292	.634	198	291	489	66	251	1	38	113	79	925	6.1	0.8	11.6
88-89–L.A. Lakers	80	8	1994	291	521	.559	0	1	.000	156	230	.678	157	310	467	48	224	0	58	97	59	738	5.8	0.6	9.2
89-90–L.A. Lakers	70	70	1883	281	562	.500	0	0	–	144	204	.706	173	304	477	43	207	0	33	79	73	706	6.8	0.6	10.1
90-91–L.A. Lakers	72	4	1077	113	228	.496	0	2	.000	62	88	.705	74	154	228	21	112	0	23	47	23	288	3.2	0.3	4.0
Reg. Season Totals	935	454	27764	5191	10306	.504	1	12	.083	2427	3707	.655	2229	4722	6951	2141	2692	27	701	2104	1073	12810	7.4	2.3	13.7
Playoff Totals	104	23	2708	449	897	.501	0	0	–	234	361	.648	224	403	627	126	309	4	56	156	106	1132	6.0	1.2	10.9

Thompson, Paul Stanford b. May 25, 1961 Ht. 6-6 Wt. 210 College: Tulane

SEASON–TEAM	G	GS	MIN	FGM	FGA	PCT	3FGM	3FGA	PCT	FTM	FTA	PCT	O-RB	D-RB	TOT	AST	PF	DQ	STL	TO	BLK	PTS	RPG	APG	PPG
83-84–Cleveland	82	10	1731	309	662	.467	9	39	.231	115	149	.772	120	192	312	122	192	2	70	73	37	742	3.8	1.5	9.0
84-85–Clev.-Milw.	49	27	942	189	459	.412	6	30	.200	69	87	.793	57	101	158	78	119	1	56	57	25	453	3.2	1.6	9.2
85-86–Philadelphia	23	8	432	70	194	.361	2	12	.167	37	43	.860	27	36	63	24	49	1	15	30	17	179	2.7	1.0	7.8
Reg. Season Totals	154	45	3105	568	1315	.432	17	81	.210	221	279	.792	204	329	533	224	360	4	141	160	79	1374	3.5	1.5	8.9
Playoff Totals	3	0	34	5	12	.417	0	2	.000	3	5	.600	1	4	5	2	3	0	4	4	1	13	1.7	0.7	4.3

Thompson, Stephen M. b. December 2, 1968 Ht. 6-4 Wt. 185 College: Syracuse

SEASON–TEAM	G	GS	MIN	FGM	FGA	PCT	3FGM	3FGA	PCT	FTM	FTA	PCT	O-RB	D-RB	TOT	AST	PF	DQ	STL	TO	BLK	PTS	RPG	APG	PPG
91-92–Orlando-Sac.	19	0	91	14	37	.378	0	1	.000	3	8	.375	11	8	19	8	9	0	6	5	3	31	1.0	0.4	1.6
Reg. Season Totals	19	0	91	14	37	.378	0	1	.000	3	8	.375	11	8	19	8	9	0	6	5	3	31	1.0	0.4	1.6

Thompson, William Stansbury (Billy, B.T. Express) b. December 1, 1963 Ht. 6-7 Wt. 220 College: Louisville

SEASON–TEAM	G	GS	MIN	FGM	FGA	PCT	3FGM	3FGA	PCT	FTM	FTA	PCT	O-RB	D-RB	TOT	AST	PF	DQ	STL	TO	BLK	PTS	RPG	APG	PPG
86-87–L.A. Lakers	59	0	762	142	261	.544	0	1	.000	48	74	.649	69	102	171	60	148	1	15	61	30	332	2.9	1.0	5.6
87-88–L.A. Lakers	9	0	38	3	13	.231	0	0	–	8	10	.800	2	7	9	1	11	0	1	6	0	14	1.0	0.1	1.6
88-89–Miami	79	58	2273	349	716	.487	0	4	.000	156	224	.696	241	331	572	176	260	8	56	189	105	854	7.2	2.2	10.8
89-90–Miami	79	45	2142	375	727	.516	2	4	.500	115	185	.622	238	313	551	166	237	1	54	156	89	867	7.0	2.1	11.0
90-91–Miami	73	46	1481	205	411	.499	0	4	.000	89	124	.718	120	192	312	111	161	3	32	117	48	499	4.3	1.5	6.8
91-92–Golden State	1	0	1	0	0	–	0	0	–	0	0	–	0	0	0	0	0	0	0	0	0	0	0.0	0.0	0.0
Reg. Season Totals	300	149	6697	1074	2128	.505	2	13	.154	416	617	.674	670	945	1615	514	817	13	158	529	272	2566	5.4	1.7	8.6
Playoff Totals	3	0	27	6	11	.545	0	0	–	2	2	1.000	3	3	6	2	2	0	4	0	0	14	2.0	0.7	4.7

Thoren, Duane W. (Skip) b. April 5, 1943 Ht. 6-10 Wt. 230 College: Illinois

SEASON–TEAM	G	GS	MIN	FGM	FGA	PCT	3FGM	3FGA	PCT	FTM	FTA	PCT	O-RB	D-RB	TOT	AST	PF	DQ	STL	TO	BLK	PTS	RPG	APG	PPG
67-68–Minnesota (A)	63	–	1203	206	475	.434	0	1	.000	102	164	.622	–	–	436	59	124	3	–	77	–	514	6.9	0.9	8.2
68-69–Miami (A)	78	–	2645	532	1100	.484	0	2	.000	241	392	.615	391	655	1046	195	324	11	–	180	–	1305	13.4	2.5	16.7
69-70–Miami (A)	29	–	1020	164	364	.451	0	2	.000	92	155	.594	–	–	393	75	112	2	–	–	–	420	13.6	2.6	14.5
Reg. ABA Totals	170	–	4868	902	1939	.465	0	5	.000	435	711	.612	391	655	1875	329	560	16	–	257	–	2239	11.0	1.9	13.2
ABA Playoff Totals	14	–	454	75	157	.478	0	0	–	42	73	.575	42	113	182	21	53	3	–	7	–	192	13.0	1.5	13.7

Thorn, Rodney King (Rod) b. May 23, 1941 Ht. 6-4 Wt. 195 College: West Virginia

SEASON–TEAM	G	GS	MIN	FGM	FGA	PCT	3FGM	3FGA	PCT	FTM	FTA	PCT	O-RB	D-RB	TOT	AST	PF	DQ	STL	TO	BLK	PTS	RPG	APG	PPG
63-64–Baltimore	75	–	2594	411	1015	.405	–	–	–	258	353	.731	–	–	360	281	187	3	–	–	–	1080	4.8	3.7	14.4
64-65–Detroit	74	–	1770	320	750	.427	–	–	–	176	243	.724	–	–	266	161	122	0	–	–	–	816	3.6	2.2	11.0
65-66–Detroit-St. L.	73	–	1739	306	728	.420	–	–	–	168	236	.712	–	–	210	145	144	0	–	–	–	780	2.9	2.0	10.7
66-67–St. Louis	67	–	1166	233	524	.445	–	–	–	125	172	.727	–	–	160	118	88	0	–	–	–	591	2.4	1.8	8.8
67-68–Seattle	66	–	1668	377	835	.451	–	–	–	252	342	.737	–	–	265	230	117	1	–	–	–	1006	4.0	3.5	15.2
68-69–Seattle	29	–	567	131	283	.463	–	–	–	71	97	.732	–	–	83	80	58	0	–	–	–	333	2.9	2.8	11.5
69-70–Seattle	19	–	105	20	45	.444	–	–	–	15	24	.625	–	–	16	17	8	0	–	–	–	55	0.8	0.9	2.9
70-71–Seattle	63	–	767	141	299	.472	–	–	–	69	102	.676	–	–	103	182	60	0	–	–	–	351	1.6	2.9	5.6
Reg. Season Totals	466	–	10376	1939	4479	.433	–	–	–	1134	1569	.723	–	–	1463	1214	784	4	–	–	–	5012	3.1	2.6	10.8
Playoff Totals	19	–	275	45	116	.388	–	–	–	39	45	.867	–	–	45	21	22	0	–	–	–	129	2.4	1.1	6.8

Thornton, Dallas **(Big D.)** b. September 1, 1946 Ht. 6-4 Wt. 190 College: Kentucky Wesleyan

SEASON–TEAM	G	GS	MIN	FGM	FGA	PCT	3FGM	3FGA	PCT	FTM	FTA	PCT	O-RB	D-RB	TOT	AST	PF	DQ	STL	TO	BLK	PTS	RPG	APG	PPG
68-69–Miami (A)	45	–	756	108	249	.434	2	9	.222	79	125	.632	–	–	119	63	92	1	–	80	–	297	2.6	1.4	6.6
69-70–Miami (A)	5	–	114	15	35	.429	0	2	.000	14	17	.824	–	–	22	11	14	0	–	–	–	44	4.4	2.2	8.8
Reg. ABA Totals	50	–	870	123	284	.433	2	11	.182	93	142	.655	–	–	141	74	106	1	–	80	–	341	2.8	1.5	6.8
ABA Playoff Totals	7	–	118	23	59	.390	0	7	.000	21	34	.618	–	–	23	6	9	0	–	–	–	67	3.3	0.9	9.6

Thornton, Robert George **(Bob)** b. July 10, 1962 Ht. 6-10 Wt. 225 College: Saddleback (Calif.) Coll. (J.C.); California-Irvine

SEASON–TEAM	G	GS	MIN	FGM	FGA	PCT	3FGM	3FGA	PCT	FTM	FTA	PCT	O-RB	D-RB	TOT	AST	PF	DQ	STL	TO	BLK	PTS	RPG	APG	PPG
85-86–New York	71	23	1323	125	274	.456	0	0	–	86	162	.531	113	177	290	43	209	5	30	83	7	336	4.1	0.6	4.7
86-87–New York	33	4	282	29	67	.433	0	1	.000	13	20	.650	18	38	56	8	48	0	4	24	3	71	1.7	0.2	2.2
87-88–N.Y.-Phil.	48	2	593	65	130	.500	0	2	.000	34	55	.618	46	66	112	15	103	1	11	35	3	164	2.3	0.3	3.4
88-89–Philadelphia	54	0	449	47	111	.423	1	3	.333	32	60	.533	36	56	92	15	87	0	8	23	7	127	1.7	0.3	2.4
89-90–Philadelphia	56	0	592	48	112	.429	1	3	.333	26	51	.510	45	88	133	17	105	1	20	35	12	123	2.4	0.3	2.2
90-91–Minnesota	12	1	110	4	13	.308	0	0	–	8	10	.800	1	14	15	1	18	0	0	9	3	16	1.3	0.1	1.3
91-92–Utah	2	0	6	1	7	.143	0	0	–	2	2	1.000	2	0	2	0	1	0	0	0	0	4	1.0	0.0	2.0
95-96–Washington	7	0	31	1	6	.167	0	0	–	1	2	.500	6	6	12	0	7	0	1	1	0	3	1.7	0.0	0.4
Reg. Season Totals	283	30	3386	320	720	.444	2	9	.222	202	362	.558	267	445	712	99	578	7	74	210	35	844	2.5	0.3	3.0
Playoff Totals	16	0	121	9	23	.391	0	0	–	8	14	.571	15	9	24	5	25	0	2	3	1	26	1.5	0.3	1.6

Thorpe, Otis Henry **(O.T.)** b. August 5, 1962 Ht. 6-10 Wt. 246 College: Providence

SEASON–TEAM	G	GS	MIN	FGM	FGA	PCT	3FGM	3FGA	PCT	FTM	FTA	PCT	O-RB	D-RB	TOT	AST	PF	DQ	STL	TO	BLK	PTS	RPG	APG	PPG
84-85–Kansas City	82	23	1918	411	685	.600	0	2	.000	230	371	.620	187	369	556	111	256	2	34	187	37	1052	6.8	1.4	12.8
85-86–Sacramento	75	18	1675	289	492	.587	0	0	–	164	248	.661	137	283	420	84	233	3	35	123	34	742	5.6	1.1	9.9
86-87–Sacramento	82	82	2956	567	1050	.540	0	3	.000	413	543	.761	259	560	819	201	292	11	46	189	60	1547	10.0	2.5	18.9
87-88–Sacramento	82	82	3072	622	1226	.507	0	6	.000	460	609	.755	279	558	837	266	264	3	62	228	56	1704	10.2	3.2	20.8
88-89–Houston	82	82	3135	521	961	.542	0	2	.000	328	450	.729	272	515	787	202	259	6	82	225	37	1370	9.6	2.5	16.7
89-90–Houston	82	82	2947	547	998	.548	0	10	.000	307	446	.688	258	476	734	261	270	5	66	229	24	1401	9.0	3.2	17.1
90-91–Houston	82	82	3039	549	988	.556	3	7	.429	334	480	.696	287	559	846	197	278	10	73	217	20	1435	10.3	2.4	17.5
91-92–Houston	82	82	3056	558	943	.592	0	7	.000	304	463	.657	285	577	862	250	307	7	52	237	37	1420	10.5	3.0	17.3
92-93–Houston	72	69	2357	385	690	.558	0	2	.000	153	256	.598	219	370	589	181	234	3	43	151	19	923	8.2	2.5	12.8
93-94–Houston	82	82	2909	449	801	.561	0	2	.000	251	382	.657	271	599	870	189	253	1	66	185	28	1149	10.6	2.3	14.0
94-95–Houston-Port.	70	35	2096	385	681	.565	0	7	.000	167	281	.594	202	356	558	112	224	3	41	132	28	937	8.0	1.6	13.4
95-96–Detroit	82	82	2841	452	853	.530	0	4	.000	257	362	.710	211	477	688	158	300	7	53	195	39	1161	8.4	1.9	14.2
96-97–Detroit	79	79	2661	419	787	.532	0	2	.000	198	303	.653	226	396	622	133	298	7	59	145	17	1036	7.9	1.7	13.1
97-98–Vanc.-Sac.	74	66	2197	294	624	.471	0	5	.000	164	240	.683	151	386	537	222	238	4	48	152	30	752	7.3	3.0	10.2
98-99–Washington	49	38	1539	240	440	.545	0	2	.000	74	106	.698	96	238	334	101	196	9	42	88	19	554	6.8	2.1	11.3
99-00–Miami	51	1	777	125	243	.514	0	3	.000	29	48	.604	56	110	166	33	136	4	26	59	9	279	3.3	0.6	5.5
Reg. Season Totals	1208	985	39175	6813	12462	.547	3	64	.047	3833	5588	.686	3396	6829	10225	2701	4038	85	828	2742	494	17462	8.5	2.2	14.5
Playoff Totals	70	54	2195	319	555	.575	1	3	.333	147	233	.631	176	354	530	128	233	4	33	115	15	786	7.6	1.8	11.2
All-Star Totals	1	0	4	1	1	1.000	0	0	–	0	0	–	0	0	0	0	0	0	0	0	0	2	0.0	0.0	2.0

Threatt, Sedale Eugene b. September 10, 1961 Ht. 6-2 Wt. 185 College: West Virginia Tech

SEASON–TEAM	G	GS	MIN	FGM	FGA	PCT	3FGM	3FGA	PCT	FTM	FTA	PCT	O-RB	D-RB	TOT	AST	PF	DQ	STL	TO	BLK	PTS	RPG	APG	PPG
83-84–Philadelphia	45	0	464	62	148	.419	1	8	.125	23	28	.821	17	23	40	41	65	1	13	33	2	148	0.9	0.9	3.3
84-85–Philadelphia	82	0	1304	188	416	.452	4	22	.182	66	90	.733	21	78	99	175	171	2	80	99	16	446	1.2	2.1	5.4
85-86–Philadelphia	70	27	1754	310	684	.453	1	24	.042	75	90	.833	21	100	121	193	157	1	93	102	5	696	1.7	2.8	9.9
86-87–Phil.-Chicago	68	8	1446	239	534	.448	7	32	.219	95	119	.798	26	82	108	259	164	0	74	89	13	580	1.6	3.8	8.5
87-88–Chi.-Seattle	71	0	1055	216	425	.508	3	27	.111	57	71	.803	23	65	88	160	100	0	60	63	8	492	1.2	2.3	6.9
88-89–Seattle	63	0	1220	235	476	.494	11	30	.367	63	77	.818	31	86	117	238	155	0	83	77	4	544	1.9	3.8	8.6
89-90–Seattle	65	18	1481	303	599	.506	8	32	.250	130	157	.828	43	72	115	216	164	0	65	77	8	744	1.8	3.3	11.4
90-91–Seattle	80	57	2066	433	835	.519	10	35	.286	137	173	.792	25	74	99	273	191	0	113	138	8	1013	1.2	3.4	12.7
91-92–L.A. Lakers	82	82	3070	509	1041	.489	20	62	.323	202	243	.831	43	210	253	593	231	1	168	182	16	1240	3.1	7.2	15.1
92-93–L.A. Lakers	82	82	2893	522	1028	.508	14	53	.264	177	215	.823	47	226	273	564	248	1	142	173	11	1235	3.3	6.9	15.1
93-94–L.A. Lakers	81	20	2278	411	852	.482	5	33	.152	138	155	.890	28	125	153	344	186	1	110	106	19	965	1.9	4.2	11.9
94-95–L.A. Lakers	59	2	1384	217	437	.497	36	95	.379	88	111	.793	21	103	124	248	139	1	54	70	12	558	2.1	4.2	9.5
95-96–L.A. Lakers	82	8	1687	241	526	.458	60	169	.355	54	71	.761	20	75	95	269	178	0	68	74	11	596	1.2	3.3	7.3
96-97–Houston	21	0	334	28	74	.378	8	20	.400	6	8	.750	5	19	24	40	29	0	15	13	3	70	1.1	1.9	3.3
Reg. Season Totals	951	304	22436	3914	8075	.485	188	642	.293	1311	1608	.815	371	1338	1709	3613	2178	8	1138	1296	136	9327	1.8	3.8	9.8
Playoff Totals	70	15	1534	251	555	.452	21	79	.266	84	103	.816	22	88	110	252	162	1	73	84	7	607	1.6	3.6	8.7

Thurmond, Nathaniel **(Nate)** b. July 25, 1941 Ht. 6-11 Wt. 230 College: Bowling Green State HOF: 1984

SEASON–TEAM	G	GS	MIN	FGM	FGA	PCT	3FGM	3FGA	PCT	FTM	FTA	PCT	O-RB	D-RB	TOT	AST	PF	DQ	STL	TO	BLK	PTS	RPG	APG	PPG
63-64–San Francisco	76	–	1966	219	554	.395	–	–	–	95	173	.549	–	–	790	86	184	2	–	–	–	533	10.4	1.1	7.0
64-65–San Francisco	77	–	3173	519	1240	.419	–	–	–	235	357	.658	–	–	1395	157	232	3	–	–	–	1273	18.1	2.0	16.5
65-66–San Francisco	73	–	2891	454	1119	.406	–	–	–	280	428	.654	–	–	1312	111	223	7	–	–	–	1188	18.0	1.5	16.3
66-67–San Francisco	65	–	2761	467	1068	.437	–	–	–	280	445	.629	–	–	1382	166	183	3	–	–	–	1214	21.3	2.6	18.7
67-68–San Francisco	51	–	2222	382	929	.411	–	–	–	282	438	.644	–	–	1121	215	137	1	–	–	–	1046	22.0	4.2	20.5
68-69–San Francisco	71	–	3208	571	1394	.410	–	–	–	382	621	.615	–	–	1402	253	171	0	–	–	–	1524	19.7	3.6	21.5
69-70–San Francisco	43	–	1919	341	824	.414	–	–	–	261	346	.754	–	–	762	150	110	1	–	–	–	943	17.7	3.5	21.9
70-71–San Francisco	82	–	3351	623	1401	.445	–	–	–	395	541	.730	–	–	1128	257	192	1	–	–	–	1641	13.8	3.1	20.0
71-72–Golden State	78	–	3362	628	1454	.432	–	–	–	417	561	.743	–	–	1252	230	214	1	–	–	–	1673	16.1	2.9	21.4
72-73–Golden State	79	–	3419	517	1159	.446	–	–	–	315	439	.718	–	–	1349	280	240	2	–	–	–	1349	17.1	3.5	17.1
73-74–Golden State	62	–	2463	308	694	.444	–	–	–	191	287	.666	249	629	878	165	179	4	41	–	179	807	14.2	2.7	13.0
74-75–Chicago	80	–	2756	250	686	.364	–	–	–	132	224	.589	259	645	904	328	271	6	46	–	195	632	11.3	4.1	7.9
75-76–Chicago-Clev.	78	–	1393	142	337	.421	–	–	–	62	123	.504	115	300	415	94	160	1	22	–	98	346	5.3	1.2	4.4
76-77–Cleveland	49	–	997	100	246	.407	–	–	–	68	106	.642	121	253	374	83	128	2	16	–	81	268	7.6	1.7	5.5
Reg. Season Totals	964	–	35881	5521	13105	.421	–	–	–	3395	5089	.667	744	1827	14464	2575	2624	34	125	–	553	14437	15.0	2.7	15.0
Playoff Totals	81	–	2875	379	912	.416	–	–	–	208	335	.621	62	143	1101	227	266	4	11	–	51	966	13.6	2.8	11.9
All-Star Totals	5	–	104	14	43	.326	–	–	–	3	8	.375	1	2	44	2	5	0	0	–	0	31	8.8	0.4	6.2

Thurston, John Melvin **(Mel)** b. January 16, 1919 d. October 8, 1997 Ht. 6-0 Wt. 175 College: Canisius

SEASON–TEAM	G	GS	MIN	FGM	FGA	PCT	3FGM	3FGA	PCT	FTM	FTA	PCT	O-RB	D-RB	TOT	AST	PF	DQ	STL	TO	BLK	PTS	RPG	APG	PPG
46-47–Tri-Cities (N)	39	–	–	39	–	–	–	–	–	36	59	.610	–	–	–	–	62	–	–	–	–	114	–	–	2.9
47-48–Tri-Cities (N)	34	–	–	36	–	–	–	–	–	38	61	.623	–	–	–	–	–	–	–	–	–	110	–	–	3.2
47-48–Providence	14	–	–	32	113	.283	–	–	–	14	28	.500	–	–	–	4	42	–	–	–	–	78	–	0.3	5.6
Reg. NBA Totals	14	–	–	32	113	.283	–	–	–	14	28	.500	–	–	–	4	42	–	–	–	–	78	–	0.3	5.6
Reg. NBL Totals	73	–	–	75	–	–	–	–	–	74	120	.617	–	–	–	–	62	–	–	–	–	224	–	–	3.1

Tidrick, Howard Benjamin **(Hal)** b. June 14, 1915 d. April 2, 1974 Ht. 6-1 Wt. 190 College: Washington & Jefferson

SEASON–TEAM	G	GS	MIN	FGM	FGA	PCT	3FGM	3FGA	PCT	FTM	FTA	PCT	O-RB	D-RB	TOT	AST	PF	DQ	STL	TO	BLK	PTS	RPG	APG	PPG
44-45–Sheboygan (N)	1	–	–	0	–	–	–	–	–	0	–	–	–	–	–	–	–	–	–	–	–	0	–	–	0.0
46-47–Toledo (N)	44	–	–	232	–	–	–	–	–	115	165	.697	–	–	–	–	105	–	–	–	–	579	–	–	13.2
47-48–Toledo (N)	59	–	–	267	–	–	–	–	–	189	243	.778	–	–	–	–	149	–	–	–	–	723	–	–	12.3
48-49–Ind.-Balt.	61	–	–	194	616	.315	–	–	–	164	205	.800	–	–	–	101	191	–	–	–	–	552	–	1.7	9.0
Reg. NBA Totals	61	–	–	194	616	.315	–	–	–	164	205	.800	–	–	–	101	191	–	–	–	–	552	–	1.7	9.0
Reg. NBL Totals	104	–	–	499	–	–	–	–	–	304	408	.745	–	–	–	–	254	–	–	–	–	1302	–	–	12.5
NBA Playoff Totals	3	–	–	5	19	.263	–	–	–	3	5	.600	–	–	–	1	16	2	–	–	–	13	–	0.3	4.3
NBL Playoff Totals	5	–	–	19	–	–	–	–	–	14	23	.609	–	–	–	–	15	–	–	–	–	52	–	–	10.4

Tieman, Daniel Theodore **(Dan)** b. November 30, 1940 Ht. 6-0 Wt. 185 College: Thomas More

SEASON–TEAM	G	GS	MIN	FGM	FGA	PCT	3FGM	3FGA	PCT	FTM	FTA	PCT	O-RB	D-RB	TOT	AST	PF	DQ	STL	TO	BLK	PTS	RPG	APG	PPG
62-63–Cincinnati	29	–	176	15	57	.263	–	–	–	4	10	.400	–	–	22	27	18	0	–	–	–	34	0.8	0.9	1.2
Reg. Season Totals	29	–	176	15	57	.263	–	–	–	4	10	.400	–	–	22	27	18	0	–	–	–	34	0.8	0.9	1.2

Tillis, Darren b. February 23, 1960 Ht. 6-11 Wt. 215 College: Cleveland State

SEASON–TEAM	G	GS	MIN	FGM	FGA	PCT	3FGM	3FGA	PCT	FTM	FTA	PCT	O-RB	D-RB	TOT	AST	PF	DQ	STL	TO	BLK	PTS	RPG	APG	PPG
82-83–Boston-Clev.	52	4	526	76	181	.420	0	1	.000	16	28	.571	41	89	130	18	76	3	8	22	30	168	2.5	0.3	3.2
83-84–Golden State	72	1	730	108	254	.425	0	2	.000	41	63	.651	75	109	184	24	176	1	12	51	60	257	2.6	0.3	3.6
Reg. Season Totals	124	5	1256	184	435	.423	0	3	.000	57	91	.626	116	198	314	42	252	4	20	73	90	425	2.5	0.3	3.4

Tingle, Robert Jackson **(Jack)** b. December 30, 1924 d. September 22, 1958 Ht. 6-4 Wt. 205 College: Kentucky

SEASON–TEAM	G	GS	MIN	FGM	FGA	PCT	3FGM	3FGA	PCT	FTM	FTA	PCT	O-RB	D-RB	TOT	AST	PF	DQ	STL	TO	BLK	PTS	RPG	APG	PPG
47-48–Washington	37	–	–	36	137	.263	–	–	–	17	33	.515	–	–	–	7	45	–	–	–	–	89	–	0.2	2.4
48-49–Minneapolis	2	–	–	1	6	.167	–	–	–	0	0	–	–	–	–	1	2	–	–	–	–	2	–	0.5	1.0
Reg. Season Totals	39	–	–	37	143	.259	–	–	–	17	33	.515	–	–	–	8	47	–	–	–	–	91	–	0.2	2.3

Tinsley, George T. b. September 19, 1946 Ht. 6-5 Wt. 205 College: Kentucky Wesleyan

SEASON–TEAM	G	GS	MIN	FGM	FGA	PCT	3FGM	3FGA	PCT	FTM	FTA	PCT	O-RB	D-RB	TOT	AST	PF	DQ	STL	TO	BLK	PTS	RPG	APG	PPG
69-70–Wash.-Ken. (A)	82	–	1446	175	407	.430	1	8	.125	162	218	.743	–	–	325	76	192	3	–	–	–	513	4.0	0.9	6.3
71-72–Floridians (A)	51	–	418	70	174	.402	5	22	.227	46	62	.742	–	–	60	38	79	–	–	26	–	191	1.2	0.7	3.7
Reg. ABA Totals	133	–	1864	245	581	.422	6	30	.200	208	280	.743	–	–	385	114	271	3	–	26	–	704	2.9	0.9	5.3
ABA Playoff Totals	15	–	284	44	96	.458	2	7	.286	32	44	.727	–	–	65	19	35	0	–	2	–	122	4.3	1.3	8.1

Tisdale, Wayman Lawrence b. June 9, 1964 Ht. 6-9 Wt. 260 College: Oklahoma

SEASON–TEAM	G	GS	MIN	FGM	FGA	PCT	3FGM	3FGA	PCT	FTM	FTA	PCT	O-RB	D-RB	TOT	AST	PF	DQ	STL	TO	BLK	PTS	RPG	APG	PPG
85-86–Indiana	81	60	2277	516	1002	.515	0	2	.000	160	234	.684	191	393	584	79	290	3	32	188	44	1192	7.2	1.0	14.7
86-87–Indiana	81	15	2159	458	892	.513	0	2	.000	258	364	.709	217	258	475	117	293	9	50	139	26	1174	5.9	1.4	14.5
87-88–Indiana	79	57	2378	511	998	.512	0	2	.000	246	314	.783	168	323	491	103	274	5	54	145	34	1268	6.2	1.3	16.1
88-89–Indiana-Sac.	79	35	2434	532	1036	.514	0	4	.000	317	410	.773	187	422	609	128	290	7	55	172	52	1381	7.7	1.6	17.5
89-90–Sacramento	79	79	2937	726	1383	.525	0	6	.000	306	391	.783	185	410	595	108	251	3	54	153	54	1758	7.5	1.4	22.3
90-91–Sacramento	33	31	1116	262	542	.483	0	1	.000	136	170	.800	75	178	253	66	99	0	23	82	28	660	7.7	2.0	20.0
91-92–Sacramento	72	71	2521	522	1043	.500	0	2	.000	151	198	.763	135	334	469	106	248	3	55	124	79	1195	6.5	1.5	16.6
92-93–Sacramento	76	75	2283	544	1068	.509	0	2	.000	175	231	.758	127	373	500	108	277	8	52	117	47	1263	6.6	1.4	16.6
93-94–Sacramento	79	77	2557	552	1102	.501	0	0	–	215	266	.808	159	401	560	139	290	4	37	124	52	1319	7.1	1.8	16.7
94-95–Phoenix	65	13	1276	278	574	.484	0	0	–	94	122	.770	83	164	247	45	190	3	29	64	27	650	3.8	0.7	10.0
95-96–Phoenix	63	6	1152	279	564	.495	0	0	–	114	149	.765	55	159	214	58	188	2	15	63	36	672	3.4	0.9	10.7
96-97–Phoenix	53	15	778	158	371	.426	0	0	–	30	48	.625	35	85	120	20	111	0	8	36	21	346	2.3	0.4	6.5
Reg. Season Totals	840	534	23868	5338	10575	.505	0	21	.000	2202	2897	.760	1617	3500	5117	1077	2801	47	464	1407	500	12878	6.1	1.3	15.3
Playoff Totals	22	4	381	67	147	.456	0	1	.000	23	39	.590	16	41	57	22	61	2	2	13	5	157	2.6	1.0	7.1

Todorovich, Marko John (Mike) b. June 11, 1923 Ht. 6-5 Wt. 220 College: Washington-St. Louis; Notre Dame; Wyoming

SEASON–TEAM	G	GS	MIN	FGM	FGA	PCT	3FGM	3FGA	PCT	FTM	FTA	PCT	O-RB	D-RB	TOT	AST	PF	DQ	STL	TO	BLK	PTS	RPG	APG	PPG
47-48–Sheboygan (N)	60	–	–	277	–	–	–	–	–	223	343	.650	–	–	–	–	182	–	–	–	–	777	–	–	13.0
48-49–Sheboygan (N)	60	–	–	239	–	–	–	–	–	170	281	.605	–	–	–	–	183	–	–	–	–	648	–	–	10.8
49-50–St. Louis-Tri-Cit	65	–	–	263	852	.309	–	–	–	266	370	.719	–	–	–	207	230	–	–	–	–	792	–	3.2	12.2
50-51–Tri-Cities	66	–	–	221	715	.309	–	–	–	211	301	.701	–	–	455	179	197	5	–	–	–	653	6.9	2.7	9.9
Reg. NBA Totals	131	–	–	484	1567	.309	–	–	–	477	671	.711	–	–	455	386	427	5	–	–	–	1445	6.9	2.9	11.0
Reg. NBL Totals	120	–	–	516	–	–	–	–	–	393	624	.630	–	–	–	–	365	–	–	–	–	1425	–	–	11.9
NBA Playoff Totals	3	–	–	6	31	.194	–	–	–	19	24	.792	–	–	–	8	14	1	–	–	–	31	–	2.7	10.3

Tolbert, Byron Thomas (Tom, Fabian) b. October 16, 1965 Ht. 6-7 Wt. 240 College: Arizona

SEASON–TEAM	G	GS	MIN	FGM	FGA	PCT	3FGM	3FGA	PCT	FTM	FTA	PCT	O-RB	D-RB	TOT	AST	PF	DQ	STL	TO	BLK	PTS	RPG	APG	PPG
88-89–Charlotte	14	0	117	17	37	.459	0	3	.000	6	12	.500	7	14	21	7	20	0	2	2	4	40	1.5	0.5	2.9
89-90–Golden State	70	21	1347	218	442	.493	5	18	.278	175	241	.726	122	241	363	58	191	0	23	79	25	616	5.2	0.8	8.8
90-91–Golden State	62	32	1371	183	433	.423	7	21	.333	127	172	.738	87	188	275	76	195	4	35	80	38	500	4.4	1.2	8.1
91-92–Golden State	35	0	310	33	86	.384	2	8	.250	22	40	.550	14	41	55	21	73	0	10	20	6	90	1.6	0.6	2.6
92-93–Orlando	72	61	1838	226	454	.498	9	28	.321	122	168	.726	133	279	412	91	192	4	33	124	21	583	5.7	1.3	8.1
93-94–L.A. Clippers	49	6	640	74	177	.418	6	16	.375	33	45	.733	36	72	108	30	61	0	13	39	15	187	2.2	0.6	3.8
94-95–Charlotte	10	0	57	6	18	.333	0	4	.000	2	2	1.000	7	10	17	2	9	0	0	3	0	14	1.7	0.2	1.4
Reg. Season Totals	312	120	5680	757	1647	.460	29	98	.296	487	680	.716	406	845	1251	285	741	8	116	347	109	2030	4.0	0.9	6.5
Playoff Totals	9	0	116	14	33	.424	1	3	.333	3	11	.273	0	18	18	8	29	0	3	4	4	32	2.0	0.9	3.6

Tolbert, Raymond Lee (Ray) b. September 10, 1958 Ht. 6-9 Wt. 225 College: Indiana

SEASON–TEAM	G	GS	MIN	FGM	FGA	PCT	3FGM	3FGA	PCT	FTM	FTA	PCT	O-RB	D-RB	TOT	AST	PF	DQ	STL	TO	BLK	PTS	RPG	APG	PPG
81-82–N.J.-Seattle	64	0	607	100	202	.495	0	2	.000	19	35	.543	50	76	126	33	83	0	12	45	15	219	2.0	0.5	3.4
82-83–Seattle-Detroit	73	2	1107	157	314	.500	0	3	.000	52	103	.505	72	170	242	50	153	1	26	83	47	366	3.3	0.7	5.0
83-84–Detroit	49	0	475	64	121	.529	0	1	.000	23	45	.511	45	53	98	26	88	1	12	26	20	151	2.0	0.5	3.1
87-88–N.Y.-Lakers	25	0	259	35	69	.507	0	0	–	19	30	.633	23	32	55	10	39	0	8	21	5	89	2.2	0.4	3.6
88-89–Atlanta	50	0	341	40	94	.426	0	0	–	23	37	.622	31	57	88	16	55	0	13	35	13	103	1.8	0.3	2.1
Reg. Season Totals	261	2	2789	396	800	.495	0	6	.000	136	250	.544	221	388	609	135	418	2	71	210	100	928	2.3	0.5	3.6
Playoff Totals	5	0	33	3	5	.600	0	0	–	4	8	.500	1	4	5	1	7	0	4	0	0	10	1.0	0.2	2.0

Tolson, Byron Dean (Dean) b. November 25, 1951 Ht. 6-8 Wt. 195 College: Arkansas

SEASON–TEAM	G	GS	MIN	FGM	FGA	PCT	3FGM	3FGA	PCT	FTM	FTA	PCT	O-RB	D-RB	TOT	AST	PF	DQ	STL	TO	BLK	PTS	RPG	APG	PPG
74-75–Seattle	19	–	87	16	37	.432	–	–	–	11	17	.647	12	10	22	5	12	0	4	–	6	43	1.2	0.3	2.3
76-77–Seattle	60	–	587	137	242	.566	–	–	–	85	159	.535	73	84	157	27	83	0	32	–	21	359	2.6	0.5	6.0
77-78–Seattle	1	–	7	0	1	.000	–	–	–	0	0	–	0	0	0	2	2	0	0	1	0	0	0.0	2.0	0.0
Reg. Season Totals	80	–	681	153	280	.546	–	–	–	96	176	.545	85	94	179	34	97	0	36	1	27	402	2.2	0.4	5.0
Playoff Totals	4	–	22	1	8	.125	–	–	–	2	2	1.000	4	3	7	1	3	0	0	–	0	4	1.8	0.3	1.0

T

Tomjanovich, Rudolph (Rudy) b. November 24, 1948 Ht. 6-8 Wt. 220 College: Michigan

SEASON–TEAM	G	GS	MIN	FGM	FGA	PCT	3FGM	3FGA	PCT	FTM	FTA	PCT	O-RB	D-RB	TOT	AST	PF	DQ	STL	TO	BLK	PTS	RPG	APG	PPG
70-71–San Diego	77	–	1062	168	439	.383	–	–	–	73	112	.652	–	–	381	73	124	0	–	–	–	409	4.9	0.9	5.3
71-72–Houston	78	–	2689	500	1010	.495	–	–	–	172	238	.723	–	–	923	117	193	2	–	–	–	1172	11.8	1.5	15.0
72-73–Houston	81	–	2972	655	1371	.478	–	–	–	250	335	.746	–	–	938	178	225	1	–	–	–	1560	11.6	2.2	19.3
73-74–Houston	80	–	3227	788	1470	.536	–	–	–	385	454	.848	230	487	717	250	230	0	89	–	66	1961	9.0	3.1	24.5
74-75–Houston	81	–	3134	694	1323	.525	–	–	–	289	366	.790	184	429	613	236	230	1	76	–	24	1677	7.6	2.9	20.7
75-76–Houston	79	–	2912	622	1202	.517	–	–	–	221	288	.767	167	499	666	188	206	1	42	–	19	1465	8.4	2.4	18.5
76-77–Houston	81	–	3130	733	1437	.510	–	–	–	287	342	.839	172	512	684	172	198	1	57	–	27	1753	8.4	2.1	21.6
77-78–Houston	23	–	849	217	447	.485	–	–	–	61	81	.753	40	98	138	32	63	0	15	38	5	495	6.0	1.4	21.5
78-79–Houston	74	–	2641	620	1200	.517	–	–	–	168	221	.760	170	402	572	137	186	0	44	138	18	1408	7.7	1.9	19.0
79-80–Houston	62	–	1834	370	778	.476	22	79	.278	118	147	.803	132	226	358	109	161	2	32	98	10	880	5.8	1.8	14.2
80-81–Houston	52	–	1264	263	563	.467	12	51	.235	65	82	.793	78	130	208	81	121	0	19	58	6	603	4.0	1.6	11.6
Reg. Season Totals	768	–	25714	5630	11240	.501	34	130	.262	2089	2666	.784	1173	2783	6198	1573	1937	8	374	332	175	13383	8.1	2.0	17.4
Playoff Totals	37	–	1041	213	436	.489	1	10	.100	84	109	.771	67	122	189	59	78	1	11	17	8	511	5.1	1.6	13.8
All-Star Totals	5	–	89	12	32	.375	0	0	–	0	0	–	10	17	27	2	9	0	1	0	1	24	5.4	0.4	4.8

Toney, Andrew (Boston Strangler) b. November 23, 1957 Ht. 6-3 Wt. 185 College: Southwestern Louisiana-Lafayette

SEASON–TEAM	G	GS	MIN	FGM	FGA	PCT	3FGM	3FGA	PCT	FTM	FTA	PCT	O-RB	D-RB	TOT	AST	PF	DQ	STL	TO	BLK	PTS	RPG	APG	PPG
80-81–Philadelphia	75	57	1768	399	806	.495	9	29	.310	161	226	.712	32	111	143	273	234	5	59	219	10	968	1.9	3.6	12.9
81-82–Philadelphia	77	1	1909	511	979	.522	25	59	.424	227	306	.742	43	91	134	283	269	5	64	214	17	1274	1.7	3.7	16.5
82-83–Philadelphia	81	81	2474	626	1250	.501	22	76	.289	324	411	.788	42	183	225	365	255	0	80	271	17	1598	2.8	4.5	19.7
83-84–Philadelphia	78	72	2556	593	1125	.527	12	38	.316	390	465	.839	57	136	193	373	251	1	70	297	23	1588	2.5	4.8	20.4
84-85–Philadelphia	70	65	2237	450	914	.492	39	105	.371	306	355	.862	35	142	177	363	211	1	65	224	24	1245	2.5	5.2	17.8
85-86–Philadelphia	6	0	84	11	36	.306	0	2	.000	3	8	.375	2	3	5	12	8	0	2	7	0	25	0.8	2.0	4.2
86-87–Philadelphia	52	12	1058	197	437	.451	22	67	.328	133	167	.796	16	69	85	188	78	0	18	112	8	549	1.6	3.6	10.6
87-88–Philadelphia	29	15	522	72	171	.421	9	27	.333	58	72	.806	8	39	47	108	35	0	11	50	6	211	1.6	3.7	7.3
Reg. Season Totals	468	246	12608	2859	5718	.500	138	403	.342	1602	2010	.797	235	774	1009	1965	1341	12	369	1394	105	7458	2.2	4.2	15.9
Playoff Totals	72	49	2146	485	1015	.478	12	51	.235	272	346	.786	56	112	168	323	265	3	58	257	18	1254	2.3	4.5	17.4
All-Star Totals	2	0	40	10	16	.625	0	1	.000	1	1	1.000	0	1	1	10	3	0	4	4	0	21	0.5	5.0	10.5

Toney, Sedric Andre b. April 13, 1962 Ht. 6-2 Wt. 180 College: Phillips; Western Nebraska (Neb.) C.C.; Dayton

SEASON–TEAM	G	GS	MIN	FGM	FGA	PCT	3FGM	3FGA	PCT	FTM	FTA	PCT	O-RB	D-RB	TOT	AST	PF	DQ	STL	TO	BLK	PTS	RPG	APG	PPG
85-86–Atlanta-Phoenix	13	0	230	28	66	.424	3	10	.300	21	31	.677	3	22	25	26	24	0	6	22	0	80	1.9	2.0	6.2
87-88–New York	21	0	139	21	48	.438	5	14	.357	10	11	.909	3	5	8	24	20	0	9	12	1	57	0.4	1.1	2.7
88-89–Indiana	2	0	9	1	5	.200	0	3	.000	0	1	.000	1	1	2	0	1	0	0	2	0	2	1.0	0.0	1.0
89-90–Atlanta-Sac.	64	9	968	87	250	.348	23	63	.365	67	83	.807	14	46	60	174	106	1	33	73	0	264	0.9	2.7	4.1
93-94–Cleveland	12	0	64	2	12	.167	0	1	.000	2	2	1.000	1	2	3	11	8	0	0	5	0	6	0.3	0.9	0.5
Reg. Season Totals	112	9	1410	139	381	.365	31	91	.341	100	128	.781	22	76	98	235	159	1	48	114	1	409	0.9	2.1	3.7
Playoff Totals	3	0	15	3	6	.500	3	6	.500	2	2	1.000	0	0	0	2	4	0	1	2	0	11	0.0	0.7	3.7

Tonkovich, Andrew Edward (Andy) b. November 1, 1922 Ht. 6-1 Wt. 185 College: Marshall

SEASON–TEAM	G	GS	MIN	FGM	FGA	PCT	3FGM	3FGA	PCT	FTM	FTA	PCT	O-RB	D-RB	TOT	AST	PF	DQ	STL	TO	BLK	PTS	RPG	APG	PPG
48-49–Providence	17	–	–	19	71	.268	–	–	–	6	9	.667	–	–	–	10	12	–	–	–	–	44	–	0.6	2.6
Reg. Season Totals	17	–	–	19	71	.268	–	–	–	6	9	.667	–	–	–	10	12	–	–	–	–	44	–	0.6	2.6

Toolson, Andrew K. (Andy) b. January 19, 1966 Ht. 6-6 Wt. 210 College: Brigham Young

SEASON–TEAM	G	GS	MIN	FGM	FGA	PCT	3FGM	3FGA	PCT	FTM	FTA	PCT	O-RB	D-RB	TOT	AST	PF	DQ	STL	TO	BLK	PTS	RPG	APG	PPG
90-91–Utah	47	15	470	50	124	.403	12	32	.375	25	33	.758	32	35	67	31	58	0	14	24	2	137	1.4	0.7	2.9
95-96–Utah	13	0	53	8	22	.364	3	12	.250	3	4	.750	0	6	6	1	12	0	0	2	0	22	0.5	0.1	1.7
Reg. Season Totals	60	15	523	58	146	.397	15	44	.341	28	37	.757	32	41	73	32	70	0	14	26	2	159	1.2	0.5	2.7
Playoff Totals	2	0	4	0	2	.000	0	1	.000	0	0	–	0	0	0	1	0	0	1	0	0	0	0.0	0.5	0.0

Toomay, John C. (Jack) b. August 9, 1922 Ht. 6-6 Wt. 215 College: U. of Pacific

SEASON–TEAM	G	GS	MIN	FGM	FGA	PCT	3FGM	3FGA	PCT	FTM	FTA	PCT	O-RB	D-RB	TOT	AST	PF	DQ	STL	TO	BLK	PTS	RPG	APG	PPG
47-48–Chicago-Prov.	23	–	–	61	191	.319	–	–	–	60	91	.659	–	–	–	7	71	–	–	–	–	182	–	0.3	7.9
48-49–Balt.-Wash.	36	–	–	32	84	.381	–	–	–	36	53	.679	–	–	–	12	65	–	–	–	–	100	–	0.3	2.8
49-50–Denver	62	–	–	204	514	.397	–	–	–	186	264	.705	–	–	–	94	213	–	–	–	–	594	–	1.5	9.6
Reg. Season Totals	121	–	–	297	789	.376	–	–	–	282	408	.691	–	–	–	113	349	–	–	–	–	876	–	0.9	7.2
Playoff Totals	1	–	–	1	5	.200	–	–	–	5	7	.714	–	–	–	–	6	1	–	–	–	7	–	0.0	7.0

Toone, Bernard b. July 14, 1956 Ht. 6-9 Wt. 210 College: Marquette

SEASON–TEAM	G	GS	MIN	FGM	FGA	PCT	3FGM	3FGA	PCT	FTM	FTA	PCT	O-RB	D-RB	TOT	AST	PF	DQ	STL	TO	BLK	PTS	RPG	APG	PPG
79-80–Philadelphia	23	0	124	23	64	.359	1	7	.143	8	10	.800	12	22	34	12	20	0	4	16	5	55	1.5	0.5	2.4
Reg. Season Totals	23	0	124	23	64	.359	1	7	.143	8	10	.800	12	22	34	12	20	0	4	16	5	55	1.5	0.5	2.4
Playoff Totals	4	–	6	0	4	.000	0	1	.000	0	0	–	0	1	1	1	1	0	0	0	0	0	0.3	0.3	0.0

Torgoff, Irving (Irv) b. March 6, 1917 d. October 21, 1993 Ht. 6-2 Wt. 195 College: Long Island University

SEASON–TEAM	G	GS	MIN	FGM	FGA	PCT	3FGM	3FGA	PCT	FTM	FTA	PCT	O-RB	D-RB	TOT	AST	PF	DQ	STL	TO	BLK	PTS	RPG	APG	PPG
39-40–Detroit (N)	26	–	–	64	–	–	–	–	–	43	67	.642	–	–	–	–	58	–	–	–	–	171	–	–	6.6
46-47–Washington	58	–	–	187	684	.273	–	–	–	116	159	.730	–	–	–	30	173	–	–	–	–	490	–	0.5	8.4
47-48–Washington	47	–	–	111	541	.205	–	–	–	117	144	.813	–	–	–	32	153	–	–	–	–	339	–	0.7	7.2
48-49–Balt.-Phil.	42	–	–	59	226	.261	–	–	–	50	64	.781	–	–	–	44	110	–	–	–	–	168	–	1.0	4.0
Reg. NBA Totals	147	–	–	357	1451	.246	–	–	–	283	367	.771	–	–	–	106	436	–	–	–	–	997	–	0.7	6.8
Reg. NBL Totals	26	–	–	64	–	–	–	–	–	43	67	.642	–	–	–	–	58	–	–	–	–	171	–	–	6.6
NBA Playoff Totals	8	–	–	13	165	.158	–	–	–	13	19	.684	–	–	–	12	24	3	–	–	–	39	–	0.9	4.9
NBL Playoff Totals	3	–	–	10	–	–	–	–	–	7	0	–	–	–	–	–	7	–	–	–	–	27	–	–	9.0

Tormohlen, Eugene R. (Gene, Bumper) b. May 12, 1937 Ht. 6-9 Wt. 250 College: Tennessee

SEASON–TEAM	G	GS	MIN	FGM	FGA	PCT	3FGM	3FGA	PCT	FTM	FTA	PCT	O-RB	D-RB	TOT	AST	PF	DQ	STL	TO	BLK	PTS	RPG	APG	PPG
62-63–St. Louis	7	–	47	5	10	.500	–	–	–	2	10	.200	–	–	15	5	11	0	–	–	–	12	2.1	0.7	1.7
63-64–St. Louis	51	–	640	94	250	.376	–	–	–	22	46	.478	–	–	216	50	128	3	–	–	–	210	4.2	1.0	4.1
65-66–St. Louis	71	–	775	144	324	.444	–	–	–	54	82	.659	–	–	314	60	138	3	–	–	–	342	4.4	0.8	4.8
66-67–St. Louis	63	–	1036	172	403	.427	–	–	–	50	84	.595	–	–	347	73	177	4	–	–	–	394	5.5	1.2	6.3
67-68–St. Louis	77	–	714	98	262	.374	–	–	–	33	56	.589	–	–	226	68	94	0	–	–	–	229	2.9	0.9	3.0
69-70–Atlanta	2	–	11	2	4	.500	–	–	–	0	0	–	–	–	4	1	3	0	–	–	–	4	2.0	0.5	2.0
Reg. Season Totals	271	–	3223	515	1253	.411	–	–	–	161	278	.579	–	–	1122	257	551	10	–	–	–	1191	4.1	0.9	4.4
Playoff Totals	26	–	169	24	60	.400	–	–	–	11	18	.611	–	–	62	21	38	0	–	–	–	59	2.4	0.8	2.3

Tosheff, William Mark (Bill) b. June 2, 1926 Ht. 6-1 Wt. 175 College: Indiana

SEASON–TEAM	G	GS	MIN	FGM	FGA	PCT	3FGM	3FGA	PCT	FTM	FTA	PCT	O-RB	D-RB	TOT	AST	PF	DQ	STL	TO	BLK	PTS	RPG	APG	PPG
51-52–Indianapolis	65	–	2055	213	651	.327	–	–	–	182	221	.824	–	–	216	222	204	7	–	–	–	608	3.3	3.4	9.4
52-53–Indianapolis	67	–	2459	253	783	.323	–	–	–	253	314	.806	–	–	229	243	243	5	–	–	–	759	3.4	3.6	11.3
53-54–Milwaukee	71	–	1825	168	578	.291	–	–	–	156	210	.743	–	–	163	196	207	3	–	–	–	492	2.3	2.8	6.9
Reg. Season Totals	203	–	6339	634	2012	.315	–	–	–	591	745	.793	–	–	608	661	654	15	–	–	–	1859	3.0	3.3	9.2
Playoff Totals	4	–	202	3	37	.081	–	–	–	10	10	1.000	–	–	17	18	14	0	–	–	–	16	2.8	3.0	4.0

Tough, Robert (Bob, Red) b. August 28, 1920 d. April 7, 1999 Ht. 6-0 Wt. 185 College: St. John's (N.Y.)

SEASON–TEAM	G	GS	MIN	FGM	FGA	PCT	3FGM	3FGA	PCT	FTM	FTA	PCT	O-RB	D-RB	TOT	AST	PF	DQ	STL	TO	BLK	PTS	RPG	APG	PPG
45-46–Fort Wayne (N)	5	–	–	12	–	–	–	–	–	5	–	–	–	–	–	–	–	–	–	–	–	29	–	–	5.8
46-47–Fort Wayne (N)	44	–	–	124	–	–	–	–	–	55	81	.679	–	–	–	–	73	–	–	–	–	303	–	–	6.9
47-48–Fort Wayne (N)	60	–	–	129	–	–	–	–	–	48	71	.676	–	–	–	–	98	–	–	–	–	306	–	–	5.1
48-49–Fort Wayne	53	–	–	183	661	.277	–	–	–	100	138	.725	–	–	–	99	101	–	–	–	–	466	–	1.9	8.8
49-50–Balt.-Wat.	29	–	–	43	153	.281	–	–	–	37	40	.925	–	–	–	38	40	–	–	–	–	123	–	1.3	4.2
Reg. NBA Totals	82	–	–	226	814	.278	–	–	–	137	178	.770	–	–	–	137	141	–	–	–	–	589	–	1.7	7.2
Reg. NBL Totals	109	–	–	265	–	–	–	–	–	108	152	.678	–	–	–	–	171	–	–	–	–	638	–	–	5.9
NBL Playoff Totals	16	–	–	35	–	–	–	–	–	23	31	.742	–	–	–	–	27	–	–	–	–	93	–	–	5.8

Towe, Monte Corwin b. September 27, 1953 Ht. 5-7 Wt. 150 College: North Carolina State

SEASON–TEAM	G	GS	MIN	FGM	FGA	PCT	3FGM	3FGA	PCT	FTM	FTA	PCT	O-RB	D-RB	TOT	AST	PF	DQ	STL	TO	BLK	PTS	RPG	APG	PPG
75-76–Denver (A)	64	–	576	72	179	.402	9	42	.214	36	44	.818	6	49	55	136	84	–	37	81	5	189	0.9	2.1	3.0
76-77–Denver	51	–	409	56	138	.406	–	–	–	18	25	.720	8	26	34	87	61	0	16	–	0	130	0.7	1.7	2.5
Reg. NBA Totals	51	–	409	56	138	.406	–	–	–	18	25	.720	8	26	34	87	61	0	16	–	0	130	0.7	1.7	2.5
Reg. ABA Totals	64	–	576	72	179	.402	9	42	.214	36	44	.818	6	49	55	136	84	–	37	81	5	189	0.9	2.1	3.0
NBA Playoff Totals	1	–	6	2	3	.667	–	–	–	0	0	–	0	0	0	1	0	0	0	–	0	4	0.0	1.0	4.0
ABA Playoff Totals	4	–	30	3	8	.375	0	0	–	4	5	.800	0	0	0	6	6	–	1	5	0	10	0.0	1.5	2.5

Tower, Keith Raymond b. May 15, 1970 Ht. 6-11 Wt. 260 College: Notre Dame

SEASON–TEAM	G	GS	MIN	FGM	FGA	PCT	3FGM	3FGA	PCT	FTM	FTA	PCT	O-RB	D-RB	TOT	AST	PF	DQ	STL	TO	BLK	PTS	RPG	APG	PPG
93-94–Orlando	11	0	32	4	9	.444	0	0	–	0	0	–	0	6	6	1	6	0	0	0	0	8	0.5	0.1	0.7
94-95–Orlando	3	0	7	0	2	.000	0	0	–	1	2	.500	1	2	3	0	1	0	0	1	0	1	1.0	0.0	0.3
95-96–L.A. Clippers	34	1	305	32	72	.444	0	1	.000	18	26	.692	22	29	51	5	50	1	4	16	11	82	1.5	0.1	2.4
96-97–Milwaukee	5	1	72	3	8	.375	0	0	–	1	8	.125	2	7	9	1	12	0	2	2	1	7	1.8	0.2	1.4
Reg. Season Totals	53	2	416	39	91	.429	0	1	.000	20	36	.556	25	44	69	7	69	1	6	19	12	98	1.3	0.1	1.8

Towery, William Carlisle (Blackie) b. June 20, 1920 Ht. 6-4 Wt. 210 College: Western Kentucky

SEASON–TEAM	G	GS	MIN	FGM	FGA	PCT	3FGM	3FGA	PCT	FTM	FTA	PCT	O-RB	D-RB	TOT	AST	PF	DQ	STL	TO	BLK	PTS	RPG	APG	PPG
41-42–Fort Wayne (N)	24	–	–	64	–	–	–	–	–	35	–	–	–	–	–	–	92	–	–	–	–	163	–	–	6.8
42-43–Fort Wayne (N)	23	–	–	53	–	–	–	–	–	33	53	.623	–	–	–	–	71	–	–	–	–	139	–	–	6.0
43-44–Fort Wayne (N)	22	–	–	48	–	–	–	–	–	33	–	–	–	–	–	–	74	–	–	–	–	129	–	–	5.9
44-45–Fort Wayne (N)	1	–	–	0	–	–	–	–	–	1	–	–	–	–	–	–	–	–	–	–	–	1	–	–	1.0
46-47–Fort Wayne (N)	41	–	–	100	–	–	–	–	–	80	134	.597	–	–	–	–	123	–	–	–	–	280	–	–	6.8
47-48–Fort Wayne (N)	59	–	–	139	–	–	–	–	–	129	187	.690	–	–	–	–	194	–	–	–	–	407	–	–	6.9
48-49–FtWayne-Ind.	60	–	–	203	771	.263	–	–	–	195	263	.741	–	–	–	171	243	–	–	–	–	601	–	2.9	10.0
49-50–Baltimore	68	–	–	222	678	.327	–	–	–	153	202	.757	–	–	–	142	244	–	–	–	–	597	–	2.1	8.8
Reg. NBA Totals	128	–	–	425	1449	.293	–	–	–	348	465	.748	–	–	–	313	487	–	–	–	–	1198	–	2.4	9.4
Reg. NBL Totals	170	–	–	404	–	–	–	–	–	311	374	.647	–	–	–	–	554	–	–	–	–	1119	–	–	6.6
NBL Playoff Totals	29	–	–	63	–	–	–	–	–	36	26	.500	–	–	–	–	90	–	–	–	–	162	–	–	5.6

Townes, Linton Rodney b. November 30, 1959 Ht. 6-7 Wt. 195 College: James Madison

SEASON–TEAM	G	GS	MIN	FGM	FGA	PCT	3FGM	3FGA	PCT	FTM	FTA	PCT	O-RB	D-RB	TOT	AST	PF	DQ	STL	TO	BLK	PTS	RPG	APG	PPG
82-83–Portland	55	0	516	105	234	.449	9	25	.360	28	38	.737	30	35	65	31	81	0	19	33	5	247	1.2	0.6	4.5
83-84–Milw.-S.D.	4	0	19	4	8	.500	0	0	–	0	0	–	0	1	1	1	4	0	1	1	2	8	0.3	0.3	2.0
84-85–San Antonio	1	0	8	0	6	.000	0	0	–	2	2	1.000	1	0	1	0	1	0	0	0	0	2	1.0	0.0	2.0
Reg. Season Totals	60	0	543	109	248	.440	9	25	.360	30	40	.750	31	36	67	32	86	0	20	34	7	257	1.1	0.5	4.3
Playoff Totals	8	0	66	17	35	.486	1	4	.250	6	7	.857	4	2	6	5	12	0	0	3	0	41	0.8	0.6	5.1

Townsend, Raymond Anthony b. December 20, 1955 Ht. 6-3 Wt. 185 College: UCLA

SEASON–TEAM	G	GS	MIN	FGM	FGA	PCT	3FGM	3FGA	PCT	FTM	FTA	PCT	O-RB	D-RB	TOT	AST	PF	DQ	STL	TO	BLK	PTS	RPG	APG	PPG
78-79–Golden State	65	–	771	127	289	.439	–	–	–	50	68	.735	11	44	55	91	70	0	27	51	6	304	0.8	1.4	4.7
79-80–Golden State	75	–	1159	171	421	.406	4	26	.154	60	84	.714	33	56	89	116	113	0	60	65	4	406	1.2	1.5	5.4
81-82–Indiana	14	0	95	11	41	.268	2	9	.222	11	20	.550	2	11	13	10	18	0	3	6	0	35	0.9	0.7	2.5
Reg. Season Totals	154	0	2025	309	751	.411	6	35	.171	121	172	.703	46	111	157	217	201	0	90	122	10	745	1.0	1.4	4.8

Trapp, George b. July 11, 1948 Ht. 6-8 Wt. 205 College: Pasadena City (Calif.) Coll. (J.C.); Long Beach State

SEASON–TEAM	G	GS	MIN	FGM	FGA	PCT	3FGM	3FGA	PCT	FTM	FTA	PCT	O-RB	D-RB	TOT	AST	PF	DQ	STL	TO	BLK	PTS	RPG	APG	PPG
71-72–Atlanta	60	–	890	144	388	.371	–	–	–	105	139	.755	–	–	183	51	144	2	–	–	–	393	3.1	0.9	6.6
72-73–Atlanta	77	–	1853	359	824	.436	–	–	–	150	194	.773	–	–	455	127	274	11	–	–	–	868	5.9	1.6	11.3
73-74–Detroit	82	–	1489	333	693	.481	–	–	–	99	134	.739	97	216	313	81	226	2	47	–	33	765	3.8	1.0	9.3
74-75–Detroit	78	–	1472	288	652	.442	–	–	–	99	131	.756	71	205	276	63	210	1	37	–	14	675	3.5	0.8	8.7
75-76–Detroit	76	–	1091	278	602	.462	–	–	–	63	88	.716	79	150	229	50	167	3	33	–	23	619	3.0	0.7	8.1
76-77–Detroit	6	–	68	15	29	.517	–	–	–	3	4	.750	4	6	10	3	13	0	0	–	1	33	1.7	0.5	5.5
Reg. Season Totals	379	–	6863	1417	3188	.444	–	–	–	519	690	.752	251	577	1466	375	1034	19	117	–	71	3353	3.9	1.0	8.8
Playoff Totals	31	–	518	115	249	.462	–	–	–	28	40	.700	21	58	118	23	89	1	4	–	9	258	3.8	0.7	8.3

Trapp, John Quincy b. October 2, 1945 Ht. 6-7 Wt. 215 College: Pasadena City (Calif.) Coll. (J.C.); Nevada-Las Vegas

SEASON–TEAM	G	GS	MIN	FGM	FGA	PCT	3FGM	3FGA	PCT	FTM	FTA	PCT	O-RB	D-RB	TOT	AST	PF	DQ	STL	TO	BLK	PTS	RPG	APG	PPG
68-69–San Diego	25	–	142	29	80	.363	–	–	–	19	29	.655	–	–	49	5	38	0	–	–	–	77	2.0	0.2	3.1
69-70–San Diego	70	–	1025	185	434	.426	–	–	–	72	104	.692	–	–	309	49	200	3	–	–	–	442	4.4	0.7	6.3
70-71–San Diego	82	–	2080	322	766	.420	–	–	–	142	188	.755	–	–	510	138	337	16	–	–	–	786	6.2	1.7	9.6
71-72–Los Angeles	58	–	759	139	314	.443	–	–	–	51	73	.699	–	–	180	42	130	3	–	–	–	329	3.1	0.7	5.7
72-73–L.A.-Phil.	44	–	889	171	420	.407	–	–	–	90	122	.738	–	–	200	49	150	4	–	–	–	432	4.5	1.1	9.8
72-73–Denver (A)	25	–	342	54	128	.422	0	2	.000	19	32	.594	27	45	72	20	76	0	–	25	–	127	2.9	0.8	5.1
Reg. NBA Totals	279	–	4895	846	2014	.420	–	–	–	374	516	.725	–	–	1248	283	855	26	–	–	–	2066	4.5	1.0	7.4
Reg. ABA Totals	25	–	342	54	128	.422	0	2	.000	19	32	.594	27	45	72	20	76	0	–	25	–	127	2.9	0.8	5.1
NBA Playoff Totals	10	–	71	8	33	.242	–	–	–	4	7	.571	–	–	16	5	9	0	–	–	–	20	1.6	0.5	2.0
ABA Playoff Totals	5	–	51	7	16	.438	0	0	–	8	12	.667	–	–	7	2	13	0	–	1	–	22	1.4	0.4	4.4

Traylor, Robert DeShaun (Tractor) b. February 1, 1977 Ht. 6-8 Wt. 284 College: Michigan

SEASON–TEAM	G	GS	MIN	FGM	FGA	PCT	3FGM	3FGA	PCT	FTM	FTA	PCT	O-RB	D-RB	TOT	AST	PF	DQ	STL	TO	BLK	PTS	RPG	APG	PPG
98-99–Milwaukee	49	43	786	108	201	.537	0	1	.000	43	80	.538	80	102	182	38	140	4	44	42	44	259	3.7	0.8	5.3
99-00–Milwaukee	44	16	447	58	122	.475	0	4	.000	41	68	.603	50	65	115	20	79	0	25	27	25	157	2.6	0.5	3.6
Reg. Season Totals	93	59	1233	166	323	.514	0	5	.000	84	148	.568	130	167	297	58	219	4	69	69	69	416	3.2	0.6	4.5
Playoff Totals	4	1	49	7	10	.700	0	0	–	2	4	.500	7	7	14	3	17	1	2	4	5	16	3.5	0.8	4.0

Trent, Gary Dajaun (Shaq of the MAC) b. September 22, 1974 Ht. 6-8 Wt. 250 College: Ohio U.

SEASON–TEAM	G	GS	MIN	FGM	FGA	PCT	3FGM	3FGA	PCT	FTM	FTA	PCT	O-RB	D-RB	TOT	AST	PF	DQ	STL	TO	BLK	PTS	RPG	APG	PPG
95-96–Portland	69	10	1219	220	429	.513	0	9	.000	78	141	.553	84	154	238	50	116	0	25	92	11	518	3.4	0.7	7.5
96-97–Portland	82	28	1918	361	674	.536	0	11	.000	160	229	.699	156	272	428	87	186	2	48	129	35	882	5.2	1.1	10.8
97-98–Port.-Toronto	54	20	1360	241	505	.477	4	12	.333	144	212	.679	123	215	338	72	161	3	35	94	27	630	6.3	1.3	11.7
98-99–Dallas	45	23	1362	287	602	.477	0	5	.000	145	235	.617	127	224	351	77	122	1	29	66	23	719	7.8	1.7	16.0
99-00–Dallas	11	11	301	70	142	.493	0	2	.000	11	21	.524	20	32	52	22	28	0	8	25	3	151	4.7	2.0	13.7
Reg. Season Totals	261	92	6160	1179	2352	.501	4	39	.103	538	838	.642	510	897	1407	308	613	6	145	406	99	2900	5.4	1.2	11.1
Playoff Totals	6	0	71	14	33	.424	0	1	.000	6	11	.545	5	8	13	4	14	0	1	6	1	34	2.2	0.7	5.7

Tresvant, John B. b. November 6, 1939 Ht. 6-7 Wt. 215 College: Seattle

SEASON–TEAM	G	GS	MIN	FGM	FGA	PCT	3FGM	3FGA	PCT	FTM	FTA	PCT	O-RB	D-RB	TOT	AST	PF	DQ	STL	TO	BLK	PTS	RPG	APG	PPG
64-65–St. Louis	4	–	35	4	11	.364	–	–	–	6	9	.667	–	–	18	6	9	0	–	–	–	14	4.5	1.5	3.5
65-66–St. L.-Detroit	61	–	969	171	400	.428	–	–	–	142	190	.747	–	–	364	72	179	2	–	–	–	484	6.0	1.2	7.9
66-67–Detroit	68	–	1553	256	585	.438	–	–	–	164	234	.701	–	–	483	88	246	8	–	–	–	676	7.1	1.3	9.9
67-68–Detroit-Cin.	85	–	2473	396	867	.457	–	–	–	250	384	.651	–	–	709	160	344	18	–	–	–	1042	8.3	1.9	12.3
68-69–Cin.-Seattle	77	–	2482	380	820	.463	–	–	–	202	330	.612	–	–	686	166	300	9	–	–	–	962	8.9	2.2	12.5
69-70–Seattle-L.A.	69	–	1499	264	595	.444	–	–	–	206	284	.725	–	–	425	112	204	4	–	–	–	734	6.2	1.6	10.6
70-71–L.A.-Balt.	75	–	1517	202	436	.463	–	–	–	146	205	.712	–	–	382	86	196	1	–	–	–	550	5.1	1.1	7.3
71-72–Baltimore	65	–	1227	162	360	.450	–	–	–	121	148	.818	–	–	323	83	175	6	–	–	–	445	5.0	1.3	6.8
72-73–Baltimore	55	–	541	85	182	.467	–	–	–	41	59	.695	–	–	156	33	101	0	–	–	–	211	2.8	0.6	3.8
Reg. Season Totals	559	–	12296	1920	4256	.451	–	–	–	1278	1843	.693	–	–	3546	806	1754	48	–	–	–	5118	6.3	1.4	9.2
Playoff Totals	40	–	862	104	251	.414	–	–	–	66	95	.695	–	–	246	44	115	3	–	–	–	274	6.2	1.1	6.9

Triptow, Richard Floyd (Dick, Tiptoe) b. November 3, 1922 Ht. 6-0 Wt. 170 College: DePaul

SEASON–TEAM	G	GS	MIN	FGM	FGA	PCT	3FGM	3FGA	PCT	FTM	FTA	PCT	O-RB	D-RB	TOT	AST	PF	DQ	STL	TO	BLK	PTS	RPG	APG	PPG
44-45–Chicago (N)	30	–	–	113	–	–	–	–	–	73	–	–	–	–	–	–	–	–	–	–	–	299	–	–	10.0
45-46–Chicago (N)	34	–	–	68	–	–	–	–	–	85	127	.669	–	–	–	–	77	–	–	–	–	221	–	–	6.5
46-47–Chicago (N)	44	–	–	59	–	–	–	–	–	60	90	.667	–	–	–	–	71	–	–	–	–	178	–	–	4.0
47-48–Tri-Cit-FtWayne (N)	57	–	–	92	–	–	–	–	–	87	138	.630	–	–	–	–	109	–	–	–	–	271	–	–	4.8
48-49–Fort Wayne	55	–	–	116	417	.278	–	–	–	102	141	.723	–	–	–	96	107	–	–	–	–	334	–	1.7	6.1
49-50–Baltimore	4	–	–	0	5	.000	–	–	–	2	2	1.000	–	–	–	1	5	–	–	–	–	2	–	0.3	0.5
Reg. NBA Totals	59	–	–	116	422	.275	–	–	–	104	143	.727	–	–	–	97	112	–	–	–	–	336	–	1.6	5.7
Reg. NBL Totals	165	–	–	332	–	–	–	–	–	305	355	.654	–	–	–	–	257	–	–	–	–	969	–	–	5.9
NBL Playoff Totals	18	–	–	39	–	–	–	–	–	22	33	.576	–	–	–	–	38	–	–	–	–	100	–	–	5.6

Tripucka, Peter Kelly (Kelly) b. February 16, 1959 Ht. 6-6 Wt. 225 College: Notre Dame

SEASON–TEAM	G	GS	MIN	FGM	FGA	PCT	3FGM	3FGA	PCT	FTM	FTA	PCT	O-RB	D-RB	TOT	AST	PF	DQ	STL	TO	BLK	PTS	RPG	APG	PPG
81-82–Detroit	82	82	3077	636	1281	.496	5	22	.227	495	621	.797	219	224	443	270	241	0	89	280	16	1772	5.4	3.3	21.6
82-83–Detroit	58	58	2252	565	1156	.489	14	37	.378	392	464	.845	126	138	264	237	157	0	67	187	20	1536	4.6	4.1	26.5
83-84–Detroit	76	75	2493	595	1296	.459	2	17	.118	426	523	.815	119	187	306	228	190	0	65	190	17	1618	4.0	3.0	21.3
84-85–Detroit	55	43	1675	396	831	.477	2	5	.400	255	288	.885	66	152	218	135	118	1	49	118	14	1049	4.0	2.5	19.1
85-86–Detroit	81	81	2626	615	1236	.498	12	25	.480	380	444	.856	116	232	348	265	167	0	93	183	10	1622	4.3	3.3	20.0
86-87–Utah	79	76	1865	291	621	.469	19	52	.365	197	226	.872	54	188	242	243	147	0	85	167	11	798	3.1	3.1	10.1
87-88–Utah	49	21	976	139	303	.459	31	74	.419	59	68	.868	30	87	117	105	68	1	34	68	4	368	2.4	2.1	7.5
88-89–Charlotte	71	65	2302	568	1215	.467	30	84	.357	440	508	.866	79	188	267	224	196	0	88	236	16	1606	3.8	3.2	22.6
89-90–Charlotte	79	73	2404	442	1029	.430	38	104	.365	310	351	.883	82	240	322	224	220	1	75	176	16	1232	4.1	2.8	15.6
90-91–Charlotte	77	1	1289	187	412	.454	15	45	.333	152	167	.910	46	130	176	159	130	0	33	92	13	541	2.3	2.1	7.0
Reg. Season Totals	707	575	20959	4434	9380	.473	168	465	.361	3106	3660	.849	937	1766	2703	2090	1634	3	678	1697	137	12142	3.8	3.0	17.2
Playoff Totals	25	23	750	145	314	.462	0	5	.000	101	118	.856	41	52	93	57	65	2	22	61	5	391	3.7	2.3	15.6
All-Star Totals	2	0	21	3	7	.429	0	0	–	1	2	.500	0	1	1	4	1	0	1	3	0	7	0.5	2.0	3.5

Truitt, Ansley Hoover b. August 24, 1950 Ht. 6-9 Wt. 215 College: California

SEASON–TEAM	G	GS	MIN	FGM	FGA	PCT	3FGM	3FGA	PCT	FTM	FTA	PCT	O-RB	D-RB	TOT	AST	PF	DQ	STL	TO	BLK	PTS	RPG	APG	PPG
72-73–Dallas (A)	16	–	86	18	42	.429	0	0	–	3	9	.333	10	28	38	2	9	0	–	7	–	39	2.4	0.1	2.4
Reg. ABA Totals	16	–	86	18	42	.429	0	0	–	3	9	.333	10	28	38	2	9	0	–	7	–	39	2.4	0.1	2.4

Tschogl, John Mark b. April 25, 1950 Ht. 6-6 Wt. 210 College: California-Santa Barbara

SEASON–TEAM	G	GS	MIN	FGM	FGA	PCT	3FGM	3FGA	PCT	FTM	FTA	PCT	O-RB	D-RB	TOT	AST	PF	DQ	STL	TO	BLK	PTS	RPG	APG	PPG
72-73–Atlanta	10	–	94	14	40	.350	–	–	–	2	4	.500	–	–	21	6	25	0	–	–	–	30	2.1	0.6	3.0
73-74–Atlanta	64	–	499	59	166	.355	–	–	–	10	17	.588	33	43	76	33	69	0	17	–	20	128	1.2	0.5	2.0
74-75–Philadelphia	39	–	623	53	148	.358	–	–	–	13	22	.591	52	59	111	30	80	2	25	–	25	119	2.8	0.8	3.1
Reg. Season Totals	113	–	1216	126	354	.356	–	–	–	25	43	.581	85	102	208	69	174	2	42	–	45	277	1.8	0.6	2.5
Playoff Totals	3	–	11	5	8	.625	–	–	–	0	0	–	0	0	4	1	0	0	0	–	0	10	1.3	0.3	3.3

Tsioropoulos, Louis C. (Lou) b. August 31, 1930 Ht. 6-5 Wt. 195 College: Kentucky

SEASON–TEAM	G	GS	MIN	FGM	FGA	PCT	3FGM	3FGA	PCT	FTM	FTA	PCT	O-RB	D-RB	TOT	AST	PF	DQ	STL	TO	BLK	PTS	RPG	APG	PPG
56-57–Boston	52	–	670	79	256	.309	–	–	–	69	89	.775	–	–	207	33	135	6	–	–	–	227	4.0	0.6	4.4
57-58–Boston	70	–	1819	198	624	.317	–	–	–	142	207	.686	–	–	434	112	242	8	–	–	–	538	6.2	1.6	7.7
58-59–Boston	35	–	488	60	190	.316	–	–	–	25	33	.758	–	–	110	20	74	0	–	–	–	145	3.1	0.6	4.1
Reg. Season Totals	157	–	2977	337	1070	.315	–	–	–	236	329	.717	–	–	751	165	451	14	–	–	–	910	4.8	1.1	5.8
Playoff Totals	11	–	239	25	85	.294	–	–	–	19	29	.655	–	–	64	14	40	4	–	–	–	69	5.8	1.3	6.3

T

Tucker, Albert Ames (Al, Tuck) b. February 24, 1943 Ht. 6-8 Wt. 190 College: Oklahoma Baptist

SEASON–TEAM	G	GS	MIN	FGM	FGA	PCT	3FGM	3FGA	PCT	FTM	FTA	PCT	O-RB	D-RB	TOT	AST	PF	DQ	STL	TO	BLK	PTS	RPG	APG	PPG
67-68–Seattle	81	–	2368	437	989	.442	–	–	–	186	263	.707	–	–	605	111	262	6	–	–	–	1060	7.5	1.4	13.1
68-69–Seattle-Cin.	84	–	1885	361	809	.446	–	–	–	158	244	.648	–	–	439	74	186	2	–	–	–	880	5.2	0.9	10.5
69-70–Chicago-Balt.	61	–	819	146	285	.512	–	–	–	70	87	.805	–	–	166	38	86	0	–	–	–	362	2.7	0.6	5.9
70-71–Baltimore	31	–	276	52	115	.452	–	–	–	25	31	.806	–	–	73	7	33	0	–	–	–	129	2.4	0.2	4.2
70-71–Floridians (A)	14	–	331	66	149	.443	3	7	.429	34	42	.810	–	–	65	12	40	–	–	–	–	169	4.6	0.9	12.1
71-72–Floridians (A)	81	–	1799	377	810	.465	30	82	.366	157	199	.789	–	–	392	100	205	–	–	129	–	941	4.8	1.2	11.6
Reg. NBA Totals	257	–	5348	996	2198	.453	–	–	–	439	625	.702	–	–	1283	230	567	8	–	–	–	2431	5.0	0.9	9.5
Reg. ABA Totals	95	–	2130	443	959	.462	33	89	.371	191	241	.793	–	–	457	112	245	–	–	129	–	1110	4.8	1.2	11.7
NBA Playoff Totals	4	–	5	2	2	1.000	–	–	–	0	0	–	–	–	0	–	0	0	–	–	–	4	0.0	0.0	1.0
ABA Playoff Totals	9	–	216	33	85	.388	1	7	.143	19	24	.792	–	–	46	16	28	–	–	3	–	86	5.1	1.8	9.6

Tucker, Anthony Glenn b. April 4, 1969 Ht. 6-8 Wt. 220 College: Wake Forest

SEASON–TEAM	G	GS	MIN	FGM	FGA	PCT	3FGM	3FGA	PCT	FTM	FTA	PCT	O-RB	D-RB	TOT	AST	PF	DQ	STL	TO	BLK	PTS	RPG	APG	PPG
94-95–Washington	62	13	982	96	210	.457	0	1	.000	51	83	.614	44	126	170	68	129	0	46	56	11	243	2.7	1.1	3.9
Reg. Season Totals	62	13	982	96	210	.457	0	1	.000	51	83	.614	44	126	170	68	129	0	46	56	11	243	2.7	1.1	3.9

Tucker, James D. (Jim) b. December 11, 1932 Ht. 6-7 Wt. 185 College: Duquesne

SEASON–TEAM	G	GS	MIN	FGM	FGA	PCT	3FGM	3FGA	PCT	FTM	FTA	PCT	O-RB	D-RB	TOT	AST	PF	DQ	STL	TO	BLK	PTS	RPG	APG	PPG
54-55–Syracuse	20	–	287	39	116	.336	–	–	–	27	38	.711	–	–	97	12	50	0	–	–	–	105	4.9	0.6	5.3
55-56–Syracuse	70	–	895	101	290	.348	–	–	–	66	83	.795	–	–	232	38	166	2	–	–	–	268	3.3	0.5	3.8
56-57–Syracuse	9	–	119	17	44	.386	–	–	–	0	1	.000	–	–	20	2	26	0	–	–	–	34	2.2	0.2	3.8
Reg. Season Totals	99	–	1301	157	450	.349	–	–	–	93	122	.762	–	–	349	52	242	2	–	–	–	407	3.5	0.5	4.1
Playoff Totals	15	–	131	21	61	.344	–	–	–	14	17	.824	–	–	40	3	28	0	–	–	–	56	2.7	0.2	3.7

Tucker, Kelvin Trent (Trent) b. December 20, 1959 Ht. 6-5 Wt. 195 College: Minnesota

SEASON–TEAM	G	GS	MIN	FGM	FGA	PCT	3FGM	3FGA	PCT	FTM	FTA	PCT	O-RB	D-RB	TOT	AST	PF	DQ	STL	TO	BLK	PTS	RPG	APG	PPG
82-83–New York	78	59	1830	299	647	.462	14	30	.467	43	64	.672	75	141	216	195	235	1	56	70	6	655	2.8	2.5	8.4
83-84–New York	63	21	1228	225	450	.500	6	16	.375	25	33	.758	43	87	130	138	124	0	63	54	8	481	2.1	2.2	7.6
84-85–New York	77	46	1819	293	606	.483	29	72	.403	38	48	.792	74	114	188	199	195	0	75	64	15	653	2.4	2.6	8.5
85-86–New York	77	23	1788	349	740	.472	41	91	.451	79	100	.790	70	99	169	192	167	0	65	70	8	818	2.2	2.5	10.6
86-87–New York	70	15	1691	325	691	.470	68	161	.422	77	101	.762	49	86	135	166	169	1	116	78	13	795	1.9	2.4	11.4
87-88–New York	71	4	1248	193	455	.424	69	167	.413	51	71	.718	32	87	119	117	158	3	53	47	6	506	1.7	1.6	7.1
88-89–New York	81	24	1824	263	579	.454	118	296	.399	43	55	.782	55	121	176	132	163	0	88	59	6	687	2.2	1.6	8.5
89-90–New York	81	2	1725	253	606	.417	95	245	.388	66	86	.767	57	117	174	173	159	0	74	73	8	667	2.1	2.1	8.2
90-91–New York	65	13	1194	191	434	.440	64	153	.418	17	27	.630	33	72	105	111	120	0	44	46	9	463	1.6	1.7	7.1
91-92–San Antonio	24	0	415	60	129	.465	19	48	.396	16	20	.800	8	29	37	27	39	0	21	14	3	155	1.5	1.1	6.5
92-93–Chicago	69	0	909	143	295	.485	52	131	.397	18	22	.818	16	55	71	82	65	0	24	18	6	356	1.0	1.2	5.2
Reg. Season Totals	756	207	15671	2594	5632	.461	575	1410	.408	473	627	.754	512	1008	1520	1532	1594	5	679	593	88	6236	2.0	2.0	8.2
Playoff Totals	66	8	1059	142	316	.449	50	120	.417	30	43	.698	30	64	94	100	107	0	44	38	5	364	1.4	1.5	5.5

Turkcan, Mirsad b. June 7, 1976 Ht. 6-9 Wt. 216 Country: Yugoslavia

SEASON–TEAM	G	GS	MIN	FGM	FGA	PCT	3FGM	3FGA	PCT	FTM	FTA	PCT	O-RB	D-RB	TOT	AST	PF	DQ	STL	TO	BLK	PTS	RPG	APG	PPG
99-00–N.Y.-Milw.	17	0	90	14	38	.368	0	6	.000	5	8	.625	13	20	33	5	14	0	3	8	1	33	1.9	0.3	1.9
Reg. Season Totals	17	0	90	14	38	.368	0	6	.000	5	8	.625	13	20	33	5	14	0	3	8	1	33	1.9	0.3	1.9
Playoff Totals	2	0	10	1	5	.200	0	1	.000	2	2	1.000	0	2	2	–	1	0	0	3	0	4	1.0	0.0	2.0

Turner, Andre D. b. December 13, 1964 Ht. 5-11 Wt. 160 College: Memphis

SEASON–TEAM	G	GS	MIN	FGM	FGA	PCT	3FGM	3FGA	PCT	FTM	FTA	PCT	O-RB	D-RB	TOT	AST	PF	DQ	STL	TO	BLK	PTS	RPG	APG	PPG
86-87–Boston	3	0	18	2	5	.400	0	1	.000	0	0	–	1	1	2	1	1	0	0	5	0	4	0.7	0.3	1.3
87-88–Houston	12	0	99	12	34	.353	1	7	.143	10	14	.714	4	4	8	23	13	0	7	12	1	35	0.7	1.9	2.9
88-89–Milwaukee	4	0	13	3	6	.500	0	0	–	0	0	–	0	3	3	0	2	0	2	4	0	6	0.8	0.0	1.5
89-90–LAClips-Cha.	11	0	115	11	38	.289	0	2	.000	4	4	1.000	4	4	8	23	6	0	8	12	0	26	0.7	2.1	2.4
90-91–Philadelphia	70	1	1407	168	383	.439	12	33	.364	64	87	.736	36	116	152	311	124	0	63	95	0	412	2.2	4.4	5.9
91-92–Washington	70	3	871	111	261	.425	1	16	.063	61	77	.792	17	73	90	177	59	0	57	84	2	284	1.3	2.5	4.1
Reg. Season Totals	170	4	2523	307	727	.422	14	59	.237	139	182	.764	62	201	263	535	205	0	137	212	3	767	1.5	3.1	4.5
Playoff Totals	8	0	189	21	48	.438	3	9	.333	13	16	.813	2	11	13	35	12	0	11	8	0	58	1.6	4.4	7.3

Turner, Elston Howard b. June 10, 1959 Ht. 6-5 Wt. 200 College: Mississippi

SEASON–TEAM	G	GS	MIN	FGM	FGA	PCT	3FGM	3FGA	PCT	FTM	FTA	PCT	O-RB	D-RB	TOT	AST	PF	DQ	STL	TO	BLK	PTS	RPG	APG	PPG
81-82–Dallas	80	62	1996	282	639	.441	0	4	.000	97	138	.703	143	158	301	189	182	1	75	116	3	661	3.8	2.4	8.3
82-83–Dallas	59	16	879	96	238	.403	2	3	.667	20	30	.667	68	84	152	88	75	0	47	59	0	214	2.6	1.5	3.6
83-84–Dallas	47	1	536	54	150	.360	1	9	.111	28	34	.824	42	51	93	59	40	0	26	29	0	137	2.0	1.3	2.9
84-85–Denver	81	2	1491	181	388	.466	1	6	.167	51	65	.785	88	128	216	158	152	0	96	70	7	414	2.7	2.0	5.1
85-86–Denver	73	0	1324	165	379	.435	0	9	.000	39	53	.736	64	137	201	165	150	1	70	80	6	369	2.8	2.3	5.1
86-87–Chicago	70	4	936	112	252	.444	1	8	.125	23	31	.742	34	81	115	102	97	1	30	31	4	248	1.6	1.5	3.5
87-88–Chicago	17	0	98	8	30	.267	0	0	–	1	2	.500	8	2	10	9	5	0	8	10	0	17	0.6	0.5	1.0
88-89–Denver	78	12	1746	151	353	.428	2	7	.286	33	56	.589	109	178	287	144	209	2	90	60	8	337	3.7	1.8	4.3
Reg. Season Totals	505	97	9006	1049	2429	.432	7	46	.152	292	409	.714	556	819	1375	914	910	5	442	455	28	2397	2.7	1.8	4.7
Playoff Totals	43	4	735	97	200	.485	3	4	.750	21	33	.636	51	79	130	86	79	1	33	35	2	218	3.0	2.0	5.1

Turner, Gary D. b. 1945 Ht. 6-7 Wt. 200 College: Texas Christian

SEASON–TEAM	G	GS	MIN	FGM	FGA	PCT	3FGM	3FGA	PCT	FTM	FTA	PCT	O-RB	D-RB	TOT	AST	PF	DQ	STL	TO	BLK	PTS	RPG	APG	PPG
67-68–Houston (A)	2	–	21	2	2	1.000	0	0	–	2	3	.667	–	–	3	0	2	0	–	2	–	6	1.5	0.0	3.0
Reg. ABA Totals	2	–	21	2	2	1.000	0	0	–	2	3	.667	–	–	3	0	2	0	–	2	–	6	1.5	0.0	3.0

Turner, Henry b. August 18, 1966 Ht. 6-7 Wt. 200 College: Cal State-Fullerton

SEASON–TEAM	G	GS	MIN	FGM	FGA	PCT	3FGM	3FGA	PCT	FTM	FTA	PCT	O-RB	D-RB	TOT	AST	PF	DQ	STL	TO	BLK	PTS	RPG	APG	PPG
89-90–Sacramento	36	1	315	58	122	.475	0	3	.000	40	65	.615	22	28	50	22	40	0	17	26	7	156	1.4	0.6	4.3
94-95–Sacramento	30	0	149	23	57	.404	2	5	.400	20	35	.571	17	11	28	7	20	0	8	12	1	68	0.9	0.2	2.3
Reg. Season Totals	66	1	464	81	179	.453	2	8	.250	60	100	.600	39	39	78	29	60	0	25	38	8	224	1.2	0.4	3.4

Turner, Herschell C. b. March 29, 1938 Ht. 6-2 Wt. 195 College: Nebraska

SEASON–TEAM	G	GS	MIN	FGM	FGA	PCT	3FGM	3FGA	PCT	FTM	FTA	PCT	O-RB	D-RB	TOT	AST	PF	DQ	STL	TO	BLK	PTS	RPG	APG	PPG
67-68–Pitt.-Anaheim (A)	41	–	500	51	159	.321	6	26	.231	23	47	.489	–	–	74	45	72	1	–	45	–	131	1.8	1.1	3.2
Reg. ABA Totals	41	–	500	51	159	.321	6	26	.231	23	47	.489	–	–	74	45	72	1	–	45	–	131	1.8	1.1	3.2

Turner, Jackie Lee (Jack) b. June 29, 1930 Ht. 6-4 Wt. 170 College: Western Kentucky

SEASON–TEAM	G	GS	MIN	FGM	FGA	PCT	3FGM	3FGA	PCT	FTM	FTA	PCT	O-RB	D-RB	TOT	AST	PF	DQ	STL	TO	BLK	PTS	RPG	APG	PPG
54-55–New York	65	–	922	111	308	.360	–	–	–	60	76	.789	–	–	154	77	76	0	–	–	–	282	2.4	1.2	4.3
Reg. Season Totals	65	–	922	111	308	.360	–	–	–	60	76	.789	–	–	154	77	76	0	–	–	–	282	2.4	1.2	4.3
Playoff Totals	2	–	16	2	6	.333	–	–	–	1	3	.333	–	–	4	2	1	0	–	–	–	5	2.0	1.0	2.5

Turner, Jeffrey Steven (Jeff) b. April 9, 1962 Ht. 6-9 Wt. 244 College: Vanderbilt

SEASON–TEAM	G	GS	MIN	FGM	FGA	PCT	3FGM	3FGA	PCT	FTM	FTA	PCT	O-RB	D-RB	TOT	AST	PF	DQ	STL	TO	BLK	PTS	RPG	APG	PPG
84-85–New Jersey	72	36	1429	171	377	.454	0	3	.000	79	92	.859	88	130	218	108	243	8	29	90	7	421	3.0	1.5	5.8
85-86–New Jersey	53	1	650	84	171	.491	0	1	.000	58	78	.744	45	92	137	14	125	4	21	49	3	226	2.6	0.3	4.3
86-87–New Jersey	76	22	1003	151	325	.465	0	1	.000	76	104	.731	80	117	197	60	200	6	33	81	13	378	2.6	0.8	5.0
89-90–Orlando	60	15	1105	132	308	.429	2	10	.200	42	54	.778	52	175	227	53	161	4	23	61	12	308	3.8	0.9	5.1
90-91–Orlando	71	43	1683	259	532	.487	6	15	.400	85	112	.759	108	255	363	97	234	5	29	126	10	609	5.1	1.4	8.6
91-92–Orlando	75	42	1591	225	499	.451	1	8	.125	79	114	.693	62	184	246	92	229	6	24	106	16	530	3.3	1.2	7.1
92-93–Orlando	75	20	1479	231	437	.529	10	17	.588	56	70	.800	74	178	252	107	192	2	19	66	9	528	3.4	1.4	7.0
93-94–Orlando	68	51	1536	199	426	.467	18	55	.327	35	45	.778	79	192	271	60	239	1	23	75	11	451	4.0	0.9	6.6
94-95–Orlando	49	5	576	73	178	.410	27	75	.360	26	29	.897	23	74	97	38	102	2	12	22	3	199	2.0	0.8	4.1
95-96–Orlando-Vanc.	13	0	192	18	51	.353	9	27	.333	2	2	1.000	10	18	28	6	33	2	2	11	1	47	2.2	0.5	3.6
Reg. Season Totals	612	235	11244	1543	3304	.467	73	212	.344	538	700	.769	621	1415	2036	635	1758	40	215	687	85	3697	3.3	1.0	6.0
Playoff Totals	24	0	218	20	48	.417	11	22	.500	5	5	1.000	6	26	32	16	57	0	4	10	3	56	1.3	0.7	2.3

Turner, John F. (Jack) b. June 5, 1939 Ht. 6-5 Wt. 200 College: Louisville

SEASON–TEAM	G	GS	MIN	FGM	FGA	PCT	3FGM	3FGA	PCT	FTM	FTA	PCT	O-RB	D-RB	TOT	AST	PF	DQ	STL	TO	BLK	PTS	RPG	APG	PPG
61-62–Chicago	42	–	567	84	221	.380	–	–	–	32	42	.762	–	–	85	44	51	0	–	–	–	200	2.0	1.0	4.8
Reg. Season Totals	42	–	567	84	221	.380	–	–	–	32	42	.762	–	–	85	44	51	0	–	–	–	200	2.0	1.0	4.8

Turner, John L. b. November 30, 1967 Ht. 6-8 Wt. 245 College: Allegany (Md.) C.C.; Georgetown; Phillips

SEASON–TEAM	G	GS	MIN	FGM	FGA	PCT	3FGM	3FGA	PCT	FTM	FTA	PCT	O-RB	D-RB	TOT	AST	PF	DQ	STL	TO	BLK	PTS	RPG	APG	PPG
91-92–Houston	42	0	345	43	98	.439	0	0	–	31	59	.525	38	40	78	12	40	0	6	32	4	117	1.9	0.3	2.8
Reg. Season Totals	42	0	345	43	98	.439	0	0	–	31	59	.525	38	40	78	12	40	0	6	32	4	117	1.9	0.3	2.8

Turner, Wayne b. March 22, 1976 Ht. 6-2 Wt. 185 College: Kentucky

SEASON–TEAM	G	GS	MIN	FGM	FGA	PCT	3FGM	3FGA	PCT	FTM	FTA	PCT	O-RB	D-RB	TOT	AST	PF	DQ	STL	TO	BLK	PTS	RPG	APG	PPG
99-00–Boston	3	0	41	1	6	.167	0	0	–	2	6	.333	1	2	3	5	4	0	0	3	0	4	1.0	1.7	1.3
Reg. Season Totals	3	0	41	1	6	.167	0	0	–	2	6	.333	1	2	3	5	4	0	0	3	0	4	1.0	1.7	1.3

Turner, William R. III (Bill) b. February 18, 1944 Ht. 6-7 Wt. 220 College: Akron

SEASON–TEAM	G	GS	MIN	FGM	FGA	PCT	3FGM	3FGA	PCT	FTM	FTA	PCT	O-RB	D-RB	TOT	AST	PF	DQ	STL	TO	BLK	PTS	RPG	APG	PPG
67-68–San Francisco	42	–	482	68	157	.433	–	–	–	36	60	.600	–	–	155	16	74	1	–	–	–	172	3.7	0.4	4.1
68-69–San Francisco	79	–	1486	222	535	.415	–	–	–	175	230	.761	–	–	380	67	231	6	–	–	–	619	4.8	0.8	7.8
69-70–S.F.-Cin.	72	–	1170	197	468	.421	–	–	–	123	167	.737	–	–	304	43	193	3	–	–	–	517	4.2	0.6	7.2
70-71–San Francisco	18	–	200	26	82	.317	–	–	–	13	20	.650	–	–	42	8	24	0	–	–	–	65	2.3	0.4	3.6
71-72–Golden State	62	–	597	71	181	.392	–	–	–	40	53	.755	–	–	131	22	67	1	–	–	–	182	2.1	0.4	2.9
72-73–Port.-L.A.	21	–	125	19	58	.328	–	–	–	4	7	.571	–	–	27	11	16	0	–	–	–	42	1.3	0.5	2.0
Reg. Season Totals	294	–	4060	603	1481	.407	–	–	–	391	537	.728	–	–	1039	167	605	11	–	–	–	1597	3.5	0.6	5.4
Playoff Totals	22	–	284	37	87	.425	–	–	–	22	31	.710	–	–	62	16	47	2	–	–	–	96	2.8	0.7	4.4

Turpin, Melvin Harrison (Mel) b. December 28, 1960 Ht. 6-11 Wt. 250 College: Kentucky

SEASON–TEAM	G	GS	MIN	FGM	FGA	PCT	3FGM	3FGA	PCT	FTM	FTA	PCT	O-RB	D-RB	TOT	AST	PF	DQ	STL	TO	BLK	PTS	RPG	APG	PPG
84-85–Cleveland	79	45	1949	363	711	.511	0	0	–	109	139	.784	155	297	452	36	211	3	38	118	87	835	5.7	0.5	10.6
85-86–Cleveland	80	69	2292	456	838	.544	0	4	.000	185	228	.811	182	374	556	55	260	6	65	134	106	1097	7.0	0.7	13.7
86-87–Cleveland	64	1	801	169	366	.462	0	0	–	55	77	.714	62	128	190	33	90	1	11	63	40	393	3.0	0.5	6.1
87-88–Utah	79	0	1011	199	389	.512	1	3	.333	71	98	.724	88	148	236	32	157	2	26	71	68	470	3.0	0.4	5.9
89-90–Washington	59	12	818	110	209	.526	0	2	.000	56	71	.789	88	133	221	27	135	0	15	45	47	276	3.7	0.5	4.7
Reg. Season Totals	361	127	6871	1297	2513	.516	1	9	.111	476	613	.777	575	1080	1655	183	853	12	155	431	348	3071	4.6	0.5	8.5
Playoff Totals	11	0	76	15	28	.536	0	0	–	3	4	.750	6	8	14	2	8	0	5	7	5	33	1.3	0.2	3.0

Twardzik, Dave John (Pinball) b. September 20, 1950 Ht. 6-1 Wt. 180 College: Old Dominion

SEASON–TEAM	G	GS	MIN	FGM	FGA	PCT	3FGM	3FGA	PCT	FTM	FTA	PCT	O-RB	D-RB	TOT	AST	PF	DQ	STL	TO	BLK	PTS	RPG	APG	PPG
72-73–Virginia (A)	80	–	1357	141	306	.461	2	9	.222	178	212	.840	45	113	158	184	202	1	–	122	–	462	2.0	2.3	5.8
73-74–Virginia (A)	57	–	1413	163	343	.475	3	15	.200	168	214	.785	52	129	181	170	173	–	60	118	8	497	3.2	3.0	8.7
74-75–Virginia (A)	76	–	2679	359	657	.546	1	6	.167	317	384	.826	94	153	247	404	238	–	132	266	11	1036	3.3	5.3	13.6
75-76–Virginia (A)	43	–	871	100	216	.463	3	16	.188	113	139	.813	28	61	89	125	107	–	62	93	3	316	2.1	2.9	7.3
76-77–Portland	74	–	1937	263	430	.612	–	–	–	239	284	.842	75	127	202	247	228	6	128	–	15	765	2.7	3.3	10.3
77-78–Portland	75	–	1820	242	409	.592	–	–	–	183	234	.782	36	98	134	244	186	2	107	158	4	667	1.8	3.3	8.9
78-79–Portland	64	–	1570	203	381	.533	–	–	–	261	299	.873	39	80	119	176	185	5	84	127	4	667	1.9	2.8	10.4
79-80–Portland	67	–	1594	183	394	.464	4	7	.571	197	252	.782	52	104	156	273	149	2	77	131	1	567	2.3	4.1	8.5
Reg. NBA Totals	280	–	6921	891	1614	.552	4	7	.571	880	1069	.823	202	409	611	940	748	15	396	416	24	2666	2.2	3.4	9.5
Reg. ABA Totals	256	–	6320	763	1522	.501	9	46	.196	776	949	.818	219	456	675	883	720	1	254	599	22	2311	2.6	3.4	9.0
NBA Playoff Totals	25	–	559	74	134	.552	0	0	–	68	85	.800	10	29	39	62	79	3	30	22	2	216	1.6	2.5	8.6
ABA Playoff Totals	7	–	112	10	24	.417	0	1	.000	17	21	.810	7	7	15	8	15	0	3	7	0	37	2.1	1.1	5.3

Twyman, John Kennedy (Jack) b. May 11, 1934 Ht. 6-6 Wt. 210 College: Cincinnati HOF: 1982

SEASON–TEAM	G	GS	MIN	FGM	FGA	PCT	3FGM	3FGA	PCT	FTM	FTA	PCT	O-RB	D-RB	TOT	AST	PF	DQ	STL	TO	BLK	PTS	RPG	APG	PPG
55-56–Rochester	72	–	2186	417	987	.422	–	–	–	204	298	.685	–	–	466	171	239	4	–	–	–	1038	6.5	2.4	14.4
56-57–Rochester	72	–	2338	449	1023	.439	–	–	–	276	363	.760	–	–	354	123	251	4	–	–	–	1174	4.9	1.7	16.3
57-58–Cincinnati	72	–	2178	465	1028	.452	–	–	–	307	396	.775	–	–	464	110	224	3	–	–	–	1237	6.4	1.5	17.2
58-59–Cincinnati	72	–	2713	710	1691	.420	–	–	–	437	558	.783	–	–	653	209	277	6	–	–	–	1857	9.1	2.9	25.8
59-60–Cincinnati	75	–	3023	870	2063	.422	–	–	–	598	762	.785	–	–	664	260	275	10	–	–	–	2338	8.9	3.5	31.2
60-61–Cincinnati	79	–	2920	796	1632	.488	–	–	–	405	554	.731	–	–	672	225	279	5	–	–	–	1997	8.5	2.8	25.3
61-62–Cincinnati	80	–	2991	739	1542	.479	–	–	–	353	435	.811	–	–	638	215	323	5	–	–	–	1831	8.0	2.7	22.9
62-63–Cincinnati	80	–	2623	641	1335	.480	–	–	–	304	375	.811	–	–	598	214	286	7	–	–	–	1586	7.5	2.7	19.8
63-64–Cincinnati	68	–	1996	447	993	.450	–	–	–	189	228	.829	–	–	364	137	267	7	–	–	–	1083	5.4	2.0	15.9
64-65–Cincinnati	80	–	2236	479	1081	.443	–	–	–	198	239	.828	–	–	383	137	239	4	–	–	–	1156	4.8	1.7	14.5
65-66–Cincinnati	73	–	943	224	498	.450	–	–	–	95	117	.812	–	–	168	60	122	1	–	–	–	543	2.3	0.8	7.4
Reg. Season Totals	823	–	26147	6237	13873	.450	–	–	–	3366	4325	.778	–	–	5424	1861	2782	56	–	–	–	15840	6.6	2.3	19.2
Playoff Totals	34	–	1095	245	556	.441	–	–	–	131	159	.824	–	–	255	62	131	2	–	–	–	621	7.5	1.8	18.3
All-Star Totals	6	–	117	38	68	.559	–	–	–	13	20	.650	–	–	21	8	14	0	–	–	–	89	3.5	1.3	14.8

Tyler, Brandon Joel (B.J.) b. April 30, 1971 Ht. 6-1 Wt. 185 College: Texas

SEASON–TEAM	G	GS	MIN	FGM	FGA	PCT	3FGM	3FGA	PCT	FTM	FTA	PCT	O-RB	D-RB	TOT	AST	PF	DQ	STL	TO	BLK	PTS	RPG	APG	PPG
94-95–Philadelphia	55	8	809	72	189	.381	16	51	.314	35	50	.700	13	49	62	174	58	0	36	97	2	195	1.1	3.2	3.5
Reg. Season Totals	55	8	809	72	189	.381	16	51	.314	35	50	.700	13	49	62	174	58	0	36	97	2	195	1.1	3.2	3.5

Tyler, Terry Christopher b. October 30, 1956 Ht. 6-7 Wt. 215 College: Detroit Mercy

SEASON–TEAM	G	GS	MIN	FGM	FGA	PCT	3FGM	3FGA	PCT	FTM	FTA	PCT	O-RB	D-RB	TOT	AST	PF	DQ	STL	TO	BLK	PTS	RPG	APG	PPG
78-79–Detroit	82	–	2560	456	946	.482	–	–	–	144	219	.658	211	437	648	89	254	3	104	141	201	1056	7.9	1.1	12.9
79-80–Detroit	82	–	2672	430	925	.465	2	12	.167	143	187	.765	228	399	627	129	237	3	107	175	220	1005	7.6	1.6	12.3
80-81–Detroit	82	–	2549	476	895	.532	0	8	.000	148	250	.592	198	369	567	136	215	2	112	163	180	1100	6.9	1.7	13.4
81-82–Detroit	82	0	1989	336	643	.523	1	4	.250	142	192	.740	154	339	493	126	182	1	77	121	160	815	6.0	1.5	9.9
82-83–Detroit	82	56	2543	421	880	.478	2	15	.133	146	196	.745	180	360	540	157	221	3	103	120	160	990	6.6	1.9	12.1
83-84–Detroit	82	7	1602	313	691	.453	2	13	.154	94	132	.712	104	181	285	76	151	1	63	78	59	722	3.5	0.9	8.8
84-85–Detroit	82	53	2004	422	855	.494	0	8	.000	106	148	.716	148	275	423	63	192	0	49	76	90	950	5.2	0.8	11.6
85-86–Sacramento	71	52	1651	295	649	.455	0	3	.000	84	112	.750	109	204	313	94	159	0	64	94	108	674	4.4	1.3	9.5
86-87–Sacramento	82	48	1930	329	664	.495	1	3	.333	101	140	.721	116	212	328	73	151	1	55	78	78	760	4.0	0.9	9.3
87-88–Sacramento	74	28	1185	184	407	.452	1	7	.143	41	64	.641	87	155	242	56	85	0	43	43	47	410	3.3	0.8	5.5
88-89–Dallas	70	11	1057	169	360	.469	1	9	.111	47	62	.758	74	135	209	40	90	0	24	51	39	386	3.0	0.6	5.5
Reg. Season Totals	871	255	21742	3831	7915	.484	10	82	.122	1196	1702	.703	1609	3066	4675	1039	1937	14	801	1140	1342	8868	5.4	1.2	10.2
Playoff Totals	17	2	272	61	134	.455	0	1	.000	31	40	.775	23	32	55	8	26	0	8	11	10	153	3.2	0.5	9.0

Tyra, Charles E. (Charlie) b. August 16, 1935 Ht. 6-8 Wt. 235 College: Louisville

SEASON–TEAM	G	GS	MIN	FGM	FGA	PCT	3FGM	3FGA	PCT	FTM	FTA	PCT	O-RB	D-RB	TOT	AST	PF	DQ	STL	TO	BLK	PTS	RPG	APG	PPG
57-58–New York	68	–	1182	175	490	.357	–	–	–	150	224	.670	–	–	480	34	175	3	–	–	–	500	7.1	0.5	7.4
58-59–New York	69	–	1586	240	606	.396	–	–	–	129	190	.679	–	–	485	33	180	2	–	–	–	609	7.0	0.5	8.8
59-60–New York	74	–	2033	406	952	.426	–	–	–	133	189	.704	–	–	598	80	258	8	–	–	–	945	8.1	1.1	12.8
60-61–New York	59	–	1404	199	549	.362	–	–	–	120	173	.694	–	–	394	82	164	7	–	–	–	518	6.7	1.4	8.8
61-62–Chicago	78	–	1606	193	534	.361	–	–	–	133	214	.621	–	–	610	86	210	7	–	–	–	519	7.8	1.1	6.7
Reg. Season Totals	348	–	7811	1213	3131	.387	–	–	–	665	990	.672	–	–	2567	315	987	27	–	–	–	3091	7.4	0.9	8.9
Playoff Totals	2	–	55	12	28	.429	–	–	–	6	9	.667	–	–	31	1	5	0	–	–	–	30	15.5	0.5	15.0

Unseld, Westley Sissel (Wes) b. March 14, 1946 Ht. 6-7 Wt. 245 College: Louisville HOF: 1987

SEASON–TEAM	G	GS	MIN	FGM	FGA	PCT	3FGM	3FGA	PCT	FTM	FTA	PCT	O-RB	D-RB	TOT	AST	PF	DQ	STL	TO	BLK	PTS	RPG	APG	PPG
68-69–Baltimore	82	–	2970	427	897	.476	–	–	–	277	458	.605	–	–	1491	213	276	4	–	–	–	1131	18.2	2.6	13.8
69-70–Baltimore	82	–	3234	526	1015	.518	–	–	–	273	428	.638	–	–	1370	291	250	2	–	–	–	1325	16.7	3.5	16.2
70-71–Baltimore	74	–	2904	424	846	.501	–	–	–	199	303	.657	–	–	1253	293	235	2	–	–	–	1047	16.9	4.0	14.1
71-72–Baltimore	76	–	3171	409	822	.498	–	–	–	171	272	.629	–	–	1336	278	218	1	–	–	–	989	17.6	3.7	13.0
72-73–Baltimore	79	–	3085	421	854	.493	–	–	–	149	212	.703	–	–	1260	347	168	0	–	–	–	991	15.9	4.4	12.5
73-74–Capital	56	–	1727	146	333	.438	–	–	–	36	55	.655	152	365	517	159	121	1	56	–	16	328	9.2	2.8	5.9
74-75–Washington	73	–	2904	273	544	.502	–	–	–	126	184	.685	318	759	1077	297	180	1	115	–	68	672	14.8	4.1	9.2
75-76–Washington	78	–	2922	318	567	.561	–	–	–	114	195	.585	271	765	1036	404	203	3	84	–	59	750	13.3	5.2	9.6
76-77–Washington	82	–	2860	270	551	.490	–	–	–	100	166	.602	243	634	877	363	253	5	87	–	45	640	10.7	4.4	7.8
77-78–Washington	80	–	2644	257	491	.523	–	–	–	93	173	.538	286	669	955	326	234	2	98	173	45	607	11.9	4.1	7.6
78-79–Washington	77	–	2406	346	600	.577	–	–	–	151	235	.643	274	556	830	315	204	2	71	156	37	843	10.8	4.1	10.9
79-80–Washington	82	–	2973	327	637	.513	1	2	.500	139	209	.665	334	760	1094	366	249	5	65	153	61	794	13.3	4.5	9.7
80-81–Washington	63	–	2032	225	429	.524	2	4	.500	55	86	.640	207	466	673	170	171	1	52	97	36	507	10.7	2.7	8.0
Reg. Season Totals	984	–	35832	4369	8586	.509	3	6	.500	1883	2976	.633	2085	4974	13769	3822	2762	29	628	579	367	10624	14.0	3.9	10.8
Playoff Totals	119	–	4889	513	1040	.493	0	1	.000	234	385	.608	306	742	1777	453	371	5	67	69	55	1260	14.9	3.8	10.6
All-Star Totals	5	–	77	14	28	.500	0	0	–	3	5	.600	2	4	36	6	10	0	2	–	0	31	7.2	1.2	6.2

Uplinger, Harold F. (Hal) b. September 30, 1929 Ht. 6-4 Wt. 185 College: Long Island University

SEASON–TEAM	G	GS	MIN	FGM	FGA	PCT	3FGM	3FGA	PCT	FTM	FTA	PCT	O-RB	D-RB	TOT	AST	PF	DQ	STL	TO	BLK	PTS	RPG	APG	PPG
53-54–Baltimore	23	–	268	33	94	.351	–	–	–	20	22	.909	–	–	31	26	42	0	–	–	–	86	1.3	1.1	3.7
Reg. Season Totals	23	–	268	33	94	.351	–	–	–	20	22	.909	–	–	31	26	42	0	–	–	–	86	1.3	1.1	3.7

Upshaw, Kelvin Parnell b. January 24, 1963 Ht. 6-2 Wt. 180 College: Northeastern State (Okla.); Utah

SEASON–TEAM	G	GS	MIN	FGM	FGA	PCT	3FGM	3FGA	PCT	FTM	FTA	PCT	O-RB	D-RB	TOT	AST	PF	DQ	STL	TO	BLK	PTS	RPG	APG	PPG
88-89–Miami-Boston	32	0	617	99	212	.467	3	15	.200	18	26	.692	10	39	49	117	80	1	26	55	3	219	1.5	3.7	6.8
89-90–Boston-Dallas-G.S.	40	0	387	64	146	.438	4	15	.267	28	37	.757	9	32	41	54	53	0	27	27	1	160	1.0	1.4	4.0
90-91–Dallas	48	1	514	104	231	.450	7	29	.241	55	64	.859	20	35	55	86	77	0	28	39	5	270	1.1	1.8	5.6
Reg. Season Totals	120	1	1518	267	589	.453	14	59	.237	101	127	.795	39	106	145	257	210	1	81	121	9	649	1.2	2.1	5.4
Playoff Totals	3	0	24	5	12	.417	0	0	–	0	0	–	0	2	2	5	4	0	1	1	0	10	0.7	1.7	3.3

Vacendak, Stephen T. (Steve) b. August 15, 1944 Ht. 6-1 Wt. 185 College: Duke

SEASON–TEAM	G	GS	MIN	FGM	FGA	PCT	3FGM	3FGA	PCT	FTM	FTA	PCT	O-RB	D-RB	TOT	AST	PF	DQ	STL	TO	BLK	PTS	RPG	APG	PPG
67-68–Pittsburgh (A)	9	–	73	13	35	.371	0	0	–	10	15	.667	–	–	15	8	14	0	–	9	–	36	1.7	0.9	4.0
68-69–Minnesota (A)	60	–	1589	288	716	.402	2	8	.250	167	215	.777	–	–	210	166	158	1	–	139	–	745	3.5	2.8	12.4
69-70–Pitt.-Miami (A)	14	–	173	15	59	.254	0	2	.000	13	22	.591	–	–	13	20	22	0	–	–	–	43	0.9	1.4	3.1
Reg. ABA Totals	83	–	1835	316	810	.390	2	10	.200	190	252	.754	–	–	238	194	194	1	–	148	–	824	2.9	2.3	9.9
ABA Playoff Totals	14	–	230	41	92	.446	0	0	–	37	41	.902	–	–	20	14	26	0	–	1	–	119	1.4	1.0	8.5

Valentine, Darnell Terrell b. February 3, 1959 Ht. 6-2 Wt. 185 College: Kansas

SEASON–TEAM	G	GS	MIN	FGM	FGA	PCT	3FGM	3FGA	PCT	FTM	FTA	PCT	O-RB	D-RB	TOT	AST	PF	DQ	STL	TO	BLK	PTS	RPG	APG	PPG
81-82–Portland	82	14	1387	187	453	.413	0	9	.000	152	200	.760	48	101	149	270	187	1	94	127	3	526	1.8	3.3	6.4
82-83–Portland	47	36	1298	209	460	.454	0	1	.000	169	213	.793	34	83	117	293	139	1	101	131	5	587	2.5	6.2	12.5
83-84–Portland	68	60	1893	251	561	.447	0	3	.000	194	246	.789	49	78	127	395	179	1	107	149	6	696	1.9	5.8	10.2
84-85–Portland	75	59	2278	321	679	.473	0	2	.000	230	290	.793	54	165	219	522	189	1	143	194	5	872	2.9	7.0	11.6
85-86–Port.-LAClips	62	29	1217	161	388	.415	4	14	.286	130	175	.743	32	93	125	246	123	0	72	115	2	456	2.0	4.0	7.4
86-87–L.A. Clippers	65	52	1759	275	671	.410	13	56	.232	163	200	.815	38	112	150	447	148	3	116	167	10	726	2.3	6.9	11.2
87-88–L.A. Clippers	79	31	1636	223	533	.418	15	33	.455	101	136	.743	37	119	156	382	135	0	122	148	8	562	2.0	4.8	7.1
88-89–Cleveland	77	4	1086	136	319	.426	3	14	.214	91	112	.813	22	81	103	174	88	0	57	83	7	366	1.3	2.3	4.8
90-91–Cleveland	65	60	1841	230	496	.464	6	25	.240	143	172	.831	37	135	172	351	170	2	98	126	12	609	2.6	5.4	9.4
Reg. Season Totals	620	345	14395	1993	4560	.437	41	157	.261	1373	1744	.787	351	967	1318	3080	1358	9	910	1240	58	5400	2.1	5.0	8.7
Playoff Totals	26	21	707	114	248	.460	1	2	.500	84	95	.884	17	33	50	177	79	3	40	56	4	313	1.9	6.8	12.0

Valentine, Ronnie L. (Ron) b. November 27, 1957 Ht. 6-7 Wt. 210 College: Old Dominion

SEASON–TEAM	G	GS	MIN	FGM	FGA	PCT	3FGM	3FGA	PCT	FTM	FTA	PCT	O-RB	D-RB	TOT	AST	PF	DQ	STL	TO	BLK	PTS	RPG	APG	PPG
80-81–Denver	24	–	123	37	98	.378	1	2	.500	9	19	.474	10	20	30	7	23	0	7	16	4	84	1.3	0.3	3.5
Reg. Season Totals	24	–	123	37	98	.378	1	2	.500	9	19	.474	10	20	30	7	23	0	7	16	4	84	1.3	0.3	3.5

Vallely, John Stephen b. October 3, 1948 Ht. 6-3 Wt. 185 College: Orange Coast (Calif.) Coll. (J.C.); UCLA

SEASON–TEAM	G	GS	MIN	FGM	FGA	PCT	3FGM	3FGA	PCT	FTM	FTA	PCT	O-RB	D-RB	TOT	AST	PF	DQ	STL	TO	BLK	PTS	RPG	APG	PPG
70-71–Atlanta	51	–	430	73	204	.358	–	–	–	45	59	.763	–	–	34	47	50	0	–	–	–	191	0.7	0.9	3.7
71-72–Atlanta-Hou.	49	–	366	69	171	.404	–	–	–	30	45	.667	–	–	32	37	50	0	–	–	–	168	0.7	0.8	3.4
Reg. Season Totals	100	–	796	142	375	.379	–	–	–	75	104	.721	–	–	66	84	100	0	–	–	–	359	0.7	0.8	3.6

Van Arsdale, Richard Albert (Dick) b. February 22, 1943 Ht. 6-5 Wt. 210 College: Indiana

SEASON–TEAM	G	GS	MIN	FGM	FGA	PCT	3FGM	3FGA	PCT	FTM	FTA	PCT	O-RB	D-RB	TOT	AST	PF	DQ	STL	TO	BLK	PTS	RPG	APG	PPG
65-66–New York	79	–	2289	359	838	.428	–	–	–	251	351	.715	–	–	376	184	235	5	–	–	–	969	4.8	2.3	12.3
66-67–New York	79	–	2892	410	913	.449	–	–	–	371	509	.729	–	–	555	247	264	3	–	–	–	1191	7.0	3.1	15.1
67-68–New York	78	–	2348	316	725	.436	–	–	–	227	339	.670	–	–	424	230	225	0	–	–	–	859	5.4	2.9	11.0
68-69–Phoenix	80	–	3388	612	1386	.442	–	–	–	454	644	.705	–	–	548	388	245	2	–	–	–	1678	6.9	4.9	21.0
69-70–Phoenix	77	–	2966	592	1166	.508	–	–	–	459	575	.798	–	–	264	338	282	5	–	–	–	1643	3.4	4.4	21.3
70-71–Phoenix	81	–	3157	609	1346	.452	–	–	–	553	682	.811	–	–	316	329	246	1	–	–	–	1771	3.9	4.1	21.9
71-72–Phoenix	82	–	3096	545	1178	.463	–	–	–	529	626	.845	–	–	334	297	232	1	–	–	–	1619	4.1	3.6	19.7
72-73–Phoenix	81	–	2979	532	1118	.476	–	–	–	426	496	.859	–	–	326	268	221	2	–	–	–	1490	4.0	3.3	18.4
73-74–Phoenix	78	78	2832	514	1028	.500	–	–	–	361	423	.853	66	155	221	324	241	2	96	–	17	1389	2.8	4.2	17.8
74-75–Phoenix	70	–	2419	421	895	.470	–	–	–	282	339	.832	52	137	189	195	177	2	81	–	11	1124	2.7	2.8	16.1
75-76–Phoenix	58	–	1870	276	570	.484	–	–	–	195	235	.830	39	98	137	140	113	2	52	–	11	747	2.4	2.4	12.9
76-77–Phoenix	78	–	1535	227	498	.456	–	–	–	145	166	.873	31	86	117	120	94	0	35	–	5	599	1.5	1.5	7.7
Reg. Season Totals	921	78	31771	5413	11661	.464	–	–	–	4253	5385	.790	188	476	3807	3060	2575	25	264	–	44	15079	4.1	3.3	16.4
Playoff Totals	34	–	968	124	294	.422	–	–	–	88	105	.838	10	13	82	94	89	1	13	–	2	336	2.4	2.8	9.9
All-Star Totals	3	–	38	8	16	.500	–	–	–	0	1	.000	0	0	8	5	1	0	0	–	0	16	2.7	1.7	5.3

Van Arsdale, Thomas Arthur (Tom) b. February 22, 1943 Ht. 6-5 Wt. 215 College: Indiana

SEASON–TEAM	G	GS	MIN	FGM	FGA	PCT	3FGM	3FGA	PCT	FTM	FTA	PCT	O-RB	D-RB	TOT	AST	PF	DQ	STL	TO	BLK	PTS	RPG	APG	PPG
65-66–Detroit	79	–	2041	312	834	.374	–	–	–	209	290	.721	–	–	309	205	251	1	–	–	–	833	3.9	2.6	10.5
66-67–Detroit	79	–	2134	347	887	.391	–	–	–	272	347	.784	–	–	341	193	241	3	–	–	–	966	4.3	2.4	12.2
67-68–Detroit-Cin.	77	–	1514	211	545	.387	–	–	–	188	252	.746	–	–	225	155	202	5	–	–	–	610	2.9	2.0	7.9
68-69–Cincinnati	77	–	3059	547	1233	.444	–	–	–	398	533	.747	–	–	356	208	300	6	–	–	–	1492	4.6	2.7	19.4
69-70–Cincinnati	71	–	2544	620	1376	.451	–	–	–	381	492	.774	–	–	463	155	247	3	–	–	–	1621	6.5	2.2	22.8
70-71–Cincinnati	82	–	3146	749	1642	.456	–	–	–	377	523	.721	–	–	499	181	294	3	–	–	–	1875	6.1	2.2	22.9
71-72–Cincinnati	73	–	2598	550	1205	.456	–	–	–	299	396	.755	–	–	350	198	241	1	–	–	–	1399	4.8	2.7	19.2
72-73–K.C.-Omaha-Phil.	79	–	2311	445	1043	.427	–	–	–	250	308	.812	–	–	358	152	224	2	–	–	–	1140	4.5	1.9	14.4
73-74–Philadelphia	78	–	3041	614	1433	.428	–	–	–	298	350	.851	88	305	393	202	300	6	62	–	3	1526	5.0	2.6	19.6
74-75–Phil.-Atlanta	82	–	2843	593	1385	.428	–	–	–	322	424	.759	77	201	278	223	257	5	91	–	3	1508	3.4	2.7	18.4
75-76–Atlanta	75	–	2026	346	785	.441	–	–	–	126	166	.759	35	151	186	146	202	5	57	–	7	818	2.5	1.9	10.9
76-77–Phoenix	77	–	1425	171	395	.433	–	–	–	102	145	.703	47	137	184	67	163	0	20	–	3	444	2.4	0.9	5.8
Reg. Season Totals	929	–	28682	5505	12763	.431	–	–	–	3222	4226	.762	247	794	3942	2085	2922	40	230	–	16	14232	4.2	2.2	15.3
All-Star Totals	3	–	23	6	16	.375	–	–	–	1	3	.333	0	0	3	2	3	0	0	–	0	13	1.0	0.7	4.3

Van Breda Kolff, Jan Michael (V.B.K.) b. December 16, 1951 Ht. 6-7 Wt. 200 College: Vanderbilt

SEASON–TEAM	G	GS	MIN	FGM	FGA	PCT	3FGM	3FGA	PCT	FTM	FTA	PCT	O-RB	D-RB	TOT	AST	PF	DQ	STL	TO	BLK	PTS	RPG	APG	PPG
74-75–Denver (A)	84	–	1639	155	342	.453	0	3	.000	177	211	.839	121	237	358	181	164	–	48	122	43	487	4.3	2.2	5.8
75-76–Vir.-Ken. (A)	80	–	1978	223	488	.457	2	6	.333	165	198	.833	144	292	436	182	164	–	65	144	96	613	5.5	2.3	7.7
76-77–New York Nets	72	–	2398	271	609	.445	–	–	–	195	228	.855	156	304	460	117	205	2	74	–	68	737	6.4	1.6	10.2
77-78–New Jersey	68	–	1419	107	292	.366	–	–	–	87	123	.707	66	178	244	105	192	8	52	73	46	301	3.6	1.5	4.4
78-79–New Jersey	80	–	1998	196	423	.463	–	–	–	146	183	.798	108	274	382	180	235	4	85	135	74	538	4.8	2.3	6.7
79-80–New Jersey	82	–	2399	212	458	.463	7	20	.350	130	155	.839	103	326	429	247	307	11	100	158	76	561	5.2	3.0	6.8
80-81–New Jersey	78	–	1426	100	245	.408	2	8	.250	98	117	.838	48	154	202	129	214	3	38	108	50	300	2.6	1.7	3.8
81-82–New Jersey	41	0	452	41	82	.500	0	2	.000	62	76	.816	17	31	48	32	63	1	12	29	13	144	1.2	0.8	3.5
82-83–New Jersey	13	0	63	5	14	.357	0	0	–	5	6	.833	2	11	13	5	9	0	2	3	2	15	1.0	0.4	1.2
Reg. NBA Totals	434	0	10155	932	2123	.439	9	30	.300	723	888	.814	500	1278	1778	815	1225	29	363	506	329	2596	4.1	1.9	6.0
Reg. ABA Totals	164	–	3617	378	830	.455	2	9	.222	342	409	.836	265	529	794	363	328	–	113	266	139	1100	4.8	2.2	6.7
NBA Playoff Totals	4	0	97	8	21	.381	0	0	–	5	6	.833	11	12	23	7	9	0	2	6	4	21	5.8	1.8	5.3
ABA Playoff Totals	22	–	378	38	80	.475	0	0	–	40	45	.889	35	41	76	31	39	–	10	25	11	116	3.5	1.4	5.3

Van Breda Kolff, Willem H. (Butch) b. October 28, 1922 Ht. 6-3 Wt. 185 College: Princeton; New York U.

SEASON–TEAM	G	GS	MIN	FGM	FGA	PCT	3FGM	3FGA	PCT	FTM	FTA	PCT	O-RB	D-RB	TOT	AST	PF	DQ	STL	TO	BLK	PTS	RPG	APG	PPG
46-47–New York	16	–	–	7	34	.206	–	–	–	11	17	.647	–	–	–	6	10	–	–	–	–	25	–	0.4	1.6
47-48–New York	44	–	–	53	192	.276	–	–	–	74	120	.617	–	–	–	29	81	–	–	–	–	180	–	0.7	4.1
48-49–New York	59	–	–	127	401	.317	–	–	–	161	240	.671	–	–	–	143	148	–	–	–	–	415	–	2.4	7.0
49-50–New York	56	–	–	55	167	.329	–	–	–	96	134	.716	–	–	–	78	111	–	–	–	–	206	–	1.4	3.7
Reg. Season Totals	175	–	–	242	794	.305	–	–	–	342	511	.669	–	–	–	256	350	–	–	–	–	826	–	1.5	4.7
Playoff Totals	15	–	–	28	99	.333	–	–	–	36	53	.736	–	–	–	14	29	–	–	–	–	92	–	0.8	6.1

Vance, Ellis Eugene (Gene) b. February 25, 1923 Ht. 6-3 Wt. 195 College: Illinois

SEASON–TEAM	G	GS	MIN	FGM	FGA	PCT	3FGM	3FGA	PCT	FTM	FTA	PCT	O-RB	D-RB	TOT	AST	PF	DQ	STL	TO	BLK	PTS	RPG	APG	PPG
47-48–Chicago	48	–	–	163	617	.264	–	–	–	76	126	.603	–	–	–	49	193	–	–	–	–	402	–	1.0	8.4
48-49–Chicago	56	–	–	222	657	.338	–	–	–	131	181	.724	–	–	–	167	217	–	–	–	–	575	–	3.0	10.3
49-50–Tri-Cities	35	–	–	110	325	.338	–	–	–	86	120	.717	–	–	–	121	145	–	–	–	–	306	–	3.5	8.7
50-51–Tri-Cities	28	–	–	44	110	.400	–	–	–	43	61	.705	–	–	88	53	91	0	–	–	–	131	3.1	1.9	4.7
51-52–Milwaukee	7	–	118	7	26	.269	–	–	–	9	14	.643	–	–	15	9	18	0	–	–	–	23	2.1	1.3	3.3
Reg. Season Totals	174	–	118	546	1735	.315	–	–	–	345	502	.687	–	–	103	399	664	0	–	–	–	1437	2.9	2.3	8.3
Playoff Totals	10	–	0	32	264	.242	–	–	–	24	33	.727	–	–	–	34	58	3	–	–	–	88	–	1.7	8.8

Vander Velden, Logan b. April 3, 1971 Ht. 6-9 Wt. 215 College: Wisconsin-Green Bay

SEASON–TEAM	G	GS	MIN	FGM	FGA	PCT	3FGM	3FGA	PCT	FTM	FTA	PCT	O-RB	D-RB	TOT	AST	PF	DQ	STL	TO	BLK	PTS	RPG	APG	PPG
95-96–L.A. Clippers	15	0	31	3	14	.214	0	5	.000	3	4	.750	1	5	6	1	4	0	0	0	0	9	0.4	0.1	0.6
Reg. Season Totals	15	0	31	3	14	.214	0	5	.000	3	4	.750	1	5	6	1	4	0	0	0	0	9	0.4	0.1	0.6

Vandeweghe, Ernest Maurice III (Kiki) b. August 1, 1958 Ht. 6-8 Wt. 220 College: UCLA

SEASON–TEAM	G	GS	MIN	FGM	FGA	PCT	3FGM	3FGA	PCT	FTM	FTA	PCT	O-RB	D-RB	TOT	AST	PF	DQ	STL	TO	BLK	PTS	RPG	APG	PPG
80-81–Denver	51	–	1376	229	537	.426	0	7	.000	130	159	.818	86	184	270	94	116	0	29	86	24	588	5.3	1.8	11.5
81-82–Denver	82	78	2775	706	1260	.560	1	13	.077	347	405	.857	149	312	461	247	217	1	52	189	29	1760	5.6	3.0	21.5
82-83–Denver	82	79	2909	841	1537	.547	15	51	.294	489	559	.875	124	313	437	203	198	0	66	177	38	2186	5.3	2.5	26.7
83-84–Denver	78	71	2734	895	1603	.558	11	30	.367	494	580	.852	84	289	373	238	187	1	53	156	50	2295	4.8	3.1	29.4
84-85–Portland	72	69	2502	618	1158	.534	11	33	.333	369	412	.896	74	154	228	106	116	0	37	116	22	1616	3.2	1.5	22.4
85-86–Portland	79	76	2791	719	1332	.540	1	8	.125	523	602	.869	92	124	216	187	161	0	54	177	17	1962	2.7	2.4	24.8
86-87–Portland	79	79	3029	808	1545	.523	39	81	.481	467	527	.886	86	165	251	220	137	0	52	139	17	2122	3.2	2.8	26.9
87-88–Portland	37	7	1038	283	557	.508	22	58	.379	159	181	.878	36	73	109	71	68	0	21	48	7	747	2.9	1.9	20.2
88-89–Port.-N.Y.	45	1	934	200	426	.469	19	48	.396	80	89	.899	26	45	71	69	78	0	19	41	11	499	1.6	1.5	11.1
89-90–New York	22	13	563	102	231	.442	10	19	.526	44	48	.917	15	38	53	41	28	0	15	26	3	258	2.4	1.9	11.7
90-91–New York	75	72	2420	458	927	.494	51	141	.362	259	288	.899	78	102	180	110	122	0	42	108	10	1226	2.4	1.5	16.3
91-92–New York	67	0	956	188	383	.491	26	66	.394	65	81	.802	31	57	88	57	87	0	15	27	8	467	1.3	0.9	7.0
92-93–L.A. Clippers	41	3	494	92	203	.453	12	37	.324	58	66	.879	12	36	48	25	45	0	13	20	7	254	1.2	0.6	6.2
Reg. Season Totals	810	548	24521	6139	11699	.525	218	592	.368	3484	3997	.872	893	1892	2785	1668	1560	2	468	1310	243	15980	3.4	2.1	19.7
Playoff Totals	68	46	1890	419	822	.510	20	58	.345	235	259	.907	53	135	188	134	132	1	39	89	27	1093	2.8	2.0	16.1
All-Star Totals	2	0	40	10	17	.588	0	0	–	1	2	.500	1	5	6	2	2	0	1	0	0	21	3.0	1.0	10.5

Vandeweghe, Ernest Maurice Jr. (Ernie, Doc) b. September 12, 1928 Ht. 6-3 Wt. 195 College: Colgate

SEASON–TEAM	G	GS	MIN	FGM	FGA	PCT	3FGM	3FGA	PCT	FTM	FTA	PCT	O-RB	D-RB	TOT	AST	PF	DQ	STL	TO	BLK	PTS	RPG	APG	PPG
49-50–New York	42	–	–	164	390	.421	–	–	–	93	140	.664	–	–	–	78	126	–	–	–	–	421	–	1.9	10.0
50-51–New York	44	–	–	135	336	.402	–	–	–	68	97	.701	–	–	195	121	144	6	–	–	–	338	4.4	2.8	7.7
51-52–New York	57	–	1507	200	457	.438	–	–	–	124	160	.775	–	–	264	164	188	3	–	–	–	524	4.6	2.9	9.2
52-53–New York	61	–	1745	272	625	.435	–	–	–	187	244	.766	–	–	342	144	242	11	–	–	–	731	5.6	2.4	12.0
53-54–New York	15	–	271	37	103	.359	–	–	–	25	31	.806	–	–	39	29	38	1	–	–	–	99	2.6	1.9	6.6
55-56–New York	5	–	77	10	31	.323	–	–	–	2	2	1.000	–	–	13	12	15	0	–	–	–	22	2.6	2.4	4.4
Reg. Season Totals	224	–	3600	818	1942	.421	–	–	–	499	674	.740	–	–	853	548	753	21	–	–	–	2135	4.7	2.4	9.5
Playoff Totals	43	–	874	146	360	.419	–	–	–	136	174	.782	–	–	199	92	179	5	–	–	–	428	5.1	2.1	10.0

Van Exel, Nickey Maxwell (Nick) b. November 27, 1971 Ht. 6-1 Wt. 190 College: Trinity Valley (Texas) C.C.; Cincinnati

SEASON–TEAM	G	GS	MIN	FGM	FGA	PCT	3FGM	3FGA	PCT	FTM	FTA	PCT	O-RB	D-RB	TOT	AST	PF	DQ	STL	TO	BLK	PTS	RPG	APG	PPG
93-94–L.A. Lakers	81	80	2700	413	1049	.394	123	364	.338	150	192	.781	47	191	238	466	154	1	85	145	8	1099	2.9	5.8	13.6
94-95–L.A. Lakers	80	80	2944	465	1107	.420	183	511	.358	235	300	.783	27	196	223	660	157	0	97	220	6	1348	2.8	8.3	16.9
95-96–L.A. Lakers	74	74	2513	396	950	.417	144	403	.357	163	204	.799	29	152	181	509	115	0	70	156	10	1099	2.4	6.9	14.9
96-97–L.A. Lakers	79	79	2937	432	1075	.402	177	468	.378	165	200	.825	44	182	226	672	110	0	75	212	10	1206	2.9	8.5	15.3
97-98–L.A. Lakers	64	46	2053	311	743	.419	123	316	.389	136	172	.791	31	163	194	442	120	0	64	104	6	881	3.0	6.9	13.8
98-99–Denver	50	50	1802	306	769	.398	72	234	.308	142	175	.811	14	99	113	368	90	0	40	121	3	826	2.3	7.4	16.5
99-00–Denver	79	79	2950	473	1213	.390	133	401	.332	196	240	.817	34	277	311	714	148	0	68	221	11	1275	3.9	9.0	16.1
Reg. Season Totals	507	488	17899	2796	6906	.405	955	2697	.354	1187	1483	.800	226	1260	1486	3831	894	1	499	1179	54	7734	2.9	7.6	15.3
Playoff Totals	36	23	1321	178	486	.366	60	196	.306	112	146	.767	28	89	117	212	92	0	41	73	4	528	3.3	5.9	14.7
All-Star Totals	1	0	20	5	14	.357	1	6	.167	2	2	1.000	1	2	3	2	0	0	0	2	0	13	3.0	2.0	13.0

Van Horn, Keith Adam b. October 23, 1975 Ht. 6-10 Wt. 250 College: Utah

SEASON–TEAM	G	GS	MIN	FGM	FGA	PCT	3FGM	3FGA	PCT	FTM	FTA	PCT	O-RB	D-RB	TOT	AST	PF	DQ	STL	TO	BLK	PTS	RPG	APG	PPG
97-98–New Jersey	62	62	2325	446	1047	.426	69	224	.308	258	305	.846	142	266	408	106	216	0	64	164	25	1219	6.6	1.7	19.7
98-99–New Jersey	42	42	1576	322	752	.428	16	53	.302	256	298	.859	114	244	358	65	134	2	43	133	53	916	8.5	1.5	21.8
99-00–New Jersey	80	80	2782	559	1257	.445	84	228	.368	333	393	.847	200	476	676	158	258	5	64	245	60	1535	8.5	2.0	19.2
Reg. Season Totals	184	184	6683	1327	3056	.434	169	505	.335	847	996	.850	456	986	1442	329	608	7	171	542	138	3670	7.8	1.8	19.9
Playoff Totals	3	3	77	13	29	.448	0	2	.000	12	15	.800	2	7	9	1	7	0	0	2	0	38	3.0	0.3	12.7

Van Lier, Norman Allen III (Norm) b. April 1, 1947 Ht. 6-2 Wt. 175 College: St. Francis (Pa.)

SEASON–TEAM	G	GS	MIN	FGM	FGA	PCT	3FGM	3FGA	PCT	FTM	FTA	PCT	O-RB	D-RB	TOT	AST	PF	DQ	STL	TO	BLK	PTS	RPG	APG	PPG
69-70–Cincinnati	81	–	2895	302	749	.403	–	–	–	166	224	.741	–	–	409	500	329	18	–	–	–	770	5.0	6.2	9.5
70-71–Cincinnati	82	–	3324	478	1138	.420	–	–	–	359	440	.816	–	–	583	832	343	12	–	–	–	1315	7.1	10.1	16.0
71-72–Cin.-Chicago	79	–	2415	334	761	.439	–	–	–	237	300	.790	–	–	357	542	239	5	–	–	–	905	4.5	6.9	11.5
72-73–Chicago	80	–	2882	474	1064	.445	–	–	–	166	211	.787	–	–	438	567	269	5	–	–	–	1114	5.5	7.1	13.9
73-74–Chicago	80	–	2863	427	1051	.406	–	–	–	288	370	.778	114	263	377	548	282	4	162	–	7	1142	4.7	6.9	14.3
74-75–Chicago	70	–	2590	407	970	.420	–	–	–	236	298	.792	86	242	328	403	246	5	139	–	14	1050	4.7	5.8	15.0
75-76–Chicago	76	–	3026	361	987	.366	–	–	–	235	319	.737	138	272	410	500	298	9	150	–	26	957	5.4	6.6	12.6
76-77–Chicago	82	–	3097	300	729	.412	–	–	–	238	306	.778	108	262	370	636	268	3	129	–	16	838	4.5	7.8	10.2
77-78–Chicago	78	–	2524	200	477	.419	–	–	–	172	229	.751	86	198	284	531	279	9	144	200	5	572	3.6	6.8	7.3
78-79–Milwaukee	38	–	555	30	77	.390	–	–	–	47	52	.904	8	32	40	158	108	4	43	49	3	107	1.1	4.2	2.8
Reg. Season Totals	746	–	26171	3313	8003	.414	–	–	–	2144	2749	.780	540	1269	3596	5217	2661	74	767	249	71	8770	4.8	7.0	11.8
Playoff Totals	38	–	1549	198	509	.389	–	–	–	134	171	.784	34	95	191	234	154	5	47	–	9	530	5.0	6.2	13.9
All-Star Totals	3	–	37	2	7	.286	–	–	–	1	2	.500	2	1	3	3	5	0	2	–	1	5	1.0	1.0	1.7

Vanos, Nicholas (Nick) b. April 13, 1963 d. August 16, 1987 Ht. 7-2 Wt. 260 College: Santa Clara

SEASON–TEAM	G	GS	MIN	FGM	FGA	PCT	3FGM	3FGA	PCT	FTM	FTA	PCT	O-RB	D-RB	TOT	AST	PF	DQ	STL	TO	BLK	PTS	RPG	APG	PPG
85-86–Phoenix	11	0	202	23	72	.319	0	0	–	8	23	.348	21	39	60	16	34	0	2	20	5	54	5.5	1.5	4.9
86-87–Phoenix	57	14	640	65	158	.411	0	2	.000	38	59	.644	67	113	180	43	94	0	19	48	23	168	3.2	0.8	2.9
Reg. Season Totals	68	14	842	88	230	.383	0	2	.000	46	82	.561	88	152	240	59	128	0	21	68	28	222	3.5	0.9	3.3

Van Zant, Dennis b. June 1, 1952 Ht. 6-9 Wt. 210 College: Azusa Pacific

SEASON–TEAM	G	GS	MIN	FGM	FGA	PCT	3FGM	3FGA	PCT	FTM	FTA	PCT	O-RB	D-RB	TOT	AST	PF	DQ	STL	TO	BLK	PTS	RPG	APG	PPG
75-76–San Antonio (A)	1	–	2	0	0	–	0	0	–	2	2	1.000	0	1	1	0	1	–	0	0	0	2	1.0	0.0	2.0
Reg. ABA Totals	1	–	2	0	0	–	0	0	–	2	2	1.000	0	1	1	0	1	–	0	0	0	2	1.0	0.0	2.0

Vaughn, Charles (Chico) b. February 19, 1940 Ht. 6-3 Wt. 215 College: Southern Illinois

SEASON–TEAM	G	GS	MIN	FGM	FGA	PCT	3FGM	3FGA	PCT	FTM	FTA	PCT	O-RB	D-RB	TOT	AST	PF	DQ	STL	TO	BLK	PTS	RPG	APG	PPG
62-63–St. Louis	77	–	1845	295	708	.417	–	–	–	188	261	.720	–	–	258	252	201	3	–	–	–	778	3.4	3.3	10.1
63-64–St. Louis	68	–	1340	238	538	.442	–	–	–	107	148	.723	–	–	126	129	166	0	–	–	–	583	1.9	1.9	8.6
64-65–St. Louis	75	–	1965	344	811	.424	–	–	–	182	242	.752	–	–	173	157	192	2	–	–	–	870	2.3	2.1	11.6
65-66–St. L.-Detroit	56	–	1219	182	474	.384	–	–	–	106	144	.736	–	–	109	140	99	1	–	–	–	470	1.9	2.5	8.4
66-67–Detroit	50	–	680	85	226	.376	–	–	–	50	74	.676	–	–	67	75	54	0	–	–	–	220	1.3	1.5	4.4
67-68–Pittsburgh (A)	74	–	2858	512	1350	.379	137	410	.334	308	416	.740	–	–	298	142	203	0	–	171	–	1469	4.0	1.9	19.9
68-69–Minnesota (A)	69	–	2301	415	1170	.355	145	523	.277	253	329	.769	–	–	165	107	178	1	–	150	–	1228	2.4	1.6	17.8
69-70–Pittsburgh (A)	21	–	401	66	180	.367	24	82	.293	48	70	.686	–	–	28	22	53	1	–	–	–	204	1.3	1.0	9.7
Reg. NBA Totals	326	–	7049	1144	2757	.415	–	–	–	633	869	.728	–	–	733	753	712	6	–	–	–	2921	2.2	2.3	9.0
Reg. ABA Totals	164	–	5560	993	2700	.368	306	1015	.301	609	815	.747	–	–	491	271	434	2	–	321	–	2901	3.0	1.7	17.7
NBA Playoff Totals	27	–	631	98	226	.434	–	–	–	44	61	.721	–	–	62	62	91	2	–	–	–	240	2.3	2.3	8.9
ABA Playoff Totals	20	–	633	101	293	.345	30	114	.263	68	85	.800	–	–	59	45	58	1	–	34	–	300	3.0	2.3	15.0

Vaughn, David b. June 4, 1952 Ht. 7-0 Wt. 220 College: Nevada-Las Vegas; Oral Roberts

SEASON–TEAM	G	GS	MIN	FGM	FGA	PCT	3FGM	3FGA	PCT	FTM	FTA	PCT	O-RB	D-RB	TOT	AST	PF	DQ	STL	TO	BLK	PTS	RPG	APG	PPG
74-75–Virginia (A)	83	–	2507	422	998	.423	0	2	.000	125	229	.546	276	618	894	132	274	–	79	195	126	969	10.8	1.6	11.7
75-76–Virginia (A)	10	–	86	12	33	.364	0	0	–	5	8	.625	8	11	19	3	15	–	0	5	2	29	1.9	0.3	2.9
Reg. ABA Totals	93	–	2593	434	1031	.421	0	2	.000	130	237	.549	284	629	913	135	289	–	79	200	128	998	9.8	1.5	10.7

Vaughn, David III b. March 23, 1973 Ht. 6-9 Wt. 240 College: Memphis

SEASON–TEAM	G	GS	MIN	FGM	FGA	PCT	3FGM	3FGA	PCT	FTM	FTA	PCT	O-RB	D-RB	TOT	AST	PF	DQ	STL	TO	BLK	PTS	RPG	APG	PPG
95-96–Orlando	33	0	266	27	80	.338	0	1	.000	10	18	.556	33	47	80	8	68	2	6	18	15	64	2.4	0.2	1.9
96-97–Orlando	35	6	298	31	72	.431	0	0	–	19	30	.633	35	60	95	7	43	0	8	29	15	81	2.7	0.2	2.3
97-98–G.S.-Chi.-N.J.	40	2	489	66	148	.446	0	1	.000	30	47	.638	53	99	152	20	83	1	15	40	10	162	3.8	0.5	4.1
98-99–New Jersey	10	0	103	13	24	.542	0	0	–	8	10	.800	13	21	34	1	22	0	2	11	8	34	3.4	0.1	3.4
Reg. Season Totals	118	8	1156	137	324	.423	0	2	.000	67	105	.638	134	227	361	36	216	3	31	98	48	341	3.1	0.3	2.9
Playoff Totals	1	0	1	0	0	–	0	0	–	0	0	–	0	0	0	–	0	0	0	0	1	0	0.0	0.0	0.0

Vaughn, Jacque b. February 11, 1975 Ht. 6-1 Wt. 190 College: Kansas

SEASON–TEAM	G	GS	MIN	FGM	FGA	PCT	3FGM	3FGA	PCT	FTM	FTA	PCT	O-RB	D-RB	TOT	AST	PF	DQ	STL	TO	BLK	PTS	RPG	APG	PPG
97-98–Utah	45	0	419	44	122	.361	3	8	.375	48	68	.706	4	34	38	84	63	1	9	56	1	139	0.8	1.9	3.1
98-99–Utah	19	0	87	11	30	.367	2	8	.250	20	24	.833	1	10	11	12	14	0	5	14	0	44	0.6	0.6	2.3
99-00–Utah	78	0	884	109	262	.416	14	34	.412	57	76	.750	11	54	65	121	92	0	32	77	0	289	0.8	1.6	3.7
Reg. Season Totals	142	0	1390	164	414	.396	19	50	.380	125	168	.744	16	98	114	217	169	1	46	147	1	472	0.8	1.5	3.3
Playoff Totals	16	0	97	13	40	.325	3	5	.600	9	10	.900	4	11	15	17	7	0	4	13	1	38	0.9	1.1	2.4

Vaughn, Virgil V. b. May 15, 1918 Ht. 6-4 Wt. 205 College: Kentucky Wesleyan

SEASON–TEAM	G	GS	MIN	FGM	FGA	PCT	3FGM	3FGA	PCT	FTM	FTA	PCT	O-RB	D-RB	TOT	AST	PF	DQ	STL	TO	BLK	PTS	RPG	APG	PPG
46-47–Boston	17	–	–	15	78	.192	–	–	–	15	28	.536	–	–	–	10	18	–	–	–	–	45	–	0.6	2.6
47-48–Syracuse (N)	11	–	–	29	–	–	–	–	–	5	9	.556	–	–	–	–	–	–	–	–	–	63	–	–	5.7
Reg. NBA Totals	17	–	–	15	78	.192	–	–	–	15	28	.536	–	–	–	10	18	–	–	–	–	45	–	0.6	2.6
Reg. NBL Totals	11	–	–	29	–	–	–	–	–	5	9	.556	–	–	–	–	–	–	–	–	–	63	–	–	5.7
NBL Playoff Totals	3	–	–	2	–	–	–	–	–	6	11	.545	–	–	–	–	3	–	–	–	–	10	–	–	3.3

Vaught, Loy Stephen b. February 27, 1968 Ht. 6-9 Wt. 240 College: Michigan

SEASON–TEAM	G	GS	MIN	FGM	FGA	PCT	3FGM	3FGA	PCT	FTM	FTA	PCT	O-RB	D-RB	TOT	AST	PF	DQ	STL	TO	BLK	PTS	RPG	APG	PPG
90-91–L.A. Clippers	73	0	1178	175	359	.487	0	2	.000	49	74	.662	124	225	349	40	135	2	20	49	23	399	4.8	0.5	5.5
91-92–L.A. Clippers	79	38	1687	271	551	.492	4	5	.800	55	69	.797	160	352	512	71	165	1	37	66	31	601	6.5	0.9	7.6
92-93–L.A. Clippers	79	4	1653	313	616	.508	1	4	.250	116	155	.748	164	328	492	54	172	2	55	83	39	743	6.2	0.7	9.4
93-94–L.A. Clippers	75	56	2118	373	695	.537	0	5	.000	131	182	.720	218	438	656	74	221	5	76	96	22	877	8.7	1.0	11.7
94-95–L.A. Clippers	80	79	2966	609	1185	.514	7	33	.212	176	248	.710	261	511	772	139	243	4	104	166	29	1401	9.7	1.7	17.5
95-96–L.A. Clippers	80	78	2966	571	1087	.525	7	19	.368	149	205	.727	204	604	808	112	241	4	87	158	40	1298	10.1	1.4	16.2
96-97–L.A. Clippers	82	82	2838	542	1084	.500	2	12	.167	134	191	.702	222	595	817	110	241	3	85	137	25	1220	10.0	1.3	14.9
97-98–L.A. Clippers	10	6	265	36	84	.429	0	2	.000	3	8	.375	16	49	65	7	33	0	4	13	2	75	6.5	0.7	7.5
98-99–Detroit	37	10	481	59	155	.381	0	1	.000	9	14	.643	36	110	146	11	54	0	15	17	6	127	3.9	0.3	3.4
99-00–Detroit	43	0	292	32	89	.360	0	3	.000	11	16	.688	26	65	91	11	45	0	6	11	4	75	2.1	0.3	1.7
Reg. Season Totals	638	353	16444	2981	5905	.505	21	86	.244	833	1162	.717	1431	3277	4708	629	1550	21	489	796	221	6816	7.4	1.0	10.7
Playoff Totals	15	3	207	34	64	.531	2	4	.500	12	16	.750	12	52	64	6	24	1	11	11	4	82	4.3	0.4	5.5

Verga, Robert Bruce (Bob) b. September 7, 1945 Ht. 6-1 Wt. 190 College: Duke

SEASON–TEAM	G	GS	MIN	FGM	FGA	PCT	3FGM	3FGA	PCT	FTM	FTA	PCT	O-RB	D-RB	TOT	AST	PF	DQ	STL	TO	BLK	PTS	RPG	APG	PPG
67-68–Dallas (A)	31	–	1285	280	633	.442	13	50	.260	162	218	.743	–	–	138	74	93	1	–	95	–	735	4.5	2.4	23.7
68-69–Den.-N.Y.-Hou. (A)	63	–	1804	416	1006	.414	19	68	.279	336	454	.740	–	–	233	188	200	1	–	195	–	1187	3.7	3.0	18.8
69-70–Carolina (A)	82	–	3411	867	1984	.437	66	215	.307	458	565	.811	–	–	430	290	268	3	–	–	–	2258	5.2	3.5	27.5
70-71–Carolina (A)	75	–	2009	550	1202	.458	10	44	.227	302	419	.721	–	–	280	182	223	–	–	–	–	1412	3.7	2.4	18.8
71-72–Car.-Pitt. (A)	70	–	2029	459	1046	.439	19	52	.365	285	398	.716	–	–	237	253	198	–	–	224	–	1222	3.4	3.6	17.5
73-74–Portland	21	–	216	42	93	.452	–	–	–	20	32	.625	11	7	18	17	22	0	12	–	0	104	0.9	0.8	5.0
Reg. NBA Totals	21	–	216	42	93	.452	–	–	–	20	32	.625	11	7	18	17	22	0	12	–	0	104	0.9	0.8	5.0
Reg. ABA Totals	321	–	10538	2572	5871	.438	127	429	.296	1543	2054	.751	–	–	1318	987	982	5	–	514	–	6814	4.1	3.1	21.2
ABA Playoff Totals	4	–	156	48	102	.471	4	16	.250	8	11	.727	–	–	11	10	14	0	–	–	–	108	2.8	2.5	27.0

Verhoeven, Peter Gerard b. February 15, 1959 Ht. 6-9 Wt. 220 College: Fresno State

SEASON–TEAM	G	GS	MIN	FGM	FGA	PCT	3FGM	3FGA	PCT	FTM	FTA	PCT	O-RB	D-RB	TOT	AST	PF	DQ	STL	TO	BLK	PTS	RPG	APG	PPG
81-82–Portland	71	22	1207	149	296	.503	0	0	–	51	72	.708	106	148	254	52	215	4	42	55	22	349	3.6	0.7	4.9
82-83–Portland	48	0	527	87	171	.509	0	1	.000	21	31	.677	44	52	96	32	95	2	18	40	9	195	2.0	0.7	4.1
83-84–Portland	43	0	327	50	100	.500	0	1	.000	17	25	.680	27	34	61	20	75	0	22	21	11	117	1.4	0.5	2.7
84-85–Kansas City	54	0	366	51	108	.472	0	0	–	21	25	.840	28	35	63	17	85	1	15	20	7	123	1.2	0.3	2.3
85-86–Golden State	61	5	749	90	167	.539	1	2	.500	25	43	.581	65	95	160	29	141	3	29	30	17	206	2.6	0.5	3.4
86-87–Indiana	5	0	44	5	14	.357	0	0	–	0	0	–	2	5	7	2	11	1	2	0	1	10	1.4	0.4	2.0
Reg. Season Totals	282	27	3220	432	856	.505	1	4	.250	135	196	.689	272	369	641	152	622	11	128	166	67	1000	2.3	0.5	3.5
Playoff Totals	3	0	19	0	0	–	0	0	–	2	2	1.000	0	0	0	–	10	0	1	1	0	2	0.0	0.0	0.7

Vetra, Gundars b. May 22, 1967 Ht. 6-6 Wt. 195 Country: Latvia

SEASON–TEAM	G	GS	MIN	FGM	FGA	PCT	3FGM	3FGA	PCT	FTM	FTA	PCT	O-RB	D-RB	TOT	AST	PF	DQ	STL	TO	BLK	PTS	RPG	APG	PPG
92-93–Minnesota	13	0	89	19	40	.475	3	3	1.000	4	6	.667	4	4	8	6	12	0	2	2	0	45	0.6	0.5	3.5
Reg. Season Totals	13	0	89	19	40	.475	3	3	1.000	4	6	.667	4	4	8	6	12	0	2	2	0	45	0.6	0.5	3.5

V

Vianna, Joao Jose b. November 15, 1966 Ht. 6-9 Wt. 215 Country: Brazil

SEASON–TEAM	G	GS	MIN	FGM	FGA	PCT	3FGM	3FGA	PCT	FTM	FTA	PCT	O-RB	D-RB	TOT	AST	PF	DQ	STL	TO	BLK	PTS	RPG	APG	PPG
91-92–Dallas	1	0	9	1	2	.500	0	0	–	0	0	–	0	0	0	2	3	0	0	1	0	2	0.0	2.0	2.0
Reg. Season Totals	1	0	9	1	2	.500	0	0	–	0	0	–	0	0	0	2	3	0	0	1	0	2	0.0	2.0	2.0

Vincent, James Samuel (Sam) b. May 18, 1963 Ht. 6-2 Wt. 185 College: Michigan State

SEASON–TEAM	G	GS	MIN	FGM	FGA	PCT	3FGM	3FGA	PCT	FTM	FTA	PCT	O-RB	D-RB	TOT	AST	PF	DQ	STL	TO	BLK	PTS	RPG	APG	PPG
85-86–Boston	57	0	432	59	162	.364	1	4	.250	65	70	.929	11	37	48	69	59	0	17	49	4	184	0.8	1.2	3.2
86-87–Boston	46	5	374	60	136	.441	0	0	–	51	55	.927	5	22	27	59	33	0	13	33	1	171	0.6	1.3	3.7
87-88–Seattle-Chi.	72	27	1501	210	461	.456	8	21	.381	145	167	.868	35	117	152	381	145	0	55	136	16	573	2.1	5.3	8.0
88-89–Chicago	70	56	1703	274	566	.484	2	17	.118	106	129	.822	34	156	190	335	124	0	53	142	10	656	2.7	4.8	9.4
89-90–Orlando	63	45	1657	258	564	.457	1	14	.071	188	214	.879	37	157	194	354	108	1	65	132	20	705	3.1	5.6	11.2
90-91–Orlando	49	17	975	152	353	.431	3	19	.158	99	120	.825	17	90	107	197	74	0	30	91	5	406	2.2	4.0	8.3
91-92–Orlando	39	18	885	150	349	.430	1	13	.077	110	130	.846	19	82	101	148	55	1	35	72	4	411	2.6	3.8	10.5
Reg. Season Totals	396	168	7527	1163	2591	.449	16	88	.182	764	885	.863	158	661	819	1543	598	2	268	655	60	3106	2.1	3.9	7.8
Playoff Totals	52	10	546	82	227	.361	1	8	.125	62	78	.795	14	32	46	87	54	0	16	47	4	227	0.9	1.7	4.4

Vincent, Jay Fletcher b. June 10, 1959 Ht. 6-8 Wt. 220 College: Michigan State

SEASON–TEAM	G	GS	MIN	FGM	FGA	PCT	3FGM	3FGA	PCT	FTM	FTA	PCT	O-RB	D-RB	TOT	AST	PF	DQ	STL	TO	BLK	PTS	RPG	APG	PPG
81-82–Dallas	81	62	2626	719	1448	.497	1	4	.250	293	409	.716	182	383	565	176	308	8	89	194	21	1732	7.0	2.2	21.4
82-83–Dallas	81	73	2726	622	1272	.489	0	3	.000	269	343	.784	217	375	592	212	295	4	70	188	45	1513	7.3	2.6	18.7
83-84–Dallas	61	5	1421	252	579	.435	0	1	.000	168	215	.781	81	166	247	114	159	1	30	113	10	672	4.0	1.9	11.0
84-85–Dallas	79	47	2543	545	1138	.479	0	4	.000	351	420	.836	185	519	704	169	226	0	48	170	22	1441	8.9	2.1	18.2
85-86–Dallas	80	3	1994	442	919	.481	0	3	.000	222	274	.810	107	261	368	180	193	2	66	145	21	1106	4.6	2.3	13.8
86-87–Washington	51	17	1386	274	613	.447	0	3	.000	130	169	.769	69	141	210	85	127	0	40	77	17	678	4.1	1.7	13.3
87-88–Denver	73	8	1755	446	958	.466	1	4	.250	231	287	.805	80	229	309	143	198	1	46	137	26	1124	4.2	2.0	15.4
88-89–Denver-S.A.	29	4	646	104	257	.405	1	3	.333	40	60	.667	38	72	110	27	63	0	6	42	4	249	3.8	0.9	8.6
89-90–Phil.-Lakers	41	6	459	86	183	.470	1	2	.500	41	49	.837	20	42	62	18	52	0	18	33	5	214	1.5	0.4	5.2
Reg. Season Totals	576	225	15556	3490	7367	.474	4	27	.148	1745	2226	.784	979	2188	3167	1124	1621	16	413	1099	171	8729	5.5	2.0	15.2
Playoff Totals	38	12	971	170	415	.410	0	2	.000	150	174	.862	65	112	177	46	107	1	24	73	9	490	4.7	1.2	12.9

Vinson, Frederick O'Neal (Fred) b. January 28, 1971 Ht. 6-4 Wt. 200 College: Georgia Tech

SEASON–TEAM	G	GS	MIN	FGM	FGA	PCT	3FGM	3FGA	PCT	FTM	FTA	PCT	O-RB	D-RB	TOT	AST	PF	DQ	STL	TO	BLK	PTS	RPG	APG	PPG
94-95–Atlanta	5	0	27	1	7	.143	1	6	.167	1	1	1.000	0	0	0	1	4	0	0	2	0	4	0.0	0.2	0.8
99-00–Seattle	8	0	40	5	17	.294	2	7	.286	1	2	.500	0	1	1	0	2	0	3	4	0	13	0.1	0.0	1.6
Reg. Season Totals	13	0	67	6	24	.250	3	13	.231	2	3	.667	0	1	1	1	6	0	3	6	0	17	0.1	0.1	1.3

Virden, Claude Felton b. November 25, 1947 Ht. 6-6 Wt. 200 College: Murray State

SEASON–TEAM	G	GS	MIN	FGM	FGA	PCT	3FGM	3FGA	PCT	FTM	FTA	PCT	O-RB	D-RB	TOT	AST	PF	DQ	STL	TO	BLK	PTS	RPG	APG	PPG
72-73–Kentucky (A)	31	–	825	130	327	.398	0	2	.000	46	59	.780	49	105	154	74	84	0	–	49	–	306	5.0	2.4	9.9
Reg. ABA Totals	31	–	825	130	327	.398	0	2	.000	46	59	.780	49	105	154	74	84	0	–	49	–	306	5.0	2.4	9.9

Voce, Gary Anthony b. November 24, 1965 Ht. 6-9 Wt. 245 College: Notre Dame

SEASON–TEAM	G	GS	MIN	FGM	FGA	PCT	3FGM	3FGA	PCT	FTM	FTA	PCT	O-RB	D-RB	TOT	AST	PF	DQ	STL	TO	BLK	PTS	RPG	APG	PPG
89-90–Cleveland	1	0	4	1	3	.333	0	0	–	0	0	–	2	0	2	0	0	0	0	0	0	2	2.0	0.0	2.0
Reg. Season Totals	1	0	4	1	3	.333	0	0	–	0	0	–	2	0	2	0	0	0	0	0	0	2	2.0	0.0	2.0

Volker, Floyd W. b. June 21, 1921 Ht. 6-4 Wt. 205 College: Wyoming

SEASON–TEAM	G	GS	MIN	FGM	FGA	PCT	3FGM	3FGA	PCT	FTM	FTA	PCT	O-RB	D-RB	TOT	AST	PF	DQ	STL	TO	BLK	PTS	RPG	APG	PPG
47-48–Oshkosh (N)	57	–	–	102	–	–	–	–	–	31	66	.470	–	–	–	–	133	–	–	–	–	235	–	–	4.1
48-49–Oshkosh (N)	64	–	–	166	–	–	–	–	–	78	134	.582	–	–	–	–	190	–	–	–	–	410	–	–	6.4
49-50–Ind.-Denver	54	–	–	163	527	.309	–	–	–	71	129	.550	–	–	–	112	169	–	–	–	–	397	–	2.1	7.4
Reg. NBA Totals	54	–	–	163	527	.309	–	–	–	71	129	.550	–	–	–	112	169	–	–	–	–	397	–	2.1	7.4
Reg. NBL Totals	121	–	–	268	–	–	–	–	–	109	200	.545	–	–	–	–	323	–	–	–	–	645	–	–	5.3
NBL Playoff Totals	11	–	–	34	–	–	–	–	–	13	21	.619	–	–	–	–	37	–	–	–	–	81	–	–	7.4

Volkov, Alexander (Sasha) b. March 29, 1964 Ht. 6-10 Wt. 235 College: Kiev Institute (Ukraine)

SEASON–TEAM	G	GS	MIN	FGM	FGA	PCT	3FGM	3FGA	PCT	FTM	FTA	PCT	O-RB	D-RB	TOT	AST	PF	DQ	STL	TO	BLK	PTS	RPG	APG	PPG
89-90–Atlanta	72	4	937	137	284	.482	13	34	.382	70	120	.583	52	67	119	83	166	3	36	52	22	357	1.7	1.2	5.0
91-92–Atlanta	77	27	1516	251	569	.441	35	110	.318	125	198	.631	103	162	265	250	178	2	66	102	30	662	3.4	3.2	8.6
Reg. Season Totals	149	31	2453	388	853	.455	48	144	.333	195	318	.613	155	229	384	333	344	5	102	154	52	1019	2.6	2.2	6.8

Von Nieda, Stanley L. Jr. (Whitey) b. June 19, 1922 Ht. 6-1 Wt. 175 College: Penn State

SEASON–TEAM	G	GS	MIN	FGM	FGA	PCT	3FGM	3FGA	PCT	FTM	FTA	PCT	O-RB	D-RB	TOT	AST	PF	DQ	STL	TO	BLK	PTS	RPG	APG	PPG
47-48–Tri-Cities (N)	60	–	–	276	–	–	–	–	–	174	287	.606	–	–	–	–	144	–	–	–	–	726	–	–	12.1
48-49–Tri-Cities (N)	64	–	–	247	–	–	–	–	–	147	226	.650	–	–	–	–	141	–	–	–	–	641	–	–	10.0
49-50–Tri-Cit-Balt.	59	–	–	120	336	.357	–	–	–	73	115	.635	–	–	–	143	127	–	–	–	–	313	–	2.4	5.3
Reg. NBA Totals	59	–	–	120	336	.357	–	–	–	73	115	.635	–	–	–	143	127	–	–	–	–	313	–	2.4	5.3
Reg. NBL Totals	124	–	–	523	–	–	–	–	–	321	513	.626	–	–	–	–	285	–	–	–	–	1367	–	–	11.0
NBL Playoff Totals	12	–	–	61	–	–	–	–	–	28	51	.549	–	–	–	–	29	–	–	–	–	150	–	–	12.5

Vranes, Daniel LaDrew (Danny) b. October 29, 1958 Ht. 6-8 Wt. 220 College: Utah

SEASON–TEAM	G	GS	MIN	FGM	FGA	PCT	3FGM	3FGA	PCT	FTM	FTA	PCT	O-RB	D-RB	TOT	AST	PF	DQ	STL	TO	BLK	PTS	RPG	APG	PPG
81-82–Seattle	77	1	1075	143	262	.546	0	1	.000	89	148	.601	71	127	198	56	150	0	28	68	22	375	2.6	0.7	4.9
82-83–Seattle	82	73	2054	226	429	.527	0	1	.000	115	209	.550	177	248	425	120	254	2	53	102	49	567	5.2	1.5	6.9
83-84–Seattle	80	72	2174	258	495	.521	0	1	.000	153	236	.648	150	245	395	132	263	4	51	121	54	669	4.9	1.7	8.4
84-85–Seattle	76	70	2163	186	402	.463	1	4	.250	67	127	.528	154	282	436	152	256	4	76	119	57	440	5.7	2.0	5.8
85-86–Seattle	80	19	1569	131	284	.461	0	4	.000	39	75	.520	115	166	281	68	218	3	63	58	31	301	3.5	0.9	3.8
86-87–Philadelphia	58	6	817	59	138	.428	1	5	.200	21	45	.467	51	95	146	30	127	0	35	26	25	140	2.5	0.5	2.4
87-88–Philadelphia	57	5	772	53	121	.438	0	3	.000	15	35	.429	45	72	117	36	100	0	27	25	33	121	2.1	0.6	2.1
Reg. Season Totals	510	246	10624	1056	2131	.496	2	19	.105	499	875	.570	763	1235	1998	594	1368	13	333	519	271	2613	3.9	1.2	5.1
Playoff Totals	15	7	235	23	61	.377	0	1	.000	5	9	.556	26	36	62	12	34	1	4	8	7	51	4.1	0.8	3.4

Vrankovic, Stojan (Stojko) b. January 22, 1964 Ht. 7-2 Wt. 270 Country: Croatia

SEASON–TEAM	G	GS	MIN	FGM	FGA	PCT	3FGM	3FGA	PCT	FTM	FTA	PCT	O-RB	D-RB	TOT	AST	PF	DQ	STL	TO	BLK	PTS	RPG	APG	PPG
90-91–Boston	31	0	166	24	52	.462	0	0	–	10	18	.556	15	36	51	4	43	1	1	24	29	58	1.6	0.1	1.9
91-92–Boston	19	0	110	15	32	.469	0	0	–	7	12	.583	8	20	28	5	22	0	0	10	17	37	1.5	0.3	1.9
96-97–Minnesota	53	35	766	78	139	.561	0	0	–	25	37	.676	57	111	168	14	121	1	10	52	67	181	3.2	0.3	3.4
97-98–L.A. Clippers	65	38	996	79	186	.425	0	0	–	37	65	.569	71	192	263	36	130	3	11	46	66	195	4.0	0.6	3.0
98-99–L.A. Clippers	2	0	12	1	4	.250	0	0	–	0	0	–	4	2	6	0	2	0	0	0	0	2	3.0	0.0	1.0
Reg. Season Totals	170	73	2050	197	413	.477	0	0	–	79	132	.598	155	361	516	59	318	5	22	132	179	473	3.0	0.3	2.8
Playoff Totals	3	0	13	2	4	.500	0	0	–	0	1	.000	1	2	3	1	2	0	0	1	0	4	1.0	0.3	1.3

Vroman, Brett Grant b. December 25, 1955 Ht. 7-0 Wt. 230 College: UCLA; Nevada-Las Vegas

SEASON–TEAM	G	GS	MIN	FGM	FGA	PCT	3FGM	3FGA	PCT	FTM	FTA	PCT	O-RB	D-RB	TOT	AST	PF	DQ	STL	TO	BLK	PTS	RPG	APG	PPG
80-81–Utah	11	–	93	10	27	.370	0	1	.000	14	19	.737	7	18	25	9	26	1	5	9	5	34	2.3	0.8	3.1
Reg. Season Totals	11	–	93	10	27	.370	0	1	.000	14	19	.737	7	18	25	9	26	1	5	9	5	34	2.3	0.8	3.1

Wade, Mark A. b. October 15, 1965 Ht. 6-1 Wt. 160 College: El Camino (Calif.) Coll. (J.C.); Oklahoma; Nevada-Las Vegas

SEASON–TEAM	G	GS	MIN	FGM	FGA	PCT	3FGM	3FGA	PCT	FTM	FTA	PCT	O-RB	D-RB	TOT	AST	PF	DQ	STL	TO	BLK	PTS	RPG	APG	PPG
87-88–Golden State	11	0	123	3	20	.150	0	2	.000	2	4	.500	3	12	15	34	13	0	7	13	1	8	1.4	3.1	0.7
89-90–Dallas	1	0	3	0	0	–	0	0	–	0	0	–	0	0	0	2	0	0	0	0	0	0	0.0	2.0	0.0
Reg. Season Totals	12	0	126	3	20	.150	0	2	.000	2	4	.500	3	12	15	36	13	0	7	13	1	8	1.3	3.0	0.7

Wager, Clinton B. (Clint) b. January 20, 1920 d. February 29, 1996 Ht. 6-6 Wt. 230 College: St. Mary's (Minn.)

SEASON–TEAM	G	GS	MIN	FGM	FGA	PCT	3FGM	3FGA	PCT	FTM	FTA	PCT	O-RB	D-RB	TOT	AST	PF	DQ	STL	TO	BLK	PTS	RPG	APG	PPG
43-44–Oshkosh (N)	22	–	–	79	–	–	–	–	–	72	–	–	–	–	–	–	–	–	–	–	–	230	–	–	10.5
44-45–Oshkosh (N)	27	–	–	70	–	–	–	–	–	28	–	–	–	–	–	–	–	–	–	–	–	168	–	–	6.2
45-46–Oshkosh (N)	34	–	–	68	–	–	–	–	–	31	48	.646	–	–	–	–	83	–	–	–	–	167	–	–	4.9
46-47–Oshkosh (N)	44	–	–	68	–	–	–	–	–	50	69	.725	–	–	–	–	142	–	–	–	–	186	–	–	4.2
47-48–Oshkosh (N)	59	–	–	90	–	–	–	–	–	56	93	.602	–	–	–	–	169	–	–	–	–	236	–	–	4.0
48-49–Hammond (N)	61	–	–	125	–	–	–	–	–	82	146	.562	–	–	–	–	236	–	–	–	–	332	–	–	5.4
49-50–Fort Wayne	63	–	–	57	203	.281	–	–	–	29	47	.617	–	–	–	90	175	–	–	–	–	143	–	1.4	2.3
Reg. NBA Totals	63	–	–	57	203	.281	–	–	–	29	47	.617	–	–	–	90	175	–	–	–	–	143	–	1.4	2.3
Reg. NBL Totals	247	–	–	500	–	–	–	–	–	319	356	.615	–	–	–	–	630	–	–	–	–	1319	–	–	5.3
NBA Playoff Totals	4	–	–	11	50	.440	–	–	–	8	10	.800	–	–	–	16	22	3	–	–	–	30	–	2.0	7.5
NBL Playoff Totals	20	–	–	41	–	–	–	–	–	24	21	.619	–	–	–	–	68	–	–	–	–	106	–	–	5.3

Wagner, Daniel Earnest (Danny) b. August 1, 1922 Ht. 6-0 Wt. 170 College: Schreiner Coll.; Texas

SEASON–TEAM	G	GS	MIN	FGM	FGA	PCT	3FGM	3FGA	PCT	FTM	FTA	PCT	O-RB	D-RB	TOT	AST	PF	DQ	STL	TO	BLK	PTS	RPG	APG	PPG
47-48–Flint (N)	50	–	–	96	–	–	–	–	–	59	92	.641	–	–	–	–	82	–	–	–	–	251	–	–	5.0
48-49–Sheboygan (N)	62	–	–	111	–	–	–	–	–	109	146	.747	–	–	–	–	120	–	–	–	–	331	–	–	5.3
49-50–Sheboygan	11	–	–	19	54	.352	–	–	–	31	35	.886	–	–	–	18	22	–	–	–	–	69	–	1.6	6.3
Reg. NBA Totals	11	–	–	19	54	.352	–	–	–	31	35	.886	–	–	–	18	22	–	–	–	–	69	–	1.6	6.3
Reg. NBL Totals	112	–	–	207	–	–	–	–	–	168	238	.706	–	–	–	–	202	–	–	–	–	582	–	–	5.2
NBL Playoff Totals	2	–	–	3	–	–	–	–	–	1	1	1.000	–	–	–	–	9	–	–	–	–	7	–	–	3.5

Wagner, Milton Jr. (Milt) b. February 20, 1963 Ht. 6-5 Wt. 185 College: Louisville

SEASON–TEAM	G	GS	MIN	FGM	FGA	PCT	3FGM	3FGA	PCT	FTM	FTA	PCT	O-RB	D-RB	TOT	AST	PF	DQ	STL	TO	BLK	PTS	RPG	APG	PPG
87-88–L.A. Lakers	40	4	380	62	147	.422	2	10	.200	26	29	.897	4	24	28	61	42	0	6	22	4	152	0.7	1.5	3.8
90-91–Miami	13	1	116	24	57	.421	6	17	.353	9	11	.818	0	7	7	15	14	0	2	12	3	63	0.5	1.2	4.8
Reg. Season Totals	53	5	496	86	204	.422	8	27	.296	35	40	.875	4	31	35	76	56	0	8	34	7	215	0.7	1.4	4.1
Playoff Totals	5	0	14	2	5	.400	0	1	.000	2	2	1.000	0	2	2	3	3	0	0	0	1	6	0.4	0.6	1.2

Wagner, Phillip C. (Phil) b. December 18, 1945 Ht. 6-2 Wt. 190 College: Georgia Tech

SEASON–TEAM	G	GS	MIN	FGM	FGA	PCT	3FGM	3FGA	PCT	FTM	FTA	PCT	O-RB	D-RB	TOT	AST	PF	DQ	STL	TO	BLK	PTS	RPG	APG	PPG
68-69–Indiana (A)	12	–	180	11	41	.268	1	4	.250	13	17	.765	–	–	23	14	28	0	–	18	–	36	1.9	1.2	3.0
Reg. ABA Totals	12	–	180	11	41	.268	1	4	.250	13	17	.765	–	–	23	14	28	0	–	18	–	36	1.9	1.2	3.0

Waiters, Granville S. b. January 8, 1961 Ht. 6-11 Wt. 225 College: Ohio State

SEASON–TEAM	G	GS	MIN	FGM	FGA	PCT	3FGM	3FGA	PCT	FTM	FTA	PCT	O-RB	D-RB	TOT	AST	PF	DQ	STL	TO	BLK	PTS	RPG	APG	PPG
83-84–Indiana	78	8	1040	123	238	.517	0	1	.000	31	51	.608	64	163	227	60	164	2	24	65	85	277	2.9	0.8	3.6
84-85–Indiana	62	5	703	85	190	.447	0	1	.000	29	50	.580	57	113	170	30	107	2	16	55	44	199	2.7	0.5	3.2
85-86–Houston	43	0	156	13	39	.333	0	1	.000	1	6	.167	15	13	28	8	30	0	4	11	10	27	0.7	0.2	0.6
86-87–Chicago	44	26	534	40	93	.430	0	1	.000	5	9	.556	38	49	87	22	83	1	10	16	31	85	2.0	0.5	1.9
87-88–Chicago	22	0	114	9	29	.310	0	1	.000	0	2	.000	9	19	28	1	26	0	2	6	15	18	1.3	0.0	0.8
Reg. Season Totals	249	39	2547	270	589	.458	0	5	.000	66	118	.559	183	357	540	121	410	5	56	153	185	606	2.2	0.5	2.4
Playoff Totals	13	0	34	4	7	.571	0	0	–	0	0	–	2	4	6	–	4	0	1	1	4	8	0.5	0.0	0.6

Wakefield, Andre b. January 11, 1955 Ht. 6-3 Wt. 175 College: Coll. of Southern Idaho (J.C.); Loyola (Chicago)

SEASON–TEAM	G	GS	MIN	FGM	FGA	PCT	3FGM	3FGA	PCT	FTM	FTA	PCT	O-RB	D-RB	TOT	AST	PF	DQ	STL	TO	BLK	PTS	RPG	APG	PPG
78-79–Chi.-Detroit	73	–	586	62	177	.350	–	–	–	48	69	.696	25	51	76	70	70	0	19	73	2	172	1.0	1.0	2.4
79-80–Utah	8	–	47	6	15	.400	0	0	–	3	3	1.000	0	4	4	3	13	0	1	8	0	15	0.5	0.4	1.9
Reg. Season Totals	81	–	633	68	192	.354	0	0	–	51	72	.708	25	55	80	73	83	0	20	81	2	187	1.0	0.9	2.3

Walk, Neal Eugene b. July 29, 1948 Ht. 6-10 Wt. 250 College: Florida

SEASON–TEAM	G	GS	MIN	FGM	FGA	PCT	3FGM	3FGA	PCT	FTM	FTA	PCT	O-RB	D-RB	TOT	AST	PF	DQ	STL	TO	BLK	PTS	RPG	APG	PPG
69-70–Phoenix	82	–	1394	257	547	.470	–	–	–	155	242	.640	–	–	455	80	225	2	–	–	–	669	5.5	1.0	8.2
70-71–Phoenix	82	–	2033	426	945	.451	–	–	–	205	268	.765	–	–	674	117	282	8	–	–	–	1057	8.2	1.4	12.9
71-72–Phoenix	81	–	2142	506	1057	.479	–	–	–	256	344	.744	–	–	665	151	295	9	–	–	–	1268	8.2	1.9	15.7
72-73–Phoenix	81	–	3114	678	1455	.466	–	–	–	279	355	.786	–	–	1006	287	323	11	–	–	–	1635	12.4	3.5	20.2
73-74–Phoenix	82	–	2549	573	1245	.460	–	–	–	235	297	.791	235	602	837	331	255	8	73	–	57	1381	10.2	4.0	16.8
74-75–N.O.-N.Y.	67	–	1125	198	473	.419	–	–	–	86	105	.819	91	248	339	123	177	3	37	–	23	482	5.1	1.8	7.2
75-76–New York	82	–	1340	262	607	.432	–	–	–	79	99	.798	98	291	389	119	209	3	26	–	22	603	4.7	1.5	7.4
76-77–N.Y. Knicks	11	–	135	28	57	.491	–	–	–	6	7	.857	5	22	27	6	22	0	4	–	3	62	2.5	0.5	5.6
Reg. Season Totals	568	–	13832	2928	6386	.459	–	–	–	1301	1717	.758	429	1163	4392	1214	1788	44	140	–	105	7157	7.7	2.1	12.6
Playoff Totals	8	–	102	22	53	.415	–	–	–	6	8	.750	0	5	40	4	17	0	1	–	2	50	5.0	0.5	6.3

Walker, Andrew Martin (Andy) b. March 25, 1955 Ht. 6-4 Wt. 190 College: Niagara

SEASON–TEAM	G	GS	MIN	FGM	FGA	PCT	3FGM	3FGA	PCT	FTM	FTA	PCT	O-RB	D-RB	TOT	AST	PF	DQ	STL	TO	BLK	PTS	RPG	APG	PPG
76-77–New Orleans	40	–	438	72	156	.462	–	–	–	36	47	.766	23	52	75	32	59	0	20	–	7	180	1.9	0.8	4.5
Reg. Season Totals	40	–	438	72	156	.462	–	–	–	36	47	.766	23	52	75	32	59	0	20	–	7	180	1.9	0.8	4.5

Walker, Antoine Devon b. August 12, 1976 Ht. 6-9 Wt. 245 College: Kentucky

SEASON–TEAM	G	GS	MIN	FGM	FGA	PCT	3FGM	3FGA	PCT	FTM	FTA	PCT	O-RB	D-RB	TOT	AST	PF	DQ	STL	TO	BLK	PTS	RPG	APG	PPG
96-97–Boston	82	68	2970	576	1354	.425	52	159	.327	231	366	.631	288	453	741	262	271	1	105	230	53	1435	9.0	3.2	17.5
97-98–Boston	82	82	3268	722	1705	.423	91	292	.312	305	473	.645	270	566	836	273	262	2	142	292	60	1840	10.2	3.3	22.4
98-99–Boston	42	41	1549	303	735	.412	65	176	.369	113	202	.559	106	253	359	130	142	2	63	119	28	784	8.5	3.1	18.7
99-00–Boston	82	82	3003	648	1506	.430	73	285	.256	311	445	.699	199	453	652	305	263	4	117	259	32	1680	8.0	3.7	20.5
Reg. Season Totals	288	273	10790	2249	5300	.424	281	912	.308	960	1486	.646	863	1725	2588	970	938	9	427	900	173	5739	9.0	3.4	19.9
All-Star Totals	1	0	15	2	8	.250	0	3	.000	0	0	–	1	2	3	3	0	0	1	1	0	4	3.0	3.0	4.0

Walker, Brady W. b. March 15, 1921 Ht. 6-6 Wt. 205 College: Brigham Young

SEASON–TEAM	G	GS	MIN	FGM	FGA	PCT	3FGM	3FGA	PCT	FTM	FTA	PCT	O-RB	D-RB	TOT	AST	PF	DQ	STL	TO	BLK	PTS	RPG	APG	PPG
48-49–Providence	59	–	–	202	556	.363	–	–	–	87	155	.561	–	–	–	68	100	–	–	–	–	491	–	1.2	8.3
49-50–Boston	68	–	–	218	583	.374	–	–	–	72	114	.632	–	–	–	109	100	–	–	–	–	508	–	1.6	7.5
50-51–Boston-Balt.	66	–	–	164	416	.394	–	–	–	72	103	.699	–	–	354	111	82	2	–	–	–	400	5.4	1.7	6.1
51-52–Baltimore	35	–	699	89	217	.410	–	–	–	26	34	.765	–	–	195	40	38	0	–	–	–	204	5.6	1.1	5.8
Reg. Season Totals	228	–	699	673	1772	.380	–	–	–	257	406	.633	–	–	549	328	320	2	–	–	–	1603	5.4	1.4	7.0

Walker, Chester (Chet, Chet the Jet) b. February 22, 1940 Ht. 6-7 Wt. 215 College: Bradley

SEASON–TEAM	G	GS	MIN	FGM	FGA	PCT	3FGM	3FGA	PCT	FTM	FTA	PCT	O-RB	D-RB	TOT	AST	PF	DQ	STL	TO	BLK	PTS	RPG	APG	PPG
62-63–Syracuse	78	–	1992	352	751	.469	–	–	–	253	362	.699	–	–	561	83	220	3	–	–	–	957	7.2	1.1	12.3
63-64–Philadelphia	76	–	2775	492	1118	.440	–	–	–	330	464	.711	–	–	784	124	232	3	–	–	–	1314	10.3	1.6	17.3
64-65–Philadelphia	79	–	2187	377	936	.403	–	–	–	288	388	.742	–	–	528	132	200	2	–	–	–	1042	6.7	1.7	13.2
65-66–Philadelphia	80	–	2603	443	982	.451	–	–	–	335	468	.716	–	–	636	201	238	3	–	–	–	1221	8.0	2.5	15.3
66-67–Philadelphia	81	–	2691	561	1150	.488	–	–	–	445	581	.766	–	–	660	188	232	4	–	–	–	1567	8.1	2.3	19.3
67-68–Philadelphia	82	–	2623	539	1172	.460	–	–	–	387	533	.726	–	–	607	157	252	3	–	–	–	1465	7.4	1.9	17.9
68-69–Philadelphia	82	–	2753	554	1145	.484	–	–	–	369	459	.804	–	–	640	144	244	0	–	–	–	1477	7.8	1.8	18.0
69-70–Chicago	78	–	2726	596	1249	.477	–	–	–	483	568	.850	–	–	604	192	203	1	–	–	–	1675	7.7	2.5	21.5
70-71–Chicago	81	–	2927	650	1398	.465	–	–	–	480	559	.859	–	–	588	179	187	2	–	–	–	1780	7.3	2.2	22.0
71-72–Chicago	78	–	2588	619	1225	.505	–	–	–	481	568	.847	–	–	473	178	171	0	–	–	–	1719	6.1	2.3	22.0
72-73–Chicago	79	–	2455	597	1248	.478	–	–	–	376	452	.832	–	–	395	179	166	1	–	–	–	1570	5.0	2.3	19.9
73-74–Chicago	82	–	2661	572	1178	.486	–	–	–	439	502	.875	131	275	406	200	201	1	68	–	4	1583	5.0	2.4	19.3
74-75–Chicago	76	–	2452	524	1076	.487	–	–	–	413	480	.860	114	318	432	169	181	0	49	–	6	1461	5.7	2.2	19.2
Reg. Season Totals	1032	–	33433	6876	14628	.470	–	–	–	5079	6384	.796	245	593	7314	2126	2727	23	117	–	10	18831	7.1	2.1	18.2
Playoff Totals	105	–	3688	687	1531	.449	–	–	–	542	689	.787	36	85	737	212	286	3	23	–	2	1916	7.0	2.0	18.2
All-Star Totals	7	–	125	20	46	.435	–	–	–	17	20	.850	0	2	18	9	11	0	0	–	0	57	2.6	1.3	8.1

Walker, Clarence (Foots) b. May 21, 1951 Ht. 6-1 Wt. 170 College: Vincennes (Ind.) (J.C.); West Georgia

SEASON–TEAM	G	GS	MIN	FGM	FGA	PCT	3FGM	3FGA	PCT	FTM	FTA	PCT	O-RB	D-RB	TOT	AST	PF	DQ	STL	TO	BLK	PTS	RPG	APG	PPG
74-75–Cleveland	72	–	1070	111	275	.404	–	–	–	80	117	.684	47	99	146	192	126	0	80	–	7	302	2.0	2.7	4.2
75-76–Cleveland	81	–	1280	143	369	.388	–	–	–	84	108	.778	53	129	182	288	136	0	98	–	5	370	2.2	3.6	4.6
76-77–Cleveland	62	–	1216	157	349	.450	–	–	–	89	115	.774	55	105	160	254	124	1	83	–	4	403	2.6	4.1	6.5
77-78–Cleveland	81	–	2496	287	641	.448	–	–	–	159	221	.719	76	218	294	453	218	0	176	181	24	733	3.6	5.6	9.0
78-79–Cleveland	55	–	1753	208	448	.464	–	–	–	137	175	.783	59	139	198	321	153	0	130	127	18	553	3.6	5.8	10.1
79-80–Cleveland	76	–	2422	258	568	.454	1	9	.111	195	243	.802	78	209	287	607	202	2	155	157	12	712	3.8	8.0	9.4
80-81–New Jersey	41	–	1172	72	169	.426	2	9	.222	88	111	.793	22	80	102	253	105	0	52	85	1	234	2.5	6.2	5.7
81-82–New Jersey	77	54	1861	156	378	.413	3	9	.333	141	194	.727	31	119	150	398	179	1	120	107	6	456	1.9	5.2	5.9
82-83–New Jersey	79	10	1388	114	250	.456	2	12	.167	116	149	.779	30	106	136	264	134	1	78	104	3	346	1.7	3.3	4.4
83-84–New Jersey	34	0	378	32	90	.356	2	5	.400	24	27	.889	8	23	31	81	37	0	20	31	3	90	0.9	2.4	2.6
Reg. Season Totals	658	64	15036	1538	3537	.435	10	44	.227	1113	1460	.762	459	1227	1686	3111	1414	5	992	792	83	4199	2.6	4.7	6.4
Playoff Totals	22	0	330	41	97	.423	0	0	–	27	33	.818	14	21	35	64	37	0	14	8	4	109	1.6	2.9	5.0

Walker, Darrell b. March 9, 1961 Ht. 6-4 Wt. 180 College: Westark (Ark.) C.C.; Arkansas

SEASON–TEAM	G	GS	MIN	FGM	FGA	PCT	3FGM	3FGA	PCT	FTM	FTA	PCT	O-RB	D-RB	TOT	AST	PF	DQ	STL	TO	BLK	PTS	RPG	APG	PPG
83-84–New York	82	0	1324	216	518	.417	4	15	.267	208	263	.791	74	93	167	284	202	1	127	194	15	644	2.0	3.5	7.9
84-85–New York	82	66	2489	430	989	.435	0	17	.000	243	347	.700	128	150	278	408	244	2	167	204	21	1103	3.4	5.0	13.5
85-86–New York	81	35	2023	324	753	.430	0	10	.000	190	277	.686	100	120	220	337	216	1	146	192	36	838	2.7	4.2	10.3
86-87–Denver	81	25	2020	358	742	.482	0	4	.000	272	365	.745	157	170	327	282	229	0	120	187	37	988	4.0	3.5	12.2
87-88–Washington	52	0	940	114	291	.392	0	6	.000	82	105	.781	43	84	127	100	105	2	62	69	10	310	2.4	1.9	6.0
88-89–Washington	79	78	2565	286	681	.420	0	9	.000	142	184	.772	135	372	507	496	215	2	155	184	23	714	6.4	6.3	9.0
89-90–Washington	81	81	2883	316	696	.454	2	21	.095	138	201	.687	173	541	714	652	220	1	139	173	30	772	8.8	8.0	9.5
90-91–Washington	71	65	2305	230	535	.430	0	9	.000	93	154	.604	140	358	498	459	199	2	78	154	33	553	7.0	6.5	7.8
91-92–Detroit	74	4	1541	161	381	.423	0	10	.000	65	105	.619	85	153	238	205	134	0	63	79	18	387	3.2	2.8	5.2
92-93–Detroit-Chi.	37	2	511	34	96	.354	0	1	.000	12	26	.462	22	36	58	53	63	0	33	25	2	80	1.6	1.4	2.2
Reg. Season Totals	720	356	18601	2469	5682	.435	6	102	.059	1445	2027	.713	1057	2077	3134	3276	1827	11	1090	1461	225	6389	4.4	4.6	8.9
Playoff Totals	34	3	508	64	174	.368	0	1	.000	49	76	.645	37	45	82	48	58	0	34	51	6	177	2.4	1.4	5.2

Walker, Horace b. April 17, 1938 Ht. 6-3 Wt. 210 College: Michigan State

SEASON–TEAM	G	GS	MIN	FGM	FGA	PCT	3FGM	3FGA	PCT	FTM	FTA	PCT	O-RB	D-RB	TOT	AST	PF	DQ	STL	TO	BLK	PTS	RPG	APG	PPG
61-62–Chicago	65	–	1331	149	439	.339	–	–	–	140	193	.725	–	–	466	69	194	2	–	–	–	438	7.2	1.1	6.7
Reg. Season Totals	65	–	1331	149	439	.339	–	–	–	140	193	.725	–	–	466	69	194	2	–	–	–	438	7.2	1.1	6.7

Walker, James (Jimmy) b. April 8, 1944 Ht. 6-3 Wt. 205 College: Providence

SEASON–TEAM	G	GS	MIN	FGM	FGA	PCT	3FGM	3FGA	PCT	FTM	FTA	PCT	O-RB	D-RB	TOT	AST	PF	DQ	STL	TO	BLK	PTS	RPG	APG	PPG
67-68–Detroit	81	–	1585	289	733	.394	–	–	–	134	175	.766	–	–	135	226	204	1	–	–	–	712	1.7	2.8	8.8
68-69–Detroit	69	–	1639	312	670	.466	–	–	–	182	229	.795	–	–	157	221	172	1	–	–	–	806	2.3	3.2	11.7
69-70–Detroit	81	–	2869	666	1394	.478	–	–	–	355	440	.807	–	–	242	248	203	4	–	–	–	1687	3.0	3.1	20.8
70-71–Detroit	79	–	2765	524	1201	.436	–	–	–	344	414	.831	–	–	207	268	173	0	–	–	–	1392	2.6	3.4	17.6
71-72–Detroit	78	–	3083	634	1386	.457	–	–	–	397	480	.827	–	–	231	315	198	2	–	–	–	1665	3.0	4.0	21.3
72-73–Houston	81	–	3079	605	1301	.465	–	–	–	244	276	.884	–	–	268	442	207	0	–	–	–	1454	3.3	5.5	18.0
73-74–Hou.-K.C.-Omaha	75	–	2958	582	1240	.469	–	–	–	273	333	.820	39	165	204	307	170	0	81	–	9	1437	2.7	4.1	19.2
74-75–K.C.-Omaha	81	–	3122	553	1164	.475	–	–	–	247	289	.855	51	188	239	226	222	2	85	–	13	1353	3.0	2.8	16.7
75-76–Kansas City	73	–	2490	459	950	.483	–	–	–	231	267	.865	49	128	177	176	186	2	87	–	14	1149	2.4	2.4	15.7
Reg. Season Totals	698	–	23590	4624	10039	.461	–	–	–	2407	2903	.829	139	481	1860	2429	1735	12	253	–	36	11655	2.7	3.5	16.7
Playoff Totals	12	–	346	70	151	.464	–	–	–	28	35	.800	1	9	19	26	29	1	5	–	1	168	1.6	2.2	14.0
All-Star Totals	2	–	30	4	12	.333	–	–	–	3	6	.500	0	0	3	1	3	0	0	–	0	11	1.5	0.5	5.5

Walker, Kenneth **(Kenny, Sky)** b. August 18, 1964 Ht. 6-8 Wt. 220 College: Kentucky

SEASON–TEAM	G	GS	MIN	FGM	FGA	PCT	3FGM	3FGA	PCT	FTM	FTA	PCT	O-RB	D-RB	TOT	AST	PF	DQ	STL	TO	BLK	PTS	RPG	APG	PPG
86-87–New York	68	64	1719	285	581	.491	0	4	.000	140	185	.757	118	220	338	75	236	7	49	75	49	710	5.0	1.1	10.4
87-88–New York	82	61	2139	344	728	.473	0	1	.000	138	178	.775	192	197	389	86	290	5	63	83	59	826	4.7	1.0	10.1
88-89–New York	79	2	1163	174	356	.489	5	20	.250	66	85	.776	101	129	230	36	190	1	41	44	45	419	2.9	0.5	5.3
89-90–New York	68	21	1595	204	384	.531	2	5	.400	125	173	.723	131	212	343	49	178	1	33	60	52	535	5.0	0.7	7.9
90-91–New York	54	8	771	83	191	.435	0	1	.000	64	82	.780	63	94	157	13	92	0	18	30	30	230	2.9	0.2	4.3
93-94–Washington	73	4	1397	132	274	.482	0	3	.000	87	125	.696	118	171	289	33	156	1	26	44	59	351	4.0	0.5	4.8
94-95–Washington	24	0	266	18	42	.429	0	0	–	21	28	.750	19	28	47	7	42	0	5	15	5	57	2.0	0.3	2.4
Reg. Season Totals	448	160	9050	1240	2556	.485	7	34	.206	641	856	.749	742	1051	1793	299	1184	15	235	351	299	3128	4.0	0.7	7.0
Playoff Totals	26	4	355	31	74	.419	0	1	.000	27	37	.730	17	40	57	15	63	0	4	9	11	89	2.2	0.6	3.4

Walker, Phillip B. **(Phil)** b. March 20, 1956 Ht. 6-3 Wt. 190 College: Millersville

SEASON–TEAM	G	GS	MIN	FGM	FGA	PCT	3FGM	3FGA	PCT	FTM	FTA	PCT	O-RB	D-RB	TOT	AST	PF	DQ	STL	TO	BLK	PTS	RPG	APG	PPG
77-78–Washington	40	–	384	57	161	.354	–	–	–	64	96	.667	21	31	52	54	39	0	14	62	5	178	1.3	1.4	4.5
Reg. Season Totals	40	–	384	57	161	.354	–	–	–	64	96	.667	21	31	52	54	39	0	14	62	5	178	1.3	1.4	4.5
Playoff Totals	4	–	17	1	8	.125	–	–	–	4	5	.800	1	1	2	2	5	0	0	3	0	6	0.5	0.5	1.5

Walker, Samaki Ijuma b. February 25, 1976 Ht. 6-9 Wt. 260 College: Louisville

SEASON–TEAM	G	GS	MIN	FGM	FGA	PCT	3FGM	3FGA	PCT	FTM	FTA	PCT	O-RB	D-RB	TOT	AST	PF	DQ	STL	TO	BLK	PTS	RPG	APG	PPG
96-97–Dallas	43	12	602	83	187	.444	0	1	.000	48	74	.649	47	100	147	17	71	0	15	39	22	214	3.4	0.4	5.0
97-98–Dallas	41	19	1027	156	321	.486	0	1	.000	53	97	.546	96	206	302	24	127	2	30	61	40	365	7.4	0.6	8.9
98-99–Dallas	39	2	568	88	190	.463	0	1	.000	53	98	.541	46	97	143	6	87	3	9	37	16	229	3.7	0.2	5.9
99-00–San Antonio	71	7	980	137	305	.449	0	0	–	86	126	.683	77	195	272	38	108	1	10	64	35	360	3.8	0.5	5.1
Reg. Season Totals	194	40	3177	464	1003	.463	0	3	.000	240	395	.608	266	598	864	85	393	6	64	201	113	1168	4.5	0.4	6.0
Playoff Totals	4	4	121	14	31	.452	0	0	–	8	12	.667	13	32	45	2	13	0	1	8	12	36	11.3	0.5	9.0

Walker, Walter Frederick **(Wally)** b. July 18, 1954 Ht. 6-8 Wt. 195 College: Virginia

SEASON–TEAM	G	GS	MIN	FGM	FGA	PCT	3FGM	3FGA	PCT	FTM	FTA	PCT	O-RB	D-RB	TOT	AST	PF	DQ	STL	TO	BLK	PTS	RPG	APG	PPG
76-77–Portland	66	–	627	137	305	.449	–	–	–	67	100	.670	45	63	108	51	92	0	14	–	2	341	1.6	0.8	5.2
77-78–Port.-Seattle	77	–	1104	204	461	.443	–	–	–	75	120	.625	87	132	219	77	138	1	26	77	10	483	2.8	1.0	6.3
78-79–Seattle	60	–	969	168	343	.490	–	–	–	58	96	.604	66	111	177	69	127	0	12	68	26	394	3.0	1.2	6.6
79-80–Seattle	70	–	844	139	274	.507	0	0	–	48	64	.750	64	106	170	53	102	0	21	50	4	326	2.4	0.8	4.7
80-81–Seattle	82	–	1796	290	626	.463	0	3	.000	109	169	.645	105	210	315	122	168	1	53	115	15	689	3.8	1.5	8.4
81-82–Seattle	70	70	1965	302	629	.480	0	2	.000	90	134	.672	108	197	305	218	215	2	36	111	28	694	4.4	3.1	9.9
82-83–Houston	82	59	2251	362	806	.449	1	4	.250	72	116	.621	137	236	373	199	202	3	37	144	22	797	4.5	2.4	9.7
83-84–Houston	58	18	612	118	241	.490	2	6	.333	6	18	.333	26	66	92	55	65	0	17	33	4	244	1.6	0.9	4.2
Reg. Season Totals	565	147	10168	1720	3685	.467	3	15	.200	525	817	.643	638	1121	1759	844	1109	7	216	598	111	3968	3.1	1.5	7.0
Playoff Totals	64	8	743	99	217	.456	0	0	–	45	65	.692	56	67	123	44	136	1	16	34	11	243	1.9	0.7	3.8

Wallace, Ben b. September 10, 1974 Ht. 6-9 Wt. 240 College: Virginia Union

SEASON–TEAM	G	GS	MIN	FGM	FGA	PCT	3FGM	3FGA	PCT	FTM	FTA	PCT	O-RB	D-RB	TOT	AST	PF	DQ	STL	TO	BLK	PTS	RPG	APG	PPG
96-97–Washington	34	0	197	16	46	.348	0	0	–	6	20	.300	25	33	58	2	27	0	8	18	11	38	1.7	0.1	1.1
97-98–Washington	67	16	1124	85	164	.518	0	0	–	35	98	.357	112	212	324	18	116	1	61	28	72	205	4.8	0.3	3.1
98-99–Washington	46	16	1231	115	199	.578	0	0	–	47	132	.356	137	247	384	18	111	0	50	36	90	277	8.3	0.4	6.0
99-00–Orlando	81	81	1959	168	334	.503	0	0	–	54	114	.474	211	454	665	67	162	0	72	67	130	390	8.2	0.8	4.8
Reg. Season Totals	228	113	4511	384	743	.517	0	0	–	142	364	.390	485	946	1431	105	416	1	191	149	303	910	6.3	0.5	4.0

Wallace, John b. February 9, 1974 Ht. 6-9 Wt. 225 College: Syracuse

SEASON–TEAM	G	GS	MIN	FGM	FGA	PCT	3FGM	3FGA	PCT	FTM	FTA	PCT	O-RB	D-RB	TOT	AST	PF	DQ	STL	TO	BLK	PTS	RPG	APG	PPG
96-97–New York	68	6	787	122	236	.517	2	4	.500	79	110	.718	51	104	155	37	102	0	21	76	25	325	2.3	0.5	4.8
97-98–Toronto	82	36	2361	468	979	.478	1	2	.500	210	293	.717	117	256	373	110	239	7	62	172	101	1147	4.5	1.3	14.0
98-99–Toronto	48	3	812	153	354	.432	0	0	–	105	150	.700	54	117	171	46	92	0	12	70	43	411	3.6	1.0	8.6
99-00–New York	60	0	798	155	332	.467	0	3	.000	82	102	.804	42	93	135	22	103	0	10	63	14	392	2.3	0.4	6.5
Reg. Season Totals	258	45	4758	898	1901	.472	3	9	.333	476	655	.727	264	570	834	215	536	7	105	381	183	2275	3.2	0.8	8.8
Playoff Totals	5	1	44	4	17	.235	0	1	.000	2	2	1.000	2	6	8	5	7	0	2	3	2	10	1.6	1.0	2.0

Wallace, Michael John **(Red)** b. July 12, 1918 d. July 7, 1977 Ht. 6-1 Wt. 185 College: Scranton

SEASON–TEAM	G	GS	MIN	FGM	FGA	PCT	3FGM	3FGA	PCT	FTM	FTA	PCT	O-RB	D-RB	TOT	AST	PF	DQ	STL	TO	BLK	PTS	RPG	APG	PPG
46-47–Boston-Toronto	61	–	–	225	809	.278	–	–	–	106	196	.541	–	–	–	58	167	–	–	–	–	556	–	1.0	9.1
Reg. Season Totals	61	–	–	225	809	.278	–	–	–	106	196	.541	–	–	–	58	167	–	–	–	–	556	–	1.0	9.1

Wallace, Rasheed Abdul b. September 17, 1974 Ht. 6-11 Wt. 225 College: North Carolina

SEASON–TEAM	G	GS	MIN	FGM	FGA	PCT	3FGM	3FGA	PCT	FTM	FTA	PCT	O-RB	D-RB	TOT	AST	PF	DQ	STL	TO	BLK	PTS	RPG	APG	PPG
95-96–Washington	65	51	1788	275	565	.487	27	82	.329	78	120	.650	93	210	303	85	206	4	42	103	54	655	4.7	1.3	10.1
96-97–Portland	62	56	1892	380	681	.558	9	33	.273	169	265	.638	122	297	419	74	198	1	48	114	59	938	6.8	1.2	15.1
97-98–Portland	77	77	2896	466	875	.533	8	39	.205	184	278	.662	132	346	478	195	268	6	75	167	88	1124	6.2	2.5	14.6
98-99–Portland	49	18	1414	242	476	.508	13	31	.419	131	179	.732	57	184	241	60	175	6	48	80	54	628	4.9	1.2	12.8
99-00–Portland	81	77	2845	542	1045	.519	8	50	.160	233	331	.704	129	437	566	142	216	2	87	157	107	1325	7.0	1.8	16.4
Reg. Season Totals	334	279	10835	1905	3642	.523	65	235	.277	795	1173	.678	533	1474	2007	556	1063	19	300	621	362	4670	6.0	1.7	14.0
Playoff Totals	37	37	1378	241	474	.508	15	32	.469	119	169	.704	63	146	209	65	135	2	39	50	35	616	5.6	1.8	16.6
All-Star Totals	1	0	21	3	6	.500	0	0	–	3	4	.750	2	2	4	0	0	0	1	0	1	9	4.0	0.0	9.0

Waller, Dwight b. October 5, 1945 Ht. 6-7 Wt. 225 College: Tennessee State

SEASON–TEAM	G	GS	MIN	FGM	FGA	PCT	3FGM	3FGA	PCT	FTM	FTA	PCT	O-RB	D-RB	TOT	AST	PF	DQ	STL	TO	BLK	PTS	RPG	APG	PPG
68-69–Atlanta	11	–	29	2	9	.222	–	–	–	3	7	.429	–	–	10	1	8	0	–	–	–	7	0.9	0.1	0.6
69-70–Denver (A)	7	–	87	10	24	.417	0	1	.000	9	19	.474	–	–	38	4	12	0	–	–	–	29	5.4	0.6	4.1
71-72–Denver (A)	2	–	10	2	4	.500	0	0	–	0	0	–	–	–	5	1	3	–	–	1	–	4	2.5	0.5	2.0
Reg. NBA Totals	11	–	29	2	9	.222	–	–	–	3	7	.429	–	–	10	1	8	0	–	–	–	7	0.9	0.1	0.6
Reg. ABA Totals	9	–	97	12	28	.429	0	1	.000	9	19	.474	–	–	43	5	15	0	–	1	–	33	4.8	0.6	3.7

Waller, Jamie Antonio b. November 20, 1964 Ht. 6-4 Wt. 215 College: Virginia Union

SEASON–TEAM	G	GS	MIN	FGM	FGA	PCT	3FGM	3FGA	PCT	FTM	FTA	PCT	O-RB	D-RB	TOT	AST	PF	DQ	STL	TO	BLK	PTS	RPG	APG	PPG
87-88–New Jersey	9	0	91	16	40	.400	0	2	.000	10	18	.556	9	4	13	3	13	0	4	11	1	42	1.4	0.3	4.7
Reg. Season Totals	9	0	91	16	40	.400	0	2	.000	10	18	.556	9	4	13	3	13	0	4	11	1	42	1.4	0.3	4.7

Walsh, James Patrick (Jim) b. August 29, 1931 d. March 4, 1976 Ht. 6-4 Wt. 195 College: Stanford

SEASON–TEAM	G	GS	MIN	FGM	FGA	PCT	3FGM	3FGA	PCT	FTM	FTA	PCT	O-RB	D-RB	TOT	AST	PF	DQ	STL	TO	BLK	PTS	RPG	APG	PPG
57-58–Philadelphia	10	–	72	5	27	.185	–	–	–	10	17	.588	–	–	15	8	9	0	–	–	–	20	1.5	0.8	2.0
Reg. Season Totals	10	–	72	5	27	.185	–	–	–	10	17	.588	–	–	15	8	9	0	–	–	–	20	1.5	0.8	2.0

Walters, Rex Andrew b. March 12, 1970 Ht. 6-4 Wt. 195 College: De Anza (Calif.) Coll. (J.C.); Northwestern; Kansas

SEASON–TEAM	G	GS	MIN	FGM	FGA	PCT	3FGM	3FGA	PCT	FTM	FTA	PCT	O-RB	D-RB	TOT	AST	PF	DQ	STL	TO	BLK	PTS	RPG	APG	PPG
93-94–New Jersey	48	0	386	60	115	.522	14	28	.500	28	34	.824	6	32	38	71	41	0	15	30	3	162	0.8	1.5	3.4
94-95–New Jersey	80	30	1435	206	469	.439	71	196	.362	40	52	.769	18	75	93	121	135	0	37	71	16	523	1.2	1.5	6.5
95-96–N.J.-Phil.	44	8	610	61	148	.412	22	66	.333	42	52	.808	13	42	55	106	53	0	25	41	4	186	1.3	2.4	4.2
96-97–Philadelphia	59	16	1041	148	325	.455	57	148	.385	49	62	.790	21	86	107	113	75	1	28	61	3	402	1.8	1.9	6.8
97-98–Phil.-Miami	38	0	235	24	53	.453	6	22	.273	26	28	.929	5	19	24	35	28	0	8	27	1	80	0.6	0.9	2.1
98-99–Miami	33	13	506	35	95	.368	12	38	.316	19	23	.826	10	40	50	58	63	0	10	32	3	101	1.5	1.8	3.1
99-00–Miami	33	0	389	38	91	.418	5	20	.250	12	16	.750	8	28	36	65	44	0	6	29	0	93	1.1	2.0	2.8
Reg. Season Totals	335	67	4602	572	1296	.441	187	518	.361	216	267	.809	81	322	403	569	439	1	129	291	30	1547	1.2	1.7	4.6
Playoff Totals	4	0	14	1	4	.250	0	2	.000	0	0	–	0	0	0	4	0	0	0	0	0	2	0.0	1.0	0.5

Walther, Paul P. (Lefty) b. March 23, 1927 Ht. 6-2 Wt. 165 College: Tennessee

SEASON–TEAM	G	GS	MIN	FGM	FGA	PCT	3FGM	3FGA	PCT	FTM	FTA	PCT	O-RB	D-RB	TOT	AST	PF	DQ	STL	TO	BLK	PTS	RPG	APG	PPG
49-50–Minn.-Ind.	53	–	–	114	290	.393	–	–	–	63	109	.578	–	–	–	56	123	–	–	–	–	291	–	1.1	5.5
50-51–Indianapolis	63	–	–	213	634	.336	–	–	–	145	209	.694	–	–	226	225	201	8	–	–	–	571	3.6	3.6	9.1
51-52–Indianapolis	55	–	1903	220	549	.401	–	–	–	231	308	.750	–	–	246	137	171	6	–	–	–	671	4.5	2.5	12.2
52-53–Indianapolis	67	–	2468	227	645	.352	–	–	–	264	354	.746	–	–	284	205	260	7	–	–	–	718	4.2	3.1	10.7
53-54–Philadelphia	64	–	2067	138	392	.352	–	–	–	145	206	.704	–	–	257	220	199	5	–	–	–	421	4.0	3.4	6.6
54-55–Fort Wayne	68	–	820	56	161	.348	–	–	–	54	88	.614	–	–	155	131	115	1	–	–	–	166	2.3	1.9	2.4
Reg. Season Totals	370	–	7258	968	2671	.362	–	–	–	902	1274	.708	–	–	1168	974	1069	27	–	–	–	2838	3.7	2.6	7.7
Playoff Totals	24	–	340	40	105	.381	–	–	–	63	87	.724	–	–	47	41	59	1	–	–	–	143	2.6	1.7	6.0
All-Star Totals	1	–	17	1	4	.250	–	–	–	0	0	–	–	–	2	2	1	0	–	–	–	2	2.0	2.0	2.0

Walthour, Isaac (Rabbit) b. 1928 Ht. 5-11 Wt. 175 College: None

SEASON–TEAM	G	GS	MIN	FGM	FGA	PCT	3FGM	3FGA	PCT	FTM	FTA	PCT	O-RB	D-RB	TOT	AST	PF	DQ	STL	TO	BLK	PTS	RPG	APG	PPG
53-54–Milwaukee	4	–	30	1	6	.167	–	–	–	0	0	–	–	–	1	2	6	0	–	–	–	2	0.3	0.5	0.5
Reg. Season Totals	4	–	30	1	6	.167	–	–	–	0	0	–	–	–	1	2	6	0	–	–	–	2	0.3	0.5	0.5

W

Walton, Lloyd b. November 23, 1953 Ht. 6-0 Wt. 160 College: Moberly Area C.C.; Marquette

SEASON–TEAM	G	GS	MIN	FGM	FGA	PCT	3FGM	3FGA	PCT	FTM	FTA	PCT	O-RB	D-RB	TOT	AST	PF	DQ	STL	TO	BLK	PTS	RPG	APG	PPG
76-77–Milwaukee	53	–	678	88	188	.468	–	–	–	53	65	.815	15	36	51	141	52	0	40	–	2	229	1.0	2.7	4.3
77-78–Milwaukee	76	–	1264	154	344	.448	–	–	–	54	83	.651	26	50	76	253	94	0	77	107	13	362	1.0	3.3	4.8
78-79–Milwaukee	75	–	1381	157	327	.480	–	–	–	61	90	.678	34	70	104	356	103	0	72	123	9	375	1.4	4.7	5.0
79-80–Milwaukee	76	–	1243	110	242	.455	1	3	.333	49	71	.690	33	58	91	285	68	0	43	112	2	270	1.2	3.8	3.6
80-81–Kansas City	61	–	821	90	218	.413	0	1	.000	26	33	.788	13	35	48	208	45	0	32	80	2	206	0.8	3.4	3.4
Reg. Season Totals	341	–	5387	599	1319	.454	1	4	.250	243	342	.711	121	249	370	1243	362	0	264	422	28	1442	1.1	3.6	4.2
Playoff Totals	18	–	201	21	51	.412	0	1	.000	11	17	.647	4	8	12	57	14	0	12	24	4	53	0.7	3.2	2.9

Walton, William Theodore III (Bill) b. November 5, 1952 Ht. 7-0 Wt. 240 College: UCLA HOF: 1993

SEASON–TEAM	G	GS	MIN	FGM	FGA	PCT	3FGM	3FGA	PCT	FTM	FTA	PCT	O-RB	D-RB	TOT	AST	PF	DQ	STL	TO	BLK	PTS	RPG	APG	PPG
74-75–Portland	35	–	1153	177	345	.513	–	–	–	94	137	.686	92	349	441	167	115	4	29	–	94	448	12.6	4.8	12.8
75-76–Portland	51	–	1687	345	732	.471	–	–	–	133	228	.583	132	549	681	220	144	4	49	–	82	823	13.4	4.3	16.1
76-77–Portland	65	–	2264	491	930	.528	–	–	–	228	327	.697	211	723	934	245	174	5	66	–	211	1210	14.4	3.8	18.6
77-78–Portland	58	–	1929	460	882	.522	–	–	–	177	246	.720	118	648	766	291	145	3	60	206	146	1097	13.2	5.0	18.9
79-80–San Diego	14	–	337	81	161	.503	0	0	–	32	54	.593	28	98	126	34	37	0	8	37	38	194	9.0	2.4	13.9
82-83–San Diego	33	32	1099	200	379	.528	0	0	–	65	117	.556	75	248	323	120	113	0	34	105	119	465	9.8	3.6	14.1
83-84–San Diego	55	46	1476	288	518	.556	0	2	.000	92	154	.597	132	345	477	183	153	1	45	177	88	668	8.7	3.3	12.1
84-85–L.A. Clippers	67	37	1647	269	516	.521	0	2	.000	138	203	.680	168	432	600	156	184	0	50	174	140	676	9.0	2.3	10.1
85-86–Boston	80	2	1546	231	411	.562	0	0	–	144	202	.713	136	408	544	165	210	1	38	151	106	606	6.8	2.1	7.6
86-87–Boston	10	0	112	10	26	.385	0	0	–	8	15	.533	11	20	31	9	23	0	1	15	10	28	3.1	0.9	2.8
Reg. Season Totals	468	117	13250	2552	4900	.521	0	4	.000	1111	1683	.660	1103	3820	4923	1590	1298	18	380	865	1034	6215	10.5	3.4	13.3
Playoff Totals	49	0	1197	230	438	.525	0	1	.000	68	101	.673	95	349	444	145	149	4	32	36	83	528	9.1	3.0	10.8
All-Star Totals	1	1	31	6	14	.429	0	0	–	3	3	1.000	2	8	10	2	3	0	3	4	2	15	10.0	2.0	15.0

Wanzer, Robert Francis (Bobby) b. June 4, 1921 Ht. 6-0 Wt. 170 College: Colgate; Seton Hall

SEASON–TEAM	G	GS	MIN	FGM	FGA	PCT	3FGM	3FGA	PCT	FTM	FTA	PCT	O-RB	D-RB	TOT	AST	PF	DQ	STL	TO	BLK	PTS	RPG	APG	PPG
47-48–Rochester (N)	40	–	–	55	–	–	–	–	–	57	69	.826	–	–	–	–	38	–	–	–	–	167	–	–	4.2
48-49–Rochester	60	–	–	202	533	.379	–	–	–	209	254	.823	–	–	–	186	132	–	–	–	–	613	–	3.1	10.2
49-50–Rochester	67	–	–	254	614	.414	–	–	–	283	351	.806	–	–	–	214	102	–	–	–	–	791	–	3.2	11.8
50-51–Rochester	68	–	–	252	628	.401	–	–	–	232	273	.850	–	–	232	181	129	0	–	–	–	736	3.4	2.7	10.8
51-52–Rochester	66	–	2498	328	772	.425	–	–	–	377	417	.904	–	–	333	262	201	5	–	–	–	1033	5.0	4.0	15.7
52-53–Rochester	70	–	2577	318	866	.367	–	–	–	384	473	.812	–	–	351	252	206	7	–	–	–	1020	5.0	3.6	14.6
53-54–Rochester	72	–	2538	322	835	.386	–	–	–	314	428	.734	–	–	392	254	171	2	–	–	–	958	5.4	3.5	13.3
54-55–Rochester	72	–	2376	324	820	.395	–	–	–	294	374	.786	–	–	374	247	163	2	–	–	–	942	5.2	3.4	13.1
55-56–Rochester	72	–	1980	245	651	.376	–	–	–	259	360	.719	–	–	272	225	151	0	–	–	–	749	3.8	3.1	10.4
56-57–Rochester	21	–	159	23	49	.469	–	–	–	36	46	.783	–	–	25	9	20	0	–	–	–	82	1.2	0.4	3.9
Reg. NBA Totals	568	–	12128	2268	5768	.393	–	–	–	2388	2976	.802	–	–	1979	1830	1275	16	–	–	–	6924	4.5	3.2	12.2
Reg. NBL Totals	40	–	–	55	–	–	–	–	–	57	69	.826	–	–	–	–	38	–	–	–	–	167	–	–	4.2
NBA Playoff Totals	38	–	1204	172	528	.420	–	–	–	212	240	.883	–	–	259	192	123	3	–	–	–	556	5.9	3.4	14.6
NBL Playoff Totals	11	–	–	21	–	–	–	–	–	24	28	.857	–	–	–	–	5	–	–	–	–	66	–	–	6.0
NBA All-Star Totals	5	–	131	17	43	.395	–	–	–	12	14	.857	–	–	17	17	17	1	–	–	–	46	3.4	3.4	9.2

Warbington, Perry b. September 7, 1952 Ht. 6-2 Wt. 165 College: Lake City (Fla.) C.C.; Georgia Southern

SEASON–TEAM	G	GS	MIN	FGM	FGA	PCT	3FGM	3FGA	PCT	FTM	FTA	PCT	O-RB	D-RB	TOT	AST	PF	DQ	STL	TO	BLK	PTS	RPG	APG	PPG
74-75–Philadelphia	5	0	70	4	21	.190	–	–	–	2	2	1.000	2	6	8	16	16	0	0	–	0	10	1.6	3.2	2.0
Reg. Season Totals	5	0	70	4	21	.190	–	–	–	2	2	1.000	2	6	8	16	16	0	0	–	0	10	1.6	3.2	2.0

Ward, Charlie b. October 12, 1970 Ht. 6-2 Wt. 190 College: Florida State

SEASON–TEAM	G	GS	MIN	FGM	FGA	PCT	3FGM	3FGA	PCT	FTM	FTA	PCT	O-RB	D-RB	TOT	AST	PF	DQ	STL	TO	BLK	PTS	RPG	APG	PPG
94-95–New York	10	0	44	4	19	.211	1	10	.100	7	10	.700	1	5	6	4	7	0	2	8	0	16	0.6	0.4	1.6
95-96–New York	62	1	787	87	218	.399	33	99	.333	37	54	.685	29	73	102	132	98	0	54	79	6	244	1.6	2.1	3.9
96-97–New York	79	21	1763	133	337	.395	48	154	.312	95	125	.760	45	175	220	326	188	2	83	147	15	409	2.8	4.1	5.2
97-98–New York	82	82	2317	235	516	.455	81	215	.377	91	113	.805	32	242	274	466	195	3	144	175	37	642	3.3	5.7	7.8
98-99–New York	50	50	1556	135	334	.404	53	149	.356	55	78	.705	23	149	172	271	105	0	103	131	8	378	3.4	5.4	7.6
99-00–New York	72	69	1986	189	447	.423	102	264	.386	48	58	.828	22	206	228	300	176	3	95	102	16	528	3.2	4.2	7.3
Reg. Season Totals	355	223	8453	783	1871	.418	318	891	.357	333	438	.760	152	850	1002	1499	769	8	481	642	82	2217	2.8	4.2	6.2
Playoff Totals	62	46	1468	135	315	.429	52	151	.344	38	56	.679	31	145	176	256	136	2	101	82	10	360	2.8	4.1	5.8

Ward, Gerald W. (Gerry) b. September 6, 1941 Ht. 6-4 Wt. 200 College: Boston College

SEASON–TEAM	G	GS	MIN	FGM	FGA	PCT	3FGM	3FGA	PCT	FTM	FTA	PCT	O-RB	D-RB	TOT	AST	PF	DQ	STL	TO	BLK	PTS	RPG	APG	PPG
63-64–St. Louis	24	–	139	16	53	.302	–	–	–	11	17	.647	–	–	21	21	26	0	–	–	–	43	0.9	0.9	1.8
64-65–Boston	3	–	30	2	18	.111	–	–	–	1	1	1.000	–	–	5	6	6	0	–	–	–	5	1.7	2.0	1.7
65-66–Philadelphia	66	–	838	67	189	.354	–	–	–	39	60	.650	–	–	89	80	163	3	–	–	–	173	1.3	1.2	2.6
66-67–Chicago	76	–	1042	117	307	.381	–	–	–	87	138	.630	–	–	179	130	169	2	–	–	–	321	2.4	1.7	4.2
Reg. Season Totals	169	–	2049	202	567	.356	–	–	–	138	216	.639	–	–	294	237	364	5	–	–	–	542	1.7	1.4	3.2
Playoff Totals	14	–	118	13	34	.382	–	–	–	3	6	.500	–	–	10	11	27	0	–	–	–	29	0.7	0.8	2.1

Ward, Henry Lorette b. January 30, 1952 Ht. 6-4 Wt. 195 College: Jackson State

SEASON–TEAM	G	GS	MIN	FGM	FGA	PCT	3FGM	3FGA	PCT	FTM	FTA	PCT	O-RB	D-RB	TOT	AST	PF	DQ	STL	TO	BLK	PTS	RPG	APG	PPG
75-76–San Antonio (A)	61	–	688	154	333	.462	6	23	.261	16	27	.593	45	95	140	35	99	–	16	45	10	330	2.3	0.6	5.4
76-77–San Antonio	27	–	171	34	90	.378	–	–	–	15	17	.882	10	23	33	6	30	0	6	–	5	83	1.2	0.2	3.1
Reg. NBA Totals	27	–	171	34	90	.378	–	–	–	15	17	.882	10	23	33	6	30	0	6	–	5	83	1.2	0.2	3.1
Reg. ABA Totals	61	–	688	154	333	.462	6	23	.261	16	27	.593	45	95	140	35	99	–	16	45	10	330	2.3	0.6	5.4
NBA Playoff Totals	1	–	1	2	3	.667	–	–	–	0	0	–	0	0	0	–	0	0	0	–	0	4	0.0	0.0	4.0
ABA Playoff Totals	5	–	18	4	12	.333	2	2	1.000	0	0	–	1	1	2	0	6	–	1	1	1	10	0.4	0.0	2.0

Ware, James Edward (Jim) b. May 2, 1944 Ht. 6-7 Wt. 210 College: Oklahoma City

SEASON–TEAM	G	GS	MIN	FGM	FGA	PCT	3FGM	3FGA	PCT	FTM	FTA	PCT	O-RB	D-RB	TOT	AST	PF	DQ	STL	TO	BLK	PTS	RPG	APG	PPG
66-67–Cincinnati	33	–	201	30	97	.309	–	–	–	10	17	.588	–	–	69	6	35	0	–	–	–	70	2.1	0.2	2.1
67-68–San Diego	30	–	228	25	97	.258	–	–	–	23	34	.676	–	–	77	7	28	1	–	–	–	73	2.6	0.2	2.4
68-69–Dallas (A)	1	–	15	3	4	.750	0	0	–	1	2	.500	–	–	7	1	4	0	–	1	–	7	7.0	1.0	7.0
Reg. NBA Totals	63	–	429	55	194	.284	–	–	–	33	51	.647	–	–	146	13	63	1	–	–	–	143	2.3	0.2	2.3
Reg. ABA Totals	1	–	15	3	4	.750	0	0	–	1	2	.500	–	–	7	1	4	0	–	1	–	7	7.0	1.0	7.0
NBA Playoff Totals	3	–	13	5	13	.385	–	–	–	0	0	–	–	–	2	–	1	0	–	–	–	10	0.7	0.0	3.3

Warley, Benjamin Vallintina (Ben) b. September 4, 1936 Ht. 6-6 Wt. 205 College: Tennessee State

SEASON–TEAM	G	GS	MIN	FGM	FGA	PCT	3FGM	3FGA	PCT	FTM	FTA	PCT	O-RB	D-RB	TOT	AST	PF	DQ	STL	TO	BLK	PTS	RPG	APG	PPG
62-63–Syracuse	26	–	206	50	111	.450	–	–	–	25	35	.714	–	–	86	4	42	1	–	–	–	125	3.3	0.2	4.8
63-64–Philadelphia	79	–	1740	215	494	.435	–	–	–	220	305	.721	–	–	619	71	274	5	–	–	–	650	7.8	0.9	8.2
64-65–Philadelphia	64	–	900	94	253	.372	–	–	–	124	176	.705	–	–	277	53	170	6	–	–	–	312	4.3	0.8	4.9
65-66–Phil.-Balt.	57	–	773	116	284	.408	–	–	–	64	97	.660	–	–	217	25	129	2	–	–	–	296	3.8	0.4	5.2
66-67–Baltimore	62	–	1037	125	312	.401	–	–	–	134	170	.788	–	–	325	51	176	6	–	–	–	384	5.2	0.8	6.2
67-68–Anaheim (A)	71	–	2297	435	985	.442	52	166	.313	313	389	.805	–	–	608	96	276	12	–	161	–	1235	8.6	1.4	17.4
68-69–Los Angeles (A)	35	–	876	172	423	.407	31	121	.256	116	155	.748	–	–	194	26	127	6	–	53	–	491	5.5	0.7	14.0
69-70–Denver (A)	42	–	475	60	170	.353	15	58	.259	58	76	.763	–	–	110	30	98	0	–	–	–	193	2.6	0.7	4.6
Reg. NBA Totals	288	–	4656	600	1454	.413	–	–	–	567	783	.724	–	–	1524	204	791	20	–	–	–	1767	5.3	0.7	6.1
Reg. ABA Totals	148	–	3648	667	1578	.423	98	345	.284	487	620	.785	–	–	912	152	501	18	–	214	–	1919	6.2	1.0	13.0
NBA Playoff Totals	10	–	109	9	32	.281	–	–	–	13	20	.650	–	–	39	3	16	0	–	–	–	31	3.9	0.3	3.1
ABA Playoff Totals	10	–	129	16	38	.421	7	16	.438	6	10	.600	–	–	29	11	27	1	–	–	–	45	2.9	1.1	4.5

Warlick, Robert Lee (Bob) b. March 20, 1941 Ht. 6-5 Wt. 205 College: Pueblo (Colo.) C.C.; Pepperdine; Denver

SEASON–TEAM	G	GS	MIN	FGM	FGA	PCT	3FGM	3FGA	PCT	FTM	FTA	PCT	O-RB	D-RB	TOT	AST	PF	DQ	STL	TO	BLK	PTS	RPG	APG	PPG
65-66–Detroit	10	–	78	11	38	.289	–	–	–	2	6	.333	–	–	16	10	8	0	–	–	–	24	1.6	1.0	2.4
66-67–San Francisco	12	–	65	15	52	.288	–	–	–	6	11	.545	–	–	20	10	4	0	–	–	–	36	1.7	0.8	3.0
67-68–San Francisco	69	–	1320	257	610	.421	–	–	–	97	171	.567	–	–	264	159	164	1	–	–	–	611	3.8	2.3	8.9
68-69–Milw.-Phoenix	66	–	997	213	509	.418	–	–	–	87	142	.613	–	–	152	132	122	0	–	–	–	513	2.3	2.0	7.8
69-70–Los Angeles (A)	29	–	711	112	309	.362	0	1	.000	65	96	.677	–	–	114	76	70	0	–	–	–	289	3.9	2.6	10.0
Reg. NBA Totals	157	–	2460	496	1209	.410	–	–	–	192	330	.582	–	–	452	311	298	1	–	–	–	1184	2.9	2.0	7.5
Reg. ABA Totals	29	–	711	112	309	.362	0	1	.000	65	96	.677	–	–	114	76	70	0	–	–	–	289	3.9	2.6	10.0
NBA Playoff Totals	12	–	234	55	120	.458	–	–	–	28	37	.757	–	–	53	25	26	2	–	–	–	138	4.4	2.1	11.5

Warner, Cornell b. August 12, 1948 Ht. 6-9 Wt. 225 College: Jackson State

SEASON–TEAM	G	GS	MIN	FGM	FGA	PCT	3FGM	3FGA	PCT	FTM	FTA	PCT	O-RB	D-RB	TOT	AST	PF	DQ	STL	TO	BLK	PTS	RPG	APG	PPG
70-71–Buffalo	65	–	1293	156	376	.415	–	–	–	79	143	.552	–	–	452	53	140	2	–	–	–	391	7.0	0.8	6.0
71-72–Buffalo	62	–	1239	162	366	.443	–	–	–	58	78	.744	–	–	379	54	125	2	–	–	–	382	6.1	0.9	6.2
72-73–Buffalo-Clev.	72	–	1370	174	421	.413	–	–	–	59	90	.656	–	–	522	72	178	3	–	–	–	407	7.3	1.0	5.7
73-74–Clev.-Milw.	72	–	1405	174	349	.499	–	–	–	85	114	.746	106	291	397	71	204	8	27	–	42	433	5.5	1.0	6.0
74-75–Milwaukee	79	–	2519	248	541	.458	–	–	–	106	155	.684	238	574	812	127	267	8	49	–	54	602	10.3	1.6	7.6
75-76–Los Angeles	81	–	2512	251	524	.479	–	–	–	89	128	.695	223	499	722	106	283	3	55	–	46	591	8.9	1.3	7.3
76-77–Los Angeles	14	–	170	25	53	.472	–	–	–	4	6	.667	21	48	69	11	28	0	1	–	2	54	4.9	0.8	3.9
Reg. Season Totals	445	–	10508	1190	2630	.452	–	–	–	480	714	.672	588	1412	3353	494	1225	26	132	–	144	2860	7.5	1.1	6.4
Playoff Totals	21	–	561	54	123	.439	–	–	–	13	19	.684	37	135	172	26	81	3	8	–	14	121	8.2	1.2	5.8

Warren, John II (Johnny) b. July 7, 1947 Ht. 6-3 Wt. 180 College: St. John's (N.Y.)

SEASON–TEAM	G	GS	MIN	FGM	FGA	PCT	3FGM	3FGA	PCT	FTM	FTA	PCT	O-RB	D-RB	TOT	AST	PF	DQ	STL	TO	BLK	PTS	RPG	APG	PPG
69-70–New York	44	–	272	44	108	.407	–	–	–	24	35	.686	–	–	40	30	53	0	–	–	–	112	0.9	0.7	2.5
70-71–Cleveland	82	–	2610	380	899	.423	–	–	–	180	217	.829	–	–	344	347	299	13	–	–	–	940	4.2	4.2	11.5
71-72–Cleveland	68	–	969	144	345	.417	–	–	–	49	58	.845	–	–	133	91	92	0	–	–	–	337	2.0	1.3	5.0
72-73–Cleveland	40	–	290	54	111	.486	–	–	–	18	19	.947	–	–	42	34	45	0	–	–	–	126	1.1	0.9	3.2
73-74–Cleveland	69	–	790	132	291	.454	–	–	–	35	41	.854	42	86	128	62	117	1	27	–	6	299	1.9	0.9	4.3
Reg. Season Totals	303	–	4931	754	1754	.430	–	–	–	306	370	.827	42	86	687	564	606	14	27	–	6	1814	2.3	1.9	6.0
Playoff Totals	10	–	22	2	5	.400	–	–	–	0	0	–	0	0	3	2	6	0	0	–	0	4	0.3	0.2	0.4

Warren, Robert G. (Bobby, Colonel) b. July 17, 1946 Ht. 6-5 Wt. 190 College: Vanderbilt

SEASON–TEAM	G	GS	MIN	FGM	FGA	PCT	3FGM	3FGA	PCT	FTM	FTA	PCT	O-RB	D-RB	TOT	AST	PF	DQ	STL	TO	BLK	PTS	RPG	APG	PPG
68-69–Los Angeles (A)	76	–	2045	285	645	.442	31	89	.348	297	385	.771	–	–	349	155	252	6	–	175	–	898	4.6	2.0	11.8
69-70–Los Angeles (A)	72	–	1672	266	647	.411	25	107	.234	176	238	.739	–	–	277	141	190	1	–	–	–	733	3.8	2.0	10.2
70-71–Memphis (A)	46	–	763	146	367	.398	21	81	.259	107	133	.805	–	–	144	85	87	–	–	–	–	420	3.1	1.8	9.1
71-72–Memphis-Car. (A)	75	–	1801	313	707	.443	11	55	.200	213	268	.795	–	–	259	182	165	–	–	140	–	850	3.5	2.4	11.3
72-73–Car.-Dallas-Utah (A)	77	–	1571	244	504	.484	5	19	.263	236	274	.861	92	150	242	147	212	2	–	143	–	729	3.1	1.9	9.5
73-74–Utah-S.A. (A)	59	–	799	110	255	.431	0	6	.000	63	73	.863	53	51	104	74	73	–	21	62	13	283	1.8	1.3	4.8
74-75–San Antonio (A)	71	–	992	127	265	.479	2	7	.286	77	91	.846	42	70	112	91	109	–	35	68	9	333	1.6	1.3	4.7
75-76–San Diego (A)	10	–	265	36	81	.444	1	3	.333	28	32	.875	27	32	59	23	35	–	9	23	6	101	5.9	2.3	10.1
Reg. ABA Totals	486	–	9908	1527	3471	.440	96	367	.262	1197	1494	.801	214	303	1546	898	1123	9	65	611	28	4347	3.2	1.8	8.9
ABA Playoff Totals	35	–	935	142	321	.442	17	58	.293	86	104	.827	9	12	187	92	108	0	2	30	2	387	5.3	2.6	11.1

Warrick, Bryan Anthony b. July 22, 1959 Ht. 6-5 Wt. 195 College: St. Joseph's (Pa.)

SEASON–TEAM	G	GS	MIN	FGM	FGA	PCT	3FGM	3FGA	PCT	FTM	FTA	PCT	O-RB	D-RB	TOT	AST	PF	DQ	STL	TO	BLK	PTS	RPG	APG	PPG
82-83–Washington	43	20	727	65	171	.380	0	5	.000	42	57	.737	15	54	69	126	103	5	21	71	8	172	1.6	2.9	4.0
83-84–Washington	32	0	254	27	66	.409	1	3	.333	8	16	.500	5	17	22	43	37	0	9	20	3	63	0.7	1.3	2.0
84-85–L.A. Clippers	58	1	713	85	173	.491	1	4	.250	44	57	.772	10	48	58	153	85	0	23	70	6	215	1.0	2.6	3.7
85-86–Milw.-Indiana	36	5	685	85	182	.467	3	12	.250	54	68	.794	10	59	69	115	79	0	27	53	2	227	1.9	3.2	6.3
Reg. Season Totals	169	26	2379	262	592	.443	5	24	.208	148	198	.747	40	178	218	437	304	5	80	214	19	677	1.3	2.6	4.0

Washburn, Christopher Scott (Chris) b. May 13, 1965 Ht. 6-11 Wt. 255 College: North Carolina State

SEASON–TEAM	G	GS	MIN	FGM	FGA	PCT	3FGM	3FGA	PCT	FTM	FTA	PCT	O-RB	D-RB	TOT	AST	PF	DQ	STL	TO	BLK	PTS	RPG	APG	PPG
86-87–Golden State	35	2	385	57	145	.393	0	1	.000	18	51	.353	36	65	101	16	51	0	6	39	8	132	2.9	0.5	3.8
87-88–G.S.-Atlanta	37	0	260	36	81	.444	0	0	–	18	31	.581	28	47	75	6	29	0	5	17	8	90	2.0	0.2	2.4
Reg. Season Totals	72	2	645	93	226	.412	0	1	.000	36	82	.439	64	112	176	22	80	0	11	56	16	222	2.4	0.3	3.1
Playoff Totals	6	0	31	3	7	.429	0	0	–	5	6	.833	0	1	1	2	2	0	0	4	0	11	0.2	0.3	1.8

Washington, Donald Maurice Jr. (Don) b. April 22, 1952 Ht. 6-8 Wt. 210 College: North Carolina

SEASON–TEAM	G	GS	MIN	FGM	FGA	PCT	3FGM	3FGA	PCT	FTM	FTA	PCT	O-RB	D-RB	TOT	AST	PF	DQ	STL	TO	BLK	PTS	RPG	APG	PPG
74-75–Denver (A)	50	–	438	79	183	.432	0	2	.000	38	56	.679	41	48	89	30	92	–	12	49	19	196	1.8	0.6	3.9
75-76–Utah (A)	6	–	58	12	18	.667	0	0	–	0	0	–	4	9	13	3	19	–	1	3	1	24	2.2	0.5	4.0
Reg. ABA Totals	56	–	496	91	201	.453	0	2	.000	38	56	.679	45	57	102	33	111	–	13	52	20	220	1.8	0.6	3.9
ABA Playoff Totals	4	–	26	5	10	.500	0	0	–	1	1	1.000	2	4	6	2	9	–	1	4	2	11	1.5	0.5	2.8

Washington, Duane E. b. August 31, 1964 Ht. 6-4 Wt. 195 College: Laredo (Texas) C.C.; Middle Tennessee State

SEASON–TEAM	G	GS	MIN	FGM	FGA	PCT	3FGM	3FGA	PCT	FTM	FTA	PCT	O-RB	D-RB	TOT	AST	PF	DQ	STL	TO	BLK	PTS	RPG	APG	PPG
87-88–New Jersey	15	0	156	18	42	.429	2	4	.500	16	20	.800	5	17	22	34	23	0	12	9	0	54	1.5	2.3	3.6
92-93–L.A. Clippers	4	0	28	0	5	.000	0	0	–	0	0	–	0	2	2	5	2	0	1	2	0	0	0.5	1.3	0.0
Reg. Season Totals	19	0	184	18	47	.383	2	4	.500	16	20	.800	5	19	24	39	25	0	13	11	0	54	1.3	2.1	2.8

Washington, Dwayne Alonzo (Pearl) b. January 6, 1964 Ht. 6-2 Wt. 195 College: Syracuse

SEASON–TEAM	G	GS	MIN	FGM	FGA	PCT	3FGM	3FGA	PCT	FTM	FTA	PCT	O-RB	D-RB	TOT	AST	PF	DQ	STL	TO	BLK	PTS	RPG	APG	PPG
86-87–New Jersey	72	61	1600	257	538	.478	4	24	.167	98	125	.784	37	92	129	301	184	5	92	175	7	616	1.8	4.2	8.6
87-88–New Jersey	68	10	1379	245	547	.448	11	49	.224	132	189	.698	54	64	118	206	163	2	91	141	4	633	1.7	3.0	9.3
88-89–Miami	54	8	1065	164	387	.424	1	14	.071	82	104	.788	49	74	123	226	101	0	73	122	4	411	2.3	4.2	7.6
Reg. Season Totals	194	79	4044	666	1472	.452	16	87	.184	312	418	.746	140	230	370	733	448	7	256	438	15	1660	1.9	3.8	8.6

Washington, Eric Maurice b. March 23, 1974 Ht. 6-4 Wt. 190 College: Alabama

SEASON–TEAM	G	GS	MIN	FGM	FGA	PCT	3FGM	3FGA	PCT	FTM	FTA	PCT	O-RB	D-RB	TOT	AST	PF	DQ	STL	TO	BLK	PTS	RPG	APG	PPG
97-98–Denver	66	36	1539	201	498	.404	44	137	.321	65	83	.783	47	80	127	78	143	0	53	72	25	511	1.9	1.2	7.7
98-99–Denver	38	6	761	73	184	.397	37	97	.381	22	32	.688	35	54	89	30	87	2	25	34	18	205	2.3	0.8	5.4
Reg. Season Totals	104	42	2300	274	682	.402	81	234	.346	87	115	.757	82	134	216	108	230	2	78	106	43	716	2.1	1.0	6.9

Washington, James H. (Jim) b. July 1, 1943 Ht. 6-7 Wt. 215 College: Villanova

SEASON–TEAM	G	GS	MIN	FGM	FGA	PCT	3FGM	3FGA	PCT	FTM	FTA	PCT	O-RB	D-RB	TOT	AST	PF	DQ	STL	TO	BLK	PTS	RPG	APG	PPG
65-66–St. Louis	65	–	1104	158	393	.402	–	–	–	68	120	.567	–	–	353	43	176	4	–	–	–	384	5.4	0.7	5.9
66-67–Chicago	77	–	1475	252	604	.417	–	–	–	88	159	.553	–	–	468	56	181	1	–	–	–	592	6.1	0.7	7.7
67-68–Chicago	82	–	2525	418	915	.457	–	–	–	187	274	.682	–	–	825	113	233	1	–	–	–	1023	10.1	1.4	12.5
68-69–Chicago	80	–	2705	440	1023	.430	–	–	–	241	356	.677	–	–	847	104	226	0	–	–	–	1121	10.6	1.3	14.0
69-70–Philadelphia	79	–	2459	401	842	.476	–	–	–	204	273	.747	–	–	734	104	262	5	–	–	–	1006	9.3	1.3	12.7
70-71–Philadelphia	78	–	2501	395	829	.476	–	–	–	259	340	.762	–	–	747	97	258	6	–	–	–	1049	9.6	1.2	13.4
71-72–Phil.-Atlanta	84	–	2961	393	885	.444	–	–	–	256	323	.793	–	–	736	146	276	3	–	–	–	1042	8.8	1.7	12.4
72-73–Atlanta	75	–	2833	308	713	.432	–	–	–	163	224	.728	–	–	801	174	252	6	–	–	–	779	10.7	2.3	10.4
73-74–Atlanta	73	–	2519	297	612	.485	–	–	–	134	196	.684	207	528	735	156	249	6	49	–	74	728	10.1	2.1	10.0
74-75–Atlanta-Buffalo	80	–	1579	191	421	.454	–	–	–	62	93	.667	110	280	390	111	167	5	34	–	26	444	4.9	1.4	5.6
75-76–Buffalo	1	–	7	0	1	.000	–	–	–	0	0	–	1	0	1	1	0	0	0	–	0	0	1.0	1.0	0.0
Reg. Season Totals	774	–	22668	3253	7238	.449	–	–	–	1662	2358	.705	318	808	6637	1105	2280	37	83	–	100	8168	8.6	1.4	10.6
Playoff Totals	42	–	1106	151	340	.444	–	–	–	67	112	.598	3	4	300	58	111	2	0	–	0	369	7.1	1.4	8.8

Washington, Kermit Alan (Special K) b. September 17, 1951 Ht. 6-8 Wt. 230 College: American International

SEASON–TEAM	G	GS	MIN	FGM	FGA	PCT	3FGM	3FGA	PCT	FTM	FTA	PCT	O-RB	D-RB	TOT	AST	PF	DQ	STL	TO	BLK	PTS	RPG	APG	PPG
73-74–Los Angeles	45	–	400	73	151	.483	–	–	–	26	49	.531	62	85	147	19	77	0	21	–	18	172	3.3	0.4	3.8
74-75–Los Angeles	55	–	949	87	207	.420	–	–	–	72	122	.590	106	244	350	66	155	2	25	–	32	246	6.4	1.2	4.5
75-76–Los Angeles	36	–	492	39	90	.433	–	–	–	45	66	.682	51	114	165	20	76	0	11	–	26	123	4.6	0.6	3.4
76-77–Los Angeles	53	–	1342	191	380	.503	–	–	–	132	187	.706	182	310	492	48	183	1	43	–	52	514	9.3	0.9	9.7
77-78–L.A.-Boston	57	–	1617	247	507	.487	–	–	–	170	246	.691	215	399	614	72	188	3	47	107	64	664	10.8	1.3	11.6
78-79–San Diego	82	–	2764	350	623	.562	–	–	–	227	330	.688	296	504	800	125	317	11	85	185	121	927	9.8	1.5	11.3
79-80–Portland	80	–	2657	421	761	.553	0	3	.000	231	360	.642	325	517	842	167	307	8	73	170	131	1073	10.5	2.1	13.4
80-81–Portland	73	–	2120	325	571	.569	0	1	.000	181	288	.628	236	450	686	149	258	5	85	144	86	831	9.4	2.0	11.4
81-82–Portland	20	4	418	38	78	.487	0	0	–	24	41	.585	40	77	117	29	56	0	9	19	16	100	5.9	1.5	5.0
87-88–Golden State	6	1	56	7	14	.500	0	0	–	2	2	1.000	9	10	19	0	13	0	4	4	4	16	3.2	0.0	2.7
Reg. Season Totals	507	5	12815	1778	3382	.526	0	4	.000	1110	1691	.656	1522	2710	4232	695	1630	30	403	629	550	4666	8.3	1.4	9.2
Playoff Totals	9	0	263	30	60	.500	0	2	.000	12	17	.706	35	58	93	14	18	0	10	11	6	72	10.3	1.6	8.0
All-Star Totals	1	0	14	1	6	.167	0	0	–	2	4	.500	4	4	8	1	4	0	0	1	1	4	8.0	1.0	4.0

Washington, Richard Lee b. July 15, 1955 Ht. 6-11 Wt. 220 College: UCLA

SEASON–TEAM	G	GS	MIN	FGM	FGA	PCT	3FGM	3FGA	PCT	FTM	FTA	PCT	O-RB	D-RB	TOT	AST	PF	DQ	STL	TO	BLK	PTS	RPG	APG	PPG
76-77–Kansas City	82	–	2265	446	1034	.431	–	–	–	177	254	.697	201	497	698	85	324	13	63	–	90	1069	8.5	1.0	13.0
77-78–Kansas City	78	–	2231	425	891	.477	–	–	–	150	199	.754	188	466	654	118	324	12	74	191	73	1000	8.4	1.5	12.8
78-79–Kansas City	18	–	161	14	41	.341	–	–	–	10	16	.625	11	37	48	7	31	0	7	15	3	38	2.7	0.4	2.1
79-80–Milwaukee	75	–	1092	197	421	.468	0	0	–	46	76	.605	95	181	276	55	166	2	26	63	48	440	3.7	0.7	5.9
80-81–Dallas-Clev.	80	–	1812	340	747	.455	1	2	.500	119	159	.748	158	295	453	129	283	3	46	129	61	800	5.7	1.6	10.0
81-82–Cleveland	18	2	313	50	115	.435	0	2	.000	9	15	.600	32	43	75	15	51	0	8	35	2	109	4.2	0.8	6.1
Reg. Season Totals	351	2	7874	1472	3249	.453	1	4	.250	511	719	.711	685	1519	2204	409	1179	30	224	433	277	3456	6.3	1.2	9.8
Playoff Totals	11	0	164	36	67	.537	0	0	–	3	6	.500	10	23	33	3	39	1	5	9	9	75	3.0	0.3	6.8

Washington, Robert (Bobby) b. July 11, 1947 Ht. 6-0 Wt. 175 College: Eastern Kentucky

SEASON–TEAM	G	GS	MIN	FGM	FGA	PCT	3FGM	3FGA	PCT	FTM	FTA	PCT	O-RB	D-RB	TOT	AST	PF	DQ	STL	TO	BLK	PTS	RPG	APG	PPG
69-70–Kentucky (A)	2	–	5	0	1	.000	0	0	–	0	0	–	–	–	0	0	0	0	–	–	–	0	0.0	0.0	0.0
70-71–Cleveland	47	–	823	123	310	.397	–	–	–	104	140	.743	–	–	105	190	105	0	–	–	–	350	2.2	4.0	7.4
71-72–Cleveland	69	–	967	123	309	.398	–	–	–	104	128	.813	–	–	129	223	135	1	–	–	–	350	1.9	3.2	5.1
Reg. NBA Totals	116	–	1790	246	619	.397	–	–	–	208	268	.776	–	–	234	413	240	1	–	–	–	700	2.0	3.6	6.0
Reg. ABA Totals	2	–	5	0	1	.000	0	0	–	0	0	–	–	–	0	0	0	0	–	–	–	0	0.0	0.0	0.0

Washington, Stanley (Stan) b. January 23, 1952 Ht. 6-4 Wt. 190 College: San Diego

SEASON–TEAM	G	GS	MIN	FGM	FGA	PCT	3FGM	3FGA	PCT	FTM	FTA	PCT	O-RB	D-RB	TOT	AST	PF	DQ	STL	TO	BLK	PTS	RPG	APG	PPG
74-75–Washington	1	–	4	0	1	.000	–	–	–	0	0	–	0	0	0	0	1	0	0	–	0	0	0.0	0.0	0.0
Reg. Season Totals	1	–	4	0	1	.000	–	–	–	0	0	–	0	0	0	0	1	0	0	–	0	0	0.0	0.0	0.0

Washington, Thomas (Trooper) b. April 21, 1944 Ht. 6-7 Wt. 225 College: Cheyney

SEASON–TEAM	G	GS	MIN	FGM	FGA	PCT	3FGM	3FGA	PCT	FTM	FTA	PCT	O-RB	D-RB	TOT	AST	PF	DQ	STL	TO	BLK	PTS	RPG	APG	PPG
67-68–Pittsburgh (A)	63	–	1844	312	596	.523	2	2	1.000	106	186	.570	303	369	672	102	189	4	–	110	–	732	10.7	1.6	11.6
68-69–Minnesota (A)	69	–	2625	421	839	.502	0	6	.000	190	316	.601	367	501	868	178	239	2	–	190	–	1032	12.6	2.6	15.0
69-70–Pitt.-L.A. (A)	81	–	2353	320	582	.550	4	8	.500	155	240	.646	–	–	822	196	285	8	–	–	–	799	10.1	2.4	9.9
70-71–Floridians (A)	57	–	1876	216	426	.507	0	2	.000	102	167	.611	–	–	606	187	184	–	–	–	–	534	10.6	3.3	9.4
71-72–New York (A)	80	–	2510	387	678	.571	0	0	–	107	166	.645	–	–	750	161	291	–	–	188	–	881	9.4	2.0	11.0
72-73–New York (A)	76	–	2027	229	425	.539	0	0	–	63	101	.624	174	379	553	203	242	5	–	183	–	521	7.3	2.7	6.9
Reg. ABA Totals	426	–	13235	1885	3546	.532	6	18	.333	723	1176	.615	844	1249	4271	1027	1430	19	–	671	–	4499	10.0	2.4	10.6
ABA Playoff Totals	66	–	2015	256	472	.542	0	2	.000	73	139	.525	169	271	748	161	218	5	–	67	–	585	11.3	2.4	8.9

Washington, Wilson Jr. b. August 3, 1955 Ht. 6-10 Wt. 235 College: Old Dominion

SEASON–TEAM	G	GS	MIN	FGM	FGA	PCT	3FGM	3FGA	PCT	FTM	FTA	PCT	O-RB	D-RB	TOT	AST	PF	DQ	STL	TO	BLK	PTS	RPG	APG	PPG
77-78–Phil.-N.J.	38	–	561	100	206	.485	–	–	–	29	53	.547	50	106	156	10	75	2	18	63	37	229	4.1	0.3	6.0
78-79–New Jersey	62	–	1139	218	434	.502	–	–	–	66	104	.635	88	206	294	47	186	5	31	98	67	502	4.7	0.8	8.1
Reg. Season Totals	100	–	1700	318	640	.497	–	–	–	95	157	.605	138	312	450	57	261	7	49	161	104	731	4.5	0.6	7.3

Watson, Jamie Lovell b. February 23, 1972 Ht. 6-7 Wt. 190 College: South Carolina

SEASON–TEAM	G	GS	MIN	FGM	FGA	PCT	3FGM	3FGA	PCT	FTM	FTA	PCT	O-RB	D-RB	TOT	AST	PF	DQ	STL	TO	BLK	PTS	RPG	APG	PPG
94-95–Utah	60	1	673	76	152	.500	5	19	.263	38	56	.679	16	58	74	59	86	0	35	51	11	195	1.2	1.0	3.3
95-96–Utah	16	0	217	18	43	.419	3	7	.429	9	13	.692	5	22	27	24	30	0	8	17	2	48	1.7	1.5	3.0
96-97–Utah-Dallas	23	6	340	31	72	.431	4	12	.333	12	16	.750	18	29	47	33	34	0	22	24	4	78	2.0	1.4	3.4
98-99–Miami	3	0	18	1	2	.500	0	0	–	0	0	–	0	1	1	1	1	0	0	1	0	2	0.3	0.3	0.7
Reg. Season Totals	102	7	1248	126	269	.468	12	38	.316	59	85	.694	39	110	149	117	151	0	65	93	17	323	1.5	1.1	3.2
Playoff Totals	5	0	57	6	9	.667	0	0	–	0	0	–	1	0	1	3	12	0	2	6	1	12	0.2	0.6	2.4

Watson, Robert E. **(Bobby)** b. March 22, 1930 Ht. 6-0 Wt. 160 College: Kentucky

SEASON–TEAM	G	GS	MIN	FGM	FGA	PCT	3FGM	3FGA	PCT	FTM	FTA	PCT	O-RB	D-RB	TOT	AST	PF	DQ	STL	TO	BLK	PTS	RPG	APG	PPG
54-55–Minn.-Milw.	63	–	702	72	223	.323	–	–	–	31	45	.689	–	–	87	79	67	0	–	–	–	175	1.4	1.3	2.8

Watts, Donald Earl **(Slick)** b. July 22, 1951 Ht. 6-1 Wt. 175 College: Xavier (La.)

SEASON–TEAM	G	GS	MIN	FGM	FGA	PCT	3FGM	3FGA	PCT	FTM	FTA	PCT	O-RB	D-RB	TOT	AST	PF	DQ	STL	TO	BLK	PTS	RPG	APG	PPG
73-74–Seattle	62	–	1424	198	510	.388	–	–	–	100	155	.645	72	110	182	351	207	8	115	–	13	496	2.9	5.7	8.0
74-75–Seattle	82	–	2056	232	551	.421	–	–	–	93	153	.608	95	167	262	499	254	7	190	–	12	557	3.2	6.1	6.8
75-76–Seattle	82	–	2776	433	1015	.427	–	–	–	199	344	.578	112	253	365	661	270	3	261	–	16	1065	4.5	8.1	13.0
76-77–Seattle	79	–	2627	428	1015	.422	–	–	–	172	293	.587	81	226	307	630	256	5	214	–	25	1028	3.9	8.0	13.0
77-78–Seattle-N.O.	71	–	1584	219	558	.392	–	–	–	92	156	.590	60	119	179	294	184	1	108	168	31	530	2.5	4.1	7.5
78-79–Houston	61	–	1046	92	227	.405	–	–	–	41	67	.612	35	68	103	243	143	1	73	71	14	225	1.7	4.0	3.7
Reg. Season Totals	437	–	11513	1602	3876	.413	–	–	–	697	1168	.597	455	943	1398	2678	1314	25	961	239	111	3901	3.2	6.1	8.9
Playoff Totals	17	–	522	79	177	.446	–	–	–	27	52	.519	19	39	58	120	66	1	43	7	7	185	3.4	7.1	10.9

Watts, Ronald Michael **(Ron)** b. May 21, 1943 Ht. 6-6 Wt. 210 College: Wake Forest

SEASON–TEAM	G	GS	MIN	FGM	FGA	PCT	3FGM	3FGA	PCT	FTM	FTA	PCT	O-RB	D-RB	TOT	AST	PF	DQ	STL	TO	BLK	PTS	RPG	APG	PPG
65-66–Boston	1	–	3	1	2	.500	–	–	–	0	0	–	–	–	1	1	1	0	–	–	–	2	1.0	1.0	2.0
66-67–Boston	27	–	89	11	44	.250	–	–	–	16	23	.696	–	–	38	1	16	0	–	–	–	38	1.4	0.0	1.4
Reg. Season Totals	28	–	92	12	46	.261	–	–	–	16	23	.696	–	–	39	2	17	0	–	–	–	40	1.4	0.1	1.4
Playoff Totals	1	–	5	1	6	.167	–	–	–	1	2	.500	–	–	2	–	3	0	–	–	–	3	2.0	0.0	3.0

Watts, Samuel D. **(Sam)** b. March 14, 1948 Ht. 6-3 Wt. 185 College: Northwest (Wyo.) Coll. (J.C.); Great Falls; Florida A&M

SEASON–TEAM	G	GS	MIN	FGM	FGA	PCT	3FGM	3FGA	PCT	FTM	FTA	PCT	O-RB	D-RB	TOT	AST	PF	DQ	STL	TO	BLK	PTS	RPG	APG	PPG
70-71–Pittsburgh (A)	54	–	650	109	287	.380	14	41	.341	49	67	.731	–	–	99	45	106	–	–	–	–	281	1.8	0.8	5.2
Reg. ABA Totals	54	–	650	109	287	.380	14	41	.341	49	67	.731	–	–	99	45	106	–	–	–	–	281	1.8	0.8	5.2

Weatherspoon, Clarence **(Spoon, Baby Barkley)** b. September 8, 1970 Ht. 6-7 Wt. 240 College: Southern Mississippi

SEASON–TEAM	G	GS	MIN	FGM	FGA	PCT	3FGM	3FGA	PCT	FTM	FTA	PCT	O-RB	D-RB	TOT	AST	PF	DQ	STL	TO	BLK	PTS	RPG	APG	PPG
92-93–Philadelphia	82	82	2654	494	1053	.469	1	4	.250	291	408	.713	179	410	589	147	188	1	85	176	67	1280	7.2	1.8	15.6
93-94–Philadelphia	82	82	3147	602	1246	.483	4	17	.235	298	430	.693	254	578	832	192	152	0	100	195	116	1506	10.1	2.3	18.4
94-95–Philadelphia	76	76	2991	543	1238	.439	4	21	.190	283	377	.751	144	382	526	215	195	1	115	191	67	1373	6.9	2.8	18.1
95-96–Philadelphia	78	75	3096	491	1015	.484	0	2	.000	318	426	.746	237	516	753	158	214	3	112	179	108	1300	9.7	2.0	16.7
96-97–Philadelphia	82	82	2949	398	811	.491	1	6	.167	206	279	.738	219	460	679	140	187	0	74	137	86	1003	8.3	1.7	12.2
97-98–Phil.-G.S.	79	49	2325	268	608	.441	0	0	–	200	277	.722	198	396	594	89	194	2	85	119	74	736	7.5	1.1	9.3
98-99–Miami	49	3	1040	141	264	.534	0	0	–	115	143	.804	72	171	243	34	107	0	28	61	17	397	5.0	0.7	8.1
99-00–Miami	78	2	1615	215	419	.513	0	0	–	135	183	.738	128	321	449	93	165	1	51	100	49	565	5.8	1.2	7.2
Reg. Season Totals	606	451	19817	3152	6654	.474	10	50	.200	1846	2523	.732	1431	3234	4665	1068	1402	8	650	1158	584	8160	7.7	1.8	13.5
Playoff Totals	15	0	282	34	86	.395	0	0	–	25	41	.610	22	40	62	3	31	0	11	11	4	93	4.1	0.2	6.2

Weatherspoon, Nick Levoter **(Spoon)** b. July 20, 1950 Ht. 6-7 Wt. 195 College: Illinois

SEASON–TEAM	G	GS	MIN	FGM	FGA	PCT	3FGM	3FGA	PCT	FTM	FTA	PCT	O-RB	D-RB	TOT	AST	PF	DQ	STL	TO	BLK	PTS	RPG	APG	PPG
73-74–Capital	65	–	1216	199	483	.412	–	–	–	96	139	.691	133	264	397	38	179	1	48	–	16	494	6.1	0.6	7.6
74-75–Washington	82	–	1347	256	562	.456	–	–	–	103	138	.746	132	214	346	51	212	2	65	–	21	615	4.2	0.6	7.5
75-76–Washington	64	–	1083	218	458	.476	–	–	–	96	137	.701	85	189	274	55	172	2	46	–	16	532	4.3	0.9	8.3
76-77–Wash.-Seattle	62	–	1657	310	690	.449	–	–	–	91	144	.632	120	308	428	53	168	1	52	–	28	711	6.9	0.9	11.5
77-78–Chicago	41	–	611	86	194	.443	–	–	–	37	42	.881	57	68	125	32	74	0	19	49	10	209	3.0	0.8	5.1
78-79–San Diego	82	–	2642	479	998	.480	–	–	–	176	238	.739	179	275	454	135	287	6	80	184	37	1134	5.5	1.6	13.8
79-80–San Diego	57	–	1124	164	378	.434	0	0	–	63	91	.692	83	125	208	54	136	1	34	86	17	391	3.6	0.9	6.9
Reg. Season Totals	453	–	9680	1712	3763	.455	0	0	–	662	929	.713	789	1443	2232	418	1228	13	344	319	145	4086	4.9	0.9	9.0
Playoff Totals	31	–	715	115	235	.489	0	0	–	51	73	.699	46	104	150	26	95	1	18	–	8	281	4.8	0.8	9.1

Webb, Anthony Jerome **(Spud)** b. July 13, 1963 Ht. 5-7 Wt. 133 College: Midland (Texas) Coll. (J.C.); North Carolina State

SEASON–TEAM	G	GS	MIN	FGM	FGA	PCT	3FGM	3FGA	PCT	FTM	FTA	PCT	O-RB	D-RB	TOT	AST	PF	DQ	STL	TO	BLK	PTS	RPG	APG	PPG
85-86–Atlanta	79	8	1229	199	412	.483	2	11	.182	216	275	.785	27	96	123	337	164	1	82	159	5	616	1.6	4.3	7.8
86-87–Atlanta	33	0	532	71	162	.438	1	6	.167	80	105	.762	6	54	60	167	65	1	34	70	2	223	1.8	5.1	6.8
87-88–Atlanta	82	1	1347	191	402	.475	1	19	.053	107	131	.817	16	130	146	337	125	0	63	131	11	490	1.8	4.1	6.0
88-89–Atlanta	81	6	1219	133	290	.459	1	22	.045	52	60	.867	21	102	123	284	104	0	70	83	6	319	1.5	3.5	3.9
89-90–Atlanta	82	46	2184	294	616	.477	1	19	.053	162	186	.871	38	163	201	477	185	0	105	141	12	751	2.5	5.8	9.2
90-91–Atlanta	75	64	2197	359	803	.447	54	168	.321	231	266	.868	41	133	174	417	180	0	118	146	6	1003	2.3	5.6	13.4
91-92–Sacramento	77	77	2724	448	1006	.445	73	199	.367	262	305	.859	30	193	223	547	193	1	125	229	24	1231	2.9	7.1	16.0
92-93–Sacramento	69	68	2335	342	789	.433	37	135	.274	279	328	.851	44	149	193	481	177	0	104	194	6	1000	2.8	7.0	14.5
93-94–Sacramento	79	62	2567	373	810	.460	55	164	.335	204	251	.813	44	178	222	528	182	1	93	168	23	1005	2.8	6.7	12.7
94-95–Sacramento	76	76	2458	302	689	.438	48	145	.331	226	242	.934	29	145	174	468	148	0	75	185	8	878	2.3	6.2	11.6
95-96–Atlanta-Minn.	77	21	1462	186	430	.433	47	129	.364	125	145	.862	26	74	100	294	109	0	52	110	7	544	1.3	3.8	7.1
97-98–Orlando	4	0	34	5	12	.417	0	1	.000	2	2	1.000	2	1	3	5	6	0	1	7	0	12	0.8	1.3	3.0
Reg. Season Totals	814	429	20288	2903	6421	.452	320	1018	.314	1946	2296	.848	324	1418	1742	4342	1638	4	922	1623	110	8072	2.1	5.3	9.9
Playoff Totals	39	6	725	114	249	.458	7	23	.304	86	105	.819	19	66	85	198	64	0	30	51	2	321	2.2	5.1	8.2

Webb, Jeffrey William **(Jeff)** b. July 6, 1948 Ht. 6-4 Wt. 170 College: Kansas State

SEASON–TEAM	G	GS	MIN	FGM	FGA	PCT	3FGM	3FGA	PCT	FTM	FTA	PCT	O-RB	D-RB	TOT	AST	PF	DQ	STL	TO	BLK	PTS	RPG	APG	PPG
70-71–Milwaukee	29	–	300	27	78	.346	–	–	–	11	15	.733	–	–	24	19	33	0	–	–	–	65	0.8	0.7	2.2
71-72–Milw.-Phoenix	46	–	238	40	100	.400	–	–	–	16	23	.696	–	–	35	23	29	0	–	–	–	96	0.8	0.5	2.1
Reg. Season Totals	75	–	538	67	178	.376	–	–	–	27	38	.711	–	–	59	42	62	0	–	–	–	161	0.8	0.6	2.1
Playoff Totals	9	–	23	4	7	.571	–	–	–	3	3	1.000	–	–	1	2	2	0	–	–	–	11	0.1	0.2	1.2

Webb, Marcus L. b. May 9, 1970 Ht. 6-9 Wt. 255 College: Alabama

SEASON–TEAM	G	GS	MIN	FGM	FGA	PCT	3FGM	3FGA	PCT	FTM	FTA	PCT	O-RB	D-RB	TOT	AST	PF	DQ	STL	TO	BLK	PTS	RPG	APG	PPG
92-93–Boston	9	0	51	13	25	.520	0	1	.000	13	21	.619	5	5	10	2	11	0	1	5	2	39	1.1	0.2	4.3
Reg. Season Totals	9	0	51	13	25	.520	0	1	.000	13	21	.619	5	5	10	2	11	0	1	5	2	39	1.1	0.2	4.3

Webber, Mayce Edward Christopher III **(Chris)** b. March 1, 1973 Ht. 6-10 Wt. 245 College: Michigan

SEASON–TEAM	G	GS	MIN	FGM	FGA	PCT	3FGM	3FGA	PCT	FTM	FTA	PCT	O-RB	D-RB	TOT	AST	PF	DQ	STL	TO	BLK	PTS	RPG	APG	PPG
93-94–Golden State	76	76	2438	572	1037	.552	0	14	.000	189	355	.532	305	389	694	272	247	4	93	206	164	1333	9.1	3.6	17.5
94-95–Washington	54	52	2067	464	938	.495	40	145	.276	117	233	.502	200	318	518	256	186	2	83	167	85	1085	9.6	4.7	20.1
95-96–Washington	15	15	558	150	276	.543	15	34	.441	41	69	.594	37	77	114	75	51	1	27	49	9	356	7.6	5.0	23.7
96-97–Washington	72	72	2806	604	1167	.518	60	151	.397	177	313	.565	238	505	743	331	258	6	122	230	137	1445	10.3	4.6	20.1
97-98–Washington	71	71	2809	647	1341	.482	65	205	.317	196	333	.589	176	498	674	273	269	4	111	185	124	1555	9.5	3.8	21.9
98-99–Sacramento	42	42	1719	378	778	.486	4	34	.118	79	174	.454	149	396	545	173	145	1	60	148	89	839	13.0	4.1	20.0
99-00–Sacramento	75	75	2880	748	1548	.483	27	95	.284	311	414	.751	189	598	787	345	264	7	120	218	128	1834	10.5	4.6	24.5
Reg. Season Totals	405	403	15277	3563	7085	.503	211	678	.311	1110	1891	.587	1294	2781	4075	1725	1420	25	616	1203	736	8447	10.1	4.3	20.9
Playoff Totals	16	16	603	119	260	.458	8	25	.320	44	77	.571	47	98	145	84	63	5	22	53	31	290	9.1	5.3	18.1
All-Star Totals	2	0	27	4	14	.286	0	0	–	0	0	–	4	8	12	6	5	0	2	5	0	8	6.0	3.0	4.0

Weber, Forest John **(Jake)** b. March 18, 1918 Ht. 6-6 Wt. 225 College: Purdue

SEASON–TEAM	G	GS	MIN	FGM	FGA	PCT	3FGM	3FGA	PCT	FTM	FTA	PCT	O-RB	D-RB	TOT	AST	PF	DQ	STL	TO	BLK	PTS	RPG	APG	PPG
45-46–Indianapolis (N)	5	–	–	7	–	–	–	–	–	4	–	–	–	–	–	–	–	–	–	–	–	18	–	–	3.6
46-47–N.Y.-Prov.	50	–	–	59	202	.292	–	–	–	55	79	.696	–	–	–	4	111	–	–	–	–	173	–	0.1	3.5
Reg. NBA Totals	50	–	–	59	202	.292	–	–	–	55	79	.696	–	–	–	4	111	–	–	–	–	173	–	0.1	3.5
Reg. NBL Totals	5	–	–	7	–	–	–	–	–	4	0	–	–	–	–	–	–	–	–	–	–	18	–	–	3.6

Webster, Elnardo b. March 6, 1948 Ht. 6-5 Wt. 200 College: Wharton Co. (Texas) J.C.; St. Peter's

SEASON–TEAM	G	GS	MIN	FGM	FGA	PCT	3FGM	3FGA	PCT	FTM	FTA	PCT	O-RB	D-RB	TOT	AST	PF	DQ	STL	TO	BLK	PTS	RPG	APG	PPG
71-72–N.Y.-Mem. (A)	19	–	237	50	109	.459	1	4	.250	21	29	.724	–	–	44	16	39	–	–	35	–	122	2.3	0.8	6.4
Reg. ABA Totals	19	–	237	50	109	.459	1	4	.250	21	29	.724	–	–	44	16	39	–	–	35	–	122	2.3	0.8	6.4

Webster, Jeffrey Tyrone **(Jeff)** b. February 19, 1971 Ht. 6-8 Wt. 232 College: Oklahoma

SEASON–TEAM	G	GS	MIN	FGM	FGA	PCT	3FGM	3FGA	PCT	FTM	FTA	PCT	O-RB	D-RB	TOT	AST	PF	DQ	STL	TO	BLK	PTS	RPG	APG	PPG
95-96–Washington	11	0	58	8	23	.348	2	6	.333	0	0	–	2	5	7	3	7	0	4	3	0	18	0.6	0.3	1.6
Reg. Season Totals	11	0	58	8	23	.348	2	6	.333	0	0	–	2	5	7	3	7	0	4	3	0	18	0.6	0.3	1.6

Webster, Marvin Nathaniel **(The Human Eraser)** b. April 13, 1952 Ht. 7-1 Wt. 235 College: Morgan State

SEASON–TEAM	G	GS	MIN	FGM	FGA	PCT	3FGM	3FGA	PCT	FTM	FTA	PCT	O-RB	D-RB	TOT	AST	PF	DQ	STL	TO	BLK	PTS	RPG	APG	PPG
75-76–Denver (A)	38	–	398	55	120	.458	0	1	.000	55	78	.705	63	111	174	30	60	–	9	38	52	165	4.6	0.8	4.3
76-77–Denver	80	–	1276	198	400	.495	–	–	–	143	220	.650	152	332	484	62	149	2	23	–	118	539	6.1	0.8	6.7
77-78–Seattle	82	–	2910	427	851	.502	–	–	–	290	461	.629	361	674	1035	203	262	8	48	257	162	1144	12.6	2.5	14.0
78-79–New York	60	–	2027	264	558	.473	–	–	–	150	262	.573	198	457	655	172	183	6	24	170	112	678	10.9	2.9	11.3
79-80–New York	20	–	298	38	79	.481	0	0	–	12	16	.750	28	52	80	9	39	1	3	20	11	88	4.0	0.5	4.4
80-81–New York	82	–	1708	159	341	.466	1	4	.250	104	163	.638	162	303	465	72	187	2	27	103	97	423	5.7	0.9	5.2
81-82–New York	82	32	1883	199	405	.491	0	0	–	108	170	.635	184	306	490	99	211	2	22	90	90	506	6.0	1.2	6.2
82-83–New York	82	0	1472	168	331	.508	0	1	.000	106	180	.589	176	267	443	49	210	3	35	102	131	442	5.4	0.6	5.4
83-84–New York	76	5	1290	112	239	.469	0	0	–	66	117	.564	146	220	366	53	187	2	34	85	100	290	4.8	0.7	3.8
86-87–Milwaukee	15	0	102	10	19	.526	1	1	1.000	6	8	.750	12	14	26	3	17	0	3	8	7	27	1.7	0.2	1.8
Reg. NBA Totals	579	37	12966	1575	3223	.489	2	6	.333	985	1597	.617	1419	2625	4044	722	1445	26	219	835	828	4137	7.0	1.2	7.1
Reg. ABA Totals	38	–	398	55	120	.458	0	1	.000	55	78	.705	63	111	174	30	60	–	9	38	52	165	4.6	0.8	4.3
NBA Playoff Totals	48	0	1382	177	365	.485	0	0	–	108	167	.647	150	273	423	68	144	2	12	83	94	462	8.8	1.4	9.6
ABA Playoff Totals	13	–	155	21	50	.420	0	0	–	15	28	.536	24	47	71	9	28	–	1	15	14	57	5.5	0.7	4.4

Wedman, Scott Dean b. July 29, 1952 Ht. 6-7 Wt. 215 College: Colorado

SEASON–TEAM	G	GS	MIN	FGM	FGA	PCT	3FGM	3FGA	PCT	FTM	FTA	PCT	O-RB	D-RB	TOT	AST	PF	DQ	STL	TO	BLK	PTS	RPG	APG	PPG
74-75–K.C.-Omaha	80	–	2554	375	806	.465	–	–	–	139	170	.818	202	288	490	129	270	2	81	–	27	889	6.1	1.6	11.1
75-76–Kansas City	82	–	2968	538	1181	.456	–	–	–	191	245	.780	199	407	606	199	280	8	103	–	36	1267	7.4	2.4	15.5
76-77–Kansas City	81	–	2743	521	1133	.460	–	–	–	206	241	.855	187	319	506	227	226	3	100	–	23	1248	6.2	2.8	15.4
77-78–Kansas City	81	–	2961	607	1192	.509	–	–	–	221	254	.870	144	319	463	201	242	2	99	158	22	1435	5.7	2.5	17.7
78-79–Kansas City	73	–	2498	561	1050	.534	–	–	–	216	271	.797	135	251	386	144	239	4	76	106	30	1338	5.3	2.0	18.3
79-80–Kansas City	68	–	2347	569	1112	.512	7	22	.318	145	181	.801	114	272	386	145	230	1	84	112	45	1290	5.7	2.1	19.0
80-81–Kansas City	81	–	2902	685	1437	.477	25	77	.325	140	204	.686	128	305	433	226	294	4	97	161	46	1535	5.3	2.8	19.0
81-82–Cleveland	54	39	1638	260	589	.441	5	23	.217	66	90	.733	128	176	304	133	189	4	73	73	14	591	5.6	2.5	10.9
82-83–Clev.-Boston	75	35	1793	374	788	.475	10	32	.313	85	107	.794	98	184	282	117	228	6	43	126	17	843	3.8	1.6	11.2
83-84–Boston	68	5	916	148	333	.444	2	13	.154	29	35	.829	41	98	139	67	107	0	27	43	7	327	2.0	1.0	4.8
84-85–Boston	78	5	1127	220	460	.478	17	34	.500	42	55	.764	57	102	159	94	111	0	23	47	10	499	2.0	1.2	6.4
85-86–Boston	79	19	1402	286	605	.473	17	48	.354	45	68	.662	66	126	192	83	127	0	38	54	22	634	2.4	1.1	8.0
86-87–Boston	6	2	78	9	27	.333	1	2	.500	1	2	.500	3	6	9	6	6	0	2	3	2	20	1.5	1.0	3.3
Reg. Season Totals	906	105	25927	5153	10713	.481	84	251	.335	1526	1923	.794	1502	2853	4355	1771	2549	34	846	883	301	11916	4.8	2.0	13.2
Playoff Totals	85	2	1961	368	812	.453	27	70	.386	119	171	.696	105	217	322	150	189	1	63	90	20	882	3.8	1.8	10.4
All-Star Totals	1	0	20	4	5	.800	0	0	–	0	0	–	0	6	6	2	2	0	1	–	0	8	6.0	2.0	8.0

Wehr, Richard Wade (Dick) b. December 9, 1925 Ht. 6-4 Wt. 180 College: Rice; Indiana

SEASON–TEAM	G	GS	MIN	FGM	FGA	PCT	3FGM	3FGA	PCT	FTM	FTA	PCT	O-RB	D-RB	TOT	AST	PF	DQ	STL	TO	BLK	PTS	RPG	APG	PPG
48-49–Indianapolis	9	–	–	5	21	.238	–	–	–	2	6	.333	–	–	–	3	12	–	–	–	–	12	–	0.3	1.3
Reg. Season Totals	9	–	–	5	21	.238	–	–	–	2	6	.333	–	–	–	3	12	–	–	–	–	12	–	0.3	1.3

Weidner, Brant Clifford b. October 28, 1960 Ht. 6-10 Wt. 230 College: William & Mary

SEASON–TEAM	G	GS	MIN	FGM	FGA	PCT	3FGM	3FGA	PCT	FTM	FTA	PCT	O-RB	D-RB	TOT	AST	PF	DQ	STL	TO	BLK	PTS	RPG	APG	PPG
83-84–San Antonio	8	0	38	2	9	.222	0	0	–	4	4	1.000	4	7	11	0	5	0	0	2	2	8	1.4	0.0	1.0
Reg. Season Totals	8	0	38	2	9	.222	0	0	–	4	4	1.000	4	7	11	0	5	0	0	2	2	8	1.4	0.0	1.0

Weiss, Robert William (Bob) b. May 7, 1942 Ht. 6-3 Wt. 180 College: Penn State

SEASON–TEAM	G	GS	MIN	FGM	FGA	PCT	3FGM	3FGA	PCT	FTM	FTA	PCT	O-RB	D-RB	TOT	AST	PF	DQ	STL	TO	BLK	PTS	RPG	APG	PPG
65-66–Philadelphia	7	–	30	3	9	.333	–	–	–	0	0	–	–	–	7	4	10	0	–	–	–	6	1.0	0.6	0.9
66-67–Philadelphia	6	–	29	5	10	.500	–	–	–	2	5	.400	–	–	3	10	8	0	–	–	–	12	0.5	1.7	2.0
67-68–Seattle	82	–	1614	295	686	.430	–	–	–	213	254	.839	–	–	150	342	137	0	–	–	–	803	1.8	4.2	9.8
68-69–Milw.-Chicago	77	–	1478	189	499	.379	–	–	–	128	160	.800	–	–	162	199	174	1	–	–	–	506	2.1	2.6	6.6
69-70–Chicago	82	–	2544	365	855	.427	–	–	–	213	253	.842	–	–	227	474	206	0	–	–	–	943	2.8	5.8	11.5
70-71–Chicago	82	–	2237	278	659	.422	–	–	–	226	269	.840	–	–	189	387	216	1	–	–	–	782	2.3	4.7	9.5
71-72–Chicago	82	–	2450	358	832	.430	–	–	–	212	254	.835	–	–	170	377	212	1	–	–	–	928	2.1	4.6	11.3
72-73–Chicago	82	–	2086	279	655	.426	–	–	–	159	189	.841	–	–	148	295	151	1	–	–	–	717	1.8	3.6	8.7
73-74–Chicago	79	–	1708	263	564	.466	–	–	–	142	170	.835	32	71	103	303	156	0	104	–	12	668	1.3	3.8	8.5
74-75–Buffalo	76	–	1338	102	261	.391	–	–	–	54	67	.806	21	83	104	260	146	0	82	–	19	258	1.4	3.4	3.4
75-76–Buffalo	66	–	995	89	183	.486	–	–	–	35	48	.729	13	53	66	150	94	0	48	–	14	213	1.0	2.3	3.2
76-77–Washington	62	–	768	62	133	.466	–	–	–	29	37	.784	15	54	69	130	66	0	53	–	7	153	1.1	2.1	2.5
Reg. Season Totals	783	–	17277	2288	5346	.428	–	–	–	1413	1706	.828	81	261	1398	2931	1576	4	287	–	52	5989	1.8	3.7	7.6
Playoff Totals	53	–	1103	167	392	.426	–	–	–	73	91	.802	8	26	89	164	111	1	14	–	2	407	1.7	3.1	7.7

Weitzman, Richard L. (Rick) b. April 30, 1946 Ht. 6-2 Wt. 185 College: Northeastern

SEASON–TEAM	G	GS	MIN	FGM	FGA	PCT	3FGM	3FGA	PCT	FTM	FTA	PCT	O-RB	D-RB	TOT	AST	PF	DQ	STL	TO	BLK	PTS	RPG	APG	PPG
67-68–Boston	25	–	75	12	46	.261	–	–	–	9	13	.692	–	–	10	8	8	0	–	–	–	33	0.4	0.3	1.3
Reg. Season Totals	25	–	75	12	46	.261	–	–	–	9	13	.692	–	–	10	8	8	0	–	–	–	33	0.4	0.3	1.3
Playoff Totals	3	–	5	2	3	.667	–	–	–	0	0	–	–	–	1	1	0	0	–	–	–	4	0.3	0.3	1.3

Wells, Charles Richard (Bubba) b. July 26, 1974 Ht. 6-5 Wt. 230 College: Austin Peay State

SEASON–TEAM	G	GS	MIN	FGM	FGA	PCT	3FGM	3FGA	PCT	FTM	FTA	PCT	O-RB	D-RB	TOT	AST	PF	DQ	STL	TO	BLK	PTS	RPG	APG	PPG
97-98–Dallas	39	2	395	48	116	.414	1	6	.167	31	43	.721	22	46	68	34	40	1	15	31	4	128	1.7	0.9	3.3
Reg. Season Totals	39	2	395	48	116	.414	1	6	.167	31	43	.721	22	46	68	34	40	1	15	31	4	128	1.7	0.9	3.3

Wells, Gawen Deangelo (Bonzi) b. September 20, 1976 Ht. 6-5 Wt. 210 College: Ball State

SEASON–TEAM	G	GS	MIN	FGM	FGA	PCT	3FGM	3FGA	PCT	FTM	FTA	PCT	O-RB	D-RB	TOT	AST	PF	DQ	STL	TO	BLK	PTS	RPG	APG	PPG
98-99–Portland	7	0	35	11	20	.550	1	3	.333	8	18	.444	4	5	9	3	5	0	1	6	1	31	1.3	0.4	4.4
99-00–Portland	66	0	1162	236	480	.492	20	53	.377	88	129	.682	78	104	182	97	153	3	69	97	12	580	2.8	1.5	8.8
Reg. Season Totals	73	0	1197	247	500	.494	21	56	.375	96	147	.653	82	109	191	100	158	3	70	103	13	611	2.6	1.4	8.4
Playoff Totals	14	0	188	37	83	.446	2	10	.200	29	41	.707	12	23	35	13	33	0	7	16	0	105	2.5	0.9	7.5

Wells, Owen b. December 9, 1950 Ht. 6-7 Wt. 200 College: Detroit Mercy

SEASON–TEAM	G	GS	MIN	FGM	FGA	PCT	3FGM	3FGA	PCT	FTM	FTA	PCT	O-RB	D-RB	TOT	AST	PF	DQ	STL	TO	BLK	PTS	RPG	APG	PPG
74-75–Houston	33	–	214	42	100	.420	–	–	–	15	22	.682	12	23	35	22	38	0	9	–	3	99	1.1	0.7	3.0
Reg. Season Totals	33	–	214	42	100	.420	–	–	–	15	22	.682	12	23	35	22	38	0	9	–	3	99	1.1	0.7	3.0
Playoff Totals	4	–	5	3	5	.600	–	–	–	0	0	–	0	1	1	1	1	0	0	–	0	6	0.3	0.3	1.5

Wells, Ralph E. b. September 3, 1940 d. August 2, 1968 Ht. 6-1 Wt. 180 College: Northwestern

SEASON–TEAM	G	GS	MIN	FGM	FGA	PCT	3FGM	3FGA	PCT	FTM	FTA	PCT	O-RB	D-RB	TOT	AST	PF	DQ	STL	TO	BLK	PTS	RPG	APG	PPG
62-63–Chicago	3	–	48	1	7	.143	–	–	–	0	7	.000	–	–	6	7	6	0	–	–	–	2	2.0	2.3	0.7
Reg. Season Totals	3	–	48	1	7	.143	–	–	–	0	7	.000	–	–	6	7	6	0	–	–	–	2	2.0	2.3	0.7

Welp, Christian Ansgar (Chris) b. January 2, 1964 Ht. 7-0 Wt. 245 College: Washington

SEASON–TEAM	G	GS	MIN	FGM	FGA	PCT	3FGM	3FGA	PCT	FTM	FTA	PCT	O-RB	D-RB	TOT	AST	PF	DQ	STL	TO	BLK	PTS	RPG	APG	PPG
87-88–Philadelphia	10	0	132	18	31	.581	0	0	–	12	18	.667	11	13	24	5	25	0	5	9	5	48	2.4	0.5	4.8
88-89–Philadelphia	72	0	843	99	222	.446	0	1	.000	48	73	.658	59	134	193	29	176	0	23	42	41	246	2.7	0.4	3.4
89-90–S.A.-G.S.	27	3	198	23	61	.377	0	0	–	19	25	.760	18	30	48	9	58	0	6	15	8	65	1.8	0.3	2.4
Reg. Season Totals	109	3	1173	140	314	.446	0	1	.000	79	116	.681	88	177	265	43	259	0	34	66	54	359	2.4	0.4	3.3
Playoff Totals	3	0	22	1	3	.333	0	0	–	0	2	.000	0	7	7	–	7	0	0	1	0	2	2.3	0.0	0.7

Wennington, William Percey (Bill) b. April 26, 1963 Ht. 7-0 Wt. 270 College: St. John's (N.Y.)

SEASON–TEAM	G	GS	MIN	FGM	FGA	PCT	3FGM	3FGA	PCT	FTM	FTA	PCT	O-RB	D-RB	TOT	AST	PF	DQ	STL	TO	BLK	PTS	RPG	APG	PPG
85-86–Dallas	56	3	562	72	153	.471	0	4	.000	45	62	.726	32	100	132	21	83	0	11	21	22	189	2.4	0.4	3.4
86-87–Dallas	58	0	560	56	132	.424	0	2	.000	45	60	.750	53	76	129	24	95	0	13	39	10	157	2.2	0.4	2.7
87-88–Dallas	30	0	125	25	49	.510	1	2	.500	12	19	.632	14	25	39	4	33	0	5	9	9	63	1.3	0.1	2.1
88-89–Dallas	65	9	1074	119	275	.433	1	9	.111	61	82	.744	82	204	286	46	211	3	16	54	35	300	4.4	0.7	4.6
89-90–Dallas	60	2	814	105	234	.449	0	4	.000	60	75	.800	64	134	198	41	144	2	20	50	21	270	3.3	0.7	4.5
90-91–Sacramento	77	23	1455	181	415	.436	1	5	.200	74	94	.787	101	239	340	69	230	4	46	51	59	437	4.4	0.9	5.7
93-94–Chicago	76	0	1371	235	482	.488	0	2	.000	72	88	.818	117	236	353	70	214	4	43	75	29	542	4.6	0.9	7.1
94-95–Chicago	73	1	956	156	317	.492	0	4	.000	51	63	.810	64	126	190	40	198	5	22	39	17	363	2.6	0.5	5.0
95-96–Chicago	71	20	1065	169	343	.493	1	1	1.000	37	43	.860	58	116	174	46	171	1	21	37	16	376	2.5	0.6	5.3
96-97–Chicago	61	19	783	118	237	.498	0	2	.000	44	53	.830	46	83	129	41	132	1	10	31	11	280	2.1	0.7	4.6
97-98–Chicago	48	8	467	75	172	.436	0	0	–	17	21	.810	32	48	80	19	77	1	4	16	5	167	1.7	0.4	3.5
98-99–Chicago	38	3	451	62	178	.348	1	1	1.000	18	22	.818	20	59	79	18	79	1	13	17	12	143	2.1	0.5	3.8
99-00–Sacramento	7	0	57	6	19	.316	0	0	–	2	2	1.000	5	14	19	1	13	0	2	1	2	14	2.7	0.1	2.0
Reg. Season Totals	720	88	9740	1379	3006	.459	5	36	.139	538	684	.787	688	1460	2148	440	1680	22	226	440	248	3301	3.0	0.6	4.6
Playoff Totals	70	0	572	79	172	.459	1	2	.500	19	28	.679	41	60	101	25	122	1	14	28	11	178	1.4	0.4	2.5

Wenstrom, Matthew William (Matt) b. November 4, 1970 Ht. 7-1 Wt. 250 College: North Carolina

SEASON–TEAM	G	GS	MIN	FGM	FGA	PCT	3FGM	3FGA	PCT	FTM	FTA	PCT	O-RB	D-RB	TOT	AST	PF	DQ	STL	TO	BLK	PTS	RPG	APG	PPG
93-94–Boston	11	0	37	6	10	.600	0	0	–	6	10	.600	6	6	12	0	7	0	0	4	2	18	1.1	0.0	1.6
Reg. Season Totals	11	0	37	6	10	.600	0	0	–	6	10	.600	6	6	12	0	7	0	0	4	2	18	1.1	0.0	1.6

Werdann, Robert b. September 12, 1970 Ht. 6-11 Wt. 260 College: St. John's (N.Y.)

SEASON–TEAM	G	GS	MIN	FGM	FGA	PCT	3FGM	3FGA	PCT	FTM	FTA	PCT	O-RB	D-RB	TOT	AST	PF	DQ	STL	TO	BLK	PTS	RPG	APG	PPG
92-93–Denver	28	0	149	18	59	.305	0	1	.000	17	31	.548	23	29	52	7	38	1	6	12	4	53	1.9	0.3	1.9
95-96–New Jersey	13	0	93	16	32	.500	0	0	–	7	13	.538	5	18	23	2	17	0	5	6	3	39	1.8	0.2	3.0
96-97–New Jersey	6	0	31	3	7	.429	0	0	–	3	3	1.000	3	3	6	0	10	0	2	2	1	9	1.0	0.0	1.5
Reg. Season Totals	47	0	273	37	98	.378	0	1	.000	27	47	.574	31	50	81	9	65	1	13	20	8	101	1.7	0.2	2.1

Wertis, Raymond A. (Ray) b. January 1, 1922 Ht. 5-11 Wt. 175 College: St. John's (N.Y.)

SEASON–TEAM	G	GS	MIN	FGM	FGA	PCT	3FGM	3FGA	PCT	FTM	FTA	PCT	O-RB	D-RB	TOT	AST	PF	DQ	STL	TO	BLK	PTS	RPG	APG	PPG
46-47–Toronto-Clev.	61	–	–	79	366	.216	–	–	–	56	91	.615	–	–	–	39	82	–	–	–	–	214	–	0.6	3.5
47-48–Providence	7	–	–	13	72	.181	–	–	–	6	14	.429	–	–	–	6	13	–	–	–	–	32	–	0.9	4.6
Reg. Season Totals	68	–	–	92	438	.210	–	–	–	62	105	.590	–	–	–	45	95	–	–	–	–	246	–	0.7	3.6
Playoff Totals	3	–	–	6	26	.231	–	–	–	4	5	.800	–	–	–	6	6	–	–	–	–	16	–	2.0	5.3

Wesley, David Barakau b. November 14, 1970 Ht. 6-1 Wt. 202 College: Temple (Texas) Coll. (J.C.); Baylor

SEASON–TEAM	G	GS	MIN	FGM	FGA	PCT	3FGM	3FGA	PCT	FTM	FTA	PCT	O-RB	D-RB	TOT	AST	PF	DQ	STL	TO	BLK	PTS	RPG	APG	PPG
93-94–New Jersey	60	0	542	64	174	.368	11	47	.234	44	53	.830	10	34	44	123	47	0	38	52	4	183	0.7	2.1	3.1
94-95–Boston	51	36	1380	128	313	.409	51	119	.429	71	94	.755	31	86	117	266	144	0	82	87	9	378	2.3	5.2	7.4
95-96–Boston	82	53	2104	338	736	.459	116	272	.426	217	288	.753	68	196	264	390	207	0	100	159	11	1009	3.2	4.8	12.3
96-97–Boston	74	73	2991	456	974	.468	103	286	.360	225	288	.781	67	197	264	537	221	1	162	211	13	1240	3.6	7.3	16.8
97-98–Charlotte	81	81	2845	383	864	.443	59	170	.347	229	288	.795	49	164	213	529	229	3	140	226	30	1054	2.6	6.5	13.0
98-99–Charlotte	50	50	1848	243	545	.446	61	170	.359	159	191	.832	23	138	161	322	130	2	100	142	10	706	3.2	6.4	14.1
99-00–Charlotte	82	82	2760	407	955	.426	88	248	.355	214	275	.778	39	186	225	463	186	2	109	159	11	1116	2.7	5.6	13.6
Reg. Season Totals	480	375	14470	2019	4561	.443	489	1312	.373	1159	1477	.785	287	1001	1288	2630	1164	8	731	1036	88	5686	2.7	5.5	11.8
Playoff Totals	16	13	455	52	138	.377	13	35	.371	26	32	.813	8	22	30	82	42	0	17	29	0	143	1.9	5.1	8.9

Wesley, Walter (Walt) b. January 25, 1945 Ht. 6-11 Wt. 230 College: Kansas

SEASON–TEAM	G	GS	MIN	FGM	FGA	PCT	3FGM	3FGA	PCT	FTM	FTA	PCT	O-RB	D-RB	TOT	AST	PF	DQ	STL	TO	BLK	PTS	RPG	APG	PPG
66-67–Cincinnati	64	–	909	131	333	.393	–	–	–	52	123	.423	–	–	329	19	161	2	–	–	–	314	5.1	0.3	4.9
67-68–Cincinnati	66	–	918	188	404	.465	–	–	–	76	152	.500	–	–	281	34	168	2	–	–	–	452	4.3	0.5	6.8
68-69–Cincinnati	82	–	1334	245	534	.459	–	–	–	134	207	.647	–	–	403	47	191	0	–	–	–	624	4.9	0.6	7.6
69-70–Chicago	72	–	1407	270	648	.417	–	–	–	145	219	.662	–	–	455	68	184	1	–	–	–	685	6.3	0.9	9.5
70-71–Cleveland	82	–	2425	565	1241	.455	–	–	–	325	473	.687	–	–	713	83	295	5	–	–	–	1455	8.7	1.0	17.7
71-72–Cleveland	82	–	2185	412	1006	.410	–	–	–	196	291	.674	–	–	711	76	245	4	–	–	–	1020	8.7	0.9	12.4
72-73–Clev.-Phoenix	57	–	474	77	202	.381	–	–	–	26	46	.565	–	–	151	31	77	1	–	–	–	180	2.6	0.5	3.2
73-74–Capital	39	–	400	71	151	.470	–	–	–	26	43	.605	63	73	136	14	74	1	9	–	20	168	3.5	0.4	4.3
74-75–Phil.-Milw.	45	–	247	42	93	.452	–	–	–	16	27	.593	18	45	63	12	51	0	7	–	5	100	1.4	0.3	2.2
75-76–Los Angeles	1	–	7	1	2	.500	–	–	–	2	4	.500	0	1	1	1	2	0	0	–	0	4	1.0	1.0	4.0
Reg. Season Totals	590	–	10306	2002	4614	.434	–	–	–	998	1585	.630	81	119	3243	385	1448	16	16	–	25	5002	5.5	0.7	8.5
Playoff Totals	8	–	83	18	41	.439	–	–	–	6	12	.500	0	0	28	2	16	0	0	–	0	42	3.5	0.3	5.3

West, Jeffery Douglas (Doug, Fresh) b. May 27, 1967 Ht. 6-6 Wt. 220 College: Villanova

SEASON–TEAM	G	GS	MIN	FGM	FGA	PCT	3FGM	3FGA	PCT	FTM	FTA	PCT	O-RB	D-RB	TOT	AST	PF	DQ	STL	TO	BLK	PTS	RPG	APG	PPG
89-90–Minnesota	52	0	378	53	135	.393	3	11	.273	26	32	.813	24	46	70	18	61	0	10	31	6	135	1.3	0.3	2.6
90-91–Minnesota	75	1	824	118	246	.480	0	1	.000	58	84	.690	56	80	136	48	115	0	35	41	23	294	1.8	0.6	3.9
91-92–Minnesota	80	72	2540	463	894	.518	4	23	.174	186	231	.805	107	150	257	281	239	1	66	120	26	1116	3.2	3.5	14.0
92-93–Minnesota	80	80	3104	646	1249	.517	2	23	.087	249	296	.841	89	158	247	235	279	1	85	165	21	1543	3.1	2.9	19.3
93-94–Minnesota	72	61	2182	434	891	.487	1	8	.125	187	231	.810	61	170	231	172	236	3	65	137	24	1056	3.2	2.4	14.7
94-95–Minnesota	71	65	2328	351	762	.461	11	61	.180	206	246	.837	60	167	227	185	250	4	65	126	24	919	3.2	2.6	12.9
95-96–Minnesota	73	16	1639	175	393	.445	1	13	.077	114	144	.792	48	113	161	119	228	2	30	81	17	465	2.2	1.6	6.4
96-97–Minnesota	68	66	1920	226	484	.467	15	45	.333	64	94	.681	37	111	148	113	218	3	61	66	24	531	2.2	1.7	7.8
97-98–Minn.-Vanc.	38	10	688	64	171	.374	0	2	.000	29	40	.725	23	59	82	45	97	1	11	21	5	157	2.2	1.2	4.1
98-99–Vancouver	14	2	294	31	65	.477	0	2	.000	19	25	.760	5	20	25	19	38	1	16	12	7	81	1.8	1.4	5.8
99-00–Vancouver	38	0	581	59	145	.407	0	3	.000	34	40	.850	18	53	71	43	80	1	12	19	8	152	1.9	1.1	4.0
Reg. Season Totals	661	373	16478	2620	5435	.482	37	192	.193	1172	1463	.801	528	1127	1655	1278	1841	17	456	819	185	6449	2.5	1.9	9.8
Playoff Totals	3	3	87	12	22	.545	0	2	.000	9	9	1.000	0	4	4	6	11	0	2	1	1	33	1.3	2.0	11.0

West, Jerry Alan b. May 28, 1938 Ht. 6-3 Wt. 180 College: West Virginia HOF: 1979

SEASON–TEAM	G	GS	MIN	FGM	FGA	PCT	3FGM	3FGA	PCT	FTM	FTA	PCT	O-RB	D-RB	TOT	AST	PF	DQ	STL	TO	BLK	PTS	RPG	APG	PPG
60-61–Los Angeles	79	–	2797	529	1264	.419	–	–	–	331	497	.666	–	–	611	333	213	1	–	–	–	1389	7.7	4.2	17.6
61-62–Los Angeles	75	–	3087	799	1795	.445	–	–	–	712	926	.769	–	–	591	402	173	4	–	–	–	2310	7.9	5.4	30.8
62-63–Los Angeles	55	–	2163	559	1213	.461	–	–	–	371	477	.778	–	–	384	307	150	1	–	–	–	1489	7.0	5.6	27.1
63-64–Los Angeles	72	–	2906	740	1529	.484	–	–	–	584	702	.832	–	–	443	403	200	2	–	–	–	2064	6.2	5.6	28.7
64-65–Los Angeles	74	–	3066	822	1655	.497	–	–	–	648	789	.821	–	–	447	364	221	2	–	–	–	2292	6.0	4.9	31.0
65-66–Los Angeles	79	–	3218	818	1731	.473	–	–	–	840	977	.860	–	–	562	480	243	1	–	–	–	2476	7.1	6.1	31.3
66-67–Los Angeles	66	–	2670	645	1389	.464	–	–	–	602	686	.878	–	–	392	447	160	1	–	–	–	1892	5.9	6.8	28.7
67-68–Los Angeles	51	–	1919	476	926	.514	–	–	–	391	482	.811	–	–	294	310	152	1	–	–	–	1343	5.8	6.1	26.3
68-69–Los Angeles	61	–	2394	545	1156	.471	–	–	–	490	597	.821	–	–	262	423	156	1	–	–	–	1580	4.3	6.9	25.9
69-70–Los Angeles	74	–	3106	831	1673	.497	–	–	–	647	785	.824	–	–	338	554	160	3	–	–	–	2309	4.6	7.5	31.2
70-71–Los Angeles	69	–	2845	667	1351	.494	–	–	–	525	631	.832	–	–	320	655	180	0	–	–	–	1859	4.6	9.5	26.9
71-72–Los Angeles	77	–	2973	735	1540	.477	–	–	–	515	633	.814	–	–	327	747	209	0	–	–	–	1985	4.2	9.7	25.8
72-73–Los Angeles	69	–	2460	618	1291	.479	–	–	–	339	421	.805	–	–	289	607	138	0	–	–	–	1575	4.2	8.8	22.8
73-74–Los Angeles	31	–	967	232	519	.447	–	–	–	165	198	.833	30	86	116	206	80	0	81	–	23	629	3.7	6.6	20.3
Reg. Season Totals	932	–	36571	9016	19032	.474	–	–	–	7160	8801	.814	30	86	5376	6238	2435	17	81	–	23	25192	5.8	6.7	27.0
Playoff Totals	153	–	6321	1622	3460	.469	–	–	–	1213	1506	.805	0	2	855	970	451	3	0	–	0	4457	5.6	6.3	29.1
All-Star Totals	12	–	341	62	137	.453	–	–	–	36	50	.720	0	0	47	55	28	0	0	–	0	160	3.9	4.6	13.3

West, Mark Andre b. November 5, 1960 Ht. 6-10 Wt. 246 College: Old Dominion

SEASON–TEAM	G	GS	MIN	FGM	FGA	PCT	3FGM	3FGA	PCT	FTM	FTA	PCT	O-RB	D-RB	TOT	AST	PF	DQ	STL	TO	BLK	PTS	RPG	APG	PPG
83-84–Dallas	34	0	202	15	42	.357	0	0	–	7	22	.318	19	27	46	13	55	0	1	12	15	37	1.4	0.4	1.1
84-85–Milw.-Clev.	66	25	888	106	194	.546	0	1	.000	43	87	.494	90	161	251	15	197	7	13	59	49	255	3.8	0.2	3.9
85-86–Cleveland	67	26	1172	113	209	.541	0	0	–	54	103	.524	97	225	322	20	235	6	27	91	62	280	4.8	0.3	4.2
86-87–Cleveland	78	13	1333	209	385	.543	0	2	.000	89	173	.514	126	213	339	41	229	5	22	106	81	507	4.3	0.5	6.5
87-88–Clev.-Phoenix	83	41	2098	316	573	.551	0	1	.000	170	285	.596	165	358	523	74	265	4	47	173	147	802	6.3	0.9	9.7
88-89–Phoenix	82	32	2019	243	372	.653	0	0	–	108	202	.535	167	384	551	39	273	4	35	103	187	594	6.7	0.5	7.2
89-90–Phoenix	82	79	2399	331	530	.625	0	0	–	199	288	.691	212	516	728	45	277	5	36	126	184	861	8.9	0.5	10.5
90-91–Phoenix	82	64	1957	247	382	.647	0	0	–	135	206	.655	171	393	564	37	266	2	32	86	161	629	6.9	0.5	7.7
91-92–Phoenix	82	11	1436	196	310	.632	0	0	–	109	171	.637	134	238	372	22	239	2	14	82	81	501	4.5	0.3	6.1
92-93–Phoenix	82	82	1558	175	285	.614	0	0	–	86	166	.518	153	305	458	29	243	3	16	93	103	436	5.6	0.4	5.3
93-94–Phoenix	82	50	1236	162	286	.566	0	0	–	58	116	.500	112	183	295	33	214	4	31	74	109	382	3.6	0.4	4.7
94-95–Detroit	67	58	1543	217	390	.556	0	0	–	66	138	.478	160	248	408	18	247	8	27	85	102	500	6.1	0.3	7.5
95-96–Detroit	47	21	682	61	126	.484	0	0	–	28	45	.622	49	84	133	6	135	2	6	35	37	150	2.8	0.1	3.2
96-97–Cleveland	70	43	959	100	180	.556	0	0	–	27	56	.482	69	117	186	19	142	0	11	52	55	227	2.7	0.3	3.2
97-98–Indiana	15	1	105	10	21	.476	0	0	–	3	6	.500	6	9	15	2	15	0	2	8	4	23	1.0	0.1	1.5
98-99–Atlanta	49	0	499	22	59	.373	0	0	–	16	45	.356	49	76	125	13	81	0	4	17	22	60	2.6	0.3	1.2
99-00–Phoenix	22	2	127	5	12	.417	0	0	–	5	8	.625	6	25	31	2	23	0	2	6	4	15	1.4	0.1	0.7
Reg. Season Totals	1090	548	20213	2528	4356	.580	0	4	.000	1203	2117	.568	1785	3562	5347	428	3136	52	326	1208	1403	6259	4.9	0.4	5.7
Playoff Totals	95	69	1755	201	355	.566	0	0	–	94	163	.577	152	270	422	36	293	8	24	81	119	496	4.4	0.4	5.2

West, Roland D. b. June 6, 1944 Ht. 6-4 Wt. 180 College: Cincinnati

SEASON–TEAM	G	GS	MIN	FGM	FGA	PCT	3FGM	3FGA	PCT	FTM	FTA	PCT	O-RB	D-RB	TOT	AST	PF	DQ	STL	TO	BLK	PTS	RPG	APG	PPG
67-68–Baltimore	4	–	14	2	5	.400	–	–	–	0	0	–	–	–	5	0	3	0	–	–	–	4	1.3	0.0	1.0
Reg. Season Totals	4	–	14	2	5	.400	–	–	–	0	0	–	–	–	5	0	3	0	–	–	–	4	1.3	0.0	1.0

Westbrook, Dexter b. 1943 Ht. 6-8 Wt. 200 College: Providence

SEASON–TEAM	G	GS	MIN	FGM	FGA	PCT	3FGM	3FGA	PCT	FTM	FTA	PCT	O-RB	D-RB	TOT	AST	PF	DQ	STL	TO	BLK	PTS	RPG	APG	PPG
67-68–N.J.-Pitt. (A)	12	–	127	19	39	.487	0	0	–	10	14	.714	–	–	23	5	30	0	–	13	–	48	1.9	0.4	4.0
Reg. ABA Totals	12	–	127	19	39	.487	0	0	–	10	14	.714	–	–	23	5	30	0	–	13	–	48	1.9	0.4	4.0

Westphal, Paul Douglas b. November 30, 1950 Ht. 6-4 Wt. 195 College: USC

SEASON–TEAM	G	GS	MIN	FGM	FGA	PCT	3FGM	3FGA	PCT	FTM	FTA	PCT	O-RB	D-RB	TOT	AST	PF	DQ	STL	TO	BLK	PTS	RPG	APG	PPG
72-73–Boston	60	–	482	89	212	.420	–	–	–	67	86	.779	–	–	67	69	88	0	–	–	–	245	1.1	1.2	4.1
73-74–Boston	82	–	1165	238	475	.501	–	–	–	112	153	.732	49	94	143	171	173	1	39	–	34	588	1.7	2.1	7.2
74-75–Boston	82	–	1581	342	670	.510	–	–	–	119	156	.763	44	119	163	235	192	0	78	–	33	803	2.0	2.9	9.8
75-76–Phoenix	82	–	2960	657	1329	.494	–	–	–	365	440	.830	74	185	259	440	218	3	210	–	38	1679	3.2	5.4	20.5
76-77–Phoenix	81	–	2600	682	1317	.518	–	–	–	362	439	.825	57	133	190	459	171	1	134	–	21	1726	2.3	5.7	21.3
77-78–Phoenix	80	–	2481	809	1568	.516	–	–	–	396	487	.813	41	123	164	437	162	0	138	280	31	2014	2.1	5.5	25.2
78-79–Phoenix	81	–	2641	801	1496	.535	–	–	–	339	405	.837	35	124	159	529	159	1	111	232	26	1941	2.0	6.5	24.0
79-80–Phoenix	82	–	2665	692	1317	.525	26	93	.280	382	443	.862	46	141	187	416	162	0	119	207	35	1792	2.3	5.1	21.9
80-81–Seattle	36	–	1078	221	500	.442	6	25	.240	153	184	.832	11	57	68	148	70	0	46	78	14	601	1.9	4.1	16.7
81-82–New York	18	12	451	86	194	.443	2	8	.250	36	47	.766	9	13	22	100	61	1	19	47	8	210	1.2	5.6	11.7
82-83–New York	80	59	1978	318	693	.459	14	48	.292	148	184	.804	19	96	115	439	180	1	87	196	16	798	1.4	5.5	10.0
83-84–Phoenix	59	2	865	144	313	.460	7	26	.269	117	142	.824	8	35	43	148	69	0	41	77	6	412	0.7	2.5	7.0
Reg. Season Totals	823	73	20947	5079	10084	.504	55	200	.275	2596	3166	.820	393	1120	1580	3591	1705	8	1022	1117	262	12809	1.9	4.4	15.6
Playoff Totals	107	8	2449	553	1149	.481	6	29	.207	225	285	.789	40	106	153	353	241	2	89	89	23	1337	1.4	3.3	12.5
All-Star Totals	5	4	128	43	68	.632	0	2	.000	11	16	.688	3	4	7	24	14	0	6	11	5	97	1.4	4.8	19.4

Wetzel, John Francis b. October 22, 1944 Ht. 6-5 Wt. 190 College: Virginia Tech

SEASON–TEAM	G	GS	MIN	FGM	FGA	PCT	3FGM	3FGA	PCT	FTM	FTA	PCT	O-RB	D-RB	TOT	AST	PF	DQ	STL	TO	BLK	PTS	RPG	APG	PPG
67-68–Los Angeles	38	–	434	52	119	.437	–	–	–	35	46	.761	–	–	84	51	55	0	–	–	–	139	2.2	1.3	3.7
70-71–Phoenix	70	–	1091	124	288	.431	–	–	–	83	101	.822	–	–	153	114	156	1	–	–	–	331	2.2	1.6	4.7
71-72–Phoenix	51	–	419	31	82	.378	–	–	–	24	30	.800	–	–	65	56	71	0	–	–	–	86	1.3	1.1	1.7
72-73–Atlanta	28	–	504	42	94	.447	–	–	–	14	17	.824	–	–	58	39	41	1	–	–	–	98	2.1	1.4	3.5
73-74–Atlanta	70	–	1232	107	252	.425	–	–	–	41	57	.719	39	131	170	138	147	1	73	–	19	255	2.4	2.0	3.6
74-75–Atlanta	63	–	785	87	204	.426	–	–	–	68	77	.883	34	80	114	77	108	1	51	–	8	242	1.8	1.2	3.8
75-76–Phoenix	37	–	249	22	46	.478	–	–	–	20	24	.833	8	30	38	19	30	0	9	–	3	64	1.0	0.5	1.7
Reg. Season Totals	357	–	4714	465	1085	.429	–	–	–	285	352	.810	81	241	682	494	608	4	133	–	30	1215	1.9	1.4	3.4
Playoff Totals	5	–	38	3	7	.429	–	–	–	2	2	1.000	0	2	4	4	8	0	0	–	0	8	0.8	0.8	1.6

Whatley, Ennis b. August 11, 1962 Ht. 6-3 Wt. 180 College: Alabama

SEASON–TEAM	G	GS	MIN	FGM	FGA	PCT	3FGM	3FGA	PCT	FTM	FTA	PCT	O-RB	D-RB	TOT	AST	PF	DQ	STL	TO	BLK	PTS	RPG	APG	PPG
83-84–Chicago	80	73	2159	261	556	.469	0	2	.000	146	200	.730	63	134	197	662	223	4	119	268	17	668	2.5	8.3	8.4
84-85–Chicago	70	44	1385	140	313	.447	1	9	.111	68	86	.791	34	67	101	381	141	1	66	144	10	349	1.4	5.4	5.0
85-86–Clev.-Wash.-S.A.	14	1	107	15	35	.429	0	0	–	5	10	.500	4	10	14	23	10	0	5	10	1	35	1.0	1.6	2.5
86-87–Washington	73	72	1816	246	515	.478	0	2	.000	126	165	.764	58	136	194	392	172	0	92	138	10	618	2.7	5.4	8.5
87-88–Atlanta	5	0	24	4	9	.444	0	0	–	3	4	.750	0	4	4	2	3	0	2	4	0	11	0.8	0.4	2.2
88-89–L.A. Clippers	8	0	90	12	33	.364	0	0	–	10	11	.909	2	14	16	22	15	0	7	11	1	34	2.0	2.8	4.3
91-92–Portland	23	0	209	21	51	.412	0	4	.000	27	31	.871	6	15	21	34	12	0	14	14	3	69	0.9	1.5	3.0
93-94–Atlanta	82	1	1004	120	236	.508	0	6	.000	52	66	.788	22	77	99	181	93	0	59	78	2	292	1.2	2.2	3.6
94-95–Atlanta	27	2	292	24	53	.453	2	8	.250	20	32	.625	9	21	30	54	37	0	19	19	0	70	1.1	2.0	2.6
96-97–Portland	3	0	22	2	4	.500	0	0	–	0	0	–	0	3	3	3	5	0	0	1	0	4	1.0	1.0	1.3
Reg. Season Totals	385	193	7108	845	1805	.468	3	31	.097	457	605	.755	198	481	679	1754	711	5	383	687	44	2150	1.8	4.6	5.6
Playoff Totals	31	2	260	18	64	.281	0	1	.000	10	12	.833	5	26	31	32	33	0	16	21	0	46	1.0	1.0	1.5

Wheat, DeJuan Shontez b. October 14, 1973 Ht. 6-0 Wt. 165 College: Louisville

SEASON–TEAM	G	GS	MIN	FGM	FGA	PCT	3FGM	3FGA	PCT	FTM	FTA	PCT	O-RB	D-RB	TOT	AST	PF	DQ	STL	TO	BLK	PTS	RPG	APG	PPG
97-98–Minnesota	34	0	150	20	50	.400	8	17	.471	9	15	.600	3	8	11	25	12	0	6	9	1	57	0.3	0.7	1.7
98-99–Vancouver	46	0	590	73	193	.378	22	60	.367	40	55	.727	11	34	45	102	59	0	26	48	2	208	1.0	2.2	4.5
Reg. Season Totals	80	0	740	93	243	.383	30	77	.390	49	70	.700	14	42	56	127	71	0	32	57	3	265	0.7	1.6	3.3
Playoff Totals	1	0	3	1	2	.500	0	0	–	0	0	–	0	1	1	–	0	0	1	0	0	2	1.0	0.0	2.0

Wheeler, Clinton b. October 27, 1959 Ht. 6-1 Wt. 185 College: William Paterson

SEASON–TEAM	G	GS	MIN	FGM	FGA	PCT	3FGM	3FGA	PCT	FTM	FTA	PCT	O-RB	D-RB	TOT	AST	PF	DQ	STL	TO	BLK	PTS	RPG	APG	PPG
87-88–Indiana	59	0	513	62	132	.470	0	0	–	25	34	.735	19	21	40	103	37	0	36	52	2	149	0.7	1.7	2.5
88-89–Miami-Port.	28	0	354	45	87	.517	0	1	.000	15	20	.750	17	14	31	54	26	0	27	24	0	105	1.1	1.9	3.8
Reg. Season Totals	87	0	867	107	219	.489	0	1	.000	40	54	.741	36	35	71	157	63	0	63	76	2	254	0.8	1.8	2.9

Wheeler, Tyson Aaron b. October 8, 1975 Ht. 5-10 Wt. 165 College: Rhode Island

SEASON–TEAM	G	GS	MIN	FGM	FGA	PCT	3FGM	3FGA	PCT	FTM	FTA	PCT	O-RB	D-RB	TOT	AST	PF	DQ	STL	TO	BLK	PTS	RPG	APG	PPG
98-99–Denver	1	0	3	1	1	1.000	1	1	1.000	1	2	.500	0	0	0	2	1	0	0	0	0	4	0.0	2.0	4.0
Reg. Season Totals	1	0	3	1	1	1.000	1	1	1.000	1	2	.500	0	0	0	2	1	0	0	0	0	4	0.0	2.0	4.0

Whitaker, Lucian Cary (Skippy) b. August 29, 1930 Ht. 6-1 Wt. 185 College: Kentucky

SEASON–TEAM	G	GS	MIN	FGM	FGA	PCT	3FGM	3FGA	PCT	FTM	FTA	PCT	O-RB	D-RB	TOT	AST	PF	DQ	STL	TO	BLK	PTS	RPG	APG	PPG
54-55–Boston	3	–	15	1	6	.167	–	–	–	0	0	–	–	–	1	1	4	0	–	–	–	2	0.3	0.3	0.7
Reg. Season Totals	3	–	15	1	6	.167	–	–	–	0	0	–	–	–	1	1	4	0	–	–	–	2	0.3	0.3	0.7

White, Eric Lance b. December 30, 1965 Ht. 6-8 Wt. 200 College: Pepperdine

SEASON–TEAM	G	GS	MIN	FGM	FGA	PCT	3FGM	3FGA	PCT	FTM	FTA	PCT	O-RB	D-RB	TOT	AST	PF	DQ	STL	TO	BLK	PTS	RPG	APG	PPG
87-88–L.A. Clippers	17	4	352	66	124	.532	1	1	1.000	45	57	.789	31	31	62	9	32	0	7	21	3	178	3.6	0.5	10.5
88-89–Utah-LAClips	38	0	436	62	120	.517	0	0	–	34	42	.810	34	36	70	17	40	0	10	26	1	158	1.8	0.4	4.2
Reg. Season Totals	55	4	788	128	244	.525	1	1	1.000	79	99	.798	65	67	132	26	72	0	17	47	4	336	2.4	0.5	6.1

White, Herbert Thomas (Herb) b. June 15, 1948 Ht. 6-2 Wt. 195 College: Georgia

SEASON–TEAM	G	GS	MIN	FGM	FGA	PCT	3FGM	3FGA	PCT	FTM	FTA	PCT	O-RB	D-RB	TOT	AST	PF	DQ	STL	TO	BLK	PTS	RPG	APG	PPG
70-71–Atlanta	38	–	315	34	84	.405	–	–	–	22	39	.564	–	–	48	47	62	2	–	–	–	90	1.3	1.2	2.4
Reg. Season Totals	38	–	315	34	84	.405	–	–	–	22	39	.564	–	–	48	47	62	2	–	–	–	90	1.3	1.2	2.4

White, Hubert Jr. (Hubie) b. January 26, 1940 Ht. 6-4 Wt. 205 College: Villanova

SEASON–TEAM	G	GS	MIN	FGM	FGA	PCT	3FGM	3FGA	PCT	FTM	FTA	PCT	O-RB	D-RB	TOT	AST	PF	DQ	STL	TO	BLK	PTS	RPG	APG	PPG
62-63–San Francisco	29	–	271	40	111	.360	–	–	–	12	18	.667	–	–	35	28	47	0	–	–	–	92	1.2	1.0	3.2
63-64–Philadelphia	23	–	196	31	105	.295	–	–	–	17	28	.607	–	–	42	12	28	0	–	–	–	79	1.8	0.5	3.4
69-70–Miami (A)	54	–	824	146	363	.402	7	43	.163	62	84	.738	–	–	155	56	147	2	–	–	–	361	2.9	1.0	6.7
70-71–Pittsburgh (A)	14	–	166	17	61	.279	2	7	.286	10	13	.769	–	–	32	14	28	–	–	–	–	46	2.3	1.0	3.3
Reg. NBA Totals	52	–	467	71	216	.329	–	–	–	29	46	.630	–	–	77	40	75	0	–	–	–	171	1.5	0.8	3.3
Reg. ABA Totals	68	–	990	163	424	.384	9	50	.180	72	97	.742	–	–	187	70	175	2	–	–	–	407	2.8	1.0	6.0

White, Jahidi b. February 19, 1976 Ht. 6-9 Wt. 290 College: Georgetown

SEASON–TEAM	G	GS	MIN	FGM	FGA	PCT	3FGM	3FGA	PCT	FTM	FTA	PCT	O-RB	D-RB	TOT	AST	PF	DQ	STL	TO	BLK	PTS	RPG	APG	PPG
98-99–Washington	20	0	191	17	32	.531	0	0	–	15	35	.429	23	35	58	1	39	1	3	16	11	49	2.9	0.1	2.5
99-00–Washington	80	59	1537	228	450	.507	0	0	–	113	211	.536	202	351	553	15	234	2	31	94	83	569	6.9	0.2	7.1
Reg. Season Totals	100	59	1728	245	482	.508	0	0	–	128	246	.520	225	386	611	16	273	3	34	110	94	618	6.1	0.2	6.2

White, Joseph Henry (Jo Jo) b. November 16, 1946 Ht. 6-3 Wt. 190 College: Kansas

SEASON–TEAM	G	GS	MIN	FGM	FGA	PCT	3FGM	3FGA	PCT	FTM	FTA	PCT	O-RB	D-RB	TOT	AST	PF	DQ	STL	TO	BLK	PTS	RPG	APG	PPG
69-70–Boston	60	–	1328	309	684	.452	–	–	–	111	135	.822	–	–	169	145	132	1	–	–	–	729	2.8	2.4	12.2
70-71–Boston	75	–	2787	693	1494	.464	–	–	–	215	269	.799	–	–	376	361	255	5	–	–	–	1601	5.0	4.8	21.3
71-72–Boston	79	–	3261	770	1788	.431	–	–	–	285	343	.831	–	–	446	416	227	1	–	–	–	1825	5.6	5.3	23.1
72-73–Boston	82	–	3250	717	1665	.431	–	–	–	178	228	.781	–	–	414	498	185	2	–	–	–	1612	5.0	6.1	19.7
73-74–Boston	82	–	3238	649	1445	.449	–	–	–	190	227	.837	100	251	351	448	185	1	105	–	25	1488	4.3	5.5	18.1
74-75–Boston	82	–	3220	658	1440	.457	–	–	–	186	223	.834	84	227	311	458	207	1	128	–	17	1502	3.8	5.6	18.3
75-76–Boston	82	–	3257	670	1492	.449	–	–	–	212	253	.838	61	252	313	445	183	2	107	–	20	1552	3.8	5.4	18.9
76-77–Boston	82	–	3333	638	1488	.429	–	–	–	333	383	.869	87	296	383	492	193	5	118	–	22	1609	4.7	6.0	19.6
77-78–Boston	46	–	1641	289	690	.419	–	–	–	103	120	.858	53	127	180	209	109	2	49	117	7	681	3.9	4.5	14.8
78-79–Boston-G.S.	76	–	2338	404	910	.444	–	–	–	139	158	.880	42	158	200	347	173	1	80	212	7	947	2.6	4.6	12.5
79-80–Golden State	78	–	2052	336	706	.476	1	6	.167	97	114	.851	42	139	181	239	186	0	88	157	13	770	2.3	3.1	9.9
80-81–Kansas City	13	–	236	36	82	.439	0	0	–	11	18	.611	3	18	21	37	21	0	11	18	1	83	1.6	2.8	6.4
Reg. Season Totals	837	–	29941	6169	13884	.444	1	6	.167	2060	2471	.834	472	1468	3345	4095	2056	21	686	504	112	14399	4.0	4.9	17.2
Playoff Totals	80	–	3428	732	1629	.449	0	0	–	256	309	.828	57	178	358	452	241	3	63	–	7	1720	4.5	5.7	21.5
All-Star Totals	7	–	124	29	60	.483	0	0	–	6	11	.545	2	7	27	21	6	0	4	–	1	64	3.9	3.0	9.1

White, Randy (Bird) b. November 4, 1967 Ht. 6-8 Wt. 240 College: Louisiana Tech

SEASON–TEAM	G	GS	MIN	FGM	FGA	PCT	3FGM	3FGA	PCT	FTM	FTA	PCT	O-RB	D-RB	TOT	AST	PF	DQ	STL	TO	BLK	PTS	RPG	APG	PPG
89-90–Dallas	55	2	707	93	252	.369	1	14	.071	50	89	.562	78	95	173	21	124	0	24	47	6	237	3.1	0.4	4.3
90-91–Dallas	79	29	1901	265	665	.398	6	37	.162	159	225	.707	173	331	504	63	308	6	81	131	44	695	6.4	0.8	8.8
91-92–Dallas	65	12	1021	145	382	.380	4	27	.148	124	162	.765	96	140	236	31	157	1	31	68	22	418	3.6	0.5	6.4
92-93–Dallas	64	20	1433	235	540	.435	10	42	.238	138	184	.750	154	216	370	49	226	4	63	108	45	618	5.8	0.8	9.7
93-94–Dallas	18	3	320	45	112	.402	6	20	.300	19	33	.576	30	53	83	11	46	0	10	18	10	115	4.6	0.6	6.4
Reg. Season Totals	281	66	5382	783	1951	.401	27	140	.193	490	693	.707	531	835	1366	175	861	11	209	372	127	2083	4.9	0.6	7.4
Playoff Totals	1	0	2	0	0	–	0	0	–	0	0	–	0	0	0	–	0	0	0	0	0	0	0.0	0.0	0.0

White, Rory Wilbur b. August 16, 1959 Ht. 6-8 Wt. 215 College: South Alabama

SEASON–TEAM	G	GS	MIN	FGM	FGA	PCT	3FGM	3FGA	PCT	FTM	FTA	PCT	O-RB	D-RB	TOT	AST	PF	DQ	STL	TO	BLK	PTS	RPG	APG	PPG
82-83–Phoenix	65	0	626	127	234	.543	0	1	.000	70	109	.642	47	58	105	30	54	0	16	51	2	324	1.6	0.5	5.0
83-84–Phoenix-Milw.-S.D.	36	2	372	80	170	.471	0	0	–	26	47	.553	37	37	74	15	31	0	15	24	3	186	2.1	0.4	5.2
84-85–L.A. Clippers	80	14	1106	144	279	.516	0	0	–	90	130	.692	94	101	195	34	115	0	35	87	20	378	2.4	0.4	4.7
85-86–L.A. Clippers	75	30	1761	355	684	.519	1	9	.111	164	222	.739	82	99	181	74	161	2	74	95	8	875	2.4	1.0	11.7
86-87–L.A. Clippers	68	35	1545	265	552	.480	0	3	.000	94	144	.653	90	104	194	79	159	1	47	73	19	624	2.9	1.2	9.2
Reg. Season Totals	324	81	5410	971	1919	.506	1	13	.077	444	652	.681	350	399	749	232	520	3	187	330	52	2387	2.3	0.7	7.4
Playoff Totals	3	0	40	7	14	.500	0	1	.000	2	4	.500	1	9	10	–	4	0	0	1	0	16	3.3	0.0	5.3

White, Rudolph (Rudy) b. June 23, 1953 Ht. 6-2 Wt. 195 College: Arizona State

SEASON–TEAM	G	GS	MIN	FGM	FGA	PCT	3FGM	3FGA	PCT	FTM	FTA	PCT	O-RB	D-RB	TOT	AST	PF	DQ	STL	TO	BLK	PTS	RPG	APG	PPG
75-76–Houston	32	–	284	42	102	.412	–	–	–	18	25	.720	13	25	38	30	32	0	19	–	5	102	1.2	0.9	3.2
76-77–Houston	46	–	368	47	106	.443	–	–	–	15	25	.600	13	28	41	35	39	0	11	–	1	109	0.9	0.8	2.4
77-78–Houston	21	–	219	31	85	.365	–	–	–	14	18	.778	8	13	21	22	24	0	8	22	0	76	1.0	1.0	3.6
79-80–Houston	9	–	106	13	24	.542	0	0	–	10	13	.769	0	9	9	5	8	0	5	8	0	36	1.0	0.6	4.0
80-81–G.S.-Seattle	16	–	208	23	65	.354	0	1	.000	15	16	.938	1	10	11	20	23	0	9	12	1	61	0.7	1.3	3.8
Reg. Season Totals	124	–	1185	156	382	.408	0	1	.000	72	97	.742	35	85	120	112	126	0	52	42	7	384	1.0	0.9	3.1
Playoff Totals	1	–	2	1	3	.333	0	0	–	0	0	–	1	0	1	–	0	0	1	–	0	2	1.0	0.0	2.0

White, Tony F. b. February 15, 1965 Ht. 6-2 Wt. 170 College: Tennessee

SEASON–TEAM	G	GS	MIN	FGM	FGA	PCT	3FGM	3FGA	PCT	FTM	FTA	PCT	O-RB	D-RB	TOT	AST	PF	DQ	STL	TO	BLK	PTS	RPG	APG	PPG
87-88–Chi.-N.Y.-G.S.	49	0	581	111	249	.446	0	6	.000	39	54	.722	12	19	31	59	57	0	20	47	2	261	0.6	1.2	5.3
Reg. Season Totals	49	0	581	111	249	.446	0	6	.000	39	54	.722	12	19	31	59	57	0	20	47	2	261	0.6	1.2	5.3

White, Willie b. August 20, 1962 Ht. 6-3 Wt. 195 College: Tennessee-Chattanooga

SEASON–TEAM	G	GS	MIN	FGM	FGA	PCT	3FGM	3FGA	PCT	FTM	FTA	PCT	O-RB	D-RB	TOT	AST	PF	DQ	STL	TO	BLK	PTS	RPG	APG	PPG
84-85–Denver	39	0	234	52	124	.419	4	11	.364	21	31	.677	15	21	36	29	24	0	5	30	2	129	0.9	0.7	3.3
85-86–Denver	43	4	343	74	168	.440	6	21	.286	19	23	.826	17	27	44	53	24	0	18	25	2	173	1.0	1.2	4.0
Reg. Season Totals	82	4	577	126	292	.432	10	32	.313	40	54	.741	32	48	80	82	48	0	23	55	4	302	1.0	1.0	3.7
Playoff Totals	14	3	144	29	64	.453	3	7	.429	7	12	.583	10	10	20	23	10	0	6	18	0	68	1.4	1.6	4.9

Whitehead, Jerome Clay b. September 30, 1956 Ht. 6-10 Wt. 220 College: Riverside (Calif.) C.C.; Marquette

SEASON–TEAM	G	GS	MIN	FGM	FGA	PCT	3FGM	3FGA	PCT	FTM	FTA	PCT	O-RB	D-RB	TOT	AST	PF	DQ	STL	TO	BLK	PTS	RPG	APG	PPG
78-79–San Diego	31	–	152	15	34	.441	–	–	–	8	18	.444	16	34	50	7	29	0	3	11	4	38	1.6	0.2	1.2
79-80–S.D.-Utah	50	–	553	58	114	.509	0	0	–	10	35	.286	56	111	167	24	97	3	8	36	17	126	3.3	0.5	2.5
80-81–Dallas-Clev.-S.D.	48	–	688	83	180	.461	0	1	.000	28	56	.500	58	156	214	26	122	2	20	56	9	194	4.5	0.5	4.0
81-82–San Diego	72	63	2214	406	726	.559	0	0	–	184	241	.763	231	433	664	102	290	16	48	141	44	996	9.2	1.4	13.8
82-83–San Diego	46	23	905	164	306	.536	0	0	–	72	87	.828	105	156	261	42	139	2	21	65	15	400	5.7	0.9	8.7
83-84–San Diego	70	1	921	144	294	.490	0	0	–	88	107	.822	94	151	245	19	159	2	17	59	12	376	3.5	0.3	5.4
84-85–Golden State	79	78	2536	421	825	.510	0	0	–	184	235	.783	219	403	622	53	322	8	45	141	43	1026	7.9	0.7	13.0
85-86–Golden State	81	3	1079	126	294	.429	0	0	–	60	97	.619	94	234	328	19	176	2	18	64	19	312	4.0	0.2	3.9
86-87–Golden State	73	1	937	147	327	.450	0	1	.000	79	113	.699	110	152	262	24	175	1	16	50	12	373	3.6	0.3	5.1
87-88–Golden State	72	27	1221	174	360	.483	0	0	–	59	82	.720	109	212	321	39	209	3	32	49	21	407	4.5	0.5	5.7
88-89–G.S.-S.A.	57	4	622	72	182	.396	0	0	–	31	47	.660	49	85	134	19	115	1	23	24	4	175	2.4	0.3	3.1
Reg. Season Totals	679	200	11828	1810	3642	.497	0	2	.000	803	1118	.718	1141	2127	3268	374	1833	40	251	696	200	4423	4.8	0.6	6.5
Playoff Totals	10	0	100	9	27	.333	0	0	–	4	10	.400	5	9	14	3	22	1	2	1	2	22	1.4	0.3	2.2

Whiteside, Donald b. April 25, 1969 Ht. 5-11 Wt. 170 College: Northern Illinois

SEASON–TEAM	G	GS	MIN	FGM	FGA	PCT	3FGM	3FGA	PCT	FTM	FTA	PCT	O-RB	D-RB	TOT	AST	PF	DQ	STL	TO	BLK	PTS	RPG	APG	PPG
96-97–Toronto	27	1	259	18	55	.327	12	36	.333	11	15	.733	2	10	12	36	23	0	11	17	0	59	0.4	1.3	2.2
97-98–Atlanta	3	0	16	1	2	.500	0	1	.000	0	2	.000	0	1	1	1	0	0	0	1	0	2	0.3	0.3	0.7
Reg. Season Totals	30	1	275	19	57	.333	12	37	.324	11	17	.647	2	11	13	37	23	0	11	18	0	61	0.4	1.2	2.0

Whitfield, Dwayne b. August 21, 1972 Ht. 6-9 Wt. 240 College: Jackson State

SEASON–TEAM	G	GS	MIN	FGM	FGA	PCT	3FGM	3FGA	PCT	FTM	FTA	PCT	O-RB	D-RB	TOT	AST	PF	DQ	STL	TO	BLK	PTS	RPG	APG	PPG
95-96–Toronto	8	1	122	13	30	.433	0	0	–	14	22	.636	9	16	25	2	14	0	3	8	2	40	3.1	0.3	5.0
Reg. Season Totals	8	1	122	13	30	.433	0	0	–	14	22	.636	9	16	25	2	14	0	3	8	2	40	3.1	0.3	5.0

Whitney, Charles Vincent (Hawkeye) b. June 22, 1957 Ht. 6-5 Wt. 235 College: North Carolina State

SEASON–TEAM	G	GS	MIN	FGM	FGA	PCT	3FGM	3FGA	PCT	FTM	FTA	PCT	O-RB	D-RB	TOT	AST	PF	DQ	STL	TO	BLK	PTS	RPG	APG	PPG
80-81–Kansas City	47	–	782	149	306	.487	2	6	.333	50	65	.769	29	77	106	68	98	0	47	48	6	350	2.3	1.4	7.4
81-82–Kansas City	23	4	266	25	71	.352	0	1	.000	4	7	.571	13	27	40	19	31	0	12	14	1	54	1.7	0.8	2.3
Reg. Season Totals	70	4	1048	174	377	.462	2	7	.286	54	72	.750	42	104	146	87	129	0	59	62	7	404	2.1	1.2	5.8

Whitney, Christofer Antoine (Chris) b. October 5, 1971 Ht. 6-0 Wt. 175 College: Lincoln Land (Ill.) C.C.; Clemson

SEASON–TEAM	G	GS	MIN	FGM	FGA	PCT	3FGM	3FGA	PCT	FTM	FTA	PCT	O-RB	D-RB	TOT	AST	PF	DQ	STL	TO	BLK	PTS	RPG	APG	PPG
93-94–San Antonio	40	4	339	25	82	.305	10	30	.333	12	15	.800	5	24	29	53	53	0	11	37	1	72	0.7	1.3	1.8
94-95–San Antonio	25	0	179	14	47	.298	3	19	.158	11	11	1.000	4	9	13	28	34	1	4	18	0	42	0.5	1.1	1.7
95-96–Washington	21	0	335	45	99	.455	19	44	.432	41	44	.932	2	31	33	51	46	0	18	23	1	150	1.6	2.4	7.1
96-97–Washington	82	1	1117	139	330	.421	58	163	.356	94	113	.832	13	91	104	182	100	0	49	68	4	430	1.3	2.2	5.2
97-98–Washington	82	6	1073	126	355	.355	52	169	.308	118	129	.915	16	99	115	196	106	0	34	65	6	422	1.4	2.4	5.1
98-99–Washington	39	1	441	64	156	.410	32	95	.337	27	31	.871	8	39	47	69	49	0	18	36	2	187	1.2	1.8	4.8
99-00–Washington	82	15	1627	217	521	.417	96	255	.376	112	132	.848	20	114	134	313	166	1	55	107	5	642	1.6	3.8	7.8
Reg. Season Totals	371	27	5111	630	1590	.396	270	775	.348	415	475	.874	68	407	475	892	554	2	189	354	19	1945	1.3	2.4	5.2
Playoff Totals	3	0	20	2	5	.400	2	4	.500	1	1	1.000	0	2	2	2	1	0	0	5	0	7	0.7	0.7	2.3

Whitney, Henry Lee (Hank) b. April 28, 1939 Ht. 6-7 Wt. 235 College: Iowa State

SEASON–TEAM	G	GS	MIN	FGM	FGA	PCT	3FGM	3FGA	PCT	FTM	FTA	PCT	O-RB	D-RB	TOT	AST	PF	DQ	STL	TO	BLK	PTS	RPG	APG	PPG
67-68–New Jersey (A)	37	–	1159	217	552	.393	0	0	–	157	220	.714	–	–	477	56	158	3	–	54	–	591	12.9	1.5	16.0
68-69–N.Y.-Houston (A)	49	–	892	131	329	.398	0	1	.000	89	130	.685	–	–	254	56	144	1	–	72	–	351	5.2	1.1	7.2
69-70–Carolina (A)	59	–	981	170	403	.422	0	0	–	57	88	.648	–	–	371	56	200	4	–	–	–	397	6.3	0.9	6.7
Reg. ABA Totals	145	–	3032	518	1284	.403	0	1	.000	303	438	.692	–	–	1102	168	502	8	–	126	–	1339	7.6	1.2	9.2
ABA Playoff Totals	4	–	60	17	33	.515	0	0	–	4	9	.444	–	–	21	2	12	0	–	–	–	38	5.3	0.5	9.5

Wicks, Sidney b. September 19, 1949 Ht. 6-9 Wt. 225 College: Santa Monica (Calif.) Coll. (J.C.); UCLA

SEASON–TEAM	G	GS	MIN	FGM	FGA	PCT	3FGM	3FGA	PCT	FTM	FTA	PCT	O-RB	D-RB	TOT	AST	PF	DQ	STL	TO	BLK	PTS	RPG	APG	PPG
71-72–Portland	82	–	3245	784	1837	.427	–	–	–	441	621	.710	–	–	943	350	186	1	–	–	–	2009	11.5	4.3	24.5
72-73–Portland	80	–	3152	761	1684	.452	–	–	–	384	531	.723	–	–	870	440	253	3	–	–	–	1906	10.9	5.5	23.8
73-74–Portland	75	–	2853	685	1492	.459	–	–	–	314	412	.762	196	488	684	326	214	2	90	–	64	1684	9.1	4.3	22.5
74-75–Portland	82	–	3162	692	1391	.497	–	–	–	394	558	.706	231	646	877	287	289	5	108	–	80	1778	10.7	3.5	21.7
75-76–Portland	79	–	3044	580	1201	.483	–	–	–	345	512	.674	245	467	712	244	250	5	77	–	53	1505	9.0	3.1	19.1
76-77–Boston	82	–	2642	464	1012	.458	–	–	–	310	464	.668	268	556	824	169	331	14	64	–	61	1238	10.0	2.1	15.1
77-78–Boston	81	–	2413	433	927	.467	–	–	–	217	329	.660	223	450	673	171	318	9	67	226	46	1083	8.3	2.1	13.4
78-79–San Diego	79	–	2022	312	676	.462	–	–	–	147	226	.650	159	246	405	126	274	4	70	180	36	771	5.1	1.6	9.8
79-80–San Diego	71	–	2146	210	496	.423	0	1	.000	83	152	.546	138	271	409	213	241	5	76	167	52	503	5.8	3.0	7.1
80-81–San Diego	49	–	1083	125	286	.437	0	1	.000	76	150	.507	79	144	223	111	168	3	40	94	40	326	4.6	2.3	6.7
Reg. Season Totals	760	–	25762	5046	11002	.459	0	2	.000	2711	3955	.685	1539	3268	6620	2437	2524	51	592	667	432	12803	8.7	3.2	16.8
Playoff Totals	9	–	261	42	81	.519	0	0	–	34	47	.723	26	57	83	16	37	2	13	–	3	118	9.2	1.8	13.1
All-Star Totals	4	–	81	18	40	.450	0	0	–	13	18	.722	5	5	17	3	10	0	2	–	1	49	4.3	0.8	12.3

Widby, George Ronald (Ron) b. March 9, 1945 Ht. 6-4 Wt. 210 College: Tennessee

SEASON–TEAM	G	GS	MIN	FGM	FGA	PCT	3FGM	3FGA	PCT	FTM	FTA	PCT	O-RB	D-RB	TOT	AST	PF	DQ	STL	TO	BLK	PTS	RPG	APG	PPG
67-68–New Orleans (A)	20	–	137	27	70	.386	0	3	.000	4	7	.571	–	–	45	4	18	0	–	7	–	58	2.3	0.2	2.9
Reg. ABA Totals	20	–	137	27	70	.386	0	3	.000	4	7	.571	–	–	45	4	18	0	–	7	–	58	2.3	0.2	2.9
ABA Playoff Totals	6	–	31	8	19	.421	2	3	.667	0	2	.000	–	–	17	1	5	0	–	2	–	18	2.8	0.2	3.0

Wier, Murray Neal b. December 12, 1926 Ht. 5-9 Wt. 155 College: Iowa

SEASON–TEAM	G	GS	MIN	FGM	FGA	PCT	3FGM	3FGA	PCT	FTM	FTA	PCT	O-RB	D-RB	TOT	AST	PF	DQ	STL	TO	BLK	PTS	RPG	APG	PPG
48-49–Tri-Cities (N)	60	–	–	80	–	–	–	–	–	79	113	.699	–	–	–	–	91	–	–	–	–	239	–	–	4.0
49-50–Tri-Cities	56	–	–	157	480	.327	–	–	–	115	166	.693	–	–	–	107	141	–	–	–	–	429	–	1.9	7.7
Reg. NBA Totals	56	–	–	157	480	.327	–	–	–	115	166	.693	–	–	–	107	141	–	–	–	–	429	–	1.9	7.7
Reg. NBL Totals	60	–	–	80	–	–	–	–	–	79	113	.699	–	–	–	–	91	–	–	–	–	239	–	–	4.0
NBA Playoff Totals	3	–	–	3	18	.333	–	–	–	4	8	.500	–	–	–	–	4	–	–	–	–	10	–	0.0	3.3
NBL Playoff Totals	6	–	–	13	–	–	–	–	–	9	13	.692	–	–	–	–	15	–	–	–	–	35	–	–	5.8

Wiesenhahn, Robert B. Jr. (Bob) b. December 22, 1938 Ht. 6-4 Wt. 215 College: Cincinnati

SEASON–TEAM	G	GS	MIN	FGM	FGA	PCT	3FGM	3FGA	PCT	FTM	FTA	PCT	O-RB	D-RB	TOT	AST	PF	DQ	STL	TO	BLK	PTS	RPG	APG	PPG
61-62–Cincinnati	60	–	326	51	161	.317	–	–	–	17	30	.567	–	–	112	23	50	0	–	–	–	119	1.9	0.4	2.0
Reg. Season Totals	60	–	326	51	161	.317	–	–	–	17	30	.567	–	–	112	23	50	0	–	–	–	119	1.9	0.4	2.0
Playoff Totals	2	–	6	1	4	.250	–	–	–	1	1	1.000	–	–	2	–	0	0	–	–	–	3	1.0	0.0	1.5

Wiggins, Mitchell Lee b. September 28, 1959 Ht. 6-4 Wt. 185 College: Truett-McConnell (Ga.) Coll. (J.C.); Clemson; Florida State

SEASON–TEAM	G	GS	MIN	FGM	FGA	PCT	3FGM	3FGA	PCT	FTM	FTA	PCT	O-RB	D-RB	TOT	AST	PF	DQ	STL	TO	BLK	PTS	RPG	APG	PPG
83-84–Chicago	82	40	2123	399	890	.448	7	29	.241	213	287	.742	138	190	328	187	278	8	106	139	11	1018	4.0	2.3	12.4
84-85–Houston	82	24	1575	318	657	.484	6	23	.261	96	131	.733	110	125	235	119	195	1	83	90	13	738	2.9	1.5	9.0
85-86–Houston	78	0	1198	222	489	.454	1	12	.083	86	118	.729	87	72	159	101	155	1	59	62	5	531	2.0	1.3	6.8
86-87–Houston	32	19	788	153	350	.437	0	5	.000	49	65	.754	74	59	133	76	82	1	44	50	3	355	4.2	2.4	11.1
89-90–Houston	66	52	1852	416	853	.488	0	3	.000	192	237	.810	133	153	286	104	165	0	85	87	1	1024	4.3	1.6	15.5
91-92–Philadelphia	49	0	569	88	229	.384	0	1	.000	35	51	.686	43	51	94	22	67	0	20	25	1	211	1.9	0.4	4.3
Reg. Season Totals	389	135	8105	1596	3468	.460	14	73	.192	671	889	.755	585	650	1235	609	942	11	397	453	34	3877	3.2	1.6	10.0
Playoff Totals	29	0	539	105	212	.495	0	3	.000	23	31	.742	45	48	93	34	55	0	19	34	3	233	3.2	1.2	8.0

Wilburn, Kenneth (Ken) b. June 8, 1944 Ht. 6-6 Wt. 195 College: Central State (Ohio)

SEASON–TEAM	G	GS	MIN	FGM	FGA	PCT	3FGM	3FGA	PCT	FTM	FTA	PCT	O-RB	D-RB	TOT	AST	PF	DQ	STL	TO	BLK	PTS	RPG	APG	PPG
67-68–Chicago	3	–	26	5	9	.556	–	–	–	1	4	.250	–	–	10	2	4	0	–	–	–	11	3.3	0.7	3.7
68-69–Chicago	4	–	14	3	8	.375	–	–	–	1	4	.250	–	–	3	1	1	0	–	–	–	7	0.8	0.3	1.8
68-69–Minn.-N.Y.-Den. (A)	47	–	465	76	198	.384	0	0	–	38	71	.535	–	–	199	26	68	1	–	47	–	190	4.2	0.6	4.0
Reg. NBA Totals	7	–	40	8	17	.471	–	–	–	2	8	.250	–	–	13	3	5	0	–	–	–	18	1.9	0.4	2.6
Reg. ABA Totals	47	–	465	76	198	.384	0	0	–	38	71	.535	–	–	199	26	68	1	–	47	–	190	4.2	0.6	4.0
ABA Playoff Totals	7	–	93	16	33	.485	0	0	–	4	16	.250	–	–	32	5	21	0	–	–	–	36	4.6	0.7	5.1

Wilcutt, D.C. b. March 25, 1923 Ht. 6-2 Wt. 165 College: St. Louis

SEASON–TEAM	G	GS	MIN	FGM	FGA	PCT	3FGM	3FGA	PCT	FTM	FTA	PCT	O-RB	D-RB	TOT	AST	PF	DQ	STL	TO	BLK	PTS	RPG	APG	PPG
48-49–St. Louis	22	–	–	18	51	.353	–	–	–	15	18	.833	–	–	–	31	9	–	–	–	–	51	–	1.4	2.3
49-50–St. Louis	37	–	–	24	73	.329	–	–	–	29	42	.690	–	–	–	49	27	–	–	–	–	77	–	1.3	2.1
Reg. Season Totals	59	–	–	42	124	.339	–	–	–	44	60	.733	–	–	–	80	36	–	–	–	–	128	–	1.4	2.2
Playoff Totals	2	–	–	3	9	.444	–	–	–	0	0	–	–	–	–	8	2	–	–	–	–	6	–	2.0	3.0

Wiley, Eugene (Gene) b. November 12, 1937 Ht. 6-10 Wt. 220 College: Wichita State

SEASON–TEAM	G	GS	MIN	FGM	FGA	PCT	3FGM	3FGA	PCT	FTM	FTA	PCT	O-RB	D-RB	TOT	AST	PF	DQ	STL	TO	BLK	PTS	RPG	APG	PPG
62-63–Los Angeles	75	–	1488	109	236	.462	–	–	–	23	68	.338	–	–	504	40	180	4	–	–	–	241	6.7	0.5	3.2
63-64–Los Angeles	78	–	1510	146	273	.535	–	–	–	45	75	.600	–	–	510	44	225	4	–	–	–	337	6.5	0.6	4.3
64-65–Los Angeles	80	–	2002	175	376	.465	–	–	–	56	111	.505	–	–	690	105	235	11	–	–	–	406	8.6	1.3	5.1
65-66–Los Angeles	67	–	1386	123	289	.426	–	–	–	43	76	.566	–	–	490	63	171	3	–	–	–	289	7.3	0.9	4.3
67-68–Oak.-Dallas (A)	9	–	85	7	20	.350	0	0	–	4	8	.500	–	–	20	2	10	0	–	2	–	18	2.2	0.2	2.0
Reg. NBA Totals	300	–	6386	553	1174	.471	–	–	–	167	330	.506	–	–	2194	252	811	22	–	–	–	1273	7.3	0.8	4.2
Reg. ABA Totals	9	–	85	7	20	.350	0	0	–	4	8	.500	–	–	20	2	10	0	–	2	–	18	2.2	0.2	2.0
NBA Playoff Totals	27	–	710	52	103	.505	–	–	–	16	37	.432	–	–	272	34	80	2	–	–	–	120	10.1	1.3	4.4

Wiley, Michael Anthony b. October 16, 1957 Ht. 6-9 Wt. 200 College: Long Beach State

SEASON–TEAM	G	GS	MIN	FGM	FGA	PCT	3FGM	3FGA	PCT	FTM	FTA	PCT	O-RB	D-RB	TOT	AST	PF	DQ	STL	TO	BLK	PTS	RPG	APG	PPG
80-81–San Antonio	33	–	271	76	138	.551	0	2	.000	36	48	.750	22	42	64	11	38	1	8	28	6	188	1.9	0.3	5.7
81-82–San Diego	61	1	1013	203	359	.565	0	5	.000	98	141	.695	67	115	182	52	127	1	40	71	16	504	3.0	0.9	8.3
Reg. Season Totals	94	1	1284	279	497	.561	0	7	.000	134	189	.709	89	157	246	63	165	2	48	99	22	692	2.6	0.7	7.4
Playoff Totals	3	0	5	0	1	.000	0	0	–	2	2	1.000	0	0	0	–	2	0	0	0	0	2	0.0	0.0	0.7

Wiley, Morlon David b. September 24, 1966 Ht. 6-4 Wt. 192 College: Long Beach State

SEASON–TEAM	G	GS	MIN	FGM	FGA	PCT	3FGM	3FGA	PCT	FTM	FTA	PCT	O-RB	D-RB	TOT	AST	PF	DQ	STL	TO	BLK	PTS	RPG	APG	PPG
88-89–Dallas	51	1	408	46	114	.404	6	24	.250	13	16	.813	13	34	47	76	61	0	25	34	6	111	0.9	1.5	2.2
89-90–Orlando	40	2	638	92	208	.442	17	46	.370	28	38	.737	13	39	52	114	65	0	45	63	3	229	1.3	2.9	5.7
90-91–Orlando	34	0	350	45	108	.417	6	12	.500	17	25	.680	4	13	17	73	37	1	24	34	0	113	0.5	2.1	3.3
91-92–Orl.-S.A.-Atlanta	53	19	870	83	193	.430	14	42	.333	24	35	.686	24	57	81	180	89	0	47	60	3	204	1.5	3.4	3.8
92-93–Atlanta-Dallas	58	15	995	96	254	.378	54	154	.351	17	26	.654	29	62	91	181	127	2	65	80	3	263	1.6	3.1	4.5
93-94–Miami-Dallas	16	0	158	9	29	.310	3	10	.300	0	0	–	0	10	10	23	21	0	15	17	0	21	0.6	1.4	1.3
94-95–Dallas-Hou.-Atlanta	43	2	424	50	117	.427	30	79	.380	7	10	.700	6	37	43	75	44	0	22	23	2	137	1.0	1.7	3.2
Reg. Season Totals	295	39	3843	421	1023	.412	130	367	.354	106	150	.707	89	252	341	722	444	3	243	311	17	1078	1.2	2.4	3.7

Wilfong, Alva Winfred (Win) b. March 18, 1932 d. May 18, 1985 Ht. 6-2 Wt. 185 College: Memphis; Missouri

SEASON–TEAM	G	GS	MIN	FGM	FGA	PCT	3FGM	3FGA	PCT	FTM	FTA	PCT	O-RB	D-RB	TOT	AST	PF	DQ	STL	TO	BLK	PTS	RPG	APG	PPG
57-58–St. Louis	71	–	1360	196	543	.361	–	–	–	163	238	.685	–	–	290	163	199	3	–	–	–	555	4.1	2.3	7.8
58-59–St. Louis	63	–	741	99	285	.347	–	–	–	62	82	.756	–	–	121	50	102	0	–	–	–	260	1.9	0.8	4.1
59-60–Cincinnati	72	–	1992	283	764	.370	–	–	–	161	207	.778	–	–	352	265	229	1	–	–	–	727	4.9	3.7	10.1
60-61–Cincinnati	62	–	717	106	305	.348	–	–	–	72	89	.809	–	–	147	87	119	1	–	–	–	284	2.4	1.4	4.6
Reg. Season Totals	268	–	4810	684	1897	.361	–	–	–	458	616	.744	–	–	910	565	649	5	–	–	–	1826	3.4	2.1	6.8
Playoff Totals	16	–	208	26	88	.295	–	–	–	28	39	.718	–	–	47	28	31	0	–	–	–	80	2.9	1.8	5.0

Wilkens, Leonard Randolph (Lenny) b. October 28, 1937 Ht. 6-1 Wt. 185 College: Providence HOF: 1989

SEASON–TEAM	G	GS	MIN	FGM	FGA	PCT	3FGM	3FGA	PCT	FTM	FTA	PCT	O-RB	D-RB	TOT	AST	PF	DQ	STL	TO	BLK	PTS	RPG	APG	PPG
60-61–St. Louis	75	–	1898	333	783	.425	–	–	–	214	300	.713	–	–	335	212	215	5	–	–	–	880	4.5	2.8	11.7
61-62–St. Louis	20	–	870	140	364	.385	–	–	–	84	110	.764	–	–	131	116	63	0	–	–	–	364	6.6	5.8	18.2
62-63–St. Louis	75	–	2569	333	834	.399	–	–	–	222	319	.696	–	–	403	381	256	6	–	–	–	888	5.4	5.1	11.8
63-64–St. Louis	78	–	2526	334	808	.413	–	–	–	270	365	.740	–	–	335	359	287	7	–	–	–	938	4.3	4.6	12.0
64-65–St. Louis	78	–	2854	434	1048	.414	–	–	–	416	558	.746	–	–	365	431	283	7	–	–	–	1284	4.7	5.5	16.5
65-66–St. Louis	69	–	2692	411	954	.431	–	–	–	422	532	.793	–	–	322	429	248	4	–	–	–	1244	4.7	6.2	18.0
66-67–St. Louis	78	–	2974	448	1036	.432	–	–	–	459	583	.787	–	–	412	442	280	6	–	–	–	1355	5.3	5.7	17.4
67-68–St. Louis	82	–	3169	546	1246	.438	–	–	–	546	711	.768	–	–	438	679	255	3	–	–	–	1638	5.3	8.3	20.0
68-69–Seattle	82	–	3463	644	1462	.440	–	–	–	547	710	.770	–	–	511	674	294	8	–	–	–	1835	6.2	8.2	22.4
69-70–Seattle	75	–	2802	448	1066	.420	–	–	–	438	556	.788	–	–	378	683	212	5	–	–	–	1334	5.0	9.1	17.8
70-71–Seattle	71	–	2641	471	1125	.419	–	–	–	461	574	.803	–	–	319	654	201	3	–	–	–	1403	4.5	9.2	19.8
71-72–Seattle	80	–	2989	479	1027	.466	–	–	–	480	620	.774	–	–	338	766	209	4	–	–	–	1438	4.2	9.6	18.0
72-73–Cleveland	75	–	2973	572	1275	.449	–	–	–	394	476	.828	–	–	346	628	221	2	–	–	–	1538	4.6	8.4	20.5
73-74–Cleveland	74	–	2483	462	994	.465	–	–	–	289	361	.801	80	197	277	522	165	2	97	–	17	1213	3.7	7.1	16.4
74-75–Portland	65	–	1161	134	305	.439	–	–	–	152	198	.768	38	82	120	235	96	1	77	–	9	420	1.8	3.6	6.5
Reg. Season Totals	1077	–	38064	6189	14327	.432	–	–	–	5394	6973	.774	118	279	5030	7211	3285	63	174	–	26	17772	4.7	6.7	16.5
Playoff Totals	64	–	2403	359	899	.399	–	–	–	313	407	.769	0	0	373	372	258	7	0	–	0	1031	5.8	5.8	16.1
All-Star Totals	9	–	182	30	75	.400	–	–	–	25	32	.781	0	0	22	26	15	0	0	–	0	85	2.4	2.9	9.4

Wilkerson, Robert Lee (Bob) b. August 15, 1954 Ht. 6-6 Wt. 195 College: Indiana

SEASON–TEAM	G	GS	MIN	FGM	FGA	PCT	3FGM	3FGA	PCT	FTM	FTA	PCT	O-RB	D-RB	TOT	AST	PF	DQ	STL	TO	BLK	PTS	RPG	APG	PPG
76-77–Seattle	78	–	1552	221	573	.386	–	–	–	84	122	.689	96	162	258	171	136	0	72	–	8	526	3.3	2.2	6.7
77-78–Denver	81	–	2780	382	936	.408	–	–	–	157	210	.748	98	376	474	439	275	3	126	294	21	921	5.9	5.4	11.4
78-79–Denver	80	–	2425	396	869	.456	–	–	–	119	173	.688	100	314	414	284	190	0	118	196	21	911	5.2	3.6	11.4
79-80–Denver	75	–	2381	430	1030	.417	7	34	.206	166	222	.748	85	231	316	243	194	1	93	193	27	1033	4.2	3.2	13.8
80-81–Chicago	80	–	2238	330	715	.462	1	10	.100	137	163	.840	86	196	282	272	170	0	102	175	23	798	3.5	3.4	10.0
81-82–Cleveland	65	38	1805	284	679	.418	3	18	.167	145	185	.784	60	190	250	237	188	3	92	138	25	716	3.8	3.6	11.0
82-83–Cleveland	77	11	1702	213	511	.417	0	4	.000	93	124	.750	62	180	242	189	157	0	68	160	16	519	3.1	2.5	6.7
Reg. Season Totals	536	49	14883	2256	5313	.425	11	66	.167	901	1199	.751	587	1649	2236	1835	1310	7	671	1156	141	5424	4.2	3.4	10.1
Playoff Totals	22	0	679	86	220	.391	0	1	.000	32	50	.640	33	80	113	107	75	2	27	42	6	204	5.1	4.9	9.3

Wilkes, Jamaal Abdul-Lateef (Silk, formerly Jackson Keith Wilkes) b. May 2, 1953 Ht. 6-6 Wt. 190 College: UCLA

SEASON–TEAM	G	GS	MIN	FGM	FGA	PCT	3FGM	3FGA	PCT	FTM	FTA	PCT	O-RB	D-RB	TOT	AST	PF	DQ	STL	TO	BLK	PTS	RPG	APG	PPG
74-75–Golden State	82	–	2515	502	1135	.442	–	–	–	160	218	.734	203	468	671	183	222	0	107	–	22	1164	8.2	2.2	14.2
75-76–Golden State	82	–	2716	617	1334	.463	–	–	–	227	294	.772	193	527	720	167	222	0	102	–	31	1461	8.8	2.0	17.8
76-77–Golden State	76	–	2579	548	1147	.478	–	–	–	247	310	.797	155	423	578	211	222	1	127	–	16	1343	7.6	2.8	17.7
77-78–Los Angeles	51	–	1490	277	630	.440	–	–	–	106	148	.716	113	267	380	182	162	1	77	107	22	660	7.5	3.6	12.9
78-79–Los Angeles	82	–	2915	626	1242	.504	–	–	–	272	362	.751	164	445	609	227	275	2	134	224	27	1524	7.4	2.8	18.6
79-80–Los Angeles	82	–	3111	726	1358	.535	3	17	.176	189	234	.808	176	349	525	250	220	1	129	157	28	1644	6.4	3.0	20.0
80-81–Los Angeles	81	–	3028	786	1495	.526	1	13	.077	254	335	.758	146	289	435	235	223	1	121	207	29	1827	5.4	2.9	22.6
81-82–Los Angeles	82	82	2906	744	1417	.525	0	4	.000	246	336	.732	153	240	393	143	240	1	89	164	24	1734	4.8	1.7	21.1
82-83–Los Angeles	80	80	2552	684	1290	.530	0	6	.000	203	268	.757	146	197	343	182	221	0	65	150	17	1571	4.3	2.3	19.6
83-84–Los Angeles	75	74	2507	542	1055	.514	2	8	.250	208	280	.743	130	210	340	214	205	0	72	137	41	1294	4.5	2.9	17.3
84-85–L.A. Lakers	42	8	761	148	303	.488	0	1	.000	51	66	.773	35	59	94	41	65	0	19	49	3	347	2.2	1.0	8.3
85-86–L.A. Clippers	13	1	195	26	65	.400	1	3	.333	22	27	.815	13	16	29	15	19	0	7	16	2	75	2.2	1.2	5.8
Reg. Season Totals	828	245	27275	6226	12471	.499	7	52	.135	2185	2878	.759	1627	3490	5117	2050	2296	7	1049	1211	262	14644	6.2	2.5	17.7
Playoff Totals	113	29	3799	785	1689	.465	0	6	.000	250	344	.727	251	467	718	246	326	3	137	145	53	1820	6.4	2.2	16.1
All-Star Totals	3	0	54	13	27	.481	0	0	–	7	7	1.000	6	8	14	7	3	0	4	4	0	33	4.7	2.3	11.0

Wilkes, James Robert b. March 12, 1958 Ht. 6-7 Wt. 200 College: UCLA

SEASON–TEAM	G	GS	MIN	FGM	FGA	PCT	3FGM	3FGA	PCT	FTM	FTA	PCT	O-RB	D-RB	TOT	AST	PF	DQ	STL	TO	BLK	PTS	RPG	APG	PPG
80-81–Chicago	48	–	540	85	184	.462	0	1	.000	29	42	.690	36	60	96	30	86	0	25	34	12	199	2.0	0.6	4.1
81-82–Chicago	57	22	862	128	266	.481	0	1	.000	58	80	.725	62	97	159	64	112	0	30	62	18	314	2.8	1.1	5.5
82-83–Detroit	9	0	129	11	34	.324	0	1	.000	12	15	.800	9	10	19	10	22	0	3	5	1	34	2.1	1.1	3.8
Reg. Season Totals	114	22	1531	224	484	.463	0	3	.000	99	137	.723	107	167	274	104	220	0	58	101	31	547	2.4	0.9	4.8
Playoff Totals	2	0	5	0	1	.000	0	0	–	0	0	–	0	1	1	1	0	0	1	2	0	0	0.5	0.5	0.0

Wilkins, Eddie Lee (Eddie Lee) b. May 7, 1962 Ht. 6-10 Wt. 265 College: Gardner-Webb

SEASON–TEAM	G	GS	MIN	FGM	FGA	PCT	3FGM	3FGA	PCT	FTM	FTA	PCT	O-RB	D-RB	TOT	AST	PF	DQ	STL	TO	BLK	PTS	RPG	APG	PPG
84-85–New York	54	16	917	116	233	.498	0	2	.000	66	122	.541	86	176	262	16	155	3	21	64	16	298	4.9	0.3	5.5
86-87–New York	24	10	454	56	127	.441	0	1	.000	27	58	.466	45	62	107	6	67	1	9	28	2	139	4.5	0.3	5.8
88-89–New York	71	2	584	114	245	.465	0	1	.000	61	111	.550	72	76	148	7	110	1	10	56	16	289	2.1	0.1	4.1
89-90–New York	79	0	972	141	310	.455	0	2	.000	89	147	.605	114	151	265	16	152	1	18	73	18	371	3.4	0.2	4.7
90-91–New York	68	1	668	114	255	.447	0	1	.000	51	90	.567	69	111	180	15	91	0	17	50	7	279	2.6	0.2	4.1
92-93–Philadelphia	26	0	192	55	97	.567	0	2	.000	48	78	.615	14	26	40	2	34	1	7	17	1	158	1.5	0.1	6.1
Reg. Season Totals	322	29	3787	596	1267	.470	0	9	.000	342	606	.564	400	602	1002	62	609	7	82	288	60	1534	3.1	0.2	4.8
Playoff Totals	15	0	93	18	35	.514	0	0	–	12	23	.522	12	12	24	–	14	0	2	8	0	48	1.6	0.0	3.2

Wilkins, Gerald Bernard (Doug E. Fresh) b. September 11, 1963 Ht. 6-6 Wt. 225 College: Moberly Area (Mo.) C.C.; Tennessee-Chattanooga

SEASON–TEAM	G	GS	MIN	FGM	FGA	PCT	3FGM	3FGA	PCT	FTM	FTA	PCT	O-RB	D-RB	TOT	AST	PF	DQ	STL	TO	BLK	PTS	RPG	APG	PPG
85-86–New York	81	53	2025	437	934	.468	7	25	.280	132	237	.557	92	116	208	161	155	0	68	157	9	1013	2.6	2.0	12.5
86-87–New York	80	73	2758	633	1302	.486	26	74	.351	235	335	.701	120	174	294	354	165	0	88	214	18	1527	3.7	4.4	19.1
87-88–New York	81	78	2703	591	1324	.446	39	129	.302	191	243	.786	106	164	270	326	183	1	90	212	22	1412	3.3	4.0	17.4
88-89–New York	81	58	2414	462	1025	.451	51	172	.297	186	246	.756	95	149	244	274	166	1	115	169	22	1161	3.0	3.4	14.3
89-90–New York	82	80	2609	472	1032	.457	39	125	.312	208	259	.803	133	238	371	330	188	0	95	194	21	1191	4.5	4.0	14.5
90-91–New York	68	56	2164	380	804	.473	9	43	.209	169	206	.820	78	129	207	275	181	0	82	161	23	938	3.0	4.0	13.8
91-92–New York	82	82	2344	431	964	.447	38	108	.352	116	159	.730	74	132	206	219	195	4	76	113	17	1016	2.5	2.7	12.4
92-93–Cleveland	80	35	2079	361	797	.453	16	58	.276	152	181	.840	74	140	214	183	154	1	78	94	18	890	2.7	2.3	11.1
93-94–Cleveland	82	82	2768	446	975	.457	84	212	.396	194	250	.776	106	197	303	255	186	0	105	131	38	1170	3.7	3.1	14.3
95-96–Vancouver	28	14	738	77	205	.376	14	64	.219	20	23	.870	22	43	65	68	55	0	22	37	2	188	2.3	2.4	6.7
96-97–Orlando	80	26	2202	323	759	.426	66	203	.325	136	190	.716	59	114	173	173	144	0	54	123	12	848	2.2	2.2	10.6
97-98–Orlando	72	16	1252	141	434	.325	29	109	.266	69	98	.704	16	74	90	78	78	0	34	79	6	380	1.3	1.1	5.3
98-99–Orlando	3	0	28	0	9	.000	0	0	–	2	2	1.000	0	1	1	1	3	0	0	3	0	2	0.3	0.3	0.7
Reg. Season Totals	900	653	26084	4754	10564	.450	418	1322	.316	1810	2429	.745	975	1671	2646	2697	1853	7	907	1687	208	11736	2.9	3.0	13.0
Playoff Totals	55	41	1686	292	661	.442	22	79	.278	105	131	.802	50	103	153	190	137	1	52	91	10	711	2.8	3.5	12.9

Wilkins, Jacques Dominique (Dominique, Human Highlight Film) b. January 12, 1960 Ht. 6-8 Wt. 230 College: Georgia

SEASON–TEAM	G	GS	MIN	FGM	FGA	PCT	3FGM	3FGA	PCT	FTM	FTA	PCT	O-RB	D-RB	TOT	AST	PF	DQ	STL	TO	BLK	PTS	RPG	APG	PPG
82-83–Atlanta	82	82	2697	601	1220	.493	2	11	.182	230	337	.682	226	252	478	129	210	1	84	180	63	1434	5.8	1.6	17.5
83-84–Atlanta	81	81	2961	684	1429	.479	0	11	.000	382	496	.770	254	328	582	126	197	1	117	215	87	1750	7.2	1.6	21.6
84-85–Atlanta	81	81	3023	853	1891	.451	25	81	.309	486	603	.806	226	331	557	200	170	0	135	225	54	2217	6.9	2.5	27.4
85-86–Atlanta	78	78	3049	888	1897	.468	13	70	.186	577	705	.818	261	357	618	206	170	0	138	251	49	2366	7.9	2.6	30.3
86-87–Atlanta	79	79	2969	828	1787	.463	31	106	.292	607	742	.818	210	284	494	261	149	0	117	215	51	2294	6.3	3.3	29.0
87-88–Atlanta	78	76	2948	909	1957	.464	38	129	.295	541	655	.826	211	291	502	224	162	0	103	218	47	2397	6.4	2.9	30.7
88-89–Atlanta	80	80	2997	814	1756	.464	29	105	.276	442	524	.844	256	297	553	211	138	0	117	181	52	2099	6.9	2.6	26.2
89-90–Atlanta	80	79	2888	810	1672	.484	59	183	.322	459	569	.807	217	304	521	200	141	0	126	174	47	2138	6.5	2.5	26.7
90-91–Atlanta	81	81	3078	770	1640	.470	85	249	.341	476	574	.829	261	471	732	265	156	0	123	201	65	2101	9.0	3.3	25.9
91-92–Atlanta	42	42	1601	424	914	.464	37	128	.289	294	352	.835	103	192	295	158	77	0	52	122	24	1179	7.0	3.8	28.1
92-93–Atlanta	71	70	2647	741	1584	.468	120	316	.380	519	627	.828	187	295	482	227	116	0	70	184	27	2121	6.8	3.2	29.9
93-94–Atlanta-LAClips	74	74	2635	698	1588	.440	85	295	.288	442	522	.847	182	299	481	169	126	0	92	172	30	1923	6.5	2.3	26.0
94-95–Boston	77	64	2423	496	1169	.424	112	289	.388	266	340	.782	157	244	401	166	130	0	61	173	14	1370	5.2	2.2	17.8
96-97–San Antonio	63	26	1945	397	953	.417	70	239	.293	281	350	.803	169	233	402	119	100	0	39	135	31	1145	6.4	1.9	18.2
98-99–Orlando	27	2	252	50	132	.379	5	19	.263	29	42	.690	30	41	71	16	19	0	4	23	1	134	2.6	0.6	5.0
Reg. Season Totals	1074	995	38113	9963	21589	.461	711	2231	.319	6031	7438	.811	2950	4219	7169	2677	2061	2	1378	2669	642	26668	6.7	2.5	24.8
Playoff Totals	56	55	2172	515	1201	.429	27	96	.281	366	444	.824	158	217	375	143	123	0	73	153	35	1423	6.7	2.6	25.4
All-Star Totals	8	3	159	38	95	.400	2	8	.250	28	38	.737	16	11	27	15	13	0	6	8	4	106	3.4	1.9	13.3

Wilkins, Jeffrey (Jeff) b. March 9, 1955 Ht. 6-10 Wt. 230 College: Black Hawk (Ill.) Coll. (J.C.); Illinois State

SEASON–TEAM	G	GS	MIN	FGM	FGA	PCT	3FGM	3FGA	PCT	FTM	FTA	PCT	O-RB	D-RB	TOT	AST	PF	DQ	STL	TO	BLK	PTS	RPG	APG	PPG
80-81–Utah	56	–	1058	117	260	.450	0	0	–	27	40	.675	62	212	274	40	169	3	32	59	46	261	4.9	0.7	4.7
81-82–Utah	82	62	2274	314	718	.437	0	3	.000	137	176	.778	120	491	611	90	248	4	32	134	77	765	7.5	1.1	9.3
82-83–Utah	81	34	2307	389	816	.477	0	3	.000	156	200	.780	154	442	596	132	251	4	41	186	42	934	7.4	1.6	11.5
83-84–Utah	81	1	1734	249	520	.479	0	3	.000	134	182	.736	109	346	455	73	205	1	27	109	42	632	5.6	0.9	7.8
84-85–Utah	79	0	1505	285	582	.490	0	1	.000	61	80	.763	78	288	366	81	173	0	35	91	18	631	4.6	1.0	8.0
85-86–Utah-S.A.	75	4	1126	147	374	.393	0	0	–	58	93	.624	74	198	272	46	157	1	11	52	21	352	3.6	0.6	4.7
Reg. Season Totals	454	101	10004	1501	3270	.459	0	10	.000	573	771	.743	597	1977	2574	462	1203	13	178	631	246	3575	5.7	1.0	7.9
Playoff Totals	24	1	478	81	176	.460	0	1	.000	44	57	.772	23	92	115	18	65	0	4	26	12	206	4.8	0.8	8.6

Wilkinson, Dale Wayne b. March 18, 1960 Ht. 6-10 Wt. 220 College: Idaho State

SEASON–TEAM	G	GS	MIN	FGM	FGA	PCT	3FGM	3FGA	PCT	FTM	FTA	PCT	O-RB	D-RB	TOT	AST	PF	DQ	STL	TO	BLK	PTS	RPG	APG	PPG
84-85–Detroit-LAClips	12	0	45	4	16	.250	0	1	.000	6	7	.857	1	3	4	2	10	0	0	4	0	14	0.3	0.2	1.2
Reg. Season Totals	12	0	45	4	16	.250	0	1	.000	6	7	.857	1	3	4	2	10	0	0	4	0	14	0.3	0.2	1.2

Williams, Aaron b. January 2, 1971 Ht. 6-9 Wt. 225 College: Xavier (Ohio)

SEASON–TEAM	G	GS	MIN	FGM	FGA	PCT	3FGM	3FGA	PCT	FTM	FTA	PCT	O-RB	D-RB	TOT	AST	PF	DQ	STL	TO	BLK	PTS	RPG	APG	PPG
93-94–Utah	6	0	12	2	8	.250	0	0	–	0	1	.000	1	2	3	1	4	0	0	1	0	4	0.5	0.2	0.7
94-95–Milwaukee	15	0	72	8	24	.333	0	1	.000	8	12	.667	5	14	19	0	14	0	2	7	6	24	1.3	0.0	1.6
96-97–Denver-Vanc.	33	1	563	85	148	.574	0	1	.000	33	49	.673	62	81	143	15	72	1	16	32	29	203	4.3	0.5	6.2
97-98–Seattle	65	9	757	115	220	.523	0	1	.000	66	85	.776	48	99	147	14	119	0	19	50	38	296	2.3	0.2	4.6
98-99–Seattle	40	2	458	52	123	.423	0	1	.000	54	74	.730	54	74	128	22	75	1	14	30	24	158	3.2	0.6	4.0
99-00–Washington	81	0	1545	235	450	.522	0	3	.000	146	201	.726	159	250	409	58	234	3	41	80	92	616	5.0	0.7	7.6
Reg. Season Totals	240	12	3407	497	973	.511	0	7	.000	307	422	.727	329	520	849	110	518	5	92	200	189	1301	3.5	0.5	5.4
Playoff Totals	3	0	7	0	3	.000	0	0	–	2	2	1.000	1	0	1	–	0	0	0	1	1	2	0.3	0.0	0.7

Williams, Alfred (Al) b. January 3, 1948 Ht. 6-6 Wt. 210 College: Drake

SEASON–TEAM	G	GS	MIN	FGM	FGA	PCT	3FGM	3FGA	PCT	FTM	FTA	PCT	O-RB	D-RB	TOT	AST	PF	DQ	STL	TO	BLK	PTS	RPG	APG	PPG
70-71–Kentucky (A)	11	–	70	19	43	.442	0	0	–	5	10	.500	–	–	26	5	13	–	–	–	–	43	2.4	0.5	3.9
Reg. ABA Totals	11	–	70	19	43	.442	0	0	–	5	10	.500	–	–	26	5	13	–	–	–	–	43	2.4	0.5	3.9

Williams, Alvin Leon b. August 6, 1974 Ht. 6-5 Wt. 185 College: Villanova

SEASON–TEAM	G	GS	MIN	FGM	FGA	PCT	3FGM	3FGA	PCT	FTM	FTA	PCT	O-RB	D-RB	TOT	AST	PF	DQ	STL	TO	BLK	PTS	RPG	APG	PPG
97-98–Port.-Toronto	54	13	1071	125	282	.443	9	28	.321	65	90	.722	24	57	81	103	79	0	38	58	3	324	1.5	1.9	6.0
98-99–Toronto	50	45	1051	95	237	.401	14	42	.333	44	52	.846	19	63	82	130	94	1	51	56	12	248	1.6	2.6	5.0
99-00–Toronto	55	28	779	114	287	.397	16	55	.291	48	65	.738	27	58	85	126	78	0	34	47	11	292	1.5	2.3	5.3
Reg. Season Totals	159	86	2901	334	806	.414	39	125	.312	157	207	.758	70	178	248	359	251	1	123	161	26	864	1.6	2.3	5.4
Playoff Totals	1	0	1	0	0	–	0	0	–	0	0	–	0	0	0	–	0	0	0	0	0	0	0.0	0.0	0.0

Williams, Arthur T. (Hambone) b. September 29, 1939 Ht. 6-2 Wt. 180 College: San Diego City (Calif.) Coll. (J.C.); Cal Poly-S.L.O.

SEASON–TEAM	G	GS	MIN	FGM	FGA	PCT	3FGM	3FGA	PCT	FTM	FTA	PCT	O-RB	D-RB	TOT	AST	PF	DQ	STL	TO	BLK	PTS	RPG	APG	PPG
67-68–San Diego	79	–	1739	265	718	.369	–	–	–	113	165	.685	–	–	286	391	204	0	–	–	–	643	3.6	4.9	8.1
68-69–San Diego	79	–	1987	227	592	.383	–	–	–	105	149	.705	–	–	364	524	238	0	–	–	–	559	4.6	6.6	7.1
69-70–San Diego	80	–	1545	189	464	.407	–	–	–	88	118	.746	–	–	292	503	168	0	–	–	–	466	3.7	6.3	5.8
70-71–Boston	74	–	1141	150	330	.455	–	–	–	60	83	.723	–	–	205	233	182	1	–	–	–	360	2.8	3.1	4.9
71-72–Boston	81	–	1326	161	339	.475	–	–	–	90	119	.756	–	–	256	327	204	2	–	–	–	412	3.2	4.0	5.1
72-73–Boston	81	–	974	110	261	.421	–	–	–	43	56	.768	–	–	182	236	136	1	–	–	–	263	2.2	2.9	3.2
73-74–Boston	67	–	617	73	168	.435	–	–	–	27	32	.844	20	95	115	163	100	0	44	–	3	173	1.7	2.4	2.6
74-75–San Diego (A)	7	–	89	8	12	.667	0	0	–	0	0	–	3	9	12	20	15	–	7	10	0	16	1.7	2.9	2.3
Reg. NBA Totals	541	–	9329	1175	2872	.409	–	–	–	526	722	.729	20	95	1700	2377	1232	4	44	–	3	2876	3.1	4.4	5.3
Reg. ABA Totals	7	–	89	8	12	.667	0	0	–	0	0	–	3	9	12	20	15	–	7	10	0	16	1.7	2.9	2.3
NBA Playoff Totals	39	–	527	68	163	.417	–	–	–	31	43	.721	4	19	95	135	90	1	7	–	0	167	2.4	3.5	4.3

Williams, Bernard (Bernie) b. December 30, 1945 Ht. 6-3 Wt. 175 College: La Salle

SEASON–TEAM	G	GS	MIN	FGM	FGA	PCT	3FGM	3FGA	PCT	FTM	FTA	PCT	O-RB	D-RB	TOT	AST	PF	DQ	STL	TO	BLK	PTS	RPG	APG	PPG
69-70–San Diego	72	–	1228	251	641	.392	–	–	–	96	122	.787	–	–	155	165	124	0	–	–	–	598	2.2	2.3	8.3
70-71–San Diego	56	–	708	112	338	.331	–	–	–	68	81	.840	–	–	85	113	76	1	–	–	–	292	1.5	2.0	5.2
71-72–Virginia (A)	78	–	1667	349	816	.428	18	65	.277	113	142	.796	–	–	154	134	178	–	–	123	–	829	2.0	1.7	10.6
72-73–Virginia (A)	71	–	1513	356	831	.428	10	58	.172	166	193	.860	60	65	125	137	150	0	–	136	–	888	1.8	1.9	12.5
73-74–Virginia (A)	6	–	51	6	19	.316	1	2	.500	2	2	1.000	0	4	4	7	3	–	1	5	0	15	0.7	1.2	2.5
Reg. NBA Totals	128	–	1936	363	979	.371	–	–	–	164	203	.808	–	–	240	278	200	1	–	–	–	890	1.9	2.2	7.0
Reg. ABA Totals	155	–	3231	711	1666	.427	29	125	.232	281	337	.834	60	69	283	278	331	0	1	264	0	1732	1.8	1.8	11.2
ABA Playoff Totals	14	–	380	87	198	.439	2	5	.400	20	28	.714	0	0	47	24	42	0	0	35	0	196	3.4	1.7	14.0

Williams, Brandon b. February 27, 1975 Ht. 6-6 Wt. 215 College: Davidson

SEASON–TEAM	G	GS	MIN	FGM	FGA	PCT	3FGM	3FGA	PCT	FTM	FTA	PCT	O-RB	D-RB	TOT	AST	PF	DQ	STL	TO	BLK	PTS	RPG	APG	PPG
97-98–Golden State	9	2	140	16	50	.320	3	9	.333	2	4	.500	4	11	15	3	18	0	6	9	3	37	1.7	0.3	4.1
98-99–San Antonio	3	0	4	0	0	–	0	0	–	2	4	.500	1	0	1	0	0	0	0	0	0	2	0.3	0.0	0.7
Reg. Season Totals	12	2	144	16	50	.320	3	9	.333	4	8	.500	5	11	16	3	18	0	6	9	3	39	1.3	0.3	3.3

Williams, Charles E. (Charlie, Toothpick) b. September 5, 1943 Ht. 6-0 Wt. 175 College: Seattle

SEASON–TEAM	G	GS	MIN	FGM	FGA	PCT	3FGM	3FGA	PCT	FTM	FTA	PCT	O-RB	D-RB	TOT	AST	PF	DQ	STL	TO	BLK	PTS	RPG	APG	PPG
67-68–Pittsburgh (A)	78	–	3042	642	1573	.408	51	178	.287	290	429	.676	–	–	377	173	295	6	–	270	–	1625	4.8	2.2	20.8
68-69–Minnesota (A)	66	–	2282	484	1298	.373	66	212	.311	203	286	.710	–	–	246	163	222	6	–	204	–	1237	3.7	2.5	18.7
69-70–Pittsburgh (A)	26	–	925	193	537	.359	16	75	.213	104	135	.770	–	–	78	94	80	1	–	–	–	506	3.0	3.6	19.5
70-71–Pitt.-Mem. (A)	88	–	2242	501	1217	.412	33	136	.243	204	291	.701	–	–	210	250	243	–	–	–	–	1239	2.4	2.8	14.1
71-72–Memphis (A)	82	–	2583	480	1258	.382	41	174	.236	294	395	.744	–	–	228	253	250	–	–	233	–	1295	2.8	3.1	15.8
72-73–Mem.-Utah (A)	32	–	370	37	115	.322	3	20	.150	41	57	.719	4	14	18	59	54	1	–	34	–	118	0.6	1.8	3.7
Reg. ABA Totals	372	–	11444	2337	5998	.390	210	795	.264	1136	1593	.713	4	14	1157	992	1144	14	–	741	–	6020	3.1	2.7	16.2
ABA Playoff Totals	30	–	1022	218	527	.414	19	79	.241	100	139	.719	–	–	103	60	107	4	–	57	–	555	3.4	2.0	18.5

Williams, Charles Leon (Chuckie) b. December 31, 1953 Ht. 6-3 Wt. 180 College: Kansas State

SEASON–TEAM	G	GS	MIN	FGM	FGA	PCT	3FGM	3FGA	PCT	FTM	FTA	PCT	O-RB	D-RB	TOT	AST	PF	DQ	STL	TO	BLK	PTS	RPG	APG	PPG
76-77–Cleveland	22	–	65	14	47	.298	–	–	–	9	12	.750	3	1	4	7	7	0	1	–	0	37	0.2	0.3	1.7
Reg. Season Totals	22	–	65	14	47	.298	–	–	–	9	12	.750	3	1	4	7	7	0	1	–	0	37	0.2	0.3	1.7

Williams, Charles Linwood (Buck) b. March 8, 1960 Ht. 6-8 Wt. 225 College: Maryland

SEASON–TEAM	G	GS	MIN	FGM	FGA	PCT	3FGM	3FGA	PCT	FTM	FTA	PCT	O-RB	D-RB	TOT	AST	PF	DQ	STL	TO	BLK	PTS	RPG	APG	PPG
81-82–New Jersey	82	82	2825	513	881	.582	0	1	.000	242	388	.624	347	658	1005	107	285	5	84	235	84	1268	12.3	1.3	15.5
82-83–New Jersey	82	82	2961	536	912	.588	0	4	.000	324	523	.620	365	662	1027	125	270	4	91	246	110	1396	12.5	1.5	17.0
83-84–New Jersey	81	81	3003	495	926	.535	0	4	.000	284	498	.570	355	645	1000	130	298	3	81	237	125	1274	12.3	1.6	15.7
84-85–New Jersey	82	82	3182	577	1089	.530	1	4	.250	336	538	.625	323	682	1005	167	293	7	63	238	110	1491	12.3	2.0	18.2
85-86–New Jersey	82	82	3070	500	956	.523	0	2	.000	301	445	.676	329	657	986	131	294	9	73	244	96	1301	12.0	1.6	15.9
86-87–New Jersey	82	82	2976	521	936	.557	0	1	.000	430	588	.731	322	701	1023	129	315	8	78	280	91	1472	12.5	1.6	18.0
87-88–New Jersey	70	70	2637	466	832	.560	1	1	1.000	346	518	.668	298	536	834	109	266	5	68	189	44	1279	11.9	1.6	18.3
88-89–New Jersey	74	72	2446	373	702	.531	0	3	.000	213	320	.666	249	447	696	78	223	0	61	142	36	959	9.4	1.1	13.0
89-90–Portland	82	82	2801	413	754	.548	0	1	.000	288	408	.706	250	550	800	116	285	4	69	168	39	1114	9.8	1.4	13.6
90-91–Portland	80	80	2582	358	595	.602	0	0	–	217	308	.705	227	524	751	97	247	2	47	137	47	933	9.4	1.2	11.7
91-92–Portland	80	80	2519	340	563	.604	0	1	.000	221	293	.754	260	444	704	108	244	4	62	130	41	901	8.8	1.4	11.3
92-93–Portland	82	82	2498	270	528	.511	0	1	.000	138	214	.645	232	458	690	75	270	0	81	101	61	678	8.4	0.9	8.3
93-94–Portland	81	81	2636	291	524	.555	0	1	.000	201	296	.679	315	528	843	80	239	1	58	111	47	783	10.4	1.0	9.7
94-95–Portland	82	82	2422	309	604	.512	1	2	.500	138	205	.673	251	418	669	78	254	2	67	119	69	757	8.2	1.0	9.2
95-96–Portland	70	10	1672	192	384	.500	2	3	.667	125	187	.668	159	245	404	42	187	1	40	90	47	511	5.8	0.6	7.3
96-97–New York	74	4	1496	175	326	.537	0	1	.000	115	179	.642	166	231	397	53	204	2	40	79	38	465	5.4	0.7	6.3
97-98–New York	41	6	738	75	149	.503	0	0	–	52	71	.732	78	105	183	21	93	1	17	38	15	202	4.5	0.5	4.9
Reg. Season Totals	1307	1140	42464	6404	11661	.549	5	30	.167	3971	5979	.664	4526	8491	13017	1646	4267	58	1080	2784	1100	16784	10.0	1.3	12.8
Playoff Totals	108	92	3710	436	839	.520	1	2	.500	338	503	.672	351	590	941	113	386	10	90	190	70	1211	8.7	1.0	11.2
All-Star Totals	3	0	61	10	19	.526	0	0	–	5	11	.455	7	17	24	6	3	0	1	4	2	25	8.0	2.0	8.3

Williams, Clifford L. (Cliff) b. April 15, 1945 Ht. 6-3 Wt. 180 College: Bowling Green State

SEASON–TEAM	G	GS	MIN	FGM	FGA	PCT	3FGM	3FGA	PCT	FTM	FTA	PCT	O-RB	D-RB	TOT	AST	PF	DQ	STL	TO	BLK	PTS	RPG	APG	PPG
68-69–Detroit	3	–	18	2	9	.222	–	–	–	0	0	–	–	–	3	2	7	0	–	–	–	4	1.0	0.7	1.3
Reg. Season Totals	3	–	18	2	9	.222	–	–	–	0	0	–	–	–	3	2	7	0	–	–	–	4	1.0	0.7	1.3

Williams, Corey b. April 24, 1970 Ht. 6-2 Wt. 190 College: Oklahoma State

SEASON–TEAM	G	GS	MIN	FGM	FGA	PCT	3FGM	3FGA	PCT	FTM	FTA	PCT	O-RB	D-RB	TOT	AST	PF	DQ	STL	TO	BLK	PTS	RPG	APG	PPG
92-93–Chicago	35	0	242	31	85	.365	1	3	.333	18	22	.818	19	12	31	23	24	0	4	11	2	81	0.9	0.7	2.3
93-94–Minnesota	4	0	46	5	13	.385	0	1	.000	1	1	1.000	1	5	6	6	6	0	2	2	0	11	1.5	1.5	2.8
Reg. Season Totals	39	0	288	36	98	.367	1	4	.250	19	23	.826	20	17	37	29	30	0	6	13	2	92	0.9	0.7	2.4

Williams, Donald Edgar (Don, Duck) b. August 2, 1956 Ht. 6-2 Wt. 180 College: Notre Dame

SEASON–TEAM	G	GS	MIN	FGM	FGA	PCT	3FGM	3FGA	PCT	FTM	FTA	PCT	O-RB	D-RB	TOT	AST	PF	DQ	STL	TO	BLK	PTS	RPG	APG	PPG
79-80–Utah	77	–	1794	232	519	.447	0	12	.000	42	60	.700	21	85	106	183	166	0	100	107	11	506	1.4	2.4	6.6
Reg. Season Totals	77	–	1794	232	519	.447	0	12	.000	42	60	.700	21	85	106	183	166	0	100	107	11	506	1.4	2.4	6.6

Williams, Earl (Earl the Twirl) b. March 24, 1951 Ht. 6-7 Wt. 230 College: Winston-Salem State

SEASON–TEAM	G	GS	MIN	FGM	FGA	PCT	3FGM	3FGA	PCT	FTM	FTA	PCT	O-RB	D-RB	TOT	AST	PF	DQ	STL	TO	BLK	PTS	RPG	APG	PPG
74-75–Phoenix	79	–	1040	163	394	.414	–	–	–	45	103	.437	156	300	456	95	146	0	28	–	32	371	5.8	1.2	4.7
75-76–Detroit	46	–	562	73	152	.480	–	–	–	22	44	.500	103	148	251	18	81	0	22	–	20	168	5.5	0.4	3.7
76-77–New York Nets	1	–	7	0	2	.000	–	–	–	3	6	.500	1	1	2	1	2	0	0	–	1	3	2.0	1.0	3.0
78-79–Boston	20	–	273	54	123	.439	–	–	–	14	24	.583	41	64	105	12	41	0	12	20	9	122	5.3	0.6	6.1
Reg. Season Totals	146	–	1882	290	671	.432	–	–	–	84	177	.475	301	513	814	126	270	0	62	20	62	664	5.6	0.9	4.5

Williams, Edward (Chuck) b. June 6, 1946 Ht. 6-2 Wt. 175 College: Colorado

SEASON–TEAM	G	GS	MIN	FGM	FGA	PCT	3FGM	3FGA	PCT	FTM	FTA	PCT	O-RB	D-RB	TOT	AST	PF	DQ	STL	TO	BLK	PTS	RPG	APG	PPG
70-71–Pittsburgh (A)	83	–	1795	268	613	.437	1	4	.250	249	317	.785	–	–	185	170	161	–	–	–	–	786	2.2	2.0	9.5
71-72–Denver (A)	84	–	1580	263	583	.451	0	4	.000	205	275	.745	–	–	157	160	144	–	–	98	–	731	1.9	1.9	8.7
72-73–San Diego (A)	83	–	3074	488	1020	.478	1	7	.143	493	623	.791	71	158	229	582	275	8	–	231	–	1470	2.8	7.0	17.7
73-74–S.D.-Ken. (A)	90	–	2876	405	918	.441	4	12	.333	299	382	.783	80	170	250	557	198	–	89	256	11	1113	2.8	6.2	12.4
74-75–Memphis (A)	81	–	3171	476	963	.494	10	24	.417	212	260	.815	60	160	220	576	165	–	115	171	18	1174	2.7	7.1	14.5
75-76–Denver (A)	79	–	2529	339	660	.514	0	4	.000	188	231	.814	41	169	210	375	215	–	115	180	7	866	2.7	4.7	11.0
76-77–Denver-Buffalo	65	–	867	78	210	.371	–	–	–	68	87	.782	26	75	101	132	60	0	32	–	3	224	1.6	2.0	3.4
77-78–Buffalo	73	–	2002	208	436	.477	–	–	–	114	138	.826	29	108	137	317	137	0	48	156	4	530	1.9	4.3	7.3
Reg. NBA Totals	138	–	2869	286	646	.443	–	–	–	182	225	.809	55	183	238	449	197	0	80	156	7	754	1.7	3.3	5.5
Reg. ABA Totals	500	–	15025	2239	4757	.471	16	55	.291	1646	2088	.788	252	657	1251	2420	1158	8	319	936	36	6140	2.5	4.8	12.3
ABA Playoff Totals	37	–	1133	162	348	.466	1	3	.333	116	133	.872	19	57	105	152	82	0	21	88	9	441	2.8	4.1	11.9

Williams, Eric C. b. July 17, 1972 Ht. 6-8 Wt. 220 College: Providence

SEASON–TEAM	G	GS	MIN	FGM	FGA	PCT	3FGM	3FGA	PCT	FTM	FTA	PCT	O-RB	D-RB	TOT	AST	PF	DQ	STL	TO	BLK	PTS	RPG	APG	PPG
95-96–Boston	64	6	1470	241	546	.441	3	10	.300	200	298	.671	92	125	217	70	147	1	56	88	11	685	3.4	1.1	10.7
96-97–Boston	72	67	2435	374	820	.456	2	8	.250	328	436	.752	126	203	329	129	213	0	72	139	13	1078	4.6	1.8	15.0
97-98–Denver	4	4	145	24	61	.393	0	0	–	31	45	.689	10	11	21	12	9	0	4	9	0	79	5.3	3.0	19.8
98-99–Denver	38	8	780	80	219	.365	6	26	.231	111	139	.799	34	47	81	37	76	0	27	49	8	277	2.1	1.0	7.3
99-00–Boston	68	17	1378	165	386	.427	25	72	.347	134	169	.793	55	101	156	93	165	3	44	66	16	489	2.3	1.4	7.2
Reg. Season Totals	246	102	6208	884	2032	.435	36	116	.310	804	1087	.740	317	487	804	341	610	4	203	351	48	2608	3.3	1.4	10.6

Williams, Eugene (Gene) b. April 1, 1947 Ht. 6-7 Wt. 235 College: Kansas State

SEASON–TEAM	G	GS	MIN	FGM	FGA	PCT	3FGM	3FGA	PCT	FTM	FTA	PCT	O-RB	D-RB	TOT	AST	PF	DQ	STL	TO	BLK	PTS	RPG	APG	PPG
69-70–Kentucky (A)	1	–	8	0	1	.000	0	0	–	0	0	–	–	–	0	0	2	0	–	–	–	0	0.0	0.0	0.0
Reg. ABA Totals	1	–	8	0	1	.000	0	0	–	0	0	–	–	–	–	0	2	0	–	–	–	0	0.0	0.0	0.0

Williams, Freeman Jr. b. May 15, 1956 Ht. 6-4 Wt. 190 College: Portland State

SEASON–TEAM	G	GS	MIN	FGM	FGA	PCT	3FGM	3FGA	PCT	FTM	FTA	PCT	O-RB	D-RB	TOT	AST	PF	DQ	STL	TO	BLK	PTS	RPG	APG	PPG
78-79–San Diego	72	–	1195	335	683	.490	–	–	–	76	98	.776	48	50	98	83	88	0	42	99	2	746	1.4	1.2	10.4
79-80–San Diego	82	–	2118	645	1343	.480	42	128	.328	194	238	.815	103	89	192	166	145	0	72	171	9	1526	2.3	2.0	18.6
80-81–San Diego	82	–	1976	642	1381	.465	48	141	.340	253	297	.852	75	54	129	164	157	0	91	166	5	1585	1.6	2.0	19.3
81-82–S.D.-Atlanta	60	10	997	276	623	.443	28	94	.298	140	166	.843	23	39	62	86	103	1	29	107	0	720	1.0	1.4	12.0
82-83–Utah	18	3	210	36	101	.356	2	7	.286	18	25	.720	3	14	17	10	30	0	6	12	1	92	0.9	0.6	5.1
85-86–Washington	9	0	110	25	67	.373	7	14	.500	12	17	.706	4	8	12	7	10	0	7	13	1	69	1.3	0.8	7.7
Reg. Season Totals	323	13	6606	1959	4198	.467	127	384	.331	693	841	.824	256	254	510	516	533	1	247	568	18	4738	1.6	1.6	14.7
Playoff Totals	1	0	4	0	2	.000	0	1	.000	0	0	–	0	0	0	–	0	0	0	0	0	0	0.0	0.0	0.0

Williams, Gus (The Wizard) b. October 10, 1953 Ht. 6-2 Wt. 175 College: USC

SEASON–TEAM	G	GS	MIN	FGM	FGA	PCT	3FGM	3FGA	PCT	FTM	FTA	PCT	O-RB	D-RB	TOT	AST	PF	DQ	STL	TO	BLK	PTS	RPG	APG	PPG
75-76–Golden State	77	–	1728	365	853	.428	–	–	–	173	233	.742	62	97	159	240	143	2	140	–	26	903	2.1	3.1	11.7
76-77–Golden State	82	–	1930	325	701	.464	–	–	–	112	150	.747	72	161	233	292	218	4	121	–	19	762	2.8	3.6	9.3
77-78–Seattle	79	–	2572	602	1335	.451	–	–	–	227	278	.817	83	173	256	294	198	2	185	189	41	1431	3.2	3.7	18.1
78-79–Seattle	76	–	2266	606	1224	.495	–	–	–	245	316	.775	111	134	245	307	162	3	158	190	29	1457	3.2	4.0	19.2
79-80–Seattle	82	–	2969	739	1533	.482	7	36	.194	331	420	.788	127	148	275	397	160	1	200	181	37	1816	3.4	4.8	22.1
81-82–Seattle	80	80	2876	773	1592	.486	9	40	.225	320	436	.734	92	152	244	549	163	0	172	197	36	1875	3.1	6.9	23.4
82-83–Seattle	80	80	2761	660	1384	.477	2	43	.047	278	370	.751	72	133	205	643	117	0	182	230	26	1600	2.6	8.0	20.0
83-84–Seattle	80	80	2818	598	1306	.458	4	25	.160	297	396	.750	67	137	204	675	151	0	189	232	25	1497	2.6	8.4	18.7
84-85–Washington	79	78	2960	638	1483	.430	51	176	.290	251	346	.725	72	123	195	608	159	1	178	213	32	1578	2.5	7.7	20.0
85-86–Washington	77	67	2284	434	1013	.428	30	116	.259	138	188	.734	52	114	166	453	113	0	96	160	15	1036	2.2	5.9	13.5
86-87–Atlanta	33	0	481	53	146	.363	5	18	.278	27	40	.675	8	32	40	139	53	0	17	54	5	138	1.2	4.2	4.2
Reg. Season Totals	825	385	25645	5793	12570	.461	108	454	.238	2399	3173	.756	818	1404	2222	4597	1637	13	1638	1646	291	14093	2.7	5.6	17.1
Playoff Totals	99	24	3215	782	1644	.476	9	39	.231	356	483	.737	136	172	308	469	243	4	174	201	40	1929	3.1	4.7	19.5
All-Star Totals	2	1	41	12	28	.429	0	1	.000	4	4	1.000	3	0	3	13	2	0	2	5	0	28	1.5	6.5	14.0

Williams, Guy Bernard b. July 1, 1960 Ht. 6-9 Wt. 200 College: San Francisco; Washington State

SEASON–TEAM	G	GS	MIN	FGM	FGA	PCT	3FGM	3FGA	PCT	FTM	FTA	PCT	O-RB	D-RB	TOT	AST	PF	DQ	STL	TO	BLK	PTS	RPG	APG	PPG
84-85–Washington	21	0	119	29	63	.460	1	4	.250	2	5	.400	15	12	27	9	17	0	5	8	2	61	1.3	0.4	2.9
85-86–Golden State	5	0	25	2	5	.400	0	0	–	3	6	.500	0	6	6	0	7	1	1	0	2	7	1.2	0.0	1.4
Reg. Season Totals	26	0	144	31	68	.456	1	4	.250	5	11	.455	15	18	33	9	24	1	6	8	4	68	1.3	0.3	2.6

Williams, Henry (Hank) b. April 28, 1952 Ht. 6-6 Wt. 215 College: Jacksonville

SEASON–TEAM	G	GS	MIN	FGM	FGA	PCT	3FGM	3FGA	PCT	FTM	FTA	PCT	O-RB	D-RB	TOT	AST	PF	DQ	STL	TO	BLK	PTS	RPG	APG	PPG
74-75–Utah (A)	40	–	468	76	173	.439	3	22	.136	18	23	.783	31	65	96	26	74	–	14	32	4	173	2.4	0.7	4.3
Reg. ABA Totals	40	–	468	76	173	.439	3	22	.136	18	23	.783	31	65	96	26	74	–	14	32	4	173	2.4	0.7	4.3
ABA Playoff Totals	2	–	7	2	6	.333	0	0	–	0	0	–	1	1	2	0	2	–	0	0	0	4	1.0	0.0	2.0

Williams, Herbert L. (Herb) b. February 16, 1958 Ht. 6-11 Wt. 260 College: Ohio State

SEASON–TEAM	G	GS	MIN	FGM	FGA	PCT	3FGM	3FGA	PCT	FTM	FTA	PCT	O-RB	D-RB	TOT	AST	PF	DQ	STL	TO	BLK	PTS	RPG	APG	PPG
81-82–Indiana	82	75	2277	407	854	.477	2	7	.286	126	188	.670	175	430	605	139	200	0	53	137	178	942	7.4	1.7	11.5
82-83–Indiana	78	74	2513	580	1163	.499	0	7	.000	155	220	.705	151	432	583	262	230	4	54	229	171	1315	7.5	3.4	16.9
83-84–Indiana	69	53	2279	411	860	.478	0	4	.000	207	295	.702	154	400	554	215	193	4	60	207	108	1029	8.0	3.1	14.9
84-85–Indiana	75	70	2557	575	1211	.475	1	9	.111	224	341	.657	154	480	634	252	218	1	54	265	134	1375	8.5	3.4	18.3
85-86–Indiana	78	74	2770	627	1275	.492	1	12	.083	294	403	.730	172	538	710	174	244	2	50	210	184	1549	9.1	2.2	19.9
86-87–Indiana	74	67	2526	451	939	.480	0	9	.000	199	269	.740	143	400	543	174	255	9	59	145	93	1101	7.3	2.4	14.9
87-88–Indiana	75	37	1966	311	732	.425	0	6	.000	126	171	.737	116	353	469	98	244	1	37	119	146	748	6.3	1.3	10.0
88-89–Indiana-Dallas	76	66	2470	322	739	.436	0	5	.000	133	194	.686	135	458	593	124	236	5	46	149	134	777	7.8	1.6	10.2
89-90–Dallas	81	19	2199	295	665	.444	2	9	.222	108	159	.679	76	315	391	119	243	4	51	106	106	700	4.8	1.5	8.6
90-91–Dallas	60	36	1832	332	655	.507	0	4	.000	83	130	.638	86	271	357	95	197	3	30	113	88	747	6.0	1.6	12.5
91-92–Dallas	75	26	2040	367	851	.431	1	6	.167	124	171	.725	106	348	454	94	189	2	35	114	98	859	6.1	1.3	11.5
92-93–New York	55	0	571	72	175	.411	0	0	–	14	21	.667	44	102	146	19	78	0	21	22	28	158	2.7	0.3	2.9
93-94–New York	70	3	774	103	233	.442	0	1	.000	27	42	.643	56	126	182	28	108	1	18	39	43	233	2.6	0.4	3.3
94-95–New York	56	3	743	82	180	.456	0	0	–	23	37	.622	23	109	132	27	108	0	13	40	45	187	2.4	0.5	3.3
95-96–Toronto-N.Y.	44	2	571	62	152	.408	1	4	.250	13	20	.650	15	75	90	27	79	0	14	22	33	138	2.0	0.6	3.1
96-97–New York	21	2	184	18	46	.391	0	1	.000	3	4	.750	9	22	31	5	18	0	4	5	5	39	1.5	0.2	1.9
97-98–New York	27	0	178	18	43	.419	0	0	–	1	8	.125	6	23	29	4	34	0	6	5	9	37	1.1	0.1	1.4
98-99–New York	6	0	34	4	8	.500	0	0	–	2	2	1.000	3	3	6	0	2	0	0	2	2	10	1.0	0.0	1.7
Reg. Season Totals	1102	607	28484	5037	10781	.467	8	84	.095	1862	2675	.696	1624	4885	6509	1856	2876	36	605	1929	1605	11944	5.9	1.7	10.8
Playoff Totals	57	4	538	61	130	.469	0	0	–	31	42	.738	25	53	78	17	83	1	10	25	25	153	1.4	0.3	2.7

Williams, James (Fly) b. February 18, 1953 Ht. 6-5 Wt. 200 College: Austin Peay State

SEASON–TEAM	G	GS	MIN	FGM	FGA	PCT	3FGM	3FGA	PCT	FTM	FTA	PCT	O-RB	D-RB	TOT	AST	PF	DQ	STL	TO	BLK	PTS	RPG	APG	PPG
74-75–St. Louis (A)	71	–	1239	297	643	.462	2	14	.143	69	101	.683	72	109	181	142	156	–	64	177	10	665	2.5	2.0	9.4
Reg. ABA Totals	71	–	1239	297	643	.462	2	14	.143	69	101	.683	72	109	181	142	156	–	64	177	10	665	2.5	2.0	9.4
ABA Playoff Totals	2	–	8	1	5	.200	0	1	.000	0	0	–	0	1	1	0	2	–	0	1	0	2	0.5	0.0	1.0

Williams, Jason Chandler (White Chocolate) b. November 18, 1975 Ht. 6-1 Wt. 190 College: Marshall; Florida

SEASON–TEAM	G	GS	MIN	FGM	FGA	PCT	3FGM	3FGA	PCT	FTM	FTA	PCT	O-RB	D-RB	TOT	AST	PF	DQ	STL	TO	BLK	PTS	RPG	APG	PPG
98-99–Sacramento	50	50	1805	231	617	.374	100	323	.310	79	105	.752	14	139	153	299	91	0	95	143	1	641	3.1	6.0	12.8
99-00–Sacramento	81	81	2760	363	973	.373	145	505	.287	128	170	.753	22	208	230	589	140	0	117	296	8	999	2.8	7.3	12.3
Reg. Season Totals	131	131	4565	594	1590	.374	245	828	.296	207	275	.753	36	347	383	888	231	0	212	439	9	1640	2.9	6.8	12.5
Playoff Totals	10	10	308	34	93	.366	17	54	.315	17	19	.895	3	23	26	32	23	0	11	21	1	102	2.6	3.2	10.2

Williams, Jayson b. February 22, 1968 Ht. 6-10 Wt. 245 College: St. John's (N.Y.)

SEASON–TEAM	G	GS	MIN	FGM	FGA	PCT	3FGM	3FGA	PCT	FTM	FTA	PCT	O-RB	D-RB	TOT	AST	PF	DQ	STL	TO	BLK	PTS	RPG	APG	PPG
90-91–Philadelphia	52	1	508	72	161	.447	1	2	.500	37	56	.661	41	70	111	16	92	1	9	40	6	182	2.1	0.3	3.5
91-92–Philadelphia	50	8	646	75	206	.364	0	0	–	56	88	.636	62	83	145	12	110	1	20	44	20	206	2.9	0.2	4.1
92-93–New Jersey	12	2	139	21	46	.457	0	0	–	7	18	.389	22	19	41	0	24	0	4	8	4	49	3.4	0.0	4.1
93-94–New Jersey	70	0	877	125	293	.427	0	0	–	72	119	.605	109	154	263	26	140	1	17	35	36	322	3.8	0.4	4.6
94-95–New Jersey	75	6	982	149	323	.461	0	5	.000	65	122	.533	179	246	425	35	160	2	26	59	33	363	5.7	0.5	4.8
95-96–New Jersey	80	6	1858	279	660	.423	2	7	.286	161	272	.592	342	461	803	47	238	4	35	106	57	721	10.0	0.6	9.0
96-97–New Jersey	41	40	1432	221	540	.409	0	4	.000	108	183	.590	242	311	553	51	158	5	24	82	36	550	13.5	1.2	13.4
97-98–New Jersey	65	65	2343	321	645	.498	0	4	.000	195	293	.666	443	440	883	67	236	7	45	95	49	837	13.6	1.0	12.9
98-99–New Jersey	30	30	1020	97	218	.445	0	2	.000	48	85	.565	147	213	360	33	126	3	24	46	60	242	12.0	1.1	8.1
Reg. Season Totals	475	158	9805	1360	3092	.440	3	24	.125	749	1236	.606	1587	1997	3584	287	1284	24	204	515	301	3472	7.5	0.6	7.3
Playoff Totals	9	2	143	13	29	.448	0	0	–	4	8	.500	25	24	49	5	14	0	2	5	3	30	5.4	0.6	3.3
All-Star Totals	1	0	19	2	3	.667	0	0	–	0	0	–	3	7	10	1	2	0	0	0	0	4	10.0	1.0	4.0

Williams, Jerome b. May 10, 1973 Ht. 6-9 Wt. 206 College: ;Georgetown

SEASON–TEAM	G	GS	MIN	FGM	FGA	PCT	3FGM	3FGA	PCT	FTM	FTA	PCT	O-RB	D-RB	TOT	AST	PF	DQ	STL	TO	BLK	PTS	RPG	APG	PPG
96-97–Detroit	33	0	177	20	51	.392	0	0	–	9	17	.529	22	28	50	7	18	0	13	13	1	49	1.5	0.2	1.5
97-98–Detroit	77	3	1305	151	288	.524	0	1	.000	108	166	.651	170	209	379	48	144	1	51	60	10	410	4.9	0.6	5.3
98-99–Detroit	50	10	1154	124	248	.500	0	0	–	107	159	.673	158	191	349	23	108	0	63	41	7	355	7.0	0.5	7.1
99-00–Detroit	82	1	2102	257	456	.564	0	3	.000	175	284	.616	277	512	789	68	196	0	95	105	21	689	9.6	0.8	8.4
Reg. Season Totals	242	14	4738	552	1043	.529	0	4	.000	399	626	.637	627	940	1567	146	466	1	222	219	39	1503	6.5	0.6	6.2
Playoff Totals	9	5	201	21	43	.488	0	0	–	8	17	.471	19	37	56	6	15	0	8	8	0	50	6.2	0.7	5.6

Williams, John (Hot Rod) b. August 9, 1962 Ht. 6-11 Wt. 245 College: Tulane

SEASON–TEAM	G	GS	MIN	FGM	FGA	PCT	3FGM	3FGA	PCT	FTM	FTA	PCT	O-RB	D-RB	TOT	AST	PF	DQ	STL	TO	BLK	PTS	RPG	APG	PPG
86-87–Cleveland	80	80	2714	435	897	.485	0	1	.000	298	400	.745	222	407	629	154	197	0	58	139	167	1168	7.9	1.9	14.6
87-88–Cleveland	77	50	2106	316	663	.477	0	1	.000	211	279	.756	159	347	506	103	203	2	61	104	145	843	6.6	1.3	10.9
88-89–Cleveland	82	10	2125	356	700	.509	1	4	.250	235	314	.748	173	304	477	108	188	1	77	102	134	948	5.8	1.3	11.6
89-90–Cleveland	82	29	2776	528	1070	.493	0	0	–	325	440	.739	220	443	663	168	214	2	86	143	167	1381	8.1	2.0	16.8
90-91–Cleveland	43	14	1293	199	430	.463	0	1	.000	107	164	.652	111	179	290	100	126	2	36	63	69	505	6.7	2.3	11.7
91-92–Cleveland	80	12	2432	341	678	.503	0	4	.000	270	359	.752	228	379	607	196	191	2	60	83	182	952	7.6	2.5	11.9
92-93–Cleveland	67	13	2055	263	560	.470	0	0	–	212	296	.716	127	288	415	152	171	2	48	116	105	738	6.2	2.3	11.0
93-94–Cleveland	76	72	2660	394	825	.478	0	0	–	252	346	.728	207	368	575	193	219	3	78	139	130	1040	7.6	2.5	13.7
94-95–Cleveland	74	73	2641	366	810	.452	1	5	.200	196	286	.685	173	334	507	192	211	2	83	149	101	929	6.9	2.6	12.6
95-96–Phoenix	62	58	1652	180	397	.453	0	1	.000	95	130	.731	129	243	372	62	170	2	46	62	90	455	6.0	1.0	7.3
96-97–Phoenix	68	66	2137	204	416	.490	0	2	.000	133	198	.672	178	384	562	100	176	1	67	66	88	541	8.3	1.5	8.0
97-98–Phoenix	71	30	1333	95	202	.470	0	0	–	65	93	.699	107	205	312	49	138	2	33	29	60	255	4.4	0.7	3.6
98-99–Dallas	25	11	403	11	33	.333	0	0	–	7	10	.700	36	47	83	15	49	0	13	13	18	29	3.3	0.6	1.2
Reg. Season Totals	887	518	26327	3688	7681	.480	2	19	.105	2406	3315	.726	2070	3928	5998	1592	2253	21	746	1208	1456	9784	6.8	1.8	11.0
Playoff Totals	57	15	1669	230	480	.479	0	1	.000	161	223	.722	122	236	358	100	180	5	47	85	70	621	6.3	1.8	10.9

Williams, John Sam (Rock) b. October 26, 1966 Ht. 6-9 Wt. 295 College: Louisiana State

SEASON–TEAM	G	GS	MIN	FGM	FGA	PCT	3FGM	3FGA	PCT	FTM	FTA	PCT	O-RB	D-RB	TOT	AST	PF	DQ	STL	TO	BLK	PTS	RPG	APG	PPG
86-87–Washington	78	6	1773	283	624	.454	8	36	.222	144	223	.646	130	236	366	191	173	1	129	122	30	718	4.7	2.4	9.2
87-88–Washington	82	37	2428	427	910	.469	5	38	.132	188	256	.734	127	317	444	232	217	3	117	145	34	1047	5.4	2.8	12.8
88-89–Washington	82	1	2413	438	940	.466	19	71	.268	225	290	.776	158	415	573	356	213	1	142	157	70	1120	7.0	4.3	13.7
89-90–Washington	18	18	632	130	274	.474	2	18	.111	65	84	.774	27	109	136	84	33	0	21	43	9	327	7.6	4.7	18.2
90-91–Washington	33	11	941	164	393	.417	10	41	.244	73	97	.753	42	135	177	133	63	0	39	68	6	411	5.4	4.0	12.5
92-93–L.A. Clippers	74	8	1638	205	477	.430	12	53	.226	70	129	.543	88	228	316	142	188	1	83	79	23	492	4.3	1.9	6.6
93-94–L.A. Clippers	34	6	725	81	188	.431	5	20	.250	24	36	.667	37	90	127	97	85	1	25	35	10	191	3.7	2.9	5.6
94-95–Indiana	34	0	402	41	115	.357	4	12	.333	14	25	.560	23	39	62	27	48	0	10	35	2	100	1.8	0.8	2.9
Reg. Season Totals	435	87	10952	1769	3921	.451	65	289	.225	803	1140	.704	632	1569	2201	1262	1020	7	566	684	184	4406	5.1	2.9	10.1
Playoff Totals	13	5	332	35	80	.438	2	5	.400	24	41	.585	20	34	54	30	38	2	15	20	4	96	4.2	2.3	7.4

Williams, Kenneth Ray (Kenny) b. June 9, 1969 Ht. 6-9 Wt. 205 College: Barton County (Kan.) C.C.; Elizabeth City State

SEASON–TEAM	G	GS	MIN	FGM	FGA	PCT	3FGM	3FGA	PCT	FTM	FTA	PCT	O-RB	D-RB	TOT	AST	PF	DQ	STL	TO	BLK	PTS	RPG	APG	PPG
90-91–Indiana	75	0	527	93	179	.520	0	3	.000	34	50	.680	56	75	131	31	81	0	11	41	31	220	1.7	0.4	2.9
91-92–Indiana	60	6	565	113	218	.518	0	4	.000	26	43	.605	64	65	129	40	99	0	20	22	41	252	2.2	0.7	4.2
92-93–Indiana	57	0	844	150	282	.532	0	3	.000	48	68	.706	102	126	228	38	87	1	21	28	45	348	4.0	0.7	6.1
93-94–Indiana	68	1	982	191	391	.488	0	4	.000	45	64	.703	93	112	205	52	99	0	24	45	49	427	3.0	0.8	6.3
Reg. Season Totals	260	7	2918	547	1070	.511	0	14	.000	153	225	.680	315	378	693	161	366	1	76	136	166	1247	2.7	0.6	4.8
Playoff Totals	17	0	105	10	26	.385	0	0	–	2	6	.333	6	11	17	7	20	0	6	6	5	22	1.0	0.4	1.3

Williams, Kevin Eugene b. September 11, 1961 Ht. 6-2 Wt. 180 College: St. John's (N.Y.)

SEASON–TEAM	G	GS	MIN	FGM	FGA	PCT	3FGM	3FGA	PCT	FTM	FTA	PCT	O-RB	D-RB	TOT	AST	PF	DQ	STL	TO	BLK	PTS	RPG	APG	PPG
83-84–San Antonio	19	0	200	25	58	.431	0	1	.000	25	32	.781	4	9	13	43	42	1	8	22	4	75	0.7	2.3	3.9
84-85–Cleveland	46	4	413	58	134	.433	0	5	.000	47	64	.734	19	44	63	61	86	1	22	49	4	163	1.4	1.3	3.5
86-87–Seattle	65	0	703	132	296	.446	0	7	.000	55	66	.833	47	36	83	66	154	1	45	63	8	319	1.3	1.0	4.9
87-88–Seattle	80	9	1084	199	450	.442	1	7	.143	103	122	.844	61	66	127	96	207	1	62	68	7	502	1.6	1.2	6.3
88-89–N.J.-LAClips	50	0	547	81	200	.405	1	6	.167	46	59	.780	28	42	70	53	91	0	30	52	11	209	1.4	1.1	4.2
Reg. Season Totals	260	13	2947	495	1138	.435	2	26	.077	276	343	.805	159	197	356	319	580	4	167	254	34	1268	1.4	1.2	4.9
Playoff Totals	21	0	332	53	112	.473	0	4	.000	30	40	.750	25	17	42	40	60	0	19	14	1	136	2.0	1.9	6.5

Williams, Lorenzo b. July 15, 1969 Ht. 6-9 Wt. 230 College: Polk (Fla.) C.C.; Stetson

SEASON–TEAM	G	GS	MIN	FGM	FGA	PCT	3FGM	3FGA	PCT	FTM	FTA	PCT	O-RB	D-RB	TOT	AST	PF	DQ	STL	TO	BLK	PTS	RPG	APG	PPG
92-93–Cha.-Orl.-Bos.	27	7	179	17	36	.472	0	0	–	2	7	.286	17	38	55	5	29	0	5	8	17	36	2.0	0.2	1.3
93-94–Orl.-Cha.-Dallas	38	11	716	49	110	.445	0	1	.000	12	28	.429	95	122	217	25	92	0	18	22	46	110	5.7	0.7	2.9
94-95–Dallas	82	81	2383	145	304	.477	0	0	–	38	101	.376	291	399	690	124	306	6	52	105	148	328	8.4	1.5	4.0
95-96–Dallas	65	61	1806	87	214	.407	0	1	.000	24	70	.343	234	287	521	85	226	9	48	78	122	198	8.0	1.3	3.0
96-97–Washington	19	0	264	20	31	.645	0	0	–	5	7	.714	28	41	69	4	49	0	6	18	8	45	3.6	0.2	2.4
97-98–Washington	14	6	111	13	17	.765	0	0	–	0	2	.000	16	10	26	3	17	0	2	2	3	26	1.9	0.2	1.9
99-00–Washington	8	0	76	7	9	.778	0	0	–	0	0	–	12	13	25	1	13	0	3	3	6	14	3.1	0.1	1.8
Reg. Season Totals	253	166	5535	338	721	.469	0	2	.000	81	215	.377	693	910	1603	247	732	15	134	236	350	757	6.3	1.0	3.0
Playoff Totals	3	0	8	1	1	1.000	0	0	–	0	0	–	1	0	1	–	1	0	0	0	0	2	0.3	0.0	0.7

Williams, Michael George (Mike) b. August 14, 1963 Ht. 6-8 Wt. 255 College: Cincinnati; Bradley

SEASON–TEAM	G	GS	MIN	FGM	FGA	PCT	3FGM	3FGA	PCT	FTM	FTA	PCT	O-RB	D-RB	TOT	AST	PF	DQ	STL	TO	BLK	PTS	RPG	APG	PPG
89-90–Sac.-Atlanta	21	0	102	6	18	.333	0	1	.000	3	6	.500	5	18	23	2	30	0	3	3	7	15	1.1	0.1	0.7
Reg. Season Totals	21	0	102	6	18	.333	0	1	.000	3	6	.500	5	18	23	2	30	0	3	3	7	15	1.1	0.1	0.7

Williams, Micheal Douglas b. July 23, 1966 Ht. 6-2 Wt. 175 College: Baylor

SEASON–TEAM	G	GS	MIN	FGM	FGA	PCT	3FGM	3FGA	PCT	FTM	FTA	PCT	O-RB	D-RB	TOT	AST	PF	DQ	STL	TO	BLK	PTS	RPG	APG	PPG
88-89–Detroit	49	0	358	47	129	.364	2	9	.222	31	47	.660	9	18	27	70	44	0	13	42	3	127	0.6	1.4	2.6
89-90–Phoenix-Cha.	28	1	329	60	119	.504	0	3	.000	36	46	.783	12	20	32	81	39	0	22	33	1	156	1.1	2.9	5.6
90-91–Indiana	73	37	1706	261	523	.499	1	7	.143	290	330	.879	49	127	176	348	202	1	150	150	17	813	2.4	4.8	11.1
91-92–Indiana	79	76	2750	404	824	.490	8	33	.242	372	427	.871	73	209	282	647	262	7	233	240	22	1188	3.6	8.2	15.0
92-93–Minnesota	76	76	2661	353	791	.446	26	107	.243	419	462	.907	84	189	273	661	268	7	165	227	23	1151	3.6	8.7	15.1
93-94–Minnesota	71	66	2206	314	687	.457	10	45	.222	333	397	.839	67	154	221	512	193	3	118	203	24	971	3.1	7.2	13.7
94-95–Minnesota	1	1	28	1	4	.250	0	0	–	4	5	.800	0	1	1	3	3	0	2	3	0	6	1.0	3.0	6.0
95-96–Minnesota	9	7	189	13	40	.325	1	3	.333	28	33	.848	3	20	23	31	37	0	5	23	3	55	2.6	3.4	6.1
97-98–Minnesota	25	0	161	16	48	.333	0	4	.000	32	33	.970	2	12	14	32	24	0	9	16	2	64	0.6	1.3	2.6
98-99–Toronto	2	0	15	1	5	.200	0	0	–	0	0	–	1	0	1	0	1	0	0	1	0	2	0.5	0.0	1.0
Reg. Season Totals	413	264	10403	1470	3170	.464	48	211	.227	1545	1780	.868	300	750	1050	2385	1073	18	717	938	95	4533	2.5	5.8	11.0
Playoff Totals	16	8	353	54	123	.439	4	12	.333	63	74	.851	11	24	35	79	50	2	27	22	1	175	2.2	4.9	10.9

Williams, Milton (Milt) b. November 22, 1945 Ht. 6-2 Wt. 185 College: Lincoln (Mo.); Campbell

SEASON–TEAM	G	GS	MIN	FGM	FGA	PCT	3FGM	3FGA	PCT	FTM	FTA	PCT	O-RB	D-RB	TOT	AST	PF	DQ	STL	TO	BLK	PTS	RPG	APG	PPG
70-71–New York	5	–	13	1	1	1.000	–	–	–	2	3	.667	–	–	0	2	3	0	–	–	–	4	0.0	0.4	0.8
71-72–Atlanta	10	–	127	23	53	.434	–	–	–	21	29	.724	–	–	4	20	18	0	–	–	–	67	0.4	2.0	6.7
73-74–Seattle	53	–	505	62	149	.416	–	–	–	41	63	.651	19	28	47	103	82	1	25	–	0	165	0.9	1.9	3.1
74-75–St. Louis (A)	4	–	95	11	19	.579	0	0	–	0	0	–	4	9	13	12	10	–	10	10	0	22	3.3	3.0	5.5
Reg. NBA Totals	68	–	645	86	203	.424	–	–	–	64	95	.674	19	28	51	125	103	1	25	–	0	236	0.8	1.8	3.5
Reg. ABA Totals	4	–	95	11	19	.579	0	0	–	0	0	–	4	9	13	12	10	–	10	10	0	22	3.3	3.0	5.5

Williams, Nathaniel Russell (Nate) b. May 2, 1950 Ht. 6-5 Wt. 220 College: Utah State

SEASON–TEAM	G	GS	MIN	FGM	FGA	PCT	3FGM	3FGA	PCT	FTM	FTA	PCT	O-RB	D-RB	TOT	AST	PF	DQ	STL	TO	BLK	PTS	RPG	APG	PPG
71-72–Cincinnati	81	–	2173	418	968	.432	–	–	–	127	172	.738	–	–	372	174	300	11	–	–	–	963	4.6	2.1	11.9
72-73–K.C.-Omaha	80	–	1979	417	874	.477	–	–	–	106	133	.797	–	–	339	128	272	9	–	–	–	940	4.2	1.6	11.8
73-74–K.C.-Omaha	82	–	2513	538	1165	.462	–	–	–	193	236	.818	118	226	344	182	290	5	149	–	34	1269	4.2	2.2	15.5
74-75–K.C.-Omaha-N.O.	85	–	1945	474	988	.480	–	–	–	181	220	.823	102	235	337	145	251	3	97	–	30	1129	4.0	1.7	13.3
75-76–New Orleans	81	–	1935	421	948	.444	–	–	–	197	239	.824	135	225	360	107	253	6	109	–	17	1039	4.4	1.3	12.8
76-77–New Orleans	79	–	1776	414	917	.451	–	–	–	146	194	.753	107	199	306	92	200	0	76	–	16	974	3.9	1.2	12.3
77-78–N.O.-G.S.	73	–	1249	312	724	.431	–	–	–	101	121	.835	65	139	204	74	181	3	57	83	34	725	2.8	1.0	9.9
78-79–Golden State	81	–	1299	284	567	.501	–	–	–	102	117	.872	68	139	207	61	169	0	55	93	5	670	2.6	0.8	8.3
Reg. Season Totals	642	–	14869	3278	7151	.458	–	–	–	1153	1432	.805	595	1163	2469	963	1916	37	543	176	136	7709	3.8	1.5	12.0

Williams, Reggie (Silk) b. March 5, 1964 Ht. 6-7 Wt. 195 College: Georgetown

SEASON–TEAM	G	GS	MIN	FGM	FGA	PCT	3FGM	3FGA	PCT	FTM	FTA	PCT	O-RB	D-RB	TOT	AST	PF	DQ	STL	TO	BLK	PTS	RPG	APG	PPG
87-88–L.A. Clippers	35	14	857	152	427	.356	13	58	.224	48	66	.727	55	63	118	58	108	1	29	63	21	365	3.4	1.7	10.4
88-89–L.A. Clippers	63	17	1303	260	594	.438	30	104	.288	92	122	.754	70	109	179	103	181	1	81	114	29	642	2.8	1.6	10.2
89-90–LAClips-Clev.-S.A.	47	17	743	131	338	.388	6	37	.162	52	68	.765	28	55	83	53	102	2	32	45	14	320	1.8	1.1	6.8
90-91–S.A.-Denver	73	46	1896	384	855	.449	57	157	.363	166	197	.843	133	173	306	133	253	9	113	112	41	991	4.2	1.8	13.6
91-92–Denver	81	80	2623	601	1277	.471	56	156	.359	216	269	.803	145	260	405	235	270	4	148	173	68	1474	5.0	2.9	18.2
92-93–Denver	79	79	2722	535	1167	.458	33	122	.270	238	296	.804	132	296	428	295	284	6	126	194	76	1341	5.4	3.7	17.0
93-94–Denver	82	68	2654	418	1014	.412	64	230	.278	165	225	.733	98	294	392	300	288	3	117	163	66	1065	4.8	3.7	13.0
94-95–Denver	74	70	2198	388	846	.459	85	266	.320	132	174	.759	94	235	329	231	264	4	114	124	67	993	4.4	3.1	13.4
95-96–Denver	52	5	817	94	254	.370	20	89	.225	33	39	.846	25	97	122	74	137	1	34	51	21	241	2.3	1.4	4.6
96-97–Indiana-N.J.	13	0	200	29	76	.382	9	34	.265	9	12	.750	5	26	31	10	33	0	8	12	4	76	2.4	0.8	5.8
Reg. Season Totals	599	396	16013	2992	6848	.437	373	1253	.298	1151	1468	.784	785	1608	2393	1492	1920	31	802	1051	407	7508	4.0	2.5	12.5
Playoff Totals	24	15	538	79	212	.373	24	65	.369	35	43	.814	28	60	88	57	72	1	14	36	13	217	3.7	2.4	9.0

Williams, Richard C. (Rickey) b. March 12, 1957 Ht. 6-1 Wt. 175 College: New Mexico; Long Beach State

SEASON–TEAM	G	GS	MIN	FGM	FGA	PCT	3FGM	3FGA	PCT	FTM	FTA	PCT	O-RB	D-RB	TOT	AST	PF	DQ	STL	TO	BLK	PTS	RPG	APG	PPG
82-83–Utah	44	0	346	56	135	.415	0	3	.000	35	53	.660	15	23	38	37	42	0	20	38	4	147	0.9	0.8	3.3
Reg. Season Totals	44	0	346	56	135	.415	0	3	.000	35	53	.660	15	23	38	37	42	0	20	38	4	147	0.9	0.8	3.3

Williams, Robert (Bob) b. May 12, 1931 Ht. 6-6 Wt. 230 College: Florida A&M

SEASON–TEAM	G	GS	MIN	FGM	FGA	PCT	3FGM	3FGA	PCT	FTM	FTA	PCT	O-RB	D-RB	TOT	AST	PF	DQ	STL	TO	BLK	PTS	RPG	APG	PPG
55-56–Minneapolis	20	–	173	21	46	.457	–	–	–	24	45	.533	–	–	54	7	36	1	–	–	–	66	2.7	0.4	3.3
56-57–Minneapolis	4	–	30	1	4	.250	–	–	–	2	3	.667	–	–	5	0	2	0	–	–	–	4	1.3	0.0	1.0
Reg. Season Totals	24	–	203	22	50	.440	–	–	–	26	48	.542	–	–	59	7	38	1	–	–	–	70	2.5	0.3	2.9

Williams, Robert Aaron (Rob) b. May 5, 1961 Ht. 6-2 Wt. 175 College: Houston

SEASON–TEAM	G	GS	MIN	FGM	FGA	PCT	3FGM	3FGA	PCT	FTM	FTA	PCT	O-RB	D-RB	TOT	AST	PF	DQ	STL	TO	BLK	PTS	RPG	APG	PPG
82-83–Denver	74	33	1443	191	468	.408	2	15	.133	131	174	.753	37	99	136	361	221	4	89	185	12	515	1.8	4.9	7.0
83-84–Denver	79	66	1924	309	671	.461	15	47	.319	171	209	.818	54	140	194	464	268	4	84	169	5	804	2.5	5.9	10.2
Reg. Season Totals	153	99	3367	500	1139	.439	17	62	.274	302	383	.789	91	239	330	825	489	8	173	354	17	1319	2.2	5.4	8.6
Playoff Totals	12	11	283	45	101	.446	7	16	.438	17	19	.895	7	25	32	61	46	2	11	27	2	114	2.7	5.1	9.5

Williams, Robert Eric (Pete) b. March 10, 1965 Ht. 6-7 Wt. 190 College: Mount San Antonio (Calif.) Coll. (J.C.); Arizona

SEASON–TEAM	G	GS	MIN	FGM	FGA	PCT	3FGM	3FGA	PCT	FTM	FTA	PCT	O-RB	D-RB	TOT	AST	PF	DQ	STL	TO	BLK	PTS	RPG	APG	PPG
85-86–Denver	53	11	573	67	111	.604	0	0	–	17	40	.425	47	99	146	14	68	1	19	19	23	151	2.8	0.3	2.8
86-87–Denver	5	0	10	1	2	.500	0	0	–	0	0	–	0	1	1	1	1	0	0	1	0	2	0.2	0.2	0.4
Reg. Season Totals	58	11	583	68	113	.602	0	0	–	17	40	.425	47	100	147	15	69	1	19	20	23	153	2.5	0.3	2.6
Playoff Totals	4	0	18	2	4	.500	0	1	.000	0	0	–	1	3	4	3	2	0	0	0	0	4	1.0	0.8	1.0

Williams, Ronald Robert (Ron, Fritz) b. September 24, 1944 Ht. 6-3 Wt. 190 College: West Virginia

SEASON–TEAM	G	GS	MIN	FGM	FGA	PCT	3FGM	3FGA	PCT	FTM	FTA	PCT	O-RB	D-RB	TOT	AST	PF	DQ	STL	TO	BLK	PTS	RPG	APG	PPG
68-69–San Francisco	75	–	1472	238	567	.420	–	–	–	109	142	.768	–	–	178	247	176	3	–	–	–	585	2.4	3.3	7.8
69-70–San Francisco	80	–	2435	452	1046	.432	–	–	–	277	337	.822	–	–	190	424	287	7	–	–	–	1181	2.4	5.3	14.8
70-71–San Francisco	82	–	2809	426	977	.436	–	–	–	331	392	.844	–	–	244	480	301	9	–	–	–	1183	3.0	5.9	14.4
71-72–Golden State	80	–	1932	291	614	.474	–	–	–	195	234	.833	–	–	147	308	232	1	–	–	–	777	1.8	3.9	9.7
72-73–Golden State	73	–	1016	180	409	.440	–	–	–	75	83	.904	–	–	81	114	108	0	–	–	–	435	1.1	1.6	6.0
73-74–Milwaukee	71	–	1130	192	393	.489	–	–	–	60	68	.882	19	50	69	153	114	1	49	–	2	444	1.0	2.2	6.3
74-75–Milwaukee	46	–	526	62	165	.376	–	–	–	24	29	.828	10	33	43	71	70	2	23	–	2	148	0.9	1.5	3.2
75-76–Los Angeles	9	–	158	17	43	.395	–	–	–	10	13	.769	2	17	19	21	15	0	3	–	0	44	2.1	2.3	4.9
Reg. Season Totals	516	–	11478	1858	4214	.441	–	–	–	1081	1298	.833	31	100	971	1818	1303	23	75	–	4	4797	1.9	3.5	9.3
Playoff Totals	32	–	671	104	248	.419	–	–	–	52	59	.881	6	21	57	94	76	2	9	–	3	260	1.8	2.9	8.1

Williams, Samuel H. (Sam) b. January 22, 1945 Ht. 6-3 Wt. 180 College: Burlington Co. Coll. N.J. (J.C.); Iowa

SEASON–TEAM	G	GS	MIN	FGM	FGA	PCT	3FGM	3FGA	PCT	FTM	FTA	PCT	O-RB	D-RB	TOT	AST	PF	DQ	STL	TO	BLK	PTS	RPG	APG	PPG
68-69–Milwaukee	55	–	628	78	228	.342	–	–	–	72	134	.537	–	–	109	61	106	1	–	–	–	228	2.0	1.1	4.1
69-70–Milwaukee	11	–	44	11	24	.458	–	–	–	5	11	.455	–	–	7	3	5	0	–	–	–	27	0.6	0.3	2.5
Reg. Season Totals	66	–	672	89	252	.353	–	–	–	77	145	.531	–	–	116	64	111	1	–	–	–	255	1.8	1.0	3.9
Playoff Totals	2	–	16	4	7	.571	–	–	–	0	2	.000	–	–	4	1	5	0	–	–	–	8	2.0	0.5	4.0

Williams, Samuel Keith b. March 7, 1959 Ht. 6-8 Wt. 215 College: Pasadena City (Calif.) Coll. (J.C.); Arizona State

SEASON–TEAM	G	GS	MIN	FGM	FGA	PCT	3FGM	3FGA	PCT	FTM	FTA	PCT	O-RB	D-RB	TOT	AST	PF	DQ	STL	TO	BLK	PTS	RPG	APG	PPG
81-82–Golden State	59	22	1073	154	277	.556	0	0	–	49	89	.551	91	217	308	38	156	0	45	64	76	357	5.2	0.6	6.1
82-83–Golden State	75	28	1533	252	479	.526	0	1	.000	123	171	.719	153	240	393	45	244	4	71	101	89	627	5.2	0.6	8.4
83-84–G.S.-Phil.	77	12	1434	204	431	.473	0	1	.000	92	140	.657	121	218	339	62	209	3	68	99	106	500	4.4	0.8	6.5
84-85–Philadelphia	46	8	488	58	148	.392	0	1	.000	28	47	.596	38	68	106	11	92	1	26	44	26	144	2.3	0.2	3.1
Reg. Season Totals	257	70	4528	668	1335	.500	0	3	.000	292	447	.653	403	743	1146	156	701	8	210	308	297	1628	4.5	0.6	6.3
Playoff Totals	9	0	81	3	14	.214	0	0	–	4	12	.333	5	13	18	3	9	0	2	9	6	10	2.0	0.3	1.1

Williams, Scott Christopher b. March 21, 1968 Ht. 6-10 Wt. 230 College: North Carolina

SEASON–TEAM	G	GS	MIN	FGM	FGA	PCT	3FGM	3FGA	PCT	FTM	FTA	PCT	O-RB	D-RB	TOT	AST	PF	DQ	STL	TO	BLK	PTS	RPG	APG	PPG
90-91–Chicago	51	0	337	53	104	.510	1	2	.500	20	28	.714	42	56	98	16	51	0	12	23	13	127	1.9	0.3	2.5
91-92–Chicago	63	0	690	83	172	.483	0	3	.000	48	74	.649	90	157	247	50	122	0	13	35	36	214	3.9	0.8	3.4
92-93–Chicago	71	5	1369	166	356	.466	0	7	.000	90	126	.714	168	283	451	68	230	3	55	73	66	422	6.4	1.0	5.9
93-94–Chicago	38	11	638	114	236	.483	1	5	.200	60	98	.612	69	112	181	39	112	1	16	44	21	289	4.8	1.0	7.6
94-95–Philadelphia	77	43	1781	206	434	.475	0	7	.000	79	107	.738	173	312	485	59	237	4	71	84	40	491	6.3	0.8	6.4
95-96–Philadelphia	13	1	193	15	29	.517	0	2	.000	10	12	.833	13	33	46	5	27	0	6	8	7	40	3.5	0.4	3.1
96-97–Philadelphia	62	52	1317	162	318	.509	0	2	.000	38	55	.691	155	242	397	41	206	5	44	50	41	362	6.4	0.7	5.8
97-98–Philadelphia	58	7	801	93	213	.437	0	5	.000	51	63	.810	87	124	211	29	132	0	17	30	21	237	3.6	0.5	4.1
98-99–Phil.-Milw.	7	0	46	5	17	.294	0	0	–	4	7	.571	3	11	14	1	9	0	3	4	2	14	2.0	0.1	2.0
99-00–Milwaukee	68	46	1488	213	426	.500	0	0	–	94	129	.729	177	271	448	28	230	3	40	65	66	520	6.6	0.4	7.6
Reg. Season Totals	508	165	8660	1110	2305	.482	2	33	.061	494	699	.707	977	1601	2578	336	1356	16	277	416	313	2716	5.1	0.7	5.3
Playoff Totals	68	0	1032	131	263	.498	0	4	.000	67	104	.644	101	192	293	45	177	2	23	56	46	329	4.3	0.7	4.8

Williams, Shammond Omar b. April 5, 1975 Ht. 6-1 Wt. 201 College: North Carolina

SEASON–TEAM	G	GS	MIN	FGM	FGA	PCT	3FGM	3FGA	PCT	FTM	FTA	PCT	O-RB	D-RB	TOT	AST	PF	DQ	STL	TO	BLK	PTS	RPG	APG	PPG
98-99–Atlanta	2	0	4	0	1	.000	0	0	–	3	4	.750	0	0	0	1	0	0	0	0	0	3	0.0	0.5	1.5
99-00–Seattle	43	5	517	84	225	.373	24	81	.296	33	51	.647	12	40	52	78	39	0	18	40	0	225	1.2	1.8	5.2
Reg. Season Totals	45	5	521	84	226	.372	24	81	.296	36	55	.655	12	40	52	79	39	0	18	40	0	228	1.2	1.8	5.1
Playoff Totals	5	2	99	18	33	.545	7	11	.636	8	11	.727	2	9	11	18	3	0	8	6	0	51	2.2	3.6	10.2

Williams, Sylvester (Sly, The Garbage Man) b. January 26, 1958 Ht. 6-7 Wt. 210 College: Rhode Island

SEASON–TEAM	G	GS	MIN	FGM	FGA	PCT	3FGM	3FGA	PCT	FTM	FTA	PCT	O-RB	D-RB	TOT	AST	PF	DQ	STL	TO	BLK	PTS	RPG	APG	PPG
79-80–New York	57	–	556	104	267	.390	0	4	.000	58	90	.644	65	56	121	36	73	0	19	49	8	266	2.1	0.6	4.7
80-81–New York	67	–	1976	349	708	.493	2	8	.250	185	268	.690	159	257	416	180	199	0	116	141	18	885	6.2	2.7	13.2
81-82–New York	60	27	1521	349	628	.556	2	9	.222	131	173	.757	100	127	227	142	153	0	77	114	16	831	3.8	2.4	13.9
82-83–New York	68	6	1385	314	647	.485	2	19	.105	176	259	.680	94	196	290	133	166	3	73	133	3	806	4.3	2.0	11.9
83-84–Atlanta	13	1	258	34	114	.298	1	9	.111	36	46	.783	19	31	50	16	33	0	14	18	1	105	3.8	1.2	8.1
84-85–Atlanta	34	20	867	167	380	.439	4	15	.267	79	123	.642	45	123	168	94	83	1	28	78	8	417	4.9	2.8	12.3
85-86–Boston	6	0	54	5	21	.238	0	4	.000	7	12	.583	7	8	15	2	15	0	1	7	1	17	2.5	0.3	2.8
Reg. Season Totals	305	54	6617	1322	2765	.478	11	68	.162	672	971	.692	489	798	1287	603	722	4	328	540	55	3327	4.2	2.0	10.9
Playoff Totals	7	0	138	29	59	.492	1	1	1.000	3	3	1.000	14	16	30	11	11	0	6	15	1	62	4.3	1.6	8.9

Williams, Tavares Montgomery (Monty) b. October 8, 1971 Ht. 6-8 Wt. 225 College: Notre Dame

SEASON–TEAM	G	GS	MIN	FGM	FGA	PCT	3FGM	3FGA	PCT	FTM	FTA	PCT	O-RB	D-RB	TOT	AST	PF	DQ	STL	TO	BLK	PTS	RPG	APG	PPG
94-95–New York	41	23	503	60	133	.451	0	8	.000	17	38	.447	42	56	98	49	87	0	20	41	4	137	2.4	1.2	3.3
95-96–N.Y.-S.A.	31	0	184	27	68	.397	0	1	.000	14	20	.700	20	20	40	8	26	0	6	18	2	68	1.3	0.3	2.2
96-97–San Antonio	65	26	1345	234	460	.509	0	1	.000	120	186	.645	98	108	206	91	161	1	55	116	52	588	3.2	1.4	9.0
97-98–San Antonio	72	16	1314	165	368	.448	1	2	.500	122	182	.670	67	112	179	89	133	1	34	82	24	453	2.5	1.2	6.3
98-99–Denver	1	0	6	0	2	.000	0	0	–	1	2	.500	0	0	0	0	0	0	0	0	0	1	0.0	0.0	1.0
99-00–Orlando	75	23	1501	263	538	.489	2	5	.400	123	166	.741	96	154	250	106	187	1	46	109	17	651	3.3	1.4	8.7
Reg. Season Totals	285	88	4853	749	1569	.477	3	17	.176	397	594	.668	323	450	773	343	594	3	161	366	99	1898	2.7	1.2	6.7
Playoff Totals	13	0	61	9	19	.474	0	0	–	5	9	.556	5	8	13	1	7	0	0	8	0	23	1.0	0.1	1.8

Williams, Thomas Ray (Ray) b. October 14, 1954 Ht. 6-3 Wt. 190 College: San Jacinto (Texas) Coll. (J.C.); Minnesota

SEASON–TEAM	G	GS	MIN	FGM	FGA	PCT	3FGM	3FGA	PCT	FTM	FTA	PCT	O-RB	D-RB	TOT	AST	PF	DQ	STL	TO	BLK	PTS	RPG	APG	PPG
77-78–New York	81	–	1550	305	689	.443	–	–	–	146	207	.705	85	124	209	363	211	4	108	242	15	756	2.6	4.5	9.3
78-79–New York	81	–	2370	575	1257	.457	–	–	–	251	313	.802	104	187	291	504	274	4	128	285	19	1401	3.6	6.2	17.3
79-80–New York	82	–	2582	687	1384	.496	7	37	.189	333	423	.787	149	263	412	512	295	5	167	256	24	1714	5.0	6.2	20.9
80-81–New York	79	–	2742	616	1335	.461	16	68	.235	312	382	.817	122	199	321	432	270	4	185	235	37	1560	4.1	5.5	19.7
81-82–New Jersey	82	69	2732	639	1383	.462	9	54	.167	387	465	.832	117	208	325	488	302	9	199	290	43	1674	4.0	6.0	20.4
82-83–Kansas City	72	68	2170	419	1068	.392	15	74	.203	256	333	.769	93	234	327	569	248	3	120	335	26	1109	4.5	7.9	15.4
83-84–New York	76	63	2230	418	939	.445	25	81	.309	263	318	.827	67	200	267	449	274	5	162	219	26	1124	3.5	5.9	14.8
84-85–Boston	23	5	459	55	143	.385	6	23	.261	31	46	.674	16	41	57	90	56	1	30	42	5	147	2.5	3.9	6.4
85-86–Atlanta-S.A.-N.J.	47	21	827	117	306	.382	6	19	.316	115	126	.913	35	51	86	187	124	2	61	101	4	355	1.8	4.0	7.6
86-87–New Jersey	32	14	800	131	290	.452	7	28	.250	49	60	.817	26	49	75	185	111	4	38	94	9	318	2.3	5.8	9.9
Reg. Season Totals	655	240	18462	3962	8794	.451	91	384	.237	2143	2673	.802	814	1556	2370	3779	2165	41	1198	2099	208	10158	3.6	5.8	15.5
Playoff Totals	40	8	889	166	412	.403	7	35	.200	86	106	.811	39	71	110	202	128	2	43	106	2	425	2.8	5.1	10.6

Williams, Travis b. May 27, 1969 Ht. 6-7 Wt. 224 College: South Carolina State

SEASON–TEAM	G	GS	MIN	FGM	FGA	PCT	3FGM	3FGA	PCT	FTM	FTA	PCT	O-RB	D-RB	TOT	AST	PF	DQ	STL	TO	BLK	PTS	RPG	APG	PPG
97-98–Charlotte	39	0	365	56	119	.471	0	1	.000	24	46	.522	53	39	92	20	55	0	18	30	5	136	2.4	0.5	3.5
98-99–Charlotte	8	0	62	6	13	.462	0	0	–	3	4	.750	6	13	19	2	10	0	2	6	1	15	2.4	0.3	1.9
Reg. Season Totals	47	0	427	62	132	.470	0	1	.000	27	50	.540	59	52	111	22	65	0	20	36	6	151	2.4	0.5	3.2
Playoff Totals	4	0	18	1	3	.333	0	0	–	3	4	.750	1	4	5	–	3	0	1	0	1	5	1.3	0.0	1.3

Williams, Walter Ander Jr. (Walt, The Wizard) b. April 16, 1970 Ht. 6-8 Wt. 230 College: Maryland

SEASON–TEAM	G	GS	MIN	FGM	FGA	PCT	3FGM	3FGA	PCT	FTM	FTA	PCT	O-RB	D-RB	TOT	AST	PF	DQ	STL	TO	BLK	PTS	RPG	APG	PPG
92-93–Sacramento	59	26	1673	358	823	.435	61	191	.319	224	302	.742	115	150	265	178	209	6	66	179	29	1001	4.5	3.0	17.0
93-94–Sacramento	57	4	1356	226	580	.390	38	132	.288	148	233	.635	71	164	235	132	200	6	52	145	23	638	4.1	2.3	11.2
94-95–Sacramento	77	77	2739	445	998	.446	103	296	.348	266	364	.731	100	245	345	316	265	3	123	243	63	1259	4.5	4.1	16.4
95-96–Sac.-Miami	73	73	2169	359	808	.444	114	293	.389	163	232	.703	99	220	319	230	238	0	85	151	58	995	4.4	3.2	13.6
96-97–Toronto	73	73	2647	419	982	.427	175	437	.400	186	243	.765	103	264	367	197	282	11	97	174	62	1199	5.0	2.7	16.4
97-98–Toronto-Port.	59	17	1470	210	544	.386	80	219	.365	108	125	.864	50	150	200	122	161	2	59	92	35	608	3.4	2.1	10.3
98-99–Portland	48	16	1044	147	347	.424	63	144	.438	89	107	.832	36	107	143	80	101	2	37	63	28	446	3.0	1.7	9.3
99-00–Houston	76	66	1859	312	681	.458	102	261	.391	101	123	.821	69	237	306	157	190	2	49	113	44	827	4.0	2.1	10.9
Reg. Season Totals	522	352	14957	2476	5763	.430	736	1973	.373	1285	1729	.743	643	1537	2180	1412	1646	32	568	1160	342	6973	4.2	2.7	13.4
Playoff Totals	20	3	357	44	107	.411	22	56	.393	20	30	.667	11	31	42	25	49	2	9	15	4	130	2.1	1.3	6.5

Williams, Ward M. b. June 26, 1923 Ht. 6-4 Wt. 195 College: Indiana

SEASON–TEAM	G	GS	MIN	FGM	FGA	PCT	3FGM	3FGA	PCT	FTM	FTA	PCT	O-RB	D-RB	TOT	AST	PF	DQ	STL	TO	BLK	PTS	RPG	APG	PPG
48-49–Fort Wayne	53	–	–	61	257	.237	–	–	–	93	124	.750	–	–	–	82	158	–	–	–	–	215	–	1.5	4.1
Reg. Season Totals	53	–	–	61	257	.237	–	–	–	93	124	.750	–	–	–	82	158	–	–	–	–	215	–	1.5	4.1

Williams, Willie Earl b. July 28, 1946 Ht. 6-7 Wt. 200 College: Florida State

SEASON–TEAM	G	GS	MIN	FGM	FGA	PCT	3FGM	3FGA	PCT	FTM	FTA	PCT	O-RB	D-RB	TOT	AST	PF	DQ	STL	TO	BLK	PTS	RPG	APG	PPG
70-71–Boston-Cin.	25	–	105	10	42	.238	–	–	–	3	5	.600	–	–	23	8	14	0	–	–	–	23	0.9	0.3	0.9
Reg. Season Totals	25	–	105	10	42	.238	–	–	–	3	5	.600	–	–	23	8	14	0	–	–	–	23	0.9	0.3	0.9

Williamson, Corliss Mondari (Big Nasty) b. December 4, 1973 Ht. 6-7 Wt. 245 College: Arkansas

SEASON–TEAM	G	GS	MIN	FGM	FGA	PCT	3FGM	3FGA	PCT	FTM	FTA	PCT	O-RB	D-RB	TOT	AST	PF	DQ	STL	TO	BLK	PTS	RPG	APG	PPG
95-96–Sacramento	53	3	609	125	268	.466	0	3	.000	47	84	.560	56	58	114	23	115	2	11	76	9	297	2.2	0.4	5.6
96-97–Sacramento	79	31	1992	371	745	.498	0	3	.000	173	251	.689	139	187	326	124	263	4	60	157	49	915	4.1	1.6	11.6
97-98–Sacramento	79	75	2819	561	1134	.495	0	9	.000	279	443	.630	162	284	446	230	252	4	76	199	48	1401	5.6	2.9	17.7
98-99–Sacramento	50	50	1374	269	555	.485	1	5	.200	120	188	.638	85	121	206	66	118	1	30	75	8	659	4.1	1.3	13.2
99-00–Sacramento	76	76	1707	311	622	.500	0	0	–	163	212	.769	122	168	290	82	192	0	38	110	19	785	3.8	1.1	10.3
Reg. Season Totals	337	235	8501	1637	3324	.492	1	20	.050	782	1178	.664	564	818	1382	525	940	11	215	617	133	4057	4.1	1.6	12.0
Playoff Totals	11	10	219	34	57	.596	0	0	–	19	23	.826	11	20	31	7	21	0	3	11	1	87	2.8	0.6	7.9

Williamson, John Lee (Super John) b. November 10, 1951 d. November 30, 1996 Ht. 6-2 Wt. 190 College: New Mexico State

SEASON–TEAM	G	GS	MIN	FGM	FGA	PCT	3FGM	3FGA	PCT	FTM	FTA	PCT	O-RB	D-RB	TOT	AST	PF	DQ	STL	TO	BLK	PTS	RPG	APG	PPG
73-74–New York (A)	77	–	2264	482	982	.491	2	11	.182	150	190	.789	68	145	213	243	254	–	86	208	27	1116	2.8	3.2	14.5
74-75–New York (A)	75	–	1872	370	768	.482	3	13	.231	123	147	.837	51	98	149	197	188	–	61	148	23	866	2.0	2.6	11.5
75-76–New York (A)	76	–	2255	519	1153	.450	8	42	.190	187	232	.806	70	120	190	188	224	–	76	185	33	1233	2.5	2.5	16.2
76-77–N.Y.-Indiana	72	–	2481	618	1347	.459	–	–	–	259	329	.787	42	151	193	201	246	4	107	–	13	1495	2.7	2.8	20.8
77-78–Indiana-N.J.	75	–	2731	723	1649	.438	–	–	–	331	391	.847	66	161	227	214	236	6	94	228	10	1777	3.0	2.9	23.7
78-79–New Jersey	74	–	2451	635	1367	.465	–	–	–	373	437	.854	53	143	196	255	215	3	89	233	12	1643	2.6	3.4	22.2
79-80–N.J.-Wash.	58	–	1374	359	817	.439	11	35	.314	116	138	.841	38	61	99	126	137	1	36	92	19	845	1.7	2.2	14.6
80-81–Washington	9	–	112	18	56	.321	1	6	.167	5	6	.833	0	7	7	17	13	0	4	12	1	42	0.8	1.9	4.7
Reg. NBA Totals	288	–	9149	2353	5236	.449	12	41	.293	1084	1301	.833	199	523	722	813	847	14	330	565	55	5802	2.5	2.8	20.1
Reg. ABA Totals	228	–	6391	1371	2903	.472	13	66	.197	460	569	.808	189	363	552	628	666	0	223	541	83	3215	2.4	2.8	14.1
NBA Playoff Totals	4	–	123	34	81	.420	2	6	.333	16	19	.842	4	4	8	9	15	0	4	18	0	86	2.0	2.3	21.5
ABA Playoff Totals	29	–	903	192	392	.490	2	10	.200	62	86	.721	31	49	80	76	101	0	21	72	12	448	2.8	2.6	15.4

Williford, Duncan Vann (Vann) b. January 26, 1948 Ht. 6-6 Wt. 195 College: North Carolina State

SEASON–TEAM	G	GS	MIN	FGM	FGA	PCT	3FGM	3FGA	PCT	FTM	FTA	PCT	O-RB	D-RB	TOT	AST	PF	DQ	STL	TO	BLK	PTS	RPG	APG	PPG
70-71–Carolina (A)	38	–	295	62	141	.440	3	9	.333	21	37	.568	–	–	68	15	34	–	–	–	–	148	1.8	0.4	3.9
Reg. ABA Totals	38	–	295	62	141	.440	3	9	.333	21	37	.568	–	–	68	15	34	–	–	–	–	148	1.8	0.4	3.9

Willis, Kevin Alvin (Devo, Fresh) b. September 6, 1962 Ht. 7-0 Wt. 245 College: Michigan State

SEASON–TEAM	G	GS	MIN	FGM	FGA	PCT	3FGM	3FGA	PCT	FTM	FTA	PCT	O-RB	D-RB	TOT	AST	PF	DQ	STL	TO	BLK	PTS	RPG	APG	PPG
84-85–Atlanta	82	19	1785	322	690	.467	2	9	.222	119	181	.657	177	345	522	36	226	4	31	104	49	765	6.4	0.4	9.3
85-86–Atlanta	82	59	2300	419	811	.517	0	6	.000	172	263	.654	243	461	704	45	294	6	66	177	44	1010	8.6	0.5	12.3
86-87–Atlanta	81	81	2626	538	1003	.536	1	4	.250	227	320	.709	321	528	849	62	313	4	65	173	61	1304	10.5	0.8	16.1
87-88–Atlanta	75	55	2091	356	687	.518	0	2	.000	159	245	.649	235	312	547	28	240	2	68	138	42	871	7.3	0.4	11.6
89-90–Atlanta	81	51	2273	418	805	.519	2	7	.286	168	246	.683	253	392	645	57	259	4	63	144	47	1006	8.0	0.7	12.4
90-91–Atlanta	80	80	2373	444	881	.504	4	10	.400	159	238	.668	259	445	704	99	235	2	60	153	40	1051	8.8	1.2	13.1
91-92–Atlanta	81	80	2962	591	1224	.483	6	37	.162	292	363	.804	418	840	1258	173	223	0	72	197	54	1480	15.5	2.1	18.3
92-93–Atlanta	80	80	2878	616	1218	.506	7	29	.241	196	300	.653	335	693	1028	165	264	1	68	213	41	1435	12.9	2.1	17.9
93-94–Atlanta	80	80	2867	627	1257	.499	9	24	.375	268	376	.713	335	628	963	150	250	2	79	188	38	1531	12.0	1.9	19.1
94-95–Atlanta-Miami	67	63	2390	473	1015	.466	3	15	.200	205	297	.690	227	505	732	86	215	3	60	162	36	1154	10.9	1.3	17.2
95-96–Miami-G.S.	75	60	2135	325	712	.456	1	9	.111	143	202	.708	208	430	638	53	253	4	32	161	41	794	8.5	0.7	10.6
96-97–Houston	75	32	1964	350	728	.481	2	14	.143	140	202	.693	146	415	561	71	216	1	42	119	32	842	7.5	0.9	11.2
97-98–Houston	81	74	2528	531	1041	.510	1	7	.143	242	305	.793	232	447	679	78	235	1	55	170	38	1305	8.4	1.0	16.1
98-99–Toronto	42	38	1216	187	447	.418	0	2	.000	130	155	.839	109	241	350	67	134	1	28	86	28	504	8.3	1.6	12.0
99-00–Toronto	79	1	1679	236	569	.415	1	3	.333	131	164	.799	201	281	482	49	256	3	36	98	48	604	6.1	0.6	7.6
Reg. Season Totals	1141	853	34067	6433	13088	.492	39	178	.219	2751	3857	.713	3699	6963	10662	1219	3613	38	825	2283	639	15656	9.3	1.1	13.7
Playoff Totals	73	54	2261	374	775	.483	2	12	.167	168	243	.691	215	385	600	58	273	3	58	121	38	918	8.2	0.8	12.6
All-Star Totals	1	0	14	4	10	.400	0	0	–	0	0	–	4	0	4	0	1	0	0	0	0	8	4.0	0.0	8.0

Willoughby, Dedric b. May 27, 1974 Ht. 6-3 Wt. 190 College: Iowa State

SEASON–TEAM	G	GS	MIN	FGM	FGA	PCT	3FGM	3FGA	PCT	FTM	FTA	PCT	O-RB	D-RB	TOT	AST	PF	DQ	STL	TO	BLK	PTS	RPG	APG	PPG
99-00–Chicago	25	1	508	61	179	.341	29	98	.296	39	51	.765	11	40	51	66	32	0	23	37	2	190	2.0	2.6	7.6
Reg. Season Totals	25	1	508	61	179	.341	29	98	.296	39	51	.765	11	40	51	66	32	0	23	37	2	190	2.0	2.6	7.6

Willoughby, William Wesley (Bill) b. May 20, 1957 Ht. 6-8 Wt. 205 High School: Dwight Morrow H.S. (Englewood, N.J.)

SEASON–TEAM	G	GS	MIN	FGM	FGA	PCT	3FGM	3FGA	PCT	FTM	FTA	PCT	O-RB	D-RB	TOT	AST	PF	DQ	STL	TO	BLK	PTS	RPG	APG	PPG
75-76–Atlanta	62	–	870	113	284	.398	–	–	–	66	100	.660	103	185	288	31	87	0	37	–	29	292	4.6	0.5	4.7
76-77–Atlanta	39	–	549	75	169	.444	–	–	–	43	63	.683	65	105	170	13	64	1	19	–	23	193	4.4	0.3	4.9
77-78–Buffalo	56	–	1079	156	363	.430	–	–	–	64	80	.800	76	143	219	38	131	2	24	56	47	376	3.9	0.7	6.7
79-80–Cleveland	78	–	1447	219	457	.479	1	9	.111	96	127	.756	122	207	329	72	189	0	32	68	62	535	4.2	0.9	6.9
80-81–Houston	55	–	1145	150	287	.523	0	3	.000	49	64	.766	74	153	227	64	102	0	18	74	31	349	4.1	1.2	6.3
81-82–Houston	69	42	1475	240	464	.517	3	7	.429	56	77	.727	107	157	264	75	146	1	31	78	60	539	3.8	1.1	7.8
82-83–S.A.-N.J.	62	0	1146	147	324	.454	6	14	.429	43	55	.782	63	138	201	64	139	0	25	61	17	343	3.2	1.0	5.5
83-84–New Jersey	67	2	936	124	258	.481	0	7	.000	55	63	.873	75	118	193	56	106	0	23	53	24	303	2.9	0.8	4.5
Reg. Season Totals	488	44	8647	1224	2606	.470	10	40	.250	472	629	.750	685	1206	1891	413	964	4	209	390	293	2930	3.9	0.8	6.0
Playoff Totals	24	0	447	44	121	.364	0	1	.000	32	42	.762	33	61	94	23	45	0	14	24	19	120	3.9	1.0	5.0

Wilson, Coatlen Othell (Othell) b. October 26, 1961 Ht. 6-0 Wt. 190 College: Virginia

SEASON–TEAM	G	GS	MIN	FGM	FGA	PCT	3FGM	3FGA	PCT	FTM	FTA	PCT	O-RB	D-RB	TOT	AST	PF	DQ	STL	TO	BLK	PTS	RPG	APG	PPG
84-85–Golden State	74	23	1260	134	291	.460	3	16	.188	54	76	.711	35	96	131	217	122	0	77	95	12	325	1.8	2.9	4.4
86-87–Sacramento	53	2	789	82	185	.443	3	18	.167	43	54	.796	28	53	81	207	67	0	42	77	4	210	1.5	3.9	4.0
Reg. Season Totals	127	25	2049	216	476	.454	6	34	.176	97	130	.746	63	149	212	424	189	0	119	172	16	535	1.7	3.3	4.2

Wilson, George (Jiff) b. May 9, 1942 Ht. 6-8 Wt. 230 College: Cincinnati

SEASON–TEAM	G	GS	MIN	FGM	FGA	PCT	3FGM	3FGA	PCT	FTM	FTA	PCT	O-RB	D-RB	TOT	AST	PF	DQ	STL	TO	BLK	PTS	RPG	APG	PPG
64-65–Cincinnati	39	–	288	41	155	.265	–	–	–	9	30	.300	–	–	102	11	59	0	–	–	–	91	2.6	0.3	2.3
65-66–Cincinnati	47	–	276	54	138	.391	–	–	–	27	42	.643	–	–	98	17	56	0	–	–	–	135	2.1	0.4	2.9
66-67–Cin.-Chicago	55	–	573	85	234	.363	–	–	–	58	86	.674	–	–	206	15	92	0	–	–	–	228	3.7	0.3	4.1
67-68–Seattle	77	–	1236	179	498	.359	–	–	–	109	155	.703	–	–	470	56	218	1	–	–	–	467	6.1	0.7	6.1
68-69–Phoenix-Phil.	79	–	1846	272	663	.410	–	–	–	153	235	.651	–	–	721	108	232	5	–	–	–	697	9.1	1.4	8.8
69-70–Philadelphia	67	–	836	118	304	.388	–	–	–	122	172	.709	–	–	317	52	145	3	–	–	–	358	4.7	0.8	5.3
70-71–Buffalo	46	–	713	92	269	.342	–	–	–	56	69	.812	–	–	230	48	99	1	–	–	–	240	5.0	1.0	5.2
Reg. Season Totals	410	–	5768	841	2261	.372	–	–	–	534	789	.677	–	–	2144	307	901	10	–	–	–	2216	5.2	0.7	5.4
Playoff Totals	12	–	101	8	31	.258	–	–	–	7	11	.636	–	–	42	10	20	0	–	–	–	23	3.5	0.8	1.9

Wilson, Isaiah (Bunny) b. May 31, 1948 Ht. 6-2 Wt. 175 College: Baltimore

SEASON–TEAM	G	GS	MIN	FGM	FGA	PCT	3FGM	3FGA	PCT	FTM	FTA	PCT	O-RB	D-RB	TOT	AST	PF	DQ	STL	TO	BLK	PTS	RPG	APG	PPG
71-72–Detroit	48	–	322	63	177	.356	–	–	–	41	56	.732	–	–	47	41	32	0	–	–	–	167	1.0	0.9	3.5
72-73–Memphis (A)	30	–	386	68	159	.428	3	8	.375	51	64	.797	18	21	39	72	46	0	–	41	–	190	1.3	2.4	6.3
Reg. NBA Totals	48	–	322	63	177	.356	–	–	–	41	56	.732	–	–	47	41	32	0	–	–	–	167	1.0	0.9	3.5
Reg. ABA Totals	30	–	386	68	159	.428	3	8	.375	51	64	.797	18	21	39	72	46	0	–	41	–	190	1.3	2.4	6.3

Wilson, James (Jim) b. 1948 Ht. 5-10 Wt. 175 College: Cheyney

SEASON–TEAM	G	GS	MIN	FGM	FGA	PCT	3FGM	3FGA	PCT	FTM	FTA	PCT	O-RB	D-RB	TOT	AST	PF	DQ	STL	TO	BLK	PTS	RPG	APG	PPG
70-71–Pittsburgh (A)	6	–	44	1	8	.125	0	0	–	4	6	.667	–	–	6	8	3	–	–	–	–	6	1.0	1.3	1.0
Reg. ABA Totals	6	–	44	1	8	.125	0	0	–	4	6	.667	–	–	6	8	3	–	–	–	–	6	1.0	1.3	1.0

Wilson, Jasper b. July 12, 1947 Ht. 6-6 Wt. 200 College: Southern University

SEASON–TEAM	G	GS	MIN	FGM	FGA	PCT	3FGM	3FGA	PCT	FTM	FTA	PCT	O-RB	D-RB	TOT	AST	PF	DQ	STL	TO	BLK	PTS	RPG	APG	PPG
68-69–New Orleans (A)	66	–	756	128	339	.378	5	12	.417	82	127	.646	–	–	173	43	127	1	–	63	–	343	2.6	0.7	5.2
69-70–New Orleans (A)	4	–	59	8	21	.381	1	2	.500	6	8	.750	–	–	14	2	6	0	–	–	–	23	3.5	0.5	5.8
Reg. ABA Totals	70	–	815	136	360	.378	6	14	.429	88	135	.652	–	–	187	45	133	1	–	63	–	366	2.7	0.6	5.2
ABA Playoff Totals	10	–	92	11	42	.262	0	5	.000	17	23	.739	–	–	26	2	20	0	–	–	–	39	2.6	0.2	3.9

Wilson, Michael (Mike) b. September 15, 1959 Ht. 6-3 Wt. 180 College: Marquette

SEASON–TEAM	G	GS	MIN	FGM	FGA	PCT	3FGM	3FGA	PCT	FTM	FTA	PCT	O-RB	D-RB	TOT	AST	PF	DQ	STL	TO	BLK	PTS	RPG	APG	PPG
83-84–Washington	6	0	26	0	2	.000	0	1	.000	1	2	.500	1	0	1	3	5	0	0	3	0	1	0.2	0.5	0.2
84-85–Clev.-N.J.	19	0	267	36	77	.468	0	0	–	27	36	.750	14	17	31	35	21	0	14	20	5	99	1.6	1.8	5.2
86-87–N.J.-Atlanta	7	0	45	3	10	.300	0	0	–	2	2	1.000	1	3	4	7	10	0	1	5	0	8	0.6	1.0	1.1
Reg. Season Totals	32	0	338	39	89	.438	0	1	.000	30	40	.750	16	20	36	45	36	0	15	28	5	108	1.1	1.4	3.4

Wilson, Nikita Franciscus b. February 25, 1964 Ht. 6-8 Wt. 200 College: Louisiana State

SEASON–TEAM	G	GS	MIN	FGM	FGA	PCT	3FGM	3FGA	PCT	FTM	FTA	PCT	O-RB	D-RB	TOT	AST	PF	DQ	STL	TO	BLK	PTS	RPG	APG	PPG
87-88–Portland	15	0	54	7	23	.304	0	0	–	5	6	.833	2	9	11	3	7	0	0	5	0	19	0.7	0.2	1.3
Reg. Season Totals	15	0	54	7	23	.304	0	0	–	5	6	.833	2	9	11	3	7	0	0	5	0	19	0.7	0.2	1.3

Wilson, Richard (Rick) b. February 7, 1956 Ht. 6-5 Wt. 200 College: Louisville

SEASON–TEAM	G	GS	MIN	FGM	FGA	PCT	3FGM	3FGA	PCT	FTM	FTA	PCT	O-RB	D-RB	TOT	AST	PF	DQ	STL	TO	BLK	PTS	RPG	APG	PPG
78-79–Atlanta	61	–	589	81	197	.411	–	–	–	24	44	.545	20	56	76	72	66	1	30	41	8	186	1.2	1.2	3.0
79-80–Atlanta	5	–	59	2	14	.143	0	0	–	4	6	.667	2	1	3	11	3	0	4	8	1	8	0.6	2.2	1.6
Reg. Season Totals	66	–	648	83	211	.393	0	0	–	28	50	.560	22	57	79	83	69	1	34	49	9	194	1.2	1.3	2.9
Playoff Totals	1	–	1	0	0	–	0	0	–	0	0	–	0	0	0	–	0	0	0	0	0	0	0.0	0.0	0.0

Wilson, Ricky b. July 16, 1964 Ht. 6-3 Wt. 195 College: George Mason

SEASON–TEAM	G	GS	MIN	FGM	FGA	PCT	3FGM	3FGA	PCT	FTM	FTA	PCT	O-RB	D-RB	TOT	AST	PF	DQ	STL	TO	BLK	PTS	RPG	APG	PPG
87-88–N.J.-S.A.	24	1	420	43	110	.391	10	26	.385	29	40	.725	2	25	27	69	40	0	23	25	3	125	1.1	2.9	5.2
Reg. Season Totals	24	1	420	43	110	.391	10	26	.385	29	40	.725	2	25	27	69	40	0	23	25	3	125	1.1	2.9	5.2
Playoff Totals	2	0	9	0	2	.000	0	0	–	0	0	–	0	0	0	1	2	0	0	1	0	0	0.0	0.5	0.0

Wilson, Robert E. (Bobby) b. January 15, 1951 Ht. 6-3 Wt. 175 College: Pasadena City (Calif.) Coll. (J.C.); Northeastern Christian J.C. (Pa.); Wichita State

SEASON–TEAM	G	GS	MIN	FGM	FGA	PCT	3FGM	3FGA	PCT	FTM	FTA	PCT	O-RB	D-RB	TOT	AST	PF	DQ	STL	TO	BLK	PTS	RPG	APG	PPG
74-75–Chicago	48	–	425	115	225	.511	–	–	–	46	58	.793	18	34	52	36	54	1	22	–	1	276	1.1	0.8	5.8
75-76–Chicago	58	–	856	197	489	.403	–	–	–	43	58	.741	32	62	94	52	96	1	25	–	2	437	1.6	0.9	7.5
76-77–Boston	25	–	131	19	59	.322	–	–	–	11	13	.846	3	6	9	14	19	0	3	–	0	49	0.4	0.6	2.0
77-78–Indiana	12	–	86	14	36	.389	–	–	–	2	3	.667	6	6	12	8	16	0	2	6	1	30	1.0	0.7	2.5
Reg. Season Totals	143	–	1498	345	809	.426	–	–	–	102	132	.773	59	108	167	110	185	2	52	6	4	792	1.2	0.8	5.5
Playoff Totals	10	–	93	17	41	.415	–	–	–	10	12	.833	2	9	11	4	10	0	4	–	0	44	1.1	0.4	4.4

Wilson, Robert F. (Bobby) b. 1944 Ht. 6-8 Wt. 215 College: Kansas

SEASON–TEAM	G	GS	MIN	FGM	FGA	PCT	3FGM	3FGA	PCT	FTM	FTA	PCT	O-RB	D-RB	TOT	AST	PF	DQ	STL	TO	BLK	PTS	RPG	APG	PPG
67-68–Dallas (A)	69	–	1562	226	581	.389	1	2	.500	163	265	.615	–	–	450	55	209	8	–	127	–	616	6.5	0.8	8.9
Reg. ABA Totals	69	–	1562	226	581	.389	1	2	.500	163	265	.615	–	–	450	55	209	8	–	127	–	616	6.5	0.8	8.9
ABA Playoff Totals	6	–	50	7	25	.280	1	1	1.000	6	13	.462	–	–	26	2	12	1	–	7	–	21	4.3	0.3	3.5

Wilson, Robert Jr. (Bob) b. March 8, 1926 Ht. 6-4 Wt. 185 College: West Virginia State

SEASON–TEAM	G	GS	MIN	FGM	FGA	PCT	3FGM	3FGA	PCT	FTM	FTA	PCT	O-RB	D-RB	TOT	AST	PF	DQ	STL	TO	BLK	PTS	RPG	APG	PPG
51-52–Milwaukee	63	–	1308	79	264	.299	–	–	–	78	135	.578	–	–	210	108	172	8	–	–	–	236	3.3	1.7	3.7
Reg. Season Totals	63	–	1308	79	264	.299	–	–	–	78	135	.578	–	–	210	108	172	8	–	–	–	236	3.3	1.7	3.7

Wilson, Stephen Earl (Steve) b. October 16, 1948 Ht. 6-5 Wt. 185 College: Hanover

SEASON–TEAM	G	GS	MIN	FGM	FGA	PCT	3FGM	3FGA	PCT	FTM	FTA	PCT	O-RB	D-RB	TOT	AST	PF	DQ	STL	TO	BLK	PTS	RPG	APG	PPG
70-71–Denver (A)	39	–	261	52	132	.394	8	33	.242	22	41	.537	–	–	48	29	43	–	–	–	–	134	1.2	0.7	3.4
71-72–Denver (A)	9	–	36	5	23	.217	0	2	.000	4	7	.571	–	–	4	6	9	–	–	3	–	14	0.4	0.7	1.6
Reg. ABA Totals	48	–	297	57	155	.368	8	35	.229	26	48	.542	–	–	52	35	52	–	–	3	–	148	1.1	0.7	3.1

Wilson, Thomas E. (Bubba) b. August 7, 1955 Ht. 6-3 Wt. 175 College: Western Carolina

SEASON–TEAM	G	GS	MIN	FGM	FGA	PCT	3FGM	3FGA	PCT	FTM	FTA	PCT	O-RB	D-RB	TOT	AST	PF	DQ	STL	TO	BLK	PTS	RPG	APG	PPG
79-80–Golden State	16	–	143	7	25	.280	0	0	–	3	6	.500	6	10	16	12	11	0	2	8	0	17	1.0	0.8	1.1
Reg. Season Totals	16	–	143	7	25	.280	0	0	–	3	6	.500	6	10	16	12	11	0	2	8	0	17	1.0	0.8	1.1

Wilson, Trevor b. March 16, 1968 Ht. 6-8 Wt. 215 College: UCLA

SEASON–TEAM	G	GS	MIN	FGM	FGA	PCT	3FGM	3FGA	PCT	FTM	FTA	PCT	O-RB	D-RB	TOT	AST	PF	DQ	STL	TO	BLK	PTS	RPG	APG	PPG
90-91–Atlanta	25	0	162	21	70	.300	0	2	.000	13	26	.500	16	24	40	11	13	0	5	17	1	55	1.6	0.4	2.2
93-94–Lakers-Sac.	57	13	1221	187	388	.482	0	2	.000	92	166	.554	120	153	273	72	123	0	38	93	11	466	4.8	1.3	8.2
94-95–Sacramento	15	0	147	18	40	.450	0	0	–	11	14	.786	10	16	26	12	12	0	4	6	2	47	1.7	0.8	3.1
95-96–Philadelphia	6	0	79	10	20	.500	0	0	–	3	4	.750	7	7	14	4	9	0	3	1	0	23	2.3	0.7	3.8
Reg. Season Totals	103	13	1609	236	518	.456	0	4	.000	119	210	.567	153	200	353	99	157	0	50	117	14	591	3.4	1.0	5.7

Winchester, Kennard Norman Jr. b. September 3, 1966 Ht. 6-5 Wt. 210 College: James Madison; Averett

SEASON–TEAM	G	GS	MIN	FGM	FGA	PCT	3FGM	3FGA	PCT	FTM	FTA	PCT	O-RB	D-RB	TOT	AST	PF	DQ	STL	TO	BLK	PTS	RPG	APG	PPG
90-91–Houston	64	1	607	98	245	.400	8	20	.400	35	45	.778	34	33	67	25	70	0	16	30	13	239	1.0	0.4	3.7
91-92–Houston-N.Y.	19	0	81	13	30	.433	1	2	.500	8	10	.800	6	9	15	8	5	0	2	2	2	35	0.8	0.4	1.8
92-93–Houston	39	0	340	61	139	.439	4	19	.211	17	22	.773	17	32	49	13	40	0	10	15	10	143	1.3	0.3	3.7
Reg. Season Totals	122	1	1028	172	414	.415	13	41	.317	60	77	.779	57	74	131	46	115	0	28	47	25	417	1.1	0.4	3.4
Playoff Totals	3	0	11	3	5	.600	0	0	–	0	1	.000	0	0	0	2	0	0	0	1	0	6	0.0	0.7	2.0

Windis, Tony John b. January 27, 1933 Ht. 6-1 Wt. 160 College: Wyoming

SEASON–TEAM	G	GS	MIN	FGM	FGA	PCT	3FGM	3FGA	PCT	FTM	FTA	PCT	O-RB	D-RB	TOT	AST	PF	DQ	STL	TO	BLK	PTS	RPG	APG	PPG
59-60–Detroit	9	–	193	16	60	.267	–	–	–	4	6	.667	–	–	47	32	20	0	–	–	–	36	5.2	3.6	4.0
Reg. Season Totals	9	–	193	16	60	.267	–	–	–	4	6	.667	–	–	47	32	20	0	–	–	–	36	5.2	3.6	4.0

Windsor, John T. b. April 3, 1940 Ht. 6-8 Wt. 220 College: Stanford

SEASON–TEAM	G	GS	MIN	FGM	FGA	PCT	3FGM	3FGA	PCT	FTM	FTA	PCT	O-RB	D-RB	TOT	AST	PF	DQ	STL	TO	BLK	PTS	RPG	APG	PPG
63-64–San Francisco	11	–	68	10	27	.370	–	–	–	7	8	.875	–	–	26	2	13	0	–	–	–	27	2.4	0.2	2.5
Reg. Season Totals	11	–	68	10	27	.370	–	–	–	7	8	.875	–	–	26	2	13	0	–	–	–	27	2.4	0.2	2.5

Winfield, Leroy (Lee) b. February 4, 1947 Ht. 6-2 Wt. 175 College: North Texas

SEASON–TEAM	G	GS	MIN	FGM	FGA	PCT	3FGM	3FGA	PCT	FTM	FTA	PCT	O-RB	D-RB	TOT	AST	PF	DQ	STL	TO	BLK	PTS	RPG	APG	PPG
69-70–Seattle	64	–	771	138	288	.479	–	–	–	87	116	.750	–	–	98	102	95	0	–	–	–	363	1.5	1.6	5.7
70-71–Seattle	79	–	1605	334	716	.466	–	–	–	162	244	.664	–	–	193	225	135	1	–	–	–	830	2.4	2.8	10.5
71-72–Seattle	81	–	2040	343	692	.496	–	–	–	175	262	.668	–	–	218	290	198	1	–	–	–	861	2.7	3.6	10.6
72-73–Seattle	53	–	1061	143	332	.431	–	–	–	62	108	.574	–	–	126	186	92	3	–	–	–	348	2.4	3.5	6.6
73-74–Buffalo	36	–	433	37	105	.352	–	–	–	33	52	.635	19	24	43	47	42	0	15	–	5	107	1.2	1.3	3.0
74-75–Buffalo	68	–	1259	164	312	.526	–	–	–	49	68	.721	45	81	126	134	106	1	43	–	30	377	1.9	2.0	5.5
75-76–Kansas City	22	–	214	32	66	.485	–	–	–	9	14	.643	8	16	24	19	14	0	10	–	6	73	1.1	0.9	3.3
Reg. Season Totals	403	–	7383	1191	2511	.474	–	–	–	577	864	.668	72	121	828	1003	682	6	68	–	41	2959	2.1	2.5	7.3
Playoff Totals	7	–	77	7	18	.389	–	–	–	4	7	.571	5	6	11	11	10	1	3	–	1	18	1.6	1.6	2.6

Wingate, David Grover Stacey Jr. b. December 15, 1963 Ht. 6-5 Wt. 187 College: Georgetown

SEASON–TEAM	G	GS	MIN	FGM	FGA	PCT	3FGM	3FGA	PCT	FTM	FTA	PCT	O-RB	D-RB	TOT	AST	PF	DQ	STL	TO	BLK	PTS	RPG	APG	PPG
86-87–Philadelphia	77	9	1612	259	602	.430	13	52	.250	149	201	.741	70	86	156	155	169	1	93	128	19	680	2.0	2.0	8.8
87-88–Philadelphia	61	22	1419	218	545	.400	10	40	.250	99	132	.750	44	57	101	119	125	0	47	104	22	545	1.7	2.0	8.9
88-89–Philadelphia	33	6	372	54	115	.470	2	6	.333	27	34	.794	12	25	37	73	43	0	9	35	2	137	1.1	2.2	4.2
89-90–San Antonio	78	2	1856	220	491	.448	0	13	.000	87	112	.777	62	133	195	208	154	2	89	127	18	527	2.5	2.7	6.8
90-91–San Antonio	25	0	563	53	138	.384	1	9	.111	29	41	.707	24	51	75	46	66	0	19	42	5	136	3.0	1.8	5.4
91-92–Washington	81	72	2127	266	572	.465	1	18	.056	105	146	.719	80	189	269	247	162	1	123	124	21	638	3.3	3.0	7.9
92-93–Charlotte	72	55	1471	180	336	.536	1	6	.167	79	107	.738	49	125	174	183	135	1	66	89	9	440	2.4	2.5	6.1
93-94–Charlotte	50	36	1005	136	283	.481	4	12	.333	34	51	.667	30	104	134	104	85	0	42	53	6	310	2.7	2.1	6.2
94-95–Charlotte	52	9	515	50	122	.410	4	22	.182	18	24	.750	11	49	60	56	60	0	19	27	6	122	1.2	1.1	2.3
95-96–Seattle	60	3	695	88	212	.415	15	34	.441	32	41	.780	17	39	56	58	66	0	20	42	4	223	0.9	1.0	3.7
96-97–Seattle	65	2	929	89	214	.416	25	71	.352	33	40	.825	23	51	74	80	108	0	44	37	5	236	1.1	1.2	3.6
97-98–Seattle	58	2	546	66	140	.471	3	7	.429	15	29	.517	19	60	79	37	58	0	21	37	3	150	1.4	0.6	2.6
98-99–New York	20	0	92	7	16	.438	0	0	–	0	0	–	3	5	8	5	10	0	4	6	0	14	0.4	0.3	0.7
99-00–New York	7	0	32	1	9	.111	0	0	–	0	0	–	1	1	2	3	7	0	1	2	2	2	0.3	0.4	0.3
Reg. Season Totals	739	218	13234	1687	3795	.445	79	290	.272	707	958	.738	445	975	1420	1374	1248	5	597	853	122	4160	1.9	1.9	5.6
Playoff Totals	59	4	884	119	262	.454	19	44	.432	44	66	.667	38	76	114	94	115	3	38	43	8	301	1.9	1.6	5.1

Wingfield, Dontonio b. June 23, 1974 Ht. 6-8 Wt. 256 College: Cincinnati

SEASON–TEAM	G	GS	MIN	FGM	FGA	PCT	3FGM	3FGA	PCT	FTM	FTA	PCT	O-RB	D-RB	TOT	AST	PF	DQ	STL	TO	BLK	PTS	RPG	APG	PPG
94-95–Seattle	20	0	81	18	51	.353	2	12	.167	8	10	.800	11	19	30	3	15	0	5	8	3	46	1.5	0.2	2.3
95-96–Portland	44	2	487	60	157	.382	19	63	.302	26	34	.765	45	59	104	28	73	1	20	31	6	165	2.4	0.6	3.8
96-97–Portland	47	0	569	79	193	.409	26	77	.338	27	40	.675	63	74	137	45	101	1	14	49	6	211	2.9	1.0	4.5
97-98–Portland	3	0	9	0	3	.000	0	0	–	1	2	.500	2	2	4	0	2	0	0	1	0	1	1.3	0.0	0.3
Reg. Season Totals	114	2	1146	157	404	.389	47	152	.309	62	86	.721	121	154	275	76	191	2	39	89	15	423	2.4	0.7	3.7
Playoff Totals	8	0	78	10	23	.435	6	10	.600	6	10	.600	10	6	16	5	13	0	1	5	0	32	2.0	0.6	4.0

Wingo, Harthorne Nathaniel (Wingy) b. September 9, 1947 Ht. 6-8 Wt. 210 College: Friends

SEASON–TEAM	G	GS	MIN	FGM	FGA	PCT	3FGM	3FGA	PCT	FTM	FTA	PCT	O-RB	D-RB	TOT	AST	PF	DQ	STL	TO	BLK	PTS	RPG	APG	PPG
72-73–New York	13	–	59	9	22	.409	–	–	–	2	6	.333	–	–	16	1	9	0	–	–	–	20	1.2	0.1	1.5
73-74–New York	60	–	536	82	172	.477	–	–	–	48	76	.632	72	94	166	25	85	0	7	–	14	212	2.8	0.4	3.5
74-75–New York	82	–	1686	233	506	.460	–	–	–	141	187	.754	163	293	456	84	215	2	48	–	35	607	5.6	1.0	7.4
75-76–New York	57	–	533	72	163	.442	–	–	–	40	60	.667	46	61	107	18	59	0	19	–	8	184	1.9	0.3	3.2
Reg. Season Totals	212	–	2814	396	863	.459	–	–	–	231	329	.702	281	448	745	128	368	2	74	–	57	1023	3.5	0.6	4.8
Playoff Totals	11	–	104	21	47	.447	–	–	–	8	12	.667	11	14	32	8	10	0	5	–	0	50	2.9	0.7	4.5

Winkler, Marvin (Marv) b. February 18, 1948 Ht. 6-1 Wt. 170 College: Louisiana-Lafayette

SEASON–TEAM	G	GS	MIN	FGM	FGA	PCT	3FGM	3FGA	PCT	FTM	FTA	PCT	O-RB	D-RB	TOT	AST	PF	DQ	STL	TO	BLK	PTS	RPG	APG	PPG
70-71–Milwaukee	3	–	14	3	10	.300	–	–	–	2	2	1.000	–	–	4	2	3	0	–	–	–	8	1.3	0.7	2.7
71-72–Indiana (A)	20	–	155	15	54	.278	2	4	.500	8	14	.571	–	–	16	12	16	–	–	12	–	40	0.8	0.6	2.0
Reg. NBA Totals	3	–	14	3	10	.300	–	–	–	2	2	1.000	–	–	4	2	3	0	–	–	–	8	1.3	0.7	2.7
Reg. ABA Totals	20	–	155	15	54	.278	2	4	.500	8	14	.571	–	–	16	12	16	–	–	12	–	40	0.8	0.6	2.0
NBA Playoff Totals	5	–	8	0	4	.000	–	–	–	0	0	–	–	–	0	1	3	0	–	–	–	0	0.0	0.2	0.0

Winslow, Rickie O'Neal b. July 26, 1964 Ht. 6-8 Wt. 225 College: Houston

SEASON–TEAM	G	GS	MIN	FGM	FGA	PCT	3FGM	3FGA	PCT	FTM	FTA	PCT	O-RB	D-RB	TOT	AST	PF	DQ	STL	TO	BLK	PTS	RPG	APG	PPG
87-88–Milwaukee	7	0	45	3	13	.231	0	1	.000	1	2	.500	3	4	7	2	9	0	1	4	0	7	1.0	0.3	1.0
Reg. Season Totals	7	0	45	3	13	.231	0	1	.000	1	2	.500	3	4	7	2	9	0	1	4	0	7	1.0	0.3	1.0

Winter, Trevor b. January 7, 1974 Ht. 7-0 Wt. 280 College: Minnesota

SEASON–TEAM	G	GS	MIN	FGM	FGA	PCT	3FGM	3FGA	PCT	FTM	FTA	PCT	O-RB	D-RB	TOT	AST	PF	DQ	STL	TO	BLK	PTS	RPG	APG	PPG
98-99–Minnesota	1	0	5	0	0	–	0	0	–	0	0	–	1	2	3	0	5	0	0	0	0	0	3.0	0.0	0.0
Reg. Season Totals	1	0	5	0	0	–	0	0	–	0	0	–	1	2	3	0	5	0	0	0	0	0	3.0	0.0	0.0

Winters, Brian Joseph b. March 1, 1952 Ht. 6-4 Wt. 185 College: South Carolina

SEASON–TEAM	G	GS	MIN	FGM	FGA	PCT	3FGM	3FGA	PCT	FTM	FTA	PCT	O-RB	D-RB	TOT	AST	PF	DQ	STL	TO	BLK	PTS	RPG	APG	PPG
74-75–Los Angeles	68	–	1516	359	810	.443	–	–	–	76	92	.826	39	99	138	195	168	1	74	–	18	794	2.0	2.9	11.7
75-76–Milwaukee	78	–	2795	618	1333	.464	–	–	–	180	217	.829	66	183	249	366	240	0	124	–	25	1416	3.2	4.7	18.2
76-77–Milwaukee	78	–	2717	652	1308	.498	–	–	–	205	242	.847	64	167	231	337	228	1	114	–	29	1509	3.0	4.3	19.3
77-78–Milwaukee	80	–	2751	674	1457	.463	–	–	–	246	293	.840	87	163	250	393	239	4	124	236	27	1594	3.1	4.9	19.9
78-79–Milwaukee	79	–	2575	662	1343	.493	–	–	–	237	277	.856	48	129	177	383	243	1	83	257	40	1561	2.2	4.8	19.8
79-80–Milwaukee	80	–	2623	535	1116	.479	38	102	.373	184	214	.860	48	175	223	362	208	0	101	186	28	1292	2.8	4.5	16.2
80-81–Milwaukee	69	–	1771	331	697	.475	18	51	.353	119	137	.869	32	108	140	229	185	2	70	136	10	799	2.0	3.3	11.6
81-82–Milwaukee	61	13	1829	404	806	.501	36	93	.387	123	156	.788	51	119	170	253	187	1	57	118	9	967	2.8	4.1	15.9
82-83–Milwaukee	57	12	1361	255	587	.434	22	68	.324	73	85	.859	35	75	110	156	132	2	45	81	4	605	1.9	2.7	10.6
Reg. Season Totals	650	25	19938	4490	9457	.475	114	314	.363	1443	1713	.842	470	1218	1688	2674	1830	12	792	1014	190	10537	2.6	4.1	16.2
Playoff Totals	41	9	1352	269	549	.490	19	48	.396	80	99	.808	26	92	118	192	123	3	52	96	16	637	2.9	4.7	15.5
All-Star Totals	2	1	30	5	12	.417	0	0	–	0	0	–	2	4	6	2	4	0	1	3	0	10	3.0	1.0	5.0

Winters, Voise Lee b. October 12, 1962 Ht. 6-8 Wt. 200 College: Bradley

SEASON–TEAM	G	GS	MIN	FGM	FGA	PCT	3FGM	3FGA	PCT	FTM	FTA	PCT	O-RB	D-RB	TOT	AST	PF	DQ	STL	TO	BLK	PTS	RPG	APG	PPG
85-86–Philadelphia	4	0	17	3	13	.231	0	1	.000	0	0	–	1	2	3	0	1	0	1	2	0	6	0.8	0.0	1.5
Reg. Season Totals	4	0	17	3	13	.231	0	1	.000	0	0	–	1	2	3	0	1	0	1	2	0	6	0.8	0.0	1.5

Wise, Allen Harper (Skip) b. July 25, 1955 Ht. 6-3 Wt. 180 College: Clemson

SEASON–TEAM	G	GS	MIN	FGM	FGA	PCT	3FGM	3FGA	PCT	FTM	FTA	PCT	O-RB	D-RB	TOT	AST	PF	DQ	STL	TO	BLK	PTS	RPG	APG	PPG
75-76–San Antonio (A)	2	–	10	2	4	.500	0	0	–	0	0	–	1	2	3	1	4	–	0	2	0	4	1.5	0.5	2.0
Reg. ABA Totals	2	–	10	2	4	.500	0	0	–	0	0	–	1	2	3	1	4	–	0	2	0	4	1.5	0.5	2.0

Wise, Willie M. b. March 3, 1947 Ht. 6-6 Wt. 220 College: Drake

SEASON–TEAM	G	GS	MIN	FGM	FGA	PCT	3FGM	3FGA	PCT	FTM	FTA	PCT	O-RB	D-RB	TOT	AST	PF	DQ	STL	TO	BLK	PTS	RPG	APG	PPG
69-70–Los Angeles (A)	82	–	2709	483	1014	.476	4	17	.235	278	427	.651	283	669	952	204	301	8	–	–	–	1248	11.6	2.5	15.2
70-71–Utah (A)	82	–	2676	491	1059	.464	5	17	.294	312	467	.668	–	–	807	204	297	–	–	–	–	1299	9.8	2.5	15.8
71-72–Utah (A)	84	–	3300	743	1471	.505	6	18	.333	459	633	.725	282	612	894	286	299	–	–	282	–	1951	10.6	3.4	23.2
72-73–Utah (A)	83	–	3131	672	1404	.479	3	18	.167	476	607	.784	217	465	682	277	278	5	–	236	–	1823	8.2	3.3	22.0
73-74–Utah (A)	82	–	3292	714	1458	.490	2	16	.125	396	501	.790	170	453	623	302	246	–	118	202	43	1826	7.6	3.7	22.3
74-75–Virginia (A)	16	–	574	128	296	.432	1	4	.250	77	111	.694	32	70	102	54	50	–	26	45	3	334	6.4	3.4	20.9
75-76–Virginia (A)	46	–	1343	247	595	.415	0	6	.000	135	175	.771	89	173	262	125	135	–	53	125	13	629	5.7	2.7	13.7
76-77–Denver	75	–	1403	237	513	.462	–	–	–	142	218	.651	76	177	253	142	180	2	60	–	18	616	3.4	1.9	8.2
77-78–Seattle	2	–	10	0	3	.000	–	–	–	1	4	.250	2	1	3	0	2	0	0	0	0	1	1.5	0.0	0.5
Reg. NBA Totals	77	–	1413	237	516	.459	–	–	–	143	222	.644	78	178	256	142	182	2	60	0	18	617	3.3	1.8	8.0
Reg. ABA Totals	475	–	17025	3478	7297	.477	21	96	.219	2133	2921	.730	1073	2442	4322	1452	1606	13	197	890	59	9110	9.1	3.1	19.2
NBA Playoff Totals	6	–	106	14	41	.341	–	–	–	17	25	.680	6	22	28	3	16	0	0	–	1	45	4.7	0.5	7.5
ABA Playoff Totals	68	–	2592	564	1120	.504	2	10	.200	292	411	.710	124	373	644	224	223	1	25	124	10	1422	9.5	3.3	20.9

Witte, Luke b. October 19, 1950 Ht. 7-0 Wt. 235 College: Ohio State

SEASON–TEAM	G	GS	MIN	FGM	FGA	PCT	3FGM	3FGA	PCT	FTM	FTA	PCT	O-RB	D-RB	TOT	AST	PF	DQ	STL	TO	BLK	PTS	RPG	APG	PPG
73-74–Cleveland	57	–	728	105	243	.432	–	–	–	46	62	.742	80	147	227	41	91	0	8	–	22	256	4.0	0.7	4.5
74-75–Cleveland	39	–	271	33	96	.344	–	–	–	19	31	.613	38	54	92	15	42	0	4	–	22	85	2.4	0.4	2.2
75-76–Cleveland	22	–	99	11	32	.344	–	–	–	9	15	.600	9	29	38	4	14	0	1	–	1	31	1.7	0.2	1.4
Reg. Season Totals	118	–	1098	149	371	.402	–	–	–	74	108	.685	127	230	357	60	147	0	13	–	45	372	3.0	0.5	3.2
Playoff Totals	7	–	28	6	11	.545	–	–	–	4	4	1.000	4	5	9	4	4	0	0	–	0	16	1.3	0.6	2.3

Wittman, H. Gregory (Greg) b. May 10, 1947 Ht. 6-8 Wt. 210 College: Western Carolina

SEASON–TEAM	G	GS	MIN	FGM	FGA	PCT	3FGM	3FGA	PCT	FTM	FTA	PCT	O-RB	D-RB	TOT	AST	PF	DQ	STL	TO	BLK	PTS	RPG	APG	PPG
69-70–Denver (A)	50	–	453	80	204	.392	4	17	.235	32	59	.542	–	–	98	15	87	2	–	–	–	196	2.0	0.3	3.9
70-71–Texas-Fla. (A)	10	–	70	6	25	.240	0	1	.000	4	9	.444	–	–	19	0	21	–	–	–	–	16	1.9	0.0	1.6
Reg. ABA Totals	60	–	523	86	229	.376	4	18	.222	36	68	.529	–	–	117	15	108	2	–	–	–	212	2.0	0.3	3.5
ABA Playoff Totals	2	–	4	1	2	.500	1	1	1.000	1	3	.333	–	–	–	0	2	0	–	–	–	4	0.0	0.0	2.0

Wittman, Randy Scott b. October 28, 1959 Ht. 6-6 Wt. 210 College: Indiana

SEASON–TEAM	G	GS	MIN	FGM	FGA	PCT	3FGM	3FGA	PCT	FTM	FTA	PCT	O-RB	D-RB	TOT	AST	PF	DQ	STL	TO	BLK	PTS	RPG	APG	PPG
83-84–Atlanta	78	1	1071	160	318	.503	2	5	.400	28	46	.609	14	57	71	71	82	0	17	32	0	350	0.9	0.9	4.5
84-85–Atlanta	41	22	1168	187	352	.531	2	7	.286	30	41	.732	16	57	73	125	58	0	28	57	7	406	1.8	3.0	9.9
85-86–Atlanta	81	79	2760	467	881	.530	5	16	.313	104	135	.770	51	119	170	306	118	0	81	114	14	1043	2.1	3.8	12.9
86-87–Atlanta	71	65	2049	398	792	.503	4	12	.333	100	127	.787	30	94	124	211	107	0	39	88	16	900	1.7	3.0	12.7
87-88–Atlanta	82	82	2412	376	787	.478	0	0	–	71	89	.798	39	131	170	302	117	0	50	82	18	823	2.1	3.7	10.0
88-89–Sac.-Indiana	64	13	1120	130	286	.455	3	6	.500	28	41	.683	26	54	80	111	43	0	23	32	2	291	1.3	1.7	4.5
89-90–Indiana	61	0	544	62	122	.508	1	2	.500	5	6	.833	4	26	30	39	21	0	7	23	4	130	0.5	0.6	2.1
90-91–Indiana	41	0	355	35	79	.443	0	5	.000	4	6	.667	6	27	33	25	9	0	10	10	4	74	0.8	0.6	1.8
91-92–Indiana	24	0	115	8	19	.421	0	0	–	1	2	.500	1	8	9	11	4	0	2	3	0	17	0.4	0.5	0.7
Reg. Season Totals	543	262	11594	1823	3636	.501	17	53	.321	371	493	.753	187	573	760	1201	559	0	257	441	65	4034	1.4	2.2	7.4
Playoff Totals	38	30	1105	225	417	.540	0	2	.000	37	50	.740	21	57	78	115	68	0	22	42	6	487	2.1	3.0	12.8

Witts, Garrett David (Garry) b. July 3, 1959 Ht. 6-7 Wt. 190 College: Holy Cross

SEASON–TEAM	G	GS	MIN	FGM	FGA	PCT	3FGM	3FGA	PCT	FTM	FTA	PCT	O-RB	D-RB	TOT	AST	PF	DQ	STL	TO	BLK	PTS	RPG	APG	PPG
81-82–Washington	46	0	493	49	84	.583	1	2	.500	33	40	.825	29	33	62	38	74	1	17	35	4	132	1.3	0.8	2.9
Reg. Season Totals	46	0	493	49	84	.583	1	2	.500	33	40	.825	29	33	62	38	74	1	17	35	4	132	1.3	0.8	2.9
Playoff Totals	4	0	28	2	2	1.000	0	0	–	1	2	.500	2	1	3	2	6	0	1	0	0	5	0.8	0.5	1.3

Wohl, David Bruce (Dave) b. November 2, 1949 Ht. 6-2 Wt. 185 College: Pennsylvania

SEASON–TEAM	G	GS	MIN	FGM	FGA	PCT	3FGM	3FGA	PCT	FTM	FTA	PCT	O-RB	D-RB	TOT	AST	PF	DQ	STL	TO	BLK	PTS	RPG	APG	PPG
71-72–Philadelphia	79	–	1628	243	567	.429	–	–	–	156	206	.757	–	–	150	228	229	2	–	–	–	642	1.9	2.9	8.1
72-73–Port.-Buffalo	78	–	1933	254	568	.447	–	–	–	103	133	.774	–	–	109	326	227	3	–	–	–	611	1.4	4.2	7.8
73-74–Buffalo-Hou.	67	–	1055	121	277	.437	–	–	–	75	102	.735	11	35	46	236	136	3	76	–	2	317	0.7	3.5	4.7
74-75–Houston	75	–	1722	203	462	.439	–	–	–	79	106	.745	26	86	112	340	184	1	75	–	9	485	1.5	4.5	6.5
75-76–Houston	50	–	700	66	163	.405	–	–	–	38	49	.776	9	47	56	112	112	2	26	–	1	170	1.1	2.2	3.4
76-77–Houston-N.Y.	51	–	986	116	290	.400	–	–	–	61	89	.685	16	65	81	142	115	2	39	–	6	293	1.6	2.8	5.7
77-78–New Jersey	10	–	118	12	34	.353	–	–	–	11	12	.917	1	3	4	13	24	0	3	16	0	35	0.4	1.3	3.5
Reg. Season Totals	410	–	8142	1015	2361	.430	–	–	–	523	697	.750	63	236	558	1397	1027	13	219	16	18	2553	1.4	3.4	6.2
Playoff Totals	4	–	8	3	3	1.000	–	–	–	0	0	–	0	1	1	2	2	0	1	–	0	6	0.3	0.5	1.5

Wolf, Joseph James (Joe) b. December 17, 1964 Ht. 6-11 Wt. 253 College: North Carolina

SEASON–TEAM	G	GS	MIN	FGM	FGA	PCT	3FGM	3FGA	PCT	FTM	FTA	PCT	O-RB	D-RB	TOT	AST	PF	DQ	STL	TO	BLK	PTS	RPG	APG	PPG
87-88–L.A. Clippers	42	26	1137	136	334	.407	3	15	.200	45	54	.833	51	136	187	98	139	8	38	76	16	320	4.5	2.3	7.6
88-89–L.A. Clippers	66	15	1450	170	402	.423	2	14	.143	44	64	.688	83	188	271	113	152	1	32	94	16	386	4.1	1.7	5.8
89-90–L.A. Clippers	77	19	1325	155	392	.395	5	25	.200	55	71	.775	63	169	232	62	129	0	30	77	24	370	3.0	0.8	4.8
90-91–Denver	74	38	1593	234	519	.451	2	15	.133	69	83	.831	136	264	400	107	244	8	60	95	31	539	5.4	1.4	7.3
91-92–Denver	67	0	1160	100	277	.361	1	11	.091	53	66	.803	97	143	240	61	124	1	32	60	14	254	3.6	0.9	3.8
92-93–Boston-Port.	23	0	165	20	44	.455	0	1	.000	13	16	.813	14	34	48	5	24	0	7	7	1	53	2.1	0.2	2.3
94-95–Charlotte	63	6	583	38	81	.469	2	6	.333	12	16	.750	34	95	129	37	101	0	9	22	6	90	2.0	0.6	1.4
95-96–Cha.-Orlando	64	8	1065	135	263	.513	0	6	.000	21	29	.724	49	138	187	63	163	4	15	42	5	291	2.9	1.0	4.5
96-97–Milwaukee	56	7	525	40	89	.449	1	7	.143	14	19	.737	32	80	112	20	105	0	14	14	11	95	2.0	0.4	1.7
97-98–Denver	57	8	621	40	121	.331	2	10	.200	5	10	.500	36	90	126	30	92	0	20	22	7	87	2.2	0.5	1.5
98-99–Charlotte	3	0	12	0	1	.000	0	0	–	0	2	.000	0	1	1	0	6	0	0	0	0	0	0.3	0.0	0.0
Reg. Season Totals	592	127	9636	1068	2523	.423	18	110	.164	331	430	.770	595	1338	1933	596	1279	22	257	509	131	2485	3.3	1.0	4.2
Playoff Totals	14	0	108	9	25	.360	1	3	.333	3	4	.750	3	7	10	2	20	0	1	4	1	22	0.7	0.1	1.6

Wood, David b. November 30, 1964 Ht. 6-9 Wt. 230 College: Nevada-Reno

SEASON–TEAM	G	GS	MIN	FGM	FGA	PCT	3FGM	3FGA	PCT	FTM	FTA	PCT	O-RB	D-RB	TOT	AST	PF	DQ	STL	TO	BLK	PTS	RPG	APG	PPG
88-89–Chicago	2	0	2	0	0	–	0	0	–	0	0	–	0	0	0	0	0	0	0	0	0	0	0.0	0.0	0.0
90-91–Houston	82	13	1421	148	349	.424	28	90	.311	108	133	.812	107	139	246	94	236	4	58	89	16	432	3.0	1.1	5.3
92-93–San Antonio	64	2	598	52	117	.444	5	21	.238	46	55	.836	38	59	97	34	93	1	13	29	12	155	1.5	0.5	2.4
93-94–Detroit	78	3	1182	119	259	.459	22	49	.449	62	82	.756	104	135	239	51	201	3	39	35	19	322	3.1	0.7	4.1
94-95–Golden State	78	13	1336	153	326	.469	31	91	.341	91	117	.778	83	158	241	65	217	4	28	53	13	428	3.1	0.8	5.5
95-96–G.S.-Phoenix-Dallas	62	0	772	75	174	.431	20	62	.323	38	50	.760	51	103	154	34	150	5	19	24	10	208	2.5	0.5	3.4
96-97–Milwaukee	46	0	240	20	38	.526	5	15	.333	12	18	.667	5	22	27	13	36	0	7	6	6	57	0.6	0.3	1.2
Reg. Season Totals	412	31	5551	567	1263	.449	111	328	.338	357	455	.785	388	616	1004	291	933	17	164	236	76	1602	2.4	0.7	3.9
Playoff Totals	8	0	64	4	7	.571	2	2	1.000	2	4	.500	2	6	8	4	15	0	3	1	0	12	1.0	0.5	1.5

Wood, James Howard (Howard) b. May 20, 1959 Ht. 6-7 Wt. 235 College: Tennessee

SEASON–TEAM	G	GS	MIN	FGM	FGA	PCT	3FGM	3FGA	PCT	FTM	FTA	PCT	O-RB	D-RB	TOT	AST	PF	DQ	STL	TO	BLK	PTS	RPG	APG	PPG
81-82–Utah	42	3	342	55	120	.458	0	1	.000	34	52	.654	22	43	65	9	37	0	8	15	6	144	1.5	0.2	3.4
Reg. Season Totals	42	3	342	55	120	.458	0	1	.000	34	52	.654	22	43	65	9	37	0	8	15	6	144	1.5	0.2	3.4

Wood, Martin Alphonzo (Al) b. June 2, 1958 Ht. 6-6 Wt. 210 College: North Carolina

SEASON–TEAM	G	GS	MIN	FGM	FGA	PCT	3FGM	3FGA	PCT	FTM	FTA	PCT	O-RB	D-RB	TOT	AST	PF	DQ	STL	TO	BLK	PTS	RPG	APG	PPG
81-82–Atlanta-S.D.	48	5	930	179	381	.470	3	24	.125	93	119	.782	51	83	134	58	108	4	31	71	9	454	2.8	1.2	9.5
82-83–San Diego	76	47	1822	343	740	.464	15	50	.300	124	161	.770	96	140	236	134	188	5	55	111	36	825	3.1	1.8	10.9
83-84–Seattle	81	81	2236	467	945	.494	3	21	.143	223	271	.823	94	181	275	166	207	1	64	126	32	1160	3.4	2.0	14.3
84-85–Seattle	80	79	2545	515	1061	.485	7	33	.212	166	214	.776	99	180	279	236	187	3	84	120	52	1203	3.5	3.0	15.0
85-86–Seattle	78	34	1749	355	817	.435	5	37	.135	187	239	.782	80	164	244	114	171	2	57	107	19	902	3.1	1.5	11.6
86-87–Dallas	54	0	657	121	310	.390	7	25	.280	109	139	.784	39	55	94	34	83	0	19	34	11	358	1.7	0.6	6.6
Reg. Season Totals	417	246	9939	1980	4254	.465	40	190	.211	902	1143	.789	459	803	1262	742	944	15	310	569	159	4902	3.0	1.8	11.8
Playoff Totals	5	5	157	26	56	.464	0	1	.000	8	12	.667	7	27	34	10	16	0	1	7	1	60	6.8	2.0	12.0

Wood, Osie Leon III (Leon) b. March 25, 1962 Ht. 6-3 Wt. 185 College: Arizona; Cal State-Fullerton

SEASON–TEAM	G	GS	MIN	FGM	FGA	PCT	3FGM	3FGA	PCT	FTM	FTA	PCT	O-RB	D-RB	TOT	AST	PF	DQ	STL	TO	BLK	PTS	RPG	APG	PPG
84-85–Philadelphia	38	1	269	50	134	.373	4	30	.133	18	26	.692	3	15	18	45	17	0	8	25	0	122	0.5	1.2	3.2
85-86–Phil.-Wash.	68	1	1198	184	466	.395	41	114	.360	123	155	.794	25	65	90	182	70	0	34	87	0	532	1.3	2.7	7.8
86-87–New Jersey	76	7	1733	187	501	.373	60	200	.300	123	154	.799	23	97	120	370	126	0	48	108	3	557	1.6	4.9	7.3
87-88–S.A.-Atlanta	52	8	909	136	312	.436	52	127	.409	76	99	.768	17	40	57	174	50	0	26	39	1	400	1.1	3.3	7.7
89-90–New Jersey	28	2	200	16	49	.327	4	21	.190	14	16	.875	1	11	12	47	16	0	6	8	0	50	0.4	1.7	1.8
90-91–Sacramento	12	0	222	25	63	.397	12	38	.316	19	21	.905	5	14	19	49	10	0	5	12	0	81	1.6	4.1	6.8
Reg. Season Totals	274	19	4531	598	1525	.392	173	530	.326	373	471	.792	74	242	316	867	289	0	127	279	4	1742	1.2	3.2	6.4
Playoff Totals	10	0	21	6	15	.400	2	3	.667	8	10	.800	0	1	1	3	0	0	0	3	0	22	0.1	0.3	2.2

Wood, Robert A. (Bob) b. October 7, 1921 Ht. 5-10 College: Northern Illinois

SEASON–TEAM	G	GS	MIN	FGM	FGA	PCT	3FGM	3FGA	PCT	FTM	FTA	PCT	O-RB	D-RB	TOT	AST	PF	DQ	STL	TO	BLK	PTS	RPG	APG	PPG
49-50–Sheboygan	6	–	–	3	14	.214	–	–	–	1	1	1.000	–	–	–	1	6	–	–	–	–	7	–	0.2	1.2
Reg. Season Totals	6	–	–	3	14	.214	–	–	–	1	1	1.000	–	–	–	1	6	–	–	–	–	7	–	0.2	1.2

Woods, James Thomas Jr. (Tommy) b. June 10, 1943 Ht. 6-10 Wt. 225 College: East Tennessee State

SEASON–TEAM	G	GS	MIN	FGM	FGA	PCT	3FGM	3FGA	PCT	FTM	FTA	PCT	O-RB	D-RB	TOT	AST	PF	DQ	STL	TO	BLK	PTS	RPG	APG	PPG
67-68–Kentucky (A)	18	–	184	14	43	.326	0	1	.000	14	16	.875	–	–	55	4	25	0	–	9	–	42	3.1	0.2	2.3
Reg. ABA Totals	18	–	184	14	43	.326	0	1	.000	14	16	.875	–	–	55	4	25	0	–	9	–	42	3.1	0.2	2.3

Woods, Randolph (Randy) b. September 23, 1970 Ht. 6-0 Wt. 185 College: La Salle

SEASON–TEAM	G	GS	MIN	FGM	FGA	PCT	3FGM	3FGA	PCT	FTM	FTA	PCT	O-RB	D-RB	TOT	AST	PF	DQ	STL	TO	BLK	PTS	RPG	APG	PPG
92-93–L.A. Clippers	41	1	174	23	66	.348	3	14	.214	19	26	.731	6	8	14	40	26	0	14	16	1	68	0.3	1.0	1.7
93-94–L.A. Clippers	40	0	352	49	133	.368	27	78	.346	20	35	.571	13	16	29	71	40	0	24	34	2	145	0.7	1.8	3.6
94-95–L.A. Clippers	62	3	495	37	117	.316	22	74	.297	28	38	.737	10	34	44	134	87	0	41	55	0	124	0.7	2.2	2.0
95-96–Denver	8	0	72	6	22	.273	5	21	.238	2	2	1.000	3	3	6	12	13	0	6	5	1	19	0.8	1.5	2.4
Reg. Season Totals	151	4	1093	115	338	.340	57	187	.305	69	101	.683	32	61	93	257	166	0	85	110	4	356	0.6	1.7	2.4

Woodson, Michael Dean (Mike) b. March 24, 1958 Ht. 6-5 Wt. 200 College: Indiana

SEASON–TEAM	G	GS	MIN	FGM	FGA	PCT	3FGM	3FGA	PCT	FTM	FTA	PCT	O-RB	D-RB	TOT	AST	PF	DQ	STL	TO	BLK	PTS	RPG	APG	PPG
80-81–New York	81	–	949	165	373	.442	1	5	.200	49	64	.766	33	64	97	75	95	0	36	54	12	380	1.2	0.9	4.7
81-82–N.J.-K.C.	83	74	2331	538	1069	.503	7	25	.280	221	286	.773	102	145	247	222	220	3	142	153	35	1304	3.0	2.7	15.7
82-83–Kansas City	81	3	2426	584	1154	.506	7	33	.212	298	377	.790	84	164	248	254	203	0	137	174	59	1473	3.1	3.1	18.2
83-84–Kansas City	71	12	1838	389	816	.477	2	8	.250	247	302	.818	62	113	175	175	174	2	83	115	28	1027	2.5	2.5	14.5
84-85–Kansas City	78	3	1998	530	1068	.496	5	21	.238	264	330	.800	69	129	198	143	216	1	117	139	28	1329	2.5	1.8	17.0
85-86–Sacramento	81	51	2417	510	1073	.475	2	13	.154	242	289	.837	94	132	226	197	215	1	92	145	37	1264	2.8	2.4	15.6
86-87–L.A. Clippers	74	66	2126	494	1130	.437	34	123	.276	240	290	.828	68	94	162	196	201	1	100	168	16	1262	2.2	2.6	17.1
87-88–L.A. Clippers	80	77	2534	562	1263	.445	18	78	.231	296	341	.868	64	126	190	273	210	1	109	186	26	1438	2.4	3.4	18.0
88-89–Houston	81	79	2259	410	936	.438	31	89	.348	195	237	.823	51	143	194	206	195	1	89	136	18	1046	2.4	2.5	12.9
89-90–Houston	61	11	972	160	405	.395	12	41	.293	62	86	.721	25	63	88	66	100	1	42	49	11	394	1.4	1.1	6.5
90-91–Houston-Clev.	15	3	171	26	77	.338	1	7	.143	11	13	.846	3	10	13	15	18	0	5	12	5	64	0.9	1.0	4.3
Reg. Season Totals	786	379	20021	4368	9364	.466	120	443	.271	2125	2615	.813	655	1183	1838	1822	1847	11	952	1331	275	10981	2.3	2.3	14.0
Playoff Totals	13	7	348	59	148	.399	3	13	.231	37	41	.902	17	13	30	34	35	0	10	23	4	158	2.3	2.6	12.2

Woollard, Robert George (Bob) b. July 27, 1940 Ht. 6-10 Wt. 225 College: Wake Forest

SEASON–TEAM	G	GS	MIN	FGM	FGA	PCT	3FGM	3FGA	PCT	FTM	FTA	PCT	O-RB	D-RB	TOT	AST	PF	DQ	STL	TO	BLK	PTS	RPG	APG	PPG
69-70–Miami (A)	19	–	234	32	82	.390	0	1	.000	20	25	.800	–	–	69	6	42	1	–	–	–	84	3.6	0.3	4.4
Reg. ABA Totals	19	–	234	32	82	.390	0	1	.000	20	25	.800	–	–	69	6	42	1	–	–	–	84	3.6	0.3	4.4

Woolridge, Orlando Vernada b. December 16, 1959 Ht. 6-9 Wt. 215 College: Notre Dame

SEASON–TEAM	G	GS	MIN	FGM	FGA	PCT	3FGM	3FGA	PCT	FTM	FTA	PCT	O-RB	D-RB	TOT	AST	PF	DQ	STL	TO	BLK	PTS	RPG	APG	PPG
81-82–Chicago	75	12	1188	202	394	.513	0	3	.000	144	206	.699	82	145	227	81	152	1	23	107	24	548	3.0	1.1	7.3
82-83–Chicago	57	38	1627	361	622	.580	0	3	.000	217	340	.638	122	176	298	97	177	1	38	157	44	939	5.2	1.7	16.5
83-84–Chicago	75	74	2544	570	1086	.525	1	2	.500	303	424	.715	130	239	369	136	253	6	71	188	60	1444	4.9	1.8	19.3
84-85–Chicago	77	76	2816	679	1225	.554	0	5	.000	409	521	.785	158	277	435	135	185	0	58	178	38	1767	5.6	1.8	22.9
85-86–Chicago	70	59	2248	540	1090	.495	4	23	.174	364	462	.788	150	200	350	213	186	2	49	174	47	1448	5.0	3.0	20.7
86-87–New Jersey	75	53	2638	556	1067	.521	1	8	.125	438	564	.777	118	249	367	261	243	4	54	213	86	1551	4.9	3.5	20.7
87-88–New Jersey	19	12	622	110	247	.445	0	2	.000	92	130	.708	31	60	91	71	73	2	13	48	20	312	4.8	3.7	16.4
88-89–L.A. Lakers	74	0	1491	231	494	.468	0	1	.000	253	343	.738	81	189	270	58	130	0	30	103	65	715	3.6	0.8	9.7
89-90–L.A. Lakers	62	2	1421	306	550	.556	0	5	.000	176	240	.733	49	136	185	96	160	2	39	73	46	788	3.0	1.5	12.7
90-91–Denver	53	50	1823	490	983	.498	0	4	.000	350	439	.797	141	220	361	119	145	2	69	152	23	1330	6.8	2.2	25.1
91-92–Detroit	82	61	2113	452	907	.498	1	9	.111	241	353	.683	109	151	260	88	154	0	41	133	33	1146	3.2	1.1	14.0
92-93–Detroit-Milw.	58	47	1555	289	599	.482	0	9	.000	120	177	.678	87	98	185	115	122	1	27	79	27	698	3.2	2.0	12.0
93-94–Philadelphia	74	1	1955	364	773	.471	1	14	.071	208	302	.689	103	195	298	139	186	1	41	142	56	937	4.0	1.9	12.7
Reg. Season Totals	851	485	24041	5150	10037	.513	8	88	.091	3315	4501	.737	1361	2335	3696	1609	2166	22	553	1747	569	13623	4.3	1.9	16.0
Playoff Totals	36	12	905	161	327	.492	0	2	.000	106	148	.716	43	87	130	42	105	2	20	55	26	428	3.6	1.2	11.9

Workman, Haywoode Wilvon (Woody) b. January 23, 1966 Ht. 6-3 Wt. 200 College: Winston-Salem State; Oral Roberts

SEASON–TEAM	G	GS	MIN	FGM	FGA	PCT	3FGM	3FGA	PCT	FTM	FTA	PCT	O-RB	D-RB	TOT	AST	PF	DQ	STL	TO	BLK	PTS	RPG	APG	PPG
89-90–Atlanta	6	0	16	2	3	.667	0	0	–	2	2	1.000	0	3	3	2	3	0	3	0	0	6	0.5	0.3	1.0
90-91–Washington	73	56	2034	234	515	.454	12	50	.240	101	133	.759	51	191	242	353	162	1	87	135	7	581	3.3	4.8	8.0
93-94–Indiana	65	52	1714	195	460	.424	18	56	.321	93	116	.802	32	172	204	404	152	0	85	151	4	501	3.1	6.2	7.7
94-95–Indiana	69	14	1028	101	269	.375	35	98	.357	55	74	.743	21	90	111	194	115	0	59	73	5	292	1.6	2.8	4.2
95-96–Indiana	77	4	1164	101	259	.390	23	71	.324	54	73	.740	27	97	124	213	152	0	65	93	4	279	1.6	2.8	3.6
96-97–Indiana	4	2	81	11	20	.550	0	3	.000	0	1	.000	4	3	7	11	10	0	3	5	0	22	1.8	2.8	5.5
98-99–Milwaukee	29	29	815	73	170	.429	17	47	.362	37	47	.787	14	88	102	172	53	0	32	63	1	200	3.5	5.9	6.9
99-00–Milw.-Toronto	36	2	350	31	90	.344	14	43	.326	10	15	.667	1	25	26	61	37	1	20	18	0	86	0.7	1.7	2.4
Reg. Season Totals	359	159	7202	748	1786	.419	119	368	.323	352	461	.764	150	669	819	1410	684	2	354	538	21	1967	2.3	3.9	5.5
Playoff Totals	41	15	892	80	225	.356	11	47	.234	66	78	.846	18	67	85	167	97	0	44	63	1	237	2.1	4.1	5.8

Workman, Mark Cecil b. March 10, 1930 d. December 21, 1983 Ht. 6-9 Wt. 215 College: West Virginia

SEASON–TEAM	G	GS	MIN	FGM	FGA	PCT	3FGM	3FGA	PCT	FTM	FTA	PCT	O-RB	D-RB	TOT	AST	PF	DQ	STL	TO	BLK	PTS	RPG	APG	PPG
52-53–Milw.-Phil.	65	–	1030	130	408	.319	–	–	–	70	113	.619	–	–	193	37	166	5	–	–	–	330	3.0	0.6	5.1
53-54–Baltimore	14	–	151	25	60	.417	–	–	–	6	10	.600	–	–	37	7	31	0	–	–	–	56	2.6	0.5	4.0
Reg. Season Totals	79	–	1181	155	468	.331	–	–	–	76	123	.618	–	–	230	44	197	5	–	–	–	386	2.9	0.6	4.9

Workman, Thomas Edwin (Tom, Hawk) b. November 14, 1944 Ht. 6-7 Wt. 225 College: Seattle

SEASON–TEAM	G	GS	MIN	FGM	FGA	PCT	3FGM	3FGA	PCT	FTM	FTA	PCT	O-RB	D-RB	TOT	AST	PF	DQ	STL	TO	BLK	PTS	RPG	APG	PPG
67-68–St. Louis-Balt.	20	–	95	19	40	.475	–	–	–	18	23	.783	–	–	25	3	17	0	–	–	–	56	1.3	0.2	2.8
68-69–Baltimore	21	–	86	22	54	.407	–	–	–	9	15	.600	–	–	27	2	16	0	–	–	–	53	1.3	0.1	2.5
69-70–Detroit	2	–	6	0	1	.000	–	–	–	0	0	–	–	–	0	0	1	0	–	–	–	0	0.0	0.0	0.0
69-70–Los Angeles (A)	26	–	445	116	251	.462	1	4	.250	77	98	.786	–	–	94	22	69	0	–	–	–	310	3.6	0.8	11.9
70-71–Utah-Denver (A)	56	–	679	133	303	.439	3	19	.158	86	105	.819	–	–	179	48	113	–	–	–	–	355	3.2	0.9	6.3
Reg. NBA Totals	43	–	187	41	95	.432	–	–	–	27	38	.711	–	–	52	5	34	0	–	–	–	109	1.2	0.1	2.5
Reg. ABA Totals	82	–	1124	249	554	.449	4	23	.174	163	203	.803	–	–	273	70	182	0	–	–	–	665	3.3	0.9	8.1
NBA Playoff Totals	1	–	2	0	1	.000	–	–	–	0	0	–	–	–	1	–	0	0	–	–	–	0	1.0	0.0	0.0
ABA Playoff Totals	3	–	9	3	7	.429	0	0	–	0	0	–	–	–	3	0	0	0	–	–	–	6	1.0	0.0	2.0

Worsley, Willie James b. November 13, 1945 Ht. 5-10 Wt. 175 College: Texas-El Paso

SEASON–TEAM	G	GS	MIN	FGM	FGA	PCT	3FGM	3FGA	PCT	FTM	FTA	PCT	O-RB	D-RB	TOT	AST	PF	DQ	STL	TO	BLK	PTS	RPG	APG	PPG
68-69–New York (A)	24	–	460	36	123	.293	10	30	.333	63	84	.750	–	–	35	39	48	0	–	32	–	145	1.5	1.6	6.0
Reg. ABA Totals	24	–	460	36	123	.293	10	30	.333	63	84	.750	–	–	35	39	48	0	–	32	–	145	1.5	1.6	6.0

Worthen, Samuel Lee (Sam) b. January 17, 1958 Ht. 6-5 Wt. 195 College: McLennan (Texas) C.C.; Marquette

SEASON–TEAM	G	GS	MIN	FGM	FGA	PCT	3FGM	3FGA	PCT	FTM	FTA	PCT	O-RB	D-RB	TOT	AST	PF	DQ	STL	TO	BLK	PTS	RPG	APG	PPG
80-81–Chicago	64	–	945	95	192	.495	0	4	.000	45	60	.750	22	93	115	115	115	0	57	91	6	235	1.8	1.8	3.7
81-82–Utah	5	0	22	2	5	.400	0	0	–	0	0	–	1	0	1	3	3	0	0	2	0	4	0.2	0.6	0.8
Reg. Season Totals	69	0	967	97	197	.492	0	4	.000	45	60	.750	23	93	116	118	118	0	57	93	6	239	1.7	1.7	3.5
Playoff Totals	1	0	1	0	0	–	0	0	–	0	0	–	0	0	0	–	0	0	0	0	0	0	0.0	0.0	0.0

Worthy, James Ager (Big Game James) b. February 27, 1961 Ht. 6-9 Wt. 225 College: North Carolina

SEASON–TEAM	G	GS	MIN	FGM	FGA	PCT	3FGM	3FGA	PCT	FTM	FTA	PCT	O-RB	D-RB	TOT	AST	PF	DQ	STL	TO	BLK	PTS	RPG	APG	PPG
82-83–Los Angeles	77	1	1970	447	772	.579	1	4	.250	138	221	.624	157	242	399	132	221	2	91	178	64	1033	5.2	1.7	13.4
83-84–Los Angeles	82	53	2415	495	890	.556	0	6	.000	195	257	.759	157	358	515	207	244	5	77	181	70	1185	6.3	2.5	14.5
84-85–L.A. Lakers	80	76	2696	610	1066	.572	0	7	.000	190	245	.776	169	342	511	201	196	0	87	198	67	1410	6.4	2.5	17.6
85-86–L.A. Lakers	75	73	2454	629	1086	.579	0	13	.000	242	314	.771	136	251	387	201	195	0	82	149	77	1500	5.2	2.7	20.0
86-87–L.A. Lakers	82	82	2819	651	1207	.539	0	13	.000	292	389	.751	158	308	466	226	206	0	108	168	83	1594	5.7	2.8	19.4
87-88–L.A. Lakers	75	72	2655	617	1161	.531	2	16	.125	242	304	.796	129	245	374	289	175	1	72	155	55	1478	5.0	3.9	19.7
88-89–L.A. Lakers	81	81	2960	702	1282	.548	2	23	.087	251	321	.782	169	320	489	288	175	0	108	182	56	1657	6.0	3.6	20.5
89-90–L.A. Lakers	80	80	2960	711	1298	.548	15	49	.306	248	317	.782	160	318	478	288	190	0	99	160	49	1685	6.0	3.6	21.1
90-91–L.A. Lakers	78	74	3008	716	1455	.492	26	90	.289	212	266	.797	107	249	356	275	117	0	104	127	35	1670	4.6	3.5	21.4
91-92–L.A. Lakers	54	54	2108	450	1007	.447	9	43	.209	166	204	.814	98	207	305	252	89	0	76	127	23	1075	5.6	4.7	19.9
92-93–L.A. Lakers	82	69	2359	510	1142	.447	30	111	.270	171	211	.810	73	174	247	278	87	0	92	137	27	1221	3.0	3.4	14.9
93-94–L.A. Lakers	80	2	1597	340	838	.406	32	111	.288	100	135	.741	48	133	181	154	80	0	45	97	18	812	2.3	1.9	10.2
Reg. Season Totals	926	717	30001	6878	13204	.521	117	486	.241	2447	3184	.769	1561	3147	4708	2791	1975	8	1041	1859	624	16320	5.1	3.0	17.6
Playoff Totals	143	125	5297	1267	2329	.544	14	67	.209	474	652	.727	257	490	747	463	352	2	177	298	96	3022	5.2	3.2	21.1
All-Star Totals	7	3	142	34	77	.442	0	3	.000	6	9	.667	12	14	26	9	10	0	7	4	4	74	3.7	1.3	10.6

Wright, Bradford William (Brad) b. March 26, 1962 Ht. 6-11 Wt. 225 College: UCLA

SEASON–TEAM	G	GS	MIN	FGM	FGA	PCT	3FGM	3FGA	PCT	FTM	FTA	PCT	O-RB	D-RB	TOT	AST	PF	DQ	STL	TO	BLK	PTS	RPG	APG	PPG
86-87–New York	14	0	138	20	46	.435	0	1	.000	12	28	.429	25	28	53	1	20	0	3	13	6	52	3.8	0.1	3.7
87-88–Denver	2	0	7	1	5	.200	0	0	–	0	0	–	0	1	1	0	3	0	0	2	0	2	0.5	0.0	1.0
Reg. Season Totals	16	0	145	21	51	.412	0	1	.000	12	28	.429	25	29	54	1	23	0	3	15	6	54	3.4	0.1	3.4

Wright, Howard Gregory b. December 20, 1967 Ht. 6-8 Wt. 220 College: Stanford

SEASON–TEAM	G	GS	MIN	FGM	FGA	PCT	3FGM	3FGA	PCT	FTM	FTA	PCT	O-RB	D-RB	TOT	AST	PF	DQ	STL	TO	BLK	PTS	RPG	APG	PPG
90-91–Atlanta-Orl.-Dallas	15	0	164	19	47	.404	0	1	.000	16	24	.667	12	33	45	3	28	0	4	11	5	54	3.0	0.2	3.6
92-93–Orlando	4	0	10	4	5	.800	0	0	–	0	2	.000	1	1	2	0	0	0	0	0	0	8	0.5	0.0	2.0
Reg. Season Totals	19	0	174	23	52	.442	0	1	.000	16	26	.615	13	34	47	3	28	0	4	11	5	62	2.5	0.2	3.3

Wright, Howard L. (Howie) b. February 22, 1947 Ht. 6-3 Wt. 185 College: Austin Peay State

SEASON–TEAM	G	GS	MIN	FGM	FGA	PCT	3FGM	3FGA	PCT	FTM	FTA	PCT	O-RB	D-RB	TOT	AST	PF	DQ	STL	TO	BLK	PTS	RPG	APG	PPG
70-71–Kentucky (A)	52	–	612	94	245	.384	9	42	.214	40	49	.816	–	–	80	63	89	–	–	–	–	237	1.5	1.2	4.6
71-72–Kentucky (A)	1	–	4	0	0	–	0	0	–	0	1	.000	–	–	0	0	0	–	–	1	–	0	0.0	0.0	0.0
Reg. ABA Totals	53	–	616	94	245	.384	9	42	.214	40	50	.800	–	–	80	63	89	–	–	1	–	237	1.5	1.2	4.5
ABA Playoff Totals	5	–	36	7	20	.350	2	8	.250	4	9	.444	–	–	2	4	6	–	–	–	–	20	0.4	0.8	4.0

Wright, Joseph A. (Joby) b. September 5, 1950 Ht. 6-8 Wt. 220 College: Indiana

SEASON–TEAM	G	GS	MIN	FGM	FGA	PCT	3FGM	3FGA	PCT	FTM	FTA	PCT	O-RB	D-RB	TOT	AST	PF	DQ	STL	TO	BLK	PTS	RPG	APG	PPG
72-73–Seattle	77	–	931	133	278	.478	–	–	–	37	89	.416	–	–	218	36	164	0	–	–	–	303	2.8	0.5	3.9
73-74–Memphis (A)	3	–	31	5	16	.313	0	0	–	2	2	1.000	9	5	14	0	7	–	0	4	1	12	4.7	0.0	4.0
75-76–S.D.-Vir. (A)	23	–	305	50	109	.459	0	0	–	21	38	.553	29	30	59	2	54	–	5	24	4	121	2.6	0.1	5.3
Reg. NBA Totals	77	–	931	133	278	.478	–	–	–	37	89	.416	–	–	218	36	164	0	–	–	–	303	2.8	0.5	3.9
Reg. ABA Totals	26	–	336	55	125	.440	0	0	–	23	40	.575	38	35	73	2	61	0	5	28	5	133	2.8	0.1	5.1

Wright, Larry Glenn b. November 23, 1954 Ht. 6-1 Wt. 170 College: Grambling State

SEASON–TEAM	G	GS	MIN	FGM	FGA	PCT	3FGM	3FGA	PCT	FTM	FTA	PCT	O-RB	D-RB	TOT	AST	PF	DQ	STL	TO	BLK	PTS	RPG	APG	PPG
76-77–Washington	78	–	1421	262	595	.440	–	–	–	88	115	.765	32	66	98	232	170	0	55	–	5	612	1.3	3.0	7.8
77-78–Washington	70	–	1466	283	570	.496	–	–	–	76	107	.710	31	71	102	260	195	3	68	134	15	642	1.5	3.7	9.2
78-79–Washington	73	–	1658	276	589	.469	–	–	–	125	168	.744	48	92	140	298	166	3	69	119	13	677	1.9	4.1	9.3
79-80–Washington	76	–	1286	229	500	.458	4	16	.250	96	108	.889	40	82	122	222	144	3	49	108	18	558	1.6	2.9	7.3
80-81–Detroit	45	–	997	140	303	.462	2	7	.286	53	66	.803	26	62	88	153	114	1	42	74	7	335	2.0	3.4	7.4
81-82–Detroit	1	0	6	0	1	.000	0	0	–	0	0	–	0	0	0	0	2	0	0	1	0	0	0.0	0.0	0.0
Reg. Season Totals	343	0	6834	1190	2558	.465	6	23	.261	438	564	.777	177	373	550	1165	791	10	283	436	58	2824	1.6	3.4	8.2
Playoff Totals	49	0	870	166	348	.477	0	1	.000	65	81	.802	21	44	65	133	131	2	37	55	7	397	1.3	2.7	8.1

Wright, Lawrence (Lonnie) b. January 23, 1944 Ht. 6-2 Wt. 205 College: Colorado State

SEASON–TEAM	G	GS	MIN	FGM	FGA	PCT	3FGM	3FGA	PCT	FTM	FTA	PCT	O-RB	D-RB	TOT	AST	PF	DQ	STL	TO	BLK	PTS	RPG	APG	PPG
67-68–Denver (A)	38	–	896	146	346	.422	2	9	.222	79	121	.653	–	–	96	68	96	0	–	43	–	373	2.5	1.8	9.8
68-69–Denver (A)	69	–	2538	453	1089	.416	19	86	.221	205	276	.743	–	–	290	175	250	2	–	160	–	1130	4.2	2.5	16.4
69-70–Denver (A)	79	–	2237	393	952	.413	54	193	.280	121	175	.691	–	–	216	149	278	7	–	–	–	961	2.7	1.9	12.2
70-71–Denver-Fla. (A)	72	–	1398	199	558	.357	17	74	.230	93	133	.699	–	–	153	116	162	–	–	–	–	508	2.1	1.6	7.1
71-72–Floridians (A)	77	–	1638	252	599	.421	19	73	.260	95	117	.812	–	–	158	133	197	–	–	89	–	618	2.1	1.7	8.0
Reg. ABA Totals	335	–	8707	1443	3544	.407	111	435	.255	593	822	.721	–	–	913	641	983	9	–	292	–	3590	2.7	1.9	10.7
ABA Playoff Totals	33	–	905	110	335	.328	6	34	.176	57	76	.750	–	–	100	78	88	0	–	19	–	283	3.0	2.4	8.6

Wright, Leroy b. May 6, 1938 Ht. 6-9 Wt. 220 College: U. of Pacific

SEASON–TEAM	G	GS	MIN	FGM	FGA	PCT	3FGM	3FGA	PCT	FTM	FTA	PCT	O-RB	D-RB	TOT	AST	PF	DQ	STL	TO	BLK	PTS	RPG	APG	PPG
67-68–Pittsburgh (A)	17	–	331	24	60	.400	0	0	–	9	22	.409	–	–	108	14	49	1	–	20	–	57	6.4	0.8	3.4
68-69–Minnesota (A)	10	–	95	4	13	.308	0	0	–	0	5	.000	–	–	30	1	15	0	–	2	–	8	3.0	0.1	0.8
Reg. ABA Totals	27	–	426	28	73	.384	0	0	–	9	27	.333	–	–	138	15	64	1	–	22	–	65	5.1	0.6	2.4
ABA Playoff Totals	14	–	195	9	31	.290	0	1	.000	8	22	.364	–	–	73	8	32	2	–	8	–	26	5.2	0.6	1.9

Wright, Lorenzen Vern-Gagne b. November 4, 1975 Ht. 6-11 Wt. 240 College: Memphis

SEASON–TEAM	G	GS	MIN	FGM	FGA	PCT	3FGM	3FGA	PCT	FTM	FTA	PCT	O-RB	D-RB	TOT	AST	PF	DQ	STL	TO	BLK	PTS	RPG	APG	PPG
96-97–L.A. Clippers	77	51	1936	236	491	.481	1	4	.250	88	150	.587	206	265	471	49	211	2	48	79	60	561	6.1	0.6	7.3
97-98–L.A. Clippers	69	38	2067	241	542	.445	0	2	.000	141	214	.659	180	426	606	55	237	2	55	81	87	623	8.8	0.8	9.0
98-99–L.A. Clippers	48	15	1135	119	260	.458	0	1	.000	81	117	.692	142	219	361	33	162	2	26	48	36	319	7.5	0.7	6.6
99-00–Atlanta	75	0	1205	180	361	.499	1	3	.333	87	135	.644	117	188	305	21	203	3	29	66	40	448	4.1	0.3	6.0
Reg. Season Totals	269	104	6343	776	1654	.469	2	10	.200	397	616	.644	645	1098	1743	158	813	9	158	274	223	1951	6.5	0.6	7.3
Playoff Totals	3	3	92	13	32	.406	0	0	–	5	5	1.000	7	15	22	2	6	0	3	1	2	31	7.3	0.7	10.3

Wright, Luther A. Jr. b. September 22, 1971 Ht. 7-2 Wt. 270 College: Seton Hall

SEASON–TEAM	G	GS	MIN	FGM	FGA	PCT	3FGM	3FGA	PCT	FTM	FTA	PCT	O-RB	D-RB	TOT	AST	PF	DQ	STL	TO	BLK	PTS	RPG	APG	PPG
93-94–Utah	15	2	92	8	23	.348	0	1	.000	3	4	.750	6	4	10	0	21	0	1	6	2	19	0.7	0.0	1.3
Reg. Season Totals	15	2	92	8	23	.348	0	1	.000	3	4	.750	6	4	10	0	21	0	1	6	2	19	0.7	0.0	1.3

Wright, Sharone Addaryl b. January 30, 1973 Ht. 6-11 Wt. 260 College: Clemson

SEASON–TEAM	G	GS	MIN	FGM	FGA	PCT	3FGM	3FGA	PCT	FTM	FTA	PCT	O-RB	D-RB	TOT	AST	PF	DQ	STL	TO	BLK	PTS	RPG	APG	PPG
94-95–Philadelphia	79	49	2044	361	776	.465	0	8	.000	182	282	.645	191	281	472	48	246	5	37	151	104	904	6.0	0.6	11.4
95-96–Phil.-Toronto	57	38	1434	248	512	.484	1	3	.333	167	259	.645	148	208	356	38	163	4	30	109	49	664	6.2	0.7	11.6
96-97–Toronto	60	28	1009	161	403	.400	0	1	.000	68	133	.511	79	107	186	28	146	3	15	93	50	390	3.1	0.5	6.5
97-98–Toronto	7	0	44	7	14	.500	0	0	–	2	4	.500	1	8	9	4	7	0	0	2	0	16	1.3	0.6	2.3
Reg. Season Totals	203	115	4531	777	1705	.456	1	12	.083	419	678	.618	419	604	1023	118	562	12	82	355	203	1974	5.0	0.6	9.7

Wuycik, Dennis Mark b. March 29, 1950 Ht. 6-6 Wt. 215 College: North Carolina

SEASON–TEAM	G	GS	MIN	FGM	FGA	PCT	3FGM	3FGA	PCT	FTM	FTA	PCT	O-RB	D-RB	TOT	AST	PF	DQ	STL	TO	BLK	PTS	RPG	APG	PPG
72-73–Carolina (A)	83	–	973	151	329	.459	0	4	.000	75	108	.694	69	110	179	79	165	3	–	116	–	377	2.2	1.0	4.5
73-74–Carolina (A)	49	–	492	88	190	.463	1	2	.500	51	77	.662	51	55	106	31	88	–	16	40	4	228	2.2	0.6	4.7
74-75–St. Louis (A)	25	–	219	34	74	.459	0	1	.000	11	19	.579	17	21	38	18	40	–	6	25	1	79	1.5	0.7	3.2
Reg. ABA Totals	157	–	1684	273	593	.460	1	7	.143	137	204	.672	137	186	323	128	293	3	22	181	5	684	2.1	0.8	4.4
ABA Playoff Totals	15	–	94	8	24	.333	0	1	.000	8	12	.667	1	2	19	3	14	0	0	9	0	24	1.3	0.2	1.6

Wydner, A.J. b. September 11, 1964 Ht. 6-2 Wt. 180 College: Massachusetts; Fairfield

SEASON–TEAM	G	GS	MIN	FGM	FGA	PCT	3FGM	3FGA	PCT	FTM	FTA	PCT	O-RB	D-RB	TOT	AST	PF	DQ	STL	TO	BLK	PTS	RPG	APG	PPG
90-91–Boston	6	0	39	3	12	.250	0	1	.000	6	8	.750	1	2	3	8	1	0	1	4	0	12	0.5	1.3	2.0
Reg. Season Totals	6	0	39	3	12	.250	0	1	.000	6	8	.750	1	2	3	8	1	0	1	4	0	12	0.5	1.3	2.0

Yardley, George Harry III b. November 3, 1928 Ht. 6-5 Wt. 195 College: Stanford HOF: 1996

SEASON–TEAM	G	GS	MIN	FGM	FGA	PCT	3FGM	3FGA	PCT	FTM	FTA	PCT	O-RB	D-RB	TOT	AST	PF	DQ	STL	TO	BLK	PTS	RPG	APG	PPG
53-54–Fort Wayne	63	–	1489	209	492	.425	–	–	–	146	205	.712	–	–	407	99	166	3	–	–	–	564	6.5	1.6	9.0
54-55–Fort Wayne	60	–	2150	363	869	.418	–	–	–	310	416	.745	–	–	594	126	205	7	–	–	–	1036	9.9	2.1	17.3
55-56–Fort Wayne	71	–	2353	434	1067	.407	–	–	–	365	492	.742	–	–	686	159	212	2	–	–	–	1233	9.7	2.2	17.4
56-57–Fort Wayne	72	–	2691	522	1273	.410	–	–	–	503	639	.787	–	–	755	147	231	2	–	–	–	1547	10.5	2.0	21.5
57-58–Detroit	72	–	2843	673	1624	.414	–	–	–	655	808	.811	–	–	768	97	226	3	–	–	–	2001	10.7	1.3	27.8
58-59–Detroit-Syr.	61	–	1839	446	1042	.428	–	–	–	317	407	.779	–	–	431	65	159	2	–	–	–	1209	7.1	1.1	19.8
59-60–Syracuse	73	–	2402	546	1205	.453	–	–	–	381	467	.816	–	–	579	122	227	3	–	–	–	1473	7.9	1.7	20.2
Reg. Season Totals	472	–	15767	3193	7572	.422	–	–	–	2677	3434	.780	–	–	4220	815	1426	22	–	–	–	9063	8.9	1.7	19.2
Playoff Totals	46	–	1800	324	798	.425	–	–	–	285	349	.817	–	–	481	115	143	2	–	–	–	933	9.6	2.3	20.3
All-Star Totals	6	–	131	26	60	.433	–	–	–	12	17	.706	–	–	35	4	13	0	–	–	–	64	5.8	0.7	10.7

Yates, Barry b. January 30, 1946 Ht. 6-7 Wt. 215 College: Nebraska; Maryland

SEASON–TEAM	G	GS	MIN	FGM	FGA	PCT	3FGM	3FGA	PCT	FTM	FTA	PCT	O-RB	D-RB	TOT	AST	PF	DQ	STL	TO	BLK	PTS	RPG	APG	PPG
71-72–Philadelphia	24	–	144	31	83	.373	–	–	–	7	11	.636	–	–	40	7	14	0	–	–	–	69	1.7	0.3	2.9
Reg. Season Totals	24	–	144	31	83	.373	–	–	–	7	11	.636	–	–	40	7	14	0	–	–	–	69	1.7	0.3	2.9

Yates, Wayne E. b. November 7, 1937 Ht. 6-8 Wt. 235 College: Memphis

SEASON–TEAM	G	GS	MIN	FGM	FGA	PCT	3FGM	3FGA	PCT	FTM	FTA	PCT	O-RB	D-RB	TOT	AST	PF	DQ	STL	TO	BLK	PTS	RPG	APG	PPG
61-62–Los Angeles	37	–	263	31	105	.295	–	–	–	10	22	.455	–	–	94	16	72	1	–	–	–	72	2.5	0.4	1.9
Reg. Season Totals	37	–	263	31	105	.295	–	–	–	10	22	.455	–	–	94	16	72	1	–	–	–	72	2.5	0.4	1.9
Playoff Totals	4	–	12	3	8	.375	–	–	–	1	2	.500	–	–	5	1	2	0	–	–	–	7	1.3	0.3	1.8

Yelverton, Charles W. (Charlie) b. December 5, 1948 Ht. 6-2 Wt. 190 College: Fordham

SEASON–TEAM	G	GS	MIN	FGM	FGA	PCT	3FGM	3FGA	PCT	FTM	FTA	PCT	O-RB	D-RB	TOT	AST	PF	DQ	STL	TO	BLK	PTS	RPG	APG	PPG
71-72–Portland	69	–	1227	206	530	.389	–	–	–	133	188	.707	–	–	201	81	145	2	–	–	–	545	2.9	1.2	7.9
Reg. Season Totals	69	–	1227	206	530	.389	–	–	–	133	188	.707	–	–	201	81	145	2	–	–	–	545	2.9	1.2	7.9

Yonakor, Richard Robert (Rich) b. October 3, 1958 Ht. 6-9 Wt. 220 College: North Carolina

SEASON–TEAM	G	GS	MIN	FGM	FGA	PCT	3FGM	3FGA	PCT	FTM	FTA	PCT	O-RB	D-RB	TOT	AST	PF	DQ	STL	TO	BLK	PTS	RPG	APG	PPG
81-82–San Antonio	10	0	70	14	26	.538	0	0	–	5	7	.714	13	14	27	3	7	0	1	2	2	33	2.7	0.3	3.3
Reg. Season Totals	10	0	70	14	26	.538	0	0	–	5	7	.714	13	14	27	3	7	0	1	2	2	33	2.7	0.3	3.3
Playoff Totals	2	0	4	1	2	.500	0	0	–	0	0	–	0	1	1	1	1	0	1	0	0	2	0.5	0.5	1.0

Young, Danny Richardson b. July 26, 1962 Ht. 6-4 Wt. 175 College: Wake Forest

SEASON–TEAM	G	GS	MIN	FGM	FGA	PCT	3FGM	3FGA	PCT	FTM	FTA	PCT	O-RB	D-RB	TOT	AST	PF	DQ	STL	TO	BLK	PTS	RPG	APG	PPG
84-85–Seattle	3	0	26	2	10	.200	0	1	.000	0	0	–	0	3	3	2	2	0	3	2	0	4	1.0	0.7	1.3
85-86–Seattle	82	29	1901	227	449	.506	24	74	.324	90	106	.849	29	91	120	303	113	0	110	92	9	568	1.5	3.7	6.9
86-87–Seattle	73	26	1482	132	288	.458	29	79	.367	59	71	.831	23	90	113	353	72	0	74	85	3	352	1.5	4.8	4.8
87-88–Seattle	77	0	949	89	218	.408	22	77	.286	43	53	.811	18	57	75	218	69	0	52	37	2	243	1.0	2.8	3.2
88-89–Portland	48	2	952	115	250	.460	17	50	.340	50	64	.781	17	57	74	123	50	0	55	45	3	297	1.5	2.6	6.2
89-90–Portland	82	8	1393	138	328	.421	16	59	.271	91	112	.813	29	93	122	231	84	0	82	80	4	383	1.5	2.8	4.7
90-91–Portland	75	1	897	103	271	.380	36	104	.346	41	45	.911	22	53	75	141	49	0	50	50	7	283	1.0	1.9	3.8
91-92–Port.-LAClips	62	5	1023	100	255	.392	23	70	.329	57	67	.851	16	59	75	172	53	0	46	47	4	280	1.2	2.8	4.5
92-93–Detroit	65	2	836	69	167	.413	22	68	.324	28	32	.875	13	34	47	119	36	0	31	30	5	188	0.7	1.8	2.9
94-95–Milw.-Lakers	7	0	77	9	17	.529	5	12	.417	1	1	1.000	1	4	5	12	8	0	4	4	0	24	0.7	1.7	3.4
Reg. Season Totals	574	73	9536	984	2253	.437	194	594	.327	460	551	.835	168	541	709	1674	536	0	507	472	37	2622	1.2	2.9	4.6
Playoff Totals	53	1	710	80	186	.430	19	59	.322	40	49	.816	20	44	64	119	59	1	32	37	4	219	1.2	2.2	4.1

Young, Michael Wayne b. January 2, 1961 Ht. 6-7 Wt. 220 College: Houston

SEASON–TEAM	G	GS	MIN	FGM	FGA	PCT	3FGM	3FGA	PCT	FTM	FTA	PCT	O-RB	D-RB	TOT	AST	PF	DQ	STL	TO	BLK	PTS	RPG	APG	PPG
84-85–Phoenix	2	0	11	2	6	.333	0	1	.000	0	0	–	1	1	2	0	0	0	0	0	0	4	1.0	0.0	2.0
85-86–Philadelphia	2	0	2	0	2	.000	0	0	–	0	0	–	0	0	0	0	0	0	0	0	0	0	0.0	0.0	0.0
89-90–L.A. Clippers	45	2	459	92	194	.474	8	26	.308	27	38	.711	36	50	86	24	47	0	25	15	3	219	1.9	0.5	4.9
Reg. Season Totals	49	2	472	94	202	.465	8	27	.296	27	38	.711	37	51	88	24	47	0	25	15	3	223	1.8	0.5	4.6
Playoff Totals	3	0	3	1	4	.250	0	0	–	0	0	–	1	0	1	–	0	0	0	0	0	2	0.3	0.0	0.7

Young, Perry b. August 4, 1963 Ht. 6-5 Wt. 210 College: Virginia Tech

SEASON–TEAM	G	GS	MIN	FGM	FGA	PCT	3FGM	3FGA	PCT	FTM	FTA	PCT	O-RB	D-RB	TOT	AST	PF	DQ	STL	TO	BLK	PTS	RPG	APG	PPG
86-87–Chicago-Port.	9	0	72	6	21	.286	0	0	–	1	2	.500	3	5	8	7	14	0	5	4	1	13	0.9	0.8	1.4
Reg. Season Totals	9	0	72	6	21	.286	0	0	–	1	2	.500	3	5	8	7	14	0	5	4	1	13	0.9	0.8	1.4

Young, Suntino Korleone (Korleone, Don) b. December 31, 1978 Ht. 6-7 Wt. 220 High School: Hargrave Military Academy (Va.)

SEASON–TEAM	G	GS	MIN	FGM	FGA	PCT	3FGM	3FGA	PCT	FTM	FTA	PCT	O-RB	D-RB	TOT	AST	PF	DQ	STL	TO	BLK	PTS	RPG	APG	PPG
98-99–Detroit	3	0	15	5	10	.500	1	4	.250	2	2	1.000	2	2	4	1	3	0	0	1	0	13	1.3	0.3	4.3
Reg. Season Totals	3	0	15	5	10	.500	1	4	.250	2	2	1.000	2	2	4	1	3	0	0	1	0	13	1.3	0.3	4.3

Young, Tim Aaron b. February 6, 1976 Ht. 7-2 Wt. 270 College: Stanford

SEASON–TEAM	G	GS	MIN	FGM	FGA	PCT	3FGM	3FGA	PCT	FTM	FTA	PCT	O-RB	D-RB	TOT	AST	PF	DQ	STL	TO	BLK	PTS	RPG	APG	PPG
99-00–Golden State	25	0	137	13	39	.333	0	0	–	28	36	.778	13	22	35	5	18	0	2	9	1	54	1.4	0.2	2.2
Reg. Season Totals	25	0	137	13	39	.333	0	0	–	28	36	.778	13	22	35	5	18	0	2	9	1	54	1.4	0.2	2.2

Zaslofsky, Max (Slats) b. December 7, 1925 d. October 15, 1985 Ht. 6-2 Wt. 170 College: Chicago; St. John's (N.Y.)

SEASON–TEAM	G	GS	MIN	FGM	FGA	PCT	3FGM	3FGA	PCT	FTM	FTA	PCT	O-RB	D-RB	TOT	AST	PF	DQ	STL	TO	BLK	PTS	RPG	APG	PPG
46-47–Chicago	61	–	–	336	1020	.329	–	–	–	205	278	.737	–	–	–	40	121	–	–	–	–	877	–	0.7	14.4
47-48–Chicago	48	–	–	373	1156	.323	–	–	–	261	333	.784	–	–	–	29	125	–	–	–	–	1007	–	0.6	21.0
48-49–Chicago	58	–	–	425	1216	.350	–	–	–	347	413	.840	–	–	–	149	156	–	–	–	–	1197	–	2.6	20.6
49-50–Chicago	68	–	–	397	1132	.351	–	–	–	321	381	.843	–	–	–	155	185	–	–	–	–	1115	–	2.3	16.4
50-51–New York	66	–	–	302	853	.354	–	–	–	231	298	.775	–	–	228	136	150	3	–	–	–	835	3.5	2.1	12.7
51-52–New York	66	–	2113	322	958	.336	–	–	–	287	380	.755	–	–	194	156	183	5	–	–	–	931	2.9	2.4	14.1
52-53–New York	29	–	722	123	320	.384	–	–	–	98	142	.690	–	–	75	55	81	1	–	–	–	344	2.6	1.9	11.9
53-54–Balt.-Milw.-FtWayne	65	–	1881	278	756	.368	–	–	–	255	357	.714	–	–	160	154	142	1	–	–	–	811	2.5	2.4	12.5
54-55–Fort Wayne	70	–	1862	269	821	.328	–	–	–	247	352	.702	–	–	191	203	130	0	–	–	–	785	2.7	2.9	11.2
55-56–Fort Wayne	9	–	182	29	81	.358	–	–	–	30	35	.857	–	–	16	16	18	1	–	–	–	88	1.8	1.8	9.8
Reg. Season Totals	540	–	6760	2854	8313	.343	–	–	–	2282	2969	.769	–	–	864	1093	1291	11	–	–	–	7990	2.8	2.0	14.8
Playoff Totals	63	–	893	305	1211	.350	–	–	–	287	376	.763	–	–	121	117	192	4	–	–	–	897	2.8	1.4	14.2
All-Star Totals	1	–	25	3	7	.429	–	–	–	5	5	1.000	–	–	4	2	0	0	–	–	–	11	4.0	2.0	11.0

Zawoluk, Robert Michael (Zeke) b. October 13, 1930 Ht. 6-7 Wt. 215 College: St. John's (N.Y.)

SEASON–TEAM	G	GS	MIN	FGM	FGA	PCT	3FGM	3FGA	PCT	FTM	FTA	PCT	O-RB	D-RB	TOT	AST	PF	DQ	STL	TO	BLK	PTS	RPG	APG	PPG
52-53–Indianapolis	41	–	622	55	150	.367	–	–	–	77	116	.664	–	–	146	31	83	1	–	–	–	187	3.6	0.8	4.6
53-54–Philadelphia	71	–	1795	203	540	.376	–	–	–	186	230	.809	–	–	330	99	220	6	–	–	–	592	4.6	1.4	8.3
54-55–Philadelphia	67	–	1117	138	375	.368	–	–	–	155	199	.779	–	–	256	87	147	3	–	–	–	431	3.8	1.3	6.4
Reg. Season Totals	179	–	3534	396	1065	.372	–	–	–	418	545	.767	–	–	732	217	450	10	–	–	–	1210	4.1	1.2	6.8
Playoff Totals	2	–	18	1	6	.167	–	–	–	0	2	.000	–	–	2	–	5	0	–	–	–	2	1.0	0.0	1.0

Zeller, David A. **(Dave)** b. June 8, 1939 Ht. 6-1 Wt. 175 College: Miami (Ohio)

SEASON–TEAM	G	GS	MIN	FGM	FGA	PCT	3FGM	3FGA	PCT	FTM	FTA	PCT	O-RB	D-RB	TOT	AST	PF	DQ	STL	TO	BLK	PTS	RPG	APG	PPG
61-62–Cincinnati	61	–	278	36	102	.353	–	–	–	18	24	.750	–	–	27	58	37	0	–	–	–	90	0.4	1.0	1.5
Reg. Season Totals	61	–	278	36	102	.353	–	–	–	18	24	.750	–	–	27	58	37	0	–	–	–	90	0.4	1.0	1.5
Playoff Totals	2	–	5	1	2	.500	–	–	–	0	0	–	–	–	1	1	0	0	–	–	–	2	0.5	0.5	1.0

Zeller, Gary Lynn b. November 20, 1947 Ht. 6-3 Wt. 205 College: Drake

SEASON–TEAM	G	GS	MIN	FGM	FGA	PCT	3FGM	3FGA	PCT	FTM	FTA	PCT	O-RB	D-RB	TOT	AST	PF	DQ	STL	TO	BLK	PTS	RPG	APG	PPG
70-71–Baltimore	50	–	226	34	115	.296	–	–	–	15	28	.536	–	–	27	7	43	0	–	–	–	83	0.5	0.1	1.7
71-72–Baltimore	28	–	471	83	229	.362	–	–	–	22	35	.629	–	–	65	30	62	0	–	–	–	188	2.3	1.1	6.7
71-72–New York (A)	12	–	82	7	30	.233	0	1	.000	4	6	.667	–	–	10	2	16	–	–	9	–	18	0.8	0.2	1.5
Reg. NBA Totals	78	–	697	117	344	.340	–	–	–	37	63	.587	–	–	92	37	105	0	–	–	–	271	1.2	0.5	3.5
Reg. ABA Totals	12	–	82	7	30	.233	0	1	.000	4	6	.667	–	–	10	2	16	–	–	9	–	18	0.8	0.2	1.5
NBA Playoff Totals	15	–	67	12	35	.343	–	–	–	2	7	.286	–	–	13	4	15	0	–	–	–	26	0.9	0.3	1.7
ABA Playoff Totals	3	–	9	1	1	1.000	0	0	–	0	1	.000	–	–	1	0	7	–	–	3	–	2	0.3	0.0	0.7

Zeller, Harry Raymond **(Hank)** b. July 10, 1918 Ht. 6-4 Wt. 210 College: Pittsburgh; Washington & Jefferson

SEASON–TEAM	G	GS	MIN	FGM	FGA	PCT	3FGM	3FGA	PCT	FTM	FTA	PCT	O-RB	D-RB	TOT	AST	PF	DQ	STL	TO	BLK	PTS	RPG	APG	PPG
46-47–Pittsburgh	48	–	–	120	382	.314	–	–	–	122	177	.689	–	–	–	31	177	–	–	–	–	362	–	0.6	7.5
Reg. Season Totals	48	–	–	120	382	.314	–	–	–	122	177	.689	–	–	–	31	177	–	–	–	–	362	–	0.6	7.5

Zeno, Anthony Michael **(Tony)** b. October 1, 1957 Ht. 6-8 Wt. 210 College: Arizona State

SEASON–TEAM	G	GS	MIN	FGM	FGA	PCT	3FGM	3FGA	PCT	FTM	FTA	PCT	O-RB	D-RB	TOT	AST	PF	DQ	STL	TO	BLK	PTS	RPG	APG	PPG
79-80–Indiana	8	–	59	6	21	.286	0	0	–	2	2	1.000	3	11	14	1	13	0	4	9	3	14	1.8	0.1	1.8
Reg. Season Totals	8	–	59	6	21	.286	0	0	–	2	2	1.000	3	11	14	1	13	0	4	9	3	14	1.8	0.1	1.8

Zevenbergen, Phil b. April 13, 1964 Ht. 6-10 Wt. 230 College: Seattle Pacific; Edmonds (Wash.) C.C; Washington

SEASON–TEAM	G	GS	MIN	FGM	FGA	PCT	3FGM	3FGA	PCT	FTM	FTA	PCT	O-RB	D-RB	TOT	AST	PF	DQ	STL	TO	BLK	PTS	RPG	APG	PPG
87-88–San Antonio	8	0	58	15	27	.556	0	0	–	0	2	.000	4	9	13	3	12	0	3	4	1	30	1.6	0.4	3.8
Reg. Season Totals	8	0	58	15	27	.556	0	0	–	0	2	.000	4	9	13	3	12	0	3	4	1	30	1.6	0.4	3.8
Playoff Totals	1	0	1	0	0	–	0	0	–	0	0	–	0	0	0	–	0	0	0	0	0	0	0.0	0.0	0.0

Zidek, Jiri **(George)** b. August 2, 1973 Ht. 7-0 Wt. 266 College: UCLA

SEASON–TEAM	G	GS	MIN	FGM	FGA	PCT	3FGM	3FGA	PCT	FTM	FTA	PCT	O-RB	D-RB	TOT	AST	PF	DQ	STL	TO	BLK	PTS	RPG	APG	PPG
95-96–Charlotte	71	21	888	105	248	.423	0	0	–	71	93	.763	69	114	183	16	170	2	9	38	7	281	2.6	0.2	4.0
96-97–Cha.-Denver	52	2	376	49	118	.415	0	2	.000	45	57	.789	35	51	86	14	61	0	5	27	3	143	1.7	0.3	2.8
97-98–Denver-Seattle	12	0	64	7	29	.241	1	2	.500	14	16	.875	4	13	17	2	10	0	0	4	2	29	1.4	0.2	2.4
Reg. Season Totals	135	23	1328	161	395	.408	1	4	.250	130	166	.783	108	178	286	32	241	2	14	69	12	453	2.1	0.2	3.4

Zoet, Jim b. December 30, 1953 Ht. 7-1 Wt. 240 College: Kent State

SEASON–TEAM	G	GS	MIN	FGM	FGA	PCT	3FGM	3FGA	PCT	FTM	FTA	PCT	O-RB	D-RB	TOT	AST	PF	DQ	STL	TO	BLK	PTS	RPG	APG	PPG
82-83–Detroit	7	0	30	1	5	.200	0	0	–	0	0	–	3	5	8	1	9	0	1	4	3	2	1.1	0.1	0.3
Reg. Season Totals	7	0	30	1	5	.200	0	0	–	0	0	–	3	5	8	1	9	0	1	4	3	2	1.1	0.1	0.3

Zopf, William Charles Jr. **(Bill, Zip)** b. June 7, 1948 Ht. 6-1 Wt. 170 College: Duquesne

SEASON–TEAM	G	GS	MIN	FGM	FGA	PCT	3FGM	3FGA	PCT	FTM	FTA	PCT	O-RB	D-RB	TOT	AST	PF	DQ	STL	TO	BLK	PTS	RPG	APG	PPG
70-71–Milwaukee	53	–	398	49	135	.363	–	–	–	20	36	.556	–	–	46	73	34	0	–	–	–	118	0.9	1.4	2.2
Reg. Season Totals	53	–	398	49	135	.363	–	–	–	20	36	.556	–	–	46	73	34	0	–	–	–	118	0.9	1.4	2.2

Zunic, Matthew **(Matt, Mad Matt)** b. December 19, 1919 Ht. 6-7 Wt. 195 College: George Washington

SEASON–TEAM	G	GS	MIN	FGM	FGA	PCT	3FGM	3FGA	PCT	FTM	FTA	PCT	O-RB	D-RB	TOT	AST	PF	DQ	STL	TO	BLK	PTS	RPG	APG	PPG
47-48–Flint (N)	57	–	–	123	–	–	–	–	–	85	128	.664	–	–	–	–	209	–	–	–	–	331	–	–	5.8
48-49–Washington	56	–	–	98	323	.303	–	–	–	77	109	.706	–	–	–	50	182	–	–	–	–	273	–	0.9	4.9
Reg. NBA Totals	56	–	–	98	323	.303	–	–	–	77	109	.706	–	–	–	50	182	–	–	–	–	273	–	0.9	4.9
Reg. NBL Totals	57	–	–	123	–	–	–	–	–	85	128	.664	–	–	–	–	209	–	–	–	–	331	–	–	5.8
NBA Playoff Totals	9	–	–	7	71	.183	–	–	–	12	19	.632	–	–	–	12	26	1	–	–	–	26	–	0.8	2.9

CHAPTER 30

ALL-TIME RECORDS

ALL-TIME TEAM RECORDS

Anderson Packers

		Reg Sea		Playoffs	
SEASON	COACH	W	L	W	L
1949-50	Howard Schultz, (21-14)				
	Ike Duffy, (1-2)				
	Doxie Moore, (15-11)	37	27	4	4

Atlanta Hawks

		Reg Sea		Playoffs	
SEASON	COACH	W	L	W	L
1949-50*	Roger Potter, (1-6)				
	Red Auerbach, (28-29)				
	3rd/Western Division	29	35	1	2
1950-51*	Dave McMillan, (9-14)				
	John Logan, (2-1)				
	M. Todorovich, (14-28)	25	43	–	–
1951-52†	Doxie Moore	17	49	–	–
1952-53†	Andrew Levane	27	44	–	–
1953-54†	Andrew Levane, (11-35)				
	Red Holzman, (10-16)	21	51	–	–
1954-55†	Red Holzman	26	46	–	–
1955-56‡	Red Holzman	33	39	4	5
1956-57‡	Red Holzman, (14-19)				
	Slater Martin, (5-3)				
	Alex Hannum, (15-16)	34	38	8	4
1957-58‡	Alex Hannum	41	31	8	3
1958-59‡	Andy Phillip, (6-4)				
	Ed Macauley, (43-19)	49	23	2	4
1959-60‡	Ed Macauley	46	29	7	7
1960-61‡	Paul Seymour	51	28	5	7
1961-62‡	Paul Seymour, (5-9)				
	Andrew Levane, (20-40)				
	Bob Pettit, (4-2)	29	51	–	–
1962-63‡	Harry Gallatin	48	32	6	5
1963-64‡	Harry Gallatin	46	34	6	6
1964-65‡	Harry Gallatin, (17-16)				
	Richie Guerin, (28-19)	45	35	1	3
1965-66‡	Richie Guerin	36	44	6	4
1966-67‡	Richie Guerin	39	42	5	4
1967-68‡	Richie Guerin	56	26	2	4
1968-69	Richie Guerin	48	34	5	6
1969-70	Richie Guerin	48	34	4	5
1970-71	Richie Guerin	36	46	1	4
1971-72	Richie Guerin	36	46	2	4
1972-73	Cotton Fitzsimmons	46	36	2	4
1973-74	Cotton Fitzsimmons	35	47	–	–
1974-75	Cotton Fitzsimmons	31	51	–	–
1975-76	C. Fitzsimmons, (28-46)				
	Gene Tormohlen, (1-7)	29	53	–	–
1976-77	Hubie Brown	31	51	–	–
1977-78	Hubie Brown	41	41	0	2
1978-79	Hubie Brown	46	36	5	4
1979-80	Hubie Brown	50	32	1	4
1980-81	Hubie Brown, (31-48)				
	Mike Fratello, (0-3)	31	51	–	–
1981-82	Kevin Loughery	42	40	0	2
1982-83	Kevin Loughery	43	39	1	2
1983-84	Mike Fratello	40	42	2	3
1984-85	Mike Fratello	34	48	–	–
1985-86	Mike Fratello	50	32	4	5
1986-87	Mike Fratello	57	25	4	5
1987-88	Mike Fratello	50	32	6	6
1988-89	Mike Fratello	52	30	2	3
1989-90	Mike Fratello	41	41	–	–
1990-91	Bob Weiss	43	39	2	3
1991-92	Bob Weiss	38	44	–	–
1992-93	Bob Weiss	43	39	0	3
1993-94	Lenny Wilkens	57	25	5	6
1994-95	Lenny Wilkens	42	40	0	3
1995-96	Lenny Wilkens	46	36	4	6
1996-97	Lenny Wilkens	56	26	4	6
1997-98	Lenny Wilkens	50	32	1	3
1998-99	Lenny Wilkens	31	19	3	6
1999-00	Lenny Wilkens	28	54	–	–
TOTALS		2049	1961	119	153

*Tri-Cities Blackhawks
†Milwaukee Hawks
‡St. Louis Hawks

Baltimore Bullets

		Reg Sea		Playoffs	
SEASON	COACH	W	L	W	L
1947-48	Buddy Jeannette	28	20	9	3
1948-49	Buddy Jeannette	29	31	1	2
1949-50	Buddy Jeannette	25	43	–	–
1950-51	Buddy Jeannette, (14-23)				
	Walter Budko, (10-19)	24	42	–	–
1951-52	Fred Scolari, (12-27)				
	Chick Reiser, (8-19)	20	46	–	–
1952-53	Chick Reiser, (0-3)				
	Clair Bee, (16-51)	16	54	0	2
1953-54	Clair Bee	16	56	–	–
1954-55*	Clair Bee, (2-9)				
	Al Barthelme, (1-2)	3	11	–	–
TOTALS		161	303	10	7

*Team disbanded November 27.

Boston Celtics

		Reg Sea		Playoffs	
SEASON	COACH	W	L	W	L
1946-47	John Russell	22	38	–	–
1947-48	John Russell	20	28	1	2
1948-49	Alvin Julian	25	35	–	–
1949-50	Alvin Julian	22	46	–	–
1950-51	Red Auerbach	39	30	0	2
1951-52	Red Auerbach	39	27	1	2
1952-53	Red Auerbach	46	25	3	3
1953-54	Red Auerbach	42	30	2	4

For additional records, please log on to NBA.com.

ALL-TIME TEAM RECORDS – Continued

SEASON	COACH	Reg Sea W	Reg Sea L	Playoffs W	Playoffs L
1954-55	Red Auerbach	36	36	3	4
1955-56	Red Auerbach	39	33	1	2
1956-57	Red Auerbach	44	28	7	3
1957-58	Red Auerbach	49	23	6	5
1958-59	Red Auerbach	52	20	8	3
1959-60	Red Auerbach	59	16	8	5
1960-61	Red Auerbach	57	22	8	2
1961-62	Red Auerbach	60	20	8	6
1962-63	Red Auerbach	58	22	8	5
1963-64	Red Auerbach	59	21	8	2
1964-65	Red Auerbach	62	18	8	4
1965-66	Red Auerbach	54	26	11	6
1966-67	Bill Russell	60	21	4	5
1967-68	Bill Russell	54	28	12	7
1968-69	Bill Russell	48	34	12	6
1969-70	Tom Heinsohn	34	48	–	–
1970-71	Tom Heinsohn	44	38	–	–
1971-72	Tom Heinsohn	56	26	5	6
1972-73	Tom Heinsohn	68	14	7	6
1973-74	Tom Heinsohn	56	26	12	6
1974-75	Tom Heinsohn	60	22	6	5
1975-76	Tom Heinsohn	54	28	12	6
1976-77	Tom Heinsohn	44	38	5	4
1977-78	Tom Heinsohn, (11-23)				
	Tom Sanders, (21-27)	32	50	–	–
1978-79	Tom Sanders, (2-12)				
	Dave Cowens, (27-41)	29	53	–	–
1979-80	Bill Fitch	61	21	5	4
1980-81	Bill Fitch	62	20	12	5
1981-82	Bill Fitch	63	19	7	5
1982-83	Bill Fitch	56	26	2	5
1983-84	K.C. Jones	62	20	15	8
1984-85	K.C. Jones	63	19	13	8
1985-86	K.C. Jones	67	15	15	3
1986-87	K.C. Jones	59	23	13	10
1987-88	K.C. Jones	57	25	9	8
1988-89	Jimmy Rodgers	42	40	0	3
1989-90	Jimmy Rodgers	52	30	2	3
1990-91	Chris Ford	56	26	5	6
1991-92	Chris Ford	51	31	6	4
1992-93	Chris Ford	48	34	1	3
1993-94	Chris Ford	32	50	–	–
1994-95	Chris Ford	35	47	1	3
1995-96	M.L. Carr	33	49	–	–
1996-97	M.L. Carr	15	67	–	–
1997-98	Rick Pitino	36	46	–	–
1998-99	Rick Pitino	19	31	–	–
1999-00	Rick Pitino	35	47	–	–
TOTALS		2527	1656	272	189

Charlotte Hornets

SEASON	COACH	Reg Sea W	Reg Sea L	Playoffs W	Playoffs L
1988-89	Dick Harter	20	62	–	–
1989-90	Dick Harter, (8-32)				
	Gene Littles, (11-31)	19	63	–	–
1990-91	Gene Littles	26	56	–	–
1991-92	Allan Bristow	31	51	–	–
1992-93	Allan Bristow	44	38	4	5
1993-94	Allan Bristow	41	41	–	–
1994-95	Allan Bristow	50	32	1	3
1995-96	Allan Bristow	41	41	–	–
1996-97	Dave Cowens	54	28	0	3
1997-98	Dave Cowens	51	31	4	5
1998-99	Dave Cowens, (4-11)				
	Paul Silas, (22-13)	26	24	–	–
1999-00	Paul Silas	49	33	1	3
TOTALS		452	500	10	19

Chicago Bulls

SEASON	COACH	Reg Sea W	Reg Sea L	Playoffs W	Playoffs L
1966-67	Red Kerr	33	48	0	3
1967-68	Red Kerr	29	53	1	4
1968-69	Dick Motta	33	49	–	–
1969-70	Dick Motta	39	43	1	4
1970-71	Dick Motta	51	31	3	4
1971-72	Dick Motta	57	25	0	4
1972-73	Dick Motta	51	31	3	4
1973-74	Dick Motta	54	28	4	7
1974-75	Dick Motta	47	35	7	6
1975-76	Dick Motta	24	58	–	–
1976-77	Ed Badger	44	38	1	2
1977-78	Ed Badger	40	42	–	–
1978-79	Larry Costello, (20-36)				
	Scotty Robertson, (11-15)	31	51	–	–
1979-80	Jerry Sloan	30	52	–	–
1980-81	Jerry Sloan	45	37	2	4
1981-82	Jerry Sloan, (19-32)				
	Phil Johnson, (0-1)				
	Rod Thorn, (15-15)	34	48	–	–
1982-83	Paul Westhead	28	54	–	–
1983-84	Kevin Loughery	27	55	–	–
1984-85	Kevin Loughery	38	44	1	3
1985-86	Stan Albeck	30	52	0	3
1986-87	Doug Collins	40	42	0	3
1987-88	Doug Collins	50	32	4	6
1988-89	Doug Collins	47	35	9	8
1989-90	Phil Jackson	55	27	10	6
1990-91	Phil Jackson	61	21	15	2
1991-92	Phil Jackson	67	15	15	7
1992-93	Phil Jackson	57	25	15	4
1993-94	Phil Jackson	55	27	6	4
1994-95	Phil Jackson	47	35	5	5
1995-96	Phil Jackson	72	10	15	3
1996-97	Phil Jackson	69	13	15	4
1997-98	Phil Jackson	62	20	15	6
1998-99	Tim Floyd	13	37	–	–
1999-00	Tim Floyd	17	65	–	–
TOTALS		1477	1278	147	106

Chicago Stags

SEASON	COACH	Reg Sea W	Reg Sea L	Playoffs W	Playoffs L
1946-47	Harold Olsen	39	22	5	6
1947-48	Harold Olsen	28	20	3	4
1948-49	Harold Olsen, (28-21)	38	22	0	2
	*P. Brownstein, (10-1)				
1949-50	Philip Brownstein	40	28	0	3
TOTALS		145	92	8	15

*Substituted during Olsen's illness.

Cleveland Cavaliers

SEASON	COACH	Reg Sea W	Reg Sea L	Playoffs W	Playoffs L
1970-71	Bill Fitch	15	67	–	–
1971-72	Bill Fitch	23	59	–	–
1972-73	Bill Fitch	32	50	–	–
1973-74	Bill Fitch	29	53	–	–
1974-75	Bill Fitch	40	42	–	–
1975-76	Bill Fitch	49	33	6	7
1976-77	Bill Fitch	43	39	1	2
1977-78	Bill Fitch	43	39	0	2
1978-79	Bill Fitch	30	52	–	–
1979-80	Stan Albeck	37	45	–	–
1980-81	Bill Musselman, (25-46)				
	Don Delaney, (3-8)	28	54	–	–
1981-82	Don Delaney, (4-11)				
	Bob Kloppenburg, (0-3)				
	Chuck Daly, (9-32)				
	Bill Musselman, (2-21)	15	67	–	–
1982-83	Tom Nissalke	23	59	–	–
1983-84	Tom Nissalke	28	54	–	–
1984-85	George Karl	36	46	1	3
1985-86	George Karl, (25-42)				
	Gene Littles, (4-11)	29	53	–	–
1986-87	Lenny Wilkens	31	51	–	–
1987-88	Lenny Wilkens	42	40	2	3
1988-89	Lenny Wilkens	57	25	2	3
1989-90	Lenny Wilkens	42	40	2	3
1990-91	Lenny Wilkens	33	49	–	–
1991-92	Lenny Wilkens	57	25	9	8
1992-93	Lenny Wilkens	54	28	3	6
1993-94	Mike Fratello	47	35	0	3
1994-95	Mike Fratello	43	39	1	3
1995-96	Mike Fratello	47	35	0	3
1996-97	Mike Fratello	42	40	–	–
1997-98	Mike Fratello	47	35	1	3
1998-99	Mike Fratello	22	28	–	–
1999-00	Randy Wittman	32	50	–	–
TOTALS		1096	1332	28	49

Cleveland Rebels

SEASON	COACH	Reg Sea W	Reg Sea L	Playoffs W	Playoffs L
1946-47	Dutch Dehnert, (17-20)				
	Roy Clifford, (13-10)	30	30	1	2

Dallas Mavericks

SEASON	COACH	Reg Sea W	Reg Sea L	Playoffs W	Playoffs L
1980-81	Dick Motta	15	67	–	–
1981-82	Dick Motta	28	54	–	–
1982-83	Dick Motta	38	44	–	–
1983-84	Dick Motta	43	39	4	6
1984-85	Dick Motta	44	38	1	3
1985-86	Dick Motta	44	38	5	5
1986-87	Dick Motta	55	27	1	3
1987-88	John MacLeod	53	29	10	7
1988-89	John MacLeod	38	44	–	–
1989-90	John MacLeod, (5-6)				
	Richie Adubato, (42-29)	47	35	0	3
1990-91	Richie Adubato	28	54	–	–
1991-92	Richie Adubato	22	60	–	–
1992-93	Richie Adubato, (2-27)				
	Gar Heard, (9-44)	11	71	–	–
1993-94	Quinn Buckner	13	69	–	–
1994-95	Dick Motta	36	46	–	–
1995-96	Dick Motta	26	56	–	–
1996-97	Jim Cleamons	24	58	–	–
1997-98	Jim Cleamons, (4-12)				
	Don Nelson, (16-50)	20	62	–	–
1998-99	Don Nelson	19	31	–	–
1999-00	Don Nelson	40	42	–	–
TOTALS		644	964	21	27

ALL-TIME TEAM RECORDS – Continued

Denver Nuggets

SEASON	COACH	Reg Sea W	Reg Sea L	Playoffs W	Playoffs L
1949-50	James Darden	11	51	–	–

Denver Nuggets

SEASON	COACH	Reg Sea W	Reg Sea L	Playoffs W	Playoffs L
1967-68*	Bob Bass	45	33	2	3
1968-69*	Bob Bass	44	34	3	4
1969-70*	John McLendon, (9-19)				
	Joe Belmont, (42-14)	51	33	5	7
1970-71*	Joe Belmont, (3-10)				
	Stan Albeck, (27-44)	30	54	–	–
1971-72*	Alex Hannum	34	50	3	4
1972-73*	Alex Hannum	47	37	1	4
1973-74*	Alex Hannum	37	47	–	–
1974-75†	Larry Brown	65	19	7	6
1975-76†	Larry Brown	60	24	6	7
1976-77	Larry Brown	50	32	2	4
1977-78	Larry Brown	48	34	6	7
1978-79	Larry Brown, (28-25)				
	Donnie Walsh, (19-10)	47	35	1	2
1979-80	Donnie Walsh	30	52	–	–
1980-81	Donnie Walsh, (11-20)				
	Doug Moe, (26-25)	37	45	–	–
1981-82	Doug Moe	46	36	1	2
1982-83	Doug Moe	45	37	3	5
1983-84	Doug Moe	38	44	2	3
1984-85	Doug Moe	52	30	8	7
1985-86	Doug Moe	47	35	5	5
1986-87	Doug Moe	37	45	0	3
1987-88	Doug Moe	54	28	5	6
1988-89	Doug Moe	44	38	0	3
1989-90	Doug Moe	43	39	0	3
1990-91	Paul Westhead	20	62	–	–
1991-92	Paul Westhead	24	58	–	–
1992-93	Dan Issel	36	46	–	–
1993-94	Dan Issel	42	40	6	6
1994-95	Dan Issel, (18-16)				
	Gene Littles, (3-13)				
	B. Bickerstaff, (20-12)	41	41	0	3
1995-96	Bernie Bickerstaff	35	47	–	–
1996-97	Bernie Bickerstaff, (4-9)				
	Dick Motta, (17-52)	21	61	–	–
1997-98	Bill Hanzlik	11	71	–	–
1998-99	Mike D'Antoni	14	36	–	–
1999-00	Dan Issel	35	47	–	–
ABA TOTALS		413	331	27	35
NBA TOTALS		897	1039	39	59

*Denver Rockets; club in ABA.
†Denver Nuggets; club in ABA.

Detroit Falcons

SEASON	COACH	Reg Sea W	Reg Sea L	Playoffs W	Playoffs L
1946-47	Glenn Curtis, (12-22)				
	Philip Sachs, (8-18)	20	40	–	–

Detroit Pistons

SEASON	COACH	Reg Sea W	Reg Sea L	Playoffs W	Playoffs L
1948-49*	Carl Bennett, (0-6)				
	Paul Armstrong, (22-32)	22	38	–	–
1949-50*	Murray Mendenhall	40	28	3	2
1950-51*	Murray Mendanhall	32	36	1	2
1951-52*	Paul Birch	29	37	0	2
1952-53*	Paul Birch	36	33	4	4
1953-54*	Paul Birch	40	32	0	4
1954-55*	Charles Eckman	43	29	6	5
1955-56*	Charles Eckman	37	35	4	6
1956-57*	Charles Eckman	34	38	0	3
1957-58	Charles Eckman, (9-16)				
	Red Rocha, (24-23)	33	39	3	4
1958-59	Red Rocha	28	44	1	2
1959-60	Red Rocha, (13-21)				
	Dick McGuire, (17-24)	30	45	0	2
1960-61	Dick McGuire	34	45	2	3
1961-62	Dick McGuire	37	43	5	5
1962-63	Dick McGuire	34	46	1	3
1963-64	Charles Wolf	23	57	–	–
1964-65	Charles Wolf, (2-9)				
	D. DeBusschere, (29-40)	31	49	–	–
1965-66	Dave DeBusschere	22	58	–	–
1966-67	D. DeBusschere, (28-45)				
	Donnis Butcher, (2-6)	30	51	–	–
1967-68	Donnis Butcher	40	42	2	4
1968-69	Donnis Butcher, (10-12)				
	Paul Seymour, (22-38)	32	50	–	–
1969-70	Bill van Breda Kolff	31	51	–	–
1970-71	Bill van Breda Kolff	45	37	–	–
1971-72	B. van Breda Kolff, (6-4)				
	Terry Dischinger, (0-2)				
	Earl Lloyd, (20-50)	26	56	–	–
1972-73	Earl Lloyd, (2-5)				
	Ray Scott, 38-37	40	42	–	–
1973-74	Ray Scott	52	30	3	4
1974-75	Ray Scott	40	42	1	2
1975-76	Ray Scott, (17-25)				
	Herb Brown, (19-21)	36	46	4	5
1976-77	Herb Brown	44	38	1	2
1977-78	Herb Brown, (9-15)				
	Bob Kauffman, (29-29)	38	44	–	–
1978-79	Dick Vitale	30	52	–	–
1979-80	Dick Vitale, (4-8)				
	Richie Adubato, (12-58)	16	66	–	–
1980-81	Scotty Robertson	21	61	–	–
1981-82	Scotty Robertson	39	43	–	–
1982-83	Scotty Robertson	37	45	–	–
1983-84	Chuck Daly	49	33	2	3
1984-85	Chuck Daly	46	36	5	4
1985-86	Chuck Daly	46	36	1	3
1986-87	Chuck Daly	52	30	10	5
1987-88	Chuck Daly	54	28	14	9
1988-89	Chuck Daly	63	19	15	2
1989-90	Chuck Daly	59	23	15	5
1990-91	Chuck Daly	50	32	7	8
1991-92	Chuck Daly	48	34	2	3
1992-93	Ron Rothstein	40	42	–	–
1993-94	Don Chaney	20	62	–	–
1994-95	Don Chaney	28	54	–	–
1995-96	Doug Collins	46	36	0	3
1996-97	Doug Collins	54	28	2	3
1997-98	Doug Collins, (21-24)				
	Alvin Gentry, (16-21)	37	45	–	–
1998-99	Alvin Gentry	29	21	2	3
1999-00	Alvin Gentry, (28-30)				
	George Irvine, (14-10)	42	40	0	3
TOTALS		1945	2127	116	118

*Fort Wayne Pistons.

Golden State Warriors

SEASON	COACH	Reg Sea W	Reg Sea L	Playoffs W	Playoffs L
1946-47*	Eddie Gottlieb	35	25	8	2
1947-48*	Eddie Gottlieb	27	21	6	7
1948-49*	Eddie Gottlieb	28	32	0	2
1949-50*	Eddie Gottlieb	26	42	0	2
1950-51*	Eddie Gottlieb	40	26	0	2
1951-52*	Eddie Gottlieb	33	33	1	2
1952-53*	Eddie Gottlieb	12	57	–	–
1953-54*	Eddie Gottlieb	29	43	–	–
1954-55*	Eddie Gottlieb	33	39	–	–
1955-56*	George Senesky	45	27	7	3
1956-57*	George Senesky	37	35	0	2
1957-58*	George Senesky	37	35	3	5
1958-59*	Al Cervi	32	40	–	–
1959-60*	Neil Johnston	49	26	4	5
1960-61*	Neil Johnston	46	33	0	3
1961-62*	Frank McGuire	49	31	6	6
1962-63†	Bob Feerick	31	49	–	–
1963-64†	Alex Hannum	48	32	5	7
1964-65†	Alex Hannum	17	63	–	–
1965-66†	Alex Hannum	35	45	–	–
1966-67†	Bill Sharman	44	37	9	6
1967-68†	Bill Sharman	43	39	4	6
1968-69†	George Lee	41	41	2	4
1969-70†	George Lee, (22-30)				
	Al Attles, (8-22)	30	52	–	–
1970-71†	Al Attles	41	41	1	4
1971-72	Al Attles	51	31	1	4
1972-73	Al Attles	47	35	5	6
1973-74	Al Attles	44	38	–	–
1974-75	Al Attles	48	34	12	5
1975-76	Al Attles	59	23	7	6
1976-77	Al Attles	46	36	5	5
1977-78	Al Attles	43	39	–	–
1978-79	Al Attles	38	44	–	–
1979-80	Al Attles, (18-43)				
	John Bach, (6-15)	24	58	–	–
1980-81	Al Attles	39	43	–	–
1981-82	Al Attles	45	37	–	–
1982-83	Al Attles	30	52	–	–
1983-84	John Bach	37	45	–	–
1984-85	John Bach	22	60	–	–
1985-86	John Bach	30	52	–	–
1986-87	George Karl	42	40	4	6
1987-88	George Karl, (16-48)				
	Ed Gregory, (4-14)	20	62	–	–
1988-89	Don Nelson	43	39	4	4
1989-90	Don Nelson	37	45	–	–
1990-91	Don Nelson	44	38	4	5
1991-92	Don Nelson	55	27	1	3
1992-93	Don Nelson	34	48	–	–
1993-94	Don Nelson	50	32	0	3
1994-95	Don Nelson, (14-31)				
	Bob Lanier, (12-25)	26	56	–	–
1995-96	Rick Adelman	36	46	–	–
1996-97	Rick Adelman	30	52	–	–
1997-98	P.J. Carlesimo	19	63	–	–
1998-99	P.J. Carlesimo	21	29	–	–
1999-00	P.J. Carlesimo, (6-21)				
	Garry St. Jean, (13-42)	19	63	–	–
TOTALS		1967	2211	99	115

*Philadelphia Warriors.
†San Francisco Warriors.

ALL-TIME TEAM RECORDS – Continued

Houston Rockets

SEASON	COACH	Reg Sea W	Reg Sea L	Playoffs W	Playoffs L
1967-68*	Jack McMahon	15	67	–	–
1968-69*	Jack McMahon	37	45	2	4
1969-70*	Jack McMahon, (9-17)				
	Alex Hannum, (18-38)	27	55	–	–
1970-71*	Alex Hannum	40	42	–	–
1971-72	Tex Winter	34	48	–	–
1972-73	Tex Winter, (17-30)				
	John Egan, (16-19)	33	49	–	–
1973-74	John Egan	32	50	–	–
1974-75	John Egan	41	41	3	5
1975-76	John Egan	40	42	–	–
1976-77	Tom Nissalke	49	33	6	6
1977-78	Tom Nissalke	28	54	–	–
1978-79	Tom Nissalke	47	35	0	2
1979-80	Del Harris	41	41	2	5
1980-81	Del Harris	40	42	12	9
1981-82	Del Harris	46	36	1	2
1982-83	Del Harris	14	68	–	–
1983-84	Bill Fitch	29	53	–	–
1984-85	Bill Fitch	48	34	2	3
1985-86	Bill Fitch	51	31	13	7
1986-87	Bill Fitch	42	40	5	5
1987-88	Bill Fitch	46	36	1	3
1988-89	Don Chaney	45	37	1	3
1989-90	Don Chaney	41	41	1	3
1990-91	Don Chaney	52	30	0	3
1991-92	Don Chaney, (26-26)				
	R. Tomjanovich, (16-14)	42	40	–	–
1992-93	Rudy Tomjanovich	55	27	6	6
1993-94	Rudy Tomjanovich	58	24	15	8
1994-95	Rudy Tomjanovich	47	35	15	7
1995-96	Rudy Tomjanovich	48	34	3	5
1996-97	Rudy Tomjanovich	57	25	9	7
1997-98	Rudy Tomjanovich	41	41	2	3
1998-99	Rudy Tomjanovich	31	19	1	3
1999-00	Rudy Tomjanovich	34	48	–	–
TOTALS		1331	1343	100	99

*San Diego Rockets.

Indiana Pacers

SEASON	COACH	Reg Sea W	Reg Sea L	Playoffs W	Playoffs L
1967-68*	Larry Staverman	38	40	0	3
1968-69*	Larry Staverman, (2-7)				
	Bob Leonard, (42-27)	44	34	9	8
1969-70*	Bob Leonard	59	25	2	3
1970-71*	Bob Leonard	58	26	7	4
1971-72*	Bob Leonard	47	37	12	8
1972-73*	Bob Leonard	51	33	12	6
1973-74*	Bob Leonard	46	38	7	7
1974-75*	Bob Leonard	45	39	9	9
1975-76*	Bob Leonard	39	45	1	2
1976-77	Bob Leonard	36	46	–	–
1977-78	Bob Leonard	31	51	–	–
1978-79	Bob Leonard	38	44	–	–
1979-80	Bob Leonard	37	45	–	–
1980-81	Jack McKinney	44	38	0	2
1981-82	Jack McKinney	35	47	–	–
1982-83	Jack McKinney	20	62	–	–
1983-84	Jack McKinney	26	56	–	–
1984-85	George Irvine	22	60	–	–
1985-86	George Irvine	26	56	–	–
1986-87	Jack Ramsay	41	41	1	3
1987-88	Jack Ramsay	38	44	–	–
1988-89	Jack Ramsay, (0-7)				
	Mel Daniels, (0-2)				
	George Irvine, (6-14)				
	Dick Versace, (22-31)	28	54	–	–
1989-90	Dick Versace	42	40	0	3
1990-91	Dick Versace, (9-16)				
	Bob Hill, (32-25)	41	41	2	3
1991-92	Bob Hill	40	42	0	3
1992-93	Bob Hill	41	41	1	3
1993-94	Larry Brown	47	35	10	6
1994-95	Larry Brown	52	30	10	7
1995-96	Larry Brown	52	30	2	3
1996-97	Larry Brown	39	43	–	–
1997-98	Larry Bird	58	24	10	6
1998-99	Larry Bird	33	17	9	4
1999-00	Larry Bird	56	26	13	10
ABA TOTALS		427	317	69	50
NBA TOTALS		923	1013	58	53

*Club in ABA.

Indianapolis Jets

SEASON	COACH	Reg Sea W	Reg Sea L	Playoffs W	Playoffs L
1948-49	Bruce Hale, (4-13)				
	Burl Friddle, (14-29)	18	42	–	–

Indianapolis Olympians

SEASON	COACH	Reg Sea W	Reg Sea L	Playoffs W	Playoffs L
1949-50	Clifford Barker	39	25	3	3
1950-51	Clifford Barker, (24-32)				
	Wallace Jones, (7-5)	31	37	1	2
1951-52	Herman Schaefer	34	32	0	2
1952-53	Herman Schaefer	28	43	0	2
TOTALS		132	137	4	9

Los Angeles Clippers

SEASON	COACH	Reg Sea W	Reg Sea L	Playoffs W	Playoffs L
1970-71*	Dolph Schayes	22	60	–	–
1971-72*	Dolph Schayes, (0-1)				
	John McCarthy, (22-59)	22	60	–	–
1972-73*	Jack Ramsay	21	61	–	–
1973-74*	Jack Ramsay	42	40	2	4
1974-75*	Jack Ramsay	49	33	3	4
1975-76*	Jack Ramsay	46	36	4	5
1976-77*	Tates Locke, (16-30)				
	Bob MacKinnon, (3-4)				
	Joe Mullaney, (11-18)	30	52	–	–
1977-78*	Cotton Fitzsimmons	27	55	–	–
1978-79†	Gene Shue	43	39	–	–
1979-80†	Gene Shue	35	47	–	–
1980-81†	Paul Silas	36	46	–	–
1981-82†	Paul Silas	17	65	–	–
1982-83†	Paul Silas	25	57	–	–
1983-84†	Jim Lynam	30	52	–	–
1984-85	Jim Lynam, (22-39)				
	Don Chaney, (9-12)	31	51	–	–
1985-86	Don Chaney	32	50	–	–
1986-87	Don Chaney	12	70	–	–
1987-88	Gene Shue	17	65	–	–
1988-89	Gene Shue, (10-28)				
	Don Casey, (11-33)	21	61	–	–
1989-90	Don Casey	30	52	–	–
1990-91	Mike Schuler	31	51	–	–
1991-92	Mike Schuler, (21-24)				
	Mack Calvin, (1-1)				
	Larry Brown, (23-12)	45	37	2	3
1992-93	Larry Brown	41	41	2	3
1993-94	Bob Weiss	27	55	–	–
1994-95	Bill Fitch	17	65	–	–
1995-96	Bill Fitch	29	53	–	–
1996-97	Bill Fitch	36	46	0	3
1997-98	Bill Fitch	17	65	–	–
1998-99	Chris Ford	9	41	–	–
1999-00	Chris Ford, (11-34)				
	Jim Todd, (4-33)	15	67	–	–
TOTALS		855	1573	13	22

*Buffalo Braves

†San Diego Clippers.

Los Angeles Lakers

SEASON	COACH	Reg Sea W	Reg Sea L	Playoffs W	Playoffs L
1948-49*	John Kundla	44	16	8	2
1949-50*	John Kundla	51	17	10	2
1950-51*	John Kundla	44	24	3	4
1951-52*	John Kundla	40	26	9	4
1952-53*	John Kundla	48	22	9	3
1953-54*	John Kundla	46	26	9	4
1954-55*	John Kundla	40	32	3	4
1955-56*	John Kundla	33	39	1	2
1956-57*	John Kundla	34	38	2	3
1957-58*	George Mikan, (9-30)				
	John Kundla, (10-23)	19	53	–	–
1958-59*	John Kundla	33	39	6	7
1959-60*	John Castellani, (11-25)				
	Jim Pollard (14-25)	25	50	5	4
1960-61	Fred Schaus	36	43	6	6
1961-62	Fred Schaus	54	26	7	6
1962-63	Fred Schaus	53	27	6	7
1963-64	Fred Schaus	42	38	2	3
1964-65	Fred Schaus	49	31	5	6
1965-66	Fred Schaus	45	35	7	7
1966-67	Fred Schaus	36	45	0	3
1967-68	Bill van Breda Kolff	52	30	10	5
1968-69	Bill van Breda Kolff	55	27	11	7
1969-70	Joe Mullaney	46	36	11	7
1970-71	Joe Mullaney	48	34	5	7
1971-72	Bill Sharman	69	13	12	3
1972-73	Bill Sharman	60	22	9	8
1973-74	Bill Sharman	47	35	1	4
1974-75	Bill Sharman	30	52	–	–
1975-76	Bill Sharman	40	42	–	–
1976-77	Jerry West	53	29	4	7
1977-78	Jerry West	45	37	1	2
1978-79	Jerry West	47	35	3	5
1979-80	Jack McKinney, (10-4)				
	Paul Westhead, (50-18)	60	22	12	4
1980-81	Paul Westhead	54	28	1	2
1981-82	Paul Westhead, (7-4)				
	Pat Riley, (50-21)	57	25	12	2
1982-83	Pat Riley	58	24	8	7
1983-84	Pat Riley	54	28	14	7
1984-85	Pat Riley	62	20	15	4
1985-86	Pat Riley	62	20	8	6
1986-87	Pat Riley	65	17	15	3
1987-88	Pat Riley	62	20	15	9
1988-89	Pat Riley	57	25	11	4
1989-90	Pat Riley	63	19	4	5
1990-91	Mike Dunleavy	58	24	12	7
1991-92	Mike Dunleavy	43	39	1	3
1992-93	Randy Pfund	39	43	2	3

ALL-TIME TEAM RECORDS – Continued

		Reg Sea		Playoffs	
SEASON	COACH	W	L	W	L
1993-94	Randy Pfund, (27-37)				
	Bill Bertka, (1-1)				
	Magic Johnson, (5-11)	33	49	–	–
1994-95	Del Harris	48	34	5	5
1995-96	Del Harris	53	29	1	3
1996-97	Del Harris	56	26	4	5
1997-98	Del Harris	61	21	7	6
1998-99	Del Harris, (6-6)				
	Bill Bertka, (1-0)				
	Kurt Rambis, (24-13)	31	19	3	5
1999-00	Phil Jackson	67	15	15	8
TOTALS		2507	1566	330	230

*Minneapolis Lakers.

Miami Heat

SEASON	COACH	W	L	W	L
1988-89	Ron Rothstein	15	67	–	–
1989-90	Ron Rothstein	18	64	–	–
1990-91	Ron Rothstein	24	58	–	–
1991-92	Kevin Loughery	38	44	0	3
1992-93	Kevin Loughery	36	46	–	–
1993-94	Kevin Loughery	42	40	2	3
1994-95	Kevin Loughery, (17-29)				
	Alvin Gentry, (15-21)	32	50	–	–
1995-96	Pat Riley	42	40	0	3
1996-97	Pat Riley	61	21	8	9
1997-98	Pat Riley	55	27	2	3
1998-99	Pat Riley	33	17	2	3
1999-00	Pat Riley	52	30	6	4
TOTALS		448	504	20	28

Milwaukee Bucks

SEASON	COACH	W	L	W	L
1968-69	Larry Costello	27	55	–	–
1969-70	Larry Costello	56	26	5	5
1970-71	Larry Costello	66	16	12	2
1971-72	Larry Costello	63	19	6	5
1972-73	Larry Costello	60	22	2	4
1973-74	Larry Costello	59	23	11	5
1974-75	Larry Costello	38	44	–	–
1975-76	Larry Costello	38	44	1	2
1976-77	Larry Costello, (3-15)				
	Don Nelson, (27-37)	30	52	–	–
1977-78	Don Nelson	44	38	5	4
1978-79	Don Nelson	38	44	–	–
1979-80	Don Nelson	49	33	3	4
1980-81	Don Nelson	60	22	3	4
1981-82	Don Nelson	55	27	2	4
1982-83	Don Nelson	51	31	5	4
1983-84	Don Nelson	50	32	8	8
1984-85	Don Nelson	59	23	3	5
1985-86	Don Nelson	57	25	7	7
1986-87	Don Nelson	50	32	6	6
1987-88	Del Harris	42	40	2	3
1988-89	Del Harris	49	33	3	6
1989-90	Del Harris	44	38	1	3
1990-91	Del Harris	48	34	0	3
1991-92	Del Harris, (8-9)				
	Frank Hamblen, (23-42)	31	51	–	–
1992-93	Mike Dunleavy	28	54	–	–
1993-94	Mike Dunleavy	20	62	–	–
1994-95	Mike Dunleavy	34	48	–	–
1995-96	Mike Dunleavy	25	57	–	–
1996-97	Chris Ford	33	49	–	–
1997-98	Chris Ford	36	46	–	–
1998-99	George Karl	28	22	0	3
1999-00	George Karl	42	40	2	3
TOTALS		1410	1182	87	90

Minnesota Timberwolves

SEASON	COACH	W	L	W	L
1989-90	Bill Musselman	22	60	–	–
1990-91	Bill Musselman	29	53	–	–
1991-92	Jimmy Rodgers	15	67	–	–
1992-93	Jimmy Rodgers, (6-23)				
	Sidney Lowe, (13-40)	19	63	–	–
1993-94	Sidney Lowe	20	62	–	–
1994-95	Bill Blair	21	61	–	–
1995-96	Bill Blair, (6-14)				
	Flip Saunders, (20-42)	26	56	–	–
1996-97	Flip Saunders	40	42	0	3
1997-98	Flip Saunders	45	37	2	3
1998-99	Flip Saunders	25	25	1	3
1999-00	Flip Saunders	50	32	1	3
TOTALS		312	558	4	12

New Jersey Nets

SEASON	COACH	W	L	W	L
1967-68*	Max Zaslofsky	36	42	–	–
1968-69†	Max Zaslofsky	17	61	–	–
1969-70†	York Larese	39	45	3	4
1970-71†	Lou Carnesecca	40	44	2	4
1971-72†	Lou Carnesecca	44	40	10	9
1972-73†	Lou Carnesecca	30	54	1	4
1973-74†	Kevin Loughery	55	29	12	2
1974-75†	Kevin Loughery	58	26	1	4
1975-76†	Kevin Loughery	55	29	8	5
1976-77‡	Kevin Loughery	22	60	–	–
1977-78	Kevin Loughery	24	58	–	–
1978-79	Kevin Loughery	37	45	0	2
1979-80	Kevin Loughery	34	48	–	–
1980-81	Kevin Loughery, (12-23)				
	Bob MacKinnon, (12-35)	24	58	–	–
1981-82	Larry Brown	44	38	0	2
1982-83	Larry Brown, (47-29)				
	Bill Blair, (2-4)	49	33	0	2
1983-84	Stan Albeck	45	37	5	6
1984-85	Stan Albeck	42	40	0	3
1985-86	Dave Wohl	39	43	0	3
1986-87	Dave Wohl	24	58	–	–
1987-88	Dave Wohl, (2-13)				
	Bob MacKinnon, (10-29)				
	Willis Reed, (7-21)	19	63	–	–
1988-89	Willis Reed	26	56	–	–
1989-90	Bill Fitch	17	65	–	–
1990-91	Bill Fitch	26	56	–	–
1991-92	Bill Fitch	40	42	1	3
1992-93	Chuck Daly	43	39	2	3
1993-94	Chuck Daly	45	37	1	3
1994-95	Butch Beard	30	52	–	–
1995-96	Butch Beard	30	52	–	–
1996-97	John Calipari	26	56	–	–
1997-98	John Calipari	43	39	0	3
1998-99	John Calipari, (3-17)				
	Don Casey, (13-17)	16	34	–	–
1999-00	Don Casey	31	51	–	–
ABA TOTALS		374	370	37	32
NBA TOTALS		776	1160	9	30

*New Jersey Americans; club in ABA.
†New York Nets; club in ABA.
‡New York Nets; club in NBA.

New York Knickerbockers

SEASON	COACH	W	L	W	L
1946-47	Neil Cohalan	33	27	2	3
1947-48	Joe Lapchick	26	22	1	2
1948-49	Joe Lapchick	32	28	3	3
1949-50	Joe Lapchick	40	28	3	2
1950-51	Joe Lapchick	36	30	8	6
1951-52	Joe Lapchick	37	29	8	6
1952-53	Joe Lapchick	47	23	6	5
1953-54	Joe Lapchick	44	28	0	4
1954-55	Joe Lapchick	38	34	1	2
1955-56	Joe Lapchick, (26-25)				
	Vince Boryla, (9-12)	35	37	–	–
1956-57	Vince Boryla	36	36	–	–
1957-58	Vince Boryla	35	37	–	–
1958-59	Andrew Levane	40	32	0	2
1959-60	Andrew Levane, (8-19)				
	Carl Braun, (19-29)	27	48	–	–
1960-61	Carl Braun	21	58	–	–
1961-62	Eddie Donovan	29	51	–	–
1962-63	Eddie Donovan	21	59	–	–
1963-64	Eddie Donovan	22	58	–	–
1964-65	Eddie Donovan, (12-26)				
	Harry Gallatin, (19-23)	31	49	–	–
1965-66	Harry Gallatin, (6-15)				
	Dick McGuire, (24-35)	30	50	–	–
1966-67	Dick McGuire	36	45	1	3
1967-68	Dick McGuire, (15-22)				
	Red Holzman, (28-17)	43	39	2	4
1968-69	Red Holzman	54	28	6	4
1969-70	Red Holzman	60	22	12	7
1970-71	Red Holzman	52	30	7	5
1971-72	Red Holzman	48	34	9	7
1972-73	Red Holzman	57	25	12	5
1973-74	Red Holzman	49	33	5	7
1974-75	Red Holzman	40	42	1	2
1975-76	Red Holzman	38	44	–	–
1976-77	Red Holzman	40	42	–	–
1977-78	Willis Reed	43	39	2	4
1978-79	Willis Reed, (6-8)				
	Red Holzman, (25-43)	31	51	–	–
1979-80	Red Holzman	39	43	–	–
1980-81	Red Holzman	50	32	0	2
1981-82	Red Holzman	33	49	–	–
1982-83	Hubie Brown	44	38	2	4
1983-84	Hubie Brown	47	35	6	6
1984-85	Hubie Brown	24	58	–	–
1985-86	Hubie Brown	23	59	–	–
1986-87	Hubie Brown, (4-12)				
	Bob Hill, (20-46)	24	58	–	–
1987-88	Rick Pitino	38	44	1	3
1988-89	Rick Pitino	52	30	5	4
1989-90	Stu Jackson	45	37	4	6
1990-91	Stu Jackson, (7-8)				
	John MacLeod, (32-35)	39	43	0	3
1991-92	Pat Riley	51	31	6	6
1992-93	Pat Riley	60	22	9	6
1993-94	Pat Riley	57	25	14	11
1994-95	Pat Riley	55	27	6	5
1995-96	Don Nelson, (34-25)				
	Jeff Van Gundy, (13-10)	47	35	4	4
1996-97	Jeff Van Gundy	57	25	6	4

ALL-TIME TEAM RECORDS – Continued

SEASON	COACH	Reg Sea W	Reg Sea L	Playoffs W	Playoffs L
1997-98	Jeff Van Gundy	43	39	4	6
1998-99	Jeff Van Gundy	27	23	12	8
1999-00	Jeff Van Gundy	50	32	9	7
TOTALS		2156	2023	177	168

Orlando Magic

SEASON	COACH	Reg Sea W	Reg Sea L	Playoffs W	Playoffs L
1989-90	Matt Guokas	18	64	–	–
1990-91	Matt Guokas	31	51	–	–
1991-92	Matt Guokas	21	61	–	–
1992-93	Matt Guokas	41	41	–	–
1993-94	Brian Hill	50	32	0	3
1994-95	Brian Hill	57	25	11	10
1995-96	Brian Hill	60	22	7	5
1996-97	Brian Hill, (24-25)				
	Richie Adubato, (21-12)	45	37	2	3
1997-98	Chuck Daly	41	41	–	–
1998-99	Chuck Daly	33	17	1	3
1999-00	Doc Rivers	41	41	–	–
TOTALS		438	432	21	24

Philadelphia 76ers

SEASON	COACH	Reg Sea W	Reg Sea L	Playoffs W	Playoffs L
1949-50*	Al Cervi	51	13	6	5
1950-51*	Al Cervi	32	34	4	3
1951-52*	Al Cervi	40	26	3	4
1952-53*	Al Cervi	47	24	0	2
1953-54*	Al Cervi	42	30	9	4
1954-55*	Al Cervi	43	29	7	4
1955-56*	Al Cervi	35	37	5	4
1956-57*	Al Cervi, (4-8)				
	Paul Seymour, (34-26)	38	34	2	3
1957-58*	Paul Seymour	41	31	1	2
1958-59*	Paul Seymour	35	37	5	4
1959-60*	Paul Seymour	45	30	1	2
1960-61*	Alex Hannum	38	41	4	4
1961-62*	Alex Hannum	41	39	2	3
1962-63*	Alex Hannum	48	32	2	3
1963-64	Dolph Schayes	34	46	2	3
1964-65	Dolph Schayes	40	40	6	5
1965-66	Dolph Schayes	55	25	1	4
1966-67	Alex Hannum	68	13	11	4
1967-68	Alex Hannum	62	20	7	6
1968-69	Jack Ramsay	55	27	1	4
1969-70	Jack Ramsay	42	40	1	4
1970-71	Jack Ramsay	47	35	3	4
1971-72	Jack Ramsay	30	52	–	–
1972-73	Roy Rubin, (4-47)				
	Kevin Loughery, (5-26)	9	73	–	–
1973-74	Gene Shue	25	57	–	–
1974-75	Gene Shue	34	48	–	–
1975-76	Gene Shue	46	36	1	2
1976-77	Gene Shue	50	32	10	9
1977-78	Gene Shue, (2-4)				
	B. Cunningham, (53-23)	55	27	6	4
1978-79	Billy Cunningham	47	35	5	4
1979-80	Billy Cunningham	59	23	12	6
1980-81	Billy Cunningham	62	20	9	7
1981-82	Billy Cunningham	58	24	12	9
1982-83	Billy Cunningham	65	17	12	1
1983-84	Billy Cunningham	52	30	2	3
1984-85	Billy Cunningham	58	24	8	5
1985-86	Matt Guokas	54	28	6	6
1986-87	Matt Guokas	45	37	2	3
1987-88	Matt Guokas, (20-23)				
	Jim Lynam, (16-23)	36	46	–	–
1988-89	Jim Lynam	46	36	0	3
1989-90	Jim Lynam	53	29	4	6
1990-91	Jim Lynam	44	38	4	4
1991-92	Jim Lynam	35	47	–	–
1992-93	Doug Moe, (19-37)				
	Fred Carter, (7-19)	26	56	–	–
1993-94	Fred Carter	25	57	–	–
1994-95	John Lucas	24	58	–	–
1995-96	John Lucas	18	64	–	–
1996-97	Johnny Davis	22	60	–	–
1997-98	Larry Brown	31	51	–	–
1998-99	Larry Brown	28	22	3	5
1999-00	Larry Brown	49	33	5	5
TOTALS		2165	1843	183	163

*Syracuse Nationals.

Phoenix Suns

SEASON	COACH	Reg Sea W	Reg Sea L	Playoffs W	Playoffs L
1968-69	Johnny Kerr	16	66	–	–
1969-70	Johnny Kerr, (15-23)				
	Jerry Colangelo, (24-20)	39	43	3	4
1970-71	Cotton Fitzsimmons	48	34	–	–
1971-72	Cotton Fitzsimmons	49	33	–	–
1972-73	B. van Breda Kolff, (3-4)				
	Jerry Colangelo, (35-40)	38	44	–	–
1973-74	John MacLeod	30	52	–	–
1974-75	John MacLeod	32	50	–	–
1975-76	John MacLeod	42	40	10	9
1976-77	John MacLeod	34	48	–	–
1977-78	John MacLeod	49	33	0	2
1978-79	John MacLeod	50	32	9	6
1979-80	John MacLeod	55	27	3	5
1980-81	John MacLeod	57	25	3	4
1981-82	John MacLeod	46	36	2	5
1982-83	John MacLeod	53	29	1	2
1983-84	John MacLeod	41	41	9	8
1984-85	John MacLeod	36	46	0	3
1985-86	John MacLeod	32	50	–	–
1986-87	John MacLeod, (22-34)				
	D. Van Arsdale, (14-12)	36	46	–	–
1987-88	John Wetzel	28	54	–	–
1988-89	Cotton Fitzsimmons	55	27	7	5
1989-90	Cotton Fitzsimmons	54	28	9	7
1990-91	Cotton Fitzsimmons	55	27	1	3
1991-92	Cotton Fitzsimmons	53	29	4	4
1992-93	Paul Westphal	62	20	13	11
1993-94	Paul Westphal	56	26	6	4
1994-95	Paul Westphal	59	23	6	4
1995-96	Paul Westphal, (14-19)				
	C. Fitzsimmons, (27-22)	41	41	1	3
1996-97	Cotton Fitzsimmons, (0-8)				
	Danny Ainge, (40-34)	40	42	2	3
1997-98	Danny Ainge	56	26	1	3
1998-99	Danny Ainge	27	23	0	3
1999-00	Danny Ainge, (13-7)				
	Scott Skiles, (40-22)	53	29	4	5
TOTALS		1422	1170	94	103

Pittsburg Ironmen

SEASON	COACH	Reg Sea W	Reg Sea L	Playoffs W	Playoffs L
1946-47	Paul Birch	15	45	–	–

Portland Trail Blazers

SEASON	COACH	Reg Sea W	Reg Sea L	Playoffs W	Playoffs L
1970-71	Rolland Todd	29	53	–	–
1971-72	Rolland Todd, (12-44)				
	Stu Inman, (6-20)	18	64	–	–
1972-73	Jack McCloskey	21	61	–	–
1973-74	Jack McCloskey	27	55	–	–
1974-75	Lenny Wilkens	38	44	–	–
1975-76	Lenny Wilkens	37	45	–	–
1976-77	Jack Ramsay	49	33	14	5
1977-78	Jack Ramsay	58	24	2	4
1978-79	Jack Ramsay	45	37	1	2
1979-80	Jack Ramsay	38	44	1	2
1980-81	Jack Ramsay	45	37	1	2
1981-82	Jack Ramsay	42	40	–	–
1982-83	Jack Ramsay	46	36	3	4
1983-84	Jack Ramsay	48	34	2	3
1984-85	Jack Ramsay	42	40	4	5
1985-86	Jack Ramsay	40	42	1	3
1986-87	Mike Schuler	49	33	1	3
1987-88	Mike Schuler	53	29	1	3
1988-89	Mike Schuler, (25-22)				
	Rick Adelman, (14-21)	39	43	0	3
1989-90	Rick Adelman	59	23	12	9
1990-91	Rick Adelman	63	19	9	7
1991-92	Rick Adelman	57	25	13	8
1992-93	Rick Adelman	51	31	1	3
1993-94	Rick Adelman	47	35	1	3
1994-95	P.J. Carlesimo	44	38	0	3
1995-96	P.J. Carlesimo	44	38	2	3
1996-97	P.J. Carlesimo	49	33	1	3
1997-98	Mike Dunleavy	46	36	1	3
1998-99	Mike Dunleavy	35	15	7	6
1999-00	Mike Dunleavy	59	23	10	6
TOTALS		1318	1110	88	93

Providence Steamrollers

SEASON	COACH	Reg Sea W	Reg Sea L	Playoffs W	Playoffs L
1946-47	Robert Morris	28	32	–	–
1947-48	Albert Soar, (2-17)				
	Nat Hickey, (4-25)	6	42	–	–
1948-49	Ken Loeffler	12	48	–	–
TOTALS		46	122	–	–

Sacramento Kings

SEASON	COACH	Reg Sea W	Reg Sea L	Playoffs W	Playoffs L
1948-49*	Les Harrison	45	15	2	2
1949-50*	Les Harrison	51	17	0	2
1950-51*	Les Harrison	41	27	9	5
1951-52*	Les Harrison	41	25	3	3
1952-53*	Les Harrison	44	26	1	2
1953-54*	Les Harrison	44	28	3	3
1954-55*	Les Harrison	29	43	1	2
1955-56*	Bob Wanzer	31	41	–	–
1956-57*	Bob Wanzer	31	41	–	–
1957-58†	Bob Wanzer	33	39	0	2
1958-59†	Bob Wanzer, (3-15)				
	Tom Marshall, (16-38)	19	53	–	–
1959-60†	Tom Marshall	19	56	–	–
1960-61†	Charles Wolf	33	46	–	–
1961-62†	Charles Wolf	43	37	1	3
1962-63†	Charles Wolf	42	38	6	6
1963-64†	Jack McMahon	55	25	4	6

ALL-TIME TEAM RECORDS – Continued

		Reg Sea		Playoffs	
SEASON	COACH	W	L	W	L
1964-65†	Jack McMahon	48	32	1	3
1965-66†	Jack McMahon	45	35	2	3
1966-67†	Jack McMahon	39	42	1	3
1967-68†	Ed Jucker	39	43	–	–
1968-69†	Ed Jucker	41	41	–	–
1969-70†	Bob Cousy	36	46	–	–
1970-71†	Bob Cousy	33	49	–	–
1971-72†	Bob Cousy	30	52	–	–
1972-73‡	Bob Cousy	36	46	–	–
1973-74‡	Bob Cousy, (6-16)				
	Draff Young, (0-3)				
	Phil Johnson, (27-30)	33	49	–	–
1974-75‡	Phil Johnson	44	38	2	4
1975-76§	Phil Johnson	31	51	–	–
1976-77§	Phil Johnson	40	42	–	–
1977-78§	Phil Johnson, (13-24)				
	L. Staverman, (18-27)	31	51	–	–
1978-79§	Cotton Fitzsimmons	48	34	1	4
1979-80§	Cotton Fitzsimmons	47	35	1	2
1980-81§	Cotton Fitzsimmons	40	42	7	8
1981-82§	Cotton Fitzsimmons	30	52	–	–
1982-83§	Cotton Fitzsimmons	45	37	–	–
1983-84§	Cotton Fitzsimmons	38	44	0	3
1984-85§	Jack McKinney, (1-8)				
	Phil Johnson, (30-43)	31	51	–	–
1985-86	Phil Johnson	37	45	0	3
1986-87	Phil Johnson, (14-32)				
	Jerry Reynolds, (15-21)	29	53	–	–
1987-88	Bill Russell, (17-41)				
	Jerry Reynolds, (7-17)	24	58	–	–
1988-89	Jerry Reynolds	27	55	–	–
1989-90	Jerry Reynolds, 7-21				
	Dick Motta, (16-38)	23	59	–	–
1990-91	Dick Motta	25	57	–	–
1991-92	Dick Motta, (7-18)				
	Rex Hughes, (22-35)	29	53	–	–
1992-93	Garry St. Jean	25	57	–	–
1993-94	Garry St. Jean	28	54	–	–
1994-95	Garry St. Jean	39	43	–	–
1995-96	Garry St. Jean	39	43	1	3
1996-97	Garry St. Jean, (28-39)				
	Eddie Jordan, (6-9)	34	48	–	–
1997-98	Eddie Jordan	27	55	–	–
1998-99	Rick Adelman	27	23	2	3
1999-00	Rick Adelman	44	38	2	3
TOTALS		1863	2210	50	78

*Rochester Royals.
†Cincinnati Royals.
‡Kansas City/Omaha Kings.
§Kansas City Kings.

St. Louis Bombers

1946-47	Ken Loeffler	38	23	1	2
1947-48	Ken Loeffler	29	19	3	4
1948-49	Grady Lewis	29	31	0	2
1949-50	Grady Lewis	26	42	–	–
TOTALS		122	115	4	8

San Antonio Spurs

		Reg Sea		Playoffs	
SEASON	COACH	W	L	W	L
1967-68*	Cliff Hagan	46	32	4	4
1968-69*	Cliff Hagan	41	37	3	4
1969-70*	Cliff Hagan, (22-21)				
	Max Williams, (23-18)	45	39	2	4
1970-71†	Max Williams, (5-14)				
	Bill Blakely, (25-40)	30	54	0	4
1971-72†	Tom Nissalke	42	42	0	4
1972-73†	Babe McCarthy, (24-48)				
	Dave Brown, (4-8)	28	56	–	–
1973-74‡	Tom Nissalke	45	39	3	4
1974-75‡	Tom Nissalke, (17-10)				
	Bob Bass, (34-23)	51	33	2	4
1975-76‡	Bob Bass	50	34	3	4
1976-77	Doug Moe	44	38	0	2
1977-78	Doug Moe	52	30	2	4
1978-79	Doug Moe	48	34	7	7
1979-80	Doug Moe, (33-33)				
	Bob Bass, (8-8)	41	41	1	2
1980-81	Stan Albeck	52	30	3	4
1981-82	Stan Albeck	48	34	4	5
1982-83	Stan Albeck	53	29	6	5
1983-84	Morris McHone, (11-20)				
	Bob Bass, (26-25)	37	45	–	–
1984-85	Cotton Fitzsimmons	41	41	2	3
1985-86	Cotton Fitzsimmons	35	47	0	3
1986-87	Bob Weiss	28	54	–	–
1987-88	Bob Weiss	31	51	0	3
1988-89	Larry Brown	21	61	–	–
1989-90	Larry Brown	56	26	6	4
1990-91	Larry Brown	55	27	1	3
1991-92	Larry Brown, (21-17)				
	Bob Bass, (26-18)	47	35	0	3
1992-93	Jerry Tarkanian, (9-11)				
	Rex Hughes, (1-0)				
	John Lucas, (39-22)	49	33	5	5
1993-94	John Lucas	55	27	1	3
1994-95	Bob Hill	62	20	9	6
1995-96	Bob Hill	59	23	5	5
1996-97	Bob Hill, (3-15)				
	Gregg Popovich, (17-47)	20	62	–	–
1997-98	Gregg Popovich	56	26	4	5
1998-99	Gregg Popovich	37	13	15	2
1999-00	Gregg Popovich	53	29	1	3
ABA TOTALS		431	395	18	35
NBA TOTALS		1080	856	72	77

*Dallas Chaparrals; club in ABA.
†Texas Chaparrals; club in ABA.
‡San Antonio Spurs; club in ABA.

Seattle SuperSonics

		Reg Sea		Playoffs	
SEASON	COACH	W	L	W	L
1967-68	Al Bianchi	23	59	–	–
1968-69	Al Bianchi	30	52	–	–
1969-70	Lenny Wilkens	36	46	–	–
1970-71	Lenny Wilkens	38	44	–	–
1971-72	Lenny Wilkens	47	35	–	–
1972-73	Tom Nissalke, (13-32)				
	B. Buckwalter, (13-24)	26	56	–	–
1973-74	Bill Russell	36	46	–	–
1974-75	Bill Russell	43	39	4	5
1975-76	Bill Russell	43	39	2	4
1976-77	Bill Russell	40	42	–	–
1977-78	Bob Hopkins, (5-17)				
	Lenny Wilkens, (42-18)	47	35	13	9
1978-79	Lenny Wilkens	52	30	12	5
1979-80	Lenny Wilkens	56	26	7	8
1980-81	Lenny Wilkens	34	48	–	–
1981-82	Lenny Wilkens	52	30	3	5
1982-83	Lenny Wilkens	48	34	0	2
1983-84	Lenny Wilkens	42	40	2	3
1984-85	Lenny Wilkens	31	51	–	–
1985-86	Bernie Bickerstaff	31	51	–	–
1986-87	Bernie Bickerstaff	39	43	7	7
1987-88	Bernie Bickerstaff	44	38	2	3
1988-89	B. Bickerstaff, (46-30)	47	35	3	5
	*Tom Newell, (0-1)				
	*Bob Kloppenburg, (1-4)				
1989-90	Bernie Bickerstaff	41	41	–	–
1990-91	K.C. Jones	41	41	2	3
1991-92	K.C. Jones, (18-18)				
	Bob Kloppenburg, (2-2)				
	George Karl, (27-15)	47	35	4	5
1992-93	George Karl	55	27	10	9
1993-94	George Karl	63	19	2	3
1994-95	George Karl	57	25	1	3
1995-96	George Karl	64	18	13	8
1996-97	George Karl	57	25	6	6
1997-98	George Karl	61	21	4	6
1998-99	Paul Westphal	25	25	–	–
1999-00	Paul Westphal	45	37	2	3
TOTALS		1441	1233	99	102

*Substituted during Bickerstaff's illness

Sheboygan Redskins

1949-50	Ken Suesens	22	40	1	2

Toronto Huskies

1946-47	Ed Sadowski, (3-9)				
	Lew Hayman, (0-1)				
	Dick Fitzgerald, (2-1)				
	Robert Rolfe, (17-27)	22	38	–	–

Toronto Raptors

1995-96	Brendan Malone	21	61	–	–
1996-97	Darrell Walker	30	52	–	–
1997-98	Darrell Walker, (11-38)				
	Butch Carter, (5-28)	16	66	–	–
1998-99	Butch Carter	23	27	–	–
1999-00	Butch Carter	45	37	0	3
TOTALS		135	243	0	3

Utah Jazz

1974-75*	Scotty Robertson, (1-14)				
	Elgin Baylor, (0-1)				
	B. van Breda Kolff, (22-44)	23	59	–	–
1975-76*	Butch van Breda Kolff	38	44	–	–
1976-77*	B. van Breda Kolff, (14-12)				
	Elgin Baylor, (21-35)	35	47	–	–
1977-78*	Elgin Baylor	39	43	–	–
1978-79*	Elgin Baylor	26	56	–	–
1979-80	Tom Nissalke	24	58	–	–
1980-81	Tom Nissalke	28	54	–	–
1981-82	Tom Nissalke, (8-12)				
	Frank Layden, (17-45)	25	57	–	–

ALL-TIME TEAM RECORDS – Continued

SEASON	COACH	Reg Sea W	Reg Sea L	Playoffs W	Playoffs L
1982-83	Frank Layden	30	52	–	–
1983-84	Frank Layden	45	37	5	6
1984-85	Frank Layden	41	41	4	6
1985-86	Frank Layden	42	40	1	3
1986-87	Frank Layden	44	38	2	3
1987-88	Frank Layden	47	35	6	5
1988-89	Frank Layden, (11-6)				
	Jerry Sloan, (40-25)	51	31	0	3
1989-90	Jerry Sloan	55	27	2	3
1990-91	Jerry Sloan	54	28	4	5
1991-92	Jerry Sloan	55	27	9	7
1992-93	Jerry Sloan	47	35	2	3
1993-94	Jerry Sloan	53	29	8	8
1994-95	Jerry Sloan	60	22	2	3
1995-96	Jerry Sloan	55	27	10	8
1996-97	Jerry Sloan	64	18	13	7
1997-98	Jerry Sloan	62	20	13	7
1998-99	Jerry Sloan	37	13	5	6
1999-00	Jerry Sloan	55	27	4	6
TOTALS		1135	965	90	89

*New Orleans Jazz.

Vancouver Grizzlies

SEASON	COACH	Reg Sea W	Reg Sea L	Playoffs W	Playoffs L
1995-96	Brian Winters	15	67	–	–
1996-97	Brian Winters, (8-35)				
	Stu Jackson, (6-33)	14	68	–	–
1997-98	Brian Hill	19	63	–	–
1998-99	Brian Hill	8	42	–	–
1999-00	Brian Hill, (4-18)				
	Lionel Hollins, (18-42)	22	60	–	–
TOTALS		78	300	–	–

Washington Capitols

SEASON	COACH	Reg Sea W	Reg Sea L	Playoffs W	Playoffs L
1946-47	Red Auerbach	49	11	2	4
1947-48	Red Auerbach	28	20	–	–
1948-49	Red Auerbach	38	22	6	5
1949-50	Robert Feerick	32	36	0	2
1950-51*	Horace McKinney	10	25	–	–
TOTALS		157	114	8	11

*Team disbanded January 9.

Washington Wizards

SEASON	COACH	Reg Sea W	Reg Sea L	Playoffs W	Playoffs L
1961-62*	Jim Pollard	18	62	–	–
1962-63†	Jack McMahon, (12-26)				
	Bob Leonard, (13-29)	25	55	–	–
1963-64‡	Bob Leonard	31	49	–	–
1964-65‡	Buddy Jeannette	37	43	5	5
1965-66‡	Paul Seymour	38	42	0	3
1966-67‡	Mike Farmer, (1-8)				
	Buddy Jeannette, (3-13)				
	Gene Shue, (16-40)	20	61	–	–
1967-68‡	Gene Shue	36	46	–	–
1968-69‡	Gene Shue	57	25	0	4
1969-70‡	Gene Shue	50	32	3	4
1970-71‡	Gene Shue	42	40	8	10
1971-72‡	Gene Shue	38	44	2	4
1972-73‡	Gene Shue	52	30	1	4
1973-74§	K. C. Jones	47	35	3	4
1974-75°	K. C. Jones	60	22	8	9
1975-76°	K. C. Jones	48	34	3	4
1976-77°	Dick Motta	48	34	4	5
1977-78°	Dick Motta	44	38	14	7
1978-79°	Dick Motta	54	28	9	10
1979-80°	Dick Motta	39	43	0	2
1980-81°	Gene Shue	39	43	–	–
1981-82°	Gene Shue	43	39	3	4
1982-83°	Gene Shue	42	40	–	–
1983-84°	Gene Shue	35	47	1	3
1984-85°	Gene Shue	40	42	1	3
1985-86°	Gene Shue, (32-37)				
	Kevin Loughery, (7-6)	39	43	2	3
1986-87°	Kevin Loughery	42	40	0	3
1987-88°	Kevin Loughery, (8-19)				
	Wes Unseld, (30-25)	38	44	2	3
1988-89°	Wes Unseld	40	42	–	–
1989-90°	Wes Unseld	31	51	–	–
1990-91°	Wes Unseld	30	52	–	–
1991-92°	Wes Unseld	25	57	–	–
1992-93°	Wes Unseld	22	60	–	–
1993-94°	Wes Unseld	24	58	–	–
1994-95°	Jim Lynam	21	61	–	–
1995-96°	Jim Lynam	39	43	–	–
1996-97°	Jim Lynam, (22-24)				
	Bob Staak, (0-1)				
	Bernie Bickerstaff, (22-13)	44	38	0	3
1997-98	Bernie Bickerstaff	42	40	–	–
1998-99	Bernie Bickerstaff, (13-19)				
	Jim Brovelli, (5-13)	18	32	–	–
1999-00	Gar Heard, (14-30)				
	Darrell Walker, (15-23)	29	53	–	–
TOTALS		1467	1688	69	97

*Chicago Packers.
†Chicago Zephyrs.
‡Baltimore Bullets.
§Capital Bullets.
°Washington Bullets.

WATERLOO HAWKS

SEASON	COACH	Reg Sea W	Reg Sea L	Playoffs W	Playoffs L
1949-50	Charles Shipp, (8-27)				
	Jack Smiley, (11-16)	19	43	–	–

NBA POSTSEASON AWARDS

NBA MOST VALUABLE PLAYER

(Maurice Podoloff Trophy)

Selected by vote of NBA players through 1979-80; by writers and broadcasters since 1980-81.

1955-56 — Bob Pettit, St. Louis
1956-57 — Bob Cousy, Boston
1957-58 — Bill Russell, Boston
1958-59 — Bob Pettit, St. Louis
1959-60 — Wilt Chamberlain, Phil.
1960-61 — Bill Russell, Boston
1961-62 — Bill Russell, Boston
1962-63 — Bill Russell, Boston
1963-64 — Oscar Robertson, Cincinnati
1964-65 — Bill Russell, Boston
1965-66 — Wilt Chamberlain, Phil.
1966-67 — Wilt Chamberlain, Phil.
1967-68 — Wilt Chamberlain, Phil.
1968-69 — Wes Unseld, Baltimore
1969-70 — Willis Reed, New York
1970-71 — Kareem Abdul-Jabbar, Milw.
1971-72 — Kareem Abdul-Jabbar, Milw.
1972-73 — Dave Cowens, Boston
1973-74 — Kareem Abdul-Jabbar, Milw.
1974-75 — Bob McAdoo, Buffalo
1975-76 — Kareem Abdul-Jabbar, L.A.
1976-77 — Kareem Abdul-Jabbar, L.A.
1977-78 — Bill Walton, Portland
1978-79 — Moses Malone, Houston
1979-80 — Kareem Abdul-Jabbar, L.A.
1980-81 — Julius Erving, Philadelphia
1981-82 — Moses Malone, Houston
1982-83 — Moses Malone, Philadelphia
1983-84 — Larry Bird, Boston
1984-85 — Larry Bird, Boston
1985-86 — Larry Bird, Boston
1986-87 — Magic Johnson, L.A. Lakers
1987-88 — Michael Jordan, Chicago
1988-89 — Magic Johnson, L.A. Lakers
1989-90 — Magic Johnson, L.A. Lakers
1990-91 — Michael Jordan, Chicago
1991-92 — Michael Jordan, Chicago
1992-93 — Charles Barkley, Phoenix
1993-94 — Hakeem Olajuwon, Houston
1994-95 — David Robinson, San Antonio
1995-96 — Michael Jordan, Chicago
1996-97 — Karl Malone, Utah
1997-98 — Michael Jordan, Chicago
1998-99 — Karl Malone, Utah
1999-00 — Shaquille O'Neal, L.A. Lakers

IBM NBA COACH OF THE YEAR

(Red Auerbach Trophy)

Selected by writers and broadcasters.

1962-63 — Harry Gallatin, St. Louis
1963-64 — Alex Hannum, San Francisco
1964-65 — Red Auerbach, Boston
1965-66 — Dolph Schayes, Philadelphia

NBA POSTSEASON AWARDS – Continued

1966-67 — Johnny Kerr, Chicago
1967-68 — Richie Guerin, St. Louis
1968-69 — Gene Shue, Baltimore
1969-70 — Red Holzman, New York
1970-71 — Dick Motta, Chicago
1971-72 — Bill Sharman, Los Angeles
1972-73 — Tom Heinsohn, Boston
1973-74 — Ray Scott, Detroit
1974-75 — Phil Johnson, K.C.-Omaha
1975-76 — Bill Fitch, Cleveland
1976-77 — Tom Nissalke, Houston
1977-78 — Hubie Brown, Atlanta
1978-79 — Cotton Fitzsimmons, K.C.
1979-80 — Bill Fitch, Boston
1980-81 — Jack McKinney, Indiana
1981-82 — Gene Shue, Washington
1982-83 — Don Nelson, Milwaukee
1983-84 — Frank Layden, Utah
1984-85 — Don Nelson, Milwaukee
1985-86 — Mike Fratello, Atlanta
1986-87 — Mike Schuler, Portland
1987-88 — Doug Moe, Denver
1988-89 — Cotton Fitzsimmons, Pho.
1989-90 — Pat Riley, L.A. Lakers
1990-91 — Don Chaney, Houston
1991-92 — Don Nelson, Golden State
1992-93 — Pat Riley, New York
1993-94 — Lenny Wilkens, Atlanta
1994-95 — Del Harris, L.A. Lakers
1995-96 — Phil Jackson, Chicago
1996-97 — Pat Riley, Miami
1997-98 — Larry Bird, Indiana
1998-99 — Mike Dunleavy, Portland
1999-00 — Doc Rivers, Orlando

SCHICK NBA ROOKIE OF THE YEAR

(Eddie Gottlieb Trophy)

Selected by writers and broadcasters.

1952-53 — Don Meineke, Fort Wayne
1953-54 — Ray Felix, Baltimore
1954-55 — Bob Pettit, Milwaukee
1955-56 — Maurice Stokes, Rochester
1956-57 — Tom Heinsohn, Boston
1957-58 — Woody Sauldsberry, Phil.
1958-59 — Elgin Baylor, Minneapolis
1959-60 — Wilt Chamberlain, Phil.
1960-61 — Oscar Robertson, Cincinnati
1961-62 — Walt Bellamy, Chicago
1962-63 — Terry Dischinger, Chicago
1963-64 — Jerry Lucas, Cincinnati
1964-65 — Willis Reed, New York
1965-66 — Rick Barry, San Francisco
1966-67 — Dave Bing, Detroit
1967-68 — Earl Monroe, Baltimore
1968-69 — Wes Unseld, Baltimore
1969-70 — Kareem Abdul-Jabbar, Milw.
1970-71 — (tie) Dave Cowens, Boston
Geoff Petrie, Portland
1971-72 — Sidney Wicks, Portland
1972-73 — Bob McAdoo, Buffalo
1973-74 — Ernie DiGregorio, Buffalo
1974-75 — Jamaal Wilkes, Golden State
1975-76 — Alvan Adams, Phoenix
1976-77 — Adrian Dantley, Buffalo
1977-78 — Walter Davis, Phoenix
1978-79 — Phil Ford, Kansas City
1979-80 — Larry Bird, Boston
1980-81 — Darrell Griffith, Utah
1981-82 — Buck Williams, New Jersey
1982-83 — Terry Cummings, San Diego
1983-84 — Ralph Sampson, Houston
1984-85 — Michael Jordan, Chicago
1985-86 — Patrick Ewing, New York
1986-87 — Chuck Person, Indiana
1987-88 — Mark Jackson, New York
1988-89 — Mitch Richmond, Golden St.
1989-90 — David Robinson, San Antonio
1990-91 — Derrick Coleman, New Jersey
1991-92 — Larry Johnson, Charlotte
1992-93 — Shaquille OÄNeal, Orlando
1993-94 — Chris Webber, Golden State
1994-95 — (tie) Grant Hill, Detroit
Jason Kidd, Dallas
1995-96 — Damon Stoudamire, Toronto
1996-97 — Allen Iverson, Philadelphia
1997-98 — Tim Duncan, San Antonio
1998-99 — Vince Carter, Toronto
1999-00 — (tie) Elton Brand, Chicago
Steve Francis, Houston

NBA MOST IMPROVED PLAYER

Selected by writers and broadcasters.

1985-86 — Alvin Robertson, San Antonio
1986-87 — Dale Ellis, Seattle
1987-88 — Kevin Duckworth, Portland
1988-89 — Kevin Johnson, Phoenix
1989-90 — Rony Seikaly, Miami
1990-91 — Scott Skiles, Orlando
1991-92 — Pervis Ellison, Washington
1992-93 — Mahmoud Abdul-Rauf, Den.
1993-94 — Don MacLean, Washington
1994-95 — Dana Barros, Philadelphia
1995-96 — Gheorghe Muresan, Was.
1996-97 — Isaac Austin, Miami
1997-98 — Alan Henderson, Atlanta
1998-99 — Darrell Armstrong, Orlando
1999-00 — Jalen Rose, Indiana

NBA EXECUTIVE OF THE YEAR

Selected by NBA executives for The Sporting News.

1972-73 — Joe Axelson, K.C.-Omaha
1973-74 — Eddie Donovan, Buffalo
1974-75 — Dick Vertlieb, Golden State
1975-76 — Jerry Colangelo, Phoenix
1976-77 — Ray Patterson, Houston
1977-78 — Angelo Drossos, San Ant.
1978-79 — Bob Ferry, Washington
1979-80 — Red Auerbach, Boston
1980-81 — Jerry Colangelo, Phoenix
1981-82 — Bob Ferry, Washington
1982-83 — Zollie Volchok, Seattle
1983-84 — Frank Layden, Utah
1984-85 — Vince Boryla, Denver
1985-86 — Stan Kasten, Atlanta
1986-87 — Stan Kasten, Atlanta
1987-88 — Jerry Krause, Chicago
1988-89 — Jerry Colangelo, Phoenix
1989-90 — Bob Bass, San Antonio
1990-91 — Bucky Buckwalter, Portland
1991-92 — Wayne Embry, Cleveland
1992-93 — Jerry Colangelo, Phoenix
1993-94 — Bob Whitsitt, Seattle
1994-95 — Jerry West, L.A. Lakers
1995-96 — Jerry Krause, Chicago
1996-97 — Bob Bass, Charlotte
1997-98 — Wayne Embry, Cleveland
1998-99 — Geoff Petrie, Sacramento
1999-00 — John Gabriel, Orlando

J. WALTER KENNEDY CITIZENSHIP AWARD

Selected by the Pro Basketball Writers Association.

1974-75 — Wes Unseld, Washington
1975-76 — Slick Watts, Seattle
1976-77 — Dave Bing, Washington
1977-78 — Bob Lanier, Detroit
1978-79 — Calvin Murphy, Houston
1979-80 — Austin Carr, Cleveland
1980-81 — Mike Glenn, New York
1981-82 — Kent Benson, Detroit
1982-83 — Julius Erving, Philadelphia
1983-84 — Frank Layden, Utah
1984-85 — Dan Issel, Denver
1985-86 — (tie) Michael Cooper, L.A. Lakers
Rory Sparrow, New York
1986-87 — Isiah Thomas, Detroit
1987-88 — Alex English, Denver
1988-89 — Thurl Bailey, Utah
1989-90 — Doc Rivers, Atlanta
1990-91 — Kevin Johnson, Phoenix
1991-92 — Magic Johnson, L.A. Lakers
1992-93 — Terry Porter, Portland
1993-94 — Joe Dumars, Detroit
1994-95 — Joe O'Toole, Atlanta
1995-96 — Chris Dudley, Portland
1996-97 — P.J. Brown, Miami
1997-98 — Steve Smith, Atlanta
1998-99 — Brian Grant, Portland
1999-00 — Vlade Divac, Sacramento

NBA DEFENSIVE PLAYER OF THE YEAR

Selected by writers and broadcasters.

1982-83 — Sidney Moncrief, Milwaukee
1983-84 — Sidney Moncrief, Milwaukee
1984-85 — Mark Eaton, Utah
1985-86 — Alvin Robertson, San Ant.
1986-87 — Michael Cooper, L.A. Lakers
1987-88 — Michael Jordan, Chicago
1988-89 — Mark Eaton, Utah
1989-90 — Dennis Rodman, Detroit
1990-91 — Dennis Rodman, Detroit
1991-92 — David Robinson, San Ant.
1992-93 — Hakeem Olajuwon, Houston
1993-94 — Hakeem Olajuwon, Houston
1994-95 — Dikembe Mutombo, Denver
1995-96 — Gary Payton, Seattle
1996-97 — Dikembe Mutombo, Atlanta
1997-98 — Dikembe Mutombo, Atlanta
1998-99 — Alonzo Mourning, Miami
1999-00 — Alonzo Mourning, Miami

NBA SIXTH MAN AWARD

Selected by writers and broadcasters.

1982-83 — Bobby Jones, Philadelphia
1983-84 — Kevin McHale, Boston
1984-85 — Kevin McHale, Boston
1985-86 — Bill Walton, Boston
1986-87 — Ricky Pierce, Milwaukee
1987-88 — Roy Tarpley, Dallas

NBA POSTSEASON AWARDS – Continued

1988-89 — Eddie Johnson, Phoenix
1989-90 — Ricky Pierce, Milwaukee
1990-91 — Detlef Schrempf, Indiana
1991-92 — Detlef Schrempf, Indiana
1992-93 — Clifford Robinson, Portland
1993-94 — Dell Curry, Charlotte
1994-95 — Anthony Mason, New York
1995-96 — Toni Kukoc, Chicago
1996-97 — John Starks, New York
1997-98 — Danny Manning, Phoenix
1998-99 — Darrell Armstrong, Orlando
1999-00 — Rodney Rogers, Phoenix

IBM AWARD

Determined by computer formula.

1983-84 — Magic Johnson, Los Angeles
1984-85 — Michael Jordan, Chicago
1985-86 — Charles Barkley, Philadelphia
1986-87 — Charles Barkley, Philadelphia
1987-88 — Charles Barkley, Philadelphia
1988-89 — Michael Jordan, Chicago
1989-90 — David Robinson, San Antonio
1990-91 — David Robinson, San Antonio
1991-92 — Dennis Rodman, Detroit
1992-93 — Hakeem Olajuwon, Houston
1993-94 — David Robinson, San Antonio
1994-95 — David Robinson, San Antonio
1995-96 — David Robinson, San Antonio
1996-97 — Grant Hill, Detroit
1997-98 — Karl Malone, Utah
1998-99 — Dikembe Mutombo, Atlanta
1999-00 — Shaquille O'Neal, L.A. Lakers

NBA FINALS MOST VALUABLE PLAYER

Selected by writers and broadcasters.

1969 — Jerry West, Los Angeles
1970 — Willis Reed, New York
1971 — Kareem Abdul-Jabbar, Milwaukee
1972 — Wilt Chamberlain, Los Angeles
1973 — Willis Reed, New York
1974 — John Havlicek, Boston
1975 — Rick Barry, Golden State
1976 — Jo Jo White, Boston
1977 — Bill Walton, Portland
1978 — Wes Unseld, Washington
1979 — Dennis Johnson, Seattle
1980 — Magic Johnson, Los Angeles
1981 — Cedric Maxwell, Boston
1982 — Magic Johnson, Los Angeles
1983 — Moses Malone, Philadelphia
1984 — Larry Bird, Boston
1985 — K. Abdul-Jabbar, L.A. Lakers
1986 — Larry Bird, Boston
1987 — Magic Johnson, L.A. Lakers
1988 — James Worthy, L.A. Lakers
1989 — Joe Dumars, Detroit
1990 — Isiah Thomas, Detroit
1991 — Michael Jordan, Chicago
1992 — Michael Jordan, Chicago
1993 — Michael Jordan, Chicago
1994 — Hakeem Olajuwon, Houston
1995 — Hakeem Olajuwon, Houston
1996 — Michael Jordan, Chicago
1997 — Michael Jordan, Chicago
1998 — Michael Jordan, Chicago
1999 — Tim Duncan, San Antonio
2000 — Shaquille O'Neal, L.A. Lakers

NBA SPORTMANSHIP AWARD

Selected by writers and broadcasters.

Inaugural — Joe Dumars

1996-97 — Terrell Brandon
1996-97 Divisional winners:
Atlantic — Buck Williams, New York
Central — Terrell Brandon, Cleveland
Midwest — Jeff Hornacek, Utah
Pacific — Mitch Richmond, Sacramento

1997-98 — Avery Johnson, San Antonio
1997-98 Divisional winners:
Atlantic — Allan Houston, New York
Central — Bobby Phills, Charlotte
Midwest — Avery Johnson, San Antonio
Pacific — Hersey Hawkins, Seattle

1998-99 — Hersey Hawkins, Seattle
1998-99 Divisional winners:
Atlantic — Eric Snow, Philadelphia
Central — Vince Carter, Toronto
Midwest — Kevin Garnett, Minnesota
Pacific — Hersey Hawkins, Seattle

1999-2000 — Eric Snow, Philadelphia
Atlantic — Eric Snow, Philadelphia
Central — LaPhonso Ellis, Atlanta
Midwest — Hakeen Olajuwon, Houston
Pacific — Jason Kidd, Phoenix

ALL-NBA TEAMS

Selected by writers and broadcasters

1946-47

FIRST
Joe Fulks, Philadelphia
Bob Feerick, Washington
Stan Miasek, Detroit
Bones McKinney, Washington
Max Zaslofsky, Chicago
SECOND
Ernie Calverley, Providence
Frank Baumholtz, Cleveland
John Logan, St. Louis
Chuck Halbert, Chicago
Fred Scolari, Washington

1947-48

FIRST
Joe Fulks, Philadelphia
Max Zaslofsky, Chicago
Ed Sadowski, Boston
Howie Dallmar, Philadelphia
Bob Feerick, Washington
SECOND
John Logan, St. Louis
Carl Braun, New York
Stan Miasek, Chicago
Fred Scolari, Washington
Buddy Jeannette, Baltimore

1948-49

FIRST
George Mikan, Minneapolis
Joe Fulks, Philadelphia
Bob Davies, Rochester
Max Zaslofsky, Chicago
Jim Pollard, Minneapolis
SECOND
Arnie Risen, Rochester
Bob Feerick, Washington
Bones McKinney, Washington
Ken Sailors, Providence
John Logan, St. Louis

1949-50

FIRST
George Mikan, Minneapolis
Jim Pollard, Minneapolis
Alex Groza, Indianapolis
Bob Davies, Rochester
Max Zaslofsky, Chicago
SECOND
Frank Brian, Anderson
Fred Schaus, Fort Wayne
Dolph Schayes, Syracuse
Al Cervi, Syracuse
Ralph Beard, Indianapolis

1950-51

FIRST
George Mikan, Minneapolis
Alex Groza, Indianapolis
Ed Macauley, Boston
Bob Davies, Rochester
Ralph Beard, Indianapolis
SECOND
Dolph Schayes, Syracuse
Frank Brian, Tri-Cities
Vern Mikkelsen, Minneapolis
Joe Fulks, Philadelphia
Dick McGuire, New York

1951-52

FIRST
George Mikan, Minneapolis
Ed Macauley, Boston
Paul Arizin, Philadelphia
Bob Cousy, Boston
Bob Davies, Rochester
Dolph Schayes, Syracuse
SECOND
Larry Foust, Fort Wayne
Vern Mikkelsen, Minneapolis
Jim Pollard, Minneapolis
Bob Wanzer, Rochester
Andy Phillip, Philadelphia

1952-53

FIRST
George Mikan, Minneapolis
Bob Cousy, Boston
Neil Johnston, Philadelphia
Ed Macauley, Boston
Dolph Schayes, Syracuse
SECOND
Bill Sharman, Boston
Vern Mikkelsen, Minneapolis
Bob Wanzer, Rochester
Bob Davies, Rochester
Andy Phillip, Philadelphia

ALL-NBA TEAMS – Continued

1953-54
FIRST
Bob Cousy, Boston
Neil Johnston, Philadelphia
George Mikan, Minneapolis
Dolph Schayes, Syracuse
Harry Gallatin, New York
SECOND
Ed Macauley, Boston
Jim Pollard, Minneapolis
Carl Braun, New York
Bob Wanzer, Rochester
Paul Seymour, Syracuse

1954-55
FIRST
Neil Johnston, Philadelphia
Bob Cousy, Boston
Dolph Schayes, Syracuse
Bob Pettit, Milwaukee
Larry Foust, Fort Wayne
SECOND
Vern Mikkelsen, Minneapolis
Harry Gallatin, New York
Paul Seymour, Syracuse
Slater Martin, Minneapolis
Bill Sharman, Boston

1955-56
FIRST
Bob Pettit, St. Louis
Paul Arizin, Philadelphia
Neil Johnston, Philadelphia
Bob Cousy, Boston
Bill Sharman, Boston
SECOND
Dolph Schayes, Syracuse
Maurice Stokes, Rochester
Clyde Lovellette, Minneapolis
Slater Martin, Minneapolis
Jack George, Philadelphia

1956-57
FIRST
Paul Arizin, Philadelphia
Dolph Schayes, Syracuse
Bob Pettit, St. Louis
Bob Cousy, Boston
Bill Sharman, Boston
SECOND
George Yardley, Fort Wayne
Maurice Stokes, Rochester
Neil Johnston, Philadelphia
Dick Garmaker, Minneapolis
Slater Martin, St. Louis

1957-58
FIRST
Dolph Schayes, Syracuse
George Yardley, Detroit
Bob Pettit, St. Louis
Bob Cousy, Boston
Bill Sharman, Boston
SECOND
Cliff Hagan, St. Louis
Maurice Stokes, Cincinnati
Bill Russell, Boston
Tom Gola, Philadelphia
Slater Martin, St. Louis

1958-59
FIRST
Bob Pettit, St. Louis
Elgin Baylor, Minneapolis
Bill Russell, Boston
Bob Cousy, Boston
Bill Sharman, Boston
SECOND
Paul Arizin, Philadelphia
Cliff Hagan, St. Louis
Dolph Schayes, Syracuse
Slater Martin, St. Louis
Richie Guerin, New York

1959-60
FIRST
Bob Pettit, St. Louis
Elgin Baylor, Minneapolis
Wilt Chamberlain, Philadelphia
Bob Cousy, Boston
Gene Shue, Detroit
SECOND
Jack Twyman, Cincinnati
Dolph Schayes, Syracuse
Bill Russell, Boston
Richie Guerin, New York
Bill Sharman, Boston

1960-61
FIRST
Elgin Baylor, Los Angeles
Bob Pettit, St. Louis
Wilt Chamberlain, Philadelphia
Bob Cousy, Boston
Oscar Robertson, Cincinnati
SECOND
Dolph Schayes, Syracuse
Tom Heinsohn, Boston
Bill Russell, Boston
Larry Costello, Syracuse
Gene Shue, Detroit

1961-62
FIRST
Bob Pettit, St. Louis
Elgin Baylor, Los Angeles
Wilt Chamberlain, Philadelphia
Jerry West, Los Angeles
Oscar Robertson, Cincinnati
SECOND
Tom Heinsohn, Boston
Jack Twyman, Cincinnati
Bill Russell, Boston
Richie Guerin, New York
Bob Cousy, Boston

1962-63
FIRST
Elgin Baylor, Los Angeles
Bob Pettit, St. Louis
Bill Russell, Boston
Oscar Robertson, Cincinnati
Jerry West, Los Angeles
SECOND
Tom Heinsohn, Boston
Bailey Howell, Detroit
Wilt Chamberlain, San Francisco
Bob Cousy, Boston
Hal Greer, Syracuse

1963-64
FIRST
Bob Pettit, St. Louis
Elgin Baylor, Los Angeles
Wilt Chamberlain, San Francisco
Oscar Robertson, Cincinnati
Jerry West, Los Angeles
SECOND
Tom Heinsohn, Boston
Jerry Lucas, Cincinnati
Bill Russell, Boston
John Havlicek, Boston
Hal Greer, Philadelphia

1964-65
FIRST
Elgin Baylor, Los Angeles
Jerry Lucas, Cincinnati
Bill Russell, Boston
Oscar Robertson, Cincinnati
Jerry West, Los Angeles
SECOND
Bob Pettit, St. Louis
Gus Johnson, Baltimore
Wilt Chamberlain, S.F.-Phila.
Sam Jones, Boston
Hal Greer, Philadelphia

1965-66
FIRST
Rick Barry, San Francisco
Jerry Lucas, Cincinnati
Wilt Chamberlain, Philadelphia
Oscar Robertson, Cincinnati
Jerry West, Los Angeles
SECOND
John Havlicek, Boston
Gus Johnson, Baltimore
Bill Russell, Boston
Sam Jones, Boston
Hal Greer, Philadelphia

1966-67
FIRST
Rick Barry, San Francisco
Elgin Baylor, Los Angeles
Wilt Chamberlain, Philadelphia
Jerry West, Los Angeles
Oscar Robertson, Cincinnati
SECOND
Willis Reed, New York
Jerry Lucas, Cincinnati
Bill Russell, Boston
Hal Greer, Philadelphia
Sam Jones, Boston

1967-68
FIRST
Elgin Baylor, Los Angeles
Jerry Lucas, Cincinnati
Wilt Chamberlain, Philadelphia
Dave Bing, Detroit
Oscar Robertson, Cincinnati
SECOND
Willis Reed, New York
John Havlicek, Boston
Bill Russell, Boston
Hal Greer, Philadelphia
Jerry West, Los Angeles

1968-69
FIRST
Billy Cunningham, Philadelphia
Elgin Baylor, Los Angeles
Wes Unseld, Baltimore
Earl Monroe, Baltimore
Oscar Robertson, Cincinnati
SECOND
John Havlicek, Boston
Dave DeBusschere, Detroit-New York
Willis Reed, New York
Hal Greer, Philadelphia
Jerry West, Los Angeles

1969-70
FIRST
Billy Cunningham, Philadelphia
Connie Hawkins, Phoenix
Willis Reed, New York
Jerry West, Los Angeles
Walt Frazier, New York
SECOND
John Havlicek, Boston
Gus Johnson, Baltimore
Kareem Abdul-Jabbar, Milwaukee
Lou Hudson, Atlanta
Oscar Robertson, Cincinnati

1970-71
FIRST
John Havlicek, Boston
Billy Cunningham, Philadelphia
Kareem Abdul-Jabbar, Milwaukee
Jerry West, Los Angeles
Dave Bing, Detroit
SECOND
Gus Johnson, Baltimore
Bob Love, Chicago
Willis Reed, New York
Walt Frazier, New York
Oscar Robertson, Milwaukee

1971-72
FIRST
John Havlicek, Boston
Spencer Haywood, Seattle
Kareem Abdul-Jabbar, Milwaukee
Jerry West, Los Angeles
Walt Frazier, New York
SECOND
Bob Love, Chicago
Billy Cunningham, Philadelphia

For additional records, please log on to NBA.com.

ALL-NBA TEAMS – Continued

Wilt Chamberlain, Los Angeles
Nate Archibald, Cincinnati
Archie Clark, Phil.-Balt.

1972-73
FIRST
John Havlicek, Boston
Spencer Haywood, Seattle
Kareem Abdul-Jabbar, Milwaukee
Nate Archibald, Kansas City-Omaha
Jerry West, Los Angeles
SECOND
Elvin Hayes, Baltimore
Rick Barry, Golden State
Dave Cowens, Boston
Walt Frazier, New York
Pete Maravich, Atlanta

1973-74
FIRST
John Havlicek, Boston
Rick Barry, Golden State
Kareem Abdul-Jabbar, Milwaukee
Walt Frazier, New York
Gail Goodrich, Los Angeles
SECOND
Elvin Hayes, Capital
Spencer Haywood, Seattle
Bob McAdoo, Buffalo
Dave Bing, Detroit
Norm Van Lier, Chicago

1974-75
FIRST
Rick Barry, Golden State
Elvin Hayes, Washington
Bob McAdoo, Buffalo
Nate Archibald, Kansas City-Omaha
Walt Frazier, New York
SECOND
John Havlicek, Boston
Spencer Haywood, Seattle
Dave Cowens, Boston
Phil Chenier, Washington
Jo Jo White, Boston

1975-76
FIRST
Rick Barry, Golden State
George McGinnis, Philadelphia
Kareem Abdul-Jabbar, Los Angeles
Nate Archibald, Kansas City
Pete Maravich, New Orleans
SECOND
Elvin Hayes, Washington
John Havlicek, Boston
Dave Cowens, Boston
Randy Smith, Buffalo
Phil Smith, Golden State

1976-77
FIRST
Elvin Hayes, Washington
David Thompson, Denver
Kareem Abdul-Jabbar, Los Angeles
Pete Maravich, New Orleans
Paul Westphal, Phoenix
SECOND
Julius Erving, Philadelphia
George McGinnis, Philadelphia
Bill Walton, Portland
George Gervin, San Antonio
Jo Jo White, Boston

1977-78
FIRST
Leonard Robinson, New Orleans
Julius Erving, Philadelphia
Bill Walton, Portland
George Gervin, San Antonio
David Thompson, Denver
SECOND
Walter Davis, Phoenix
Maurice Lucas, Portland
Kareem Abdul-Jabbar, Los Angeles
Paul Westphal, Phoenix
Pete Maravich, New Orleans

1978-79
FIRST
Marques Johnson, Milwaukee
Elvin Hayes, Washington
Moses Malone, Houston
George Gervin, San Antonio
Paul Westphal, Phoenix
SECOND
Walter Davis, Phoenix
Bobby Dandridge, Washington
Kareem Abdul-Jabbar, Los Angeles
World B. Free, San Diego
Phil Ford, Kansas City

1979-80
FIRST
Julius Erving, Philadelphia
Larry Bird, Boston
Kareem Abdul-Jabbar, Los Angeles
George Gervin, San Antonio
Paul Westphal, Phoenix
SECOND
Dan Roundfield, Atlanta
Marques Johnson, Milwaukee
Moses Malone, Houston
Dennis Johnson, Seattle
Gus Williams, Seattle

1980-81
FIRST
Julius Erving, Philadelphia
Larry Bird, Boston
Kareem Abdul-Jabbar, Los Angeles
George Gervin, San Antonio
Dennis Johnson, Phoenix
SECOND
Marques Johnson, Milwaukee
Adrian Dantley, Utah
Moses Malone, Houston
Otis Birdsong, Kansas City
Nate Archibald, Boston

1981-82
FIRST
Larry Bird, Boston
Julius Erving, Philadelphia
Moses Malone, Houston
George Gervin, San Antonio
Gus Williams, Seattle
SECOND
Alex English, Denver
Bernard King, Golden State
Robert Parish, Boston
Magic Johnson, Los Angeles
Sidney Moncrief, Milwaukee

1982-83
FIRST
Larry Bird, Boston
Julius Erving, Philadelphia
Moses Malone, Philadelphia
Magic Johnson, Los Angeles
Sidney Moncrief, Milwaukee
SECOND
Alex English, Denver
Buck Williams, New Jersey
Kareem Abdul-Jabbar, Los Angeles
George Gervin, San Antonio
Isiah Thomas, Detroit

1983-84
FIRST
Larry Bird, Boston
Bernard King, New York
Kareem Abdul-Jabbar, Los Angeles
Magic Johnson, Los Angeles
Isiah Thomas, Detroit
SECOND
Julius Erving, Philadelphia
Adrian Dantley, Utah
Moses Malone, Philadelphia
Sidney Moncrief, Milwaukee
Jim Paxson, Portland

1984-85
FIRST
Larry Bird, Boston
Bernard King, New York
Moses Malone, Philadelphia
Magic Johnson, L.A. Lakers
Isiah Thomas, Detroit
SECOND
Terry Cummings, Milwaukee
Ralph Sampson, Houston
Kareem Abdul-Jabbar, L.A. Lakers
Michael Jordan, Chicago
Sidney Moncrief, Milwaukee

1985-86
FIRST
Larry Bird, Boston
Dominique Wilkins, Atlanta
Kareem Abdul-Jabbar, L.A. Lakers
Magic Johnson, L.A. Lakers
Isiah Thomas, Detroit
SECOND
Charles Barkley, Philadelphia
Alex English, Denver
Hakeem Olajuwon, Houston
Sidney Moncrief, Milwaukee
Alvin Robertson, San Antonio

1986-87
FIRST
Larry Bird, Boston
Kevin McHale, Boston
Hakeem Olajuwon, Houston
Magic Johnson, L.A. Lakers
Michael Jordan, Chicago
SECOND
Dominique Wilkins, Atlanta
Charles Barkley, Philadelphia
Moses Malone, Washington
Isiah Thomas, Detroit
Fat Lever, Denver

1987-88
FIRST
Larry Bird, Boston
Charles Barkley, Philadelphia
Hakeem Olajuwon, Houston
Michael Jordan, Chicago
Magic Johnson, L.A. Lakers
SECOND
Karl Malone, Utah
Dominique Wilkins, Atlanta
Patrick Ewing, New York
Clyde Drexler, Portland
John Stockton, Utah

1988-89
FIRST
Karl Malone, Utah
Charles Barkley, Philadelphia
Hakeem Olajuwon, Houston
Magic Johnson, L.A. Lakers
Michael Jordan, Chicago
SECOND
Tom Chambers, Phoenix
Chris Mullin, Golden State
Patrick Ewing, New York
John Stockton, Utah
Kevin Johnson, Phoenix
THIRD
Dominique Wilkins, Atlanta
Terry Cummings, Milwaukee
Robert Parish, Boston
Dale Ellis, Seattle
Mark Price, Cleveland

1989-90
FIRST
Karl Malone, Utah
Charles Barkley, Philadelphia
Patrick Ewing, New York
Magic Johnson, L.A. Lakers
Michael Jordan, Chicago
SECOND
Larry Bird, Boston
Tom Chambers, Phoenix
Hakeem Olajuwon, Houston
John Stockton, Utah
Kevin Johnson, Phoenix

ALL-NBA TEAMS – Continued

THIRD
James Worthy, L.A. Lakers
Chris Mullin, Golden State
David Robinson, San Antonio
Clyde Drexler, Portland
Joe Dumars, Detroit

1990-91
FIRST
Karl Malone, Utah
Charles Barkley, Philadelphia
David Robinson, San Antonio
Michael Jordan, Chicago
Magic Johnson, L.A. Lakers
SECOND
Dominique Wilkins, Atlanta
Chris Mullin, Golden State
Patrick Ewing, New York
Kevin Johnson, Phoenix
Clyde Drexler, Portland
THIRD
James Worthy, L.A. Lakers
Bernard King, Washington
Hakeem Olajuwon, Houston
John Stockton, Utah
Joe Dumars, Detroit

1991-92
FIRST
Karl Malone, Utah
Chris Mullin, Golden State
David Robinson, San Antonio
Michael Jordan, Chicago
Clyde Drexler, Portland
SECOND
Scottie Pippen, Chicago
Charles Barkley, Philadelphia
Patrick Ewing, New York
Tim Hardaway, Golden State
John Stockton, Utah
THIRD
Dennis Rodman, Detroit
Kevin Willis, Atlanta
Brad Daugherty, Cleveland
Mark Price, Cleveland
Kevin Johnson, Phoenix

1992-93
FIRST
Charles Barkley, Phoenix
Karl Malone, Utah
Hakeem Olajuwon, Houston
Michael Jordan, Chicago
Mark Price, Cleveland
SECOND
Dominique Wilkins, Atlanta
Larry Johnson, Charlotte
Patrick Ewing, New York
John Stockton, Utah
Joe Dumars, Detroit
THIRD
Scottie Pippen, Chicago
Derrick Coleman, New Jersey
David Robinson, San Antonio
Tim Hardaway, Golden State
Drazen Petrovic, New Jersey

1993-94
FIRST
Scottie Pippen, Chicago
Karl Malone, Utah
Hakeem Olajuwon, Houston
John Stockton, Utah
Latrell Sprewell, Golden State
SECOND
Shawn Kemp, Seattle
Charles Barkley, Phoenix
David Robinson, San Antonio
Mitch Richmond, Sacramento
Kevin Johnson, Phoenix
THIRD
Derrick Coleman, New Jersey
Dominique Wilkins, Atl.-LAC
Shaquille OÄNeal, Orlando
Mark Price, Cleveland
Gary Payton, Seattle

1994-95
FIRST
Scottie Pippen, Chicago
Karl Malone, Utah
David Robinson, San Antonio
John Stockton, Utah
Anfernee Hardaway, Orlando
SECOND
Shawn Kemp, Seattle
Charles Barkley, Phoenix
Shaquille OÄNeal, Orlando
Mitch Richmond, Sacramento
Gary Payton, Seattle
THIRD
Detlef Schrempf, Seattle
Dennis Rodman, San Antonio
Hakeem Olajuwon, Houston
Reggie Miller, Indiana
Clyde Drexler, Portland-Houston

1995-96
FIRST
Scottie Pippen, Chicago
Karl Malone, Utah
David Robinson, San Antonio
Michael Jordan, Chicago
Anfernee Hardaway, Orlando
SECOND
Shawn Kemp, Seattle
Grant Hill, Detroit
Hakeem Olajuwon, Houston
Gary Payton, Seattle
John Stockton, Utah
THIRD
Charles Barkley, Phoenix
Juwan Howard, Washington
Shaquille OÄNeal, Orlando
Mitch Richmond, Sacramento
Reggie Miller, Indiana

1996-97
FIRST
Grant Hill, Detroit
Karl Malone, Utah
Hakeem Olajuwon, Houston
Michael Jordan, Chicago
Tim Hardaway, Miami
SECOND
Scottie Pippen, Chicago
Glen Rice, Charlotte
Patrick Ewing, New York
Gary Payton, Seattle
Mitch Richmond, Sacramento
THIRD
Anthony Mason, Charlotte
Vin Baker, Milwaukee
Shaquille OÄNeal, L.A. Lakers
John Stockton, Utah
Anfernee Hardaway, Orlando

1997-98
FIRST
Karl Malone, Utah
Tim Duncan, San Antonio
Shaquille OÄNeal, L.A. Lakers
Michael Jordan, Chicago
Gary Payton, Seattle
SECOND
Grant Hill, Detroit
Vin Baker, Seattle
David Robinson, San Antonio
Tim Hardaway, Miami
Rod Strickland, Washington
THIRD
Scottie Pippen, Chicago
Glen Rice, Charlotte
Dikembe Mutombo, Atlanta
Mitch Richmond, Sacramento
Reggie Miller, Indiana

1998-99
FIRST
Karl Malone, Utah
Tim Duncan, San Antonio
Alonzo Mourning, Miami
Allen Iverson, Philadelphia
Jason Kidd, Phoenix
SECOND
Chris Webber, Sacramento
Grant Hill, Detroit
Shaquille OÄNeal, L.A. Lakers
Gary Payton, Seattle
Tim Hardaway, Miami
THIRD
Kevin Garnett, Minnesota
Antonio McDyess, Denver
Hakeem Olajuwon, Houston
Kobe Bryant, L.A. Lakers
John Stockton, Utah

1999-00
FIRST
Kevin Garnett, Minnesota
Tim Duncan, San Antonio
Shaquille O'Neal, L.A. Lakers
Gary Payton, Seattle
Jason Kidd, Phoenix
SECOND
Karl Malone, Utah
Grant Hill, Detroit
Alonzo Mourning, Miami
Allen Iverson, Philadelphia
Kobe Bryant, L.A. Lakers
THIRD
Chris Webber, Sacramento
Vince Carter, Toronto
David Robinson, San Antonio
Eddie Jones, Charlotte
Stephon Marbury, New Jersey

PLAYERS WHO HAVE MADE ALL-NBA TEAMS
(Official All-NBA teams at end of season; active 1999-00 players in CAPS.)

Player	1st	2nd	3rd
KARL MALONE	11	2	0
Kareem Abdul-Jabbar	10	5	0
Bob Cousy	10	2	0
Jerry West	10	2	0
Michael Jordan	10	1	0
Bob Pettit	10	1	0
Elgin Baylor	10	0	0
Oscar Robertson	9	2	0
Larry Bird	9	1	0
Magic Johnson	9	1	0
Wilt Chamberlain	7	3	0
Dolph Schayes	6	6	0
HAKEEM OLAJUWON	6	3	3
George Mikan	6	0	0
CHARLES BARKLEY	5	5	1
Julius Erving	5	2	0
George Gervin	5	2	0
Rick Barry	5	1	0
John Havlicek	4	7	0
Moses Malone	4	4	0
Bill Sharman	4	3	0
DAVID ROBINSON	4	2	3
Walt Frazier	4	2	0
Bob Davies	4	1	0

PLAYERS WHO HAVE MADE ALL-NBA TEAMS – Continued

Player	1st	2nd	3rd
Neil Johnston	4	1	0
Max Zaslofsky	4	0	0
Bill Russell	3	8	0
Elvin Hayes	3	3	0
SCOTTIE PIPPEN	3	2	2
Nate Archibald	3	2	0
Jerry Lucas	3	2	0
Isiah Thomas	3	2	0
Paul Arizin	3	1	0
Billy Cunningham	3	1	0
Joe Fulks	3	1	0
Ed Macauley	3	1	0
Paul Westphal	3	1	0
TIM DUNCAN	3	0	0
JOHN STOCKTON	2	6	3
GARY PAYTON	2	4	1
Spencer Haywood	2	2	0
Pete Maravich	2	2	0
SHAQUILLE O'NEAL	2	2	3
Jim Pollard	2	2	0
Bernard King	2	1	1
Dave Bing	2	1	0
Bob Feerick	2	1	0
ANFERNEE HARDAWAY	2	0	1
Alex Groza	2	0	0
JASON KIDD	2	0	0
David Thompson	2	0	0
PATRICK EWING	1	6	0
Dominique Wilkins	1	4	2
Sidney Moncrief	1	4	0
Willis Reed	1	4	0
GRANT HILL	1	4	0
Clyde Drexler	1	2	2
TIM HARDAWAY	1	2	1
CHRIS MULLIN	1	2	1
Marques Johnson	1	2	0
SHAWN KEMP	1	2	0
Ralph Beard	1	1	0
Larry Foust	1	1	0
Harry Gallatin	1	1	0
ALLEN IVERSON	1	1	0
Dennis Johnson	1	1	0
Bob McAdoo	1	1	0
George McGinnis	1	1	0
Bones McKinney	1	1	0
Stan Miasek	1	1	0
ALONZO MOURNING	1	1	0
Gene Shue	1	1	0
Bill Walton	1	1	0
Gus Williams	1	1	0
George Yardley	1	1	0
Mark Price	1	0	3
KEVIN GARNETT	1	0	1
Howie Dallmar	1	0	0
Gail Goodrich	1	0	0
Connie Hawkins	1	0	0
Kevin McHale	1	0	0
Earl Monroe	1	0	0
Truck Robinson	1	0	0
LATRELL SPREWELL	1	0	0
Wes Unseld	1	0	0
Hal Greer	0	7	0
Slater Martin	0	5	0
KEVIN JOHNSON	0	4	1
Tom Heinsohn	0	4	0
Gus Johnson	0	4	0
Vern Mikkelsen	0	4	0
MITCH RICHMOND	0	3	2
Dave Cowens	0	3	0
Alex English	0	3	0
Richie Guerin	0	3	0
Sam Jones	0	3	0
John Logan	0	3	0
Maurice Stokes	0	3	0
Bob Wanzer	0	3	0
Carl Braun	0	2	0
Frank Brian	0	2	0
Tom Chambers	0	2	0
Adrian Dantley	0	2	0
Walter Davis	0	2	0
Cliff Hagan	0	2	0
Bob Love	0	2	0
Andy Phillip	0	2	0
Fred Scolari	0	2	0
Paul Seymour	0	2	0
Jack Twyman	0	2	0
Jo Jo White	0	2	0
Joe Dumars	0	1	2
VIN BAKER	0	1	1
KOBE BRYANT	0	1	1
TERRY CUMMINGS	0	1	1
Robert Parish	0	1	1
GLEN RICE	0	1	1
CHRIS WEBBER	0	1	1
Frank Baumholtz	0	1	0
Otis Birdsong	0	1	0
Ernie Calverley	0	1	0
Al Cervi	0	1	0
Phil Chenier	0	1	0
Archie Clark	0	1	0
Larry Costello	0	1	0
Bobby Dandridge	0	1	0
Dave DeBusschere	0	1	0
Phil Ford	0	1	0
World B. Free	0	1	0
Dick Garmaker	0	1	0
Jack George	0	1	0
Tom Gola	0	1	0
Chuck Halbert	0	1	0
Bailey Howell	0	1	0
Lou Hudson	0	1	0
Buddy Jeannette	0	1	0
LARRY JOHNSON	0	1	0
Fat Lever	0	1	0
Clyde Lovellette	0	1	0
Maurice Lucas	0	1	0
Dick McGuire	0	1	0
Jim Paxson	0	1	0
Arnie Risen	0	1	0
Alvin Robertson	0	1	0
Dan Roundfield	0	1	0
Ken Sailors	0	1	0
Ralph Sampson	0	1	0
Fred Schaus	0	1	0
Phil Smith	0	1	0
Randy Smith	0	1	0
ROD STRICKLAND	0	1	0
Norm Van Lier	0	1	0
Buck Williams	0	1	0
REGGIE MILLER	0	0	3
DERRICK COLEMAN	0	0	2
DENNIS RODMAN	0	0	2
James Worthy	0	0	2
VINCE CARTER	0	0	1
Brad Daugherty	0	0	1
DALE ELLIS	0	0	1
JUWAN HOWARD	0	0	1
EDDIE JONES	0	0	1
STEPHON MARBURY	0	0	1
ANTHONY MASON	0	0	1
ANTONIO McDYESS	0	0	1
DIKEMBE MUTOMBO	0	0	1
Drazen Petrovic	0	0	1
DETLEF SCHREMPF	0	0	1
KEVIN WILLIS	0	0	1

SCHICK ALL-ROOKIE TEAMS

Selected by NBA coaches.

1962-63
Terry Dischinger, Chicago
Chet Walker, Syracuse
Zelmo Beaty, St. Louis
John Havlicek, Boston
Dave DeBusschere, Detroit

1963-64
Jerry Lucas, Cincinnati
Gus Johnson, Baltimore
Nate Thurmond, San Francisco
Art Heyman, New York
Rod Thorn, Baltimore

1964-65
Willis Reed, New York
Jim Barnes, New York
Howard Komives, New York
Lucious Jackson, Philadelphia
Wally Jones, Baltimore
Joe Caldwell, Detroit

1965-66
Rick Barry, San Francisco
Billy Cunningham, Philadelphia
Tom Van Arsdale, Detroit
Dick Van Arsdale, New York
Fred Hetzel, San Francisco

1966-67
Lou Hudson, St. Louis
Jack Marin, Baltimore
Erwin Mueller, Chicago
Cazzie Russell, New York
Dave Bing, Detroit

1967-68
Earl Monroe, Baltimore
Bob Rule, Seattle
Walt Frazier, New York
Al Tucker, Seattle
Phil Jackson, New York

1968-69
Wes Unseld, Baltimore
Elvin Hayes, San Diego
Bill Hewitt, Los Angeles
Art Harris, Seattle
Gary Gregor, Phoenix

1969-70
Kareem Abdul-Jabbar, Milwaukee
Bob Dandridge, Milwaukee
Jo Jo White, Boston
Mike Davis, Baltimore
Dick Garrett, Los Angeles

1970-71
Geoff Petrie, Portland
Dave Cowens, Boston
Pete Maravich, Atlanta
Calvin Murphy, San Diego
Bob Lanier, Detroit

1971-72
Elmore Smith, Buffalo
Sidney Wicks, Portland
Austin Carr, Cleveland
Phil Chenier, Baltimore
Clifford Ray, Chicago

1972-73
Bob McAdoo, Buffalo
Lloyd Neal, Portland
Fred Boyd, Philadelphia
Dwight Davis, Cleveland
Jim Price, Los Angeles

1973-74
Ernie DiGregorio, Buffalo
Ron Behagen, Kansas City-Omaha
Mike Bantom, Phoenix
John Brown, Atlanta
Nick Weatherspoon, Capital

SCHICK ALL-ROOKIE TEAMS – Continued

1974-75
Jamaal Wilkes, Golden State
John Drew, Atlanta
Scott Wedman, Kansas City-Omaha
Tom Burleson, Seattle
Brian Winters, Los Angeles

1975-76
Alvan Adams, Phoenix
Gus Williams, Golden State
Joe Meriweather, Houston
John Shumate, Phoenix-Buffalo
Lionel Hollins, Portland

1976-77
Adrian Dantley, Buffalo
Scott May, Chicago
Mitch Kupchak, Washington
John Lucas, Houston
Ron Lee, Phoenix

1977-78
Walter Davis, Phoenix
Marques Johnson, Milwaukee
Bernard King, New Jersey
Jack Sikma, Seattle
Norm Nixon, Los Angeles

1978-79
Phil Ford, Kansas City
Mychal Thompson, Portland
Ron Brewer, Portland
Reggie Theus, Chicago
Terry Tyler, Detroit

1979-80
Larry Bird, Boston
Magic Johnson, Los Angeles
Bill Cartwright, New York
Calvin Natt, New Jersey-Portland
David Greenwood, Chicago

1980-81
Joe Barry Carroll, Golden State
Darrell Griffith, Utah
Larry Smith, Golden State
Kevin McHale, Boston
Kelvin Ransey, Portland

1981-82
Kelly Tripucka, Detroit
Jay Vincent, Dallas
Isiah Thomas, Detroit
Buck Williams, New Jersey
Jeff Ruland, Washington

1982-83
Terry Cummings, San Diego
Clark Kellogg, Indiana
Dominique Wilkins, Atlanta
James Worthy, Los Angeles
Quintin Dailey, Chicago

1983-84
Ralph Sampson, Houston
Steve Stipanovich, Indiana
Byron Scott, Los Angeles
Jeff Malone, Washington
Thurl Bailey, Utah
Darrell Walker, New York

1984-85
Michael Jordan, Chicago
Hakeem Olajuwon, Houston
Sam Bowie, Portland
Charles Barkley, Philadelphia
Sam Perkins, Dallas

1985-86
Xavier McDaniel, Seattle
Patrick Ewing, New York
Karl Malone, Utah
Joe Dumars, Detroit
Charles Oakley, Chicago

1986-87
Brad Daugherty, Cleveland
Ron Harper, Cleveland
Chuck Person, Indiana
Roy Tarpley, Dallas
John Williams, Cleveland

1987-88
Mark Jackson, New York
Armon Gilliam, Phoenix
Kenny Smith, Sacramento
Greg Anderson, San Antonio
Derrick McKey, Seattle

1988-89
FIRST
Mitch Richmond, Golden State
Willie Anderson, San Antonio
Hersey Hawkins, Philadelphia
Rik Smits, Indiana
Charles Smith, L.A. Clippers
SECOND
Brian Shaw, Boston
Rex Chapman, Charlotte
Chris Morris, New Jersey
Rod Strickland, New York
Kevin Edwards, Miami

1989-90
FIRST
David Robinson, San Antonio
Tim Hardaway, Golden State
Vlade Divac, L.A. Lakers
Sherman Douglas, Miami
Pooh Richardson, Minnesota
SECOND
J.R. Reid, Charlotte
Sean Elliott, San Antonio
Stacey King, Chicago
Blue Edwards, Utah
Glen Rice, Miami

1990-91
FIRST
Kendall Gill, Charlotte
Dennis Scott, Orlando
Dee Brown, Boston
Lionel Simmons, Sacramento
Derrick Coleman, New Jersey
SECOND
Chris Jackson, Denver
Gary Payton, Seattle
Felton Spencer, Minnesota
Travis Mays, Sacramento
Willie Burton, Miami

1991-92
FIRST
Larry Johnson, Charlotte
Dikembe Mutombo, Denver
Billy Owens, Golden State
Steve Smith, Miami
Stacey Augmon, Atlanta
SECOND
Rick Fox, Boston
Terrell Brandon, Cleveland
Larry Stewart, Washington
Stanley Roberts, Orlando
Mark Macon, Denver

1992-93
FIRST
Shaquille O'Neal, Orlando
Alonzo Mourning, Charlotte
Christian Laettner, Minnesota
Tom Gugliotta, Washington
LaPhonso Ellis, Denver
SECOND
Walt Williams, Sacramento
Robert Horry, Houston
Latrell Sprewell, Golden State
Clarence Weatherspoon, Philadelphia
Richard Dumas, Phoenix

1993-94
FIRST
Chris Webber, Golden State
Anfernee Hardaway, Orlando
Vin Baker, Milwaukee
Jamal Mashburn, Dallas
Isaiah Rider, Minnesota
SECOND
Dino Radja, Boston
Nick Van Exel, L.A. Lakers
Shawn Bradley, Philadelphia
Toni Kukoc, Chicago
Lindsey Hunter, Detroit

1994-95
FIRST
Jason Kidd, Dallas
Grant Hill, Detroit
Glenn Robinson, Milwaukee
Eddie Jones, L.A. Lakers
Brian Grant, Sacramento
SECOND
Juwan Howard, Washington
Eric Montross, Boston
Wesley Person, Phoenix
Jalen Rose, Denver
Donyell Marshall, Minnesota-Golden St.
Sharone Wright, Philadelphia

1995-96
FIRST
Damon Stoudamire, Toronto
Joe Smith, Golden State
Jerry Stackhouse, Philadelphia
Antonio McDyess, Denver
Arvydas Sabonis, Portland
Michael Finley, Phoenix
SECOND
Kevin Garnett, Minnesota
Bryant Reeves, Vancouver
Brent Barry, L.A. Clippers
Rasheed Wallace, Washington
Tyus Edney, Sacramento

1996-97
FIRST
Shareef Abdur-Rahim, Vancouver
Allen Iverson, Philadelphia
Stephon Marbury, Minnesota
Marcus Camby, Toronto
Antoine Walker, Boston
SECOND
Kerry Kittles, New Jersey
Ray Allen, Milwaukee
Travis Knight, L.A. Lakers
Kobe Bryant, L.A. Lakers
Matt Maloney, Houston

1997-98
FIRST
Tim Duncan, San Antonio
Keith Van Horn, New Jersey
Brevin Knight, Cleveland
Zydrunas Ilgauskas, Cleveland
Ron Mercer, Boston
SECOND
Tim Thomas, Philadelphia
Cedric Henderson, Cleveland
Derek Anderson, Cleveland
Maurice Taylor, L.A. Clippers
Bobby Jackson, Denver

1998-99
FIRST
Vince Carter, Toronto
Paul Pierce, Boston
Jason Williams, Sacramento
Mike Bibby, Vancouver
Matt Harpring, Orlando
SECOND
Michael Dickerson, Houston
Michael Doleac, Orlando
Cuttino Mobley, Houston
Michael Olowokandi, L.A. Clippers
Antawn Jamison, Golden State

SCHICK ALL-ROOKIE TEAMS – Continued

1999-00

FIRST
Elton Brand, Chicago
Steve Francis, Houston
Lamar Odom, L.A. Clippers
Wally Szczerbiak, Minnesota
Andre Miller, Cleveland

SECOND
Shawn Marion, Phoenix
Ron Artest, Chicago
James Posey, Denver
Jason Terry, Atlanta
Chucky Atkins, Orlando

ALL-DEFENSIVE TEAMS

Selected by NBA coaches.

1968-69

FIRST
Dave DeBusschere, Detroit-New York
Nate Thurmond, San Francisco
Bill Russell, Boston
Walt Frazier, New York
Jerry Sloan, Chicago

SECOND
Rudy LaRusso, San Francisco
Tom Sanders, Boston
John Havlicek, Boston
Jerry West, Los Angeles
Bill Bridges, Atlanta

1969-70

FIRST
Dave DeBusschere, New York
Gus Johnson, Baltimore
Willis Reed, New York
Walt Frazier, New York
Jerry West, Los Angeles

SECOND
John Havlicek, Boston
Bill Bridges, Atlanta
Kareem Abdul-Jabbar, Milwaukee
Joe Caldwell, Atlanta
Jerry Sloan, Chicago

1970-71

FIRST
Dave DeBusschere, New York
Gus Johnson, Baltimore
Nate Thurmond, San Francisco
Walt Frazier, New York
Jerry West, Los Angeles

SECOND
John Havlicek, Boston
Paul Silas, Phoenix
Kareem Abdul-Jabbar, Milwaukee
Jerry Sloan, Chicago
Norm Van Lier, Cincinnati

1971-72

FIRST
Dave DeBusschere, New York
John Havlicek, Boston
Wilt Chamberlain, Los Angeles
Jerry West, Los Angeles
Walt Frazier, New York
Jerry Sloan, Chicago

SECOND
Paul Silas, Phoenix
Bob Love, Chicago
Nate Thurmond, Golden State
Norm Van Lier, Chicago
Don Chaney, Boston

1972-73

FIRST
Dave DeBusschere, New York
John Havlicek, Boston
Wilt Chamberlain, Los Angeles
Jerry West, Los Angeles
Walt Frazier, New York

SECOND
Paul Silas, Boston
Mike Riordan, Baltimore
Nate Thurmond, Golden State
Norm Van Lier, Chicago
Don Chaney, Boston

1973-74

FIRST
Dave DeBusschere, New York
John Havlicek, Boston
Kareem Abdul-Jabbar, Milwaukee
Norm Van Lier, Chicago
Walt Frazier, New York
Jerry Sloan, Chicago

SECOND
Elvin Hayes, Capital
Bob Love, Chicago
Nate Thurmond, Golden State
Don Chaney, Boston
Dick Van Arsdale, Phoenix
Jim Price, Los Angeles

1974-75

FIRST
John Havlicek, Boston
Paul Silas, Boston
Kareem Abdul-Jabbar, Milwaukee
Jerry Sloan, Chicago
Walt Frazier, New York

SECOND
Elvin Hayes, Washington
Bob Love, Chicago
Dave Cowens, Boston
Norm Van Lier, Chicago
Don Chaney, Boston

1975-76

FIRST
Paul Silas, Boston
John Havlicek, Boston
Dave Cowens, Boston
Norm Van Lier, Chicago
Don Watts, Seattle

SECOND
Jim Brewer, Cleveland
Jamaal Wilkes, Golden State
Kareem Abdul-Jabbar, Los Angeles
Jim Cleamons, Cleveland
Phil Smith, Golden State

1976-77

FIRST
Bobby Jones, Denver
E.C. Coleman, New Orleans
Bill Walton, Portland
Don Buse, Indiana
Norm Van Lier, Chicago

SECOND
Jim Brewer, Cleveland
Jamaal Wilkes, Golden State
Kareem Abdul-Jabbar, Los Angeles
Brian Taylor, Kansas City
Don Chaney, Los Angeles

1977-78

FIRST
Bobby Jones, Denver
Maurice Lucas, Portland
Bill Walton, Portland
Lionel Hollins, Portland
Don Buse, Phoenix

SECOND
E.C. Coleman, Golden State
Bob Gross, Portland
Kareem Abdul-Jabbar, Los Angeles
Artis Gilmore, Chicago
Norm Van Lier, Chicago
Quinn Buckner, Milwaukee

1978-79

FIRST
Bobby Jones, Philadelphia
Bobby Dandridge, Washington
Kareem Abdul-Jabbar, Los Angeles
Dennis Johnson, Seattle
Don Buse, Phoenix

SECOND
Maurice Lucas, Portland
M.L. Carr, Detroit
Moses Malone, Houston
Lionel Hollins, Portland
Eddie Johnson, Atlanta

1979-80

FIRST
Bobby Jones, Philadelphia
Dan Roundfield, Atlanta
Kareem Abdul-Jabbar, Los Angeles
Dennis Johnson, Seattle
Don Buse, Phoenix
Micheal Ray Richardson, New York

SECOND
Scott Wedman, Kansas City
Kermit Washington, Portland
Dave Cowens, Boston
Quinn Buckner, Milwaukee
Eddie Johnson, Atlanta

1980-81

FIRST
Bobby Jones, Philadelphia
Caldwell Jones, Philadelphia
Kareem Abdul-Jabbar, Los Angeles
Dennis Johnson, Phoenix
Micheal Ray Richardson, New York

SECOND
Dan Roundfield, Atlanta
Kermit Washington, Portland
George Johnson, San Antonio
Quinn Buckner, Milwaukee
Dudley Bradley, Indiana
Michael Cooper, Los Angeles

1981-82

FIRST
Bobby Jones, Philadelphia
Dan Roundfield, Atlanta
Caldwell Jones, Philadelphia
Michael Cooper, Los Angeles
Dennis Johnson, Phoenix

SECOND
Larry Bird, Boston
Lonnie Shelton, Seattle
Jack Sikma, Seattle
Quinn Buckner, Milwaukee
Sidney Moncrief, Milwaukee

ALL-DEFENSIVE TEAMS – Continued

1982-83
FIRST
Bobby Jones, Philadelphia
Dan Roundfield, Atlanta
Moses Malone, Philadelphia
Sidney Moncrief, Milwaukee
Dennis Johnson, Phoenix
Maurice Cheeks, Philadelphia
SECOND
Larry Bird, Boston
Kevin McHale, Boston
Tree Rollins, Atlanta
Michael Cooper, Los Angeles
T.R. Dunn, Denver

1983-84
FIRST
Bobby Jones, Philadelphia
Michael Cooper, Los Angeles
Tree Rollins, Atlanta
Maurice Cheeks, Philadelphia
Sidney Moncrief, Milwaukee
SECOND
Larry Bird, Boston
Dan Roundfield, Atlanta
Kareem Abdul-Jabbar, Los Angeles
Dennis Johnson, Boston
T.R. Dunn, Denver

1984-85
FIRST
Sidney Moncrief, Milwaukee
Paul Pressey, Milwaukee
Mark Eaton, Utah
Michael Cooper, L.A. Lakers
Maurice Cheeks, Philadelphia
SECOND
Bobby Jones, Philadelphia
Danny Vranes, Seattle
Hakeem Olajuwon, Houston
Dennis Johnson, Boston
T.R. Dunn, Denver

1985-86
FIRST
Paul Pressey, Milwaukee
Kevin McHale, Boston
Mark Eaton, Utah
Sidney Moncrief, Milwaukee
Maurice Cheeks, Philadelphia
SECOND
Michael Cooper, L.A. Lakers
Bill Hanzlik, Denver
Manute Bol, Washington
Alvin Robertson, San Antonio
Dennis Johnson, Boston

1986-87
FIRST
Kevin McHale, Boston
Michael Cooper, L.A. Lakers
Hakeem Olajuwon, Houston
Alvin Robertson, San Antonio
Dennis Johnson, Boston
SECOND
Paul Pressey, Milwaukee
Rodney McCray, Houston
Mark Eaton, Utah
Maurice Cheeks, Philadelphia
Derek Harper, Dallas

1987-88
FIRST
Kevin McHale, Boston
Rodney McCray, Houston
Hakeem Olajuwon, Houston
Michael Cooper, L.A. Lakers
Michael Jordan, Chicago
SECOND
Buck Williams, New Jersey
Karl Malone, Utah
Mark Eaton, Utah
Patrick Ewing, New York
Alvin Robertson, San Antonio
Fat Lever, Denver

1988-89
FIRST
Dennis Rodman, Detroit
Larry Nance, Cleveland
Mark Eaton, Utah
Michael Jordan, Chicago
Joe Dumars, Detroit
SECOND
Kevin McHale, Boston
A.C. Green, L.A. Lakers
Patrick Ewing, New York
John Stockton, Utah
Alvin Robertson, San Antonio

1989-90
FIRST
Dennis Rodman, Detroit
Buck Williams, Portland
Hakeem Olajuwon, Houston
Michael Jordan, Chicago
Joe Dumars, Detroit
SECOND
Kevin McHale, Boston
Rick Mahorn, Philadelphia
David Robinson, San Antonio
Derek Harper, Dallas
Alvin Robertson, Milwaukee

1990-91
FIRST
Michael Jordan, Chicago
Alvin Robertson, Milwaukee
David Robinson, San Antonio
Dennis Rodman, Detroit
Buck Williams, Portland
SECOND
Joe Dumars, Detroit
John Stockton, Utah
Hakeem Olajuwon, Houston
Scottie Pippen, Chicago
Dan Majerle, Phoenix

1991-92
FIRST
Dennis Rodman, Detroit
Scottie Pippen, Chicago
David Robinson, San Antonio
Michael Jordan, Chicago
Joe Dumars, Detroit
SECOND
Larry Nance, Cleveland
Buck Williams, Portland
Patrick Ewing, New York
John Stockton, Utah
Micheal Williams, Indiana

1992-93
FIRST
Scottie Pippen, Chicago
Dennis Rodman, Detroit
Hakeem Olajuwon, Houston
Michael Jordan, Chicago
Joe Dumars, Detroit
SECOND
Horace Grant, Chicago
Larry Nance, Cleveland
David Robinson, San Antonio
Dan Majerle, Phoenix
John Starks, New York

1993-94
FIRST
Scottie Pippen, Chicago
Charles Oakley, New York
Hakeem Olajuwon, Houston
Gary Payton, Seattle
Mookie Blaylock, Atlanta
SECOND
Dennis Rodman, San Antonio
Horace Grant, Chicago
David Robinson, San Antonio
Nate McMillan, Seattle
Latrell Sprewell, Golden State

1994-95
FIRST
Scottie Pippen, Chicago
Dennis Rodman, San Antonio
David Robinson, San Antonio
Gary Payton, Seattle
Mookie Blaylock, Atlanta
SECOND
Horace Grant, Chicago
Derrick McKey, Indiana
Dikembe Mutombo, Denver
John Stockton, Utah
Nate McMillan, Seattle

1995-96
FIRST
Scottie Pippen, Chicago
Dennis Rodman, Chicago
David Robinson, San Antonio
Gary Payton, Seattle
Michael Jordan, Chicago
SECOND
Horace Grant, Orlando
Derrick McKey, Indiana
Hakeem Olajuwon, Houston
Mookie Blaylock, Atlanta
Bobby Phills, Cleveland

1996-97
FIRST
Scottie Pippen, Chicago
Karl Malone, Utah
Dikembe Mutombo, Atlanta
Michael Jordan, Chicago
Gary Payton, Seattle
SECOND
Anthony Mason, Charlotte
P.J. Brown, Miami
Hakeem Olajuwon, Houston
Mookie Blaylock, Atlanta
John Stockton, Utah

1997-98
FIRST
Scottie Pippen, Chicago
Karl Malone, Utah
Dikembe Mutombo, Atlanta
Michael Jordan, Chicago
Gary Payton, Seattle
SECOND
Tim Duncan, San Antonio
Charles Oakley, New York
David Robinson, San Antonio
Mookie Blaylock, Atlanta
Eddie Jones, L.A. Lakers

1998-99
FIRST
Tim Duncan, San Antonio
Karl Malone, Utah
Scottie Pippen, Houston
Alonzo Mourning, Miami
Gary Payton, Seattle
Jason Kidd, Phoenix
SECOND
P.J. Brown, Miami
Theo Ratliff, Philadelphia
Dikembe Mutombo, Atlanta
Mookie Blaylock, Atlanta
Eddie Jones, L.A.Lakers-Charlotte

1999-00
FIRST
Tim Duncan, San Antonio
Kevin Garnett, Minnesota
Alonzo Mourning, Miami
Gary Payton, Seattle
Kobe Bryant, L.A. Lakers
SECOND
Scottie Pippen, Portland
Clifford Robinson, Phoenix
Shaquille O'Neal, L.A. Lakers
Eddie Jones, Charlotte
Jason Kidd, Phoenix

INDIVIDUAL LEADERS

SCORING

1946-47 — 1,389 Joe Fulks, Philadelphia
1947-48 — 1,007 Max Zaslofsky, Chicago
1948-49 — 1,698 George Mikan, Minneapolis
1949-50 — 1,865 George Mikan, Minneapolis
1950-51 — 1,932 George Mikan, Minneapolis
1951-52 — 1,674 Paul Arizin, Philadelphia
1952-53 — 1,564 Neil Johnston, Philadelphia
1953-54 — 1,759 Neil Johnston, Philadelphia
1954-55 — 1,631 Neil Johnston, Philadelphia
1955-56 — 1,849 Bob Pettit, St. Louis
1956-57 — 1,817 Paul Arizin, Philadelphia
1957-58 — 2,001 George Yardley, Detroit
1958-59 — 2,105 Bob Pettit, St. Louis
1959-60 — 2,707 Wilt Chamberlain, Philadelphia
1960-61 — 3,033 Wilt Chamberlain, Philadelphia
1961-62 — 4,029 Wilt Chamberlain, Philadelphia
1962-63 — 3,586 Wilt Chamberlain, San Francisco
1963-64 — 2,948 Wilt Chamberlain, San Francisco
1964-65 — 2,534 Wilt Chamberlain, S.F.-Phil.
1965-66 — 2,649 Wilt Chamberlain, Philadelphia
1966-67 — 2,775 Rick Barry, San Francisco
1967-68 — 2,142 Dave Bing, Detroit
1968-69 — 2,327 Elvin Hayes, San Diego
1969-70 — 31.2* Jerry West, Los Angeles
1970-71 — 31.7* Kareem Abdul-Jabbar, Milwaukee
1971-72 — 34.8* Kareem Abdul-Jabbar, Milwaukee
1972-73 — 34.0* Nate Archibald, K.C./Omaha
1973-74 — 30.6* Bob McAdoo, Buffalo
1974-75 — 34.5* Bob McAdoo, Buffalo
1975-76 — 31.1* Bob McAdoo, Buffalo
1976-77 — 31.1* Pete Maravich, New Orleans
1977-78 — 27.2* George Gervin, San Antonio
1978-79 — 29.6* George Gervin, San Antonio
1979-80 — 33.1* George Gervin, San Antonio
1980-81 — 30.7* Adrian Dantley, Utah
1981-82 — 32.3* George Gervin, San Antonio
1982-83 — 28.4* Alex English, Denver
1983-84 — 30.6* Adrian Dantley, Utah
1984-85 — 32.9* Bernard King, New York
1985-86 — 30.3* Dominique Wilkins, Atlanta
1986-87 — 37.1* Michael Jordan, Chicago
1987-88 — 35.0* Michael Jordan, Chicago
1988-89 — 32.5* Michael Jordan, Chicago
1989-90 — 33.6* Michael Jordan, Chicago
1990-91 — 31.5* Michael Jordan, Chicago
1991-92 — 30.1* Michael Jordan, Chicago
1992-93 — 32.6* Michael Jordan, Chicago
1993-94 — 29.8* David Robinson, San Antonio
1994-95 — 29.3* Shaquille O'Neal, Orlando
1995-96 — 30.4* Michael Jordan, Chicago
1996-97 — 29.6* Michael Jordan, Chicago
1997-98 — 28.7* Michael Jordan, Chicago
1998-99 — 26.8* Allen Iverson, Philadelphia
1999-00 — 29.7* Shaquille O'Neal, L.A. Lakers
Based on average per game.

FIELD-GOAL PERCENTAGE

1946-47 — .401 Bob Feerick, Washington
1947-48 — .340 Bob Feerick, Washington
1948-49 — .423 Arnie Risen, Rochester
1949-50 — .478 Alex Groza, Indianapolis
1950-51 — .470 Alex Groza, Indianapolis
1951-52 — .448 Paul Arizin, Philadelphia
1952-53 — .452 Neil Johnston, Philadelphia
1953-54 — .486 Ed Macauley, Boston
1954-55 — .487 Larry Foust, Fort Wayne
1955-56 — .457 Neil Johnston, Philadelphia
1956-57 — .447 Neil Johnston, Philadelphia
1957-58 — .452 Jack Twyman, Cincinnati
1958-59 — .490 Ken Sears, New York
1959-60 — .477 Ken Sears, New York
1960-61 — .509 Wilt Chamberlain, Philadelphia
1961-62 — .519 Walt Bellamy, Chicago
1962-63 — .528 Wilt Chamberlain, San Francisco
1963-64 — .527 Jerry Lucas, Cincinnati
1964-65 — .510 Wilt Chamberlain, S.F.-Phil.
1965-66 — .540 Wilt Chamberlain, Philadelphia
1966-67 — .683 Wilt Chamberlain, Philadelphia
1967-68 — .595 Wilt Chamberlain, Philadelphia
1968-69 — .583 Wilt Chamberlain, Los Angeles
1969-70 — .559 Johnny Green, Cincinnati
1970-71 — .587 Johnny Green, Cincinnati
1971-72 — .649 Wilt Chamberlain, Los Angeles
1972-73 — .727 Wilt Chamberlain, Los Angeles
1973-74 — .547 Bob McAdoo, Buffalo
1974-75 — .539 Don Nelson, Boston
1975-76 — .561 Wes Unseld, Washington
1976-77 — .579 Kareem Abdul-Jabbar, Los Angeles
1977-78 — .578 Bobby Jones, Denver
1978-79 — .584 Cedric Maxwell, Boston
1979-80 — .609 Cedric Maxwell, Boston
1980-81 — .670 Artis Gilmore, Chicago
1981-82 — .652 Artis Gilmore, Chicago
1982-83 — .626 Artis Gilmore, San Antonio
1983-84 — .631 Artis Gilmore, San Antonio
1984-85 — .637 James Donaldson, L.A. Clippers
1985-86 — .632 Steve Johnson, San Antonio
1986-87 — .604 Kevin McHale, Boston
1987-88 — .604 Kevin McHale, Boston
1988-89 — .595 Dennis Rodman, Detroit
1989-90 — .625 Mark West, Phoenix
1990-91 — .602 Buck Williams, Portland
1991-92 — .604 Buck Williams, Portland
1992-93 — .576 Cedric Ceballos, Phoenix
1993-94 — .599 Shaquille O'Neal, Orlando
1994-95 — .633 Chris Gatling, Golden State
1995-96 — .584 Gheorghe Muresan, Washington
1996-97 — .604 Gheorghe Muresan, Washington
1997-98 — .584 Shaquille O'Neal, L.A. Lakers
1998-99 — .576 Shaquille O'Neal, L.A. Lakers
1999-00 — .574 Shaquille O'Neal L.A. Lakers

FREE-THROW PERCENTAGE

1946-47 — .811 Fred Scolari, Washington
1947-48 — .788 Bob Feerick, Washington
1948-49 — .859 Bob Feerick, Washington
1949-50 — .843 Max Zaslofsky, Chicago
1950-51 — .855 Joe Fulks, Philadelphia
1951-52 — .904 Bob Wanzer, Rochester
1952-53 — .850 Bill Sharman, Boston
1953-54 — .844 Bill Sharman, Boston
1954-55 — .897 Bill Sharman, Boston
1955-56 — .867 Bill Sharman, Boston
1956-57 — .905 Bill Sharman, Boston
1957-58 — .904 Dolph Schayes, Syracuse
1958-59 — .932 Bill Sharman, Boston
1959-60 — .892 Dolph Schayes, Syracuse
1960-61 — .921 Bill Sharman, Boston
1961-62 — .896 Dolph Schayes, Syracuse
1962-63 — .881 Larry Costello, Syracuse
1963-64 — .853 Oscar Robertson, Cincinnati
1964-65 — .877 Larry Costello, Philadelphia
1965-66 — .881 Larry Siegfried, Boston
1966-67 — .903 Adrian Smith, Cincinnati
1967-68 — .873 Oscar Robertson, Cincinnati
1968-69 — .864 Larry Siegfried, Boston
1969-70 — .898 Flynn Robinson, Milwaukee
1970-71 — .859 Chet Walker, Chicago
1971-72 — .894 Jack Marin, Baltimore
1972-73 — .902 Rick Barry, Golden State
1973-74 — .902 Ernie DiGregorio, Buffalo
1974-75 — .904 Rick Barry, Golden State
1975-76 — .923 Rick Barry, Golden State
1976-77 — .945 Ernie DiGregorio, Buffalo
1977-78 — .924 Rick Barry, Golden State
1978-79 — .947 Rick Barry, Houston
1979-80 — .935 Rick Barry, Houston
1980-81 — .958 Calvin Murphy, Houston
1981-82 — .899 Kyle Macy, Phoenix
1982-83 — .920 Calvin Murphy, Houston
1983-84 — .888 Larry Bird, Boston
1984-85 — .907 Kyle Macy, Phoenix
1985-86 — .896 Larry Bird, Boston
1986-87 — .910 Larry Bird, Boston
1987-88 — .922 Jack Sikma, Milwaukee
1988-89 — .911 Magic Johnson, L.A. Lakers
1989-90 — .930 Larry Bird, Boston
1990-91 — .918 Reggie Miller, Indiana
1991-92 — .947 Mark Price, Cleveland
1992-93 — .948 Mark Price, Cleveland
1993-94 — .956 Mahmoud Abdul-Rauf, Denver
1994-95 — .934 Spud Webb, Sacramento
1995-96 — .930 Mahmoud Abdul-Rauf, Denver
1996-97 — .906 Mark Price, Golden State
1997-98 — .939 Chris Mullin, Indiana
1998-99 — .915 Reggie Miller, Indiana
1999-00 — .950 Jeff Hornacek, Utah

THREE-POINT FIELD-GOAL PERCENTAGE

1979-80 — .443 Fred Brown, Seattle
1980-81 — .383 Brian Taylor, San Diego
1981-82 — .439 Campy Russell, New York
1982-83 — .345 Mike Dunleavy, San Antonio
1983-84 — .361 Darrell Griffith, Utah
1984-85 — .433 Byron Scott, L.A. Lakers
1985-86 — .451 Craig Hodges, Milwaukee
1986-87 — .481 Kiki Vandeweghe, Portland
1987-88 — .491 Craig Hodges, Mil.-Pho.
1988-89 — .522 Jon Sundvold, Miami
1989-90 — .507 Steve Kerr, Cleveland
1990-91 — .461 Jim Les, Sacramento
1991-92 — .446 Dana Barros, Seattle
1992-93 — .453 B.J. Armstrong, Chicago
1993-94 — .459 Tracy Murray, Portland
1994-95 — .524 Steve Kerr, Chicago
1995-96 — .522 Tim Legler, Washington
1996-97 — .470 Glen Rice, Charlotte
1997-98 — .464 Dale Ellis, Seattle
1998-99 — .476 Dell Curry, Milwaukee
1999-00 — .491 Hubert Davis, Dallas

MINUTES

1951-52 — 2,939 Paul Arizin, Philadelphia
1952-53 — 3,166 Neil Johnston, Philadelphia
1953-54 — 3,296 Neil Johnston, Philadelphia
1954-55 — 2,953 Paul Arizin, Philadelphia
1955-56 — 2,838 Slater Martin, Minneapolis

INDIVIDUAL LEADERS – Continued

1956-57 — 2,851 Dolph Schayes, Syracuse
1957-58 — 2,918 Dolph Schayes, Syracuse
1958-59 — 2,979 Bill Russell, Boston
1959-60 — 3,338 (tie) Wilt Chamberlain, Philadelphia
Gene Shue, Detroit
1960-61 — 3,773 Wilt Chamberlain, Philadelphia
1961-62 — 3,882 Wilt Chamberlain, Philadelphia
1962-63 — 3,806 Wilt Chamberlain, San Francisco
1963-64 — 3,689 Wilt Chamberlain, San Francisco
1964-65 — 3,466 Bill Russell, Boston
1965-66 — 3,737 Wilt Chamberlain, Philadelphia
1966-67 — 3,682 Wilt Chamberlain, Philadelphia
1967-68 — 3,836 Wilt Chamberlain, Philadelphia
1968-69 — 3,695 Elvin Hayes, San Diego
1969-70 — 3,665 Elvin Hayes, San Diego
1970-71 — 3,678 John Havlicek, Boston
1971-72 — 3,698 John Havlicek, Boston
1972-73 — 3,681 Nate Archibald, K.C./Omaha
1973-74 — 3,602 Elvin Hayes, Capital
1974-75 — 3,539 Bob McAdoo, Buffalo
1975-76 — 3,379 Kareem Abdul-Jabbar, Los Angeles
1976-77 — 3,364 Elvin Hayes, Washington
1977-78 — 3,638 Len Robinson, New Orleans
1978-79 — 3,390 Moses Malone, Houston
1979-80 — 3,226 Norm Nixon, Los Angeles
1980-81 — 3,417 Adrian Dantley, Utah
1981-82 — 3,398 Moses Malone, Houston
1982-83 — 3,093 Isiah Thomas, Detroit
1983-84 — 3,082 Jeff Ruland, Washington
1984-85 — 3,182 Buck Williams, New Jersey
1985-86 — 3,270 Maurice Cheeks, Philadelphia
1986-87 — 3,281 Michael Jordan, Chicago
1987-88 — 3,311 Michael Jordan, Chicago
1988-89 — 3,255 Michael Jordan, Chicago
1989-90 — 3,238 Rodney McCray, Sacramento
1990-91 — 3,315 Chris Mullin, Golden State
1991-92 — 3,346 Chris Mullin, Golden State
1992-93 — 3,323 Larry Johnson, Charlotte
1993-94 — 3,533 Latrell Sprewell, Golden State
1994-95 — 3,361 Vin Baker, Milwaukee
1995-96 — 3,457 Anthony Mason, New York
1996-97 — 3,362 Glen Rice, Charlotte
1997-98 — 3,394 Michael Finley, Dallas
1998-99 — 2,060 Jason Kidd, Phoenix
1999-00 — 3,464 Michael Finley, Dallas

REBOUNDING

1950-51 — 1,080 Dolph Schayes, Syracuse
1951-52 — 880 (tie) Larry Foust, Fort Wayne
Mel Hutchins, Milwaukee
1952-53 — 1,007 George Mikan, Minneapolis
1953-54 — 1,098 Harry Gallatin, New York
1954-55 — 1,085 Neil Johnston, Philadelphia
1955-56 — 1,164 Bob Pettit, St. Louis
1956-57 — 1,256 Maurice Stokes, Rochester
1957-58 — 1,564 Bill Russell, Boston
1958-59 — 1,612 Bill Russell, Boston
1959-60 — 1,941 Wilt Chamberlain, Philadelphia
1960-61 — 2,149 Wilt Chamberlain, Philadelphia
1961-62 — 2,052 Wilt Chamberlain, Philadelphia
1962-63 — 1,946 Wilt Chamberlain, San Francisco
1963-64 — 1,930 Bill Russell, Boston
1964-65 — 1,878 Bill Russell, Boston
1965-66 — 1,943 Wilt Chamberlain, Philadelphia
1966-67 — 1,957 Wilt Chamberlain, Philadelphia
1967-68 — 1,952 Wilt Chamberlain, Philadelphia
1968-69 — 1,712 Wilt Chamberlain, Los Angeles
1969-70 — 16.9* Elvin Hayes, San Diego
1970-71 — 18.2* Wilt Chamberlain, Los Angeles
1971-72 — 19.2* Wilt Chamberlain, Los Angeles
1972-73 — 18.6* Wilt Chamberlain, Los Angeles
1973-74 — 18.1* Elvin Hayes, Capital
1974-75 — 14.8* Wes Unseld, Washington
1975-76 — 16.9* Kareem Abdul-Jabbar, Los Angeles
1976-77 — 14.4* Bill Walton, Portland
1977-78 — 15.7* Len Robinson, New Orleans
1978-79 — 17.6* Moses Malone, Houston
1979-80 — 15.0* Swen Nater, San Diego
1980-81 — 14.8* Moses Malone, Houston
1981-82 — 14.7* Moses Malone, Houston
1982-83 — 15.3* Moses Malone, Philadelphia
1983-84 — 13.4* Moses Malone, Philadelphia
1984-85 — 13.1* Moses Malone, Philadelphia
1985-86 — 13.1* Bill Laimbeer, Detroit
1986-87 — 14.6* Charles Barkley, Philadelphia
1987-88 — 13.03* Michael Cage, L.A. Clippers
1988-89 — 13.5* Hakeem Olajuwon, Housto
1989-90 — 14.0* Hakeem Olajuwon, Houston
1990-91 — 13.0* David Robinson, San Antonio
1991-92 — 18.7* Dennis Rodman, Detroit
1992-93 — 18.3* Dennis Rodman, Detroit
1993-94 — 17.3* Dennis Rodman, San Antonio
1994-95 — 16.8* Dennis Rodman, San Antonio
1995-96 — 14.9* Dennis Rodman, Chicago
1996-97 — 16.1* Dennis Rodman, Chicago
1997-98 — 15.0* Dennis Rodman, Chicago
1998-99 — 13.0* Chris Webber, Sacramento
1999-00 — 14.1 Dikembe Mutombo, Atlanta
**Based on average per game.*

ASSISTS

1946-47 — 202 Ernie Calverly, Providence
1947-48 — 120 Howie Dallmar, Philadelphia
1948-49 — 321 Bob Davies, Rochester
1949-50 — 396 Dick McGuire, New York
1950-51 — 414 Andy Phillip, Philadelphia
1951-52 — 539 Andy Phillip, Philadelphia
1952-53 — 547 Bob Cousy, Boston
1953-54 — 518 Bob Cousy, Boston
1954-55 — 557 Bob Cousy, Boston
1955-56 — 642 Bob Cousy, Boston
1956-57 — 478 Bob Cousy, Boston
1957-58 — 463 Bob Cousy, Boston
1958-59 — 557 Bob Cousy, Boston
1959-60 — 715 Bob Cousy, Boston
1960-61 — 690 Oscar Robertson, Cincinnati
1961-62 — 899 Oscar Robertson, Cincinnati
1962-63 — 825 Guy Rodgers, San Francisco
1963-64 — 868 Oscar Robertson, Cincinnati
1964-65 — 861 Oscar Robertson, Cincinnati
1965-66 — 847 Oscar Robertson, Cincinnati
1966-67 — 908 Guy Rodgers, Chicago
1967-68 — 702 Wilt Chamberlain, Philadelphia
1968-69 — 772 Oscar Robertson, Cincinnati
1969-70 — 9.1* Lenny Wilkens, Seattle
1970-71 — 10.1* Norm Van Lier, Cincinnati
1971-72 — 9.7* Jerry West, Los Angeles
1972-73 — 11.4* Nate Archibald, K.C./Omaha
1973-74 — 8.2* Ernie DiGregorio, Buffalo
1974-75 — 8.0* Kevin Porter, Washington
1975-76 — 8.1* Don Watts, Seattle
1976-77 — 8.5* Don Buse, Indiana
1977-78 — 10.2* Kevin Porter, Detroit-New Jersey
1978-79 — 13.4* Kevin Porter, Detroit
1979-80 — 10.1* Micheal Ray Richardson, New York
1980-81 — 9.1* Kevin Porter, Washington
1981-82 — 9.6* Johnny Moore, San Antonio
1982-83 — 10.5* Magic Johnson, Los Angeles
1983-84 — 13.1* Magic Johnson, Los Angeles
1984-85 — 13.98* Isiah Thomas, Detroit
1985-86 — 12.6* Magic Johnson, L.A. Lakers
1986-87 — 12.2* Magic Johnson, L.A. Lakers
1987-88 — 13.8* John Stockton, Utah
1988-89 — 13.6* John Stockton, Utah
1989-90 — 14.5* John Stockton, Utah
1990-91 — 14.2* John Stockton, Utah
1991-92 — 13.7* John Stockton, Utah
1992-93 — 12.0* John Stockton, Utah
1993-94 — 12.6* John Stockton, Utah
1994-95 — 12.3* John Stockton, Utah
1995-96 — 11.2* John Stockton, Utah
1996-97 — 11.4* Mark Jackson, Denver-Indiana
1997-98 — 10.5* Rod Strickland, Washington
1998-99 — 10.8* Jason Kidd, Phoenix
1999-00 — 10.1* Jason Kidd, Phoenix
**Based on average per game.*

STEALS

1973-74 — 2.68* Larry Steele, Portland
1974-75 — 2.85* Rick Barry, Golden State
1975-76 — 3.18* Don Watts, Seattle
1976-77 — 3.47* Don Buse, Indiana
1977-78 — 2.74* Ron Lee, Phoenix
1978-79 — 2.46* M.L. Carr, Detroit
1979-80 — 3.23* Micheal Ray Richardson, New York
1980-81 — 3.43* Magic Johnson, L.A. Lakers
1981-82 — 2.67* Magic Johnson, L.A. Lakers
1982-83 — 2.84* Micheal Ray Richardson, G.S.-N.J.
1983-84 — 2.65* Rickey Green, Utah
1984-85 — 2.96* Micheal Ray Richardson, New Jersey
1985-86 — 3.67* Alvin Robertson, San Antonio
1986-87 — 3.21* Alvin Robertson, San Antonio
1987-88 — 3.16* Michael Jordan, Chicago
1988-89 — 3.21* John Stockton, Utah
1989-90 — 2.77* Michael Jordan, Chicago
1990-91 — 3.04* Alvin Robertson, Milwaukee
1991-92 — 2.98* John Stockton, Utah
1992-93 — 2.83* Michael Jordan, Chicago
1993-94 — 2.96* Nate McMillan, Seattle
1994-95 — 2.94* Scottie Pippen, Chicago
1995-96 — 2.85* Gary Payton, Seattle
1996-97 — 2.72* Mookie Blaylock, Atlanta
1997-98 — 2.61* Mookie Blaylock, Atlanta
1998-99 — 2.68* Kendall Gill, New Jersey
1999-00 — 2.67* Eddie Jones, Charlotte
**Based on average per game.*

BLOCKED SHOTS

1973-74 — 4.85* Elmore Smith, Los Angeles
1974-75 — 3.26* Kareem Abdul-Jabbar, Milwaukee
1975-76 — 4.12* Kareem Abdul-Jabbar, Los Angeles
1976-77 — 3.25* Bill Walton, Portland
1977-78 — 3.38* George Johnson, New Jersey
1978-79 — 3.95* Kareem Abdul-Jabbar, Los Angeles
1979-80 — 3.41* Kareem Abdul-Jabbar, Los Angeles

INDIVIDUAL LEADERS – Continued

1980-81 — 3.39* George Johnson, San Antonio
1981-82 — 3.12* George Johnson, San Antonio
1982-83 — 4.29* Tree Rollins, Atlanta
1983-84 — 4.28* Mark Eaton, Utah
1984-85 — 5.56* Mark Eaton, Utah
1985-86 — 4.96* Manute Bol, Washington
1986-87 — 4.06* Mark Eaton, Utah
1987-88 — 3.71* Mark Eaton, Utah
1988-89 — 4.31* Manute Bol, Golden State
1989-90 — 4.59* Hakeem Olajuwon, Houston
1990-91 — 3.95* Hakeem Olajuwon, Houston
1991-92 — 4.49* David Robinson, San Antonio
1992-93 — 4.17* Hakeem Olajuwon, Houston
1993-94 — 4.10* Dikembe Mutombo, Denver
1994-95 — 3.91* Dikembe Mutombo, Denver
1995-96 — 4.49* Dikembe Mutombo, Denver
1996-97 — 3.40* Shawn Bradley, New Jersey-Dallas
1997-98 — 3.65* Marcus Camby, Toronto
1998-99 — 3.91* Alonzo Mourning, Miami
1999-00 — 3.72* Alonzo Mourning, Miami
**Based on average per game.*

ALL-TIME TOP TENS

(Active 1999-00 players in CAPS.)

MOST GAMES PLAYED

Robert Parish	1,611
Kareem Abdul-Jabbar	1,560
Moses Malone	1,329
Buck Williams	1,307
Elvin Hayes	1,303
John Havlicek	1,270
JOHN STOCKTON	1,258
Paul Silas	1,254
SAM PERKINS	1,222
DALE ELLIS	1,209

MOST MINUTES PLAYED

Kareem Abdul-Jabbar	57,446
Elvin Hayes	50,000
Wilt Chamberlain	47,859
John Havlicek	46,471
Robert Parish	45,704
Moses Malone	45,071
KARL MALONE	44,608
Oscar Robertson	43,886
Buck Williams	42,464
HAKEEM OLAJUWON	41,299

MOST FIELD GOALS MADE

Kareem Abdul-Jabbar	15,837
Wilt Chamberlain	12,681
KARL MALONE	11,435
Elvin Hayes	10,976
Michael Jordan	10,962
Alex English	10,659
John Havlicek	10,513
HAKEEM OLAJUWON	10,272
Dominique Wilkins	9,963
Robert Parish	9,614

MOST FIELD GOALS ATTEMPTED

Kareem Abdul-Jabbar	28,307
Elvin Hayes	24,272
John Havlicek	23,930
Wilt Chamberlain	23,497
KARL MALONE	21,777
Michael Jordan	21,686
Dominique Wilkins	21,589
Alex English	21,036
Elgin Baylor	20,171
HAKEEM OLAJUWON	20,005

HIGHEST FIELD GOAL PERCENTAGE

(2,000 FGM minimum)

PLAYER	FGM	FGA	Pct
Artis Gilmore	5,732	9,570	.599
MARK WEST	2,528	4,356	.580
SHAQUILLE O'NEAL	5,896	10,210	.577
Steve Johnson	2,841	4,965	.572
Darryl Dawkins	3,477	6,079	.572
James Donaldson	3,105	5,442	.571
Jeff Ruland	2,105	3,734	.564
Kareem Abdul-Jabbar	15,837	28,307	.559
Kevin McHale	6,830	12,334	.554
Bobby Jones	3,412	6,199	.550

MOST FREE THROWS MADE

Moses Malone	8,531
KARL MALONE	8,100
Oscar Robertson	7,694
Jerry West	7,160
Dolph Schayes	6,979
Adrian Dantley	6,832
Michael Jordan	6,798
Kareem Abdul-Jabbar	6,712
CHARLES BARKLEY	6,349
Bob Pettit	6,182

MOST FREE THROWS ATTEMPTED

Wilt Chamberlain	11,862
Moses Malone	11,090
KARL MALONE	11,027
Kareem Abdul-Jabbar	9,304
Oscar Robertson	9,185
Jerry West	8,801
CHARLES BARKLEY	8,643
Adrian Dantley	8,351
Dolph Schayes	8,274
Bob Pettit	8,119

HIGHEST FREE THROW PERCENTAGE

(1,200 FTM minimum)

PLAYER	FTM	FTA	Pct
Mark Price	2,135	2,362	.904
Rick Barry	3,818	4,243	.900
Calvin Murphy	3,445	3,864	.892
Scott Skiles	1,548	1,741	.889
Larry Bird	3,960	4,471	.886
Bill Sharman	3,143	3,559	.883
REGGIE MILLER	5,015	5,690	.881
JEFF HORNACEK	2,973	3,390	.877
Ricky Pierce	3,389	3,871	.875
Kiki Vandeweghe	3,484	3,997	.872

MOST 3-PT. FIELD GOALS MADE

REGGIE MILLER	1,867
DALE ELLIS	1,719
GLEN RICE	1,353
MITCH RICHMOND	1,263
DAN MAJERLE	1,224
VERNON MAXWELL	1,222
CHUCK PERSON	1,220
TIM HARDAWAY	1,219
DENNIS SCOTT	1,214
HERSEY HAWKINS	1,209

MOST 3-PT. FIELD GOALS ATTEMPTED

REGGIE MILLER	4,629
DALE ELLIS	4,266
VERNON MAXWELL	3,820
MOOKIE BLAYLOCK	3,549
TIM HARDAWAY	3,443
DAN MAJERLE	3,382
CHUCK PERSON	3,370
GLEN RICE	3,339
JOHN STARKS	3,314
MITCH RICHMOND	3,222

HIGHEST 3-POINT FIELD GOAL PERCENTAGE

(250 3FGM Minimum)

PLAYER	3FGM	3FGA	Pct
STEVE KERR	618	1,332	.464
HUBERT DAVIS	581	1,317	.441
Drazen Petrovic	255	583	.437
TIM LEGLER	260	603	.431
B.J. ARMSTRONG	436	1,026	.425
DANA BARROS	1,022	2,476	.413
WESLEY PERSON	777	1,890	.411
Trent Tucker	575	1,410	.408
ALLAN HOUSTON	777	1,917	.405
GLEN RICE	1,353	3,339	.405

MOST OFFENSIVE REBOUNDS

Moses Malone	6,731
Robert Parish	4,598
Buck Williams	4,526
DENNIS RODMAN	4,329
CHARLES BARKLEY	4,260
HAKEEM OLAJUWON	3,812
KEVIN WILLIS	3,699
CHARLES OAKLEY	3,673
Larry Smith	3,401
OTIS THORPE	3,396

MOST DEFENSIVE REBOUNDS

Robert Parish	10,117
KARL MALONE	9,486
Moses Malone	9,481
Kareem Abdul-Jabbar	9,394
HAKEEM OLAJUWON	9,139

ALL-TIME TOP TENS – Continued

Buck Williams 8,491
CHARLES BARKLEY 8,286
Jack Sikma 8,274
PATRICK EWING 8,191
DENNIS RODMAN 7,625

MOST TOTAL REBOUNDS

Wilt Chamberlain 23,924
Bill Russell 21,620
Kareem Abdul-Jabbar 17,440
Elvin Hayes 16,279
Moses Malone 16,212
Robert Parish 14,715
Nate Thurmond 14,464
Walt Bellamy 14,241
Wes Unseld 13,769
Buck Williams 13,017

MOST ASSISTS

JOHN STOCKTON 13,790
Magic Johnson 10,141
Oscar Robertson 9,887
Isiah Thomas 9,061
MARK JACKSON 8,574
Maurice Cheeks 7,392
Lenny Wilkens 7,211
Bob Cousy 6,955
Guy Rodgers 6,917
ROD STRICKLAND 6,723

MOST PERSONAL FOULS

Kareem Abdul-Jabbar 4,657
Robert Parish 4,443
Buck Williams 4,267
Elvin Hayes 4,193
HAKEEM OLAJUWON 4,095
James Edwards 4,042
OTIS THORPE 4,038
CHARLES OAKLEY 3,890
Jack Sikma 3,879
Hal Greer 3,855

MOST DISQUALIFICATIONS

Vern Mikkelsen 127
Walter Dukes 121
SHAWN KEMP 109
Charlie Share 105
Paul Arizin 101
Darryl Dawkins 100
James Edwards 96
Tom Gola 94
Tom Sanders 94
Steve Johnson 93

MOST STEALS

JOHN STOCKTON 2,844
Maurice Cheeks 2,310
Michael Jordan 2,306
Clyde Drexler 2,207
Alvin Robertson 2,112
HAKEEM OLAJUWON 2,018
SCOTTIE PIPPEN 1,986
Derek Harper 1,957
MOOKIE BLAYLOCK 1,888
Isiah Thomas 1,861

MOST BLOCKED SHOTS

HAKEEM OLAJUWON 3,652
Kareem Abdul-Jabbar 3,189
Mark Eaton 3,064
PATRICK EWING 2,758
Tree Rollins 2,542
DAVID ROBINSON 2,506
DIKEMBE MUTOMBO 2,443
Robert Parish 2,361
Manute Bol 2,086
George T. Johnson 2,082

HIGHEST SCORING AVERAGE

(400 Games or 10,000 Points Minimum)

PLAYER	G	FTM	FGM	PTS	AVG
Michael Jordan	930	6,798	10,962	29,277	31.5
Wilt Chamberlain	1045	6,057	12,681	31,419	30.1
SHAQUILLE O'NEAL	534	2,894	5,896	14,687	27.5
Elgin Baylor	846	5,763	8,693	23,149	27.4
Jerry West	932	7,160	9,016	25,192	27.0
Bob Pettit	792	6,182	7,349	20,880	26.4
George Gervin	791	4,541	8,045	20,708	26.2
KARL MALONE	1192	8,100	11,435	31,041	26.0
Oscar Robertson	1040	7,694	9,508	26,710	25.7
Dominique Wilkins	1074	6,031	9,963	26,668	24.8

POINTS

Kareem Abdul-Jabbar 38,387
Wilt Chamberlain 31,419
KARL MALONE 31,041
Michael Jordan 29,277
Moses Malone 27,409
Elvin Hayes 27,313
Oscar Robertson 26,710
Dominique Wilkins 26,668
John Havlicek 26,395
HAKEEM OLAJUWON 25,822

ALL-TIME REGULAR-SEASON NBA RECORDS: INDIVIDUAL

Compiled by Elias Sports Bureau

Throughout this all-time NBA Record section, records for 'fewest' and 'lowest' exclude games and seasons before 1954-55, when the 24-second clock was introduced.

SEASONS

Most seasons

21 — Robert Parish, Golden State, 1976-77 — 1979-80; Boston, 1980-81 — 1993-94; Charlotte, 1994-95 — 1995-96; Chicago, 1996-97

20 — Kareem Abdul-Jabbar, Milwaukee, 1969-70 — 1974-75; L.A. Lakers, 1975-76 — 1988-89

19 — James Edwards, Los Angeles, 1977-78; Indiana, 1977-78 — 1980-81; Cleveland, 1981-82 — 1982-83; Phoenix, 1982-83 — 1987-88; Detroit, 1987-88 — 1990-91; L.A. Clippers, 1991-92; L.A. Lakers, 1992-93 — 1993-94; Portland, 1994-95; Chicago, 1995-96
Moses Malone, Buffalo, 1976-77; Houston, 1976-77 — 1981-82; Philadelphia, 1982-83 — 1985-86; Washington, 1986-87 — 1987-88; Atlanta, 1988-89 — 1990-91; Milwaukee, 1991-92 — 1992-93; Philadelphia, 1993-94; San Antonio, 1994-95

GAMES

Most games, career

1,611 — Robert Parish, Golden State, 1976-77 — 1979-80; Boston, 1980-81 — 1993-94; Charlotte, 1994-95 — 1995-96; Chicago, 1996-97

1,560 — Kareem Abdul-Jabbar, Milwaukee, 1969-70 — 1974-75; L.A. Lakers, 1975-76 — 1988-89

1,329 — Moses Malone, Buffalo, 1976-77; Houston, 1976-77 — 1981-82; Philadelphia, 1982-83 — 1985-86; Washington, 1986-87 — 1987-88; Atlanta, 1988-89 — 1990-91; Milwaukee, 1991-92 — 1992-93; Philadelphia, 1993-94; San Antonio, 1994-95

Most consecutive games, career

1,110 — A.C. Green, L.A. Lakers, Phoenix, Dallas, November 19, 1986 — April 19, 2000 (current)

906 — Randy Smith, Buffalo, San Diego, Cleveland, New York, San Diego, February 18, 1972 — March 13, 1983

844 — John Kerr, Syracuse, Philadelphia, Baltimore, October 31, 1954 — November 4, 1965

Most games, season

88 — Walt Bellamy, New York, Detroit, 1968-69

87 — Tom Henderson, Atlanta, Washington, 1976-77

86 — McCoy McLemore, Cleveland, Milwaukee, 1970-71
Garfield Heard, Buffalo, Phoenix, 1975-76

MINUTES

Minutes have been compiled since 1951-52

Most seasons leading league, minutes

8 — Wilt Chamberlain, Philadelphia, 1959-60 — 1961-62; San Francisco,

For additional records, please log on to NBA.com.

ALL-TIME REGULAR-SEASON NBA RECORDS: INDIVIDUAL – Continued

1962-63 — 1963-64; Philadelphia, 1965-66 — 1967-68
4 — Elvin Hayes, San Diego, 1968-69 — 1969-70; Capital, 1973-74; Washington, 1976-77
3 — Michael Jordan, Chicago, 1986-87 — 1988-89

Most consecutive seasons leading league, minutes
5 — Wilt Chamberlain, Philadelphia, 1959-60 — 1961-62; San Francisco, 1962-63 — 1963-64
3 — Wilt Chamberlain, Philadelphia, 1965-66 — 1967-68
Michael Jordan, Chicago, 1986-87 — 1988-89

Most minutes, career
57,446 — Kareem Abdul-Jabbar, Milwaukee, 1969-70 — 1974-75; L.A. Lakers, 1975-76 — 1988-89
50,000 — Elvin Hayes, San Diego, 1968-69 — 1970-71; Houston, 1971-72; Baltimore, 1972-73; Capital, 1973-74; Washington, 1974-75 — 1980-81; Houston, 1981-82 — 1983-84
47,859 — Wilt Chamberlain, Philadelphia, 1959-60 — 1961-62; San Francisco, 1962-63 — 1964-65; Philadelphia, 1964-65 — 1967-68; Los Angeles, 1968-69 — 1972-73
46,471 — John Havlicek, Boston, 1962-63 — 1977-78
45,704 — Robert Parish, Golden State, 1976-77 — 1979-80; Boston, 1980-81 — 1993-94; Charlotte, 1994-95 — 1995-96; Chicago, 1996-97

Highest average, minutes per game, career
(minimum: 400 games)
45.8 — Wilt Chamberlain, Philadelphia, 1959-60 — 1961-62; San Francisco, 1962-63 — 1964-65; Philadelphia, 1964-65 — 1967-68; Los Angeles, 1968-69 — 1972-73 (47,859/1,045)
42.3 — Bill Russell, Boston, 1956-57 — 1968-69 (40,726/963)
42.2 — Oscar Robertson, Cincinnati, 1960-61 — 1969-70; Milwaukee, 1970-71 — 1973-74 (43,866/1,040)

Most minutes, season
3,882 — Wilt Chamberlain, Philadelphia, 1961-62
3,836 — Wilt Chamberlain, Philadelphia, 1967-68
3,806 — Wilt Chamberlain, San Francisco, 1962-63
3,773 — Wilt Chamberlain, Philadelphia, 1960-61
3,737 — Wilt Chamberlain, Philadelphia, 1965-66
3,698 — John Havlicek, Boston, 1971-72

Highest average, minutes per game, season
48.5 — Wilt Chamberlain, Philadelphia, 1961-62 (3,882/80)
47.8 — Wilt Chamberlain, Philadelphia, 1960-61 (3,773/79)
47.6 — Wilt Chamberlain, San Francisco, 1962-63 (3,806/80)
47.3 — Wilt Chamberlain, Philadelphia, 1965-66 (3,737/79)
46.8 — Wilt Chamberlain, Philadelphia, 1967-68 (3,836/82)
46.4 — Wilt Chamberlain, Philadelphia, 1959-60 (3,338/72)
46.1 — Wilt Chamberlain, San Francisco, 1963-64 (3,689/80)
46.0 — Nate Archibald, K.C.-Omaha, 1972-73 (3,681/80)

Most minutes, game
69 — Dale Ellis, Seattle at Milwaukee, November 9, 1989 (5 ot)
68 — Xavier McDaniel, Seattle at Milwaukee, November 9, 1989 (5 ot)
64 — Norm Nixon, Los Angeles at Cleveland, January 29, 1980 (4 ot)
Eric Floyd, Golden State vs. New Jersey, February 1, 1987 (4 ot)

COMPLETE GAMES

Most complete games, season
79 — Wilt Chamberlain, Philadelphia, 1961-62

Most consecutive complete games, season
47 — Wilt Chamberlain, Philadelphia, January 5 — March 14, 1962

SCORING

Most seasons leading league
10 — Michael Jordan, Chicago, 1986-87 — 1992-93, 1995-96 — 1997-98
7 — Wilt Chamberlain, Philadelphia, 1959-60 — 1961-62; San Francisco, 1962-63 — 1963-64; San Francisco, Philadelphia, 1964-65; Philadelphia, 1965-66
4 — George Gervin, San Antonio, 1977-78 — 1979-80, 1981-82

Most consecutive seasons leading league
7 — Wilt Chamberlain, Philadelphia, 1959-60 — 1961-62; San Francisco, 1962-63 — 1963-64; San Francisco, Philadelphia, 1964-65; Philadelphia, 1965-66
Michael Jordan, Chicago, 1986-87 — 1992-93

Most points, lifetime
38,387 — Kareem Abdul-Jabbar, Milwaukee, 1969-70 — 1974-75; L.A. Lakers, 1975-76 — 1988-89
31,419 — Wilt Chamberlain, Philadelphia, 1959-60 — 1961-62; San Francisco, 1962-63 — 1964-65; Philadelphia, 1964-65 — 1967-68; Los Angeles, 1968-69 — 1972-73
31,041 — Karl Malone, Utah, 1985-86 — 1999-00
29,277 — Michael Jordan, Chicago, 1984-85 — 1992-93, 1994-95 — 1997-98
27,409 — Moses Malone, Buffalo, 1976-77; Houston, 1976-77 — 1981-82; Philadelphia, 1982-83 — 1985-86; Washington, 1986-87 — 1987-88; Atlanta, 1988-89 — 1990-91; Milwaukee, 1991-92 — 1992-93; Philadelphia, 1993-94; San Antonio, 1994-95

Highest average, points per game, career
(minimum: 400 games)
31.5 — Michael Jordan, Chicago, 1984-85 — 1992-93, 1994-95 — 1997-98 (29,277/930)
30.1 — Wilt Chamberlain, Philadelphia, 1959-60 — 1961-62; San Francisco, 1962-63 — 1964-65; Philadelphia, 1964-65 — 1967-68; Los Angeles, 1968-69 — 1972-73 (31,419/1,045)
27.5 — Shaquille O'Neal, Orlando, 1992-93 — 1995-96; L.A. Lakers, 1996-97 — 1999-00 (14,687/534)
27.4 — Elgin Baylor, Minneapolis, 1958-59 — 1959-60; Los Angeles, 1960-61 — 1971-72 (23,149/846)
27.0 — Jerry West, Los Angeles, 1960-61 — 1973-74 (25,192/932)

Most points, season
4,029 — Wilt Chamberlain, Philadelphia, 1961-62
3,586 — Wilt Chamberlain, San Francisco, 1962-63
3,041 — Michael Jordan, Chicago, 1986-87
3,033 — Wilt Chamberlain, Philadelphia, 1960-61

Highest average, points per game, season
(minimum: 70 games)
50.4 — Wilt Chamberlain, Philadelphia, 1961-62 (4,029/80)
44.8 — Wilt Chamberlain, San Francisco, 1962-63 (3,586/80)
38.4 — Wilt Chamberlain, Philadelphia, 1960-61 (3,033/79)
37.6 — Wilt Chamberlain, Philadelphia, 1959-60 (2,707/72)
37.1 — Michael Jordan, Chicago, 1986-87 (3,041/82)

Highest average, points per game, rookie, season
37.6 — Wilt Chamberlain, Philadelphia, 1959-60 (2,707/72)
31.6 — Walt Bellamy, Chicago, 1961-62 (2,495/79)
30.5 — Oscar Robertson, Cincinnati, 1960-61 (2,165/71)

Most seasons, 2,000-or-more points
12 — Karl Malone, Utah, 1987-88 — 1997-98, 1999-00
11 — Michael Jordan, Chicago, 1984-85, 1986-87 — 1992-93, 1995-96 — 1997-98
9 — Kareem Abdul-Jabbar, Milwaukee, 1969-70 — 1973-74; Los Angeles, 1975-76 — 1976-77, 1979-80 — 1980-81

Most consecutive seasons, 2,000-or-more points
11 — Karl Malone, Utah, 1987-88 — 1997-98

ALL-TIME REGULAR-SEASON NBA RECORDS: INDIVIDUAL – Continued

8 — Alex English, Denver, 1981-82 — 1988-89
7 — Wilt Chamberlain, Philadelphia, 1959-60 — 1961-62; San Francisco, 1962-63 — 1963-64; San Francisco, Philadelphia, 1964-65; Philadelphia, 1965-66
Oscar Robertson, Cincinnati, 1960-61 — 1966-67
Dominique Wilkins, Atlanta, 1984-85 — 1990-91
Michael Jordan, Chicago, 1986-87 — 1992-93

Most points, game

100 — Wilt Chamberlain, Philadelphia vs. New York, at Hershey, Pa., March 2, 1962
78 — Wilt Chamberlain, Philadelphia vs. Los Angeles, December 8, 1961 (3 ot)
73 — Wilt Chamberlain, Philadelphia vs. Chicago, January 13, 1962
Wilt Chamberlain, San Francisco at New York, November 16, 1962
David Thompson, Denver at Detroit, April 9, 1978
72 — Wilt Chamberlain, San Francisco at Los Angeles, November 3, 1962
71 — Elgin Baylor, Los Angeles at New York, November 15, 1960
David Robinson, San Antonio at L.A. Clippers, April 24, 1994

Most games, 50-or-more points, career

118 — Wilt Chamberlain, Philadelphia, 1959-60 — 1961-62; San Francisco, 1962-63 — 1964-65; Philadelphia, 1964-65 — 1967-68; Los Angeles, 1968-69 — 1972-73
30 — Michael Jordan, Chicago, 1984-85 — 1992-93, 1994-95 — 1996-97
18 — Elgin Baylor, Minneapolis, 1958-59 — 1959-60; Los Angeles, 1960-61 — 1971-72
14 — Rick Barry, San Francisco, 1965-66 — 1966-67; Golden State, 1972-73 — 1977-78; Houston, 1978-79 — 1979-80

Most games, 50-or-more points, season

45 — Wilt Chamberlain, Philadelphia, 1961-62
30 — Wilt Chamberlain, San Francisco, 1962-63
9 — Wilt Chamberlain, San Francisco, 1963-64
Wilt Chamberlain, San Francisco, Philadelphia, 1964-65

Most consecutive games, 50-or-more points

7 — Wilt Chamberlain, Philadelphia, December 16 — December 29, 1961
6 — Wilt Chamberlain, Philadelphia, January 11 — January 19, 1962
5 — Wilt Chamberlain, Philadelphia, December 8 — December 13, 1961
Wilt Chamberlain, Philadelphia, February 25 — March 4, 1962

Most games, 40-or-more points, career

271 — Wilt Chamberlain, Philadelphia, 1959-60 — 1961-62; San Francisco, 1962-63 — 1964-65; Philadelphia, 1964-65 — 1967-68; Los Angeles, 1968-69 — 1972-73
165 — Michael Jordan, Chicago, 1984-85 — 1992-93, 1994-95 — 1997-98
87 — Elgin Baylor, Minneapolis, 1958-59 — 1959-60; Los Angeles, 1960-61 — 1971-72

Most games, 40-or-more points, season

63 — Wilt Chamberlain, Philadelphia, 1961-62
52 — Wilt Chamberlain, San Francisco, 1962-63
37 — Michael Jordan, Chicago, 1986-87

Most consecutive games, 40-or-more points

14 — Wilt Chamberlain, Philadelphia, December 8 — December 30, 1961
Wilt Chamberlain, Philadelphia, January 11 — February 1, 1962
10 — Wilt Chamberlain, San Francisco, November 9 — November 25, 1962
9 — Michael Jordan, Chicago, November 28 — December 12, 1986

Most consecutive games, 30-or-more points

65 — Wilt Chamberlain, Philadelphia, November 4, 1961 — February 22, 1962
31 — Wilt Chamberlain, Philadelphia, San Francisco, February 25 — December 8, 1962
25 — Wilt Chamberlain, Philadelphia, November 11 — December 27, 1960

Most consecutive games, 20-or-more points

126 — Wilt Chamberlain, Philadelphia, San Francisco, October 19, 1961 — January 19, 1963
92 — Wilt Chamberlain, San Francisco, February 26, 1963 — March 18, 1964

Most consecutive games, 10-or-more points

840 — Michael Jordan, Chicago, March 25, 1986 — April 18, 1998
787 — Kareem Abdul-Jabbar, L.A. Lakers, December 4, 1977 — December 2, 1987

Most points, one half

59 — Wilt Chamberlain, Philadelphia vs. New York, at Hershey, Pa., March 2, 1962 (2nd Half)
53 — David Thompson, Denver at Detroit, April 9, 1978 (1st Half)
George Gervin, San Antonio at New Orleans, April 9, 1978 (1st Half)
47 — David Robinson, San Antonio at L.A. Clippers, April 24, 1994 (2nd Half)

Most points, one quarter

33 — George Gervin, San Antonio at New Orleans, April 9, 1978 (2nd Qtr.)
32 — David Thompson, Denver at Detroit, April 9, 1978 (1st Qtr.)
31 — Wilt Chamberlain, Philadelphia vs. New York, at Hershey, Pa., March 2, 1962 (4th Qtr.)

Most points, overtime period

14 — Butch Carter, Indiana vs. Boston, March 20, 1984
13 — Earl Monroe, Baltimore vs. Detroit, February 6, 1970
Joe Caldwell, Atlanta vs. Cincinnati, at Memphis, February 18, 1970
Steve Smith, Atlanta vs. Washington, January 24, 1997

FIELD GOAL PERCENTAGE

Most seasons, leading league

9 — Wilt Chamberlain, Philadelphia, 1960-61; San Francisco, 1962-63; San Francisco, Philadelphia, 1964-65; Philadelphia, 1965-66 — 1967-68; Los Angeles, 1968-69, 1971-72 — 1972-73
4 — Artis Gilmore, Chicago, 1980-81 — 1981-82; San Antonio, 1982-83 — 1983-84;
Shaquille O'Neal, Orlando, 1993-94; L.A. Lakers, 1997-98 — 1999-00

Most consecutive seasons leading league

5 — Wilt Chamberlain, San Francisco, Philadelphia, 1964-65; Philadelphia, 1965-66 — 1967-68; Los Angeles, 1968-69
4 — Artis Gilmore, Chicago, 1980-81 — 1981-82; San Antonio, 1982-83 — 1983-84
3 — Shaquille O'Neal, L.A. Lakers, 1997-98 — 1999-00

Highest field goal percentage, career
(minimum: 2,000 field goals)

.599 — Artis Gilmore, Chicago, 1976-77 — 1981-82; San Antonio, 1982-83 — 1986-87; Chicago, 1987-88; Boston, 1987-88 (5,732/9,570)
.580 — Mark West, Dallas, 1983-84; Milwaukee, 1984-85; Cleveland, 1984-85 — 1987-88; Phoenix, 1987-88 — 1993-94; Detroit, 1994-95 — 1995-96; Cleveland, 1996-97; Indiana, 1997-98; Atlanta, 1998-99; Phoenix, 1999-00 (2,528/4,356)
.577 — Shaquille O'Neal, Orlando, 1992-93 — 1995-96; L.A. Lakers, 1996-97 — 1999-00 (5,896/10,210)

Highest field goal percentage, season (qualifiers)

.727 — Wilt Chamberlain, Los Angeles, 1972-73 (426/586)
.683 — Wilt Chamberlain, Philadelphia, 1966-67 (785/1,150)
.670 — Artis Gilmore, Chicago, 1980-81 (547/816)

Highest field goal percentage, game
(minimum: 15 field goals)

1.000 — Wilt Chamberlain, Philadelphia vs. Los Angeles, January 20, 1967 (15/15)
Wilt Chamberlain, Philadelphia vs. Baltimore, at Pittsburgh, February 24, 1967 (18/18)
Wilt Chamberlain, Philadelphia at Baltimore, March 19, 1967 (16/16)
.947 — Wilt Chamberlain, San Francisco vs. New York, at Boston, November 27,

ALL-TIME REGULAR-SEASON NBA RECORDS: INDIVIDUAL – Continued

1963 (18/19)
.944 — George Gervin, San Antonio vs. Chicago, February 18, 1978 (17/18)

Most field goals, no misses, game
18 — Wilt Chamberlain, Philadelphia vs. Baltimore, at Pittsburgh, February 24, 1967
16 — Wilt Chamberlain, Philadelphia at Baltimore, March 19, 1967
15 — Wilt Chamberlain, Philadelphia vs. Los Angeles, January 20, 1967
14 — Bailey Howell, Baltimore vs. San Francisco, January 3, 1965
Wilt Chamberlain, Los Angeles vs. Detroit, March 11, 1969
Billy McKinney, Kansas City vs. Boston, at St. Louis, December 27, 1978
Gary Payton, Seattle at Cleveland, January 4, 1995

Most field goal attempts, none made, game
17 — Tim Hardaway, Golden State at Minnesota, December 27, 1991 (ot)
15 — Howie Dallmar, Philadelphia vs. New York, November 27, 1947
Howie Dallmar, Philadelphia vs. Washington, November 25, 1948
Dick Ricketts, Rochester vs. St. Louis, March 7, 1956
Corky Devlin, Ft. Wayne vs. Minneapolis, at Rochester, December 25, 1956
Charlie Tyra, New York at Philadelphia, November 7, 1957
Frank Ramsey, Boston vs. Cincinnati, at Philadelphia, December 8, 1960
Bob Love, Chicago vs. Kansas City, March 12, 1976
Ray Williams, New Jersey vs. Indiana, December 28, 1981
Rodney McCray, Sacramento at Utah, November 9,1988

FIELD GOALS

Most seasons leading league
10 — Michael Jordan, Chicago, 1986-87 — 1992-93, 1995-96 — 1997-98
7 — Wilt Chamberlain, Philadelphia, 1959-60 — 1961-62; San Francisco, 1962-63 — 1963-64; San Francisco, Philadelphia, 1964-65; Philadelphia, 1965-66

Most consecutive seasons leading league
7 — Wilt Chamberlain, Philadelphia, 1959-60 — 1961-62; San Francisco, 1962-63 — 1963-64; San Francisco, Philadelphia, 1964-65; Philadelphia, 1965-66
Michael Jordan, Chicago, 1986-87 — 1992-93
3 — George Mikan, Minneapolis, 1948-49 — 1950-51
Kareem Abdul-Jabbar, Milwaukee, 1969-70 — 1971-72
George Gervin, San Antonio, 1977-78 — 1979-80
Michael Jordan, Chicago, 1995-96 — 1997-98

Most field goals, career
15,837 — Kareem Abdul-Jabbar, Milwaukee, 1969-70 — 1974-75; L.A. Lakers, 1975-76 — 1988-89
12,681 — Wilt Chamberlain, Philadelphia, 1959-60 — 1961-62; San Francisco, 1962-63 — 1964-65; Philadelphia, 1964-65 — 1967-68; Los Angeles, 1968-69 — 1972-73
11,435 — Karl Malone, Utah, 1985-86 — 1999-00

Most field goals, season
1,597 — Wilt Chamberlain, Philadelphia, 1961-62
1,463 — Wilt Chamberlain, San Francisco, 1962-63
1,251 — Wilt Chamberlain, Philadelphia, 1960-61

Most consecutive field goals, no misses, season
35 — Wilt Chamberlain, Philadelphia, February 17 — February 28, 1967

Most field goals, game
36 — Wilt Chamberlain, Philadelphia vs. New York, at Hershey, Pa., March 2, 1962
31 — Wilt Chamberlain, Philadelphia vs. Los Angeles, December 8, 1961 (3 ot)

Most field goals, one half
22 — Wilt Chamberlain, Philadelphia vs. New York, at Hershey, Pa., March 2, 1962 (2nd Half)
21 — Rick Barry, Golden State vs. Portland, March 26, 1974 (2nd Half)
20 — David Thompson, Denver at Detroit, April 9, 1978 (1st Half)

Most field goals, one quarter
13 — David Thompson, Denver at Detroit, April 9, 1978 (1st Qtr.)
12 — Cliff Hagan, St. Louis at New York, February 4, 1958 (4th Qtr.)
Wilt Chamberlain, Philadelphia vs. New York, at Hershey, Pa., March 2, 1962 (4th Qtr.)
George Gervin, San Antonio at New Orleans, April 9, 1978 (2nd Qtr.)
Jeff Malone, Washington at Phoenix, February 27, 1988 (3rd Qtr.)

FIELD GOAL ATTEMPTS

Most seasons leading league
9 — Michael Jordan, Chicago, 1986-87 — 1987-88, 1989-90 — 1992-93, 1995-96 — 1997-98
7 — Wilt Chamberlain, Philadelphia, 1959-60 — 1961-62; San Francisco, 1962-63 — 1963-64; San Francisco, Philadelphia, 1964-65; Philadelphia, 1965-66
3 — Joe Fulks, Philadelphia, 1946-47 — 1948-49
George Mikan, Minneapolis, 1949-50 — 1951-52
Elvin Hayes, San Diego, 1968-69 — 1970-71
George Gervin, San Antonio, 1978-79 — 1979-80, 1981-82

Most consecutive seasons leading league
7 — Wilt Chamberlain, Philadelphia, 1959-60 — 1961-62; San Francisco, 1962-63 — 1963-64; San Francisco, Philadelphia, 1964-65; Philadelphia, 1965-66
4 — Michael Jordan, Chicago, 1989-90 — 1992-93
3 — Joe Fulks, Philadelphia, 1946-47 — 1948-49
George Mikan, Minneapolis, 1949-50 — 1951-52
Elvin Hayes, San Diego, 1968-69 — 1970-71
Michael Jordan, Chicago, 1995-96 — 1997-98

Most field goal attempts, career
28,307 — Kareem Abdul-Jabbar, Milwaukee, 1969-70 — 1974-75; L.A. Lakers, 1975-76 — 1988-89
24,272 — Elvin Hayes, San Diego, 1968-69 — 1970-71; Houston, 1971-72; Baltimore, 1972-73; Capital, 1973-74; Washington, 1974-75 — 1980-81; Houston, 1981-82 — 1983-84
23,930 — John Havlicek, Boston, 1962-63 — 1977-78

Most field goal attempts, season
3,159 — Wilt Chamberlain, Philadelphia, 1961-62
2,770 — Wilt Chamberlain, San Francisco, 1962-63
2,457 — Wilt Chamberlain, Philadelphia, 1960-61

Most field goal attempts, game
63 — Wilt Chamberlain, Philadelphia vs. New York, at Hershey, Pa., March 2, 1962
62 — Wilt Chamberlain, Philadelphia vs. Los Angeles, December 8, 1961 (3 ot)
60 — Wilt Chamberlain, San Francisco at Cincinnati, October 28, 1962 (ot)

Most field goal attempts, one half
37 — Wilt Chamberlain, Philadelphia vs. New York, at Hershey, Pa., March 2, 1962 (2nd Half)
34 — George Gervin, San Antonio at New Orleans, April 9, 1978 (1st Half)
32 — Wilt Chamberlain, Philadelphia vs. Chicago, at Boston, January 24, 1962

Most field goal attempts, one quarter
21 — Wilt Chamberlain, Philadelphia vs. New York, at Hershey, Pa., March 2, 1962 (4th Qtr.)
20 — Wilt Chamberlain, Philadelphia vs. Chicago, at Boston, January 24, 1962
George Gervin, San Antonio at New Orleans, April 9, 1978 (2nd Qtr.)
19 — Bob Pettit, St. Louis at Philadelphia, December 6, 1961

THREE-POINT FIELD GOAL PERCENTAGE

Most seasons leading league
2 — Craig Hodges, Milwaukee, 1985-86; Milwaukee, Phoenix, 1987-88
Steve Kerr, Cleveland, 1989-90; Chicago, 1994-95

Highest three-point field goal percentage, career
(minimum: 250 three-point FGs)
.464 — Steve Kerr, Phoenix, 1988-89; Cleveland, 1989-90 — 1992-93, Orlando,

ALL-TIME REGULAR-SEASON NBA RECORDS: INDIVIDUAL – Continued

1992-93; Chicago, 1993-94 — 1997-98; San Antonio, 1998-99 — 1999-00 (618/1,332)
.441 — Hubert Davis, New York, 1992-93 — 1995-96; Toronto, 1996-97; Dallas, 1997-98 — 1999-00
.437 — Drazen Petrovic, Portland, 1989-90 — 1990-91; New Jersey, 1990-91 — 1992-93 (255/583)

Highest three-point field goal percentage, season (qualifiers)
.524 — Steve Kerr, Chicago, 1994-95 (89/170)
.5224 — Tim Legler, Washington, 1995-96 (128/245)
.5217 — Jon Sundvold, Miami, 1988-89 (48/92)

Most three-point field goals, no misses, game
8 — Jeff Hornacek, Utah vs. Seattle, November 23, 1994
Sam Perkins, Seattle vs. Toronto, January 15, 1997
7 — Terry Porter, Portland at Golden State, November 14, 1992
Sam Perkins, Seattle vs. Denver, November 9, 1993
Sasha Danilovic, Miami at New York, December 3, 1996
Mitch Richmond, Sacramento at Boston, February 26, 1997

Most three-point field goal attempts, none made, game
10 — George McCloud, Dallas at Toronto, March 10, 1996
9 — Isiah Thomas, Detroit vs. Milwaukee, November 6, 1992
John Starks, New York vs. Sacramento, February 23, 1995
Dana Barros, Boston vs. New York, January 12, 1996

THREE-POINT FIELD GOALS

Most seasons leading league
2 — Darrell Griffith, Utah, 1983-84 — 1984-85
Larry Bird, Boston, 1985-86 — 1986-87
Michael Adams, Denver, 1988-89 — 1989-90
Vernon Maxwell, Houston, 1990-91 — 1991-92
Dan Majerle, Phoenix, 1992-93 — 1993-94
Reggie Miller, Indiana, 1992-93, 1996-97

Most three-point field goals, career
1,867 — Reggie Miller, Indiana, 1987-88 — 1999-00
1,719 — Dale Ellis, Dallas, 1983-84 — 1985-86; Seattle, 1986-87 — 1990-91; Milwaukee, 1990-91 — 1991-92; San Antonio, 1992-93 — 1993-94; Denver, 1994-95 — 1996-97; Seattle, 1997-98 — 1998-99; Milwaukee, 1999-00; Charlotte, 1999-00

Most three-point field goals, season
267 — Dennis Scott, Orlando, 1995-96
257 — George McCloud, Dallas, 1995-96
231 — Mookie Blaylock, Atlanta, 1995-96

Most consecutive three-point field goals, no misses, season
13 — Brent Price, Washington, January 15 — January 19, 1996
Terry Mills, Detroit, December 4 — December 7, 1996
11 — Scott Wedman, Boston, December 21, 1984 — March 31, 1985
Jeff Hornacek, Utah, December 30, 1994 — January 11, 1995

Most three-point field goals, game
11 — Dennis Scott, Orlando vs. Atlanta, April 18, 1996
10 — Brian Shaw, Miami at Milwaukee, April 8, 1993
Joe Dumars, Detroit vs. Minnesota, November 8, 1994
George McCloud, Dallas vs. Phoenix, December 16, 1995 (ot)

Most consecutive games, three-point field goals made
89 — Dana Barros, Philadelphia, Boston, December 23, 1994 — January 10, 1996 (58 games in 1994-95; 31 games in 1995-96)
79 — Michael Adams, Denver, January 28, 1988 — January 23, 1989 (43 games in 1987-88; 36 games in 1988-89)
78 — Dennis Scott, Orlando, April 17, 1995 — April 4, 1996 (4 games in 1994-95; 74 games in 1995-96)

Most three-point field goals made, one half
7 — John Roche, Denver vs. Seattle, January 9, 1982
Michael Adams, Denver vs. Milwaukee, January 21, 1989
John Starks, New York vs. Miami, November 22, 1993
Allan Houston, Detroit at Chicago, February 17, 1995
Joe Dumars, Detroit at Orlando, April 5, 1995
George McCloud, Dallas vs. Phoenix, December 16, 1995
George McCloud, Dallas vs. Philadelphia, February 27, 1996
Dennis Scott, Orlando vs. Atlanta, April 18, 1996
Steve Smith, Atlanta vs. Seattle, March 14, 1997
Henry James, Atlanta vs. New Jersey, April 15, 1997
Glen Rice, L.A. Lakers vs. Portland, May 5, 1999

Most three-point field goals made, one quarter
7 — John Roche, Denver vs. Seattle, January 9, 1982
Steve Smith, Atlanta vs. Seattle, March 14, 1997
Henry James, Atlanta vs. New Jersey, April 15, 1997
6 — Brian Shaw, Miami at Milwaukee, April 8, 1993
Allan Houston, Detroit vs. Denver, March 10, 1995
George McCloud, Dallas vs. Phoenix, December 16, 1995
George McCloud, Dallas at Vancouver, March 1, 1996
James Robinson, Minnesota at Cleveland, December 30, 1996
Cliff Robinson, Portland vs. Vancouver, March 28, 1997
Dee Brown, Boston vs. Dallas, February 4, 1998
Dee Brown, Toronto at Washington, April 21, 1999
Glen Rice, L.A. Lakers vs. Portland, May 5, 1999

THREE-POINT FIELD GOAL ATTEMPTS

Most seasons leading league
4 — Michael Adams, Denver, 1987-88 — 1990-91
2 — Darrell Griffith, Utah, 1983-84 — 1984-85
Dan Majerle, Phoenix, 1992-93 — 1993-94

Most three-point field goal attempts, career
4,629 — Reggie Miller, Indiana, 1987-88 — 1999-00
4,266 — Dale Ellis, Dallas, 1983-84 — 1985-86; Seattle, 1986-87 — 1990-91; Milwaukee, 1990-91 — 1991-92; San Antonio, 1992-93 — 1993-94; Denver, 1994-95 — 1996-97; Seattle, 1997-98 — 1998-99; Milwaukee, 1999-00; Charlotte, 1999-00
3,820 — Vernon Maxwell, San Antonio, 1988-89 — 1989-90; Houston, 1989-90 — 1994-95; Philadelphia, 1995-96; San Antonio, 1996-97; Orlando, 1997-98; Charlotte, 1997-98; Sacramento, 1998-99; Seattle, 1999-00

Most three-point field goal attempts, season
678 — George McCloud, Dallas, 1995-96
628 — Dennis Scott, Orlando, 1995-96
623 — Mookie Blaylock, Atlanta, 1995-96

Most three-point field goal attempts, game
20 — Michael Adams, Denver at L.A. Clippers, April 12, 1991
George McCloud, Dallas vs. New Jersey, March 5, 1996
19 — Dennis Scott, Orlando vs. Milwaukee, April 13, 1993

Most three-point field goal attempts, one half
13 — Michael Adams, Denver at L.A. Clippers, April 12, 1991
12 — Manute Bol, Philadelphia at Phoenix, March 3, 1993
Dennis Scott, Orlando vs. Milwaukee, April 13, 1993
Allan Houston, Detroit vs. Denver, March 10, 1995
Vernon Maxwell, Philadelphia vs. New Jersey, April 8, 1996
Jason Williams, Sacramento vs. Minnesota, April 23, 1999

FREE THROW PERCENTAGE

Most seasons leading league
7 — Bill Sharman, Boston, 1952-53 — 1956-57, 1958-59, 1960-61
6 — Rick Barry, Golden State, 1972-73, 1974-75 — 1975-76, 1977-78; Houston, 1978-79 — 1979-80
4 — Larry Bird, Boston, 1983-84, 1985-86 — 1986-87, 1989-90

ALL-TIME REGULAR-SEASON NBA RECORDS: INDIVIDUAL – Continued

Most consecutive seasons leading league
5 — Bill Sharman, Boston, 1952-53 — 1956-57
3 — Rick Barry, Golden State, 1977-78; Houston, 1978-79 — 1979-80

Highest free throw percentage, career
(minimum: 1,200 free throws made)
.904 — Mark Price, Cleveland, 1986-87 — 1994-95; Washington, 1995-96; Golden State, 1996-97; Orlando, 1997-98 (2,135/2,362)
.900 — Rick Barry, San Francisco, 1965-66 — 1966-67; Golden State, 1972-73 — 1977-78; Houston, 1978-79 — 1979-80 (3,818/4,243)
.892 — Calvin Murphy, San Diego, 1970-71; Houston, 1971-72 — 1982-83 (3,445/3,864)

Highest free throw percentage, season (qualifiers)
.958 — Calvin Murphy, Houston, 1980-81 (206/215)
.956 — Mahmoud Abdul-Rauf, Denver, 1993-94 (219/229)
.950 — Jeff Hornacek, Utah, 1999-00 (171/180)

Most free throws made, no misses, game
23 — Dominique Wilkins, Atlanta vs. Chicago, December 8, 1992
19 — Bob Pettit, St. Louis at Boston, November 22, 1961
Bill Cartwright, New York vs. Kansas City, November 17, 1981
Adrian Dantley, Detroit vs. Chicago, December 15, 1987 (ot)

Most free throw attempts, none made, game
10 — Wilt Chamberlain, Philadelphia vs. Detroit, November 4, 1960
9 — Wilt Chamberlain, Philadelphia at St. Louis, February 19, 1967
Truck Robinson, Phoenix vs. Chicago, November 28, 1980

FREE THROWS MADE

Most seasons leading league
8 — Karl Malone, Utah, 1988-89 — 1992-93, 1996-97 — 1998-99
5 — Adrian Dantley, Indiana, Los Angeles, 1977-78; Utah, 1980-81 — 1981-82; 1983-84, 1985-86

Most free throws made, career
8,531 — Moses Malone, Buffalo, 1976-77; Houston, 1976-77 — 1981-82; Philadelphia, 1982-83 — 1985-86; Washington, 1986-87 — 1987-88; Atlanta, 1988-89 — 1990-91; Milwaukee, 1991-92 — 1992-93; Philadelphia, 1993-94; San Antonio, 1994-95
8,100 — Karl Malone, Utah, 1985-86 — 1999-00
7,694 — Oscar Robertson, Cincinnati, 1960-61 — 1969-70; Milwaukee, 1970-71 — 1973-74

Most free throws made, season
840 — Jerry West, Los Angeles, 1965-66
835 — Wilt Chamberlain, Philadelphia, 1961-62
833 — Michael Jordan, Chicago, 1986-87

Most consecutive free throws made
97 — Micheal Williams, Minnesota, March 24, 1993 — November 9, 1993
81 — Mahmoud Abdul-Rauf, Denver, March 15, 1993 — November 16, 1993
78 — Calvin Murphy, Houston, December 27, 1980 — February 28, 1981

Most free throws made, game
28 — Wilt Chamberlain, Philadelphia vs. New York, at Hershey, Pa., March 2, 1962
Adrian Dantley, Utah vs. Houston, at Las Vegas, January 4, 1984
27 — Adrian Dantley, Utah vs. Denver, November 25, 1983

Most free throws made, one half
20 — Michael Jordan, Chicago at Miami, December 30, 1992 (2nd Half)
19 — Oscar Robertson, Cincinnati at Baltimore, December 27, 1964

Most free throws made, one quarter
14 — Rick Barry, San Francisco at New York, December 6, 1966 (3rd Qtr.)
Pete Maravich, Atlanta vs. Buffalo, November 28, 1973 (3rd Qtr.)
Adrian Dantley, Detroit vs. Sacramento, December 10, 1986 (4th Qtr.)
Michael Jordan, Chicago at Utah, November 15, 1989 (4th Qtr.)
Michael Jordan, Chicago at Miami, December 30, 1992 (4th Qtr.)
Johnny Newman, Denver vs. Boston, February 10, 1998 (4th Qtr.)

FREE THROW ATTEMPTS

Most seasons leading league
9 — Wilt Chamberlain, Philadelphia, 1959-60 — 1961-62; San Francisco, 1962-63 — 1963-64; San Francisco, Philadelphia, 1964-65; Philadelphia, 1966-67 — 1967-68; Los Angeles, 1968-69
7 — Karl Malone, Utah, 1988-89 — 1992-93, 1996-97 — 1997-98
5 — Moses Malone, Houston, 1979-80 — 1981-82; Philadelphia, 1982-83, 1984-85

Most consecutive seasons leading league
6 — Wilt Chamberlain, Philadelphia, 1959-60 — 1961-62; San Francisco, 1962-63 — 1963-64; San Francisco, Philadelphia, 1964-65
5 — Karl Malone, Utah, 1988-89 — 1992-93

Most free throw attempts, career
11,862 — Wilt Chamberlain, Philadelphia, 1959-60 — 1961-62; San Francisco, 1962-63 — 1964-65; Philadelphia, 1964-65 — 1967-68; Los Angeles, 1968-69 — 1972-73
11,090 — Moses Malone, Buffalo, 1976-77; Houston, 1976-77 — 1981-82; Philadelphia, 1982-83 — 1985-86; Washington, 1986-87 — 1987-88; Atlanta, 1988-89 — 1990-91; Milwaukee, 1991-92 — 1992-93; Philadelphia, 1993-94; San Antonio, 1994-95
11,027 — Karl Malone, Utah, 1985-86 — 1999-00

Most free throw attempts, season
1,363 — Wilt Chamberlain, Philadelphia, 1961-62
1,113 — Wilt Chamberlain, San Francisco, 1962-63

Most free throw attempts, game
34 — Wilt Chamberlain, Philadelphia vs. St. Louis, February 22, 1962
32 — Wilt Chamberlain, Philadelphia vs. New York, at Hershey, Pa., March 2, 1962
31 — Adrian Dantley, Utah vs. Denver, November 25, 1983
Shaquille O'Neal, L.A. Lakers vs. Chicago, November 19, 1999

Most free throw attempts, one half
23 — Michael Jordan, Chicago at Miami, December 30, 1992
22 — Oscar Robertson, Cincinnati at Baltimore, December 27, 1964
Tony Campbell, Minnesota vs. L.A. Clippers, March 8, 1990
Willie Burton, Philadelphia vs. Miami, December 13, 1994

Most free throw attempts, one quarter
16 — Oscar Robertson, Cincinnati at Baltimore, December 27, 1964
Stan McKenzie, Phoenix at Philadelphia, February 15, 1970
Pete Maravich, Atlanta at Chicago, January 2, 1973 (2nd Qtr.)
Michael Jordan, Chicago at Miami, December 30, 1992
Willie Burton, Philadelphia vs. Miami, December 13, 1994
Johnny Newman, Denver vs. Boston, February 10, 1998

REBOUNDS

Rebounds have been compiled since 1950-51

Most seasons leading league
11 — Wilt Chamberlain, Philadelphia, 1959-60 — 1961-62; San Francisco, 1962-63; Philadelphia, 1965-66 — 1967-68; Los Angeles, 1968-69, 1970-71 — 1972-73
7 — Dennis Rodman, Detroit, 1991-92 — 1992-93; San Antonio, 1993-94 — 1994-95; Chicago, 1995-96 — 1997-98
6 — Moses Malone, Houston, 1978-79, 1980-81 — 1981-82; Philadelphia, 1982-83 — 1984-85

ALL-TIME REGULAR-SEASON NBA RECORDS: INDIVIDUAL – Continued

Most consecutive seasons leading league

7 — Dennis Rodman, Detroit, 1991-92 — 1992-93; San Antonio, 1993-94 — 1994-95; Chicago, 1995-96 — 1997-98
5 — Moses Malone, Houston, 1980-81 — 1981-82; Philadelphia, 1982-83 — 1984-85
4 — Wilt Chamberlain, Philadelphia, 1959-60 — 1961-62; San Francisco, 1962-63
Wilt Chamberlain, Philadelphia, 1965-66 — 1967-68; Los Angeles, 1968-69

Most rebounds, career

23,924 — Wilt Chamberlain, Philadelphia, 1959-60 — 1961-62; San Francisco, 1962-63 — 1964-65; Philadelphia, 1964-65 — 1967-68; Los Angeles, 1968-69 — 1972-73
21,620 — Bill Russell, Boston 1956-57 — 1968-69
17,440 — Kareem Abdul-Jabbar, Milwaukee, 1969-70 — 1974-75; L.A. Lakers, 1975-76 — 1988-89

Highest average, rebounds per game, career
(minimum: 400 games)

22.9 — Wilt Chamberlain, Philadelphia, 1959-60 — 1961-62; San Francisco, 1962-63 — 1964-65; Philadelphia, 1964-65 — 1967-68; Los Angeles, 1968-69 — 1972-73 (23,924/1,045)
22.5 — Bill Russell, Boston 1956-57 — 1968-69 (21,620/963)
16.2 — Bob Pettit, Milwaukee, 1954-55; St. Louis, 1955-56 — 1964-65 (12,849/792)

Most rebounds, season

2,149 — Wilt Chamberlain, Philadelphia, 1960-61
2,052 — Wilt Chamberlain, Philadelphia, 1961-62
1,957 — Wilt Chamberlain, Philadelphia, 1966-67

Most seasons, 1,000-or-more rebounds

13 — Wilt Chamberlain, Philadelphia, 1959-60 — 1961-62; San Francisco, 1962-63 — 1963-64; San Francisco, Philadelphia, 1964-65; Philadelphia 1965-66 — 1967-68; Los Angeles, 1968-69, 1970-71 — 1972-73
12 — Bill Russell, Boston, 1957-58 — 1968-69
9 — Bob Pettit, St. Louis, 1955-56 — 1963-64
Walt Bellamy, Chicago, 1961-62 — 1962-63; Baltimre, 1963-64 — 1964-65; Baltimore, New York, 1965-66; New York, 1966-67; New York, Detroit, 1968-69; Atlanta, 1970-71 — 1971-72
Elvin Hayes, San Diego, 1968-69 — 1970-71; Houston, 1971-72; Baltimore, 1972-73; Capital, 1973-74;
Washington, 1974-75, 1976-77 — 1977-78

Most consecutive seasons, 1,000-or-more rebounds

12 — Bill Russell, Boston, 1957-58 — 1968-69
10 — Wilt Chamberlain, Philadelphia, 1959-60 — 1961-62; San Francisco, 1962-63 — 1963-64; San Francisco, Philadelphia, 1964-65; Philadelphia 1965-66 — 1967-68; Los Angeles, 1968-69
9 — Bob Pettit, St. Louis, 1955-56 — 1963-64

Highest average, rebounds per game, season

27.2 — Wilt Chamberlain, Philadelphia, 1960-61 (2,149/79)
27.0 — Wilt Chamberlain, Philadelphia, 1959-60 (1,941/72)
25.7 — Wilt Chamberlain, Philadelphia, 1961-62 (2,052/80)
24.7 — Bill Russell, Boston, 1963-64 (1,930/78)

Most rebounds, game

55 — Wilt Chamberlain, Philadelphia vs. Boston, November 24, 1960
51 — Bill Russell, Boston vs. Syracuse, February 5, 1960
49 — Bill Russell, Boston vs. Philadelphia, November 16, 1957
Bill Russell, Boston vs. Detroit, at Providence, March 11, 1965

Most rebounds, one half

32 — Bill Russell, Boston vs. Philadelphia, November 16, 1957
31 — Wilt Chamberlain, Philadelphia vs. Boston, November 24, 1960
28 — Wilt Chamberlain, Philadelphia vs. Syracuse, February 6, 1960

Most rebounds, one quarter

18 — Nate Thurmond, San Francisco at Baltimore, February 28, 1965
17 — Bill Russell, Boston vs. Philadelphia, November 16, 1957
Bill Russell, Boston vs. Cincinnati, December 12, 1958
Bill Russell, Boston vs. Syracuse, February 5, 1960
Wilt Chamberlain, Philadelphia vs. Syracuse, February 6, 1960

ASSISTS

Most seasons leading league

9 — John Stockton, Utah, 1987-88 — 1995-96
8 — Bob Cousy, Boston, 1952-53 — 1959-60
6 — Oscar Robertson, Cincinnati, 1960-61 — 1961-62, 1963-64 — 1965-66, 1968-69

Most consecutive seasons leading league

9 — John Stockton, Utah, 1987-88 — 1995-96
8 — Bob Cousy, Boston, 1952-53 — 1959-60
3 — Oscar Robertson, Cincinnati, 1963-64 — 1965-66

Most assists, career

13,790 — John Stockton, Utah, 1984-85 — 1999-00
10,141 — Magic Johnson, L.A. Lakers, 1979-80 — 1990-91, 1995-96
9,887 — Oscar Robertson, Cincinnati, 1960-61 — 1969-70; Milwaukee, 1970-71 — 1973-74

Highest average, assists per game, career
(minimum:400 games)

11.2 — Magic Johnson, L.A. Lakers, 1979-80 — 1990-91, 1995-96 (10,141/906)
11.0 — John Stockton, Utah, 1984-85 — 1999-00 (13,790/1,258)
9.5 — Oscar Robertson, Cincinnati, 1960-61 — 1969-70; Milwaukee, 1970-71 — 1973-74 (9,887/1,040)

Most assists, season

1,164 — John Stockton, Utah, 1990-91
1,134 — John Stockton, Utah, 1989-90
1,128 — John Stockton, Utah, 1987-88

Highest average, assists per game, season
(minimum: 70 games)

14.5 — John Stockton, Utah, 1989-90 (1,134/78)
14.2 — John Stockton, Utah, 1990-91 (1,164/82)
13.9 — Isiah Thomas, Detroit, 1984-85 (1,123/81)

Most assists, game

30 — Scott Skiles, Orlando vs. Denver, December 30, 1990
29 — Kevin Porter, New Jersey vs. Houston, February 24, 1978
28 — Bob Cousy, Boston vs. Minneapolis, February 27, 1959
Guy Rodgers, San Francisco vs. St. Louis, March 14, 1963
John Stockton, Utah vs. San Antonio, January 15, 1991

Most assists, one half

19 — Bob Cousy, Boston vs. Minneapolis, February 27, 1959
18 — Magic Johnson, Los Angeles vs. Seattle, February 21, 1984 (1st Half)
17 — Nate McMillan, Seattle vs. L.A. Clippers, February 23, 1987 (2nd Half)

Most assists, one quarter

14 — John Lucas, San Antonio vs. Denver, April 15, 1984 (2nd Qtr.)
12 — Bob Cousy, Boston vs. Minneapolis, February 27, 1959
John Lucas, Houston vs. Milwaukee, October 27, 1977 (3rd Qtr.)
John Lucas, Golden State vs. Chicago, November 17, 1978 (1st Qtr.)
Magic Johnson, Los Angeles vs. Seattle, February 21, 1984 (1st Qtr.)
Mark Jackson, Denver vs. New Jersey, January 20, 1997
Avery Johnson, San Antonio vs. L.A. Clippers, December 10, 1997

ALL-TIME REGULAR-SEASON NBA RECORDS: INDIVIDUAL – Continued

PERSONAL FOULS

Most seasons leading league

3 — George Mikan, Minneapolis, 1949-50 — 1951-52
Vern Mikkelsen, Minneapolis, 1954-55 — 1956-57
Darryl Dawkins, Philadelphia, 1979-80; New Jersey, 1982-83 — 1983-84
Shawn Kemp, Seattle, 1993-94, 1996-97; Cleveland, 1999-00

Most consecutive seasons leading league

3 — George Mikan, Minneapolis, 1949-50 — 1951-52
Vern Mikkelsen, Minneapolis, 1954-55 — 1956-57

Most personal fouls, career

4,657 — Kareem Abdul-Jabbar, Milwaukee, 1969-70 — 1974-75; L.A. Lakers, 1975-76 — 1988-89
4,443 — Robert Parish, Golden State, 1976-77 — 1979-80; Boston, 1980-81 — 1993-94; Charlotte, 1994-95 — 1995-96; Chicago, 1996-97

Most personal fouls, season

386 — Darryl Dawkins, New Jersey, 1983-84
379 — Darryl Dawkins, New Jersey, 1982-83

Most personal fouls, game

8 — Don Otten, Tri-Cities at Sheboygan, November 24, 1949
7 — Alex Hannum, Syracuse at Boston, December 26, 1950
Cal Bowdler, Atlanta at Portland, November 13, 1999

DISQUALIFICATIONS

Disqualifications have been compiled since 1950-51

Most seasons leading league

5 — Shawn Kemp, Seattle, 1991-92, 1993-94, 1996-97; Cleveland, 1997-98, 1999-00
4 — Walter Dukes, Detroit, 1958-59 — 1961-62
3 — Vern Mikkelsen, Minneapolis, 1955-56 — 1957-58
Steve Johnson, Kansas City, 1981-82; San Antonio, 1985-86; Portland, 1986-87
Rik Smits, Indiana, 1988-89 — 1989-90, 1993-94

Most consecutive seasons leading league

4 — Walter Dukes, Detroit, 1958-59 — 1961-62
3 — Vern Mikkelsen, Minneapolis, 1955-56 — 1957-58

Most disqualifications, career

127 — Vern Mikkelsen, Minneapolis, 1950-51 — 1958-59
121 — Walter Dukes, New York, 1955-56; Minneapolis, 1956-57; Detroit, 1957-58 — 1962-63
109 — Shawn Kemp, Seattle, 1989-90 — 1996-97; Cleveland, 1997-98 — 1999-00

Most consecutive games without disqualification, career

1,212 — Moses Malone, Houston, Philadelphia, Washington, Atlanta, Milwaukee, Philadelphia, San Antonio, January 7, 1978 — December 27, 1994
1,045 — Wilt Chamberlain, Philadelphia, San Francisco, Philadelphia, Los Angeles, October 24, 1959 — March 28, 1973
957 — Dominique Wilkins, Atlanta, L.A. Clippers, Boston, San Antonio, Orlando, January 12, 1984 — May 5, 1999 (current)

Most disqualifications, season

26 — Don Meineke, Ft. Wayne, 1952-53
25 — Steve Johnson, Kansas City, 1981-82
23 — Darryl Dawkins, New Jersey, 1982-83

Fewest minutes, disqualified, game

3 — Bubba Wells, Dallas at Chicago, December 29, 1997
5 — Dick Farley, Syracuse at St. Louis, March 12, 1956

STEALS

Steals have been compiled since 1973-74

Most seasons leading league

3 — Micheal Ray Richardson, New York, 1979-80; Golden State, New Jersey, 1982-83; New Jersey, 1984-85
Alvin Robertson, San Antonio, 1985-86 — 1986-87; Milwaukee, 1990-91
Michael Jordan, Chicago, 1987-88, 1989-90, 1992-93
2 — Magic Johnson, Los Angeles, 1980-81 — 1981-82
John Stockton, Utah, 1988-89, 1991-92
Mookie Blaylock, Atlanta, 1996-97 — 1997-98

Most consecutive seasons leading league

2 — Magic Johnson, Los Angeles, 1980-81 — 1981-82
Alvin Robertson, San Antonio, 1985-86 — 1986-87
Mookie Blaylock, Atlanta, 1996-97 — 1997-98

Most steals, career

2,844 — John Stockton, Utah, 1984-85 — 1999-00
2,310 — Maurice Cheeks, Philadelphia, 1978-79 — 1988-89; San Antonio, 1989-90; New York, 1989-90 — 1990-91; Atlanta, 1991-92; New Jersey, 1992-93
2,306 — Michael Jordan, Chicago, 1984-85 — 1992-93, 1994-95 — 1997-98

Highest average, steals per game, career

(minimum: 400 games)

2.71 — Alvin Robertson, San Antonio, 1984-85 — 1988-89; Milwaukee, 1989-90 — 1992-93; Detroit, 1992-93; Toronto, 1995-96 (2,112/779)
2.63 — Micheal Ray Richardson, New York, 1978-79 — 1981-82; Golden State, New Jersey, 1982-83; New Jersey, 1983-84 — 1985-86 (1,463/556)
2.48 — Michael Jordan, Chicago, 1984-85 — 1992-93, 1994-95 — 1997-98 (2,306/930)

Most steals, season

301 — Alvin Robertson, San Antonio, 1985-86
281 — Don Buse, Indiana, 1976-77
265 — Micheal Ray Richardson, New York, 1979-80

Highest average, steals per game, season (qualifiers)

3.67 — Alvin Robertson, San Antonio, 1985-86 (301/82)
3.47 — Don Buse, Indiana, 1976-77 (281/81)
3.43 — Magic Johnson, Los Angeles, 1980-81 (127/37)

Highest average, steals per game, rookie, season (qualifiers)

2.57 — Dudley Bradley, Indiana, 1979-80 (211/82)
2.55 — Ron Harper, Cleveland, 1986-87 (209/82)
2.50 — Mark Jackson, New York, 1987-88 (205/82)

Most steals, game

11 — Larry Kenon, San Antonio at Kansas City, December 26, 1976
Kendall Gill, New Jersey vs. Miami, April 3, 1999
10 — Jerry West, Los Angeles vs. Seattle, December 7, 1973
Larry Steele, Portland vs. Los Angeles, November 16, 1974
Fred Brown, Seattle at Philadelphia, December 3, 1976
Gus Williams, Seattle at New Jersey, February 22, 1978
Eddie Jordan, New Jersey at Philadelphia, March 23, 1979
Johnny Moore, San Antonio vs. Indiana, March 6, 1985
Lafayette Lever, Denver vs. Indiana, March 9, 1985
Clyde Drexler, Portland at Milwaukee, January 10, 1986
Alvin Robertson, San Antonio vs. Phoenix, February 18, 1986
Alvin Robertson, San Antonio at L.A. Clippers, November 22, 1986
Ron Harper, Cleveland vs. Philadelphia, March 10, 1987
Michael Jordan, Chicago vs. New Jersey, January 29, 1988
Alvin Robertson, San Antonio vs. Houston, January 11, 1989 (ot)
Alvin Robertson, Milwaukee vs. Utah, November 19, 1990
Kevin Johnson, Phoenix vs. Washington, December 9, 1993
Clyde Drexler, Houston vs. Sacramento, November 1, 1996
Mookie Blaylock, Atlanta vs. Philadelphia, April 14, 1998

ALL-TIME REGULAR-SEASON NBA RECORDS: INDIVIDUAL – Continued

Most steals, one half
8 — Quinn Buckner, Milwaukee vs. N.Y. Nets, November 27, 1976
Fred Brown, Seattle at Philadelphia, December 3, 1976
Gus Williams, Seattle at Washington, January 23, 1979
Eddie Jordan, New Jersey at Chicago, October 23, 1979
Dudley Bradley, Indiana at Utah, November 10, 1980
Rob Williams, Denver at New Jersey, February 17, 1983
Lafayette Lever, Denver vs. Indiana, March 9, 1985
Michael Jordan, Chicago at Boston, November 9, 1988
Clyde Drexler, Houston vs. Sacramento, November 1, 1996
Doug Christie, Toronto at Philadelphia, April 2, 1997

Most steals, one quarter
8 — Lafayette Lever, Denver vs. Indiana, March 9, 1985
7 — Quinn Buckner, Milwaukee vs. N.Y. Nets, November 27, 1976
Alvin Robertson, San Antonio vs. Detroit, March 25, 1988
Michael Adams, Washington at Atlanta, November 26, 1993
Tom Gugliotta, Minnesota at Portland, February 21, 1995

BLOCKED SHOTS

Blocked Shots have been compiled since 1973-74

Most seasons leading league
4 — Kareem Abdul-Jabbar, Milwaukee, 1974-75; Los Angeles, 1975-76, 1978-79 — 1979-80
Mark Eaton, Utah, 1983-84 — 1984-85; 1986-87 — 1987-88
3 — George T. Johnson, New Jersey, 1977-78; San Antonio, 1980-81 — 1981-82
Hakeem Olajuwon, Houston, 1989-90 — 1990-91, 1992-93
Dikembe Mutombo, Denver, 1993-94 — 1995-96

Most blocked shots, career
3,652 — Hakeem Olajuwon, Houston, 1984-85 — 1999-00
3,189 — Kareem Abdul-Jabbar, Milwaukee, 1973-74 — 1974-75; L.A. Lakers, 1975-76 — 1988-89
3,064 — Mark Eaton, Utah, 1982-83 — 1992-93

Highest average, blocked shots per game, career
(minimum: 400 games)
3.57 — Dikembe Mutombo, Denver, 1991-92 — 1995-96; Atlanta, 1996-97 — 1999-00 (2,443/685)
3.50 — Mark Eaton, Utah, 1982-83 — 1992-93 (3,064/875)
3.34 — Manute Bol, Washington, 1985-86 — 1987-88; Golden State, 1988-89 — 1989-90; Philadelphia, 1990-91 — 1992-93; Miami, 1993-94; Washington, 1993-94; Philadelphia, 1993-94; Golden State, 1994-95 (2,086/624)

Most blocked shots, season
456 — Mark Eaton, Utah, 1984-85
397 — Manute Bol, Washington, 1985-86
393 — Elmore Smith, Los Angeles, 1973-74

Highest average, blocked shots per game, season (qualifiers)
5.56 — Mark Eaton, Utah, 1984-85 (456/82)
4.97 — Manute Bol, Washington, 1985-86 (397/80)
4.85 — Elmore Smith, Los Angeles, 1973-74 (393/81)

Most blocked shots, game
17 — Elmore Smith, Los Angeles vs. Portland, October 28, 1973
15 — Manute Bol, Washington vs. Atlanta, January 25, 1986
Manute Bol, Washington vs. Indiana, February 26, 1987
Shaquille O'Neal, Orlando at New Jersey, November 20, 1993
14 — Elmore Smith, Los Angeles vs. Detroit, October 26, 1973
Elmore Smith, Los Angeles vs. Houston, November 4, 1973
Mark Eaton, Utah vs. Portland, January 18, 1985
Mark Eaton, Utah vs. San Antonio, February 18, 1989

Most blocked shots, one half
11 — Elmore Smith, Los Angeles vs. Portland, October 28, 1973
George Johnson, San Antonio vs. Golden State, February 24, 1981
Manute Bol, Washington vs. Milwaukee, December 12, 1985
10 — Harvey Catchings, Philadelphia vs. Atlanta, March 21, 1975
Manute Bol, Washington vs. Indiana, February 26, 1987

Most blocked shots, one quarter
8 — Manute Bol, Washington vs. Milwaukee, December 12, 1985
Manute Bol, Washington vs. Indiana, February 26, 1987

TURNOVERS

Turnovers have been compiled since 1977-78

Most turnovers, career
3,804 — Moses Malone, Houston, 1977-78 — 1981-82; Philadelphia, 1982-83 — 1985-86; Washington, 1986-87 — 1987-88; Atlanta, 1988-89 — 1990-91; Milwaukee, 1991-92 — 1992-93; Philadelphia, 1993-94; San Antonio, 1994-95
3,704 — Karl Malone, Utah, 1985-86 — 1999-00
3,682 — Isiah Thomas, Detroit, 1981-82 — 1993-94

Most turnovers, season
366 — Artis Gilmore, Chicago, 1977-78
360 — Kevin Porter, Detroit, New Jersey, 1977-78
359 — Micheal Ray Richardson, New York, 1979-80

Most turnovers, game
14 — John Drew, Atlanta at New Jersey, March 1, 1978
13 — Chris Mullin, Golden State at Utah, March 31, 1988
12 — Kevin Porter, New Jersey at Philadelphia, November 9, 1977
Artis Gilmore, Chicago vs. Atlanta, January 31, 1978 (ot)
Kevin Porter, Detroit at Philadelphia, February 7, 1979
Maurice Lucas, Portland vs. Phoenix, November 25, 1979
Moses Malone, Houston at Phoenix, February 6, 1981
Eric Floyd, Golden State vs. Denver, October 25, 1985
Scottie Pippen, Chicago at New Jersey, February 25, 1990 (ot)
Scottie Pippen, Chicago at Houston, January 30, 1996
Damon Stoudamire, Toronto at Chicago, January 25, 1997

ALL-TIME REGULAR-SEASON NBA RECORDS: TEAM (OFFENSE)

SCORING

Highest average, points per game, season
126.5 — Denver, 1981-82 (10,371/82)

Lowest average, points per game, season
81.9 — Chicago, 1998-99 (4,095/50)

Most consecutive games, 100 or more points
136 — Denver, January 21, 1981-December 8, 1982

Most consecutive games, 100 or more points, season
82 — Denver, October 30, 1981- April 17, 1982 (entire season)

Most consecutive games, fewer than 100 points, season
29 — Orlando, December 13, 1997-February 16, 1998 Chicago, November 3, 1999-January 5, 2000

Most points, game
186 — Detroit at Denver, December 13, 1983 (3 OT)

ALL-TIME REGULAR-SEASON NBA RECORDS: TEAM (OFFENSE) – Continued

Fewest points, game
49 — Chicago vs. Miami, April 10, 1999

Most points, both teams, game
370 — Detroit (186) at Denver (184), December 13, 1983 (3 OT)

Fewest points, both teams, game
119 — Milwaukee (57) vs. Boston (62), at Providence, February 27, 1955

Largest margin of victory, game
68 — Cleveland vs. Miami, December 17, 1991 (148-80)

PLAYERS SCORING

Most players, 2,000 or more points, season
2 — Los Angeles, 1964-65 (West 2,292, Baylor 2,009)

Most players, 1,000 or more points, season
6 — Syracuse, 1960-61 (Schayes 1,868, Greer 1,551, Barnett 1,320, Gambee 1,085, Costello 1,084, Kerr 1, 056)

Most players, 40 or more points, game
2 — Baltimore vs. Los Angeles, November 14, 1964 (Johnson 41, Bellamy 40)

Most players, 40 or more points, both teams, game
4 — Denver vs. Detroit, December 13, 1983 (3 OT) (Detroit: Thomas 47, Long 41; Denver: Vandeweghe 51, English 47)

FIELD GOAL PERCENTAGE

Highest field goal percentage, season
.545 — L.A. Lakers, 1984-85 (3,952/7,254)

Lowest field goal percentage, season
.362 — Milwaukee, 1954-55 (2,187/6,041)

Highest field goal percentage, game
.707 — San Antonio at Dallas, April 16, 1983 (53/75)

Lowest field goal percentage, game
.229 — Milwaukee vs. Minneapolis, at Buffalo, November 6, 1954 (22/96)

Highest field goal percentage, both teams, game
.632 — Boston (.650) vs. New Jersey (.615) at Hartford, December 11, 1984 (108/171)

Lowest field goal percentage, both teams, game
.246 — Milwaukee (.229) vs. Minneapolis (.263), at Buffalo, November 6,1954 (48/195)

FIELD GOALS

Most field goals per game, season
49.9 — Boston, 1959-60 (3,744/75)

Fewest field goals per game, season
30.4 — Milwaukee, 1954-55 (2,187/72)

Most field goals, game
74 — Detroit at Denver, December 13, 1983 (3 OT)

Fewest field goals, game
18 — Chicago vs. Miami, April 10, 1999

Most field goals, both teams, game
142 — Detroit (74) at Denver (68), December 13, 1983 (3 OT)

Fewest field goals, both teams, game
45 — Minnesota (22) vs. Atlanta (23), April 12, 1997

FIELD GOAL ATTEMPTS

Most field goal attempts per game, season
119.6 — Boston, 1959-60 (8,971/75)

Fewest field goal attempts per game, season
71.22 — Cleveland, 1998-99 (3,561/50)

Most field goal attempts, game
153 — Philadelphia vs. Los Angeles, December 8, 1961 (3 OT)

Fewest field goal attempts, game
53 — Cleveland vs. Boston, November 29, 1997

Most field goal attempts, both teams, game
291 — Philadelphia (153) vs. Los Angeles (138), December 8, 1961 (3 OT)

Fewest field goal attempts, both teams, game
116 — Utah (53) vs. Dallas (63), December 12, 1997

THREE-POINT FIELD GOAL PERCENTAGE

(Three-point field goal percentages have been compiled since 1979-80)

Highest three-point field goal percentage, season
.428-Charlotte, 1996-97 (591/1,382)

Lowest three-point field goal percentage, season
.104 — Los Angeles, 1982-83 (10/96)

Most three-point field goals, none missed, game
7 — Indiana vs. Atlanta, January 20, 1995

Most three-point field goals, both teams, none missed, game
5 — San Antonio (4) at Philadelphia (1), December 19, 1984

Most three-point field goal attempts, none made, game
15 — Houston at Orlando, March 30, 1991

THREE-POINT FIELD GOALS

(Three-point field goals have been compiled since 1979-80)

Most three-point field goals per game, season
8.96 — Dallas, 1995-96 (735/82)

Fewest three-point field goals per game, season
0.12 — Atlanta, 1980-81 (10/82)

Most three-point field goals, game
19 — Atlanta at Dallas, December 17, 1996

Most three-point field goals, both teams, game
29 — Denver (16) at Seattle (13), March 20, 1997

THREE-POINT FIELD GOAL ATTEMPTS

(Three-point field goal attempts have been compiled since 1979-80)

Most three-point field goal attempts per game, season
24.87 — Dallas, 1995-96 (2,039/82)

Fewest three-point field goal attempts per game, season
0.91 — Atlanta, 1979-80 (75/82)

Most three-point field goal attempts, game
49-Dallas vs. New Jersey, March 5, 1996

Most three-point field goal attempts, both teams, game
64 — Houston (33) vs. Dallas (31), April 11, 1995 (2 OT)
Cleveland (40) vs. Portland (24), December 30, 1995 (2 OT)
Houston (37) vs. L.A. Lakers (27), November 12, 1996 (2 OT)

ALL-TIME REGULAR-SEASON NBA RECORDS: TEAM (OFFENSE) – Continued

FREE THROW PERCENTAGE

Highest free throw percentage, season
.832 — Boston, 1989-90 (1,791/2,153)

Lowest free throw percentage, season
.635 — Philadelphia, 1967-68 (2,121/3,338)

Most free throws made, none missed, game
39 — Utah at Portland, December 7, 1982

Lowest free throw percentage, game
.000 — Toronto vs. Charlotte, January 9, 1996 (0/3)

Highest free throw percentage, both teams, game
.973 — Denver (1.000) vs. Phoenix (.938), April 4, 1997 (36/37)

Lowest free throw percentage, both teams, game
.410 — Los Angeles (.386) at Chicago (.471), December 7, 1968 (25/61)

FREE THROWS MADE

Most free throws made per game, season
31.9 — New York, 1957-58 (2,300/72)

Fewest free throws made per game, season
14.9-Boston, 1998-99 (745/50)

Most free throws made, game
61 — Phoenix vs. Utah, April 9, 1990 (OT)

Fewest free throws made, game
0 — Toronto vs. Charlotte, January 9, 1996

Most free throws made, both teams, game
116 — Syracuse (59) vs. Anderson (57), November 24, 1949 (5 OT)

Fewest free throws made, both teams, game
7 — Milwaukee (3) vs. Baltimore (4), January 1, 1973

FREE THROW ATTEMPTS

Most free throw attempts per game, season
42.4 — New York, 1957-58 (3,056/72)

Fewest free throw attempts per game, season
20.6-Milwaukee, 1972-73 (1,687/82)

Most free throw attempts, game
86 — Syracuse vs. Anderson, November 24, 1949 (5 OT)

Fewest free throw attempts, game
2 — Cleveland vs. Golden State, November 26, 1994

Most free throw attempts, both teams, game
160 — Syracuse (86) vs. Anderson (74), November 24, 1949 (5 OT)

Fewest free throw attempts, both teams, game
12 — Los Angeles (3) vs. San Diego (9), March 28, 1980

REBOUNDS

(Rebounds have been compiled since 1950-51; team rebounds not included.)

Most rebounds per game, season
71.5 — Boston, 1959-60 (5,365/75)

Fewest rebounds per game, season
35.6 — Cleveland, 1995-96 (2,922/82)

Most rebounds, game
109 — Boston vs. Detroit, December 24, 1960

For additional records, please log on to NBA.com.

Fewest rebounds, game
19 — Seattle vs. Phoenix, April 14, 1999

Most rebounds, both teams, game
188 — Philadelphia (98) vs. Los Angeles (90), December 8, 1961 (3 OT)

Fewest rebounds, both teams, game
48 — New York (20) vs. Fort Wayne (28), at Miami, February 14, 1955

ASSISTS

Most assists per game, season
31.4 — L.A. Lakers, 1984-85 (2,575/82)

Fewest assists per game, season
15.6 — Atlanta, 1998-99 (782/50)

Most assists, game
53 — Milwaukee vs. Detroit, December 26, 1978

Fewest assists, game
3 — Boston vs. Minneapolis, at Louisville, November 28, 1956
Baltimore vs. Boston, October 16, 1963
Cincinnati vs. Chicago, at Evansville, December 5, 1967
New York at Boston, March 28, 1976

Most assists, both teams, game
93 — Detroit (47) at Denver (46), December 13, 1983 (3 OT)

Fewest assists, both teams, game
10 — Boston (3) vs. Minneapolis (7), at Louisville, November 28, 1956

PERSONAL FOULS

Most personal fouls per game, season
32.1 — Tri-Cities, 1949-50 (2,057/64)

Fewest personal fouls per game, season
18.1 — Philadelphia, 1993-94 (1,488/82)

Most personal fouls, game
66 — Anderson at Syracuse, November 24, 1949 (5 OT)

Fewest personal fouls, game
5 — Dallas at San Antonio, November 20, 1999

Most personal fouls, both teams, game
122 — Anderson (66) at Syracuse (56), November 24, 1949 (5 OT)

Fewest personal fouls, both teams, game
22 — New Jersey (10) at Philadelphia (12), December 22, 1984
Dallas (10) at New York (12), December 22, 1997

DISQUALIFICATIONS

(Disqualifications have been compiled since 1950-51.)

Most disqualifications per game, season
1.53 — Rochester, 1952-53 (107/70)

Fewest disqualifications per game, season
0.02 — L.A. Lakers, 1988-89 (2/82)

Most disqualifications, game
8 — Syracuse at Baltimore, November 15, 1952 (OT)

Most disqualifications, both teams, game
13 — Syracuse (8) at Baltimore (5), November 15, 1952 (OT)

ALL-TIME REGULAR-SEASON NBA RECORDS: TEAM (OFFENSE) – Continued

STEALS

(Steals have been compiled since 1973-74.)

Most steals per game, season
12.9 — Phoenix, 1977-78 (1,059/82)

Fewest steals per game, season
5.94 — Detroit, 1990-91 (487/82)

Most steals, game
27 — Seattle vs. Toronto, January 15, 1997

Fewest steals, game
0 — Accomplished 14 times. Most recent: Atlanta at Charlotte, December 21, 1996

Most steals, both teams, game
40 — Golden State (24) vs. Los Angeles (16), January 21, 1975
Philadelphia (24) vs. Detroit (16), November 11, 1978
Golden State (25) vs. San Antonio (15), February 15, 1989

Fewest steals, both teams, game
2 — Detroit (1) at New York (1), October 9, 1973
San Antonio (1) at Charlotte (1), February 6, 1996

BLOCKED SHOTS

(Blocked shots have been compiled since 1973-74.)

Most blocked shots per game, season
8.7 — Washington, 1985-86 (716/82)

Fewest blocked shots per game, season
2.6 — Dallas, 1980-81 (214/82)

Most blocked shots, game
22 — New Jersey vs. Denver, December 12, 1991

Fewest blocked shots, game
0 — By many teams

Most blocked shots, both teams, game
34 — Detroit (19) vs. Washington (15), November 19, 1981

Fewest blocked shots, both teams, game
0 — Seattle at Portland, November 22, 1973
Atlanta at Phoenix, December 3, 1974
Kansas City at New York, October 30, 1975
Detroit at New York, November 29, 1975
Houston at Los Angeles, January 22, 1978
Buffalo at Atlanta, January 29, 1978
Phoenix at Portland, November 25, 1979
Washington at Dallas, February 10, 1982
Miami at Detroit, January 2, 1994
San Antonio at Milwaukee, November 14, 1995

TURNOVERS

(Turnovers have been compiled since 1970-71.)

Most turnovers per game, season
24.5 — Denver, 1976-77 (2,011/82)

Fewest turnovers per game, season
12.7 — Detroit, 1996-97 (1,041/82)

Most turnovers, game
43 — Los Angeles vs. Seattle, February 15, 1974

Fewest turnovers, game
3 — Portland vs. Phoenix, February 22, 1991
Orlando vs. New York, March 31, 1996

Most turnovers, both teams, game
73 — Philadelphia (38) vs. San Antonio (35), October 22, 1976
Denver (38) vs. Phoenix (35), October 24, 1980

Fewest turnovers, both teams, game
12 — Cleveland (6) at Boston (6), March 7, 1993

ALL-TIME REGULAR-SEASON NBA RECORDS: TEAM (DEFENSE)

POINTS

Fewest points allowed per game, season
83.4 — Atlanta, 1998-99 (4,170/50)

Most points allowed per game, season
130.8 — Denver, 1990-91 (10,723/82)

Most consecutive games, fewer than 100 points allowed, season
28 — Fort Wayne, October 30-December 30, 1954

Most consecutive games, 100 or more points allowed, season
82 — Denver, October 30, 1981-April 17, 1982 (entire season)
Denver, November 2, 1990-April 21, 1991 (entire season)

FIELD GOAL PERCENTAGE

(Opponents' field goal percentage has been compiled since 1970-71.)

Lowest opponents' field goal percentage, season
.402 — San Antonio, 1998-99 (1,631/4,061)

Highest opponents' field goal percentage, season
.536 — Golden State, 1984-85 (3,839/7,165)

TURNOVERS

(Opponents' turnovers have been compiled since 1970-71.)

Most opponents' turnovers per game, season
24.1 — Atlanta, 1977-78 (1,980/82)

Fewest opponents' turnovers per game, season
12.21 — Atlanta, 1999-00 (1,001/82)

ALL-TIME PLAYOFF RECORDS: INDIVIDUAL

MINUTES

Most minutes, game
67 — Red Rocha, Syracuse at Boston, March 21, 1953 (4 OT)
Paul Seymour, Syracuse at Boston, March 21, 1953 (4 OT)
66 — Bob Cousy, Boston vs. Syracuse, March 21, 1953 (4 OT)

Highest average, minutes per game, one playoff series
49.33 — Wilt Chamberlain, Philadelphia vs. New York, 1968 (296/6)
49.29 — Kareem Abdul-Jabbar, Milwaukee vs. Boston, 1974 (345/7)
48.75 — Wilt Chamberlain, Philadelphia vs. Cincinnati, 1965 (195/4)
Jerry Lucas, Cincinnati vs. Philadelphia, 1965 (195/4)
Oscar Robertson, Cincinnati vs. Philadelphia, 1965 (195/4)
Wilt Chamberlain, Los Angeles vs. Atlanta, 1970 (195/4)

ALL-TIME PLAYOFF RECORDS: INDIVIDUAL - Continued

SCORING

Highest scoring average, one playoff series
46.3 — Jerry West, Los Angeles vs. Baltimore, 1965 (278/6)
45.2 — Michael Jordan, Chicago vs. Cleveland, 1988 (226/5)
45.0 — Michael Jordan, Chicago vs. Miami, 1992 (135/3)

Most points, game
63 — Michael Jordan, Chicago at Boston, April 20, 1986 (2 OT)
61 — Elgin Baylor, Los Angeles at Boston, April 14, 1962
56 — Wilt Chamberlain, Philadelphia vs. Syracuse, March 22, 1962
Michael Jordan, Chicago at Miami, April 29, 1992
Charles Barkley, Phoenix at Golden State, May 4, 1994

Most consecutive games, 20 or more points
60 — Michael Jordan, Chicago, June 2, 1989-May 11, 1993
57 — Kareem Abdul-Jabbar, Milwaukee, Los Angeles, April 13, 1973-April 5, 1981
49 — Elgin Baylor, Minneapolis, Los Angeles, March 17, 1960-March 30, 1964

Most consecutive games, 30 or more points
11 — Elgin Baylor, Los Angeles, March 27, 1962-April 18, 1962
9 — Kareem Abdul-Jabbar, Milwaukee, March 25, 1970-April 19, 1970
Bob McAdoo, Buffalo, April 12, 1974-April 15, 1976
8 — Michael Jordan, Chicago, April 23, 1987-May 8, 1988
Michael Jordan, Chicago, June 9, 1993-April 30, 1995

Most consecutive games, 40 or more points
6 — Jerry West, Los Angeles, April 3-April 13, 1965
4 — Bernard King, New York, April 19-April 27, 1984
Michael Jordan, Chicago, June 11, 1993-June 18, 1993
3 — Kareem Abdul-Jabbar, Los Angeles, April 26-May 1, 1977
Michael Jordan, Chicago, May 3-May 7, 1989
Michael Jordan, Chicago, May 9-May 13, 1990

Most points, one half
39 — Sleepy Floyd, Golden State vs. L.A. Lakers, May 10, 1987
38 — Charles Barkley, Phoenix at Golden State, May 4, 1994

Most points, one quarter
29 — Sleepy Floyd, Golden State vs. L.A. Lakers, May 10, 1987
27 — Mark Aguirre, Dallas at Houston, May 5, 1988
Charles Barkley, Phoenix at Golden State, May 4, 1994

Most points, overtime period
13 — Clyde Drexler, Portland at L.A. Lakers, April 29, 1992

FIELD GOALS

Highest field goal percentage, game
(minimum 8 made)
1.000 — Wilt Chamberlain, Los Angeles at Atlanta, April 17, 1969 (9/9)
Don Nelson, Boston at Buffalo, April 6, 1974 (10/10)
Tom Kozelko, Capital at New York, April 12, 1974 (8/8)
Larry McNeill, Kansas City/Omaha vs. Chicago, April 13, 1975 (12/12)
Clifford Ray, Golden State at Detroit, April 14, 1977 (8/8)
Scott Wedman, Boston vs. L.A. Lakers, May 27, 1985 (11/11)
Brad Davis, Dallas at Utah, April 25, 1986 (8/8)
Bob Hansen, Utah vs. Dallas, April 25, 1986 (9/9)
Robert Parish, Boston at Atlanta, May 16, 1988 (8/8)
John Paxson, Chicago vs. L.A. Lakers, June 5, 1991 (8/8)
Horace Grant, Chicago vs. Cleveland, May 13, 1993 (8/8)

Most field goals, none missed, game
12 — Larry McNeill, Kansas City/Omaha vs. Chicago, April 13, 1975
11 — Scott Wedman, Boston vs. L.A. Lakers, May 27, 1985
10 — Don Nelson, Boston at Buffalo, April 6, 1974

Most field goals, game
24 — Wilt Chamberlain, Philadelphia vs. Syracuse, March 14, 1960
John Havlicek, Boston vs. Atlanta, April 1, 1973
Michael Jordan, Chicago vs. Cleveland, May 1, 1988
23 — Charles Barkley, Phoenix at Golden State, May 4, 1994

Most field goals, one half
15 — Sleepy Floyd, Golden State vs. L.A. Lakers, May 10, 1987
Charles Barkley, Phoenix at Golden State, May 4, 1994
14 — John Havlicek, Boston vs. Atlanta, April 1, 1973
Gus Williams, Seattle at Dallas, April 17, 1984
Michael Jordan, Chicago vs. Cleveland, May 1, 1988
Isiah Thomas, Detroit at L.A. Lakers, June 19, 1988
Michael Jordan, Chicago at Philadelphia, May 11, 1990
Michael Jordan, Chicago vs. Portland, June 3, 1992
Michael Jordan, Chicago vs. Phoenix, June 16, 1993

Most field goals, one quarter
12 — Sleepy Floyd, Golden State vs. L.A. Lakers, May 10, 1987
11 — Gus Williams, Seattle at Dallas, April 17, 1984
Isiah Thomas, Detroit at L.A. Lakers, June 19, 1988
Charles Barkley, Phoenix at Golden State, May 4, 1994

Most field goal attempts, game
48 — Wilt Chamberlain, Philadelphia vs. Syracuse, March 22, 1962
Rick Barry, San Francisco vs. Philadelphia, April 18, 1967
46 — Elgin Baylor, Los Angeles at Boston, April 14, 1962
45 — Elgin Baylor, Los Angeles at St. Louis, March 27, 1961
Michael Jordan, Chicago vs. Cleveland, May 1, 1988

Most field goal attempts, none made, game
14 — Chick Reiser, Baltimore at Philadelphia, April 10, 1948
Dennis Johnson, Seattle vs. Washington, June 7, 1978
12 — Tom Gola, Philadelphia at Boston, March 23, 1958
Guy Rodgers, San Francisco at Boston, April 18, 1964
Paul Pressey, Milwaukee at Boston, May 5, 1987

THREE-POINT FIELD GOALS

Most three-point field goals, none missed, game
7 — Robert Horry, L.A. Lakers at Utah, May 6, 1997
5 — Brad Davis, Dallas at Utah, April 25, 1986
Byron Scott, L.A. Lakers vs. Golden State, May 5, 1991
Nate McMillan, Seattle vs. Houston, May 6, 1996
Mario Elie, Houston vs. Seattle, May 5, 1997
Larry Johnson, New York vs. Indiana, May 29, 2000

Most three-point field goals, game
9 — Rex Chapman, Phoenix at Seattle, April 25, 1997
8 — Dan Majerle, Phoenix vs. Seattle, June 1, 1993
Gary Payton, Seattle at Phoenix, April 29, 1997
Mookie Blaylock, Atlanta at Chicago, May 8, 1997
Matt Maloney, Houston at Seattle, May 11, 1997 (OT)

Most three-point field goals, one half
6 — Michael Jordan, Chicago vs. Portland, June 3, 1992
Reggie Miller, Indiana at New York, June 1, 1994
Kenny Smith, Houston at Utah, April 29, 1995
Reggie Miller, Indiana vs. Atlanta, April 29, 1995
John Starks, New York at Indiana, May 11, 1995
Kenny Smith, Houston at Orlando, June 7, 1995
Mookie Blaylock, Atlanta at Chicago, May 8, 1997

Most three-point field goals, one quarter
5 — Reggie Miller, Indiana at New York, June 1, 1994

ALL-TIME PLAYOFF RECORDS: INDIVIDUAL – Continued

Kenny Smith, Houston at Orlando, June 7, 1995
Robert Horry, Houston vs. Seattle, May 12, 1996
Gary Payton, Seattle at Phoenix, April 29, 1997
Ray Allen, Milwaukee at Indiana, May 11, 1999

Most three-point field goal attempts, game
17 — Rex Chapman, Phoenix at Seattle, April 25, 1997
16 — Reggie Miller, Indiana vs. Milwaukee, May 11, 1999 (OT)

Most three-point field goal attempts, one half
11 — Gary Payton, Seattle vs. Houston, May 4, 1996

FREE THROWS

Most free throws made, none missed, game
18 — Karl Malone, Utah at L.A. Lakers, May 10, 1997
17 — Gail Goodrich, Los Angeles at Chicago, March 28, 1971
Bob Love, Chicago at Golden State, April 27, 1975
Reggie Miller, Indiana at New York, April 30, 1993

Most free throws made, game
30 — Bob Cousy, Boston vs. Syracuse, March 21, 1953 (4 OT)
23 — Michael Jordan, Chicago vs. New York, May 14, 1989
22 — Michael Jordan, Chicago vs. Cleveland, May 5, 1989 (OT)
Karl Malone, Utah at L.A. Clippers, May 3, 1992

Most free throws made, one half
19 — Magic Johnson, L.A. Lakers vs. Golden State, May 8, 1991
Karl Malone, Utah at Portland, May 9, 1991
Charles Barkley, Phoenix vs. Seattle, June 5, 1993

Most free throws made, one quarter
13 — Michael Jordan, Chicago vs. Detroit, May 21, 1991
12 — Reggie Miller, Indiana at New York, April 30, 1993
Shaquille O'Neal, L.A. Lakers vs. Portland, May 20, 2000

Most free throw attempts, game
39 — Shaquille O'Neal, L.A. Lakers vs. Indiana, June 9, 2000
32 — Bob Cousy, Boston vs. Syracuse, March 21, 1953 (4 OT)

Most free throw attempts, one half
27 — Shaquille O'Neal, L.A. Lakers vs. Portland, May 20, 2000
22 — Shaquille O'Neal, L.A. Lakers vs. Indiana, June 9, 2000

Most free throw attempts, one quarter
25 — Shaquille O'Neal, L.A. Lakers vs. Portland, May 20, 2000
16 — Shaquille O'Neal, L.A. Lakers vs. Indiana, June 9, 2000

REBOUNDS

Most rebounds, game
41 — Wilt Chamberlain, Philadelphia vs. Boston, April 5, 1967
40 — Bill Russell, Boston vs. Philadelphia, March 23, 1958
Bill Russell, Boston vs. St. Louis, March 29, 1960
Bill Russell, Boston vs. Los Angeles, April 18, 1962 (OT)

Most rebounds, one half
26 — Wilt Chamberlain, Philadelphia vs. San Francisco, April 16, 1967

Most rebounds, one quarter
19 — Bill Russell, Boston vs. Los Angeles, April 18, 1962

ASSISTS

Highest average, assists per game, one playoff series
17.0 — Magic Johnson, L.A. Lakers vs. Portland, 1985 (85/5)
16.4 — John Stockton, Utah vs. L.A. Lakers, 1988 (115/7)
16.2 — Magic Johnson, L.A. Lakers vs. Houston, 1986 (81/5)

Most assists, game
24 — Magic Johnson, Los Angeles vs. Phoenix, May 15, 1984
John Stockton, Utah at L.A. Lakers, May 17, 1988
23 — Magic Johnson, L.A. Lakers at Portland, May 3, 1985
John Stockton, Utah vs. Portland, April 25, 1996
22 — Doc Rivers, Atlanta vs. Boston, May 16, 1988

Most assists, one half
15 — Magic Johnson, L.A. Lakers at Portland, May 3, 1985
Doc Rivers, Atlanta vs. Boston, May 16, 1988

Most assists, one quarter
11 — John Stockton, Utah vs. San Antonio, May 5, 1994

PERSONAL FOULS

Most personal fouls, game
8 — Jack Toomay, Baltimore at New York, March 26, 1949 (OT)
7 — Al Cervi, Syracuse at Boston, March 21, 1953 (4 OT)
6 — By many players

DISQUALIFICATIONS

Fewest minutes played, disqualified player, game
6 — Travis Knight, L.A. Lakers vs. San Antonio, May 23, 1999
7 — Bob Lochmueller, Syracuse vs. Boston, March 19, 1953
Will Perdue, Chicago at New York, May 14, 1992
Scot Pollard, Sacramento vs. L.A. Lakers, April 30, 2000
Brian Shaw, L.A. Lakers vs. Portland, May 30, 2000

STEALS

Most steals, game
10 — Allen Iverson, Philadelphia vs. Orlando, May 13, 1999
8 — Rick Barry, Golden State vs. Seattle, April 14, 1975
Lionel Hollins, Portland at Los Angeles, May 8, 1977
Maurice Cheeks, Philadelphia vs. New Jersey, April 11, 1979
Craig Hodges, Milwaukee at Philadelphia, May 9, 1986
Tim Hardaway, Golden State at L.A. Lakers, May 8, 1991
Tim Hardaway, Golden State at Seattle, April 30, 1992
Mookie Blaylock, Atlanta vs. Indiana, April 29, 1996

BLOCKED SHOTS

Most blocked shots, game
10 — Mark Eaton, Utah vs. Houston, April 26, 1985
Hakeem Olajuwon, Houston at L.A. Lakers, April 29, 1990
9 — Kareem Abdul-Jabbar, Los Angeles vs. Golden State, April 22, 1977
Manute Bol, Washington at Philadelphia, April 18, 1986
Hakeem Olajuwon, Houston vs. L.A. Clippers, April 29, 1993
Derrick Coleman, New Jersey vs. Cleveland, May 7, 1993
Greg Ostertag, Utah vs. L.A. Lakers, May 12, 1997 (OT)
Alonzo Mourning, Miami vs. Detroit, April 22, 2000

TURNOVERS

Most turnovers, game
11 — John Williamson, New Jersey at Philadelphia, April 11, 1979
10 — Quinn Buckner, Milwaukee vs. Phoenix, April 14, 1978
Magic Johnson, Los Angeles vs. Philadelphia, May 14, 1980
Larry Bird, Boston vs. Chicago, April 7, 1981
Moses Malone, Philadelphia at New Jersey, April 24, 1984
Kevin Johnson, Phoenix at L.A. Lakers, May 23, 1989
Anfernee Hardaway, Orlando at Indiana, May 2, 1994
Kevin Garnett, Minnesota at Seattle, May 2, 1998

ALL-TIME NBA PLAYOFF RECORDS: INDIVIDUAL (SERIES)

MOST POINTS

2-game series
68 — Bob McAdoo, New York vs. Cleveland 1978

3-game series
135 — Michael Jordan, Chicago vs. Miami 1992

4-game series
150 — Hakeem Olajuwon, Houston vs. Dallas 1988

5-game series
226 — Michael Jordan, Chicago vs. Cleveland 1988

6-game series
278 — Jerry West, Los Angeles vs. Baltimore 1965

7-game series
284 — Elgin Baylor, Los Angeles vs. Boston 1962

MOST MINUTES PLAYED

2-game series
95 — Red Kerr, Syracuse vs. New York, 1959

3-game series
144 — Wilt Chamberlain, Philadelphia vs. Syracuse 1961

4-game series
195 — Wilt Chamberlain, Philadelphia vs. Cincinnati 1965
Jerry Lucas, Cincinnati vs. Philadelphia 1965
Oscar Robertson, Cincinnati vs. Philadelphia 1965
Wilt Chamberlain, Los Angeles vs. Atlanta 1970

5-game series
243 — Oscar Robertson, Cincinnati vs. Syracuse 1963

6-game series
296 — Wilt Chamberlain, Philadelphia vs. New York 1968

7-game series
345 — Kareem Abdul-Jabbar, Milwaukee vs. Boston 1974

MOST FIELD GOALS

2-game series
28 — Bob McAdoo, New York vs. Cleveland 1978

3-game series
53 — Michael Jordan, Chicago vs. Miami 1992

4-game series
65 — Kareem Abdul-Jabbar, Milwaukee vs. Chicago 1974

5-game series
86 — Michael Jordan, Chicago vs. Philadelphia 1990

6-game series
101 — Michael Jordan, Chicago vs. Phoenix 1993

7-game series
113 — Wilt Chamberlain, San Francisco vs. St. Louis 1964

MOST FIELD GOAL ATTEMPTS

2-game series
62 — John Williamson, New Jersey vs. Philadelphia 1979

3-game series
104 — Wilt Chamberlain, Philadelphia vs. Syracuse 1960

4-game series
116 — Hakeem Olajuwon, Houston vs. Orlando, 1995

5-game series
159 — Wilt Chamberlain, Philadelphia vs. Syracuse 1962

6-game series
235 — Rick Barry, San Francisco vs. Philadelphia 1967

7-game series
235 — Elgin Baylor, Los Angeles vs. Boston 1962

MOST THREE-POINT FIELD GOALS MADE, NONE MISSED

2-game series
4 — Kevin Grevey, Washington vs. New Jersey 1982

3-game series
3 — Pat Garrity, Phoenix vs. Portland 1999

4-game series
4 — Dana Barros, Seattle vs. Golden State 1992

5-game series
4 — Ricky Pierce, Milwaukee vs. Atlanta 1989

6-game series
3 — Norm Nixon, Los Angeles vs. San Antonio 1983
Fat Lever, Denver vs. Dallas 1988

7-game series
2 — David Wingate, San Antonio vs. Portland 1990

MOST THREE-POINT FIELD GOALS MADE

2-game series
5 — Kevin Grevey, Washington vs. Philadelphia 1980

3-game series
14 — John Starks, New York vs. Cleveland 1996

4-game series
14 — Nick Van Exel, L.A. Lakers vs. Seattle 1995
Robert Horry, Houston vs. Seattle 1996

5-game series
22 — Rex Chapman, Phoenix vs. Seattle 1997

6-game series
18 — Terry Porter, Portland vs. Utah 1992

7-game series
28 — Dennis Scott, Orlando vs. Indiana 1995

MOST THREE-POINT FIELD GOAL ATTEMPTS

2-game series
10 — Kevin Grevey, Washington vs. Philadelphia 1980

3-game series
35 — Reggie Miller, Indiana vs. Milwaukee 1999

4-game series
42 — Nick Anderson, Orlando vs. Philadelphia 1999

5-game series
48 — Rex Chapman, Phoenix vs. Seattle 1997

6-game series
43 — Dennis Scott, Orlando vs. Chicago 1995

7-game series
65 — Dennis Scott, Orlando vs. Indiana 1995

MOST FREE THROWS MADE, NONE MISSED

2-game series
8 — Jo Jo White, Boston vs. Seattle 1977
Rick Barry, Houston vs. Atlanta 1979
Caldwell Jones, Philadelphia vs. New Jersey 1979
Mike Newlin, Houston vs. Atlanta 1979
Bobby Jones, Philadelphia vs. Washington 1980

3-game series
18 — Kiki Vandeweghe, Denver vs. Phoenix 1982

4-game series
32 — Kiki Vandeweghe, Portland vs. Denver 1986

5-game series
30 — Mark Price, Cleveland vs. Philadelphia 1990

6-game series
17 — Bob Lanier, Milwaukee vs. New Jersey 1984

7-game series
35 — Jack Sikma, Milwaukee vs. Boston 1987

MOST FREE THROWS MADE

2-game series
21 — George Yardley, Detroit vs. Cincinnati 1958

3-game series
43 — Kevin Johnson, Phoenix vs. Denver 1989

4-game series
49 — Jerry West, Los Angeles vs. Atlanta 1970

5-game series
62 — Oscar Robertson, Cincinnati vs. Philadelphia 1964

6-game series
86 — Jerry West, Los Angeles vs. Baltimore, 1965

7-game series
83 — Dolph Schayes, Syracuse vs. Boston 1959

MOST FREE THROW ATTEMPTS

2-game series
24 — George Yardley, Detroit vs. Cincinnati 1958
Bernard King, New Jersey vs. Philadelphia 1979
Calvin Natt, Portland vs. Seattle 1983

3-game series
47 — Dolph Schayes, Syracuse vs. Boston 1957

4-game series
61 — Shaquille O'Neal, L.A. Lakers vs. San Antonio 1999

5-game series
79 — Karl Malone, Utah vs. L.A. Clippers 1992

6-game series
95 — Jerry West, Los Angeles vs. Baltimore 1965

ALL-TIME NBA PLAYOFF RECORDS: INDIVIDUAL (SERIES) – Continued

7-game series
100 — Charles Barkley, Philadelphia vs. Milwaukee 1986

MOST REBOUNDS

2-game series
41 — Moses Malone, Houston vs. Atlanta 1979

3-game series
84 — Bill Russell, Boston vs. Syracuse 1957

4-game series
118 — Bill Russell, Boston vs. Minneapolis 1959

5-game series
160 — Wilt Chamberlain, Philadelphia vs. Boston 1967

6-game series
171 — Wilt Chamberlain, Philadelphia vs. San Francisco 1967

7-game series
220 — Wilt Chamberlain, Philadelphia vs. Boston 1965

MOST ASSISTS

2-game series
20 — Frank Johnson, Washington vs. New Jersey 1982

3-game series
48 — Magic Johnson, L.A. Lakers vs. San Antonio 1986

4-game series
57 — Magic Johnson, L.A. Lakers vs. Phoenix 1989

5-game series
85 — Magic Johnson, L.A. Lakers vs. Portland 1985

6-game series
90 — Johnny Moore, San Antonio vs. Los Angeles 1983

7-game series
115 — John Stockton, Utah vs. L.A. Lakers 1988

MOST STEALS

2-game series
10 — Maurice Cheeks, Philadelphia vs. New Jersey 1979

3-game series
13 — Clyde Drexler, Portland vs. Dallas 1990
Hersey Hawkins, Philadelphia vs. Milwaukee 1991

4-game series
17 — Lionel Hollins, Portland vs. Los Angeles 1977

5-game series
21 — Micheal Ray Richardson, New Jersey vs. Philadelphia 1984

6-game series
19 — Rick Barry, Golden State vs. Seattle 1975

7-game series
28 — John Stockton, Utah vs. L.A. Lakers 1988

MOST BLOCKED SHOTS

2-game series
10 — Darryl Dawkins, Philadelphia vs. Atlanta 1982

3-game series
18 — Manute Bol, Golden State vs. Utah 1989

4-game series
23 — Hakeem Olajuwon, Houston vs. L.A. Lakers 1990

5-game series
31 — Dikembe Mutombo, Denver vs. Seattle 1994

6-game series
27 — Marvin Webster, Seattle vs. Denver 1978

7-game series
38 — Dikembe Mutombo, Denver vs. Utah 1994

MOST TURNOVERS

2-game series
14 — John Williamson, New Jersey vs. Philadelphia 1979

3-game series
20 — Anfernee Hardaway, Orlando vs. Indiana 1994

4-game series
25 — Darrell Armstrong, Orlando vs. Philadelphia 1999

5-game series
29 — Larry Bird, Boston vs. Milwaukee 1984

6-game series
30 — Magic Johnson, Los Angeles vs. Philadelphia 1980
Sidney Moncrief, Milwaukee vs. New Jersey 1984

7-game series
37 — Charles Barkley, Philadelphia vs. Milwaukee 1986

ALL-TIME PLAYOFF RECORDS: TEAM (SERIES)

MOST POINTS

2-game series
260 — Syracuse vs. New York 1959

3-game series
408 — L.A. Lakers vs. Phoenix 1985

4-game series
498 — Philadelphia vs. New York 1978

5-game series
664 — San Antonio vs. Denver 1983

6-game series
747 — Philadelphia vs. San Francisco 1967

7-game series
869 — Boston vs. Syracuse 1959

FEWEST POINTS

2-game series
171 — Atlanta vs. Philadelphia 1982

3-game series
239 — Cleveland vs. New York 1996
Detroit vs. Miami 2000

4-game series
304 — Portland vs. San Antonio 1999

5-game series
393 — Miami vs. Chicago 1997

6-game series
481 — Utah vs. Chicago 1998

7-game series
562 — Miami vs. New York 2000
568 — New York vs. Miami 2000

HIGHEST FIELD GOAL PERCENTAGE

2-game series
.555 — New York vs. Cleveland 1978

3-game series
.600 — L.A. Lakers vs. Phoenix 1985

4-game series
.561 — Milwaukee vs. Chicago 1974

5-game series
.565 — L.A. Lakers vs. Denver 1985

6-game series
.536 — Los Angeles vs. Phoenix 1984

7-game series
.534 — L.A. Lakers vs. Dallas 1988

LOWEST FIELD GOAL PERCENTAGE

2-game series
.321 — Cincinnati vs. Detroit 1958

3-game series
.308 — Syracuse vs. Boston 1957

4-game series
.316 — Atlanta vs. New York 1999

5-game series
.348 — Syracuse vs. Boston 1961

6-game series
.355 — Boston vs. St. Louis 1958

7-game series
.339 — Syracuse vs. Fort Wayne 1955

MOST FIELD GOALS

2-game series
101 — New York vs. Cleveland 1978

3-game series
165 — L.A. Lakers vs. Phoenix 1985

4-game series
206 — Portland vs. Dallas 1985

5-game series
274 — San Antonio vs. Denver 1983
L.A. Lakers vs. Denver 1985

6-game series
293 — Boston vs. Atlanta 1972

ALL-TIME PLAYOFF RECORDS: TEAM (SERIES) – Continued

7-game series
333 — Boston vs. Cincinnati 1963

FEWEST FIELD GOALS

2-game series
63 — Atlanta vs. Philadelphia 1982

3-game series
83 — Toronto vs. New York 2000

4-game series
101 — Atlanta vs. New York 1999

5-game series
131 — Miami vs. Chicago 1997

6-game series
164 — Portland vs. Utah 1999

7-game series
204 — Miami vs. New York 1997
New York vs. Miami 2000
206 — Miami vs. New York 2000

MOST FIELD GOAL ATTEMPTS

2-game series
248 — New York vs. Syracuse 1959

3-game series
349 — Philadelphia vs. Syracuse 1960

4-game series
464 — Minneapolis vs. Boston 1959

5-game series
568 — Boston vs. Los Angeles 1965

6-game series
743 — San Francisco vs. Philadelphia 1967

7-game series
835 — Boston vs. Syracuse 1959

FEWEST FIELD GOAL ATTEMPTS

2-game series
150 — Atlanta vs. Philadelphia 1982
157 — Milwaukee vs. Phoenix 1978
Philadelphia vs. Atlanta 1982

3-game series
199 — Portland vs. Phoenix 1999

4-game series
246 — Cleveland vs. Indiana 1998

5-game series
337 — San Antonio vs. New York 1999

6-game series
408 — San Antonio vs. Utah 1996

7-game series
454 — Seattle vs. Utah 1996

MOST THREE-POINT FIELD GOALS MADE

2-game series
7 — Washington vs. Philadelphia 1980

3-game series
35 — Houston vs. Minnesota 1997

4-game series
43 — Houston vs. Seattle 1996
41 — Orlando vs. Houston 1995
Seattle vs. Houston 1996

5-game series
54 — Seattle vs. Phoenix 1997
51 — Phoenix vs. Seattle 1997

6-game series
49 — Indiana vs. L.A. Lakers 2000

7-game series
77 — Orlando vs. Indiana 1995

MOST THREE-POINT FIELD GOAL ATTEMPTS

2-game series
19 — Washington vs. Philadelphia 1980

3-game series
85 — Indiana vs. Milwaukee 1999

4-game series
118 — Orlando vs. Houston 1995
Houston vs. Seattle 1996

5-game series
145-Phoenix vs. Seattle 1997

6-game series
137 — Chicago vs. Seattle 1996

7-game series
180 — Houston vs. Seattle 1997

HIGHEST FREE THROW PERCENTAGE

2-game series
.865 — Syracuse vs. New York 1959

3-game series
.872 — Denver vs. San Antonio 1990

4-game series
.882 — Houston vs. Boston 1980

5-game series
.894 — Dallas vs. Seattle 1984

6-game series
.852 — Indiana vs. L.A. Lakers 2000

7-game series
.840 — Syracuse vs. Boston 1959

LOWEST FREE THROW PERCENTAGE

2-game series
.610 — New Jersey vs. Washington 1982

3-game series
.611 — Baltimore vs. St. Louis 1966

4-game series
.543 — Orlando vs. Chicago 1996

5-game series
.567 — Houston vs. Utah 1985

6-game series
.570 — L.A. Lakers vs. Indiana 2000

7-game series
.582 — San Francisco vs. St. Louis 1964

MOST FREE THROWS MADE

2-game series
90 — Syracuse vs. New York 1959

3-game series
131 — Minneapolis vs. St. Louis 1956
121 — St. Louis vs. Minneapolis 1956

4-game series
144 — L.A. Lakers vs. Seattle 1987

5-game series
183 — Philadelphia vs. Syracuse 1956

6-game series
232 — Boston vs. St. Louis 1958
215 — St. Louis vs. Boston 1958

7-game series
244 — St. Louis vs. Boston 1957

FEWEST FREE THROWS MADE

2-game series
25 — New Jersey vs. Washington 1982

3-game series
35 — Cleveland vs. New York 1996
New York vs. Charlotte 1997

4-game series
46 — Milwaukee vs. Chicago 1974

5-game series
57 — Detroit vs. Atlanta 1999

6-game series
82 — New York vs. Indiana 2000
82 — Chicago vs. Phoenix 1993
84 — Cleveland vs. Boston 1976

7-game series
100 — Milwaukee vs. Boston 1974

MOST FREE THROW ATTEMPTS

2-game series
104 — Syracuse vs. New York 1959

3-game series
174 — St. Louis vs. Minneapolis 1956
173 — Minneapolis vs. St. Louis 1956

4-game series
186 — Syracuse vs. Boston 1955

5-game series
238 — Philadelphia vs. Syracuse 1956

6-game series
298 — Boston vs. St. Louis 1958
292 — St. Louis vs. Boston 1958

7-game series
341 — St. Louis vs. Boston 1957

FEWEST FREE THROW ATTEMPTS

2-game series
38 — Phoenix vs. Milwaukee 1978

3-game series
45 — Cleveland vs. New York 1996

4-game series
57 — Milwaukee vs. Chicago 1974

5-game series
72 — Detroit vs. Atlanta 1999

6-game series
105 — Boston vs. Buffalo 1974

7-game series
128 — New York vs. Capital 1974

HIGHEST REBOUND PERCENTAGE

2-game series
.585 — Boston vs. San Antonio 1977

3-game series
.652 — L.A. Lakers vs. San Antonio 1986

4-game series
.597 — Chicago vs. Orlando 1996

5-game series
.591 — Boston vs. New York 1974

6-game series
.580 — Los Angeles vs. Philadelphia 1980

7-game series
.5561 — San Francisco vs. St. Louis 1964
.5556 — Seattle vs. Phoenix 1979

MOST REBOUNDS

2-game series
137 — New York vs. Syracuse 1959
127 — Cincinnati vs. Detroit 1958
Detroit vs. Cincinnati 1958

3-game series
225 — Philadelphia vs. Syracuse 1960

4-game series
295 — Boston vs. Minneapolis 1959
268 — Minneapolis vs. Boston 1959

ALL-TIME PLAYOFF RECORDS: TEAM (SERIES) – Continued

5-game series
396 — Boston vs. Syracuse 1961

6-game series
457 — Boston vs. Philadelphia 1960

7-game series
525 — Boston vs. Syracuse 1959

FEWEST REBOUNDS

2-game series
71 — Atlanta vs. Philadelphia 1982

3-game series
79 — San Antonio vs. L.A. Lakers 1986

4-game series
115 — Cleveland vs. New York 1995

5-game series
159 — Detroit vs. Atlanta 1997

6-game series
201 — Chicago vs. New York 1993

7-game series
240 — Orlando vs. Indiana 1995

MOST ASSISTS

2-game series
62 — New York vs. Cleveland 1978
Philadelphia vs. New Jersey 1979

3-game series
107 — L.A. Lakers vs. Denver 1987

4-game series
129 — Los Angeles vs. San Antonio 1982

5-game series
181 — San Antonio vs. Denver 1983

6-game series
197 — Los Angeles vs. Phoenix 1984

7-game series
233 — Milwaukee vs. Denver 1978

FEWEST ASSISTS

2-game series
24 — Cincinnati vs. Detroit 1958

3-game series
36 — Syracuse vs. Philadelphia 1958
New York vs. Toronto 2000

4-game series
44 — Atlanta vs. New York 1999

5-game series
64 — New York vs. Miami 1999

6-game series
91 — Portland vs. Utah 1999

7-game series
95 — New York vs. Miami 2000

MOST PERSONAL FOULS

2-game series
70 — New York vs. Syracuse 1959

3-game series
105 — Denver vs. San Antonio 1995

4-game series
126 — Detroit vs. Chicago 1991

5-game series
165 — Syracuse vs. Boston 1961

6-game series
197 — Milwaukee vs. New Jersey 1984

7-game series
221 — Boston vs. St. Louis 1957

FEWEST PERSONAL FOULS

2-game series
40 — Milwaukee vs. Phoenix 1978

3-game series
51 — New York vs. Cleveland 1996

4-game series
69 — Chicago vs. Milwaukee 1974

5-game series
86 — Atlanta vs. Detroit 1999

6-game series
108 — Los Angeles vs. Milwaukee 1972

7-game series
124 — Cleveland vs. Boston 1992

MOST STEALS

2-game series
23 — Philadelphia vs. Washington 1980

3-game series
38 — Indiana vs. Orlando 1994

4-game series
57 — Portland vs. Los Angeles 1977

5-game series
66 — Kansas City vs. Phoenix 1979

6-game series
81 — Golden State vs. Seattle 1975

7-game series
94 — Golden State vs. Phoenix 1976

FEWEST STEALS

2-game series
10 — New York vs. Cleveland 1978
Atlanta vs. Philadelphia 1982

3-game series
8 — Detroit vs. Orlando 1996

4-game series
10 — Detroit vs. Milwaukee 1989

5-game series
17 — Dallas vs. Seattle 1984

6-game series
24 — Detroit vs. Boston 1991

7-game series
21 — Milwaukee vs. Boston 1974

MOST BLOCKED SHOTS

2-game series
22 — Philadelphia vs. Atlanta 1982

3-game series
34 — L.A. Lakers vs. Denver 1987
Golden State vs. Utah 1989

4-game series
39 — Phoenix vs. San Antonio 2000

5-game series
53 — Boston vs. Washington 1982

6-game series
60 — Philadelphia vs. Los Angeles 1980

7-game series
71 — Denver vs. Utah 1994

FEWEST BLOCKED SHOTS

2-game series
4 — New York vs. Chicago 1981

3-game series
3 — Cleveland vs. Chicago 1994

4-game series
6 — Indiana vs. Atlanta 1987

5-game series
7 — New York vs. Miami 1998

6-game series
10 — Boston vs. Phoenix 1976

7-game series
7 — Boston vs. Milwaukee 1974

MOST TURNOVERS

2-game series
47 — Boston vs. San Antonio 1977

3-game series
82 — Chicago vs. Portland 1977

4-game series
94 — Golden State vs. Washington 1975

5-game series
128 — Phoenix vs. Kansas City 1979

6-game series
149 — Portland vs. Philadelphia 1977

7-game series
147 — Phoenix vs. Golden State 1976

FEWEST TURNOVERS

2-game series
23 — Seattle vs. Portland 1983

3-game series
28 — Houston vs. Seattle 1982
Minnesota vs. Houston 1997

4-game series
36 — Milwaukee vs. Detroit 1989

5-game series
48 — Detroit vs. Atlanta 1997

6-game series
46 — Detroit vs. Boston 1991

7-game series
76 — Atlanta vs. Boston 1988

ALL-TIME NBA PLAYOFF RECORDS: TEAM

WON-LOST

Most consecutive games won, all playoff series
13 — L.A. Lakers, 1988-89
12 — Detroit, 1989-90
San Antonio, 1999

Most consecutive games won, one playoff series
12 — San Antonio, 1999
11 — L.A. Lakers, 1989

Most consecutive games won at home, all playoff series
15 — Chicago, 1990-91

Most consecutive games won at home, one playoff series
10 — Portland, 1977
Boston, 1986
L.A. Lakers, 1987
Detroit, 1990
Chicago, 1996
Utah, 1997

Most consecutive games won on road, all playoff series
8 — Chicago, 1991-92
Houston, 1995-96

Most consecutive games won on road, one playoff series
7 — Houston, 1995

Most consecutive games lost, all playoff series
11 — Baltimore, 1965-66, 1969-70
Denver, 1988-90, 1994

Most consecutive games lost at home, all playoff series
9 — Philadelphia, 1968-71

Most consecutive games lost at home, one playoff series
4 — Los Angeles, 1983
San Antonio, 1995

Most consecutive games lost on road, all playoff series
18 — Chicago, 1967-68, 1970-73

Most consecutive games lost on road, one playoff series
7 — Boston, 1987

Most games, one postseason
25 — New York, 1994
24 — L.A. Lakers, 1988
Phoenix, 1993

Most home games, one postseason
14 — L.A. Lakers, 1988

Most road games, one postseason
12 — Houston, 1981
New York, 1994
Houston, 1995

Most wins, one postseason
15 — By many teams. Most recently:
L.A. Lakers, 2000

Most wins at home, one postseason
12 — Boston, 1984
L.A. Lakers, 1988

Most wins on road, one postseason
9 — Houston, 1995

Most games lost, one postseason
11 — Phoenix, 1993
New York, 1994

Most games lost at home, one postseason
6 — Phoenix, 1993
5 — Washington, 1979
Houston, 1981

Most losses on road, one postseason
9 — New York, 1994
8 — Boston, 1987

Highest won-lost pct., one postseason
.923 — Philadelphia, 1983 (12-1)
.883 — Detroit, 1989 (15-2)
Chicago, 1991 (15-2)
San Antonio, 1999 (15-2)

SCORING

Most points, game
157 — Boston vs. New York, April 28, 1990

Fewest points, game
54 — Utah at Chicago, June 7, 1998

Most points, both teams, game
304 — Portland (153) at Phoenix (151),
May 11, 1992 (2 OT)

Fewest points, both teams, game
142 — Atlanta (63) at Detroit (79), May 12, 1999
Miami (70) at New York (72), May 19, 2000
San Antonio (70) vs. Phoenix (72), April 22, 2000

Largest margin of victory, game
58 — Minneapolis vs. St. Louis,
March 19, 1956 (133-75)

BY HALF

Most points, first half
82 — San Antonio vs. Denver, April 26, 1983
L.A. Lakers vs. Denver, April 23, 1987

Fewest points, first half
23 — Phoenix at L.A. Lakers, May 16, 2000

Most points, both teams, first half
150 — San Antonio (82) vs. Denver (68), April 26, 1983

Fewest points, both teams, first half
63 — Philadelphia (27) at Orlando (36), May 11, 1999
Utah (31) vs. Portland (32), May 20, 1999

Largest lead at halftime
40 — Detroit vs. Washington, April 26, 1987
(led 76-36; won 128-85)

Largest deficit at halftime overcome to win game
21 — Baltimore at Philadelphia, April 13, 1948
(trailed 20-41; won 66-63)

Most points, second half
87 — Milwaukee vs. Denver, April 23, 1978

Fewest points, second half
23 — Utah at Chicago, June 7, 1998

Most points, both teams, second half
158 — Milwaukee (79) at Philadelphia (79),
March 30, 1970

Fewest points, both teams, second half
60 — Atlanta (29) at New York (31), May 24, 1999

PLAYERS SCORING

Most players, 40 or more points, game
2 — Los Angeles at Detroit, March 29, 1962
(Baylor 45, West 41)
Houston at Dallas, April 30, 1988
(Floyd 42, Olajuwon 41)
Houston vs. Utah, May 5, 1995
(Drexler 41, Olajuwon 40)
Indiana vs. Philadelphia, May 6, 2000
(Miller 40, Rose 40)

Most players, 30 or more points, game
3 — Denver at Utah, April 19, 1984
San Antonio vs. Golden State, April 25, 1991

Most players, 30 or more points, both teams, game
4 — Houston (2) at Orlando (2), June 9, 1995

Most players, 20 or more points, game
5 — Boston vs. Los Angeles, April 19, 1965
Philadelphia vs. Boston, April 11, 1967
Phoenix at Los Angeles, May 23, 1984
Boston vs. Milwaukee, May 15, 1986
L.A. Lakers vs. Boston, June 4, 1987
Boston vs. L.A. Lakers, June 11, 1987

Most players, 20 or more points, both teams, game
8 — Cincinnati (4) at Detroit (4), March 16, 1962
Boston (4) at Los Angeles (4), April 26, 1966
Phoenix (5) at Los Angeles (3), May 23, 1984
Boston (5) vs. Milwaukee (3), May 15, 1986
L.A. Lakers (5) vs. Boston (3), June 4, 1987
Portland (4) at Phoenix (4), May 11, 1992 (2 OT)

Most players, 10 or more points, game
10 — Minneapolis vs. St. Louis, March 19, 1956

Most players, 10 or more points, both teams, game
15 — Philadelphia (8) vs. Milwaukee (7), March 30, 1970
L.A. Lakers (8) vs. Phoenix (7), April 18, 1985
Dallas (9) vs. Seattle (6), April 23, 1987
Dallas (8) vs. Houston (7), April 28, 1988

Fewest players, 10 or more points, game
1 — Golden State vs. Los Angeles, April 21, 1973

ALL-TIME NBA PLAYOFF RECORDS: TEAM – Continued

Phoenix vs. Kansas City, April 8, 1981
Utah at San Antonio, April 28, 1994
Utah at San Antonio, May 9, 1998
Utah at Chicago, June 7, 1998
Detroit at Atlanta, May 8, 1999
Sacramento at L.A. Lakers, May 5, 2000
Phoenix at L.A. Lakers, May 16, 2000

Fewest players, 10 or more points, both teams, game
4 — Chicago (2) at Miami (2), May 24, 1997
Utah (2) at Chicago (2), June 10, 1998
Utah (2) at Chicago (2), June 12, 1998
Phoenix (1) at L.A. Lakers (3), May 16, 2000

FIELD GOAL PERCENTAGE

Highest field goal percentage, game
.670 — Boston vs. New York, April 28, 1990 (63-94)

Lowest field goal percentage, game
.233 — Golden State vs. Los Angeles, April 21, 1973 (27-116)

Highest field goal percentage, both teams, game
.591 — L.A. Lakers (.640) vs. Denver (.543), May 11, 1985

Lowest field goal percentage, both teams, game
.277 — Syracuse (.275) vs. Fort Wayne (.280) at Indianapolis, April 7, 1955

FIELD GOALS

Most field goals, game
67 — Milwaukee at Philadelphia, March 30, 1970
San Antonio vs. Denver, May 4, 1983
L.A. Lakers vs. Denver, May 22, 1985

Fewest field goals, game
19 — Portland vs. San Antonio, June 4, 1999

Most field goals, both teams, game
119 — Milwaukee (67) at Philadelphia (52), March 30, 1970

Fewest field goals, both teams, game
48 — Fort Wayne (23) vs. Syracuse (25) at Indianapolis, April 7, 1955
Cleveland (21) vs. New York (27), May 1, 1995
Chicago (23) vs. Miami (25), May 22, 1997
Portland (19) vs. San Antonio (29), June 4, 1999

FIELD GOAL ATTEMPTS

Most field goal attempts, game
140 — Boston vs. Syracuse, March 18, 1959
San Francisco at Philadelphia, April 14, 1967 (OT)

Fewest field goal attempts, game
53 — Cleveland at New York, April 29, 1995
Seattle at Utah, May 26, 1996

Most field goal attempts, both teams, game
257 — Boston (135) vs. Philadelphia (122), March 22, 1960

Fewest field goal attempts, both teams, game
113 — Cleveland (53) at New York (60), April 29, 1995

THREE-POINT FIELD GOALS

Most three-point field goals, game
20 — Seattle vs. Houston, May 6, 1996

Most three-point field goals, both teams, game
33 — Seattle (20) vs. Houston (13), May 6, 1996

Most three-point field goals, one half
11— Houston at Utah, April 29, 1995
New York at Cleveland, April 25, 1996

Most three-point field goals, one quarter
8 — New York at Cleveland, April 25, 1996
L.A. Lakers at Portland, June 2, 2000

Most three-point field goals, none missed, game
5 — Dallas at Utah, April 25, 1986
Dallas vs. L.A. Lakers, May 4, 1986

THREE-POINT FIELD GOAL ATTEMPTS

Most three-point field goal attempts, game
34 — Houston vs. Seattle, May 12, 1996 (OT)

Most three-point field goal attempts, both teams, game
63 — Seattle (33) at Phoenix (30), May 1, 1997 (OT)

Most three-point field goal attempts, one half
20 — Seattle at Phoenix, April 29, 1997

FREE THROW PERCENTAGE

Highest free throw percentage, game
1.000 — Detroit at Milwaukee, April 18, 1976 (15-15)
Dallas vs. Seattle, April 19, 1984 (24-24)
Detroit vs. Chicago, May 18, 1988 (23-23)
Phoenix vs. Golden State, May 9, 1989 (28-28)
Chicago vs. Cleveland, May 19, 1992 (19-19)
Portland at Chicago, June 14, 1992 (21-21)
New Jersey vs. Cleveland, May 7, 1993 (3-3)
Indiana at New York, June 11, 1999 (9-9)
Indiana vs. New York, May 23, 2000 (12-12)

Lowest free throw percentage, game
.261 — Philadelphia at Boston, March 19, 1960 (6-23)

Highest free throw percentage, both teams, game
.957 — Chicago (.964) at Boston (.947), April 23, 1987

Lowest free throw percentage, both teams, game
.444 — Orlando (.333) at Chicago (.667), May 19, 1996

FREE THROWS MADE

Most free throws made, game
57 — Boston vs. Syracuse, March 21, 1953 (4 OT)
Phoenix vs. Seattle, June 5, 1993

Fewest free throws made, game
3 — Houston vs. Washington, April 19, 1977
Los Angeles at Philadelphia, May 26, 1983
New Jersey vs. Cleveland, May 7, 1993

Most free throws made, both teams, game
108 — Boston (57) vs. Syracuse (51), March 21, 1953 (4 OT)

Fewest free throws made, both teams, game
12 — Boston (6) at Buffalo (6), April 6, 1974

FREE THROW ATTEMPTS

Most free throw attempts, game
70 — St. Louis vs. Minneapolis, March 17, 1956

Fewest free throw attempts, game
3 — New Jersey vs. Cleveland, May 7, 1993

Most free throw attempts, both teams, game
128 — Boston (64) vs. Syracuse (64), March 21, 1953 (4 OT)

Fewest free throw attempts, both teams, game
16 — New Jersey (3) vs. Cleveland (13), May 7, 1993

TOTAL REBOUNDS

(Team rebounds not included.)

Most rebounds, game
97 — Boston vs. Philadelphia, March 19, 1960

Fewest rebounds, game
18 — San Antonio at L.A. Lakers, April 17, 1986

Most rebounds, both teams, game
169 — Boston (89) vs. Philadelphia (80), March 22, 1960
Philadelphia (93) vs. San Francisco (76), April 16, 1967

Fewest rebounds, both teams, game
51 — Milwaukee (25) vs. Philadelphia (26), May 1, 1982

ASSISTS

Most assists, game
51 — San Antonio vs. Denver, May 4, 1983

Fewest assists, game
5 — Boston at St. Louis, April 3, 1960
Detroit at Chicago, April 5, 1974

Most assists, both teams, game
79 — L.A. Lakers (44) vs. Boston (35), June 4, 1987

Fewest assists, both teams, game
16 — Chicago (6) vs. Los Angeles (10), March 29, 1968

PERSONAL FOULS

Most personal fouls, game
55 — Syracuse at Boston, March 21, 1953 (4 OT)

Fewest personal fouls, game
9 — Cleveland vs. Boston, May 2, 1992

Most personal fouls, both teams, game
106 — Syracuse (55) at Boston (51), March 21, 1953 (4 OT)

Fewest personal fouls, both teams, game
25 — Cleveland (10) at New Jersey (15), May 7, 1993

DISQUALIFICATIONS

Most disqualifications, game
7 — Syracuse at Boston, March 21, 1953 (4 OT)

ALL-TIME NBA PLAYOFF RECORDS: TEAM – Continued

Most disqualifications, both teams, game
12 — Syracuse (7) at Boston (5), March 21, 1953 (4 OT)

STEALS

Most steals, game
22 — Golden State vs. Seattle, April 14, 1975

Fewest steals game
0 — Buffalo at Boston, March 30, 1974
Phoenix at Seattle, April 15, 1976
Indiana vs. Orlando, May 27, 1995

Most steals, both teams, game
35 — Golden State (22) vs. Seattle (13), April 14, 1975

Fewest steals, both teams, game
2 — Phoenix (0) at Seattle (2), April 15, 1976

BLOCKED SHOTS

Most blocked shots, game
20 — Philadelphia vs. Milwaukee, April 5, 1981

Fewest blocked shots, game
0 — Accomplished 47 times. Most recent:
New York vs. Miami, May 19, 2000

Most blocked shots, both teams, game
29 — Philadelphia (20) vs. Milwaukee (9), April 5, 1981

Fewest blocked shots, both teams, game
1 — Portland (0) vs. Dallas (1), April 25, 1985
Houston (0) vs. Seattle (1), May 17, 1997
New York (0) vs. Miami (1), April 30, 1998

TURNOVERS

Most turnovers, game
36 — Chicago at Portland, April 17, 1977

Fewest turnovers, game
4 — Detroit at Boston, May 9, 1991

Most turnovers, both teams, game
60 — Golden State (31) at Washington (29), May 25, 1975

Fewest turnovers, both teams, game
13 — Detroit (4) at Boston (9), May 9, 1991
Portland (6) at Minnesota (7), April 30, 2000

ALL-TIME NBA FINALS RECORDS: INDIVIDUAL

MINUTES

Most minutes, game
62 — Kevin Johnson, Phoenix at Chicago, June 13, 1993 (3 OT)
61 — Garfield Heard, Phoenix at Boston, June 4, 1976 (3 OT)
60 — Jo Jo White, Boston vs. Phoenix, June 4, 1976 (3 OT)

Most minutes per game, one championship series
49.3 — Kareem Abdul-Jabbar, Milwaukee vs. Boston, 1974 (345/7)
48.7 — Bill Russell, Boston vs. Los Angeles, 1968 (292/6)
48.5 — John Havlicek, Boston vs. Los Angeles, 1968 (291/6)

SCORING

Most points, game
61 — Elgin Baylor, Los Angeles at Boston, April 14, 1962
55 — Rick Barry, San Francisco vs. Philadelphia, April 18, 1967
Michael Jordan, Chicago vs. Phoenix, June 16, 1993
53 — Jerry West, Los Angeles vs. Boston, April 23, 1969

Most points, rookie, game
42 — Magic Johnson, Los Angeles at Philadelphia, May 16, 1980
37 — Joe Fulks, Philadelphia vs. Chicago, April 16, 1947
Tom Heinsohn, Boston vs. St. Louis, April 13, 1957 (2 OT)
34 — Joe Fulks, Philadelphia vs. Chicago, April 22, 1947
Elgin Baylor, Minneapolis at Boston, April 4, 1959

Highest scoring average, one championship series
41.0 — Michael Jordan, Chicago vs. Phoenix, 1993 (246/6)
40.8 — Rick Barry, San Francisco vs. Philadelphia, 1967 (245/6)
40.6 — Elgin Baylor, Los Angeles vs. Boston, 1962 (284/7)

For additional records, please log on to NBA.com.

Highest scoring average, rookie, one championship series
26.2 — Joe Fulks, Philadelphia vs. Chicago, 1947 (131/5)
24.0 — Tom Heinsohn, Boston vs. St. Louis, 1957 (168/7)
23.0 — Alvan Adams, Phoenix vs. Boston, 1976 (138/6)

Most consecutive games, 20 or more points
35 — Michael Jordan, Chicago, June 2, 1991-June 14, 1998
25 — Jerry West, Los Angeles, April 20, 1966-May 8, 1970
19 — Julius Erving, Philadelphia, May 22, 1977-May 22, 1983

Most consecutive games, 30 or more points
13 — Elgin Baylor, Minneapolis-Los Angeles, April 9, 1959-April 21, 1963
9 — Michael Jordan, June 10, 1992-June 20, 1993
6 — Rick Barry, San Francisco, April 14, 1967-April 24, 1967
Shaquille O'Neal, L.A. Lakers, June 7, 2000-June 19, 2000 (current)

Most consecutive games, 40 or more points
4 — Michael Jordan, June 11, 1993-June 18, 1993
2 — Jerry West, Los Angeles, April 19-21, 1965
Rick Barry, San Francisco, April 18-20, 1967
Jerry West, Los Angeles, April 23-25, 1969
Shaquille O'Neal, L.A. Lakers, June 7-9, 2000

Scoring 30 or more points in all games in championship series
— Elgin Baylor, Los Angeles vs. Boston, 1962 (7-game series)
— Rick Barry, San Francisco vs. Philadelphia, 1967 (6-game series)
— Michael Jordan, Chicago vs. Phoenix, 1993 (6-game series)
— Hakeem Olajuwon, Houston vs. Orlando, 1995 (4-game series)
— Shaquille O'Neal, L.A. Lakers vs. Indiana, 2000 (6-game series)

Scoring 20 or more points in all games of 7-game championship series
Bob Pettit, St. Louis vs. Boston, 1960
Elgin Baylor, Los Angeles vs. Boston, 1962
Jerry West, Los Angeles vs. Boston, 1962
Jerry West, Los Angeles vs. Boston, 1969
Jerry West, Los Angeles vs. New York, 1970
Kareem Abdul-Jabbar, Milwaukee vs. Boston, 1974
Larry Bird, Boston vs. Los Angeles, 1984
Hakeem Olajuwon, Houston vs. New York, 1994

Most points, one half
35 — Michael Jordan, Chicago vs. Portland, June 3, 1992

Most points, one quarter
25 — Isiah Thomas, Detroit at L.A. Lakers, June 19, 1988

Most points, overtime period
9 — John Havlicek, Boston vs. Milwaukee, May 10, 1974 (2nd OT)
Bill Laimbeer, Detroit vs. Portland, June 7, 1990
Danny Ainge, Portland at Chicago, June 5, 1992

FIELD GOALS

Highest field goal percentage, game
(minimum 8 made)
1.000 — Scott Wedman, Boston vs. L.A. Lakers, May 27, 1985 (11/11)
John Paxson, Chicago vs. L.A. Lakers, June 5, 1991 (8/8)
.917 — Bill Bradley, New York at Los Angeles, April 26, 1972 (11/12)
James Worthy, Los Angeles at Boston, May 31, 1984 (11/12) (OT)

Most field goals, game
22 — Elgin Baylor, Los Angeles at Boston, April 14, 1962
Rick Barry, San Francisco vs. Philadelphia, April 18, 1967
21 — Jerry West, Los Angeles vs. Boston, April 23, 1969
Michael Jordan, Chicago vs. Phoenix, June 16, 1993
Shaquille O'Neal, L.A. Lakers vs. Indiana, June 7, 2000

ALL-TIME NBA FINALS RECORDS: INDIVIDUAL – Continued

Most field goal attempts, game
48 — Rick Barry, San Francisco vs. Philadelphia, April 18, 1967
46 — Elgin Baylor, Los Angeles at Boston, April 14, 1962
43 — Rick Barry, San Francisco at Philadelphia, April 14, 1967 (OT)
Michael Jordan, Chicago vs. Phoenix, June 13, 1993 (3 OT)

Most field goal attempts, one half
25 — Elgin Baylor, Los Angeles at Boston, April 14, 1962

Most field goal attempts, one quarter
17 — Rick Barry, San Francisco at Philadelphia, April 14, 1967

THREE-POINT FIELD GOALS

Most three-point field goals, none missed, game
4 — Scott Wedman, Boston vs. L.A. Lakers, May 27, 1985
3 — Danny Ainge, Boston at L.A. Lakers, June 2, 1987
Isiah Thomas, Detroit at Portland, June 14, 1990
Sam Cassell, Houston at New York, June 12, 1994
Glen Rice, L.A. Lakers vs. Indiana, June 19, 2000

Most three-point field goals, game
7 — Kenny Smith, Houston at Orlando, June 7, 1995 (OT)
Scottie Pippen, Chicago at Utah, June 6, 1997
6 — Michael Cooper, L.A. Lakers vs. Boston, June 4, 1987
Bill Laimbeer, Detroit vs. Portland, June 7, 1990 (OT)
Michael Jordan, Chicago vs. Portland, June 3, 1992
Dan Majerle, Phoenix at Chicago, June 13, 1993 (3 OT)
Reggie Miller, Indiana vs. L.A. Lakers, June 14, 2000 (OT)

Most three-point field goals, one half
6 — Michael Jordan, Chicago vs. Portland, June 3, 1992
Kenny Smith, Houston at Orlando, June 7, 1995

Most three-point field goals, one quarter
5 — Kenny Smith, Houston at Orlando, June 7, 1995

Most three-point field goal attempts, game
12 — Nick Anderson, Orlando at Houston, June 11, 1995
11 — John Starks, New York at Houston, June 22, 1994
Kenny Smith, Houston at Orlando, June 7, 1995 (OT)
Brian Shaw, Orlando at Houston, June 14, 1995
Scottie Pippen, Chicago at Utah, June 6, 1997

Most three-point field goal attempts, one half
10 — John Starks, New York at Houston, June 22, 1994

FREE THROWS

Most free throws made, none missed, game
15 — Terry Porter, Portland at Detroit, June 7, 1990 (OT)
14 — Magic Johnson, Los Angeles at Philadelphia, May 16, 1980

Most free throws made, game
19 — Bob Pettit, St. Louis at Boston, April 9, 1958
18 — Shaquille O'Neal, L.A. Lakers vs. Indiana, June 9, 2000

Most free throws made, one half
13 — Shaquille O'Neal, L.A. Lakers vs. Indiana, June 9, 2000

Most free throws made, one quarter
9 — Frank Ramsey, Boston vs. Minneapolis, April 4, 1959
Michael Jordan, Chicago at Utah, June 11, 1997
Shaquille O'Neal, L.A. Lakers vs. Indiana, June 9, 2000
Austin Croshere, Indiana vs. L.A. Lakers, June 16, 2000

Most free throw attempts, game
39 — Shaquille O'Neal, L.A. Lakers vs. Indiana, June 9, 2000
24 — Bob Pettit, St. Louis at Boston, April 9, 1958

Most free throw attempts, one half
22 — Shaquille O'Neal, L.A. Lakers vs. Indiana, June 9, 2000

Most free throw attempts, one quarter
16 — Shaquille O'Neal, L.A. Lakers vs. Indiana, June 9, 2000

REBOUNDS

Most rebounds, game
40 — Bill Russell, Boston vs. St. Louis, March 29, 1960
Bill Russell, Boston vs. Los Angeles, April 18, 1962 (OT)
38 — Bill Russell, Boston vs. St. Louis, April 11, 1961
Bill Russell, Boston vs. Los Angeles, April 16, 1963
Wilt Chamberlain, San Francisco vs. Boston, April 24, 1964
Wilt Chamberlain, Philadelphia vs. San Francisco, April 16, 1967

Most consecutive games, 20 or more rebounds
15 — Bill Russell, Boston, April 9, 1960-April 16, 1963
12 — Wilt Chamberlain, San Francisco, Philadelphia, Los Angeles, April 18, 1964-April 23, 1969

Most consecutive games, 30 or more rebounds
3 — Bill Russell, Boston, April 5, 1959-April 9, 1959
2 — Bill Russell, Boston, April 9, 1960-April 2, 1961
Wilt Chamberlain, Philadelphia, April 14, 1967-April 16, 1967
Wilt Chamberlain, Los Angeles, April 29, 1969-May 1, 1969

Most rebounds, one half
26 — Wilt Chamberlain, Philadelphia vs. San Francisco, April 16, 1967

Most rebounds, one quarter
19 — Bill Russell, Boston vs. Los Angeles, April 18, 1962

ASSISTS

Most assists, game
21 — Magic Johnson, Los Angeles vs. Boston, June 3, 1984
20 — Magic Johnson, L.A. Lakers vs. Boston, June 4, 1987
Magic Johnson, L.A. Lakers vs. Chicago, June 12, 1991

Highest average, assists per game, one championship series
14.0 — Magic Johnson, L.A. Lakers vs. Boston, 1985 (84/6)
13.6 — Magic Johnson, Los Angeles vs. Boston, 1984 (95/7)
13.0 — Magic Johnson, L.A. Lakers vs. Boston, 1987 (78/6)
Magic Johnson, L.A. Lakers vs. Detroit, 1988 (91/7)

Most consecutive games, 10 or more assists
13 — Magic Johnson, L.A. Lakers, June 3, 1984-June 4, 1987
6 — Magic Johnson, Los Angeles, June 8, 1982-May 27, 1984

PERSONAL FOULS

Most minutes played, no personal fouls, game
59 — Dan Majerle, Phoenix at Chicago, June 13, 1993 (3 OT)
50 — Jo Jo White, Boston at Milwaukee, April 30, 1974 (OT)
Nick Anderson, Orlando vs. Houston, June 7, 1995 (OT)

DISQUALIFICATIONS

Most consecutive games disqualified
5 — Art Hillhouse, Philadelphia, 1947
Charlie Scott, Boston, 1976
4 — Arnie Risen, Boston, 1957

Fewest minutes played, disqualified player, game
9 — Bob Harrison, Minneapolis vs. New York, April 13, 1952
10 — Bob Harrison, Minneapolis vs. New York, April 4, 1953

STEALS

Most steals, game
7 — Robert Horry, Houston at Orlando, June 9, 1995
6 — John Havlicek, Boston vs. Milwaukee, May 3, 1974
Steve Mix, Philadelphia vs. Portland, May 22, 1977
Maurice Cheeks, Philadelphia at Los Angeles, May 7, 1980
Isiah Thomas, Detroit at L.A. Lakers, June 19, 1988

BLOCKED SHOTS

Most blocked shots, game
8 — Bill Walton, Portland vs. Philadelphia, June 5, 1977
Hakeem Olajuwon, Houston vs. Boston, June 5, 1986
Patrick Ewing, New York vs. Houston, June 17, 1994
7 — Dennis Johnson, Seattle at Washington, May 28, 1978
Patrick Ewing, New York vs. Houston, June 12, 1994
Hakeem Olajuwon, Houston at New York, June 12, 1994

TURNOVERS

Most turnovers, game
10 — Magic Johnson, Los Angeles vs. Philadelphia, May 14, 1980

ALL-TIME NBA FINALS RECORDS: INDIVIDUAL (SERIES)

MOST POINTS

4-game series
131— Hakeem Olajuwon, Houston 1995
118 — Rick Barry, Golden State 1975

5-game series
169 — Jerry West, Los Angeles 1965
156 — Michael Jordan, Chicago 1991

6-game series
246 — Michael Jordan, Chicago 1993
245 — Rick Barry, San Francisco 1967

7-game series
284 — Elgin Baylor, Los Angeles 1962
265 — Jerry West, Los Angeles 1969

MOST MINUTES PLAYED

4-game series
187 — Robert Horry, Houston 1995

5-game series
240 — Wilt Chamberlain, Los Angeles 1973

6-game series
292 — Bill Russell, Boston 1968

7-game series
345 — Kareem Abdul-Jabbar, Milwaukee 1974

HIGHEST FIELD GOAL PERCENTAGE

(minimum 4 made per game)

4-game series
.739 — Derrek Dickey, Golden State 1975

5-game series
.702 — Bill Russell, Boston 1965

6-game series
.667 — Bob Gross, Portland 1977

7-game series
.638 — James Worthy, Los Angeles 1984

MOST FIELD GOALS

4-game series
56 — Hakeem Olajuwon, Houston 1995

5-game series
63 — Michael Jordan, Chicago 1991

6-game series
101 — Michael Jordan, Chicago 1993

7-game series
101 — Elgin Baylor, Los Angeles 1962

MOST FIELD GOAL ATTEMPTS

4-game series
116 — Hakeem Olajuwon, Houston 1995

5-game series
139 — Jerry West, Los Angeles 1965

6-game series
235 — Rick Barry, San Francisco 1967

7-game series
235 — Elgin Baylor, Los Angeles 1962

MOST THREE-POINT FIELD GOALS MADE

4-game series
11 — Anfernee Hardaway, Orlando 1995
Robert Horry, Houston 1995

5-game series
11 — Isiah Thomas, Detroit 1990

6-game series
17 — Dan Majerle, Phoenix 1993

7-game series
17 — Derek Harper, New York 1994

MOST THREE-POINT FIELD GOAL ATTEMPTS

4-game series
31 — Nick Anderson, Orlando 1995

5-GAME SERIES
25 — Terry Porter, Portland 1990

6-game series
40 — Reggie Miller, Indiana 2000

7-game series
50 — John Starks, New York 1994
40 — Vernon Maxwell, Houston 1994

HIGHEST FREE THROW PERCENTAGE

(minimum 2 made per game)

4-game series
1.000 — Dennis Scott, Orlando 1995

5-game series
1.000 — Bill Laimbeer, Detroit 1990
Vlade Divac, L.A. Lakers 1991

6-game series
.978 — Reggie Miller, Indiana 2000

7-game series
.959 — Bill Sharman, Boston 1957

MOST FREE THROWS MADE

4-game series
34 — Phil Chenier, Washington 1975

5-game series
51 — Jerry West, Los Angeles 1965

6-game series
67 — George Mikan, Minneapolis 1950

7-game series
82 — Elgin Baylor, Los Angeles 1962

MOST FREE THROW ATTEMPTS

4-game series
47 — Moses Malone, Philadelphia 1983

5-game series
60 — Bob Pettit, St. Louis 1961

6-game series
93 — Shaquille O'Neal, L.A. Lakers 2000

7-game series
99 — Elgin Baylor, Los Angeles 1962

MOST REBOUNDS

4-game series
118 — Bill Russell, Boston 1959

5-game series
144 — Bill Russell, Boston 1961

6-game series
171 — Wilt Chamberlain, Philadelphia 1967

7-game series
189 — Bill Russell, Boston 1962

MOST ASSISTS

4-game series
51 — Bob Cousy, Boston 1959

5-game series
62 — Magic Johnson, L.A. Lakers 1991

6-game series
84 — Magic Johnson, L.A. Lakers 1985

7-game series
95 — Magic Johnson, Los Angeles 1984

MOST PERSONAL FOULS

4-game series
20 — Michael Cooper, Los Angeles 1983

5-game series
27 — George Mikan, Minneapolis 1953

6-game series
35 — Charlie Scott, Boston 1976

7-game series
37 — Arnie Risen, Boston 1957

MOST DISQUALIFICATIONS

4-game series
1 — John Tresvant, Baltimore 1971
Elvin Hayes, Washington 1975
George Johnson, Golden State 1975
Kevin Porter, Washington 1975
Marc Iavaroni, Philadelphia 1983
Michael Cooper, Los Angeles 1983
Tony Campbell, L.A. Lakers 1989
A.C. Green, L.A. Lakers 1989
Rick Mahorn, Detroit 1989

5-game series
5 — Art Hillhouse, Philadelphia 1947

6-game series
5 — Charlie Scott, Boston 1976

7-game series
5 — Arnie Risen, Boston 1957

ALL-TIME NBA FINALS RECORDS: INDIVIDUAL (SERIES) – Continued

MOST STEALS

4-game series
14 — Rick Barry, Golden State 1975

5-game series
14 — Michael Jordan, Chicago 1991

6-game series
16 — Julius Erving, Philadelphia 1977
Magic Johnson, Los Angeles 1980
Larry Bird, Boston 1986

7-game series
20 — Isiah Thomas, Detroit 1988

MOST BLOCKED SHOTS

4-game series
11 — Elvin Hayes, Washington 1975
George Johnson, Golden State 1975
Julius Erving, Philadelphia 1983
John Salley, Detroit 1989
10 — Shaquille O'Neal, Orlando 1995

5-game series
16 — Jack Sikma, Seattle 1979

6-game series
23 — Kareem Abdul-Jabbar, Los Angeles 1980

7-game series
30 — Patrick Ewing, New York 1994

MOST TURNOVERS

4-game series
24 — Magic Johnson, Los Angeles 1983
21 — Shaquille O'Neal, Orlando 1995

5-game series
25 — Isiah Thomas, Detroit 1990

6-game series
30 — Magic Johnson, Los Angeles 1980

7-game series
31 — Magic Johnson, Los Angeles 1984

ALL-TIME NBA FINALS RECORDS: TEAM (SERIES)

MOST POINTS

4-game series
487 — Boston vs. Minneapolis 1959

5-game series
617 — Boston vs. Los Angeles 1965

6-game series
747 — Philadelphia vs. San Francisco 1967

7-game series
827 — Boston vs. Los Angeles 1966

FEWEST POINTS

4-game series
376 — Baltimore vs. Milwaukee 1971

5-game series
399 — New York vs. San Antonio 1999

6-game series
481 — Utah vs. Chicago 1998

7-game series
603 — Houston vs. New York 1994

HIGHEST FIELD GOAL PERCENTAGE

4-game series
.527 — Detroit vs. L.A. Lakers 1989

5-game series
.527 — Chicago vs. L.A. Lakers 1991

6-game series
.515 — L.A. Lakers vs. Boston 1987

7-game series
.515 — Los Angeles vs. Boston 1984

MOST FIELD GOALS

4-game series
188 — Boston vs. Minneapolis 1959

5-game series
243 — Boston vs. Los Angeles 1965

6-game series
287 — Philadelphia vs. San Francisco 1967
San Francisco vs. Philadelphia 1967

7-game series
332 — New York vs. Los Angeles 1970

FEWEST FIELD GOALS

4-game series
144 — L.A. Lakers vs. Detroit 1989

5-game series
150 — San Antonio vs. New York 1999
154 — New York vs. San Antonio 1999

6-game series
185 — Utah vs. Chicago 1997

7-game series
207 — Syracuse vs. Fort Wayne 1955

MOST THREE-POINT FIELD GOALS MADE

4-game series
41 — Orlando vs. Houston 1995
37 — Houston vs. Orlando 1995

5-game series
25 — Detroit vs. Portland 1990

6-game series
49 — Indiana vs. L.A. Lakers 2000

7-game series
37 — Houston vs. New York 1994
36 — New York vs. Houston 1994

MOST THREE-POINT FIELD GOAL ATTEMPTS

4-game series
118 — Orlando vs. Houston 1995
92 — Houston vs. Orlando 1995

5-game series
62 — San Antonio vs. New York 1999

6-game series
137 — Chicago vs. Seattle 1996

7-game series
121 — Houston vs. New York 1994
105 — New York vs. Houston 1994

HIGHEST FREE THROW PERCENTAGE

4-game series
.785 — Los Angeles vs. Philadelphia 1983

5-game series
.826 — Chicago vs. L.A. Lakers 1991
.810 — L.A. Lakers vs. Chicago 1991

6-game series
.852 — Indiana vs. L.A. Lakers 2000

7-game series
.827 — Boston vs. Los Angeles 1966

LOWEST FREE THROW PERCENTAGE

4-game series
.675 — Baltimore vs. Milwaukee 1971

5-game series
.616 — San Francisco vs. Boston 1964

6-game series
.570 — L.A. Lakers vs. Indiana 2000

7-game series
.641 — Los Angeles vs. Boston 1969

MOST REBOUNDS

4-game series
295 — Boston vs. Minneapolis 1959
268 — Minneapolis vs. Boston 1959

5-game series
369 — Boston vs. St. Louis 1961

6-game series
435 — San Francisco vs. Philadelphia 1967
425 — Philadelphia vs. San Francisco 1967

ALL-TIME NBA FINALS RECORDS: TEAM (SERIES) – Continued

7-game series
487 — Boston vs. St. Louis 1957

FEWEST REBOUNDS

4-game series
145 — L.A. Lakers vs. Detroit 1989
160 — Detroit vs. L.A. Lakers 1989

5-game series
178 — L.A. Lakers vs. Chicago 1991

6-game series
223 — Philadelphia vs. Los Angeles 1980
Seattle vs. Chicago 1996

7-game series
263 — L.A. Lakers vs. Detroit 1988

MOST ASSISTS

4-game series
114 — Boston vs. Minneapolis 1959

5-game series
139 — Chicago vs. L.A. Lakers 1991

6-game series
192 — L.A. Lakers vs. Boston 1985

7-game series
198 — Los Angeles vs. Boston 1984

MOST STEALS

4-game series
55 — Golden State vs. Washington 1975
45 — Washington vs. Golden State 1975

5-game series
49 — Chicago vs. L.A. Lakers 1991

6-game series
71 — Philadelphia vs. Portland 1977
64 — Portland vs. Philadelphia 1977
Los Angeles vs. Philadelphia 1982

7-game series
65 — Boston vs. Los Angeles 1984
59 — Los Angeles vs. Boston 1984

FEWEST STEALS

4-game series
16 — Detroit vs. L.A. Lakers 1989

5-game series
28 — Detroit vs. Portland 1990

6-game series
30 — Boston vs. L.A. Lakers 1987

7-game series
21 — Milwaukee vs. Boston 1974

MOST BLOCKED SHOTS

4-game series
32 — Golden State vs. Washington 1975
Philadelphia vs. Los Angeles 1983

5-game series
39 — Seattle vs. Washington 1979
29 — San Antonio vs. New York 1999

6-game series
60 — Philadelphia vs. Los Angeles 1980
51 — Philadelphia vs. Los Angeles 1982
29 — Los Angeles vs. Philadelphia 1983

7-game series
49 — Seattle vs. Washington 1978

MOST TURNOVERS

4-game series
94 — Golden State vs. Washington 1975

5-game series
104-Los Angeles vs. New York 1973

6-game series
149 — Portland vs. Philadelphia 1977

7-game series
142 — Milwaukee vs. Boston 1974

FEWEST TURNOVERS

4-game series
41 — Houston vs. Orlando 1995

5-game series
64 — New York vs. San Antonio 1999

6-game series
68 — L.A. Lakers vs. Boston 1987
L.A. Lakers vs. Indiana 2000

7-game series
87 — Detroit vs. L.A. Lakers 1988

ALL-TIME NBA FINALS RECORDS: TEAM

WON-LOST

Most consecutive games won, all championship series
6 — Houston, 1994-95 (current)

Most consecutive games won, one championship series
4 — Minneapolis vs. New York, 1953 (5-game series)
Boston vs. Minneapolis, 1959 (4-game series)
Milwaukee vs. Baltimore, 1971 (4-game series)
Los Angeles vs. New York, 1972 (5-game series)
New York vs. Los Angeles, 1973 (5-game series)
Golden State vs. Washington, 1975 (4-game series)
Portland vs. Philadelphia, 1977 (6-game series)
Seattle vs. Washington, 1979 (5-game series)
Philadelphia vs. Los Angeles, 1983 (4-game series)
Detroit vs. L.A. Lakers, 1989 (4-game series)
Chicago vs. L.A. Lakers, 1991 (5-game series)
Houston vs. Orlando, 1995 (4-game series)

Most consecutive games won at home, all championship series
8 — Chicago, 1996-98
7 — Minneapolis, 1949-52

Most consecutive games won at home, one championship series
4 — Syracuse vs. Fort Wayne, 1955 (7-game series)

Most consecutive games won on road, all championship series
5 — Detroit, 1989-90
Chicago, 1992-93, 1996

Most consecutive games won on road, one championship series
3 — Minneapolis vs. New York, 1953 (5-game series)
Detroit vs. Portland, 1990 (5-game series)
Chicago vs. L.A. Lakers, 1991 (5-game series)
Chicago vs. Phoenix, 1993 (6-game series)

Most consecutive games lost, all championship series
9 — Baltimore/Washington, 1971-78

Most consecutive games lost at home, all championship series
5 — L.A. Lakers, 1989-91 (current)

Most consecutive games lost on road, all championship series
7 — Fort Wayne, 1955-56

SCORING

Most points, game
148 — Boston vs. L.A. Lakers (114), May 27, 1985

Fewest points, game
54 — Utah at Chicago (96), June 7, 1998
67 — New York at San Antonio (80), June 18, 1999

Most points, both teams, game
276 — Philadelphia (141) vs. San Francisco (135), April 14, 1967 (OT)

Fewest points, both teams, game
145 — Syracuse (71) vs. Fort Wayne (74) at Indianapolis, April 7, 1955
147 — New York (67) at San Antonio (80), June 18, 1999

Largest margin of victory, game
42 — Chicago vs. Utah, June 7, 1998 (96-54)

ALL-TIME NBA FINALS RECORDS: TEAM – Continued

BY HALF

Most points, first half
79 — Boston vs. L.A. Lakers, May 27, 1985

Fewest points, first half
30 — Houston vs. Boston, May 9, 1981
Utah at Chicago, June 12, 1998

Most points, both teams, first half
140 — San Francisco (72) vs. Philadelphia (68), April 24, 1967

Fewest points, both teams, first half
66 — Utah (30) at Chicago (36), June 12, 1998

Largest lead at halftime
30 — Boston vs. L.A. Lakers, May 27, 1985 (led 79-49; won 148-114)

Largest deficit at halftime, overcome to win game
21 — Baltimore at Philadelphia, April 13, 1948 (trailed 20-41; won 66-63)

Most points, second half
81 — Philadelphia vs. Los Angeles, June 6, 1982

Fewest points, second half
23 — Utah at Chicago, June 7, 1998

Most points, both teams, second half
139 — Boston (78) vs. Los Angeles (61), April 18, 1965
138 — Los Angeles (71) at Boston (67), April 21, 1963
Los Angeles (80) vs. Boston (58), June 3, 1984

Fewest points, both teams, second half
63 — Houston (31) vs. New York (32), June 8, 1994

Most points, overtime period
22 — Los Angeles vs. New York, May 1, 1970

Fewest points, overtime period
4 — Boston vs. Milwaukee, May 10, 1974 (1st OT)
Milwaukee at Boston, May 10, 1974 (1st OT)
L.A. Lakers vs. Chicago, June 7, 1991
Chicago vs. Phoenix, June 13, 1993 (1st OT)
Phoenix at Chicago, June 13, 1993 (1st OT)

Most points, both teams, overtime period
38 — Los Angeles (22) vs. New York (16), May 1, 1970
30 — Boston (16) vs. Phoenix (14), June 4, 1976 (3rd OT)
L.A. Lakers (16) at Indiana (14), June 14, 2000

Fewest points, both teams, overtime period
8 — Boston (4) vs. Milwaukee (4), May 10, 1974 (1st OT)
Chicago (4) vs. Phoenix (4), June 13, 1993 (1st OT)

100-POINT GAMES

Most consecutive games, 100 or more points, all championship series
20 — Minneapolis/Los Angeles, 1959-65
L.A. Lakers, 1983-87

Most consecutive games scoring fewer than 100 points, all championship series
15 — Chicago, 1996-98 (current)

PLAYERS SCORING

Most players, 30 or more points, game
2 — Accomplished 27 times. Most recent:
Houston at Orlando, June 9, 1995
Orlando at Houston, June 9, 1995

Most players, 30 or more points, both teams, game
4 — Houston (2) at Orlando (2), June 9, 1995

Most players, 20 or more points, game
5 — Boston vs. Los Angeles, April 19, 1965
L.A. Lakers vs. Boston, June 4, 1987
Boston vs. L.A. Lakers, June 11, 1987

Most players, 20 or more points, both teams, game
8 — Boston (4) at Los Angeles (4), April 26, 1966
L.A. Lakers (5) vs. Boston (3), June 4, 1987

Most players, 10 or more points, game
8 — Boston vs. Los Angeles, May 31, 1984 (OT)

Most players, 10 or more points, both teams, game
14 — Boston (7) vs. St. Louis (7), March 27, 1960

Fewest players, 10 or more points, game
1 — Utah at Chicago, June 7, 1998

Fewest players, 10 or more points, both teams, game
4 — Utah (2) at Chicago (2), June 10, 1998
Utah (2) at Chicago (2), June 12, 1998

FIELD GOAL PERCENTAGE

Highest field goal percentage, game
.617 — Chicago vs. L.A. Lakers, June 5, 1991 (50/81)

Lowest field goal percentage, game
.275 — Syracuse vs. Fort Wayne at Indianapolis, April 7, 1955 (25-91)

Highest field goal percentage, both teams, game
.582 — L.A. Lakers (.615) vs. Boston (.548), June 4, 1987 (107-184)
.553 — L.A. Lakers (.556) vs. Boston (.549), June 2, 1987 (100-181)

Lowest field goal percentage, both teams, game
.277— Syracuse (.275) vs. Fort Wayne (.280) at Indianapolis, April 7, 1955 (48-173)

Highest field goal percentage, one half
.706 — Philadelphia vs. Los Angeles, June 6, 1982 (36/51)

Highest field goal percentage, one quarter
.850 — Chicago vs. L.A. Lakers, June 5, 1991 (17/20)

FIELD GOALS

Most field goals, game
62 — Boston vs. L.A. Lakers, May 27, 1985

Fewest field goals, game
21 — Utah at Chicago, June 7, 1998

Most field goals, both teams, game
112 — Philadelphia (57) vs. San Francisco (55), April 14, 1967 (OT)

Fewest field goals, both teams, game
48 — Fort Wayne (23) vs. Syracuse (25) at Indianapolis, April 7, 1955
54 — San Antonio (27) vs. New York (27), June 18, 1999

FIELD GOAL ATTEMPTS

Most field goal attempts, game
140 — San Francisco at Philadelphia, April 14, 1967 (OT)

Fewest field goal attempts, game
60 — Seattle vs. Chicago, June 9, 1996

Most field goal attempts, both teams, game
256 — San Francisco (140) at Philadelphia (116), April 14, 1967 (OT)

Fewest field goal attempts, both teams, game
131 — Utah (64) vs. Chicago (67), June 14, 1998

THREE-POINT FIELD GOALS MADE

Most three-point field goals made, game
14 — Houston at Orlando, June 7, 1995 (OT)
Orlando at Houston, June 14, 1995
12 — Chicago at Utah, June 6, 1997
Indiana at L.A. Lakers, June 19, 2000

Most three-point field goals, both teams, game
25 — Orlando (14) at Houston (11), June 14, 1995
23 — Houston (14) at Orlando (9), June 7, 1995 (OT)

Most three-point field goals made, one half
9 — Houston at Orlando, June 7, 1995
Orlando at Houston, June 14, 1995

Most three-point field goals made, one quarter
7 — Houston at Orlando, June 7, 1995
Orlando at Houston, June 14, 1995

THREE-POINT FIELD GOAL ATTEMPTS

Most three-point field goal attempts, game
32 — Houston at Orlando, June 7, 1995 (OT)
Chicago at Utah, June 6, 1997
31 — Orlando at Houston, June 11, 1995
Orlando at Houston, June 14, 1995

Most three-point field goal attempts, both teams, game
62 — Houston (32) at Orlando (30), June 7, 1995 (OT)
58 — Orlando (31) at Houston (27), June 14, 1995

Most three-point field goal attempts, one half
19 — Chicago vs. Seattle, June 16, 1996

FREE THROW PERCENTAGE

Highest free throw percentage, game
1.000 — Portland at Chicago, June 14, 1992 (21-21)
.958 — Boston vs. Houston, May 29, 1986 (23-24)

Lowest free throw percentage, game
.417 — Chicago at Utah, June 8, 1997 (5/12)
.421 — L.A. Lakers at Indiana, June 11, 2000 (8/19)

ALL-TIME NBA FINALS RECORDS: TEAM – Continued

Highest free throw percentage, both teams, game
.933 — L.A. Lakers (.955) at Chicago (.875), June 5, 1991 (28-30)

Lowest free throw percentage, both teams, game
.538 — Philadelphia (.444) vs. San Francisco (.655), April 16, 1967 (35-65)

FREE THROWS MADE

Most free throws made, game
45 — St. Louis at Boston, April 13, 1957 (2 OT)

Fewest free throws made, game
3 — Los Angeles at Philadelphia, May 26, 1983

Most free throws made, both teams, game
80 — St. Louis (44) at Boston (36), April 9, 1958

Fewest free throws made, both teams, game
17 — Utah (7) at Chicago (10), June 1, 1997

FREE THROW ATTEMPTS

Most free throw attempts, game
64 — Philadelphia at San Francisco, April 24, 1967

Fewest free throw attempts, game
5 — Los Angeles at Philadelphia, May 26, 1983

Most free throw attempts, both teams, game
116 — St. Louis (62) at Boston (54), April 13, 1957 (2 OT)

Fewest free throw attempts, both teams, game
26 — Utah (11) at Chicago (15), June 1, 1997

TOTAL REBOUNDS

(Rebounds have been compiled since 1950-51; team rebounds not included.)

Most rebounds, game
93 — Philadelphia vs. San Francisco, April 16, 1967

Fewest rebounds, game
22 — Chicago at Utah, June 14, 1998

Most rebounds, both teams, game
169 — Philadelphia (93) vs. San Francisco (76), April 16, 1967

Fewest rebounds, both teams, game
55 — Chicago (22) at Utah (33), June 14, 1998

ASSISTS

Most assists, game
44 — Los Angeles vs. New York, May 6, 1970
L.A. Lakers vs. Boston, June 4, 1987
43 — Boston vs. L.A. Lakers, May 27, 1985

Fewest assists, game
5 — Boston at St. Louis, April 3, 1960
8 — New York at San Antonio, June 18, 1999

Most assists, both teams, game
79 — L.A. Lakers (44) vs. Boston (35), June 4, 1987

Fewest assists, both teams, game
21 — Los Angeles (10) at Boston (11), April 29, 1969

PERSONAL FOULS

Most personal fouls, game
42 — Minneapolis vs. Syracuse, April 23, 1950

Fewest personal fouls, game
13 — L.A. Lakers at Detroit, June 12, 1988
San Antonio vs. New York, June 18, 1999

Most personal fouls, both teams, game
77 — Minneapolis (42) vs. Syracuse (35), April 23, 1950

Fewest personal fouls, both teams, game
35 — Boston (17) at Milwaukee (18), April 28, 1974
Boston (17) at Houston (18), June 3, 1986
L.A. Lakers (15) at Chicago (20), June 5, 1991
Chicago (15) vs. Seattle (20), June 16, 1996

DISQUALIFICATIONS

Most disqualifications, game
4 — Minneapolis vs. Syracuse, April 23, 1950
Minneapolis vs. New York, April 4, 1953
New York vs. Minneapolis, April 10, 1953
St. Louis at Boston, April 13, 1957 (2 OT)
Boston vs. Los Angeles, April 18, 1962 (OT)

Most disqualifications, both teams, game
7 — Boston (4) vs. Los Angeles (3), April 18, 1962 (OT)

STEALS

Most steals, game
17 — Golden State vs. Washington, May 23, 1975

Fewest steals, game
1 — Milwaukee at Boston, May 10, 1974 (2 OT)
Boston vs. Phoenix, May 23, 1976

Most steals, both teams, game
31 — Golden State (17) vs. Washington (14), May 23, 1975
28 — Golden State (15) at Washington (13), May 25, 1975

Fewest steals, both teams, game
6 — Detroit (3) vs. L.A. Lakers (3), June 8, 1989
L.A. Lakers (3) vs. Detroit (3), June 13, 1989
7 — Chicago (3) at Seattle (4), June 14, 1996
Indiana (2) at L.A. Lakers (5), June 19, 2000

BLOCKED SHOTS

Most blocked shots, game
13 — Seattle at Washington, May 28, 1978
Philadelphia at Los Angeles, May 4, 1980
Philadelphia vs. Los Angeles, June 6, 1982
Philadelphia vs. Los Angeles, May 22, 1983
Houston vs. Boston, June 5, 1986

Fewest blocked shots, game
0 — Boston vs. Milwaukee, May 5, 1974
Boston vs. Milwaukee, May 10, 1974 (2 OT)
Boston vs. Phoenix, June 4, 1976 (3 OT)
Philadelphia vs. Portland, May 22, 1977
Washington at Seattle, May 21, 1978
Boston at Houston, May 14, 1981
L.A. Lakers vs. Boston, June 5, 1985
L.A. Lakers vs. Detroit, June 7, 1988
Utah at Chicago, June 1, 1997
Utah at Chicago, June 4, 1997
Utah vs. Chicago, June 14, 1998

Most blocked shots, both teams, game
22 — Philadelphia (13) at Los Angeles (9), May 4, 1980
Philadelphia (13) vs. Los Angeles (9), June 6, 1982

Fewest blocked shots, both teams, game
2 — Boston (0) at Houston (2), May 14, 1981

TURNOVERS

Most turnovers, game
34 — Portland at Philadelphia, May 22, 1977

Fewest turnovers, game
5 — Chicago at L.A. Lakers, June 9, 1991
L.A. Lakers vs. Indiana, June 19, 2000
6 — Indiana at L.A. Lakers, June 9, 2000

Most turnovers, both teams, game
60 — Golden State (31) at Washington (29), May 25, 1975

Fewest turnovers, both teams, game
14 — L.A. Lakers (5) vs. Indiana (9), June 19, 2000

ATTENDANCE: TOP SINGLE-GAME CROWDS

REGULAR SEASON

62,046 — March 27, 1998, Chicago at Atlanta (Georgia Dome)
61,983 — January 29, 1988, Boston at Detroit (Silverdome)
52,745 — February 14, 1987, Philadelphia at Detroit (Silverdome)
49,551 — April 17, 1990, Denver at Minnesota (Metrodome)
47,692 — March 30, 1988, Atlanta at Detroit (Silverdome)
45,790 — November 7, 1997, Chicago at Atlanta (Georgia Dome)
45,458 — April 13, 1990, Orlando at Minnesota (Metrodome)
44,970 — February 21, 1987, Atlanta at Detroit (Silverdome)
44,180 — February 15, 1986, Philadelphia at Detroit (Silverdome)
43,816 — February 16, 1985, Philadelphia at Detroit (Silverdome)

PLAYOFFS

41,732 — June 16, 1988, L.A. Lakers at Detroit (Silverdome), 1988 NBA Finals, Game 5
40,172 — April 15, 1980, Milwaukee at Seattle (Kingdome), 1980 West Semifinals, Game 5
39,554 — June 18, 1999, New York at San Antonio (Alamodome), 1999 NBA Finals, Game 2
39,514 — June 16, 1999, New York at San Antonio (Alamodome), 1999 NBA Finals, Game 1
39,457 — May 30, 1978, Washington at Seattle (Kingdome), 1978 NBA Finals, Game 4

CHAPTER 31

NBA TIMELINE

DECEMBER 1891—Dr. James Naismith, an instructor at the Springfield Men's Christian Association Training School (now Springfield College) in Springfield, Mass., invents the game of basketball.

1896—The first known professional basketball game is played, in Trenton, N.J.

JUNE 6, 1946—The Basketball Association of America, the forerunner of the National Basketball Association, is founded at the Commodore Hotel in New York. Maurice Podoloff is the league's first president.

NOVEMBER 1, 1946—The Basketball Association of America begins play as the New York Knickerbockers defeat the Toronto Huskies 68-66 in Toronto. Any fan taller than Huskie center George Nostrand (6-8) got in free.

JANUARY 11, 1947—The Basketball Association of America outlaws the use of zone defenses.

APRIL 22, 1947—Philadelphia beats Chicago 83-80 to claim the first championship of the BAA, four games to one.

AUGUST 3, 1949—Six surviving teams from the midwest-based National Basketball League join the Basketball Association of America. The resulting 17-team league is renamed the National Basketball Association, with Maurice Podoloff as president.

APRIL 23, 1950—The Minneapolis Lakers become the first team to win back-to-back NBA championships by defeating Syracuse in six games.

NOVEMBER 22, 1950—The Fort Wayne Pistons beat the Minneapolis Lakers 19-18 in the lowest scoring game in NBA history.

MARCH 2, 1951—The East defeats the West 111-94 in the first NBA All-Star Game, held at Boston Garden.

1952—The NBA widens the foul lane from six to 12 feet.

APRIL 12, 1954—The Minneapolis Lakers become the first team to win three NBA championships in a row by defeating Syracuse 87-80 in Game 7.

1954-55—The NBA adopts two playing rules that revolutionize the game of basketball: the introduction of the 24-second clock and the awarding of a penalty shot following a team's fifth foul in any one period.

OCTOBER 30, 1954—The 24-second clock is used in an NBA game for the first time in Rochester, N.Y., with the host Royals beating the Boston Celtics 98-95.

APRIL 9, 1959—The Boston Celtics win their first of eight consecutive NBA championships with a 118-113 victory over Minneapolis for a four-game sweep of the NBA Finals.

JANUARY 25, 1960—Wilt Chamberlain sets rookie scoring record with 58 points for Philadelphia in a 127-117 win over Detroit. He would tie his record less than a month later.

OCTOBER 19, 1960—Relocated to the West Coast after 13 years in Minneapolis, the Lakers open their inaugural season as the Los Angeles Lakers with a 140-123 loss at Cincinnati.

NOVEMBER 24, 1960—Philadelphia's Wilt Chamberlain sets a record by grabbing 55 rebounds in a 132-129 loss to the Boston Celtics.

1961—The Chicago Packers enter the NBA as an expansion team, the league's ninth franchise, only to move to Baltimore two years later.

MARCH 2,1962—Wilt Chamberlain scores an NBA record 100 points as the Philadelphia Warriors beat the New York Knicks 169-147 in Hershey, Pa.

MARCH 10,1962—Oscar Robertson of Cincinnati finishes the season with averages of 30.8 points, 12.5 rebounds and a league-leading 11.4 assists per game, the only time an NBA player has averaged a triple-double for a full season.

SEPTEMBER 1, 1963—Walter Kennedy succeeds Maurice Podoloff as the president of the NBA. The job title is changed to commissioner in 1967.

1964—The NBA widens its foul lane from 12 to 16 feet.

APRIL 28, 1966—The Boston Celtics win their eighth straight NBA title, the longest streak in league history.

1966—The third NBA team to call Chicago home, the Bulls, enters the league as its 10th franchise.

FEBRUARY 1, 1967—The formation of the American Basketball Association (ABA) is announced at a press conference at the Carlyle Hotel in New York. George Mikan is named commissioner of the league, scheduled to begin play in October 1967.

FEBRUARY 24, 1967—Wilt Chamberlain of Philadelphia sinks all 18 of his shot attempts in a 149-118 win over Baltimore, setting a record for most baskets in a game without a miss.

1967—San Diego and Seattle enter the NBA as the league's 11th and 12th franchises.

OCTOBER 13, 1967—The ABA opens its inaugural season as the Oakland Oaks beat the Anaheim Amigos 134-129.

FEBRUARY 17, 1968—The Naismith Memorial Basketball Hall of Fame opens in Springfield, Mass., on the Springfield College campus, where the game was invented by Dr. James Naismith.

1968—The NBA expands to 14 teams with the addition of Milwaukee and Phoenix.

MAY 5, 1969—Bill Russell and the Boston Celtics end their spectacular run of 11 NBA titles in 13 seasons by outlasting the Los Angeles Lakers 108-106 in Game 7 of the 1969 NBA Finals.

1970—Expansion franchises begin play in Buffalo, Cleveland and Portland, bringing the number of NBA teams to 17.

LONG BEFORE THE TERM "TRIPLE-DOUBLE" BECAME PART OF THE NBA LEXICON, OSCAR ROBERTSON HAD MANY GAMES WHEN HE REACHED DOUBLE FIGURES IN POINTS, REBOUNDS AND ASSISTS. IN 1961-62, IN FACT, HE AVERAGED A TRIPLE-DOUBLE.

It was fitting that when Kareem Abdul-Jabbar passed Wilt Chamberlain as the NBA's all-time leading scorer that he did it with his signature shot. Abdul-Jabbar's skyhook (above) was one of the most potent offensive moves in NBA history. decorated players of all time.

JANUARY 7, 1972—The Los Angeles Lakers defeat the Atlanta Hawks, 134-90 for their 33rd straight win, an NBA record.

MARCH 26, 1972—The Los Angeles Lakers finished the season at 69-13, the best record in NBA history.

OCTOBER 28, 1973—Elmore Smith of the Los Angeles Lakers blocks a record 17 shots in a 111-98 victory over the Portland Trail Blazers.

1974—ABA/USA officially forms to become the United States' representative in FIBA, the International Basketball Federation.

MARCH 7, 1974—New Orleans becomes the NBA's 18th franchise, bought by a nine-man group for $6.15 million.

AUGUST 1974—Moses Malone signs with the Utah Stars of the ABA to become the first professional basketball player of the modern era to go directly from high school to the pros.

APRIL 30, 1975—Larry O'Brien is named the third commissioner of the NBA, succeeding Walter Kennedy.

JUNE 17, 1976—Four former ABA teams — San Antonio, Denver, New York and Indiana — are admitted into the NBA, raising the league to 22 teams.

JULY 7, 1978—The NBA approves a franchise swap in which Buffalo Braves owners John Y. Brown and Harry Mangurian acquire the Celtics, while Celtics owner Irv Levin acquires the Braves. He soon moved them to San Diego to become the Clippers.

1978-79—The NBA adds a third referee on a one-year experimental basis.

1979-80—The NBA adopts the three-point field goal and votes to eliminate the third referee.

OCTOBER 12, 1979—Chris Ford of the Boston Celtics scores the first official three-point field goal in the NBA as the Celtics defeat Houston 114-106 in Boston Garden.

MAY 1, 1980—Dallas is granted an expansion franchise, bringing the number of NBA teams to 23.

DECEMBER 13, 1983—The Detroit Pistons defeat the Denver Nuggets 186-184 in triple overtime in the highest scoring game in NBA history.

FEBRUARY 1, 1984—David J. Stern succeeds Larry O'Brien and becomes the fourth commissioner of the NBA.

APRIL 5, 1984—Kareem Abdul-Jabbar surpasses Wilt Chamberlain's 31,419 points to become the NBA's all-time scoring leader, hitting a sky-hook against the Utah Jazz in Las Vegas. Abdul-Jabbar concluded his career five years later with 38,387 points.

MAY 12, 1985—The New York Knicks win the first-ever NBA Draft Lottery, enabling them to select Patrick Ewing with the first pick in the NBA Draft.

JUNE 18, 1985—At the annual NBA Draft, the number of rounds is reduced from 10 to seven.

JUNE 30, 1985—The new Naismith Memorial Basketball Hall of Fame in downtown Springfield, Mass., is officially dedicated and opened to the public.

APRIL 13, 1986—The Boston Celtics close out the regular season with a 135-107 win over New Jersey, giving the

Celtics a 40-1 record at home. This sets a record for most home-court wins and highest home winning percentage (.976) in a season in NBA history.

APRIL 20, 1986—Michael Jordan of Chicago scores a playoff-record 63 points, but the Bulls lose to the Boston Celtics 135-131 in double overtime.

APRIL 22, 1987—The NBA grants expansion franchises to Charlotte, Miami, Minnesota and Orlando, raising the number of teams to 27.

OCTOBER 23-25, 1987—The first McDonald's Championship is played in Milwaukee involving the NBA's Milwaukee Bucks, the Soviet Union's National Team and the Italian League champion, Tracer Milan. This is the first tournament involving NBA teams to be sanctioned by FIBA.

APRIL 26, 1988—The NBA permanently adds a third referee in games. It had previously experimented with a third referee during the 1978-79 season.

JULY 25, 1988—The Atlanta Hawks become the first NBA team to play in the Soviet Union as they defeat the Soviet Georgia All-Stars 85-84 in an exhibition game.

APRIL 8, 1989—FIBA votes to allow NBA players to participate in international events, including the Olympic Games and the World Championship of Basketball. The final tally was 56 countries in favor of opening the competition, 13 opposed and one abstaining.

NOVEMBER 9, 1989—Dale Ellis of Seattle sets a record by playing 69 of a possible 73 minutes in a five-overtime game won by Milwaukee 155-154.

NOVEMBER 2, 1990—The Phoenix Suns defeat the Utah Jazz at the Tokyo Metropolitan Gym in Japan in the first regular-season game played outside North America by any major professional sports league.

DECEMBER 30, 1990—Scott Skiles of Orlando dishes 30 assists in a 155-116 rout of Denver to set an NBA record.

JUNE 24, 1992—The city of Portland becomes the first city besides New York to host the annual NBA Draft.

AUGUST 8, 1992—In Barcelona, Spain, the USA Olympic Men's Basketball Team, nicknamed the Dream Team, defeats Croatia 117-85 for the gold medal. This is the first time NBA players are allowed to compete in the Olympics.

MARCH 24, 1993—Micheal Williams of Minnesota begins a streak of 97 consecutive free throws made, an NBA record. He would not miss again until November 9, 1993.

NOVEMBER 4, 1993—The NBA Board of Governors awards an expansion team to Toronto, Canada, bringing the total of teams to 28.

APRIL 27, 1994—The NBA Board of Governors awards an expansion franchise to Vancouver, Canada, raising the number of NBA teams to 29. Both Toronto and Vancouver will begin play in the 1995-96 season.

JANUARY 6, 1995—With his 939th victory — an 112-90 Atlanta Hawks win over the Washington Bullets — Lenny Wilkens surpasses Red Auerbach to become the NBA's all-time winningest coach. Wilkens lights a cigar — Auerbach's trademark — to mark the occasion.

FEBRUARY 1, 1995—During an 129-88 victory over Denver, Utah Jazz point guard John Stockton surpasses Magic Johnson to become the NBA's all-time assists leader.

FEBRUARY 20, 1996—During an 112-98 victory over Boston, Utah Jazz point guard John Stockton became the NBA's most successful ball thief, surpassing Maurice Cheeks' record for steals.

APRIL 21, 1996—The Chicago Bulls defeat the Washington Bullets 103-93, to complete the 1995-96 season with a 72-10 record, establishing a new NBA record for victories in a season.

APRIL 24, 1996—The NBA Board of Governors approves the Women's National Basketball Association (WNBA) concept. The first game of the new league is played on June 21, 1997, in Los Angeles between the New York Liberty and the Los Angeles Sparks.

FEBRUARY 9, 1997—The 50 Greatest Players in NBA History are honored at the NBA All-Star Weekend in Cleveland.

OCTOBER 31, 1997—Violet Palmer becomes the first female referee to officiate an NBA game. Palmer is joined by Dee Kantner during the 1997-98 season.

MARCH 27, 1998—A crowd of 62,046, largest in NBA history, turns out at the Georgia Dome in Atlanta as the Hawks bow to the Chicago Bulls and Michael Jordan 89-74.

JUNE 14, 1998—Michael Jordan of the Chicago Bulls closes out his career with a game-winning shot against the Utah Jazz in Game 6 of the 1998 NBA Finals. Chicago wins 87-86 to capture its sixth NBA title in eight seasons.

All persons who appear in the encyclopedia are indexed with the exception of those who only appear in box scores or statistical listings. Page numbers of photographs appear in italics.

ABA. *See* American Basketball Association (ABA)
Abdul-Jabbar, Kareem, 17–18, 122, 166
- All-Time Team, 154
- background of, 27
- as college player, 27
- draft and, 310
- fined after punching incident, 160
- Hall of Fame Profile, 216
- last season, 138
- Los Angeles Lakers and, 34, 35, 82–85, *84*, 136, 138, 140, 146, 156, 164
- Mikan, George, and, 26–29
- Milwaukee Bucks and, 164, 168, *168*, 172, 174, *174*, 208
- most prolific scorer in NBA, 27, 138, 148, 174
- MVP awards, 138, 164, 168, 174
- NBA 50 greatest players profile and career highlights, 230–31, *230*
- Olympic boycott, 230
- plays on six NBA title teams, 138
- size of, 174
- sky-hook, 27, 28, 174
- volunteer coach at Alchesay Falcons High School, 26, 29

Abdur-Rahim, Shareef, 122
ABL. *See* American Basketball League
Ackerman, Val, 306–7, *307*, 309
Adams, Alvan, 164, *164*
Adelman, Rick, 106, *106*
African-Americans in basketball
- above the rim play or walking on air, 60–61, 62, 66
- Chamberlain, first African-American scoring champion, 60
- coaches, 11–12, *12*, 15, 52, 61, *61*, 71, 102–3, *103*, 106, *106*, 108, *108*
- college teams, integration of, 58–59
- Douglas, father of black basketball, 52, 53
- first general manager, 61, *61*
- first players on NBA championship team, 59
- Harlem Globetrotters, 42, 47, 45, 52, 54–57, *52, 54, 55, 56, 57*
- influence on NBA, 58–61
- integration of NBA, 56, 57, 58–59, *58*, 87, 196
- MVPs, dominance of, 60
- NBL all-black team competes against all-white, 45
- NBL, opportunities in, 1942–43, 45
- New England League, first African-American plays professional basketball in, 42–43
- New York Renaissance Five (Rens), 42, 45, 47, 52–54, *52*, 60
- Olympics, first African-American in, 58
- Russell, first African-American coach in major sports league, 61, *61* , 87, 179
- Russell, first African-American MVP, 60
- Russell, first African-American superstar, 60
- scoring titles, dominance in, 60
- style of play, 58–59

Aguirre, Mark, 136, 138
Ainge, Danny, 142, 146
Akron Firestone Non-Skids, 43
Akron Goodyear Wingfoots, 43
Albany Patroons, 77
Albeck, Stan, 110
Alcindor, Lew. *See* Abdul-Jabbar, Kareem
Alford, Steve, 146
Allen, Forrest "Phog," 12
Allen, Lucius, 174
Allen, Ray, 17, 122
Allmen Transfers. *See* Cleveland Allmen Transfers
All-Star Franca (Brazil), 304
All-Star experience, 256–87
- ABA ex-players in, 62
- ABA Games, 68
- ABA Games Profiles, 1968–76, 267
- ABA Games Results, 267
- AT&T Shootout results, 261
- Carter, Vince, dunk, at All-Star 2000, 256, *256*
- Game profiles, 2000–1951, 264–66
- Game Records, Individual, 262
- Game Records, Team, 263
- Game Results, 260–61
- Game Stats, 2000–1951, 268–87
- Jam Session, *258*, 259
- Johnson, Magic, 1992 game, 258–59, *259*
- Legends Classic, 259
- NBA first game, 1951, 196, 256
- NBA at 50, lineup at game, 1997, 228, *229*
- NBA 1987 record 303 points, 258
- NBA.com Slam Dunk results, 261
- Rookie Game, 259
- Schick Legends Classic results, 261
- Schick Rookie Challenge results, 261
- Slam Dunk contest ABA, Erving's famous half-court dunk, 1976, 65–66, 257
- Slam Dunk contest NBA, added 1984, 66, 256–57, *257*
- Sony All-Star 2ball results, 261
- TeamUp Celebration, 259
- three-point shooting contest, 258, *258*
- 2ball, 259
- 2000, expansion of activities to a full week, 257, 259
- Weekend, ABA, 1976, 65–66
- Weekend, NBA, 257

All-Time Team, 154
Amateur Athletic Union (AAU), 40, 91
Amateur Basketball Association of the USA (ABAUSA), 259
American League, 40
American Basketball Association (ABA), 62–71
- All-ABA Teams, 68
- All-Rookie Teams, 67
- All-Star Games, 68
- Career Scoring stats, 69
- Champions, 67, 201
- coaches, stats, 70
- dispersal draft and NBA absorption of teams, 36–37, 62, 66, 162, 162, 164, 205

early entry rules, 203
Erving and, 62–66, *63*, 162
expansion, 205, 207
final Finals, 202
final season, 62, 164, 202
franchise relocations, 207, 208, 209
franchises, 63–64, *63, 64*, 95, 178, 205
franchises lost, 202, 205
gate receipts, 203
Highest Field Goal Percentage stats, 69
Highest Free Throw Percentage stats, 69
Highest Scoring Average stats, 69
Highest Three-Point Field Goal Percentage stats, 69
interleague exhibition games, 64, 65, *66*
legal disputes, 204, 205, 207
logo, *62*
Mikan commissioner, 63, 178, 210
origins, 62, 63, 73, 178
painted basketball, 62, 63, 209, 210
player stats, 70
Postseason Awards, 67
quality of players, 62, 64–65
salaries, 207
seasons in review, ABA champions 1975-1967, 201–10
Slam Dunk contest, 65–66
three-point shot, 62, 100
American Basketball League (ABL), 42, 45–46, 47, 52, 54, 100
American Basketball League (ABL), 1961, 71
American Basketball League (Women's), 308–9
Americans. *See* New Jersey Americans
Anaheim Amigos, 63, *64*, 209
Anderson Duffey Packers, 45, 196
Anderson, Nick, 126
Anderson, Shandon, 310
Arapovic, Franjo, 299
Arcadians. *See* Brooklyn Arcadians
Archibald, Nate "Tiny," 156, 170, *170*, 310
Hall of Fame profile, 216
NBA 50 greatest players profile and career highlights, 231, *231*
Arizin, Paul, 34, 190, 191, 192, 195, *195*
Hall of Fame profile, 216
NBA 50 greatest players profile and career highlights, 231, *231*
Armstrong, B. J., 132
Armstrong, Scott, 43
Armstrong, Warren, 201, *201*
Arnold, Steve, 64
AT&T Shootout results, 261
Atlanta Hawks
international players, 297–98
London exhibition game, 305
nickname, 94
Vilnius, Lithuania trip, 296, 297
Attles, Al, 61, 72, 106, *106*, 166
Auerbach, Arnold "Red," 12, 30, *102*, 194
coach Celtics, 86, *86*, 87, 88, *88*, 89, 102, 180, *180*, 181, 182, 190
coach Capitols, 92, 102, 196, 198, 200
coach NBA'S All-Time Team, 154
coach Tri-Cities, 196
on consistency of the game, 12
draft of Sam Jones, 311–12
games won, 102
general manager Celtics, 154, 168, 180
Hall of Fame profile, 224
integration of NBA and, 59, *59*, 196
on Russell blocking shots, 60

BAA. *See* Basketball Association of America
Ballard, Greg, 160
Baltimore Bullets, 40, 72, 97, 179, 182, 191
NBA Championship 1947–48, 199
NBA Finals 1970–71, 174–75
Baltimore Claws, 202
Baranova, Elena, 308
Barkley, Charles, 32, 126, 128, 130, 146, *229*
NBA 50 greatest players profile and career highlights, 232, *232*
Olympics, 1992, Dream Team, 290, *290*, 291, 292, 293
Barksdale, Don, 58
Barnett, Dick, 71, 176
Barnhill, John, 208
Barnhorst, Leo, 195
Barnstorming teams, 42, 46–47
Buffalo Germans, 14, 42, *42*, 47
Carlisle Indians, 47
Harlem Globetrotters, 42, 47, 52, 54–57
Indianapolis Kautskys, 14
New York Renaissance Five, 42, 47, 52–54
New York Trojans, 47
Original Celtics, 10, 42, 47
Philadelphia SPHAs, 47
Barry, Pete, *44*, 46, 47
Barry, Rick, 106, 164, 166
ABA and, 64, 178, 201, *201*, 208
Hall of Fame profile, 216
NBA 50 greatest players profile and career highlights, 232, *232*
scoring titles, 60, 179
Basketball Association of American (BAA), 37, 38–41, 198
absorbs NBL, 37, 40–41, 45, 92, 197
first game, 38, *38*
first season, 38, 40, 200
first title, 200
formed, 39
franchises lost, second season, 199
name change to NBA, 37, 41, 197
NBL rivalry, 40–41, 198
rules and, 99–100
salary caps in, 38
segregation in, 58
slowness of game, 200
teams in, still in NBA, 40
Basketball, history of the game. *See also* Basketball plays; National Basketball Association (NBA)

ABA history, 62–71
ABA influence on the game, 62, 66
ABA-NBA dispersal draft and teams absorbed, 36–37, 62, 66
abandons center jump and creates "racehorse" style of play, 39
above the rim play or walking on air, 60–61, 62, 66
African-American player in game, 1902, 42–43, *see also* African-Americans in basketball
African-Americans in NBL, 1940s, 45
American Basketball League (ABL), 40, 42, 45–46, 47, 52
BAA, 38–41
BAA absorbs NBL, becomes NBA, 37, 45
barnstorming teams, 10, 14, 42, 46–47, 52–57, *see also specific teams*
big arenas and promotion of, 38, 39, *39*, 40
"black style" and African-American influence on game, 59–61
cage era ("cagers"), 14, 42, 45, 48–49, *48*
college scandals and public's switch to pro basketball, 41, 195
consistency, unchanging aspects of, 10–15
early leagues, 46, 47
early superstars, 17–18
first basket ever made, 12, 51
first professional game played, 42
free agency system, 36
games piggybacked with dances or other events, 45–46
industrial teams, 40
integration of the NBA, 56, 57, 58–59, *58*, 196
Mikan drill and, 11, *11*, 26, 27
migration of teams from smaller towns to big cities, 41
Naismith's first team, players in, *51*
National Basketball League (NBL), 39–41, 43–45, *43, 45*
NBL all-black team plays all-white, 45
Olympics, 1936, first inclusion of sport, 14, 50
Olympics, 1992, first inclusion of professional players, 36, *see also* Olympic Games
Original Celtics, impact on the game, 47
origins, 1891, 12–13, 50–51
player contracts, first, 47
player salary, bonus, or game stipend, 36, 38, 46, 47, 52, 53, 64, 170, 200
players union, 36, 37
players who advanced level of game, 14, 20–25, 26–29
"Power in the Paint" game, 60
pre-league games, 38–39
professional league, first, 42
professional leagues, early, 42–51, *see also specific leagues*
professional players, first, 1890s, 13–14
rules and regulations, evolution of, 10, 12–13, 14, 26, 27–28, 37, 45, 57, 66, 92, 98–101, *99*, 112, 156, 191, 192, 195, 199
rules, 13 original, 50, 51
salary cap and revenue sharing, 36
24-second shot clock, 26, 27–28, 37, 60, 98–100, *99*, 191, 192
violence of early game, 13–14, 48–49
women's basketball, 306, *306*
Basketball Federation of the USA (BFUSA), 289
Basketball plays
blocked shots, 60
dunk, 9, 11, 15, 63, 65–66
"flop," 47
full court press, 60
hook shot and sky-hook, 27, 28, *28*, 35
layup, 49
Original Celtics, innovations of, 47
pick and roll, 10–11, *10*
pivot pass, 47
playing above the rim, 9
Triangle Offense, 78–79
two-handed set shot, 49
Basloe, Frank, 48
Bavetta, Dick, 114
Baylor, Elgin, 13, 18, 19, 34, 100, 172, 181, 183, 184, 188, *188, 229*
All-NBA First Team, 172
All-Star Game 1959, 257
All-Time Team, 154
Hall of Fame profile, 216
NBA 50 greatest players profile and career highlights, 232–33, *232*
scoring record, 184
Beard, Alfred, Jr., "Butch," 166
Beard, Ralph, 195
Beaty, Zelmo, 183, 207
Beck, Byron, 64
Beckman, Johnny, *44*, 46, 47
Bee, Clair, Hall of Fame profile, 225
Bellamy, Walt, 177, 184
Hall of Fame profile, 216
Benson, Kent, 160
Berenson, Senda, 306
Berger, Ben, 37
Bertka, Bill, *115*
Biasatti, Hank Arcado, 297
Biasone, Danny, 98–99, *100*, 192, *192*
Hall of Fame profile, 225
Bickerstaff, Bernie, 110
Binelli, Augusto, 298
Bing, Dave, *178*
Hall of Fame profile, 216
NBA 50 greatest players profile and career highlights, 233–34, *234*
scoring record as guard, 178
Bird, Larry, *229*
All-NBA First Team, 32
All-NBA Second Team, 32
All-Star Game, 1980, first three-point shot, 257
best shot, 154
in Big Three, 154, *154*
career playoff highs, 148
championship games, 33, 34–35, 142, 144, 146, 148, 154
coach of Pacers, 81, 116, 118, 120

college play, Indiana State, 31
first season Celtics, 156
Hall of Fame profile, 216–17
injuries, 132, 291
Johnson rivalry with, 16, 20, 22, 30–35, *34, 35, 84*, 85, 142, 148, 156
Jordan influenced by, 8
last season, 1991–92, 132
MVP awards, 32, 60, 144
NBA 50 greatest players profile and career highlights, 234, *234*
Olympics, 1992 Dream Team, 24–25, *24*, 290, *290, 291*, 292, *292*
popularity of, 74
quotes about Jordan, 21, 144, 146
Rookie of the Year, 156
three-point shooting contest debut All Star Game 1986, 258
three-point shot, 101, *101*
Black, Hughie, 47
Blackhawks. *See* Tri-Cities Blackhawks
Blackman, Rolando, *140*
Blake, Marty, 298, 310–12, *311*
Boe, Roy, 204
Boozer, Bob, 174
Borgia, Sid, 114
Borrell, Lazaro, 299
Boston Celtics, *76*, 84, 86–89, *86, 87, 88, 89*
Big Three, 154
Bird-Magic rivalry, 16, 20, 22, 30–35, *34, 35, 84*, 85, 142, 148, 156
coach Auerbach, Red, 86, *86*, 87, 88, *88*, 89, 102, *102*, 180, *180*, 181, 182, 183, 187, 190, 196, 200
coach Heinsohn, Tommy, 164, 168
coach Russell, Bill, 87, 89, 178, 179, 180
first team averaging more than 100 points per game, 99
first team scoring triple digits, 192
fouls and free throws, 1953 game, 98
franchise-best record, 1985-86, 144
"Havlicek Stole the Ball," 89, 181
history of, 40
integration of, 59, *59*, 87, 196
jerseys retired, 87
league records, 1959, 188
McDonald's Championship 1988, 304
MVP, record number, 89
nickname, 94
NBA Championship 1956–57, 190
NBA Championship 1958–59, 188
NBA Championship 1959–60, 187
NBA Championship 1960–61, 186
NBA Championship 1961–62, 184
NBA Championship 1962–63, 183
NBA Championship 1963–64, 182
NBA Championship 1964–65, 181
NBA Championship 1965–66, 180
NBA Championship 1967–68, 178
NBA Championship 1968–69, 177
NBA Championship 1973–74, 168–69
NBA Championship 1975–76, 164–65
NBA Championship 1980–81, 154–55
NBA Championship 1983–84, 148–49
NBA Championship 1985–86, 144–45
NBA Finals 1957–58, 189
NBA Finals 1984–85, 146–47
NBA Finals 1986–87, 142–43
record number of titles, 177, 181, 182
regular-season records, 89
rivalry with LA Lakers, 31, *84*, 85, 86, 142, 146, 148, 183
Russell-Chamberlain rivalry and, 30–35, *30, 31, 32, 33*, 86, 89, 177
Russell era, 16, 20, 30–35, 61, *61*, 86, *86*,, 87–89, 111, 177, 178, 179, 180, 181, 182, 183, 184, 186, 187, 188, 189, 190, *190*
Boston Garden, 37, 39, 85
Boswell, Sonny, 56
Bowie, Sam, 312
Bradds, Gary, 201, *201*
Bradley, Bill, 170, 176
Hall of Fame profile, 217
Brand, Elton, 17, 18, *18*
Brandon, Terrell, 10
Braun, Carl, 30, 194, *194*
Braves. *See* Buffalo Braves
Bridges, Bill, 71
Brisker, John, 207
Brooklyn Spartan Braves and Spartan Five, 52
Brown, Bill, 57
Brown, "Downtown" Fred, 158
Brown, Hillary, 56
Brown, Hubie, 106–7, *106*
Brown, Larry, 107, *107*, 201, *201*, 205
Brown, P. J., 310
Brown, Rickey, 154
Brown, Roger, 63, *63*, *64*, 206, 208
Brown, Walter, 39, 88, *88*, 89, 94, 181, 256
Hall of Fame profile, 225
Bryant, Kobe, 15, *16*, 18, *115*, 116, 122, 132
Buccaneers. *See* New Orleans Buccaneers
Bucks. *See* Milwaukee Bucks
Buffalo Braves, 75, 95, 174, 310
Buffalo Germans, 14, 42, *42*, 47
Bufman, Zev, 96
Bullets. *See* Baltimore Bullets; Washington Bullets
Bulls. *See* Chicago Bulls
Buss, Jerry, 83, *115*, 152

"Cagers" and cages, 14, 42, 45, 48–49, *48*
Calling the Shots (Strom), 113
Calverley, Ernest, 200
Calvin, Mack, 203
Canadian basketball, 74. *See also* Toronto Huskies; Toronto Raptors; Vancouver Grizzlies
Capitols. *See* Washington Capitols
Carlisle Indians, 47
Carlson, Don "Swede," 91
Carolina Cougars, 205, 208

Carril, Pete, Hall of Fame profile, 224
Carroll, Joe Barry, 154
Carter, Vince, 11, *13*, 16, 18, 118, 259
  All-Star Weekend 2000, dunk, 256, *256*
  dunk and, 15
  Rookie of the Year, 118
  walking on air, 60
Cavaliers. *See* Cleveland Cavaliers
Celestand, John, *115*
Celtics. *See* Boston Celtics; New York Celtics; Original Celtics
Cervi, Al, 111, 192, 197
  Hall of Fame profile, 217
Chamberlain, Wilt, *5*, 17, 27, 29, 33, 170, 172, 176
  All-Star Games, 33, 257
  All-Time Team, 154
  championship titles, 33, 179
  death, 185
  first African-American scoring champ, 60
  foul lane widened because of, 100, 181
  Globetrotters and, 57, *57*
  Hall of Fame profile, 217
  influence of, 30, 60
  leads league in scoring, 21, 88, 130, 148, 168, 180, 181, 183, 184, 185, 187
  MVP awards, 177, 187
  NBA 50 greatest players ceremony, 228, *229*
  NBA 50 greatest players profile and career highlights, 234–35, *234*
  Philadelphia 76ers and, 89, 179
  rebounding, 31, 32
  records, various, 30, 31, 179, 186
  retirement of, 168
  Rookie of the Year, 177, 187
  Russell rivalry, 16, 20, 30–35, *30, 31, 32, 33*, 86, 88, 181
  San Francisco Warriors/Philadelphia Warriors and, 181, 182, 183, 184, 185
  scores 100, 185, *185*
  size and weight, 30, 187
  teams played on, 32, 33
Chaney, Don, 160, 164, 168, 170
Chaparrals. *See* Dallas Chaparrals; Texas Chaparrals
Charlotte Hornets, 75
  internationally held games, 305
  nickname, 94
Charlotte Sting (WNBA), 308
Chase, William R., 12, 51, *51*
Chenier, Phil, 166
Chicago American Gears, 26–27, 40–41, 45, *45*
Chicago Bulls, 20–21, *76*, 77–81, *77, 78, 79, 80, 81*, 122, 124, 130, 132, 166
  coach Jackson, Phil, 77–78, *78*, 80, 103, *103*, 120, 122, 124, 130, 132, 134, 136
  coach Motta, Dick, 166
  coach Sloan, Jerry, 154
  consecutive NBA titles, 130
  creation of, 72–73, *73*
  dispersal draft, Gilmore acquired, 162
  facts, 75
  Jordan and, 77–81, *77, 79, 81*, 120, 130, 132, 134, 136, 304
  McDonald's Championship 1997, 304
  "Miracle on Madison," 162
  NBA Championship 1990–91, 134–35
  NBA Championship 1991–92, 132–33
  NBA Championship 1992–93, 130–31
  NBA Championship 1995–96, 124–25
  NBA Championship 1996–97, 122–23
  NBA Championship 1997–98, 120–21
  NBA franchise granted, 179
  nickname, 94
  rebuilding effort, 18
  Triangle Offence and, 78–79, 80
Chicago Duffy Florals, 43
Chicago Packers, 72, 75, 97, 160, 183, 184
Chicago, the Stadium, 39
Chicago Stags, 91
Chicago Studebakers, 45
Chicago World Tournament, 92
Chicago Zephyrs, 72, 97, 182, 183, 196
  NBA Finals, 1946–47, 200
Childs, Chris, 122
Chones, Jim, 64
Christodoulou, Theo, 298
Cincinnati Royals, 170, 184, 189
Clawson, John, 201, *201*
Cleamons, Jim, *115*
Cleveland Allmen Transfers, 43
Cleveland Cavaliers, 75, 77, 174
  "miracle of Richfield," 106
  nickname, 94
Cleveland Pipers, 71
Cleveland Rockers (WNBA), 308
Cleveland Rosenblums, 46, 47, *47*
Clifton, Nat "Sweetwater," 59, 60, *60*, 194, 196
Clippers. *See* Los Angeles Clippers; San Diego Clippers
Coaches, 102–11
  ABA stats, 70
  Adelman, Rick, 106, *106*
  African-American, 11–12, *12*, 15, 52, 61, *61*, 71, 102–3, *103*, 106, *106*, 108, *108*
  Albeck, Stan, 110
  Attles, Al, 61, 72, 106, *106*, 166
  Auerbach, Red, 86, *86*, 87, 88, *88*, 89, 92, 102, *102*, 154, 180, *180*, 181, 182, 190, 194
  Bickerstaff, Bernie, 110
  Bird, Larry, 81
  Brown, Hubie, 106–7, *106*
  Brown, Larry, 107, *107*, 201, *201*, 205
  Cervi, Al, 111, 192, 197
  Collins, Doug, 77, 111
  Costello, Larry, 107, *107*, 174
  Cunningham, Billy, 34, 104, 107, *107*
  Daly, Chuck, 104, *104*, 140
  Dunleavy, Mike, 111
  Fitch, Bill, 105–6, *106*, 144
  Fitzsimmons, Cotton, 107, *107*

Ford, Chris, 111
Fratello, Mike, 107, *107*, 298, 299
Gottlieb, Eddie, 40, *40*, 46, 47, 111, 200
Guerin, Richie, 111
Hall of Fame enshrinee list, 214–15
Hall of Fame profiles, 224–25
Hannum, Alex, 107–8, *108*, 179, 182, 201, *201, 209*
Harris, Del, 108, *108*, 124
Harrison, Lester, 111, 196
Heinsohn, Tom, 87, 108, *108*, 124, 164
Holzman, William "Red," 41, 104–5, *105*
Jackson, Phil, 77–78, *78*, 80, 103, *103*, *115*, 116, 120, 122, 130, 132, 136
Jones, K. C., 108, *108*, 166
Karl, George, 25, 108–9, *108*
Kundla, John, 91–92, 93, 105, *105*, 194
Lapchick, Joe, *44*, 46, 47, 60, *60*, 111, 199, *199*
Layden, Frank, 111
Loughery, Kevin, 63, 109, *109*
Lynam, Jim, 111
MacLeod, John, 109, *109*
McMahon, Jack, 111
Moe, Doug, 63, 109, *109*, 201, *201*
Motta, Dick, 100, 109–10, *109*, 160, 166
Nelson, Don, 106, *106*
Ramsay, Jack, 105, *105*, 162
Riley, Pat, 74, *74*, 83, *83*, 84–85, 103–4, *104*, 122, 124, 128, 130, 140, 146, *146*
Russell, Bill, 61, *61*, 87, 111, 166, 179
Schaus, Fred, 111
Seymour, Paul, 111, 197
Sharman, Bill, 110, *110*, 172
Shue, Gene, 110, *110*
Sloan, Jerry, 110, *110*
Tomjanovich, Rudy, 110, *110*
van Breda Kolff, Butch, 111
Westphal, Paul, 111, 130, 164
Wilkens, Lenny, 61, 102–3, *103*, 158
winningest, 103
Cohen, Haskell, 256
Colangelo, Jerry, 73, *73*, 74
Collins, Doug, 77, 111, 156
Colonels. *See* Kentucky Colonels
Commissioners, NBA
Kennedy, J. Walter, 36–37, *37*, 39, 164, 166, 182
O'Brien, Larry, 36–37, *37*, 148, 160, 164, 166
Podoloff, Maurice, 36–37, *37*, 39, 41, 182, 188, 256
Stern, David J., *4*, 5, 36–37, *36*, 74, 82, 148, 296–97, 303, 304–5, 306
Condors. *See* Pittsburgh Condors
Conley, Gene, *88*, 187
Connors, Chuck, 41
Conquistadors. *See* San Diego Conquistadors
Continental Basketball Association (CBA), 77
Cooke, Jack Kent, 177
Cooper, Charles "Chuck," 59, *59*, 87, 196, *196*
Cooper, Charles "Tarzan," 53, *53*
Cooper, Cynthia, 308–9, *308*
Cooper, Fred, 42, 49
Cooper, Michael, 34, 83, 84, 85, 101, 140
Costas, Bob, 62
Costello, Larry, 107, *107*, 174
Cotta, Jim, *115*
Cougars. *See* Carolina Cougars
Cousy, Bob, 17, 87–89, *87, 88*, 98, 182, 183, 187, 190, 192, 193, *193*, 194, 195
All-Star Game, *257*
All-Time Team, 154
50 point game, 194
Hall of Fame profile, 217
NBA 50 greatest players profile and career highlights, 235–36, *235*
Cowens, Dave, 27, 60, 87, 156, 164, 166, 168, *168*, 170
Hall of Fame profile, 217
NBA 50 greatest players profile and career highlights, 236, *236*
Crawford, Joe, 114
Crider, Josh, 57
Critchfield, Russ, 201, *201*
Cunningham, Billy, 34, 104, 107, *107*, 170, 179, 180
in ABA, 205, *205*
Hall of Fame profile, 217
NBA 50 greatest players profile and career highlights, 236, *236*

Dallas Chaparrals, 63, *64*
Dallas Mavericks, 74, 75
Mexico regular season game, 305
nickname, 95
Dallmar, Howie, 40, *40*, 200
Daly, Chuck, 24, 104, *104*, 140
Hall of Fame profile, 224
Olympic Games, 1992, 290, *290*, 291, 293
Dampier, Louie, 64
Dandridge, Bob, 158, 160, 174
Daniels, Mel, 64, *64*, 206, 208, 209
Dantley, Adrian, 31, 85, 138, 140
Daugherty, Brad, 128, 132
Davies, Bob, 37, 98, 195, 196
Hall of Fame profile, 217
Davis, Antonio, 310
Davis, Walter "Buddy," 7, *7*, 8
Dawkins, Darryl, 203
Dayton Rens, 45, 54
DeBusschere, Dave, 168, 170, 176, 183, *183*, *312*
Hall of Fame profile, 217–18
NBA 50 greatest players profile and career highlights, 236–37, *236*
Dehnert, Henry "Dutch," 10–11, *44*, 46, 47
Denver Nuggets, 54, 63, 65, *66*, 203
ABA Finals, 1976, 202
NBA admittance of, 66, 162, 164, 202
McDonald's Championship 1989, 304
NBA scoring record 1981–82, 152
nickname, 95
Denver Rockets, 63, 64, *64*, 95, 196

Detroit Eagles, 43, *43*
Detroit Gems, 91
Detroit Olympia (stadium), 39
Detroit Pistons, 77, 84, 85
  coach Daly, Chuck, 104, *104*, 140
  history of, 46, 189, *see also* Fort Wayne Zollner Pistons
  NBA Championship 1988–89, 138–39
  NBA Championship 1989–90, 136–37
  NBA Finals 1987–88, 140–41
  nickname, 95
Detroit Shock (WNBA), 308
Detroit Vagabond Kings, 54
Dierking, Connie, 181
Divac, Vlade, 136
Douglas, Robert J., 52, 53
Draft (NBA), 310–12, *310, 311, 312*
Dream Teams. *See* Olympic Games
Drexler, Clyde, 126, 136, *229*
  NBA 50 greatest players profile and career highlights, 237, *237*
  Olympics, 1992, Dream Team, *290*, 291, 292, *292*
Drucker, Norm, 114
Dukes, Walter, 183
Dumars, Joe, 138, *138*, 140, 295, 311
Duncan, Tim, 16, 116, 118, *118*
Dunk, 9, 11, 15, 63, 65–66. *See also* All-Star Experience
  Carter, Vince, at All-Star 2000, 256, *256*
  college no-dunk rule, 63
  Erving's famous half-court, 65–66
  first 360-degree, 65
  Jordan and, 9, 11, 15, 142, 146
Dunleavy, Mike, 111

Eakins, Jim, 201, *201*
Eagles. *See* Detroit Eagles
Eastern League, 42, 47
Eckman, Charley, 191, 192
Edwards, James, 136
Edwards, Leroy "Cowboy," 44
Ehlo, Craig, 77, *77*
Elliott, Sean, 118
Embry, Wayne, 61, *61*
  Hall of Fame profile, 225–26
English, Alex, 211–12
  Hall of Fame profile, 218
Enright, Jim, Hall of Fame profile, 227
Erickson, John, 96
Erving, Julius "Dr. J," *5,* 13, 18, 113
  ABA and, 62–66, 202, *202*, 204, *204*, 206
  ABA championships, MVP awards, titles, 63, 150, 202, 204
  ABA game average, 63
  All-Time Team, 154
  college career, 206
  contributions to game, 14, 206
  "Dr. J" nickname, 63
  dunk and, 11, 15
  endorsements and marketing, 61
  foreword, previous NBA encyclopedia, 5
  Hall of Fame profile, 218
  Jordan influenced by, 8
  NBA 50 greatest players, 19, 228, *229*
  NBA 50 greatest players profile and career highlights, 237–38, *237*
  New York/New Jersey Nets and, 63–66, *63*, 162
  Philadelphia 76ers and, 66, 150, 156, 162
  Slam Dunk Contest, ABA 1976, famous shot, 65–66
  Slam Dunk Contest, NBA 1984, 257
  Virginia Squires and, 63
  walking on air, 60
Evans, Hugh, 114
Ewing, Patrick, 31, 118, 128, 130, 136, 297, 310, *312*
  NBA 50 greatest players profile and career highlights, 238–39, *238*
  Olympics, 1992, Dream Team, *290*, 291, 292
Expansion of NBA, 36, 37, 41, 66, 72–75, 124, 136, 138, 140, 174, 178, 179
  Draft, 136
  facts, 75
  playoff system, 148
  team prices, 75

Falk, David, 124
Federation de Basketball Internationale (FIBA), 289, 296–97
  eliminates distinction between amateurs and professionals, 297
  NBA in first competition sanctioned by, 303
Feerick, Bob, 199, 200
FIBA. *See* International Basketball Federation
Fisher, Derek, *115*
Fitch, Bill, 105–6, *106*, 144
Fitzsimmons, Cotton, 107, *107*, 311
Fleisher, Larry, 170
  Hall of Fame profile, 226
Fleishman, Jerry, 40, *40*
Floridians. *See* Miami Floridians
Ford, Chris, 111, 156
Fort Wayne General Electrics, 43
Fort Wayne Pistons (Fort Wayne Zollner Pistons), 37, 41, 44, 91, 95, 98, 189, 197, 198
  NBA Finals 1954–55, 192
  NBA Finals 1955–56, 191
Foust, Larry, 91, 196
Fox, Rick, *115*
Francis, Steve, 17, 19, *19*
Fratello, Mike, 107, *107*, 298, 299
Frazier, Walt "Clyde," 170, 176
  Hall of Fame profile, 218
  NBA 50 greatest players profile and career highlights, 239–49, *239*
Fredman, Dave, 73, 74
Free agency system, 36
Free throws, consecutive, 14
Fulks, Joe, 14, 40, *40*, 198, 199, 200, *200*
  Hall of Fame profile, 218
Furey, Jim, 46, 47

Gallatin, Harry, 194
  Hall of Fame profile, 218
Garciduenas, Rudy, *115*
Garnett, Kevin, 10, 15, 16–17, *17*, 302, *303*
Gates, William "Pop," 52, *52*
Gears. *See* Chicago Gears
General Electrics. *See* Fort Wayne General Electrics
George, Devean, *115*
Germans. *See* Buffalo Germans
Gervin, George, 19, 32, 63, 64, 65, 158, *158*
  Hall of Fame profile, 218
  NBA 50 greatest players profile and career highlights, 240, *240*
  scoring titles, 158, 160
Gibson, Don, 211–13
Gilmore, Artis, 64, 65, 162, 203, 206
Ginobili, Emanuel, 299
Glickman, Harry, 97
Global games. *See also* Japan Games
  Dream Teams, *see* Olympic Games
  McDonald's Championship games, 122, 296–97, *302*, 303, 304
  McDonald's Championship games, Drazen Petrovic Trophy for MVP, 304–5
  Olympic Games, *see* Olympic Games
  Pan American Games, 289
  World Championship, 1994, 295
  World Championship, 1994, stats, 295
  World Championship for Young Men, 289
Glouchkov, Georgi Nikolov, 299, *299*
Gola, Tom, 34, 191
  Hall of Fame profile, 218
Golden State Warriors, 40
  coach Attles, Al, 166
  internationally held games, 305
  international players, 296, *296*, 310
  Mexican exhibition game, 305
  NBA Championship 1974–75, 166–67
  nickname, 95
Gonzalez, Jorge, 299
Goodrich, Gail, 156, 170, 172
  Hall of Fame profile, 218–19
Gottlieb, Eddie, 40, *40*, 46, 47, 111, 191, 200
  Hall of Fame profile, 226
Graham, Otto, 41
Granik, Russ, 288–89, *289*, 291
Grant, Harry "Bud," 28, 126, 132
Grant, Horace, 79, 80
Green, A.C., *115*, 140
  consecutive games, 120
Green, Sidney, 144
Greer, Hal, 34, 61, 89, 310
  Hall of Fame profile, 219
  NBA 50 greatest players profile and career highlights, 241, *241*
Grevey, Kevin, 158, 160
Griffith, Yolanda, 309
Grimstead, Swede, 47
Gross, Bobby, 162
Groza, Alex, 195, 197
Guarillia, Gene, 88
Guerin, Richie, 111
Gulick, Jr., Luther Halsey, 50
Guokas, Matt, 40, *40*

Hagan, Cliff, 190
  Hall of Fame profile, 219
Haggerty, Horse, 47
Hairston, Harold "Happy," 170, 172
Hakoahs. *See* New York Hakoahs
Halbert, Chuck, 200
Hale, Bruce, 64
Hall of Fame (Naismith Memorial Basketball Hall of Fame)
  coach enshrinee list, 214–15
  coach profiles, 224–25
  contributor enshrinee list, 215
  contributor profiles, 225–27
  directory of members, 214–15
  eligibility requirements, 213
  facts about and description of contents, 211–13, *211, 212, 213, 227*
  first class of inductees, 1959, 212
  Gibson, Don, Chief Operating Officer, 211–13
  Honors Court, 211
  location, 211
  plaque inscription in, violence of early game, 14
  player enshrinee list, 214
  player profiles, 216–24
  referee enshrinee list, 215
  referee profiles, 227
  teams enshrined, list, 215
Hannum, Alex, 107–8, *108*, 179, 182, 201, *201*, 209
  Hall of Fame profile, 224
Hansen, Bobby, 78, 132
Hardaway, Anfernee, 116, 126
  Olympics, 1996, Dream Team, 294
Hardaway, Tim, 213
Harge, Ira, 201, *201*
Harlem Globetrotters, 42, 52, *52*, 59
  barnstorming of, 47, 54–55
  Berlin trip, 1951, 55, *55*, 56
  "black" style of play, 60
  Chamberlain plays for, 57, *57*
  as cultural icons, 57
  entertaining style, 54–55, 56
  exhibition game, defeat Mikan, 57
  first outside U.S. trip, 55
  movies on, 56, 57
  origins of, 54
  team members join white NBL's Chicago Studebakers, 45
  theme song, 57
  world trips, 56, 57
Harp, Dick, 174
Harper, Derek, *140*
Harper, Ron, 81, *115*
Harris, Del, 108, *108*, 124

Harris, John, 39
Harrison, Lester, 111, 196
  Hall of Fame profile, 226
Harrison, Tex, 54
Hartman, Sid, 91
Havlicek, John, 88–89, *89*, 156, 164, 168, 170, 181, *181*, 183, *229*
  All-Time Team, 154
  Hall of Fame profile, 219
  NBA 50 greatest players profile and career highlights, 241, *241*
Hawkins, Connie, 13, 18, 19, 54, 63, 71, 208, 209, 210, *210*
  Hall of Fame profile, 219
Hawks. *See* Atlanta Hawks; Milwaukee Hawks; St. Louis Hawks; Waterloo Hawks
Hayes, Elvin, 158, 160, *160*, 166, 177
  Hall of Fame profile, 219
  NBA 50 greatest players profile and career highlights, 241–42, *241*
Haynes, Marques, 17, 56, 57
Haywood, Spencer, 64, 174, *208*
Heard, Gar, 164
Heat. *See* Miami Heat
Heathcote, Jud, 156
Heinsohn, Tom, 87, 108, *108*, 124, 164, 187, 190
  Hall of Fame profile, 219
Henderson, Gerald, 148
Henderson, Tommy, 160
Hermsen, Clarence "Kleggie," 199
Herring, Clifton, 6
Hill, Grant, 17
Hilliard, Leon, 57
Hillhouse, Art, 40, *40*
Hodges, Craig, 101, 258
Hoffman, Paul, 199
Holdsclaw, Chamique, 309, *309*
Hollins, Hue, 114
Hollins, Lionel, 162
Holman, Nat, 10–11, *44*, 46, 47
Holt, John, 53, *53*
Holzman, William "Red," 41, 104–5, *105*
  Hall of Fame profile, 224
Hoosiers. *See* Fort Wayne Hoosiers
Hornacek, Jeff, 258, *258*, 259, 310, 312
Hornets. *See* Charlotte Hornets
Horry, Robert, *115*
Houbregs, Robert, Hall of Fame profile, 219
Houston, Allan, 17, 118, 122
Houston Comets (WNBA), 308
Houston Mavericks, 63, 208
Houston Rockets. *See also* Malone, Moses
  coach Fitch, Bill, 105–6, *106*, 144
  McDonald's Championship 1995, 304
  Mexico regular season game, 305
  NBA Championship 1993–94, 128–29
  NBA Championship 1994–95, 126–27
  NBA Finals 1980–81, 154–55
  NBA Finals 1985–86, 144–45
  nickname, 95
Howell, Bailey, 178
  Hall of Fame profile, 219
Hudson, Lou, 160
Hudson River League, 42
Hundley, Rodney "Hot Rod,"
Huskies. *See* Toronto Huskies
Husta, Carl, 46

Ilgauskas, Zydrunas, 296, 297, 299
Illidge, Eric, 53, 54
Indiana Fever (WNBA), 309
Indiana Pacers
  ABA Championship 1969-70, 208
  ABA Championship 1972-73, 205
  ABA Finals 1968-69, 208
  ABA Finals 1975-76, 64, *64*, 203
  as ABA team, 63, *63*, 64, *64*, 66
  Bird coaches, 81, 116
  internationally held games, 305
  NBA Finals 1999–2000, 81, 116–17
  NBA admittance of, 66, 162, 202
  nickname, 95
Indianapolis Kautskys, 14, 37, 41, 43
Indianapolis Olympians, 195, 197, 198
Indians. *See* Carlisle Indians
International basketball. *See* Global games
International Basketball Federation, 36
International players. *See also individuals*
  added to NBA, 296–299, *296, 297, 298, 299*
  All-Time List, 300–301
  draft and, 311–12
Interstate League, 42
Irish, Edward S. "Ned," 39, 96
  Hall of Fame profile, 226
Ironmen. *See* Pittsburgh Ironmen
Issel, Dan, 64, 203, 206, 207, *207*
  Hall of Fame profile, 219
Iverson, Allen, 17, 19, *19*, 118, 122

Jackson, Inman, 54, 56
Jackson, Phil, 21–22, 77–78, *78*, 80, 103, *103*, *115*, 116, 120, 122, 130, 132, 136, 170
Japan Games, 302–3, *303*, *304*
Jaros, Tony, 91
Javie, Steve, 114
Jazz. *See* New Orleans Jazz; Utah Jazz
Jeannette, Buddy, 44, 199
  Hall of Fame profile, 220
Jenkins, Clarence "Fat," 53, *53*
Jim White Chevrolets. *See* Toledo Jim White Chevrolets
Johnson, Avery, 118
Johnson, Charles, 160
Johnson, Dennis, 34, 142, 146, 158, 310
Johnson, Earvin "Magic," *142*
  All-NBA First Team, 32
  All-NBA Second Team, 32
  All-Star Game 1992, 258–59, *259*

assists, 82
basketball players who inspired, influenced, 12
Bird rivalry, 16, 20, 22, 30–35, *34, 35*, *84*, 85, 142, 148
championship title games, 33, 34–35, 134, 136, 142, 148, 152
college play, Michigan State, 31, 156
comeback 1995, 124, 132
first season with Lakers, 156, *156*
greatness of, 156
HIV diagnosis and retirement, 132, 257, 291
Jordan and, 8, 79, *79*, 134
Lakers and, 82–85, *82, 83*, 124, 136, 140, 142, 148, 152, 154
McDonald's Championship, 1991, *302*
MVP awards, 32, 138, 152
NBA 50 greatest players profile and career highlights, 242, *242*
Olympics, 1992 Dream Team, 24–25, *24*, 290, *290*, 291, *291*, 292
popularity of, 74
sky-hook, 35
Thomas, Isiah, friendship, 136
three-point shot and, 101
Johnson, Gus, 174, 310
Johnson, John, 158
Johnson, Kevin, 128
Johnson, Larry, 122
Johnson, Vinnie, 140
Johnston, Neil, 191, 192, 193, 194
Hall of Fame profile, 220
Jones, Bill, 45
Jones, Bobby, 150, 203
Jones, Caldwell, 150
Jones, Eddie, 17
Jones, James, 209
Jones, K. C., 60, 61, 87, 88, *88*, 108, *108*, 166, 179, 182, 187
Hall of Fame profile, 220
Jones, Larry, 209
Jones, Sam, 34, 60, 88, *88*, 184, 187, 312
Hall of Fame profile, 220
NBA 50 greatest players profile and career highlights, 242, *242*
Jones, Wali, 179
Jordan, Michael, 6–9, *6*, 13, 19, *20, 21, 22, 23, 25*, *134*, 136, *229*
All-Defensive First Team, 22, 120, 124
All-Star MVP, 120
appearance and personal style, 22
baseball hiatus and comeback, 124, 126, 128
basketball players who inspired and influenced, *7*, 8, 9, *9*, 15, 28
Bird on, 21, 144, 146
championship games, 21, 120, 122
Chicago Bulls and, 20, 21–22, 77–80, *77, 79, 81*, 120, 122, 134, 136, 144, 146
competitiveness, 24, 144
cultural icon/superstar status, 18, 20–25, 74
cut from high school team, 6
Defensive Player of the Year, 22
determination of, 6, 144
draft, 1984, 146
dunk and, 9, 11, 15, 142, 146
evolution of the game and, 8
father's murder, 80, 128
foreword, previous edition NBA encyclopedia, 5
future of the game and, 8, 9
golf and, 24
international popularity, 22, 23, 25
Johnson, Magic and, 79, *79*, 134
last play of, 21, 120
leadership and character, 134, 142
love of the game, 6–7, 9
marketing by, 22, 23, 61
MVP awards, 21, *21*, 120, 128, 132
NBA 50 greatest players profile, 20–25
North Carolina, NCAA championship, 21
Olympics, 1992 Dream Team, 24–25, *24*, 130, 290, *290, 291,* 292, 293
personality, 23, 24
playing above the rim and walking on air, 9, 60, 144
playoffs, 1986, Game 2 stats, 24
pro career, span of, 20
record, consecutive games scoring, 25
retirement, 1998, 22, 116, 118
retirement to play baseball, 20, 80, 126, 128
scoring titles, 21, 22, 120, 130, 132, 138, 142, 144
size of, 21
Sporting News ranks No. 1, 23–24
tops 50-point mark in playoffs, 23
Washington Wizards president, 6, *8*, 25
Jucker, Ed, 174
Julian, Alvin "Doggie," Hall of Fame profile, 225
Junior National Teams, 289

Kaner, Richard, 298
Kansas City Kings, 97, 170
Kaplowitz, Ralph, 40, *40*
Karl, George, 25, 108–9, *108*
Karnisovas, Arturas, 290, 291
Kaselman, Cy, 40, *40*
Kasten, Stan, 298
Kautskys. *See* Indianapolis Kautskys
Kennedy, J. Walter, 36–37, *37*, 39, 164, 166, 182
Hall of Fame profile, 226
Kennedy, Matthew "Pat," 114, *114*
Hall of Fame profile, 227
Kenon, Larry, 65, 204
Kentucky Colonels, 63, 64, 65, 66, 162, 206
ABA Championship 1975, 203
ABA Finals 1971, 207
ABA Finals 1973, 205
Kerr, Johnny "Red," 9, 73, *73*, 188
Kerr, Steve, 24, 80, 126
Kersey, Jess, 114
Keye, Julius, 205
Kidd, Jason, 16, 17

King, Bernard, 146, 148, *148*
King, George, 192
King, Stacey, 132
Kings. *See* Kansas City Kings; Sacramento Kings
Klein, Dick, 73, *73*, 94
Knicks (Knickerbockers). *See* New York Knicks
Knight, Travis, *115*
Koppett, Leonard, 192
Kosloff, Irv, 96
Krause, Jerry, 80, 124
Kukoc, Toni, 81, 310
Kundla, John, 91–92, *90*, 93, 105, *105*, 194
  Hall of Fame profile, 225
Kunnert, Kevin, 160
Kupchak, Mitch, 160

Lacey, Sam, 166
Laettner, Christian, Olympics, 1992, Dream Team, *290*, 291, 292
Laimbeer, Bill, 136, 138, 140
Lakers. *See* Los Angeles Lakers; Minneapolis Lakers
Lanier, Bob, 213
  Hall of Fame profile, 220
Lantz, Stu, 160
Lapchick, Joe, *44*, 46, 47, 60, *60*, 111, 199, *199*
  Hall of Fame profile, 220
Layden, Frank, 111
Lemon, Meadowlark, 57
LeRoux, Buddy, *88*
Leslie, Lisa, 307, *307*
Lew, Harry "Bucky," 42–43
Lewin, Leonard, 11
Lewis, Freddie, 206, 208
Llamas, Horacio, 299
Lloyd, Earl, 58–59, *58*, 196
Lobo, Rebecca, 307, *307*
Loeffler, Ken, Hall of Fame profile, 225
Logan, Henry, 201, *201*
Long, Byron "Fats," 54
Longley, Luc, 298
Los Angeles Clippers, nickname, 95
Los Angeles Forum, 85
Los Angeles Lakers, 33, 34, *76*, 82–85, *82, 83, 84, 85*
  Abdul-Jabbar and, 34, 35, 82, 83, 84, *84*, 85, 136, 138, 140, 146, 156
  coach Harris, Del, 124
  coach, Jackson, Phil, *115*, 116
  coach Mullaney, Joe, 172
  coach Riley, Pat, 74, *74*, 83, *83*, 84–85, 103–4, *104*, 140, 142, 146, *146*, 152
  coach Sharman, Bill, 172
  coach Westhead, Paul, 152
  field goal percentage record, 146
  Johnson, Magic and, 79, 82–85, *82, 83*, 142, 152, 156, *156*
  McDonald's Championship, 1991, *302*, 304
  Memorial Day Massacre, 146
  move from Minneapolis, 72, 186
  NBA Championship 1971–72, 172–73
  NBA Championship 1979–80, 156–57
  NBA Championship 1981–82, 152–53
  NBA Championship 1984–85, 146–47
  NBA Championship 1986–87, 142–43
  NBA Championship 1987–88, 140–41
  NBA Championship 2000, 16, *115*, 116
  NBA Finals, 1961–62, 184
  NBA Finals, 1962–63, 183
  NBA Finals, 1964–65, 181
  NBA Finals, 1965–66, 180
  NBA Finals, 1967–68, 178
  NBA Finals, 1968–69, 177
  NBA Finals, 1969–70, 176
  NBA Finals, 1972–73, 170–71
  NBA Finals, 1982–83, 150–51
  NBA Finals, 1983–84, 148–49
  NBA Finals, 1988–89, 138–39
  NBA Finals, 1990–91, 79, 134–35
  new dynasty, 16
  nickname, 95
  record for consecutive victories, 14, 172
  records broken, 1971-72, 172
  rivalry with Boston Celtics, 31, 85, 142, 146, 156, 172, 183
  "showtime" style, 85, *85*, 142
  three-point field goals, 1982–83, 150
Los Angeles Sparks (WNBA), 308, 309
Los Angeles Stars, 207, 209
  ABA Finals 1970, 208
Loscutoff, "Jungle Jim," 87, *88*, 181, 187, 190
Loughery, Kevin, 63, 109, *109*
Love, Bob, 170
Lovellette, Clyde, 12, 91, *91*, 93
  Hall of Fame profile, 220
Lucas, Jerry, 168, 170, 182, *182*
  Hall of Fame profile, 220
  NBA 50 greatest players profile and career highlights, 243, *243*
Lucas, Maurice, 62, 162
Lue, Tyronn, *115*
Lynam, Jim, 111

McAdoo, Bob, 83, 150, 152, 166, *166*
  Hall of Fame profile, 221
Macauley, Ed, 190, 195
  All-Star Game, *257*
  Hall of Fame profile, 220
McCloskey, Jack, 140
McCloy, John J., 56
McCollum, Grady, 54, *54*
McDaniels, Jim, 64
McDermott, Bobby, 44
McDonald, Glenn, 164
McDonald's Championship
  Drazen Petrovic Trophy for MVP, 304–5
  1987 (first), 296–97, 303
  1988, 297, 304
  1989, 304

1990, 304
1991, 122, *302*, 304
1993, 304
1995, 304
1997, 304
1999, 304
McGinnis, George, 64, *64*, 66, 206, *206*
McGlocklin, Jon, 174
McGrady, Tracy, 17
McGuire, Dick, 98, 194
Hall of Fame profile, 221
McGuire, Frank, Hall of Fame profile, 225
McHale, Kevin, 34, 35, 142, 144, 146, 154
Hall of Fame profile, 221
NBA 50 greatest players profile and career highlights, 245–46, *245*
McKinney, Horace "Bones," 198, 200, 312
MacLeod, John, 109, *109*, 299
McMahon, Jack, 111
McMillian, Jim, 172
Maccabi Tel Aviv (Israel), 305
Madison Square Garden, 37, 38, 39, *39*, 40
Magic. *See* Orlando Magic
Mahorn, Derrick "Rick," 136, 140
Malone, Karl, 10, *10*, 32, 120, 122, *122*, 132, 136, 311
All Star Games, 259
MVP awards, 118, 122, 259
NBA 50 greatest players profile and career highlights, 243–44, *243*
Olympics, 1992, Dream Team, 290, *290*, 292, *292*
Malone, Moses, 27, 64, 150, *150*, 154, 203, *203*
drafted from high school, 203
MVP, 150
NBA 50 greatest players profile and career highlights, 245, *245*
Maravich, Pete
Hall of Fame profile, 220
NBA 50 greatest players profile and career highlights, 245, *245*
scoring title, 60
Marbury, Stephon, 122
Marciulionis, Sarunas, 296, *296*, 297, 299, 310
Marks, Sean, 299
Martin, Kenyon, 310, *310*
Martin, Slater "Dugie," 91, *91*, 93, 98, 197
Hall of Fame profile, 221
Mathis, Mike, 114
Mavericks. *See* Dallas Mavericks; Houston Mavericks
Maxwell, Cedric, 148, 154, 156
Memphis Pros, 202, 207
Meneghin, Dino, 298, 310
Metropolitan League, 47
Meyer, Ray, 11, 26, 27
Miami Floridians, 205, 207, 209
Miami Heat, 74, 75, 116, 122
coach/owner, Riley, Pat, 104, 124
internationally held games, 305
nickname, 96
rivalry with Knicks, 120
Miami Sol (WNBA), 309
Miasek, Stan, 200
Mikan, George, *5*, 26–29, *26, 27*, 90, 92, 93, 192, 194
ABA commissioner, 63, 178, 210
All-NBA First Team, 195
All-Time Team, 154
background, 27
center position, 27
Chicago American Gears and, 26–27, 40–41, 45, *45*, 192
college basketball, DePaul Blue Demons, 26, 27, 29, 40
cut from playing high school ball, 28–29
drill, 11, *11*, 26, 27
endorsements and marketing by, 28
Hall of Fame, 91, *91,* 93
Hall of Fame profile, 221
height and weight, 26, 27, 28–29
hook shot, 27, 28, *28*
Minneapolis Lakers and, 12, 27, 29, 37, 41, 45, 57, 90–93, *90, 91, 92, 93*, 192, 193, 194, 195, 196, 198, *198*
NBA 50 greatest players, 26–29, 228, *229*
NBL era and, 44–45, *45*, 192
rebound record, 28
retirement, 29, 192
rules changed because of (foul lane widened), 26, 27–28, 92, 98–100, *99*, 193, 195
scoring titles, 27, 28, 189
skills of, 27, 198
star status of, 17, 28, 29, *29*
Mikkelsen, Vern, 28, 91, *91*, 92, *92*, 93, 194, 197
Hall of Fame profile, 221
Milanesio, Marcelo, 291
Miller, Reggie, 120
Olympics, 1996, Dream Team, 294
World Championships, 1994, 295
Milton, DeLisha, 309
Milwaukee Bucks, 61, 75
coach Costello, Larry, 174
McDonald's Championship, 1987, 303–4
NBA Championship 1970–71, 174–75
NBA Finals 1973–74, 168–69
nickname, 96
Milwaukee Hawks, 191
Minneapolis Lakers, 12, 27, 37, 41, 45, 57, 72, *76*, 90–93, *90, 91, 92, 93*
coach, Kundla, John, 91–92, 93, 105, *105*, 194
Hall of Famers and, *91,* 93, 197
high scoring game, 191
home court advantage (narrow court), 92, 197
lowest-scoring game, 98, 196
Mikan and, 12, 27, 29, 37, 41, 45, 57, 90–93, *90, 91, 92, 93*, 193, 194, 197, 198
move to BAA, 198
move to Los Angeles, 90
NBA Championship 1948–49, 198
NBA Championship 1949–50, 197
NBA Championship 1951–52, 195
NBA Championship 1952–53, 194

NBA Championship 1953–54, 193
NBA Finals 1958–59, 188
origins, 91
Minnesota Lynx (WNBA), 308
Minnesota Muskies, 63, 209
Minnesota Pipers, 208, 209
Minnesota Timberwolves, 14, 74, 75, 136
Japan Games, 302, *303*
nickname, 96
Moe, Doug, 63, 109, *109*, 201, *201*
Mokray, Bill, Hall of Fame profile, 226
Molinas, Jack, 193
Monroe, Earl "the Pearl," 17, 170, 174
Hall of Fame profile, 221
NBA 50 greatest players profile and career highlights, 239–40, *239*
Montero, Jose-Antonio, 298
Morandoti, Ricardo, 298–99
Most, Johnny, 89, 181
Motta, Dick
coaching of, 109–10, *109*, 160, 166
on long ball, 100
Mount, Rick, 64, 206
Mourning, Alonzo, 17, 120, 124
Mullin, Chris, Olympics, 1992, Dream Team, *290*, 291, 292
Murphy, Calvin, 154, 310
Hall of Fame profile, 221
Murphy, Dennis, 63
Musi, Angelo, 40, *40*, 200
Muskies. *See* Minnesota Muskies
Mutombo, Dikembe, 122, 298

Naismith, James A., 50–51, *50*, 74
backboard instituted by, 1893, 12–13
coach of UK, 12, 51
football helmet invented by, 51
Hall of Fame and, 212
Olympics trip, 212
original 13 rules, 50, 51
originator of game, 1891, 12, 50, 212
players in first game, 51, *51*
Nance, Larry, 257, *257*
National Basketball Association. *See also* Basketball, history of the game
ABA, dispersal draft and absorption of teams, 36–37, 62, 66, 162, 164
ABA influence on style of play, 62
ABA-NBA exhibition games, 64, 65, *66*
ABA rules and Slam-Dunk contest adopted, 66
ABA threat and decision to expand NBA, 73
African-American influence on, 58–61
All-Star Games begun, 1951, 196, 256
All-Star Game 1987, record high score, 142
anti-drug program, 36, 37
back-to-back repeat champions, 136, 140
betting scandals avoided, 193, 195
bicoastal status, 186
Bird-Johnson rivalry and popularity of, 31, 34
club nicknames, 94–97
collective bargaining agreement, 36, 37, 170
competitive 1970s, 158
current and upcoming stars, 16–19, *16, 17, 18, 19*
"Dark Days" of 1980s, 74, 82
Director of Scouting, 310–12
draft, 310–12, *310, 311, 312*
draft eligibility guidelines revised, 174
expansion, 36, 37, 41, 66, 72–75, 124, 136, 138, 140, 174, 178, 179
expansion draft, 136
expansion facts, 75
expansion playoff system, 148
expansion team prices, 75
Fiftieth Anniversary, 228–29, *229*
first game in league history, 305
four divisions created, 174
free agency system, 36
future of, 16–19
global games, 302–5
globalization of, 36, 212, 288–89, 296–305
greatest players, first 35 years, 154
greatest players, first 50 years, 228–29, *229*
greatest players, first 50 years, profiles, 230–55
high school players drafted, 203
integration of, 56, 57, 58–59, *58*, 196
international players, 296–299, *296, 297, 298, 299*
international players, all-time list, 300–301
Internet site, 5
Jordan's contributions to popularity of, 22–23
Kennedy, Commissioner J. Walter, 36–37, *37*, 39, 164, 166, 182
labor lockout 1998, 118
loss of franchises, 1950s, 196
lowest-scoring game and Mikan, 27, 196
marketing players, 7
O'Brien, Commissioner Larry, 36–37, *37*, 148, 160, 164, 166
origins of, in BAA and NBL, 37, 38–41, 197
"Oscar Robertson Suit," 37
pension plan, 37
Podoloff, President Maurice, 36–37, *37*, 39, 41, 182, 188, 256
players salaries, 7, 40, 170
players union, 37, 170
Pre-Draft Camp, 312
season by season review 1946 to 2000, 115–200
schedule change, 1960, 186
schedule change, 1979, 156
slow pace and financial struggles, 1950s, 193
steals and blocked shots first recorded, 168
Stern, Commissioner David J., *4,* 5, 36–37, *36*, 74, 82, 148, 296–96, 303, 304–5, 306
up-tempo game begun, 191, *see also* 24-second shot clock
violent incidents, 1977-78, 160
Women's National Basketball Association (WNBA) created, 306–7
Zollner's financial support of, 44

National Basketball League (NBL), 26–27, 37, 39–41, 42–45. *43, 45*, 90–92, 197, 198
African-Americans given opportunities in, 45
all-black team competes against all-white, 45
first pro league, 42
founding of, six teams, 42, 94
industrial teams in, 43
lack of playing arenas, 44, 47
Mikan and, 44, 45, *45*, 90, 198
three eras of, 43–44
National Basketball Players Association, 37, 170
National Professional Basketball League, 45
Nats (Nationals). *See* Syracuse Nats
NBA. *See* National Basketball Association
NBA.com, 5, 36
NBA.comTV, 36
NBA Entertainment, 36
NBA Properties, 36
NBL. *See* National Basketball League
Neal, Curly, 57
Nelson, Don, 106, *106*, 164, 170, 177
World Championships, 1994, 295
Netolicky, Bob, 208
Nets. *See* New Jersey Nets; New York Nets
Neumann, Paul, 181
New England League, first African-American plays professional basketball, 42–43
Newell, Pete, 160, 174
Hall of Fame profile, 226
New Jersey Americans, 63, *64*, 96, 209
New Jersey Nets, 64
Japan Games, *304*
Mexican exhibition game, 305
nickname, 96
New Orleans Buccaneers, 63, *64*, 207
ABA Finals 1967-68, 210
New Orleans Jazz, 73, 75, 95, 156
New York Celtics, 47
New York Knicks, 116, 148
coach, Holzman, William "Red," 41, 104–5, *105*
coach, Riley, Pat, 104, 128, 130
coach, Van Gundy, Jeff, 120
early, in Madison Square Garden and 69th Regiment Armory, 39
history of, 40, 41
integration of, 59, 196
McDonald's Championship 1990, 304
NBA Championship 1969–70, 176
NBA Championship 1972–73, 170–71
NBA Finals 1950–51, 196
NBA Finals 1951–52, 195
NBA Finals 1952–53, 194
NBA Finals 1971–72, 172–73
NBA Finals, 1993–94, 128–29
NBA Finals, 1998–99, 118–19
nickname, 96
playoff 1999, 118
playoff, free throws outnumber baskets, 98
records set, 176
New York Liberty (WNBA), 307, 308, 309
New York Nets, 63, *63*, 65, 96, 209
ABA Championship 1976, 202
ABA Championship 1974, 204
ABA Finals 1971, 206
Erving acquired, 203
NBA admittance of, 66, 162, 164, 202
New York Renaissance Five (Rens), 42, 45, 52–54, *52*, 92
all-black team in all-white league, 45
barnstorming of, 47, 52, 53
"black" style of play, 60
discrimination and, 54
game record of, 53, 54
last game, 54
origins, 53
New York State League, 42, 46
New York Trojans, 47
Nicola, Marcelo, 299
Nike Desert Classic, 312
Nixon, Norm, 34, 83, 150
Nucatola, John, Hall of Fame profile, 227
Nuggets. *See* Denver Nuggets
Nunn, Ronnie, 114

Oakland Bittners, 91
Oakland Oaks, 63, *63*, 64, *64*, 208
ABA Champions 1968-69, *201*, 209, *209*
coach Hannum, Alex, 201, *201*, 209
impact on NBA, 201
Oakley, Charles, 130
O'Brien, Jim, 63, 64
O'Brien, Larry, 36–37, *37*, 148, 160, 164, 166
Hall of Fame profile, 226
Odom, Lamar, 11, *11*, 12
O'Donnell, Jake, 114
Officials. *See* Referees
Oilers, *See* Warren Penn Oilers
Olajuwon, Hakeem, 17, 29, 124, 126, 128, *128*, 136, 144, 297, *297*
MVP awards, 128
NBA 50 greatest players profile and career highlights, 246, *246*
Oliver, Willis "Kid," 54
Olsen, Harold, Hall of Fame profile, 226
Olympians. *See* Indianapolis Olympians
Olympic Games. *See also* USA Basketball
1936, first inclusion of basketball in, 14, 50
1948, first African-American on U.S. team, 58
1956, Russell on, 190
1960, West and Robertson in, 186
1968, Abdul-Jabbar boycotts, 230
1984, Jordan in, 146
1988, loss to Soviet Team, 297
1989, rules changed to allow professional players, 297
1992, coaches, 290, 293
1992, Dream Team, 24–25, *24*, 104, 130, 288, 290–93, *290, 291*

1992 Final Standings, 293
1992 Men's Cumulative Statistics, 293
1992 USA Results, 293
1996, Dream Team, gold medal, 288, *288*, 294
1996, U.S. Women's National Team, gold medal, 289, *289*, 306, 307
1996 Final Standings, 294
1996 Men's Cumulative Statistics, 294
1996 USA Results, 294
2000, 110
U.S. Team medals, 14
O'Neal, Shaquille, 16, 17, *17*, *116*, 120, 310
"Hack-a-Shaq" fouls, 116
Laker championship 2000, 18, *115*, 116
McDonald's Championship, *305*
leaves Orlando, signs Lakers, 122, 124
most points scored during a game record, 14
MVP 2000, *4*, 18, 116
NBA 50 greatest players profile and career highlights, 246–47, *246*
Olympics, 1996, Dream Team, 294
Orlando and, 126
rivalry with Duncan or Ewing, 16, 31
World Championship, 1994, 295
Original Celtics, *44*
ABL and, 46
ahead of their time, 44
arena rented by, 47
barnstorming, 47
founding of, 47
leagues joined, 47
nickname, 94
play style and inventions, 10–11
player contracts, first, 47
playing all-black teams, 52, 55
record of wins, 1920s, 45
world's best team, 46
Orlando Magic, 74, 75, 136
Japan Games, *304*
London exhibition game, 305
NBA Finals 1994–95, 126–27
nickname, 96
Orlando Miracle (WNBA), 308
"Oscar Robertson Suit," 37
Oshkosh All-Stars, 44
Owens, Jesse, 55, 56

Pacers. *See* Indiana Pacers
Packers. *See* Anderson Packers; Chicago Packers
Paderatz, Fred, 49
Pan American Games, 289
Parish, Robert, 34, 35, 84, *84*, 142, 144, 146, 154
most NBA seasons, 122
NBA 50 greatest players profile and career highlights, 247, *247*
Paspalj, Zarko, 297
Passon, Harry, 47
Paultz, Billy, 204
Payton, Gary, 17, 81, 124
Paxson, James J. "Jim," 130, 134, 142
Paxson, John, 80
Perkins, Sam, 134
Peterson, Mel, 201, *201*
Petrovic, Drazen, 292, *292*, 293, 297, *297*, 304–5, 310
Pettit, Bob
in All-Star Games, 257, 259
on "All-Time NBA Team," 154
career scoring record of, 180
championship series games, 189, 190
Hall of Fame profile, 221
with Hawks, 182, 189, 190, 191, *191*
inner fire of, 189
MVP awards, 60, 257
NBA 50 greatest players profile and career highlights, 247–48, *248*
Philadelphia Basketball League, 42, 47
Philadelphia 76ers, 41. *See also* Syracuse Nationals
ABA players bought, 66, 162
best season record, 39
Chamberlain and, 89, 179
coach, Cunningham, Billy, 150
coach, Hannum, Alex, 179, 201
Erving, Julius and, 150, 162
Malone, Moses and, 150, *150*
move to Philadelphia from Syracuse, 72, 182
nickname, 96
NBA Championship 1966–67, 179
NBA Championship 1982–83, 150–51
NBA Finals 1976–77, 162–63
NBA Finals 1979–80, 156–57
NBA Finals 1981–82, 152–53
Philadelphia SPHAs, 46, 47, 56, *56*
Philadelphia Warriors, 40, *40*, 41, 46, 72, 183, 191
NBA Championship, 1946–47, 200
NBA Championship 1955–56, 191
NBA Finals 1947–48, 199
Phillip, Andy, 98, 195
Hall of Fame profile, 222
Phoenix Mercury (WNBA), 308
Phoenix Suns, 14, 25, 73, 75, 116
highest scoring playoffs, 132
international players, 299
Japan Games, 303
McDonald's Championship 1993, 304
NBA Finals 1975–76, 164–65
NBA Finals 1992–93, 130–31
nickname, 96
Pierce, Paul, 312
Pieri, Lou, 88, *88*
Pipers. *See* Cleveland Pipers; Minnesota Pipers; Pittsburgh Pipers
Pippen, Scottie, 21, 77, 78, 116, 120, *120*, 122, 132, 134
All-Defensive Team, 124
NBA 50 greatest players profile and career highlights, 248–49, *248*
Olympics, 1992, Dream Team, 130, 290, *290*, 292

Olympics, 1996, Dream Team, 294
Pistons. *See* Detroit Pistons; Fort Wayne Pistons
Pitino, Rick, 312
Pittsburgh Condors, 205, 207
Pittsburgh Pipers, 63, *64*, 207, 208, 209
ABA Championship 1967-68, 210
Podestra, Fred, 96
Podoloff, Maurice, 36–37, *37*, 39, 41, 182, 188, 256
Hall of Fame profile, 226
Pollack, Harvey, 185
Pollard, Jim "The Kangaroo Kid," 11, 41, 45, 90, *90*, 91, *91*, 92, *92*, 93, 194
Hall of Fame profile, 222
Pollin, Abe, 97
Popovich, Gregg, 118
Porter, Kevin, 166
Portland Fire (WNBA), 309
Portland Trail Blazers, 75, 116, 174
coach, Ramsay, Jack, 162
first championship title and ABA players, 62, 162
highest scoring playoffs, 132
international players, 297, 298
NBA Championship 1976–77, 162–63
NBA Finals 1989–90, 136–37
NBA Finals 1991–92, 132–33
nickname, 97
Rip City, 162
Portsmouth Invitational Tournament, 312
Powers, Richie, 114
Pressley, Babe, 56, 57
Price, Bernie, 56
Price, Mark, 132, *132*, 295, 310
Pros. *See* Memphis Pros
Providence Steamrollers, 200
Pullins, Al "Runt," 54

Radja, Dino, 292, *292*
Raga, Manuel, 310
Rambis, Kurt, 140
Ramsay, Jack, 105, *105*, 162
Hall of Fame profile, 225
Ramsey, Frank, 88, *88*, 181, 187, 190
Hall of Fame profile, 222
Ray, Clifford, 166
Redskins. *See* Sheboygan Redskins
Reed, Willis, 27, 168, 170, 172, 176, *176*
draft and, 310
Hall of Fame profile, 222
NBA 50 greatest players profile and career highlights, 249, *249*
Referees, 112–14, *112, 113, 114*
Hall of Fame enshrinee list, 215
Hall of Fame profiles, 227
Reinsdorf, Jerry, 22–23, 122, 144
Reiser, Chick, 199
Rice, Glen, *115*
Richman, Ike, 96
Ricks, James "Pappy," 53, *53*
Riley, Pat, 74, *74*, 83, *83*, 84–85, 103–4, *104*, 122, 124, 128, 130, 140, 146, *146*, 152, 172
Riordan, Mike, 166, 170
Risen, Arnie, 196
Hall of Fame profile, 222
Rivers, Doc, 11–12, *12*, 15
Robertson, Oscar, *5*, 20, 61, 166, 168, 174, 183, 184, *184*, 186
All-Time Team, 154
championship team 1970-71, 174
Hall of Fame profile, 222
NBA 50 greatest players ceremony, 228
NBA 50 greatest players profile and career highlights, 249–50, *249*
Olympic team, 186
Rookie of the Year, 174
scoring and assists records, 174
triple-double seasons, 174, 184
Robinson, David, 118, 120, 126, 128
NBA 50 greatest players profile and career highlights, 250–51, *250*
Olympics, 1992, Dream Team, *290*, 291, 292
Olympics, 1996, Dream Team, 294
Robinson, Ermer, 57
Robinson, Glenn, 17
Rochester Royals, 37, 41, 92, 93, 97, 189, 198
NBA Championship 1950–51, 196
Rockets. *See* Denver Rockets; Houston Rockets; San Diego Rockets
Rodgers, Guy, 34, 61
Rodman, Dennis, 80–81, *81*, 120, 122, 124, *124*, 138, 140
All-Defensive Team, 124
rebounding titles, 120, 124, 130
Rose, Jalen, 17
Rosenberg, Petey, 40, *40*
Royals. *See* Cincinnati Royals; Rochester Royals
Rudolph, Mendy, 114
Rudoy, Herb, 299
Ruklick, Joe, 185
Rules, official
ABA three-point shot adopted, 66, 100–101, 156
ABL and changes in, 45
BAA and, 99–100
college, 100
court dimensions, 100
early entry, 57, 203
evolution of, 10, 12–13, 14, 26, 27–28, 37, 45, 57, 66, 92, 98–101, *99*, 156
foul lane, 26, 27–28, 100, 195
fouls and disqualification, 199
fouls limited, 98–101, 192, 193
illegal defenses, 100
original 13, 50, 51
number of players, 199
seasonal changes by NBA, 13
third official, 112
three-point shot, 66, 71, 100–101, 156
24-second shot clock, 26, 27–28, 37, 92, 98–100, *99*, 191, 192

zone defense outlawed, 47, 200
Rullo, Jerry, 40, *40*
Rupp, Adolph, 14
Rush, Ed, 112, *113*, 114
Russell, Bill, *5*, 17, 33, 34, 87–89, 177, 178, 179, 180, 181, 182, 183, 184, 186, 187, 188, 189, 190, *229*
All-Star games, 33
All-Time Team, 154
coach Seattle SuperSonics, 166
basketball players influenced by, 12
Celtics and, 16, 20, 30–35, 61, *61*, 87–89, 111, 177, 178, 179, 180, 181, 182, 183, 184, 186, 187, 188, 189, 190, *190*
Chamberlain rivalry, 16, 20, 30–35, *30, 31, 32, 33*
Finals record, rebounds, 187
first African-American coach in major sports league, 61, *61*, 87, 111, 179
first African-American MVP, 60
first African-American superstar, 60
Hall of Fame profile, 222
Jordan and, 9, *9*
Mikan and, 12, 27, 29
NBA 50 greatest players ceremony, 228, *229*
NBA 50 greatest players profile and career highlights, 251, *251*
Olympics, 1956, 190
rebounding, 32, 190
retirement from Celtics, 168, 176
Russell, Byron, 120
Russell, John "Honey," 46, 54

Sabonis, Arvydas, 297, *297*, 298, 299, 310
Sacramento Kings, 92, 116
Japan Games, 302, *303*
nickname, 97
Sacramento Monarchs (WNBA), 308
Sadowski, Ed, 41
St. Louis Hawks, 60, 94, 187, 189, 190, 191, 196, 201
NBA Championship 1957–58, 189
NBA Finals 1956–57, 190
NBA Finals 1959–60, 187
NBA Finals 1960–61, 186
St. Louis Spirits. *See* Spirits of St. Louis
Saitch, Eyre "Bruiser," 53, *53*
Salley, John, *115*, 140
Salvatore, Bennett, 114
Sampson, Ralph, 144
San Antonio Spurs, 63
failure to defend championship, 116
international player added, 297
McDonald's Championship 1999, 304
NBA admittance of, 66, 162, 202
NBA Championship, 1998–99, 118–19
nickname, 97
Sanders, Tom "Satch," 88, *88*, 170
San Diego Clippers, 95
San Diego Conquistadors, 202, 205
San Diego Rockets, 74, 75, 177, 178
San Francisco Warriors, 41, 64, 72, 95, 181, 182, 183
NBA Finals 1963–64, 182
NBA Finals 1966–67, 179
Saperstein, Abe, 54, *54*
founds new ABL, 71, *71*
Savoy Big Five, 54
Schaefer, Chip, *115*, 122
Schanwald, Steve, 132
Schaus, Fred, 111, 195
Schayes, Dolph, 188, 191, 192, 195, 197, *197*
Hall of Fame profile, 222
NBA 50 greatest players profile and career highlights, 251, *251*
scoring record, 189
Schick Legends Classic results, 261
Schick Rookie Challenge results, 261
Schmidt, Oscar, 294
Schrempf, Detlef, 297, 298, *298*
Scott, Byron, 34, 83, 85, 101, 136, 138, 140
Scott, Charlie, 64, 160, 164
Season on the Reservation, A (Abdul-Jabbar), 26
Seattle Storm (WNBA), 309
Seattle SuperSonics, 14, 25, 75, 81, 103
coach Wilkens, Lenny, 158
NBA Championship 1978–79, 158–59
NBA Finals 1977–78, 160–61
NBA Finals 1995–96, 124–25
installed in NBA, 178
internationally held games, 305
nickname, 97
Sedran, Barney, 43, 46, 49, *49*
Selvy, Frank, 88, 184
Senesky, George, 40, *40*, 191
76ers. *See* Philadelphia 76ers
Seymour, Paul, 111, 192, 197
Shaffer, Lee, 181
Sharman, Bill
in ABL, 71
in All-Star Game, *257*
as Celtics player, 87–88, *88*, 187, *187*, 190, 194
as coach, 110, *110*, 172
draft and, 310
Hall of Fame profile, 222–23
Lakers and, 83, 172
NBA 50 greatest players profile and career highlights, 252, *252*
Shaw, Brian, *115*
Sheboygan Redskins, 43, *43*, 196
Sheffer, Doron, 299
Shelton, Lonnie, 158
Shirley, J. Dallas, Hall of Fame profile, 227
Shue, Gene, 110, *110*
Sichting, Jerry, 144
Sikma, Jack, 158
Silas, Paul, 158, 168
Simmons, Connie, 199
Simpson, Ralph, 203
Slam Dunk Contest. *See* All-Star Experience

Sloan, Jerry, 110, *110*, 122, 166, 170
Smith, Alan, 204
Smith, Adrian, 180
Smith, Charles, 130
Smith, Dean, 8
Smith, Elmore, 168
Smith, Greg, 174
Smith, Kenny, 126, *126*
Smith, Randy, 120
Smith, Wee Willie, 53, *53*
Smits, Rik, 297
Sojourner, Willie, 63
Sony All-Star 2ball results, 261
Soviet National Team, 296–97, 303–4
Spahn, Moe, 45–46
SPHAs. *See* Philadelphia SPHAs
Spirits of St. Louis, 62, 66
Spivey, Bill, 193
Sprewell, Latrell, 17, 118
Spurs. *See* San Antonio Spurs
Squires. *See* Virginia Squires
Stallworth, Dave, 170
Stankovic, Borislav, 296–97
Starks, John, 128
Stars. *See* Los Angeles Stars; Utah Stars
Staverman, Larry, 71
Steamrollers. *See* Providence Steamrollers
Steele, Larry, 168
Steinbrenner, George, 71
Stern, David J., *4*
  as commissioner, NBA, 5, 36–37, *36*, 74, 82, 148, 296–97, 303, 304–5, 306
  length of career in NBA, 5, 37
Stockton, John, 10, *10*, 120, 130, 132, 136, *136*, 146
  All-Star Games, 259
  assists record, 124, 136
  NBA 50 greatest players profile and career highlights, 243–44, *243*
  Olympics, 1992, Dream Team, *290*, 291, 292
Strom, Earl, *112*, 113, 114
  Hall of Fame profile, 227
Strong, Ted, 56
Suns. *See* Phoenix Suns
SuperSonics. *See* Seattle SuperSonics
Sutphin, Al, 39
Swoopes, Sheryl, 307, *307*
Syracuse Nationals, *58*, 59, 72, 91, 92, 96, 98, 182, 191
  NBA Championship 1954–55, 192
  NBA Finals 1949–50, 197
  NBA Finals 1953–54, 193

Tao, Song, 298
Tatum, Reece "Goose," 56, *56*, 57
Taylor, Brian, 204
Texas Chaparrals, 65, 95, 207
Thomas, Isiah, 136, 138, 140
  Hall of Fame profile, 223
  NBA 50 greatest players profile and career highlights, 252, *252*
Thompson, David, 7, *7*, 8, 65, 160
  Hall of Fame profile, 223
Thompson, Mychal, 84, 136, 140
Thompson, Tina, 309
Thorpe, Jim, 47
Thorpe, Otis, 126
"Three-peat," 93
Three-point shot, 66, 100–101, 126, 156
Thurmond, Nate, 27, 34, 166, 182
  Hall of Fame profile, 223
  NBA 50 greatest players profile and career highlights, 252–53, *252*
Tikhonenko, Valery, 298
Timberwolves. *See* Minnesota Timberwolves
Timms, Michele, 308
Toledo Jim White Chevrolets, 43, 45
Tomjanovich, Rudy, 110, *110*, 160
Toler, Penny, 307
Tormohlen, Gene, 71
Toronto Huskies, 41, 74, 297, 305
Toronto Maple Leaf Gardens, 39, 305
Toronto Raptors, 74, 75, 103, 305
  nickname, 97
Tracer Milan (Italy), 296, 303–4
Trail Blazers. *See* Portland Trail Blazers
Trenton Basketball Team, 42, 47
Triangle Offense, 78–79, 116
Tri-Cities Blackhawks, 94, 196
Tri-County League, 46
Trojans. *See* New York Trojans
Tucker, Jim, 59
Turkcan, Mirsad, 299
Twardzik, Dave, 162
24-second shot clock, 26, 27–28, 37, 60, 98–100, *99*, 191, 192
Twyman, Jack, Hall of Fame profile, 223
Tyrell, Peter A., 40, *40*

Unseld, Wes, 9, 160, 166, 174, 177, *177*
  Hall of Fame profile, 223
  NBA 50 greatest players profile and career highlights, 253, *253*
U.S. Women's National Team, 289, *289*
USA Basketball, 288–89, *288, 289*
  Select Teams, 289
  Women's National Team, 1995–96, 307
Utah Jazz, 74, 120
  Japan Games, 303
  NBA Finals 1996–97, 122–23
  NBA Finals 1997–98, 120–21
  nickname, 97
Utah Stars, 64, 207
  ABA Championship 1971, 172, 207
  ABA Finals 1974, 204
  disbanded, 202
Utah Starzz (WNBA), 259, 308

Vagabond Kings. *See* Detroit Vagabond Kings
van Breda Kolff, Butch, 111
Vancouver Grizzlies, 74, 75, 305
 nickname, 97
Van Exel, Nick, 124, 310
Van Gundy, Jeff, 120
Virginia Squires, 63, 64, 66, 204, 207
Vitti, Gary, *115*
Volkov, Alexander, 297, 298

Walker, Antoine, 122
Walker, Chet, 34, 166, 170, 179, *179*, 310
Wallace, Chris, 312
Wallace, Rasheed, 116
Walton, Bill, 14, 27, 29, 34, 60, 142, 144, *144*, 160, 162, *162*, 211
 Hall of Fame profile, 223
 NBA 50 greatest players profile and career highlights, 253, *253*
Wang, Zhi Zhi, 299
Wanzer, Bobby, 195
 Hall of Fame profile, 223
Warley, Ben, 71
Warriors. *See* Golden State Warriors; Philadelphia Warriors; San Francisco Warriors
Washington, Andy, 54
Washington, Kermit, 160
Washington Bullets
 coach Jones, K. C., 166
 coach Motta, Dick, 160
 NBA Championship 1977–78, 160–61
 NBA Finals 1974–75, 166–67
 NBA Finals 1978–79, 158–59
Washington Capitols, 39, 58–59, *58*, 92, 196, 200, 207, 208
 NBA Finals 1948–49, 198
Washington Generals, 54
Washington Mystics (WNBA), 308, 309
Washington Wizards
 Jordan president, 6, *8*, 25
 nickname, 97
Waterloo Hawks, 196
Weatherspoon, Teresa, 309
Webber, Chris, 10, 17, 18, *18*, 116, 302, *303*
Wedman, Scott, 142, 144
West, Jerry, 20, 34, 168, 170, 172, *172*, 177, 181, 183, 186, *186*
 All-Star Game, 1972, 257
 All-Time Team, 154
 Hall of Fame profile, 223–24
 Jordan influenced by, 8
 Lakers front office and, 83, 152
 MVP, first Finals honor to member of a losing team, 177
 NBA 50 greatest players profile and career highlights, 254–55, *254*
 Olympic team, 186
 retirement from play, 166
 scoring title, 60, 176, 181
Westhead, Paul, 152
Westphal, Paul, 111, 130, 164
White, Jo Jo, 164, 168, 170
White, Maurice, 45
Wilkens, Lenny, 61, 186, 212
 coaching career, 102–3, *102*, 158
 Hall of Fame coach profile, 225
 Hall of Fame player profile, 224
 NBA 50 greatest players profile and career highlights, 255, *255*
 Olympics, 1996, Dream Team, 294
 winningest coach in NBA, 103
Wilkes, Jamaal, 34, 83, 84, 152, *152*, 156, 166
Wilkins, Dominique, 18, 130, *130*, 295, 296
Williams, Gus, 32, 158
Williams, Lee, 212–13
Williams, Jason, 10, 17
Williams, Micheal, 14, 128
Williams, Natalie, 259, 309
Williams, Pat, 74, 162
Williams, Scott, 132
Williamson, John, 204
Wilson, Clarence, 57
Winter, Max, 37, 91
Winter, Tex, 14, 77, 78, *115*
Women's National Basketball Association (WNBA), 306–9
 Ackerman, Val, and, 306–7, *307*, 309
 All-Star 2ball, 259
 Cooper, Cynthia, first superstar, 308–9, *308*
 creation of league, 306–8
 expansion of, 308
 first basket scored, 307
 franchises, 306, 308
 Sony All-Star 2ball results, 261
 television broadcast deals, 307
 "We Got Next" slogan, 307
Wooden, John, 14, 15, *15*, 162, 212
World Championship for Young Men, 289
World University Games, 289
Worthy, James, 34, 83, 85, *85*, 140, 146, 148, 150
 NBA 50 greatest players profile and career highlights, 255, *255*
Wright, Larry, 158, 160
Wright, Walter "Toots," 54

Yancey, Bill, 53, *53*
Yardley, George, 71, 188, 189, *189*, 191
 Hall of Fame profile, 224
Youth Development Festival, 289

Zaslofsky, Max, 200
Zephyrs. *See* Chicago Zephyrs
Zheng, Haixia, 308
Zollner, Fred, 44, 46, *46*, 95
 Hall of Fame profile, 227
Zollner Pistons. *See* Fort Wayne Pistons

Designed and Produced by: Rare Air Media
1711 N. Paulina, Suite 311, Chicago, IL 60622

THE OFFICIAL NBA ENCYCLOPEDIA

Published by Doubleday
a division of Random House, Inc.
1540 Broadway, New York, NY 10036

Library of Congress Cataloging-in-Publication Data is available from the Publisher.

ISBN 0-385-501307

Printed in the United States of America

First English Edition published by Doubleday, November 2000

9 8 7 6 5 4 3 2

Third Edition

PHOTOGRAPHY CREDITS

Bill Baptist	3, 104, 246, 250, 308
AndrewBernstein	2, 3, 4, 16, 17, 19, 20, 22, 24, 34, 35, 61, 76, 78, 79, 83, 84, 85, 101, 104, 108, 114, 115, 128, 134, 136, 142, 144, 146, 148, 150, 229, 230, 232, 242, 245, 246, 247, 248, 252, 255, 258, 289, 290, 291, 292, 296, 297, 302, 305
Bruce Bennett	297
Nathaniel S. Butler	2, 6, 21, 25, 81, 103, 109, 113, 126, 130, 132, 138, 238, 259, 288, 307
Lou Capozzola	23, 79, 80, 106
Richard Clarkson/SI	156
Jerry Colangelo	2, 73
Chris Covatta	298, 303
Jim Cummins	63, 106, 202, 237
Scott Cunningham	103, 106, 107, 109, 110, 120, 124, 234, 245, 311
Tim Defrisco	106
Gary Dineen	19
Garrett Ellwood	110, 256
D. Clarke Evans	17, 118
Sam Forencich	2, 10, 11
Steve Freeman	3, 5, 99, 289
Jesse Garrabrant	3, 310
Barry Gossage	107, 309
Andy Hayt	108, 122
Ron Hoskins	258, 304
Walter Iooss Jr./SI	31, 32, 172, 177
Glenn James	107, 243
George Kalinsky	239, 241, 247
Heinz Kluetmeier/SI	168
Ron Koch	254
David Liam Kyle	61
Mitchell Layton	8, 309
Neil Leifer	2, 102, 170, 180, 232, 251
Fernando Medina	9, 12, 13, 21, 229
Manny Millan/SI	77
Peter Read Miller	231
Robert Mora	116
Layne Murdoch	3, 113, 140
Anthony Neste	109, 152
Richard Pilling	253
Dick Raphael	2, 30, 59, 86, 89, 162, 232
Ken Regan	105, 109, 234, 253
Jeff Reinking	298
Wen Roberts	176, 236, 243, 249, 255
Sheedy & Long/SI	33
Charles Smith	307
Jerry Wachter	154, 160, 166, 241
Rocky Widner	18, 110, 258
Steve Woltman	23
University of North Carolina	7
North Carolina State University	7
AP Wide World	2, 3, 11, 28, 91, 93, 100, 112, 183, 184, 185, 187, 189, 193, 312
Minnesota Historical Society	2, 26, 29, 76, 90
Sports Illustrated	82, 87
Sporting News	34, 196
NBA Photo Library	36, 37, 39, 40, 88, 99, 105, 106, 107, 108, 110, 158, 174, 182, 190, 194, 195, 197, 231, 235, 237, 240, 241, 245, 251, 257, 299
Naismith Memorial Basketball Hall of Fame, Springfield, Mass.	2, 3, 15, 27, 37, 38, 42, 43, 44, 45, 46, 47, 48, 49, 50, 51, 52, 53, 54, 55, 56, 57, 58, 60, 65, 66, 71, 74, 92, 108, 114, 178, 179, 181, 186, 188, 191, 192, 198, 199, 200, 201, 203, 204, 205, 207, 208, 209, 210, 211, 212, 213, 227, 236, 242, 252, 306
Detroit Pistons	233
Indiana Pacers	64, 206

COLOR PHOTO ESSAY

Bill Baptist	30
Andrew Bernstein	5, 7, 9, 15, 18, 19, 20, 21, 22, 23, 27, 31, 32
Nathaniel S. Butler	9, 13, 17, 27
Chris Covatta	27
Jim Cummins	22
Scott Cunningham	6, 11, 26
Gary Dineen	31
Sam Forencich	30
Jesse Garrabrant	4, 8
Don Grayston	29
Andy Hayt	22, 25, 30
Walter Iooss Jr./SI	13, 24
Glenn James	22
George Kalinsky	11, 25
Ron Koch	26
Fernando Medina	23, 31
Manny Millan/SI	19
Robert Mora	19
Layne Murdoch	22
Hy Peskin/SI	7
Dick Raphael	17, 26
Ken Regan	23,
Jeff Reinking	23, 31
Wen Roberts	23
Tony Tomsic/SI	21
Noren Trotman	13, 30, 31
Jerry Wachter	19
Rocky Widner	7, 31
AP Wide World	6, 12, 25, 28, 32
Sports Illustrated	16
NBA Photo Library	6, 18, 23
Naismith Memorial Basketball Hall of Fame, Springfield, Mass.	2, 3, 4, 5, 6, 8, 10, 13, 14, 18, 22, 26

Acknowledgements

The collective goal of everyone who contributed to the third edition of *The Official NBA Encyclopedia* was to revisit the history and retrace the ancestry of the league in a unique and innovative manner. We wanted to give basketball fans the staple of any Encyclopedia — statistics and more statistics — and we also wanted to present a visual history of our sport. We were able to utilize the extraordinary talents of the best basketball writers in the world, the staff at NBA Photos and photo journalists dating all the way back to when the game was invented. An enterprising photographer snapped the picture that opens this book, a photo of the gymnasium where the first game was played in 1891, and we are indebted to the Naismith Memorial Basketball Hall of Fame for allowing us to use the photo.

To properly thank everyone would take much more than a few kind words. The "special thanks" section reflects the monumental effort of all contributors. But a few deserve to be singled out, particularly the day-to-day manager of the project John Hareas, who attacked the assignment in relentless and meticulous manner. Veteran basketball experts helped us check the facts, notably Alex Sachare (who edited the previous NBA Encyclopedias), John Fawaz, Zelda Spoelstra and Harvey Pollack, who was the Philadelphia Warriors PR director in 1962 and once scribbled "100" on a piece of paper and handed it to Wilt Chamberlain. That unforgettable photo is on page 185 and also in the opening photo section.

The crews at NBA Photos and NBA Editorial worked a staggering number of hours on the project and their contributions are greatly appreciated. Thanks to David Stern for his input and direction; Russ Granik for his guidance and basketball expertise; my boss Brian McIntyre and my cohort Terry Lyons, for their friendship and timely contributions.

At Doubleday, Peter Gethers was incredibly enthusiastic and supportive, and Michael Palgon came up big in the late stages of the project to increase the size of the book because we told him it was necessary. It was the equivalent of a last-second, game-winning, three-pointer in the great tradition of the other Michael, and we're still cheering.

Thanks to everyone at Rare Air Media, particularly the designers in the trenches — Steve Polacek and Shereen Boury, who were directed with great humility and flourish by John Vieceli.

To embrace a historical project like this usually means the passion for the subject began at an early age and was fueled by many people and institutions. My hometown of Dallas was football country, but it is where I found my inspiration for basketball. So, in no particular order, thanks to: the *Dallas Morning News* and defunct *Dallas Times Herald* because during my youth, long before the Mavericks and the NBA came to Dallas, they not only provided NBA box scores, but also box scores of the ABL. That allowed me to keep up with the exploits of Connie Hawkins and Dick Barnett, which seemed very important at the time. Thanks to Jim Krebs, Max Williams, Jan Loudermilk (love the name) and all of the 1950s and early '60s SMU Mustangs; Slater Martin of the University of Texas because he proved that a player from the Southwest Conference could be a top player in the NBA; the St. James Red Raiders; the Dallas Chaparrals; Terry Stembridge; Randy Galloway and Beckley-Saner Recreation Center. And last but not least, thanks to Msgr. Francis L. Becker, who during my childhood continually provided me with the necessary tools — discipline, morality, love, a passion for sport and even a pair of new basketball shoes — to succeed on and off the court.

JAN HUBBARD

—

AUGUST 2000

Special Thanks

NBA EDITORIAL: Jeanne Tang, Chris Ekstrand, Rita Sullivan, Barry Rubinstein, John Gardella, Tracey Reavis, Rob Reheuser, Philip Mirrer-Singer, April Bulger.

NBA PHOTOS: Carmin Romanelli, Joe Amati, Mike Klein, Scott Yurdin, David Bonilla and all of the sensational photographers listed on the photo credits page.

NBA ENTERTAINMENT: Adam Silver, Heidi Ueberroth, Charles Rosenzweig, Paul Hirschheimer, Marc Hirschheimer, Michael Levine, M.J. Morse, Meredith Tanchum, Nathalie Maurice.

RARE AIR MEDIA: Mark Vancil, Jim Forni, Andrew Pipitone, Dennis Carlson, Melinda Fry, Elizabeth Fulton, John Arthurs.

ELIAS SPORTS BUREAU: Steve Hirdt, Chris Thorn, Santo Labombarda, John Carson, and Bob Rosen.

NAISMITH MEMORIAL BASKETBALL HALL OF FAME: Robin Deutsch and Doug Stark, whose historical expertise and incredible photo library were invaluable.

PROFESSIONAL GRAPHICS INC.: Dave, Pat and Steve Goley, Vince Llamzon, Greg Whitmer, David Iben, Keith Long, Jamie Stukenberg, Teri North and Lynn Manis.

ALSO: Michael Jordan, Jerry West, Julius Erving, Red Auerbach, Doc Rivers, Pat Riley, Doug Collins, Bill Walton, Don Chaney, Kevin Garnett, Ian Naismith, Lamar Odom, Rena Leinberger, Josh Hirsch, Seth Guge, Mark Alper, Charlee Trantino and all contributing writers.

Contributing Writers

DAN BARREIRO is a general sports columnist for the *Minneapolis Star-Tribune* and KFAN Radio. Barreiro was the lead feature writer and Olympic writer for the *Dallas Morning News*. He also worked for the *Atlanta Constitution*.

FRAN BLINEBURY currently serves as a general sports columnist for the *Houston Chronicle*, where he began in 1982, covering the Houston Rockets until 1986. Blinebury covered the Philadelphia 76ers for the *Philadelphia Journal* from 1977-81. He served as President of the Pro Basketball Writers Association (PBWA) from 1982-86. Blinebury also worked on "Sports Talk" for KPRC Radio in Houston from 1995-2000, and writes about the NBA for a variety of publications, including *Street & Smith* and *Hoop* magazine.

MARY SCHMITT BOYER has covered the Cleveland Cavaliers for the *Cleveland Plain Dealer* since 1996. She also covered the first four seasons of the Minnesota Timberwolves for the *St. Paul Pioneer Press*. Schmitt Boyer has also worked for the *Milwaukee Sentinel*, the *Milwaukee Journal*, the *Washington Post*, the *Eugene Register-Guard* and the *Kansas City Star*. Primarily a basketball writer, she also has covered the Minnesota Vikings of the NFL and four Olympics. Schmitt Boyer graduated from Marquette University in 1977, the same year the basketball team won the NCAA title. She is married to Gene Boyer, principal of St. Edward High School in Lakewood, Ohio.

CURTIS BUNN has covered the NBA for 15 years. Currently, he is a general sports columnist and national NBA writer for the *Atlanta Journal-Constitution*. Bunn covered the New York Knicks for eight years for *Newsday* and the *New York Daily News*, and the New Jersey Nets for three years while at *Newsday*. He has also contributed to *The Sporting News*, *Basketball News*, *Hoop* magazine and *The Source Sports*.

BRYAN BURWELL currently serves as a senior correspondent for HoopsTV.com and a correspondent for HBO Sports, and writes a monthly column for *Sports Business Journal.* He has also commented for Turner Sports and CNN. Burwell served as a columnist for *USA Today* and *The Sporting News*, and covered a variety of sports for the *New York Daily News*, *Detroit News*, *Newsday*, *Washington Star* and the *Baltimore Sun*.

ROBIN JONATHAN DEUTSCH is the Director of Publishing & New Media at the Naismith Memorial Basketball Hall of Fame. He has been at the Hall of Fame for nine years and oversees all publishing and Internet ventures. He is a columnist for *Eastern Basketball* and contributor to *Basketball Times*, *USA Basketball News*, www.MassLive.com and the *Springfield Union-News* and *Sunday Republican*. He has also written for *Street & Smith*, *ESPN The Magazine*, *The Associated Press*, the *Boston Globe* and *Boston Herald*.

DAVID DUPREE is a veteran basketball writer who has been covering the NBA for 25 years. DuPree is currently the national NBA writer for *USA Today*. He also covered the Washington Bullets for the *Washington Post*. DuPree has written for a variety of basketball publications. He also played college football at the University of Washington.

CHRIS EKSTRAND has been with the NBA since 1990. Currently with NBA Editorial, Ekstrand is a frequent contributor to *Hoop* magazine and NBA.com, serves as editor of the *NBA Draft Media Guide* and is a contributing editor of *The Sporting News Official NBA Guide* and *The Sporting News Official NBA Register*. Ekstrand previously wrote news and sports for *The Associated Press* and the *Newark Star-Ledger*.

JOHN GARDELLA has been with NBA Editorial since January 2000, contributing to *Hoop* magazine and NBA.com. Gardella was a senior editor for *American Metal Market* and a sports editor for the *Benicia Herald*. He has also contributed articles to *ESPN The Magazine*.

SAM GOLDAPER retired in 1991 after nearly half a century as a sportswriter, spending the last 24 years of his career at the *New York Times*. He covered the NBA extensively, contributing to numerous books, magazines and other publications. In 1992, Goldaper was the recipient of the prestigious Curt Gowdy Award, presented by the Naismith Memorial Basketball Hall of Fame.

MARK HALE recently graduated from Cornell University, where he served as the sports editor for the *Cornell Daily Sun* and as a contributing writer for the sports site SuperCornell.com. He previously interned at *Sports Illustrated* and the NBA, where he contributed research to publications including the 1998 NBA Finals book, *Six Times as Sweet*, and *For the Love of the Game: My Story*, by Michael Jordan. Hale has also been a frequent contributor to *Hoop* magazine.

JOHN HAREAS joined NBA Editorial in July 1996. He is the managing editor of *Hoop* magazine, the All-Star Game, the NBA Finals Programs, *The Sporting News Official NBA Guide* and *The Sporting News Official NBA Register*. He also edits the NBA Scholastic books and authored one title, *NBA Slam*. Hareas previously was a senior associate editor for *Inside Sports* and *Basketball Digest*.

JAN HUBBARD, NBA Vice President, Editorial, joined the NBA in 1993 after a 16-year career as a newspaper writer. Hubbard covered the NBA for 13 years for *Newsday*, the *Dallas Morning News* and the *Fort Worth Star-Telegram*. He also wrote an NBA column for *The Sporting News* for 10 years and appeared on the NBA Beat on ESPN during the 1992-93 NBA season. He has written two books on the NBA Finals: *Six Times as Sweet* (the Chicago Bulls' 1998 championship) and *One For San Antonio* (the Spurs' 1999 championship).

FRED KERBER has been a sports writer for the *New York Post* for 10 years and previously worked at the *New York Daily News* for 16 years. He has been covering the NBA since 1984. Kerber contributes to a variety of sports publications, including *Hoop* magazine, and served as president of the Pro Basketball Writers Association (PBWA) from 1992-93.

LEONARD KOPPETT actively covered the NBA during the first 30 years of the league's existence for the *New York Post*, *New York Times* and *New York Herald Tribune*. He is a member of the writer's wing of the Naismith Memorial Basketball Hall of Fame. Koppett is also the author of four books about basketball, including *24 Seconds to Shoot: The Birth and Improbable Rise of the National Basketball Association*.

PAUL LADEWSKI has been with the *Daily Southtown* since 1972. He has covered the NBA and the Chicago Bulls since 1978, beginning as a rookie with Reggie Theus. Ladewski also serves as a general correspondent for *Sports Illustrated* and a frequent contributor to *Hoop* magazine. Ladewski can also be heard as a weekend co-host on WSCR Radio in Chicago.

ROLAND LAZENBY is the author of many books, including *Blood on the Horns*; *Three Peat!*; *And Now, Your Chicago Bulls!*; *Yo, Baby, It's Attitude!!!*; *The NBA Finals, A 50 Year Celebration*; and *Bull Run!*, which was named the Sports Book of the Year for 1997. His work has appeared in a number of publications, including *Sport* and *The Sporting News*.

JACKIE MACMULLAN spent five years as a senior writer for *Sports Illustrated* covering the NBA. MacMullan previously spent 13 years at the *Boston Globe*. She recently collaborated with Larry Bird on his biography, *Bird Watching*.

JACK MCCALLUM, a senior writer at *Sports Illustrated*, has been with the magazine since 1981. He covered the NBA from 1985 through 1993 and continues to write frequently about pro and college basketball. He has written two books about pro basketball — *Unfinished Business: A Year with the 1990-91Boston Celtics*, and *Shaq Attaq!* with Shaquille O'Neal — as well as three other books.

MIKE MONROE is NBA senior writer for FoxSports. A 1971 graduate of the University of Colorado, Monroe was a sports reporter at the *Denver Post* for 29 years, covering the NBA for 15 years beginning in 1985. He also worked at the *Colorado Springs Free Press* and the *Colorado Springs Gazette-Telegraph*. A past president of the Professional Basketball Writers Association (PBWA), Monroe has written two books about professional basketball: *Hardwood Gold*, a history of the Denver Nuggets franchise; and *NBA Rookie Experience*, about key rookies from the draft class of 1997.

BRUCE NEWMAN is currently a film critic with the *San Jose Mercury News*, after spending the majority of a 20-year career at *Sports Illustrated* as a senior writer, covering the NBA for the last four. After leaving *SI*, Newman contributed to a number of publications as an entertainment writer, including the *New York Times*, *Los Angeles Times*, *US* magazine and *TV Guide*, before joining the *Mercury-News* in 2000.

SCOTT OSTLER currently serves as a columnist for the *San Francisco Chronicle*, where he has worked since 1992. He also serves as the "Answer Man" on MSNBC.com, where he answers fans' sports questions. Ostler also writes about the NFL and NBA for various publications, including *Hoop* magazine. Before joining the *Chronicle*, Ostler wrote for the *National Sports Daily* and at the *Los Angeles Times* for 12 years, serving as the Lakers beat writer from 1979-81.

TRACEY REAVIS joined NBA Editorial in 1999. She has written for *Hoop* magazine and has contributed to NBA.com and WNBA.com. Before joining the NBA, Reavis spent three years as a reporter for *Sports Illustrated* and was the Director of Research at Callaway Golf Publishing Ventures. She has also covered high school sports for *Newsday*.

ROB REHEUSER joined NBA Editorial in October 1999, working on various league publications including *Hoop* magazine and *NBA News*. He is also a frequent contributor to NBA.com. Before joining the NBA, Reheuser covered high school and college sports for *Newsday* and was a business reporter for *Homeworld Business Magazine*. He also contributed articles to *New York Sportscene* magazine.

BARRY RUBINSTEIN joined NBA Editorial in 1999. He is a frequent contributor to *Hoop* magazine and other NBA publications, and co-authored *The Big Title, the Official NBA Finals 2000 Retrospective*. Before working for the NBA, Rubinstein covered the NBA and Major League Baseball for the *Newark Star-Ledger*, where he spent eight years, including three on the New York Knicks beat. He also covered the NHL for the *Morristown (N.J.) Daily Record*.

BOB RYAN is a general sports columnist for the *Boston Globe*, where he has worked for more than 30 years, beginning in 1968, covering the Boston Celtics for 14 seasons. He has written or co-authored 10 books, including collaborations with Bob Cousy, John Havlicek and Larry Bird. Ryan has been a regular panelist on ESPN's "The Sports Reporters" since 1989, and has appeared on numerous other television and radio broadcasts.

ALEX SACHARE currently serves as the Director of Communications for the Columbia College Office of Alumni Affairs and Development, where he serves as editor and publisher of *Columbia College Today*, his alma mater's alumni magazine. He also is a frequent contributor to NBA.com, *Hoop* magazine and other sports media outlets. Sachare was a sports writer for *The Associated Press* for 10 years, including five as the pro basketball editor. He subsequently worked at the NBA for 15 years, serving as Director of Information, Executive Editor and Vice President, Editorial. Sachare has authored or co-authored several books about basketball including *When Seconds Count*, his most recent, which is a countdown of the most exciting endings and amazing buzzer-beaters in basketball.

DAN SHAUGHNESSY has been with the *Boston Globe* since 1981, where he currently serves as a general sports columnist. He worked as a Celtics beat writer from 1982-86. Shaughnessy has penned two basketball books: *Seeing Red*, the Red Auerbach story; and *Ever Green*, a history of the Celtics.

JOHN SMALLWOOD is a general sports columnist for the *Philadelphia Daily News*, where he has worked for the past six years. Smallwood writes extensively about the NBA, and has covered the NBA Finals for the past five seasons. He also has written *Yesterday's Heroes*, a book on the history of African-Americans in the NBA.

LYLE SPENCER is a general sports columnist for the *Riverside Press-Enterprise*. He has covered the NBA since 1971, working for the *Santa Monica Evening Outlook*, *Los Angeles Herald Examiner*, *Rocky Mountain News*, *San Antonio Light*, *New York Post* and the *National Sports Daily*.

DOUGLAS STARK has been the Librarian and Archivist at the Naismith Memorial Basketball Hall of Fame since January 1998. He is responsible for maintaining and making accessible the library, archival, photograph, film and oral history collections. Before the Hall of Fame, he was an intern at the Chicago Historical Society and a consulting archivist at the Whitney Museum of American Art. He has also contributed to *Basketball Digest*, *Basketball Times*, *Museum News* and *The American Archivist*.

RITA SULLIVAN joined NBA Editorial in 1999. She contributes to *Hoop* magazine, NBA.com and WNBA.com, and is a contributing editor for *The Sporting News Official WNBA Guide and Register* and *WNBA News*. Sullivan played Division I basketball at the University of Maine.

JEANNE TANG joined NBA Editorial in 1993. She is the Deputy Editor of *Hoop* magazine as well as a host of other NBA publications, including books, newsletters and on-line material. In addition to her NBA responsibilities, Tang handles WNBA publications, serving as Editor of the *WNBA Yearbook*, *The Sporting News Official WNBA Guide and Register* and *WNBA News*.

ART THIEL has been with the *Seattle Post-Intelligencer* for 20 years, working as a general sports columnist for the last 13. He covered the SuperSonics from 1982-84. Thiel has also contributed to *Hoop* magazine, *Sport*, *Inside Sports* and *Outside* magazine, and is a regular on radio station KZOK.

NBA
DVD
AVAILABLE IN OCTOBER 2000
ORDER YOURS TODAY BY CALLING 1-888-742-4NBA OR VISIT
nba.com
GREATEST NBA FINALS MOMENTS
•DVD-ROM WITH ACCESS TO NBA PHOTO GALLERY
• CUSTOMIZABLE SCREEN SAVER, STATS, PLAY ANIMATIONS AND MORE
•SIX CHANNEL SURROUND SOUND
•MULTIPLE CAMERA ANGLES OF MAJOR PLAYS
ENHANCED DVD EDITION
SPECIAL FEATURES INCLUD
• DVD ROM WITH ACCESS TO NBA PHOTO GALLERY
• CUSTOMIZABLE SCREEN SAVER, STATS, PLAY ANIMATIONS AND MORE
• SIX CHANNEL SURROUND SOUND
• MULTIPLE CAMERA ANGLE OF MAJOR PLAYS
NBA on DVD... There's Nothing Else Like It!
NBA UNDER PRESSURE
UPSETS & UNDERDOGS
Hosted by Bill Walton
NBA VIDEO
Nothing Gets You Closer to the Game!
inside STUFF
SHOWMEN OF TODAY
USA HOME ENTERTAINMENT

The great thing about basketball is that it is a game that you can practice alone to get better. And if you have an imagination, you can entertain yourself for hours, playing against the greatest players in the NBA. I remember growing up as a kid and playing alone in my backyard. I would always imagine that I was playing against Jerry West. I had read his book where he talked about how he would take a hard step that powered him into his jump shot for a quick release. When I played him in my backyard, I'd use that move. And I would always find a way to beat him.

Doug Collins